Federal Acquisition Regulation

as of January 1, 2020

Compiled from CCH Government Contracts Reporter
(As of January 1, 2020)

2700 Lake Cook Road
Riverwoods, IL, 60015
866 529 6600
www.WoltersKluwerLR.com

Printed in the United States of America
ISBN 978-1-5438-1940-3
Media Issue 10030148-0011

Federal Acquisition Regulation

Table of Contents

	Page
Sources	9
SUBCHAPTER A—GENERAL	
Part 1—Federal Acquisition Regulations System	19
Part 2—Definitions of Words and Terms	43
Part 3—Improper Business Practices and Personal Conflicts of Interest	73
Part 4—Administrative and Information Matters	113
SUBCHAPTER B—ACQUISITION PLANNING	
Part 5—Publicizing Contract Actions	159
Part 6—Competition Requirements	179
Part 7—Acquisition Planning	197
Part 8—Required Sources of Supplies and Services	219
Part 9—Contractor Qualifications	255
Part 10—Market Research	301
Part 11—Describing Agency Needs	307
Part 12—Acquisition of Commercial Items	325
SUBCHAPTER C—CONTRACTING METHODS AND CONTRACT TYPES	
Part 13—Simplified Acquisition Procedures	347
Part 14—Sealed Bidding	371
Part 15—Contracting by Negotiation	403
Part 16—Types of Contracts	465
Part 17—Special Contracting Methods	505
Part 18—Emergency Acquisitions	525
SUBCHAPTER D—SOCIOECONOMIC PROGRAMS	
Part 19—Small Business Programs	535
Part 20—[Reserved]	
Part 21—[Reserved]	
Part 22—Application of Labor Laws to Government Acquisitions	621

Page

Part 23—Environment, Energy and Water Efficiency, Renewable Energy Technologies, Occupational Safety, and Drug-Free Workplace . . . 723
Part 24—Protection of Privacy and Freedom of Information . . . 745
Part 25—Foreign Acquisition . . . 751
Part 26—Other Socioeconomic Programs . . . 799

SUBCHAPTER E—GENERAL CONTRACTING REQUIREMENTS

Part 27—Patents, Data, and Copyrights . . . 809
Part 28—Bonds and Insurance . . . 841
Part 29—Taxes . . . 865
Part 30—Cost Accounting Standards Administration . . . 873
Part 31—Contract Cost Principles and Procedures . . . 893
Part 32—Contract Financing . . . 953
Part 33—Protests, Disputes, and Appeals . . . 1031

SUBCHAPTER F—SPECIAL CATEGORIES OF CONTRACTING

Part 34—Major System Acquisition . . . 1049
Part 35—Research and Development Contracting . . . 1057
Part 36—Construction and Architect-Engineer Contracts . . . 1071
Part 37—Service Contracting . . . 1093
Part 38—Federal Supply Schedule Contracting . . . 1109
Part 39—Acquisition of Information Technology . . . 1113
Part 40—[Reserved]
Part 41—Acquisition of Utility Services . . . 1121

SUBCHAPTER G—CONTRACT MANAGEMENT

Part 42—Contract Administration and Audit Services . . . 1135
Part 43—Contract Modifications . . . 1181
Part 44—Subcontracting Policies and Procedures . . . 1189
Part 45—Government Property . . . 1199
Part 46—Quality Assurance . . . 1215
Part 47—Transportation . . . 1237

Page

Part 48—Value Engineering 1279
Part 49—Termination of Contracts 1291
Part 50—Extraordinary Contractual Actions and the SAFETY ACT 1341
Part 51—Use of Government Sources by Contractors 1357

SUBCHAPTER H—CLAUSES AND FORMS

Part 52—Solicitation Provisions and Contract Clauses 1367
Part 53—Forms 2035

TOPICAL INDEX

Topical Index 2223

SOURCES

Federal Acquisition Regulation, 1984 edition, effective 4-1-84.

FAC 2020-03, 84 FR 68314, 12-13-2019; see ¶ 70,002.214.
FAC 2020-02, 84 FR 64680, 11-22-2019; see ¶ 70,002.213.
FAC 2020-01, 84 FR 54760, 10-10-2019; see ¶ 70,002.212.
FAC 2019-06, 84 FR 47860, 9-10-2019; see ¶ 70,002.211.
FAC 2019-05, 84 FR 40216, 8-13-2019; see ¶ 70,002.210.
FAC 2019-04, 84 FR 38838, 8-7-2019; see ¶ 70,002.209.
FAC 2019-03, 84 FR 27494, 6-12-2019; see ¶ 70,002.208.
FAC 2019-02, 84 FR 19834, 5-6-2019; see ¶ 70,002.207.
FAC 2019-01, 83 FR 65466, 12-20-2018; see ¶ 70,002.206.
FAC 2005-101, 83 FR 48690, 9-26-2018; see ¶ 70,002.205.
FAC 2005-100, 83 FR 42568, 8-22-2018; see ¶ 70,002.204.
FAC 2005-99, 83 FR 28140, 6-15-2018; see ¶ 70,002.203.
FAC 2005-98, 83 FR 19144, 5-1-2018; see ¶ 70,002.202.
FAC 2005-97, 83 FR 3396, 1-24-2018; see ¶ 70,002.201.
FAC 2005-96, 82 FR 51526, 11-6-2017; see ¶ 70,002.200.
FAC 2005-95, 82 FR 4708, 1-13-2017; see ¶ 70,002.199.
FAC 2005-94, 81 FR 93476, 12-20-2016; see ¶ 70,002.198.
FAC 2005-93, 81 FR 91626, 12-16-2016; see ¶ 70,002.197.
FAC 2005-92, 81 FR 83092, 11-18-2016; see ¶ 70,002.196.
Correction, 81 FR 72738, 10-21-2016; see ¶ 70,002.195.
Correction, 81 FR 71384, 10-17-2016; see ¶ 70,002.194.
FAC 2005-91, 81 FR 67726, 9-30-2016; see ¶ 70,002.193.
FAC 2005-90, 81 FR 58561, 8-25-2016; see ¶ 70,002.192.
FAC 2005-89, 81 FR 45832, 7-14-2016; see ¶ 70,002.191.
FAC 2005-88, 81 FR 30427, 5-16-2016; see ¶ 70,002.190.
Correction, 81 FR 13998, 3-16-2016; see ¶ 70,002.189.
FAC 2005-87, 81 FR 11988, 3-7-2016; see ¶ 70,002.188.
FAC 2005-86, 80 FR 81885, 12-31-2015; see ¶ 70,002.187.
FAC 2005-85, 80 FR 75901, 12-4-2015; see ¶ 70,002.186.
Final rule, 80 FR 53753, 9-8-2015; see ¶ 70,002.185.
FAC 2005-84, 80 FR 53435, 9-3-2015; see ¶ 70,002.184.
FAC 2005-83, 80 FR 38291, 7-2-2015; see ¶ 70,002.183.
FAC 2005-82, 80 FR 26421, 5-7-2015; see ¶ 70,002.182.
FAC 2005-81, 80 FR 19504, 4-10-2015; see ¶ 70,002.181.
Correction, 80 FR 6909, 2-92015; see ¶ 70,002.180.
Correction, 80 FR 6909, 2-92015; see ¶ 70,002.179.
Correction, 80 FR 6908, 2-9-2015; see ¶ 70,002.178.
FAC 2005-80, 80 FR 4965, 1-29-2015; see ¶ 70,002.177.
Correction, 79 FR 75434, 12-18-2014; see ¶ 70,002.176.
FAC 2005-79, 79 FR 74543, 12-15-2014; see ¶ 70,002.175.
FAC 2005-78, 79 FR 70339, 11-25-2014; see ¶ 70,002.174.
Correction, 79 FR 63562, 10-24-2014; see ¶ 70,002.173.
FAC 2005-77, 79 FR 61737, 10-14-2014; see ¶ 70,002.172.
Correction, 79 FR 46375, 8-8-2014; see ¶ 70,002.171.

FAC 2005-76, 79 FR 43573, 7-25-2014; see ¶ 70,002.170.
FAC 2005-75, 79 FR 35857, 6-24-2014; see ¶ 70,002.169.
FAC 2005-74, 79 FR 31185, 5-30-2014; see ¶ 70,002.168.
FAC 2005-73, 79 FR 24191, 4-29-2014; see ¶ 70,002.167.
Final rule, 79 FR 4630, 1-29-2014; see ¶ 70,002.166.
Final rule, 79 FR 4630, 1-29-2014; see ¶ 70,002.165.
FAC 2005-72, 78 FR 80367, 12-31-2013; see ¶ 70,002.164.
FAC 2005-71, 78 FR 70475, 10-25-2013; see ¶ 70,002.163.
FAC 2005-70, 78 FR 60167, 9-30-2013; see ¶ 70,002.162.
FAC 2005-69, 78 FR 46779, 8-1-2013; see ¶ 70,002.161.
FAC 2005-68, 78 FR 38533, 6-26-2013; see ¶ 70,002.160.
FAC 2005-67, 78 FR 37667, 6-21-2013; see ¶ 70,002.159.
CFR Correction, 78 FR 26518, 5-7-2013; see ¶ 70,002.158.
FAC 2005-66, 78 FR 13763, 2-28-2013; see ¶ 70,002.157.
FAC 2005-65, 78 FR 6183, 1-29-2013; see ¶ 70,002.156.
Correction, 78 FR 2893, 1-15-2013; see ¶ 70,002.155.
FAC 2005-64, 77 FR 75765, 12-21-2012; see ¶ 70,002.154.
FAC 2005-63, 77 FR 73515, 12-10-2012; see ¶ 70,002.153.
FAC 2005-62, 77 FR 69713, 11-20-2012; see ¶ 70,002.152.
FAC 2005-61, 77 FR 56737, 9-13-2012; see ¶ 70,002.151.
FAC 2005-60, 77 FR 44045, 7-26-2012; see ¶ 70,002.150.
Correction, 77 FR 35624, 6-14-2012; see ¶ 70,002.149.
FAC 2005-59, 77 FR 27546, 5-9-2012; see ¶ 70,002.148.
FAC 2005-58, 77 FR 23364, 4-18-2012; see ¶ 70,002.147.
Correction, 77 FR 17353, 3-26-2012; see ¶ 70,002.146.
Correction, 77 FR 17352, 3-26-2012; see ¶ 70,002.145.
Correction, 77 FR 14303, 3-9-2012; see ¶ 70,002.144.
Correction, 77 FR 14303, 3-9-2012; see ¶ 70,002.143.
FAC 2005-57, 77 FR 13952, 3-7-2012; see ¶ 70,002.142.
FAC 2005-56, 77 FR 12912, 3-2-2012; see ¶ 70,002.141.
Interim rule, 77 FR 1889, 1-12-2012; see ¶ 70,002.139.
Correction, 77 FR 1640, 1-11-2012; see ¶ 70,002.138.
FAC 2005-55, 77 FR 182, 1-3-2011; see ¶ 70,002.137.
Correcting amendment (FAC 2005-54), 76 FR 76899, 12-9-2011; see ¶ 70,002.136.
FAC 2005-54, 76 FR 68014, 11-2-2011; see ¶ 70,002.135.
FAC 2005-53, 76 FR 39232, 7-5-2011; see ¶ 70,002.134.
FAC 2005-52, 76 FR 31394, 5-31-2011; see ¶ 70,002.133.
Correcting amendment (FAC 2005-50), 76 FR 26220, 5-6-2011; see ¶ 70,002.132.
FAC 2005-51, 76 FR 18303, 4-1-2011; see ¶ 70,002.131.
FAC 2005-50, 76 FR 14541, 3-16-2010; see ¶ 70,002.130.
FAC 2005-49, 76 FR 4187, 1-24-2010; see ¶ 70,002.129.
FAC 2005-48, 75 FR 82565, 12-30-2010; see ¶ 70,002.128.
FAC 2005-47, 75 FR 77721, 12-13-2010; see ¶ 70,002.127.
FAC 2005-46, 75 FR 60247, 9-29-2010; see ¶ 70,002.126.
FAC 2005-45, 75 FR 53135, 8-30-2010; see ¶ 70,002.125.
CFR correction, 75 FR 43090, 7-23-2010; see ¶ 70,002.124.
FAC 2005-44, 75 FR 39413, 7-8-2010; see ¶ 70,002.123.

FAC 2005-43, 75 FR 38673, 7-2-2010; see ¶ 70,002.122.
FAC 2005-42, 75 FR 34255, 6-16-2010; see ¶ 70,002.121.
FAC 2005-41, 75 FR 19168, 4-13-2010; see ¶ 70,002.120.
FAC 2005-40, 75 FR 14057, 3-23-2010; see ¶ 70,002.119.
FAC 2005-39, 75 FR 13411, 3-19-2010; see ¶ 70,002.118.
FAC 2005-38, 74 FR 65597, 12-10-2009; see ¶ 70,002.117.
FAC 2005-37, 74 FR 52845, 10-14-2009; see ¶ 70,002.116.
CFR correction, 74 FR 49825, 9-29-2009; see ¶ 70,002.115.
CFR correction, 74 FR 48421, 9-23-2009; see ¶ 70,002.114.
FAC 2005-36, 74 FR 40457, 8-11-2009; see ¶ 70,002.113.
FAC 2005-35, 74 FR 34206, 7-14-2009; see ¶ 70,002.112.
FAC 2005-34, 74 FR 31556, 7-1-2009; see ¶ 70,002.111.
FAC 2005-33, 74 FR 28426, 6-15-2009; see ¶ 70,002.110.
Amendment-4 (FAC 2005-29) 74 FR 26981, 6-5-2009; see ¶ 70,002.109.
Technical Amendment (FAC 2005-32), 74 FR 22809, 5-14-2009; see ¶ 70,002.109.
Amendment-3 (FAC 2005-29) 74 FR 17793, 4-17-2009; see ¶ 70,007.17.
FAC 2005-32, 74 FR 14621, 3-31-2009; see ¶ 70,002.108.
Correction, 74 FR 14492, 3-31-2009; see ¶ 70,002.107.
FAC 2005-31, 74 FR 11819, 3-19-2009; see ¶ 70,002.106.
Amendment-2 (FAC 2005-29), 74 FR 5621, 1-30-2009; see ¶ 70,007.16.
FAC 2005-30, 74 FR 2710, 1-15-2009; see ¶ 70,002.105.
Amendment-1 (FAC 2005-29), 74 FR 1937, 1-14-2009; see ¶ 70,007.15.
Correction, 73 FR 72242, 11-26-2008; see ¶ 70,002.104.
FAC 2005-29, 73 FR 67651, 11-14-2008; see ¶ 70,002.103.
FAC 2005-28, 73 FR 67064, 11-12-2008; see ¶ 70,002.102.
FAC 2005-27, 73 FR 53989, 9-17-2008; see ¶ 70,002.101.
FAC 2005-26, 73 FR 33635, 6-12-2008; see ¶ 70,002.100.
FAC 2005-25, 73 FR 21771, 4-28-2008; see ¶ 70,002.99.
Correction, 73 FR 16747, 3-28-2008; see ¶ 70,002.98.
FAC 2005-24, 73 FR 10942, 2-28-2008; see ¶ 70,002.97.
FAC 2005-23, 72 FR 73213, 12-26-2007; see ¶ 70,002.96.
FAC 2005-22, 72 FR 65868, 11-7-2007; see ¶ 70,002.95.
FAC 2005-21, 72 FR 63025, 11-23-2007; see ¶ 70,002.94.
Correction, 72 FR 55089, 9-28-2007; see ¶ 70,002.93.
FAC 2005-20, 72 FR 51305, 9-6-2007; see ¶ 70,002.92.
FAC 2005-19, 72 FR 46324, 8-17-2007; see ¶ 70,002.91.
FAC 2005-18, 72 FR 36852, 7-5-2007; see ¶ 70,002.90.
FAC 2005-17, 72 FR 27363, 5-15-2007; see ¶ 70,002.89.
FAC 2005-16, 72 FR 13583, 3-22-2007; see ¶ 70,002.88.
Final rule, 72 FR 6881, 2-13-2007 see ¶ 70,002.87.
FAC 2005-15, 71 FR 74655, 12-12-2006; see ¶ 70,002.86.
FAC 2005-14, 71 FR 67769, 11-22-2006; see ¶ 70,002.85.
FAC 2005-13, 71 FR 57357, 9-28-2006; see ¶ 70,002.84.
Correction, 71 FR 50862, 8-28-2006; see ¶ 70,002.83.
FAC 2005-12, 71 FR 44545, 8-4-2006; see ¶ 70,002.82.
FAC 2005-11, 71 FR 38238, 7-5-2006; see ¶ 70,002.81.
FAC 2005-10, 71 FR 36922, 7-28-2006; see ¶ 70,002.80.

Correction, 71 FR 25507, 5-1-2006; see ¶ 70,002.79.
FAC 2005-09, 71 FR 20293, 4-19-2006; see ¶ 70,002.78.
FAC 2005-08, 71 FR 863, 1-5-2006; see ¶ 70,002.77.
FAC 2005-07, 71 FR 197, 1-3-2006; see ¶ 70,002.76.
Correction, 70 FR 69100, 11-14-2005; see ¶ 70,002.75.
FAC 2005-06, 70 FR 57445, 9-30-2005; see ¶ 70,002.74.
Correction, 70 FR 46776, 8-11-2005; see ¶ 70,002.73.
FAC 2005-05, 70 FR 43575, 7-27-2005; see ¶ 70,002.72.
FAC 2005-04, 70 FR 33653, 6-8-2005; see ¶ 70,002.71.
FAC 2005-03, 70 FR 18953, 4-11-2005; see ¶ 70,002.70.
FAC 2005-02, 70 FR 14950, 3-23-2005; see ¶ 70,002.69.
FAC 2005-01, 70 FR 11735, 3-9-2005; see ¶ 70,002.68.
FAC 2001-27, 69 FR 77869, 12-28-2004; see ¶ 70,002.67.
FAC 2001-26, 69 FR 76339, 12-20-2004; see ¶ 70,002.66.
FAC 2001-25, Correcting Amendments, 69 FR 60967, 10-14-2004; see ¶ 70,002.65.
FAC 2001-25, 69 FR 59697, 10-5-2004; see ¶ 70,002.64.
FAC 2001-24, 69 FR 34228, 6-18-2004; see ¶ 70,002.63.
FAC 2001-19, revised pages, 5-28-2004; see ¶ 70,002.62.
FAC 2001-23, 69 FR 25273, 5-5-2004; see ¶ 70,002.61.
FAC 2001-22, 69 FR 17741, 4-5-2004; see ¶ 70,002.60.
FAC 2001-21, 69 FR 16147, 3-26-2004; see ¶ 70,002.59.
FAC 2001-20, 69 FR 8311, 2-23-2004; see ¶ 70,002.58.
FAC 2001-19, 69 FR 1050, 1-7-2003; see ¶ 70,002.57.
FAC 2001-18, 68 FR 69226, 12-11-2003; see ¶ 70,002.56.
FAC 2001-17, 68 FR 59999, 10-20-2003; see ¶ 70,002.55.
FAC 2001-16, 68 FR 56667, 10-1-2003; see ¶ 70,002.54.
FAC 2001-15, 68 FR 43853, 7-24-2003; see ¶ 70,002.53.
FAC 2001-14, 68 FR 28077, 5-22-2003; see ¶ 70,002.52.
FAC 2001-13, 68 FR 13199, 3-18-2003; see ¶ 70,002.51.
FAC 2001-12, 68 FR 4047, 1-27-2003; see ¶ 70,002.50.
FAC 2001-11; 67 FR 80319, 12-31-2002; see ¶ 70,002.49.
FAC 2001-10; 67 FR 70515, 11-22-2002; see ¶ 70,002.48.
FAC 2001-09; 67 FR 56115, 8-30-2002; see ¶ 70,002.47.
FAC 2001-08; 67 FR 43511, 6-27-2002; see ¶ 70,002.46.
FAC 2001-07, 67 FR 21531, 4-30-2002; see ¶ 70,002.45.
FAC 2001-06, 67 FR 13048, 3-20-2002; see ¶ 70,002.44.
Interim rule, 67 FR 10528, 3-7-2002; see ¶ 70,002.43.
FAC 2001-04, 67 FR 6112, 2-8-2002; see ¶ 70,002.42.
FAC 2001-01 Correcting Amendments, 67 FR 1857, 1-14-2002; see ¶ 70,002.41.
FAC 2001-03, 66 FR 66984, 12-27-2001; see ¶ 70,002.40.
FAC 2001-02, 66 FR 65347, 12-18-2001; see ¶ 70,002.39.
FAC 2001-01, 66 FR 53478, 10-22-2001; see ¶ 70,002.38.
FAC 97-26, 66 FR 27405, 5-16-2001; see ¶ 70,002.37.
FAC 97-25, 66 FR 22081, 5-2-2001; see ¶ 70,002.36.
FAC 97-27, 66 FR 20894, 4-25-2001; see ¶ 70,002.35.
FAC 97-24, 66 FR 17753, 4-3-2001; see ¶ 70,002.34.
FAC 97-23, 66 FR 5345, 1-18-2001; see ¶ 70,002.33.

FAC 97-22, 66 FR 2116, 1-10-2001; see ¶ 70,002.32; corrected 66 FR 27011, 5-15-2001.

FAC 97-21, 65 FR 80255, 12-20-2000; see ¶ 70,002.31.

FAC 97-20, 65 FR 60542, 10-11-2000; see ¶ 70,002.30.

FAC 97-19, 65 FR 46052, 7-26-2000; see ¶ 70,002.29.

FAC 97-18, 65 FR 36014, 6-6-2000; see ¶ 70,002.28.

FAC 97-17, 65 FR 24316, 4-25/2000; see ¶ 70,002.27.

FAC 97-16, 65 FR 16274, 3-27/2000; see ¶ 70,002.26.

FAC 97-15, 64 FR 72414, 12-27-99, corrected 65 FR 4633, 1-31-2000; see ¶ 70,002.25.

FAC 97-14, 64 FR 51828, 9-24-99; see ¶ 70,002.24.

FAC 97-13, 64 FR 36222, 7-2-99; see ¶ 70,002.23.

FAC 97-12, 64 FR 32740, 6-17-99; see ¶ 70,002.22.

FAC 97-11, 64 FR 10530, 3-4-99; see ¶ 70,002.21; corrected 64 FR 30103, 6-4-99.

Interim rule, 63 FR 71721, 12-29-98; see ¶ 70,002.20.

FAC 97-10, 63 FR 70264, 12-18-98, see ¶ 99,999.276; ¶ 70,002.19; corrected 64 FR 3195, 1-20-99.

FAC 97-9, 63 FR 58587, 10-30-98, see ¶ 99,999.238; ¶ 70,002.18.

FAC 97-8, 63 FR 52425, 9-30-98, see ¶ 99,999.224; ¶ 70,002.17.

FAC 97-7, 63 FR 36120, 7-1-98, corrected 63 FR 56738, 10-22-98, see ¶ 99,999.182; ¶ 70,002.16; corrected 12-29-98, effective 1-1-99, ¶ 70,002.20.

FAC 97-6, 63 FR 35719, 6-30-98, see ¶ 99,999.181; ¶ 70,002.15.

FAC 97-5, 63 FR 34058, 6-22-98, see ¶ 99,999.177; ¶ 70,002.14.

FAC 97-4, 63 FR 9048, 2-23-98, see ¶ 99,999.120; ¶ 70,002.13.

FAC 97-3, 62 FR 64912, 12-9-97, see ¶ 99,999.098; ¶ 70,002.12.

Corrections and technical amendments, 62 FR 51379, 10-1-97; ¶ 70,002.11.

FAC 97-2, 62 FR 51224, 9-30-97, see ¶ 99,999.078; ¶ 70,002.10.

FAC 97-1, 62 FR 44802, 8-22-97, see ¶ 99,999.063; ¶ 70,002.09; corrected 62 FR 51379, 10-1-97.

Final rule, 62 FR 40236, 7-25-97, see ¶ 99,999.049; ¶ 70,002.08; corrected 62 FR 51379, 10-1-97.

FAC 90-46, 62 FR 12690, 3-17-97, see ¶ 99,999; ¶ 70,002.07.

FAC 90-45, 62 FR 224, 1-2-97; corrected 62 FR 10709, 3-10-97; see ¶ 99,998.66; ¶ 70,002.06.

FAC 90-44, 61 FR 69286, 12-31-96, see ¶ 99,998.64; ¶ 70,002.05.

FAC 90-43, 61 FR 67408, 12-20-96, see ¶ 99,998.60; ¶ 70,002.04.

FAC 90-42, 61 FR 45769, 8-29-96; see ¶ 99,998.04; ¶ 70,002.03.

FAC 90-41, 61 FR 41466, 8-8-96; see ¶ 99,997.92; ¶ 70,002.02.

FAC 90-40, 61 FR 39186, 7-26-96; see ¶ 99,997.80; ¶ 70,002.

FAC 90-39, 61 FR 31612, 6-20-96; see ¶ 99,997.57; ¶ 70,001.99.

FAC 90-38, 61 FR 18914, 4-29-96; see ¶ 99,997.32; ¶ 70,001.98.

FAC 90-37, 61 FR 2626, 1-26-96; see ¶ 99,996.99; ¶ 70,001.97.

FAC 90-36, 60 FR 67514, 12-29-95; see ¶ 99,996.90; ¶ 70,001.96.

FAC 90-35, 60 FR 64254, 12-14-95; see ¶ 99,996.77; ¶ 70,001.95.

FAC 90-34, 60 FR 55306, 10-30-95; see ¶ 99,996.56; ¶ 70,001.94.

FAC 90-33, 60 FR 49706, 9-26-95; see ¶ 99,996.29; ¶ 70,001.93.

FAC 90-32, 60 FR 48206, 9-18-95; see ¶ 99,996.27; ¶ 70,001.92.

FAC 90-31, 60 FR 42648, 8-16-95; see ¶ 99,996.07; ¶ 70,001.91.

FAC 90-30, 60 FR 37772, 7-21-95; see ¶ 70,001.90.
FAC 90-29, 60 FR 34732, 7-3-95; see ¶ 70,001.89.
FAC 90-28, 60 FR 33064, 6-26-95; see ¶ 70,001.88.
FAC 90-27, 60 FR 28492, 5-31-95; see ¶ 70,001.87.
FAC 90-26, 60 FR 16718, 3-31-95; see ¶ 70,001.86.
FAC 90-25, 60 FR 3314, 1-13-95; corrected 60 FR 7133, 2-7-95; see ¶ 70,001.85.
FAC 90-24, 59 FR 64784, 12-15-94; see ¶ 70,001.84.
FAC 90-23, 59 FR 67010, 12-28-94; see ¶ 70,001.83.
FAC 90-22, 59 FR 62498, 12-5-94; see ¶ 70,001.82.
FAC 90-21, 59 FR 53716, 10-25-94; corrected, 59 FR 60319, 11-23-94; see ¶ 70,001.81.
FAC 90-20, 59 FR 11368, 3-10-94; corrected, 59 FR 17722, 4-14-94; see ¶ 70,001.80.
FAC 90-19, 59 FR 544, 1-5-94; see ¶ 70,001.79.
FAC 90-18, 58 FR 31140, 5-28-93; see ¶ 70,001.78.
FAC 90-17, 58 FR 12140, 3-2-93; see ¶ 70,001.77.
FAC 90-16, 57 FR 60570, 12-21-92; see ¶ 70,001.76.
FAC 90-15, 57 FR 55470, 11-25-92; see ¶ 70,001.75.
FAC 90-14, 57 FR 48470, 10-26-92; see ¶ 70,001.74.
FAC 90-13, 57 FR 44259, 9-24-92; see ¶ 70,001.73.
FAC 90-12, 57 FR 39586, 8-31-92; see ¶ 70,001.72.
FAC 90-11, 57 FR 20373, 5-12-92; see ¶ 70,001.71.
FAC 90-10, 56 FR 67412, 12-30-91; see ¶ 70,001.70.
FAC 90-9, 56 FR 67126, 12-27-91; see ¶ 70,001.69.
FAC 90-8, 56 FR 55370, 10-25-91; see ¶ 70,001.68.
FAC 90-7, 56 FR 41728, 8-22-91; see ¶ 70,001.67.
FAC 90-6, 56 FR 37259, 8-5-91; see ¶ 70,001.66.
FAC 90-5, 56 FR 29124, 6-25-91; see ¶ 70,001.65.
FAC 90-4, 56 FR 15142, 4-15-91; see ¶ 70,001.64.
FAC 90-3, 55 FR 52782, 12-21-90; see ¶ 70,001.63.
FAC 90-2, 55 FR 49852, 11-30-90; see ¶ 70,001.62.
FAC 90-1, 55 FR 42684, 10-22-90; see ¶ 70,001.61.
FAC 84-60, 55 FR 36782, 9-6-90; see ¶ 70,001.60.
FAC 84-59, 55 FR 34864, 8-24-90; see ¶ 70,001.59.
FAC 84-58, 55 FR 25522, 6-21-90; see ¶ 70,001.58.
FAC 84-57, 55 FR 21706, 5-25-90; see ¶ 70,001.57.
FAC 84-56, 55 FR 3878, 2-5-90; see ¶ 70,001.56.
FAC 84-55, 55 FR 3190, 1-30-90; see ¶ 70,001.55.
FAC 84-54, 54 FR 50718, 12-8-89; see ¶ 70,001.54.
FAC 84-53, 54 FR 48978, 11-28-89; see ¶ 70,001.53.
FAC 84-52, 54 FR 46004, 10-31-89; see ¶ 70,001.52.
FAC 84-51, 54 FR 34750, 8-21-89; see ¶ 70,001.51.
FAC 84-50, 54 FR 30708, 7-21-89; see ¶ 70,001.50.
FAC 84-49, 54 FR 29278, 7-11-89; see ¶ 70,001.49.
FAC 84-48, 54 FR 25060, 6-12-89; see ¶ 70,001.48.
FAC 84-47, 54 FR 20488, 5-11-89; see ¶ 70,001.47.
FAC 84-46, 54 FR 19812, 5-8-89; see ¶ 70,001.46.
FAC 84-45, 54 FR 13332, 3-31-89; see ¶ 70,001.45.
FAC 84-44, 54 FR 13022, 3-29-89; see ¶ 70,001.44.

FAC 84-43, 54 FR 4967, 1-31-89; see ¶ 70,001.43.
FAC 84-42, 54 FR 5052, 1-31-89; see ¶ 70,001.42.
FAC 84-41, 54 FR 53340, 12-30-88; see ¶ 70,001.41.
FAC 84-40, 53 FR 43386, 10-26-88; see ¶ 70,001.40.
FAC 84-39, 53 FR 34224, 9-2-88; see ¶ 70,001.39.
FAC 84-38, 53 FR 27460, 7-20-88; see ¶ 70,001.38.
FAC 84-37, 53 FR 17854, 5-18-88; see ¶ 70,001.37.
FAC 84-36, 53 FR 12128, 4-12-88; see ¶ 70,001.36.
FAC 84-35, 53 FR 10828, 4-1-88; see ¶ 70,001.35.
FAC 84-34, 53 FR 4934, 2-18-88; see ¶ 70,001.34.
FAC 84-33, 53 FR 3688, 2-8-88; see ¶ 70,001.33.
FAC 84-32, 53 FR 660, 1-11-88; see ¶ 70,001.32.
FAC 84-31, 52 FR 38188, 10-14-87; see ¶ 70,001.31.
FAC 84-30, 52 FR 35612, 9-22-87; see ¶ 70,001.30.
FAC 84-29, 52 FR 30074, 8-12-87; see ¶ 70,001.29.
FAC 84-28, 52 FR 21884, 6-9-87; see ¶ 70,001.28.
FAC 84-27, 52 FR 18140, 5-13-87; see ¶ 70,001.27.
FAC 84-26, 52 FR 19800, 5-27-87; see ¶ 70,001.26.
FAC 84-25, 52 FR 9036, 3-20-87; see ¶ 70,001.25.
FAC 84-24, 52 FR 6120, 2-27-87; see ¶ 70,001.24.
FAC 84-23, 51 FR 36970, 10-16-86; see ¶ 70,001.23.
FAC 84-22, 51 FR 30618, 8-27-86; see ¶ 70,001.22.
FAC 84-21, 51 FR 31424, 9-3-86; see ¶ 70,001.21.
FAC 84-20, 51 FR 29188, 8-14-86; see ¶ 70,001.20.
FAC 84-19, 51 FR 27488, 7-31-86; see ¶ 70,001.19.
FAC 84-18, 51 FR 27115, 7-29-86; see ¶ 70,001.18.
FAC 84-17, 51 FR 16802, 5-6-86; see ¶ 70,001.17.
FAC 84-16, 51 FR 19712, 5-30-86; see ¶ 70,001.16.
FAC 84-15, 51 FR 12296, 4-9-86; see ¶ 70,001.15.
FAC 84-14, 51 FR 12292, 4-9-86; see ¶ 70,001.14.
FAC 84-13, 50 FR 52428, 12-23-85; see ¶ 70,001.13.
FAC 84-12, 51 FR 2648, 1-17-86; see ¶ 70,001.12.
FAC 84-11, 50 FR 35474, 8-30-85; see ¶ 70,001.11.
FAC 84-10, 50 FR 27560, 7-3-85; see ¶ 70,001.10.
FAC 84-9, 50 FR 25680, 6-20-85; see ¶ 70,001.09.
FAC 84-8, 50 FR 26902, 6-28-85; see ¶ 70,001.08.
FAC 84-7, 50 FR 23604, 6-4-85; see ¶ 70,001.07.
FAC 84-6, 50 FR 2268, 1-15-85; see ¶ 70,001.06.
FAC 84-5, 50 FR 1726, 1-11-85; see ¶ 70,001.05.
FAC 84-4, 49 FR 34487, 8-31-84; see ¶ 70,001.04.
FAC 84-3, 49 FR 26740, 6-29-84; see ¶ 70,001.03.
FAC 84-2, 49 FR 18278, 4-27-84; see ¶ 70,001.02.
FAC 84-1, 49 FR 12997, 3-30-84; see ¶ 70,001.01.

Note: The ¶ 70, ___._ citations in the Sources list refer to the location of the source documents in **Government Contracts Reporter**, which is also available from **Wolters Kluwer Law and Business**.

Federal Acquisition Regulation Parts 1—12 General Acquisition Planning

Table of Contents

Page

SUBCHAPTER A—GENERAL

Part 1—Federal Acquisition Regulations System 19
Part 2—Definitions of Words and Terms 43
Part 3—Improper Business Practices and Personal Conflicts of Interest 73
Part 4—Administrative and Information Matters 113

SUBCHAPTER B—ACQUISITION PLANNING

Part 5—Publicizing Contract Actions 159
Part 6—Competition Requirements 179
Part 7—Acquisition Planning 197
Part 8—Required Sources of Supplies and Services 219
Part 9—Contractor Qualifications 255
Part 10—Market Research 301
Part 11—Describing Agency Needs 307
Part 12—Acquisition of Commercial Items 325

PART 1—FEDERAL ACQUISITION REGULATIONS SYSTEM

Table of Contents

Scope of part 1.000

Subpart 1.1—Purpose, Authority, Issuance

Purpose 1.101
Statement of guiding principles for the Federal Acquisition System 1.102
Discussion 1.102-1
Performance standards 1.102-2
Acquisition team 1.102-3
Role of the acquisition team 1.102-4
Authority 1.103
Applicability 1.104
Issuance 1.105
Publication and code arrangement 1.105-1
Arrangement of regulations 1.105-2
Copies 1.105-3
OMB approval under the Paperwork Reduction Act 1.106
Certifications 1.107
FAR conventions 1.108
Statutory acquisition-related dollar thresholds—adjustment for inflation 1.109
Positive law codification 1.110

Subpart 1.2—Administration

Maintenance of the FAR 1.201
The two councils 1.201-1
FAR Secretariat 1.201-2
Agency compliance with the FAR 1.202

Subpart 1.3—Agency Acquisition Regulations

Policy 1.301
Limitations 1.302
Publication and codification 1.303
Agency control and compliance procedures 1.304

Subpart 1.4—Deviations from the FAR

Scope of subpart 1.400
Definition 1.401
Policy 1.402
Individual deviations 1.403
Class deviations 1.404
Deviations pertaining to treaties and executive agreements 1.405

Subpart 1.5—Agency and Public Participation

Solicitation of agency and public views 1.501
Definition 1.501-1
Opportunity for public comments 1.501-2
Exceptions 1.501-3
Unsolicited proposed revisions 1.502
Public meetings 1.503

Subpart 1.6—Career Development, Contracting Authority, and Responsibilities

General 1.601
Contracting officers 1.602
Authority 1.602-1
Responsibilities 1.602-2
Ratification of unauthorized commitments 1.602-3

Selection, appointment, and termination of appointment for contracting officers 1.603
General 1.603-1
Selection 1.603-2
Appointment 1.603-3
Termination 1.603-4
Contracting Officer's Representative (COR) 1.604

Subpart 1.7—Determinations and Findings

Scope of subpart 1.700
Definition 1.701
General 1.702
Class determinations and findings 1.703
Content 1.704
Supersession and modification 1.705
Expiration 1.706
Signatory authority 1.707

FEDERAL ACQUISITION REGULATION (FAR)

SUBCHAPTER A—GENERAL (Parts 1-4)

PART 1—FEDERAL ACQUISITION REGULATIONS SYSTEM

1.000 Scope of part.

This part sets forth basic policies and general information about the Federal Acquisition Regulations System including purpose, authority, applicability, issuance, arrangement, numbering, dissemination, implementation, supplementation, maintenance, administration, and deviation. Subparts 1.2, 1.3, and 1.4 prescribe administrative procedures for maintaining the FAR System.

SUBPART 1.1—PURPOSE, AUTHORITY, ISSUANCE

1.101 Purpose.

The Federal Acquisition Regulations System is established for the codification and publication of uniform policies and procedures for acquisition by all executive agencies. The Federal Acquisition Regulations System consists of the Federal Acquisition Regulation (FAR), which is the primary document, and agency acquisition regulations that implement or supplement the FAR. The FAR System does not include internal agency guidance of the type described in 1.301(a)(2).

[FAC 84-18, 51 FR 27116, 7/29/86, effective 7/30/86]

1.102 Statement of guiding principles for the Federal Acquisition System.

(a) The vision for the Federal Acquisition System is to deliver on a timely basis the best value product or service to the customer, while maintaining the public's trust and fulfilling public policy objectives. Participants in the acquisition process should work together as a team and should be empowered to make decisions within their area of responsibility.

(b) The Federal Acquisition System will—

(1) Satisfy the customer in terms of cost, quality, and timeliness of the delivered product or service by, for example—

(i) Maximizing the use of commercial products and services;

(ii) Using contractors who have a track record of successful past performance or who demonstrate a current superior ability to perform; and

(iii) Promoting competition;

(2) Minimize administrative operating costs;

(3) Conduct business with integrity, fairness, and openness; and

(4) Fulfill public policy objectives.

(c) The Acquisition Team consists of all participants in Government acquisition including not only representatives of the technical, supply, and procurement communities but also the customers they serve, and the contractors who provide the products and services.

(d) The role of each member of the Acquisition Team is to exercise personal initiative and sound business judgment in providing the best value product or service to meet the customer's needs. In exercising initiative, Government members of the Acquisition Team may assume if a specific strategy, practice, policy or procedure is in the best interests of the Government and is not addressed in the FAR, nor prohibited by law (statute or case law), Executive order or other regulation, that the strategy, practice, policy or procedure is a permissible exercise of authority.

[FAC 90-29, 60 FR 34732, 7/3/95, effective 7/3/95]

1.102-1 Discussion.

(a) *Introduction*. The statement of Guiding Principles for the Federal Acquisition System (System) represents a concise statement designed to be user-friendly for all participants in Government acquisition. The following discussion of the principles is provided in order to illuminate the meaning of the terms and phrases used. The framework for the System includes the Guiding Principles for the System and the supporting policies and procedures in the FAR.

(b) *Vision.* All participants in the System are responsible for making acquisition decisions that deliver the best value product or service to the customer. Best value must be viewed from a broad perspective and is achieved by balancing the many competing interests in the System. The result is a system which works better and costs less.

[FAC 90-29, 60 FR 34732, 7/3/95, effective 7/3/95]

1.102-2 Performance standards.

(a) *Satisfy the customer in terms of cost, quality, and timeliness of the delivered product or service.*

(1) The principal customers for the product or service provided by the System are the users and line managers, acting on behalf of the American taxpayer.

(2) The System must be responsive and adaptive to customer needs, concerns, and feedback. Implementation of acquisition policies and procedures, as well as consideration of timeliness, quality, and cost throughout the process, must take into account the perspective of the user of the product or service.

(3) When selecting contractors to provide products or perform services, the Government will use contractors who have a track record of successful past performance or who demonstrate a current superior ability to perform.

(4) The Government must not hesitate to communicate with the commercial sector as early as possible in the acquisition cycle to help the Government determine the capabilities available in the commercial marketplace. The Government will maximize its use of commercial products and services in meeting Government requirements.

(5) It is the policy of the System to promote competition in the acquisition process.

(6) The System must perform in a timely, high quality, and cost effective manner.

(7) All members of the Team are required to employ planning as an integral part of the overall process of acquiring products or services. Although advance planning is required, each member of the Team must be flexible in order to accommodate changing or unforeseen mission needs. Planning is a tool for the accomplishment of tasks, and application of its discipline should be commensurate with the size and nature of a given task.

(b) *Minimize administrative operating costs.*

(1) In order to ensure that maximum efficiency is obtained, rules, regulations, and policies should be promulgated only when their benefits clearly exceed the costs of their development, implementation, administration, and enforcement. This applies to internal administrative processes, including reviews, and to rules and procedures applied to the contractor community.

(2) The System must provide uniformity where it contributes to efficiency or where fairness or predictability is essential. The System should also, however, encourage innovation, and local adaptation where uniformity is not essential.

(c) *Conduct business with integrity, fairness, and openness.*

(1) An essential consideration in every aspect of the System is maintaining the public's trust. Not only must the System have integrity, but the actions of each member of the Team must reflect integrity, fairness, and openness. The foundation of integrity within the System is a competent, experienced, and well-trained, professional workforce. Accordingly, each member of the Team is responsible and accountable for the wise use of public resources as well as acting in a manner which maintains the public's trust. Fairness and openness require open communication among team members, internal and external customers, and the public.

(2) To achieve efficient operations, the System must shift its focus from "risk avoidance" to one of "risk management." The cost to the taxpayer of attempting to eliminate all risk is prohibitive. The Executive Branch will accept and manage the risk associated with empowering local procurement officials to take independent action based on their professional judgment.

(3) The Government shall exercise discretion, use sound business judgment, and comply with applicable laws and regulations in

dealing with contractors and prospective contractors. All contractors and prospective contractors shall be treated fairly and impartially but need not be treated the same.

(d) *Fulfill public policy objectives*. The System must support the attainment of public policy goals adopted by the Congress and the President. In attaining these goals, and in its overall operations, the process shall ensure the efficient use of public resources.

[FAC 90-29, 60 FR 34732, 7/3/95, effective 7/3/95; FAC 97-2, 62 FR 51224, 9/30/97, effective 10/10/97]

1.102-3 Acquisition team.

The purpose of defining the Federal Acquisition Team (Team) in the Guiding Principles is to ensure that participants in the System are identified beginning with the customer and ending with the contractor of the product or service. By identifying the team members in this manner, teamwork, unity of purpose, and open communication among the members of the Team in sharing the vision and achieving the goal of the System are encouraged. Individual team members will participate in the acquisition process at the appropriate time.

[FAC 90-29, 60 FR 34732, 7/3/95, effective 7/3/95]

1.102-4 Role of the acquisition team.

(a) Government members of the Team must be empowered to make acquisition decisions within their areas of responsibility, including selection, negotiation, and administration of contracts consistent with the Guiding Principles. In particular, the contracting officer must have the authority to the maximum extent practicable and consistent with law, to determine the application of rules, regulations, and policies, on a specific contract.

(b) The authority to make decisions and the accountability for the decision made will be delegated to the lowest level within the System, consistent with law.

(c) The Team must be prepared to perform the functions and duties assigned. The Government is committed to provide training, professional development, and other resources necessary for maintaining and improving the knowledge, skills, and abilities for all Government participants on the Team, both with regard to their particular area of responsibility within the System, and their respective role as a team member. The contractor community is encouraged to do likewise.

(d) The System will foster cooperative relationships between the Government and its contractors consistent with its overriding responsibility to the taxpayers.

(e) The FAR outlines procurement policies and procedures that are used by members of the Acquisition Team. If a policy or procedure, or a particular strategy or practice, is in the best interest of the Government and is not specifically addressed in the FAR, nor prohibited by law (statute or case law), Executive order or other regulation, Government members of the Team should not assume it is prohibited. Rather, absence of direction should be interpreted as permitting the Team to innovate and use sound business judgment that is otherwise consistent with law and within the limits of their authority. Contracting officers should take the lead in encouraging business process innovations and ensuring that business decisions are sound.

[FAC 90-29, 60 FR 34732, 7/3/95, effective 7/3/95; FAC 97-1, 62 FR 44802, 8/22/97, effective 10/21/97]

1.103 Authority.

(a) The development of the FAR System is in accordance with the requirements of 41 U.S.C. chapter 13, Acquisition Councils.

(b) The FAR is prepared, issued, and maintained, and the FAR System is prescribed jointly by the Secretary of Defense, the Administrator of General Services, and the Administrator, National Aeronautics and Space Administration, under their several statutory authorities.

[FAC 84-18, 51 FR 27116, 7/29/86, effective 7/30/86; FAC 90-29, 60 FR 34732, 7/3/95, effective 7/3/95; FAC 97-18, 65 FR 36014, 6/6/2000, effective 6/6/2000; FAC 2005-73, 79 FR 24192, 4/29/2014, effective 5/29/2014]

1.104 Applicability.

The FAR applies to all acquisitions as defined in Part 2 of the FAR, except where expressly excluded.

[FAC 90-29, 60 FR 34732, 7/3/95, effective 7/3/95]

1.105 Issuance. (No Text)

1.105-1 Publication and code arrangement.

(a) The FAR is published in—

(1) the daily issue of the *Federal Register*;

(2) cumulated form in the *Code of Federal Regulations* (CFR); and

(3) a separate loose-leaf edition.

(b) The FAR is issued as Chapter 1 of Title 48, CFR. Subsequent chapters are reserved for agency acquisition regulations that implement or supplement the FAR (see Subpart 1.3). The CFR Staff will assign chapter numbers to requesting agencies.

(c) Each numbered unit or segment (*e.g.*, part, subpart, section, etc.) of an agency acquisition regulation that is codified in the CFR shall begin with the chapter number. However, the chapter number assigned to the FAR will not be included in the numbered units or segments of the FAR.

[FAC 90-29, 60 FR 34732, 7/3/95, effective 7/3/95]

1.105-2 Arrangement of regulations.

(a) *General.* The FAR is divided into subchapters, parts (each of which covers a separate aspect of acquisition), subparts, sections, and subsections.

(b) *Numbering.*

(1) The numbering system permits the discrete identification of every FAR paragraph. The digits to the left of the decimal point represent the part number. The numbers to the right of the decimal point and to the left of the dash represent, in order, the subpart (one or two digits), and the section (two digits). The number to the right of the dash represents the subsection. Subdivisions may be used at the section and subsection level to identify individual paragraphs. The following example illustrates the makeup of a FAR number citation (note that subchapters are not used with citations):

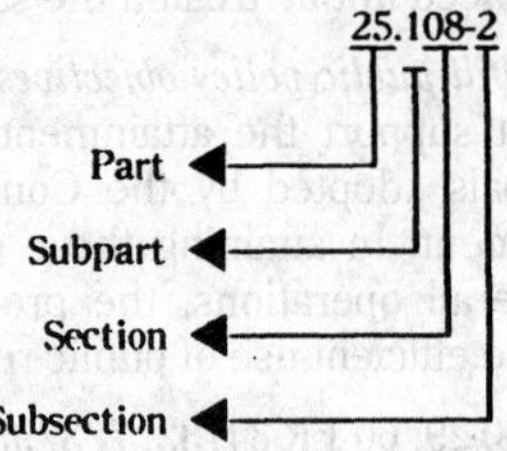

(2) Subdivisions below the section or subsection level consist of parenthetical alpha numerics using the following sequence: (a) (1) (i) (A) (*1*) (*i*).

(c) *References and citations.*

(1) Unless otherwise stated, cross-references indicate parts, subparts, sections, subsections, paragraphs, subparagraphs, or subdivisions of this regulation.

(2) This regulation may be referred to as the Federal Acquisition Regulation or the FAR.

(3) Using the FAR coverage at 9.106-4(d) as a typical illustration, reference to the—

(i) Part would be "FAR part 9" outside the FAR and "part 9" within the FAR.

(ii) Subpart would be "FAR subpart 9.1" outside the FAR and "subpart 9.1" within the FAR.

(iii) Section would be "FAR 9.106" outside the FAR and "9.106" within the FAR.

(iv) Subsection would be "FAR 9.106-4" outside the FAR and "9.106-4" within the FAR.

(v) Paragraph would be "FAR 9.106-4(d)" outside the FAR and "9.106-4(d)" within the FAR.

(4) Citations of authority (*e.g.*, statutes or Executive orders) in the FAR shall follow the Federal Register form guides.

[FAC 90-29, 60 FR 34732, 7/3/95, effective 7/3/95; FAC 97-18, 65 FR 36014, 6/6/2000, effective 8/7/2000; FAC 2005-60, 77 FR 44065, 7/26/2012, effective 7/26/2012]

1.105-3 Copies.

Copies of the FAR in CFR form may be purchased from the Bookstore of the Government Publishing Office (GPO), Washington, DC 20402.

[FAC 90-29, 60 FR 34732, 7/3/95, effective 7/3/95; Final rule, 62 FR 40236, 7/25/97, effective 6/30/97; FAC 2019-02, 84 FR 19839, 5/6/2019, effective 5/6/2019]

1.106 OMB Approval under the Paperwork Reduction Act.

The Paperwork Reduction Act of 1980 (44 U.S.C. chapter 35) imposes a requirement on Federal agencies to obtain approval from the Office of Management and Budget (OMB) before collecting information from 10 or more members of the public. The information collection and recordkeeping requirements contained in this regulation have been approved by the OMB. The following OMB control numbers apply:

FAR segment	OMB Control Number
3.103	9000-0018
3.11	9000-0183
4.102	9000-0033
4.5	9000-0137
4.605	9000-0145
4.607	9000-0145
4.7	9000-0034
4.9	9000-0097
4.14	9000-0177
4.17	9000-0179
4.21	9000-0199
5.405	9000-0036
7.2	9000-0082
8.5	9000-0113
9.1	9000-0011
9.2	9000-0083
14.201	9000-0034
14.202-4	9000-0040
14.202-5	9000-0039
14.205	9000-0037
14.407	9000-0038
14.5	9000-0041
15.2	9000-0037
15.209	9000-0034
15.4	9000-0013
15.404-1(f)	9000-0080
15.407-2	9000-0078
15.408	9000-0115
19.7	9000–0192, 9000–0006, and 9000–0007
22.5	9000-0175
22.8	1250-0003
22.11	9000-0066
22.12	1235-0007 and 1235-0025
22.14	1250-0005
22.16	1245-0004
22.17	9000-0188
22.103	9000-0065
23.602	9000-0107
24.3	9000-0182
25.302	9000-0184
27.2	9000-0096
27.3	9000-0095
27.4	9000-0090
28.1	9000-0045
28.2	9000-0045
29.304	9000-0059
30.6	9000-0129
31.205-46	9000-0079
31.205-46(a)(3)	9000-0088
32.000	9000-0138
32.1	9000-0070
	9000-0138
32.2	9000-0138
32.4	9000-0073
32.5	9000-0010
	9000-0138
32.7	9000-0074
32.9	9000-0102
32.10	9000-0138
33	9000-0035
36.213-2	9000-0037
36.603	9000-0157
41.202(c)	9000-0125
42.205(f)	9000-0026
42.7	9000-0013
42.12	9000-0076
42.13	9000-0076
42.15	9000-0142
43.205(f)	9000-0026
44.305	9000-0132
45	9000-0075
46	9000-0077
47	9000-0061
47.208	9000-0056
48	9000-0027
49	9000-0028
50	9000-0029
51.1	9000-0031
51.2	9000-0032
52.203-2	9000-0018
52.203-7	9000-0091
52.203-13	9000-0164
52.203-16	9000-0183
52.204-3	9000-0097
52.204-6	9000-0145
52.204-7	9000-0159
52.204-10	9000-0177
52.204-12	9000-0145
52.204-13	9000-0159
52.204-14	9000-0179
52.204-15	9000-0179
52.204-16	9000-0185
52.204-17	9000-0185
52.204-18	9000-0185
52.204-18	9000-0185
52.204-20	9000-0189
52.204-23	9000-0197
52.204-24	9000-0199
52.204-25	9000-0199
52.207-3	9000-0114
52.207-4	9000-0082
52.209-1	9000-0083
52.209-2	9000-0190
52.209-5	9000-0094

FAR segment	OMB Control Number
52.209-6	9000-0094
52.209-9	9000-0174
52.209-10	9000-0190
52.209–11	9000–0193
52.209–12	9000–0193
52.209–13	9000–0198
52.211-8	9000-0043
52.211-9	9000-0043
52.211-7	9000-0153
52.212-3	9000-0136
52.212-3 (h)	9000-0094
52.212-5	9000-0034
52.214-14	9000-0047
52.214-15	9000-0044
52.214-16	9000-0044
52.214-21	9000-0039
52.214-26	9000-0034
52.214-28	9000-0013
52.215-1 (c) (2) (iv)	9000-0048
52.215-1 (d)	9000-0044
52.215-2	9000-0034
52.215-6	9000-0047
52.215-9	9000-0078
52.215-12	9000-0013
52.215-13	9000-0013
52.215-14	9000-0080
52.215-19	9000-0015
52.215-20	9000-0013
52.215-21	9000-0013
52.215-22	9000-0173
52.215-23	9000-0173
52.216-2	9000-0068
52.216-3	9000-0068
52.216-4	9000-0068
52.216-5	9000-0071
52.216-6	9000-0071
52.216-7	9000-0069
52.216-10	9000-0067
52.216-15	9000-0069
52.216-16	9000-0067
52.216-17	9000-0067
52.219-9	9000–0192, 9000–0006, and 9000–0007
52.219-10	9000-0006
52.219-28	9000-0163
52.219-29	3245-0374
52.219-30	3245-0374
52.222-2	9000-0065
52.222-4	1235-0023
52.222-6	1235-0023
52.222-8	1235-0008 1235-0018
52.222-11	9000-0014
52.222-17	1235-0007 and 1235-0025
52.222-18	9000-0155
52.222-21	1250-0003
52.222-22	1250-0003
52.222-23	1250-0003
52.222-25	1250-0003
52.222-26	1250-0001, 1250-0003, and 1250-0008
52.222-27	1250-0003
52.222-32	9000-0154
52.222-35	1250-0004
52.222-36	1250-0005
52.222-37	1250-0004
52.222-38	1293-0005
52.222-40	1245-0004
52.222-41	1235-0018 1235-0007
52.222-46	9000-0066
52.222-50	9000-0188
52.222-54	1615-0092
52.222-55	1235-0018
52.222-56	9000-0188
52.222-62	1235-0018, 1235-0021, 1235-0029
52.223-2	9000-0180
52.223-4	9000-0134
52.223-5	9000-0147
52.223-6 (b) (5)	9000-0101
52.223-7	9000-0107
52.223-9	9000-0134
52.223-11	9000-0191
52.223-12	9000-0191
52.223-22	9000-0194
52.224-3	9000-0182
52.225-2	9000-0024
52.225-4	9000-0024
52.225-6	9000-0024
52.225-8	9000-0022
52.225-9	9000-0024
52.225-10	9000-0024
52.225-11	9000-0024
52.225-12	9000-0024
52.225-21	9000-0024
52.225-23	9000-0024
52.225-26	9000-0184
52.227-2	9000-0096
52.227-6	9000-0096
52.227-9	9000-0096
52.227-11	9000-0095
52.227-13	9000-0095
52.227-18	9000-0161
52.227-15	9000-0090
52.227-16	9000-0090
52.227-17	9000-0090
52.227-18	9000-0090
52.227-19	9000-0090
52.227-20	9000-0090
52.227-21	9000-0090
52.227-22	9000-0090
52.227-23	9000-0090
52.228-1	9000-0045
52.228-2	9000-0045
52.228-12	9000-0135
52.228-13	9000-0045
52.228-14	9000-0045
52.228-15	9000-0045
52.228-16	9000-0045
52.229-2	9000-0059
52.230-6	9000-0129
52.232-1	9000-0070
52.232-2	9000-0070
52.232-3	9000-0070
52.232-4	9000-0070
52.232-5	9000-0102

FAR segment	OMB Control Number
52.232-6	9000-0070
52.232-7	9000-0070
52.232-8	9000-0070
52.232-9	9000-0070
52.232-10	9000-0070
52.232-11	9000-0070
52.232-12	9000-0073
52.232-13	9000-0010
52.232-14	9000-0010
52.232-15	9000-0010
52.232-16	9000-0010
52.232-20	9000-0074
52.232-22	9000-0074
52.232-27	9000-0102
52.232-29	9000-0138
52.232-30	9000-0138
52.232-31	9000-0138
52.232-32	9000-0138
52.232-33	9000-0144
52.232-34	9000-0144
52.233-1	9000-0035
52.236-5	9000-0062
52.236-13	9000-0060
52.236-15	9000-0058
52.236-19	9000-0064
52.237-10	9000-0152
52.241-3	9000-0122
52.241-7	9000-0123
52.241-1	9000-0126
52.241-13	9000-0124
52.242-5	9000-0196
52.242-13	9000-0108
52.243-1	9000-0026
52.243-2	9000-0026
52.243-3	9000-0026
52.243-4	9000-0026
52.243-6	9000-0026
52.243-7	9000-0026
52.244-2	9000-0149
52.244-2(i)	9000-0132
52.245-1	9000-0075
52.245-9	9000-0075
52.246-2	9000-0077
52.246-3	9000-0077
52.246-4	9000-0077
52.246-5	9000-0077
52.246-6	9000-0077
52.246-7	9000-0077
52.246-8	9000-0077
52.246-12	9000-0077
52.246-15	9000-0077
52.246-26	9000-0187
52.247-2	9000-0053
52.247-6	9000-0061
52.247-29	9000-0061
52.247-30	9000-0061
52.247-31	9000-0061
52.247-32	9000-0061
52.247-33	9000-0061
52.247-34	9000-0061
52.247-35	9000-0061
52.247-36	9000-0061
52.247-37	9000-0061
52.247-38	9000-0061
52.247-39	9000-0061
52.247-40	9000-0061
52.247-41	9000-0061
52.247-42	9000-0061
52.247-43	9000-0061
52.247-44	9000-0061
52.247-48	9000-0061
52.247-51	9000-0057
52.247-52	9000-0061
52.247-53	9000-0055
52.247-57	9000-0061
52.247-63	9000-0054
52.247-64	9000-0061
52.247-68	9000-0056
52.248-1	9000-0027
52.248-2	9000-0027
52.248-3	9000-0027
52.249-2	9000-0028
52.249-3	9000-0028
52.249-5	9000-0028
52.249-6	9000-0028
52.250-1	9000-0029
52.251-2	9000-0032
SF 24	9000-0045
SF 25	9000-0045
SF 25-A	9000-0045
SF 28	9000-0001
SF 34	9000-0045
SF 35	9000-0045
SF 273	9000-0045
SF 274	9000-0045
SF 275	9000-0045
SF 294	9000-0006
SF 295	9000-0007
SF 330	9000-0157
SF 1403	9000-0011
SF 1404	9000-0011
SF 1405	9000-0011
SF 1406	9000-0011
SF 1407	9000-0011
SF 1408	9000-0011
SF 1413	9000-0014
SF 1416	9000-0045
SF 1418	9000-0045
SF 1428	9000-0075
SF 1429	9000-0075
SF 1435	9000-0012
SF 1436	9000-0012
SF 1437	9000-0012
SF 1438	9000-0012
SF 1439	9000-0012
SF 1440	9000-0012
SF 1443	9000-0010
SF 1444	9000-0089
SF 1445	9000-0089
SF 1446	9000-0089
0F 312	9000-0150

[FAC 84-7, 50 FR 23605, 6/4/85, effective 4/30/85; FAC 84-15, 51 FR 12298, 4/9/86, effective 4/7/86; FAC 84-18, 51 FR 27116, 7/29/86, effective 7/30/86; FAC 84-23, 51 FR 36971, 10/16/86, effective 9/30/86; FAC 84-27, 52 FR 18140, 5/13/87, effective 6/1/87; FAC 84-26, 52 FR 19803, 5/27/87, effective 7/30/87; 84-27 52 FR 18150, 5/13/87, effective 6/1/87; FAC 84-29, 52 FR 30076, 8/12/87, effective 8/24/87; FAC

84-30, 9/30/87, effective 9/30/87; FAC 84-34, 53 FR 4934, 2/18/88, effective 2/29/88; FAC 84-39, 53 FR 34226, 9/2/88, effective 10/3/88; FAC 84-43, 54 FR 4968, 1/31/89, effective 3/18/89; FAC 84-45, 54 FR 13333, 3/31/89, effective 4/1/89; FAC 84-46, 54 FR 19813, 5/8/89, effective 6/7/89; FAC 84-47, 54 FR 20491, 5/11/89, effective date delayed to 7/16/89, 54 FR 22282, 5/23/89; Interim rule, FAC 84-48, 54 FR 25061, 6/12/89, effective 6/12/89; FAC 84-49, 54 FR 29280, 7/11/89, effective 8/10/89; FAC 84-54, 54 FR 50718, 12/8/89, effective 12/1/89; FAC 84-58, 55 FR 25525, 6/21/90, effective 7/23/90; FAC 90-3, 55 FR 52788, 12/21/90, effective 1/22/91; FAC 90-4, 56 FR 15148, 4/15/91, effective 5/15/91; FAC 90-23, 59 FR 67010, 12/28/94, effective 12/28/94; FAC 90-29, 60 FR 34732, 7/3/95, effective 7/3/95; FAC 90-31, 60 FR 42648, 8/16/95, effective 8/16/95 and 10/1/95; FAC 90-32, 60 FR 48206, 9/18/95, effective 10/1/95; FAC 90-33, 60 FR 49706, 9/26/95, effective 10/1/95; FAC 90-38, 61 FR 18914, 4/29/96, effective 4/29/96; FAC 90-40, 61 FR 39186, 7/26/96, effective 9/24/96; FAC 90-43, Interim rule, 61 FR 67408, 12/20/96, effective 12/20/96, finalized without change, FAC 97-1, 62 FR 44802, 8/22/97, effective 10/21/97; FAC 90-44, Interim rule, 61 FR 69286, 12/31/96, effective 12/31/96, finalized without change, FAC 97-1, 62 FR 44802, 8/22/97, effective 10/21/97; FAC 90-45, Final rule, 62 FR 224, 1/2/97, effective 1/1/97; FAC 97-1, 62 FR 44802, 8/22/97, effective 10/21/97; FAC 97-2, 62 FR 51224, 9/30/97, effective 10/10/97; FAC 97-4, 63 FR 9048, 2/23/98, effective 4/24/98; FAC 97-6, 63 FR 35719, 6/30/98, effective 6/30/98, finalized without change, FAC 97-13, 7/2/99; FAC 97-7, 63 FR 36120, 7/1/98, effective 1/1/99, finalized without change, FAC 97-13, 7/2/99; FAC 97-9, 63 FR 58587, 10/30/98, effective 10/30/98, finalized without change, FAC 97-12, 64 FR 32740, 6/17/99; FAC 97-10, 63 FR 70264, 12/18/98, effective 1/4/99; FAC 97-11, 64 FR 10530, 3/4/99, effective 3/4/99, 52.212-3 effective 5/3/99, SF 1418 effective 3/4/99; FAC 97-12, 64 FR 32740, 6/17/99, effective 6/17/99; FAC 97-14, 64 FR 51828, 9/24/99, effective 9/24/99; FAC 97-15, 64 FR 72414, 12/27/99, effective 2/25/2000; FAC 97-16, 65 FR 16274, 3/27/2000, effective 3/27/2000; FAC 97-22, 66 FR 2117, 1/10/2001, effective 1/10/2001; FAC 2001-01, 66 FR 53478, 10/22/2001, effective 12/21/2001; FAC 2001-06, 67 FR 13048, 3/20/2002, effective 4/4/2002; FAC 2001-15, 68 FR 43854, 7/24/2003, effective 8/25/2003; FAC 2001-16, Final rule, 68 FR 56669, 10/1/2003, effective 10/1/2003; FAC 2001-18, Final rule, 68 FR 69227, 12/11/2003, effective 1/12/2004, delay of effective date, 6/8/2004; FAC 2001-19, Final rule, 69 FR 1050, 1/7/2004, effective 1/7/2004; FAC 2001-22, Final rule, 69 FR 17741, 4/5/2004, effective 5/5/2004; FAC 2001-25, Final rule, 69 FR 59699, 10/5/2004, effective 11/4/2004; FAC 2005-07, 71 FR 200, 1/3/2006, effective 2/2/2006; FAC 2005-17, 72 FR 27364, 5/15/2007, effective 6/14/2007; FAC 2005-19, 72 FR 46326, 8/17/2007, effective 8/17/2007; FAC 2005-21, 72 FR 63089, 11/7/2007, effective 11/7/2007; FAC 2005-25, 73 FR 21773, 21779, 4/22/2008, effective 4/22/2008; FAC 2005-30, 74 FR 2712, 1/15/2009, effective 2/17/2009; FAC 2005-31, 74 FR 11821, 3/19/2009, effective 4/20/2009; FAC 2005-32, 74 FR 14623, 3/31/2009, effective 3/31/2009; FAC 2005-42, 75 FR 34260, 6/16/2010, effective 7/16/2010; FAC 2005-45, 75 FR 53153, 8/30/2010, effective 10/1/2010; FAC 2005-46, 75 FR 60249, 9/29/2010, effective 9/29/2010; FAC 2005-47, 75 FR 77723, 12/13/2010, effective 12/13/2010; FAC 2005-48, 75 FR 82567, 12/30/2010, effective 1/31/2011; FAC 2005-49, 76 FR 4188, 1/24/2011, effective 1/24/2011; FAC 2005-52, 76 FR 31395, 5/31/2011, effective 5/31/2011; FAC 2005-53, 76 FR 39233, 7/5/2011, effective 8/4/2011; FAC 2005-54, 76 FR 68015, 11/2/2011, effective 11/2/2011; 76 FR 68017, 11/2/2011, effective 12/2/2011; 76 FR 68043, 11/2/2011, effective 11/2/2011; FAC 2005-55, 77 FR 197, 1/3/2012, effective 1/3/2012; FAC 2005-56, 77 FR 12913, 3/2/2012, effective 4/2/2012; FAC 2005-58, 77 FR 23365, 4/18/2012, effective 5/18/2012; FAC 2005-60, 77 FR 44047, 7/26/2012, effective 8/27/2012; FAC 2005-62, 77 FR 69715, 11/20/2012, effective 12/20/2012; FAC 2005-64, 77 FR 75766, 12/21/2012, effective 1/18/2013; FAC

2005-65, 78 FR 6191, 1/29/2013, effective 1/29/2013; FAC 2005-67, 78 FR 37670, 6/21/2013, effective 7/22/2013; FAC 2005-72, 78 FR 80369, 12/31/2013, effective 1/30/2014; FAC 2005-73, 79 FR 24192, 4/29/2014, effective 5/29/2014; FAC 2005-74, 79 FR 31187, 5/30/2014, effective 11/1/2014; FAC 2005-76, 79 FR 43575, 7/25/2014, effective 7/25/2014; FAC 2005-77, 79 FR 61746, 10/14/2014, effective 10/14/2014; 79 FR 61743, 10/14/2014, effective 11/13/2014; FAC 2005-78, 79 FR 70348, 11/25/2014, effective 11/25/2014; FAC 2005-79, 79 FR 74544, 12/15/2014, effective 12/15/2014; FAC 2005-80, 80 FR 4967, 1/29/2015, effective 3/2/2015; FAC 2005-81, 80 FR 19504, 4/10/2015, effective 4/10/2015; FAC 2005-82, 80 FR 26423, 5/7/2015, effective 5/7/2015; FAC 2005-83, 80 FR 38306, 7/2/2015, effective 11/1/2015;FAC 2005-85, 80 FR 75907, 80 FR 75915, 80 FR 75918, 12/4/2015, effective 12/4/2015; FAC 2005-85, 80 FR 75903, 80 FR 75907, 80 FR 75908, 80 FR 75918, 12/4/2015, effective 12/4/2015 and 2/26/2016; FAC 2005-87, 81 FR 11988, 3/7/2016, effective 4/6/2016; FAC 2005-88, 81 FR 30429, 5/16/2016, effective 6/5/2016; 81 FR 30448, 5/16/2016, effective 5/16/2016; FAC 2005-89, 81 FR 45833, 7/14/2016, effective 11/1/2016; FAC 2005-90, 81 FR 58562, 8/25/2016, effective 10/25/2016; FAC 2005-91, 81 FR 67728, 9/30/2016, effective 9/30/2016; FAC 2005-91, 81 FR 67731, 9/30/2016, effective 9/30/2016; FAC 2005-91, 81 FR 67732, 9/30/2016, effective 9/30/2016; FAC 2005-92, 81 FR 83092, 11/18/2016, effective 12/19/2016; FAC 2005-93, 81 FR 91636, 12/16/2016, effective 12/16/2016; FAC 2005-93, 81 FR 91627, 12/16/2016, effective 1/1/2017; FAC 2005-94, 81 FR 93476, 12/20/2016, effective 1/19/2017; FAC 2005-94, 81 FR 93481, 12/20/2016, effective 1/19/2017; FAC 2005-96, 82 FR 51773, 11/8/2017, effective 11/6/2017; FAC 2005-99, 83 FR 28141, 6/15/2018, effective 7/16/2018; FAC 2005-99, 83 FR 28145, 6/15/2018, effective 6/15/2018; FAC 2005-100, 83 FR 42569, 8/22/2018, effective 8/22/2018; FAC 2005-100, 83 FR 42570, 8/22/2018, effective 8/22/2018; FAC 2005-101, 83 FR 48691, 9/26/2018, effective 10/26/2018; FAC 2019-05, 84 FR 40216, 8/13/2019, effective 8/13/2019; FAC 2019-06, 84 FR 47861, 9/10/2019, effective 9/10/2019; FAC 2020-02, 84 FR 64680, 11/22/2019, effective 12/23/2019]

1.107 Certifications.

In accordance with 41 U.S.C. 1304, a new requirement for a certification by a contractor or offeror may not be included in this chapter unless—

(a) The certification requirement is specifically imposed by statute; or

(b) Written justification for such certification is provided to the Administrator for Federal Procurement Policy by the Federal Acquisition Regulatory Council, and the Administrator approves in writing the inclusion of such certification requirement.

[FAC 97-1, 62 FR 44802, 8/22/97, effective 10/21/97; FAC 2005-73, 79 FR 24192, 4/29/2014, effective 5/29/2014]

1.108 FAR conventions.

The following conventions provide guidance for interpreting the FAR:

(a) *Words and terms*. Definitions in Part 2 apply to the entire regulation unless specifically defined in another part, subpart, section, provision, or clause. Words or terms defined in a specific part, subpart, section, provision, or clause have that meaning when used in that part, subpart, section, provision, or clause. Undefined words retain their common dictionary meaning.

(b) *Delegation of authority*. Each authority is delegable unless specifically stated otherwise (see 1.102-4(b)).

(c) *Dollar thresholds*. Unless otherwise specified, a specific dollar threshold for the purpose of applicability is the final anticipated dollar value of the action, including the dollar value of all options. If the action establishes a maximum quantity of supplies or services to be acquired or establishes a ceiling price or establishes the final price to be based on future events, the final anticipated dollar value must be the highest final priced alternative to the Government, including the dollar value of all options.

(d) *Application of FAR changes to solicitations and contracts.* Unless otherwise specified—

(1) FAR changes apply to solicitations issued on or after the effective date of the change;

(2) Contracting officers may, at their discretion, include the FAR changes in solicitations issued before the effective date, provided award of the resulting contract(s) occurs on or after the effective date; and

(3) Contracting officers may, at their discretion, include the changes in any existing contract with appropriate consideration.

(e) *Citations.* When the FAR cites a statute, Executive order, Office of Management and Budget circular, Office of Federal Procurement Policy policy letter, or relevant portion of the Code of Federal Regulations, the citation includes all applicable amendments, unless otherwise stated.

(f) *Imperative sentences.* When an imperative sentence directs action, the contracting officer is responsible for the action, unless another party is expressly cited.

[FAC 97-18, 65 FR 36014, 6/6/2000, effective 8/7/2000]

1.109 Statutory acquisition-related dollar thresholds—adjustment for inflation.

(a) 41 U.S.C. 1908 requires that the FAR Council periodically adjust all statutory acquisition-related dollar thresholds in the FAR for inflation, except as provided in paragraph (c) of this section. This adjustment is calculated every 5 years, starting in October 2005, using the Consumer Price Index (CPI) for all-urban consumers, and supersedes the applicability of any other provision of law that provides for the adjustment of such acquisition-related dollar thresholds.

(b) The statute defines an acquisition-related dollar threshold as a dollar threshold that is specified in law as a factor in defining the scope of the applicability of a policy, procedure, requirement, or restriction provided in that law to the procurement of supplies or services by an executive agency, as determined by the FAR Council.

(c) The statute does not permit escalation of acquisition-related dollar thresholds established by:

(1) 40 U.S.C. chapter 31, subchapter IV, Wage Rate Requirements (Construction);

(2) 41 U.S.C. chapter 67, Service Contract Labor Standards; or

(3) The United States Trade Representative pursuant to the authority of the Trade Agreements Act of 1979 (19 U.S.C. 2511 *et seq.*).

(d) A matrix showing calculation of the most recent escalation adjustments of statutory acquisition-related dollar thresholds is available via the Internet at *http://www.regulations.gov* (search FAR Case 2014-022).

[FAC 2005-13, 71 FR 57363, 9/28/2006, effective 9/28/2006; FAC 2005-45, 75 FR 53129, 8/30/2010, effective 10/1/2010; FAC 2005-73, 79 FR 24192, 4/29/2014, effective 5/29/2014; FAC 2005-83, 80 FR 38293, 7/2/2015, effective 10/1/2015]

1.110 Positive law codification.

(a) Public Law 107-217 revised, codified, and enacted as title 40, United States Code, Public Buildings, Property, and Works, certain general and permanent laws of the United States.

(b) Public Law 111-350 revised, codified, and enacted as title 41, United States Code, Public Contracts, certain general and permanent laws of the United States.

(c) The following table provides cross references between the historical titles of the acts, and the current reference in title 40 or title 41.

Historical title of act	Division/chapter/ subchapter	Title
Anti-Kickback Act	41 U.S.C. chapter 87	Kickbacks.
Brooks Architect-Engineer Act	40 U.S.C. chapter 11	Selection of Architects and Engineers.
Buy American Act	41 U.S.C. chapter 83	Buy American.
Contract Disputes Act of 1978	41 U.S.C. chapter 71	Contract Disputes.
Contract Work Hours and Safety Standards Act	40 U.S.C. chapter 37	Contract Work Hours and Safety Standards.
Davis-Bacon Act	40 U.S.C. chapter 31, Subchapter IV.	Wage Rate Requirements (Construction).
Drug-Free Workplace Act	41 U.S.C. chapter 81	Drug-Free Workplace.
Federal Property and Administrative Services Act of 1949, Title III.	41 U.S.C. Div. C of subtitle I[1]	Procurement.
Javits-Wagner-O'Day Act	41 U.S.C. chapter 85	Committee for Purchase from People Who Are Blind or Severely Disabled.
Miller Act	40 U.S.C. chapter 31, subchapter III.	Bonds.
Office of Federal Procurement Policy Act	41 U.S.C. Div. B of subtitle I[2]	Office of Federal Procurement Policy.
Procurement Integrity Act	41 U.S.C. chapter 21	Restrictions on Obtaining and Disclosing Certain Information.
Service Contract Act of 1965	41 U.S.C. chapter 67	Service Contract Labor Standards.
Truth in Negotiations Act	41 U.S.C. chapter 35	Truthful Cost or Pricing Data.
Walsh-Healey Public Contracts Act	41 U.S.C. chapter 65	Contracts for Materials, Supplies, Articles, and Equipment Exceeding $15,000.

[1] Except sections 3302, 3501(b), 3509, 3906, 4710, and 4711.
[2] Except sections 1704 and 2303.

[FAC 2005-73, 79 FR 24192, 4/29/2014, effective 5/29/2014]

SUBPART 1.2—ADMINISTRATION

1.201 Maintenance of the FAR. (No Text)

1.201-1 The two councils.

(a) Subject to the authorities discussed in 1.103, revisions to the FAR will be prepared and issued through the coordinated action of two councils, the Defense Acquisition Regulations Council (DAR Council) and the Civilian Agency Acquisition Council (CAA Council). Members of these councils shall—

(1) Represent their agencies on a full-time basis;

(2) Be selected for their superior qualifications in terms of acquisition experience and demonstrated professional expertise; and

(3) Be funded by their respective agencies.

(b) The chairperson of the CAA Council shall be the representative of the Administrator of General Services. The other members of this council shall be one each representative from the—

(1) Departments of Agriculture, Commerce, Education, Energy, Health and Human Services, Homeland Security, Housing and Urban Development, Interior, Justice, Labor, State, Transportation, Treasury, and Veterans Affairs; and

(2) Environmental Protection Agency, National Aeronautics and Space Administration, Social Security Administration, Small Business Administration, and U.S. Agency for International Development.

(c) The Director of the DAR Council shall be the representative of the Secretary of Defense. The operation of the DAR Council will be as prescribed by the Secretary of Defense.

Membership shall include representatives of the military departments, the Defense Logistics Agency, and the Defense Contract Management Agency.

(d) Responsibility for processing revisions to the FAR is apportioned by the two councils so that each council has cognizance over specified parts or subparts.

(e) Each council shall be responsible for—

(1) Agreeing on all revisions with the other council;

(2) Submitting to the FAR Secretariat (see 1.201-2) the information required under paragraphs 1.501-2(b) and (e) for publication in the *Federal Register* of a notice soliciting comments on a proposed revision to the FAR;

(3) Considering all comments received in response to notice of proposed revisions;

(4) Arranging for public meetings;

(5) Preparing any final revision in the appropriate FAR format and language; and

(6) Submitting any final revision to the FAR Secretariat for publication in the *Federal Register* and printing for distribution.

[FAC 84-6, 50 FR 2269, 1/15/85, effective 11/29/84; FAC 84-8, 50 FR 26903, 6/28/85, effective 7/1/85; FAC 84-12, 51 FR 2649, 1/17/86, effective 1/20/86; FAC 84-49, 54 FR 29280, 7/11/89, effective 8/10/89; FAC 97-3, 62 FR 64912, 12/9/97, effective 12/9/97; FAC 97-4, 63 FR 9048, 2/23/98, effective 2/23/98; FAC 97-16, 65 FR 16274, 3/27/2000, effective 3/27/2000; FAC 2001-18, 68 FR 69258, 12/11/2003, effective 12/11/2003; FAC 2005-58, 77 FR 23370, 4/18/2012, effective 4/18/2012; FAC 2019-02, 84 FR 19839, 5/6/2019, effective 5/6/2019; FAC 2019-04, 84 FR 38838, 8/7/2019, effective 8/7/2019]

1.201-2 FAR Secretariat.

(a) The General Services Administration is responsible for establishing and operating the FAR Secretariat to print, publish, and distribute the FAR through the *Code of Federal Regulations* system (including a loose-leaf edition with periodic updates).

(b) Additionally, the FAR Secretariat shall provide the two councils with centralized services for—

(1) Keeping a synopsis of current FAR cases and their status;

(2) Maintaining official files;

(3) Assisting parties interested in reviewing the files on completed cases; and

(4) Performing miscellaneous administrative tasks pertaining to the maintenance of the FAR.

[Final rule, 62 FR 40236, 7/25/97, effective 6/30/97]

1.202 Agency compliance with the FAR.

Agency compliance with the FAR (see 1.304) is the responsibility of the Secretary of Defense (for the military departments and defense agencies), the Administrator of General Services (for civilian agencies other than NASA), and the Administrator of NASA (for NASA activities).

SUBPART 1.3—AGENCY ACQUISITION REGULATIONS

1.301 Policy.

(a) (1) Subject to the authorities in paragraph (c) of this section and other statutory authority, an agency head may issue or authorize the issuance of agency acquisition regulations that implement or supplement the FAR and incorporate, together with the FAR, agency policies, procedures, contract clauses, solicitation provisions, and forms that govern the contracting process or otherwise control the relationship between the agency, including any of its suborganizations, and contractors or prospective contractors.

(2) Subject to the authorities in paragraph (c) of this section and other statutory authority, an agency head may issue or authorize the issuance of internal agency guidance at any organizational level (*e.g.*, designations and delegations of authority, assignments of responsibilities, work-flow procedures, and internal reporting requirements).

(b) Agency heads shall establish procedures to ensure that agency acquisition regulations are published for comment in the *Federal Register* in conformance with the procedures in subpart 1.5 and as required by 41 U.S.C. 1707, and other applicable statutes, when they have a significant effect beyond the internal operating procedures of the agency or have a significant cost or administrative impact on contractors or offerors. However, publication is not required for issuances that merely implement or supplement higher level issuances that have previously undergone the public comment process, unless such implementation or supplementation results in an additional significant cost or administrative impact on contractors or offerors or effect beyond the internal operating procedures of the issuing organization. Issuances under 1.301(a)(2) need not be publicized for public comment.

(c) When adopting acquisition regulations, agencies shall ensure that they comply with the Paperwork Reduction Act (44 U.S.C. 3501, *et seq.*) as implemented in 5 CFR 1320 (see 1.106) and the Regulatory Flexibility Act (5 U.S.C. 601, *et seq.*). Normally, when a law requires publication of a proposed regulation, the Regulatory Flexibility Act applies and agencies must prepare written analyses, or certifications as provided in the law.

(d) Agency acquisition regulations implementing or supplementing the FAR are, for—

(1) The military departments and defense agencies, issued subject to the authority of the Secretary of Defense;

(2) NASA activities, issued subject to the authorities of the Administrator of NASA; and

(3) The civilian agencies other than NASA, issued by the heads of those agencies subject to the overall authority of the Administrator of General Services or independent authority the agency may have.

[FAC 84-6, 50 FR 2269, 1/15/85, effective 11/29/84; FAC 84-42, 54 FR 5054, 1/31/89, effective 3/2/89; FAC 2005-73, 79 FR 24192, 4/29/2014, effective 5/29/2014]

1.302 Limitations.

Agency acquisition regulations shall be limited to—

(a) Those necessary to implement FAR policies and procedures within the agency; and

(b) Additional policies, procedures, solicitation provisions, or contract clauses that supplement the FAR to satisfy the specific needs of the agency.

1.303 Publication and codification.

(a) Agency-wide acquisition regulations shall be published in the *Federal Register* as required by law, shall be codified under an assigned chapter in Title 48, *Code of Federal Regulations*, and shall parallel the FAR in format, arrangement, and numbering system (but see 1.105-1(c)). Coverage in an agency acquisition regulation that implements a specific part, subpart, section, or subsection of the FAR shall be numbered and titled to correspond to the appropriate FAR number and title. Supplementary material for which there is no counterpart in the FAR shall be codified using chapter, part, subpart, section, or subsection numbers of 70 and up (*e.g.*, for the Department of Interior, whose assigned chapter number in Title 48 is 14, Part 1470, Subpart 1401.70, section 1401.370, or subsection 1401.301-70).

(b) Issuances under 1.301(a)(2) need not be published in the *Federal Register*.

[FAC 84-6, 50 FR 2269, 1/15/85, effective 11/29/85]

1.304 Agency control and compliance procedures.

(a) Under the authorities of 1.301(d), agencies shall control and limit issuance of agency acquisition regulations and, in particular, local agency directives that restrain the flexibilities found in the FAR, and shall establish formal procedures for the review of these documents to assure compliance with this Part 1.

(b) Agency acquisition regulations shall not—

(1) Unnecessarily repeat, paraphrase, or otherwise restate material contained in the FAR or higher-level agency acquisition regulations; or

(2) Except as required by law or as provided in Subpart 1.4, conflict or be inconsistent with FAR content.

(c) Agencies shall evaluate all regulatory coverage in agency acquisition regulations to determine if it could apply to other agencies. Coverage that is not peculiar to one agency shall be recommended for inclusion in the FAR.

[FAC 90-40, 61 FR 39186, 7/26/96, effective 8/26/96; FAC 97-16, 65 FR 16274, 3/27/2000, effective 3/27/2000]

SUBPART 1.4—DEVIATIONS FROM THE FAR

1.400 Scope of subpart.

This subpart prescribes the policies and procedures for authorizing deviations from the FAR. Exceptions pertaining to the use of forms prescribed by the FAR are covered in Part 53 rather than in this subpart.

1.401 Definition.

Deviation means any one or combination of the following:

(a) The issuance or use of a policy, procedure, solicitation provision (see definition in 2.101), contract clause (see definition in 2.101), method, or practice of conducting acquisition actions of any kind at any stage of the acquisition process that is inconsistent with the FAR.

(b) The omission of any solicitation provision or contract clause when its prescription requires its use.

(c) The use of any solicitation provision or contract clause with modified or alternate language that is not authorized by the FAR (see definition of *modification* in 52.101(a) and definition of *alternate* in 2.101(a)).

(d) The use of a solicitation provision or contract clause prescribed by the FAR on a *substantially as follows* or *substantially the same as* basis (see definitions in 2.101 and 52.101(a)), if such use is inconsistent with the intent, principle, or substance of the prescription or related coverage on the subject matter in the FAR.

(e) The authorization of lesser or greater limitations on the use of any solicitation provision, contract clause, policy, or procedure prescribed by the FAR.

(f) The issuance of policies or procedures that govern the contracting process or otherwise control contracting relationships that are not incorporated into agency acquisition regulations in accordance with 1.301(a).

[FAC 97-22, 66 FR 2116, 1/10/2001, effective 3/12/2001; Delay of effective date, 66 FR 14259, 3/9/2001, effective 5/11/2001]

1.402 Policy.

Unless precluded by law, executive order, or regulation, deviations from the FAR may be granted as specified in this subpart when necessary to meet the specific needs and requirements of each agency. The development and testing of new techniques and methods of acquisition should not be stifled simply because such action would require a FAR deviation. The fact that deviation authority is required should not, of itself, deter agencies in their development and testing of new techniques and acquisition methods. Refer to 31.101 for instructions concerning deviations pertaining to the subject matter of Part 31, Contract Cost Principles and Procedures. Deviations are not authorized with respect to 30.201-3 and 30.201-4, or the requirements of the Cost Accounting Standards Board (CASB) rules and regulations (48 CFR Chapter 99 (FAR Appendix)). Refer to 30.201-5for instructions concerning waivers pertaining to Cost Accounting Standards.

[FAC 84-30, 9/30/87, effective 9/30/87; FAC 97-3, 62 FR 64912, 12/9/97, effective 2/9/98]

1.403 Individual deviations.

Individual deviations affect only one contract action, and, unless 1.405(e) is applicable, may be authorized by the agency head. The contracting officer must document the justification and agency approval in the contract file.

[FAC 2001-06, 67 FR 13048, 3/202/2002, effective 4/4/2002]

1.404 Class deviations.

Class deviations affect more than one contract action. When an agency knows that it will require a class deviation on a permanent basis, it should propose a FAR revision, if appropriate. Civilian agencies, other than NASA, must furnish a copy of each approved class deviation to the FAR Secretariat.

(a) For civilian agencies except NASA, class deviations may be authorized by agency heads or their designees, unless 1.405(e) is applicable. Delegation of this authority shall not be made below the head of a contracting activity. Authorization of class deviations by agency officials is subject to the following limitations:

(1) An agency official who may authorize a class deviation, before doing so, shall consult with the chairperson of the Civilian Agency Acquisition Council (CAA Council), unless that agency official determines that urgency precludes such consultation.

(2) Recommended revisions to the FAR shall be transmitted to the FAR Secretariat by agency heads or their designees for authorizing class deviations.

(b) For DOD, class deviations shall be controlled, processed, and approved in accordance with the Defense FAR supplement.

(c) For NASA, class deviations shall be controlled and approved by the Assistant Administrator for Procurement. Deviations shall be processed in accordance with agency regulations.

[FAC 90-4, 56 FR 15148, 4/15/91, effective 5/15/91; Interim rule, FAC 90-20, 59 FR 11368, 3/10/94, effective 3/10/94; FAC 90-43, Final rule, 61 FR 67408, 12/20/96, effective 2/18/97; FAC 2001-06, 67 FR 13048, 3/20/2002, effective 4/4/2002]

1.405 Deviations pertaining to treaties and executive agreements.

(a) *Executive agreements*, as used in this section, means Government-to-Government agreements, including agreements with international organizations, to which the United States is a party.

(b) Any deviation from the FAR required to comply with a treaty to which the United States is a party is authorized, unless the deviation would be inconsistent with FAR coverage based on a law enacted after the execution of the treaty.

(c) Any deviation from the FAR required to comply with an executive agreement is authorized unless the deviation would be inconsistent with FAR coverage based on law.

(d) For civilian agencies other than NASA, a copy of the text deviation authorized under paragraph (b) or (c) of this section shall be transmitted to the FAR Secretariat through a central agency control point.

(e) For civilian agencies other than NASA, if a deviation required to comply with a treaty or an executive agreement is not authorized by paragraph (b) or (c) of this section, then the request for deviation shall be processed through the FAR Secretariat to the Civilian Agency Acquisition Council.

[FAC 90-43, Final rule, 61 FR 67408, 12/20/96, effective 2/18/97]

SUBPART 1.5—AGENCY AND PUBLIC PARTICIPATION

1.501 Solicitation of agency and public views. (No Text)

1.501-1 Definition.

Significant revisions, as used in this subpart, means revisions that alter the substantive meaning of any coverage in the FAR System and which have a significant cost or administrative impact on contractors or offerors, or a significant effect beyond the internal operating procedures of the issuing agency. This expression, for example, does not include editorial, stylistic, or other revisions that have no impact on the basic meaning of the coverage being revised.

[FAC 84-6, 50 FR 2269, 1/15/85, effective 11/29/84; FAC 2005-73, 79 FR 24192, 4/29/2014, effective 5/29/2014]

1.501-2 Opportunity for public comments.

(a) Views of agencies and nongovernmental parties or organizations will be considered in formulating acquisition policies and procedures.

(b) The opportunity to submit written comments on proposed significant revisions shall be provided by placing a notice in the *Federal Register*. Each of these notices shall include—

(1) The text of the revision or, if it is impracticable to publish the full text, a summary of the proposal;

(2) The address and telephone number of the individual from whom copies of the revision, in full text, can be requested and to whom comments thereon should be addressed; and

(3) When 1.501-3(b) is applicable, a statement that the revision is effective on a temporary basis pending completion of the public comment period.

(c) A minimum of 30 days and, normally, at least 60 days will be given for the receipt of comments.

[FAC 84-6, 50 FR 2269, 1/15/85, effective 12/29/84]

1.501-3 Exceptions.

(a) Comments need not be solicited when the proposed coverage does not constitute a significant revision.

(b) Advance comments need not be solicited when urgent and compelling circumstances make solicitation of comments impracticable prior to the effective date of the coverage, such as when a new statute must be implemented in a relatively short period of time. In such case, the coverage shall be issued on a temporary basis and shall provide for at least a 30 day public comment period.

[FAC 84-6, 50 FR 2269, 1/15/85, effective 11/29/84]

1.502 Unsolicited proposed revisions.

Consideration shall also be given to unsolicited recommendations for revisions that have been submitted in writing with sufficient data and rationale to permit their evaluation.

[FAC 84-6, 50 FR 2269, 1/15/85, effective 11/29/84]

1.503 Public meetings.

Public meetings may be appropriate when a decision to adopt, amend, or delete FAR coverage is likely to benefit from significant additional views and discussion.

[FAC 84-6, 50 FR 2269, 1/15/85, effective 11/29/84]

SUBPART 1.6—CAREER DEVELOPMENT, CONTRACTING AUTHORITY, AND RESPONSIBILITIES

1.601 General.

(a) Unless specifically prohibited by another provision of law, authority and responsibility to contract for authorized supplies and services are vested in the agency head.

The agency head may establish contracting activities and delegate broad authority to manage the agency's contracting functions to heads of such contracting activities. Contracts may be entered into and signed on behalf of the Government only by contracting officers. In some agencies, a relatively small number of high level officials are designated contracting officers solely by virtue of their positions. Contracting officers below the level of a head of a contracting activity shall be selected and appointed under 1.603.

(b) Agency heads may mutually agree to—

(1) Assign contracting functions and responsibilities from one agency to another; and

(2) Create joint or combined offices to exercise acquisition functions and responsibilities.

[FAC 90-33, 60 FR 49706, 9/26/95, effective 10/1/95]

1.602 Contracting officers. (No Text)

1.602-1 Authority.

(a) Contracting officers have authority to enter into, administer, or terminate contracts and make related determinations and findings. Contracting officers may bind the Government only to the extent of the authority delegated to them. Contracting officers shall receive from the appointing authority (see 1.603-1) clear instructions in writing regarding the limits of their authority. Information on the limits of the contracting officers' authority shall be readily available to the public and agency personnel.

(b) No contract shall be entered into unless the contracting officer ensures that all requirements of law, executive orders, regulations, and all other applicable procedures, including clearances and approvals, have been met.

1.602-2 Responsibilities.

Contracting officers are responsible for ensuring performance of all necessary actions for effective contracting, ensuring compliance with the terms of the contract, and safeguarding the interests of the United States in its contractual relationships. In order to perform these responsibilities, contracting officers should be allowed wide latitude to exercise business judgment. Contracting officers shall—

(a) Ensure that the requirements of 1.602-1(b) have been met, and that sufficient funds are available for obligation;

(b) Ensure that contractors receive impartial, fair, and equitable treatment;

(c) Request and consider the advice of specialists in audit, law, engineering, information security, transportation, and other fields, as appropriate; and

(d) Designate and authorize, in writing and in accordance with agency procedures, a contracting officer's representative (COR) on all contracts and orders other than those that are firm-fixed price, and for firm-fixed-price contracts and orders as appropriate, unless the contracting officer retains and executes the COR duties. See 7.104(e). A COR—

(1) Shall be a Government employee, unless otherwise authorized in agency regulations;

(2) Shall be certified and maintain certification in accordance with the current Office of Management and Budget memorandum on the Federal Acquisition Certification for Contracting Officer Representatives (FAC–COR) guidance, or for DoD, in accordance with the current applicable DoD policy guidance;

(3) Shall be qualified by training and experience commensurate with the responsibilities to be delegated in accordance with agency procedures;

(4) May not be delegated responsibility to perform functions that have been delegated under 42.202 to a contract administration office, but may be assigned some duties at 42.302 by the contracting officer;

(5) Has no authority to make any commitments or changes that affect price, quality, quantity, delivery, or other terms and conditions of the contract nor in any way direct the contractor or its subcontractors to operate in conflict with the contract terms and conditions;

(6) Shall be nominated either by the requiring activity or in accordance with agency procedures; and

(7) Shall be designated in writing, with copies furnished to the contractor and the contract administration office—

(i) Specifying the extent of the COR's authority to act on behalf of the contracting officer;

(ii) Identifying the limitations on the COR's authority;

(iii) Specifying the period covered by the designation;

(iv) Stating the authority is not redelegable; and

(v) Stating that the COR may be personally liable for unauthorized acts.

[FAC 2005-06, 70 FR 57449, 9/30/2005, effective 9/30/2005; FAC 2005-13, 71 FR 57360, 9/28/2006, effective 9/28/2006; FAC 2005-50, 76 FR 14543, 3/16/2011, effective 3/16/2011; FAC 2005-56, 77 FR 12925, 3/2/2012, effective 4/2/2012; FAC 2005-67, 78 FR 37675, 6/21/2013, effective 7/22/2013]

1.602-3 Ratification of unauthorized commitments.

(a) *Definitions.*

Ratification, as used in this subsection, means the act of approving an unauthorized commitment by an official who has the authority to do so.

Unauthorized commitment, as used in this subsection, means an agreement that is not binding solely because the Government representative who made it lacked the authority to enter into that agreement on behalf of the Government.

(b) *Policy.* (1) Agencies should take positive action to preclude, to the maximum extent possible, the need for ratification actions. Although procedures are provided in this section for use in those cases where the ratification of an unauthorized commitment is necessary, these procedures may not be used in a manner that encourages such commitments being made by Government personnel.

(2) Subject to the limitations in paragraph (c) of this subsection, the head of the contracting activity, unless a higher level official is designated by the agency, may ratify an unauthorized commitment.

(3) The ratification authority in subparagraph (b)(2) of this subsection may be delegated in accordance with agency procedures, but in no case shall the authority be delegated below the level of chief of the contracting office.

(4) Agencies should process unauthorized commitments using the ratification authority of this subsection instead of referring such actions to the Government Accountability Office for resolution. (See 1.602-3(d).)

(5) Unauthorized commitments that would involve claims subject to resolution under 41 U.S.C. chapter 71, Contract Disputes, should be processed in accordance with Subpart 33.2, Disputes and Appeals.

(c) *Limitations.* The authority in subparagraph (b)(2) of this subsection may be exercised only when—

(1) Supplies or services have been provided to and accepted by the Government, or the Government otherwise has obtained or will obtain a benefit resulting from performance of the unauthorized commitment;

(2) The ratifying official has the authority to enter into a contractual commitment;

(3) The resulting contract would otherwise have been proper if made by an appropriate contracting officer;

(4) The contracting officer reviewing the unauthorized commitment determines the price to be fair and reasonable;

(5) The contracting officer recommends payment and legal counsel concurs in the recommendation, unless agency procedures expressly do not require such concurrence;

(6) Funds are available and were available at the time the unauthorized commitment was made; and

(7) The ratification is in accordance with any other limitations prescribed under agency procedures.

(d) *Nonratifiable commitments.* Cases that are not ratifiable under this subsection may be subject to resolution as recommended by the Government Accountability Office under its claim procedure (GAO Policy and Procedures Manual for Guidance of Federal Agencies, Title 4, Chapter 2), or as authorized by FAR Subpart 50.1. Legal advice should be obtained in these cases.

[FAC 84-33, 53 FR 3689, 2/8/88, effective 2/22/88; FAC 90-32, 60 FR 48206, 9/18/95, effective 10/1/95; FAC 2005-13, Final rule 71 FR 57380, 9/28/2006, effective 9/28/2006; FAC 2005-21, 72 FR 63027, 11/7/2007, effective 11/7/2007; FAC 2005-30, 74 FR 2733, 1/15/2009, effective 2/17/2009; FAC 2005-73, 79 FR 24192, 4/29/2014, effective 5/29/2014]

1.603 Selection, appointment, and termination of appointment for contracting officers. (No Text)

[FAC 2005-50, 76 FR 14543, 3/16/2011, effective 3/16/2011; FAC 2005-56, 77 FR 12925, 3/2/2012, effective 4/2/2012]

1.603-1 General.

41 U.S.C. 1702(b)(3)(G), requires agency heads to establish and maintain a procurement career management program and a system for the selection, appointment, and termination of appointment of contracting officers. Agency heads or their designees may select and appoint contracting officers and terminate their appointments. These selections and appointments shall be consistent with Office of Federal Procurement Policy's (OFPP) standards for skill-based training in performing contracting and purchasing duties as published in OFPP Policy Letter No. 05-01, Developing and Managing the Acquisition Workforce, April 15, 2005.

[FAC 90-23, 59 FR 67010, 12/28/94, effective 2/27/95; FAC 2005-25, 73 FR 21800, 4/22/2008, effective 4/22/2008; FAC 2005-73, 79 FR 24192, 4/29/2014, effective 5/29/2014; FAC 2005-91, 81 FR 67781, 9/30/2016, effective 9/30/2016]

1.603-2 Selection.

In selecting contracting officers, the appointing official shall consider the complexity and dollar value of the acquisitions to be assigned and the candidate's experience, training, education, business acumen, judgment, character, and reputation. Examples of selection criteria include—

(a) Experience in Government contracting and administration, commercial purchasing, or related fields;

(b) Education or special training in business administration, law, accounting, engineering, or related fields;

(c) Knowledge of acquisition policies and procedures, including this and other applicable regulations;

(d) Specialized knowledge in the particular assigned field of contracting; and

(e) Satisfactory completion of acquisition training courses.

1.603-3 Appointment.

(a) Contracting officers shall be appointed in writing on an SF 1402, Certificate of Appointment, which shall state any limitations on the scope of authority to be exercised, other than limitations contained in applicable law or regulation. Appointing officials shall maintain files containing copies of all appointments that have not been terminated.

(b) Agency heads are encouraged to delegate micro-purchase authority to individuals who are employees of an executive agency or members of the Armed Forces of the United States who will be using the supplies or services being purchased. Individuals delegated this authority are not required to be appointed on an SF 1402, but shall be appointed in writing in accordance with agency procedures.

[FAC 90-40, 61 FR 39186, 7/26/96, effective 8/26/96]

1.603-4 Termination.

Termination of a contracting officer appointment will be by letter, unless the Certificate of Appointment contains other provisions for automatic termination. Terminations may be for reasons such as reassignment, termination of employment, or unsatisfactory performance. No termination shall operate retroactively.

1.604 Contracting Officer's Representative (COR).

A contracting officer's representative (COR) assists in the technical monitoring or administration of a contract (*see* 1.602-2(d)). The COR shall maintain a file for each assigned contract. The file must include, at a minimum—

(a) A copy of the contracting officer's letter of designation and other documents describing the COR's duties and responsibilities;

(b) A copy of the contract administration functions delegated to a contract administration office which may not be delegated to the COR (*see* 1.602-2(d)(4)); and

(c) Documentation of COR actions taken in accordance with the delegation of authority.

[FAC 2005-50, 76 FR 14543, 3/16/2011, effective 3/16/2011; FAC 2005-56, 77 FR 12925, 3/2/2012, effective 4/2/2012]

SUBPART 1.7—DETERMINATIONS AND FINDINGS

1.700 Scope of subpart.

This subpart prescribes general policies and procedures for the use of determinations and findings (D&F's). Requirements for specific types of D&F's can be found with the appropriate subject matter.

[FAC 84-5, 50 FR 1726, 1/11/85, effective 4/1/85]

1.701 Definition.

Determination and Findings (D&F) means a special form of written approval by an authorized official that is required by statute or regulation as a prerequisite to taking certain contract actions. The *determination* is a conclusion or decision supported by the *findings*. The findings are statements of fact or rationale essential to support the determination and must cover each requirement of the statute or regulation.

[FAC 84-5, 50 FR 1726, 1/11/85, effective 4/1/85; FAC 2001-06, 67 FR 13048, 3/20/2002, effective 4/4/2002]

1.702 General.

(a) A D&F shall ordinarily be for an individual contract action. Unless otherwise prohibited, class D&F's may be executed for classes of contract actions (see 1.703). The approval granted by a D&F is restricted to the proposed contract action(s) reasonably described in that D&F. D&F's may provide for a reasonable degree of flexibility. Furthermore, in their application, reasonable variations in estimated quantities or prices are permitted, unless the D&F specifies otherwise.

(b) When an option is anticipated, the D&F shall state the approximate quantity to be awarded initially and the extent of the increase to be permitted by the option.

[FAC 84-5, 50 FR 1726, 1/11/85, effective 4/1/85]

1.703 Class determinations and findings.

(a) A class D&F provides authority for a class of contract actions. A class may consist of contract actions for the same or related supplies or services or other contract actions that require essentially identical justification.

(b) The findings in a class D&F shall fully support the proposed action either for the class as a whole or for each action. A class D&F shall be for a specified period, with the expiration date stated in the document.

(c) The contracting officer shall ensure that individual actions taken pursuant to the authority of a class D&F are within the scope of the D&F.

[FAC 84-5, 50 FR 1726, 1/11/85, effective 4/1/85; FAC 2001-06, 67 FR 13048, 3/20/2002, effective 4/4/2002]

1.704 Content.

Each D&F shall set forth enough facts and circumstances to clearly and convincingly justify the specific determination made. As a minimum, each D&F shall include, in the prescribed agency format, the following information:

(a) Identification of the agency and of the contracting activity and specific identification of the document as a "Determination and Findings."

(b) Nature and/or description of the action being approved.

(c) Citation of the appropriate statute and/or regulation upon which the D&F is based.

(d) Findings that detail the particular circumstances, facts, or reasoning essential to support the determination. Necessary supporting documentation shall be obtained from appropriate requirements and technical personnel.

(e) A determination, based on the findings, that the proposed action is justified under the applicable statute or regulation.

(f) Expiration date of the D&F, if required (see 1.706).

(g) The signature of the official authorized to sign the D&F (see 1.707) and the date signed.

[FAC 84-5, 50 FR 1726, 1/11/85, effective 4/1/85]

1.705 Supersession and modification.

(a) If a D&F is superseded by another D&F, that action shall not render invalid any action taken under the original D&F prior to the date of its supersession.

(b) The contracting officer need not cancel the solicitation if the D&F, as modified, supports the contract action.

[FAC 84-5, 50 FR 1726, 1/11/85, effective 4/1/85; FAC 2001-06, 67 FR 13048, 3/20/2002, effective 4/4/2002]

1.706 Expiration.

Expiration dates are required for class D&F's and are optional for individual D&F's. Authority to act under an individual D&F expires when it is exercised or on an expiration date specified in the document, whichever occurs first. Authority to act under a class D&F expires on the expiration date specified in the document. When a solicitation has been furnished to prospective offerors before the expiration date, the authority under the D&F will continue until award of the contract(s) resulting from the solicitation.

[FAC 84-5, 50 FR 1726, 1/11/85, effective 4/1/85]

1.707 Signatory authority.

When a D&F is required, it shall be signed by the appropriate official in accordance with agency regulations. Authority to sign or delegate signature authority for the various D&F's is as shown in the applicable FAR part.

[FAC 84-5, 50 FR 1726, 1/11/85, effective 4/1/85]

PART 2—DEFINITIONS OF WORDS AND TERMS

Table of Contents

Scope of part 2.000

Subpart 2.1—Definitions

Definitions 2.101

Subpart 2.2—Definitions Clause

Contract clause 2.201

PART 2—DEFINITIONS WORDS AND TERMS

2.000 Scope of part.

(a) This part—

(1) Defines words and terms that are frequently used in the FAR;

(2) Provides cross-references to other definitions in the FAR of the same word or term; and

(3) Provides for the incorporation of these definitions in solicitations and contracts by reference.

(b) Other parts, subparts, and sections of this regulation (48 CFR chapter 1) may define other words or terms and those definitions only apply to the part, subpart, or section where the word or term is defined.

[FAC 97-22, 66 FR 2116, 1/10/2001, effective 3/12/2001; Delay of effective date, 66 FR 14259, 3/9/2001, effective 5/11/2001; FAC 2005-65, 78 FR 6191, 1/29/2013, effective 1/29/2013]

SUBPART 2.1—DEFINITIONS

2.101 Definitions.

(a) A word or a term, defined in this section, has the same meaning throughout this regulation (48 CFR chapter 1), unless—

(1) The context in which the word or term is used clearly requires a different meaning; or

(2) Another FAR part, subpart, or section provides a different definition for the particular part or portion of the part.

(b) If a word or term that is defined in this section is defined differently in another part, subpart, or section of this regulation (48 CFR chapter 1), the definition in—

(1) This section includes a cross-reference to the other definitions; and

(2) That part, subpart, or section applies to the word or term when used in that part, subpart, or section.

Acquisition means the acquiring by contract with appropriated funds of supplies or services (including construction) by and for the use of the Federal Government through purchase or lease, whether the supplies or services are already in existence or must be created, developed, demonstrated, and evaluated. Acquisition begins at the point when agency needs are established and includes the description of requirements to satisfy agency needs, solicitation and selection of sources, award of contracts, contract financing, contract performance, contract administration, and those technical and management functions directly related to the process of fulfilling agency needs by contract.

Acquisition planning means the process by which the efforts of all personnel responsible for an acquisition are coordinated and integrated through a comprehensive plan for fulfilling the agency need in a timely manner and at a reasonable cost. It includes developing the overall strategy for managing the acquisition.

Activity Address Code (AAC) means a distinct six-position code consisting of a combination of alpha and/or numeric characters assigned to identify specific agency offices, units, activities, or organizations by the General Services Administration for civilian agencies and by the Department of Defense for defense agencies.

Adequate evidence means information sufficient to support the reasonable belief that a particular act or omission has occurred.

Advisory and assistance services means those services provided under contract by nongovernmental sources to support or improve: organizational policy development; decision-making; management and administration; program and/or project management and administration; or R&D activities. It can also mean the furnishing of professional advice or assistance rendered to improve the effectiveness of Federal management processes or procedures (including those of an engineering and technical nature). In rendering the foregoing services, outputs may take the form of information, advice, opinions, alternatives, analyses, evaluations, recommendations, training and the day-to-day aid of support personnel needed for the successful performance of ongoing Federal operations. All advisory and assistance services are classified in one of the following definitional subdivisions:

(1) Management and professional support services, i.e., contractual services that provide assistance, advice or training for the efficient and effective management and operation of organizations, activities (including management and support services for R&D activities), or systems. These services are normally closely related to the basic responsibilities and mission of the agency originating the requirement for the acquisition of services by contract. Included are efforts that support or contribute to improved organization of program management, logistics management, project monitoring and reporting, data collection, budgeting, accounting, performance auditing, and administrative technical support for conferences and training programs.

(2) Studies, analyses and evaluations, i.e., contracted services that provide organized, analytical assessments/evaluations in support of policy development, decision-making, management, or administration. Included are studies in support of R&D activities. Also included are acquisitions of models, methodologies, and related software supporting studies, analyses or evaluations.

(3) Engineering and technical services, i.e., contractual services used to support the program office during the acquisition cycle by providing such services as systems engineering and technical direction (see 9.505-1(b)) to ensure the effective operation and maintenance of a weapon system or major system as defined in OMB Circular No. A-109 or to provide direct support of a weapon system that is essential to research, development, production, operation or maintenance of the system.

Affiliates means associated business concerns or individuals if, directly or indirectly either one controls or can control the other; or third party controls or can control both, except as follows:

(1) For the use in subpart 9.4, see the definition at 9.403.

(2) For the use in subpart 19.1, see the definition at 19.101.

Agency head or *head of the agency* means the Secretary, Attorney General, Administrator, Governor, Chairperson, or other chief official of an executive agency, unless otherwise indicated, including any deputy or assistant chief official of an executive agency.

Alternate means a substantive variation of a basic provision or clause prescribed for use in a defined circumstance. It adds wording to, deletes wording from, or substitutes specified wording for a portion of the basic provision or clause. The alternate version of a provision or clause is the basic provision or clause as changed by the addition, deletion, or substitution (see 52.105(a)).

Architect-engineer services, as defined in 40 U.S.C. 1102, means—

(1) Professional services of an architectural or engineering nature, as defined by State law, if applicable, that are required to be performed or approved by a person licensed, registered, or certified to provide those services;

(2) Professional services of an architectural or engineering nature performed by contract that are associated with research, planning, development, design, construction, alteration, or repair of real property; and

(3) Those other professional services of an architectural or engineering nature, or incidental services, that members of the architectural and engineering professions (and individuals in their employ) may logically or justifiably perform, including studies, investigations, surveying and mapping, tests, evaluations, consultations, comprehensive planning, program management, conceptual designs, plans and specifications, value engineering, construction phase services, soils engineering, drawing reviews, preparation of operating and maintenance manuals, and other related services.

Assignment of claims means the transfer or making over by the contractor to a bank, trust company, or other financing institution, as security for a loan to the contractor, of its right to be paid by the Government for contract performance.

Assisted acquisition means a type of interagency acquisition where a servicing agency performs acquisition activities on a requesting agency's behalf, such as awarding and administering a contract, task order, or delivery order.

Basic research means that research directed toward increasing knowledge in science. The primary aim of basic research is a fuller knowledge or understanding of the subject under study, rather than any practical application of that knowledge.

Best value means the expected outcome of an acquisition that, in the Government's estimation, provides the greatest overall benefit in response to the requirement.

Bid sample means a product sample required to be submitted by an offeror to show characteristics of the offered products that cannot adequately be described by specifications, purchase descriptions, or the solicitation (e.g., balance, facility of use, or pattern).

Biobased product means a product determined by the U.S. Department of Agriculture to be a commercial or industrial product (other than food or feed) that is composed, in whole or in significant part, of biological products, including renewable domestic agricultural materials and forestry materials.

Broad agency announcement means a general announcement of an agency's research interest including criteria for selecting proposals and soliciting the participation of all offerors capable of satisfying the Government's needs (see 6.102(d)(2)).

Building or *work* means construction activity as distinguished from manufacturing, furnishing of materials, or servicing and maintenance work. The terms include, without limitation, buildings, structures, and improvements of all types, such as bridges, dams, plants, highways, parkways, streets, subways, tunnels, sewers, mains, power lines, pumping stations, heavy generators, railways, airports, terminals, docks, piers, wharves, ways, lighthouses, buoys, jetties, breakwaters, levees, canals, dredging, shoring, rehabilitation and reactivation of plants, scaffolding, drilling, blasting, excavating, clearing, and landscaping. The manufacture or furnishing of materials, articles, supplies, or equipment (whether or not a Federal or State agency acquires title to such materials, articles, supplies, or equipment during the course of the manufacture or furnishing, or owns the materials from which they are manufactured or furnished) is not "building" or "work" within the meaning of this definition unless conducted in connection with and at the site of such building or work as is described in the foregoing sentence, or under the United States Housing Act of 1937 and the Housing Act of 1949 in the construction or development of the project.

Bundling—

(1) Means a subset of consolidation that combines two or more requirements for supplies or services, previously provided or performed under separate smaller contracts (see paragraph (2) of this definition), into a solicitation for a single contract, a multiple-award contract, or a task or delivery order that is likely to be unsuitable for award to a small business concern (even if it is suitable for award to a small business with a Small Business Teaming Arrangement) due to—

(i) The diversity, size, or specialized nature of the elements of the performance specified;

(ii) The aggregate dollar value of the anticipated award;

(iii) The geographical dispersion of the contract performance sites; or

(iv) Any combination of the factors described in paragraphs (1)(i), (ii), and (iii) of this definition.

(2) *Separate smaller contract* as used in this definition, means a contract that has been performed by one or more small business concerns or that was suitable for award to one or more small business concerns.

(3) This definition does not apply to a contract that will be awarded and performed entirely outside of the United States.

Business unit means any segment of an organization, or an entire business organization that is not divided into segments.

Certified cost or pricing data means *cost or pricing data* that were required to be submitted in accordance with FAR 15.403-4 and 15.403-5 and have been certified, or are required to be certified, in accordance with 15.406-2. This certification states that, to the best of the person's knowledge and belief, the cost or pricing data are accurate, complete, and current as of a date certain before contract award. Cost or pricing data are required to be certified in certain procurements (10 U.S.C. 2306a and 41 U.S.C. chapter 35).

Change-of-name agreement means a legal instrument executed by the contractor and the Government that recognizes the legal change of name of the contractor without disturbing the original contractual rights and obligations of the parties.

Change order means a written order, signed by the contracting officer, directing the contractor to make a change that the Changes clause authorizes the contracting officer to order without the contractor's consent.

Chief Acquisition Officer means an executive level acquisition official responsible for agency performance of acquisition activities and acquisition programs created pursuant to 41 U.S.C. 1702.

Chief of mission means the principal officer in charge of a diplomatic mission of the United States or of a United States office abroad which is designated by the Secretary of State as diplomatic in nature, including any individual assigned under section 502 (c) of the Foreign Service Act of 1980 (Public Law 96-645) to be temporarily in charge of such a mission or office.

Claim means a written demand or written assertion by one of the contracting parties seeking, as a matter of right, the payment of money in a sum certain, the adjustment or interpretation of contract terms, or other relief arising under or relating to the contract. However, a written demand or written assertion by the contractor seeking the payment of money exceeding $100,000 is not a claim under 41 U.S.C. Chapter 71, Contract Disputes, until certified as required by the statute. A voucher, invoice, or other routine request for payment that is not in dispute when submitted is not a claim. The submission may be converted to a claim, by written notice to the contracting officer as provided in 33.206(a), if it is disputed either as to liability or amount or is not acted upon in a reasonable time.

Classified acquisition means an acquisition in which offerors must have access to classified information to properly submit an offer or quotation, to understand the performance requirements, or to perform the contract.

Classified contract means any contract in which the contractor or its employees must have access to classified information during contract performance. A contract may be a classified contract even though the contract document itself is unclassified.

Classified information means any knowledge that can be communicated or any documentary material, regardless of its physical form or characteristics, that—

(1) (i) Is owned by, is produced by or for, or is under the control of the United States Government; or

(ii) Has been classified by the Department of Energy as privately generated restricted data following the procedures in 10 CFR 1045.21; and

(2) Must be protected against unauthorized disclosure according to Executive Order 12958, Classified National Security Information, April 17, 1995, or classified in accordance with the Atomic Energy Act of 1954.

Cognizant Federal agency means the Federal agency that, on behalf of all Federal agencies, is responsible for establishing final indirect cost rates and forward pricing rates, if applicable, and administering cost accounting standards for all contracts in a business unit.

Combatant commander means the commander of a unified of specified combatant command established in accordance with 10 U.S.C. 161.

Commercial component means any component that is a commercial item.

Commercial computer software means any computer software that is a commercial item.

Commercial item means—

(1) Any item, other than real property, that is of a type customarily used by the general public or by non-governmental entities for purposes other than governmental purposes, and—

(i) Has been sold, leased, or licensed to the general public; or

(ii) Has been offered for sale, lease, or license to the general public;

(2) Any item that evolved from an item described in paragraph (1) of this definition through advances in technology or performance and that is not yet available in the commercial marketplace, but will be available in the commercial marketplace in time to satisfy the delivery requirements under a Government solicitation;

(3) Any item that would satisfy a criterion expressed in paragraphs (1) or (2) of this definition, but for—

(i) Modifications of a type customarily available in the commercial marketplace; or

(ii) Minor modifications of a type not customarily available in the commercial marketplace made to meet Federal Government requirements. Minor modifications means modifications that do not significantly alter the nongovernmental function or essential physical characteristics of an item or component, or change the purpose of a process. Factors to be considered in determining whether a modification is minor include the value and size of the modification and the comparative value and size of the final product. Dollar values and percentages may be used as guideposts, but are not conclusive evidence that a modification is minor;

(4) Any combination of items meeting the requirements of paragraphs (1), (2), (3), or (5) of this definition that are of a type customarily combined and sold in combination to the general public;

(5) Installation services, maintenance services, repair services, training services, and other services if—

(i) Such services are procured for support of an item referred to in paragraph (1), (2), (3), or (4) of this definition, regardless of whether such services are provided by the same source or at the same time as the item; and

(ii) The source of such services provides similar services contemporaneously to the general public under terms and conditions similar to those offered to the Federal Government;

(6) Services of a type offered and sold competitively in substantial quantities in the commercial marketplace based on established catalog or market prices for specific tasks performed or specific outcomes to be achieved and under standard commercial terms and conditions. For purposes of these services—

(i) *Catalog price* means a price included in a catalog, price list, schedule, or other form that is regularly maintained by the manufacturer or vendor, is either published or otherwise available for inspection by customers, and states prices at which sales are currently, or were last, made to a significant number of buyers constituting the general public; and

(ii) *Market prices* means current prices that are established in the course of ordinary trade between buyers and sellers free to bargain and that can be substantiated through competition or from sources independent of the offerors.

(7) Any item, combination of items, or service referred to in paragraphs (1) through (6) of this definition, notwithstanding the fact that the item, combination of items, or service is transferred between or among separate divisions, subsidiaries, or affiliates of a contractor; or

(8) A nondevelopmental item, if the procuring agency determines the item was developed exclusively at private expense and sold in substantial quantities, on a competitive basis, to multiple State and local governments or to multiple foreign governments.

Commercially available off-the-shelf (COTS) item— (1) Means any item of supply (including construction material) that is—

(i) A commercial item (as defined in paragraph (1) of the definition in this section);

(ii) Sold in substantial quantities in the commercial marketplace; and

(iii) Offered to the Government, under a contract or subcontract at any tier, without modification, in the same form in which it is sold in the commercial marketplace; and

(2) Does not include bulk cargo, as defined in 46 U.S.C. 40102(4), such as agricultural products and petroleum products.

Common item means material that is common to the applicable Government contract and the contractor's other work, except that for use in the clause at 52.246-26, see the definition in paragraph (a) of that clause.

Component means any item supplied to the Government as part of an end item or of another component, except that for use in—

(1) Part 25, see the definition in 25.003;

(2) 52.225-1 and 52.225-3, see the definition in 52.225-1(a) and 52.225-3(a);

(3) 52.225-9 and 52.225-11, see the definition in 52.225-9(a) and52.225-11(a); and

(4) FAR 52.225-21 and FAR 52.225-23, see the definition in FAR 52.225-21(a) and FAR 52.225-23(a).

Computer database or *database* means a collection of recorded information in a form capable of, and for the purpose of, being stored in, processed, and operated on by a computer. The term does not include computer software.

Computer software —(1) Means—

(i) Computer programs that comprise a series of instructions, rules, routines, or statements, regardless of the media in which recorded, that allow or cause a computer to perform a specific operation or series of operations; and

(ii) Recorded information comprising source code listings, design details, algorithms, processes, flow charts, formulas, and related material that would enable the computer program to be produced, created, or compiled.

(2) Does not include computer databases or computer software documentation.

Computer software documentation means owner's manuals, user's manuals, installation instructions, operating instructions, and other similar items, regardless of storage medium, that explain the capabilities of the computer software or provide instructions for using the software.

Consent to subcontract means the contracting officer's written consent for the prime contractor to enter into a particular subcontract.

Consolidation, or consolidated requirement —

(1) Means a solicitation for a single contract, a multiple-award contract, a task order, or a delivery order to satisfy—

(i) Two or more requirements of the Federal agency for supplies or services that have been provided to or performed for the Federal agency under two or more separate contracts, each of which was lower in cost than the total cost of the contract for which offers are solicited; or

(ii) Requirements of the Federal agency for construction projects to be performed at two or more discrete sites.

(2) *Separate contract* as used in this definition, means a contract that has been performed by any business, including small and other than small business concerns.

Construction means construction, alteration, or repair (including dredging, excavating, and painting) of buildings, structures, or other real property. For purposes of this definition, the terms *buildings, structures,* or *other real property* include, but are not limited to, improvements of all types, such as bridges, dams, plants, highways, parkways, streets, subways, tunnels, sewers, mains, power lines, cemeteries, pumping stations, railways, airport facilities, terminals, docks, piers, wharves, ways, lighthouses, buoys, jetties, breakwaters, levees, canals, and channels. Construction does not include the manufacture, production, furnishing, construction, alteration, repair, processing, or assembling of vessels, aircraft, or other kinds of personal property (except that for use in subpart 22.5, see the definition at 22.502).

Contiguous United States (CONUS) means the 48 contiguous States and the District of Columbia.

Contingency operation (10 U.S.C. 101(a)(13)) means a military operation that:

(1) Is designated by the Secretary of Defense as an operation in which members of the armed forces are or may become in-

volved in military actions, operations, or hostilities against an enemy of the United States or against an opposing military force; or

(2) Results in the call or order to, or retention on, active duty of members of the uniformed services under section 688, 12301(a), 12302, 12304, 12304 (a), 12305, or 12406 of title 10 of the United States Code, Chapter 15 of title 10 of the United States Code, or any other provision of law during a war or during a national emergency declared by the President or Congress.

Continued portion of the contract means the portion of a contract that the contractor must continue to perform following a partial termination.

Contract means a mutually binding legal relationship obligating the seller to furnish the supplies or services (including construction) and the buyer to pay for them. It includes all types of commitments that obligate the Government to an expenditure of appropriated funds and that, except as otherwise authorized, are in writing. In addition to bilateral instruments, contracts include (but are not limited to) awards and notices of awards; job orders or task letters issued under basic ordering agreements; letter contracts; orders, such as purchase orders, under which the contract becomes effective by written acceptance or performance; and bilateral contract modifications. Contracts do not include grants and cooperative agreements covered by 31 U.S.C. 6301, et seq. For discussion of various types of contracts, see part 16.

Contract administration office means an office that performs—

(1) Assigned postaward functions related to the administration of contracts; and

(2) Assigned preaward functions.

Contract clause or *clause* means a term or condition used in contracts or in both solicitations and contracts, and applying after contract award or both before and after award.

Contract modification means any written change in the terms of a contract (see 43.103).

Contracting means purchasing, renting, leasing, or otherwise obtaining supplies or services from nonfederal sources. Contracting includes description (but not determination) of supplies and services required, selection and solicitation of sources, preparation and award of contracts, and all phases of contract administration. It does not include making grants or cooperative agreements.

Contracting activity means an element of an agency designated by the agency head and delegated broad authority regarding acquisition functions.

Contracting office means an office that awards or executes a contract for supplies or services and performs postaward functions not assigned to a contract administration office (except for use in part 48, see also 48.001).

Contracting officer means a person with the authority to enter into, administer, and/or terminate contracts and make related determinations and findings. The term includes certain authorized representatives of the contracting officer acting within the limits of their authority as delegated by the contracting officer. *Administrative contracting officer (ACO)* refers to a contracting officer who is administering contracts. *Termination contracting officer (TCO)* refers to a contracting officer who is settling terminated contracts. A single contracting officer may be responsible for duties in any or all of these areas. Reference in this regulation (48 CFR chapter 1) to administrative contracting officer or termination contracting officer does not—

(1) Require that a duty be performed at a particular office or activity; or

(2) Restrict in any way a contracting officer in the performance of any duty properly assigned.

Contracting officer's representative (COR) means an individual, including a contracting officer's technical representative (COTR), designated and authorized in writing by the contracting officer to perform specific technical or administrative functions.

Conviction means a judgment or conviction of a criminal offense by any court of competent jurisdiction, whether entered upon a verdict or a plea, and includes a conviction entered upon a plea of nolo contendere. For use in subpart 23.5, see the definition at 23.503.

Cost or pricing data (10 U.S.C. 2306a(h)(1) and 41 U.S.C. chapter 35) means all facts that, as of the date of price agreement, or, if applicable, an earlier date agreed upon between the parties that is as close as practicable to the date of agreement on price, prudent buyers and sellers would reasonably expect to affect price negotiations significantly. Cost or pricing data are factual, not judgmental; and are verifiable. While they do not indicate the accuracy of the prospective contractor's judgment about estimated future costs or projections, they do include the data forming the basis for that judgment. Cost or pricing data are more than historical accounting data; they are all the facts that can be reasonably expected to contribute to the soundness of estimates of future costs and to the validity of determinations of costs already incurred. They also include, but are not limited to, such factors as—

(1) Vendor quotations;

(2) Nonrecurring costs;

(3) Information on changes in production methods and in production or purchasing volume;

(4) Data supporting projections of business prospects and objectives and related operations costs;

(5) Unit-cost trends such as those associated with labor efficiency;

(6) Make-or-buy decisions;

(7) Estimated resources to attain business goals; and

(8) Information on management decisions that could have a significant bearing on costs.

Cost realism means that the costs in an offeror's proposal—

(1) Are realistic for the work to be performed;

(2) Reflect a clear understanding of the requirements; and

(3) Are consistent with the various elements of the offeror's technical proposal.

Cost sharing means an explicit arrangement under which the contractor bears some of the burden of reasonable, allocable, and allowable contract cost.

Customs territory of the United States means the 50 States, the District of Columbia, and Puerto Rico.

Data other than certified cost or pricing data means pricing data, cost data, and judgmental information necessary for the contracting officer to determine a fair and reasonable price or to determine cost realism. Such data may include the identical types of data as certified cost or pricing data, consistent with Table 15-2 of 15.408, but without the certification. The data may also include, for example, sales data and any information reasonably required to explain the offeror's estimating process, including, but not limited to—

(1) The judgmental factors applied and the mathematical or other methods used in the estimate, including those used in projecting from known data; and

(2) The nature and amount of any contingencies included in the proposed price.

Day means, unless otherwise specified, a calendar day.

Debarment means action taken by a debarring official under 9.406 to exclude a contractor from Government contracting and Government-approved subcontracting for a reasonable, specified period; a contractor that is excluded is *debarred.*

Delivery order means an order for supplies placed against an established contract or with Government sources.

Depreciation means a charge to current operations that distributes the cost of a tangible capital asset, less estimated residual value, over the estimated useful life of the asset in a systematic and logical manner. It does not involve a process of valuation. Useful life refers to the prospective period of economic usefulness in a particular contractor's operations as distinguished from physical life; it is evidenced by the actual or estimated retirement and replacement practice of the contractor.

Descriptive literature means information provided by an offeror, such as cuts, illustrations, drawings, and brochures, that shows a product's characteristics or construction of a product or explains its operation. The term includes only that information needed to evaluate the acceptability of the product and excludes other information for operating or maintaining the product.

Design-to-cost means a concept that establishes cost elements as management goals to achieve the best balance between life-cycle cost, acceptable performance, and schedule. Under this concept, cost is a design constraint during the design and development phases and a management discipline throughout the acquisition and operation of the system or equipment.

Designated operational area means a geographic area designated by the combatant commander or subordinate joint force commander for the conduct or support of specified military operations.

Direct acquisition means a type of interagency acquisition where a requesting agency places an order directly against a servicing agency's indefinite-delivery contract. The servicing agency manages the indefinite-delivery contract but does not participate in the placement or administration of an order.

Direct cost means any cost that is identified specifically with a particular final cost objective. Direct costs are not limited to items that are incorporated in the end product as material or labor. Costs identified specifically with a contract are direct costs of that contract. All costs identified specifically with other final cost objectives of the contractor are direct costs of those cost objectives.

Disaster Response Registry means a voluntary registry of contractors who are willing to perform debris removal, distribution of supplies, reconstruction, and other disaster or emergency relief activities established in accordance with 6 U.S.C. 796, Registry of Disaster Response Contractors. The Registry contains information on contractors who are willing to perform disaster or emergency relief activities within the United States and its outlying areas. The Registry is accessed via the Internet at *https://www.sam.gov*, Search Records, Advanced Search, Disaster Response Registry Search. (See 26.205.)

Drug-free workplace means the site(s) for the performance of work done by the contractor in connection with a specific contract where employees of the contractor are prohibited from engaging in the unlawful manufacture, distribution, dispensing, possession, or use of a controlled substance.

Earned value management system means a project management tool that effectively integrates the project scope of work with cost, schedule and performance elements for optimum project planning and control. The qualities and operating characteristics of an earned value management system are described in Electronic Industries Alliance Standard 748 (EIA-748), Earned Value Management Systems. (See OMB Circular A-11, Part 7.)

Economically disadvantaged women-owned small business (EDWOSB) concern—(see definition of *Women-Owned Small Business (WOSB) Program* in this section).

Effective date of termination means the date on which the notice of termination requires the contractor to stop performance under the contract. If the contractor receives the termination notice after the date fixed for termination, then the effective date of termination means the date the contractor receives the notice.

Electronic and information technology (EIT) has the same meaning as *information technology* except EIT also includes any equipment or interconnected system or subsystem of equipment that is used in the creation, conversion, or duplication of data or information. The term EIT, includes, but is not limited to, telecommunication products (such as telephones), information kiosks and transaction machines, worldwide websites, multimedia, and office equipment (such as copiers and fax machines).

Electronic commerce means electronic techniques for accomplishing business transactions including electronic mail or messaging, World Wide Web technology, electronic bulletin boards, purchase cards, electronic funds transfer, and electronic data interchange.

Electronic data interchange (EDI) means a technique for electronically transferring and storing formatted information between computers utilizing established and published formats and codes, as authorized by the applicable Federal Information Processing Standards.

Electronic Funds Transfer (EFT) means any transfer of funds, other than a transaction originated by cash, check, or similar paper instrument, that is initiated through an electronic terminal, telephone, computer, or magnetic tape, for the purpose of ordering, instructing, or authorizing a financial institution to debit or credit an account. The term includes Automated Clearing House transfers, Fedwire transfers, and transfers made at automatic teller machines and point-of-sale terminals. For purposes of compliance with 31 U.S.C. 3332 and implementing regulations at 31 CFR part 208, the term "electronic funds transfer" includes a Governmentwide commercial purchase card transaction.

Electronic Funds Transfer (EFT) indicator means a four-character suffix to the unique entity identifier. The suffix is assigned at the discretion of the commercial, nonprofit, or Government entity to establish additional System for Award Management records for identifying alternative EFT accounts (see subpart 32.11) for the same entity.

Emergency, as used in 6.208, 13.201, 13.500, 18.001, 18.202, 18.203, and subpart 26.2, means any occasion or instance for which, in the determination of the President, Federal assistance is needed to supplement State and local efforts and capabilities to save lives and to protect property and public health and safety, or to lessen or avert the threat of a catastrophe in any part of the United States (42 U.S.C. 5122).

End product means supplies delivered under a line item of a Government contract, except for use in part 25 and the associated clauses at 52.225-1, 52.225-3, and 52.225-5, see the definitions in 25.003, 52.225-1(a), 52.225-3(a), and 52.225-5(a).

Energy-efficient product— (1) Means a product that—

(i) Meets Department of Energy and Environmental Protection Agency criteria for use of the Energy Star trademark label; or

(ii) Is in the upper 25 percent of efficiency for all similar products as designated by the Department of Energy's Federal Energy Management Program.

(2) As used in this definition, the term *product* does not include any energy-consuming product or system designed or procured for combat or combat-related missions (42 U.S.C. 8259b).

Energy-efficient standby power devices means products that use—

(1) External standby power devices, or that contain an internal standby power function; and

(2) No more than one watt of electricity in their standby power consuming mode or meet recommended low standby levels as designated by the Department of Energy Federal Energy Management Program.

Energy-savings performance contract means a contract that requires the contractor to—

(1) Perform services for the design, acquisition, financing, installation, testing, operation, and where appropriate, maintenance and repair, of an identified energy conservation measure or series of measures at one or more locations;

(2) Incur the costs of implementing the energy savings measures, including at least the cost (if any) incurred in making energy audits, acquiring and installing equipment, and training personnel in exchange for a predetermined share of the value of the energy savings directly resulting from implementation of such measures during the term of the contract; and

(3) Guarantee future energy and cost savings to the Government.

Environmentally preferable means products or services that have a lesser or reduced effect on human health and the environment when compared with competing products or services that serve the same purpose. This comparison may consider raw materials acquisition, production, manufacturing, packaging, distribution, reuse, operation, maintenance, or disposal of the product or service.

Excess personal property means any personal property under the control of a Federal agency that the agency head determines is not required for its needs or for the discharge of its responsibilities.

Executive agency means an executive department, a military department, or any independent establishment within the meaning of 5 U.S.C. 101, 102, and 104(1), respectively, and any wholly owned Government corporation within the meaning of 31 U.S.C. 9101.

Facilities capital cost of money means *cost of money as an element of the cost of facilities capital* as used at 48 CFR 9904.414—Cost Accounting Standard—Cost of Money as an Element of the Cost of Facilities Capital.

Federal agency means any executive agency or any independent establishment in the legislative or judicial branch of the Government (except the Senate, the House of Representatives, the Architect of the Capitol, and any activities under the Architect's direction).

Federal Technical Data Solution (FedTeDS) is a web application integrated with the Governmentwide Point of Entry (GPE) and the Central Contractor Registration (CCR) system for distribution of information related to contract opportunities. It is designed to enhance controls on the access and distribution of solicitation requirements or other documents when controls are necessary according to agency procedures. FedTeDS may be found on the Internet at *https://www.fedteds.gov*.

Federally-controlled facilities means—

(1) Federally-owned buildings or leased space, whether for single or multi-tenant occupancy, and its grounds and approaches, all or any portion of which is under the jurisdiction, custody or control of a department or agency;

(2) Federally-controlled commercial space shared with non-government tenants. For example, if a department or agency leased the 10th floor of a commercial building, the Directive applies to the 10th floor only;

(3) Government-owned, contractor-operated facilities, including laboratories engaged in national defense research and production activities; and

(4) Facilities under a management and operating contract, such as for the operation, maintenance, or support of a Government-owned or Government-controlled research, development, special production, or testing establishment.

Federally-controlled information system means an information system (44 U.S.C. 3502(8) used or operated by a Federal agency, or a contractor or other organization on behalf of the agency (44 U.S.C. 3544(a)(1)(A)).

Federally Funded Research and Development Centers (FFRDC's) means activities that are sponsored under a broad charter by a Government agency (or agencies) for the purpose of performing, analyzing, integrating, supporting, and/or managing basic or applied research and/or development, and that receive 70 percent or more of their financial support from the Government; and—

(1) A long-term relationship is contemplated;

(2) Most or all of the facilities are owned or funded by the Government; and

(3) The FFRDC has access to Government and supplier data, employees, and facilities beyond that common in a normal contractual relationship.

Final indirect cost rate means the indirect cost rate established and agreed upon by the Government and the contractor as not subject to change. It is usually established after the close of the contractor's fiscal year (unless the parties decide upon a different period) to which it applies. For cost-reimbursement research and development contracts with educational institutions, it may be predetermined; that is, established for a future period on the basis of cost experience with similar contracts, together with supporting data.

First article means a preproduction model, initial production sample, test sample, first lot, pilot lot, or pilot models.

First article testing means testing and evaluating the first article for conformance with specified contract requirements before or in the initial stage of production.

F.o.b. means free on board. This term is used in conjunction with a physical point to determine—

(1) The responsibility and basis for payment of freight charges; and

(2) Unless otherwise agreed, the point where title for goods passes to the buyer or consignee.

F.o.b. destination means free on board at destination; i.e., the seller or consignor delivers the goods on seller's or consignor's conveyance at destination. Unless the contract provides otherwise, the seller or consignor is responsible for the cost of shipping and risk of loss. For use in the clause at 52.247-34, see the definition at 52.247-34(a).

F.o.b. origin means free on board at origin; i.e., the seller or consignor places the goods on the conveyance. Unless the contract provides otherwise, the buyer or consignee is responsible for the cost of shipping and risk of loss. For use in the clause at 52.247-29, see the definition at 52.247-29(a).

F.o.b. (For other types of F.o.b., see 47.303).

Forward pricing rate agreement means a written agreement negotiated between a contractor and the Government to make certain rates available during a specified period for use in pricing contracts or modifications. These rates represent reasonable projections of specific costs that are not easily estimated for, identified with, or generated by a specific contract, contract end item, or task. These projections may include rates for such things as labor, indirect costs, material obsolescence and usage, spare parts provisioning, and material handling.

Forward pricing rate recommendation means a rate set unilaterally by the administrative contracting officer for use by the Government in negotiations or other contract actions when forward pricing rate agreement negotiations have not been completed or when the contractor will not agree to a forward pricing rate agreement.

Freight means supplies, goods, and transportable property.

Full and open competition, when used with respect to a contract action, means that all responsible sources are permitted to compete.

General and administrative (G&A) expense means any management, financial, and other expense which is incurred by or allocated to a business unit and which is for the general management and administration of the business unit as a whole. G&A expense does not include those management expenses whose beneficial or causal relationship to cost objectives can be more directly measured by a base other than a cost input base representing the total activity of a business unit during a cost accounting period.

Global warming potential means how much a given mass of a chemical contributes to global warming over a given time period compared to the same mass of carbon dioxide. Carbon dioxide's global warming potential is defined as 1.0.

Governmentwide acquisition contract (GWAC) means a task-order or delivery-order contract for information technology established by one agency for Governmentwide use that is operated—

(1) By an executive agent designated by the Office of Management and Budget pursuant to 40 U.S.C. 11302(e); or

(2) Under a delegation of procurement authority issued by the General Services Administration (GSA) prior to August 7, 1996, under authority granted GSA by former section 40 U.S.C. 759, repealed by Public Law 104-106. The Economy Act does not apply to orders under a Governmentwide acquisition contract.

Governmentwide point of entry (GPE) means the single point where Government business opportunities greater than $25,000, including synopses of proposed contract actions, solicitations, and associated information, can be accessed electronically by the public. The GPE is located at *https://www.fbo.gov*.

Head of the agency (see *agency head*).

Head of the contracting activity means the official who has overall responsibility for managing the contracting activity.

High global warming potential hydrofluorocarbons means any hydrofluorocarbons in a particular end use for which EPA's Significant New Alternatives Policy (SNAP) program has identified other acceptable alternatives that have lower global warming potential. The SNAP list of alternatives is found at 40 CFR part 82, subpart G, with supplemental tables of alternatives available at *http://www.epa.gov/snap/*).

Historically black college or university means an institution determined by the Secretary of Education to meet the requirements of 34 CFR 608.2.

HUBZone means a historically underutilized business zone that is an area located within one or more qualified census tracts, qualified nonmetropolitan counties, lands within the external boundaries of an Indian reservation, qualified base closure areas, or redesignated areas, as defined in 13 CFR 126.103.

HUBZone contract means a contract awarded to a Small Business Administration certified "HUBZone small business concern" through any of the following procurement methods:

(1) A sole source award to a HUBZone small business concern.

(2) Set-aside awards based on competition restricted to HUBZone small business concerns.

(3) Awards to HUBZone small business concerns through full and open competition after a price evaluation preference in favor of HUBZone small business concerns.

HUBZone small business concern means a small business concern, certified by the Small Business Administration (SBA), that appears on the List of Qualified HUBZone Small Business Concerns maintained by the SBA (13 CFR 126.103).

Humanitarian or peacekeeping operation means a military operation in support of the provision of humanitarian or foreign disaster assistance or in support of a peacekeeping operation under chapter VI or VII of the Charter of the United Nations. The term does not include routine training, force rotation, or stationing (10 U.S.C. 2302(8) and 41 U.S.C. 153(2)).

Hydrofluorocarbons means compounds that contain only hydrogen, fluorine, and carbon.

In writing, writing, or *written* means any worded or numbered expression that can be read, reproduced, and later communicated, and includes electronically transmitted and stored information.

Indirect cost means any cost not directly identified with a single, final cost objective, but identified with two or more final cost objectives or with at least one intermediate cost objective.

Indirect cost rate means the percentage or dollar factor that expresses the ratio of indirect expense incurred in a given period to direct labor cost, manufacturing cost, or another appropriate base for the same period (see also *final indirect cost rate*).

Ineligible means excluded from Government contracting (and subcontracting, if appropriate) pursuant to statutory, Executive order, or regulatory authority other than this regulation (48 CFR chapter 1) and its implementing and supplementing regulations; for example, pursuant to—

(1) 40 U.S.C. chapter 31, subchapter IV, Wage Rate Requirements (Construction), and its related statutes and implementing regulations;

(2) 41 U.S.C. chapter 67, Service Contract Labor Standards;

(3) The Equal Employment Opportunity Acts and Executive orders;

(4) 41 U.S.C. chapter 65, Contracts for Material, Supplies, Articles, and Equipment Exceeding $15,000;

(5) 41 U.S.C. chapter 83, Buy American; or

(6) The Environmental Protection Acts and Executive orders.

Information security means protecting information and information systems from unauthorized access, use, disclosure, disruption, modification, or destruction in order to provide—

(1) *Integrity*, which means guarding against improper information modification or destruction, and includes ensuring information nonrepudiation and authenticity;

(2) *Confidentiality*, which means preserving authorized restrictions on access and disclosure, including means for protecting personal privacy and proprietary information; and

(3) *Availability*, which means ensuring timely and reliable access to, and use of, information.

Information technology means any equipment, or interconnected system(s) or subsystem(s) of equipment, that is used in the automatic acquisition, storage, analysis, evaluation, manipulation, management, movement, control, display, switching, interchange, transmission, or reception of data or information by the agency.

(1) For purposes of this definition, equipment is used by an agency if the equipment is used by the agency directly or is used by a contractor under a contract with the agency that requires—

(i) Its use; or

(ii) To a significant extent, its use in the performance of a service or the furnishing of a product.

(2) The term *information technology* includes computers, ancillary equipment (including imaging peripherals, input, output, and storage devices necessary for security and surveillance), peripheral equipment designed to be controlled by the central processing unit of a computer, software, firmware and similar procedures, services (including support services), and related resources.

(3) The term *information technology* does not include any equipment that—

(i) Is acquired by a contractor incidental to a contract; or

(ii) Contains imbedded information technology that is used as an integral part of the product, but the principal function of which is not the acquisition, storage, analysis, evaluation, manipulation, management, movement, control, display, switching, interchange, transmission, or reception of data or information. For example, HVAC (heating, ventilation, and air conditioning) equipment, such as thermostats or temperature control devices, and medical equipment where information technology is integral to its operation, are not information technology.

Inherently governmental function means, as a matter of policy, a function that is so intimately related to the public interest as to mandate performance by Government employees. This definition is a policy determination, not a legal determination. An inherently governmental function includes activities that require either the exercise of discretion in applying Government authority, or the making of value judgments in making decisions for the Government. Governmental functions normally fall into two categories: the act of governing, *i.e.*, the discretionary exercise of Government authority, and monetary transactions and entitlements.

(1) An inherently governmental function involves, among other things, the interpretation and execution of the laws of the United States so as to—

(i) Bind the United States to take or not to take some action by contract, policy, regulation, authorization, order, or otherwise;

(ii) Determine, protect, and advance United States economic, political, territorial, property, or other interests by military or diplomatic action, civil or criminal judicial proceedings, contract management, or otherwise;

(iii) Significantly affect the life, liberty, or property of private persons;

(iv) Commission, appoint, direct, or control officers or employees of the United States; or

(v) Exert ultimate control over the acquisition, use, or disposition of the property, real or personal, tangible or intangible, of the United States, including the collection, control, or disbursement of Federal funds.

(2) Inherently governmental functions do not normally include gathering information for or providing advice, opinions, recommendations, or ideas to Government officials. They also do not include functions that are primarily ministerial and internal in nature, such as building security, mail operations, operation of cafeterias, housekeeping, facilities operations and maintenance, warehouse

operations, motor vehicle fleet management operations, or other routine electrical or mechanical services.

Inspection means examining and testing supplies or services (including, when appropriate, raw materials, components, and intermediate assemblies) to determine whether they conform to contract requirements.

Insurance means a contract that provides that for a stipulated consideration, one party undertakes to indemnify another against loss, damage, or liability arising from an unknown or contingent event.

Interagency acquisition means a procedure by which an agency needing supplies or services (the requesting agency) obtains them from another agency (the servicing agency), by an assisted acquisition or a direct acquisition. The term includes—

(1) Acquisitions under the Economy Act (31 U.S.C. 1535); and

(2) Non-Economy Act acquisitions completed under other statutory authorities (*e.g.,* General Services Administration Federal Supply Schedules in subpart 8.4 and Governmentwide acquisition contracts (GWACs)).

Invoice means a contractor's bill or written request for payment under the contract for supplies delivered or services performed (see also *proper invoice*).

Irrevocable letter of credit means a written commitment by a federally insured financial institution to pay all or part of a stated amount of money, until the expiration date of the letter, upon the Government's (the beneficiary) presentation of a written demand for payment. Neither the financial institution nor the offeror/contractor can revoke or condition the letter of credit.

Labor surplus area means a geographical area identified by the Department of Labor in accordance with 20 CFR part 654, subpart A, as an area of concentrated unemployment or underemployment or an area of labor surplus.

Labor surplus area concern means a concern that together with its first-tier subcontractors will perform substantially in labor surplus areas. Performance is substantially in labor surplus areas if the costs incurred under the contract on account of manufacturing, production, or performance of appropriate services in labor surplus areas exceed 50 percent of the contract price.

Latent defect means a defect that exists at the time of acceptance but cannot be discovered by a reasonable inspection.

Line item means the basic structural element in a procurement instrument that describes and organizes the required product or service for pricing, delivery, inspection, acceptance, invoicing, and payment. The use of the term *line item* includes *subline item,* as applicable.

Line item number means either a numeric or alphanumeric format to identify a line item.

Major disaster, as used in 6.208, 13.201, 13.500, 18.001, 18.202, 18.203, and subpart 26.2, means any natural catastrophe (including any hurricane, tornado, storm, high water, winddriven water, tidal wave, tsunami, earthquake, volcanic eruption, landslide, mudslide, snowstorm, or drought), or regardless of cause, any fire, flood, or explosion, in any part of the United States, which, in the determination of the President, causes damage of sufficient severity and magnitude to warrant major disaster assistance under the Stafford Act to supplement the efforts and available resources of States, local governments, and disaster relief organizations in alleviating the damage, loss, hardship, or suffering caused thereby (42 U.S.C. 5122).

Major system means that combination of elements that will function together to produce the capabilities required to fulfill a mission need. The elements may include hardware, equipment, software, or any combination thereof, but exclude construction or other improvements to real property. A system is a major system if—

(1) The Department of Defense is responsible for the system and the total expenditures for research, development, test, and evaluation for the system are estimated to be more than $185 million based on Fiscal Year 2014 constant dollars or the eventual total expenditure for the acquisition exceeds $835 million based on Fiscal Year 2014 constant dollars (or any update of these thresholds

based on a more recent fiscal year, as specified in the DoD Instruction 5000.02, "Operation of the Defense Acquisition System");

(2) A civilian agency is responsible for the system and total expenditures for the system are estimated to exceed $2 million or the dollar threshold for a *major system* established by the agency pursuant to Office of Management and Budget Circular A-109, entitled "Major System Acquisitions," whichever is greater; or

(3) The system is designated a *major system* by the head of the agency responsible for the system (10 U.S.C. 2302 and 41 U.S.C. 109).

Make-or-buy program means that part of a contractor's written plan for a contract identifying those major items to be produced or work efforts to be performed in the prime contractor's facilities and those to be subcontracted.

Manufactured end product means any end product in product and service codes (PSC) 1000-9999, except—

(1) PSC 5510, Lumber and Related Basic Wood Materials;

(2) Product or service group (PSG) 87, Agricultural Supplies;

(3) PSG 88, Live Animals;

(4) PSG 89, Subsistence;

(5) PSC 9410, Crude Grades of Plant Materials;

(6) PSC 9430, Miscellaneous Crude Animal Products, Inedible;

(7) PSC 9440, Miscellaneous Crude Agricultural and Forestry Products;

(8) PSC 9610, Ores;

(9) PSC 9620, Minerals, Natural and Synthetic; and

(10) PSC 9630, Additive Metal Materials.

Market research means collecting and analyzing information about capabilities within the market to satisfy agency needs.

Master solicitation means a document containing special clauses and provisions that have been identified as essential for the acquisition of a specific type of supply or service that is acquired repetitively.

May denotes the permissive. However, the words "no person may . . . " mean that no person is required, authorized, or permitted to do the act described.

Micro-purchase means an acquisition of supplies or services using simplified acquisition procedures, the aggregate amount of which does not exceed the micro-purchase threshold.

Micro-purchase threshold means $3,500, except it means—

(1) For acquisitions of construction subject to 40 U.S.C. chapter 31, subchapter IV, Wage Rate Requirements (Construction), $2,000;

(2) For acquisitions of services subject to 41 U.S.C. chapter 67, Service Contract Labor Standards, $2,500; and

(3) For acquisitions of supplies or services that, as determined by the head of the agency, are to be used to support a contingency operation; to facilitate defense against or recovery from cyber, nuclear, biological, chemical or radiological attack; to support a request from the Secretary of State or the Administrator of the United States Agency for International Development to facilitate provision of international disaster assistance pursuant to 22 U.S.C. 2292 *et seq.*; or to support response to an emergency or major disaster (42 U.S.C. 5122), as described in 13.201(g)(1), except for construction subject to 40 U.S.C. chapter 31, subchapter IV, Wage Rate Requirements (Construction) (41 U.S.C. 1903)—

(i) $20,000 (41 U.S.C. 134), in the case of any contract to be awarded and performed, or purchase to be made, inside the United States; and

(ii) $30,000 in the case of any contract to be awarded and performed, or purchase to be made, outside the United States.

Minority Institution means an institution of higher education meeting the requirements of Section 365(3) of the Higher Education Act of 1965 (20 U.S.C. 1067k), including a Hispanic-serving institution of higher education, as defined in Section 502(a) of the Act (20 U.S.C. 1101a).

Multi-agency contract (MAC) means a task-order or delivery-order contract established by one agency for use by Government agencies to obtain supplies and services, consistent with the Economy Act (see 17.502-2). Multi-agency contracts include contracts for information technology established pursuant to 40 U.S.C. 11314(a)(2).

Multiple-award contract means a contract that is—

(1) A Multiple Award Schedule contract issued by GSA (*e.g.*, GSA Schedule Contract) or agencies granted Multiple Award Schedule contract authority by GSA (*e.g.*, Department of Veterans Affairs) as described in FAR part 38;

(2) A multiple-award task-order or delivery-order contract issued in accordance with FAR subpart 16.5, including Governmentwide acquisition contracts; or

(3) Any other indefinite-delivery, indefinite-quantity contract entered into with two or more sources pursuant to the same solicitation.

Must (see *shall*).

National defense means any activity related to programs for military or atomic energy production or construction, military assistance to any foreign nation, stockpiling, or space, except that for use in Subpart 11.6, see the definition in 11.601.

Neutral person means an impartial third party, who serves as a mediator, fact finder, or arbitrator, or otherwise functions to assist the parties to resolve the issues in controversy. A neutral person may be a permanent or temporary officer or employee of the Federal Government or any other individual who is acceptable to the parties. A neutral person must have no official, financial, or personal conflict of interest with respect to the issues in controversy, unless the interest is fully disclosed in writing to all parties and all parties agree that the neutral person may serve (5 U.S.C. 583).

Nondevelopmental item means—

(1) Any previously developed item of supply used exclusively for governmental purposes by a Federal agency, a State or local government, or a foreign government with which the United States has a mutual defense cooperation agreement;

(2) Any item described in paragraph (1) of this definition that requires only minor modification or modifications of a type customarily available in the commercial marketplace in order to meet the requirements of the procuring department or agency; or

(3) Any item of supply being produced that does not meet the requirements of paragraphs (1) or (2) solely because the item is not yet in use.

Novation agreement means a legal instrument—

(1) Executed by the—

(i) Contractor (transferor);

(ii) Successor in interest (transferee); and

(iii) Government; and

(2) By which, among other things, the transferor guarantees performance of the contract, the transferee assumes all obligations under the contract, and the Government recognizes the transfer of the contract and related assets.

Offer means a response to a solicitation that, if accepted, would bind the offeror to perform the resultant contract. Responses to invitations for bids (sealed bidding) are offers called *bids* or *sealed bids*; responses to requests for proposals (negotiation) are offers called *proposals*; however, responses to requests for quotations (simplified acquisition) are *quotations*, not offers. For unsolicited proposals, see subpart 15.6.

Offeror means offeror or bidder.

Office of Small and Disadvantaged Business Utilization means the Office of Small Business Programs when referring to the Department of Defense.

OMB Uniform Guidance at 2 CFR part 200 is the abbreviated title for Uniform Administrative Requirements, Cost Principles, and Audit Requirements for Federal Awards (2 CFR part 200), which supersedes OMB Circulars A-21, A-87, A-89, A-102, A-110, A-122, and A-133, and the guidance in Circular A-50 on Audit Followup.

Option means a unilateral right in a contract by which, for a specified time, the Government may elect to purchase additional supplies or services called for by the contract, or may elect to extend the term of the contract.

Organizational conflict of interest means that because of other activities or relationships with other persons, a person is unable or potentially unable to render impartial assistance or advice to the Government, or the person's objectivity in performing the contract work is or might be otherwise impaired, or a person has an unfair competitive advantage.

Outlying areas means—

(1) Commonwealths. (i) Puerto Rico.

(ii) The Northern Mariana Islands;

(2) Territories. (i) American Samoa.

(ii) Guam.

(iii) U.S. Virgin Islands; and

(3) Minor outlying islands. (i) Baker Island.

(ii) Howland Island.

(iii) Jarvis Island.

(iv) Johnston Atoll.

(v) Kingman Reef.

(vi) Midway Islands.

(vii) Navassa Island.

(viii) Palmyra Atoll.

(ix) Wake Atoll.

Overtime means time worked by a contractor's employee in excess of the employee's normal workweek.

Overtime premium means the difference between the contractor's regular rate of pay to an employee for the shift involved and the higher rate paid for overtime. It does not include shift premium, i.e., the difference between the contractor's regular rate of pay to an employee and the higher rate paid for extra-pay-shift work.

Ozone-depleting substance means any substance the Environmental Protection Agency designates in 40 CFR part 82 as—

(1) Class I, including, but not limited to, chlorofluorocarbons, halons, carbon tetrachloride, and methyl chloroform; or

(2) Class II, including, but not limited to, hydrochlorofluorocarbons.

Partial termination means the termination of a part, but not all, of the work that has not been completed and accepted under a contract.

Past performance means an offeror's or contractor's performance on active and physically completed contracts (see 4.804-4).

Performance-based acquisition (PBA) means an acquisition structured around the results to be achieved as opposed to the manner by which the work is to be performed.

Performance Work Statement (PWS) means a statement of work for performance-based acquisitions that describes the required results in clear, specific and objective terms with measurable outcomes.

Personal property means property of any kind or interest in it except real property, records of the Federal Government, and naval vessels of the following categories:

(1) Battleships;

(2) Cruisers;

(3) Aircraft carriers;

(4) Destroyers; and

(5) Submarines.

Personal services contract means a contract that, by its express terms or as administered, makes the contractor personnel appear to be, in effect, Government employees (see 37.104).

Plant clearance officer means an authorized representative of the contracting officer, appointed in accordance with agency procedures, responsible for screening, redistributing, and disposing of contractor inventory from a contractor's plant or work site. The term *Contractor's plant* includes, but is not limited to, Government-owned contractor-operated plants, Federal installations, and Federal and non-Federal industrial operations, as may be required under the scope of the contract.

Pollution prevention means any practice that—

(1) (i) Reduces the amount of any hazardous substance, pollutant, or contaminant en-

tering any waste stream or otherwise released into the environment (including fugitive emissions) prior to recycling, treatment, or disposal; and

(ii) Reduces the hazards to public health and the environment associated with the release of such substances, pollutants, and contaminants;

(2) Reduces or eliminates the creation of pollutants through increased efficiency in the use of raw materials, energy, water, or other resources; or

(3) Protects natural resources by conservation.

Power of attorney means the authority given one person or corporation to act for and obligate another, as specified in the instrument creating the power; in corporate suretyship, an instrument under seal that appoints an attorney-in-fact to act in behalf of a surety company in signing bonds (see also *attorney-in-fact* at 28.001).

Preaward survey means an evaluation of a prospective contractor's capability to perform a proposed contract.

Preponderance of the evidence means proof by information that, compared with that opposing it, leads to the conclusion that the fact at issue is more probably true than not.

Pricing means the process of establishing a reasonable amount or amounts to be paid for supplies or services.

Principal means an officer, director, owner, partner, or a person having primary management or supervisory responsibilities within a business entity (e.g., general manager; plant manager; head of a division or business segment; and similar positions).

Procurement (see *acquisition*).

Procuring activity means a component of an executive agency having a significant acquisition function and designated as such by the head of the agency. Unless agency regulations specify otherwise, the term *procuring activity* is synonymous with *contracting activity.*

Products has the same meaning as *supplies.*

Projected average loss means the estimated long-term average loss per period for periods of comparable exposure to risk of loss.

Proper invoice means an invoice that meets the minimum standards specified in 32.905(b).

Purchase order, when issued by the Government, means an offer by the Government to buy supplies or services, including construction and research and development, upon specified terms and conditions, using simplified acquisition procedures.

Qualification requirement means a Government requirement for testing or other quality assurance demonstration that must be completed before award of a contract.

Qualified products list (QPL) means a list of products that have been examined, tested, and have satisfied all applicable qualification requirements.

Receiving report means written evidence that indicates Government acceptance of supplies delivered or services performed (see subpart 46.6). Receiving reports must meet the requirements of 32.905(c).

Recovered material means waste materials and by-products recovered or diverted from solid waste, but the term does not include those materials and by-products generated from, and commonly reused within, an original manufacturing process. For use in subpart 11.3 for paper and paper products, see the definition at 11.301.

Registered in the System for Award Management (SAM) means that—

(1) The Contractor has entered all mandatory information, including the unique entity identifier and the Electronic Funds Transfer indicator (if applicable), the Commercial and Government Entity (CAGE) code, as well as data required by the Federal Funding Accountability and Transparency Act of 2006 (see subpart 4.14), into SAM;

(2) The Contractor has completed the Core, Assertions, Representations and Certifications, and Points of Contract sections of the registration in SAM;

(3) The Government validated all mandatory data fields, to include validation of the Taxpayer Identification Number (TIN)

with the Internal Revenue Service (IRS). The contractor will be required to provide consent for TIN validation to the Government as a part of the SAM registration process; and

(4) The Government has marked the record "Active".

Renewable energy means energy produced by solar, wind, geothermal, biomass, landfill gas, ocean (including tidal, wave, current, and thermal), municipal solid waste, or new hydroelectric generation capacity achieved from increased efficiency or additions of new capacity at an existing hydroelectric project (Energy Policy Act of 2005, 42 U.S.C. 15852).

Renewable energy technology means—

(1) Technologies that use renewable energy to provide light, heat, cooling, or mechanical or electrical energy for use in facilities or other activities; or

(2) The use of integrated whole-building designs that rely upon renewable energy resources, including passive solar design.

Requesting agency means the agency that has the requirement for an interagency acquisition.

Residual value means the proceeds, less removal and disposal costs, if any, realized upon disposition of a tangible capital asset. It usually is measured by the net proceeds from the sale or other disposition of the asset, or its fair value if the asset is traded in on another asset. The estimated residual value is a current forecast of the residual value.

Responsible audit agency means the agency that is responsible for performing all required contract audit services at a business unit.

Responsible prospective contractor means a contractor that meets the standards in 9.104.

Scrap means personal property that has no value except its basic metallic, mineral, or organic content.

Segment means one of two or more divisions, product departments, plants, or other subdivisions of an organization reporting directly to a home office, usually identified with responsibility for profit and/or producing a product or service. The term includes—

(1) Government-owned contractor-operated (GOCO) facilities; and

(2) Joint ventures and subsidiaries (domestic and foreign) in which the organization has—

(i) A majority ownership; or

(ii) Less than a majority ownership, but over which it exercises control.

Self-insurance means the assumption or retention of the risk of loss by the contractor, whether voluntarily or involuntarily. Self-insurance includes the deductible portion of purchased insurance.

Senior procurement executive means the individual appointed pursuant to 41 U.S.C. 1702(c) who is responsible for management direction of the acquisition system of the executive agency, including implementation of the unique acquisition policies, regulations, and standards of the executive agency.

Service-disabled veteran-owned small business concern—

(1) Means a small business concern—

(i) Not less than 51 percent of which is owned by one or more service-disabled veterans or, in the case of any publicly owned business, not less than 51 percent of the stock of which is owned by one or more service-disabled veterans; and

(ii) The management and daily business operations of which are controlled by one or more service-disabled veterans or, in the case of a service-disabled veteran with permanent and severe disability, the spouse or permanent caregiver of such veteran.

(2) *Service-disabled veteran* means a veteran, as defined in 38 U.S.C. 101(2), with a disability that is service-connected, as defined in 38 U.S.C. 101(16).

Servicing agency means the agency that will conduct an assisted acquisition on behalf of the requesting agency.

Shall means the imperative.

Shipment means freight transported or to be transported.

Shop drawings means drawings submitted by the construction contractor or a subcontractor at any tier or required under a construction contract, showing in detail either or both of the following:

(1) The proposed fabrication and assembly of structural elements.

(2) The installation (i.e., form, fit, and attachment details) of materials or equipment.

Should means an expected course of action or policy that is to be followed unless inappropriate for a particular circumstance.

Signature or *signed* means the discrete, verifiable symbol of an individual that, when affixed to a writing with the knowledge and consent of the individual, indicates a present intention to authenticate the writing. This includes electronic symbols.

Simplified acquisition procedures means the methods prescribed in Part 13 for making purchases of supplies or services.

Simplified acquisition threshold means $150,000, except for—

(1) Acquisitions of supplies or services that, as determined by the head of the agency, are to be used to support a contingency operation; to facilitate defense against or recovery from cyber, nuclear, biological, chemical, or radiological attack; to support a request from the Secretary of State or the Administrator of the United States Agency for International Development to facilitate provision of international disaster assistance pursuant to 22 U.S.C. 2292 *et seq.*; or to support response to an emergency or major disaster (42 U.S.C. 5122), (41 U.S.C. 1903), the term means—

(i) $750,000 for any contract to be awarded and performed, or purchase to be made, inside the United States; and

(ii) $1.5 million for any contract to be awarded and performed, or purchase to be made, outside the United States; and

(2) Acquisitions of supplies or services that, as determined by the head of the agency, are to be used to support a humanitarian or peacekeeping operation (10 U.S.C. 2302), the term means $300,000 for any contract to be awarded and performed, or purchase to be made, outside the United States.

Single, Government wide point of entry, means the one point of entry to be designated by the Administrator of OFPP that will allow the private sector to electronically access procurement opportunities Government wide.

Small business concern means a concern, including its affiliates, that is independently owned and operated, not dominant in the field of operation in which it is bidding on Government contracts, and qualified as a small business under the criteria and size standards in 13 CFR part 121 (see 19.102). Such a concern is "not dominant in its field of operation" when it does not exercise a controlling or major influence on a national basis in a kind of business activity in which a number of business concerns are primarily engaged. In determining whether dominance exists, consideration must be given to all appropriate factors, including volume of business, number of employees, financial resources, competitive status or position, ownership or control of materials, processes, patents, license agreements, facilities, sales territory, and nature of business activity. (see 15 U.S.C. 632.)

Small business subcontractor means a concern that does not exceed the size standard for the North American Industry Classification Systems code that the prime contractor determines best describes the product or service being acquired by the subcontract.

Small Business Teaming Arrangement —

(1) Means an arrangement where—

(i) Two or more small business concerns have formed a joint venture; or

(ii) A small business offeror agrees with one or more other small business concerns to have them act as its subcontractors under a specified Government contract. A Small Business Teaming Arrangement between the offeror and its small business subcontractor(s) exists through a written agreement between the parties that—

(A) Is specifically referred to as a "Small Business Teaming Arrangement"; and

(B) Sets forth the different responsibilities, roles, and percentages (or other allocations) of work as it relates to the acquisition;

(2) (i) For civilian agencies, may include two business concerns in a mentor-protégé

relationship when both the mentor and the protégé are small or the protégé is small and the concerns have received an exception to affiliation pursuant to 13 CFR 121.103(h)(3)(ii) or (iii).

(ii) For DoD, may include two business concerns in a mentor-protégé relationship in the Department of Defense Pilot Mentor-Protégé Program (see section 831 of the National Defense Authorization Act for Fiscal Year 1991 (Pub. L. 101-510; 10 U.S.C. 2302 note)) when both the mentor and the protégé are small. There is no exception to joint venture size affiliation for offers received from teaming arrangements under the Department of Defense Pilot Mentor-Protégé Program; and

(3) See 13 CFR 121.103(b)(9) regarding the exception to affiliation for offers received from Small Business Teaming Arrangements in the case of a solicitation of offers for a bundled contract with a reserve.

Small disadvantaged business concern, consistent with 13 CFR 124.1002, means a small business concern under the size standard applicable to the acquisition, that

(1) Is at least 51 percent unconditionally and directly owned (as defined at 13 CFR 124.105) by—

(i) One or more socially disadvantaged (as defined at 13 CFR 124.103) and economically disadvantaged (as defined at 13 CFR 124.104) individuals who are citizens of the United States; and

(ii) Each individual claiming economic disadvantage has a net worth not exceeding $750,000 after taking into account the applicable exclusions set forth at 13 CFR 124.104(c)(2); and

(2) The management and daily business operations of which are controlled (as defined at 13 CFR 124.106) by individuals who meet the criteria in paragraphs (1)(i) and (ii) of this definition.

Sole source acquisition means a contract for the purchase of supplies or services that is entered into or proposed to be entered into by an agency after soliciting and negotiating with only one source.

Solicitation means any request to submit offers or quotations to the Government. Solicitations under sealed bid procedures are called *invitations for bids*. Solicitations under negotiated procedures are called *requests for proposals*. Solicitations under simplified acquisition procedures may require submission of either a quotation or an offer.

Solicitation provision or *provision* means a term or condition used only in solicitations and applying only before contract award.

Source selection information means any of the following information that is prepared for use by an agency for the purpose of evaluating a bid or proposal to enter into an agency procurement contract, if that information has not been previously made available to the public or disclosed publicly:

(1) Bid prices submitted in response to an agency invitation for bids, or lists of those bid prices before bid opening.

(2) Proposed costs or prices submitted in response to an agency solicitation, or lists of those proposed costs or prices.

(3) Source selection plans.

(4) Technical evaluation plans.

(5) Technical evaluations of proposals.

(6) Cost or price evaluations of proposals.

(7) Competitive range determinations that identify proposals that have a reasonable chance of being selected for award of a contract.

(8) Rankings of bids, proposals, or competitors.

(9) Reports and evaluations of source selection panels, boards, or advisory councils.

(10) Other information marked as "Source Selection Information—See FAR 2.101 and 3.104" based on a case-by-case determination by the head of the agency or the contracting officer, that its disclosure would jeopardize the integrity or successful completion of the Federal agency procurement to which the information relates.

Special competency means a special or unique capability, including qualitative aspects, developed incidental to the primary functions of the Federally Funded Research and Development Centers to meet some special need.

Special test equipment means either single or multipurpose integrated test units engineered, designed, fabricated, or modified to accomplish special purpose testing in performing a contract. It consists of items or assemblies of equipment including foundations and similar improvements necessary for installing special test equipment, and standard or general purpose items or components that are interconnected and interdependent so as to become a new functional entity for special testing purposes. Special test equipment does not include material, special tooling, real property, and equipment items used for general testing purposes or property that with relatively minor expense can be made suitable for general purpose use.

Special tooling means jigs, dies, fixtures, molds, patterns, taps, gauges, and all components of these items including foundations and similar improvements necessary for installing special tooling, and which are of such a specialized nature that without substantial modification or alteration their use is limited to the development or production of particular supplies or parts thereof or to the performance of particular services. Special tooling does not include material, special test equipment, real property, equipment, machine tools, or similar capital items.

State and local taxes means taxes levied by the States, the District of Columbia, outlying areas of the United States, or their political subdivisions.

Statement of Objectives (SOO) means a Government-prepared document incorporated into the solicitation that states the overall performance objectives. It is used in solicitations when the Government intends to provide the maximum flexibility to each offeror to propose an innovative approach.

Subline item means a subset of a line item.

Substantial evidence means information sufficient to support the reasonable belief that a particular act or omission has occurred.

Substantially as follows or *substantially the same as*, when used in the prescription and introductory text of a provision or clause, means that authorization is granted to prepare and utilize a variation of that provision or clause to accommodate requirements that are peculiar to an individual acquisition; provided that the variation includes the salient features of the FAR provision or clause, and is not inconsistent with the intent, principle, and substance of the FAR provision or clause or related coverage of the subject matter.

Supplemental agreement means a contract modification that is accomplished by the mutual action of the parties.

Supplies means all property except land or interest in land. It includes (but is not limited to) public works, buildings, and facilities; ships, floating equipment, and vessels of every character, type, and description, together with parts and accessories; aircraft and aircraft parts, accessories, and equipment; machine tools; and the alteration or installation of any of the foregoing.

Supporting a diplomatic or consular mission means performing outside the United States under a contract administered by Federal agency personnel who are subject to the direction of a Chief of Mission.

Surety means an individual or corporation legally liable for the debt, default, or failure of a principal to satisfy a contractual obligation. The types of sureties referred to are as follows:

(1) An individual surety is one person, as distinguished from a business entity, who is liable for the entire penal amount of the bond.

(2) A corporate surety is licensed under various insurance laws and, under its charter, has legal power to act as surety for others.

(3) A cosurety is one of two or more sureties that are jointly liable for the penal sum of the bond. A limit of liability for each surety may be stated.

Surplus property means personal property not required by any Federal agency as determined by the Administrator of the General Services Administration (GSA). (see 41 CFR 102-36.40).

Suspension means action taken by a suspending official under 9.407 to disqualify a contractor temporarily from Government contracting and Government-approved subcontracting; a contractor that is disqualified is *suspended*.

Sustainable acquisition means acquiring goods and services in order to create and maintain conditions—

(1) Under which humans and nature can exist in productive harmony; and

(2) That permit fulfilling the social, economic, and other requirements of present and future generations.

System for Award Management (SAM) means the primary Government repository for prospective Federal awardee and Federal awardee information and the centralized Government system for certain contracting, grants, and other assistance related processes. It includes—

(1) Data collected from prospective Federal awardees required for the conduct of business with the Government;

(2) Prospective contractor-submitted annual representations and certifications in accordance with FAR subpart 4.12; and

(3) Identification of those parties excluded from receiving Federal contracts, certain subcontracts, and certain types of Federal financial and non-financial assistance and benefits.

Task order means an order for services placed against an established contract or with Government sources.

Taxpayer Identification Number (TIN) means the number required by the IRS to be used by the offeror in reporting income tax and other returns. The TIN may be either a Social Security Number or an Employer Identification Number.

Technical data means recorded information (regardless of the form or method of the recording) of a scientific or technical nature (including computer databases and computer software documentation). This term does not include computer software or financial, administrative, cost or pricing, or management data or other information incidental to contract administration. The term includes recorded information of a scientific or technical nature that is included in computer databases (see 41 U.S.C. 116).

Termination for convenience means the exercise of the Government's right to completely or partially terminate performance of work under a contract when it is in the Government's interest.

Termination for default means the exercise of the Government's right to completely or partially terminate a contract because of the contractor's actual or anticipated failure to perform its contractual obligations.

Termination inventory means any property purchased, supplied, manufactured, furnished, or otherwise acquired for the performance of a contract subsequently terminated and properly allocable to the terminated portion of the contract. It includes Government-furnished property. It does not include any facilities, material, special test equipment, or special tooling that are subject to a separate contract or to a special contract requirement governing their use or disposition.

Terminated portion of the contract means the portion of a contract that the contractor is not to perform following a partial termination. For construction contracts that have been completely terminated for convenience, it means the entire contract, notwithstanding the completion of, and payment for, individual items of work before termination.

Unallowable cost means any cost that, under the provisions of any pertinent law, regulation, or contract, cannot be included in prices, cost-reimbursements, or settlements under a Government contract to which it is allocable.

Unique and innovative concept, when used relative to an unsolicited research proposal, means that—

(1) In the opinion and to the knowledge of the Government evaluator, the meritorious proposal—

(i) Is the product of original thinking submitted confidentially by one source;

(ii) Contains new, novel, or changed concepts, approaches, or methods;

(iii) Was not submitted previously by another; and

(iv) Is not otherwise available within the Federal Government.

(2) In this context, the term does not mean that the source has the sole capability of performing the research.

Unique entity identifier means a number or other identifier used to identify a specific commercial, nonprofit, or Government entity. See *www.sam.gov* for the designated entity for establishing unique entity identifiers.

United States, when used in a geographic sense, means the 50 States and the District of Columbia, except as follows:

(1) For use in subpart 3.10, see the definition at 3.1001.

(2) For use in subpart 22.8, see the definition at 22.801.

(3) For use in subpart 22.10, see the definition at 22.1001.

(4) For use in subpart 22.12, see the definition at 22.1201.

(5) For use in subpart 22.13, see the definition at 22.1301.

(6) For use in subpart 22.16, see the definition at 22.1601.

(7) For use in subpart 22.17, see the definition at 22.1702.

(8) For use in subpart 22.18, see the definition at 22.1801.

(9) For use in part 23, see definition at 23.001.

(10) For use in part 25, see the definition at 25.003.

(11) For use in part 27, see the definition at 27.001.

(12) For use in subpart 47.4, see the definition at 47.401.

Unsolicited proposal means a written proposal for a new or innovative idea that is submitted to an agency on the initiative of the offeror for the purpose of obtaining a contract with the Government, and that is not in response to a request for proposals, Broad Agency Announcement, Small Business Innovation Research topic, Small Business Technology Transfer Research topic, Program Research and Development Announcement, or any other Government-initiated solicitation or program.

Value engineering means an analysis of the functions of a program, project, system, product, item of equipment, building, facility, service, or supply of an executive agency, performed by qualified agency or contractor personnel, directed at improving performance, reliability, quality, safety, and life-cycle costs (41 U.S.C. 1711). For use in the clause at 52.248-2, see the definition at 52.248-2(b).

Value engineering change proposal (VECP)—(1) Means a proposal that—

(i) Requires a change to the instant contract to implement; and

(ii) Results in reducing the overall projected cost to the agency without impairing essential functions or characteristics, provided, that it does not involve a change—

(A) In deliverable end item quantities only;

(B) In research and development (R&D) items or R&D test quantities that are due solely to results of previous testing under the instant contract; or

(C) To the contract type only.

(2) For use in the clauses at—

(i) 52.248-2, see the definition at 52.248-2(b); and

(ii) 52.248-3, see the definition at 52.248-3(b).

Veteran-owned small business concern means a small business concern—

(1) Not less than 51 percent of which is owned by one or more veterans (as defined at 38 U.S.C. 101(2)) or, in the case of any publicly owned business, not less than 51 percent of the stock of which is owned by one or more veterans; and

(2) The management and daily business operations of which are controlled by one or more veterans.

Virgin material means—

(1) Previously unused raw material, including previously unused copper, aluminum, lead, zinc, iron, other metal or metal ore; or

(2) Any undeveloped resource that is, or with new technology will become, a source of raw materials.

Voluntary consensus standards means common and repeated use of rules, conditions, guidelines or characteristics for products, or related processes and production methods and related management systems. Voluntary Consensus Standards are developed or adopted by domestic and international voluntary consensus standard making bodies (e.g., International Organization for Standardization (ISO) and ASTM-International). See OMB Circular A-119.

Warranty means a promise or affirmation given by a contractor to the Government regarding the nature, usefulness, or condition of the supplies or performance of services furnished under the contract.

Waste reduction means preventing or decreasing the amount of waste being generated through waste prevention, recycling, or purchasing recycled and environmentally preferable products.

Water consumption intensity means water consumption per square foot of building space.

Women-owned small business concern means—

(1) A small business concern—

(i) That is at least 51 percent owned by one or more women; or, in the case of any publicly owned business, at least 51 percent of the stock of which is owned by one or more women; and

(ii) Whose management and daily business operations are controlled by one or more women; or

(2) A small business concern eligible under the Women-Owned Small Business Program in accordance with 13 CFR part 127 (see subpart 19.15).

Women-Owned Small Business (WOSB) Program. (1) *Women-Owned Small Business Program (WOSB) Program* means a program that authorizes contracting officers to limit competition, including award on a sole source basis, to—

(i) Economically disadvantaged women-owned small business (EDWOSB) concerns eligible under the WOSB Program for Federal contracts assigned a North American Industry Classification Systems (NAICS) code in an industry in which the Small Business Administration (SBA) has determined that WOSB concerns are underrepresented in Federal procurement; and

(ii) WOSB concerns eligible under the WOSB Program for Federal contracts assigned a NAICS code in an industry in which SBA has determined that WOSB concerns are substantially underrepresented in Federal procurement; and

(2) *Economically disadvantaged women-owned small business (EDWOSB) concern* means a small business concern that is at least 51 percent directly and unconditionally owned by, and the management and daily business operations of which are controlled by, one or more women who are citizens of the United States and who are economically disadvantaged in accordance with 13 CFR part 127. It automatically qualifies as a women-owned small business (WOSB) concern eligible under the WOSB Program.

(3) *Women-owned small business (WOSB) concern eligible under the WOSB Program* means a small business concern that is at least 51 percent directly and unconditionally owned by, and the management and daily business operations of which are controlled by, one or more women who are citizens of the United States (13 CFR part 127).

Writing or *written* (see *In writing*).

[FAC 84-5, 50 FR 1727, 1/11/85, effective 4/1/85; FAC 84-8, 50 FR 26903, 6/28/85, effective 7/1/85; FAC 84-12, 51 FR 2649, 1/17/86, effective 1/20/86; FAC 84-26, 52 FR 19802, 5/27/87, effective 7/30/87; FAC 84-53, 54 FR 48981, 11/28/89, effective 12/28/89; FAC 90-7, 56 FR 41744, 8/22/91, effective 9/23/91; FAC 90-29, 60 FR 34732, 7/3/95, effective 7/3/95; FAC 90-31, 60 FR 42648, 8/16/95, effective 10/1/95; FAC 90-32, 60 FR 48206, 9/18/95, effective 10/1/95; FAC 90-40, 61 FR 39186, 7/26/96, effective 8/26/96; FAC 90-41, 61 FR 41466, 8/8/96, effective 8/8/96; FAC 90-44, 61 FR 69286, 12/31/96, effective 12/31/96; FAC 90-45, 62 FR 224, 1/2/97, effective 1/1/97; FAC 97-2, 62 FR 51224, 9/30/97, effective 10/10/97; FAC 97-3, 62 FR 64912, 12/9/97, effective 2/9/98; FAC 97-9, 63 FR 58587, 10/30/98, effective 10/30/98; FAC 97-15, 64 FR 72414, 12/27/99, effective 12/27/99; FAC 97-15, 64 FR 72414, 12/27/99, effective 2/25/2000; FAC 97-17, 65 FR 24316, 4/25/2000, effective 4/25/2000; FAC 97-18, 65 FR 36014, 6/6/2000, effective 8/7/2000; FAC 97-19, 65 FR 46052, 7/26/2000, effective 7/26/2000; FAC 97-20, 65 FR 60542 10/11/2000, effective 10/11/2000; FAC 97-22, 66 FR 2116, 1/10/2001, effective 3/12/2001, corrected 66 FR 27011, 5/15/2001; Delay of effective date, 66 FR 14259, 3/9/2001, effective 5/11/2001; FAC 97-27, 66 FR 20894, 4/25/2001, effective 6/25/2001; FAC 97-25, 66 FR 22081, 5/2/2001, effective 5/2/2001; FAC 97-26, 66 FR 27405, 5/16/2001, effective 5/16/2001; FAC 2001-01, 66 FR 53478, 10/22/2001, effective 10/22/2001 and 12/21/2001; FAC 2001-02, 66 FR 65347, 12/18/2001, effective 2/19/2002; FAC 2001-04, 67 FR 6112, 2/8/2002, effective 2/20/2002; FAC 2001-06, 67 FR 13048, 3/20/2002, effective 4/4/2002; FAC 2001-08, 67 FR 43513, 6/27/2002, effective 7/29/2002; FAC 2001-09, 67 FR 56115, 8/30/2002, effective 8/30/2002; FAC 2001-12, 68 FR 4047, 1/27/2003, effective 1/24/2003; FAC 2001-14, 68 FR 28079, 5/22/2003, effective 5/22/2003; FAC 2001-14, 68 FR 28091, 5/22/2003, effective 6/23/2003; FAC 2001-14, 68 FR 28092, 5/22/2003, effective 5/22/2003; FAC 2001-15, 68 FR 43857, 7/24/2003, effective 8/25/2003; FAC 2001-16, 68 FR 56669, 10/1/2003, effective 10/1/2003; FAC 2001-16, 68 FR 56676, 10/1/2003, effective 10/1/2003; FAC 2001-17, 68 FR 59999, 10/20/2003, effective 10/20/2003; FAC 2001-18, 68 FR 69246, 12/11/2003, effective 1/12/2004; FAC 2001-20, 69 FR 8311, 2/23/2004, effective 2/23/2004; FAC 2001-22, 69 FR 17741, 17764, 4/5/2004, effective 5/5/2004; FAC 2001-23, 69 FR 25273, 5/5/2004, effective 5/5/2004; FAC 2001-24, 69 FR 34225, 6/18/2004, effective 6/18/2004; FAC 2001-26, 69 FR 76341, 12/20/2004, effective 1/1/2005, 69 FR 76347, 12/20/2004, effective 1/19/2005, 69 FR 76350, 12/20/2004, effective 1/19/2005, 69 FR 76352, 12/20/2004, effective 12/20/2004; FAC 2005-01, 70 FR 11737, 3/9/2005, effective 3/9/2005; FAC 2005-02, 70 FR 14950, 3/23/2005, effective 3/23/2005; FAC 2005-04, 70 FR 33655, 6/8/2005, effective 6/8/2005; 70 FR 33657, 6/8/2005, effective 6/8/2005; FAC 2005-05, 70 FR 43577, 7/27/2005, effective 7/27/2005; FAC 2005-06, 70 FR 57449, 9/30/2005, effective 9/30/2005; 70 FR 57452, 9/30/2005, effective 9/30/2005; 70 FR 57453, 9/30/2005, effective 9/30/2005; correction, 70 FR 69100, 11/14/2005, effective 11/14/2005; FAC 2005-07, 71 FR 208, 1/3/2006, effective 1/3/2006; FAC 2005-07, 71 FR 211, 1/3/2006, effective 2/2/2006; FAC 2005-09, 71 FR 20295, 4/19/2006, effective 5/19/2006; FAC 2005-09, 71 FR 20298, 4/19/2006, effective 4/19/2006; FAC 2005-09, 71 FR 20299, 04/19/2006, effective 5/19/2006; FAC 2005-10, 71 FR 36923, 6/28/2006, effective 7/28/2-06; FAC 2005-11, 71 FR 38238, 7/5/2006, effective 7/5/2006; FAC 2005-13, 71 FR 57363, 9/28/2006, effective 9/28/2006; FAC 2005-13, 71 FR 57360, 9/28/2006, effective 9/28/2006; FAC 2005-14, 71 FR 67771, 11/22/2006, effective 11/22/2006; FAC 2005-15, 71 FR 74667, 12/12/2006, effective 2/12/2007; FAC 2005-17, 72 FR 27364, 5/15/2007, effective 6/14/2007; FAC 2005-21, 71 FR 63040, 63045, 63075, 11/7/2007, effective 12/7/2007; FAC 2005-22, 72 FR 65868, 65873, 11/23/2007, effective 12/24/2007; FAC 2005-24, 73 FR 10943, 2/28/2008, effective 3/31/2008; FAC 2005-25, 73 FR 21773, 21783, 4/22/2008, effective 4/22/2008; FAC 2005-27, 73 FR 53992, 53993, 9/17/2008, effective 10/17/2008; FAC 2005-28, 73 FR 67064, 11/12/2008, effective 12/12/2008; FAC 2005-29, 73 FR 67651, 11/14/2008, effective 1/15/2009; Correction, 73 FR 72242, 11/26/2008, effective 1/15/2009; Amendment-1, FAC 2005-29, 74 FR 1937, 1/14/2009, effective 1/19/2009; FAC 2005-30, 74 FR 2712, 2713, 1/15/2009, effective 2/17/2009; Amendment-2, FAC 2005-29, 74 FR 5621, 1/30/2009, effective 5/21/2009; Amendment-3, FAC 2005-29, 74 FR 1773, 4/17/2009, effective 6/30/2009; Amendment-4, FAC 2005-29, 74 FR 26981, 6/5/2009, effective 9/8/2009; FAC 2005-34, 74 FR 31557, 7/1/2009, effective 7/1/2009; FAC 2005-37, 74 FR 52847, 10/14/2009, effective 10/14/2009; FAC 2005-38, 74 FR

65599, 12/10/2009, effective 12/10/2009; FAC 2005-40, 75 FR 14059, 3/23/2010, effective 4/22/2010; FAC 2005-41, 75 FR 19168, 4/13/2010, effective 5/13/2010; FAC 2005-43, 75 FR 38675, 38683, 7/2/2010, effective 8/2/2010; FAC 2005-45, 75 FR 53129, 53135, 53153, 8/30/2010, effective 10/1/2010; FAC 2005-47, 75 FR 77723, 12/13/2010, effective 12/13/2010; 75 FR 77727, 12/13/2010, effective 1/12/2011; 75 FR 77733, 77737, 12/13/2010, effective 12/13/2010; FAC 2005-50, 76 FR 14543, 3/16/2011, effective 3/16/2011; FAC 2005-51, 76 FR 18304, 4/1/2011, effective 4/1/2011; FAC 2005-52, 76 FR 31395, 5/31/2011, effective 5/31/2011; FAC 2005-54, 76 FR 68015, 68026, 11/2/2011, effective 11/2/2011; FAC 2005-55, 77 FR 183, 187, 1/3/2012, effective 2/2/2012; FAC 2005-56, 77 FR 12913, 12925, 12937, 3/2/2012, effective 4/2/2012; FAC 2005-58, 77 FR 23365, 4/18/2012, effective 5/18/2012; FAC 2005-60, 77 FR 44047, 7/26/2012, effective 8/27/2012; FAC 2005-64, 77 FR 75766, 12/21/2012, effective 1/18/2013; FAC 2005-66, 78 FR 13765, 2/28/2012, effective 2/28/2013; FAC 2005-67, 78 FR 37676, 6/21/2013, effective 7/22/2013; FAC 2005-69, 78 FR 46781, 8/1/2013, effective 8/1/2013; 78 FR 46795, 8/1/2013, effective 8/1/2013; FAC 2005-73, 79 FR 24192, 4/29/2014, effective 5/29/2014; FAC 2005-75, 79 FR 35859, 6/24/2014, effective 6/24/2014; FAC 2005-77, 79 FR 61746, 10/14/2014, effective 10/14/2014; 79 FR 61739, 10/14/2014, effective 11/13/2014; FAC 2005-80, 80 FR 4967, 1/29/2015, effective 3/2/2015; FAC 2005-83, 80 FR 38293, 7/2/2015, effective 10/1/2015; FAC 2005-84, 80 FR 53436, 9/3/2015, effective 10/5/2015; FAC 2005-86, 80 FR 81887, 12/31/2015, effective 2/1/2016; FAC 2005-86, 80 FR 81888, 12/31/2015, effective 12/31/2015; FAC 2005-88, 81 FR 30429, 5/16/2016, effective 6/15/2016; FAC 2005-88, 81 FR 30438, 5/16/2016, effective 6/15/2016; FAC 2005-89, 81 FR 45833, 7/14/2016, effective 11/1/2016; FAC 2005-89, 81 FR 45852, 7/14/2016, effective 8/15/2016; FAC 2005-91, 81 FR 67735, 9/30/2016, effective 9/30/2016; FAC 2005-91, 81 FR 67736, 9/30/2016, effective 10/31/2016; FAC 2005-91, 81 FR 67763, 9/30/2016, effective 10/31/2016; FAC 2005-92 81 FR 83103, 11/18/2016, effective 11/18/2016; FAC 2005-95, 82 FR 4709, 1/13/2017, effective 1/13/2017; FAC 2005-95, 82 FR 4716, 1/13/2017, effective 1/13/2017; FAC 2005-100, 83 FR 42571, 8/22/2018, effective 8/22/2018; FAC 2005-101, 83 FR 48691, 9/26/2018, effective 10/26/2018; FAC 2019-02, 84 FR 19835, 5/6/2019, effective 6/5/2019; FAC 2019-02, 84 FR 19839, 5/6/2019, effective 5/6/2019; FAC 2019-06, 84 FR 47862, 9/10/2019, effective 10/10/2019; FAC 2020-01, 84 FR 54760, 10/10/2019, effective 11/12/2019; FAC 2020-02, 84 FR 64680, 11/22/2019, effective 12/23/2019]

SUBPART 2.2—DEFINITIONS CLAUSE

2.201 Contract clause.

Insert the clause at 52.202-1, Definitions, in solicitations and contracts that exceed the simplified acquisition threshold.

[FAC 97-22, 66 FR 2116, 1/10/2001, effective 3/12/2001; Delay of effective date, 66 FR 14259, 3/9/2001, effective 5/11/2001; FAC 2001-24, 69 FR 34228, 6/18/2004, effective 7/19/2004]

PART 3—IMPROPER BUSINESS PRACTICES AND PERSONAL CONFLICTS OF INTERESTS

Table of Contents

Scope of part . . . 3.000

Subpart 3.1—Safeguards

Standards of conduct . . . 3.101
General . . . 3.101-1
Solicitation and acceptance of gratuities by Government personnel . . . 3.101-2
Agency regulations . . . 3.101-3
[Reserved] . . . 3.102
Independent pricing . . . 3.103
Solicitation provision . . . 3.103-1
Evaluating the certification . . . 3.103-2
The need for further certifications . . . 3.103-3
Procurement integrity . . . 3.104
Definitions . . . 3.104-1
General . . . 3.104-2
Statutory and related prohibitions, restrictions, and requirements . . . 3.104-3
Disclosure, protection, and marking of contractor bid or proposal information and source selection information . . . 3.104-4
Disqualification . . . 3.104-5
Ethics advisory opinions regarding prohibitions on a former official's acceptance of compensation from a contractor . . . 3.104-6
Violations or possible violations . . . 3.104-7
Criminal and civil penalties, and further administrative remedies . . . 3.104-8
Contract clauses . . . 3.104-9

Subpart 3.2—Contractor Gratuities to Government Personnel

Applicability . . . 3.201
Contract clause . . . 3.202
Reporting suspected violations of the Gratuities clause . . . 3.203
Treatment of violations . . . 3.204

Subpart 3.3—Reports of Suspected Antitrust Violations

General . . . 3.301
Definitions . . . 3.302
Reporting suspected antitrust violations . . . 3.303

Subpart 3.4—Contingent Fees

Scope of subpart . . . 3.400
Definitions . . . 3.401
Statutory requirements . . . 3.402
Applicability . . . 3.403
Contract clause . . . 3.404
Misrepresentations or violations of the Covenant Against Contingent Fees . . . 3.405
Records . . . 3.406

Subpart 3.5—Other Improper Business Practices

Buying-in . . . 3.501
Definition . . . 3.501-1
General . . . 3.501-2
Subcontractor kickbacks . . . 3.502
Definitions . . . 3.502-1
Subcontractor kickbacks . . . 3.502-2
Contract clause . . . 3.502-3
Unreasonable restrictions on subcontractor sales . . . 3.503
Policy . . . 3.503-1

Contract clause 3.503-2

Subpart 3.6—Contracts with Government Employees or Organizations Owned or Controlled by Them

Policy 3.601
Exceptions 3.602
Responsibilities of the contracting officer 3.603

Subpart 3.7—Voiding and Rescinding Contracts

Scope of subpart 3.700
Purpose 3.701
Definition 3.702
Authority 3.703
Policy 3.704
Procedures 3.705

Subpart 3.8—Limitation on the Payment of Funds to Influence Federal Transactions

Scope of subpart 3.800
Definitions 3.801
Statutory prohibition and requirement 3.802
Exceptions 3.803
Policy 3.804
Exemption 3.805
Processing suspected violations 3.806
Civil penalties 3.807
Solicitation provision and contract clause 3.808

Subpart 3.9—Whistleblower Protections for Contractor Employees

Scope of subpart. 3.900
Definitions 3.901
[Removed and Reserved] 3.902
Policy 3.903
Procedures for filing complaints 3.904
Procedures for investigating complaints 3.905
Remedies 3.906
Whistleblower Protections under the American Recovery and Reinvestment Act of 2009 (the Recovery Act) 3.907
Definitions 3.907-1
Policy 3.907-2
Procedures for filing complaints 3.907-3
Procedures for investigating complaints 3.907-4
Access to investigative file of Inspector General 3.907-5
Remedies and enforcement authority 3.907-6
Contract clause 3.907-7
Pilot program for enhancement of contractor employee whistleblower protections 3.908
Scope of section 3.908-1
Definitions 3.908-2
Policy 3.908-3
Filing complaints 3.908-4
Procedures for investigating complaints 3.908-5
Remedies 3.908-6
Enforcement of orders 3.908-7
Classified information 3.908-8
Contract clause 3.908-9
Prohibition on providing funds to an entity that requires certain internal confidentiality agreements or statements. 3.909

Prohibition. 3.909-1
Representation by the offeror. 3.909-2
Solicitation provision and contract clause. 3.909-3

Subpart 3.10—Contractor Code of Business Ethics and Conduct

Scope of subpart. 3.1000
Definitions 3.1001
Policy 3.1002
Requirements 3.1003
Contract clauses 3.1004

Subpart 3.11—Preventing Personal Conflicts of Interest for Contractor Employees Performing Acquisition Functions

Scope of subpart. 3.1100
Definitions 3.1101
Policy 3.1102
Procedures 3.1103
Mitigation or waiver 3.1104
Violations 3.1105
Contract clause 3.1106

PART 3—IMPROPER BUSINESS PRACTICES AND PERSONAL CONFLICTS OF INTERESTS

3.000 Scope of part.

This part prescribes policies and procedures for avoiding improper business practices and personal conflicts of interest and for dealing with their apparent or actual occurrence.

SUBPART 3.1—SAFEGUARDS

3.101 Standards of conduct. (No Text)

3.101-1 General.

Government business shall be conducted in a manner above reproach and, except as authorized by statute or regulation, with complete impartiality and with preferential treatment for none. Transactions relating to the expenditure of public funds require the highest degree of public trust and an impeccable standard of conduct. The general rule is to avoid strictly any conflict of interest or even the appearance of a conflict of interest in Government-contractor relationships. While many Federal laws and regulations place restrictions on the actions of Government personnel, their official conduct must, in addition, be such that they would have no reluctance to make a full public disclosure of their actions.

3.101-2 Solicitation and acceptance of gratuities by Government personnel.

As a rule, no Government employee may solicit or accept, directly or indirectly, any gratuity, gift, favor, entertainment, loan, or anything of monetary value from anyone who (a) has or is seeking to obtain Government business with the employee's agency, (b) conducts activities that are regulated by the employee's agency, or (c) has interests that may be substantially affected by the performance or nonperformance of the employee's official duties. Certain limited exceptions are authorized in agency regulations.

3.101-3 Agency regulations.

(a) Agencies are required by E.O. 11222 of May 8, 1965, and 5 CFR 735 to prescribe *Standards of Conduct*. These agency standards contain—

(1) Agency-authorized exceptions to 3.101-2; and

(2) Disciplinary measures for persons violating the standards of conduct.

(b) Requirements for employee financial disclosure and restrictions on private employment for former Government employees are in Office of Personnel Management and agency regulations implementing Public Law 95-521, which amended 18 U.S.C. 207.

3.102 [Reserved]

[Reserved, FAC 91-30, 60 FR 37772, 7/21/95, effective 9/19/95]

3.103 Independent pricing. (No Text)

3.103-1 Solicitation provision.

The contracting officer shall insert the provision at 52.203-2, Certificate of Independent Price Determination, in solicitations when a firm-fixed-price contract or fixed-price contract with economic price adjustment is contemplated, unless—

(a) The acquisition is to be made under the simplified acquisition procedures in Part 13;

(b) [Reserved]

(c) The solicitation is a request for technical proposals under two-step sealed bidding procedures; or

(d) The solicitation is for utility services for which rates are set by law or regulation.

[FAC 84-5, 50 FR 1727, 1/11/85, effective 4/1/85; FAC 84-58, 55 FR 25526, 6/21/90, effective 7/23/90; FAC 90-29, 60 FR 34732, 7/3/95, effective 7/3/95]

3.103-2 Evaluating the certification.

(a) *Evaluation guidelines*. (1) None of the following, in and of itself, constitutes "disclosure" as it is used in paragraph (a) (2) of the Certificate of Independent Price Determination (hereafter, the certificate):

(i) The fact that a firm has published price lists, rates, or tariffs covering items being acquired by the Government.

(ii) The fact that a firm has informed prospective customers of proposed or pending publication of new or revised price lists for items being acquired by the Government.

(iii) The fact that a firm has sold the same items to commercial customers at the same prices being offered to the Government.

(2) For the purpose of paragraph (b) (2) of the certificate, an individual may use a blanket authorization to act as an agent for the person(s) responsible for determining the offered prices if—

(i) The proposed contract to which the certificate applies is clearly within the scope of the authorization; and

(ii) The person giving the authorization is the person within the offeror's organization who is responsible for determining the prices being offered at the time the certification is made in the particular offer.

(3) If an offer is submitted jointly by two or more concerns, the certification provided by the representative of each concern applies only to the activities of that concern.

(b) *Rejection of offers suspected of being collusive.* (1) If the offeror deleted or modified paragraph (a) (1) or (3) or paragraph (b) of the certificate, the contracting officer shall reject the offeror's bid or proposal.

(2) If the offeror deleted or modified paragraph (a) (2) of the certificate, the offeror must have furnished with its offer a signed statement of the circumstances of the disclosure of prices contained in the bid or proposal. The chief of the contracting office shall review the altered certificate and the statement and shall determine, in writing, whether the disclosure was made for the purpose or had the effect of restricting competition. If the determination is positive, the bid or proposal shall be rejected; if it is negative, the bid or proposal shall be considered for award.

(3) Whenever an offer is rejected under paragraph (b) (1) or (2) of this section, or the certificate is suspected of being false, the contracting officer shall report the situation to the Attorney General in accordance with 3.303.

(4) The determination made under paragraph (2) of this section shall not prevent or inhibit the prosecution of any criminal or civil actions involving the occurrences or transactions to which the certificate relates.

[FAC 84-58, 55 FR 25526, 6/21/90, effective 7/23/90; FAC 2019-02, 84 FR 19839, 5/6/2019, effective 5/6/2019]

3.103-3 The need for further certifications.

A contractor that properly executed the certificate before award does not have to submit a separate certificate with each proposal to perform a work order or similar ordering instrument issued pursuant to the terms of the contract, where the Government's requirements cannot be met from another source.

3.104 Procurement integrity. (No Text)

3.104-1 Definitions.

As used in this section—

Agency ethics official means the designated agency ethics official described in 5 CFR 2638.201 or other designated person, including—

(1) Deputy ethics officials described in 5 CFR 2638.204, to whom authority under 3.104-6 has been delegated by the designated agency ethics official; and

(2) Alternate designated agency ethics officials described in 5 CFR 2638.202(b).

Compensation means wages, salaries, honoraria, commissions, professional fees, and any other form of compensation, provided directly or indirectly for services rendered. Compensation is indirectly provided if it is paid to an entity other than the individual, specifically in exchange for services provided by the individual.

Contractor bid or proposal information means any of the following information submitted to a Federal agency as part of or in connection with a bid or proposal to enter into a Federal agency procurement contract, if that information has not been previously made available to the public or disclosed publicly:

(1) Cost or pricing data (as defined by 10 U.S.C. 2306a(h)) with respect to procurements subject to that section, and 41 U.S.C. 3501(a)(2), with respect to procurements subject to that section.

(2) Indirect costs and direct labor rates.

(3) Proprietary information about manufacturing processes, operations, or techniques marked by the contractor in accordance with applicable law or regulation.

(4) Information marked by the contractor as *contractor bid or proposal information* in accordance with applicable law or regulation.

(5) Information marked in accordance with 52.215-1(e).

Decision to award a subcontract or modification of subcontract means a decision to designate award to a particular source.

Federal agency procurement means the acquisition (by using competitive procedures and awarding a contract) of goods or services (including construction) from non-Federal sources by a Federal agency using appropriated funds. For broad agency announcements and small business innovation research programs, each proposal received by an agency constitutes a separate procurement for purposes of 41 U.S.C. chapter 21.

In excess of $10,000,000 means—

(1) The value, or estimated value, at the time of award, of the contract, including all options;

(2) The total estimated value at the time of award of all orders under an indefinite-delivery, indefinite-quantity, or requirements contract;

(3) Any multiple award schedule contract, unless the contracting officer documents a lower estimate;

(4) The value of a delivery order, task order, or an order under a Basic Ordering Agreement;

(5) The amount paid or to be paid in settlement of a claim; or

(6) The estimated monetary value of negotiated overhead or other rates when applied to the Government portion of the applicable allocation base.

Official means—

(1) An officer, as defined in 5 U.S.C. 2104;

(2) An employee, as defined in 5 U.S.C. 2105;

(3) A member of the uniformed services, as defined in 5 U.S.C. 2101(3); or

(4) A special Government employee, as defined in 18 U.S.C. 202.

Participating personally and substantially in a Federal agency procurement means—

(1) Active and significant involvement of an official in any of the following activities directly related to that procurement:

(i) Drafting, reviewing, or approving the specification or statement of work for the procurement.

(ii) Preparing or developing the solicitation.

(iii) Evaluating bids or proposals, or selecting a source.

(iv) Negotiating price or terms and conditions of the contract.

(v) Reviewing and approving the award of the contract.

(2) *Participating personally* means participating directly, and includes the direct and active supervision of a subordinate's participation in the matter.

(3) *Participating substantially* means that the official's involvement is of significance to the matter. Substantial participation requires more than official responsibility, knowledge, perfunctory involvement, or involvement on an administrative or peripheral issue. Participation may be substantial even though it is not determinative of the outcome of a particular matter. A finding of substantiality should be based not only on the effort devoted to a matter, but on the importance of the effort. While a series of peripheral involvements may be insubstantial, the single act of approving or participating in a critical step may be substantial. However, the review of procurement documents solely to determine compliance with regulatory, ad-

ministrative, or budgetary procedures, does not constitute substantial participation in a procurement.

(4) Generally, an official will not be considered to have participated personally and substantially in a procurement solely by participating in the following activities:

(i) Agency-level boards, panels, or other advisory committees that review program milestones or evaluate and make recommendations regarding alternative technologies or approaches for satisfying broad agency-level missions or objectives.

(ii) The performance of general, technical, engineering, or scientific effort having broad application not directly associated with a particular procurement, notwithstanding that such general, technical, engineering, or scientific effort subsequently may be incorporated into a particular procurement.

(iii) Clerical functions supporting the conduct of a particular procurement.

(iv) For procurements to be conducted under the procedures of OMB Circular A-76, participation in management studies, preparation of in-house cost estimates, preparation of "most efficient organization" analyses, and furnishing of data or technical support to be used by others in the development of performance standards, statements of work, or specifications.

Source selection evaluation board means any board, team, council, or other group that evaluates bids or proposals.

[FAC 2001-06, 67 FR 13048, 3/20/2002, effective 4/4/2002; FAC 2005-47, 75 FR 77745, 12/13/2010, effective 12/13/2010; FAC 2005-73, 79 FR 24192, 4/29/2014, effective 5/29/2014]

3.104-2 General.

(a) This section implements 41 U.S.C. chapter 21, Restrictions on Obtaining and Disclosing Certain Information. Agency supplementation of 3.104, including specific definitions to identify individuals who occupy positions specified in 3.104-3(d)(1)(ii), and any clauses required by 3.104 must be approved by the senior procurement executive of the agency, unless a law establishes a higher level of approval for that agency.

(b) Agency officials are reminded that there are other statutes and regulations that deal with the same or related prohibited conduct, for example—

(1) The offer or acceptance of a bribe or gratuity is prohibited by 18 U.S.C. 201 and 10 U.S.C. 2207. The acceptance of a gift, under certain circumstances, is prohibited by 5 U.S.C. 7353 and 5 CFR part 2635;

(2) Contacts with an offeror during the conduct of an acquisition may constitute "seeking employment,"(see subpart F of 5 CFR part 2636 and 3.104-3(c)(2)). Government officers and employees (employees) are prohibited by 18 U.S.C. 208 and 5 CFR part 2635 from participating personally and substantially in any particular matter that would affect the financial interests of any person with whom the employee is seeking employment. An employee who engages in negotiations or is otherwise seeking employment with an offeror or who has an arrangement concerning future employment with an offeror must comply with the applicable disqualification requirements of 5 CFR 2635.604 and 2635.606. The statutory prohibition in 18 U.S.C. 208 also may require an employee's disqualification from participation in the acquisition even if the employee's duties may not be considered "participating personally and substantially," as this term is defined in 3.104-1;

(3) Post-employment restrictions are covered by 18 U.S.C. 207 and 5 CFR parts 2637 and 2641, that prohibit certain activities by former Government employees, including representation of a contractor before the Government in relation to any contract or other particular matter involving specific parties on which the former employee participated personally and substantially while employed by the Government. Additional restrictions apply to certain senior Government employees and for particular matters under an employee's official responsibility;

(4) Parts 14 and 15 place restrictions on the release of information related to procurements and other contractor information that must be protected under 18 U.S.C. 1905;

(5) Release of information both before and after award (see 3.104-4) may be prohibited by the Privacy Act (5 U.S.C. 552a), the Trade

Secrets Act (18 U.S.C. 1905), and other laws; and

(6) Using nonpublic information to further an employee's private interest or that of another and engaging in a financial transaction using nonpublic information are prohibited by 5 CFR 2635.703.

[FAC 2001-06, 67 FR 13048, 3/20/2002, effective 4/4/2002; FAC 2005-73, 79 FR 24192, 4/29/2014, effective 5/29/2014]

3.104-3 Statutory and related prohibitions, restrictions, and requirements.

(a) Prohibition on disclosing procurement information (41 U.S.C. 2102).

(1) A person described in paragraph (a)(2) of this subsection must not, other than as provided by law, knowingly disclose contractor bid or proposal information or source selection information before the award of a Federal agency procurement contract to which the information relates. (See 3.104-4(a).)

(2) Paragraph (a)(1) of this subsection applies to any person who—

(i) Is a present or former official of the United States, or a person who is acting or has acted for or on behalf of, or who is advising or has advised the United States with respect to, a Federal agency procurement; and

(ii) By virtue of that office, employment, or relationship, has or had access to contractor bid or proposal information or source selection information.

(b) Prohibition on obtaining procurement information (41 U.S.C. 2102). A person must not, other than as provided by law, knowingly obtain contractor bid or proposal information or source selection information before the award of a Federal agency procurement contract to which the information relates.

(c) Actions required when an agency official contacts or is contacted by an offeror regarding non-Federal employment (41 U.S.C. 2103). (1) If an agency official, participating personally and substantially in a Federal agency procurement for a contract in excess of the simplified acquisition threshold, contacts or is contacted by a person who is an offeror in that Federal agency procurement regarding possible non-Federal employment for that official, the official must—

(i) Promptly report the contact in writing to the official's supervisor and to the agency ethics official; and

(ii) Either reject the possibility of non-Federal employment or disqualify himself or herself from further personal and substantial participation in that Federal agency procurement (see 3.104-5) until such time as the agency authorizes the official to resume participation in that procurement, in accordance with the requirements of 18 U.S.C. 208 and applicable agency regulations, because—

(A) The person is no longer an offeror in that Federal agency procurement; or

(B) All discussions with the offeror regarding possible non-Federal employment have terminated without an agreement or arrangement for employment.

(2) A contact is any of the actions included as "seeking employment" in 5 CFR 2635.603(b). In addition, unsolicited communications from offerors regarding possible employment are considered contacts.

(3) Agencies must retain reports of employment contacts for 2 years from the date the report was submitted.

(4) Conduct that complies with 41 U.S.C. 2103 may be prohibited by other criminal statutes and the Standards of Ethical Conduct for Employees of the Executive Branch. See 3.104-2(b)(2).

(d) Prohibition on former official's acceptance of compensation from a contractor (41 U.S.C. 2104). (1) A former official of a Federal agency may not accept compensation from a contractor that has been awarded a competitive or sole source contract, as an employee, officer, director, or consultant of the contractor within a period of 1 year after such former official—

(i) Served, at the time of selection of the contractor or the award of a contract to that contractor, as the procuring contracting officer, the source selection authority, a member of a source selection evaluation board, or the chief of a financial or technical evaluation team in a procurement in which that contractor was selected for award of a contract in excess of $10,000,000;

(ii) Served as the program manager, deputy program manager, or administrative contracting officer for a contract in excess of $10,000,000 awarded to that contractor; or

(iii) Personally made for the Federal agency a decision to—

(A) Award a contract, subcontract, modification of a contract or subcontract, or a task order or delivery order in excess of $10,000,000 to that contractor;

(B) Establish overhead or other rates applicable to a contract or contracts for that contractor that are valued in excess of $10,000,000;

(C) Approve issuance of a contract payment or payments in excess of $10,000,000 to that contractor; or

(D) Pay or settle a claim in excess of $10,000,000 with that contractor.

(2) The 1-year prohibition begins on the date—

(i) Of contract award for positions described in paragraph (d) (1) (i) of this subsection, or the date of contractor selection if the official was not serving in the position on the date of award;

(ii) The official last served in one of the positions described in paragraph (d) (1) (ii) of this subsection; or

(iii) The official made one of the decisions described in paragraph (d) (1) (iii) of this subsection.

(3) Nothing in paragraph (d) (1) of this subsection may be construed to prohibit a former official of a Federal agency from accepting compensation from any division or affiliate of a contractor that does not produce the same or similar products or services as the entity of the contractor that is responsible for the contract referred to in paragraph (d) (1) of this subsection.

[FAC 2001-06, 67 FR 13048, 3/20/2002, effective 4/4/2002; FAC 2005-73, 79 FR 24192, 4/29/2014, effective 5/29/2014; FAC 2019-02, 84 FR 19839, 5/6/2019, effective 5/6/2019]

3.104-4 Disclosure, protection, and marking of contractor bid or proposal information and source selection information.

(a) Except as specifically provided for in this subsection, no person or other entity may disclose contractor bid or proposal information or source selection information to any person other than a person authorized, in accordance with applicable agency regulations or procedures, by the agency head or the contracting officer to receive such information.

(b) Contractor bid or proposal information and source selection information must be protected from unauthorized disclosure in accordance with 14.401, 15.207, applicable law, and agency regulations.

(c) Individuals unsure if particular information is source selection information, as defined in 2.101, should consult with agency officials as necessary. Individuals responsible for preparing material that may be source selection information as described at paragraph (10) of the "source selection information" definition in 2.101 must mark the cover page and each page that the individual believes contains source selection information with the legend "Source Selection Information—See FAR 2.101 and 3.104." Although the information in paragraphs (1) through (9) of the definition in 2.101 is considered to be source selection information whether or not marked, all reasonable efforts must be made to mark such material with the same legend.

(d) Except as provided in paragraph (d) (3) of this subsection, the contracting officer must notify the contractor in writing if the contracting officer believes that proprietary information, contractor bid or proposal information, or information marked in accordance with 52.215-1(e) has been inappropriately marked. The contractor that has affixed the marking must be given an opportunity to justify the marking.

(1) If the contractor agrees that the marking is not justified, or does not respond within the time specified in the notice, the contracting officer may remove the marking and release the information.

(2) If, after reviewing the contractor's justification, the contracting officer determines that the marking is not justified, the contracting officer must notify the contractor in writing before releasing the information.

(3) For technical data marked as proprietary by a contractor, the contracting officer must follow the procedures in 27.404-5.

(e) This section does not restrict or prohibit—

(1) A contractor from disclosing its own bid or proposal information or the recipient from receiving that information;

(2) The disclosure or receipt of information, not otherwise protected, relating to a Federal agency procurement after it has been canceled by the Federal agency, before contract award, unless the Federal agency plans to resume the procurement;

(3) Individual meetings between a Federal agency official and an offeror or potential offeror for, or a recipient of, a contract or subcontract under a Federal agency procurement, provided that unauthorized disclosure or receipt of contractor bid or proposal information or source selection information does not occur; or

(4) The Government's use of technical data in a manner consistent with the Government's rights in the data.

(f) This section does not authorize—

(1) The withholding of any information pursuant to a proper request from the Congress, any committee or subcommittee thereof, a Federal agency, the Comptroller General, or an Inspector General of a Federal agency, except as otherwise authorized by law or regulation. Any release containing contractor bid or proposal information or source selection information must clearly identify the information as contractor bid or proposal information or source selection information related to the conduct of a Federal agency procurement and notify the recipient that the disclosure of the information is restricted by 41 U.S.C. chapter 21;

(2) The withholding of information from, or restricting its receipt by, the Comptroller General in the course of a protest against the award or proposed award of a Federal agency procurement contract;

(3) The release of information after award of a contract or cancellation of a procurement if such information is contractor bid or proposal information or source selection information that pertains to another procurement; or

(4) The disclosure, solicitation, or receipt of bid or proposal information or source selection information after award if disclosure, solicitation, or receipt is prohibited by law. (See 3.104-2(b)(5) and subpart 24.2.).

[FAC 2001-06, 67 FR 13048, 3/20/2002, effective 4/4/2002; FAC 2005-21, 72 FR 63045, 11/7/2007, effective 12/7/2007; FAC 2005-73, 79 FR 24192, 4/29/2014, effective 5/29/2014]

3.104-5 Disqualification.

(a) *Contacts through agents or other intermediaries.* Employment contacts between the employee and the offeror, that are conducted through agents, or other intermediaries, may require disqualification under 3.104-3(c)(1). These contacts may also require disqualification under other statutes and regulations. (See 3.104-2(b)(2).)

(b) *Disqualification notice.* In addition to submitting the contact report required by 3.104-3(c)(1), an agency official who must disqualify himself or herself pursuant to 3.104-3(c)(1)(ii) must promptly submit written notice of disqualification from further participation in the procurement to the contracting officer, the source selection authority if other than the contracting officer, and the agency official's immediate supervisor. As a minimum, the notice must—

(1) Identify the procurement;

(2) Describe the nature of the agency official's participation in the procurement and specify the approximate dates or time period of participation; and

(3) Identify the offeror and describe its interest in the procurement.

(c) *Resumption of participation in a procurement.* (1) The official must remain disqualified until such time as the agency, at its sole and exclusive discretion, authorizes the official to resume participation in the procurement in accordance with 3.104-3(c)(1)(ii).

(2) After the conditions of 3.104-3(c)(1)(ii)(A) or (B) have been met, the head of the contracting activity (HCA), after consultation with the agency ethics official, may authorize the disqualified official to resume participation in the procurement, or may determine that an additional disqualification period is necessary to protect the integrity of the procurement process. In determining the disqualification period, the HCA must consider any factors that create an appearance that the disqualified official acted without complete impartiality in the procurement. The HCA's reinstatement decision should be in writing.

(3) Government officer or employee must also comply with the provisions of 18 U.S.C. 208 and 5 CFR part 2635 regarding any resumed participation in a procurement matter. Government officer or employee may not be reinstated to participate in a procurement matter affecting the financial interest of someone with whom the individual is seeking employment, unless the individual receives—

(i) A waiver pursuant to 18 U.S.C. 208(b)(1) or (b)(3); or

(ii) An authorization in accordance with the requirements of subpart F of 5 CFR part 2635.

[FAC 2001-06, 67 FR 13048, 3/20/2002, effective 4/4/2002]

3.104-6 Ethics advisory opinions regarding prohibitions on a former official's acceptance of compensation from a contractor.

(a) An official or former official of a Federal agency who does not know whether he or she is or would be precluded by 41 U.S.C. 2104 (see 3.104-3(d)) from accepting compensation from a particular contractor may request advice from the appropriate agency ethics official before accepting such compensation.

(b) The request for an advisory opinion must be in writing, include all relevant information reasonably available to the official or former official, and be dated and signed. The request must include information about the—

(1) Procurement(s), or decision(s) on matters under 3.104-3(d)(1)(iii), involving the particular contractor, in which the individual was or is involved, including contract or solicitation numbers, dates of solicitation or award, a description of the supplies or services procured or to be procured, and contract amount;

(2) Individual's participation in the procurement or decision, including the dates or time periods of that participation, and the nature of the individual's duties, responsibilities, or actions; and

(3) Contractor, including a description of the products or services produced by the division or affiliate of the contractor from whom the individual proposes to accept compensation.

(c) Within 30 days after receipt of a request containing complete information, or as soon thereafter as practicable, the agency ethics official should issue an opinion on whether the proposed conduct would violate 41 U.S.C. 2104.

(d)(1) If complete information is not included in the request, the agency ethics official may ask the requester to provide more information or request information from other persons, including the source selection authority, the contracting officer, or the requester's immediate supervisor.

(2) In issuing an opinion, the agency ethics official may rely upon the accuracy of information furnished by the requester or other agency sources, unless he or she has reason to believe that the information is fraudulent, misleading, or otherwise incorrect.

(3) If the requester is advised in a written opinion by the agency ethics official that the requester may accept compensation from a particular contractor, and accepts such compensation in good faith reliance on that advisory opinion, then neither the requester nor the contractor will be found to have knowingly violated 41 U.S.C. 2104. If the requester or the contractor has actual knowledge or reason to believe that the opinion is based upon fraudulent, mislead-

ing, or otherwise incorrect information, their reliance upon the opinion will not be deemed to be in good faith.

[FAC 2001-06, 67 FR 13048, 3/20/2002, effective 4/4/2002; FAC 2005-73, 79 FR 24192, 4/29/2014, effective 5/29/2014]

3.104-7 Violations or possible violations.

(a) A contracting officer who receives or obtains information of a violation or possible violation of 41 U.S.C. 2102, 2103, or 2104 (see 3.104-3) must determine if the reported violation or possible violation has any impact on the pending award or selection of the contractor.

(1) If the contracting officer concludes that there is no impact on the procurement, the contracting officer must forward the information concerning the violation or possible violation and documentation supporting a determination that there is no impact on the procurement to an individual designated in accordance with agency procedures.

(i) If that individual concurs, the contracting officer may proceed with the procurement.

(ii) If that individual does not concur, the individual must promptly forward the information and documentation to the HCA and advise the contracting officer to withhold award.

(2) If the contracting officer concludes that the violation or possible violation impacts the procurement, the contracting officer must promptly forward the information to the HCA.

(b) The HCA must review all information available and, in accordance with agency procedures, take appropriate action, such as—

(1) Advise the contracting officer to continue with the procurement;

(2) Begin an investigation;

(3) Refer the information disclosed to appropriate criminal investigative agencies;

(4) Conclude that a violation occurred; or

(5) Recommend that the agency head determine that the contractor, or someone acting for the contractor, has engaged in conduct constituting an offense punishable under 41 U.S.C. 2105, for the purpose of voiding or rescinding the contract.

(c) Before concluding that an offeror, contractor, or person has violated 41 U.S.C. chapter 21, the HCA may consider that the interests of the Government are best served by requesting information from appropriate parties regarding the violation or possible violation.

(d) If the HCA concludes that 41 U.S.C. chapter 21 has been violated, the HCA may direct the contracting officer to—

(1) If a contract has not been awarded—

(i) Cancel the procurement;

(ii) Disqualify an offeror; or

(iii) Take any other appropriate actions in the interests of the Government.

(2) If a contract has been awarded—

(i) Effect appropriate contractual remedies, including profit recapture under the clause at 52.203-10, Price or Fee Adjustment for Illegal or Improper Activity, or, if the contract has been rescinded under paragraph (d)(2)(ii) of this subsection, recovery of the amount expended under the contract;

(ii) Void or rescind the contract with respect to which—

(A) The contractor or someone acting for the contractor has been convicted for an offense where the conduct constitutes a violation of 41 U.S.C. 2102 for the purpose of either—

(1) Exchanging the information covered by the subsections for anything of value; or

(2) Obtaining or giving anyone a competitive advantage in the award of a Federal agency procurement contract; or

(B) The agency head has determined, based upon a preponderance of the evidence, that the contractor or someone acting for the contractor has engaged in conduct constituting an offense punishable under 41 U.S.C. 2105(a); or

(iii) Take any other appropriate actions in the best interests of the Government.

(3) Refer the matter to the agency suspending or debarring official.

(e) The HCA should recommend or direct an administrative or contractual remedy commensurate with the severity and effect of the violation.

(f) If the HCA determines that urgent and compelling circumstances justify an award, or award is otherwise in the interests of the Government, the HCA, in accordance with agency procedures, may authorize the contracting officer to award the contract or execute the contract modification after notifying the agency head.

(g) The HCA may delegate his or her authority under this subsection to an individual at least one organizational level above the contracting officer and of General Officer, Flag, Senior Executive Service, or equivalent rank.

[FAC 2001-06, 67 FR 13048, 3/2002, effective 4/4/2002; FAC 2005-73, 79 FR 24192, 4/29/2014, effective 5/29/2014]

3.104-8 Criminal and civil penalties, and further administrative remedies.

Criminal and civil penalties, and administrative remedies, may apply to conduct that violates 41 U.S.C. chapter 21 (see 3.104-3). See 33.102(f) for special rules regarding bid protests. See 3.104-7 for administrative remedies relating to contracts.

(a) An official who knowingly fails to comply with the requirements of 3.104-3 is subject to the penalties and administrative action set forth in 41 U.S.C. 2105.

(b) An offeror who engages in employment discussion with an official subject to the restrictions of 3.104-3, knowing that the official has not complied with 3.104-3(c)(1), is subject to the criminal, civil, or administrative penalties set forth in 41 U.S.C. 2105.

(c) An official who refuses to terminate employment discussions (see 3.104-5) may be subject to agency administrative actions under 5 CFR 2635.604(d) if the official's disqualification from participation in a particular procurement interferes substantially with the individual's ability to perform assigned duties.

[FAC 2001-06, 67 FR 13048, 3/20/2002, effective 4/4/2002; FAC 2005-73, 79 FR 24192, 4/29/2014, effective 5/29/2014]

3.104-9 Contract clauses.

In solicitations and contracts for other than commercial items that exceed the simplified acquisition threshold, insert the clauses at—

(a) 52.203-8, Cancellation, Rescission, and Recovery of Funds for Illegal or Improper Activity; and

(b) 52.203-10, Price or Fee Adjustment for Illegal or Improper Activity.

[FAC 2001-06, 67 FR 13048, 3/20/2002, effective 4/4/2002]

3.104-10 [Removed]

[FAC 2001-06, 67 FR 13048, 3/20/2002, effective 4/4/2002]

3.104-11 [Removed]

[FAC 2001-06, 67 FR 13048, 3/20/2002, effective 4/4/2002]

SUBPART 3.2—CONTRACTOR GRATUITIES TO GOVERNMENT PERSONNEL

3.201 Applicability.

This subpart applies to all executive agencies, except that coverage concerning exemplary damages applies only to the Department of Defense (10 U.S.C. 2207).

3.202 Contract clause.

The contracting officer shall insert the clause at 52.203-3, Gratuities, in solicitations and contracts with a value exceeding the simplified acquisition threshold, except those for personal services and those between military departments or defense agencies and foreign governments that do not obligate any funds appropriated to the Department of Defense.

[FAC 90-40, 61 FR 39186, 7/26/96, effective 8/26/96, finalized without change, FAC 90-46, 62 FR 12690, 3/17/97, effective 5/16/97]

3.203 Reporting suspected violations of the Gratuities clause.

Agency personnel shall report suspected violations of the Gratuities clause to the contracting officer or other designated official in accordance with agency procedures. The agency reporting procedures shall be published as an implementation of this section 3.203and shall clearly specify—

(a) What to report and how to report it; and

(b) The channels through which reports must pass, including the function and authority of each official designated to review them.

3.204 Treatment of violations.

(a) Before taking any action against a contractor, the agency head or a designee shall determine, after notice and hearing under agency procedures, whether the contractor, its agent, or another representative, under a contract containing the Gratuities clause—

(1) Offered or gave a gratuity (*e.g.*, an entertainment or gift) to an officer, official, or employee of the Government; and

(2) Intended by the gratuity to obtain a contract or favorable treatment under a contract (intent generally must be inferred).

(b) Agency procedures shall afford the contractor an opportunity to appear with counsel, submit documentary evidence, present witnesses, and confront any person the agency presents. The procedures should be as informal as practicable, consistent with principles of fundamental fairness.

(c) When the agency head or designee determines that a violation has occurred, the Government may—

(1) Terminate the contractor's right to proceed;

(2) Initiate debarment or suspension measures as set forth in Subpart 9.4; and

(3) Assess exemplary damages, if the contract uses money appropriated to the Department of Defense.

SUBPART 3.3—REPORTS OF SUSPECTED ANTITRUST VIOLATIONS

3.301 General.

(a) Practices that eliminate competition or restrain trade usually lead to excessive prices and may warrant criminal, civil, or administrative action against the participants. Examples of anticompetitive practices are collusive bidding, follow-the-leader pricing, rotated low bids, collusive price estimating systems, and sharing of the business.

(b) Contracting personnel are an important potential source of investigative leads for antitrust enforcement and should therefore be sensitive to indications of unlawful behavior by offerors and contractors. Agency personnel shall report, in accordance with agency regulations, evidence of suspected antitrust violations in acquisitions for possible referral to—

(1) The Attorney General under 3.303; and

(2) The agency office responsible for contractor debarment and suspension under subpart 9.4.

[FAC 84-5, 50 FR 1727, 1/11/85, effective 4/1/85; FAC 2019-02, 84 FR 19839, 5/6/2019, effective 5/6/2019]

3.302 Definitions.

As used in this subpart—

Identical bids means bids for the same line item that are determined to be identical as to unit price or total line item amount, with or without the application of evaluation factors (*e.g.*, discount or transportation cost).

[FAC 84-1, 49 FR 12974, 3/30/84, effective 4/1/84; FAC 97-22, 66 FR 2116, 1/10/2001, effective 3/12/2001; Delay of effective date, 66 FR 14259, 3/9/2001, effective 5/11/2001; FAC 2001-06, 67 FR 13048, 3/20/2002, effective 4/4/2002; FAC 2005-95, 82 FR 4709, 1/13/2017, effective 1/13/2017]

3.303 Reporting suspected antitrust violations.

(a) Agencies are required by 41 U.S.C. 3707 and 10 U.S.C. 2305(b)(9) to report to the Attorney General any bids or proposals that evidence a violation of the antitrust laws. These reports are in addition to those required by Subpart 9.4.

(b) The antitrust laws are intended to ensure that markets operate competitively. Any agreement or mutual understanding among competing firms that restrains the natural operation of market forces is suspect. Paragraph (c) of this section identifies behavior patterns that are often associated with antitrust violations. Activities meeting the descriptions in paragraph (c) are not necessarily improper, but they are sufficiently questionable to warrant notifying the appropriate authorities, in accordance with agency procedures.

(c) Practices or events that may evidence violations of the antitrust laws include—

(1) The existence of an *industry price list* or *price agreement* to which contractors refer in formulating their offers;

(2) A sudden change from competitive bidding to identical bidding;

(3) Simultaneous price increases or follow-the-leader pricing;

(4) Rotation of bids or proposals, so that each competitor takes a turn in sequence as low bidder, or so that certain competitors bid low only on some sizes of contracts and high on other sizes;

(5) Division of the market, so that certain competitors bid low only for contracts awarded by certain agencies, or for contracts in certain geographical areas, or on certain products, and bid high on all other jobs;

(6) Establishment by competitors of a collusive price estimating system;

(7) The filing of a joint bid by two or more competitors when at least one of the competitors has sufficient technical capability and productive capacity for contract performance;

(8) Any incidents suggesting direct collusion among competitors, such as the appearance of identical calculation or spelling errors in two or more competitive offers or the submission by one firm of offers for other firms; and

(9) Assertions by the employees, former employees, or competitors of offerors, that an agreement to restrain trade exists.

(d) Identical bids shall be reported under this section if the agency has some reason to believe that the bids resulted from collusion.

(e) For offers from foreign contractors for contracts to be performed outside the United States and its outlying areas, contracting officers may refer suspected collusive offers to the authorities of the foreign government concerned for appropriate action.

(f) Agency reports shall be addressed to the Attorney General, U.S. Department of Justice, Washington, DC 20530, Attention: Assistant Attorney General, Antitrust Division, and shall include—

(1) A brief statement describing the suspected practice and the reason for the suspicion; and

(2) The name, address, and telephone number of an individual in the agency who can be contacted for further information.

(g) Questions concerning this reporting requirement may be communicated by telephone directly to the Office of the Assistant Attorney General, Antitrust Division.

[FAC 84-1, 49 FR 12974, 3/30/84, effective 4/1/84; FAC 84-5, 50 FR 1727, 1/11/85, effective 4/1/85; FAC 84-58, 55 FR 25526, 6/21/90, effective 7/23/90; FAC 97-18, 65 FR 36014, 6/6/2000, effective 6/6/2000; FAC 2001-14, 5/22/2003, effective 6/23/2003; FAC 2005-73, 79 FR 24192, 4/29/2014, effective 5/29/2014; FAC 2019-02, 84 FR 19839, 5/6/2019, effective 5/6/2019]

SUBPART 3.4—CONTINGENT FEES

3.400 Scope of subpart.

This subpart prescribes policies and procedures that restrict contingent fee arrangements for soliciting or obtaining Government contracts to those permitted by 10 U.S.C. 2306(b) and 41 U.S.C. 3901.

[FAC 2005-73, 79 FR 24192, 4/29/2014, effective 5/29/2014]

3.401 Definitions.

As used in this subpart—

Bona fide agency means an established commercial or selling agency, maintained by a contractor for the purpose of securing business, that neither exerts nor proposes to exert improper influence to solicit or obtain Government contracts nor holds itself out as being able to obtain any Government contract or contracts through improper influence.

Bona fide employee means a person, employed by a contractor and subject to the contractor's supervision and control as to time, place, and manner of performance, who neither exerts nor proposes to exert improper influence to solicit or obtain Government contracts nor holds out as being able to obtain any Government contract or contracts through improper influence.

Contingent fee means any commission, percentage, brokerage, or other fee that is contingent upon the success that a person or concern has in securing a Government contract.

Improper influence means any influence that induces or tends to induce a Government employee or officer to give consideration or to act regarding a Government contract on any basis other than the merits of the matter.

[FAC 97-22, 66 FR 2116, 1/10/2001, effective 3/12/2001; Delay of effective date, 66 FR 14259, 3/9/2001, effective 5/11/2001]

3.402 Statutory requirements.

Contractors' arrangements to pay contingent fees for soliciting or obtaining Government contracts have long been considered contrary to public policy because such arrangements may lead to attempted or actual exercise of improper influence. In 10 U.S.C. 2306(b) and 41 U.S.C. 3901, Congress affirmed this public policy but permitted certain exceptions. These statutes—

(a) Require in every negotiated contract a warranty by the contractor against contingent fees;

(b) Permit, as an exception to the warranty, contingent fee arrangements between contractors and bona fide employees or bona fide agencies; and

(c) Provide that, for breach or violation of the warranty by the contractor, the Government may annul the contract without liability or deduct from the contract price or consideration, or otherwise recover, the full amount of the contingent fee.

[FAC 2005-73, 79 FR 24192, 4/29/2014, effective 5/29/2014]

3.403 Applicability.

This subpart applies to all contracts. Statutory requirements for negotiated contracts are, as a matter of policy, extended to sealed bid contracts.

[FAC 84-5, 50 FR 1727, 1/11/85, effective 4/1/85]

3.404 Contract clause.

The contracting officer shall insert the clause at 52.203-5, Covenant Against Contingent Fees, in all solicitations and contracts exceeding the simplified acquisition threshold, other than those for commercial items (see Parts 2 and 12).

[FAC 90-40, 61 FR 39186, 7/26/96, effective 9/24/96]

3.405 Misrepresentations or violations of the Covenant Against Contingent Fees.

(a) Government personnel who suspect or have evidence of attempted or actual exercise of improper influence, misrepresentation of a contingent fee arrangement, or other violation of the Covenant Against Contingent Fees shall report the matter promptly to the contracting officer or appropriate higher authority in accordance with agency procedures.

(b) When there is specific evidence or other reasonable basis to suspect one or more of the violations in paragraph (a) of this section, the chief of the contracting office shall review the facts and, if appropriate, take or direct one or more of the following, or other, actions:

(1) If before award, reject the bid or proposal.

(2) If after award, enforce the Government's right to annul the contract or to recover the fee.

(3) Initiate suspension or debarment action under Subpart 9.4.

(4) Refer suspected fraudulent or criminal matters to the Department of Justice, as prescribed in agency regulations.

[Redesignated from 3.409, FAC 90-40, 61 FR 39186, 7/26/96, effective 9/24/96; FAC 2019-02, 84 FR 19839, 5/6/2019, effective 5/6/2019]

3.406 Records.

For enforcement purposes, agencies shall preserve any specific evidence of one or more of the violations in 3.405(a), together with all other pertinent data, including a record of actions taken. Contracting offices shall not retire or destroy these records until it is certain that they are no longer needed for enforcement purposes. If the original record is maintained in a central file, a copy must be retained in the contract file.

[Redesignated from 3.410, FAC 90-40, 61 FR 39186, 7/26/96, effective 9/24/96]

SUBPART 3.5—OTHER IMPROPER BUSINESS PRACTICES

3.501 Buying-in. (No Text)

3.501-1 Definition.

Buying-in, as used in this section, means submitting an offer below anticipated costs, expecting to—

(1) Increase the contract amount after award (*e.g.*, through unnecessary or excessively priced change orders); or

(2) Receive follow-on contracts at artificially high prices to recover losses incurred on the buy-in contract.

[FAC 97-22, 66 FR 2116, 1/10/2011, effective 3/12/2001; Delay of effective date, 66 FR 14259, 3/9/2001, effective 5/11/2001]

3.501-2 General.

(a) Buying-in may decrease competition or result in poor contract performance. The contracting officer must take appropriate action to ensure buying-in losses are not recovered by the contractor through the pricing of—

(1) Change orders; or

(2) Follow-on contracts subject to cost analysis.

(b) The Government should minimize the opportunity for buying-in by seeking a price commitment covering as much of the entire program concerned as is practical by using—

(1) Multiyear contracting, with a requirement in the solicitation that a price be submitted only for the total multiyear quantity; or

(2) Priced options for additional quantities that, together with the firm contract quantity, equal the program requirements (see Subpart 17.2).

(c) Other safeguards are available to the contracting officer to preclude recovery of buying-in losses *e.g.*, amortization of nonrecurring costs (see 15.408, Table 15-2, paragraph A, column (2) under "Formats for Submission of Line Item Summaries") and treatment of unreasonable price quotations (see 15.405).

[FAC 97-2, 62 FR 51224, 9/30/97, effective 10/10/97; FAC 2019-02, 84 FR 19839, 5/6/2019, effective 5/6/2019]

3.502 Subcontractor kickbacks. (No Text)

3.502-1 Definitions.

As used in this section—

Kickback means any money, fee, commission, credit, gift, gratuity, thing of value, or compensation of any kind which is provided to any prime contractor, prime contractor employee, subcontractor, or subcontractor employee for the purpose of improperly obtaining or rewarding favorable treatment in connection with a prime contract or in connection with a subcontract relating to a prime contract.

Person means a corporation, partnership, business association of any kind, trust, joint-stock company, or individual.

Prime contract means a contract or contractual action entered into by the United States for the purpose of obtaining supplies, materials, equipment, or services of any kind.

Prime Contractor means a person who has entered into a prime contract with the United States.

Prime Contractor employee means any officer, partner, employee, or agent of a prime contractor.

Subcontract means a contract or contractual action entered into by a prime contractor or subcontractor for the purpose of obtaining supplies, materials, equipment, or services of any kind under a prime contract.

Subcontractor —

(1) Means any person, other than the prime contractor, who offers to furnish or furnishes any supplies, materials, equipment, or services of any kind under a prime contract or a subcontract entered into in connection with such prime contract; and

(2) Includes any person who offers to furnish or furnishes general supplies to the prime contractor or a higher tier subcontractor.

[FAC 84-24, 52 FR 6121, 2/27/87, effective 2/6/87; FAC 84-39, 53 FR 34226, 9/2/88, effective 10/3/88; FAC 97-22, 66 FR 2116, 1/10/2001, effective 3/12/2001, delay of effective date, 66 FR 14259, 3/9/2001, effective 5/11/2001; FAC 2005-73, 79 FR 24192, 4/29/2014, effective 5/29/2014; FAC 2019-02, 84 FR 19839, 5/6/2019, effective 5/6/2019]

3.502-2 Subcontractor kickbacks.

The Anti-Kickback Act of 1986 (now codified at 41 U.S.C. chapter 87, Kickbacks,) was passed to deter subcontractors from making payments and contractors from accepting payments for the purpose of improperly obtaining or rewarding favorable treatment in connection with a prime contract or a subcontract relating to a prime contract. The Kickbacks statute—

(a) Prohibits any person from—

(1) Providing, attempting to provide, or offering to provide any kickback;

(2) Soliciting, accepting, or attempting to accept any kickback; or

(3) Including, directly or indirectly, the amount of any kickback in the contract price charged by a subcontractor to a prime contractor or a higher tier subcontractor or in the contract price charged by a prime contractor to the United States.

(b) Imposes criminal penalties on any person who knowingly and willfully engages in the prohibited conduct addressed in paragraph (a) of this section.

(c) Provides for the recovery of civil penalties by the United States from any person who knowingly engages in such prohibited conduct and from any person whose employee, subcontractor, or subcontractor employee provides, accepts, or charges a kickback.

(d) Provides that—

(1) The contracting officer may offset the amount of a kickback against monies owed by the United States to the prime contractor under the prime contract to which such kickback relates;

(2) The contracting officer may direct a prime contractor to withhold from any sums owed to a subcontractor under a subcontract of the prime contract the amount of any kickback which was or may be offset against the prime contractor under paragraph (d)(1) of this section; and

(3) An offset under paragraph (d)(1) or a direction under paragraph (d)(2) of this section is a claim by the Government for the purposes of 41 U.S.C. chapter 71, Contract Disputes.

(e) Authorizes contracting officers to order that sums withheld under paragraph (d)(2) of this section be paid to the contracting agency, or if the sum has already been offset against the prime contractor, that it be retained by the prime contractor.

(f) Requires the prime contractor to notify the contracting officer when the withholding under paragraph (d)(2) of this section has been accomplished unless the amount withheld has been paid to the Government.

(g) Requires a prime contractor or subcontractor to report in writing to the inspector general of the contracting agency, the head of the contracting agency if the agency does not have an inspector general, or the Attorney General any possible violation of the Kickbacks statute when the prime contractor or subcontractor has reasonable grounds to believe such violation may have occurred.

(h) Provides that, for the purpose of ascertaining whether there has been a violation of the Kickbacks statute with respect to any prime contract, the Government Accountability Office and the inspector general of the contracting agency, or a representative of such contracting agency designated by the head of the agency if the agency does not have an inspector general, shall have access to and may inspect the facilities and audit the books and records, including any electronic data or records, of any prime contractor or subcontractor under a prime contract awarded by such agency.

(i) Requires each contracting agency to include in each prime contract exceeding $150,000 for other than commercial items (see Part 12), a requirement that the prime contractor shall—

(1) Have in place and follow reasonable procedures designed to prevent and detect violations of the Kickbacks statute in its own operations and direct business relationships (*e.g.*, company ethics rules prohibiting kickbacks by employees, agents, or subcontractors; education programs for new employees and subcontractors, explaining policies about kickbacks, related company procedures and the consequences of detection; procurement procedures to minimize the opportunity for kickbacks; audit procedures designed to detect kickbacks; periodic surveys of subcontractors to elicit information about kickbacks; procedures to report kickbacks to law enforcement officials; annual declarations by employees of gifts or gratuities received from subcontractors; annual employee declarations that they have violated no company ethics rules; personnel practices that document unethical or illegal behavior and make such information available to prospective employers); and

(2) Cooperate fully with any Federal agency investigating a possible violation of the Kickbacks statute.

(j) Notwithstanding paragraph (i) of this section, a prime contractor shall cooperate fully with any Federal Government agency investigating a violation of 41 U.S.C. 8702 (see 41 U.S.C. 8703(b)).

[FAC 84-24, 52 FR 6121, 2/27/87, effective 2/6/87, corrected 52 FR 9989, 3/27/87; FAC 84-39, 53 FR 34226, 9/2/88, effective 10/3/88; FAC 90-32, 60 FR 48206, 9/18/95, effective 10/1/95; FAC 90-40, 61 FR 39186, 7/26/96, effective 8/26/96; FAC 90-45, Final rule, 62 FR 224, 1/2/97, effective 1/1/97; FAC 2005-13, Final rule 71 FR 57380, 9/28/2006, effective 9/28/2006; FAC 2005-45, 75 FR 53129, 8/30/2010, effective 10/1/2010; FAC 2005-73, 79 FR 24192, 4/29/2014, effective 5/29/2014; FAC 2019-02, 84 FR 19839, 5/6/2019, effective 5/6/2019]

3.502-3 Contract clause.

The contracting officer shall insert the clause at 52.203-7, Anti-Kickback Procedures, in solicitations and contracts exceeding the simplified acquisition threshold, other than those for commercial items (see Part 12).

[FAC 90-32, 60 FR 48206, 9/18/95, effective 10/1/95; FAC 90-40, 61 FR 39186, 7/26/96, effective 8/26/96; FAC 2005-13, 71 FR 57380, 9/28/2006, effective 9/28/2006]

3.503 Unreasonable restrictions on subcontractor sales. (No Text)

3.503-1 Policy.

10 U.S.C. 2402 and 41 U.S.C. 4704 require that subcontractors not be unreasonably precluded from making direct sales to the Government of any supplies or services made or furnished under a contract. However, this does not preclude contractors from asserting rights that are otherwise authorized by law or regulation.

[FAC 84-11, 50 FR 35475, 8/30/85, effective 8/30/85; FAC 2005-73, 79 FR 24192, 4/29/2014, effective 5/29/2014]

3.503-2 Contract clause.

The contracting officer shall insert the clause at 52.203-6, Restrictions on Subcontractor Sales to the Government, in solicitations and contracts exceeding the simplified acquisition threshold. For the acquisition of commercial items, the contracting officer shall use the clause with its Alternate I.

[FAC 90-32, 60 FR 48206, 9/18/95, effective 10/1/95; FAC 90-40, 61 FR 39186, 7/26/96, effective 8/26/96; FAC 2005-30, 74 FR 2713, 1/15/2009, effective 2/17/2009; FAC 2005-31, 74 FR 11832, 3/19/2009, effective 3/19/2009]

SUBPART 3.6—CONTRACTS WITH GOVERNMENT EMPLOYEES OR

ORGANIZATIONS OWNED OR CONTROLLED BY THEM

3.601 Policy.

(a) Except as specified in 3.602, a contracting officer shall not knowingly award a contract to a Government employee or to a business concern or other organization owned or substantially owned or controlled by one or more Government employees. This policy is intended to avoid any conflict of interest that might arise between the employees' interests and their Government duties, and to avoid the appearance of favoritism or preferential treatment by the Government toward its employees.

(b) For purposes of this subpart, special Government employees (as defined in 18 U.S.C. 202) performing services as experts, advisors, or consultants, or as members of advisory committees, are not considered Government employees unless—

(1) The contract arises directly out of the individual's activity as a special Government employee;

(2) In the individual's capacity as a special Government employee, the individual is in a position to influence the award of the contract; or

(3) Another conflict of interest is determined to exist.

[FAC 84-59, 55 FR 34864, 8/24/90, effective 9/24/90]

3.602 Exceptions.

The agency head, or a designee not below the level of the head of the contracting activity, may authorize an exception to the policy in 3.601 only if there is a most compelling reason to do so, such as when the Government's needs cannot reasonably be otherwise met.

3.603 Responsibilities of the contracting officer.

(a) Before awarding a contract, the contracting officer shall obtain an authorization under 3.602 if—

(1) The contracting officer knows, or has reason to believe, that a prospective contractor is one to which award is otherwise prohibited under FAR 3.601; and

(2) There is a most compelling reason to make an award to that prospective contractor.

(b) The contracting officer shall comply with the requirements and guidance in Subpart 9.5 before awarding a contract to an organization owned or substantially owned or controlled by Government employees.

SUBPART 3.7—VOIDING AND RESCINDING CONTRACTS

3.700 Scope of subpart.

(a) This subpart prescribes Governmentwide policies and procedures for exercising discretionary authority to declare void and rescind contracts in relation to which—

(1) There has been a final conviction for bribery, conflict of interest, disclosure or receipt of contractor bid or proposal information or source selection information in exchange for a thing of value or to give anyone a competitive advantage in the award of a Federal agency procurement contract, or similar misconduct; or

(2) There has been an agency head determination that contractor bid or proposal information or source selection information has been disclosed or received in exchange for a thing of value, or for the purpose of obtaining or giving anyone a competitive advantage in the award of a Federal agency procurement contract.

(b) This subpart does not prescribe policies or procedures for, or govern the exercise of, any other remedy available to the Government with respect to such contracts, including but not limited to, the common law right of avoidance, rescission, or cancellation.

[FAC 84-18, 51 FR 27116, 7/29/86, effective 7/30/86; FAC 90-45, Final rule, 62 FR 224, 1/2/97, effective 1/1/97]

3.701 Purpose.

This subpart provides—

(a) An administrative remedy with respect to contracts in relation to which there has been—

(1) A final conviction for bribery, conflict of interest, disclosure or receipt of contractor bid or proposal information or source

selection information in exchange for a thing of value or to give anyone a competitive advantage in the award of a Federal agency procurement contract, or similar misconduct; or

(2) An agency head determination that contractor bid or proposal information or source selection information has been disclosed or received in exchange for a thing of value, or for the purpose of obtaining or giving anyone a competitive advantage in the award of a Federal agency procurement contract; and

(b) A means to deter similar misconduct in the future by those who are involved in the award, performance, and administration of Government contracts.

[FAC 90-45, Final rule, 62 FR 224, 1/2/97, effective 1/1/97]

3.702 Definition.

Final conviction means a conviction, whether entered on a verdict or plea, including a plea of nolo contendere, for which a sentence has been imposed.

[FAC 84-18, 51 FR 27116, 7/29/86, effective 7/30/86]

3.703 Authority.

(a) Section 1(e) of Public Law 87-849, 18 U.S.C. 218 ("the Act"), empowers the President or the heads of executive agencies acting under regulations prescribed by the President, to declare void and rescind contracts and other transactions enumerated in the Act, in relation to which there has been a final conviction for bribery, conflict of interest, or any other violation of Chapter 11 of Title 18 of the United States Code (18 U.S.C. 201-224). E.O. 12448, November 4, 1983, delegates the President's authority under the Act to the heads of the executive agencies and military departments.

(b) 41 U.S.C. 2105(c) requires a Federal agency, upon receiving information that a contractor or a person has violated 41 U.S.C. 2102, to consider rescission of a contract with respect to which—

(1) The contractor or someone acting for the contractor has been convicted for an offense punishable under 41 U.S.C. 2105(a); or

(2) The head of the agency, or designee, has determined, based upon a preponderance of the evidence, that the contractor or someone acting for the contractor has engaged in conduct constituting such an offense.

[FAC 84-18, 51 FR 27116, 7/29/86, effective 7/30/86; FAC 90-45, Final rule, 62 FR 224, 1/2/97, effective 1/1/97; FAC 2005-73, 79 FR 24192, 4/29/2014, effective 5/29/2014]

3.704 Policy.

(a) In cases in which there is a final conviction for any violation of 18 U.S.C. 201-224 involving or relating to contracts awarded by an agency, the agency head or designee, shall consider the facts available and, if appropriate, may declare void and rescind contracts, and recover the amounts expended and property transferred by the agency in accordance with the policies and procedures of this subpart.

(b) Since a final conviction under 18 U.S.C. 201-224 relating to a contract also may justify the conclusion that the party involved is not presently responsible, the agency should consider initiating debarment proceedings in accordance with Subpart 9.4, Debarment, Suspension, and Ineligibility, if debarment has not been initiated, or is not in effect at the time the final conviction is entered.

(c) If there is a final conviction for an offense punishable under 41 U.S.C. 2105, or if the head of the agency, or designee, has determined, based upon a preponderance of the evidence, that the contractor or someone acting for the contractor has engaged in conduct constituting such an offense, then the head of the contracting activity shall consider, in addition to any other penalty prescribed by law or regulation—

(1) Declaring void and rescinding contracts, as appropriate, and recovering the amounts expended under the contracts by using the procedures at 3.705(see 3.104-7); and

(2) Recommending the initiation of suspension or debarment proceedings in accordance with Subpart 9.4.

[FAC 84-18, 51 FR 27116, 7/29/86, effective 7/30/86; FAC 90-45, Final rule, 62 FR 224, 1/2/97, effective 1/1/97; FAC 2001-06, 67 FR 13048, 3/20/2002, effective 4/4/2002; FAC 2005-73, 79 FR 24192, 4/29/2014, effective 5/29/2014]

3.705 Procedures.

(a) *Reporting.* The facts concerning any final conviction for any violation of 18 U.S.C. 201-224 involving or relating to agency contracts shall be reported promptly to the agency head or designee for that official's consideration. The agency head or designee shall promptly notify the Civil Division, Department of Justice, that the action is being considered under this subpart.

(b) *Decision.* Following an assessment of the facts, the agency head or designee may declare void and rescind contracts with respect to which a final conviction has been entered, and recover the amounts expended and the property transferred by the agency under the terms of the contracts involved.

(c) *Decision-making process.* Agency procedures governing the voiding and rescinding decision-making process shall be as informal as practicable, consistent with the principles of fundamental fairness. As a minimum, however, agencies shall provide the following:

(1) A notice of proposed action to declare void and rescind the contract shall be made in writing and sent by certified mail, return receipt requested.

(2) A thirty calendar day period after receipt of the notice, for the contractor to submit pertinent information before any final decision is made.

(3) Upon request made within the period for submission of pertinent information, an opportunity shall be afforded for a hearing at which witnesses may be presented, and any witness the agency presents may be confronted. However, no inquiry shall be made regarding the validity of a conviction.

(4) If the agency head or designee decides to declare void and rescind the contracts involved, that official shall issue a written decision which—

(i) States that determination;

(ii) Reflects consideration of the fair value of any tangible benefits received and retained by the agency; and

(iii) States the amount due and the property to be returned to the agency.

(d) *Notice of proposed action.* The notice of the proposed action, as a minimum shall—

(1) Advise that consideration is being given to declaring void and rescinding contracts awarded by the agency, and recovering the amounts expended and property transferred therefor, under the provisions of 18 U.S.C. 218;

(2) Specifically identify the contracts affected by the action;

(3) Specifically identify the offense or final conviction on which the action is based;

(4) State the amounts expended and property transferred under each of the contracts involved, and the money and the property demanded to be returned;

(5) Identify any tangible benefits received and retained by the agency under the contract, and the value of those benefits, as calculated by the agency;

(6) Advise that pertinent information may be submitted within 30 calendar days after receipt of the notice, and that, if requested within that time, a hearing shall be held at which witnesses may be presented and any witness the agency presents may be confronted; and

(7) Advise that action shall be taken only after the agency head or designee issues a final written decision on the proposed action.

(e) *Final agency decision.* The final agency decision shall be based on the information available to the agency head or designee, including any pertinent information submitted or, if a hearing was held, presented at the hearing. If the agency decision declares void and rescinds the contract, the final decision shall specify the amounts due and property to be returned to the agency, and reflect consideration of the fair value of any tangible benefits received and retained by the agency. Notice of the decision shall be sent promptly by certified mail, return receipt requested. Rescission of contracts under the authority of the Act and demand for recovery of the amounts expended and property transferred therefor, is not a claim within the meaning of 41 U.S.C. chapter 71, Contract Disputes, or part 33. Therefore, the procedures required by the statute and the FAR for the issuance of a final contracting officer decision are not applicable to final agency decisions under this subpart, and shall not be followed.

[FAC 84-18, 51 FR 27116, 7/29/86, effective 7/30/86; FAC 90-45, Final rule, 62 FR 224, 1/2/97, effective 1/1/97; FAC 2005-73, 79 FR 24192, 4/29/2014, effective 5/29/2014]

SUBPART 3.8—LIMITATION ON THE PAYMENT OF FUNDS TO INFLUENCE FEDERAL TRANSACTIONS

3.800 Scope of subpart.

This subpart prescribes policies and procedures implementing 31 U.S.C. 1352, "Limitation on use of appropriated funds to influence certain Federal contracting and financial transactions."

[FAC 84-55, 55 FR 3191, 1/30/90, effective 1/30/90; FAC 2005-06, 70 FR 57455, 9/30/2005, effective 9/30/2005; FAC 2005-19, 72 FR 46327, 8/17/2007, effective 9/17/2007]

3.801 Definitions.

As used in this subpart—

Agency means executive agency as defined in 2.101.

Covered Federal action means any of the following actions:

(1) Awarding any Federal contract.

(2) Making any Federal grant.

(3) Making any Federal loan.

(4) Entering into any cooperative agreement.

(5) Extending, continuing, renewing, amending, or modifying any Federal contract, grant, loan, or cooperative agreement.

Indian tribe and *tribal organization* have the meaning provided in section 4 of the Indian Self-Determination and Education Assistance Act (25 U.S.C. 450b) and include Alaskan Natives.

Influencing or attempting to influence means making, with the intent to influence, any communication to or appearance before an officer or employee of any agency, a Member of Congress, an officer or employee of Congress, or an employee of a Member of Congress in connection with any covered Federal action.

Local government means a unit of government in a State and, if chartered, established, or otherwise recognized by a State for the performance of a governmental duty, including a local public authority, a special district, an intrastate district, a council of governments, a sponsor group representative organization, and any other instrumentality of a local government.

Officer or employee of an agency includes the following individuals who are employed by an agency:

(1) An individual who is appointed to a position in the Government under Title 5, United States Code, including a position under a temporary appointment.

(2) A member of the uniformed services, as defined in subsection 101(3), Title 37, United States Code.

(3) A special Government employee, as defined in section 202, Title 18, United States Code.

(4) An individual who is a member of a Federal advisory committee, as defined by the Federal Advisory Committee Act, Title 5, United States Code, appendix 2.

Person means an individual, corporation, company, association, authority, firm, partnership, society, State, and local government, regardless of whether such entity is operated for profit or not for profit. This term excludes an Indian tribe, tribal organization, or any other Indian organization eligible to receive Federal contracts, grants, cooperative agreements, or loans from an agency, but only with respect to expenditures by such tribe or organization that are made for purposes specified in paragraph 3.802(a) and are permitted by other Federal law.

Reasonable compensation means, with respect to a regularly employed officer or employee of any person, compensation that is consistent with the normal compensation for such officer or employee for work that is not furnished to, not funded by, or not furnished in cooperation with the Federal Government.

Reasonable payment means, with respect to professional and other technical services, a payment in an amount that is consistent with the amount normally paid for such services in the private sector.

Recipient includes the contractor and all subcontractors. This term excludes an Indian tribe, tribal organization, or any other Indian organization eligible to receive Federal contracts, grants, cooperative agreements, or loans from an agency, but only with respect to expenditures by such tribe or organization that are made for purposes specified in paragraph 3.802(a) and are permitted by other Federal law.

Regularly employed means, with respect to an officer or employee of a person requesting or receiving a Federal contract, an officer or employee who is employed by such person for at least 130 working days within 1 year immediately preceding the date of the submission that initiates agency consideration of such person for receipt of such contract. An officer or employee who is employed by such person for less than 130 working days within 1 year immediately preceding the date of the submission that initiates agency consideration of such person shall be considered to be regularly employed as soon as he or she is employed by such person for 130 working days.

State means a State of the United States, the District of Columbia, an outlying area of the United States, an agency or instrumentality of a State, and multi-State, regional, or interstate entity having governmental duties and powers.

[FAC 84-55, 55 FR 3191, 1/30/90, effective 1/30/90; FAC 2001-14, 68 FR 28079, 5/23/2003, effective 6/23/2003; FAC 2005-06, 70 FR 57455, 9/30/2005, effective 9/30/2005; FAC 2005-19, 72 FR 43627, 8/17/2007, effective 9/17/2007]

3.802 Statutory prohibition and requirement.

(a) 31 U.S.C. 1352 prohibits a recipient of a Federal contract, grant, loan, or cooperative agreement from using appropriated funds to pay any person for influencing or attempting to influence an officer or employee of any agency, a Member of Congress, an officer or employee of Congress, or an employee of a Member of Congress in connection with any covered Federal actions.

(1) For purposes of this subpart the term *appropriated funds* does not include profit or fee from a covered Federal action.

(2) To the extent a person can demonstrate that the person has sufficient monies, other than Federal appropriated funds, the Government shall assume that these other monies were spent for any influencing activities that would be unallowable if paid for with Federal appropriated funds.

(b) 31 U.S.C. 1352 also requires offerors to furnish a declaration consisting of both a certification and a disclosure, with periodic updates of the disclosure after contract award. These requirements are contained in the provision at 52.203-11, Certification and Disclosure Regarding Payments to Influence Certain Federal Transactions, and the clause at 52.203-12, Limitation on Payments to Influence Certain Federal Transactions.

[FAC 84-55, 55 FR 3191, 1/30/90, effective 1/30/90; corrected, 55 FR 4836, 2/12/90; FAC 2005-06, 70 FR 57455, 9/30/2005, effective 9/30/2005; FAC 2005-19, 72 FR 46327, 8/17/2007, effective 9/17/2007]

3.803 Exceptions.

(a) The prohibition of paragraph 3.802(a) does not apply under the following conditions:

(1) *Agency and legislative liaison by own employees.* (i) Payment of reasonable compensation made to an officer or employee of a person requesting or receiving a covered Federal action if the payment is for agency and legislative liaison activities not directly related to a covered Federal action. For purposes of this paragraph, providing any information specifically requested by an agency or Congress is permitted at any time.

(ii) Participating with an agency in discussions that are not related to a specific solicitation for any covered Federal action, but that concern—

(A) The qualities and characteristics (including individual demonstrations) of the person's products or services, conditions or terms of sale, and service capabilities; or

(B) The application or adaptation of the person's products or services for an agency's use.

(iii) Providing prior to formal solicitation of any covered Federal action any information not specifically requested but necessary for an agency to make an informed decision about initiation of a covered Federal action.

(iv) Participating in technical discussions regarding the preparation of an unsolicited proposal prior to its official submission.

(v) Making capability presentations prior to formal solicitation of any covered Federal action when seeking an award from an agency pursuant to the provisions of the Small Business Act, as amended by Pub. L. 95-507, and subsequent amendments.

(2) *Professional and technical services.* (i) Payment of reasonable compensation made to an officer or employee of a person requesting or receiving a covered Federal action, if payment is for professional or technical services rendered directly in the preparation, submission, or negotiation of any bid, proposal, or application for that Federal action or for meeting requirements imposed by or pursuant to law as a condition for receiving that Federal action;

(ii) Any reasonable payment to a person, other than an officer or employee of a person requesting or receiving a covered Federal action, if the payment is for professional or technical services rendered directly in the preparation, submission, or negotiation of any bid, proposal, or application for that Federal action, or for meeting requirements imposed by or pursuant to law as a condition for receiving that Federal action. Persons other than officers or employees of a person requesting or receiving a covered Federal action include consultants and trade associations.

(iii) As used in paragraph (a)(2) of this section "professional and technical services" are limited to advice and analysis directly applying any professional or technical discipline. For example, drafting of a legal document accompanying a bid or proposal by a lawyer is allowable. Similarly, technical advice provided by an engineer on the performance or operational capability of a piece of equipment rendered directly in the negotiation of a contract is allowable. However, communications with the intent to influence made by a professional or a technical person are not allowable under this section unless they provide advice and analysis directly applying their professional or technical expertise and unless the advice or analysis is rendered directly and solely in the preparation, submission or negotiation of a covered Federal action. Thus, for example, communications with the intent to influence made by a lawyer that do not provide legal advice or analysis directly and solely related to the legal aspects of his or her client's proposal, but generally advocate one proposal over another, are not allowable under this section because the lawyer is not providing professional legal services. Similarly, communications with the intent to influence made by an engineer providing an engineering analysis prior to the preparation or submission of a bid or proposal are not allowable under this section since the engineer is providing technical services but not directly in the preparation, submission or negotiation of a covered Federal action.

(iv) Requirements imposed by or pursuant to law as a condition for receiving a covered Federal award include those required by law or regulation and any other requirements in the actual award documents.

(b) Only those communications and services expressly authorized by paragraph (a) of this section are permitted.

(c) The disclosure requirements of paragraph 3.802(b) do not apply with respect to payments of reasonable compensation made to regularly employed officers or employees of a person.

[FAC 84-55, 55 FR 3191, 1/30/90, effective 1/30/90; FAC 2005-06, 70 FR 57455, 9/30/2005, effective 9/30/2005; FAC 2005-19, 72 FR 46327, 8/17/2007, effective 9/17/2007]

3.804 Policy.

The contracting officer shall obtain certifications and disclosures as required by the provision at 52.203-11, Certification and Disclosure Regarding Payments to Influence Certain Federal Transactions, prior to the award of any contract exceeding $150,000.

[FAC 84-55, 55 FR 3191, 1/30/90, effective 1/30/90; FAC 2005-06, 70 FR 57455, 9/30/2005, effective 9/30/2005; FAC 2005-19, 72 FR 46327, 8/17/2007, effective 9/17/2007; FAC 2005-45, 75 FR 53129, 8/30/2010, effective 10/1/2010]

3.805 Exemption.

The Secretary of Defense may exempt, on a case-by-case basis, a covered Federal action from the prohibitions of this subpart whenever the Secretary determines, in writing, that such an exemption is in the national interest. The Secretary shall transmit a copy of the exemption to Congress immediately after making the determination.

[FAC 84-55, 55 FR 3191, 1/30/90, effective 1/30/90; FAC 2005-06, 70 FR 57455, 9/30/2005, effective 9/30/2005; FAC 2005-19, 72 FR 46327, 8/17/2007, effective 9/17/2007]

3.806 Processing suspected violations.

The contracting officer shall report suspected violations of the requirements of 31 U.S.C. 1352 in accordance with agency procedures.

[FAC 84-55, 55 FR 3191, 1/30/90, effective 1/30/90; FAC 2005-06, 70 FR 57455, 9/30/2005, effective 9/30/2005; FAC 2005-19, 72 FR 46327, 8/17/2007, effective 9/17/2007]

3.807 Civil penalties.

Agencies shall impose and collect civil penalties pursuant to the provisions of the Program Fraud and Civil Remedies Act, 31 U.S.C. 3803 (except subsection (c)), 3804-3808, and 3812, insofar as the provisions therein are not inconsistent with the requirements of this subpart.

[FAC 84-55, 55 FR 3191, 1/30/90, effective 1/30/90; FAC 2001-04, 67 FR 6112, 2/8/2002, effective 2/8/2002; FAC 2005-06, 70 FR 57455, 9/30/2005, effective 9/30/2005]

3.808 Solicitation provision and contract clause.

(a) Insert the provision at 52.203-11, Certification and Disclosure Regarding Payments to Influence Certain Federal Transactions, in solicitations expected to exceed $150,000.

(b) Insert the clause at 52.203-12, Limitation on Payments to Influence Certain Federal Transactions, in solicitations and contracts expected to exceed $150,000.

[FAC 84-55, 55 FR 3191, 1/30/90, effective 1/30/90; FAC 2005-06, 70 FR 57455, 9/30/2005, effective 9/30/2005; FAC 2005-19, 72 FR 46327, 8/17/2007, effective 9/17/2007; FAC 2005-45, 75 FR 53129, 8/30/2010, effective 10/1/2010]

SUBPART 3.9—WHISTLEBLOWER PROTECTIONS FOR CONTRACTOR EMPLOYEES

3.900 Scope of subpart.

This subpart implements various statutory whistleblower programs. This subpart does not implement 10 U.S.C. 2409, which is applicable only to DoD, NASA, and the Coast Guard.

(a) *41 U.S.C. 4705 (in effect before July 1, 2013 and on or after January 2, 2017)*. Sections 3.901 through 3.906 of this subpart implement 41 U.S.C. 4705, applicable to civilian agencies other than NASA and the Coast Guard, except as provided in paragraph (c) of this section. These sections are not in effect for the duration of the pilot program described in paragraph (b) of this section.

(b) *41 U.S.C. 4712 (in effect on July 1, 2013 through January 1, 2017)*. Section 3.908 of this subpart implements the pilot program, applicable to civilian agencies other than NASA and the Coast Guard, except as provided in paragraph (c) of this section.

(c) Section 743 of Division E, Title VII, of the Consolidated and Further Continuing Appropriations Act, 2015 (Pub. L. 113-235) and its successor provisions in subsequent appropriations acts (and as extended in continuing resolutions), implemented in 3.909, applicable to all agencies.

(d) *Contracts funded by the American Recovery and Reinvestment Act.* Section 3.907 of this subpart implements section 1553 of the American Recovery and Reinvestment Act of 2009 (Pub. L. 111-5), and applies to all contracts funded in whole or in part by that Act.

[FAC 90-30, 60 FR 37772, 7/21/95, effective 9/19/95; FAC 2005-32, 74 FR 14633, 3/31/2009, effective 3/31/2009; FAC 2005-42, 75 FR 34258, 6/16/2010, effective 6/16/2010; FAC 2005-70, 78 FR 60169, 9/30/2013, effective 9/30/2013; FAC 2005-85, 80 FR 75911, 12/4/2015, effective 12/4/2015; FAC 2005-95, 82 FR 4717, 1/13/2017, effective 1/19/2017]

3.901 Definitions.

As used in this subpart—

Authorized official of an agency means an officer or employee responsible for contracting, program management, audit, inspection, investigation, or enforcement of any law or regulation relating to Government procurement or the subject matter of the contract.

Authorized official of the Department of Justice means any person responsible for the investigation, enforcement, or prosecution of any law or regulation.

Inspector General means an Inspector General appointed under the Inspector General Act of 1978, as amended. In the Department of Defense that is the DoD Inspector General. In the case of an executive agency that does not have an Inspector General, the duties shall be performed by an official designated by the head of the executive agency.

Internal confidentiality agreement or statement means a confidentiality agreement or any other written statement that the contractor requires any of its employees or subcontractors to sign regarding nondisclosure of contractor information, except that it does not include confidentiality agreements arising out of civil litigation or confidentiality agreements that contractor employees or subcontractors sign at the behest of a Federal agency.

Subcontract means any contract as defined in subpart 2.1 entered into by a subcontractor to furnish supplies or services for performance of a prime contract or a subcontract. It includes but is not limited to purchase orders, and changes and modifications to purchase orders.

Subcontractor means any supplier, distributor, vendor, or firm (including a consultant) that furnishes supplies or services to or for a prime contractor or another subcontractor.

[FAC 90-30, 60 FR 37772, 7/21/95, effective 9/19/95; FAC 97-22, 66 FR 2116, 1/10/2001, effective 3/12/2001; Delay of effective date, 66 FR 14259, 3/9/2001, effective 5/11/2001; FAC 2005-95, 82 FR 4717, 1/13/2017, effective 1/19/2017; FAC 2019-02, 84 FR 19839, 5/6/2019, effective 5/6/2019]

3.902 [Removed and Reserved]

[FAC 90-30, 60 FR 37772, 7/21/95, effective 9/19/95; FAC 2005-32, 74 FR 14633, 3/31/2009, effective 3/31/2009; FAC 2005-42, 75 FR 34258, 6/16/2010, effective 6/16/2010]

3.903 Policy.

Government contractors shall not discharge, demote or otherwise discriminate against an employee as a reprisal for disclosing information to a Member of Congress, or an authorized official of an agency or of the Department of Justice, relating to a substantial violation of law related to a contract (including the competition for or negotiation of a contract).

[FAC 90-30, 60 FR 37772, 7/21/95, effective 9/19/95]

3.904 Procedures for filing complaints.

(a) Any employee of a contractor who believes that he or she has been discharged, demoted, or otherwise discriminated against contrary to the policy in 3.903 may file a complaint with the Inspector General of the agency that awarded the contract.

(b) The complaint shall be signed and shall contain—

(1) The name of the contractor;

(2) The contract number, if known; if not, a description reasonably sufficient to identify the contract(s) involved;

(3) The substantial violation of law giving rise to the disclosure;

(4) The nature of the disclosure giving rise to the discriminatory act; and

(5) The specific nature and date of the reprisal.

[FAC 90-30, 60 FR 37772, 7/21/95, effective 9/19/95]

3.905 Procedures for investigating complaints.

(a) Upon receipt of a complaint, the Inspector General shall conduct an initial inquiry. If the Inspector General determines that the complaint is frivolous or for other reasons does not merit further investigation, the Inspector General shall advise the complainant that no further action on the complaint will be taken.

(b) If the Inspector General determines that the complaint merits further investigation, the Inspector General shall notify the complainant, contractor, and head of the contracting activity. The Inspector General shall conduct an investigation and provide a written report of findings to the head of the agency or designee.

(c) Upon completion of the investigation, the head of the agency or designee shall ensure that the Inspector General provides the report of findings to—

(1) The complainant and any person acting on the complainant's behalf;

(2) The contractor alleged to have committed the violation; and

(3) The head of the contracting activity.

(d) The complainant and contractor shall be afforded the opportunity to submit a written response to the report of findings within 30 days to the head of the agency or designee. Extensions of time to file a written response may be granted by the head of the agency or designee.

(e) At any time, the head of the agency or designee may request additional investigative work be done on the complaint.

[FAC 90-30, 60 FR 37772, 7/21/95, effective 9/19/95]

3.906 Remedies.

(a) If the head of the agency or designee determines that a contractor has subjected one of its employees to a reprisal for providing information to a Member of Congress, or an authorized official of an agency or of the Department of Justice, the head of the agency or designee may take one or more of the following actions:

(1) Order the contractor to take affirmative action to abate the reprisal.

(2) Order the contractor to reinstate the person to the position that the person held before the reprisal, together with the compensation (including back pay), employment benefits, and other terms and conditions of employment that would apply to the person in that position if the reprisal had not been taken.

(3) Order the contractor to pay the complainant an amount equal to the aggregate amount of all costs and expenses (including attorneys' fees and expert witnesses' fees) that were reasonably incurred by the complainant for, or in connection with, bringing the complaint regarding the reprisal.

(b) Whenever a contractor fails to comply with an order, the head of the agency or designee shall request the Department of Justice to file an action for enforcement of such order in the United States district court for a district in which the reprisal was found to have occurred. In any action brought under this section, the court may grant appropriate relief, including injunctive relief and compensatory and exemplary damages.

(c) Any person adversely affected or aggrieved by an order issued under this section may obtain review of the order's conformance with the law, and this subpart, in the United States Court of Appeals for a circuit in which the reprisal is alleged in the order to have occurred. No petition seeking such review may be filed more than 60 days after issuance of the order by the head of the agency or designee. Review shall conform to Chapter 7 of Title 5, United States Code.

[FAC 90-30, 60 FR 37772, 7/21/95, effective 9/19/95]

3.907 Whistleblower Protections Under the American Recovery and Reinvestment Act of 2009 (the Recovery Act). (No Text)

[FAC 2005-32, 74 FR 14633, 3/31/2009, effective 3/31/2009; FAC 2005-42, 75 FR 34258, 6/16/2010, effective 6/16/2010]

3.907-1 Definitions.

As used in this section—

Board means the Recovery Accountability and Transparency Board established by Section 1521 of the Recovery Act.

Covered funds means any contract payment, grant payment, or other payment received by a contractor if—

(1) The Federal Government provides any portion of the money or property that is provided, requested, or demanded; and

(2) At least some of the funds are appropriated or otherwise made available by the Recovery Act.

Covered information means information that the employee reasonably believes is evidence of gross mismanagement of the contract or subcontract related to covered funds, gross waste of covered funds, a substantial and specific danger to public health or safety related to the implementation or use of covered funds, an abuse of authority related to the implementation or use of covered funds, or a violation of law, rule, or regulation related to an agency contract (including the competition for or negotiation of a contract) awarded or issued relating to covered funds.

Inspector General means an Inspector General appointed under the Inspector General Act of 1978. In the Department of Defense that is the DoD Inspector General. In the case of an executive agency that does not have an Inspector General, the duties shall be performed by an official designated by the head of the executive agency.

Non-Federal employer, as used in this section, means any employer that receives Recovery Act funds, including a contractor, subcontractor, or other recipient of funds pursuant to a contract or other agreement awarded and administered in accordance with the Federal Acquisition Regulation.

[FAC 2005-32, 74 FR 14633, 3/31/2009, effective 3/31/2009; FAC 2005-42, 75 FR 34258, 6/16/2010, effective 6/16/2010; FAC 2005-42, 75 FR 34258, 6/16/2010, effective 6/16/2010]

3.907-2 Policy.

Non-Federal employers are prohibited from discharging, demoting, or otherwise discriminating against an employee as a reprisal for disclosing covered information to any of the following entities or their representatives:

(1) The Board.

(2) An Inspector General.

(3) The Comptroller General.

(4) A member of Congress.

(5) A State or Federal regulatory or law enforcement agency.

(6) A person with supervisory authority over the employee or such other person working for the employer who has the authority to investigate, discover, or terminate misconduct.

(7) A court or grand jury.

(8) The head of a Federal agency.

[FAC 2005-32, 74 FR 14633, 3/31/2009, effective 3/31/2009; FAC 2005-42, 75 FR 34258, 6/16/2010, effective 6/16/2010]

3.907-3 Procedures for filing complaints.

(a) An employee who believes that he or she has been subjected to reprisal prohibited by the Recovery Act, Section 1553 as set forth in 3.907-2, may submit a complaint regarding the reprisal to the Inspector General of the agency that awarded the contract.

(b) The complaint shall be signed and shall contain—

(1) The name of the contractor;

(2) The contract number, if known; if not, a description reasonably sufficient to identify the contract(s) involved;

(3) The covered information giving rise to the disclosure;

(4) The nature of the disclosure giving rise to the discriminatory act; and

(5) The specific nature and date of the reprisal.

(c) A contracting officer who receives a complaint of reprisal of the type described in 3.907-2 shall forward it to the Office of Inspector General and to other designated officials in accordance with agency procedures (*e.g.*, agency legal counsel).

[FAC 2005-32, 74 FR 14633, 3/31/2009, effective 3/31/2009; FAC 2005-42, 75 FR 34258, 6/16/2010, effective 6/16/2010]

3.907-4 Procedures for investigating complaints.

Investigation of complaints will be in accordance with section 1553 of the Recovery Act.

[FAC 2005-32, 74 FR 14633, 3/31/2009, effective 3/31/2009; FAC 2005-42, 75 FR 34258, 6/16/2010, effective 6/16/2010]

3.907-5 Access to investigative file of Inspector General.

(a) The employee alleging reprisal under this section shall have access to the investigation file of the Inspector General, in accordance with the Privacy Act, 5 U.S.C. 552a. The investigation of the Inspector General shall be deemed closed for the purposes of disclosure under such section when an employee files an appeal to the agency head or a court of competent jurisdiction.

(b) In the event the employee alleging reprisal brings a civil action under section 1553(c)(3) of the Recovery Act, the employee alleging the reprisal and the non-Federal employer shall have access to the investigative file of the Inspector General in accordance with the Privacy Act.

(c) The Inspector General may exclude from disclosures made under 3.907-5(a) or (b)—

(1) Information protected from disclosure by a provision of law; and

(2) Any additional information the Inspector General determines disclosure of which would impede a continuing investigation, provided that such information is disclosed once such disclosure would no longer impede such investigation, unless the Inspector General determines that the disclosure of law enforcement techniques, procedures, or information could reasonably be expected to risk circumvention of the law or disclose the identity of a confidential source.

(d) An Inspector General investigating an alleged reprisal under this section may not respond to any inquiry or disclose any information from or about any person alleging such reprisal, except in accordance with 5 U.S.C. 552a or as required by any other applicable Federal law.

[FAC 2005-32, 74 FR 14633, 3/31/2009, effective 3/31/2009; FAC 2005-42, 75 FR 34258, 6/16/2010, effective 6/16/2010]

3.907-6 Remedies and enforcement authority.

(a) *Burden of Proof.* (1) Disclosure as contributing factor in reprisal.

(i) An employee alleging a reprisal under this section shall be deemed to have affirmatively established the occurrence of the reprisal if the employee demonstrates that a disclosure described in section 3.907-2 was a contributing factor in the reprisal.

(ii) A disclosure may be demonstrated as a contributing factor in a reprisal for purposes of this paragraph by circumstantial evidence, including—

(A) Evidence that the official undertaking the reprisal knew of the disclosure; or

(B) Evidence that the reprisal occurred within a period of time after the disclosure such that a reasonable person could conclude that the disclosure was a contributing factor in the reprisal.

(2) *Opportunity for rebuttal.* The head of an agency may not find the occurrence of a reprisal with respect to a reprisal that is affirmatively established under section 3.907-6(a)(1) if the non-Federal employer demonstrates by clear and convincing evidence that the non-Federal employer would have taken the action constituting the reprisal in the absence of the disclosure.

(b) No later than 30 days after receiving an Inspector General report in accordance with section 1553 of the Recovery Act, the head of the agency concerned shall determine whether there is sufficient basis to conclude that the non-Federal employer has subjected the complainant to a reprisal prohibited by subsection 3.907-2 and shall either issue an order denying relief in whole or in part or shall take one or more of the following actions:

(1) Order the employer to take affirmative action to abate the reprisal.

(2) Order the employer to reinstate the person to the position that the person held before the reprisal, together with the compensation (including back pay), compensatory damages, employment benefits, and other terms and conditions of employment that would apply to the person in that position if the reprisal had not been taken.

(3) Order the employer to pay the complainant an amount equal to the aggregate amount of all costs and expenses (including attorneys' fees and expert witnesses' fees) that were reasonably incurred by the complainant for, or in connection with, bringing the complaint regarding the reprisal.

(c)(1) The complainant shall be deemed to have exhausted all administrative remedies with respect to the complaint, and the complainant may bring a de novo action at law or equity against the employer to seek compensatory damages and other relief available under this section in the appropriate district court of United States, which shall have jurisdiction over such an action without regard to the amount in controversy if

(i) The head of an agency—

(A) Issues an order denying relief in whole or in part under paragraph (a) of this section;

(B) Has not issued an order within 210 days after the submission of a complaint in accordance with section 1553 of the Recovery Act, or in the case of an extension of time in accordance with section 1553 of the Recovery Act, within 30 days after the expiration of the extension of time; or

(C) Decides in accordance with section 1553 of the Recovery Act not to investigate or to discontinue an investigation; and

(ii) There is no showing that such delay or decision is due to the bad faith of the complainant.

(2) Such an action shall, at the request of either party to the action, be tried by the court with a jury.

(d) Whenever an employer fails to comply with an order issued under this section, the head of the agency shall request the Department of Justice to file an action for enforcement of such order in the United States district court for a district in which the reprisal was found to have occurred. In any action brought under this section, the court may grant appropriate relief, including injunctive relief, compensatory and exemplary damages, and attorneys fees and costs.

(e) Any person adversely affected or aggrieved by an order issued under paragraph (b) of this subsection may obtain review of the order's conformance with the law, and this section, in the United States Court of Appeals for a circuit in which the reprisal is alleged in the order to have occurred. No petition seeking such review may be filed more than 60 days after issuance of the order by the head of the agency.

[FAC 2005-32, 74 FR 14633, 3/31/2009, effective 3/31/2009; FAC 2005-42, 75 FR 34258, 6/16/2010, effective 6/16/2010]

3.907-7 Contract clause.

Use the clause at 52.203-15, Whistleblower Protections Under the American Recovery and Reinvestment Act of 2009 in all solicitations and contracts funded in whole or in part with Recovery Act funds.

[FAC 2005-32, 74 FR 14633, 3/31/2009, effective 3/31/2009; FAC 2005-42, 75 FR 34258, 6/16/2010, effective 6/16/2010; FAC 2019-02, 84 FR 19839, 5/6/2019, effective 5/6/2019]

3.908 Pilot program for enhancement of contractor employee whistleblower protections. (No Text)

[FAC 2005-70, 78 FR 60169, 9/30/2013, effective 9/30/2013; FAC 2005-85, 80 FR 75911, 12/4/2015, effective 12/4/2015]

3.908-1 Scope of section.

(a) This section implements 41 U.S.C. 4712.

(b) This section does not apply to—

(1) DoD, NASA, and the Coast Guard; or

(2) Any element of the intelligence community, as defined in section 3(4) of the National Security Act of 1947 (50 U.S.C. 3003(4)). This section does not apply to any disclosure made by an employee of a contractor or subcontractor of an element of the intelligence community if such disclosure—

(i) Relates to an activity of an element of the intelligence community; or

(ii) Was discovered during contract or subcontract services provided to an element of the intelligence community.

[FAC 2005-70, 78 FR 60169, 9/30/2013, effective 9/30/2013; FAC 2005-85, 80 FR 75911, 12/4/2015, effective 12/4/2015]

3.908-2 Definitions.

As used in this section—

Abuse of authority means an arbitrary and capricious exercise of authority that is inconsistent with the mission of the executive agency concerned or the successful performance of a contract of such agency.

Inspector General means an Inspector General appointed under the Inspector General Act of 1978 and any Inspector General that receives funding from, or has oversight over contracts awarded for, or on behalf of, the executive agency concerned.

[FAC 2005-70, 78 FR 60169, 9/30/2013, effective 9/30/2013; FAC 2005-85, 80 FR 75911, 12/4/2015, effective 12/4/2015]

3.908-3 Policy.

(a) Contractors and subcontractors are prohibited from discharging, demoting, or otherwise discriminating against an employee as a reprisal for disclosing, to any of the entities listed at paragraph (b) of this subsection, information that the employee reasonably believes is evidence of gross mismanagement of a Federal contract, a gross waste of Federal funds, an abuse of authority relating to a Federal contract, a substantial and specific danger to public health or safety, or a violation of law, rule, or regulation related to a Federal contract (including the competition for or negotiation of a contract). A reprisal is prohibited even if it is undertaken at the request of an executive branch official, unless the request takes the form of a non-discretionary directive and is within the authority of the executive branch official making the request.

(b) *Entities to whom disclosure may be made.*

(1) A Member of Congress or a representative of a committee of Congress.

(2) An Inspector General.

(3) The Government Accountability Office.

(4) A Federal employee responsible for contract oversight or management at the relevant agency.

(5) An authorized official of the Department of Justice or other law enforcement agency.

(6) A court or grand jury.

(7) A management official or other employee of the contractor or subcontractor who has the responsibility to investigate, discover, or address misconduct.

(c) An employee who initiates or provides evidence of contractor or subcontractor misconduct in any judicial or administrative proceeding relating to waste, fraud, or abuse on a Federal contract shall be deemed to have made a disclosure.

[FAC 2005-70, 78 FR 60169, 9/30/2013, effective 9/30/2013; FAC 2005-85, 80 FR 75911, 12/4/2015, effective 12/4/2015]

3.908-4 Filing complaints.

A contractor or subcontractor employee who believes that he or she has been discharged, demoted, or otherwise discriminated against contrary to the policy in 3.908-3 of this section may submit a complaint with the Inspector General of the agency concerned. Procedures for submitting fraud, waste, abuse, and whistleblower complaints are generally accessible on agency Office of Inspector General Hotline or Whistleblower Internet sites. A complaint by the employee may not be brought under 41 U.S.C. 4712 more than three years after the date on which the alleged reprisal took place.

[FAC 2005-70, 78 FR 60169, 9/30/2013, effective 9/30/2013; FAC 2005-85, 80 FR 75911, 12/4/2015, effective 12/4/2015]

3.908-5 Procedures for investigating complaints.

(a) Investigation of complaints will be in accordance with 41 U.S.C. 4712(b).

(b) Upon completion of the investigation, the head of the agency or designee shall ensure that the Inspector General provides the report of findings to—

(1) The complainant and any person acting on the complainant's behalf;

(2) The contractor alleged to have committed the violation; and

(3) The head of the contracting activity.

(c) The complainant and contractor shall be afforded the opportunity to submit a written response to the report of findings within 30 days to the head of the agency or designee. Extensions of time to file a written response may be granted by the head of the agency or designee.

(d) At any time, the head of the agency or designee may request additional investigative work be done on the complaint.

[FAC 2005-70, 78 FR 60169, 9/30/2013, effective 9/30/2013; FAC 2005-85, 80 FR 75911, 12/4/2015, effective 12/4/2015]

3.908-6 Remedies.

(a) *Agency response to Inspector General report.* Not later than 30 days after receiving an Inspector General report in accordance with 41 U.S.C. 4712, the head of the agency shall—

(1) Determine whether sufficient basis exists to conclude that the contractor or subcontractor has subjected the employee who submitted the complaint to a reprisal as prohibited by 3.908-3; and

(2) Issue an order denying relief or take one or more of the following actions:

(i) Order the contractor to take affirmative action to abate the reprisal.

(ii) Order the contractor or subcontractor to reinstate the complainant-employee to the position that the person held before the reprisal, together with compensatory damages (including back pay), employment benefits, and other terms and conditions of employment that would apply to the person in that position if the reprisal had not been taken.

(iii) Order the contractor or subcontractor to pay the complainant- employee an amount equal to the aggregate amount of all costs and expenses (including attorneys' fees and expert witnesses' fees) that were reasonably incurred by the complainant for, or in connection with, bringing the complaint regarding the reprisal, as determined by the head of the agency.

(b) *Complainant's right to go to court.* If the head of the agency issues an order denying relief or has not issued an order within 210 days after the submission of the complaint or within 30 days after the expiration of an extension of time granted in accordance with 41 U.S.C. 4712(b)(2)(B) for the submission of the Inspector General's report on the investigative findings of the complaint to the head of the agency, the contractor or subcontractor, and the complainant, and there is no showing that such delay is due to the bad faith of the complainant—

(1) The complainant shall be deemed to have exhausted all administrative remedies with respect to the complaint; and

(2) The complainant may bring a de novo action at law or equity against the contractor or subcontractor to seek compensatory damages and other relief available under 41 U.S.C. 4712 in the appropriate district court of the United States, which shall have jurisdiction over such an action without regard to the amount in controversy. Such an action shall, at the request of either party to the action, be tried by the court with a jury. An action under this authority may not be brought more than two years after the date on which remedies are deemed to have been exhausted.

(c) *Admissibility in evidence.* An Inspector General determination and an agency head order denying relief under this section shall be admissible in evidence in any de novo action at law or equity brought pursuant to 41 U.S.C. 4712.

(d) *No waiver.* The rights and remedies provided for in 41 U.S.C. 4712 may not be waived by any agreement, policy, form, or condition of employment.

[FAC 2005-70, 78 FR 60169, 9/30/2013, effective 9/30/2013; FAC 2005-85, 80 FR 75911, 12/4/2015, effective 12/4/2015]

3.908-7 Enforcement of orders.

(a) Whenever a contractor or subcontractor fails to comply with an order issued under 3.908-6(a)(2) of this section, the head of the agency concerned shall file an action for enforcement of the order in the U.S. district court for a district in which the reprisal was found to have occurred. In any action brought pursuant to this authority, the court may grant appropriate relief, including injunctive relief, compensatory and exemplary damages, and attorney fees and costs. The complainant-employee upon whose behalf an order was issued may also file such an action or join in an action filed by the head of the agency.

(b) Any person adversely affected or aggrieved by an order issued under 3.908-6(a)(2) may obtain review of the order's conformance with 41 U.S.C. 4712 and its implementing regulations, in the U.S. court of appeals for a circuit in which the reprisal is alleged in the order to have occurred. No petition seeking such review may be filed more than 60 days after issuance of the order by the head of the agency. Filing such an appeal shall not act to stay the enforcement of the order of the head of an agency, unless a stay is specifically entered by the court.

[FAC 2005-70, 78 FR 60169, 9/30/2013, effective 9/30/2013; FAC 2005-85, 80 FR 75911, 12/4/2015, effective 12/4/2015]

3.908-8 Classified information.

41 U.S.C. 4712 does not provide any right to disclose classified information not otherwise provided by law.

[FAC 2005-70, 78 FR 60169, 9/30/2013, effective 9/30/2013]

3.908-9 Contract clause.

The contracting officer shall insert the clause at 52.203-17, Contractor Employee Whistleblower Rights and Requirement to Inform Employees of Whistleblower Rights, in all solicitations and contracts that exceed the simplified acquisition threshold.

[FAC 2005-70, 78 FR 60169, 9/30/2013, effective 9/30/2013; FAC 2005-85, 80 FR 75911, 12/4/2015, effective 12/4/2015]

3.909 Prohibition on providing funds to an entity that requires certain internal confidentiality agreements or statements. (No Text)

[FAC 2005-95, 82 FR 4717, 1/13/2017, effective 1/19/2017]

3.909-1 Prohibition.

(a) The Government is prohibited from using fiscal year 2015 and subsequent fiscal year funds for a contract with an entity that requires employees or subcontractors of such entity seeking to report waste, fraud, or abuse to sign internal confidentiality agreements or statements prohibiting or otherwise restricting such employees or subcontractors from lawfully reporting such waste, fraud, or abuse to a designated investigative or law enforcement representative of a Federal department or agency authorized to receive such information. See section 743 of Division E, Title VII, of the Consolidated and Further Continuing Appropriations Act, 2015 (Pub. L. 113-235) and its successor provisions in subsequent appropriations acts (and as extended in continuing resolutions.)

(b) The prohibition in paragraph (a) of this section does not contravene requirements applicable to Standard Form 312 (Classified Information Nondisclosure Agreement), Form 4414 (Sensitive Compartmented Information Nondisclosure Agreement), or any other form issued by a Federal department or agency governing the nondisclosure of classified information.

[FAC 2005-95, 82 FR 4717, 1/13/2017, effective 1/19/2017]

3.909-2 Representation by the offeror.

(a) In order to be eligible for contract award, an offeror must represent that it will not require its employees or subcontractors to sign internal confidentiality agreements or statements prohibiting or otherwise restricting such employees or subcontractors from lawfully reporting waste, fraud, or abuse related to the performance of a Government contract to a designated investigative or law enforcement representative of a Federal department or agency authorized to receive such information (e.g., agency Office of the Inspector General). Any offeror that does not so represent is ineligible for award of a contract.

(b) The contracting officer may rely on an offeror's representation unless the contracting officer has reason to question the representation.

[FAC 2005-95, 82 FR 4717, 1/13/2017, effective 1/19/2017]

3.909-3 Solicitation provision and contract clause.

When using funding subject to the prohibitions in 3.909-1(a), the contracting officer shall—

(a) (1) Include the provision at 52.203-18, Prohibition on Contracting with Entities that Require Certain Internal Confidentiality Agreements or Statements—Representation, in all solicitations, except as provided in paragraph (a) (2) of this section; and

(2) Do not insert the provision in solicitations for a personal services contract with an individual if the services are to be performed entirely by the individual, rather than by an employee of the contractor or a subcontractor.

(b) (1) Include the clause at 52.203-19, Prohibition on Requiring Certain Internal Confidentiality Agreements or Statements, in all solicitations and resultant contracts, other than personal services contracts with individuals.

(2) Modify existing contracts, other than personal services contracts with individuals, to include the clause before obligating FY 2015 or subsequent FY funds that are subject to the same prohibition on internal confidentiality agreements or statements.

[FAC 2005-95, 82 FR 4717, 1/13/2017, effective 1/19/2017]

SUBPART 3.10—CONTRACTOR CODE OF BUSINESS ETHICS AND CONDUCT

3.1000 Scope of subpart.

This subpart—

(a) Implements 41 U.S.C. 3509, Notification of Violations of Federal Criminal Law or Overpayments; and

(b) Prescribes policies and procedures for the establishment of contractor codes of business ethics and conduct, and display of agency Office of Inspector General (OIG) fraud hotline posters.

[FAC 2005-22, 72 FR 65873, 11/23/2007, effective 12/24/2007; FAC 2005-73, 79 FR 24192, 4/29/2014, effective 5/29/2014]

3.1001 Definitions.

As used in this subpart—

Subcontract means any contract entered into by a subcontractor to furnish supplies or services for performance of a prime contract or a subcontract.

Subcontractor means any supplier, distributor, vendor, or firm that furnished supplies or services to or for a prime contractor or another subcontractor.

United States means the 50 States, the District of Columbia, and outlying areas.

[FAC 2005-22, 72 FR 65873, 11/23/2007, effective 12/24/2007; FAC 2005-28, 73 FR 67064, 11/12/2008, effective 12/12/2008]

3.1002 Policy.

(a) Government contractors must conduct themselves with the highest degree of integrity and honesty.

(b) Contractors should have a written code of business ethics and conduct. To promote compliance with such code of business ethics and conduct, contractors should have an employee business ethics and compliance training program and an internal control system that—

(1) Are suitable to the size of the company and extent of its involvement in Government contracting;

(2) Facilitate timely discovery and disclosure of improper conduct in connection with Government contracts; and

(3) Ensure corrective measures are promptly instituted and carried out.

[FAC 2005-22, 72 FR 65873, 11/23/2007, effective 12/24/2007]

3.1003 Requirements.

(a) *Contractor requirements.* (1) Although the policy at 3.1002 applies as guidance to all Government contractors, the contractual requirements set forth in the clauses at 52.203-13, Contractor Code of Business Ethics and Conduct, and 52.203-14, Display of Hotline Poster(s), are mandatory if the contracts meet the conditions specified in the clause prescriptions at 3.1004.

(2) Whether or not the clause at 52.203-13 is applicable, a contractor may be suspended and/or debarred for knowing failure by a principal to timely disclose to the Government, in connection with the award, performance, or closeout of a Government contract performed by the contractor or a subcontract awarded thereunder, credible evidence of a violation of Federal criminal law involving fraud, conflict of interest, bribery, or gratuity violations found in Title 18 of the United States Code or a violation of the civil False Claims Act. Knowing failure to timely disclose credible evidence of any of the above violations remains a cause for suspension and/or debarment until 3 years after final payment on a contract (see 9.406-2(b)(1)(vi) and 9.407-2(a)(8)).

(3) The Payment clauses at FAR 52.212-4(i)(5), 52.232-25(d), 52.232-26(c), and 52.232-27(l) require that, if the contractor becomes aware that the Government has overpaid on a contract financing or invoice payment, the contractor shall remit the overpayment amount to the Government. A contractor may be suspended and/or debarred for knowing failure by a principal to timely disclose credible evidence of a significant overpayment, other than overpayments resulting from contract financing payments as defined in 32.001 (see 9.406-2(b)(1)(vi) and 9.407-2(a)(8)).

(b) *Notification of possible contractor violation.* If the contracting officer is notified of possible contractor violation of Federal criminal law involving fraud, conflict of interest, bribery, or gratuity violations found in Title 18 U.S.C.; or a violation of the civil False Claims Act, the contracting officer shall—

(1) Coordinate the matter with the agency Office of the Inspector General; or

(2) Take action in accordance with agency procedures.

(c) *Fraud Hotline Poster.* (1) Agency OIGs are responsible for determining the need for, and content of, their respective agency OIG fraud hotline poster(s).

(2) When requested by the Department of Homeland Security, agencies shall ensure that contracts funded with disaster assistance funds require display of any fraud hotline poster applicable to the specific contract. As established by the agency OIG, such posters may be displayed in lieu of, or in addition to, the agency's standard poster.

[FAC 2005-22, 72 FR 65873, 11/23/2007, effective 12/24/2007; FAC 2005-28, 73 FR 67064, 11/12/2008, effective 12/12/2008]

3.1004 Contract clauses.

(a) Insert the clause at FAR 52.203-13, Contractor Code of Business Ethics and Conduct, in solicitations and contracts if the value of the contract is expected to exceed $5.5 million and the performance period is 120 days or more.

(b)(1) Unless the contract is for the acquisition of a commercial item or will be performed entirely outside the United States, insert the clause at FAR 52.203-14, Display of Hotline Poster(s), if—

(i) The contract exceeds $5.5 million or a lesser amount established by the agency; and

(ii)(A) The agency has a fraud hotline poster; or

(B) The contract is funded with disaster assistance funds.

(2) In paragraph (b)(3) of the clause, the contracting officer shall—

(i) Identify the applicable posters; and

(ii) Insert the website link(s) or other contact information for obtaining the agency and/or Department of Homeland Security poster.

(3) In paragraph (d) of the clause, if the agency has established policies and procedures for display of the OIG fraud hotline poster at a lesser amount, the contracting officer shall replace $5.5 million with the

lesser amount that the agency has established.

[FAC 2005-22, 72 FR 65873, 11/23/2007, effective 12/24/2007; FAC 2005-28, 73 FR 67064, 11/12/2008, effective 12/12/2008; FAC 2005-83, 80 FR 38293, 7/2/2015, effective 10/1/2015]

SUBPART 3.11—PREVENTING PERSONAL CONFLICTS OF INTEREST FOR CONTRACTOR EMPLOYEES PERFORMING ACQUISITION FUNCTIONS

3.1100 Scope of subpart.

This subpart implements policy on personal conflicts of interest by employees of Government contractors as required by 41 U.S.C. 2303.

[FAC 2005-54, 76 FR 68017, 11/2/2011, effective 12/2/2011; FAC 2005-73, 79 FR 24192, 4/29/2014, effective 5/29/2014]

3.1101 Definitions.

As used in this subpart—

Acquisition function closely associated with inherently governmental functions means supporting or providing advice or recommendations with regard to the following activities of a Federal agency:

(1) Planning acquisitions.

(2) Determining what supplies or services are to be acquired by the Government, including developing statements of work.

(3) Developing or approving any contractual documents, to include documents defining requirements, incentive plans, and evaluation criteria.

(4) Evaluating contract proposals.

(5) Awarding Government contracts.

(6) Administering contracts (including ordering changes or giving technical direction in contract performance or contract quantities, evaluating contractor performance, and accepting or rejecting contractor products or services).

(7) Terminating contracts.

(8) Determining whether contract costs are reasonable, allocable, and allowable.

Covered employee means an individual who performs an acquisition function closely associated with inherently governmental functions and is—

(1) An employee of the contractor; or

(2) A subcontractor that is a self-employed individual treated as a covered employee of the contractor because there is no employer to whom such an individual could submit the required disclosures.

Personal conflict of interest means a situation in which a covered employee has a financial interest, personal activity, or relationship that could impair the employee's ability to act impartially and in the best interest of the Government when performing under the contract. (A *de minimis* interest that would not "impair the employee's ability to act impartially and in the best interest of the Government" is not covered under this definition.)

(1) Among the sources of personal conflicts of interest are—

(i) Financial interests of the covered employee, of close family members, or of other members of the covered employee's household;

(ii) Other employment or financial relationships (including seeking or negotiating for prospective employment or business); and

(iii) Gifts, including travel.

(2) For example, financial interests referred to in paragraph (1) of this definition may arise from—

(i) Compensation, including wages, salaries, commissions, professional fees, or fees for business referrals;

(ii) Consulting relationships (including commercial and professional consulting and service arrangements, scientific and technical advisory board memberships, or serving as an expert witness in litigation);

(iii) Services provided in exchange for honorariums or travel expense reimbursements;

(iv) Research funding or other forms of research support;

(v) Investment in the form of stock or bond ownership or partnership interest (excluding diversified mutual fund investments);

(vi) Real estate investments;

(vii) Patents, copyrights, and other intellectual property interests; or

(viii) Business ownership and investment interests.

[FAC 2005-54, 76 FR 68017, 11/2/2011, effective 12/2/2011]

3.1102 Policy.

The Government's policy is to require contractors to—

(a) Identify and prevent personal conflicts of interest of their covered employees; and

(b) Prohibit covered employees who have access to non-public information by reason of performance on a Government contract from using such information for personal gain.

[FAC 2005-54, 76 FR 68017, 11/2/2011, effective 12/2/2011]

3.1103 Procedures.

(a) By use of the contract clause at 52.203-16, as prescribed at 3.1106, the contracting officer shall require each contractor whose employees perform acquisition functions closely associated with inherently Government functions to—

(1) Have procedures in place to screen covered employees for potential personal conflicts of interest by—

(i) Obtaining and maintaining from each covered employee, when the employee is initially assigned to the task under the contract, a disclosure of interests that might be affected by the task to which the employee has been assigned, as follows:

(A) Financial interests of the covered employee, of close family members, or of other members of the covered employee's household.

(B) Other employment or financial relationships of the covered employee (including seeking or negotiating for prospective employment or business).

(C) Gifts, including travel; and

(ii) Requiring each covered employee to update the disclosure statement whenever the employee's personal or financial circumstances change in such a way that a new personal conflict of interest might occur because of the task the covered employee is performing.

(2) For each covered employee—

(i) Prevent personal conflicts of interest, including not assigning or allowing a covered employee to perform any task under the contract for which the Contractor has identified a personal conflict of interest for the employee that the Contractor or employee cannot satisfactorily prevent or mitigate in consultation with the contracting agency;

(ii) Prohibit use of non-public information accessed through performance of a Government contract for personal gain; and

(iii) Obtain a signed non-disclosure agreement to prohibit disclosure of non-public information accessed through performance of a Government contract.

(3) Inform covered employees of their obligation—

(i) To disclose and prevent personal conflicts of interest;

(ii) Not to use non-public information accessed through performance of a Government contract for personal gain; and

(iii) To avoid even the appearance of personal conflicts of interest;

(4) Maintain effective oversight to verify compliance with personal conflict-of-interest safeguards;

(5) Take appropriate disciplinary action in the case of covered employees who fail to comply with policies established pursuant to this section; and

(6) Report to the contracting officer any personal conflict-of-interest violation by a covered employee as soon as identified. This report shall include a description of the violation and the proposed actions to be taken by the contractor in response to the violation, with follow-up reports of corrective actions taken, as necessary.

(b) If a contractor reports a personal conflict-of-interest violation by a covered employee to the contracting officer in accordance with paragraph (b)(6) of the clause at 52.203-16, Preventing Personal Conflicts of Interest, the contracting officer shall—

(1) Review the actions taken by the contractor;

(2) Determine whether any action taken by the contractor has resolved the violation satisfactorily; and

(3) If the contracting officer determines that the contractor has not resolved the violation satisfactorily, take any appropriate action in consultation with agency legal counsel.

[FAC 2005-54, 76 FR 68017, 11/2/2011, effective 12/2/2011]

3.1104 Mitigation or waiver.

(a) In exceptional circumstances, if the contractor cannot satisfactorily prevent a personal conflict of interest as required by paragraph (b)(2)(i) of the clause at 52.203-16, Preventing Personal Conflicts of Interest, the contractor may submit a request, through the contracting officer, for the head of the contracting activity to—

(1) Agree to a plan to mitigate the personal conflict of interest; or

(2) Waive the requirement to prevent personal conflicts of interest.

(b) If the head of the contracting activity determines in writing that such action is in the best interest of the Government, the head of the contracting activity may impose conditions that provide mitigation of a personal conflict of interest or grant a waiver.

(c) This authority shall not be redelegated.

[FAC 2005-54, 76 FR 68017, 11/2/2011, effective 12/2/2011]

3.1105 Violations.

If the contracting officer suspects violation by the contractor of a requirement of paragraph (b), (c)(3), or (d) of the clause at 52.203-16, Preventing Personal Conflicts of Interest, the contracting officer shall contact the agency legal counsel for advice and/or recommendations on a course of action.

[FAC 2005-54, 76 FR 68017, 11/2/2011, effective 12/2/2011]

3.1106 Contract clause.

(a) Insert the clause at 52.203-16, Preventing Personal Conflicts of Interest, in solicitations and contracts that—

(1) Exceed the simplified acquisition threshold; and

(2) Include a requirement for services by contractor employee(s) that involve performance of acquisition functions closely associated with inherently governmental functions for, or on behalf of, a Federal agency or department.

(b) If only a portion of a contract is for the performance of acquisition functions closely associated with inherently governmental functions, then the contracting officer shall still insert the clause, but shall limit applicability of the clause to that portion of the contract that is for the performance of such services.

(c) Do not insert the clause in solicitations or contracts with a self-employed individual if the acquisition functions closely associated with inherently governmental functions are to be performed entirely by the self-employed individual, rather than an employee of the contractor.

[FAC 2005-54, 76 FR 68017, 11/2/2011, effective 12/2/2011]

PART 4—ADMINISTRATIVE AND INFORMATION MATTERS

Table of Contents

Scope of part 4.000
Definitions 4.001

Subpart 4.1—Contract Execution

Contracting officer's signature 4.101
Contractor's signature 4.102
Contract clause 4.103

Subpart 4.2—Contract Distribution

Procedures 4.201
Agency distribution requirements 4.202
Taxpayer identification information 4.203

Subpart 4.3—Paper Documents

Scope of subpart 4.300
Definition 4.301
Policy 4.302
Contract clause 4.303

Subpart 4.4—Safeguarding Classified Information Within Industry

[Removed and Reserved] 4.401
General 4.402
Responsibilities of contracting officers 4.403
Contract clause 4.404

Subpart 4.5—Electronic Commerce in Contracting

Scope of subpart 4.500
[Reserved] 4.501
Policy 4.502

Subpart 4.6—Contract Reporting

Scope of subpart 4.600
Definitions 4.601
General 4.602
Policy 4.603
Responsibilities 4.604
Procedures 4.605
Reporting data 4.606
Solicitation provisions and contract clause 4.607

Subpart 4.7—Contractor Records Retention

Scope of subpart 4.700
Purpose 4.701
Applicability 4.702
Policy 4.703
Calculation of retention periods 4.704
Specific retention periods 4.705
Financial and cost accounting records 4.705-1
Pay administration records 4.705-2
Acquisition and supply records 4.705-3
[Reserved] 4.706

Subpart 4.8—Government Contract Files

Scope of subpart 4.800
General 4.801
Contract files 4.802
Contents of contract files 4.803
Closeout of contract files 4.804
Closeout by the office administering the contract 4.804-1

Closeout of the contracting office files if another office administers the contract 4.804-2
Closeout of paying office contract files 4.804-3
Physically completed contracts 4.804-4
Procedures for closing out contract files 4.804-5
Storage, handling, and disposal of contract files 4.805

Subpart 4.9—Taxpayer Identification Number Information

Scope of subpart 4.900
Definition 4.901
General 4.902
Reporting contract information to the IRS 4.903
Reporting payment information to the IRS 4.904
Solicitation provision 4.905

Subpart 4.10—Uniform Use of Line Items

Scope 4.1000
Policy 4.1001
Applicability 4.1002
Establishing line items 4.1003
Establishing subline items 4.1004
Data elements for line items and subline items 4.1005
Required data elements 4.1005-1
Exceptions 4.1005-2
Modifications 4.1006
Solicitation alternative line item proposal 4.1007
Solicitation provision 4.1008

Subpart 4.11—System for Award Management

Scope 4.1100
Definitions 4.1101
Policy 4.1102
Procedures 4.1103
Disaster Response Registry 4.1104
Solicitation provision and contract clauses 4.1105

Subpart 4.12—Representations and Certifications

Scope 4.1200
Policy 4.1201
Solicitation provision and contract clause 4.1202

Subpart 4.13—Personal Identity Verification

Scope of subpart 4.1300
Policy 4.1301
Acquisition of approved products and services for personal identity verification 4.1302
Contract clause 4.1303

Subpart 4.14—Reporting Executive Compensation and First-Tier Subcontract Awards

Scope of subpart 4.1400
Applicability 4.1401
Procedures 4.1402
Contract clause 4.1403

Subpart 4.15—[Reserved]

[Removed and Reserved] 4.1500
[Removed and Reserved] 4.1501
[Removed and Reserved] 4.1502

Subpart 4.16—Unique Procurement Instrument Identifiers

Scope of subpart 4.1600
Policy 4.1601
Identifying the PIID and supplementary PIID 4.1602
Procedures 4.1603

Subpart 4.17—Service Contracts Inventory

Scope of subpart 4.1700
Definitions 4.1701
Applicability 4.1702
Reporting requirements 4.1703
Contracting officer responsibilities 4.1704
Contract clauses 4.1705

Subpart 4.18—Commercial and Government Entity Code

Scope of subpart 4.1800
Definitions 4.1801
Policy 4.1802
Verifying CAGE codes prior to award 4.1803
Solicitation provisions and contract clause 4.1804

Subpart 4.19—Basic Safeguarding of Covered Contractor Information Systems

Definitions 4.1901
Applicability 4.1902
Contract clause 4.1903

Subpart 4.20—Prohibition on Contracting for Hardware, Software, and Services Developed or Provided by Kaspersky Lab

Definitions 4.2001
Prohibition 4.2002
Notification 4.2003
Contract clause 4.2004

Subpart 4.21—Prohibition on Contracting for Certain Telecommunications and Video Surveillance Services or Equipment

Scope of subpart 4.2100
Definitions 4.2101
Prohibition 4.2102
Procedures 4.2103
Waivers 4.2104
Solicitation provisions and contract clause 4.2105

PART 4—ADMINISTRATIVE AND INFORMATION MATTERS

4.000 Scope of part.

This part prescribes policies and procedures relating to the administrative aspects of contract execution, contractor-submitted paper documents, distribution, reporting, retention, and files.

[FAC 90-27, 60 FR 28492, 5/31/95, effective 5/31/95]

4.001 Definitions.

As used in this part—

Procurement Instrument Identifier (PIID) means the Government-unique identifier for each solicitation, contract, agreement, or order. For example, an agency may use as its PIID for procurement actions, such as delivery and task orders or basic ordering agreements, the order or agreement number in conjunction with the contract number (see 4.1602).

Supplementary procurement instrument identifier means the non-unique identifier for a procurement action that is used in conjunction with the Government-unique identifier. For example, an agency may use as its PIID for an amended solicitation, the Government-unique identifier for a solicitation number (*e.g.*, N0002309R0009) in conjunction with a non-unique amendment number (*e.g.*, 0001). The non-unique amendment number represents the supplementary PIID.

[FAC 2005-53, 76 FR 39234, 7/5/2011, effective 8/4/2011]

SUBPART 4.1—CONTRACT EXECUTION

4.101 Contracting officer's signature.

Only contracting officers shall sign contracts on behalf of the United States. The contracting officer's name and official title shall be typed, stamped, or printed on the contract. The contracting officer normally signs the contract after it has been signed by the contractor. The contracting officer shall ensure that the signer(s) have authority to bind the contractor (see specific requirements in 4.102 of this subpart).

[FAC 90-29, 60 FR 34732, 7/3/95, effective 7/3/95]

4.102 Contractor's signature.

(a) *Individuals.* A contract with an individual shall be signed by that individual. A contract with an individual doing business as a firm shall be signed by that individual, and the signature shall be followed by the individual's typed, stamped, or printed name and the words, "an individual doing business as ________________________" [*insert name of firm*].

(b) *Partnerships.* A contract with a partnership shall be signed in the partnership name. Before signing for the Government, the contracting officer shall obtain a list of all partners and ensure that the individual(s) signing for the partnership have authority to bind the partnership.

(c) *Corporations.* A contract with a corporation shall be signed in the corporate name, followed by the word "by" and the signature and title of the person authorized to sign. The contracting officer shall ensure that the person signing for the corporation has authority to bind the corporation.

(d) *Joint venturers.* A contract with joint venturers may involve any combination of individuals, partnerships, or corporations. The contract shall be signed by each participant in the joint venture in the manner prescribed in paragraphs (a) through (c) of this section for each type of participant. When a corporation is participating, the contracting officer shall verify that the corporation is authorized to participate in the joint venture.

(e) *Agents.* When an agent is to sign the contract, other than as stated in paragraphs (a) through (d) of this section, the agent's authorization to bind the principal must be established by evidence satisfactory to the contracting officer.

[FAC 90-45, Final rule, 62 FR 224, 1/2/97, effective 1/1/97; FAC 2019-02, 84 FR 19839, 5/6/2019, effective 5/6/2019]

4.103 Contract clause.

The contracting officer shall insert the clause at 52.204-1, Approval of Contract, in solicitations and contracts if required by agency procedures.

[FAC 84-3, 49 FR 26741, 6/29/84, effective 10/1/84]

SUBPART 4.2—CONTRACT DISTRIBUTION

4.201 Procedures.

Contracting officers shall distribute copies of contracts or modifications within 10 working days after execution by all parties. As a minimum, the contracting officer shall—

(a) Distribute simultaneously one signed copy or reproduction of the signed contract to the contractor and the paying office;

(b) When a contract is assigned to another office for contract administration (see Subpart 42.2), provide to that office—

(1) One copy or reproduction of the signed contract and of each modification; and

(2) A copy of the contract distribution list, showing those offices that should receive copies of modifications, and any changes to the list as they occur;

(c) Distribute one copy to each accounting and finance office (funding office) whose funds are cited in the contract;

(d) When the contract is not assigned for administration but contains a Cost Accounting Standards clause, provide one copy of the contract to the cognizant administrative contracting officer and mark the copy "FOR COST ACCOUNTING STANDARDS ADMINISTRATION ONLY" (see 30.601(b));

(e) Provide one copy of each contract or modification that requires audit service to the appropriate field audit office listed in the "Directory of Federal Contract Audit Offices" (see 42.103); and

(f) Provide copies of contracts and modifications to those organizations required to perform contract administration support functions (e.g., when manufacturing is performed at multiple sites, the contract administration office cognizant of each location).

[FAC 90-29, 60 FR 34732, 7/3/95, effective 7/3/95; FAC 2019-02, 84 FR 19839, 5/6/2019, effective 5/6/2019]

4.202 Agency distribution requirements.

Agencies shall limit additional distribution requirements to the minimum necessary for proper performance of essential functions. When contracts are assigned for administration to a contract administration office located in an agency different from that of the contracting office (see Part 42), the two agencies shall agree on any necessary distribution in addition to that prescribed in 4.201.

[FAC 2019-02, 84 FR 19839, 5/6/2019, effective 5/6/2019]

4.203 Taxpayer identification information.

(a) If the contractor has furnished a Taxpayer Identification Number (TIN) when completing the solicitation provision at 52.204-3, Taxpayer Identification, or paragraph (l) of the solicitation provision at 52.212-3, Offeror Representations and Certifications—Commercial Items, the contracting officer shall, unless otherwise provided in agency procedures, attach a copy of the completed solicitation provision as the last page of the copy of the contract sent to the payment office.

(b) If the TIN or type of organization is derived from a source other than the provision at 52.204-3 or 52.212-3(l), the contracting officer shall annotate the last page of the contract or order forwarded to the payment office to state the contractor's TIN and type of organization, unless this information is otherwise provided to the payment office in accordance with agency procedures.

(c) If the contractor provides its TIN or type of organization to the contracting officer after award, the contracting officer shall forward the information to the payment office within 7 days of its receipt.

(d) Federal Supply Schedule contracts. Each contracting officer that places an order under a Federal Supply Schedule contract (see Subpart 8.4) shall provide the TIN and type of organization information to the payment office in accordance with paragraph (b) of this section.

(e) Basic ordering agreements and indefinite-delivery contracts (other than Federal Supply Schedule contracts).

(1) Each contracting officer that issues a basic ordering agreement or indefinite-delivery contract (other than a Federal Supply Schedule contract) shall provide to contracting officers placing orders under the agreement or contract (if the contractor is not required to provide this information to the System for Award Management)—

(i) A copy of the agreement or contract with a copy of the completed solicitation provision at 52.204-3 or 52.212-3(l) as the last page of the agreement or contract; or

(ii) The contractor's TIN and type of organization information.

(2) Each contracting officer that places an order under a basic ordering agreement or indefinite-delivery contract (other than a Federal Supply Schedule contract) shall provide the TIN and type of organization information to the payment office in accordance with paragraph (a) or (b) of this section.

[FAC 97-9, 63 FR 58587, 10/30/98, effective 10/30/98, finalized without change, FAC 97-12, 64 FR 32740, 6/17/99; FAC 2001-16, Final rule, 68 FR 56669, 10/1/2003, effective 10/1/2003; FAC 2005-26, 73 FR 33636, 6/12/2008, effective 6/12/2008; FAC 2005-36, 74 FR 40463, 8/11/2009, effective 8/11/2009; FAC 2005-67, 78 FR 37676, 6/21/2013, effective 7/22/2013]

SUBPART 4.3—PAPER DOCUMENTS

4.300 Scope of subpart.

This subpart provides policies and procedures on contractor-submitted paper documents.

[FAC 90-27, 60 FR 28492, 5/31/95, effective 5/31/95, adopted as final, FAC 90-39, 61 FR 31612, 6/20/96]

4.301 Definition.

Printed or copied double-sided, as used in this subpart, means printing or reproducing a document so that information is on both sides of a sheet of paper.

[Redesignated from 4.302, FAC 97-18, 65 FR 36014, 6/6/2000, effective 8/7/2000]

4.302 Policy.

(a) Section 3(a) of E.O. 13423, Strengthening Federal Environmental, Energy, and Transportation Management, directs agencies to implement waste prevention. In addition, section 2(e) of E.O. 13514, Federal Leadership in Environmental, Energy, and Economic Performance, directs agencies to eliminate waste. Electronic commerce methods (see 4.502) and double-sided printing and copying are best practices for waste prevention.

(b) When electronic commerce methods (see 4.502) are not used, agencies shall require contractors to submit paper documents to the Government relating to an acquisition printed or copied double-sided on at least 30 percent postconsumer fiber paper whenever practicable. If the contractor cannot print or copy double-sided, it shall print or copy single-sided on at least 30 percent postconsumer fiber paper.

[Redesignated from 4.303, FAC 97-18, 65 FR 36014, 6/6/2000, effective 8/7/2000; FAC 2005-52, 76 FR 31395, 5/31/2011, effective 5/31/2011]

4.303 Contract clause.

Insert the clause at 52.204-4, Printed or Copied Double-Sided on Recycled Paper, in solicitations and contracts that exceed the simplified acquisition threshold.

[Redesignated from 4.304, FAC 97-18, 65 FR 36014, 6/6/2000, effective 8/7/2000]

SUBPART 4.4—SAFEGUARDING CLASSIFIED INFORMATION WITHIN INDUSTRY

4.401 [Removed and Reserved]

[Removed and reserved by FAC 2001-04, 67 FR 6112, 2/8/2002, effective 2/20/2002]

4.402 General.

(a) Executive Order 12829, January 6, 1993 (58 FR 3479, January 8, 1993), entitled "National Industrial Security Program" (NISP), establishes a program to safeguard Federal Government classified information that is released to contractors, licensees, and grantees of the United States Government. Executive Order 12829 amends Executive Order 10865, February 20, 1960 (25 FR 1583,

February 25, 1960), entitled "Safeguarding Classified Information Within Industry," as amended by Executive Order 10909, January 17, 1961 (26 FR 508, January 20, 1961).

(b) The National Industrial Security Program Operating Manual (NISPOM) incorporates the requirements of these Executive orders. The Secretary of Defense, in consultation with all affected agencies and with the concurrence of the Secretary of Energy, the Chairman of the Nuclear Regulatory Commission, and the Director of Central Intelligence, is responsible for issuance and maintenance of this Manual. The following DoD publications implement the program:

(1) National Industrial Security Program Operating Manual (NISPOM) (DoD 5220.22-M).

(2) Industrial Security Regulation (DoD 5220.22-R).

(c) Procedures for the protection of information relating to foreign classified contracts awarded to U.S. industry, and instructions for the protection of U.S. information relating to classified contracts awarded to foreign firms, are prescribed in Chapter 10 of the NISPOM.

(d) Part 27, Patents, Data, and Copyrights, contains policy and procedures for safeguarding classified information in patent applications and patents.

[FAC 90-39, 61 FR 31612, 6/20/96, effective 8/19/96; FAC 2005-25, 73 FR 21779, 4/22/2008, effective 4/22/2008; FAC 2005-42, 75 FR 34260, 6/16/2010, effective 7/16/2010; FAC 2019-02, 84 FR 19839, 5/6/2019, effective 5/6/2019]

4.403 Responsibilities of contracting officers.

(a) *Presolicitation phase*. Contracting officers shall review all proposed solicitations to determine whether access to classified information may be required by offerors, or by a contractor during contract performance.

(1) If access to classified information of another agency may be required, the contracting officer shall—

(i) Determine if the agency is covered by the NISP; and

(ii) Follow that agency's procedures for determining the security clearances of firms to be solicited.

(2) If the classified information required is from the contracting officer's agency, the contracting officer shall follow agency procedures.

(b) *Solicitation phase*. Contracting officers shall—

(1) Ensure that the classified acquisition is conducted as required by the NISP or agency procedures, as appropriate; and

(2) Include—

(i) An appropriate Security Requirements clause in the solicitation (see 4.404); and

(ii) As appropriate, in solicitations and contracts when the contract may require access to classified information, a requirement for security safeguards in addition to those provided in the clause (52.204-2, Security Requirements).

(c) *Award phase*. Contracting officers shall inform contractors and subcontractors of the security classifications and requirements assigned to the various documents, materials, tasks, subcontracts, and components of the classified contract as follows:

(1) Agencies covered by the DISP shall use the Contract Security Classification Specification, DD Form 254. The contracting officer, or authorized representative, is the approving official for the form and shall ensure that it is prepared and distributed in accordance with the Industrial Security Regulation.

(2) Contracting officers in agencies not covered by the NISP shall follow agency procedures.

[FAC 90-39, 61 FR 61312, 6/20/96, effective 8/19/96; FAC 2005-25, 73 FR 21779, 4/22/2008, effective 4/22/2008; FAC 2005-42, 75 FR 34260, 6/16/2010, effective 7/16/2010; FAC 2019-02, 84 FR 19839, 5/6/2019, effective 5/6/2019]

4.404 Contract clause.

(a) The contracting officer shall insert the clause at 52.204-2, Security Requirements, in solicitations and contracts when the contract may require access to classified information, unless the conditions specified in paragraphs (d) of this section apply.

(b) If a cost contract (see 16.302) for research and development with an educational institution is contemplated, the contracting officer shall use the clause with its Alternate I.

(c) If a construction or architect-engineer contract where employee identification is required for security reasons is contemplated, the contracting officer shall use the clause with its Alternate II.

(d) If the contracting agency is not covered by the NISP and has prescribed a clause and alternates that are substantially the same as those at 52.204-2, the contracting officer shall use the agency-prescribed clause as required by agency procedures.

[FAC 90-39, 61 FR 61312, 6/20/96, effective 8/19/96; FAC 2019-02, 84 FR 19839, 5/6/2019, effective 5/6/2019]

SUBPART 4.5—ELECTRONIC COMMERCE IN CONTRACTING

4.500 Scope of subpart.

This subpart provides policy and procedures for the establishment and use of electronic commerce in Federal acquisition as required by 41 U.S.C. 2301.

[FAC 97-9, 63 FR 58587, 10/30/98, effective 10/30/98; FAC 2005-73, 79 FR 24192, 4/29/2014, effective 5/29/2014]

4.501 [Reserved]

[Removed and reserved, FAC 97-22, 66 FR 2116, 1/10/2001, effective 3/12/2001; Delay of effective date, 66 FR 14259, 3/9/2001, effective 5/11/2001]

4.502 Policy.

(a) The Federal Government shall use electronic commerce whenever practicable or cost-effective. The use of terms commonly associated with paper transactions (e.g., *copy, document, page, printed, sealed envelope,* and *stamped*) shall not be interpreted to restrict the use of electronic commerce. Contracting officers may supplement electronic transactions by using other media to meet the requirements of any contract action governed by the FAR (*e.g.*, transmit hard copy of drawings).

(b) Agencies may exercise broad discretion in selecting the hardware and software that will be used in conducting electronic commerce. However, as required by 41 U.S.C. 2301, the head of each agency, after consulting with the Administrator of OFPP, shall ensure that systems, technologies, procedures, and processes used by the agency to conduct electronic commerce—

(1) Are implemented uniformly throughout the agency, to the maximum extent practicable;

(2) Are implemented only after considering the full or partial use of existing infrastructures;

(3) Facilitate access to Government acquisition opportunities by small business concerns, small disadvantaged business concerns, women-owned, veteran-owned, HUBZone, and service-disabled veteran-owned small business concerns;

(4) Include a single means of providing widespread public notice of acquisition opportunities through the Governmentwide point of entry and a means of responding to notices or solicitations electronically; and

(5) Comply with nationally and internationally recognized standards that broaden interoperability and ease the electronic interchange of information, such as standards established by the National Institute of Standards and Technology.

(c) Before using electronic commerce, the agency head shall ensure that the agency systems are capable of ensuring authentication and confidentiality commensurate with the risk and magnitude of the harm from loss, misuse, or unauthorized access to or modification of the information.

(d) Agencies may accept electronic signatures and records in connection with Government contracts.

[FAC 97-9, 63 FR 58587, 10/30/98, effective 10/30/98; FAC 97-26, 66 FR 27405, 5/16/2001, effective 5/16/2001; FAC 2001-14, 68 FR 28093, 5/22/2003, effective 6/23/2003; FAC 2005-02, 70 FR 14950, 3/23/2005, effective 3/23/2005; FAC

2005-21, 72 FR 63075, 11/7/2007, effective 12/7/2007; FAC 2005-73, 79 FR 24192, 4/29/2014, effective 5/29/2014]

SUBPART 4.6—CONTRACT REPORTING

4.600 Scope of subpart.

This subpart prescribes uniform reporting requirements for the Federal Procurement Data System (FPDS).

[FAC 2005-25, 73 FR 21773, 4/22/2008, effective 4/22/2008; FAC 2005-30, 74 FR 2712, 1/15/2009, effective 2/17/2009]

4.601 Definitions.

As used in this subpart—

Contract action means any oral or written action that results in the purchase, rent, or lease of supplies or equipment, services, or construction using appropriated dollars over the micro-purchase threshold, or modifications to these actions regardless of dollar value. Contract action does not include grants, cooperative agreements, other transactions, real property leases, requisitions from Federal stock, training authorizations, or other non-FAR based transactions.

Contract action report (CAR) means contract action data required to be entered into the Federal Procurement Data System (FPDS).

Definitive contract means any contract that must be reported to FPDS other than an indefinite delivery vehicle. This definition is only for FPDS, and is not intended to apply to Part 16.

Entitlement program means a Federal program that guarantees a certain level of benefits to persons or other entities who meet requirements set by law, such as Social Security, farm price supports, or unemployment benefits.

Generic entity identifier means a number or other identifier assigned to a category of vendors and not specific to any individual or entity.

Indefinite delivery vehicle (IDV) means an indefinite delivery contract or agreement that has one or more of the following clauses:

(1) 52.216-18, Ordering.

(2) 52.216-19, Order Limitations.

(3) 52.216-20, Definite Quantity.

(4) 52.216-21, Requirements.

(5) 52.216-22, Indefinite Quantity.

(6) Any other clause allowing ordering.

[FAC 84-13, 50 FR 52429, 12/23/85, effective 2/3/86; FAC 84-26, 52 FR 19800, 5/27/87, effective 7/30/87; FAC 90-31, 60 FR 42648, 8/16/95, effective 10/1/95; FAC 97-15, 64 FR 72414, 12/27/99, effective 12/27/99, finalized without change, FAC 97-19, 65 FR 46052, 7/26/2000; FAC 2001-18, 68 FR 69248, 12/11/2003; effective 12/11/2003; FAC 2001-24, 69 FR 34225, 6/18/2004, effective 6/18/2004; FAC 2005-04, 70 FR 33657, 6/8/2005, effective 6/8/2005; FAC 2005-13, 71 FR 57363, 9/28/2006, effective 9/28/2006; FAC 2005-25, 73 FR 21773, 4/22/2008, effective 4/22/2008; FAC 2005-30, 74 FR 2712, 1/15/2009, effective 2/17/2009; FAC 2005-47, 75 FR 77733, 12/13/2010, effective 12/13/2010; FAC 2005-55, 77 FR 183, 1/3/2012, effective 2/2/2012; FAC 2005-91, 81 FR 67736, 9/30/2016, effective 10/31/2016]

4.602 General.

(a) The FPDS provides a comprehensive web-based tool for agencies to report contract actions. The resulting data provides—

(1) A basis for recurring and special reports to the President, the Congress, the Government Accountability Office, Federal executive agencies, and the general public;

(2) A means of measuring and assessing the effect of Federal contracting on the Nation's economy and the extent to which small, veteran owned small, service-disabled veteran owned small, HUBZone small, small disadvantaged, women-owned small business concerns, and AbilityOne nonprofit agencies operating under 41 U.S.C. chapter 85, Committee for Purchase from People Who Are Blind or Severely Disabled, are sharing in Federal contracts;

(3) A means of measuring and assessing the effect of Federal contracting for promoting sustainable technologies, materials, products, and high-performance sustainable

buildings. This is accomplished by collecting and reporting agency data on sustainable acquisition, including types of products purchased, the purchase costs, and the exceptions used for other than sustainable acquisition; and

(4) A means of measuring and assessing the effect of other policy and management initiatives (*e.g.*, performance based acquisitions and competition).

(b) FPDS does not provide reports for certain acquisition information used in the award of a contract action (*e.g.*, subcontracting data, funding data, or accounting data).

(c) The FPDS Web site, *https://www.fpds.gov*, provides instructions for submitting data. It also provides—

(1) A complete list of departments, agencies, and other entities that submit data to the FPDS;

(2) Technical and end-user guidance;

(3) A computer-based tutorial; and

(4) Information concerning reports not generated in FPDS.

[FAC 84-13, 50 FR 52429, 12/23/85, effective 2/3/86; FAC 84-40, 53 FR 43388, 10/26/88, effective 11/25/88; FAC 84-49, 54 FR 29280, 7/11/89, effective 8/10/89; FAC 90-3, 55 FR 52788, 12/21/90, effective 1/22/91; FAC 90-7, 56 FR 41744, 8/22/91, effective 9/23/91; FAC 90-16, 57 FR 60572, 12/21/92, effective 10/1/92; FAC 90-32, 60 FR 48206, 9/18/95, effective 10/1/95; FAC 90-43, Interim rule, 61 FR 67408, 12/20/96, effective 12/20/96; Final rule, 62 FR 40236, 7/25/97, effective 6/30/97; FAC 97-20, 65 FR 60542, 10/11/2000, effective 10/11/2000; FAC 2001-16, 68 FR 56669, 10/1/2003, effective 10/1/2003; FAC 2001-18, 68 FR 69248, 12/11/2003; effective 12/11/2003; FAC 2001-22, Final rule, 69 FR 17768, 4/5/2004, effective 4/5/2004; FAC 2005-13, 71 FR 57363, 9/28/2006, effective 9/28/2006; FAC 2005-13, 71 FR 57380, 9/28/2006, effective 9/28/2006; FAC 2005-18, Interim rule, 72 FR 36852, 7/5/2007, effective 6/30/2007; FAC 2005-25, 73 FR 21773, 4/22/2008, effective 4/22/2008; FAC 2005-27, 73 FR 53994, 9/17/2008, effective 10/17/2008; FAC 2005-30, 74 FR 2712, 1/15/2009, effective 2/17/2009, FAC 2005-31, 74 FR 11821, 3/19/2009, effective 4/20/2009; FAC 2005-52, 76 FR 31395, 5/31/2011, effective 5/31/2011; FAC 2005-73, 79 FR 24192, 4/29/2014, effective 5/29/2014]

4.603 Policy.

(a) In accordance with the Federal Funding Accountability and Transparency Act of 2006 (Pub. L. 109–282), all unclassified Federal award data must be publicly accessible.

(b) Executive agencies shall use FPDS to maintain publicly available information about all unclassified contract actions exceeding the micropurchase threshold, and any modifications to those actions that change previously reported contract action report data, regardless of dollar value.

(c) Agencies awarding assisted acquisitions or direct acquisitions must report these actions and identify the Program/Funding Agency and Office Codes from the applicable agency codes maintained by each agency at FPDS. These codes represent the agency and office that has provided the predominant amount of funding for the contract action. For assisted acquisitions, the requesting agency will receive socioeconomic credit for meeting agency small business goals, where applicable. Requesting agencies shall provide the appropriate agency/bureau component code as part of the written interagency agreement between the requesting and servicing agencies (see 17.502-1(a)(1)). For assisted acquisitions, the requesting agency will receive socioeconomic credit for meeting agency small business goals, where applicable. Requesting agencies shall provide the appropriate agency/bureau component code as part of the written interagency agreement between the requesting and servicing agencies (see 17.502-1(a)(1)).

(d) Agencies awarding contract actions with a mix of appropriated and non-appropriated funding shall only report the full appropriated portion of the contract action in FPDS.

[FAC 90-43, Interim rule, 61 FR 67408, 12/20/96, effective 12/20/96; FAC 97-4, 63 FR 9048, 2/23/98, effective 4/24/98; FAC 97-11, 64 FR 10530, 3/4/99, effective 5/3/99; FAC 2001-14, 68 FR 28079, 5/22/2003, effective 6/23/2003; FAC 2001-16, 68 FR 56679,

10/1/2003, effective 10/1/2003; FAC 2001-18, 68 FR 69248, 12/11/2003; effective 12/11/2003; FAC 2005-25, 73 FR 21773, 4/22/2008, effective 4/22/2008; FAC 2005-30, 74 FR 2712, 1/15/2009, effective 2/17/2009; FAC 2005-48, 75 FR 82567, 12/20/2010, effective 1/31/2011; FAC 2005-55, 77 FR 187, 1/3/2012, effective 2/2/2012, 77 FR 204, 1/3/2012, effective 1/3/2012; FAC 2005-62, 77 FR 69715, 11/20/2012, effective 12/20/2012; 77 69720, 11/20/2012, effective 11/20/2012; FAC 2005-67, 78 FR 37684, 6/21/2013, effective 7/22/2013; FAC 2019-02, 84 FR 19837, 5/6/2019, effective 6/5/2019]

4.604 Responsibilities.

(a) The Senior Procurement Executive in coordination with the head of the contracting activity is responsible for developing and monitoring a process to ensure timely and accurate reporting of contractual actions to FPDS.

(b)(1) The responsibility for the completion and accuracy of the individual contract action report (CAR) resides with the contracting officer who awarded the contract action. CARs in a draft or error status in FPDS are not considered complete.

(2) The CAR must be confirmed for accuracy by the contracting officer prior to release of the contract award. The CAR must then be completed in FPDS within three business days after contract award.

(3) For any action awarded in accordance with 6.302–2 or pursuant to any of the authorities listed at subpart 18.2, the CAR must be completed in FPDS within 30 days after contract award.

(4) When the contracting office receives written notification that a contractor has changed its size status in accordance with the clause at 52.219-28, Post-Award Small Business Program Rerepresentation, the contracting officer shall update the size status in FPDS within 30 days after receipt of contractor's notification of rerepresentation.

(5) If after award of a contract, the contracting officer receives written notification of SBA's final decision on a protest concerning a size determination, the contracting officer shall update FPDS to reflect the final decision.

(c) The chief acquisition officer of each agency required to report its contract actions must submit to the General Services Administration (GSA), in accordance with FPDS guidance, within 120 days after the end of each fiscal year, an annual certification of whether, and to what degree, agency CAR data for the preceding fiscal year is complete and accurate.

[FAC 2005-25, 73 FR 21773, 4/22/2008, effective 4/22/2008; FAC 2005-30, 74 FR 2712, 1/15/2009, effective 2/17/2009; FAC 2005-54, 76 FR 68043, 11/2/2011, effective 11/2/2011; FAC 2005-62, 77 FR 69715, 11/20/2012, effective 12/20/2012; FAC 2005-76, 79 FR 43580, 7/25/2014, effective 8/25/2014; FAC 2019-02, 84 FR 19839, 5/6/2019, effective 5/6/2019]

4.605 Procedures.

(a) *Procurement Instrument Identifier (PIID)*. Agencies shall have in place a process that ensures that each PIID reported to FPDS is unique Governmentwide, for all solicitations, contracts, blanket purchase agreements, basic agreements, basic ordering agreements, or orders in accordance with 4.1601 to 4.1603, and will remain so for at least 20 years from the date of contract award. Other pertinent PIID instructions for FPDS reporting can be found at ***https://www.fpds.gov***.

(b) *Unique entity identifier*. The contracting officer shall identify and report a unique entity identifier for the successful offeror on a contract action. The unique entity identifier shall correspond to the successful offeror's name and address as stated in the offer and resultant contract, and as registered in the System for Award Management in accordance with the provision at 52.204-7, System for Award Management. The contracting officer shall ask the offeror to provide its unique entity identifier by using either the provision at 52.204-6, Unique Entity Identifier, the provision at 52.204-7, System for Award Management, or the provision at 52.212-1, Instructions to Offerors—Commercial Items. (For a discussion of the Commercial and Government Entity

(CAGE) Code, which is a different identifier, see subpart 4.18.)

(c) *Generic entity identifier.* (1) The use of a generic entity identifier should be limited, and only used in the situations described in paragraph (c)(2) of this section. Use of a generic entity identifier does not supersede the requirements of provisions 52.204-6, Unique Entity Identifier or 52.204-7, System for Award Management (if present in the solicitation) for the contractor to have a unique entity identifier assigned.

(2) Authorized generic entity identifiers, maintained by the Integrated Award Environment (IAE) program office (*http://www.gsa.gov/portal/content/105036*), may be used to report contracts in lieu of the contractor's actual unique entity identifier only for—

(i) Contract actions valued at or below $30,000 that are awarded to a contractor that is—

(A) A student;

(B) A dependent of either a veteran, foreign service officer, or military member assigned outside the United States and its outlying areas (as defined in 2.101); or

(C) Located outside the United States and its outlying areas for work to be performed outside the United States and its outlying areas and the contractor does not otherwise have a unique entity identifier;

(ii) Contracts valued above $30,000 awarded to individuals located outside the United States and its outlying areas for work to be performed outside the United States and its outlying areas; or

(iii) Contracts when specific public identification of the contracted party could endanger the mission, contractor, or recipients of the acquired goods or services. The contracting officer must include a written determination in the contract file of a decision applicable to authority under this paragraph (c)(2)(iii).

(d) *American Recovery and Reinvestment Act actions.* The contracting officer, when entering data in FPDS, shall use the instructions at *https://www.fpds.gov* to identify any action funded in whole or in part by the American Recovery and Reinvestment Act of 2009 (Pub. L. 111–5).

(e) *Office codes.* Agencies shall by March 31, 2016—

(1) Use the Activity Address Code (AAC), as defined in 2.101, assigned to the issuing contracting office as the contracting office code, and

(2) Use the AAC assigned to the program/funding office providing the predominance of funding for the contract action as the program/funding office code.

[FAC 2005-25, 73 FR 21773, 4/22/2008, effective 4/22/2008; FAC 2005-30, 74 FR 2712, 1/15/2009, effective 2/17/2009; FAC 2005-32, 74 FR 14636, 3/31/2009, effective 3/31/2009; FAC 2005-42, 75 FR 34271, 6/16/2010, effective 7/16/2010; FAC 2005-53, 76 FR 39234, 7/5/2011, effective 8/4/2011; FAC 2005-62, 76 FR 69715, 11/20/2011, effective 12/20/2011; FAC 2005-67, 78 FR 37676, 6/21/2013, effective 7/22/2013; FAC 2005-74, 79 FR 31187, 5/30/2014, effective 11/1/2014; FAC 2005-76, 79 FR 43590, 7/25/2014, effective 7/25/2014; FAC 2005-77, 79 FR 61739, 10/14/2014, effective 11/13/2014; Correction, 79 FR 63562, 10/24/2014, effective 11/13/2014; FAC 2005-83, 80 FR 38293, 7/2/2015, effective 10/1/2015; FAC 2005-84, 80 FR 53439, 9/3/2015, effective 9/3/2015; FAC 2005-91, 81 FR 67736, 9/30/2016, effective 10/31/2016; FAC 2005-101, 83 FR 48691, 9/26/2018, effective 10/26/2018]

4.606 Reporting data.

(a) *Actions required to be reported to FPDS.* (1) As a minimum, agencies must report the following contract actions over the micro-purchase threshold, regardless of solicitation process used, and agencies must report any modification to these contract actions that change previously reported contract action data, regardless of dollar value:

(i) Definitive contracts, including purchase orders and imprest fund buys over the micro-purchase threshold awarded by a contracting officer.

(ii) Indefinite delivery vehicle (identified as an "IDV" in FPDS). Examples of IDVs include the following:

(A) Task and Delivery Order Contracts (see Subpart 16.5), including—

(*1*) Government-wide acquisition contracts.

(*2*) Multi-agency contracts.

(B) GSA Federal supply schedules.

(C) Blanket Purchase Agreements (see 13.303).

(D) Basic Ordering Agreements (see 16.703).

(E) Any other agreement or contract against which individual orders or purchases may be placed.

(iii) All calls and orders awarded under the indefinite delivery vehicles identified in paragraph (a)(1)(ii) of this section.

(2) The GSA Office of Charge Card Management will provide the Government purchase card data, at a minimum annually, and GSA will incorporate that data into FPDS for reports.

(3) Agencies may use the FPDS Express Reporting capability for consolidated multiple action reports for a vendor when it would be overly burdensome to report each action individually. When used, Express Reporting should be done at least monthly.

(b) *Reporting other actions.* Agencies may submit actions other than those listed at paragraph (a)(1) of this section only if they are able to be segregated from FAR-based actions and this is approved in writing by the FPDS Program Office. Prior to the commencement of reporting, agencies must contact the FPDS Program Office if they desire to submit any of the following types of activity:

(1) Transactions at or below the micro-purchase threshold, except as provided in paragraph (a)(2) of this section.

(2) Any non-appropriated fund (NAF) or NAF portion of a contract action using a mix of appropriated and nonappropriated funding.

(3) Lease and supplemental lease agreements for real property.

(4) Grants and entitlement actions.

(c) *Actions not reported.* The following types of contract actions are not to be reported to FPDS:

(1) Imprest fund transactions below the micro-purchase threshold, including those made via the Government purchase card (unless specific agency procedures prescribe reporting these actions).

(2) Orders from GSA stock and the GSA Global Supply Program.

(3) Purchases made at GSA or AbilityOne service stores, as these items stocked for resale have already been reported by GSA.

(4) Purchases made using nonappropriated fund activity cards, chaplain fund cards, individual Government personnel training orders, and Defense Printing orders.

(5) Actions that, pursuant to other authority, will not be entered in FPDS (*e.g.*, reporting of the information would compromise national security).

(6) Contract actions in which the required data would constitute classified information.

(7) Resale activity (*i.e.*, commissary or exchange activity).

(8) Revenue generating arrangements (*i.e.*, concessions).

(9) Training expenditures not issued as orders or contracts.

(10) Interagency agreements other than inter-agency acquisitions required to be reported at 4.606(a)(1).

(11) Letters of obligation used in the A–76 process.

(d) *Agencies not subject to the FAR.* Agencies not subject to the FAR may be required by other authority (*e.g.*, statute, OMB, or internal agency policy) to report certain information to FPDS. Those agencies not subject to the FAR must first receive approval from the FPDS Program Office prior to reporting to FPDS.

[FAC 2005-25, 73 FR 21773, 4/22/2008, effective 4/22/2008; FAC 2005-27, 73 FR 53994, 9/17/2008, effective 10/17/2008; FAC 2005-30, 74 FR 2712, 1/15/2009, effective 2/17/2009; FAC 2005-42, 75 FR 34260, 6/16/2010, effective 7/16/2010; FAC

2005-48, 75 FR 82567, 12/20/2010, effective 1/31/2011; FAC 2005-62, 75 FR 69715, 11/20/2012, effective 12/20/2012]

4.607 Solicitation provisions and contract clause.

(a) Insert the provision at 52.204-5, Women-Owned Business (Other Than Small Business), in all solicitations that—

(1) Are not set aside for small business concerns;

(2) Exceed the simplified acquisition threshold; and

(3) Are for contracts that will be performed in the United States or its outlying areas.

(b) Insert the provision at 52.204-6, Unique Entity Identifier, in solicitations that do not contain the provision at 52.204-7, System for Award Management, or meet a condition at 4.605(c)(2).

(c) Insert the clause at 52.204-12, Unique Entity Identifier Maintenance, in solicitations and resulting contracts that contain the provision at 52.204-6, Unique Entity Identifier.

[FAC 2005-25, 73 FR 21773, 4/22/2008, effective 4/22/2008; FAC 2005-30, 74 FR 2712, 1/15/2009, effective 2/17/2009; FAC 2005-62, 77 FR 69715, 11/20/2009, effective 12/20/2009; FAC 2005-67, 78 FR 37676, 6/21/2013, effective 7/22/2013; FAC 2005-91, 81 FR 67736, 9/30/2016, effective 10/31/2016; FAC 2019-02, 84 FR 19839, 5/6/2019, effective 5/6/2019]

SUBPART 4.7—CONTRACTOR RECORDS RETENTION

4.700 Scope of subpart.

This subpart provides policies and procedures for retention of records by contractors to meet the records review requirements of the Government. In this subpart, the terms *contracts* and *contractors* include *subcontracts* and *subcontractors*.

4.701 Purpose.

The purpose of this subpart is to generally describe records retention requirements and to allow reductions in the retention period for specific classes of records under prescribed circumstances.

4.702 Applicability.

(a) This subpart applies to records generated under contracts that contain one of the following clauses:

(1) Audit and Records—Sealed Bidding (52.214-26).

(2) Audit and Records—Negotiation (52.215-2).

(b) This subpart is not mandatory on Department of Energy contracts for which the Comptroller General allows alternative records retention periods. Apart from this exception, this subpart applies to record retention periods under contracts that are subject to Chapter 137, Title 10, U.S.C., or 40 U.S.C. 101 *et seq*.

[FAC 84-5, 50 FR 1727, 1/11/85, effective 4/1/85; FAC 90-31, 60 FR 42648, 8/16/95, effective 10/1/95; FAC 90-32, 60 FR 48206, 9/18/95, effective 10/1/95; FAC 90-45, Final rule, 62 FR 224, 1/2/97, effective 1/1/97; FAC 2005-06, 70 FR 57453, 9/30/2005, effective 9/30/2005]

4.703 Policy.

(a) Except as stated in 4.703(b), contractors shall make available records, which includes books, documents, accounting procedures and practices, and other data, regardless of type and regardless of whether such items are in written form, in the form of computer data, or in any other form, and other supporting evidence to satisfy contract negotiation, administration, and audit requirements of the contracting agencies and the Comptroller General for—

(1) 3 years after final payment; or

(2) For certain records, the period specified in 4.705 through 4.705-3, whichever of these periods expires first.

(b) Contractors shall make available the foregoing records and supporting evidence for a longer period of time than is required in 4.703(a) if—

(1) A retention period longer than that cited in 4.703(a) is specified in any contract clause; or

(2) The contractor, for its own purposes, retains the foregoing records and supporting evidence for a longer period. Under this circumstance, the retention period shall be the period of the contractor's retention or 3 years after final payment, whichever period expires first.

(3) The contractor does not meet the original due date for submission of final indirect cost rate proposals specified in paragraph (d)(2) of the clause at 52.216-7, Allowable Cost and Payment. Under these circumstances, the retention periods in 4.705 shall be automatically extended one day for each day the proposal is not submitted after the original due date.

(c) Nothing in this section shall be construed to preclude a contractor from duplicating or storing original records in electronic form unless they contain significant information not shown on the record copy. Original records need not be maintained or produced in an audit if the contractor or subcontractor provides photographic or electronic images of the original records and meets the following requirements:

(1) The contractor or subcontractor has established procedures to ensure that the imaging process preserves accurate images of the original records, including signatures and other written or graphic images, and that the imaging process is reliable and secure so as to maintain the integrity of the records.

(2) The contractor or subcontractor maintains an effective indexing system to permit timely and convenient access to the imaged records.

(3) The contractor or subcontractor retains the original records for a minimum of one year after imaging to permit periodic validation of the imaging systems.

(d) If the information described in paragraph (a) of this section is maintained on a computer, contractors shall retain the computer data on a reliable medium for the time periods prescribed. Contractors may transfer computer data in machine readable form from one reliable computer medium to another. Contractors' computer data retention and transfer procedures shall maintain the integrity, reliability, and security of the original computer data. Contractors shall also retain an audit trail describing the data transfer. For the record retention time periods prescribed, contractors shall not destroy, discard, delete, or write over such computer data.

[FAC 84-12, 51 FR 2649, 1/17/86, effective 1/20/86; FAC 84-40, 53 FR 43388, 10/26/88, effective 11/25/88; FAC 84-53, 54 FR 48982, 11/28/89, effective 12/28/89; FAC 90-23, 59 FR 67010, 12/28/94, effective 2/27/95; FAC 90-31, 60 FR 42648, 8/16/95, effective 10/1/95; FAC 97-3, 62 FR 64912, 12/9/97, effective 2/9/98; FAC 2005-17, 72 FR 27364, 5/15/2007, effective 6/14/2007; FAC 2019-02, 84 FR 19839, 5/6/2019, effective 5/6/2019]

4.704 Calculation of retention periods.

(a) The retention periods in 4.705 are calculated from the end of the contractor's fiscal year in which an entry is made charging or allocating a cost to a Government contract or subcontract. If a specific record contains a series of entries, the retention period is calculated from the end of the contractor's fiscal year in which the final entry is made. The contractor should cut off the records in annual blocks and retain them for block disposal under the prescribed retention periods.

(b) When records generated during a prior contract are relied upon by a contractor for certified cost or pricing data in negotiating a succeeding contract, the prescribed periods shall run from the date of the succeeding contract.

(c) If two or more of the record categories described in 4.705 are interfiled and screening for disposal is not practical, the contractor shall retain the entire record series for the longest period prescribed for any category of records.

[FAC 2005-45, 75 FR 53135, 8/30/2010, effective 10/1/2010]

4.705 Specific retention periods.

The contractor shall retain the records identified in 4.705-1 through 4.705-3 for the periods designated, provided retention is required under 4.702. Records are identified in this subpart in terms of their purpose or use and not by specific name or form number. Although the descriptive identifications may not conform to normal contractor usage or filing practices, these identifications apply to all contractor records that come within the description.

4.705-1 Financial and cost accounting records.

(a) Accounts receivable invoices, adjustments to the accounts, invoice registers, carrier freight bills, shipping orders, and other documents which detail the material or services billed on the related invoices: Retain 4 years.

(b) Material, work order, or service order files, consisting of purchase requisitions or purchase orders for material or services, or orders for transfer of material or supplies: Retain 4 years.

(c) Cash advance recapitulations, prepared as posting entries to accounts receivable ledgers for amounts of expense vouchers prepared for employees' travel and related expenses: Retain 4 years.

(d) Paid, canceled, and voided checks, other than those issued for the payment of salary and wages: Retain 4 years.

(e) Accounts payable records to support disbursements of funds for materials, equipment, supplies, and services, containing originals or copies of the following and related documents: remittance advices and statements, vendors' invoices, invoice audits and distribution slips, receiving and inspection reports or comparable certifications of receipt and inspection of material or services, and debit and credit memoranda: Retain 4 years.

(f) Labor cost distribution cards or equivalent documents: Retain 2 years.

(g) Petty cash records showing description of expenditures, to whom paid, name of person authorizing payment, and date, including copies of vouchers and other supporting documents: Retain 2 years.

4.705-2 Pay administration records.

(a) Payroll sheets, registers, or their equivalent, of salaries and wages paid to individual employees for each payroll period; change slips; and tax withholding statements: Retain 4 years.

(b) Clock cards or other time and attendance cards: Retain 2 years.

(c) Paid checks, receipts for wages paid in cash, or other evidence of payments for services rendered by employees: Retain 2 years.

[FAC 97-5, 63 FR 34058, 6/22/98, effective 8/21/98; FAC 97-18, 65 FR 36014, 6/6/2000, effective 8/7/2000; FAC 2001-10, 67 FR 70517, 11/22/2002, effective 12/23/2002]

4.705-3 Acquisition and supply records.

(a) Store requisitions for materials, supplies, equipment, and services: Retain 2 years.

(b) Work orders for maintenance and other services: Retain 4 years.

(c) Equipment records, consisting of equipment usage and status reports and equipment repair orders: Retain 4 years.

(d) Expendable property records, reflecting accountability for the receipt and use of material in the performance of a contract: Retain 4 years.

(e) Receiving and inspection report records, consisting of reports reflecting receipt and inspection of supplies, equipment, and materials: Retain 4 years.

(f) Purchase order files for supplies, equipment, material, or services used in the performance of a contract; supporting documentation and backup files including, but not limited to, invoices, and memoranda; *e.g.*, memoranda of negotiations showing the principal elements of subcontract price negotiations (see 52.244-2): Retain 4 years.

(g) Production records of quality control, reliability, and inspection: Retain 4 years.

(h) Property records (see FAR 45.101 and 52.245-1): Retain 4 years.

[FAC 97-5, 63 FR 34058, 6/22/98, effective 8/21/98; FAC 2005-43, 75 FR 38675, 7/2/2010, effective 8/2/2010]

4.706 [Reserved]

SUBPART 4.8—GOVERNMENT CONTRACT FILES

4.800 Scope of subpart.

This subpart prescribes requirements for establishing, maintaining, and disposing of contract files.

[FAC 97-18, 65 FR 36014, 6/6/2000, effective 8/7/2000]

4.801 General.

(a) The head of each office performing contracting, contract administration, or paying functions shall establish files containing the records of all contractual actions.

(b) The documentation in the files (see 4.803) shall be sufficient to constitute a complete history of the transaction for the purpose of—

(1) Providing a complete background as a basis for informed decisions at each step in the acquisition process;

(2) Supporting actions taken;

(3) Providing information for reviews and investigations; and

(4) Furnishing essential facts in the event of litigation or congressional inquiries.

(c) The files to be established include—

(1) A file for cancelled solicitations;

(2) A file for each contract; and

(3) A file such as a contractor general file, containing documents relating, for example, to—

(i) No specific contract;

(ii) More than one contract; or

(iii) The contractor in a general way (*e.g.*, contractor's management systems, past performance, or capabilities).

[FAC 2019-02, 84 FR 19839, 5/6/2019, effective 5/6/2019]

4.802 Contract files.

(a) A contract file should generally consist of—

(1) The contracting office contract file, that documents the basis for the acquisition and the award, the assignment of contract administration (including payment responsibilities), and any subsequent actions taken by the contracting office;

(2) The contract administration office contract file, that documents actions reflecting the basis for and the performance of contract administration responsibilities; and

(3) The paying office contract file, that documents actions prerequisite to, substantiating, and reflecting contract payments.

(b) Normally, each file should be kept separately; however, if appropriate, any or all of the files may be combined; *e.g.*, if all functions or any combination of the functions are performed by the same office.

(c) Files must be maintained at organizational levels that ensure—

(1) Effective documentation of contract actions;

(2) Ready accessibility to principal users;

(3) Minimal establishment of duplicate and working files;

(4) The safeguarding of classified documents; and

(5) Conformance with agency regulations for file location and maintenance.

(d) If the contract files or file segments are decentralized (*e.g.*, by type or function) to various organizational elements or to other outside offices, responsibility for their maintenance must be assigned. A central control and, if needed, a locator system should be established to ensure the ability to locate promptly any contract files.

(e) Contents of contract files that are contractor bid or proposal information or source selection information as defined in 2.101 must be protected from disclosure to unauthorized persons (see 3.104-4).

(f) Agencies may retain contract files in any medium (paper, electronic, microfilm, etc.) or any combination of media, as long as the requirements of this subpart are satisfied.

[FAC 84-47, 54 FR 20496, 5/11/89, effective date delayed to 7/16/89, 54 FR 22282, 5/23/89; FAC 85-54, 54 FR 50718, 12/8/89, effective 12/1/89; FAC 84-60, 55 FR 36794, 9/6/90, effective 9/6/90; FAC 90-23, 59 FR 67010, 12/28/94, effective 2/27/95; FAC

90-45, Final rule, 62 FR 224, 1/2/97, effective 1/1/97; FAC 2001-06, 67 FR 13048, 3/20/2002, effective 4/4/2002]

4.803 Contents of contract files.

The following are examples of the records normally contained, if applicable, in contract files:

(a) *Contracting office contract file.* (1) Purchase request, acquisition planning information, and other presolicitation documents.

(2) Justifications and approvals, determinations and findings, and associated documents.

(3) Evidence of availability of funds.

(4) Synopsis of proposed acquisition as required by part 5 or a reference to the synopsis.

(5) The list of sources solicited, and a list of any firms or persons whose requests for copies of the solicitation were denied, together with the reasons for denial.

(6) Set-aside decision including the type and extent of market research conducted.

(7) Government estimate of contract price.

(8) A copy of the solicitation and all amendments thereto.

(9) Security requirements and evidence of required clearances.

(10) A copy of each offer or quotation, the related abstract, and records of determinations concerning late offers or quotations. Unsuccessful offers or quotations may be maintained separately, if cross-referenced to the contract file. The only portions of the unsuccessful offer or quotation that need be retained are—

(i) Completed solicitation sections A, B, and K;

(ii) Technical and management proposals;

(iii) Cost/price proposals; and

(iv) Any other pages of the solicitation that the offeror or quoter has altered or annotated.

(11) Contractor's representations and certifications (see 4.1201(c)).

(12) Preaward survey reports or reference to previous preaward survey reports relied upon.

(13) Source selection documentation.

(14) Contracting officer's determination of the contractor's responsibility.

(15) Small Business Administration Certificate of Competency.

(16) Records of contractor's compliance with labor policies including equal employment opportunity policies.

(17) Data and information related to the contracting officer's determination of a fair and reasonable price. This may include—

(i) Certified cost or pricing data;

(ii) Data other than certified cost or pricing data;

(iii) Justification for waiver from the requirement to submit certified cost or pricing data; or

(iv) Certificates of Current Cost or Pricing Data.

(18) Packaging and transportation data.

(19) Cost or price analysis.

(20) Audit reports or reasons for waiver.

(21) Record of negotiation.

(22) Justification for type of contract.

(23) Authority for deviations from this regulation, statutory requirements, or other restrictions.

(24) Required approvals of award and evidence of legal review.

(25) Notice of award.

(26) The original of—

(i) The signed contract or award;

(ii) All contract modifications; and

(iii) Documents supporting modifications executed by the contracting office.

(27) Synopsis of award or reference thereto.

(28) Notice to unsuccessful quoters or offerors and record of any debriefing.

(29) Acquisition management reports (see Subpart 4.6).

(30) Bid, performance, payment, or other bond documents, or a reference thereto, and notices to sureties.

(31) Report of postaward conference.

(32) Notice to proceed, stop orders, and any overtime premium approvals granted at the time of award.

(33) Documents requesting and authorizing modification in the normal assignment of contract administration functions and responsibility.

(34) Approvals or disapprovals of requests for waivers or deviations from contract requirements.

(35) Rejected engineering change proposals.

(36) Royalty, invention, and copyright reports (including invention disclosures) or reference thereto.

(37) Contract completion documents.

(38) Documentation regarding termination actions for which the contracting office is responsible.

(39) Cross-references to pertinent documents that are filed elsewhere.

(40) Any additional documents on which action was taken or that reflect actions by the contracting office pertinent to the contract.

(41) A current chronological list identifying the awarding and successor contracting officers, with inclusive dates of responsibility.

(42) When limiting competition, or awarding on a sole source basis, to economically disadvantaged women- owned small business (EDWOSB) concerns or women-owned small business (WOSB) concerns eligible under the WOSB Program in accordance with subpart 19.15, include documentation—

(i) Of the type and extent of market research; and

(ii) That the NAICS code assigned to the acquisition is for an industry that SBA has designated as—

(A) Underrepresented for EDWOSB concerns; or

(B) Substantially underrepresented for WOSB concerns.

(b) *Contract administration office contract file*. (1) Copy of the contract and all modifications, together with official record copies of supporting documents executed by the contract administration office.

(2) Any document modifying the normal assignment of contract administration functions and responsibility.

(3) Security requirements.

(4) Certified cost or pricing data, Certificates of Current Cost or Pricing Data, or data other than certified cost or pricing data; cost or price analysis; and other documentation supporting contractual actions executed by the contract administration office.

(5) Preaward survey information.

(6) Purchasing system information.

(7) Consent to subcontract or purchase.

(8) Performance and payment bonds and surety information.

(9) Postaward conference records.

(10) Orders issued under the contract.

(11) Notice to proceed and stop orders.

(12) Insurance policies or certificates of insurance or references to them.

(13) Documents supporting advance or progress payments.

(14) Progressing, expediting, and production surveillance records.

(15) Quality assurance records.

(16) Property administration records.

(17) Documentation regarding termination actions for which the contract administration office is responsible.

(18) Cross reference to other pertinent documents that are filed elsewhere.

(19) Any additional documents on which action was taken or that reflect actions by the contract administration office pertinent to the contract.

(20) Contract completion documents.

(c) *Paying office contract file*. (1) Copy of the contract and any modifications.

(2) Bills, invoices, vouchers, and supporting documents.

(3) Record of payments or receipts.

(4) Other pertinent documents.

[FAC 84-5, 50 FR 1727, 1/11/85, effective 4/1/85; FAC 84-42, 54 FR 5054, 1/31/89,

effective 3/2/89; FAC 84-60, 55 FR 38795, 9/6/90, effective 9/6/90; FAC 90-32, 60 FR 48206, 9/18/95, effective 10/1/95; FAC 90-40, 61 FR 39186, 7/26/96, effective 9/24/96; FAC 90-43,61 FR 67408, 12/20/96, effective 12/20/96; FAC 90-45, Final rule, 62 FR 224, 1/2/97 effective 1/1/97; FAC 97-4, 63 FR 9048, 2/23/98, effective 4/24/98; FAC 97-19, 65 FR 46052, 7/26/2000, effective 7/26/2000; FAC 97-26, 66 FR 27405, 5/16/2001, effective 5/16/2001; FAC 2005-13, 71 FR 57362, 9/28/2006, effective 9/28/2006; FAC 2005-19, 72 FR 46333, 8/17/2007, effective 8/17/2007; FAC 2005-45, 75 FR 53135, 8/30/2010, effective 10/1/2010; FAC 2005-51, 76 FR 18304, 4/1/2011, effective 4/1/2011; FAC 2005-56, 77 FR 12913, 3/2/2012, effective 4/2/2012; FAC 2005-86, 80 FR 81888, 12/31/2015, effective 12/31/2015; FAC 2005-91, 81 FR 67735, 9/30/2016, effective 9/30/2016; FAC 2019-02, 84 FR 19839, 5/6/2019, effective 5/6/2019]

4.804 Closeout of contract files. (No Text)

4.804-1 Closeout by the office administering the contract.

(a) Except as provided in paragraph (c) of this section, time standards for closing out contract files are as follows:

(1) Files for contracts using simplified acquisition procedures should be considered closed when the contracting officer receives evidence of receipt of property and final payment, unless otherwise specified by agency regulations.

(2) Files for firm-fixed-price contracts, other than those using simplified acquisition procedures, should be closed within 6 months after the date on which the contracting officer receives evidence of physical completion.

(3) Files for contracts requiring settlement of indirect cost rates should be closed within 36 months of the month in which the contracting officer receives evidence of physical completion.

(4) Files for all other contracts should be closed within 20 months of the month in which the contracting officer receives evidence of physical completion.

(b) When closing out the contract files at 4.804-1(a)(2), (3), and (4), the contracting officer shall use the closeout procedures at 4.804-5. However, these closeout actions may be modified to reflect the extent of administration that has been performed. Quick closeout procedures (see 42.708) should be used, when appropriate, to reduce administrative costs and to enable deobligation of excess funds.

(c) A contract file shall not be closed if—

(1) The contract is in litigation or under appeal; or

(2) In the case of a termination, all termination actions have not been completed.

[FAC 84-51, 54 FR 34752, 8/21/89, effective 9/20/89; FAC 90-29, 60 FR 34732, 7/3/95, effective 7/3/95; FAC 2019-02, 84 FR 19839, 5/6/2019, effective 5/6/2019]

4.804-2 Closeout of the contracting office files if another office administers the contract.

(a) Contract files for contracts using simplified acquisition procedures should be considered closed when the contracting officer receives evidence of receipt of property and final payment, unless otherwise specified by agency regulation.

(b) All other contract files shall be closed as soon as practicable after the contracting officer receives a contract completion statement from the contract administration office. The contracting officer shall ensure that all contractual actions required have been completed and shall prepare a statement to that effect. This statement is authority to close the contract file and shall be made a part of the official contract file.

[FAC 90-29, 60 FR 34732, 7/3/95, effective 7/3/95]

4.804-3 Closeout of paying office contract files.

The paying office shall close the contract file upon issuance of the final payment voucher.

4.804-4 Physically completed contracts.

(a) Except as provided in paragraph (b) of this section, a contract is considered to be physically completed when—

(1) (i) The contractor has completed the required deliveries and the Government has inspected and accepted the supplies;

(ii) The contractor has performed all services and the Government has accepted these services; and

(iii) All option provisions, if any, have expired; or

(2) The Government has given the contractor a notice of complete contract termination.

(b) Rental, use, and storage agreements are considered to be physically completed when—

(1) The Government has given the contractor a notice of complete contract termination; or

(2) The contract period has expired.

[FAC 2005-17, 72 FR 27364, 5/15/2007, effective 6/14/2007; FAC 2019-02, 84 FR 19839, 5/6/2019, effective 5/6/2019]

4.804-5 Procedures for closing out contract files.

(a) The contract administration office is responsible for initiating (automated or manual) administrative closeout of the contract after receiving evidence of its physical completion. At the outset of this process, the contract administration office must review the contract funds status and notify the contracting office of any excess funds the contract administration office might deobligate. When complete, the administrative closeout procedures must ensure that—

(1) Disposition of classified material is completed;

(2) *Final patent report is cleared.* If a final patent report is required, the contracting officer may proceed with contract closeout in accordance with the following procedures, or as otherwise prescribed by agency procedures:

(i) Final patent reports should be cleared within 60 days of receipt.

(ii) If the final patent report is not received, the contracting officer shall notify the contractor of the contractor's obligations and the Government's rights under the applicable patent rights clause, in accordance with 27.303. If the contractor fails to respond to this notification, the contracting officer may proceed with contract closeout upon consultation with the agency legal counsel responsible for patent matters regarding the contractor's failure to respond.

(3) Final royalty report is cleared;

(4) There is no outstanding value engineering change proposal;

(5) Plant clearance report is received;

(6) Property clearance is received;

(7) All interim or disallowed costs are settled;

(8) Price revision is completed;

(9) Subcontracts are settled by the prime contractor;

(10) Prior year indirect cost rates are settled;

(11) Termination docket is completed;

(12) Contract audit is completed;

(13) Contractor's closing statement is completed;

(14) Contractor's final invoice has been submitted; and

(15) Contract funds review is completed and excess funds deobligated.

(b) When the actions in paragraph (a) of this section have been verified, the contracting officer administering the contract shall ensure that a contract completion statement, containing the following information, is prepared:

(1) Contract administration office name and address (if different from the contracting office).

(2) Contracting office name and address.

(3) Contract number.

(4) Last modification number.

(5) Last call or order number.

(6) Contractor name and address.

(7) Dollar amount of excess funds, if any.

(8) Voucher number and date, if final payment has been made.

(9) Invoice number and date, if the final approved invoice has been forwarded to a disbursing office of another agency or activity and the status of the payment is unknown.

(10) A statement that all required contract administration actions have been fully and satisfactorily accomplished.

(11) Name and signature of the contracting officer.

(12) Date.

(c) When the statement is completed, the contracting officer shall ensure that—

(1) The signed original is placed in the contracting office contract file (or forwarded to the contracting office for placement in the files if the contract administration office is different from the contracting office); and

(2) A signed copy is placed in the appropriate contract administration file if administration is performed by a contract administration office.

[FAC 84-51, 54 FR 34752, 8/21/89, effective 9/20/89; FAC 97-15, 64 FR 72414, 12/27/99, effective 2/25/2000; FAC 2005-52, 76 FR 31402, 5/31/2011, effective 6/30/2011; FAC 2019-02, 84 FR 19839, 5/6/2019, effective 5/6/2019]

4.805 Storage, handling, and disposal of contract files.

(a) Agencies must prescribe procedures for the handling, storing, and disposing of contract files, in accordance with the National Archives and Records Administration (NARA) General Records Schedule 1.1, Financial Management and Reporting Records. The Financial Management and Reporting Records can be found at *http://www.archives.gov/records-mgmt/grs.html.* These procedures must take into account documents held in all types of media, including microfilm and various electronic media. Agencies may change the original medium to facilitate storage as long as the requirements of this part, law, and other regulations are satisfied. The process used to create and store records must record and reproduce the original document, including signatures and other written and graphic images completely, accurately, and clearly. Data transfer, storage, and retrieval procedures must protect the original data from alteration. Unless law or other regulations require signed originals to be kept, they may be destroyed after the responsible agency official verifies that record copies on alternate media and copies reproduced from the record copy are accurate, complete, and clear representations of the originals. When original documents have been converted to alternate media for storage, the requirements in Table 4-1 of this section also apply to the record copies in the alternate media.

(b) If administrative records are mixed with program records and cannot be economically segregated, the entire file should be kept for the period of time approved for the program records. Similarly, if documents described in the following table are part of a subject or case file that documents activities that are not described in the table, they should be treated in the same manner as the files of which they are a part.

(c) An agency that requires a shorter retention period than those identified in Table 4-1 shall request approval from NARA through the agency's records officer.

TABLE 4-1—RETENTION PERIODS

Record	Retention period
(1) Contracts (and related records or documents, including successful and unsuccessful proposals, except see paragraph (c)(2) of this section regarding contractor payrolls submitted under construction contracts).	6 years after final payment.
(2) Contractor's payrolls submitted under construction contracts in accordance with Department of Labor regulations (29 CFR 5.5(a)(3)), with related certifications, anti-kickback affidavits, and other related records.	3 years after contract completion unless contract performance is the subject of an enforcement action on that date (see paragraph (c)(8) of this section).
(3) Unsolicited proposals not accepted by a department or agency.	Retain in accordance with agency procedures.
(4) Files for canceled solicitations.	6 years after cancellation.
(5) Other copies of procurement file records used for administrative purposes.	When business use ceases.
(6) Documents pertaining generally to the contractor as described at 4.801(c)(3).	Until superseded or obsolete.
(7) Data submitted to the Federal Procurement Data System (FPDS). Electronic data file maintained by fiscal year, containing unclassified records of all procurements exceeding the micro-purchase threshold, and information required under 4.603.	6 years after submittal to FPDS.
(8) Investigations, cases pending or in litigation (including protests), or similar matters (including enforcement actions).	Until final clearance or settlement, or, if related to a document identified in paragraphs (c)(1) through (7) of this section, for the retention period specified for the related document, whichever is later.

[FAC 97-18, 65 FR 36014, 6/6/2000, effective 8/7/2000; FAC 2005-25, 73 FR 21773, 4/22/2008, effective 4/22/2008; FAC 2005-30, 74 FR 2712, 1/15/2009, effective 2/17/2009; FAC 2005-73, 79 FR 24192, 4/29/2014, effective 5/29/2014; FAC 2005-85, 80 FR 75913, 12/4/2015, effective 1/4/2016; FAC 2019-02, 84 FR 19839, 5/6/2019, effective 5/6/2019]

SUBPART 4.9—TAXPAYER IDENTIFICATION NUMBER INFORMATION

4.900 Scope of subpart.

This subpart provides policies and procedures for obtaining—

(a) Taxpayer Identification Number (TIN) information that may be used for debt collection purposes; and

(b) Contract information and payment information for submittal to the payment office for Internal Revenue Service (IRS) reporting purposes.

[FAC 97-9, 63 FR 58587, 10/30/98, effective 10/30/98; finalized without change, FAC 97-12, 64 FR 32740, 6/17/99]

4.901 Definition.

Common parent, as used in this subpart, means that corporate entity that owns or controls an affiliated group of corporations that files its Federal income tax returns on a consolidated basis, and of which the offeror is a member.

[FAC 97-9, 63 FR 58587, 10/30/98, effective 10/30/98, finalized without change, FAC 97-12, 64 FR 32740, 6/17/99; FAC 97-22, 66 FR 2116, 1/10/2001, effective 3/12/2001; Delay of effective date, 66 FR 14259, 3/9/2001, effective 5/11/2001]

4.902 General.

(a) *Debt collection.* 31 U.S.C. 7701(c) requires each contractor doing business with a Government agency to furnish its TIN to that agency. 31 U.S.C. 3325(d) requires the Government to include, with each certified voucher prepared by the Government payment office and submitted to a disbursing official, the TIN of the contractor receiving payment under the voucher. The TIN may be used by the Government to collect and report on any delinquent amounts arising out of the contractor's relationship with the Government.

(b) *Information reporting to the IRS.* The TIN is also required for Government reporting of certain contract information (see 4.903) and payment information (see 4.904) to the IRS.

[FAC 97-9, 63 FR 58587, 10/30/98, effective 10/30/98, finalized without change, FAC 97-12, 64 FR 32740, 6/17/99]

4.903 Reporting contract information to the IRS.

(a) 26 U.S.C. 6050M, as implemented in 26 CFR, requires heads of Federal executive agencies to report certain information to the IRS.

(b) (1) The required information applies to contract modifications—

(i) Increasing the amount of a contract awarded before January 1, 1989, by $50,000 or more; and

(ii) Entered into on or after April 1, 1990.

(2) The reporting requirement also applies to certain contracts and modifications thereto in excess of $25,000 entered into on or after January 1, 1989.

(c) The information to report is—

(1) Name, address, and TIN of the contractor;

(2) Name and TIN of the common parent (if any);

(3) Date of the contract action;

(4) Amount obligated on the contract action; and

(5) Estimated contract completion date.

(d) Transmit the information to the IRS through the Federal Procurement Data System (see Subpart 4.6 and implementing instructions).

[FAC 97-9, 63 FR 58587, 10/30/98, effective 10/30/98, finalized without change, FAC 97-12, 64 FR 32740, 6/17/99]

4.904 Reporting Payment Information to the IRS.

26 U.S.C.6041 and 6041A, as implemented in 26 CFR, in part, require payors, including Government agencies, to report to the IRS on Form 1099, payments made to certain contractors. 26 U.S.C. 6109 requires a contractor to provide its TIN of a Form 1099 is required. The payment office is responsible for submitting reports to the IRS.

[FAC 97-9, 63 FR 58587, 10/30/98, effective 10/30/98, finalized without change, FAC 97-12, 64 FR 32740, 6/17/99]

4.905 Solicitation provision.

The contracting officer shall insert the provision at 52.204-3, Taxpayer Identification, in solicitations that—

(a) Do not include the provision at 52.204-7, System for Award Management; and

(b) Are not conducted under the procedures of part 12.

[FAC 97-9, 63 FR 58587, 10/30/98, effective 10/30/98, finalized without change, FAC 97-12, 64 FR 32740, 6/17/99; FAC 2001-16, Final rule, 68 FR 56669, 10/1/2003, effective 10/1/2003; FAC 2005-62, 77 FR 69715, 11/20/2012, effective 12/20/2012; FAC 2005-67, 78 FR 37676, 6/21/2013, effective 7/22/2013; FAC 2005-82, 80 FR 26427, 5/7/2015, effective 5/7/2015]

SUBPART 4.10—UNIFORM USE OF LINE ITEMS

4.1000 Scope.

This subpart prescribes policies and procedures for assigning line items and subline items and their identifiers. However, in order to provide agencies with time to transition their information systems, agencies have until October 1, 2019, to apply the requirements of 4.1002 through 4.1008.

[FAC 2005-95, 82 FR 4709, 1/13/2017, effective 1/13/2017]

4.1001 Policy.

In order to improve the accuracy, traceability, and usability of procurement data, procurement instruments shall identify the supplies or services to be acquired as separately identified line items and, as needed, subline items.

(a) Line items are established to define deliverables or organize information about deliverables. Each line item describes characteristics for the item purchased, e.g., pricing, delivery, and funding information.

(b) Each line item may be subdivided into separate unique subsets (called subline items) to ease administration. If a line item has deliverable subline items, the line item is informational. Subline items differentiate between or among certain characteristics of the line item, such as colors or sizes, dates of delivery, destinations, or places of performance. Subline items are established to define deliverables or organize information about deliverables.

[FAC 97-2, 62 FR 51224, 9/30/97, effective 10/10/97; FAC 2005-95, 82 FR 4709, 1/13/2017, effective 1/13/2017]

4.1002 Applicability.

The policies of this subpart shall apply to the following procurement instruments, to include amendments, modifications, and change orders thereto:

(a) Solicitations.

(b) Contracts, including, but not limited to, Governmentwide acquisition contracts (GWACs), multi-agency contracts (MACs), Federal Supply Schedule (FSS) contracts, indefinite-delivery contracts, and purchase orders.

(c) Agreements that include pre-priced supplies or services.

(d) Task and delivery orders.

[FAC 2005-95, 82 FR 4709, 1/13/2017, effective 1/13/2017]

4.1003 Establishing line items.

Establish separate line items for deliverables that have the following characteristics except as provided at 4.1005-2:

(a) Separately identifiable.

(1) A supply is separately identifiable if it has its own identification (e.g., national stock number (NSN), item description, manufacturer's part number).

(2) Services are separately identifiable if they have no more than one statement of work or performance work statement.

(3) If the procurement instrument involves a first article (see subpart 9.3), establish a separate line item for each item requiring a separate approval. If the first article consists of a lot composed of a mixture of items that will be approved as a single lot, a single line item may be used.

(b) Single unit price or total price.

(c) Single accounting classification citation. A single deliverable may be funded by multiple accounting classifications when the deliverable effort cannot be otherwise subdivided.

(d) Separate delivery schedule, destination, period of performance, or place of performance.

(e) Single contract pricing type (e.g., fixed-price or cost-reimbursement).

[FAC 2005-95, 82 FR 4709, 1/13/2017, effective 1/13/2017]

4.1004 Establishing subline items.

Subline items may be used to facilitate tracking of performance, deliverables, payment, and contract funds accounting or for other management purposes. Subline items may be either deliverable or informational. The list of characteristics at 4.1003 applies to deliverable subline items, but it is not applicable to informational subline items. A line item with subline items shall contain only that information that is common to all subline items thereunder. All subline items under one line item shall be the same contract type as the line item.

(a) *Deliverable subline items.* Deliverable subline items may be used for several related items that require separate identification. For example, instead of establishing multiple separate line items, subline items may be established for—

(1) Items that are basically the same, except for minor variations such as—

(i) Size or color;

(ii) Accounting classification, but see also 4.1005-1(a)(4); or

(iii) Date of delivery, destination, or period or place of performance;

(2) Separately priced collateral functions that relate to the primary product, such as packaging and handling, or transportation; or

(3) Items to be separately identified at the time of shipment or performance.

(b) *Informational subline items.*

(1) Informational subline items may be used by agencies for administrative purposes. This type of subline item identifies information that relates directly to the line item and is an integral part of it (e.g., parts of an assembly or parts of a kit).

(2) Position informational subline items within the line item description, not in the quantity or price fields.

[FAC 2005-95, 82 FR 4709, 1/13/2017, effective 1/13/2017]

4.1005 Data elements for line items and subline items. (No Text)

4.1005-1 Required data elements.

(a) Except as provided in 4.1005-2, each line item or subline item shall include in the schedule (described at 12.303(b)(4), 14.201-2, or 15.204-2, or in a comparable section of the procurement instrument), at a minimum, the following information as separate, distinct data elements:

(1) Line item or subline item number established in accordance with agency procedures.

(2) Description of what is being purchased.

(3) Product or Service Code (PSC).

(4) Accounting classification citation.

(i) Line items or deliverable subline items. If multiple accounting classifications for a single deliverable apply, include the dollar amount for each accounting classification in the schedule (or a comparable section of the procurement instrument).

(ii) Informational subline items. An accounting classification citation is not required. (See 4.1004).

(5)(i) For fixed-price line items:

(A) Unit of measure.

(B) Quantity.

(C) Unit price.

(D) Total price.

(ii) For cost-reimbursement line items:

(A) Unit of measure.

(B) Quantity.

(C) Estimated cost.

(D) Fee (if any).

(E) Total estimated cost plus any fee.

(b) If a contract contains a combination of fixed-price, time-and-materials, labor-hour, or cost-reimbursable line items, identify the contract type for each line item in the schedule (or a comparable section of the procurement instrument) to facilitate payment.

(c) Each deliverable line item or deliverable subline item shall have its own delivery schedule, destination, period of performance, or place of performance expressly stated in the appropriate section of the procurement instrument ("as required" constitutes an expressly stated delivery term). When a line item has deliverable subline items, the delivery schedule, destination, period of performance, or place of performance shall be identified at the subline item level, rather than the line item level.

(d) Terms and conditions in other sections of the contract (such as contract clauses or payment instructions) shall also specify applicability to individual line items if not applicable to the contract as a whole.

[FAC 2005-95, 82 FR 4709, 1/13/2017, effective 1/13/2017]

4.1005-2 Exceptions.

(a) *Indefinite-delivery contracts*—

(1) *General.* The following required data elements are not known at time of issuance of an indefinite-delivery contract, but shall be provided in each order at the time of issuance: accounting classification, delivery date and destination, or period and place of performance.

(2) *Indefinite-delivery indefinite-quantity (IDIQ) and requirements contracts.* IDIQ and requirements contracts may omit the quantity at the line item level for the base award provided that the total contract minimum and maximum, or the estimate, respectively, is stated.

(b) *Item description and PSC.* These data elements are not required in the line item if there are associated deliverable subline items that include the actual detailed identification. When this exception applies, use a general narrative description for the line item.

(c) *Single unit price or single total price.* The requirement for a single unit price or single total price at the line item level does not apply if any of the following conditions are present:

(1) There are associated deliverable subline items that are priced.

(2) The line item or subline item is not separately priced.

(3) The supplies or services are being acquired on a cost-reimbursement, time-and-materials, or labor-hour basis.

(4) The procurement instrument is for services and firm prices have been established for elements of the total price, but the actual number of the elements is not known until performance (e.g., a labor-hour contract for maintenance/repair). The contracting officer may structure these procurement instruments to reflect a firm or estimated total amount for each line item.

[FAC 2005-95, 82 FR 4709, 1/13/2017, effective 1/13/2017; FAC 2019-02, 84 FR 19839, 5/6/2019, effective 5/6/2019]

4.1006 Modifications.

(a) When a new item (such as an increased quantity) is added to the procurement instrument, assign a new line item number.

(b) If the modification relates to existing line items, the modification shall refer to those items.

[FAC 2005-95, 82 FR 4709, 1/13/2017, effective 1/13/2017]

4.1007 Solicitation alternative line item proposal.

Solicitations should be structured to allow offerors to propose alternative line items (see 4.1008 and 52.212- 1(e)). For example, when soliciting certain items using units of measure such as kit, set, or lot, the offeror may not be able to group and deliver all items in a single shipment.

[FAC 2005-95, 82 FR 4709, 1/13/2017, effective 1/13/2017]

4.1008 Solicitation provision.

Insert the provision at 52.204-22, Alternative Line Item Proposal, in all solicitations.

[FAC 2005-95, 82 FR 4709, 1/13/2017, effective 1/13/2017]

SUBPART 4.11 — SYSTEM FOR AWARD MANAGEMENT

4.1100 Scope.

This subpart prescribes policies and procedures for requiring contractor registration in the System for Award Management (SAM) to—

(a) Increase visibility of vendor sources (including their geographical locations) for specific supplies and services; and

(b) Establish a common source of vendor data for the Government.

[FAC 2001-16, Final rule, 68 FR 56669, 10/1/2003, effective 10/1/2003; FAC 2005-55, 77 FR 187, 1/3/2012, effective 2/2/2012; FAC 2005-67, 78 FR 37676, 6/21/2013, effective 7/22/2013; FAC

2005-101, 83 FR 48691, 9/26/2018, effective 10/26/2018]

4.1101 Definition.

As used in this subpart—

Agreement means basic agreement, basic ordering agreement, or blanket purchase agreement.

[FAC 2001-16, Final rule, 68 FR 56669, 10/1/2003, effective 10/1/2003; FAC 2001-26, 69 FR 76341, 12/20/2004, effective 1/1/2005]

4.1102 Policy.

(a) Offerors and quoters are required to be registered in SAM at the time an offer or quotation is submitted in order to comply with the annual representations and certifications requirements except for—

(1) Purchases under the micropurchase threshold that use a Governmentwide commercial purchase card as both the purchasing and payment mechanism, as opposed to using the purchase card for payment only;

(2) Classified contracts (see 2.101) when registration in SAM, or use of SAM data, could compromise the safeguarding of classified information or national security;

(3) Contracts awarded by—

(i) Deployed contracting officers in the course of military operations, including, but not limited to, contingency operations as defined in 10 U.S.C. 101(a)(13) or humanitarian or peacekeeping operations as defined in 10 U.S.C. 2302(8);

(ii) Contracting officers located outside the United States and its outlying areas, as defined in 2.101, for work to be performed in support of diplomatic or developmental operations, including those performed in support of foreign assistance programs overseas, in an area that has been designated by the Department of State as a danger pay post (see *http://aoprals.state.gov/Web920/danger_pay_all.asp*); or

(iii) Contracting officers in the conduct of emergency operations, such as responses to natural or environmental disasters or national or civil emergencies, e.g., Robert T. Stafford Disaster Relief and Emergency Assistance Act (42 U.S.C. 5121);

(4) Contracts with individuals for performance outside the United States and its outlying areas;

(5) Contracts awarded without providing for full and open competition due to unusual or compelling urgency (see 6.302-2);

(6) Contract actions at or below $30,000 awarded to foreign vendors for work performed outside the United States, if it is impractical to obtain SAM registration; and

(7) Micro-purchases that do not use the electronic funds transfer (EFT) method for payment and are not required to be reported (see Subpart 4.6).

(b) If practical, the contracting officer shall modify the contract or agreement awarded under paragraph (a)(3) of this section to require SAM registration.

(c) Contracting officers shall use the legal business name or "doing business as" name and physical address from the contractor's SAM registration for the provided unique entity identifier to identify the contractor in section A of the contract schedule, similar sections of non-uniform contract formats and agreements, and all corresponding forms and data exchanges. Contracting officers shall make no changes to the data retrieved from SAM.

(d)(1)(i) If a contractor has legally changed its business name or "doing business as" name (whichever is shown on the contract), or has transferred the assets used in performing the contract, but has not completed the necessary requirements regarding novation and change-of-name agreements in subpart 42.12, the contractor is required to provide the responsible contracting officer a minimum of one business day's written notification of its intention to change the name in SAM, comply with the requirements of subpart 42.12, and agree in writing to the timeline and procedures specified by the responsible contracting officer. Along with the notification, the contractor is required to provide the contracting officer sufficient documentation to support the legally changed name.

(ii) If the contractor fails to comply with the requirements of paragraph (d)(1)(i) of the clause at 52.204-13, System for Award

Management Maintenance, or fails to perform the agreement at 52.204-13, paragraph (d)(1)(i)(C), and, in the absence of a properly executed novation or change-of-name agreement, the SAM information that shows the contractor to be other than the contractor indicated in the contract will be considered to be incorrect information within the meaning of the "Suspension of Payment" paragraph of the EFT clause of the contract.

(2) The contractor shall not change the name or address for electronic funds transfer payments (EFT) or manual payments, as appropriate, in the SAM record to reflect an assignee for the purpose of assignment of claims (see subpart 32.8, Assignment of Claims).

(3) Assignees shall be separately registered in SAM. Information provided to the contractor's SAM record that indicates payments, including those made by EFT, to an ultimate recipient other than that contractor will be considered to be incorrect information within the meaning of the "Suspension of payment" paragraph of the EFT clause of the contract.

[FAC 2001-16, Final rule, 68 FR 56669, 10/1/2003, effective 10/1/2003; FAC 2005-05, 70 FR 43586, 7/27/2005, effective 7/27/2005; FAC 2005-62, 77 FR 69715, 11/20/2012, effective 12/20/2012; FAC 2005-67, 78 FR 37676, 6/21/2013, effective 7/22/2013; FAC 2005-83, 80 FR 38293, 7/2/2015, effective 10/1/2015; FAC 2005-88, 81 FR 30438, 5/16/2016, effective 6/15/2016; FAC 2005-101, 83 FR 48691, 9/26/2018, effective 10/26/2018]

4.1103 Procedures.

(a) Unless the acquisition is exempt under 4.1102(a), the contracting officer—

(1) Shall verify that the offeror or quoter is registered in SAM (see paragraph (b) of this section) at the time an offer or quotation is submitted;

(2) Should use the unique entity identifier to verify SAM registration—

(i) Via *https://www.sam.gov;* or

(ii) As otherwise provided by agency procedures; or

(3) Need not verify SAM registration before placing an order or call if the contract or agreement includes the provision at 52.204-7, System for Award Management, or the clause at 52.212-4, Contract Terms and Conditions—Commercial Items, or a similar agency clause, except when use of the Governmentwide commercial purchase card is contemplated as a method of payment. (See 32.1108(b)(2).)

(b) If the contract action is being awarded in accordance with 4.1102(a)(5), the contractor is required to be registered in SAM within 30 days after contract award, or at least three days prior to submission of the first invoice, whichever occurs first.

(c) Agencies shall protect against improper disclosure of information contained in SAM.

(d) The contracting officer shall, on contractual documents transmitted to the payment office, provide the unique entity identifier, or, if applicable, the Electronic Funds Transfer indicator, in accordance with agency procedures.

[FAC 2001-16, Final rule, 68 FR 56669, 10/1/2003, effective 10/1/2003; FAC 2005-10, 71 FR 36923, 6/28/2006, effective 7/28/2006; FAC 2005-38, 74 FR 65600, 12/10/2009, effective 2/1/2010; FAC 2005-55, 77 FR 187, 1/3/2012, effective 2/2/2012; FAC 2005-62, 77 FR 69715, 11/20/2012, effective 12/20/2012; FAC 2005-67, 78 FR 37676, 6/21/2013, effective 7/22/2013; FAC 2005-91, 81 FR 67736, 9/30/2016, effective 10/31/2016; FAC 2005-101, 83 FR 48691, 9/26/2018, effective 10/26/2018]

4.1104 Disaster Response Registry.

Contracting officers shall consult the Disaster Response Registry via *https://www.sam.gov*, Search Records, Advanced Search, Disaster Response Registry Search when contracting for debris removal, distribution of supplies, reconstruction, and other disaster or emergency relief activities inside the United States and outlying areas. (See 26.205).

[FAC 2005-43, 75 FR 38683, 7/2/2010, effective 8/2/2010; FAC 2005-55, 77 FR 187, 1/3/2012, effective 2/2/2012; FAC 2005-101,

83 FR 48691, 9/26/2018, effective 10/26/2018]

4.1105 Solicitation provision and contract clauses.

(a) (1) Insert the provision at 52.204-7, System for Award Management, in all solicitations except when the conditions in 4.1102(a) apply.

(2) Insert the provision at 52.204-7, System for Award Management, with its Alternate I when the solicitation is anticipated to be awarded in accordance with 4.1102(a)(5).

(b) Insert the clause at 52.204-13, System for Award Management Maintenance, in solicitations that contain the provision at 52.204-7, and resulting contracts.

[FAC 2001-16, Final rule, 68 FR 56669, 10/1/2003, effective 10/1/2003; FAC 2005-10, 71 FR 36923, 6/28/2006, effective 7/28/2006; FAC 2005-37, 74 FR 52847, 10/14/2009, effective 10/14/2009; FAC 2005-43, 75 FR 38683, 7/2/2010, effective 8/2/2010; FAC 2005-62, 77 FR 69715, 11/20/2012, effective 12/20/2012; FAC 2005-67, 78 FR 37676, 6/21/2013, effective 7/22/2013; FAC 2005-101, 83 FR 48691, 9/26/2018, effective 10/26/2018]

SUBPART 4.12—REPRESENTATIONS AND CERTIFICATIONS

4.1200 Scope.

This subpart prescribes policies and procedures for requiring submission and maintenance of representations and certifications via the System for Award Management (SAM) to—

(a) Eliminate the administrative burden for contractors of submitting the same information to various contracting offices;

(b) Establish a common source for this information to procurement offices across the Government; and

(c) Incorporate by reference the contractor's representations and certifications in the awarded contract.

[FAC 2001-26, 69 FR 76341, 12/20/2004, effective 1/1/2005; FAC 2005-18, Interim rule, 72 FR 36852, 7/5/2007, effective 6/30/2007; FAC 2005-31, 74 FR 11821, 3/19/2009, effective 4/20/2009; FAC 2005-67, 78 FR 37676, 6/21/2013, effective 7/22/2013; FAC 2005-78, 79 FR 70341, 11/25/2014, effective 12/26/2014; FAC 2019-02, 84 FR 19839, 5/6/2019, effective 5/6/2019]

4.1201 Policy.

(a) Offerors and quoters are required to complete electronic annual representations and certifications in SAM accessed via *https://www.sam.gov* as a part of required registration (see FAR 4.1102).

(b) (1) All registrants are required to review and update the representations and certifications submitted to SAM as necessary, but at least annually, to ensure they are kept current, accurate, and complete. The representations and certifications are effective until one year from date of submission or update to SAM.

(2) A contractor that represented itself as a small business prior to award of a contract must update the representations and certifications in SAM in accordance with 52.219-28. A contractor that represented itself as other than small business before contract award and qualifies as a small business may update its representations and certifications in SAM in accordance with 52.219-28.

(c) Data in SAM is archived and is electronically retrievable. Therefore, when a prospective contractor has completed representations and certifications electronically in SAM, the contracting officer must reference the date of SAM verification in the contract file to satisfy contract file documentation requirements of 4.803(a)(11). However, if an offeror identifies changes to SAM data pursuant to the FAR provisions at 52.204-8(d) or 52.212-3(b), the contracting officer must include a copy of the changes in the contract file.

(d) The contracting officer shall incorporate the representations and certifications by reference in the contract (see 52.204-19, or for acquisitions of commercial items see 52.212-4(v)).

[FAC 2001-26, 69 FR 76341, 12/20/2004, effective 1/1/2005; FAC 2005-13, Interim rule 71 FR 57362, 9/28/2006, effective 9/28/2006; FAC 2005-18, 72 FR 36852, 7/5/2007, effective 6/30/2007; FAC 2005-19,

72 FR 46333, 8/17/2007, effective 8/17/2007; FAC-2005-21, 72 FR 63040, 63076, 11/7/2007, effective 11/7/2007; FAC 2005-26, 73 FR 33636, 6/12/2008, effective 6/12/2008; FAC 2005-30, 74 FR 2724, 1/15/2009, effective 2/17/2009; FAC 2005-31, 74 FR 11821, 3/19/2009, effective 4/20/2009; FAC 2005-36, 74 FR 40463, 8/11/2009, effective 8/11/2009; FAC 2005-55, 77 FR 187, 1/3/2012, effective 2/2/2012; FAC 2005-67, 78 FR 37676, 6/21/2013, effective 7/22/2013; FAC 2005-78, 79 FR 70341, 11/25/2014, effective 12/26/2014; FAC 2005-101, 83 FR 48691, 9/26/2018, effective 10/26/2018]

4.1202 Solicitation provision and contract clause.

(a) Insert the provision at 52.204-8, Annual Representations and Certifications, in solicitations, except for commercial item solicitations issued under FAR part 12. The contracting officer shall check the applicable provisions at 52.204-8(c)(2). When the provision at 52.204-7, System for Award Management, is included in the solicitation, do not separately include the following representations and certifications:

(1) 52.203-2, Certificate of Independent Price Determination.

(2) 52.203-11, Certification and Disclosure Regarding Payments to Influence Certain Federal Transactions.

(3) 52.203-18, Prohibition on Contracting with Entities that Require Certain Internal Confidentiality Agreements or Statements—Representation.

(4) 52.204-3, Taxpayer Identification.

(5) 52.204-5, Women-Owned Business (Other Than Small Business).

(6) 52.204-17, Ownership or Control of Offeror.

(7) 52.204–20, Predecessor of Offeror.

(8) 52.204–26, Covered Telecommunications Equipment or Services—Representation.

(9) 52.209-2, Prohibition on Contracting with Inverted Domestic Corporations—Representation.

(10) 52.209-5, Certification Regarding Responsibility Matters.

(11) 52.209-11, Representation by Corporations Regarding Delinquent Tax Liability or a Felony Conviction under any Federal Law.

(12) 52.214-14, Place of Performance—Sealed Bidding.

(13) 52.215-6, Place of Performance.

(14) 52.219-1, Small Business Program Representations (Basic & Alternate I).

(15) [Removed and Reserved]

(16) 52.219-22, Small Disadvantaged Business Status (Basic & Alternate I).

(17) 52.222-18, Certification Regarding Knowledge of Child Labor for Listed End Products.

(18) 52.222-22, Previous Contracts and Compliance Reports.

(19) 52.222-25, Affirmative Action Compliance.

(20) 52.222-38, Compliance with Veterans' Employment Reporting Requirements.

(21) 52.222-48, Exemption from Application of the Service Contract Labor Standards to Contracts for Maintenance, Calibration, or Repair of Certain Equipment-Certification.

(22) 52.222-52, Exemption from Application of the Service Contract Labor Standards to Contracts for Certain Services—Certification.

(23) 52.223-1, Biobased Product Certification.

(24) 52.223-4, Recovered Material Certification.

(25) 52.223-9, Estimate of Percentage of Recovered Material Content for EPA-Designated Items (Alternate I only).

(26) 52.223-22, Public Disclosure of Greenhouse Gas Emissions and Reduction Goals—Representation.

(27) 52.225-2, Buy American Certificate.

(28) 52.225-4, Buy American—Free Trade Agreements—Israeli Trade Act Certificate (Basic, Alternates I, II, and III).

(29) 52.225-6, Trade Agreements Certificate.

(30) 52.225-20, Prohibition on Conducting Restricted Business Operations in Sudan—Certification.

(31) 52.225-25, Prohibition on Contracting with Entities Engaging in Certain Activities or Transactions Relating to Iran—Representation and Certifications.

(32) 52.226-2, Historically Black College or University and Minority Institution Representation.

(33) 52.227-6, Royalty Information (Basic & Alternate I).

(34) 52.227-15, Representation of Limited Rights Data and Restricted Computer Software.

(b) The contracting officer shall insert the clause at 52.204-19, Incorporation by Reference of Representations and Certifications, in solicitations and contracts.

[FAC 2001-26, 69 FR 76341, 12/20/2004, effective 1/1/2005; FAC 2005-10, 71 FR 36930, 6/28/2006, effective 6/28/2006; FAC 2005-16, 72 FR 13585, 3/22/2007, effective 3/22/2007; FAC 2005-21, 72 FR 63040, 63076, 11/7/2007, effective 12/7/2007; FAC 2005-25, 73 FR 21789, 21791, 4/22/2008, effective 5/22/2008; FAC 2005-26, 73 FR 33636, 6/12/2008, effective 6/12/2008; FAC 2005-30, 74 FR 2724, 1/15/2009, effective 2/17/2009; FAC 2005-34, 74 FR 31561, 7/1/2009, effective 7/1/2009; FAC 2005-36, 74 FR 40463, 8/11/2009, effective 8/11/2009; FAC 2005-46, 75 FR 60254, 9/29/2010, effective 9/29/2010; FAC 2005-48, 75 FR 82567, 12/20/2010, effective 1/31/2011; FAC 2005-52, 76 FR 31395, 31410, 5/31/2011, effective 5/31/2011; FAC 2005-54, 76 FR 68027, 68028, 11/2/2011, effective 11/2/2011; FAC 2005-57, 77 FR 13952, 3/7/2012, effective 3/15/2012; FAC 2005-58, 77 FR 23368, 4/18/2012, effective 5/18/2012; FAC 2005-61, 77 FR 56739, 9/13/2012, effective 9/13/2012; FAC 2005-62, 77 FR 69715, 11/20/2012, effective 12/20/2012; FAC 2005-63, 77 FR 73516, 12/10/2012, effective 12/10/2012; FAC 2005-67, 78 FR 37676, 6/21/2013, effective 7/22/2013; FAC 2005-69, 78 FR 46782, 8/1/2013, effective 8/1/2013; FAC 2005-73, 79 FR 24192, 4/29/2014, effective 5/29/2014; FAC 2005-74, 79 FR 31187, 5/30/2014, effective 11/1/2014; FAC 2005-77, 79 FR 61746, 10/14/2014, effective 10/14/2014; FAC 2005-78, 79 FR 70341, 11/25/2014, effective 12/26/2014; FAC 2005-85, 80 FR 75903, 12/4/2015, effective 2/26/2016; FAC 2005-87, 81 FR 11988, 3/7/2016, effective 4/6/2016; FAC 2005-90, 81 FR 58562, 8/25/2016, effective 10/25/2016; FAC 2005-91, 81 FR 67728, 9/30/2016, effective 9/30/2016; FAC 2005-92, 81 FR 83092, 11/18/2016, effective 12/19/2016; FAC 2005-93, 81 FR 91636, 12/16/2016, effective 12/16/2016; FAC 2005-95, 82 FR 4717, 1/13/2017, effective 1/19/2017; FAC 2005-96, 82 FR 51773, 11/8/2017, effective 11/6/2017; FAC 2005-101, 83 FR 48691, 9/26/2018, effective 10/26/2018; FAC 2020-03, 84 FR 68314, 12/13/2019, effective 12/13/2019]

SUBPART 4.13—PERSONAL IDENTITY VERIFICATION

4.1300 Scope of subpart.

This subpart provides policy and procedures associated with Personal Identity Verification as required by—

(a) Federal Information Processing Standards Publication (FIPS PUB) Number 201, "Personal Identity Verification of Federal Employees and Contractors"; and

(b) Office of Management and Budget (OMB) Guidance M-05-24, dated August 5, 2005, "Implementation of Homeland Security Presidential Directive (HSPD) 12—Policy for a Common Identification Standard for Federal Employees and Contractors."

[FAC 2005-07, 71 FR 208, 1/3/2006, effective 1/3/2006; FAC 2005-14, 71 FR 67771, 11/22/2006, effective 11/22/2006; FAC 2005-19, 72 FR 46333, 8/17/2007, effective 9/17/2007]

4.1301 Policy.

(a) Agencies must follow FIPS PUB Number 201 and the associated OMB implementation guidance for personal identity verification for all affected contractor and subcontractor personnel when contract performance requires contractors to have routine physical access to a Federally-controlled facility and/or routine access to a Federally-controlled information system.

(b) Agencies must include their implementation of FIPS PUB 201 and Guidance M-05-24 in solicitations and contracts that require the contractor to have routine physical access to a Federally-controlled facility and/or routine access to a Federally-controlled information system.

(c) Agencies must designate an official responsible for verifying contractor employee personal identity.

(d) (1) Agency procedures for the return of Personal Identity Verification (PIV) products shall ensure that Government contractors account for all forms of Government-provided identification issued to Government contractor employees under a contract, *i.e.*, the PIV cards or other similar badges, and shall ensure that contractors return such identification to the issuing agency as soon as any of the following occurs, unless otherwise determined by the agency:

(i) When no longer needed for contract performance.

(ii) Upon completion of a contractor employee's employment.

(iii) Upon contract completion or termination.

(2) The contracting officer may delay final payment under a contract if the contractor fails to comply with these requirements.

[FAC 2005-07, 71 FR 208, 1/3/2006, effective 1/3/2006; FAC 2005-14, 71 FR 67771, 11/22/2006, effective 11/22/2006; FAC 2005-19, 72 FR 46333, 8/17/2007, effective 9/17/2007; FAC 2005-48, 75 FR 82575, 12/30/2010, effective 1/31/2011]

4.1302 Acquisition of approved products and services for personal identity verification.

(a) In order to comply with FIPS PUB 201, agencies must purchase only approved personal identity verification products and services.

(b) Agencies may acquire the approved products and services from the GSA, Federal Supply Schedule 70, Special Item Number (SIN) 132-62, HSPD-12 Product and Service Components, in accordance with ordering procedures outlined in FAR Subpart 8.4.

(c) When acquiring personal identity verification products and services not using the process in paragraph (b) of this section, agencies must ensure that the applicable products and services are approved as compliant with FIPS PUB 201 including—

(1) Certifying the products and services procured meet all applicable Federal standards and requirements;

(2) Ensuring interoperability and conformance to applicable Federal standards for the lifecycle of the components; and

(3) Maintaining a written plan for ensuring ongoing conformance to applicable Federal standards for the lifecycle of the components.

(d) For more information on personal identity verification products and services see *http://www.idmanagement.gov*.

[FAC 2005-19, 72 FR 46333, 8/17/2007, effective 9/17/2007]

4.1303 Contract clause.

The contracting officer shall insert the clause at 52.204-9, Personal Identity Verification of Contractor Personnel, in solicitations and contracts when contract performance requires contractors to have routine physical access to a Federally-controlled facility and/or routine access to a Federally-controlled information system. The clause shall not be used when contractors require only intermittent access to Federally-controlled facilities.

[FAC 2005-19, 72 FR 46333, 8/17/2007, effective 9/17/2007]

SUBPART 4.14—REPORTING EXECUTIVE COMPENSATION AND FIRST-TIER SUBCONTRACT AWARDS

4.1400 Scope of subpart.

This subpart implements section 2 of the Federal Funding Accountability and Transparency Act of 2006 (Pub. L. 109- 282), as amended by section 6202 of the Government Funding Transparency Act of 2008 (Pub. L. 110-252), which requires contractors to report subcontract award data and the total compensation of the five most highly compensated executives of the contractor and subcontractor. The public may view first-tier subcontract award data at *https://www.usaspending.gov*.

[FAC 2005-20, 72 FR 51306, 9/6/2007, effective 9/6/2007; FAC 2005-44, 75 FR 39414, 7/8/2010, effective 7/8/2010; FAC 2005-60, 77 FR 44047, 7/26/2012, effective 8/27/2012; FAC 2005-91, 81 FR 67781, 9/30/2016, effective 9/30/2016]

4.1401 Applicability.

(a) This subpart applies to all contracts with a value of $30,000 or more. Nothing in this subpart requires the disclosure of classified information.

(b) Reporting of subcontract information will be limited to the first-tier subcontractor.

[FAC 2005-20, 72 FR 51306, 9/6/2007, effective 9/6/2007; FAC 2005-44, 75 FR 39414, 7/8/2010, effective 7/8/2010; FAC 2005-60, 77 FR 44047, 7/26/2012, effective 8/27/2012; FAC 2005-83, 80 FR 38293, 7/2/2015, effective 10/1/2015]

4.1402 Procedures.

(a) Agencies shall ensure that contractors comply with the reporting requirements of 52.204-10, Reporting Executive Compensation and First-Tier Subcontract Awards. Agencies shall review contractor reports on a quarterly basis to ensure the information is consistent with contract information. The agency is not required to address data for which the agency would not normally have supporting information, such as the compensation information required of contractors and first-tier subcontractors. However, the agency shall inform the contractor of any inconsistencies with the contract information and require that the contractor correct the report, or provide a reasonable explanation as to why it believes the information is correct. Agencies may review the reports at *http://www.fsrs.gov*.

(b) When contracting officers report the contract action to the Federal Procurement Data System (FPDS) in accordance with FAR subpart 4.6, certain data will then prepopulate from FPDS, to assist contractors in completing and submitting their reports. If data originating from FPDS is found by the contractor to be in error when the contractor completes the subcontract report, the contractor should notify the Government contracting officer, who is responsible for correcting the data in FPDS. Contracts reported using the generic entity identifier allowed at FAR 4.605(c)(2) will interfere with the contractor's ability to comply with this reporting requirement, because the data will not pre-populate from FPDS.

(c) If the contractor fails to comply with the reporting requirements, the contracting officer shall exercise appropriate contractual remedies. In addition, the contracting officer shall make the contractor's failure to comply with the reporting requirements a part of the contractor's performance information under Subpart 42.15.

(d) There is a reporting exception in 52.204-10(g) for contractors and subcontractors who had gross income in the previous tax year under $300,000.

[FAC 2005-20, 72 FR 51306, 9/6/2007, effective 9/6/2007; FAC 2005-44, 75 FR 39414, 7/8/2010, effective 7/8/2010; FAC 2005-60, 77 FR 44047, 7/26/2012, effective 8/27/2012; FAC 2005-62, 77 FR 69715, 11/20/2012, effective 12/20/2012; FAC 2005-91, 81 FR 67736, 9/30/2016, effective 10/31/2016]

4.1403 Contract clause.

(a) Except as provided in paragraph (b) of this section, the contracting officer shall insert the clause at 52.204-10, Reporting Executive Compensation and First-Tier Subcontract Awards, in all solicitations and contracts of $30,000 or more.

(b) The clause is not prescribed for contracts that are not required to be reported in the Federal Procurement Data System (FPDS) (see subpart 4.6).

[FAC 2005-20, 72 FR 51306, 9/6/2007, effective 9/6/2007; FAC 2005-44, 75 FR 39414, 7/8/2010, effective 7/8/2010; FAC 2005-60, 77 FR 44047, 7/26/2012, effective 8/27/2012; FAC 2005-83, 80 FR 38293, 7/2/2015, effective 10/1/2015]

SUBPART 4.15—[RESERVED]

4.1500 [Removed and Reserved]

[FAC 2005-32, 74 FR 14639, 3/31/2009, effective 3/31/2009; FAC 2005-74, 79 FR 31193, 5/30/2014, effective 5/30/2014]

4.1501 [Removed and Reserved]

[FAC 2005-32, 74 FR 14639, 3/31/2009, effective 3/31/2009; FAC 2005-74, 79 FR 31193, 5/30/2014, effective 5/30/2014]

4.1502 [Removed and Reserved]

[FAC 2005-32, 74 FR 14639, 3/31/2009, effective 3/31/2009; FAC 2005-43, 75 FR 38684, 7/2/2010, effective 7/2/2010; FAC 2005-74, 79 FR 31193, 5/30/2014, effective 5/30/2014]

SUBPART 4.16—UNIQUE PROCUREMENT INSTRUMENT IDENTIFIERS

4.1600 Scope of subpart.

This subpart prescribes policies and procedures for assigning unique Procurement Instrument Identifiers (PIID) for each solicitation, contract, agreement, or order and related procurement instrument.

[FAC 2005-53, 76 FR 39234, 7/5/2011, effective 8/4/2011]

4.1601 Policy.

(a) *Establishment of a Procurement Instrument Identifier (PIID).* Agencies shall have in place a process that ensures that each PIID used to identify a solicitation or contract action is unique Governmentwide, and will remain so for at least 20 years from the date of contract award. The PIID shall be used to identify all solicitation and contract actions. The PIID shall also be used to identify solicitation and contract actions in designated support and reporting systems (*e.g.,* Federal Procurement Data System, System for Award Management), in accordance with regulations, applicable authorities, and agency policies and procedures.)

(b) *Transition of PIID numbering.* No later than October 1, 2017, agencies shall comply with paragraph (a) of this section and use the requirements in 4.1602 and 4.1603 for all new solicitations and contract awards. Until an agency's transition is complete, it shall maintain its 2013 PIID format that is on record with the General Services Administration's Integrated Award Environment Program Office (which maintains a registry of the agency unique identifier scheme). The 2013 PIID format consisted of alpha characters in the first positions to indicate the agency, followed by alpha-numeric characters; the 2017 format instead has the AAC in the beginning 6 positions.

(c) *Change in the Procurement Instrument Identifier after its assignment.* (1) Agencies shall not change the PIID unless one of the following two circumstances apply:

(i) The PIID serial numbering system is exhausted. In this instance, the contracting officer may assign a new PIID by issuing a contract modification.

(ii) Continued use of a PIID is administratively burdensome (*e.g.,* for implementations of new agency contract writing systems). In this instance, the contracting officer may assign a new PIID by issuing a contract modification.

(2) The modification shall clearly identify both the original and the newly assigned PIID. Issuance of a new PIID is an administrative change (see 43.101).

[FAC 2005-53, 76 FR 39234, 7/5/2011, effective 8/4/2011; FAC 2005-76, 79 FR 43590, 7/25/2014, effective 7/25/2014; FAC 2005-77, 79 FR 61739, 10/14/2014, effective 11/13/2014]

4.1602 Identifying the PIID and supplementary PIID.

(a) *Identifying the PIID in solicitation and contract award documentation (including forms and electronic generated formats).* Agencies shall include all PIIDs for all related procurement actions as identified in paragraphs (a)(1) through (5) of this section.

(1) *Solicitation.* Identify the PIID for all solicitations. For amendments to solicitations, identify a supplementary PIID, in conjunction with the PIID for the solicitation.

(2) *Contracts and purchase orders.* Identify the PIID for contracts and purchase orders.

(3) *Delivery and task orders.* For delivery and task orders placed by an agency under a contract (*e.g.,* indefinite delivery indefinite quantity (IDIQ) contracts, multi-agency contracts (MAC), Governmentwide acquisition contracts (GWACs), or Multiple Award Schedule (MAS) contracts), identify the PIID for the delivery and task order and the PIID for the contract.

(4) *Blanket purchase agreements and basic ordering agreements.* Identify the PIID for blanket purchase agreements issued in accordance with 13.303, and for basic agreements and basic ordering agreements issued in accordance with subpart 16.7. For blanket purchase agreements issued in accordance with subpart 8.4 under a MAS contract, identify the PIID for the blanket purchase agreement and the PIID for the MAS contract.

(i) *Orders.* For orders against basic ordering agreements or blanket purchase agreements issued in accordance with 13.303, identify the PIID for the order and the PIID for the blanket purchase agreement or basic ordering agreement.

(ii) *Orders under subpart 8.4.* For orders against a blanket purchase agreement established under a MAS contract, identify the PIID for the order, the PIID for the blanket purchase agreement, and the PIID for the MAS contract.

(5) *Modifications.* For modifications to actions described in paragraphs (a)(2) through (4) of this section, and in accordance with agency procedures, identify a supplementary PIID for the modification in conjunction with the PIID for the contract, order, or agreement being modified.

(b) *Placement of the PIID on forms.* When the form (including electronic generated format) does not provide spaces or fields for the PIID or supplementary PIID required in paragraph (a) of this section, identify the PIID in accordance with agency procedures.

(c) *Additional agency specific identification information.* If agency procedures require additional identification information in solicitations, contracts, or other related procurement instruments for administrative purposes, separate and clearly identify the additional information from the PIID.

[FAC 2005-53, 76 FR 39234, 7/5/2011, effective 8/4/2011; FAC 2005-77, 79 FR 61739, 10/14/2014, effective 11/13/2014]

4.1603 Procedures.

(a) *Elements of a PIID.* The PIID consists of a combination of thirteen to seventeen alpha and/or numeric characters sequenced to convey certain information. Do not use special characters (such as hyphens, dashes, or spaces).

(1) *Positions 1 through 6.* The first six positions identify the department/agency and office issuing the instrument. Use the AAC assigned to the issuing office for positions 1 through 6. Civilian agency points of contact for obtaining an AAC are on the AAC Contact list maintained by the General Services Administration and can be found at *http://www.gsa.gov/graphics/fas/Civilian contacts.pdf.* For Department of Defense (DoD) inquiries, contact the service/agency Central Service Point or DoDAAC Monitor, or if unknown, email *DODAADHQ@DLA.MIL* for assistance.

(2) *Positions 7 through 8.* The seventh and eighth positions are the last two digits of the fiscal year in which the procurement instrument is issued or awarded. This is the date the action is signed, not the effective date if the effective date is different.

(3) *Position 9.* Indicate the type of instrument by entering one of the following upper case letters in position nine. Departments and independent agencies may assign those letters identified for department use below in accordance with their agency policy; however, any use must be applied to the entire department or agency.

Instrument	Letter designation
(i) Blanket purchase agreements	A
(ii) Invitations for bids	B

Instrument	Letter designation
(iii) Contracts of all types except indefinite-delivery contracts (see subpart 16.5)	C
(iv) Indefinite-delivery contracts (including Federal Supply Schedules, Governmentwide acquisition contracts (GWACs), and multi-agency contracts)	D
(v) Reserved for future Federal Governmentwide use	E
(vi) Task orders, delivery orders or calls under— • Indefinite-delivery contracts (including Federal Supply Schedules, Governmentwide acquisition contracts (GWACs), and multi-agency contracts); • Blanket purchase agreements; or • Basic ordering agreements.	F
(vii) Basic ordering agreements	G
(viii) Agreements, including basic agreements and loan agreements, but excluding blanket purchase agreements, basic ordering agreements, and leases. Do not use this code for contracts or agreements with provisions for orders or calls	H
(ix) Do not use this letter	I
(x) Reserved for future Federal Governmentwide use	J
(xi) Reserved for departmental or agency use	K
(xii) Lease agreements	L
(xiii) Reserved for departmental or agency use	M
(xiv) Reserved for departmental or agency use	N
(xv) Do not use this letter	O
(xvi) Purchase orders (assign V if numbering capacity of P is exhausted during a fiscal year)	P
(xvii) Requests for quotations (assign U if numbering capacity of Q is exhausted during a fiscal year)	Q
(xviii) Requests for proposals	R
(xix) Reserved for departmental or agency use	S
(xx) Reserved for departmental or agency use	T
(xxi) See Q, requests for quotations	U
(xxii) See P, purchase orders	V
(xxiii) Reserved for future Federal Governmentwide use	W
(xxiv) Reserved for future Federal Governmentwide use	X
(xxv) Imprest fund	Y
(xxvi) Reserved for future Federal Governmentwide use	Z

(4) *Positions 10 through 17.* Enter the number assigned by the issuing agency in these positions. Agencies may choose a minimum of four characters up to a maximum of eight characters to be used, but the same number of characters must be used agency-wide. If a number less than the maximum is used, do not use leading or trailing zeroes to make it equal the maximum in any system or data transmission. A separate series of numbers may be used for any type of instrument listed in paragraph (a)(3) of this section. An agency may reserve blocks of numbers or

alpha-numeric numbers for use by its various components.

Position	Contents
1-6	Identification of department/agency office (AAC)
7-8	Last two digits of the fiscal year in which the procurement instrument is issued or awarded
9	Type of instrument
10-13	Four position agency assigned number

(5) *Illustration of PIID*. The following illustrates a properly configured PIID using four characters in the final positions:

N00062 17 C 0001

(b) *Elements of a supplementary PIID*. Use the supplementary PIID to identify amendments to solicitations and modifications to contracts, orders, and agreements. The supplementary PIID is reported as a separate data element used in conjunction with, but not appended to, the PIID.

(1) *Amendments to solicitations*. Number amendments to solicitations sequentially using a four position numeric serial number in addition to the 13-17 character PIID beginning with 0001.

(2) *Modifications to contracts, orders, and agreements*. Number modifications to contracts, orders, and agreements using a six position alpha or numeric, or a combination thereof, in addition to the 13-17 character PIID. For example, a modification could be numbered P00001. This would be in addition to the 13-17 character PIID illustrated in paragraph (a)(5) of this section.

(i) *Position 1*. Identify the office issuing the modification. The letter P shall be designated for modifications issued by the procuring contracting office. The letter A shall be used for modifications issued by the contract administration office (if other than the procuring contracting office).

(ii) *Positions 2 through 6*. These positions may be alpha, numeric, or a combination thereof, in accordance with agency procedures.

(iii) Each office authorized to issue modifications shall assign the supplementary identification numbers in sequence (unless provided otherwise in agency procedures). Do not assign the numbers until it has been determined that a modification is to be issued.

[FAC 2005-77, 79 FR 61739, 10/14/2014, effective 11/13/2014; FAC 2005-100, 83 FR 42571, 8/22/2018, effective 8/22/2018]

SUBPART 4.17—SERVICE CONTRACTS INVENTORY

4.1700 Scope of subpart.

This subpart implements section 743(a) of Division C of the Consolidated Appropriations Act, 2010 (Pub. L. 111-117), which requires agencies to report annually to the Office of Management and Budget (OMB) on activities performed by service contractors. Section 743(a) applies to executive agencies, other than the Department of Defense (DoD), covered by the Federal Activities Inventory Reform Act (Pub. L. 105-270)

(FAIR Act). The information reported in the inventory will be publicly accessible.

[FAC 2005-72, 78 FR 80369, 12/31/2013, effective 1/30/2014]

4.1701 Definitions.

As used in this subpart—

FAIR Act agencies means the agencies required under the FAIR Act to submit inventories annually of the activities performed by Government personnel.

First-tier subcontract means a subcontract awarded directly by the contractor for the purpose of acquiring supplies or services (including construction) for performance of a prime contract. It does not include the contractor's supplier agreements with vendors, such as long-term arrangements for materials or supplies that benefit multiple contracts and/or the costs of which are normally applied to a contractor's general and administrative expenses or indirect costs.

[FAC 2005-72, 78 FR 80369, 12/31/2013, effective 1/30/2014]

4.1702 Applicability.

(a) This subpart applies to—

(1) All FAIR Act agencies, except DoD as specified in 4.1705;

(2) Solicitations, contracts, and orders for services (including construction) that meet or exceed the thresholds at 4.1703; and

(3) Contractors and first-tier subcontractors.

(b) Procedures for compiling and submitting agency service contract inventories are governed by section 743(a)(3) of Division C of Pub. L. 111-117 and Office of Federal Procurement Policy (OFPP) guidance. The guidance is available at the following Web site: ***https://www.whitehouse.gov/sites/whitehouse.gov/files/omb/procurement/memo/service-contract-inventory-guidance.pdf.***

(c) This subpart addresses requirements for obtaining information from, and reporting by, agency service contractors.

[FAC 2005-72, 78 FR 80369, 12/31/2013, effective 1/30/2014; FAC 2005-100, 83 FR 42571, 8/22/2018, effective 8/22/2018]

4.1703 Reporting requirements.

(a) *Thresholds.* (1) Except as exempted by OFPP guidance, service contractor reporting shall be required for contracts and first-tier subcontracts for services based on type of contract and estimated total value. For indefinite-delivery contracts, reporting shall be determined based on the type and estimated total value of the each order under the contract. Indefinite-delivery contracts include, but are not limited to, contracts such as indefinite-delivery indefinite-quantity (IDIQ) contracts, Federal Supply Schedule contracts (FSSs), Governmentwide acquisition contracts (GWACs), and multi-agency contracts.

(2) Reporting is required according to the following thresholds:

(i) All cost-reimbursement, time-and-materials, and labor-hour service contracts and orders with an estimated total value above the simplified acquisition threshold.

(ii) All fixed-price service contracts awarded and orders issued according to the following thresholds:

(A) Awarded or issued in Fiscal Year 2014, with an estimated total value of $2.5 million or greater.

(B) Awarded or issued in Fiscal Year 2015, with an estimated total value of $1 million or greater.

(C) Awarded or issued in Fiscal Year 2016, and subsequent years, with an estimated total value of $500,000 or greater.

(3) Reporting is required for all first-tier subcontracts for services as prescribed in paragraphs (a)(2)(i) and (ii) of this section.

(b) *Agency reporting responsibilities.* (1) Agencies shall ensure that contractors comply with the reporting requirements of 52.204-14, Service Contract Reporting Requirements and 52.204-15, Service Contract Reporting Requirements for Indefinite-Delivery Contracts. Agencies shall review contractor reported information for reasonableness and consistency with available contract information. The agency is not required to address data for which the agency would not normally have supporting information. In the event the agency believes that revisions to the contractor reported information are warranted, the agency shall notify the contractor no later than November 15. By November 30, the contractor shall revise the report, or document its rationale for the agency. Authorized agency officials may review the reports at *www.sam.gov.*

(2) Agencies are required to compile annually an inventory of service contracts performed for, or on behalf of, the agency during the prior fiscal year in order to determine the extent of the agency's reliance on service contractors. Agencies shall submit a service contract inventory to OMB by January 15 annually. Then, each agency must post the inventory on its Web site and publish a Federal Register Notice of Availability by February 15 annually.

(3) Most of the required information is already collected in the Federal Procurement Data System (FPDS). Information not collected in FPDS will be provided by the contractor, as specified in 52.204-14, Service Contract Reporting Requirements and 52.204-15, Service Contract Reporting Requirements for Indefinite-Delivery Contracts.

[FAC 2005-72, 78 FR 80369, 12/31/2013, effective 1/30/2014; FAC 2005-87, 81 FR 11988, 3/7/2016, effective 4/6/2016; FAC 2005-87, 81 FR 11992, 3/7/2016, effective 3/7/2016]

4.1704 Contracting officer responsibilities.

(a) For other than indefinite-delivery contracts, the contracting officer shall ensure that 52.204-14, Service Reporting Requirement, is included in solicitations, contracts, and orders as prescribed at 4.1705. For indefinite-delivery contracts, the contracting officer who awarded the contract shall ensure that 52.204-15, Service Contract Reporting Requirements for Indefinite-Delivery Contracts, is included in solicitations and contracts as prescribed at 4.1705. The contracting officer at the order level shall verify the clause's inclusion in the contract.

(b) If the contractor fails to submit a report in a timely manner, the contracting officer shall exercise appropriate contractual remedies. In addition, the contracting officer shall make the contractor's failure to comply with the reporting requirements a part of the contractor's performance information under subpart 42.15.

[FAC 2005-72, 78 FR 80369, 12/31/2013, effective 1/30/2014]

4.1705 Contract clauses.

(a) The contracting officer shall insert the clause at 52.204-14, Service Contract Reporting Requirements, in solicitations and contracts for services (including construction) that meet or exceed the thresholds at 4.1703, except for indefinite-delivery contracts. This clause is not required for actions entirely funded by DoD, contracts awarded with a generic entity identifier, or in classified solicitations, contracts, or orders.

(b) The contracting officer shall insert the clause at 52.204-15, Service Contract Reporting Requirements for Indefinite-Delivery Contracts, in solicitations and indefinite-delivery contracts for services (including construction) where one or more orders issued thereunder are expected to each meet or exceed the thresholds at 4.1703. This clause is not required for actions entirely funded by DoD, contracts awarded with a generic entity identifier, or in classified solicitations, contracts, or orders.

[FAC 2005-72, 78 FR 80369, 12/31/2013, effective 1/30/2014; FAC 2005-91, 81 FR 67736, 9/30/2016, effective 10/31/2016]

SUBPART 4.18—COMMERCIAL AND GOVERNMENT ENTITY CODE

4.1800 Scope of subpart.

(a) This subpart prescribes policies and procedures for identification of commercial and government entities. The Commercial and Government Entity (CAGE) code system may be used, among other things, to—

(1) Exchange data with another contracting activity, including contract administration activities and contract payment activities;

(2) Exchange data with another system that requires the unique identification of a contractor entity; or

(3) Identify when offerors are owned or controlled by another entity.

(b) For information on the unique entity identifier, which is a different identifier, see 4.605 and the provisions at 52.204-6, Unique Entity Identifier, and 52.204-7, System for Award Management.

[FAC 2005-74, 79 FR 31187, 5/30/2014, effective 11/1/2014; FAC 2005-91, 81 FR 67736, 9/30/2016, effective 10/31/2016]

4.1801 Definitions.

As used in this part—

Commercial and Government Entity (CAGE) code means-

(1) An identifier assigned to entities located in the United States or its outlying areas by the Defense Logistics Agency (DLA) Commercial and Government Entity (CAGE) Branch to identify a commercial or government entity; or

(2) An identifier assigned by a member of the North Atlantic Treaty Organization (NATO) or by the NATO Support and Procurement Agency (NSPA) to entities located outside the United States and its outlying areas that the DLA Commercial and Government Entity (CAGE) Branch records and maintains in the CAGE master file. This type of code is known as a NATO CAGE (NCAGE) code.

Highest-level owner means the entity that owns or controls an immediate owner of the offeror, or that owns or controls one or more entities that control an immediate owner of the offeror. No entity owns or exercises control of the highest level owner.

Immediate owner means an entity, other than the offeror, that has direct control of the offeror. Indicators of control include, but are not limited to, one or more of the following: ownership or interlocking management, identity of interests among family members, shared facilities and equipment, and the common use of employees.

[FAC 2005-74, 79 FR 31187, 5/30/2014, effective 11/1/2014; FAC 2005-89, 81 FR 45866, 7/14/2016, effective 7/14/2016; FAC 2019-02, 84 FR 19839, 5/6/2019, effective 5/6/2019]

4.1802 Policy.

(a) *Commercial and Government Entity code.* (1) Offerors shall provide the contracting officer the CAGE code assigned to that offeror's location prior to the award of a contract action above the micro-purchase threshold, when there is a requirement to be registered in the System for Award Management (SAM) or a requirement to have a unique entity identifier in the solicitation.

(2) The contracting officer shall include the contractor's CAGE code in the contract and in any electronic transmissions of the contract data to other systems when it is provided in accordance with paragraph (a)(1) of this section.

(b) *Ownership or control of offeror.* Offerors, if owned or controlled by another entity, shall provide the contracting officer with the CAGE code and legal name of that entity prior to the award of a contract action above the micro-purchase threshold, when there is a requirement to be registered in SAM or a requirement to have a unique entity identifier in the solicitation.

[FAC 2005-74, 79 FR 31187, 5/30/2014, effective 11/1/2014; FAC 2005-91, 81 FR 67736, 9/30/2016, effective 10/31/2016]

4.1803 Verifying CAGE codes prior to award.

(a) Contracting officers shall verify the offeror's CAGE code by reviewing the entity's registration in the System for Award Management (SAM). Active registrations in SAM have had the associated CAGE codes verified.

(b) For entities not required to be registered in SAM, the contracting officer shall validate the CAGE code using the CAGE code search feature at ***https://cage.dla.mil.***

[FAC 2005-74, 79 FR 31187, 5/30/2014, effective 11/1/2014; FAC 2005-89, 81 FR 45866, 7/14/2016, effective 7/14/2016]

4.1804 Solicitation provisions and contract clause.

(a) Insert the provision at 52.204-16, Commercial and Government Entity Code Reporting, in all solicitations that include—

(1) 52.204-6, Unique Entity Identifier; or

(2) 52.204-7, System for Award Management.

(b) Insert the provision at 52.204-17, Ownership or Control of Offeror, in all solicitations that include the provision at 52.204-16, Commercial and Government Entity Code Reporting.

(c) Insert the clause at 52.204-18, Commercial and Government Entity Code Maintenance, in all solicitations and contracts when the solicitation contains the provision at 52.204-16, Commercial and Government Entity Code Reporting.

(d) Insert the provision at 52.204–20, Predecessor of Offeror, in all solicitations that include the provision at 52.204–16, Commercial and Government Entity Code Reporting.

[FAC 2005-74, 79 FR 31187, 5/30/2014, effective 11/1/2014; FAC 2005-87, 81 FR 11988, 3/7/2016, effective 4/6/2016; FAC 2005-91, 81 FR 67736, 9/30/2016, effective 10/31/2016]

SUBPART 4.19—BASIC SAFEGUARDING OF COVERED CONTRACTOR INFORMATION SYSTEMS

4.1901 Definitions.

As used in this subpart—

Covered contractor information system means an information system that is owned or operated by a contractor that processes, stores, or transmits Federal contract information.

Federal contract information means information, not intended for public release, that is provided by or generated for the Government under a contract to develop or deliver a product or service to the Government, but not including information provided by the Government to the public (such as that on public Web sites) or simple transactional information, such as that necessary to process payments.

Information means any communication or representation of knowledge such as facts, data, or opinions in any medium or form, including textual, numerical, graphic, cartographic, narrative, or audiovisual (Committee on National Security Systems Instruction (CNSSI) 4009).

Information system means a discrete set of information resources organized for the collection, processing, maintenance, use, sharing, dissemination, or disposition of information (44 U.S.C. 3502).

Safeguarding means measures or controls that are prescribed to protect information systems.

[FAC 2005-88, 81 FR 30439, 5/16/2016, effective 6/15/2016]

4.1902 Applicability.

This subpart applies to all acquisitions, including acquisitions of commercial items other than commercially available off-the-shelf items, when a contractor's information system may contain Federal contract information.

[FAC 2005-88, 81 FR 30439, 5/16/2016, effective 6/15/2016]

4.1903 Contract clause.

The contracting officer shall insert the clause at 52.204-21, Basic Safeguarding of Covered Contractor Information Systems, in solicitations and contracts when the contractor or a subcontractor at any tier may have Federal contract information residing in or transiting through its information system.

[FAC 2005-88, 81 FR 30439, 5/16/2016, effective 6/15/2016]

SUBPART 4.20—PROHIBITION ON CONTRACTING FOR HARDWARE, SOFTWARE, AND SERVICES DEVELOPED OR PROVIDED BY KASPERSKY LAB

4.2001 Definitions.

As used in this subpart—

Covered article means any hardware, software, or service that—

(1) Is developed or provided by a covered entity;

(2) Includes any hardware, software, or service developed or provided in whole or in part by a covered entity; or

(3) Contains components using any hardware or software developed in whole or in part by a covered entity.

Covered entity means—

(1) Kaspersky Lab;

(2) Any successor entity to Kaspersky Lab;

(3) Any entity that controls, is controlled by, or is under common control with Kaspersky Lab; or

(4) Any entity of which Kaspersky Lab has a majority ownership.

[FAC 2005-99, 83 FR 28141, 6/15/2018, effective 7/16/2018; FAC 2019-06, 84 FR 47861, 9/10/2019, effective 9/10/2019]

4.2002 Prohibition.

Section 1634 of Division A of the National Defense Authorization Act for Fiscal Year 2018 (Pub. L. 115-91) prohibits Government use on or after October 1, 2018, of any hardware, software, or services developed or provided, in whole or in part, by a covered entity. Contractors are prohibited from—

(a) Providing any covered article that the Government will use on or after October 1, 2018; and

(b) Using any covered article on or after October 1, 2018, in the development of data or deliverables first produced in the performance of the contract.

[FAC 2005-99, 83 FR 28141, 6/15/2018, effective 7/16/2018; FAC 2019-06, 84 FR 47861, 9/10/2019, effective 9/10/2019]

4.2003 Notification.

When a contractor provides notification pursuant to 52.204-23, follow agency procedures.

[FAC 2005-99, 83 FR 28141, 6/15/2018, effective 7/16/2018; FAC 2019-06, 84 FR 47861, 9/10/2019, effective 9/10/2019]

4.2004 Contract clause.

The contracting officer shall insert the clause at 52.204-23, Prohibition on Contracting for Hardware, Software, and Services Developed or Provided by Kaspersky Lab and Other Covered Entities, in all solicitations and contracts.

[FAC 2005-99, 83 FR 28141, 6/15/2018, effective 7/16/2018; FAC 2019-06, 84 FR 47861, 9/10/2019, effective 9/10/2019]

SUBPART 4.21—PROHIBITION ON CONTRACTING FOR CERTAIN TELECOMMUNICATIONS AND VIDEO SURVEILLANCE SERVICES OR EQUIPMENT

4.2100 Scope of subpart.

This subpart implements paragraph (a) (1) (A) of section 889 of the John S. McCain National Defense Authorization Act for Fiscal Year 2019 (Pub. L. 115-232).

[FAC 2019-05, 84 FR 40216, 8/13/2019, effective 8/13/2019]

4.2101 Definitions.

As used in this subpart—

Covered foreign country means The People's Republic of China.

Covered telecommunications equipment or services means—

(1) Telecommunications equipment produced by Huawei Technologies Company or ZTE Corporation, (or any subsidiary or affiliate of such entities);

(2) For the purpose of public safety, security of Government facilities, physical security surveillance of critical infrastructure, and other national security purposes, video surveillance and telecommunications equipment produced by Hytera Communications Corporation, Hangzhou Hikvision Digital Technology Company, or Dahua Technology Company (or any subsidiary or affiliate of such entities);

(3) Telecommunications or video surveillance services provided by such entities or using such equipment; or

(4) Telecommunications or video surveillance equipment or services produced or provided by an entity that the Secretary of Defense, in consultation with the Director of National Intelligence or the Director of the Federal Bureau of Investigation, reasonably believes to be an entity owned or controlled by, or otherwise connected to, the government of a covered foreign country.

Critical technology means—

(1) Defense articles or defense services included on the United States Munitions List set forth in the International Traffic in Arms

Regulations under subchapter M of chapter I of title 22, Code of Federal Regulations;

(2) Items included on the Commerce Control List set forth in Supplement No. 1 to part 774 of the Export Administration Regulations under subchapter C of chapter VII of title 15, Code of Federal Regulations, and controlled—

(i) Pursuant to multilateral regimes, including for reasons relating to national security, chemical and biological weapons proliferation, nuclear nonproliferation, or missile technology; or

(ii) For reasons relating to regional stability or surreptitious listening;

(3) Specially designed and prepared nuclear equipment, parts and components, materials, software, and technology covered by part 810 of title 10, Code of Federal Regulations (relating to assistance to foreign atomic energy activities);

(4) Nuclear facilities, equipment, and material covered by part 110 of title 10, Code of Federal Regulations (relating to export and import of nuclear equipment and material);

(5) Select agents and toxins covered by part 331 of title 7, Code of Federal Regulations, part 121 of title 9 of such Code, or part 73 of title 42 of such Code; or

(6) Emerging and foundational technologies controlled pursuant to section 1758 of the Export Control Reform Act of 2018 (50 U.S.C. 4817).

Substantial or essential component means any component necessary for the proper function or performance of a piece of equipment, system, or service.

[FAC 2019-05, 84 FR 40216, 8/13/2019, effective 8/13/2019]

4.2102 Prohibition.

(a) *Prohibited equipment, systems, or services.* On or after August 13, 2019, agencies are prohibited from procuring or obtaining, or extending or renewing a contract to procure or obtain, any equipment, system, or service that uses covered telecommunications equipment or services as a substantial or essential component of any system, or as critical technology as part of any system, unless an exception at paragraph (b) of this section applies or the covered telecommunications equipment or services are covered by a waiver described in 4.2104.

(b) *Exceptions.* This subpart does not prohibit agencies from procuring or contractors from providing—

(1) A service that connects to the facilities of a third-party, such as backhaul, roaming, or interconnection arrangements; or

(2) Telecommunications equipment that cannot route or redirect user data traffic or permit visibility into any user data or packets that such equipment transmits or otherwise handles.

(c) *Contracting Officers.* Contracting officers shall not procure or obtain, or extend or renew a contract (*e.g.*, exercise an option) to procure or obtain, any equipment, system, or service that uses covered telecommunications equipment or services as a substantial or essential component of any system, or as critical technology as part of any system, unless an exception at paragraph (b) of this section applies or the covered telecommunications equipment or services are covered by a waiver described in 4.2104.

(d) *Recording prohibitions in the System for Award Management (SAM).*

(1) Prohibitions on purchases of products or services produced or provided by entities identified in paragraphs (1) and (2) of the definition of "covered telecommunications equipment or services" (including known subsidiaries or affiliates) at 4.2101 will be recorded in SAM (see 9.404).

(2) Prohibitions on purchases of products or services produced or provided by entities identified pursuant to paragraph (4) of the definition of "covered telecommunications equipment or services" (including known subsidiaries or affiliates) at 4.2101 are recorded by the Department of Defense in SAM (see 9.404).

FAC 2019-05, 84 FR 40216, 8/13/2019, effective 8/13/2019; FAC 2020-03, 84 FR 68314, 12/13/2019, effective 12/13/2019]

4.2103 Procedures.

(a) *Representations.*

(1) (i) If the offeror selects "does not" in response to the provision at 52.204–26 or

52.212–3(v), the contracting officer may rely on the representation, unless the contracting officer has reason to question the representation. If the contracting officer has a reason to question the representation, the contracting officer shall follow agency procedures.

(ii) If the offeror selects "does" in response to the provision at 52.204–26 or 52.212–3(v), the offeror must complete the representation at 52.204–24.

(2) (i) If the offeror selects "will not" in paragraph (d) of the provision at 52.204–24, the contracting officer may rely on the representation, unless the contracting officer has reason to question the representation. If the contracting officer has a reason to question the representation, the contracting officer shall follow agency procedures.

(ii) If an offeror selects "will" in paragraph (d) of the provision at 52.204–24, the offeror must provide the information required by paragraph 52.204–24(e), and the contracting officer shall follow agency procedures.

(b) *Reporting*. If a contractor provides a report pursuant to paragraph (d) of the clause at 52.204-25, Prohibition on Contracting for Certain Telecommunications and Video Surveillance Services or Equipment, follow agency procedures.

[FAC 2019-05, 84 FR 40216, 8/13/2019, effective 8/13/2019; FAC 2020-03, 84 FR 68314, 12/13/2019, effective 12/13/2019]

4.2104 Waivers.

(a) *Executive agencies*. The head of an executive agency may, on a one-time basis, waive the prohibition at 4.2102(a) with respect to a Government entity (*e.g.*, requirements office, contracting office) that requests such a waiver.

(1) The waiver may be provided, for a period not to extend beyond August 13, 2021, if the Government entity seeking the waiver submits to the head of the executive agency—

(i) A compelling justification for the additional time to implement the requirements under 4.2102(a), as determined by the head of the executive agency; and

(ii) A full and complete laydown or description of the presences of covered telecommunications or video surveillance equipment or services in the relevant supply chain and a phase-out plan to eliminate such covered telecommunications or video surveillance equipment or services from the relevant systems.

(2) The head of the executive agency shall, not later than 30 days after approval, submit to the appropriate congressional committees the full and complete laydown or description of the presences of covered telecommunications or video surveillance equipment or services in the relevant supply chain and the phase-out plan to eliminate such covered telecommunications or video surveillance equipment or services from the relevant systems.

(b) *Director of National Intelligence*. The Director of National Intelligence may provide a waiver if the Director determines the waiver is in the national security interests of the United States.

[FAC 2019-05, 84 FR 40216, 8/13/2019, effective 8/13/2019]

4.2105 Solicitation provisions and contract clause.

(a) The contracting officer shall insert the provision at 52.204-24, Representation Regarding Certain Telecommunications and Video Surveillance Services or Equipment—

(1) In all solicitations for contracts; and

(2) Under indefinite delivery contracts, in all notices of intent to place an order, or solicitations for an order (*e.g.*, subpart 8.4 and 16.505).

(b) The contracting officer shall insert the clause at 52.204-25, Prohibition on Contracting for Certain Telecommunications and Video Surveillance Services or Equipment, in all solicitations and contracts.

(c) The contracting officer shall insert the provision at 52.204–26, Covered Telecommunications Equipment or Services—Representation, in all solicitations.

[FAC 2019-05, 84 FR 40216, 8/13/2019, effective 8/13/2019; FAC 2020-03, 84 FR 68314, 12/13/2019, effective 12/13/2019]

PART 5—PUBLICIZING CONTRACT ACTIONS

Table of Contents

Scope of part 5.000
Definition 5.001
Policy 5.002
Governmentwide point of entry 5.003

Subpart 5.1—Dissemination of Information

Methods of disseminating information 5.101
Availability of solicitations 5.102

Subpart 5.2—Synopses of Proposed Contract Actions

General 5.201
Exceptions 5.202
Publicizing and response time 5.203
Presolicitation notices 5.204
Special situations 5.205
Notices of subcontracting opportunities 5.206
Preparation and transmittal of synopses 5.207

Subpart 5.3—Synopses of Contract Awards

General 5.301
Preparation and transmittal of synopses of awards 5.302
Announcement of contract awards 5.303

Subpart 5.4—Release of Information

General 5.401
General public 5.402
Requests from Members of Congress 5.403
Release of long-range acquisition estimates 5.404
Release procedures 5.404-1
Announcements of long-range acquisition estimates 5.404-2
Exchange of acquisition information 5.405
Public disclosure of justification documents for certain contract actions 5.406

Subpart 5.5—Paid Advertisements

Definitions 5.501
Authority 5.502
Procedures 5.503
Use of advertising agencies 5.504

Subpart 5.6—Publicizing Multi-Agency Use Contracts

Governmentwide database of contracts 5.601

Subpart 5.7—Publicizing Requirements under the American Recovery and Reinvestment Act of 2009

Scope 5.701
Applicability 5.702
Definitions 5.703
Publicizing preaward 5.704
Publicizing postaward 5.705

SUBCHAPTER B—ACQUISITION PLANNING (Parts 5-12)

PART 5—PUBLICIZING CONTRACT ACTIONS

5.000 Scope of part.

This part prescribes policies and procedures for publicizing contract opportunities and award information.

5.001 Definition.

Contract action, as used in this part, means an action resulting in a contract, as defined in subpart 2.1, including actions for additional supplies or services outside the existing contract scope, but not including actions that are within the scope and under the terms of the existing contract, such as contract modifications issued pursuant to the Changes clause, or funding and other administrative changes.

[FAC 2001-06, 67 FR 13048, 3/20/2002, effective 4/4/2002]

5.002 Policy.

Contracting officers must publicize proposed contract actions in order to—

(a) Increase competition;

(b) Broaden industry participation in meeting Government requirements; and

(c) Assist small business concerns, veteran-owned small business concerns, service-disabled veteran-owned small business concerns, HUBZone small business concerns, small disadvantaged business concerns, and women-owned small business concerns in obtaining contracts and subcontracts.

[FAC 84-13, 50 FR 52429, 12/23/85, effective 2/3/86; FAC 90-32, 60 FR 48206, 9/18/95, effective 10/1/95; FAC 97-20, 65 FR 60542, 10/11/2000, effective 10/11/2000]

5.003 Governmentwide point of entry.

For any requirement in the FAR to publish a notice, the contracting officer must transmit the notices to the GPE.

[FAC 97-26, 66 FR 27405, 5/16/2001, effective 5/16/2001; FAC 2001-16, Interim/Final rule, 68 FR 56676, 10/1/2003, effective 10/1/2003]

SUBPART 5.1—DISSEMINATION OF INFORMATION

5.101 Methods of disseminating information.

(a) As required by the Small Business Act (15 U.S.C. 637(e)) and 41 U.S.C. 1708, contracting officers must disseminate information on proposed contract actions as follows:

(1) For proposed contract actions expected to exceed $25,000, by synopsizing in the GPE (see 5.201).

(2) For proposed contract actions expected to exceed $15,000, but not expected to exceed $25,000, by displaying in a public place, or by any appropriate electronic means, an unclassified notice of the solicitation or a copy of the solicitation satisfying the requirements of 5.207(c). The notice must include a statement that all responsible sources may submit a response which, if timely received, must be considered by the agency. The information must be posted not later than the date the solicitation is issued, and must remain posted for at least 10 days or until after quotations have been opened, whichever is later.

(i) If solicitations are posted instead of a notice, the contracting officer may employ various methods of satisfying the requirements of 5.207(c). For example, the contracting officer may meet the requirements of 5.207(c) by stamping the solicitation, by a cover sheet to the solicitation, or by placing a general statement in the display room.

(ii) The contracting officer need not comply with the display requirements of this section when the exemptions at 5.202(a)(1), (a)(4) through (a)(9), or (a)(11) apply, when oral solicitations are used, or when providing access to a notice of proposed contract action and solicitation through the GPE and the notice permits the public to respond to the solicitation electronically.

(iii) Contracting officers may use electronic posting of requirements in a place accessible by the general public at the Government installation to satisfy the public display requirement. Contracting offices using electronic systems for public posting that are not accessible outside the installation must periodically publicize the methods for accessing the information.

(b) In addition, one or more of the following methods may be used:

(1) Preparing periodic handouts listing proposed contracts, and displaying them as in 5.101(a)(2).

(2) Assisting local trade associations in disseminating information to their members.

(3) Making brief announcements of proposed contracts to newspapers, trade journals, magazines, or other mass communication media for publication without cost to the Government.

(4) Placing paid advertisements in newspapers or other communications media, subject to the following limitations:

(i) Contracting officers shall place paid advertisements of proposed contracts only when it is anticipated that effective competition cannot be obtained otherwise (see 5.205(d)).

(ii) Contracting officers shall not place advertisements of proposed contracts in a newspaper published and printed in the District of Columbia unless the supplies or services will be furnished, or the labor performed, in the District of Columbia or adjoining counties in Maryland or Virginia (44 U.S.C. 3701).

(iii) Advertisements published in newspapers must be under proper written authority in accordance with 44 U.S.C. 3702 (see 5.502(a)).

[FAC 84-5, 50 FR 1728, 1/11/85, effective 4/1/85; FAC 84-13, 50 FR 52429, 12/23/85, effective 2/3/86; FAC 84-18, 51 FR 27117, 7/29/86, effective 7/30/86; FAC 84-28, 52 FR 21885, 6/9/87, effective 4/16/87; FAC 90-7, Interim rule, 56 FR 41731, 8/22/91, effective 8/22/91; FAC 90-29, 60 FR 34732, 7/3/95, effective 7/3/95; FAC 90-40, 61 FR 39186, 7/26/96, effective 8/26/96; FAC 90-46, 62 FR 12690, 3/17/97, effective 5/16/97; FAC 97-9, 63 FR 58587, 10/30/98, effective 10/30/98; FAC 97-26, 66 FR 27405, 5/16/2001, effective 5/16/2001; FAC 2001-16, Interim/Final rule, 68 FR 56676, 10/1/2003, effective 10/1/2003; FAC 2005-21, 72 FR 63075, 11/7/2007, effective 12/7/2007; FAC 2005-45, 75 FR 53129, 8/30/2010, effective 10/1/2010; FAC 2005-73, 79 FR 24192, 4/29/2014, effective 5/29/2014]

5.102 Availability of solicitations.

(a)(1) Except as provided in paragraph (a)(5) of this section, the contracting officer must make available through the GPE solicitations synopsized through the GPE, including specifications, technical data, and other pertinent information determined necessary by the contracting officer. Transmissions to the GPE must be in accordance with the interface description available via the Internet at *https://www.fbo.gov*.

(2) The contracting officer is encouraged, when practicable and cost-effective, to make accessible through the GPE additional information related to a solicitation.

(3) The contracting officer must ensure that solicitations transmitted using electronic commerce are forwarded to the GPE to satisfy the requirements of paragraph (a)(1) of this section.

(4) When an agency determines that a solicitation contains information that requires additional controls to monitor access and distribution (e.g., technical data, specifications, maps, building designs, schedules, etc.), the information shall be made available through the enhanced controls of the GPE, unless an exception in paragraph (a)(5) of this section applies. The GPE meets the synopsis and advertising requirements of this part.

(5) The contracting officer need not make a solicitation available through the GPE as required in paragraph (a)(4) of this section, when—

(i) Disclosure would compromise the national security (e.g., would result in disclosure of classified information, or information subject to export controls) or create other security risks. The fact that access to classified matter may be necessary to submit a proposal or perform the contract does not, in itself, justify use of this exception;

(ii) The nature of the file (e.g., size, format) does not make it cost-effective or practicable for contracting officers to provide access to the solicitation through the GPE; or

(iii) The agency's senior procurement executive makes a written determination that access through the GPE is not in the Government's interest.

(6) When an acquisition contains brand name specifications, the contracting officer shall include with the solicitation the justification or documentation required by 6.302-1(c), 13.106-1(b), or 13.501, redacted as necessary (see 6.305).

(b) When the contracting officer does not make a solicitation available through the GPE pursuant to paragraph (a)(5) of this section, the contracting officer—

(1) Should employ other electronic means (e.g., CD-ROM or electronic mail) whenever practicable and cost-effective. When solicitations are provided electronically on physical media (e.g., disks) or in paper form, the contracting officer must—

(i) Maintain a reasonable number of copies of solicitations, including specifications and other pertinent information determined necessary by the contracting officer (upon request, potential sources not initially solicited should be mailed or provided copies of solicitations, if available);

(ii) Provide copies on a "first-come-first-served" basis, for pickup at the contracting office, to publishers, trade associations, information services, and other members of the public having a legitimate interest (for construction, see 36.211); and

(iii) Retain a copy of the solicitation and other documents for review by and duplication for those requesting copies after the initial number of copies is exhausted; and

(2) May require payment of a fee, not exceeding the actual cost of duplication, for a copy of the solicitation document.

(c) In addition to the methods of disseminating proposed contract information in 5.101(a) and (b), provide, upon request to small business concerns, as required by 15 U.S.C. 637(b)—

(1) A copy of the solicitation and specifications. In the case of solicitations disseminated by electronic data interchange, solicitations may be furnished directly to the electronic address of the small business concern;

(2) The name and telephone number of an employee of the contracting office who will answer questions on the solicitation; and

(3) Adequate citations to each applicable major Federal law or agency rule with which small business concerns must comply in performing the contract.

(d) When electronic commerce (see subpart 4.5) is used in the solicitation process, availability of the solicitation may be limited to the electronic medium.

(e) Provide copies of a solicitation issued under other than full and open competition to firms requesting copies that were not initially solicited, but only after advising the requester of the determination to limit the solicitation to a specified firm or firms as authorized under part 6.

(f) This section 5.102 applies to classified contracts to the extent consistent with agency security requirements (see 5.202(a)(1)).

[FAC 97-26, 66 FR 27405, 5/16/2001, effective 5/16/2001; FAC 2005-09, 71 FR 20295, 4/19/2006, effective 5/19/2006; FAC 2005-13, 71 FR 57357, 9/28/2006, effective 9/28/2006; FAC 2005-21, 72 FR 63075, 11/7/2007, effective 12/7/2007; FAC 2005-36, 74 FR 40459, 8/11/2009, effective 9/10/2009; FAC 2005-37, 74 FR 52860, 10/14/2009, effective 10/14/2009; FAC 2005-55, 77 FR 189, 1/3/2012, effective 2/2/2012; FAC 2005-100, 83 FR 42571, 8/22/2018, effective 8/22/2018]

SUBPART 5.2—SYNOPSES OF PROPOSED CONTRACT ACTIONS

5.201 General.

(a) As required by the Small Business Act (15 U.S.C. 637(e)) and 41 U.S.C. 1708, agencies must make notices of proposed contract actions available as specified in paragraph (b) of this section.

(b)(1) For acquisitions of supplies and services, other than those covered by the exceptions in 5.202 and the special situations in 5.205, the contracting officer must transmit a notice to the GPE, for each proposed—

(i) Contract action meeting the threshold in 5.101(a)(1);

(ii) Modification to an existing contract for additional supplies or services that meets the threshold in 5.101(a)(1); or

(iii) Contract action in any amount when advantageous to the Government.

(2) When transmitting notices using electronic commerce, contracting officers must ensure the notice is forwarded to the GPE.

(c) The primary purposes of the notice are to improve small business access to acquisition information and enhance competition by identifying contracting and subcontracting opportunities.

(d) The GPE may be accessed via the Internet at *https://www.fbo.gov*.

[FAC 97-26, 66 FR 27405, 5/16/2001, effective 5/16/2001; FAC 2001-16, Interim/Final rule, 68 FR 56676, 10/1/2003, effective 10/1/2003; FAC 2005-21, 72 FR 63075, 11/7/2007, effective 12/7/2007; FAC 2005-73, 79 FR 24192, 4/29/2014, effective 5/29/2014; FAC 2005-100, 83 FR 42571, 8/22/2018, effective 8/22/2018]

5.202 Exceptions.

The contracting officer need not submit the notice required by 5.201 when—

(a) The contracting officer determines that—

(1) The synopsis cannot be worded to preclude disclosure of an agency's needs and such disclosure would compromise the national security (e.g., would result in disclosure of classified information). The fact that a proposed solicitation or proposed contract action contains classified information, or that access to classified matter may be necessary to submit a proposal or perform the contract does not, in itself, justify use of this exception to synopsis;

(2) The proposed contract action is made under the conditions described in 6.302-2(or, for purchases conducted using simplified acquisition procedures, if unusual and compelling urgency precludes competition to the maximum extent practicable) and the Government would be seriously injured if the agency complies with the time periods specified in 5.203;

(3) The proposed contract action is one for which either the written direction of a foreign government reimbursing the agency for the cost of the acquisition of the supplies or services for such government, or the terms of an international agreement or treaty between the United States and a foreign government or international organizations, has the effect of requiring that the acquisition shall be from specified sources;

(4) The proposed contract action is expressly authorized or required by a statute to be made through another Government agency, including acquisitions from the Small Business Administration (SBA) using the authority of section 8(a) of the Small Business Act (but see 5.205(f)), or from a specific source such as a workshop for the blind under the rules of the Committee for Purchase from People Who Are Blind or Severely Disabled;

(5) The proposed contract action is for utility services other than telecommunications services and only one source is available;

(6) The proposed contract action is an order placed under Subpart 16.5. When the order contains brand-name specifications, see especially 16.505(a)(4);

(7) The proposed contract action results from acceptance of a proposal under the Small Business Innovation Development Act of 1982 (Pub. L. 97-219);

(8) The proposed contract action results from the acceptance of an unsolicited research proposal that demonstrates a unique and innovative concept (see 2.101) and publication of any notice complying with 5.207 would improperly disclose the originality of thought or innovativeness of the proposed research, or would disclose proprietary information associated with the proposal. This exception does not apply if the proposed contract action results from an unsolicited research proposal and acceptance is based solely upon the unique capability of the

source to perform the particular research services proposed (see 6.302-1(a)(2)(i));

(9) The proposed contract action is made for perishable subsistence supplies, and advance notice is not appropriate or reasonable;

(10) The proposed contract action is made under conditions described in 6.302-3, or 6.302-5 with regard to brand name commercial items for authorized resale, or 6.302-7, and advance notice is not appropriate or reasonable;

(11) The proposed contract action is made under the terms of an existing contract that was previously synopsized in sufficient detail to comply with the requirements of 5.207 with respect to the current proposed contract action;

(12) The proposed contract action is by a Defense agency and the proposed contract action will be made and performed outside the United States and its outlying areas, and only local sources will be solicited. This exception does not apply to proposed contract actions covered by the World Trade Organization Government Procurement Agreement or a Free Trade Agreement (see Subpart 25.4);

(13) The proposed contract action—

(i) Is for an amount not expected to exceed the simplified acquisition threshold;

(ii) Will be made through a means that provides access to the notice of proposed contract action through the GPE; and

(iii) Permits the public to respond to the solicitation electronically; or

(14) The proposed contract action is made under conditions described in 6.302-3 with respect to the services of an expert to support the Federal Government in any current or anticipated litigation or dispute.

(b) The head of the agency determines in writing after consultation with the Administrator for Federal Procurement Policy and the Administrator of the Small Business Administration, that advance notice is not appropriate or reasonable.

[FAC 84-5, 50 FR 1728, 1/11/85, effective 4/1/85; FAC 84-13, 50 FR 52430, 12/23/85, effective 2/3/86; FAC 84-18, 51 FR 27117, 7/29/86, effective 7/30/86; FAC 84-38, 53 FR 27462, 7/20/88, effective 8/19/88; FAC 84-52, 54 FR 46004, 10/31/89, effective 11/30/89; FAC 90-4, 56 FR 15148, 4/15/91, effective 5/15/91; FAC 90-7, 56 FR 8/22/91, effective 9/23/91; Interim rule, FAC 90-19, 59 FR 544, 1/5/94, effective 1/1/94, interim rule finalized without change, FAC 90-45, 62 FR 224, 1/2/97, effective 1/1/97; FAC 90-29, 60 FR 34732, 7/3/95, effective 7/3/95; FAC 90-31, 60 FR 42648, 8/16/95, effective 10/1/95; FAC 90-33, 60 FR 49706, 9/26/95, effective 10/1/95; FAC 90-40, 61 FR 39186, 7/26/96, effective 8/26/96; FAC 97-9, 63 FR 58587, 10/30/98, effective 10/30/98; FAC 97-22, 66 FR 2116, 1/10/2001, effective 3/12/2001; Delay of effective date, 66 FR 14259, 3/9/2001, effective 5/11/2001; FAC 97-26, 66 FR 27405, 5/16/2001, effective 5/16/2001; FAC 2001-14, 68 FR 28079, 5/22/2003, effective 6/23/2003; FAC 2001-27, interim rule, 69 FR 77870, 12/28/2004, effective 1/1/2005; FAC 2005-07, 71 FR 219, 1/3/2006, effective 1/3/2006; FAC 2005-55, 77 FR 189, 1/3/2012, effective 2/2/2012; FAC 2005-73, 79 FR 24192, 4/29/2014, effective 5/29/2014]

5.203 Publicizing and response time.

Whenever agencies are required to publicize notice of proposed contract actions under 5.201, they must proceed as follows:

(a) An agency must transmit a notice of proposed contract action to the GPE (see 5.201). All publicizing and response times are calculated based on the date of publication. The publication date is the date the notice appears on the GPE. The notice must be published at least 15 days before issuance of a solicitation, or a proposed contract action the Government intends to solicit and negotiate with only one source under the authority of 6.302, except that, for acquisitions of commercial items, the contracting officer may—

(1) Establish a shorter period for issuance of the solicitation; or

(2) Use the combined synopsis and solicitation procedure (see 12.603).

(b) The contracting officer must establish a solicitation response time that will afford potential offerors a reasonable opportunity to respond to each proposed contract action, (including actions where the notice of proposed contract action and solicitation information is accessible through the GPE), in an amount estimated to be greater than $25,000, but not greater than the simplified acquisition threshold; or each contract action for the acquisition of commercial items in an amount estimated to be greater than $25,000. The contracting officer should consider the circumstances of the individual acquisition, such as the complexity, commerciality, availability, and urgency, when establishing the solicitation response time.

(c) Except for the acquisition of commercial items (see 5.203 (b)), agencies shall allow at least a 30-day response time for receipt of bids or proposals from the date of issuance of a solicitation, if the proposed contract action is expected to exceed the simplified acquisition threshold.

(d) Agencies shall allow at least a 30 day response time from the date of publication of a proper notice of intent to contract for architect-engineer services or before issuance of an order under a basic ordering agreement or similar arrangement if the proposed contract action is expected to exceed the simplified acquisition threshold.

(e) Agencies must allow at least a 45-day response time for receipt of bids or proposals from the date of publication of the notice required in 5.201 for proposed contract actions categorized as research and development if the proposed contract action is expected to exceed the simplified acquisition threshold.

(f) Nothing in this subpart prohibits officers or employees of agencies from responding to requests for information.

(g) Contracting officers may, unless they have evidence to the contrary, presume the notice was published one day after transmission to the GPE. This presumption does not negate the mandatory waiting or response times specified in paragraphs (a) through (d) of this section. Upon learning that a particular notice has not in fact been published within the presumed time frames, contracting officers should consider whether the date for receipt of offers can be extended or whether circumstances have become sufficiently compelling to justify proceeding with the proposed contract action under the authority of 5.202(a)(2).

(h) In addition to other requirements set forth in this section, for acquisitions covered by the World Trade Organization Government Procurement Agreement Act or a Free Trade Agreement (see subpart 25.4), the period of time between publication of the synopsis notice and receipt of offers must be no less than 40 days. However, if the acquisition falls within a general category identified in an annual forecast, the availability of which is published, the contracting officer may reduce this time period to as few as 10 days.

[FAC 84-13, 50 FR 52430, 12/23/85, effective 2/3/86; FAC 84-21, 51 FR 31425, 9/3/86, effective 8/29/86; FAC 90-29, 60 FR 34732, 7/3/95, effective 7/3/95; FAC 90-32, 60 FR 48206, 9/18/95, effective 10/1/95; FAC 90-40, 61 FR 39186, 7/26/96, effective 8/26/96; FAC 90-45, Final rule, 62 FR 224, 1/2/97, effective 1/1/97, corrected 62 FR 10709, 3/10/97; FAC 97-9, 63 FR 58587, 10/30/98, effective 10/30/98; FAC 97-26, 66 FR 27405, 5/16/2001, effective 5/16/2001; FAC 2001-16, Interim/Final rule, 68 FR 56676, 10/1/2003, effective 10/1/2003; FAC 2001-19, Interim rule, 69 FR 1051, 1/7/2004, effective 1/1/2004; FAC 2001-25, Final rule, 69 FR 59700, 10/5/2004, effective 10/5/2004; FAC 2001-27, interim rule, 69 FR 77870, 12/28/2004, effective 1/1/2005; FAC 2005-07, 71 FR 219, 1/3/2006, effective 1/3/2006; FAC 2005-21, 72 FR 63075, 11/7/2007, effective 12/7/2007; FAC 2005-24, 73 FR 10960, 2/28/2008, effective 3/31/2008]

5.204 Presolicitation notices.

Contracting officers must provide access to presolicitation notices through the GPE (see 15.201 and 36.213-2). The contracting officer must synopsize a proposed contract action before issuing any resulting solicitation (see 5.201 and 5.203).

[FAC 97-26, 66 FR 27405, 5/16/2001, effective 5/16/2001]

5.205 Special situations.

(a) *Research and development (R&D) advance notices.* Contracting officers may transmit to the GPE advance notices of their interest in potential R&D programs whenever market research does not produce a sufficient number of concerns to obtain adequate competition. Advance notices must not be used where security considerations prohibit such publication. Contracting officers must consider potential sources which respond to advance notices for a subsequent solicitation. Potential sources which respond to advance notices must be added to the appropriate solicitation mailing list for subsequent solicitation. Advance notices must be entitled "Research and Development Sources Sought" and include the name and telephone number of the contracting officer or other contracting activity official from whom technical details of the project can be obtained. This will enable sources to submit information for evaluation of their R&D capabilities. Contracting officers must synopsize (see 5.201) all subsequent solicitations for R&D contracts, including those resulting from a previously synopsized advance notice, unless one of the exceptions in 5.202 applies.

(b) *Federally Funded Research and Development Centers.* Before establishing a Federally Funded Research and Development Center (FFRDC) (see Part 35) or before changing its basic purpose and mission, the sponsor must transmit at least three notices over a 90-day period to the GPE and the Federal Register, indicating the agency's intention to sponsor an FFRDC or change the basic purpose and mission of an FFRDC. The notice must indicate the scope and nature of the effort to be performed and request comments. Notice is not required where the action is required by law.

(c) *Special notices.* Contracting officers may transmit to the GPE special notices of procurement matters such as business fairs, long-range procurement estimates, prebid or preproposal conferences, meetings, and the availability of draft solicitations or draft specifications for review.

(d) *Architect-engineering services.* Contracting officers must publish notices of intent to contract for architect-engineering services as follows:

(1) Except when exempted by 5.202, contracting officers must transmit to the GPE a synopsis of each proposed contract action for which the total fee (including phases and options) is expected to exceed $25,000.

(2) When the total fee is expected to exceed $15,000 but not exceed $25,000, the contracting officer must comply with 5.101(a)(2). When the proposed contract action is not required to be synopsized under paragraph (d)(1) of this section, the contracting officer must display a notice of the solicitation or a copy of the solicitation in a public place at the contracting office. Other optional publicizing methods are authorized in accordance with 5.101(b).

(e) *Public-private competitions under OMB Circular A-76.*

(1) The contracting officer shall make a formal public announcement for each streamlined or standard competition. The public announcement shall include, at a minimum, the agency, agency component, location, type of competition (streamlined or standard), activity being competed, incumbent service providers, number of Government personnel performing the activity, name of the Competitive Sourcing Official, name of the contracting officer, name of the Agency Tender Official, and projected end date of the competition.

(2) The contracting officer shall announce the end of the streamlined or standard competition by making a formal public announcement of the performance decision. (See OMB Circular A-76.)

(f) *Section 8(a) competitive acquisition.* When a national buy requirement is being considered for competitive acquisition limited to eligible 8(a) participants under subpart 19.8, the contracting officer must transmit a synopsis of the proposed contract action to the GPE. The synopsis may be transmitted to the GPE concurrent with submission of the agency offering (see 19.804-2) to the Small Business Administration (SBA). The synopsis should also include information—

(1) Advising that the acquisition is being offered for competition limited to eligible 8(a) participants;

(2) Specifying the North American Industry Classification System (NAICS) code;

(3) Advising that eligibility to participate may be restricted to 8(a) participants in either the developmental stage or the developmental and transitional stages; and

(4) Encouraging interested 8(a) participants to request a copy of the solicitation as expeditiously as possible since the solicitation will be issued without further notice upon SBA acceptance of the requirement for the section 8(a) program.

(g) *Notification to the public of rationale for bundled requirement*. The agency is encouraged to provide notification of the rationale for any bundled requirement to the GPE before issuing the solicitation of any bundled requirement (see 7.107-5(b)(2)).

[FAC 97-26, 66 FR 27405, 5/16/2001, effective 5/16/2001, finalized without change by 66 FR 65347, 12/18/2001, effective 12/18/2001; FAC 2001-15, 68 FR 43854, 7/24/2003, effective 8/25/2003; FAC 2001-16, Interim/Final rule, 68 FR 56676, 10/1/2003, effective 10/1/2003; FAC 2005-09, Final rule, 71 FR 20299, 04/19/2006, effective 5/19/2006; FAC 2005-24, 73 FR 10960, 2/28/2008, effective 3/31/2008; FAC 2005-45, 75 FR 53129, 8/30/2010, effective 10/1/2010; FAC 2005-91, 81 FR 67763, 9/30/2016, effective 10/31/2016; FAC 2005-95, 82 FR 4724, 1/13/2017, effective 1/13/2017]

5.206 Notices of subcontracting opportunities.

(a) The following entities may transmit a notice to the GPE to seek competition for subcontracts, to increase participation by qualified HUBZone small business, small, small disadvantaged, women-owned small business, veteran-owned small business and service-disabled veteran-owned small business concerns, and to meet established subcontracting plan goals:

(1) A contractor awarded a contract exceeding $150,000 that is likely to result in the award of any subcontracts.

(2) A subcontractor or supplier, at any tier, under a contract exceeding $150,000, that has a subcontracting opportunity exceeding $15,000.

(b) The notices must describe—

(1) The business opportunity;

(2) Any prequalification requirements; and

(3) Where to obtain technical data needed to respond to the requirement.

[FAC 97-15, 64 FR 72414,12/27/99, effective 12/27/99; FAC 97-19, 65 FR 46052, 7/26/2000, effective 7/26/2000; FAC 97-26, 66 FR 27405, 5/16/2001, effective 5/16/2001; FAC 2001-16, Interim/Final rule, 68 FR 56676, 10/1/2003, effective 10/1/2003; FAC 2001-23, 69 FR 25273, 5/5/2004, effective 5/5/2004; FAC 2005-02, 70 FR 14950, 3/23/2005, effective 3/23/2005; FAC 2005-45, 75 FR 53129, 8/30/2010, effective 10/1/2010]

5.207 Preparation and transmittal of synopses.

(a) *Content*. Each synopsis transmitted to the GPE must address the following data elements, as applicable:

(1) Action Code.

(2) Date.

(3) Year.

(4) Contracting Office ZIP Code.

(5) Product or Service Code.

(6) Contracting Office Address.

(7) Subject.

(8) Proposed Solicitation Number.

(9) Closing Response Date.

(10) Contact Point or Contracting Officer.

(11) Contract Award and Solicitation Number.

(12) Contract Award Dollar Amount.

(13) Line Item Number.

(14) Contract Award Date.

(15) Contractor.

(16) Description.

(17) Place of Contract Performance.

(18) Set-aside Status.

(b) *Transmittal.* Transmissions to the GPE must be in accordance with the interface description available via the Internet at *https://www.fbo.gov.*

(c) *General format for "Description."* Prepare a clear and concise description of the supplies or services that is not unnecessarily restrictive of competition and will allow a prospective offeror to make an informed business judgment as to whether a copy of the solicitation should be requested including the following, as appropriate:

(1) National Stock Number (NSN) if assigned.

(2) Specification and whether an offeror, its product, or service must meet a qualification requirement in order to be eligible for award, and identification of the office from which additional information about the qualification requirement may be obtained (see subpart 9.2).

(3) Manufacturer, including part number, drawing number, etc.

(4) Size, dimensions, or other form, fit or functional description.

(5) Predominant material of manufacture.

(6) Quantity, including any options for additional quantities.

(7) Unit of issue.

(8) Destination information.

(9) Delivery schedule.

(10) Duration of the contract period.

(11) Sustainable acquisition requirements (or a description of high-performance sustainable building practices required, if for design, construction, renovation, repair, or deconstruction) (see parts 23 or 36).

(12) For a proposed contract action in an amount estimated to be greater than $25,000 but not greater than the simplified acquisition threshold, enter—

(i) A description of the procedures to be used in awarding the contract (e.g., request for oral or written quotation or solicitation); and

(ii) The anticipated award date.

(13) For Architect-Engineer projects and other projects for which the product or service codes are insufficient, provide brief details with respect to: location, scope of services required, cost range and limitations, type of contract, estimated starting and completion dates, and any significant evaluation factors.

(14) (i) If the solicitation will include the FAR clause at 52.225-3, Buy American-Free Trade Agreements-Israeli Trade Act, or an equivalent agency clause, insert the following notice in the synopsis: "One or more of the items under this acquisition is subject to Free Trade Agreements."

(ii) If the solicitation will include the FAR clause at 52.225-5, Trade Agreements, or an equivalent agency clause, insert the following notice in the synopsis: "One or more of the items under this acquisition is subject to World Trade Organization Government Procurement Agreement and Free Trade Agreements."

(iii) If the solicitation will include the FAR clause at 52.225-11, Buy American-Construction Materials under Trade Agreements, 52.225-23, Required Use of American Iron, Steel, and Manufactured Goods—Buy American Statute—Construction Materials under Trade Agreements, or an equivalent agency clause, insert the following notice in the synopsis: "One or more of the items under this acquisition is subject to the World Trade Organization Government Procurement Agreement and Free Trade Agreements."

(15) In the case of noncompetitive contract actions (including those that do not exceed the simplified acquisition threshold), identify the intended source and insert a statement of the reason justifying the lack of competition.

(16) (i) Except when using the sole source authority at 6.302-1, insert a statement that all responsible sources may submit a bid, proposal, or quotation which shall be considered by the agency.

(ii) When using the sole source authority at 6.302-1, insert a statement that all responsible sources may submit a capability statement, proposal, or quotation which shall be considered by the agency.

(17) If solicitations synopsized through the GPE will not be made available through

the GPE, provide information on how to obtain the solicitation.

(18) If the solicitation will be made available to interested parties through electronic data interchange, provide any information necessary to obtain and respond to the solicitation electronically.

(19) If the technical data required to respond to the solicitation will not be furnished as part of such solicitation, identify the source in the Government, such as *https://www.fbo.gov*, from which the technical data may be obtained.

(d) *Set-asides.* When the proposed acquisition provides for a total or partial small business set-aside, or when the proposed acquisition provides for a local area set-aside (see Subpart 26.2), the contracting officer shall identify the type of set-aside in the synopsis and in the solicitation.

(e) *Codes to be used in Synopses to identify services or supplies.* Contracting officers must use one of the classification codes identified at *https://www.fbo.gov* to identify services or supplies in synopses.

(f) *Notice of solicitation cancellation.* Contracting officers may publish notices of solicitation cancellations (or indefinite suspensions) of proposed contract actions in the GPE.

[FAC 84-5, 50 FR 1729, 1/11/85, effective 4/1/85; corrected 50 FR 4221, 1/30/85; FAC 84-13, 50 FR 52430, 12/23/85, effective 2/3/86; FAC 84-18, 51 FR 27117, 7/29/86, effective 7/30/86; FAC 84-37, 53 FR 17856, 5/18/88 effective 6/17/88; FAC 84-46, 54 FR 19813, 5/8/89, effective 6/7/89; FAC 84-48, 54 FR 25061, 6/12/89, effective 7/12/89; FAC 90-3, 55 FR 52789, 12/21/90, effective 1/22/91; FAC 90-9, 56 FR 67128, 12/27/91, effective 2/25/92; Interim rule, FAC 90-20, 59 FR 11368, 3/10/94, effective 3/10/94; FAC 90-29, 60 FR 34732, 7/3/95, effective 7/3/95; FAC 90-32, 60 FR 48206, 9/18/95, effective 10/1/95; FAC 90-40, 61 FR 39186, 7/26/96, effective 8/26/96; FAC 90-41, 61 FR 41466, 8/8/96, effective 8/8/96, finalized without change, FAC 97-3, 62 FR 64912, 12/9/97, effective 2/9/98; FAC 90-45, Final rule, 62 FR 224, 1/2/97, effective 1/1/97; Final rule, 62 FR 40236, 7/25/97, effective 6/30/97; FAC 97-9, 63 FR 58587, 10/30/98, effective 10/30/98; FAC 97-10, 63 FR 70264, 12/18/98, effective 1/4/99; FAC 97-11, 64 FR 10530, 3/4/99, effective 3/4/99; FAC 97-26, 66 FR 27405, 5/16/2001, effective 5/16/2001; FAC 2001-06, 67 FR 13048, 3/20/2002, effective 4/4/2002; FAC 2001-16, Interim/Final rule, 68 FR 56676, 10/1/2003, effective 10/1/2003; FAC 2001-23, 69 FR 25273, 5/5/2004, effective 5/5/2004; FAC 2005-02, 70 FR 14950, 3/23/2005, effective 3/23/2005; FAC 2005-07, 71 FR 219, 220, 1/3/2006, effective 1/3/2006; FAC 2005-09, 71 FR 20295, 4/19/2006, effective 5/19/2006; FAC 2005-21, 72 FR 63084, 11/7/2007, effective 11/7/2007; FAC 2005-24, 73 FR 10960, 2/28/2008, effective 3/31/2008; FAC 2005-27, 73 FR 53995, 9/17/2008, effective 10/17/2008; FAC 2005-32, 74 FR 14623, 3/31/2009, effective 3/31/2009; FAC 2005-36, 74 FR 40459, 8/11/2009, effective 9/10/2009; FAC 2005-45, 75 FR 53153, 8/30/2010, effective 10/1/2010; FAC 2005-52, 76 FR 31395, 5/31/2011, effective 5/31/2011; FAC 2005-73, 79 FR 24192, 4/29/2014, effective 5/29/2014; FAC 2005-83, 80 FR 38307, 7/2/2015, effective 8/3/2015; FAC 2005-95, 82 FR 4709, 1/13/2017, effective 1/13/2017; FAC 2005-100, 83 FR 42571, 8/22/2018, effective 8/22/2018; FAC 2019-02, 84 FR 19839, 5/6/2019, effective 5/6/2019]

SUBPART 5.3—SYNOPSES OF CONTRACT AWARDS

5.301 General.

(a) Except for contract actions described in paragraph (b) of this section and as provided in 5.003, contracting officers must synopsize through the GPE the following:

(1) Contract awards exceeding $25,000 that are—

(i) Covered by the World Trade Organization Government Procurement Agreement or a Free Trade Agreement (*see* subpart 25.4); or

(ii) Likely to result in the award of any subcontracts. However, the dollar threshold is not a prohibition against publicizing an award of a smaller amount when publicizing would be advantageous to industry or to the Government.

(2) Certain contract actions greater than the simplified acquisition threshold as follows—

(i) Federal Supply Schedule (FSS) orders or Blanket Purchase Agreements supported by a limited-source justification (excluding brand name) in accordance with 8.405-6; or

(ii) Task or delivery orders awarded without providing fair opportunity in accordance with 16.505(b)(2).

(3) A notice is not required under this section if the notice would disclose the executive agency's needs and the disclosure of such needs would compromise the national security.

(b) A notice is not required under paragraph (a)(1) of this section if—

(1) The award results from acceptance of an unsolicited research proposal that demonstrates a unique and innovative research concept and publication of any notice would disclose the originality of thought or innovativeness of the proposed research or would disclose proprietary information associated with the proposal;

(2) The award results from a proposal submitted under the Small Business Innovation Development Act of 1982 (Pub. L. 97-219);

(3) The contract action is an order placed under subpart 16.5 or 8.4, except *see* paragraph (a)(2) of this section;

(4) The award is made for perishable subsistence supplies;

(5) The award is for utility services, other than telecommunications services, and only one source is available;

(6) The contract action—

(i) Is for an amount not greater than the simplified acquisition threshold;

(ii) Was made through a means where access to the notice of proposed contract action was provided through the GPE; and

(iii) Permitted the public to respond to the solicitation electronically; or

(7) The award is for the services of an expert to support the Federal Government in any current or anticipated litigation or dispute pursuant to the exception to full and open competition authorized at 6.302-3.

(c) With respect to acquisitions covered by the World Trade Organization Government Procurement Agreement or a Free Trade Agreement, contracting officers must submit synopses in sufficient time to permit their publication in the GPE not later than 60 days after award.

(d) Posting is required of the justifications for—

(1) Contracts awarded using other than full and open competition in accordance with 6.305;

(2) FSS orders or Blanket Purchase Agreements with an estimated value greater than the simplified acquisition threshold and supported by a limited-sources justification (*see* 8.405-6(a)); or

(3) Task or delivery orders greater than the simplified acquisition threshold and awarded without providing for fair opportunity in accordance with 16.505(b)(2)(ii)(B) and (D).

[FAC 84-26, 52 FR 19802, 5/27/87, effective 7/30/87; FAC 84-38, interim rule, 53 FR 27463, 7/20/88, effective 8/1/88; FAC 90-29, 60 FR 34732, 7/3/95, effective 7/3/95; FAC 90-31, 60 FR 42648, 8/16/95, effective 10/1/95; FAC 90-33, 60 FR 49706, 9/26/95, effective 10/1/95; FAC 97-9, 63 FR 58587, 10/30/98, effective 10/30/98; FAC 97-15, 64 FR 72414, 12/27/99, effective 2/25/2000; FAC 97-26, 66 FR 27405, 5/16/2001, effective 5/16/2001; FAC 2001-16, Interim/Final rule, 68 FR 56676, 10/1/2003, effective 10/1/2003; FAC 2001-27, interim rule 69 FR 77870, 12/28/2004, effective 1/1/2005; FAC 2005-07, 71 FR 219, 1/3/2006, effective 1/3/2006; FAC 2005-30, 1/15/2009, effective 2/17/2009; FAC 2005-42, 75 FR 34273, 6/16/2010, effective 7/16/2010; FAC 2005-50, 76 FR 14548, 3/16/2011, effective 5/16/2011; FAC 2005-56, 77 FR 12927, 3/2/2012, effective 4/2/2012]

5.302 Preparation and transmittal of synopses of awards.

Contracting officers shall transmit synopses of contract awards in the same manner as prescribed in 5.207.

[FAC 90-3, 55 FR 52790, 12/21/90, effective 1/22/91]

5.303 Announcement of contract awards.

(a) *Public announcement.* Contracting officers shall make information available on awards over $4 million (unless another dollar amount is specified in agency acquisition regulations) in sufficient time for the agency concerned to announce it by 5 p.m. Washington, DC, time on the day of award. Agencies shall not release information on awards before the public release time of 5 p.m. Washington, DC time. Contracts excluded from this reporting requirement include—

(1) Those placed with the Small Business Administration under section 8(a) of the Small Business Act;

(2) Those placed with foreign firms when the place of delivery or performance is outside the United States and its outlying areas; and

(3) Those for which synopsis was exempted under 5.202(a)(1).

(b) *Local announcement.* Agencies may also release information on contract awards to the local press or other media. When local announcements are made for contract awards in excess of the simplified acquisition threshold, they shall include—

(1) For awards after sealed bidding, a statement that the contract was awarded after competition by sealed bidding, the number of offers solicited and received, and the basis for selection (e.g., the lowest responsible bidder); or

(2) For awards after negotiation, the information prescribed by 15.503(b), and after competitive negotiation (either price or design competition), a statement to this effect, and in general terms the basis for selection.

[FAC 84-5, 50 FR 1729, 1/11/85, effective 4/1/85; FAC 84-29, 52 FR 30076, 8/12/87, effective 8/24/87; FAC 84-56, 55 FR 3881, 2/5/90, effective 3/7/90; FAC 90-9, 56 FR 67128, 12/27/91, effective 2/25/92; FAC 90-23, 59 FR 67010, 12/28/94, effective 2/27/95; FAC 90-29, 60 FR 34732, 7/3/95, effective 7/3/95; FAC 90-31, 60 FR 42648, 8/16/95, effective 10/1/95; FAC 90-40, 61 FR 39186, 7/26/96, effective 8/26/96; FAC 90-44, Final rule, 61 FR 69286, 12/31/96, effective 1/1/97; FAC 97-2, 62 FR 51224, 9/30/97, effective 10/10/97; FAC 2001-14, 68 FR 28079, 5/22/2003, effective 6/23/2003; FAC 2005-13, 71 FR 57363, 9/28/2006, effective 9/28/2006; FAC 2005-45, 75 FR 53129, 8/30/2010, effective 10/1/2010]

SUBPART 5.4—RELEASE OF INFORMATION

5.401 General.

(a) A high level of business security must be maintained in order to preserve the integrity of the acquisition process. When it is necessary to obtain information from potential contractors and others outside the Government for use in preparing Government estimates, contracting officers shall ensure that the information is not publicized or discussed with potential contractors.

(b) Contracting officers may make available maximum information to the public, except information—

(1) On plans that would provide undue or discriminatory advantage to private or personal interests;

(2) Received in confidence from an offeror;

(3) Otherwise requiring protection under Freedom of Information Act (see Subpart 24.2) or Privacy Act (see Subpart 24.1); or

(4) Pertaining to internal agency communications (e.g., technical reviews, contracting authority or other reasons, or recommendations referring thereto).

(c) This policy applies to all Government personnel who participate directly or indirectly in any stage of the acquisition cycle.

5.402 General public.

Contracting officers shall process requests for specific information from the general public, including suppliers, in accordance with Subpart 24.1 or 24.2, as appropriate.

5.403 Requests from Members of Congress.

(a) Contracting officers shall give Members of Congress, upon their request, detailed information regarding any particular contract. When responsiveness would result in disclosure of classified matter, business confidential information, or information prejudicial to competitive acquisition, the contracting officer shall refer the proposed reply, with full documentation, to the agency head and inform the legislative liaison office of the action.

[FAC 84-5, 50 FR 1729, 1/11/85, effective 4/1/85; FAC 2001-15, 68 FR 43854, 7/24/2003, effective 8/25/2003]

5.404 Release of long-range acquisition estimates.

To assist industry planning and to locate additional sources of supply, it may be desirable to publicize estimates of unclassified long-range acquisition requirements. Estimates may be publicized as far in advance as possible.

5.404-1 Release procedures.

(a) *Application*. The agency head, or a designee, may release long-range acquisition estimates if the information will—

(1) Assist industry in its planning and facilitate meeting the acquisition requirements;

(2) Not encourage undesirable practices (e.g., attempts to corner the market or hoard industrial materials); and

(3) Not indicate the existing or potential mobilization of the industry as a whole.

(b) *Conditions*. The agency head shall ensure that—

(1) Classified information is released through existing security channels in accordance with agency security regulations;

(2) The information is publicized as widely as practicable to all parties simultaneously by any of the means described in this part;

(3) Each release states that—

(i) The estimate is based on the best information available;

(ii) The information is subject to modification and is in no way binding on the Government; and

(iii) More specific information relating to any individual item or class of items will not be furnished until the proposed action is synopsized through the GPE or the solicitation is issued;

(4) Each release contains the name and address of the contracting officer that will process the acquisition;

(5) Modifications to the original release are publicized as soon as possible, in the same manner as the original; and

(6) Each release—

(i) Is coordinated in advance with small business, public information, and public relations personnel, as appropriate;

(ii) Contains, if applicable, a statement that small business set-asides may be involved, but that a determination can be made only when acquisition action is initiated; and

(iii) Contains the name or description of the item, and the estimated quantity to be acquired by calendar quarter, fiscal year, or other period. It may also contain such additional information as the number of units last acquired, the unit price, and the name of the last supplier.

[FAC 90-32, 60 FR 48206, 9/18/95, effective 10/1/95; FAC 97-26, 66 FR 27405, 5/16/2001, effective 5/16/2001; FAC 2019-02, 84 FR 19839, 5/6/2019, effective 5/6/2019]

5.404-2 Announcements of long-range acquisition estimates.

Further publicizing, consistent with the needs of the individual case, may be accomplished by announcing through the GPE that long-range acquisition estimates have been published and are obtainable, upon request, from the contracting officer.

[FAC 97-26, 66 FR 27405, 5/16/2001, effective 5/16/2001]

5.405 Exchange of acquisition information.

(a) When the same item or class of items is being acquired by more than one agency, or by more than one contracting activity within an agency, the exchange and coordination of pertinent information, particularly cost and pricing data, between these agencies or contracting activities is necessary to promote uniformity of treatment of major issues and the resolution of particularly difficult or controversial issues. The exchange and coordination of information is particularly beneficial during the period of acquisition planning, presolicitation, evaluation, and pre-award survey.

(b) When substantial acquisitions of major items are involved or when the contracting activity deems it desirable, the contracting activity shall request appropriate information (on both the end item and on major subcontracted components) from other agencies or contracting activities responsible for acquiring similar items. Each agency or contracting activity receiving such a request shall furnish the information requested. The contracting officer, early in a negotiation of a contract, or in connection with the review of a subcontract, shall request the contractor to furnish information as to the contractor's or subcontractor's previous Government contracts and subcontracts for the same or similar end items and major subcontractor components.

5.406 Public disclosure of justification documents for certain contract actions.

(a) Justifications and approvals for other than full and open competition must be posted in accordance with 6.305.

(b) Limited-source justifications (excluding brand name) for FSS orders or blanket purchase agreements with an estimated value greater than the simplified acquisition threshold must be posted in accordance with 8.405-6(a)(2).

(c) Justifications for task or delivery orders greater than the simplified acquisition threshold and awarded without providing for fair opportunity must be posted in accordance with 16.505(b)(2)(ii)(D).

[FAC 2005-30, 74 FR 2731, 1/15/2009, effective 2/17/2009; FAC 2005-42, 75 FR 34273, 6/16/2010, effective 7/16/2010; FAC 2005-50, 76 FR 14548, 3/16/2011, effective 5/16/2011; FAC 2005-56, 77 FR 12927, 3/2/2012, effective 4/2/2012]

SUBPART 5.5—PAID ADVERTISEMENTS

5.501 Definitions.

As used in this subpart—

Advertisement means any single message prepared for placement in communication media, regardless of the number of placements.

Publication means—

(1) The placement of an advertisement in a newspaper, magazine, trade or professional journal, or any other printed medium; or

(2) The broadcasting of an advertisement over radio or television.

[FAC 97-22, 66 FR 2116, 1/10/2001, effective 3/12/2001; Delay of effective date, 66 FR 14259, 3/9/2001, effective 5/11/2001; FAC 2019-02, 84 FR 19839, 5/6/2019, effective 5/6/2019]

5.502 Authority.

(a) *Newspapers.* Authority to approve the publication of paid advertisements in newspapers is vested in the head of each agency (44 U.S.C. 3702). This approval authority may be delegated (5 U.S.C. 302 (b)). Contracting officers shall obtain written authorization in accordance with agency procedures before advertising in newspapers.

(b) *Other media.* Unless the agency head determines otherwise, advance written authorization is not required to place advertisements in media other than newspapers.

5.503 Procedures.

(a) *General.* (1) Orders for paid advertisements may be placed directly with the media or through an advertising agency. Contracting officers shall give small, small disadvantaged, women-owned, veteran-owned, HUBZone, and service-disabled veteran-owned small business concerns maximum opportunity to participate in these acquisitions.

(2) The contracting officer shall use the SF 1449 for paper solicitations. The SF 1449 shall be used to make awards or place orders unless the award/order is made by using electronic commerce or by using the

Governmentwide commercial purchase card for micropurchases.

(b) *Rates.* Advertisements may be paid for at rates not over the commercial rates charged private individuals, with the usual discounts (44 U.S.C. 3703).

(c) *Proof of advertising.* Every invoice for advertising shall be accompanied by a copy of the advertisement or an affidavit of publication furnished by the publisher, radio or television station, or advertising agency concerned (44 U.S.C. 3703). Paying offices shall retain the proof of advertising until the Government Accountability Office settles the paying office's account.

(d) *Payment.* Upon receipt of an invoice supported by proof of advertising, the contracting officer shall attach a copy of the written authority (see 5.502(a)) and submit the invoice for payment under agency procedures.

[FAC 84-53, 54 FR 48978, 11/28/89, effective 12/28/89; FAC 90-29, 60 FR 34732, 7/3/95, effective 7/3/95; FAC 90-32, 60 FR 48206, 9/18/95, effective 10/1/95; FAC 90-40, 61 FR 39186, 7/26/96, effective 8/26/96; FAC 97-9, 63 FR 58587, 10/30/98, effective 10/30/98; FAC 2005-02, 70 FR 14950, 3/23/2005, effective 3/23/2005; FAC 2005-13, 71 FR 57380, 9/28/2006, effective 9/28/2006]

5.504 Use of advertising agencies.

(a) *General.* Basic ordering agreements may be placed with advertising agencies for assistance in producing and placing advertisements when a significant number will be placed in several publications and in national media. Services of advertising agencies include, but are not limited to, counseling as to selection of the media for placement of the advertisement, contacting the media in the interest of the Government, placing orders, selecting and ordering typography, copywriting, and preparing rough layouts.

(b) *Use of commission-paying media.* The services of advertising agencies in placing advertising with media often can be obtained at no cost to the Government, over and above the space cost, as many media give advertising agencies a commission or discount on the space cost that is not given to the Government.

(c) *Use of noncommission-paying media.* Some media do not grant advertising agencies a commission or discount, meaning the Government can obtain the same rate as the advertising agency. If the advertising agency agrees to place advertisements in noncommission-paying media as a no-cost service, the basic ordering agreement shall so provide. If the advertising agency will not agree to place advertisements at no cost, the agreement shall—

(1) Provide that the Government may place orders directly with the media; or

(2) Specify an amount that the Government will pay if the agency places the orders.

(d) *Art work, supplies, and incidentals.* The basic ordering agreement also may provide for the furnishing by the advertising agency of art work, supplies, and incidentals, including brochures and pamphlets, but not their printing. "Incidentals" may include telephone calls, and postage incurred by the advertising agency on behalf of the Government.

[FAC 2005-92, 81 FR 83097, 11/18/2016, effective 12/19/2016; FAC 2019-02, 84 FR 19839, 5/6/2019, effective 5/6/2019]

SUBPART 5.6—PUBLICIZING MULTI-AGENCY USE CONTRACTS

5.601 Governmentwide database of contracts.

(a) A Governmentwide database of contracts and other procurement instruments intended for use by multiple agencies is available via the Internet at *https://www.contractdirectory.gov/contractdirecotry/*. This searchable database is a tool that may be used to identify existing contracts and other procurement instruments that may be used to fulfill Government needs.

(b) The contracting activity shall—

(1) Enter the information specified at *https://www.contractdirectory.gov/contractdirecotry/*, in accordance with the instructions on that Web site, within ten days of award of a Governmentwide acquisition contract (GWAC), multi-agency contract,

Federal Supply Schedule contract, or any other procurement instrument intended for use by multiple agencies, including blanket purchase agreements (BPAs) under Federal Supply Schedule contracts.

(2) Enter the information specified at *https://www.contractdirectory.gov/contractdirecotry/* in accordance with the instructions on that Web site by October 31, 2003, for all contracts and other procurement instruments intended for use by multiple agencies that were awarded before July 24, 2003.

[FAC 2001-15, 68 FR 43859, 7/24/2003, effective 7/24/2003; FAC 2005-47, 75 FR 77745, 12/13/2010, effective 12/13/2010; FAC 2005-66, 78 FR 13768, 2/28/2013, effective 2/28/2013; Correction 78 FR 41331, 7/10/2013, effective 7/10/2013; FAC 2019-02, 84 FR 19839, 5/6/2019, effective 5/6/2019]

SUBPART 5.7—PUBLICIZING REQUIREMENTS UNDER THE AMERICAN RECOVERY AND REINVESTMENT ACT OF 2009

5.701 Scope.

This subpart prescribes posting requirements for presolicitation and award notices for actions funded in whole or in part by the American Recovery and Reinvestment Act of 2009 (Pub. L. 111-5) (Recovery Act). The requirements of this subpart enhance transparency to the public.

[FAC 2005-32, 74 FR 14636, 3/31/2009, effective 3/31/2009; FAC 2005-42, 75 FR 34271, 6/16/2010, effective 7/16/2010]

5.702 Applicability.

This subpart applies to all actions expected to exceed $25,000 funded in whole or in part by the Recovery Act. Unlike subparts 5.2 and 5.3, this subpart includes additional requirements for orders and for actions that are not both fixed-price and competitive.

[FAC 2005-32, 74 FR 14636, 3/31/2009, effective 3/31/2009; FAC 2005-42, 75 FR 34271, 6/16/2010, effective 7/16/2010]

5.703 Definition.

As used in this subpart—

Task or delivery order contract means a *delivery order contract*, and a *task order contract*, as defined in 16.501-1. For example, it includes Governmentwide Acquisition Contracts (GWACs), multi-agency contracts (MACs), and other indefinite-delivery/indefinite-quantity contracts, whether single award or multiple award. It also includes Federal Supply Schedule contracts (including Blanket Purchase Agreements under Subpart 8.4).

[FAC 2005-32, 74 FR 14636, 3/31/2009, effective 3/31/2009; FAC 2005-42, 75 FR 34271, 6/16/2010, effective 7/16/2010]

5.704 Publicizing preaward.

(a) (1) Follow the publication procedures at 5.201.

(2) In addition, notices of proposed contract actions are required for orders exceeding $25,000, funded in whole or in part by the Recovery Act, which are issued under task or delivery order contracts. This does not include modifications to existing orders, but these modifications are covered postaward, see 5.705. These notices are for "informational purposes only," therefore, 5.203 does not apply. Contracting officers should concurrently use their usual solicitation practice (*e.g.*, e-Buy).

(b) Contracting officers shall identify proposed contract actions, funded in whole or in part by the Recovery Act, by using the following instructions which are also available in the Recovery FAQs under "Buyers/Engineers" at the Governmentwide Point of Entry (GPE) (*https://www.fbo.gov*):

(1) If submitting notices electronically via ftp or email, enter the word "Recovery" as the first word in the title field.

(2) If using the GPE directly, select the "yes" radio button for the "Is this a Recovery and Reinvestment Act action" field on the "Notice Details" form (Step 2) located below the "NAICS Code" field. In addition, enter the word "Recovery" as the first word in the title field.

(c) In preparing the description required by 5.207(a)(16), use clear and concise language to describe the planned procurement. Use descriptions of the goods and services (including construction), that can be understood by the general public. Avoid the use of acronyms or terminology that is not widely understood by the general public.

[FAC 2005-32, 74 FR 14636, 3/31/2009, effective 3/31/2009; FAC 2005-42, 75 FR 34271, 6/16/2010, effective 7/16/2010; FAC 2005-100, 83 FR 42571, 8/22/2018, effective 8/22/2018]

5.705 Publicizing postaward.

Follow usual publication procedures at 5.301, except that the following supersede the exceptions at 5.301(b)(2) through (7):

(a)(1) Publicize the award notice for any action exceeding $500,000, funded in whole or in part by the Recovery Act, including—

(i) Contracts;

(ii) Modifications to existing contracts;

(iii) Orders which are issued under task or delivery order contracts; and

(iv) Modifications to orders under task or delivery order contracts.

(2) Contracting officers shall identify contract actions, funded in whole or in part by the Recovery Act, by using the following instructions which are also available in the Recovery FAQS under "Buyers/Engineers" at the Governmentwide Point of Entry (GPE) (*https://www.fbo.gov*):

(i) If submitting notices electronically via ftp or email, enter the word "Recovery" as the first word in the title field.

(ii) If using the GPE directly, select the "yes" radio button for the "Is this a Recovery and Reinvestment Act action" field on the "Notice Details" form (Step 2) located below the "NAICS Code" field. In addition, enter the word "Recovery" as the first word in the title field.

(3) In preparing the description required by 5.207(a)(16), use clear and concise language to describe the planned procurement. Use descriptions of the goods and services (including construction), that can be understood by the general public. Avoid the use of acronyms or terminology that is not widely understood by the general public.

(b) Regardless of dollar value, if the contract action, including all modifications and orders under task or delivery order contracts, is not both fixed-price and competitively awarded, publicize the award notice and include in the description the rationale for using other than a fixed-priced and/or competitive approach. Include in the description a statement specifically noting if the contract action was not awarded competitively, or was not fixed-price, or was neither competitive nor fixed-price. These notices and the rationale will be available to the public at the GPE, so do not include any proprietary information or information that would compromise national security. The following table provides examples for when a rationale is required.

POSTING OF RATIONALE—EXAMPLES

Description of contract action	Rationale Required
(1) A contract is competitively awarded and is fixed-price.	Not required.
(2) A contract is awarded that is not fixed-price.	Required.
(3) A contract is awarded without competition.	Required.
(4) An order is issued under a new or existing single award IDIQ contract.	Required if order is made under a contract described in paragraph (b)(2) or (3) of this section.
(5) An order is issued under a new or existing multiple award IDIQ contract.	Required if one or both of the following conditions exist:

Description of contract action	Rationale Required
	(i) The order is not fixed-price. (ii) The order is awarded pursuant to an exception to the competition requirements applicable to the underlying vehicle (*e.g.*, award is made pursuant to an exception to the fair opportunity process).
(6) A modification is issued.	Required if modification is made— (i) To a contract described in paragraph (b)(2) or (3) of this section; or (ii) To an order requiring posting as described in paragraph (b)(4) or (5) of this section.
(7) A contract or order is awarded pursuant to a small business contracting authority (*e.g.*, SBA's section 8(a) program).	Required if one or both of the following conditions exist: (i) The contract or order is not fixed-price; (ii) The contract or order was not awarded using competition (*e.g.*, a noncompetitive 8(a) award).

(c) Contracting officers shall use the instructions available in the Recovery FAQs under "Buyers/Engineers" at the GPE (*https://www.fbo.gov*) to identify actions funded in whole or in part by the Recovery Act.

[FAC 2005-32, 74 FR 14636, 3/31/2009, effective 3/31/2009; Technical amendment, 74 FR 22809, 5/14/2009, effective 5/14/2009; FAC 2005-42, 75 FR 34271, 6/16/2010, effective 7/16/2010; FAC 2005-50, 76 FR 14548, 3/16/2011, effective 5/16/2011; FAC 2005-56, 77 FR 12927, 3/2/2012, effective 4/2/2012; FAC 2005-100, 83 FR 42571, 8/22/2018, effective 8/22/2018; FAC 2019-02, 84 FR 19839, 5/6/2019, effective 5/6/2019]

PART 6—COMPETITION REQUIREMENTS

Table of Contents

Scope of part 6.000
Applicability 6.001
Limitations 6.002
[Reserved] 6.003

Subpart 6.1—Full and Open Competition

Scope of subpart 6.100
Policy 6.101
Use of competitive procedures 6.102

Subpart 6.2—Full and Open Competition After Exclusion of Sources

Scope of subpart 6.200
Policy 6.201
Establishing or maintaining alternative sources 6.202
Set-asides for small business concerns 6.203
Section 8(a) competition 6.204
Set-asides for HUBZone small business concerns 6.205
Set-asides for service-disabled veteran-owned small business concerns 6.206
Set-asides for economically disadvantaged women-owned small business (EDWOSB) concerns or women-owned small business (WOSB) concerns eligible under the WOSB Program 6.207
Set-asides for local firms during a major disaster or emergency 6.208

Subpart 6.3—Other Than Full and Open Competition

Scope of subpart 6.300
Policy 6.301
Circumstances permitting other than full and open competition 6.302
Only one responsible source and no other supplies or services will satisfy agency requirements 6.302-1
Unusual and compelling urgency 6.302-2
Industrial mobilization; engineering, developmental, or research capability; or expert services 6.302-3
International agreement 6.302-4
Authorized or required by statute 6.302-5
National security 6.302-6
Public interest 6.302-7
Justifications 6.303
Requirements 6.303-1
Content 6.303-2
Approval of the justification 6.304
Availability of the justification 6.305

Subpart 6.4—Sealed Bidding and Competitive Proposals

Sealed bidding and competitive proposals 6.401

Subpart 6.5—Advocates for Competition

Requirement 6.501
Duties and responsibilities 6.502

PART 6—COMPETITION REQUIREMENTS

6.000 Scope of part.

This part prescribes policies and procedures to promote full and open competition in the acquisition process and to provide for full and open competition, full and open competition after exclusion of sources, other than full and open competition, and advocates for competition. This part does not deal with the results of competition (e.g., adequate price competition), that are addressed in other parts (e.g., part 15).

[FAC 97-22, 66 FR 2116, 1/10/2001, effective 3/12/2001; Delay of effective date, 66 FR 14259, 3/9/2001, effective 5/11/2001; FAC 2005-73, 79 FR 24192, 4/29/2014, effective 5/29/2014]

6.001 Applicability.

This part applies to all acquisitions except—

(a) Contracts awarded using the simplified acquisition procedures of Part 13 (but see 13.501 for requirements pertaining to sole source acquisitions of commercial items under Subpart 13.5);

(b) Contracts awarded using contracting procedures (other than those addressed in this part) that are expressly authorized by statute;

(c) Contract modifications, including the exercise of priced options that were evaluated as part of the initial competition (see 17.207(f)), that are within the scope and under the terms of an existing contract;

(d) Orders placed under requirements contracts or definite-quantity contracts;

(e) Orders placed under indefinite-quantity contracts that were entered into pursuant to this part when—

(1) The contract was awarded under Subpart 6.1 or 6.2 and all responsible sources were realistically permitted to compete for the requirements contained in the order; or

(2) The contract was awarded under Subpart 6.3 and the required justification and approval adequately covers the requirements contained in the order; or

(f) Orders placed against task order and delivery order contracts entered into pursuant to Subpart 16.5.

[FAC 84-5, 50 FR 1729, 1/11/85, effective 4/1/85; FAC 84-13, 50 FR 52431, 12/23/85, effective 2/3/86; FAC 90-3, 55 FR 52790, 12/21/90, effective 1/22/91; FAC 90-29, 60 FR 34732, 7/3/95, effective 7/3/95; FAC 90-33, 60 FR 49706, 9/26/95, effective 10/1/95; FAC 90-45, Final rule, 62 FR 224, 1/2/97, effective 1/1/97, corrected 62 FR 10709, 3/10/97; FAC 97-3, 62 FR 64912, 12/9/97, effective 2/9/98; FAC 2019-02, 84 FR 19839, 5/6/2019, effective 5/6/2019]

6.002 Limitations.

No agency shall contract for supplies or services from another agency for the purpose of avoiding the requirements of this part.

[FAC 84-5, 50 FR 1729, 1/11/85, effective 4/1/85]

6.003 [Reserved]

[Removed and reserved, FAC 97-22, 66 FR 2116, 1/10/2001, effective 3/12/2001; Delay of effective date, 66 FR 14259, 3/9/2001, effective 5/11/2001]

SUBPART 6.1—FULL AND OPEN COMPETITION

6.100 Scope of subpart.

This subpart prescribes the policy and procedures that are to be used to promote and provide for full and open competition.

[FAC 84-5, 50 FR 1729, 1/11/85, effective 4/1/85; corrected 50 FR 4221, 1/30/85]

6.101 Policy.

(a) 10 U.S.C. 2304 and 41 U.S.C. 3301 require, with certain limited exceptions (see Subparts 6.2 and 6.3), that contracting officers shall promote and provide for full and open competition in soliciting offers and awarding Government contracts.

(b) Contracting officers shall provide for full and open competition through use of the competitive procedure(s) contained in this subpart that are best suited to the circumstances of the contract action and consistent with the need to fulfill the Government's requirements efficiently (10 U.S.C. 2304 and 41 U.S.C. 3301).

[FAC 84-5, 50 FR 1729, 1/11/85, effective 4/1/85; FAC 97-2, 62 FR 51224, 9/30/97, effective 10/10/97; FAC 2005-73, 79 FR 24192, 4/29/2014, effective 5/29/2014]

6.102 Use of competitive procedures.

The competitive procedures available for use in fulfilling the requirement for full and open competition are as follows:

(a) *Sealed bids.* (See 6.401(a).)

(b) *Competitive proposals.* (See 6.401(b).) If sealed bids are not appropriate under paragraph (a) of this section, contracting officers shall request competitive proposals or use the other competitive procedures under paragraph (c) or (d) of this section.

(c) *Combination of competitive procedures.* If sealed bids are not appropriate, contracting officers may use any combination of competitive procedures (*e.g.*, two-step sealed bidding).

(d) *Other competitive procedures.*

(1) Selection of sources for architect-engineer contracts in accordance with the provisions of 40 U.S.C. 1102 *et seq.* is a competitive procedure (see Subpart 36.6 for procedures).

(2) Competitive selection of basic and applied research and that part of development not related to the development of a specific system or hardware procurement is a competitive procedure if award results from—

(i) A broad agency announcement that is general in nature identifying areas of research interest, including criteria for selecting proposals, and soliciting the participation of all offerors capable of satisfying the Government's needs; and

(ii) A peer or scientific review.

(3) Use of multiple award schedules issued under the procedures established by the Administrator of General Services consistent with the requirement of 41 U.S.C. 152(3)(A) for the multiple award schedule program of the General Services Administration is a competitive procedure.

[FAC 84-5, 50 FR 1729, 1/11/85, effective 4/1/85; FAC 84-18, 51 FR 27119, 7/29/86, effective 7/30/86; FAC 84-38, 53 FR 27463, 7/20/88, effective 8/19/88; FAC 90-21, 59 FR 53716, 10/25/94, effective 10/25/94; FAC 2005-06, 70 FR 57453, 9/30/2005, effective 9/30/2005; FAC 2005-73, 79 FR 24192, 4/29/2014, effective 5/29/2014; FAC 2019-02, 84 FR 19839, 5/6/2019, effective 5/6/2019]

SUBPART 6.2—FULL AND OPEN COMPETITION AFTER EXCLUSION OF SOURCES

6.200 Scope of subpart.

This subpart prescribes policies and procedures for providing for full and open competition after excluding one or more sources. [FAC 84-5, 50 FR 1729, 1/11/85, effective 4/1/85]

6.201 Policy.

Acquisitions made under this subpart require use of the competitive procedures prescribed in 6.102.

[FAC 97-14, 64 FR 51828, 9/24/99, effective 11/23/99]

6.202 Establishing or maintaining alternative sources.

(a) Agencies may exclude a particular source from a contract action in order to establish or maintain an alternative source or sources for the supplies or services being acquired if the agency head determines that to do so would—

(1) Increase or maintain competition and likely result in reduced overall costs for the acquisition, or for any anticipated acquisition;

(2) Be in the interest of national defense in having a facility (or a producer, manufacturer, or other supplier) available for furnishing the supplies or services in case of a national emergency or industrial mobilization;

(3) Be in the interest of national defense in establishing or maintaining an essential engineering, research, or development capability to be provided by an educational or other nonprofit institution or a federally funded research and development center;

(4) Ensure the continuous availability of a reliable source of supplies or services;

(5) Satisfy projected needs based on a history of high demand; or

(6) Satisfy a critical need for medical, safety, or emergency supplies.

(b) (1) Every proposed contract action under the authority of paragraph (a) of this section shall be supported by a determination and findings (D&F) (see Subpart 1.7) signed by the head of the agency or designee. This D&F shall not be made on a class basis.

(2) Technical and requirements personnel are responsible for providing all necessary data to support their recommendation to exclude a particular source.

(3) When the authority in paragraph (a) (1) of this section is cited, the findings shall include a description of the estimated reduction in overall costs and how the estimate was derived.

[FAC 84-5, 50 FR 1729, 1/11/85, effective 4/1/85; FAC 90-31, 60 FR 42648, 8/16/95, effective 10/1/95; FAC 2019-02, 84 FR 19839, 5/6/2019, effective 5/6/2019]

6.203 Set-asides for small business concerns.

(a) To fulfill the statutory requirements relating to small business concerns, contracting officers may set aside solicitations to allow only such business concerns to compete. This includes contract actions conducted under the Small Business Innovation Research Program established under Pub. L. 97-219.

(b) No separate justification or determination and findings is required under this part to set aside a contract action for small business concerns.

(c) Subpart 19.5 prescribes policies and procedures that shall be followed with respect to set-asides.

[FAC 90-32, 60 FR 48206, 9/18/95, effective 10/1/95]

6.204 Section 8(a) competition.

(a) To fulfill statutory requirements relating to section 8(a) of the Small Business Act, as amended by Public Law 100-656, contracting officers may limit competition to eligible 8(a) participants (see subpart 19.8).

(b) No separate justification or determination and findings is required under this part to limit competition to eligible 8(a) participants. (But see 6.302-5 and 6.303- 1 for sole source 8(a) awards over $22 million.)

[FAC 84-5, 50 FR 1729, 1/11/85, effective 4/1/85; FAC 84-52, 54 FR 46005, 10/31/89, effective 11/30/89; FAC 2005-50, 76 FR 14559, 3/16/2011, effective 3/16/2011; FAC 2005-58, 77 FR 23369, 4/18/2012, effective 4/18/2012; FAC 2005-83, 80 FR 38293, 7/2/2015, effective 10/1/2015; FAC 2005-95, 82 FR 4724, 1/13/2017, effective 1/13/2017]

6.205 Set-asides for HUBZone small business concerns.

(a) To fulfill the statutory requirements relating to the HUBZone Act of 1997 (15 U.S.C. 631 note), contracting officers in participating agencies (see 19.1302) may set aside solicitations to allow only qualified HUBZone small business concerns to compete (see 19.1305).

(b) No separate justification or determination and findings is required under this part to set aside a contract action for qualified HUBZone small business concerns.

[FAC 97-10, 63 FR 70264, 12/18/98, effective 1/4/99]

6.206 Set-asides for service-disabled veteran-owned small business concerns.

(a) To fulfill the statutory requirements relating to the Veterans Benefits Act of 2003 (15 U.S.C. 657f), contracting officers may set-aside solicitations to allow only service-disabled veteran-owned small business concerns to compete (see 19.1405).

(b) No separate justification or determination and findings are required under this part to set aside a contract action for service-disabled veteran-owned small business concerns.

[FAC 2001-23, 69 FR 25273, 5/5/2004, effective 5/5/2004; FAC 2005-02, 70 FR 14950, 3/23/2005, effective 3/23/2005]

6.207 Set-asides for economically disadvantaged women-owned small

business (EDWOSB) concerns or women-owned small business (WOSB) concerns eligible under the WOSB Program.

(a) To fulfill the statutory requirements relating to 15 U.S.C. 637(m), contracting officers may set aside solicitations for only EDWOSB concerns or WOSB concerns eligible under the WOSB Program (see 19.1505).

(b) No separate justification or determination and findings is required under this part to set aside a contract action for EDWOSB concerns or WOSB concerns eligible under the WOSB Program.

[FAC 2005-51, 76 FR 18304, 4/1/2011, effective 4/1/2011; FAC 2005-56, 77 FR 12913, 3/2/2012, effective 4/2/2012]

6.208 Set-asides for local firms during a major disaster or emergency.

(a) To fulfill the statutory requirements relating to 42 U.S.C. 5150, contracting officers may set aside solicitations to allow only offerors residing or doing business primarily in the area affected by such major disaster or emergency to compete (see Subpart 26.2).

(b) No separate justification or determination and findings is required under this part to set aside a contract action. The set-aside area specified by the contracting officer shall be a geographic area within the area identified in a Presidential declaration(s) of major disaster or emergency and any additional geographic areas identified by the Department of Homeland Security.

[FAC 2005-21, 72 FR 63084, 11/7/2007, effective 11/7/2007; FAC 2005-27, 73 FR 53995, 9/17/2008, effective 10/17/2008; Redesignated from 6.207, FAC 2005-51, 76 FR 18304, 4/1/2011, effective 4/1/2011; FAC 2005-56, 77 FR 12913, 3/2/2012, effective 4/2/2012]

SUBPART 6.3—OTHER THAN FULL AND OPEN COMPETITION

6.300 Scope of subpart.

This subpart prescribes policies and procedures, and identifies the statutory authorities, for contracting without providing for full and open competition.

[FAC 84-5, 50 FR 1729, 1/11/85, effective 4/1/85]

6.301 Policy.

(a) 41 U.S.C. 253(c) and 10 U.S.C. 2304(c) each authorize, under certain conditions, contracting without providing for full and open competition. The Department of Defense, Coast Guard, and National Aeronautics and Space Administration are subject to 10 U.S.C. 2304(c). Contracting without providing for full and open competition or full and open competition after exclusion of sources is a violation of statute, unless permitted by one of the exceptions in 6.302.

(b) Each contract awarded without providing for full and open competition shall contain a reference to the specific authority under which it was so awarded. Contracting officers shall use the U.S. Code citation applicable to their agency. (See 6.302.)

(c) Contracting without providing for full and open competition shall not be justified on the basis of—

(1) A lack of advance planning by the requiring activity; or

(2) Concerns related to the amount of funds available (*e.g.*, funds will expire) to the agency or activity for the acquisition of supplies or services.

(d) When not providing for full and open competition, the contracting officer shall solicit offers from as many potential sources as is practicable under the circumstances.

(e) For contracts under this subpart, the contracting officer shall use the contracting procedures prescribed in 6.102(a) or (b), if appropriate, or any other procedures authorized by this regulation.

[FAC 84-5, 50 FR 1729, 1/11/85, effective 4/1/85; FAC 2005-73, 79 FR 24192, 4/29/2014, effective 5/29/2014; FAC 2019-02, 84 FR 19839, 5/6/2019, effective 5/6/2019]

6.302 Circumstances permitting other than full and open competition.

The following statutory authorities (including applications and limitations) permit contracting without providing for full and open competition. Requirements for justifications to support the use of these authorities are in 6.303.

[FAC 84-5, 50 FR 1729, 1/11/85, effective 4/1/85; FAC 84-13, 50 FR 52431, 12/23/85, effective 2/3/86]

6.302-1 Only one responsible source and no other supplies or services will satisfy agency requirements.

(a) *Authority.*

(1) Citations: 10 U.S.C. 2304(c)(1) or 41 U.S.C. 3304(a)(1).

(2) When the supplies or services required by the agency are available from only one responsible source, or, for DoD, NASA, and the Coast Guard, from only one or a limited number of responsible sources, and no other type of supplies or services will satisfy agency requirements, full and open competition need not be provided for.

(i) Supplies or services may be considered to be available from only one source if the source has submitted an unsolicited research proposal that—

(A) Demonstrates a unique and innovative concept (see definition at 2.101), or, demonstrates a unique capability of the source to provide the particular research services proposed;

(B) Offers a concept or services not otherwise available to the Government; and

(C) Does not resemble the substance of a pending competitive acquisition. (See 10 U.S.C. 2304(d)(1)(A) and 41 U.S.C. 3304(b)(1)).

(ii) Supplies may be deemed to be available only from the original source in the case of a follow-on contract for the continued development or production of a major system or highly specialized equipment, including major components thereof, when it is likely that award to any other source would result in—

(A) Substantial duplication of cost to the Government that is not expected to be recovered through competition; or

(B) Unacceptable delays in fulfilling the agency's requirements. (See 10 U.S.C. 2304(d)(1)(B) or 41 U.S.C. 3304(b)(2).)

(iii) For DoD, NASA, and the Coast Guard, services may be deemed to be available only from the original source in the case of follow-on contracts for the continued provision of highly specialized services when it is likely that award to any other source would result in—

(A) Substantial duplication of cost to the Government that is not expected to be recovered through competition; or

(B) Unacceptable delays in fulfilling the agency's requirements. (See 10 U.S.C. 2304(d)(1)(B).)

(b) *Application.* This authority shall be used, if appropriate, in preference to the authority in 6.302-7; it shall not be used when any of the other circumstances is applicable. Use of this authority may be appropriate in situations such as the following (these examples are not intended to be all-inclusive and do not constitute authority in and of themselves):

(1) When there is a reasonable basis to conclude that the agency's minimum needs can only be satisfied by—

(i) Unique supplies or services available from only one source or only one supplier with unique capabilities; or

(ii) For DoD, NASA, and the Coast Guard, unique supplies or services available from only one or a limited number of sources or from only one or a limited number of suppliers with unique capabilities.

(2) The existence of limited rights in data, patent rights, copyrights, or secret processes; the control of basic raw material; or similar circumstances, make the supplies and services available from only one source (however, the mere existence of such rights or circumstances does not in and of itself justify the use of these authorities) (see Part 27).

(3) When acquiring utility services (see 41.101), circumstances may dictate that only one supplier can furnish the service (see 41.202); or when the contemplated contract is for construction of a part of a utility sys-

tem and the utility company itself is the only source available to work on the system.

(4) When the agency head has determined in accordance with the agency's standardization program that only specified makes and models of technical equipment and parts will satisfy the agency's needs for additional units or replacement items, and only one source is available.

(c) *Application for brand-name descriptions.* (1) An acquisition or portion of an acquisition that uses a brand-name description or other purchase description to specify a particular brand-name, product, or feature of a product, peculiar to one manufacturer—

(i) Does not provide for full and open competition, regardless of the number of sources solicited; and

(ii) Shall be justified and approved in accordance with 6.303 and 6.304.

(A) If only a portion of the acquisition is for a brand-name product or item peculiar to one manufacturer, the justification and approval is to cover only the portion of the acquisition which is brand-name or peculiar to one manufacturer. The justification should state it is covering only the portion of the acquisition which is brand-name or peculiar to one manufacturer, and the approval level requirements will then only apply to that portion;

(B) The justification should indicate that the use of such descriptions in the acquisition or portion of an acquisition is essential to the Government's requirements, thereby precluding consideration of a product manufactured by another company; and

(C) The justification shall be posted with the solicitation (see 5.102(a)(6)).

(2) Brand-name or equal descriptions, and other purchase descriptions that permit prospective contractors to offer products other than those specifically referenced by brand-name, provide for full and open competition and do not require justifications and approvals to support their use.

(d) *Limitations.*

(1) Contracts awarded using this authority shall be supported by the written justifications and approvals described in 6.303 and 6.304.

(2) For contracts awarded using this authority, the notices required by 5.201 shall have been published and any bids, proposals, quotations, or capability statements must have been considered.

[FAC 84-5, 50 FR 1729, 1/11/85, effective 4/1/85; corrected 50 FR 4221, 1/30/85; FAC 84-13, 50 FR 52431, 12/23/85, effective 2/3/86; FAC 84-28, 52 FR 21886, 6/9/87, effective 4/16/87; FAC 84-38, 53 FR 27463, 7/20/88, effective 8/19/88; FAC 90-5, 56 FR 29127, 6/25/91, effective 7/25/91; FAC 90-23,59 FR 67010, 12/28/94, effective 2/27/95; FAC 97-2, 62 FR 51224, 9/30/97, effective 10/10/97; FAC 97-22, 66 FR 2116, 1/10/2001, effective 3/12/2001; Delay of effective date, 66 FR 14259, 3/9/2001, effective 5/11/2001; FAC 2005-13, 71 FR 57357, 9/28/2006, effective 9/28/2006; FAC 2005-24, 73 FR 10960, 2/28/2008, effective 3/31/2008; FAC 2005-55, 77 FR 189, 1/3/2012, effective 2/2/2012; FAC 2005-73, 79 FR 24192, 4/29/2014, effective 5/29/2014; FAC 2019-02, 84 FR 19839, 5/6/2019, effective 5/6/2019]

6.302-2 Unusual and compelling urgency.

(a) *Authority.*

(1) Citations: 10 U.S.C. 2304(c)(2) or 41 U.S.C. 3304(a)(2).

(2) When the agency's need for the supplies or services is of such an unusual and compelling urgency that the Government would be seriously injured unless the agency is permitted to limit the number of sources from which it solicits bids or proposals, full and open competition need not be provided for.

(b) *Application.* This authority applies in those situations where—

(1) An unusual and compelling urgency precludes full and open competition; and

(2) Delay in award of a contract would result in serious injury, financial or other, to the Government.

(c) *Limitations.*

(1) Contracts awarded using this authority shall be supported by the written justifica-

tions and approvals described in 6.303 and FAR 6.304. These justifications may be made and approved after contract award when preparation and approval prior to award would unreasonably delay the acquisition.

(2) This statutory authority requires that agencies shall request offers from as many potential sources as is practicable under the circumstances.

(d) *Period of Performance.* (1) The total period of performance of a contract awarded or modified using this authority—

(i) May not exceed the time necessary—

(A) To meet the unusual and compelling requirements of the work to be performed under the contract; and

(B) For the agency to enter into another contract for the required goods and services through the use of competitive procedures; and

(ii) May not exceed one year, including all options, unless the head of the agency determines that exceptional circumstances apply. This determination must be documented in the contract file.

(2) (i) Any subsequent modification using this authority, which will extend the period of performance beyond one year under this same authority, requires a separate determination. This determination is only required if the cumulative period of performance using this authority exceeds one year. This requirement does not apply to the exercise of options previously addressed in the determination required at paragraph (d) (1) (ii) of this section.

(ii) The determination shall be approved at the same level as the level to which the agency head authority in paragraph (d) (1) (ii) of this section is delegated.

(3) The requirements in paragraphs (d) (1) and (2) of this section shall apply to any contract in an amount greater than the simplified acquisition threshold.

(4) The determination of exceptional circumstances is in addition to the approval of the justification in 6.304.

(5) The determination may be made after contract award when making the determination prior to award would unreasonably delay the acquisition.

[FAC 84-5, 50 FR 1729, 1/11/85, effective 4/1/85; FAC 84-13, 50 FR 52431, 12/23/85, effective 2/3/86; FAC 2005-37, 74 FR 52849, 10/14/2009, effective 10/14/2009; FAC 2005-38, 74 FR 65614, 12/10/2009, effective 12/10/2009; FAC 2005-73, 79 FR 24192, 4/29/2014, effective 5/29/2014; FAC 2005-83, 80 FR 38308, 7/2/2015, effective 8/3/2015; FAC 2019-02, 84 FR 19839, 5/6/2019, effective 5/6/2019]

6.302-3 Industrial mobilization; engineering, developmental, or research capability; or expert services.

(a) *Authority.*

(1) Citations: 10 U.S.C. 2304(c)(3) or 41 U.S.C. 3304(a)(3).

(2) Full and open competition need not be provided for when it is necessary to award the contract to a particular source or sources in order—

(i) To maintain a facility, producer, manufacturer, or other supplier available for furnishing supplies or services in case of a national emergency or to achieve industrial mobilization;

(ii) To establish or maintain an essential engineering, research, or development capability to be provided by an educational or other nonprofit institution or a federally funded research and development center;

(iii) To acquire the services of an expert or neutral person for any current or anticipated litigation or dispute.

(b) *Application.*

(1) Use of the authority in (a) (2) (i) of this section may be appropriate when it is necessary to—

(i) Keep vital facilities or suppliers in business or make them available in the event of a national emergency;

(ii) Train a selected supplier in the furnishing of critical supplies or services, prevent the loss of a supplier's ability and employees' skills, or maintain active engineering, research, or development work;

(iii) Maintain properly balanced sources of supply for meeting the requirements of acquisition programs in the interest of industrial mobilization (when the quantity required is substantially larger than the quantity that must be awarded in order to meet the objectives of this authority, that portion not required to meet such objectives will be acquired by providing for full and open competition as appropriate under this part);

(iv) Create or maintain the required domestic capability for production of critical supplies by limiting competition to items manufactured in—

(A) The United States or its outlying areas; or

(B) The United States, its outlying areas, or Canada.

(v) Continue in production, contractors that are manufacturing critical items, where there would otherwise be a break in production; or

(vi) Divide current production requirements among two or more contractors to provide for an adequate industrial mobilization base.

(2) Use of the authority in paragraph (a)(2)(ii) of this section may be appropriate when it is necessary to—

(i) Establish or maintain an essential capability for theoretical analyses, exploratory studies, or experiments in any field of science or technology;

(ii) Establish or maintain an essential capability for engineering or developmental work calling for the practical application of investigative findings and theories of a scientific or technical nature; or

(iii) Contract for supplies or services as are necessary incident to paragraph (b)(2)(i) or (ii) of this section.

(3) Use of the authority in paragraph (a)(2)(iii) of this section may be appropriate when it is necessary to acquire the services of either—

(i) An expert to use, in any litigation or dispute (including any reasonably foreseeable litigation or dispute) involving the Government in any trial, hearing, or proceeding before any court, administrative tribunal, or agency, whether or not the expert is expected to testify. Examples of such services include, but are not limited to:

(A) Assisting the Government in the analysis, presentation, or defense of any claim or request for adjustment to contract terms and conditions, whether asserted by a contractor or the Government, which is in litigation or dispute, or is anticipated to result in dispute or litigation before any court, administrative tribunal, or agency, or

(B) Participating in any part of an alternative dispute resolution process, including but not limited to evaluators, fact finders, or witnesses, regardless of whether the expert is expected to testify; or

(ii) A neutral person, e.g., mediators or arbitrators, to facilitate the resolution of issues in an alternative dispute resolution process.

(c) *Limitations.* Contracts awarded using this authority shall be supported by the written justifications and approvals described in 6.303 and 6.304.

[FAC 84-5, 50 FR 1729, 1/11/85, effective 4/1/85; FAC 84-13, 50 FR 52431, 12/23/85, effective 2/3/86; [FAC 90-31, 60 FR 42648, 8/16/95, effective 10/1/95, corrected 60 FR 44548, 8/28/95; FAC 90-45, Final rule, 62 FR 224, 1/2/97, effective 1/1/97; FAC 97-9, 63 FR 58587, 10/30/98, (a)(2)(i) and (a)(2)(ii) effective 10/30/98, (a)(2)(iii) effective 12/29/98; FAC 97-22,66 FR 2116, 1/10/2001, effective 3/12/2001; Delay of effective date, 66 FR 14259, 3/9/2001, effective 5/11/2001; FAC 2001-14, 68 FR 28079, 5/22/2003, effective 6/23/2003; FAC 2005-61, 77 FR 56740, 9/13/2012, effective 10/15/2012; FAC 2005-73, 79 FR 24192, 4/29/2014, effective 5/29/2014; FAC 2019-02, 84 FR 19839, 5/6/2019, effective 5/6/2019]

6.302-4 International agreement.

(a) *Authority.*

(1) Citations: 10 U.S.C. 2304(c)(4) or 41 U.S.C. 3304(a)(4).

(2) Full and open competition need not be provided for when precluded by the terms of an international agreement or a treaty between the United States and a foreign gov-

ernment or international organization, or the written directions of a foreign government reimbursing the agency for the cost of the acquisition of the supplies or services of such government.

(b) *Application.* This authority may be used in circumstances such as—

(1) When a contemplated acquisition is to be reimbursed by a foreign country that requires that the product be obtained from a particular firm as specified in official written direction such as a Letter of Offer and Acceptance; or

(2) When a contemplated acquisition is for services to be performed, or supplies to be used, in the sovereign territory of another country and the terms of a treaty or agreement specify or limit the sources to be solicited.

(c) *Limitations.* Except for DOD, NASA, and the Coast Guard, contracts awarded using this authority shall be supported by written justifications and approvals described in 6.303 and 6.304.

[FAC 84-5, 50 FR 1729, 1/11/85, effective 4/1/85; FAC 84-13, 50 FR 52432, 12/23/85, effective 2/3/86; FAC 90-3, 55 FR 52790, 12/21/90, effective 1/22/91; FAC 2005-73, 79 FR 24192, 4/29/2014, effective 5/29/2014]

6.302-5 Authorized or required by statute.

(a) *Authority.*

(1) Citations: 10 U.S.C. 2304(c)(5) or 41 U.S.C. 3304(a)(5).

(2) Full and open competition need not be provided for when—

(i) A statute expressly authorizes or requires that the acquisition be made through another agency or from a specified source; or

(ii) The agency's need is for a brand name commercial item for authorized resale.

(b) *Application.* This authority may be used when statutes, such as the following, expressly authorize or require that acquisition be made from a specified source or through another agency:

(1) Federal Prison Industries (UNICOR)—18 U.S.C. 4124 (see Subpart 8.6).

(2) Qualified nonprofit agencies for the blind or other severely disabled—41 U.S.C. chapter 85, Committee for Purchase From People Who Are Blind or Severely Disabled (see subpart 8.7).

(3) Government Printing and Binding—44 U.S.C. 501-504, 1121 (see Subpart 8.8).

(4) Sole source awards under the 8(a) Program (15 U.S.C. 637), but *see* 6.303 for requirements for justification and approval of sole-source 8(a) awards over $22 million. (*See* subpart 19.8.)

(5) Sole source awards under the HUBZone Act of 1997—15 U.S.C. 657a (see 19.1306).

(6) Sole source awards under the Veterans Benefits Act of 2003 (15 U.S.C. 657f).

(7) Sole source awards under the WOSB Program-15 U.S.C. 637(m) (see 19.1506).

(c) *Limitations.*

(1) This authority shall not be used when a provision of law requires an agency to award a new contract to a specified non-Federal Government entity unless the provision of law specifically—

(i) Identifies the entity involved;

(ii) Refers to 10 U.S.C. 2304(k) for armed services acquisitions or 41 U.S.C. 3105 for civilian agency acquisitions; and

(iii) States that award to that entity shall be made in contravention of the merit-based selection procedures in 10 U.S.C. 2304(k) or 41 U.S.C. 3105, as appropriate. However, this limitation does not apply—

(A) When the work provided for in the contract is a continuation of the work performed by the specified entity under a preceding contract; or

(B) To any contract requiring the National Academy of Sciences to investigate, examine, or experiment upon any subject of science or art of significance to an executive agency and to report on those matters to the Congress or any agency of the Federal Government.

(2) Contracts awarded using this authority shall be supported by the written justifications and approvals described in 6.303 and 6.304, except for—

(i) Contracts awarded under paragraph (a)(2)(ii) or (b)(2) of this section;

(ii) Contracts awarded under paragraph (a)(2)(i) of this section when the statute expressly requires that the procurement be made from a specified source. (Justification and approval requirements apply when the statute authorizes, but does not require, that the procurement be made from a specified source); or

(iii) Contracts less than or equal to $22 million awarded under paragraph (b)(4) of this section.

(3) The authority in paragraph (a)(2)(ii) of this section may be used only for purchases of brand-name commercial items for resale through commissaries or other similar facilities. Ordinarily, these purchases will involve articles desired or preferred by customers of the selling activities (but see 6.301(d)).

[FAC 84-5, 50 FR 1729, 1/11/85, effective 4/1/85; FAC 84-13, 50 FR 52432, 12/23/85, effective 2/3/86; FAC 84-23, 51 FR 36971, 10/16/86, effective 9/30/86; FAC 84-52, 54 FR 46005, 10/31/89, effective 11/30/89; FAC 90-31, 60 FR 42648, 8/16/95, effective 10/1/95; FAC 90-40, 61 FR 39186, 7/26/96, effective 9/24/96; FAC 97-10, 63 FR 70264, 12/18/98, effective 1/4/99; FAC 2001-06, 67 FR 13048, 3/20/2002, effective 4/4/2002; FAC 2001-23, 69 FR 25273, 5/5/2004, effective 5/5/2004; FAC 2005-02, 70 FR 14950, 3/23/2005, effective 3/23/2005; FAC 2005-12, 71 FR 44546, 8/4/2006, effective 8/4/2006; FAC 2005-27, 73 FR 53995, 9/17/2008, effective 10/17/2008; FAC 2005-50, 76 FR 14559, 3/16/2011, effective 3/16/2011; FAC 2005-58, 77 FR 23369, 4/18/2012, effective 4/18/2012; FAC 2005-73, 79 FR 24192, 4/29/2014, effective 5/29/2014; FAC 2005-83, 80 FR 38293, 7/2/2015, effective 10/1/2015; FAC 2005-86, 80 FR 81888, 12/31/2015, effective 12/31/2015; FAC 2005-91, 81 FR 67735, 9/30/2016, effective 9/30/2016; FAC 2019-02, 84 FR 19839, 5/6/2019, effective 5/6/2019]

6.302-6 National security.

(a) *Authority.*

(1) Citations: 10 U.S.C. 2304(c)(6) or 41 U.S.C. 3304(a)(6).

(2) Full and open competition need not be provided for when the disclosure of the agency's needs would compromise the national security unless the agency is permitted to limit the number of sources from which it solicits bids or proposals.

(b) *Application.* This authority may be used for any acquisition when disclosure of the Government's needs would compromise the national security (e.g., would violate security requirements); it shall not be used merely because the acquisition is classified, or merely because access to classified matter will be necessary to submit a proposal or to perform the contract.

(c) *Limitations.*

(1) Contracts awarded using this authority shall be supported by the written justifications and approvals described in 6.303 and 6.304.

(2) See 5.202(a)(1) for synopsis requirements.

(3) This statutory authority requires that agencies shall request offers from as many potential sources as is practicable under the circumstances.

[FAC 84-5, 50 FR 1729, 1/11/85, effective 4/1/85; FAC 84-13, 50 FR 52432, 12/23/85, effective 2/3/86; FAC 2005-73, 79 FR 24192, 4/29/2014, effective 5/29/2014]

6.302-7 Public interest.

(a) *Authority.*

(1) Citations: 10 U.S.C. 2304(c)(7) or 41 U.S.C. 3304(a)(7).

(2) Full and open competition need not be provided for when the agency head determines that it is not in the public interest in the particular acquisition concerned.

(b) *Application.* This authority may be used when none of the other authorities in 6.302 apply.

(c) *Limitations.*

(1) A written determination to use this authority shall be made in accordance with Subpart 1.7, by—

(i) the Secretary of Defense, the Secretary of the Army, the Secretary of the Navy, the Secretary of the Air Force, the Secretary of Homeland Security for the Coast Guard, or the Administrator of the National Aeronautics and Space Administration; or

(ii) the head of any other executive agency. This authority may not be delegated.

(2) The Congress shall be notified in writing of such determination not less than 30 days before award of the contract.

(3) If required by the head of the agency, the contracting officer shall prepare a justification to support the determination under (c)(1) above.

(4) This Determination and Finding (D&F) shall not be made on a class basis.

[FAC 84-5, 50 FR 1729, 1/11/85, effective 4/1/85; FAC 84-13, 50 FR 52432, 12/23/85, effective 2/3/86; FAC 2001-18, FR 69258, 12/11/2003; effective 12/11/2003; FAC 2005-73, 79 FR 24192, 4/29/2014, effective 5/29/2014]

6.303 Justifications. (No Text)

6.303-1 Requirements.

(a) A contracting officer shall not commence negotiations for a sole source contract, commence negotiations for a contract resulting from an unsolicited proposal, or award any other contract without providing for full and open competition unless the contracting officer—

(1) Justifies, if required in 6.302, the use of such actions in writing;

(2) Certifies the accuracy and completeness of the justification; and

(3) Obtains the approval required by 6.304.

(b) The contracting officer shall not award a sole-source contract under the 8(a) authority (15 U.S.C. 637(a)) for an amount exceeding $22 million unless—

(1) The contracting officer justifies the use of a sole-source contract in writing in accordance with 6.303-2;

(2) The justification is approved by the appropriate official designated at 6.304; and

(3) The justification and related information are made public after award in accordance with 6.305.

(c) Technical and requirements personnel are responsible for providing and certifying as accurate and complete necessary data to support their recommendation for other than full and open competition.

(d) Justifications required by paragraph (a) of this section may be made on an individual or class basis. Any justification for contracts awarded under the authority of 6.302-7 shall only be made on an individual basis. Whenever a justification is made and approved on a class basis, the contracting officer must ensure that each contract action taken pursuant to the authority of the class justification and approval is within the scope of the class justification and approval and shall document the contract file for each contract action accordingly.

(e) The justifications for contracts awarded under the authority cited in 6.302-2 may be prepared and approved within a reasonable time after contract award when preparation and approval prior to award would unreasonably delay the acquisitions.

[FAC 84-5, 50 FR 1729, 1/11/85, effective 4/1/85; FAC 84-13, 50 FR 52433, 12/23/85, effective 2/3/86; FAC 84-58, 55 FR 25526, 6/21/90, effective 7/23/90; FAC 97-15, 64 FR 72414, 12/27/99, effective 2/25/2000; FAC 2001-27, 69 FR 77870, 12/28/2004, effective 1/1/2005; FAC 2005-07, 71 FR 219, 1/3/2006, effective 1/3/2006; FAC 2005-50, 76 FR 14559, 3/16/2011, effective 3/16/2011; FAC 2005-58, 77 FR 23369, 4/18/2012, effective 4/18/2012; FAC 2005-83, 80 FR 38293, 7/2/2015, effective 10/1/2015; FAC 2019-02, 84 FR 19839, 5/6/2019, effective 5/6/2019]

6.303-2 Content.

(a) Each justification shall contain sufficient facts and rationale to justify the use of the specific authority cited.

(b) As a minimum, each justification, except those for sole-source 8(a) contracts over $22 million (*see* paragraph (d) of this section), shall include the following information:

(1) Identification of the agency and the contracting activity, and specific identification of the document as a "Justification for other than full and open competition."

(2) Nature and/or description of the action being approved.

(3) A description of the supplies or services required to meet the agency's needs (including the estimated value).

(4) An identification of the statutory authority permitting other than full and open competition.

(5) A demonstration that the proposed contractor's unique qualifications or the nature of the acquisition requires use of the authority cited.

(6) A description of efforts made to ensure that offers are solicited from as many potential sources as is practicable, including whether a notice was or will be publicized as required by Subpart 5.2 and, if not, which exception under 5.202 applies.

(7) A determination by the contracting officer that the anticipated cost to the Government will be fair and reasonable.

(8) A description of the market research conducted (see Part 10) and the results or a statement of the reason market research was not conducted.

(9) Any other facts supporting the use of other than full and open competition, such as:

(i) Explanation of why technical data packages, specifications, engineering descriptions, statements of work, or purchase descriptions suitable for full and open competition have not been developed or are not available.

(ii) When 6.302-1 is cited for follow-on acquisitions as described in 6.302-1(a)(2)(ii), an estimate of the cost to the Government that would be duplicated and how the estimate was derived.

(iii) When 6.302-2 is cited, data, estimated cost, or other rationale as to the extent and nature of the harm to the Government.

(10) A listing of the sources, if any, that expressed, in writing, an interest in the acquisition.

(11) A statement of the actions, if any, the agency may take to remove or overcome any barriers to competition before any subsequent acquisition for the supplies or services required.

(12) Contracting officer certification that the justification is accurate and complete to the best of the contracting officer's knowledge and belief.

(c) Each justification shall include evidence that any supporting data that is the responsibility of technical or requirements personnel (*e.g.*, verifying the Government's minimum needs or schedule requirements or other rationale for other than full and open competition) and which form a basis for the justification have been certified as complete and accurate by the technical or requirements personnel.

(d) As a minimum, each justification for a sole-source 8(a) contract over $22 million shall include the following information:

(1) A description of the needs of the agency concerned for the matters covered by the contract.

(2) A specification of the statutory provision providing the exception from the requirement to use competitive procedures in entering into the contract (*see* 19.805-1).

(3) A determination that the use of a sole-source contract is in the best interest of the agency concerned.

(4) A determination that the anticipated cost of the contract will be fair and reasonable.

(5) Such other matters as the head of the agency concerned shall specify for purposes of this section.

[FAC 84-5, 50 FR 1729, 1/11/85, effective 4/1/85; FAC 84-13, 50 FR 52433, 12/23/85, effective 2/3/86; FAC 90-32, 60 FR 48206, 9/18/95, effective 10/1/95; FAC 97-26, 66 FR 27405, 5/16/2001, effective 5/16/2001; FAC 2005-50, 76 FR 14559, 3/16/2011, effective 3/16/2011; FAC 2005-58, 77 FR 23369, 4/18/2012, effective 4/18/2012; FAC 2005-83, 80 FR 38293, 7/2/2015, effective 10/1/2015; FAC 2019-02, 84 FR 19839, 5/6/2019, effective 5/6/2019]

6.304 Approval of the justification.

(a) Except for paragraph (b) of this section, the justification for other than full and open competition shall be approved in writing—

(1) For a proposed contract not exceeding $700,000, the contracting officer's certification required by 6.303-2(b)(12) will serve as approval unless a higher approving level is established in agency procedures.

(2) For a proposed contract over $700,000 but not exceeding $13.5 million, by the advocate for competition for the procuring activity designated pursuant to 6.501 or an official described in paragraph (a)(3) or (4) of this section. This authority is not delegable.

(3) For a proposed contract over $13.5 million but not exceeding $68 million or, for DoD, NASA, and the Coast Guard, not exceeding $93 million, by the head of the procuring activity, or a designee who—

(i) If a member of the armed forces, is a general or flag officer; or

(ii) If a civilian, is serving in a position in a grade above GS-15 under the General Schedule (or in a comparable or higher position under another schedule).

(4) For a proposed contract over $68 million, or, for DoD, NASA, and the Coast Guard, over $93 million, by the senior procurement executive of the agency designated pursuant to 41 U.S.C. 1702(c) in accordance with agency procedures. This authority is not delegable except in the case of the Under Secretary of Defense for Acquisition and Sustainment, acting as the senior procurement executive for the Department of Defense.

(b) Any justification for a contract awarded under the authority of 6.302-7, regardless of dollar amount, shall be considered approved when the determination required by 6.302-7(c)(1) is made.

(c) A class justification for other than full and open competition shall be approved in writing in accordance with agency procedures. The approval level shall be determined by the estimated total value of the class.

(d) The estimated dollar value of all options shall be included in determining the approval level of a justification.

[FAC 84-5, 50 FR 1729, 1/11/85, effective 4/1/85; FAC 84-13, 50 FR 52433, 12/23/85, effective 2/3/86; FAC 84-44, 54 FR 13023, 3/29/89, effective 4/28/89; FAC 84-56, 55 FR 3881, 2/5/90, effective 3/7/90; FAC 90-3, 55 FR 52790, 12/21/90, effective 1/22/91; FAC 90-31,60 FR 42648, 8/16/95, effective 8/16/95 and 10/1/95; FAC 90-39, 61 FR 31612, 6/20/96, effective 8/19/96; FAC 97-17, 65 FR 24316, 4/25/2000, effective 4/25/2000; FAC 2005-01, 70 FR 11739, 3/9/2005, effective 3/9/2005; FAC 2005-06, 70 FR 57457, 9/30/2005, effective 9/30/2005; FAC 2005-13, 71 FR 57363, 9/28/2006, effective 9/28/2006; FAC 2005-45, 75 FR 53129, 8/30/2010, effective 10/1/2010; FAC 2005-50, 76 FR 14559, 3/16/2011, effective 3/16/2011; FAC 2005-58, 77 FR 23369, 4/18/2012, effective 4/18/2012; FAC 2005-73, 79 FR 24192, 4/29/2014, effective 5/29/2014; FAC 2005-83, 80 FR 38293, 7/2/2015, effective 10/1/2015; FAC 2019-02, 84 FR 19839, 5/6/2019, effective 5/6/2019]

6.305 Availability of the justification.

(a) The agency shall make publicly available the justification required by 6.303-1 as required by 10 U.S.C. 2304(l) and 41 U.S.C. 3304(f). Except for the circumstances in paragraphs (b) and (c) of this section, the justification shall be made publicly available within 14 days after contract award.

(b) In the case of a contract award permitted under 6.302-2, the justification shall be posted within 30 days after contract award.

(c) In the case of a brand name justification under 6.302-1(c), the justification shall be posted with the solicitation (see 5.102(a)(6)).

(d) The justifications shall be made publicly available—

(1) At the Government Point of Entry (GPE) *https://www.fbo.gov*;

(2) On the website of the agency, which may provide access to the justifications by linking to the GPE; and

(3) Must remain posted for a minimum of 30 days.

(e) Contracting officers shall carefully screen all justifications for contractor proprietary data and remove all such data, and such references and citations as are necessary to protect the proprietary data, before making the justifications available for public inspection. Contracting officers shall also be guided by the exemptions to disclosure of information contained in the Freedom of Information Act (5 U.S.C. 552) and the prohibitions against disclosure in 24.202 in determining whether the justification, or portions of it, are exempt from posting. Although the submitter notice process set out in EO 12600, entitled "Predisclosure Notification Procedures for Confidential Commercial Information," does not apply, if the justification appears to contain proprietary data, the contracting officer should provide the contractor that submitted the information an opportunity to review the justification for proprietary data, before making the justification available for public inspection, redacted as necessary. This process must not prevent or delay the posting of the justification in accordance with the timeframes required in paragraphs (a) through (c).

(f) The requirements of paragraphs (a) through (d) do not apply if posting the justification would disclose the executive agency's needs and disclosure of such needs would compromise national security or create other security risks.

[FAC 84-5, 50 FR 1729, 1/11/85, effective 4/1/85; FAC 90-45, Final rule, 62 FR 224, 1/2/97, effective 1/1/97;FAC 97-16, 65 FR 16274, 3/27/2000, effective 3/27/2000; FAC 2005-30, 74 FR 2731, 1/15/2009, effective 2/17/2009; FAC 2005-42, 75 FR 34273, 6/16/2010, effective 7/16/2010; FAC 2005-73, 79 FR 24192, 4/29/2014, effective 5/29/2014; FAC 2005-100, 83 FR 42571, 8/22/2018, effective 8/22/2018]

SUBPART 6.4—SEALED BIDDING AND COMPETITIVE PROPOSALS

6.401 Sealed bidding and competitive proposals.

Sealed bidding and competitive proposals, as described in parts 14 and 15, are both acceptable procedures for use under subparts 6.1, 6.2; and, when appropriate, under subpart 6.3.

(a) *Sealed bids.* (See Part 14 for procedures.) Contracting officers shall solicit sealed bids if—

(1) Time permits the solicitation, submission, and evaluation of sealed bids;

(2) The award will be made on the basis of price and other price-related factors;

(3) It is not necessary to conduct discussions with the responding offerors about their bids; and

(4) There is a reasonable expectation of receiving more than one sealed bid.

(b) *Competitive proposals.* (See Part 15 for procedures.)

(1) Contracting officers may request competitive proposals if sealed bids are not appropriate under paragraph (a) of this section.

(2) Because of differences in areas such as law, regulations, and business practices, it is generally necessary to conduct discussions with offerors relative to proposed contracts to be made and performed outside the United States, and its outlying areas. Competitive proposals will therefore be used for these contracts unless discussions are not required and the use of sealed bids is otherwise appropriate.

[FAC 84-5, 50 FR 1729, 1/11/85, effective 4/1/85; corrected 50 FR 4221, 1/30/85; FAC 84-42, 54 FR 5054, 1/31/89, effective 3/2/89; FAC 97-14, 64 FR 51828, 9/24/99, effective 11/23/99; FAC 2001-14, 68 FR 28079, 5/22/2003, effective 6/23/2003; FAC 2019-02, 84 FR 19839, 5/6/2019, effective 5/6/2019]

SUBPART 6.5—ADVOCATES FOR COMPETITION

6.501 Requirement.

As required by 41 U.S.C. 1705, the head of each executive agency shall designate an advocate for competition for the agency and for each procuring activity of the agency. The advocates for competition shall—

(a) Be in positions other than that of the agency senior procurement executive;

(b) Not be assigned any duties or responsibilities that are inconsistent with 6.502; and

(c) Be provided with staff or assistance (*e.g.*, specialists in engineering, technical operations, contract administration, financial management, supply management, and utilization of small business concerns), as may be necessary to carry out the advocate's duties and responsibilities.

[FAC 84-5, 50 FR 1729, 1/11/85, effective 4/1/85; FAC 90-32, 60 FR 48206, 9/18/95, effective 10/1/95; FAC 2005-73, 79 FR 24192, 4/29/2014, effective 5/29/2014; FAC 2019-02, 84 FR 19839, 5/6/2019, effective 5/6/2019]

6.502 Duties and responsibilities.

(a) Agency and procuring activity advocates for competition are responsible for promoting the acquisition of commercial items, promoting full and open competition, challenging requirements that are not stated in terms of functions to be performed, performance required or essential physical characteristics, and challenging barriers to the acquisition of commercial items and full and open competition such as unnecessarily restrictive statements of work, unnecessarily detailed specifications, and unnecessarily burdensome contract clauses.

(b) Agency advocates for competition shall—

(1) Review the contracting operations of the agency and identify and report to the agency senior procurement executive and the chief acquisition officer—

(i) Opportunities and actions taken to acquire commercial items to meet the needs of the agency;

(ii) Opportunities and actions taken to achieve full and open competition in the contracting operations of the agency;

(iii) Actions taken to challenge requirements that are not stated in terms of functions to be performed, performance required or essential physical characteristics;

(iv) Any condition or action that has the effect of unnecessarily restricting the acquisition of commercial items or competition in the contract actions of the agency;

(2) Prepare and submit an annual report to the agency senior procurement executive and the chief acquisition officer in accordance with agency procedures, describing—

(i) Such advocate's activities under this subpart;

(ii) New initiatives required to increase the acquisition of commercial items;

(iii) New initiatives required to increase competition;

(iv) New initiatives to ensure requirements are stated in terms of functions to be performed, performance required or essential physical characteristics;

(v) Any barriers to the acquisition of commercial items or competition that remain;

(vi) Other ways in which the agency has emphasized the acquisition of commercial items and competition in areas such as acquisition training and research; and

(vii) Initiatives that ensure task and delivery orders over $1,000,000 issued under multiple award contracts are properly planned, issued, and comply with 8.405 and 16.505.

(3) Recommend goals and plans for increasing competition on a fiscal year basis to the agency senior procurement executive and the chief acquisition officer; and

(4) Recommend to the agency senior procurement executive and the chief acquisition officer a system of personal and organizational accountability for competition, which may include the use of recognition and awards to motivate program managers, contracting officers, and others in authority to promote competition in acquisition.

[FAC 90-32, 60 FR 48206, 9/18/95, effective 10/1/95; FAC 2001-06, 67 FR 13048,

3/20/2002, effective 4/4/2002.; FAC 2005-27, 73 FR 53996, 9/17/2008, effective 10/17/2008; FAC 2005-73, 79 FR 24192, 4/29/2014, effective 5/29/2014]

PART 7—ACQUISITION PLANNING

Table of Contents

Scope of part 7.000

Subpart 7.1—Acquisition Plans

Definitions 7.101
Policy 7.102
Agency-head responsibilities 7.103
General procedures 7.104
Contents of written acquisition plans 7.105
Additional requirements for major systems 7.106
Additional requirements for acquisitions involving consolidation, bundling, or substantial bundling 7.107
General 7.107-1
Consolidation 7.107-2
Bundling 7.107-3
Substantial bundling 7.107-4
Notifications 7.107-5
Solicitation provision 7.107-6
Additional requirements for telecommuting 7.108

Subpart 7.2—Planning for the Purchase of Supplies in Economic Quantities

Scope of subpart 7.200
[Reserved] 7.201
Policy 7.202
Solicitation provision 7.203
Responsibilities of contracting officers 7.204

Subpart 7.3—Contractor Versus Government Performance

[Reserved] 7.300
Definitions 7.301
Policy 7.302
[Reserved] 7.303
[Reserved] 7.304
Solicitation provisions and contract clause 7.305
[Removed] 7.306
[Removed] 7.307

Subpart 7.4—Equipment Lease or Purchase

Scope of subpart 7.400
Acquisition considerations 7.401
Acquisition methods 7.402
General Services Administration assistance 7.403
Contract clause 7.404

Subpart 7.5—Inherently Governmental Functions

Scope of subpart 7.500
[Reserved] 7.501
Applicability 7.502
Policy 7.503

PART 7—ACQUISITION PLANNING

7.000 Scope of part.

This part prescribes policies and procedures for—

(a) Developing acquisition plans;

(b) Determining whether to use commercial or Government resources for acquisition of supplies or services;

(c) Deciding whether it is more economical to lease equipment rather than purchase it; and

(d) Determining whether functions are inherently governmental.

[FAC 90-37, 61 FR 2626, 1/26/96, effective 3/26/96]

SUBPART 7.1—ACQUISITION PLANS

7.101 Definitions.

As used in this subpart—

Acquisition streamlining means any effort that results in more efficient and effective use of resources to design and develop, or produce quality systems. This includes ensuring that only necessary and cost-effective requirements are included, at the most appropriate time in the acquisition cycle, in solicitations and resulting contracts for the design, development, and production of new systems, or for modifications to existing systems that involve redesign of systems or subsystems.

Life-cycle cost means the total cost to the Government of acquiring, operating, supporting, and (if applicable) disposing of the items being acquired.

Order means an order placed under a—

(1) Federal Supply Schedule contract; or

(2) Task-order contract or delivery-order contract awarded by another agency, (i.e., Governmentwide acquisition contract or multi-agency contract).

Planner means the designated person or office responsible for developing and maintaining a written plan, or for the planning function in those acquisitions not requiring a written plan.

[FAC 84-5, 50 FR 1734, 1/11/85, effective 4/1/85; FAC 84-39, 53 FR 34226, 9/2/88, effective 10/3/88; FAC 90-32, 60 FR 48206, 9/18/95, effective 10/1/95; FAC 97-22, 66 FR 2116, 1/10/2001, effective 3/12/2001; Delay of effective date, 66 FR 14259, 3/9/2001, effective 5/11/2001; FAC 2001-09, 67 FR 56115, 8/30/2002, effective 9/30/2002]

7.102 Policy.

(a) Agencies shall perform acquisition planning and conduct market research (see part 10) for all acquisitions in order to promote and provide for—

(1) Acquisition of commercial items or, to the extent that commercial items suitable to meet the agency's needs are not available, nondevelopmental items, to the maximum extent practicable (10 U.S.C. 2377 and 41 U.S.C. 3307);

(2) Full and open competition (see part 6) or, when full and open competition is not required in accordance with part 6, to obtain competition to the maximum extent practicable, with due regard to the nature of the supplies or services to be acquired (10 U.S.C. 2305(a)(1)(A) and 41 U.S.C. 3306(a)(1));

(3) Selection of appropriate contract type in accordance with part 16; and

(4) Appropriate consideration of the use of pre-existing contracts, including interagency and intra-agency contracts, to fulfill the requirement, before awarding new contracts. (See 8.002 through 8.004 and subpart 17.5).

(b) This planning shall integrate the efforts of all personnel responsible for significant aspects of the acquisition. The purpose of this planning is to ensure that the Government meets its needs in the most effective, economical, and timely manner. Agencies that have a detailed acquisition planning system in place that generally meets the requirements of 7.104 and 7.105 need not revise their system to specifically meet all of these requirements.

[FAC 90-32, 60 FR 48206, 9/18/95, effective 10/1/95; FAC 2005-50, 76 FR 14543, 3/16/2011, effective 3/16/2011; FAC 2005-56, 77 FR 12925, 3/2/2012, effective 4/2/2012; FAC 2005-72, 78 FR 80376,

12/31/2013, effective 1/30/2014; FAC 2005-73, 79 FR 24192, 4/29/2014, effective 5/29/2014; FAC 2019-02, 84 FR 19839, 5/6/2019, effective 5/6/2019]

7.103 Agency-head responsibilities.

The agency head or a designee shall prescribe procedures for the following:

(a) Promoting and providing for full and open competition (see Part 6) or, when full and open competition is not required in accordance with Part 6, for obtaining competition to the maximum extent practicable, with due regard to the nature of the supplies and services to be acquired (10 U.S.C. 2305(a)(1)(A) and 41 U.S.C. 3306(a)(1)).

(b) Encouraging offerors to supply commercial items, or to the extent that commercial items suitable to meet the agency needs are not available, nondevelopmental items in response to agency solicitations (10 U.S.C. 2377 and 41 U.S.C. 3307).

(c) Ensuring that acquisition planners address the requirement to specify needs, develop specifications, and to solicit offers in such a manner to promote and provide for full and open competition with due regard to the nature of the supplies and services to be acquired (10 U.S.C. 2305(a)(1)(A) and 41 U.S.C. 3306(a)(1)). (See Part 6 and 10.002.)

(d) Ensuring that acquisition planners document the file to support the selection of the contract type in accordance with subpart 16.1.

(e) Establishing criteria and thresholds at which increasingly greater detail and formality in the planning process is required as the acquisition becomes more complex and costly, including for cost-reimbursement and other high-risk contracts (*e.g.*, other than firm-fixed-price contracts) requiring a written acquisition plan. A written plan shall be prepared for cost reimbursement and other high-risk contracts other than firm-fixed-price contracts, although written plans may be required for firm-fixed-price contracts as appropriate.

(f) Ensuring that the statement of work is closely aligned with performance outcomes and cost estimates.

(g) Writing plans either on a systems basis, on an individual contract basis, or on an individual order basis, depending upon the acquisition.

(h) Ensuring that the principles of this subpart are used, as appropriate, for those acquisitions that do not require a written plan as well as for those that do.

(i) Designating planners for acquisitions.

(j) Reviewing and approving acquisition plans and revisions to these plans to ensure compliance with FAR requirements including 7.104 and part 16. For other than firm-fixed-price contracts, ensuring that the plan is approved and signed at least one level above the contracting officer.

(k) Establishing criteria and thresholds at which design-to-cost and life-cycle-cost techniques will be used.

(l) Establishing standard acquisition plan formats, if desired, suitable to agency needs.

(m) Waiving requirements of detail and formality, as necessary, in planning for acquisitions having compressed delivery or performance schedules because of the urgency of the need.

(n) Assuring that the contracting officer, prior to contracting, reviews:

(1) The acquisition history of the supplies and services; and

(2) A description of the supplies, including, when necessary for adequate description, a picture, drawing, diagram, or other graphic representation.

(o) Ensuring that agency planners include use of the metric system of measurement in proposed acquisitions in accordance with 15 U.S.C. 205b (see 11.002(b)) and agency metric plans and guidelines.

(p) Ensuring that agency planners—

(1) Specify needs for printing and writing paper consistent with the 30 percent postconsumer fiber minimum content standards specified in section 2(d)(ii) of E.O. Executive Order 13423 of January 24, 2007, Strengthening Federal Environmental, Energy, and Transportation Management, and section 2(e)(iv) of E.O. Executive Order 13514 of October 5, 2009 (see 11.303);

(2) Comply with the policy in 11.002(d) regarding procurement of biobased products, products containing recovered materials, environmentally preferable products and services (including Electronic Product Environmental Assessment Tool (EPEAT®)-registered electronic products, nontoxic or low-toxic alternatives), ENERGY STAR® and Federal Energy Management Program-designated products, renewable energy, water-efficient products, non-ozone-depleting products, and products and services that minimize or eliminate, when feasible, the use, release, or emission of high global warming potential hydrofluorocarbons, such as by using reclaimed instead of virgin hydrofluorocarbons;

(3) Comply with the Guiding Principles for Federal Leadership in High-Performance and Sustainable Buildings (Guiding Principles), for the design, construction, renovation, repair, or deconstruction of Federal buildings. The Guiding Principles can be accessed at *https://www.epa.gov/greeningepa/guiding-principles-federal-leadership-high-performance-and-sustainable-buildings*; and

(4) Require contractor compliance with Federal environmental requirements, when the contractor is operating Government-owned facilities or vehicles, to the same extent as the agency would be required to comply if the agency operated the facilities or vehicles.

(q) Ensuring that acquisition planners specify needs and develop plans, drawings, work statements, specifications, or other product descriptions that address Electronic and Information Technology Accessibility Standards (see 36 CFR part 1194) in proposed acquisitions (see 11.002(e)) and that these standards are included in requirements planning, as appropriate (see Subpart 39.2).

(r) Making a determination, prior to issuance of a solicitation for advisory and assistance services involving the analysis and evaluation of proposals submitted in response to a solicitation, that a sufficient number of covered personnel with the training and capability to perform an evaluation and analysis of proposals submitted in response to a solicitation are not readily available within the agency or from another Federal agency in accordance with the guidelines at 37.204.

(s) Ensuring that no purchase request is initiated or contract entered into that would result in the performance of an inherently governmental function by a contractor and that all contracts or orders are adequately managed so as to ensure effective official control over contract or order performance.

(t) Ensuring that knowledge gained from prior acquisitions is used to further refine requirements and acquisition strategies. For services, greater use of performance-based acquisition methods should occur for follow-on acquisitions.

(u) Ensuring that acquisition planners, to the maximum extent practicable—

(1) Structure contract requirements to facilitate competition by and among small business concerns; and

(2) Avoid unnecessary and unjustified consolidation or bundling (see 7.107) (15 U.S.C. 631(j) and 15 U.S.C. 657q).

(v) Ensuring that agency planners on information technology acquisitions comply with the capital planning and investment control requirements in 40 U.S.C. 11312 and OMB Circular A-130.

(w) Ensuring that agency planners on information technology acquisitions comply with the information technology security requirements in the Federal Information Security Management Act (44 U.S.C. 3544), OMB's implementing policies including Appendix III of OMB Circular A-130, and guidance and standards from the Department of Commerce's National Institute of Standards and Technology.

(x) Encouraging agency planners to consider the use of a project labor agreement (see subpart 22.5).

(y) Ensuring that contracting officers consult the Disaster Response Registry via *https://www.sam.gov*, Search Records, Advanced Search, Disaster Response Registry Search as a part of acquisition planning for debris removal, distribution of supplies, reconstruction, and other disaster or emergency relief activities inside the United States and outlying areas. (See 26.205).

[FAC 84-5, 50 FR 1735, 1/11/85, effective 4/1/85; FAC 84-10, 50 FR 27561, 7/3/85, effective 7/3/85; FAC 90-16, 57 FR 60574, 12/21/92, effective 2/19/93; FAC 90-27, 60 FR 28492, 5/31/95, effective 5/31/95; FAC 90-32, 60 FR 48206, 9/18/95, effective 10/1/95; FAC 90-33, 60 FR 49706, 9/26/95, effective 10/1/95; FAC 90-37, 61 FR 2626, 1/26/96, effective 3/26/96; Final rule, 62 FR 40236, 7/25/97, effective 6/30/97; FAC 97-1, 62 FR 44802, 8/22/97, effective 10/21/97; FAC 97-15, 64 FR 72414, 12/27/99, effective 12/27/99, finalized without change, FAC 97-19, 65 FR 46052, 7/26/2000; FAC 97-18, 65 FR 36014, 6/6/2000, effective 8/7/2000; FAC 97-27, 66 FR 20894, 4/25/2001, effective 6/25/2001; FAC 2001-09, 67 FR 56115, 8/30/2002, effective 9/30/2002; FAC 2005-06, 70 FR 57449, 9/30/2005, effective 9/30/2005; 70 FR 57453, 9/30/2005, effective 9/30/2005; FAC 2005-07, 71 FR 211, 1/3/2006, effective 2/2/2006; FAC 2005-13, 71 FR 57360, 9/28/2006, effective 9/28/2006; FAC 2005-21, 72 FR 63040, 11/7/2007, effective 12/7/2007; FAC 2005-37, 74 FR 52847, 10/14/2009, effective 10/14/2009; FAC 2005-41, 75 FR 19168, 4/13/2010, effective 5/13/2010; FAC 2005-43, 75 FR 38683, 7/2/2010, effective 8/2/2010; FAC 2005-50, 76 FR 14543, 3/16/2011, effective 3/16/2011; FAC 2005-52, 76 FR 31395, 5/31/2011, effective 5/31/2011; FAC 2005-55, 77 FR 187, 1/3/2012, effective 2/2/2012; FAC 2005-56, 77 FR 12925, 3/2/2012, effective 4/2/2012; FAC 2005-73, 79 FR 24192, 4/29/2014, effective 5/29/2014; FAC 2005-75, 79 FR 35859, 6/24/2014, effective 6/24/2014; FAC 2005-84, 80 FR 53436, 9/3/2015, effective 10/5/2015; FAC 2005-88, 81 FR 30429, 5/16/2016, effective 6/15/2016; FAC 2005-91, 81 FR 67763, 9/30/2016, effective 10/31/2016; FAC 2005-100, 83 FR 42571, 8/22/2018, effective 8/22/2018; FAC 2005-101, 83 FR 48691, 9/26/2018, effective 10/26/2018; FAC 2019-02, 84 FR 19839, 5/6/2019, effective 5/6/2019]

7.104 General procedures.

(a) Acquisition planning should begin as soon as the agency need is identified, preferably well in advance of the fiscal year in which contract award or order placement is necessary. In developing the plan, the planner shall form a team consisting of all those who will be responsible for significant aspects of the acquisition, such as contracting, small business, fiscal, legal, and technical personnel. If contract performance is to be in a designated operational area or supporting a diplomatic or consular mission, the planner shall also consider inclusion of the combatant commander or chief of mission, as appropriate. The planner should review previous plans for similar acquisitions and discuss them with the key personnel involved in those acquisitions. At key dates specified in the plan or whenever significant changes occur, and no less often than annually, the planner shall review the plan and, if appropriate, revise it.

(b) Requirements and logistics personnel should avoid issuing requirements on an urgent basis or with unrealistic delivery or performance schedules, since it generally restricts competition and increases prices. Early in the planning process, the planner should consult with requirements and logistics personnel who determine type, quality, quantity, and delivery requirements.

(c) The planner shall coordinate with and secure the concurrence of the contracting officer in all acquisition planning. If the plan proposes using other than full and open competition when awarding a contract, the plan shall also be coordinated with the cognizant advocate for competition.

(d) The planner shall coordinate the acquisition plan or strategy with the cognizant small business specialist when the strategy contemplates an acquisition meeting the thresholds in 7.107-4 for substantial bundling unless the contract or task order or delivery order is entirely reserved or set-aside for small business under part 19. The small business specialist shall notify the agency Office of Small and Disadvantaged Business Utilization or the Office of Small Business Programs if the strategy involves—

(1) Bundling that is unnecessary or unjustified; or

(2) Bundled or consolidated requirements not identified as such by the agency (see 7.107).

(e) The planner shall ensure that a COR is nominated as early as practicable in the acquisition process by requirements officials or in accordance with agency procedures. The contracting officer shall designate and authorize a COR as early as practicable after the nomination. See 1.602-2(d).

[FAC 84-5, 50 FR 1735, 1/11/85, effective 4/1/85; FAC 84-13, 50 FR 52433, 12/23/85, effective 2/3/86; FAC 2001-09, 67 FR 56115, 8/30/2002, effective 9/30/2002; FAC 2001-17, 68 FR 59999, 10/20/2003, effective date 10/20/2003; FAC 2005-13, 71 FR 57363, 9/28/2006, effective 9/28/2006; FAC 2005-24, 73 FR 10943, 2/28/2008, effective 3/31/2008; FAC 2005-45, 75 FR 53129, 8/30/2010, effective 10/1/2010; FAC 2005-50, 76 FR 14543, 3/16/2011, effective 3/16/2011; FAC 2005-56, 77 FR 12925, 3/2/2012, effective 4/2/2012; FAC 2005-67, 78 FR 37675, 6/21/2013, effective 7/22/2013; FAC 2005-73, 79 FR 24192, 4/29/2014, effective 5/29/2014; FAC 2005-83, 80 FR 38293, 7/2/2015, effective 10/1/2015; Final rule, 80 FR 53753, 9/8/2015, effective 10/1/2015; FAC 2005-91, 81 FR 67763, 9/30/2016, effective 10/31/2016]

7.105 Contents of written acquisition plans.

In order to facilitate attainment of the acquisition objectives, the plan must identify those milestones at which decisions should be made (see paragraph (b)(21) of this section). The plan must address all the technical, business, management, and other significant considerations that will control the acquisition. The specific content of plans will vary, depending on the nature, circumstances, and stage of the acquisition. In preparing the plan, the planner must follow the applicable instructions in paragraphs (a) and (b) of this section, together with the agency's implementing procedures. Acquisition plans for service contracts or orders must describe the strategies for implementing performance-based acquisition methods or must provide rationale for not using those methods (see subpart 37.6).

(a) *Acquisition background and objectives.*

(1) *Statement of need.* Introduce the plan by a brief statement of need. Summarize the technical and contractual history of the acquisition. Discuss feasible acquisition alternatives, the impact of prior acquisitions on those alternatives, and any related in-house effort.

(2) *Applicable conditions.* State all significant conditions affecting the acquisition, such as—

(i) Requirements for compatibility with existing or future systems or programs; and

(ii) Any known cost, schedule, and capability or performance constraints.

(3) *Cost.* Set forth the established cost goals for the acquisition and the rationale supporting them, and discuss related cost concepts to be employed, including, as appropriate, the following items:

(i) *Life-cycle cost.* Discuss how life-cycle cost will be considered. If it is not used, explain why. If appropriate, discuss the cost model used to develop life-cycle-cost estimates.

(ii) *Design-to-cost.* Describe the design-to-cost objective(s) and underlying assumptions, including the rationale for quantity, learning-curve, and economic adjustment factors. Describe how objectives are to be applied, tracked, and enforced. Indicate specific related solicitation and contractual requirements to be imposed.

(iii) *Application of should-cost.* Describe the application of should-cost analysis to the acquisition (see 15.407-4).

(4) *Capability or performance.* Specify the required capabilities or performance characteristics of the supplies or the performance standards of the services being acquired and state how they are related to the need.

(5) *Delivery or performance-period requirements.* Describe the basis for establishing delivery or performance-period requirements (see Subpart 11.4). Explain and provide reasons for any urgency if it results in concurrency of development and production or constitutes justification for not providing for full and open competition.

(6) *Trade-offs*. Discuss the expected consequences of trade-offs among the various cost, capability or performance, and schedule goals.

(7) *Risks*. Discuss technical, cost, and schedule risks and describe what efforts are planned or underway to reduce risk and the consequences of failure to achieve goals. If concurrency of development and production is planned, discuss its effects on cost and schedule risks.

(8) *Acquisition streamlining.* If specifically designated by the requiring agency as a program subject to acquisition streamlining, discuss plans and procedures to—

(i) Encourage industry participation by using draft solicitations, presolicitation conferences, and other means of stimulating industry involvement during design and development in recommending the most appropriate application and tailoring of contract requirements;

(ii) Select and tailor only the necessary and cost-effective requirements; and

(iii) State the timeframe for identifying which of those specifications and standards, originally provided for guidance only, shall become mandatory.

(b) *Plan of action* —(1) *Sources.* (i) Indicate the prospective sources of supplies or services that can meet the need.

(ii) Consider required sources of supplies or services (see part 8) and sources identifiable through databases including the Governmentwide database of contracts and other procurement instruments intended for use by multiple agencies available at *https://www.contractdirectory.gov/contractdirectory/*.

(iii) Include consideration of small business, veteran-owned small business, service-disabled veteran-owned small business, HUBZone small business, small disadvantaged business, and women-owned small business concerns (see part 19).

(iv) Consider the impact of any consolidation or bundling that might affect participation of small businesses in the acquisition (see 7.107) (15 U.S.C. 644(e) and 15 U.S.C. 657q). When the proposed acquisition strategy involves bundling, identify the incumbent contractors and contracts affected by the bundling.

(v) Address the extent and results of the market research and indicate their impact on the various elements of the plan (see part 10).

(2) *Competition.*

(i) Describe how competition will be sought, promoted, and sustained throughout the course of the acquisition. If full and open competition is not contemplated, cite the authority in 6.302, discuss the basis for the application of that authority, identify the source(s), and discuss why full and open competition cannot be obtained.

(ii) Identify the major components or subsystems. Discuss component breakout plans relative to these major components or subsystems. Describe how competition will be sought, promoted, and sustained for these components or subsystems.

(iii) Describe how competition will be sought, promoted, and sustained for spares and repair parts. Identify the key logistic milestones, such as technical data delivery schedules and acquisition method coding conferences, that affect competition.

(iv) When effective subcontract competition is both feasible and desirable, describe how such subcontract competition will be sought, promoted, and sustained throughout the course of the acquisition. Identify any known barriers to increasing subcontract competition and address how to overcome them.

(3) *Contract type selection.* Discuss the rationale for the selection of contract type. For other than firm-fixed-price contracts, *see* 16.103(d) for additional documentation guidance. Acquisition personnel shall document the acquisition plan with findings that detail the particular facts and circumstances, (*e.g.*, complexity of the requirements, uncertain duration of the work, contractor's technical capability and financial responsibility, or adequacy of the contractor's accounting system), and associated reasoning essential to support the contract type selection. The contracting officer shall ensure that requirements and technical personnel provide the

necessary documentation to support the contract type selection.

(4) *Source-selection procedures.* Discuss the source-selection procedures for the acquisition, including the timing for submission and evaluation of proposals, and the relationship of evaluation factors to the attainment of the acquisition objectives (see subpart 15.3). When an EVMS is required (see FAR 34.202(a)) and a pre-award IBR is contemplated, the acquisition plan must discuss—

(i) How the pre-award IBR will be considered in the source selection decision;

(ii) How it will be conducted in the source selection process (see FAR 15.306); and

(iii) Whether offerors will be directly compensated for the costs of participating in a pre-award IBR.

(5) *Acquisition considerations.* (i) For each contract contemplated, discuss use of multi-year contracting, options, or other special contracting methods (see Part 17); any special clauses, special solicitation provisions, or FAR deviations required (see Subpart 1.4); whether sealed bidding or negotiation will be used and why; whether equipment will be acquired by lease or purchase (see Subpart 7.4) and why; and any other contracting considerations. Provide rationale if a performance-based acquisition will not be used or if a performance-based acquisition for services is contemplated on other than a firm-fixed-price basis (see 37.102(a), 16.103(d), and 16.505(a)(3)).

(ii) For each order contemplated, discuss—

(A) For information technology acquisitions, how the capital planning and investment control requirements of 40 U.S.C. 11312 and OMB Circular A-130 will be met (see 7.103(v) and part 39); and

(B) Why this action benefits the Government, such as when—

(1) The agency can accomplish its mission more efficiently and effectively (e.g., take advantage of the servicing agency's specialized expertise; or gain access to contractors with needed expertise); or

(2) Ordering through an indefinite delivery contract facilitates access to small business concerns, including small disadvantaged business concerns, 8(a) contractors, women-owned small business concerns, HUBZone small business concerns, veteran-owned small business concerns, or service-disabled veteran-owned small business concerns.

(iii) For information technology acquisitions using Internet Protocol, discuss whether the requirements documents include the Internet Protocol compliance requirements specified in 11.002(g) or a waiver of these requirements has been granted by the agency's Chief Information Officer.

(iv) For each contract (and order) contemplated, discuss the strategy to transition to firm-fixed-price contracts to the maximum extent practicable. During the requirements development stage, consider structuring the contract requirements, *i.e.*, line items, in a manner that will permit some, if not all, of the requirements to be awarded on a firm-fixed-price basis, either in the current contract, future option years, or follow-on contracts. This will facilitate an easier transition to a firm-fixed-price contract, because a cost history will be developed for a recurring definitive requirement.

(6) *Budgeting and funding.* Include budget estimates, explain how they were derived, and discuss the schedule for obtaining adequate funds at the time they are required (see Subpart 32.7).

(7) *Product or service descriptions.* Explain the choice of product or service description types (including performance-based acquisition descriptions) to be used in the acquisition.

(8) *Priorities, allocations, and allotments.* When urgency of the requirement dictates a particularly short delivery or performance schedule, certain priorities may apply. If so, specify the method for obtaining and using priorities, allocations, and allotments, and the reasons for them (see Subpart 11.6).

(9) *Contractor versus Government performance.* Address the consideration given to OMB Circular No. A-76 (see Subpart 7.3).

(10) *Inherently governmental functions.* Address the consideration given to subpart 7.5.

(11) *Management information requirements.* Discuss, as appropriate, what management system will be used by the Government to monitor the contractor's effort. If an Earned Value Management System is to be used, discuss the methodology the Government will employ to analyze and use the earned value data to assess and monitor contract performance. In addition, discuss how the offeror's/contractor's EVMS will be verified for compliance with the Electronic Industries Alliance Standard 748 (EIA-748), and the timing and conduct of integrated baseline reviews (whether prior to or post award). (See 34.202.)

(12) *Make or buy.* Discuss any consideration given to make-or-buy programs (see Subpart 15.407-2).

(13) *Test and evaluation.* To the extent applicable, describe the test program of the contractor and the Government. Describe the test program for each major phase of a major system acquisition. If concurrency is planned, discuss the extent of testing to be accomplished before production release.

(14) *Logistics considerations.* Describe—(i) The assumptions determining contractor or agency support, both initially and over the life of the acquisition, including consideration of contractor or agency maintenance and servicing (see subpart 7.3), support for contracts to be performed in a designated operational area or supporting a diplomatic or consular mission (see 25.301-3); and distribution of commercial items;

(ii) The reliability, maintainability, and quality assurance requirements, including any planned use of warranties (see Part 46);

(iii) The requirements for contractor data (including repurchase data) and data rights, their estimated cost, and the use to be made of the data (see Part 27); and

(iv) Standardization concepts, including the necessity to designate, in accordance with agency procedures, technical equipment as "standard" so that future purchases of the equipment can be made from the same manufacturing source.

(15) *Government-furnished property.* Indicate any Government property to be furnished to contractors, and discuss any associated considerations, such as its availability or the schedule for its acquisition (see Part 45.102).

(16) *Government-furnished information.* Discuss any Government information, such as manuals, drawings, and test data, to be provided to prospective offerors and contractors. Indicate which information that requires additional controls to monitor access and distribution (e.g., technical specifications, maps, building designs, schedules, etc.), as determined by the agency, is to be posted via the enhanced controls of the GPE at *https://www.fbo.gov* (see 5.102(a)).

(17) *Environmental and energy conservation objectives.* Discuss all applicable environmental and energy conservation objectives associated with the acquisition (see Part 23), the applicability of an environmental assessment or environmental impact statement (see 40 CFR Part 1502), the proposed resolution of environmental issues, and any environmentally-related requirements to be included in solicitations and contracts (see 11.002 and 11.303).

(18) *Security considerations.* (i) For acquisitions dealing with classified matters, discuss how adequate security will be established, maintained, and monitored (see subpart 4.4).

(ii) For information technology acquisitions, discuss how agency information security requirements will be met.

(iii) For acquisitions requiring routine contractor physical access to a Federally-controlled facility and/or routine access to a Federally-controlled information system, discuss how agency requirements for personal identity verification of contractors will be met (see subpart 4.13).

(iv) For acquisitions that may require Federal contract information to reside in or transit through contractor information systems, discuss compliance with subpart 4.19.

(19) *Contract administration.* Describe how the contract will be administered. In contracts for services, include how inspection and acceptance corresponding to the

work statement's performance criteria will be enforced. In contracts for supplies or service contracts that include supplies, address whether higher-level quality standards are necessary (46.202) and whether the supplies to be acquired are critical items (46.101).

(20) *Other considerations.* Discuss, as applicable:

(i) Standardization concepts;

(ii) The industrial readiness program;

(iii) The Defense Production Act;

(iv) The Occupational Safety and Health Act;

(v) Support Anti-terrorism by Fostering Effective Technologies Act of 2002 (SAFETY Act) (see subpart 50.2);

(vi) Foreign sales implications;

(vii) Special requirements for contracts to be performed in a designated operational area or supporting a diplomatic or consular mission; and

(viii) Any other matters germane to the plan not covered elsewhere.

(21) *Milestones for the acquisition cycle.* Address the following steps and any others appropriate:

Acquisition plan approval.

Statement of work.

Specifications.

Data requirements.

Completion of acquisition-package preparation.

Purchase request.

Justification and approval for other than full and open competition where applicable and/or any required D&F approval.

Issuance of synopsis.

Issuance of solicitation.

Evaluation of proposals, audits, and field reports.

Beginning and completion of negotiations.

Contract preparation, review, and clearance.

Contract award.

(22) *Identification of participants in acquisition plan preparation.* List the individuals who participated in preparing the acquisition plan, giving contact information for each.

[FAC 84-5, 50 FR 1735, 1/11/85, effective 4/1/85; FAC 84-37, 53 FR 17856, 5/18/88, effective 6/17/88; FAC 84-39, 53 FR 34226, 9/2/88, effective 10/3/88; FAC 90-27, 60 FR 28492, 5/31/95, effective 5/31/95; FAC 90-32, 60 FR 48206, 9/18/95, effective 10/1/95; FAC 90-37, 61 FR 2626, 1/26/96, effective 3/26/96; Final rule, 62 FR 40236, 7/25/97, effective 6/30/97; FAC 97-1, 62 FR 44802, 8/22/97, effective 10/21/97; FAC 97-2, 62 FR 51224, 9/30/97, effective 10/10/97; FAC 97-10, 63 FR 70264, 12/18/98, effective 1/4/99; FAC 97-15, 64 FR 72414, 12/27/99, effective 12/27/99; finalized without change, FAC 97-19, 65 FR 46052, 7/26/2000; FAC 97-20, 65 FR 60542, 10/11/2000, effective 10/11/2000; FAC 2001-07, 67 FR 21533, 4/30/2002, effective 5/15/2002; FAC 2001-09, 67 FR 56115, 8/30/2002, effective 9/30/2002; FAC 2001-10, 67 FR 70522, 11/22/2002; FAC 2001-15, 68 FR 43859, 7/24/2003, effective 7/24/2003; FAC 2001-17, 68 FR 59999, 10/20/2003, effective date 10/20/2003; FAC 2005-06, 70 FR 57449, 9/30/2005, effective 9/30/2005; 70 FR 57453, 9/30/2005, effective 9/30/2005; FAC 2005-07, 71 FR 208, 1/3/2006, effective 1/3/2006; FAC 2005-07, 71 FR 211, 1/3/2006, effective 2/2/2006; FAC 2005-09, 71 FR 20295, 4/19/2006, effective 5/19/2006; FAC 2005-09, 71 FR 20299, 4/19/2006, effective 5/19/2006; FAC 2005-11, 71 FR 38238, 7/5/2006, effective 7/5/2006; FAC 2005-13, 71 FR 57360, 9/28/2006, effective 9/28/2006;FAC 2005-14, 71 FR 67771, 11/22/2006, effective 11/22/2006; FAC 2005-17, 72 FR 27364, 5/15/2007, effective 6/14/2007; FAC 2005-21, 72 FR 63027, 11/7/2007, effective 11/7/2007; FAC 2005-24, 73 FR 10943, 2/28/2008, effective 3/31/2008; FAC 2005-30, 74 FR 2733, 1/15/2009, effective 2/17/2009; FAC 2005-36, 74 FR 40459, 8/11/2009, effective 9/10/2009; FAC 2005-38, 74 FR 65605, 12/10/2009, effective 12/10/2009; FAC 2005-47, 75 FR 77745, 12/13/2010, effective 12/13/2010; FAC 2005-50, 76 FR 14543, 3/16/2011, effective 3/16/2011; FAC 2005-52, 76 FR 31395, 5/31/2011, effective 5/31/2011; FAC 2005-56, 77 FR 12925, 3/2/2012, effective

4/2/2012; FAC 2005-66, 78 FR 13768, 2/28/2013, effective 2/28/2013; FAC 2005-88, 81 FR 30439, 5/16/2016, effective 6/15/2016; FAC 2005-91, 81 FR 67763, 9/30/2016, effective 10/31/2016; FAC 2005-92 81 FR 83103, 11/18/2016, effective 11/18/2016; FAC 2005-95, 82 FR 4709, 1/13/2017, effective 1/13/2017; FAC 2005-100, 83 FR 42571, 8/22/2018, effective 8/22/2018; FAC 2019-02, 84 FR 19839, 5/6/2019, effective 5/6/2019; FAC 2020-02, 84 FR 64680, 11/22/2019, effective 12/23/2019]

7.106 Additional requirements for major systems.

(a) In planning for the solicitation of a major system (see Part 34) development contract, planners shall consider requiring offerors to include, in their offers, proposals to incorporate in the designs of a major system—

(1) Items which are currently available within the supply system of the agency responsible for the major system, available elsewhere in the national supply system, or commercially available from more than one source; and

(2) Items which the Government will be able to acquire competitively in the future if they are likely to be needed in substantial quantities during the system's service life.

(b) In planning for the solicitation of a major system (see Part 34) production contract, planners shall consider requiring offerors to include, in their offers, proposals identifying opportunities to assure that the Government will be able to obtain, on a competitive basis, items acquired in connection with the system that are likely to be acquired in substantial quantities during the service life of the system. Proposals submitted in response to such requirements may include the following:

(1) Proposals to provide the Government the right to use technical data to be provided under the contract for competitive future acquisitions, together with the cost to the Government, if any, of acquiring such technical data and the right to use such data.

(2) Proposals for the qualification or development of multiple sources of supply for competitive future acquisitions.

(c) In determining whether to apply paragraphs (a) and (b) of this section, planners shall consider the purposes for which the system is being acquired and the technology necessary to meet the system's required capabilities. If such proposals are required, the contracting officer shall consider them in evaluating competing offers. In noncompetitive awards, the factors in paragraphs (a) and (b) of this section, may be considered by the contracting officer as objectives in negotiating the contract.

[FAC 84-10, 50 FR 27561, 7/3/85, effective 7/3/85; FAC 2019-02, 84 FR 19839, 5/6/2019, effective 5/6/2019]

7.107 Additional requirements for acquisitions involving consolidation, bundling, or substantial bundling. (No Text)

[FAC 97-15, 64 FR 72414, 12/27/99, effective 12/27/99; FAC 97-19, 65 FR 46052, 7/26/2000, effective 7/26/2000; FAC 2001-17, 68 FR 59999, 10/20/2003, effective date 10/20/2003; FAC 2005-13, 71 FR 57363, 9/28/2006, effective 9/28/2006; FAC 2005-45, 75 FR 53129, 8/30/2010, effective 10/1/2010; FAC 2005-83, 80 FR 38293, 7/2/2015, effective 10/1/2015; Final rule, 80 FR 53753, 9/8/2015, effective 10/1/2015; FAC 2005-91, 81 FR 67763, 9/30/2016, effective 10/31/2016]

7.107-1 General.

(a) If the requirement is considered both consolidated and bundled, the agency shall follow the guidance regarding bundling in 7.107-3 and 7.107-4.

(b) The requirements of this section 7.107 do not apply—

(1) If a cost comparison analysis will be performed in accordance with OMB Circular A-76 (except 7.107-4 still applies);

(2) To orders placed under single-agency task-order contracts or delivery-order contracts, when the requirement was considered in determining that the consolidation or bundling of the underlying contract was necessary and justified; or

(3) To requirements for which there is a mandatory source (see 8.002 or 8.003), including supplies and services that are on the Procurement List maintained by the Committee for Purchase From People Who Are Blind or Severely Disabled or the Schedule of Products issued by Federal Prison Industries, Inc. This exception does not apply—

(i) When the requiring agency obtains a waiver in accordance with 8.604 or an exception in accordance with 8.605 or 8.706; or

(ii) When optional acquisitions of supplies and services permitted under 8.713 are included.

[FAC 2005-91, 81 FR 67763, 9/30/2016, effective 10/31/2016]

7.107-2 Consolidation.

(a) Consolidation may provide substantial benefits to the Government. However, because of the potential impact on small business participation, before conducting an acquisition that is a consolidation of requirements with an estimated total dollar value exceeding $2 million, the senior procurement executive or chief acquisition officer shall make a written determination that the consolidation is necessary and justified in accordance with 15 U.S.C. 657q, after ensuring that—

(1) Market research has been conducted;

(2) Any alternative contracting approaches that would involve a lesser degree of consolidation have been identified;

(3) The determination is coordinated with the agency's Office of Small Disadvantaged Business Utilization or the Office of Small Business Programs;

(4) Any negative impact by the acquisition strategy on contracting with small business concerns has been identified; and

(5) Steps are taken to include small business concerns in the acquisition strategy.

(b) The senior procurement executive or chief acquisition officer may determine that the consolidation is necessary and justified if the benefits of the acquisition would substantially exceed the benefits that would be derived from each of the alternative contracting approaches identified under paragraph (a)(2) of this subsection, including benefits that are quantifiable in dollar amounts as well as any other specifically identified benefits.

(c) Such benefits may include cost savings or price reduction and, regardless of whether quantifiable in dollar amounts—

(1) Quality improvements that will save time or improve or enhance performance or efficiency;

(2) Reduction in acquisition cycle times;

(3) Better terms and conditions; or

(4) Any other benefit.

(d) *Benefits.* (1) Benefits that are quantifiable in dollar amounts are substantial if individually, in combination, or in the aggregate the anticipated financial benefits are equivalent to—

(i) Ten percent of the estimated contract or order value (including options) if the value is $94 million or less; or

(ii) Five percent of the estimated contract or order value (including options) or $9.4 million, whichever is greater, if the value exceeds $94 million.

(2) Benefits that are not quantifiable in dollar amounts shall be specifically identified and otherwise quantified to the extent feasible.

(3) Reduction of administrative or personnel costs alone is not sufficient justification for consolidation unless the cost savings are expected to be at least 10 percent of the estimated contract or order value (including options) of the consolidated requirements, as determined by the senior procurement executive or chief acquisition officer (15 U.S.C. 657q(c)(2)(B)).

(e)(1) Notwithstanding paragraphs (a) through (d) of this subsection, the approving authority identified in paragraph (e)(2) of this subsection may determine that consolidation is necessary and justified when—

(i) The expected benefits do not meet the thresholds for a substantial benefit at paragraph (d)(1) of this subsection but are critical to the agency's mission success; and

(ii) The procurement strategy provides for maximum practicable participation by small business.

(2) The approving authority is—

(i) For the Department of Defense, the senior procurement executive; or

(ii) For the civilian agencies, the Deputy Secretary or equivalent.

(f) If a determination is made that consolidation is necessary and justified, the contracting officer shall include it in the acquisition strategy documentation and provide it to the Small Business Administration (SBA) upon request.

[FAC 2005-91, 81 FR 67763, 9/30/2016, effective 10/31/2016]

7.107-3 Bundling.

(a) Bundling may provide substantial benefits to the Government. However, because of the potential impact on small business participation, before conducting an acquisition strategy that involves bundling, the agency shall make a written determination that the bundling is necessary and justified in accordance with 15 U.S.C. 644(e). A bundled requirement is considered necessary and justified if the agency would obtain measurably substantial benefits as compared to meeting its agency's requirements through separate smaller contracts or orders.

(b) The agency shall quantify the specific benefits identified through the use of market research and other techniques to explain how their impact would be measurably substantial (see 10.001(a)(2)(iv) and (a)(3)(vii)).

(c) Such benefits may include, but are not limited to—

(1) Cost savings;

(2) Price reduction;

(3) Quality improvements that will save time or improve or enhance performance or efficiency;

(4) Reduction in acquisition cycle times, or

(5) Better terms and conditions.

(d) Benefits are measurably substantial if individually, in combination, or in the aggregate the anticipated financial benefits are equivalent to—

(1) Ten percent of the estimated contract or order value (including options) if the value is $94 million or less; or

(2) Five percent of the estimated contract or order value (including options) or $9.4 million, whichever is greater, if the value exceeds $94 million.

(e) Reduction of administrative or personnel costs alone is not sufficient justification for bundling unless the cost savings are expected to be at least ten percent of the estimated contract or order value (including options) of the bundled requirements.

(f)(1) Notwithstanding paragraphs (a) through (e) of this subsection, the approving authority identified in paragraph (f)(2) of this subsection may determine that bundling is necessary and justified when—

(i) The expected benefits do not meet the thresholds for a substantial benefit but are critical to the agency's mission success; and

(ii) The acquisition strategy provides for maximum practicable participation by small business concerns.

(2) The approving authority, without power of delegation, is—

(i) For the Department of Defense, the senior procurement executive; or

(ii) For the civilian agencies is the Deputy Secretary or equivalent.

(g) In assessing whether cost savings and/or price reduction would be achieved through bundling, the agency and SBA shall—

(1) Compare the price that has been charged by small businesses for the work that they have performed; or

(2) Where previous prices are not available, compare the price, based on market research, that could have been or could be charged by small businesses for the work previously performed by other than a small business.

(h) If a determination is made that bundling is necessary and justified, the contracting officer shall include it in the acquisition strategy documentation and provide it to SBA upon request.

[FAC 2005-91, 81 FR 67763, 9/30/2016, effective 10/31/2016]

7.107-4 Substantial bundling.

(a) (1) Substantial bundling is any bundling that results in a contract or task or delivery order with an estimated value of—

(i) $8 million or more for the Department of Defense;

(ii) $6 million or more for the National Aeronautics and Space Administration, the General Services Administration, and the Department of Energy; or

(iii) $2.5 million or more for all other agencies.

(2) These thresholds apply to the cumulative estimated dollar value (including options) of—

(i) Multiple-award contracts;

(ii) Task orders or delivery orders issued against a GSA Schedule contract; or

(iii) Task orders or delivery orders issued against a task-order or delivery-order contract awarded by another agency.

(b) In addition to addressing the requirements for bundling (see 7.107-3), when the proposed acquisition strategy involves substantial bundling, the agency shall document in its strategy—

(1) The specific benefits anticipated to be derived from substantial bundling;

(2) An assessment of the specific impediments to participation by small business concerns as contractors that result from substantial bundling;

(3) Actions designed to maximize small business participation as contractors, including provisions that encourage small business teaming;

(4) Actions designed to maximize small business participation as subcontractors (including suppliers) at any tier under the contract, or order, that may be awarded to meet the requirements;

(5) The determination that the anticipated benefits of the proposed bundled contract or order justify its use; and

(6) Alternative strategies that would reduce or minimize the scope of the bundling, and the rationale for not choosing those alternatives.

[FAC 2005-91, 81 FR 67763, 9/30/2016, effective 10/31/2016; FAC 2005-100, 83 FR 42571, 8/22/2018, effective 8/22/2018]

7.107-5 Notifications.

(a) *Notifications to current small business contractors of agency's intent to bundle.* (1) The contracting officer shall notify each small business performing a contract that it intends to bundle the requirement at least 30 days prior to the issuance of the solicitation for the bundled requirement.

(2) The notification shall provide the name, phone number and address of the applicable SBA procurement center representative (PCR), or if an SBA PCR is not assigned to the procuring activity, the SBA Office of Government Contracting Area Office serving the area in which the buying activity is located.

(3) This notification shall be documented in the contract file.

(b) *Notification to public of rationale for bundled requirement.* (1) The agency shall publish on its website a list and rationale for any bundled requirement for which the agency solicited offers or issued an award. The notification shall be made within 30 days of the agency's data certification regarding the validity and verification of data entered in the Federal Procurement Data System to the Office of Federal Procurement Policy (see 4.604).

(2) In addition, the agency is encouraged to provide notification of the rationale for any bundled requirement to the GPE, before issuance of the solicitation (see 5.201).

(c) *Notification to SBA of follow-on bundled or consolidated requirements.* For each follow-on bundled or consolidated requirement, the contracting officer shall obtain the following from the requiring activity and notify the SBA PCR no later than 30 days prior to issuance of the solicitation:

(1) The amount of savings and benefits achieved under the prior consolidation or bundling.

(2) Whether such savings and benefits will continue to be realized if the contract remains consolidated or bundled.

(3) Whether such savings and benefits would be greater if the procurement requirements were divided into separate solicitations suitable for award to small business concerns.

(4) List of requirements that have been added or deleted for the follow-on.

(d) *Public notification of bundling policy.* In accordance with 15 U.S.C. 644(q)(2)(A)(ii), agencies shall publish the Governmentwide policy regarding contract bundling, including regarding the solicitation of teaming and joint ventures, on their agency website.

[FAC 2005-91, 81 FR 67763, 9/30/2016, effective 10/31/2016; FAC 2019-02, 84 FR 19839, 5/6/2019, effective 5/6/2019]

7.107-6 Solicitation provision.

The contracting officer shall insert the provision at 52.207-6, Solicitation of Offers from Small Business Concerns and Small Business Teaming Arrangements or Joint Ventures (Multiple-Award Contracts), in solicitations for multiple-award contracts above the substantial bundling threshold of the agency (see 7.107-4(a)).

[FAC 2005-91, 81 FR 67763, 9/30/2016, effective 10/31/2016]

7.108 Additional requirements for telecommuting.

In accordance with section 41 U.S.C. 3306(f), an agency shall generally not discourage a contractor from allowing its employees to telecommute in the performance of Government contracts. Therefore, agencies shall not—

(a) Include in a solicitation a requirement that prohibits an offeror from permitting its employees to telecommute unless the contracting officer first determines that the requirements of the agency, including security requirements, cannot be met if telecommuting is permitted. The contracting officer shall document the basis for the determination in writing and specify the prohibition in the solicitation; or

(b) When telecommuting is not prohibited, unfavorably evaluate an offer because it includes telecommuting, unless the contracting officer first determines that the requirements of the agency, including security requirements, would be adversely impacted if telecommuting is permitted. The contracting officer shall document the basis for the determination in writing and address the evaluation procedures in the solicitation.

[FAC 2001-25, 69 FR 59701, 10/5/2004, effective 10/5/2004; FAC 2005-04, 70 FR 33656, 6/8/2005, effective 6/8/2005; FAC 2005-73, 79 FR 24192, 4/29/2014, effective 5/29/2014]

SUBPART 7.2—PLANNING FOR THE PURCHASE OF SUPPLIES IN ECONOMIC QUANTITIES

7.200 Scope of subpart.

This subpart prescribes policies and procedures for gathering information from offerors to assist the Government in planning the most advantageous quantities in which supplies should be purchased.

[FAC 84-11, 50 FR 35475, 8/30/85, effective 8/30/85]

7.201 [Reserved]

[Reserved, FAC 84-11, 50 FR 35475, 8/30/85, effective 8/30/85]

7.202 Policy.

(a) Agencies are required by 10 U.S.C. 2384a and 41 U.S.C. 3310 to procure supplies in such quantity as—

(1) Will result in the total cost and unit cost most advantageous to the Government, where practicable; and

(2) Does not exceed the quantity reasonably expected to be required by the agency.

(b) Each solicitation for a contract for supplies is required, if practicable, to include a provision inviting each offeror responding to the solicitation—

(1) To state an opinion on whether the quantity of the supplies proposed to be acquired is economically advantageous to the Government; and

(2) If applicable, to recommend a quantity or quantities which would be more economi-

cally advantageous to the Government. Each such recommendation is required to include a quotation of the total price and the unit price for supplies procured in each recommended quantity.

[FAC 84-11, 50 FR 35475, 8/30/85, effective 8/30/85; FAC 2005-73, 79 FR 24192, 4/29/2014, effective 5/29/2014; FAC 2019-02, 84 FR 19839, 5/6/2019, effective 5/6/2019]

7.203 Solicitation provision.

Contracting officers shall insert the provision at 52.207-4, Economic Purchase Quantity—Supplies, in solicitations for supplies. The provision need not be inserted if the solicitation is for a contract under the General Services Administration's multiple award schedule contract program, or if the contracting officer determines that—

(a) The Government already has the data;

(b) The data is otherwise readily available; or

(c) It is impracticable for the Government to vary its future requirements.

[FAC 84-11, 50 FR 35475, 8/30/85, effective 8/30/85; FAC 84-29, 52 FR 30076, 8/12/87, effective 8/24/87; FAC 2019-02, 84 FR 19839, 5/6/2019, effective 5/6/2019]

7.204 Responsibilities of contracting officers.

(a) Contracting officers are responsible for transmitting offeror responses to the solicitation provision at 52.207-4 to appropriate inventory management/requirements development activities in accordance with agency procedures. The economic purchase quantity data so obtained are intended to assist inventory managers in establishing and evaluating economic order quantities for supplies under their cognizance.

(b) In recognition of the fact that economic purchase quantity data furnished by offerors are only one of many data inputs required for determining the most economical order quantities, contracting officers should generally take no action to revise quantities to be acquired in connection with the instant procurement. However, if a significant price variation is evident from offeror responses, and the potential for significant savings is apparent, the contracting officer shall consult with the cognizant inventory manager or requirements development activity before proceeding with an award or negotiations. If this consultation discloses that the Government should be ordering an item of supply in different quantities and the inventory manager/requirements development activity concurs, the solicitation for the item should be amended or canceled and a new requisition should be obtained.

[FAC 84-11, 50 FR 35475, 8/30/85, effective 8/30/85]

SUBPART 7.3—CONTRACTOR VERSUS GOVERNMENT PERFORMANCE

7.300 [Reserved]

[FAC 90-16, 57 FR 60575, 12/21/92, effective 2/19/93; FAC 2005-09, 71 FR 20299, 4/19/2006, effective 5/19/2006]

7.301 Definitions.

Definitions of *inherently governmental activity* and other terms applicable to this subpart are set forth at Attachment D of the Office of Management and Budget Circular No. A-76 (Revised), Performance of Commercial Activities, dated May 29, 2003 (the Circular).

[FAC 2005-09, 71 FR 20299, 4/19/2006, effective 5/19/2006]

7.302 Policy.

(a) The Circular provides that it is the policy of the Government to—

(1) Perform inherently governmental activities with Government personnel; and

(2) Subject commercial activities to the forces of competition.

(b) As provided in the Circular, agencies shall—

(1) Not use contractors to perform inherently governmental activities;

(2) Conduct public-private competitions in accordance with the provisions of the Circular and, as applicable, these regulations;

(3) Give appropriate consideration relative to cost when making performance decisions between agency and contractor performance in public-private competitions;

(4) Consider the Agency Tender Official an interested party in accordance with 31 U.S.C. 3551 to 3553 for purposes of filing a protest at the Government Accountability Office; and

(5) Hear contests in accordance with OMB Circular A-76, Attachment B, Paragraph F.

(c) When using sealed bidding in public-private competitions under OMB Circular A-76, contracting officers shall not hold discussions to correct deficiencies.

[FAC 84-37, 53 FR 17856, 5/18/88, effective 6/17/88; FAC 84-58, 55 FR 25526, 6/21/90, effective 7/23/90; FAC 90-16, 57 FR 60575, 12/21/92, effective 2/19/93; FAC 2005-09, 71 FR 20299, 4/19/2006, effective 5/19/2006]

7.303 [Reserved]

[FAC 84-58, 55 FR 25526, 6/21/90, effective 7/23/90; FAC 90-16, 57 FR 60575, 12/21/92, effective 2/19/93; FAC 97-26, 66 FR 27405, 5/16/2001, effective 5/16/2001; FAC 2005-09, 71 FR 20299, 4/19/2006, effective 5/19/2006]

7.304 [Reserved]

[FAC 84-5, 50 FR 1735, 1/11/85, effective 4/1/85; FAC 84-58, 55 FR 25526, 6/21/90, effective 7/23/90; FAC 90-16, 57 FR 60575, 12/21/92, effective 2/19/93; FAC 90-29, 60 FR 34732, 7/3/95, effective 7/3/95; FAC 2005-09, 71 FR 20299, 4/19/2006, effective 5/19/2006]

7.305 Solicitation provisions and contract clause.

(a) The contracting officer shall, when soliciting offers and tenders, insert in solicitations issued for standard competitions the provision at 52.207-1, Notice of Standard Competition.

(b) The contracting officer shall, when soliciting offers, insert in solicitations issued for streamlined competitions the provision at 52.207-2, Notice of Streamlined Competition.

(c) The contracting officer shall insert the clause at 52.207-3, Right of First Refusal of Employment, in all solicitations which may result in a conversion from in-house performance to contract performance of work currently being performed by the Government and in contracts that result from the solicitations, whether or not a public-private competition is conducted. The 10-day period in the clause may be varied by the contracting officer up to a period of 90 days.

[FAC 84-5, 50 FR 1735, 1/11/85, effective 4/1/85; FAC 84-25, 52 FR 9037, 3/20/87, effective 7/1/87; FAC 90-8, 56 FR 55371, 10/25/91, effective 11/25/91; FAC 2005-09, 71 FR 20299, 4/19/2006, effective 5/19/2006]

7.306 [Removed]

[FAC 84-5, 50 FR 1735, 1/11/85, effective 4/1/85; FAC 84-21, 51 FR 31425, 9/3/86, effective 8/29/86; FAC 84-32, 53 FR 661, 1/11/88, effective 1/29/88; FAC 84-58, 55 FR 25526, 6/21/90, effective 7/23/90; FAC 90-7, 56 FR 41744, 8/22/91, effective 9/23/91; FAC 90-16,57 FR 60575, 12/21/92, effective 2/19/93; FAC 90-29, 60 FR 34732, 7/3/95, effective 7/3/95; FAC 97-2, 62 FR 51224, 9/30/97, effective 10/10/97; FAC 2005-09, Final rule, 71 FR 20299, 4/19/2006, effective 5/19/2006]

7.307 [Removed]

[FAC 84-58, 55 FR 25526, 6/21/90, effective 7/23/90; FAC 90-16, 57 FR 60575, 12/21/92, effective 2/19/93; FAC 90-29, 60 FR 34732, 7/3/95, effective 7/3/95; Final rule, 62 FR 40236, 7/25/97, effective 6/30/97; FAC 2005-09, Final rule, 71 FR 20299, 4/19/2006, effective 5/19/2006]

SUBPART 7.4—EQUIPMENT LEASE OR PURCHASE

7.400 Scope of subpart.

This subpart provides guidance pertaining to the decision to acquire equipment by lease or purchase. It applies to both the initial acquisition of equipment and the renewal or extension of existing equipment leases.

7.401 Acquisition considerations.

(a) Agencies should consider whether to lease or purchase equipment based on a case-by-case evaluation of comparative costs and other factors. The following factors are the minimum that should be considered:

(1) Estimated length of the period the equipment is to be used and the extent of use within that period.

(2) Financial and operating advantages of alternative types and makes of equipment.

(3) Cumulative rental payments for the estimated period of use.

(4) Net purchase price.

(5) Transportation and installation costs.

(6) Maintenance and other service costs.

(7) Potential obsolescence of the equipment because of imminent technological improvements.

(b) The following additional factors should be considered, as appropriate, depending on the type, cost, complexity, and estimated period of use of the equipment:

(1) Availability of purchase options.

(2) Potential for use of the equipment by other agencies after its use by the acquiring agency is ended.

(3) Trade-in or salvage value.

(4) Imputed interest.

(5) Availability of a servicing capability, especially for highly complex equipment; *e.g.*, can the equipment be serviced by the Government or other sources if it is purchased?

7.402 Acquisition methods.

(a) *Purchase method.*

(1) Generally, the purchase method is appropriate if the equipment will be used beyond the point in time when cumulative leasing costs exceed the purchase costs.

(2) Agencies should not rule out the purchase method of equipment acquisition in favor of leasing merely because of the possibility that future technological advances might make the selected equipment less desirable.

(b) *Lease method.* (1) The lease method is appropriate if it is to the Government's advantage under the circumstances. The lease method may also serve as an interim measure when the circumstances—

(i) Require immediate use of equipment to meet program or system goals; but

(ii) Do not currently support acquisition by purchase.

(2) If a lease is justified, a lease with option to purchase is preferable.

(3) Generally, a long term lease should be avoided, but may be appropriate if an option to purchase or other favorable terms are included.

(4) If a lease with option to purchase is used, the contract shall state the purchase price or provide a formula which shows how the purchase price will be established at the time of purchase.

[FAC 90-23, 59 FR 67010, 12/28/94, effective 2/27/95]

7.403 General Services Administration assistance.

(a) When requested by an agency, the General Services Administration (GSA) will assist in lease or purchase decisions by providing information such as—

(1) Pending price adjustments to Federal Supply Schedule contracts;

(2) Recent or imminent technological developments;

(3) New techniques; and

(4) Industry or market trends.

(b) Agencies may request information from the following GSA office: U.S. General Services Administration, Federal Acquisition Service, Office of Acquisition Management, 2200 Crystal Drive, Room 806, Arlington, VA. 22202. Email: *fasam@gsa.gov*.

(1) Center for Strategic IT Analysis (MKS), Washington, DC 20405, for information on acquisition of information technology.

(2) Federal Supply Service, Office of Acquisition (FC), Washington, DC 20406, for information on other types of equipment.

[FAC 84-49, 54 FR 29280, 7/11/89, effective 8/10/89; FAC 90-41, 61 FR 41466, 8/8/96, effective 8/8/96, finalized without change, FAC 97-3, 62 FR 64912, 12/9/97, effective 2/9/98; Final rule, 62 FR 40236, 7/25/97, effective 6/30/97; FAC 2005-61, 77 FR 56743, 9/13/2012, effective 9/13/2012]

7.404 Contract clause.

The contracting officer shall insert a clause substantially the same as the clause in 52.207-5, Option to Purchase Equipment, in solicitations and contracts involving a lease with option to purchase.

[FAC 90-23, 59 FR 67010, 12/28/94, effective 2/27/95]

SUBPART 7.5—INHERENTLY GOVERNMENTAL FUNCTIONS

7.500 Scope of subpart.

The purpose of this subpart is to prescribe policies and procedures to ensure that inherently governmental functions are not performed by contractors.

[FAC 90-37, 61 FR 2626, 1/26/96, effective 3/26/96; FAC 2005-09, 71 FR 20299, 4/19/2006, effective 5/19/2006]

7.501 [Reserved]

[Removed and reserved, FAC 97-22, 66 FR 2116, 1/10/2001, effective 3/12/2001; Delay of effective date, 66 FR 14259, 3/9/2001, effective 5/11/2001]

7.502 Applicability.

The requirements of this subpart apply to all contracts for services. This subpart does not apply to services obtained through either personnel appointments, advisory committees, or personal services contracts issued under statutory authority.

[FAC 90-37, 61 FR 2626, 1/26/96, effective 3/26/96]

7.503 Policy.

(a) Contracts shall not be used for the performance of inherently governmental functions.

(b) Agency decisions which determine whether a function is or is not an inherently governmental function may be reviewed and modified by appropriate Office of Management and Budget officials.

(c) The following is a list of examples of functions considered to be inherently governmental functions or which shall be treated as such. This list is not all inclusive:

(1) The direct conduct of criminal investigations.

(2) The control of prosecutions and performance of adjudicatory functions other than those relating to arbitration or other methods of alternative dispute resolution.

(3) The command of military forces, especially the leadership of military personnel who are members of the combat, combat support, or combat service support role.

(4) The conduct of foreign relations and the determination of foreign policy.

(5) The determination of agency policy, such as determining the content and application of regulations, among other things.

(6) The determination of Federal program priorities for budget requests.

(7) The direction and control of Federal employees.

(8) The direction and control of intelligence and counter-intelligence operations.

(9) The selection or non-selection of individuals for Federal Government employment, including the interviewing of individuals for employment.

(10) The approval of position descriptions and performance standards for Federal employees.

(11) The determination of what Government property is to be disposed of and on what terms (although an agency may give contractors authority to dispose of property at prices within specified ranges and subject to other reasonable conditions deemed appropriate by the agency).

(12) In Federal procurement activities with respect to prime contracts—

(i) Determining what supplies or services are to be acquired by the Government (although an agency may give contractors authority to acquire supplies at prices within specified ranges and subject to other reasonable conditions deemed appropriate by the agency);

(ii) Participating as a voting member on any source selection boards;

(iii) Approving any contractual documents, to include documents defining requirements, incentive plans, and evaluation criteria;

(iv) Awarding contracts;

(v) Administering contracts (including ordering changes in contract performance or contract quantities, taking action based on evaluations of contractor performance, and accepting or rejecting contractor products or services);

(vi) Terminating contracts;

(vii) Determining whether contract costs are reasonable, allocable, and allowable; and

(viii) Participating as a voting member on performance evaluation boards.

(13) The approval of agency responses to Freedom of Information Act requests (other than routine responses that, because of statute, regulation, or agency policy, do not require the exercise of judgment in determining whether documents are to be released or withheld), and the approval of agency responses to the administrative appeals of denials of Freedom of Information Act requests.

(14) The conduct of administrative hearings to determine the eligibility of any person for a security clearance, or involving actions that affect matters of personal reputation or eligibility to participate in Government programs.

(15) The approval of Federal licensing actions and inspections.

(16) The determination of budget policy, guidance, and strategy.

(17) The collection, control, and disbursement of fees, royalties, duties, fines, taxes, and other public funds, unless authorized by statute, such as 31 U.S.C. 3718 (relating to private collection contractors and private attorney collection services), but not including—

(i) Collection of fees, fines, penalties, costs, or other charges from visitors to or patrons of mess halls, post or base exchange concessions, national parks, and similar entities or activities, or from other persons, where the amount to be collected is easily calculated or predetermined and the funds collected can be easily controlled using standard case management techniques; and

(ii) Routine voucher and invoice examination.

(18) The control of the treasury accounts.

(19) The administration of public trusts.

(20) The drafting of Congressional testimony, responses to Congressional correspondence, or agency responses to audit reports from the Inspector General, the Government Accountability Office, or other Federal audit entity.

(d) The following is a list of examples of functions generally not considered to be inherently governmental functions. However, certain services and actions that are not considered to be inherently governmental functions may approach being in that category because of the nature of the function, the manner in which the contractor performs the contract, or the manner in which the Government administers contractor performance. This list is not all inclusive:

(1) Services that involve or relate to budget preparation, including workload modeling, fact finding, efficiency studies, and should-cost analyses, etc.

(2) Services that involve or relate to reorganization and planning activities.

(3) Services that involve or relate to analyses, feasibility studies, and strategy options to be used by agency personnel in developing policy.

(4) Services that involve or relate to the development of regulations.

(5) Services that involve or relate to the evaluation of another contractor's performance.

(6) Services in support of acquisition planning.

(7) Contractors providing assistance in contract management (such as where the contractor might influence official evaluations of other contractors).

(8) Contractors providing technical evaluation of contract proposals.

(9) Contractors providing assistance in the development of statements of work.

(10) Contractors providing support in preparing responses to Freedom of Information Act requests.

(11) Contractors working in any situation that permits or might permit them to gain access to confidential business information

and/or any other sensitive information (other than situations covered by the National Industrial Security Program described in 4.402(b)).

(12) Contractors providing information regarding agency policies or regulations, such as attending conferences on behalf of an agency, conducting community relations campaigns, or conducting agency training courses.

(13) Contractors participating in any situation where it might be assumed that they are agency employees or representatives.

(14) Contractors participating as technical advisors to a source selection board or participating as voting or nonvoting members of a source evaluation board.

(15) Contractors serving as arbitrators or providing alternative methods of dispute resolution.

(16) Contractors constructing buildings or structures intended to be secure from electronic eavesdropping or other penetration by foreign governments.

(17) Contractors providing inspection services.

(18) Contractors providing legal advice and interpretations of regulations and statutes to Government officials.

(19) Contractors providing special non-law enforcement, security activities that do not directly involve criminal investigations, such as prisoner detention or transport and non-military national security details.

(e) Agency implementation shall include procedures requiring the agency head or designated requirements official to provide the contracting officer, concurrent with transmittal of the statement of work (or any modification thereof), a written determination that none of the functions to be performed are inherently governmental. This assessment should place emphasis on the degree to which conditions and facts restrict the discretionary authority, decision-making responsibility, or accountability of Government officials using contractor services or work products. Disagreements regarding the determination will be resolved in accordance with agency procedures before issuance of a solicitation.

[FAC 90-37, 61 FR 2626, 1/26/96, effective 3/26/96; Final rule, 62 FR 40236, 7/25/97, effective 6/30/97; FAC 2005-13, 71 FR 57380, 9/28/2006, effective 9/28/2006; FAC 2019-02, 84 FR 19839, 5/6/2019, effective 5/6/2019]

PART 8—REQUIRED SOURCES OF SUPPLIES AND SERVICES

Table of Contents

Scope of part 8.000
General 8.001
Priorities for use of mandatory Government sources 8.002
Use of other mandatory sources 8.003
Use of other sources 8.004
Contract clause 8.005

Subpart 8.1—Excess Personal Property

[Reserved] 8.101
Policy 8.102
Information on available excess personal property 8.103
Obtaining nonreportable property 8.104

Subpart 8.2—[Reserved]

Subpart 8.3—[Reserved]

Subpart 8.4—Federal Supply Schedules

Definitions 8.401
General 8.402
Applicability 8.403
Use of Federal Supply Schedules 8.404
Ordering procedures for Federal Supply Schedules 8.405
Ordering procedures for supplies, and services not requiring a statement of work 8.405-1
Ordering procedures for services requiring a statement of work 8.405-2
Blanket purchase agreements (BPAs) 8.405-3
Price reductions 8.405-4
Small business 8.405-5
Limiting sources 8.405-6
Payment 8.405-7
[Redesignated] 8.405-8
Ordering activity responsibilities 8.406
Order placement 8.406-1
Inspection and acceptance 8.406-2
Remedies for nonconformance 8.406-3
Termination for cause 8.406-4
Termination for the Government's convenience 8.406-5
Disputes 8.406-6
Contractor Performance Evaluation 8.406-7

Subpart 8.5—Acquisition of Helium

Scope of subpart 8.500
Definitions 8.501
Policy 8.502
Exception 8.503
Procedures 8.504
Contract clause 8.505

Subpart 8.6—Acquisition from Federal Prison Industries, Inc.

General 8.601
Policy 8.602
Purchase priorities 8.603
Waivers 8.604
Exceptions 8.605
Evaluating FPI performance 8.606
Performance as a subcontractor 8.607

Protection of classified and sensitive information 8.608

Subpart 8.7—Acquisition from Nonprofit Agencies Employing People Who Are Blind or Severely Disabled

Scope of subpart 8.700
Definitions 8.701
General 8.702
Procurement List 8.703
Purchase priorities 8.704
Procedures 8.705
General 8.705-1
Direct-order process 8.705-2
Allocation process 8.705-3
Compliance with orders 8.705-4
Purchase exceptions 8.706
Prices 8.707
Shipping 8.708
Payments 8.709
Quality of merchandise 8.710
Quality complaints 8.711
Specification changes 8.712
Optional acquisition of supplies and services 8.713
Communications with the central nonprofit agencies and the Committee 8.714
Replacement commodities 8.715
Change-of-name and successor in interest procedures 8.716

Subpart 8.8—Acquisition of Printing and Related Supplies

Scope of subpart 8.800
Definitions 8.801
Policy 8.802

Subpart 8.9—[Reservedl]

Subpart 8.10—[Reserved]

Subpart 8.11—Leasing of Motor Vehicles

Scope of subpart 8.1100
Definitions 8.1101
Presolicitation requirements 8.1102
Contract requirements 8.1103
Contract clauses 8.1104

PART 8—REQUIRED SOURCES OF SUPPLIES AND SERVICES

8.000 Scope of part.

This part deals with prioritizing sources of supplies and services for use by the Government.

[FAC 2005-72, 78 FR 80376, 12/31/2013, effective 1/30/2014]

8.001 General.

Regardless of the source of supplies or services to be acquired, information technology acquisitions shall comply with capital planning and investment control requirements in 40 U.S.C. 11312 and OMB Circular A-130.

[FAC 2001-09, 67 FR 56115, 8/30/2002, effective 9/30/2002; FAC 2005-06, 70 FR 57453, 9/30/2005, effective 9/30/2005]

8.002 Priorities for use of mandatory Government sources.

(a) Except as required by 8.003, or as otherwise provided by law, agencies shall satisfy requirements for supplies and services from or through the mandatory Government sources and publications listed below in descending order of priority:

(1) *Supplies.* (i) Inventories of the requiring agency.

(ii) Excess from other agencies (see subpart 8.1).

(iii) Federal Prison Industries, Inc. (see subpart 8.6).

(iv) Supplies that are on the Procurement List maintained by the Committee for Purchase From People Who Are Blind or Severely Disabled (see Subpart 8.7).

(v) Wholesale supply sources, such as stock programs of the General Services Administration (GSA) (see 41 CFR 101-26.3), the Defense Logistics Agency (see 41 CFR 101-26.6), the Department of Veterans Affairs (see 41 CFR 101-26.704), and military inventory control points.

(2) *Services.* Services that are on the Procurement List maintained by the Committee for Purchase From People Who Are Blind or Severely Disabled (see subpart 8.7).

(b) Sources other than those listed in paragraph (a) of this section may be used as prescribed in 41 CFR 101-26.301 and in an unusual and compelling urgency as prescribed in 6.302-2 and in 41 CFR 101-25.101-5.

(c) The statutory obligation for Government agencies to satisfy their requirements for supplies or services available from the Committee for Purchase From People Who Are Blind or Severely Disabled also applies when contractors purchase the supplies or services for Government use.

[FAC 84-5, 50 FR 1735, 1/11/85, effective 4/1/85; FAC 84-49, 54 FR 29280, 7/11/89, effective 8/10/89; FAC 90-4, 56 FR 15148, 4/15/91, effective 5/15/91; FAC 90-21, 59 FR 53716, 10/25/94, effective 10/25/94; FAC 90-23, 59 FR 67010, 12/28/94, effective 2/27/95; FAC 90-37, 61 FR 2626, 1/26/96, effective 3/26/96; FAC 2001-02, 66 FR 65347, 12/18/2001, effective 2/19/2002; FAC 2001-09, 67 FR 56115, 8/30/2002, effective 9/30/2002; FAC 2001-24, 69 FR 34229, 6/18/2004, effective 7/19/2004; FAC 2005-72, 78 FR 80376, 12/31/2013, effective 1/30/2014]

8.003 Use of other mandatory sources.

Agencies shall satisfy requirements for the following supplies or services from or through specified sources, as applicable:

(a) Public utility services (see part 41).

(b) Printing and related supplies (see subpart 8.8).

(c) Leased motor vehicles (see subpart 8.11).

(d) Strategic and critical materials (*e.g.*, metals and ores) from inventories exceeding Defense National Stockpile requirements (detailed information is available from the DLA Strategic Materials, 8725 John J. Kingman Rd., Suite 3229, Fort Belvoir, VA 22060-6223.

(e) Helium (see subpart 8.5—Acquisition of Helium).

[FAC 90-16, 57 FR 60576, 12/21/92, effective 2/19/93; FAC 90-23, 59 FR 67010, 12/28/94, effective 2/27/95; FAC 90-41, 61 FR 41466, 8/8/96, effective 8/8/96, finalized without change, FAC 97-3, 62 FR 64912, 12/9/97, effective 2/9/98; FAC 90-45, Final rule, 62 FR 224, 1/2/97, effective 1/1/97; FAC 2001-09, 67 FR 56115, 8/30/2002, effective 9/30/2002; FAC 2001-24, 69 FR 34244, 6/18/2004, effective 6/18/2004; FAC 2005-72, 78 FR 80376, 12/31/2013, effective 1/30/2014]

8.004 Use of other sources.

If an agency is unable to satisfy requirements for supplies and services from the mandatory sources listed in 8.002 and 8.003, agencies are encouraged to consider satisfying requirements from or through the non-mandatory sources listed in paragraph (a) of this section (not listed in any order of priority) before considering the non-mandatory source listed in paragraph (b) of this section. When satisfying requirements from non-mandatory sources, see 7.105(b) and part 19 regarding consideration of small business, veteran-owned small business, service-disabled veteran-owned small business, HUBZone small business, small disadvantaged business (including 8(a) participants), and women-owned small business concerns.

(a) (1) *Supplies.* Federal Supply Schedules, Governmentwide acquisition contracts, multi-agency contracts, and any other procurement instruments intended for use by multiple agencies, including blanket purchase agreements (BPAs) under Federal Supply Schedule contracts (*e.g.,* Federal Strategic Sourcing Initiative (FSSI) agreements accessible at *http://www.gsa.gov/fssi* (see also 5.601)).

(2) *Services.* Agencies are encouraged to consider Federal Prison Industries, Inc., as well as the sources listed in paragraph (a)(1) of this section (see subpart 8.6).

(b) Commercial sources (including educational and non-profit institutions) in the open market.

[FAC 2005-72, 78 FR 80376, 12/31/2013, effective 1/30/2014]

8.005 Contract clause.

Insert the clause at 52.208-9, Contractor Use of Mandatory Sources of Supply and Services, in solicitations and contracts that require a contractor to provide supplies or services for Government use that are on the Procurement List maintained by the Committee for Purchase From People Who Are Blind or Severely Disabled. The contracting officer shall identify in the contract schedule the supplies or services that shall be purchased from a mandatory source and the specific source.

[FAC 2001-02, 66 FR 65347, 12/18/2001, effective 2/19/2002; FAC 2001-09, 67 FR 56115, 8/30/2002, effective 9/30/2002; FAC 2001-24, 69 FR 34229, 6/18/2004, effective 7/19/2004; FAC 2005-72, 78 FR 80376, 12/31/2013, effective 1/30/2014; FAC 2019-02, 84 FR 19839, 5/6/2019, effective 5/6/2019]

SUBPART 8.1—EXCESS PERSONAL PROPERTY

8.101 [Reserved]

[FAC 2001-22, 69 FR 17741, 4/5/2004, effective 5/5/2004]

8.102 Policy.

When practicable, agencies must use excess personal property as the first source of supply for agency and cost-reimbursement contractor requirements. Agency personnel must make positive efforts to satisfy agency requirements by obtaining and using excess personal property (including that suitable for adaptation or substitution) before initiating a contract action.

[FAC 2001-06, 67 FR 13048, 3/20/2002, effective 4/4/2002]

8.103 Information on available excess personal property.

Information regarding the availability of excess personal property can be obtained through—

(a) Review of excess personal property catalogs and bulletins issued by the General Services Administration (GSA);

(b) Personal contact with GSA or the activity holding the property;

(c) Submission of supply requirements to the regional offices of GSA (GSA Form 1539, Request for Excess Personal Property, is available for this purpose); and

(d) Examination and inspection of reports and samples of excess personal property in GSA regional offices.

8.104 Obtaining nonreportable property.

GSA will assist agencies in meeting their requirements for supplies of the types excepted from reporting as excess by the Federal Management Regulations (41 CFR 102-36.90). Federal agencies requiring such supplies should contact the appropriate GSA regional office.

[FAC 2001-22, 69 FR 17741, 4/5/2004, effective 5/5/2004]

SUBPART 8.2—[RESERVED]

SUBPART 8.3—[RESERVED]

SUBPART 8.4—FEDERAL SUPPLY SCHEDULES

8.401 Definitions.

As used in this subpart—

Ordering activity means an activity that is authorized to place orders, or establish blanket purchase agreements (BPA), against the General Services Administration's (GSA) Multiple Award Schedule contracts. A list of eligible ordering activities is available at *http://www.gsa.gov/schedules* (click "For Customers Ordering from Schedules" and then "Eligibility to Use GSA Sources").

Multiple Award Schedule (MAS) means contracts awarded by GSA or the Department of Veterans Affairs (VA) for similar or comparable supplies, or services, established with more than one supplier, at varying prices. The primary statutory authorities for the MAS program are 41 U.S.C. 152(3), Competitive Procedures, and 40 U.S.C. 501, Services for Executive Agencies.

Requiring agency means the agency needing the supplies or services.

Schedules e-Library means the on-line source for GSA and VA Federal Supply Schedule contract award information. Schedules e-Library may be accessed at *http://www.gsa.gov/elibrary.*

Special Item Number (SIN) means a group of generically similar (but not identical) supplies or services that are intended to serve the same general purpose or function.

[FAC 97-1, 62 FR 44802, 8/22/97, effective 10/21/97; FAC 2001-08, 67 FR 43514, 6/27/2002, effective 7/29/2002; FAC 2001-09, 67 FR 56115, 8/30/2002, effective 9/30/2002; FAC 2001-24, 69 FR 34231, 6/18/2004, effective 7/19/2004; FAC 2005-05, 70 FR 43578, 7/27/2005, effective 7/27/2005; FAC 2005-73, 79 FR 24192, 4/29/2014, effective 5/29/2014]

8.402 General.

(a) The Federal Supply Schedule program is also known as the GSA Schedules Program or the Multiple Award Schedule Program. The Federal Supply Schedule program is directed and managed by GSA and provides Federal agencies (see 8.004) with a simplified process for obtaining commercial supplies and services at prices associated with volume buying. Indefinite delivery contracts are awarded to provide supplies and services at stated prices for given periods of time. GSA may delegate certain responsibilities to other agencies (e.g., GSA has delegated authority to the VA to procure medical supplies under the VA Federal Supply Schedules program). Orders issued under the VA Federal Supply Schedule program are covered by this subpart. Additionally, the Department of Defense (DoD) manages similar systems of schedule-type contracting for military items; however, DoD systems are not covered by this subpart.

(b) GSA schedule contracts require all schedule contractors to publish an "Authorized Federal Supply Schedule Pricelist" (pricelist). The pricelist contains all supplies and services offered by a schedule contractor. In addition, each pricelist contains the pricing and the terms and conditions pertaining to each Special Item Number that is on schedule. The schedule contractor is required to provide one copy of its pricelist to any ordering activity upon request. Also, a copy of the pricelist may be obtained from the Federal Supply Service by submitting a written e-mail request to *schedules.infocenter@gsa.gov* or by telephone at 1-800-488-3111. This subpart, together with the pricelists, contain necessary information for placing delivery or task orders with schedule contractors. In addition, the GSA schedule contracting office issues Federal Supply Schedules publications that contain a general overview of the Federal Supply Schedule (FSS) program and address pertinent topics. Ordering activities may request copies of schedules publications by contacting the Centralized Mailing List Service through the Internet at *http://www.gsa.gov/cmls*, submitting written e-mail requests to *CMLS@gsa.gov*; or by completing GSA Form 457, FSS Publications Mailing List Application, and mailing it to the GSA Centralized Mailing List Service (7SM), P.O. Box 6477, Fort Worth, TX 76115. Copies of GSA Form 457 may also be obtained from the above-referenced points of contact.

(c) (1) GSA offers an on-line shopping service called "GSA Advantage!" through which ordering activities may place orders against Schedules. (Ordering activities may also use GSA Advantage! to place orders through GSA's Global Supply System, a GSA wholesale supply source, formerly known as "GSA Stock" or the "Customer Supply Center." FAR subpart 8.4 is not applicable to orders placed through the GSA Global Supply System.) Ordering activities may access GSA Advantage! through the GSA Federal Supply Service Home Page (*http://www.gsa.gov/fas*) or the GSA Federal Supply Schedule Home Page at *http://www.gsa.gov/schedules*.

(2) GSA Advantage! enables ordering activities to search specific information (i.e., national stock number, part number, common name), review delivery options, place orders directly with Schedule contractors (except see 8.405-6) and pay for orders using the Governmentwide commercial purchase card.

(d) (1) *e-Buy,* GSA's electronic Request for Quotation (RFQ) system, is a part of a suite of on-line tools which complement GSA Advantage!. E-Buy allows ordering activities to post requirements, obtain quotes, and issue orders electronically. Posting an RFQ on e-Buy—

(i) Is one medium for providing fair notice to all schedule contractors offering such supplies and services as required by 8.405-1, 8.405-2, and 8.405-3; and

(ii) Is required when an order contains brand-name specifications (*see* 8.405-6).

(2) Ordering activities may access e-Buy at *http://www.ebuy.gsa.gov*. For more information or assistance on either GSA Advantage! or e-Buy, contact GSA at Internet e-mail address *gsa.advantage@gsa.gov*.

(e) For more information or assistance regarding the Federal Supply Schedule Program, review the following website: *http://www.gsa.gov/schedules*. Additionally, for on-line training courses regarding the Schedules Program, review the following website: *http://www.gsa.gov/training*.

(f) For administrative convenience, an ordering activity contracting officer may add items not on the Federal Supply Schedule (also referred to as open market items) to a Federal Supply Schedule blanket purchase agreement (BPA) or an individual task or delivery order only if—

(1) All applicable acquisition regulations pertaining to the purchase of the items not on the Federal Supply Schedule have been followed (e.g., publicizing (part 5), competition requirements (part 6), acquisition of commercial items (part 12), contracting methods (parts 13, 14, and 15), and small business programs (part 19));

(2) The ordering activity contracting officer has determined the price for the items not on the Federal Supply Schedule is fair and reasonable;

(3) The items are clearly labeled on the order as items not on the Federal Supply Schedule and they conform to the rules for numbering line items at subpart 4.10; and

(4) All clauses applicable to items not on the Federal Supply Schedule are included in the order.

(g) When using the Governmentwide commercial purchase card as a method of payment, orders at or below the micro-purchase threshold are exempt from verification in the System for Award Management as to whether the contractor has a delinquent debt subject to collection under the Treasury Offset Program (TOP).

[FAC 97-18, 65 FR 36014, 6/6/2000, effective 8/7/2000; FAC 2001-24, 69 FR 34231,

6/18/2004, effective 7/19/2004; FAC 2005-13, 71 FR 57357, 9/28/2006, effective 9/28/2006; FAC 2005-38, 74 FR 65600, 12/10/2009, effective 2/1/2010; FAC 2005-50, 76 FR 14548, 3/16/2011, effective 5/16/2011; FAC 2005-55, 77 FR 189, 1/3/2012, effective 2/2/2012, 77 FR 204, 1/3/2012, effective 1/3/2012; FAC 2005-56, 77 FR 12927, 3/2/2012, effective 4/2/2012; FAC 2005-67, 78 FR 37676, 6/21/2013, effective 7/22/2013; FAC 2005-72, 78 FR 80376, 12/31/2014, effective 1/30/2014; FAC 2005-95, 82 FR 4709, 1/13/2017, effective 1/13/2017; FAC 2005-101, 83 FR 48691, 9/26/2018, effective 10/26/2018; FAC 2019-02, 84 FR 19839, 5/6/2019, effective 5/6/2019]

8.403 Applicability.

(a) Procedures in this subpart apply to—

(1) Individual orders for supplies or services placed against Federal Supply Schedules contracts; and

(2) BPAs established against Federal Supply Schedule contracts.

(b) GSA may establish special ordering procedures for a particular schedule. In this case, that schedule will specify those special ordering procedures. Unless otherwise noted, special ordering procedures established for a Federal Supply Schedule take precedence over the procedures in 8.405.

(c) In accordance with section 1427(b) of Public Law 108-136 (40 U.S.C. 1103 note), for requirements that substantially or to a dominant extent specify performance of architect-engineer services (as defined in 2.101), agencies—

(1) Shall use the procedures at Subpart 36.6; and

(2) Shall not place orders for such requirements under a Federal Supply Schedule.

[FAC 2001-24, 69 FR 34231, 6/18/2004, effective 7/19/2004; FAC 2005-01, 70 FR 11737, 3/9/2005, effective 3/9/2005; FAC 2005-06, 70 FR 57452, 9/30/2005, effective 9/30/2005; FAC 2005-73, 79 FR 24192, 4/29/2014, effective 5/29/2014]

8.404 Use of Federal Supply Schedules.

(a) *General.* Parts 13 (except 13.303-2(c)(3)), 14, 15, and 19 (except for the requirement at 19.202-1(e)(1)(iii)) do not apply to BPAs or orders placed against Federal Supply Schedules contracts (but see 8.405-5). BPAs and orders placed against a MAS, using the procedures in this subpart, are considered to be issued using full and open competition (see 6.102(d)(3)). Therefore, when establishing a BPA (as authorized by 13.303-2(c)(3)), or placing orders under Federal Supply Schedule contracts using the procedures of 8.405, ordering activities shall not seek competition outside of the Federal Supply Schedules or synopsize the requirement; but *see* paragraph (g) of this section.

(b)(1) The contracting officer, when placing an order or establishing a BPA, is responsible for applying the regulatory and statutory requirements applicable to the agency for which the order is placed or the BPA is established. The requiring agency shall provide the information on the applicable regulatory and statutory requirements to the contracting officer responsible for placing the order.

(2) For orders over $550,000, *see* subpart 17.5 for additional requirements for interagency acquisitions.

(c) *Acquisition planning.* Orders placed under a Federal Supply Schedule contract—

(1) Are not exempt from the development of acquisition plans (see subpart 7.1), and an information technology acquisition strategy (see Part 39);

(2) Shall comply with all FAR requirements for a consolidated or bundled contract when the order meets the definition at 2.101(b) of *consolidation* or *bundling*; and

(3) Must, whether placed by the requiring agency, or on behalf of the requiring agency, be consistent with the requiring agency's statutory and regulatory requirements applicable to the acquisition of the supply or service.

(d) *Pricing.* Supplies offered on the schedule are listed at fixed prices. Services offered on the schedule are priced either at hourly rates, or at a fixed price for performance of a specific task (e.g., installation, maintenance, and repair). GSA has already determined the prices of supplies and fixed-price services, and rates for services offered at hourly rates, under schedule contracts to be fair and reasonable. Therefore, ordering activities are not required to make a separate determination of fair and reasonable pricing, except for a price evaluation as required by 8.405-2(d). By placing an order against a schedule contract using the procedures in 8.405, the ordering activity has concluded that the order represents the best value (as defined in FAR 2.101) and results in the lowest overall cost alternative (considering price, special features, administrative costs, etc.) to meet the Government's needs. Although GSA has already negotiated fair and reasonable pricing, ordering activities may seek additional discounts before placing an order (see 8.405-4).

(e) The procedures under subpart 33.1 are applicable to the issuance of an order or the establishment of a BPA against a schedule contract.

(f) If the ordering activity issues an RFQ, the ordering activity shall provide the RFQ to any schedule contractor that requests a copy of it.

(g) (1) Ordering activities shall publicize contract actions funded in whole or in part by the American Recovery and Reinvestment Act of 2009 (Pub. L. 111-5):

(i) Notices of proposed MAS orders (including orders issued under BPAs) that are for "informational purposes only" exceeding $25,000 shall follow the procedures in 5.704 for posting orders.

(ii) Award notices for MAS orders (including orders issued under BPAs) shall follow the procedures in 5.705.

(2) When an order is awarded or a Blanket Purchase Agreement is established with an estimated value greater than the simplified acquisition threshold and supported by a limited-source justification at 8.405-6(a), the ordering activity contracting officer must—

(i) Publicize the action (*see* 5.301); and

(ii) Post the justification in accordance with 8.405-6(a)(2).

(h) *Type-of-order preference for services.* (1) The ordering activity shall specify the order type (*i.e.,* firm-fixed price, time-and-materials, or labor-hour) for the services offered on the schedule priced at hourly rates.

(2) Agencies shall use fixed-price orders for the acquisition of commercial services to the maximum extent practicable.

(3) (i) A time-and-materials or labor-hour order may be used for the acquisition of commercial services only when it is not possible at the time of placing the order to estimate accurately the extent or duration of the work or to anticipate costs with any reasonable degree of confidence.

(ii) Prior to the issuance of a time-and-materials or labor-hour order, the contracting officer shall—

(A) Execute a determination and findings (D&F) for the order, in accordance with paragraph (h)(3)(iii) of this section that a fixed-price order is not suitable;

(B) Include a ceiling price in the order that the contractor exceeds at its own risk; and

(C) When the total performance period, including options, is more than three years, the D&F prepared in accordance with this paragraph shall be signed by the contracting officer and approved by the head of the contracting activity prior to the execution of the base period.

(iii) The D&F required by paragraph (h)(3)(ii)(A) of this section shall contain sufficient facts and rationale to justify that a fixed-price order is not suitable. At a minimum, the D&F shall—

(A) Include a description of the market research conducted (see 8.404(c) and 10.002(e));

(B) Establish that it is not possible at the time of placing the order to accurately estimate the extent or duration of the work or anticipate costs with any reasonable degree of confidence;

(C) Establish that the current requirement has been structured to maximize the use of fixed-price orders (*e.g.,* by limiting the value or length of the time-and-materials/labor-hour order; or, establishing fixed prices for portions of the requirement) on future acquisitions for the same or similar requirements; and

(D) Describe actions to maximize the use of fixed-price orders on future acquisitions for the same requirements.

(iv) Prior to an increase in the ceiling price of a time-and-materials or labor-hour order, the ordering activity shall—

(A) Conduct an analysis of pricing and other relevant factors to determine if the action is in the best interest of the Government and document the order file;

(B) Follow the procedures at 8.405-6 for a change that modifies the general scope of the order; and

(C) Comply with the requirements at 8.402(f) when modifying an order to add open market items.

(i) Ensure that service contractor reporting requirements are met in accordance with subpart 4.17, Service Contracts Inventory.

(j) *Line items.* When placing orders or establishing BPAs, ordering activities shall reference the special item number and the corresponding line or subline item awarded (established per 4.1005) in the schedule. If an ordering activity contracting officer adds an item not on the Federal Supply Schedule in accordance with FAR 8.402(f), establish a new line item in accordance with subpart 4.10.

[FAC 84-49, 54 FR 29280, 7/11/89, effective 8/10/89; Final rule, 55 FR 38516, 9/18/90; FAC 90-7, 56 FR 41744, 8/22/91, effective 9/23/91; FAC 90-21, 59 FR 53716, 10/25/94, effective 10/25/94, corrected, 59 FR 60319, 11/23/94; FAC 90-29, 60 FR 34732, 7/3/95, effective 7/3/95; FAC 97-1, 62 FR 44802, 8/22/97, effective 10/21/97; FAC 97-3, 62 FR 64912, 12/9/97, effective 2/9/98; FAC 97-5, 63 FR 34058, 6/22/98, effective 6/22/98; FAC 97-10, 63 FR 70264, 12/18/98, effective 1/4/99; FAC 97-11, 64 FR 10530, 3/4/99, effective 3/4/99; FAC 97-18, 65 FR 36014, 6/6/2000, effective 8/7/2000; FAC 2001-09, 67 FR 56115, 8/30/2002, effective 9/30/2002; FAC 2001-16, 68 FR 56688, 10/1/2003, effective 10/1/2003; FAC 2001-16, 67 FR 56688, 10/1/2003, 10/1/2003; FAC 2001-17, 68 FR 59999, 10/20/2003, effective 10/20/2003; FAC 2001-24, 69 FR 34231, 6/18/2004, effective 7/19/2004; FAC 2005-32, 74 FR 14636, 3/31/2009, effective 3/31/2009; FAC 2005-42, 75 FR 34271, 6/16/2010, effective 7/16/2010; FAC 2005-47, 75 FR 77733, 12/13/2010, effective 12/13/2010; FAC 2005-50, 76 FR 14548, 3/16/2011, effective 5/16/2011; FAC 2005-55, 77 FR 183, 194, 1/3/2012, effective 2/2/2012; FAC 2005-56, 77 FR 12927, 3/2/2012, effective 4/2/2012; FAC 2005-66, 78 FR 13766, 2/28/2013, effective 4/1/2013; FAC 2005-72, 78 FR 80369, 12/31/2013, effective 1/30/2014; FAC 2005-83, 80 FR 38293, 7/2/2015, effective 10/1/2015; FAC 2005-91, 81 FR 67763, 9/30/2016, effective 10/31/2016; FAC 2005-95, 82 FR 4709, 1/13/2017, effective 1/13/2017; FAC 2019-02, 84 FR 19837, 5/6/2019, effective 6/5/2019]

8.405 Ordering procedures for Federal Supply Schedules.

Ordering activities shall use the ordering procedures of this section when placing an order or establishing a BPA for supplies or services. The procedures in this section apply to all schedules. For establishing BPAs and for orders under BPAs *see* 8.405-3.

[FAC 2001-24, 69 FR 34231, 6/18/2004, effective 7/19/2004; FAC 2005-50, 76 FR 14548, 3/16/2011, effective 5/16/2011; FAC 2005-56, 77 FR 12927, 3/2/2012, effective 4/2/2012]

8.405-1 Ordering procedures for supplies, and services not requiring a statement of work.

(a) Ordering activities shall use the procedures of this subsection when ordering supplies and services that are listed in the schedules contracts at a fixed price for the performance of a specific task, where a statement of work is not required (e.g., installation, maintenance, and repair). For establishing BPAs and for orders under BPAs *see* 8.405-3.

(b) *Orders at or below the micro-purchase threshold.* Ordering activities may place orders at, or below, the micro-purchase threshold with any Federal Supply Schedule contractor that can meet the agency's needs. Although not required to solicit from a specific number of schedule contractors, ordering activities should attempt to distribute orders among contractors.

(c) *Orders exceeding the micro-purchase threshold but not exceeding the simplified acquisition threshold.* Ordering activities shall place orders with the schedule contractor that can provide the supply or service that represents the best value. Before placing an order, an ordering activity shall:

(1) Consider reasonably available information about the supply or service offered under MAS contracts by surveying at least three schedule contractors through the GSA Advantage! on-line shopping service, by reviewing the catalogs or pricelists of at least three schedule contractors, or by requesting quotations from at least three schedule contractors (*see* 8.405-5); or

(2) Document the circumstances for restricting consideration to fewer than three schedule contractors based on one of the reasons at 8.405-6(a).

(d) *For proposed orders exceeding the simplified acquisition threshold.* (1) Each order shall be placed on a competitive basis in accordance with (d)(2) and (3) of this section, unless this requirement is waived on the basis of a justification that is prepared and approved in accordance with 8.405-6.

(2) The ordering activity contracting officer shall provide an RFQ that includes a description of the supplies to be delivered or the services to be performed and the basis upon which the selection will be made (*see* 8.405-1(f)).

(3) The ordering activity contracting officer shall—

(i) Post the RFQ on e-Buy to afford all schedule contractors offering the required supplies or services under the appropriate multiple award schedule(s) an opportunity to submit a quote; or

(ii) Provide the RFQ to as many schedule contractors as practicable, consistent with market research appropriate to the circumstances, to reasonably ensure that quotes will be received from at least three contractors that can fulfill the requirements. When fewer than three quotes are received from schedule contractors that can fulfill the requirement, the contracting officer shall prepare a written determination explaining that no additional contractors capable of fulfilling the requirement could be identified despite reasonable efforts to do so. The determination must clearly explain efforts made to obtain quotes from at least three schedule contractors.

(4) The ordering activity contracting officer shall ensure that all quotes received are fairly considered and award is made in accordance with the basis for selection in the RFQ.

(e) When an order contains brand-name specifications, the contracting officer shall post the RFQ on e-Buy along with the justification or documentation, as required by 8.405-6. An RFQ is required when a purchase description specifies a brand-name.

(f) In addition to price (*see* 8.404(d) and 8.405-4), when determining best value, the ordering activity may consider, among other factors, the following:

(1) Past performance.

(2) Special features of the supply or service required for effective program performance.

(3) Trade-in considerations.

(4) Probable life of the item selected as compared with that of a comparable item.

(5) Warranty considerations.

(6) Maintenance availability.

(7) Environmental and energy efficiency considerations.

(8) Delivery terms.

(g) *Minimum documentation.* The ordering activity shall document—

(1) The schedule contracts considered, noting the contractor from which the supply or service was purchased;

(2) A description of the supply or service purchased;

(3) The amount paid;

(4) When an order exceeds the simplified acquisition threshold, evidence of compliance with the ordering procedures at 8.405-1(d); and

(5) The basis for the award decision.

[Reserved, FAC 90-21, 59 FR 53716, 10/25/94, effective 10/25/94; FAC 2001-24, 69 FR 34231, 6/18/2004, effective 7/19/2004; FAC 2005-05, 70 FR 43578, 7/27/2005, effective 7/27/2005; FAC 2005-13, 71 FR 57357, 9/28/2006, effective 9/28/2006; FAC 2005-50, 76 FR 14548, 3/16/2011, effective 5/16/2011; FAC 2005-55, 77 FR 189, 1/3/2012, effective 2/2/2012; FAC 2005-56, 77 FR 12927, 3/2/2012, effective 4/2/2012]

8.405-2 Ordering procedures for services requiring a statement of work.

(a) *General.* Ordering activities shall use the procedures in this subsection when ordering services priced at hourly rates as established by the schedule contracts. The applicable services will be identified in the Federal Supply Schedule publications and the contractor's pricelists. For establishing BPAs and for orders under BPAs *see* 8.405-3.

(b) *Statements of Work (SOWs).* All Statements of Work shall include a description of work to be performed; location of work; period of performance; deliverable schedule; applicable performance standards; and any special requirements (e.g., security clearances, travel, special knowledge). To the maximum extent practicable, agency requirements shall be performance-based statements (see subpart 37.6).

(c) *Request for Quotation procedures.* The ordering activity must provide the Request for Quotation (RFQ), which includes the statement of work and evaluation criteria (e.g., experience and past performance), to schedule contractors that offer services that will meet the agency's needs. The RFQ may be posted to GSA's electronic RFQ system, e-Buy (see 8.402(d)).

(1) Orders at, or below, the micro-purchase threshold. Ordering activities may place orders at, or below, the micro-purchase threshold with any Federal Supply Schedule contractor that can meet the agency's needs. The ordering activity should attempt to distribute orders among contractors.

(2) For orders exceeding the micro-purchase threshold, but not exceeding the simplified acquisition threshold.

(i) The ordering activity shall develop a statement of work, in accordance with 8.405-2(b).

(ii) The ordering activity shall provide the RFQ (including the statement of work and evaluation criteria) to at least three schedule contractors that offer services that will meet the agency's needs or document the circumstances for restricting consideration to fewer than three schedule contractors based on one of the reasons at 8.405-6(a).

(iii) The ordering activity shall specify the type of order (*i.e.*, firm-fixed-price, labor-hour) for the services identified in the statement of work. The contracting officer should establish firm-fixed-prices, as appropriate.

(3) *For proposed orders exceeding the simplified acquisition threshold.* In addition to meeting the requirements of 8.405-2(c)(2)(i) and (iii), the following procedures apply:

(i) Each order shall be placed on a competitive basis in accordance with (c)(3)(ii) and (iii) of this section, unless this requirement is waived on the basis of a justification that is prepared and approved in accordance with 8.405-6.

(ii) The ordering activity contracting officer shall provide an RFQ that includes a statement of work and the evaluation criteria.

(iii) The ordering activity contracting officer shall—

(A) Post the RFQ on e-Buy to afford all schedule contractors offering the required services under the appropriate multiple-award schedule(s) an opportunity to submit a quote; or

(B) Provide the RFQ to as many schedule contractors as practicable, consistent with market research appropriate to the circumstances, to reasonably ensure that quotes will be received from at least three contractors that can fulfill the requirements. When fewer than three quotes are received from schedule contractors that can fulfill the requirements, the contracting officer shall prepare a written determination to explain that no additional contractors capable of fulfilling the requirements could be identified despite reasonable efforts to do so. The determination must clearly explain efforts made to obtain quotes from at least three schedule contractors.

(C) Ensure all quotes received are fairly considered and award is made in accordance with the evaluation criteria in the RFQ.

(4) The ordering activity shall provide the RFQ (including the statement of work and the evaluation criteria) to any schedule contractor who requests a copy of it.

(d) *Evaluation*. The ordering activity shall evaluate all responses received using the evaluation criteria provided to the schedule contractors. The ordering activity is responsible for considering the level of effort and the mix of labor proposed to perform a specific task being ordered, and for determining that the total price is reasonable. Place the order with the schedule contractor that represents the best value (*see* 8.404(d) and 8.405-4). After award, ordering activities should provide timely notification to unsuccessful offerors. If an unsuccessful offeror requests information on an award that was based on factors other than price alone, a brief explanation of the basis for the award decision shall be provided.

(e) *Use of time-and-materials and labor-hour orders for services*. When placing a time-and-materials or labor-hour order for services, see 8.404(h).

(f) *Minimum documentation*. The ordering activity shall document—

(1) The schedule contracts considered, noting the contractor from which the service was purchased;

(2) A description of the service purchased;

(3) The amount paid;

(4) The evaluation methodology used in selecting the contractor to receive the order;

(5) The rationale for any tradeoffs in making the selection;

(6) The price reasonableness determination required by paragraph (d) of this subsection;

(7) The rationale for using other than—

(i) A firm-fixed price order; or

(ii) A performance-based order; and

(8) When an order exceeds the simplified acquisition threshold, evidence of compliance with the ordering procedures at 8.405-2(c).

[FAC 90-29, 60 FR 34732, 7/3/95, effective 7/3/95; FAC 2001-24, 69 FR 34231, 6/18/2004, effective 7/19/2004; FAC 2005-05, 70 FR 43578, 7/27/2005, effective 7/27/2005; FAC 2005-50, 76 FR 14548, 3/16/2011, effective 5/16/2011; FAC 2005-55, 77 FR 194, 1/3/2012, effective 2/2/2012; FAC 2005-56, 77 FR 12927, 3/2/2012, effective 4/2/2012]

8.405-3 Blanket purchase agreements (BPAs).

(a) *Establishment*. (1) Ordering activities may establish BPAs under any schedule contract to fill repetitive needs for supplies or services. Ordering activities shall establish the BPA with the schedule contractor(s) that can provide the supply or service that represents the best value.

(2) In addition to price (*see* 8.404(d) and 8.405-4), when determining best value, the ordering activity may consider, among other factors, the following:

(i) Past performance.

(ii) Special features of the supply or service required for effective program performance.

(iii) Trade-in considerations.

(iv) Probable life of the item selected as compared with that of a comparable item.

(v) Warranty considerations.

(vi) Maintenance availability.

(vii) Environmental and energy efficiency considerations.

(viii) Delivery terms.

(3) (i) The ordering activity contracting officer shall, to the maximum extent practicable, give preference to establishing multiple-award BPAs, rather than establishing a single-award BPA.

(ii) No single-award BPA with an estimated value exceeding $112 million (including any options), may be awarded unless the head of the agency determines in writing that—

(A) The orders expected under the BPA are so integrally related that only a single source can reasonably perform the work;

(B) The BPA provides only for firm-fixed priced orders for—

(*1*) Products with unit prices established in the BPA; or

(*2*) Services with prices established in the BPA for specific tasks to be performed;

(C) Only one source is qualified and capable of performing the work at a reasonable price to the Government; or

(D) It is necessary in the public interest to award the BPA to a single source for exceptional circumstances.

(iii) The requirement for a determination for a single-award BPA greater than $112 million is in addition to any applicable requirement for a limited-source justification at 8.405-6. However, the two documents may be combined into one document.

(iv) In determining how many multiple-award BPAs to establish or that a single-award BPA is appropriate, the contracting officer should consider the following factors and document the decision in the acquisition plan or BPA file:

(A) The scope and complexity of the requirement(s);

(B) The benefits of on-going competition and the need to periodically compare multiple technical approaches or prices;

(C) The administrative costs of BPAs; and

(D) The technical qualifications of the schedule contractor(s).

(4) BPAs shall address the frequency of ordering, invoicing, discounts, requirements (*e.g.*, estimated quantities, work to be performed), delivery locations, and time.

(5) When establishing multiple-award BPAs, the ordering activity shall specify the procedures for placing orders under the BPAs in accordance with 8.405-3(c)(2).

(6) Establishment of a multi-agency BPA against a Federal Supply Schedule contract is permitted if the multi-agency BPA identifies the participating agencies and their estimated requirements at the time the BPA is established.

(7) *Minimum documentation.* The ordering activity contracting officer shall include in the BPA file documentation the—

(i) Schedule contracts considered, noting the contractor to which the BPA was awarded;

(ii) Description of the supply or service purchased;

(iii) Price;

(iv) Required justification for a limited-source BPA (*see* 8.405-6), if applicable;

(v) Determination for a single-award BPA exceeding $112 million, if applicable (see (a)(3)(ii)) of this section);

(vi) Documentation supporting the decision to establish multiple-award BPAs or a single-award BPA (*see* (a)(3)(iv));

(vii) Evidence of compliance with paragraph (b) of this section, for competitively awarded BPAs, if applicable; and

(viii) *Basis for the award decision.* This should include the evaluation methodology used in selecting the contractor, the rationale for any tradeoffs in making the selection, and a price reasonableness determination for services requiring a statement of work.

(b) *Competitive procedures for establishing a BPA.* This paragraph applies to the establishment of a BPA, in addition to applicable instructions in paragraph (a).

(1) *For supplies, and for services not requiring a statement of work.* The procedures of this paragraph apply when establishing a BPA for supplies and services that are listed in the schedule contract at a fixed price for the performance of a specific task, where a statement of work is not required (*e.g.*, installation, maintenance, and repair).

(i) *If the estimated value of the BPA does not exceed the simplified acquisition threshold.* (A) The ordering activity shall:

(*1*) Consider reasonably available information about the supply or service offered under MAS contracts by surveying at least three schedule contractors through the GSA Advantage! on-line shopping service, by reviewing the catalogs or pricelists of at least three schedule contractors, or by requesting quotations from at least three schedule contractors (*see* 8.405-5); or

(*2*) Document the circumstances for restricting consideration to fewer than three schedule contractors based on one of the reasons at 8.405-6(a).

(B) The ordering activity shall establish the BPA with the schedule contractor(s) that can provide the best value.

(ii) *If the estimated value of the BPA exceeds the simplified acquisition threshold.* The ordering activity contracting officer:

(A) Shall provide an RFQ that includes a description of the supplies to be delivered or the services to be performed and the basis upon which the selection will be made.

(B)(*1*) Shall post the RFQ on e-Buy to afford all schedule contractors offering the required supplies or services under the appropriate multiple award schedule(s) an opportunity to submit a quote; or

(*2*) Shall provide the RFQ to as many schedule contractors as practicable, consistent with market research appropriate to the circumstances, to reasonably ensure that quotes will be received from at least three contractors that can fulfill the requirements. When fewer than three quotes are received from schedule contractors that can fulfill the requirements, the contracting officer shall prepare a written determination explaining that no additional contractors capable of fulfilling the requirements could be identified despite reasonable efforts to do so. The determination must clearly explain efforts made to obtain quotes from at least three schedule contractors.

(C) Shall ensure all quotes received are fairly considered and award is made in accordance with the basis for selection in the RFQ. After seeking price reductions (*see* 8.405-4), establish the BPA with the schedule contractor(s) that provides the best value.

(D) The BPA must be established in accordance with paragraphs (b)(1)(ii)(B) and (C) of this section, unless the requirement is waived on the basis of a justification that is prepared and approved in accordance with 8.405-6.

(2) *For services requiring a statement of work.* This applies when establishing a BPA that requires services priced at hourly rates, as provided by the schedule contract. The applicable services will be identified in the Federal Supply Schedule publications and the contractor's pricelists.

(i) *Statements of Work (SOWs).* The ordering activity shall develop a statement of work. All Statements of Work shall include a description of work to be performed; location of work; period of performance; deliverable schedule; applicable performance standards; and any special requirements (*e.g.,* security clearances, travel, and special knowledge). To the maximum extent practicable, agency requirements shall be performance-based statements (*see* subpart 37.6).

(ii) *Type-of-order preference.* The ordering activity shall specify the order type (*i.e.,* firm-fixed price, time-and-materials, or labor-hour) for the services identified in the statement of work. The contracting officer should establish firm-fixed priced orders to the maximum extent practicable. For time-and-materials and labor-hour orders, the contracting officer shall follow the procedures at 8.404(h).

(iii) *Request for Quotation procedures.* The ordering activity must provide a RFQ, which includes the statement of work and evaluation criteria (*e.g.,* experience and past performance), to schedule contractors that offer services that will meet the agency's needs. The RFQ may be posted to GSA's electronic RFQ system, e-Buy (*see* 8.402(d)).

(iv) *If the estimated value of the BPA does not exceed the simplified acquisition threshold.* The ordering activity shall provide the RFQ (including the statement of work and evaluation criteria) to at least three schedule contractors that offer services that will meet the agency's needs.

(v) *If estimated value of the BPA exceeds the simplified acquisition threshold.* The ordering activity contracting officer—

(A) Shall post the RFQ on e-Buy to afford all schedule contractors offering the required supplies or services under the appropriate multiple-award schedule an opportunity to submit a quote; or

(B) Shall provide the RFQ, which includes the statement of work and evaluation criteria, to as many schedule contractors as practicable, consistent with market research appropriate to the circumstances, to reasonably ensure that quotes will be received from at least three contractors that can fulfill the requirements. When fewer than three quotes are received from schedule contractors that can fulfill the requirements, the contracting officer shall document the file. The contracting officer shall prepare a written determination explaining that no additional contractors capable of fulfilling the requirements could be identified despite reasonable efforts to do so. The determination must clearly explain efforts made to obtain quotes from at least three schedule contractors.

(vi) The ordering activity contracting officer shall ensure all quotes received are fairly considered and award is made in accordance with the basis for selection in the RFQ. The ordering activity is responsible for considering the level of effort and the mix of labor proposed to perform, and for determining that the proposed price is reasonable.

(vii) The BPA must be established in accordance with paragraph (b)(2)(iv) or (v), and with paragraph (b)(2)(vi) of this section, unless the requirement is waived on the basis of a justification that is prepared and approved in accordance with 8.405-6.

(viii) The ordering activity contracting officer shall establish the BPA with the schedule contractor(s) that represents the best value (*see* 8.404(d) and 8.405-4).

(3) After award, ordering activities should provide timely notification to unsuccessful offerors. If an unsuccessful offeror requests information on an award that was based on factors other than price alone, a brief explanation of the basis for the award decision shall be provided.

(c) *Ordering from BPAs.* The procedures in this paragraph (c) are not required for BPAs established on or before May 16, 2011. However, ordering activities are encouraged to use the procedures for such BPAs.

(1) *Single-award BPA.* If the ordering activity establishes a single-award BPA, authorized users may place the order directly under the established BPA when the need for the supply or service arises.

(2) *Multiple-award BPAs.* (i) *Orders at or below the micro-purchase threshold.* The ordering activity may place orders at or below the micro-purchase threshold with any BPA holder that can meet the agency needs. The ordering activity should attempt to distribute any such orders among the BPA holders.

(ii) *Orders exceeding the micro-purchase threshold but not exceeding the simplified acquisition threshold.* (A) The ordering activity must provide each multiple-award BPA holder a fair opportunity to be considered for each order exceeding the micro-purchase threshold, but not exceeding the simplified acquisition threshold unless one of the exceptions at 8.405-6(a)(1)(i) applies.

(B) The ordering activity need not contact each of the multiple-award BPA holders before placing an order if information is available to ensure that each BPA holder is provided a fair opportunity to be considered for each order.

(C) The ordering activity contracting officer shall document the circumstances when restricting consideration to less than all multiple-award BPA holders offering the required supplies and services.

(iii) *Orders exceeding the simplified acquisition threshold.* (A) The ordering activity shall place an order in accordance with paragraphs (c)(2)(iii)(A)(*1*), (*2*) and (*3*) of this paragraph, unless the requirement is waived on the basis of a justification that is prepared and approved in accordance with 8.405-6. The ordering activity shall—

(*1*) Provide an RFQ to all BPA holders offering the required supplies or services under the multiple-award BPAs, to include a description of the supplies to be delivered or the services to be performed and the basis upon which the selection will be made;

(*2*) Afford all BPA holders responding to the RFQ an opportunity to submit a quote; and

(*3*) Fairly consider all responses received and make award in accordance with the selection procedures.

(B) The ordering activity shall document evidence of compliance with these procedures and the basis for the award decision.

(3) *BPAs for hourly-rate services.* If the BPA is for hourly-rate services, the ordering activity shall develop a statement of work for each order covered by the BPA. Ordering activities should place these orders on a firm-fixed price basis to the maximum extent practicable. For time-and-materials and labor-hour orders, the contracting officer shall follow the procedures at 8.404(h). All orders under the BPA shall specify a price for the performance of the tasks identified in the statement of work. The ordering activity is responsible for considering the level of effort and the mix of labor proposed to perform a specific task being ordered, and for determining that the total price is reasonable through appropriate analysis techniques, and documenting the file accordingly.

(d) *Duration of BPAs.* (1) Multiple-award BPAs generally should not exceed five years in length, but may do so to meet program requirements.

(2) A single-award BPA shall not exceed one year. It may have up to four one-year options. *See* paragraph (e) of this section for requirements associated with option exercise.

(3) Contractors may be awarded BPAs that extend beyond the current term of their GSA Schedule contract, so long as there are option periods in their GSA Schedule contract that, if exercised, will cover the BPA's period of performance.

(e) *Review of BPAs.* (1) The ordering activity contracting officer shall review the BPA and determine in writing, at least once a year (*e.g.,* at option exercise), whether—

(i) The schedule contract, upon which the BPA was established, is still in effect;

(ii) The BPA still represents the best value (*see* 8.404(d)); and

(iii) Estimated quantities/amounts have been exceeded and additional price reductions can be obtained.

(2) The determination shall be included in the BPA file documentation.

[FAC 2001-24, 69 FR 34231, 6/18/2004, effective 7/19/2004; FAC 2005-05, 70 FR 43578, 7/27/2005, effective 7/27/2005; FAC 2005-50, 76 FR 14548, 3/16/2011, effective 5/16/2011; FAC 2005-55, 77 FR 194, 1/3/2012, effective 2/2/2012; FAC 2005-56, 77 FR 12927, 3/2/2012, effective 4/2/2012; FAC 2005-83, 80 FR 38293, 7/2/2015, effective 10/1/2015]

8.405-4 Price reductions.

Ordering activities may request a price reduction at any time before placing an order, establishing a BPA, or in conjunction with the annual BPA review. However, the ordering activity shall seek a price reduction when the order or BPA exceeds the simplified acquisition threshold. Schedule contractors are not required to pass on to all schedule users a price reduction extended only to an individual ordering activity for a specific order or BPA.

[FAC 90-21, 59 FR 53716, 10/25/94, effective 10/25/94; FAC 2001-24, 69 FR 34231, 6/18/2004, effective 7/19/2004; FAC 2005-50, 76 FR 14548, 3/16/2011, effective 5/16/2011; FAC 2005-56, 77 FR 12927, 3/2/2012, effective 4/2/2012]

8.405-5 Small business.

(a) Although the preference programs of part 19 are not mandatory in this subpart, in accordance with section 1331 of Public Law 111-240 (15 U.S.C. 644(r))—

(1) Ordering activity contracting officers may, at their discretion—

(i) Set aside orders for any of the small business concerns identified in 19.000(a)(3); and

(ii) Set aside BPAs for any of the small business concerns identified in 19.000(a)(3).

(2) When setting aside orders and BPAs—

(i) Follow the ordering procedures for Federal Supply Schedules at 8.405-1, 8.405-2, and 8.405-3; and

(ii) The specific small business program eligibility requirements identified in part 19 apply.

(b) Orders placed against schedule contracts may be credited toward the ordering activity's small business goals. For purposes of reporting an order placed with a small business schedule contractor, an ordering agency may only take credit if the awardee meets a size standard that corresponds to the work performed. Ordering activities should rely on the small business representations made by schedule contractors at the contract level.

(c) Ordering activities may consider socioeconomic status when identifying contractor(s) for consideration or competition for award of an order or BPA. At a minimum, ordering activities should consider, if available, at least one small business, veteran-owned small business, service disabled veteran-owned small business, HUBZone small business, women-owned small business, or small disadvantaged business schedule contractor(s). GSA Advantage! and Schedules e-Library at *http://www.gsa.gov/fas* contain information on the small business representations of Schedule contractors.

(d) For orders exceeding the micro-purchase threshold, ordering activities should give preference to the items of small business concerns when two or more items at the same delivered price will satisfy the requirement.

[FAC 90-21, 59 FR 53716, 10/25/94, effective 10/25/94; FAC 2001-24, 69 FR 34231, 6/18/2004, effective 7/19/2004; FAC 2005-54, 76 FR 68032, 11/2/2011, effective 11/2/2011; FAC 2005-55, 77 FR 204, 1/3/2012, effective 1/3/2012; Interim rule, 77 FR 1889, 1/12/2012, effective 2/13/2012]

8.405-6 Limiting sources.

Orders placed or BPAs established under Federal Supply Schedules are exempt from the requirements in part 6. However, an ordering activity must justify its action when restricting consideration in accordance with paragraph (a) or (b) of this section—

(a) *Orders or BPAs exceeding the micro-purchase threshold based on a limited sources justification.* (1) *Circumstances justifying limiting the source.* (i) For a proposed order or BPA with an estimated value exceeding the micro-purchase threshold not placed or established in accordance with the procedures in 8.405-1, 8.405-2 or 8.405-3, the only circumstances that may justify the action are—

(A) An urgent and compelling need exists, and following the procedures would result in unacceptable delays;

(B) Only one source is capable of providing the supplies or services required at the level of quality required because the supplies or services are unique or highly specialized; or

(C) In the interest of economy and efficiency, the new work is a logical follow-on to an original Federal Supply Schedule order provided that the original order was placed in accordance with the applicable Federal Supply Schedule ordering procedures. The original order or BPA must not have been previously issued under sole-source or limited-sources procedures.

(ii) *See* 8.405-6(c) for the content of the justification for an order or BPA exceeding the simplified acquisition threshold.

(2) *Posting.* (i) Within 14 days after placing an order or establishing a BPA exceeding the simplified acquisition threshold that is supported by a limited-sources justification permitted under any of the circumstances under paragraph (a)(1) of this section, the ordering activity shall—

(A) Publish a notice in accordance with 5.301; and

(B) Post the justification—

(*1*) At the GPE *https://www.fbo.gov;*

(*2*) On the Web site of the ordering activity agency, which may provide access to the justification by linking to the GPE; and

(*3*) For a minimum of 30 days.

(ii) In the case of an order or BPA permitted under paragraph (a)(1)(i)(A) of this section, the justification shall be posted within 30 days after award.

(iii) Contracting officers shall carefully screen all justifications for contractor proprietary data and remove all such data, and such references and citations as are necessary to protect the proprietary data, before making the justifications available for public inspection. Contracting officers shall also be guided by the exemptions to disclosure of information contained in the Freedom of Information Act (5 U.S.C. 552) and the prohibitions against disclosure in 24.202 in determining whether other data should be removed. Although the submitter notice process set out in Executive Order 12600 "Predisclosure Notification Procedures for Confidential Commercial Information" does not apply, if the justification appears to contain proprietary data, the contracting officer should provide the contractor that submitted the information an opportunity to review the justification for proprietary data before making the justification available for public inspection, redacted as necessary. This process must not prevent or delay the posting of the justification in accordance with the timeframes required in paragraphs (a)(2)(i) and (ii) of this section.

(iv) This posting requirement does not apply when disclosure would compromise the national security (*e.g.,* would result in disclosure of classified information) or create other security risks.

(b) *Items peculiar to one manufacturer.* An item peculiar to one manufacturer can be a particular brand name, product, or a feature of a product, peculiar to one manufacturer. A brand name item, whether available on one or more schedule contracts, is an item peculiar to one manufacturer.

(1) Brand name specifications shall not be used unless the particular brand name, product, or feature is essential to the Government's requirements, and market research indicates other companies' similar products, or products lacking the particular feature, do not meet, or cannot be modified to meet, the agency's needs.

(2) *Documentation.* (i) For proposed orders or BPAs with an estimated value exceeding the micro-purchase threshold, but not exceeding the simplified acquisition threshold, the ordering activity contracting officer shall document the basis for restricting consideration to an item peculiar to one manufacturer.

(ii) For proposed orders or BPAs with an estimated value exceeding the simplified acquisition threshold, *see* paragraph (c) of this section.

(iii) The documentation or justification must be completed and approved at the time the requirement for a brand-name item is determined. In addition, the justification for a brand-name item is required at the order level when a justification for the brand-name item was not completed for the BPA or does not adequately cover the requirements in the order.

(3) *Posting.* (i) The ordering activity shall post the following information along with the Request for Quotation (RFQ) to e-Buy (*http://www.ebuy.gsa.gov*):

(A) For proposed orders or BPAs with an estimated value exceeding $25,000, but not exceeding the simplified acquisition threshold, the documentation required by paragraph (b)(2)(i) of this section.

(B) For proposed orders or BPAs with an estimated value exceeding the simplified acquisition threshold, the justification required by paragraph (c) of this section.

(C) The documentation in paragraph (b)(2)(i) of this section and the justification in paragraph (c) of this section is subject to the screening requirement in paragraph (a)(2)(iii) of this section.

(ii) The posting requirement of paragraph (b)(3)(i) of this section does not apply when—

(A) Disclosure would compromise the national security (*e.g.,* would result in disclosure of classified information) or create other security risks. The fact that access to classified matter may be necessary to submit a proposal or perform the contract does not, in itself, justify use of this exception;

(B) The nature of the file (*e.g.,* size, format) does not make it cost-effective or practicable for contracting officers to provide access through e-Buy; or

(C) The agency's senior procurement executive makes a written determination that access through e-Buy is not in the Government's interest.

(4) When applicable, the documentation and posting requirements in paragraphs (b)(2) and (3) of this section apply only to the portion of the order or BPA that requires a brand-name item. If the justification and

approval is to cover only the portion of the acquisition which is brand-name, then it should so state; the approval level requirements will then only apply to that portion.

(c) *An order or BPA with an estimated value exceeding the simplified acquisition threshold.* (1) For a proposed order or BPA exceeding the simplified acquisition threshold, the requiring activity shall assist the ordering activity contracting officer in the preparation of the justification. The justification shall cite that the acquisition is conducted under the authority of the Multiple-Award Schedule Program (*see* 8.401).

(2) At a minimum, each justification shall include the following information:

(i) Identification of the agency and the contracting activity, and specific identification of the document as a "Limited-Sources Justification."

(ii) Nature and/or description of the action being approved.

(iii) A description of the supplies or services required to meet the agency's needs (including the estimated value).

(iv) The authority and supporting rationale (*see* 8.405-6(a)(1)(i) and (b)(1)) and, if applicable, a demonstration of the proposed contractor's unique qualifications to provide the required supply or service.

(v) A determination by the ordering activity contracting officer that the order represents the best value consistent with 8.404(d).

(vi) A description of the market research conducted among schedule holders and the results or a statement of the reason market research was not conducted.

(vii) Any other facts supporting the justification.

(viii) A statement of the actions, if any, the agency may take to remove or overcome any barriers that led to the restricted consideration before any subsequent acquisition for the supplies or services is made.

(ix) The ordering activity contracting officer's certification that the justification is accurate and complete to the best of the contracting officer's knowledge and belief.

(x) Evidence that any supporting data that is the responsibility of technical or requirements personnel (*e.g.*, verifying the Government's minimum needs or requirements or other rationale for limited sources) and which form a basis for the justification have been certified as complete and accurate by the technical or requirements personnel.

(xi) For justifications under 8.405-6(a)(1), a written determination by the approving official identifying the circumstance that applies.

(d) *Justification approvals.* (1) For a proposed order or BPA with an estimated value exceeding the simplified acquisition threshold, but not exceeding $700,000, the ordering activity contracting officer's certification that the justification is accurate and complete to the best of the ordering activity contracting officer's knowledge and belief will serve as approval, unless a higher approval level is established in accordance with agency procedures.

(2) For a proposed order or BPA with an estimated value exceeding $700,000, but not exceeding $13.5 million, the justification must be approved by the advocate for competition of the activity placing the order, or by an official named in paragraph (d)(3) or (4) of this section. This authority is not delegable.

(3) For a proposed order or BPA with an estimated value exceeding $13.5 million, but not exceeding $68 million (or, for DoD, NASA, and the Coast Guard, not exceeding $93 million), the justification must be approved by—

(i) The head of the procuring activity placing the order;

(ii) A designee who—

(A) If a member of the armed forces, is a general or flag officer; or

(B) If a civilian, is serving in a position in a grade above GS-15 under the General Schedule (or in a comparable or higher position under another schedule); or

(iii) An official named in paragraph (d)(4) of this section.

(4) For a proposed order or BPA with an estimated value exceeding $68 million (or, for DoD, NASA, and the Coast Guard, over $93 million), the justification must be ap-

proved by the senior procurement executive of the agency placing the order. This authority is not delegable, except in the case of the Under Secretary of Defense for Acquisition and Sustainment, acting as the senior procurement executive for the Department of Defense.

[FAC 2001-24, 69 FR 34231, 6/18/2004, effective 7/19/2004; FAC 2005-05, 70 FR 43578, 7/27/2005, effective 7/27/2005; FAC 2005-13, 71 FR 57357, 9/28/2006, effective 9/28/2006; FAC 2005-13, 71 FR 57363, 9/28/2006, effective 9/28/2006; FAC 2005-45, 75 FR 53129, 8/30/2010, effective 10/1/2010; FAC 2005-50, 76 FR 14548, 3/16/2011, effective 5/16/2011; FAC 2005-55, 77 FR 189, 1/3/2012, effective 2/2/2012; FAC 2005-56, 77 FR 12927, 3/2/2012, effective 4/2/2012; FAC 2005-73, 79 FR 24192, 4/29/2014, effective 5/29/2014; FAC 2005-83, 80 FR 38293, 7/2/2015, effective 10/1/2015; FAC 2005-100, 83 FR 42571, 8/22/2018, effective 8/22/2018; FAC 2019-02, 84 FR 19839, 5/6/2019, effective 5/6/2019]

8.405-7 Payment.

Agencies may make payments for oral or written orders by any authorized means, including the Governmentwide commercial purchase card (but see 32.1108(b) (2)).

[FAC 2001-24, 69 FR 34231, 6/18/2004, effective 7/19/2004; FAC 2005-05, 70 FR 43578, 7/27/2005, effective 7/27/2005; FAC 2005-38, 74 FR 65600, 12/10/2009, effective 2/1/2010]

8.405-8 [Redesignated]

[FAC 2001-24, 69 FR 34231, 6/18/2004, effective 7/19/2004; Redesignated as 8.405-7, FAC 2005-05, 70 FR 43578, 7/27/2005, effective 7/27/2005]

8.406 Ordering activity responsibilities. (No Text)

[FAC 2001-24, 69 FR 34231, 6/18/2004, effective 7/19/2004]

8.406-1 Order placement.

(a) Ordering activities may place orders orally, except for—

(1) Supplies and services not requiring a statement of work exceeding the simplified acquisition threshold;

(2) Services requiring a statement of work (SOW); and

(3) Orders containing brand-name specifications that exceed $25,000.

(b) Ordering activities may use Optional Form 347, an agency-prescribed form, or an established electronic communications format to order supplies or services from schedule contracts.

(c) The ordering activity shall place an order directly with the contractor in accordance with the terms and conditions of the pricelists (*see* 8.402(b)). Prior to placement of the order, the ordering activity shall ensure that the regulatory and statutory requirements of the requiring agency have been applied.

(d) Orders shall include the following information in addition to any information required by the schedule contract:

(1) Complete shipping and billing addresses.

(2) Contract number and date.

(3) Agency order number.

(4) F.o.b. delivery point; *i.e.,* origin or destination.

(5) Discount terms.

(6) Delivery time or period of performance.

(7) Special item number or national stock number.

(8) Line item or subline item.

(9) A statement of work for services, when required, or a brief, complete description of each item (when ordering by model number, features and options such as color, finish, and electrical characteristics, if available, must be specified).

(10) Quantity and any variation in quantity.

(11) Number of units.

(12) Unit price.

(13) Total price of order.

(14) Points of inspection and acceptance.

(15) Other pertinent data; *e.g.,* delivery instructions or receiving hours and size-of-truck limitation.

(16) Marking requirements.

(17) Level of preservation, packaging, and packing.

[FAC 2001-24, 69 FR 34231, 6/18/2004, effective 7/19/2004; FAC 2005-13, 71 FR 57357, 9/28/2006, effective 9/28/2006; FAC 2005-50, 76 FR 14548, 3/16/2011, effective 5/16/2011; FAC 2005-55, 77 FR 189, 1/3/2012, effective 2/2/2012; FAC 2005-56, 77 FR 12927, 3/2/2012, effective 4/2/2012; FAC 2005-95, 82 FR 4709, 1/13/2017, effective 1/13/2017]

8.406-2 Inspection and acceptance.

(a) *Supplies.* (1) Consignees shall inspect supplies at destination except when—

(i) The schedule contract indicates that mandatory source inspection is required by the schedule contracting agency; or

(ii) A schedule item is covered by a product description, and the ordering activity determines that the schedule contracting agency's inspection assistance is needed (based on the ordering volume, the complexity of the supplies, or the past performance of the supplier).

(2) When the schedule contracting agency performs the inspection, the ordering activity will provide two copies of the order specifying source inspection to the schedule contracting agency. The schedule contracting agency will notify the ordering activity of acceptance or rejection of the supplies.

(3) Material inspected at source by the schedule contracting agency, and determined to conform with the product description of the schedule, shall not be reinspected for the same purpose. The consignee shall limit inspection to kind, count, and condition on receipt.

(4) Unless otherwise provided in the schedule contract, acceptance is conclusive, except as regards latent defects, fraud, or such gross mistakes as amount to fraud.

(b) *Services.* The ordering activity has the right to inspect all services in accordance with the contract requirements and as called for by the order. The ordering activity shall perform inspections and tests as specified in the order's quality assurance surveillance plan in a manner that will not unduly delay the work.

[FAC 2001-24, 69 FR 34231, 6/18/2004, effective 7/19/2004]

8.406-3 Remedies for nonconformance.

(a) If a contractor delivers a supply or service, but it does not conform to the order requirements, the ordering activity shall take appropriate action in accordance with the inspection and acceptance clause of the contract, as supplemented by the order.

(b) If the contractor fails to perform an order, or take appropriate corrective action, the ordering activity may terminate the order for cause or modify the order to establish a new delivery date (after obtaining consideration, as appropriate). Ordering activities shall follow the procedures at 8.406-4 when terminating an order for cause.

[FAC 2001-24, 69 FR 34231, 6/18/2004, effective 7/19/2004]

8.406-4 Termination for cause.

(a)(1) An ordering activity contracting officer may terminate individual orders for cause. Termination for cause shall comply withFAR 12.403, and may include charging the contractor with excess costs resulting from repurchase.

(2) The schedule contracting office shall be notified of all instances where an ordering activity contracting officer has terminated for cause an individual order to a Federal Supply Schedule contractor, or if fraud is suspected.

(b) If the contractor asserts that the failure was excusable, the ordering activity contracting officer shall follow the procedures at 8.406-6, as appropriate.

(c) If the contractor is charged excess costs, the following apply:

(1) Any repurchase shall be made at as low a price as reasonable, considering the quality required by the Government, delivery requirement, and administrative expenses. Copies of all repurchase orders, except the copy furnished to the contractor

or any other commercial concern, shall include the notation:

Repurchase against the account of ________ [*insert contractor's name*] under Order ________ [*insert number*] under Contract ________ [*insert number*].

(2) When excess costs are anticipated, the ordering activity may withhold funds due the contractor as offset security. Ordering activities shall minimize excess costs to be charged against the contractor and collect or set-off any excess costs owed.

(3) If an ordering activity is unable to collect excess repurchase costs, it shall notify the schedule contracting office after final payment to the contractor.

(i) The notice shall include the following information about the terminated order:

(A) Name and address of the contractor.

(B) Schedule, contract, and order number.

(C) Line item number(s) and a brief description of the item(s).

(D) Cost of schedule items involved.

(E) Excess costs to be collected.

(F) Other pertinent data.

(ii) The notice shall also include the following information about the purchase contract:

(A) Name and address of the contractor.

(B) Item repurchase cost.

(C) Repurchase order number and date of payment.

(D) Contract number, if any.

(E) Other pertinent data.

(d) Only the schedule contracting officer may modify the contract to terminate for cause any, or all, supplies or services covered by the schedule contract. If the schedule contracting officer has terminated any supplies or services covered by the schedule contract, no further orders may be placed for those items. Orders placed prior to termination for cause shall be fulfilled by the contractor, unless terminated for the convenience of the Government by the ordering activity contracting officer.

(e) *Reporting.* An ordering activity contracting officer, in accordance with agency procedures, shall ensure that information related to termination for cause notices and any amendments are reported. In the event the termination for cause is subsequently converted to a termination for convenience, or is otherwise withdrawn, the contracting officer shall ensure that a notice of the conversion or withdrawal is reported. All reporting shall be in accordance with 42.1503(h).

[FAC 2001-24, 69 FR 34231, 6/18/2004, effective 7/19/2004; FAC 2005-46, 75 FR 60258, 9/29/2010, effective 10/29/2010; FAC 2005-69, 78 FR 46783, 8/1/2013, effective 9/3/2013; FAC 2005-95, 82 FR 4709, 1/13/2017, effective 1/13/2017]

8.406-5 Termination for the Government's convenience.

(a) An ordering activity contracting officer may terminate individual orders for the Government's convenience. Terminations for the Government's convenience shall comply withFAR 12.403.

(b) Before terminating orders for the Government's convenience, the ordering activity contracting officer shall endeavor to enter into a "no cost" settlement agreement with the contractor.

(c) Only the schedule contracting officer may modify the schedule contract to terminate any, or all, supplies or services covered by the schedule contract for the Government's convenience.

[FAC 2001-24, 69 FR 34231, 6/18/2004, effective 7/19/2004]

8.406-6 Disputes.

(a) *Disputes pertaining to the performance of orders under a schedule contract.* (1) Under the Disputes clause of the schedule contract, the ordering activity contracting officer may—

(i) Issue final decisions on disputes arising from performance of the order (but see paragraph (b) of this section); or

(ii) Refer the dispute to the schedule contracting officer.

(2) The ordering activity contracting officer shall notify the schedule contracting officer promptly of any final decision.

(b) *Disputes pertaining to the terms and conditions of schedule contracts.* The ordering activity contracting officer shall refer all disputes that relate to the contract terms and conditions to the schedule contracting officer for resolution under the Disputes clause of the contract and notify the schedule contractor of the referral.

(c) *Appeals.* Contractors may appeal final decisions to either the Board of Contract Appeals servicing the agency that issued the final decision or the U.S. Court of Federal Claims.

(d) *Alternative dispute resolution.* The contracting officer should use the alternative dispute resolution (ADR) procedures, to the maximum extent practicable (see 33.204 and 33.214).

[FAC 2001-24, 69 FR 34231, 6/18/2004, effective 7/19/2004]

8.406-7 Contractor Performance Evaluation.

Ordering activities must prepare at least annually and at the time the work under the order is completed, an evaluation of contractor performance for each order that exceeds the simplified acquisition threshold in accordance with 42.1502(c).

[FAC 2005-34, 74 FR 31557, 7/1/2009, effective 7/1/2009; FAC 2005-69, 78 FR 46783, 8/1/2013, effective 9/3/2013]

SUBPART 8.5—ACQUISITION OF HELIUM

8.500 Scope of subpart.

This subpart implements the requirements of the Helium Act (50 U.S.C. 167, et seq.) concerning the acquisition of liquid or gaseous helium by Federal agencies or by Government contractors or subcontractors for use in the performance of a Government contract (also see 43 CFR part 3195).

[FAC 2001-06, 67 FR 13048, 3/20/2002, effective 4/4/2002]

8.501 Definitions.

As used in this subpart—

Bureau of Land Management means the Department of the Interior, Bureau of Land Management, Amarillo Field Office, Helium Operations, 801 South Fillmore Street, Suite 500, Amarillo, TX 79101-3545.

Federal helium supplier means a private helium vendor that has an in-kind crude helium sales contract with the Bureau of Land Management (BLM) and that is on the BLM Amarillo Field Office's Authorized List of Federal Helium Suppliers available via the Internet at *https://www.blm.gov/programs/energy-and-minerals/helium/partners*.

Major helium requirement means an estimated refined helium requirement greater than 200,000 standard cubic feet (scf) (measured at 14.7 pounds per square inch absolute pressure and 70 degrees Fahrenheit temperature) of gaseous helium or 7510 liters of liquid helium delivered to a helium use location per year.

[FAC 2001-06, 67 FR 13048, 3/20/2002, effective 4/4/2002; FAC 2005-54, 76 FR 68043, 11/2/2011, effective 11/2/2011; FAC 2005-100, 83 FR 42571, 8/22/2018, effective 8/22/2018]

8.502 Policy.

Agencies and their contractors and subcontractors must purchase major helium requirements from Federal helium suppliers, to the extent that supplies are available.

[FAC 2001-06, 67 FR 13048, 3/20/2002, effective 4/4/2002]

8.503 Exception.

The requirements of this subpart do not apply to contracts or subcontracts in which the helium was acquired by the contractor prior to award of the contract or subcontract.

[FAC 2001-06, 67 FR 13048, 3/20/2002, effective 4/4/2002]

8.504 Procedures.

The contracting officer must forward the following information to the Bureau of Land Management within 45 days of the close of each fiscal quarter:

(a) The name of any company that supplied a major helium requirement.

(b) The amount of helium purchased.

(c) The delivery date(s).

(d) The location where the helium was used.

[FAC 2001-06, 67 FR 13048, 3/20/2002, effective 4/4/2002]

8.505 Contract clause.

Insert the clause at 52.208-8, Required Sources for Helium and Helium Usage Data, in solicitations and contracts if it is anticipated that performance of the contract involves a major helium requirement.

[FAC 2001-06, 67 FR 13048, 3/20/2002, effective 4/4/2002]

SUBPART 8.6—ACQUISITION FROM FEDERAL PRISON INDUSTRIES, INC.

8.601 General.

(a) Federal Prison Industries, Inc. (FPI), also referred to as UNICOR, is a self-supporting, wholly owned Government corporation of the District of Columbia.

(b) FPI provides training and employment for prisoners confined in Federal penal and correctional institutions through the sale of its supplies and services to Government agencies (18 U.S.C. 4121-4128).

(c) FPI diversifies its supplies and services to minimize adverse impact on private industry.

(d) Supplies manufactured and services performed by FPI are listed in the FPI Schedule, which can be accessed at *http://www.unicor.gov* or by submitting a written request to Federal Prison Industries, Inc., Department of Justice, Washington, DC 20534.

(e) Agencies are encouraged to purchase FPI supplies and services to the maximum extent practicable.

[FAC 90-4, 56 FR 15148, 4/15/91, effective 5/15/91; FAC 2001-21, 69 FR 16147, 3/26/2004, effective 3/26/2004; FAC 2005-03, 70 FR 18954, 4/11/2005, effective 4/11/2005; FAC 2005-07, 71 FR 221, 1/3/2006, effective 1/3/2006]

8.602 Policy.

(a) In accordance with 10 U.S.C. 2410n and Section 637 of Division H of the Consolidated Appropriations Act, 2005 (Pub. L. 108-447) (18 U.S.C. 4124 note), and except as provided in paragraph (b) of this section, agencies shall—

(1) Before purchasing an item of supply listed in the FPI Schedule, conduct market research to determine whether the FPI item is comparable to supplies available from the private sector that best meet the Government's needs in terms of price, quality, and time of delivery. This is a unilateral determination made at the discretion of the contracting officer. The arbitration provisions of 18 U.S.C. 4124(b) do not apply;

(2) Prepare a written determination that includes supporting rationale explaining the assessment of price, quality, and time of delivery, based on the results of market research comparing the FPI item to supplies available from the private sector;

(3) If the FPI item is comparable, purchase the item from FPI following the ordering procedures at *http://www.unicor.gov*, unless a waiver is obtained in accordance with 8.604; and

(4) If the FPI item is not comparable in one or more of the areas of price, quality, and time of delivery—

(i) Acquire the item using—

(A) Competitive procedures (e.g., the procedures in 6.102, the set-aside procedures in subpart 19.5, or competition conducted in accordance with part 13); or

(B) The fair opportunity procedures in 16.505, if placing an order under a multiple award delivery-order contract;

(ii) Include FPI in the solicitation process and consider a timely offer from FPI for award in accordance with the item description or specifications, and evaluation factors in the solicitation—

(A) If the solicitation is available through the Governmentwide point of entry (FedBizOpps, also known as FBO), it is not necessary to provide a separate copy of the solicitation to FPI;

(B) If the solicitation is not available through FedBizOpps, also known as FBO, provide a copy of the solicitation to FPI;

(iii) When using a multiple award schedule issued under the procedures in Subpart 8.4 or when using the fair opportunity procedures in 16.505—

(A) Establish and communicate to FPI the item description or specifications, and evaluation factors that will be used as the basis for selecting a source, so that an offer from FPI can be evaluated on the same basis as the contract or schedule holder; and

(B) Consider a timely offer from FPI;

(iv) Award to the source offering the item determined by the agency to provide the best value to the Government; and

(v) When the FPI item is determined to provide the best value to the Government as a result of FPI's response to a competitive solicitation, follow the ordering procedures at *http://www.unicor.gov*.

(b) The procedures in paragraph (a) of this section do not apply if an exception in 8.605(b) through (g) applies.

(c) In some cases where FPI and an AbilityOne participating nonprofit agency produce identical items (see 8.603), FPI grants a waiver to permit the Government to purchase a portion of its requirement from the AbilityOne participating nonprofit agency. When this occurs, the portion of the requirement for which FPI has granted a waiver—

(1) Shall be purchased from the AbilityOne participating nonprofit agency using the procedures in Subpart 8.7; and

(2) Shall not be subject to the procedures in paragraph (a) of this section.

(d) Disputes regarding price, quality, character, or suitability of supplies produced by FPI, except for determinations under paragraph (a)(1) of this section, are subject to arbitration as specified in 18 U.S.C. 4124. The statute provides that the arbitration shall be conducted by a board consisting of the Comptroller General of the United States, the Administrator of General Services, and the President, or their representatives. The decisions of the board are final and binding on all parties.

[FAC 90-4, 56 FR 15148, 4/15/91, effective 5/15/91; FAC 2001-09, 67 FR 56115, 8/30/2002, effective 9/30/2002; FAC 2001-21, 69 FR 16147, 3/26/2004, effective 3/26/2004; FAC 2005-03, 70 FR 18954, 4/11/2005, effective 4/11/2005; FAC 2005-07, 71 FR 221, 1/3/2006, effective 1/3/2006; FAC 2005-27, 73 FR 53994, 9/17/2008, effective 10/17/2008; FAC 2005-73, 79 FR 24192, 4/29/2014, effective 5/29/2014; FAC 2005-100, 83 FR 42571, 8/22/2018, effective 8/22/2018]

8.603 Purchase priorities.

FPI and nonprofit agencies participating in the AbilityOne Program under 41 U.S.C. chapter 85, Committee for Purchase from People Who Are Blind or Severely Disabled (see subpart 8.7), may produce identical supplies or services. When this occurs, ordering offices shall purchase supplies and services in the following priorities:

(a) *Supplies*:

(1) Federal Prison Industries, Inc. (41 U.S.C. 8504).

(2) AbilityOne participating nonprofit agencies.

(3) Commercial sources.

(b) *Services*:

(1) AbilityOne participating nonprofit agencies.

(2) Federal Prison Industries, Inc., or commercial sources.

[FAC 90-4, 56 FR 15149, 4/15/91, effective 5/15/91; FAC 90-23, 59 FR 67010, 12/28/94, effective 2/27/95; FAC 2001-21, 69 FR 16147, 3/26/2004, effective 3/26/2004; FAC 2005-07, 71 FR 221, 1/3/2006, effective 1/3/2006; FAC 2005-27, 73 FR 53994, 9/17/2008, effective 10/17/2008; FAC 2005-73, 79 FR 24192, 4/29/2014, effective 5/29/2014]

8.604 Waivers.

FPI may grant a waiver for purchase of supplies in the FPI Schedule from another source. FPI waivers ordinarily are of the following types:

(a) General or blanket waivers issued when classes of supplies are not available from FPI.

(b) Formal waivers issued in response to requests from offices desiring to acquire, from other sources, supplies listed in the FPI Schedule and not covered by a general waiver. Agencies shall process waiver requests in accordance with the procedures at *http://www.unicor.gov*.

[FAC 2001-21, 69 FR 16147, 3/26/2004, effective 3/26/2004]

8.605 Exceptions.

Purchase from FPI is not mandatory and a waiver is not required if—

(a) (1) The contracting officer makes a determination that the FPI item of supply is not comparable to supplies available from the private sector that best meet the Government's needs in terms of price, quality, and time of delivery; and

(2) The item is acquired in accordance with 8.602(a)(4);

(b) Public exigency requires immediate delivery or performance;

(c) Suitable used or excess supplies are available;

(d) The supplies are acquired and used outside the United States;

(e) Acquiring listed items totaling $3,500 or less;

(f) Acquiring items that FPI offers exclusively on a competitive (non-mandatory) basis, as identified in the FPI Schedule; or

(g) Acquiring services.

[FAC 90-4, 56 FR 15149, 4/15/91, effective 5/15/91; FAC 2001-21, 69 FR 16147, 3/26/2004, effective 3/26/2004; FAC 2005-03, 70 FR 18954, 4/11/2005, effective 4/11/2005; FAC 2005-07, 71 FR 221, 1/3/2006, effective 1/3/2006; FAC 2005-27, 73 FR 53994, 9/17/2008, effective 10/17/2008; FAC 2005-89, 81 FR 45854, 7/14/2016, effective 8/15/2016]

8.606 Evaluating FPI performance.

Agencies shall evaluate FPI contract performance in accordance with subpart 42.15. Performance evaluations do not negate the requirements of 8.602 and 8.604, but they may be used to support a waiver request in accordance with 8.604.

[FAC 90-4, 56 FR 15149, 4/15/91, effective 5/15/91; FAC 2001-14, 68 FR 28094, 5/22/2003, effective 5/22/2003; FAC 2001-18, 68 FR 69249, 12/11/2003, effective 12/11/2003, finalized without change; FAC 2001-21, 69 FR 16147, 3/26/2004, effective 3/26/2004; FAC 2005-07, 71 FR 221, 1/3/2006, effective 1/3/2006]

8.607 Performance as a subcontractor.

Agencies shall not require a contractor, or subcontractor at any tier, to use FPI as a subcontractor for performance of a contract by any means, including means such as—

(a) A solicitation provision requiring a potential contractor to offer to make use of FPI supplies or services;

(b) A contract specification requiring the contractor to use specific supplies or services (or classes of supplies or services) offered by FPI; or

(c) Any contract modification directing the use of FPI supplies or services.

[FAC 2001-14, 68 FR 28095, 5/22/2003, effective 6/23/2003; FAC 2001-21, 69 FR 16147, 3/26/2004, effective 3/26/2004; FAC 2005-07, 71 FR 221, 1/3/2006, effective 1/3/2006]

8.608 Protection of classified and sensitive information.

Agencies shall not enter into any contract with FPI that allows an inmate worker access to any—

(a) Classified data;

(b) Geographic data regarding the location of—

(1) Surface and subsurface infrastructure providing communications or water or electrical power distribution;

(2) Pipelines for the distribution of natural gas, bulk petroleum products, or other commodities; or

(3) Other utilities; or

(c) Personal or financial information about any individual private citizen, including information relating to such person's real property however described, without the prior consent of the individual.

[FAC 2001-21, 69 FR 16147, 3/26/2004, effective 3/26/2004]

SUBPART 8.7—ACQUISITION FROM NONPROFIT AGENCIES EMPLOYING

PEOPLE WHO ARE BLIND OR SEVERELY DISABLED

8.700 Scope of subpart.

This subpart prescribes the policies and procedures for implementing—

(a) 41 U.S.C. chapter 85, Committee for Purchase from People Who Are Blind or Severely Disabled; and

(b) The rules of the Committee for Purchase from People Who Are Blind or Severely Disabled (41 CFR Chapter 51), which implements the AbilityOne program.

[FAC 90-23, 59 FR 67010, 12/28/94, effective 2/27/95; FAC 2005-27, 73 FR 53994, 9/17/2008, effective 10/17/2008; FAC 2005-73, 79 FR 24192, 4/29/2014, effective 5/29/2014]

8.701 Definitions.

As used in this subpart—

Allocation means an action taken by a central nonprofit agency to designate the AbilityOne participating nonprofit agencies that will furnish definite quantities of supplies or perform specific services upon receipt of orders from ordering offices.

Central nonprofit agency means National Industries for the Blind (NIB), which has been designated to represent people who are blind; or NISH, which has been designated to represent AbilityOne participating nonprofit agencies serving people with severe disabilities other than blindness.

Committee means the Committee for Purchase From People Who Are Blind or Severely Disabled.

Government or *entity of the Government* means any entity of the legislative or judicial branch, any executive agency, military department, Government corporation, or independent establishment, the U.S. Postal Service, or any nonappropriated-fund instrumentality of the Armed Forces.

Ordering office means any activity in an entity of the Government that places orders for the purchase of supplies or services under the AbilityOne Program.

Procurement List means a list of supplies (including military resale commodities) and services that the Committee has determined are suitable for purchase by the Government under 41 U.S.C. chapter 85.

Nonprofit agency serving people who are blind or *nonprofit agency serving people with other severe disabilities* (referred to jointly as AbilityOne participating nonprofit agencies) means a qualified nonprofit agency employing people who are blind or have other severe disabilities approved by the Committee to furnish a commodity or a service to the Government under 41 U.S.C. chapter 85.

[FAC 90-23, 59 FR 67010, 12/28/94, effective 2/27/95; FAC 97-22, 66 FR 2116, 1/10/2001, effective 3/12/2001; Delay of effective date, 66 FR 14259, 3/9/2001, effective 5/11/2001; FAC 2005-27, 73 FR 53994, 9/17/2008, effective 10/17/2008; FAC 2005-73, 79 FR 24192, 4/29/2014, effective 5/29/2014; FAC 2019-02, 84 FR 19839, 5/6/2019, effective 5/6/2019]

8.702 General.

The Committee is an independent Government activity with members appointed by the President of the United States. It is responsible for—

(a) Determining those supplies and services to be purchased by all entities of the Government from AbilityOne participating nonprofit agencies;

(b) Establishing prices for the supplies and services; and

(c) Establishing rules and regulations to implement 41 U.S.C. chapter 85.

[FAC 90-23, 59 FR 67010, 12/28/94, effective 2/27/95; FAC 2005-27, 73 FR 53994, 9/17/2008, effective 10/17/2008; FAC 2005-73, 79 FR 24192, 4/29/2014, effective 5/29/2014]

8.703 Procurement list.

The Committee maintains a Procurement List of all supplies and services required to be purchased from AbilityOne participating nonprofit agencies. The Procurement List may be accessed at: *http://www.abilityone.gov.*

Questions concerning whether a supply item or service is on the Procurement List may be submitted at Internet e-mail address *info@abilityone.gov* or referred to the Committee offices at the following address and telephone number: Committee for Purchase From People Who Are Blind or Severely Disabled, 1401 S. Clark Street, Suite 10800, Arlington, VA 22202-3259, (703) 603-7740.

Many items on the Procurement List are identified in the General Services Administration (GSA) Supply Catalog and GSA's Customer Service Center Catalogs with a black square and the words "NIB/NISH Mandatory Source," and in similar catalogs issued by the Defense Logistics Agency (DLA) and the Department of Veterans Affairs (VA). GSA, DLA, and VA are central supply agencies from which other Federal agencies are required to purchase certain supply items on the Procurement List.

[FAC 90-23, 59 FR 67010, 12/28/94, effective 2/27/95; FAC 2001-24, 69 FR 34229, 6/18/2004, effective 7/19/2004; FAC 2005-27, 73 FR 53994, 9/17/2008, effective 10/17/2008; FAC 2005-38, 74 FR 65614, 12/10/2009, effective 12/10/2009; FAC 2005-55, 77 FR 204, 1/3/2012, effective 1/3/2012; FAC 2005-67, 78 FR 37697, 6/21/2013, effective 6/21/2013; FAC 2019-02, 84 FR 19839, 5/6/2019, effective 5/6/2019]

8.704 Purchase priorities.

(a) 41 U.S.C. chapter 85 requires the Government to purchase supplies or services on the Procurement List, at prices established by the Committee, from AbilityOne participating nonprofit agencies if they are available within the period required. When identical supplies or services are on the Procurement List and the Schedule of Products issued by Federal Prison Industries, Inc., ordering offices shall purchase supplies and services in the following priorities:

(1) *Supplies*:

(i) Federal Prison Industries, Inc. (41 U.S.C. 8504).

(ii) AbilityOne participating nonprofit agencies.

(iii) Commercial sources.

(2) *Services*:

(i) AbilityOne participating nonprofit agencies.

(ii) Federal Prison Industries, Inc., or commercial sources.

(b) No other provision of the FAR shall be construed as permitting an exception to the mandatory purchase of items on the Procurement List.

(c) The Procurement List identifies those supplies for which the ordering office must obtain a formal waiver (8.604) from Federal Prison Industries, Inc., before making any purchases from AbilityOne participating nonprofit agencies.

[FAC 84-16, 51 FR 19713, 5/30/86, effective 5/30/86; FAC 90-4, 56 FR 15149, 4/15/91, effective 5/15/91; FAC 90-23, 59 FR 67010, 12/28/94, effective 2/27/95; FAC 2001-21, 69 FR 16147, 3/26/2004, effective 3/26/2004; FAC 2005-07, 71 FR 221, 1/3/2006, effective 1/3/2006; FAC 2005-27, 73 FR 53994, 9/17/2008, effective 10/17/2008; FAC 2005-73, 79 FR 24192, 4/29/2014, effective 5/29/2014]

8.705 Procedures. (No Text)

8.705-1 General.

(a) Ordering offices shall obtain supplies and services on the Procurement List from the central nonprofit agency or its designated AbilityOne participating nonprofit agencies, except that supplies identified on the Procurement List as available from DLA, GSA, or VA supply distribution facilities shall be obtained through DLA, GSA, or VA procedures. If a distribution facility cannot provide the supplies, it shall inform the ordering office, which shall then order from the AbilityOne participating nonprofit agency designated by the Committee.

(b) Supply distribution facilities in DLA and GSA shall obtain supplies on the Procurement List from the central nonprofit agency identified or its designated AbilityOne participating nonprofit agency.

[FAC 90-23, 59 FR 67010, 12/28/94, effective 2/27/95; FAC 2005-27, 73 FR 53994, 9/17/2008, effective 10/17/2008]

8.705-2 Direct-order process.

Central nonprofit agencies may authorize ordering offices to transmit orders for specific supplies or services directly to an AbilityOne participating nonprofit agency. The written authorization remains valid until it is revoked by the central nonprofit agency or the Committee. The central nonprofit agency shall specify the normal delivery or performance lead time required by the nonprofit agency. The ordering office shall reflect this lead time in its orders.

[FAC 90-9, 56 FR 67136, 12/27/91, effective 2/25/92; FAC 90-23, 59 FR 67010, 12/28/94, effective 2/27/95; FAC 2005-27, 73 FR 53994, 9/17/2008, effective 10/17/2008; FAC 2019-02, 84 FR 19839, 5/6/2019, effective 5/6/2019]

8.705-3 Allocation process.

(a) When the direct order process has not been authorized, the ordering office shall submit a letter request for allocation (requesting the designation of the AbilityOne participating nonprofit agency to produce the supplies or perform the service) to the central nonprofit agency designated in the Procurement List. Ordering offices shall request allocations in sufficient time for a reply, for orders to be placed, and for the nonprofit agency to produce the supplies or provide the service within the required delivery or performance schedule.

(b) The ordering office's request to the central nonprofit agency for allocation shall include the following information:

(1) For supplies—Item name, stock number, latest specification, quantity, unit price, date delivery is required, and destination to which delivery is to be made.

(2) For services—Type and location of service required, latest specification, work to be performed, estimated volume, and required date or dates for completion.

(3) Other requirements; *e.g.*, packing, marking, as necessary.

(c) When an allocation is received, the ordering office shall promptly issue an order to the specified AbilityOne participating nonprofit agency or to the central nonprofit agency, as instructed by the allocation. If the issuance of an order is to be delayed for more than 15 days beyond receipt of the allocation, or canceled, the ordering office shall advise the central nonprofit agency immediately.

(d) Ordering offices may issue orders without limitation as to dollar amount and shall record them upon issuance as obligations. Each order shall include, as a minimum, the information contained in the request for allocation. Ordering offices shall also include additional instructions necessary for performance under the order; *e.g.*, on the handling of Government-furnished property, reports required, and notification of shipment.

[FAC 90-23, 59 FR 67010, 12/28/94, effective 2/27/95; FAC 90-29, 60 FR 34732, 7/3/95, effective 7/3/95; FAC 2005-27, 73 FR 53994, 9/17/2008, effective 10/17/2008]

8.705-4 Compliance with orders.

(a) The central nonprofit agency shall inform the ordering office of changes in lead time experienced by its AbilityOne participating nonprofit agencies to minimize requests for extensions once the ordering office places an order.

(b) The ordering office shall grant a request by a central nonprofit agency or AbilityOne participating nonprofit agency for revision in the delivery or completion schedule, if feasible. If extension of the delivery or completion date is not feasible, the ordering office shall notify the appropriate central nonprofit agency and request that it reallocate the order, or grant a purchase exception authorizing acquisition from commercial sources.

(c) When an AbilityOne participating nonprofit agency fails to perform under the terms of an order, the ordering office shall make every effort to resolve the noncompliance with the nonprofit agency involved and to negotiate an adjustment before taking action to cancel the order. If the problem cannot be resolved with the nonprofit agency, the ordering office shall refer the matter for resolution first to the central nonprofit agency and then, if necessary, to the Committee.

(d) When, after complying with 8.705-4(c), the ordering office determines that it must cancel an order, it shall notify the central nonprofit agency and, if practical, request a reallocation of the order. When the central nonprofit agency cannot reallocate the order, it shall grant a purchase exception permitting use of commercial sources, subject to approval by the Committee when the value of the purchase exception is $25,000 or more.

[FAC 90-9, 56 FR 67136, 12/27/91, effective 2/25/92; FAC 90-23, 59 FR 67010, 12/28/94, effective 2/27/95; FAC 2005-27, 73 FR 53994, 9/17/2008, effective 10/17/2008]

8.706 Purchase exceptions.

(a) Ordering offices may acquire supplies or services on the Procurement List from commercial sources only if the acquisition is specifically authorized in a purchase exception granted by the designated central nonprofit agency.

(b) The central nonprofit agency shall promptly grant purchase exceptions when—

(1) The AbilityOne participating nonprofit agencies cannot provide the supplies or services within the time required, and commercial sources can provide them significantly sooner in the quantities required; or

(2) The quantity required cannot be produced or provided economically by the AbilityOne participating nonprofit agencies.

(c) The central nonprofit agency granting the exception shall specify the quantity and delivery or performance period covered by the exception.

(d) When a purchase exception is granted, the contracting officer shall—

(1) Initiate purchase action within 15 days following the date of the exception or any extension granted by the central nonprofit agency; and

(2) Provide a copy of the solicitation to the central nonprofit agency when it is issued.

(e) The Committee may also grant a purchase exception, under any circumstances it considers appropriate.

[FAC 90-23, 59 FR 67010, 12/28/94, effective 2/27/95; FAC 2005-27, 73 FR 53994, 9/17/2008, effective 10/17/2008]

8.707 Prices.

(a) The prices of items on the Procurement List are fair market prices established by the Committee. All prices for supplies ordered under this subpart are f.o.b. origin.

(b) Prices for supplies are normally adjusted semiannually. Prices for services are normally adjusted annually.

(c) The Committee may request the agency responsible for acquiring the supplies or service to assist it in establishing or revising the fair market price. The Committee has the authority to establish prices without prior coordination with the responsible contracting office.

(d) Price changes shall normally apply to all orders received by the AbilityOne participating nonprofit agency on or after the effective date of the change. In special cases, after considering the views of the ordering office, the Committee may make price changes applicable to orders received by the AbilityOne participating nonprofit agency prior to the effective date of the change.

(e) If an ordering office desires packing, packaging, or marking of supplies other than the standard pack as provided on the Procurement List, any difference in costs shall be included as a separate item on the nonprofit agency's invoice. The ordering office shall reimburse the nonprofit agency for these costs.

(f) Ordering offices may make recommendations to the Committee at any time for price revisions for supplies and services on the Procurement List.

[FAC 90-23, 59 FR 67010, 12/28/94, effective 2/27/95; FAC 2005-27, 73 FR 53994, 9/17/2008, effective 10/17/2008]

8.708 Shipping.

(a) Delivery is accomplished when a shipment is placed aboard the vehicle of the initial carrier. The time of delivery is the date shipment is released to and accepted by the initial carrier.

(b) Shipment is normally under Government bills of lading. However, for small orders, ordering offices may specify other shipment methods.

(c) When shipments are under Government bills of lading, the bills of lading may accompany orders or be otherwise furnished promptly. Failure of an ordering office to furnish bills of lading or to designate a method of transportation may result in an excusable delay in delivery.

(d) AbilityOne participating nonprofit agencies shall include transportation costs for small shipments paid by the nonprofit agencies as an item on the invoice. The ordering office shall reimburse the nonprofit agencies for these costs.

[FAC 84-16, 51 FR 19713, 5/30/86, effective 5/30/86; FAC 90-23, 59 FR 67010, 12/28/94, effective 2/27/95; FAC 2005-27, 73 FR 53994, 9/17/2008, effective 10/17/2008]

8.709 Payments.

The ordering office shall make payments for supplies or services on the Procurement List within 30 days after shipment or after receipt of a proper invoice or voucher.

[FAC 90-23, 59 FR 67010, 12/28/94, effective 2/27/95]

8.710 Quality of merchandise.

Supplies and services provided by AbilityOne participating nonprofit agencies shall comply with the applicable Government specifications and standards cited in the order. When no specifications or standards exist—

(a) Supplies shall be of the highest quality and equal to similar items available on the commercial market; and

(b) Services shall conform to good commercial practices.

[FAC 90-23, 59 FR 67010, 12/28/94, effective 2/27/95; FAC 2005-27, 73 FR 53994, 9/17/2008, effective 10/17/2008]

8.711 Quality complaints.

(a) When the quality of supplies or services received is unsatisfactory, the using activity shall take the following actions:

(1) For supplies received from DLA supply centers, GSA supply distribution facilities, or Department of Veterans Affairs distribution division, notify the supplying agency.

(2) For supplies or services received from AbilityOne participating nonprofit agencies, address complaints to the individual nonprofit agency involved, with a copy to the appropriate central nonprofit agency.

(b) When quality problems cannot be resolved by the AbilityOne participating nonprofit agency and the ordering office, the ordering office shall first contact the central nonprofit agency and then, if necessary, the Committee for resolution.

[FAC 90-23, 59 FR 67010, 12/28/94, effective 2/27/95; FAC 2005-27, 73 FR 53994, 9/17/2008, effective 10/17/2008]

8.712 Specification changes.

(a) The contracting activity shall notify the AbilityOne participating nonprofit agency and appropriate central nonprofit agency of any change in specifications or descriptions. In the absence of such written notification, the AbilityOne participating nonprofit agency shall furnish the supplies or services under the specification or description cited in the order.

(b) The contracting activity shall provide 90-days advance notification to the Committee and the central nonprofit agency on actions that affect supplies on the Procurement List and shall permit them to comment before action is taken, particularly when it involves—

(1) Changes that require new national stock numbers or item designations;

(2) Deleting items from the supply system;

(3) Standardization; or

(4) Developing new items to replace items on the Procurement List.

(c) For services, the contracting activity shall notify the AbilityOne participating nonprofit agency and central nonprofit agency concerned at least 90 days prior to the date that any changes in the scope of work or other conditions will be required.

(d) When, in order to meet its emergency needs, a contracting activity is unable to give the 90-day notification required in paragraphs (b) and (c) of this section, the contracting activity shall, at the time it places the order or change notice, inform the AbilityOne participating nonprofit agency and the central nonprofit agency in writing of the reasons that it cannot meet the 90-day notification requirement.

[FAC 84-16, 51 FR 19713, 5/30/86, effective 5/30/86; FAC 90-23, 59 FR 67010, 12/28/94, effective 2/27/95; FAC 2005-27, 73 FR 53994, 9/17/2008, effective 10/17/2008]

8.713 Optional acquisition of supplies and services.

(a) Ordering offices may acquire supplies and services not included on the Procurement List from an AbilityOne participating nonprofit agency that is the low responsive, responsible offeror under a solicitation issued by other authorized acquisition methods.

(b) Ordering offices should forward solicitations to AbilityOne participating nonprofit agencies that may be qualified to provide the supplies or services required.

[FAC 90-23, 59 FR 67010, 12/28/94, effective 2/27/95; FAC 2005-27, 73 FR 53994, 9/17/2008, effective 10/17/2008]

8.714 Communications with the central nonprofit agencies and the Committee.

(a) The addresses of the central nonprofit agencies are:

(1) National Industries for the Blind, 1310 Braddock Place, Alexandria, VA 22314-1691, (703) 310-0500; and

(2) NISH, 8401 Old Courthouse Road, Vienna, VA 22182, (571) 226- 4660.

(b) Any matter requiring referral to the Committee shall be addressed to: Executive Director of the Committee, 1401 S. Clark, Suite 10800, Arlington, VA 22202-3259.

[FAC 90-23, 59 FR 67010, 12/28/94, effective 2/27/95; FAC 2001-24, 69 FR 34229, 6/18/2004, effective 7/19/2004; FAC 2005-10, 71 FR 36941, 6/28/2006, effective 6/28/2006; FAC 2005-67, 78 FR 37697, 6/21/2013, effective 6/21/2013; FAC 2019-02, 84 FR 19839, 5/6/2019, effective 5/6/2019]

8.715 Replacement commodities.

When a commodity on the Procurement List is replaced by another commodity which has not been previously acquired, and a qualified AbilityOne participating nonprofit agency can furnish the replacement commodity in accordance with the Government's quality standards and delivery schedules and at a fair market price, the replacement commodity is automatically on the Procurement List and shall be acquired from the AbilityOne participating nonprofit agency designated by the Committee. The commodity being replaced shall continue to be included on the Procurement List until there is no longer a requirement for that commodity.

[FAC 2005-27, 73 FR 53994, 9/17/2008, effective 10/17/2008]

8.716 Change-of-name and successor in interest procedures.

When the Committee recognizes a name change or a successor in interest for an AbilityOne participating nonprofit agency providing supplies or services on the Procurement List—

(a) The Committee will provide a notice of a change to the Procurement List to the cognizant contracting officers; and

(b) Upon receipt of a notice of a change to the Procurement List from the Committee, the contracting officer must—

(1) Prepare a Standard Form (SF) 30, Amendment of Solicitation/Modification of Contract, incorporating a summary of the notice and attaching a list of contracts affected; and

(2) Distribute the SF 30, including a copy to the Committee.

[FAC 97-14, 64 FR 51828, 9/24/99, effective, 11/23/99; FAC 2005-27, 73 FR 53994, 9/17/2008, effective 10/17/2008]

SUBPART 8.8—ACQUISITION OF PRINTING AND RELATED SUPPLIES

8.800 Scope of subpart.

This subpart provides policy for the acquisition of Government printing and related supplies.

[FAC 84-25, 52 FR 9037, 3/20/87, effective 7/1/87]

8.801 Definitions.

As used in this subpart—

Government printing means printing, binding, and blankbook work for the use of an executive department, independent agency, or establishment of the Government.

Related supplies means supplies that are used and equipment that is usable in printing and binding operations.

[FAC 84-25, 52 FR 9037, 3/20/87, effective 7/1/87; FAC 97-22, 66 FR 2116, 1/10/2001, effective 3/12/2001; Delay of effective date, 66 FR 14259, 3/9/2001, effective 5/11/2001]

8.802 Policy.

(a) Government printing must be done by or through the Government Publishing Office (GPO) (44 U.S.C. 501), unless—

(1) The GPO cannot provide the printing service (44 U.S.C. 504);

(2) The printing is done in field printing plants operated by an executive agency (44 U.S.C. 501(2));

(3) The printing is acquired by an executive agency from allotments for contract field printing (44 U.S.C. 501(2)); or

(4) The printing is specifically authorized by statute to be done other than by the GPO.

(b) The head of each agency shall designate a central printing authority; that central printing authority may serve as the liaison with the Congressional Joint Committee on Printing (JCP) and the Public Printer on matters related to printing. Contracting officers shall obtain approval from their designated central printing authority before contracting in any manner, whether directly or through contracts for other supplies or services, for the items defined in 8.801 and for composition, platemaking, presswork, binding, and micrographics (when used as a substitute for printing).

(c)(1) Further, 44 U.S.C. 1121 provides that the Public Printer may acquire and furnish paper and envelopes (excluding envelopes printed in the course of manufacture) in common use by two or more Government departments, establishments, or services within the District of Columbia, and provides for reimbursement of the Public Printer from available appropriations or funds. Paper and envelopes that are furnished by the Public Printer may not be acquired in any other manner.

(2) Paper and envelopes for use by Executive agencies outside the District of Columbia and stocked by GSA shall be requisitioned from GSA in accordance with the procedures listed in Federal Property Management Regulations (FPMR) Subpart 101-26.3.

[FAC 84-25, 52 FR 9037, 3/20/87, effective 7/1/87; FAC 84-53, 54 FR 48982, 11/28/89, effective 12/28/89; FAC 90-23, 59 FR 67010, 12/28/94, effective 2/27/95; FAC 2019-02, 84 FR 19839, 5/6/2019, effective 5/6/2019]

SUBPART 8.9—[RESERVED]

[Removed and Reserved, FAC 97-15, 64 FR 72414, 12/27/99, effective 2/25/2000]

SUBPART 8.10—[RESERVED]

SUBPART 8.11—LEASING OF MOTOR VEHICLES

8.1100 Scope of subpart.

This subpart covers the procedures for the leasing, from commercial concerns, of motor vehicles that comply with Federal Motor Vehicle Safety Standards and applicable State motor vehicle safety regulations. It does not apply to motor vehicles leased outside the United States and its outlying areas.

[FAC 2001-14, 68 FR 28079, 5/22/2003, effective 6/23/2003]

8.1101 Definitions.

As used in this subpart—

Leasing means the acquisition of motor vehicles, other than by purchase from private or commercial sources, and includes the synonyms *hire* and *rent*.

Motor vehicle means an item of equipment, mounted on wheels and designed for highway and/or land use, that—

(1) Derives power from a self-contained power unit; or

(2) Is designed to be towed by and used in conjunction with self-propelled equipment.

[FAC 97-22, 66 FR 2116, 1/10/2001, effective 3/12/2001; Delay of effective date, 66 FR 14259, 3/9/2001, effective 5/11/2001; FAC 2019-02, 84 FR 19839, 5/6/2019, effective 5/6/2019]

8.1102 Presolicitation requirements.

(a) Except as specified in 8.1102(b), before preparing solicitations for leasing of motor vehicles, contracting officers shall obtain from the requiring activity a written certification that—

(1) The vehicles requested are of maximum fuel efficiency and minimum body size, engine size, and equipment (if any) necessary to fulfill operational needs, and meet prescribed fuel economy standards;

(2) The head of the requiring agency, or a designee, has certified that the requested passenger automobiles (sedans and station wagons) larger than Type IA, IB, or II (small, subcompact, or compact) are essential to the agency's mission;

(3) Internal approvals have been received; and

(4) The General Services Administration has advised that it cannot furnish the vehicles.

(b) With respect to requirements for leasing motor vehicles for a period of less than 60 days, the contracting officer need not obtain the certification specified in 8.1102(a)—

(1) If the requirement is for type 1A, 1B, or II vehicles, which are by definition fuel efficient; or

(2) If the requirement is for passenger vehicles larger than 1A, 1B, or II, and the agency has established procedures for advance approval, on a case-by-case basis, of such requirements.

(c) Generally, solicitations shall not be limited to current-year production models. However, with the prior approval of the head of the contracting office, solicitations may be limited to current models on the basis of overall economy.

[FAC 84-58, 55 FR 25527, 6/21/90, effective 7/23/90]

8.1103 Contract requirements.

Contracting officers shall include the following items in each contract for leasing motor vehicles:

(a) Scope of contract.

(b) Method of computing payments.

(c) A listing of the number and type of vehicles required, and the equipment and accessories to be provided with each vehicle.

(d) Responsibilities of the contractor or the Government for furnishing gasoline, motor oil, antifreeze, and similar items.

(e) Unless it is determined that it will be more economical for the Government to perform the work, a statement that the contractor shall perform all maintenance on the vehicles.

(f) A statement as to the applicability of pertinent State and local laws and regulations, and the responsibility of each party for compliance with them.

(g) Responsibilities of the contractor or the Government for emergency repairs and services.

8.1104 Contract clauses.

Insert the following clauses in solicitations and contracts for leasing of motor vehicles, unless the motor vehicles are leased in foreign countries:

(a) The clause at 52.208-4, Vehicle Lease Payments.

(b) The clause at 52.208-5, Condition of Leased Vehicles.

(c) The clause at 52.208-6, Marking of Leased Vehicles.

(d) A clause substantially the same as the clause at 52.208-7, Tagging of Leased Vehicles, for vehicles leased over 60 days (see subpart B of 41 CFR part 102-34).

(e) The provisions and clauses prescribed elsewhere in the FAR for solicitations and contracts for supplies when a fixed-price contract is contemplated, but excluding—

(1) The clause at 52.211-16, Variation in Quantity;

(2) The clause at 52.232-1, Payments;

(3) The clause at 52.222-20, Contracts for Materials, Supplies, Articles, and Equipment Exceeding $15,000; and

(4) The clause at 52.246-16, Responsibility for Supplies.

[FAC 84-16, 51 FR 19714, 5/30/86, effective 5/30/86; FAC 90-32, 60 FR 48206, 9/18/95, effective 10/1/95; FAC 2001-14, 68 FR 28079, 5/22/2003, effective 6/23/2003; FAC 2005-73, 79 FR 24192, 4/29/2014, effective 5/29/2014; FAC 2019-02, 84 FR 19839, 5/6/2019, effective 5/6/2019]

PART 9—CONTRACTOR QUALIFICATIONS

Table of Contents

Scope of part 9.000

Subpart 9.1—Responsible Prospective Contractors

Scope of subpart 9.100
Definitions 9.101
Applicability 9.102
Policy 9.103
Standards 9.104
General standards 9.104-1
Special standards 9.104-2
Application of standards 9.104-3
Subcontractor responsibility 9.104-4
Representation and certifications regarding responsibility matters 9.104-5
Federal Awardee Performance and Integrity Information System 9.104-6
Solicitation provisions and contract clauses 9.104-7
Procedures 9.105
Obtaining information 9.105-1
Determinations and documentation 9.105-2
Disclosure of preaward information 9.105-3
Preaward surveys 9.106
Conditions for preaward surveys 9.106-1
Requests for preaward surveys 9.106-2
Interagency preaward surveys 9.106-3
Reports 9.106-4
Surveys of nonprofit agencies participating in the AbilityOne Program 9.107
Prohibition on contracting with inverted domestic corporations 9.108
Definitions 9.108-1
Prohibition 9.108-2
Representation by the offeror 9.108-3
Waiver 9.108-4
Solicitation provision and contract clause 9.108-5
Prohibition on contracting with an entity involved in activities that violate arms control treaties or agreements with the United States 9.109
Authority 9.109-1
Prohibition 9.109-2
Exception 9.109-3
Certification by the offeror 9.109-4
Solicitation provision 9.109-5

Subpart 9.2—Qualifications Requirements

Scope of subpart 9.200
Definitions 9.201
Policy 9.202
QPL's, QML's and QBL's 9.203
Responsibilities for establishment of a qualification requirement 9.204
Opportunity for qualification before award 9.205
Acquisitions subject to qualification requirements 9.206
General 9.206-1
Contract clause 9.206-2
Competition 9.206-3
Changes in status regarding qualification requirements 9.207

Subpart 9.3—First Article Testing and Approval

Definition 9.301

General . . . 9.302
Use . . . 9.303
Exceptions . . . 9.304
Risk . . . 9.305
Solicitation requirements . . . 9.306
Government administration procedures . . . 9.307
Contract clauses . . . 9.308
Testing performed by the contractor . . . 9.308-1
Testing performed by the Government . . . 9.308-2

Subpart 9.4—Debarment, Suspension, and Ineligibility

Scope of subpart . . . 9.400
Applicability . . . 9.401
Policy . . . 9.402
Definitions . . . 9.403
Exclusions in the System for Award Management . . . 9.404
Effect of listing . . . 9.405
Continuation of current contracts . . . 9.405-1
Restrictions on subcontracting . . . 9.405-2
Debarment . . . 9.406
General . . . 9.406-1
Causes for debarment . . . 9.406-2
Procedures . . . 9.406-3
Period of debarment . . . 9.406-4
Scope of debarment . . . 9.406-5
Suspension . . . 9.407
General . . . 9.407-1
Causes for suspension . . . 9.407-2
Procedures . . . 9.407-3
Period of suspension . . . 9.407-4
Scope of suspension . . . 9.407-5
[Removed and Reserved] . . . 9.408
Contract clause . . . 9.409

Subpart 9.5—Organizational and Consultant Conflicts of Interest

Scope of subpart . . . 9.500
Definition . . . 9.501
Applicability . . . 9.502
Waiver . . . 9.503
Contracting officer responsibilities . . . 9.504
General rules . . . 9.505
Providing systems engineering and technical direction . . . 9.505-1
Preparing specifications or work statements . . . 9.505-2
Providing evaluation services . . . 9.505-3
Obtaining access to proprietary information . . . 9.505-4
Procedures . . . 9.506
Solicitation provisions and contract clause . . . 9.507
Solicitation provisions . . . 9.507-1
Contract clause . . . 9.507-2
Examples . . . 9.508

Subpart 9.6—Contractor Team Arrangements

Definition . . . 9.601
General . . . 9.602
Policy . . . 9.603
Limitations . . . 9.604

Subpart 9.7—Defense Production Pools and Research and Development Pools

Definition 9.701
Contracting with pools 9.702
Contracting with individual pool members 9.703

PART 9—CONTRACTOR QUALIFICATIONS

9.000 Scope of part.

This part prescribes policies, standards, and procedures pertaining to prospective contractors' responsibility; debarment, suspension, and ineligibility; qualified products; first article testing and approval; contractor team arrangements; defense production pools and research and development pools; and organizational conflicts of interest.

SUBPART 9.1—RESPONSIBLE PROSPECTIVE CONTRACTORS

9.100 Scope of subpart.

This subpart prescribes policies, standards, and procedures for determining whether prospective contractors and subcontractors are responsible.

9.101 Definitions.

Administrative proceeding means a non-judicial process that is adjudicatory in nature in order to make a determination of fault or liability (*e.g.*, Securities and Exchange Commission Administrative Proceedings, Civilian Board of Contract Appeals Proceedings, and Armed Services Board of Contract Appeals Proceedings). This includes administrative proceedings at the Federal and state level but only in connections with performance of a Federal contract or grant. It does not include agency actions such as contract audits, site visits, corrective plans, or inspection of deliverables.

Surveying activity, as used in this subpart, means the cognizant contract administration office or, if there is no such office, another organization designated by the agency to conduct preaward surveys.

[FAC 97-22, 66 FR 2116, 1/10/2001, effective 3/12/2001, delay of effective date, 66 FR 14259, 3/9/2001, effective 5/11/2001; FAC 2005-40, 75 FR 14059, 3/23/2010, effective 4/22/2010]

9.102 Applicability.

(a) This subpart applies to all proposed contracts with any prospective contractor that is located—

(1) In the United States, or its outlying areas; or

(2) Elsewhere, unless application of the subpart would be inconsistent with the laws or customs where the contractor is located.

(b) This subpart does not apply to proposed contracts with—

(1) Foreign, State, or local governments;

(2) Other U.S. Government agencies or their instrumentalities; or

(3) Agencies for people who are blind or severely disabled (see subpart 8.7).

[FAC 2001-14, 68 FR 28079, 5/22/2003, effective 6/23/2003; FAC 2005-73, 79 FR 24192, 4/29/2014, effective 5/29/2014; FAC 2019-02, 84 FR 19839, 5/6/2019, effective 5/6/2019]

9.103 Policy.

(a) Purchases shall be made from, and contracts shall be awarded to, responsible prospective contractors only.

(b) No purchase or award shall be made unless the contracting officer makes an affirmative determination of responsibility. In the absence of information clearly indicating that the prospective contractor is responsible, the contracting officer shall make a determination of nonresponsibility. If the prospective contractor is a small business concern, the contracting officer shall comply with subpart 19.6, Certificates of Competency and Determinations of Responsibility. (If Section 8(a) of the Small Business Act (15 U.S.C. 637) applies, see subpart 19.8)

(c) The award of a contract to a supplier based on lowest evaluated price alone can be false economy if there is subsequent default, late deliveries, or other unsatisfactory performance resulting in additional contractual or administrative costs. While it is important that Government purchases be made at the lowest price, this does not require an award to a supplier solely because that supplier submits the lowest offer. A prospective contractor must affirmatively demonstrate its responsibility, including, when necessary, the responsibility of its proposed subcontractors.

[FAC 90-43, 61 FR 67408, 12/20/96, effective 12/20/96, finalized without change, FAC

97-1, 62 FR 44802, 8/22/97, effective 10/21/97; FAC 97-1, 62 FR 44819, 8/22/97, effective 8/22/97, finalized without change, FAC 97-4, 63 FR 9048, 2/23/98, effective 4/24/98; FAC 97-21, 65 FR 80255, 12/20/2000, effective 1/19/2001, stayed FAC 97-24,66 FR 17753, 4/3/2001, effective 4/3/2001, finalized with changes FAC 2001-03, 66 FR 66984, 12/27/2001, effective 12/27/2001]

9.104 Standards. (No Text)

9.104-1 General standards.

To be determined responsible, a prospective contractor must—

(a) Have adequate financial resources to perform the contract, or the ability to obtain them (see 9.104-3(a));

(b) Be able to comply with the required or proposed delivery or performance schedule, taking into consideration all existing commercial and governmental business commitments;

(c) Have a satisfactory performance record (see 9.104-3(b) and subpart 42.15). A prospective contractor shall not be determined responsible or nonresponsible solely on the basis of a lack of relevant performance history, except as provided in 9.104-2;

(d) Have a satisfactory record of integrity and business ethics (for example, see subpart 42.15);

(e) Have the necessary organization, experience, accounting and operational controls, and technical skills, or the ability to obtain them (including, as appropriate, such elements as production control procedures, property control systems, quality assurance measures, and safety programs applicable to materials to be produced or services to be performed by the prospective contractor and subcontractors) (see 9.104-3(a));

(f) Have the necessary production, construction, and technical equipment and facilities, or the ability to obtain them (see 9.104-3(a)); and

(g) Be otherwise qualified and eligible to receive an award under applicable laws and regulations (see also inverted domestic corporation prohibition at 9.108).

[FAC 84-18, 51 FR 27119, 7/29/86, effective 7/30/86; FAC 90-8, 56 FR 55374, 10/25/91 effective 11/25/91; FAC 90-26, 60 FR 16718, 3/31/95, effective 5/30/95; FAC 90-43, Interim rule, 61 FR 67408, 12/20/96, effective 12/20/96, finalized without change, FAC 97-1, 62 FR 44802, 8/22/97, effective 10/21/97; FAC 97-21,65 FR 80255, 12/20/2000, effective 1/19/2001, stayed FAC 97-24, 66 FR 17753, 4/3/2001, effective 4/3/2001, finalized with changes FAC 2001-03, 66 FR 66984, 12/27/2001, effective 12/27/2001; FAC 2005-28, 73 FR 67064, 11/12/2008, effective 12/12/2008; FAC 2005-34, 74 FR 31561, 7/1/2009, effective 7/1/2009; FAC 2005-52, 76 FR 31410, 5/31/2011, effective 5/31/2011; FAC 2019-02, 84 FR 19839, 5/6/2019, effective 5/6/2019]

9.104-2 Special standards.

(a) When it is necessary for a particular acquisition or class of acquisitions, the contracting officer shall develop, with the assistance of appropriate specialists, special standards of responsibility. Special standards may be particularly desirable when experience has demonstrated that unusual expertise or specialized facilities are needed for adequate contract performance. The special standards shall be set forth in the solicitation (and so identified) and shall apply to all offerors.

(b) Contracting officers shall award contracts for subsistence only to those prospective contractors that meet the general standards in 9.104-1 and are approved in accordance with agency sanitation standards and procedures.

9.104-3 Application of standards.

(a) *Ability to obtain resources.* Except to the extent that a prospective contractor has sufficient resources or proposes to perform the contract by subcontracting, the contracting officer shall require acceptable evidence of the prospective contractor's ability to obtain required resources (see 9.104-1(a), (e), and (f)). Acceptable evidence normally consists of a commitment or explicit arrangement, that will be in existence at the time of contract award, to rent, purchase, or otherwise acquire the needed facilities, equipment, other resources, or personnel. Consideration of a prime contractor's compliance with limitations on subcontracting shall take into account the time period covered by the contract base period or quantities plus option periods or quantities, if such options are considered when evaluating offers for award.

(b) *Satisfactory performance record.* A prospective contractor that is or recently has been seriously deficient in contract performance shall be presumed to be nonresponsible, unless the contracting officer determines that the circumstances were properly beyond the contractor's control, or that the contractor has taken appropriate corrective action. Past failure to apply sufficient tenacity and perseverance to perform acceptably is strong evidence of nonresponsibility. Failure to meet the quality requirements of the contract is a significant factor to consider in determining satisfactory performance. The contracting officer shall consider the number of contracts involved and the extent of deficient performance in each contract when making this determination. If the pending contract requires a subcontracting plan pursuant to Subpart 19.7, The Small Business Subcontracting Program, the contracting officer shall also consider the prospective contractor's compliance with subcontracting plans under recent contracts.

(c) *Affiliated concerns.* Affiliated concerns (see Concern in 19.001 and Affiliates in 19.101) are normally considered separate entities in determining whether the concern that is to perform the contract meets the applicable standards for responsibility. However, the contracting officer shall consider the affiliate's past performance and integrity when they may adversely affect the prospective contractor's responsibility.

(d) (1) *Small business concerns.* Upon making a determination of nonresponsibility with regard to a small business concern, the contracting officer shall refer the matter to the Small Business Administration, which will decide whether to issue a Certificate of Competency (see subpart 19.6).

(2) A small business that is unable to comply with the limitations on subcontracting at 52.219-14 may be considered nonresponsible.

[FAC 84-38, 53 FR 27463, 7/20/88, effective 8/19/88; FAC 84-39, 53 FR 34226, 9/2/88, effective 10/3/88; FAC 90-8, 56 FR 55378, 10/25/91, effective 11/25/91; FAC 90-32, 60 FR 48206, 9/18/95, effective 10/1/95; FAC 90-43, 61 FR 67408, 12/20/96, effective 12/20/96, finalized without change, FAC 97-1,62 FR 44802, 8/22/97, effective 10/21/97; FAC 97-1, 62 FR 44802, 8/22/97, effective 8/22/97, finalized without change, FAC 97-4, 63 FR 9048, 2/23/98, effective 4/24/98; FAC 97-10, 63 FR 70264, 12/18/98, effective 1/4/99; FAC 97-21, 65 FR 80255, 12/20/2000, effective 1/19/2001, stayed FAC 97-24, 66 FR 17753, 4/3/2001, effective 4/3/2001, finalized with changes FAC 2001-03, 66 FR 66984, 12/27/2001, effective 12/27/2001; FAC 2001-06, 67 FR 13048, 3/20/2002, effective 4/4/2002; FAC 2005-40, 75 FR 14059, 3/23/2010, effective 4/22/2010]

9.104-4 Subcontractor responsibility.

(a) Generally, prospective prime contractors are responsible for determining the responsibility of their prospective subcontractors (but see 9.405 and 9.405-2 regarding debarred, ineligible, or suspended firms). Determinations of prospective subcontractor responsibility may affect the Government's determination of the prospective prime contractor's responsibility. A prospective contractor may be required to provide written evidence of a proposed subcontractor's responsibility.

(b) When it is in the Government's interest to do so, the contracting officer may directly determine a prospective subcontractor's responsibility (*e.g.*, when the prospective contract involves medical supplies, urgent requirements, or substantial subcontracting). In this case, the same standards used to determine a prime contractor's responsibility shall be used by the Government to determine subcontractor responsibility.

[FAC 2005-90, 81 FR 58562, 8/25/2016, effective 10/25/2016; FAC 2005-93, 81 FR 91636, 12/16/2016, effective 12/16/2016;

FAC 2005-96, 82 FR 51773, 11/8/2017, effective 11/6/2017]

9.104-5 Representation and certifications regarding responsibility matters.

(a) When an offeror provides an affirmative response in paragraph (a)(1) of the provision at 52.209-5, Certification Regarding Responsibility Matters, or paragraph (h) of provision 52.212-3, the contracting officer shall—

(1) Promptly, upon receipt of offers, request such additional information from the offeror as the offeror deems necessary in order to demonstrate the offeror's responsibility to the contracting officer (but see 9.405); and

(2) Notify, prior to proceeding with award, in accordance with agency procedures (see 9.406-3(a) and 9.407-3(a)), the agency official responsible for initiating debarment or suspension action, where an offeror indicates the existence of an indictment, charge, conviction, or civil judgment, or Federal tax delinquency in an amount that exceeds $3,500.

(b) The provision at 52.209–11, Representation by Corporations Regarding Delinquent Tax Liability or a Felony Conviction under any Federal Law, implements sections 744 and 745 of Division E of the Consolidated and Further Continuing Appropriations Act, 2015 (Pub. L. 113–235) (and similar provisions in subsequent appropriations acts). When an offeror provides an affirmative response in paragraph (b)(1) or (2) of the provision at 52.209–11 or paragraph (q)(2)(i) or (ii) of provision 52.212–3, the contracting officer shall—

(1) Promptly, upon receipt of offers, request such additional information from the offeror as the offeror deems necessary in order to demonstrate the offeror's responsibility to the contracting officer (but see 9.405);

(2) Notify, in accordance with agency procedures (see 9.406–3(a) and 9.407–3(a)), the agency official responsible for initiating debarment or suspension action; and

(3) Not award to the corporation unless an agency suspending or debarring official has considered suspension or debarment of the corporation and made a determination that suspension or debarment is not necessary to protect the interests of the Government.

(c) If the provision at 52.209–12, Certification Regarding Tax Matters, is applicable (see 9.104–7(e)), then the contracting officer shall not award any contract in an amount greater than $5,000,000, unless the offeror affirmatively certified in its offer, as required by paragraph (b)(1), (2), and (3) of the provision.

(d) Offerors who do not furnish the representation or certifications or such information as may be requested by the contracting officer shall be given an opportunity to remedy the deficiency. Failure to furnish the representation or certifications or such information may render the offeror nonresponsible.

[FAC 2005-25, 73 FR 21791, 4/22/2008, effective 5/22/2008; FAC 2005-83, 80 FR 38293, 7/2/2015, effective 10/1/2015; FAC 2005-85, 80 FR 75903, 12/4/2015, effective 2/26/2016; FAC 2005-90, 81 FR 58562, 8/25/2016, effective 10/25/2016; FAC 2005-91, 81 FR 67728, 9/30/2016, effective 9/30/2016; FAC 2005-93, 81 FR 91636, 12/16/2016, effective 12/16/2016; FAC 2005-96, 82 FR 51773, 11/8/2017, effective 11/6/2017]

9.104-6 Federal Awardee Performance and Integrity Information System.

(a)(1) Before awarding a contract in excess of the simplified acquisition threshold, the contracting officer shall review the performance and integrity information available in the Federal Awardee Performance and Integrity Information System (FAPIIS), (available at *https://www.cpars.gov*), including FAPIIS information from the System for Award Management (SAM) Exclusions and the Contractor Performance Assessment Reporting System (CPARS).

(2) In accordance with 41 U.S.C. 2313(d)(3), FAPIIS also identifies—

(i) An affiliate that is an immediate owner or subsidiary of the offeror, if any (see 52.204–17, Ownership or Control of Offeror); and

(ii) All predecessors of the offeror that held a Federal contract or grant within the last three years (see 52.204–20, Predecessor of Offeror).

(b)(1) When making a responsibility determination, the contracting officer shall consider all the information available through FAPIIS with regard to the offeror and any immediate owner, predecessor, or subsidiary identified for that offeror in FAPIIS, as well as other past performance information on the offeror (see subpart 42.15).

(2) For evaluation of information available through FAPIIS relating to an affiliate of the offeror, see 9.104–3(c).

(3) For source selection evaluations of past performance, see 15.305(a)(2). Contracting officers shall use sound judgment in determining the weight and relevance of the information contained in FAPIIS and how it relates to the present acquisition.

(4) Since FAPIIS may contain information on any of the offeror's previous contracts and information covering a five-year period, some of that information may not be relevant to a determination of present responsibility, *e.g.*, a prior administrative action such as debarment or suspension that has expired or otherwise been resolved, or information relating to contracts for completely different products or services.

(5) Because FAPIIS is a database that provides information about prime contractors, the contracting officer posts information required to be posted about a subcontractor, such as trafficking in persons violations, to the record of the prime contractor (see 42.1503(h)(1)(v)). The prime contractor has the opportunity to post in FAPIIS any mitigating factors. The contracting officer shall consider any mitigating factors posted in FAPIIS by the prime contractor, such as degree of compliance by the prime contractor with the terms of FAR clause 52.222–50.

(c) If the contracting officer obtains relevant information from FAPIIS regarding criminal, civil, or administrative proceedings in connection with the award or performance of a Government contract; terminations for default or cause; determinations of nonresponsibility because the contractor does not have a satisfactory performance record or a satisfactory record of integrity and business ethics; or comparable information relating to a grant, the contracting officer shall, unless the contractor has already been debarred or suspended—

(1) Promptly request such additional information from the offeror as the offeror deems necessary in order to demonstrate the offeror's responsibility to the contracting officer (but see 9.405); and

(2) Notify, prior to proceeding with award, in accordance with agency procedures (see 9.406-3(a) and 9.407-3(a)), the agency official responsible for initiating debarment or suspension action, if the information appears appropriate for the official's consideration.

(d) The contracting officer shall document the contract file for each contract in excess of the simplified acquisition threshold to indicate how the information in FAPIIS was considered in any responsibility determination, as well as the action that was taken as a result of the information. A contracting officer who makes a nonresponsibility determination is required to document that information in FAPIIS in accordance with 9.105-2(b)(2).

[FAC 2005-40, 75 FR 14059, 3/23/2010, effective 4/22/2010; FAC 2005-80, 80 FR 4967, 1/29/2015, effective 3/2/2015; FAC 2005-87, 81 FR 11988, 3/7/2016, effective 4/6/2016; FAC 2005-90, 81 FR 58562, 8/25/2016, effective 10/25/2016; FAC 2005-93, 81 FR 91636, 12/16/2016, effective 12/16/2016; FAC 2005-96, 82 FR 51773, 11/8/2017, effective 11/6/2017; FAC 2019-06, 84 FR 47865, 9/10/2019, effective 10/10/2019]

9.104-7 Solicitation provisions and contract clauses.

(a) The contracting officer shall insert the provision at 52.209-5, Certification Regarding Responsibility Matters, in solicitations where the contract value is expected to exceed the simplified acquisition threshold.

(b) The contracting officer shall insert the provision at 52.209-7, Information Regarding Responsibility Matters, in solicitations where the resultant contract value is expected to exceed $550,000.

(c) The contracting officer shall insert the clause at 52.209-9, Updates of Publicly Available Information Regarding Responsibility Matters—

(1) In solicitations where the resultant contract value is expected to exceed $550,000; and

(2) In contracts in which the offeror checked "has" in paragraph (b) of the provision at 52.209-7.

(d) The contracting officer shall insert the provision 52.209–11, Representation by Corporations Regarding Delinquent Tax Liability or a Felony Conviction under any Federal Law, in all solicitations.

(e) For agencies receiving funds subject to section 523 of Division B of the Consolidated and Further Continuing Appropriations Act, 2015 (Pub. L. 113–235) and similar provisions in subsequent appropriations acts, the contracting officer shall insert the provision 52.209–12, Certification Regarding Tax Matters, in solicitations for which the resultant contract (including options) may have a value greater than $5,000,000. Division B of the Consolidated and Continuing Further Appropriations Act, 2015 appropriates funds for the following agencies: the Department of Commerce, the Department of Justice, the National Aeronautics and Space Administration, the Office of Science and Technology Policy, the National Science Foundation, the Commission on Civil Rights, the Equal Employment Opportunity Commission, the U.S. International Trade Commission, the Legal Services Corporation, the Marine Mammal Commission, the Office of the United States Trade Representative, and the State Justice Institute.

[FAC 2005-25, 73 FR 21791, 4/22/2008, effective 5/22/2008; FAC 2005-40, 75 FR 14059, 3/23/2010, effective 4/22/2010; FAC 2005-49, 76 FR 4188, 1/24/2011, effective 1/24/2011; FAC 2005-55, 77 FR 197, 1/3/2012, effective 1/3/2012; FAC 2005-83, 80 FR 38293, 7/2/2015, effective 10/1/2015; FAC 2005-85, 80 FR 75903, 12/4/2015, effective 2/26/2016; FAC 2005-91, 81 FR 67728, 9/30/2016, effective 9/30/2016; FAC 2019-02, 84 FR 19839, 5/6/2019, effective 5/6/2019]

9.105 Procedures. (No Text)

9.105-1 Obtaining information.

(a) Before making a determination of responsibility, the contracting officer shall possess or obtain information sufficient to be satisfied that a prospective contractor currently meets the applicable standards in 9.104.

(b) (1) Generally, the contracting officer shall obtain information regarding the responsibility of prospective contractors, including requesting preaward surveys when necessary (see 9.106), promptly after a bid opening or receipt of offers. However, in negotiated contracting, especially when research and development is involved, the contracting officer may obtain this information before issuing the request for proposals. Requests for information shall ordinarily be limited to information concerning—

(i) The low bidder; or

(ii) Those offerors in range for award.

(2) Preaward surveys shall be managed and conducted by the surveying activity.

(i) If the surveying activity is a contract administration office—

(A) That office shall advise the contracting officer on prospective contractors' financial competence and credit needs; and

(B) The administrative contracting officer shall obtain from the auditor any information required concerning the adequacy of prospective contractors' accounting systems and these systems' suitability for use in administering the proposed type of contract.

(ii) If the surveying activity is not a contract administration office, the contracting officer shall obtain from the auditor any information required concerning prospective contractors' financial competence and credit needs, the adequacy of their accounting systems, and these systems' suitability for use in administering the proposed type of contract.

(3) Information on financial resources and performance capability shall be obtained or updated on as current a basis as is feasible up to the date of award.

(c) In making the determination of responsibility, the contracting officer shall consider information available through FAPIIS (see 9.104-6), i with regard to the offeror and any immediate owner, predecessor, or subsidiary identified for that offeror in FAPIIS, including information that is linked to FAPIIS such as from SAM, and CPARS, as well as any other relevant past performance information on the offeror (see 9.104-1(c) and subpart 42.15). In addition, the contracting officer should use the following sources of information to support such determinations:

(1) Records and experience data, including verifiable knowledge of personnel within the contracting office, audit offices, contract administration offices, and other contracting offices.

(2) The prospective contractor—including bid or proposal information (including the certification at 52.209-5 or 52.212-3(h) (see 9.104-5)), questionnaire replies, financial data, information on production equipment, and personnel information.

(3) Commercial sources of supplier information of a type offered to buyers in the private sector.

(4) Preaward survey reports (see 9.106).

(5) Other sources such as publications; suppliers, subcontractors, and customers of the prospective contractor; financial institutions; Government agencies; and business and trade associations.

(d) Contracting offices and cognizant contract administration offices that become aware of circumstances casting doubt on a contractor's ability to perform contracts successfully shall promptly exchange relevant information.

[FAC 84-18, 51 FR 27119, 7/29/86, effective 7/30/86; FAC 84-25, 52 FR 9038, 3/20/87, effective 7/1/87; FAC 84-46, 54 FR 19813, 5/8/89, effective 6/7/89; FAC 90-26, 60 FR 16718, 3/31/95, effective 5/30/95; FAC 90-28, 60 FR 33064, 6/26/95, effective 8/25/95; FAC 90-40, 61 FR 39186, 7/26/96, effective 9/24/96; FAC 2001-26, 69 FR 76347, 12/20/2004, effective 1/19/2005; FAC 2005-25, 73 FR 21791, 4/22/2008, effective 5/22/2008; FAC 2005-34, 74 FR 31557, 7/1/2009, effective 7/1/2009; FAC 2005-40, 75 FR 14059, 3/23/2010, effective 4/22/2010; FAC 2005-67, 78 FR 37676, 6/21/2013, effective 7/22/2013; FAC 2005-87, 81 FR 11988, 3/7/2016, effective 4/6/2016; FAC 2005-90, 81 FR 58562, 8/25/2016, effective 10/25/2016; FAC 2005-93, 81 FR 91636, 12/16/2016, effective 12/16/2016; FAC 2005-96, 82 FR 51773, 11/8/2017, effective 11/6/2017; FAC 2019-02, 84 FR 19839, 5/6/2019, effective 5/6/2019; FAC 2019-06, 84 FR 47865, 9/10/2019, effective 10/10/2019]

9.105-2 Determinations and documentation.

(a) *Determinations.*

(1) The contracting officer's signing of a contract constitutes a determination that the prospective contractor is responsible with respect to that contract. When an offer on which an award would otherwise be made is rejected because the prospective contractor is found to be nonresponsible, the contracting officer shall make, sign, and place in the contract file a determination of nonresponsibility, which shall state the basis for the determination.

(2) If the contracting officer determines that a responsive small business lacks certain elements of responsibility, the contracting officer shall comply with the procedures in subpart 19.6. When a Certificate of Competency is issued for a small business concern (see subpart 19.6), the contracting officer shall accept the Small Business Administration's decision to issue a Certificate of Competency and award the contract to the concern.

(b) *Support documentation.* (1) Documents and reports supporting a determination of responsibility or nonresponsibility, including any preaward survey reports, the use of FAPIIS information (see 9.104-6), and any applicable Certificate of Competency, must be included in the contract file.

(2)(i) The contracting officer shall document the determination of nonresponsibility in FAPIIS (available at *https://www.cpars.gov*) if—

(A) The contract is valued at more than the simplified acquisition threshold;

(B) The determination of nonresponsibility is based on lack of satisfactory performance record or satisfactory record of integrity and business ethics; and

(C) The Small Business Administration does not issue a Certificate of Competency.

(ii) The contracting officer is responsible for the timely submission, within 3 working days, and sufficiency, and accuracy of the documentation regarding the nonresponsibility determination.

(iii) As required by section 3010 of the Supplemental Appropriations Act, 2010 (Pub. L. 111-212), all information posted in FAPIIS on or after April 15, 2011, except past performance reviews, will be publicly available. FAPIIS consists of two segments—

(A) The non-public segment, into which Government officials and contractors post information, which can only be viewed by—

(*1*) Government personnel and authorized users performing business on behalf of the Government; or

(*2*) An offeror or contractor, when viewing data on itself; and

(B) The publicly-available segment, to which all data in the non-public segment of FAPIIS is automatically transferred after a waiting period of 14 calendar days, except for—

(*1*) Past performance reviews required by subpart 42.15;

(*2*) Information that was entered prior to April 15, 2011; or

(*3*) Information that is withdrawn during the 14-calendar-day waiting period by the Government official who posted it in accordance with paragraph (b)(2)(iv) of this section.

(iv) The contracting officer, or any other Government official, shall not post any information in the non-public segment of FAPIIS that is covered by a disclosure exemption under the Freedom of Information Act. If the contractor asserts within 7 calendar days, to the Government official who posted the information, that some of the information posted to the non-public segment of FAPIIS is covered by a disclosure exemption under the Freedom of Information Act, the Government official who posted the information must within 7 calendar days remove the posting from FAPIIS and resolve the issue in accordance with agency Freedom of Information Act procedures, prior to reposting the releasable information.

[FAC 2005-40, 75 FR 14059, 3/23/2010, effective 4/22/2010; FAC 2005-55, 77 FR 197, 1/3/2012, effective 1/3/2012; FAC 2005-73, 79 FR 24253, 4/29/2014, effective 4/29/2014; FAC 2019-06, 84 FR 47865, 9/10/2019, effective 10/10/2019]

9.105-3 Disclosure of preaward information.

(a) Except as provided in subpart 24.2, Freedom of Information Act, information (including the preaward survey report) accumulated for purposes of determining the responsibility of a prospective contractor shall not be released or disclosed outside the Government.

(b) The contracting officer may discuss preaward survey information with the prospective contractor before determining responsibility. After award, the contracting officer or, if it is appropriate, the head of the surveying activity or a designee may discuss the findings of the preaward survey with the company surveyed.

(c) Preaward survey information may contain proprietary or source selection information and should be marked with the appropriate legend and protected accordingly (see 3.104-4).

[FAC 84-4754 FR 20496, 5/11/89, effective date delayed to 7/16/89, 54 FR 22282, 5/23/89; FAC 84-54, 54 FR 50718, 12/8/89, effective 12/1/89; FAC 90-45, Final rule, 62 FR 224, 1/2/97, effective 1/1/97; FAC 2001-06, 67 FR 13048, 3/20/2002, effective 4/4/2002; FAC 2005-90, 81 FR 58562, 8/25/2016, effective 10/25/2016; FAC 2005-96, 82 FR 51773, 11/8/2017, effective 11/6/2017]

9.106 Preaward surveys. (No Text)

9.106-1 Conditions for preaward surveys.

(a) A preaward survey is normally required only when the information on hand or readily available to the contracting officer, including information from commercial sources, is not sufficient to make a determination regarding responsibility. In addition, if the contemplated contract will have a fixed price at or below the simplified acquisition threshold or will involve the acquisition of commercial items (see Part 12), the contracting officer should not request a preaward survey unless circumstances justify its cost.

(b) When a cognizant contract administration office becomes aware of a prospective award to a contractor about which unfavorable information exists and no preaward survey has been requested, it shall promptly obtain and transmit details to the contracting officer.

(c) Before beginning a preaward survey, the surveying activity shall ascertain whether the prospective contractor is debarred, suspended, or ineligible (see Subpart 9.4). If the prospective contractor is debarred, suspended, or ineligible, the surveying activity shall advise the contracting officer promptly and not proceed with the preaward survey unless specifically requested to do so by the contracting officer.

[FAC 84-19, 51 FR 27489, 7/31/86, effective 7/31/86; FAC 90-32, 60 FR 48206, 9/18/95, effective 10/1/95; FAC 90-40, 61 FR 30186, 7/26/96, effective 9/24/96]

9.106-2 Requests for preaward surveys.

The contracting officer's request to the surveying activity (Preaward Survey of Prospective Contractor (General), SF 1403) shall—

(a) Identify additional factors about which information is needed;

(b) Include the complete solicitation package (unless it has previously been furnished), and any information indicating prior unsatisfactory performance by the prospective contractor;

(c) State whether the contracting office will participate in the survey;

(d) Specify the date by which the report is required. This date should be consistent with the scope of the survey requested and normally shall allow at least 7 working days to conduct the survey; and

(e) When appropriate, limit the scope of the survey.

9.106-3 Interagency preaward surveys.

When the contracting office and the surveying activity are in different agencies, the procedures of this section 9.106 and Subpart 42.1 shall be followed along with the regulations of the agency in which the surveying activity is located, except that reasonable special requests by the contracting office shall be accommodated (also see subpart 17.5).

[FAC 84-4754 FR 20496, 5/11/89, effective date delayed to 7/16/89, 54 FR 22282, 5/23/89; FAC 84-54, 54 FR 50718, 12/8/89, effective 12/1/89; FAC 84-60, 55 FR 36795, 9/6/90, effective 9/6/90; FAC 90-45, Final rule, 62 FR 224, 1/2/97, effective 1/1/97; FAC 2005-47, 75 FR 77733, 12/13/2010, effective 12/13/2010; FAC 2005-55, 77 FR 183, 1/3/2012, effective 2/2/2012]

9.106-4 Reports.

(a) The surveying activity shall complete the applicable parts of SF 1403, Preaward Survey of Prospective Contractor (General); SF 1404, Preaward Survey of Prospective Contractor—Technical; SF 1405, Preaward Survey of Prospective Contractor—Production; SF 1406, Preaward Survey of Prospective Contractor—Quality Assurance; SF 1407, Preaward Survey of Prospective Contractor—Financial Capability; and SF 1408, Preaward Survey of Prospective Contractor—Accounting System; and provide a narrative discussion sufficient to support both the evaluation ratings and the recommendations.

(b) When the contractor surveyed is a small business that has received preferential treatment on an ongoing contract under Section 8(a) of the Small Business Act (15 U.S.C. 637) or has received a Certificate of Competency during the last 12 months, the surveying activity shall consult the appropriate Small Business Administration field office before making an affirmative recommendation regarding the contractor's responsibility or nonresponsibility.

(c) When a preaward survey discloses previous unsatisfactory performance, the surveying activity shall specify the extent to which the prospective contractor plans, or has taken, corrective action. Lack of evidence that past failure to meet contractual requirements was the prospective contractor's fault does not necessarily indicate satisfactory performance. The narrative shall report any persistent pattern of need for costly and burdensome Government assistance (*e.g.*, engineering, inspection, or testing) provided in the Government's interest but not contractually required.

(d) When the surveying activity possesses information that supports a recommendation of complete award without an on-site survey and no special areas for investigation have been requested, the surveying activity may provide a short-form preaward survey report. The short-form report shall consist solely of the Preaward Survey of Prospective Contractor (General), SF 1403. Sections III and IV of this form shall be completed and block 21 shall be checked to show that the report is a short-form preaward report.

9.107 Surveys of nonprofit agencies participating in the AbilityOne Program.

(a) The Committee for Purchase From People Who Are Blind or Severely Disabled (Committee), as authorized by 41 U.S.C. chapter 85, determines what supplies and services Federal agencies are required to purchase from AbilityOne participating nonprofit agencies serving people who are blind or have other severe disabilities (see Subpart 8.7). The Committee is required to find an AbilityOne participating nonprofit agency capable of furnishing the supplies or services before the nonprofit agency can be designated as a mandatory source under the AbilityOne Program. The Committee may request a contracting office to assist in assessing the capabilities of a nonprofit agency.

(b) The contracting office, upon request from the Committee, shall request a capability survey from the activity responsible for performing preaward surveys, or notify the Committee that the AbilityOne participating nonprofit agency is capable, with supporting rationale, and that the survey is waived. The capability survey will focus on the technical and production capabilities and applicable preaward survey elements to furnish specific supplies or services being considered for addition to the Procurement List.

(c) The contracting office shall use the Standard Form 1403 to request a capability survey of organizations employing people who are blind or have other severe disabilities.

(d) The contracting office shall furnish a copy of the completed survey, or notice that the AbilityOne participating nonprofit agency is capable and the survey is waived, to the Executive Director, Committee for Purchase From People Who Are Blind or Severely Disabled.

[FAC 90-23, 59 FR 67010, 12/28/94, effective 2/27/95; FAC 2005-27, 73 FR 53994, 9/17/2008, effective 10/17/2008; FAC 2005-73, 79 FR 24192, 4/29/2014, effective 5/29/2014; FAC 2019-02, 84 FR 19839, 5/6/2019, effective 5/6/2019]

9.108 Prohibition on contracting with inverted domestic corporations. (No Text)

[FAC 2005-34, 74 FR 31561, 7/1/2009, effective 7/1/2009]

9.108-1 Definitions.

As used in this section—

Inverted domestic corporation means a foreign incorporated entity that meets the definition of an inverted domestic corporation under 6 U.S.C. 395(b), applied in accordance with the rules and definitions of 6 U.S.C. 395(c).

Subsidiary means an entity in which more than 50 percent of the entity is owned—

(1) Directly by a parent corporation; or

(2) Through another subsidiary of a parent corporation.

[FAC 2005-34, 74 FR 31561, 7/1/2009, effective 7/1/2009; FAC 2005-52, 76 FR 31410, 5/31/2011, effective 5/31/2011; FAC 2005-79, 79 FR 74554, 12/15/2014, effective

12/15/2014; FAC 2005-83, 80 FR 38309, 7/2/2015, effective 7/2/2015]

9.108-2 Prohibition.

(a) Section 745 of Division D of the Consolidated Appropriations Act, 2008 (Pub. L. 110-161) and its successor provisions in subsequent appropriations acts (and as extended in continuing resolutions) prohibit, on a Governmentwide basis, the use of appropriated (or otherwise made available) funds for contracts with either an inverted domestic corporation, or a subsidiary of such a corporation, except as provided in paragraph (b) of this section and in 9.108-4 Waiver.

(b) (1) Section 745 and its successor provisions include the following exception: This section shall not apply to any Federal Government contract entered into before the date of the enactment of this Act, or to any task order issued pursuant to such contract.

(2) To ensure appropriate application of the prohibition and this exception, contracting officers should consult with legal counsel if, during the performance of a contract, a contractor becomes an inverted domestic corporation or a subsidiary of one.

[FAC 2005-34, 74 FR 31561, 7/1/2009, effective 7/1/2009; FAC 2005-52, 76 FR 31410, 5/31/2011, effective 5/31/2011; FAC 2005-59, 77 FR 27547, 5/10/2012, effective 5/10/2012; FAC 2005-65, 78 FR 6185, 1/29/2013, effective 1/29/2013; FAC 2005-79, 79 FR 74554, 12/15/2014, effective 12/15/2014; FAC 2005-83, 80 FR 38309, 7/2/2015, effective 7/2/2015]

9.108-3 Representation by the offeror.

(a) In order to be eligible for contract award, an offeror must represent that it is neither an inverted domestic corporation, nor a subsidiary of an inverted domestic corporation. Any offeror that cannot so represent is ineligible for award of a contract, unless waived in accordance with the procedures at 9.108-4.

(b) The contracting officer may rely on an offeror's representation that it is not an inverted domestic corporation unless the contracting officer has reason to question the representation.

[FAC 2005-34, 74 FR 31561, 7/1/2009, effective 7/1/200; FAC 2005-52, 76 FR 31410, 5/31/2011, effective 5/31/2011; FAC 2005-59, 77 FR 27547, 5/10/2012, effective 5/10/2012; FAC 2005-65, 78 FR 6185, 1/29/2013, effective 1/29/2013; FAC 2005-79, 79 FR 74554, 12/15/2014, effective 12/15/2014; FAC 2005-83, 80 FR 38309, 7/2/2015, effective 7/2/2015]

9.108-4 Waiver.

Any agency head may waive the prohibition in subsection 9.108-2 and the requirement of subsection 9.108-3 for a specific contract if the agency head determines in writing that the waiver is required in the interest of national security, documents the determination, and reports it to the Congress.

[FAC 2005-34, 74 FR 31561, 7/1/2009, effective 7/1/2009; FAC 2005-52, 76 FR 31410, 5/31/2011, effective 5/31/2011]

9.108-5 Solicitation provision and contract clause.

The contracting officer shall—

(a) Include the provision at 52.209-2, Prohibition on Contracting with Inverted Domestic Corporations—Representation, in each solicitation for the acquisition of products or services (including construction); and

(b) Include the clause at 52.209-10, Prohibition on Contracting with Inverted Domestic Corporations, in each solicitation and contract for the acquisition of products or services (including construction).

[FAC 2005-34, 74 FR 31561, 7/1/2009, effective 7/1/2009; FAC 2005-52, 76 FR 31410, 5/31/2011, effective 5/31/2011; FAC 2005-59, 77 FR 27547, 5/10/2012, effective 5/10/2012; FAC 2005-65, 78 FR 6185, 1/29/2013, effective 1/29/2013; FAC 2005-79, 79 FR 74554, 12/15/2014, effective 12/15/2014; FAC 2005-83, 80 FR 38309, 7/2/2015, effective 7/2/2015]

9.109 Prohibition on contracting with an entity involved in activities that violate arms control treaties or

agreements with the United States. (No Text)

[FAC 2005-99, 83 FR 28145, 6/15/2018, effective 6/15/2018]

9.109-1 Authority.

This section implements 22 U.S.C. 2593e.

[FAC 2005-99, 83 FR 28145, 6/15/2018, effective 6/15/2018]

9.109-2 Prohibition.

Contracting officers shall not award, renew, or extend a contract for the procurement of products or services with an entity identified as excluded in the System for Award Management, specifically for this subpart, on the basis of involvement in activities that violate arms control treaties or agreements with the United States.

[FAC 2005-99, 83 FR 28145, 6/15/2018, effective 6/15/2018; FAC 2005-101, 83 FR 48691, 9/26/2018, effective 10/26/2018]

9.109-3 Exception.

The prohibition in 9.109-2 does not apply to contracts for the procurement of products or services along a major route of supply to a zone of active combat or major contingency operation, as specified in statute or by the cognizant Combatant Commander, in consultation with the Chief of Mission. As of May 10, 2018, countries along the major route of supply to support operations in Afghanistan are Afghanistan, Georgia, the Kyrgyz Republic, Pakistan, the Republic of Armenia, the Republic of Azerbaijan, the Republic of Kazakhstan, the Republic of Tajikistan, the Republic of Uzbekistan, and Turkmenistan.

[FAC 2005-99, 83 FR 28145, 6/15/2018, effective 6/15/2018]

9.109-4 Certification by the offeror.

(a) In order to be eligible for contract award, an offeror is required to—

(1) (i) Certify that it does not engage and has not engaged in any activity that contributed to or was a significant factor in the President's or Secretary of State's determination that a foreign country is in violation of its obligations undertaken in any arms control, nonproliferation, or disarmament agreement to which the United States is a party, or is not adhering to its arms control, nonproliferation, or disarmament commitments in which the United States is a participating state. The determinations are described in the most recent unclassified annual report provided to Congress pursuant to section 403 of the Arms Control and Disarmament Act (22 U.S.C. 2593a). The report is available via the internet at *https://www.state.gov/t/avc/rls/rpt/*; and

(ii) Similarly certify with regard to any entity owned or controlled by the offeror; or

(2) Provide with its offer information that the President of the United States has—

(i) Waived application under 22 U.S.C. 2593e(d) or (e); or

(ii) Determined under 22 U.S.C. 2593e(g)(2) that the entity has ceased all activities for which measures were imposed under 22 U.S.C. 2593e(b).

(b) If certifying in accordance with 52.209-13(b)(1), the Offeror is required to submit the certification with the offer. It is not included in the annual representations and certifications in the System for Award Management.

(c) The contracting officer may rely on an offeror's certification unless the contracting officer has reason to question the certification.

(d) An offeror that falsely certifies under 52.209-13 will be subject to such remedies as suspension or debarment for a period of not less than 2 years, subject to the procedures set forth in subpart 9.4 (including 9.406-1 or 9.407-1), or termination of any contract resulting from the false certification.

[FAC 2005-99, 83 FR 28145, 6/15/2018, effective 6/15/2018; FAC 2005-101, 83 FR 48691, 9/26/2018, effective 10/26/2018]

9.109-5 Solicitation provision.

Unless the exception at 9.109-3 applies, the contracting officer shall include the provision at 52.209-13, Violation of Arms Control Treaties or Agreements—Certification, in each solicitation for the acquisition of products or services (including construction) that exceeds the simplified acquisition threshold, other than solicitations for the acquisition of commercial items.

[FAC 2005-99, 83 FR 28145, 6/15/2018, effective 6/15/2018]

SUBPART 9.2—QUALIFICATIONS REQUIREMENTS

9.200 Scope of subpart.

This subpart implements 10 U.S.C. 2319 and 41 U.S.C. 3311 and prescribes policies and procedures regarding qualification requirements and the acquisitions that are subject to such requirements.

[FAC 84-11, 50 FR 35476, 8/30/85, effective 8/30/85; FAC 2005-73, 79 FR 24192, 4/29/2014, effective 5/29/2014]

9.201 Definitions.

As used in this subpart—

Qualified bidders list (QBL) means a list of bidders who have had their products examined and tested and who have satisfied all applicable qualification requirements for that product or have otherwise satisfied all applicable qualification requirements.

Qualified manufacturers list (QML) means a list of manufacturers who have had their products examined and tested and who have satisfied all applicable qualification requirements for that product.

[FAC 84-11, 50 FR 35476, 8/30/85, effective 8/30/85; FAC 84-39, 53 FR 34227, 9/2/88, effective 10/3/88; FAC 97-22, 66 FR 2116, 1/10/2001, effective 3/12/2001; Delay of effective date, 66 FR 14259, 3/9/2001, effective 5/11/2001]

9.202 Policy.

(a) (1) The head of the agency or designee shall, before establishing a qualification requirement, prepare a written justification—

(i) Stating the necessity for establishing the qualification requirement and specifying why the qualification requirement must be demonstrated before contract award;

(ii) Estimating the likely costs for testing and evaluation which will be incurred by the potential offeror to become qualified; and

(iii) Specifying all requirements that a potential offeror (or its product) must satisfy in order to become qualified. Only those requirements which are the least restrictive to meet the purposes necessitating the establishment of the qualification requirements shall be specified.

(2) Upon request to the contracting activity, potential offerors shall be provided—

(i) All requirements that they or their products must satisfy to become qualified; and

(ii) At their expense (but see 9.204(a)(2) with regard to small businesses), a prompt opportunity to demonstrate their abilities to meet the standards specified for qualification using qualified personnel and facilities of the agency concerned, or of another agency obtained through interagency agreements, or under contract, or other methods approved by the agency (including use of approved testing and evaluation services not provided under contract to the agency).

(3) If the services in paragraph (a)(2)(ii) of this section are provided by contract, the contractors selected to provide testing and evaluation services shall be—

(i) Those that are not expected to benefit from an absence of additional qualified sources; and

(ii) Required by their contracts to adhere to any restriction on technical data asserted by the potential offeror seeking qualification.

(4) A potential offeror seeking qualification shall be promptly informed as to whether qualification is attained and, in the event it is not, promptly furnished specific reasons why qualification was not attained.

(b) When justified under the circumstances, the agency activity responsible for establishing a qualification requirement shall submit to the advocate for competition for the procuring activity responsible for purchasing the item subject to the qualification requirement, a determination that it is unreasonable to specify the standards for qualification which a prospective offeror (or its product) must satisfy. After considering any comments of the advocate for competition reviewing the determination, the head of the procuring activity may waive the requirements of 9.202 (a)(1)(ii) through (a)(4) of this section for up to 2 years with respect to the item subject to the qualification requirement. A copy of the waiver shall be furnished to the head of the agency or other official responsible for actions under 9.202 paragraph (a)(1) of this section. The waiver authority provided in this paragraph does not apply with respect to qualification requirements contained in a QPL, QML, or QBL.

(c) If a potential offeror can demonstrate to the satisfaction of the contracting officer that the potential offeror (or its product) meets the standards established for qualification or can meet them before the date specified for award of the contract, a potential offeror may not be denied the opportunity to submit and have considered an offer for a contract solely because the potential offeror—

(1) Is not on a QPL, QML, or QBL maintained by the Department of Defense (DoD) or the National Aeronautics and Space Administration (NASA); or

(2) Has not been identified as meeting a qualification requirement established after October 19, 1984, by DoD or NASA; or

(3) Has not been identified as meeting a qualification requirement established by a civilian agency (not including NASA).

(d) The procedures in Subpart 19.6 for referring matters to the Small Business Administration are not mandatory on the contracting officer when the basis for a referral would involve a challenge by the offeror to either the validity of the qualification requirement or the offeror's compliance with such requirement.

(e) The contracting officer need not delay a proposed award in order to provide a potential offeror with an opportunity to demonstrate its ability to meet the standards specified for qualification. In addition, when approved by the head of an agency or designee, a procurement need not be delayed in order to comply with paragraph (a) of this section.

(f) Within 7 years following enforcement of a QPL, QML, or QBL by DoD or NASA, or within 7 years after any qualification requirement was originally established by a civilian agency other than NASA, the qualification requirement shall be examined and revalidated in accordance with the requirements of paragraph (a) of this section. For DoD and NASA, qualification requirements other than QPL's, QML's and QBL's shall be examined and revalidated within 7 years after establishment of the requirement under paragraph (a) of this section. Any periods for which a waiver under paragraph (b) of this section is in effect shall be excluded in computing the 7 years within which review and revalidation must occur.

[FAC 84-11, 50 FR 35476, 8/30/85, effective 8/30/85; FAC 84-39, 53 FR 34227, 9/2/88, effective 10/3/88; FAC 2005-73, 79 FR 24192, 4/29/2014, effective 5/29/2014; FAC 2019-02, 84 FR 19839, 5/6/2019, effective 5/6/2019]

9.203 QPL's, QML's, and QBL's.

(a) Qualification and listing in a QPL, QML, or QBL is the process by which products are obtained from manufacturers or distributors, examined and tested for compliance with specification requirements, or manufacturers or potential offerors, are provided an opportunity to demonstrate their abilities to meet the standards specified for qualification. The names of successful products, manufacturers, or potential offerors are included on lists evidencing their status. Generally, qualification is performed in advance and independently of any specific acquisition action. After qualification, the products, manufacturers, or potential offerors are included in a Federal or Military QPL, QML, or QBL. (See 9.202(a)(2) with regard to any product, manufacturer, or potential offeror not yet included on an applicable list.)

(b) Specifications requiring a qualified product are included in the following publications:

(1) GSA Index of Federal Specifications, Standards and Commercial Item Descriptions, FPMR 101-29.1.

(2) Department of Defense Acquisition Streamlining and Standardization Information System (ASSIST) at (*https://assist.dla.mil/online/start/*).

(c) Instructions concerning qualification procedures are included in the following publications:

(1) Federal Standardization Manual, FSPM-0001.

(2) Defense Standardization Manual 4120.24-M, Appendix 2, as amended by Military Standards 961 and 962.

(d) The publications listed in paragraphs (b) and (c) of this section are sold to the public. The publications in paragraphs (b) (1) and (c) (1) of this section may be obtained from the addressee in 11.201(d) (1). The publications in paragraphs (b) (2) and (c) (2) of this section may be obtained from the addressee in 11.201(d) (2).

[FAC 84-11, 50 FR 35476, 8/30/85, effective 8/30/85; FAC 84-37, 53 FR 17857, 5/18/88, effective 6/17/88; FAC 97-5, 63 FR 34058, 6/22/98, effective 8/21/98; FAC 2001-04, 67 FR 6112, 2/8/2002, effective 2/8/2002; FAC 2005-07, 71 FR 227, 1/3/2006, effective 1/3/2006; FAC 2005-73, 79 FR 24253, 4/29/2014, effective 4/29/2014]

9.204 Responsibilities for establishment of a qualification requirement.

The responsibilities of agency activities that establish qualification requirements include the following:

(a) Arranging publicity for the qualification requirements. If active competition on anticipated future qualification requirements is likely to be fewer than two manufacturers or the products of two manufacturers, the activity responsible for establishment of the qualification requirements must—

(1) Periodically furnish through the Governmentwide point of entry (GPE) a notice seeking additional sources or products for qualification unless the contracting officer determines that such publication would compromise the national security.

(2) Bear the cost of conducting the specified testing and evaluation (excluding the costs associated with producing the item or establishing the production, quality control, or other system to be tested and evaluated) for a small business concern or a product manufactured by a small business concern which has met the standards specified for qualification and which could reasonably be expected to compete for a contract for that requirement. However, such costs may be borne only if it is determined in accordance with agency procedures that such additional qualified sources or products are likely to result in cost savings from increased competition for future requirements sufficient to amortize the costs incurred by the agency within a reasonable period of time, considering the duration and dollar value of anticipated future requirements. A prospective contractor requesting the United States to bear testing and evaluation costs must certify as to its status as a small business concern under Section 3 of the Small Business Act in order to receive further consideration.

(b) Qualifying products that meet specification requirements.

(c) Listing manufacturers and suppliers whose products are qualified in accordance with agency procedures.

(d) Furnishing QPL's, QML's, or QBL's or the qualification requirements themselves to prospective offerors and the public upon request (see 9.202(a) (2) (i)).

(e) Clarifying, as necessary, qualification requirements.

(f) In appropriate cases, when requested by the contracting officer, providing concurrence in a decision not to enforce a qualification requirement for a solicitation.

(g) Withdrawing or omitting qualification of a listed product, manufacturer or offeror, as necessary.

(h) Advising persons furnished any list of products, manufacturers or offerors meeting a qualification requirement and suppliers whose products are on any such list that—

(1) The list does not constitute endorsement of the product, manufacturer, or other source by the Government;

(2) The products or sources listed have been qualified under the latest applicable specification;

(3) The list may be amended without notice;

(4) The listing of a product or source does not release the supplier from compliance with the specification; and

(5) Use of the list for advertising or publicity is permitted. However, it must not be stated or implied that a particular product or source is the only product or source of that type qualified, or that the Government in any way recommends or endorses the products or the sources listed.

(i) Reexamining a qualified product or manufacturer when—

(1) The manufacturer has modified its product, or changed the material or the processing sufficiently so that the validity of previous qualification is questionable;

(2) The requirements in the specification have been amended or revised sufficiently to affect the character of the product; or

(3) It is otherwise necessary to determine that the quality of the product is maintained in conformance with the specification.

[FAC 84-11, 50 FR 35476, 8/30/85, effective 8/30/85; FAC 97-26, 66 FR 27405, 5/16/2001, effective 5/16/2001; FAC 2001-16, Interim/Final rule, 68 FR 56676, 10/1/2003, effective 10/1/2003; FAC 2019-02, 84 FR 19839, 5/6/2019, effective 5/6/2019]

9.205 Opportunity for qualification before award.

(a) If an agency determines that a qualification requirement is necessary, the agency activity responsible for establishing the requirement must urge manufacturers and other potential sources to demonstrate their ability to meet the standards specified for qualification and, when possible, give sufficient time to arrange for qualification before award. The responsible agency activity must, before establishing any qualification requirement, furnish notice through the GPE. The notice must include—

(1) Intent to establish a qualification requirement;

(2) The specification number and name of the product;

(3) The name and address of the activity to which a request for the information and opportunity described in 9.202(a)(2) should be submitted;

(4) The anticipated date that the agency will begin awarding contracts subject to the qualification requirement;

(5) A precautionary notice that when a product is submitted for qualification testing, the applicant must furnish any specific information that may be requested of the manufacturer before testing will begin; and

(6) The approximate time period following submission of a product for qualification testing within which the applicant will be notified whether the product passed or failed the qualification testing (see 9.202(a)(4)).

(b) The activity responsible for establishing a qualification requirement must keep any list maintained of those already qualified open for inclusion of additional products, manufacturers, or other potential sources.

[FAC 84-11, 50 FR 35476, 8/30/85, effective 8/30/85; FAC 97-15, 64 FR 72414, 12/27/99, effective 2/25/2000; FAC 97-26, 66 FR 27405, 5/16/2001, effective 5/16/2001; FAC 2001-16, Interim/Final rule, 68 FR 56676, 10/1/2003, effective 10/1/2003; FAC 2001-27, interim rule, 69 FR 77870, 12/28/2004, effective 1/1/2005; FAC 2005-07, 71 FR 219, 1/3/2006, effective 1/3/2006]

9.206 Acquisitions subject to qualification requirements. (No Text)

9.206-1 General.

(a) Agencies may not enforce any QPL, QML, or QBL without first complying with the requirements of 9.202(a). However, qualification requirements themselves, whether or not previously embodied in a QPL, QML, or QBL, may be enforced without regard to 9.202(a) if they are in either of the following categories:

(1) Any qualification requirement established by statute prior to October 30, 1984, for civilian agencies (not including NASA); or

(2) Any qualification requirement established by statute or administrative action prior to October 19, 1984, for DOD or NASA. Qualification requirements established after the above dates must comply with 9.202(a) to be enforceable.

(b) Except when the agency head or designee determines that an emergency exists, whenever an agency elects, whether before or after award, not to enforce a qualification requirement which it established, the requirement may not thereafter be enforced unless the agency complies with 9.202(a).

(c) If a qualification requirement applies, the contracting officer need consider only those offers identified as meeting the requirement or included on the applicable QPL, QML, or QBL, unless an offeror can satisfactorily demonstrate to the contracting officer that it or its product or its subcontractor or its product can meet the standards established for qualification before the date specified for award.

(d) If a product subject to a qualification requirement is to be acquired as a component of an end item, the contracting officer must ensure that all such components and their qualification requirements are properly identified in the solicitation since the product or source must meet the standards specified for qualification before award.

(e) In acquisitions subject to qualification requirements, the contracting officer shall take the following steps:

(1) Use presolicitation notices in appropriate cases to advise potential suppliers before issuing solicitations involving qualification requirements. The notices shall identify the specification containing the qualification requirement and establish an allowable time period, consistent with delivery requirements, for prospective offerors to demonstrate their abilities to meet the standards specified for qualification. The notice shall be publicized in accordance with 5.204. Whether or not a presolicitation notice is used, the general synopsizing requirements of Subpart 5.2 apply.

(2) Distribute solicitations to prospective contractors whether or not they have been identified as meeting applicable qualification requirements.

(3) When appropriate, request in accordance with agency procedures that a qualification requirement not be enforced in a particular acquisition and, if granted, so specify in the solicitation (see 9.206-1(b)).

(4) Forward requests from potential suppliers for information on a qualification requirement to the agency activity responsible for establishing the requirement.

(5) Allow the maximum time, consistent with delivery requirements, between issuing the solicitation and the contract award. As a minimum, contracting officers shall comply with the time frames specified in 5.203 when applicable.

[FAC 84-11, 50 FR 35476, 8/30/85, effective 8/30/85; FAC 84-39, 53 FR 34227, 9/2/88, effective 10/3/88]

9.206-2 Contract clause.

The contracting officer shall insert the clause at 52.209-1, Qualification Requirements, in solicitations and contracts when the acquisition is subject to a qualification requirement.

[FAC 84-11, 50 FR 35476, 8/30/85, effective 8/30/85; FAC 84-39, 53 FR 34227, 9/2/88, effective 10/3/88]

9.206-3 Competition.

(a) *Presolicitation.* If a qualification requirement applies to an acquisition, the contracting officer shall review the applicable QPL, QML, or QBL or other identification of those sources which have met the requirement before issuing a solicitation to ascertain whether the number of sources is adequate for competition. (See 9.204(a) for duties of the agency activity responsible for establishment of the qualification requirement.) If the number of sources is inadequate, the contracting officer shall request the agency activity which established the requirement to—

(1) Indicate the anticipated date on which any sources presently undergoing evaluation will have demonstrated their abilities to meet the qualification requirement so that the solicitation could be rescheduled to allow as many additional sources as possible to qualify; or

(2) Indicate whether a means other than the qualification requirement is feasible for testing or demonstrating quality assurance.

(b) *Postsolicitation.* The contracting officer shall submit to the agency activity which established the qualification requirement the names and addresses of concerns which expressed interest in the acquisition but are not included on the applicable QPL, QML, or QBL or identified as meeting the qualification requirement. The activity will then assist interested concerns in meeting the standards specified for qualification (see 9.202(a)(2) and (4)).

[FAC 84-11, 50 FR 35476, 8/30/85, effective 8/30/85; FAC 90-29, 60 FR 34732, 7/3/95, effective 7/3/95]

9.207 Changes in status regarding qualification requirements.

(a) The contracting officer shall promptly report to the agency activity which established the qualification requirement any conditions which may merit removal or omission from a QPL, QML, or QBL or affect whether a source should continue to be otherwise identified as meeting the requirement. These conditions exist when—

(1) Products or services are submitted for inspection or acceptance that do not meet the qualification requirement;

(2) Products or services were previously rejected and the defects were not corrected when submitted for inspection or acceptance;

(3) A supplier fails to request reevaluation following change of location or ownership of the plant where the product which met the qualification requirement was manufactured (see the clause at 52.209-1, Qualification Requirements);

(4) A manufacturer of a product which met the qualification requirement has discontinued manufacture of the product;

(5) A source requests removal from a QPL, QML, or QBL;

(6) A condition of meeting the qualification requirement was violated; *e.g.*, advertising or publicity contrary to 9.204(h)(5);

(7) A revised specification imposes a new qualification requirement;

(8) Manufacturing or design changes have been incorporated in the qualification requirement;

(9) The source is listed in the System for Award Management Exclusions (see Subpart 9.4); or

(10) Performance of a contract subject to a qualification requirement is otherwise unsatisfactory.

(b) After considering any of the above or other conditions reasonably related to whether a product or source continues to meet the standards specified for qualification, an agency may take appropriate action without advance notification. The agency shall, however, promptly notify the affected parties if a product or source is removed from a QPL, QML, or QBL, or will no longer be identified as meeting the standards specified for qualification. This notice shall contain specific information why the product or source no longer meets the qualification requirement.

[FAC 84-11, 50 FR 35476, 8/30/85, effective 8/30/85; FAC 84-39, 53 FR 34226, 9/2/88, effective 10/3/88; FAC 90-4, 56 FR 15149, 4/15/91, effective 5/15/91; FAC 90-28, 60 FR 33064, 6/26/95, effective 8/25/95; FAC 2001-26, 69 FR 76347, 12/20/2004, effective 1/19/2005; FAC 2005-67, 78 FR 37676, 6/21/2013, effective 7/22/2013]

SUBPART 9.3—FIRST ARTICLE TESTING AND APPROVAL

9.301 Definition.

Approval, as used in this subpart, means the contracting officer's written notification to the contractor accepting the test results of the first article.

[FAC 97-22, 66 FR 2116, 1/10/2001, effective 3/12/2001; Delay of effective date, 66 FR 14259, 3/9/2001, effective 5/11/2001]

9.302 General.

First article testing and approval (hereafter referred to as testing and approval) ensures that the contractor can furnish a product that conforms to all contract requirements for acceptance. Before requiring testing and approval, the contracting officer shall consider the—

(a) Impact on cost or time of delivery;

(b) Risk to the Government of foregoing such test; and

(c) Availability of other, less costly, methods of ensuring the desired quality.

9.303 Use.

Testing and approval may be appropriate when—

(a) The contractor has not previously furnished the product to the Government;

(b) The contractor previously furnished the product to the Government, but—

(1) There have been subsequent changes in processes or specifications;

(2) Production has been discontinued for an extended period of time; or

(3) The product acquired under a previous contract developed a problem during its life;

(c) The product is described by a performance specification; or

(d) It is essential to have an approved first article to serve as a manufacturing standard.

9.304 Exceptions.

Normally, testing and approval is not required in contracts for—

(a) Research or development;

(b) Products requiring qualification before award (*e.g.*, when an applicable qualified products list exists (see Subpart 9.2));

(c) Products normally sold in the commercial market; or

(d) Products covered by complete and detailed technical specifications, unless the requirements are so novel or exacting that it is questionable whether the products would meet the requirements without testing and approval.

9.305 Risk.

Before first article approval, the acquisition of materials or components, or commencement of production, is normally at the sole risk of the contractor. To minimize this risk, the contracting officer shall provide sufficient time in the delivery schedule for acquisition of materials and components, and for production after receipt of first article approval. When Government requirements preclude this action, the contracting officer may, before approval of the first article, authorize the contractor to acquire specific materials or components or commence production to the extent essential to meet the delivery schedule (see Alternate II of the clause at 52.209-3, First Article Approval—Contractor Testing, and Alternate II of the clause at 52.209-4, First Article Approval—Government Testing). Costs incurred based on this authorization are allocable to the contract for—

(a) Progress payments; and

(b) Termination settlements if the contract is terminated for the convenience of the Government.

[FAC 2019-02, 84 FR 19839, 5/6/2019, effective 5/6/2019]

9.306 Solicitation requirements.

Solicitations containing a testing and approval requirement shall—

(a) Provide, in the circumstance where the contractor is to be responsible for the first article approval testing—

(1) The performance or other characteristics that the first article must meet for approval;

(2) The detailed technical requirements for the tests that must be performed for approval; and

(3) The necessary data that must be submitted to the Government in the first article approval test report;

(b) Provide, in the circumstance where the Government is to be responsible for the first article approval testing—

(1) The performance or other characteristics that the first article must meet for approval; and

(2) The tests to which the first article will be subjected for approval;

(c) Inform offerors that the requirement may be waived when supplies identical or similar to those called for have previously been delivered by the offeror and accepted by the Government (see 52.209-3(h) and 52.209-4(i));

(d) Permit the submission of alternative offers, one including testing and approval and the other excluding testing and approval (if eligible under paragraph (c) of this section);

(e) State clearly the first article's relationship to the contract quantity (see paragraph (e) of the clause at 52.209-3, First Article Approval—Contractor Testing, or 52.209-4, First Article Approval—Government Testing);

(f) Contain a delivery schedule for the production quantity (see 11.403). The delivery schedule may—

(1) Be the same whether or not testing and approval is waived; or

(2) Provide for earlier delivery when testing and approval is waived and the Government desires earlier delivery. In the latter case, any resulting difference in delivery schedules shall not be a factor in evaluation for award. The clause at 52.209-4, First Article Approval—Government Testing, shall contain the delivery schedule for the first article;

(g) Provide for the submission of contract numbers, if any, to document the offeror's eligibility under paragraph (c) of this section;

(h) State whether the approved first article will serve as a manufacturing standard;

(i) Include, when the Government is responsible for first article testing, the Government's estimated testing costs as a factor for use in evaluating offers (when appropriate); and

(j) Inform offerors that the prices for first articles and first article tests in relation to production quantities shall not be materially unbalanced (see 15.404-1(g)) if first article test items or tests are to be separately priced.

[FAC 84-51, 54 FR 34753, 8/21/89, effective 9/20/89; FAC 84-58, 55 FR 25527, 6/21/90, effective 7/23/90; FAC 90-32, 60 FR 48206, 9/18/95, effective 10/1/95; FAC 97-2, 62 FR 51224, 9/30/97, effective 10/10/97; FAC 2019-02, 84 FR 19839, 5/6/2019, effective 5/6/2019]

9.307 Government administration procedures.

(a) Before the contractor ships the first article, or the first article test report, to the Government laboratory or other activity responsible for approval at the address specified in the contract, the contract administration office shall provide that activity with as much advance notification as is feasible of the forthcoming shipment, and—

(1) Advise that activity of the contractual requirements for testing and approval, or evaluation, as appropriate;

(2) Call attention to the notice requirement in paragraph (b) of the clause at 52.209-3, First Article Approval—Contractor Testing, or 52.209-4, First Article Approval—Government Testing; and

(3) Request that the activity inform the contract administration office of the date when testing or evaluation will be completed.

(b) The Government laboratory or other activity responsible for first article testing or evaluation shall inform the contracting office whether to approve, conditionally approve, or disapprove the first article. The contracting officer shall then notify the contractor of the action taken and furnish a copy of the notice to the contract administration office. The notice shall include the first article shipment number, when available, and the applicable line item number. Any changes in the drawings, designs, or specifications determined by the contracting officer to be necessary shall be made under the Changes clause, and not by the notice of approval, conditional approval, or disapproval furnished the contractor.

[FAC 2005-95, 82 FR 4709, 1/13/2017, effective 1/13/2017]

9.308 Contract clauses. (No Text)

9.308-1 Testing performed by the contractor.

(a)(1) The contracting officer shall insert the clause at 52.209-3, First Article Approval—Contractor Testing, in solicitations and contracts when a fixed-price contract is contemplated and it is intended that the contract require—

(i) First article approval; and

(ii) That the contractor be required to conduct the first article testing.

(2) If it is intended that the contractor be required to produce the first article and the production quantity at the same facility, the contracting officer shall use the clause with its Alternate I.

(3) If it is necessary to authorize the contractor to purchase material or to commence production before first article approval, the contracting officer shall use the clause with its Alternate II.

(b) (1) The contracting officer shall insert a clause substantially the same as the clause at 52.209-3, First Article Approval—Contractor Testing, in solicitations and contracts when a cost-reimbursement contract is contemplated and it is intended that the contract require—

(i) First article approval; and

(ii) That the contractor be required to conduct the first article test.

(2) If it is intended that the contractor be required to produce the first article and the production quantity at the same facility, the contracting officer shall use a clause substantially the same as the clause at 52.209-3, First Article Approval—Contractor Testing, with its Alternate I.

(3) If it is necessary to authorize the contractor to purchase material or to commence production before first article approval, the contracting officer shall use a clause substantially the same as the clause at 52.209-3, First Article Approval—Contractor Testing, with its Alternate II.

[FAC 2019-02, 84 FR 19839, 5/6/2019, effective 5/6/2019]

9.308-2 Testing performed by the Government.

(a) (1) The contracting officer shall insert the clause at 52.209-4, First Article Approval—Government Testing, in solicitations and contracts when a fixed-price contract is contemplated and it is intended that the contract require first article approval and that the Government will be responsible for conducting the first article test.

(2) If it is intended that the contractor be required to produce the first article and the production quantity at the same facility, the contracting officer shall use the basic clause with its Alternate I.

(3) If it is necessary to authorize the contractor to purchase material or to commence production before first article approval, the contracting officer shall use the basic clause with its Alternate II.

(b) (1) The contracting officer shall insert a clause substantially the same as the clause at 52.209-4, First Article Approval—Government Testing, in solicitations and contracts when a cost-reimbursement contract is contemplated and it is intended that the contract require first article approval and that the Government be responsible for conducting the first article test.

(2) If it is intended that the contractor be required to produce the first article and the production quantity at the same facility, the contracting officer shall use a clause substantially the same as the clause at 52.209-4, First Article Approval—Government Testing, with its Alternate I.

(3) If it is necessary to authorize the contractor to purchase material or to commence production before first article approval, the contracting officer shall use a clause substantially the same as the clause at 52.209-4, First Article Approval—Government Testing, with its Alternate II.

SUBPART 9.4—DEBARMENT, SUSPENSION, AND INELIGIBILITY

9.400 Scope of subpart.

(a) This subpart—

(1) Prescribes policies and procedures governing the debarment and suspension of contractors by agencies for the causes given in 9.406-2 and 9.407-2;

(2) Provides for the listing of contractors debarred, suspended, proposed for debarment, and declared ineligible (see the definition of *ineligible* in 2.101); and

(3) Sets forth the consequences of this listing.

(b) Although this subpart does cover the listing of ineligible contractors (9.404) and the effect of this listing (9.405(b)), it does not prescribe policies and procedures governing declarations of ineligibility.

[FAC 84-46, 54 FR 19814, 5/8/89, effective 6/7/89; FAC 97-22, 66 FR 2116, 1/10/2001, effective 3/12/2001; Delay of effective date, 66 FR 14259, 3/9/2001, effective 5/11/2001]

9.401 Applicability.

In accordance with Public Law 103-355, Section 2455 (31 U.S.C. 6101, note), and Executive Order 12689, any debarment, suspension or other Governmentwide exclusion initiated under the Nonprocurement Common Rule implementing Executive Order 12549 on or after August 25, 1995, shall be recognized by and effective for Executive Branch agencies as a debarment or suspension under this subpart. Similarly, any debarment, suspension, proposed debarment or other Governmentwide exclusion initiated on or after August 25, 1995, under this subpart shall also be recognized by and effective for those agencies and participants as an exclusion under the Nonprocurement Common Rule.

[FAC 90-28, 60 FR 33064, 6/26/95, effective 8/25/95; FAC 2019-02, 84 FR 19839, 5/6/2019, effective 5/6/2019]

9.402 Policy.

(a) Agencies shall solicit offers from, award contracts to, and consent to subcontracts with responsible contractors only. Debarment and suspension are discretionary actions that, taken in accordance with this subpart, are appropriate means to effectuate this policy.

(b) The serious nature of debarment and suspension requires that these sanctions be imposed only in the public interest for the Government's protection and not for purposes of punishment. Agencies shall impose debarment or suspension to protect the Government's interest and only for the causes and in accordance with the procedures set forth in this subpart.

(c) Agencies are encouraged to establish methods and procedures for coordinating their debarment or suspension actions.

(d) When more than one agency has an interest in the debarment or suspension of a contractor, the Interagency Committee on Debarment and Suspension, established under Executive Order 12549, and authorized by Section 873 of the National Defense Authorization Act for Fiscal Year 2009 (Pub. L. 110-417) (31 U.S.C. 6101 note), shall resolve the lead agency issue and coordinate such resolution among all interested agencies prior to the initiation of any suspension, debarment, or related administrative action by any agency.

(e) Agencies shall establish appropriate procedures to implement the policies and procedures of this subpart.

[FAC 84-46, 54 FR 19814, 5/8/89, effective 6/7/89; FAC 2005-34, 74 FR 31564, 7/1/2009, effective 7/31/2009; FAC 2005-73, 79 FR 24192, 4/29/2014, effective 5/29/2014]

9.403 Definitions.

As used in this subpart—

Affiliates. (1) Business concerns, organizations, or individuals are affiliates of each other if, directly or indirectly—

(i) Either one controls or has the power to control the other; or

(ii) A third party controls or has the power to control both.

(2) Indicia of control include, but are not limited to, interlocking management or ownership, identity of interests among family members, shared facilities and equipment, common use of employees, or a business entity organized following the debarment, suspension, or proposed debarment of a contractor which has the same or similar management, ownership, or principal employees as the contractor that was debarred, suspended, or proposed for debarment.

Agency means any executive department, military department or defense agency, or other agency or independent establishment of the executive branch.

Civil judgment means a judgment or finding of a civil offense by any court of competent jurisdiction.

Contractor means any individual or other legal entity that—

(1) Directly or indirectly (*e.g.*, through an affiliate), submits offers for or is awarded, or reasonably may be expected to submit offers for or be awarded, a Government contract,

including a contract for carriage under Government or commercial bills of lading, or a subcontract under a Government contract; or

(2) Conducts business, or reasonably may be expected to conduct business, with the Government as an agent or representative of another contractor.

Debarring official means—

(1) An agency head; or

(2) A designee authorized by the agency head to impose debarment.

Indictment means indictment for a criminal offense. An information or other filing by competent authority charging a criminal offense is given the same effect as an indictment.

Legal proceedings means any civil judicial proceeding to which the Government is a party or any criminal proceeding. The term includes appeals from such proceedings.

Nonprocurement Common Rule means the procedures used by Federal Executive Agencies to suspend, debar, or exclude individuals or entities from participation in nonprocurement transactions under Executive Order 12549. Examples of nonprocurement transactions are grants, cooperative agreements, scholarships, fellowships, contracts of assistance, loans, loan guarantees, subsidies, insurance, payments for specified use, and donation agreements.

Suspending official means—

(1) An agency head; or

(2) A designee authorized by the agency head to impose suspension.

Unfair trade practices means the commission of any of the following acts by a contractor:

(1) A violation of Section 337 of the Tariff Act of 1930 (19 U.S.C. 1337) as determined by the International Trade Commission.

(2) A violation, as determined by the Secretary of Commerce, of any agreement of the group known as the "Coordination Committee" for purposes of the Export Administration Act of 1979 (50 U.S.C. App. 2401, *et seq.*) or any similar bilateral or multilateral export control agreement.

(3) A knowingly false statement regarding a material element of a certification concerning the foreign content of an item of supply, as determined by the Secretary of the Department or the head of the agency to which such certificate was furnished.

[FAC 84-46, 54 FR 19814, 5/8/89, effective 6/7/89; FAC 90-4, 56 FR 15149, 4/15/91, effective 5/15/91; Interim rule, FAC 90-20, 59 FR 11368, 3/10/94, effective 3/10/94, finalized without change, FAC 90-37, 61 FR 2626, 1/26/96, effective date 1/26/96; FAC 90-28, 60 FR 33064, 6/26/95, effective 8/25/95; FAC 97-22, 66 FR 2116, 1/10/2001, effective 3/12/2001; Delay of effective date, 66 FR 14259, 3/9/2001, effective 5/11/2001; FAC 2019-02, 84 FR 19839, 5/6/2019, effective 5/6/2019]

9.404 Exclusions in the System for Award Management.

(a) The General Services Administration (GSA)—

(1) Operates the web-based System for Award Management (SAM), which contains exclusion records; and

(2) Provides technical assistance to Federal agencies in the use of SAM.

(b) An exclusion record in SAM contains the—

(1) Names and addresses of the entities debarred, suspended, proposed for debarment, declared ineligible, or excluded or disqualified under the nonprocurement common rule, with cross-references when more than one name is involved in a single action;

(2) Name of the agency or other authority taking the action;

(3) Cause for the action (see 9.406-2 and 9.407-2 for causes authorized under this subpart) or other statutory or regulatory authority;

(4) Effect of the action;

(5) Termination date for each listing;

(6) Unique Entity Identifier;

(7) Social Security Number (SSN), Employer Identification Number (EIN), or other Taxpayer Identification Number (TIN), if available; and

(8) Name and telephone number of the agency point of contact for the action.

(c) Each agency shall—

(1) Identify the individual(s) responsible for entering and updating exclusions data in SAM and assign the appropriate roles;

(2) Remove the exclusion roles in SAM when the individual leaves the organization or changes functions;

(3) For each exclusion accomplished by the Agency—

(i) Enter the information required by paragraph (b) of this section within 3 working days after the action becomes effective;

(ii) Determine whether it is legally permitted to enter the SSN, EIN, or other TIN, under agency authority to suspend or debar; and

(iii) Update the exclusion record in SAM, generally within 5 working days after modifying or rescinding an action;

(4) In accordance with internal retention procedures, maintain records relating to each debarment, suspension, or proposed debarment taken by the agency;

(5) Establish procedures to ensure that the agency does not solicit offers from, award contracts to, or consent to subcontracts with contractors who have an active exclusion record in SAM, except as otherwise provided in this subpart;

(6) Direct inquiries concerning listed contractors and other entities to the agency or other authority that took the action; and

(7) Contact GSA for technical assistance with SAM, via the support email address or on the technical support phone line.

(d) SAM is available via *https://www.sam.gov*.

[FAC 97-16, 65 FR 16274, 3/27/2000, effective 3/27/2000; FAC 2001-26, 69 FR 76347, 12/20/2004, effective 1/19/2005; FAC 2005-40, 75 FR 14059, 3/23/2010, effective 4/22/2010; FAC 2005-55, 77 FR 187, 1/3/2012, effective 2/2/2012; FAC 2005-67, 78 FR 37676, 6/21/2013, effective 7/22/2013; FAC 2005-91, 81 FR 67736, 9/30/2016, effective 10/31/2016; FAC 2005-101, 83 FR 48691, 9/26/2018, effective 10/26/2018]

9.405 Effect of listing.

(a) Contractors debarred, suspended, or proposed for debarment are excluded from receiving contracts, and agencies shall not solicit offers from, award contracts to, or consent to subcontracts with these contractors, unless the agency head determines that there is a compelling reason for such action (see 9.405-1(b), 9.405-2, 9.406-1(c), 9.407-1(d), and 23.506(e)). Contractors debarred, suspended, or proposed for debarment are also excluded from conducting business with the Government as agents or representatives of other contractors.

(b) Contractors and other entities that have an active exclusion record in SAM because they have been declared ineligible on the basis of statutory or other regulatory procedures are excluded from receiving contracts, and if applicable, subcontracts, under the conditions and for the period set forth in the statute or regulation. Agencies shall not solicit offers from, award contracts to, or consent to subcontracts with these contractors under those conditions and for that period. In addition, agencies shall not extend contracts with contractors that have been declared ineligible pursuant to 22 U.S.C. 2593e.

(c) Contractors debarred, suspended, or proposed for debarment are excluded from acting as individual sureties (see Part 28).

(d) (1) After the opening of bids or receipt of proposals or quotes, the contracting officer shall review the exclusion records in SAM.

(2) Bids received from any listed contractor in response to an invitation for bids shall be entered on the abstract of bids, and rejected unless the agency head determines in writing that there is a compelling reason to consider the bid.

(3) Proposals, quotations, or offers received from any listed contractor shall not be evaluated for award or included in the competitive range, nor shall discussions be conducted with a listed offeror during a period of ineligibility, unless the agency head determines, in writing, that there is a com-

pelling reason to do so. If the period of ineligibility expires or is terminated prior to award, the contracting officer may, but is not required to, consider such proposals, quotations, or offers.

(4) Immediately prior to award, the contracting officer shall again review the exclusion records in SAM to ensure that no award is made to a listed contractor.

[FAC 84-25, 52 FR 9038, 3/20/87, effective 7/1/87; Interim rule, FAC 84-43, 54 FR 4968, 1/31/89, effective 3/18/89 for contracts issued on or after that date; FAC 84-46, 54 FR 19315, 5/8/89, effective 6/7/89; FAC 84-53, 54 FR 48982, 11/28/89, effective 2/26/90; FAC 84-57, 55 FR 21707, 5/25/90, effective 7/24/90; FAC 90-5, 56 FR 29127, 6/25/91, effective 7/25/91; FAC 90-23, 59 FR 67010, 12/28/94, effective 2/27/95; FAC 90-28, 60 FR 33064, 6/26/95, effective 8/25/95; FAC 97-16, 65 FR 16274, 3/27/2000, effective 3/27/2000; FAC 2001-18, 68 FR 69250, 12/11/2003; effective 1/12/2004; FAC 2001-26, 69 FR 76347, 12/20/2004, effective 1/19/2005; FAC 2005-67, 78 FR 37676, 6/21/2013, effective 7/22/2013; FAC 2005-99, 83 FR 28145, 6/15/2018, effective 6/15/2018; FAC 2005-101, 83 FR 48691, 9/26/2018, effective 10/26/2018]

9.405-1 Continuation of current contracts.

(a) Notwithstanding the debarment, suspension, or proposed debarment of a contractor, agencies may continue contracts or subcontracts in existence at the time the contractor was debarred, suspended, or proposed for debarment unless the agency head directs otherwise. A decision as to the type of termination action, if any, to be taken should be made only after review by agency contracting and technical personnel and by counsel to ensure the propriety of the proposed action.

(b) For contractors debarred, suspended, or proposed for debarment, unless the agency head makes a written determination of the compelling reasons for doing so, ordering activities shall not—

(1) Place orders exceeding the guaranteed minimum under indefinite quantity contracts;

(2) Place orders under Federal Supply Schedule contracts, blanket purchase agreements, or basic ordering agreements; or

(3) Add new work, exercise options, or otherwise extend the duration of current contracts or orders.

[FAC 84-46, 54 FR 19315, 5/8/89, effective 6/7/89; FAC 90-23, 59 FR 67010, 12/28/94, effective 2/27/95; FAC 2001-18, 68 FR 69250, 12/11/2003, effective 1/12/2004; FAC 2005-72, 78 FR 80376, 12/31/2013, effective 1/30/2014]

9.405-2 Restrictions on subcontracting.

(a) When a contractor debarred, suspended, or proposed for debarment is proposed as a subcontractor for any subcontract subject to Government consent (see Subpart 44.2), contracting officers shall not consent to subcontracts with such contractors unless the agency head states in writing the compelling reasons for this approval action. (See 9.405(b) concerning declarations of ineligibility affecting subcontracting.)

(b) The Government suspends or debars contractors to protect the Government's interests. By operation of the clause at 52.209-6, Protecting the Government's Interests When Subcontracting with Contractors Debarred, Suspended or Proposed for Debarment, contractors shall not enter into any subcontract in excess of $35,000, other than a subcontract for a commercially available off-the-shelf item, with a contractor that has been debarred, suspended, or proposed for debarment unless there is a compelling reason to do so. If a contractor intends to enter into a subcontract in excess of $35,000, other than a subcontract for a commercially available off-the-shelf item, with a party that is debarred, suspended, or proposed for debarment as evidenced by the party's having an active exclusion record in SAM (*see* 9.404), a corporate officer or designee of the contractor is required by operation of the clause at 52.209-6, Protecting the Government's Interests when Subcontracting with Contractors Debarred, Suspended, or Proposed for Debarment, to notify the contracting officer, in writing, before entering into such subcontract. For contracts for the acquisition of commercial items, the notification requirement applies only for first-tier subcontracts. For all other contracts, the notification requirement applies to subcontracts at any tier. The notice must provide the following:

(1) The name of the subcontractor;

(2) The contractor's knowledge of the reasons for the subcontractor's having an active exclusion record in SAM;

(3) The compelling reason(s) for doing business with the subcontractor notwithstanding its inclusion in having an active exclusion record in SAM; and

(4) The systems and procedures the contractor has established to ensure that it is fully protecting the Government's interests when dealing with such subcontractor in view of the specific basis for the party's debarment, suspension, or proposed debarment.

(c) The contractor's compliance with the requirements of 52.209-6will be reviewed during Contractor Purchasing System Reviews (see Subpart 44.3).

[FAC 84-46, 54 FR 19315, 5/8/89, effective 6/7/89; FAC 90-5, 56 FR 29127, 6/25/91, effective 7/25/91; FAC 90-23, 59 FR 67010, 12/28/94, effective 2/27/95; FAC 90-29, 60 FR 34732, 7/3/95, effective 7/3/95; FAC 90-28, 60 FR 33064, 6/26/95, effective 8/25/95; FAC 90-32, 60 FR 48206, 9/18/95, effective 10/1/95; FAC 2001-18, 68 FR 69250, 12/11/2003, effective 1/12/2004; FAC 2001-26, 69 FR 76347, 12/20/2004, effective 1/19/2005; FAC 2005-13, 71 FR 57363, 9/28/2006, effective 9/28/2006; FAC 2005-47, 75 FR 77739, 12/13/2010, effective 12/13/2010; FAC 2005-53, 76 FR 39236, 7/5/2011, effective 8/4/2011; FAC 2005-67, 78 FR 37676, 6/21/2013, effective 7/22/2013; FAC 2005-83, 80 FR 38293, 7/2/2015, effective 10/1/2015; FAC 2005-101, 83 FR 48691, 9/26/2018, effective 10/26/2018]

9.406 Debarment. (No Text)

9.406-1 General.

(a) It is the debarring official's responsibility to determine whether debarment is in the Government's interest. The debarring official may, in the public interest, debar a contractor for any of the causes in 9.406-2, using the procedures in 9.406-3. The existence of a cause for debarment, however, does not necessarily require that the contractor be debarred; the seriousness of the contractor's acts or omissions and any remedial measures or mitigating factors should be considered in making any debarment decision. Before arriving at any debarment decision, the debarring official should consider factors such as the following:

(1) Whether the contractor had effective standards of conduct and internal control systems in place at the time of the activity which constitutes cause for debarment or had adopted such procedures prior to any Government investigation of the activity cited as a cause for debarment.

(2) Whether the contractor brought the activity cited as a cause for debarment to the attention of the appropriate Government agency in a timely manner.

(3) Whether the contractor has fully investigated the circumstances surrounding the cause for debarment and, if so, made the result of the investigation available to the debarring official.

(4) Whether the contractor cooperated fully with Government agencies during the investigation and any court or administrative action.

(5) Whether the contractor has paid or has agreed to pay all criminal, civil, and administrative liability for the improper activity, including any investigative or administrative costs incurred by the Government, and has made or agreed to make full restitution.

(6) Whether the contractor has taken appropriate disciplinary action against the individuals responsible for the activity which constitutes cause for debarment.

(7) Whether the contractor has implemented or agreed to implement remedial measures, including any identified by the Government.

(8) Whether the contractor has instituted or agreed to institute new or revised review and control procedures and ethics training programs.

(9) Whether the contractor has had adequate time to eliminate the circumstances within the contractor's organization that led to the cause for debarment.

(10) Whether the contractor's management recognizes and understands the seriousness of the misconduct giving rise to the cause for debarment and has implemented programs to prevent recurrence.

The existence or nonexistence of any mitigating factors or remedial measures such as set forth in this paragraph (a) is not necessarily determinative of a contractor's present responsibility. Accordingly, if a cause for debarment exists, the contractor has the burden of demonstrating, to the satisfaction of the debarring official, its present responsibility and that debarment is not necessary.

(b) Debarment constitutes debarment of all divisions or other organizational elements of the contractor, unless the debarment decision is limited by its terms to specific divisions, organizational elements, or commodities. The debarring official may extend the debarment decision to include any affiliates of the contractor if they are—

(1) Specifically named; and

(2) Given written notice of the proposed debarment and an opportunity to respond (see 9.406-3(c)).

(c) A contractor's debarment, or proposed debarment, shall be effective throughout the executive branch of the Government, unless the agency head or a designee (except see 23.506(e)) states in writing the compelling reasons justifying continued business dealings between that agency and the contractor.

(d) (1) When the debarring official has authority to debar contractors from both acquisition contracts pursuant to this regulation and contracts for the purchase of Federal personal property pursuant to the Federal Property Management Regulations (FPMR) 101-45.6, that official shall consider simultaneously debarring the contractor from the award of acquisition contracts and from the purchase of Federal personal property.

(2) When debarring a contractor from the award of acquisition contracts and from the purchase of Federal personal property, the debarment notice shall so indicate and the appropriate FAR and FPMR citations shall be included.

[FAC 84-24, 52 FR 6122, 2/27/87, effective 2/6/87; Interim rule, FAC 84-43, 54 FR 4968, 1/31/89, effective 3/18/89 for contracts issued on or after that date; FAC 84-46, 54 FR 19315, 5/8/89, effective 6/7/89; FAC 84-57, 55 FR 21707, 5/25/90, effective 7/24/90, corrected, 55 FR 30465, 7/26/90; FAC 90-9, 56 FR 67129, 12/27/91, effective 2/25/92; FAC 90-23, 59 FR 67010, 12/28/94, effective 2/27/95; FAC 2019-02, 84 FR 19839, 5/6/2019, effective 5/6/2019]

9.406-2 Causes for debarment.

The debarring official may debar—

(a) A contractor for a conviction of or civil judgment for—

(1) Commission of fraud or a criminal offense in connection with—

(i) Obtaining;

(ii) Attempting to obtain; or

(iii) Performing a public contract or subcontract;

(2) Violation of Federal or State antitrust statutes relating to the submission of offers;

(3) Commission of embezzlement, theft, forgery, bribery, falsification or destruction of records, making false statements, tax evasion, violating Federal criminal tax laws, or receiving stolen property;

(4) Intentionally affixing a label bearing a "Made in America" inscription (or any inscription having the same meaning) to a product sold in or shipped to the United States or its outlying areas, when the product was not made in the United States or its outlying areas (see Section 202 of the Defense Production Act (Public Law 102-558)); or

(5) Commission of any other offense indicating a lack of business integrity or business honesty that seriously and directly affects the present responsibility of a Government contractor or subcontractor.

(b) (1) A contractor, based upon a preponderance of the evidence, for any of the following—

(i) Violation of the terms of a Government contract or subcontract so serious as to justify debarment, such as—

(A) Willful failure to perform in accordance with the terms of one or more contracts; or

(B) A history of failure to perform, or of unsatisfactory performance of, one or more contracts.

(ii) Violations of 41 U.S.C. chapter 81, Drug-Free Workplace, as indicated by—

(A) Failure to comply with the requirements of the clause at 52.223-6, Drug-Free Workplace; or

(B) Such a number of contractor employees convicted of violations of criminal drug statutes occurring in the workplace as to indicate that the contractor has failed to make a good faith effort to provide a drug-free workplace (see 23.504).

(iii) Intentionally affixing a label bearing a "Made in America" inscription (or any inscription having the same meaning) to a product sold in or shipped to the United States or its outlying areas, when the product was not made in the United States or its outlying areas (see Section 202 of the Defense Production Act (Public Law 102-558)).

(iv) Commission of an unfair trade practice as defined in 9.403(see Section 201 of the Defense Production Act (Pub. L. 102-558)).

(v) Delinquent Federal taxes in an amount that exceeds $3,500.

(A) Federal taxes are considered delinquent for purposes of this provision if both of the following criteria apply:

(1) The tax liability is finally determined. The liability is finally determined if it has been assessed. A liability is not finally determined if there is a pending administrative or judicial challenge. In the case of a judicial challenge to the liability, the liability is not finally determined until all judicial appeal rights have been exhausted.

(2) The taxpayer is delinquent in making payment. A taxpayer is delinquent if the taxpayer has failed to pay the tax liability when full payment was due and required. A taxpayer is not delinquent in cases where enforced collection action is precluded.

(B) *Examples.* (1) The taxpayer has received a statutory notice of deficiency, under I.R.C. Sec. 6212, which entitles the taxpayer to seek Tax Court review of a proposed tax deficiency. This is not a delinquent tax because it is not a final tax liability. Should the taxpayer seek Tax Court review, this will not be a final tax liability until the taxpayer has exercised all judicial appeal rights.

(2) The IRS has filed a notice of Federal tax lien with respect to an assessed tax liability, and the taxpayer has been issued a notice under I.R.C. Sec. 6320 entitling the taxpayer to request a hearing with the IRS Office of Appeals contesting the lien filing, and to further appeal to the Tax Court if the IRS determines to sustain the lien filing. In the course of the hearing, the taxpayer is entitled to contest the underlying tax liability because the taxpayer has had no prior opportunity to contest the liability. This is not a delinquent tax because it is not a final tax liability. Should the taxpayer seek tax court review, this will not be a final tax liability until the taxpayer has exercised all judicial appeal rights.

(3) *The taxpayer has entered into an installment agreement pursuant to I.R.C. Sec. 6159.* The taxpayer is making timely payments and is in full compliance with the agreement terms. The taxpayer is not delinquent because the taxpayer is not currently required to make full payment.

(4) *The taxpayer has filed for bankruptcy protection.* The taxpayer is not delinquent because enforced collection action is stayed under 11 U.S.C. 362 (the Bankruptcy Code).

(vi) Knowing failure by a principal, until 3 years after final payment on any Government contract awarded to the contractor, to timely disclose to the Government, in connection with the award, performance, or closeout of the contract or a subcontract thereunder, credible evidence of—

(A) Violation of Federal criminal law involving fraud, conflict of interest, bribery, or gratuity violations found in Title 18 of the United States Code;

(B) Violation of the civil False Claims Act (31 U.S.C. 3729-3733); or

(C) Significant overpayment(s) on the contract, other than overpayments resulting from contract financing payments as defined in 32.001.

(2) A contractor, based on a determination by the Secretary of Homeland Security or the Attorney General of the United States, that the contractor is not in compliance with Immigration and Nationality Act employment provisions (see Executive Order 12989, as amended by Executive Order 13286). Such determination is not reviewable in the debarment proceedings.

(c) A contractor or subcontractor based on any other cause of so serious or compelling a nature that it affects the present responsibility of the contractor or subcontractor.

[Interim rule, FAC 84-43, 54 FR 4968, 1/31/89, effective 3/18/89 for contracts issued on or after that date; FAC 84-46, 54 FR 19315, 5/8/89, effective 6/7/89; FAC 84-57, 55 FR 21707, 5/25/90, effective 7/24/90; Interim rule, FAC 90-20, 59 FR 11368, 3/10/94, effective 3/10/94, finalized without change, FAC 90-37, 61 FR 2626, 1/26/96, effective date 1/26/96; FAC 90-37, 61 FR 2626, 1/26/96, effective 3/26/96; FAC 90-41, 61 FR 41466, 8/8/96, effective 8/8/96, finalized without change, FAC 90-45, 62 FR 224, 1/2/97, effective 1/1/97; FAC 90-44, Final rule, 61 FR 69286, 12/31/96, effective 1/1/97; FAC 2001-14, 68 FR 28079, 5/22/2003, effective 6/23/2003; FAC 2001-24, 69 FR 34230, 6/18/2004, effective 6/18/2004; FAC 2005-25, 73 FR 21791, 4/22/2008, effective 5/22/2008; FAC 2005-28, 73 FR 67064, 11/12/2008, effective 12/12/2008; FAC 2005-73, 79 FR 24192, 4/29/2014, effective 5/29/2014; FAC 2005-83, 80 FR 38293, 7/2/2015, effective 10/1/2015; FAC 2019-02, 84 FR 19839, 5/6/2019, effective 5/6/2019]

9.406-3 Procedures.

(a) *Investigation and referral*. Agencies shall establish procedures for the prompt reporting, investigation, and referral to the debarring official of matters appropriate for that official's consideration.

(b) *Decisionmaking process*.

(1) Agencies shall establish procedures governing the debarment decisionmaking process that are as informal as is practicable, consistent with principles of fundamental fairness. These procedures shall afford the contractor (and any specifically named affiliates) an opportunity to submit, in person, in writing, or through a representative, information and argument in opposition to the proposed debarment.

(2) In actions not based upon a conviction or civil judgment, if it is found that the contractor's submission in opposition raises a genuine dispute over facts material to the proposed debarment, agencies shall also—

(i) Afford the contractor an opportunity to appear with counsel, submit documentary evidence, present witnesses, and confront any person the agency presents; and

(ii) Make a transcribed record of the proceedings and make it available at cost to the contractor upon request, unless the contractor and the agency, by mutual agreement, waive the requirement for a transcript.

(c) *Notice of proposal to debar*. A notice of proposed debarment shall be issued by the debarring official advising the contractor and any specifically named affiliates, by certified mail, return receipt requested—

(1) That debarment is being considered;

(2) Of the reasons for the proposed debarment in terms sufficient to put the contractor on notice of the conduct or transaction(s) upon which it is based;

(3) Of the cause(s) relied upon under 9.406-2for proposing debarment;

(4) That, within 30 days after receipt of the notice, the contractor may submit, in person, in writing, or through a representative, information and argument in opposition to the proposed debarment, including any additional specific information that raises a genuine dispute over the material facts;

(5) Of the agency's procedures governing debarment decisionmaking;

(6) Of the effect of the issuance of the notice of proposed debarment; and

(7) Of the potential effect of an actual debarment.

(d) *Debarring official's decision.*

(1) In actions based upon a conviction or civil judgment, or in which there is no genuine dispute over material facts, the debarring official shall make a decision on the basis of all the information in the administrative record, including any submission made by the contractor. If no suspension is in effect, the decision shall be made within 30 working days after receipt of any information and argument submitted by the contractor, unless the debarring official extends this period for good cause.

(2) (i) In actions in which additional proceedings are necessary as to disputed material facts, written findings of fact shall be prepared. The debarring official shall base the decision on the facts as found, together with any information and argument submitted by the contractor and any other information in the administrative record.

(ii) The debarring official may refer matters involving disputed material facts to another official for findings of fact. The debarring official may reject any such findings, in whole or in part, only after specifically determining them to be arbitrary and capricious or clearly erroneous.

(iii) The debarring official's decision shall be made after the conclusion of the proceedings with respect to disputed facts.

(3) In any action in which the proposed debarment is not based upon a conviction or civil judgment, the cause for debarment must be established by a preponderance of the evidence.

(e) *Notice of debarring official's decision.* (1) If the debarring official decides to impose debarment, the contractor and any affiliates involved shall be given prompt notice by certified mail, return receipt requested—

(i) Referring to the notice of proposed debarment;

(ii) Specifying the reasons for debarment;

(iii) Stating the period of debarment, including effective dates; and

(iv) Advising that the debarment is effective throughout the executive branch of the Government unless the head of an agency or a designee makes the statement called for by 9.406-1(c).

(2) If debarment is not imposed, the debarring official shall promptly notify the contractor and any affiliates involved, by certified mail, return receipt requested.

(f) (1) If the contractor enters into an administrative agreement with the Government in order to resolve a debarment proceeding, the debarring official shall access the website (available at *https://www.cpars.gov*, then select FAPIIS) and enter the requested information.

(2) The debarring official is responsible for the timely submission, within 3 working days, and accuracy of the documentation regarding the administrative agreement.

(3) With regard to information that may be covered by a disclosure exemption under the Freedom of Information Act, the debarring official shall follow the procedures at 9.105-2(b)(2)(iv).

[FAC 84-46, 54 FR 19815, 5/8/89, effective 6/7/89; FAC 90-23, 59 FR 67010, 12/28/94, effective 2/27/95; FAC 2005-40, 75 FR 14059, 3/23/2010, effective 4/22/2010; FAC 2005-55, 77 FR 197, 1/3/2012, effective 1/3/2012; FAC 2005-100, 83 FR 42571, 8/22/2018, effective 8/22/2018; FAC 2019-02, 84 FR 19839, 5/6/2019, effective 5/6/2019]

9.406-4 Period of debarment.

(a) (1) Debarment shall be for a period commensurate with the seriousness of the cause(s). Generally, debarment should not exceed 3 years, except that—

(i) Debarment for violation of the provisions of 41 U.S.C. chapter 81, Drug-Free Workplace (see 23.506) may be for a period not to exceed 5 years;

(ii) Debarments under 9.406-2(b)(2) shall be for 1 year unless extended pursuant to paragraph (b) of this section; and

(iii) Debarments pursued as a remedy under 9.109-4(d), for a false certification regarding violations of arms control treaties or agreements with the United States, shall be for a period of not less than 2 years.

(2) If suspension precedes a debarment, the suspension period shall be considered in determining the debarment period.

(b) The debarring official may extend the debarment for an additional period, if that official determines that an extension is necessary to protect the Government's interest. However, a debarment may not be extended solely on the basis of the facts and circumstances upon which the initial debarment action was based. Debarments under 9.406-2(b)(2) may be extended for additional periods of one year if the Secretary of Homeland Security or the Attorney General determines that the contractor continues to be in violation of the employment provisions of the Immigration and Nationality Act. If debarment for an additional period is determined to be necessary, the procedures of 9.406-3 shall be followed to extend the debarment.

(c) The debarring official may reduce the period or extent of debarment, upon the contractor's request, supported by documentation, for reasons such as—

(1) Newly discovered material evidence;

(2) Reversal of the conviction or civil judgment upon which the debarment was based;

(3) Bona fide change in ownership or management;

(4) Elimination of other causes for which the debarment was imposed; or

(5) Other reasons the debarring official deems appropriate.

[Interim rule, FAC 84-43, 54 FR 4968, 1/31/89, effective 3/18/89 for contracts issued on or after that date; FAC 84-46, 54 FR 19815, 5/8/89, effective 6/7/89; FAC 84-57, 55 FR 21707, 5/25/90, effective 7/24/90; FAC 90-41, 61 FR 41466, 8/8/96, effective 8/8/96; finalized without change, FAC 90-45, 62 FR 224, 1/2/97, effective 1/1/97; FAC 2001-24, 69 FR 34230, 6/18/2004, effective 6/18/2004; FAC 2005-73, 79 FR 24192, 4/29/2014, effective 5/29/2014; FAC 2005-99, 83 FR 28145, 6/15/2018, effective 6/15/2018; FAC 2019-02, 84 FR 19839, 5/6/2019, effective 5/6/2019]

9.406-5 Scope of debarment.

(a) The fraudulent, criminal, or other seriously improper conduct of any officer, director, shareholder, partner, employee, or other individual associated with a contractor may be imputed to the contractor when the conduct occurred in connection with the individual's performance of duties for or on behalf of the contractor, or with the contractor's knowledge, approval, or acquiescence. The contractor's acceptance of the benefits derived from the conduct shall be evidence of such knowledge, approval, or acquiescence.

(b) The fraudulent, criminal, or other seriously improper conduct of a contractor may be imputed to any officer, director, shareholder, partner, employee, or other individual associated with the contractor who participated in, knew of, or had reason to know of the contractor's conduct.

(c) The fraudulent, criminal, or other seriously improper conduct of one contractor participating in a joint venture or similar arrangement may be imputed to other participating contractors if the conduct occurred for or on behalf of the joint venture or similar arrangement, or with the knowledge, approval, or acquiescence of these contractors. Acceptance of the benefits derived from the conduct shall be evidence of such knowledge, approval, or acquiescence.

9.407 Suspension. (No Text)

9.407-1 General.

(a) The suspending official may, in the public interest, suspend a contractor for any of the causes in 9.407-2, using the procedures in 9.407-3.

(b)(1) Suspension is a serious action to be imposed on the basis of adequate evidence, pending the completion of investigation or legal proceedings, when it has been determined that immediate action is necessary to protect the Government's interest. In assessing the adequacy of the evidence, agencies should consider how much information is available, how credible it is given the circumstances, whether or not important allegations are corroborated, and what inferences can reasonably be drawn as a result. This assessment should include an examination of basic documents such as contracts, inspection reports, and correspondence.

(2) The existence of a cause for suspension does not necessarily require that the contractor be suspended. The suspending official should consider the seriousness of the contractor's acts or omissions and may, but is not required to, consider remedial measures or mitigating factors, such as those set forth in 9.406-1(a). A contractor has the burden of promptly presenting to the suspending official evidence of remedial measures or mitigating factors when it has reason to know that a cause for suspension exists. The existence or nonexistence of any remedial measures or mitigating factors is not necessarily determinative of a contractor's present responsibility.

(c) Suspension constitutes suspension of all divisions or other organizational elements of the contractor, unless the suspension decision is limited by its terms to specific divisions, organizational elements, or commodities. The suspending official may extend the suspension decision to include any affiliates of the contractor if they are—

(1) Specifically named; and

(2) Given written notice of the suspension and an opportunity to respond (see 9.407-3(c)).

(d) A contractor's suspension shall be effective throughout the executive branch of the Government, unless the agency head or a designee (except see 23.506(e)) states in writing the compelling reasons justifying continued business dealings between that agency and the contractor.

(e)(1) When the suspending official has authority to suspend contractors from both acquisition contracts pursuant to this regulation and contracts for the purchase of Federal personal property pursuant to FPMR 101-45.6, that official shall consider simultaneously suspending the contractor from the award of acquisition contracts and from the purchase of Federal personal property.

(2) When suspending a contractor from the award of acquisition contracts and from the purchase of Federal personal property, the suspension notice shall so indicate and the appropriate FAR and FPMR citations shall be included.

[Interim rule, FAC 84-43, 54 FR 4968, 1/31/89, effective 3/18/89 for contracts issued on or after that date; FAC 84-46, 54 FR 19816, 5/8/89, effective 6/7/89; FAC 90-9, 56 FR 67130, 12/27/91, effective 2/25/92; FAC 90-23, 59 FR 67010, 12/28/94, effective 2/27/95; FAC 2019-02, 84 FR 19839, 5/6/2019, effective 5/6/2019]

9.407-2 Causes for suspension.

(a) The suspending official may suspend a contractor suspected, upon adequate evidence, of—

(1) Commission of fraud or a criminal offense in connection with—

(i) Obtaining;

(ii) Attempting to obtain; or

(iii) Performing a public contract or subcontract;

(2) Violation of Federal or State antitrust statutes relating to the submission of offers;

(3) Commission of embezzlement, theft, forgery, bribery, falsification or destruction of records, making false statements, tax evasion, violating Federal criminal tax laws, or receiving stolen property;

(4) Violations of 41 U.S.C. chapter 81, Drug-Free Workplace, as indicated by—

(i) Failure to comply with the requirements of the clause at 52.223-6, Drug-Free Workplace; or

(ii) Such a number of contractor employees convicted of violations of criminal drug statutes occurring in the workplace as to indicate that the contractor has failed to make a good faith effort to provide a drug-free workplace (see 23.504);

(5) Intentionally affixing a label bearing a "Made in America" inscription (or any inscription having the same meaning) to a product sold in or shipped to the United States or its outlying areas, when the product was not made in the United States or its outlying areas (see Section 202 of the Defense Production Act (Public Law 102-558));

(6) Commission of an unfair trade practice as defined in 9.403 (see section 201 of the Defense Production Act (Pub. L. 102-558));

(7) Delinquent Federal taxes in an amount that exceeds $3,500. See the criteria at 9.406-2(b)(1)(v) for determination of when taxes are delinquent;

(8) Knowing failure by a principal, until 3 years after final payment on any Government contract awarded to the contractor, to timely disclose to the Government, in connection with the award, performance, or closeout of the contract or a subcontract thereunder, credible evidence of—

(i) Violation of Federal criminal law involving fraud, conflict of interest, bribery, or gratuity violations found in Title 18 of the United States Code;

(ii) Violation of the civil False Claims Act (31 U.S.C. 3729-3733); or

(iii) Significant overpayment(s) on the contract, other than overpayments resulting from contract financing payments as defined in 32.001; or

(9) Commission of any other offense indicating a lack of business integrity or business honesty that seriously and directly affects the present responsibility of a Government contractor or subcontractor.

(b) Indictment for any of the causes in paragraph (a) of this section constitutes adequate evidence for suspension.

(c) The suspending official may upon adequate evidence also suspend a contractor for any other cause of so serious or compelling a nature that it affects the present responsibility of a Government contractor or subcontractor.

[Interim rule, FAC 84-43, 54 FR 4968, 1/31/89, effective 3/18/89 for contracts issued on or after that date; FAC 84-57, 55 FR 21707, 5/25/90, effective 7/24/90; Interim rule, FAC 90-20, 59 FR 11368, 3/10/94, effective 3/10/94, finalized without change, FAC 90-37, 61 FR 2626, 1/26/96, effective date 1/26/96; FAC 90-37, 61 FR 2626, 1/26/96, effective 3/26/96; FAC 90-44, Final rule, 61 FR 69286, 12/31/96, effective 1/1/97; FAC 2001-14, 68 FR 28079, 5/22/2003, effective 6/23/2003; FAC 2005-25, 73 FR 21791, 4/22/2008, effective 5/22/2008; FAC 2005-28, 73 FR 67064, 11/12/2008, effective 12/12/2008; FAC 2005-73, 79 FR 24192, 4/29/2014, effective 5/29/2014; FAC 2005-83, 80 FR 38293, 7/2/2015, effective 10/1/2015; FAC 2019-02, 84 FR 19839, 5/6/2019, effective 5/6/2019]

9.407-3 Procedures.

(a) *Investigation and referral.* Agencies shall establish procedures for the prompt reporting, investigation, and referral to the suspending official of matters appropriate for that official's consideration.

(b) *Decisionmaking process.* (1) Agencies shall establish procedures governing the suspension decisionmaking process that are as informal as is practicable, consistent with principles of fundamental fairness. These procedures shall afford the contractor (and any specifically named affiliates) an opportunity, following the imposition of suspension, to submit, in person, in writing, or through a representative, information and argument in opposition to the suspension.

(2) In actions not based on an indictment, if it is found that the contractor's submission in opposition raises a genuine dispute over facts material to the suspension and if no determination has been made, on the basis of Department of Justice advice, that substantial interests of the Government in pending or contemplated legal proceedings based on the same facts as the suspension would be prejudiced, agencies shall also—

(i) Afford the contractor an opportunity to appear with counsel, submit documentary evidence, present witnesses, and confront any person the agency presents; and

(ii) Make a transcribed record of the proceedings and make it available at cost to the contractor upon request, unless the contractor and the agency, by mutual agreement, waive the requirement for a transcript.

(c) *Notice of suspension.* When a contractor and any specifically named affiliates are suspended, they shall be immediately advised by certified mail, return receipt requested—

(1) That they have been suspended and that the suspension is based on an indictment or other adequate evidence that the contractor has committed irregularities—

(i) Of a serious nature in business dealings with the Government or

(ii) Seriously reflecting on the propriety of further Government dealings with the contractor—any such irregularities shall be described in terms sufficient to place the contractor on notice without disclosing the Government's evidence;

(2) That the suspension is for a temporary period pending the completion of an investigation and such legal proceedings as may ensue;

(3) Of the cause(s) relied upon under 9.407-2 for imposing suspension;

(4) Of the effect of the suspension;

(5) That, within 30 days after receipt of the notice, the contractor may submit, in person, in writing, or through a representative, information and argument in opposition to the suspension, including any additional specific information that raises a genuine dispute over the material facts; and

(6) That additional proceedings to determine disputed material facts will be conducted unless—

(i) The action is based on an indictment; or

(ii) A determination is made, on the basis of Department of Justice advice, that the substantial interests of the Government in pending or contemplated legal proceedings based on the same facts as the suspension would be prejudiced.

(d) *Suspending official's decision.* (1) In actions—

(i) based on an indictment;

(ii) In which the contractor's submission does not raise a genuine dispute over material facts; or

(iii) In which additional proceedings to determine disputed material facts have been denied on the basis of Department of Justice advice, the suspending official's decision shall be based on all the information in the administrative record, including any submission made by the contractor.

(2) (i) In actions in which additional proceedings are necessary as to disputed material facts, written findings of fact shall be prepared. The suspending official shall base the decision on the facts as found, together with any information and argument submitted by the contractor and any other information in the administrative record.

(ii) The suspending official may refer matters involving disputed material facts to another official for findings of fact. The suspending official may reject any such findings, in whole or in part, only after specifically determining them to be arbitrary and capricious or clearly erroneous.

(iii) The suspending official's decision shall be made after the conclusion of the proceedings with respect to disputed facts.

(3) The suspending official may modify or terminate the suspension or leave it in force (for example, see 9.406-4(c) for the reasons for reducing the period or extent of debarment). However, a decision to modify or terminate the suspension shall be without prejudice to the subsequent imposition of—

(i) suspension by any other agency; or

(ii) debarment by any agency.

(4) Prompt written notice of the suspending official's decision shall be sent to the contractor and any affiliates involved, by certified mail, return receipt requested.

(e) (1) If the contractor enters into an administrative agreement with the Government in order to resolve a suspension proceeding, the suspending official shall access the website (available at *https://www.cpars.gov*, then select FAPIIS) and enter the requested information.

(2) The suspending official is responsible for the timely submission, within 3 working days, and accuracy of the documentation regarding the administrative agreement.

(3) With regard to information that may be covered by a disclosure exemption under the Freedom of Information Act, the suspending official shall follow the procedures at 9.105-2(b)(2)(iv).

[FAC 84-12, 51 FR 2649, 1/17/86, effective 1/20/86; FAC 2005-40, 75 FR 14059, 3/23/2010, effective 4/22/2010; FAC 2005-55, 77 FR 197, 1/3/2012, effective 1/3/2012; FAC 2005-100, 83 FR 42571, 8/22/2018, effective 8/22/2018]

9.407-4 Period of suspension.

(a) Suspension shall be for a temporary period pending the completion of investigation and any ensuing legal proceedings, unless sooner terminated by the suspending official or as provided in this subsection.

(b) If legal proceedings are not initiated within 12 months after the date of the suspension notice, the suspension shall be terminated unless an Assistant Attorney General requests its extension, in which case it may be extended for an additional 6 months. In no event may a suspension extend beyond 18 months, unless legal proceedings have been initiated within that period.

(c) The suspending official shall notify the Department of Justice of the proposed termination of the suspension, at least 30 days before the 12-month period expires, to give that Department an opportunity to request an extension.

[FAC 84-12, 51 FR 2649, 1/17/86, effective 1/20/86]

9.407-5 Scope of suspension.

The scope of suspension shall be the same as that for debarment (see 9.406-5), except that the procedures of 9.407-3 shall be used in imposing suspension.

9.408 [Removed and Reserved]

[FAC 84-46, 54 FR 19816, 5/8/89, effective 6/7/89; FAC 2005-25, 73 FR 21791, 4/22/2008, effective 5/22/2008]

9.409 Contract clause.

The contracting officer shall insert the clause at 52.209-6, Protecting the Government's Interests when Subcontracting with Contractors Debarred, Suspended, or Proposed for Debarment, in solicitations and contracts where the contract value exceeds $35,000.

[FAC 90-29, 60 FR 34732, 7/3/95, effective 7/3/95; FAC 2005-13, 71 FR 57363, 9/28/2006, effective 9/28/2006; FAC 2005-25, 73 FR 21791, 4/22/2008, effective 5/22/2008; FAC 2005-83, 80 FR 38293, 7/2/2015, effective 10/1/2015]

SUBPART 9.5—ORGANIZATIONAL AND CONSULTANT CONFLICTS OF INTEREST

9.500 Scope of subpart.

This subpart—

(a) Prescribes responsibilities, general rules, and procedures for identifying, evaluating, and resolving organizational conflicts of interest;

(b) Provides examples to assist contracting officers in applying these rules and procedures to individual contracting situations; and

(c) Implements section 8141 of the 1989 Department of Defense Appropriation Act, Pub. L. 100-463, 102 Stat. 2270-47 (1988).

[FAC 90-1, 55 FR 42685, 10/22/90, effective 10/22/90; FAC 97-18, 65 FR 36014, 6/6/2000, effective 6/6/2000]

9.501 Definition.

Marketing consultant, as used in this subpart, means any independent contractor who furnishes advice, information, direction, or assistance to an offeror or any other contractor in support of the preparation or submission of an offer for a Government contract by that offeror. An independent contractor is not a marketing consultant when rendering—

(1) Services excluded in Subpart 37.2;

(2) Routine engineering and technical services (such as installation, operation, or maintenance of systems, equipment, software, components, or facilities);

(3) Routine legal, actuarial, auditing, and accounting services; and

(4) Training services.

[FAC 90-1, 55 FR 42685, 10/22/90, effective 10/22/90; FAC 97-22, 66 FR 2116, 1/10/2001, effective 3/12/2001; Delay of effective date, 66 FR 14259, 3/9/2001, effective 5/11/2001]

9.502 Applicability.

(a) This subpart applies to contracts with either profit or nonprofit organizations, including nonprofit organizations created largely or wholly with Government funds.

(b) The applicability of this subpart is not limited to any particular kind of acquisition. However, organizational conflicts of interest are more likely to occur in contracts involving—

(1) Management support services;

(2) Consultant or other professional services;

(3) Contractor performance of or assistance in technical evaluations; or

(4) Systems engineering and technical direction work performed by a contractor that does not have overall contractual responsibility for development or production.

(c) An organizational conflict of interest may result when factors create an actual or potential conflict of interest on an instant contract, or when the nature of the work to be performed on the instant contract creates an actual or potential conflict of interest on a future acquisition. In the latter case, some restrictions on future activities of the contractor may be required.

(d) Acquisitions subject to unique agency organizational conflict of interest statutes are excluded from the requirements of this subpart.

[FAC 90-8, 56 FR 55377, 10/25/91, effective 11/25/91; FAC 2019-02, 84 FR 19839, 5/6/2019, effective 5/6/2019]

9.503 Waiver.

The agency head or a designee may waive any general rule or procedure of this subpart by determining that its application in a particular situation would not be in the Government's interest. Any request for waiver must be in writing, shall set forth the extent of the conflict, and requires approval by the agency head or a designee. Agency heads shall not delegate waiver authority below the level of head of a contracting activity.

9.504 Contracting officer responsibilities.

(a) Using the general rules, procedures, and examples in this subpart, contracting officers shall analyze planned acquisitions in order to—

(1) Identify and evaluate potential organizational conflicts of interest as early in the acquisition process as possible; and

(2) Avoid, neutralize, or mitigate significant potential conflicts before contract award.

(b) Contracting officers should obtain the advice of counsel and the assistance of appropriate technical specialists in evaluating potential conflicts and in developing any necessary solicitation provisions and contract clauses (see 9.506).

(c) Before issuing a solicitation for a contract that may involve a significant potential conflict, the contracting officer shall recommend to the head of the contracting activity a course of action for resolving the conflict (see 9.506).

(d) In fulfilling their responsibilities for identifying and resolving potential conflicts, contracting officers should avoid creating unnecessary delays, burdensome information requirements, and excessive documentation. The contracting officer's judgment need be formally documented only when a substantive issue concerning potential organizational conflict of interest exists.

(e) The contracting officer shall award the contract to the apparent successful offeror unless a conflict of interest is determined to exist that cannot be avoided or mitigated. Before determining to withhold award based on conflict of interest considerations, the contracting officer shall notify the contractor, provide the reasons therefor, and allow the contractor a reasonable opportunity to respond. If the contracting officer finds that it is in the best interest of the United States to award the contract notwithstanding a conflict of interest, a request for waiver shall be submitted in accordance with 9.503. The waiver request and decision shall be included in the contract file.

[FAC 90-1, 55 FR 42686, 10/22/90, effective 10/22/90; FAC 90-8, 56 FR 55377, 10/25/91, effective 11/25/91]

9.505 General rules.

The general rules in 9.505-1 through 9.505-4 prescribe limitations on contracting as the means of avoiding, neutralizing, or mitigating organizational conflicts of interest that might otherwise exist in the stated situations. Some illustrative examples are provided in 9.508. Conflicts may arise in situations not expressly covered in this section 9.505 or in the examples in 9.508. Each individual contracting situation should be examined on the basis of its particular facts and the nature of the proposed contract. The exercise of common sense, good judgment, and sound discretion is required in both the decision on whether a significant potential conflict exists and, if it does, the development of an appropriate means for resolving it. The two underlying principles are—

(a) Preventing the existence of conflicting roles that might bias a contractor's judgment; and

(b) Preventing unfair competitive advantage. In addition to the other situations described in this subpart, an unfair competitive advantage exists where a contractor competing for award of any Federal contract possesses—

(1) Proprietary information (that was obtained from a Government official without proper authorization; or

(2) Source selection information (as defined in 2.101) that is relevant to the contract but is not available to all competitors, and such information would assist that contractor in obtaining the contract.

[FAC 90-1, 55 FR 42686, 10/22/90, effective 10/22/90; FAC 90-8, 56 FR 55377, 10/25/91, effective 11/25/91; FAC 90-45, Final rule, 62 FR 224, 1/2/97, effective 1/1/97; FAC 97-12, 64 FR 32740, 6/17/99, effective 6/17/99; FAC 2001-06, 67 FR 13048, 3/20/2002, effective 4/4/2002; FAC 2019-02, 84 FR 19839, 5/6/2019, effective 5/6/2019]

9.505-1 Providing systems engineering and technical direction.

(a) A contractor that provides systems engineering and technical direction for a system but does not have overall contractual responsibility for its development, its integration, assembly, and checkout, or its production shall not—

(1) Be awarded a contract to supply the system or any of its major components; or

(2) Be a subcontractor or consultant to a supplier of the system or any of its major components.

(b) Systems engineering includes a combination of substantially all of the following activities: determining specifications, identifying and resolving interface problems, developing test requirements, evaluating test data, and supervising design. Technical direction includes a combination of substantially all of the following activities: developing work statements, determining parameters, directing other contractors' operations, and resolving technical controversies. In performing these activities, a contractor occupies a highly influential and responsible position in determining a system's basic concepts and supervising their execution by other contractors. Therefore this contractor should not be in a position to make decisions favoring its own products or capabilities.

[FAC 2019-02, 84 FR 19839, 5/6/2019, effective 5/6/2019]

9.505-2 Preparing specifications or work statements.

(a) (1) If a contractor prepares and furnishes complete specifications covering nondevelopmental items, to be used in a competitive acquisition, that contractor shall not be allowed to furnish these items, either as a prime contractor or as a subcontractor, for a reasonable period of time including, at least, the duration of the initial production contract. The restriction in this paragraph (a) (1) shall not apply to—

(i) Contractors that furnish at Government request specifications or data regarding a product they provide, even though the specifications or data may have been paid for separately or in the price of the product; or

(ii) Situations in which contractors, acting as industry representatives, help Government agencies prepare, refine, or coordinate specifications, regardless of source, provided this assistance is supervised and controlled by Government representatives.

(2) If a single contractor drafts complete specifications for nondevelopmental equipment, it should be eliminated for a reasonable time from competition for production

based on the specifications. This should be done in order to avoid a situation in which the contractor could draft specifications favoring its own products or capabilities. In this way the Government can be assured of getting unbiased advice as to the content of the specifications and can avoid allegations of favoritism in the award of production contracts.

(3) In development work, it is normal to select firms that have done the most advanced work in the field. These firms can be expected to design and develop around their own prior knowledge. Development contractors can frequently start production earlier and more knowledgeably than firms that did not participate in the development, and this can affect the time and quality of production, both of which are important to the Government. In many instances the Government may have financed the development. Thus, while the development contractor has a competitive advantage, it is an unavoidable one that is not considered unfair; hence no prohibition should be imposed.

(b) (1) If a contractor prepares, or assists in preparing, a work statement to be used in competitively acquiring a system or services—or provides material leading directly, predictably, and without delay to such a work statement—that contractor may not supply the system, major components of the system, or the services unless—

(i) It is the sole source;

(ii) It has participated in the development and design work; or

(iii) More than one contractor has been involved in preparing the work statement.

(2) Agencies should normally prepare their own work statements. When contractor assistance is necessary, the contractor might often be in a position to favor its own products or capabilities. To overcome the possibility of bias, contractors are prohibited from supplying a system or services acquired on the basis of work statements growing out of their services, unless excepted in paragraph (b)(1) of this section.

(3) For the reasons given in paragraph (a)(3) of this section, no prohibitions are imposed on development and design contractors.

[FAC 2019-02, 84 FR 19839, 5/6/2019, effective 5/6/2019]

9.505-3 Providing evaluation services.

Contracts for the evaluation of offers for products or services shall not be awarded to a contractor that will evaluate its own offers for products or services, or those of a competitor, without proper safeguards to ensure objectivity to protect the Government's interests.

[FAC 90-46, 62 FR 12690, 3/17/97, effective 5/16/97]

9.505-4 Obtaining access to proprietary information.

(a) When a contractor requires proprietary information from others to perform a Government contract and can use the leverage of the contract to obtain it, the contractor may gain an unfair competitive advantage unless restrictions are imposed. These restrictions protect the information and encourage companies to provide it when necessary for contract performance. They are not intended to protect information—

(1) Furnished voluntarily without limitations on its use; or

(2) Available to the Government or contractor from other sources without restriction.

(b) A contractor that gains access to proprietary information of other companies in performing advisory and assistance services for the Government must agree with the other companies to protect their information from unauthorized use or disclosure for as long as it remains proprietary and refrain from using the information for any purpose other than that for which it was furnished. The contracting officer shall obtain copies of these agreements and ensure that they are properly executed.

(c) Contractors also obtain proprietary and source selection information by acquiring the services of marketing consultants which, if used in connection with an acquisition, may give the contractor an unfair competitive advantage. Contractors should make inquiries of marketing consultants to ensure that the marketing consultant has provided no unfair competitive advantage.

[FAC 90-1, 55 FR 42686, 10/22/90, effective 10/22/90; FAC 90-8, 56 FR 55377, 10/25/91, effective 11/25/91; FAC 90-45, Final rule, 62 FR 224, 1/2/97, effective 1/1/97; FAC 2019-02, 84 FR 19839, 5/6/2019, effective 5/6/2019]

9.506 Procedures.

(a) If information concerning prospective contractors is necessary to identify and evaluate potential organizational conflicts of interest or to develop recommended actions, contracting officers first should seek the information from within the Government or from other readily available sources. Government sources include the files and the knowledge of personnel within the contracting office, other contracting offices, the cognizant contract administration and audit activities and offices concerned with contract financing. Non-Government sources include publications and commercial services, such as credit rating services, trade and financial journals, and business directories and registers.

(b) If the contracting officer decides that a particular acquisition involves a significant potential organizational conflict of interest, the contracting officer shall, before issuing the solicitation, submit for approval to the chief of the contracting office (unless a higher level official is designated by the agency)—

(1) A written analysis, including a recommended course of action for avoiding, neutralizing, or mitigating the conflict, based on the general rules in 9.505 or on another basis not expressly stated in that section;

(2) A draft solicitation provision (see 9.507-1); and

(3) If appropriate, a proposed contract clause (see 9.507-2).

(c) The approving official shall—

(1) Review the contracting officer's analysis and recommended course of action, including the draft provision and any proposed clause;

(2) Consider the benefits and detriments to the Government and prospective contractors; and

(3) Approve, modify, or reject the recommendations in writing.

(d) The contracting officer shall—

(1) Include the approved provision(s) and any approved clause(s) in the solicitation or the contract, or both;

(2) Consider additional information provided by prospective contractors in response to the solicitation or during negotiations; and

(3) Before awarding the contract, resolve the conflict or the potential conflict in a manner consistent with the approval or other direction by the head of the contracting activity.

(e) If, during the effective period of any restriction (see 9.507), a contracting office transfers acquisition responsibility for the item or system involved, it shall notify the successor contracting office of the restriction, and send a copy of the contract under which the restriction was imposed.

[FAC 90-1, 55 FR 42686, 10/22/90, effective 10/22/90; FAC 90-45, Final rule, 62 FR 224, 1/2/97, effective 1/1/97]

9.507 Solicitation provisions and contract clause. (No Text)

9.507-1 Solicitation provisions.

As indicated in the general rules in 9.505, significant potential organizational conflicts of interest are normally resolved by imposing some restraint, appropriate to the nature of the conflict, upon the contractor's eligibility for future contracts or subcontracts. Therefore, affected solicitations shall contain a provision that—

(a) Invites offerors' attention to this subpart;

(b) States the nature of the potential conflict as seen by the contracting officer;

(c) States the nature of the proposed restraint upon future contractor activities; and

(d) Depending on the nature of the acquisition, states whether or not the terms of any proposed clause and the application of this subpart to the contract are subject to negotiation.

[FAC 90-1, 55 FR 42687, 10/22/90, effective 10/22/90; FAC 90-8, 56 FR 55377, 10/25/91, effective 11/25/91; FAC 90-29, 60 FR 34732, 7/3/95, effective 7/3/95; FAC 90-33, 60 FR 49706, 9/26/95, effective 10/1/95; FAC 90-45, Final rule, 62 FR 224, 1/2/97, effective 1/1/97, corrected, 62 FR 10709, 3/10/97; FAC 2019-02, 84 FR 19839, 5/6/2019, effective 5/6/2019]

9.507-2 Contract clause.

(a) If, as a condition of award, the contractor's eligibility for future prime contract or subcontract awards will be restricted or the contractor must agree to some other restraint, the solicitation shall contain a proposed clause that specifies both the nature and duration of the proposed restraint. The contracting officer shall include the clause in the contract, first negotiating the clause's final terms with the successful offeror, if it is appropriate to do so (see 9.506(d) of this subsection).

(b) The restraint imposed by a clause shall be limited to a fixed term of reasonable duration, sufficient to avoid the circumstance of unfair competitive advantage or potential bias. This period varies. It might end, for example, when the first production contract using the contractor's specifications or work statement is awarded, or it might extend through the entire life of a system for which the contractor has performed systems engineering and technical direction. In every case, the restriction shall specify termination by a specific date or upon the occurrence of an identifiable event.

[FAC 90-1, 55 FR 42687, 10/22/90, effective 10/22/90; FAC 2019-02, 84 FR 19839, 5/6/2019, effective 5/6/2019]

9.508 Examples.

The examples in paragraphs (a) through (i) of this section illustrate situations in which questions concerning organizational conflicts of interest may arise. They are not all inclusive, but are intended to help the contracting officer apply the general rules in 9.505 to individual contract situations.

(a) Company A agrees to provide systems engineering and technical direction for the Navy on the powerplant for a group of submarines (*i.e.*, turbines, drive shafts, propellers, etc.). Company A should not be allowed to supply any powerplant components. Company A can, however, supply components of the submarine unrelated to the powerplant (*e.g.*, fire control, navigation, etc.). In this example, the system is the powerplant, not the submarine, and the ban on supplying components is limited to those for the system only.

(b) Company A is the systems engineering and technical direction contractor for system X. After some progress, but before completion, the system is canceled. Later, system Y is developed to achieve the same purposes as system X, but in a fundamentally different fashion. Company B is the systems engineering and technical direction contractor for system Y. Company A may supply system Y or its components.

(c) Company A develops new electronic equipment and, as a result of this development, prepares specifications. Company A may supply the equipment.

(d) XYZ Tool Company and PQR Machinery Company, representing the American Tool Institute, work under Government supervision and control to refine specifications or to clarify the requirements of a specific acquisition. These companies may supply the item.

(e) Before an acquisition for information technology is conducted, Company A is awarded a contract to prepare data system specifications and equipment performance criteria to be used as the basis for the equipment competition. Since the specifications are the basis for selection of commercial hardware, a potential conflict of interest exists. Company A should be excluded from the initial follow-on information technology hardware acquisition.

(f) Company A receives a contract to define the detailed performance characteristics an agency will require for purchasing rocket fuels. Company A has not developed the particular fuels. When the definition contract is awarded, it is clear to both parties that the agency will use the performance characteristics arrived at to choose competitively a contractor to develop or produce the fuels. Company A may not be awarded this follow-on contract.

(g) Company A receives a contract to prepare a detailed plan for scientific and technical training of an agency's personnel. It suggests a curriculum that the agency endorses and incorporates in its request for proposals to institutions to establish and conduct the training. Company A may not be awarded a contract to conduct the training.

(h) Company A is selected to study the use of lasers in communications. The agency intends to ask that firms doing research in the field make proprietary information available to Company A. The contract must require Company A to—

(1) Enter into agreements with these firms to protect any proprietary information they provide; and

(2) Refrain from using the information in supplying lasers to the Government or for any purpose other than that for which it was intended.

(i) An agency that regulates an industry wishes to develop a system for evaluating and processing license applications. Contractor X helps develop the system and process the applications. Contractor X should be prohibited from acting as a consultant to any of the applicants during its period of performance and for a reasonable period thereafter.

[FAC 90-1, 55 FR 42687, 10/22/90, effective 10/22/90; FAC 90-41, 61 FR 41466, 8/8/96, effective 8/8/96, finalized without change, FAC 97-3, 62 FR 64912, 12/9/97, effective 2/9/98; FAC 2019-02, 84 FR 19839, 5/6/2019, effective 5/6/2019]

SUBPART 9.6—CONTRACTOR TEAM ARRANGEMENTS

9.601 Definition.

Contractor team arrangement, as used in this subpart, means an arrangement in which—

(1) Two or more companies form a partnership or joint venture to act as a potential prime contractor; or

(2) A potential prime contractor agrees with one or more other companies to have them act as its subcontractors under a specified Government contract or acquisition program.

[FAC 97-22, 66 FR 2116, 1/10/2001, effective 3/12/2001; Delay of effective date, 66 FR 14259, 3/9/2001, effective 5/11/2001]

9.602 General.

(a) Contractor team arrangements may be desirable from both a Government and industry standpoint in order to enable the companies involved to—

(1) Complement each other's unique capabilities; and

(2) Offer the Government the best combination of performance, cost, and delivery for the system or product being acquired.

(b) Contractor team arrangements may be particularly appropriate in complex research and development acquisitions, but may be used in other appropriate acquisitions, including production.

(c) The companies involved normally form a contractor team arrangement before submitting an offer. However, they may enter into an arrangement later in the acquisition process, including after contract award.

[FAC 2019-02, 84 FR 19839, 5/6/2019, effective 5/6/2019]

9.603 Policy.

The Government will recognize the integrity and validity of contractor team arrangements; *provided*, the arrangements are identified and company relationships are fully disclosed in an offer or, for arrangements entered into after submission of an offer, before the arrangement becomes effective. The Government will not normally require or encourage the dissolution of contractor team arrangements.

9.604 Limitations.

Nothing in this subpart authorizes contractor team arrangements in violation of antitrust statutes or limits the Government's rights to—

(a) Require consent to subcontracts (see Subpart 44.2);

(b) Determine, on the basis of the stated contractor team arrangement, the responsibility of the prime contractor (see Subpart 9.1);

(c) Provide to the prime contractor data rights owned or controlled by the Government;

(d) Pursue its policies on competitive contracting, subcontracting, and component breakout after initial production or at any other time; and

(e) Hold the prime contractor fully responsible for contract performance, regardless of any team arrangement between the prime contractor and its subcontractors.

SUBPART 9.7—DEFENSE PRODUCTION POOLS AND RESEARCH AND DEVELOPMENT POOLS

9.701 Definition.

Pool, as used in this subpart, means a group of concerns (see 19.001) that have—

(1) Associated together in order to obtain and perform, jointly or in conjunction with each other, defense production or research and development contracts;

(2) Entered into an agreement governing their organization, relationship, and procedures; and

(3) Obtained approval of the agreement by either—

(i) The Small Business Administration (SBA) under section 9 or 11 of the Small Business Act (15 U.S.C. 638 or 640) (see 13 CFR 125); or

(ii) A designated official under Part V of Executive Order 10480, August 14, 1953 (18 FR 4939, August 20, 1953) and section 708 of the Defense Production Act of 1950 (50 U.S.C. App. 2158).

[FAC 84-12, 51 FR 2648, 1/17/86, effective 1/20/86; FAC 97-22, 66 FR 2116, 1/10/2001, effective 3/12/2001; Delay of effective date, 66 FR 14259, 3/9/2001, effective 5/11/2001]

9.702 Contracting with pools.

(a) Except as specified in this subpart, a pool shall be treated the same as any other prospective or actual contractor.

(b) The contracting officer shall not award a contract to a pool unless the offer leading to the contract is submitted by the pool in its own name or by an individual pool member expressly stating that the offer is on behalf of the pool.

(c) Upon receipt of an offer submitted by a group representing that it is a pool, the contracting officer shall verify its approved status with the SBA District Office Director or other approving agency and document the contract file that the verification was made.

(d) Pools approved by the SBA under the Small Business Act are entitled to the preferences and privileges accorded to small business concerns. Approval under the Defense Production Act does not confer these preferences and privileges.

(e) Before awarding a contract to an unincorporated pool, the contracting officer shall require each pool member participating in the contract to furnish a certified copy of a power of attorney identifying the agent authorized to sign the offer or contract on that member's behalf. The contracting officer shall attach a copy of each power of attorney to each signed copy of the contract retained by the Government.

[FAC 90-43, Interim rule, 61 FR 67408, 12/20/96, effective 12/20/96, finalized without change, FAC 97-1, 62 FR 44802, 8/22/97, effective 10/21/97]

9.703 Contracting with individual pool members.

(a) Pool members may submit individual offers, independent of the pool. However, the contracting officer shall not consider an independent offer by a pool member if that pool member participates in a competing offer submitted by the pool.

(b) If a pool member submits an individual offer, independent of the pool, the contracting officer shall consider the pool agreement, along with other factors, in determining whether that pool member is a responsible prospective contractor under Subpart 9.1.

[FAC 2005-83, 80 FR 38309, 7/2/2015, effective 7/2/2015]

PART 10—MARKET RESEARCH

Table of Contents

Scope of part 10.000
Policy 10.001
Procedures 10.002
Contract clause 10.003

PART 10—MARKET RESEARCH

10.000 Scope of part.

This part prescribes policies and procedures for conducting market research to arrive at the most suitable approach to acquiring, distributing, and supporting supplies and services. This part implements requirements of 41 U.S.C. 3306(a)(1), 41 U.S.C. 3307, 10 U.S.C. 2377, and 6 U.S.C. 796.

[FAC 90-32, 60 FR 48206, 9/18/95, effective 10/1/95; FAC 2005-37, 74 FR 52847, 10/14/2009, effective 10/14/2009; FAC 2005-43, 75 FR 38683, 7/2/2010, effective 8/2/2010; FAC 2005-73, 79 FR 24192, 4/29/2014, effective 5/29/2014]

10.001 Policy.

(a) Agencies shall—

(1) Ensure that legitimate needs are identified and trade-offs evaluated to acquire items that meet those needs;

(2) Conduct market research appropriate to the circumstances—

(i) Before developing new requirements documents for an acquisition by that agency;

(ii) Before soliciting offers for acquisitions with an estimated value in excess of the simplified acquisition threshold;

(iii) Before soliciting offers for acquisitions with an estimated value less than the simplified acquisition threshold when adequate information is not available and the circumstances justify its cost;

(iv) Before soliciting offers for acquisitions that could lead to consolidation or bundling (15 U.S.C. 644(e)(2)(A) and 15 U.S.C. 657q);

(v) Before awarding a task or delivery order under an indefinite-delivery-indefinite-quantity (ID/IQ) contract (*e.g.*, GWACs, MACs) for a noncommercial item in excess of the simplified acquisition threshold (10 U.S.C. 2377(c)); and

(vi) On an ongoing basis, take advantage (to the maximum extent practicable) of commercially available market research methods in order to effectively identify the capabilities of small businesses and new entrants into Federal contracting that are available in the marketplace for meeting the requirements of the agency in furtherance of—

(A) A contingency operation or defense against or recovery from cyber, nuclear, biological, chemical, or radiological attack; and

(B) Disaster relief to include debris removal, distribution of supplies, reconstruction, and other disaster or emergency relief activities (see 26.205); and

(3) Use the results of market research to—

(i) Determine if sources capable of satisfying the agency's requirements exist;

(ii) Determine if commercial items or, to the extent commercial items suitable to meet the agency's needs are not available, nondevelopmental items are available that—

(A) Meet the agency's requirements;

(B) Could be modified to meet the agency's requirements; or

(C) Could meet the agency's requirements if those requirements were modified to a reasonable extent;

(iii) Determine the extent to which commercial items or nondevelopmental items could be incorporated at the component level;

(iv) Determine the practices of firms engaged in producing, distributing, and supporting commercial items, such as type of contract, terms for warranties, buyer financing, maintenance and packaging, and marking;

(v) Ensure maximum practicable use of recovered materials (see Subpart 23.4) and promote energy conservation and efficiency;

(vi) Determine whether consolidation is necessary and justified (see 7.107-2) (15 U.S.C. 657q);

(vii) Determine whether bundling is necessary and justified (see 7.107-3) (15 U.S.C. 644(e)(2)(A)); and

(b) When conducting market research, agencies should not request potential sources to submit more than the minimum information necessary.

(c) If an agency contemplates consolidation or bundling, the agency—

(1) When performing market research, should consult with the agency small business specialist and the local Small Business Administration procurement center representative (PCR). If a PCR is not assigned, see 19.402(a); and

(2) Shall notify any affected incumbent small business concerns of the Government's intention to bundle the requirement and how small business concerns may contact the appropriate Small Business Administration procurement center representative (see 7.107-5(a)).

(d) *See* 10.003 for the requirement for a prime contractor to perform market research in contracts in excess of $5.5 million for the procurement of items other than commercial items in accordance with section 826 of Public Law 110-181.

[FAC 90-32, 60 FR 48206, 9/18/95, effective 10/1/95; FAC 97-15, 64 FR 72414, 12/27/99, effective 12/27/99; FAC 97-19, 65 FR 46052, 7/26/2000, effective 7/26/2000; FAC 97-27, 66 FR 20894, 4/25/2001, effective 6/25/2001; FAC 2001-12, 1/27/2003, effective 1/24/2003; FAC 2001-17, 68 FR 59999, 10/20/2003, effective 10/20/2003; FAC 2001-20, 69 FR 8311, 2/23/2004, effective 2/23/2004; FAC 2001-26, 69 FR 76350, 12/20/2004, effective 1/19/2005; FAC 2005-10, 71 FR 36925, 6/28/2006, effective 7/28/2006; FAC 2005-15, 71 FR 74667, 12/12/2006, effective 2/12/2007; FAC 2005-37, 74 FR 52847, 10/14/2009, effective 10/14/2009; FAC 2005-42, 75 FR 34277, 6/16/2010, effective 6/16/2010; FAC 2005-43, 75 FR 38683, 7/2/2010, effective 8/2/2010; FAC 2005-50, 76 FR 14562, 3/16/2011, effective 4/15/2011; FAC 2005-83, 80 FR 38293, 7/2/2015, effective 10/1/2015; FAC 2005-91, 81 FR 67763, 9/30/2016, effective 10/31/2016; FAC 2019-02, 84 FR 19835, 5/6/2019, effective 6/5/2019]

10.002 Procedures.

(a) Acquisitions begin with a description of the Government's needs stated in terms sufficient to allow conduct of market research.

(b) Market research is then conducted to determine if commercial items or nondevelopmental items are available to meet the Government's needs or could be modified to meet the Government's needs.

(1) The extent of market research will vary, depending on such factors as urgency, estimated dollar value, complexity, and past experience. The contracting officer may use market research conducted within 18 months before the award of any task or delivery order if the information is still current, accurate, and relevant. Market research involves obtaining information specific to the item being acquired and should include—

(i) Whether the Government's needs can be met by—

(A) Items of a type customarily available in the commercial marketplace;

(B) Items of a type customarily available in the commercial marketplace with modifications; or

(C) Items used exclusively for governmental purposes;

(ii) Customary practices regarding customizing, modifying or tailoring of items to meet customer needs and associated costs;

(iii) Customary practices, including warranty, buyer financing, discounts, contract type considering the nature and risk associated with the requirement, etc., under which commercial sales of the products or services are made;

(iv) The requirements of any laws and regulations unique to the item being acquired;

(v) The availability of items that contain recovered materials and items that are energy efficient;

(vi) The distribution and support capabilities of potential suppliers, including alternative arrangements and cost estimates; and

(vii) Size and status of potential sources (see Part 19).

(2) Techniques for conducting market research may include any or all of the following:

(i) Contacting knowledgeable individuals in Government and industry regarding market capabilities to meet requirements.

(ii) Reviewing the results of recent market research undertaken to meet similar or identical requirements.

(iii) Publishing formal requests for information in appropriate technical or scientific journals or business publications.

(iv) Querying the Governmentwide database of contracts and other procurement instruments intended for use by multiple agencies available at *https://www.contractdirectory.gov/contractdirectory/* and other Government and commercial databases that provide information relevant to agency acquisitions.

(v) Participating in interactive, on-line communication among industry, acquisition personnel, and customers.

(vi) Obtaining source lists of similar items from other contracting activities or agencies, trade associations or other sources.

(vii) Reviewing catalogs and other generally available product literature published by manufacturers, distributors, and dealers or available on-line.

(viii) Conducting interchange meetings or holding presolicitation conferences to involve potential offerors early in the acquisition process.

(c) If market research indicates commercial or nondevelopmental items might not be available to satisfy agency needs, agencies shall reevaluate the need in accordance with 10.001(a)(3)(ii) and determine whether the need can be restated to permit commercial or nondevelopmental items to satisfy the agency's needs.

(d)(1) If market research establishes that the Government's need may be met by a type of item or service customarily available in the commercial marketplace that would meet the definition of a commercial item at Subpart 2.1, the contracting officer shall solicit and award any resultant contract using the policies and procedures in Part 12.

(2) If market research establishes that the Government's need cannot be met by a type of item or service customarily available in the marketplace, Part 12 shall not be used. When publication of the notice at 5.201 is required, the contracting officer shall include a notice to prospective offerors that the Government does not intend to use Part 12 for the acquisition.

(e) Agencies should document the results of market research in a manner appropriate to the size and complexity of the acquisition.

[FAC 90-32, 60 FR 48206, 9/18/95, effective 10/1/95; FAC 2001-15, 68 FR 43859, 7/24/2003, effective 7/24/2003; FAC 2001-16, 68 FR 56681, 10/1/2003, effective 10/1/2003; FAC 2001-16, Interim/Final rule, 68 FR 56676, 10/1/2003, effective 10/1/2003; FAC 2005-15, 71 FR 74667, 12/12/2006, effective 2/12/2007; FAC 2005-24, 73 FR 10960, 2/28/2008, effective 3/31/2008; FAC 2005-42, 75 FR 34277, 6/16/2010, effective 6/16/2010; FAC 2005-47, 75 FR 77745, 12/13/2010, effective 12/13/2010; FAC 2005-50, 76 FR 14562, 3/16/2011, effective 4/15/2011; FAC 2005-66, 78 FR 13768, 2/28/2013, effective 2/28/2013]

10.003 Contract clause.

The contracting officer shall insert the clause at 52.210-1, Market Research, in solicitations and contracts over $5.5 million for the procurement of items other than commercial items.

[FAC 2005-50, 76 FR 14562, 3/16/2011, effective 4/15/2011; FAC 2005-83, 80 FR 38293, 7/2/2015, effective 10/1/2015]

PART 11—DESCRIBING AGENCY NEEDS

Table of Contents

Scope of part 11.000
Definitions 11.001
Policy 11.002

Subpart 11.1—Selecting and Developing Requirements Documents

Order of precedence for requirements documents 11.101
Standardization program 11.102
Market acceptance 11.103
Use of brand name or equal purchase descriptions 11.104
Items peculiar to one manufacturer 11.105
Purchase descriptions for service contracts 11.106
Solicitation provision 11.107

Subpart 11.2—Using and Maintaining Requirements Documents

Identification and availability of specifications 11.201
Maintenance of standardization documents 11.202
Customer satisfaction 11.203
Solicitation provisions and contract clauses 11.204

Subpart 11.3—Acceptable Material

Definitions 11.301
Policy 11.302
Special requirements for printing and writing paper 11.303
Contract clause 11.304

Subpart 11.4—Delivery or Performance Schedules

General 11.401
Factors to consider in establishing schedules 11.402
Supplies or services 11.403
Contract clauses 11.404

Subpart 11.5—Liquidated Damages

Scope 11.500
Policy 11.501
Procedures 11.502
Contract clauses 11.503

Subpart 11.6—Priorities and Allocations

Scope of subpart 11.600
Definitions 11.601
General 11.602
Procedures 11.603
Solicitation provision and contract clause 11.604

Subpart 11.7—Variation in Quantity

Supply contracts 11.701
Construction contracts 11.702
Contract clauses 11.703

Subpart 11.8—Testing

Preaward in-use evaluation 11.801

PART 11—DESCRIBING AGENCY NEEDS

11.000 Scope of part.

This part prescribes policies and procedures for describing agency needs.

[FAC 90-32, 60 FR 48206, 9/18/95, effective 10/1/95]

11.001 Definitions.

As used in this part—

Reconditioned means restored to the original normal operating condition by readjustments and material replacement.

Remanufactured means factory rebuilt to original specifications.

[FAC 97-1, 62 FR 44802, 8/22/97, effective 10/21/97; FAC 97-4, 63 FR 9048, 2/23/98, effective 4/24/98; FAC 97-18, 65 FR 36014, 6/6/2000, effective 8/7/2000]

11.002 Policy.

(a) In fulfilling requirements of 10 U.S.C. 2305(a)(1), 10 U.S.C. 2377, 41 U.S.C. 3306(a), and 41 U.S.C. 3307, agencies shall—

(1) Specify needs using market research in a manner designed to—

(i) Promote full and open competition (see Part 6), or maximum practicable competition when using simplified acquisition procedures, with due regard to the nature of the supplies or services to be acquired; and

(ii) Only include restrictive provisions or conditions to the extent necessary to satisfy the needs of the agency or as authorized by law.

(2) To the maximum extent practicable, ensure that acquisition officials—

(i) State requirements with respect to an acquisition of supplies or services in terms of—

(A) Functions to be performed;

(B) Performance required; or

(C) Essential physical characteristics;

(ii) Define requirements in terms that enable and encourage offerors to supply commercial items, or, to the extent that commercial items suitable to meet the agency's needs are not available, nondevelopmental items, in response to the agency solicitations;

(iii) Provide offerors of commercial items and nondevelopmental items an opportunity to compete in any acquisition to fill such requirements;

(iv) Require prime contractors and subcontractors at all tiers under the agency contracts to incorporate commercial items or nondevelopmental items as components of items supplied to the agency; and

(v) Modify requirements in appropriate cases to ensure that the requirements can be met by commercial items or, to the extent that commercial items suitable to meet the agency's needs are not available, nondevelopmental items.

(b) The Metric Conversion Act of 1975, as amended by the Omnibus Trade and Competitiveness Act of 1988 (15 U.S.C. 205a, *et seq.*), designates the metric system of measurement as the preferred system of weights and measures for United States trade and commerce, and it requires that each agency use the metric system of measurement in its acquisitions, except to the extent that such use is impracticable or is likely to cause significant inefficiencies or loss of markets to United States firms. Requiring activities are responsible for establishing guidance implementing this policy in formulating their requirements for acquisitions.

(c) To the extent practicable and consistent with Subpart 9.5, potential offerors should be given an opportunity to comment on agency requirements or to recommend application and tailoring of requirements documents and alternative approaches. Requiring agencies should apply specifications, standards, and related documents initially for guidance only, making final decisions on the application and tailoring of these documents as a product of the design and development process. Requiring agencies should not dictate detailed design solutions prematurely (see 7.101 and 7.105(a)(8)).

(d)(1) When agencies acquire products and services, various statutes and executive orders (identified in part 23) require consideration of sustainable acquisition (see subpart 23.1) including—

(i) Energy-efficient and water-efficient services and products (including products containing energy-efficient standby power devices) (subpart 23.2);

(ii) Products and services that utilize renewable energy technologies (subpart 23.2);

(iii) Products containing recovered materials (subpart 23.4);

(iv) Biobased products (subpart 23.4);

(v) Environmentally preferable products and services, including EPEAT® -registered electronic products and non-toxic or low-toxic alternatives (subpart 23.7); and

(vi) Non-ozone-depleting substances, and products and services that minimize or eliminate, when feasible, the use, release, or emission of high global warming potential hydrofluorocarbons, such as by using reclaimed instead of virgin hydrofluorocarbons (subpart 23.8).

(2) Unless an exception applies and is documented by the requiring activity, Executive agencies shall, to the maximum practicable, require the use of products and services listed in paragraph (d)(1) of this section when—

(i) Developing, reviewing, or revising Federal and military specifications, product descriptions (including commercial item descriptions) and standards;

(ii) Describing Government requirements for products and services; and

(iii) Developing source-selection factors.

(e) Some or all of the performance levels or performance specifications in a solicitation may be identified as targets rather than as fixed or minimum requirements.

(f) In accordance with Section 508 of the Rehabilitation Act of 1973 (29 U.S.C. 794d), requiring activities must prepare requirements documents for electronic and information technology that comply with the applicable accessibility standards issued by the Architectural and Transportation Barriers Compliance Board at 36 CFR part 1194 (see subpart 39.2).

(g) Unless the agency Chief Information Officer waives the requirement, when acquiring information technology using Internet Protocol, the requirements documents must include reference to the appropriate technical capabilities defined in the USGv6 Profile (NIST Special Publication 500-267) and the corresponding declarations of conformance defined in the USGv6 Test Program. The applicability of IPv6 to agency networks, infrastructure, and applications specific to individual acquisitions will be in accordance with the agency's Enterprise Architecture (see OMB Memorandum M-05-22 dated August 2, 2005).

(h) Agencies shall not include in a solicitation a requirement that prohibits an offeror from permitting its employees to telecommute unless the contracting officer executes a written determination in accordance with FAR 7.108(a).

[FAC 90-32, 60 FR 48206, 9/18/95, effective 10/1/95; FAC 90-40, 61 FR 39186, 7/26/96, effective 8/26/96; FAC 90-45, Final rule, 62 FR 224, 1/2/97, effective 1/1/97; FAC 97-1, 62 FR 44802, 8/22/97, effective 10/21/97; FAC 97-2, 62 FR 51224, 9/30/97, effective 10/10/97; FAC 97-18,65 FR 36014, 6/6/2000, effective 8/7/2000; FAC 97-27, 66 FR 20894, 4/25/2001, effective 6/25/2001; FAC 2001-02, 66 FR 65347, 12/18/2001, effective 2/19/2002; FAC 2001-15, 68 FR 43857, 7/24/2003, effective 8/25/2003; FAC 2001-25, 69 FR 59701, 10/5/2004, effective 10/5/2004; FAC 2005-04, 70 FR 33656, 6/8/2005, effective 6/8/2005; FAC 2005-21, 72 FR 63040, 11/7/2007, effective 12/7/2007; FAC 2005-38, 74 FR 65605, 12/10/2009, effective 12/10/2009; FAC 2005-52, 76 FR 31395, 5/31/2011, effective 5/31/2011; FAC 2005-73, 79 FR 24192, 4/29/2014, effective 5/29/2014; FAC 2005-75, 79 FR 35859, 6/24,2014, effective 6/24/2014; FAC 2005-84, 80 FR 53436, 9/3/2015, effective 10/5/2015; FAC 2005-88, 81 FR 30429, 5/16/2016, effective 6/15/2016]

SUBPART 11.1—SELECTING AND DEVELOPING REQUIREMENTS DOCUMENTS

11.101 Order of precedence for requirements documents.

(a) Agencies may select from existing requirements documents, modify or combine existing requirements documents, or create new requirements documents to meet agency needs, consistent with the following order of precedence:

(1) Documents mandated for use by law.

(2) Performance-oriented documents (e.g., a PWS or SOO). (See 2.101.)

(3) Detailed design-oriented documents.

(4) Standards, specifications and related publications issued by the Government outside the Defense or Federal series for the non-repetitive acquisition of items.

(b) In accordance with OMB Circular A-119, "Federal Participation in the Development and Use of Voluntary Consensus Standards and in Conformity Assessment Activities," and section 12(d) of the National Technology Transfer and Advancement Act of 1995, Pub. L. 104-113 (15 U.S.C. 272 note), agencies must use voluntary consensus standards, when they exist, in lieu of Government-unique standards, except where inconsistent with law or otherwise impractical. The private sector manages and administers voluntary consensus standards. Such standards are not mandated by law (e.g., industry standards such as ISO 9000, and IEEE 1680).

[FAC 90-32, 60 FR 48206, 9/18/95, effective 10/1/95; FAC 97-1, 62 FR 44802, 8/22/97, effective 10/21/97; FAC 97-14, 64 FR 51828, 9/24/99, effective 11/23/99; FAC 2001-02, 66 FR 65347, 12/18/2001, effective 2/19/2002; FAC 2001-15, 68 FR 43857, 7/24/2003, effective 8/25/2003; FAC 2005-07, 71 FR 211, 1/3/2006, effective 2/2/2006; FAC 2005-21, 72 FR 63040, 11/7/2007, effective 12/7/2007; FAC 2005-23, 72 FR 73215, 12/26/2007, effective 12/26/2007; FAC 2005-30, 74 FR 2740, 1/15/2009, effective 2/17/2009]

11.102 Standardization program.

Agencies shall select existing requirements documents or develop new requirements documents that meet the needs of the agency in accordance with the guidance contained in the Federal Standardization Manual, FSPM-0001; for DoD components, DoD 4120.24-M, Defense Standardization Program Policies and Procedures; and for IT standards and guidance, the Federal Information Processing Standards Publications (FIPS PUBS). The Federal Standardization Manual may be obtained from the General Services Administration (see address in 11.201(d)(1)). DoD 4120.24-M may be obtained from DoD (see 11.201(d)(2) or (3)). FIPS PUBS may be obtained from the Government Publishing Office (GPO), or the Department of Commerce's National Technical Information Service (NTIS) (see address in 11.201(d)(4)).

[FAC 97-5, 63 FR 34058, 6/22/98, effective 8/21/98; FAC 2001-24, 69 34244, 6/18/2004, effective 6/18/2004; FAC 2005-06, 70 FR 57449, 9/30/2005, effective 9/30/2005; FAC 2005-07, 71 FR 227, 1/3/2006, effective 1/3/2006; FAC 2005-13, 71 FR 57360, 9/28/2006, effective 9/28/2006; FAC 2019-02, 84 FR 19839, 5/6/2019, effective 5/6/2019]

11.103 Market acceptance.

(a) 41 U.S.C. 3307(e) provides that, in accordance with agency procedures, the head of an agency may, under appropriate circumstances, require offerors to demonstrate that the items offered—

(1) Have either—

(i) Achieved commercial market acceptance; or

(ii) Been satisfactorily supplied to an agency under current or recent contracts for the same or similar requirements; and

(2) Otherwise meet the item description, specifications, or other criteria prescribed in the public notice and solicitation.

(b) Appropriate circumstances may, for example, include situations where the agency's minimum need is for an item that has a demonstrated reliability, performance or product support record in a specified environment. Use of market acceptance is inappropriate when new or evolving items may meet the agency's needs.

(c) In developing criteria for demonstrating that an item has achieved commercial market acceptance, the contracting officer shall ensure the criteria in the solicitation—

(1) Reflect the minimum need of the agency and are reasonably related to the demonstration of an item's acceptability to meet the agency's minimum need;

(2) Relate to an item's performance and intended use, not an offeror's capability;

(3) Are supported by market research;

(4) Include consideration of items supplied satisfactorily under recent or current Government contracts, for the same or similar items; and

(5) Consider the entire relevant commercial market, including small business concerns.

(d) Commercial market acceptance shall not be used as a sole criterion to evaluate whether an item meets the Government's requirements.

(e) When commercial market acceptance is used, the contracting officer shall document the file to—

(1) Describe the circumstances justifying the use of commercial market acceptance criteria; and

(2) Support the specific criteria being used.

[FAC 90-32, 60 FR 48206, 9/18/95, effective 10/1/95; FAC 2005-73, 79 FR 24192, 4/29/2014, effective 5/29/2014]

11.104 Use of brand name or equal purchase descriptions.

(a) While the use of performance specifications is preferred to encourage offerors to propose innovative solutions, the use of brand name or equal purchase descriptions may be advantageous under certain circumstances.

(b) Brand name or equal purchase descriptions must include, in addition to the brand name, a general description of those salient physical, functional, or performance characteristics of the brand name item that an "equal" item must meet to be acceptable for award. Use brand name or equal descriptions when the salient characteristics are firm requirements.

[FAC 97-12, 64 FR 32740, 6/17/99, effective 8/16/99]

11.105 Items peculiar to one manufacturer.

Agency requirements shall not be written so as to require a particular brand-name, product, or a feature of a product, peculiar to one manufacturer, thereby precluding consideration of a product manufactured by another company, unless—

(a) (1) The particular brand name, product, or feature is essential to the Government's requirements, and market research indicates other companies' similar products, or products lacking the particular feature, do not meet, or cannot be modified to meet, the agency's needs;

(2) (i) The authority to contract without providing for full and open competition is supported by the required justifications and approvals (see 6.302-1); or

(ii) The basis for not providing for maximum practicable competition is documented in the file (see 13.106-1(b)) or justified (see 13.501) when the acquisition is awarded using simplified acquisition procedures.

(3) The documentation or justification is posted for acquisitions over $25,000. (See 5.102(a)(6).)

(b) For multiple award schedule orders, see 8.405-6.

(c) For orders under indefinite-quanity contracts, see 16.505(a)(4).

[FAC 90-32, 60 FR 48206, 9/18/95, effective 10/1/95; FAC 90-40, 61 FR 39186, 7/26/96, effective 8/26/96; FAC 90-45, Final rule, 62 FR 224, 1/2/97, effective 1/1/97, corrected 62 FR 10709, 3/10/97; redesignated from 11.104, FAC 97-12, 64 FR 32740, 6/17/99, effective 8/16/99; FAC 2005-13, 71 FR 57357, 9/28/2006, effective 9/28/2006; FAC 2005-55, 77 FR 189, 1/3/2012, effective 2/2/2012]

11.106 Purchase descriptions for service contracts.

In drafting purchase descriptions for service contracts, agency requiring activities shall ensure that inherently governmental functions (see Subpart 7.5) are not assigned to a contractor. These purchase descriptions shall—

(a) Reserve final determination for Government officials;

(b) Require proper identification of contractor personnel who attend meetings, answer Government telephones, or work in situations where their actions could be construed as acts of Government officials unless, in the judgment of the agency, no harm can come from failing to identify themselves; and

(c) Require suitable marking of all documents or reports produced by contractors.

[FAC 90-37, 61 FR 2626, 1/26/96, effective 3/26/96; redesignated from 11.105, FAC 97-12, 64 FR 32740, 6/17/99, effective 8/16/99]

11.107 Solicitation provision.

(a) Insert the provision at 52.211-6, Brand Name or Equal, when brand name or equal purchase descriptions are included in a solicitation.

(b) Insert the provision at 52.211-7, Alternatives to Government-Unique Standards, in solicitations that use Government-unique standards when the agency uses the transaction-based reporting method to report its use of voluntary consensus standards to the National Institute of Standards and Technology (see OMB Circular A-119, "Federal Participation in the Development and Use of Voluntary Consensus Standards and in Conformity Assessment Activities"). Use of the provision is optional for agencies that report their use of voluntary consensus standards to the National Institute of Standards and Technology using the categorical reporting method. Agencies that manage their specifications on a contract-by-contract basis use the transaction-based method of reporting. Agencies that manage their specifications centrally use the categorical method of reporting. Agency regulations regarding specification management describe which method is used.

[FAC 97-14, 64 FR 51828, 9/24/99, effective 11/23/99]

SUBPART 11.2—USING AND MAINTAINING REQUIREMENTS DOCUMENTS

11.201 Identification and availability of specifications.

(a) Solicitations citing requirements documents listed in the General Services Administration (GSA) Index of Federal Specifications, Standards and Commercial Item Descriptions, the DoD Acquisition Streamlining and Standardization Information System (ASSIST), or other agency index shall identify each document's approval date and the dates of any applicable amendments and revisions. Do not use general identification references, such as "the issue in effect on the date of the solicitation." Contracting offices will not normally furnish these cited documents with the solicitation, except when—

(1) The requirements document must be furnished with the solicitation to enable prospective contractors to make a competent evaluation of the solicitation;

(2) In the judgment of the contracting officer, it would be impracticable for prospective contractors to obtain the documents in reasonable time to respond to the solicitation; or

(3) A prospective contractor requests a copy of a Government promulgated requirements document.

(b) Contracting offices shall clearly identify in the solicitation any pertinent documents not listed in the GSA Index of Federal Specifications, Standards and Commercial Item Descriptions or ASSIST. Such documents shall be furnished with the solicitation or specific instructions shall be furnished for obtaining or examining such documents.

(c) When documents refer to other documents, such references shall—

(1) Be restricted to documents, or appropriate portions of documents, that apply in the acquisition;

(2) Cite the extent of their applicability;

(3) Not conflict with other documents and provisions of the solicitation; and

(4) Identify all applicable first tier references.

(d) (1) The GSA Index of Federal Specifications, Standards and Commercial Item Descriptions, FPMR Part 101-29, may be purchased from the—General Services Administration, Federal Supply Service, Specifications Section, Suite 8100, 470 East L'Enfant Plaza, SW, Washington, DC 20407, Telephone (202) 619-8925.

(2) Most unclassified Defense specifications and standards may be downloaded from the following ASSIST websites:

(i) ASSIST (*https://assist.dla.mil/online/start/*).

(ii) Quick Search (*http://quicksearch.dla.mil/*).

(iii) ASSISTdocs.com (*http://assistdocs.com*).

(3) Documents not available from ASSIST may be ordered from the Department of Defense Single Stock Point (DoDSSP) by—

(i) Using the ASSIST Shopping Wizard (*https://assist.dla.mil/wizard/index.cfm*);

(ii) Phoning the DoDSSP Customer Service Desk, (215) 697-2179, Mon–Fri, 0730 to 1600 EST; or

(iii) Ordering from DoDSSP, Building 4, Section D, 700 Robbins Avenue, Philadelphia, PA 19111-5094, Telephone (215) 697-2667/2179, Facsimile (215) 697-1462.

(4) The FIPS PUBS may be obtained from *http://www.itl.nist.gov/fipspubs/*, or purchased from the Superintendent of Documents, U.S. Government Publishing Office, Washington, DC 20402, Telephone (202) 512- 1800, Facsimile (202) 512-2250; or National Technical Information Service (NTIS), 5285 Port Royal Road, Springfield, VA 22161, Telephone (703) 605-6000, Facsimile (703) 605-6900, Email: *orders@ntis.gov*.

(e) Agencies may purchase some nongovernment standards, including voluntary consensus standards, from the National Technical Information Service's Fedworld Information Network. Agencies may also obtain nongovernment standards from the standards developing organization responsible for the preparation, publication, or maintenance of the standard, or from an authorized document reseller. The National Institute of Standards and Technology can assist agencies in identifying sources for, and content of, nongovernment standards. DoD activities may obtain from the DoDSSP those nongovernment standards, including voluntary consensus standards, adopted for use by defense activities.

[FAC 90-32, 60 FR 48206, 9/18/95, effective 10/1/95; Final rule, 62 FR 40236, 7/25/97, effective 6/30/97, FAC 97-5, 63 FR 34058, 6/22/98, effective 8/21/98; FAC 97-14, 64 FR 51828, 9/24/99, effective 11/23/99; FAC 97-15, 64 FR 72414, 12/27/99, effective 12/27/99; FAC 2001-26, 69 FR 76358, 12/20/2004, effective 12/20/2004; FAC 2005-06, 70 FR 57449, 9/30/2005, effective 9/30/2005; FAC 2005-07, 71 FR 227, 1/3/2006, effective 1/3/2006; FAC 2005-13, 71 FR 57360, 9/28/2006, effective 9/28/2006; FAC 2005-73, 79 FR 24253, 4/29/2014, effective 4/29/2014; FAC 2019-02, 84 FR 19839, 5/6/2019, effective 5/6/2019]

11.202 Maintenance of standardization documents.

(a) Recommendations for changes to standardization documents listed in the GSA Index of Federal Specifications, Standards and Commercial Item Descriptions should be submitted to the General Services Administration, Federal Supply Service, Office of Acquisition, Washington, DC 20406. Agencies shall submit recommendations for changes to standardization documents listed in the DoDISS to the cognizant preparing activity.

(b) When an agency cites an existing standardization document but modifies it to meet its needs, the agency shall follow the guidance in Federal Standardization Manual and, for Defense components, DoD 4120.24-M, Defense Standardization Program Policies and Procedures.

[FAC 90-32, 60 FR 48206, 9/18/95, effective 10/1/95; FAC 2001-24, 69 FR 34244, 6/18/2004, effective 6/18/2004]

11.203 Customer satisfaction.

Acquisition organizations shall communicate with customers to determine how well the requirements document reflects the customer's needs and to obtain suggestions for corrective actions. Whenever practicable, the agency may provide affected industry an opportunity to comment on the requirements documents.

[FAC 90-32, 60 FR 48206, 9/18/95, effective 10/1/95]

11.204 Solicitation provisions and contract clauses.

(a) The contracting officer shall insert the provision at 52.211-1, Availability of Specifications Listed in the GSA Index of Federal Specifications, Standards and Commercial Item Descriptions, FPMR Part 101-29, in solicitations that cite specifications listed in the Index that are not furnished with the solicitation.

(b) The contracting officer shall insert the provision at 52.211-2, Availability of Specifications, Standards, and Data Item Description Listed in the Acquisition Streamlining and Standardization Information System (ASSIST), in solicitations that cite specifications listed in the ASSIST that are not furnished with the solicitation.

(c) The contracting officer shall insert a provision substantially the same as the provision at 52.211-3, Availability of Specifications Not Listed in the GSA Index of Federal Specifications, Standards and Commercial Item Descriptions, in solicitations that cite specifications that are not listed in the Index and are not furnished with the solicitation, but may be obtained from a designated source.

(d) The contracting officer shall insert a provision substantially the same as the provision at 52.211-4, Availability for Examination of Specifications Not Listed in the GSA Index of Federal Specifications, Standards and Commercial Item Descriptions, in solicitations that cite specifications that are not listed in the Index and are available for examination at a specified location.

[FAC 90-32, 60 FR 48206, 9/18/95, effective 10/1/95, FAC 97-5, 63 FR 34058, 6/22/98, effective 8/21/98; FAC 2005-07, 71 FR 227, 1/3/2006, effective 1/3/2006]

SUBPART 11.3—ACCEPTABLE MATERIAL

11.301 Definitions.

As used in this subpart—

Postconsumer material means a material or finished product that has served its intended use and has been discarded for disposal or recovery, having completed its life as a consumer item. Postconsumer material is a part of the broader category of *recovered material*. For paper and paper products, postconsumer material means *postconsumer fiber* defined by the U.S. Environmental Protection Agency (EPA) as—

(1) Paper, paperboard, and fibrous materials from retail stores, office buildings, homes, and so forth, after they have passed through their end-usage as a consumer item, including: used corrugated boxes; old newspapers; old magazines; mixed waste paper; tabulating cards; and used cordage; or

(2) All paper, paperboard, and fibrous materials that enter and are collected from municipal solid waste; but not

(3) Fiber derived from printers' over-runs, converters' scrap, and over-issue publications.

Recovered material for paper and paper products, is defined by EPA in its Comprehensive Procurement Guideline as "recovered fiber" and means the following materials:

(1) Postconsumer fiber.

(2) Manufacturing wastes such as—

(i) Dry paper and paperboard waste generated after completion of the papermaking process (that is, those manufacturing operations up to and including the cutting and trimming of the paper machine reel into smaller rolls or rough sheets) including: envelope cuttings, bindery trimmings, and other paper and paperboard waste resulting from printing, cutting, forming, and other converting operations; bag, box, and carton manufacturing wastes; and butt rolls, mill wrappers, and rejected unused stock; and

(ii) Repulped finished paper and paperboard from obsolete inventories of paper and paperboard manufacturers, merchants, wholesalers, dealers, printers, converters, or others.

[FAC 97-18, 65 FR 36014, 6/6/2000, effective 8/7/2000]

11.302 Policy.

(a) Agencies must not require virgin material or supplies composed of or manufactured using virgin material unless compelled by law or regulation or unless virgin material is vital for safety or meeting performance requirements of the contract.

(b) (1) When acquiring other than commercial items, agencies must require offerors to identify used, reconditioned, or remanufactured supplies; or unused former Government surplus property proposed for use under the contract. These supplies or property may not be used in contract performance unless authorized by the contracting officer.

(2) When acquiring commercial items, the contracting officer must consider the customary practices in the industry for the item being acquired. The contracting officer may require offerors to provide information on used, reconditioned, or remanufactured supplies, or unused former Government surplus property proposed for use under the contract. The request for the information must be included in the solicitation, and to the maximum extent practicable must be limited to information or standards consistent with normal commercial practices.

(c) (1) When the contracting officer needs additional information to determine whether supplies meet minimum recovered material or biobased standards stated in the solicitation, the contracting officer may require offerors to submit additional information on the recycled or biobased content or related standards. The request for the information must be included in the solicitation. When acquiring commercial items, limit the information to the maximum extent practicable to that available under normal commercial practices.

(2) For biobased products, agencies may not require, as a condition of purchase of such products, the vendor or manufacturer to provide more data than would typically be provided by other business entities offering products for sale to the agency, other than data confirming the biobased content of a product (see 7 CFR 3201.8).

[FAC 97-18, 65 FR 36014, 6/6/2000, effective 8/7/2000; FAC 2005-21, 72 FR 63040, 11/7/2007, effective 12/7/2007; FAC 2005-58, 77 FR 23365, 4/18/2012, effective 5/18/2012]

11.303 Special requirements for printing and writing paper.

(a) The following applies when agencies acquire paper in the United States (as defined in 23.001):

(1) Section 2(d) (ii) of Executive Order 13423, Strengthening Federal Environmental, Energy, and Transportation Management, establishes a 30 percent postconsumer fiber content standards for agency paper use. Section 2(d) (ii) requires that an agency's paper products must meet or exceed the minimum content standard.

(2) Section 2(e) (iv) of Executive Order 13514 requires acquisition of uncoated printing and writing paper containing at least 30 percent postconsumer fiber.

(b) Exceptions. If paper under paragraphs (a) (1) or (a) (2) of this section containing at least 30 percent postconsumer fiber is not reasonably available, does not meet reasonable performance requirements, or is only available at an unreasonable price, then the agency must purchase—

(1) Printing and writing paper containing no less than 20 percent postconsumer fiber; or

(2) Paper, other than printing and writing paper, with the maximum practicable percentage of postconsumer fiber that is reasonably available at a reasonable price and that meets reasonable performance requirements.

[FAC 97-18, 65 FR 36014, 6/6/2000, effective 8/7/2000; FAC 2005-52, 76 FR 31395, 5/31/2011, effective 5/31/2011]

11.304 Contract clause.

Insert the clause at 52.211-5, Material Requirements, in solicitations and contracts for supplies that are not commercial items.

[FAC 97-18, 65 FR 36014, 6/6/2000, effective 8/7/2000]

SUBPART 11.4—DELIVERY OR PERFORMANCE SCHEDULES

11.401 General.

(a) The time of delivery or performance is an essential contract element and shall be clearly stated in solicitations. Contracting officers shall ensure that delivery or performance schedules are realistic and meet the requirements of the acquisition. Schedules that are unnecessarily short or difficult to attain—

(1) Tend to restrict competition,

(2) Are inconsistent with small business policies, and

(3) May result in higher contract prices.

(b) Solicitations shall, except when clearly unnecessary, inform bidders or offerors of the basis on which their bids or proposals will be evaluated with respect to time of delivery or performance.

(c) If timely delivery or performance is unusually important to the Government, liquidated damages clauses may be used (see Subpart 11.5).

[Redesignated from 12.101, FAC 90-32, 60 FR 48206, 9/18/95, effective 10/1/95]

11.402 Factors to consider in establishing schedules.

(a) *Supplies or services.* When establishing a contract delivery or performance schedule, consideration shall be given to applicable factors such as the—

(1) Urgency of need;

(2) Industry practices;

(3) Market conditions;

(4) Transportation time;

(5) Production time;

(6) Capabilities of small business concerns;

(7) Administrative time for obtaining and evaluating offers and for awarding contracts;

(8) Time for contractors to comply with any conditions precedent to contract performance; and

(9) Time for the Government to perform its obligations under the contract; *e.g.*, furnishing Government property.

(b) *Construction.* When scheduling the time for completion of a construction contract, the contracting officer shall consider applicable factors such as the—

(1) Nature and complexity of the project;

(2) Construction seasons involved;

(3) Required completion date;

(4) Availability of materials and equipment;

(5) Capacity of the contractor to perform; and

(6) Use of multiple completion dates. (In any given contract, separate completion dates may be established for separable items of work. When multiple completion dates are used, requests for extension of time must be evaluated with respect to each item, and the affected completion dates modified when appropriate.)

[Redesignated from 12.102, FAC 90-32, 60 FR 48206, 9/18/95, effective 10/1/95]

11.403 Supplies or services.

(a) The contracting officer may express contract delivery or performance schedules in terms of—

(1) Specific calendar dates;

(2) Specific periods from the date of the contract; *i.e.*, from the date of award or acceptance by the Government, or from the date shown as the effective date of the contract;

(3) Specific periods from the date of receipt by the contractor of the notice of award or acceptance by the Government (including notice by receipt of contract document executed by the Government); or

(4) Specific time for delivery after receipt by the contractor of each individual order issued under the contract, as in indefinite delivery type contracts and GSA schedules.

(b) The time specified for contract performance should not be curtailed to the prejudice of the contractor because of delay by the Government in giving notice of award.

(c) If the delivery schedule is based on the date of the contract, the contracting officer shall mail or otherwise furnish to the contractor the contract, notice of award, acceptance of proposal, or other contract document not later than the date of the contract.

(d) If the delivery schedule is based on the date the contractor receives the notice of award, or if the delivery schedule is expressed in terms of specific calendar dates on the assumption that the notice of award will be received by a specified date, the contracting officer shall send the contract, notice of award, acceptance of proposal, or other contract document by certified mail, return receipt requested, or by any other method that will provide evidence of the date of receipt.

(e) In invitations for bids, if the delivery schedule is based on the date of the contract, and a bid offers delivery based on the date the contractor receives the contract or notice of award, the contracting officer shall evaluate the bid by adding 5 calendar days (as representing the normal time for arrival through ordinary mail). If the contract or notice of award will be transmitted electronically, (1) the solicitation shall so state; and (2) the contracting officer shall evaluate delivery schedule based on the date of contract receipt or notice of award, by adding one working day. (The term "working day" excludes weekends and U.S. Federal holidays.) If the offered delivery date computed with mailing or transmittal time is later than the delivery date required by the invitation for bids, the bid shall be considered nonresponsive and rejected. If award is made, the delivery date will be the number of days offered in the bid after the contractor actually receives the notice of award.

[Redesignated from 12.103, FAC 90-32, 60 FR 48206, 9/18/95, effective 10/1/95]

11.404 Contract clauses.

(a) *Supplies or services.*

(1) The contracting officer may use a time of delivery clause to set forth a required delivery schedule and to allow an offeror to propose an alternative delivery schedule. The clauses and their alternates may be used in solicitations and contracts for other than construction and architect-engineering substantially as shown, or they may be changed or new clauses written.

(2) The contracting officer may insert in solicitations and contracts other than those for construction and architect-engineering, a clause substantially the same as the clause at 52.211-8, Time of Delivery, if the Government requires delivery by a particular time and the delivery schedule is to be based on the date of the contract. If the delivery schedule is expressed in terms of specific calendar dates or specific periods and is based on an assumed date of award, the contracting officer may use the clause with its Alternate I. If the delivery schedule is expressed in terms of specific calendar dates or specific periods and is based on an assumed date the contractor will receive notice of award, the contracting officer may use the clause with its Alternate II. If the delivery schedule is to be based on the actual date the contractor receives a written notice of award, the contracting officer may use the clause with its Alternate III.

(3) The contracting officer may insert in solicitations and contracts other than those for construction and architect-engineering, a clause substantially the same as the clause at 52.211-9, Desired and Required Time of Delivery, if the Government desires delivery by a certain time but requires delivery by a specified later time, and the delivery schedule is to be based on the date of the contract. If the delivery schedule is expressed in terms of specific calendar dates or specific periods and is based on an assumed date of award, the contracting officer may use the clause with its Alternate I. If the delivery schedule is expressed in terms of specific calendar dates or specific periods and is based on an assumed date the contractor will receive notice of award, the contracting officer may use the clause with its Alternate II. If the delivery schedule is to be based on the actual date the contractor receives a writ-

ten notice of award, the contracting officer may use the clause with its Alternate III.

(b) *Construction*. The contracting officer shall insert the clause at 52.211-10, Commencement, Prosecution, and Completion of Work, in solicitations and contracts when a fixed-price construction contract is contemplated. The clause may be changed to accommodate the issuance of orders under indefinite-delivery contracts. If the completion date is expressed as a specific calendar date, computed on the basis of the contractor receiving the notice to proceed by a certain day, the contracting officer may use the clause with its Alternate I.

[Redesignated from 12.104, FAC 90-32, 60 FR 48206, 9/18/95, effective 10/1/95]

SUBPART 11.5—LIQUIDATED DAMAGES

11.500 Scope.

(a) This subpart prescribes policies and procedures for using liquidated damages clauses in solicitations and contracts for supplies, services, research and development, and construction.

(b) This subpart does not apply to liquidated damages—

(1) For subcontracting plans (see 19.705-7);

(2) Related to the Contract Work Hours and Safety Standards statute (see subpart 22.3); or

(3) Related to paid sick leave for Federal contractors (see subpart 22.21)

[FAC 97-19, 65 FR 46052, 7/26/2000, effective 9/25/2000; FAC 2005-73, 79 FR 24192, 4/29/2014, effective 5/29/2014; FAC 2005-93, 81 FR 91627, 12/16/2016, effective 1/1/2017; FAC 2005-100, 83 FR 42569, 8/22/2018, effective 8/22/2018]

11.501 Policy.

(a) The contracting officer must consider the potential impact on pricing, competition, and contract administration before using a liquidated damages clause. Use liquidated damages clauses only when—

(1) The time of delivery or timely performance is so important that the Government may reasonably expect to suffer damage if the delivery or performance is delinquent; and

(2) The extent or amount of such damage would be difficult or impossible to estimate accurately or prove.

(b) Liquidated damages are not punitive and are not negative performance incentives (see 16.402-2). Liquidated damages are used to compensate the Government for probable damages. Therefore, the liquidated damages rate must be a reasonable forecast of just compensation for the harm that is caused by late delivery or untimely performance of the particular contract. Use a maximum amount or a maximum period for assessing liquidated damages if these limits reflect the maximum probable damage to the Government. Also, the contracting officer may use more than one liquidated damages rate when the contracting officer expects the probable damage to the Government to change over the contract period of performance.

(c) The contracting officer must take all reasonable steps to mitigate liquidated damages. If the contract contains a liquidated damages clause and the contracting officer is considering terminating the contract for default, the contracting officer should seek expeditiously to obtain performance by the contractor or terminate the contract and repurchase (see subpart 49.4). Prompt contracting officer action will prevent excessive loss to defaulting contractors and protect the interests of the Government.

(d) The head of the agency may reduce or waive the amount of liquidated damages assessed under a contract, if the Commissioner, Financial Management Service, or designee approves (see Treasury Order 145-10).

[FAC 97-19, 65 FR 46052, 7/26/2000, effective 9/25/2000]

11.502 Procedures.

(a) Include the applicable liquidated damages clause and liquidated damages rates in solicitations when the contract will contain liquidated damages provisions.

(b) Construction contracts with liquidated damages provisions must describe the rate(s) of liquidated damages assessed per day of delay. The rate(s) should include the estimated daily cost of Government inspection and superintendence. The rate(s) should also include an amount for other expected expenses associated with delayed completion such as—

(1) Renting substitute property; or

(2) Paying additional allowance for living quarters.

[FAC 97-19, 65 FR 46052, 7/26/2000, effective 9/25/2000]

11.503 Contract clauses.

(a) Use the clause at 52.211-11, Liquidated Damages—Supplies, Services, or Research and Development, in fixed-price solicitations and contracts for supplies, services, or research and development when the contracting officer determines that liquidated damages are appropriate (see 11.501(a)).

(b) Use the clause at 52.211-12, Liquidated Damages—Construction, in solicitations and contracts for construction, other than cost-plus-fixed-fee, when the contracting officer determines that liquidated damages are appropriate (see 11.501(a)). If the contract specifies more than one completion date for separate parts or stages of the work, revise paragraph (a) of the clause to state the amount of liquidated damages for delay of each separate part or stage of the work.

(c) Use the clause at 52.211-13, Time Extensions, in solicitations and contracts for construction that use the clause at 52.211-12, Liquidated Damages—Construction, when that clause has been revised as provided in paragraph (b) of this section.

[FAC 97-19, 65 FR 46052, 7/26/2000, effective 9/25/2000]

SUBPART 11.6—PRIORITIES AND ALLOCATIONS

11.600 Scope of subpart.

This subpart implements the Defense Priorities and Allocations System (DPAS), a Department of Commerce regulation in support of approved national defense, emergency preparedness, and energy programs (see 15 CFR part 700).

[Redesignated from 12.300, FAC 90-32, 60 FR 48206, 9/18/95, effective 10/1/95; FAC 2005-25, 73 FR 21783, 4/22/2008, effective 4/22/2008]

11.601 Definitions.

As used in this subpart—

Approved program means a program determined as necessary or appropriate for priorities and allocations support to promote the national defense by the Secretary of Defense, the Secretary of Energy, or the Secretary of Homeland Security, under the authority of the Defense Production Act, the Stafford Act, and Executive Order 12919, or the Selective Service Act and related statutes and Executive Order 12742.

Delegate Agency means a Government agency authorized by delegation from the Department of Commerce to place priority ratings on contracts or orders needed to support approved programs.

National defense means programs for military and energy production or construction, military assistance to any foreign nation, stockpiling, space, and any directly related activity. Such term includes emergency preparedness activities conducted pursuant to title VI of The Robert T. Stafford Disaster Relief and Emergency Assistance Act (42 U.S.C. 5195 *et seq.*) and critical infrastructure protection and restoration. (50 U.S.C. App. § 2152).

Rated order means a prime contract, a subcontract, or a purchase order in support of an approved program issued in accordance with the provisions of the DPAS regulation (15 CFR part 700).

[Redesignated from 12.301, FAC 90-32, 60 FR 48206, 9/18/95, effective 10/1/95; FAC 97-22, 66 FR 2116, 1/10/2001, effective 3/12/2001; Delay of effective date, 66 FR 14259, 3/9/2001, effective 5/11/2001; FAC 2005-25, 73 FR 21783, 4/22/2008, effective 4/22/2008]

11.602 General.

(a) Under Title I of the Defense Production Act of 1950 (50 U.S.C. App. 2061, *et seq.*), the President is authorized to require preferential acceptance and performance of contracts and orders supporting certain approved national defense and energy programs and to allocate materials, services, and facilities in such a manner as to promote these approved programs.

(b) The President delegated the priorities and allocations authorities of the Defense Production Act in Executive Order 12919. As part of that delegation, the President designated the Secretary of Commerce to administer the DPAS. For more information, check the DPAS website at: *www.bis.doc.gov/dpas.*

[Redesignated from 12.302, FAC 90-32, 60 FR 48206, 9/18/95, effective 10/1/95; FAC 2005-25, 73 FR 21783, 4/22/2008, effective 4/22/2008]

11.603 Procedures.

(a) There are two levels of priority for rated orders established by the DPAS, identified by the rating symbols "DO" and "DX". All DO rated orders have equal priority with each other and take preference over unrated orders. All DX rated orders have equal priority with each other and take preference over DO rated and unrated orders (see 15 CFR 700.11). The DPAS regulation contains provisions concerning the elements of a rated order (see 15 CFR 700.12); acceptance and rejection of rated orders (see 15 CFR 700.13); preferential scheduling (see 15 CFR 700.14); extension of priority ratings (flowdown) (see 15 CFR 700.15); changes or cancellations of priority ratings and rated orders (see 15 CFR 700.16); use of rated orders (see 15 CFR 700.17); and limitations on placing rated orders (see 15 CFR 700.18).

(b) The Delegate Agencies have been given authority by the Department of Commerce to place rated orders in support of approved programs (see Schedule I of the DPAS). Other U.S. Government agencies, Canada, and foreign nations may apply for priority rating authority.

(c) Rated orders shall be placed in accordance with the provisions of the DPAS.

(d) Agency heads shall ensure compliance with the DPAS by contracting activities within their agencies.

(e) Agency heads shall provide contracting activities with specific guidance on the issuance of rated orders in support of approved agency programs, including the general limitations and jurisdictional limitations on placing rated orders (see 15 CFR 700.18 and Executive Order 12919).

(f) Contracting officers shall follow agency procedural instructions concerning the use of rated orders in support of approved agency programs.

(g) Contracting officers, contractors, or subcontractors at any tier, that experience difficulty placing rated orders, obtaining timely delivery under rated orders, locating a contractor or supplier to fill a rated order, ensuring that rated orders receive preferential treatment by contractors or suppliers, or require rating authority for items not automatically ratable under the DPAS, should promptly seek special priorities assistance in accordance with agency procedures (see 15 CFR 700.50—700.55 and 700.80).

(h) The Department of Commerce may take specific official actions (Ratings Authorizations, Directives, Letters of Understanding, Administrative Subpoenas, Demands for Information, and Inspection Authorizations) to implement or enforce the provisions of the DPAS (see 15 CFR 700.60-700.71).

(i) Contracting officers shall report promptly any violations of the DPAS in accordance with agency procedures to the Office of Strategic Industries and Economic Security, U.S. Department of Commerce, Room 3876, Washington, DC 20230, Ref: DPAS; telephone: (202) 482-3634 or fax: (202) 482-5650.

[Redesignated from 12.303, FAC 90-32, 60 FR 48206, 9/18/95, effective 10/1/95; FAC 2005-25, 73 FR 21783, 4/22/2008, effective 4/22/2008]

11.604 Solicitation provision and contract clause.

(a) Contracting officers shall insert the provision at 52.211-14, Notice of Priority Rating for National Defense Emergency Preparedness, and Energy Program Use, in solicitations when the contract to be awarded will be a rated order.

(b) Contracting officers shall insert the clause at 52.211-15, Defense Priority and Allocation Requirements, in contracts that are rated orders.

[Redesignated from 12.304, FAC 90-32, 60 FR 48206, 9/18/95, effective 10/1/95; FAC 2005-25, 73 FR 21783, 4/22/2008, effective 4/22/2008; FAC 2019-02, 84 FR 19839, 5/6/2019, effective 5/6/2019]

SUBPART 11.7—VARIATION IN QUANTITY

11.701 Supply contracts.

(a) A fixed-price supply contract may authorize Government acceptance of a variation in the quantity of items called for if the variation is caused by conditions of loading, shipping, or packing, or by allowances in manufacturing processes. Any permissible variation shall be stated as a percentage and it may be an increase, a decrease, or a combination of both; however, contracts for subsistence items may use other applicable terms of variation in quantity.

(b) There should be no standard or usual variation percentage. The overrun or underrun permitted in each contract should be based upon the normal commercial practices of a particular industry for a particular item, and the permitted percentage should be no larger than is necessary to afford a contractor reasonable protection. The permissible variation shall not exceed plus or minus 10 percent unless a different limitation is established in agency regulations. Consideration shall be given to the quantity to which the percentage variation applies. For example, when delivery will be made to multiple destinations and it is desired that the quantity variation apply to the item quantity for each destination, this requirement must be stated in the contract.

(c) Contractors are responsible for delivery of the specified quantity of items in a fixed-price contract, within allowable variations, if any. If a contractor delivers a quantity of items in excess of the contract requirements plus any allowable variation in quantity, particularly small dollar value overshipments, it results in unnecessary administrative costs to the Government in determining disposition of the excess quantity. Accordingly, the contract may include the clause at 52.211-17, Delivery of Excess Quantities, to provide that—

(1) Excess quantities of items totaling up to $250 in value may be retained without compensating the contractor; and

(2) Excess quantities of items totaling over $250 in value may, at the Government's option, be either returned at the contractor's expense or retained and paid for at the contract unit price.

[Redesignated from 12.701, FAC 90-32, 60 FR 48206, 9/18/95, effective 10/1/95; Final rule, 62 FR 40236, 7/25/97, effective 6/30/97]

11.702 Construction contracts.

Construction contracts may authorize a variation in estimated quantities of unit-priced items. When the variation between the estimated quantity and the actual quantity of a unit-priced item is more than plus or minus 15 percent, an equitable adjustment in the contract price shall be made upon the demand of either the Government or the contractor. The contractor may request an extension of time if the quantity variation is such as to cause an increase in the time necessary for completion. The contracting officer must receive the request in writing within 10 days from the beginning of the period of delay. However, the contracting officer may extend this time limit before the date of final settlement of the contract. The contracting officer shall ascertain the facts and make any adjustment for extending the completion date that the findings justify.

[Redesignated from 12.702, FAC 90-32, 60 FR 48206, 9/18/95, effective 10/1/95]

11.703 Contract clauses.

(a) The contracting officer shall insert the clause at 52.211-16, Variation in Quantity, in solicitations and contracts, if authorizing a variation in quantity in fixed-price contracts for supplies or for services that involve the furnishing of supplies.

(b) The contracting officer may insert the clause at 52.211-17, Delivery of Excess Quantities, in solicitations and contracts when a fixed-price supply contract is contemplated.

(c) The contracting officer shall insert the clause at 52.211-18, Variation in Estimated Quantity, in solicitations and contracts when a fixed-price construction contract is contemplated that authorizes a variation in the estimated quantity of unit-priced items.

[Redesignated from 12.403, FAC 90-32, 60 FR 48206, 9/18/95, effective 10/1/95; FAC 97-11, 64 FR 10530, 3/4/99, effective 5/3/99]

SUBPART 11.8—TESTING

11.801 Preaward in-use evaluation.

Supplies may be evaluated under comparable in-use conditions without a further test plan, provided offerors are so advised in the solicitation. The results of such tests or demonstrations may be used to rate the proposal, to determine technical acceptability, or otherwise to evaluate the proposal (see 15.305).

[FAC 97-2, 62 FR 51224, 9/30/97, effective 10/10/97]

PART 12—ACQUISITION OF COMMERCIAL ITEMS

Table of Contents

Scope of part 12.000
Definition 12.001

Subpart 12.1—Acquisition of Commercial Items—General

Policy 12.101
Applicability 12.102
Commercially available off-the-shelf (COTS) items 12.103

Subpart 12.2—Special Requirements for the Acquisition of Commercial Items

General 12.201
Market research and description of agency need 12.202
Procedures for solicitation, evaluation, and award 12.203
Solicitation/contract form 12.204
Offers 12.205
Use of past performance 12.206
Contract type 12.207
Contract quality assurance 12.208
Determination of price reasonableness 12.209
Contract financing 12.210
Technical data 12.211
Computer software 12.212
Other commercial practices 12.213
Cost accounting standards 12.214
Notification of overpayment 12.215
Unenforceability of unauthorized obligations 12.216

Subpart 12.3—Solicitation Provisions and Contract Clauses for the Acquisition of Commercial Items

Scope of subpart 12.300
Solicitation provisions and contract clauses for acquisition of commercial items 12.301
Tailoring of provisions and clauses for the acquisition of commercial items . . . 12.302
Contract format 12.303

Subpart 12.4—Unique Requirements Regarding Terms and Conditions for Commercial Items

General 12.401
Acceptance 12.402
Termination 12.403
Warranties 12.404

Subpart 12.5—Applicability of Certain Laws to the Acquisition of Commercial Items and Commercially Available Off-The-Shelf Items

Scope of subpart 12.500
Applicability 12.501
Procedures 12.502
Applicability of certain laws to Executive agency contracts for the acquisition of commercial items 12.503
Applicability of certain laws to subcontracts for the acquisition of commercial items 12.504
Applicability of certain laws to contracts for the acquisition of COTS items 12.505

Subpart 12.6—Streamlined Procedures for Evaluation and Solicitation for Commercial Items

General 12.601
Streamlined evaluation of offers 12.602
Streamlined solicitation for commercial items 12.603

PART 12—ACQUISITION OF COMMERCIAL ITEMS

12.000 Scope of part.

This part prescribes policies and procedures unique to the acquisition of commercial items. It implements the Federal Government's preference for the acquisition of commercial items contained in 41 U.S.C. 1906, 1907, and 3307 and 10 U.S.C. 2375-2377 by establishing acquisition policies more closely resembling those of the commercial marketplace and encouraging the acquisition of commercial items and components.

[FAC 90-32, 60 FR 48206, 9/18/95, effective 10/1/95; FAC 2005-73, 79 FR 24192, 4/29/2014, effective 5/29/2014]

12.001 Definition.

Subcontract, as used in this part, includes, but is not limited to, a transfer of commercial items between divisions, subsidiaries, or affiliates of a contractor or subcontractor.

[FAC 90-32, 60 FR 48206, 9/18/95, effective 10/1/95]

SUBPART 12.1—ACQUISITION OF COMMERCIAL ITEMS—GENERAL

12.101 Policy.

Agencies shall—

(a) Conduct market research to determine whether commercial items or nondevelopmental items are available that could meet the agency's requirements;

(b) Acquire commercial items or nondevelopmental items when they are available to meet the needs of the agency; and

(c) Require prime contractors and subcontractors at all tiers to incorporate, to the maximum extent practicable, commercial items or nondevelopmental items as components of items supplied to the agency.

[FAC 90-32, 60 FR 48206, 9/18/95, effective 10/1/95]

12.102 Applicability.

(a) This part shall be used for the acquisition of supplies or services that meet the definition of commercial items at 2.101.

(b) Contracting officers shall use the policies in this part in conjunction with the policies and procedures for solicitation, evaluation and award prescribed in Part 13, Simplified Acquisition Procedures; Part 14, Sealed Bidding; or Part 15, Contracting by Negotiation, as appropriate for the particular acquisition.

(c) Contracts for the acquisition of commercial items are subject to the policies in other parts of the FAR. When a policy in another part of the FAR is inconsistent with a policy in this part, this part 12 shall take precedence for the acquisition of commercial items.

(d) The definition of commercial item in section 2.101 uses the phrase "purposes other than governmental purposes." These purposes are those that are not unique to a government.

(e) This part shall not apply to the acquisition of commercial items—

(1) At or below the micro-purchase threshold;

(2) Using the Standard Form 44 (see 13.306);

(3) Using the imprest fund (see 13.305);

(4) Using the Governmentwide commercial purchase card as a method of purchase rather than only as a method of payment; or

(5) Directly from another Federal agency.

(f) (1) Contracting officers may treat any acquisition of supplies or services that, as determined by the head of the agency, are to be used to facilitate defense against or recovery from cyber, nuclear, biological, chemical, or radiological attack, as an acquisition of commercial items.

(2) A contract in an amount greater than $19 million that is awarded on a sole source basis for an item or service treated as a commercial item under paragraph (f) (1) of this section but does not meet the definition of a commercial item as defined at FAR 2.101 shall not be exempt from—

(i) Cost accounting standards (see Subpart 30.2); or

(ii) Certified cost or pricing data requirements (see 15.403).

(g) (1) In accordance with 41 U.S.C. 2310, the contracting officer also may use Part 12 for any acquisition for services that does not meet the definition of commercial item in FAR 2.101, if the contract or task order—

(i) Is entered into on or before November 24, 2013;

(ii) Has a value of $29.5 million or less;

(iii) Meets the definition of performance-based acquisition at FAR 2.101;

(iv) Uses a quality assurance surveillance plan;

(v) Includes performance incentives where appropriate;

(vi) Specifies a firm-fixed price for specific tasks to be performed or outcomes to be achieved; and

(vii) Is awarded to an entity that provides similar services to the general public under terms and conditions similar to those in the contract or task order.

(2) In exercising the authority specified in paragraph (g) (1) of this section, the contracting officer may tailor paragraph (a) of the clause at FAR 52.212-4 as may be necessary to ensure the contract's remedies adequately protect the Government's interests.

[FAC 90-32, 60 FR 48206, 9/18/95, effective 10/1/95; FAC 90-40, 61 FR 39186, 7/26/96, effective 8/26/96; FAC 97-3, 62 FR 64912, 12/9/97, effective 2/9/98; FAC 97-12, 64 FR 32740, 6/17/99, effective 6/17/99, finalized without change, FAC 97-15, 64 FR 72414, 12/27/99; FAC 2001-01, 66 FR 53478, 10/22/2001, effective 12/21/2001, FAC 2001-09, 67 FR 56115, 8/30/2002, effective 8/30/2002; FAC 2001-12, 1/27/2003, effective 1/27/2003; FAC 2001-20, 69 FR 8311, 2/23/2004, effective 2/23/2004; FAC 2001-24, 69 FR 34225 6/18/2004, effective 6/18/2004; correction, 69 FR 38955, 6/29/2004; FAC 2001-26, 69 FR 76350, 12/20/2004, effective 1/19/2005; FAC 2005-04, 70 FR 33657, 6/8/2005, effective 6/8/2005; FAC 2005-07, 71 FR 211, 1/3/2006, effective 2/2/2006; FAC 2005-13, 71 FR 57363, 9/28/2006, effective 9/28/2006; FAC 2005-45, 75 FR 53129, 53135, 8/30/2010, effective 10/1/2010; FAC 2005-52, 76 FR 31395, 5/31/2011, effective 5/31/2011; FAC 2005-67, 78 FR 37686, 6/21/2013, effective 6/21/2013; FAC 2005-72, 78 FR 80382,12/31/2013, effective 12/31/2013; FAC 2005-73, 79 FR 24192, 4/29/2014, effective 5/29/2014; FAC 2005-83, 80 FR 38293, 7/2/2015, effective 10/1/2015; FAC 2019-02, 84 FR 19835, 5/6/2019, effective 6/5/2019]

12.103 Commercially available off-the-shelf (COTS) items.

Commercially available off-the-shelf (COTS) items are defined in 2.101. Unless indicated otherwise, all of the policies that apply to commercial items also apply to COTS items. Section 12.505 lists the laws that are not applicable to COTS items (in addition to 12.503 and 12.504).

[FAC 2005-30, 74 FR 2713, 1/15/2009, effective 2/17/2009; FAC 2005-73, 79 FR 24192, 4/29/2014, effective 5/29/2014; FAC 2005-80, 80 FR 4967, 1/29/2015, effective 3/2/2015]

SUBPART 12.2—SPECIAL REQUIREMENTS FOR THE ACQUISITION OF COMMERCIAL ITEMS

12.201 General.

This subpart identifies those special requirements as well as other considerations necessary for proper planning, solicitation, evaluation and award of contracts for commercial items.

[FAC 90-32, 60 FR 48206, 9/18/95, effective 10/1/95; FAC 2005-73, 79 FR 24192, 4/29/2014, effective 5/29/2014]

12.202 Market research and description of agency need.

(a) Market research (see 10.001) is an essential element of building an effective strategy for the acquisition of commercial items and establishes the foundation for the agency description of need (see Part 11), the solicitation, and resulting contract.

(b) The description of agency need must contain sufficient detail for potential offerors of commercial items to know which commercial products or services may be suitable. Generally, for acquisitions in excess of the simplified acquisition threshold, an agency's statement of need for a commercial item will describe the type of product or service to be acquired and explain how the agency intends to use the product or service in terms of function to be performed, performance requirement or essential physical characteristics. Describing the agency's needs in these terms allows offerors to propose methods that will best meet the needs of the Government.

(c) Follow the procedures in Subpart 11.2 regarding the identification and availability of specifications, standards and commercial item descriptions.

(d) Requirements documents for electronic and information technology must comply with the applicable accessibility standards issued by the Architectural and Transportation Barriers Compliance Board at 36 CFR part 1194 (see subpart 39.2).

(e) When acquiring information technology using Internet Protocol, agencies must include the appropriate Internet Protocol compliance requirements in accordance with 11.002(g).

[FAC 90-32, 60 FR 48206, 9/18/95, effective 10/1/95; FAC 90-45, Final rule, 62 FR 224, 1/2/97, effective 1/1/97; FAC 97-27, 66 FR 20894, 4/25/2001, effective 6/25/2001; FAC 2005-38, 74 FR 65605, 12/10/2009, effective 12/10/2009]

12.203 Procedures for solicitation, evaluation, and award.

Contracting officers shall use the policies unique to the acquisition of commercial items prescribed in this part in conjunction with the policies and procedures for solicitation, evaluation and award prescribed in Part 13, Simplified Acquisition Procedures; Part 14, Sealed Bidding; or Part 15, Contracting by Negotiation, as appropriate for the particular acquisition. The contracting officer may use the streamlined procedure for soliciting offers for commercial items prescribed in 12.603. For acquisitions of commercial items exceeding the simplified acquisition threshold but not exceeding $7 million ($13 million for acquisitions as described in 13.500(c)), including options, contracting activities may use any of the simplified procedures authorized by subpart 13.5.

[FAC 90-32, 60 FR 48206, 9/18/95, effective 10/1/95; FAC 90-45, Final rule, 62 FR 224, 1/2/97, effective 1/1/97; FAC 97-3, 62 FR 64912, 12/9/97, effective 2/9/98; FAC 2001-20, 69 FR 8311, 2/23/2004, effective 2/23/2004; FAC 2001-26, 69 FR 76350, 12/20/2004, effective 1/19/2005; FAC 2005-13, 71 FR 57363, 9/28/2006, effective 9/28/2006; FAC 2005-45, 75 FR 53129, 8/30/2010, effective 10/1/2010; FAC 2005-83, 80 FR 38293, 7/2/2015, effective 10/1/2015, FAC 2005-83, 80 FR 38311, 7/2/2015, effective 8/3/2015]

12.204 Solicitation/contract form.

(a) The contracting officer shall use the Standard Form 1449, Solicitation/Contract/Order for Commercial Items, if

(1) the acquisition is expected to exceed the simplified acquisition threshold;

(2) a paper solicitation or contract is being issued; and

(3) procedures at 12.603 are not being used. Use of the SF 1449 is nonmandatory but encouraged for commercial acquisitions not exceeding the simplified acquisition threshold.

(b) Consistent with the requirements at 5.203(a) and (h), the contracting officer may allow fewer than 15 days before issuance of the solicitation.

[FAC 90-45, Final rule, 62 FR 224, 1/2/97, effective 1/1/97]

12.205 Offers.

(a) Where technical information is necessary for evaluation of offers, agencies should, as part of market research, review existing product literature generally available in the industry to determine its adequacy for purposes of evaluation. If adequate, contracting officers shall request existing product literature from offerors of commercial items in lieu of unique technical proposals.

(b) Contracting officers should allow offerors to propose more than one product that will meet a Government need in response to solicitations for commercial items. The contracting officer shall evaluate each product as a separate offer.

(c) Consistent with the requirements at 5.203(b), the contracting officer may allow fewer than 30 days response time for receipt of offers for commercial items, unless the acquisition is covered by the World Trade Organization Government Procurement Agreement or a Free Trade Agreement (see 5.203(h)).

[FAC 90-32, 60 FR 48206, 9/18/95, effective 10/1/95; FAC 90-45, Final rule, 62 FR 224, 1/2/97, effective 1/1/97; FAC 97-15, 64 FR 72414, 12/27/99, effective 2/25/2000; FAC 2001-19, Interim rule, 69 FR 1051, 1/7/2004, effective 1/1/2004; FAC 2001-25, Final rule, 69 FR 59700, 10/5/2004, effective 10/5/2004; FAC 2001-27, interim rule, 69 FR 77870, 12/28/2004, effective 1/1/2005; FAC 2005-07, 71 FR 219, 1/3/2006, effective 1/3/2006]

12.206 Use of past performance.

Past performance should be an important element of every evaluation and contract award for commercial items. Contracting officers should consider past performance data from a wide variety of sources both inside and outside the Federal Government in accordance with the policies and procedures contained in Subpart 9.1, 13.106, or Subpart 15.3, as applicable.

[FAC 90-32, 60 FR 48206, 9/18/95, effective 10/1/95; FAC 90-40, 61 FR 39186, 7/26/96, effective 8/26/96; FAC 97-2, 62 FR 51224, 9/30/97, effective 10/10/97; FAC 97-3, 62 FR 64912, 12/9/97, effective 2/9/98]

12.207 Contract type.

(a) Except as provided in paragraph (b) of this section, agencies shall use firm-fixed-price contracts or fixed-price contracts with economic price adjustment for the acquisition of commercial items.

(b) (1) A time-and-materials contract or labor-hour contract (see Subpart 16.6) may be used for the acquisition of commercial services when—

(i) The service is acquired under a contract awarded using—

(A) Competitive procedures (e.g., the procedures in 6.102, the set-aside procedures in Subpart 19.5, or competition conducted in accordance with Part 13);

(B) The procedures for other than full and open competition in 6.3 provided the agency receives offers that satisfy the Government's expressed requirement from two or more responsible offerors; or

(C) The fair opportunity procedures in 16.505 (including discretionary small business set-asides under 16.505(b) (2) (i) (F)), if placing an order under a multiple award delivery-order contract; and

(ii) The contracting officer—

(A) Executes a determination and findings (D&F) for the contract, in accordance with paragraph (b) (2) of this section (but see paragraph (c) of this section for indefinite-delivery contracts), that no other contract type authorized by this subpart is suitable;

(B) Includes a ceiling price in the contract or order that the contractor exceeds at its own risk; and

(C) Prior to increasing the ceiling price of a time-and-materials or labor-hour contract or order, shall—

(1) Conduct an analysis of pricing and other relevant factors to determine if the action is in the best interest of the Government;

(2) Document the decision in the contract or order file; and

(3) When making a change that modifies the general scope of—

(i) A contract, follow the procedures at 6.303;

(ii) An order issued under the Federal Supply Schedules, follow the procedures at 8.405–6; or

(iii) An order issued under multiple award task and delivery order contracts, follow the procedures at 16.505(b) (2).

(2) Each D&F required by paragraph (b) (1) (ii) (A) of this section shall contain sufficient facts and rationale to justify that no other contract type authorized by this subpart is suitable. At a minimum, the D&F shall—

(i) Include a description of the market research conducted (see 10.002(e));

(ii) Establish that it is not possible at the time of placing the contract or order to accurately estimate the extent or duration of the work or to anticipate costs with any reasonable degree of confidence;

(iii) Establish that the requirement has been structured to maximize the use of firm-fixed-price or fixed-price with economic price adjustment contracts (e.g., by limiting the value or length of the time-and-material/labor-hour contract or order; establishing fixed prices for portions of the requirement) on future acquisitions for the same or similar requirements; and

(iv) Describe actions planned to maximize the use of firm-fixed-price or fixed-price with economic price adjustment contracts on future acquisitions for the same requirements.

(3) See 16.601(d)(1) for additional approval required for contracts expected to extend beyond three years.

(4) See 8.404(h) for the requirement for determination and findings when using Federal Supply Schedules.

(c)(1) Indefinite-delivery contracts (see Subpart 16.5) may be used when—

(i) The prices are established based on a firm-fixed-price or fixed-price with economic price adjustment; or

(ii) Rates are established for commercial services acquired on a time-and-materials or labor-hour basis.

(2) When an indefinite-delivery contract is awarded with services priced on a time-and-materials or labor-hour basis, contracting officers shall, to the maximum extent practicable, also structure the contract to allow issuance of orders on a firm-fixed-price or fixed-price with economic price adjustment basis. For such contracts, the contracting officer shall execute the D&F required by paragraph (b)(2) of this section, for each order placed on a time-and-materials or labor-hour basis. Placement of orders shall be in accordance with Subpart 8.4 or 16.5, as applicable.

(3) If an indefinite-delivery contract only allows for the issuance of orders on a time-and-materials or labor-hour basis, the D&F required by paragraph (b)(2) of this section shall be executed to support the basic contract and shall also explain why providing for an alternative firm-fixed-price or fixed-price with economic price adjustment pricing structure is not practicable. The D&F for this contract shall be approved one level above the contracting officer. Placement of orders shall be in accordance with Subpart 16.5.

(d) The contract types authorized by this subpart may be used in conjunction with an award fee and performance or delivery incentives when the award fee or incentive is based solely on factors other than cost (see 16.202-1 and 16.203-1).

(e) Use of any contract type other than those authorized by this subpart to acquire commercial items is prohibited.

[FAC 90-32, 60 FR 48206, 9/18/95, effective 10/1/95; FAC 2001-13, 68 FR 13201, 3/18/2003, effective 4/17/2003; FAC 2005-15, 71 FR 74667, 12/12/2006, effective 2/12/2007; Final rule, 72 FR 6881, 2/13/2007, effective 2/12/2007; FAC 2005-54, 76 FR 68032, 11/2/2011, effective 11/2/2011; FAC 2005-55, 77 FR 194, 1/3/2012, effective 2/2/2012; Interim rule, 77 FR 1889 77 FR 1889, 1/12/2012, effective 2/13/2012; FAC 2005-66, 78 FR 13766, 2/28/2013, effective 4/1/2013]

12.208 Contract quality assurance.

Contracts for commercial items shall rely on contractors' existing quality assurance systems as a substitute for Government inspection and testing before tender for acceptance unless customary market practices for the commercial item being acquired include in-process inspection. Any in-process inspection by the Government shall be conducted in a manner consistent with commercial practice.

[FAC 90-32, 60 FR 48206, 9/18/95, effective 10/1/95]

12.209 Determination of price reasonableness.

While the contracting officer must establish price reasonableness in accordance with 13.106-3, 14.408-2, or subpart 15.4, as applicable, the contracting officer should be aware of customary commercial terms and conditions when pricing commercial items. Commercial item prices are affected by factors that include, but are not limited to, speed of delivery, length and extent of warranty, limitations of seller's liability, quantities ordered, length of the performance period, and specific performance requirements. The contracting officer must ensure that contract terms, conditions, and prices are commensurate with the Government's need.

[FAC 2001-01, 66 FR 53478, 10/22/2001, effective 12/21/2001]

12.210 Contract financing.

Customary market practice for some commercial items may include buyer contract financing. The contracting officer may offer Government financing in accordance with the policies and procedures in Part 32.

[FAC 90-32, 60 FR 48206, 9/18/95, effective 10/1/95]

12.211 Technical data.

Except as provided by agency-specific statutes, the Government shall acquire only the technical data and the rights in that data customarily provided to the public with a commercial item or process. The contracting officer shall presume that data delivered under a contract for commercial items was developed exclusively at private expense. When a contract for commercial items requires the delivery of technical data, the contracting officer shall include appropriate provisions and clauses delineating the rights in the technical data in addenda to the solicitation and contract (see Part 27 or agency FAR supplements).

[FAC 90-32, 60 FR 48206, 9/18/95, effective 10/1/95]

12.212 Computer software.

(a) Commercial computer software or commercial computer software documentation shall be acquired under licenses customarily provided to the public to the extent such licenses are consistent with Federal law and otherwise satisfy the Government's needs. Generally, offerors and contractors shall not be required to—

(1) Furnish technical information related to commercial computer software or commercial computer software documentation that is not customarily provided to the public; or

(2) Relinquish to, or otherwise provide, the Government rights to use, modify, reproduce, release, perform, display, or disclose commercial computer software or commercial computer software documentation except as mutually agreed to by the parties.

(b) With regard to commercial computer software and commercial computer software documentation, the Government shall have only those rights specified in the license contained in any addendum to the contract. For additional guidance regarding the use and negotiation of license agreements for commercial computer software, see 27.405-3.

[FAC 90-32, 60 FR 48206, 9/18/95, effective 10/1/95; FAC 2005-21, 72 FR 63045, 11/7/2007, effective 12/7/2007]

12.213 Other commercial practices.

It is a common practice in the commercial marketplace for both the buyer and seller to propose terms and conditions written from their particular perspectives. The terms and conditions prescribed in this part seek to balance the interests of both the buyer and seller. These terms and conditions are generally appropriate for use in a wide range of acquisitions. However, market research may indicate other commercial practices that are appropriate for the acquisition of the particular item. These practices should be considered for incorporation into the solicitation and contract if the contracting officer determines them appropriate in concluding a business arrangement satisfactory to both parties and not otherwise precluded by law or Executive order.

[FAC 90-45, Final rule, 62 FR 224, 1/2/97, effective 1/1/97]

12.214 Cost Accounting Standards.

Cost Accounting Standards (CAS) do not apply to contracts and subcontracts for the acquisition of commercial items when these contracts and subcontracts are firm-fixed-price or fixed-price with economic price adjustment (provided that the price adjustment is not based on actual costs incurred). See 30.201-1 for CAS applicability to fixed-price with economic price adjustment contracts and subcontracts for commercial items when the price adjustment is based on actual costs incurred. When CAS applies, the contracting officer shall insert the appropriate provisions and clauses as prescribed in 30.201.

12.215 Notification of overpayment.

If the contractor notifies the contracting officer of a duplicate contract payment or that the Government has otherwise overpaid, the contracting officer shall follow the procedures at 32.604.

[FAC 97-4, 63 FR 9048, 2/23/98, effective 4/24/98; FAC 2001-16, 68 FR 56682, 10/1/2003, effective 10/31/2003; FAC 2007-27, 73 FR 53997, 9/17/2008, effective 10/17/2008]

12.216 Unenforceability of unauthorized obligations.

Many supplies or services are acquired subject to supplier license agreements. These are particularly common in information technology acquisitions, but they may apply to any supply or service. For example, computer software and services delivered through the internet (web services) are often subject to license agreements, referred to as End User License Agreements (EULA), Terms of Service (TOS), or other similar legal instruments or agreements. Many of these agreements contain indemnification clauses that are inconsistent with Federal law and unenforceable, but which could create a violation of the Anti-Deficiency Act (31 U.S.C. 1341) if agreed to by the Government. Paragraph (u) of the clause at 52.212–4 prevents any such violations.

[FAC 2005-67, 78 FR 37686, 6/21/2013, effective 6/21/2013; FAC 2005-72, 78 FR 80382,12/31/2013, effective 12/31/2013]

SUBPART 12.3—SOLICITATION PROVISIONS AND CONTRACT CLAUSES FOR THE ACQUISITION OF COMMERCIAL ITEMS

12.300 Scope of subpart.

This subpart establishes provisions and clauses to be used when acquiring commercial items.

[FAC 90-32, 60 FR 48206, 9/18/95, effective 10/1/95]

12.301 Solicitation provisions and contract clauses for acquisition of commercial items.

(a) In accordance with 41 U.S.C. 3307, contracts for the acquisition of commercial items shall, to the maximum extent practicable, include only those clauses—

(1) Required to implement provisions of law or executive orders applicable to the acquisition of commercial items; or

(2) Determined to be consistent with customary commercial practice.

(b) Insert the following provisions in solicitations for the acquisition of commercial items, and clauses in solicitations and contracts for the acquisition of commercial items:

(1) *The provision at 52.212-1, Instructions to Offerors—Commercial Items.* This provision provides a single, streamlined set of instructions to be used when soliciting offers for commercial items and is incorporated in the solicitation by reference (see Block 27a, SF 1449). The contracting officer may tailor these instructions or provide additional instructions tailored to the specific acquisition in accordance with 12.302.

(2) *The provision at 52.212-3, Offeror Representations and Certifications—Commercial Items.* This provision provides a single, consolidated list of representations and certifications for the acquisition of commercial items and is attached to the solicitation for offerors to complete. This provision may not be tailored except in accordance with Subpart 1.4. Use the provision with its Alternate I in solicitations issued by DoD, NASA, or the Coast Guard.

(3) *The clause at 52.212-4, Contract Terms and Conditions—Commercial Items.* This clause includes terms and conditions which are, to the maximum extent practicable, consistent with customary commercial practices and is incorporated in the solicitation and contract by reference (see Block 27, SF 1449). Use this clause with its Alternate I when a time-and-materials or labor-hour contract will be awarded. The contracting officer may tailor this clause in accordance with 12.302.

(4) *The clause at 52.212-5, Contract Terms and Conditions Required to Implement Statutes or Executive Orders—Commercial Items.* This clause incorporates by reference only those clauses required to implement provisions of law or Executive orders applicable to the acquisition of commercial items. The contracting officer shall attach this clause to the solicitation and contract and, using the appropriate clause prescriptions, indicate which, if any, of the additional clauses cited in 52.212-5(b) or (c) are applicable to the specific acquisition. Some of the clauses require fill-in; the fill-in language should be inserted as directed by 52.104(d). When cost information is obtained pursuant to Part 15 to establish the reasonableness of prices for commercial items, the contracting officer shall insert the clauses prescribed for this purpose in an addendum to the solicitation and contract. This clause may not be tailored.

(i) Use the clause with its Alternate I when the head of the agency has waived the examination of records by the Comptroller General in accordance with 25.1001.

(ii)(A) If the acquisition will use funds appropriated or otherwise made available by the American Recovery and Reinvestment Act of 2009 (Pub. L. 111-5), the contracting officer shall use the clause with its Alternate II.

(B)(*1*) In the case of a bilateral contract modification that will use funds appropriated or otherwise made available by the American Recovery and Reinvestment Act of 2009, the contracting officer shall specify applicability of Alternate II to that modification.

(*2*) In the case of a task- or delivery-order contract in which not all orders will use funds appropriated or otherwise made available by the American Recovery and Reinvestment Act of 2009, the contracting officer shall specify the task or delivery orders to which Alternate II applies.

(C) The contracting officer may not use Alternate I when Alternate II applies.

(c) When the use of evaluation factors is appropriate, the contracting officer may—

(1) Insert the provision at 52.212-2, Evaluation—Commercial Items, in solicitations for commercial items (see 12.602); or

(2) Include a similar provision containing all evaluation factors required by 13.106, Subpart 14.2 or Subpart 15.3, as an addendum (see 12.302(d)).

(d) *Other required provisions and clauses.* Notwithstanding prescriptions contained elsewhere in the FAR, when acquiring commercial items, contracting officers shall be required to use only those provisions and clauses prescribed in this part. The provisions and clauses prescribed in this part shall be revised, as necessary, to reflect the applicability of statutes and executive orders to the acquisition of commercial items.

(1) Insert the provision at 52.204-7, System for Award Management, as prescribed in 4.1105(a).

(2) Insert the clause at 52.204-13, System for Award Management Maintenance, as prescribed in 4.1105(b).

(3) Insert the provision at 52.204-16, Commercial and Government Entity Code Reporting, as prescribed in 4.1804(a).

(4) Insert the clause at 52.204-18, Commercial and Government Entity Code Maintenance, as prescribed in 4.1804(c).

(5) Insert the clause at 52.204-21, Basic Safeguarding of Covered Contractor Information Systems, in solicitations and contracts (except for acquisitions of COTS items), as prescribed in 4.1903.

(6) Insert the provision at 52.204-24, Representation Regarding Certain Telecommunications and Video Surveillance Services or Equipment, as prescribed in 4.2105(a).

(7) Insert the provision at 52.207-6, Solicitation of Offers from Small Business Concerns and Small Business Teaming Arrangements or Joint Ventures (Multiple-Award Contracts), as prescribed at 7.107-6.

(8) Insert the provision at 52.209-7, Information Regarding Responsibility Matters, as prescribed in 9.104-7(b).

(9) Insert the provision at 52.209–12, Certification Regarding Tax Matters, as prescribed at 9.104–7(e).

(10) Insert the provision at 52.222-56, Certification Regarding Trafficking in Persons Compliance Plan, in solicitations as prescribed at 22.1705(b).

(11) Insert the clause at 52.225-19, Contractor Personnel in a Designated Operational Area or Supporting a Diplomatic or Consular Mission outside the United States, as prescribed in 25.301-4.

(12) Insert the clause at 52.232-40, Providing Accelerated Payments to Small Business Subcontractors, as prescribed in 32.009-2.

(e) *Discretionary use of FAR provisions and clauses.* The contracting officer may include in solicitations and contracts by addendum other FAR provisions and clauses when their use is consistent with the limitations contained in 12.302. For example:

(1) The contracting officer may include appropriate clauses when an indefinite-delivery type of contract will be used. The clauses prescribed at 16.506 may be used for this purpose.

(2) The contracting officer may include appropriate provisions and clauses when the use of options is in the Government's interest. The provisions and clauses prescribed in 17.208 may be used for this purpose. If the provision at 52.212-2 is used, paragraph (b) provides for the evaluation of options.

(3) The contracting officer may use the provisions and clauses contained in Part 23 regarding the use of products containing recovered materials and biobased products when appropriate for the item being acquired.

(4) When setting aside under the Stafford Act (Subpart 26.2), include the provision at 52.226-3, Disaster or Emergency Area Representation, in the solicitation. The representation in this provision is not in the System for Award Management.

(f) Agencies may supplement the provisions and clauses prescribed in this part (to require use of additional provisions and clauses) only as necessary to reflect agency unique statutes applicable to the acquisition of commercial items or as may be approved by the agency senior procurement executive, or the individual responsible for representing the agency on the FAR Council, without power of delegation.

[FAC 90-32, 60 FR 48206, 9/18/95, effective 10/1/95; FAC 90-40, 61 FR 39186, 7/26/96, effective 8/26/96; FAC 90-43, 61 FR 67408, 12/20/96, effective 12/20/96; FAC 97-2, 62 FR 51224, 9/30/97, effective 10/10/97; FAC 97-3, 62 FR 64912, 12/9/97, effective 2/9/98; FAC 97-6, 63 FR 35719, 6/30/98, effective 10/1/98, finalized without change, FAC 97-13, 7/2/99; FAC 97-8, 63 FR 52425, 9/30/98, effective 10/1/98, finalized without change, FAC 97-13, 7/2/99; FAC 97-10, 63 FR 70264, 12/18/98, effective 1/4/99; FAC 97-12, 64 FR 32740, 6/17/99, effective 6/17/99; FAC 97-15, 64 FR 72414, 12/27/99, effective 2/25/2000; FAC 2001-04, 67 FR 6112, 2/8/2002, effective 2/8/2002; FAC 2001-06, 67 FR 13048, 3/20/2002, effective 4/4/2002; FAC 2001-07, 67 FR 21538, 4/30/2002, effective 5/15/2002; FAC 2005-12, 71 FR 44546, 8/4/2006, effective 8/4/2006; FAC 2005-13, 71 FR 57362, 9/28/2006, effective 9/28/2006; FAC 2005-15, 71 FR 74667, 12/12/2006, effective 2/12/2007; FAC 2005-19, 72 FR 46333, 8/17/2007, effective 8/17/2007; FAC 2005-21, 72 FR 63040, 63084, 11/7/2007, effective 11/7/2007, 12/7/2007; FAC 2005-24, 73 FR 10943, 2/28/2008, effective 3/31/2008; FAC 2005-25, 73 FR 21773, 21789, 4/22/2008, effective 4/22/2008, 5/22/2008; FAC 2005-27, 73 FR 53995, 9/17/2008, effective 10/17/2008; FAC 2005-30, 74 FR 2712, 2713, 1/15/2009, effective 2/17/2009; FAC 2005-32, 74 FR 14646, 3/31/2009, effective 3/31/2009; FAC 2005-40, 75 FR 14059, 3/23/2010, effective 4/22/2010; FAC 2005-42, 75 FR 34279, 6/16/2010, effective 7/16/2010; FAC 2005-49, 76 FR 4188, 1/24/2011, effective 1/24/2011; FAC 2005-55, 77 FR 194, 1/3/2012, effective 2/2/2012, 77 FR 197, 1/3/2012, effective 1/3/2012; FAC 2005-67, 78 FR 37676, 6/21/2013, effective 7/22/2013; FAC 2005-71, 78 FR 70477, 11/25/2013, effective 12/26/2013; FAC 2005-73, 79 FR 24192, 4/29/2014, effective 5/29/2014; FAC 2005-74, 79 FR 31187, 5/30/2014, effective 11/1/2014; FAC 2005-77, 79 FR 61746, 10/14/2014, effective 10/14/2014; FAC 2005-80, 80 FR 4967, 1/29/2015, effective 3/2/2015; FAC 2005-85,

80 FR 75903, 12/4/2015, effective 2/26/2016; FAC 2005-88, 81 FR 30439, 5/16/2016, effective 6/15/2016; FAC 2005-91, 81 FR 67728, 9/30/2016, effective 9/30/2016; FAC 2005-91, 81 FR 67736, 9/30/2016, effective 10/31/2016; FAC 2005-91, 81 FR 67763, 9/30/2016, effective 10/31/2016; FAC 2005-101, 83 FR 48691, 9/26/2018, effective 10/26/2018; FAC 2019-05, 84 FR 40216, 8/13/2019, effective 8/13/2019]

12.302 Tailoring of provisions and clauses for the acquisition of commercial items.

(a) *General.* The provisions and clauses established in this subpart are intended to address, to the maximum extent practicable, commercial market practices for a wide range of potential Government acquisitions of commercial items. However, because of the broad range of commercial items acquired by the Government, variations in commercial practices, and the relative volume of the Government's acquisitions in the specific market, contracting officers may, within the limitations of this subpart, and after conducting appropriate market research, tailor the provision at 52.212-1, Instructions to Offerors—Commercial Items, and the clause at 52.212-4, Contract Terms and Conditions—Commercial Items, to adapt to the market conditions for each acquisition.

(b) *Tailoring 52.212-4, Contract Terms and Conditions—Commercial Items.* The following paragraphs of the clause at 52.212-4, Contract Terms and Conditions—Commercial Items, implement statutory requirements and shall not be tailored—

(1) Assignments;

(2) Disputes;

(3) Payment (except as provided in Subpart 32.11);

(4) Invoice;

(5) Other compliances;

(6) Compliance with laws unique to Government contracts; and

(7) Unauthorized obligations.

(c) *Tailoring inconsistent with customary commercial practice.* The contracting officer shall not tailor any clause or otherwise include any additional terms or conditions in a solicitation or contract for commercial items in a manner that is inconsistent with customary commercial practice for the item being acquired unless a waiver is approved in accordance with agency procedures. The request for waiver must describe the customary commercial practice found in the marketplace, support the need to include a term or condition that is inconsistent with that practice and include a determination that use of the customary commercial practice is inconsistent with the needs of the Government. A waiver may be requested for an individual or class of contracts for that specific item.

(d) *Tailoring shall be by addenda to the solicitation and contract.* The contracting officer shall indicate in Block 27a of the SF 1449 if addenda are attached. These addenda may include, for example, a continuation of the schedule of supplies/services to be acquired from blocks 18 through 21 of the SF 1449; a continuation of the description of the supplies/services being acquired; further elaboration of any other item(s) on the SF 1449; any other terms or conditions necessary for the performance of the proposed contract (such as options, ordering procedures for indefinite-delivery type contracts, warranties, contract financing arrangements, etc.).

[FAC 90-32, 60 FR 48206, 9/18/95, effective 10/1/95; FAC 90-42, 61 FR 45769, 8/29/96, effective 8/29/96; FAC 90-43, 61 FR 67408, 12/20/96, effective 12/20/96; FAC 90-45, Final rule, 62 FR 224, 1/2/97, effective 1/1/97; FAC 2005-67, 78 FR 37686, 6/21/2013, effective 6/21/2013; FAC 2005-72, 78 FR 80382,12/31/2013, effective 12/31/2013]

12.303 Contract format.

Solicitations and contracts for the acquisition of commercial items prepared using this Part 12 shall be assembled, to the maximum extent practicable, using the following format:

(a) Standard Form (SF) 1449;

(b) Continuation of any block from SF 1449, such as—

(1) Block 10 if an incentive subcontracting clause is used (the contracting officer shall indicate the applicable percentage);

(2) Block 18B for remittance address;

(3) Block 19 for line item numbers;

(4) Block 20 for schedule of supplies/ services;

(5) Block 25 for accounting data;

(c) Contract clauses—

(1) 52.212-4, Contract Terms and Conditions—Commercial Items, by reference (see SF 1449, Block 27a);

(2) Any addendum to 52.212-4; and

(3) 52.212-5, Contract Terms and Conditions Required to Implement Statutes and Executive Orders;

(d) Any contract documents, exhibits or attachments; and

(e) Solicitation provisions—

(1) 52.212-1, Instructions to Offerors—Commercial Items, by reference (see SF 1449, Block 27a);

(2) Any addendum to 52.212-1;

(3) 52.212-2, Evaluation—Commercial Items, or other description of evaluation factors for award, if used; and

(4) 52.212-3, Offeror Representations and Certifications—Commercial Items.

[FAC 90-32, 60 FR 48206, 9/18/95, effective 10/1/95, corrected 60 FR 54817, 10/26/95; FAC 90-43, 61 FR 67408, 12/20/96, effective 12/20/96; FAC 97-6, 63 FR 35719, 6/30/98, effective 10/1/98, finalized without change, FAC 97-13, 7/2/99; FAC 97-7, 63 FR 36120, 7/1/98, effective 1/1/99, finalized without change, FAC 97-13, 7/2/99; FAC 97-11, 64 FR 10530, 3/4/99, effective 3/4/99; FAC 2005-07, 71 FR 220, 1/3/2006, effective 1/3/2006; FAC 2005-48, 75 FR 82567, 12/30/2010, effective 1/31/2011; FAC 2005-77, 79 FR 61746, 10/14/2014, effective 10/14/2014; FAC 2005-95, 82 FR 4709, 1/13/2017, effective 1/13/2017]

SUBPART 12.4—UNIQUE REQUIREMENTS REGARDING TERMS AND CONDITIONS FOR COMMERCIAL ITEMS

12.401 General.

This subpart provides—

(a) Guidance regarding tailoring of the paragraphs in the clause at 52.212-4, Contract Terms and Conditions—Commercial Items, when the paragraphs do not reflect the customary practice for a particular market; and

(b) Guidance on the administration of contracts for commercial items in those areas where the terms and conditions in 52.212-4 differ substantially from those contained elsewhere in the FAR.

[FAC 90-32, 60 FR 48206, 9/18/95, effective 10/1/95]

12.402 Acceptance.

(a) The acceptance paragraph in 52.212-4 is based upon the assumption that the Government will rely on the contractor's assurances that the commercial item tendered for acceptance conforms to the contract requirements. The Government inspection of commercial items will not prejudice its other rights under the acceptance paragraph. Additionally, although the paragraph does not address the issue of rejection, the Government always has the right to refuse acceptance of nonconforming items. This paragraph is generally appropriate when the Government is acquiring noncomplex commercial items.

(b) Other acceptance procedures may be more appropriate for the acquisition of complex commercial items or commercial items used in critical applications. In such cases, the contracting officer shall include alternative inspection procedure(s) in an addendum and ensure these procedures and the post-award remedies adequately protect the interests of the Government. The contracting officer must carefully examine the terms and conditions of any express warranty with regard to the effect it may have on the Government's available post-award remedies (see 12.404).

(c) The acquisition of commercial items under other circumstances such as on an "as is" basis may also require acceptance procedures different from those contained in 52.212-4. The contracting officer should consider the effect the specific circumstances will have on the acceptance paragraph as well as other paragraphs of the clause.

[FAC 90-32, 60 FR 48206, 9/18/95, effective 10/1/95]

12.403 Termination.

(a) *General.* The clause at 52.212-4 permits the Government to terminate a contract for commercial items either for the convenience of the Government or for cause. However, the paragraphs in 52.212-4 entitled "Termination for the Government's Convenience" and "Termination for Cause" contain concepts which differ from those contained in the termination clauses prescribed in Part 49. Consequently, the requirements of Part 49 do not apply when terminating contracts for commercial items and contracting officers shall follow the procedures in this section. Contracting officers may continue to use Part 49 as guidance to the extent that Part 49 does not conflict with this section and the language of the termination paragraphs in 52.212-4.

(b) *Policy.* The contracting officer should exercise the Government's right to terminate a contract for commercial items either for convenience or for cause only when such a termination would be in the best interests of the Government. The contracting officer should consult with counsel prior to terminating for cause.

(c) *Termination for cause.*

(1) The paragraph in 52.212-4 entitled "Excusable Delay" requires contractors notify the contracting officer as soon as possible after commencement of any excusable delay. In most situations, this requirement should eliminate the need for a show cause notice prior to terminating a contract. The contracting officer shall send a cure notice prior to terminating a contract for a reason other than late delivery.

(2) The Government's rights after a termination for cause shall include all the remedies available to any buyer in the marketplace. The Government's preferred remedy will be to acquire similar items from another contractor and to charge the defaulted contractor with any excess reprocurement costs together with any incidental or consequential damages incurred because of the termination.

(3) When a termination for cause is appropriate, the contracting officer shall send the contractor a written notification regarding the termination. At a minimum, this notification shall—

(i) Indicate the contract is terminated for cause;

(ii) Specify the reasons for the termination;

(iii) Indicate which remedies the Government intends to seek or provide a date by which the Government will inform the contractor of the remedy; and

(iv) State that the notice constitutes a final decision of the contracting officer and that the contractor has the right to appeal under the Disputes clause (see 33.211).

(4) The contracting officer, in accordance with agency procedures, shall ensure that information related to termination for cause notices and any amendments are reported. In the event the termination for cause is subsequently converted to a termination for convenience, or is otherwise withdrawn, the contracting officer shall ensure that a notice of the conversion or withdrawal is reported. All reporting shall be in accordance with 42.1503(h).

(d) *Termination for the Government's convenience.* (1) When the contracting officer terminates a contract for commercial items for the Government's convenience, the contractor shall be paid—

(i) (A) The percentage of the contract price reflecting the percentage of the work performed prior to the notice of the termination for fixed-price or fixed-price with economic price adjustment contracts; or

(B) An amount for direct labor hours (as defined in the Schedule of the contract) determined by multiplying the number of direct labor hours expended before the effective date of termination by the hourly rate(s) in the Schedule; and

(ii) Any charges the contractor can demonstrate directly resulted from the termination. The contractor may demonstrate such charges using its standard record keeping system and is not required to comply with the cost accounting standards or the contract cost principles in Part 31. The Government does not have any right to audit the contractor's records solely because of the termination for convenience.

(2) Generally, the parties should mutually agree upon the requirements of the termination proposal. The parties must balance the Government's need to obtain sufficient documentation to support payment to the contractor against the goal of having a simple and expeditious settlement.

[FAC 90-32, 60 FR 48206, 9/18/95, effective 10/1/95; FAC 2005-15, 71 FR 74667, 12/12/2006, effective 2/12/2007; FAC 2005-46, 75 FR 60258, 9/29/2010, effective 10/29/2010; FAC 2005-69, 78 FR 46783, 8/1/2013, effective 9/3/2013]

12.404 Warranties.

(a) *Implied warranties.* The Government's post award rights contained in 52.212-4 are the implied warranty of merchantability, the implied warranty of fitness for particular purpose and the remedies contained in the acceptance paragraph.

(1) The implied warranty of merchantability provides that an item is reasonably fit for the ordinary purposes for which such items are used. The items must be of at least average, fair or medium-grade quality and must be comparable in quality to those that will pass without objection in the trade or market for items of the same description.

(2) The implied warranty of fitness for a particular purpose provides that an item is fit for use for the particular purpose for which the Government will use the items. The Government can rely upon an implied warranty of fitness for particular purpose when—

(i) The seller knows the particular purpose for which the Government intends to use the item; and

(ii) The Government relied upon the contractor's skill and judgment that the item would be appropriate for that particular purpose.

(3) Contracting officers should consult with legal counsel prior to asserting any claim for a breach of an implied warranty.

(b) *Express warranties.* 41 U.S.C. 3307(e)(5)(B) requires contracting officers to take advantage of commercial warranties. To the maximum extent practicable, solicitations for commercial items shall require offerors to offer the Government at least the same warranty terms, including offers of extended warranties, offered to the general public in customary commercial practice. Solicitations may specify minimum warranty terms, such as minimum duration, appropriate for the Government's intended use of the item.

(1) Any express warranty the Government intends to rely upon must meet the needs of the Government. The contracting officer should analyze any commercial warranty to determine if—

(i) The warranty is adequate to protect the needs of the Government, *e.g.*, items covered by the warranty and length of warranty;

(ii) The terms allow the Government effective post-award administration of the warranty to include the identification of warranted items, procedures for the return of warranted items to the contractor for repair or replacement, and collection of product performance information; and

(iii) The warranty is cost-effective.

(2) In some markets, it may be customary commercial practice for contractors to exclude or limit the implied warranties contained in 52.212-4 in the provisions of an express warranty. In such cases, the contracting officer shall ensure that the express warranty provides for the repair or replacement of defective items discovered within a reasonable period of time after acceptance.

(3) Express warranties shall be included in the contract by addendum (see 12.302).

[FAC 90-32, 60 FR 48206, 9/18/95, effective 10/1/95; FAC 2005-73, 79 FR 24192, 4/29/2014, effective 5/29/2014]

SUBPART 12.5—APPLICABILITY OF CERTAIN LAWS TO THE ACQUISITION OF COMMERCIAL ITEMS AND

COMMERCIALLY AVAILABLE OFF-THE-SHELF ITEMS

12.500 Scope of subpart.

(a) As required by 41 U.S.C. 1906 and 1907, this subpart lists provisions of law that are not applicable to—

(1) Contracts for the acquisition of commercial items;

(2) Subcontracts, at any tier, for the acquisition of commercial items; and

(3) Contracts and subcontracts, at any tier, for the acquisition of COTS items.

(b) This subpart also lists provisions of law that have been amended to eliminate or modify their applicability to either contracts or subcontracts for the acquisition of commercial items.

[FAC 90-32, 60 FR 48206, 9/18/95, effective 10/1/95; FAC 2005-30, 74 FR 2713, 1/15/2009, effective 2/17/2009; FAC 2005-73, 79 FR 24192, 4/29/2014, effective 5/29/2014]

12.501 Applicability.

(a) This subpart applies to any contract or subcontract at any tier for the acquisition of commercial items.

(b) Nothing in this Subpart shall be construed to authorize the waiver of any provision of law with respect to any subcontract if the prime contractor is reselling or distributing commercial items of another contractor without adding value. This limitation is intended to preclude establishment of unusual contractual arrangements solely for the purpose of Government sales.

(c) For purposes of this subpart, contractors awarded subcontracts under Subpart 19.8, Contracting with the Small Business Administration (the 8(a) Program), shall be considered prime contractors.

[FAC 90-32, 60 FR 48206, 9/18/95, effective 10/1/95]

12.502 Procedures.

(a) The FAR prescription for the provision or clause for each of the laws listed in 12.503 has been revised in the appropriate part to reflect its proper application to prime contracts for the acquisition of commercial items.

(b) For subcontracts for the acquisition of commercial items or commercial components, the clauses at 52.212-5, Contract Terms and Conditions Required to Implement Statutes or Executive Orders—Commercial Items, and 52.244-6, Subcontracts for Commercial Items, reflect the applicability of the laws listed in 12.504 by identifying the only provisions and clauses that are required to be included in a subcontract at any tier for the acquisition of commercial items or commercial components.

(c) The FAR prescription for the provision or clause for each of the laws listed in 12.505 has been revised in the appropriate part to reflect its proper application to contracts and subcontracts for the acquisition of COTS items.

[FAC 90-32, 60 FR 48206, 9/18/95, effective 10/1/95; FAC 2005-30, 74 FR 2713, 1/15/2009, effective 2/17/2009; FAC 2005-73, 79 FR 24192, 4/29/2014, effective 5/29/2014]

12.503 Applicability of certain laws to Executive agency contracts for the acquisition of commercial items.

(a) The following laws are not applicable to Executive agency contracts for the acquisition of commercial items:

(1) 41 U.S.C. chapter 65, Contracts for Materials, Supplies, Articles, and Equipment Exceeding $15,000 (see subpart 22.6).

(2) 41 U.S.C. 3901(b) and 10 U.S.C. 2306(b), Contingent Fees (see 3.404).

(3) 41 U.S.C. 1708(e)(3), Minimum Response Time for Offers (see 5.203).

(4) 41 U.S.C. chapter 81, Drug-Free Workplace (see 23.501).

(5) 31 U.S.C. 1354(a), Limitation on use of appropriated funds for contracts with entities not meeting veterans employment reporting requirements (see 22.1302).

(6) [Removed and reserved]

(7) Section 806(a)(3) of Pub. L. 102–190, as amended by sections 2091 and 8105 of Pub. L. 103–355 (10 U.S.C. 2302 note), Pay-

ment Protections for Subcontractors and Suppliers (see 28.106-6).

(8) 41 U.S.C. 4706(d)(1) and 10 U.S.C. 2313(c)(1), GAO Access to Contractor Employees, section 871 of Pub. L. 110–417 (see 52.214-26 and 52.215-2).

(9) 41 U.S.C. 2303(b), Policy on Personal Conflicts of Interest by Contractor Employees (see subpart 3.11).

(b) Certain requirements of the following laws are not applicable to executive agency contracts for the acquisition of commercial items:

(1) 22 U.S.C. 2593e, Requirement for a certification under Measures Against Persons Involved in Activities that Violate Arms Control Treaties or Agreements with the United States (see 9.109).

(2) 40 U.S.C. chapter 37, Requirement for a certificate and clause under the Contract Work Hours and Safety Standards statute (see 22.305).

(3) 41 U.S.C. 8703 and 8704, Requirement for a clause and certain other requirements related to kickbacks (see 3.502).

(4) 49 U.S.C. 40118, Requirement for a clause under the Fly American provisions (see 47.405).

(c) The applicability of the following laws has been modified in regards to Executive agency contracts for the acquisition of commercial items:

(1) 41 U.S.C. 4704 and 10 U.S.C. 4704, Prohibition on Limiting Subcontractor Direct Sales to the United States (see 3.503).

(2) 41 U.S.C. chapter 35, Truthful Cost or Pricing Data, and 10 U.S.C. 2306a, Truth in Negotiations (see 15.403).

(3) 41 U.S.C. chapter 15, Cost Accounting Standards (48 CFR chapter 99) (see 12.214).

(7) Section 806(a)(3) of Pub. L. 102-190, as amended by Sections 2091 and 8105 of Pub. L. 103-355, Payment Protections for Subcontractors and Suppliers (see 28.106-6).

[FAC 90-32, 60 FR 48206, 9/18/95, effective 10/1/95; FAC 90-43, Final rule, 61 FR 67408, 12/20/96, effective 1/1/97; FAC 90-45, Final rule, 62 FR 224, 1/2/97, effective 1/1/97, corrected 62 FR 10709, 3/10/97; FAC 97-2, 62 FR 51224, 9/30/97, effective 10/10/97; FAC 97-11, 64 FR 10530, 3/4/99, effective 5/3/99; FAC 97-15, 64 FR 72414, 12/27/99, effective 2/25/2000; FAC 2001-01, 66 FR 53478, 10/22/2001, effective 12/21/2001; FAC 2005-06, 70 FR 57453, 9/30/2005, effective 9/30/2005; FAC 2005-09, Interim rule, 71 FR 20301, 4/19/2006, effective 4/19/2006; FAC 2005-19, 72 FR 46335, 8/17/2007, effective 8/17/2007; FAC 2005-20, 72 FR 51306, 9/6/2007, effective 9/6/2007; FAC 2007-27, 73 FR 54007, 9/17/2008, effective 9/17/2008; FAC 2005-30, 74 FR 2741, 1/15/2009, effective 2/17/2009; FAC 2005-32, 74 FR 14649, 3/31/2009, effective 3/31/2009; FAC 2005-37, 74 FR 52851, 10/14/2009, effective 10/14/2009; FAC 2005-44, 75 FR 39414, 7/8/2010, effective 7/8/2010; FAC 2005-54, 76 FR 68017, 11/2/2011, effective 12/2/2011; FAC 2005-60, 77 FR 44047, 7/26/2012, effective 8/27/2012; FAC 2005-73, 79 FR 24192, 4/29/2014, effective 5/29/2014; FAC 2005-99, 83 FR 28145, 6/15/2018, effective 6/15/2018]

12.504 Applicability of certain laws to subcontracts for the acquisition of commercial items.

(a) The following laws are not applicable to subcontracts at any tier for the acquisition of commercial items or commercial components at any tier:

(1) 10 U.S.C. 2631, Transportation of Supplies by Sea (except for the types of subcontracts listed at 47.504(d)).

(2) 15 U.S.C. 644(d), Requirements relative to labor surplus areas under the Small Business Act (see Subpart 19.2).

(3) [Reserved].

(4) 41 U.S.C. 6505, Contracts for Materials, Supplies, Articles, and Equipment Exceeding $15,000 (see subpart 22.6).

(5) 41 U.S.C. 4703, Validation of Proprietary Data restrictions (see subpart 27.4).

(6) 41 U.S.C. 3901(b) and 10 U.S.C. 2306(b), Contingent Fees (see subpart 3.4).

(7) 41 U.S.C. 4706(d) and 10 U.S.C. 2313(c), Examination of Records of Contractor, when a subcontractor is not required to

provide certified cost or pricing data (see 15.209(b)), unless using funds appropriated or otherwise made available by the American Recovery and Reinvestment Act of 2009 (Pub. L. 111–5).

(8) 41 U.S.C. 1708(e)(3), Minimum Response Time for Offers (see subpart 5.2).

(9) 41 U.S.C. 2302, Rights in Technical Data (see subpart 27.4).

(10) 41 U.S.C. chapter 81, Drug-Free Workplace (see subpart 23.5).

(11) 46 U.S.C. Appx 1241 (b), Transportation in American Vessels of Government Personnel and Certain Cargo (see Subpart 47.5) (except for the types of subcontracts listed at 47.504(d)).

(12) 49 U.S.C. 40118, Fly American provisions (see Subpart 47.4).

(13) Section 806(a)(3) of Pub. L. 102-190, as amended by Sections 2091 and 8105 of Pub. L. 103-355 (10 U.S.C. 2302 note), Payment Protections for Subcontractors and Suppliers (see 28.106-6).

(b) The requirements for a certificate and clause under the Contract Work Hours and Safety Standards statute, 40 U.S.C. chapter 37 (see Subpart 22.3) are not applicable to subcontracts at any tier for the acquisition of commercial items or commercial components.

(c) The applicability of the following laws has been modified in regards to subcontracts at any tier for the acquisition of commercial items or commercial components:

(1) 41 U.S.C. 4704 and 10 U.S.C. 2402, Prohibition on Limiting Subcontractor Direct Sales to the United States (see subpart 3.5).

(2) 41 U.S.C. chapter 35, Truthful Cost or Pricing Data, and 10 U.S.C. 2306a, Truth in Negotiations (see subpart 15.4).

(3) 41 U.S.C. chapter 15, Cost Accounting Standards (48 CFR chapter 99) (see 12.214).

[FAC 90-32, 60 FR 48206, 9/18/95, effective 10/1/95; FAC 90-43, Final rule, 61 FR 67408, 12/20/96, effective 1/1/97; FAC 90-45, Final rule, 62 FR 224, 1/2/97, effective 1/1/97; FAC 97-2, 62 FR 51224, 9/30/97, effective 10/10/97; FAC 97-15, 64 FR 72414, 12/27/99, effective 2/25/2000; FAC 97-19, 65 FR 46052, 7/26/2000, effective 8/25/2000; FAC 2001-13, 68 FR 13202, 3/18/2003, effective 4/17/2003; FAC 2005-06, 70 FR 57453, 9/30/2005, effective 9/30/2005; FAC 2005-19, 72 FR 46327, 8/17/2007, effective 9/17/2007; FAC 2005-27, 73 FR 54007, 9/17/2008, effective 9/17/2008; FAC 2005-32, 74 FR 14646, 3/31/2009, effective 3/31/2009; FAC 2005-42, 75 FR 34279, 6/16/2010, effective 7/16/2010; FAC 2005-45, 75 FR 53135, 8/30/2010, effective 10/1/2010; FAC 2005-73, 79 FR 24192, 4/29/2014, effective 5/29/2014]

12.505 Applicability of certain laws to contracts for the acquisition of COTS items.

COTS items are a subset of commercial items. Therefore, any laws listed in sections 12.503 and 12.504 are also inapplicable or modified in their applicability to contracts or subcontracts for the acquisition of COTS items. In addition, the following laws are not applicable to contracts for the acquisition of COTS items:

(a)(1) The portion of 41 U.S.C. 8302(a)(1) that reads "substantially all from articles, materials, or supplies mined, produced, or manufactured in the United States," Buy American—Supplies, component test (see 52.225-1 and 52.225-3).

(2) The portion of 41 U.S.C. 8303(a)(2) that reads "substantially all from articles, materials, or supplies mined, produced, or manufactured in the United States," Buy American—Construction Materials, component test (see 52.225-9 and 52.225-11).

(b) 42 U.S.C. 6962(c)(3)(A), Certification and Estimate of Percentage of Recovered Material.

(c) Compliance Plan and Certification Requirement, section 1703 of the National Defense Authorization Act for Fiscal Year 2013 (Pub. L. 112-239), Title XVII, Ending trafficking in Government Contracting (see 52.222-50(h) and 52.222-56).

[FAC 2005-30, 74 FR 2713, 1/15/2009, effective 2/17/2009; FAC 2005-73, 79 FR 24192, 4/29/2014, effective 5/29/2014; FAC 2005-80, 80 FR 4967, 1/29/2015, effective 3/2/2015]

SUBPART 12.6—STREAMLINED PROCEDURES FOR EVALUATION AND SOLICITATION FOR COMMERCIAL ITEMS

12.601 General.

This subpart provides optional procedures for—

(a) Streamlined evaluation of offers for commercial items; and

(b) Streamlined solicitation of offers for commercial items for use where appropriate.

These procedures are intended to simplify the process of preparing and issuing solicitations, and evaluating offers for commercial items consistent with customary commercial practices.

[FAC 90-32, 60 FR 48206, 9/18/95, effective 10/1/95]

12.602 Streamlined evaluation of offers.

(a) When evaluation factors are used, the contracting officer may insert a provision substantially the same as the provision at 52.212-2, Evaluation—Commercial Items, in solicitations for commercial items or comply with the procedures in 13.106 if the acquisition is being made using simplified acquisition procedures. When the provision at 52.212-2 is used, paragraph (a) of the provision shall be tailored to the specific acquisition to describe the evaluation factors and relative importance of those factors. However, when using the simplified acquisition procedures in Part 13, contracting officers are not required to describe the relative importance of evaluation factors.

(b) Offers shall be evaluated in accordance with the criteria contained in the solicitation. For many commercial items, the criteria need not be more detailed than technical (capability of the item offered to meet the agency need), price and past performance. Technical capability may be evaluated by how well the proposed products meet the Government requirement instead of predetermined subfactors. Solicitations for commercial items do not have to contain subfactors for technical capability when the solicitation adequately describes the item's intended use. A technical evaluation would normally include examination of such things as product literature, product samples (if requested), technical features and warranty provisions. Past performance shall be evaluated in accordance with the procedures in 13.106 or Subpart 15.3, as applicable. The contracting officer shall ensure the instructions provided in the provision at 52.212-1, Instructions to Offerors—Commercial Items, and the evaluation criteria provided in the provision at 52.212-2, Evaluation—Commercial Items, are in agreement.

(c) Select the offer that is most advantageous to the Government based on the factors contained in the solicitation. Fully document the rationale for selection of the successful offeror including discussion of any trade-offs considered.

[FAC 90-32, 60 FR 48206, 9/18/95, effective 10/1/95; FAC 90-40, 61 FR 39186, 7/26/96, effective 8/26/96; FAC 90-45, Final rule, 62 FR 224, 1/2/97, effective 1/1/97; FAC 97-2, 62 FR 51224, 9/30/97, effective 10/10/97; FAC 97-3, 62 FR 64912, 12/9/97, effective 2/9/98]

12.603 Streamlined solicitation for commercial items.

(a) When a written solicitation will be issued, the contracting officer may use the following procedure to reduce the time required to solicit and award contracts for the acquisition of commercial items. This procedure combines the synopsis required by 5.203 and the issuance of the solicitation into a single document.

(b) When using the combined synopsis/solicitation procedure, the SF 1449 is not used for issuing the solicitation.

(c) To use these procedures, the contracting officer shall—

(1) Prepare the synopsis as described at 5.207.

(2) In the Description, include the following additional information:

(i) The following statement:

This is a combined synopsis/solicitation for commercial items prepared in accordance with the format in Subpart 12.6, as supplemented with additional information included in this notice. This announcement constitutes the only solicitation; proposals are being requested and a written solicitation will not be issued.

(ii) The solicitation number and a statement that the solicitation is issued as an invitation to bid (IFB), request for quotation (RFQ) or request for proposal (RFP).

(iii) A statement that the solicitation document and incorporated provisions and clauses are those in effect through Federal Acquisition Circular____

(iv) A notice regarding any set-aside and the associated NAICS code and small business size standard.

(v) A list of line item number(s) and items, quantities, and units of measure (including option(s), if applicable).

(vi) Description of requirements for the items to be acquired.

(vii) Date(s) and place(s) of delivery and acceptance and FOB point.

(viii) A statement that the provision at 52.212-1, Instructions to Offerors—Commercial, applies to this acquisition and a statement regarding any addenda to the provision.

(ix) A statement regarding the applicability of the provision at 52.212-2, Evaluation—Commercial Items, if used, and the specific evaluation criteria to be included in paragraph (a) of that provision. If this provision is not used, describe the evaluation procedures to be used.

(x) A statement advising offerors to include a completed copy of the provision at 52.212-3, Offeror Representations and Certifications—Commercial Items, with its offer.

(xi) A statement that the clause at 52.212-4, Contract Terms and Conditions—Commercial Items, applies to this acquisition and a statement regarding any addenda to the clause.

(xii) A statement that the clause at 52.212-5, Contract Terms and Conditions Required To Implement Statutes Or Executive Orders—Commercial Items, applies to this acquisition and a statement regarding which, if any, of the additional FAR clauses cited in the clause are applicable to the acquisition.

(xiii) A statement regarding any additional contract requirement(s) or terms and conditions (such as contract financing arrangements or warranty requirements) determined by the contracting officer to be necessary for this acquisition and consistent with customary commercial practices.

(xiv) A statement regarding the Defense Priorities and Allocations System (DPAS) and assigned rating, if applicable.

(xv) The date, time and place offers are due.

(xvi) The name and telephone number of the individual to contact for information regarding the solicitation.

(3) Allow response time for receipt of offers as follows:

(i) Because the synopsis and solicitation are contained in a single document, it is not necessary to publicize a separate synopsis 15 days before the issuance of the solicitation.

(ii) When using the combined synopsis and solicitation, contracting officers must establish a response time in accordance with 5.203(b) (but see 5.203(h)).

(4) Publicize amendments to solicitations in the same manner as the initial synopsis and solicitation.

[FAC 90-32, 60 FR 48206, 9/18/95, effective 10/1/95; FAC 90-41, 61 FR 41466, 8/8/96, effective 8/8/96, finalized without change, FAC 97-3, 62 FR 64912, 12/9/97, effective 2/9/98; FAC 90-45, Final rule, 62 FR 224, 1/2/97, effective 1/1/97; FAC 97-19, 65 FR 46052, 7/26/2000, effective 10/1/2000, interim rule adopted as final by FAC 2001-02, 66 FR 65347, 12/18/2001, effective 12/18/2001; FAC 97-26, 66 FR 27405, 5/16/2001, effective 5/16/2001; FAC 2001-16, Interim/Final rule, 68 FR 56676, 10/1/2003, effective 10/1/2003; FAC 2005-24, 73 FR 10960, 2/28/2008, effective 3/31/2008; FAC 2005-48, 75 FR 82567, 12/30/2010, effective 1/31/2011; FAC 2005-95, 82 FR 4709, 1/13/2017, effective 1/13/2017]

Federal Acquisition Regulation Parts 13—18 Contracting Methods and Contract Types

---

Table of Contents

SUBCHAPTER C—CONTRACTING METHODS AND CONTRACT TYPES

Part 13—Simplified Acquisition Procedures 347
Part 14—Sealed Bidding 371
Part 15—Contracting by Negotiation 403
Part 16—Types of Contracts 465
Part 17—Special Contracting Methods 505
Part 18—Emergency Acquisitions 525

PART 13—SIMPLIFIED ACQUISITION PROCEDURES

Table of Contents

Scope of part 13.000
Definitions 13.001
Purpose 13.002
Policy 13.003
Legal effect of quotations 13.004
List of laws inapplicable to contracts and subcontracts at or below the simplified acquisition threshold 13.005
Inapplicable provisions and clauses 13.006

Subpart 13.101—Procedures

General 13.101
Source list 13.102
Use of standing price quotations 13.103
Promoting competition 13.104
Synopsis and posting requirements 13.105
Soliciting competition, evaluation of quotations or offers, award and documentation 13.106
Soliciting competition 13.106-1
Evaluation of quotations or offers 13.106-2
Award and documentation 13.106-3

Subpart 13.2—Actions at or Below the Micro-Purchase Threshold

General 13.201
Unenforceability of unauthorized obligations in micro-purchases 13.202
Purchase guidelines 13.203

Subpart 13.3—Simplified Acquisition Methods

Governmentwide commercial purchase card 13.301
Purchase orders 13.302
General 13.302-1
Unpriced purchase orders 13.302-2
Obtaining contractor acceptance and modifying purchase orders 13.302-3
Termination or cancellation of purchase orders 13.302-4
Clauses 13.302-5
Blanket purchase agreements (BPAs) 13.303
General 13.303-1
Establishment of BPAs 13.303-2
Preparation of BPAs 13.303-3
Clauses 13.303-4
Purchases under BPAs 13.303-5
Review procedures 13.303-6
Completion of BPAs 13.303-7
Optional clause 13.303-8
[Reserved] 13.304
Imprest funds and third party drafts 13.305
General 13.305-1
Agency responsibilities 13.305-2
Conditions for use 13.305-3
Procedures 13.305-4
SF 44, Purchase Order—Invoice—Voucher 13.306
Forms 13.307

Subpart 13.4—Fast Payment Procedure

General 13.401
Conditions for use 13.402
Preparation and execution of orders 13.403

Contract clause 13.404

Subpart 13.5—Simplified Procedures for Certain Commercial Items

General 13.500
Special documentation requirements 13.501

SUBCHAPTER C—CONTRACTING METHODS AND CONTRACT TYPES (Parts 13-18)

PART 13—SIMPLIFIED ACQUISITION PROCEDURES

13.000 Scope of part.

This part prescribes policies and procedures for the acquisition of supplies and services, including construction, research and development, and commercial items, the aggregate amount of which does not exceed the simplified acquisition threshold (see 2.101). Subpart 13.5 provides special authority for acquisitions of commercial items exceeding the simplified acquisition threshold but not exceeding $7 million ($13 million for acquisitions as described in 13.500(c)), including options. See part 12 for policies applicable to the acquisition of commercial items exceeding the micro-purchase threshold. See 36.602-5 for simplified procedures to be used when acquiring architect-engineer services.

[FAC 97-3, 62 FR 64912, 12/9/97, effective 2/9/98; FAC 2001-20, 69 FR 8311, 2/23/2004, effective 2/23/2004; FAC 2001-26, 69 FR 76350, 12/20/2004, effective 1/19/2005; FAC 2005-13, 71 FR 57363, 9/28/2006, effective 9/28/2006; FAC 2005-45, 75 FR 53129, 8/30/2010, effective 10/1/2010; FAC 2005-83, 80 FR 38293, 7/2/2015, effective 10/1/2015, 80 FR 38311, 7/2/2015, effective 8/3/2015]

13.001 Definitions.

As used in this part—

Authorized individual means a person who has been granted authority, in accordance with agency procedures, to acquire supplies and services in accordance with this part.

Governmentwide commercial purchase card means a purchase card, similar in nature to a commercial credit card, issued to authorized agency personnel to use to acquire and to pay for supplies and services.

Imprest fund means a cash fund of a fixed amount established by an advance of funds, without charge to an appropriation, from an agency finance or disbursing officer to a duly appointed cashier, for disbursement as needed from time to time in making payment in cash for relatively small amounts.

Third party draft means an agency bank draft, similar to a check, that is used to acquire and to pay for supplies and services. (See Treasury Financial Management Manual, Section 3040.70.)

[FAC 97-3, 62 FR 64912, 12/9/97, effective 2/9/98; FAC 97-22, 66 FR 2116, 1/10/2001, effective 3/12/2001; Delay of effective date, 66 FR 14259, 3/9/2001, effective 5/11/2001]

13.002 Purpose.

The purpose of this part is to prescribe simplified acquisition procedures in order to—

(a) Reduce administrative costs;

(b) Improve opportunities for small, small disadvantaged, women-owned, veteran-owned, HUBZone, and service-disabled veteran-owned small business concerns to obtain a fair proportion of Government contracts;

(c) Promote efficiency and economy in contracting; and

(d) Avoid unnecessary burdens for agencies and contractors.

[FAC 97-3, 62 FR 64912, 12/9/97, effective 2/9/98; FAC 2005-02, 70 FR 14950, 3/23/2005, effective 3/23/2005]

13.003 Policy.

(a) Agencies shall use simplified acquisition procedures to the maximum extent practicable for all purchases of supplies or services not exceeding the simplified acquisition threshold (including purchases at or below the micro-purchase threshold). This policy does not apply if an agency can meet its requirement using—

(1) Required sources of supply under part 8 (e.g., Federal Prison Industries, Committee for Purchase from People Who are Blind or Severely Disabled, and Federal Supply Schedule contracts);

(2) Existing indefinite delivery/indefinite quantity contracts; or

(3) Other established contracts.

(b) (1) Acquisitions of supplies or services that have an anticipated dollar value exceeding $3,500 ($20,000 for acquisitions as described in 13.201(g)(1)) but not exceeding $150,000 ($750,000 for acquisitions described in paragraph (1)(i) of the simplified acquisition threshold definition at 2.101) are reserved exclusively for small business concerns and shall be set aside (see 19.000, 19.203, and subpart 19.5).

(2) The contracting officer may make an award to a small business concern under the—

(i) 8(a) Program (see subpart 19.8);

(ii) Historically Underutilized Business Zone (HUBZone) Program (but see 19.1305 and 19.1306(a)(4));

(iii) Service-Disabled Veteran-Owned Small Business (SDVOSB) Program (see subpart 19.14); or

(iv) Women-Owned Small Business (WOSB) Program (see subpart 19.15).

(3) The following contracting officer's decisions for acquisitions at or below the simplified acquisition threshold are not subject to review under subpart 19.4:

(i) A decision not to make an award under the 8(a) Program.

(ii) A decision not to set aside an acquisition for HUBZone small business concerns, service-disabled veteran-owned small business concerns, or EDWOSB concerns and WOSB concerns eligible under the WOSB Program.

(4) Each written solicitation under a set-aside shall contain the appropriate provisions prescribed by part 19. If the solicitation is oral, however, information substantially identical to that in the provision shall be given to potential quoters.

(c) (1) The contracting officer shall not use simplified acquisition procedures to acquire supplies and services if the anticipated award will exceed—

(i) The simplified acquisition threshold; or

(ii) $7 million ($13 million for acquisitions as described in 13.500(c)), including options, for acquisitions of commercial items using Subpart 13.5.

(2) Do not break down requirements aggregating more than the simplified acquisition threshold (or for commercial items, the threshold in Subpart 13.5) or the micro-purchase threshold into several purchases that are less than the applicable threshold merely to—

(i) Permit use of simplified acquisition procedures; or

(ii) Avoid any requirement that applies to purchases exceeding the micro-purchase threshold.

(d) An agency that has specific statutory authority to acquire personal services (see 37.104) may use simplified acquisition procedures to acquire those services.

(e) Agencies shall use the Governmentwide commercial purchase card and electronic purchasing techniques to the maximum extent practicable in conducting simplified acquisitions (but see 32.1108(b)(2)).

(f) Agencies shall maximize the use of electronic commerce when practicable and cost-effective (see Subpart 4.5). Drawings and lengthy specifications can be provided off-line in hard copy or through other appropriate means.

(g) Authorized individuals shall make purchases in the simplified manner that is most suitable, efficient, and economical based on the circumstances of each acquisition. For acquisitions not expected to exceed—

(1) The simplified acquisition threshold for other than commercial items, use any appropriate combination of the procedures in parts 13, 14, 15, 35, or 36, including the use of Standard Form 1442, Solicitation, Offer, and Award (Construction, Alteration, or Repair), for construction contracts (see 36.701(a)); or

(2) $7 million ($13 million for acquisitions as described in 13.500(c)) for commercial items, use any appropriate combination of the procedures in Parts 12, 13, 14, and 15 (see paragraph (d) of this section).

(h) In addition to other considerations, contracting officers shall—

(1) Promote competition to the maximum extent practicable (see 13.104);

(2) Establish deadlines for the submission of responses to solicitations that afford suppliers a reasonable opportunity to respond (see 5.203);

(3) Consider all quotations or offers that are timely received. For evaluation of quotations or offers received electronically, see 13.106-2(b)(3); and

(4) Use innovative approaches, to the maximum extent practicable, in awarding contracts using simplified acquisition procedures.

[FAC 97-3, 62 FR 64912, 12/9/97, effective 2/9/98; FAC 97-9, 63 FR 58587, 10/30/98, effective 10/30/98; FAC 97-10, 63 FR 70264, 12/18/98, effective 1/4/99; FAC 2001-09, 67 FR 56115, 8/30/2002, effective 8/30/2002; FAC 2001-12, 68 FR 4047, 1/27/2003, effective 1/24/2003; FAC 2001-20, 69 FR 8311, 2/23/2004, effective 2/23/2004; FAC 2001-23, 69 FR 25273, 5/5/2004, effective 5/5/2004; FAC 2001-25, 69 FR 59699, 10/5/2004, effective 11/4/2004; FAC 2001-26, 69 FR 76350, 12/20/2004, effective 1/19/2005; FAC 2005-02, 70 FR 14950, 3/23/2005, effective 3/23/2005; FAC 2005-13, 71 FR 57363, 9/28/2006, effective 9/28/2006; FAC 2005-38, 74 FR 65600, 12/10/2009, effective 2/1/2010; FAC 2005-45, 75 FR 53129, 8/30/2010, effective 10/1/2010; FAC 2005-50, 76 FR 14566, 3/16/2011, effective 3/16/2011; FAC 2005-51, 76 FR 18304, 4/1/2011, effective 4/1/2011; FAC 2005-56, 77 FR 12913, 12930, 3/2/2012, effective 4/2/2012; FAC 2005-83, 80 FR 38293, 7/2/2015, effective 10/1/2015, 80 FR 38311, 7/2/2015, effective 8/3/2015; Final rule, 80 FR 53753, 9/8/2015, effective 10/1/2015; FAC 2005-88, 81 FR 30438, 5/16/2016, effective 6/15/2016; FAC 2005-95, 82 FR 4716, 1/13/2017, effective 1/13/2017]

13.004 Legal effect of quotations.

(a) A quotation is not an offer and, consequently, cannot be accepted by the Government to form a binding contract. Therefore, issuance by the Government of an order in response to a supplier's quotation does not establish a contract. The order is an offer by the Government to the supplier to buy certain supplies or services upon specified terms and conditions. A contract is established when the supplier accepts the offer.

(b) When appropriate, the contracting officer may ask the supplier to indicate acceptance of an order by notification to the Government, preferably in writing, as defined at 2.101. In other circumstances, the supplier may indicate acceptance by furnishing the supplies or services ordered or by proceeding with the work to the point where substantial performance has occurred.

(c) If the Government issues an order resulting from a quotation, the Government may (by written notice to the supplier, at any time before acceptance occurs) withdraw, amend, or cancel its offer. (See 13.302-4for procedures on termination or cancellation of purchase orders.)

[FAC 97-3, 62 FR 64912, 12/9/97, effective 2/9/98]

13.005 List of laws inapplicable to contracts and subcontracts at or below the simplified acquisition threshold.

(a) The following laws are inapplicable to all contracts and subcontracts (if otherwise applicable to subcontracts) at or below the simplified acquisition threshold pursuant to 41 U.S.C. 1905:

(1) 41 U.S.C 8703 (Kickbacks statute). (Only the requirement for the incorporation of the contractor procedures for the prevention and detection of violations, and the contractual requirement for contractor cooperation in investigations are inapplicable.).

(2) 40 U.S.C. 3131 (Bonds statue). (Although the Bonds statute does not apply to contracts at or below the simplified acquisition threshold, alternative forms of payment protection for suppliers of labor and material (see 28.102) are still required if the contract exceeds $35,000 (40 U.S.C. 3132)).

(3) 40 U.S.C. chapter 37 (Contract Work Hours and Safety Standards—Overtime Compensation).

(4) 41 U.S.C. 8102(a)(1) (Drug-Free Workplace), except for individuals.

(5) 42 U.S.C. 6962 (Solid Waste Disposal Act). (The requirement to provide an estimate of recovered material utilized in contract performance does not apply unless the contract value exceeds $150,000.)

(6) 10 U.S.C. 2306(b) and 41 U.S.C. 3901(b) (Contract Clause Regarding Contingent Fees).

(7) 10 U.S.C. 2313 and 41 U.S.C. 4706 (Authority to Examine Books and Records of Contractors).

(8) 10 U.S.C. 2402 and 41 U.S.C. 4704 (Prohibition on Limiting Subcontractors Direct Sales to the United States).

(9) 15 U.S.C. 631 note (HUBZone Act of 1997), except for 15 U.S.C. 657a(b)(2)(B), which is optional for the agencies subject to the requirements of the Act.

(10) 31 U.S.C. 1354(a) (Limitation on use of appropriated funds for contracts with entities not meeting veterans employment reporting requirements).

(11) 22 U.S.C. 2593e (Measures Against Persons Involved in Activities that Violate Arms Control Treaties or Agreements with the United States). (The requirement at 22 U.S.C. 2593e(c)(3)(B) to provide a certification does not apply).

(b) The Federal Acquisition Regulatory (FAR) Council will include any law enacted after October 13, 1994, that sets forth policies, procedures, requirements, or restrictions for the acquisition of property or services, on the list set forth in paragraph (a) of this section. The FAR Council may make exceptions when it determines in writing that it is in the best interest of the Government that the enactment should apply to contracts or subcontracts not greater than the simplified acquisition threshold.

(c) The provisions of paragraph (b) of this section do not apply to laws that—

(1) Provide for criminal or civil penalties; or

(2) Specifically state that notwithstanding the language of 41 U.S.C. 1905, the enactment will be applicable to contracts or subcontracts in amounts not greater than the simplified acquisition threshold.

(d) Any individual may petition the Administrator, Office of Federal Procurement Policy (OFPP), to include any applicable provision of law not included on the list set forth in paragraph (a) of this section unless the FAR Council has already determined in writing that the law is applicable. The Administrator, OFPP, will include the law on the list in paragraph (a) of this section unless the FAR Council makes a determination that it is applicable within 60 days of receiving the petition.

[FAC 97-3, 62 FR 64912, 12/9/97, effective 2/9/98; FAC 97-10, 63 FR 70264, 12/18/98, effective 1/4/99; FAC 97-18, 65 FR 36014, 6/6/2000, effective 8/7/2000; FAC 2001-01, 66 FR 53478, 10/22/2001, effective 12/21/2001; Interim rule, 69 FR 4050, 1/27/2003, effective 1/27/2003; FAC 2005-06, 70 FR 57453, 9/30/2005, effective 9/30/2005; FAC 2005-13, 71 FR 57363, 9/28/2006, effective 9/28/2006; FAC 2005-45, 75 FR 53129, 8/30/2010, effective 10/1/2010; FAC 2005-73, 79 FR 24192, 4/29/2014, effective 5/29/2014; FAC 2005-83, 80 FR 38293, 7/2/2015, effective 10/1/2015; FAC 2005-99, 83 FR 28145, 6/15/2018, effective 6/15/2018]

13.006 Inapplicable provisions and clauses.

While certain statutes still apply, pursuant to Public Law 103-355, the following provisions and clauses are inapplicable to contracts and subcontracts at or below the simplified acquisition threshold:

(a) 52.203-5, Covenant Against Contingent Fees.

(b) 52.203-6, Restrictions on Subcontractor Sales to the Government.

(c) 52.203-7, Anti-Kickback Procedures.

(d) 52.215-2, Audits and Records—Negotiation, except as used with its Alternative I, when using funds appropriated or otherwise made available by the American Recovery and Reinvestment Act of 2009 (Pub. L. 111-5).

(e) 52.222-4, Contract Work Hours and Safety Standards—Overtime Compensation.

(f) 52.223-6, Drug-Free Workplace, except for individuals.

(g) 52.223-9, Estimate of Percentage of Recovered Material Content for EPA Designated Items.

[FAC 97-3, 62 FR 64912, 12/9/97, effective 2/9/98; FAC 97-18, 65 FR 36014, 6/6/2000, effective 8/7/2000; FAC 2005-25, 73 FR 21789, 4/22/2008, effective 5/22/2008; FAC 2005-32, 74 FR 14646, 3/31/2009, effective 3/31/2009; FAC 2005-42, 75 FR 34279, 6/16/2010, effective 7/16/2010; FAC 2005-73, 79 FR 24192, 4/29/2014, effective 5/29/2014]

SUBPART 13.1—PROCEDURES

13.101 General.

(a) In making purchases, contracting officers shall—

(1) Comply with the policy in 7.202 relating to economic purchase quantities, when practicable;

(2) Satisfy the procedures described in subpart 19.6 with respect to Certificates of Competency before rejecting a quotation, oral or written, from a small business concern determined to be nonresponsible (see subpart 9.1); and

(3) Provide for the inspection of supplies or services as prescribed in 46.404.

(b) In making purchases, contracting officers should—

(1) Include related items (such as small hardware items or spare parts for vehicles) in one solicitation and make award on an "all-or-none" or "multiple award" basis provided suppliers are so advised when quotations or offers are requested;

(2) Incorporate provisions and clauses by reference in solicitations and in awards under requests for quotations, provided the requirements in 52.102 are satisfied;

(3) Make maximum effort to obtain trade and prompt payment discounts (see 14.408-3). Prompt payment discounts shall not be considered in the evaluation of quotations; and

(4) Use bulk funding to the maximum extent practicable. Bulk funding is a system whereby the contracting officer receives authorization from a fiscal and accounting officer to obligate funds on purchase documents against a specified lump sum of funds reserved for the purpose for a specified period of time rather than obtaining individual obligational authority on each purchase document. Bulk funding is particularly appropriate if numerous purchases using the same type of funds are to be made during a given period.

[FAC 97-3, 62 FR 64912, 12/9/97, effective 2/9/98; FAC 97-15, 64 FR 72414, 12/27/99, effective 2/25/2000]

13.102 Source list.

(a) Contracting officers should use the System for Award Management (see subpart 4.11) via *https://www.sam.gov* as their primary sources of vendor information. Offices maintaining additional vendor source files or listings should identify the status of each source (when the status is made known to the contracting office) in the following categories:

(1) Small business.

(2) Small disadvantaged business.

(3) Women-owned small business concern, including economically disadvantaged women-owned small business concerns and women-owned small business concerns eligible under the Women-owned Small Business (WOSB) Program.

(4) HUBZone small business.

(5) Service-disabled veteran-owned small business.

(6) Veteran-owned small business.

(b) The status information may be used as the basis to ensure that small business concerns are provided the maximum practicable opportunities to respond to solicitations issued using simplified acquisition procedures.

[FAC 97-3, 62 FR 64912, 12/9/97, effective 2/9/98; FAC 97-9, 63 FR 58587, 10/30/98, effective 10/30/98; FAC 2001-16, Final rule, 68 FR 56669, 10/1/2003, effective 10/1/2003; FAC 2005-51, 76 FR 18304, 4/1/2011, effective 4/1/2011; FAC 2005-55, 77 FR 187, 1/3/2012, effective 2/2/2012; FAC 2005-56, 77 FR 12913, 3/2/2012, effective 4/2/2012; FAC 2005-67, 78 FR 37676, 6/21/2013, effective 7/22/2013; FAC 2005-76, 79 FR 43580, 7/25/2014, effective

8/25/2014; FAC 2005-101, 83 FR 48691, 9/26/2018, effective 10/26/2018]

13.103 Use of standing price quotations.

Authorized individuals do not have to obtain individual quotations for each purchase. Standing price quotations may be used if—

(a) The pricing information is current; and

(b) The Government obtains the benefit of maximum discounts before award.

[FAC 97-3, 62 FR 64912, 12/9/97, effective 2/9/98]

13.104 Promoting competition.

The contracting officer must promote competition to the maximum extent practicable to obtain supplies and services from the source whose offer is the most advantageous to the Government, considering the administrative cost of the purchase.

(a) The contracting officer must not—

(1) Solicit quotations based on personal preference; or

(2) Restrict solicitation to suppliers of well-known and widely distributed makes or brands.

(b) If using simplified acquisition procedures and not providing access to the notice of proposed contract action and solicitation information through the Governmentwide point of entry (GPE), maximum practicable competition ordinarily can be obtained by soliciting quotations or offers from sources within the local trade area. Unless the contract action requires synopsis pursuant to 5.101 and an exception under 5.202 is not applicable, consider using solicitation of at least three sources to promote competition to the maximum extent practicable. Whenever practicable, request quotations or offers from two sources not included in the previous solicitation.

[FAC 97-3, 62 FR 64912, 12/9/97, effective 2/9/98; FAC 97-9, 63 FR 58587, 10/30/98, effective 10/30/98; FAC 97-26, 66 FR 27405, 5/16/2001, effective 5/16/2001; FAC 2001-16, Interim/Final rule, 68 FR 56676, 10/1/2003, effective 10/1/2003; FAC 2005-21, 72 FR 63075, 11/7/2007, effective 12/7/2007]

13.105 Synopsis and posting requirements.

(a) The contracting officer must comply with the public display and synopsis requirements of 5.101 and 5.203 unless an exception in 5.202 applies.

(b) When acquiring commercial items or supplies or services procured in accordance with 12.102(f)(1), the contracting officer may use a combined synopsis and solicitation. In these cases, a separate solicitation is not required. The contracting officer must include enough information to permit suppliers to develop quotations or offers.

(c) See 5.102(a)(6) for the requirement to post a brand name justification or documentation required by 13.106-1(b) or 13.501.

(d) When publicizing contract actions funded in whole or in part by the American Recovery and Reinvestment Act of 2009 (Pub. L. 111-5):

(1) Notices of proposed contract actions shall follow the procedures in 5.704 for posting orders.

(2) Award notices shall follow the procedures in 5.705.

[FAC 97-3, 62 FR 64912, 12/9/97, effective 2/9/98; FAC 97-9, 63 FR 58587, 10/30/98, effective 10/30/98; FAC 97-26, 66 FR 27405, 5/16/2001, effective 5/16/2001; FAC 2001-12, 68 FR 4047, 1/27/2003, effective 1/24/2003; FAC 2001-20, 69 FR 8311, 2/23/2004, effective 2/23/2004; FAC 2001-26, 69 FR 76350, 12/20/2004, effective 1/19/2005; FAC 2005-13, 71 FR 57357, 9/28/2006, effective 9/28/2006; FAC 2005-21, 72 FR 63075, 11/7/2007, effective 12/7/2007; FAC 2005-32, 74 FR 14636, 3/31/2009, effective 3/31/2009; FAC 2005-42, 75 FR 34271, 6/16/2010, effective 7/16/2010; FAC 2005-55, 77 FR 189, 1/3/2012, effective 2/2/2012]

13.106 Soliciting competition, evaluation of quotations or offers, award and documentation. (No Text)

13.106-1 Soliciting competition.

(a) *Considerations.* In soliciting competition, the contracting officer shall consider the guidance in 13.104 and the following before requesting quotations or offers:

(1) (i) The nature of the article or service to be purchased and whether it is highly competitive and readily available in several makes or brands, or is relatively noncompetitive.

(ii) An electronic commerce method that employs widespread electronic public notice is not available; and

(iii) The urgency of the proposed purchase.

(iv) The dollar value of the proposed purchase.

(v) Past experience concerning specific dealers' prices.

(2) When soliciting quotations or offers, the contracting officer shall notify potential quoters or offerors of the basis on which award will be made (price alone or price and other factors, e.g., past performance and quality). Contracting officers are encouraged to use best value. Solicitations are not required to state the relative importance assigned to each evaluation factor and subfactor, nor are they required to include subfactors.

(b) *Soliciting from a single source.* (1) *For purchases not exceeding the simplified acquisition threshold.* (i) Contracting officers may solicit from one source if the contracting officer determines that the circumstances of the contract action deem only one source reasonably available (e.g., urgency, exclusive licensing agreements, brand name or industrial mobilization).

(ii) Where a single source is identified to provide a purchase because that portion of the purchase specifies a particular brand-name item, the documentation in paragraph (b) (1) (i) of this section only applies to the portion of the purchase requiring the brand-name item. The documentation should state it is covering only the portion of the acquisition which is brand-name.

(2) *For purchases exceeding the simplified acquisition threshold.* The requirements at 13.501 (a) apply to sole-source (including brand-name) acquisitions of commercial items conducted pursuant to subpart 13.5.

(3) See 5.102 (a) (6) for the requirement to post the brand name justification or documentation.

(c) *Soliciting orally.* (1) The contracting officer shall solicit quotations orally to the maximum extent practicable, if—

(i) The acquisition does not exceed the simplified acquisition threshold;

(ii) Oral solicitation is more efficient than soliciting through available electronic commerce alternatives; and

(iii) Notice is not required under 5.101.

(2) However, an oral solicitation may not be practicable for contract actions exceeding $25,000 unless covered by an exception in 5.202.

(d) *Written solicitations.* If obtaining electronic or oral quotations is uneconomical or impracticable, the contracting officer should issue paper solicitations for contract actions likely to exceed $25,000. The contracting officer shall issue a written solicitation for construction requirements exceeding $2,000.

(e) *Use of options.* Options may be included in solicitations, provided the requirements of subpart 17.2 are met and the aggregate value of the acquisition and all options does not exceed the dollar threshold for use of simplified acquisition procedures.

(f) *Inquiries.* An agency should respond to inquiries received through any medium (including electronic commerce) if doing so would not interfere with the efficient conduct of the acquisition.

[FAC 97-3, 62 FR 64912, 12/9/97, effective 2/9/98; FAC 97-9, 63 FR 58587, 10/30/98, effective 10/30/98; FAC 2005-13, 71 FR 57357, 9/28/2006, effective 9/28/2006; FAC 2005-13, 71 FR 57363, 9/28/2006, effective 9/28/2006; FAC 2005-21, 72 FR 63075, 11/7/2007, effective 12/7/2007; FAC 2005-55, 77 FR 189, 1/3/2012, effective 2/2/2012; FAC 2005-83, 80 FR 38293, 7/2/2015, effective 10/1/2015]

13.106-2 Evaluation of quotations or offers.

(a) *General.* (1) The contracting officer shall evaluate quotations or offers—

(i) In an impartial manner; and

(ii) Inclusive of transportation charges from the shipping point of the supplier to the delivery destination.

(2) Quotations or offers shall be evaluated on the basis established in the solicitation.

(3) All quotations or offers shall be considered (see paragraph (b) of this subsection).

(b) *Evaluation procedures.* (1) The contracting officer has broad discretion in fashioning suitable evaluation procedures. The procedures prescribed in parts 14 and 15 are not mandatory. At the contracting officer's discretion, one or more, but not necessarily all, of the evaluation procedures in part 14 or 15 may be used.

(2) If telecommuting is not prohibited, agencies shall not unfavorably evaluate an offer that includes telecommuting unless the contracting officer executes a written determination in accordance with FAR 7.108(b).

(3) If using price and other factors, ensure that quotations or offers can be evaluated in an efficient and minimally burdensome fashion. Formal evaluation plans and establishing a competitive range, conducting discussions, and scoring quotations or offers are not required. Contracting offices may conduct comparative evaluations of offers. Evaluation of other factors, such as past performance—

(i) Does not require the creation or existence of a formal data base; and

(ii) May be based on one or more of the following:

(A) The contracting officer's knowledge of and previous experience with the supply or service being acquired;

(B) Customer surveys, and past performance questionnaire replies;

(C) The Contractor Performance Assessment Reporting System (CPARS) at *https://www.cpars.gov*; or

(D) Any other reasonable basis.

(4) For acquisitions conducted using a method that permits electronic response to the solicitation, the contracting officer may—

(i) After preliminary consideration of all quotations or offers, identify from all quotations or offers received one that is suitable to the user, such as the lowest priced brand name product, and quickly screen all lower priced quotations or offers based on readily discernible value indicators, such as past performance, warranty conditions, and maintenance availability; or

(ii) Where an evaluation is based only on price and past performance, make an award based on whether the lowest priced of the quotations or offers having the highest past performance rating possible represents the best value when compared to any lower priced quotation or offer.

[FAC 97-3, 62 FR 64912, 12/9/97, effective 2/9/98; FAC 97-9, 63 FR 58587, 10/30/98, effective 10/30/98; FAC 2001-25, 69 FR 59701, 10/5/2004, effective 10/5/2004; FAC 2005-04, 70 FR 33656, 6/8/2005, effective 6/8/2005; FAC 2005-21, 72 FR 63075, 11/7/2007, effective 12/7/2007; FAC 2005-34, 74 FR 31557, 7/1/2009, effective 7/1/2009; FAC 2019-06, 84 FR 47865, 9/10/2019, effective 10/10/2019]

13.106-3 Award and documentation.

(a) *Basis for award.* Before making award, the contracting officer must determine that the proposed price is fair and reasonable.

(1) Whenever possible, base price reasonableness on competitive quotations or offers.

(2) If only one response is received, include a statement of price reasonableness in the contract file. The contracting officer may base the statement on—

(i) Market research;

(ii) Comparison of the proposed price with prices found reasonable on previous purchases;

(iii) Current price lists, catalogs, or advertisements. However, inclusion of a price in a price list, catalog, or advertisement does not, in and of itself, establish fairness and reasonableness of the price;

(iv) A comparison with similar items in a related industry;

(v) The contracting officer's personal knowledge of the item being purchased;

(vi) Comparison to an independent Government estimate; or

(vii) Any other reasonable basis.

(3) Occasionally an item can be obtained only from a supplier that quotes a minimum order price or quantity that either unreasonably exceeds stated quantity requirements or results in an unreasonable price for the quantity required. In these instances, the contracting officer should inform the requiring activity of all facts regarding the quotation or offer and ask it to confirm or alter its requirement. The file shall be documented to support the final action taken.

(b) *File documentation and retention.* Keep documentation to a minimum. Purchasing offices shall retain data supporting purchases (paper or electronic) to the minimum extent and duration necessary for management review purposes (see subpart 4.8). The following illustrate the extent to which quotation or offer information should be recorded:

(1) *Oral solicitations.* The contracting office should establish and maintain records of oral price quotations in order to reflect clearly the propriety of placing the order at the price paid with the supplier concerned. In most cases, this will consist merely of showing the names of the suppliers contacted and the prices and other terms and conditions quoted by each.

(2) *Written solicitations* (see 2.101). For acquisitions not exceeding the simplified acquisition threshold, limit written records of solicitations or offers to notes or abstracts to show prices, delivery, references to printed price lists used, the supplier or suppliers contacted, and other pertinent data.

(3) *Special situations.* Include additional statements—

(i) Explaining the absence of competition (see 13.106-1for brand name purchases) if only one source is solicited and the acquisition does not exceed the simplified acquisition threshold (does not apply to an acquisition of utility services available from only one source); or

(ii) Supporting the award decision if other than price-related factors were considered in selecting the supplier.

(c) *Notification.* For acquisitions that do not exceed the simplified acquisition threshold and for which automatic notification is not provided through an electronic commerce method that employs widespread electronic public notice, notification to unsuccessful suppliers shall be given only if requested or required by 5.301.

(d) *Request for information.* If a supplier requests information on an award that was based on factors other than price alone, a brief explanation of the basis for the contract award decision shall be provided (see 15.503(b)(2)).

(e) *Taxpayer Identification Number.* If an used, the contracting officer shall ensure that the copy of the award document sent to the payment office is annotated with the contractor's Taxpayer Identification Number (TIN) and type of organization (see 4.203), unless this information will be obtained from some other source (e.g., centralized database). The contracting officer shall disclose to the contractor that the TIN may be used by the Government to collect and report on any delinquent amounts arising out of the contractor's relationship with the Government (31 U.S.C. 7701(c)(3)).

[FAC 97-3, 62 FR 64912, 12/9/97, effective 2/9/98; FAC 97-9, 63 FR 58587, 10/30/98, effective 10/30/98, finalized without change, FAC 97-12, 64 FR 32740, 6/17/99; FAC 97-14, 64 FR 51828, 9/24/99, effective 9/24/99, finalized without change, FAC 97-17, 65 FR 24316, 4/25/2000; FAC 2005-13, 71 FR 57357, 9/28/2006, effective 9/28/2006; FAC 2005-21, 72 FR 63075, 11/7/2007, effective 12/7/2007; FAC 2005-55, 77 FR 189, 1/3/2012, effective 2/2/2012]

SUBPART 13.2—ACTIONS AT OR BELOW THE MICRO-PURCHASE THRESHOLD

13.201 General.

(a) Agency heads are encouraged to delegate micro-purchase authority (see 1.603-3).

(b) The Governmentwide commercial purchase card shall be the preferred method to purchase and to pay for micro-purchases (see 2.101).

(c) Purchases at or below the micro-purchase threshold may be conducted using any of the methods described in subpart 13.3, provided the purchaser is authorized and trained, pursuant to agency procedures, to use those methods.

(d) Micro-purchases do not require provisions or clauses, except as provided at 13.202 and 32.1110. This paragraph takes precedence over any other FAR requirement to the contrary, but does not prohibit the use of any clause.

(e) The requirements in part 8 apply to purchases at or below the micro-purchase threshold.

(f) The procurement requirements in subparts 23.1, 23.2, 23.4, and 23.7 apply to purchases at or below the micro-purchase threshold.

(g)(1) For acquisitions of supplies or services that, as determined by the head of the agency, are to be used to support a contingency operation; to facilitate defense against or recovery from cyber, nuclear, biological, chemical, or radiological attack; to support a request from the Secretary of State or the Administrator of the United States Agency for International Development to facilitate provision of international disaster assistance pursuant to 22 U.S.C. 2292 *et seq.*; or to support response to an emergency or major disaster (42 U.S.C. 5122), the micro-purchase threshold is—

(i) $20,000 in the case of any contract to be awarded and performed, or purchase to be made, inside the United States; and

(ii) $30,000 in the case of any contract to be awarded and performed, or purchase to be made, outside the United States.

(2) Purchases using this authority must have a clear and direct relationship to the support of a contingency operation; or the defense against or recovery from cyber, nuclear, biological, chemical, or radiological attack; international disaster assistance; or an emergency or major disaster.

(h) When using the Governmentwide commercial purchase card as a method of payment, purchases at or below the micro-purchase threshold are exempt from verification in the System for Award Management as to whether the contractor has a delinquent debt subject to collection under the Treasury Offset Program (TOP).

(i) Do not purchase any hardware, software, or services developed or provided by Kaspersky Lab that the Government will use on or after October 1, 2018. (See 4.2002.)

(j) On or after August 13, 2019, do not procure or obtain, or extend or renew a contract to procure or obtain, any equipment, system, or service that uses covered telecommunications equipment or services as a substantial or essential component of any system, or as critical technology as part of any system, unless an exception applies or a waiver is granted. (See subpart 4.21.)

[FAC 97-3, 62 FR 64912, 12/9/97, effective 2/9/98; FAC 97-11, 64 FR 10530, 3/4/99, effective 5/3/99; FAC 97-18, 65 FR 36014, 6/6/2000, effective 8/7/2000; FAC 2001-09, 67 FR 56115, 8/30/2002, effective 8/30/2002; FAC 2001-12, 68 FR 4047, 1/27/2003, effective 1/24/2003; FAC 2001-16, Final rule, 68 FR 56669, 10/1/2003, effective 10/1/2003; FAC 2001-20, 69 FR 8311, 2/23/2004, effective 2/23/2004; FAC 2001-26, 69 FR 76350, 12/20/2004, effective 1/19/2005; FAC 2005-21, 72 FR 63040, 11/7/2007, effective 12/7/2007; FAC 2005-37, 74 FR 52847, 10/14/2009, effective 10/14/2009; FAC 2005-38, 74 FR 65600, 12/10/2009, effective 2/1/2010; FAC 2005-43, 75 FR 38683, 7/2/2010, effective 8/2/2010; FAC 2005-45, 75 FR 53129, 8/30/2010, effective 10/1/2010; FAC 2005-52, 76 FR 31395, 5/31/2011, effective 5/31/2011; FAC 2005-62, 77 FR 69715, 11/20/2012, effective 12/20/2012; FAC 2005-67, 78 FR 37676, 6/21/2013, effective 7/22/2013; 78 FR 37686, 6/21/2013, effective 6/21/2013; FAC 2005-72, 78FR 80382, 12/31/2013, effective 12/31/2013; FAC 2005-83, 80 FR 38293, 7/2/2015, effective 10/1/2015; FAC 2005-99, 83 FR 28141, 6/15/2018, effective 7/16/2018; FAC 2005-101, 83 FR 48691, 9/26/2018, effective 10/26/2018; FAC 2019-02, 84 FR 19835, 5/6/2019, effective 6/5/2019; FAC 2019-05, 84 FR 40216, 8/13/2019, effective 8/13/2019; FAC 2019-06, 84 FR 47861, 9/10/2019, effective 9/10/2019]

13.202 Unenforceability of unauthorized obligations in micro-purchases.

Many supplies or services are acquired subject to supplier license agreements. These are particularly common in information technology acquisitions, but they may apply to any supply or service. For example, computer software and services delivered through the internet (web services) are often subject to license agreements, referred to as End User License Agreements (EULA), Terms of Service (TOS), or other similar legal instruments or agreements. Many of these agreements contain indemnification clauses that are inconsistent with Federal law and unenforceable, but which could create a violation of the Anti-Deficiency Act (31 U.S.C. 1341) if agreed to by the Government. The clause at 52.232–39, Unenforceability of Unauthorized Obligations, automatically applies to any micro-purchase, including those made with the Governmentwide purchase card. This clause prevents such violations of the Anti-Deficiency Act.

[FAC 2005-67, 78 FR 37686, 6/21/2013, effective 6/21/2013; FAC 2005-72, 78 FR 80382, 12/31/2013, effective 12/31/2013]

13.203 Purchase guidelines.

(a) *Solicitation, evaluation of quotations, and award.* (1) To the extent practicable, micro-purchases shall be distributed equitably among qualified suppliers.

(2) Micro-purchases may be awarded without soliciting competitive quotations if the contracting officer or individual appointed in accordance with 1.603-3(b) considers the price to be reasonable.

(3) The administrative cost of verifying the reasonableness of the price for purchases may more than offset potential savings from detecting instances of overpricing. Therefore, action to verify price reasonableness need only be taken if—

(i) The contracting officer or individual appointed in accordance with 1.603-3(b) suspects or has information to indicate that the price may not be reasonable (e.g., comparison to the previous price paid or personal knowledge of the supply or service); or

(ii) Purchasing a supply or service for which no comparable pricing information is readily available (e.g., a supply or service that is not the same as, or is not similar to, other supplies or services that have recently been purchased on a competitive basis).

(b) *Documentation.* If competitive quotations were solicited and award was made to other than the low quoter, documentation to support the purchase may be limited to identification of the solicited concerns and an explanation for the award decision.

[FAC 97-3, 62 FR 64912, 12/9/97, effective 2/9/98; Redesignate, FAC 2005-67, 78 FR 37686, 6/21/2013, effective 6/21/2013; FAC 2005-72, 78 FR 80382,12/31/2013, effective 12/31/2013; FAC 2005-72, 78 FR 80382, 12/31/2013, effective 12/31/2013]

SUBPART 13.3—SIMPLIFIED ACQUISITION METHODS

13.301 Governmentwide commercial purchase card.

(a) Except as provided in 32.1108(b)(2), the Governmentwide commercial purchase card is authorized for use in making and/or paying for purchases of supplies, services, or construction. The Governmentwide commercial purchase card may be used by contracting officers and other individuals designated in accordance with 1.603-3. The card may be used only for purchases that are otherwise authorized by law or regulation.

(b) Agencies using the Governmentwide commercial purchase card shall establish procedures for use and control of the card that comply with the Treasury Financial Manual for Guidance of Departments and Agencies (TFM 4-4500) and that are consistent with the terms and conditions of the current GSA credit card contract. Agency procedures should not limit the use of the Governmentwide commercial purchase card to micro-purchases. Agency procedures should encourage use of the card in greater dollar amounts by contracting officers to place orders and to pay for purchases against contracts established under part 8 procedures, when authorized; and to place orders and/or make payment under other contractual instruments, when agreed to by the contractor. See 32.1110(d) for instructions for use of the appropriate clause when payment under a written contract will be made through use of the card.

(c) The Governmentwide commercial purchase card may be used to—

(1) Make micro-purchases;

(2) Place a task or delivery order (if authorized in the basic contract, basic ordering agreement, or blanket purchase agreement); or

(3) Make payments, when the contractor agrees to accept payment by the card (but see 32.1108(b)(2)).

[FAC 97-3, 62 FR 64912, 12/9/97, effective 2/9/98; FAC 97-11, 64 FR 10530, 3/4/99, effective 5/3/99; FAC 2001-04, 67 FR 6112, 2/8/2002, effective 2/8/2002; FAC 2005-38, 74 FR 65600, 12/10/2009, effective 2/1/2010]

13.302 Purchase orders. (No Text)

13.302-1 General.

(a) Except as provided under the unpriced purchase order method (see 13.302-2), purchase orders generally are issued on a fixed-price basis. See 12.207 for acquisition of commercial items.

(b) Purchase orders shall—

(1) Specify the quantity of supplies or scope of services ordered;

(2) Contain a determinable date by which delivery of the supplies or performance of the services is required;

(3) Provide for inspection as prescribed in Part 46. Generally, inspection and acceptance should be at destination. Source inspection should be specified only if required by Part 46. When inspection and acceptance will be performed at destination, advance copies of the purchase order or equivalent notice shall be furnished to the consignee(s) for material receipt purposes. Receiving reports shall be accomplished immediately upon receipt and acceptance of supplies;

(4) Specify f.o.b. destination for supplies to be delivered within the United States, except Alaska or Hawaii, unless there are valid reasons to the contrary; and

(5) Include any trade and prompt payment discounts that are offered, consistent with the applicable principles at 14.408-3.

(c) The contracting officer's signature on purchase orders shall be in accordance with 4.101 and the definitions at 2.101. Facsimile and electronic signature may be used in the production of purchase orders by automated methods.

(d) Limit the distribution of copies of purchase orders and related forms to the minimum deemed essential for administration and transmission of contractual information.

(e) In accordance with 31 U.S.C. 3332, electronic funds transfer (EFT) is required for payments except as provided in 32.1110. See Subpart 32.11 for instructions for use of the appropriate clause in purchase orders. When obtaining oral quotes, the contracting officer shall inform the quoter of the EFT clause that will be in any resulting purchase order.

[FAC 97-3, 62 FR 64912, 12/9/97, effective 2/9/98; FAC 97-11, 64 FR 10530, 3/4/99, effective 5/3/99]

13.302-2 Unpriced purchase orders.

(a) An unpriced purchase order is an order for supplies or services, the price of which is not established at the time of issuance of the order.

(b) An unpriced purchase order may be used only when—

(1) It is impractical to obtain pricing in advance of issuance of the purchase order; and

(2) The purchase is for—

(i) Repairs to equipment requiring disassembly to determine the nature and extent of repairs;

(ii) Material available from only one source and for which cost cannot readily be established; or

(iii) Supplies or services for which prices are known to be competitive, but exact prices are not known (*e.g.*, miscellaneous repair parts, maintenance agreements).

(c) Unpriced purchase orders may be issued on paper or electronically. A realistic monetary limitation, either for each line item or for the total order, shall be placed on each unpriced purchase order. The monetary limitation shall be an obligation subject to adjustment when the firm price is established. The contracting office shall follow up on each order to ensure timely pricing. The contracting officer or the contracting officer's designated representative shall review the invoice price and, if reasonable (see 13.106-3(a)), process the invoice for payment.

[FAC 97-3, 62 FR 64912, 12/9/97, effective 2/9/98]

13.302-3 Obtaining contractor acceptance and modifying purchase orders.

(a) When it is desired to consummate a binding contract between the parties before the contractor undertakes performance, the contracting officer shall require written (see 2.101) acceptance of the purchase order by the contractor.

(b) Each purchase order modification shall identify the order it modifies and shall contain an appropriate modification number.

(c) A contractor's written acceptance of a purchase order modification may be required only if—

(1) Determined by the contracting officer to be necessary to ensure the contractor's compliance with the purchase order as revised; or

(2) Required by agency regulations.

[FAC 97-3, 62 FR 64912, 12/9/97, effective 2/9/98]

13.302-4 Termination or cancellation of purchase orders.

(a) If a purchase order that has been accepted in writing by the contractor is to be terminated, the contracting officer shall process the termination in accordance with—

(1) 12.403 and 52.212-4(l) or (m) for commercial items; or

(2) Part 49 or 52.213-4 for other than commercial items.

(b) If a purchase order that has not been accepted in writing by the contractor is to be canceled, the contracting officer shall notify the contractor in writing that the purchase order has been canceled, request the contractor's written acceptance of the cancellation, and proceed as follows:

(1) If the contractor accepts the cancellation and does not claim that costs were incurred as a result of beginning performance under the purchase order, no further action is required (*i.e.*, the purchase order shall be considered canceled).

(2) If the contractor does not accept the cancellation or claims that costs were incurred as a result of beginning performance under the purchase order, the contracting officer shall process the action as a termination prescribed in paragraph (a) of this subsection.

[FAC 97-3, 62 FR 64912, 12/9/97, effective 2/9/98; FAC 2005-16, 72 FR 13586, 3/22/2007, effective 3/22/2007]

13.302-5 Clauses.

(a) Each purchase order (and each purchase order modification (see 13.302-3)) shall incorporate all clauses prescribed for the particular acquisition.

(b) The contracting officer shall insert the clause at 52.213-2, Invoices, in purchase orders that authorize advance payments (see 31 U.S.C. 3324(d)(2)) for subscriptions or other charges for newspapers, magazines, periodicals, or other publications (*i.e.*, any publication printed, microfilmed, photocopied, or magnetically or otherwise recorded for auditory or visual usage).

(c) The contracting officer shall insert the clause at 52.213-3, Notice to Supplier, in unpriced purchase orders.

(d)(1) The contracting officer may use the clause at 52.213-4, Terms and Conditions—Simplified Acquisitions (Other Than Commercial Items), in simplified acquisitions exceeding the micro-purchase threshold that are for other than commercial items (see 12.301).

(2) The clause—

(i) Is a compilation of the most commonly used clauses that apply to simplified acquisitions; and

(ii) May be modified to fit the individual acquisition to add other needed clauses, or those clauses may be added separately. Modifications (i.e., additions, deletions, or substitutions) must not create a void or internal contradiction in the clause. For example, do not add an inspection and acceptance or termination for convenience requirement unless the existing requirement is deleted. Also, do not delete a paragraph without providing for an appropriate substitute.

(3) (i) When an acquisition for supplies for use within the United States cannot be set aside for small business concerns and trade agreements apply (see Subpart 25.4), substitute the clause at FAR 52.225-3, Buy American-Free Trade Agreements, used with Alternate I or Alternate II, if appropriate, instead of the clause at FAR 52.225-1, Buy American-Supplies.

(ii) When acquiring supplies for use outside the United States, delete clause 52.225-1 from the clause list at 52.213-4(b).

[FAC 97-3, 62 FR 64912, 12/9/97, effective 2/9/98; FAC 97-15, 64 FR 72414, 12/27/99, effective 2/25/2000; FAC 2001-07, 67 FR 21534, 4/30/2002, effective 5/15/2002; FAC 2001-19, Interim Rule, 69 FR 1051, 1/7/2004, effective 1/1/2004; FAC 2001-25, Final rule, 69 FR 59700, 10/5/2004, effective 10/5/2004; FAC 2005-73, 79 FR 24192, 4/29/2014, effective 5/29/2014]

13.303 Blanket purchase agreements (BPAs). (No Text)

13.303-1 General.

(a) A blanket purchase agreement (BPA) is a simplified method of filling anticipated repetitive needs for supplies or services by establishing "charge accounts" with qualified sources of supply (see Subpart 16.7 for additional coverage of agreements).

(b) BPAs should be established for use by an organization responsible for providing supplies for its own operations or for other offices, installations, projects, or functions. Such organizations, for example, may be organized supply points, separate independent or detached field parties, or one-person posts or activities.

(c) The use of BPAs does not exempt an agency from the responsibility for keeping obligations and expenditures within available funds.

[FAC 97-3, 62 FR 64912, 12/9/97, effective 2/9/98]

13.303-2 Establishment of BPAs.

(a) The following are circumstances under which contracting officers may establish BPAs:

(1) There is a wide variety of items in a broad class of supplies or services that are generally purchased, but the exact items, quantities, and delivery requirements are not known in advance and may vary considerably.

(2) There is a need to provide commercial sources of supply for one or more offices or projects in a given area that do not have or need authority to purchase otherwise.

(3) The use of this procedure would avoid the writing of numerous purchase orders.

(4) There is no existing requirements contract for the same supply or service that the contracting activity is required to use.

(b) After determining a BPA would be advantageous, contracting officers shall—

(1) Establish the parameters to limit purchases to individual items or commodity groups or classes, or permit the supplier to furnish unlimited supplies or services; and

(2) Consider suppliers whose past performance has shown them to be dependable, who offer quality supplies or services at consistently lower prices, and who have provided numerous purchases at or below the simplified acquisition threshold.

(c) BPAs may be established with—

(1) More than one supplier for supplies or services of the same type to provide maximum practicable competition;

(2) A single firm from which numerous individual purchases at or below the simplified acquisition threshold will likely be made in a given period; or

(3) Federal Supply Schedule contractors, if not inconsistent with the terms of the applicable schedule contract.

(d) BPAs should be prepared without a purchase requisition and only after contacting suppliers to make the necessary arrangements for—

(1) Securing maximum discounts;

(2) Documenting individual purchase transactions;

(3) Periodic billings; and

(4) Incorporating other necessary details.

[FAC 97-3, 62 FR 64912, 12/9/97, effective 2/9/98]

13.303-3 Preparation of BPAs.

Prepare BPAs on the forms specified in 13.307. Do not cite accounting and appropriation data (see 13.303-5(e)(4)).

(a) The following terms and conditions are mandatory:

(1) *Description of agreement.* A statement that the supplier shall furnish supplies or services, described in general terms, if and when requested by the contracting officer (or the authorized representative of the contracting officer) during a specified period and within a stipulated aggregate amount, if any.

(2) *Extent of obligation.* A statement that the Government is obligated only to the extent of authorized purchases actually made under the BPA.

(3) *Purchase limitation.* A statement that specifies the dollar limitation for each individual purchase under the BPA (see 13.303-5(b)).

(4) *Individuals authorized to purchase under the BPA.* A statement that a list of individuals authorized to purchase under the BPA, identified either by title of position or by name of individual, organizational component, and the dollar limitation per purchase for each position title or individual shall be furnished to the supplier by the contracting officer.

(5) *Delivery tickets.* A requirement that all shipments under the agreement, except those for newspapers, magazines, or other periodicals, shall be accompanied by delivery tickets or sales slips that shall contain the following minimum information:

(i) Name of supplier.

(ii) BPA number.

(iii) Date of purchase.

(iv) Purchase number.

(v) Itemized list of supplies or services furnished.

(vi) Quantity, unit price, and extension of each item, less applicable discounts (unit prices and extensions need not be shown when incompatible with the use of automated systems, provided that the invoice is itemized to show this information).

(vii) Date of delivery or shipment.

(6) *Invoices.* One of the following statements shall be included (except that the statement in paragraph (a)(6)(iii) of this subsection should not be used if the accumulation of the individual invoices by the Government materially increases the administrative costs of this purchase method):

(i) A summary invoice shall be submitted at least monthly or upon expiration of this BPA, whichever occurs first, for all deliveries made during a billing period, identifying the delivery tickets covered therein, stating their total dollar value, and supported by receipt copies of the delivery tickets.

(ii) An itemized invoice shall be submitted at least monthly or upon expiration of this BPA, whichever occurs first, for all deliveries made during a billing period and for which payment has not been received. These invoices need not be supported by copies of delivery tickets.

(iii) When billing procedures provide for an individual invoice for each delivery, these invoices shall be accumulated, provided that—

(A) A consolidated payment will be made for each specified period; and

(B) The period of any discounts will commence on the final date of the billing period or on the date of receipt of invoices for all deliveries accepted during the billing period, whichever is later.

(iv) An invoice for subscriptions or other charges for newspapers, magazines, or other periodicals shall show the starting and ending dates and shall state either that ordered subscriptions have been placed in effect or will be placed in effect upon receipt of payment.

(b) If the fast payment procedure is used, include the requirements stated in 13.403.

[FAC 97-3, 62 FR 64912, 12/9/97, effective 2/9/98]

13.303-4 Clauses.

(a) The contracting officer shall insert in each BPA the clauses prescribed elsewhere in this part that are required for or applicable to the particular BPA.

(b) Unless a clause prescription specifies otherwise (*e.g.*, see 22.305(a), 22.605(a)(5), or 22.1006), if the prescription includes a dollar threshold, the amount to be compared to that threshold is that of any particular order under the BPA.

[FAC 97-3, 62 FR 64912, 12/9/97, effective 2/9/98]

13.303-5 Purchases under BPAs.

(a) Use a BPA only for purchases that are otherwise authorized by law or regulation.

(b) Individual purchases shall not exceed the simplified acquisition threshold. However, agency regulations may establish a higher threshold consistent with the following:

(1) The simplified acquisition threshold and the $7 million limitation for individual purchases ($13 million for purchases entered into under the authority of 12.102(f)(1)) do not apply to BPAs established in accordance with 13.303-2(c)(3).

(2) The limitation for individual purchases for commercial item acquisitions conducted under Subpart 13.5 is $7 million ($13 million for acquisitions as described in 13.500(c)).

(c) The existence of a BPA does not justify purchasing from only one source or avoiding small business set-asides. The requirements of 13.003(b) and Subpart 19.5 also apply to each order.

(d) If, for a particular purchase greater than the micro-purchase threshold, there is an insufficient number of BPAs to ensure maximum practicable competition, the contracting officer shall—

(1) Solicit quotations from other sources (see 13.105) and make the purchase as appropriate; and

(2) Establish additional BPAs to facilitate future purchases if—

(i) Recurring requirements for the same or similar supplies or services seem likely;

(ii) Qualified sources are willing to accept BPAs; and

(iii) It is otherwise practical to do so.

(e) Limit documentation of purchases to essential information and forms as follows:

(1) Purchases generally should be made electronically, or orally when it is not considered economical or practical to use electronic methods.

(2) A paper purchase document may be issued if necessary to ensure that the supplier and the purchaser agree concerning the transaction.

(3) Unless a paper document is issued, record essential elements (*e.g.*, date, supplier, supplies or services, price, delivery date) on the purchase requisition, in an informal memorandum, or on a form developed locally for the purpose.

(4) Cite the pertinent purchase requisitions and the accounting and appropriation data.

(5) When delivery is made or the services are performed, the supplier's sales document, delivery document, or invoice may (if it reflects the essential elements) be used for the purpose of recording receipt and acceptance of the supplies or services. However, if the purchase is assigned to another activity for administration, the authorized Government representative shall document receipt and acceptance of supplies or services by signing and dating the agency specified form after verification and after notation of any exceptions.

[FAC 97-3, 62 FR 64912, 12/9/97, effective 2/9/98; FAC 2001-20, 69 FR 8311, 2/23/2004, effective 2/23/2004; FAC 2001-26, 69 FR 76350, 12/20/2004, effective 1/19/2005; FAC 2005-13, 71 FR 57363, 9/28/2006, effective 9/28/2006; FAC 2005-45, 75 FR 53129, 8/30/2010, effective 10/1/2010; FAC 2005-83, 80 FR 38293, 7/2/2015, effective 10/1/2015, 80 FR 38311, 7/2/2015, effective 8/3/2015]

13.303-6 Review procedures.

(a) The contracting officer placing orders under a BPA, or the designated representative of the contracting officer, shall review a sufficient random sample of the BPA files at least annually to ensure that authorized procedures are being followed.

(b) The contracting officer that entered into the BPA shall—

(1) Ensure that each BPA is reviewed at least annually and, if necessary, updated at that time; and

(2) Maintain awareness of changes in market conditions, sources of supply, and other pertinent factors that may warrant making new arrangements with different suppliers or modifying existing arrangements.

(c) If an office other than the purchasing office that established a BPA is authorized to make purchases under that BPA, the agency that has jurisdiction over the office authorized to make the purchases shall ensure that the procedures in paragraph (a) of this subsection are being followed.

[FAC 97-3, 62 FR 64912, 12/9/97, effective 2/9/98]

13.303-7 Completion of BPAs.

An individual BPA is considered complete when the purchases under it equal its total dollar limitation, if any, or when its stated time period expires.

[FAC 97-3, 62 FR 64912, 12/9/97, effective 2/9/98]

13.303-8 Optional clause.

The clause at 52.213-4, Terms and Conditions—Simplified Acquisitions (Other Than Commercial Items), may be used in BPAs established under this section.

[FAC 97-3, 62 FR 64912, 12/9/97, effective 2/9/98]

13.304 [Reserved]

[Reserved, FAC 97-3, 62 FR 64912, 12/9/97, effective 2/9/98]

13.305 Impress funds and third party drafts. (No Text)

13.305-1 General.

Imprest funds and third party drafts may be used to acquire and to pay for supplies or services. Policies and regulations concerning the establishment of and accounting for imprest funds and third party drafts, including the responsibilities of designated cashiers and alternates, are contained in Part IV of the Treasury Financial Manual for Guidance of Departments and Agencies, Title 7 of the GAO Policy and Procedures Manual for Guidance of Federal Agencies, and the agency implementing regulations. Agencies also shall be guided by the Manual of Procedures and Instructions for Cashiers, issued by the Financial Management Service, Department of the Treasury.

[FAC 97-3, 62 FR 64912, 12/9/97, effective 2/9/98; FAC 2005-13, 71 FR 57380, 9/28/2006, effective 9/28/2006]

13.305-2 Agency responsibilities.

Each agency using imprest funds and third party drafts shall—

(a) Periodically review and determine whether there is a continuing need for each fund or third party draft account established, and that amounts of those funds or accounts are not in excess of actual needs;

(b) Take prompt action to have imprest funds or third party draft accounts adjusted to a level commensurate with demonstrated needs whenever circumstances warrant such action; and

(c) Develop and issue appropriate implementing regulations. These regulations shall include (but are not limited to) procedures covering—

(1) Designation of personnel authorized to make purchases using imprest funds or third party drafts; and

(2) Documentation of purchases using imprest funds or third party drafts, including documentation of—

(i) Receipt and acceptance of supplies and services by the Government;

(ii) Receipt of cash or third party draft payments by the suppliers; and

(iii) Cash advances and reimbursements.

[FAC 97-3, 62 FR 64912, 12/9/97, effective 2/9/98]

13.305-3 Conditions for use.

Imprest funds or third party drafts may be used for purchases when—

(a) The imprest fund transaction does not exceed $500 or such other limits as have been approved by the agency head;

(b) The third party draft transaction does not exceed $2,500, unless authorized at a higher level in accordance with Treasury restrictions;

(c) The use of imprest funds or third party drafts is considered to be advantageous to the Government; and

(d) The use of imprest funds or third party drafts for the transaction otherwise complies with any additional conditions established by agencies and with the policies and regulations referenced in 13.305-1.

[FAC 97-3, 62 FR 64912, 12/9/97, effective 2/9/98]

13.305-4 Procedures.

(a) Each purchase using imprest funds or third party drafts shall be based upon an authorized purchase requisition, contracting officer verification statement, or other agency approved method of ensuring that adequate funds are available for the purchase.

(b) Normally, purchases should be placed orally and without soliciting competition if prices are considered reasonable.

(c) Since there is, for all practical purposes, simultaneous placement of the order and delivery of the items, clauses are not required for purchases using imprest funds or third party drafts.

(d) Forms prescribed at 13.307(e) may be used if a written order is considered necessary (*e.g.*, if required by the supplier for discount, tax exemption, or other reasons). If a purchase order is used, endorse it "Payment to be made from Imprest Fund" (or "Payment to be made from Third Party Draft," as appropriate).

(e) The individual authorized to make purchases using imprest funds or third party drafts shall—

(1) Furnish to the imprest fund or third party draft cashier a copy of the document required under paragraph (a) of this subsection annotated to reflect—

(i) That an imprest fund or third party draft purchase has been made;

(ii) The unit prices and extensions; and

(iii) The supplier's name and address; and

(2) Require the supplier to include with delivery of the supplies an invoice, packing slip, or other sales instrument giving—

(i) The supplier's name and address;

(ii) List and quantity of items supplied;

(iii) Unit prices and extensions; and

(iv) Cash discount, if any.

[FAC 97-3, 62 FR 64912, 12/9/97, effective 2/9/98]

13.306 SF 44, Purchase Order—Invoice—Voucher.

The SF 44, Purchase Order—Invoice—Voucher, is a multipurpose pocket-size purchase order form designed primarily for on-the-spot, over-the-counter purchases of supplies and nonpersonal services while away from the purchasing office or at isolated activities. It also can be used as a receiving report, invoice, and public voucher.

(a) This form may be used if all of the following conditions are satisfied:

(1) The amount of the purchase is at or below the micro-purchase threshold, except for purchases made under unusual and compelling urgency or in support of contingency operations. Agencies may establish higher dollar limitations for specific activities or items;

(2) The supplies or services are immediately available;

(3) One delivery and one payment will be made; and

(4) Its use is determined to be more economical and efficient than use of other simplified acquisition procedures.

(b) General procedural instructions governing the form's use are printed on the form and on the inside front cover of each book of forms.

(c) Since there is, for all practical purposes, simultaneous placement of the order and delivery of the items, clauses are not required for purchases using this form.

(d) Agencies shall provide adequate safeguards regarding the control of forms and accounting for purchases.

[FAC 97-3, 62 FR 64912, 12/9/97, effective 2/9/98]

13.307 Forms.

(a) *Commercial items.* For use of the SF 1449, Solicitation/Contract/Order for Commercial Items, see 12.204.

(b) *Other than commercial items.*

(1) Except when quotations are solicited electronically or orally, the SF 1449; SF 18, Request for Quotations; or an agency form/automated format may be used. Each agency request for quotations form/automated format should conform with the SF 18 or SF 1449 to the maximum extent practicable.

(2) Both SF 1449 and OF 347, Order for Supplies or Services, are multipurpose forms used for negotiated purchases of supplies or services, delivery or task orders, inspection and receiving reports, and invoices. An agency form/automated format also may be used.

(c) *Forms used for both commercial and other than commercial items.*

(1) OF 336, Continuation Sheet, or an agency form/automated format may be used when additional space is needed.

(2) OF 348, Order for Supplies or Services Schedule—Continuation, or an agency form/automated format may be used for negotiated purchases when additional space is needed. Agencies may print on these forms the clauses considered to be generally suitable for purchases.

(3) SF 30, Amendment of Solicitation/Modification of Contract, or a purchase order form may be used to modify a purchase order, unless an agency form/automated format is prescribed in agency regulations.

(d) SF 44, Purchase Order—Invoice—Voucher, is a multipurpose pocket-size purchase order form that may be used as outlined in 13.306.

(e) SF 1165, Receipt for Cash—Subvoucher, or an agency purchase order form may be used for purchases using imprest funds or third party drafts.

[FAC 97-3, 62 FR 64912, 12/9/97, effective 2/9/98; FAC 97-9, 63 FR 58587, 10/30/98, effective 10/30/98; FAC 2005-21, 72 FR 63075, 11/7/2007, effective 12/7/2007]

SUBPART 13.4—FAST PAYMENT PROCEDURE

13.401 General.

(a) The fast payment procedure allows payment under limited conditions to a contractor prior to the Government's verification that supplies have been received and accepted. The procedure provides for payment for supplies based on the contractor's submission of an invoice that constitutes a certification that the contractor—

(1) Has delivered the supplies to a post office, common carrier, or point of first receipt by the Government; and

(2) Shall replace, repair, or correct supplies not received at destination, damaged in transit, or not conforming to purchase agreements.

(b) The contracting officer shall be primarily responsible for determining the amount of debts resulting from failure of contractors to properly replace, repair, or correct supplies lost, damaged, or not conforming to purchase requirements (see 32.602and 32.603).

[FAC 97-3, 62 FR 64912, 12/9/97, effective 2/9/98; FAC 2005-27, 73 FR 53997, 9/17/2008, effective 10/17/2008]

13.402 Conditions for use.

If the conditions in paragraphs (a) through (f) of this section are present, the fast payment procedure may be used, provided that use of the procedure is consistent with the other conditions of the purchase. The conditions for use of the fast payment procedure are as follows:

(a) Individual purchasing instruments do not exceed $35,000, except that executive agencies may permit higher dollar limitations for specified activities or items on a case-by-case basis.

(b) Deliveries of supplies are to occur at locations where there is both a geographical separation and a lack of adequate communications facilities between Government receiving and disbursing activities that will make it impractical to make timely payment based on evidence of Government acceptance.

(c) Title to the supplies passes to the Government—

(1) Upon delivery to a post office or common carrier for mailing or shipment to destination; or

(2) Upon receipt by the Government if the shipment is by means other than Postal Service or common carrier.

(d) The supplier agrees to replace, repair, or correct supplies not received at destination, damaged in transit, or not conforming to purchase requirements.

(e) The purchasing instrument is a firm-fixed-price contract, a purchase order, or a delivery order for supplies.

(f) A system is in place to ensure—

(1) Documentation of evidence of contractor performance under fast payment purchases;

(2) Timely feedback to the contracting officer in case of contractor deficiencies; and

(3) Identification of suppliers that have a current history of abusing the fast payment procedure (also see subpart 9.1).

[FAC 97-3, 62 FR 64912, 12/9/97, effective 2/9/98; FAC 2005-13, 71 FR 57363, 9/28/2006, effective 9/28/2006; FAC 2005-83, 80 FR 38293, 7/2/2015, effective 10/1/2015]

13.403 Preparation and execution of orders.

Priced or unpriced contracts, purchase orders, or BPAs using the fast payment procedure shall include the following:

(a) A requirement that the supplies be shipped transportation or postage prepaid.

(b) A requirement that invoices be submitted directly to the finance or other office designated in the order, or in the case of unpriced purchase orders, to the contracting officer (see 13.302-2(c)).

(c) The following statement on the consignee's copy:

Consignee's Notification to Purchasing Activity of Nonreceipt, Damage, or Nonconformance

The consignee shall notify the purchasing office promptly after the specified date of delivery of supplies not received, damaged intransit, or not conforming to specifications of the purchase order. Unless extenuating circumstances exist, the notification should be made not later than 60 days after the specified date of delivery.

[FAC 97-3, 62 FR 64912, 12/9/97, effective 2/9/98]

13.404 Contract clause.

The contracting officer shall insert the clause at 52.213-1, Fast Payment Procedure, in solicitations and contracts when the conditions in 13.402 are applicable and it is intended that the fast payment procedure be used in the contract (in the case of BPAs, the contracting officer may elect to insert the clause either in the BPA or in orders under the BPA).

[FAC 97-3, 62 FR 64912, 12/9/97, effective 2/9/98]

SUBPART 13.5—SIMPLIFIED PROCEDURES FOR CERTAIN COMMERCIAL ITEMS

13.500 General.

(a) This subpart authorizes the use of simplified procedures for the acquisition of supplies and services in amounts greater than the simplified acquisition threshold but not exceeding $7 million ($13 million for acquisitions as described in 13.500(c)), including options, if the contracting officer reasonably expects, based on the nature of the supplies or services sought, and on market research, that offers will include only commercial items. Contracting officers may use any simplified acquisition procedure in this part, subject to any specific dollar limitation applicable to the particular procedure. The purpose of these simplified procedures is to vest contracting officers with additional procedural discretion and flexibility, so that commercial item acquisitions in this dollar range may be solicited, offered, evaluated, and awarded in a simplified manner that maximizes efficiency and economy and minimizes burden and administrative costs for both the Government and industry (10 U.S.C. 2304(g) and 2305 and 41 U.S.C. 3305, 3306, and chapter 37, Awarding of Contracts.

(b) When acquiring commercial items using the procedures in this part, the requirements of part 12 apply subject to the order of precedence provided at 12.102(c). This includes use of the provisions and clauses in subpart 12.3.

(c) Under 41 U.S.C. 1903, the simplified acquisition procedures authorized in this subpart may be used for acquisitions that do not exceed $13 million when—

(1) The acquisition is for commercial items that, as determined by the head of the agency, are to be used in support of a contingency operation; to facilitate the defense against or recovery from cyber, nuclear, biological, chemical, or radiological attack; to support a request from the Secretary of State or the Administrator of the United States Agency for International Development to facilitate provision of international disaster assistance; or to support response to an emergency or major disaster, or

(2) The acquisition will be treated as an acquisition of commercial items in accordance with 12.102(f)(1).

[FAC 2001-20, 69 FR 8311, 2/23/2004, effective 2/23/2004; FAC 2001-26, 69 FR 76350, 12/20/2004, effective 1/19/2005; FAC 2005-01, 70 FR 11739, 3/9/2005, effective 4/8/2005; FAC 2005-13, 71 FR 57363, 9/28/2006, effective 9/28/2006; FAC 2005-27, 73 FR 54008, 9/17/2008, effective 9/17/2008; FAC 2005-39, 75 FR 13413, 3/19/2010, effective 3/19/2010; FAC 2005-45, 75 FR 53129, 8/30/2010, effective 10/1/2010; FAC 2005-66, 78 FR 13767, 2/28/2013, effective 2/28/2013; FAC 2005-73, 79 FR 24192, 4/29/2014, effective 5/29/2014; FAC 2005-83, 80 FR 38293, 7/2/2015, effective 10/1/2015, 80 FR 38311, 7/2/2015, effective 8/3/2015; FAC 2019-02, 84 FR 19835, 5/6/2019, effective 6/5/2019]

13.501 Special documentation requirements.

(a) *Sole source (including brand name) acquisitions.*

(1) Acquisitions conducted under simplified acquisition procedures are exempt from the requirements in Part 6. However, contracting officers must—

(i) Conduct sole source acquisitions, as defined in 2.101, (including brand name) under this subpart only if the need to do so is justified in writing and approved at the levels specified in paragraphs (a)(2) of this section;

(ii) Prepare sole source (including brand name) justifications using the format at 6.303-2, modified to reflect that the procedures in FAR subpart 13.5 were used in accordance with 41 U.S.C. 1901 or the authority of 41 U.S.C. 1903;

(iii) Make publicly available the justifications (excluding brand name) required by 6.305(a) within 14 days after contract award or in the case of unusual and compelling urgency within 30 days after contract award, in accordance with 6.305 procedures at paragraphs (b), (d), (e), and (f); and

(iv) Make publicly available brand name justifications with the solicitation, in accordance with 5.102(a)(6).

(2) Justifications and approvals are required under this subpart only for sole source (including brand name) acquisitions or portions of an acquisition requiring a brand-name. If the justification is to cover only the portion of the acquisition which is brand-name, then it should so state; the approval level requirements will then only apply to that portion.

(i) For a proposed contract exceeding $150,000, but not exceeding $700,000, the contracting officer's certification that the justification is accurate and complete to the best of the contracting officer's knowledge and belief will serve as approval, unless a higher approval level is established in accordance with agency procedures.

(ii) For a proposed contract exceeding $700,000, but not exceeding $13.5 million, the advocate for competition for the procuring activity, designated pursuant to 6.501, or an official described in 6.304(a)(3) or (a)(4) must approve the justification and approval. This authority is not delegable.

(iii) For a proposed contract exceeding $13.5 million but not exceeding $68 million or, for DoD, NASA, and the Coast Guard, not exceeding $93 million. The head of the procuring activity or the official described in 6.304(a)(3) or (a)(4) must approve the justification and approval. This authority is not delegable.

(iv) For a proposed contract exceeding $68 million or, for DoD, NASA, and the Coast Guard, $93 million, the official described in 6.304(a)(4) must approve the justification and approval. This authority is not delegable except as provided in 6.304(a)(4).

(b) *Contract file documentation*. The contract file must include—

(1) A brief written description of the procedures used in awarding the contract, including the fact that the procedures in FAR Subpart 13.5 were used;

(2) The number of offers received;

(3) An explanation, tailored to the size and complexity of the acquisition, of the basis for the contract award decision; and

(4) Any justification approved under paragraph (a) of this section.

[FAC 97-3, 62 FR 64912, 12/9/97, effective 2/9/98; FAC 97-15, 64 FR 72414, 12/27/99, effective 12/27/99; FAC 97-22, 66 FR 2116, 1/10/2001, effective 3/12/2001; Delay of effective date, 66 FR 14259, 3/9/2001, effective 5/11/2001; FAC 2001-12, 68 FR 4047, 1/27/2003, effective 1/24/2003; FAC 2001-20, 69 FR 8311, 2/23/2004, effective 2/23/2004; FAC 2001-26, 69 FR 76350, 12/20/2004, effective 1/19/2005; FAC 2005-06, 70 FR 57457, 9/30/2005, effective 9/30/2005; FAC 2005-13, 71 FR 57357, 9/28/2006, effective 9/28/2006; FAC 2005-13, 71 FR 57363, 9/28/2006, effective 9/28/2006; FAC 2005-42, 75 FR 34271, 34273, 6/16/2010, effective 7/16/2010; FAC 2005-45, 75 FR 53129, 8/30/2010, effective 10/1/2010; FAC 2005-55, 77 FR 189, 1/3/2012, effective 2/2/2012; FAC 2005-73, 79 FR 24192, 4/29/2014, effective 5/29/2014; FAC 2005-83, 80 FR 38293, 7/2/2015, effective 10/1/2015, 80 FR 38311, 7/2/2015, effective 8/3/2015]

PART 14—SEALED BIDDING

Table of Contents

Scope of part 14.000

Subpart 14.1—Use of Sealed Bidding

Elements of sealed bidding 14.101
[Reserved] 14.102
Policy 14.103
General 14.103-1
Limitations 14.103-2
Types of contracts 14.104
Solicitations for informational or planning purposes 14.105

Subpart 14.2—Solicitation of Bids

Preparation of invitations for bids 14.201
Uniform contract format 14.201-1
Part I—The Schedule 14.201-2
Part II—Contract clauses 14.201-3
Part III—Documents, exhibits, and other attachments 14.201-4
Part IV—Representations and instructions 14.201-5
Solicitation provisions 14.201-6
Contract clauses 14.201-7
Price-related factors 14.201-8
Simplified contract format 14.201-9
General rules for solicitation of bids 14.202
Bidding time 14.202-1
[Removed and Reserved] 14.202-2
Bid envelopes 14.202-3
Bid samples 14.202-4
Descriptive literature 14.202-5
Final review of invitations for bids 14.202-6
Facsimile bids 14.202-7
Electronic bids 14.202-8
Methods of soliciting bids 14.203
Transmittal to prospective bidders 14.203-1
Dissemination of information concerning invitations for bids 14.203-2
Master solicitation 14.203-3
Records of invitations for bids and records of bids 14.204
Presolicitation notices 14.205
[Removed] 14.205-1
[Removed] 14.205-2
[Removed] 14.205-3
[Removed] 14.205-4
[Removed] 14.205-5
[Removed and Reserved] 14.206
Pre-bid conference 14.207
Amendment of invitation for bids 14.208
Cancellation of invitations before opening 14.209
Qualified products 14.210
Release of acquisition information 14.211
Economic purchase quantities (supplies) 14.212
[Removed] 14.213

Subpart 14.3—Submission of Bids

Responsiveness of bids 14.301
Bid submission 14.302
Modification or withdrawal of bids 14.303

Submission, modification, and withdrawal of bids 14.304

Subpart 14.4—Opening of Bids and Award of Contract

Scope of subpart 14.400
Receipt and safeguarding of bids 14.401
Opening of bids 14.402
Unclassified bids 14.402-1
Classified bids 14.402-2
Postponement of openings 14.402-3
Recording of bids 14.403
Rejection of bids 14.404
Cancellation of invitations after opening 14.404-1
Rejection of individual bids 14.404-2
Notice to bidders of rejection of all bids 14.404-3
Restrictions on disclosure of descriptive literature 14.404-4
All or none qualifications 14.404-5
Minor informalities or irregularities in bids 14.405
Receipt of an unreadable electronic bid 14.406
Mistakes in bids 14.407
General 14.407-1
Apparent clerical mistakes 14.407-2
Other mistakes disclosed before award 14.407-3
Mistakes after award 14.407-4
Award 14.408
General 14.408-1
Responsible bidder—reasonableness of price 14.408-2
Prompt payment discounts 14.408-3
Economic price adjustment 14.408-4
Reserved 14.408-5
Equal low bids 14.408-6
Documentation of award 14.408-7
Protests against award 14.408-8
Information to bidders 14.409
Award of unclassified contracts 14.409-1
Award of classified contracts 14.409-2

Subpart 14.5—Two-Step Sealed Bidding

General 14.501
Conditions for use 14.502
Procedures 14.503
Step one 14.503-1
Step two 14.503-2

PART 14—SEALED BIDDING

14.000 Scope of part.

This part prescribes—

(a) The basic requirements of contracting for supplies and services (including construction) by sealed bidding;

(b) The information to be included in the solicitation (invitation for bids);

(c) Procedures concerning the submission of bids;

(d) Requirements for opening and evaluating bids and awarding contracts; and

(e) Procedures for two-step sealed bidding.

[FAC 84-5, 50 FR 1737, 1/11/85, effective 4/1/85]

SUBPART 14.1—USE OF SEALED BIDDING

14.101 Elements of sealed bidding.

Sealed bidding is a method of contracting that employs competitive bids, public opening of bids, and awards. The following steps are involved:

(a) *Preparation of invitations for bids.* Invitations must describe the requirements of the Government clearly, accurately, and completely. Unnecessarily restrictive specifications or requirements that might unduly limit the number of bidders are prohibited. The invitation includes all documents (whether attached or incorporated by reference) furnished prospective bidders for the purpose of bidding.

(b) *Publicizing the invitation for bids.* Invitations must be publicized through distribution to prospective bidders, posting in public places, and such other means as may be appropriate. Publicizing must occur a sufficient time before public opening of bids to enable prospective bidders to prepare and submit bids.

(c) *Submission of bids.* Bidders must submit sealed bids to be opened at the time and place stated in the solicitation for the public opening of bids.

(d) *Evaluation of bids.* Bids shall be evaluated without discussions.

(e) *Contract award.* After bids are publicly opened, an award will be made with reasonable promptness to that responsible bidder whose bid, conforming to the invitation for bids, will be most advantageous to the Government, considering only price and the price-related factors included in the invitation.

[FAC 84-5, 50 FR 1737, 1/11/85, effective 4/1/85; Final rule, 50 FR 52429, 12/23/85, effective 12/23/85]

14.102 [Reserved]

14.103 Policy. (No Text)

14.103-1 General.

(a) Sealed bidding shall be used whenever the conditions in 6.401(a) are met. This requirement applies to any proposed contract action under Part 6.

(b) Sealed bidding may be used for classified acquisitions if its use does not violate agency security requirements.

(c) The policy for pricing modifications of sealed bid contracts appears in 15.403-4(a)(1)(iii).

[FAC 84-5, 50 FR 1737, 1/11/85, effective 4/1/85; FAC 97-2, 62 FR 51224, 9/30/97, effective 10/10/97; FAC 2001-04, 67 FR 6112, 2/8/2002, effective 2/20/2002; FAC 2001-15, 68 FR 43854, 7/24/2003, effective 8/25/2003]

14.103-2 Limitations.

No awards shall be made as a result of sealed bidding unless—

(a) Bids have been solicited as required by Subpart 14.2;

(b) Bids have been submitted as required by Subpart 14.3;

(c) The requirements of 1.602-1(b) and Part 6 have been met; and

(d) An award is made to the responsible bidder (see 9.1) whose bid is responsive to the terms of the invitation for bids and is most advantageous to the Government, considering only price and the price-related factors included in the invitation, as provided in Subpart 14.4.

[FAC 84-5, 50 FR 1737, 1/11/85, effective 4/1/85; Final rule, 50 FR 52429, 12/23/85, effective 12/23/85]

14.104 Types of contracts.

Firm-fixed-price contracts shall be used when the method of contracting is sealed bidding, except that fixed-price contracts with economic price adjustment clauses may be used if authorized in accordance with 16.203 when some flexibility is necessary and feasible. Such clauses must afford all bidders an equal opportunity to bid.

[FAC 84-5, 50 FR 1737, 1/11/85, effective 4/1/85; Final rule, 50 FR 52429, 12/23/85, effective 12/23/85]

14.105 Solicitations for informational or planning purposes.

(See 15.201(e).)

[FAC 84-5, 50 FR 1737, 1/11/85, effective 4/1/85; FAC 97-2, 62 FR 51224, 9/30/97, effective 10/10/97]

SUBPART 14.2—SOLICITATION OF BIDS

14.201 Preparation of invitations for bids. (No Text)

14.201-1 Uniform contract format.

(a) Contracting officers shall prepare invitations for bids and contracts using the uniform contract format outlined in Table 14-1 to the maximum practicable extent. The use of the format facilitates preparation of the solicitation and contract as well as reference to, and use of, those documents by bidders and contractors. It need not be used for acquisition of the following:

(1) Construction (see Part 36).

(2) Shipbuilding (including design, construction, and conversion), ship overhaul, and ship repair.

(3) Subsistence items.

(4) Supplies or services requiring special contract forms prescribed elsewhere in this regulation that are inconsistent with the uniform contract format.

(5) Firm-fixed-price or fixed-price with economic price adjustment acquisitions that use the simplified contract format (see 14.201-9).

(b) Information suitable for inclusion in invitations for bids under the uniform contract format shall also be included in invitations for bids not subject to that format if applicable.

(c) Solicitations to which the uniform contract format applies shall include Parts I, II, III, and IV. If any section of the uniform contract format does not apply, the contracting officer should so mark that section in the solicitation. Upon award, the contracting officer shall not physically include Part IV in the resulting contract, but shall retain it in the contract file. (See 4.1201(c).)Award by acceptance of a bid on the award portion of Standard Form 33, Solicitation, Offer and Award (SF 33), Standard Form 26, Award/Contract (SF 26), or Standard Form 1447, Solicitation/Contract (SF 1447), incorporates Section K, Representations, certifications, and other statements of bidders, in the resultant contract even though not physically attached. The representations and certifications shall be incorporated by reference in the contract by using 52.204-19 (see 4.1202(b)) or for acquisitions of commercial items see 52.212-4(v).

TABLE 14-1
Uniform Contract Format

Section	Title
Part I - - The Schedule	
A	Solicitation/contract form
B	Supplies or services and prices
C	Description/specifications
D	Packaging and marking
E	Inspection and acceptance
F	Deliveries or performance
G	Contract administration data
H	Special contract requirements
Part II - - Contract Clauses	
I	Contract clauses
Part III - - List of Documents, Exhibits, and Other Attachments	

Section	Title
J	List of documents, exhibits, and other attachments
Part IV- -Representations and Instructions	
K	Representations, certifications, and other statements of bidders
L	Instructions, conditions, and notices to bidders
M	Evaluation factors for award

[FAC 84-5, 50 FR 1737, 1/11/85, effective 4/1/85; FAC 84-53, 54 FR 48982, 11/28/89, effective 12/28/89; FAC 2005-13, 71 FR 57362, 9/28/2006, effective 9/28/2006; FAC 2005-19, 72 FR 46333, 8/17/2007, effective 8/17/2007; FAC 2005-78, 79 FR 70341, 11/25/2014, effective 12/26/2014]

14.201-2 Part I—The Schedule.

The contracting officer shall prepare the Schedule as follows:

(a) *Section A, Solicitation/contract form.*

(1) Prepare the invitation for bids on SF 33, or the SF 1447, unless otherwise permitted by this regulation. The SF 33 is the first page of the solicitation and includes Section A of the uniform contract format. When the SF 1447 is used as the solicitation document, the information in subdivisions (a) (2) (i) and (a) (2) (iv) of this subsection shall be inserted in block 9 of the SF 1447.

(2) When the SF 33 or SF 1447 is not used, include the following on the first page of the invitation for bids:

(i) Name, address, and location of issuing activity, including room and building where bids must be submitted.

(ii) Invitation for bids number.

(iii) Date of issuance.

(iv) Time specified for receipt of bids.

(v) Number of pages.

(vi) Requisition or other purchase authority.

(vii) Requirement for bidder to provide its name and complete address, including street, city, county, State, and ZIP code.

(viii) A statement that bidders should include in the bid the address to which payment should be mailed, if that address is different from that of the bidder.

(b) *Section B, Supplies or services and prices.* Include a brief description of the supplies or services; e.g., line item number, national stock number/part number if applicable, title or name identifying the supplies or services, and quantities (see part 11). The SF 33 and SF 1447 may be supplemented as necessary by the Optional Form 336(OF 336), Continuation Sheet.

(c) *Section C, Description/specifications.* Include any description or specifications needed in addition to Section B to permit full and open competition (see Part 11).

(d) *Section D, Packaging and marking.* Provide packaging, packing, preservation, and marking requirements, if any.

(e) *Section E, Inspection and acceptance.* Include inspection, acceptance, quality assurance, and reliability requirements (see Part 46, Quality Assurance).

(f) *Section F, Deliveries or performance.* Specify the requirements for time, place, and method of delivery or performance (see Subpart 11.4, Delivery or Performance Schedules).

(g) *Section G, Contract administration data.* Include any required accounting and appropriation data and any required contract administration information or instructions other than those on the solicitation form.

(h) *Section H, Special contract requirements.* Include a clear statement of any special contract requirements that are not included in Section I, Contract clauses, or in other sections of the uniform contract format.

[FAC 84-5, 50 FR 1737, 1/11/85, effective 4/1/85; FAC 84-18, 51 FR 27119, 7/29/86, effective 7/30/86; FAC 84-53, 54 FR 48982, 11/28/89, effective 12/28/89; Final rule, 55 FR 38516, 9/18/90; FAC 90-32, 60 FR 48206, 9/18/95, effective 10/1/95; FAC 2005-95, 82 FR 4709, 1/13/2017, effective 1/13/2017; FAC 2005-100, 83 FR 42571, 8/22/2018, effective 8/22/2018]

14.201-3 Part II—Contract clauses.

Section I, Contract clauses. The contracting officer shall include in this section the clauses required by law or by this regulation and any additional clauses expected to apply to any resulting contract, if these clauses are not required to be included in any other section of the uniform contract format.

[FAC 84-5, 50 FR 1737, 1/11/85, effective 4/1/85; FAC 84-37, 53 FR 17857, 5/18/88, effective 6/17/88]

14.201-4 Part III—Documents, exhibits, and other attachments.

Section J, List of documents, exhibits, and other attachments. The contracting officer shall list the title, date, and number of pages for each attached document.

[FAC 84-5, 50 FR 1737, 1/11/85, effective 4/1/85]

14.201-5 Part IV—Representations and instructions.

The contracting officer shall prepare the representations and instructions as follows:

(a) *Section K, Representations, certifications, and other statements of bidders.* Include in this section those solicitation provisions that require representations, certifications, or the submission of other information by bidders.

(b) *Section L, Instructions, conditions, and notices to bidders.* Insert in this section solicitation provisions and other information and instructions not required elsewhere to guide bidders. Invitations shall include the time and place for bid openings, and shall advise bidders that bids will be evaluated without discussions (see 52.214-10 and, for construction contracts, 52.214-19).

(c) *Section M, Evaluation factors for award.* Identify the price-related factors other than the bid price that will be considered in evaluating bids and awarding the contract. (See 14.201-8.)

[FAC 84-5, 50 FR 1737, 1/11/85, effective 4/1/85; FAC 84-37, 53 FR 17857, 5/18/88, effective 6/17/88]

14.201-6 Solicitation provisions.

(a) The provisions prescribed in this subsection apply to preparation and submission of bids in general. See other FAR parts for provisions and clauses related to specific acquisition requirements.

(b) Insert in all invitations for bids the provisions at—

(1) 52.214-3, Amendments to Invitations for Bids; and

(2) 52.214-4, False Statements in Bids.

(c) Insert the following provisions in invitations for bids:

(1) 52.214-5, Submission of Bids.

(2) 52.214-6, Explanation to Prospective Bidders.

(3) 52.214-7, Late Submissions, Modifications, and Withdrawals of Bids.

(d) [Reserved]

(e) Insert in all invitations for bids, except those for construction, the provision at 52.214-10, Contract Award—Sealed Bidding.

(f) Insert in invitations for bids to which the uniform contract format applies, the provision at 52.214-12, Preparation of Bids.

(g) [Removed and Reserved]

(h) Insert the provision at 52.214-14, Place of Performance—Sealed Bidding, in invitations for bids except those in which the place of performance is specified by the Government.

(i) Insert the provision at 52.214-15, Period for Acceptance of Bids, in invitations for bids (IFB's) that are not issued on SF 33 or SF 1447 except IFB's

(1) for construction work or

(2) in which the Government specifies a minimum acceptance period.

(j) Insert the provision at 52.214-16, Minimum Bid Acceptance Period, in invitations for bids, except for construction, if the contracting officer determines that a minimum acceptance period must be specified.

(k) [Reserved].

(l) Insert the provision at 52.214-18, Preparation of Bids—Construction, in invitations for bids for construction work.

(m) Insert the provision at 52.214-19, Contract Award—Sealed Bidding—Construction, in all invitations for bids for construction work.

(n) [Reserved].

(o) (1) Insert the provision at 52.214-20, Bid Samples, in invitations for bids if bid samples are required.

(2) If it appears that the conditions in 14.202-4(e)(1) will apply and the contracting officer anticipates granting waivers and—

(i) If the nature of the required product does not necessitate limiting the grant of a waiver to a product produced at the same plant in which the product previously acquired or tested was produced, use the provision with its Alternate I; or

(ii) If the nature of the required product necessitates limiting the grant of a waiver to a product produced at the same plant in which the product previously acquired or tested was produced, use the provision with its Alternate II.

(3) See 14.202-4(e)(2) regarding waiving the requirement for all bidders.

(p) (1) Insert the provision at 52.214-21, Descriptive Literature, in invitations for bids if—

(i) Descriptive literature is required to evaluate the technical acceptability of an offered product and

(ii) The required information will not be readily available unless it is submitted by bidders.

(2) Use the basic clause with its Alternate I if the possibility exists that the contracting officer may waive the requirement for furnishing descriptive literature for a bidder offering a previously supplied product that meets specification requirements of the current solicitation.

(3) See 14.202-5(d)(2) regarding waiving the requirement for all bidders.

(q) Insert the provision at 52.214-22, Evaluation of Bids for Multiple Awards, in invitations for bids if the contracting officer determines that multiple awards might be made if doing so is economically advantageous to the Government.

(r) Insert the provision at 52.214-23, Late Submissions, Modifications, Revisions, and Withdrawals of Technical Proposals under Two-Step Sealed Bidding, in solicitations for technical proposals in step one of two-step sealed bidding.

(s) Insert the provision at 52.214-24, Multiple Technical Proposals, in solicitations for technical proposals in step one of two-step sealed bidding if the contracting officer permits the submission of multiple technical proposals.

(t) Insert the provision at 52.214-25, Step Two of Two-Step Sealed Bidding, in invitations for bids issued under step two of two-step sealed bidding.

(u) [Reserved]

(v) Insert the provision at 52.214-31, Facsimile Bids, in solicitations if facsimile bids are authorized (see 14.202-7).

(w) Insert the provision at 52.214-34, Submission of Offers in the English Language, in solicitations that include any of the clauses prescribed in 25.1101 or 25.1102. It may be included in other solicitations when the contracting officer decides that it is necessary.

(x) Insert the provision at 52.214-35, Submission of Offers in U.S. Currency, in solicitations that include any of the clauses prescribed in 25.1101 or 25.1102, unless the contracting officer includes the clause at 52.225-17, Evaluation of Foreign Currency Offers, as prescribed in 25.1103(d). It may be included in other solicitations when the contracting officer decides that it is necessary.

[FAC 84-5, 50 FR 1737, 1/11/85, effective 4/1/85; FAC 84-12, 51 FR 2649, 1/17/86, effective 1/20/86; FAC 84-40, 53 FR 43390, 10/26/88, effective 11/25/88; FAC 84-42, 54 FR 5054, 1/31/89, effective 3/2/89; FAC 84-53, 54 FR 48982, 11/28/89, effective 12/28/89; FAC 84-58,55 FR 25527, 6/21/90, effective 7/23/90; FAC 90-4, 56 FR 15149, 4/15/91, effective 5/15/91; interim rule, FAC 90-18, 58 FR 31140, 5/28/93, effective 5/28/93; interim rule, FAC 90-19, 59 FR 544, 1/5/94, effective 1/1/94, interim rule finalized without change, FAC 90-45, 62 FR 224, 1/2/97, effective 1/1/97; FAC 90-29, 60 FR

34732, 7/3/95, effective 7/3/95; FAC 97-2, 62 FR 51224, 9/30/97, effective 10/10/97; FAC 97-9, 63 FR 58587, 10/30/98, effective 10/30/98, finalized without change, FAC 97-12, 64 FR 32740, 6/17/99; FAC 97-11, 64 FR 10530, 3/4/99, effective 5/3/99; FAC 97-14, 64 FR 51828, 9/24/99, effective 11/23/99; FAC 97-15, 64 FR 72414, 12/27/99, effective 12/27/99; FAC 97-15, 64 FR 72414, 12/27/99, effective 2/25/2000; FAC 2001-06, 67 FR 13048, 3/20/2002, effective 4/4/2002; FAC 2001-1, 68 FR 43854, 7/24/2003, effective 8/25/2003; FAC 2001-26, 69 FR 76341, 12/20/2004, effective 1/1/2005; FAC 2005-92, 81 FR 83097, 11/18/2016, effective 12/19/2016]

14.201-7 Contract clauses.

(a) When contracting by sealed bidding, the contracting officer shall insert the clause at 52.214-26, Audit and Records-Sealed Bidding, in solicitations and contracts as follows:

(1) Use the basic clause if—

(i) The acquisition will not use funds appropriated or otherwise made available by the American Recovery and Reinvestment Act of 2009 (Pub. L. 111-5); and

(ii) The contract amount is expected to exceed the threshold at 15.403-4(a)(1) for submission of certified cost or pricing data.

(2)(i) If the acquisition will use funds appropriated or otherwise made available by the American Recovery and Reinvestment Act of 2009, use the clause with its Alternate I in all solicitations and contracts.

(ii)(A) In the case of a bilateral contract modification that will use funds appropriated or otherwise made available by the American Recovery and Reinvestment Act of 2009, the contracting officer shall specify applicability of Alternate I to that modification.

(B) In the case of a task- or delivery-order contract in which not all orders will use funds appropriated or otherwise made available by the American Recovery and Reinvestment Act of 2009, the contracting officer shall specify the task or delivery orders to which Alternate I applies.

(b)(1) When contracting by sealed bidding, the contracting officer shall insert the clause at 52.214-27, Price Reduction for Defective Certified Cost or Pricing Data—Modifications—Sealed Bidding, in solicitations and contracts if the contract amount is expected to exceed the threshold for submission of certified cost or pricing data at 15.403-4(a)(1).

(2) In exceptional cases, the head of the contracting activity may waive the requirement for inclusion of the clause in a contract with a foreign government or agency of that government. The authorizations for the waiver and the reasons for granting it shall be in writing.

(c)(1) When contracting by sealed bidding, the contracting officer shall insert the clause at 52.214-28, Subcontractor Certified Cost or Pricing Data—Modifications—Sealed Bidding, in solicitations and contracts if the contract amount is expected to exceed the threshold for submission of certified cost or pricing data at 15.403-4(a)(1).

(2) In exceptional cases, the head of the contracting activity may waive the requirement for inclusion of the clause in a contract with a foreign government or agency of that government. The authorizations for the waiver and the reasons for granting it shall be in writing.

(d) When contracting by sealed bidding, the contracting officer shall insert the clause at 52.214-29, Order of Precedence—Sealed Bidding, in solicitations and contracts to which the uniform contract format applies.

[FAC 84-5, 50 FR 1738, 1/11/85, effective 4/1/85; FAC 84-12, 51 FR 2649, 1/17/86, effective 1/20/86; Interim rule, FAC 90-10, 56 FR 67413, 12/30/91, effective 12/30/91; Final rule, FAC 90-20, 59 FR 11368, 3/10/94, effective 3/10/94; FAC 90-22, 59 FR 62498, 12/5/94, effective 12/5/94; FAC 90-31,60 FR 42648, 8/16/95, effective 10/1/95; FAC 90-32, 60 FR 48206, 9/18/95, effective 10/1/95; FAC 97-2, 62 FR 51224, 9/30/97, effective 10/10/97; FAC 2005-32, 74 FR 14646, 3/31/2009, effective 3/31/2009; FAC 2005-42, 75 FR 34279, 6/16/2010, effective 7/16/2010; FAC 2005-45, 75 FR 53135, 8/30/2010, effective 10/1/2010]

14.201-8 Price-related factors.

The factors set forth in paragraphs (a) through (e) below may be applicable in evaluation of bids for award and shall be included in the solicitation when applicable. (See 14.201-5(c).)

(a) Foreseeable costs or delays to the Government resulting from such factors as differences in inspection, locations of supplies, and transportation. If bids are on an f.o.b. origin basis (see 47.303 and 47.305), transportation costs to the designated points shall be considered in determining the lowest cost to the Government.

(b) Changes made, or requested by the bidder, in any of the provisions of the invitation for bids, if the change does not constitute a ground for rejection under 14.404.

(c) Advantages or disadvantages to the Government that might result from making more than one award (see 14.201-6(q)). The contracting officer shall assume, for the purpose of making multiple awards, that $500 would be the administrative cost to the Government for issuing and administering each contract awarded under a solicitation. Individual awards shall be for the items or combinations of items that result in the lowest aggregate cost to the Government, including the assumed administrative costs.

(d) Federal, state, and local taxes (see Part 29).

(e) Origin of supplies, and, if foreign, the application of the Buy American statute or any other prohibition on foreign purchases (see Part 25).

[FAC 84-5, 50 FR 1738, 1/11/85, effective 4/1/85; FAC 84-58, 55 FR 25527, 6/21/90, effective 7/23/90; FAC 2005-73, 79 FR 24192, 4/29/2014, effective 5/29/2014]

14.201-9 Simplified contract format.

Policy. For firm-fixed-price or fixed-price with economic price adjustment acquisitions of supplies and services, the contracting officer may use the simplified contract format in lieu of the uniform contract format (see 14.201-1). The contracting officer has flexibility in preparation and organization of the simplified contract format. However, the following format should be used to the maximum practical extent:

(a) *Solicitation/contract form.* Standard Form (SF) 1447, Solicitation/Contract, shall be used as the first page of the solicitation.

(b) *Contract schedule.* Include the following for each line item:

(1) Line item number.

(2) Description of supplies or services, or data sufficient to identify the requirement.

(3) Quantity and unit of issue.

(4) Unit price and amount.

(5) Packaging and marking requirements.

(6) Inspection and acceptance, quality assurance, and reliability requirements.

(7) Place of delivery, performance and delivery dates, period of performance, and f.o.b. point.

(8) Other item-peculiar information as necessary (*e.g.*, individual fund citations).

(c) *Clauses.* Include the clauses required by this regulation. Additional clauses shall be incorporated only when considered absolutely necessary to the particular acquisition.

(d) *List of documents and attachments.* Include if necessary.

(e) *Representations and instructions*—

(1) *Representations and certifications.* Insert those solicitation provisions that require representations, certifications, or the submission of other information by offerors.

(2) *Instructions, conditions, and notices.* Include the solicitation provisions required by 14.201-6. Include any other information/instructions necessary to guide offerors.

(3) *Evaluation factors for award.* Insert all evaluation factors and any significant subfactors for award.

(4) Upon award, the contracting officer need not physically include the provisions in subparagraphs (e)(1), (2), and (3) of this subsection in the resulting contract, but shall retain them in the contract file. Award by acceptance of a bid on the award portion of SF 1447 incorporates the representations, certifications, and other statements of bidders in the resultant contract even though not physically attached.

[FAC 84-53, 54 FR 48983, 11/28/89, effective 12/28/89; Interim rule, FAC 90-7, 56 FR 41733, 8/22/91, effective 8/22/91; FAC 2005-95, 82 FR 4709, 1/13/2017, effective 1/13/2017]

14.202 General rules for solicitation of bids. (No Text)

14.202-1 Bidding time.

(a) *Policy.* A reasonable time for prospective bidders to prepare and submit bids shall be allowed in all invitations, consistent with the needs of the Government. (For construction contracts, see 36.213-3(a)). A bidding time (*i.e.*, the time between issuance of the solicitation and opening of bids) of at least 30 calendar days shall be provided, when synopsis is required by Subpart 5.2.

(b) *Factors to be considered.* Because of unduly limited bidding time, some potential sources may be precluded from bidding and others may be forced to include amounts for contingencies that, with additional time, could be eliminated. To avoid unduly restricting competition or paying higher-than-necessary prices, consideration shall be given to such factors as the following in establishing a reasonable bidding time:

(1) degree of urgency;

(2) complexity of requirement;

(3) anticipated extent of subcontracting;

(4) whether use was made of presolicitation notices;

(5) geographic distribution of bidders; and

(6) normal transmittal time for both invitations and bids.

[FAC 84-5, 50 FR 1738, 1/11/85, effective 4/1/85; FAC 90-29, 60 FR 34732, 7/3/95, effective 7/3/95; FAC 90-45, Final rule, 62 FR 224, 1/2/97, effective 1/1/97]

14.202-2 [Removed and Reserved]

[FAC 90-29, 60 FR 34732, 7/3/95, effective 7/3/95; FAC 2005-92, 81 FR 83097, 11/18/2016, effective 12/19/2016]

14.202-3 Bid envelopes.

(a) Postage or envelopes bearing "Postage and Fees Paid" indicia shall not be distributed with the invitation for bids or otherwise supplied to prospective bidders.

(b) To provide for ready identification and proper handling of bids, Optional Form 17, Offer Label, may be furnished with each bid set. The form may be obtained from the General Services Administration (see 53.107).

[FAC 84-5, 50 FR 1737, 1/11/85, effective 4/1/85; FAC 90-23, 59 FR 67010, 12/28/94, effective 2/27/95]

14.202-4 Bid samples.

(a) *Policy.*

(1) Bidders shall not be required to furnish bid samples unless there are characteristics of the product that cannot be described adequately in the specification or purchase description.

(2) Bid samples will be used only to determine the responsiveness of the bid and will not be used to determine a bidder's ability to produce the required items.

(3) Bid samples may be examined for any required characteristic, whether or not such characteristic is adequately described in the specification, if listed in accordance with paragraph (d) (1) (ii) of this section.

(4) Bids will be rejected as nonresponsive if the sample fails to conform to each of the characteristics listed in the invitation.

(b) *When to use.* The use of bid samples would be appropriate for products that must be suitable from the standpoint of balance, facility of use, general "feel," color, pattern, or other characteristics that cannot be described adequately in the specification. However, when more than a minor portion of the characteristics of the product cannot be adequately described in the specification, products should be acquired by two-step sealed bidding or negotiation, as appropriate.

(c) *Justification.* The reasons why acceptable products cannot be acquired without the submission of bid samples shall be set forth in the contract file, except where the submission is required by the formal specifications (Federal, Military, or other) applicable to the acquisition.

(d) *Requirements for samples in invitations for bids.*

(1) Invitations for bids shall—

(i) State the number and, if appropriate, the size of the samples to be submitted and otherwise fully describe the samples required; and

(ii) List all the characteristics for which the samples will be examined.

(2) If bid samples are required, see 14.201-6(o).

(e) *Waiver of requirement for bid samples.*

(1) The requirement for furnishing bid samples may be waived when a bidder offers a product previously or currently being contracted for or tested by the Government and found to comply with specification requirements conforming in every material respect with those in the current invitation for bids. When the requirement may be waived, see 14.201-6(o)(2).

(2) Where samples required by a Federal, Military, or other formal specification are not considered necessary and a waiver of the sample requirements of the specification has been authorized, a statement shall be included in the invitation that notwithstanding the requirements of the specification, samples will not be required.

(f) *Unsolicited samples.* Bid samples furnished with a bid that are not required by the invitation generally will not be considered as qualifying the bid and will be disregarded. However, the bid sample will not be disregarded if it is clear from the bid or accompanying papers that the bidder's intention was to qualify the bid. (See 14.404-2(d) if the qualification does not conform to the solicitation.)

(g) *Handling bid samples.*

(1) Samples that are not destroyed in testing shall be returned to bidders at their request and expense, unless otherwise specified in the invitation.

(2) Disposition instructions shall be requested from bidders and samples disposed of accordingly.

(3) Samples ordinarily will be returned collect to the address from which received if disposition instructions are not received within 30 days. Small items may be returned by mail, postage prepaid.

(4) Samples that are to be retained for inspection purposes in connection with deliveries shall be transmitted to the inspecting activity concerned, with instructions to retain the sample until completion of the contract or until disposition instructions are furnished.

(5) Where samples are consumed or their usefulness is impaired by tests, they will be disposed of as scrap unless the bidder requests their return.

[FAC 84-5, 50 FR 1738, 1/11/85, effective 4/1/85; FAC 2001-06, 67 FR 13048, 3/20/2002, effective 4/4/2002; FAC 2005-39, 75 FR 13425, 3/19/2010, effective 3/19/2010]

14.202-5 Descriptive literature.

(a) *Policy.* Contracting officers must not require bidders to furnish descriptive literature unless it is needed before award to determine whether theproducts offered meet the specification and to establish exactly what the bidder proposes to furnish.

(b) *Justification.* The contracting officer must document in the contract file the reasons why product acceptability cannot be determined without the submission of descriptive literature, except when the contract specifications require submission.

(c) *Requirements of invitation for bids.* (1) The invitation must clearly state—

(i) What descriptive literature the bidders must furnish;

(ii) The purpose for requiring the literature;

(iii) The extent of its consideration in the evaluation of bids; and

(iv) The rules that will apply if a bidder fails to furnish the literature before bid opening or if the literature provided does not comply with the requirements of the invitation.

(2) If bidders must furnish descriptive literature, see 14.201-6(p).

(d) *Waiver of requirement for descriptive literature.* (1) The contracting officer may waive the requirement for descriptive literature if—

(i) The bidder states in the bid that the product being offered is the same as a product previously or currently being furnished to the contracting activity; and

(ii) The contracting officer determines that the product offered by the bidder complies with the specification requirements of the current invitation for bids. When the contracting officer waives the requirement, see 14.201-6(p)(2).

(2) When descriptive literature is not necessary and a waiver of literature requirements of a specification has been authorized, the contracting officer must include a statement in the invitation that, despite the requirements of the specifications, descriptive literature will not be required.

(3) If the solicitation provides for a waiver, a bidder may submit a bid on the basis of either the descriptive literature furnished with the bid or a previously furnished product. If the bid is submitted on one basis, the bidder may not have it considered on the other basis after bids are opened.

(e) *Unsolicited descriptive literature.* If descriptive literature is furnished when it is not required by the invitation for bids, the procedures set forth in 14.202-4(f) must be followed.

[FAC 2001-06, 67 FR 13048, 3/20/2002, effective 4/4/2002]

14.202-6 Final review of invitations for bids.

Each invitation for bids shall be thoroughly reviewed before issuance to detect and correct discrepancies or ambiguities that could limit competition or result in the receipt of nonresponsive bids. Contracting officers are responsible for the reviews.

[FAC 84-5, 50 FR 1737, 1/11/85, effective 4/1/85]

14.202-7 Facsimile bids.

(a) Unless prohibited or otherwise restricted by agency procedures, contracting officers may authorize facsimile bids (see 14.201-6(v)). In determining whether or not to authorize facsimile bids, the contracting officer shall consider factors such as—

(1) Anticipated bid size and volume;

(2) Urgency of the requirement;

(3) Frequency of price changes;

(4) Availability, reliability, speed, and capacity of the receiving facsimile equipment; and

(5) Adequacy of administrative procedures and controls for receiving, identifying, recording, and safeguarding facsimile bids, and ensuring their timely delivery to the bids opening location.

(b) If facsimile bids are authorized, contracting officers may, after the date set for bid opening, request the apparently successful offeror to provide the complete, original signed bid.

[FAC 84-53, 54 FR 48983, 11/28/89, effective 12/28/89; FAC 97-14, 64 FR 51828, 9/24/99, effective 11/23/99]

14.202-8 Electronic bids.

In accordance with Subpart 4.5, contracting officers may authorize use of electronic commerce for submission of bids. If electronic bids are authorized, the solicitation shall specify the electronic commerce method(s) that bidders may use.

[FAC 90-29, 60 FR 34732, 7/3/95, effective 7/3/95]

14.203 Methods of soliciting bids. (No Text)

14.203-1 Transmittal to prospective bidders.

Invitations for bids or presolicitation notices must be provided in accordance with 5.102. When a contracting office is located in the United States, any solicitation sent to a prospective bidder located outside the United States shall be sent by electronic data interchange or air mail if security classification permits.

[FAC 90-29, 60 FR 34732, 7/3/95, effective 7/3/95; FAC 2001-14, 68 FR 28079, 5/22/2003, effective 6/23/2003; FAC 2001-15, 68 FR 43854, 7/24/2003, effective 8/25/2003]

14.203-2 Dissemination of information concerning invitations for bids.

Procedures concerning display of invitations for bids in a public place, information releases to newspapers and trade journals, paid advertisements, and synopsizing through the Governmentwide point of entry (GPE) are set forth in 5.101 and Subpart 5.2.

[FAC 97-26, 66 FR 27405, 5/16/2001, effective 5/16/2001; FAC 2005-09, 71 FR 20299, 4/19/2006, effective 5/19/2006]

14.203-3 Master solicitation.

The master solicitation is provided to potential sources who are requested to retain it for continued and repetitive use. Individual solicitations must reference the date of the current master solicitation and identify any changes. The contracting officer must—

(a) Make available copies of the master solicitation on request; and

(b) Provide the cognizant contract administration activity a current copy of the master solicitation.

[FAC 97-22, 66 FR 2116, 1/10/2001, effective 3/12/2001; Delay of effective date, 66 FR 14259, 3/9/2001, effective 5/11/2001]

14.204 Records of invitations for bids and records of bids.

(a) Each contracting office shall retain a record of each invitation that it issues and each abstract or record of bids. Contracting officers shall review and utilize the information available in connection with subsequent acquisitions of the same or similar items.

(b) The file for each invitation shall show the distribution that was made and the date the invitation was issued. The names and addresses of prospective bidders who requested the invitation and were not included on the original solicitation list shall be added to the list and made a part of the record.

[FAC 84-5, 50 FR 1737, 1/11/85, effective 4/1/85]

14.205 Presolicitation notices.

In lieu of initially forwarding complete bid sets, the contracting officer may send presolicitation notices to concerns. The notice shall—

(a) Specify the final date for receipt of requests for a complete bid set;

(b) Briefly describe the requirement and furnish other essential information to enable concerns to determine whether they have an interest in the invitation; and

(c) Normally not include drawings, plans, and specifications. The return date of the notice must be sufficiently in advance of the mailing date of the invitation for bids to permit an accurate estimate of the number of bid sets required. Bid sets shall be sent to concerns that request them in response to the notice.

[FAC 2001-15, 68 FR 43854, 7/24/2003, effective 8/25/2003]

14.205-1 [Removed]

[FAC 90-29, 60 FR 34732, 7/3/95, effective 7/3/95; FAC 90-32, 60 FR 48206, 9/18/95, effective 10/1/95; FAC 90-43, Interim rule, 61 FR 67408, 12/20/96, effective 12/20/96, finalized without change, FAC 97-1, 62 FR 44802, 8/22/97, effective 10/21/97; FAC 97-9, 63 FR 58587, 10/30/98, effective 10/30/98; FAC 2001-15, 68 FR 43854, 7/24/2003, effective 8/25/2003]

14.205-2 [Removed]

[FAC 84-5, 50 FR 1738, 1/11/85, effective 4/1/85; FAC 2001-15, 68 FR 43854, 7/24/2003, effective 8/25/2003]

14.205-3 [Removed]

[FAC 84-5, 50 FR 1737, 1/11/85, effective 4/1/85; FAC 2001-15, 68 FR 43854, 7/24/2003, effective 8/25/2003]

14.205-4 [Removed]

[FAC 84-5, 50 FR 1738 1/11/85, effective 4/1/85; FAC 90-32, 60 FR 48206, 9/18/95, effective 10/1/95; FAC 2001-15, 68 FR 43854, 7/24/2003, effective 8/25/2003]

14.205-5 [Removed]

[FAC 84-31, 52 FR 38189, 10/14/87, effective 10/1/87; FAC 84-32, 53 FR 661, 1/11/88, effective 1/29/88; FAC 84-40, 53 FR 43390, 10/26/88, effective 11/25/88; FAC 2001-15, 68 FR 43854, 7/24/2003, effective 8/25/2003]

14.206 [Removed and Reserved]

[Removed and Reserved, FAC 97-10, 63 FR 70264, 12/18/98, effective 1/4/99]

14.207 Pre-bid conference.

A pre-bid conference may be used, generally in a complex acquisition, as a means of briefing prospective bidders and explaining complicated specifications and requirements to them as early as possible after the invitation has been issued and before the bids are opened. It shall never be used as a substitute for amending a defective or ambiguous invitation. The conference shall be conducted in accordance with the procedure prescribed in 15.201.

[FAC 84-5, 50 FR 1737, 1/11/85, effective 4/1/85; FAC 97-2, 62 FR 51224, 9/30/97, effective 10/10/97]

14.208 Amendment of invitation for bids.

(a) If it becomes necessary to make changes in quantity, specifications, delivery schedules, opening dates, etc., or to correct a defective or ambiguous invitation, such changes shall be accomplished by amendment of the invitation for bids using Standard Form 30, Amendment of Solicitation/Modification of Contract. The fact that a change was mentioned at a pre-bid conference does not relieve the necessity for issuing an amendment. Amendments shall be sent, before the time for bid opening, to everyone to whom invitations have been furnished and shall be displayed in the bid room.

(b) Before amending an invitation for bids, the contracting officer shall consider the period of time remaining until bid opening and the need to extend this period.

(c) Any information given to a prospective bidder concerning an invitation for bids shall be furnished promptly to all other prospective bidders as an amendment to the invitation—

(1) if such information is necessary for bidders to submit bids or

(2) if the lack of such information would be prejudicial to uninformed bidders. The information shall be furnished even though a pre-bid conference is held. No award shall be made on the invitation unless such amendment has been issued in sufficient time to permit all prospective bidders to consider such information in submitting or modifying their bids.

[FAC 84-5, 50 FR 1737, 1/11/85, effective 4/1/85; FAC 2005-92, 81 FR 83097, 11/18/2016, effective 12/19/2016]

14.209 Cancellation of invitations before opening.

(a) The cancellation of an invitation for bids usually involves a loss of time, effort, and money spent by the Government and bidders. Invitations should not be cancelled unless cancellation is clearly in the public interest; *e.g.*,—

(1) where there is no longer a requirement for the supplies or services or

(2) where amendments to the invitation would be of such magnitude that a new invitation is desirable.

(b) When an invitation issued other than electronically is cancelled, bids that have been received shall be returned unopened to the bidders and notice of cancellation shall be sent to all prospective bidders to whom invitations were issued. When an invitation issued electronically is cancelled, a general notice of cancellation shall be posted electronically, the bids received shall not be viewed, and the bids shall be purged from primary and backup data storage systems.

(c) The notice of cancellation shall—

(1) identify the invitation for bids by number and short title or subject matter,

(2) briefly explain the reason the invitation is being cancelled, and

(3) where appropriate, assure prospective bidders that they will be given an opportunity to bid on any resolicitation of bids or any future requirements for the type of supplies or services involved. Cancellations shall be recorded in accordance with 14.403(d).

[FAC 90-29, 60 FR 34732, 7/3/95, effective 7/3/95; FAC 90-46, 62 FR 12690, 3/17/97, effective 5/16/97]

14.210 Qualified products.

See Subpart 9.2.

[FAC 84-5, 50 FR 1737, 1/11/85, effective 4/1/85]

14.211 Release of acquisition information.

(a) *Before solicitation.* Information concerning proposed acquisitions shall not be released outside the Government before solicitation except for presolicitation notices in accordance with 14.205 or 36.213-2, or long-range acquisition estimates in accordance with 5.404, or synopses in accordance with 5.201. Within the Government, such information shall be restricted to those having a legitimate interest. Releases of information shall be made—

(1) to all prospective bidders, and

(2) as nearly as possible at the same time, so that one prospective bidder shall not be given unfair advantage over another. See 3.104 regarding requirements for proprietary and source selection information including access to and disclosure thereof.

(b) *After solicitation.* Discussions with prospective bidders regarding a solicitation shall be conducted and technical or other information shall be transmitted only by the contracting officer or superiors having contractual authority or by others specifically authorized. Such personnel shall not furnish any information to a prospective bidder that alone or together with other information may afford an advantage over others. However, general information that would not be prejudical to other prospective bidders may be furnished upon request; *e.g.,* explanation of a particular contract clause or a particular condition of the schedule in the invitation for bids, and more specific information or clarifications may be furnished by amending the solicitation (see 14.208).

[FAC 84-5, 50 FR 1738, 1/11/85, effective 4/1/85; FAC 84-60, 55 FR 36795, 9/6/90, effective 9/6/90; FAC 90-45, Final rule, 62 FR 224, 1/2/97, effective 1/1/97; FAC 2001-15, 68 FR 43854, 7/24/2003, effective 8/25/2003]

14.212 Economic purchase quantities (supplies).

Contracting officers shall comply with the economic purchase quantity planning requirements for supplies in Subpart 7.2. See 7.203 for instructions regarding use of the provision at 52.207-4, Economic Purchase Quantity—Supplies, and 7.204for guidance on handling responses to that provision.

[FAC 84-5, 50 FR 1737, 1/11/85, effective 4/1/85; FAC 84-11, 50 FR 35479, 8/30/85, effective 8/30/85]

14.213 [Removed]

[FAC 84-53, 54 FR 48983, 11/28/89, effective 12/28/89; FAC 2001-26, 69 FR 76341, 12/20/2004, effective 1/1/2005]

SUBPART 14.3—SUBMISSION OF BIDS

14.301 Responsiveness of bids.

(a) To be considered for award, a bid must comply in all material respects with the invitation for bids. Such compliance enables bidders to stand on an equal footing and maintain the integrity of the sealed bidding system.

(b) Facsimile bids shall not be considered unless permitted by the solicitation (see 14.202-7).

(c) Bids should be filled out, executed, and submitted in accordance with the instructions in the invitation. If a bidder uses its own bid form or a letter to submit a bid, the bid may be considered only if—

(1) The bidder accepts all the terms and conditions of the invitation; and

(2) Award on the bid would result in a binding contract with terms and conditions that do not vary from the terms and conditions of the invitation.

(d) Bids submitted by electronic commerce shall be considered only if the electronic commerce method was specifically stipulated or permitted by the solicitation.

[FAC 84-5, 50 FR 1738, 1/11/85, effective 4/1/85; FAC 84-53, 54 FR 48983, 11/28/89, effective 12/28/89; FAC 90-29, 60 FR 34732, 7/3/95, effective 7/3/95; FAC 2005-92, 81 FR 83097, 11/18/2016, effective 12/19/2016]

14.302 Bid submission.

Bids shall be submitted so that they will be received in the office designated in the invitation for bids not later than the exact time set for opening of bids.

[FAC 84-5, 50 FR 1737, 1/11/85, effective 4/1/85; FAC 2005-92, 81 FR 83097, 11/18/2016, effective 12/19/2016]

14.303 Modification or withdrawal of bids.

(a) Bids may be modified or withdrawn by any method authorized by the solicitation, if notice is received in the office designated in the solicitation not later than the exact time set for opening of bids. If the solicitation authorizes facsimile bids, bids may be modified or withdrawn via facsimile received at any time before the exact time set for receipt of bids, subject to the conditions specified in the provision prescribed in 14.201-6(v). Modifications received by facsimile shall be sealed in an envelope by a proper official.

(1) The official shall—

(i) Write on the envelope—

(A) The date and time of receipt and by whom; and

(B) The number of invitation for bids; and

(ii) Sign the envelope.

(2) No information contained in the envelope shall be disclosed before the time set for bid opening.

(b) A bid may be withdrawn in person by a bidder or its authorized representative if, before the exact time set for opening of bids, the identity of the persons requesting withdrawal is established and that person signs a receipt for the bid.

(c) Upon withdrawal of an electronically transmitted bid, the data received shall not be viewed and shall be purged from primary and backup data storage systems.

[FAC 84-53, 54 FR 48983, 11/28/89, effective 12/28/89; FAC 90-29, 60 FR 34732, 7/3/95, effective 7/3/95; FAC 97-14, 64 FR 51828, 9/24/99, effective 11/23/99; FAC 2005-92, 81 FR 83097, 11/18/2016, effective 12/19/2016]

14.304 Submission, modification, and withdrawal of bids.

(a) Bidders are responsible for submitting bids, and any modifications or withdrawals, so as to reach the Government office designated in the invitation for bid (IFB) by the time specified in the IFB. They may use any transmission method authorized by the IFB (i.e., regular mail, electronic commerce, or facsimile). If no time is specified in the IFB, the time for receipt is 4:30 p.m., local time, for the designated Government office on the date that bids are due.

(b) (1) Any bid, modification, or withdrawal of a bid received at the Government office designated in the IFB after the exact time specified for receipt of bids is "late" and will not be considered unless it is received before award is made, the contracting officer determines that accepting the late bid would not unduly delay the acquisition; and—

(i) If it was transmitted through an electronic commerce method authorized by the IFB, it was received at the initial point of entry to the Government infrastructure not later than 5:00 p.m. one working day prior to the date specified for receipt of bids; or

(ii) There is acceptable evidence to establish that it was received at the Government installation designated for receipt of bids and was under the Government's control prior to the time set for receipt of bids.

(2) However, a late modification of an otherwise successful bid, that makes its terms more favorable to the Government, will be considered at any time it is received and may be accepted.

(c) Acceptable evidence to establish the time of receipt at the Government installation includes the time/date stamp of that installation on the bid wrapper, other documentary evidence of receipt maintained by the installation, or oral testimony or statements of Government personnel.

(d) If an emergency or unanticipated event interrupts normal Government processes so that bids cannot be received at the Government office designated for receipt of bids by the exact time specified in the IFB, and urgent Government requirements preclude amendment of the bid opening date, the time specified for receipt of bids will be deemed to be extended to the same time of day specified in the IFB on the first work day on which normal Government processes resume.

(e) Bids may be withdrawn by written notice received at any time before the exact time set for receipt of bids. If the IFB authorizes facsimile bids, bids may be withdrawn via facsimile received at any time before the exact time set for receipt of bids, subject to the conditions specified in the provision at 52.214-31, Facsimile Bids. A bid may be withdrawn in person by a bidder or its authorized representative if, before the exact time set for receipt of bids, the identity of the person requesting withdrawal is established and the person signs a receipt for the bid. Upon withdrawal of an electronically transmitted bid, the data received must not be viewed and, where practicable, must be purged from primary and backup data storage systems.

(f) The contracting officer must promptly notify any bidder if its bid, modification, or withdrawal was received late, and must inform the bidder whether its bid will be considered, unless contract award is imminent and the notices prescribed in 14.409 would suffice.

(g) Late bids and modifications that are not considered must be held unopened, unless opened for identification, until after award and then retained with other unsuccessful bids. However, any bid bond or guarantee must be returned.

(h) If available, the following must be included in the contract files for each late bid, modification, or withdrawal:

(1) The date and hour of receipt.

(2) A statement, with supporting rationale, regarding whether the bid was considered for award.

(3) The envelope, wrapper, or other evidence of the date of receipt.

[FAC 97-14, 64 FR 51828, 9/24/99, effective 11/23/99]

SUBPART 14.4—OPENING OF BIDS AND AWARD OF CONTRACT

14.400 Scope of subpart.

This subpart contains procedures for the receipt, handling, opening, and disposition of bids including mistakes in bids, and subsequent award of contracts.

[FAC 84-5, 50 FR 1737, 1/11/85, effective 4/1/85; FAC 97-9, 63 FR 58587, 10/30/98, effective 10/30/98]

14.401 Receipt and safeguarding of bids.

(a) All bids (including modifications) received before the time set for the opening of bids shall be kept secure. Except as provided in paragraph (b) of this section, the bids shall not be opened or viewed, and shall remain in a locked bid box, a safe, or in a secured, restricted-access electronic bid box. If an invitation for bids is cancelled, bids shall be returned to the bidders. Necessary precautions shall be taken to ensure the security of the bid box or safe. Before bid opening, information concerning the identity and number of bids received shall be made available only to Government employees. Such disclosure shall be only on a "need to know" basis. When bid samples are submitted, they shall be handled with sufficient care to prevent disclosure of characteristics before bid opening.

(b) Envelopes marked as bids but not identifying the bidder or the solicitation may be opened solely for the purpose of identification, and then only by an official designated for this purpose. If a sealed bid is opened by mistake (e.g., because it is not marked as being a bid), the envelope shall be signed by the opener, whose position shall also be written thereon, and delivered to the designated official. This official shall immediately write on the envelope—

(1) an explanation of the opening,

(2) the date and time opened, and

(3) the invitation for bids number, and shall sign the envelope. The official shall then immediately reseal the envelope.

[FAC 90-29, 60 FR 34732, 7/3/95, effective 7/3/95]

14.402 Opening of bids. (No Text)

14.402-1 Unclassified bids.

(a) The bid opening officer shall decide when the time set for opening bids has arrived and shall inform those present of that decision. The officer shall then—

(1) personally and publicly open all bids received before that time,

(2) if practical, read the bids aloud to the persons present, and

(3) have the bids recorded. The original of each bid shall be carefully safeguarded, particularly until the abstract of bids required by 14.403 has been made and its accuracy verified.

(b) Performance of the procedure in paragraph (a) above may be delegated to an assistant, but the bid opening officer remains fully responsible for the actions of the assistant.

(c) Examination of bids by interested persons shall be permitted if it does not interfere unduly with the conduct of Government business. Original bids shall not be allowed to pass out of the hands of a Government official unless a duplicate bid is not available for public inspection. The original bid may be examined by the public only under the immediate supervision of a Government official and under conditions that preclude possibility of a substitution, addition, deletion, or alteration in the bid.

[FAC 84-5, 50 FR 1737, 1/11/85, effective 4/1/85]

14.402-2 Classified bids.

The general public may not attend bid openings for classified acquisitions. A bidder or its representative may attend and record the results if the individual has the appropriate security clearnace. The contracting officer also may make the bids available at a later time to properly cleared individuals who represent bidders. No public record shall be made of bids or bid prices received in reponse to classified invitations for bids.

[FAC 84-5, 50 FR 1737; 1/11/85, effective 4/1/85; 67 FR 6114, 2/8/2002, effective 2/28/2002]

14.402-3 Postponement of openings.

(a) A bid opening may be postponed even after the time scheduled for bid opening (but otherwise in accordance with 14.208) when—

(1) The contracting officer has reason to believe that the bids of an important segment of bidders have been delayed in the mails, or in the communications system specified for transmission of bids, for causes beyond their control and without their fault or negligence (e.g., flood, fire, accident, weather conditions, strikes, or Government equipment blackout or malfunction when bids are due); or

(2) Emergency or unanticipated events interrupt normal governmental processes so that the conduct of bid openings as scheduled is impractical.

(b) At the time of a determination to postpone a bid opening under subparagraph (a)(1) of this section, an announcement of the determination shall be publicly posted. If practical before issuance of a formal amendment of the invitation, the determination shall be otherwise communicated to prospective bidders who are likely to attend the scheduled bid opening.

(c) In the case of paragraph (a)(2) of this section, and when urgent Government requirements preclude amendment of the solicitation as prescribed in 14.208, the time specified for opening of bids will be deemed to be extended to the same time of day specified in the solicitation on the first work day on which normal Government processes resume. In such cases, the time of actual bid opening shall be deemed to be the time set for bid opening for the purpose of determining "late bids" under 14.304. A note should be made on the abstract of bids or otherwise added to the file explaining the circumstances of the postponement.

[FAC 90-29, 60 FR 34732, 7/3/95, effective 7/3/95; FAC 90-39, 61 FR 31612, 6/20/96, effective 8/19/96]

14.403 Recording of bids.

(a) Standard Form 1409, Abstract of Offers, or Optional Form 1419, Abstract of Offers—Construction (or automated equivalent), shall be completed and certified as to its accuracy by the bid opening officer as soon after bid opening as practicable. Where bid items are too numerous to warrant complete recording of all bids, abstract entries for individual bids may be limited to item numbers and bid prices. In preparing these forms, the extra columns and SF 1410, Abstract of Offer—Continuation, and OF 1419A, Abstract of Offers—Construction, Continuation Sheet, may be used to label and record such information as the contracting activity deems necessary.

(b) Abstracts of offers for unclassified acquisitions shall be available for public inspection. Such abstracts shall not contain information regarding failure to meet minimum standards of responsibility, apparent collusion of bidders, or other notations properly exempt from disclosure to the public in accordance with agency regulations implementing Subpart 24.2.

(c) The forms identified in paragraph (a) of this section need not be used by the Defense energy Support Center for acquisitions of coal or petroleum products or by the Defense Supply Center Philadelphia for perishable subsistence items.

(d) If an invitation for bids is cancelled before the time set for bid opening, this fact shall be recorded together with a statement of the number of bids invited and the number of bids received.

[FAC 84-5, 50 FR 1737, 1/11/85, effective 4/1/85; FAC 84-49, 54 FR 29280, 7/11/89, effective 8/10/89; FAC 2001-25, 69 FR 59703, 10/5/2004, effective 10/5/2004]

14.404 Rejection of bids. (No Text)

14.404-1 Cancellation of invitations after opening.

(a) (1) Preservation of the integrity of the competitive bid system dictates that, after bids have been opened, award must be made to that responsible bidder who submitted the lowest responsive bid, unless there is a compelling reason to reject all bids and cancel the invitation.

(2) Every effort shall be made to anticipate changes in a requirement before the date of opening and to notify all prospective bidders of any resulting modification or cancellation. This will permit bidders to change their bids and prevent unnecessary exposure of bid prices.

(3) As a general rule, after the opening of bids, an invitation should not be cancelled and resolicited due solely to increased requirements for the items being acquired. Award should be made on the initial invitation for bids and the additional quantity should be treated as a new acquisition.

(b) When it is determined before award but after opening that the requirements of 11.201 (relating to the availability and identification of specifications) have not been met, the invitation shall be cancelled.

(c) Invitations may be cancelled and all bids rejected before award but after opening when, consistent with subparagraph (a)(1) of this section, the agency head determines in writing that—

(1) Inadequate or ambiguous specifications were cited in the invitation;

(2) Specifications have been revised;

(3) The supplies or services being contracted for are no longer required;

(4) The invitation did not provide for consideration of all factors of cost to the Government, such as cost of transporting Government-furnished property to bidders' plants;

(5) Bids received indicate that the needs of the Government can be satisfied by a less expensive article differing from that for which the bids were invited;

(6) All otherwise acceptable bids received are at unreasonable prices, or only one bid is received and the contracting officer cannot determine the reasonableness of the bid price;

(7) The bids were not independently arrived at in open competition, were collusive, or were submitted in bad faith (see Subpart 3.3 for reports to be made to the Department of Justice);

(8) No responsive bid has been received from a responsible bidder;

(9) A cost comparison as prescribed in OMB Circular A-76 and Subpart 7.3 shows that performance by the Government is more economical; or

(10) For other reasons, cancellation is clearly in the public's interest.

(d) Should administrative difficulties be encountered after bid opening that may delay award beyond bidders' acceptance periods, the several lowest bidders whose bids have not expired (irrespective of the acceptance period specified in the bid) should be requested, before expiration of their bids, to extend in writing the bid acceptance period (with consent of sureties, if any) in order to avoid the need for resoliciting.

(e) Under some circumstances, completion of the acquisition after cancellation of the invitation for bids may be appropriate.

(1) If the invitation for bids has been cancelled for the reasons specified in subparagraphs (c)(6), (7), or (8) of this subsection, and the agency head has authorized, in the determination in paragraph (c) of this subsection, the completion of the acquisition through negotiation, the contracting officer shall proceed in accordance with paragraph (f) of this subsection.

(2) If the invitation for bids has been cancelled for the reasons specified in subparagraphs (c)(1), (2), (4), (5), or (10) of this subsection, or for the reasons in subparagraphs (c)(6), (7), or (8) of this subsection and completion through negotiation is not authorized under subparagraph (e)(1) of this subsection, the contracting officer shall proceed with a new acquisition.

(f) When the agency head has determined, in accordance with paragraph (e)(1) of this subsection, that an invitation for bids should be canceled and that use of negotiation is in the Government's interest, the contracting officer may negotiate (in accordance with Part 15, as appropriate) and make award without issuing a new solicitation provided—

(1) Each responsible bidder in the sealed bid acquisition has been given notice that negotiations will be conducted and has been given an opportunity to participate in negotiations; and

(2) The award is made to the responsible bidder offering the lowest negotiated price.

[FAC 84-5, 50 FR 1738, 1/11/85, effective 4/1/85; FAC 90-3, 55 FR 52790, 12/21/90, effective 1/22/91; FAC 90-32, 60 FR 48206, 9/18/95, effective 10/1/95; FAC 97-2, 62 FR 51224, 9/30/97, effective 10/10/97]

14.404-2 Rejection of individual bids.

(a) Any bid that fails to conform to the essential requirements of the invitation for bids shall be rejected.

(b) Any bid that does not conform to the applicable specifications shall be rejected unless the invitation authorized the submission of alternate bids and the supplies offered as alternates meet the requirements specified in the invitation.

(c) Any bid that fails to conform to the delivery schedule or permissible alternates stated in the invitation shall be rejected.

(d) A bid shall be rejected when the bidder imposes conditions that would modify requirements of the invitation or limit the bidder's liability to the Government, since to allow the bidder to impose such conditions would be prejudicial to other bidders. For example, bids shall be rejected in which the bidder—

(1) Protects against future changes in conditions, such as increased costs, if total possible costs to the Government cannot be determined;

(2) Fails to state a price and indicates that price shall be "price in effect at time of delivery";

(3) States a price but qualifies it as being subject to "price in effect at time of delivery";

(4) When not authorized by the invitation, conditions or qualifies a bid by stipulating that it is to be considered only if, before date of award, the bidder receives (or does not receive) award under a separate solicitation;

(5) Requires that the Government is to determine that the bidder's product meets applicable Government specifications; or

(6) Limits rights of the Government under any contract clause.

(e) A low bidder may be requested to delete objectionable conditions from a bid provided the conditions do not go to the substance, as distinguished from the form, of the bid, or work an injustice on other bidders. A condition goes to the substance of a bid where it affects price, quantity, quality, or delivery of the items offered.

(f) Any bid may be rejected if the contracting officer determines in writing that it is unreasonable as to price. Unreasonableness of price includes not only the total price of the bid, but the prices for individual line items as well.

(g) Any bid may be rejected if the prices for any line items or subline items are materially unbalanced (see 15.404-1(g)).

(h) Bids received from any person or concern that is suspended, debarred, proposed for debarment, or declared ineligible as of the bid opening date shall be rejected unless a compelling reason determination is made (see subpart 9.4).

(i) Low bids received from concerns determined to be not responsible pursuant to subpart 9.1 shall be rejected (but if a bidder is a small business concern, see 19.6 with respect to certificates of competency).

(j) When a bid guarantee is required and a bidder fails to furnish the guarantee in accordance with the requirements of the invitation for bids, the bid shall be rejected, except as otherwise provided in 28.101-4.

(k) The originals of all rejected bids, and any written findings with respect to such rejections, shall be preserved with the papers relating to the acquisition.

(l) After submitting a bid, if all of a bidder's assets or that part related to the bid are transferred during the period between the bid opening and the award, the transferee may not be able to take over the bid. Accordingly, the contracting officer shall reject the bid unless the transfer is effected by merger, operation of law, or other means not barred by 41 U.S.C. 6305 or 31 U.S.C. 3727.

[FAC 84-5, 50 FR 1737, 1/11/85, effective 4/1/85; FAC 84-12, 51 FR 2649, 1/17/86, effective 1/20/86; FAC 84-58, 55 FR 25527, 6/21/90, effective 7/23/90; FAC 84-60, 55 FR 36795, 9/6/90, effective 9/6/90; FAC 90-5, 56 FR 29127, 6/25/91, effective 7/25/91; FAC 90-45,Final rule, 62 FR 224, 1/2/97, effective 1/1/97; FAC 97-2, 62 FR 51224, 9/30/97, effective 10/10/97; FAC 97-21, 65 FR 80255, 12/20/2000, effective 1/19/2001, stayed FAC 97-24, 66 FR 17753, 4/3/2001, effective 4/3/2001, finalized with changes FAC 2001-03, 66 FR 66984, 12/27/2001, effective 12/27/2001; FAC 2005-73, 79 FR 24192, 4/29/2014, effective 5/29/2014]

14.404-3 Notice to bidders of rejection of all bids.

When it is determined necessary to reject all bids, the contracting officer shall notify each bidder that all bids have been rejected and shall state the reason for such action.

[FAC 84-5, 50 FR 1737, 1/11/85, effective 4/1/85]

14.404-4 Restrictions on disclosure of descriptive literature.

When a bid is accompanied by descriptive literature (as defined in 2.101), and the bidder imposes a restriction that prevents the public disclosure of such literature, the restriction may render the bid nonresponsive. The restriction renders the bid nonresponsive if it prohibits the disclosure of sufficient information to permit competing bidders to know the essential nature and type of the products offered or those elements of the bid that relate to quantity, price, and delivery terms. The provisions of this paragraph do not apply to unsolicited descriptive literature submitted by a bidder if such literature does not qualify the bid (see 14.202-5(e)).

[FAC 84-5, 50 FR 1737, 1/11/85, effective 4/1/85; FAC 2001-06, 67 FR 13048, 3/20/2002, effective 4/4/2002]

14.404-5 All or none qualifications.

Unless the solicitation provides otherwise, a bid may be responsive notwithstanding that the bidder specifies that award will be accepted only on all, or a specified group, of the items. Bidders shall not be permitted to withdraw or modify "all or none" qualifications after bid opening since such qualifications are substantive and affect the rights of other bidders.

[FAC 84-5, 50 FR 1737, 1/11/85, effective 4/1/85]

14.405 Minor informalities or irregularities in bids.

A minor informality or irregularity is one that is merely a matter of form and not of substance. It also pertains to some immaterial defect in a bid or variation of a bid from the exact requirements of the invitation that can be corrected or waived without being prejudicial to other bidders. The defect or variation is immaterial when the effect on price, quantity, quality, or delivery is negligible when contrasted with the total cost or scope of the supplies or services being acquired. The contracting officer either shall give the bidder an opportunity to cure any deficiency resulting from a minor informality or irregularity in a bid or waive the deficiency, whichever is to the advantage of the Government. Examples of minor informalities or irregularities include failure of a bidder to—

(a) Return the number of copies of signed bids required by the invitation;

(b) Furnish required information concerning the number of its employees;

(c) Sign its bid, but only if—

(1) The unsigned bid is accompanied by other material indicating the bidder's intention to be bound by the unsigned bid (such as the submission of a bid guarantee or a letter signed by the bidder, with the bid, referring to and clearly identifying the bid itself); or

(2) The firm submitting a bid has formally adopted or authorized, before the date set for opening of bids, the execution of documents by typewritten, printed, or stamped signature and submits evidence of such authorization and the bid carries such a signature;

(d) Acknowledge receipt of an amendment to an invitation for bids, but only if—

(1) The bid received clearly indicates that the bidder received the amendment, such as where the amendment added another item to the invitation and the bidder submitted a bid on the item; or

(2) The amendment involves only a matter of form or has either no effect or merely a negligible effect on price, quantity, quality, or delivery of the item bid upon and

(e) Execute the representations with respect to Equal Opportunity and Affirmative Action Programs, as set forth in the clauses at 52.222-22, Previous Contracts and Compliance Reports, and 52.222-25, Affirmative Action Compliance.

[FAC 84-5, 50 FR 1737, 1/11/85, effective 4/1/85; FAC 84-58, 55 FR 25527, 6/21/90, effective 7/23/90; FAC 90-45, Final rule, 62 FR 224, 1/2/97, effective 1/1/97; FAC 97-11, 64 FR 10530, 3/4/99, effective 5/3/99]

14.406 Receipt of an unreadable electronic bid.

If a bid received at the Government facility by electronic data interchange is unreadable to the degree that conformance to the essential requirements of the invitation for bids cannot be ascertained, the contracting officer immediately shall notify the bidder that the bid will be rejected unless the bidder provides clear and convincing evidence—

(a) Of the content of the bid as originally submitted; and

(b) That the unreadable condition of the bid was caused by Government software or hardware error, malfunction, or other Government mishandling.

[FAC 90-29, 60 FR 34732, 7/3/95, effective 7/3/95]

14.407 Mistakes in bids. (No Text)

[Redesignated from 14.406, FAC 90-29, 60 FR 34732, 7/3/95, effective 7/3/95]

14.407-1 General.

After the opening of bids, contracting officers shall examine all bids for mistakes. In cases of apparent mistakes and in cases where the contracting officer has reason to believe that a mistake may have been made, the contracting officer shall request from the bidder a verification of the bid, calling attention to the suspected mistake. If the bidder alleges a mistake, the matter shall be processed in accordance with this section 14.407. Such actions shall be taken before award.

[FAC 84-5, 50 FR 1737, 1/11/85, effective 4/1/85; Redesignated from 14.406-1, FAC 90-29, 60 FR 34732, 7/3/95, effective 7/3/95]

14.407-2 Apparent clerical mistakes.

(a) Any clerical mistake, apparent on its face in the bid, may be corrected by the contracting officer before award. The contracting officer first shall obtain from the bidder a verification of the bid intended. Examples of apparent mistakes are—

(1) Obvious misplacement of a decimal point;

(2) Obviously incorrect discounts (for example, 1 percent 10 days, 2 percent 20 days, 5 percent 30 days);

(3) Obvious reversal of the price f.o.b. destination and price f.o.b. origin; and

(4) Obvious mistake in designation of unit.

(b) Correction of the bid shall be effected by attaching the verification to the original bid and a copy of the verification to the duplicate bid. Correction shall not be made on the face of the bid; however, it shall be reflected in the award document.

(c) Correction of bids submitted by electronic data interchange shall be effected by including in the electronic solicitation file the original bid, the verification request, and the bid verification.

[Redesignated from 14.406-2, FAC 90-29, 60 FR 34732, 7/3/95, effective 7/3/95]

14.407-3 Other mistakes disclosed before award.

In order to minimize delays in contract awards, administrative determinations may be made as described in this 14.407-3 in connection with mistakes in bids alleged after opening of bids and before award. The authority to permit correction of bids is limited to bids that, as submitted, are responsive to the invitation and may not be used to permit correction of bids to make them responsive. This authority is in addition to that in 14.407-2 or that may be otherwise available.

(a) If a bidder requests permission to correct a mistake and clear and convincing evidence establishes both the existence of the mistake and the bid actually intended, the agency head may make a determination permitting the bidder to correct the mistake; provided, that if this correction would result in displacing one or more lower bids, such a determination shall not be made unless the existence of the mistake and the bid actually intended are ascertainable substantially from the invitation and the bid itself.

(b) If—

(1) A bidder requests permission to withdraw a bid rather than correct it;

(2) The evidence is clear and convincing both as to the existence of a mistake and as to the bid actually intended; and

(3) The bid, both as uncorrected and as corrected, is the lowest received, the agency head may make a determination to correct the bid and not permit its withdrawal.

(c) If, under paragraph (a) or (b) of this subsection,

(1) the evidence of a mistake is clear and convincing only as to the mistake but not as to the intended bid, or

(2) the evidence reasonably supports the existence of a mistake but is not clear and convincing, an official above the contracting officer, unless otherwise provided by agency procedures, may make a determination permitting the bidder to withdraw the bid.

(d) If the evidence does not warrant a determination under paragraph (a), (b), or (c) of this section, the agency head may make a determination that the bid be neither withdrawn nor corrected.

(e) Heads of agencies may delegate their authority to make the determinations under paragraphs (a), (b), (c), and (d) of this 14.407-3 to a central authority, or a limited number of authorities as necessary, in their agencies, without power of redelegation.

(f) Each proposed determination shall have the concurrence of legal counsel within the agency concerned before issuance.

(g) Suspected or alleged mistakes in bids shall be processed as follows. A mere statement by the administrative officials that they are satisfied that an error was made is insufficient.

(1) The contracting officer shall immediately request the bidder to verify the bid. Action taken to verify bids must be sufficient to reasonably assure the contracting officer that the bid as confirmed is without error, or

to elicit the allegation of a mistake by the bidder. To assure that the bidder will be put on notice of a mistake suspected by the contracting officer, the bidder should be advised as appropriate—

(i) That its bid is so much lower than the other bids or the Government's estimate as to indicate a possibility of error;

(ii) Of important or unusual characteristics of the specifications;

(iii) Of changes in requirements from previous purchases of a similar item; or

(iv) Of any other information, proper for disclosure, that leads the contracting officer to believe that there is a mistake in bid.

(2) If the bid is verified, the contracting officer shall consider the bid as originally submitted. If the time for acceptance of bids is likely to expire before a decision can be made, the contracting officer shall request all bidders whose bids may become eligible for award to extend the time for acceptance of their bids in accordance with 14.404-1(d). If the bidder whose bid is believed erroneous does not (or cannot) grant an extension of time, the bid shall be considered as originally submitted (but see subparagraph (5) of this section). If the bidder alleges a mistake, the contracting officer shall advise the bidder to make a written request to withdraw or modify the bid. The request must be supported by statements (sworn statements, if possible) and shall include all pertinent evidence such as the bidder's file copy of the bid, the original worksheets and other data used in preparing the bid, subcontractors' quotations, if any, published price lists, and any other evidence that establishes the existence of the error, the manner in which it occurred, and the bid actually intended.

(3) When the bidder furnishes evidence supporting an alleged mistake, the contracting officer shall refer the case to the appropriate authority (see paragraph (e) of this section) together with the following data:

(i) A signed copy of the bid involved.

(ii) A copy of the invitation for bids and any specifications or drawings relevant to the alleged mistake.

(iii) An abstract or record of the bids received.

(iv) The written request by the bidder to withdraw or modify the bid, together with the bidder's written statement and supporting evidence.

(v) A written statement by the contracting officer setting forth—

(A) A description of the supplies or services involved;

(B) The expiration date of the bid in question and of the other bids submitted;

(C) Specific information as to how and when the mistake was alleged;

(D) A summary of the evidence submitted by the bidder;

(E) In the event only one bid was received, a quotation of the most recent contract price for the supplies or services involved or, in the absence of a recent comparable contract, the contracting officer's estimate of a fair price for the supplies or services;

(F) Any additional pertinent evidence; and

(G) A recommendation that either the bid be considered for award in the form submitted, or the bidder be authorized to withdraw or modify the bid.

(4) Where the bidder fails or refuses to furnish evidence in support of a suspected or alleged mistake, the contracting officer shall consider the bid as submitted unless (1) the amount of the bid is so far out of line with the amounts of other bids received, or with the amount estimated by the agency or determined by the contracting officer to be reasonable, or (ii) there are other indications of error so clear, as to reasonably justify the conclusion that acceptance of the bid would be unfair to the bidder or to other bona fide bidders. Attempts made to obtain the information required and the action taken with respect to the bid shall be fully documented.

(h) Each agency shall maintain records of all determinations made in accordance with this subsection 14.407-3, the facts involved, and the action taken in each case. Copies of all such determinations shall be included in the file.

(i) Nothing contained in this subsection 14.407-3 prevents an agency from submitting doubtful cases to the Comptroller General for advance decision.

[FAC 84-37, 53 FR 17857, 5/18/88, effective 6/17/88; FAC 84-44, 54 FR 13023, 3/29/89, effective 4/28/89; Redesignated from 14.406-3, FAC 90-29, 60 FR 34732, 7/3/95, effective 7/3/95; FAC 2005-92, 81 FR 83097, 11/18/2016, effective 12/19/2016]

14.407-4 Mistakes after award.

If a contractor's discovery and request for correction of a mistake in bid is not made until after the award, it shall be processed under the procedures of Subpart 33.2 and the following:

(a) When a mistake in a contractor's bid is not discovered until after award, the mistake may be corrected by contract modification if correcting the mistake would be favorable to the Government without changing the essential requirements of the specifications.

(b) In addition to the cases contemplated in paragraph (a) above or as otherwise authorized by law, agencies are authorized to make a determination—

(1) To rescind a contract;

(2) To reform a contract—

(i) to delete the items involved in the mistake or

(ii) to increase the price if the contract price, as corrected, does not exceed that of the next lowest acceptable bid under the original invitation for bids; or

(3) That no change shall be made in the contract as awarded, if the evidence does not warrant a determination under subparagraphs (1) or (2) above.

(c) Determinations under subparagraphs (b) (1) and (2) above may be made only on the basis of clear and convincing evidence that a mistake in bid was made. In addition, it must be clear that the mistake was—

(1) mutual, or

(2) if unilaterally made by the contractor, so apparent as to have charged the contracting officer with notice of the probability of the mistake.

(d) Each proposed determination shall be coordinated with legal counsel in accordance with agency procedures.

(e) Mistakes alleged or disclosed after award shall be processed as follows:

(1) The contracting officer shall request the contractor to support the alleged mistake by submission of written statements and pertinent evidence, such as—

(i) the contractor's file copy of the bid,

(ii) the contractor's original worksheets and other data used in preparing the bid,

(iii) subcontractors' and suppliers' quotations, if any,

(iv) published price lists, and

(v) any other evidence that will serve to establish the mistake, the manner in which the mistake occurred, and the bid actually intended.

(2) The case file concerning an alleged mistake shall contain the following:

(i) All evidence furnished by the contractor in support of the alleged mistake.

(ii) A signed statement by the contracting officer—

(A) Describing the supplies or services involved;

(B) Specifying how and when the mistake was alleged or disclosed;

(C) Summarizing the evidence submitted by the contractor and any additional evidence considered pertinent;

(D) Quoting, in cases where only one bid was received, the most recent contract price for the supplies or services involved, or in the absence of a recent comparable contract, the contracting officer's estimate of a fair price for the supplies or services and the basis for the estimate;

(E) Setting forth the contracting officer's opinion whether a bona fide mistake was made and whether the contracting officer was, or should have been, on constructive notice of the mistake before the award, together with the reasons for, or data in support of, such opinion;

(F) Setting forth the course of action with respect to the alleged mistake that the contracting officer considers proper on the basis of the evidence, and if other than a change in contract price is recommended, the manner by which the supplies or services will otherwise be acquired; and

(G) Disclosing the status of performance and payments under the contract, including contemplated performance and payments.

(iii) A signed copy of the bid involved.

(iv) A copy of the invitation for bids and any specifications or drawings relevant to the alleged mistake.

(v) An abstract of written record of the bids received.

(vi) A written request by the contractor to reform or rescind the contract, and copies of all other relevant correspondence between the contracting officer and the contractor concerning the alleged mistake.

(vii) A copy of the contract and any related change orders or supplemental agreements.

(f) Each agency shall include in the contract file a record of—

(1) all determinations made in accordance with this 14.407-4,

(2) the facts involved, and

(3) the action taken in each case.

[FAC 84-5, 50 FR 1738, 1/11/85, effective 4/1/85; Redesignated from 14.406-4, FAC 90-29, 60 FR 34732, 7/3/95, effective 7/3/95; FAC 97-9, 63 FR 58587, 10/30/98, effective 10/30/98.]

14.408 Award. (No Text)

14.408-1 General.

(a) The contracting officer shall make a contract award

(1) by written or electronic notice,

(2) within the time for acceptance specified in the bid or an extension (see 14.404-1(d)), and

(3) to that responsible bidder whose bid, conforming to the invitation, will be most advantageous to the Government, considering only price and the price-related factors (see 14.201-8) included in the invitation. Award shall not be made until all required approvals have been obtained and the award otherwise conforms with 14.103-2.

(b) If less than three bids have been received, the contracting officer shall examine the situation to ascertain the reasons for the small number of responses. Award shall be made notwithstanding the limited number of bids. However, the contracting officer shall initiate, if appropriate, corrective action to increase competition in future solicitations for the same or similar items, and include a notation of such action in the records of the invitation for bids (see 14.204).

(c) (1) Award shall be made by mailing or otherwise furnishing a properly executed award document to the successful bidder.

(2) When a notice of award is issued, it shall be followed as soon as possible by the formal award.

(3) When more than one award results from any single invitation for bids, separate award documents shall be suitably numbered and executed.

(4) When an award is made to a bidder for less than all of the items that may be awarded to that bidder and additional items are being withheld for subsequent award, the award shall state that the Government may make subsequent awards on those additional items within the bid acceptance period.

(5) All provisions of the invitation for bids, including any acceptable additions or changes made by a bidder in the bid, shall be clearly and accurately set forth (either expressly or by reference) in the award document. The award is an acceptance of the bid, and the bid and the award constitute the contract.

(d) (1) Award is generally made by using the Award portion of Standard Form (SF) 33, Solicitation, Offer, and Award, or SF 1447, Solicitation/Contract (see 53.214). If an offer on an SF 33 leads to further changes, the resulting contract shall be prepared as a bilateral document on SF 26, Award/Contract.

(2) Use of the Award portion of SF 33, SF 26, or SF 1447, does not preclude the additional use of informal documents, including electronic communications, as notices of awards.

[FAC 84-5, 50 FR 1738, 1/1/85, effective 4/1/85; FAC 84-53, 54 FR 48984, 11/28/89, effective 12/28/89; FAC 84-56, 55 FR 3881, 2/5/90, effective 3/7/90; Redesignated from 14.407-1, FAC 90-29, 60 FR 34732, 7/3/95, effective 7/3/95; FAC 90-31, 60 FR 42648, 8/16/95, effective 10/1/95; FAC 2005-92, 81 FR 83097, 11/18/2016, effective 12/19/2016]

14.408-2 Responsible bidder—reasonableness of price.

(a) The contracting officer shall determine that a prospective contractor is responsible (see Subpart 9.1) and that the prices offered are reasonable before awarding the contract. The price analysis techniques in 15.404-1(b) may be used as guidelines. In each case the determination shall be made in the light of all prevailing circumstances. Particular care must be taken in cases where only a single bid is received.

(b) The price analysis shall consider whether bids are materially unbalanced (see 15.404-1(g)).

[FAC 84-58, 55 FR 25527, 6/21/90, effective 7/23/90; Redesignated from 14.407-2, FAC 90-29, 60 FR 34732, 7/3/95, effective 7/3/95; FAC 97-2, 62 FR 51224, 9/30/97, effective 10/10/97]

14.408-3 Prompt payment discounts.

(a) Prompt payment discounts shall not be considered in the evaluation of bids. However, any discount offered will form a part of the award, and will be taken by the payment center if payment is made within the discount period specified by the bidder. As an alternative to indicating a discount in conjunction with the offer, bidders may prefer to offer discounts on individual invoices.

(b) See 32.111(b)(1), which prescribes the contract clause at 52.232-8, Discounts for Prompt Payment.

[FAC 84-8, 50 FR 26903, 6/28/85, effective 7/1/85; Redesignated from 14.407-3, FAC 90-29, 60 FR 34732, 7/3/95, effective 7/3/95; FAC 2005-05, 70 FR 43580, 7/27/2005, effective 8/26/2005]

14.408-4 Economic price adjustment.

(a) *Bidder proposes economic price adjustment.*

(1) When a solicitation does not contain an economic price adjustment clause but a bidder proposes one with a ceiling that the price will not exceed, the bid shall be evaluated on the basis of the maximum possible economic price adjustment of the quoted base price.

(2) If the bid is eligible for award, the contracting officer shall request the bidder to agree to the inclusion in the award of an approved economic price adjustment clause (see 16.203) that is subject to the same ceiling. If the bidder will not agree to an approved clause, the award may be made on the basis of the bid as originally submitted.

(3) Bids that contain economic price adjustments with no ceiling shall be rejected unless a clear basis for evaluation exists.

(b) *Government proposes economic price adjustment.*

(1) When an invitation contains an economic price adjustment clause and no bidder takes exception to the provisions, bids shall be evaluated on the basis of the quoted prices without the allowable economic price adjustment being added.

(2) When a bidder increases the maximum percentage of economic price adjustment stipulated in the invitation or limits the downward economic price adjustment provisions of the invitation, the bid shall be rejected as nonresponsive.

(3) When a bid indicates deletion of the economic price adjustment clause, the bid shall be rejected as nonresponsive since the downward economic price adjustment provisions are thereby limited.

(4) When a bidder decreases the maximum percentage of economic price adjustment stipulated in the invitation, the bid shall be evaluated at the base price on an equal basis with bids that do not reduce the stipulated ceiling. However, after evaluation, if the bidder offering the lower ceiling is in a position to receive the award, the award shall reflect the lower ceiling.

[Redesignated from 14.407-4, FAC 90-29, 60 FR 34732, 7/3/95, effective 7/3/95]

14.408-5 [Reserved]

[Reserved, FAC 84-5, 50 FR 1737, 1/11/85, effective 4/1/85; Redesignated from 14.407-5, FAC 90-29, 60 FR 34732, effective 7/3/95]

14.408-6 Equal low bids.

(a) Contracts shall be awarded in the following order of priority when two or more low bids are equal in all respects:

(1) Small business concerns that are also labor surplus area concerns.

(2) Other small business concerns.

(3) Other business concerns.

(b) If two or more bidders still remain equally eligible after application of paragraph (a) of this section, award shall be made by a drawing by lot limited to those bidders. If time permits, the bidders involved shall be given an opportunity to attend the drawing. The drawing shall be witnessed by at least three persons, and the contract file shall contain the names and addresses of the witnesses and the person supervising the drawing.

(c) When an award is to be made by using the priorities under this 14.408-6, the contracting officer shall include a written agreement in the contract that the contractor will perform, or cause to be performed, the contract in accordance with the circumstances justifying the priority used to break the tie or select bids for a drawing by lot.

[Redesignated from 14.407-6, FAC 90-29, 60 FR 34732, 7/3/95, effective 7/3/95; FAC 90-32, 60 FR 48206, 9/18/95, effective 10/1/95]

14.408-7 Documentation of award.

(a) The contracting officer shall document compliance with 14.103-2 in the contract file.

(b) The documentation shall either state that the accepted bid was the lowest bid received, or list all lower bids with reasons for their rejection in sufficient detail to justify the award.

(c) When an award is made after receipt of equal low bids, the documentation shall describe how the tie was broken.

[Redesignated from 14.407-7, FAC 90-29, 60 FR 34732, 7/3/95, effective 7/3/95]

14.408-8 Protests against award.

(See Subpart 33.1, Protests.)

[FAC 84-6, 50 FR 2268, 1/15/86, effective 1/15/85; FAC 84-7, 50 FR 23606, 6/4/85, effective 4/30/85; Redesignated from 14.407-7, FAC 90-29, 60 FR 34732, 7/3/95, effective 7/3/95]

14.409 Information to bidders. (No Text)

14.409-1 Award of unclassified contracts.

(a) (1) The contracting officer shall as a minimum (subject to any restrictions in Subpart 9.4)—

(i) Notify each unsuccessful bidder in writing or electronically within three days after contract award, that its bid was not accepted. *Day*, for purposes of the notification process, means calendar day, except that the period will run until a day which is not a Saturday, Sunday, or legal holiday;

(ii) Extend appreciation for the interest the unsuccessful bidder has shown in submitting a bid; and

(iii) When award is made to other than a low bidder, state the reason for rejection in the notice to each of the unsuccessful low bidders.

(2) For acquisitions covered by the World Trade Organization Government Procurement Agreement or a Free Trade Agreement (see 25.408(a)(5)), agencies must include in notices given unsuccessful bidders from World Trade Organization Government Procurement Agreement or Free Trade Agreement countries—

(i) The dollar amount of the successful bid; and

(ii) The name and address of the successful bidder.

(b) Information included in paragraph (a)(2) of this subsection shall be provided to any unsuccessful bidder upon request except when multiple awards have been made and furnishing information on the successful bids would require so much work as to interfere with normal operations of the contracting office. In such circumstances, only information concerning location of the abstract of offers need be given.

(c) When a request is received concerning an unclassified invitation from an inquirer who is neither a bidder nor a representative of a bidder, the contracting officer should make every effort to furnish the names of successful bidders and, if requested, the prices at which awards were made. However, when such requests require so much work as to interfere with the normal operations of the contracting office, the inquirer will be advised where a copy of the abstract of offers may be seen.

(d) Requests for records shall be governed by agency regulations implementing Subpart 24.2.

[FAC 90-31, 60 FR 42648, 8/16/95, effective 10/1/95; FAC 97-15, 64 FR 72414, 12/27/99, effective 2/25/2000; FAC 2001-04, 67 FR 6112, 2/8/2002, effective 2/8/2002; FAC 2001-19, Interim rule, 69 FR 1051, 1/7/2004, effective 1/1/2004; FAC 2001-25, Final rule, 69 FR 59700, 10/5/2004, effective 10/5/2004; FAC 2001-27, interim rule, 69 FR 77870, 12/28/2004, effective 1/1/2005; FAC 2005-07, 71 FR 219, 1/3/2006, effective 1/3/2006]

14.409-2 Award of classified contracts.

In addition to 14.409-1, if classified information was furnished or created in connection with the solicitation, the contracting officer shall advise the unsuccessful bidders, including any who did not bid, to take disposition action in accordance with agency procedures. The name of the successful bidder and the contract price will be furnished to unsuccessful bidders only upon request. Information regarding a classified award shall not be furnished by telephone.

[Redesignated from 14.408-2, FAC 90-29, 60 FR 34732, 7/3/95, effective 7/3/95]

SUBPART 14.5—TWO-STEP SEALED BIDDING

14.501 General.

Two-step sealed bidding is a combination of competitive procedures designed to obtain the benefits of sealed bidding when adequate specifications are not available. An objective is to permit the development of a sufficiently descriptive and not unduly restrictive statement of the Government's requirements, including an adequate technical data package, so that subsequent acquisitions may be made by conventional sealed bidding. This method is especially useful in acquisitions requiring technical proposals, particularly those for complex items. It is conducted in two steps:

(a) Step one consists of the request for, submission, evaluation, and (if necessary) discussion of a technical proposal. No pricing is involved. The objective is to determine the acceptability of the supplies or services offered. As used in this context, the word "technical" has a broad connotation and includes, among other things, the engineering approach, special manufacturing processes, and special testing techniques. It is the proper step for clarification of questions relating to technical requirements. Conformity to the technical requirements is resolved in this step, but not responsibility as defined in 9.1.

(b) Step two involves the submission of sealed priced bids by those who submitted acceptable technical proposals in step one. Bids submitted in step two are evaluated and the awards made in accordance with Subparts 14.3 and 14.4.

[FAC 84-5, 50 FR 1739, 1/11/85, effective 4/1/85]

14.502 Conditions for use.

(a) Unless other factors require the use of sealed bidding, two-step sealed bidding may be used in preference to negotiation when all of the following conditions are present:

(1) Available specifications or purchase descriptions are not definite or complete or may be too restrictive without technical evaluation, and any necessary discussion, of the technical aspects of the requirement to en-

sure mutual understanding between each source and the Government.

(2) Definite criteria exist for evaluating technical proposals.

(3) More than one technically qualified source is expected to be available.

(4) Sufficient time will be available for use of the two-step method.

(5) A firm-fixed-price contract or a fixed-price contract with economic price adjustment will be used.

(b) None of the following precludes the use of two-step sealed bidding:

(1) Multi-year contracting.

(2) Government property to be made available to the successful bidder.

(3) A total small business set-aside (see 19.502-2).

(4) The use of a set-aside or price evaluation preference for HUBZone small business concerns (see subpart 19.13).

(5) The use of a set-aside for service-disabled veteran-owned small business concerns (see subpart 19.14).

(6) The use of a set-aside for economically disadvantaged woman-owned small business concerns and women-owned small business concerns eligible under the Women-Owned Small Business Program (*see* subpart 19.15).

(7) A first or subsequent production quantity is being acquired under a performance specification.

[FAC 84-5, 50 FR 1739, 1/11/85, effective 4/1/85; FAC 90-32, 60 FR 48206, 9/18/95, effective 10/1/95; FAC 97-6, 63 FR 35719, 6/30/98, effective 10/1/98, finalized without change, FAC 97-13, 7/2/99; FAC 97-10, 63 FR 70264, 12/18/98, effective 1/4/99; FAC 2001-23, 69 FR 25273, 5/5/2004, effective 5/5/2004; FAC 2005-02, 70 FR 14950, 3/23/2005, effective 3/23/2005; FAC 2005-17, 72 FR 27364, 5/15/2007, effective 6/14/2007; FAC 2005-51, 76 FR 18304, 4/1/2011, effective 4/1/2011; FAC 2005-56, 77 FR 12913, 3/2/2012, effective 4/2/2012; FAC 2005-76, 79 FR 43580, 7/25/2014, effective 8/25/2014; FAC 2005-77, 79 FR 61746, 10/14/2014, effective 10/14/2014]

14.503 Procedures. (No Text)

14.503-1 Step one.

(a) Requests for technical proposals shall be synopsized in accordance with Part 5. The request must include, as a minimum, the following:

(1) A description of the supplies or services required.

(2) A statement of intent to use the two-step method.

(3) The requirements of the technical proposal.

(4) The evaluation criteria, to include all factors and any significant subfactors.

(5) A statement that the technical proposals shall not include prices or pricing information.

(6) The date, or date and hour, by which the proposal must be received (see 14.201-6(r).

(7) A statement that—

(*i*) In the second step, only bids based upon technical proposals determined to be acceptable, either initially or as a result of discussions, will be considered for awards, and

(*ii*) Each bid in the second step must be based on the bidder's own technical proposals.

(8) A statement that—

(*i*) Offerors should submit proposals that are acceptable without additional explanation or information,

(*ii*) The Government may make a final determination regarding a proposal's acceptability solely on the basis of the proposal as submitted; and

(*iii*) The Government may proceed with the second step without requesting further information from any offeror; however, the Government may request additional information from offerors of proposals that it considers reasonably susceptible of being made acceptable, and may discuss proposals with their offerors.

(9) A statement that a notice of unacceptability will be forwarded to the offeror

upon completion of the proposal evaluation and final determination of unacceptability.

(10) A statement either that only one technical proposal may be submitted by each offeror or that multiple technical proposals may be submitted. When specifications permit different technical approaches, it is generally in the Government's interest to authorize multiple proposals. If multiple proposals are authorized, see 14.201-6(s).

(b) Information on delivery or performance requirements may be of assistance to bidders in determining whether or not to submit a proposal and may be included in the request. The request shall also indicate that the information is not binding on the Government and that the actual delivery or performance requirements will be contained in the invitation issued under step two.

(c) Upon receipt, the contracting officer shall—

(1) Safeguard proposals against disclosure to unauthorized persons;

(2) Accept and handle data marked in accordance with 15.609 as provided in that section; and

(3) Remove any reference to price or cost.

(d) The contracting officer shall establish a time period for evaluating technical proposals. The period may vary with the complexity and number of proposals involved. However, the evaluation should be completed quickly.

(e) (1) Evaluations shall be based on the criteria in the request for proposals but not consideration of responsibility as defined in 9.1, Proposals, shall be categorized as—

(i) Acceptable;

(ii) Reasonably susceptible of being made acceptable; or

(iii) Unacceptable.

(2) Any proposal which modifies, or fails to conform to the essential requirements or specifications of, the request for technical proposals shall be considered nonresponsive and categorized as unacceptable.

(f) (1) The contracting officer may proceed directly with step two if there are sufficient acceptable proposals to ensure adequate price competition under step two, and if further time, effort and delay to make additional proposals acceptable and thereby increase competition would not be in the Government's interest. If this is not the case, the contracting officer shall request bidders whose proposals may be made acceptable to submit additional clarifying or supplementing information. The contracting officer shall identify the nature of the deficiencies in the proposal or the nature of the additional information required. The contracting officer may also arrange discussions for this purpose. No proposal shall be discussed with any offeror other than the submitter.

(2) In initiating requests for additional information, the contracting officer shall fix an appropriate time for bidders to conclude discussions, if any, submit all additional information, and incorporate such additional information as part of their proposals submitted. Such time may be extended in the discretion of the contracting officer. If the additional information incorporated as part of a proposal within the final time fixed by the contracting officer establishes that the proposal is acceptable, it shall be so categorized. Otherwise, it shall be categorized as unacceptable.

(g) When a technical proposal is found unacceptable (either initially or after clarification), the contracting officer shall promptly notify the offeror of the basis of the determination and that a revision of the proposal will not be considered. Upon written request, the contracting officer shall debrief unsuccessful offerors (see 15.505 and 15.506).

(h) Late technical proposals are governed by 15.208(b), (c), and (f).

(i) If it is necessary to discontinue two-step sealed bidding, the contracting officer shall include a statement of the facts and circumstances in the contract file. Each offeror shall be notified in writing. When step one results in no acceptable technical proposal or only one acceptable technical proposal, the acquisition may be continued by negotiation.

[FAC 84-5, 50 FR 1739, 1/11/85, effective 4/1/85; FAC 84-12, 51 FR 2649, 1/17/86, effective 1/20/86; Interim rule, FAC 90-7, 56

FR 41733, 8/22/91, effective 8/22/91; FAC 90-31, 60 FR 42648, 8/16/95, effective 10/1/95; FAC 90-44, Final rule, 61 FR 69286, 12/31/96, effective 1/1/97; FAC 97-2, 62 FR 51224, 9/30/97, effective 10/10/97; FAC 97-14, 64 FR 51828, 9/24/99, effective 11/23/99; FAC 2001-15, 68 FR 43854, 7/24/2003, effective 8/25/2003]

14.503-2 Step two.

(a) Sealed bidding procedures shall be followed except that invitations for bids shall—

(1) Be issued only to those offerors submitting acceptable technical proposals in step one;

(2) Include the provision prescribed in 14.201-6(t);

(3) Prominently state that the bidder shall comply with the specifications and the bidder's technical proposal; and

(4) Not be synopsized through the Governmentwide point of entry (GPE) as an acquisition opportunity nor publicly posted (see 5.101(a)).

(b) The names of firms that submitted acceptable proposals in step one will be listed through the GPE for the benefit of prospective subcontractors (see 5.207).

[FAC 84-5, 50 FR 1739, 1/11/85, effective 4/1/85; FAC 90-4, 56 FR 15149, 4/15/91, effective 5/15/91; FAC 97-26, 66 FR 27405, 5/16/2001, effective 5/16/2001; FAC 2001-16, Interim/Final rule, 68 FR 56676, 10/1/2003, effective 10/1/2003]

PART 15—CONTRACTING BY NEGOTIATION

Table of Contents

Scope of part . . . 15.000
Definitions . . . 15.001
Types of negotiated acquisition . . . 15.002

Subpart 15.1—Source Selection Processes and Techniques

Scope of subpart . . . 15.100
Best value continuum . . . 15.101
Tradeoff process . . . 15.101-1
Lowest price technically acceptable source selection process . . . 15.101-2
Oral presentations . . . 15.102

Subpart 15.2—Solicitation and Receipt of Proposals and Information

Scope of subpart . . . 15.200
Exchanges with industry before receipt of proposals . . . 15.201
Advisory multi-step process . . . 15.202
Requests for proposals . . . 15.203
Contract format . . . 15.204
Uniform contract format . . . 15.204-1
Part I—The Schedule . . . 15.204-2
Part II—Contract Clauses . . . 15.204-3
Part III—List of Documents, Exhibits, and Other Attachments . . . 15.204-4
Part IV—Representations and Instructions . . . 15.204-5
Issuing solicitations . . . 15.205
Amending the solicitation . . . 15.206
Handling proposals and information . . . 15.207
Submission, modification, revision, and withdrawal of proposals . . . 15.208
Solicitation provisions and contract clauses . . . 15.209
Forms . . . 15.210

Subpart 15.3—Source Selection

Scope of subpart . . . 15.300
[Removed and Reserved] . . . 15.301
Source selection objective . . . 15.302
Responsibilities . . . 15.303
Evaluation factors and significant subfactors . . . 15.304
Proposal evaluation . . . 15.305
Exchanges with offerors after receipt of proposals . . . 15.306
Proposal revisions . . . 15.307
Source selection decision . . . 15.308

Subpart 15.4—Contract Pricing

Scope of subpart . . . 15.400
Definitions . . . 15.401
Pricing policy . . . 15.402
Obtaining certified cost or pricing data . . . 15.403
Prohibition on obtaining certified cost or pricing data (10 U.S.C. 2306a and 41 U.S.C. chapter 35) . . . 15.403-1
Other circumstances where certified cost or pricing data are not required . . . 15.403-2
Requiring data other than certified cost or pricing data . . . 15.403-3
Requiring certified cost or pricing data (10 U.S.C. 2306a and 41 U.S.C. chapter 35) . . . 15.403-4
Instructions for submission of certified cost or pricing data other than cost or pricing data . . . 15.403-5
Proposal analysis . . . 15.404
Proposal analysis techniques . . . 15.404-1
Data to support proposal analysis . . . 15.404-2

Subcontract pricing considerations 15.404-3
Profit 15.404-4
Price negotiation 15.405
Documentation 15.406
Prenegotiation objectives 15.406-1
Certificate of Current Cost or Pricing Data 15.406-2
Documenting the negotiation 15.406-3
Special cost or pricing areas 15.407
Defective certified cost or pricing data 15.407-1
Make-or-buy programs 15.407-2
Forward pricing rate agreements 15.407-3
Should-cost review 15.407-4
Estimating systems 15.407-5
Solicitation provisions and contract clauses 15.408

Subpart 15.5—Preaward, Award, and Postaward Notifications, Protests, and Mistakes

Definition 15.501
Applicability 15.502
Notifications to unsuccessful offerors 15.503
Award to successful offeror 15.504
Preaward debriefing of offerors 15.505
Postaward debriefing of offerors 15.506
Protests against award 15.507
Discovery of mistakes 15.508
Forms 15.509

Subpart 15.6—Unsolicited Proposals

Scope of subpart 15.600
Definitions 15.601
Policy 15.602
General 15.603
Agency points of contact 15.604
Content of unsolicited proposals 15.605
Agency procedures 15.606
Receipt and initial review 15.606-1
Evaluation 15.606-2
Criteria for acceptance and negotiation of an unsolicited proposal 15.607
Prohibitions 15.608
Limited use of data 15.609

PART 15—CONTRACTING BY NEGOTIATION

15.000 Scope of part.

This part prescribes policies and procedures governing competitive and noncompetitive negotiated acquisitions. A contract awarded using other than sealed bidding procedures is a negotiated contract (see 14.101).

[FAC 97-2, 62 FR 51224, 9/30/97, effective 10/10/97]

15.001 Definitions.

As used in this part—

Deficiency is a material failure of a proposal to meet a Government requirement or a combination of significant weaknesses in a proposal that increases the risk of unsuccessful contract performance to an unacceptable level.

Proposal modification is a change made to a proposal before the solicitation closing date and time, or made in response to an amendment, or made to correct a mistake at any time before award.

Proposal revision is a change to a proposal made after the solicitation closing date, at the request of or as allowed by a contracting officer, as the result of negotiations.

Weakness means a flaw in the proposal that increases the risk of unsuccessful contract performance. A *significant weakness* in the proposal is a flaw that appreciably increases the risk of unsuccessful contract performance.

[FAC 97-2, 62 FR 51224, 9/30/97, effective 10/10/97; FAC 97-22, 66 FR 2116, 1/10/2001, effective 3/12/2001; Delay of effective date, 66 FR 14259, 3/9/2001, effective 5/11/2001]

15.002 Types of negotiated acquisition.

(a) *Sole source acquisitions.* When contracting in a sole source environment, the request for proposals (RFP) should be tailored to remove unnecessary information and requirements; *e.g.*, evaluation criteria and voluminous proposal preparation instructions.

(b) *Competitive acquisitions.* When contracting in a competitive environment, the procedures of this part are intended to minimize the complexity of the solicitation, the evaluation, and the source selection decision, while maintaining a process designed to foster an impartial and comprehensive evaluation of offerors' proposals, leading to selection of the proposal representing the best value to the Government (see 2.101).

[FAC 97-2, 62 FR 51224, 9/30/97, effective 10/10/97]

SUBPART 15.1—SOURCE SELECTION PROCESSES AND TECHNIQUES

15.100 Scope of subpart.

This subpart describes some of the acquisition processes and techniques that may be used to design competitive acquisition strategies suitable for the specific circumstances of the acquisition.

[FAC 97-2, 62 FR 51224, 9/30/97, effective 10/10/97]

15.101 Best value continuum.

An agency can obtain best value in negotiated acquisitions by using any one or a combination of source selection approaches. In different types of acquisitions, the relative importance of cost or price may vary. For example, in acquisitions where the requirement is clearly definable and the risk of unsuccessful contract performance is minimal, cost or price may play a dominant role in source selection. The less definitive the requirement, the more development work required, or the greater the performance risk, the more technical or past performance considerations may play a dominant role in source selection.

[FAC 97-2, 62 FR 51224, 9/30/97, effective 10/10/97]

15.101-1 Tradeoff process.

(a) A tradeoff process is appropriate when it may be in the best interest of the Government to consider award to other than the lowest priced offeror or other than the highest technically rated offeror.

(b) When using a tradeoff process, the following apply:

(1) All evaluation factors and significant subfactors that will affect contract award and their relative importance shall be clearly stated in the solicitation; and

(2) The solicitation shall state whether all evaluation factors other than cost or price, when combined, are significantly more important than, approximately equal to, or significantly less important than cost or price.

(c) This process permits tradeoffs among cost or price and non-cost factors and allows the Government to accept other than the lowest priced proposal. The perceived benefits of the higher priced proposal shall merit the additional cost, and the rationale for tradeoffs must be documented in the file in accordance with 15.406.

[FAC 97-2, 62 FR 51224, 9/30/97, effective 10/10/97]

15.101-2 Lowest price technically acceptable source selection process.

(a) The lowest price technically acceptable source selection process is appropriate when best value is expected to result from selection of the technically acceptable proposal with the lowest evaluated price.

(b) When using the lowest price technically acceptable process, the following apply:

(1) The evaluation factors and significant subfactors that establish the requirements of acceptability shall be set forth in the solicitation. Solicitations shall specify that award will be made on the basis of the lowest evaluated price of proposals meeting or exceeding the acceptability standards for non-cost factors. If the contracting officer documents the file pursuant to 15.304(c)(3)(iii), past performance need not be an evaluation factor in lowest price technically acceptable source selections. If the contracting officer elects to consider past performance as an evaluation factor, it shall be evaluated in accordance with 15.305. However, the comparative assessment in 15.305(a)(2)(i) does not apply. If the contracting officer determines that a small business's past performance is not acceptable, the matter shall be referred to the Small Business Administration for a Certificate of Competency determination, in accordance with the procedures contained in Subpart 19.6 and 15 U.S.C. 637(b)(7).

(2) Tradeoffs are not permitted.

(3) Proposals are evaluated for acceptability but not ranked using the non-cost/price factors.

(4) Exchanges may occur (see 15.306).

[FAC 97-2, 62 FR 51224, 9/30/97, effective 10/10/97; FAC 97-15, 64 FR 72414, 12/27/99, effective 12/27/99; finalized without change, FAC 97-19, 65 FR 46052, 7/26/2000; FAC 2005-30, 74 FR 2746, 1/15/2009, effective 1/15/2009]

15.102 Oral presentations.

(a) Oral presentations by offerors as requested by the Government may substitute for, or augment, written information. Use of oral presentations as a substitute for portions of a proposal can be effective in streamlining the source selection process. Oral presentations may occur at any time in the acquisition process, and are subject to the same restrictions as written information, regarding timing (see 15.208) and content (see 15.306). Oral presentations provide an opportunity for dialogue among the parties. Pre-recorded videotaped presentations that lack real-time interactive dialogue are not considered oral presentations for the purposes of this section, although they may be included in offeror submissions, when appropriate.

(b) The solicitation may require each offeror to submit part of its proposal through oral presentations. However, representations and certifications, shall be submitted as required in the FAR provisions at FAR 52.204-8(d) or FAR 52.212-3(b), and a signed offer sheet (including any exceptions to the Government's terms and conditions) shall be submitted in writing.

(c) Information pertaining to areas such as an offeror's capability, past performance, work plans or approaches, staffing resources, transition plans, or sample tasks (or other types of tests) may be suitable for oral presentations. In deciding what information to obtain through an oral presentation, consider the following:

(1) The Government's ability to adequately evaluate the information;

(2) The need to incorporate any information into the resultant contract;

(3) The impact on the efficiency of the acquisition; and

(4) The impact (including cost) on small businesses. In considering the costs of oral presentations, contracting officers should also consider alternatives to on-site oral presentations (*e.g.*, teleconferencing, video teleconferencing).

(d) When oral presentations are required, the solicitation shall provide offerors with sufficient information to prepare them. Accordingly, the solicitation may describe—

(1) The types of information to be presented orally and the associated evaluation factors that will be used;

(2) The qualifications for personnel that will be required to provide the oral presentation(s);

(3) The requirements for, and any limitations and/or prohibitions on, the use of written material or other media to supplement the oral presentations;

(4) The location, date, and time for the oral presentations;

(5) The restrictions governing the time permitted for each oral presentation; and

(6) The scope and content of exchanges that may occur between the Government's participants and the offeror's representatives as part of the oral presentations, including whether or not discussions (see 15.306(d)) will be permitted during oral presentations.

(e) The contracting officer shall maintain a record of oral presentations to document what the Government relied upon in making the source selection decision. The method and level of detail of the record (*e.g.*, videotaping, audio tape recording, written record, Government notes, copies of offeror briefing slides or presentation notes) shall be at the discretion of the source selection authority. A copy of the record placed in the file may be provided to the offeror.

(f) When an oral presentation includes information that the parties intend to include in the contract as material terms or conditions, the information shall be put in writing. Incorporation by reference of oral statements is not permitted.

(g) If, during an oral presentation, the Government conducts discussions (see 15.306(d)), the Government must comply with 15.306 and 15.307.

[FAC 97-2, 62 FR 51224, 9/30/97, effective 10/10/97; FAC 2005-13, 71 FR 57362, 9/28/2006, effective 9/28/2006; FAC 2005-19, 72 FR 46333, 8/17/2007, effective 8/17/2007; FAC 2005-21, 72 FR 63076, 11/7/2007, effective 11/7/2007; FAC 2005-26, 73 FR 33636, 6/12/2008, effective 6/12/2008; FAC 2005-30, 74 FR 2724, 1/15/2009, effective 2/17/2009; FAC 2005-36, 74 FR 40463, 8/11/2009, effective 8/11/2009]

SUBPART 15.2—SOLICITATION AND RECEIPT OF PROPOSALS AND INFORMATION

15.200 Scope of subpart.

This subpart prescribes policies and procedures for—

(a) Exchanging information with industry prior to receipt of proposals;

(b) Preparing and issuing requests for proposals (RFPs) and requests for information (RFIs); and

(c) Receiving proposals and information.

[FAC 97-2, 62 FR 51224, 9/30/97, effective 10/10/97]

15.201 Exchanges with industry before receipt of proposals.

(a) Exchanges of information among all interested parties, from the earliest identification of a requirement through receipt of proposals, are encouraged. Any exchange of information must be consistent with procurement integrity requirements (see 3.104). Interested parties include potential offerors, end users, Government acquisition and supporting personnel, and others involved in the conduct or outcome of the acquisition.

(b) The purpose of exchanging information is to improve the understanding of Government requirements and industry capabilities, thereby allowing potential offerors to judge whether or how they can satisfy the Government's requirements, and enhancing the Government's ability to obtain quality supplies and services, including construction, at reasonable prices, and increase efficiency in proposal preparation, proposal evaluation, negotiation, and contract award.

(c) Agencies are encouraged to promote early exchanges of information about future acquisitions. An early exchange of information among industry and the program manager, contracting officer, and other participants in the acquisition process can identify and resolve concerns regarding the acquisition strategy, including proposed contract type, terms and conditions, and acquisition planning schedules; the feasibility of the requirement, including performance requirements, statements of work, and data requirements; the suitability of the proposal instructions and evaluation criteria, including the approach for assessing past performance information; the availability of reference documents; and any other industry concerns or questions. Some techniques to promote early exchanges of information are—

(1) Industry or small business conferences;

(2) Public hearings;

(3) Market research, as described in Part 10;

(4) One-on-one meetings with potential offerors (any that are substantially involved with potential contract terms and conditions should include the contracting officer; also see paragraph (f) of this section regarding restrictions on disclosure of information);

(5) Presolicitation notices;

(6) Draft RFPs;

(7) RFIs;

(8) Presolicitation or preproposal conferences; and

(9) Site visits.

(d) The special notices of procurement matters at 5.205(c), or electronic notices, may be used to publicize the Government's requirement or solicit information from industry.

(e) RFIs may be used when the Government does not presently intend to award a contract, but wants to obtain price, delivery, other market information, or capabilities for planning purposes. Responses to these notices are not offers and cannot be accepted by the Government to form a binding contract. There is no required format for RFIs.

(f) General information about agency mission needs and future requirements may be disclosed at any time. After release of the solicitation, the contracting officer must be the focal point of any exchange with potential offerors. When specific information about a proposed acquisition that would be necessary for the preparation of proposals is disclosed to one or more potential offerors, that information must be made available to the public as soon as practicable, but no later than the next general release of information, in order to avoid creating an unfair competitive advantage. Information provided to a potential offeror in response to its request must not be disclosed if doing so would reveal the potential offeror's confidential business strategy, and is protected under 3.104 or subpart 24.2. When conducting a presolicitation or preproposal conference, materials distributed at the conference should be made available to all potential offerors, upon request.

[FAC 97-2, 62 FR 51224, 9/30/97, effective 10/10/97; FAC 2001-06, 67 FR 13048, 3/20/2002, effective 4/4/2002]

15.202 Advisory multi-step process.

(a) The agency may publish a presolicitation notice (see 5.204) that provides a general description of the scope or purpose of the acquisition and invites potential offerors to submit information that allows the Government to advise the offerors about their potential to be viable competitors. The presolicitation notice should identify the information that must be submitted and the criteria that will be used in making the initial evaluation. Information sought may be limited to a statement of qualifications and other appropriate information (*e.g.*, proposed technical concept, past performance, and limited pricing information). At a minimum, the notice shall contain sufficient information to permit a potential offeror to make an informed decision about whether to participate in the acquisition. This process should not be used for multi-step acquisitions where it would result in offerors being required to submit identical information in response to the notice and in response to the initial step of the acquisition.

(b) The agency shall evaluate all responses in accordance with the criteria stated in the notice, and shall advise each respondent in writing either that it will be invited to participate in the resultant acquisition or, based on the information submitted, that it is unlikely to be a viable competitor. The agency shall advise respondents considered not to be viable competitors of the general basis for that opinion. The agency shall inform all respondents that, notwithstanding the advice provided by the Government in response to their submissions, they may participate in the resultant acquisition.

[FAC 97-2, 62 FR 51224, 9/30/97, effective 10/10/97]

15.203 Requests for proposals.

(a) Requests for proposals (RFPs) are used in negotiated acquisitions to communicate Government requirements to prospective contractors and to solicit proposals. RFPs for competitive acquisitions shall, at a minimum, describe the—

(1) Government's requirement;

(2) Anticipated terms and conditions that will apply to the contract. The solicitation may authorize offerors to propose alternative terms and conditions. If the solicitation permits offerors to submit one or more additional proposals with alternative line items (see 52.204-22 or 52.212-1(e)), the evaluation approach should consider the potential impact of the alternative line items on other terms and conditions or the requirement (e.g., place of performance or payment and funding requirements) (see 15.206);

(i) The solicitation may authorize offerors to propose alternative terms and conditions, including the contract line item number (CLIN) structure; and

(ii) When alternative CLIN structures are permitted, the evaluation approach should consider the potential impact on other terms and conditions or the requirement (*e.g.*, place of performance or payment and funding requirements) (see 15.206);

(3) Information required to be in the offeror's proposal; and

(4) Factors and significant subfactors that will be used to evaluate the proposal and their relative importance.

(b) An RFP may be issued for OMB Circular A-76 studies. See Subpart 7.3 for additional information regarding cost comparisons between Government and contractor performance.

(c) Electronic commerce may be used to issue RFPs and to receive proposals, modifications, and revisions. In this case, the RFP shall specify the electronic commerce method(s) that offerors may use (See Subpart 4.5).

(d) Contracting officers may issue RFPs and/or authorize receipt of proposals, modifications, or revisions by facsimile.

(1) In deciding whether or not to use facsimiles, the contracting officer should consider factors such as—

(i) Anticipated proposal size and volume;

(ii) Urgency of the requirement;

(iii) Availability and suitability of electronic commerce methods; and

(iv) Adequacy of administrative procedures and controls for receiving, identifying, recording, and safeguarding facsimile proposals, and ensuring their timely delivery to the designated proposal delivery location.

(2) If facsimile proposals are authorized, contracting officers may request offeror(s) to provide the complete, original signed proposal at a later date.

(e) Letter RFPs may be used in sole source acquisitions and other appropriate circumstances. Use of a letter RFP does not relieve the contracting officer from complying with other FAR requirements. Letter RFPs should be as complete as possible and, at a minimum, should contain the following:

(1) RFP number and date;

(2) Name, address (including electronic address and facsimile address, if appropriate), and telephone number of the contracting officer;

(3) Type of contract contemplated;

(4) Quantity, description, and required delivery dates for the item;

(5) Applicable certifications and representations;

(6) Anticipated contract terms and conditions;

(7) Instructions to offerors and evaluation criteria for other than sole source actions;

(8) Proposal due date and time; and

(9) Other relevant information; *e.g.*, incentives, variations in delivery schedule, cost proposal support, and data requirements.

(f) Oral RFPs are authorized when processing a written solicitation would delay the acquisition of supplies or services to the detriment of the Government and a notice is not required under 5.202 (*e.g.*, perishable items and support of contingency operations or other emergency situations). Use of an oral RFP does not relieve the contracting officer from complying with other FAR requirements.

(1) The contract files supporting oral solicitations should include—

(i) A description of the requirement;

(ii) Rationale for use of an oral solicitation;

(iii) Sources solicited, including the date, time, name of individuals contacted, and prices offered; and

(iv) The solicitation number provided to the prospective offerors.

(2) The information furnished to potential offerors under oral solicitations should include appropriate items from paragraph (e) of this section.

[FAC 97-2, 62 FR 51224, 9/30/97, effective 10/10/97; FAC 2005-95, 82 FR 4709, 1/13/2017, effective 1/13/2017]

15.204 Contract format.

The use of a uniform contract format facilitates preparation of the solicitation and contract as well as reference to, and use of, those documents by offerors, contractors, and contract administrators. The uniform contract format need not be used for the following:

(a) Construction and architect-engineer contracts (see Part 36).

(b) Subsistence contracts.

(c) Supplies or services contracts requiring special contract formats prescribed elsewhere in this part that are inconsistent with the uniform format.

(d) Letter requests for proposals (see 15.203(e)).

(e) Contracts exempted by the agency head or designee.

[FAC 97-2, 62 FR 51224, 9/30/97, effective 10/10/97]

15.204-1 Uniform contract format.

(a) Contracting officers shall prepare solicitations and resulting contracts using the uniform contract format outlined in Table 15-1 of this subsection.

(b) Solicitations using the uniform contract format shall include Parts I, II, III, and IV (see 15.204-2 through 15.204-5). Upon award, contracting officers shall not physically include Part IV in the resulting contract, but shall retain it in the contract file, (See 4.1201(c).) Section K shall be incorporated by reference in the contract. The representations and certifications are incorporated by reference in the contract by using 52.204-19 (see 4.1202(b)) or for acquisitions of commercial items see 52.212-4(v).

Table 15-1.—Uniform Contract Format

Section	Title
	Part I—The Schedule
A.	Solicitation/contract form.
B	Supplies or services and prices/costs.
C	Description/specifications/statement of work.
D	Packaging and marking.
E.	Inspection and acceptance.
F	Deliveries or performance.
G	Contract administration data.
H	Special contract requirements.
	Part II—Contract Clauses

Section	Title
I	Contract clauses.
Part III—List of Documents, Exhibits, and Other Attachments	
J	List of attachments.
Part IV—Representations and Instructions.	
K	Representations, certifications, and other statements of offerors or respondents.
L......	Instructions, conditions, and notices to offerors or respondents.
M	Evaluation factors for award.

[FAC 97-2, 62 FR 51224, 9/30/97, effective 10/10/97; FAC 2005-13, 71 FR 57362, 9/28/2006, effective 9/28/2006; FAC 2005-19, 72 FR 46333, 8/17/2007, effective 8/17/2007; FAC 2005-78, 79 FR 70341 11/25/22014, effective 12/26/2014]

15.204-2 Part I—The Schedule.

The contracting officer shall prepare the contract Schedule as follows:

(a) *Section A, Solicitation/contract form.* (1) Optional Form (OF) 308, Solicitation and Offer—Negotiated Acquisition, or Standard Form (SF) 33, Solicitation, Offer and Award, may be used to prepare RFPs.

(2) When other than OF 308 or SF 33 is used, include the following information on the first page of the solicitation:

(i) Name, address, and location of issuing activity, including room and building where proposals or information must be submitted.

(ii) Solicitation number.

(iii) Date of issuance.

(iv) Closing date and time.

(v) Number of pages.

(vi) Requisition or other purchase authority.

(vii) Brief description of item or service.

(viii) Requirement for the offeror to provide its name and complete address, including street, city, county, state, and zip code, and electronic address (including facsimile address), if appropriate.

(ix) Offer expiration date.

(b) *Section B, Supplies or services and prices/costs.* Include a brief description of the supplies or services; *e.g.*, item number, national stock number/part number if applicable, nouns, nomenclature, and quantities. (This includes incidental deliverables such as manuals and reports.)

(c) *Section C, Description/specifications/statement of work.* Include any description or specifications needed in addition to Section B (see Part 11, Describing Agency Needs).

(d) *Section D, Packaging and marking.* Provide packaging, packing, preservation, and marking requirements, if any.

(e) *Section E, Inspection and acceptance.* Include inspection, acceptance, quality assurance, and reliability requirements (see Part 46, Quality Assurance).

(f) *Section F, Deliveries or performance.* Specify the requirements for time, place, and method of delivery or performance (see Subpart 11.4, Delivery or Performance Schedules, and 47.301-1).

(g) *Section G, Contract administration data.* Include any required accounting and appropriation data and any required contract administration information or instructions other than those on the solicitation form. Include a statement that the offeror should include the payment address in the proposal, if it is different from that shown for the offeror.

(h) *Section H, Special contract requirements.* Include a clear statement of any special contract requirements that are not included in Section I, Contract clauses, or in other sections of the uniform contract format.

[FAC 97-2, 62 FR 51224, 9/30/97, effective 10/10/97]

15.204-3 Part II—Contract Clauses.

Section I, Contract clauses. The contracting officer shall include in this section the clauses required by law or by this part and any additional clauses expected to be included in any resulting contract, if these clauses are not required in any other section of the uniform contract format. An index may be inserted if this section's format is particularly complex.

[FAC 97-2, 62 FR 51224, 9/30/97, effective 10/10/97]

15.204-4 Part III—List of Documents, Exhibits, and Other Attachments.

Section J, List of attachments. The contracting officer shall list the title, date, and number of pages for each attached document, exhibit, and other attachment. Cross-references to material in other sections may be inserted, as appropriate.

[FAC 97-2, 62 FR 51224, 9/30/97, effective 10/10/97]

15.204-5 Part IV—Representations and Instructions.

The contracting officer shall prepare the representations and instructions as follows:

(a) *Section K, Representations, certifications, and other statements of offerors.* Include in this section those solicitation provisions that require representations, certifications, or the submission of other information by offerors.

(b) *Section L, Instructions, conditions, and notices to offerors or respondents.* Insert in this section solicitation provisions and other information and instructions not required elsewhere to guide offerors or respondents in preparing proposals or responses to requests for information. Prospective offerors or respondents may be instructed to submit proposals or information in a specific format or severable parts to facilitate evaluation. The instructions may specify further organization of proposal or response parts, such as—

(1) Administrative;

(2) Management;

(3) Technical;

(4) Past performance; and

(5) Certified cost or pricing data (see Table 15-2 of 15.408) or data other than certified cost or pricing data.

(c) *Section M, Evaluation factors for award.* Identify all significant factors and any significant subfactors that will be considered in awarding the contract and their relative importance (see 15.304(d)). The contracting officer shall insert one of the phrases in 15.304(e).

[FAC 97-2, 62 FR 51224, 9/30/97, effective 10/10/97; FAC 2005-45, 75 FR 53135, 8/30/2010, effective 10/1/2010]

15.205 Issuing solicitations.

(a) The contracting officer shall issue solicitations to potential sources in accordance with the policies and procedures in 5.102, 19.202-4, and Part 6.

(b) A master solicitation, as described in 14.203-3, may also be used for negotiated acquisitions.

[FAC 97-2, 62 FR 51224, 9/30/97, effective 10/10/97]

15.206 Amending the solicitation.

(a) When, either before or after receipt of proposals, the Government changes its requirements or terms and conditions, the contracting officer shall amend the solicitation.

(b) Amendments issued before the established time and date for receipt of proposals shall be issued to all parties receiving the solicitation.

(c) Amendments issued after the established time and date for receipt of proposals shall be issued to all offerors that have not been eliminated from the competition.

(d) If a proposal of interest to the Government involves a departure from the stated requirements, the contracting officer shall amend the solicitation, provided this can be done without revealing to the other offerors the alternate solution proposed or any other information that is entitled to protection (see 15.207(b) and 15.306(e)).

(e) If, in the judgment of the contracting officer, based on market research or otherwise, an amendment proposed for issuance after offers have been received is so substantial as to exceed what prospective offerors reasonably could have anticipated, so that additional sources likely would have submitted offers had the substance of the amendment been known to them, the contracting officer shall cancel the original solicitation and issue a new one, regardless of the stage of the acquisition.

(f) Oral notices may be used when time is of the essence. The contracting officer shall document the contract file and formalize the notice with an amendment (see Subpart 4.5, Electronic Commerce in Contracting).

(g) At a minimum, the following information should be included in each amendment:

(1) Name and address of issuing activity.

(2) Solicitation number and date.

(3) Amendment number and date.

(4) Number of pages.

(5) Description of the change being made.

(6) Government point of contact and phone number (and electronic or facsimile address, if appropriate).

(7) Revision to solicitation closing date, if applicable.

[FAC 97-2, 62 FR 51224, 9/30/97, effective 10/10/97]

15.207 Handling proposals and information.

(a) Upon receipt at the location specified in the solicitation, proposals and information received in response to a request for information (RFI) shall be marked with the date and time of receipt and shall be transmitted to the designated officials.

(b) Proposals shall be safeguarded from unauthorized disclosure throughout the source selection process. (See 3.104 regarding the disclosure of source selection information (41 U.S.C. chapter 21, Restrictions on Obtaining and Disclosing Certain Information)). Information received in response to an RFI shall be safeguarded adequately from unauthorized disclosure.

(c) If any portion of a proposal received by the contracting officer electronically or by facsimile is unreadable, the contracting officer immediately shall notify the offeror and permit the offeror to resubmit the unreadable portion of the proposal. The method and time for resubmission shall be prescribed by the contracting officer after consultation with the offeror, and documented in the file. The resubmission shall be considered as if it were received at the date and time of the original unreadable submission for the purpose of determining timeliness under 15.208(a), provided the offeror complies with the time and format requirements for resubmission prescribed by the contracting officer.

[FAC 97-2, 62 FR 51224, 9/30/97, effective 10/10/97; FAC 2005-73, 79 FR 24192, 4/29/2014, effective 5/29/2014]

15.208 Submission, modification, revision, and withdrawal of proposals.

(a) Offerors are responsible for submitting proposals, and any revisions, and modifications, so as to reach the Government office designated in the solicitation by the time specified in the solicitation. Offerors may use any transmission method authorized by the solicitation (i.e., regular mail, electronic commerce, or facsimile). If no time is specified in the solicitation, the time for receipt is 4:30 p.m., local time, for the designated Government office on the date that proposals are due.

(b)(1) Any proposal, modification, or revision, that is received at the designated Government office after the exact time specified for receipt of proposals is "late" and will not be considered unless it is received before award is made, the contracting officer determines that accepting the late proposal would not unduly delay the acquisition; and—

(i) If it was transmitted through an electronic commerce method authorized by the solicitation, it was received at the initial point of entry to the Government infrastructure not later than 5:00 p.m. one working day prior to the date specified for receipt of proposals; or

(ii) There is acceptable evidence to establish that it was received at the Government installation designated for receipt of proposals and was under the Government's control prior to the time set for receipt of proposals; or

(iii) It was the only proposal received.

(2) However, a late modification of an otherwise successful proposal, that makes its terms more favorable to the Government,

will be considered at any time it is received and may be accepted.

(c) Acceptable evidence to establish the time of receipt at the Government installation includes the time/date stamp of that installation on the proposal wrapper, other documentary evidence of receipt maintained by the installation, or oral testimony or statements of Government personnel.

(d) If an emergency or unanticipated event interrupts normal Government processes so that proposals cannot be received at the Government office designated for receipt of proposals by the exact time specified in the solicitation, and urgent Government requirements preclude amendment of the solicitation closing date, the time specified for receipt of proposals will be deemed to be extended to the same time of day specified in the solicitation on the first work day on which normal Government processes resume.

(e) Proposals may be withdrawn by written notice at any time before award. Oral proposals in response to oral solicitations may be withdrawn orally. The contracting officer must document the contract file when oral withdrawals are made. One copy of withdrawn proposals should be retained in the contract file (see 4.803(a)(10)). Extra copies of the withdrawn proposals may be destroyed or returned to the offeror at the offerors request. Where practicable, electronically transmitted proposals that are withdrawn must be purged from primary and backup data storage systems after a copy is made for the file. Extremely bulky proposals must only be returned at the offeror's request and expense.

(f) The contracting officer must promptly notify any offeror if its proposal, modification, or revision was received late, and must inform the offeror whether its proposal will be considered, unless contract award is imminent and the notice prescribed in 15.503(b) would suffice.

(g) Late proposals and modifications that are not considered must be held unopened, unless opened for identification, until after award and then retained with other unsuccessful proposals.

(h) If available, the following must be included in the contracting office files for each late proposal, modification, revision, or withdrawal:

(1) The date and hour of receipt.

(2) A statement regarding whether the proposal was considered for award, with supporting rationale.

(3) The envelope, wrapper, or other evidence of date of receipt.

[FAC 97-14, 64 FR 51828, 9/24/99, effective 11/23/99; FAC 97-15, 64 FR 72414, 12/27/99, effective 12/27/99]

15.209 Solicitation provisions and contract clauses.

When contracting by negotiation—

(a) The contracting officer shall insert the provision at 52.215-1, Instructions to Offerors—Competitive Acquisition, in all competitive solicitations where the government intends to award a contract without discussions.

(1) If the Government intends to make award after discussions with offerors within the competitive range, the contracting officer shall use the basic provision with its Alternate I.

(2) If the Government would be willing to accept alternate proposals, the contracting officer shall alter the basic clause to add a new paragraph (c)(9) substantially the same as Alternate II.

(b)(1) Except as provided in paragraph (b)(2) of this section, the contracting officer shall insert the clause at 52.215-2, Audit and Records-Negotiation (10 U.S.C. 2313, 41 U.S.C. 4706, and Audit Requirements in the OMB Uniform Guidance at 2 CFR part 200, subpart F), in solicitations and contracts except those for—

(i) Acquisitions not exceeding the simplified acquisition threshold;

(ii) The acquisition of utility services at rates not exceeding those established to apply uniformly to the general public, plus any applicable reasonable connection charge; or

(iii) The acquisition of commercial items exempted under 15.403-1.

(2) (i) When using funds appropriated or otherwise made available by the American Recovery and Reinvestment Act of 2009 (Pub. L. 111-5)—

(A) The exceptions in paragraphs (b) (1) (i) through (b) (1) (iii) are not applicable; and

(B) Use the clause with its Alternate I.

(ii) (A) In the case of a bilateral contract modification that will use funds appropriated or otherwise made available by the American Recovery and Reinvestment Act of 2009, the contracting officer shall specify applicability of Alternate I to that modification.

(B) In the case of a task- or delivery-order contract in which not all orders will use funds appropriated or otherwise made available by the American Recovery and Reinvestment Act of 2009, the contracting officer shall specify the task or delivery orders to which Alternate I applies.

(3) For cost-reimbursement contracts with State and local Governments, educational institutions, and other nonprofit organizations, the contracting officer shall use the clause with its Alternate II.

(4) When the head of the agency has waived the examination of records by the Comptroller General in accordance with 25.1001, use the clause with its Alternate III.

(c) When issuing a solicitation for information or planning purposes, the contracting officer shall insert the provision at 52.215-3, Request for Information or Solicitation for Planning Purposes, and clearly mark on the face of the solicitation that it is for information or planning purposes.

(d) [Reserved]

(e) The contracting officer shall insert the provision at 52.215-5, Facsimile Proposals, in solicitations if facsimile proposals are authorized (see 15.203(d)).

(f) The contracting officer shall insert the provision at 52.215-6, Place of Performance, in solicitations unless the place of performance is specified by the Government.

(g) [Reserved]

(h) The contracting officer shall insert the clause at 52.215-8, Order of Precedence—Uniform Contract Format, in solicitations and contracts using the format at 15.204.

[FAC 97-2, 62 FR 51224, 9/30/97, effective 10/10/97; FAC 97-4, 63 FR 9048, 2/23/98, effective 4/24/98; FAC 97-9, 63 FR 58587, 10/30/98, effective 10/30/98, finalized without change, FAC 97-12, 64 FR 32740, 6/17/99; FAC 97-15, 64 FR 72414, 12/27/99, effective 2/25/2000; FAC 2001-26, 69 FR 76341, 12/20/2004, effective 1/1/2005; FAC 2005-17, 72 FR 27364, 5/15/2007, effective 6/14/2007; FAC 2005-32, 74 FR 14646, 3/31/2009, effective 3/31/2009; FAC 2005-42, 75 FR 34279, 6/16/2010, effective 7/16/2010; FAC 2005-73, 79 FR 24192, 4/29/2014, effective 5/29/2014; FAC 2005-89, 81 FR 45852, 7/14/2016, effective 8/15/2016]

15.210 Forms.

Prescribed forms are not required to prepare solicitations described in this part. The following forms may be used at the discretion of the contracting officer:

(a) Standard Form 33, Solicitation, Offer and Award, and Optional Form 308, Solicitation and Offer—Negotiated Acquisition, may be used to issue RFPs and RFIs.

(b) Standard Form 30, Amendment of Solicitation/Modification of Contract, and Optional Form 309, Amendment of Solicitation, may be used to amend solicitations of negotiated contracts.

(c) Optional Form 17, Offer Label, may be furnished with each request for proposal.

[FAC 97-2, 62 FR 51224, 9/30/97, effective 10/10/97]

SUBPART 15.3—SOURCE SELECTION

15.300 Scope of subpart.

This subpart prescribes policies and procedures for selection of a source or sources in competitive negotiated acquisitions.

[FAC 97-2, 62 FR 51224, 9/30/97, effective 10/10/97]

15.301 [Removed and Reserved]

[Removed and Reserved, FAC 97-22, 66 FR 2116, 1/10/2001, effective 3/12/2001; Delay of effective date, 66 FR 14259, 3/9/2001, effective 5/11/2001]

15.302 Source selection objective.

The objective of source selection is to select the proposal that represents the best value.

[FAC 97-2, 62 FR 51224, 9/30/97, effective 10/10/97]

15.303 Responsibilities.

(a) Agency heads are responsible for source selection. The contracting officer is designated as the source selection authority, unless the agency head appoints another individual for a particular acquisition or group of acquisitions.

(b) The source selection authority shall—

(1) Establish an evaluation team, tailored for the particular acquisition, that includes appropriate contracting, legal, logistics, technical, and other expertise to ensure a comprehensive evaluation of offers;

(2) Approve the source selection strategy or acquisition plan, if applicable, before solicitation release;

(3) Ensure consistency among the solicitation requirements, notices to offerors, proposal preparation instructions, evaluation factors and subfactors, solicitation provisions or contract clauses, and data requirements;

(4) Ensure that proposals are evaluated based solely on the factors and subfactors contained in the solicitation (10 U.S.C. 2305(b)(1)(C) and 41 U.S.C. 3703(c));

(5) Consider the recommendations of advisory boards or panels (if any); and

(6) Select the source or sources whose proposal is the best value to the Government (10 U.S.C. 2305(b)(4)(C) and 41 U.S.C. 3703(c)).

(c) The contracting officer shall—

(1) After release of a solicitation, serve as the focal point for inquiries from actual or prospective offerors;

(2) After receipt of proposals, control exchanges with offerors in accordance with 15.306; and

(3) Award the contract(s).

[FAC 97-2, 62 FR 51224, 9/30/97, effective 10/10/97; FAC 2005-73, 79 FR 24192, 4/29/2014, effective 5/29/2014]

15.304 Evaluation factors and significant subfactors.

(a) The award decision is based on evaluation factors and significant subfactors that are tailored to the acquisition.

(b) Evaluation factors and significant subfactors must—

(1) Represent the key areas of importance and emphasis to be considered in the source selection decision; and

(2) Support meaningful comparison and discrimination between and among competing proposals.

(c) The evaluation factors and significant subfactors that apply to an acquisition and their relative importance are within the broad discretion of agency acquisition officials, subject to the following requirements:

(1) Price or cost to the Government shall be evaluated in every source selection (10 U.S.C. 2305(a)(3)(A) (ii) and 41 U.S.C. 3306(c)(1)(B)) (also see Part 36 for architect-engineer contracts).

(2) The quality of the product or service shall be addressed in every source selection through consideration of one or more non-cost evaluation factors such as past performance, compliance with solicitation requirements, technical excellence, management capability, personnel qualifications, and prior experience (10 U.S.C. 2305(a)(3) (A)(i) and 41 U.S.C. 3306(c)(1)(A)); and

(3)(i) Past performance, except as set forth in paragraph (c)(3)(iii) of this section, shall be evaluated in all source selections for negotiated competitive acquisitions expected to exceed the simplified acquisition threshold.

(ii) For solicitations that are not set aside for small business concerns, involving consolidation or bundling, that offer a significant opportunity for subcontracting, the contracting officer shall include a factor to evaluate past performance indicating the extent to which the offeror attained applicable goals for small business participation under contracts that required subcontracting plans (15 U.S.C. 637(d)(4)(G)(ii)).

(iii) Past performance need not be evaluated if the contracting officer documents the reason past performance is not an appropriate evaluation factor for the acquisition.

(4) For solicitations, that are not set aside for small business concerns, involving consolidation or bundling, that offer a significant opportunity for subcontracting, the contracting officer shall include proposed small business subcontracting participation in the subcontracting plan as an evaluation factor (15 U.S.C. 637(d)(4)(G)(i)).

(5) If telecommuting is not prohibited, agencies shall not unfavorably evaluate an offer that includes telecommuting unless the contracting officer executes a written determination in accordance with FAR 7.108(b).

(d) All factors and significant subfactors that will affect contract award and their relative importance shall be stated clearly in the solicitation (10 U.S.C. 2305(a)(2)(A)(i) and 41 U.S.C. 3306(b)(1)(A)) (see 15.204-5(c)). The rating method need not be disclosed in the solicitation. The general approach for evaluating past performance information shall be described.

(e) The solicitation shall also state, at a minimum, whether all evaluation factors other than cost or price, when combined, are—

(1) Significantly more important than cost or price;

(2) Approximately equal to cost or price; or

(3) Significantly less important than cost or price (10 U.S.C. 2305(a)(3)(A)(iii) and 41 U.S.C. 3306(c)(1)(C)).

[FAC 97-2, 62 FR 51224, 9/30/97, effective 10/10/97; FAC 97-7, 63 FR 36120, 7/1/98, effective 1/1/99, finalized without change, FAC 97-13, 7/2/99; FAC 97-15, 64 FR 72414, 12/27/99, effective 12/27/99, finalized without change, FAC 97-19, 65 FR 46052, 7/26/2000; FAC 97-18, 65 FR 36014, 6/6/2000, effective 6/6/2000; FAC 2001-25, 69 FR 59701, 10/5/2004, effective 10/5/2004; FAC 2005-04, 70 FR 33656, 6/8/2005, effective 6/8/2005; FAC 2005-13, 71 FR 57363, 9/28/2006, effective 9/28/2006; FAC 2005-45, 75 FR 53129, 8/30/2010, effective 10/1/2010; FAC 2005-73, 79 FR 24192, 4/29/2014, effective 5/29/2014; FAC 2005-77, 79 FR 61746, 10/14/2014, effective 10/14/2014; FAC 2005-89, 81 FR 45833, 7/14/2016, effective 11/1/2016; FAC 2005-91, 81 FR 67763, 9/30/2016, effective 10/31/2016]

15.305 Proposal evaluation.

(a) Proposal evaluation is an assessment of the proposal and the offeror's ability to perform the prospective contract successfully. An agency shall evaluate competitive proposals and then assess their relative qualities solely on the factors and subfactors specified in the solicitation. Evaluations may be conducted using any rating method or combination of methods, including color or adjectival ratings, numerical weights, and ordinal rankings. The relative strengths, deficiencies, significant weaknesses, and risks supporting proposal evaluation shall be documented in the contract file.

(1) *Cost or price evaluation.* Normally, competition establishes price reasonableness. Therefore, when contracting on a firm-fixed-price or fixed-price with economic price adjustment basis, comparison of the proposed prices will usually satisfy the requirement to perform a price analysis, and a cost analysis need not be performed. In limited situations, a cost analysis may be appropriate to establish reasonableness of the otherwise successful offeror's price (see 15.403-1(c)(1)(i)(C)). When contracting on a cost-reimbursement basis, evaluations shall include a cost realism analysis to determine what the Government should realistically expect to pay for the proposed effort, the offeror's understanding of the work, and the offeror's ability to perform the contract. Cost realism analyses may also be used on fixed-price incentive contracts or, in exceptional cases, on other competitive fixed-price-type contracts (see 15.404-1(d)(3)) (See 37.115 for uncompensated overtime evaluation.). The contracting officer shall document the cost or price evaluation.

(2) *Past performance evaluation.*

(i) Past performance information is one indicator of an offeror's ability to perform the contract successfully. The currency and relevance of the information, source of the information, context of the data, and general trends in contractor's performance shall be considered. This comparative assessment of past performance information is separate from the responsibility determination required under Subpart 9.1.

(ii) The solicitation shall describe the approach for evaluating past performance, including evaluating offerors with no relevant performance history, and shall provide offerors an opportunity to identify past or current contracts (including Federal, State, and local government and private) for efforts similar to the Government requirement. The solicitation shall also authorize offerors to provide information on problems encountered on the identified contracts and the offeror's corrective actions. The Government shall consider this information, as well as information obtained from any other sources, when evaluating the offeror's past performance. The source selection authority shall determine the relevance of similar past performance information.

(iii) The evaluation should take into account past performance information regarding predecessor companies, key personnel who have relevant experience, or subcontractors that will perform major or critical aspects of the requirement when such information is relevant to the instant acquisition.

(iv) In the case of an offeror without a record of relevant past performance or for whom information on past performance is not available, the offeror may not be evaluated favorably or unfavorably on past performance.

(v) The evaluation should include the past performance of offerors in complying with subcontracting plan goals for small disadvantaged business (SDB) concerns (see subpart 19.7).

(3) *Technical evaluation.* When tradeoffs are performed (see 15.101-1), the source selection records shall include—

(i) An assessment of each offeror's ability to accomplish the technical requirements; and

(ii) A summary, matrix, or quantitative ranking, along with appropriate supporting narrative, of each technical proposal using the evaluation factors.

(4) *Cost information.* Cost information may be provided to members of the technical evaluation team in accordance with agency procedures.

(5) *Small business subcontracting evaluation.* Solicitations must be structured to give offers from small business concerns the highest rating for the evaluation factors in 15.304(c)(3)(ii) and (c)(4).

(b) The source selection authority may reject all proposals received in response to a solicitation, if doing so is in the best interest of the Government.

(c) For restrictions on the use of support contractor personnel in proposal evaluation, see 37.203(d).

[FAC 97-2, 62 FR 51224, 9/30/97, effective 10/10/97; FAC 97-7, 63 FR 36120, 7/1/98, effective 1/1/99, finalized without change, FAC 97-13, 7/2/99; FAC 97-14, 64 FR 51828, 9/24/99, effective 11/23/99; FAC 97-15, 64 FR 72414, 12/27/99, effective 12/27/99; FAC 97-19, 65 FR 46052, 7/26/2000, effective 7/26/2000; FAC 2005-38, 74 FR 65614, 12/10/2009, effective 12/10/2009; FAC 2005-77, 79 FR 61746, 10/14/2014, effective 10/14/2014; FAC 2019-03, 84 FR 27494, 6/12/2019, effective 7/12/2019]

15.306 Exchanges with offerors after receipt of proposals.

(a) *Clarifications and award without discussions.*

(1) Clarifications are limited exchanges, between the Government and offerors, that may occur when award without discussions is contemplated.

(2) If award will be made without conducting discussions, offerors may be given the opportunity to clarify certain aspects of proposals (e.g., the relevance of an offeror's past performance information and adverse past performance information to which the offeror has not previously had an opportunity to respond) or to resolve minor or clerical errors.

(3) Award may be made without discussions if the solicitation states that the Government intends to evaluate proposals and make award without discussions. If the solicitation contains such a notice and the Gov-

ernment determines it is necessary to conduct discussions, the rationale for doing so shall be documented in the contract file (see the provision at 52.215-1) (10 U.S.C. 2305(b)(4)(A)(ii) and 41 U.S.C. 3703(a)(2)).

(b) *Communications with offerors before establishment of the competitive range.* Communications are exchanges, between the Government and offerors, after receipt of proposals, leading to establishment of the competitive range. If a competitive range is to be established, these communications—

(1) Shall be limited to the offerors described in paragraphs (b)(1)(i) and (b)(1)(ii) of this section and—

(i) Shall be held with offerors whose past performance information is the determining factor preventing them from being placed within the competitive range. Such communications shall address adverse past performance information to which an offeror has not had a prior opportunity to respond; and

(ii) May only be held with those offerors (other than offerors under paragraph (b)(1)(i) of this section) whose exclusion from, or inclusion in, the competitive range is uncertain;

(2) May be conducted to enhance Government understanding of proposals; allow reasonable interpretation of the proposal; or facilitate the Government's evaluation process. Such communications shall not be used to cure proposal deficiencies or material omissions, materially alter the technical or cost elements of the proposal, and/or otherwise revise the proposal. Such communications may be considered in rating proposals for the purpose of establishing the competitive range;

(3) Are for the purpose of addressing issues that must be explored to determine whether a proposal should be placed in the competitive range. Such communications shall not provide an opportunity for the offeror to revise its proposal, but may address—

(i) Ambiguities in the proposal or other concerns (e.g., perceived deficiencies, weaknesses, errors, omissions, or mistakes (see 14.407)); and

(ii) Information relating to relevant past performance; and

(4) Shall address adverse past performance information to which the offeror has not previously had an opportunity to comment.

(c) *Competitive range.*

(1) Agencies shall evaluate all proposals in accordance with 15.305(a), and, if discussions are to be conducted, establish the competitive range. Based on the ratings of each proposal against all evaluation criteria, the contracting officer shall establish a competitive range comprised of all of the most highly rated proposals, unless the range is further reduced for purposes of efficiency pursuant to paragraph (c)(2) of this section.

(2) After evaluating all proposals in accordance with 15.305(a) and paragraph (c)(1) of this section, the contracting officer may determine that the number of most highly rated proposals that might otherwise be included in the competitive range exceeds the number at which an efficient competition can be conducted. Provided the solicitation notifies offerors that the competitive range can be limited for purposes of efficiency (see 52.215-1(f)(4)), the contracting officer may limit the number of proposals in the competitive range to the greatest number that will permit an efficient competition among the most highly rated proposals (10 U.S.C. 2305(b)(4) and 41 U.S.C. 3703).

(3) If the contracting officer, after complying with paragraph (d)(3) of this section, decides that an offeror's proposal should no longer be included in the competitive range, the proposal shall be eliminated from consideration for award. Written notice of this decision shall be provided to unsuccessful offerors in accordance with 15.503.

(4) Offerors excluded or otherwise eliminated from the competitive range may request a debriefing (see 15.505 and 15.506).

(d) *Exchanges with offerors after establishment of the competitive range.* Negotiations are exchanges, in either a competitive or sole source environment, between the Government and offerors, that are undertaken with the intent of allowing the offeror to revise its proposal. These negotiations may include bargaining. Bargaining includes persuasion, alteration of assumptions and positions, give-and-take, and may apply to price, schedule, technical requirements, type of contract, or other terms of a proposed contract. When negotiations are conducted in a competitive acquisition, they take place after establishment of the competitive range and are called discussions.

(1) Discussions are tailored to each offeror's proposal, and must be conducted by the contracting officer with each offeror within the competitive range.

(2) The primary objective of discussions is to maximize the Government's ability to obtain best value, based on the requirement and the evaluation factors set forth in the solicitation.

(3) At a minimum, the contracting officer must, subject to paragraphs (d)(5) and (e) of this section and 15.307(a), indicate to, or discuss with, each offeror still being considered for award, deficiencies, significant weaknesses, and adverse past performance information to which the offeror has not yet had an opportunity to respond. The contracting officer also is encouraged to discuss other aspects of the offeror's proposal that could, in the opinion of the contracting officer, be altered or explained to enhance materially the proposal's potential for award. However, the contracting officer is not required to discuss every area where the proposal could be improved. The scope and extent of discussions are a matter of contracting officer judgment.

(4) In discussing other aspects of the proposal, the Government may, in situations where the solicitation stated that evaluation credit would be given for technical solutions exceeding any mandatory minimums, negotiate with offerors for increased performance beyond any mandatory minimums, and the Government may suggest to offerors that have exceeded any mandatory minimums (in ways that are not integral to the design), that their proposals would be more competitive if the excesses were removed and the offered price decreased.

(5) If, after discussions have begun, an offeror originally in the competitive range is no longer considered to be among the most highly rated offerors being considered for award, that offeror may be eliminated from the competitive range whether or not all material aspects of the proposal have been discussed, or whether or not the offeror has been afforded an opportunity to submit a proposal revision (see 15.307(a) and 15.503(a)(1)).

(e) *Limits on exchanges.* Government personnel involved in the acquisition shall not engage in conduct that—

(1) Favors one offeror over another;

(2) Reveals an offeror's technical solution, including unique technology, innovative and unique uses of commercial items, or any information that would compromise an offeror's intellectual property to another offeror;

(3) Reveals an offeror's price without that offeror's permission. However, the contracting officer may inform an offeror that its price is considered by the Government to be too high, or too low, and reveal the results of the analysis supporting that conclusion. It is also permissible, at the Government's discretion, to indicate to all offerors the cost or price that the Government's price analysis, market research, and other reviews have identified as reasonable (41 U.S.C. 2102 and 2107);

(4) Reveals the names of individuals providing reference information about an offeror's past performance; or

(5) Knowingly furnishes source selection information in violation of 3.104 and 41 U.S.C. 2102 and 2107.

[FAC 97-2, 62 FR 51224, 9/30/97, effective 10/10/97; FAC 2001-02, 66 FR 65347, 12/18/2001, effective 2/19/2002; FAC 2005-73, 79 FR 24192, 4/29/2014, effective 5/29/2014]

15.307 Proposal revisions.

(a) If an offeror's proposal is eliminated or otherwise removed from the competitive range, no further revisions to that offeror's proposal shall be accepted or considered.

(b) The contracting officer may request or allow proposal revisions to clarify and document understandings reached during negotiations. At the conclusion of discussions, each offeror still in the competitive range shall be given an opportunity to submit a final proposal revision. The contracting officer is required to establish a common cut-off date only for receipt of final proposal revisions. Requests for final proposal revisions shall advise offerors that the final proposal revisions shall be in writing and that the Government intends to make award without obtaining further revisions.

[FAC 97-2, 62 FR 51224, 9/30/97, effective 10/10/97]

15.308 Source selection decision.

The source selection authority's (SSA) decision shall be based on a comparative assessment of proposals against all source selection criteria in the solicitation. While the SSA may use reports and analyses prepared by others, the source selection decision shall represent the SSA's independent judgment. The source selection decision shall be documented, and the documentation shall include the rationale for any business judgments and tradeoffs made or relied on by the SSA, including benefits associated with additional costs. Although the rationale for the selection decision must be documented, that documentation need not quantify the tradeoffs that led to the decision.

[FAC 97-2, 62 FR 51224, 9/30/97, effective 10/10/97]

SUBPART 15.4—CONTRACT PRICING

15.400 Scope of subpart.

This subpart prescribes the cost and price negotiation policies and procedures for pricing negotiated prime contracts (including subcontracts) and contract modifications, including modifications to contracts awarded by sealed bidding.

[FAC 97-2, 62 FR 51224, 9/30/97, effective 10/10/97]

15.401 Definitions.

As used in this subpart—

Price means cost plus any fee or profit applicable to the contract type.

Subcontract (except as used in 15.407-2) also includes a transfer of commercial items between divisions, subsidiaries, or affiliates of a contractor or a subcontractor (10 U.S.C. 2306a(h)(2) and 41 U.S.C. 3501(a)(3)).

[FAC 97-2, 62 FR 51224, 9/30/97, effective 10/10/97; FAC 97-22, 66 FR 2116, 1/10/2001, effective 3/12/2001; Delay of effective date, 66 FR 14259, 3/9/2001, effective 5/11/2001; FAC 2001-02, 66 FR 65347, 12/18/2001, effective 2/19/2002; FAC 2005-73, 79 FR 24192, 4/29/2014, effective 5/29/2014]

15.402 Pricing policy.

Contracting officers shall—

(a) Purchase supplies and services from responsible sources at fair and reasonable prices. In establishing the reasonableness of the offered prices, the contracting officer—

(1) Shall obtain certified cost or pricing data when required by 15.403-4, along with data other than certified cost or pricing data as necessary to establish a fair and reasonable price; or

(2) When certified cost or pricing data are not required by 15.403-4, shall obtain data other than certified cost or pricing data as necessary to establish a fair and reasonable price, generally using the following order of preference in determining the type of data required:

(i) No additional data from the offeror, if the price is based on adequate price competition, except as provided by 15.403-3(b).

(ii) Data other than certified cost or pricing data such as—

(A) Data related to prices (*e.g.*, established catalog or market prices, sales to non-governmental and governmental entities), relying first on data available within the Government; second, on data obtained from sources other than the offeror; and, if necessary, on data obtained from the offeror. When obtaining data from the offeror is necessary, unless an exception under 15.403-1(b)(1) or (2) applies, such data submitted by the offeror shall include, at a minimum, appropriate data on the prices at which the same or similar items have been sold previously, adequate for evaluating the reasonableness of the price.

(B) Cost data to the extent necessary for the contracting officer to determine a fair and reasonable price.

(3) Obtain the type and quantity of data necessary to establish a fair and reasonable price, but not more data than is necessary. Requesting unnecessary data can lead to increased proposal preparation costs, generally extend acquisition lead time, and consume additional contractor and Government resources. Use techniques such as, but not limited to, price analysis, cost analysis, and/or cost realism analysis to establish a fair and reasonable price. If a fair and reasonable price cannot be established by the contracting officer from the analyses of the data obtained or submitted to date, the contracting officer shall require the submission of additional data sufficient for the contracting officer to support the determination of the fair and reasonable price.

(b) Price each contract separately and independently and not—

(1) Use proposed price reductions under other contracts as an evaluation factor; or

(2) Consider losses or profits realized or anticipated under other contracts.

(c) Not include in a contract price any amount for a specified contingency to the extent that the contract provides for a price adjustment based upon the occurrence of that contingency.

[FAC 97-2, 62 FR 51224, 9/30/97, effective 10/10/97; FAC 97-22, 66 FR 2116, 1/10/2001, effective 3/12/2001; Delay of effective date, 66 FR 14259, 3/9/2001, effective 5/11/2001; FAC 2005-45, 75 FR 53135, 8/30/2010, effective 10/1/2010; FAC 2005-55, 77 FR 204, 1/3/2012, effective 1/3/2012]

15.403 Obtaining certified cost or pricing data. (No Text)

15.403-1 Prohibition on obtaining certified cost or pricing data (10 U.S.C. 2306a and 41 U.S.C. chapter 35).

(a) Certified cost or pricing data shall not be obtained for acquisitions at or below the simplified acquisition threshold.

(b) *Exceptions to certified cost or pricing data requirements.* The contracting officer shall not require certified cost or pricing data to support any action (contracts, subcontracts, or modifications) (but may require data other than certified cost or pricing data as defined in FAR 2.101 to support a determination of a fair and reasonable price or cost realism)—

(1) When the contracting officer determines that prices agreed upon are based on adequate price competition (see standards in paragraph (c)(1) of this subsection);

(2) When the contracting officer determines that prices agreed upon are based on prices set by law or regulation (see standards in paragraph (c)(2) of this subsection);

(3) When a commercial item is being acquired (see standards in paragraph (c)(3) of this subsection);

(4) When a waiver has been granted (see standards in paragraph (c)(4) of this subsection); or

(5) When modifying a contract or subcontract for commercial items (see standards in paragraph (c)(3) of this subsection).

(c) *Standards for exceptions from certified cost or pricing data requirements—*

(1) *Adequate price competition.* (i) A price is based on adequate price competition when—

(A) Two or more responsible offerors, competing independently, submit priced offers that satisfy the Government's expressed requirement;

(B) Award will be made to the offeror whose proposal represents the best value (see 2.101) where price is a substantial factor in source selection; and

(C) There is no finding that the price of the otherwise successful offeror is unreasonable. Any finding that the price is unreasonable must be supported by a statement of the facts and approved at a level above the contracting officer.

(ii) For agencies other than DoD, NASA, and the Coast Guard, a price is also based on adequate price competition when-

(A) There was a reasonable expectation, based on market research or other assessment, that two or more responsible offerors, competing independently, would submit priced offers in response to the solicitation's expressed requirement, even though only one offer is received from a responsible offeror and if—

(1) Based on the offer received, the contracting officer can reasonably conclude that the offer was submitted with the expectation of competition, *e.g.*, circumstances indicate that—

(i) The offeror believed that at least one other offeror was capable of submitting a meaningful offer; and

(ii) The offeror had no reason to believe that other potential offerors did not intend to submit an offer; and

(2) The determination that the proposed price is based on adequate price competition and is reasonable has been approved at a level above the contracting officer; or

(B) Price analysis clearly demonstrates that the proposed price is reasonable in comparison with current or recent prices for the same or similar items, adjusted to reflect changes in market conditions, economic conditions, quantities, or terms and conditions under contracts that resulted from adequate price competition.

(2) *Prices set by law or regulation.* Pronouncements in the form of periodic rulings, reviews, or similar actions of a governmental body, or embodied in the laws, are sufficient to set a price.

(3) *Commercial items.*

(i) Any acquisition of an item that the contracting officer determines meets the commercial item definition in 2.101, or any modification, as defined in paragraph (3)(i) of that definition, that does not change the item from a commercial item to a noncommercial item, is exempt from the requirement for certified cost or pricing data. If the contracting officer determines that an item claimed to be commercial is, in fact, not commercial and that no other exception or waiver applies, (*e.g.* the acquisition is not based on adequate price competition; the acquisition is not based on prices set by law or regulation; and the acquisition exceeds the threshold for the submission of certified cost or pricing data at 15.403-4(a)(1)) the contracting officer shall require submission of certified cost or pricing data.

(ii) In accordance with 41 U.S.C. 3501:

(A) When purchasing services that are not offered and sold competitively in substantial quantities in the commercial marketplace, but are of a type offered and sold competitively in substantial quantities in the commercial marketplace, they may be considered commercial items (thus meeting the purpose of 41 U.S.C chapter 35 and 10 U.S.C. 2306a for truth in negotiations) only if the contracting officer determines in writing that the offeror has submitted sufficient information to evaluate, through price analysis, the reasonableness of the price of such services.

(B) In order to make this determination, the contracting officer may request the offeror to submit prices paid for the same or similar commercial items under comparable terms and conditions by both Government and commercial customers; and

(C) If the contracting officer determines that the information described in paragraph (c)(3)(ii)(B) of this section is not sufficient to determine the reasonableness of price, other relevant information regarding the basis for price or cost, including information on labor costs, material costs and overhead rates may be requested.

(iii) The following requirements apply to minor modifications defined in paragraph (3)(ii) of the definition of a commercial item at 2.101 that do not change the item from a commercial item to a noncommercial item:

(A) For acquisitions funded by any agency other than DoD, NASA, or Coast Guard, such modifications of a commercial item are exempt from the requirement for submission of certified cost or pricing data.

(B) For acquisitions funded by DoD, NASA, or Coast Guard, such modifications of a commercial item are exempt from the requirement for submission of certified cost or pricing data provided the total price of all such modifications under a particular contract action does not exceed the greater of the threshold for obtaining certified cost or pricing data in 15.403-4 or 5 percent of the total price of the contract at the time of contract award.

(C) For acquisitions funded by DoD, NASA, or Coast Guard such modifications of a commercial item are not exempt from the requirement for submission of certified cost or pricing data on the basis of the exemption provided for at 15.403-1(c)(3) if the total price of all such modifications under a particular contract action exceeds the greater of the threshold for obtaining certified cost or pricing data in 15.403-4 or 5 percent of the total price of the contract at the time of contract award.

(iv) Any acquisition for noncommercial supplies or services treated as commercial items at 12.102(f)(1), except sole source contracts greater than $19 million, is exempt from the requirements for certified cost or pricing data (41 U.S.C. 1903).

(4) *Waivers.* The head of the contracting activity (HCA) may, without power of delegation, waive the requirement for submission of certified cost or pricing data in exceptional cases. The authorization for the waiver and the supporting rationale shall be in writing. The HCA may consider waiving the requirement if the price can be determined to be fair and reasonable without submission of certified cost or pricing data. For example, if certified cost or pricing data were furnished on previous production buys and the contracting officer determines such data are sufficient, when combined with updated data, a waiver may be granted. If the HCA has waived the requirement for submission of certified cost or pricing data, the contractor or higher-tier subcontractor to whom the waiver relates shall be considered as having been required to provide certified cost or pricing data. Consequently, award of any lower-tier subcontract expected to exceed the certified cost or pricing data threshold requires the submission of certified cost or pricing data unless—

(i) An exception otherwise applies to the subcontract; or

(ii) The waiver specifically includes the subcontract and the rationale supporting the waiver for that subcontract.

[FAC 97-2, 62 FR 51224, 9/30/97, effective 10/10/97; FAC 97-11, 64 FR 10530, 3/4/99, effective 5/3/99; FAC 97-14, 64 FR 51828, 9/24/99, effective 9/24/99, finalized without change, FAC 97-17, 65 FR 24316, 4/25/2000; FAC 97-22, 66 FR 2116, 1/10/2001, effective 3/12/2001; Delay of effective date, 66 FR 14259, 3/9/2001, effective 5/11/2001; FAC 2001-20, 69 FR 8311, 2/23/2004, effective 2/23/2004; FAC 2001-26, 69 FR 76350, 12/20/2004, effective 1/19/2005; FAC 2005-04, 70 FR 33659, 6/8/2005, effective 6/8/2005; FAC 2005-10, 71 FR 36927, 6/28/2006, effective 7/28/2006; FAC 2005-13, 71 FR 57363, 9/28/2006, effective 9/28/2006; FAC 2005-31, 74 FR 11826, 3/19/2009, effective 3/19/2009; FAC 2005-37, 74 FR 52852, 10/14/2009, effective 10/14/2009; FAC 2005-39, 75 FR 13414, 3/19/2010, effective 3/19/2010; FAC 2005-45, 75 FR 53129, 53135, 8/30/2010, effective 10/1/2010; FAC 2005-50, 76 FR 14568, 3/16/2011, effective 3/16/2011; FAC 2005-55, 77 FR 204, 1/3/2012, effective 1/3/2012; FAC 2005-73, 79 FR 24192, 4/29/2014, effective 5/29/2014; FAC 2005-83, 80 FR 38293, 7/2/2015, effective 10/1/2015; FAC 2019-03, 84 FR 27494, 6/12/2019, effective 7/12/2019]

15.403-2 Other circumstances where certified cost or pricing data are not required.

(a) The exercise of an option at the price established at contract award or initial negotiation does not require submission of certified cost or pricing data.

(b) Certified cost or pricing data are not required for proposals used solely for overrun funding or interim billing price adjustments.

[FAC 97-2, 62 FR 51224, 9/30/97, effective 10/10/97; FAC 2005-45, 75 FR 53135, 8/30/2010, effective 10/1/2010]

15.403-3 Requiring data other than certified cost or pricing data.

(a)(1) In those acquisitions that do not require certified cost or pricing data, the contracting officer shall—

(i) Obtain whatever data are available from Government or other secondary sources and use that data in determining a fair and reasonable price;

(ii) Require submission of data other than certified cost or pricing data, as defined in 2.101, from the offeror to the extent necessary to determine a fair and reasonable price (10 U.S.C. 2306a(d)(1) and 41 U.S.C. 3505(a)) if the contracting officer determines that adequate data from sources other than the offeror are not available. This includes requiring data from an offeror to support a cost realism analysis;

(iii) Consider whether cost data are necessary to determine a fair and reasonable price when there is not adequate price competition;

(iv) Require that the data submitted by the offeror include, at a minimum, appropriate data on the prices at which the same item or similar items have previously been sold, adequate for determining the reasonableness of the price unless an exception under 15.403-1(b)(1) or (2) applies; and

(v) Consider the guidance in section 3.3, chapter 3, volume I, of the Contract Pricing Reference Guide cited at 15.404-1(a)(7) to determine the data an offeror shall be required to submit.

(2) The contractor's format for submitting the data should be used (see 15.403-5(b)(2)).

(3) The contracting officer shall ensure that data used to support price negotiations are sufficiently current to permit negotiation of a fair and reasonable price. Requests for updated offeror data should be limited to data that affect the adequacy of the proposal for negotiations, such as changes in price lists.

(4) As specified in section 808 of the Strom Thurmond National Defense Authorization Act for Fiscal Year 1999 (Pub. L. 105-261), an offeror who does not comply with a requirement to submit data for a contract or subcontract in accordance with paragraph (a)(1) of this subsection is ineligible for award unless the HCA determines that it is in the best interest of the Government to make the award to that offeror, based on consideration of the following:

(i) The effort made to obtain the data.

(ii) The need for the item or service.

(iii) Increased cost or significant harm to the Government if award is not made.

(b) *Adequate price competition.* When adequate price competition exists (see 15.403-1(c)(1)), generally no additional data are necessary to determine the reasonableness of price. However, if there are unusual circumstances where it is concluded that additional data are necessary to determine the reasonableness of price, the contracting officer shall, to the maximum extent practicable, obtain the additional data from sources other than the offeror. In addition, the contracting officer should request data to determine the cost realism of competing offers or to evaluate competing approaches.

(c) *Commercial items.* (1) At a minimum, the contracting officer must use price analysis to determine whether the price is fair and reasonable whenever the contracting officer acquires a commercial item (see 15.404-1(b)). The fact that a price is included in a catalog does not, in and of itself, make it fair and reasonable. If the contracting officer cannot determine whether an offered price is fair and reasonable, even after obtaining additional data from sources other than the offeror, then the contracting officer shall require the offeror to submit data other than certified cost or pricing data to support further analysis (see 15.404-1). This data may include history of sales to non-governmental and governmental entities, cost data, or any other information the contracting officer requires to determine the price is fair and reasonable. Unless an exception under 15.403-1(b)(1) or (2) applies, the contracting officer shall require that the data submitted by the offeror include, at a minimum, appropriate data on the prices at which the same item or similar items have previously been sold, adequate for determining the reasonableness of the price.

(2) *Limitations relating to commercial items (10 U.S.C. 2306a(d)(2) and 41 U.S.C. 3505(b)).* (i) The contracting officer shall limit requests for sales data relating to commercial items to data for the same or similar items during a relevant time period.

(ii) The contracting officer shall, to the maximum extent practicable, limit the scope of the request for data relating to commercial items to include only data that are in the form regularly maintained by the offeror as part of its commercial operations.

(iii) The Government shall not disclose outside the Government data obtained relating to commercial items that is exempt from disclosure under 24.202(a) or the Freedom of Information Act (5 U.S.C. 552(b)).

(3) For services that are not offered and sold competitively in substantial quantities in the commercial marketplace, but are of a type offered and sold competitively in substantial quantities in the commercial marketplace, see 15.403-1(c)(3)(ii).

[FAC 97-2, 62 FR 51224, 9/30/97, effective 10/10/97; FAC 97-14, 64 FR 51828, 9/24/99, effective 9/24/99; FAC 97-17, 65 FR 24316, 4/25/2000, effective 4/25/2000; FAC 2005-37, 74 FR 52852, 10/14/2009, effective 10/14/2009; FAC 2005-45, 75 FR 53135, 8/30/2010, effective 10/1/2010; FAC 2005-50, 76 FR 14568, 3/16/2011, effective 3/16/2011; FAC 2005-73, 79 FR 24192, 4/29/2014, effective 5/29/2014]

15.403-4 Requiring certified cost or pricing data (10 U.S.C. 2306a and 41 U.S.C. chapter 35).

(a)(1) The contracting officer shall obtain certified cost or pricing data only if the contracting officer concludes that none of the exceptions in 15.403-1(b) applies. However, if the contracting officer has reason to believe exceptional circumstances exist and has sufficient data available to determine a fair and reasonable price, then the contracting officer should consider requesting a waiver under the exception at 15.403-1(b)(4). The threshold for obtaining certified cost or pricing data is $750,000. Unless an exception applies, certified cost or pricing data are required before accomplishing any of the following actions expected to exceed the current threshold or, in the case of existing contracts, the threshold specified in the contract:

(i) The award of any negotiated contract (except for undefinitized actions such as letter contracts).

(ii) The award of a subcontract at any tier, if the contractor and each higher-tier subcontractor were required to furnish certified cost or pricing data (but see waivers at 15.403-1(c)(4)).

(iii) The modification of any sealed bid or negotiated contract (whether or not certified cost or pricing data were initially required) or any subcontract covered by paragraph (a)(1)(ii) of this subsection. Price adjustment amounts must consider both increases and decreases (*e.g.,* a $200,000 modification resulting from a reduction of $500,000 and an increase of $300,000 is a pricing adjustment exceeding $750,000). This requirement does not apply when unrelated and separately priced changes for which certified cost or pricing data would not otherwise be required are included for administrative convenience in the same modification. Negotiated final pricing actions (such as termination settlements and total final price agreements for fixed-price incentive and redeterminable contracts) are contract modifications requiring certified cost or pricing data if—

(A) The total final price agreement for such settlements or agreements exceeds the pertinent threshold set forth at paragraph (a)(1) of this subsection; or

(B) The partial termination settlement plus the estimate to complete the continued portion of the contract exceeds the pertinent threshold set forth at paragraph (a)(1) of this subsection (see 49.105(c)(15)).

(2) Unless prohibited because an exception at 15.403-1(b) applies, the head of the contracting activity, without power of delegation, may authorize the contracting officer to obtain certified cost or pricing data for pricing actions below the pertinent threshold in paragraph (a)(1) of this subsection, provided the action exceeds the simplified acquisition threshold. The head of the contracting activity shall justify the requirement for certified cost or pricing data. The documentation shall include a written finding that certified cost or pricing data are necessary to determine whether the price is fair and reasonable and the facts supporting that finding.

(b) When certified cost or pricing data are required, the contracting officer shall require the contractor or prospective contractor to submit to the contracting officer (and to have any subcontractor or prospective subcontractor submit to the prime contractor or appropriate subcontractor tier) the following in support of any proposal:

(1) The certified cost or pricing data and data other than certified cost or pricing data required by the contracting officer to determine that the price is fair and reasonable.

(2) A Certificate of Current Cost or Pricing Data, in the format specified in 15.406-2, certifying that to the best of its knowledge and belief, the cost or pricing data were accurate, complete, and current as of the date of agreement on price or, if applicable, an earlier date agreed upon between the parties that is as close as practicable to the date of agreement on price.

(c) If certified cost or pricing data are requested and submitted by an offeror, but an exception is later found to apply, the data must not be considered certified cost or pricing data as defined in 2.101 and must not be certified in accordance with 15.406-2.

(d) The requirements of this subsection also apply to contracts entered into by an agency on behalf of a foreign government.

[FAC 97-2, 62 FR 51224, 9/30/97, effective 10/10/97; FAC 97-20, 65 FR 60542, 10/11/2000, effective 10/11/2000; FAC 97-22, 66 FR 2116, 1/10/2001, effective 3/12/2001; Delay of effective date, 66 FR 14259, 3/9/2001, effective 5/11/2001; FAC 2005-13, 71 FR 57363, 9/28/2006, effective 9/28/2006; FAC 2005-45, 75 FR 53129, 8/30/2010, effective 10/1/2010; FAC 2005-73, 79 FR 24192, 4/29/2014, effective 5/29/2014; FAC 2005-83, 80 FR 38293, 7/2/2015, effective 10/1/2015]

15.403-5 Instructions for submission of certified cost or pricing data other than certified cost or pricing data.

(a) Taking into consideration the policy at 15.402, the contracting officer shall specify in the solicitation (see 15.408 (l) and (m))—

(1) Whether certified cost or pricing data are required;

(2) That, in lieu of submitting certified cost or pricing data, the offeror may submit a request for exception from the requirement to submit certified cost or pricing data;

(3) Any requirement for data other than certified cost or pricing data; and

(4) The requirement for necessary preaward or postaward access to offeror's records.

(b) (1) *Format for submission of certified cost or pricing data.* When certification is required, the contracting officer may require submission of certified cost or pricing data in the format indicated in Table 15-2 of 15.408, specify an alternative format, or permit submission in the contractor's format (See 15.408 (l) (1)), unless the data are required to be submitted on one of the termination forms specified in subpart 49.6.

(2) *Format for submission of data other than certified cost or pricing data.* When required by the contracting officer, data other than certified cost or pricing data may be submitted in the offeror's own format unless the contracting officer decides that use of a specific format is essential for evaluating and determining that the price is fair and reasonable and the format has been described in the solicitation.

(3) *Format for submission of data supporting forward pricing rate agreements.* Data supporting forward pricing rate agreements or final indirect cost proposals shall be submitted in a form acceptable to the contracting officer.

[FAC 97-2, 62 FR 51224, 9/30/97, effective 10/10/97; FAC 2005-45, 75 FR 53129, 8/30/2010, effective 10/1/2010]

15.404 Proposal analysis. (No Text)

15.404-1 Proposal analysis techniques.

(a) *General.* The objective of proposal analysis is to ensure that the final agreed-to price is fair and reasonable.

(1) The contracting officer is responsible for evaluating the reasonableness of the offered prices. The analytical techniques and procedures described in this section may be used, singly or in combination with others, to ensure that the final price is fair and reasonable. The complexity and circumstances of each acquisition should determine the level of detail of the analysis required.

(2) Price analysis shall be used when certified cost or pricing data are not required (see paragraph (b) of this subsection and 15.404-3).

(3) Cost analysis shall be used to evaluate the reasonableness of individual cost elements when certified cost or pricing data are required. Price analysis should be used to verify that the overall price offered is fair and reasonable.

(4) Cost analysis may also be used to evaluate data other than certified cost or pricing data to determine cost reasonableness or cost realism when a fair and reasonable price cannot be determined through price analysis alone for commercial or non-commercial items.

(5) The contracting officer may request the advice and assistance of other experts to ensure that an appropriate analysis is performed.

(6) Recommendations or conclusions regarding the Government's review or analysis of an offeror's or contractor's proposal shall not be disclosed to the offeror or contractor without the concurrence of the contracting officer. Any discrepancy or mistake of fact (such as duplications, omissions, and errors in computation) contained in the certified cost or pricing data or data other than certified cost or pricing data submitted in support of a proposal shall be brought to the contracting officer's attention for appropriate action.

(7) The Air Force Institute of Technology (AFIT) and the Federal Acquisition Institute (FAI) jointly prepared a five-volume set of Contract Pricing Reference Guides to guide pricing and negotiation personnel. The five guides are: I Price Analysis, II Quantitative Techniques for Contract Pricing, III Cost Analysis, IV Advanced Issues in Contract Pricing, and V Federal Contract Negotiation Techniques. These references provide detailed discussion and examples applying pricing policies to pricing problems. They are to be used for instruction and professional guidance. However, they are not directive and should be considered informational only. They are available via the internet at *http://www.acq.osd.mil/dpap/cpic/cp/contract_pricing_reference guides.html.*

(b) *Price analysis for commercial and non-commercial items* (1) Price analysis is the process of examining and evaluating a proposed price without evaluating its separate cost elements and proposed profit. Unless an exception from the requirement to obtain certified cost or pricing data applies under 15.403-1(b)(1) or (b)(2), at a minimum, the contracting officer shall obtain appropriate data, without certification, on the prices at which the same or similar items have previously been sold and determine if the data is adequate for evaluating the reasonableness of the price. Price analysis may include evaluating data other than certified cost or pricing data obtained from the offeror or contractor when there is no other means for determining a fair and reasonable price. Contracting officers shall obtain data other than certified cost or pricing data from the offeror or contractor for all acquisitions (including commercial item acquisitions), if that is the contracting officer's only means to determine the price to be fair and reasonable.

(2) The Government may use various price analysis techniques and procedures to ensure a fair and reasonable price. Examples of such techniques include, but are not limited to, the following:

(i) Comparison of proposed prices received in response to the solicitation. Normally, adequate price competition establishes a fair and reasonable price (see 15.403-1(c)(1)).

(ii) Comparison of the proposed prices to historical prices paid, whether by the Government or other than the Government, for the same or similar items. This method may be used for commercial items including those "of a type" or requiring minor modifications.

(A) The prior price must be a valid basis for comparison. If there has been a significant time lapse between the last acquisition and the present one, if the terms and conditions of the acquisition are significantly different, or if the reasonableness of the prior price is uncertain, then the prior price may not be a valid basis for comparison.

(B) The prior price must be adjusted to account for materially differing terms and conditions, quantities and market and economic factors. For similar items, the contracting officer must also adjust the prior price to account for material differences between the similar item and the item being procured.

(C) Expert technical advice should be obtained when analyzing similar items, or commercial items that are "of a type" or requiring minor modifications, to ascertain the magnitude of changes required and to assist in pricing the required changes.

(iii) Use of parametric estimating methods/application of rough yardsticks (such as dollars per pound or per horsepower, or other units) to highlight significant inconsistencies that warrant additional pricing inquiry.

(iv) Comparison with competitive published price lists, published market prices of commodities, similar indexes, and discount or rebate arrangements.

(v) Comparison of proposed prices with independent Government cost estimates.

(vi) Comparison of proposed prices with prices obtained through market research for the same or similar items.

(vii) Analysis of data other than certified cost or pricing data (as defined at 2.101) provided by the offeror.

(3) The first two techniques at 15.404-1(b)(2) are the preferred techniques. However, if the contracting officer determines that information on competitive proposed prices or previous contract prices is not available or is insufficient to determine that the price is fair and reasonable, the contracting officer may use any of the remaining techniques as appropriate to the circumstances applicable to the acquisition.

(4) Value analysis can give insight into the relative worth of a product and the Government may use it in conjunction with the price analysis techniques listed in paragraph (b)(2) of this section.

(c) *Cost analysis.*

(1) Cost analysis is the review and evaluation of any separate cost elements and profit or fee in an offeror's or contractor's proposal, as needed to determine a fair and reasonable price or to determine cost realism, and the application of judgment to determine how well the proposed costs represent what the cost of the contract should be, assuming reasonable economy and efficiency.

(2) The Government may use various cost analysis techniques and procedures to ensure a fair and reasonable price, given the circumstances of the acquisition. Such techniques and procedures include the following:

(i) Verification of cost data or pricing data and evaluation of cost elements, including—

(A) The necessity for, and reasonableness of, proposed costs, including allowances for contingencies;

(B) Projection of the offeror's cost trends, on the basis of current and historical cost data or pricing data;

(C) Reasonableness of estimates generated by appropriately calibrated and validated parametric models or cost-estimating relationships; and

(D) The application of audited or negotiated indirect cost rates, labor rates, and cost of money or other factors.

(ii) Evaluating the effect of the offeror's current practices on future costs. In conducting this evaluation, the contracting officer shall ensure that the effects of inefficient or uneconomical past practices are not projected into the future. In pricing production of recently developed complex equipment, the contracting officer should perform a trend analysis of basic labor and materials, even in periods of relative price stability.

(iii) Comparison of costs proposed by the offeror for individual cost elements with—

(A) Actual costs previously incurred by the same offeror;

(B) Previous cost estimates from the offeror or from other offerors for the same or similar items;

(C) Other cost estimates received in response to the Government's request;

(D) Independent Government cost estimates by technical personnel; and

(E) Forecasts of planned expenditures.

(iv) Verification that the offeror's cost submissions are in accordance with the contract cost principles and procedures in part 31 and, when applicable, the requirements and procedures in 48 CFR Chapter 99 (Appendix to the FAR looseleaf edition), Cost Accounting Standards.

(v) Review to determine whether any cost data or pricing data, necessary to make the offeror's proposal suitable for negotiation, have not been either submitted or identified in writing by the offeror. If there are such data, the contracting officer shall attempt to obtain and use them in the negotiations or make satisfactory allowance for the incomplete data.

(vi) Analysis of the results of any make-or-buy program reviews, in evaluating subcontract costs (see 15.407-2).

(d) *Cost realism analysis*.

(1) Cost realism analysis is the process of independently reviewing and evaluating specific elements of each offeror's proposed cost estimate to determine whether the estimated proposed cost elements are realistic for the work to be performed; reflect a clear understanding of the requirements; and are consistent with the unique methods of performance and materials described in the offeror's technical proposal.

(2) Cost realism analyses shall be performed on cost-reimbursement contracts to determine the probable cost of performance for each offeror.

(i) The probable cost may differ from the proposed cost and should reflect the Government's best estimate of the cost of any contract that is most likely to result from the offeror's proposal. The probable cost shall be used for purposes of evaluation to determine the best value.

(ii) The probable cost is determined by adjusting each offeror's proposed cost, and fee when appropriate, to reflect any additions or reductions in cost elements to realistic levels based on the results of the cost realism analysis.

(3) Cost realism analyses may also be used on competitive fixed-price incentive contracts or, in exceptional cases, on other competitive fixed-price-type contracts when new requirements may not be fully understood by competing offerors, there are quality concerns, or past experience indicates that contractors' proposed costs have resulted in quality or service shortfalls. Results of the analysis may be used in performance risk assessments and responsibility determinations. However, proposals shall be evaluated using the criteria in the solicitation, and the offered prices shall not be adjusted as a result of the analysis.

(e) *Technical analysis*.

(1) The contracting officer should request that personnel having specialized knowledge, skills, experience, or capability in engineering, science, or management perform a technical analysis of the proposed types and quantities of materials, labor, processes, special tooling, equipment or real property, the reasonableness of scrap and spoilage, and other associated factors set forth in the proposal(s) in order to determine the need for and reasonableness of the proposed resources, assuming reasonable economy and efficiency.

(2) At a minimum, the technical analysis should examine the types and quantities of material proposed and the need for the types and quantities of labor hours and the labor mix. Any other data that may be pertinent to an assessment of the offeror's ability to accomplish the technical requirements or to the cost or price analysis of the service or product being proposed should also be included in the analysis.

(3) The contracting officer should request technical assistance in evaluating pricing related to items that are "similar to" items being purchased, or commercial items that are "of a type" or requiring minor modifications, to ascertain the magnitude of changes required and to assist in pricing the required changes.

(f) *Unit prices*.

(1) Except when pricing an item on the basis of adequate price competition or catalog or market price, unit prices shall reflect the intrinsic value of an item or service and shall be in proportion to an item's base cost

(*e.g.*, manufacturing or acquisition costs). Any method of distributing costs to line items that distorts the unit prices shall not be used. For example, distributing costs equally among line items is not acceptable except when there is little or no variation in base cost.

(2) Except for the acquisition of commercial items, contracting officers shall require that offerors identify in their proposals those items of supply that they will not manufacture or to which they will not contribute significant value, unless adequate price competition is expected (10 U.S.C. 2306a(b)(1)(A)(i) and 41 U.S.C. 3503(a)(1)(A)). Such information shall be used to determine whether the intrinsic value of an item has been distorted through application of overhead and whether such items should be considered for breakout. The contracting officer should require such information in all other negotiated contracts when appropriate.

(g) *Unbalanced pricing.*

(1) Unbalanced pricing may increase performance risk and could result in payment of unreasonably high prices. Unbalanced pricing exists when, despite an acceptable total evaluated price, the price of one or more line items is significantly over or understated as indicated by the application of cost or price analysis techniques. The greatest risks associated with unbalanced pricing occur when—

(i) Startup work, mobilization, first articles, or first article testing are separate line items;

(ii) Base quantities and option quantities are separate line items; or

(iii) The evaluated price is the aggregate of estimated quantities to be ordered under separate line items of an indefinite-delivery contract.

(2) All offers with separately priced line items or subline items shall be analyzed to determine if the prices are unbalanced. If cost or price analysis techniques indicate that an offer is unbalanced, the contracting officer shall—

(i) Consider the risks to the Government associated with the unbalanced pricing in determining the competitive range and in making the source selection decision; and

(ii) Consider whether award of the contract will result in paying unreasonably high prices for contract performance.

(3) An offer may be rejected if the contracting officer determines that the lack of balance poses an unacceptable risk to the Government.

(h) *Review and justification of pass-through contracts.* (1) The requirements of this paragraph (h) are applicable to all agencies. The requirements apply by law to the Department of Defense, the Department of State, and the United States Agency for International Development, per section 802 of the National Defense Authorization Act (NDAA) for Fiscal Year 2013. The requirements apply as a matter of policy to other Federal agencies.

(2) Except as provided in paragraph (h)(3) of this section, when an offeror for a contract or a task or delivery order informs the contracting officer pursuant to 52.215–22 that it intends to award subcontracts for more than 70 percent of the total cost of work to be performed under the contract, task or delivery order, the contracting officer shall—

(i) Consider the availability of alternative contract vehicles and the feasibility of contracting directly with a subcontractor or subcontractors that will perform the bulk of the work. If such alternative approaches are selected, any resulting solicitations shall be issued in accordance with the competition requirements under FAR part 6;

(ii) Make a written determination that the contracting approach selected is in the best interest of the Government; and

(iii) Document the basis for such determination.

(3) Contract actions awarded pursuant to subparts 19.5, 19.8, 19.13, 19.14, or 19.15 are exempt from the requirements of this paragraph (h) (see section 1615 of the National Defense Authorization Act for Fiscal Year 2014 (Pub. L. 113–66)).

[FAC 97-2, 62 FR 51224, 9/30/97, effective 10/10/97; FAC 97-9, 63 FR 58587, 10/30/98,

effective 10/30/98; FAC 97-14, 64 FR 51828, 9/24/99, effective 9/24/99, finalized without change, FAC 97-17, 65 FR 24316, 4/25/2000; FAC 97-16, 65 FR 16274, 3/27/2000, effective 3/27/2000; FAC 2005-14, 71 FR 67779, 11/22/2006, effective 11/22/2006; FAC 2005-17, 72 FR 27364, 5/15/2007, effective 6/14/2007; FAC 2005-27, 73 FR 54016, 9/17/2008, effective 9/17/2008; FAC 2005-45, 75 FR 53129, 8/30/2010, effective 10/1/2010; FAC 2005-61, 77 FR 56743, 9/13/2012, effective 9/13/2012; FAC 2005-67, 78 FR 37690, 6/21/2013, effective 7/22/2013; FAC 2005-73, 79 FR 24192, 4/29/2014, effective 5/29/2014; FAC 2005-82, 80 FR 26424, 5/7/2015, effective 6/8/2015; FAC 2005-95, 82 FR 4709, 1/13/2017, effective 1/13/2017; FAC 2019-03, 84 FR 27494, 6/12/2019, effective 7/12/2019]

15.404-2 Data to support proposal analysis.

(a) *Field pricing assistance.*

(1) The contracting officer should request field pricing assistance when the information available at the buying activity is inadequate to determine a fair and reasonable price. The contracting officer shall tailor requests to reflect the minimum essential supplementary information needed to conduct a technical or cost or pricing analysis.

(2) The contracting officer shall tailor the type of information and level of detail requested in accordance with the specialized resources available at the buying activity and the magnitude and complexity of the required analysis. Field pricing assistance is generally available to provide—

(i) Technical, audit, and special reports associated with the cost elements of a proposal, including subcontracts;

(ii) Information on related pricing practices and history;

(iii) Information to help contracting officers determine commerciality and a fair and reasonable price, including—

(A) Verifying sales history to source documents;

(B) Identifying special terms and conditions;

(C) Identifying customarily granted or offered discounts for the item;

(D) Verifying the item to an existing catalog or price list;

(E) Verifying historical data for an item previously not determined commercial that the offeror is now trying to qualify as a commercial item; and

(F) Identifying general market conditions affecting determinations of commerciality and a fair and reasonable price.

(iv) Information relative to the business, technical, production, or other capabilities and practices of an offeror.

(3) When field pricing assistance is requested, contracting officers are encouraged to team with appropriate field experts throughout the acquisition process, including negotiations. Early communication with these experts will assist in determining the extent of assistance required, the specific areas for which assistance is needed, a realistic review schedule, and the information necessary to perform the review.

(4) When requesting field pricing assistance on a contractor's request for equitable adjustment, the contracting officer shall provide the information listed in 43.204(b)(5).

(5) Field pricing information and other reports may include proprietary or source selection information (see 2.101). This information must be appropriately identified and protected accordingly.

(b) *Reporting field pricing information.*

(1) Depending upon the extent and complexity of the field pricing review, results, including supporting rationale, may be reported directly to the contracting officer orally, in writing, or by any other method acceptable to the contracting officer.

(i) Whenever circumstances permit, the contracting officer and field pricing experts are encouraged to use telephonic and/or electronic means to request and transmit pricing information.

(ii) When it is necessary to have written technical and audit reports, the contracting officer shall request that the audit agency concurrently forward the audit report to the requesting contracting officer and the administrative contracting officer (ACO). The completed field pricing assistance results may reference audit information, but need not reconcile the audit recommendations and technical recommendations. A copy of the information submitted to the contracting officer by field pricing personnel shall be provided to the audit agency.

(2) Audit and field pricing information, whether written or reported telephonically or electronically, shall be made a part of the official contract file (see 4.803(a)(19)).

(c) *Audit assistance for prime contracts or subcontracts.*

(1) The contracting officer may contact the cognizant audit office directly, particularly when an audit is the only field pricing support required. The audit office shall send the audit report, or otherwise transmit the audit recommendations, directly to the contracting officer.

(i) The auditor shall not reveal the audit conclusions or recommendations to the offeror/contractor without obtaining the concurrence of the contracting officer. However, the auditor may discuss statements of facts with the contractor.

(ii) The contracting officer should be notified immediately of any information disclosed to the auditor after submission of a report that may significantly affect the audit findings and, if necessary, a supplemental audit report shall be issued.

(2) The contracting officer shall not request a separate preaward audit of indirect costs unless the information already available from an existing audit, completed within the preceding 12 months, is considered inadequate for determining the reasonableness of the proposed indirect costs (41 U.S.C. 4706 and 10 U.S.C. 2313).

(3) The auditor is responsible for the scope and depth of the audit. Copies of updated information that will significantly affect the audit should be provided to the auditor by the contracting officer.

(4) General access to the offeror's books and financial records is limited to the auditor. This limitation does not preclude the contracting officer or the ACO, or their representatives, from requesting that the offeror provide or make available any data or records necessary to analyze the offeror's proposal.

(d) *Deficient proposals.* The ACO or the auditor, as appropriate, shall notify the contracting officer immediately if the data provided for review is so deficient as to preclude review or audit, or if the contractor or offeror has denied access to any records considered essential to conduct a satisfactory review or audit. Oral notifications shall be confirmed promptly in writing, including a description of deficient or denied data or records. The contracting officer immediately shall take appropriate action to obtain the required data. Should the offeror/contractor again refuse to provide adequate data, or provide access to necessary data, the contracting officer shall withhold the award or price adjustment and refer the contract action to a higher authority, providing details of the attempts made to resolve the matter and a statement of the practicability of obtaining the supplies or services from another source.

[FAC 97-2, 62 FR 51224, 9/30/97, effective 10/10/97; FAC 97-14, 64 FR 51828, 9/24/99, effective 9/24/99, finalized without change, FAC 97-17, 65 FR 24316, 4/25/2000; FAC 2001-06, 67 FR 13048, 3/20/2002, effective 4/4/2002; FAC 2005-45, 75 FR 53129, 53135, 8/30/2010, effective 10/1/2010; FAC 2005-73, 79 FR 24192, 4/29/2014, effective 5/29/2014; FAC 2005-83, 80 FR 38312, 7/2/2015, effective 7/2/2015]

15.404-3 Subcontract pricing considerations.

(a) The contracting officer is responsible for the determination of a fair and reasonable price for the prime contract, including subcontracting costs. The contracting officer should consider whether a contractor or subcontractor has an approved purchasing system, has performed cost or price analysis of proposed subcontractor prices, or has negotiated the subcontract prices before negotiation of the prime contract, in determining the reasonableness of the prime contract price. This does not relieve the contracting officer from the responsibility to analyze the contractor's submission, including subcontractor's certified cost or pricing data.

(b) The prime contractor or subcontractor shall—

(1) Conduct appropriate cost or price analyses to establish the reasonableness of proposed subcontract prices;

(2) Include the results of these analyses in the price proposal; and

(3) When required by paragraph (c) of this subsection, submit subcontractor certified cost or pricing data to the Government as part of its own certified cost or pricing data.

(c) Any contractor or subcontractor that is required to submit certified cost or pricing data also shall obtain and analyze certified cost or pricing data before awarding any subcontract, purchase order, or modification expected to exceed the certified cost or pricing data threshold, unless an exception in 15.403-1(b) applies to that action.

(1) The contractor shall submit, or cause to be submitted by the subcontractor(s), certified cost or pricing data to the Government for subcontracts that are the lower of either—

(i) $13.5 million or more; or

(ii) Both more than the pertinent certified cost or pricing data threshold and more than 10 percent of the prime contractor's proposed price, unless the contracting officer believes such submission is unnecessary.

(2) The contracting officer should require the contractor or subcontractor to submit to the Government (or cause submission of) subcontractor certified cost or pricing data below the thresholds in paragraph (c)(1) of this subsection and data other than certified cost or pricing data that the contracting officer considers necessary for adequately pricing the prime contract.

(3) Subcontractor certified cost or pricing data shall be submitted in the format provided in Table 15-2 of 15.408 or the alternate format specified in the solicitation.

(4) Subcontractor certified cost or pricing data shall be current, accurate, and complete as of the date of price agreement, or, if applicable, an earlier date agreed upon by the parties and specified on the contractor's Certificate of Current Cost or Pricing Data. The contractor shall update subcontractor's data, as appropriate, during source selection and negotiations.

(5) If there is more than one prospective subcontractor for any given work, the contractor need only submit to the Government certified cost or pricing data for the prospective subcontractor most likely to receive the award.

[FAC 97-2, 62 FR 51224, 9/30/97, effective 10/10/97; FAC 2005-13, 71 FR 57363, 9/28/2006, effective 9/28/2006; FAC 2005-45, 75 FR 53129, 53135, 8/30/2010, effective 10/1/2010; FAC 2005-83, 80 FR 38293, 7/2/2015, effective 10/1/2015]

15.404-4 Profit.

(a) *General*. This subsection prescribes policies for establishing the profit or fee portion of the Government prenegotiation objective in price negotiations based on cost analysis.

(1) Profit or fee prenegotiation objectives do not necessarily represent net income to contractors. Rather, they represent that element of the potential total remuneration that contractors may receive for contract performance over and above allowable costs. This potential remuneration element and the Government's estimate of allowable costs to be incurred in contract performance together equal the Government's total prenegotiation objective. Just as actual costs may vary from estimated costs, the contractor's actual realized profit or fee may vary from negotiated profit or fee, because of such factors as efficiency of performance, incurrence of costs the Government does not recognize as allowable, and the contract type.

(2) It is in the Government's interest to offer contractors opportunities for financial rewards sufficient to stimulate efficient contract performance, attract the best capabilities of qualified large and small business concerns to Government contracts, and maintain a viable industrial base.

(3) Both the Government and contractors should be concerned with profit as a motivator of efficient and effective contract performance. Negotiations, aimed merely at reducing prices by reducing profit, without

proper recognition of the function of profit, are not in the Government's interest. Negotiation of extremely low profits, use of historical averages, or automatic application of predetermined percentages to total estimated costs do not provide proper motivation for optimum contract performance.

(b) *Policy.*

(1) Structured approaches (see paragraph (d) of this subsection) for determining profit or fee prenegotiation objectives provide a discipline for ensuring that all relevant factors are considered. Subject to the authorities in 1.301(c), agencies making noncompetitive contract awards over $100,000 totaling $50 million or more a year—

(i) Shall use a structured approach for determining the profit or fee objective in those acquisitions that require cost analysis; and

(ii) May prescribe specific exemptions for situations in which mandatory use of a structured approach would be clearly inappropriate.

(2) Agencies may use another agency's structured approach.

(c) *Contracting officer responsibilities.*

(1) When the price negotiation is not based on cost analysis, contracting officers are not required to analyze profit.

(2) When the price negotiation is based on cost analysis, contracting officers in agencies that have a structured approach shall use it to analyze profit. When not using a structured approach, contracting officers shall comply with paragraph (d)(1) of this subsection in developing profit or fee prenegotiation objectives.

(3) Contracting officers shall use the Government prenegotiation cost objective amounts as the basis for calculating the profit or fee prenegotiation objective. Before applying profit or fee factors, the contracting officer shall exclude from the pre-negotiation cost objective amounts the purchase cost of contractor-acquired property that is categorized as equipment, as defined in FAR 45.101, and where such equipment is to be charged directly to the contract. Before applying profit or fee factors, the contracting officer shall exclude any facilities capital cost of money included in the cost objective amounts. If the prospective contractor fails to identify or propose facilities capital cost of money in a proposal for a contract that will be subject to the cost principles for contracts with commercial organizations (see Subpart 31.2), facilities capital cost of money will not be an allowable cost in any resulting contract (see 15.408(i)).

(4) (i) The contracting officer shall not negotiate a price or fee that exceeds the following statutory limitations, imposed by 10 U.S.C. 2306(d) and 41 U.S.C. 3905:

(A) For experimental, developmental, or research work performed under a cost-plus-fixed-fee contract, the fee shall not exceed 15 percent of the contract's estimated cost, excluding fee.

(B) For architect-engineer services for public works or utilities, the contract price or the estimated cost and fee for production and delivery of designs, plans, drawings, and specifications shall not exceed 6 percent of the estimated cost of construction of the public work or utility, excluding fees.

(C) For other cost-plus-fixed-fee contracts, the fee shall not exceed 10 percent of the contract's estimated cost, excluding fee.

(ii) The contracting officer's signature on the price negotiation memorandum or other documentation supporting determination of fair and reasonable price documents the contracting officer's determination that the statutory price or fee limitations have not been exceeded.

(5) The contracting officer shall not require any prospective contractor to submit breakouts or supporting rationale for its profit or fee objective but may consider it, if it is submitted voluntarily.

(6) If a change or modification calls for essentially the same type and mix of work as the basic contract and is of relatively small dollar value compared to the total contract value, the contracting officer may use the basic contract's profit or fee rate as the prenegotiation objective for that change or modification.

(d) *Profit-analysis factors*—

(1) *Common factors.* Unless it is clearly inappropriate or not applicable, each factor outlined in paragraphs (d)(1)(i) through (vi) of this subsection shall be considered by agencies in developing their structured approaches and by contracting officers in analyzing profit, whether or not using a structured approach.

(i) *Contractor effort.* This factor measures the complexity of the work and the resources required of the prospective contractor for contract performance. Greater profit opportunity should be provided under contracts requiring a high degree of professional and managerial skill and to prospective contractors whose skills, facilities, and technical assets can be expected to lead to efficient and economical contract performance. The subfactors in paragraphs (d)(1)(i)(A) through (D) of this subsection shall be considered in determining contractor effort, but they may be modified in specific situations to accommodate differences in the categories used by prospective contractors for listing costs—

(A) *Material acquisition.* This subfactor measures the managerial and technical effort needed to obtain the required purchased parts and material, subcontracted items, and special tooling. Considerations include the complexity of the items required, the number of purchase orders and subcontracts to be awarded and administered, whether established sources are available or new or second sources must be developed, and whether material will be obtained through routine purchase orders or through complex subcontracts requiring detailed specifications. Profit consideration should correspond to the managerial and technical effort involved.

(B) *Conversion direct labor.* This subfactor measures the contribution of direct engineering, manufacturing, and other labor to converting the raw materials, data, and subcontracted items into the contract items. Considerations include the diversity of engineering, scientific, and manufacturing labor skills required and the amount and quality of supervision and coordination needed to perform the contract task.

(C) *Conversion-related indirect costs.* This subfactor measures how much the indirect costs contribute to contract performance. The labor elements in the allocable indirect costs should be given the profit consideration they would receive if treated as direct labor. The other elements of indirect costs should be evaluated to determine whether they merit only limited profit consideration because of their routine nature, or are elements that contribute significantly to the proposed contract.

(D) *General management.* This subfactor measures the prospective contractor's other indirect costs and general and administrative (G&A) expense, their composition, and how much they contribute to contract performance. Considerations include how labor in the overhead pools would be treated if it were direct labor, whether elements within the pools are routine expenses or instead are elements that contribute significantly to the proposed contract, and whether the elements require routine as opposed to unusual managerial effort and attention.

(ii) *Contract cost risk.*

(A) This factor measures the degree of cost responsibility and associated risk that the prospective contractor will assume as a result of the contract type contemplated and considering the reliability of the cost estimate in relation to the complexity and duration of the contract task. Determination of contract type should be closely related to the risks involved in timely, cost-effective, and efficient performance. This factor should compensate contractors proportionately for assuming greater cost risks.

(B) The contractor assumes the greatest cost risk in a closely priced firm-fixed-price contract under which it agrees to perform a complex undertaking on time and at a predetermined price. Some firm-fixed-price contracts may entail substantially less cost risk than others because, for example, the contract task is less complex or many of the contractor's costs are known at the time of price agreement, in which case the risk factor should be reduced accordingly. The contractor assumes the least cost risk in a cost-plus-fixed-fee level-of-effort contract, under which it is reimbursed those costs determined to be allocable and allowable, plus the fixed fee.

(C) In evaluating assumption of cost risk, contracting officers shall, except in unusual circumstances, treat time-and-materials, labor-hour, and firm-fixed-price, level-of-effort term contracts as cost-plus-fixed-fee contracts.

(iii) *Federal socioeconomic programs.*. This factor measures the degree of support given by the prospective contractor to Federal socioeconomic programs, such as those involving small business concerns, small business concerns owned and controlled by socially and economically disadvantaged individuals, women-owned small business concerns, veteran-owned, HUBZone, service-disabled veteran-owned small business concerns, sheltered workshops for workers with disabilities, and energy conservation. Greater profit opportunity should be provided contractors that have displayed unusual initiative in these programs.

(iv) *Capital investments*. This factor takes into account the contribution of contractor investments to efficient and economical contract performance.

(v) *Cost-control and other past accomplishments*. This factor allows additional profit opportunities to a prospective contractor that has previously demonstrated its ability to perform similar tasks effectively and economically. In addition, consideration should be given to measures taken by the prospective contractor that result in productivity improvements, and other cost-reduction accomplishments that will benefit the Government in follow-on contracts.

(vi) *Independent development*. Under this factor, the contractor may be provided additional profit opportunities in recognition of independent development efforts relevant to the contract end item without Government assistance. The contracting officer should consider whether the development cost was recovered directly or indirectly from Government sources.

(2) *Additional factors*. In order to foster achievement of program objectives, each agency may include additional factors in its structured approach or take them into account in the profit analysis of individual contract actions.

[FAC 97-2, 62 FR 51224, 9/30/97, effective 10/10/97; FAC 2001-04, 67 FR 6112, 2/8/2002, effective 2/8/2002; FAC 2005-02, 70 FR 14950, 3/23/2005, effective 3/23/2005; FAC 2005-43, 75 FR 38675, 7/2/2010, effective 8/2/2010; FAC 2005-73, 79 FR 24192, 4/29/2014, effective 5/29/2014]

15.405 Price negotiation.

(a) The purpose of performing cost or price analysis is to develop a negotiation position that permits the contracting officer and the offeror an opportunity to reach agreement on a fair and reasonable price. A fair and reasonable price does not require that agreement be reached on every element of cost, nor is it mandatory that the agreed price be within the contracting officer's initial negotiation position. Taking into consideration the advisory recommendations, reports of contributing specialists, and the current status of the contractor's purchasing system, the contracting officer is responsible for exercising the requisite judgment needed to reach a negotiated settlement with the offeror and is solely responsible for the final price agreement. However, when significant audit or other specialist recommendations are not adopted, the contracting officer should provide rationale that supports the negotiation result in the price negotiation documentation.

(b) The contracting officer's primary concern is the overall price the Government will actually pay. The contracting officer's objective is to negotiate a contract of a type and with a price providing the contractor the greatest incentive for efficient and economical performance. The negotiation of a contract type and a price are related and should be considered together with the issues of risk and uncertainty to the contractor and the Government. Therefore, the contracting officer should not become preoccupied with any single element and should balance the contract type, cost, and profit or fee negotiated to achieve a total result—a price that is fair and reasonable to both the Government and the contractor.

(c) The Government's cost objective and proposed pricing arrangement directly affect the profit or fee objective. Because profit or fee is only one of several interrelated variables, the contracting officer shall not agree on profit or fee without concurrent agreement on cost and type of contract.

(d) If, however, the contractor insists on a price or demands a profit or fee that the contracting officer considers unreasonable, and the contracting officer has taken all authorized actions (including determining the feasibility of developing an alternative source) without success, the contracting officer shall refer the contract action to a level above the contracting officer. Disposition of the action should be documented.

[FAC 97-2, 62 FR 51224, 9/30/97, effective 10/10/97]

15.406 Documentation. (No Text)

15.406-1 Prenegotiation objectives.

(a) The prenegotiation objectives establish the Government's initial negotiation position. They assist in the contracting officer's determination of fair and reasonable price. They should be based on the results of the contracting officer's analysis of the offeror's proposal, taking into consideration all pertinent information including field pricing assistance, audit reports and technical analysis, fact-finding results, independent Government cost estimates and price histories.

(b) The contracting officer shall establish prenegotiation objectives before the negotiation of any pricing action. The scope and depth of the analysis supporting the objectives should be directly related to the dollar value, importance, and complexity of the pricing action. When cost analysis is required, the contracting officer shall document the pertinent issues to be negotiated, the cost objectives, and a profit or fee objective.

[FAC 97-2, 62 FR 51224, 9/30/97, effective 10/10/97]

15.406-2 Certificate of current cost or pricing data.

(a) When certified cost or pricing data are required, the contracting officer shall require the contractor to execute a Certificate of Current Cost or Pricing Data, using the format in this paragraph, and must include the executed certificate in the contract file.

CERTIFICATE OF CURRENT COST OR PRICING DATA

This is to certify that, to the best of my knowledge and belief, the cost or pricing data (as defined in section 2.101 of the Federal Acquisition Regulation (FAR) and required under FAR subsection 15.403-4) submitted, either actually or by specific identification in writing, to the Contracting Officer or to the Contracting Officer's representative in support of ____* are accurate, complete, and current as of ____**. This certification includes the cost or pricing data supporting any advance agreements and forward pricing rate agreements between the offeror and the Government that are part of the proposal.

Firm____________________

Signature____________________

Name____________________

Title____________________

Date of execution***____________________

* Identify the proposal, request for price adjustment, or other submission involved, giving the appropriate identifying number (*e.g.*, RFP No.).

** Insert the day, month, and year when price negotiations were concluded and price agreement was reached or, if applicable, an earlier date agreed upon between the parties that is as close as practicable to the date of agreement on price.

*** Insert the day, month, and year of signing, which should be as close as practicable to the date when the price negotiations were concluded and the contract price was agreed to.

(End of certificate)

(b) The certificate does not constitute a representation as to the accuracy of the contractor's judgment on the estimate of future costs or projections. It applies to the data upon which the judgment or estimate was based. This distinction between fact and judgment should be clearly understood. If the contractor had information reasonably available at the time of agreement showing that the negotiated price was not based on accurate, complete, and current data, the contractor's responsibility is not limited by any lack of personal knowledge of the information on the part of its negotiators.

(c) The contracting officer and contractor are encouraged to reach a prior agreement on criteria for establishing closing or cutoff dates when appropriate in order to minimize delays associated with proposal updates. Closing or cutoff dates should be included as part of the data submitted with the proposal and, before agreement on price, data should be updated by the contractor to the latest closing or cutoff dates for which the data are available. Use of cutoff dates coinciding with reports is acceptable, as certain data may not be reasonably available before normal periodic closing dates (*e.g.*, actual indirect costs). Data within the contractor's or a subcontractor's organization on matters significant to contractor management and to the Government will be treated as reasonably available. What is significant depends upon the circumstances of each acquisition.

(d) Possession of a Certificate of Current Cost or Pricing Data is not a substitute for examining and analyzing the contractor's proposal.

(e) If certified cost or pricing data are requested by the Government and submitted by an offeror, but an exception is later found to apply, the data shall not be considered certified cost or pricing data and shall not be certified in accordance with this subsection.

[FAC 97-2, 62 FR 51224, 9/30/97, effective 10/10/97; FAC 97-22, 66 FR 2116, 1/10/2001, effective 3/12/2001; Delay of effective date, 66 FR 14259, 3/9/2001, effective 5/11/2001; FAC 2005-45, 75 FR 53129, 53135, 8/30/2010, effective 10/1/2010]

15.406-3 Documenting the negotiation.

(a) The contracting officer shall document in the contract file the principal elements of the negotiated agreement. The documentation (*e.g.*, price negotiation memorandum (PNM)) shall include the following:

(1) The purpose of the negotiation.

(2) A description of the acquisition, including appropriate identifying numbers (*e.g.*, RFP No.).

(3) The name, position, and organization of each person representing the contractor and the Government in the negotiation.

(4) The current status of any contractor systems (*e.g.*, purchasing, estimating, accounting, and compensation) to the extent they affected and were considered in the negotiation.

(5) If certified cost or pricing data were not required in the case of any price negotiation exceeding the certified cost or pricing data threshold, the exception used and the basis for it.

(6) If certified cost or pricing data were required, the extent to which the contracting officer—

(i) Relied on the certified cost or pricing data submitted and used them in negotiating the price;

(ii) Recognized as inaccurate, incomplete, or noncurrent any certified cost or pricing data submitted; the action taken by the contracting officer and the contractor as a result; and the effect of the defective data on the price negotiated; or

(iii) Determined that an exception applied after the data were submitted and, therefore, considered not to be certified cost or pricing data.

(7) A summary of the contractor's proposal, any field pricing assistance recommendations, including the reasons for any pertinent variances from them, the Government's negotiation objective, and the negotiated position. Where the determination of a fair and reasonable price is based on cost analysis, the summary shall address each major cost element. When determination of a fair and reasonable price is based on price analysis, the summary shall include the source and type of data used to support the determination.

(8) The most significant facts or considerations controlling the establishment of the prenegotiation objectives and the negotiated agreement including an explanation of any significant differences between the two positions.

(9) To the extent such direction has a significant effect on the action, a discussion and quantification of the impact of direction given by Congress, other agencies, and higher-level officials (*i.e.*, officials who would not normally exercise authority during the award and review process for the instant contract action).

(10) The basis for the profit or fee prenegotiation objective and the profit or fee negotiated.

(11) Documentation of fair and reasonable pricing.

(b) Whenever field pricing assistance has been obtained, the contracting officer shall forward a copy of the negotiation documentation to the office(s) providing assistance. When appropriate, information on how advisory field support can be made more effective should be provided separately.

[FAC 97-2, 62 FR 51224, 9/30/97, effective 10/10/97; FAC 2005-45, 75 FR 53129, 53135, 8/30/2010, effective 10/1/2010]

15.407 Special cost or pricing areas. (No Text)

15.407-1 Defective certified cost or pricing data.

(a) If, before agreement on price, the contracting officer learns that any certified cost or pricing data submitted are inaccurate, incomplete, or noncurrent, the contracting officer shall immediately bring the matter to the attention of the prospective contractor, whether the defective data increase or decrease the contract price. The contracting officer shall consider any new data submitted to correct the deficiency, or consider the inaccuracy, incompleteness, or noncurrency of the data when negotiating the contract price. The price negotiation memorandum shall reflect the adjustments made to the data or the corrected data used to negotiate the contract price.

(b) (1) If, after award, certified cost or pricing data are found to be inaccurate, incomplete, or noncurrent as of the date of final agreement on price or an earlier date agreed upon by the parties given on the contractor's or subcontractor's Certificate of Current Cost or Pricing Data, the Government is entitled to a price adjustment, including profit or fee, of any significant amount by which the price was increased because of the defective data. This entitlement is ensured by including in the contract one of the clauses prescribed in 15.408(b) and (c) and is set forth in the clauses at 52.215-10, Price Reduction for Defective Certified Cost or Pricing Data, and 52.215-11, Price Reduction for Defective Certified Cost or Pricing Data—Modifications. The clauses give the Government the right to a price adjustment for defects in certified cost or pricing data submitted by the contractor, a prospective subcontractor, or an actual subcontractor.

(2) In arriving at a price adjustment, the contracting officer shall consider the time by which the certified cost or pricing data became reasonably available to the contractor, and the extent to which the Government relied upon the defective data.

(3) The clauses referred to in paragraph (b)(1) of this subsection recognize that the Government's right to a price adjustment is not affected by any of the following circumstances:

(i) The contractor or subcontractor was a sole source supplier or otherwise was in a superior bargaining position;

(ii) The contracting officer should have known that the certified cost or pricing data in issue were defective even though the contractor or subcontractor took no affirmative action to bring the character of the data to the attention of the contracting officer;

(iii) The contract was based on an agreement about the total cost of the contract and there was no agreement about the cost of each item procured under such contract; or

(iv) Certified cost or pricing data were required; however, the contractor or subcontractor did not submit a Certificate of Current Cost or Pricing Data relating to the contract.

(4) Subject to paragraphs (b)(5) and (6) of this subsection, the contracting officer shall allow an offset for any understated certified cost or pricing data submitted in support of price negotiations, up to the amount of the Government's claim for overstated pricing data arising out of the same pricing action (*e.g.*, the initial pricing of the same contract or the pricing of the same change order).

(5) An offset shall be allowed only in an amount supported by the facts and if the contractor—

(i) Certifies to the contracting officer that, to the best of the contractor's knowledge and belief, the contractor is entitled to the offset in the amount requested; and

(ii) Proves that the certified cost or pricing data were available before the "as of" date specified on the Certificate of Current Cost or Pricing Data but were not submitted. Such offsets need not be in the same cost groupings (*e.g.*, material, direct labor, or indirect costs).

(6) An offset shall not be allowed if—

(i) The understated data were known by the contractor to be understated before the "as of" date specified on the Certificate of Current Cost or Pricing Data; or

(ii) The Government proves that the facts demonstrate that the price would not have increased in the amount to be offset even if the available data had been submitted before the "as of" date specified on the Certificate of Current Cost or Pricing Data.

(7)(i) In addition to the price adjustment, the Government is entitled to recovery of any overpayment plus interest on the overpayments. The Government is also entitled to penalty amounts on certain of these overpayments. Overpayment occurs only when payment is made for supplies or services accepted by the Government. Overpayments do not result from amounts paid for contract financing, as defined in 32.001.

(ii) In calculating the interest amount due, the contracting officer shall—

(A) Determine the defective pricing amounts that have been overpaid to the contractor;

(B) Consider the date of each overpayment (the date of overpayment for this interest calculation shall be the date payment was made for the related completed and accepted contract items; or for subcontract defective pricing, the date payment was made to the prime contractor, based on prime contract progress billings or deliveries, which included payments for a completed and accepted subcontract item); and

(C) Apply the underpayment interest rate(s) in effect for each quarter from the time of overpayment to the time of repayment, utilizing rate(s) prescribed by the Secretary of the Treasury under 26 U.S.C. 6621(a)(2).

(iii) In arriving at the amount due for penalties on contracts where the submission of defective certified cost or pricing data was a knowing submission, the contracting officer shall obtain an amount equal to the amount of overpayment made. Before taking any contractual actions concerning penalties, the contracting officer shall obtain the advice of counsel.

(iv) In the demand letter, the contracting officer shall separately include—

(A) The repayment amount;

(B) The penalty amount (if any);

(C) The interest amount through a specified date; and

(D) A statement that interest will continue to accrue until repayment is made.

(c) If, after award, the contracting officer learns or suspects that the data furnished were not accurate, complete, and current, or were not adequately verified by the contractor as of the time of negotiation, the contracting officer shall request an audit to evaluate the accuracy, completeness, and currency of the data. The Government may evaluate the profit-cost relationships only if the audit reveals that the data certified by the contractor were defective. The contracting officer shall not reprice the contract solely because the profit was greater than forecast or because a contingency specified in the submission failed to materialize.

(d) For each advisory audit received based on a postaward review that indicates defective pricing, the contracting officer shall make a determination as to whether or not the data submitted were defective and relied upon. Before making such a determination, the contracting officer should give the contractor an opportunity to support the accuracy, completeness, and currency of the data in question. The contracting officer shall prepare a memorandum documenting both the determination and any corrective action taken as a result. The contracting officer shall send one copy of this memorandum to the auditor and, if the contract has been assigned for administration, one copy to the administrative contracting officer (ACO). A copy of the memorandum or other notice of the contracting officer's determination shall be provided to the contractor. When the contracting officer determines that the contractor submitted defective cost or pricing data, the contracting officer, in accordance with agency procedures, shall ensure that information relating to the contracting officer's final determination is reported in accordance with 42.1503(h). Agencies shall ensure updated information that changes a contracting officer's prior final determination is reported into the FAPIIS module of Contractor Performance Assessment Reporting System (CPARS) in the event of a—

(1) Contracting officer's decision in accordance with the Contract Disputes statute;

(2) Board of Contract Appeals decision; or

(3) Court decision.

(e) If both the contractor and subcontractor submitted, and the contractor certified, or should have certified, cost or pricing data, the Government has the right, under the clauses at 52.215-10, Price Reduction for Defective Certified Cost or Pricing Data, and 52.215-11, Price Reduction for Defective Certified Cost or Pricing Data—Modifications, to reduce the prime contract price if it was significantly increased because a subcontractor submitted defective data. This right applies whether these data supported subcontract cost estimates or supported firm agreements between subcontractor and contractor.

(f) If Government audit discloses defective subcontractor certified cost or pricing data, the information necessary to support a reduction in prime contract and subcontract prices may be available only from the Government. To the extent necessary to secure a prime contract price reduction, the contracting officer should make this information available to the prime contractor or appropriate subcontractors, upon request. If release of the information would compromise Government security or disclose trade secrets or confidential business information, the contracting officer shall release it only under conditions that will protect it from improper disclosure. Information made available under this paragraph shall be limited to that used as the basis for the prime contract price reduction. In order to afford an opportunity for corrective action, the contracting officer should give the prime contractor reasonable advance notice before determining to reduce the prime contract price.

(1) When a prime contractor includes defective subcontract data in arriving at the price but later awards the subcontract to a lower priced subcontractor (or does not subcontract for the work), any adjustment in the prime contract price due to defective subcontract data is limited to the difference (plus applicable indirect cost and profit markups) between the subcontract price used for pricing the prime contract, and either the actual subcontract price or the actual cost to the contractor, if not subcontracted, provided the data on which the actual subcontract price is based are not themselves defective.

(2) Under cost-reimbursement contracts and under all fixed-price contracts except firm-fixed-price contracts and fixed-price contracts with economic price adjustment, payments to subcontractors that are higher than they would be had there been no defective subcontractor certified cost or pricing data shall be the basis for disallowance or nonrecognition of costs under the clauses prescribed in 15.408 (b) and (c). The Government has a continuing and direct financial interest in such payments that is unaffected by the initial agreement on prime contract price.

[FAC 97-2, 62 FR 51224, 9/30/97, effective 10/10/97; FAC 2001-02, 66 FR 65347,

12/18/2001, effective 2/19/2002; FAC 2005-45, 75 FR 53129, 53135, 8/30/2010, effective 10/1/2010; FAC 2005-46, 75 FR 60258, 9/29/2010, efffective 10/29/2010; FAC 2005-69, 78 FR 46783, 8/1/2013, effective 9/3/2013; FAC 2005-73, 79 FR 24192, 4/29/2014, effective 5/29/2014; FAC 2019-06, 84 FR 47865, 9/10/2019, effective 10/10/2019]

15.407-2 Make-or-buy programs.

(a) *General.* The prime contractor is responsible for managing contract performance, including planning, placing, and administering subcontracts as necessary to ensure the lowest overall cost and technical risk to the Government. When make-or-buy programs are required, the Government may reserve the right to review and agree on the contractor's make-or-buy program when necessary to ensure negotiation of reasonable contract prices, satisfactory performance, or implementation of socioeconomic policies. Consent to subcontracts and review of contractors' purchasing systems are separate actions covered in Part 44.

(b) *Definition.* Make item, as used in this subsection, means an item or work effort to be produced or performed by the prime contractor or its affiliates, subsidiaries, or divisions.

(c) *Acquisitions requiring make-or-buy programs.*

(1) Contracting officers may require prospective contractors to submit make-or-buy program plans for negotiated acquisitions requiring certified cost or pricing data whose estimated value is $13.5 million or more, except when the proposed contract is for research or development and, if prototypes or hardware are involved, no significant follow-on production is anticipated.

(2) Contracting officers may require prospective contractors to submit make-or-buy programs for negotiated acquisitions whose estimated value is under $13.5 million only if the contracting officer—

(i) Determines that the information is necessary; and

(ii) Documents the reasons in the contract file.

(d) *Solicitation requirements.* When prospective contractors are required to submit proposed make-or-buy programs, the solicitation shall include—

(1) A statement that the program and required supporting information must accompany the offer; and

(2) A description of factors to be used in evaluating the proposed program, such as capability, capacity, availability of small, small disadvantaged, women-owned, veteran-owned, HUBZone, and service-disabled veteran-owned small business concerns for subcontracting, establishment of new facilities in or near labor surplus areas, delivery or performance schedules, control of technical and schedule interfaces, proprietary processes, technical superiority or exclusiveness, and technical risks involved.

(e) *Program requirements.* To support a make-or-buy program, the following information shall be supplied by the contractor in its proposal:

(1) *Items and work included.* The information required from a contractor in a make-or-buy program shall be confined to those major items or work efforts that normally would require company management review of the make-or-buy decision because they are complex, costly, needed in large quantities, or require additional equipment or real property to produce. Raw materials, commercial items (see 2.101), and off-the-shelf items (see 46.101) shall not be included, unless their potential impact on contract cost or schedule is critical. Normally, make-or-buy programs should not include items or work efforts estimated to cost less than 1 percent of the total estimated contract price or any minimum dollar amount set by the agency.

(2) The offeror's program should include or be supported by the following information:

(i) A description of each major item or work effort.

(ii) Categorization of each major item or work effort as "must make," "must buy," or "can either make or buy."

(iii) For each item or work effort categorized as "can either make or buy," a proposal either to "make" or to "buy."

(iv) Reasons for categorizing items and work efforts as "must make" or "must buy," and proposing to "make" or to "buy" those categorized as "can either make or buy." The reasons must include the consideration given to the evaluation factors described in the solicitation and must be in sufficient detail to permit the contracting officer to evaluate the categorization or proposal.

(v) Designation of the plant or division proposed to make each item or perform each work effort, and a statement as to whether the existing or proposed new facility is in or near a labor surplus area.

(vi) Identification of proposed subcontractors, if known, and their location and size status (also see Subpart 19.7 for subcontracting plan requirements).

(vii) Any recommendations to defer make-or-buy decisions when categorization of some items or work efforts is impracticable at the time of submission.

(viii) Any other information the contracting officer requires in order to evaluate the program.

(f) *Evaluation, negotiation, and agreement.* Contracting officers shall evaluate and negotiate proposed make-or-buy programs as soon as practicable after their receipt and before contract award.

(1) When the program is to be incorporated in the contract and the design status of the product being acquired does not permit accurate precontract identification of major items or work efforts, the contracting officer shall notify the prospective contractor in writing that these items or efforts, when identifiable, shall be added under the clause at 52.215-9, Changes or Additions to Make-or-Buy Program.

(2) Contracting officers normally shall not agree to proposed "make items" when the products or services are not regularly manufactured or provided by the contractor and are available—quality, quantity, delivery, and other essential factors considered—from another firm at equal or lower prices, or when they are regularly manufactured or provided by the contractor, but are available—quality, quantity, delivery, and other essential factors considered—from another firm at lower prices. However, the contracting officer may agree to these as "make items" if an overall lower Governmentwide cost would result or it is otherwise in the best interest of the Government. If this situation occurs in any fixed-price incentive or cost-plus-incentive-fee contract, the contracting officer shall specify these items in the contract and state that they are subject to paragraph (d) of the clause at 52.215-9, Changes or Additions to Make-or-Buy Program (see 15.408(a)). If the contractor proposes to reverse the categorization of such items during contract performance, the contract price shall be subject to equitable reduction.

(g) *Incorporating make-or-buy programs in contracts.* The contracting officer may incorporate the make-or-buy program in negotiated contracts for—

(1) Major systems (see Part 34) or their subsystems or components, regardless of contract type; or

(2) Other supplies and services if—

(i) The contract is a cost-reimbursable contract, or a cost-sharing contract in which the contractor's share of the cost is less than 25 percent; and

(ii) The contracting officer determines that technical or cost risks justify Government review and approval of changes or additions to the make-or-buy program.

[FAC 97-2, 62 FR 51224, 9/30/97, effective 10/10/97; FAC 97-22, 66 FR 2116, 1/10/2001, effective 3/12/2001; Delay of effective date, 66 FR 14259, 3/9/2001, effective 5/11/2001; FAC 2005-02, 70 FR 14950, 3/23/2005, effective 3/23/2005; FAC 2005-13, 71 FR 57363, 9/28/2006, effective 9/28/2006; FAC 2005-17, 72 FR 27364, 5/15/2007, effective 6/14/2007; FAC 2005-45, 75 FR 53129, 53135, 8/30/2010, effective 10/1/2010; FAC 2005-83, 80 FR 38293, 7/2/2015, effective 10/1/2015]

15.407-3 Forward pricing rate agreements.

(a) When certified cost or pricing data are required, offerors are required to describe any forward pricing rate agreements (FPRAs) in each specific pricing proposal to which the rates apply and to identify the latest cost or pricing data already submitted in accordance with the FPRA. All data submitted in connection with the FPRA, updated as necessary, form a part of the total data that the offeror certifies to be accurate, complete, and current at the time of agreement on price for an initial contract or for a contract modification. (See the Certificate of Current Cost or Pricing Data at 15.406-2.)

(b) Contracting officers will use FPRA rates as bases for pricing all contracts, modifications, and other contractual actions to be performed during the period covered by the agreement. Conditions that may affect the agreement's validity shall be reported promptly to the ACO. If the ACO determines that a changed condition invalidates the agreement, the ACO shall notify all interested parties of the extent of its effect and status of efforts to establish a revised FPRA.

(c) Contracting officers shall not require certification at the time of agreement for data supplied in support of FPRA's or other advance agreements. When a forward pricing rate agreement or other advance agreement is used to price a contract action that requires a certificate, the certificate supporting that contract action shall cover the data supplied to support the FPRA or other advance agreement, and all other data supporting the action.

[FAC 97-2, 62 FR 51224, 9/30/97, effective 10/10/97; FAC 2005-45, 75 FR 53135, 8/30/2010, effective 10/1/2010]

15.407-4 Should-cost review.

(a) *General.*

(1) Should-cost reviews are a specialized form of cost analysis. Should-cost reviews differ from traditional evaluation methods because they do not assume that a contractor's historical costs reflect efficient and economical operation. Instead, these reviews evaluate the economy and efficiency of the contractor's existing work force, methods, materials, equipment, real property, operating systems, and management. These reviews are accomplished by a multi-functional team of Government contracting, contract administration, pricing, audit, and engineering representatives. The objective of should-cost reviews is to promote both short and long-range improvements in the contractor's economy and efficiency in order to reduce the cost of performance of Government contracts. In addition, by providing rationale for any recommendations and quantifying their impact on cost, the Government will be better able to develop realistic objectives for negotiation.

(2) There are two types of should-cost reviews—program should-cost review (see paragraph (b) of this subsection) and overhead should-cost review (see paragraph (c) of this subsection). These should-cost reviews may be performed together or independently. The scope of a should-cost review can range from a large-scale review examining the contractor's entire operation (including plant-wide overhead and selected major subcontractors) to a small-scale tailored review examining specific portions of a contractor's operation.

(b) *Program should-cost review.*

(1) A program should-cost review is used to evaluate significant elements of direct costs, such as material and labor, and associated indirect costs, usually associated with the production of major systems. When a program should-cost review is conducted relative to a contractor proposal, a separate audit report on the proposal is required.

(2) A program should-cost review should be considered, particularly in the case of a major system acquisition (see Part 34), when—

(i) Some initial production has already taken place;

(ii) The contract will be awarded on a sole source basis;

(iii) There are future year production requirements for substantial quantities of like items;

(iv) The items being acquired have a history of increasing costs;

(v) The work is sufficiently defined to permit an effective analysis and major changes are unlikely;

(vi) Sufficient time is available to plan and adequately conduct the should-cost review; and

(vii) Personnel with the required skills are available or can be assigned for the duration of the should-cost review.

(3) The contracting officer should decide which elements of the contractor's operation have the greatest potential for cost savings and assign the available personnel resources accordingly. The expertise of on-site Government personnel should be used, when appropriate. While the particular elements to be analyzed are a function of the contract work task, elements such as manufacturing, pricing and accounting, management and organization, and subcontract and vendor management are normally reviewed in a should-cost review.

(4) In acquisitions for which a program should-cost review is conducted, a separate program should-cost review team report, prepared in accordance with agency procedures, is required. The contracting officer shall consider the findings and recommendations contained in the program should-cost review team report when negotiating the contract price. After completing the negotiation, the contracting officer shall provide the ACO a report of any identified uneconomical or inefficient practices, together with a report of correction or disposition agreements reached with the contractor. The contracting officer shall establish a follow-up plan to monitor the correction of the uneconomical or inefficient practices.

(5) When a program should-cost review is planned, the contracting officer should state this fact in the acquisition plan or acquisition plan updates (see Subpart 7.1) and in the solicitation.

(c) *Overhead should-cost review.*

(1) An overhead should-cost review is used to evaluate indirect costs, such as fringe benefits, shipping and receiving, real property and equipment, depreciation, plant maintenance and security, taxes, and general and administrative activities. It is normally used to evaluate and negotiate an FPRA with the contractor. When an overhead should-cost review is conducted, a separate audit report is required.

(2) The following factors should be considered when selecting contractor sites for overhead should-cost reviews:

(i) Dollar amount of Government business.

(ii) Level of Government participation.

(iii) Level of noncompetitive Government contracts.

(iv) Volume of proposal activity.

(v) Major system or program.

(vi) Corporate reorganizations, mergers, acquisitions, or takeovers.

(vii) Other conditions (*e.g.*, changes in accounting systems, management, or business activity).

(3) The objective of the overhead should-cost review is to evaluate significant indirect cost elements in-depth, and identify and recommend corrective actions regarding inefficient and uneconomical practices. If it is conducted in conjunction with a program should-cost review, a separate overhead should-cost review report is not required. However, the findings and recommendations of the overhead should-cost team, or any separate overhead should-cost review report, shall be provided to the ACO. The ACO should use this information to form the basis for the Government position in negotiating an FPRA with the contractor. The ACO shall establish a follow-up plan to monitor the correction of the uneconomical or inefficient practices.

[FAC 97-2, 62 FR 51224, 9/30/97, effective 10/10/97; FAC 2005-17, 72 FR 27364, 5/15/2007, effective 6/14/2007]

15.407-5 Estimating systems.

(a) Using an acceptable estimating system for proposal preparation benefits both the Government and the contractor by increasing the accuracy and reliability of individual proposals. Cognizant audit activities, when it is appropriate to do so, shall establish and manage regular programs for reviewing selected contractors' estimating systems or methods, in order to reduce the scope of reviews to be performed on individual proposals, expedite the negotiation process, and increase the reliability of proposals. The results of estimating system reviews shall be documented in survey reports.

(b) The auditor shall send a copy of the estimating system survey report and a copy of the official notice of corrective action required to each contracting office and contract administration office having substantial business with that contractor. Significant deficiencies not corrected by the contractor shall be a consideration in subsequent proposal analyses and negotiations.

[FAC 97-2, 62 FR 51224, 9/30/97, effective 10/10/97]

15.408 Solicitation provisions and contract clauses.

(a) *Changes or Additions to Make-or-Buy Program*. The contracting officer shall insert the clause at 52.215-9, Changes or Additions to Make-or-Buy Program, in solicitations and contracts when it is contemplated that a make-or-buy program will be incorporated in the contract. If a less economical "make" or "buy" categorization is selected for one or more items of significant value, the contracting officer shall use the clause with—

(1) Its Alternate I, if a fixed-price incentive contract is contemplated; or

(2) Its Alternate II, if a cost-plus-incentive-fee contract is contemplated.

(b) *Price Reduction for Defective Certified Cost or Pricing Data*. The contracting officer shall, when contracting by negotiation, insert the clause at 52.215-10, Price Reduction for Defective Certified Cost or Pricing Data, in solicitations and contracts when it is contemplated that certified cost or pricing data will be required from the contractor or any subcontractor (see 15.403-4).

(c) *Price Reduction for Defective Certified Cost or Pricing Data—Modifications*. The contracting officer shall, when contracting by negotiation, insert the clause at 52.215-11, Price Reduction for Defective Certified Cost or Pricing Data—Modifications, in solicitations and contracts when it is contemplated that certified cost or pricing data will be required from the contractor or any subcontractor (see 15.403-4) for the pricing of contract modifications, and the clause prescribed in paragraph (b) of this section has not been included.

(d) *Subcontractor Certified Cost or Pricing Data*. The contracting officer shall insert the clause at 52.215-12, Subcontractor Certified Cost or Pricing Data, in solicitations and contracts when the clause prescribed in paragraph (b) of this section is included.

(e) *Subcontractor Certified Cost or Pricing Data—Modifications*. The contracting officer shall insert the clause at 52.215-13, Subcontractor Certified Cost or Pricing Data—Modifications, in solicitations and contracts when the clause prescribed in paragraph (c) of this section is included.

(f) *Integrity of Unit Prices*.

(1) The contracting officer shall insert the clause at 52.215-14, Integrity of Unit Prices, in solicitations and contracts except for—

(i) Acquisitions at or below the simplified acquisition threshold;

(ii) Construction or architect-engineer services under Part 36;

(iii) Utility services under Part 41;

(iv) Service contracts where supplies are not required;

(v) Acquisitions of commercial items; and

(vi) Contracts for petroleum products.

(2) The contracting officer shall insert the clause with its Alternate I when contracting without adequate price competition or when prescribed by agency regulations.

(g) *Pension Adjustments and Asset Reversions*. The contracting officer shall insert the clause at 52.215-15, Pension Adjustments and Asset Reversions, in solicitations and contracts for which it is anticipated that certified cost or pricing data will be required or for which any preaward or postaward cost determinations will be subject to part 31.

(h) *Facilities Capital Cost of Money*. The contracting officer shall insert the provision at 52.215-16, Facilities Capital Cost of Money, in solicitations expected to result in contracts that are subject to the cost principles for contracts with commercial organizations (see Subpart 31.2).

(i) *Waiver of Facilities Capital Cost of Money*. If the prospective contractor does not propose facilities capital cost of money in its offer, the contracting officer shall insert the clause at 52.215-17, Waiver of Facilities Capital Cost of Money, in the resulting contract.

(j) *Reversion or Adjustment of Plans for Postretirement Benefits (PRB) Other Than Pensions.* The contracting officer shall insert the clause at 52.215-18, Reversion or Adjustment of Plans for Postretirement Benefits (PRB) Other Than Pensions, in solicitations and contracts for which it is anticipated that certified cost or pricing data will be required or for which any preaward or postaward cost determinations will be subject to Part 31.

(k) *Notification of Ownership Changes.* The contracting officer shall insert the clause at 52.215-19, Notification of Ownership Changes, in solicitations and contracts for which it is contemplated that certified cost or pricing data will be required or for which any preaward or postaward cost determination will be subject to subpart 31.2.

(l) *Requirements for Certified Cost or Pricing Data and Data Other Than Certified Cost or Pricing Data.* Considering the hierarchy at 15.402, the contracting officer shall insert the provision at 52.215-20, Requirements for Certified Cost or Pricing Data and Data Other Than Certified Cost or Pricing Data, in solicitations if it is reasonably certain that certified cost or pricing data or data other than certified cost or pricing data will be required. This provision also provides instructions to offerors on how to request an exception from the requirement to submit certified cost or pricing data. The contracting officer shall—

(1) Use the provision with its Alternate I to specify a format for certified cost or pricing data other than the format required by Table 15-2 of this section;

(2) Use the provision with its Alternate II if copies of the proposal are to be sent to the ACO and contract auditor;

(3) Use the provision with its Alternate III if submission via electronic media is required; and

(4) Replace the basic provision with its Alternate IV if certified cost or pricing data are not expected to be required because an exception may apply, but data other than certified cost or pricing data will be required as described in 15.403-3.

(m) *Requirements for Certified Cost or Pricing Data and Data Other Than Certified Cost or Pricing Data—Modifications.* Considering the hierarchy at 15.402, the contracting officer shall insert the clause at 52.215-21, Requirements for Certified Cost or Pricing Data and Data Other Than Certified Cost or Pricing Data—Modifications, in solicitations and contracts if it is reasonably certain that certified cost or pricing data or data other than certified cost or pricing data will be required for modifications. This clause also provides instructions to contractors on how to request an exception from the requirement to submit certified cost or pricing data. The contracting officer shall—

(1) Use the clause with its Alternate I to specify a format for certified cost or pricing data other than the format required by Table 15-2 of this section;

(2) Use the clause with its Alternate II if copies of the proposal are to be sent to the ACO and contract auditor;

(3) Use the clause with its Alternate III if submission via electronic media is required; and

(4) Replace the basic clause with its Alternate IV if certified cost or pricing data are not expected to be required because an exception may apply, but data other than certified cost or pricing data will be required as described in 15.403-3.

(n) *Limitations on Pass-Through Charges.* (1) The contracting officer shall insert the provision at 52.215-22, Limitations on Pass-Through Charges—Identification of Subcontract Effort, in solicitations containing the clause at 52.215-23.

(2) (i) Except as provided in paragraph (n) (2) (ii) of this section, the contracting officer shall insert the clause 52.215-23, Limitations on Pass-Through Charges, in solicitations and contracts including task or delivery orders as follows:

(A) For civilian agencies, insert the clause when—

(*1*) The total estimated contract or order value exceeds the simplified acquisition threshold as defined in section 2.101 and

(*2*) The contemplated contract type is expected to be a cost-reimbursement type contract as defined in Subpart 16.3; or

(B) For DoD, insert the clause when—

(*1*) The total estimated contract or order value exceeds the threshold for obtaining cost or pricing data in 15.403- 4; and

(*2*) The contemplated contract type is expected to be any contract type except—

(*i*) A firm-fixed-price contract awarded on the basis of adequate price competition;

(*ii*) A fixed-price contract with economic price adjustment awarded on the basis of adequate price competition;

(*iii*) A firm-fixed-price contract for the acquisition of a commercial item;

(*iv*) A fixed-price contract with economic price adjustment, for the acquisition of a commercial item;

(*v*) A fixed-price incentive contract awarded on the basis of adequate price competition; or

(*vi*) A fixed-price incentive contract for the acquisition of a commercial item.

(ii) The clause may be used when the total estimated contract or order value is below the thresholds identified in 15.408(n)(2)(i) and for any contract type, when the contracting officer determines that inclusion of the clause is appropriate.

(iii) Use the clause 52.215-23 with its Alternate I when the contracting officer determines that the prospective contractor has demonstrated that its functions provide added value to the contracting effort and there are no excessive pass-through charges.

Table 15-2—Instructions for Submitting Cost/Price Proposals When Certified Cost or Pricing Data Are Required

This document provides instructions for preparing a contract pricing proposal when certified cost or pricing data are required.

Note 1: There is a clear distinction between submitting certified cost or pricing data and merely making available books, records, and other documents without identification. The requirement for submission of certified cost or pricing data is met when all accurate certified cost or pricing data reasonably available to the offeror have been submitted, either actually or by specific identification, to the Contracting Officer or an authorized representative. As later data come into your possession, it should be submitted promptly to the Contracting Officer in a manner that clearly shows how the data relate to the offeror's price proposal. The requirement for submission of certified cost or pricing data continues up to the time of agreement on price, or an earlier date agreed upon between the parties if applicable.

Note 2: By submitting your proposal, you grant the Contracting Officer or an authorized representative the right to examine records that formed the basis for the pricing proposal. That examination can take place at any time before award. It may include those books, records, documents, and other types of factual data (regardless of form or whether the data are specifically referenced or included in the proposal as the basis for pricing) that will permit an adequate evaluation of the proposed price.

I. General Instructions

A. You must provide the following information on the first page of your pricing proposal:

(1) Solicitation, contract, and/or modification number;

(2) Name and address of offeror;

(3) Name and telephone number of point of contact;

(4) Name of contract administration office (if available);

(5) Type of contract action (that is, new contract, change order, price revision/redetermination, letter contract, unpriced order, or other);

(6) Proposed cost; profit or fee; and total;

(7) Whether you will require the use of Government property in the performance of the contract, and, if so, what property;

(8) Whether your organization is subject to cost accounting standards; whether your organization has submitted a CASB Disclo-

sure Statement, and if it has been determined adequate; whether you have been notified that you are or may be in noncompliance with your Disclosure Statement or CAS (other than a noncompliance that the cognizant Federal agency official has determined to have an immaterial cost impact), and, if yes, an explanation; whether any aspect of this proposal is inconsistent with your disclosed practices or applicable CAS, and, if so, an explanation; and whether the proposal is consistent with your established estimating and accounting principles and procedures and FAR Part 31, Cost Principles, and, if not, an explanation;

(9) The following statement: This proposal reflects our estimates and/or actual costs as of this date and conforms with the instructions in FAR 15.403-5(b)(1) and Table 15-2. By submitting this proposal, we grant the Contracting Officer and authorized representative(s) the right to examine, at any time before award, those records, which include books, documents, accounting procedures and practices, and other data, regardless of type and form or whether such supporting information is specifically referenced or included in the proposal as the basis for pricing, that will permit an adequate evaluation of the proposed price.

(10) Date of submission; and

(11) Name, title, and signature of authorized representative.

B. In submitting your proposal, you must include an index, appropriately referenced, of all the certified cost or pricing data and information accompanying or identified in the proposal. In addition, you must annotate any future additions and/or revisions, up to the date of agreement on price, or an earlier date agreed upon by the parties, on a supplemental index.

C. As part of the specific information required, you must submit, with your proposal—

(1) Certified cost or pricing data (as defined at FAR 2.101). You must clearly identify on your cover sheet that certified cost or pricing data are included as part of the proposal.

(2) Information reasonably required to explain your estimating process, including—

(i) The judgmental factors applied and the mathematical or other methods used in the estimate, including those used in projecting from known data; and

(ii) The nature and amount of any contingencies included in the proposed price.

D. You must show the relationship between line item prices and the total contract price. You must attach cost-element breakdowns for each proposed line item, using the appropriate format prescribed in the "Formats for Submission of Line Item Summaries" section of this table. You must furnish supporting breakdowns for each cost element, consistent with your cost accounting system.

E. When more than one line item is proposed, you must also provide summary total amounts covering all line items for each element of cost.

F. Whenever you have incurred costs for work performed before submission of a proposal, you must identify those costs in your cost/price proposal.

G. If you have reached an agreement with Government representatives on use of forward pricing rates/factors, identify the agreement, include a copy, and describe its nature.

H. As soon as practicable after final agreement on price or an earlier date agreed to by the parties, but before the award resulting from the proposal, you must, under the conditions stated in FAR 15.406-2, submit a Certificate of Current Cost or Pricing Data.

II. Cost Elements

Depending on your system, you must provide breakdowns for the following basic cost elements, as applicable:

A. *Materials and services.* Provide a consolidated priced summary of individual material quantities included in the various tasks, orders, or line items being proposed and the basis for pricing (vendor quotes, invoice prices, etc.). Include raw materials, parts, components, assemblies, and services to be produced or performed by others. For all items proposed, identify the item and show the source, quantity, and price. Conduct price analyses of all subcontractor proposals. Conduct cost analyses for all subcontracts when certified cost or pricing data are submitted by the subcontractor. Include these analyses as part of your own certified cost or pricing data submissions for subcontracts expected to exceed the appropriate threshold in FAR 15.403-4. Submit the subcontractor certified cost or pricing data and data other than certified cost or pricing data as part of your own certified cost or pricing data as required in paragraph IIA(2) of this table. These requirements also apply to all subcontractors if required to submit certified cost or pricing data.

(1) *Adequate Price Competition*. Provide data showing the degree of competition and the basis for establishing the source and reasonableness of price for those acquisitions (such as subcontracts, purchase orders, material order, *etc.*) exceeding, or expected to exceed, the appropriate threshold set forth at FAR 15.403-4 priced on the basis of adequate price competition. For interorganizational transfers priced at other than the cost of comparable competitive commercial work of the division, subsidiary, or affiliate of the contractor, explain the pricing method (see FAR 31.205-26(e)).

(2) *All Other*. Obtain certified cost or pricing data from prospective sources for those acquisitions (such as subcontracts, purchase orders, material order, etc.) exceeding the threshold set forth in FAR 15.403-4 and not otherwise exempt, in accordance with FAR 15.403-1(b) (*i.e.*, adequate price competition, commercial items, prices set by law or regulation or waiver). Also provide data showing the basis for establishing source and reasonableness of price. In addition, provide a summary of your cost analysis and a copy of certified cost or pricing data submitted by the prospective source in support of each subcontract, or purchase order that is the lower of either $13.5 million or more, or both more than the pertinent certified cost or pricing data threshold and more than 10 percent of the prime contractor's proposed price. Also submit any information reasonably required to explain your estimating process (including the judgmental factors applied and the mathematical or other methods used in the estimate, including those used in projecting from known data, and the nature and amount of any contingencies included in the price). The Contracting Officer may require you to submit cost or pricing data in support of proposals in lower amounts. Subcontractor certified cost or pricing data must be accurate, complete and current as of the date of final price agreement, or an earlier date agreed upon by the parties, given on the prime contractor's Certificate of Current Cost or Pricing Data. The prime contractor is responsible for updating a prospective subcontractor's data. For standard commercial items fabricated by the offeror that are generally stocked in inventory, provide a separate cost breakdown, if priced based on cost. For interorganizational transfers priced at cost, provide a separate breakdown of cost elements. Analyze the certified cost or pricing data and submit the results of your analysis of the prospective source's proposal. When submission of a prospective source's certified cost or pricing data is required as described in this paragraph, it must be included as part of your own certified cost or pricing data. You must also submit any data other than certified cost or pricing data obtained from a subcontractor, either actually or by specific identification, along with the results of any analysis performed on that data.

B. *Direct Labor*. Provide a time-phased (*e.g.*, monthly, quarterly, *etc.*) breakdown of labor hours, rates, and cost by appropriate category, and furnish bases for estimates.

C. *Indirect Costs*. Indicate how you have computed and applied your indirect costs, including cost breakdowns. Show trends and budgetary data to provide a basis for evaluating the reasonableness of proposed rates. Indicate the rates used and provide an appropriate explanation.

D. *Other Costs*. List all other costs not otherwise included in the categories described above (*e.g.*, special tooling, travel, computer and consultant services, preservation, packaging and packing, spoilage and rework, and Federal excise tax on finished articles) and provide bases for pricing.

E. *Royalties.* If royalties exceed $1,500, you must provide the following information on a separate page for each separate royalty or license fee:

(1) Name and address of licensor.

(2) Date of license agreement.

(3) Patent numbers.

(4) Patent application serial numbers, or other basis on which the royalty is payable.

(5) Brief description (including any part or model numbers of each contract item or component on which the royalty is payable).

(6) Percentage or dollar rate of royalty per unit.

(7) Unit price of contract item.

(8) Number of units.

(9) Total dollar amount of royalties.

(10) If specifically requested by the Contracting Officer, a copy of the current license agreement and identification of applicable claims of specific patents (see FAR 27.202 and 31.205-37).

F. *Facilities Capital Cost of Money.* When you elect to claim facilities capital cost of money as an allowable cost, you must submit Form CASB-CMF and show the calculation of the proposed amount (see FAR 31.205-10).

III. Formats for Submission of Line Item Summaries

A. New Contracts (Including Letter Contracts)

Cost elements (1)	Proposed contract estimate—total cost (2)	Proposed contract estimate—unit cost (3)	Reference (4)

Column and Instruction.

(1) Enter appropriate cost elements.

(2) Enter those necessary and reasonable costs that, in your judgment, will properly be incurred in efficient contract performance. When any of the costs in this column have already been incurred (*e.g.*, under a letter contract), describe them on an attached supporting page. When preproduction or startup costs are significant, or when specifically requested to do so by the Contracting Officer, provide a full identification and explanation of them.

(3) Optional, unless required by the Contracting Officer.

(4) Identify the attachment in which the information supporting the specific cost element may be found. (Attach separate pages as necessary.)

B. Change Orders, Modifications, and Claims

Cost elements (1)	Estimated cost of all work deleted (2)	Cost of deleted work already performed (3)	Net cost to be deleted (4)	Cost of work added (5)	Net cost of change (6)	Reference (7)

Column and Instruction.

(1) Enter appropriate cost elements.

(2) Include the current estimates of what the cost would have been to complete the deleted work not yet performed (not the original proposal estimates), and the cost of deleted work already performed.

(3) Include the incurred cost of deleted work already performed, using actuals incurred if possible, or, if actuals are not available, estimates from your accounting records. Attach a detailed inventory of work, materials, parts, components, and hardware already purchased, manufactured, or performed and deleted by the change, indicat-

ing the cost and proposed disposition of each line item. Also, if you desire to retain these items or any portion of them, indicate the amount offered for them.

(4) Enter the net cost to be deleted, which is the estimated cost of all deleted work less the cost of deleted work already performed. Column (2) minus Column (3) equals Column (4).

(5) Enter your estimate for cost of work added by the change. When nonrecurring costs are significant, or when specifically requested to do so by the Contracting Officer, provide a full identification and explanation of them. When any of the costs in this column have already been incurred, describe them on an attached supporting schedule.

(6) Enter the net cost of change, which is the cost of work added, less the net cost to be deleted. Column (5) minus Column (4) equals Column (6). When this result is negative, place the amount in parentheses.

(7) Identify the attachment in which the information supporting the specific cost element may be found. (Attach separate pages as necessary.)

C. Price Revision/Redetermination

Cutoff date	Number of units completed	Number of units to be completed	Contract amount	Redetermination proposal amount	Difference	Cost elements	Incurred cost—preproduction	Incurred cost—completed units	Incurred cost—work in process	Total incurred cost	Estimated cost to complete	Estimated total cost	Reference
(1)	(2)	(3)	(4)	(5)	(6)	(7)	(8)	(9)	(10)	(11)	(12)	(13)	(14)

(1) Enter the cutoff date required by the contract, if applicable.

(2) Enter the number of units completed during the period for which experienced costs of production are being submitted.

(3) Enter the number of units remaining to be completed under the contract.

(4) Enter the cumulative contract amount.

(5) Enter your redetermination proposal amount.

(6) Enter the difference between the contract amount and the redetermination proposal amount. When this result is negative, place the amount in parentheses. Column (4) minus Column (5) equals Column (6).

(7) Enter appropriate cost elements. When residual inventory exists, the final costs established under fixed-price-incentive and fixed-price-redeterminable arrangements should be net of the fair market value of such inventory. In support of subcontract costs, submit a listing of all subcontracts subject to repricing action, annotated as to their status.

(8) Enter all costs incurred under the contract before starting production and other nonrecurring costs (usually referred to as startup costs) from your books and records as of the cutoff date. These include such costs as preproduction engineering, special plant rearrangement, training program, and any identifiable nonrecurring costs such as initial rework, spoilage, pilot runs, etc. In the event the amounts are not segregated in or otherwise available from your records, enter in this column your best estimates. Explain the basis for each estimate and how the costs are charged on your accounting records (*e.g.*, included in production costs as direct engineering labor, charged to manufacturing overhead). Also show how the costs would be allocated to the units at their various stages of contract completion.

(9) Enter in Column (9) the production costs from your books and records (exclusive of preproduction costs reported in Column (8)) of the units completed as of the cutoff date.

(10) Enter in Column (10) the costs of work in process as determined from your records or inventories at the cutoff date. When the amounts for work in process are not available in your records but reliable estimates for them can be made, enter the estimated amounts in Column (10) and enter in Column (9) the differences between the total incurred costs (exclusive of preproduction costs) as of the cutoff date and these estimates. Explain the basis for the estimates, including identification of any provi-

sion for experienced or anticipated allowances, such as shrinkage, rework, design changes, etc. Furnish experienced unit or lot costs (or labor hours) from inception of contract to the cutoff date, improvement curves, and any other available production cost history pertaining to the item(s) to which your proposal relates.

(11) Enter total incurred costs (Total of Columns (8), (9), and (10)).

(12) Enter those necessary and reasonable costs that in your judgment will properly be incurred in completing the remaining work to be performed under the contract with respect to the item(s) to which your proposal relates.

(13) Enter total estimated cost (Total of Columns (11) and (12)).

(14) Identify the attachment in which the information supporting the specific cost element may be found. (Attach separate pages as necessary.)

[FAC 97-2, 62 FR 51224, 9/30/97, effective 10/10/97; FAC 97-9, 63 FR 58587, 10/30/98, effective 12/29/98; FAC 97-22, 66 FR 2116, 1/10/2001, effective 3/12/2001; Delay of effective date, 66 FR 14259, 3/9/2001, effective 5/11/2001; FAC 2001-04, 67 FR 6112, 2/8/2002, effective 2/20/2002; FAC 2005-13, 71 FR 57363, 9/28/2006, effective 9/28/2006; FAC 2005-21, 72 FR 63045, 11/7/2007, effective 12/7/2007; FAC 2005-37, 74 FR 52853, 10/14/2009, effective 10/14/2009; FAC 2005-45, 75 FR 53129, 53135, 8/30/2010, effective 10/1/2010; FAC 2005-47, 75 FR 77741, 12/13/2010, effective 1/12/2011; FAC 2005-83, 80 FR 38293, 7/2/2015, effective 10/1/2015; FAC 2005-95, 82 FR 4709, 1/13/2017, effective 1/13/2017]

SUBPART 15.5—PREAWARD, AWARD, AND POSTAWARD NOTIFICATIONS, PROTESTS, AND MISTAKES

15.501 Definition.

Day, as used in this subpart, has the meaning set forth at 33.101.

[FAC 97-2, 62 FR 51224, 9/30/97, effective 10/10/97]

15.502 Applicability.

This subpart applies to competitive proposals, as described in 6.102(b), and a combination of competitive procedures, as described in 6.102(c). The procedures in 15.504, 15.506, 15.507, 15.508, and 15.509, with reasonable modification, should be followed for sole source acquisitions and acquisitions described in 6.102(d)(1) and (2).

[FAC 97-2, 62 FR 51224, 9/30/97, effective 10/10/97]

15.503 Notifications to unsuccessful offerors.

(a) *Preaward notices*—(1) *Preaward notices* of exclusion from competitive range. The contracting officer shall notify offerors promptly in writing when their proposals are excluded from the competitive range or otherwise eliminated from the competition. The notice shall state the basis for the determination and that a proposal revision will not be considered.

(2) *Preaward notices* for small business programs.

(i) In addition to the notice in paragraph (a)(1) of this section, the contracting officer shall notify each offeror in writing prior to award and upon completion of negotiations and determinations of responsibility—

(A) When using a small business set-aside (see subpart 19.5);

(B) When using the HUBZone procedures in 19.1305 or 19.1307;

(C) When using the service-disabled veteran-owned small business procedures in 19.1405; or

(D) When using the Women-Owned Small Business Program procedures in 19.1505.

(ii) The notice shall state—

(A) The name and address of the apparently successful offeror;

(B) That the Government will not consider subsequent revisions of the offeror's proposal; and

(C) That no response is required unless a basis exists to challenge the size status or small business status of the apparently successful offeror (*e.g.,* small business concern, small disadvantaged business concern,

HUBZone small business concern, service-disabled veteran-owned small business concern, economically disadvantaged women-owned small business concern, or women-owned small business concern eligible under the Women-Owned Small Business Program).

(iii) The notice is not required when the contracting officer determines in writing that the urgency of the requirement necessitates award without delay or when the contract is entered into under the 8(a) program (see 19.805-2).

(b) *Postaward notices.* (1) Within 3 days after the date of contract award, the contracting officer shall provide written notification to each offeror whose proposal was in the competitive range but was not selected for award (10 U.S.C. 2305(b)(5) and 41 U.S.C. 3704) or had not been previously notified under paragraph (a) of this section. The notice shall include—

(i) The number of offerors solicited;

(ii) The number of proposals received;

(iii) The name and address of each offeror receiving an award;

(iv) The items, quantities, and any stated unit prices of each award. If the number of items or other factors makes listing any stated unit prices impracticable at that time, only the total contract price need be furnished in the notice. However, the items, quantities, and any stated unit prices of each award shall be made publicly available, upon request; and

(v) In general terms, the reason(s) the offeror's proposal was not accepted, unless the price information in paragraph (b)(1)(iv) of this section readily reveals the reason. In no event shall an offeror's cost breakdown, profit, overhead rates, trade secrets, manufacturing processes and techniques, or other confidential business information be disclosed to any other offeror.

(2) Upon request, the contracting officer shall furnish the information described in paragraph (b)(1) of this section to unsuccessful offerors in solicitations using simplified acquisition procedures in Part 13.

(3) Upon request, the contracting officer shall provide the information in paragraph (b)(1) of this section to unsuccessful offerors that received a preaward notice of exclusion from the competitive range.

[FAC 97-2, 62 FR 51224, 9/30/97, effective 10/10/97; FAC 97-6, 63 FR 35719, 6/30/98, effective 10/1/98, finalized without change, FAC 97-13, 7/2/99; FAC 97-7, 63 FR 36120, 7/1/98, effective 1/1/99, finalized without change, FAC 97-13, 7/2/99; FAC 97-10,63 FR 70264, 12/18/98, effective 1/4/99; FAC 97-21, 65 FR 80255, 12/20/2000, effective 1/19/2001, stayed FAC 97-24, 66 FR 17753, 4/3/2001, effective 4/3/2001, finalized with changes FAC 2001-03, 66 FR 66984, 12/27/2001, effective 12/27/2001; FAC 2001-23, 69 FR 25273, 5/5/2004, effective 5/5/2004; FAC 2005-02, 70 FR 14950, 3/23/2005, effective 3/23/2005; FAC 2005-51, 76 FR 18304, 4/1/2011, effective 4/1/2011; FAC 2005-56, 77 FR 12913, 3/2/2012, effective 4/2/2012; FAC 2005-73, 79 FR 24192, 4/29/2014, effective 5/29/2014; FAC 2005-76, 79 FR 43580, 7/25/2014, effective 8/25/2014; FAC 2005-77, 79 FR 61746, 10/14/2014, effective 10/14/2014]

15.504 Award to successful offeror.

The contracting officer shall award a contract to the successful offeror by furnishing the executed contract or other notice of the award to that offeror.

(a) If the award document includes information that is different than the latest signed proposal, as amended by the offeror's written correspondence, both the offeror and the contracting officer shall sign the contract award.

(b) When an award is made to an offeror for less than all of the items that may be awarded and additional items are being withheld for subsequent award, each notice shall state that the Government may make subsequent awards on those additional items within the proposal acceptance period.

(c) If the Optional Form (OF) 307, Contract Award, Standard Form (SF) 26, Award/Contract, or SF 33, Solicitation, Offer and Award, is not used to award the contract, the first page of the award document shall contain the Government's acceptance statement from Block 15 of that form, exclusive of the Item 3 reference language, and shall contain the contracting officer's name, signature, and date. In addition, if the award document includes information that is different than the signed proposal, as amended by the offeror's written correspondence, the first page shall include the contractor's agreement statement from Block 14 of the OF 307 and the signature of the contractor's authorized representative.

[FAC 97-2, 62 FR 51224, 9/30/97, effective 10/10/97]

15.505 Preaward debriefing of offerors.

Offerors excluded from the competitive range or otherwise excluded from the competition before award may request a debriefing before award (10 U.S.C. 2305(b)(6)(A) and 41 U.S.C. 3705).

(a)(1) The offeror may request a preaward debriefing by submitting a written request for debriefing to the contracting officer within 3 days after receipt of the notice of exclusion from the competition.

(2) At the offeror's request, this debriefing may be delayed until after award. If the debriefing is delayed until after award, it shall include all information normally provided in a postaward debriefing (see 15.506(d)). Debriefings delayed pursuant to this paragraph could affect the timeliness of any protest filed subsequent to the debriefing.

(3) If the offeror does not submit a timely request, the offeror need not be given either a preaward or a postaward debriefing. Offerors are entitled to no more than one debriefing for each proposal.

(b) The contracting officer shall make every effort to debrief the unsuccessful offeror as soon as practicable, but may refuse the request for a debriefing if, for compelling reasons, it is not in the best interests of the Government to conduct a debriefing at that time. The rationale for delaying the debriefing shall be documented in the contract file. If the contracting officer delays the debriefing, it shall be provided no later than the time postaward debriefings are provided under 15.506. In that event, the contracting officer shall include the information at 15.506(d) in the debriefing.

(c) Debriefings may be done orally, in writing, or by any other method acceptable to the contracting officer.

(d) The contracting officer should normally chair any debriefing session held. Individuals who conducted the evaluations shall provide support.

(e) At a minimum, preaward debriefings shall include—

(1) The agency's evaluation of significant elements in the offeror's proposal;

(2) A summary of the rationale for eliminating the offeror from the competition; and

(3) Reasonable responses to relevant questions about whether source selection procedures contained in the solicitation, applicable regulations, and other applicable authorities were followed in the process of eliminating the offeror from the competition.

(f) Preaward debriefings shall not disclose—

(1) The number of offerors;

(2) The identity of other offerors;

(3) The content of other offerors proposals;

(4) The ranking of other offerors;

(5) The evaluation of other offerors; or

(6) Any of the information prohibited in 15.506(e).

(g) An official summary of the debriefing shall be included in the contract file.

[FAC 97-2, 62 FR 51224, 9/30/97, effective 10/10/97; FAC 2005-73, 79 FR 24192, 4/29/2014, effective 5/29/2014]

15.506 Postaward debriefing of offerors.

(a)(1) An offeror, upon its written request received by the agency within 3 days after the date on which that offeror has received notification of contract award in accordance with 15.503(b), shall be debriefed and furnished the basis for the selection decision and contract award.

(2) To the maximum extent practicable, the debriefing should occur within 5 days after receipt of the written request. Offerors

that requested a postaward debriefing in lieu of a preaward debriefing, or whose debriefing was delayed for compelling reasons beyond contract award, also should be debriefed within this time period.

(3) An offeror that was notified of exclusion from the competition (see 15.505(a)), but failed to submit a timely request, is not entitled to a debriefing.

(4) (i) Untimely debriefing requests may be accommodated.

(ii) Government accommodation of a request for delayed debriefing pursuant to 15.505(a) (2), or any untimely debriefing request, does not automatically extend the deadlines for filing protests. Debriefings delayed pursuant to 15.505(a) (2) could affect the timeliness of any protest filed subsequent to the debriefing.

(b) Debriefings of successful and unsuccessful offerors may be done orally, in writing, or by any other method acceptable to the contracting officer.

(c) The contracting officer should normally chair any debriefing session held. Individuals who conducted the evaluations shall provide support.

(d) At a minimum, the debriefing information shall include—

(1) The Government's evaluation of the significant weaknesses or deficiencies in the offeror's proposal, if applicable;

(2) The overall evaluated cost or price (including unit prices), and technical rating, if applicable, of the successful offeror and the debriefed offeror, and past performance information on the debriefed offeror;

(3) The overall ranking of all offerors, when any ranking was developed by the agency during the source selection;

(4) A summary of the rationale for award;

(5) For acquisitions of commercial items, the make and model of the item to be delivered by the successful offeror; and

(6) Reasonable responses to relevant questions about whether source selection procedures contained in the solicitation, applicable regulations, and other applicable authorities were followed.

(e) The debriefing shall not include point-by-point comparisons of the debriefed offeror's proposal with those of other offerors. Moreover, the debriefing shall not reveal any information prohibited from disclosure by 24.202 or exempt from release under the Freedom of Information Act (5 U.S.C. 552) including—

(1) Trade secrets;

(2) Privileged or confidential manufacturing processes and techniques;

(3) Commercial and financial information that is privileged or confidential, including cost breakdowns, profit, indirect cost rates, and similar information; and

(4) The names of individuals providing reference information about an offeror's past performance.

(f) An official summary of the debriefing shall be included in the contract file.

[FAC 97-2, 62 FR 51224, 9/30/97, effective 10/10/97]

15.507 Protests against award.

(a) Protests against award in negotiated acquisitions shall be handled in accordance with Part 33. Use of agency protest procedures that incorporate the alternative dispute resolution provisions of Executive Order 12979 is encouraged for both preaward and postaward protests.

(b) If a protest causes the agency, within 1 year of contract award, to—

(1) Issue a new solicitation on the protested contract award, the contracting officer shall provide the information in paragraph (c) of this section to all prospective offerors for the new solicitation; or

(2) Issue a new request for revised proposals on the protested contract award, the contracting officer shall provide the information in paragraph (c) of this section to offerors that were in the competitive range and are requested to submit revised proposals.

(c) The following information will be provided to appropriate parties:

(1) Information provided to unsuccessful offerors in any debriefings conducted on the original award regarding the successful offeror's proposal; and

(2) Other nonproprietary information that would have been provided to the original offerors.

[FAC 97-2, 62 FR 51224, 9/30/97, effective 10/10/97]

15.508 Discovery of mistakes.

Mistakes in a contractor's proposal that are disclosed after award shall be processed substantially in accordance with the procedures for mistakes in bids at 14.407-4.

[FAC 97-2, 62 FR 51224, 9/30/97, effective 10/10/97]

15.509 Forms.

Optional Form 307, Contract Award, Standard Form (SF) 26, Award/Contract, or SF 33, Solicitation, Offer and Award, may be used to award negotiated contracts in which the signature of both parties on a single document is appropriate. Note however, if using the SF 26 for a negotiated procurement, block 18 is not to be used. If these forms are not used, the award document shall incorporate the agreement and award language from the OF 307.

[FAC 97-2, 62 FR 51224, 9/30/97, effective 10/10/97; FAC 2005-39, 75 FR 13415, 3/19/2010, effective 4/19/2010]

SUBPART 15.6—UNSOLICITED PROPOSALS

15.600 Scope of subpart.

This subpart sets forth policies and procedures concerning the submission, receipt, evaluation, and acceptance or rejection of unsolicited proposals.

[FAC 97-2, 62 FR 51224, 9/30/97, effective 10/10/97]

15.601 Definitions.

As used in this subpart—

Advertising material means material designed to acquaint the Government with a prospective contractor's present products, services, or potential capabilities, or designed to stimulate the Government's interest in buying such products or services.

Commercial item offer means an offer of a commercial item that the vendor wishes to see introduced in the Government's supply system as an alternate or a replacement for an existing supply item. This term does not include innovative or unique configurations or uses of commercial items that are being offered for further development and that may be submitted as an unsolicited proposal.

Contribution means a concept, suggestion, or idea presented to the Government for its use with no indication that the source intends to devote any further effort to it on the Government's behalf.

[FAC 97-2, 62 FR 51224, 9/30/97, effective 10/10/97; FAC 97-22, 66 FR 2116, 1/10/2001, effective 3/12/2001; Delay of effective date, 66 FR 14259, 3/9/2001, effective 5/11/2001]

15.602 Policy.

It is the policy of the Government to encourage the submission of new and innovative ideas in response to Broad Agency Announcements, Small Business Innovation Research topics, Small Business Technology Transfer Research topics, Program Research and Development Announcements, or any other Government-initiated solicitation or program. When the new and innovative ideas do not fall under topic areas publicized under those programs or techniques, the ideas may be submitted as unsolicited proposals.

[FAC 97-2, 62 FR 51224, 9/30/97, effective 10/10/97]

15.603 General.

(a) Unsolicited proposals allow unique and innovative ideas or approaches that have been developed outside the Government to be made available to Government agencies for use in accomplishment of their missions. Unsolicited proposals are offered with the intent that the Government will enter into a contract with the offeror for research and development or other efforts supporting the Government mission, and often represent a substantial investment of time and effort by the offeror.

(b) Advertising material, commercial item offers, or contributions, as defined in 15.601, or routine correspondence on technical issues, are not unsolicited proposals.

(c) A valid unsolicited proposal must—

(1) Be innovative and unique;

(2) Be independently originated and developed by the offeror;

(3) Be prepared without Government supervision, endorsement, direction, or direct Government involvement;

(4) Include sufficient detail to permit a determination that Government support could be worthwhile and the proposed work could benefit the agency's research and development or other mission responsibilities;

(5) Not be an advance proposal for a known agency requirement that can be acquired by competitive methods; and

(6) Not address a previously published agency requirement.

(d) Unsolicited proposals in response to a publicized general statement of agency needs are considered to be independently originated.

(e) Agencies must evaluate unsolicited proposals for energy-savings performance contracts in accordance with the procedures in 10 CFR 436.33(b).

[FAC 97-2, 62 FR 51224, 9/30/97, effective 10/10/97; FAC 2001-02, 66 FR 65347, 12/18/2001, effective 2/19/2002; FAC 2001-22, 69 FR 17768, 4/5/2004, effective 5/5/2004]

15.604 Agency points of contact.

(a) Preliminary contact with agency technical or other appropriate personnel before preparing a detailed unsolicited proposal or submitting proprietary information to the Government may save considerable time and effort for both parties (see 15.201). Agencies must make available to potential offerors of unsolicited proposals at least the following information:

(1) Definition (see 2.101) and content (see 15.605) of an unsolicited proposal acceptable for formal evaluation.

(2) Requirements concerning responsible prospective contractors (see Subpart 9.1), and organizational conflicts of interest (see Subpart 9.5).

(3) Guidance on preferred methods for submitting ideas/concepts to the Government, such as any agency: upcoming solicitations; Broad Agency Announcements; Small Business Innovation Research programs; Small Business Technology Transfer Research programs; Program Research and Development Announcements; or grant programs.

(4) Agency points of contact for information regarding advertising, contributions, and other types of transactions similar to unsolicited proposals.

(5) Information sources on agency objectives and areas of potential interest.

(6) Procedures for submission and evaluation of unsolicited proposals.

(7) Instructions for identifying and marking proprietary information so that it is protected and restrictive legends conform to 15.609.

(b) Only the cognizant contracting officer has the authority to bind the Government regarding unsolicited proposals.

[FAC 97-2, 62 FR 51224, 9/30/97, effective 10/10/97; FAC 97-22, 66 FR 2116, 1/10/2001, effective 3/12/2001; Delay of effective date, 66 FR 14259, 3/9/2001, effective 5/11/2001]

15.605 Content of unsolicited proposals.

Unsolicited proposals should contain the following information to permit consideration in an objective and timely manner:

(a) Basic information including—

(1) Offeror's name and address and type of organization; *e.g.*, profit, nonprofit, educational, small business;

(2) Names and telephone numbers of technical and business personnel to be contacted for evaluation or negotiation purposes;

(3) Identification of proprietary data to be used only for evaluation purposes;

(4) Names of other Federal, State, or local agencies or parties receiving the proposal or funding the proposed effort;

(5) Date of submission; and

(6) Signature of a person authorized to represent and contractually obligate the offeror.

(b) Technical information including—

(1) Concise title and abstract (approximately 200 words) of the proposed effort;

(2) A reasonably complete discussion stating the objectives of the effort or activity, the method of approach and extent of effort to be employed, the nature and extent of the anticipated results, and the manner in which the work will help to support accomplishment of the agency's mission;

(3) Names and biographical information on the offeror's key personnel who would be involved, including alternates; and

(4) Type of support needed from the agency; *e.g.*, Government property, or personnel resources.

(c) Supporting information including—

(1) Proposed price or total estimated cost for the effort in sufficient detail for meaningful evaluation;

(2) Period of time for which the proposal is valid (a 6-month minimum is suggested);

(3) Type of contract preferred;

(4) Proposed duration of effort;

(5) Brief description of the organization, previous experience, relevant past performance, and facilities to be used;

(6) Other statements, if applicable, about organizational conflicts of interest, security clearances, and environmental impacts; and

(7) The names and telephone numbers of agency technical or other agency points of contact already contacted regarding the proposal.

[FAC 97-2, 62 FR 51224, 9/30/97, effective 10/10/97; FAC 2005-17, 72 FR 27364, 5/15/2007, effective 6/14/2007]

15.606 Agency procedures.

(a) Agencies shall establish procedures for controlling the receipt, evaluation, and timely disposition of unsolicited proposals consistent with the requirements of this subpart. The procedures shall include controls on the reproduction and disposition of proposal material, particularly data identified by the offeror as subject to duplication, use, or disclosure restrictions.

(b) Agencies shall establish agency points of contact (see 15.604) to coordinate the receipt and handling of unsolicited proposals.

[FAC 97-2, 62 FR 51224, 9/30/97, effective 10/10/97]

15.606-1 Receipt and initial review.

(a) Before initiating a comprehensive evaluation, the agency contact point shall determine if the proposal—

(1) Is a valid unsolicited proposal, meeting the requirements of 15.603(c);

(2) Is suitable for submission in response to an existing agency requirement (see 15.602);

(3) Is related to the agency mission;

(4) Contains sufficient technical information and cost-related or price-related information for evaluation;

(5) Has overall scientific, technical, or socioeconomic merit;

(6) Has been approved by a responsible official or other representative authorized to obligate the offeror contractually; and

(7) Complies with the marking requirements of 15.609.

(b) If the proposal meets these requirements, the contact point shall promptly acknowledge receipt and process the proposal.

(c) If a proposal is rejected because the proposal does not meet the requirements of paragraph (a) of this subsection, the agency contact point shall promptly inform the offeror of the reasons for rejection in writing and of the proposed disposition of the unsolicited proposal.

[FAC 97-2, 62 FR 51224, 9/30/97, effective 10/10/97; FAC 2001-22, 69 FR 17768, 4/5/2004, effective 5/5/2004]

15.606-2 Evaluation.

(a) Comprehensive evaluations shall be coordinated by the agency contact point, who shall attach or imprint on each unsolicited proposal, circulated for evaluation, the legend required by 15.609(d). When performing a comprehensive evaluation of an unsolicited proposal, evaluators shall consider the following factors, in addition to any others appropriate for the particular proposal:

(1) Unique, innovative, and meritorious methods, approaches, or concepts demonstrated by the proposal;

(2) Overall scientific, technical, or socioeconomic merits of the proposal;

(3) Potential contribution of the effort to the agency's specific mission;

(4) The offeror's capabilities, related experience, facilities, techniques, or unique combinations of these that are integral factors for achieving the proposal objectives;

(5) The qualifications, capabilities, and experience of the proposed principal investigator, team leader, or key personnel critical to achieving the proposal objectives; and

(6) The realism of the proposed cost.

(b) The evaluators shall notify the agency point of contact of their recommendations when the evaluation is completed.

[FAC 97-2, 62 FR 51224, 9/30/97, effective 10/10/97]

15.607 Criteria for acceptance and negotiation of an unsolicited proposal.

(a) A favorable comprehensive evaluation of an unsolicited proposal does not, in itself, justify awarding a contract without providing for full and open competition. The agency point of contact shall return an unsolicited proposal to the offeror, citing reasons, when its substance—

(1) Is available to the Government without restriction from another source;

(2) Closely resembles a pending competitive acquisition requirement;

(3) Does not relate to the activity's mission; or

(4) Does not demonstrate an innovative and unique method, approach, or concept, or is otherwise not deemed a meritorious proposal.

(b) The contracting officer may commence negotiations on a sole source basis only when—

(1) An unsolicited proposal has received a favorable comprehensive evaluation;

(2) A justification and approval has been obtained (see 6.302-1(a)(2)(i) for research proposals or other appropriate provisions of Subpart 6.3, and 6.303-2(c));

(3) The agency technical office sponsoring the contract furnishes the necessary funds; and

(4) The contracting officer has complied with the synopsis requirements of Subpart 5.2.

[FAC 97-2, 62 FR 51224, 9/30/97, effective 10/10/97; FAC 2005-50, 76 FR 14559, 3/16/2011, effective 3/16/2011; FAC 2005-58, 77 FR 23369, 4/18/2012, effective 4/18/2012]

15.608 Prohibitions.

(a) Government personnel shall not use any data, concept, idea, or other part of an unsolicited proposal as the basis, or part of the basis, for a solicitation or in negotiations with any other firm unless the offeror is notified of and agrees to the intended use. However, this prohibition does not preclude using any data, concept, or idea in the proposal that also is available from another source without restriction.

(b) Government personnel shall not disclose restrictively marked information (see 3.104 and 15.609) included in an unsolicited proposal. The disclosure of such information concerning trade secrets, processes, operations, style of work, apparatus, and other matters, except as authorized by law, may result in criminal penalties under 18 U.S.C. 1905.

[FAC 97-2, 62 FR 51224, 9/30/97, effective 10/10/97]

15.609 Limited use of data.

(a) An unsolicited proposal may include data that the offeror does not want disclosed to the public for any purpose or used by the Government except for evaluation purposes. If the offeror wishes to restrict the data, the title page must be marked with the following legend:

Use and Disclosure of Data

This proposal includes data that shall not be disclosed outside the Government and shall not be duplicated, used, or disclosed—

in whole or in part—for any purpose other than to evaluate this proposal. However, if a contract is awarded to this offeror as a result of—or in connection with—the submission of these data, the Government shall have the right to duplicate, use, or disclose the data to the extent provided in the resulting contract. This restriction does not limit the Government's right to use information contained in these data if they are obtained from another source without restriction. The data subject to this restriction are contained in Sheets *[insert numbers or other identification of sheets]*.

(b) The offeror shall also mark each sheet of data it wishes to restrict with the following legend: Use or disclosure of data contained on this sheet is subject to the restriction on the title page of this proposal.

(c) The agency point of contact shall return to the offeror any unsolicited proposal marked with a legend different from that provided in paragraph (a) of this section. The return letter will state that the proposal cannot be considered because it is impracticable for the Government to comply with the legend and that the agency will consider the proposal if it is resubmitted with the proper legend.

(d) The agency point of contact shall place a cover sheet on the proposal or clearly mark it as follows, unless the offeror clearly states in writing that no restrictions are imposed on the disclosure or use of the data contained in the proposal:

Unsolicited Proposal—Use of Data Limited

All Government personnel must exercise extreme care to ensure that the information in this proposal is not disclosed to an individual who has not been authorized access to such data in accordance with FAR 3.104, and is not duplicated, used, or disclosed in whole or in part for any purpose other than evaluation of the proposal, without the written permission of the offeror. If a contract is awarded on the basis of this proposal, the terms of the contract shall control disclosure and use. This notice does not limit the Government's right to use information contained in the proposal if it is obtainable from another source without restriction. This is a Government notice, and shall not by itself be construed to impose any liability upon the Government or Government personnel for disclosure or use of data contained in this proposal.

(e) Use the notice in paragraph (d) of this section solely as a manner of handling unsolicited proposals that will be compatible with this subpart. However, do not use this notice to justify withholding of a record, or to improperly deny the public access to a record, where an obligation is imposed by the Freedom of Information Act (5 U.S.C. 552). An offeror should identify trade secrets, commercial or financial information, and privileged or confidential information to the Government (see paragraph (a) of this section).

(f) When an agency receives an unsolicited proposal without any restrictive legend from an educational or nonprofit organization or institution, and an evaluation outside the Government is necessary, the agency point of contact shall—

(1) Attach a cover sheet clearly marked with the legend in paragraph (d) of this section;

(2) Change the beginning of this legend to read "All Government and non-Government personnel . . ."; and

(3) Require any non-Government evaluator to agree in writing that data in the proposal will not be disclosed to others outside the Government.

(g) If the proposal is received with the restrictive legend (see paragraph (a) of this section), the modified cover sheet shall also be used and permission shall be obtained from the offeror before release of the proposal for evaluation by non-Government personnel.

(h) When an agency receives an unsolicited proposal with or without a restrictive legend from other than an educational or nonprofit organization or institution, and evaluation by Government personnel outside the agency or by experts outside of the Government is necessary, written permission must be obtained from the offeror before release of the proposal for evaluation. The agency point of contact shall—

(1) Clearly mark the cover sheet with the legend in paragraph (d) or as modified in paragraph (f) of this section; and

(2) Obtain a written agreement from any non-Government evaluator stating that data in the proposal will not be disclosed to persons outside the Government.

[FAC 97-2, 62 FR 51224, 9/30/97, effective 10/10/97; FAC 2001-06, 67 FR 13048, 3/20/2002, effective 4/4/2002]

PART 16—TYPES OF CONTRACTS

Table of Contents

Scope of part 16.000
Definitions 16.001

Subpart 16.1—Selecting Contract Types

General 16.101
Policies 16.102
Negotiating contract type 16.103
Factors in selecting contract types 16.104
Solicitation provision 16.105

Subpart 16.2—Fixed-Price Contracts

General 16.201
Firm-fixed-price contracts 16.202
Description 16.202-1
Application 16.202-2
Fixed-price contracts with economic price adjustment 16.203
Description 16.203-1
Application 16.203-2
Limitations 16.203-3
Contract clauses 16.203-4
Fixed-price incentive contracts 16.204
Fixed-price contracts with prospective price redetermination 16.205
Description 16.205-1
Application 16.205-2
Limitations 16.205-3
Contract clause 16.205-4
Fixed-ceiling-price contracts with retroactive price redetermination 16.206
Description 16.206-1
Application 16.206-2
Limitations 16.206-3
Contract clause 16.206-4
Firm-fixed-price, level-of-effort term contracts 16.207
Description 16.207-1
Application 16.207-2
Limitations 16.207-3

Subpart 16.3—Cost-Reimbursement Contracts

General 16.301
Description 16.301-1
Application 16.301-2
Limitations 16.301-3
Cost contracts 16.302
Cost-sharing contracts 16.303
Cost-plus-incentive-fee contracts 16.304
Cost-plus-award-fee contracts 16.305
Cost-plus-fixed-fee contracts 16.306
Contract clauses 16.307

Subpart 16.4—Incentive Contracts

General 16.401
Application of predetermined, formula-type incentives 16.402
Cost incentives 16.402-1
Performance incentives 16.402-2
Delivery incentives 16.402-3
Structuring multiple-incentive contracts 16.402-4
Fixed-price incentive contracts 16.403

Fixed-price incentive (firm target) contracts 16.403-1
Fixed-price incentive (successive targets) contracts 16.403-2
Fixed-price contracts with award fees 16.404
Cost-reimbursement incentive contracts 16.405
Cost-plus-incentive-fee contracts 16.405-1
Cost-plus-award-fee contracts 16.405-2
Contract clauses 16.406

Subpart 16.5—Indefinite-Delivery Contracts

Scope of subpart 16.500
Definitions 16.501-1
General 16.501-2
Definite-quantity contracts 16.502
Requirements contracts 16.503
Indefinite-quantity contracts 16.504
Ordering 16.505
Solicitation provisions and contract clauses 16.506

Subpart 16.6—Time-And-Materials, Labor-Hour, And Letter Contracts

Scope 16.600
Time-and-materials contracts 16.601
Labor-hour contracts 16.602
Letter contracts 16.603
Description 16.603-1
Application 16.603-2
Limitations 16.603-3
Contract clauses 16.603-4

Subpart 16.7—Agreements

Scope 16.701
Basic agreements 16.702
Basic ordering agreements 16.703

PART 16—TYPES OF CONTRACTS

16.000 Scope of part.

This part describes types of contracts that may be used in acquisitions. It prescribes policies and procedures and provides guidance for selecting a contract type appropriate to the circumstances of the acquisition.

[FAC 90-29, 60 FR 34732, 7/3/95, effective 7/3/95; FAC 90-40, 61 FR 39186, 7/26/96, effective 8/26/96]

16.001 Definitions.

As used in this part—

Award-Fee Board means the team of individuals identified in the award-fee plan who have been designated to assist the Fee-Determining Official in making award-fee determinations.

Fee-Determining Official (FDO) means the designated Agency official(s) who reviews the recommendations of the Award-Fee Board in determining the amount of award fee to be earned by the contractor for each evaluation period.

Rollover of unearned award fee means the process of transferring unearned award fee, which the contractor had an opportunity to earn, from one evaluation period to a subsequent evaluation period, thus allowing the contractor an additional opportunity to earn that previously unearned award fee.

[FAC 2005-37, 74 FR 52856, 10/14/2009, effective 10/14/2009; FAC 2005-46, 75 FR 60261, 9/29/2010, effective 10/29/2010]

SUBPART 16.1—SELECTING CONTRACT TYPES

16.101 General.

(a) A wide selection of contract types is available to the Government and contractors in order to provide needed flexibility in acquiring the large variety and volume of supplies and services required by agencies. Contract types vary according to—

(1) The degree and timing of the responsibility assumed by the contractor for the costs of performance; and

(2) The amount and nature of the profit incentive offered to the contractor for achieving or exceeding specified standards or goals.

(b) The contract types are grouped into two broad categories: fixed-price contracts (see Subpart 16.2) and cost-reimbursement contracts (see Subpart 16.3). The specific contract types range from firm-fixed-price, in which the contractor has full responsibility for the performance costs and resulting profit (or loss), to cost-plus-fixed-fee, in which the contractor has minimal responsibility for the performance costs and the negotiated fee (profit) is fixed. In between are the various incentive contracts (see Subpart 16.4), in which the contractor's responsibility for the performance costs and the profit or fee incentives offered are tailored to the uncertainties involved in contract performance.

16.102 Policies.

(a) Contracts resulting from sealed bidding shall be firm-fixed-price contracts or fixed-price contracts with economic price adjustment.

(b) Contracts negotiated under Part 15 may be of any type or combination of types that will promote the Government's interest, except as restricted in this part (see 10 U.S.C. 2306(a) and 41 U.S.C. 3901). Contract types not described in this regulation shall not be used, except as a deviation under Subpart 1.4.

(c) The cost-plus-a-percentage-of-cost system of contracting shall not be used (see 10 U.S.C. 2306(a) and 41 U.S.C. 3905(a)). Prime contracts (including letter contracts) other than firm-fixed-price contracts shall, by an appropriate clause, prohibit cost-plus-a-percentage-of-cost subcontracts (see clauses prescribed in Subpart 44.2 for cost-reimbursement contracts and Subparts 16.2 and 16.4 for fixed-price contracts).

(d) No contract may be awarded before the execution of any determination and findings (D&F's) required by this part. Minimum requirements for the content of D&F's required by this part are specified in 1.704.

[FAC 84-5, 50 FR 1741, 1/11/85, effective 4/1/85; FAC 2005-73, 79 FR 24192, 4/29/2014, effective 5/29/2014]

16.103 Negotiating contract type.

(a) Selecting the contract type is generally a matter for negotiation and requires the exercise of sound judgment. Negotiating the contract type and negotiating prices are closely related and should be considered together. The objective is to negotiate a contract type and price (or estimated cost and fee) that will result in reasonable contractor risk and provide the contractor with the greatest incentive for efficient and economical performance.

(b) A firm-fixed-price contract, which best utilizes the basic profit motive of business enterprise, shall be used when the risk involved is minimal or can be predicted with an acceptable degree of certainty. However, when a reasonable basis for firm pricing does not exist, other contract types should be considered, and negotiations should be directed toward selecting a contract type (or combination of types) that will appropriately tie profit to contractor performance.

(c) In the course of an acquisition program, a series of contracts, or a single long-term contract, changing circumstances may make a different contract type appropriate in later periods than that used at the outset. In particular, contracting officers should avoid protracted use of a cost-reimbursement or time-and-materials contract after experience provides a basis for firmer pricing.

(1) Each contract file shall include documentation to show why the particular contract type was selected. This shall be documented in the acquisition plan, or in the contract file if a written acquisition plan is not required by agency procedures.

(i) Explain why the contract type selected must be used to meet the agency need.

(ii) Discuss the Government's additional risks and the burden to manage the contract type selected (*e.g.,* when a cost-reimbursement contract is selected, the Government incurs additional cost risks, and the Government has the additional burden of managing the contractor's costs). For such instances, acquisition personnel shall discuss—

(A) How the Government identified the additional risks (*e.g.,* pre-award survey, or past performance information);

(B) The nature of the additional risks (*e.g.,* inadequate contractor's accounting system, weaknesses in contractor's internal control, non-compliance with Cost Accounting Standards, or lack of or inadequate earned value management system); and

(C) How the Government will manage and mitigate the risks.

(iii) Discuss the Government resources necessary to properly plan for, award, and administer the contract type selected (*e.g.,* resources needed and the additional risks to the Government if adequate resources are not provided).

(iv) For other than a firm-fixed price contract, at a minimum the documentation should include—

(A) An analysis of why the use of other than a firm-fixed-price contract (*e.g.,* cost reimbursement, time and materials, labor hour) is appropriate;

(B) Rationale that detail the particular facts and circumstances (*e.g.,* complexity of the requirements, uncertain duration of the work, contractor's technical capability and financial responsibility, or adequacy of the contractor's accounting system), and associated reasoning essential to support the contract type selection;

(C) An assessment regarding the adequacy of Government resources that are necessary to properly plan for, award, and administer other than firm-fixed-price contracts; and

(D) A discussion of the actions planned to minimize the use of other than firm-fixed-price contracts on future acquisitions for the same requirement and to transition to firm-fixed-price contracts to the maximum extent practicable.

(v) A discussion of why a level-of-effort, price redetermination, or fee provision was included.

(2) Exceptions to the requirements at (d)(1) of this section are—

(i) Fixed-price acquisitions made under simplified acquisition procedures;

(ii) Contracts on a firm-fixed-price basis other than those for major systems or research and development; and

(iii) Awards on the set-aside portion of sealed bid partial set-asides for small business.

[FAC 84-5, 50 FR 1742, 1/11/85, effective 4/1/85; FAC 84-42, 54 FR 5054, 1/31/89, effective 3/2/89; FAC 90-29, 60 FR 34732, 7/3/95, effective 7/3/95; FAC 90-32, 60 FR 48206, 9/18/95, effective 10/1/95; FAC 90-40, 61 FR 39186, 7/26/96, effective 8/26/96; FAC 2005-50, 76 FR 14543, 3/16/2011, effective 3/16/2011; FAC 2005-56, 77 FR 12925, 3/2/2012, effective 4/2/2012; FAC 2005-78, 79 FR 70348, 11/25/2014, effective 11/25/2014]

16.104 Factors in selecting contract types.

There are many factors that the contracting officer should consider in selecting and negotiating the contract type. They include the following:

(a) *Price competition*. Normally, effective price competition results in realistic pricing, and a fixed-price contract is ordinarily in the Government's interest.

(b) *Price analysis*. Price analysis, with or without competition, may provide a basis for selecting the contract type. The degree to which price analysis can provide a realistic pricing standard should be carefully considered. (See 15.404-1(b).)

(c) *Cost analysis*. In the absence of effective price competition and if price analysis is not sufficient, the cost estimates of the offeror and the Government provide the bases for negotiating contract pricing arrangements. It is essential that the uncertainties involved in performance and their possible impact upon costs be identified and evaluated, so that a contract type that places a reasonable degree of cost responsibility upon the contractor can be negotiated.

(d) *Type and complexity of the requirement*. Complex requirements, particularly those unique to the Government, usually result in greater risk assumption by the Government. This is especially true for complex research and development contracts, when performance uncertainties or the likelihood of changes makes it difficult to estimate performance costs in advance. As a requirement recurs or as quantity production begins, the cost risk should shift to the contractor, and a fixed-price contract should be considered.

(e) *Combining contract types*. If the entire contract cannot be firm-fixed-price, the contracting officer shall consider whether or not a portion of the contract can be established on a firm-fixed-price basis.

(f) *Urgency of the requirement*. If urgency is a primary factor, the Government may choose to assume a greater proportion of risk or it may offer incentives tailored to performance outcomes to ensure timely contract performance.

(g) *Period of performance or length of production run*. In times of economic uncertainty, contracts extending over a relatively long period may require economic price adjustment or price redetermination clauses.

(h) *Contractor's technical capability and financial responsibility*.

(i) *Adequacy of the contractor's accounting system*. Before agreeing on a contract type other than firm-fixed-price, the contracting officer shall ensure that the contractor's accounting system will permit timely development of all necessary cost data in the form required by the proposed contract type. This factor may be critical—

(1) When the contract type requires price revision while performance is in progress; or

(2) When a cost-reimbursement contract is being considered and all current or past experience with the contractor has been on a fixed-price basis. *See* 42.302(a)(12).

(j) *Concurrent contracts*. If performance under the proposed contract involves concurrent operations under other contracts, the impact of those contracts, including their pricing arrangements, should be considered.

(k) *Extent and nature of proposed subcontracting*. If the contractor proposes extensive subcontracting, a contract type reflecting the actual risks to the prime contractor should be selected.

(l) *Acquisition history*. Contractor risk usually decreases as the requirement is repetitively acquired. Also, product descriptions or descriptions of services to be performed can be defined more clearly.

[FAC 84-5, 50 FR 1742, 1/11/85, effective 4/1/85; FAC 97-1, 62 FR 44802, 8/22/97, effective 10/21/97; FAC 97-2, 62 FR 51224, 9/30/97, effective 10/10/97; FAC 2005-50, 76 FR 14543, 3/16/2011, effective 3/16/2011; FAC 2005-56, 77 FR 12925, 3/2/2012, effective 4/2/2012]

16.105 Solicitation provision.

The contracting officer shall complete and insert the provision at 52.216-1, Type of Contract, in a solicitation unless it is for—

(a) A fixed-price acquisition made under simplified acquisition procedures; or

(b) Information or planning purposes.

[FAC 90-29, 60 FR 34732, 7/3/95, effective 7/3/95; FAC 90-40, 61 FR 39186, 7/26/96, effective 8/26/96]

SUBPART 16.2—FIXED-PRICE CONTRACTS

16.201 General.

(a) Fixed-price types of contracts provide for a firm price or, in appropriate cases, an adjustable price. Fixed-price contracts providing for an adjustable price may include a ceiling price, a target price (including target cost), or both. Unless otherwise specified in the contract, the ceiling price or target price is subject to adjustment only by operation of contract clauses providing for equitable adjustment or other revision of the contract price under stated circumstances. The contracting officer shall use firm-fixed-price or fixed-price with economic price adjustment contracts when acquiring commercial items, except as provided in 12.207(b).

(b) Time-and-materials contracts and labor-hour contracts are not fixed-price contracts.

[FAC 90-32, 60 FR 48206, 9/18/95, effective 10/1/95; FAC 2005-55, 77 FR 194, 1/3/2012, effective 2/2/2012]

16.202 Firm-fixed-price contracts. (No Text)

16.202-1 Description.

A firm-fixed-price contract provides for a price that is not subject to any adjustment on the basis of the contractor's cost experience in performing the contract. This contract type places upon the contractor maximum risk and full responsibility for all costs and resulting profit or loss. It provides maximum incentive for the contractor to control costs and perform effectively and imposes a minimum administrative burden upon the contracting parties. The contracting officer may use a firm-fixed-price contract in conjunction with an award-fee incentive (see 16.404) and performance or delivery incentives (see 16.402-2 and 16.402-3) when the award fee or incentive is based solely on factors other than cost. The contract type remains firm-fixed price when used with these incentives.

[FAC 2001-13, 68 FR 13201, 3/18/2003, effective 4/17/2003]

16.202-2 Application.

A firm-fixed-price contract is suitable for acquiring commercial items (see Parts 2 and 12) or for acquiring other supplies or services on the basis of reasonably definite functional or detailed specifications (see Part 11) when the contracting officer can establish fair and reasonable prices at the outset, such as when—

(a) There is adequate price competition;

(b) There are reasonable price comparisons with prior purchases of the same or similar supplies or services made on a competitive basis or supported by valid certified cost or pricing data;

(c) Available cost or pricing information permits realistic estimates of the probable costs of performance; or

(d) Performance uncertainties can be identified and reasonable estimates of their cost impact can be made, and the contractor is willing to accept a firm fixed price representing assumption of the risks involved.

[FAC 90-32, 60 FR 48206, 9/18/95, effective 10/1/95; FAC 2005-45, 75 FR 53135, 8/30/2010, effective 10/1/2010]

16.203 Fixed-price contracts with economic price adjustment. (No Text)

16.203-1 Description.

(a) A fixed-price contract with economic price adjustment provides for upward and downward revision of the stated contract price upon the occurrence of specified contingencies. Economic price adjustments are of three general types:

(1) *Adjustments based on established prices.* These price adjustments are based on increases or decreases from an agreed-upon level in published or otherwise established prices of specific items or the contract end items.

(2) *Adjustments based on actual costs of labor or material.* These price adjustments are based on increases or decreases in specified costs of labor or material that the contractor actually experiences during contract performance.

(3) *Adjustments based on cost indexes of labor or material.* These price adjustments are based on increases or decreases in labor or material cost standards or indexes that are specifically identified in the contract.

(b) The contracting officer may use a fixed-price contract with economic price adjustment in conjunction with an award-fee incentive (see 16.404) and performance or delivery incentives (see 16.404-2 and 16.402-3) when the award fee or incentive is based solely on factors other than cost. The contract type remains fixed-price with economic price adjustment when used with these incentives.

[FAC 2001-13, 68 FR 13201, 3/18/2003, effective 4/17/2003]

16.203-2 Application.

A fixed-price contract with economic price adjustment may be used when

(i) there is serious doubt concerning the stability of market or labor conditions that will exist during an extended period of contract performance, and

(ii) contingencies that would otherwise be included in the contract price can be identified and covered separately in the contract. Price adjustments based on established prices should normally be restricted to industry-wide contingencies. Price adjustments based on labor and material costs should be limited to contingencies beyond the contractor's control. For use of economic price adjustment in sealed bid contracts, see 14.408-4.

(a) In establishing the base level from which adjustment will be made, the contracting officer shall ensure that contingency allowances are not duplicated by inclusion in both the base price and the adjustment requested by the contractor under economic price adjustment clause.

(b) In contracts that do not require submission of certified cost or pricing data, the contracting officer shall obtain adequate data to establish the base level from which adjustment will be made and may require verification of data submitted.

[FAC 84-5, 50 FR 1742, 1/11/85, effective 4/1/85; FAC 90-29, 60 FR 34732, 7/3/95, effective 7/3/95; FAC 2005-45, 75 FR 53135, 8/30/2010, effective 10/1/2010]

16.203-3 Limitations.

A fixed-price contract with economic price adjustment shall not be used unless the contracting officer determines that it is necessary either to protect the contractor and the Government against significant fluctuations in labor or material costs or to provide for contract price adjustment in the event of changes in the contractor's established prices.

16.203-4 Contract clauses.

(a) *Adjustment based on established prices—standard supplies.* (1) The contracting officer shall, when contracting by negotiation, insert the clause at 52.216-2, Economic Price Adjustment—Standard Supplies, or an agency-prescribed clause as authorized in subparagraph (a)(2) of this subsection, in solicitations and contracts when all of the following conditions apply:

(i) A fixed-price contract is contemplated.

(ii) The requirement is for standard supplies that have an established catalog or market price.

(iii) The contracting officer has made the determination specified in 16.203-3.

(2) If all the conditions in subparagraph (a)(1) of this subsection apply and the contracting officer determines that the use of the clause at 52.216-2 is inappropriate, the contracting officer may use an agency-prescribed clause instead of the clause at FAR 52.216-2.

(3) If the negotiated unit price reflects a net price after applying a trade discount from a catalog or list price, the contracting officer shall document in the contract file both the catalog or list price and the discount. (This does not apply to prompt payment or cash discounts.)

(b) *Adjustment based on established prices—semistandard supplies.* (1) The contracting officer shall, when contracting by negotiation, insert the clause at 52.216-3, Economic Price Adjustment—Semistandard Supplies, or an agency-prescribed clause as authorized in subparagraph (b)(2) below, in solicitations and contracts when all of the following conditions apply:

(i) A fixed price contract is contemplated.

(ii) The requirement is for semistandard supplies for which the prices can be reasonably related to the prices of nearly equivalent standard supplies that have an established catalog or market price.

(iii) The contracting officer has made the determination specified in 16.203-3.

(2) If all conditions in subparagraph (b)(1) of this subsection apply and the contracting officer determines that the use of the clause at 52.216-3 is inappropriate, the contracting officer may use an agency-prescribed clause instead of the clause at 52.216-3.

(3) If the negotiated unit price reflects a net price after applying a trade discount from a catalog or list price, the contracting officer shall document in the contract file both the catalog or list price and the discount. (This does not apply to prompt payment or cash discounts.)

(4) Before entering into the contract, the contracting officer and contractor must agree in writing on the identity of the standard supplies and the corresponding line items to which the clause applies.

(5) If the supplies are standard, except for preservation, packaging, and packing requirements, the clause prescribed in 16.203-4(a) shall be used rather than this clause.

(c) *Adjustments based on actual cost of labor or material.* (1) The contracting officer shall, when contracting by negotiation, insert a clause that is substantially the same as the clause at 52.216-4, Economic Price Adjustment—Labor and Material, or an agency-prescribed clause as authorized in subparagraph (c)(2) below, in solicitations and contracts when all of the following conditions apply:

(i) A fixed-price contract is contemplated.

(ii) There is no major element of design engineering or development work involved.

(iii) One or more identifiable labor or material cost factors are subject to change.

(iv) The contracting officer has made the determination specified in 16.203-3.

(2) If all conditions in subparagraph (c)(1) above apply and the contracting officer determines that the use of the clause at 52.216-4 is inappropriate, the contracting officer may use an agency-prescribed clause instead of the clause at 52.216-4.

(3) The contracting officer shall describe in detail in the contract Schedule—

(i) The types of labor and materials subject to adjustment under the clause;

(ii) The labor rates, including fringe benefits (if any) and unit prices of materials that may be increased or decreased; and

(iii) The quantities of the specified labor and materials allocable to each unit to be delivered under the contract.

(4) In negotiating adjustments under the clause, the contracting officer shall—

(i) Consider work in process and materials on hand at the time of changes in labor rates, including fringe benefits (if any) or material prices;

(ii) Not include in adjustments any indirect cost (except fringe benefits as defined in 31.205-6(m)) or profit; and

(iii) Consider only those fringe benefits specified in the contract Schedule.

(d) *Adjustments based on cost indexes of labor or material.* The contracting officer should consider using an economic price adjustment clause based on cost indexes of labor or material under the circumstances and subject to approval as described in subparagraphs (d) (1) and (d) (2) below.

(1) A clause providing adjustment based on cost indexes of labor or materials may be appropriate when—

(i) The contract involves an extended period of performance with significant costs to be incurred beyond 1 year after performance begins;

(ii) The contract amount subject to adjustment is substantial; and

(iii) The economic variables for labor and materials are too unstable to permit a reasonable division of risk between the Government and the contractor, without this type of clause.

(2) Any clause using this method shall be prepared and approved under agency procedures. Because of the variations in circumstances and clause wording that may arise, no standard clause is prescribed.

[FAC 84-26, 52 FR 19803, 5/27/87, effective 7/30/87; FAC 90-32, 60 FR 48206, 9/18/95, effective 10/1/95; FAC 90-45, 62 FR 224, 1/2/97, effective 1/1/97; FAC 2005-95, 82 FR 4709, 1/13/2017, effective 1/13/2017]

16.204 Fixed-price incentive contracts.

A fixed-price incentive contract is a fixed-price contract that provides for adjusting profit and establishing the final contract price by a formula based on the relationship of final negotiated total cost to total target cost. Fixed-price incentive contracts are covered in Subpart 16.4, Incentive Contracts. See 16.403 for more complete descriptions, application, and limitations for these contracts. Prescribed clauses are found at 16.406.

[Interim rule, FAC 90-20, 59 FR 11368, 3/10/94, effective 3/10/94; Final rule, FAC 90-46, 62 FR 12690, 3/17/97, effective 5/16/97]

16.205 Fixed-price contracts with prospective price redetermination. (No Text)

16.205-1 Description.

A fixed-price contract with prospective price redetermination provides for—

(a) A firm fixed price for an initial period of contract deliveries or performance; and

(b) Prospective redetermination, at a stated time or times during performance, of the price for subsequent periods of performance.

16.205-2 Application.

A fixed-price contract with prospective price redetermination may be used in acquisitions of quantity production or services for which it is possible to negotiate a fair and reasonable firm fixed price for an initial period, but not for subsequent periods of contract performance.

(a) The initial period should be the longest period for which it is possible to negotiate a fair and reasonable firm fixed price. Each subsequent pricing period should be at least 12 months.

(b) The contract may provide for a ceiling price based on evaluation of the uncertainties involved in performance and their possible cost impact. This ceiling price should provide for assumption of a reasonable proportion of the risk by the contractor and, once established, may be adjusted only by operation of contract clauses providing for equitable adjustment or other revision of the contract price under stated circumstances.

16.205-3 Limitations.

This contract type shall not be used unless—

(a) Negotiations have established that—

(1) The conditions for use of a firm-fixed-price contract are not present (see 16.202-2); and

(2) A fixed-price incentive contract would not be more appropriate;

(b) The contractor's accounting system is adequate for price redetermination;

(c) The prospective pricing periods can be made to conform with operation of the contractor's accounting system; and

(d) There is reasonable assurance that price redetermination actions will take place promptly at the specified times.

16.205-4 Contract clause.

The contracting officer shall, when contracting by negotiation, insert the clause at 52.216-5, Price Redetermination—Prospective, in solicitations and contracts when a fixed-price contract is contemplated and the conditions specified in 16.205-2 and 16.205-3(a) through (d) apply.

16.206 Fixed-ceiling-price contracts with retroactive price redetermination. (No Text)

16.206-1 Description.

A fixed-ceiling-price contract with retroactive price redetermination provides for—

(a) A fixed ceiling price; and

(b) Retroactive price redetermination within the ceiling after completion of the contract.

16.206-2 Application.

A fixed-ceiling-price contract with retroactive price redetermination is appropriate for research and development contracts estimated at $150,000 or less when it is established at the outset that a fair and reasonable firm fixed price cannot be negotiated and that the amount involved and short performance period make the use of any other fixed-price contract type impracticable.

(a) A ceiling price shall be negotiated for the contract at a level that reflects a reasonable sharing of risk by the contractor. The established ceiling price may be adjusted only if required by the operation of contract clauses providing for equitable adjustment or other revision of the contract price under stated circumstances.

(b) The contract should be awarded only after negotiation of a billing price that is as fair and reasonable as the circumstances permit.

(c) Since this contract type provides the contractor no cost control incentive except the ceiling price, the contracting officer should make clear to the contractor during discussion before award that the contractor's management effectiveness and ingenuity will be considered in retroactively redetermining the price.

[FAC 2005-45, 75 FR 53129, 8/30/2010, effective 10/1/2010]

16.206-3 Limitations.

This contract type shall not be used unless—

(a) The contract is for research and development and the estimated cost is $150,000 or less;

(b) The contractor's accounting system is adequate for price redetermination;

(c) There is reasonable assurance that the price redetermination will take place promptly at the specified time; and

(d) The head of the contracting activity (or a higher-level official, if required by agency procedures) approves its use in writing.

[FAC 2005-45, 75 FR 53129, 8/30/2010, effective 10/1/2010]

16.206-4 Contract clause.

The contracting officer shall, when contracting by negotiation, insert the clause at 52.216-6, Price Redetermination—Retroactive, in solicitations and contracts when a fixed-price contract is contemplated and the conditions in 16.206-2 and 16.206-3(a) through (d) apply.

16.207 Firm-fixed-price, level-of-effort term contracts. (No Text)

16.207-1 Description.

A firm-fixed-price, level-of-effort term contract requires—

(a) The contractor to provide a specified level of effort, over a stated period of time, on work that can be stated only in general terms; and

(b) The Government to pay the contractor a fixed dollar amount.

16.207-2 Application.

A firm-fixed-price, level-of-effort term contract is suitable for investigation or study in a specific research and development area. The product of the contract is usually a report showing the results achieved through application of the required level of effort. However, payment is based on the effort expended rather than on the results achieved.

16.207-3 Limitations.

This contract type may be used only when—

(a) The work required cannot otherwise be clearly defined;

(b) The required level of effort is identified and agreed upon in advance;

(c) There is reasonable assurance that the intended result cannot be achieved by expending less than the stipulated effort; and

(d) The contract price is $150,000 or less, unless approved by the chief of the contracting office.

[FAC 2005-45, 75 FR 53129, 8/30/2010, effective 10/1/2010]

SUBPART 16.3—COST-REIMBURSEMENT CONTRACTS

16.301 General. (No Text)

16.301-1 Description.

Cost-reimbursement types of contracts provide for payment of allowable incurred costs, to the extent prescribed in the contract. These contracts establish an estimate of total cost for the purpose of obligating funds and establishing a ceiling that the contractor may not exceed (except at its own risk) without the approval of the contracting officer.

16.301-2 Application.

(a) The contracting officer shall use cost-reimbursement contracts only when—

(1) Circumstances do not allow the agency to define its requirements sufficiently to allow for a fixed-price type contract (*see* 7.105); or

(2) Uncertainties involved in contract performance do not permit costs to be estimated with sufficient accuracy to use any type of fixed-price contract.

(b) The contracting officer shall document the rationale for selecting the contract type in the written acquisition plan and ensure that the plan is approved and signed at least one level above the contracting officer (*see* 7.103(j) and 7.105).

[FAC 2005-50, 76 FR 14543, 3/16/2011, effective 3/16/2011; FAC 2005-56, 77 FR 12925, 3/2/2012, effective 4/2/2012]

16.301-3 Limitations.

(a) A cost-reimbursement contract may be used only when—

(1) The factors in 16.104 have been considered;

(2) A written acquisition plan has been approved and signed at least one level above the contracting officer;

(3) The contractor's accounting system is adequate for determining costs applicable to the contract or order; and

(4) Prior to award of the contract or order, adequate Government resources are available to award and manage a contract other than firm-fixed-priced (see 7.104(e)). This includes appropriate Government surveillance during performance in accordance with 1.602-2, to provide reasonable assurance that efficient methods and effective cost controls are used.

(b) The use of cost-reimbursement contracts is prohibited for the acquisition of commercial items (see Parts 2 and 12).

[FAC 84-5, 50 FR 1742, 1/11/85, effective 4/1/85; FAC 90-24, interim rule, 59 FR 64784, 12/15/94, effective 12/15/94; FAC 90-30, 60 FR 37772, 7/21/95, effective 9/19/95; FAC 90-32, 60 FR 48206, 9/18/95, effective 10/1/95; FAC 97-2, 62 FR 51224, 9/30/97, effective 10/10/97; FAC 97-5, 63 FR 34058, 6/22/98, effective 8/21/98; FAC 2005-50, 76 FR 14543, 3/16/2011, effective 3/16/2011; FAC 2005-56, 77 FR 12925, 3/2/2012, effective 4/2/2012; FAC 2005-60, 77 FR 44065, 7/26/2012, effective 7/26/2012]

16.302 Cost contracts.

(a) *Description*. A cost contract is a cost-reimbursement contract in which the contractor receives no fee.

(b) *Application*. A cost contract may be appropriate for research and development work, particularly with nonprofit educational institutions or other nonprofit organizations.

(c) *Limitations*. See 16.301-3.

[FAC 2005-17, 72 FR 27364, 5/15/2007, effective 6/14/2007]

16.303 Cost-sharing contracts.

(a) *Description*. A cost-sharing contract is a cost-reimbursement contract in which the contractor receives no fee and is reimbursed only for an agreed-upon portion of its allowable costs.

(b) *Application*. A cost-sharing contract may be used when the contractor agrees to absorb a portion of the costs, in the expectation of substantial compensating benefits.

(c) *Limitations*. See 16.301-3.

16.304 Cost-plus-incentive-fee contracts.

A cost-plus-incentive-fee contract is a cost-reimbursement contract that provides for an initially negotiated fee to be adjusted later by a formula based on the relationship of total allowable costs to total target costs. Cost-plus-incentive-fee contracts are covered in Subpart 16.4, Incentive Contracts. See 16.405-1 for a more complete description and discussion of application of these contracts. See 16.301-3 for limitations.

[FAC 90-46, 62 FR 12690, 3/17/97, effective 5/16/97]

16.305 Cost-plus-award-fee contracts.

A cost-plus-award-fee contract is a cost-reimbursement contract that provides for a fee consisting of

(a) a base amount (which may be zero) fixed at inception of the contract and

(b) an award amount, based upon a judgmental evaluation by the Government, sufficient to provide motivation for excellence in contract performance. Cost-plus-award-fee contracts are covered in Subpart 16.4, Incentive Contracts. See 16.401(e) for a more complete description and discussion of application of these contracts. See 16.301-3 and 16.401(e)(5) for limitations.

[FAC 90-46, 62 FR 12690, 3/17/97, effective 5/16/97; FAC 2005-37, 74 FR 52856, 10/14/2009, effective 10/14/2009; FAC 2005-46, 75 FR 60261, 9/29/2010, effective 10/29/2010]

16.306 Cost-plus-fixed-fee contracts.

(a) *Description*. A cost-plus-fixed-fee contract is a cost-reimbursement contract that provides for payment to the contractor of a negotiated fee that is fixed at the inception of the contract. The fixed fee does not vary with actual cost, but may be adjusted as a result of changes in the work to be performed under the contract. This contract type permits contracting for efforts that might otherwise present too great a risk to contractors, but it provides the contractor only a minimum incentive to control costs.

(b) *Application*. (1) A cost-plus-fixed-fee contract is suitable for use when the conditions of 16.301-2 are present and, for example—

(i) The contract is for the performance of research or preliminary exploration or study, and the level of effort required is unknown; or

(ii) The contract is for development and test, and using a cost-plus- incentive-fee contract is not practical.

(2) A cost-plus-fixed-fee contract normally should not be used in development of major systems (see Part 34) once preliminary exploration, studies, and risk reduction have indicated a high degree of probability that the development is achievable and the Government has established reasonably firm performance objectives and schedules.

(c) *Limitations*. No cost-plus-fixed-fee contract shall be awarded unless the contracting officer complies with all limitations in 15.404-4(c)(4)(i) and 16.301-3.

(d) *Completion and term forms*. A cost-plus-fixed-fee contract may take one of two basic forms—completion or term.

(1) The completion form describes the scope of work by stating a definite goal or target and specifying an end product. This form of contract normally requires the contractor to complete and deliver the specified end product (*e.g.*, a final report of research accomplishing the goal or target) within the estimated cost, if possible, as a condition for payment of the entire fixed fee. However, in the event the work cannot be completed within the estimated cost, the Government may require more effort without increase in fee, provided the Government increases the estimated cost.

(2) The term form describes the scope of work in general terms and obligates the contractor to devote a specified level of effort for a stated time period. Under this form, if the performance is considered satisfactory by the Government, the fixed fee is payable at the expiration of the agreed-upon period, upon contractor statement that the level of effort specified in the contract has been expended in performing the contract work. Renewal for further periods of performance is a new acquisition that involves new cost and fee arrangements.

(3) Because of the differences in obligation assumed by the contractor, the completion form is preferred over the term form whenever the work, or specific milestones for the work, can be defined well enough to permit development of estimates within which the contractor can be expected to complete the work.

(4) The term form shall not be used unless the contractor is obligated by the contract to provide a specific level of effort within a definite time period.

[FAC 84-5, 50 FR 1742, 1/11/85, effective 4/1/85; FAC 90-30, 60 FR 37772, 7/21/95, effective 9/19/95; FAC 90-45, 62 FR 224, 1/2/97, effective 1/1/97; FAC 97-2, 62 FR 51224, 9/30/97, effective 10/10/97; FAC 97-5, 63 FR 34058, 6/22/98, effective 8/21/98]

16.307 Contract clauses.

(a)(1) The contracting officer shall insert the clause at 52.216-7, Allowable Cost and Payment, in solicitations and contracts when a cost-reimbursement contract or a time-and-materials contract (other than a contract for a commercial item) is contemplated. If the contract is a time-and-materials contract, the clause at 52.216-7 applies in conjunction with the clause at 52.232-7, but only to the portion of the contract that provides for reimbursement of materials (as defined in the clause at 52.232-7) at actual cost. Further, the clause at 52.216-7 does not apply to labor-hour contracts.

(2) If the contract is a construction contract and contains the clause at 52.232-27, Prompt Payment for Construction Contracts, the contracting officer shall use the clause at 52.216-7 with its Alternate I.

(3) If the contract is with an educational institution, the contracting officer shall use the clause at 52.216-7 with its Alternate II.

(4) If the contract is with a State or local government, the contracting officer shall use the clause at 52.216-7 with its Alternate III.

(5) If the contract is with a nonprofit organization other than an educational institution, a State or local government, or a nonprofit organization exempted under the OMB Uniform Guidance at 2 CFR part 200, appendix VIII, the contracting officer shall use the clause at 52.216-7 with its Alternate IV.

(b) The contracting officer shall insert the clause at 52.216-8, Fixed Fee, in solicitations and contracts when a cost-plus-fixed-fee contract (other than a construction contract) is contemplated.

(c) The contracting officer shall insert the clause at 52.216-9, Fixed-Fee—Construction, in solicitations and contracts when a cost-plus-fixed-fee construction contract is contemplated.

(d) The contracting officer shall insert the clause at 52.216-10, Incentive Fee, in solicitations and contracts when a cost-plus-incentive-fee contract is contemplated.

(e) (1) The contracting officer shall insert the clause at 52.216-11, Cost Contract—No Fee, in solicitations and contracts when a cost-reimbursement contract is contemplated that provides no fee and is not a cost-sharing contract.

(2) If a cost-reimbursement research and development contract with an educational institution or a nonprofit organization that provides no fee or other payment above cost and is not a cost-sharing contract is contemplated, and if the contracting officer determines that withholding of a portion of allowable costs is not required, the contracting officer shall use the clause with its Alternate I.

(f) (1) The contracting officer shall insert the clause at 52.216-12, Cost-Sharing Contract—No Fee, in solicitations and contracts when a cost-sharing contract is contemplated.

(2) If a cost-sharing research and development contract with an educational institution or a nonprofit organization is contemplated, and if the contracting officer determines that withholding of a portion of allowable costs is not required, the contracting officer shall use the clause with its Alternate I.

(g) The contracting officer shall insert the clause at 52.216-15, Predetermined Indirect Cost Rates, in solicitations and contracts when a cost-reimbursement research and development contract with an educational institution (see 42.705-3(b)) is contemplated and predetermined indirect cost rates are to be used.

[FAC 84-7, 50 FR 23604, 6/4/85, effective 4/30/85; FAC 90-39, 61 FR 31612, 6/20/96, effective 8/19/96; FAC 90-43, 61 FR 67408, 12/20/96, effective 2/18/97; FAC 2005-15, 71 FR 74656, 12/12/2006, effective 2/12/2007; FAC 2005-17, 72 FR 27364, 5/15/2007, effective 6/14/2007; FAC 2005-60, 77 FR 44059, 7/26/2012, effective 8/27/2012; FAC 2005-89, 81 FR 45852, 7/14/2016, effective 8/15/2016]

SUBPART 16.4—INCENTIVE CONTRACTS

16.401 General.

(a) Incentive contracts as described in this subpart are appropriate when a firm-fixed-price contract is not appropriate and the required supplies or services can be acquired at lower costs and, in certain instances, with improved delivery or technical performance, by relating the amount of profit or fee payable under the contract to the contractor's performance. Incentive contracts are designed to obtain specific acquisition objectives by—

(1) Establishing reasonable and attainable targets that are clearly communicated to the contractor; and

(2) Including appropriate incentive arrangements designed to—

(i) Motivate contractor efforts that might not otherwise be emphasized; and

(ii) Discourage contractor inefficiency and waste.

(b) When predetermined, formula-type incentives on technical performance or delivery are included, increases in profit or fee are provided only for achievement that surpasses the targets, and decreases are provided for to the extent that such targets are not met. The incentive increases or decreases are applied to performance targets rather than minimum performance requirements.

(c) The two basic categories of incentive contracts are fixed-price incentive contracts (see 16.403 and 16.404) and cost-reimbursement incentive contracts (see 16.405). Since it is usually to the Government's advantage for the contractor to assume substantial cost responsibility and an appropriate share of the cost risk, fixed-price incentive contracts are preferred when contract costs and performance requirements are reasonably certain. Cost-reimbursement incentive contracts are subject to the overall limitations in 16.301 that apply to all cost-reimbursement contracts.

(d) A determination and finding, signed by the head of the contracting activity, shall be completed for all incentive- and award-fee contracts justifying that the use of this type of contract is in the best interest of the Government. This determination shall be documented in the contract file and, for award-fee contracts, shall address all of the suitability items in 16.401(e)(1).

(e) Award-fee contracts are a type of incentive contract.

(1) *Application*. An award-fee contract is suitable for use when—

(i) The work to be performed is such that it is neither feasible nor effective to devise predetermined objective incentive targets applicable to cost, schedule, and technical performance;

(ii) The likelihood of meeting acquisition objectives will be enhanced by using a contract that effectively motivates the contractor toward exceptional performance and provides the Government with the flexibility to evaluate both actual performance and the conditions under which it was achieved; and

(iii) Any additional administrative effort and cost required to monitor and evaluate performance are justified by the expected benefits as documented by a risk and cost benefit analysis to be included in the Determination and Findings referenced in 16.401(e)(5)(iii).

(2) *Award-fee amount*. The amount of award fee earned shall be commensurate with the contractor's overall cost, schedule, and technical performance as measured against contract requirements in accordance with the criteria stated in the award-fee plan. Award fee shall not be earned if the contractor's overall cost, schedule, and technical performance in the aggregate is below satisfactory. The basis for all award-fee determinations shall be documented in the contract file to include, at a minimum, a determination that overall cost, schedule and technical performance in the aggregate is or is not at a satisfactory level. This determination and the methodology for determining the award fee are unilateral decisions made solely at the discretion of the Government.

(3) *Award-fee plan*. All contracts providing for award fees shall be supported by an award-fee plan that establishes the procedures for evaluating award fee and an Award-Fee Board for conducting the award-fee evaluation. Award-fee plans shall—

(i) Be approved by the FDO unless otherwise authorized by agency procedures;

(ii) Identify the award-fee evaluation criteria and how they are linked to acquisition objectives which shall be defined in terms of contract cost, schedule, and technical performance. Criteria should motivate the contractor to enhance performance in the areas rated, but not at the expense of at least minimum acceptable performance in all other areas;

(iii) Describe how the contractor's performance will be measured against the award-fee evaluation criteria;

(iv) Utilize the adjectival rating and associated description as well as the award-fee pool earned percentages shown below in Table 16-1. Contracting officers may supplement the adjectival rating description. The method used to determine the adjectival rating must be documented in the award-fee plan;

TABLE 16-1

Award-Fee Adjectival Rating	Award-Fee Pool Available To Be Earned	Description
Excellent	91%—100%	Contractor has exceeded almost all of the significant award-fee criteria and has met overall cost, schedule, and technical performance requirements of the contract in the aggregate as defined and measured against the criteria in the award-fee plan for the award-fee evaluation period.
Very Good	76%—90%	Contractor has exceeded many of the significant award-fee criteria and has met overall cost, schedule, and technical performance requirements of the contract in the aggregate as defined and measured against the criteria in the award-fee plan for the award-fee evaluation period.

Award-Fee Adjectival Rating	Award-Fee Pool Available To Be Earned	Description
Good	51%—75%	Contractor has exceeded some of the significant award-fee criteria and has met overall cost, schedule, and technical performance requirements of the contract in the aggregate as defined and measured against the criteria in the award-fee plan for the award-fee evaluation period.
Satisfactory	No Greater Than 50%	Contractor has met overall cost, schedule, and technical performance requirements of the contract in the aggregate as defined and measured against the criteria in the award-fee plan for the award-fee evaluation period.
Unsatisfactory	0%	Contractor has failed to meet overall cost, schedule, and technical performance requirements of the contract in the aggregate as defined and measured against the criteria in the award-fee plan for the award-fee evaluation period.

(v) Prohibit earning any award fee when a contractor's overall cost, schedule, and technical performance in the aggregate is below satisfactory;

(vi) Provide for evaluation period(s) to be conducted at stated intervals during the contract period of performance so that the contractor will periodically be informed of the quality of its performance and the areas in which improvement is expected (*e.g.* six months, nine months, twelve months, or at specific milestones); and

(vii) Define the total award-fee pool amount and how this amount is allocated across each evaluation period.

(4) *Rollover of unearned award fee.* The use of rollover of unearned award fee is prohibited.

(5) *Limitations.* No award-fee contract shall be awarded unless—

(i) All of the limitations in 16.301-3, that are applicable to cost-reimbursement contracts only, are complied with;

(ii) An award-fee plan is completed in accordance with the requirements in 16.401(e)(3); and

(iii) A determination and finding is completed in accordance with 16.401(d) addressing all of the suitability items in 16.401(e)(1).

(f) *Incentive- and Award-Fee Data Collection and Analysis.* Each agency shall collect relevant data on award fee and incentive fees paid to contractors and include performance measures to evaluate such data on a regular basis to determine effectiveness of award and incentive fees as a tool for improving contractor performance and achieving desired program outcomes. This information should be considered as part of the acquisition planning process (see 7.105) in determining the appropriate type of contract to be utilized for future acquisitions.

(g) *Incentive- and Award-Fee Best Practices.* Each agency head shall provide mechanisms for sharing proven incentive strategies for the acquisition of different types of products and services among contracting and program management officials.

[FAC 90-46, 62 FR 12690, 3/17/97, effective 5/16/97; FAC 2005-37, 74 FR 52856, 10/14/2009, effective 10/14/2009; FAC 2005-46, 75 FR 60261, 9/29/2010, effective 10/29/2010]

16.402 Application of predetermined, formula-type incentives. (No Text)

16.402-1 Cost incentives.

(a) Most incentive contracts include only cost incentives, which take the form of a profit or fee adjustment formula and are intended to motivate the contractor to effectively manage costs. No incentive contract may provide for other incentives without also providing a cost incentive (or constraint).

(b) Except for award-fee contracts (see 16.404 and 16.401(e)), incentive contracts include a target cost, a target profit or fee, and a profit or fee adjustment formula that (within the constraints of a price ceiling or minimum and maximum fee) provides that—

(1) Actual cost that meets the target will result in the target profit or fee;

(2) Actual cost that exceeds the target will result in downward adjustment of target profit or fee; and

(3) Actual cost that is below the target will result in upward adjustment of target profit or fee.

[FAC 90-46, 62 FR 12690, 3/17/97, effective 5/16/97; Technical correction, 62 FR 51379, 10/1/97, effective 10/1/97; FAC 2005-37, 74 FR 52856, 10/14/2009, effective 10/14/2009; FAC 2005-46, 75 FR 60261, 9/29/2010, effective 10/29/2010]

16.402-2 Performance incentives.

(a) Performance incentives may be considered in connection with specific product characteristics (*e.g.*, a missile range, an aircraft speed, an engine thrust, or a vehicle maneuverability) or other specific elements of the contractor's performance. These incentives should be designed to relate profit or fee to results achieved by the contractor, compared with specified targets.

(b) To the maximum extent practicable, positive and negative performance incentives shall be considered in connection with service contracts for performance of objectively measurable tasks when quality of performance is critical and incentives are likely to motivate the contractor.

(c) Technical performance incentives may be particularly appropriate in major systems contracts, both in development (when performance objectives are known and the fabrication of prototypes for test and evaluation is required) and in production (if improved performance is attainable and highly desirable to the Government).

(d) Technical performance incentives may involve a variety of specific characteristics that contribute to the overall performance of the end item. Accordingly, the incentives on individual technical characteristics must be balanced so that no one of them is exaggerated to the detriment of the overall performance of the end item.

(e) Performance tests and/or assessments of work performance are generally essential in order to determine the degree of attainment of performance targets. Therefore, the contract must be as specific as possible in establishing test criteria (such as testing conditions, instrumentation precision, and data interpretation) and performance standards (such as the quality levels of services to be provided).

(f) Because performance incentives present complex problems in contract administration, the contracting officer should negotiate them in full coordination with Government engineering and pricing specialists.

(g) It is essential that the Government and contractor agree explicitly on the effect that contract changes (e.g., pursuant to the Changes clause) will have on performance incentives.

(h) The contracting officer must exercise care, in establishing performance criteria, to recognize that the contractor should not be rewarded or penalized for attainments of Government-furnished components.

[FAC 97-1, 62 FR 44802, 8/22/97, effective 10/21/97]

16.402-3 Delivery incentives.

(a) Delivery incentives should be considered when improvement from a required delivery schedule is a significant Government objective. It is important to determine the

Government's primary objectives in a given contract (*e.g.*, earliest possible delivery or earliest quantity production).

(b) Incentive arrangements on delivery should specify the application of the reward-penalty structure in the event of Government-caused delays or other delays beyond the control, and without the fault or negligence, of the contractor or subcontractor.

16.402-4 Structuring multiple-incentive contracts.

A properly structured multiple-incentive arrangement should—

(a) Motivate the contractor to strive for outstanding results in all incentive areas; and

(b) Compel trade-off decisions among the incentive areas, consistent with the Government's overall objectives for the acquisition. Because of the interdependency of the Government's cost, the technical performance, and the delivery goals, a contract that emphasizes only one of the goals may jeopardize control over the others. Because outstanding results may not be attainable for each of the incentive areas, all multiple-incentive contracts must include a cost incentive (or constraint) that operates to preclude rewarding a contractor for superior technical performance or delivery results when the cost of those results outweighs their value to the Government.

16.403 Fixed-price incentive contracts.

(a) *Description*. A fixed-price incentive contract is a fixed-price contract that provides for adjusting profit and establishing the final contract price by application of a formula based on the relationship of total final negotiated cost to total target cost. The final price is subject to a price ceiling, negotiated at the outset. The two forms of fixed-price incentive contracts, firm target and successive targets, are further described in 16.403-1 and 16.403-2below.

(b) *Application*. A fixed-price incentive contract is appropriate when—

(1) A firm-fixed-price contract is not suitable;

(2) The nature of the supplies or services being acquired and other circumstances of the acquisition are such that the contractor's assumption of a degree of cost responsibility will provide a positive profit incentive for effective cost control and performance; and

(3) If the contract also includes incentives on technical performance and/or delivery, the performance requirements provide a reasonable opportunity for the incentives to have a meaningful impact on the contractor's management of the work.

(c) *Billing prices*. In fixed-price incentive contracts, billing prices are established as an interim basis for payment. These billing prices may be adjusted, within the ceiling limits, upon request of either party to the contract, when it becomes apparent that final negotiated cost will be substantially different from the target cost.

[FAC 90-24, interim rule, 59 FR 64784, 12/15/94, effective 12/15/94; FAC 90-30, 60 FR 37772, 7/21/95, effective 9/19/95]

16.403-1 Fixed-price incentive (firm target) contracts.

(a) *Description*. A fixed-price incentive (firm target) contract specifies a target cost, a target profit, a price ceiling (but not a profit ceiling or floor), and a profit adjustment formula. These elements are all negotiated at the outset. The price ceiling is the maximum that may be paid to the contractor, except for any adjustment under other contract clauses. When the contractor completes performance, the parties negotiate the final cost, and the final price is established by applying the formula. When the final cost is less than the target cost, application of the formula results in a final profit greater than the target profit; conversely, when final cost is more than target cost, application of the formula results in a final profit less than the target profit, or even a net loss. If the final negotiated cost exceeds the price ceiling, the contractor absorbs the difference as a loss. Because the profit varies inversely with the cost, this contract type provides a positive, calculable profit incentive for the contractor to control costs.

(b) *Application*. A fixed-price incentive (firm target) contract is appropriate when the parties can negotiate at the outset a firm target cost, target profit, and profit adjustment formula that will provide a fair and reasonable incentive and a ceiling that provides for the contractor to assume an appropriate share of the risk. When the contractor assumes a considerable or major share of the cost responsibility under the adjustment formula, the target profit should reflect this responsibility.

(c) *Limitations.* This contract type may be used only when—

(1) The contractor's accounting system is adequate for providing data to support negotiation of final cost and incentive price revision; and

(2) Adequate cost or pricing information for establishing reasonable firm targets is available at the time of initial contract negotiation.

(d) *Contract Schedule.* The contracting officer shall specify in the contract Schedule the target cost, target profit, and target price for each item subject to incentive price revision.

[FAC 90-24, interim rule, 59 FR 64784, 12/15/94, effective 12/15/94; FAC 90-30, 60 FR 37772, 7/21/95, effective 9/19/95]

16.403-2 Fixed-price incentive (successive targets) contracts.

(a) *Description.* (1) A fixed-price incentive (successive targets) contract specifies the following elements, all of which are negotiated at the outset:

(i) An initial target cost.

(ii) An initial target profit.

(iii) An initial profit adjustment formula to be used for establishing the firm target profit, including a ceiling and floor for the firm target profit. (This formula normally provides for a lesser degree of contractor cost responsibility than would a formula for establishing final profit and price.)

(iv) The production point at which the firm target cost and firm target profit will be negotiated (usually before delivery or shop completion of the first item).

(v) A ceiling price that is the maximum that may be paid to the contractor, except for any adjustment under other contract clauses providing for equitable adjustment or other revision of the contract price under stated circumstances.

(2) When the production point specified in the contract is reached, the parties negotiate the firm target cost, giving consideration to cost experience under the contract and other pertinent factors. The firm target profit is established by the formula. At this point, the parties have two alternatives, as follows:

(i) They may negotiate a firm fixed price, using the firm target cost plus the firm target profit as a guide.

(ii) If negotiation of a firm fixed price is inappropriate, they may negotiate a formula for establishing the final price using the firm target cost and firm target profit. The final cost is then negotiated at completion, and the final profit is established by formula, as under the fixed-price incentive (firm target) contract (see 16.403-1 above).

(b) *Application.* A fixed-price incentive (successive targets) contract is appropriate when—

(1) Available cost or pricing information is not sufficient to permit the negotiation of a realistic firm target cost and profit before award;

(2) Sufficient information is available to permit negotiation of initial targets; and

(3) There is reasonable assurance that additional reliable information will be available at an early point in the contract performance so as to permit negotiation of either

(i) a firm fixed price or

(ii) firm targets and a formula for establishing final profit and price that will provide a fair and reasonable incentive. This additional information is not limited to experience under the contract, itself, but may be drawn from other contracts for the same or similar items.

(c) *Limitations.* This contract type may be used only when—

(1) The contractor's accounting system is adequate for providing data for negotiating firm targets and a realistic profit adjustment formula, as well as later negotiation of final costs; and

(2) Cost or pricing information adequate for establishing a reasonable firm target cost is reasonably expected to be available at an early point in contract performance.

(d) *Contract Schedule*. The contracting officer shall specify in the contract Schedule the initial target cost, initial target profit, and initial target price for each item subject to incentive price revision.

[FAC 90-24, interim rule, 59 FR 64784, 12/15/94, effective 12/15/94; FAC 90-30, 60 FR 37772, 7/21/95, effective 9/19/95]

16.404 Fixed-price contracts with award fees.

Award-fee provisions may be used in fixed-price contracts when the Government wishes to motivate a contractor and other incentives cannot be used because contractor performance cannot be measured objectively. Such contracts shall establish a fixed price (including normal profit) for the effort. This price will be paid for satisfactory contract performance. Award fee earned (if any) will be paid in addition to that fixed price. See 16.401(e) for the requirements relative to utilizing this contract type.

[FAC 90-46, 62 FR 12690, 3/17/97, effective 5/16/97; FAC 2005-37, 74 FR 52856, 10/14/2009, effective 10/14/2009; FAC 2005-46, 75 FR 60261, 9/29/2010, effective 10/29/2010]

16.405 Cost-reimbursement incentive contracts.

See 16.301 for requirements applicable to all cost-reimbursement contracts, for use in conjunction with the following subsections.

[Redesignated from 16.404, FAC 90-46, 62 FR 12690, 3/17/97, effective 5/16/97]

16.405-1 Cost-plus-incentive-fee contracts.

(a) *Description*. The cost-plus-incentive-fee contract is a cost-reimbursement contract that provides for the initially negotiated fee to be adjusted later by a formula based on the relationship of total allowable costs to total target costs. This contract type specifies a target cost, a target fee, minimum and maximum fees, and a fee adjustment formula. After contract performance, the fee payable to the contractor is determined in accordance with the formula. The formula provides, within limits, for increases in fee above target fee when total allowable costs are less than target costs, and decreases in fee below target fee when total allowable costs exceed target costs. This increase or decrease is intended to provide an incentive for the contractor to manage the contract effectively. When total allowable cost is greater than or less than the range of costs within which the fee-adjustment formula operates, the contractor is paid total allowable costs, plus the minimum or maximum fee.

(b) *Application*.

(1) A cost-plus-incentive-fee contract is appropriate for services or development and test programs when—

(i) A cost-reimbursement contract is necessary (see 16.301-2); and

(ii) A target cost and a fee adjustment formula can be negotiated that are likely to motivate the contractor to manage effectively.

(2) The contract may include technical performance incentives when it is highly probable that the required development of a major system is feasible and the Government has established its performance objectives, at least in general terms. This approach also may apply to other acquisitions, if the use of both cost and technical performance incentives is desirable and administratively practical.

(3) The fee adjustment formula should provide an incentive that will be effective over the full range of reasonably foreseeable variations from target cost. If a high maximum fee is negotiated, the contract shall also provide for a low minimum fee that may be a zero fee or, in rare cases, a negative fee.

(c) *Limitations*. No cost-plus-incentive-fee contract shall be awarded unless all limitations in 16.301-3 are complied with.

[Redesignated from 16.404-1, FAC 90-46, 62 FR 12690, 3/17/97, effective 5/16/97; FAC 97-1, 62 FR 44802, 8/22/97, effective 10/21/97]

16.405-2 Cost-plus-award-fee contracts.

A cost-plus-award-fee contract is a cost-reimbursement contract that provides for a fee consisting of (1) a base amount fixed at inception of the contract, if applicable and at the discretion of the contracting officer, and (2) an award amount that the contractor may earn in whole or in part during performance and that is sufficient to provide motivation for excellence in the areas of cost, schedule, and technical performance. See 16.401(e) for the requirements relative to utilizing this contract type.

[Redesignated from 16.404-2, FAC 90-46, 62 FR 12690, 3/17/97, effective 5/16/97; FAC 97-5, 63 FR 34058, 6/22/98, effective 8/21/98; FAC 97-15, 64 FR 72414, 12/27/99, effective 2/25/2000; FAC 2005-37, 74 FR 52856, 10/14/2009, effective 10/14/2009; FAC 2005-46, 75 FR 60261, 9/29/2010, effective 10/29/2010]

16.406 Contract clauses.

(a) Insert the clause at 52.216-16, Incentive Price Revision—Firm Target, in solicitations and contracts when a fixed-price incentive (firm target) contract is contemplated. If the contract calls for supplies or services to be ordered under a provisioning document or Government option and the prices are to be subject to the incentive price revision under the clause, the contracting officer shall use the clause with its Alternate I.

(b) Insert the clause at 52.216-17, Incentive Price Revision—Successive Targets, in solicitations and contracts when a fixed-price incentive (successive targets) contract is contemplated. If the contract calls for supplies or services to be ordered under a provisioning document or Government option and the prices are to be subject to incentive price revision under the clause, the contracting officer shall use the clause with its Alternate I.

(c) The clause at 52.216-7, Allowable Cost and Payment, is prescribed in 16.307(a) for insertion in solicitations and contracts when a cost-plus-incentive-fee contract or a cost-plus-award-fee contract is contemplated.

(d) The clause at 52.216-10, Incentive Fee, is prescribed in 16.307(d) for insertion in solicitations and contracts when a cost-plus-incentive-fee contract is contemplated.

(e) Insert an appropriate award-fee clause in solicitations and contracts when an award-fee contract is contemplated, provided that the clause—

(1) Is prescribed by or approved under agency acquisition regulations;

(2) Is compatible with the clause at 52.216-7, Allowable Cost and Payment; and

(3) Expressly provides that the award amount and the award-fee determination methodology are unilateral decisions made solely at the discretion of the Government.

[Redesignated from 16.405, FAC 90-46, 62 FR 12690, 3/17/97, effective 5/16/97; FAC 97-15, 64 FR 72414, 12/27/99, effective 2/25/2000]

SUBPART 16.5—INDEFINITE-DELIVERY CONTRACTS

16.500 Scope of subpart.

(a) This subpart prescribes policies and procedures for making awards of indefinite-delivery contracts and establishes a preference for making multiple awards of indefinite-quantity contracts.

(b) This subpart does not limit the use of other than competitive procedures authorized by part 6.

(c) Nothing in this subpart restricts the authority of the General Services Administration (GSA) to enter into schedule, multiple award, or task or delivery order contracts under any other provision of law. Therefore, GSA regulations and the coverage for the Federal Supply Schedule program in subpart 8.4 and part 38 take precedence over this subpart.

(d) The statutory multiple award preference implemented by this subpart does not apply to architect-engineer contracts subject to the procedures in subpart 36.6. However, agencies are not precluded from making multiple awards for architect-engineer services using the procedures in this subpart, provided the selection of contractors and placement of orders are consistent with subpart 36.6.

[FAC 97-17, 65 FR 24316, 4/25/2000, effective 4/25/2000]

16.501-1 Definitions.

As used in this subpart—

Delivery-order contract means a contract for supplies that does not procure or specify a firm quantity of supplies (other than a minimum or maximum quantity) and that provides for the issuance of orders for the delivery of supplies during the period of the contract.

Task-order contract means a contract for services that does not procure or specify a firm quantity of services (other than a minimum or maximum quantity) and that provides for the issuance of orders for the performance of tasks during the period of the contract.

[FAC 90-33, 60 FR 49706, 9/26/95, effective 10/1/95; FAC 97-17, 65 FR 24316, 4/25/2000, effective 4/25/2000; FAC 2005-39, 75 FR 13416, 3/19/2010, effective 4/19/2010]

16.501-2 General.

(a) There are three types of indefinite-delivery contracts: Definite-quantity contracts, requirements contracts, and indefinite-quantity contracts. The appropriate type of indefinite-delivery contract may be used to acquire supplies and/or services when the exact times and/or exact quantities of future deliveries are not known at the time of contract award. Pursuant to 10 U.S.C. 2304d and 41 U.S.C. 4101, requirements contracts and indefinite-quantity contracts are also known as delivery-order contracts or task-order contracts.

(b) The various types of indefinite-delivery contracts offer the following advantages:

(1) All three types permit—

(i) Government stocks to be maintained at minimum levels; and

(ii) Direct shipment to users.

(2) Indefinite-quantity contracts and requirements contracts also permit—

(i) Flexibility in both quantities and delivery scheduling; and

(ii) Ordering of supplies or services after requirements materialize.

(3) Indefinite-quantity contracts limit the Government's obligation to the minimum quantity specified in the contract.

(4) Requirements contracts may permit faster deliveries when production lead time is involved, because contractors are usually willing to maintain limited stocks when the Government will obtain all of its actual purchase requirements from the contractor.

(c) Indefinite-delivery contracts may provide for any appropriate cost or pricing arrangement under Part 16. Cost or pricing arrangements that provide for an estimated quantity of supplies or services (*e.g.*, estimated number of labor hours) must comply with the appropriate procedures of this subpart.

[FAC 90-32, 60 FR 48206, 9/18/95, effective 10/1/95; FAC 90-33, 60 FR 49706, 9/26/95, effective 10/1/95; FAC 2005-39, 75 FR 13416, 3/19/2010, effective 4/19/2010; FAC 2005-73, 79 FR 24192, 4/29/2014, effective 5/29/2014]

16.502 Definite-quantity contracts.

(a) *Description*. A definite-quantity contract provides for delivery of a definite quantity of specific supplies or services for a fixed period, with deliveries or performance to be scheduled at designated locations upon order.

(b) *Application*. A definite-quantity contract may be used when it can be determined in advance that—

(1) A definite quantity of supplies or services will be required during the contract period; and

(2) The supplies or services are regularly available or will be available after a short lead time.

[FAC 90-33, 60 FR 49706, 9/26/95, effective 10/1/95]

16.503 Requirements contracts.

(a) *Description*. A requirements contract provides for filling all actual purchase requirements of designated Government activities for supplies or services during a specified contract period (from one contractor), with deliveries or performance to be scheduled by placing orders with the contractor.

(1) For the information of offerors and contractors, the contracting officer shall state a realistic estimated total quantity in the solicitation and resulting contract. This estimate is not a representation to an offeror or contractor that the estimated quantity will be required or ordered, or that conditions affecting requirements will be stable or normal. The contracting officer may obtain the estimate from records of previous requirements and consumption, or by other means, and should base the estimate on the most current information available.

(2) The contract shall state, if feasible, the maximum limit of the contractor's obligation to deliver and the Government's obligation to order. The contract may also specify maximum or minimum quantities that the Government may order under each individual order and the maximum that it may order during a specified period of time.

(b) *Application.* (1) A requirements contract may be appropriate for acquiring any supplies or services when the Government anticipates recurring requirements but cannot predetermine the precise quantities of supplies or services that designated Government activities will need during a definite period.

(2) No requirements contract in an amount estimated to exceed $112 million (including all options) may be awarded to a single source unless a determination is executed in accordance with 16.504(c)(1)(ii)(D).

(c) *Government property furnished for repair.* When a requirements contract is used to acquire work (*e.g.*, repair, modification, or overhaul) on existing items of Government property, the contracting officer shall specify in the Schedule that failure of the Government to furnish such items in the amounts or quantities described in the Schedule as "estimated" or "maximum" will not entitle the contractor to any equitable adjustment in price under the Government Property clause of the contract.

(d) *Limitations on use of requirements contracts for advisory and assistance services.*

(1) Except as provided in paragraph (d)(2) of this section, no solicitation for a requirements contract for advisory and assistance services in excess of three years and $13.5 million (including all options) may be issued unless the contracting officer or other official designated by the head of the agency determines in writing that the services required are so unique or highly specialized that it is not practicable to make multiple awards using the procedures in 16.504.

(2) The limitation in paragraph (d)(1) of this section is not applicable to an acquisition of supplies or services that includes the acquisition of advisory and assistance services, if the contracting officer or other official designated by the head of the agency determines that the advisory and assistance services are necessarily incident to, and not a significant component of, the contract.

[FAC 90-4, 56 FR 15150, 4/15/91, effective 5/15/91; FAC 90-33, 60 FR 49706, 9/26/95, effective 10/1/95; FAC 2005-13, 71 FR 57363, 9/28/2006, effective 9/28/2006; FAC 2005-27, 73 FR 54008, 9/17/2008, effective 9/17/2008; FAC 2005-39, 75 FR 13416, 3/19/2010, effective 4/19/2010; FAC 2005-45, 75 FR 53129, 8/30/2010, effective 10/1/2010; FAC 2005-83, 80 FR 38293, 7/2/2015, effective 10/1/2015]

16.504 Indefinite-quantity contracts.

(a) *Description.* An indefinite-quantity contract provides for an indefinite quantity, within stated limits, of supplies or services during a fixed period. The Government places orders for individual requirements. Quantity limits may be stated as number of units or as dollar values.

(1) The contract must require the Government to order and the contractor to furnish at least a stated minimum quantity of supplies or services. In addition, if ordered, the contractor must furnish any additional quantities, not to exceed the stated maximum. The contracting officer should establish a reasonable maximum quantity based on market research, trends on recent contracts for similar supplies or services, survey of potential users, or any other rational basis.

(2) To ensure that the contract is binding, the minimum quantity must be more than a nominal quantity, but it should not exceed the amount that the Government is fairly certain to order.

(3) The contract may also specify maximum or minimum quantities that the Government may order under each task or delivery order and the maximum that it may order during a specific period of time.

(4) A solicitation and contract for an indefinite quantity must—

(i) Specify the period of the contract, including the number of options and the period for which the Government may extend the contract under each option;

(ii) Specify the total minimum and maximum quantity of supplies or services the Government will acquire under the contract;

(iii) Include a statement of work, specifications, or other description, that reasonably describes the general scope, nature, complexity, and purpose of the supplies or services the Government will acquire under the contract in a manner that will enable a prospective offeror to decide whether to submit an offer;

(iv) State the procedures that the Government will use in issuing orders, including the ordering media, and, if multiple awards may be made, state the procedures and selection criteria that the Government will use to provide awardees a fair opportunity to be considered for each order (see 16.505(b)(1));

(v) Include a description of the activities authorized to issue orders; and

(vi) Include authorization for placing oral orders, if appropriate, provided that the Government has established procedures for obligating funds and that oral orders are confirmed in writing.

(b) *Application.* Contracting officers may use an indefinite-quantity contract when the Government cannot predetermine, above a specified minimum, the precise quantities of supplies or services that the Government will require during the contract period, and it is inadvisable for the Government to commit itself for more than a minimum quantity. The contracting officer should use an indefinite-quantity contract only when a recurring need is anticipated.

(c) *Multiple award preference—*

(1) *Planning the acquisition.*

(i) Except for indefinite-quantity contracts for advisory and assistance services as provided in paragraph (c)(2) of this section, the contracting officer must, to the maximum extent practicable, give preference to making multiple awards of indefinite-quantity contracts under a single solicitation for the same or similar supplies or services to two or more sources.

(ii) (A) The contracting officer must determine whether multiple awards are appropriate as part of acquisition planning. The contracting officer must avoid situations in which awardees specialize exclusively in one or a few areas within the statement of work, thus creating the likelihood that orders in those areas will be awarded on a sole-source basis; however, each awardee need not be capable of performing every requirement as well as any other awardee under the contracts. The contracting officer should consider the following when determining the number of contracts to be awarded:

(1) The scope and complexity of the contract requirement.

(2) The expected duration and frequency of task or delivery orders.

(3) The mix of resources a contractor must have to perform expected task or delivery order requirements.

(4) The ability to maintain competition among the awardees throughout the contracts' period of performance.

(B) The contracting officer must not use the multiple award approach if—

(1) Only one contractor is capable of providing performance at the level of quality required because the supplies or services are unique or highly specialized;

(2) Based on the contracting officer's knowledge of the market, more favorable terms and conditions, including pricing, will be provided if a single award is made;

(3) The expected cost of administration of multiple contracts outweighs the expected benefits of making multiple awards;

(4) The projected orders are so integrally related that only a single contractor can reasonably perform the work;

(5) The total estimated value of the contract is less than the simplified acquisition threshold; or

(6) Multiple awards would not be in the best interests of the Government.

(C) The contracting officer must document the decision whether or not to use multiple awards in the acquisition plan or contract file. The contracting officer may determine that a class of acquisitions is not appropriate for multiple awards (see subpart 1.7).

(D) (1) No task or delivery order contract in an amount estimated to exceed $112 million (including all options) may be awarded to a single source unless the head of the agency determines in writing that—

(i) The task or delivery orders expected under the contract are so integrally related that only a single source can reasonably perform the work;

(ii) The contract provides only for firm-fixed price (see 16.202) task or delivery orders for—

(A) Products for which unit prices are established in the contract; or

(B) Services for which prices are established in the contract for the specific tasks to be performed;

(iii) Only one source is qualified and capable of performing the work at a reasonable price to the Government; or

(iv) It is necessary in the public interest to award the contract to a single source due to exceptional circumstances.

(2) The head of the agency must notify Congress within 30 days after any determination under paragraph (c) (1) (ii) (D) (1) (iv) of this section.

(3) The requirement for a determination for a single-award contract greater than $112 million—

(i) Is in addition to any applicable requirements of Subpart 6.3; and

(ii) Is not applicable for architect-engineer services awarded pursuant to Subpart 36.6.

(2) *Contracts for advisory and assistance services.* (i) Except as provided in paragraph (c) (2) (ii) of this section, if an indefinite-quantity contract for advisory and assistance services exceeds 3 years and $13.5 million, including all options, the contracting officer must make multiple awards unless—

(A) The contracting officer or other official designated by the head of the agency determines in writing, as part of acquisition planning, that multiple awards are not practicable. The contracting officer or other official must determine that only one contractor can reasonably perform the work because either the scope of work is unique or highly specialized or the tasks so integrally related;

(B) The contracting officer or other official designated by the head of the agency determines in writing, after the evaluation of offers, that only one offeror is capable of providing the services required at the level of quality required; or

(C) Only one offer is received.

(ii) The requirements of paragraph (c) (2) (i) of this section do not apply if the contracting officer or other official designated by the head of the agency determines that the advisory and assistance services are incidental and not a significant component of the contract.

[FAC 97-17, 65 FR 24316, 4/25/2000, effective 4/25/2000; FAC 2005-13, 71 FR 57363, 9/28/2006, effective 9/28/2006; FAC 2005-27, 73 FR 54008, 9/17/2008, effective 9/17/2008; FAC 2005-39, 75 FR 13416, 3/19/2010, effective 4/19/2010; FAC 2005-45, 75 FR 53129, 8/30/2010, effective 10/1/2010; FAC 2005-66, 78 FR 13766, 2/28/2013, effective 4/1/2013; FAC 2005-83, 80 FR 38293, 7/2/2015, effective 10/1/2015; FAC 2019-04, 84 FR 38836, 8/7/2019, effective 9/6/2019]

16.505 Ordering.

(a) *General.* (1) In general, the contracting officer does not synopsize orders under indefinite-delivery contracts; except *see*

16.505(a)(4) and (11), under 16.505(b)(2)(ii)(D).

(2) Individual orders shall clearly describe all services to be performed or supplies to be delivered so the full cost or price for the performance of the work can be established when the order is placed. Orders shall be within the scope, issued within the period of performance, and be within the maximum value of the contract.

(3) Performance-based acquisition methods must be used to the maximum extent practicable, if the contract or order is for services (see 37.102(a) and subpart 37.6).

(4) The following requirements apply when procuring items peculiar to one manufacturer:

(i) The contracting officer must justify restricting consideration to an item peculiar to one manufacturer (*e.g.,* a particular brand-name, product, or a feature of a product that is peculiar to one manufacturer). A brand-name item, even if available on more than one contract, is an item peculiar to one manufacturer. Brand-name specifications shall not be used unless the particular brand-name, product, or feature is essential to the Government's requirements and market research indicates other companies' similar products, or products lacking the particular feature, do not meet, or cannot be modified to meet, the agency's needs.

(ii) Requirements for use of items peculiar to one manufacturer shall be justified and approved using the format(s) and requirements from paragraphs (b)(2)(ii)(A), (B), and (C) of this section, modified to show the brand-name justification. A justification is required unless a justification covering the requirements in the order was previously approved for the contract in accordance with 6.302-1(c) or unless the base contract is a single-award contract awarded under full and open competition. Justifications for the use of brand-name specifications must be completed and approved at the time the requirement for a brand-name is determined.

(iii)(A) For an order in excess of $30,000, the contracting officer shall—

(*1*) Post the justification and supporting documentation on the agency Web site used (if any) to solicit offers for orders under the contract; or

(*2*) Provide the justification and supporting documentation along with the solicitation to all contract awardees.

(B) The justifications for brand-name acquisitions may apply to the portion of the acquisition requiring the brand-name item. If the justification is to cover only the portion of the acquisition which is brand-name, then it should so state; the approval level requirements will then only apply to that portion.

(C) The requirements in paragraph (a)(4)(iii)(A) of this section do not apply when disclosure would compromise the national security (*e.g.,* would result in disclosure of classified information) or create other security risks.

(D) The justification is subject to the screening requirement in paragraph (b)(2)(ii)(D)(*4*) of this section.

(5) When acquiring information technology and related services, consider the use of modular contracting to reduce program risk (see 39.103(a)).

(6) Orders may be placed by using any medium specified in the contract.

(7) Orders placed under indefinite-delivery contracts must contain the following information:

(i) Date of order.

(ii) Contract number and order number.

(iii) For supplies and services, line item number, subline item number (if applicable), description, quantity, and unit price or estimated cost and fee (as applicable). The corresponding line item number and subline item number from the base contract shall also be included.

(iv) Delivery or performance schedule.

(v) Place of delivery or performance (including consignee).

(vi) Any packaging, packing, and shipping instructions.

(vii) Accounting and appropriation data.

(viii) Method of payment and payment office, if not specified in the contract (see 32.1110(e)).

(8) Orders placed under a task-order contract or delivery-order contract awarded by another agency (i.e., a Governmentwide acquisition contract, or multi-agency contract)—

(i) Are not exempt from the development of acquisition plans (see subpart 7.1), and an information technology acquisition strategy (see part 39);

(ii) May not be used to circumvent conditions and limitations imposed on the use of funds (e.g., 31 U.S.C. 1501(a)(1)); and

(iii) Shall comply with all FAR requirements for a consolidated or bundled contract when the order meets the definition at 2.101(b) of *consolidation* or *bundling*.

(9) In accordance with section 1427(b) of Public Law 108-136 (40 U.S.C. 1103 note), orders placed under multi-agency contracts for services that substantially or to a dominant extent specify performance of architect-engineer services, as defined in 2.101, shall—

(i) Be awarded using the procedures at subpart 36.6; and

(ii) Require the direct supervision of a professional architect or engineer licensed, registered or certified in the State, Federal District, or outlying area, in which the services are to be performed.

(10)(i) No protest under subpart 33.1 is authorized in connection with the issuance or proposed issuance of an order under a task-order contract or delivery-order contract, except—

(A) A protest on the grounds that the order increases the scope, period, or maximum value of the contract; or

(B)(*1*) For agencies other than DoD, NASA, and the Coast Guard, a protest of an order valued in excess of $10 million (41 U.S.C. 4106(f)); or

(*2*) For DoD, NASA, or the Coast Guard, a protest of an order valued in excess of $25 million (10 U.S.C. 2304c(e)).

(ii) Protests of orders in excess of the thresholds stated in 16.505(a)(10)(i)(B) may only be filed with the Government Accountability Office, in accordance with the procedures at 33.104.

(11) Publicize orders funded in whole or in part by the American Recovery and Reinvestment Act of 2009 (Pub. L. 111-5) as follows:

(i) Notices of proposed orders shall follow the procedures in 5.704 for posting orders.

(ii) Award notices for orders shall follow the procedures in 5.705.

(12) When using the Governmentwide commercial purchase card as a method of payment, orders at or below the micro-purchase threshold are exempt from verification in the System for Award Management as to whether the contractor has a delinquent debt subject to collection under the Treasury Offset Program (TOP).

(b) *Orders under multiple-award contracts*—

(1) *Fair opportunity.*

(i) The contracting officer must provide each awardee a fair opportunity to be considered for each order exceeding $3,500 issued under multiple delivery-order contracts or multiple task-order contracts, except as provided for in paragraph (b)(2) of this section.

(ii) The contracting officer may exercise broad discretion in developing appropriate order placement procedures. The contracting officer should keep submission requirements to a minimum. Contracting officers may use streamlined procedures, including oral presentations. If the order does not exceed the simplified acquisition threshold, the contracting officer need not contact each of the multiple awardees under the contract before selecting an order awardee if the contracting officer has information available to ensure that each awardee is provided a fair opportunity to be considered for each order. The competition requirements in part 6 and the policies in subpart 15.3 do not apply to the ordering process. However, the contracting officer must—

(A) Develop placement procedures that will provide each awardee a fair opportunity to be considered for each order and that reflect the requirement and other aspects of the contracting environment;

(B) Not use any method (such as allocation or designation of any preferred awardee) that would not result in fair consideration being given to all awardees prior to placing each order;

(C) Tailor the procedures to each acquisition;

(D) Include the procedures in the solicitation and the contract; and

(E) Consider price or cost under each order as one of the factors in the selection decision.

(iii) *Orders exceeding the simplified acquisition threshold.* (A) Each order exceeding the simplified acquisition threshold shall be placed on a competitive basis in accordance with paragraph (b) (1) (iii) (B) of this section, unless supported by a written determination that one of the circumstances described at 16.505(b) (2) (i) applies to the order and the requirement is waived on the basis of a justification that is prepared in accordance with 16.505(b) (2) (ii) (B);

(B) The contracting officer shall—

(*1*) Provide a fair notice of the intent to make a purchase, including a clear description of the supplies to be delivered or the services to be performed and the basis upon which the selection will be made to all contractors offering the required supplies or services under the multiple-award contract; and

(*2*) Afford all contractors responding to the notice a fair opportunity to submit an offer and have that offer fairly considered.

(iv) *Orders exceeding $5.5 million.* For task or delivery orders in excess of $5.5 million, the requirement to provide all awardees a fair opportunity to be considered for each order shall include, at a minimum—

(A) A notice of the task or delivery order that includes a clear statement of the agency's requirements;

(B) A reasonable response period;

(C) Disclosure of the significant factors and subfactors, including cost or price, that the agency expects to consider in evaluating proposals, and their relative importance.

(D) Where award is made on a best value basis, a written statement documenting the basis for award and the relative importance of quality and price or cost factors; and

(E) An opportunity for a postaward debriefing in accordance with paragraph (b) (6) of this section.

(v) The contracting officer should consider the following when developing the procedures:

(A) *(1)* Past performance on earlier orders under the contract, including quality, timeliness and cost control.

(2) Potential impact on other orders placed with the contractor.

(3) Minimum order requirements.

(4) The amount of time contractors need to make informed business decisions on whether to respond to potential orders.

(5) Whether contractors could be encouraged to respond to potential orders by outreach efforts to promote exchanges of information, such as—

(i) Seeking comments from two or more contractors on draft statement of work; or

(ii) Using a multiphased approach when effort required to a potential order may be resource intensive (*e.g.*, requirements are complex or need continued development), where all contractors are initially considered on price considerations (*e.g.*, rough estimates), and other considerations as appropriate (*e.g.*, proposed conceptual approach, past performance). The contractors most likely to submit the highest value solutions are then selected for one-on-one session with the Government to increase their understanding of the requirements, provide suggestions fopr refining requirements, and discuss risk reduction measures,

(B) Formal evaluation plans or scoring of quotes or offers are not required.

(2) *Exceptions to the fair opportunity process.* (i) The contracting officer shall give every awardee a fair opportunity to be considered for a delivery-order or task-order exceeding $3,500 unless one of the following statutory exceptions applies:

(A) The agency need for the supplies or services is so urgent that providing a fair opportunity would result in unacceptable delays.

(B) Only one awardee is capable of providing the supplies or services required at the level of quality required because the supplies or services ordered are unique or highly specialized.

(C) The order must be issued on a sole-source basis in the interest of economy and efficiency because it is a logical follow-on to an order already issued under the contract, provided that all awardees were given a fair opportunity to be considered for the original order.

(D) It is necessary to place an order to satisfy a minimum guarantee.

(E) For orders exceeding the simplified acquisition threshold, a statute expressly authorizes or requires that the purchase be made from a specified source.

(F) In accordance with section 1331 of Public Law 111-240 (15 U.S.C. 644(r)), contracting officers may, at their discretion, set aside orders for any of the small business concerns identified in 19.000(a)(3). When setting aside orders for small business concerns, the specific small business program eligibility requirements identified in part 19 apply.

(ii) The justification for an exception to fair opportunity shall be in writing as specified in paragraph (b)(2)(ii)(A) or (B) of this section. No justification is needed for the exception described in paragraph (b)(2)(i)(F) of this section.

(A) *Orders exceeding $3,500, but not exceeding the simplified acquisition threshold.* The contracting officer shall document the basis for using an exception to the fair opportunity process. If the contracting officer uses the logical follow-on exception, the rationale shall describe why the relationship between the initial order and the follow-on is logical (*e.g.,* in terms of scope, period of performance, or value).

(B) *Orders exceeding the simplified acquisition threshold.* As a minimum, each justification shall include the following information and be approved in accordance with paragraph (b)(2)(ii)(C) of this section:

(*1*) Identification of the agency and the contracting activity, and specific identification of the document as a "Justification for an Exception to Fair Opportunity."

(*2*) Nature and/or description of the action being approved.

(*3*) A description of the supplies or services required to meet the agency's needs (including the estimated value).

(*4*) Identification of the exception to fair opportunity (*see* 16.505(b)(2)) and the supporting rationale, including a demonstration that the proposed contractor's unique qualifications or the nature of the acquisition requires use of the exception cited. If the contracting officer uses the logical follow-on exception, the rationale shall describe why the relationship between the initial order and the follow-on is logical (*e.g.,* in terms of scope, period of performance, or value).

(*5*) A determination by the contracting officer that the anticipated cost to the Government will be fair and reasonable.

(*6*) Any other facts supporting the justification.

(*7*) A statement of the actions, if any, the agency may take to remove or overcome any barriers that led to the exception to fair opportunity before any subsequent acquisition for the supplies or services is made.

(*8*) The contracting officer's certification that the justification is accurate and complete to the best of the contracting officer's knowledge and belief.

(*9*) Evidence that any supporting data that is the responsibility of technical or requirements personnel (*e.g.,* verifying the Government's minimum needs or requirements or other rationale for an exception to fair opportunity) and which form a basis for the justification have been certified as complete and accurate by the technical or requirements personnel.

(*10*) A written determination by the approving official that one of the circumstances in paragraphs (b)(2)(i)(A) through (E) of this section applies to the order.

(C) *Approval.* (*1*) For proposed orders exceeding the simplified acquisition threshold, but not exceeding $700,000, the ordering activity contracting officer's certification that the justification is accurate and complete to the best of the ordering activity contracting officer's knowledge and belief will serve as approval, unless a higher approval level is established in accordance with agency procedures.

(*2*) For a proposed order exceeding $700,000, but not exceeding $13.5 million, the justification must be approved by the advocate for competition of the activity placing the order, or by an official named in paragraph (b)(2)(ii)(C)(*3*) or (*4*) of this section. This authority is not delegable.

(*3*) For a proposed order exceeding $13.5 million, but not exceeding $68 million (or, for DoD, NASA, and the Coast Guard, not exceeding $93 million), the justification must be approved by—

(*i*) The head of the procuring activity placing the order;

(*ii*) A designee who—

(*A*) If a member of the armed forces, is a general or flag officer;

(*B*) If a civilian, is serving in a position in a grade above GS-15 under the General Schedule (or in a comparable or higher position under another schedule); or

(*iii*) An official named in paragraph (b)(2)(ii)(C)(*4*) of this section.

(*4*) For a proposed order exceeding $68 million (or, for DoD, NASA, and the Coast Guard, over $93 million), the justification must be approved by the senior procurement executive of the agency placing the order. This authority is not delegable, except in the case of the Under Secretary of Defense for Acquisition and Sustainment, acting as the senior procurement executive for the Department of Defense.

(D) *Posting.* (*1*) Except as provided in paragraph (b)(2)(ii)(D)(*5*) of this section, within 14 days after placing an order exceeding the simplified acquisition threshold that does not provide for fair opportunity in accordance with 16.505(b), the contract officer shall—

(*i*) Publish a notice in accordance with 5.301; and

(*ii*) Make publicly available the justification required at paragraph (b)(2)(ii)(B) of this section.

(*2*) The justification shall be made publicly available—

(*i*) At the GPE *https://www.fbo.gov;*

(*ii*) On the Web site of the agency, which may provide access to the justifications by linking to the GPE; and

(*iii*) Must remain posted for a minimum of 30 days.

(*3*) In the case of an order permitted under paragraph (b)(2)(i)(A) of this section, the justification shall be posted within 30 days after award of the order.

(*4*) Contracting officers shall carefully screen all justifications for contractor proprietary data and remove all such data, and such references and citations as are necessary to protect the proprietary data, before making the justifications available for public inspection. Contracting officers shall also be guided by the exemptions to disclosure of information contained in the Freedom of Information Act (5 U.S.C. 552) and the prohibitions against disclosure in 24.202 in determining whether other data should be removed. Although the submitter notice process set out in Executive Order 12600 "Predisclosure Notification Procedures for Confidential Commercial Information" does not apply, if the justification appears to contain proprietary data, the contracting officer should provide the contractor that submitted the information an opportunity to review the justification for proprietary data before making the justification available for public inspection, redacted as necessary. This process must not prevent or delay the posting of the justification in accordance with the timeframes required in paragraphs (b)(2)(ii)(D)(*1*) and (*3*) of this section).

(*5*) The posting requirement of this section does not apply—

(*i*) When disclosure would compromise the national security (*e.g.*, would result in disclosure of classified information) or create other security risks; or

(*ii*) To a small business set-aside under paragraph (b)(2)(i)(F) of this section.

(3) *Pricing orders.* If the contract did not establish the price for the supply or service, the contracting officer must establish prices for each order using the policies and methods in subpart 15.4.

(4) For additional requirements for cost reimbursement orders see 16.301–3.

(5) For additional requirements for time-and-materials or labor-hour orders, see 16.601(e).

(6) *Postaward Notices and Debriefing of Awardees for Orders Exceeding $5.5 million.* The contracting officer shall notify unsuccessful awardees when the total price of a task or delivery order exceeds $5.5 million.

(i) The procedures at 15.503(b)(1) shall be followed when providing postaward notification to unsuccessful awardees.

(ii) The procedures at 15.506 shall be followed when providing postaward debriefing to unsuccessful awardees.

(iii) A summary of the debriefing shall be included in the task or delivery order file.

(7) *Decision documentation for orders.* (i) The contracting officer shall document in the contract file the rationale for placement and price of each order, including the basis for award and the rationale for any tradeoffs among cost or price and non-cost considerations in making the award decision. This documentation need not quantify the tradeoffs that led to the decision.

(ii) The contract file shall also identify the basis for using an exception to the fair opportunity process (*see* paragraph (b)(2) of this section).

(8) *Task and Delivery Order Ombudsman.* The head of the agency shall designate a task-order and delivery-order ombudsman. The ombudsman must review complaints from contractors and ensure they are afforded a fair opportunity to be considered, consistent with the procedures in the contract. The ombudsman must be a senior agency official who is independent of the contracting officer and may be the agency's advocate for competition.

(c) *Limitation on ordering period for task-order contracts for advisory and assistance services.*

(1) Except as provided for in paragraphs (c)(2) and (3) of this section, the ordering period of a task-order contract for advisory and assistance services, including all options or modifications, normally may not exceed 5 years.

(2) The 5-year limitation does not apply when—

(i) A longer ordering period is specifically authorized by a statute; or

(ii) The contract is for an acquisition of supplies or services that includes the acquisition of advisory and assistance services and the contracting officer, or other official designated by the head of the agency, determines that the advisory and assistance services are incidental and not a significant component of the contract.

(3) The contracting officer may extend the contract on a sole-source basis only once for a period not to exceed 6 months if the contracting officer, or other official designated by the head of the agency, determines that—

(i) The award of a follow-on contract is delayed by circumstances that were not reasonably foreseeable at the time the initial contract was entered into; and

(ii) The extension is necessary to ensure continuity of services, pending the award of the follow-on contract.

[FAC 97-17, 65 FR 24316, 4/25/2000, effective 4/25/2000; FAC 2001-09, 67 FR 56115, 8/30/2002, effective 9/30/2002; FAC 2001-17, 68 FR 59999, 10/20/2003, effective 10/20/2003; FAC 2005-01, 70 FR 11737, 3/9/2005, effective 3/9/2005; FAC 2005-06, 70 FR 57452, 9/30/2005, effective 9/30/2005; FAC 2005-07, 71 FR 211, 1/3/2006, effective 2/2/2006; FAC 2005-13, 71 FR 57363, 9/28/2006, effective 9/28/2006; FAC 2005-27, 73 FR 54008, 9/17/2008, effective 9/17/2008; FAC 2005-32, 74 FR 14636, 3/31/2009, effective 3/31/2009; FAC 2005-38, 74 FR 65600, 12/10/2009, effective 2/1/2010; FAC 2005-39, 75 FR 13416, 3/19/2010, effective 4/19/2010; FAC 2005-42, 75 FR 34271, 6/16/2010, effective 7/16/2010; FAC 2005-50, 76 FR 14548, 3/16/2011, effective 5/16/2011; FAC 2005-53, 76 FR 39238, 7/5/2011, effective 7/5/2011; FAC 2005-54, 76 FR 68032, 11/2/2011, effective 11/2/2011; FAC 2005-55, 77 FR 189, 1/3/2012, effective 2/2/2012; Interim rule,

77 FR 1889, 1/12/2012, effective 2/13/2012; Correction, 77 FR 3636, 1/25/2012, 2/2/2012; FAC 2005-56, 77 FR 12927, 3/2/2012, effective 4/2/2012; FAC 2005-60, 77 FR 44062, 7/26/2012, effective 7/26/2012; FAC 2005-65, 78 FR 6187, 1/29/2013, effective 1/29/2013; FAC 2005-66, 78 FR 13766, 2/28/2013, effective 4/1/2013; FAC 2005-67, 78 FR 37676, 6/21/2013, effective 7/22/2013; FAC 2005-69, 78 FR 46792, 8/1/2013, effective 9/3/2013; FAC 2005-73, 79 FR 24192, 4/29/2014, effective 5/29/2014; FAC 2005-83, 80 FR 38293, 7/2/2015, effective 10/1/2015; FAC 2005-91, 81 FR 67763, 9/30/2016, effective 10/31/2016; FAC 2005-95, 82 FR 4709, 1/13/2017, effective 1/13/2017; FAC 2005-98, 83 FR 19145, 5/1/2018, effective 5/31/2018; FAC 2005-100, 83 FR 42571, 8/22/2018, effective 8/22/2018; FAC 2005-101, 83 FR 48691, 9/26/2018, effective 10/26/2018; FAC 2019-02, 84 FR 19839, 5/6/2019, effective 5/6/2019]

16.506 Solicitation provisions and contract clauses.

(a) Insert the clause at 52.216-18, Ordering, in solicitations and contracts when a definite-quantity contract, a requirements contract, or an indefinite-quantity contract is contemplated.

(b) Insert a clause substantially the same as the clause at 52.216-19, Order Limitations, in solicitations and contracts when a definite-quantity contract, a requirements contract, or an indefinite-quantity contract is contemplated.

(c) Insert the clause at 52.216-20, Definite Quantity, in solicitations and contracts when a definite-quantity contract is contemplated.

(d) (1) Insert the clause at 52.216-21, Requirements, in solicitations and contracts when a requirements contract is contemplated.

(2) If the contract is for nonpersonal services and related supplies and covers estimated requirements that exceed a specific Government activity's internal capability to produce or perform, use the clause with its Alternate I.

(3) If the contract includes subsistence for both Government use and resale in the same Schedule, and similar products may be acquired on a brand-name basis, use the clause with its Alternate II (but see paragraph (d)(5) of this section).

(4) If the contract involves a partial small business set-aside, use the clause with its Alternate III (but see paragraph (d)(5) of this section).

(5) If the contract—

(i) Includes subsistence for Government use and resale in the same schedule and similar products may be acquired on a brand-name basis; and

(ii) Involves a partial small business set-aside, use the clause with its Alternate IV.

(e) Insert the clause at 52.216-22, Indefinite Quantity, in solicitations and contracts when an indefinite-quantity contract is contemplated.

(f) Insert the provision at 52.216-27, Single or Multiple Awards, in solicitations for indefinite-quantity contracts that may result in multiple contract awards. Modify the provision to specify the estimated number of awards. Do not use this provision for advisory and assistance services contracts that exceed 3 years and $13.5 million (including all options).

(g) Insert the provision at 52.216-28, Multiple Awards for Advisory and Assistance Services, in solicitations for task-order contracts for advisory and assistance services that exceed 3 years and $13.5 million (including all options), unless a determination has been made under 16.504(c)(2)(i)(A). Modify the provision to specify the estimated number of awards.

(h) *See* 10.001(d) for insertion of the clause at 52.210-1, Market Research, when the contract is over $5.5 million for the procurement of items other than commercial items.

(i) See 7.107-6 for use of 52.207-6, Solicitation of Offers from Small Business Concerns and Small Business Teaming Arrangement or Joint Ventures (Multiple-Award Contracts) in solicitations for multiple-award contracts above the substantial bundling threshold of the agency.

(j) Insert the clause at 52.216-32, Task-Order and Delivery-Order Ombudsman, in solicitations and contracts when a multiple-award indefinite-delivery indefinite-quantity contract is contemplated. Use the clause with its Alternate I when the contract will be available for use by multiple agencies (*e.g.*, Governmentwide acquisition contracts or multi-agency contracts). When placing orders under the multiple-award contract available for use by multiple agencies, the ordering activity's contracting officer shall complete paragraph (d)(2) and include Alternate I in the notice of intent to place an order, and in the resulting order.

[FAC 90-32, 60 FR 48206, 9/18/95, effective 10/1/95; Redesignated from 16.505, FAC 90-33, 60 FR 49706, 9/26/95, effective 10/1/95; FAC 97-17, 65 FR 24316, 4/25/2000, effective 4/25/2000; FAC 2005-13, 71 FR 57363, 9/28/2006, effective 9/28/2006; FAC 2005-45, 75 FR 53129, 8/30/2010, effective 10/1/2010; FAC 2005-50, 76 FR 14562, 3/16/2011, effective 4/15/2011; FAC 2005-83, 80 FR 38293, 7/2/2015, effective 10/1/2015; FAC 2005-91, 81 FR 67763, 9/30/2016, effective 10/31/2016; FAC 2019-04, 84 FR 38836, 8/7/2019, effective 9/6/2019]

SUBPART 16.6—TIME-AND-MATERIALS, LABOR-HOUR, AND LETTER CONTRACTS

16.600 Scope.

Time-and-materials contracts and labor-hour contracts are not fixed-price contracts.

[FAC 2005-55, 77 FR 194, 1/3/2012, effective 2/2/2012]

16.601 Time-and-materials contracts.

(a) Definitions for the purposes of Time-and-Materials Contracts.

Direct materials means those materials that enter directly into the end product, or that are used or consumed directly in connection with the furnishing of the end product or service.

Hourly rate means the rate(s) prescribed in the contract for payment for labor that meets the labor category qualifications of a labor category specified in the contract that are—

(1) Performed by the contractor;

(2) Performed by the subcontractors; or

(3) Transferred between divisions, subsidiaries, or affiliates of the contractor under a common control.

Materials means—

(1) Direct materials, including supplies transferred between divisions, subsidiaries, or affiliates of the contractor under a common control;

(2) Subcontracts for supplies and incidental services for which there is not a labor category specified in the contract;

(3) Other direct costs (e.g., incidental services for which there is not a labor category specified in the contract, travel, computer usage charges, etc.); and

(4) Applicable indirect costs.

(b) *Description.* A time-and-materials contract provides for acquiring supplies or services on the basis of—

(1) Direct labor hours at specified fixed hourly rates that include wages, overhead, general and administrative expenses, and profit; and

(2) Actual cost for materials (except as provided for in 31.205- 26(e) and (f)).

(c)*Application.* A time-and-materials contract may be used only when it is not possible at the time of placing the contract to estimate accurately the extent or duration of the work or to anticipate costs with any reasonable degree of confidence. See 12.207(b) for the use of time-and-material contracts for certain commercial services.

(1) *Government surveillance.* A time-and-materials contract provides no positive profit incentive to the contractor for cost control or labor efficiency. Therefore, appropriate Government surveillance of contractor performance is required to give reasonable assurance that efficient methods and effective cost controls are being used.

(2) *Fixed hourly rates.* (i) The contract shall specify separate fixed hourly rates that include wages, overhead, general and administrative expenses, and profit for each category of labor (see 16.601(f)(1)).

(ii) For acquisitions of noncommercial items awarded without adequate price competition (see 15.403-1(c)(1)), the contract shall specify separate fixed hourly rates that include wages, overhead, general and administrative expenses, and profit for each category of labor to be performed by—

(A) The contractor;

(B) Each subcontractor; and

(C) Each division, subsidiary, or affiliate of the contractor under a common control.

(iii) For contract actions that are not awarded using competitive procedures, unless exempt under paragraph (c)(2)(iv) of this section, the fixed hourly rates for services transferred between divisions, subsidiaries, or affiliates of the contractor under a common control—

(A) Shall not include profit for the transferring organization; but

(B) May include profit for the prime contractor.

(iv) For contract actions that are not awarded using competitive procedures, the fixed hourly rates for services that meet the definition of commercial item at 2.101 that are transferred between divisions, subsidiaries, or affiliates of the contractor under a common control may be the established catalog or market rate when—

(A) It is the established practice of the transferring organization to price interorganizational transfers at other than cost for commercial work of the contractor or any division, subsidiary or affiliate of the contractor under a common control; and

(B) The contracting officer has not determined the price to be unreasonable.

(3) *Material handling costs.* When included as part of material costs, material handling costs shall include only costs clearly excluded from the labor-hour rate. Material handling costs may include all appropriate indirect costs allocated to direct materials in accordance with the contractor's usual accounting procedures consistent with Part 31.

(d) *Limitations.* A time-and-materials contract or order may be used only if—

(1) The contracting officer prepares a determination and findings that no other contract type is suitable. The determination and finding shall be—

(i) Signed by the contracting officer prior to the execution of the base period or any option periods of the contracts; and

(ii) Approved by the head of the contracting activity prior to the execution of the base period when the base period plus any option periods exceeds three years; and

(2) The contract or order includes a ceiling price that the contractor exceeds at its own risk. Also see 12.207(b) for further limitations on use of time-andmaterials or labor-hour contracts for acquisition of commercial items.

(e) *Post award requirements.* Prior to an increase in the ceiling price of a time-and-materials or labor-hour shall—

(1) Conduct an analysis of pricing and other relevant factors to determine if the action is in the best interest of the Government;

(2) Document the decision in the contract or order file; and

(3) When making a change that modifies the general scope of—

(i) A contract, follow the procedures at 6.303;

(ii) An order issued under the Federal Supply Schedules, follow the procedures at 8.405–6; or

(iii) An order issued under multiple award task and delivery order contracts, follow the procedures at 16.505(b)(2).

(f) *Solicitation provisions.* (1) The contracting officer shall insert the provision at 52.216-29, Time-and-Materials/Labor-Hour Proposal Requirements—Non-Commercial Item Acquisitions With Adequate Price Competition, in solicitations contemplating use of a Time-and-Materials or Labor-Hour type of contract for noncommercial items, if the price is expected to be based on adequate price competition. If authorized by agency procedures, the contracting officer may amend the provision to make mandatory one of the three approaches in paragraph (c) of the provision, and/or to require the identification of all subcontractors, divisions, subsidiaries, or affiliates included in a blended labor rate.

(2) The contracting officer shall insert the provision at 52.216- 30, Time-and-Materials/ Labor-Hour Proposal Requirements—Non-Commercial Item Acquisitions without Adequate Price Competition, in solicitations for noncommercial items contemplating use of a Time-and-Materials or Labor-Hour type of contract if the price is not expected to be based on adequate price competition.

(3) The contracting officer shall insert the provision at 52.216- 31, Time-and-Materials/ Labor-Hour Proposal Requirements—Commercial Item Acquisitions, in solicitations contemplating use of a Commercial Time-and-Materials or Labor-Hour contract.

[FAC 2005-13, 71 FR 57363, 9/28/2006, effective 9/28/2006; FAC 2005-15, 71 FR 74656, 12/12/2006, effective 2/12/2007; 71 FR 74667, 12/12/2006, effective 2/12/2007; FAC 2005-66, 78 FR 13766, 2/28/2013, effective 4/1/2013]

16.602 Labor-hour contracts.

Description. A labor-hour contract is a variation of the time-and-materials contract, differing only in that materials are not supplied by the contractor. See 12.207(b), 16.601(c), and 16.601(d) for application and limitations, for time-and-materials contracts that also apply to labor-hour contracts. See 12.207(b) for the use of labor-hour contracts for certain commercial services.

[FAC 2005-15, 71 FR 74667, 12/12/2006, effective 2/12/2007]

16.603 Letter contracts. (No Text)

16.603-1 Description.

A letter contract is a written preliminary contractual instrument that authorizes the contractor to begin immediately manufacturing supplies or performing services.

16.603-2 Application.

(a) A letter contract may be used when—

(1) the Government's interests demand that the contractor be given a binding commitment so that work can start immediately and

(2) negotiating a definitive contract is not possible in sufficient time to meet the requirement. However, a letter contract should be as complete and definite as feasible under the circumstances.

(b) When a letter contract award is based on price competition, the contracting officer shall include an overall price ceiling in the letter contract.

(c) Each letter contract shall, as required by the clause at 52.216-25, Contract Definitization, contain a negotiated definitization schedule including—(1) dates for submission of the contractor's price proposal, required cost or pricing data, and, if required, make-or-buy and subcontracting plans, (2) a date for the start of negotiations, and (3) a target date for definitization, which shall be the earliest practicable date for definitization.

The schedule will provide for definitization of the contract within 180 days after the date of the letter contract or before completion of 40 percent of the work to be performed, whichever occurs first. However, the contracting officer may, in extreme cases and according to agency procedures, authorize an additional period. If, after exhausting all reasonable efforts, the contracting officer and the contractor cannot negotiate a definitive contract because of failure to reach agreement as to price or fee, the clause at 52.216-25 requires the contractor to proceed with the work and provides that the contracting officer may, with the approval of the head of the contracting activity, determine a reasonable price or fee in accordance with Subpart 15.4 and Part 31, subject to appeal as provided in the Disputes clause.

(d) The maximum liability of the Government inserted in the clause at 52.216-24, Limitation of Government Liability, shall be the estimated amount necessary to cover the contractor's requirements for funds before definitization. However, it shall not exceed

50 percent of the estimated cost of the definitive contract unless approved in advance by the official that authorized the letter contract.

(e) The contracting officer shall assign a priority rating to the letter contract if it is appropriate under 11.604.

[FAC 90-32, 60 FR 48206, 9/18/95, effective 10/1/95; FAC 97-2, 62 FR 51224, 9/30/97, effective 10/10/97; FAC 2005-45, 75 FR 53135, 8/30/2010, effective 10/1/2010]

16.603-3 Limitations.

A letter contract may be used only after the head of the contracting activity or a designee determines in writing that no other contract is suitable. Letter contracts shall not—

(a) Commit the Government to a definitive contract in excess of the funds available at the time the letter contract is executed;

(b) Be entered into without competition when competition is required by Part 6; or

(c) Each letter contract shall, as required by the clause at 52.216-25, Contract Definitization, contain a negotiated definitization schedule including (1) dates for submission of the contractor's price proposal, required certified cost or pricing data and data other than certified cost or pricing data; and, if required, make-or-buy and subcontracting plans, (2) a date for the start of negotiations, and (3) a target date for definitization, which shall be the earliest practicable date for definitization. Any such amendment is subject to the same requirements and limitations as a new letter contract.

[FAC 84-5, 50 FR 1742, 1/11/85, effective 4/1/85; FAC 84-21, 51 FR 31425, 9/3/86, effective 8/29/86; FAC 2005-45, 75 FR 53135, 8/30/2010, effective 10/1/2010]

16.603-4 Contract clauses.

(a) The contracting officer shall include in each letter contract the clauses required by this regulation for the type of definitive contract contemplated and any additional clauses known to be appropriate for it.

(b) In addition, the contracting officer shall insert the following clauses in solicitations and contracts when a letter contract is contemplated:

(1) The clause at 52.216-23, Execution and Commencement of Work, except that this clause may be omitted from letter contracts awarded on SF 26;

(2) The clause at 52.216-24, Limitation of Government Liability, with dollar amounts completed in a manner consistent with 16.603-2(d); and

(3) The clause at 52.216-25, Contract Definitization, with its paragraph (b) completed in a manner consistent with 16.603-2(c). If at the time of entering into the letter contract, the contracting officer knows that the definitive contract will be based on adequate price competition or will otherwise meet the criteria of FAR 15.403-1 for not requiring submission of certified cost or pricing data, the words "and certified cost or pricing data in accordance with FAR 15.408, Table 15-2 supporting its proposal" may be deleted from paragraph (a) of the clause. If the letter contract is being awarded on the basis of price competition, the contracting officer shall use the clause with its Alternate I.

(c) The contracting officer shall also insert the clause at 52.216-26, Payments of Allowable Costs Before Definitization, in solicitations and contracts if a cost-reimbursement definitive contract is contemplated, unless the acquisition involves conversion, alteration, or repair of ships.

[FAC 90-32, 60 FR 48206, 9/18/95, effective 10/1/95; FAC 97-2, 62 FR 51224, 9/30/97, effective 10/10/97; FAC 2005-45, 75 FR 53135, 8/30/2010, effective 10/1/2010]

SUBPART 16.7—AGREEMENTS

16.701 Scope.

This subpart prescribes policies and procedures for establishing and using basic agreements and basic ordering agreements. (See 13.303 for blanket purchase agreements (BPA's) and see 35.015(b) for additional coverage of basic agreements with educational institutions and nonprofit organizations.)

[FAC 97-3, 62 FR 64912, 12/9/97, effective 2/9/98]

16.702 Basic agreements.

(a) *Description.* A basic agreement is a written instrument of understanding, negotiated between an agency or contracting activity and a contractor, that—

(1) contains contract clauses applying to future contracts between the parties during its term and

(2) contemplates separate future contracts that will incorporate by reference or attachment the required and applicable clauses agreed upon in the basic agreement. A basic agreement is not a contract.

(b) *Application.* A basic agreement should be used when a substantial number of separate contracts may be awarded to a contractor during a particular period and significant recurring negotiating problems have been experienced with the contractor. Basic agreements may be used with negotiated fixed-price or cost-reimbursement contracts.

(1) Basic agreements shall contain—

(i) Clauses required for negotiated contracts by statute, executive order, and this regulation; and

(ii) Other clauses prescribed in this regulation or agency acquisition regulations that the parties agree to include in each contract as applicable.

(2) Each basic agreement shall provide for discontinuing its future applicability upon 30 days' written notice by either party.

(3) Each basic agreement shall be reviewed annually before the anniversary of its effective date and revised as necessary to conform to the requirements of this regulation. Basic agreements may need to be revised before the annual review due to mandatory statutory requirements. A basic agreement may be changed only by modifying the agreement itself and not by a contract incorporating the agreement.

(4) Discontinuing or modifying a basic agreement shall not affect any prior contract incorporating the basic agreement.

(5) Contracting officers of one agency should obtain and use existing basic agreements of another agency to the maximum practical extent.

(c) *Limitations.* A basic agreement shall not—

(1) Cite appropriations or obligate funds;

(2) State or imply any agreement by the Government to place future contracts or orders with the contractor; or

(3) Be used in any manner to restrict competition.

(d) *Contracts incorporating basic agreements.*

(1) Each contract incorporating a basic agreement shall include a scope of work and price, delivery, and other appropriate terms that apply to the particular contract. The basic agreement shall be incorporated into the contract by specific reference (including reference to each amendment) or by attachment.

(2) The contracting officer shall include clauses pertaining to subjects not covered by the basic agreement, but applicable to the contract being negotiated, in the same manner as if there were no basic agreement.

(3) If an existing contract is modified to effect new acquisition, the modification shall incorporate the most recent basic agreement, which shall apply only to work added by the modification, except that this action is not mandatory if the contract or modification includes all clauses required by statute, executive order, and this regulation as of the date of the modification. However, if it is in the Government's interest and the contractor agrees, the modification may incorporate the most recent basic agreement for application to the entire contract as of the date of the modification.

16.703 Basic ordering agreements.

(a) *Description.* A basic ordering agreement is a written instrument of understanding, negotiated between an agency, contracting activity, or contracting office and a contractor, that contains—

(1) terms and clauses applying to future contracts (orders) between the parties during its term,

(2) a description, as specific as practicable, of supplies or services to be provided, and

(3) methods for pricing, issuing, and delivering future orders under the basic ordering agreement. A basic ordering agreement is not a contract.

(b) *Application*. A basic ordering agreement may be used to expedite contracting for uncertain requirements for supplies or services when specific items, quantities, and prices are not known at the time the agreement is executed, but a substantial number of requirements for the type of supplies or services covered by the agreement are anticipated to be purchased from the contractor. Under proper circumstances, the use of these procedures can result in economies in ordering parts for equipment support by reducing administrative lead-time, inventory investment, and inventory obsolescence due to design changes.

(c) *Limitations*. A basic ordering agreement shall not state or imply any agreement by the Government to place future contracts or orders with the contractor or be used in any manner to restrict competition.

(1) Each basic ordering agreement shall—

(i) Describe the method for determining prices to be paid to the contractor for the supplies or services;

(ii) Include delivery terms and conditions or specify how they will be determined;

(iii) List one or more Government activities authorized to issue orders under the agreement;

(iv) Specify the point at which each order becomes a binding contract (*e.g.*, issuance of the order, acceptance of the order in a specified manner, or failure to reject the order within a specified number of days);

(v) Provide that failure to reach agreement on price for any order issued before its price is established (see paragraph (d) (3) of this section) is a dispute under the Disputes clause included in the basic ordering agreement; and

(vi) If fast payment procedures will apply to orders, include the special data required by 13.403.

(2) Each basic ordering agreement shall be reviewed annually before the anniversary of its effective date and revised as necessary to conform to the requirements of this regulation. Basic ordering agreements may need to be revised before the annual review due to mandatory statutory requirements. A basic ordering agreement shall be changed only by modifying the agreement itself and not by individual orders issued under it. Modifying a basic ordering agreement shall not retroactively affect orders previously issued under it.

(d) *Orders*. A contracting officer representing any Government activity listed in a basic ordering agreement may issue orders for required supplies or services covered by that agreement.

(1) Before issuing an order under a basic ordering agreement, the contracting officer shall—

(i) Obtain competition in accordance with Part 6;

(ii) If the order is being placed after competition, ensure that use of the basic ordering agreement is not prejudicial to other offerors; and

(iii) Sign or obtain any applicable justifications and approvals, and any determination and findings, and comply with other requirements in accordance with 1.602-1(b), as if the order were a contract awarded independently of a basic ordering agreement.

(2) Contracting officers shall—

(i) Issue orders under basic ordering agreements on Optional Form (OF) 347, Order for Supplies or Services, or on any other appropriate contractual instrument;

(ii) Incorporate by reference the provisions of the basic ordering agreement;

(iii) If applicable, cite the authority under 6.302 in each order; and

(iv) Comply with 5.203 when synopsis is required by FAR 5.201.

(3) The contracting officer shall neither make any final commitment nor authorize the contractor to begin work on an order under a basic ordering agreement until prices have been established, unless the or-

der establishes a ceiling price limiting the Government's obligation and either—

(i) The basic ordering agreement provides adequate procedures for timely pricing of the order early in its performance period; or

(ii) The need for the supplies or services is compelling and unusually urgent (*i.e.*, when the Government would be seriously injured, financially or otherwise, if the requirement is not met sooner than would be possible if prices were established before the work began). The contracting officer shall proceed with pricing as soon as practical. In no event shall an entire order be priced retroactively.

[FAC 84-5, 50 FR 1742, 1/11/85, effective 4/1/85; FAC 90-40, 61 FR 39186, 7/26/96, effective 8/26/96; FAC 97-3, 62 FR 64912, 12/9/97, effective 2/9/98]

PART 17—SPECIAL CONTRACTING METHODS

Table of Contents

Scope of part 17.000

Subpart 17.1—Multiyear Contracting

Authority 17.101
Applicability 17.102
Definitions 17.103
General 17.104
Policy 17.105
Uses 17.105-1
Objectives 17.105-2
Procedures 17.106
General 17.106-1
Solicitations 17.106-2
Special procedures applicable to DoD, NASA, and the Coast Guard 17.106-3
Options 17.107
Congressional notification 17.108
Contract clauses 17.109

Subpart 17.2—Options

Scope of subpart 17.200
[Removed and Reserved] 17.201
Use of options 17.202
Solicitations 17.203
Contracts 17.204
Documentation 17.205
Evaluation 17.206
Exercise of options 17.207
Solicitation provisions and contract clauses 17.208

Subpart 17.3—[Reserved]

Subpart 17.4—Leader Company Contracting

General 17.401
Limitations 17.402
Procedures 17.403

Subpart 17.5—Interagency Acquisitions

Scope of subpart 17.500
General 17.501
Procedures 17.502
General 17.502-1
The Economy Act 17.502-2
Ordering procedures 17.503
Reporting requirements 17.504

Subpart 17.6—Management and Operating Contracts

Scope of subpart 17.600
Definition 17.601
Policy 17.602
Limitations 17.603
Identifying management and operating contracts 17.604
Award, renewal, and extension 17.605

Subpart 17.7—Interagency Acquisitions: Acquisitions by Nondefense Agencies on Behalf of the Department of Defense

Scope of subpart 17.700
Definitions 17.701
Applicability 17.702

Policy 17.703

PART 17—SPECIAL CONTRACTING METHODS

17.000 Scope of part.

This part prescribes policies and procedures for the acquisition of supplies and services through special contracting methods, including—

(a) Multi-year contracting;

(b) Options; and

(c) Leader company contracting.

SUBPART 17.1—MULTIYEAR CONTRACTING

17.101 Authority.

This subpart implements 41 U.S.C. 3903 and 10 U.S.C. 2306b and provides policy and procedures for the use of multi-year contracting.

[FAC 90-40, 61 FR 39186, 7/26/96, effective 7/26/96; FAC 2005-73, 79 FR 24192, 4/29/2014, effective 5/29/2014]

17.102 Applicability.

For DoD, NASA, and the Coast Guard, the authorities cited in 17.101 do not apply to contracts for the purchase of supplies to which 40 U.S.C. 759 applies (information resource management supply contracts).

[FAC 90-40, 61 FR 39186, 7/26/96, effective 7/26/96]

17.103 Definitions.

As used in this subpart—

Cancellation means the cancellation (within a contractually specified time) of the total requirements of all remaining program years. Cancellation results when the contracting officer—

(1) Notifies the contractor of nonavailability of funds for contract performance for any subsequent program year, or

(2) Fails to notify the contractor that funds are available for performance of the succeeding program year requirement.

Cancellation ceiling means the maximum cancellation charge that the contractor can receive in the event of cancellation.

Cancellation charge means the amount of unrecovered costs which would have been recouped through amortization over the full term of the contract, including the term canceled.

Multi-year contract means a contract for the purchase of supplies or services for more than 1, but not more than 5, program years. A multi-year contract may provide that performance under the contract during the second and subsequent years of the contract is contingent upon the appropriation of funds, and (if it does so provide) may provide for a cancellation payment to be made to the contractor if appropriations are not made. The key distinguishing difference between multi-year contracts and multiple year contracts is that multi-year contracts, defined in the statutes cited at 17.101, buy more than 1 year's requirement (of a product or service) without establishing and having to exercise an option for each program year after the first.

Nonrecurring costs means those costs which are generally incurred on a one-time basis and include such costs as plant or equipment relocation, plant rearrangement, special tooling and special test equipment, preproduction engineering, initial spoilage and rework, and specialized work force training.

Recurring costs means costs that vary with the quantity being produced, such as labor and materials.

[FAC 90-40, 61 FR 39186, 7/26/96, effective 7/26/96; FAC 97-22, 66 FR 2116, 1/10/2001, effective 3/12/2001; Delay of effective date, 66 FR 14259, 3/9/2001, effective 5/11/2001; FAC 2001-08, 67 FR 43513, 6/27/2002, effective 7/29/2002]

17.104 General.

(a) Multi-year contracting is a special contracting method to acquire known requirements in quantities and total cost not over planned requirements for up to 5 years unless otherwise authorized by statute, even though the total funds ultimately to be obligated may not be available at the time of contract award. This method may be used in sealed bidding or contracting by negotiation.

(b) Multi-year contracting is a flexible contracting method applicable to a wide range of acquisitions. The extent to which cancellation terms are used in multi-year contracts will depend on the unique circumstances of each contract. Accordingly, for multi-year contracts, the agency head may authorize modification of the requirements of this subpart and the clause at 52.217-2, Cancellation Under Multi-year Contracts.

(c) Agency funding of multi-year contracts shall conform to the policies in OMB Circulars A-11 (Preparation and Submission of Budget Estimates) and A-34 (Instructions on Budget Execution) and other applicable guidance regarding the funding of multi-year contracts. As provided by that guidance, the funds obligated for multi-year contracts must be sufficient to cover any potential cancellation and/or termination costs; and multi-year contracts for the acquisition of fixed assets should be fully funded or funded in stages that are economically or programmatically viable.

(d) The termination for convenience procedure may apply to any Government contract, including multiyear contracts. As contrasted with cancellation, termination can be effected at any time during the life of the contract (cancellation is effected between fiscal years) and can be for the total quantity or partial quantity (where as cancellation must be for all subsequent fiscal years' quantities).

[FAC 90-40, 61 FR 39186, 7/26/96, effective 7/26/96; FAC 2001-0667 FR 13048, 3/20/2002, effective 4/4/2002FAC 2001-08, 67 FR 43513, 6/27/2002, effective 7/29/2002]

17.105 Policy. (No Text)

17.105-1 Uses.

(a) Except for DoD, NASA, and the Coast Guard, the contracting officer may enter into a multi-year contract if the head of the contracting activity determines that—

(1) The need for the supplies or services is reasonably firm and continuing over the period of the contract; and

(2) A multi-year contract will serve the best interests of the United States by encouraging full and open competition or promoting economy in administration, performance, and operation of the agency's programs.

(b) For DoD, NASA, and the Coast Guard, the head of the agency may enter into a multi-year contract for supplies if—

(1) The use of such a contract will result in significant savings of the total estimated costs of carrying out the program through annual contracts;

(2) The minimum need to be purchased is expected to remain substantially unchanged during the contemplated contract period in terms of production rate, procurement rate, and total quantities;

(3) There is a stable design for the supplies to be acquired, and the technical risks associated with such supplies are not excessive;

(4) There is a reasonable expectation that, throughout the contemplated contract period, the head of the agency will request funding for the contract at a level to avoid contract cancellation; and

(5) The estimates of both the cost of the contract and the cost avoidance through the use of a multi-year contract are realistic.

(c) The multi-year contracting method may be used for the acquisition of supplies or services.

(d) If funds are not appropriated to support the succeeding years' requirements, the agency must cancel the contract.

[FAC 90-40, 61 FR 39186, 7/26/96, effective 7/26/96; FAC 2005-91, 81 FR 67773, 9/30/2016, effective 10/31/2016]

17.105-2 Objectives.

Use of multi-year contracting is encouraged to take advantage of one or more of the following:

(a) Lower costs.

(b) Enhancement of standardization.

(c) Reduction of administrative burden in the placement and administration of contracts.

(d) Substantial continuity of production or performance, thus avoiding annual startup costs, preproduction testing costs, make-ready expenses, and phaseout costs.

(e) Stabilization of contractor work forces.

(f) Avoidance of the need for establishing quality control techniques and procedures for a new contractor each year.

(g) Broadening the competitive base with opportunity for participation by firms not otherwise willing or able to compete for lesser quantities, particularly in cases involving high startup costs.

(h) Providing incentives to contractors to improve productivity through investment in capital facilities, equipment, and advanced technology.

[FAC 90-40, 61 FR 39186, 7/26/96, effective 7/26/96]

17.106 Procedures. (No Text)

17.106-1 General.

(a) *Method of contracting.* The nature of the requirement should govern the selection of the method of contracting, since the multi-year procedure is compatible with sealed bidding, including two-step sealed bidding, and negotiation.

(b) *Type of contract.* Given the longer performance period associated with multi-year acquisition, consideration in pricing fixed-priced contracts should be given to the use of economic price adjustment terms and profit objectives commensurate with contractor risk and financing arrangements.

(c) *Cancellation procedures.* (1) All program years except the first are subject to cancellation. For each program year subject to cancellation, the contracting officer shall establish a cancellation ceiling. Ceilings must exclude amounts for requirements included in prior program years. The contracting officer shall reduce the cancellation ceiling for each program year in direct proportion to the remaining requirements subject to cancellation. For example, consider that the total nonrecurring costs (see 15.408, Table 15-2, III. Formats for Submission of Line Item Summaries C(8)) are estimated at 10 percent of the total multi-year price, and the percentages for each of the program year requirements for 5 years are (i) 30 in the first year, (ii) 30 in the second, (iii) 20 in the third, (iv) 10 in the fourth, and (v) 10 in the fifth. The cancellation percentages, after deducting 3 percent for the first program year, would be 7, 4, 2, and 1 percent of the total price applicable to the second, third, fourth, and fifth program years, respectively.

(2) In determining cancellation ceilings, the contracting officer must estimate reasonable preproduction or startup, labor learning, and other nonrecurring costs to be incurred by an "average" prime contractor or subcontractor, which would be applicable to, and which normally would be amortized over, the items or services to be furnished under the multi-year requirements. Nonrecurring costs include such costs, where applicable, as plant or equipment relocation or rearrangement, special tooling and special test equipment, preproduction engineering, initial rework, initial spoilage, pilot runs, allocable portions of the costs of facilities to be acquired or established for the conduct of the work, costs incurred for the assembly, training, and transportation to and from the job site of a specialized work force, and unrealized labor learning. They shall not include any costs of labor or materials, or other expenses (except as indicated above), which might be incurred for performance of subsequent program year requirements. The total estimate of the above costs must then be compared with the best estimate of the contract cost to arrive at a reasonable percentage or dollar figure. To perform this calculation, the contracting officer should obtain in-house engineering cost estimates identifying the detailed recurring and nonrecurring costs, and the effect of labor learning.

(3) The contracting officer shall establish cancellation dates for each program year's requirements regarding production lead time and the date by which funding for these requirements can reasonably be established. The contracting officer shall include these dates in the schedule, as appropriate.

(d) *Cancellation ceilings.* Cancellation ceilings and dates may be revised after issuing the solicitation if necessary. In sealed bidding, the contracting officer shall change the ceiling by amending the solicitation before bid opening. In two-step sealed bidding, discussions conducted during the first step may indicate the need for revised ceilings and dates which may be incorporated in step two. In a negotiated acquisition, negotiations with offerors may provide information requiring a change in cancellation ceilings and dates before final negotiation and contract award.

(e) *Payment of cancellation charges.* If cancellation occurs, the Government's liability will be determined by the terms of the applicable contract.

(f) *Presolicitation or pre-bid conferences.* To ensure that all interested sources of supply are thoroughly aware of how multi-year contracting is accomplished, use of presolicitation or pre-bid conferences may be advisable.

(g) *Payment limit.* The contracting officer shall limit the Government's payment obligation to an amount available for contract performance. The contracting officer shall insert the amount for the first program year in the contract upon award and modify it for successive program years upon availability of funds.

(h) *Termination payment.* If the contract is terminated for the convenience of the Government in whole, including requirements subject to cancellation, the Government's obligation shall not exceed the amount specified in the Schedule as available for contract performance, plus the cancellation ceiling.

[FAC 90-40, 61 FR 39186, 7/26/96, effective 7/26/96; FAC 97-2, 62 FR 51224, 9/30/97, effective 10/10/97; FAC 2005-95, 82 FR 4709, 1/13/2017, effective 1/13/2017]

17.106-2 Solicitations.

Solicitations for multi-year contracts shall reflect all the factors to be considered for evaluation, specifically including the following:

(a) The requirements, by item of supply or service, for the—

(1) First program year; and

(2) Multi-year contract including the requirements for each program year.

(b) Criteria for comparing the lowest evaluated submission on the first program year requirements to the lowest evaluated submission on the multi-year requirements.

(c) A provision that, if the Government determines before award that only the first program year requirements are needed, the Government's evaluation of the price or estimated cost and fee shall consider only the first year.

(d) A provision specifying a separate cancellation ceiling (on a percentage or dollar basis) and dates applicable to each program year subject to a cancellation (see 17.106-1(c) and (d)).

(e) A statement that award will not be made on less than the first program year requirements.

(f) The Government's administrative costs of annual contracting may be used as a factor in the evaluation only if they can be reasonably established and are stated in the solicitation.

(g) The cancellation ceiling shall not be an evaluation factor.

[FAC 90-40, 61 FR 39186, 7/26/96, effective 7/26/96]

17.106-3 Special procedures applicable to DoD, NASA, and the Coast Guard.

(a) *Participation by subcontractors, suppliers, and vendors.* In order to broaden the defense industrial base, to the maximum extent practicable—

(1) Multi-year contracting shall be used in such a manner as to seek, retain, and promote the use under such contracts of companies that are subcontractors, suppliers, and vendors; and

(2) Upon accrual of any payment or other benefit under such a multi-year contract to any subcontractor, supplier, or vendor company participating in such contract, such payment or benefits shall be delivered to such company in the most expeditious manner practicable.

(b) *Protection of existing authority.* To the extent practicable, multi-year contracting shall not be carried out in a manner to preclude or curtail the existing ability of the Department or agency to provide for termination of a prime contract, the performance of which is deficient with respect to cost, quality, or schedule.

(c) *Cancellation or termination for insufficient funding.* In the event funds are not made available for the continuation of a multi-year contract awarded using the procedures in this section, the contract shall be canceled or terminated.

(d) Contracts awarded under the multi-year procedure shall be firm-fixed-price, fixed-price with economic price adjustment, or fixed-price incentive.

(e) *Recurring costs in cancellation ceiling.* The inclusion of recurring costs in cancellation ceilings is an exception to normal contract financing arrangements and requires approval by the agency head.

(f) *Annual and multi-year proposals.* Obtaining both annual and multi-year offers provides reduced lead time for making an annual award in the event that the multi-year award is not in the Government's interest. Obtaining both also provides a basis for the computation of savings and other benefits. However, the preparation and evaluation of dual offers may increase administrative costs and workload for both offerors and the Government, especially for large or complex acquisitions. The head of a contracting activity may authorize the use of a solicitation requesting only multi-year prices, provided it is found that such a solicitation is in the Government's interest, and that dual proposals are not necessary to meet the objectives in 17.105-2.

(g) *Level unit prices.* Multi-year contract procedures provide for the amortization of certain costs over the entire contract quantity resulting in identical (level) unit prices (except when the economic price adjustment terms apply) for all items or services under the multi-year contract. If level unit pricing is not in the Government's interest, the head of a contracting activity may approve the use of variable unit prices, provided that for competitive proposals there is a valid method of evaluation.

[FAC 90-40, 61 FR 39186, 7/26/96, effective 7/26/96]

17.107 Options.

Benefits may accrue by including options in a multi-year contract. In that event, contracting officers must follow the requirements of Subpart 17.2. Options should not include charges for plant and equipment already amortized, or other nonrecurring charges which were included in the basic contract.

[FAC 90-40, 61 FR 39186, 7/26/96, effective 7/26/96]

17.108 Congressional notification.

(a) Except for DoD, NASA, and the Coast Guard, a multi-year contract which includes a cancellation ceiling in excess of $13.5 million may not be awarded until the head of the agency gives written notification of the proposed contract and of the proposed cancellation ceiling for that contract to the committees on appropriations of the House of Representatives and Senate and the appropriate oversight committees of the House and Senate for the agency in question. Information on such committees may not be readily available to contracting officers. Accordingly, agencies should provide such information through its internal regulations. The contract may not be awarded until the thirty-first day after the date of notification.

(b) For DoD, NASA, and the Coast Guard, a multi-year contract which includes a cancellation ceiling in excess of $135.5 million may not be awarded until the head of the agency gives written notification of the proposed contract and of the proposed cancellation ceiling for that contract to the committees on armed services and on appropriations of the House of Representatives and Senate. The contract may not be awarded until the thirty-first day after the date of notification.

[FAC 90-40, 61 FR 39186, 7/26/96, effective 7/26/96; FAC 2005-13, 71 FR 57363, 9/28/2006, effective 9/28/2006; FAC 2005-45, 75 FR 53129, 8/30/2010, effective 10/1/2010; FAC 2005-83, 80 FR 38293, 7/2/2015, effective 10/1/2015]

17.109 Contract clauses.

(a) The contracting officer shall insert the clause at 52.217-2, Cancellation Under Multi-year Contracts, in solicitations and contracts when a multi-year contract is contemplated.

(b) *Economic price adjustment clauses.* Economic price adjustment clauses are adaptable to multi-year contracting needs. When the period of production is likely to warrant a labor and material costs contingency in the contract price, the contracting officer should normally use an economic price adjustment clause (see 16.203). When contracting for services, the contracting officer—

(1) Shall add the clause at 52.222-43, Fair Labor Standards Act and Service Contract Labor Standards—Price Adjustment (Multiple Year and Option Contracts), when the contract includes the clause at 52.222-41, Service Contract Labor Standards,

(2) May modify the clause at 52.222-43 in overseas contracts when laws, regulations, or international agreements require contractors to pay higher wage rates; or

(3) May use an economic price adjustment clause authorized by 16.203, when potential fluctuations require coverage and are not included in cost contingencies provided for by the clause at 52.222-43.

[FAC 90-40, 61 FR 39186, 7/26/96, effective 7/26/96; FAC 2005-21, 72 FR 63076, 11/7/2007, effective 11/7/2007; FAC 2005-30, 74 FR 2724, 1/15/2009, effective 2/17/2009; FAC 2005-73, 79 FR 24192, 4/29/2014, effective 5/29/2014]

SUBPART 17.2—OPTIONS

17.200 Scope of subpart.

This subpart prescribes policies and procedures for the use of option solicitation provisions and contract clauses. Except as provided in agency regulations, this subpart does not apply to contracts for

(a) services involving the construction, alteration, or repair (including dredging, excavating, and painting) of buildings, bridges, roads, or other kinds of real property;

(b) architect-engineer services; and

(c) research and development services. However, it does not preclude the use of options in those contracts.

[FAC 90-41, 61 FR 41466, 8/8/96, effective 8/8/96, finalized without change, FAC 97-3, 62 FR 64912, 12/9/97, effective 2/9/98]

17.201 [Removed and Reserved]

[Removed and Reserved, FAC 97-22, 66 FR 2116, 1/10/2001, effective 3/12/2001; Delay of effective date, 66 FR 14259, 3/9/2001, effective 5/11/2001]

17.202 Use of options.

(a) Subject to the limitations of paragraphs (b) and (c) of this section, for both sealed bidding and contracting by negotiation, the contracting officer may include options in contracts when it is in the Government's interest. When using sealed bidding, the contracting officer shall make a written determination that there is a reasonable likelihood that the options will be exercised before including the provision at 52.217-5, Evaluation of Options, in the solicitation. (See 17.207(f) with regard to the exercise of options.)

(b) Inclusion of an option is normally not in the Government's interest when, in the judgment of the contracting officer—

(1) The foreseeable requirements involve—

(i) Minimum economic quantities (*i.e.*, quantities large enough to permit the recovery of startup costs and the production of the required supplies at a reasonable price); and

(ii) Delivery requirements far enough into the future to permit competitive acquisition, production, and delivery.

(2) An indefinite quantity or requirements contract would be more appropriate than a contract with options. However, this does not preclude the use of an indefinite quantity contract or requirements contract with options.

(c) The contracting officer shall not employ options if—

(1) The contractor will incur undue risks; *e.g.*, the price or availability of necessary materials or labor is not reasonably foreseeable;

(2) Market prices for the supplies or services involved are likely to change substantially; or

(3) The option represents known firm requirements for which funds are available unless—

(i) The basic quantity is a learning or testing quantity; and

(ii) Competition for the option is impracticable once the initial contract is awarded.

(d) In recognition of—

(1) The Government's need in certain service contracts for continuity of operations; and

(2) The potential cost of disrupted support, options may be included in service contracts if there is an anticipated need for a similar service beyond the first contract period.

[FAC 84-37, 53 FR 17858, 5/18/88, effective 6/17/88; FAC 90-4, 56 FR 15150, 4/15/91, effective 5/15/91; FAC 90-31, 60 FR 42648, 8/16/95, effective 10/1/95]

17.203 Solicitations.

(a) Solicitations shall include appropriate option provisions and clauses when resulting contracts will provide for the exercise of options (see 17.208).

(b) Solicitations containing option provisions shall state the basis of evaluation, either exclusive or inclusive of the option and, when appropriate, shall inform offerors that it is anticipated that the Government may exercise the option at time of award.

(c) Solicitations normally should allow option quantities to be offered without limitation as to price, and there shall be no limitation as to price if the option quantity is to be considered in the evaluation for award (see 17.206).

(d) Solicitations that allow the offer of options at unit prices which differ from the unit prices for the basic requirement shall state that offerors may offer varying prices for options, depending on the quantities actually ordered and the dates when ordered.

(e) If it is anticipated that the Government may exercise an option at the time of award and if the condition specified in paragraph (d) above applies, solicitations shall specify the price at which the Government will evaluate the option (highest option price offered or option price for specified requirements).

(f) Solicitations may, in unusual circumstances, require that options be offered at prices no higher than those for the initial requirement; *e.g.*, when—

(1) The option cannot be evaluated under 17.206; or

(2) Future competition for the option is impracticable.

(g) Solicitations that require the offering of an option at prices no higher than those for the initial requirement shall—

(1) Specify that the Government will accept an offer containing an option price higher than the base price only if the acceptance does not prejudice any other offeror; and

(2) Limit option quantities for additional supplies to not more than 50 percent of the initial quantity of the same line item. In unusual circumstances, an authorized person at a level above the contracting officer may approve a greater percentage of quantity.

(h) Include the value of options in determining if the acquisition will exceed the World Trade Organization Government Procurement Agreement or Free Trade Agreement thresholds.

[FAC 84-38, interim rule, 53 FR 27464, 7/20/88, effective 8/1/88; Interim rule, FAC 90-18, 58 FR 31140, 5/28/93, effective 5/28/93, Interim rule finalized without change, FAC 90-39, 61 FR 31612, 6/20/96; Interim rule, FAC 90-19, 59 FR 544, 1/5/94, effective 1/1/94; FAC 97-15, 64 FR 72414, 12/27/99, effective 2/25/2000; FAC 2001-19, Interim rule, 69 FR 1051, 1/7/2004, effective 1/1/2004; FAC 2001-25, Final rule, 69 FR 59700, 10/5/2004, effective 10/5/2004; FAC 2001-27, interim rule, 69 FR 77870, 12/28/2004, effective 1/1/2005; FAC 2005-07, 71 FR 219, 1/3/2006, effective 1/3/2006; FAC 2005-95, 82 FR 4709, 1/13/2017, effective 1/13/2017]

17.204 Contracts.

(a) The contract shall specify limits on the purchase of additional supplies or services, or the overall duration of the term of the contract, including any extension.

(b) The contract shall state the period within which the option may be exercised.

(c) The period shall be set so as to provide the contractor adequate lead time to ensure continuous production.

(d) The period may extend beyond the contract completion date for service contracts. This is necessary for situations when exercise of the option would result in the obligation of funds that are not available in the fiscal year in which the contract would otherwise be completed.

(e) Unless otherwise approved in accordance with agency procedures, the total of the basic and option periods shall not exceed 5 years in the case of services, and the total of the basic and option quantities shall not exceed the requirement for 5 years in the case of supplies. These limitations do not apply to information technology contracts. However, statutes applicable to various classes of contracts, for example, the Service Contract Labor Standards statute (see 22.1002-1), may place additional restrictions on the length of contracts.

(f) Contracts may express options for increased quantities of supplies or services in terms of—

(1) Percentage of specific line items;

(2) Increase in specific line items; or

(3) Additional numbered line items identified as the option.

(g) Contracts may express extensions of the term of the contract as an amended completion date or as additional time for performance; *e.g.*, days, weeks, or months.

[FAC 84-42, 54 FR 5055, 1/31/89, effective 3/2/89; FAC 90-41, 61 FR 41466, 8/8/96, effective 8/8/96, finalized without change, FAC 97-3, 62 FR 64912, 12/9/97, effective 2/9/98; FAC 2005-73, 79 FR 24192, 4/29/2014, effective 5/29/2014]

17.205 Documentation.

(a) The contracting officer shall justify in writing the quantities or the term under option, the notification period for exercising the option, and any limitation on option price under 17.203(g); and shall include the justification document in the contract file.

(b) Any justifications and approvals and any determination and findings required by Part 6 shall specify both the basic requirement and the increase permitted by the option.

[FAC 84-5, 50 FR 1742, 1/11/85, effective 4/1/85]

17.206 Evaluation.

(a) In awarding the basic contract, the contracting officer shall, except as provided in paragraph (b) of this section, evaluate offers for any option quantities or periods contained in a solicitation when it has been determined prior to soliciting offers that the Government is likely to exercise the options. (See 17.208.)

(b) The contracting officer need not evaluate offers for any option quantities when it is determined that evaluation would not be in the best interests of the Government and this determination is approved at a level above the contracting officer. An example of a circumstance that may support a determination not to evaluate offers for option quantities is when there is a reasonable certainty that funds will be unavailable to permit exercise of the option.

[FAC 84-37, 53 FR 17858, 5/18/88, effective 6/17/88]

17.207 Exercise of options.

(a) When exercising an option, the contracting officer shall provide written notice to the contractor within the time period specified in the contract.

(b) When the contract provides for economic price adjustment and the contractor requests a revision of the price, the contracting officer shall determine the effect of the adjustment on prices under the option before the option is exercised.

(c) The contracting officer may exercise options only after determining that—

(1) Funds are available;

(2) The requirement covered by the option fulfills an existing Government need;

(3) The exercise of the option is the most advantageous method of fulfilling the Government's need, price and other factors (see paragraphs (d) and (e) of this section) considered;

(4) The option was synopsized in accordance with Part 5 unless exempted by

5.202(a)(11) or other appropriate exemptions in 5.202;

(5) The contractor does not have an active exclusion record in the System for Award Management (see FAR 9.405-1);

(6) The contractor's past performance evaluations on other contract actions have been considered; and

(7) The contractor's performance on this contract has been acceptable, *e.g.*, received satisfactory ratings.

(d) The contracting officer, after considering price and other factors, shall make the determination on the basis of one of the following:

(1) A new solicitation fails to produce a better price or a more advantageous offer than that offered by the option. If it is anticipated that the best price available is the option price or that this is the more advantageous offer, the contracting officer should not use this method of testing the market.

(2) An informal analysis of prices or an examination of the market indicates that the option price is better than prices available in the market or that the option is the more advantageous offer.

(3) The time between the award of the contract containing the option and the exercise of the option is so short that it indicates the option price is the lowest price obtainable or the more advantageous offer. The contracting officer shall take into consideration such factors as market stability and comparison of the time since award with the usual duration of contracts for such supplies or services.

(e) The determination of other factors under paragraph (c)(3) of this section—

(1) Should take into account the Government's need for continuity of operations and potential costs of disrupting operations; and

(2) May consider the effect on small business.

(f) Before exercising an option, the contracting officer shall make a written determination for the contract file that exercise is in accordance with the terms of the option, the requirements of this section, and Part 6. To satisfy requirements of Part 6 regarding full and open competition, the option must have been evaluated as part of the initial competition and be exercisable at an amount specified in or reasonably determinable from the terms of the basic contract, *e.g.*—

(1) A specific dollar amount;

(2) An amount to be determined by applying provisions (or a formula) provided in the basic contract, but not including renegotiation of the price for work in a fixed-price type contract;

(3) In the case of a cost-type contract, if—

(i) The option contains a fixed or maximum fee; or

(ii) The fixed or maximum fee amount is determinable by applying a formula contained in the basic contract (but see 16.102(c));

(4) A specific price that is subject to an economic price adjustment provision; or

(5) A specific price that is subject to change as the result of changes to prevailing labor rates provided by the Secretary of Labor.

(g) The contract modification or other written document which notifies the contractor of the exercise of the option shall cite the option clause as authority.

[FAC 84-5, 50 FR 1742, 1/11/85, effective 4/1/85; FAC 84-13, 50 FR 52434, 12/23/85, effective 2/3/86; FAC 84-37, 53 FR 17858, 5/18/88, effective 6/17/88; FAC 2005-18, Interim rule, 72 FR 36852, 7/5/2007, effective 6/30/2007; FAC 2005-31, 74 FR 11821, 3/19/2009, effective 4/20/2009; FAC 2005-34, 74 FR 31557, 7/1/2009, effective 7/1/2009; FAC 2005-67, 78 FR 37676, 6/21/2013, effective 7/22/2013; FAC 2005-69, 78 FR 46783, 8/1/2013, effective 9/3/2013; FAC 2005-90, 81 FR 58562, 8/25/2016, effective 10/25/2016; FAC 2005-93, 81 FR 91636, 12/16/2016, effective 12/16/2016; FAC 2005-96, 82 FR 51773, 11/8/2017, effective 11/6/2017; FAC 2005-101, 83 FR 48691, 9/26/2018, effective 10/26/2018]

17.208 Solicitation provisions and contract clauses.

(a) Insert a provision substantially the same as the provision at 52.217-3, Evaluation

Exclusive of Options, in solicitations when the solicitation includes an option clause and does not include one of the provisions prescribed in paragraph (b) or (c) of this section.

(b) Insert a provision substantially the same as the provision at 52.217-4, Evaluation of Options Exercised at Time of Contract Award, in solicitations when the solicitation includes an option clause, the contracting officer has determined that there is a reasonable likelihood that the option will be exercised, and the option may be exercised at the time of contract award.

(c) Insert a provision substantially the same as the provision at 52.217-5, Evaluation of Options, in solicitations when—

(1) The solicitation contains an option clause;

(2) An option is not to be exercised at the time of contract award;

(3) A firm-fixed-price contract, a fixed-price contract with economic price adjustment, or other type of contract approved under agency procedures is contemplated; and

(4) The contracting officer has determined that there is a reasonable likelihood that the option will be exercised. For sealed bids, the determination shall be in writing.

(5) The contractor is not listed in the System for Award Management Exclusions (see FAR 9.405–1).

(d) Insert a clause substantially the same as the clause at 52.217-6, Option for Increased Quantity, in solicitations and contracts, other than those for services, when the inclusion of an option is appropriate (see 17.200 and 17.202) and the option quantity is expressed as a percentage of the basic contract quantity or as an additional quantity of a specific line item.

(e) Insert a clause substantially the same as the clause at 52.217-7, Option for Increased Quantity—Separately Priced Line Item, in solicitations and contracts, other than those for services, when the inclusion of an option is appropriate (see 17.200 and 17.202) and the option quantity is identified as a separately priced line item having the same nomenclature as a corresponding line item.

(f) Insert a clause substantially the same as the clause at 52.217-8, Option to Extend Services, in solicitations and contracts for services when the inclusion of an option is appropriate (See 17.200, 17.202, and 37.111.)

(g) Insert a clause substantially the same as the clause at 52.217-9, Option to Extend the Term of the Contract, in solicitations and contracts when the inclusion of an option is appropriate (see 17.200 and 17.202) and it is necessary to include in the contract any or all of the following:

(1) A requirement that the Government must give the contractor a preliminary written notice of its intent to extend the contract.

(2) A statement that an extension of the contract includes an extension of the option.

(3) A specified limitation on the total duration of the contract.

[FAC 84-37, 53 FR 17858, 5/18/88, effective 6/17/88; FAC 84-42, 54 FR 5055, 1/31/89, effective 3/2/89; FAC 84-49, 54 FR 29281, 7/11/89, effective 8/10/89; Final rule, 55 FR 38516, 9/18/90; FAC 90-31, 60 FR 42648, 8/16/95, effective 10/1/95; FAC 97-14, 64 FR 51828, 9/24/99, effective 11/23/99; FAC 2005-95, 82 FR 4709, 1/13/2017, effective 1/13/2017]

SUBPART 17.3—[RESERVED]

SUBPART 17.4—LEADER COMPANY CONTRACTING

17.401 General.

Leader company contracting is an extraordinary acquisition technique that is limited to special circumstances and utilized only when its use is in accordance with agency procedures. A developer or sole producer of a product or system is designated under this acquisition technique to be the leader company, and to furnish assistance and know-how under an approved contract to one or more designated follower companies, so they can become a source of supply. The objectives of this technique are one or more of the following:

(a) Reduce delivery time.

(b) Achieve geographic dispersion of suppliers.

(c) Maximize the use of scarce tooling or special equipment.

(d) Achieve economies in production.

(e) Ensure uniformity and reliability in equipment, compatibility or standardization of components, and interchangeability of parts.

(f) Eliminate problems in the use of proprietary data that cannot be resolved by more satisfactory solutions.

(g) Facilitate the transition from development to production and to subsequent competitive acquisition of end items or major components.

17.402 Limitations.

(a) Leader company contracting is to be used only when—

(1) The leader company has the necessary production know-how and is able to furnish required assistance to the follower(s);

(2) No other source can meet the Government's requirements without the assistance of a leader company;

(3) The assistance required of the leader company is limited to that which is essential to enable the follower(s) to produce the items; and

(4) Its use is authorized in accordance with agency procedures.

(b) When leader company contracting is used, the Government shall reserve the right to approve subcontracts between the leader company and the follower(s).

17.403 Procedures.

(a) The contracting officer may award a prime contract to a—

(1) Leader company, obligating it to subcontract a designated portion of the required end items to a specified follower company and to assist it to produce the required end items;

(2) Leader company, for the required assistance to a follower company, and a prime contract to the follower for production of the items; or

(3) Follower company, obligating it to subcontract with a designated leader company for the required assistance.

(b) The contracting officer shall ensure that any contract awarded under this arrangement contains a firm agreement regarding disclosure, if any, of contractor trade secrets, technical designs or concepts, and specific data, or software, of a proprietary nature.

SUBPART 17.5—INTERAGENCY ACQUISITIONS

17.500 Scope of subpart.

(a) This subpart prescribes policies and procedures applicable to all interagency acquisitions under any authority, except as provided for in paragraph (c) of this section. In addition to complying with the interagency acquisition policy and procedures in this subpart, nondefense agencies acquiring supplies and services on behalf of the Department of Defense shall also comply with the policy and procedures at subpart 17.7.

(b) This subpart applies to interagency acquisitions, see 2.101 for definition, when—

(1) An agency needing supplies or services obtains them using another agency's contract; or

(2) An agency uses another agency to provide acquisition assistance, such as awarding and administering a contract, a task order, or delivery order.

(c) This subpart does not apply to—

(1) Interagency reimbursable work performed by Federal employees (other than acquisition assistance), or interagency activities where contracting is incidental to the purpose of the transaction; or

(2) Orders of $550,000 or less issued against Federal Supply Schedules.

[FAC 90-33, 60 FR 49706, 9/26/95, effective 10/1/95; FAC 2001-09, 67 FR 56115, 8/30/2002, effective 9/30/2002; FAC 2005-47, 75 FR 77733, 12/13/2010, effective 12/13/2010; FAC 2005-55, 77 FR 183, 1/3/2012, effective 2/2/2012; FAC 2005-62, 77 FR 69720, 11/20/2012, effective 11/20/2012; FAC 2005-67, 78 FR 37684, 6/21/2013, effective 7/22/2013; FAC

2005-83, 80 FR 38293, 7/2/2015, effective 10/1/2015]

17.501 General.

(a) Interagency acquisitions are commonly conducted through indefinite-delivery contracts, such as task- and delivery-order contracts. The indefinite-delivery contracts used most frequently to support interagency acquisitions are Federal Supply Schedules (FSS), Governmentwide acquisition contracts (GWACs), and multi-agency contracts (MACs).

(b) An agency shall not use an interagency acquisition to circumvent conditions and limitations imposed on the use of funds.

(c) An interagency acquisition is not exempt from the requirements of subpart 7.3, Contractor Versus Government Performance.

(d) An agency shall not use an interagency acquisition to make acquisitions conflicting with any other agency's authority or responsibility (for example, that of the Administrator of General Services under title 40, United States Code, "Public Buildings, Property and Works" and 41 U.S.C. division C of subtitle I, Procurement).

[FAC 90-33, 60 FR 49706, 9/26/95, effective 10/1/95; FAC 97-22, 66 FR 2116, 1/10/2001, effective 3/12/2001; Delay of effective date, 66 FR 14259, 3/9/2001, effective 5/11/2001; FAC 2005-47, 75 FR 77733, 12/13/2010, effective 12/13/2010; FAC 2005-55, 77 FR 183, 1/3/2012, effective 2/2/2012; FAC 2005-73, 79 FR 24192, 4/29/2014, effective 5/29/2014]

17.502 Procedures. (No Text)

[FAC 90-33, 60 FR 49706, 9/26/95, effective 10/1/95; FAC 2005-47, 75 FR 77733, 12/13/2010, effective 12/13/2010; FAC 2005-55, 77 FR 183, 1/3/2012, effective 2/2/2012]

17.502-1 General.

(a) *Written agreement on responsibility for management and administration*—

(1) *Assisted acquisitions.*

(i) Prior to the issuance of a solicitation, the servicing agency and the requesting agency shall both sign a written interagency agreement that establishes the general terms and conditions governing the relationship between the parties, including roles and responsibilities for acquisition planning, contract execution, and administration and management of the contract(s) or order(s). The requesting agency shall provide to the servicing agency any unique terms, conditions, and applicable agency-specific statutes, regulations, directives, and other applicable requirements for incorporation into the order or contract. In the event there are no agency unique requirements beyond the FAR, the requesting agency shall so inform the servicing agency contracting officer in writing. For acquisitions on behalf of the Department of Defense, also see subpart 17.7. For patent rights, see 27.304-2. In preparing interagency agreements to support assisted acquisitions, agencies should review the Office of Federal Procurement Policy guidance, Interagency Acquisitions, available at *https://www.whitehouse.gov/sites/whitehouse.gov/files/omb/assets/OMB/procurement/interagency_acq/iac_revised.pdf.*

(ii) Each agency's file shall include the interagency agreement between the requesting and servicing agency, and shall include sufficient documentation to ensure an adequate audit consistent with 4.801(b).

(2) *Direct acquisitions.* The requesting agency administers the order; therefore, no written agreement with the servicing agency is required.

(b) *Business-case analysis requirements for multi-agency contracts and governmentwide acquisition contracts.* In order to establish a multi-agency or governmentwide acquisition contract, a business-case analysis must be prepared by the servicing agency and approved in accordance with the Office of Federal Procurement Policy (OFPP) business case guidance, available at *https://www.whitehouse.gov/sites/whitehouse.gov/files/omb/procurement/memo/development-review-and-approval-of-business-cases-for-certain-interagency-and-agency-specific-acquisitions-memo.pdf.* The business-case analysis shall—

(1) Consider strategies for the effective participation of small businesses during acquisition planning (see 7.103(u));

(2) Detail the administration of such contract, including an analysis of all direct and indirect costs to the Government of awarding and administering such contract;

(3) Describe the impact such contract will have on the ability of the Government to leverage its purchasing power, *e.g.,* will it have a negative effect because it dilutes other existing contracts;

(4) Include an analysis concluding that there is a need for establishing the multi-agency contract; and

(5) Document roles and responsibilities in the administration of the contract.

[FAC 2005-47, 75 FR 77733, 12/13/2010, effective 12/13/2010; FAC 2005-55, 77 FR 183, 1/3/2012, effective 2/2/2012; FAC 2005-62, 77 FR 69720, 11/20/2012, effective 11/20/2012; FAC 2005-67, 78 FR 37684, 6/21/2013, effective 7/22/2013; FAC 2005-100, 83 FR 42571, 8/22/2018, effective 8/22/2018; FAC 2019-02, 84 FR 19837, 5/6/2019, effective 6/5/2019]

17.502-2 The Economy Act.

(a) The Economy Act (31 U.S.C. 1535) authorizes agencies to enter into agreements to obtain supplies or services from another agency. The FAR applies when one agency uses another agency's contract to obtain supplies or services. If the interagency business transaction does not result in a contract or an order, then the FAR does not apply. The Economy Act also provides authority for placement of orders between major organizational units within an agency; procedures for such intra-agency transactions are addressed in agency regulations.

(b) The Economy Act applies when more specific statutory authority does not exist. Examples of more specific authority are 40 U.S.C. 501 for the Federal Supply Schedules (subpart 8.4), and 40 U.S.C. 11302(e) for Governmentwide acquisition contracts (GWACs).

(c) *Requirements for determinations and findings.* (1) Each Economy Act order to obtain supplies or services by interagency acquisition shall be supported by a determination and findings (D&F). The D&F shall—

(i) State that use of an interagency acquisition is in the best interest of the Government;

(ii) State that the supplies or services cannot be obtained as conveniently or economically by contracting directly with a private source; and

(iii) Include a statement that at least one of the following circumstances applies:

(A) The acquisition will appropriately be made under an existing contract of the servicing agency, entered into before placement of the order, to meet the requirements of the servicing agency for the same or similar supplies or services.

(B) The servicing agency has the capability or expertise to enter into a contract for such supplies or services that is not available within the requesting agency.

(C) The servicing agency is specifically authorized by law or regulation to purchase such supplies or services on behalf of other agencies.

(2) The D&F shall be approved by a contracting officer of the requesting agency with authority to contract for the supplies or services to be ordered, or by another official designated by the agency head, except that, if the servicing agency is not covered by the FAR, approval of the D&F may not be delegated below the senior procurement executive of the requesting agency.

(3) The requesting agency shall furnish a copy of the D&F to the servicing agency with the request for order.

(d) *Payment.* (1) The servicing agency may ask the requesting agency, in writing, for advance payment for all or part of the estimated cost of furnishing the supplies or services. Adjustment on the basis of actual costs shall be made as agreed to by the agencies.

(2) If approved by the servicing agency, payment for actual costs may be made by the requesting agency after the supplies or services have been furnished.

(3) Bills rendered or requests for advance payment shall not be subject to audit or certification in advance of payment.

(4) In no event shall the servicing agency require, or the requesting agency pay, any fee or charge in excess of the actual cost (or estimated cost if the actual cost is not known) of entering into and administering the contract or other agreement under which the order is filled.

[FAC 2005-47, 75 FR 77733, 12/13/2010, effective 12/13/2010; FAC 2005-55, 77 FR 183, 1/3/2012, effective 2/2/2012]

17.503 Ordering procedures.

(a) Before placing an order for supplies or services with another Government agency, the requesting agency shall follow the procedures in 17.502-1 and, if under the Economy Act, also 17.502-2.

(b) The order may be placed on any form or document that is acceptable to both agencies. The order should include—

(1) A description of the supplies or services required;

(2) Delivery requirements;

(3) A funds citation;

(4) A payment provision (*see* 17.502-2(d) for Economy Act orders); and

(5) Acquisition authority as may be appropriate (*see* 17.503(d)).

(c) The requesting and servicing agencies should agree to procedures for the resolution of disagreements that may arise under interagency acquisitions, including, in appropriate circumstances, the use of a third-party forum. If a third party is proposed, consent of the third party should be obtained in writing.

(d) When an interagency acquisition requires the servicing agency to award a contract, the following procedures also apply:

(1) If a justification and approval or a D&F (other than the requesting agency's D&F required in 17.502-2(c)) is required by law or regulation, the servicing agency shall execute and issue the justification and approval or D&F. The requesting agency shall furnish the servicing agency any information needed to make the justification and approval or D&F.

(2) The requesting agency shall also be responsible for furnishing other assistance that may be necessary, such as providing information or special contract terms needed to comply with any condition or limitation applicable to the funds of the requesting agency.

(3) The servicing agency is responsible for compliance with all other legal or regulatory requirements applicable to the contract, including—

(i) Having adequate statutory authority for the contractual action; and

(ii) Complying fully with the competition requirements of part 6 (*see* 6.002). However, if the servicing agency is not subject to the Federal Acquisition Regulation, the requesting agency shall verify that contracts utilized to meet its requirements contain provisions protecting the Government from inappropriate charges (for example, provisions mandated for FAR agencies by part 31), and that adequate contract administration will be provided.

(e) Nonsponsoring Federal agencies may use a Federally Funded Research and Development Center (FFRDC) only if the terms of the FFRDC's sponsoring agreement permit work from other than a sponsoring agency. Work placed with the FFRDC is subject to the acceptance by the sponsor and must fall within the purpose, mission, general scope of effort, or special competency of the FFRDC. (*See* 35.017; *see also* 6.302 for procedures to follow where using other than full and open competition.) The nonsponsoring agency shall provide to the sponsoring agency necessary documentation that the requested work would not place the FFRDC in direct competition with domestic private industry.

[FAC 90-33, 60 FR 49706, 9/26/95, effective 10/1/95; FAC 2005-47, 75 FR 77733, 12/13/2010, effective 12/13/2010; FAC 2005-55, 77 FR 183, 1/3/2012, effective 2/2/2012]

17.504 Reporting requirements.

(a) The senior procurement executive for each executive agency shall submit to the Director of OMB an annual report on interagency acquisitions, as directed by OMB.

(b) The contracting officer for the servicing agency shall ensure that service contractor reporting requirements are met in accordance with subpart 4.17, Service Contracts Inventory.

[FAC 90-33, 60 FR 49706, 9/26/95, effective 10/1/95; FAC 2005-47, 75 FR 77733, 12/13/2010, effective 12/13/2010; FAC 2005-55, 77 FR 183, 1/3/2012, effective 2/2/2012; FAC 2005-72, 78 FR 80369, 12/31/2013, effective 1/30/2014]

SUBPART 17.6—MANAGEMENT AND OPERATING CONTRACTS

17.600 Scope of subpart.

This subpart prescribes policies and procedures for management and operating contracts for the Department of Energy and any other agency having requisite statutory authority.

17.601 Definition.

Management and operating contract means an agreement under which the Government contracts for the operation, maintenance, or support, on its behalf, of a Government-owned or -controlled research, development, special production, or testing establishment wholly or principally devoted to one or more major programs of the contracting Federal agency.

17.602 Policy.

(a) Heads of agencies, with requisite statutory authority, may determine in writing to authorize contracting officers to enter into or renew any management and operating contract in accordance with the agency's statutory authority, or 41 U.S.C. chapter 33, and the agency's regulations governing such contracts. This authority shall not be delegated. Every contract so authorized shall show its authorization upon its face.

(b) Agencies may authorize management and operating contracts only in a manner consistent with the guidance of this subpart and only if they are consistent with the situations described in 17.604.

(c) Within 2 years of the effective date of this regulation, agencies shall review their current contractual arrangements in the light of the guidance of this subpart, in order to—

(1) Identify, modify as necessary, and authorize management and operating contracts; and

(2) Modify as necessary or terminate contracts not so identified and authorized, except that any contract with less than 4 years remaining as of the effective date of this regulation need not be terminated, nor need it be identified, modified, or authorized unless it is renewed or its terms are substantially renegotiated.

[FAC 84-13, 50 FR 52434, 12/23/85, effective 2/3/86; FAC 2005-73, 79 FR 24192, 4/29/2014, effective 5/29/2014]

17.603 Limitations.

(a) Management and operating contracts shall not be authorized for—

(1) Functions involving the direction, supervision, or control of Government personnel, except for supervision incidental to training;

(2) Functions involving the exercise of police or regulatory powers in the name of the Government, other than guard or plant protection services;

(3) Functions of determining basic Government policies;

(4) Day-to-day staff or management functions of the agency or of any of its elements; or

(5) Functions that can more properly be accomplished in accordance with Subpart 45.3, Authorizing the Use and Rental of Government Property.

(b) Since issuance of an authorization under 17.602(a) is deemed sufficient proof of compliance with paragraph (a) immediately above, nothing in paragraph (a) immediately above shall affect the validity or legality of such an authorization.

(c) For use of project labor agreements, see Subpart 22.5.

[FAC 97-26, 66 FR 27405, 5/16/2001, effective 5/16/2001; FAC 2001-10, 67 FR 70518, 11/22/2002, effective 11/22/2002; FAC 2005-17, 72 FR 27364, 5/15/2007, effective 6/14/2007; FAC 2005-35, 74 FR 34206, 7/14/2009, effective 7/14/2009; FAC 2005-41, 75 FR 19168, 4/13/2010, effective 5/13/2010]

17.604 Identifying management and operating contracts.

A management and operating contract is characterized both by its purpose (see 17.601) and by the special relationship it creates between Government and contractor. The following criteria can generally be applied in identifying management and operating contracts:

(a) Government-owned or -controlled facilities must be utilized; for instance—

(1) In the interest of national defense or mobilization readiness;

(2) To perform the agency's mission adequately; or

(3) Because private enterprise is unable or unwilling to use its own facilities for the work.

(b) Because of the nature of the work, or because it is to be performed in Government facilities, the Government must maintain a special, close relationship with the contractor and the contractor's personnel in various important areas (*e.g.*, safety, security, cost control, site conditions).

(c) The conduct of the work is wholly or at least substantially separate from the contractor's other business, if any.

(d) The work is closely related to the agency's mission and is of a long-term or continuing nature, and there is a need—

(1) To ensure its continuity; and

(2) For special protection covering the orderly transition of personnel and work in the event of a change in contractors.

17.605 Award, renewal, and extension.

(a) Effective work performance under management and operating contracts usually involves high levels of expertise and continuity of operations and personnel. Because of program requirements and the unusual (sometimes unique) nature of the work performed under management and operating contracts, the Government is often limited in its ability to effect competition or to replace a contractor. Therefore contracting officers should take extraordinary steps before award to assure themselves that the prospective contractor's technical and managerial capacity are sufficient, that organizational conflicts of interest are adequately covered, and that the contract will grant the Government broad and continuing rights to involve itself, if necessary, in technical and managerial decision making concerning performance.

(b) The contracting officer shall review each management and operating contract, following agency procedures, at appropriate intervals and at least once every 5 years. The review should determine whether meaningful improvement in performance or cost might reasonably be achieved. Any extension or renewal of an operating and management contract must be authorized at a level within the agency no lower than the level at which the original contract was authorized in accordance with 17.602(a).

(c) Replacement of an incumbent contractor is usually based largely upon expectation of meaningful improvement in performance or cost. Therefore, when reviewing contractor performance, contracting officers should consider—

(1) The incumbent contractor's overall performance, including, specifically, technical, administrative, and cost performance;

(2) The potential impact of a change in contractors on program needs, including safety, national defense, and mobilization considerations; and

(3) Whether it is likely that qualified offerors will compete for the contract.

SUBPART 17.7—INTERAGENCY ACQUISITIONS: ACQUISITIONS BY NONDEFENSE AGENCIES ON

BEHALF OF THE DEPARTMENT OF DEFENSE

17.700 Scope of subpart.

(a) Compliance with this subpart is in addition to the policies and procedures for interagency acquisitions set forth in subpart 17.5. This subpart prescribes policies and procedures specific to acquisitions of supplies and services by nondefense agencies on behalf of the Department of Defense (DoD).

(b) This subpart implements Public Law 110-181, section 801, as amended (10 U.S.C. 2304 Note).

[FAC 2005-62, 77 FR 69720, 11/20/2012, effective 11/20/2012; FAC 2005-67, 78 FR 37684, 6/21/2013, effective 7/22/2013]

17.701 Definitions.

As used in this subpart—

Department of Defense (DoD) acquisition official means—

(1) A DoD contracting officer; or

(2) Any other DoD official authorized to approve a direct acquisition or an assisted acquisition on behalf of DoD.

Nondefense agency means any department or agency of the Federal Government other than the Department of Defense.

Nondefense agency that is an element of the intelligence community means the agencies identified in 50 U.S.C. 401a(4), which include the—

(1) Office of the Director of National Intelligence;

(2) Central Intelligence Agency;

(3) Intelligence elements of the Federal Bureau of Investigation, Department of Energy, and Drug Enforcement Agency;

(4) Bureau of Intelligence and Research of the Department of State;

(5) Office of Intelligence and Analysis of the Department of the Treasury;

(6) The Office of Intelligence and Analysis of the Department of Homeland Security and the Office of Intelligence of the Coast Guard; and

(7) Such other elements of any department or agency as have been designated by the President, or designated jointly by the Director of National Intelligence and the head of the department or agency concerned, as an element of the intelligence community.

[FAC 2005-62, 77 FR 69720, 11/20/2012, effective 11/20/2012; FAC 2005-67, 78 FR 37684, 6/21/2013, effective 7/22/2013]

17.702 Applicability.

This subpart applies to all acquisitions made by nondefense agencies on behalf of DoD. It does not apply to contracts entered into by a nondefense agency that is an element of the intelligence community for the performance of a joint program conducted to meet the needs of DoD and the nondefense agency.

[FAC 2005-62, 77 FR 69720, 11/20/2012, effective 11/20/2012; FAC 2005-67, 78 FR 37684, 6/21/2013, effective 7/22/2013]

17.703 Policy.

(a) A DoD acquisition official may request a nondefense agency to conduct an acquisition on behalf of DoD in excess of the simplified acquisition threshold *only if* the head of the nondefense agency conducting the acquisition on DoD's behalf has certified that the agency will comply with applicable procurement requirements for that fiscal year except when waived in accordance with paragraph (e) of this section.

(b) A nondefense agency is compliant with applicable procurement requirements if the procurement policies, procedures, and internal controls of the nondefense agency applicable to the procurement of supplies and services on behalf of DoD, and the manner in which they are administered, are adequate to ensure the compliance of the nondefense department or agency with—

(1) The Federal Acquisition Regulation and other laws and regulations that apply to procurements of supplies and services by Federal agencies; and

2) Laws and regulations that apply to procurements of supplies and services made by DoD through other Federal agencies, including DoD financial management regula-

tions, the Defense Federal Acquisition Regulation Supplement (DFARS), DoD class deviations, and the DFARS Procedures, Guidance, and Information (PGI). (The DFARS, DoD class deviations, and PGI are accessible at: *http://www.acq.osd.mil/dpap/dars*).

(c) Within 30 days of the beginning of each fiscal year, submit nondefense agency certifications of compliance to the Principal Director, Defense Pricing and Contracting at: Department of Defense, Office of the Under Secretary of Defense (Acquisition and Sustainment), Defense Pricing and Contracting, Contract Policy, Room 3B938, 3060 Defense Pentagon, Washington DC 20301-3060.

(d) The DoD acquisition official, as defined at 17.701, shall provide to the servicing nondefense agency contracting officer any DoD-unique terms, conditions, other related statutes, regulations, directives, and other applicable requirements for incorporation into the order or contract. In the event there are no DoD-unique requirements beyond the FAR, the DoD acquisition official shall so inform the servicing nondefense agency contracting officer in writing. Nondefense agency contracting officers are responsible for ensuring support provided in response to DoD's request complies with paragraph (b) of this section.

(e) *Waiver.* The limitation in paragraph (a) of this section shall not apply to the acquisition of supplies and services on behalf of DoD by a nondefense agency during any fiscal year for which the Under Secretary of Defense for Acquisition and Sustainment has determined in writing that it is necessary in the interest of DoD to acquire supplies and services through the nondefense agency during the fiscal year. The written determination shall identify the acquisition categories to which the Waiver applies.

(f) Nondefense agency certifications, waivers, and additional information are available at *http://www.acq.osd.mil/dpap/cpic/cp/interagency_acquisition.html*.

[FAC 2005-62, 77 FR 69720, 11/20/2012, effective 11/20/2012; FAC 2005-67, 78 FR 37684, 6/21/2013, effective 7/22/2013; FAC 2019-02, 84 FR 19839, 5/6/2019, effective 5/6/2019]

PART 18—EMERGENCY ACQUISITIONS

Table of Contents

Scope of part 18.000
Definition 18.001

Subpart 18.1 Available Acquisition Flexibilities

General 18.101
System for Award Management 18.102
Synopses of proposed contract actions 18.103
Unusual and compelling urgency 18.104
Federal Supply Schedules (FSSs), multi-agency blanket purchase agreements (BPAs), and multi-agency indefinite delivery contracts 18.105
Acquisitions from Federal Prison Industries, Inc. (FPI) 18.106
AbilityOne specification changes 18.107
Qualifications requirements 18.108
Priorities and allocations 18.109
Soliciting from a single source 18.110
Oral requests for proposals 18.111
Letter contracts 18.112
Interagency acquisitions 18.113
Contracting with the Small Business Administration (The 8(a) Program) 18.114
HUBZone sole source awards 18.115
Service-disabled Veteran-owned Small Business (SDVOSB) sole source awards 18.116
Awards to economically disadvantaged women-owned small business concerns and women-owned small business concerns eligible under the Women-Owned Small Business Program 18.117
Overtime approvals 18.118
Trade agreements 18.119
Use of patented technology under the North American Free Trade Agreement 18.120
Bid guarantees 18.121
Advance payments 18.122
Assignment of claims 18.123
Electronic funds transfer 18.124
Protest to GAO 18.125
Contractor rent-free use of Government property 18.126
Extraordinary contractual actions 18.127

Subpart 18.2 Emergency Acquisition Flexibilities

Contingency operation 18.201
Defense or recovery from certain events 18.202
Emergency declaration or major disaster declaration 18.203
Humanitarian or peacekeeping operation 18.204
Resources 18.205

PART 18—EMERGENCY ACQUISITIONS

18.000 Scope of part.

(a) This part identifies acquisition flexibilities that are available for emergency acquisitions. These flexibilities are specific techniques or procedures that may be used to streamline the standard acquisition process. This part includes—

(1) Generally available flexibilities; and

(2) Emergency acquisition flexibilities that are available only under prescribed circumstances.

(b) The acquisition flexibilities in this part are not exempt from the requirements and limitations set forth in FAR Part 3, Improper Business Practices and Personal Conflicts of Interest.

(c) Additional flexibilities may be authorized in an executive agency supplement to the FAR.

[FAC 2005-11, 71 FR 38247, 7/5/2006, effective 7/5/2006; FAC 2005-19, 72 FR 46342, 8/17/2007, effective 9/17/2007]

18.001 Definition.

Emergency acquisition flexibilities, as used in this part, means flexibilities provided with respect to any acquisition of supplies or services by or for an executive agency that, as determined by the head of an executive agency, may be used—

(a) In support of a contingency operation as defined in 2.101;

(b) To facilitate the defense against or recovery from cyber, nuclear, biological, chemical, or radiological attack against the United States;

(c) In support of a request from the Secretary of State or the Administrator of the United States Agency for International Development to facilitate the provision of international disaster assistance; or

(d) When the President issues an emergency declaration, or a major disaster declaration.

[FAC 2005-11, 71 FR 38247, 7/5/2006, effective 7/5/2006; FAC 2005-19, 72 FR 46342, 8/17/2007, effective 9/17/2007; FAC 2005-37, 74 FR 52859, 10/14/2009, effective 11/13/2009; FAC 2019-02, 84 FR 19835, 5/6/2019, effective 6/5/2019]

SUBPART 18.1—AVAILABLE ACQUISITION FLEXIBILITIES

18.101 General.

The FAR includes many acquisition flexibilities that are available to the contracting officer when certain conditions are met. These acquisition flexibilities do not require an emergency declaration or designation of contingency operation.

[FAC 2005-11, 71 FR 38247, 7/5/2006, effective 7/5/2006; FAC 2005-19, 72 FR 46342, 8/17/2007, effective 9/17/2007]

18.102 System for Award Management.

(a) In accordance with 4.1102, contractors are not required to be registered in the System for Award Management (SAM) at the time of submission of offers or quotations for—

(1) Contracts awarded without providing for full and open competition due to unusual and compelling urgency (see 6.302-2); or

(2) Contracts awarded by a contracting officer—

(i) Deployed in the course of military operations;

(ii) Located outside the United States and its outlying areas, for work to be performed in support of diplomatic or developmental operations, in an area that has been designated by the Department of State as a danger pay post; or

(iii) In the conduct of emergency operations.

(b) However, contractors are required to be registered in SAM in order to gain access to the Disaster Response Registry.

(c) Contracting officers shall consult the Disaster Response Registry via *https://www.sam.gov*, Search Records, Advanced Search, Disaster Response Registry Search to determine the availability of contractors for debris removal, distribution of supplies, reconstruction, and other disaster or emergency relief activities inside the United States and outlying areas. (See 26.205).

[FAC 2005-11, 71 FR 38247, 7/5/2006, effective 7/5/2006; FAC 2005-19, 72 FR 46342, 8/17/2007, effective 9/17/2007; FAC 2005-37, 74 FR 52847, 10/14/2009, effective 10/14/2009; FAC 2005-43, 75 FR 38683, 7/2/2010, effective 8/2/2010; FAC 2005-55, 77 FR 187, 1/3/2012, effective 2/2/2012; FAC 2005-67, 78 FR 37676, 6/21/2013, effective 7/22/2013; FAC 2005-101, 83 FR 48691, 9/26/2018, effective 10/26/2018]

18.103 Synopses of proposed contract actions.

Contracting officers need not submit a synopsis notice when there is an unusual and compelling urgency and the Government would be seriously injured if the agency complied with the notice time periods. (See 5.202(a)(2).)

[FAC 2005-11, 71 FR 38247, 7/5/2006, effective 7/5/2006; FAC 2005-19, 72 FR 46342, 8/17/2007, effective 9/17/2007]

18.104 Unusual and compelling urgency.

Agencies may limit the number of sources and full and open competition need not be provided for contracting actions involving urgent requirements. (see 6.302-2.)

[FAC 2005-11, 71 FR 38247, 7/5/2006, effective 7/5/2006; FAC 2005-19, 72 FR 46342, 8/17/2007, effective 9/17/2007]

18.105 Federal Supply Schedules (FSSs), multi-agency blanket purchase agreements (BPAs), and multi-agency indefinite delivery contracts.

Streamlined procedures and a broad range of goods and services may be available under Federal Supply Schedule contracts (see Subpart 8.4), multi-agency BPAs (See 8.405-3(a)(6)), or multi-agency, indefinite-delivery contracts (see 16.505(a)(8)). These contracting methods may offer agency advance planning, pre-negotiated line items, and special terms and conditions that permit rapid response.

[FAC 2005-11, 71 FR 38247, 7/5/2006, effective 7/5/2006; FAC 2005-19, 72 FR 46342, 8/17/2007, effective 9/17/2007; FAC 2005-50, 76 FR 14548, 3/16/2011, effective 5/16/2011; FAC 2005-55, 77 FR 189, 1/3/2012, effective 2/2/2012; FAC 2005-56, 77 FR 12927, 3/2/2012, effective 4/2/2012]

18.106 Acquisitions from Federal Prison Industries, Inc. (FPI).

Purchase from FPI is not mandatory and a waiver is not required if public exigency requires immediate delivery or performance (see 8.605(b)).

[FAC 2005-19, 72 FR 46342, 8/17/2007, effective 9/17/2007]

18.107 AbilityOne specification changes.

Contracting officers are not held to the notification required when changes in AbilityOne specifications or descriptions are required to meet emergency needs. (See 8.712(d).)

[FAC 2005-11, 71 FR 38247, 7/5/2006, effective 7/5/2006; FAC 2005-19, 72 FR 46342, 8/17/2007, effective 9/17/2007; FAC 2005-27, 73 FR 53994, 9/17/2008, effective 10/17/2008]

18.108 Qualifications requirements.

Agencies may determine not to enforce qualification requirements when an emergency exists. (See 9.206-1.)

[FAC 2005-11, 71 FR 38247, 7/5/2006, effective 7/5/2006; FAC 2005-19, 72 FR 46342, 8/17/2007, effective 9/17/2007]

18.109 Priorities and allocations.

The Defense Priorities and Allocations System (DPAS) supports approved national defense, emergency preparedness, and energy programs and was established to facilitate rapid industrial mobilization in case of a national emergency. (See Subpart 11.6.)

[FAC 2005-11, 71 FR 38247, 7/5/2006, effective 7/5/2006; FAC 2005-19, 72 FR 46342, 8/17/2007, effective 9/17/2007; FAC 2005-25, 73 FR 21783, 4/22/2008, effective 4/22/2008]

18.110 Soliciting from a single source.

For purchases not exceeding the simplified acquisition threshold, contracting officers may solicit from one source under certain circumstances. (See 13.106-1(b).)

[FAC 2005-11, 71 FR 38247, 7/5/2006, effective 7/5/2006; FAC 2005-19, 72 FR 46342, 8/17/2007, effective 9/17/2007]

18.111 Oral requests for proposals.

Oral requests for proposals are authorized under certain conditions. (See 15.203(f).)

[FAC 2005-11, 71 FR 38247, 7/5/2006, effective 7/5/2006; FAC 2005-19, 72 FR 46342, 8/17/2007, effective 9/17/2007]

18.112 Letter contracts.

Letter contracts may be used when contract performance must begin immediately. (See 16.603.)

[FAC 2005-11, 71 FR 38247, 7/5/2006, effective 7/5/2006; FAC 2005-19, 72 FR 46342, 8/17/2007, effective 9/17/2007]

18.113 Interagency acquisitions.

Interagency acquisitions are authorized under certain conditions. (See Subpart 17.5.)

[FAC 2005-11, 71 FR 38247, 7/5/2006, effective 7/5/2006; FAC 2005-19, 72 FR 46342, 8/17/2007, effective 9/17/2007; FAC 2005-47, 75 FR 77733, 12/13/2010, effective 12/13/2010; FAC 2005-55, 77 FR 183, 1/3/2012, effective 2/2/2012]

18.114 Contracting with the Small Business Administration (The 8(a) Program).

Contracts may be awarded to the Small Business Administration (SBA) for performance by eligible 8(a) participants on either a sole source or competitive basis. (See Subpart 19.8.)

[FAC 2005-11, 71 FR 38247, 7/5/2006, effective 7/5/2006; FAC 2005-19, 72 FR 46342, 8/17/2007, effective 9/17/2007; FAC 2005-95, 82 FR 4724, 1/13/2017, effective 1/13/2017]

18.115 HUBZone sole source awards.

Contracts may be awarded to Historically Underutilized Business Zone (HUBZone) small business concerns on a sole source basis. (See 19.1306.)

[FAC 2005-11, 71 FR 38247, 7/5/2006, effective 7/5/2006; FAC 2005-19, 72 FR 46342, 8/17/2007, effective 9/17/2007]

18.116 Service-disabled Veteran-owned Small Business (SDVOSB) sole source awards.

Contracts may be awarded to Service-disabled Veteran-owned Small Business (SDVOSB) concerns on a sole source basis. (See 19.1406.)

[FAC 2005-11, 71 FR 38247, 7/5/2006, effective 7/5/2006; FAC 2005-19, 72 FR 46342, 8/17/2007, effective 9/17/2007]

18.117 Awards to economically disadvantaged women-owned small business concerns and women-owned small business concerns eligible under the women-owned small business program.

Contracts may be awarded to economically disadvantaged women-owned small business (EDWOSB) concerns and women-owned small business (WOSB) concerns eligible under the WOSB Program on a competitive or sole source basis. (See subpart 19.15.)

[FAC 2005-51, 76 FR 18304, 4/1/2011, effective 4/1/2011; FAC 2005-56, 77 FR 12913, 3/2/2012, effective 4/2/2012; FAC 2005-86, 80 FR 81888, 12/31/2015, effective 12/31/2015; FAC 2005-91, 81 FR 67735, 9/30/2016, effective 9/30/2016]

18.118 Overtime approvals.

Overtime approvals may be retroactive if justified by emergency circumstances. (See 22.103-4(i).)

[FAC 2005-11, 71 FR 38247, 7/5/2006, effective 7/5/2006; FAC 2005-19, 72 FR 46342, 8/17/2007, effective 9/17/2007; FAC 2005-51, 76 FR 18304, 4/1/2011, effective 4/1/2011; FAC 2005-56, 77 FR 12913, 3/2/2012, effective 4/2/2012]

18.119 Trade agreements.

The policies and procedures of FAR 25.4 may not apply to acquisitions not awarded under full and open competition (see 25.401(a)(5)).

[FAC 2005-19, 72 FR 46342, 8/17/2007, effective 9/17/2007; FAC 2005-51, 76 FR 18304, 4/1/2011, effective 4/1/2011; FAC 2005-56, 77 FR 12913, 3/2/2012, effective 4/2/2012]

18.120 Use of patented technology under the North American Free Trade Agreement.

Requirement to obtain authorization prior to use of patented technology may be waived in circumstances of extreme urgency or national emergency. (See 27.204-1.)

[FAC 2005-11, 71 FR 38247, 7/5/2006, effective 7/5/2006; FAC 2005-19, 72 FR 46342, 8/17/2007, effective 9/17/2007; FAC 2005-21, 72 FR 63045, 11/7/2007, effective 12/7/2007; FAC 2005-51, 76 FR 18304, 4/1/2011, effective 4/1/2011; FAC 2005-56, 77 FR 12913, 3/2/2012, effective 4/2/2012]

18.121 Bid guarantees.

The chief of the contracting office may waive the requirement to obtain a bid guarantee for emergency acquisitions when a performance bond or a performance bond and payment bond is required. (See 28.101-1(c).)

[FAC 2005-11, 71 FR 38247, 7/5/2006, effective 7/5/2006; FAC 2005-19, 72 FR 46342, 8/17/2007, effective 9/17/2007; FAC 2005-51, 76 FR 18304, 4/1/2011, effective 4/1/2011; FAC 2005-56, 77 FR 12913, 3/2/2012, effective 4/2/2012]

18.122 Advance payments.

Agencies may authorize advance payments to facilitate the national defense for actions taken under Public Law 85-804 (see Subpart 50.1, Extraordinary Contractual Actions). These advance payments may be made at or after award of sealed bid contracts, as well as negotiated contracts. (See 32.405.)

[FAC 2005-11, 71 FR 38247, 7/5/2006, effective 7/5/2006; FAC 2005-19, 72 FR 46342, 8/17/2007, effective 9/17/2007; FAC 2005-21, 72 FR 63027, 11/7/2007, effective 11/7/2007; FAC 2005-30, 74 FR 2733, 1/15/2009, effective 2/17/2009; FAC 2005-51, 76 FR 18304, 4/1/2011, effective 4/1/2011; FAC 2005-56, 77 FR 12913, 3/2/2012, effective 4/2/2012]

18.123 Assignment of claims.

The use of the no-setoff provision may be appropriate to facilitate the national defense in the event of a national emergency or natural disaster. (See 32.803(d).)

[FAC 2005-11, 71 FR 38247, 7/5/2006, effective 7/5/2006; FAC 2005-19, 72 FR 46342, 8/17/2007, effective 9/17/2007; FAC 2005-51, 76 FR 18304, 4/1/2011, effective 4/1/2011; FAC 2005-56, 77 FR 12913, 3/2/2012, effective 4/2/2012]

18.124 Electronic funds transfer.

Electronic funds transfer payments may be waived for acquisitions to support unusual and compelling needs or emergency acquisitions. (See 32.1103(e).)

[FAC 2005-11, 71 FR 38247, 7/5/2006, effective 7/5/2006; FAC 2005-19, 72 FR 46342, 8/17/2007, effective 9/17/2007; FAC 2005-51, 76 FR 18304, 4/1/2011, effective 4/1/2011; FAC 2005-56, 77 FR 12913, 3/2/2012, effective 4/2/2012]

18.125 Protest to GAO.

When urgent and compelling circumstances exist, agency protest override procedures allow the head of the contracting activity to determine that the contracting process may continue after GAO has received a protest. (See 33.104(b) and (c).)

[FAC 2005-11, 71 FR 38247, 7/5/2006, effective 7/5/2006; FAC 2005-19, 72 FR 46342, 8/17/2007, effective 9/17/2007; FAC 2005-51, 76 FR 18304, 4/1/2011, effective 4/1/2011; FAC 2005-56, 77 FR 12913, 3/2/2012, effective 4/2/2012]

18.126 Contractor rent-free use of Government property.

Rental requirements do not apply to items of Government production and research property that are part of a general program approved by the Federal Emergency Management Agency and meet certain criteria. (See 45.301.)

[FAC 2005-11, 71 FR 38247, 7/5/2006, effective 7/5/2006; FAC 2005-17, 72 FR 27364, 5/15/2007, effective 6/14/2007; FAC 2005-19, 72 FR 46342, 8/17/2007, effective 9/17/2007; FAC 2005-51, 76 FR 18304,

4/1/2011, effective 4/1/2011; FAC 2005-56, 77 FR 12913, 3/2/2012, effective 4/2/2012]

18.127 Extraordinary contractual actions.

Subpart 50.1 prescribes policies and procedures for entering into, amending, or modifying contracts in order to facilitate the national defense under the extraordinary emergency authority granted by Public Law 85-804 (50 U.S.C. 1431-1434). This includes—

(a) Amending contracts without consideration (see 50.103-2(a));

(b) Correcting or mitigating mistakes in a contract (see 50.103-2(b)); and

(c) Formalizing informal commitments (See 50.103-2(c)).

[FAC 2005-11, 71 FR 38247, 7/5/2006, effective 7/5/2006; FAC 2005-19, 72 FR 46342, 8/17/2007, effective 9/17/2007; FAC 2005-21, 72 FR 63027, 11/7/2007, effective 11/7/2007; FAC 2005-30, 74 FR 2733, 1/15/2009, effective 2/17/2009; FAC 2005-51, 76 FR 18304, 4/1/2011, effective 4/1/2011; FAC 2005-56, 77 FR 12913, 3/2/2012, effective 4/2/2012]

SUBPART 18.2—EMERGENCY ACQUISITION FLEXIBILITIES

18.201 Contingency operation.

(a) *Contingency operation* is defined in 2.101.

(b) *Micro-purchase threshold.* The threshold increases when the head of the agency determines the supplies or services are to be used to support a contingency operation. (See 2.101 and 13.201(g).)

(c) *Simplified acquisition threshold.* The threshold increases when the head of the agency determines the supplies or services are to be used to support a contingency operation. (See 2.101.)

(d) *SF 44, Purchase Order-Invoice-Voucher.* The normal threshold for the use of the SF 44 is at or below the micro-purchase threshold. Agencies may, however, establish higher dollar limitations for purchases made to support a contingency operation. (See 13.306.)

(e) *Simplified procedures for certain commercial items.* The threshold limits authorized for use of this authority may be increased for acquisitions to support a contingency operation. (See 13.500(c)).

[FAC 2005-11, 71 FR 38247, 7/5/2006, effective 7/5/2006; FAC 2005-19, 72 FR 46342, 8/17/2007, effective 9/17/2007; FAC 2005-83, 80 FR 38311, 7/2/2015, effective 8/3/2015]

18.202 Defense or recovery from certain events.

(a) *Micro-purchase threshold.* The threshold increases when the head of the agency determines the supplies or services are to be used to facilitate defense against or recovery from cyber, nuclear, biological, chemical, or radiological attack; to facilitate provision of international disaster assistance; or to support response to an emergency or major disaster. (See 2.101.)

(b) *Simplified acquisition threshold.* The threshold increases when the head of the agency determines the supplies or services are to be used to facilitate defense against or recovery from cyber, nuclear, biological, chemical, or radiological attack; to facilitate provision of international disaster assistance; or to support response to an emergency or major disaster. (See 2.101.)

(c) *Treating certain items as commercial.* Contracting officers may treat any acquisition of supplies or services as an acquisition of commercial items if the head of the agency determines the acquisition is to be used to facilitate the defense against or recovery from cyber, nuclear, biological, chemical, or radiological attack. (See 12.102(f)(1) and 13.500(c)(2).)

(d) *Simplified procedures for certain commercial items.* The threshold limits authorized for use of this authority may be increased when it is determined the acquisition is to facilitate defense against or recovery from cyber, nuclear, biological, chemical, or radiological attack; to facilitate provision of international disaster assistance; or to support response to an emergency or major disaster. (See 13.500(c).)

[FAC 2005-11, 71 FR 38247, 7/5/2006, effective 7/5/2006; FAC 2005-19, 72 FR 46342,

8/17/2007, effective 9/17/2007; FAC 2005-83, 80 FR 38311, 7/2/2015, effective 8/3/2015; FAC 2019-02, 84 FR 19835, 5/6/2019, effective 6/5/2019]

18.203 Emergency declaration or major disaster declaration.

(a) *Disaster or emergency assistance activities.* Preference will be given to local organizations, firms, and individuals when contracting for major disaster or emergency assistance activities when the President has made a declaration under the Robert T. Stafford Disaster Relief and Emergency Assistance Act. Preference may take the form of local area set-asides or an evaluation preference. (See 6.208 and Subpart 26.2.)

(b) *Ocean transportation by U.S. flag vessels.* The provisions of the Cargo Preference Act of 1954 may be waived in emergency situations. (See 47.502(c).)

[FAC 2005-11, 71 FR 38247, 752006, effective 752006; FAC 2005-19, 72 FR 46342, 8172007, effective 9172007; FAC 2005-21, 72 FR 63084, 1172007, effective 1172007; FAC 2005-27, 73 FR 53995, 9/17/2008, effective 10/17/2008; FAC 2005-37, 74 FR 52859, 10/14/2009, effective 11/13/2009; FAC 2005-51, 76 FR 18304, 4/1/2011, effective 4/1/2011; FAC 2005-56, 77 FR 12913, 3/2/2012, effective 4/2/2012]

18.204 Humanitarian or peacekeeping operation.

(a) A humanitarian or peacekeeping operation is defined in 2.101.

(b) *Simplified acquisition threshold.* The threshold increases when the head of the agency determines the supplies or services are to be used to support a humanitarian or peacekeeping operation. (See 2.101.)

[FAC 2005-88, 81 FR 30438, 5/16/2016, effective 6/15/2016]

18.205 Resources.

(a) *National Response Framework.* The National Response Framework (NRF) is a guide to how the Nation conducts all-hazards response. This key document establishes a comprehensive, national, all-hazards approach to domestic incident response. The Framework identifies the key response principles, roles and structures that organize national response. It describes how communities, States, the Federal Government, the private-sector, and nongovernmental partners apply these principles for a coordinated, effective national response. It also describes special circumstances where the Federal Government exercises a larger role, including incidents where Federal interests are involved and catastrophic incidents where a State would require significant support. The NRF is available at *http://www.fema.gov/emergency/nrf/*.

(b) *OFPP Guidelines.* The Office of Federal Procurement Policy (OFPP) "Emergency Acquisitions Guide" is available at *https://www.whitehouse.gov/sites/whitehouse.gov/files/omb/assets/procurement_guides/emergency_acquisitions_guide.pdf.*

[FAC 2005-11, 71 FR 38247, 7/5/2006, effective 7/5/2006; FAC 2005-19, 72 FR 46342, 8/17/2007, effective 9/17/2007; FAC 2005-37, 74 FR 52859, 10/14/2009, effective 11/13/2009; FAC 2005-50, 76 FR 14572, 3/16/2011, effective 3/16/2011; FAC 2005-88, 81 FR 30438, 5/16/2016, effective 6/15/2016; FAC 2005-100, 83 FR 42571, 8/22/2018, effective 8/22/2018]

Federal Acquisition Regulation Parts 19—26 Socioeconomic Programs

---

Table of Contents

SUBCHAPTER D—SOCIOECONOMIC PROGRAMS

Part 19—Small Business Programs 535
Part 20—[Reserved]
Part 21—[Reserved]
Part 22—Application of Labor Laws to Government Acquisitions 621
Part 23—Environment, Energy and Water Efficiency, Renewable Energy Technologies, Occupational Safety, and Drug-Free Workplace 723
Part 24—Protection of Privacy and Freedom of Information 745
Part 25—Foreign Acquisition 751
Part 26—Other Socioeconomic Programs 799

PART 19—SMALL BUSINESS PROGRAMS

Table of Contents

Scope of part 19.000
Definitions 19.001

Subpart 19.1—Size Standards

Definitions 19.101
Size standards 19.102

Subpart 19.2—Policies

General policy 19.201
Specific policies 19.202
Encouraging small business participation in acquisitions 19.202-1
Locating small business sources 19.202-2
Equal low bids 19.202-3
Solicitation 19.202-4
Data collection and reporting requirements 19.202-5
Determination of fair market price 19.202-6
Relationship among small business programs 19.203

Subpart 19.3—Determination of Small Business Status for Small Business Programs

Representations and rerepresentations 19.301
Representation by the offeror 19.301-1
Rerepresentation by a contractor that represented itself as a small business concern 19.301-2
Rerepresentation by a contractor that represented itself as other than a small business concern 19.301-3
Protesting a small business representation or rerepresentation 19.302
Determining North American Industry Classification System codes and size standards 19.303
Small disadvantaged business status 19.304
Reviews and protests of SDB status 19.305
Protesting a firm's status as a HUBZone small business concern 19.306
Protesting a firm's status as a service-disabled veteran-owned small business concern 19.307
Protesting a firm's status as an economically disadvantaged women-owned small business concern or women-owned small business concern eligible under the Women-Owned Small Business Program 19.308
Solicitation provisions and contract clauses 19.309

Subpart 19.4—Cooperation with the Small Business Administration

General 19.401
Small Business Administration procurement center representatives 19.402
Small Business Administration breakout procurement center representative. 19.403

Subpart 19.5—Set-Asides for Small Business

General 19.501
Setting aside acquisitions 19.502
Requirements for setting aside acquisitions 19.502-1
Total small business set-asides 19.502-2
Partial set-asides 19.502-3
Multiple-award contracts and small business set-asides 19.502-4
Methods of conducting set- asides 19.502-5
Insufficient causes for not setting aside an acquisition 19.502-6
Setting aside a class of acquisitions for small business 19.503

Inclusion of Federal Prison Industries, Inc 19.504
Rejecting Small Business Administration recommendations 19.505
Withdrawing or modifying small business set-asides 19.506
Automatic dissolution of a small business set-aside 19.507
Solicitation provisions and contract clauses 19.508

Subpart 19.6—Certificates of Competency and Determinations of Responsibility

General 19.601
Procedures 19.602
Referral 19.602-1
Issuing or denying a Certificate of Competency (COC) 19.602-2
Resolving differences between the agency and the Small Business Administration 19.602-3
Awarding the contract 19.602-4

Subpart 19.7—The Small Business Subcontracting Program

Definitions 19.701
Statutory requirements 19.702
Eligibility requirements for participating in the program 19.703
Subcontracting plan requirements 19.704
Responsibilities of the contracting officer under the subcontracting assistance program 19.705
General 19.705-1
Determining the need for a subcontracting plan 19.705-2
Preparing the solicitation 19.705-3
Reviewing the subcontracting plan 19.705-4
Awards involving subcontracting plans 19.705-5
Postaward responsibilities of the contracting officer 19.705-6
Liquidated damages 19.705-7
Responsibilities of the cognizant administrative contracting officer 19.706
The Small Business Administration's role in carrying out the program 19.707
Contract clauses 19.708

Subpart 19.8—Contracting with the Small Business Administration (The 8(a) Program)

General 19.800
[Reserved] 19.801
Determining eligibility for the 8(a) program 19.802
Selecting acquisitions for the 8(a) program 19.803
Evaluation, offering, and acceptance 19.804
Agency evaluation 19.804-1
Agency offering 19.804-2
SBA acceptance 19.804-3
Repetitive acquisitions 19.804-4
Basic ordering agreements 19.804-5
Indefinite-delivery contracts 19.804-6
Competitive 8(a) 19.805
General 19.805-1
Procedures 19.805-2
Pricing the 8(a) contract 19.806
Estimating fair market price 19.807
Contract negotiation 19.808
Sole source 19.808-1
Competitive 19.808-2
Preaward considerations 19.809
SBA appeals 19.810

Preparing the contracts 19.811
Sole source 19.811-1
Competitive 19.811-2
Contract clauses 19.811-3
Contract administration 19.812
Protesting an 8(a) participant's eligibility or size status 19.813
Requesting a formal size determination (8(a) sole source requirements) . . . 19.814
Release for non-8(a) procurement 19.815
Exiting the 8(a) program 19.816

Subpart 19.9—[Reserved]

Subpart 19.10—[Removed and Reserved]

[Removed and Reserved] 19.1001
[Removed and Reserved] 19.1002
[Removed and Reserved] 19.1003
[Removed and Reserved] 19.1004
[Removed and Reserved] 19.1005
[Removed and Reserved] 19.1006
[Removed and Reserved] 19.1007
[Removed and Reserved] 19.1008

Subpart 19.11—[Removed and Reserved]

[Removed and Reserved] 19.1101
[Removed and Reserved] 19.1102
[Removed and Reserved] 19.1103
[Removed and Reserved] 19.1104

Subpart 19.12—[Removed and Reserved]

[Removed and Reserved] 19.1201
[Removed and Reserved] 19.1202
[Removed and Reserved] 19.1202-1
[Removed and Reserved] 19.1202-2
[Removed and Reserved] 19.1202-3
[Removed and Reserved] 19.1202-4
[Removed and Reserved] 19.1203
[Removed and Reserved] 19.1204

Subpart 19.13—Historically Underutilized Business Zone (Hubzone) Program

General 19.1301
Applicability 19.1302
Status as a HUBZone small business concern 19.1303
Exclusions 19.1304
HUBZone set-aside procedures 19.1305
HUBZone sole source awards 19.1306
Price evaluation preference for HUBZone small business concerns 19.1307
Performance of work requirements (limitations on subcontracting) for general construction or construction by special trade contractors 19.1308
Contract clauses 19.1309

Subpart 19.14—Service-Disabled Veteran-Owned Small Business Procurement Program

General 19.1401
Applicability 19.1402
Status as a service-disabled veteran-owned small business concern 19.1403
Exclusions 19.1404
Service-disabled veteran-owned small business set-aside procedures 19.1405

Sole source awards to service-disabled veteran-owned small business concerns 19.1406
Contract clauses 19.1407

Subpart 19.15—Women-Owned Small Business Program

General 19.1500
Definition 19.1501
Applicability 19.1502
Status 19.1503
Exclusions 19.1504
Set-aside procedures 19.1505
Women-Owned Small Business Program sole source awards 19.1506
Contract clauses 19.1507

SUBCHAPTER D—SOCIOECONOMIC PROGRAMS (Parts 19-26)

PART 19—SMALL BUSINESS PROGRAMS

19.000 Scope of part.

(a) This part implements the acquisition-related sections of the Small Business Act (15 U.S.C. 631, *et seq.*), applicable sections of the Armed Services Procurement Act (10 U.S.C. 2302, *et seq.*), 41 U.S.C. 3104, and Executive Order 12138, May 18, 1979. It covers—

(1) The determination that a concern is eligible for participation in the programs identified in this part;

(2) The respective roles of executive agencies and the Small Business Administration (SBA) in implementing the programs;

(3) Setting acquisitions aside for exclusive competitive participation by small business, 8(a) participants, HUBZone small business concerns, service-disabled veteran-owned small business concerns, and economically disadvantaged women-owned small business (EDWOSB) concerns and women-owned small business (WOSB) concerns eligible under the WOSB Program;

(4) The certificate of competency program;

(5) The subcontracting assistance program;

(6) The "8(a)" business development program (hereafter referred to as 8(a) program), under which agencies contract with the SBA for goods or services to be furnished under a subcontract by a small disadvantaged business concern;

(7) The use of a price evaluation preference for HUBZone small business concerns;

(8) The use of veteran-owned small business concerns; and

(9) Sole source awards to HUBZone small business concerns, service-disabled veteran-owned small business concerns, and EDWOSB concerns and WOSB concerns eligible under the WOSB Program.

(b) This part, except for subpart 19.6, applies only in the United States or its outlying areas. Subpart 19.6 applies worldwide.

[FAC 90-24, interim rule, 59 FR 64784, 12/15/94, effective 12/15/94; FAC 90-23, 59 FR 67010, 12/28/94, effective 2/27/95; FAC 90-30, 60 FR 37772, 7/21/95, effective 9/19/95; FAC 97-6, 63 FR 35719, 6/30/98, effective 10/1/98, finalized without change, FAC 97-13, 7/2/99; FAC 97-7, 63 FR 36120, 7/1/98, effective 1/1/99, finalized without change, FAC 97-13, 7/2/99; FAC 97-10, 63 FR 70264, 12/18/98, effective 1/4/99; FAC 97-11, 64 FR 10530, 3/4/99, effective 3/4/99; FAC 97-20, 65 FR 60542, 10/11/2000, effective 10/11/2000; FAC 2001-14, 68 FR 28079, 5/22/2003, effective 6/23/2003; FAC 2001-23, 69 FR 25273, 5/5/2004, effective 5/5/2004; FAC 2005-02, 70 FR 14950, 3/23/2005, effective 3/23/2005; FAC 2005-07, 71 FR 220, 1/3/2006, effective 1/3/2006; FAC 2005-47, 75 FR 77727, 12/13/2010, effective 1/12/2011; FAC 2005-51, 76 FR 18304, 4/1/2011, effective 4/1/2011; FAC 2005-56, 77 FR 12913, 3/2/2012, effective 4/2/2012; FAC 2005-73, 79 FR 24192, 4/29/2014, effective 5/29/2014; FAC 2005-77, 79 FR 61746, 10/14/2014, effective 10/14/2014; FAC 2005-86, 80 FR 81888, 12/31/2015, effective 12/31/2015; FAC 2005-91, 81 FR 67735, 9/30/2016, effective 9/30/2016; FAC 2005-95, 82 FR 4724, 1/13/2017, effective 1/13/2017]

19.001 Definitions.

As used in this part—

Concern means any business entity organized for profit (even if its ownership is in the hands of a nonprofit entity) with a place of business located in the United States or its outlying areas and that makes a significant contribution to the U.S. economy through payment of taxes and/or use of American products, material and/or labor, etc. *Concern* includes but is not limited to an individual, partnership, corporation, joint venture, association, or cooperative. For more information, see 13 CFR 121.105.

Fair market price means a price based on reasonable costs under normal competitive conditions and not on lowest possible cost (see 19.202-6).

Industry means all concerns primarily engaged in similar lines of activity, as listed and described in the North American Industry Classification system (NAICS) manual.

Nonmanufacturer rule means that a contractor under a small business set-aside or 8(a) contract shall be a small business under the applicable size standard and shall provide either its own product or that of another domestic small business manufacturing or processing concern (see 13 CFR 121.406).

[FAC 84-12, 51 FR 2650, 1/17/86, effective 1/20/86; FAC 84-31, 52 FR 38189, 10/14/87, effective 10/1/87; FAC 84-48, 54 FR 25062, 6/12/89, effective 6/12/89; FAC 84-56, 55 FR 3881, 2/5/90, effective 2/5/90; FAC 90-16, 57 FR 60580, 12/21/92, effective 12/21/92; FAC 90-20, 59 FR 11368, 3/10/94, effective 3/10/94; FAC 90-32, 60 FR 48206, 9/18/95, effective 10/1/95; FAC 90-43, 61 FR 67408, 12/20/96, effective 12/20/96, finalized without change, FAC 97-1, 62 FR 44802, 8/22/97, effective 10/21/97; FAC 90-45, 62 FR 224, 1/2/97, effective 1/1/97; FAC 97-1, 62 FR 44802, 8/22/97, effective 10/21/97, finalized without change, FAC 97-4, 63 FR 9048, 2/23/98, effective 4/24/98; FAC 97-6, 63 FR 35719, 6/30/98, effective 10/1/98; FAC 97-7, 63 FR 36120, 7/1/98, effective 1/1/99, corrected, interim rule, 63 FR 71721, 12/29/98; FAC 97-10, 63 FR 70264, 12/18/98, effective 1/4/99; FAC 97-11, 64 FR 10530, 3/4/99, effective 3/4/99; FAC 97-13, 64 FR 36222, 7/2/99, effective 10/1/99; FAC 97-19, 65 FR 46052, 7/26/2000, effective 10/1/2000; FAC 97-20, 65 FR 60542, 10/11/2000, effective 10/11/2000; FAC 97-22, 66 FR 2116, 1/10/2001, effective 3/12/2001; Delay of effective date, 66 FR 14259, 3/9/2001, effective 5/11/2001; Delay of effective date, 66 FR 14259, 3/9/2001, effective 5/11/2001; FAC 2001-02, 66 FR 65347, 12/18/2001, effective 2/19/2002; FAC 2001-14, 68 FR 28079, 5/22/2003, effective 6/23/2003; FAC 2005-07, 71 FR 220, 1/3/2006, effective 1/3/2006; FAC 2005-21, 72 FR 63045, 11/7/2007, effective 12/7/2007; FAC 2005-61, 77 FR 56741, 9/13/2012, effective 10/15/2012; FAC 2019-06, 84 FR 47862, 9/10/2019, effective 10/10/2019]

SUBPART 19.1—SIZE STANDARDS

19.101 Definitions.

As used in this subpart—

Affiliates means business concerns, one of whom directly or indirectly controls or has the power to control the others, or a third party or parties control or have the power to control the others. In determining whether affiliation exists, consideration is given to all appropriate factors including common ownership, common management, and contractual relationships. SBA determines affiliation based on the factors set forth at 13 CFR 121.103.

(1) *Nature of control.* Every business concern is considered as having one or more parties who directly or indirectly control or have the power to control it. Control may be affirmative or negative and it is immaterial whether it is exercised so long as the power to control exists.

(2) *Meaning of party or parties.* The term *party* or *parties* includes, but is not limited to, two or more persons with an identity of interest such as members of the same family or persons with common investments in more than one concern. In determining who controls or has the power to control a concern, persons with an identity of interest may be treated as though they were one person.

(3) *Control through stock ownership.*

(i) A party is considered to control or have the power to control a concern, if the party controls or has the power to control 50 percent or more of the concern's voting stock.

(ii) A party is considered to control or have the power to control a concern, even though the party owns, controls, or has the power to control less than 50 percent of the concern's voting stock, if the block of stock the party owns, controls, or has the power to control is large, as compared with any other outstanding block of stock. If two or more parties each owns, controls, or has the power to control, less than 50 percent of the voting stock of a concern, and such minority block is equal or substantially equal in size, and large as compared with any other block outstanding, there is a presumption that each such party controls or has the power to control such concern; however, such presumption may be rebutted by a showing that such control or power to control, in fact, does not exist.

(iii) If a concern's voting stock is distributed other than as described above, its management (officers and directors) is deemed to be in control of such concern.

(4) *Stock options and convertible debentures.* Stock options and convertible debentures exercisable at the time or within a relatively short time after a size determination and agreements to merge in the future, are considered as having a present effect on the power to control the concern. Therefore, in making a size determination, such options, debentures, and agreements are treated as though the rights held thereunder had been exercised.

(5) *Voting trusts.* If the purpose of a voting trust, or similar agreement, is to separate voting power from beneficial ownership of voting stock for the purpose of shifting control of or the power to control a concern in order that such concern or another concern may qualify as a small business within the size regulations, such voting trust shall not be considered valid for this purpose regardless of whether it is or is not valid within the appropriate jurisdiction. However, if a voting trust is entered into for a legitimate purpose other than that described above, and it is valid within the appropriate jurisdiction, it may be considered valid for the purpose of a size determination, provided such consideration is determined to be in the best interest of the small business program.

(6) *Control through common management.* A concern may be found as controlling or having the power to control another concern when one or more of the following circumstances are found to exist, and it is reasonable to conclude that under the circumstances, such concern is directing or influencing, or has the power to direct or influence, the operation of such other concern.

(i) *Interlocking management.* Officers, directors, employees, or principal stockholders of one concern serve as a working majority of the board of directors or officers of another concern.

(ii) *Common facilities.* One concern shares common office space and/or employees and/or other facilities with another concern, particularly where such concerns are in the same or related industry or field of operation, or where such concerns were formerly affiliated.

(iii) *Newly organized concern.* Former officers, directors, principal stockholders, and/or key employees of one concern organize a new concern in the same or a related industry or field operation, and serve as its officers, directors, principal stockholders, and/or key employees, and one concern is furnishing or will furnish the other concern with subcontracts, financial or technical assistance, and/or facilities, whether for a fee or otherwise.

(7) *Control through contractual relationships*—(i) *Definition of a joint venture for size determination purposes.* A joint venture for size determination purposes is an association of persons or concerns with interests in any degree or proportion by way of contract, express or implied, consorting to engage in and carry out a single specific business venture for joint profit, for which purpose they combine their efforts, property, money, skill, or knowledge, but not on a continuing or permanent basis for conducting business generally. A joint venture is viewed as a business entity in determining power to control its management.

(A) For bundled requirements, apply size standards for the requirement to individual persons or concerns, not to the combined assets, of the joint venture.

(B) For other than bundled requirements, apply size standards for the requirement to individual persons or concerns, not to the combined assets, of the joint venture, if—

(1) A revenue-based size standard applies to the requirement and the estimated contract value, including options, exceeds one-half the applicable size standard; or

(2) An employee-based size standard applies to the requirement and the estimated

contract value, including options, exceeds $10 million.

(ii) *HUBZone joint venture.* A HUBZone joint venture of two or more HUBZone small business concerns may submit an offer for a HUBZone contract as long as each concern is small under the size standard corresponding to the NAICS code assigned to the contract, provided one of the following conditions apply:

(A) The aggregate total of the joint venture is small under the size standard corresponding to the NAICS code assigned to the contract.

(B) The aggregate total of the joint venture is not small under the size standard corresponding to the NAICS code assigned to the contract and either—

(*1*) For a revenue-based size standard, the estimated contract value exceeds half the size standard corresponding to the NAICS code assigned to the contract; or

(*2*) For an employee-based size standard, the estimated contract value exceeds $10 million.

(iii) *Joint venture.* Concerns submitting offers on a particular acquisition as joint ventures are considered as affiliated and controlling or having the power to control each other with regard to performance of the contract. Moreover, an ostensible subcontractor which is to perform primary or vital requirements of a contract may have a controlling role such to be considered a joint venturer affiliated on the contract with the prime contractor. A joint venture affiliation finding is limited to particular contracts unless the SBA size determination finds general affiliation between the parties. The rules governing 8(a) Program joint ventures are described in 13 CFR 124.513.

(iv) Where a concern is not considered as being an affiliate of a concern with which it is participating in a joint venture, it is necessary, nevertheless, in computing annual receipts, etc., for the purpose of applying size standards, to include such concern's share of the joint venture receipts (as distinguished from its share of the profits of such venture).

(v) *Franchise and license agreements.* If a concern operates or is to operate under a franchise (or a license) agreement, the following policy is applicable: In determining whether the franchisor controls or has the power to control and, therefore, is affiliated with the franchisee, the restraints imposed on a franchisee by its franchise agreement shall not be considered, provided that the franchisee has the right to profit from its effort and the risk of loss or failure, commensurate with ownership. Even though a franchisee may not be controlled by the franchisor by virtue of the contractual relationship between them, the franchisee may be controlled by the franchisor or others through common ownership or common management, in which case they would be considered as affiliated.

(vi) Size determination for teaming arrangements. For size determination purposes, apply the size standard tests in paragraphs (7)(i)(A) and (B) of this section when a teaming arrangement of two or more business concerns submits an offer, as appropriate.

Annual receipts.

(1) Annual receipts of a concern which has been in business for 3 or more complete fiscal years means the annual average gross revenue of the concern taken for the last 3 fiscal years. For the purpose of this definition, gross revenue of the concern includes revenues from sales of products and services, interest, rents, fees, commissions and/or whatever other sources derived, but less returns and allowances, sales of fixed assets, interaffiliate transactions between a concern and its domestic and foreign affiliates, and taxes collected for remittance (and if due, remitted) to a third party. Such revenues shall be measured as entered on the regular books of account of the concern whether on a cash, accrual, or other basis of accounting acceptable to the U.S. Treasury Department for the purpose of supporting Federal income tax returns, except when a change in accounting method from cash to accrual or accrual to cash has taken place during such 3-year period, or when the completed contract method has been used.

(i) In any case of a change in accounting method from cash to accrual or accrual to cash, revenues for such 3-year period shall, prior to the calculation of the annual average, be restated to the accrual method. In any case, where the completed contract method has been used to account for revenues in such 3-year period, revenues must be restated on an accrual basis using the percentage of completion method.

(ii) In the case of a concern which does not keep regular books of accounts, but which is subject to U.S. Federal income taxation, "annual receipts" shall be measured as reported, or to be reported to the U.S. Treasury Department, Internal Revenue Service, for Federal income tax purposes, except that any return based on a change in accounting method or on the completed contract method of accounting must be restated as provided for in the preceding paragraphs.

(2) Annual receipts of a concern that has been in business for less than 3 complete fiscal years means its total receipts for the period it has been in business, divided by the number of weeks including fractions of a week that it has been in business, and multiplied by 52. In calculating total receipts, the definitions and adjustments related to a change of accounting method and the completed contract method of paragraph (1) of this section, are applicable.

Number of employees is a measure of the average employment of a business concern and means its average employment, including the employees of its domestic and foreign affiliates, based on the number of persons employed on a full-time, part-time, temporary, or other basis during each of the pay periods of the preceding 12 months. If a business has not been in existence for 12 months, "number of employees" means the average employment of such concern and its affiliates during the period that such concern has been in existence based on the number of persons employed during each of the pay periods of the period that such concern has been in business. If a business has acquired an affiliate during the applicable 12-month period, it is necessary, in computing the applicant's number of employees, to include the affiliate's number of employees during the entire period, rather than only its employees during the period in which it has been an affiliate. The employees of a former affiliate are not included, even if such concern had been an affiliate during a portion of the period.

[FAC 84-12, 51 FR 2650, 1/17/86, effective 1/20/86; FAC 97-12, 64 FR 32740, 6/17/99, effective 6/17/99, finalized without change, FAC 97-15, 64 FR 72414, 12/27/99; FAC 97-15, 64 FR 72414, 12/27/99, effective 12/27/99; FAC 97-19, 65 FR 46052, 7/26/2000, effective 7/26/2000; FAC 97-22, 66 FR 2116, 1/10/01, effective 3/12/01; Delay of effective date, 66 FR 14259, 3/9/2001, effective 5/11/2001; FAC 2001-14, 68 FR 28079, 5/22/2003, effective 6/23/2003; FAC 2005-47, 75 FR 77727, 12/13/2010, effective 1/12/2011; FAC 2019-06, 84 FR 47862, 9/10/2019, effective 10/10/2019]

19.102 Size standards.

(a) (1) The SBA establishes small business size standards on an industry-by-industry basis. (See 13 CFR 121). Small business size standards matched to industry NAICS codes are published by the Small Business Administration and are available at *http://www.sba.gov/content/table-small-business-size-standards*.

(2) NAICS codes are updated by the Office of Management and Budget through its Economic Classification Policy Committee every five years. New NAICS codes are not available for use in Federal contracting until the Small Business Administration publishes corresponding industry size standards (see 19.102(a)(1)).

(b) Small business size standards are applied by—

(1) Classifying the product or service being acquired in the industry whose definition, as found in the North American Industry Classification System (NAICS) Manual (available at *http://www.census.gov/eos/www/naics/*), best describes the principal nature of the product or service being acquired;

(2) Identifying the size standard SBA established for that industry; and

(3) Specifying the size standard in the solicitation, so that offerors can appropriately represent themselves as small or large.

(c) For size standard purposes, a product or service shall be classified in only one industry, whose definition best describes the principal nature of the product or service being acquired even though for other purposes it could be classified in more than one.

(d) When acquiring a product or service that could be classified in two or more industries with different size standards, contracting officers shall apply the size standard for the industry accounting for the greatest percentage of the contract price.

(e) If a solicitation calls for more than one item and allows offers to be submitted on any or all of the items, an offeror must meet the size standard for each item it offers to furnish. If a solicitation calling for more than one item requires offers on all or none of the items, an offeror may qualify as a small business by meeting the size standard for the item accounting for the greatest percentage of the total contract price.

(f) Any concern submitting a bid or offer in its own name, other than on a construction or service contract, that proposes to furnish an end product it did not manufacture (a "nonmanufacturer"), is a small business if it has no more than 500 employees, and—

(1) Except as provided in paragraphs (f)(4) through (f)(7) of this section, in the case of Government acquisitions set-aside for small businesses, furnishes in the performance of the contract, the product of a small business manufacturer or producer. The end product furnished must be manufactured or produced in the United States or its outlying areas. The term "nonmanufacturer" includes a concern that can, but elects not to, manufacture or produce the end product for the specific acquisition. For size determination purposes, there can be only one manufacturer of the end product being acquired. The manufacturer of the end product being acquired is the concern that, with its own forces, transforms inorganic or organic substances including raw materials and/or miscellaneous parts or components into the end product. However, see the limitations on subcontracting at 52.219-14 that apply to any small business offeror other than a nonmanufacturer for purposes of set-asides and 8(a) awards, 52.219-3 for HUBZone set-asides and HUBZone sole source awards, 52.219-27 for SDVOSB set-asides and SDVOSB sole source awards, 52.219-29 for economically disadvantaged women-owned small business (EDWOSB) set-asides and EDWOSB sole source awards, and 52.219-30 for set-asides and sole source awards to women- owned small business (WOSB) concerns eligible under the WOSB Program.

(2) A concern which purchases items and packages them into a kit is considered to be a nonmanufacturer small business and can qualify as such for a given acquisition if it meets the size qualifications of a small nonmanufacturer for the acquisition, and if more than 50 percent of the total value of the kit and its contents are accounted for by items manufactured by small business.

(3) For the purpose of receiving a Certificate of Competency on an unrestricted acquisition, a small business nonmanufacturer may furnish any domestically produced or manufactured product.

(4) In the case of acquisitions set aside for small business or awarded under section 8(a) of the Small Business Act, when the acquisition is for a specific product (or a product in a class of products) for which the SBA has determined that there are no small business manufacturers or processors in the Federal market, then the SBA may grant a class waiver so that a nonmanufacturer does not have to furnish the product of a small business. For the most current listing of classes for which SBA has granted a waiver, contact an SBA Office of Government Contracting. A listing is also available on SBA's Internet Homepage at *http://www.sba.gov/content/class-waivers.* Contracting officers may request that the SBA waive the nonmanufacturer rule for a particular class of products. For procedures in requesting a waiver see 13 CFR 121.1204.

(5) For a specific solicitation, a contracting officer may request a waiver of that part of the nonmanufacturer rule which requires that the actual manufacturer or processor be a small business concern if the contracting

officer determines that no known domestic small business manufacturers or processors can reasonably be expected to offer a product meeting the requirements of the solicitation.

(6) Requests for waivers shall be sent to the Associate Administrator for Government Contracting, United States Small Business Administration, Mail Code 6250, 409 Third Street, SW., Washington, DC 20416.

(7) The SBA provides for an exception to the nonmanufacturer rule if—

(i) The procurement of a manufactured end product processed under the procedures set forth in part 13—

(A) Is set aside for small business; and

(B) Is not anticipated to exceed $25,000; and

(ii) The offeror supplies an end product that is manufactured or produced in the United States or its outlying areas.

(8) For nonmanufacturer rules pertaining to HUBZone contracts, *see* 19.1303(e).

[FAC 90-39, 61 FR 31612, 6/20/96, effective 6/20/96; FAC 90-40, 61 FR 39186, 7/26/96, effective 7/26/96; FAC 90-43, 61 FR 67408, 12/20/96, effective 12/20/96; finalized without change, FAC 97-1, 62 FR 44802, 8/22/97, effective 10/21/97; FAC 97-9, 63 FR 58587, 10/30/98, effective 10/30/98; FAC 97-10, 63 FR 70264, 12/18/98, effective 1/4/99; FAC 97-11, 64 FR 10530, 3/4/99, effective 3/4/99; FAC 97-14, 64 FR 51828, 9/24/99, effective 11/23/99, corrected, 64 FR 53264, 10/7/99; FAC 97-19, 65 FR 46052, 7/26/2000, effective 10/1/2000; FAC 2001-02, 66 FR 65347, 12/18/2001, effective 12/18/2001; FAC 2001-14, 68 FR 28079, 5/22/2003, effective 6/23/2003; FAC 2005-07, 71 FR 220, 1/3/2006, effective 1/3/2006; FAC 2005-47, 75 FR 77727, 12/13/2010, effective 1/12/2011; FAC 2005-55, 77 FR 204, 1/3/2012, effective 1/3/2012; FAC 2005-61, 77 FR 56741, 9/13/2012, effective 10/15/2012; FAC 2005-76, 79 FR 43580, 7/25/2014, effective 8/25/2014; FAC 2005-86, 80 FR 81888, 12/31/2015, effective 12/31/2015; FAC 2005-91, 81 FR 67735, 9/30/2016, effective 9/30/2016]

SUBPART 19.2—POLICIES

19.201 General policy.

(a) It is the policy of the Government to provide maximum practicable opportunities in its acquisitions to small business, veteran-owned small business, service-disabled veteran-owned small business, HUBZone small business, small disadvantaged business, and women-owned small business concerns. Such concerns must also have the maximum practicable opportunity to participate as subcontractors in the contracts awarded by any executive agency, consistent with efficient contract performance. The Small Business Administration (SBA) counsels and assists small business concerns and assists contracting personnel to ensure that a fair proportion of contracts for supplies and services is placed with small business.

(b) Heads of contracting activities are responsible for effectively implementing the small business programs within their activities, including achieving program goals. They are to ensure that contracting and technical personnel maintain knowledge of small business program requirements and take all reasonable action to increase participation in their activities' contracting processes by these businesses.

(c) The Small Business Act requires each agency with contracting authority to establish an Office of Small and Disadvantaged Business Utilization (see section 15(k) of the Small Business Act). For the Department of Defense, in accordance with section 904 of the National Defense Authorization Act for Fiscal Year 2006 (Pub. L. 109-163) (10 U.S.C. 144 note), the Office of Small and Disadvantaged Business Utilization has been redesignated as the Office of Small Business Programs. Management of the office is the responsibility of an officer or employee of the agency who, in carrying out the purposes of the Act—

(1) Is known as the Director of Small and Disadvantaged Business Utilization, or for the Department of Defense, the Director of Small Business Programs;

(2) Is appointed by the agency head;

(3) Is responsible to and reports directly to the agency head or the deputy to the agency head;

(4) Is responsible for the agency carrying out the functions and duties in sections 8, 15, 31, 36, and 44 of the Small Business Act;

(5) Works with the SBA procurement center representative (or, if a procurement center representative is not assigned, see 19.402(a)(2)) to identify proposed solicitations that involve bundling and work with the agency acquisition officials and SBA to revise the acquisition strategies for such proposed solicitations to increase the probability of participation by small businesses;

(6) Assists small business concerns in obtaining payments under their contracts, late payment interest penalties, or information on contractual payment provisions;

(7) Has supervisory authority over agency personnel to the extent that their functions and duties relate to sections 8, 15, 31, 36, and 44 of the Small Business Act;

(8) Assigns a small business technical advisor to each contracting activity within the agency to which the SBA has assigned a representative (see 19.402)—

(i) Who is a full-time employee of the contracting activity, well qualified, technically trained, and familiar with the supplies or services contracted for by the activity; and

(ii) Whose principal duty is to assist the SBA's assigned representative in performing functions and duties relating to sections 8, 15, 31, 36, and 44 of the Small Business Act;

(9) Cooperates and consults on a regular basis with the SBA in carrying out the agency's functions and duties in sections 8, 15, 31, 36, and 44 of the Small Business Act;

(10) Makes recommendations in accordance with agency procedures as to whether a particular acquisition should be awarded under subpart 19.5 as a small business set-aside, under subpart 19.8 as a section 8(a) award, under subpart 19.13 as a HUBZone set-aside, under subpart 19.14 as a service-disabled veteran-owned small business set-aside, or under subpart 19.15 as a set-aside for economically disadvantaged women-owned small business (EDWOSB) concerns or women-owned small business (WOSB) concerns eligible under the WOSB Program;

(11) Conducts annual reviews to assess the—

(i) Extent to which small businesses are receiving a fair share of Federal procurements, including contract opportunities under the programs administered under the Small Business Act;

(ii) Adequacy of consolidated or bundled contract documentation and justifications; and

(iii) Actions taken to mitigate the effects of necessary and justified consolidation or bundling on small businesses;

(12) Provides a copy of the assessment made under paragraph (c)(11) of this section to the Agency Head and SBA Administrator;

(13) Provides to the chief acquisition officer and senior procurement executive advice and comments on acquisition strategies, market research, and justifications related to consolidation of contract requirements;

(14) When notified by a small business concern prior to the award of a contract that the small business concern believes that a solicitation, request for proposal, or request for quotation unduly restricts the ability of the small business concern to compete for the award—

(i) Submits the notification by the small business concern to the contracting officer and, if necessary, recommends ways in which the solicitation, request for proposal, or request for quotation may be altered to increase the opportunity for competition; and

(ii) Informs the advocate for competition of such agency (as established under 41 U.S.C 1705 or 10 U.S.C. 2318) of such notification;

(15) Ensures agency purchases using the Governmentwide purchase card that are greater than the micro-purchase threshold and less than the simplified acquisition threshold were made in compliance with the Small Business Act and were properly re-

corded in accordance with subpart 4.6 in the Federal Procurement Data System;

(16) Assists small business contractors and subcontractors in finding resources for education and training on compliance with contracting regulations;

(17) Reviews all subcontracting plans required by 19.702(a) to ensure the plan provides maximum practicable opportunity for small business concerns to participate in the performance of the contract; and

(18) Performs other duties listed at 15 U.S.C. 644(k).

(d) Small Business Specialists must be appointed and act in accordance with agency regulations.

[FAC 84-10, 50 FR 27562, 7/3/85, effective 7/3/85; FAC 84-45, 54 FR 13333, 3/31/89, effective 4/1/89; FAC 84-48, 54 FR 25062, 6/12/89, effective 6/12/89; FAC 90-32, 60 FR 48206, 9/18/95, effective 10/1/95; FAC 97-1, 62 FR 44802, 8/22/97, effective 8/22/97, finalized without change, FAC 97-4, 63 FR 9048, 2/23/98, effective 4/24/98; FAC 97-6, 63 FR 35719, 6/30/98, effective 10/1/98, finalized without change, FAC 97-13, 7/2/99; FAC 97-7, 63 FR 36120, 7/1/98, effective 1/1/99, corrected 63 FR 56738, 10/22/98, finalized without change, FAC 97-13, 7/2/99; FAC 97-8, 63 FR 52425, 9/30/98, effective 10/1/98, finalized without change, FAC 97-13, 7/2/99; FAC 97-10, 63 FR 70264,12/18/98, effective 1/4/99; FAC 97-15, 64 FR 72414, 12/27/99, effective 12/27/99; FAC 97-19, 65 FR 46052, 7/26/2000, effective 7/26/2000; FAC 97-20, 65 FR 60542, 10/11/2000, effective 10/11/2000; FAC 2001-02, 66 FR 65347, 12/18/2001, effective 2/19/2002; FAC 2001-17, 68 FR 59999, 10/20/2003, effective 10/20/2003; FAC 2001-23, 69 FR 25273, 5/5/2004, effective 5/5/2004; FAC 2005-02, 70 FR 14950, 3/23/2005, effective 3/23/2005; FAC 2005-10, 71 FR 36925, 6/28/2006, effective 7/28/2006; FAC 2005-27, 73 FR 53993, 9/17/2008, effective 10/17/2008; FAC 2005-50, 76 FR 14572, 3/16/2011, effective 3/16/2011; FAC 2005-51, 76 FR 18304, 4/1/2011, effective 4/1/2011; FAC 2005-56, 77 FR 12913, 3/2/2012, effective 4/2/2012; FAC 2005-73, 79 FR 24192, 4/29/2014, effective 5/29/2014; FAC 2005-77, 79 FR 61746, 10/14/2014, effective 10/14/2014; FAC 2005-91, 81 FR 67763, 9/30/2016, effective 10/31/2016; FAC 2005-98, 83 FR 19146, 5/1/2018, effective 5/31/2018]

19.202 Specific policies.

In order to further the policy in 19.201(a), contracting officers shall comply with the specific policies listed in this section and shall consider recommendations of the agency Director of Small and Disadvantaged Business Utilization, or the Director's designee, as to whether a particular acquisition should be awarded under subpart 19.5, 19.8, 19.13, 19.14, or 19.15. Agencies shall establish procedures including dollar thresholds for review of acquisitions by the Director or the Director's designee for the purpose of making these recommendations. The contracting officer shall document the contract file whenever the Director's recommendations are not accepted.

[FAC 84-48, 54 FR 25062, 6/12/89, effective 6/12/89; FAC 90-32, 60 FR 48206, 9/18/95, effective 10/1/95; FAC 97-10, 63 FR 70264, 12/18/98, effective 1/4/99; FAC 2001-17, 68 FR 59999, 10/20/2003, effective 10/20/2003; FAC 2005-50, 76 FR 14566, 3/16/2011, effective 3/16/2011; FAC 2005-51, 76 FR 18304, 4/1/2011, effective 4/1/2011; FAC 2005-56, 77 FR 12913, 3/2/2012, effective 4/2/2012]

19.202-1 Encouraging small business participation in acquisitions.

Small business concerns shall be afforded an equitable opportunity to compete for all contracts that they can perform to the extent consistent with the Government's interest. When applicable, the contracting officer shall take the following actions:

(a) Divide proposed acquisitions of supplies and services (except construction) into reasonably small lots (not less than economic production runs) to permit offers on quantities less than the total requirement.

(b) Plan acquisitions such that, if practicable, more than one small business concern may perform the work, if the work exceeds the amount for which a surety may be guaranteed by SBA against loss under 15 U.S.C. 694b.

(c) Ensure that delivery schedules are established on a realistic basis that will encourage small business participation to the extent consistent with the actual requirements of the Government.

(d) Encourage prime contractors to subcontract with small business concerns (see Subpart 19.7).

(e) (1) Provide a copy of the proposed acquisition package to the SBA procurement center representative (or, if a procurement center representative is not assigned, see 19.402(a)) at least 30 days prior to the issuance of the solicitation if—

(i) The proposed acquisition is for supplies or services currently being provided by a small business and the proposed acquisition is of a quantity or estimated dollar value, the magnitude of which makes it unlikely that small businesses can compete for the prime contract;

(ii) The proposed acquisition is for construction and seeks to package or consolidate discrete construction projects and the magnitude of this consolidation makes it unlikely that small businesses can compete for the prime contract, or

(iii) The proposed acquisition is for a consolidated or bundled requirement. (See 7.107-5(a) for mandatory 30-day notice requirement to incumbent small business concerns.) The contracting officer shall provide all information relative to the justification for the consolidation or bundling, including the acquisition plan or strategy, and if the acquisition involves substantial bundling, the information identified in 7.107-4. The contracting officer shall also provide the same information to the agency Office of Small and Disadvantaged Business Utilization.

(2) Provide a statement explaining why the—

(i) Proposed acquisition cannot be divided into reasonably small lots (not less than economic production runs) to permit offers on quantities less than the total requirement;

(ii) Delivery schedules cannot be established on a realistic basis that will encourage small business participation to the extent consistent with the actual requirements of the Government;

(iii) Proposed acquisition cannot be structured so as to make it likely that small businesses can compete for the prime contract;

(iv) Consolidated construction project cannot be acquired as separate discrete projects; or

(v) Consolidation or bundling is necessary and justified.

(3) Process the 30-day notification concurrently with other processing steps required prior to the issuance of the solicitation.

(4) If the contracting officer rejects the SBA procurement center representative's recommendation made in accordance with 19.402(c)(2), document the basis for the rejection and notify the SBA procurement center representative in accordance with 19.505.

[Interim rule, FAC 90-9, 56 FR 67132, 12/27/91, effective 12/27/91; FAC 90-16, 57 FR 60581, 12/21/92, effective 2/19/93; FAC 97-15, 64 FR 72414, 12/27/99, effective 12/27/99; FAC 97-19, 65 FR 46052, 7/26/2000, effective 7/26/2000; FAC 2001-17, 68 FR 59999, 10/20/2003, effective 10/20/2003; FAC 2005-10, 71 FR 36925, 6/28/2006, effective 7/28/2006; FAC 2005-91, 81 FR 67763, 9/30/2016, effective 10/31/2016]

19.202-2 Locating small business sources.

The contracting officer must, to the extent practicable, encourage maximum participation by small business, veteran-owned small business, service-disabled veteran-owned small business, HUBZone small business, small disadvantaged business, and women-owned small business concerns in acquisitions by taking the following actions:

(a) Before issuing solicitations, make every reasonable effort to find additional small business concerns, unless lists are already excessively long and only some of the concerns on the list will be solicited. This effort should include contacting the SBA procurement center representative (or, if a procurement center representative is not assigned, see 19.402(a)).

(b) Publicize solicitations and contract awards through the Governmentwide point of entry (see subparts 5.2 and 5.3).

[FAC 97-10, 63 FR 70264, 12/18/98, effective 1/4/99; FAC 97-20, 65 FR 60542, 10/11/2000, effective 10/11/2000; FAC 97-26, 66 FR 27405, 5/16/2001, effective 5/16/2001; FAC 2001-15, 68 FR 43854, 7/24/2003, effective 8/25/2003; FAC 2005-10, 71 FR 36925, 6/28/2006, effective 7/28/2006]

19.202-3 Equal low bids.

In the event of equal low bids (see 14.408-6), awards shall be made first to small business concerns which are also labor surplus area concerns, and second to small business concerns which are not also labor surplus area concerns.

[FAC 90-32, 60 FR 48206, 9/18/95, effective 10/1/95]

19.202-4 Solicitation.

The contracting officer must encourage maximum response to solicitations by small business, veteran-owned small business, service-disabled veteran-owned small business, HUBZone small business, small disadvantaged business, and women-owned small business concerns by taking the following actions:

(a) Allow the maximum amount of time practicable for the submission of offers.

(b) Furnish specifications, plans, and drawings with solicitations, or furnish information as to where they may be obtained or examined.

(c) Provide to any small business concern, upon its request, a copy of bid sets and specifications with respect to any contract to be let, the name and telephone number of an agency contact to answer questions related to such prospective contract and adequate citations to each major Federal law or agency rule with which such business concern must comply in performing such contract other than laws or agency rules with which the small business must comply when doing business with other than the Government.

[FAC 97-10, 63 FR 70264, 12/18/98, effective 1/4/99; FAC 97-20, 65 FR 60542, 10/11/2000, effective 10/11/2000; FAC 2001-15, 68 FR 43854, 7/24/2003, effective 8/25/2003]

19.202-5 Data collection and reporting requirements.

Agencies must measure the extent of small business participation in their acquisition programs by taking the following actions:

(a) Require each prospective contractor to represent whether it is a small business, veteran-owned small business, service-disabled veteran-owned small business, HUBZone small business, small disadvantaged business, women-owned small business, EDWOSB concern, or WOSB concern eligible under the WOSB Program (see the provision at 52.219-1, Small Business Program Representations).

(b) Accurately measure the extent of participation by small business, veteran-owned small business, service-disabled veteran-owned small business, HUBZone small business, small disadvantaged business, and women-owned small business concerns in Government acquisitions in terms of the total value of contracts placed during each fiscal year, and report data to the SBA at the end of each fiscal year (see subpart 4.6).

(c) When the contract includes the clause at 52.219-28, Post Award Small Business Program Rerepresentation, and the conditions in the clause for rerepresenting are met—

(1) Require a contractor that represented itself as a small business concern prior to award of the contract to rerepresent its size status; and

(2) Permit a contractor that represented itself as other than a small business concern prior to award to rerepresent its size status.

[FAC 90-32, 60 FR 48206, 9/18/95, effective 10/1/95; FAC 97-10, 63 FR 70264, 12/18/98, effective 1/4/99; FAC 97-20, 65 FR 60542, 10/11/2000, effective 10/11/2000; FAC 2005-18, Interim rule, 72 FR 36852, 7/5/2007, effective 6/30/2007; FAC 2005-31,

74 FR 11821, 3/19/2009, effective 4/20/2009; FAC 2005-51, 76 FR 18304, 4/1/2011, effective 4/1/2011; FAC 2005-56, 77 FR 12913, 3/2/2012, effective 4/2/2012]

19.202-6 Determination of fair market price.

(a) The fair market price shall be the price achieved in accordance with the reasonable price guidelines in 15.404-1(b) for—

(1) Total and partial small business set-asides (*see* subpart 19.5);

(2) HUBZone set-asides (*see* subpart 19.13);

(3) Contracts utilizing the price evaluation preference for HUBZone small business concerns (*see* subpart 19.13);

(4) Service-disabled veteran-owned small business set-asides (*see* subpart 19.14); and

(5) Set-asides for EDWOSB concerns and WOSB concerns eligible under the WOSB Program (*see* subpart 19.15).

(b) For 8(a) contracts, both with respect to meeting the requirement at 19.806(b) and in order to accurately estimate the current fair market price, contracting officers shall follow the procedures at 19.807.

[FAC 84-31, 52 FR 38189, 10/14/87, effective 10/1/87; FAC 84-40, 53 FR 43390, 10/26/88, effective 11/25/88; FAC 84-52, 54 FR 46005, 10/31/89, effective 11/30/89; FAC 97-2, 62 FR 51224, 9/30/97, effective 10/10/97; FAC 97-6, 63 FR 35719, 6/30/98, effective 10/1/98, finalized without change, FAC 97-13, 7/2/99; FAC 97-10, 63 FR 70264, 12/18/98, effective 1/4/99; FAC 2001-23, 69 FR 25273, 5/5/2004, effective 5/5/2004; FAC 2005-02, 70 FR 14950, 3/23/2005, effective 3/23/2005; FAC 2005-51, 76 FR 18304, 4/1/2011, effective 4/1/2011; FAC 2005-56, 77 FR 12913, 12930, 3/2/2012, effective 4/2/2012; FAC 2005-77, 79 FR 61746, 10/14/2014, effective 10/14/2014]

19.203 Relationship among small business programs.

(a) There is no order of precedence among the 8(a) Program (subpart 19.8), HUBZone Program (subpart 19.13), Service-Disabled Veteran-Owned Small Business (SDVOSB) Procurement Program (subpart 19.14), or the Women-Owned Small Business (WOSB) Program (subpart 19.15).

(b) *At or below the simplified acquisition threshold.* For acquisitions of supplies or services that have an anticipated dollar value exceeding $3,500 ($20,000 for acquisitions as described in 13.201(g)(1)), but not exceeding $150,000 ($750,000 for acquisitions described in paragraph (1)(i) of the simplified acquisition threshold definition at 2.101), the requirement at 19.502-2(a) to exclusively reserve acquisitions for small business concerns does not preclude the contracting officer from awarding a contract to a small business under the 8(a) Program, HUBZone Program, SDVOSB Program, or WOSB Program.

(c) *Above the simplified acquisition threshold.* For acquisitions of supplies or services that have an anticipated dollar value exceeding the simplified acquisition threshold definition at 2.101, the contracting officer shall first consider an acquisition for the small business socioeconomic contracting programs (*i.e.,* 8(a), HUBZone, SDVOSB, or WOSB programs) before considering a small business set-aside (see 19.502-2(b)). However, if a requirement has been accepted by the SBA under the 8(a) Program, it must remain in the 8(a) Program unless the SBA agrees to its release in accordance with 13 CFR parts 124, 125, and 126.

(d) In determining which socioeconomic program to use for an acquisition, the contracting officer should consider, at a minimum—

(1) Results of market research that was done to determine if there are socioeconomic firms capable of satisfying the agency's requirement; and

(2) Agency progress in fulfilling its small business goals.

(e) Small business set-asides have priority over acquisitions using full and open competition. *See* requirements for establishing a small business set-aside at subpart 19.5.

[FAC 2005-50, 76 FR 14566, 3/16/2011, effective 3/16/2011; FAC 2005-51, 76 FR 18304, 4/1/2011, effective 4/1/2011; FAC 2005-56, 77 FR 12913, 12930, 3/2/2012, effective 4/2/2012; FAC 2005-83, 80 FR 38293,

7/2/2015, effective 10/1/2015; FAC 2005-88, 81 FR 30438, 5/16/2016, effective 6/15/2016; FAC 2005-95, 82 FR 4716, 1/13/2017, effective 1/13/2017]

SUBPART 19.3—DETERMINATION OF SMALL BUSINESS STATUS FOR SMALL BUSINESS PROGRAMS

19.301 Representations and rerepresentations. (No Text)

19.301-1 Representation by the offeror.

(a) To be eligible for award as a small business, an offeror must represent in good faith that it is a small business at the time of its written representation. An offeror may represent that it is a small business concern in connection with a specific solicitation if it meets the definition of a small business concern applicable to the solicitation and has not been determined by the Small Business Administration (SBA) to be other than a small business.

(b) The contracting officer shall accept an offeror's representation in a specific bid or proposal that it is a small business unless—

(1) another offeror or interested party challenges the concern's small business representation; or

(2) the contracting officer has a reason to question the representation. Challenges of and questions concerning a specific representation shall be referred to the SBA in accordance with 19.302.

(c) An offeror's representation that it is a small business is not binding on the SBA. If an offeror's small business status is challenged, the SBA will evaluate the status of the concern and make a determination, which will be binding on the contracting officer, as to whether the offeror is a small business. A concern cannot become eligible for a specific award by taking action to meet the definition of a small business concern after the SBA has determined that it is not a small business.

(d) If the SBA determines that the status of a concern as a small business, veteran-owned small business, service-disabled veteran-owned small business, HUBZone small business, small disadvantaged business, or women-owned small business has been misrepresented in order to obtain a set-aside contract, an 8(a) subcontract, a subcontract that is to be included as part or all of a goal contained in a subcontracting plan, or a prime or subcontract to be awarded as a result, or in furtherance of any other provision of Federal law that specifically references Section 8(d) of the Small Business Act for a definition of program eligibility, the SBA may take action as specified in Sections 16(a) or 16(d) of the Act. If the SBA declines to take action, the agency may initiate the process. The SBA's regulations on penalties for misrepresentations and false statements are contained in 13 CFR 121.108 for small business, 13 CFR 124.501 for 8(a) small business, 13 CFR 124.1004 for small disadvantaged business, 13 CFR 125.29 for veteran or service-disabled veteran-owned small business, 13 CFR 126.900 for HUBZone small business, and 13 CFR 127.700 for economically disadvantaged women-owned small business concerns and women-owned small business (WOSB) concerns eligible under the WOSB Program.

[FAC 84-56, 55 FR 3882, 2/5/90, effective 2/5/90; FAC 90-32, 60 FR 48206, 9/18/95, effective 10/1/95; FAC 90-45, Final rule, 62 FR 224, 1/2/97, effective 1/1/97; FAC 97-10, 63 FR 70264, 12/18/98, effective 1/4/99; FAC 97-20, 65 FR 60542, 10/11/2000, effective 10/11/2000; FAC 2001-23, 69 FR 25273, 5/5/2004, effective 5/5/2004; FAC 2005-02, 70 FR 14950, 3/23/2005, effective 3/23/2005; FAC 2005-18, Interim rule, 72 FR 36852, 7/5/2007, effective 6/30/2007; FAC 2005-31, 74 FR 11821, 3/19/2009, effective 4/20/2009; FAC 2005-47, 75 FR 77737, 12/13/2010, effective 12/13/2010; FAC 2005-51, 76 FR 18304, 4/1/2011, effective 4/1/2011; FAC 2005-54, 76 FR 68026, 11/2/2011, effective 11/2/2011; FAC 2005-56, 77 FR 12913, 3/2/2012, effective 4/2/2012]

19.301-2 Rerepresentation by a contractor that represented itself as a small business concern.

(a) *Definition*. As used in this subsection—

Long-term contract means a contract of more than five years in duration, including options. However, the term does not include contracts that exceed five years in duration because the period of performance has been extended for a cumulative period not to exceed six months under the clause at 52.217-8, Option to Extend Services, or other appropriate authority.

(b) A contractor that represented itself as a small business concern before contract award must rerepresent its size status for the North American Industry Classification System (NAICS) code in the contract upon the occurrence of any of the following:

(1) Within 30 days after execution of a novation agreement or within 30 days after modification of the contract to include the clause at 52.219-28, Post-Award Small Business Program Rerepresentation, if the novation agreement was executed prior to inclusion of this clause in the contract.

(2) Within 30 days after a merger or acquisition of the contractor that does not require novation or within 30 days after modification of the contract to include the clause at 52.219-28, Post-Award Small Business Program Rerepresentation, if the merger or acquisition occurred prior to inclusion of this clause in the contract.

(3) For long-term contracts—

(i) Within 60 to 120 days prior to the end of the fifth year of the contract; and

(ii) Within 60 to 120 days prior to the date specified in the contract for exercising any option thereafter.

(c) A contractor must rerepresent its size status in accordance with the size standard in effect at the time of its rerepresentation that corresponds to the NAICS code that was initially assigned to the contract.

(d) After a contractor rerepresents it is other than small in accordance with 52.219-28, the agency may no longer include the value of options exercised, modifications issued, orders issued, or purchases made under blanket purchase agreements on that contract in its small business prime contracting goal achievements. Agencies should issue a modification to the contract capturing the rerepresentation and report it to FPDS within 30 days after notification of the rerepresentation.

(e) A change in size status does not change the terms and conditions of the contract. However, the contracting officer may require a subcontracting plan for a contract containing 52.219-9, Small Business Subcontracting Plan, if a prime contractor's size status changes from small to other than small as a result of a size rerepresentation (see 19.705-2(b)(3)).

[FAC 2005-18, Interim rule, 72 FR 36852, 7/5/2007, effective 6/30/2007; FAC 2005-31, 74 FR 11821, 3/19/2009, effective 4/20/2009; FAC 2005-89, 81 FR 45833, 7/14/2016, effective 11/1/2016]

19.301-3 Rerepresentation by a contractor that represented itself as other than a small business concern.

A contractor that represented itself as other than small before contract award may, but is not required to, rerepresent its size status when—

(a) The conditions in 19.301-2(b) apply; and

(b) The contractor qualifies as a small business concern under the applicable size standard in effect at the time of its rerepresentation.

[FAC 2005-18, Interim rule, 72 FR 36852, 7/5/2007, effective 6/30/2007; FAC 2005-31, 74 FR 11821, 3/19/200, effective 4/20/2009]

19.302 Protesting a small business representation or rerepresentation.

(a)(1) The Small Business Administration (SBA) regulations on small business size and size protests are found at 13 CFR part 121.

(2) An offeror, the SBA, or another interested party may protest the small business representation of an offeror in a specific offer. However, for competitive 8(a) contracts, the filing of a protest is limited to an offeror, the contracting officer, or the SBA.

(b) Any time after offers are opened, the contracting officer may question the small business representation of any offeror in a specific offer by filing a contracting officer's protest (see paragraph (c)).

(c)(1) Any contracting officer who receives a protest, whether timely or not, or who, as the contracting officer, wishes to protest the small business representation of an offeror, or rerepresentation of a contractor, shall promptly forward the protest to the SBA Government Contracting Area Director at the Government Contracting Area Office serving the area in which the headquarters of the offeror is located.

(2) The protest, or confirmation if the protest was initiated orally, shall be in writing and shall contain the basis for the protest with specific, detailed evidence to support the allegation that the offeror is not small. The SBA will dismiss any protest that does not contain specific grounds for the protest.

(3) The protest shall include a referral letter written by the contracting officer with information pertaining to the solicitation. The referral letter must include the following information to allow SBA to determine timeliness and standing:

(i) The protest and any accompanying materials.

(ii) A copy of the size self-certification.

(iii) Identification of the applicable size standard.

(iv) A copy or an electronic link to the solicitation and any amendments.

(v) The name, address, telephone number, email address, and fax number of the contracting officer.

(vi) Identification of the bid opening date or the date of notification provided to unsuccessful offerors.

(vii) The date the contracting officer received the protest.

(viii) A complete address and point of contact for the protested concern.

(d) In order to affect a specific solicitation, a protest must be timely. SBA's regulations on timeliness are contained in 13 CFR 121.1004. SBA's regulations on timeliness related to protests of disadvantaged status are contained in 13 CFR 124, Subpart B.

(1) To be timely, a protest by any concern or other interested party must be received by the contracting officer (see (d)(1) (i) and (ii) of this section) by the close of business of the fifth business day after bid opening (in sealed bid acquisitions) or receipt of the special notification from the contracting officer that identifies the apparently successful offeror (in negotiated acquisitions) (see 15.503(a)(2)).

(i) A protest may be made orally if it is confirmed in writing and received by the contracting officer within the 5-day period or by letter postmarked no later than 1 business day after the oral protest.

(ii) A protest may be made in writing if it is delivered to the contracting officer by hand, mail, facsimile, email, express or overnight delivery service.

(2) Except as provided in paragraph (d)(4) of this section, a protest filed by the contracting officer or SBA is always considered timely whether filed before or after award.

(3) A protest under a Multiple Award Schedule will be timely if received by SBA at any time prior to the expiration of the contract period, including renewals.

(4) A protest filed before bid opening, or notification to offerors of the selection of the apparent successful offeror, will be dismissed as premature by SBA.

(e) Upon receipt of a protest from or forwarded by the Contracting Office, the SBA will—

(1) Notify the contracting officer and the protester of the date it was received, and that the size of the concern being challenged is under consideration by the SBA; and

(2) Furnish to the concern whose representation is being protested a copy of the protest and a blank SBA Form 355, Application for Small Business Determination, by certified mail, return receipt requested.

(f)(1) Within 15 business days after receipt of a protest or request for a formal size determination or within any extension of time granted by the contracting officer the SBA Area Office will determine the size status of the challenged concern. The SBA Area Office will notify the contracting officer, the protester, and the challenged concern of its decision by a verifiable means, which may include facsimile, electronic mail, or overnight delivery service.

(2) Award may be made to a protested concern after the SBA Area Office has determined that either the protested concern is an eligible small business or has dismissed all protests against it.

(3) If SBA's Office of Hearings and Appeals (OHA) subsequently overturns the Area Office's determination of eligibility or dismissal, and contract award has not been made, the contracting officer may apply the OHA decision to the procurement in question.

(g)(1) After receiving a protest involving an offeror being considered for award, the contracting officer shall not award the contract until the SBA has made a size determination or 15 business days have expired since SBA's receipt of a protest, whichever occurs first; however, award shall not be withheld when the contracting officer determines in writing that an award must be made to protect the public interest.

(2) If SBA has not made a determination within 15 business days, or within any extension of time granted by the contracting officer, the contracting officer may award the contract after determining in writing that there is an immediate need to award the contract and that waiting until SBA makes its determination will be disadvantageous to the Government.

(3) SBA may, at its sole discretion, reopen a formal size determination to correct an error or mistake, if it is within the appeal period and no appeal has been filed with OHA or, a final decision has not been rendered by the SBA Area Office or OHA.

(4) If a protest is received that challenges the small business status of an offeror not being considered for award, the contracting officer is not required to suspend contract action. The contracting officer shall forward the protest to the SBA (see paragraph (c)(1) of this section) with a notation that the concern is not being considered for award, and shall notify the protester of this action.

(h) An appeal from an SBA size determination may be filed by any concern or other interested party whose protest of the small business representation of another concern has been denied by an SBA Government Contracting Area Director, any concern or other interested party that has been adversely affected by an SBA Government Contracting Area Director's decision, or the SBA Associate Administrator for the SBA program involved. The appeal must be filed with the Office of Hearings and Appeals, Small Business Administration, Suite 5900, 409 3rd Street, SW., Washington, DC 20416, within the time limits and in strict accordance with the procedures contained in Subpart C of 13 CFR part 134. It is within the discretion of the SBA Judge whether to accept an appeal from a size determination. If a post-award appeal is submitted to OHA within the time limits specified in Subpart C of 13 CFR part 134, the contracting officer shall consider suspending contract performance until an SBA Judge decides the appeal. SBA will inform the contracting officer of its ruling on the appeal. SBA's decision, if received before award, will apply to the pending acquisition. If the contracting officer has made a written determination in accordance with (g)(1) or (2) of this section, the contract has been awarded, the SBA rulings is received after award, and OHA finds the protested concern to be ineligible for award, the contracting officer shall terminate the contract unless termination is not in the best interests of the Government, in keeping with the circumstances described in the written determination. However, the contracting officer shall not exercise any options or award further task or delivery orders.

(i) SBA will dismiss untimely protests. A protest that is not timely, even though received before award, shall be forwarded to the SBA Government Contracting Area Office (see paragraph (c)(1) of this section), with a notation on it that the protest is not timely. A protest received by a contracting officer after award of a contract shall be forwarded to the SBA Government Contracting Area Office with a notation that award has been made.

(j) When a concern is found to be other than small under a protest concerning a size status rerepresentation made in accordance with the clause at 52.219-28, Post-Award Small Business Program Rerepresentation, a contracting officer may permit contract performance to continue, issue orders, or exercise option(s), because the contract remains a valid contract.

[FAC 84-5, 50 FR 1743, 1/11/85, effective 4/1/85; FAC 84-12, 51 FR 2664, 1/17/86, effective 1/20/86; FAC 90-31, 60 FR 42648, 8/16/95, effective 10/1/95; FAC 90-44, 61 FR 69286, 12/31/96, effective 1/1/97; FAC 97-1, 62 FR 44802, 8/22/97, effective 8/22/97; FAC 97-2, 62 FR 51224, 9/30/97, effective 10/10/97; FAC 97-4, 63 FR 9048, 2/23/98, effective 4/24/98; FAC 97-6, 63 FR 35719, 6/30/98, effective 10/1/98, finalized without change, FAC 97-13, 7/2/99; FAC 97-12, 64 FR 32740, 6/17/99, effective 6/17/99, finalized without change, FAC 97-15, 64 FR 72414, 12/27/99; FAC 2001-06, 67 FR 13048, 3/20/2002, effective 4/4/2002; FAC 2005-18, Interim rule, 72 FR 36852, 7/5/2007, effective 6/30/2007; FAC 2005-31, 74 FR 11821, 3/19/2009, effective 4/20/2009; FAC 2005-76, 79 FR 43580, 7/25/2014, effective 8/25/2014; FAC 2005-92, 81 FR 83097, 11/18/2016, effective 12/19/2016]

19.303 Determining North American Industry Classification System codes and size standards.

(a) (1) The contracting officer shall determine the appropriate North American Industry Classification System (NAICS) code and related small business size standard and include them in solicitations above the micro-purchase threshold. For information on size standards matched to industry NAICS codes, including the use of new NAICS codes, see also 19.102(a).

(2) The contracting officer shall select the NAICS code which best describes the principal purpose of the product or service being acquired. Primary consideration is given to the industry descriptions in the U.S. NAICS Manual, the product or service description in the solicitation and any attachments to it, the relative value and importance of the components of the procurement making up the end item being procured, and the function of the goods or services being purchased. A procurement is usually classified according to the component which accounts for the greatest percentage of contract value. A concern that submits an offer or quote for a contract where the NAICS code assigned to the contract is one for supplies, and furnishes a product it did not itself manufacture or produce, is categorized as a nonmanufacturer and deemed small if it meets the requirements of 19.102(f).

(b) If different products or services are required in the same solicitation, the solicitation shall identify the appropriate small business size standard for each product or service.

(c) The contracting officer's determination is final unless appealed as follows:

(1) An appeal from a contracting officer's NAICS code designation and the applicable size standard must be served and filed within 10 calendar days after the issuance of the initial solicitation or any amendment affecting the NAICS code or size standard. However, SBA may file a NAICS code appeal at any time before offers are due.

(2) Appeals from a contracting officer's NAICS code designation or applicable size standard may be filed with SBA's Office of Hearings and Appeals by—

(i) Any person adversely affected by a NAICS code designation or applicable size standard. However, with respect to a particular sole source 8(a) contract, only the SBA Associate Administrator for Business Development may appeal a NAICS code designation; or

(ii) The Associate or Assistant Director for the SBA program involved, through SBA's Office of General Counsel.

(3) Contracting officers shall advise the public, by amendment to the solicitation, of the existence of a NAICS code appeal (see 5.102(a)(1)). Such notices shall include the procedures and the deadline for interested parties to file and serve arguments concerning the appeal.

(4) SBA's Office of Hearings and Appeals (OHA) will dismiss summarily an untimely NAICS code appeal.

(5) (i) The appeal petition must be in writing and must be addressed to the Office of Hearings and Appeals, Small Business Administration, Suite 5900, 409 3rd Street SW., Washington, DC 20416.

(ii) There is no required format for the appeal; however, the appeal must include—

(A) The solicitation or contract number and the name, address, email address, and telephone number of the contracting officer;

(B) A full and specific statement as to why the NAICS code designation is allegedly erroneous and argument supporting the allegation; and

(C) The name, address, telephone number, and signature of the appellant or its attorney.

(6) The appellant must serve the appeal petition upon—

(i) The contracting officer who assigned the NAICS code to the acquisition; and

(ii) SBA's Office of General Counsel, Associate General Counsel for Procurement Law, 409 Third Street SW., Washington, DC 20416, facsimile 202-205-6873, or email at *OPLService@sba.gov.*

(7) Upon receipt of a NAICS code appeal, OHA will notify the contracting officer by a notice and order of the date OHA received the appeal, the docket number, and Judge assigned to the case. The contracting officer's response to the appeal, if any, must include argument and evidence (see 13 CFR Part 134), and must be received by OHA within 15 calendar days from the date of the docketing notice and order, unless otherwise specified by the Administrative Judge. Upon receipt of OHA's docketing notice and order, the contracting officer must withhold award, unless withholding award is not in the best interests of the Government, and immediately send to OHA an electronic link to or a paper copy of both the original solicitation and all amendments relating to the NAICS code appeal. The contracting officer will inform OHA of any amendments, actions, or developments concerning the procurement in question.

(8) After close of record, OHA will issue a decision and inform the contracting officer. If OHA's decision is received by the contracting officer before the date the offers are due, the decision shall be final and the solicitation must be amended to reflect the decision, if appropriate. OHA's decision received after the due date of the initial offers shall not apply to the pending solicitation but shall apply to future solicitations of the same products or services.

(d) SBA's regulations concerning appeals of NAICS code designations are found at 13 CFR 121.1101 to 121.1103 and 13 CFR part 134.

[FAC 84-12, 51 FR 2664, 1/17/86, effective 1/20/86; Final rule, 55 FR 38516, 9/18/90; 1990 FAR edition, 10/1/90; FAC 90-3 55 FR 52791, 12/21/90, effective 1/22/91; FAC 90-29, 60 FR 34732, 7/3/95, effective 7/3/95; FAC 90-40, 61 FR 39186, 7/26/96, effective 8/26/96; FAC 90-45, Final rule, 62 FR 224, 1/2/97, effective 1/1/97, corrected 62 FR 10709, 3/10/97; FAC 97-4, 63 FR 9048, 2/23/98, effective 4/24/98; FAC 97-19, 65 FR 46052, 7/26/2000, effective 10/1/2000, finalized without change, FAC 2001-02, 12/18/2001, effective 12/18/2001; FAC 2005-61, 77 FR 56741, 9/13/2012, effective 10/15/2012; FAC 2005-76, 79 FR 43580, 7/25/2014, effective 8/25/2014]

19.304 Small disadvantaged business status.

(a) The contracting officer may accept an offeror's representation that it is a small disadvantaged business concern (SDB) concern.

(b) The provision at 52.219-1, Small Business Program Representations, or 52.212-3(c)(4), Offeror Representations and Certifications—Commercial Items, is used to collect SDB data.

(c) A representation of SDB status on a Federal prime contract will be deemed a misrepresentation of SDB status if the firm does not meet the requirements of 13 CFR 124.1001(b).

(d) Any person or entity that misrepresents a firm's status as an SDB concern in order to obtain a contracting opportunity in accordance with section 8(d) of the Small Business Act, (15 U.S.C. 637(d)) will be subject to the penalties imposed by section 16(d) of the Small Business Act, (15 U.S.C. 645(d)), as well as any other penalty authorized by law.

[FAC 97-6, 63 FR 35719, 6/30/98, effective 10/1/98; FAC 97-7, 63 FR 36120, 7/1/98,

effective 1/1/99; FAC 97-13, 64 FR 36222, 7/2/99, effective 10/1/99; FAC 97-20, 65 FR 60542, 10/11/2000, effective 10/11/2000; FAC 2005-48, 75 FR 82567, 12/30/2010, effective 1/31/2011; FAC 2005-77, 79 FR 61746, 10/14/2014, effective 10/14/2014]

19.305 Reviews and protests of SDB status.

This section applies to reviews and protests of a small business concern's SDB status as a prime contractor or subcontractor.

(a) SBA may initiate the review of SDB status on any firm that has represented itself to be an SDB on a prime contract or subcontract to a Federal prime contract whenever it receives credible information calling into question the SDB status of the firm.

(b) Requests for an SBA review of SDB status may be forwarded to the Small Business Administration, Assistant Administrator for SDBCE, 409 Third Street SW., Washington, DC 20416.

(c) An SBA review of a subcontractor's SDB status differs from a formal protest. Protests of a small business concern's SDB status as a subcontractor are processed under 19.703(e). Protests of a concern's size as a prime contractor are processed under 19.302. Protests of a concern's size as a subcontractor are processed under 19.703(b).

[FAC 97-6, 63 FR 35719, 6/30/98, effective 10/1/98, finalized without change, FAC 97-13, 7/2/99; finalized without change, FAC 97-7, 63 FR 36120, 7/1/98, effective 1/1/99, finalized without change, FAC 97-13, 7/2/99; FAC 2005-77, 79 FR 61746, 10/14/2014, effective 10/14/2014; FAC 2005-89, 81 FR 45833, 7/14/2016, effective 11/1/2016]

19.306 Protesting a firm's status as a HUBZone small business concern.

(a) *Definition.* As used in this section—

Interested party has the meaning given in 13 CFR 126.103.

(b)(1) An offeror that is an interested party, the contracting officer, or the SBA may protest the apparently successful offeror's status as a qualified historically underutilized business zone (HUBZone) small business concern (see 13 CFR 126.800).

(2) SBA's protest regulations are found in subpart H "Protests" at 13 CFR 126.800 through 126.805.

(c) Protests relating to small business size status are subject to the procedures of 19.302. An interested party seeking to protest both the small business size and HUBZone status of an apparent successful offeror shall file two separate protests. Protests relating to small business size status for the acquisition and the HUBZone qualifying requirements will be processed concurrently by SBA.

(d) All protests must be in writing and must state all specific grounds for the protest.

(1) SBA will consider protests challenging the status of a concern if the protest presents evidence that—

(i) The concern is not a qualified HUBZone small business concern as described at 13 CFR 126.103 and 13 CFR 126.200;

(ii) The principal office is not located in a HUBZone; or

(iii) At least 35 percent of the employees do not reside in a HUBZone.

(2) Assertions that a protested concern is not a qualified HUBZone small business concern, without setting forth specific facts or allegations, will not be considered by SBA (see 13 CFR 126.801(b)).

(e) *Protest by an interested party.* (1) An interested party shall submit its protest to the contracting officer—

(i) For sealed bids—

(A) By the close of business on the fifth business day after bid opening; or

(B) By the close of business on the fifth business day from the date of identification of the apparent successful offeror, if the price evaluation preference was not applied at the time of bid opening; or

(ii) For negotiated acquisitions, by the close of business on the fifth business day after notification by the contracting officer of the apparently successful offeror.

(2) Any protest received after the designated time limits is untimely, unless it is from the contracting officer or SBA.

(f) (1) The contracting officer shall forward all protests to SBA. The protests are to be submitted to the Director, HUBZone Program, U.S. Small Business Administration, 409 Third Street SW., Washington, DC 20416 or by fax to 202-205-7167, Attn: HUBZone Small Business Status Protest.

(2) The protest shall include a referral letter written by the contracting officer with information pertaining to the solicitation. The referral letter must include the following information to allow SBA to determine timeliness and standing:

(i) The solicitation number (or an electronic link to or a paper copy of the solicitation).

(ii) The name, address, telephone number, fax number, and email address, of the contracting officer.

(iii) The type of HUBZone contract.

(iv) Whether the procurement was conducted using full and open competition with a HUBZone price evaluation preference, and whether the protester's opportunity for award was affected by the preference.

(v) If a HUBZone set-aside, whether the protester submitted an offer.

(vi) Whether the protested concern was the apparent successful offeror.

(vii) Whether the procurement was conducted using sealed bid or negotiated procedures.

(viii) The bid opening date, if applicable. If a price evaluation preference was applied after the bid opening date, also provide the date of identification of the apparent successful offeror.

(ix) The date the contracting officer received the protest.

(x) Whether a contract has been awarded.

(g) SBA will notify the protester and the contracting officer of the date SBA received the protest.

(h) *Before SBA decision.* (1) After receiving a protest involving the apparent successful offeror's status as a HUBZone small business concern, the contracting officer shall either—

(i) Withhold award of the contract until SBA determines the status of the protested concern; or

(ii) Award the contract after receipt of the protest but before SBA issues its decision if the contracting officer determines in writing that an award must be made to protect the public interest.

(2) SBA will determine the merits of the status protest within 15 business days after receipt of a protest, or within any extension of time granted by the contracting officer.

(3) If SBA does not issue its determination within 15 business days, or within any extension of time granted, the contracting officer may award the contract after determining in writing that there is an immediate need to award the contract and that waiting until SBA makes its determination will be disadvantageous to the Government. This determination shall be provided to the SBA's HUBZone Program Director.

(i) *After SBA decision.* The HUBZone Program Director will notify the contracting officer, the protester, and the protested concern of the SBA determination. The determination is effective immediately and is final unless overturned on appeal by SBA's Associate Administrator, Office of Government Contracting and Business Development (AA/GCBD).

(1) If the contracting officer has withheld contract award and SBA has determined that the protested concern is an eligible HUBZone or dismissed all protests against the protested concern, the contracting officer may award the contract to the protested concern. If AA/GCBD subsequently overturns the decision of the HUBZone Program Director, the contracting officer may apply the AA/GCBD decision to the procurement in question.

(2) If the contracting officer has withheld award and the HUBZone Program Director has determined that the protested concern is ineligible, and a timely AA/GCBD appeal has not been filed, then the contracting officer shall not award the contract to the protested concern.

(3) If the contracting officer has made a written determination in accordance with (h)(1)(ii) or (h)(3) of this section, awarded the contract, and the HUBZone Program Director's ruling sustaining the protest is received after award—

(i) The contracting officer shall terminate the contract, unless the contracting officer has made a written determination that termination is not in the best interests of the Government. However, the contracting officer shall not exercise any options or award further task or delivery orders under the contract;

(ii) The contracting officer shall update the Federal Procurement Data System to reflect the final decision of the HUBZone Program Director if no appeal is filed; and

(iii) The concern's designation as a certified HUBZone small business concern will be removed by SBA from the Dynamic Small Business Database. The concern shall not submit an offer as a HUBZone small business concern, until SBA issues a decision that the ineligibility is resolved.

(4) If the contracting officer has made a written determination in accordance with (h)(1)(ii) or (h)(3) of this section, awarded the contract, SBA has sustained the protest and determined that the concern is not a HUBZone small business, and a timely AA/GCBD appeal has been filed, then the contracting officer shall consider whether performance can be suspended until an AA/GCBD decision is rendered.

(5) If AA/GCBD affirms the decision of the HUBZone Program Director, finding the protested concern is ineligible, and contract award has occurred—

(i) The contracting officer shall terminate the contract, unless the contracting officer has made a written determination that termination is not in the best interest of the Government. However, the contracting officer shall not exercise any options or award further task or delivery orders.

(ii) The contracting officer shall update the FPDS to reflect the AA/GCBD decision; and

(iii) The SBA will remove the concern's designation as a certified HUBZone small business concern. The concern shall not submit an offer as a HUBZone small business concern until SBA issues a decision that the ineligibility is resolved or AA/GCBD finds the concern is eligible on appeal.

(6) A concern found to be ineligible during a HUBZone status protest is precluded from applying for HUBZone certification for 90 calendar days from the date of the SBA final decision.

(j) *Appeals of HUBZone status determinations.* The protested HUBZone small business concern, the protester, or the contracting officer may file appeals of protest determinations with SBA's AA/GC&BD. The AA/GC&BD must receive the appeal no later than 5 business days after the date of receipt of the protest determination. SBA will dismiss any untimely appeal.

(k) *The appeal must be in writing.* The appeal must identify the protest determination being appealed and must set forth a full and specific statement as to why the decision is erroneous or what significant fact the HUBZone Program Director failed to consider.

(l)(1) The party appealing the decision must provide notice of the appeal to—

(i) The contracting officer;

(ii) HUBZone Program Director, U.S. Small Business Administration, 409 Third Street SW., Washington, DC 20416 or by fax to 202-205-7167; and

(iii) The protested HUBZone small business concern or the original protester, as appropriate.

(2) SBA will not consider additional information or changed circumstances that were not disclosed at the time of the Director/HUB's decision or that are based on disagreement with the findings and conclusions contained in the determination.

(m) The AA/GCBD will make its decision within 5 business days of the receipt of the appeal, if practicable, and will base its decision only on the information and documentation in the protest record as supplemented by the appeal. SBA will provide a copy of the decision to the contracting officer, the protester, and the protested HUBZone small business concern. The SBA decision, if received before award, will apply to the pending acquisition. The AA/GCBD's decision is the final decision.

[FAC 97-10, 63 FR 70264, 12/18/98, effective 1/4/99; FAC 97-14, 64 FR 51828, 9/24/99, effective 11/23/99; FAC 2005-47, 75 FR 77727, 12/13/2010, effective 1/12/2011; FAC 2005-76, 79 FR 43580, 7/25/2014, effective 8/25/2014]

19.307 Protesting a firm's status as a service-disabled veteran-owned small business concern.

(a) *Definition. Interested party,* as used in this section, has the meaning given in 13 CFR 125.8(b).

(b) (1) An offeror that is an interested party, the contracting officer, or the SBA may protest the apparently successful offeror's status as a service-disabled veteran-owned small business (SDVOSB) concern (see 13 CFR 125.24).

(2) SBA's protest regulations are found in subpart D "Protests" at 13 CFR 125.24 through 125.28.

(c) Protests relating to small business size status are subject to the procedures of 19.302. An interested party seeking to protest both the small business size and service-disabled veteran-owned small business status of an apparent successful offeror shall file two separate protests.

(d) All protests must be in writing and must state all specific grounds for the protest.

(1) SBA will consider protests challenging the service disabled veteran-owned status or the ownership and control of a concern if—

(i) For status protests, the protester presents evidence supporting the contention that the owner(s) cannot provide documentation from the Department of Veterans Affairs, Department of Defense determinations, or the U.S. National Archives and Records Administration to show that they meet the definition of "service-disabled veteran" or "service disabled veteran with a permanent and severe disability" as set forth in 13 CFR 125.8; or

(ii) For ownership and control protests, the protester presents evidence that the concern is not 51 percent owned and controlled by one or more service-disabled veterans. In the case of a veteran with a permanent and severe disability, the protester presents evidence that the concern is not controlled by the veteran, spouse, or permanent caregiver of such veteran.

(2) Assertions that a protested concern is not a service-disabled veteran-owned small business concern, without setting forth specific facts or allegations, will not be considered by SBA (see 13 CFR 125.25(b)).

(e) *Protest by an interested party.* (1) An offeror shall submit its protest to the contracting officer—

(i) To be received by close of business on the fifth business day after bid opening (in sealed bid acquisitions); or

(ii) To be received by close of business on the fifth business day after notification by the contracting officer of the apparently successful offeror for negotiated acquisitions).

(2) Any protest received after the designated time limits is untimely, unless it is from the contracting officer or SBA.

(f) (1) The contracting officer shall forward all protests to SBA. The protests are to be submitted to SBA's Director, Office of Government Contracting, U.S. Small Business Administration, 409 Third Street SW., Washington, DC 20416 or by fax to 202-205-6390, Attn: Service-Disabled Veteran Status Protest.

(2) The protest shall include a referral letter written by the contracting officer with information pertaining to the solicitation. The referral letter must include the following information to allow SBA to determine timeliness and standing:

(i) The solicitation number (or an electronic link to or a paper copy of the solicitation).

(ii) The name, address, telephone number, fax number, and email address of the contracting officer.

(iii) Whether the contract was sole-source or set-aside.

(iv) Whether the protestor submitted an offer.

(v) Whether the protested concern was the apparent successful offeror.

(vi) When the protested concern submitted its offer.

(vii) Whether the acquisition was conducted using sealed bid or negotiated procedures.

(viii) The bid opening date, if applicable.

(ix) The date the contracting officer received the protest.

(x) The date the protestor received notification about the apparent successful offeror, if applicable.

(xi) Whether a contract has been awarded.

(g) SBA will notify the protester and the contracting officer of the date SBA received the protest.

(h) *Before SBA decision.* (1) After receiving a protest involving the apparent successful offeror's status as a service-disabled veteran-owned small business concern, the contracting officer shall either—

(i) Withhold award of the contract until SBA determines the status of the protested concern; or

(ii) Award the contract after receipt of the protest but before SBA issues its decision if the contracting officer determines in writing that an award must be made to protect the public interest.

(2) SBA will determine the merits of the status protest within 15 business days after receipt of a protest, or within any extension of time granted by the contracting officer.

(3) If SBA does not issue its determination within 15 business days, or within any extension of time that is granted, the contracting officer may award the contract after determining in writing that there is an immediate need to award the contract and that waiting until SBA makes its determination will be disadvantageous to the government. This determination shall be provided to the SBA's Director, Office of Government Contracting and a copy shall be included in the contract file.

(i) *After SBA decision.* SBA will notify the contracting officer, the protester, and the protested concern of its determination. The determination is effective immediately and is final unless overturned on appeal by SBA's Office of Hearings and Appeals (OHA) pursuant to 13 CFR part 134.

(1) If the contracting officer has withheld contract award and SBA has determined that the protested concern is an eligible SDVOSB or dismissed all protests against the protested concern, the contracting officer may award the contract to the protested concern. If OHA subsequently overturns the SBA Director for Government Contracting's determination or dismissal, the contracting officer may apply the OHA decision to the procurement in question.

(2) If the contracting officer has withheld contract award, SBA has sustained the protest and determined that the concern is not an SDVOSB, and no OHA appeal has been filed, then the contracting officer shall not award the contract to the protested concern.

(3) If the contracting officer has made a written determination in accordance with (h)(1)(ii) or (h)(3) of this section, the contract has been awarded, and SBA's ruling sustaining the protest is received after award—

(i) The contracting officer shall terminate the contract, unless the contracting officer has made a written determination that termination is not in the best interests of the Government. However, the contracting officer shall not exercise any options or award further task or delivery orders;

(ii) The contracting officer shall update the FPDS to reflect the final SBA decision; and

(iii) The concern must remove its designation in the System for Award Management (SAM) as a SDVOSB concern, and shall not submit an offer as a SDVOSB concern, until SBA issues a decision that the ineligibility is resolved.

(4) If the contracting officer has made a written determination in accordance with (h)(1)(ii) or (h)(3) of this section and awarded the contract to the protested firm, SBA has sustained the protest and deter-

mined that the concern is not a SDVOSB, and a timely OHA appeal has been filed, then the contracting officer shall consider whether performance can be suspended until an OHA decision is rendered.

(5) If OHA affirms the SBA Director for Government Contracting's determination finding the protested concern is ineligible—

(i) The contracting officer shall terminate the contract unless the contracting officer has made a written determination that it is not in the best interest of the Government. However, the contracting officer shall not exercise any options or award further task or delivery orders;

(ii) The contracting officer shall update the FPDS to reflect OHA's decision; and

(iii) The concern shall remove its designation in SAM as a SDVOSB concern, until SBA issues a decision that the ineligibility is resolved or OHA finds the concern is eligible on appeal.

(6) A concern found to be ineligible may not submit future offers as an SDVOSB concern until the concern demonstrates to SBA's satisfaction that it has overcome the reason for the protest and SBA issues a decision to this effect.

(j) *Appeals of SDVOSB status determinations.* The protested SDVOSB small business concern, the protester, or the contracting officer may file appeals of protest determinations to OHA. OHA must receive the appeal no later than 10 business days after the date of receipt of the protest determination. SBA will dismiss an untimely appeal. See Subpart E "Rules of Practice for Appeals From Service-Disabled Veteran Owned Small Business Concerns Protests" at 13 CFR 134.501 through 134.515 for SBA's appeals regulations.

(k) *The appeal must be in writing.* The appeal must identify the protest determination being appealed and must set forth a full and specific statement as to why the SDVOSB protest determination is alleged to be based on a clear error of fact or law, together with an argument supporting such allegation.

(l) The party appealing the decision must provide notice of the appeal to—

(1) The contracting officer;

(2) Director, Office of Government Contracting, U.S. Small Business Administration, 409 Third Street SW., Washington, DC 20416, facsimile 202-205-6390;

(3) The protested SDVOSB concern or the original protester, as appropriate; and

(4) Associate General Counsel for Procurement Law, U.S. Small Business Administration, 409 Third Street SW., Washington, DC 20416, facsimile 202-205-6873, or email at *OPLService@sba.gov.*

(m) OHA will make its decision within 15 business days of the receipt of the appeal, if practicable. SBA will provide a copy of the decision to the contracting officer, the protester, and the protested SDVOSB small business concern. The OHA decision regarding the status of the concern is final and is binding on the parties.

[FAC 2001-23, 69 FR 25273, 5/5/2004, effective 5/5/2004; FAC 2005-02, 70 FR 14950, 3/23/2005, effective 3/23/2005; FAC 2005-76, 79 FR 43580, 7/25/2014, effective 8/25/2014; Correction, 79 FR 46375, 8/8/2014, effective 8/8/2014]

19.308 Protesting a firm's status as an economically disadvantaged women-owned small business concern or women-owned small business concern eligible under the Women-Owned Small Business Program.

(a) *Definition. Interested party,* as used in this section, has the meaning given in 13 CFR 127.102.

(b)(1) For sole source acquisitions, the contracting officer or SBA may protest the offeror's status as an economically disadvantaged women-owned small business (EDWOSB) concern or as a WOSB concern eligible under the WOSB Program. For all other acquisitions, an interested party (see 13 CFR 127.102) may protest the apparent successful offeror's EDWOSB or WOSB status.

(2) SBA's protest regulations are found in subpart F "Protests" at 13 CFR 127.600 through 127.605.

(c) Protests relating to small business size status are subject to the procedures of 19.302. An interested party seeking to protest both the small business size and WOSB or EDWOSB status of an apparent successful offeror shall file two separate protests.

(d) All protests shall be in writing and must state all specific grounds for the protest.

(1) SBA will consider protests challenging the status of a concern if—

(i) The protest presents evidence that the concern is not at least 51 percent owned and controlled by one or more women who are United States citizens; or

(ii) The protest presents evidence that the concern is not at least 51 percent owned and controlled by one or more economically disadvantaged women, when it is in connection with an EDWOSB contract.

(2) SBA shall consider protests by a contracting officer when the apparent successful offeror has failed to provide all of the required documents, as set forth in 19.1503(c).

(3) Assertions that a protested concern is not a EDWOSB or WOSB concern eligible under the WOSB Program, without setting forth specific facts or allegations, will not be considered by SBA (see 13 CFR 127.603(a)).

(e) *Protest by an interested party.* (1) An offeror shall submit its protest to the contracting officer—

(i) To be received by the close of business by the fifth business day after bid opening (in sealed bid acquisitions); or

(ii) To be received by the close of business by the fifth business day after notification by the contracting officer of the apparent successful offeror (in negotiated acquisitions).

(2) Any protest received after the designated time limit is untimely, unless it is from the contracting officer or SBA.

(f) (1) The contracting officer shall forward all protests to SBA. The protests are to be submitted to SBA's Director for Government Contracting, U.S. Small Business Administration, 409 Third Street SW., Washington, DC 20416 or by fax to 202-205-6390, Attn: Women-owned Small Business Status Protest.

(2) The protest shall include a referral letter written by the contracting officer with information pertaining to the solicitation. The referral letter must include the following information to allow SBA to determine timeliness and standing:

(i) The solicitation number or electronic link to or a paper copy of the solicitation.

(ii) The name, address, telephone number, email address, and facsimile number of the contracting officer.

(iii) Whether the protestor submitted an offer.

(iv) Whether the protested concern was the apparent successful offeror.

(v) When the protested concern submitted its offer.

(vi) Whether the acquisition was conducted using sealed bid or negotiated procedures.

(vii) The bid opening date, if applicable.

(viii) The date the contracting officer received the protest.

(ix) The date the protestor received notification about the apparent successful offeror, if applicable.

(x) Whether a contract has been awarded.

(g) SBA will notify the protester and the contracting officer of the date SBA received the protest.

(h) *Before SBA decision.* (1) After receiving a protest involving the apparent successful offeror's status as an EDWOSB or WOSB concern eligible under the WOSB Program, the contracting officer shall either—

(i) Withhold award of the contract until SBA determines the status of the protested concern; or

(ii) Award the contract after receipt of the protest but before SBA issues its decision if the contracting officer determines in writing that an award must be made to protect the public interest.

(2) SBA will determine the merits of the status protest within 15 business days after receipt of a protest, or within any extension

of that time granted by the contracting officer.

(3) If SBA does not issue its determination within 15 business days, or within any extension of time granted, the contracting officer may award the contract after determining in writing that there is an immediate need to award the contract and that waiting until SBA makes its determination will be disadvantageous to the Government. This determination shall be provided to the SBA Director for Government Contracting and a copy shall be included in the contract file.

(i) *After SBA decision.* SBA will notify the contracting officer, the protester, and the protested concern of its determination. The determination is effective immediately and is final unless overturned on appeal by SBA's Office of Hearings and Appeals (OHA) pursuant to 13 CFR part 134.

(1) If the contracting officer has withheld contract award and SBA has denied or dismissed the protest, the contracting officer may award the contract to the protested concern. If OHA subsequently overturns the SBA Director for Government Contracting's determination or dismissal, the contracting officer may apply the OHA decision to the procurement in question.

(2) If the contracting officer has withheld contract award, SBA has sustained the protest and determined that the concern is not eligible under the WOSB Program, and no OHA appeal has been filed, then the contracting officer shall not award the contract to the protested concern.

(3) If the contracting officer has made a written determination in accordance with (h)(1)(ii) or (h)(3) of this section, awarded the contract, and SBA's ruling is received after award, and no OHA appeal has been filed, then—

(i) The contracting officer shall terminate the contract, unless the contracting officer has made a written determination that termination is not in the best interests of the Government. However, the contracting officer shall not exercise any options or award further task or delivery orders;

(ii) The contracting officer shall update the FPDS to reflect the final SBA decision; and

(iii) The concern must remove its designation in SAM as an EDWOSB or WOSB concern eligible under the WOSB Program, and shall not submit an offer as an EDWOSB concern or WOSB concern eligible under the WOSB Program, until SBA issues a decision that the ineligibility is resolved.

(4) If the contracting officer has made a written determination in accordance with (h)(1)(ii) or (h)(3) of this section, contract award has occurred, SBA has sustained the protest and determined that the concern is not eligible under the WOSB Program, and a timely OHA appeal has been filed, then the contracting officer shall consider whether performance can be suspended until an OHA decision is rendered.

(5) If OHA affirms the SBA Director for Government Contracting's determination finding the protested concern is ineligible, then—

(i) The contracting officer shall terminate the contract, unless the contracting officer has made a written determination that termination is not in the best interests of the Government. However, the contracting officer shall not exercise any options or award further task or delivery orders;

(ii) The contracting officer shall update the FPDS to reflect OHA's decision; and

(iii) The concern must remove its designation in SAM as an EDWOSB or WOSB concern eligible under the WOSB Program, and shall not submit an offer as an EDWOSB concern or WOSB concern eligible under the WOSB Program, until SBA issues a decision that the ineligibility is resolved or OHA finds the concern is eligible on appeal.

(j) *Appeals of EDWOSB or WOSB concerns eligible under the WOSB Program status determinations.* (1) The protested EDWOSB concern or WOSB concern eligible under the WOSB program, the protester, or the contracting officer may file an appeal of a WOSB or EDWOSB status protest determination with OHA.

(2) OHA must receive the appeal no later than 10 business days after the date of re-

ceipt of the protest determination. SBA will dismiss an untimely appeal.

(3) See subpart G "Rules of Practice for Appeals From Women-Owned Small Business Concerns (WOSB) and Economically Disadvantaged WOSB Concern (EDWOSB) Protests" at 13 CFR 134.701 through 134.715 for SBA's appeals regulations.

(k) *The appeal must be in writing.* The appeal must identify the protest determination being appealed and must set forth a full and specific statement as to why the EDWOSB concern or WOSB concern eligible under the WOSB program protest determination is alleged to be based on a clear error of fact or law, together with an argument supporting such allegation.

(l) The party appealing the decision must provide notice of the appeal to—

(1) The contracting officer;

(2) Director, Office of Government Contracting, U.S. Small Business Administration, 409 Third Street SW., Washington, DC 20416, facsimile 202-205-6390;

(3) The protested EDWOSB concern or WOSB concern eligible under the WOSB program, or the original protester, as appropriate; and

(4) SBA's Office of General Counsel, Associate General Counsel for Procurement Law, U.S. Small Business Administration, 409 Third Street SW., Washington, DC 20416, facsimile 202-205-6873, or email at *OPLService@sba.gov*.

(m) OHA will make its decision within 15 business days of the receipt of the appeal, if practicable. SBA will provide a copy of the decision to the contracting officer, the protester, and the protested EDWOSB concern or WOSB concern eligible under the WOSB program. The OHA decision is the final agency decision and is binding on the parties.

[FAC 2005-51, 76 FR 18304, 4/1/2011, effective 4/1/2011; FAC 2005-56, 77 FR 12913, 3/2/2012, effective 4/2/2012; FAC 2005-67, 78 FR 37676, 6/21/2013, effective 7/22/2013; FAC 2005-76, 79 FR 43580, 7/25/2014, effective 8/25/2014; FAC 2005-86, 80 FR 81888, 12/31/2015, effective 12/31/2015; FAC 2005-91, 81 FR 67735, 9/30/2016, effective 9/30/2016; FAC 2005-101, 83 FR 48691, 9/26/2018, effective 10/26/2018]

19.309 Solicitation provisions and contract clauses.

(a) (1) Insert the provision at 52.219-1, Small Business Program Representations, in solicitations exceeding the micro-purchase threshold when the contract will be performed in the United States or its outlying areas.

(2) Use the provision with its Alternate I in solicitations issued by DoD, NASA, or the Coast Guard.

(b) When contracting by sealed bidding, insert the provision at 52.219-2, Equal Low Bids, in solicitations when the contract will be performed in the United States or its outlying areas.

(c) Insert the clause at 52.219-28, Post-Award Small Business Program Rerepresentation, in solicitations and contracts exceeding the micro-purchase threshold when the contract will be performed in the United States or its outlying areas.

[FAC 97-14, 64 FR 51828, 9/24/99, effective 11/23/99; FAC 2001-06, 67 FR 13048, 3/20/2002, effective 4/4/2002; FAC 2001-14, 68 FR 28079, 5/22/2003, effective 6/23/2003; FAC 2005-18, Interim rule, 72 FR 36852, 7/5/2007, effective 6/30/2007; FAC 2005-31, 74 FR 11821, 3/19/2009, effective 4/20/2009; Redesignated from 19.308, FAC 2005-51, 76 FR 18304, 4/1/2011, effective 4/1/2011; FAC 2005-56, 77 FR 12913, 3/2/2012, effective 4/2/2012; FAC 2005-77, 79 FR 61746, 10/14/2014, effective 10/14/2014]

SUBPART 19.4—COOPERATION WITH THE SMALL BUSINESS ADMINISTRATION

19.401 General.

(a) The Small Business Act is the authority under which the Small Business Administration (SBA) and agencies consult and cooperate with each other in formulating policies to ensure that small business interests will be recognized and protected.

(b) The Director of Small and Disadvantaged Business Utilization serves as the agency focal point for interfacing with SBA.

[FAC 90-32, 60 FR 48206, 9/18/95, effective 10/1/95]

19.402 Small Business Administration procurement center representatives.

(a)(1) The SBA may assign one or more procurement center representatives to any contracting activity or contract administration office to carry out SBA policies and programs. Assigned SBA procurement center representatives are required to comply with the contracting agency's directives governing the conduct of contracting personnel and the release of contract information. The SBA must obtain for its procurement center representatives security clearances required by the contracting agency.

(2) If a SBA procurement center representative is not assigned to the procuring activity or contract administration office, contact the SBA Office of Government Contracting Area Office serving the area in which the procuring activity is located for assistance in carrying out SBA policies and programs. See *http://www.sba.gov/content/procurement-center-representatives* for the location of the SBA office servicing the activity.

(b) Upon their request and subject to applicable acquisition and security regulations, contracting officers shall give SBA procurement center representatives (or, if a procurement center representative is not assigned, see paragraph (a) of this section) access to all reasonably obtainable contract information that is directly pertinent to their official duties.

(c) The duties assigned by SBA to its procurement center representatives include the following:

(1) Reviewing proposed acquisitions to recommend—

(i) The setting aside of selected acquisitions not unilaterally set aside by the contracting officer;

(ii) New qualified small business sources, including veteran-owned small, service-disabled veteran-owned small, HUBZone small, small disadvantaged, economically disadvantaged women-owned small, and women-owned small eligible under the Women-Owned Small Business Program; and

(iii) Breakout of components for competitive acquisitions.

(2) Reviewing proposed acquisition packages provided in accordance with 19.202-1(e). If the SBA procurement center representative (or, if a procurement center representative is not assigned, see paragraph (a) of this section) believes that the acquisition, as proposed, makes it unlikely that small businesses can compete for the prime contract, the representative shall recommend any alternate contracting method that the representative reasonably believes will increase small business prime contracting opportunities. The recommendation shall be made to the contracting officer within 15 days after receipt of the package.

(3) Recommending concerns for inclusion on a list of concerns to be solicited in a specific acquisition.

(4) Appealing to the chief of the contracting office any contracting officer's determination not to solicit a concern recommended by the SBA for a particular acquisition, when not doing so results in no small business being solicited.

(5) Conducting periodic reviews of the contracting activity to which assigned to ascertain whether it is complying with the small business policies in this regulation.

(6) Sponsoring and participating in conferences and training designed to increase small business participation in the contracting activities of the office.

[FAC 84-16, 51 FR 19715, 5/30/86, effective 5/30/86; Interim rule, FAC 90-9, 56 FR 67132, 12/27/91, effective 12/27/91; FAC 90-32, 60 FR 48206, 9/18/95, effective 10/1/95; FAC 97-10, 63 FR 70264, 12/18/98, effective 1/4/99; FAC 97-20, 65 FR 60542, 10/11/2000, effective 10/11/2000; FAC 2001-15, 68 FR 43854, 7/24/2003, effective 8/25/2003; FAC 2005-10, 71 FR 36925, 6/28/2006, effective 7/28/2006; FAC 2005-51, 76 FR 18304, 4/1/2011, effective 4/1/2011; FAC 2005-55, 77 FR 204,

1/3/2012, effective 1/3/2012; FAC 2005-56, 77 FR 12913, 3/2/2012, effective 4/2/2012; FAC 2005-76, 79 FR 43580, 7/25/2014, effective 8/25/2014]

19.403 Small Business Administration breakout procurement center representative.

(a) The SBA is required by section 403 of Pub. L. 98-577 to assign a breakout procurement center representative to each major procurement center. A major procurement center means a procurement center that, in the opinion of the administrator, purchases substantial dollar amounts of other than commercial items, and which has the potential to incur significant savings as a result of the placement of a breakout procurement representative. The SBA breakout procurement center representative is an advocate for—

(1) the appropriate use of full and open competition, and

(2) the breakout of items, when appropriate and while maintaining the integrity of the system in which such items are used. The SBA breakout procurement center representative is in addition to the SBA procurement center representative (see 19.402). When an SBA breakout procurement center representative is assigned, the SBA is required to assign at least two collocated small business technical advisors. Assigned SBA breakout procurement center representatives and technical advisors are required to comply with the contracting agency's directives governing the conduct of contracting personnel and the release of contract information. The SBA must obtain for its breakout procurement center representatives and technical advisors security clearances required by the contracting agency.

(b) Contracting officers shall comply with 19.402(b) in their relationships with SBA breakout procurement center representatives and SBA small business technical advisors.

(c) The SBA breakout procurement center representative is authorized to—

(1) Attend any provisioning conference or similar evaluation session during which determinations are made as to whether requirements are to be acquired using other than full and open competition and make recommendations with respect to such requirements to the members of such conference or session;

(2) Review, at any time, restrictions on competition previously imposed on items through acquisition method coding or similar procedures and recommend to personnel of the appropriate activity the prompt reevaluation of such limitations;

(3) Review restrictions on competition arising out of restrictions on the rights of the United States in technical data and, when appropriate, recommend that personnel of the appropriate activity initiate a review of the validity of such an asserted restriction;

(4) Obtain from any governmental source, and make available to personnel of the appropriate center, technical data necessary for the preparation of a competitive solicitation package for any item of supply or service previously acquired noncompetitively due to the unavailability of such technical data;

(5) Have access to procurement records and other data of the procurement center commensurate with the level of such representative's approved security clearance classification;

(6) Receive unsolicited engineering proposals and, when appropriate—

(i) Conduct a value analysis of such proposal to determine whether it, if adopted, will result in lower costs to the United States without substantially impeding legitimate acquisition objectives and forward to personnel of the appropriate center recommendations with respect to such proposal; or

(ii) Forward such proposals without analysis to personnel of the center responsible for reviewing them who shall furnish the breakout procurement center representative with information regarding the proposal's disposition;

(7) Review the systems that account for the acquisition and management of technical data within the procurement center to ensure that such systems provide the maximum availability and access to data needed

for the preparation of offers to sell to the United States those supplies to which such data pertain which potential offerors are entitled to receive;

(8) Appeal the failure by the procurement center to act favorably on any recommendation made pursuant to subparagraphs (c)(1) through (7) of this section. Such appeal must be in writing and shall be filed and processed in accordance with the appeal procedures set out in 19.505;

(9) Conduct familiarization sessions for contracting officers and other appropriate personnel of the procurement center to which assigned. Such sessions shall acquaint the participants with the duties and objectives of the representative and shall instruct them in the methods designed to further the breakout of items for procurement through full and open competition; and

(10) Prepare and personally deliver an annual briefing and report to the head of the procurement center to which assigned. Such briefing and report shall detail the past and planned activities of the representative and shall contain recommendations for improvement in the operation of the center as may be appropriate. The head of such center shall personally receive the briefing and report and shall, within 60 calendar days after receipt, respond, in writing, to each recommendation made by the representative.

(d) The duties of the SBA small business technical advisors are to assist the SBA breakout procurement center representative in carrying out the activities described in (c)(1) through (7) above to assist the SBA procurement center representatives (see FAR 19.402).

[FAC 84-16, 51 FR 19715, 5/30/86, effective 5/30/86; FAC 84-48, 54 FR 25062, 6/12/89, effective 6/12/89]

SUBPART 19.5—SET-ASIDES FOR SMALL BUSINESS

19.501 General.

(a) The purpose of small business set-asides is to award certain acquisitions exclusively to small business concerns. A "set-aside for small business" is the reserving of an acquisition exclusively for participation by small business concerns. A small business set-aside may be open to all small businesses. A small business set-aside of a single acquisition or a class of acquisitions may be total or partial.

(b) The determination to make a small business set-aside may be unilateral or joint. A unilateral determination is one that is made by the contracting officer. A joint determination is one that is recommended by the Small Business Administration (SBA) procurement center representative (or, if a procurement center representative is not assigned, see 19.402(a)) and concurred in by the contracting officer.

(c) The contracting officer shall review acquisitions to determine if they can be set aside for small business, giving consideration to the recommendations of agency personnel having cognizance of the agency's small business programs. The contracting officer shall perform market research and document why a small business set-aside is inappropriate when an acquisition is not set aside for small business, unless an award is anticipated to a small business under the 8(a), HUBZone, SDVOSB, or WOSB Programs. If the acquisition is set aside for small business based on this review, it is a unilateral set-aside by the contracting officer. Agencies may establish threshold levels for this review depending upon their needs.

(d) At the request of an SBA procurement center representative, (or, if a procurement center representative is not assigned, see 19.402(a)) the contracting officer shall make available for review at the contracting office (to the extent of the SBA representative's security clearance) all proposed acquisitions in excess of the micro-purchase threshold that have not been unilaterally set aside for small business.

(e) To the extent practicable, unilateral determinations initiated by a contracting officer shall be used as the basis for small business set-asides rather than joint determinations by an SBA procurement center representative and a contracting officer.

(f) All solicitations involving set-asides must specify the applicable small business size standard and NAICS code (see 19.303).

(g) Except as authorized by law, a contract may not be awarded as a result of a small business set-aside if the cost to the awarding agency exceeds the fair market price.

[FAC 84-5, 50 FR 1743, 1/11/85, effective 4/1/85; FAC 84-12, 51 FR 2664, 1/17/86, effective 1/20/86; FAC 84-28, 52 FR 21902, 6/9/87, effective 4/16/87; FAC 84-31, 52 FR 38189, 10/14/87, effective 10/1/87; FAC 84-37, 53 FR 17858, 5/18/88, effective 6/17/88; FAC 84-40, 53 FR 43390, 10/26/88, effective 11/25/88; Interim Rule, FAC 84-48, 54 FR 25063, 6/12/89, effective 6/12/89; FAC 90-3, 55 FR 52792, 12/21/90, effective 1/22/91; FAC 90-4, 56 FR 15150, 4/15/91, effective 5/15/91; FAC 90-29, 60 FR 34732, 7/3/95, effective 7/3/95; FAC 90-31, 60 FR 42648, 8/16/95, effective 10/1/95; FAC 90-32, 60 FR 48206, 9/18/95, effective 10/1/95; FAC 90-40, 61 FR 39186, 7/26/96, effective 8/24/96; FAC 90-44, Final rule, 61 FR 69286, 12/31/96, effective 1/1/97; FAC 90-45, Final rule, 62 FR 224, 1/2/97, effective 1/1/97; FAC 97-10, 63 FR 70264, 12/18/98, effective 1/4/99; FAC 97-19, 65 FR 46052, 7/26/2000, effective 10/1/2000, finalized without change by FAC 2001-02, 66 FR 65347, 12/18/2001, effective 12/18/2001; FAC 2001-23, 69 FR 25273, 5/5/2004, effective 5/5/2004; FAC 2005-02, 70 FR 14950, 3/23/2005, effective 3/23/2005; FAC 2005-10, 71 FR 36925, 6/28/2006, effective 7/28/2006; FAC 2005-50, 76 FR 14566, 3/16/2011, effective 3/16/2011; FAC 2005-51, 76 FR 18304, 4/1/2011, effective 4/1/2011; FAC 2005-56, 77 FR 12913, 12930, 3/2/2012, effective 4/2/2012]

19.502 Setting aside acquisitions. (No Text)

19.502-1 Requirements for setting aside acquisitions.

(a) The contracting officer shall set aside an individual acquisition or class of acquisitions for competition among small businesses when—

(1) It is determined to be in the interest of maintaining or mobilizing the Nations full productive capacity, war or national defense programs; or

(2) Assuring that a fair proportion of Government contracts in each industry category is placed with small business concerns; and the circumstances described in 19.502-2 or 19.502-3(a) exist.

(b) This requirement does not apply to purchases of $3,500 or less ($20,000 or less for acquisitions as described in 13.201(g)(1)), or purchases from required sources of supply under Part 8 (e.g., Committee for Purchase From People Who are Blind or Severely Disabled, and Federal Supply Schedule contracts).

[FAC 97-10, 63 FR 70264, 12/18/98, effective 1/4/99; FAC 2001-09, 67 FR 56115, 8/30/2002, effective 8/30/2002; FAC 2001-12, 68 FR 4047, 1/27/2003, effective 1/24/2003; FAC 2001-20, 69 FR 8311, 2/23/2004, effective 2/23/2004; FAC 2001-21, 69 FR 16147, 3/26/2004, effective 3/26/2004; FAC 2001-26, 69 FR 76350, 12/20/2004, effective 1/19/2005; FAC 2005-07, 71 FR 221, 1/3/2006, effective 1/3/2006; FAC 2005-13, 71 FR 57363, 9/28/2006, effective 9/28/2006; FAC 2005-83, 80 FR 38293, 7/2/2015, effective 10/1/2015]

19.502-2 Total small business set-asides.

(a) Before setting aside an acquisition under this paragraph, refer to 19.203(b). Each acquisition of supplies or services that has an anticipated dollar value exceeding $3,500 ($20,000 for acquisitions described in 13.201(g)(1)), but not over $150,000 ($750,000 for acquisitions described in paragraph (1)(i) of the simplified acquisition threshold definition at 2.101), is automatically reserved exclusively for small business concerns and shall be set aside for small business unless the contracting officer determines there is not a reasonable expectation of obtaining offers from two or more responsible small business concerns that are competitive in terms of market prices, quality, and delivery. If the contracting officer does not proceed with the small business set-aside and purchases on an unrestricted basis, the contracting officer shall include in the contract file the reason for this unrestricted purchase. If the contracting officer receives only one acceptable offer from a responsible small business concern in response to a set-aside, the contracting officer should make an award to that firm. If the contracting officer receives no acceptable offers from responsible small business concerns, the set-aside shall be withdrawn and the requirement, if still valid, shall be resolicited on an unrestricted basis. The small business reservation does not preclude the award of a contract as described in 19.203.

(b) Before setting aside an acquisition under this paragraph, refer to 19.203(c). The contracting officer shall set aside any acquisition over $150,000 for small business participation when there is a reasonable expectation that—

(1) Offers will be obtained from at least two responsible small business concerns offering the products of different small business concerns (see paragraph (c) of this section); and

(2) Award will be made at fair market prices. Total small business set-asides shall not be made unless such a reasonable expectation exists (see 19.502-3 as to partial set-asides). Although past acquisition history of an item or similar items is always important, it is not the only factor to be considered in determining whether a reasonable expectation exists. In making R&D small business set-asides, there must also be a reasonable expectation of obtaining from small businesses the best scientific and technological sources consistent with the demands of the proposed acquisition for the best mix of cost, performances, and schedules.

(c) For small business set-asides other than for construction or services, any concern proposing to furnish a product that it did not itself manufacture must furnish the product of a small business manufacturer unless the SBA has granted either a waiver or exception to the nonmanufacturer rule (see 19.102(f)). In industries where the SBA finds that there are no small business manufacturers, it may issue a waiver to the nonmanufacturer rule (see 19.102(f) (4) and (5)). In addition, SBA has excepted procurements processed under simplified acquisition procedures (see part 13), where the anticipated cost of the procurement will not exceed $25,000, from the nonmanufacturer rule. Waivers permit small businesses to provide any firm's product. The exception permits small businesses to provide any domestic firm's product. In both of these cases, the contracting officer's determination in paragraph (b)(1) of this subsection or the decision not to set aside a procurement reserved for small business under paragraph (a) of this subsection will be based on the expectation of receiving offers from at least two responsible small businesses, including nonmanufacturers, offering the products of different concerns.

[FAC 90-29, 60 FR 34732, 7/3/95, effective 7/3/95; FAC 90-40, 61 FR 39186, 7/26/96, effective 7/26/96; FAC 97-10, 63 FR 70264, 12/18/98, effective 1/4/99; FAC 97-11, 64 FR 10530, 3/4/99, effective 3/4/99; FAC 97-16, 65 FR 16274, 3/27/2000, effective 3/27/2000, finalized without change, FAC 97-19, 65 FR 46052, 7/26/2000; FAC 2001-09, 67 FR 56115, 8/30/2002, effective 8/30/2002; FAC 2001-10, 67 FR 70522, 11/22/2002, effective 11/22/2002; FAC 2001-12, 68 FR 4047, 1/27/2003, effective 1/24/2003; FAC 2001-20, 69 FR 8311, 2/23/2004, effective 2/23/2004; FAC 2001-26, 69 FR 76350, 12/20/2004, effective 1/19/2005; FAC 2005-01, 70 FR 11740, 3/9/2005, effective 3/9/2005; FAC 2005-06, 70 FR 57458, 9/30/2005, effective 9/30/2005; FAC 2005-07, 71 FR 220, 1/3/2006, effective 1/3/2006; FAC 2005-13, 71 FR 57363, 9/28/2006, effective 9/28/2006; FAC 2005-45, 75 FR 53129, 8/30/2010, effective 10/1/2010; FAC 2005-48, 75 FR 82567, 12/30/2010, effective 1/31/2011; FAC 2005-50, 76 FR 14566, 3/16/2011, effective 3/16/2011; Correction, 76 FR 26220, 5/6/2011, effective 5/6/2011; FAC 2005-56, 77 FR 12930, 3/2/2012, effective 4/2/2012; FAC 2005-83, 80 FR 38293, 7/2/2015, effective 10/1/2015; FAC 2005-88, 81 FR 30438, 5/16/2016, effective 6/15/2016; FAC 2005-95, 82 FR 4716, 1/13/2017, effective 1/13/2017]

19.502-3 Partial set-asides.

(a) The contracting officer shall set aside a portion of an acquisition, except for construction, for exclusive small business participation when—

(1) A total set-aside is not appropriate (see 19.502-2);

(2) The requirement is severable into two or more economic production runs or reasonable lots;

(3) One or more small business concerns are expected to have the technical competence and productive capacity to satisfy the set-aside portion of the requirement at a fair market price;

(4) The acquisition is not subject to simplified acquisition procedures; and

(5) A partial set-aside shall not be made if there is a reasonable expectation that only two concerns (one large and one small) with capability will respond with offers unless authorized by the head of a contracting activity on a case-by-case basis. Similarly, a class of acquisitions, not including construction, may be partially set aside. Under certain specified conditions, partial set-asides may be used in conjunction with multiyear contracting procedures.

(b) When the contracting officer determines that a portion of an acquisition is to be set aside, the requirement shall be divided into a set-aside portion and a non-set-aside portion, each of which shall—

(1) be an economic production run or reasonable lot and

(2) have terms and a delivery schedule comparable to the other. When practicable, the set-aside portion should make maximum use of small business capacity.

(c) (1) The contracting officer shall award the non-set-aside portion using normal contracting procedures.

(2) (i) After all awards have been made on the non-set-aside portion, the contracting officer shall negotiate with eligible concerns on the set-aside portion, as provided in the solicitation, and make award. Negotiations shall be conducted only with those offerors who have submitted responsive offers on the non- set-aside portion. Negotiations shall be conducted with small business concerns in the order of priority as indicated in the solicitation (but see (ii) below). The set-aside portion shall be awarded as provided in the solicitation. An offeror entitled to receive the award for quantities of an item under the non-set-aside portion and who accepts the award of additional quantities under the set-aside portion shall not be requested to accept a lower price because of the increased quantities of the award, nor shall negotiation be conducted with a view to obtaining such a lower price based solely upon receipt of award of both portions of the acquisition. This does not prevent acceptance by the contracting officer of voluntary reductions in the price from the low eligible offeror before award, acceptance of voluntary refunds, or the change of prices after award by negotiation of a contract modification.

(ii) If equal low offers are received on the non-set-aside portion from concerns eligible for the set-aside portion, the concern that is awarded the non-set-aside part of the acquisition shall have first priority with respect to negotiations for the set-aside.

[FAC 84-40, 53 FR 43390, 10/26/88, effective 11/25/88; FAC 90-29, 60 FR 34732, 7/3/95, effective 7/3/95]

19.502-4 Multiple-award contracts and small business set-asides.

In accordance with section 1331 of Public Law 111-240 (15 U.S.C. 644(r)) contracting officers may, at their discretion—

(a) When conducting multiple-award procurements using full and open competition, reserve one or more contract awards for any of the small business concerns identified in 19.000(a)(3). The specific program eligibility requirements identified in this part apply;

(b) Set aside part or parts of a multiple-award contract for any of the small business concerns identified in 19.000(a)(3). The specific program eligibility requirements identified in this part apply; or

(c) Set aside orders placed under multiple-award contracts for any of the small business concerns identified in 19.000(a)(3). For orders placed under the Federal Supply Schedules Program see 8.405-5. For all other multiple-award contracts see 16.505.

[FAC 2005-54, 76 FR 68032, 11/2/2011, effective 11/2/2011; Interim rule, 77 FR 1889, 1/12/2012, effective 2/13/2012]

19.502-5 Methods of conducting set-asides.

(a) Total small business set-asides may be conducted by using simplified acquisition procedures (see part 13), sealed bids (see part 14), or competitive proposals (see part 15). Partial small business set-asides may be conducted using sealed bids (see part 14), or competitive proposals (see part 15).

(b) Except for offers on the non-set-aside portion of partial set-asides, offers received from concerns that do not qualify as small business concerns shall be considered nonresponsive and shall be rejected. However, before rejecting an offer otherwise eligible for award because of questions concerning the size representation, an SBA determination must be obtained (see subpart 19.3).

[FAC 84-5, 50 FR 1743, 1/11/85, effective 4/1/85; FAC 90-23, 59 FR 67010, 12/28/94, effective 2/27/95; FAC 90-29, 60 FR 34732, 7/3/95, effective 7/3/95; FAC 97-10, 63 FR 70264, 12/18/98, effective 1/4/99; Redesignated, FAC 2005-54, 76 FR 68032, 11/2/2011, effective 11/2/2011; Interim rule, 77 FR 1889, 1/12/2012, effective 2/13/2012]

19.502-6 Insufficient causes for not setting aside an acquisition.

None of the following is, in itself, sufficient cause for not setting aside an acquisition:

(a) A large percentage of previous contracts for the required item(s) has been placed with small business concerns.

(b) The item is on an established planning list under the Industrial Readiness Planning Program. However, a total small business set- aside shall not be made when the list contains a large business Planned Emergency Producer of the item(s) who has conveyed a desire to supply some or all of the required items.

(c) The item is on a Qualified Products List. However, a total small business set-aside shall not be made if the list contains the products of large businesses unless none of the large businesses desire to participate in the acquisition.

(d) A period of less than 30 days is available for receipt of offers.

(e) The acquisition is classified.

(f) Small business concerns are already receiving a fair proportion of the agency's contracts for supplies and services.

(g) A class small business set-aside of the item or service has been made by another contracting activity.

(h) A "brand name or equal" product description will be used in the solicitation.

[FAC 97-10, 63 FR 70264, 12/18/98, effective 1/4/99; Redesignated, FAC 2005-54, 76 FR 68032, 11/2/2011, effective 11/2/2011; Interim rule, 77 FR 1889, 1/12/2012, effective 2/13/2012]

19.503 Setting aside a class of acquisitions for small business.

(a) A class of acquisitions of selected products or services, or a portion of the acquisitions, may be set aside for exclusive participation by small business concerns if individual acquisitions in the class will meet the criteria in 19.502-1, 19.502-2, or 19.502-3(a). The determination to make a class small business set-aside shall not depend on the existence of a current acquisition if future acquisitions can be clearly foreseen.

(b) The determination to set aside a class of acquisitions for small business may be either unilateral or joint.

(c) Each class small business set-aside determination shall be in writing and must—

(1) Specifically identify the product(s) and service(s) it covers;

(2) Provide that the set-aside does not apply to any acquisition automatically reserved for small business concerns under 19.502-2(a).

(3) Provide that the set-aside applies only to the (named) contracting office(s) making the determination; and

(4) Provide that the set-aside does not apply to any individual acquisition if the requirement is not severable into two or more economic production runs or reasonable lots, in the case of a partial class set-aside.

(d) The contracting officer shall review each individual acquisition arising under a class small business set-aside to identify any changes in the magnitude of requirements, specifications, delivery requirements, or competitive market conditions that have occurred since the initial approval of the class small business set-aside. If there are any changes of such a material nature as to result in probable payment of more than a fair market price by the Government or in a change in the capability of small business concerns to satisfy the requirements, the contracting officer may withdraw or modify (see 19.506(a)) the unilateral or joint set-aside by giving written notice to the SBA procurement center representative (or, if a procurement center representative is not assigned, see 19.402(a)) stating the reasons.

[FAC 84-40, 53 FR 43390, 10/26/88 effective 11/25/88; FAC 90-29, 60 FR 34732, 7/3/95, effective 7/3/95; FAC 97-10, 63 FR 70264, 12/18/98, effective 1/4/99; FAC 2005-10, 71 FR 36925, 6/28/2006, effective 7/28/2006]

19.504 Inclusion of Federal Prison Industries, Inc.

When using competitive procedures in accordance with 8.602(a)(4), agencies shall include Federal Prison Industries, Inc. (FPI), in the solicitation process and consider a timely offer from FPI.

[FAC 90-32, 60 FR 48206, 9/18/95, effective 10/1/95; FAC 2001-21, 69 FR 16147, 3/26/2004, effective 3/26/2004; FAC 2005-07, 71 FR 221, 1/3/2006, effective 1/3/2006]

19.505 Rejecting Small Business Administration recommendations.

(a) If the contracting officer rejects a recommendation of the SBA procurement center representative (or, if a procurement center representative is not assigned, see 19.402(a)) or breakout procurement center representative, written notice shall be furnished to the appropriate SBA representative within 5 working days of the contracting officer's receipt of the recommendation.

(b) The SBA procurement center representative (or, if a procurement center representative is not assigned, see 19.402(a)) may appeal the contracting officer's rejection to the head of the contracting activity (or designee) within 2 working days after receiving the notice. The head of the contracting activity (or designee) shall render a decision in writing, and provide it to the SBA representative within 7 working days. Pending issuance of a decision to the SBA representative, the contracting officer shall suspend action on the acquisition.

(c) If the head of the contracting activity agrees that the contracting officer's rejection was appropriate—

(1) Within 2 working days, the SBA procurement center representative (or, if a procurement center representative is not assigned, see 19.402(a)) may request the contracting officer to suspend action on the acquisition until the SBA Administrator appeals to the agency head (see paragraph (f) of this section); and

(2) The SBA must be allowed 15 working days after making such a written request, within which the Administrator of SBA—

(i) May appeal to the Secretary of the Department concerned; and

(ii) Must notify the contracting officer whether the further appeal has, in fact, been taken. If notification is not received by the contracting officer within the 15-day period, it is deemed that the SBA request to suspend the contract action has been withdrawn and that an appeal to the Secretary was not taken.

(d) When the contracting officer has been notified within the 15-day period that the SBA has appealed to the agency head, the head of the contracting activity (or designee) shall forward justification for its decision to the agency head. The contracting officer shall suspend contract action until notification is received that the SBA appeal has been settled.

(e) The agency head shall reply to the SBA within 30 working days after receiving the appeal. The decision of the agency head shall be final.

(f) A request to suspend action on an acquisition need not be honored if the contracting officer determines that proceeding to contract award and performance is in the public interest. The contracting officer shall include in the contract file a statement of the facts justifying the determination, and shall promptly notify the SBA representative of the determination and provide a copy of the justification.

[FAC 90-32, 60 FR 48206, 9/18/95, effective 10/1/95; FAC 2001-06, 67 FR 13048, 3/20/2002, effective 4/4/2002; FAC 2005-10, 71 FR 36925, 6/28/2006, effective 7/28/2006]

19.506 Withdrawing or modifying small business set-asides.

(a) If, before award of a contract involving a small business set-aside, the contracting officer considers that award would be detrimental to the public interest (*e.g.*, payment of more than a fair market price), the contracting officer may withdraw the small business set-aside determination whether it was unilateral or joint. The contracting officer shall initiate a withdrawal of an individual small business set-aside by giving written notice to the agency small business specialist and the SBA procurement center representative (or, if a procurement center representative is not assigned, see 19.402(a)) stating the reasons. In a similar manner, the contracting officer may modify a unilateral or joint class small business set-aside to withdraw one or more individual acquisitions.

(b) If the agency small business specialist does not agree to a withdrawal or modification, the case shall be promptly referred to the SBA representative (or, if a procurement center representative is not assigned, see 19.402(a)) for review.

(c) The contracting officer shall prepare a written statement supporting any withdrawal or modification of a small business set-aside and include it in the contract file.

[FAC 90-32, 60 FR 48206, 9/18/95, effective 10/1/95; FAC 97-10, 63 FR 70264, 12/18/98, effective 1/4/99; FAC 2005-10, 71 FR 36925, 6/28/2006, effective 7/28/2006]

19.507 Automatic dissolution of a small business set-aside.

(a) If a small business set-aside acquisition or portion of an acquisition is not awarded, the unilateral or joint determination to set the acquisition aside is automatically dissolved for the unawarded portion of the set- aside. The required supplies and/or services for which no award was made may be acquired by sealed bidding or negotiation, as appropriate.

(b) Before issuing a solicitation for the items called for in a small business set-aside that was dissolved, the contracting officer shall ensure that the delivery schedule is realistic in the light of all relevant factors, including the capabilities of small business concerns.

[FAC 84-5, 50 FR 1743, 1/11/85, effective 4/1/85; FAC 97-10, 63 FR 70264, 12/18/98, effective 1/4/99]

19.508 Solicitation provisions and contract clauses.

(a) [Reserved]

(b) [Reserved]

(c) The contracting officer shall insert the clause at 52.219-6, Notice of Total Small Business Set-Aside, in solicitations and contracts involving total small business set-asides or reserves. This includes multiple-award contracts when orders may be set aside for any of the small business concerns identified in 19.000(a)(3), as described in 8.405-5 and 16.505(b)(2)(i)(F). The clause at 52.219-6 with its Alternate I will be used when the acquisition is for a product in a class for which the Small Business Administration has waived the nonmanufacturer rule (see 19.102(f)(4) and (5)). Use the clause at 52.219-6 with its Alternate II when including FPI in the competition in accordance with 19.504.

(d) The contracting officer shall insert the clause at 52.219-7, Notice of Partial Small Business Set-Aside, in solicitations and contracts involving partial small business set-asides. This includes part or parts of multiple-award contracts, including those described in 38.101. The clause at 52.219-7 with its Alternate I will be used when the acquisition is for a product in a class for which the Small Business Administration has waived the nonmanufacturer rule (see 19.102(f)(4) and (5)). Use the clause at 52.219-7 with its Alternate II when including FPI in the competition in accordance with 19.504.

(e) The contracting officer shall insert the clause at 52.219-14, Limitations on Subcontracting, in solicitations and contracts for supplies, services, and construction, if any portion of the requirement is to be set aside or reserved for small business and the contract amount is expected to exceed $150,000. This includes multiple-award contracts when orders may be set aside for small business concerns, as described in 8.405-5 and 16.505(b)(2)(i)(F).

(f) The contracting officer shall insert the clause at 52.219-13, Notice of Set-Aside of Orders, in solicitations and contracts to notify offerors if an order or orders are to be set aside for any of the small business concerns identified in 19.000(a)(3).

[FAC 84-28, 52 FR 21902, 6/9/87, effective 4/16/87; FAC 84-31, 52 FR 38189, 10/14/87, effective 10/1/87; FAC 84-38, 53 FR 27464, 7/20/88, effective 8/19/88; FAC 84-40, 53 FR 43390, 10/26/88, effective 11/25/88; FAC 84-48, 54 FR 25063, 6/12/89, effective 6/12/89; FAC 84-58, 55 FR 25529, 6/21/90, effective 7/23/90; Final rule, 55 FR 38516, 9/18/90; FAC 90-29, 60 FR 34732, 7/3/95, effective 7/3/95; FAC 90-32, 60 FR 48206, 9/18/95, effective 10/1/95; FAC 90-40, 61 FR 39186, 7/26/96, effective 7/26/96; FAC 90-43, 61 FR 67408, 12/20/96, effective 12/20/96; FAC 90-45, 62 FR 224, 1/2/97, effective 1/1/97; FAC 97-1, 62 FR 44802, 8/22/97, effective 8/22/97, finalized without change, FAC 97-4, 63 FR 9048, 2/23/98, effective 4/24/98; FAC 2001-21, 69 FR 16147, 3/26/2004, effective 3/26/2004; FAC 2005-07, 71 FR 221, 1/3/2006, effective 1/3/2006; FAC 2005-45, 75 FR 53129, 8/30/2010, effective 10/1/2010; FAC 2005-54, 76 FR 68032, 11/2/2011, effective 11/2/2011; Interim rule, 77 FR 1889, 1/12/2012, effective 2/13/2012]

SUBPART 19.6—CERTIFICATES OF COMPETENCY AND DETERMINATIONS OF RESPONSIBILITY

19.601 General.

(a) A Certificate of Competency (COC) is the certificate issued by the Small Business Administration (SBA) stating that the holder is responsible (with respect to all elements of responsibility, including, but not limited to, capability, competency, capacity, credit, integrity, perseverance, tenacity, and limitations on subcontracting) for the purpose of receiving and performing a specific Government contract.

(b) The COC program empowers the Small Business Administration (SBA) to certify to Government contracting officers as to all elements of responsibility of any small business concern to receive and perform a specific Government contract. The COC program does not extend to questions concerning regulatory requirements imposed and enforced by other Federal agencies.

(c) The COC program is applicable to all Government acquisitions. A contracting officer shall, upon determining an apparent successful small business offeror to be nonresponsible, refer that small business to the SBA for a possible COC, even if the next acceptable offer is also from a small business.

(d) When a solicitation requires a small business to adhere to the limitations on subcontracting, a contracting officer's finding that a small business cannot comply with the limitation shall be treated as an element of responsibility and shall be subject to the COC process. When a solicitation requires a small business to adhere to the definition of a nonmanufacturer, a contracting officer's determination that the small business does not comply shall be processed in accordance with Subpart 19.3.

(e) Contracting officers, including those located overseas, are required to comply with this subpart for U.S. small business concerns.

[FAC 84-12, 51 FR 2664, 1/17/86, effective 1/20/86; FAC 84-51, 54 FR 34754, 8/21/89, effective 9/20/89; FAC 90-23, 59 FR 67010, 12/28/94, effective 2/27/95; FAC 90-43, 61 FR 67408, 12/20/96, effective 12/20/96, finalized without change, FAC 97-1, 62 FR 44802, 8/22/97, effective 10/21/97; FAC 97-1, 62 FR 44802, 8/22/97, effective 8/22/97, finalized without change, FAC 97-4, 63 FR 9048, 2/23/98, effective 4/24/98]

19.602 Procedures. (No Text)

19.602-1 Referral.

(a) Upon determining and documenting that an apparent successful small business offeror lacks certain elements of responsibility (including, but not limited to, capability, competency, capacity, credit, integrity, perseverance, tenacity, and limitations on subcontracting, but for sureties see 28.101-3(f) and 28.203(c)), the contracting officer shall—

(1) Withhold contract award (see 19.602-3); and

(2) Refer the matter to the cognizant SBA Government Contracting Area Office (Area Office) serving the area in which the headquarters of the offeror is located, in accordance with agency procedures, except that referral is not necessary if the small business concern—

(i) Is determined to be unqualified and ineligible because it does not meet the standard in 9.104-1(g); *provided*, that the determination is approved by the chief of the contracting office; or

(ii) Is suspended or debarred under Executive Order 11246 or Subpart 9.4.

(b) If a partial set-aside is involved, the contracting officer shall refer to the SBA the entire quantity to which the concern may be entitled, if responsible.

(c) The referral shall include—

(1) A notice that a small business concern has been determined to be nonresponsible, specifying the elements of responsibility the contracting officer found lacking; and

(2) If applicable, a copy of the following:

(i) Solicitation.

(ii) Final offer submitted by the concern whose responsibility is at issue for the procurement.

(iii) Abstract of bids or the contracting officer's price negotiation memorandum.

(iv) Preaward survey.

(v) Technical data package (including drawings, specifications and statement of work).

(vi) Any other justification and documentation used to arrive at the nonresponsibility determination.

(d) For any single acquisition, the contracting officer shall make only one referral at a time regarding a determination of nonresponsibility.

(e) Contract award shall be withheld by the contracting officer for a period of 15 business days (or longer if agreed to by the SBA and the contracting officer) following receipt by the appropriate SBA Area Office of a referral that includes all required documentation.

[FAC 84-19, 51 FR 27489, 7/31/86, effective 7/31/86; FAC 97-1, 62 FR 44802, 8/22/97, effective 8/22/97, finalized without change, FAC 97-4, 63 FR 9048, 2/23/98, effective 4/24/98; FAC 2005-06, 70 FR 57459, 9/30/2005, effective 9/30/2005]

19.602-2 Issuing or denying a Certificate of Competency (COC).

Within 15 business days (or a longer period agreed to by the SBA and the contracting agency) after receiving a notice that a small business concern lacks certain elements of responsibility, the SBA Area Office will take the following actions:

(a) Inform the small business concern of the contracting officer's determination and offer it an opportunity to apply to the SBA for a COC. (A concern wishing to apply for a COC should notify the SBA Area Office serving the geographical area in which the headquarters of the offeror is located.)

(b) Upon timely receipt of a complete and acceptable application, elect to visit the applicant's facility to review its responsibility.

(1) The COC review process is not limited to the areas of nonresponsibility cited by the contracting officer.

(2) The SBA may, at its discretion, independently evaluate the COC applicant for all elements of responsibility, but may presume responsibility exists as to elements other than those cited as deficient.

(c) Consider denying a COC for reasons of nonresponsibility not originally cited by the contracting officer.

(d) When the Area Director determines that a COC is warranted (for contracts valued at $25,000,000 or less), notify the contracting officer and provide the following options:

(1) Accept the Area Director's decision to issue a COC and award the contract to the concern. The COC issuance letter will then be sent, including as an attachment a detailed rationale for the decision; or

(2) Ask the Area Director to suspend the case for one or more of the following purposes:

(i) To permit the SBA to forward a detailed rationale for the decision to the contracting officer for review within a specified period of time.

(ii) To afford the contracting officer the opportunity to meet with the Area Office to review all documentation contained in the case file and to attempt to resolve any issues.

(iii) To submit any information to the SBA Area Office that the contracting officer believes the SBA did not consider (at which time, the SBA Area Office will establish a new suspense date mutually agreeable to the contracting officer and the SBA).

(iv) To permit resolution of an appeal by the contracting agency to SBA Headquarters under 19.602-3. However, there is no contracting officer's appeal when the Area Office proposes to issue a COC valued at $100,000 or less.

(e) At the completion of the process, notify the concern and the contracting officer that the COC is denied or is being issued.

(f) Refer recommendations for issuing a COC on contracts greater than $25,000,000 to SBA Headquarters.

[FAC 97-1, 62 FR 44802, 8/22/97, effective 8/22/97, finalized without change, FAC 97-4, 63 FR 9048, 2/23/98, effective 4/24/98]

19.602-3 Resolving differences between the agency and the Small Business Administration.

(a) *COCs valued between $100,000 and $25,000,000.*

(1) When disagreements arise about a concern's ability to perform, the contracting officer and the SBA shall make every effort to reach a resolution before the SBA takes final action on a COC. This shall be done through the complete exchange of information and in accordance with agency procedures. If agreement cannot be reached between the contracting officer and the SBA Area Office, the contracting officer shall request that the Area Office suspend action and refer the matter to SBA Headquarters for review. The SBA Area Office shall honor the request for a review if the contracting officer agrees to withhold award until the review process is concluded. Without an agreement to withhold award, the SBA Area Office will issue the COC in accordance with applicable SBA regulations.

(2) SBA Headquarters will furnish written notice to the procuring agency's Director, Office of Small and Disadvantaged Business Utilization (OSDBU) or other designated official (with a copy to the contracting officer) that the case file has been received and that an appeal decision may be requested by an authorized official.

(3) If the contracting agency decides to file an appeal, it must notify SBA Headquarters through its procuring agency's Director, OSDBU, or other designated official, within 10 business days (or a time period agreed upon by both agencies) that it intends to appeal the issuance of the COC.

(4) The appeal and any supporting documentation shall be filed by the procuring agency's Director, OSDBU, or other designated official, within 10 business days (or a period agreed upon by both agencies) after SBA Headquarters receives the agency's notification in accordance with paragraph (a)(3) of this subsection.

(5) The SBA Associate Administrator for Government Contracting will make a final determination, in writing, to issue or to deny the COC.

(b) *SBA Headquarters' decisions on COCs valued over $25,000,000.* (1) Prior to taking final action, SBA Headquarters will contact the contracting agency and offer it the following options:

(i) To request that the SBA suspend case processing to allow the agency to meet with SBA Headquarters personnel and review all documentation contained in the case file; or

(ii) To submit to SBA Headquarters for evaluation any information that the contracting agency believes has not been considered.

(2) After reviewing all available information, the SBA will make a final decision to either issue or deny the COC.

(c) *Reconsideration of a COC after issuance.* (1) The SBA reserves the right to reconsider its issuance of a COC, prior to contract award, if—

(i) The COC applicant submitted false information or omitted materially adverse information; or

(ii) The COC has been issued for more than 60 days (in which case the SBA may investigate the firm's current circumstances).

(2) When the SBA reconsiders and reaffirms the COC, the procedures in subsection 19.602-2 do not apply.

(3) Denial of a COC by the SBA does not preclude a contracting officer from awarding a contract to the referred concern, nor does it prevent the concern from making an offer on any other procurement.

[FAC 97-1, 62 FR 44802, 8/22/97, effective 8/22/97, finalized without change, FAC 97-4, 63 FR 9048, 2/23/98, effective 4/24/98]

19.602-4 Awarding the contract.

(a) If new information causes the contracting officer to determine that the concern referred to the SBA is actually responsible to perform the contract, and award has not already been made under paragraph (c) of this subsection, the contracting officer shall reverse the determination of nonresponsibility, notify the SBA of this action, withdraw the referral, and proceed to award the contract.

(b) The contracting officer shall award the contract to the concern in question if the SBA issues a COC after receiving the referral. An SBA-certified concern shall not be required to meet any other requirements of responsibility. SBA COC's are conclusive with respect to all elements of responsibility of prospective small business contractors.

(c) The contracting officer shall proceed with the acquisition and award the contract to another appropriately selected and responsible offeror if the SBA has not issued a COC within 15 business days (or a longer period of time agreed to with the SBA) after receiving the referral.

SUBPART 19.7—THE SMALL BUSINESS SUBCONTRACTING PROGRAM

19.701 Definitions.

As used in this subpart—

Alaska Native Corporation (ANC) means any Regional Corporation, Village corporation, Urban Corporation, or Group Corporation organized under the laws of the State of Alaska in accordance with the Alaska Native Claims Settlement Act, as amended (43 U.S.C.A. 1601, *et seq.*) and which is considered a minority and economically disadvantaged concern under the criteria at 43 U.S.C. 1626(e) (1). This definition also includes ANC direct and indirect subsidiary corporations, joint ventures, and partnerships that meet the requirements of 43 U.S.C. 1626(e)(2).

Commercial plan means a subcontracting plan (including goals) that covers the offeror's fiscal year and that applies to the entire production of commercial items sold by either the entire company or a portion thereof (e.g., division, plant, or product line).

Electronic Subcontracting Reporting System (eSRS) means the Governmentwide, electronic, web-based system for small business subcontracting program reporting.

Failure to make a good faith effort to comply with the subcontracting plan means willful or intentional failure to perform in accordance with the requirements of the subcontracting plan, or willful or intentional action to frustrate the plan.

Indian tribe means any Indian tribe, band, group, pueblo, or community, including native villages and native groups (including corporations organized by Kenai, Juneau, Sitka, and Kodiak) as defined in the Alaska Native Claims Settlement Act (43 U.S.C.A. 1601 *et seq.*), that is recognized by the Federal Government as eligible for services from the Bureau of Indian Affairs in accordance with 25 U.S.C. 1452(c). This definition also includes Indian-owned economic enterprises that meet the requirements of 25 U.S.C. 1452(e).

Individual subcontracting plan means a subcontracting plan that covers the entire contract period (including option periods), applies to a specific contract, and has goals that are based on the offeror's planned subcontracting in support of the specific contract, except that indirect costs incurred for common or joint purposes may be allocated on a prorated basis to the contract.

Master subcontracting plan means a subcontracting plan that contains all the required elements of an individual subcontracting plan, except goals, and may be incorporated into individual subcontracting plans, provided the master subcontracting plan has been approved.

Reduced payment means a payment that is for less than the amount agreed upon in a subcontract in accordance with its terms and conditions, for supplies and services for which the Government has paid the prime contractor.

Subcontract means any agreement (other than one involving an employer-employee relationship) entered into by a Government prime contractor or subcontractor calling for supplies and/or services required for performance of the contract, contract modification, or subcontract.

Total contract dollars means the final anticipated dollar value, including the dollar value of all options.

Untimely payment means a payment to a subcontractor that is more than 90 days past due under the terms and conditions of a subcontract for supplies and services for which the Government has paid the prime contractor.

[FAC 97-5, 63 FR 34058, 6/22/98, effective 8/21/98; FAC 97-22, 66 FR 2116, 1/10/2001, effective 3/12/2001, delay of effective date, 66 FR 14259, 3/9/2001, effective 5/11/2001; FAC 2005-19, 72 FR 46345, 8/17/2007, effective 9/17/2007; FAC 2005-25, 73 FR 21779, 4/22/2008, effective 4/22/2008; FAC 2005-42, 75 FR 34260, 6/16/2010, effective 7/16/2010; FAC 2005-89, 81 FR 45833, 7/14/2016, effective 11/1/2016; FAC 2005-94, 81 FR 93481, 12/20/2016, effective 1/19/2017]

19.702 Statutory requirements.

Any contractor receiving a contract with a value greater than the simplified acquisition threshold must agree in the contract that small business, veteran-owned small business, service-disabled veteran-owned small business, HUBZone small business, small disadvantaged business, and women-owned small business concerns will have the maximum practicable opportunity to participate in contract performance consistent with its efficient performance. It is further the policy of the United States that its prime contractors establish procedures to ensure the timely payment of amounts due pursuant to the terms of their subcontracts with small business, veteran-owned small business, service-disabled veteran-owned small business, HUBZone small business, small disadvantaged business, and women-owned small business concerns.

(a) Except as stated in paragraph (b) of this section, section 8(d) of the Small Business Act (15 U.S.C. 637(d)) imposes the following requirements regarding subcontracting with small businesses and small business subcontracting plans:

(1) In negotiated acquisitions, each solicitation of offers to perform a contract that is expected to exceed $700,000 ($1.5 million for construction) and that has subcontracting possibilities, shall require the apparently successful offeror to submit an acceptable subcontracting plan. If the apparently successful offeror fails to negotiate a subcontracting plan acceptable to the contracting officer within the time limit prescribed by the contracting officer, the offeror will be ineligible for award.

(2) In sealed bidding acquisitions, each invitation for bids to perform a contract that is expected to exceed $700,000 ($1.5 million for construction) and that has subcontracting possibilities, shall require the bidder selected for award to submit a subcontracting plan. If the selected bidder fails to submit a plan within the time limit prescribed by the contracting officer, the bidder will be ineligible for award.

(3) Each contract modification that causes the value of a contract without a subcontracting plan to exceed $700,000 ($1.5 million for construction), shall require the contractor to submit a subcontracting plan for the contract, if the contracting officer determines that subcontracting opportunities exist.

(b) Subcontracting plans (see paragraphs (a)(1) and (2) of this section) are not required—

(1) From small business concerns;

(2) For personal services contracts;

(3) For contracts or contract modifications that will be performed entirely outside of the United States and its outlying areas; or

(4) For modifications that are within the scope of the contract and the contract does not contain the clause at 52.219-8, Utilization of Small Business Concerns.

(c) As stated in 15 U.S.C. 637(d)(9), any contractor or subcontractor failing to comply in good faith with the requirements of the subcontracting plan is in material breach of its contract. Further, 15 U.S.C. 637(d)(4)(F) directs that a contractor's failure to make a good faith effort to comply with the requirements of the subcontracting plan shall result in the imposition of liquidated damages.

(d) As authorized by 15 U.S.C. 637(d)(12), certain costs incurred by a mentor firm in providing developmental assistance to a Protege firm under the Department of Defense Pilot Mentor-Protege Program, may be credited as if they were subcontract awards to a protege firm for the purpose of determining whether the mentor firm attains the applicable goals under any subcontracting plan entered into with any executive agency. However, the mentor-protégé agreement must have been approved by the Director, Small Business Programs of the cognizant DoD military department or defense agency, before developmental assistance costs may be credited against subcontract goals. A list of approved agreements may be obtained at *http://www.acq.osd.mil/osbp/mentor protege/*.

[FAC 84-5, 50 FR 1743, 1/11/85, effective 4/1/85; FAC 84-10, 50 FR 27562, 7/3/85, effective 7/3/85; Interim rule, FAC 84-50, 54 FR 30709, 7/21/89, effective 8/15/89; Interim rule, FAC 90-7, 56 FR 41731, 8/22/91, effective 8/22/91; FAC 90-29, 60 FR 34732, 7/3/95, effective 7/3/95; FAC 90-32, 60 FR 48206, 9/18/95, effective 10/1/95; FAC 90-37, 61 FR 2626, 1/26/96, effective 1/26/96; FAC 90-40, 61 FR 39186, 7/26/96, effective 8/26/96; FAC 90-43, Interim rule, 61 FR 67408, 12/20/96, effective 2/18/97; Final rule, 62 FR 40236, 7/25/97, effective 6/30/97; FAC 97-5, 63 FR 34058, 6/22/98, effective 8/21/98; FAC 97-10, 63 FR 70264, 12/18/98, effective 1/4/99; FAC 97-15, 64 FR 72414, 12/27/99, effective 12/27/99; FAC 97-20, 65 FR 60542, 10/11/2000, effective 10/11/2000; FAC 2001-14, 68 FR 28079, 5/22/2003, effective 6/23/2003; FAC 2001-26, 69 FR 76355, 12/20/2004, effective 1/19/2005; FAC 2005-13, 71 FR 57363, 9/28/2006, effective 9/28/2006; FAC 2005-27, 73 FR 53993, 9/17/2008, effective 10/17/2008; FAC 2005-45, 75 FR 53129, 8/30/2010, effective 10/1/2010; FAC 2005-83, 80 FR 38293, 7/2/2015, effective 10/1/2015; FAC 2005-89, 81 FR 45833, 7/14/2016, effective 11/1/2016; FAC 2019-02, 84 FR 19839, 5/6/2019, effective 5/6/2019]

19.703 Eligibility requirements for participating in the program.

(a) Except as provided in paragraph (c) of this section, to be eligible as a subcontractor under the program, a concern must represent itself as a small business, veteran-owned small business, service-disabled veteran-owned small business, HUBZone small business, small disadvantaged business, or women-owned small business concern.

(1) To represent itself as a small business, veteran-owned small business, service-disabled veteran-owned small business, HUBZone small business, small disadvantaged business, or women-owned small busi-

ness concern, a concern must meet the appropriate definition (see 2.101 and 19.001). For subcontracting purposes, a concern is small if it does not exceed the size standard for the NAICS code that the prime contractor determines best describes the product or service being acquired by the subcontract.

(2) (i) The prime contractor may accept a subcontractor's written representations of its size and socioeconomic status as a small business, small disadvantaged business, veteran-owned small business, service-disabled veteran-owned small business, or a women-owned small business, if the subcontractor represents that the size and socioeconomic status representation with its offer are current, accurate, and complete as of the date of the offer for the subcontracts; or

(ii) The prime contractor may accept a subcontractor's representation of its size and socioeconomic status as a small business, small disadvantaged business, veteran-owned small business, service-disabled veteran-owned small business, or a women-owned small business in the System for Award Management (SAM) if—

(A) The subcontractor is registered in SAM; and

(B) The subcontractor represents that the size and socioeconomic status representations made in SAM are current, accurate and complete as of the date of the offer for the subcontract.

(iii) The prime contractor may not require the use of SAM for the purposes of representing size or socioeconomic status in connection with a subcontract.

(iv) In accordance with 13 CFR 121.411, 124.1015, 125.29, 126.900, and 127.700, a prime contractor acting in good faith is not liable for misrepresentations made by its subcontractors regarding the subcontractor's size or socioeconomic status.

(b) The contractor, the contracting officer, or any other interested party can challenge a subcontractor's size status representation by filing a protest, in accordance with 13 CFR 121.1001 through 121.1008.

(c) (1) In accordance with 43 U.S.C. 1626, the following procedures apply:

(i) Subcontracts awarded to an ANC or Indian tribe shall be counted towards the subcontracting goals for small business and small disadvantaged business (SDB) concerns, regardless of the size or Small Business Administration certification status of the ANC or Indian tribe.

(ii) Where one or more subcontractors are in the subcontract tier between the prime contractor and the ANC or Indian tribe, the ANC or Indian tribe shall designate the appropriate contractor(s) to count the subcontract towards its small business and small disadvantaged business subcontracting goals.

(A) In most cases, the appropriate contractor is the contractor that awarded the subcontract to the ANC or Indian tribe.

(B) If the ANC or Indian tribe designates more than one contractor to count the subcontract toward its goals, the ANC or Indian tribe shall designate only a portion of the total subcontract award to each contractor. The sum of the amounts designated to various contractors cannot exceed the total value of the subcontract.

(C) The ANC or Indian tribe shall give a copy of the written designation to the contracting officer, the prime contractor, and the subcontractors in between the prime contractor and the ANC or Indian tribe within 30 days of the date of the subcontract award.

(D) If the contracting officer does not receive a copy of the ANC's or the Indian tribe's written designation within 30 days of the subcontract award, the contractor that awarded the subcontract to the ANC or Indian tribe will be considered the designated contractor.

(2) A contractor acting in good faith may rely on the written representation of an ANC or an Indian tribe as to the status of the ANC or Indian tribe unless an interested party challenges its status or the contracting officer has independent reason to question its status. In the event of a challenge of a representation of an ANC or Indian tribe, the interested parties shall follow the procedures at 26.103(b) through (e).

(d) (1) The contractor shall confirm that a subcontractor representing itself as a HUBZone small business concern is certified by SBA as a HUBZone small business concern by accessing the SAM or by contacting the SBA. Options for contacting the SBA include—

(i) HUBZone small business database search application Web page at *http://dsbs.sba.gov/dsbs/dsp_searchhubzone.cfm*.

(ii) In writing to the Director/HUBZone Program, U.S. Small Business Administration, 409 3rd Street, SW., Washington DC 20416; or

(iii) E-mail at *hubzone@sba.gov*.

(2) Protests challenging the socioeconomic status of a HUBZone small business concern must be filed in accordance with 13 CFR 126.801.

(e) The contracting officer or the SBA may protest the disadvantaged status of a proposed subcontractor. Protests challenging a subcontractor's small disadvantaged business representation must be filed in accordance with 13 CFR 124.1007 through 124.1014. Other interested parties may submit information to the contracting officer or the SBA in an effort to persuade the contracting officer or the SBA to initiate a protest. Such protests, in order to be considered timely, must be submitted to the SBA prior to completion of performance by the intended subcontractor.

[FAC 84-12, 51 FR 2664, 1/17/86, effective 1/20/86; FAC 84-56, 55 FR 3882, 2/5/90, effective 2/5/90; FAC 90-3, 55 FR 52792, 12/21/90, effective 1/22/91; FAC 90-32, 60 FR 48206, 9/18/95, effective 10/1/95; FAC 90-45, Final rule, 62 FR 224, 1/2/97, effective 1/1/97; FAC 97-5, 63 FR 34058, 6/22/98, effective 8/21/98; FAC 97-7, 63 FR 36120, 7/1/98, effective 1/1/99, corrected, interim final rule, 63 FR 71721, 12/29/98, FAC 97-13, 7/2/99; FAC 97-10, 63 FR 70264, 12/18/98, effective 1/4/99; FAC 97-13, 64 FR 36222, 7/2/99, effective 10/1/99; FAC 97-20, 65 FR 60542, 10/11/2000, effective 10/11/2000; FAC 97-22, 66 FR 2116, 1/10/2001, effective 3/12/2001; Delay of effective date, 66 FR 14259, 3/9/2001, effective 5/11/2001; FAC 2001-09, 67 FR 56115, 8/30/2002, effective 8/30/2002; FAC 2005-05, 70 FR 43581, 7/27/2005, effective 7/27/2005; FAC 2005-09, Final rule, 71 FR 20303, 4/19/2006, effective 4/19/2006; FAC 2005-19, 72 FR 46345, 8/17/2007, effective 9/17/2007; FAC 2005-47, 75 FR 77727, 12/13/2010, effective 1/12/2011; 75 FR 77737, 12/13/2010, effective 12/13/2010; FAC 2005-54, 76 FR 68026, 11/2/2011, effective 11/2/2011; FAC 2005-67, 78 FR 37676, 6/21/2013, effective 7/22/2013; FAC 2005-76, 79 FR 43580, 7/25/2014, effective 8/25/2014; FAC 2005-77, 79 FR 61746, 10/14/2014, effective 10/14/2014; FAC 2005-89, 81 FR 45833, 7/14/2016, effective 11/1/2016; FAC 2005-101, 83 FR 48691, 9/26/2018, effective 10/26/2018]

19.704 Subcontracting plan requirements.

(a) Each subcontracting plan required under 19.702(a) (1) and (2) must include—

(1) Separate percentage goals for using small business (including ANCs and Indian tribes), veteran-owned small business, service-disabled veteran-owned small business, HUBZone small business, small disadvantaged business (including ANCs and Indian tribes), and women-owned small business concerns as subcontractors;

(2) A statement of the total dollars planned to be subcontracted and a statement of the total dollars planned to be subcontracted to small business (including ANCs and Indian tribes), veteran-owned small business, service-disabled veteran-owned small business, HUBZone small business, small disadvantaged business (including ANCs and Indian tribes) and women-owned small business concerns, as a percentage of total subcontract dollars. For individual subcontracting plans only, a contracting officer may require the goals referenced in paragraph (a) (1) of this section to be calculated as a percentage of total contract dollars, in addition to the goals established as a percentage of total subcontract dollars;

(3) A description of the principal types of supplies and services to be subcontracted and an identification of types of supplies or services planned for subcontracting to small business (including ANCs and Indian

tribes), veteran-owned small business, service-disabled veteran-owned small business, HUBZone small business, small disadvantaged business (including ANCs and Indian tribes), and women-owned small business concerns;

(4) A description of the method used to develop the subcontracting goals;

(5) A description of the method used to identify potential sources for solicitation purposes;

(6) A statement as to whether or not the offeror included indirect costs in establishing subcontracting goals, and a description of the method used to determine the proportionate share of indirect costs to be incurred with small business (including ANCs and Indian tribes), veteran-owned small business, service-disabled veteran-owned small business, HUBZone small business, small disadvantaged business (including ANCs and Indian tribes), and women-owned small business concerns;

(7) The name of an individual employed by the offeror who will administer the offeror's subcontracting program, and a description of the duties of the individual;

(8) A description of the efforts the offeror will make to ensure that small business, veteran-owned small business, service-disabled veteran-owned small business, HUBZone small business, small disadvantaged business, and women-owned small business concerns have an equitable opportunity to compete for subcontracts;

(9) Assurances that the offeror will include the clause at 52.219-8, Utilization of Small Business Concerns (see 19.708(a)), in all subcontracts that offer further subcontracting opportunities, and that the offeror will require all subcontractors (except small business concerns) that receive subcontracts in excess of $700,000 ($1.5 million for construction) to adopt a plan that complies with the requirements of the clause at 52.219-9, Small Business Subcontracting Plan (see 19.708(b));

(10) Assurances that the offeror will—

(i) Cooperate in any studies or surveys as may be required;

(ii) Submit periodic reports so that the Government can determine the extent of compliance by the offeror with the subcontracting plan;

(iii) After November 30, 2017, include subcontracting data for each order when reporting subcontracting achievements for indefinite-delivery, indefinite-quantity contracts with individual subcontracting plans where the contract is intended for use by multiple agencies;

(iv) Submit the Individual Subcontract Report (ISR), and the Summary Subcontract Report (SSR) using the Electronic Subcontracting Reporting System (eSRS) (*http://www.esrs.gov*), following the instructions in the eSRS.

(A) The ISR shall be submitted semiannually during contract performance for the periods ending March 31 and September 30. A report is also required for each contract within 30 days of contract completion. Reports are due 30 days after the close of each reporting period, unless otherwise directed by the contracting officer. Reports are required when due, regardless of whether there has been any subcontracting activity since the inception of the contract or the previous reporting period. When a contracting officer rejects an ISR, the contractor is required to submit a revised ISR within 30 days of receiving the notice of the ISR rejection.

(B) The SSR shall be submitted annually by October 30 for the twelve-month period ending September 30. When an SSR is rejected, the contractor is required to submit a revised SSR within 30 days of receiving the notice of SSR rejection;

(v) Ensure that its subcontractors with subcontracting plans agree to submit the ISR and/or the SSR using the eSRS;

(vi) Provide its prime contract number, its unique entity identifier, and the e-mail address of the offeror's official responsible for acknowledging receipt of or rejecting the ISRs to all first-tier subcontractors with subcontracting plans so they can enter this information into the eSRS when submitting their ISRs; and

(vii) Require that each subcontractor with a subcontracting plan provide the prime contract number, its own unique entity identifier number, and the e-mail address of the subcontractor's official responsible for acknowledging receipt of or rejecting the ISRs, to its subcontractors with subcontracting plans;

(11) A description of the types of records that will be maintained concerning procedures adopted to comply with the requirements and goals in the plan, including establishing source lists; and a description of the offeror's efforts to locate small business, veteran-owned small business, service-disabled veteran-owned small business, HUBZone small business, small disadvantaged business, and women-owned small business concerns and to award subcontracts to them;

(12) Assurances that the offeror will make a good faith effort to acquire articles, equipment, supplies, services, or materials, or obtain the performance of construction work from the small business concerns that the offeror used in preparing the bid or proposal, in the same or greater scope, amount, and quality used in preparing and submitting the bid or proposal. Responding to a request for a quote does not constitute use in preparing a bid or proposal. An offeror used a small business concern in preparing the bid or proposal if—

(i) The offeror identifies the small business concern as a subcontractor in the bid or proposal or associated small business subcontracting plan, to furnish certain supplies or perform a portion of the contract; or

(ii) The offeror used the small business concern's pricing or cost information or technical expertise in preparing the bid or proposal, where there is written evidence of an intent or understanding that the small business concern will be awarded a subcontract for the related work if the offeror is awarded the contract;

(13) Assurances that the contractor will provide the contracting officer with a written explanation if the contractor fails to acquire articles, equipment, supplies, services or materials or obtain the performance of construction work as described in (a) (12) of this section. This written explanation will be submitted to the contracting officer within 30 days of contract completion;

(14) Assurances that the contractor will not prohibit a subcontractor from discussing with the contracting officer any material matter pertaining to payment to or utilization of a subcontractor; and

(15) Assurances that the offeror will pay its small business subcontractors on time and in accordance with the terms and conditions of the subcontract, and notify the contracting officer if the offeror pays a reduced or an untimely payment to a small business subcontractor (see 52.242-5).

(b) Contractors may establish, on a plant or division-wide basis, a master subcontracting plan (see 19.701) that contains all the elements required by the clause at 52.219-9, Small Business Subcontracting Plan, except goals. master subcontracting plans shall be effective for a 3-year period after approval by the contracting officer; however, it is incumbent upon contractors to maintain and update master subcontracting plans. Changes required to update master plans are not effective until approved by the contracting officer. A master plan, when incorporated in an individual plan, shall apply to that contract throughout the life of the contract.

(c) For multiyear contracts or contracts containing options, the cumulative value of the basic contract and all options is considered in determining whether a subcontracting plan is necessary. If a subcontracting plan is necessary and the offeror is submitting an individual subcontracting plan, the individual subcontracting plan shall contain all the elements required by paragraph (a) of this section and shall contain separate statements and goals based on total subcontract dollars for the basic contract and for each option.

(d) A commercial plan (as defined in 19.701) is the preferred type of subcontracting plan for contractors furnishing commercial items. Once a contractor's commercial plan has been approved, the Government shall not require another subcontracting plan from the same contractor while the plan remains in effect, as long as the product or service being provided by the contractor continues to meet the definition of a commercial item. The contractor shall—

(1) Submit the commercial plan to either the first contracting officer awarding a contract subject to the plan during the contractor's fiscal year, or, if the contractor has ongoing contracts with commercial plans, to the contracting officer responsible for the contract with the latest completion date. The contracting officer shall negotiate the commercial plan for the Government. The approved commercial plan shall remain in effect during the contractor's fiscal year for all Government contracts in effect during that period;

(2) Submit a new commercial plan, 30 working days before the end of the Contractor's fiscal year, to the contracting officer responsible for the uncompleted Government contract with the latest completion date. The contractor must provide to each contracting officer responsible for an ongoing contract subject to the plan, the identity of the contracting officer that will be negotiating the new plan;

(3) When the new commercial plan is approved, provide a copy of the approved plan to each contracting officer responsible for an ongoing contract that is subject to the plan; and

(4) Comply with the reporting requirements stated in paragraph (a)(10) of this section by submitting one SSR in eSRS, for all contracts covered by its commercial plan. This report will be acknowledged or rejected in eSRS by the contracting officer who approved the plan. The report shall be submitted within 30 days after the end of the Government's fiscal year.

[FAC 84-12, 51 FR 2664, 1/17/86, effective 1/20/86; FAC 84-49, 54 FR 29281, 7/11/89, effective 8/10/89; FAC 90-32, 60 FR 48206, 9/18/95, effective 10/1/95; FAC 90-39, 61 FR 31612, 6/20/96, effective 8/19/96; FAC 97-5, 63 FR 34058, 6/22/98, effective 8/21/98; FAC 97-10, 63 FR 70264, 12/18/98, effective 1/4/99; FAC 97-20, 65 FR 60542, 10/11/2000, effective 10/11/2000; FAC 2001-01, 66 FR 53478, 10/22/2001, effective 10/22/2001, corrected 67 FR 1858, 1/14/2002, effective 1/14/2002; FAC 2001-09, 67 FR 56115, 8/30/2002, effective 8/30/2002; FAC 2005-13, 71 FR 57363, 9/28/2006, effective 9/28/2006; FAC 2005-19, 72 FR 46345, 8/17/2007, effective 9/17/2007; FAC 2005-25, 73 FR 21779, 4/22/2008, effective 4/22/2008; FAC 2005-42, 75 FR 34260, 6/16/2010, effective 7/16/2010; FAC 2005-45, 75 FR 53129, 8/30/2010, effective 10/1/2010; FAC 2005-83, 80 FR 38293, 7/2/2015, effective 10/1/2015; FAC 2005-89, 81 FR 45833, 7/14/2016, effective 11/1/2016; FAC 2005-91, 81 FR 67736, 9/30/2016, effective 10/31/2016; FAC 2005-94, 81 FR 93481, 12/20/2016, effective 1/19/2017; FAC 2005-100, 83 FR 42571, 8/22/2018, effective 8/22/2018]

19.705 Responsibilities of the contracting officer under the subcontracting assistance program. (No Text)

19.705-1 General.

(a) The contracting officer may encourage the development of increased subcontracting opportunities in negotiated acquisition by providing monetary incentives such as payments based on actual subcontracting achievement or award-fee contracting (see the clause at 52.219-10, Incentive Subcontracting Program, and 19.708(c)). When using any contractual incentive provision based upon rewarding the contractor monetarily for exceeding goals in the subcontracting plan, the contracting officer must ensure that (a) the goals are realistic and (b) any rewards for exceeding the goals are commensurate with the efforts the contractor would not have otherwise expended. Incentive provisions should normally be negotiated after reaching final agreement with the contractor on the subcontracting plan.

(b)(1) Except where a contractor has a commercial plan, the contracting officer shall require a subcontracting plan for each indefinite-delivery, indefinite-quantity contract (including task or delivery order contracts, FSS, GWACs, and MACs), when the estimated value of the contract meets the subcontracting plan thresholds at 19.702(a)(1) and small business subcontracting opportunities exist.

(2) Contracting officers placing orders may establish small business subcontracting goals for each order. Establishing goals shall not be in the form of a new subcontracting plan as a contract may not have more than one plan (19.705-2(e)).

[FAC 90-32, 60 FR 48206, 9/18/95, effective 10/1/95; FAC 97-5, 63 FR 34058, 6/22/98, effective 8/21/98; FAC 97-7, 63 FR 36120, 7/1/98, effective 1/1/99, finalized without change, FAC 97-13, 7/2/99; FAC 2005-77, 79 FR 61746, 10/14/2014, effective 10/14/2014; FAC 2005-89, 81 FR 45833, 7/14/2016, effective 11/1/2016]

19.705-2 Determining the need for a subcontracting plan.

The contracting officer must take the following actions to determine whether a proposed contractual action requires a subcontracting plan:

(a) (1) Determine whether the proposed total contract-dollars will exceed the subcontracting plan threshold in 19.702(a).

(2) Determine whether a proposed modification will cause the total contract dollars to exceed the subcontracting plan threshold (see 19.702(a)).

(b) Determine whether subcontracting possibilities exist by considering relevant factors such as—

(1) Whether firms engaged in the business of furnishing the types of items to be acquired customarily contract for performance of part of the work or maintain sufficient in-house capability to perform the work; and

(2) Whether there are likely to be product prequalification requirements.

(3) Whether the firm can acquire any portion of the work with minimal or no disruption to performance (with consideration given to the time remaining until contract completion), and at fair market value, when a determination is made in accordance with paragraph (a)(2).

(c) If it is determined that there are no subcontracting possibilities, the determination-shall include a detailed rationale, be approved at a level above the contracting officer, and placed in the contract file.

(d) In solicitations for negotiated acquisitions, the contracting officer may require the submission of subcontracting plans with initial offers, or at any other time prior to award. In determining when subcontracting plans should be required, as well as when and with whom plans should be negotiated, the contracting officer must consider the integrity of the competitive process, the goal of affording maximum practicable opportunity for small business, veteran-owned small business, service-disabled veteran-owned small business, HUBZone small business, small disadvantaged business, and women-owned small business concerns to participate, and the burden placed on offerors.

(e) A contract may not have more than one subcontracting plan. However, a contracting officer may establish separate subcontracting goals for each order under an indefinite-delivery, indefinite-quantity contract (19.705-1(b)(2)). When a contract modification exceeds the subcontracting plan threshold (see 19.702(a)) or an option is exercised, the goals of an existing subcontracting plan shall be amended to reflect any new subcontracting opportunities not envisioned at the time of contract award. These goal changes do not apply retroactively.

(f) If a subcontracting plan has been added to the contract due to a modification (see 19.702(a)(3)) or a size re-representation (see 19.301-2(e)), the subcontracting goals apply from the date of incorporation of the subcontracting plan into the contract and the contractor's achievements must be reported on the ISR (or the SF-294, if applicable) on a cumulative basis from the date of incorporation of the subcontracting plan into the contract.

[FAC 84-12, 51 FR 2664, 1/17/86, effective 1/20/86; FAC 84-16, 51 FR 19716, 5/30/86, effective 5/30/86; FAC 90-32, 60 FR 48206, 9/18/95, effective 10/1/95; FAC 90-37, 61 FR 2626, 1/26/96, effective 3/26/96; FAC 97-10, 63 FR 70264, 12/18/98, effective 1/4/99; FAC 97-20, 65 FR 60542, 10/11/2000, effective 10/11/2000; FAC 2001-01, 66 FR 53478, 10/22/2001, effective 10/22/2001; FAC 2005-25, 73 FR 21779, 4/22/2008, effective 4/22/2008; FAC 2005-42, 75 FR 34260, 6/16/2010, effective

7/16/2010; FAC 2005-89, 81 FR 45833, 7/14/2016, effective 11/1/2016]

19.705-3 Preparing the solicitation.

The contracting officer shall provide the Small Business Administration's (SBA's) procurement center representative (or, if a procurement center representative is not assigned, see 19.402(a)) a reasonable period of time to review any solicitation requiring submission of a subcontracting plan and to submit advisory findings before the solicitation is issued.

[FAC 2005-10, 71 FR 36925, 6/28/2006, effective 7/28/2006]

19.705-4 Reviewing the subcontracting plan.

The contracting officer shall review the subcontracting plan for adequacy, ensuring that the required information, goals, and assurances are included (see 19.704).

(a) No detailed standards apply to every subcontracting plan. Instead, the contracting officer shall consider each plan in terms of the circumstances of the particular acquisition, including—

(1) Previous involvement of small business concerns as prime contractors or subcontractors in similar acquisitions;

(2) Proven methods of involving small business concerns as subcontractors in similar acquisitions; and

(3) The relative success of methods the contractor intends to use to meet the goals and requirements of the plan, as evidenced by records maintained by contractors.

(b) If, under a sealed bid solicitation, a bidder submits a plan that does not cover each of the 15 required elements (see 19.704), the contracting officer shall advise the bidder of the deficiency and request submission of a revised plan by a specific date. If the bidder does not submit a plan that incorporates the required elements within the time allotted, the bidder shall be ineligible for award. If the plan, although responsive, evidences the bidder's intention not to comply with its obligations under the clause at 52.219-8, Utilization of Small Business Concerns, the contracting officer may find the bidder nonresponsible.

(c) In negotiated acquisitions, the contracting officer shall determine whether the plan is acceptable based on the negotiation of each of the 15 elements of the plan (see 19.704). Subcontracting goals should be set at a level that the parties reasonably expect can result from the offeror expending good faith efforts to use small business, veteran-owned small business, service-disabled veteran-owned small business, HUBZone small business, small disadvantaged business, and women-owned small business subcontractors to the maximum practicable extent. The contracting officer shall take particular care to ensure that the offeror has not submitted unreasonably low goals to minimize exposure to liquidated damages and to avoid the administrative burden of substantiating good faith efforts. Additionally, particular attention should be paid to the identification of steps that, if taken, would be considered a good faith effort. No goal should be negotiated upward if it is apparent that a higher goal will significantly increase the Government's cost or seriously impede the attainment of acquisition objectives. An incentive subcontracting clause (see 52.219-10, Incentive Subcontracting Program), may be used when additional and unique contract effort, such as providing technical assistance, could significantly increase subcontract awards to small business, small disadvantaged business, veteran-owned small business, service-disabled veteran-owned small business, HUBZone small business, or women-owned small business concerns.

(d) In determining the acceptability of a proposed subcontracting plan, the contracting officer should take the following actions:

(1) Obtain information available from the cognizant contract administration office, as provided for in 19.706(a), and evaluate the offeror's past performance in awarding subcontracts for the same or similar products or services to small business, veteran-owned small business, service-disabled veteran-owned small business, HUBZone small business, small disadvantaged business, and women-owned small business concerns. If information is not available on a specific type of product or service, evaluate the offeror's

overall past performance and consider the performance of other contractors on similar efforts.

(2) In accordance with 15 U.S.C. 637(d)(4)(F)(iii), ensure that the goals offered are attainable in relation to—

(i) The subcontracting opportunities available to the contractor, commensurate with the efficient and economical performance of the contract;

(ii) The pool of eligible subcontractors available to fulfill the subcontracting opportunities; and

(iii) The actual performance of such contractor in fulfilling the subcontracting goals specified in prior plans.

(3) Ensure that the subcontracting goals are consistent with the offeror's certified cost or pricing data or data other than certified cost or pricing data.

(4) Evaluate the offeror's make-or-buy policy or program to ensure that it does not conflict with the offeror's proposed subcontracting plan and is in the Government's interest. If the contract involves products or services that are particularly specialized or not generally available in the commercial market, consider the offeror's current capacity to perform the work and the possibility of reduced subcontracting opportunities.

(5) Evaluate subcontracting potential, considering the offeror's make-or-buy policies or programs, the nature of the supplies or services to be subcontracted, the known availability of small business, veteran-owned small business, service-disabled veteran- owned small business, HUBZone small business, small disadvantaged business, and women-owned small business concerns in the geographical area where the work will be performed, and the potential contractor's long-standing contractual relationship with its suppliers.

(6) Advise the offeror of available sources of information on potential small business, veteran-owned small business, service-disabled veteran-owned small business, HUBZone small business, small disadvantaged business, and women-owned small business subcontractors, as well as any specific concerns known to be potential subcontractors. If the offerors proposed goals are questionable, the contracting officer must emphasize that the information should be used to develop realistic and acceptable goals.

(7) Obtain advice and recommendations from the SBA procurement center representative (or, if a procurement center representative is not assigned, see 19.402(a)) and the agency small business specialist.

[FAC 84-5, 50 FR 1743, 1/11/85, effective 4/1/85; FAC 84-16, 51 FR 19716, 5/30/86, effective 5/30/86; Interim rule, FAC 84-50, 54 FR 30709, 7/21/89, effective 8/15/89; FAC 90-3, 55 FR 52792, 12/21/90, effective 1/22/91; FAC 90-32, 60 FR 48206, 9/18/95, effective 10/1/95; FAC 97-5, 63 FR 34058, 6/22/98, effective 8/21/98; FAC 97-7, 63 FR 36120, 7/1/98, effective 1/1/99, finalized without change, FAC 97-13, 7/2/99; FAC 97-10, 63 FR 70264, 12/18/98, effective 1/4/99; FAC 97-20, 65 FR 60542, 10/11/2000, effective 10/11/2000; FAC 2001-01, 66 FR 53478, 10/22/2001, effective 10/22/2001, corrected 67 FR 1858, 1/14/2002, effective 1/14/2002; FAC 2005-10, 71 FR 36925, 6/28/2006, effective 7/28/2006; FAC 2005-45, 75 FR 53135, 8/30/2010, effective 10/1/2010; FAC 2005-77, 79 FR 61746, 10/14/2014, effective 10/14/2014; FAC 2005-89, 81 FR 45833, 7/14/2016, effective 11/1/2016; FAC 2005-94, 81 FR 93481, 12/20/2016, effective 1/19/2017]

19.705-5 Awards involving subcontracting plans.

(a) In making an award that requires a subcontracting plan, the contracting officer shall be responsible for the following:

(1) Consider the contractor's compliance with the subcontracting plans submitted on previous contracts as a factor in determining contractor responsibility.

(2) Assure that a subcontracting plan was submitted when required.

(3) Notify the SBA procurement center representative (or, if a procurement center representative is not assigned, see 19.402(a)) of the opportunity to review the proposed contract (including the plan and supporting documentation). The notice shall

be issued in sufficient time to provide the representative a reasonable time to review the material and submit advisory recommendations to the contracting officer. Failure of the representative to respond in a reasonable period of time shall not delay contract award.

(4) Determine any fee that may be payable if an incentive is used in conjunction with the subcontracting plan.

(5) Ensure that an acceptable plan is incorporated into and made a material part of the contract.

(b) Letter contracts and similar undefinitized instruments, which would otherwise meet the requirements of 19.702(a)(1) and (2), shall contain at least a preliminary basic plan addressing the requirements of 19.704 and in such cases require the negotiation of the final plan within 90 days after award or before definitization, whichever occurs first.

[FAC 84-5, 50 FR 1743, 1/11/85, effective 4/1/85; FAC 2005-10, 71 FR 36925, 6/28/2006, effective 7/28/2006]

19.705-6 Postaward responsibilities of the contracting officer.

After a contract or contract modification containing a subcontracting plan is awarded or an existing subcontracting plan is amended, the contracting officer shall do the following:

(a) Notify the SBA of the award by sending a copy of the award document to the Area Director, Office of Government Contracting, in the SBA area office where the contract will be performed.

(b) Forward a copy of each commercial plan and any associated approvals to the Area Director, Office of Government Contracting, in the SBA area office where the contractor's headquarters is located.

(c) Give to the SBA procurement center representative (or, if a procurement center representative is not assigned, see 19.402(a)) a copy of—

(1) Any subcontracting plan submitted in response to a sealed bid solicitation; and

(2) The final negotiated subcontracting plan that was incorporated into a negotiated contract or contract modification.

(d) Notify the SBA procurement center representative (or, if a procurement center representative is not assigned, see 19.402(a)) of the opportunity to review subcontracting plans in connection with contract modifications.

(e) Forward a copy of each plan, or a determination that there is no requirement for a subcontracting plan, to the cognizant contract administration office.

(f) Monitor the prime contractor's compliance with its subcontracting plan, to include the following:

(1) Ensure that subcontracting reports are submitted into the eSRS within 30 days after the report ending date (*e.g.*, by October 30th for the fiscal year ended September 30th).

(2) Review ISRs, and where applicable, SSRs, in eSRS within 60 days of the report ending date (*e.g.*, by November 30th for a report submitted for the fiscal year ended September 30th).

(3) Either acknowledge receipt of or reject the reports in accordance with subpart 19.7, 52.219-9, Small Business Subcontracting Plan, and the eSRS instructions (*www.esrs.gov*).

(i) The authority to acknowledge or reject SSRs for commercial plans resides with the contracting officer who approved the commercial plan.

(ii) If a report is rejected, the contracting officer must provide an explanation for the rejection to allow the prime contractor the opportunity to respond specifically to identified deficiencies.

(g) Evaluate the prime contractor's compliance with its subcontracting plan, to include the following:

(1) Assess whether the prime contractor made a good faith effort to comply with its small business subcontracting plan (see 13 CFR 125.3(d)(3)).

(2) Assess the prime contractor's written explanation concerning the prime contractor's failure to use a small business concern in the performance of the contract in the same scope, amount, and quality used in preparing and submitting the bid or proposal, if applicable.

(h) Initiate action to assess liquidated damages in accordance with 19.705-7 upon a recommendation by the administrative contracting officer or receipt of other reliable evidence to indicate that such action is warranted.

(i) Take action to enforce the terms of the contract upon receipt of a notice under 19.706(f).

(j) Acknowledge receipt of or reject the ISR and the SSR in the eSRS. Acknowledge receipt does not mean acceptance or approval of the report. The report shall be reject if it is not adequately completed, for instance, if there are errors, omissions, or incomplete data. Failure to meet the goals of the subcontracting plan is not a valid reason for reject the report.

[FAC 84-26, 52 FR 19803, 5/27/87, effective 7/30/87; FAC 84-38, 53 FR 27464, 7/20/88, effective 8/19/88; FAC 84-39, 53 FR 34228, 9/2/88, effective 10/3/88; Interim rule, FAC 84-50, 54 FR 30709, 7/21/89, effective 8/15/89; FAC 90-3, 55 FR 52792, 12/21/90, effective 1/22/91; FAC 97-5, 63 FR 34058, 6/22/98, effective 8/21/98; FAC 97-10, 63 FR 70264, 12/18/98, effective 1/4/99; FAC 2005-10, 71 FR 36925, 6/28/2006, effective 7/28/2006; FAC 2005-25, 73 FR 21779, 4/22/2008, effective 4/22/2008; FAC 2005-42, 75 FR 34260, 6/16/2010, effective 7/16/2010; FAC 2005-89, 81 FR 45833, 7/14/2016, effective 11/1/2016]

19.705-7 Liquidated damages.

(a) Maximum practicable utilization of small business, veteran-owned small business, service-disabled veteran-owned small business, HUBZone small business, small disadvantaged business and women-owned small business concerns as subcontractors in Government contracts is a matter of national interest with both social and economic benefits. When a contractor fails to make a good faith effort to comply with a subcontracting plan, these objectives are not achieved, and 15 U.S.C. 637(d)(4)(F) directs that liquidated damages shall be paid by the contractor.

(b) The amount of damages attributable to the contractor's failure to comply shall be an amount equal to the actual dollar amount by which the contractor failed to achieve each subcontracting goal.

(c) If, at completion of the basic contract or any option, or in the case of a commercial plan, at the close of the fiscal year for which the plan is applicable, a contractor has failed to meet its subcontracting goals, the contracting officer shall review all available information for an indication that the contractor has not made a good faith effort to comply with the plan. If no such indication is found, the contracting officer shall document the file accordingly. If the contracting officer decides in accordance with paragraph (d) of this subsection that the contractor failed to make a good faith effort to comply with its subcontracting plan, the contracting officer shall give the contractor written notice specifying the failure, advising the contractor of the possibility that the contractor may have to pay to the Government liquidated damages, and providing a period of 15 working days (or longer period as necessary) within which to respond. The notice shall give the contractor an opportunity to demonstrate what good faith efforts have been made before the contracting officer issues the final decision, and shall further state that failure of the contractor to respond may be taken as an admission that no valid explanation exists.

(d) In determining whether a contractor failed to make a good faith effort to comply with its subcontracting plan, a contracting officer must look to the totality of the contractor's actions, consistent with the information and assurances provided in its plan. The fact that the contractor failed to meet its subcontracting goals does not, in and of itself, constitute a failure to make a good faith effort. For example, notwithstanding a contractor's diligent effort to identify and solicit offers from small business, veteran-owned small business, service-disabled veteran-owned small business, HUBZone small business, small disadvantaged business and women-owned small business concerns, factors such as unavailability of anticipated sources or unreasonable prices may frustrate achievement of the contractor's goals. However, when considered in the context of the contractor's total effort in accordance with its plan, the following, though not all inclusive, may be considered as indicators of a failure to make a good faith effort: a failure to attempt to identify, contact, solicit, or consider for contract award small business, veteran-owned small business service-disabled veteran-owned small business, HUBZone small business, small disadvantaged or women-owned small business concerns; a failure to designate and maintain a company official to administer the subcontracting program and monitor and enforce compliance with the plan; a failure to submit the ISR, or the SSR, using the eSRS, or as provided in agency regulations; a failure to maintain records or otherwise demonstrate procedures adopted to comply with the plan; or the adoption of company policies or procedures that have as their objectives the frustration of the objectives of the plan.

(e) If, after consideration of all the pertinent data, the contracting officer finds that the contractor failed to make a good faith effort to comply with its subcontracting plan, the contracting officer shall issue a final decision to the contractor to that effect and require the payment of liquidated damages in an amount stated. The contracting officer's final decision shall state that the contractor has the right to appeal under the clause in the contract entitled Disputes.

(f) With respect to commercial plans approved under the clause at 52.219-9, Small Business Subcontracting Plan, the contracting officer that approved the plan shall—

(1) Perform the functions of the contracting officer under this subsection on behalf of all agencies with contracts covered by the commercial plan;

(2) Determine whether or not the goals in the commercial plan were achieved and, if they were not achieved, review all available information for an indication that the contractor has not made a good faith effort to comply with the plan, and document the results of the review;

(3) If a determination is made to assess liquidated damages, in order to calculate and assess the amount of damages, the contracting officer shall ask the contractor to provide—

(i) Contract numbers for the Government contracts subject to the plan;

(ii) The total Government sales during the contractor's fiscal year; and

(iii) The amount of payments made under the Government contracts subject to that plan that contributed to the contractor's total sales during the contractor's fiscal year; and

(4) When appropriate, assess liquidated damages on the Government's behalf, based on the pro rata share of subcontracting attributable to the Government contracts. For example: The contractor's total actual sales were $50 million and its actual subcontracting was $20 million. The Government's total payments under contracts subject to the plan contributing to the contractor's total sales were $5 million, which accounted for 10 percent of the contractor's total sales. Therefore, the pro rata share of subcontracting attributable to the Government contracts would be 10 percent of $20 million, or $2 million. To continue the example, if the contractor failed to achieve its small business goal by 1 percent, the liquidated damages would be calculated as 1 percent of $2 million, or $20,000. The contracting officer shall make similar calculations for each category of small business where the contractor failed to achieve its goal and the sum of the dollars for all of the categories equals the amount of the liquidated damages to be assessed. A copy of the contracting officer's final decision assessing liquidated damages shall be provided to other contracting officers with contracts subject to the commercial plan.

(g) Liquidated damages shall be in addition to any other remedies that the Government may have.

(h) Every contracting officer with a contract that is subject to a commercial plan shall include in the contract file a copy of the approved plan and a copy of the final decision assessing liquidating damages, if applicable.

[Interim rule, FAC 84-50, 54 FR 30709, 7/21/89, effective 8/15/89; FAC 90-32, 60 FR 48206, 9/18/95, effective 10/1/95; FAC 97-5, 63 FR 34058, 6/22/98, effective

8/21/98; FAC 97-10, 63 FR 70264, 12/18/98, effective 1/4/99; FAC 97-20, 65 FR 60542, 10/11/2000, effective 10/11/2000; FAC 2001-01, 66 FR 53478, 10/22/2001, effective 10/22/2001; FAC 2005-25, 73 FR 21779, 4/22/2008, effective 4/22/2008; FAC 2005-42, 75 FR 34260, 6/16/2010, effective 7/16/2010]

19.706 Responsibilities of the cognizant administrative contracting officer.

The administrative contracting officer is responsible for assisting in evaluating subcontracting plans, and for monitoring, evaluating, and documenting contractor performance under the clause prescribed in 19.708(b) and any subcontracting plan included in the contract. The contract administration office shall provide the necessary information and advice to support the contracting officer, as appropriate, by furnishing—

(a) Documentation on the contractor's performance and compliance with subcontracting plans under previous contracts;

(b) Information on the extent to which the contractor is meeting the plan's goals for subcontracting with eligible small business, veteran-owned small business, service-disabled veteran-owned small business, HUBZone small business, small disadvantaged business, and women-owned small business concerns;

(c) Information on whether the contractor's efforts to ensure the participation of small business, veteran-owned small business, service-disabled veteran-owned small business, HUBZone small business, small disadvantaged business, and women-owned small business concerns are in accordance with its subcontracting plan;

(d) Information on whether the contractor is requiring its subcontractors to adopt similar subcontracting plans;

(e) Immediate notice if, during performance, the contractor is failing to meet its commitments under the clause prescribed in 19.708(b) or the subcontracting plan;

(f) Immediate notice and rationale if, during performance, the contractor is failing to comply in good faith with the subcontracting plan; and

(g) Immediate notice that performance under a contract is complete, that the goals were or were not met, and, if not met, whether there is any indication of a lack of a good faith effort to comply with the subcontracting plan.

[Interim rule, FAC 84-50, 54 FR 30710, 7/21/89, effective 8/15/89; FAC 90-32, 60 FR 48206, 9/18/95, effective 10/1/95; FAC 97-5, 63 FR 34058, 6/22/98, effective 8/21/98; FAC 97-10, 63 FR 70264, 12/18/98, effective 1/4/99; FAC 97-20, 65 FR 60542, 10/11/2000, effective 10/11/2000; FAC 2001-01, 66 FR 53478, 10/22/2001, effective 10/22/2001]

19.707 The Small Business Administration's role in carrying out the program.

(a) Under the program, the SBA may—

(1) Assist both Government agencies and contractors in carrying out their responsibilities with regard to subcontracting plans;

(2) Review (within 5 working days) any solicitation that meets the dollar threshold in 19.702(a)(1) or (2) before the solicitation is issued;

(3) Review (within 5 working days) before execution any negotiated contractual document requiring a subcontracting plan, including the plan itself, and submit recommendations to the contracting officer, which shall be advisory in nature; and

(4) Evaluate compliance with subcontracting plans, either on a contract-by-contract basis, or, in the case of contractors having multiple contracts, on an aggregate basis.

(b) The SBA is not authorized to—

(1) Prescribe the extent to which any contractor or subcontractor shall subcontract,

(2) Specify concerns to which subcontracts will be awarded, or

(3) Exercise any authority regarding the administration of individual prime contracts or subcontracts.

[FAC 84-12, 51 FR 2664, 1/17/86, effective 1/20/86]

19.708 Contract clauses.

(a) Insert the clause at 52.219-8, Utilization of Small Business Concerns, in solicitations and contracts when the contract amount is expected to exceed the simplified acquisition threshold unless—

(1) A personal services contract is contemplated (see 37.104); or

(2) The contract, together with all of its subcontracts, will be performed entirely outside of the United States and its outlying areas.

(b)(1) Insert the clause at 52.219-9, Small Business Subcontracting Plan, in solicitations and contracts that offer subcontracting possibilities, are expected to exceed $700,000 ($1.5 million for construction of any public facility), and are required to include the clause at 52.219-8, Utilization of Small Business Concerns, unless the acquisition is set aside or is to be accomplished under the 8(a) program. When—

(i) Contracting by sealed bidding rather than by negotiation, the contracting officer shall use the clause with its Alternate I;

(ii) Contracting by negotiation, and subcontracting plans are required with initial proposals as provided for in 19.705-2(d), the contracting officer shall use the clause with its Alternate II;

(iii) The contract action will not be reported in the Federal Procurement Data System pursuant to 4.606(c)(5) or (c)(6), the contracting officer shall use the clause with its Alternate III; or

(iv) Incorporating a subcontracting plan due to a modification as provided for in 19.702(a)(3), the contracting officer shall use the clause with its Alternate IV.

(2) Insert the clause at 52.219-16, Liquidated Damages—Subcontracting Plan, in all solicitations and contracts containing the clause at 52.219-9, Small Business Subcontracting Plan, or the clause with its Alternate I, II, III, or IV.

(c)(1) The contracting officer may, when contracting by negotiation, insert in solicitations and contracts a clause substantially the same as the clause at 52.219-10, Incentive Subcontracting Program, when a subcontracting plan is required (see 19.702), and inclusion of a monetary incentive is, in the judgment of the contracting officer, necessary to increase subcontracting opportunities for small business, veteran-owned small business, service-disabled veteran-owned small business, HUBZone small business, small disadvantaged business, and women-owned small business concerns, and is commensurate with the efficient and economical performance of the contract; unless the conditions in paragraph (c)(3) of this section are applicable. The contracting officer may vary the terms of the clause as specified in paragraph (c)(2) of this section.

(2) Various approaches may be used in the development of small business, veteran-owned small business, service-disabled veteran-owned small business, HUBZone small business, small disadvantaged business, and women-owned small business concerns' subcontracting incentives. They can take many forms, from a fully quantified schedule of payments based on actual subcontract achievement to an award-fee approach employing subjective evaluation criteria (see paragraph (c)(3) of this section). The incentive should not reward the contractor for results other than those that are attributable to the contractor's efforts under the incentive subcontracting program.

(3) As specified in paragraph (c)(2) of this section, the contracting officer may include small business, veteran-owned small business, service-disabled veteran-owned small business, HUBZone small business, small disadvantaged business, and women-owned small business subcontracting as one of the factors to be considered in determining the award fee in a cost-plus-award-fee contract; in such cases, however, the contracting officer shall not use the clause at 52.219-10, Incentive Subcontracting Program.

[FAC 84-5, 50 FR 1743, 1/11/85, effective 4/11/85; FAC 84-12, 51 FR 2664, 1/17/86 effective 1/20/86; Interim rule, FAC 84-50, 54 FR 30710, 7/21/89, effective 8/15/89; Interim rule, FAC 90-7, 56 FR 41731, 8/22/91, effective 8/22/91; FAC 90-29, 60 FR 34732, 7/3/95, effective 7/3/95; FAC 90-32, 60 FR 48206, 9/18/95, effective 10/1/95; FAC 90-37, 61 FR 2626, 1/26/96, effective

3/26/96; FAC 90-40, 61 FR 39186, 7/26/96, effective 8/26/96; FAC 97-5, 63 FR 34058, 6/22/98, effective 8/21/98; FAC 97-7, 63 FR 36120, 7/1/98, effective 1/1/99, finalized without change, FAC 97-13, 7/2/99; FAC 97-10, 63 FR 70264, 12/18/98, effective 1/4/99; FAC 97-20, 65 FR 60542, 10/11/2000, effective 10/11/2000; FAC 2001-01, 66 FR 53478, 10/22/2001, effective 10/22/2001; FAC 2001-14, 68 FR 28079, 5/22/2003, effective 6/23/2003; FAC 2005-13, 71 FR 57363, 9/28/2006, effective 9/28/2006; FAC 2005-42; 75 FR 34260, 6/16/2010, effective 7/16/2010; FAC 2005-45, 75 FR 53129, 8/30/2010, effective 10/1/2010; FAC 2005-62, 77 FR 69715, 11/20/2012, effective 12/20/2012; FAC 2005-77, 79 FR 61746, 10/14/2014, effective 10/14/2014; FAC 2005-83, 80 FR 38293, 7/2/2015, effective 10/1/2015; FAC 2005-89, 81 FR 45833, 7/14/2016, effective 11/1/2016]

SUBPART 19.8—CONTRACTING WITH THE SMALL BUSINESS ADMINISTRATION (THE 8(a) PROGRAM)

19.800 General.

(a) Section 8(a) of the Small Business Act (15 U.S.C. 637(a)) established a program that authorizes the Small Business Administration (SBA) to enter into all types of contracts with other agencies and award subcontracts for performing those contracts to firms eligible for program participation. This program is the "8(a) Business Development Program," commonly referred to as the "8(a) program." A small business that is accepted into the 8(a) program is known as a "participant." SBA's subcontractors are referred to as "8(a) contractors." As used in this subpart, an 8(a) contractor is an 8(a) participant that is currently performing on a Federal contract or order that was set aside for 8(a) participants.

(b) Contracts may be awarded to the SBA for performance by eligible 8(a) participants on either a sole source or competitive basis.

(c) Acting under the authority of the program, the SBA certifies to an agency that SBA is competent and responsible to perform a specific contract. The contracting officer has the discretion to award the contract to the SBA based upon mutually agreeable terms and conditions.

(d) The contracting officer shall comply with 19.203 before deciding to offer an acquisition to a small business concern under the 8(a) program. For acquisitions above the simplified acquisition threshold, the contracting officer shall consider 8(a) set-asides or sole source awards before considering small business set-asides.

(e) When SBA has delegated its 8(a) program contract execution authority to an agency, the contracting officer must refer to its agency supplement or other policy directives for appropriate guidance.

[FAC 84-52, 54 FR 46005, 10/31/89, effective 11/30/89; FAC 97-10, 63 FR 70264, 12/18/98, effective 1/4/99; FAC 97-12, 64 FR 32740, 6/17/99, effective 6/17/99, finalized without change, FAC 97-15, 64 FR 72414, 12/27/99; FAC 97-14, 64 FR 51828, 9/24/99, effective 11/23/99; FAC 2001-23, 69 FR 25273, 5/5/2004, effective 5/5/2004; FAC 2005-02, 70 FR 14950, 3/23/2005, effective 3/23/2005; FAC 2005-47, 75 FR 77727, 12/13/2010, effective 1/12/2011; FAC 2005-50, 76 FR 14566, 3/16/2011, effective 3/16/2011; FAC 2005-56, 77 FR 12930, 3/2/2012, effective 4/2/2012; FAC 2005-73, 79 FR 24192, 4/29/2014, effective 5/29/2014; FAC 2005-95, 82 FR 4724, 1/13/2017, effective 1/13/2017]

19.801 [Reserved]

[Reserved, FAC 90-43, Interim rule, 61 FR 67408, 12/20/96, effective 12/20/96]

19.802 Determining eligibility for the 8(a) program.

Determining the eligibility of a small business to be a participant in the 8(a) program is the responsibility of the SBA. SBA's regulations on eligibility requirements for participation in the 8(a) program are found at 13 CFR 124.101 through 124.112.

[FAC 84-52, 54 FR 46005, 10/31/89, effective 11/30/89; FAC 97-12, 64 FR 32740, 6/17/99, effective 6/17/99, finalized without change, FAC 97-15, 64 FR 72414, 12/27/99; FAC 2005-95, 82 FR 4724, 1/13/2017, effective 1/13/2017]

19.803 Selecting acquisitions for the 8(a) program.

Through their cooperative efforts, the SBA and an agency match the agency's requirements with the capabilities of 8(a) participants to establish a basis for the agency to contract with the SBA under the program. Selection is initiated in one of three ways:

(a) The SBA advises the contracting activity of an 8(a) participant's capabilities through a search letter and requests the contracting activity to identify acquisitions to support the participant's business plans. In these instances, the SBA will provide at a minimum the following information in order to enable the contracting activity to match an acquisition to the participant's capabilities:

(1) Identification of the participant and its owners.

(2) Background information on the participant, including any and all information pertaining to the participant's technical ability and capacity to perform.

(3) The participant's present production capacity and related facilities.

(4) The extent to which contracting assistance is needed in the present and the future, described in terms that will enable the agency to relate the participant's plans to present and future agency requirements.

(5) If construction is involved, the request shall also include the following:

(i) A participant's capabilities in and qualifications for accomplishing various categories of construction work typically found in North American Industrial Category System subsector 236 (construction of buildings), subsector 237 (heavy and civil engineering construction), or subsector 238 (specialty trade contractors).

(ii) The participant's capacity in each construction category in terms of estimated dollar value (e.g., electrical, up to $100,000).

(b) The SBA identifies a specific requirement for one or more 8(a) participant(s) and sends a requirements letter to the agency's Office of Small and Disadvantaged Business Utilization, or for the Department of Defense, Office of Small Business Programs, requesting the contracting office offer the acquisition to the 8(a) program. In these instances, in addition to the information in paragraph (a) of this section, the SBA will provide—

(1) A clear identification of the acquisition sought; e.g., project name or number;

(2) A statement as to how the required equipment and real property will be provided in order to ensure that the participant will be fully capable of satisfying the agency's requirements;

(3) If construction, information as to the bonding capability of the participant(s); and

(4) Either—

(i) If a sole source request—

(A) The reasons why the participant is considered suitable for this particular acquisition; e.g., previous contracts for the same or similar supply or service; and

(B) A statement that the participant is eligible in terms of its small business size status relative to the assigned NAICS code, business support levels, and business activity targets; or

(ii) If competitive, a statement that at least two 8(a) participants are considered capable of satisfying the agency's requirements and a statement that the participants are also eligible in terms of their small business size status relative to the assigned NAICS code, business support levels, and business activity targets. If requested by the contracting office, SBA will identify at least two such participants and provide information concerning the participants' capabilities.

(c) Agencies may also review other proposed acquisitions for the purpose of identifying requirements which may be offered to the SBA. Where agencies independently, or through the self marketing efforts of an 8(a) participant, identify a requirement for the 8(a) program, they may offer on behalf of a specific 8(a) participant, for the 8(a) program in general, or for 8(a) competition.

[FAC 84-52, 54 FR 46005, 10/31/89, effective 11/30/89; FAC 84-56, 55 FR 3882, 2/5/90, effective 2/5/90; FAC 90-43, Interim rule, 61 FR 67408, 12/20/96, effective 12/20/96; finalized without change, FAC 97-1, 62 FR 44802, 8/22/97, effective

10/21/97; FAC 97-10, 63 FR 70264, 12/18/98, effective 1/4/99; FAC 97-12, 64 FR 32740, 6/17/99, effective 6/17/99; FAC 97-19, 65 FR 46052, 7/26/2000, effective 10/1/2000; FAC 2001-02, 66 FR 65347, 12/18/2001, effective 2/19/2002; FAC 2005-17, 72 FR 27364, 5/15/2007, effective 6/14/2007; FAC 2005-47, 75 FR 77727, 12/13/2010, effective 1/12/2011; FAC 2005-95, 82 FR 4724, 1/13/2017, effective 1/13/2017]

19.804 Evaluation, offering, and acceptance. (No Text)

19.804-1 Agency evaluation.

In determining the extent to which a requirement should be offered in support of the 8(a) program, the agency should evaluate—

(a) Current and future plans to acquire the specific items or work that 8(a) participants are seeking to provide, identified in terms of—

(1) Estimated quantities of the supplies or services required or the estimated number of construction projects planned; and

(2) Performance or delivery requirements, including-

(i) Required monthly production rates, when applicable; and

(ii) For construction, the geographical location where work is to be performed;

(b) The impact of any delay in delivery;

(c) Whether the items or work have previously been acquired using small business set-asides, and the date the items or work were acquired;

(d) Problems encountered in previous acquisitions of the items or work from the 8(a) participants or other contractors; and

(e) Any other pertinent information about known 8(a) participants, the items, or the work. This includes any information concerning the participants' products or capabilities. When necessary, the contracting agency shall make an independent review of the factors in 19.803(a) and other aspects of the participants' capabilities which would ensure the satisfactory performance of the requirement being considered for commitment to the 8(a) program.

[FAC 84-52, 54 FR 46006, 10/31/89, effective 11/30/89; FAC 2005-95, 82 FR 4724, 1/13/2017, effective 1/13/2017]

19.804-2 Agency offering.

(a) After completing its evaluation, the contracting office shall notify the SBA of the extent of its plans to place 8(a) contracts with the SBA for specific quantities of items or work. The notification, referred to as an offering letter, shall identify the time frames within which resulting 8(a) awards must be completed in order for the agency to meet its responsibilities. The offering letter shall also contain the following information applicable to each prospective contract:

(1) A description of the work to be performed or items to be delivered, and a copy of the statement of work, if available.

(2) The estimated period of performance.

(3) The NAICS code that applies to the principal nature of the acquisition.

(4) The anticipated dollar value of the requirement, including options, if any.

(5) Any special restrictions or geographical limitations on the requirement (for construction, include the location of the work to be performed).

(6) Any special capabilities or disciplines needed for contract performance.

(7) The type of contract anticipated.

(8) The acquisition history, if any, of the requirement, including the names and addresses of any small business contractors that have performed this requirement during the previous 24 months.

(9) A statement that prior to the offering no solicitation for the specific acquisition has been issued as a small business, HUBZone, service-disabled veteran-owned small business set-aside, or a set-aside under the Women-Owned Small Business (WOSB) Program, and that no other public communication (such as a notice through the Governmentwide point of entry (GPE)) has been made showing the contracting agency's clear intention to set-aside the acquisition for small business, HUBZone small business,

service-disabled veteran-owned small business concerns, or a set-aside under the WOSB Program.

(10) Identification of any particular 8(a) participant designated for consideration, including a brief justification, such as—

(i) The 8(a) participant, through its own efforts, marketed the requirement and caused it to be reserved for the 8(a) program; or

(ii) The acquisition is a follow-on or renewal contract and the nominated 8(a) participant is the incumbent.

(11) Bonding requirements, if applicable.

(12) Identification of all 8(a) participants which have expressed an interest in being considered for the acquisition.

(13) Identification of all SBA field offices that have asked for the acquisition for the 8(a) program.

(14) A request, if appropriate, that a requirement with an estimated contract value under the applicable competitive threshold be awarded as an 8(a) competitive contract (see 19.805-1(d)).

(15) A request, if appropriate, that a requirement with a contract value over the applicable competitive threshold be awarded as a sole source contract (see 19.805-1(b)).

(16) Any other pertinent and reasonably available data.

(b)(1) An agency offering a construction requirement for which no specific offeror is nominated should submit it to the SBA District Office for the geographical area where the work is to be performed.

(2) An agency offering a construction requirement on behalf of a specific offeror should submit it to the SBA District Office servicing that concern.

(3) Sole source requirements, other than construction, should be forwarded directly to the district office that services the nominated 8(a) participant. If the contracting officer is not nominating a specific 8(a) participant, the offering letter should be forwarded to the district office servicing the geographical area in which the contracting office is located.

(c) All requirements for 8(a) competition, other than construction, should be forwarded to the district office servicing the geographical area in which the contracting office is located. All requirements for 8(a) construction competition should be forwarded to the district office servicing the geographical area in which all or the major portion of the construction is to be performed. All requirements, including construction, must be synopsized through the GPE. For construction, the synopsis must include the geographical area of the competition set forth in the SBA's acceptance letter.

[FAC 84-52, 54 FR 46006, 10/31/89, effective 11/30/89; FAC 90-43, Interim rule, 61 FR 67408, 12/20/96, effective 12/20/96; FAC 97-1, 62 FR 44802, 8/22/97, effective 10/21/97; FAC 97-10, 63 FR 70264, 12/18/98, effective 1/4/99; FAC 97-12, 64 FR 32740, 6/17/99, effective 6/17/99, finalized without change, FAC 97-15, 64 FR 72414, 12/27/99; FAC 97-19, 65 FR 46052, 7/26/2000, effective 10/1/2000; FAC 97-26, 66 FR 27405, 5/16/2001, effective 5/16/2001; FAC 2001-02, 66 FR 65347, 12/18/2001, effective 2/19/2002; FAC 2001-23, 69 FR 25273, 5/5/2004, effective 5/5/2004; FAC 2005-02, 70 FR 14950, 3/23/2005, effective 3/23/2005; FAC 2005-46, 75 FR 60263, 9/29/2010, effective 10/29/2010; FAC 2005-50, 76 FR 14566, 3/16/2011, effective 3/16/2011; FAC 2005-51, 76 FR 18304, 4/1/2011, effective 4/1/2011; FAC 2005-56, 77 FR 12913, 12930, 3/2/2012, effective 4/2/2012; FAC 2005-95, 82 FR 4724, 1/13/2017, effective 1/13/2017]

19.804-3 SBA acceptance.

(a) Upon receipt of the contracting office's offering letter, SBA will determine whether to accept the requirement for the 8(a) program. SBA's decision whether to accept the requirement will be transmitted to the contracting office in writing within 10 working days of receipt of the offer if the contract is likely to exceed the simplified acquisition threshold and within two working days of receipt if the contract is at or below the simplified acquisition threshold. The contracting office may grant an extension of these time periods, if requested by SBA.

(1) For acquisitions exceeding the simplified acquisition threshold, if SBA does not respond to an offering letter within ten working days, the contracting office may seek SBA's acceptance through the Associate Administrator for Business Development. The contracting office may assume that SBA has accepted the requirement into the 8(a) program if it does not receive a reply from the Associate Administrator for Business Development within five calendar days of receipt of the contracting office's request.

(2) For acquisitions not exceeding the simplified acquisition threshold, when the contracting office makes an offer to the 8(a) program on behalf of a specific 8(a) participant and does not receive a reply to its offering letter within two working days, the contracting office may assume the offer is accepted and proceed with award of an 8(a) contract.

(b) As part of the acceptance process, SBA will review the appropriateness of the NAICS code designation assigned to the requirement by the contracting officer.

(1) SBA will not challenge the NAICS code assigned to the requirement by the contracting officer if it is reasonable, even though other NAICS codes may also be reasonable.

(2) If SBA and the contracting officer are unable to agree on a NAICS code designation for the requirement, SBA may refuse to accept the requirement for the 8(a) program, appeal the contracting officer's determination to the head of the agency pursuant to 19.810, or appeal the NAICS code designation to the SBA Office of Hearings and Appeals under subpart C of 13 CFR part 134.

(c) *Sole source 8(a) awards.* If an appropriate match exists, SBA will advise the contracting officer whether it will participate in contract negotiations or whether SBA will authorize the contracting officer to negotiate directly with the identified 8(a) participant. Where SBA has delegated its contract execution functions to a contracting agency, SBA will also identify that delegation in its acceptance letter.

(1) *Sole source award where the contracting officer nominates a specific 8(a) participant.* SBA will determine whether an appropriate match exists where the contracting officer identifies a particular participant for a sole source award.

(i) Once SBA determines that a procurement is suitable to be accepted as an 8(a) sole source contract, SBA will normally accept it on behalf of the 8(a) participant recommended by the contracting officer, provided that the 8(a) participant complies with the requirements of 13 CFR 124.503(c)(1).

(ii) If an appropriate match does not exist, SBA will notify the 8(a) participant and the contracting officer, and may then nominate an alternate 8(a) participant.

(2) *Sole source award where the contracting officer does not nominate a specific 8(a) participant.* When a contracting officer does not nominate an 8(a) participant for performance of a sole source 8(a) contract, SBA will select an 8(a) participant for possible award from among two or more eligible and qualified 8(a) participants. The selection will be based upon relevant factors, including business development needs, compliance with competitive business mix requirements (if applicable), financial condition, management ability, technical capability, and whether award will promote the equitable distribution of 8(a) contracts. (For construction requirements see 13 CFR 124.503(d)(1)).

[FAC 84-52, 54 FR 46006, 10/31/89, effective 11/30/89; FAC 90-8, 56 FR 55380, 10/25/91, effective 10/25/91; FAC 90-43, Interim rule, 61 FR 67408, 12/20/96, effective 12/20/96; FAC 97-12, 64 FR 32740, 6/17/99, effective 6/17/99, finalized without change, FAC 97-15, 64 FR 72414, 12/27/99; FAC 97-19, 65 FR 46052, 7/26/2000, effective 10/1/2000; FAC 2001-02, 66 FR 65347, 12/18/2001, effective 2/19/2002; FAC 2005-47, 75 FR 77727, 12/13/2010, effective 1/12/2011; FAC 2005-95, 82 FR 4724, 1/13/2017, effective 1/13/2017]

19.804-4 Repetitive acquisitions.

In order for repetitive acquisitions to be awarded through the 8(a) program, there must be separate offers and acceptances. This allows the SBA to determine—

(a) Whether the requirement should be a competitive 8(a) award;

(b) A nominated 8(a) participant's eligibility, and whether or not it is the same 8(a) participant that performed the previous contract;

(c) The effect that contract award would have on the equitable distribution of 8(a) contracts; and

(d) Whether the requirement should continue under the 8(a) program.

[FAC 97-12, 64 FR 32740, 6/17/99, effective 6/17/99, finalized without change, FAC 97-15, 64 FR 72414, 12/27/99; FAC 2005-95, 82 FR 4724, 1/13/2017, effective 1/13/2017]

19.804-5 Basic ordering agreements.

(a) The contracting office shall submit an offering letter for, and SBA must accept, each order under a basic ordering agreement (BOA) in addition to the agency offering and SBA accepting the BOA itself.

(b) SBA will not accept for award on a sole-source basis any order that would cause the total dollar amount of orders issued under a specific BOA to exceed the competitive threshold amount in 19.805-1.

(c) Once an 8(a) participant's program term expires, the participant otherwise exits the 8(a) program, or becomes other than small for the NAICS code assigned under the BOA, SBA will not accept new orders for the participant.

[FAC 97-12, 64 FR 32740, 6/17/99, effective 6/17/99, finalized without change, FAC 97-15, 64 FR 72414, 12/27/99; FAC 97-19, 65 FR 46052, 7/26/2000, effective 10/1/2000; FAC 2001-02, 66 FR 65347, 12/18/2001, effective 2/19/2002; FAC 2005-95, 82 FR 4724, 1/13/2017, effective 1/13/2017]

19.804-6 Indefinite-delivery contracts.

(a) Separate offers and acceptances are not required for individual orders under multiple-award contracts (including the Federal Supply Schedules managed by GSA, multi-agency contracts or Governmentwide acquisition contracts, or indefinite-delivery, indefinite-quantity (IDIQ) contracts) that have been set aside for exclusive competition among 8(a) contractors. SBA's acceptance of the original contract is valid for the term of the contract. Offers and acceptances are required for individual orders under multiple-award contracts that have not been set aside for exclusive competition among 8(a) contractors.

(b) An 8(a) contractor may continue to accept new orders under the contract, even if it exits the 8(a) program, or becomes other than small for the NAICS code assigned to the contract.

(c) Agencies may continue to take credit toward their prime contracting small disadvantaged business or small business goals for orders awarded to 8(a) participants, even after the contractor's 8(a) program term expires, the contractor otherwise exits the 8(a) program, or the contractor becomes other than small for the NAICS code assigned under the 8(a) contract. However, if an 8(a) contractor rerepresents that it is other than small for the NAICS code assigned under the contract in accordance with 19.301-2 or, where ownership or control of the 8(a) contractor has changed and SBA has granted a waiver to allow the contractor to continue performance (see 13 CFR 124.515), the agency may not credit any subsequent orders awarded to the contractor towards its small disadvantaged business or small business goals.

[FAC 97-12, 64 FR 32740, 6/17/99, effective 6/17/99, finalized without change, FAC 97-15, 64 FR 72414, 12/27/99; FAC 97-19, 65 FR 46052, 7/26/2000, effective 10/1/2000; FAC 2001-02, 66 FR 65347, 12/18/2001, effective 2/19/2002; FAC 2005-18, Interim rule, 72 FR 36852, 7/5/2007, effective 6/30/2007; FAC 2005-31, 74 FR 11821, 3/19/2009, effective 4/20/2009; FAC 2005-95, 82 FR 4724, 1/13/2017, effective 1/13/2017]

19.805 Competitive 8(a). (No Text)

19.805-1 General.

(a) Except as provided in paragraph (b) of this section, an acquisition offered to the SBA under the 8(a) program shall be awarded on the basis of competition limited to eligible 8(a) participants when—

(1) There is a reasonable expectation that at least two eligible and responsible 8(a) participants will submit offers and that award can be made at a fair market price; and

(2) The anticipated total value of the contract, including options, will exceed $7 million for acquisitions assigned manufacturing North American Industry Classification System (NAICS) codes and $4 million for all other acquisitions.

(b) Where an acquisition exceeds the competitive threshold (see paragraph (a)(2) of this section), the SBA may accept the requirement for a sole source 8(a) award if—

(1) There is not a reasonable expectation that at least two eligible and responsible 8(a) participants will submit offers at a fair market price; or

(2) SBA accepts the requirement on behalf of a concern owned by an Indian tribe or an Alaska Native Corporation.

(c) A proposed 8(a) requirement with an estimated value exceeding the applicable competitive threshold amount shall not be divided into several requirements for lesser amounts in order to use 8(a) sole source procedures for award to a single firm.

(d) The SBA Associate Administrator for Business Development may approve a contracting office's request for a competitive 8(a) award below the competitive thresholds. Such requests will be approved only on a limited basis and will be primarily granted where technical competitions are appropriate or where a large number of responsible 8(a) participants are available for competition. In determining whether a request to compete below the threshold will be approved, the SBA Associate Administrator for Business Development will, in part, consider the extent to which the contracting activity is supporting the 8(a) program on a noncompetitive basis. The agency may include recommendations for competition below the threshold in the offering letter or by separate correspondence to the SBA Associate Administrator for Business Development.

[FAC 84-52, 54 FR 46007, 10/31/89, effective 11/30/89; FAC 90-43, Interim rule, 61 FR 67408, 12/20/96, effective 12/20/96; FAC 97-12, 64 FR 32740, 6/17/99, effective 6/17/99, finalized without change, FAC 97-15, 64 FR 72414, 12/27/99; FAC 97-19, 65 FR 46052, 7/26/2000, effective 10/1/2000; FAC 2001-02, 66 FR 65347, 12/18/2001, effective 2/19/2002; FAC 2001-12, 68 FR 4047, 1/27/2003, effective 1/24/2003; FAC 2001-20, 69 FR 8311, 2/23/2004, effective 2/23/2004; FAC 2001-26, 69 FR 76350, 12/20/2004, effective 1/19/2005; FAC 2005-13, 71 FR 57363, 9/28/2006, effective 9/28/2006; FAC 2005-45, 75 FR 53129, 8/30/2010, effective 10/1/2010; FAC 2005-47, 75 FR 77727, 12/13/2010, effective 1/12/2011; FAC 2005-83, 80 FR 38293, 7/2/2015, effective 10/1/2015; FAC 2005-95, 82 FR 4724, 1/13/2017, effective 1/13/2017]

19.805-2 Procedures.

(a) Offers shall be solicited from those sources identified in accordance with 19.804-3.

(b) The SBA will determine the eligibility of the participants for award of the contract. Eligibility will be determined by the SBA as of the time of submission of initial offers which include price. Eligibility is based on Section 8(a) program criteria. An 8(a) participant must represent that it is a small business in accordance with the size standard corresponding to the NAICS code assigned to the contract.

(1) In either negotiated or sealed bid competitive 8(a) acquisitions SBA will determine the eligibility of the apparent successful offeror and advise the contracting office within 5 working days after receipt of the contracting office's request for an eligibility determination.

(i) If SBA determines that the apparent successful offeror is ineligible, the contracting office will then send to SBA the identity of the next highest evaluated offeror for an eligibility determination. The process is repeated until SBA determines that an identified offeror is eligible for award.

(ii) If the contracting officer believes that the apparent successful offeror (or the offeror SBA has determined eligible for award) is not responsible to perform the contract, the contracting officer must refer the matter to SBA for Certificate of Competency consideration under subpart 19.6.

(2) In any case in which an 8(a) participant is determined to be ineligible, SBA will notify the 8(a) participant of that determination.

(c) Any party with information questioning the eligibility of an 8(a) participant to continue participation in the 8(a) program or for the purposes of a specific 8(a) award may submit such information to the SBA in accordance with 13 CFR 124.112(c).

[FAC 84-52, 54 FR 46007, 10/31/89/ effective 11/30/89; FAC 90-43, Interim rule, 61 FR 67408, 12/20/96, effective 12/20/96; FAC 97-12, 64 FR 32740, 6/17/99, effective 6/17/99, finalized without change, FAC 97-15, 64 FR 72414, 12/27/99; FAC 2005-95, 82 FR 4724, 1/13/2017, effective 1/13/2017]

19.806 Pricing the 8(a) contract.

(a) The contracting officer shall price the 8(a) contract in accordance with Subpart 15.4. If required by Subpart 15.4, the SBA shall obtain cost or pricing data from the 8(a) contractor. If required by subpart 15.4, the SBA shall obtain certified cost or pricing data from the 8(a) contractor. If the SBA requests audit assistance to determine the proposed price to be fair and reasonable in a sole source acquisition, the contracting activity shall furnish it to the extent it is available.

(b) An 8(a) contract, sole source or competitive, may not be awarded if the price of the contract results in a cost to the contracting agency which exceeds a fair market price.

(c) If requested by the SBA, the contracting officer shall make available the data used to estimate the fair market price within 10 working days.

(d) The negotiated contract price and the estimated fair market price are subject to the concurrence of the SBA. In the event of a disagreement between the contracting officer and the SBA, the SBA may appeal in accordance with 19.810.

[FAC 84-52, 54 FR 46007, 10/31/89, effective 11/30/89; FAC 97-2, 62 FR 51224, 9/30/97, effective 10/10/97; FAC 97-12, 64 FR 32740, 6/17/99, effective 6/17/99, finalized without change, FAC 97-15, 64 FR 72414, 12/27/99; FAC 2005-45, 75 FR 53135, 8/30/2010, effective 10/1/2010]

19.807 Estimating fair market price.

(a) The contracting officer shall estimate the fair market price of the work to be performed by the 8(a) contractor.

(b) In estimating the fair market price for an acquisition other than those covered in paragraph (c) of this section, the contracting officer shall use cost or price analysis and consider commercial prices for similar products and services, available in-house cost estimates, data (including certified cost or pricing data) submitted by the SBA or the 8(a) contractor, and data obtained from any other Government agency.

(c) In estimating a fair market price for a repeat purchase, the contracting officer shall consider recent award prices for the same items or work if there is comparability in quantities, conditions, terms, and performance times. The estimated price should be adjusted to reflect differences in specifications, plans, transportation costs, packaging and packing costs, and other circumstances. Price indices may be used as guides to determine the changes in labor and material costs. Comparison of commercial prices for similar items may also be used.

[FAC 84-52, 54 FR 46007, 10/31/89, effective 11/30/89; FAC 2005-45, 75 FR 53135, 8/30/2010, effective 10/1/2010]

19.808 Contract negotiation. (No Text)

19.808-1 Sole source.

(a) The SBA may not accept for negotiation a sole-source 8(a) contract that exceeds $22 million unless the requesting agency has completed a justification in accordance with the requirements of 6.303.

(b) The SBA is responsible for initiating negotiations with the agency within the time established by the agency. If the SBA does not initiate negotiations within the agreed time and the agency cannot allow additional time, the agency may, after notifying the

SBA, proceed with the acquisition from other sources.

(c) The SBA should participate, whenever practicable, in negotiating the contracting terms. When mutually agreeable, the SBA may authorize the contracting officer to negotiate directly with the 8(a) participant. Whether or not direct negotiations take place, the SBA is responsible for approving the resulting contract before award.

(d) An 8(a) participant must represent that it is a small business in accordance with the size standard corresponding to the NAICS code assigned to the contract.

(e) An 8(a) participant owned by an Alaska Native Corporation, Indian Tribe, Native Hawaiian Organization, or Community Development Corporation may not receive an 8(a) sole source award that is a follow-on contract to an 8(a) contract, if the predecessor contract was performed by another 8(a) participant (or former 8(a) participant) owned by the same Alaska Native Corporation, Indian Tribe, Native Hawaiian Organization, or Community Development Corporation (See 13 CFR 124.109 through 124.111).

[FAC 84-52, 54 FR 46008, 10/31/89, effective 11/30/89; FAC 84-56, 55 FR 3882, 2/5/90, effective 2/5/90; FAC 90-8, 56 FR 55378, 10/25/91, effective 11/25/91; FAC 90-43, Interim rule, 61 FR 67408, 12/20/96, effective 12/20/96; FAC 2005-50, 76 FR 14559, 3/16/2011, effective 3/16/2011; FAC 2005-58, 77 FR 23369, 4/18/2012, effective 4/18/2012; FAC 2005-83, 80 FR 38293, 7/2/2015, effective 10/1/2015; FAC 2005-95, 82 FR 4724, 1/13/2017, effective 1/13/2017]

19.808-2 Competitive.

In competitive 8(a) acquisitions subject to part 15, the contracting officer conducts negotiations directly with the competing 8(a) participants. Conducting competitive negotiations among 8(a) participants prior to SBA's formal acceptance of the acquisition for the 8(a) program may be grounds for SBA's not accepting the acquisition for the 8(a) program.

[FAC 97-12, 64 FR 32740, 6/17/99, effective 6/17/99, finalized without change, FAC 97-15, 64 FR 72414, 12/27/99; FAC 2005-95, 82 FR 4724, 1/13/2017, effective 1/13/2017]

19.809 Preaward considerations.

The contracting officer should request a preaward survey of the 8(a) participant whenever considered useful. If the results of the preaward survey or other information available to the contracting officer raise substantial doubt as to the participant's ability to perform, the contracting officer must refer the matter to SBA for Certificate of Competency consideration under subpart 19.6.

[FAC 97-12, 64 FR 32740, 6/17/99, effective 6/17/99, finalized without change, FAC 97-15, 64 FR 72414, 12/27/99; FAC 2005-95, 82 FR 4724, 1/13/2017, effective 1/13/2017]

19.810 SBA appeals.

(a) The SBA Administrator may submit the following matters for determination to the agency head if the SBA and the contracting officer fail to agree on them:

(1) The decision not to make a particular acquisition available for award under the 8(a) Program.

(2) A contracting officer's decision to reject a specific 8(a) participant for award of an 8(a) contract after SBA's acceptance of the requirement for the 8(a) program.

(3) The terms and conditions of a proposed 8(a) contract, including the contracting officer's NAICS code designation and estimate of the fair market price.

(b) (1) Notification by SBA of an intent to appeal to the agency head—

(i) Must be received by the contracting officer within 5 working days after SBA is formally notified of the contracting officer's decision; and

(ii) Must be provided to the contracting agency Director for Small and Disadvantaged Business Utilization or, for the Department of Defense, the Director of Small Business Programs.

(2) SBA must send the written appeal to the agency head within 15 working days of SBA's notification of intent to appeal or the appeal may be considered withdrawn. Pending issuance of a decision by the agency head, the contracting officer shall suspend

action on the acquisition. The contracting officer need not suspend action on the acquisition if the contracting officer makes a written determination that urgent and compelling circumstances that significantly affect the interests of the United States will not permit waiting for a decision.

(c) If the SBA appeal is denied, the decision of the agency head shall specify the reasons for the denial, including the reasons why the selected participant was determined incapable of performance, if appropriate. The decision shall be made a part of the contract file.

[FAC 84-52, 54 FR 46008, 10/31/89, effective 11/30/89; FAC 97-12, 64 FR 32740, 6/17/99, effective 6/17/99, finalized without change, FAC 97-15, 64 FR 72414, 12/27/99; FAC 97-19, 65 FR 46052, 7/26/2000, effective 10/1/2000, finalized without change by FAC 2001-02, 66 FR 65347, 12/18/2001, effective 12/18/2001; FAC 2005-95, 82 FR 4724, 1/13/2017, effective 1/13/2017]

19.811 Preparing the contracts. (No Text)

19.811-1 Sole source.

(a) The contract to be awarded by the agency to the SBA shall be prepared in accordance with agency procedures and in the same detail as would be required in a contract with a business concern. The contracting officer shall use the Standard Form 26 as the award form, except for construction contracts, in which case the Standard Form 1442 shall be used as required in 36.701(a).

(b) The contracting officer shall prepare the contract that the SBA will award to the 8(a) participant in accordance with agency procedures, as if awarding the contract directly to the 8(a) participant, except for the following:

(1) The award form shall cite 41 U.S.C. 3304 (a)(5) or 10 U.S.C. 2304(c)(5) (as appropriate) as the authority for use of other than full and open competition.

(2) Appropriate clauses shall be included, as necessary, to reflect that the contract is between the SBA and the 8(a) contractor.

(3) The following items shall be inserted by the SBA:

(i) The SBA contract number.

(ii) The effective date.

(iii) The typed name of the SBA's contracting officer.

(iv) The signature of the SBA's contracting officer.

(v) The date signed.

(4) The SBA will obtain the signature of the 8(a) contractor prior to signing and returning the prime contract to the contracting officer for signature. The SBA will make every effort to obtain signatures and return the contract, and any subsequent bilateral modification, to the contracting officer within a maximum of 10 working days.

(c) Except in procurements where the SBA will make advance payments to its 8(a) contractor, the agency contracting officer may, as an alternative to the procedures in paragraphs (a) and (b) of this subsection, use a single contract document for both the prime contract between the agency and the SBA and its 8(a) contractor. The single contract document shall contain the information in paragraphs (b) (1), (2), and (3) of this subsection. Appropriate blocks on the Standard Form (SF) 26 or 1442 will be asterisked and a continuation sheet appended as a tripartite agreement which includes the following:

(1) Agency acquisition office, prime contract number, name of agency contracting officer and lines for signature, date signed, and effective date.

(2) The SBA office, the SBA contract number, name of the SBA contracting officer, and lines for signature and date signed.

(3) Name and lines for the 8(a) subcontractor's signature and date signed.

(d) For acquisitions not exceeding the simplified acquisition threshold, the contracting officer may use the alternative procedures in paragraph (c) of this subsection with the appropriate simplified acquisition forms.

[FAC 84-52, 54 FR 46008, 10/31/89, effective 11/30/89; FAC 84-56, 55 FR 3883, 2/5/90, effective 2/5/90; FAC 90-43, Interim rule, 61 FR 67408, 12/20/96, effective 12/20/96; FAC 90-45, Final rule, 62 FR 224, 1/2/97, effective 1/1/97; FAC 97-3, 62 FR 64912, 12/9/97, effective 12/9/97; FAC 97-12, 64 FR 32740, 6/17/99, effective 6/17/99, finalized without change, FAC 97-15, 64 FR 72414, 12/27/99; FAC 2001-25, 69 FR 59699, 10/5/2004, effective 11/4/2004; FAC 2005-73, 79 FR 24192, 4/29/2014, effective 5/29/2014; FAC 2005-95, 82 FR 4724, 1/13/2017, effective 1/13/2017]

19.811-2 Competitive.

(a) The contract will be prepared in accordance with 14.408-1(d), except that appropriate blocks on the Standard Form 26 or 1442 will be asterisked and a continuation sheet appended as a tripartite agreement which includes the following:

(1) The agency contracting activity, prime contract number, name of agency contracting officer, and lines for signature, date signed, and effective date.

(2) The SBA office, the SBA subcontract number, name of the SBA contracting officer and lines for signature and date signed.

(b) The process for obtaining signatures shall be as specified in 19.811-1(b)(4).

[FAC 84-52, 54 FR 46008, 10/31/89, effective 11/30/89; FAC 90-29, 60 FR 34732, 7/3/95, effective 7/3/95; FAC 90-45, Final rule, 62 FR 224, 1/2/97, effective 1/1/97; FAC 97-12, 64 FR 32740, 6/17/99, effective 6/17/99, finalized without change, FAC 97-15, 64 FR 72414, 12/27/99]

19.811-3 Contract clauses.

(a) The contracting officer shall insert the clause at 52.219-11, Special 8(a) Contract Conditions, in contracts between the SBA and the agency when the acquisition is accomplished using the procedures of 19.811-1(a) and (b).

(b) The contracting officer shall insert the clause at 52.219-12, Special 8(a) Subcontract Conditions, in contracts between the SBA and its 8(a) contractor when the acquisition is accomplished using the procedures of 19.811-1(a) and (b).

(c) The contracting officer shall insert the clause at 52.219-17, Section 8(a) Award, in competitive solicitations and contracts when the acquisition is accomplished using the procedures of 19.805 and in sole source awards which utilize the alternative procedure in 19.811-1(c).

(d) The contracting officer shall insert the clause at 52.219-18, Notification of Competition Limited to Eligible 8(a) Participants, in competitive solicitations and contracts when the acquisition is accomplished using the procedures of 19.805.

(1) The clause at 52.219-18 with its Alternate I will be used when competition is to be limited to 8(a) participants within one or more specific SBA districts pursuant to 19.804-2.

(2) The clause at 52.219-18 with its Alternate II will be used when the acquisition is for a product in a class for which the Small Business Administration has waived the nonmanufacturer rule (see 19.102(f) (4) and (5)).

(e) The contracting officer shall insert the clause at 52.219-14, Limitations on Subcontracting, in any solicitation and contract resulting from this subpart. This includes multiple-award contracts when orders may be set aside for 8(a) participants as described in 8.405-5 and 16.505(b)(2)(i)(F).

[FAC 84-52, 54 FR 46009, 10/31/89, effective 11/30/89; FAC 84-56, 55 FR 3883, 2/5/90, effective 2/5/90; FAC 84-58, 55 FR 25529, 6/21/90, effective 7/23/90; FAC 90-32, 60 FR 48206, 9/18/95, effective 10/1/95; FAC 90-40, 61 FR 39186, 7/26/96, effective 7/26/96; FAC 90-43, Interim rule, 61 FR 67408, 12/20/96, effective 12/20/96; FAC 2005-54, 76 FR 68032, 11/2/2011, effective 11/2/2011; Interim rule, 77 FR 1889, 1/12/2012, effective 2/13/2012; FAC 2005-95, 82 FR 4724, 1/13/2017, effective 1/13/2017]

19.812 Contract administration.

(a) The contracting officer shall assign contract administration functions, as required, based on the location of the 8(a) contractor (see Federal Directory of Contract Administration Services Components (available via the Internet at *https://pubapp.dcma.mil/CASD/main.jsp*).

(b) The agency shall distribute copies of the contract(s) in accordance with Part 4. All contracts and modifications, if any, shall be distributed to both the SBA and the 8(a) contractor in accordance with the timeframes set forth in 4.201.

(c) To the extent consistent with the contracting activity's capability and resources, 8(a) contractors furnishing requirements shall be afforded production and technical assistance, including, when appropriate, identification of causes of deficiencies in their products and suggested corrective action to make such products acceptable.

(d) An 8(a) contract, whether in the base or an option year, must be terminated for convenience if the 8(a) contractor to which it was awarded transfers ownership or control of the firm or if the contract is transferred or novated for any reason to another firm, unless the Administrator of the SBA waives the requirement for contract termination (13 CFR 124.515). The Administrator may waive the termination requirement only if certain conditions exist. Moreover, a waiver of the requirement for termination is permitted only if the 8(a) contractor's request for waiver is made to the SBA prior to the actual relinquishment of ownership or control, except in the case of death or incapacity where the waiver must be submitted within 60 calendar days after such an occurrence. The clauses in the contract entitled "Special 8(a) Contract Conditions" and "Special 8(a) Subcontract Conditions" require the SBA and the 8(a) subcontractor to notify the contracting officer when ownership of the firm is being transferred. When the contracting officer receives information that an 8(a) contractor is planning to transfer ownership or control to another firm, the contracting officer shall take action immediately to preserve the option of waiving the termination requirement. The contracting officer shall determine the timing of the proposed transfer and its effect on contract performance and mission support. If the contracting officer determines that the SBA does not intend to waive the termination requirement, and termination of the contract would severely impair attainment of the agency's program objectives or mission, the contracting officer shall immediately notify the SBA in writing that the agency is requesting a waiver. Within 15 business days thereafter, or such longer period as agreed to by the agency and the SBA, the agency head must either confirm or withdraw the request for waiver. Unless a waiver is approved by the SBA, the contracting officer must terminate the contract for convenience upon receipt of a written request by the SBA. This requirement for a convenience termination does not affect the Government's right to terminate for default if the cause for termination of an 8(a) contract is other than the transfer of ownership or control.

[FAC 84-52, 54 FR 46009, 10/31/89, effective 11/30/89; FAC 84-56, 55 FR 3883, 2/5/90, effective 2/5/90; FAC 84-58, 55 FR 25530, 6/21/90, effective 7/23/90; FAC 90-4, 56 FR 15151, 4/15/91, effective 5/15/91; FAC 97-12, 64 FR 32740, 6/17/99, effective 6/17/99, finalized without change, FAC 97-15, 64 FR 72414, 12/27/99; FAC 97-22, 66 FR 2116, 1/10/2001, effective 1/10/2001; FAC 2005-56, 77 FR 12948, 3/2/2012, effective 3/2/2012; FAC 2005-95, 82 FR 4724, 1/13/2017, effective 1/13/2017]

19.813 Protesting an 8(a) participant's eligibility or size status.

(a) The eligibility of an 8(a) participant for a sole source or competitive 8(a) requirement may not be challenged by another 8(a) participant or any other party, either to SBA or any administrative forum as part of a bid or other contract protest (see 13 CFR 124.517).

(b) The size status of an 8(a) participant nominated for an 8(a) sole source contract may not be protested by another 8(a) participant or any other party.

(c) The size status of the apparent successful offeror for competitive 8(a) awards may be protested. The filing of a size status protest is limited to—

(1) Any offeror whom the contracting officer has not eliminated for reasons unrelated to size;

(2) The contracting officer; or

(3) The SBA District Director in either the district office serving the geographical area

in which the contracting activity is located or the district office that services the apparent successful offeror, or the Associate Administrator for Business Development.

(d) Protests of competitive 8(a) awards shall follow the procedures at 19.302. For additional information, refer to 13 CFR 121.1001.

[FAC 2005-95, 82 FR 4724, 1/13/2017, effective 1/13/2017]

19.814 Requesting a formal size determination (8(a) sole source requirements).

(a) If the size status of an 8(a) participant nominated for award of an 8(a) sole source contract is called into question, a request for a formal size determination may be submitted to SBA pursuant to 13 CFR 121.1001(b)(2)(ii) by—

(1) The 8(a) participant nominated for award of the particular sole source contract;

(2) The contracting officer who has been delegated SBA's 8(a) contract execution functions, where applicable, or the SBA program official with authority to execute the 8(a) contract;

(3) The SBA District Director in the district office that services the 8(a) participant or the Associate Administrator for Business Development; or

(4) The SBA Inspector General.

(b) SBA's Government Contracting Area Director will issue a formal size determination within 15 business days, if possible, after SBA receives the request for a formal size determination.

(c) An appeal of an SBA size determination shall follow the procedures at 19.302.

[FAC 2005-95, 82 FR 4724, 1/13/2017, effective 1/13/2017]

19.815 Release for non-8(a) procurement.

(a) Once a requirement has been accepted by SBA into the 8(a) program, any follow-on requirements shall remain in the 8(a) program unless there is a mandatory source (see 8.002 or 8.003) or SBA agrees to release the requirement from the 8(a) program in accordance with 13 CFR 124.504(d).

(b) To obtain release of a requirement for a non-8(a) procurement (other than a mandatory source listed at 8.002 or 8.003), the contracting officer shall make a written request to, and receive concurrence from, the SBA Associate Administrator for Business Development.

(c)(1) The written request to the SBA Associate Administrator for Business Development shall indicate?

(i) Whether the agency has achieved its small disadvantaged business goal;

(ii) Whether the agency has achieved its HUBZone, SDVOSB, WOSB, or small business goal(s); and

(iii) Whether the requirement is critical to the business development of the 8(a) contractor that is currently performing the requirement.

(2) Generally, a requirement that was previously accepted into the 8(a) program will only be released for procurements outside the 8(a) program when the contracting activity agency agrees to set aside the requirement under the small business, HUBZone, SDVOSB, or WOSB programs.

(3) The requirement that a follow-on procurement must be released from the 8(a) program in order for it to be fulfilled outside the 8(a) program does not apply to task or delivery orders offered to and accepted into the 8(a) program, where the basic contract was not accepted into the 8(a) program.

[FAC 2005-95, 82 FR 4724, 1/13/2017, effective 1/13/2017]

19.816 Exiting the 8(a) program.

(a) Except as provided in paragraph (c) of this section, when a contractor exits the 8(a) program, it is no longer eligible to receive new 8(a) contracts. However, the contractor remains under contractual obligation to complete existing contracts, and any priced options that may be exercised.

(b) If an 8(a) contractor is suspended from the program (see 13 CFR 124.305), it may not receive any new 8(a) contracts unless the head of the contracting agency makes a determination that it is in the best interest of the Government to issue the award and SBA adopts that determination.

(c) A contractor that has completed its term of participation in the 8(a) program may be awarded a competitive 8(a) contract if it was an 8(a) participant eligible for award of the contract on the initial date specified for receipt of offers contained in the solicitation, and if the contractor continues to meet all other applicable eligibility criteria.

(d) SBA's regulations on exiting the 8(a) program are found at 13 CFR 124.301 through 124.305, and 13 CFR 124.507(d).

[FAC 2005-95, 82 FR 4724, 1/13/2017, effective 1/13/2017]

SUBPART 19.9—[RESERVED]

SUBPART 19.10—[REMOVED AND RESERVED]

19.1001 [Removed and Reserved]

[FAC 97-4, 63 FR 9048, 2/23/98, effective 2/23/98; FAC 97-16, 65 FR 16274, 3/27/2000, effective 3/27/2000, finalized without change, FAC 97-19, 65 FR 46052, 7/26/2000; FAC 2005-01, 70 FR 11740, 3/9/2005, effective 3/9/2005; FAC 2005-06, 70 FR 57458, 9/30/2004, effective 9/30/2005; FAC 2005-48, 75 FR 82567, 12/30/2010, effective 1/31/2011]

19.1002 [Removed and Reserved]

[FAC 84-42, 54 FR 5055, 1/31/89, effective 1/31/89; FAC 97-16, 65 FR 16274, 3/27/2000, effective 3/27/2000, finalized without change, FAC 97-19, 65 FR 46052, 7/26/2000; FAC 97-19, 65 FR 46052, 7/26/2000, effective 10/1/2000, finalized without change by FAC 2001-02, 12/18/2001, effective 12/18/2001; FAC 2005-01, 70 FR 11740, 3/9/2005, effective 3/9/2005; FAC 2005-06, 70 FR 57458, 9/30/2005, effective 9/30/2005; FAC 2005-13, 71 FR 57363, 9/28/2006, effective 9/28/2006; FAC 2005-48, 75 FR 82567, 12/30/2010, effective 1/31/2011]

19.1003 [Removed and Reserved]

[FAC 84-42, 54 FR 5055, 1/31/89, effective 1/31/89; FAC 90-3, 55 FR 52792, 12/21/90, effective 1/22/91; FAC 97-4, 63 FR 9048, 2/23/98, effective 2/23/98; FAC 97-16, 65 FR 16274, 3/27/2000, effective 3/27/2000, finalized without change, FAC 97-19, 65 FR 46052, 7/26/2000; FAC 2005-01, 70 FR 11740, 3/9/2005, effective 3/9/2005; FAC 2005-06, 70 FR 57458, 9/30/2004, effective 9/30/2005; FAC 2005-48, 75 FR 82567, 12/30/2010, effective 1/31/2011]

19.1004 [Removed and Reserved]

[FAC 84-42, 54 FR 5055, 1/31/89, effective 1/31/89; FAC 84-49, 54 FR 29281, 7/11/89, effective 8/10/89; Final rule, 55 FR 38516, 9/19/90; FAC 97-9, 63 FR 58587, 10/30/98, effective 10/30/98; FAC 2005-48, 75 FR 82567, 12/30/2010, effective 1/31/2011]

19.1005 [Removed and Reserved]

[FAC 90-3, 55 FR 52792, 12/21/90, effective 1/22/91; FAC 90-23, 59 FR 67010, 12/28/94, effective 12/28/94, finalized without change, FAC 90-39, 61 FR 31612, 6/20/96, effective 6/20/96; FAC 97-16, 65 FR 16274, 3/27/2000, effective 3/27/2000, finalized without change, FAC 97-19, 65 FR 46052, 7/26/2000; FAC 97-19, 65 FR 46052, 7/26/2000, effective 10/1/2000, finalized with minor changes by FAC 2001-02, 12/18/2001, effective 12/18/2001; FAC 2001-15, 68 FR 43873, 7/24/2003, effective 7/24/2003; FAC 2005-01, 70 FR 11740, 3/9/2005, effective 3/9/2005; FAC 2005-06, 70 FR 57458, 9/30/2005, effective 9/30/2005; FAC 2005-09, Final rule, 71 FR 20309, 4/19/2006, effective 4/19/2006; FAC 2005-48, 75 FR 82567, 12/30/2010, effective 1/31/2011]

19.1006 [Removed and Reserved]

[FAC 97-16, 65 FR 16274, 3/27/2000, effective 3/27/2000, finalized without change, FAC 97-19, 65 FR 46052, 7/26/2000; FAC 2005-48, 75 FR 82567, 12/30/2010, effective 1/31/2011]

19.1007 [Removed and Reserved]

[FAC 90-3, 55 FR 52792, 12/21/90, effective 1/22/91; Final rule, FAC 90-20, 59 FR 11368, 3/10/94, effective 5/9/94; FAC 90-23, 59 FR 67010, 12/28/94, effective 12/28/94, finalized without change, FAC 90-39, 61 FR 31612, 6/20/96, effective 6/20/96; FAC 90-29, 60 FR 34732, 7/3/95, effective 7/3/95; FAC 90-43, Final rule, 61 FR 67408, 12/20/96, effective 12/20/96; FAC 97-3, 62

FR 64912, 12/9/97, effective 2/9/98; FAC 97-4, 63 FR 9048, 2/23/98, effective 2/23/98; FAC 97-10, 63 FR 70264, 12/18/98, effective 1/4/99; Redesignated from 19.1006, FAC 97-16, 65 FR 16274, 3/27/2000, effective 3/27/2000, finalized without change, FAC 97-19, 65 FR 46052, 7/26/2000; FAC 97-19, 65 FR 46052, 7/26/2000, effective 10/1/2000, finalized without change by FAC 2001-02, 66 FR 65347, 12/18/2001, effective 12/18/2001; FAC 2001-23, 69 FR 25273, 5/5/2004, effective 5/5/2004; FAC 2005-01, 70 FR 11740, 3/9/2005, effective 3/9/2005; FAC 2005-02, 70 FR 14950, 3/23/2005, effective 3/23/2005; FAC 2005-06, 70 FR 57458, 9/30/2004, effective 9/30/2005; FAC 2005-13, 71 FR 57363, 9/28/2006, effective 9/28/2006; FAC 2005-48, 75 FR 82567, 12/30/2010, effective 1/31/2011]

19.1008 [Removed and Reserved]

[FAC 90-3, 55 FR 52793, 12/21/90, effective 1/22/91; Redesignated from 19.1007, FAC 97-16, 65 FR 16274, 3/27/2000, effective 3/27/2000, finalized without change, FAC 97-19, 65 FR 46052, 7/26/2000; FAC 2005-01, 70 FR 11740, 3/9/2005, effective 3/9/2005; FAC 2005-06, 70 FR 57458, 9/30/2004, effective 9/30/2005; FAC 2005-13, 71 FR 57363, 9/28/2006, effective 9/28/2006; FAC 2005-48, 75 FR 82567, 12/30/2010, effective 1/31/2011]

SUBPART 19.11—[REMOVED AND RESERVED]

19.1101 [Removed and Reserved]

[FAC 97-6, 63 FR 35719, 6/30/98, effective 10/1/98, finalized without change, FAC 97-13, 7/2/99; FAC 2005-77, 79 FR 61746, 10/14/2014, effective 10/14/2014]

19.1102 [Removed and Reserved]

[FAC 97-13, 64 FR 36222, 7/2/99, effective 10/1/99; FAC 97-19, 65 FR 46052, 7/26/2000, effective 10/1/2000, finalized without change by FAC 2001-02, 66 FR 65347, 12/18/2001, effective 12/18/2001; FAC 2001-23, 69 FR 25273, 5/5/2004, effective 5/5/2004; FAC 2005-02, 70 FR 14950, 3/23/2005, effective 3/23/2005; FAC 2005-06, 70 FR 57462, 9/30/2005, effective 9/30/2005; FAC 2005-09, 71 FR 20304, 04/19/2006, effective 4/19/2006; FAC 2005-77, 79 FR 61746, 10/14/2014, effective 10/14/2014]

19.1103 [Removed and Reserved]

[FAC 97-6, 63 FR 35719, 6/30/98, effective 10/1/98; FAC 97-8, 63 FR 52425, 9/30/98, effective 10/1/98; FAC 97-13, 64 FR 36222, 7/2/99, effective 10/1/99; FAC 97-15, 64 FR 72414, 12/27/99, effective 2/25/2000; FAC 2001-19, 69 FR 1051, 1/7/2004, effective 1/1/2004; FAC 2001-25, Final rule, 69 FR 59700, 10/5/2004, effective 10/5/2004; FAC 2005-04, 70 FR 33661, 6/8/2005, effective 7/8/2005; FAC 2005-06, 70 FR 57462, 9/30/2005, effective 9/30/2005; FAC 2005-09, 71 FR 20304, 4/19/2006, effective 4/19/2006; FAC 2005-17, 72 FR 27364, 5/15/2007, effective 6/14/2007; FAC 2005-77, 79 FR 61746, 10/14/2014, effective 10/14/2014]

19.1104 [Removed and Reserved]

[FAC 97-8, 63 FR 52425, 9/30/98, effective 10/1/98; FAC 97-13, 64 FR 36222, 7/2/99, effective 10/1/99; FAC 2005-77, 79 FR 61746, 10/14/2014, effective 10/14/2014]

SUBPART 19.12—[REMOVED AND RESERVED]

19.1201 [Removed and Reserved]

[FAC 97-7, 63 FR 36120, 7/1/98, effective 1/1/99, finalized without change, FAC 97-13, 64 FR 36222, 7/2/99; FAC 97-19, 65 FR 46052, 7/26/2000, effective 10/1/2000, finalized without change by FAC 2001-02, 66 FR 65347, 12/18/2001, effective 12/18/2001; FAC 2005-77, 79 FR 61746, 10/14/2014, effective 10/14/2014]

19.1202 [Removed and Reserved]

19.1202-1 [Removed and Reserved]

[FAC 97-7, 63 FR 36120, 7/1/98, effective 1/1/99, finalized without change, FAC 97-13, 7/2/99; FAC 97-19, 65 FR 46052, 7/26/2000, effective 10/1/2000, finalized without change by FAC 2001-02, 66 FR 65347, 12/18/2001, effective 12/18/2001; FAC 2005-77, 79 FR 61746, 10/14/2014, effective 10/14/2014]

19.1202-2 [Removed and Reserved]

[FAC 97-7, 63 FR 36120, 7/1/98, effective 1/1/99, finalized without change, FAC 97-13, 7/2/99; FAC 97-10, 63 FR 70264, 12/18/98, effective 1/4/99; FAC 97-19, 65 FR 46052, 7/26/2000, effective 10/1/2000, finalized without change by FAC 2001-02, 66 FR 65347, 12/18/2001, effective 12/18/2001; FAC 2001-14, 68 FR 28079, 5/22/2003, effective 6/23/2003; FAC 2001-23, 69 FR 25273, 5/5/2004, effective 5/5/2004; FAC 2005-02, 70 FR 14950, 3/23/2005, effective 3/23/2005; FAC 2005-13, 71 FR 57363, 9/28/2006, effective 9/28/2006; FAC 2005-45, 75 FR 53129, 8/30/2010, effective 10/1/2010; FAC 2005-51, 76 FR 18304, 4/1/2011, effective 4/1/2011; FAC 2005-56, 77 FR 12913, 3/2/2012, effective 4/2/2012; FAC 2005-77, 79 FR 61746, 10/14/2014, effective 10/14/2014]

19.1202-3 [Removed and Reserved]

[FAC 97-7, 63 FR 36120, 7/1/98, effective 1/1/99; FAC 97-13, 64 FR 36222, 7/2/99, effective 10/1/99; FAC 2005-77, 79 FR 61746, 10/14/2014, effective 10/14/2014; FAC 2005-77, 79 FR 61746, 10/14/2014, effective 10/14/2014]

19.1202-4 [Removed and Reserved]

[FAC 97-7, 63 FR 36120, 7/1/98, effective 1/1/99, corrected 63 FR 71721, 12/29/98; FAC 97-13, 64 FR 36222, 7/2/99, effective 10/1/99; FAC 97-19, 65 FR 46052, 7/26/2000, effective 10/1/2000, finalized without change by FAC 2001-02, 66 FR 65347, 12/18/2001, effective 12/18/2001; FAC 2005-77, 79 FR 61746, 10/14/2014, effective 10/14/2014]

19.1203 [Removed and Reserved]

[FAC 97-7, 63 FR 36120, 7/1/98, effective 1/1/99, finalized without change, FAC 97-13, 7/2/99; FAC 97-19, 65 FR 46052, 7/26/2000, effective 10/1/2000, finalized without change by FAC 2001-02, 66 FR 65347, 12/18/2001, effective 12/18/2001; FAC 2005-77, 79 FR 61746, 10/14/2014, effective 10/14/2014]

19.1204 [Removed and Reserved]

[FAC 97-7, 63 FR 36120, 7/1/98, effective 1/1/99, finalized without change, FAC 97-13, 7/2/99; FAC 2005-77, 79 FR 61746, 10/14/2014, effective 10/14/2014]

SUBPART 19.13—HISTORICALLY UNDERUTILIZED BUSINESS ZONE (HUBZONE) PROGRAM

19.1301 General.

(a) The Historically Underutilized Business Zone (HUBZone) Act of 1997 (15 U.S.C. 631 note) created the HUBZone Program.

(b) The purpose of the HUBZone Program is to provide Federal contracting assistance for qualified small business concerns located in historically underutilized business zones, in an effort to increase employment opportunities, investment, and economic development in those areas.

[FAC 97-10, 63 FR 70264, 12/18/98, effective 1/4/99; FAC 2005-47, 75 FR 77727, 12/13/2010, effective 1/12/2011]

19.1302 Applicability.

The procedures in this subpart apply to all Federal agencies that employ one or more contracting officers.

[FAC 2001-06, 67 FR 13048, 3/20/2002, effective 4/4/2002]

19.1303 Status as a HUBZone small business concern.

(a) Status as a HUBZone small business concern is determined by the Small Business Administration (SBA) in accordance with 13 CFR part 126.

(b) If the SBA determines that a concern is a HUBZone small business concern, it will issue a certification to that effect and will add the concern to the List of Qualified HUBZone Small Business Concerns at *http://dsbs.sba.gov/dsbs/search/dsp_searchhubzone.cfm*. Only firms on the list are HUBZone small business concerns, eligible for HUBZone preferences. HUBZone preferences apply without regard to the place of performance. Information on HUBZone small business concerns can also be obtained at *http://www.sba.gov/hubzone* or by writing to the Director for the HUBZone Program (Director/HUB) at U.S. Small Business Administration, 409 3rd

Street, SW., Washington, DC 20416 or at *hubzone@sba.gov*.

(c) A joint venture may be considered a HUBZone small business concern if it meets the criteria in 13 CFR 121.103(h).

(d) To be eligible for a HUBZone contract under this section, a HUBZone small business concern must be a HUBZone small business concern both at the time of its initial offer and at the time of contract award.

(e) A HUBZone small business concern may submit an offer for supplies as a nonmanufacturer if it meets the requirements of the nonmanufacturer rule set forth at 13 CFR 121.406(b)(1) and if the small business manufacturer providing the end item is also a HUBZone small business concern.

(1) There are no waivers to the nonmanufacturer rule for HUBZone contracts.

(2) For HUBZone contracts at or below $25,000 in total value, a HUBZone small business concern may supply the end item of any manufacturer, including a large business, so long as the product acquired is manufactured or produced in the United States.

[FAC 97-10, 63 FR 70264, 12/18/98, effective 1/4/99; FAC 97-14, 64 FR 51828, 9/24/99, effective 11/23/99; FAC 2005-47, 75 FR 77727, 12/13/2010, effective 1/12/2011; FAC 2019-06, 84 FR 47862, 9/10/2019, effective 10/10/2019]

19.1304 Exclusions.

This subpart does not apply to—

(a) Requirements that can be satisfied through award to—

(1) Federal Prison Industries, Inc. (see subpart 8.6); or

(2) AbilityOne participating non-profit agencies for the blind or severely disabled (see subpart 8.7);

(b) Orders under indefinite-delivery contracts (see subpart 16.5). (But see 16.505(b)(2)(i)(F) for discretionary set-asides of orders);

(c) Orders against Federal Supply Schedules (see subpart 8.4). (But see 8.405-5 for discretionary set-asides of orders);

(d) Requirements currently being performed by an 8(a) participant or requirements SBA has accepted for performance under the authority of the 8(a) program, unless SBA has consented to release the requirements from the 8(a) program;

(e) Requirements that do not exceed the micro-purchase threshold; or

(f) Requirements for commissary or exchange resale items.

[FAC 97-10, 63 FR 70264, 12/18/98, effective 1/4/99; FAC 2005-54, 76 FR 68032, 11/2/2011, effective 11/2/2011; Interim rule, 77 FR 1889, 1/12/2012, effective 2/13/2012; FAC 2005-73, 79 FR 24192, 4/29/2014, effective 5/29/2014; FAC 2005-95, 82 FR 4724, 1/13/2017, effective 1/13/2017]

19.1305 HUBZone set-aside procedures.

(a) The contracting officer—

(1) Shall comply with 19.203 before deciding to set aside an acquisition under the HUBZone Program;

(2) May set aside acquisitions exceeding the micro-purchase threshold for competition restricted to HUBZone small business concerns when the requirements of paragraph (b) of this section can be satisfied; and

(3) Shall consider HUBZone set-asides before considering HUBZone sole source awards (see 19.1306) or small business set-asides (see subpart 19.5).

(b) To set aside an acquisition for competition restricted to HUBZone small business concerns, the contracting officer must have a reasonable expectation that—

(1) Offers will be received from two or more HUBZone small business concerns; and

(2) Award will be made at a fair market price.

(c) If the contracting officer receives only one acceptable offer from a qualified HUBZone small business concern in response to a set aside, the contracting officer should make an award to that concern. If the contracting officer receives no acceptable offers from HUBZone small business concerns, the HUBZone set-aside shall be withdrawn and the requirement, if still valid, set aside for small business concerns, as appropriate (see 19.203).

(d) The procedures at 19.202-1 and, except for acquisitions not exceeding the simplified acquisition threshold, at 19.402 apply to this section.

(1) When the SBA intends to appeal a contracting officer's decision to reject a recommendation of the SBA procurement center representative (or, if a procurement center representative is not assigned, *see* 19.402(a)) to set aside an acquisition for competition restricted to HUBZone small business concerns, the SBA procurement center representative shall notify the contracting officer, in writing, of its intent within 5 business days of receiving the contracting officer's notice of rejection.

(2) Upon receipt of notice of SBA's intent to appeal, the contracting officer shall suspend action on the acquisition unless the head of the contracting activity makes a written determination that urgent and compelling circumstances, which significantly affect the interests of the Government, exist.

(3) Within 15 business days of SBA's notification to the contracting officer, SBA must file its formal appeal with the head of the agency, or the appeal will be deemed withdrawn. The head of the agency shall reply to SBA within 15 business days of receiving the appeal. The decision of the head of the agency shall be final.

[FAC 97-10, 63 FR 70264, 12/18/98, effective 1/4/99; FAC 2005-10, 71 FR 36925, 6/28/2006, effective 7/28/2006; FAC 2005-47, 75 FR 77727, 12/13/2010, effective 1/12/2011; FAC 2005-50, 76 FR 14566, 3/16/2011, effective 3/16/2011; FAC 2005-56, 77 FR 12930, 3/2/2012, effective 4/2/2012]

19.1306 HUBZone sole source awards.

(a) A contracting officer shall consider a contract award to a HUBZone small business concern on a sole source basis (see 6.302-5(b)(5)) before considering a small business set-aside (see 19.203 and subpart 19.5), provided none of the exclusions at 19.1304 apply; and—

(1) The contracting officer does not have a reasonable expectation that offers would be received from two or more HUBZone small business concerns;

(2) The anticipated price of the contract, including options, will not exceed—

(i) $7 million for a requirement within the North American Industry Classification System (NAICS) codes for manufacturing; or

(ii) $4 million for a requirement within all other NAICS codes;

(3) The requirement is not currently being performed by an 8(a) participant under the provisions of subpart 19.8 or has been accepted as a requirement by SBA under subpart 19.8.

(4) The acquisition is greater than the simplified acquisition threshold (see part 13);

(5) The HUBZone small business concern has been determined to be a responsible contractor with respect to performance; and

(6) Award can be made at a fair and reasonable price.

(b) The SBA has the right to appeal the contracting officer's decision not to make a HUBZone sole source award.

[FAC 97-10, 63 FR 70264, 12/18/98, effective 1/4/99; FAC 97-19, 65 FR 46052, 7/26/2000, effective 10/1/2000, finalized without change by FAC 2001-02, 66 FR 65347, 12/18/2001, effective 12/18/2001; FAC 2001-12, 1/27/2003, effective 1/24/2003; FAC 2001-20, 69 FR 8311, 2/23/2004, effective 2/23/2004; FAC 2001-26, 69 FR 76350, 12/20/2004, effective 1/19/2005; FAC 2005-13, 71 FR 57363, 9/28/2006, effective 9/28/2006; FAC 2005-43, 75 FR 38687, 7/2/2010, effective 8/2/2010; FAC 2005-45, 75 FR 53129, 8/30/2010, effective 10/1/2010; FAC 2005-47, 75 FR 77727, 12/13/2010, effective 1/12/2011; FAC 2005-50, 76 FR 14566, 3/16/2011, effective 3/16/2011; FAC 2005-56, 77 FR 12930, 3/2/2012, effective

4/2/2012; FAC 2005-83, 80 FR 38293, 7/2/2015, effective 10/1/2015]

19.1307 Price evaluation preference for HUBZone small business concerns.

(a) The price evaluation preference for HUBZone small business concerns shall be used in acquisitions conducted using full and open competition. The preference shall not be used—

(1) Where price is not a selection factor so that a price evaluation preference would not be considered (e.g., Architect/Engineer acquisitions); or

(2) Where all fair and reasonable offers are accepted (e.g., the award of multiple award schedule contracts).

(b) The contracting officer shall give offers from HUBZone small business concerns a price evaluation preference by adding a factor of 10 percent to all offers, except—

(1) Offers from HUBZone small business concerns that have not waived the evaluation preference; or

(2) Otherwise successful offers from small business concerns.

(c) The factor of 10 percent shall be applied on a line item basis or to any group of items on which award may be made. Other evaluation factors, such as transportation costs or rent-free use of Government property, shall be added to the offer to establish the base offer before adding the factor of 10 percent.

(d) When the two highest rated offerors are a HUBZone small business concern and a large business, and the evaluated offer of the HUBZone small business concern is equal to the evaluated offer of the large business after considering the price evaluation preference, the contracting officer shall award the contract to the HUBZone small business concern.

[FAC 97-10, 63 FR 70264, 12/18/98, effective 1/4/99; FAC 97-15, 64 FR 72414, 12/27/99, effective 2/25/2000; FAC 2001-19, 69 FR 1051, 1/7/2004, effective 1/1/2004; FAC 2001-25, Final rule, 69 FR 59700, 10/5/2004, effective 10/5/2004; FAC 2005-04, 70 FR 33661, 6/8/2005, effective 7/8/2005; FAC 2005-17, 72 FR 27364, 5/15/2007, effective 6/14/2007; FAC 2005-47, 75 FR 77727, 12/13/2010, effective 1/12/2011; FAC 2005-77, 79 FR 61746, 10/14/2014, effective 10/14/2014]

19.1308 Performance of work requirements (limitations on subcontracting) for general construction or construction by special trade contractors.

(a) Before issuing a solicitation for general construction or construction by special trade contractors, the contracting officer shall determine if at least two HUBZone small business concerns can spend at least 50 percent of the cost of contract performance to be incurred for personnel on their own employees or subcontract employees of other HUBZone small business concerns.

(b) The clause at 52.219-3, Notice of HUBZone Set-Aside or Sole Source Award, or 52.219-4, Notice of Price Evaluation Preference for HUBZone Small Business Concerns, shall be used, as applicable, with its Alternate I to waive the 50 percent requirement (*see* 19.1309) if at least two HUBZone small business concerns cannot meet the conditions of paragraph (a); but, the HUBZone prime contractor can still meet the following—

(1) For general construction, at least 15 percent of the cost of the contract performance to be incurred for personnel using the concern's employees; or

(2) For construction by special trade contractors, at least 25 percent of the cost of contract performance to be incurred for personnel using the concern's employees.

(c) *See* 13 CFR 125.6 for definitions of terms used in paragraph (a) of this section.

[FAC 2005-47, 75 FR 77727, 12/13/2010, effective 1/12/2011; FAC 2005-54, 76 FR 68032, 11/2/2011, effective 11/2/2011; Interim rule, 77 FR 1889, 1/12/2012, effective 2/13/2012]

19.1309 Contract clauses.

(a) The contracting officer shall insert the clause 52.219-3, Notice of HUBZone Set-Aside or Sole Source Award, in solicitations and contracts for acquisitions that are set aside, or reserved for, or awarded on a sole source basis to, HUBZone small business concerns under 19.1305 or 19.1306. This includes multiple-award contracts when orders may be set aside for HUBZone small business concerns as described in 8.405-5 and 16.505(b)(2)(i)(F).

(1) The contracting officer shall use the clause with its Alternate I to waive the 50 percent requirement if the conditions at 19.1308(b) apply.

(2) If a waiver is granted, the HUBZone small business prime contractor must still meet the performance of work requirements set forth in 13 CFR 125.6(c).

(b) The contracting officer shall insert the clause at FAR 52.219-4, Notice of Price Evaluation Preference for HUBZone Small Business Concerns, in solicitations and contracts for acquisitions conducted using full and open competition.

(1) The contracting officer shall use the clause with its Alternate I to waive the 50 percent requirement if the conditions at 19.1308(b) apply.

(2) If a waiver is granted, the HUBZone small business prime contractor must still meet the performance of work requirements set forth in 13 CFR 125.6(c).

[FAC 97-10, 63 FR 70264, 12/18/98, effective 1/4/99; Redesignated from 19.1308, FAC 2005-47, 75 FR 77727, 12/13/2010, effective 1/12/2011; FAC 2005-54, 76 FR 68032, 11/2/2011, effective 11/2/2011; Interim rule, 77 FR 1889, 1/12/2012, effective 2/13/2012]

SUBPART 19.14—SERVICE-DISABLED VETERAN-OWNED SMALL BUSINESS PROCUREMENT PROGRAM

19.1401 General.

(a) The Veterans Benefit Act of 2003 (15 U.S.C. 657f) created the procurement program for small business concerns owned and controlled by service-disabled veterans (commonly referred to as the "Service-Disabled Veteran-owned Small Business (SDVOSB) Procurement Program").

(b) The purpose of the Service-Disabled Veteran-Owned Small Business Program is to provide Federal contracting assistance to service-disabled veteran-owned small business concerns.

[FAC 2001-23, 69 FR 25273, 5/5/2004, effective 5/5/2004]

19.1402 Applicability.

The procedures in this subpart apply to all Federal agencies that employ one or more contracting officers.

[FAC 2001-23, 69 FR 25273, 5/5/2004, effective 5/5/2004]

19.1403 Status as a service-disabled veteran-owned small business concern.

(a) Status as a service-disabled veteran-owned small business concern is determined in accordance with 13 CFR parts 125.8 through 125.13; also see 19.307.

(b) At the time that a service-disabled veteran-owned small business concern submits its offer, it must represent to the contracting officer that it is a—

(1) Service-disabled veteran-owned small business concern; and

(2) Small business concern under the North American Industry Classification System (NAICS) code assigned to the procurement.

(c) A joint venture may be considered a service-disabled veteran owned small business concern if—

(1) At least one member of the joint venture is a service-disabled veteran-owned small business concern, and makes the representations in paragraph (b) of this section;

(2) Each other concern is small under the size standard corresponding to the NAICS code assigned to the procurement;

(3) The joint venture meets the requirements in 13 CFR 121.103(h); and

(4) The joint venture meets the requirements of 13 CFR 125.15(b).

(d) Any service-disabled veteran-owned small business concern (nonmanufacturer) must meet the requirements in 19.102(f) to receive a benefit under this program.

[FAC 2001-23, 69 FR 25273, 5/5/2004, effective 5/5/2004; FAC 2019-06, 84 FR 47862, 9/10/2019, effective 10/10/2019]

19.1404 Exclusions.

This subpart does not apply to—

(a) Requirements that can be satisfied through award to—

(1) Federal Prison Industries, Inc. (see Subpart 8.6);

(2) AbilityOne participating non-profit agencies for the blind or severely disabled (see Subpart 8.7);

(b) Orders under indefinite-delivery contracts (see subpart 16.5). (But see 16.505(b)(2)(i)(F) for discretionary set-asides of orders);

(c) Orders against Federal Supply Schedules (see subpart 8.4). (But see 8.405-5 for discretionary set-asides of orders); or

(d) Requirements currently being performed by an 8(a) participant or requirements SBA has accepted for performance under the authority of the 8(a) program, unless SBA has consented to release the requirements from the 8(a) program.

[FAC 2001-23, 69 FR 25273, 5/5/2004, effective 5/5/2004; FAC 2005-02, 70 FR 14950, 3/23/2005, effective 3/23/2005; FAC 2005-54, 76 FR 68032, 11/2/2011, effective 11/2/2011; Interim rule, 77 FR 1889, 1/12/2012, effective 2/13/2012; FAC 2005-73, 79 FR 24192, 4/29/2014, effective 5/29/2014; FAC 2005-95, 82 FR 4724, 1/13/2017, effective 1/13/2017]

19.1405 Service-disabled veteran-owned small business set-aside procedures.

(a) The contracting officer—

(1) Shall comply with 19.203 before deciding to set aside an acquisition under the SDVOSB Program;

(2) May set-aside acquisitions exceeding the micro-purchase threshold for competition restricted to SDVOSB concerns when the requirements of paragraph (b) of this section can be satisfied; and

(3) Shall consider SDVOSB set-asides before considering SDVOSB sole source awards (see 19.1406) or small business set-asides (see subpart 19.5).

(b) To set aside an acquisition for competition restricted to service-disabled veteran-owned small business concerns, the contracting officer must have a reasonable expectation that—

(1) Offers will be received from two or more service-disabled veteran-owned small business concerns; and

(2) Award will be made at a fair market price.

(c) If the contracting officer receives only one acceptable offer from a service-disabled veteran-owned small business concern in response to a set-aside, the contracting officer should make an award to that concern. If the contracting officer receives no acceptable offers from service-disabled veteran-owned small business concerns, the service-disabled veteran-owned set-aside shall be withdrawn and the requirement, if still valid, set aside for small business concerns, as appropriate (see 19.203).

(d) The procedures at 19.202-1 and, except for acquisitions not exceeding the simplified acquisition threshold, at 19.402 apply to this section. When the SBA intends to appeal a contracting officer's decision to reject a recommendation of the SBA procurement center representative (or, if a procurement center representative is not assigned, see 19.402(a)) to set aside an acquisition for competition restricted to service-disabled veteran-owned small business concerns, the SBA procurement center representative shall notify the contracting officer, in writing, of its intent within 5 working days of receiving the contracting officer's notice of rejection. Within 15 working days of SBA's notification to the contracting officer, SBA shall file its formal appeal with the head of the contracting activity, or that agency may consider the appeal withdrawn. The head of the contracting activity shall reply to SBA within 15 working days of receiving the appeal. The decision of the head of the contracting activity shall be final.

[FAC 2001-23, 69 FR 25273, 5/5/2004, effective 5/5/2004; FAC 2005-10, 71 FR 36925, 6/28/2006, effective 7/28/2006; FAC 2005-50, 76 FR 14566, 3/16/2011, effective 3/16/2011; FAC 2005-56, 77 FR 12930, 3/2/2012, effective 4/2/2012]

19.1406 Sole source awards to service-disabled veteran-owned small business concerns.

(a) A contracting officer shall consider a contract award to a SDVOSB concern on a sole source basis (see 6.302-5(b)(6)), before considering small business set-asides (see 19.203 and subpart 19.5) provided none of the exclusions of 19.1404 apply and—

(1) The contracting officer does not have a reasonable expectation that offers would be received from two or more service-disabled veteran-owned small business concerns;

(2) The anticipated award price of the contract, including options, will not exceed—

(i) $6.5 million for a requirement within the NAICS codes for manufacturing; or

(ii) $4 million for a requirement within any other NAICS code;

(3) The requirement is not currently being performed by an 8(a) participant under the provisions of subpart 19.8 or has been accepted as a requirement by SBA under subpart 19.8;

(4) The service-disabled veteran-owned small business concern has been determined to be a responsible contractor with respect to performance; and

(5) Award can be made at a fair and reasonable price.

(b) The SBA has the right to appeal the contracting officer's decision not to make a service-disabled veteran-owned small business sole source award.

[FAC 2001-23, 69 FR 25273, 5/5/2004, effective 5/5/2004; FAC 2005-13, 71 FR 57363, 9/28/2006, effective 9/28/2006; FAC 2005-43, 75 FR 38687, 7/2/2010, effective 8/2/2010; FAC 2005-45, 75 FR 53129, 8/30/2010, effective 10/1/2010; FAC 2005-50, 76 FR 14566, 3/16/2011, effective 3/16/2011; FAC 2005-56, 77 FR 12930, 3/2/2012, effective 4/2/2012; FAC 2005-83, 80 FR 38293, 7/2/2015, effective 10/1/2015]

19.1407 Contract clauses.

The contracting officer shall insert the clause 52.219-27, Notice of Service-Disabled Veteran-Owned Small Business Set-Aside, in solicitations and contracts for acquisitions that are set aside or reserved for, or awarded on a sole source basis to, service-disabled veteran-owned small business concerns under 19.1405 and 19.1406. This includes multiple-award contracts when orders may be set aside for service-disabled veteran-owned small business concerns as described in 8.405-5 and 16.505(b)(2)(i)(F).

[FAC 2001-23, 69 FR 25273, 5/5/2004, effective 5/5/2004; FAC 2005-54, 76 FR 68032, 11/2/2011, effective 11/2/2011; Interim rule, 77 FR 1889, 1/12/2012, effective 2/13/2012]

SUBPART 19.15—WOMEN-OWNED SMALL BUSINESS PROGRAM

19.1500 General.

(a) Section 8(m) of the Small Business Act (15 U.S.C. 637(m)) created the Women-Owned Small Business (WOSB) Program.

(b) The purpose of the WOSB Program is to ensure women-owned small business concerns have an equal opportunity to participate in Federal contracting and to assist agencies in achieving their women-owned small business participation goals (see 13 part CFR 127).

(c) An economically disadvantaged women-owned small business (EDWOSB) concern or WOSB concern eligible under the WOSB Program is a subcategory of *women-owned small business concern* as defined in 2.101.

[FAC 2005-51, 76 FR 18304, 4/1/2011, effective 4/1/2011; FAC 2005-56, 77 FR 12913, 3/2/2012, effective 4/2/2012]

19.1501 Definition.

WOSB Program Repository means a secure, Web-based application that collects, stores, and disseminates documents to the contracting community and SBA, which verify the eligibility of a business concern for a contract to be awarded under the WOSB Program.

[FAC 2005-51, 76 FR 18304, 4/1/2011, effective 4/1/2011; FAC 2005-56, 77 FR 12913, 3/2/2012, effective 4/2/2012]

19.1502 Applicability.

The procedures in this subpart apply to all Federal agencies that employ one or more contracting officers.

[FAC 2005-51, 76 FR 18304, 4/1/2011, effective 4/1/2011; FAC 2005-56, 77 FR 12913, 3/2/2012, effective 4/2/2012]

19.1503 Status.

(a) Status as an EDWOSB concern or WOSB concern eligible under the WOSB Program is determined in accordance with 13 CFR part 127.

(b) The contracting officer shall verify that the offeror—

(1) Is registered in the System for Award Management (SAM);

(2) Is self-certified as an EDWOSB or WOSB concern in SAM; and

(3) Has submitted documents verifying its eligibility at the time of initial offer to the WOSB Program Repository. The contract shall not be awarded until all required documents are received.

(c)(1) An EDWOSB concern or WOSB concern eligible under the WOSB Program that has been certified by a SBA approved third party certifier, (which includes SBA certification under the 8(a) Program), must provide the following eligibility requirement documents—

(i) The third-party certification;

(ii) SBA's WOSB Program Certification form (SBA Form 2413 for WOSB concerns eligible under the WOSB Program and SBA Form 2414 for EDWOSB concerns); and

(iii) The joint venture agreement, if applicable.

(2) An EDWOSB concern or WOSB concern eligible under the WOSB Program that has not been certified by an SBA approved third party certifier or by SBA under the 8(a) Program, must provide the following documents:

(i) The U.S. birth certificate, naturalization documentation, or unexpired U.S. passport for each woman owner.

(ii) The joint venture agreement, if applicable.

(iii) For limited liability companies, Articles of organization (also referred to as certificate of organization or articles of formation) and any amendments, and the operating agreement and any amendments.

(iv) For corporations, articles of incorporation and any amendments, by-laws and any amendments, all issued stock certificates, including the front and back copies, signed in accord with the by-laws, stock ledger, and voting agreements, if any.

(v) For partnerships, the partnership agreement and any amendments.

(vi) For sole proprietorships, corporations, limited liability companies and partnerships if applicable, the assumed/fictitious name certificate(s).

(vii) SBA's WOSB Program Certification form (SBA Form 2413 for WOSB concerns eligible under the WOSB Program and SBA Form 2414 for EDWOSB concerns).

(viii) For EDWOSB concerns, in addition to the above, the SBA Form 413, Personal Financial Statement, available to the public at *https://www.sba.gov/managing-business/forms/small-business-forms/financial-assistance-forms/personal-financial-statement,* for each woman claiming economic disadvantage.

(d)(1) A contracting officer may accept a concern's self-certification as accurate for a specific procurement reserved for award under this subpart if—

(i) The apparent successful WOSB eligible under the WOSB Program or EDWOSB offeror provided the required documents;

(ii) There has been no protest or other credible information that calls into question the concern's eligibility as an EDWOSB concern or WOSB concern eligible under the WOSB Program; and

(iii) There has been no decision issued by SBA as a result of a current eligibility examination finding the concern did not qualify as an EDWOSB concern or WOSB concern eligible under the WOSB Program at the time it submitted its initial offer.

(2) The contracting officer shall file a status protest in accordance with 19.308 if—

(i) There is information that questions the eligibility of a concern; or

(ii) The concern fails to provide all of the required documents to verify its eligibility.

(e) If there is a decision issued by SBA as a result of a current eligibility examination finding that the concern did not qualify as an EDWOSB concern or WOSB concern eligible under the WOSB Program, the contracting officer may terminate the contract, and shall not exercise any option nor award further task or delivery orders. The contracting officer shall not count or include the award toward the small business accomplishments for an EDWOSB concern or WOSB concern eligible under the WOSB Program and must update FPDS from the date of award.

(f) A joint venture may be considered an EDWOSB concern or WOSB concern eligible under the WOSB Program if it meets the requirements of 13 CFR 127.506.

(g) An EDWOSB concern or WOSB concern eligible under the WOSB Program that is a non-manufacturer, as defined in 13 CFR 121.406(b), may submit an offer on a requirement set aside for an EDWOSB concern or a WOSB concern eligible under the WOSB Program with a NAICS code for supplies, if it meets the requirements under the non-manufacturer rule set forth in that regulation.

[FAC 2005-51, 76 FR 18304, 4/1/2011, effective 4/1/2011; FAC 2005-56, 77 FR 12913, 3/2/2012, effective 4/2/2012; FAC 2005-67, 78 FR 37676, 6/21/2013, effective 7/22/2013; FAC 2005-100, 83 FR 42571, 8/22/2018, effective 8/22/2018]

19.1504 Exclusions.

This subpart does not apply to—

(a) Requirements that an 8(a) contractor is currently performing under the 8(a) program or that SBA has accepted for performance under the authority of the 8(a) program, unless SBA has consented to release the requirements from the 8(a) program;

(b) Requirements that can be satisfied through award to—

(1) Federal Prison Industries, Inc. (see subpart 8.6); or

(2) AbilityOne participating non-profit agencies for the blind or severely disabled (see subpart 8.7);

(c) Orders under indefinite-delivery contracts (see subpart 16.5). (But see 16.505(b)(2)(i)(F) for discretionary set-asides of orders); or

(d) Orders against Federal Supply Schedules (see subpart 8.4). (But see 8.405-5 for discretionary set-asides of orders.)

[FAC 2005-51, 76 FR 18304, 4/1/2011, effective 4/1/2011; FAC 2005-54, 76 FR 68032, 11/2/2011, effective 11/2/2011; Interim rule, 77 FR 1889, 1/12/2012, effective 2/13/2012; FAC 2005-56, 77 FR 12913, 3/2/2012, effective 4/2/2012; FAC 2005-73, 79 FR 24192, 4/29/2014, effective 5/29/2014; FAC 2005-95, 82 FR 4724, 1/13/2017, effective 1/13/2017]

19.1505 Set-aside procedures.

(a) The contracting officer—

(1) Shall comply with 19.203 before deciding to set aside an acquisition under the WOSB Program; and

(2) May set aside acquisitions exceeding the micro-purchase threshold for competition restricted to EDWOSB concerns or WOSB concerns eligible under the WOSB Program when the acquisition—

(i) Is assigned a NAICS code in which SBA has determined that WOSB concerns are underrepresented in Federal procurement; or

(ii) Is assigned a NAICS code in which SBA has determined that WOSB concerns are substantially underrepresented in Federal procurement, as specified on SBA's Web site at *http://www.sba.gov/WOSB*.

(b) For requirements in NAICS codes designated by SBA as underrepresented, a contracting officer may restrict competition to EDWOSB concerns if the contracting officer has a reasonable expectation based on market research that—

(1) Two or more EDWOSB concerns will submit offers for the contract and;

(2) Contract award will be made at a fair and reasonable price.

(c) A contracting officer may restrict competition to WOSB concerns eligible under the WOSB Program (including EDWOSB concerns), for requirements in NAICS codes designated by SBA as substantially underrepresented if there is a reasonable expectation based on market research that—

(1) Two or more WOSB concerns eligible under the WOSB Program (including EDWOSB concerns), will submit offers and;

(2) Contract award may be made at a fair and reasonable price.

(d) The contracting officer may make an award, if only one acceptable offer is received from a qualified EDWOSB concern or WOSB concern eligible under the WOSB Program.

(e) The contracting officer must check whether the apparently successful offeror filed all the required eligibility documents, and file a status protest if any documents are missing. *See* 19.1503(d)(2).

(f) If no acceptable offers are received from an EDWOSB concern or WOSB concern eligible under the WOSB Program, the set-aside shall be withdrawn and the requirement, if still valid, must be considered for set aside in accordance with 19.203 and subpart 19.5.

(g) If the contracting officer rejects a recommendation by SBA's Procurement Center Representative—

(1) The contracting officer shall notify the procurement center representative as soon as practicable;

(2) SBA shall notify the contracting officer of its intent to appeal the contracting officer's decision no later than five business days after receiving notice of the contracting officer's decision;

(3) The contracting officer shall suspend further action regarding the procurement until the head of the agency issues a written decision on the appeal, unless the head of the agency makes a written determination that urgent and compelling circumstances which significantly affect the interests of the United States compel award of the contract;

(4) Within 15 business days of SBA's notification to the head of the contracting activity, SBA shall file a formal appeal to the head of the agency, or the appeal will be determined withdrawn; and

(5) The head of the agency, or designee, shall specify in writing the reasons for a denial of an appeal brought under this section.

[FAC 2005-51, 76 FR 18304, 4/1/2011, effective 4/1/2011; FAC 2005-56, 77 FR 12913, 3/2/2012, effective 4/2/2012; FAC 2005-67, 78 FR 37692, 6/21/2013, effective 6/21/2013; FAC 2005-75, 79 FR 35864, 6/24/2014, effective 6/24/2014; FAC 2005-86, 80 FR 81888, 12/31/2015, effective 12/31/2015; FAC 2005-91, 81 FR 67735, 9/30/2016, effective 9/30/2016]

19.1506 Women-Owned Small Business Program sole source awards.

(a) A contracting officer shall consider a contract award to an EDWOSB concern on a sole source basis (see 6.302-5(b)(7)) before considering small business set-asides (see 19.203 and subpart 19.5) provided none of the exclusions at 19.1504 apply and—

(1) The acquisition is assigned a NAICS code in which SBA has determined that WOSB concerns are underrepresented in Federal procurement;

(2) The contracting officer does not have a reasonable expectation that offers would be received from two or more EDWOSB concerns; and

(3) The conditions in paragraph (c) of this section exist.

(b) A contracting officer shall consider a contract award to a WOSB concern (including EDWOSB concerns) eligible under the WOSB Program on a sole source basis (see 6.302-5(b)(7)) before considering small business set-asides (see 19.203 and subpart 19.5) provided none of the exclusions at FAR 19.1504 apply and—

(1) The acquisition is assigned a NAICS code in which SBA has determined that WOSB concerns are substantially underrepresented in Federal procurement;

(2) The contracting officer does not have a reasonable expectation that offers would be received from two or more WOSB concerns (including EDWOSB concerns); and

(3) The conditions in paragraph (c) of this section exist.

(c) (1) The anticipated award price of the contract, including options, will not exceed—

(i) $6.5 million for a requirement within the NAICS codes for manufacturing; or

(ii) $4 million for a requirement within any other NAICS codes.

(2) The EDWOSB concern or WOSB concern has been determined to be a responsible contractor with respect to performance.

(3) The award can be made at a fair and reasonable price.

(d) The SBA has the right to appeal the contracting officer's decision not to make a sole source award to either an EDWOSB concern or WOSB concern eligible under the WOSB program.

[FAC 2005-86, 80 FR 81888, 12/31/2015, effective 12/31/2015; FAC 2005-91, 81 FR 67735, 9/30/2016, effective 9/30/2016; FAC 2005-92 81 FR 83103, 11/18/2016, effective 11/18/2016]

19.1507 Contract clauses.

(a) The contracting officer shall insert the clause 52.219-29, Notice of Set-Aside for, or Sole Source Award to, Economically Disadvantaged Women-owned Small Business Concerns, in solicitations and contracts for acquisitions that are set aside or reserved for, or awarded on a sole source basis to, EDWOSB concerns under 19.1505(b) or 19.1506(a). This includes multiple-award contracts when orders may be set aside for EDWOSB concerns as described in 8.405-5 and 16.505(b) (2) (i) (F).

(b) The contracting officer shall insert the clause 52.219-30, Notice of Set-Aside for, or Sole Source Award to, Women-Owned Small Business Concerns Eligible Under the Women-Owned Small Business Program, in solicitations and contracts for acquisitions that are set aside or reserved for, or awarded on a sole source basis to WOSB concerns under 19.1505(c) or 19.1506(b). This includes multiple- award contracts when orders may be set aside for WOSB concerns eligible under the WOSB Program as described in 8.405-5 and 16.505(b) (2) (i) (F).

[FAC 2005-51, 76 FR 18304, 4/1/2011, effective 4/1/2011; FAC 2005-54, 76 FR 68032, 11/2/2011, effective 11/2/2011; Interim rule, 77 FR 1889, 1/12/2012, effective 2/13/2012; FAC 2005-56, 77 FR 12913, 3/2/2012, effective 4/2/2012; FAC 2005-86, 80 FR 81888, 12/31/2015, effective 12/31/2015; FAC 2005-91, 81 FR 67735, 9/30/2016, effective 9/30/2016]

PART 20—[RESERVED]

PART 21—[RESERVED]

PART 22—APPLICATION OF LABOR LAWS TO GOVERNMENT ACQUISITIONS

Table of Contents

Scope of part 22.000
Definition 22.001

Subpart 22.1—Basic Labor Policies

Labor relations 22.101
General 22.101-1
Contract pricing and administration 22.101-2
Reporting labor disputes 22.101-3
Removal of items from contractors' facilities affected by work stoppages 22.101-4
Federal and State labor requirements 22.102
Policy 22.102-1
Administration 22.102-2
Overtime 22.103
Definition 22.103-1
Policy 22.103-2
Procedures 22.103-3
Approvals 22.103-4
Contract clauses 22.103-5
[Removed] 22.104

Subpart 22.2—Convict Labor

General 22.201
Contract clause 22.202

Subpart 22.3—Contract Work Hours and Safety Standards Act

Scope of subpart 22.300
Statutory requirement 22.301
Liquidated damages and overtime pay 22.302
Administration and enforcement 22.303
Variations, tolerances, and exemptions 22.304
Contract clause 22.305

Subpart 22.4—Labor Standards for Contracts Involving Construction

Scope of subpart 22.400
Definitions 22.401
Applicability 22.402
Statutory, Executive order, and regulatory requirements 22.403
Construction Wage Rate Requirements statute 22.403-1
Copeland Act 22.403-2
Contract Work Hours and Safety Standards Act 22.403-3
Executive Order 13658 . . . . 22.403-4
Executive Order 13706 . . . . 22.403-5
Department of Labor regulations involving construction 22.403-6
Construction Wage Rate Requirements statute wage determinations 22.404
Types of wage determinations 22.404-1
General requirements 22.404-2
Procedures for requesting wage determinations 22.404-3
Solicitations issued without wage determinations for the primary site of the work 22.404-4
Expiration of project wage determinations 22.404-5
Modifications of wage determinations 22.404-6
Correction of wage determinations containing clerical errors 22.404-7
Notification of improper wage determination before award 22.404-8
Award of contract without required wage determination 22.404-9
Posting wage determinations and notice 22.404-10

Wage determination appeals 22.404-11
Labor standards for contracts containing construction requirements and option provisions that extend the term of the contract 22.404-12
[Removed and Reserved] 22.405
Administration and enforcement 22.406
Policy 22.406-1
Wages, fringe benefits, and overtime 22.406-2
Additional classifications 22.406-3
Apprentices and trainees 22.406-4
Subcontracts 22.406-5
Payrolls and statements 22.406-6
Compliance checking 22.406-7
Investigations 22.406-8
Withholding from or suspension of contract payments 22.406-9
Disposition of disputes concerning construction contract labor standards enforcement 22.406-10
Contract terminations 22.406-11
Cooperation with the Department of Labor 22.406-12
Semiannual enforcement reports 22.406-13
Solicitation provision and contract clauses 22.407

Subpart 22.5—Use of Project Labor Agreements for Federal Construction Projects

Scope of subpart 22.501
Definitions 22.502
Policy 22.503
General requirements for project labor agreements 22.504
Solicitation provision and contract clause 22.505

Subpart 22.6—Contracts for Materials, Supplies, Articles, and Equipment Exceeding $15,000

[Reserved] 22.601
Statutory requirements 22.602
Applicability 22.603
Exemptions 22.604
Statutory exemptions 22.604-1
Regulatory exemptions 22.604-2
Rulings and interpretations of the statute 22.605
[Reserved] 22.606
[Reserved] 22.607
Procedures 22.608
[Removed and Reserved] 22.609
Contract clause 22.610

Subpart 22.7—[Reserved]

Subpart 22.8—Equal Employment Opportunity

Scope of subpart 22.800
Definitions 22.801
General 22.802
Responsibilities 22.803
Affirmative action programs 22.804
Nonconstruction 22.804-1
Construction 22.804-2
Procedures 22.805
Inquiries 22.806
Exemptions 22.807
Complaints 22.808

Enforcement . . . 22.809
Solicitation provisions and contract clauses . . . 22.810

Subpart 22.9—Nondiscrimination Because of Age

Policy . . . 22.901
Handling complaints . . . 22.902

Subpart 22.10—Service Contract Labor Standards

Scope of subpart . . . 22.1000
Definitions . . . 22.1001
Statutory and Executive order requirements . . . 22.1002
General . . . 22.1002-1
Wage determinations based on prevailing rates . . . 22.1002-2
Wage determinations based on collective bargaining agreements . . . 22.1002-3
Application of the Fair Labor Standards Act minimum wage . . . 22.1002-4
Executive Order 13658 . . . 22.1002-5
Executive Order 13706 . . . 22.1002-6
Applicability . . . 22.1003
General . . . 22.1003-1
Geographical coverage of the Service Contract Labor Standards statute . . . 22.1003-2
Statutory exemptions . . . 22.1003-3
Administrative limitations, variations, tolerances, and exemptions . . . 22.1003-4
Some examples of contracts covered . . . 22.1003-5
Repair distinguished from remanufacturing of equipment . . . 22.1003-6
Questions concerning applicability of the Service Contract Labor Standards statute . . . 22.1003-7
Department of Labor responsibilities and regulations . . . 22.1004
[Reserved] . . . 22.1005
Solicitation provisions and contract clauses . . . 22.1006
Requirement to obtain wage determinations . . . 22.1007
Procedures for obtaining wage determinations . . . 22.1008
Obtaining wage determinations . . . 22.1008-1
Successorship with incumbent contractor collective bargaining agreement . . . 22.1008-2
[Removed] . . . 22.1008-4
[Removed] . . . 22.1008-5
[Removed] . . . 22.1008-6
[Removed] . . . 22.1008-7
Place of performance unknown . . . 22.1009
General . . . 22.1009-1
Attempt to identify possible places of performance . . . 22.1009-2
All possible places of performance identified . . . 22.1009-3
All possible places of performance not identified . . . 22.1009-4
Notification to interested parties under collective bargaining agreements . . . 22.1010
[Removed and Reserved] . . . 22.1011
[Removed and Reserved] . . . 22.1011-1
[Removed and Reserved] . . . 22.1011-2
Applicability of revisions to wage determinations . . . 22.1012
Prevailing wage determinations . . . 22.1012-1
Wage determinations based on collective bargaining agreements . . . 22.1012-2
[Removed] . . . 22.1012-4
[Removed] . . . 22.1012-5
Review of wage determination . . . 22.1013
Delay over 60 days in bid opening or commencement of work . . . 22.1014
Discovery of errors by the Department of Labor . . . 22.1015
Statement of equivalent rates for Federal hires . . . 22.1016
[Removed and Reserved] . . . 22.1017
Notification to contractors and employees . . . 22.1018

Additional classes of service employees 22.1019
Seniority lists 22.1020
Request for hearing 22.1021
Withholding of contract payments 22.1022
Termination for default 22.1023
Cooperation with the Department of Labor 22.1024
Ineligibility of violators 22.1025
Disputes concerning labor standards 22.1026

Subpart 22.11—Professional Employee Compensation

Applicability 22.1101
Definition 22.1102
Policy, procedures, and solicitation provision 22.1103

Subpart 22.12—Nondisplacement of Qualified Workers Under Service Contracts

Scope of subpart 22.1200
Definitions 22.1201
Policy 22.1202
Applicability 22.1203
General 22.1203-1
Exemptions 22.1203-2
Waiver 22.1203-3
Method of job offer 22.1203-4
Exceptions 22.1203-5
Reduced staffing 22.1203-6
Certified service employee lists 22.1204
Notification to contractors and service employees 22.1205
Remedies and sanctions for violations of this subpart 22.1206
Contract clause 22.1207

Subpart 22.13—Equal Opportunity for Veterans

Scope of subpart 22.1300
Definitions 22.1301
Policy 22.1302
Applicability 22.1303
Procedures 22.1304
Waivers 22.1305
Department of Labor notices and reports 22.1306
Collective bargaining agreements 22.1307
Complaint procedures 22.1308
Actions because of noncompliance 22.1309
Solicitation provision and contract clauses 22.1310

Subpart 22.14—Employment of Workers with Disabilities

Scope of subpart 22.1400
Policy 22.1401
Applicability 22.1402
Waivers 22.1403
Department of Labor notices 22.1404
Collective bargaining agreements 22.1405
Complaint procedures 22.1406
Actions because of noncompliance 22.1407
Contract clause 22.1408

Subpart 22.15—Prohibition of Acquisition of Products Produced By Forced or Indentured Child Labor

Scope 22.1500
Definitions 22.1501

Policy 22.1502
Procedures for acquiring end products on the List of Products Requiring Contractor Certification as to Forced or Indentured Child Labor 22.1503
Violations and Remedies 22.1504
Solicitation provision and contract clause 22.1505

Subpart 22.16—Notification of Employee Rights Under the National Labor Relations Act

Scope of subpart 22.1600
Definitions 22.1601
Policy 22.1602
Exceptions 22.1603
Compliance evaluation and complaint investigations and sanctions for violations 22.1604
Contract clause 22.1605

Subpart 22.17—Combating Trafficking in Persons

Scope of subpart 22.1700
Applicability 22.1701
Definitions 22.1702
Policy 22.1703
Violations and remedies 22.1704
Solicitation provision and contract clause 22.1705

Subpart 22.18—Employment Eligibility Verification

Scope 22.1800
Definitions 22.1801
Policy 22.1802
Contract clause 22.1803

Subpart 22.19—Establishing a Minimum Wage for Contractors

Scope of subpart 22.1900
Definition 22.1901
Policy 22.1902
Applicability 22.1903
Annual Executive Order Minimum Wage Rate 22.1904
Enforcement of Executive Order Minimum Wage Requirements 22.1905
Contract clause 22.1906

Subpart 22.20—[Removed and Reserved]

Subpart 22.21—Establishing Paid Sick Leave for Federal Contractors

Scope of subpart 22.2100
Definitions 22.2101
Policy 22.2102
Applicability 22.2103
Exclusions 22.2104
Paid sick leave for Federal contractors and subcontractors 22.2105
Prohibited acts 22.2106
Waiver of rights 22.2107
Multiemployer plans or other funds, plans, or programs 22.2108
Enforcement of Executive Order 13706 paid sick leave requirements 22.2109
Contract clause 22.2110

PART 22—APPLICATION OF LABOR LAWS TO GOVERNMENT ACQUISITIONS

22.000 Scope of part.

This part—

(a) Deals with general policies regarding contractor labor relations as they pertain to the acquisition process;

(b) Prescribes contracting policy and procedures for implementing pertinent labor laws; and

(c) Prescribes contract clauses with respect to each pertinent labor law.

[FAC 2005-90, 81 FR 58562, 8/25/2016, effective 10/25/2016; FAC 2005-96, 82 FR 51773, 11/8/2017, effective 11/6/2017]

22.001 Definitions.

Administrator or *Administrator, Wage and Hour Division,* as used in this part, means the Administrator, Wage and Hour Division, U.S. Department of Labor, Washington, DC 20210 or an authorized representative.

Agency labor advisor means an individual responsible for advising contracting agency officials on Federal contract labor matters.

e98 means the Department of Labor's approved electronic application (*http://www.wdol.gov*), whereby a contracting officer submits pertinent information to the Department of Labor and requests a Service Contract Labor Standards statute wage determination directly from the Wage and Hour Division.

Service contract means any Government contract, or subcontract thereunder, the principal purpose of which is to furnish services in the United States through the use of service employees, except as exempted by 41 U.S.C. chapter 67, Service Contract Labor Standards; see 22.1003-3 and 22.1003-4. See 22.1003-5 and 29 CFR 4.130 for a partial list of services covered by the Service Contract Labor Standards statute.

Service employee means any person engaged in the performance of a service contract other than any person employed in a bona fide executive, administrative, or professional capacity, as those terms are defined in 29 CFR part 541. The term *service employee* includes all such persons regardless of any contractual relationship that may be alleged to exist between a contractor or subcontractor and such persons.

Wage Determinations OnLine (WDOL) means the Government Internet Website for both Construction Wage Rate Requirements statute and Service Contract Labor Standards statute wage determinations available at *http://www.wdol.gov*.

[FAC 84-34, 53 FR 4935, 2/18/88, effective 2/29/88; FAC 2005-10, 71 FR 36930, 6/28/2006, effective 6/28/2006; FAC 2005-16, 72 FR 13585, 3/22/2007, effective 3/22/2007; FAC 2005-64, 77 FR 75766, 12/21/2012, effective 1/18/2013; FAC 2005-73, 79 FR 24192, 4/29/2014, effective 5/29/2014; FAC 2005-79, 79 FR 74544, 12/15/2014, effective 12/15/2014; FAC 2005-85, 80 FR 75915, 12/4/2015, effective 12/4/2015; FAC 2005-100, 83 FR 42571, 8/22/2018, effective 8/22/2018]

SUBPART 22.1—BASIC LABOR POLICIES

22.101 Labor relations. (No Text)

22.101-1 General.

(a) Agencies shall maintain sound relations with industry and labor to ensure—

(1) Prompt receipt of information involving labor relations that may adversely affect the Government acquisition process and

(2) That the Government obtains needed supplies and services without delay. All matters regarding labor relations shall be handled in accordance with agency procedures.

(b) (1) Agencies shall remain impartial concerning any dispute between labor and contractor management and not undertake the conciliation, mediation, or arbitration of a labor dispute. To the extent practicable, agencies should ensure that the parties to the dispute use all available methods for resolving the dispute, including the services of the National Labor Relations Board, Federal Mediation and Conciliation Service, the National Mediation Board and other appropriate Federal, State, local, or private agencies.

(2) For use of project labor agreements, see subpart 22.5.

(c) Agencies should, when practicable, exchange information concerning labor matters with other affected agencies to ensure a uniform Government approach concerning a particular plant or labor-management dispute.

(d) Agencies should take other actions concerning labor relations problems to the extent consistent with their acquisition responsibilities. For example, agencies should—

(1) Notify the agency responsible for conciliation, mediation, arbitration, or other related action of the existence of any labor dispute affecting or threatening to affect agency acquisition programs;

(2) Furnish to the parties to a dispute factual information pertinent to the dispute's potential or actual adverse impact on these programs, to the extent consistent with security regulations; and

(3) Seek a voluntary agreement between management and labor, notwithstanding the continuance of the dispute, to permit uninterrupted acquisition of supplies and services. This shall only be done, however, if the attempt to obtain voluntary agreement does not involve the agency in the merits of the dispute and only after consultation with the agency responsible for conciliation, mediation, arbitration, or other related action.

(e) The head of the contracting activity may designate programs or requirements for which it is necessary that contractors be required to notify the Government of actual or potential labor disputes that are delaying or threaten to delay the timely contract performance (see 22.103-5(a)).

[FAC 97-26, 66 FR 27405, 5/16/2001, effective 5/16/2001; FAC 2001-10, 67 FR 70518, 11/22/2002, effective 11/22/2002; FAC 2005-35, 74 FR 34206, 7/14/2009, effective 7/14/2009; FAC 2005-41, 75 FR 19168, 4/13/2010, effective 5/13/2010]

22.101-2 Contract pricing and administration.

(a) Contractor labor policies and compensation practices, whether or not included in labor-management agreements, are not acceptable bases for allowing costs in cost-reimbursement contracts or for recognition of costs in pricing fixed-price contracts if they result in unreasonable costs to the Government. For a discussion of allowable costs resulting from labor-management agreements, see 31.205-6(b).

(b) Labor disputes may cause work stoppages that delay the performance of Government contracts. Contracting officers shall impress upon contractors that each contractor shall be held accountable for reasonably avoidable delays. Standard contract clauses dealing with default, excusable delays, etc., do not relieve contractors or subcontractors from the responsibility for delays that are within the contractors' or their subcontractors' control. A delay caused by a strike that the contractor or subcontractor could not reasonably prevent can be excused; however, it cannot be excused beyond the point at which a reasonably diligent contractor or subcontractor could have acted to end the strike by actions such as—

(1) Filing a charge with the National Labor Relations Board to permit the Board to seek injunctive relief in court;

(2) Using other available Government procedures;

(3) Using private boards or organizations to settle disputes.

(c) Strikes normally result in changing patterns of cost incurrence and therefore may have an impact on the allowability of costs for cost-reimbursement contracts or for recognition of costs in pricing fixed-price contracts. Certain costs may increase because of strikes; *e.g.*, guard services and attorney's fees. Other costs incurred during a strike may not fluctuate (*e.g.*, "fixed costs" such as rent and depreciation), but because of reduced production, their proportion of the unit cost of items produced increases. All costs incurred during strikes shall be carefully examined to ensure recognition of only those costs necessary for performing the contract in accordance with the Government's essential interest.

(d) If, during a labor dispute, the inspectors' safety is not endangered, the normal functions of inspection at the plant of a Government contractor shall be continued without regard to the existence of a labor dispute, strike, or picket line.

[FAC 2001-15, 68 FR 43863, 7/24/2003, effective 8/25/2003]

22.101-3 Reporting labor disputes.

The office administering the contract shall report, in accordance with agency procedures, any potential or actual labor disputes that may interfere with performing any contracts under its cognizance. If a contract contains the clause at 52.222-1, Notice to the Government of Labor Disputes, the contractor also must report any actual or potential dispute that may delay contract performance.

22.101-4 Removal of items from contractors' facilities affected by work stoppages.

(a) Items shall be removed from contractors' facilities affected by work stoppages in accordance with agency procedures. Agency procedures should allow for the following:

(1) Determine whether removal of items is in the Government's interest. Normally the determining factor is the critical needs of an agency program.

(2) Attempt to arrange with the contractor and the union representative involved their approval of the shipment of urgently required items.

(3) Obtain appropriate approvals from within the agency.

(4) Determine who will remove the items from the plant(s) involved.

(b) Avoid the use or appearance of force and prevent incidents that might detrimentally affect labor-management relations.

(c) When two or more agencies' requirements are or may become involved in the removal of items, the contract administration office shall ensure that the necessary coordination is accomplished.

22.102 Federal and State labor requirements. (No Text)

22.102-1 Policy.

Agencies shall cooperate, and encourage contractors to cooperate with Federal and State agencies responsible for enforcing labor requirements such as—

(a) Safety;

(b) Health and sanitation;

(c) Maximum hours and minimum wages;

(d) Equal employment opportunity;

(e) Child and convict labor;

(f) Age discrimination;

(g) Disabled and Vietnam veteran employment;

(h) Employment of workers with disabilities; and

(i) Eligibility for employment under United States immigration law.

[FAC 90-8, 56 FR 55374, 10/25/91, effective 11/25/91; FAC 2005-29, 73 FR 67651, 11/14/2008, effective 1/15/2009; FAC 2005-29, 74 FR 1937, 1/14/2009, effective 1/19/2009; FAC 2005-29, 74 FR 5621, 1/30/2009, effective 5/21/2009; FAC 2005-29, 74 FR 17793, 4/17/2009, effective 6/30/2009; FAC 2005-29, 74 FR 26981, 6/5/2009, effective 9/8/2009; FAC 2005-73, 79 FR 24192, 4/29/2014, effective 5/29/2014]

22.102-2 Administration.

(a) Agencies shall cooperate with, and encourage contractors to use to the fullest extent practicable, the DOL Employment and Training Administration (DOLETA) at *http://www.doleta.gov*, and its affiliated local offices in meeting contractors' labor requirements. These requirements may be to staff new or expanding plant facilities, including requirements for workers in all occupations and skills from local labor market areas or through the Federal-State employment clearance system.

(b) Local State employment offices are operated throughout the United States, Puerto Rico, Guam, and the U.S. Virgin Islands. In addition to providing recruitment assistance to contractors, cooperation with the local

State Employment Service offices will further the national program of maintaining continuous assessment of manpower requirements and resources on a national and local basis.

(c)(1) The U.S. Department of Labor is responsible for the administration and enforcement of the Occupational Safety and Health Act. The Department of Labor's Wage and Hour Division is responsible for administration and enforcement of numerous wage and hour statutes including—

(i) 40 U.S.C. chapter 31, subchapter IV, Wage Rate Requirements (Construction);

(ii) 40 U.S.C. chapter 37, Contract Work Hours and Safety Standards;

(iii) The Copeland Act (18 U.S.C. 874 and 40 U.S.C. 3145);

(iv) 41 U.S.C. chapter 65, Contracts for Materials, Supplies, Articles, and Equipment Exceeding $15,000;

(v) 41 U.S.C. chapter 67, Service Contract Labor Standards.

(2) Contracting officers should contact the Wage and Hour Division's regional offices when required by the subparts relating to these statutes unless otherwise specified. Addresses for these offices may be found at Appendix B to 29 CFR Part 1.

[FAC 90-8, 56 FR 55374, 10/25/91, effective 11/25/91; FAC 2001-14, 68 FR 28079, 5/22/2003, effective 6/23/2003; FAC 2005-10, 71 FR 36930, 6/28/2006, effective 6/28/2006; FAC 2005-16, 72 FR 13585, 3/22/2007, effective 3/22/2007; FAC 2005-73, 79 FR 24192, 4/29/2014, effective 5/29/2014; FAC 2005-82, 80 FR 26427, 5/7/2015, effective 5/7/2015; FAC 2005-90, 81 FR 58562, 8/25/2016, effective 10/25/2016; FAC 2005-93, 81 FR 91636, 12/16/2016, effective 12/16/2016; FAC 2005-96, 82 FR 51773, 11/8/2017, effective 11/6/2017]

22.103 Overtime. (No Text)

22.103-1 Definition.

Normal workweek, as used in this subpart, means, generally, a workweek of 40 hours. Outside the United States and its outlying areas, a workweek longer than 40 hours is considered normal if—

(1) The workweek does not exceed the norm for the area, as determined by local custom, tradition, or law; and

(2) The hours worked in excess of 40 in the workweek are not compensated at a premium rate of pay.

[FAC 84-14, interim, 51 FR 12293, 4/9/86, effective 4/7/86; FAC 97-22, 66 FR 2116, 1/10/2001, effective 3/12/2001; Delay of effective date, 66 FR 14259, 3/9/2001, effective 5/11/2001; FAC 2001-14, 68 FR 28079, 5/22/2003, effective 6/23/2003]

22.103-2 Policy.

Contractors shall perform all contracts, so far as practicable, without using overtime, particularly as a regular employment practice, except when lower overall costs to the Government will result or when it is necessary to meet urgent program needs. Any approved overtime, extra-pay shifts, and multishifts should be scheduled to achieve these objectives.

22.103-3 Procedures.

(a) Solicitations normally shall not specify delivery or performance schedules that may require overtime at Government expense.

(b) In negotiating contracts, contracting officers should, consistent with the Government's needs, attempt to—

(1) Ascertain the extent that offers are based on the payment of overtime and shift premiums; and

(2) Negotiate contract prices or estimated costs without these premiums or obtain the requirement from other sources.

(c) When it becomes apparent during negotiations of applicable contracts (see 22.103-5(b)) that overtime will be required in contract performance, the contracting officer shall secure from the contractor a request for all overtime to be used during the life of the contract, to the extent that the overtime can be estimated with reasonable certainty. The contractor's request shall contain the information required by paragraph (b) of the clause at 52.222-2, Payment for Overtime Premiums.

22.103-4 Approvals.

(a) The contracting officer shall review the contractor's request for overtime. Approval of the use of overtime may be granted by an agency approving official after determining in writing that overtime is necessary to—

(1) Meet essential delivery or performance schedules;

(2) Make up for delays beyond the control and without the fault or negligence of the contractor; or

(3) Eliminate foreseeable extended production bottlenecks that cannot be eliminated in any other way.

(b) Approval by the designated official of use and total dollar amount of overtime is required before inclusion of an amount in paragraph (a) of the clause at 52.222-2, Payment for Overtime Premiums.

(c) Contracting officer approval of payment of overtime premiums is required for time-and-materials and labor-hour contracts (see sub paragraph (a)(8) of the clause at 52.232-7, Payments Under Time-and-Materials and Labor-Hour Contracts).

(d) No approvals are required for paying overtime premiums under other types of contracts.

(e) Approvals by the agency approving official (see 22.103-4(a)) may be for an individual contract, project, program, plant, division, or company, as practical.

(f) During contract performance, contractor requests for overtime exceeding the amount authorized by paragraph (a) of the clause at 52.222-2, Payment for Overtime Premiums, shall be submitted as stated in paragraph (b) of the clause to the office administering the contract. That office will review the request and if it approves, send the request to the contracting officer. If the contracting officer determines that the requested overtime should be approved in whole or in part, the contracting officer shall request the approval of the agency's designated approving official and modify paragraph (a) of the clause to reflect any approval.

(g) Overtime premiums at Government expense should not be approved when the contractor is already obligated, without the right to additional compensation, to meet the required delivery date.

(h) When the use of overtime is authorized under a contract, the office administering the contract and the auditor should periodically review the use of overtime to ensure that it is allowable in accordance with the criteria in Part 31. Only overtime premiums for work in those departments, sections, etc., of the contractor's plant that have been individually evaluated and the necessity for overtime confirmed shall be considered for approval.

(i) Approvals for using overtime shall ordinarily be prospective, but, if justified by emergency circumstances, approvals may be retroactive.

[FAC 2005-13, 71 FR 57363, 9/28/2006, effective 9/28/2006; Final rule, 72 FR 6881, 2/13/2007, effective 2/12/2007]

22.103-5 Contract clauses.

(a) The contracting officer shall insert the clause at 52.222-1, Notice to the Government of Labor Disputes, in solicitations and contracts that involve programs or requirements that have been designated under 22.101-1(e).

(b) The contracting officer shall include the clause at 52.222-2, Payment for Overtime Premiums, in solicitations and contracts when a cost-reimbursement contract is contemplated and the contract amount is expected to exceed the simplified acquisition threshold, unless—

(1) A cost-reimbursement contract for operation of vessels is contemplated; or

(2) A cost-plus-incentive-fee contract that will provide a swing from the target fee of at least plus or minus 3 percent and a contractor's share of at least 10 percent is contemplated.

[FAC 2005-13, 71 FR 57363, 9/28/2006, effective 9/28/2006]

22.104 [Removed]

[FAC 2005-90, 81 FR 58562, 8/25/2016, effective 10/25/2016; FAC 2005-93, 81 FR

91636, 12/16/2016, effective 12/16/2016; FAC 2005-96, 82 FR 51773, 11/8/2017, effective 11/6/2017]

SUBPART 22.2—CONVICT LABOR

22.201 General.

(a) Executive Order 11755, December 29, 1973, as amended by Executive Order 12608, September 9, 1987, and Executive Order 12943, December 13, 1994, states: "The development of the occupational and educational skills of prison inmates is essential to their rehabilitation and to their ability to make an effective return to free society. Meaningful employment serves to develop those skills. It is also true, however, that care must be exercised to avoid either the exploitation of convict labor or any unfair competition between convict labor and free labor in the production of goods and services." The Executive order does not prohibit the contractor, in performing the contract, from employing—

(1) Persons on parole or probation;

(2) Persons who have been pardoned or who have served their terms;

(3) Federal prisoners; or

(4) Nonfederal prisoners authorized to work at paid employment in the community under the laws of a jurisdiction listed in the Executive order if—

(i) The worker is paid or is in an approved work training program on a voluntary basis;

(ii) Representatives of local union central bodies or similar labor union organizations have been consulted;

(iii) Paid employment will not—

(A) Result in the displacement of employed workers;

(B) Be applied in skills, crafts, or trades in which there is a surplus of available gainful labor in the locality; or

(C) Impair existing contracts for services;

(iv) The rates of pay and other conditions of employment will not be less than those for work of a similar nature in the locality where the work is being performed; and

(v) The Attorney General of the United States has certified that the work-release laws or regulations of the jurisdiction involved are in conformity with the requirements of Executive Order 11755, as amended.

(b) Department of Justice regulations authorize the Director of the Bureau of Justice Assistance to exercise the power and authority vested in the Attorney General by the Executive order to certify and to revoke the certification of work-release laws or regulations (see 28 CFR 0.94-1(b)).

[FAC 90-39, 61 FR 31612, 6/20/96, effective 8/19/96]

22.202 Contract clause.

Insert the clause at 52.222-3, Convict Labor, in solicitations and contracts above the micro-purchase threshold, when the contract will be performed in the United States, Puerto Rico, the Northern Mariana Islands, American Samoa, Guam, or the U.S. Virgin Islands; unless—

(a) The contract will be subject to 41 U.S.C. chapter 65, Contracts for Materials, Supplies, Articles, and Equipment Exceeding $15,000 (see subpart 22.6), which contains a separate prohibition against the employment of convict labor;

(b) The supplies or services are to be purchased from Federal Prison Industries, Inc. (see Subpart 8.6); or

(c) The acquisition involves the purchase, from any State prison, of finished supplies that may be secured in the open market or from existing stocks, as distinguished from supplies requiring special fabrication.

[FAC 90-29, 60 FR 34732, 7/3/95, effective 7/3/95; FAC 90-39, 61 FR 31612, 6/20/96, effective 8/19/96; FAC 2001-14, 68 FR 28079, 5/22/2003, effective 6/23/2003; FAC 2005-73, 79 FR 24192, 4/29/2014, effective 5/29/2014]

SUBPART 22.3—CONTRACT WORK HOURS AND SAFETY STANDARDS ACT

22.300 Scope of subpart.

This subpart prescribes policies and procedures for applying the requirements of 40 U.S.C. chapter 37, Contract Work Hours and Safety Standards (the statute) to contracts that may require or involve laborers or mechanics. In this subpart, the term *laborers or mechanics* includes apprentices, trainees, helpers, watchmen, guards, firefighters, fireguards, and workmen who perform services in connection with dredging or rock excavation in rivers or harbors, but does not include any employee employed as a seaman.

[FAC 84-14, interim, 51 FR 12293, 4/9/86, effective 4/7/86; FAC 2005-06, 70 FR 57453, 9/30/2005, effective 9/30/2005; FAC 2005-73, 79 FR 24192, 4/29/2014, effective 5/29/2014]

22.301 Statutory requirement.

The statute requires that certain contracts contain a clause specifying that no laborer or mechanic doing any part of the work contemplated by the contract shall be required or permitted to work more than 40 hours in any workweek unless paid for all such overtime hours at not less than 1½ times the basic rate of pay.

[FAC 84-14, interim, 51 FR 12293, 4/9/86, effective 4/7/86; FAC 2005-73, 79 FR 24192, 4/29/2014, effective 5/29/2014]

22.302 Liquidated damages and overtime pay.

(a) When an overtime computation discloses underpayments, the responsible contractor or subcontractor must pay the affected employee any unpaid wages and pay liquidated damages to the Government. The contracting officer must assess liquidated damages at the rate specified at 29 CFR 5.5(b)(2) per affected employee for each calendar day on which the employer required or permitted the employee to work in excess of the standard workweek of 40 hours without paying overtime wages required by the statute. In accordance with the Federal Civil Penalties Inflation Adjustment Act of 1990 (28 U.S.C. 2461 Note), the Department of Labor adjusts this civil monetary penalty for inflation no later than January 15 each year.

(b) If the contractor or subcontractor fails or refuses to comply with overtime pay requirements of the statute and the funds withheld by Federal agencies for labor standards violations do not cover the unpaid wages due laborers and mechanics and the liquidated damages due the Government, make payments in the following order—

(1) Pay laborers and mechanics the wages they are owed (or prorate available funds if they do not cover the entire amount owed); and

(2) Pay liquidated damages.

(c) If the head of an agency finds that the administratively determined liquidated damages due under paragraph (a) of this section are incorrect, or that the contractor or subcontractor inadvertently violated the statute despite the exercise of due care, the agency head may—

(1) Reduce the amount of liquidated damages assessed for liquidated damages of $500 or less;

(2) Release the contractor or subcontractor from the liability for liquidated damages of $500 or less; or

(3) Recommend that the Secretary of Labor reduce or waive liquidated damages over $500.

(d) After the contracting officer determines the liquidated damages and the contractor makes appropriate payments, disburse any remaining assessments in accordance with agency procedures.

[FAC 97-19, 65 FR 46052, 7/26/2000, effective 9/25/2000; FAC 2005-73, 79 FR 24192, 4/29/2014, effective 5/29/2014; FAC 2005-98, 83 FR 19148, 5/1/2018, effective 5/31/2018]

22.303 Administration and enforcement.

The procedures and reports required for construction contracts in Subpart 22.4 also apply to investigations of alleged violations of the statute on other than construction contracts.

[FAC 2005-73, 79 FR 24192, 4/29/2014, effective 5/29/2014]

22.304 Variations, tolerances, and exemptions.

(a) The Secretary of Labor, under 40 U.S.C. 3706, upon the Secretary's initiative or at the request of any Federal agency, may provide reasonable limitations and allow variations, tolerances, and exemptions to and from any or all provisions of the statute (see 29 CFR 5.15).

(b) The Secretary of Labor may make variations, tolerances, and exemptions from the regulatory requirements of applicable parts of 29 CFR when the Secretary finds that such action is necessary and proper in the public interest or to prevent injustice and undue hardship (see 29 CFR 5.14).

[FAC 84-14, interim, 51 FR 12293, 4/9/86, effective 4/7/86; FAC 2005-06, 70 FR 57453, 9/30/2005, effective 9/30/2005; FAC 2005-73, 79 FR 24192, 4/29/2014, effective 5/29/2014]

22.305 Contract clause.

Insert the clause at 52.222-4, Contract Work Hours and Safety Standards—Overtime Compensation, in solicitations and contracts (including, for this purpose, basic ordering agreements) when the contract may require or involve the employment of laborers or mechanics. However, do not include the clause in solicitations and contracts—

(a) Valued at or below $150,000;

(b) For commercial items;

(c) For transportation or the transmission of intelligence;

(d) To be performed outside the United States, Puerto Rico, American Samoa, Guam, the U.S. Virgin Islands, Johnston Island, Wake Island, and the outer Continental Shelf as defined in the Outer Continental Shelf Lands Act (43 U.S.C. 1331) (29 CFR 5.15);

(e) For work to be done solely in accordance with 41 U.S.C. chapter 65, Contracts for Materials, Supplies, Articles, and Equipment Exceeding $15,000 (see subpart 22.6);

(f) For supplies that include incidental services that do not require substantial employment of laborers or mechanics; or

(g) Exempt under regulations of the Secretary of Labor (29 CFR 5.15).

[FAC 84-14, interim, 51 FR 12293, 4/9/86, effective 4/7/86; FAC 84-32, 53 FR 661, 1/11/88, effective 1/29/88; FAC 90-29, 60 FR 34732, 7/3/95, effective 7/3/95; FAC 90-32, 60 FR 48206, 9/18/95, effective 10/1/95; FAC 2001-14, 68 FR 28079, 5/22/2003, effective 6/23/2003; FAC 2005-13, 71 FR 57363, 9/28/2006, effective 9/28/2006; FAC 2005-45, 75 FR 53129, 8/30/2010, effective 10/1/2010; FAC 2005-73, 79 FR 24192, 4/29/2014, effective 5/29/2014]

SUBPART 22.4—LABOR STANDARDS FOR CONTRACTS INVOLVING CONSTRUCTION

22.400 Scope of subpart.

This subpart implements the statutes which prescribe labor standards requirements for contracts in excess of $2,000 for construction, alteration, or repair, including painting and decorating, of public buildings and public works. (See definition of *Construction, alteration, or repair* in section 22.401.) Labor relations requirements prescribed in other subparts of Part 22 may also apply.

[FAC 84-34, 53 FR 4935, 2/18/88, effective 2/29/88; FAC 97-19, 65 FR 46052, 7/26/2000, effective 7/26/2000]

22.401 Definitions.

As used in this subpart—

Apprentice means a person—

(1) Employed and individually registered in a bona fide apprenticeship program registered with the U.S. Department of Labor, Employment and Training Administration, Office of Apprenticeship Training, Employer, and Labor Services (OATELS), or with a State Apprenticeship Agency recognized by OATELS; or

(2) Who is in the first 90 days of probationary employment as an apprentice in an apprenticeship program, and is not individually registered in the program, but who has been certified by the OATELS or a State Apprenticeship Agency (where appropriate) to be eligible for probationary employment as an apprentice.

Construction, alteration, or repair means all types of work done by laborers and mechanics employed by the construction contractor or construction subcontractor on a particular building or work at the site thereof, including without limitations—

(1) Altering, remodeling, installation (if appropriate) on the site of the work of items fabricated off-site;

(2) Painting and decorating;

(3) Manufacturing or furnishing of materials, articles, supplies, or equipment on the site of the building or work;

(4) Transportation of materials and supplies between the site of the work within the meaning of paragraphs (1)(i) and (ii) of the *site of the work* definition of this section, and a facility which is dedicated to the construction of the building or work and is deemed part of the site of the work within the meaning of paragraph (2) of the *site of the work* definition of this section; and

(5) Transportation of portions of the building or work between a secondary site where a significant portion of the building or work is constructed, which is part of the *site of the work* definition in paragraph (1)(ii) of this section, and the physical place or places where the building or work will remain (paragraph (1)(i) in the *site of the work* definition of this section).

Laborers or mechanics.—(1) Means—

(i) Workers, utilized by a contractor or subcontractor at any tier, whose duties are manual or physical in nature (including those workers who use tools or who are performing the work of a trade), as distinguished from mental or managerial;

(ii) Apprentices, trainees, helpers, and, in the case of contracts subject to the Contract Work Hours and Safety Standards statute, watchmen and guards;

(iii) Working foremen who devote more than 20 percent of their time during a workweek performing duties of a laborer or mechanic, and who do not meet the criteria of 29 CFR part 541, for the time so spent; and

(iv) Every person performing the duties of a laborer or mechanic, regardless of any contractual relationship alleged to exist between the contractor and those individuals; and

(2) Does not include workers whose duties are primarily executive, supervisory (except as provided in paragraph (1)(iii) of this definition), administrative, or clerical, rather than manual. Persons employed in a bona fide executive, administrative, or professional capacity as defined in 29 CFR part 541 are not deemed to be laborers or mechanics.

Public building or *public work* means building or work, the construction, prosecution, completion, or repair of which, as defined in this section, is carried on directly by authority of, or with funds of, a Federal agency to serve the interest of the general public regardless of whether title thereof is in a Federal agency.

Site of the work.—(1) Means—

(i) *The primary site of the work.* The physical place or places where the construction called for in the contract will remain when work on it is completed; and

(ii) *The secondary site of the work, if any.* Any other site where a significant portion of the building or work is constructed, provided that such site is—

(A) Located in the United States; and

(B) Established specifically for the performance of the contract or project;

(2) Except as provided in paragraph (3) of this definition, includes fabrication plants, mobile factories, batch plants, borrow pits, job headquarters, tool yards, etc., provided—

(i) They are dedicated exclusively, or nearly so, to performance of the contract or project; and

(ii) They are adjacent or virtually adjacent to the *primary site of the work* as defined in paragraphs (1)(i) of *the secondary site of the work* as defined in paragraph (1)(ii) of this definition;

(3) Does not include permanent home offices, branch plant establishments, fabrication plants, or tool yards of a contractor or subcontractor whose locations and continuance in operation are determined wholly without regard to a particular Federal contract or project. In addition, fabrication plants, batch plants, borrow pits, job headquarters, yards, etc., of a commercial or material supplier which are established by a supplier of materials for the project before opening of bids and not on the project site,

are not included in the *site of the work*. Such permanent, previously established facilities are not a part of the *site of the work*, even if the operations for a period of time may be dedicated exclusively, or nearly so, to the performance of a contract.

Trainee means a person registered and receiving on-the-job training in a construction occupation under a program which has been approved in advance by the U.S. Department of Labor, Employment and Training Administration, Office of Apprenticeship Training, Employer, and Labor Services (OATELS), as meeting its standards for on-the-job training programs and which has been so certified by that Administration.

Wages means the basic hourly rate of pay; any contribution irrevocably made by a contractor or subcontractor to a trustee or to a third person pursuant to a bona fide fringe benefit fund, plan, or program; and the rate of costs to the contractor or subcontractor which may be reasonably anticipated in providing bona fide fringe benefits to laborers and mechanics pursuant to an enforceable commitment to carry out a financially responsible plan or program, which was communicated in writing to the laborers and mechanics affected. The fringe benefits enumerated in the Construction Wage Rate Requirements statute include medical or hospital care, pensions on retirement or death, compensation for injuries or illness resulting from occupational activity, or insurance to provide any of the foregoing; unemployment benefits; life insurance, disability insurance, sickness insurance, or accident insurance; vacation or holiday pay; defraying costs of apprenticeship or other similar programs; or other bona fide fringe benefits. Fringe benefits do not include benefits required by other Federal, State, or local law.

[FAC 84-34, 53 FR 4935, 2/18/88, effective 2/29/88; FAC 90-13, 57 FR 44263, 9/24/92, effective 11/23/92; FAC 90-23, 59 FR 67010, 12/28/94, effective 2/27/95; FAC 97-22, 66 FR 2116, 1/10/2001, effective 3/12/2001; Delay of effective date, 66 FR 14259, 3/9/2001, effective 5/11/2001; FAC 2005-04, 70 FR 33662, 6/8/2005, effective 7/8/2005; FAC 2005-22, 72 FR 65868, 11/23/2007, effective 12/24/2007; FAC 2005-73, 79 FR 24192, 4/29/2014, effective 5/29/2014]

22.402 Applicability.

(a) *Contracts for construction work.*

(1) The requirements of this subpart apply—

(i) Only if the construction work is, or reasonably can be foreseen to be, performed at a particular site so that wage rates can be determined for the locality, and only to construction work that is performed by laborers and mechanics at the site of the work;

(ii) To dismantling, demolition, or removal of improvements if a part of the construction contract, or if construction at that site is anticipated by another contract as provided in Subpart 37.3;

(iii) To the manufacture or fabrication of construction materials and components conducted in connection with the construction and on the site of the work by the contractor or a subcontractor under a contract otherwise subject to this subpart; and

(iv) To painting of public buildings or public works, whether performed in connection with the original construction or as alteration or repair of an existing structure.

(2) The requirements of this subpart do not apply to—

(i) The manufacturing of components or materials off the site of the work or their subsequent delivery to the site by the commercial supplier or materialman;

(ii) Contracts requiring construction work that is so closely related to research, experiment, and development that it cannot be performed separately, or that is itself the subject of research, experiment, or development (see paragraph (b) of this section for applicability of this subpart to research and development contracts or portions thereof involving construction, alteration, or repair of a public building or public work);

(iii) Employees of railroads operating under collective bargaining agreements that are subject to the Railway Labor Act; or

(iv) Employees who work at contractors' or subcontractors' permanent home offices, fabrication shops, or tool yards not located at the site of the work. However, if the employees go to the site of the work and perform construction activities there, the requirements of this subpart are applicable for the actual time so spent, not including travel unless the employees transport materials or supplies to or from the site of the work.

(b) *Nonconstruction contracts involving some construction work.*

(1) The requirements of this subpart apply to construction work to be performed as part of nonconstruction contracts (supply, service, research and development, etc.) if—

(i) The construction work is to be performed on a public building or public work;

(ii) The contract contains specific requirements for a substantial amount of construction work exceeding the monetary threshold for application of the Construction Wage Rate Requirements statute (the word "substantial" relates to the type and quantity of construction work to be performed and not merely to the total value of construction work as compared to the total value of the contract); and

(iii) The construction work is physically or functionally separate from, and is capable of being performed on a segregated basis from, the other work required by the contract.

(2) The requirements of this subpart do not apply if—

(i) The construction work is incidental to the furnishing of supplies, equipment, or services (for example, the requirements do not apply to simple installation or alteration at a public building or public work that is incidental to furnishing supplies or equipment under a supply contract; however, if a substantial and segregable amount of construction, alteration, or repair is required, such as for installation of heavy generators or large refrigerator systems or for plant modification or rearrangement, the requirements of this subpart apply); or

(ii) The construction work is so merged with nonconstruction work or so fragmented in terms of the locations or time spans in which it is to be performed, that it is not capable of being segregated as a separate contractual requirement.

[FAC 84-34, 53 FR 4935, 2/18/88, effective 2/29/88; FAC 2005-73, 79 FR 24192, 4/29/2014, effective 5/29/2014]

22.403 Statutory, Executive order, and regulatory requirements. (No Text)

[FAC 2005-79, 79 FR 74544, 12/15/2014, effective 12/15/2014; FAC 2005-85, 80 FR 75915, 12/4/2015, effective 12/4/2015; FAC 2005-93, 81 FR 91627, 12/16/2016, effective 1/1/2017; FAC 2005-100, 83 FR 42569, 8/22/2018, effective 8/22/2018]

22.403-1 Construction Wage Rate Requirements statute.

40 U.S.C. chapter 31, subchapter IV, Wage Rate Requirements (Construction), formerly known as the Davis-Bacon Act, provides that contracts in excess of $2,000 to which the United States or the District of Columbia is a party for construction, alteration, or repair (including painting and decorating) of public buildings or public works within the United States, shall contain a clause (see 52.222-6) that no laborer or mechanic employed directly upon the site of the work shall receive less than the prevailing wage rates as determined by the Secretary of Labor.

[FAC 84-34, 53 FR 4935, 2/18/88, effective 2/29/88; FAC 2005-06, 70 FR 57453, 9/30/2005, effective 9/30/2005; FAC 2005-73, 79 FR 24192, 4/29/2014, effective 5/29/2014]

22.403-2 Copeland Act.

The Copeland (Anti-Kickback) Act (18 U.S.C. 874 and 40 U.S.C. 3145) makes it unlawful to induce, by force, intimidation, threat of procuring dismissal from employment, or otherwise, any person employed in the construction or repair of public buildings or public works, financed in whole or in part by the United States, to give up any part of the compensation to which that person is entitled under a contract of employment. The Copeland Act also requires each contractor and subcontractor to furnish weekly a statement of compliance with respect to the wages paid each employee during the preceding week. Contracts subject to the Copeland Act shall contain a clause (see 52.222-10) requiring contractors and subcontractors to comply with the regulations issued by the Secretary of Labor under the Copeland Act.

[FAC 84-34, 53 FR 4935, 2/18/88, effective 2/29/88; FAC 2005-06, 70 FR 57453, 9/30/2005, effective 9/30/2005]

22.403-3 Contract Work Hours and Safety Standards Act.

40 U.S.C. chapter 37, Contract Work Hours and Safety Standards, requires that certain contracts (see 22.305) contain a clause (see 52.222-4) specifying that no laborer or mechanic doing any part of the work contemplated by the contract shall be required or permitted to work more than 40 hours in any workweek unless paid for all additional hours at not less than 1 1/2 times the basic rate of pay (see 22.301).

[FAC 84-34, 53 FR 4935, 2/18/88, effective 2/29/88; FAC 2005-06, 70 FR 57453, 9/30/2005, effective 9/30/2005; FAC 2005-73, 79 FR 24192, 4/29/2014, effective 5/29/2014]

22.403-4 Executive Order 13658.

Executive Order 13658 establishes minimum wages for certain workers. The wage rate is subject to annual increases by an amount determined by the Secretary of Labor. See subpart 22.19. The clause at 52.222-55, Minimum Wages under Executive Order 13658, requires the Executive Order 13658 minimum wage rate to be paid if it is higher than other minimum wage rates, such as the subpart 22.4 statutory wage determination amount.

[FAC 2005-79, 79 FR 74544, 12/15/2014, effective 12/15/2014; FAC 2005-85, 80 FR 75915, 12/4/2015, effective 12/4/2015; FAC 2005-93, 81 FR 91627, 12/16/2016, effective 1/1/2017; FAC 2005-100, 83 FR 42569, 8/22/2018, effective 8/22/2018]

22.403-5 Executive Order 13706.

Executive Order 13706 establishes paid sick leave for employees of certain Federal contractors. See subpart 22.21 and the clause at 52.222-62, Paid Sick Leave under Executive Order 13706.

[FAC 2005-93, 81 FR 91627, 12/16/2016, effective 1/1/2017; FAC 2005-100, 83 FR 42569, 8/22/2018, effective 8/22/2018]

22.403-6 Department of Labor regulations involving construction.

(a) Under the statutes and Executive orders referred to in 22.403 and Reorganization Plan No. 14 of 1950 (3 CFR 1949-53 Comp., p. 1007), the Secretary of Labor has issued regulations in title 29, subtitle A, Code of Federal Regulations, prescribing standards and procedures to be observed by the Department of Labor and the Federal contracting agencies. Those standards and procedures applicable to contracts involving construction are implemented in this subpart.

(b) The Department of Labor regulations include—

(1) Part 1, relating to Construction Wage Rate Requirements statute minimum wage rates;

(2) Part 3, relating to the Copeland (Anti-Kickback) Act and requirements for submission of weekly statements of compliance and the preservation and inspection of weekly payroll records;

(3) Part 5, relating to enforcement of the—

(i) Construction Wage Rate Requirements statute;

(ii) Contract Work Hours and Safety Standards statute; and

(iii) Copeland (Anti-Kickback) Act;

(4) Part 6, relating to rules of practice for appealing the findings of the Administrator, Wage and Hour Division, in enforcement cases under the various labor statutes, and by which Administrative Law Judge hearings are held;

(5) Part 7, relating to rules of practice by which contractors and other interested parties may appeal to the Department of Labor Administrative Review Board, decisions issued by the Administrator, Wage and Hour Division, or administrative law judges under the various labor statutes;

(6) Part 10, relating to establishing a minimum wage for Federal contractors; and

(7) Part 13, relating to establishing paid sick leave for Federal contractors.

(c) Refer all questions relating to the application and interpretation of wage determinations (including the classifications therein) and the interpretation of the Department of Labor regulations in this subsection to the Administrator, Wage and Hour Division.

[FAC 2005-93, 81 FR 91627, 12/16/2016, effective 1/1/2017; FAC 2005-100, 83 FR 42569, 8/22/2018, effective 8/22/2018]

22.404 Construction Wage Rate Requirements statute wage determinations.

The Department of Labor is responsible for issuing wage determinations reflecting prevailing wages, including fringe benefits. The wage determinations apply only to those laborers and mechanics employed by a contractor upon the site of the work including drivers who transport to or from the site materials and equipment used in the course of contract operations. Determinations are issued for different types of construction, such as building, heavy, highway, and residential (referred to as rate schedules), and apply only to the types of construction designated in the determination.

[FAC 84-34, 53 FR 4935, 2/18/88, effective 2/29/88; FAC 2005-73, 79 FR 24192, 4/29/2014, effective 5/29/2014]

22.404-1 Types of wage determinations.

(a) *General wage determinations.* (1) A general wage determination contains prevailing wage rates for the types of construction designated in the determination, and is used in contracts performed within a specified geographical area. General wage determinations contain no expiration date and remain valid until modified, superseded, or canceled by the Department of Labor. Once incorporated in a contract, a general wage determination normally remains effective for the life of the contract, unless the contracting officer exercises an option to extend the term of the contract (see 22.404-12). These determinations shall be used whenever possible. They are issued at the discretion of the Department of Labor either upon receipt of an agency request or on the Department of Labor's own initiative.

(2) General wage determinations are published on the WDOL website. General wage determinations are effective on the publication date of the wage determination or upon receipt of the wage determination by the contracting agency, whichever occurs first. *Publication* within the meaning of this section shall occur on the first date the wage determination is published on the WDOL. Archived Construction Wage Rate Requirements statute general wage determinations that are no longer current may be accessed in the "Archived DB WD" database on WDOL for information purposes only. Contracting officers may not use an archived wage determination in a contract action without obtaining prior approval of the Department of Labor. To obtain prior approval, contact the Department of Labor, Wage and Hour Division, using *http://www.wdol.gov*, or contact the procurement agency labor advisor listed on *http://www.wdol.gov*.

(b) *Project wage determinations.* A project wage determination is issued at the specific request of a contracting agency. It is used only when no general wage determination applies, and is effective for 180 calendar days from the date of the determination. However, if a determination expires before contract award, it may be possible to obtain an extension to the 180-day life of the determination (see 22.404-5(b)(2)). Once incorporated in a contract, a project wage determination normally remains effective for the life of the contract, unless the contracting officer exercises an option to extend the term of the contract (see 22.404-12).

[FAC 84-34, 53 FR 4935, 2/18/88, effective 2/29/88; FAC 2001-01, 66 FR 53478, 10/22/2001, effective 12/21/2001; FAC 2005-10, 71 FR 36930, 6/28/2006, effective 6/28/2006; FAC 2005-16, 72 FR 13585, 3/22/2007, effective 3/22/2007; FAC 2005-55, 77 FR 204, 1/3/2012, effective 1/3/2012; FAC 2005-73, 79 FR 24192, 4/29/2014, effective 5/29/2014]

22.404-2 General requirements.

(a) The contracting officer must incorporate only the appropriate wage determinations in solicitations and contracts and must designate the work to which each determination or part thereof applies. The contracting officer must not include project wage determinations in contracts or options other than those for which they are issued. When exercising an option to extend the term of a contract, the contracting officer must select the most current wage determination(s) from the same schedule(s) as the wage determination(s) incorporated into the contract.

(b) If the wage determination is a general wage determination or a project wage determination containing more than one rate schedule, the contracting officer shall either include only the rate schedules that apply to the particular types of construction (building, heavy, highway, etc.) or include the entire wage determination and clearly indicate the parts of the work to which each rate schedule shall be applied. Inclusion by reference is not permitted.

(c) The Wage and Hour Division has issued the following general guidelines for use in selecting the proper schedule(s) of wage rates:

(1) *Building* construction is generally the construction of sheltered enclosures with walk-in access, for housing persons, machinery, equipment, or supplies. It typically includes all construction of such structures, installation of utilities and equipment (both above and below grade level), as well as incidental grading, utilities and paving, unless there is an established area practice to the contrary.

(2) *Residential* construction is generally the construction, alteration, or repair of single family houses or apartment buildings of no more than four (4) stories in height, and typically includes incidental items such as site work, parking areas, utilities, streets and sidewalks, unless there is an established area practice to the contrary.

(3) *Highway* construction is generally the construction, alteration, or repair of roads, streets, highways, runways, taxiways, alleys, parking areas, and other similar projects that are not incidental to *building*, *residential*, or *heavy* construction.

(4) *Heavy* construction includes those projects that are not properly classified as either "building," "residential," or "highway," and is of a catch-all nature. Such heavy projects may sometimes be distinguished on the basis of their individual characteristics, and separate schedules issued (*e.g.*, "dredging," "water and sewer line," "dams," "flood control," etc.).

(5) When the nature of a project is not clear, it is necessary to look at additional factors, with primary consideration given to locally established area practices. If there is any doubt as to the proper application of wage rate schedules to the type or types of construction involved, guidance shall be sought before the opening of bids, or receipt of best and final offers, from the Administrator, Wage and Hour Division. Further examples are contained in Department of Labor All Agency Memoranda Numbers 130 and 131.

[FAC 84-34, 53 FR 4935, 2/18/88, effective 2/29/88; FAC 2001-01, 66 FR 53478, 10/22/2001, effective 12/21/2001]

22.404-3 Procedures for requesting wage determinations.

(a) *General wage determinations.* If there is a general wage determination on the WDOL website applicable to the project, the agency may use it without notifying the Department of Labor. When necessary, a request for a general wage determination may be made by submitting Standard Form (SF) 308, Request for Determination and Response to Request, to the Administrator, Wage and Hour Division, Attention: Branch of Construction Contract Wage Determinations, 200 Constitution Avenue, NW, Washington, DC 20210.

(b) *Project wage determinations.* If a general wage determination is not available on WDOL, a contracting agency shall submit requests for project wage determinations on SF 308 to the Department of Labor.

(1) The location, including the county (or other civil subdivision) and State in which the proposed project is located.

(2) The name of the project and a sufficiently detailed description of the work to indicate the types of construction involved

(*e.g.*, building, heavy, highway, residential, or other type).

(3) Any available pertinent wage payment information, unless wage patterns in the area are clearly established.

(4) The estimated cost of each project.

(5) All the classifications of laborers and mechanics likely to be employed.

(c) *Time for submission of requests.* (1) The time required by the Department of Labor for processing requests for project wage determinations varies according to the facts and circumstances in each case. An agency should expect the processing to take at least 30 days. Accordingly, agencies should submit requests for project wage determinations for the primary site of the work to the Department of Labor at least 45 days (60 days if possible) before issuing the solicitation or exercising an option to extend the term of a contract.

(2) Agencies should promptly submit to the Department of Labor an offeror's request for a project wage determination for a secondary site of the work.

(d) *Review of wage determinations.* Immediately upon receipt, the contracting agency shall examine the wage determination and inform the Department of Labor of any changes necessary or appropriate to correct errors. Private parties requesting changes should be advised to submit their requests to the Department of Labor.

[FAC 84-34, 53 FR 4935, 2/18/88, effective 2/29/88; FAC 2001-01, 66 FR 53478, 10/22/2001, effective 12/21/2001; FAC 2005-04, 70 FR 33662, 6/8/2005, effective 7/8/2005; FAC 2005-10, 71 FR 36930, 6/28/2006, effective 6/28/2006; FAC 2005-16, 72 FR 13585, 3/22/2007, effective 3/22/2007; FAC 2005-100, 83 FR 42571, 8/22/2018, effective 8/22/2018]

22.404-4 Solicitations issued without wage determinations for the primary site of the work.

(a) If a solicitation is issued before the wage determination for the primary site of the work is obtained, a notice shall be included in the solicitation that the schedule of minimum wage rates to be paid under the contract will be issued as an amendment to the solicitation.

(b) In sealed bidding, bids may not be opened until a reasonable time after the wage determination for the primary site of the work has been furnished to all bidders.

(c) In negotiated acquisitions, the contracting officer may open proposals and conduct negotiations before obtaining the wage determination for the primary site of the work. However, the contracting officer shall incorporate the wage determination into the solicitation before submission of best and final offers.

[FAC 84-34, 53 FR 4935, 2/18/88, effective 2/29/88; FAC 2005-04, 70 FR 33662, 6/8/2005, effective 7/8/2005]

22.404-5 Expiration of project wage determinations.

(a) The contracting officer shall make every effort to ensure that contract award is made before expiration of the project wage determination included in the solicitation.

(b) The following procedure applies when contracting by sealed bidding:

(1) If a project wage determination for the primary site of the work expires before bid opening, or if it appears before bid opening that a project wage determination may expire before award, the contracting officer shall request a new determination early enough to ensure its receipt before bid opening. If necessary, the contracting officer shall postpone the bid opening date to allow a reasonable time to obtain the determination, amend the solicitation to incorporate the new determination, and permit bidders to amend their bids. If the new determination does not change the wage rates and would not warrant amended bids, the contracting officer shall amend the solicitation to include the number and date of the new determination.

(2) If a project wage determination for the primary site of the work expires after bid opening but before award, the contracting officer shall request an extension of the project wage determination expiration date from the Administrator, Wage and Hour Division. The request for extension shall be supported

by a written finding, which shall include a brief statement of factual support, that the extension is necessary and proper in the public interest to prevent injustice or undue hardship or to avoid serious impairment of the conduct of Government business. If necessary, the contracting officer shall delay award to permit either receipt of the extension or receipt and processing of a new determination. If the request is granted, the contracting officer shall award the contract and modify it to apply the extended expiration date to the already incorporated project wage determination. (See 43.103(b)(1).) If the request is denied, the Administrator will proceed to issue a new project wage determination. Upon receipt, the contracting officer shall process the new determination as follows:

(i) If the new determination for the primary site of the work changes any wage rates for classifications to be used in the contract, the contracting officer may cancel the solicitation only in accordance with 14.404-1. Otherwise the contracting officer shall award the contract and incorporate the new determination to be effective on the date of contract award. The contracting officer shall equitably adjust the contract price for any increased or decreased cost of performance resulting from any changed wage rates.

(ii) If the new determination for the primary site of the work does not change any wage rates, the contracting officer shall award the contract and modify it to include the number and date of the new determination. (See 43.103(b)(1).)

(c) The following procedure applies when contracting by negotiation:

(1) If a project wage determination will or does expire before contract award, the contracting officer shall request a new wage determination from the Department of Labor. If necessary, the contracting officer shall delay award while the new determination is obtained and processed.

(2) The contracting officer need not delay opening and reviewing proposals or discussing them with the offerors while a new determination for the primary site of the work is being obtained. The contracting officer shall request offerors to extend the period for acceptance of any proposal if that period expires or may expire before receipt and full processing of the new determination.

(3) If the new determination for the primary site of the work changes any wage rates, the contracting officer shall amend the solicitation to incorporate the new determination, and furnish the wage rate information to all prospective offerors that were sent a solicitation if the closing date for receipt of proposals has not yet occurred, or to all offerors that have not been eliminated from the competition if the closing date has passed. All offerors to whom wage rate information has been furnished shall be given reasonable opportunity to amend their proposals.

(4) If the new determination for the primary site of the work does not change any wage rates, the contracting officer shall amend the solicitation to include the number and date of the new determination and award the contract.

[FAC 84-34, 53 FR 4935, 2/18/88, effective 2/29/88; FAC 2005-04, 70 FR 33662, 6/8/2005, effective 7/8/2005; FAC 2005-31, 74 FR 11827, 3/19/2009, effective 4/20/2009]

22.404-6 Modifications of wage determinations.

(a) *General.* (1) The Department of Labor may modify a wage determination to make it current by specifying only the items being changed or by reissuing the entire determination with changes incorporated.

(2) All project wage determination modifications expire on the same day as the original determination. The need to include a modification of a project wage determination for the primary site of the work in a solicitation is determined by the time of receipt of the modification by the contracting agency. Therefore, the contracting agency must annotate the modification of the project wage determination with the date and time immediately upon receipt.

(3) The need for inclusion of the modification of a general wage determination for the primary site of the work in a solicitation is determined by the date the modified wage

determination is published on the WDOL, or by the date the agency receives actual written notice of the modification from the Department of Labor, whichever occurs first. (Note the distinction between receipt by the agency (modification is effective) and receipt by the contracting officer, which may occur later.) During the course of the solicitation, the contracting officer shall monitor the WDOL website to determine whether the applicable wage determination has been revised. Revisions published on the WDOL website or otherwise communicated to the contracting officer within the timeframes prescribed at 22.404-6(b) and (c) are applicable and must be included in the resulting contract. Monitoring can be accomplished by use of the WDOL website's "Alert Service".

(b) The following applies when contracting by sealed bidding:

(1) A written action modifying a wage determination shall be effective if:

(i) It is received by the contracting agency, or is published on the WDOL, 10 or more calendar days before the date of bid opening; or

(ii) It is received by the contracting agency, or is published on the WDOL, less than 10 calendar days before the date of bid opening, unless the contracting officer finds that there is not reasonable time available before bid opening to notify the prospective bidders. (If the contracting officer finds that there is not reasonable time to notify bidders, a written report of the finding shall be placed in the contract file and shall be made available to the Department of Labor upon request.)

(2) All written actions modifying wage determinations received by the contracting agency after bid opening, or modifications to general wage determinations published on the WDOL after bid opening, shall not be effective and shall not be included in the solicitation (but see paragraph (b)(6) of this subsection).

(3) If an effective modification of the wage determination for the primary site of the work is received by the contracting officer before bid opening, the contracting officer shall postpone the bid opening, if necessary, to allow a reasonable time to amend the solicitation to incorporate the modification and permit bidders to amend their bids. If the modification does not change the wage rates and would not warrant amended bids, the contracting officer shall amend the solicitation to include the number and date of the modification.

(4) If an effective modification of the wage determination for the primary site of the work is received by the contracting officer after bid opening, but before award, the contracting officer shall follow the procedures in 22.404-5(b)(2)(i) or (ii).

(5) If an effective modification is received by the contracting officer after award, the contracting officer shall modify the contract to incorporate the wage modification retroactive to the date of award and equitably adjust the contract price for any increased or decreased cost of performance resulting from any changed wage rates. If the modification does not change any wage rates and would not warrant contract price adjustment, the contracting officer shall modify the contract to include the number and date of the modification.

(6) If an award is not made within 90 days after bid opening, any modification to a general wage determination which is published on the WDOL before award, shall be effective for any resultant contract unless an extension of the 90-day period is obtained from the Administrator, Wage and Hour Division. An agency head may request such an extension from the Administrator. The request must be supported by a written finding, which shall include a brief statement of factual support, that the extension is necessary and proper in the public interest to prevent injustice, undue hardship, or to avoid serious impairment in the conduct of Government business. The contracting officer shall follow the procedures in 22.404-5(b)(2).

(c) The following applies when contracting by negotiation:

(1) All written actions modifying wage determinations received by the contracting agency before contract award, or modifications to general wage determinations pub-

lished on the WDOL before award, shall be effective.

(2) If an effective wage modification is received by the contracting officer before award, the contracting officer shall follow the procedures in 22.404-5(c)(3) or (4).

(3) If an effective wage modification is received by the contracting officer after award, the contracting officer shall follow the procedures in 22.404-6(b)(5).

(d) The following applies when modifying a contract to exercise an option to extend the term of a contract:

(1) A modified wage determination is effective if—

(i) The contracting agency receives a written action from the Department of Labor prior to exercise of the option, or within 45 days after submission of a wage determination request (22.404-3(c)), whichever is later; or

(ii) The Department of Labor publishes the modification to a general wage determination on the WDOL before exercise of the option.

(2) If the contracting officer receives an effective modified wage determination either before or after execution of the contract modification to exercise the option, the contracting officer must modify the contract to incorporate the modified wage determination, and any changed wage rates, effective as of the date that the option to extend was effective.

[FAC 84-34, 53 FR 4935, 2/18/88, effective 2/29/88; FAC 2001-01, 66 FR 53478, 10/22/2001, effective 12/21/2001; FAC 2005-04, 70 FR 33662, 6/8/2005, effective 7/8/2005; FAC 2005-10, 71 FR 36930, 6/28/2006, effective 6/28/2006; FAC 2005-16, 72 FR 13585, 3/22/2007, effective 3/22/2007]

22.404-7 Correction of wage determinations containing clerical errors.

Upon the Department of Labor's own initiative or at the request of the contracting agency, the Administrator, Wage and Hour Division, may correct any wage determination found to contain clerical errors. Such corrections will be effective immediately, and will apply to any solicitation or active contract. Before contract award, the contracting officer must follow the procedures in 22.404-5(b)(1) or (2)(i) or (ii) in sealed bidding, and the procedures in 22.404-5(c)(3) or (4) in negotiations. After contract award, the contracting officer must follow the procedures at 22.404-6(b)(5), except that for contract modifications to exercise an option to extend the term of the contract, the contracting officer must follow the procedures at 22.404-6(d)(2).

[FAC 2001-01, 66 FR 53478, 10/22/2001, effective 12/21/2001]

22.404-8 Notification of improper wage determination before award.

(a) The following written notifications by the Department of Labor shall be effective immediately without regard to 22.404-6 if received by the contracting officer prior to award:

(1) A solicitation includes the wrong wage determination or the wrong rate schedule; or

(2) A wage determination is withdrawn by the Administrative Review Board.

(b) In sealed bidding, the contracting officer shall proceed in accordance with the following:

(1) If the notification of an improper wage determination for the primary site of the work reaches the contracting officer before bid opening, the contracting officer shall postpone the bid opening date, if necessary, to allow a reasonable time to—

(i) Obtain the appropriate determination if a new wage determination is required;

(ii) Amend the solicitation to incorporate the determination (or rate schedule); and

(iii) Permit bidders to amend their bids. If the appropriate wage determination does not change any wage rates and would not warrant amended bids, the contracting officer shall amend the solicitation to include the number and date of the new determination.

(2) If the notification of an improper wage determination for the primary site of the work reaches the contracting officer after bid opening but before award, the contracting officer shall delay awarding the con-

tract, if necessary, and if required, obtain the appropriate wage determination. The appropriate wage determination shall be processed in accordance with 22.404-5(b)(2)(i) or (ii).

(c) In negotiated acquisitions, the contracting officer shall delay award, if necessary, and process the notification of an improper wage determination for the primary site of the work in the manner prescribed for a new wage determination at 22.404-5(c)(3).

[FAC 84-34, 53 FR 4935, 2/18/88, effective 2/29/88; FAC 2005-04, 70 FR 33662, 6/8/2005, effective 7/8/2005]

22.404-9 Award of contract without required wage determination.

(a) If a contract is awarded without the required wage determination (*i.e.*, incorporating no determination, containing a clearly inapplicable general wage determination, or containing a project determination which is inapplicable because of an inaccurate description of the project or its location), the contracting officer shall initiate action to incorporate the required determination in the contract immediately upon discovery of the error. If a required wage determination (valid determination in effect on the date of award) is not available, the contracting officer shall expeditiously request a wage determination from the Department of Labor, including a statement explaining the circumstances and giving the date of the contract award.

(b) The contracting officer shall—

(1) Modify the contract to incorporate the required wage determination (retroactive to the date of award) and equitably adjust the contract price if appropriate; or

(2) Terminate the contract.

[FAC 84-34, 53 FR 4935, 2/18/88, effective 2/29/88]

22.404-10 Posting wage determinations and notice.

The contractor must keep a copy of the applicable wage determination (and any approved additional classifications) posted at the site of the work in a prominent place where the workers can easily see it. The contracting officer shall furnish to the contractor, Department of Labor Form WH-1321, Notice to Employees Working on Federal and Federally Financed Construction Projects, for posting with the wage rates. The name, address, and telephone number of the Government officer responsible for the administration of the contract shall be indicated in the poster to inform workers to whom they may submit complaints or raise questions concerning labor standards.

[FAC 84-34, 53 FR 4935, 2/18/88, effective 2/29/88; FAC 2001-01, 66 FR 53478, 10/22/2001, effective 12/21/2001]

22.404-11 Wage determination appeals.

The Secretary of Labor has established an Administrative Review Board which decides appeals of final decisions made by the Department of Labor concerning Construction Wage Rate Requirements statute wage determinations. A contracting agency or other interested party may file a petition for review under the procedures in 29 CFR Part 7 if reconsideration by the Administrator has been sought pursuant to 29 CFR 1.8 and denied.

[FAC 84-34, 53 FR 4935, 2/18/88, effective 2/29/88; FAC 2001-01, 66 FR 53478, 10/22/2001, effective 12/21/2001; FAC 2005-73, 79 FR 24192, 4/29/2014, effective 5/29/2014]

22.404-12 Labor standards for contracts containing construction requirements and option provisions that extend the term of the contract.

(a) Each time the contracting officer exercises an option to extend the term of a contract for construction, or a contract that includes substantial and segregable construction work, the contracting officer must modify the contract to incorporate the most current wage determination.

(b) If a contract with an option to extend the term of the contract has indefinite-delivery or indefinite-quantity construction requirements, the contracting officer must incorporate the wage determination incorporated into the contract at the exercise of the option into task orders issued during that option period. The wage determination will be effective for the complete period of performance of those task orders without further revision.

(c) The contracting officer must include in fixed-price contracts a clause that specifies one of the following methods, suitable to the interest of the Government, to provide an allowance for any increases or decreases in labor costs that result from the inclusion of the current wage determination at the exercise of an option to extend the term of the contract:

(1) The contracting officer may provide the offerors the opportunity to bid or propose separate prices for each option period. The contracting officer must not further adjust the contract price as a result of the incorporation of a new or revised wage determination at the exercise of each option to extend the term of the contract. Generally, this method is used in construction-only contracts (with options to extend the term) that are not expected to exceed a total of 3 years.

(2) The contracting officer may include in the contract a separately specified pricing method that permits an adjustment to the contract price or contract labor unit price at the exercise of each option to extend the term of the contract. At the time of option exercise, the contracting officer must incorporate a new wage determination into the contract, and must apply the specific pricing method to calculate the contract price adjustment. An example of a contract pricing method that the contracting officer might separately specify is in the incorporation in the solicitation and resulting contract of the pricing data from an annually published unit pricing book (e.g., the U.S. Army Computer-Aided Cost Estimating System or similar commercial product), which is multiplied in the contract by a factor proposed by the contractor (e.g., .95 or 1.1). At option exercise, the contracting officer incorporates the pricing data from the latest annual edition of the unit pricing book, multiplied by the factor agreed to in the basic contract. The contracting officer must not further adjust the contract price as a result of the incorporation of the new or revised wage determination.

(3) The contracting officer may provide for a contract price adjustment based solely on a percentage rate determined by the contracting officer using a published economic indicator incorporated into the solicitation and resulting contract. At the exercise of each option to extend the term of the contract, the contracting officer will apply the percentage rate, based on the economic indicator, to the portion of the contract price or contract unit price designated in the contract clause as labor costs subject to the provisions of the Construction Wage Rate Requirements statute. The contracting officer must insert 50 percent as the estimated portion of the contract price that is labor unless the contracting officer determines, prior to issuance of the solicitation, that a different percentage is more appropriate for a particular contract or requirement. This percentage adjustment to the designated labor costs must be the only adjustment made to cover increases in wages and/or benefits resulting from the incorporation of a new or revised wage determination at the exercise of the option.

(4) The contracting officer may provide a computation method to adjust the contract price to reflect the contractor's actual increase or decrease in wages and fringe benefits (combined) to the extent that the increase is made to comply with, or the decrease is voluntarily made by the contractor as a result of incorporation of, a new or revised wage determination at the exercise of the option to extend the term of the contract. Generally, this method is appropriate for use only if contract requirements are predominately services subject to the Service Contract Labor Standards statute and the construction requirements are substantial and segregable. The methods used to adjust the contract price for the service requirements and the construction requirements would be similar.

[FAC 2001-01, 66 FR 53478, 10/22/2001, effective 12/21/2001; FAC 2005-21, 72 FR 63088, 11/7/2007, effective 12/7/2007; FAC 2005-73, 79 FR 24192, 4/29/2014, effective 5/29/2014]

22.405 [Removed and Reserved]

[FAC 84-34, 53 FR 4935, 2/18/88, effective 2/29/88; FAC 2005-17, 72 FR 27364, 5/15/2007, effective 6/14/2007]

22.406 Administration and enforcement. (No Text)

22.406-1 Policy.

(a) *General.* Contracting agencies are responsible for ensuring the full and impartial enforcement of labor standards in the administration of construction contracts. Contracting agencies shall maintain an effective program that shall include—

(1) Ensuring that contractors and subcontractors are informed, before commencement of work, of their obligations under the labor standards clauses of the contract;

(2) Adequate payroll reviews, on-site inspections, and employee interviews to determine compliance by the contractor and subcontractors, and prompt initiation of corrective action when required;

(3) Prompt investigation and disposition of complaints; and

(4) Prompt submission of all reports required by this subpart.

(b) *Preconstruction letters and conferences.* Before construction begins, the contracting officer shall inform the contractor of the labor standards clauses and wage determination requirements of the contract and of the contractor's and any subcontractor's responsibilities under the contract. Unless it is clear that the contractor is fully aware of the requirements, the contracting officer shall issue an explanatory letter and/or arrange a conference with the contractor promptly after award of the contract.

[FAC 84-34, 53 FR 4935, 2/18/88, effective 2/29/88]

22.406-2 Wages, fringe benefits, and overtime.

(a) In computing wages paid to a laborer or mechanic, the contractor may include only the following items:

(1) Amounts paid in cash to the laborer or mechanic, or deducted from payments under the conditions set forth in 29 CFR 3.5.

(2) Contributions (except those required by Federal, State, or local law) the contractor makes irrevocably to a trustee or a third party under any bona fide plan or program to provide for medical or hospital care, pensions, compensation for injuries or illness resulting from occupational activity, unemployment benefits, life insurance, disability and sickness insurance, accident insurance, or any other bona fide fringe benefit.

(3) Other contributions or anticipated costs for bona fide fringe benefits to the extent expressly approved by the Secretary of Labor.

(b) (1) The contractor may satisfy the obligation under the clause at 52.222-6, Construction Wage Rate Requirements, by providing wages consisting of any combination of contributions or costs as specified in paragraph (a) of this subsection, if the total cost of the combination is not less than the total of the basic hourly rate and fringe benefits payments prescribed in the wage determination for the classification of laborer or mechanic concerned.

(2) Wages provided by the contractor and fringe benefits payments required by the wage determination may include items that are not stated as exact cash amounts. In these cases, the hourly cash equivalent of the cost of these items shall be determined by dividing the employer's contributions or costs by the employee's hours worked during the period covered by the costs or contributions. For example, if a contractor pays a monthly health insurance premium of $112 for a particular employee who worked 125 hours during the month, the hourly cash equivalent is determined by dividing $112 by 125 hours, which equals $0.90 per hour. Similarly, the calculation of hourly cash equivalent for nine paid holidays per year for an employee with an hourly rate of pay of $5.00 is determined by multiplying $5.00 by 72 (9 days at 8 hours each), and dividing the result of $360 by the number of hours worked by the employee during the year. If the interested parties (contractor, contracting officer, and employees or their representative) cannot agree on the cash equivalent, the contracting officer shall submit the question for final determination to

the Department of Labor as prescribed by agency procedures. The information submitted shall include—

(i) A comparison of the payments, contributions, or costs in the wage determination with those made or proposed as equivalents by the contractor; and

(ii) The comments and recommendations of the contracting officer.

(c) In computing required overtime payments, (*i.e.*, 1½ times the basic hourly rate of pay) the contractor shall use the basic hourly rate of pay in the wage determination, or the basic hourly rate actually paid by the contractor, if higher. The basic rate of pay includes employee contributions to fringe benefits, but excludes the contractor's contributions, costs, or payment of cash equivalents for fringe benefits. Overtime shall not be computed on a rate lower than the basic hourly rate in the wage determination.

[FAC 84-34, 53 FR 4935, 2/18/88, effective 2/29/88; FAC 2005-73, 79 FR 24192, 4/29/2014, effective 5/29/2014]

22.406-3 Additional classifications.

(a) If any laborer or mechanic is to be employed in a classification that is not listed in the wage determination applicable to the contract, the contracting officer, pursuant to the clause at 52.222-6, Construction Wage Rate Requirements, shall require that the contractor submit to the contracting officer, Standard Form (SF) 1444, Request for Authorization of Additional Classification and Rate, which, along with other pertinent data, contains the proposed additional classification and minimum wage rate including any fringe benefits payments.

(b) Upon receipt of SF 1444 from the contractor, the contracting officer shall review the request to determine whether it meets the following criteria:

(1) The classification is appropriate and the work to be performed by the classification is not performed by any classification contained in the applicable wage determination.

(2) The classification is utilized in the area by the construction industry.

(3) The proposed wage rate, including any fringe benefits, bears a reasonable relationship to the wage rates in the wage determination in the contract.

(c) (1) If the criteria in paragraph (b) of this subsection are met and the contractor and the laborers or mechanics to be employed in the additional classification (if known) or their representatives agree to the proposed additional classification, and the contracting officer approves, the contracting officer shall submit a report (including a copy of SF 1444) of that action to the Administrator, Wage and Hour Division, for approval, modification, or disapproval of the additional classification and wage rate (including any amount designated for fringe benefits); or

(2) If the contractor, the laborers or mechanics to be employed in the classification or their representatives, and the contracting officer do not agree on the proposed additional classification, or if the criteria are not met, the contracting officer shall submit a report (including a copy of SF 1444) giving the views of all interested parties and the contracting officer's recommendation to the Administrator, Wage and Hour Division, for determination of appropriate classification and wage rate.

(d) (1) Within 30 days of receipt of the report, the Administrator, Wage and Hour Division, will complete action and so advise the contracting officer, or will notify the contracting officer that additional time is necessary.

(2) Upon receipt of the Department of Labor's action, the contracting officer shall forward a copy of the action to the contractor, directing that the classification and wage rate be posted in accordance with paragraph (a) of the clause at 52.222-6 and that workers in the affected classification receive no less than the minimum rate indicated from the first day on which work under the contract was performed in the classification.

(e) In each option to extend the term of the contract, if any laborer or mechanic is to be employed during the option in a classification that is not listed (or no longer listed) on the wage determination incorporated in that option, the contracting officer must require that the contractor submit a request for conformance using the procedures noted in paragraphs (a) through (d) of this section.

[FAC 84-34, 53 FR 4935, 2/18/88, effective 2/29/88; FAC 90-13, 57 FR 44263, 9/24/92, effective 11/23/92; FAC 90-23, 59 FR 67010, 12/28/94, effective 2/27/95; FAC 2001-01, 66 FR 53478, 10/22/2001, effective 12/21/2001; FAC 2005-73, 79 FR 24192, 4/29/2014, effective 5/29/2014]

22.406-4 Apprentices and trainees.

(a) The contracting officer shall review the contractor's employment and payment records of apprentices and trainees made available pursuant to the clause at 52.222-8, Payrolls and Basic Records, to ensure that the contractor has complied with the clause at 52.222-9, Apprentices and Trainees.

(b) If a contractor has classified employees as apprentices, trainees, helpers without complying with the requirements of the clause at 52.222-9, the contracting officer shall reject the classification and require the contractor to pay the affected employees at the rates applicable to the classification of the work actually performed.

[FAC 84-34, 53 FR 4935, 2/18/88, effective 2/29/88]

22.406-5 Subcontracts.

In accordance with the requirements of the clause at 52.222-11, Subcontracts (Labor Standards), the contractor and subcontractors at any tier are required to submit a fully executed SF 1413, Statement and Acknowledgment, upon award of each subcontract.

[FAC 84-34, 53 FR 4935, 2/18/88, effective 2/29/88]

22.406-6 Payrolls and statements.

(a) *Submission.* In accordance with the clause at 52.222-8, Payrolls and Basic Records, the contractor must submit or cause to be submitted, within 7 calendar days after the regular payment date of the payroll week covered, for the contractor and each subcontractor, (1) copies of weekly payrolls applicable to the contract, and (2) weekly payroll statements of compliance. The contractor may use the Department of Labor Form WH-347, Payroll (For Contractor's Optional Use), or a similar form that provides the same data and identical representation.

(b) *Withholding for nonsubmission.* If the contractor fails to submit copies of its or its subcontractors' payrolls promptly, the contracting officer shall, from any payment due to the contractor, withhold approval of an amount that the contracting officer considers necessary to protect the interest of the Government and the employees of the contractor or any subcontractor.

(c) *Examination.* (1) The contracting officer shall examine the payrolls and payroll statements to ensure compliance with the contract and any statutory or regulatory requirements. Particular attention should be given to—

(i) The correctness of classifications and rates;

(ii) Fringe benefits payments;

(iii) Hours worked;

(iv) Deductions; and

(v) Disproportionate employment ratios of laborers, apprentices or trainees to journeymen.

(2) Fringe benefits payments, contributions made, or costs incurred on other than a weekly basis shall be considered as a part of weekly payments to the extent they are creditable to the particular weekly period involved and are otherwise acceptable.

(d) *Preservation.* The contracting agency shall retain payrolls and statements of compliance for 3 years after completion of the contract and make them available when requested by the Department of Labor at any time during that period. Submitted payrolls shall not be returned to a contractor or subcontractor for any reason, but copies thereof may be furnished to the contractor or subcontractor who submitted them, or to a higher tier contractor or subcontractor.

(e) *Disclosure of payroll records.* Contractor payroll records in the Government's possession must be carefully protected from any public disclosure which is not required by law, since payroll records may contain information in which the contractor's employees have a privacy interest, as well as information in which the contractor may have a proprietary interest that the Government may be obliged to protect. Questions concerning release of this information may involve the Freedom of Information Act (FOIA).

[FAC 84-34, 53 FR 4935, 2/18/88, effective 2/29/88]

22.406-7 Compliance checking.

(a) *General.* The contracting officer shall make checks and investigations on all contracts covered by this subpart as may be necessary to ensure compliance with the labor standards requirements of the contract.

(b) *Regular compliance checks.* Regular compliance checking includes the following activities:

(1) Employee interviews to determine correctness of classifications, rates of pay, fringe benefits payments, and hours worked. (See Standard Form 1445.)

(2) On-site inspections to check type of work performed, number and classification of workers, and fulfillment of posting requirements.

(3) Payroll reviews to ensure that payrolls of prime contractors and subcontractors have been submitted on time and are complete and in compliance with contract requirements.

(4) Comparison of the information in this paragraph (b) with available data, including daily inspector's report and daily logs of construction, to ensure consistency.

(c) *Special compliance checks.* Situations that may require special compliance checks include—

(1) Inconsistencies, errors, or omissions detected during regular compliance checks; or

(2) Receipt of a complaint alleging violations. If the complaint is not specific enough, the complainant shall be so advised and invited to submit additional information.

[FAC 84-34, 53 FR 4935, 2/18/88, effective 2/29/88]

22.406-8 Investigations.

Conduct labor standards investigations when available information indicates such action is warranted. In addition, the Department of Labor may conduct an investigation on its own initiative or may request a contracting agency to do so.

(a) *Contracting agency responsibilities.* Conduct an investigation when a compliance check indicates that substantial or willful violations may have occurred or violations have not been corrected.

(1) The investigation must—

(i) Include all aspects of the contractor's compliance with contract labor standards requirements;

(ii) Not be limited to specific areas raised in a complaint or uncovered during compliance checks; and

(iii) Use personnel familiar with labor laws and their application to contracts.

(2) Do not disclose contractor employees' oral or written statements taken during an investigation or the employee's identity to anyone other than an authorized Government official without that employee's prior signed consent.

(3) Send a written request to the Administrator, Wage and Hour Division, to obtain—

(i) Investigation and enforcement instructions; or

(ii) Available pertinent Department of Labor files.

(4) Obtain permission from the Department of Labor before disclosing material obtained from Labor Department files, other than computations of back wages and liquidated damages and summaries of back wages due, to anyone other than Government contract administrators.

(b) *Investigation report.* The contracting officer must review the investigation report on receipt and make preliminary findings. The contracting officer normally must not base adverse findings solely on employee statements that the employee does not wish to have disclosed. However, if the investigation establishes a pattern of possible violations that are based on employees' statements that are not authorized for disclosure, the pattern itself may support a finding of noncompliance.

(c) *Contractor notification.* After completing the review, the contracting officer must—

(1) Provide the contractor any written preliminary findings and proposed corrective actions, and notice that the contractor has the right to request that the basis for the findings be made available and to submit written rebuttal information.

(2) Upon request, provide the contractor with rationale for the findings. However, under no circumstances will the contracting officer permit the contractor to examine the investigation report. Also, the contracting officer must not disclose the identity of any employee who filed a complaint or who was interviewed, without the prior consent of the employee.

(3) (i) The contractor may rebut the findings in writing within 60 days after it receives a copy of the preliminary findings. The rebuttal becomes part of the official investigation record. If the contractor submits a rebuttal, evaluate the preliminary findings and notify the contractor of the final findings.

(ii) If the contracting officer does not receive a timely rebuttal, the contracting officer must consider the preliminary findings final.

(4) If appropriate, request the contractor to make restitution for underpaid wages and assess liquidated damages. If the request includes liquidated damages, the request must state that the contractor has 60 days to request relief from such assessment.

(d) *Contracting officer's report.* After taking the actions prescribed in paragraphs (b) and (c) of this subsection—

(1) The contracting officer must prepare and forward a report of any violations, including findings and supporting evidence, to the agency head. Standard Form 1446, Labor Standards Investigation Summary Sheet, is the first page of the report; and

(2) The agency head must process the report as follows:

(i) The contracting officer must send a detailed enforcement report to the Administrator, Wage and Hour Division, within 60 days after completion of the investigation, if—

(A) A contractor or subcontractor underpaid by $1,000 or more;

(B) The contracting officer believes that the violations are aggravated or willful (or there is reason to believe that the contractor has disregarded its obligations to employees and subcontractors under the Construction Wage Rate Requirements statute);

(C) The contractor or subcontractor has not made restitution; or

(D) Future compliance has not been assured.

(ii) If the Department of Labor expressly requested the investigation and none of the conditions in paragraph (d) (2) (i) of this subsection exist, submit a summary report to the Administrator, Wage and Hour Division. The report must include—

(A) A summary of any violations;

(B) The amount of restitution paid;

(C) The number of workers who received restitution;

(D) The amount of liquidated damages assessed under the Contract Work Hours and Safety Standards statute;

(E) Corrective measures taken; and

(F) Any information that may be necessary to review any recommendations for an appropriate adjustment in liquidated damages.

(iii) If none of the conditions in paragraphs (d) (2) (i) or (ii) of this subsection are present, close the case and retain the report in the appropriate contract file.

(iv) If substantial evidence is found that violations are willful and in violation of a criminal statute, (generally 18 U.S.C. 874 or 1001), forward the report (supplemented if necessary) to the Attorney General of the United States for prosecution if the facts warrant. Notify the Administrator, Wage and Hour Division, when the report is forwarded for the Attorney General's consideration.

(e) *Department of Labor investigations.* The Department of Labor will furnish the contracting officer an enforcement report detailing violations found and any corrective action taken by the contractor, in investigations that disclose—

(1) Underpayments totaling $1,000 or more;

(2) Aggravated or willful violations (or, when the contracting officer believes that the contractor has disregarded its obligations to employees and subcontractors under the Construction Wage Rate Requirements statute); or

(3) Potential assessment of liquidated damages under the Contract Work Hours and Safety Standards statute.

(f) *Other investigations.* The Department of Labor will provide a letter summarizing the findings of the investigation to the contracting officer for all investigations that are not described in paragraph (e) of this subsection.

[FAC 97-19, 65 FR 46052, 7/26/2000, effective 9/25/2000; FAC 2005-73, 79 FR 24192, 4/29/2014, effective 5/29/2014]

22.406-9 Withholding from or suspension of contract payments.

(a) *Withholding from contract payments.* If the contracting officer believes a violation exists (see 22.406-8), or upon request of the Department of Labor, the contracting officer must withhold from payments due the contractor an amount equal to the estimated wage underpayment and estimated liquidated damages due the United States under the Contract Work Hours and Safety Standards statute. (See 22.302.)

(1) If the contracting officer believes a violation exists or upon request of the Department of Labor, the contracting officer must withhold funds from any current Federal contract or Federally assisted contract with the same prime contractor that is subject to either Construction Wage Rate Requirements statute or Contract Work Hours and Safety Standards statute requirements.

(2) If a subsequent investigation confirms violations, the contracting officer must adjust the withholding as necessary. However, if the Department of Labor requested the withholding, the contracting officer must not reduce or release the withholding without written approval of the Department of Labor.

(3) Use withheld funds as provided in paragraph (c) of this subsection to satisfy assessed liquidated damages, and unless the contractor makes restitution, validated wage underpayments.

(b) *Suspension of contract payments.* If a contractor or subcontractor fails or refuses to comply with the labor standards clauses of the Construction Wage Rate Requirements statute and related statutes, the agency, upon its own action or upon the written request of the Department of Labor, must suspend any further payment, advance, or guarantee of funds until the violations cease or until the agency has withheld sufficient funds to compensate employees for back wages, and to cover any liquidated damages which may be due.

(c) *Disposition of contract payments withheld or suspended*—(1) *Forwarding wage underpayments to the Secretary of Labor.* Upon final administrative determination, if the contractor or subcontractor has not made restitution, the contracting officer must follow the Department of Labor guidance published in Wage and Hour Division, All Agency Memorandum (AAM) No. 215, Streamlining Claims for Federal Contractor Employees Act. The AAM No. 215 can be obtained at *http://www.dol.gov/whd/govcontracts/dbra.htm*; under Guidance there is a link for All Agencies Memoranda (AAMs).

(2) *Returning of withheld funds to contractor.* When funds withheld exceed the amount required to satisfy validated wage underpayments and assessed liquidated damages, return the funds to the contractor.

(3) *Limitation on returning funds.* If the Department of Labor requested the withholding or if the findings are disputed (see 22.406-10(e)), the contracting officer must not return the funds to the contractor without approval by the Department of Labor.

(4) *Liquidated damages.* Upon final administrative determination, the contracting officer must dispose of funds withheld or

collected for liquidated damages in accordance with agency procedures.

[FAC 97-19, 65 FR 46052, 7/26/2000, effective 9/25/2000; FAC 2005-04, 70 FR 33662, 6/8/2005, effective 7/8/2005; FAC 2005-73, 79 FR 24192, 4/29/2014, effective 5/29/2014; FAC 2005-78, 79 FR 70342, 11/25/2014, effective 12/26/2014]

22.406-10 Disposition of disputes concerning construction contract labor standards enforcement.

(a) The areas of possible differences of opinion between contracting officers and contractors in construction contract labor standards enforcement include—

(1) Misclassification of workers;

(2) Hours of work;

(3) Wage rates and payment;

(4) Payment of overtime;

(5) Withholding practices; and

(6) The applicability of the labor standards requirements under varying circumstances.

(b) Generally, these differences are settled administratively at the project level by the contracting agency. If necessary, these differences may be settled with assistance from the Department of Labor.

(c) When requesting the contractor to take corrective action in labor violation cases, the contracting officer shall inform the contractor of the following:

(1) Disputes concerning the labor standards requirements of the contract are handled under the contract clause at 52.222-14, Disputes Concerning Labor Standards, and not under the clause at 52.233-1, Disputes.

(2) The contractor may appeal the contracting officer's findings or part thereof by furnishing the contracting officer a complete statement of the reasons for the disagreement with the findings.

(d) The contracting officer shall promptly transmit the contracting officer's findings and the contractor's statement to the Administrator, Wage and Hour Division.

(e) The Administrator, Wage and Hour Division, will respond directly to the contractor or subcontractor, with a copy to the contracting agency. The contractor or subcontractor may appeal the Administrator's findings in accordance with the procedures outlined in Labor Department Regulations (29 CFR 5.11). Hearings before administrative law judges are conducted in accordance with 29 CFR Part 6, and hearings before the Labor Department Administrative Review Board are conducted in accordance with 29 CFR Part 7.

(f) The Administrator, Wage and Hour Division, may institute debarment proceedings against the contractor or subcontractor if the Administrator finds reasonable cause to believe that the contractor or subcontractor has committed willful or aggravated violations of the Contract Work Hours and Safety Standards statute or the Copeland (Anti-Kickback) Act, or any of the applicable statutes listed in 29 CFR 5.1 other than the Construction Wage Rate Requirements statute, or has committed violations of the Construction Wage Rate Requirements statute that constitute a disregard of its obligations to employees or subcontractors under 40 U.S.C. 3144.

[FAC 84-34, 53 FR 4935, 2/18/88, effective 2/29/88; FAC 2001-01, 66 FR 53478, 10/22/2001, effective 12/21/2001; FAC 2005-73, 79 FR 24192, 4/29/2014, effective 5/29/2014]

22.406-11 Contract terminations.

If a contract or subcontract is terminated for violation of the labor standards clauses, the contracting agency shall submit a report to the Administrator, Wage and Hour Division. The report shall include—

(a) The number of the terminated contract;

(b) The name and address of the terminated contractor or subcontractor.

(c) The name and address of the contractor or subcontractor, if any, who is to complete the work;

(d) The amount and number of the replacement contract, if any; and

(e) A description of the work.

[FAC 84-34, 53 FR 4935, 2/18/88, effective 2/29/88; FAC 2005-78, 79 FR 70342, 11/25/2014, effective 12/26/2014]

22.406-12 Cooperation with the Department of Labor.

(a) The contracting agency shall cooperate with representatives of the Department of Labor in the inspection of records, interviews with workers, and all other aspects of investigations undertaken by the Department of Labor. When requested, the contracting agency shall furnish to the Secretary of Labor any available information on contractors, subcontractors, current and previous contracts, and the nature of the contract work.

(b) If a Department of Labor representative undertakes an investigation at a construction project, the contracting officer shall inquire into the scope of the investigation, and request to be notified immediately of any violations discovered under the Construction Wage Rate Requirements statute, the Contract Work Hours and Safety Standards statute, or the Copeland (Anti-Kickback) Act.

[FAC 84-34, 53 FR 4935, 2/18/88, effective 2/29/88; FAC 2005-73, 79 FR 24192, 4/29/2014, effective 5/29/2014]

22.406-13 Semiannual enforcement reports.

A semiannual report on compliance with and enforcement of the construction labor standards requirements of the Construction Wage Rate Requirements statute and Contract Work Hours and Safety Standards is required from each contracting agency. The reporting periods are October 1 through March 31 and April 1 through September 30. The reports shall only contain information as to the enforcement actions of the contracting agency and shall be prepared as prescribed in Department of Labor memoranda and submitted to the Department of Labor within 30 days after the end of the reporting period. This report has been assigned interagency report control number 1482-DOL-SA.

[FAC 84-34, 53 FR 4935, 2/18/88, effective 2/29/88; FAC 2005-73, 79 FR 24192, 4/29/2014, effective 5/29/2014]

22.407 Solicitation provision and contract clauses.

(a) Insert the following clauses in solicitations and contracts in excess of $2,000 for construction within the United States:

(1) 52.222-6, Construction Wage Rate Requirements.

(2) 52.222-7, Withholding of Funds.

(3) 52.222-8, Payrolls and Basic Records.

(4) 52.222-9, Apprentices and Trainees.

(5) 52.222-10, Compliance with Copeland Act Requirements.

(6) 52.222-11, Subcontracts (Labor Standards).

(7) 52.222-12, Contract Termination-Debarment.

(8) 52.222-13, Compliance with Construction Wage Rate Requirements statute and Related Act Regulations.

(9) 52.222-14, Disputes Concerning Labor Standards.

(10) 52.222-15, Certification of Eligibility.

(b) Insert the clause at 52.222-16, Approval of Wage Rates, in solicitations and contracts in excess of $2,000 for cost-reimbursement construction to be performed within the United States, except for contracts with a State or political subdivision thereof.

(c) A contract that is not primarily for construction may contain a requirement for some construction work to be performed in the United States. If under22.402(b) the requirements of this subpart apply to the construction work, insert in such solicitations and contracts the applicable construction labor standards clauses required in this section and identify the item or items of construction work to which the clauses apply.

(d) [Removed and reserved]

(e) Insert the clause at 52.222-30, Construction Wage Rate Requirements—Price Adjustment (None or Separately Specified Pricing Method), in solicitations and contracts if the contract is expected to be—

(1) A fixed-price contract subject to the Construction Wage Rate Requirements statute that will contain option provisions by

which the contracting officer may extend the term of the contract, and the contracting officer determines the most appropriate contract price adjustment method is the method at 22.404-12(c)(1) or (2); or

(2) A cost-reimbursable type contract subject to the Construction Wage Rate Requirements statute that will contain option provisions by which the contracting officer may extend the term of the contract.

(f) Insert the clause at 52.222-31, Construction Wage Rate Requirements—Price Adjustment (Percentage Method), in solicitations and contracts if the contract is expected to be a fixed-price contract subject to the Construction Wage Rate Requirements statute that will contain option provisions by which the contracting officer may extend the term of the contract, and the contracting officer determines the most appropriate contract price adjustment method is the method at 22.404-12(c)(3).

(g) Insert the clause at 52.222-32, Construction Wage Rate Requirements—Price Adjustment (Actual Method), in solicitations and contracts if the contract is expected to be a fixed-price contract subject to the Construction Wage Rate Requirements statute that will contain option provisions by which the contracting officer may extend the term of the contract, and the contracting officer determines the most appropriate method to establish contract price is the method at 22.404-12(c)(4).

(h) Insert the provision at 52.222-5, Construction Wage Rate Requirements—Secondary Site of the Work, in solicitations in excess of $2,000 for construction within the United States.

[FAC 84-34, 53 FR 4935, 2/18/88, effective 2/29/88; FAC 2001-01, 66 FR 53478, 10/22/2001, effective 12/21/2001; FAC 2005-04, 70 FR 33662, 6/8/2005, effective 7/8/2005; FAC 2005-17, 72 FR 27364, 5/15/2007, effective 6/14/2007; FAC 2005-73, 79 FR 24192, 4/29/2014, effective 5/29/2014]

SUBPART 22.5—USE OF PROJECT LABOR AGREEMENTS FOR FEDERAL CONSTRUCTION PROJECTS

22.501 Scope of subpart.

This subpart prescribes policies and procedures to implement Executive Order 13502, February 6, 2009.

[FAC 2005-41, 75 FR 19168, 4/13/2010, effective 5/13/2010]

22.502 Definitions.

As used in this subpart—

Construction means construction, rehabilitation, alteration, conversion, extension, repair, or improvement of buildings, highways, or other real property.

Labor organization means a labor organization as defined in 29 U.S.C. 152(5).

Large-scale construction project means a construction project where the total cost to the Federal Government is $25 million or more.

Project labor agreement means a pre-hire collective bargaining agreement with one or more labor organizations that establishes the terms and conditions of employment for a specific construction project and is an agreement described in 29 U.S.C. 158(f).

[FAC 2005-41, 75 FR 19168, 4/13/2010, effective 5/13/2010]

22.503 Policy.

(a) Project labor agreements are a tool that agencies may use to promote economy and efficiency in Federal procurement. Pursuant to Executive Order 13502, agencies are encouraged to consider requiring the use of project labor agreements in connection with large-scale construction projects.

(b) An agency may, if appropriate, require that every contractor and subcontractor engaged in construction on the project agree, for that project, to negotiate or become a party to a project labor agreement with one or more labor organizations if the agency decides that the use of project labor agreements will—

(1) Advance the Federal Government's interest in achieving economy and efficiency in Federal procurement, producing labor-man-

agement stability, and ensuring compliance with laws and regulations governing safety and health, equal employment opportunity, labor and employment standards, and other matters; and

(2) Be consistent with law.

(c) Agencies may also consider the following factors in deciding whether the use of a project labor agreement is appropriate for the construction project:

(1) The project will require multiple construction contractors and/or subcontractors employing workers in multiple crafts or trades.

(2) There is a shortage of skilled labor in the region in which the construction project will be sited.

(3) Completion of the project will require an extended period of time.

(4) Project labor agreements have been used on comparable projects undertaken by Federal, State, municipal, or private entities in the geographic area of the project.

(5) A project labor agreement will promote the agency's long term program interests, such as facilitating the training of a skilled workforce to meet the agency's future construction needs.

(6) Any other factors that the agency decides are appropriate.

[FAC 2005-41, 75 FR 19168, 4/13/2010, effective 5/13/2010]

22.504 General requirements for project labor agreements.

(a) *General*. Project labor agreements established under this subpart shall fully conform to all statutes, regulations, and Executive orders.

(b) *Requirements*. The project labor agreement shall—

(1) Bind all contractors and subcontractors engaged in construction on the construction project to comply with the project labor agreement;

(2) Allow all contractors and subcontractors to compete for contracts and subcontracts without regard to whether they are otherwise parties to collective bargaining agreements;

(3) Contain guarantees against strikes, lockouts, and similar job disruptions;

(4) Set forth effective, prompt, and mutually binding procedures for resolving labor disputes arising during the term of the project labor agreement;

(5) Provide other mechanisms for labor-management cooperation on matters of mutual interest and concern, including productivity, quality of work, safety, and health; and

(6) Include any additional requirements as the agency deems necessary to satisfy its needs.

(c) *Terms and conditions*. As appropriate to advance economy and efficiency in the procurement, an agency may specify the terms and conditions of the project labor agreement in the solicitation and require the successful offeror to become a party to a project labor agreement containing these terms and conditions as a condition of receiving a contract award. An agency may seek the views of, confer with, and exchange information with prospective bidders and union representatives as part of the agency's effort to identify appropriate terms and conditions of a project labor agreement for a particular construction project and facilitate agreement on those terms and conditions.

[FAC 2005-41, 75 FR 19168, 4/13/2010, effective 5/13/2010]

22.505 Solicitation provision and contract clause.

For acquisition of large-scale construction projects, if the agency decides pursuant to this subpart that a project labor agreement will be required, the contracting officer shall—

(a) Insert the provision at 52.222-33, Notice of Requirement for Project Labor Agreement, in all solicitations associated with the construction project.

(1) Use the provision with its Alternate I if the agency decides to require the submission of a project labor agreement from only the apparent successful offeror, prior to contract award.

(2) Use the provision with its Alternate II if an agency allows submission of a project labor agreement after contract award.

(b) (1) Insert the clause at 52.222-34, Project Labor Agreement, in all solicitations and contracts associated with the construction project.

(2) Use the clause with its Alternate I if an agency allows submission of the project labor agreement after contract award.

[FAC 2005-41, 75 FR 19168, 4/13/2010, effective 5/13/2010]

SUBPART 22.6—CONTRACTS FOR MATERIALS, SUPPLIES, ARTICLES, AND EQUIPMENT EXCEEDING $15,000

22.601 [Reserved]

[Reserved, FAC 90-43, Interim rule, 61 FR 67408, 12/20/96, effective 12/20/96, finalized without change, FAC 97-1, 62 FR 44802, 8/22/97, effective 10/21/97]

22.602 Statutory requirements.

Except for the exemptions at 22.604, all contracts subject to 41 U.S.C. chapter 65, Contracts for Materials, Supplies, Articles, and Equipment Exceeding $15,000 (the statute), and entered into by any executive department, independent establishment, or other agency or instrumentality of the United States, or by the District of Columbia, or by any corporation (all the stock of which is beneficially owned by the United States) for the manufacture or furnishing of materials, supplies, articles, and equipment (referred to in this subpart as supplies) in any amount exceeding $15,000, shall include or incorporate by reference the stipulations required by the statute pertaining to such matters as minimum wages, maximum hours, child labor, convict labor, and safe and sanitary working conditions.

[FAC 90-43, Interim rule, 61 FR 67408, 12/20/96, effective 12/20/96, finalized without change, FAC 97-1, 62 FR 44802, 8/22/97, effective 10/21/97; FAC 2005-45, 75 FR 53129, 8/30/2010, effective 10/1/2010; FAC 2005-73, 79 FR 24192, 4/29/2014, effective 5/29/2014]

22.603 Applicability.

The requirements in 22.602 apply to contracts (including for this purpose, indefinite-delivery contracts, basic ordering agreements, and blanket purchase agreements) and subcontracts under Section 8(a) of the Small Business Act, for the manufacture or furnishing of supplies that—

(a) Will be performed in the United States, Puerto Rico, or the U.S. Virgin Islands;

(b) Exceed or may exceed $15,000; and

(c) Are not exempt under 22.604.

[FAC 2001-14, 68 FR 28079, 5/22/2003, effective 6/23/2003; FAC 2005-45, 75 FR 53129, 8/30/2010, effective 10/1/2010]

22.604 Exemptions. (No Text)

22.604-1 Statutory exemptions.

Contracts for acquisition of the following supplies are exempt from the statute:

(a) Any item in those situations where the contracting officer is authorized by the express language of a statute to purchase "in the open market" generally (such as commercial items, see Part 12); or where a specific purchase is made under the conditions described in 6.302-2 in circumstances where immediate delivery is required by the public exigency.

(b) Perishables, including dairy, livestock, and nursery products.

(c) Agricultural or farm products processed for first sale by the original producers.

(d) Agricultural commodities or the products thereof purchased under contract by the Secretary of Agriculture.

[FAC 84-34, 53 FR 4944, 2/18/88, effective 2/29/88; FAC 90-32, 60 FR 48206, 9/18/95, effective 10/1/95; FAC 2005-73, 79 FR 24192, 4/29/2014, effective 5/29/2014]

22.604-2 Regulatory exemptions.

(a) Contracts for the following acquisitions are fully exempt from the statute (see 41 CFR 50-201.603):

(1) Public utility services.

(2) Supplies manufactured outside the United States, Puerto Rico, and the U.S. Virgin Islands.

(3) Purchases against the account of a defaulting contractor where the stipulations

of the statute were not included in the defaulted contract.

(4) Newspapers, magazines, or periodicals, contracted for with sales agents or publisher representatives, which are to be delivered by the publishers thereof.

(b) (1) Upon the request of the agency head, the Secretary of Labor may exempt specific contracts or classes of contracts from the inclusion or application of one or more of the Act's stipulations; provided, that the request includes a finding by the agency head stating the reasons why the conduct of Government business will be seriously impaired unless the exemption is granted.

(2) Those requests for exemption that relate solely to safety and health standards shall be transmitted to the Assistant Secretary for Occupational Safety and Health, U.S. Department of Labor, Washington, DC 20210. All other requests shall be transmitted to the Administrator of the Wage and Hour Division, U.S. Department of Labor, Washington, DC 20210.

[FAC 90-43, Interim rule, 61 FR 67408, 12/20/96, effective 12/20/96, finalized without change, FAC 97-1, 62 FR 44802, 8/22/97, effective 10/21/97; FAC 2001-14, 68 FR 28079, 5/22/2003, effective 6/23/2003; FAC 2005-73, 79 FR 24192, 4/29/2014, effective 5/29/2014]

22.605 Rulings and interpretations of the statute.

(a) As authorized by the statute, the Secretary of Labor has issued rulings and interpretations concerning the administration of the statute (see 41 CFR 50-206). The substance of certain rulings and interpretations is as follows:

(1) If a contract for $15,000 or less is subsequently modified to exceed $15,000, the contract becomes subject to the statute for work performed after the date of the modification.

(2) If a contract for more than $15,000 is subsequently modified by mutual agreement to $15,000 or less, the contract is not subject to the statute for work performed after the date of the modification.

(3) If a contract awarded to a prime contractor contains a provision whereby the prime contractor is made an agent of the Government, the prime contractor is required to include the stipulations of the statute in contracts in excess of $15,000 awarded for and on behalf of the Government for supplies that are to be used in the construction and equipment of Government facilities.

(4) If a contract subject to the statute is awarded to a contractor operating Government-owned facilities, the stipulations of the statute affect the employees of that contractor the same as employees of contractors operating privately owned facilities.

(5) Indefinite-delivery contracts, including basic ordering agreements and blanket purchase agreements, are subject to the statute unless it can be determined in advance that the aggregate amount of all orders estimated to be placed thereunder for 1 year after the effective date of the agreement will not exceed $15,000. A determination shall be made annually thereafter if the contract or agreement is extended, and the contract or agreement modified if necessary.

(b) [Reserved.]

[FAC 2005-45, 75 FR 53129, 8/30/2010, effective 10/1/2010; FAC 2005-73, 79 FR 24192, 4/29/2014, effective 5/29/2014]

22.606 [Reserved]

[Reserved, FAC 90-43, Interim rule, 61 FR 67408, 12/20/96, effective 12/20/96, finalized without change, FAC 97-1, 62 FR 44802, 8/22/97, effective 10/21/97]

22.607 [Reserved]

[Reserved, FAC 90-43, Interim rule, 61 FR 67408, 12/20/96, effective 12/20/96, finalized without change, FAC 97-1, 62 FR 44802, 8/22/97, effective 10/21/97]

22.608 Procedures.

(a) *Award.* When a contract subject to the statute is awarded, the contracting officer, in accordance with regulations or instructions issued by the Secretary of Labor and individual agency procedures, shall furnish to the contractor DOL publication WH-1313, Notice to Employees Working on Government Contracts.

(b) *Breach of stipulation*. In the event of a violation of a stipulation required under the statute, the contracting officer shall, in accordance with agency procedures, notify the appropriate regional office of the DOL, Wage and Hour Division (see 29 CFR part 1, Appendix B), and furnish any information available.

[FAC 90-43, Interim rule, 61 FR 67408, 12/20/96, effective 12/20/96, finalized without change, FAC 97-1, 62 FR 44802, 8/22/97, effective 10/21/97; FAC 2005-10, 71 FR 36930, 6/28/2006, effective 6/28/2006; FAC 2005-16, 72 FR 13585, 3/22/2007, effective 3/22/2007; FAC 2005-73, 79 FR 24192, 4/29/2014, effective 5/29/2014]

22.609 [Removed and Reserved]

[FAC 97-12, 64 FR 32740, 6/17/99, effective 6/17/99; FAC 2005-10, 71 FR 36930, 6/28/2006, effective 6/28/2006; FAC 2005-16, 72 FR 13585, 3/22/2007, effective 3/22/2007]

22.610 Contract clause.

The contracting officer shall insert the clause at 52.222-20, Contracts for Materials, Supplies, Articles, and Equipment Exceeding $15,000, in solicitations and contracts covered by the statute (see 22.603, 22.604, and 22.605).

[FAC 90-43, Interim rule, 61 FR 67408, 12/20/96, effective 12/20/96, finalized without change, FAC 97-1, 62 FR 44802, 8/22/97, effective 10/21/97; FAC 2005-73, 79 FR 24192, 4/29/2014, effective 5/29/2014]

SUBPART 22.7—[RESERVED]

SUBPART 22.8—EQUAL EMPLOYMENT OPPORTUNITY

22.800 Scope of subpart.

This subpart prescribes policies and procedures pertaining to nondiscrimination in employment by contractors and subcontractors.

[FAC 97-10, 63 FR 70264, 12/18/98, effective 2/16/99]

22.801 Definitions.

As used in this subpart—

Affirmative action program means a contractor's program that complies with Department of Labor regulations to ensure equal opportunity in employment to minorities and women.

Compliance evaluation means any one or combination of actions that the Office of Federal Contract Compliance Programs (OFCCP) may take to examine a Federal contractor's compliance with one or more of the requirements of E.O. 11246.

Contractor includes the terms *prime contractor* and *subcontractor*.

Deputy Assistant Secretary means the Deputy Assistant Secretary for Federal Contract Compliance, U.S. Department of Labor, or a designee.

Equal Opportunity clause means the clause at 52.222-26, Equal Opportunity, as prescribed in 22.810(e).

E.O. 11246 means Parts II and IV of Executive Order 11246, September 24, 1965 (30 FR 12319), and any Executive order amending or superseding this order (see 22.802). This term specifically includes the Equal Opportunity clause at 52.222-26, and the rules, regulations, and orders issued pursuant to E.O. 11246 by the Secretary of Labor or a designee.

Gender identity has the meaning given by the Department of Labor's Office of Federal Contract Compliance Programs, and is found at *www.dol.gov/ofccp/LGBT/LGBT_FAQs.html*.

Prime contractor means any person who holds, or has held, a Government contract subject to E.O. 11246.

Recruiting and training agency means any person who refers workers to any contractor or provides or supervises apprenticeship or training for employment by any contractor.

Sexual orientation has the meaning given by the Department of Labor's Office of Federal Contract Compliance Programs, and is found at *www.dol.gov/ofccp/LGBT/LGBT_FAQs.html*.

Site of construction means the general physical location of any building, highway, or other change or improvement to real property that is undergoing construction, rehabilitation, alteration, conversion, extension, demolition, or repair; and any temporary location or facility at which a contractor or other participating party meets a demand or performs a function relating to a Government contract or subcontract.

Subcontract means any agreement or arrangement between a contractor and any person (in which the parties do not stand in the relationship of an employer and an employee)—

(1) For the purchase, sale, or use of personal property or nonpersonal services that, in whole or in part, are necessary to the performance of any one or more contracts; or

(2) Under which any portion of the contractor's obligation under any one or more contracts is performed, undertaken, or assumed.

Subcontractor means any person who holds, or has held, a subcontract subject to E.O. 11246. The term first-tier subcontractor means a subcontractor holding a subcontract with a prime contractor.

United States means the 50 States, the District of Columbia, Puerto Rico, the Northern Mariana Islands, American Samoa, Guam, the U.S. Virgin Islands, and Wake Island.

[FAC 97-10, 63 FR 70264, 12/18/98, effective 2/16/99; FAC 2001-14, 68 FR 28079, 5/22/2003, effective 6/23/2003; FAC 2005-81, 80 FR 19504, 4/10/2015, effective 4/10/2015; FAC 2005-85, 80 FR 75907, 12/4/2015, effective 12/4/2015]

22.802 General.

(a) Executive Order 11246, as amended, sets forth the Equal Opportunity clause and requires that all agencies—

(1) include this clause in all nonexempt contracts and subcontracts (see 22.807); and

(2) Act to ensure compliance with the clause and the regulations of the Secretary of Labor—

(i) To promote the full realization of equal employment opportunity for all persons, regardless of race, color, religion, sex, sexual orientation, gender identity, or national origin; and

(ii) To prohibit contractors from discharging, or in any other manner discriminating against, any employee or applicant for employment because the employee or applicant inquired about, discussed, or disclosed the compensation of the employee or applicant or another employee or applicant. This prohibition against discrimination does not apply to instances in which an employee who has access to the compensation information of other employees or applicants as a part of such employee's essential job functions discloses the compensation of such other employees or applicants to individuals who do not otherwise have access to such information, unless such disclosure is in response to a formal complaint or charge, in furtherance of an investigation, proceeding, hearing, or action, including an investigation conducted by the employer, or is consistent with the contractor's legal duty to furnish information.

(b) No contract or modification involving new acquisition shall be entered into, and no subcontract shall be approved by a contracting officer, with a person who has been found ineligible by the Deputy Assistant Secretary for reasons of noncompliance with the requirements of E.O. 11246.

(c) No contracting officer or contractor shall contract for supplies or services in a manner so as to avoid applicability of the requirements of E.O. 11246.

(d) Contractor disputes related to compliance with its obligation shall be handled according to the rules, regulations, and relevant orders of the Secretary of Labor (see 41 CFR 60-1.1).

[FAC 97-10, 63 FR 70264, 12/18/98, effective 2/16/99; FAC 2005-81, 80 FR 19504, 4/10/2015, effective 4/10/2015; FAC 2005-85, 80 FR 75907, 12/4/2015, effective 12/4/2015; FAC 2005-91, 81 FR 67732, 9/30/2016, effective 9/30/2016; FAC 2005-100, 83 FR 42570, 8/22/2018, effective 8/22/2018]

22.803 Responsibilities.

(a) The Secretary of Labor is responsible for the—

(1) Administration and enforcement of prescribed parts of E.O. 11246; and

(2) Adoption of rules and regulations and the issuance of orders necessary to achieve the purposes of E.O. 11246.

(b) The Secretary of Labor has delegated authority and assigned responsibility to the Deputy Assistant Secretary for carrying out the responsibilities assigned to the Secretary by E.O. 11246, except for the issuance of rules and regulations of a general nature.

(c) The head of each agency is responsible for ensuring that the requirements of this subpart are carried out within the agency, and for cooperating with and assisting the OFCCP in fulfilling its responsibilities.

(d) In the event the applicability of E.O. 11246 and implementing regulations is questioned, the contracting officer shall forward the matter to the Deputy Assistant Secretary, through agency channels, for resolution.

[FAC 97-10, 63 FR 70264, 12/18/98, effective 2/16/99]

22.804 Affirmative action programs. (No Text)

22.804-1 Nonconstruction.

Except as provided in 22.807, each nonconstruction prime contractor and each subcontractor with 50 or more employees and either a contract or subcontract of $50,000 or more, or Government bills of lading that in any 12-month period total, or can reasonably be expected to total, $50,000 or more, is required to develop a written affirmative action program for each of its establishments. Each contractor and subcontractor shall develop its written affirmative action programs within 120 days from the commencement of its first such Government contract, subcontract, or Government bill of lading.

[FAC 97-10, 63 FR 70264, 12/18/98, effective 2/16/99]

22.804-2 Construction.

(a) Construction contractors that hold a nonexempt (see 22.807) Government construction contract are required to meet (1) the contract terms and conditions citing affirmative action requirements applicable to covered geographical areas or projects and (2) applicable requirements of 41 CFR 60-1 and 60-4.

(b) Each agency shall maintain a listing of covered geographical areas that are subject to affirmative action requirements that specify goals for minorities and women in covered construction trades. Information concerning, and additions to, this listing will be provided to the principally affected contracting officers in accordance with agency procedures. Any contracting officer contemplating a construction project in excess of $10,000 within a geographic area not known to be covered by specific affirmative action goals shall request instructions on the most current information from the OFCCP regional office, or as otherwise specified in agency regulations, before issuing the solicitation.

(c) Contracting officers shall give written notice to the OFCCP regional office within 10 working days of award of a construction contract subject to these affirmative action requirements. The notification shall include the name, address, and telephone number of the contractor; employer identification number; dollar amount of the contract; estimated starting and completion dates of the contract; the contract number; and the geographical area in which the contract is to be performed. When requested by the OFCCP regional office, the contracting officer shall arrange a conference among contractor, contracting activity, and compliance personnel to discuss the contractor's compliance responsibilities.

[FAC 97-10, 63 FR 70264, 12/18/98, effective 2/16/99]

22.805 Procedures.

(a) *Preaward clearances for contracts and subcontracts of $10 million or more (excluding construction).*

(1) Except as provided in paragraphs (a)(4) and (a)(8) of this section, if the estimated amount of the contract or subcontract is $10 million or more, the contracting officer shall request clearance from the appropriate OFCCP regional office before—

(i) Award of any contract, including any indefinite delivery contract or letter contract; or

(ii) Modification of an existing contract for new effort that would constitute a contract award.

(2) Preaward clearance for each proposed contract and for each proposed first-tier subcontract of $10 million or more shall be requested by the contracting officer directly from the OFCCP regional office(s). Verbal requests shall be confirmed by letter or facsimile transmission.

(3) When the contract work is to be performed outside the United States with employees recruited within the United States, the contracting officer shall send the request for a preaward clearance to the OFCCP regional office serving the area where the proposed contractor's corporate home or branch office is located in the United States, or the corporate location where personnel recruiting is handled, if different from the contractor's corporate home or branch office. If the proposed contractor has no corporate office or location within the United States, the preaward clearance request action should be based on the location of the recruiting and training agency in the United States.

(4) The contracting officer does not need to request a preaward clearance if—

(i) The specific proposed contractor is listed in OFCCP's National Preaward Registry via the Internet at *https://ofccp.dol-esa.gov/preaward/pa_reg.html*;

(ii) The projected award date is within 24 months of the proposed contractor's Notice of Compliance completion date in the Registry; and

(iii) The contracting officer documents the Registry review in the contract file.

(5) The contracting officer shall include the following information in the preaward clearance request:

(i) Name, address, and telephone number of the prospective contractor and of any corporate affiliate at which work is to be performed.

(ii) Name, address, and telephone number of each proposed first-tier subcontractor with a proposed subcontract estimated at $10 million or more.

(iii) Anticipated date of award.

(iv) Information as to whether the contractor and first-tier subcontractors have previously held any Government contracts or subcontracts.

(v) Place or places of performance of the prime contract and first-tier subcontracts estimated at $10 million or more, if known.

(vi) The estimated dollar amount of the contract and each first-tier subcontract, if known.

(6) The contracting officer shall allow as much time as feasible before award for the conduct of necessary compliance evaluation by OFCCP. As soon as the apparently successful offeror can be determined, the contracting officer shall process a preaward clearance request in accordance with agency procedures, assuring, if possible, that the preaward clearance request is submitted to the OFCCP regional office at least 30 days before the proposed award date.

(7) Within 15 days of the clearance request, OFCCP will inform the awarding agency of its intention to conduct a preaward compliance evaluation. If OFCCP does not inform the awarding agency within that period of its intention to conduct a preaward compliance evaluation, clearance shall be presumed and the awarding agency is authorized to proceed with the award. If OFCCP informs the awarding agency of its intention to conduct a preaward compliance evaluation, OFCCP shall be allowed an additional 20 days after the date that it so informs the awarding agency to provide its conclusions. If OFCCP does not provide the awarding agency with its conclusions within that period, clearance shall be presumed and the awarding agency is authorized to proceed with the award.

(8) If the procedures specified in paragraphs (a)(6) and (a)(7) of this section would delay award of an urgent and critical contract beyond the time necessary to make award or beyond the time specified in the offer or extension thereof, the contracting officer shall immediately inform the OFCCP regional office of the expiration date of the offer or the required date of award and request clearance be provided before that

date. If the OFCCP regional office advises that a preaward evaluation cannot be completed by the required date, the contracting officer shall submit written justification for the award to the head of the contracting activity, who, after informing the OFCCP regional office, may then approve the award without the preaward clearance. If an award is made under this authority, the contracting officer shall immediately request a postaward evaluation from the OFCCP regional office.

(9) If, under the provisions of paragraph (a)(8) of this section, a postaward evaluation determines the contractor to be in noncompliance with E.O. 11246, the Deputy Assistant Secretary may authorize the use of the enforcement procedures at 22.809 against the noncomplying contractor.

(b) *Furnishing posters.* The contracting officer shall furnish to the contractor appropriate quantities of the poster entitled "Equal Employment Opportunity Is The Law." These shall be obtained in accordance with agency procedures.

[FAC 97-10, 63 FR 70264, 12/18/98, effective 2/16/99; FAC 2005-91, 81 FR 67781, 9/30/2016, effective 9/30/2016]

22.806 Inquiries.

(a) An inquiry from a contractor regarding status of its compliance with E.O. 11246, or rights of appeal to any of the actions in 22.809, shall be referred to the OFCCP regional office.

(b) Labor union inquiries regarding the revision of a collective bargaining agreement in order to comply with E.O. 11246 shall be referred to the Deputy Assistant Secretary.

[FAC 97-10, 63 FR 70264, 12/18/98, effective 2/16/99]

22.807 Exemptions.

(a) Under the following exemptions, all or part of the requirements of E.O. 11246 may be excluded from a contract subject to E.O. 11246:

(1) *National security.* The agency head may determine that a contract is essential to the national security and that the award of the contract without complying with one or more of the requirements of this subpart is necessary to the national security. Upon making such a determination, the agency shall notify the Deputy Assistant Secretary in writing within 30 days.

(2) *Specific contracts.* The Deputy Assistant Secretary may exempt an agency from requiring the inclusion of one or more of the requirements of E.O. 11246 in any contract if the Deputy Assistant Secretary deems that special circumstances in the national interest so require. Groups or categories of contracts of the same type may also be exempted if the Deputy Assistant Secretary finds it impracticable to act upon each request individually or if group exemptions will contribute to convenience in the administration of E.O. 11246.

(b) The following exemptions apply even though a contract or subcontract contains the Equal Opportunity clause:

(1) *Transactions of $10,000 or less.* The Equal Opportunity clause is required to be included in prime contracts and subcontracts by 22.802(a). Individual prime contracts or subcontracts of $10,000 or less are exempt from application of the Equal Opportunity clause, unless the aggregate value of all prime contracts or subcontracts awarded to a contractor in any 12-month period exceeds, or can reasonably be expected to exceed, $10,000. (Note: Government bills of lading, regardless of amount, are not exempt.)

(2) *Work outside the United States.* Contracts are exempt from the requirements of E.O. 11246 for work performed outside the United States by employees who were not recruited within the United States.

(3) *Contracts with State or local governments.* The requirements of E.O. 11246 in any contract with a State or local government (or any agency, instrumentality, or subdivision thereof) shall not be applicable to any agency, instrumentality, or subdivision of such government that does not participate in work on or under the contract.

(4) *Work on or near Indian reservations.* It shall not be a violation of E.O. 11246 for a contractor to extend a publicly announced preference in employment to Indians living on or near an Indian reservation in connec-

tion with employment opportunities on or near an Indian reservation. This applies to that area where a person seeking employment could reasonably be expected to commute to and from in the course of a work day. Contractors extending such a preference shall not, however, discriminate among Indians on the basis of religion, sex, sexual orientation, gender identity, or tribal affiliation, and the use of such preference shall not excuse a contractor from complying with E.O. 11246, rules and regulations of the Secretary of Labor, and applicable clauses in the contract.

(5) *Facilities not connected with contracts.* The Deputy Assistant Secretary may exempt from the requirements of E.O. 11246 any of a contractor's facilities that the Deputy Assistant Secretary finds to be in all respects separate and distinct from activities of the contractor related to performing the contract, provided, that the Deputy Assistant Secretary also finds that the exemption will not interfere with, or impede the effectiveness of, E.O. 11246.

(6) *Indefinite-quantity contracts.* With respect to indefinite-quantity contracts and subcontracts, the Equal Opportunity clause applies unless the contracting officer has reason to believe that the amount to be ordered in any year under the contract will not exceed $10,000. The applicability of the Equal Opportunity clause shall be determined by the contracting officer at the time of award for the first year, and annually thereafter for succeeding years, if any. Notwithstanding the above, the Equal Opportunity clause shall be applied to the contract whenever the amount of a single order exceeds $10,000. Once the Equal Opportunity clause is determined to be applicable, the contract shall continue to be subject to such clause for its duration regardless of the amounts ordered, or reasonably expected to be ordered, in any year.

(7) *Contracts with religious entities.* Pursuant to E.O. 13279, Section 202 of E.O. 11246, shall not apply to a Government contractor or subcontractor that is a religious corporation, association, educational institution, or society, with respect to the employment of individuals of a particular religion to perform work connected with the carrying on by such corporation, association, educational institution, or society of its activities. Such contractors and subcontractors are not exempted or excused from complying with the other requirements contained in the order.

(c) To request an exemption under paragraph (a)(2) or (b)(5) of this section, the contracting officer shall submit, under agency procedures, a detailed justification for omitting all, or part of, the requirements of E.O. 11246. Requests for exemptions under paragraph (a)(2) or (b)(5) of this section shall be submitted to the Deputy Assistant Secretary for approval.

(d) The Deputy Assistant Secretary may withdraw the exemption for a specific contract, or group of contracts, if the Deputy Assistant Secretary deems that such action is necessary and appropriate to achieve the purposes of E.O. 11246. Such withdrawal shall not apply—

(1) To contracts awarded before the withdrawal; or

(2) To any sealed bid contract (including restricted sealed bidding), unless the withdrawal is made more than 10 days before the bid opening date.

[FAC 84-26, 52 FR 19803, 5/27/87, effective 7/30/87; FAC 97-10, 63 FR 70264, 12/18/98, effective 2/16/99; FAC 2005-16, 72 FR 13586, 3/22/2007, effective 3/22/2007; FAC 2005-23, 72 FR 73218, 12/26/2007, effective 12/26/2007; FAC 2005-81, 80 FR 19504, 4/10/2015, effective 4/10/2015; FAC 2005-85, 80 FR 75907, 12/4/2015, effective 12/4/2015]

22.808 Complaints.

Complaints received by the contracting officer alleging violation of the requirements of E.O. 11246 shall be referred immediately to the OFCCP regional office. The complainant shall be advised in writing of the referral. The contractor that is the subject of a complaint shall not be advised in any manner or for any reason of the complainant's name, the nature of the complaint, or the fact that the complaint was received.

[FAC 97-10, 63 FR 70264, 12/18/98, effective 2/16/99]

22.809 Enforcement.

Upon written notification to the contracting officer, the Deputy Assistant Secretary may direct one or more of the following actions, as well as administrative sanctions and penalties, be taken against contractors found to be in violation of E.O. 11246, the regulations of the Secretary of Labor, or the applicable contract clauses:

(a) Publication of the names of the contractor or its unions.

(b) Cancellation, termination, or suspension of the contractor's contracts or portion thereof.

(c) Debarment from future Government contracts, or extensions or modifications of existing contracts, until the contractor has established and carried out personnel and employment policies in compliance with E.O. 11246 and the regulations of the Secretary of Labor.

(d) Referral by the Deputy Assistant Secretary of any matter arising under E.O. 11246 to the Department of Justice or to the Equal Employment Opportunity Commission (EEOC) for the institution of appropriate civil or criminal proceedings.

[FAC 97-10, 63 FR 70264, 12/18/98, effective 2/16/99; FAC 2005-91, 81 FR 67732, 9/30/2016, effective 9/30/2016; FAC 2005-100, 83 FR 42570, 8/22/2018, effective 8/22/2018]

22.810 Solicitation provisions and contract clauses.

(a) When a contract is contemplated that will include the clause at 52.222-26, Equal Opportunity, the contracting officer shall insert—

(1) The clause at 52.222-21, Prohibition of Segregated Facilities, in the solicitation and contract; and

(2) The provision at 52.222-22, Previous Contracts and Compliance Reports, in the solicitation.

(b) The contracting officer shall insert the provision at 52.222-23, Notice of Requirement for Affirmative Action to Ensure Equal Employment Opportunity for Construction, in solicitations for construction when a contract is contemplated that will include the clause at 52.222-26, Equal Opportunity, and the amount of the contract is expected to be in excess of $10,000.

(c) The contracting officer shall insert the provision at 52.222-24, Preaward On-Site Equal Opportunity Compliance Evaluation, in solicitations other than those for construction when a contract is contemplated that will include the clause at 52.222-26, Equal Opportunity, and the amount of the contract is expected be $10 million or more.

(d) The contracting officer shall insert the provision at 52.222-25, Affirmative Action Compliance, in solicitations, other than those for construction, when a contract is contemplated that will include the clause at 52.222-26, Equal Opportunity.

(e) The contracting officer shall insert the clause at 52.222-26, Equal Opportunity, in solicitations and contracts (see 22.802) unless the contract is exempt from all of the requirements of E.O. 11246 (see 22.807(a)). If the contract is exempt from one or more, but not all, of the requirements of E.O. 11246, the contracting officer shall use the clause with its Alternate I.

(f) The contracting officer shall insert the clause at 52.222-27, Affirmative Action Compliance Requirements for Construction, in solicitations and contracts for construction that will include the clause at 52.222-26, Equal Opportunity, when the amount of the contract is expected to be in excess of $10,000.

(g) The contracting officer shall insert the clause at 52.222-29, Notification of Visa Denial, in contracts that will include the clause at 52.222-26, Equal Opportunity, if the contractor is required to perform in or on behalf of a foreign country.

[FAC 84-7, 50 FR 23606, 6/4/85, effective 4/30/85; FAC 84-26, 52 FR 19803, 5/27/87, effective 7/30/87; FAC 97-5, 63 FR 34058, 6/22/98, effective 8/21/98; FAC 97-10, 63 FR 70264, 12/18/98, effective 2/16/99]

SUBPART 22.9—NONDISCRIMINATION BECAUSE OF AGE

22.901 Policy.

Executive Order 11141, February 12, 1964 (29 FR 2477), states that the Government policy is as follows:

(a) Contractors and subcontractors shall not, in connection with employment, advancement, or discharge of employees, or the terms, conditions, or privileges of their employment, discriminate against persons because of their age except upon the basis of a bona fide occupational qualification, retirement plan, or statutory requirement.

(b) Contractors and subcontractors, or persons acting on their behalf, shall not specify in solicitations or advertisements for employees to work on Government contracts, a maximum age limit for employment unless the specified maximum age limit is based upon a bona fide occupational qualification, retirement plan, or statutory requirement.

(c) Agencies will bring this policy to the attention of contractors. The use of contract clauses is not required.

22.902 Handling complaints.

Agencies shall bring complaints regarding a contractor's compliance with this policy to that contractor's attention (in writing, if appropriate), stating the policy, indicating that the contractor's compliance has been questioned, and requesting that the contractor take any appropriate steps that may be necessary to comply.

SUBPART 22.10—SERVICE CONTRACT LABOR STANDARDS

22.1000 Scope of subpart.

This subpart prescribes policies and procedures implementing the provisions of 41 U.S.C. chapter 67, Service Contract Labor Standards (formerly known as the Service Contract Act of 1965), the applicable provisions of the Fair Labor Standards Act of 1938, as amended (29 U.S.C. 201, et seq.), and related Secretary of Labor regulations and instructions (29 CFR parts 4, 6, 8, and 1925).

[FAC 84-46, 54 FR 19816, 5/8/89, effective 6/7/89; FAC 2005-73, 79 FR 24192, 4/29/2014, effective 5/29/2014]

22.1001 Definitions.

As used in this subpart—

Contractor includes a subcontractor at any tier whose subcontract is subject to the provisions of the statute.

Multiple year contracts means contracts having a term of more than 1 year regardless of fiscal year funding. The term includes multiyear contracts (see 17.103).

United States means the 50 States, the District of Columbia, Puerto Rico, the Northern Mariana Islands, American Samoa, Guam, the U.S. Virgin Islands, Johnston Island, Wake Island, and the outer Continental Shelf as defined in the Outer Continental Shelf Lands Act (43 U.S.C. 1331, *et seq.*), but does not include any other place subject to U.S. jurisdiction or any U.S. base or possession within a foreign country (29 CFR 4.112).

Wage and Hour Division means the unit in the Department of Labor to which is assigned functions of the Secretary of Labor under the Service Contract Labor Standards statute.

Wage determination means a determination of minimum wages or fringe benefits made under 41 U.S.C. 6703 or 6707(c) applicable to the employment in a given locality of one or more classes of service employees.

[FAC 84-46, 54 FR 19816, 5/8/89, effective 6/7/89; FAC 90-40, 61 FR 39186, 7/26/96, effective 7/26/96; FAC 97-22, 66 FR 2116, 1/10/2001, effective 3/12/2001; Delay of effective date, 66 FR 14259, 3/9/2001, effective 5/11/2001; FAC 2001-14, 68 FR 28079, 5/22/2003, effective 6/23/2003; FAC 2005-10, 71 FR 36930, 6/28/2006, effective 6/28/2006; FAC 2005-16, 72 FR 13585, 3/22/2007, effective 3/22/2007; FAC 2005-64, 77 FR 75766, 12/21/2012, effective 1/18/2013; FAC 2005-73, 79 FR 24192, 4/29/2014, effective 5/29/2014; FAC 2005-79, 79 FR 74544, 12/15/2014, effective 12/15/2014; FAC 2005-85, 80 FR 75915, 12/4/2015, effective 12/4/2015; FAC 2005-100, 83 FR 42571, 8/22/2018, effective 8/22/2018]

22.1002 Statutory and Executive order requirements. (No Text)

[FAC 2005-85, 80 FR 75915, 12/4/2015, effective 12/4/2015; FAC 2005-93, 81 FR 91627, 12/16/2016, effective 1/1/2017; FAC 2005-100, 83 FR 42569, 8/22/2018, effective 8/22/2018]

22.1002-1 General.

Service contracts over $2,500 shall contain mandatory provisions regarding minimum wages and fringe benefits, safe and sanitary working conditions, notification to employees of the minimum allowable compensation, and equivalent Federal employee classifications and wage rates. Under 41 U.S.C. 6707(d), service contracts may not exceed 5 years.

[FAC 84-46, 54 FR 19816, 5/8/89, effective 6/7/89; FAC 2005-73, 79 FR 24192, 4/29/2014, effective 5/29/2014]

22.1002-2 Wage determinations based on prevailing rates.

Contractors performing on service contracts in excess of $2,500 to which no predecessor contractor's collective bargaining agreement applies shall pay their employees at least the wages and fringe benefits found by the Department of Labor to prevail in the locality or, in the absence of a wage determination, the minimum wage set forth in the Fair Labor Standards Act.

[FAC 84-46, 54 FR 19816, 5/8/89, effective 6/7/89; FAC 2005-85, 80 FR 75915, 12/4/2015, effective 12/4/2015]

22.1002-3 Wage determinations based on collective bargaining agreements.

(a) Successor contractors performing on contracts in excess of $2,500 for substantially the same services performed in the same locality must pay wages and fringe benefits (including accrued wages and benefits and prospective increases) at least equal to those contained in any bona fide collective bargaining agreement entered into under the predecessor contract. This requirement is self- executing and is not contingent upon incorporating a wage determination or the wage and fringe benefit terms of the predecessor contractor's collective bargaining agreement in the successor contract. This requirement will not apply if the Secretary of Labor determines—

(1) After a hearing, that the wages and fringe benefits are substantially at variance with those which prevail for services of a similar character in the locality or

(2) that the wages and fringe benefits are not the result of arm's length negotiations.

(b) Paragraphs in this Subpart 22.10 which deal with this statutory requirement and the Department of Labor's implementing regulations are 22.1010, concerning notification to contractors and bargaining representatives of procurement dates; 22.1012-2, explaining when a collective bargaining agreement will not apply due to late receipt by the contracting officer; and 22.1013and 22.1021, explaining when the application of a collective bargaining agreement can be challenged due to a variance with prevailing rates or lack of arm's length bargaining.

[5/8/89, effective 6/7/89; FAC 90-23, 59 FR 67010, 12/28/94, effective 2/27/95; FAC 2005-10, 71 FR 36930, 6/28/2006, effective 6/28/2006; FAC 2005-16, 72 FR 13585, 3/22/2007, effective 3/22/2007]

22.1002-4 Application of the Fair Labor Standards Act minimum wage.

No contractor or subcontractor holding a service contract for any dollar amount shall pay any of its employees working on the contract less than the minimum wage specified in section 6(a)(1) of the Fair Labor Standards Act (29 U.S.C. 206).

[FAC 84-46, 54 FR 19816, 5/8/89, effective 6/7/89]

22.1002-5 Executive Order 13658.

Executive Order 13658 establishes minimum wages for certain workers. The wage rate is subject to annual increases by an amount determined by the Secretary of Labor. See subpart 22.19. The clause at 52.222-55, Minimum Wages under Executive Order 13658, requires the Executive Order 13658 minimum wage rate to be paid if it is higher than other minimum wage rates, such as the subpart 22.10 statutory wage determination amount.

[FAC 2005-79, 79 FR 74544, 12/15/2014, effective 12/15/2014; FAC 2005-85, 80 FR 75915, 12/4/2015, effective 12/4/2015]

22.1002-6 Executive Order 13706.

Executive Order 13706 establishes paid sick leave for employees of certain Federal contractors. See subpart 22.21 and the clause at 52.222-62, Paid Sick Leave under Executive Order 13706.

[FAC 2005-93, 81 FR 91627, 12/16/2016, effective 1/1/2017; FAC 2005-100, 83 FR 42569, 8/22/2018, effective 8/22/2018]

22.1003 Applicability. (No Text)

22.1003-1 General.

This Subpart 22.10 applies to all Government contracts, the principal purpose of which is to furnish services in the United States through the use of service employees, except as exempted in 22.1003-3 and 22.1003-4of this section, or any subcontract at any tier thereunder. This subpart does not apply to individual contract requirements for services in contracts not having as their principal purpose the furnishing of services. The nomenclature, type, or particular form of contract used by contracting agencies is not determinative of coverage.

[FAC 84-46, 54 FR 19816, 5/8/89, effective 6/7/89]

22.1003-2 Geographical coverage of the Service Contract Labor Standards statute.

The Service Contract Labor Standards statute applies to service contracts performed in the United States (see 22.1001). The Service Contract Labor Standards statute does not apply to contracts performed outside the United States.

[FAC 84-46, 54 FR 19816, 5/8/89, effective 6/7/89; FAC 2005-73, 79 FR 24192, 4/29/2014, effective 5/29/2014]

22.1003-3 Statutory exemptions.

The Service Contract Labor Standards statute does not apply to—

(a) Any contract for construction, alteration, or repair of public buildings or public works, including painting and decorating;

(b) Any work required to be done in accordance with the provisions of 41 U.S.C. chapter 65, Contracts for Materials, Supplies, Articles, and Equipment Exceeding $15,000;

(c) Any contract for transporting freight or personnel by vessel, aircraft, bus, truck, express, railroad, or oil or gas pipeline where published tariff rates are in effect;

(d) Any contract for furnishing services by radio, telephone, or cable companies subject to the Communications Act of 1934;

(e) Any contract for public utility services;

(f) Any employment contract providing for direct services to a Federal agency by an individual or individuals; or

(g) Any contract for operating postal contract stations for the U.S. Postal Service.

[FAC 84-46, 54 FR 19816, 5/8/89, effective 6/7/89; FAC 2005-73, 79 FR 24192, 4/29/2014, effective 5/29/2014; FAC 2005-92, 81 FR 83097, 11/18/2016, effective 12/19/2016]

22.1003-4 Administrative limitations, variations, tolerances, and exemptions.

(a) The Secretary of Labor may provide reasonable limitations and may make rules and regulations allowing reasonable variations, tolerances, and exemptions to and from any or all provisions of the Service Contract Labor Standards statute other than 41 U.S.C. 6707(f). These will be made only in special circumstances where it has been determined that the limitation, variation, tolerance, or exemption is necessary and proper in the public interest or to avoid the serious impairment of Government business, and is in accord with the remedial purpose of the Service Contract Labor Standards statute to protect prevailing labor standards (41 U.S.C. 6707(b)). See 29 CFR 4.123 for a listing of administrative exemptions, tolerances, and variations. Requests for limitations, variances, tolerances, and exemptions from the Service Contract Labor Standards statute shall be submitted in writing through contracting channels and the agency labor advisor to the Wage and Hour Administrator.

(b) In addition to the statutory exemptions cited in 22.1003-3 of this subsection, the Secretary of Labor has exempted the following types of contracts from all provisions of the Service Contract Labor Standards statute:

(1) Contracts entered into by the United States with common carriers for the carriage of mail by rail, air (except air star routes), bus, and ocean vessel, where such carriage is performed on regularly scheduled runs of the trains, airplanes, buses, and vessels over regularly established routes and accounts for an insubstantial portion of the revenue therefrom.

(2) Any contract entered into by the U.S. Postal Service with an individual owner-operator for mail service if it is not contemplated at the time the contract is made that the owner-operator will hire any service employee to perform the services under the contract except for short periods of vacation time or for unexpected contingencies or emergency situations such as illness, or accident.

(3) Contracts for the carriage of freight or personnel if such carriage is subject to rates covered by section 10721 of the Interstate Commerce Act.

(c) *Contracts for maintenance, calibration or repair of certain equipment.*— (1) *Exemption.* The Secretary of Labor has exempted from the Service Contract Labor Standards statute contracts and subcontracts in which the primary purpose is to furnish maintenance, calibration, or repair of the following types of equipment, if the conditions at paragraph (c) (2) of this subsection are met:

(i) Automated data processing equipment and office information/word processing systems.

(ii) Scientific equipment and medical apparatus or equipment if the application of micro-electronic circuitry or other technology of at least similar sophistication is an essential element (for example, Product or Service Code (PSC) 6515, "Medical and Surgical Instruments, Equipment, and Supplies;" PSC 6525, "Imaging Equipment and Supplies: Medical, Dental, Veterinary;" PSC 6630, "Chemical Analysis Instruments;" and PSC 6655, "Geophysical Instruments," are largely composed of the types of equipment exempted in this paragraph).

(iii) Office/business machines not otherwise exempt pursuant to paragraph (c) (1) (i) of this subsection, if such services are performed by the manufacturer or supplier of the equipment.

(2) *Conditions.* The exemption at paragraph (c) (1) of this subsection applies if all the following conditions are met for a contract (or a subcontract):

(i) The items of equipment to be serviced under the contract are used regularly for other than Government purposes and are sold or traded by the contractor in substantial quantities to the general public in the course of normal business operations.

(ii) The services will be furnished at prices which are, or are based on, established catalog or market prices for the maintenance, calibration, or repair of such equipment. As defined at 29 CFR 4.123(e) (1) (ii) (B)—

(A) An established catalog price is a price included in a catalog price list, schedule, or other form that is regularly maintained by the manufacturer or the contractor, is either published or otherwise available for inspection by customers, and states prices at which sales currently, or were last, made to a significant number of buyers constituting the general public.

(B) An established market price is a current price, established in the usual course of trade between buyers and sellers free to bargain, which can be substantiated from sources independent of the manufacturer or contractor.

(iii) The contractor will use the same compensation (wage and fringe benefits) plan for all service employees performing work under the contract as the contractor uses for these employees and equivalent employees servicing the same equipment of commercial customers.

(iv) The apparent successful offeror certifies to the conditions in paragraph (c) (2) (i) through (iii) of this subsection. (See 22.1006(e).)

(3) *Affirmative determination and contract award.* (i) For source selections where the contracting officer has established a competitive range, if the contracting officer determines that one or more of the conditions in paragraphs 22.1003-4 (c)(2)(i) through (iii) of an offeror's certification will not be met, the contracting officer shall identify the deficiency to the offeror before receipt of the final proposal revisions. Unless the offeror provides a revised offer acknowledging applicability of the Service Contract Labor Standards statute or demonstrating to the satisfaction of the contracting officer an ability to meet all required conditions for exemption, the offer will not be further considered for award.

(ii) The contracting officer shall determine in writing the applicability of this exemption to the contract before contract award. If the apparent successful offeror will meet all conditions in paragraph (c)(2) of this subsection, the contracting officer shall make an affirmative determination and award the contract without the otherwise applicable Service Contract Labor Standards clause(s).

(iii) If the apparent successful offeror does not certify to the conditions in paragraph (c)(2)(i) through (iii) of this subsection, the contracting officer shall incorporate in the contract the Service Contract Labor Standards clause (see 22.1006(a)) and, if the contract will exceed $2,500, the appropriate Department of Labor wage determination (see 22.1007).

(4) *Department of Labor determination.* (i) If the Department of Labor determines after award of the contract that any condition for exemption in paragraph (c)(2) of this subsection has not been met, the exemption shall be deemed inapplicable, and the contract shall become subject to the Service Contract Labor Standards statute, effective as of the date of the Department of Labor determination. In such case, the procedures at 29 CFR 4.123(e)(1)(iv) and 29 CFR 4.5(c) shall be followed.

(ii) If the Department of Labor determines that any conditions in paragraph (d)(2) of this subsection have not been met with respect to a subcontract, the exemption shall be deemed inapplicable. The contractor may be responsible for ensuring that the subcontractor complies with the Service Contract Labor Standards statute, effective as of the date of the subcontract award.

(d) *Contracts for certain services.*— (1) *Exemption.* Except as provided in paragraph (d)(5) of this subsection, the Secretary of Labor has exempted from the Service Contract Labor Standards statute contracts and subcontracts in which the primary purpose is to provide the following services, if the conditions in paragraph (d)(2) of this subsection are met:

(i) Automobile or other vehicle (*e.g.*, aircraft) maintenance services (other than contracts or subcontracts to operate a Government motor pool or similar facility).

(ii) Financial services involving the issuance and servicing of cards (including credit cards, debit cards, purchase cards, smart cards, and similar card services).

(iii) Hotel/motel services for conferences, including lodging and/or meals, that are part of the contract or subcontract for the conference (which must not include ongoing contracts for lodging on an as needed or continuing basis).

(iv) Maintenance, calibration, repair, and/or installation (where the installation is not subject to the Construction Wage Rate Requirements statute, as provided in 29 CFR 4.116(c)(2)) services for all types of equipment where the services are obtained from the manufacturer or supplier of the equipment under a contract awarded on a sole source basis.

(v) Transportation by common carrier of persons by air, motor vehicle, rail, or marine vessel on regularly scheduled routes or via standard commercial services (not including charter services).

(vi) Real estate services, including real property appraisal services, related to housing Federal agencies or disposing of real property owned by the Government.

(vii) Relocation services, including services of real estate brokers and appraisers to assist Federal employees or military personnel in buying and selling homes (which shall not include actual moving or storage of household goods and related services).

(2) *Conditions.* The exemption for the services in paragraph (d)(1) of this subsection applies if all the following conditions are met for a contract (or for a subcontract):

(i)(A) The contract will be awarded on a sole-source basis; or

(B) Except for services identified in paragraph (d)(1)(iv) of this subsection, the contractor will be selected for award based on other factors in addition to price or cost, with the combination of other factors at least as important as price or cost in selecting the contractor.

(ii) The services under the contract are offered and sold regularly to non-Governmental customers, and are provided by the contractor (or subcontractor in the case of an exempt subcontract) to the general public in substantial quantities in the course of normal business operations.

(iii) The contract services are furnished at prices that are, or are based on, established catalog or market prices. As defined at 29 CFR 4.123(e)(2)(ii)(C)—

(A) An established catalog price is a price included in a catalog, price list, schedule, or other form that is regularly maintained by the contractor, is either published or otherwise available for inspection by customers, and states prices at which sales are currently, or were last, made to a significant number of buyers constituting the general public; and

(B) An established market price is a current price, established in the usual course of trade between buyers and sellers free to bargain, which can be substantiated from sources independent of the manufacturer or contractor.

(iv) Each service employee who will perform the services under the contract will spend only a small portion of his or her time (a monthly average of less than 20 percent of the available hours on an annualized basis, or less than 20 percent of available hours during the contract period if the contract period is less than a month) servicing the Government contract.

(v) The contractor will use the same compensation (wage and fringe benefits) plan for all service employees performing work under the contract as the contractor uses for these employees and equivalent employees servicing commercial customers.

(vi) The contracting officer (or contractor with respect to a subcontract) determines in advance before issuing the solicitation, based on the nature of the contract requirements and knowledge of the practices of likely offerors, that all or nearly all offerors will meet the conditions in paragraph (d)(2)(ii) through (v) of this subsection. If the services are currently being performed under contract, the contracting officer (or contractor with respect to a subcontract) shall consider the practices of the existing contractor in making a determination regarding the conditions in paragraphs (d)(2)(ii) through (v) of this subsection.

(vii)(A) The apparent successful offeror certifies that the conditions in paragraphs (d)(2)(ii) through (v) will be met; and

(B) For other than sole source awards, the contracting officer determines that the same certification is obtained from substantially all other offerors that are—

(1) In the competitive range, if discussions are to be conducted (see FAR 15.306(c)); or

(2) Considered responsive, if award is to be made without discussions (see FAR 15.306(a)).

(3) *Contract award or resolicitation.* (i) If the apparent successful offeror does not certify to the conditions, the contracting officer shall insert in the contract the applicable Service Contract Labor Standards clause(s) (see 22.1006(a)) and, if the contract will exceed $2,500, the appropriate Department of Labor wage determination (see 22.1007).

(ii) The contracting officer shall award the contract without the otherwise applicable Service Contract Labor Standards clause(s) if—

(A) The apparent successful offeror certifies to the conditions in paragraphs (d)(2)(ii) through (v) of this subsection;

(B) The contracting officer determines that the same certification is obtained from substantially all other offerors that are—

(1) In the competitive range, if discussions are to be conducted (see FAR 15.306); or

(2) Considered responsive, if award is to be made without discussions (see FAR 15.306(a)); and

(C) The contracting officer has no reason to doubt the certification.

(iii) If the conditions in paragraph (d)(3)(ii) of this subsection are not met, then the contracting officer shall resolicit, amending the solicitation by removing the exemption provision from the solicitation as prescribed at 22.1006(e)(3). The contract will include the applicable Service Contract Labor Standards clause(s) as prescribed at 22.1006 and, if the contract will exceed $2,500, the appropriate Department of Labor wage determination (see 22.1007).

(4) *Department of Labor determination.* (i) If the Department of Labor determines after award of the contract that any conditions for exemption at paragraph (d)(2) of this subsection have not been met, the exemption shall be deemed inapplicable, and the contract shall become subject to the Service Contract Labor Standards statute. In such case, the procedures at 29 CFR 4.123(e)(2)(iii) and 29 CFR 4.5(c) shall be followed.

(ii) If the Department of Labor determines that any conditions in paragraph (d)(2) of this subsection have not been met with respect to a subcontract, the exemption shall be deemed inapplicable. The contractor may be responsible for ensuring that the subcontractor complies with the Act, effective as of the date of the subcontract award.

(5) *Exceptions.* The exemption at paragraph (d)(1) of this subsection does not apply to solicitations and contracts (subcontracts)—

(i) Awarded under 41 U.S.C. chapter 85, Committee for Purchase from People Who Are Blind or Severely Disabled (see subpart 8.7).

(ii) For the operation of a Government facility, or part of a Government facility (but may be applicable to subcontracts for services); or

(iii) Subject to 41 U.S.C. 6707(c) (see 22.1002-3).

[FAC 84-46, 54 FR 19816, 5/8/89, effective 6/7/89; FAC 90-40, 61 FR 39186, 7/26/96, effective 8/26/96; FAC 2005-10, 71 FR 36930, 6/28/2006, effective 6/28/2006; FAC 2005-16, 72 FR 13585, 3/22/2007, effective 3/22/2007; FAC 2005-21, 72 FR 63076, 11/7/2007, effective 11/7/2007; FAC 2005-30, 74 FR 2724, 1/15/2009, effective 2/15/2009; FAC 2005-73, 79 FR 24192, 4/29/2014, effective 5/29/2014; FAC 2005-83, 80 FR 38307, 7/2/2015, effective 8/3/2015]

22.1003-5 Some examples of contracts covered.

The following examples, while not definitive or exclusive, illustrate some of the types of services that have been found to be covered by the Service Contract Labor Standards statute (see 29 CFR 4.130 for additional examples):

(a) Motor pool operation, parking, taxicab, and ambulance services.

(b) Packing, crating, and storage.

(c) Custodial, janitorial, housekeeping, and guard services.

(d) Food service and lodging.

(e) Laundry, dry-cleaning, linen-supply, and clothing alteration and repair services.

(f) Snow, trash, and garbage removal.

(g) Aerial spraying and aerial reconnaissance for fire detection.

(h) Some support services at installations, including grounds maintenance and landscaping.

(i) Certain specialized services requiring specific skills, such as drafting, illustrating, graphic arts, stenographic reporting, or mortuary services.

(j) Electronic equipment maintenance and operation and engineering support services.

(k) Maintenance and repair of all types of equipment, for example, aircraft, engines, electrical motors, vehicles, and electronic, office and related business and construction equipment. (But see 22.1003-4(c)(1) and (d)(1)(iv).)

(l) Operation, maintenance, or logistics support of a Federal facility.

(m) Data collection, processing and analysis services.

[FAC 84-46, 54 FR 19816, 5/8/89, effective 6/7/89; FAC 90-9, 56 FR 67136, 12/27/91, effective 2/25/92; FAC 2005-21, 72 FR 63076, 11/7/2007, effective 11/7/2007; FAC 2005-30, 74 FR 2724, 1/15/2009, effective 2/17/2009; FAC 2005-73, 79 FR 24192, 4/29/2014, effective 5/29/2014]

22.1003-6 Repair distinguished from remanufacturing of equipment.

(a) Contracts principally for remanufacturing of equipment which is so extensive as to be equivalent to manufacturing are subject to 41 U.S.C. chapter 65, Contracts for Materials, Supplies, Articles, and Equipment Exceeding $15,000, rather than to the Service Contract Labor Standards statute. Remanufacturing shall be deemed to be manufacturing when the criteria in either paragraphs (a)(1) or (a)(2) of this subsection are met.

(1) Major overhaul of an item, piece of equipment, or material which is degraded or inoperable, and under which all of the following conditions exist:

(i) The item or equipment is required to be completely or substantially torn down into individual component parts.

(ii) Substantially all of the parts are reworked, rehabilitated, altered and/or replaced.

(iii) The parts are reassembled so as to furnish a totally rebuilt item or piece of equipment.

(iv) Manufacturing processes similar to those which were used in the manufacturing of the item or piece of equipment are utilized.

(v) The disassembled components, if usable (except for situations where the number of items or pieces of equipment involved are too few to make it practicable) are commingled with existing inventory and, as such, lose their identification with respect to a particular piece of equipment.

(vi) The items or equipment overhauled are restored to original life expectancy, or nearly so.

(vii) Such work is performed in a facility owned or operated by the contractor.

(2) Major modification of an item, piece of equipment, or material which is wholly or partially obsolete, and under which all of the following conditions exist:

(i) The item or equipment is required to be completely or substantially torn down.

(ii) Outmoded parts are replaced.

(iii) The item or equipment is rebuilt or reassembled.

(iv) The contract work results in the furnishing of a substantially modified item in a usable and serviceable condition.

(v) The work is performed in a facility owned or operated by the contractor.

(b) Remanufacturing does not include the repair of damaged or broken equipment which does not require a complete teardown, overhaul, and rebuild as described in subparagraphs (a)(1) and (a)(2) of this subsection, or the periodic and routine maintenance, preservation, care, adjustment, upkeep, or servicing of equipment to keep it in usable, serviceable, working order. Such contracts typically are billed on an hourly rate (labor plus materials and parts) basis. Any contract principally for this type of work is subject to the Service Contract Labor Standards statute. Examples of such work include the following:

(1) Repair of an automobile, truck, or other vehicle, construction equipment, tractor, crane, aerospace, air conditioning and refrigeration equipment, electric motors, and ground powered industrial or vehicular equipment.

(2) Repair of typewriters and other office equipment (but see 22.1003-4(c)(1) and (d)(1)(iv)).

(3) Repair of appliances, radios, television sets, calculators, and other electronic equipment.

(4) Inspecting, testing, calibration, painting, packaging, lubrication, tune-up, or replacement of internal parts of equipment

listed in subparagraphs (b)(1), (b)(2), and (b)(3) of this subsection.

(5) Reupholstering, reconditioning, repair, and refinishing of furniture.

[FAC 84-46, 54 FR 19816, 5/8/89, effective 6/7/89; FAC 2005-21, 72 FR 63076, 11/7/2007, effective 11/7/2007; FAC 2005-30, 74 FR 2724, 1/15/2009, effective 2/17/2009; FAC 2005-73, 79 FR 24192, 4/29/2014, effective 5/29/2014]

22.1003-7 Questions concerning applicability of the Service Contract Labor Standards statute.

If the contracting officer questions the applicability of the Service Contract Labor Standards statute to an acquisition, the contracting officer shall request the advice of the agency labor advisor. Unresolved questions shall be submitted in a timely manner to the Administrator, Wage and Hour Division, for determination.

[FAC 84-46, 54 FR 19816, 5/8/89, effective 6/7/89; FAC 2005-73, 79 FR 24192, 4/29/2014, effective 5/29/2014]

22.1004 Department of Labor responsibilities and regulations.

Under the Service Contract Labor Standards statute, the Secretary of Labor is authorized and directed to enforce the provisions of the Service Contract Labor Standards statute, make rules and regulations, issue orders, hold hearings, make decisions, and take other appropriate action. The Department of Labor has issued implementing regulations on such matters as—

(a) Service contract labor standards provisions and procedures (29 CFR Part 4, Subpart A);

(b) Wage determination procedures (29 CFR Part 4, Subparts A and B);

(c) Application of Service Contract Labor Standards statute (rulings and interpretations) (29 CFR Part 4, Subpart C);

(d) Compensation standards (29 CFR Part 4, Subpart D);

(e) Enforcement (29 CFR Part 4, Subpart E);

(f) Safe and sanitary working conditions (29 CFR Part 1925);

(g) Rules of practice for administrative proceedings enforcing service contract labor standards (29 CFR Part 6); and

(h) Practice before the Administrative Review Board (29 CFR part 8).

[FAC 84-46, 54 FR 19816, 5/8/89, effective 6/7/89; FAC 2005-10, 71 FR 36930, 6/28/2006, effective 6/28/2006; FAC 2005-16, 72 FR 13585, 3/22/2007, effective 3/22/2007; FAC 2005-21, 72 FR 63076, 11/7/2007, effective 11/7/2007; FAC 2005-30, 74 FR 2724, 1/15/2009, effective 2/17/2009; FAC 2005-73, 79 FR 24192, 4/29/2014, effective 5/29/2014]

22.1005 [Reserved]

[Reserved, FAC 90-40, 61 FR 39186, 7/26/96, effective 8/26/96]

22.1006 Solicitation provisions and contract clauses.

(a)(1) The contracting officer shall insert the clause at 52.222-41, Labor Standards, in solicitations and contracts (except as provided in paragraph (a)(2) of this section) if the contract is subject to the Service Contract Labor Standards statute and is—

(i) Over $2,500; or

(ii) For an indefinite dollar amount and the contracting officer does not know in advance that the contract amount will be $2,500 or less.

(2) The contracting officer shall not insert the clause at 52.222-41 (or any of the associated Service Contract Labor Standards statute clauses as prescribed in this section for possible use when 52.222-41 applies) in the resultant contract if—

(i) The solicitation includes the provision at—

(A) 52.222-48, Exemption from Application of the Service Contract Labor Standards to Contracts for Maintenance, Calibration, or Repair of Certain Equipment—Certification;

(B) 52.222-52, Exemption from Application of the Service Contract Labor Standards to Contracts for Certain Services—Certification; or

(C) Either of the comparable certifications is checked as applicable in the provision at 52.204-8(c)(2) or 52.212-3(k); and

(ii) The contracting officer has made the determination, in accordance with paragraphs (c)(3) or (d)(3) of subsection 22.1003-4, that the Service Contract Labor Standards statute does not apply to the contract. (In such case, insert the clause at 52.222-51, Exemption from Application of the Service Contract Labor Standards to Contracts for Maintenance, Calibration, or Repair of Certain Equipment—Requirements, or 52.222-53, Exemption from Application of the Service Contract Labor Standards to Contracts for Certain Services—Requirements, in the contract, in accordance with the prescription at paragraph (e)(2)(ii) or (e)(4)(ii) of this subsection).

(b) The contracting officer shall insert the clause at 52.222-42, Statement of Equivalent Rates for Federal Hires, in solicitations and contracts if the contracts amount is expected to be over $2,500 and the Service Contract Labor Standards statute is applicable. (See 22.1016.)

(c)(1) The contracting officer shall insert the clause at 52.222-43, Fair Labor Standards Act and Service Contract Labor Standards—Price Adjustment (Multiple Year and Option Contracts), or another clause which accomplishes the same purpose, in solicitations and contracts if the contract is expected to be a fixed-price, time-and-materials, or labor-hour service contract containing the clause at 52.222-41, Service Contract Labor Standards, and is a multiple year contract or is a contract with options to renew which exceeds the simplified acquisition threshold. The clause may be used in contracts that do not exceed the simplified acquisition threshold. The clause at 52.222-43, Fair Labor Standards Act and Service Contract Labor Standards—Price Adjustment (Multiple Year and Option Contracts), applies to both contracts subject to area prevailing wage determinations and contracts subject to the incumbent contractor's collective bargaining agreement in effect during this contract's preceding contract period (see 22.1002-2 and 22.1002-3). Contracting officers shall ensure that contract prices or contract unit price labor rates are adjusted only to the extent that a contractor's increases or decreases in applicable wages and fringe benefits are made to comply with the requirements set forth in the clauses at 52.222-43(subparagraphs (d)(1), (2) and (3)), or 52.222-44(subparagraphs (b)(1) and (2)). (For example, the prior year wage determination required a minimum wage rate of $4.00 per hour. The contractor actually paid $4.10. The new wage determination increases the minimum rate to $4.50. The contractor increases the rate actually paid to $4.75 per hour. The allowable price adjustment is $.40 per hour.)

(2) The contracting officer shall insert the clause at 52.222-44, Fair Labor Standards Act and Service Contract Labor Standards—Price Adjustment, in solicitations and contracts if the contract is expected to be a fixed-price, time-and-materials, or labor-hour service contract containing the clause at 52.222-41, Service Contract Labor Standards, exceeds the simplified acquisition threshold, and is not a multiple year contract or is not a contract with options to renew. The clause may be used in contracts that do not exceed the simplified acquisition threshold. The clause at 52.222-44, Fair Labor Standards Act and Service Contract Labor Standards—Price Adjustment, applies to both contracts subject to area prevailing wage determinations and contracts subject to contractor collective bargaining agreements (see 22.1002-2 and 22.1002-3).

(3) The clauses prescribed in paragraph 22.1006(c)(1) cover situations in which revised minimum wage rates are applied to contracts by operation of law, or by revision of a wage determination in connection with (i) exercise of a contract option or (ii) extension of a multiple year contract into a new program year. If a clause prescribed in 16.203-4(d) is used, it must not conflict with, or duplicate payment under, the clauses prescribed in this paragraph 22.1006(c).

(d) [Reserved]

(e)(1) The contracting officer shall insert the provision at 52.222-48, Exemption from Application of the Service Contract Labor Standards to Contracts for Maintenance, Calibration, or Repair of Certain Equipment—Certification, in solicitations that—

(i) Include the clause at 52.222-41, Service Contract Labor Standards; and

(ii) The contract may be exempt from the Service Contract Labor Standards statute in accordance with 22.1003-4(c).

(2) The contracting officer shall insert the clause at 52.222-51, Exemption from Application of the Service Contract Labor Standards to Contracts for Maintenance, Calibration, or Repair of Certain Equipment—Requirements—

(i) In solicitations that include the provision at 52.222-48, or the comparable provision is checked as applicable in the clause at 52.204-8(c)(2) or 52.212-3(k)(1); and

(ii) In resulting contracts in which the contracting officer has determined, in accordance with 22.1003-4(c)(3), that the Service Contract Labor Standards statute does not apply.

(3)(i) Except as provided in paragraph (e)(3)(ii) of this section, the contracting officer shall insert the provision at 52.222-52, Exemption from Application of the Service Contract Labor Standards to Contracts for Certain Services—Certification, in solicitations that—

(A) Include the clause at 52.222-41, Service Contract Labor Standards, and

(B) The contract may be exempt from the Service Contract Labor Standards statute in accordance with 22.1003-4(d).

(A) Include the clause at 52.222-41, Service Contract Act of 1965; and

(B) The contract may be exempt from the Service Contract Act in accordance with 22.1003-4(d).

(ii) When resoliciting in accordance with 22.1003-4(d)(3)(iii), amend the solicitation by removing the provision at 52.222-52 from the solicitation.

(4) The contracting officer shall insert the clause at 52.222-53, Exemption from Application of the Service Contract Labor Standards to Contracts for Certain Services—Requirements—

(i) In solicitations that include the provision at 52.222-52, or the comparable provision is checked as applicable in 52.204-8(c)(2) or 52.212-3(k)(2); and

(ii) In resulting contracts in which the contracting officer has determined, in accordance with 22.1003-4(d)(3), that the Service Contract Labor Standards statute does not apply.

(f) The contracting officer shall insert the clause at 52.222-49, Service Contract Labor Standards—Place of Performance Unknown, if using the procedures prescribed in 22.1009-4.

[FAC 84-46, 54 FR 19816, 5/8/89, effective 6/7/89; FAC 90-29, 60 FR 34732, 7/3/95, effective 7/3/95; FAC 90-41, 61 FR 41466, 8/8/96, effective 8/8/96, finalized without change, FAC 97-3, 62 FR 64912, 12/9/97, effective 2/9/98; FAC 2005-10, 71 FR 36930, 6/28/2006, effective 6/28/2006; FAC 2005-14, 71 FR 67779, 11/22/2006, effective 11/22/2006; FAC 2005-16, 72 FR 13585, 3/22/2007, effective 3/22/2007; FAC 2005-21, 72 FR 63076, 11/7/2007, effective 11/7/2007; FAC 2005-30, 74 FR 2724, 1/15/2009, effective 2/17/2009; FAC 2005-36, 74 FR 40460, 8/11/2009, effective 9/10/2009; FAC 2005-48, 75 FR 82567, 12/30/2010, effective 1/31/2011; FAC 2005-73, 79 FR 24192, 4/29/2014, effective 5/29/2014; FAC 2005-74, 79 FR 31187, 5/30/2014, effective 11/1/2014; FAC 2005-77, 79 FR 61746, 10/14/2014, effective 10/14/2014; FAC 2005-78, 79 FR 70348, 11/25/2014, effective 11/25/2014; FAC 2005-87, 81 FR 11988, 3/7/2016, effective 4/6/2016]

22.1007 Requirement to obtain wage determinations.

The contracting officer shall obtain wage determinations for the following service contracts:

(a) Each new solicitation and contract in excess of $2,500.

(b) Each contract modification which brings the contract above $2,500 and—

(1) Extends the existing contract pursuant to an option clause or otherwise; or

(2) Changes the scope of the contract whereby labor requirements are affected significantly.

(c) Each multiple year contract in excess of $2,500 upon—

(1) Annual anniversary date if the contract is subject to annual appropriations; or

(2) Biennial anniversary date if the contract is not subject to annual appropriations and its proposed term exceeds 2 years—unless otherwise advised by the Wage and Hour Division.

[FAC 84-46, 54 FR 19816, 5/8/89, effective 6/7/89; FAC 2005-10, 71 FR 36930, 6/28/2006, effective 6/28/2006; FAC 2005-16, 72 FR 13585, 3/22/2007, effective 3/22/2007]

22.1008 Procedures for obtaining wage determinations. (No Text)

[FAC 2005-10, 71 FR 36930, 6/28/2006, effective 6/28/2006; FAC 2005-16, 72 FR 13585, 3/22/2007, effective 3/22/2007]

22.1008-1 Obtaining wage determinations.

(a) Contracting officers may obtain most prevailing wage determinations using the WDOL website. Contracting officers may also use the Department of Labor's e98 electronic process, located on the WDOL website, to request a wage determination directly from the Department of Labor. If the WDOL database does not contain the applicable prevailing wage determination for a contract action, the contracting officer must use the e98 process to request a wage determination from the Department of Labor.

(b) In using the e98 process to obtain prevailing wage determinations, contracting officers shall provide as complete and accurate information on the e98 as possible. Contracting officers shall ensure that the email address submitted on an e98 request is accurate.

(c) The contracting officer must anticipate the amount of time required to gather the information necessary to obtain a wage determination, including sufficient time, if necessary, to contact the Department of Labor to request wage determinations that are not available through use of the WDOL.

(d) Although the WDOL website provides assistance to the contracting agency to select the correct wage determination, the contracting agency remains responsible for the wage determination selected. If the contracting agency has used the e98 process, the Department of Labor will respond to the contracting agency based on the information provided on the e98. The contracting agency may rely upon the Department of Labor response as the correct wage determination for the contract.

(e) To obtain the applicable wage determination for each contract action, the contracting officer shall determine the following information concerning the service employees expected to be employed by the contractor and any subcontractors in performing the contract:

(1) Determine the classes of service employees to be utilized in performance of the contract using the Wage and Hour Division's Service Contract Act Directory of Occupations (Directory). The Directory can be found on WDOL's Library Page, and is for sale by the Superintendent of Documents, U.S. Government Publishing Office.

(2) Determine the locality where the services will be performed (see 22.1009).

(3) Determine whether Section 41 U.S.C. 6707(c) applies of the Act applies (see 22.1008-2, 22.1010 and 22.1012-2).

(4) Determine the wage rate that would be paid each class if employed by the agency and subject to the wage provisions of 5 U.S.C. 5341 and/or 5332 (see 22.1016).

(f) If the contracting officer has questions regarding the procedures for obtaining a wage determination, or questions regarding the selection of a wage determination, the contracting officer should request assistance from the agency labor advisor.

[FAC 84-46, 54 FR 19816, 5/8/89, effective 6/7/89; FAC 2005-10, 71 FR 36930, 6/28/2006, effective 6/28/2006; FAC 2005-16, 72 FR 13585, 3/22/2007, effective 3/22/2007; FAC 2005-73, 79 FR 24192, 4/29/2014, effective 5/29/2014; FAC 2019-02, 84 FR 19839, 5/6/2019, effective 5/6/2019]

22.1008-2 Successorship with incumbent contractor collective bargaining agreement.

(a) Early in the acquisition cycle, the contracting officer shall determine whether 41 U.S.C. 6707(c) affects the new acquisition. The contracting officer shall determine whether there is a predecessor contract covered by the Service Contract Labor Standards statute and, if so, whether the incumbent prime contractor or its subcontractors and any of their employees have a collective bargaining agreement.

(b) 41 U.S.C. 6707(c) provides that a successor contractor must pay wages and fringe benefits (including accrued wages and benefits and prospective increases) to service employees at least equal to those agreed upon by a predecessor contractor under the following conditions:

(1) The services to be furnished under the proposed contract will be substantially the same as services being furnished by an incumbent contractor whose contract the proposed contract will succeed.

(2) The services will be performed in the same locality.

(3) The incumbent prime contractor or subcontractor is furnishing such services through the use of service employees whose wages and fringe benefits are the subject of one or more collective bargaining agreements.

(c) The application of 41 U.S.C. 6707(c) is subject to the following limitations:

(1) 41 U.S.C. 6707(c) will not apply if the incumbent contractor enters into a collective bargaining agreement for the first time and the agreement does not become effective until after the expiration of the incumbent's contract.

(2) If the incumbent contractor enters into a new or revised collective bargaining agreement during the period of the incumbent's performance on the current contract, the terms of the new or revised agreement shall not be effective for the purposes of 41 U.S.C. 6707(c) under the following conditions:

(i)(A) In sealed bidding, the contracting agency receives notice of the terms of the collective bargaining agreement less than 10 days before bid opening and finds that there is not reasonable time still available to notify bidders (see 22.1012-2); or

(B) For contractual actions other than sealed bidding, the contracting agency receives notice of the terms of the collective bargaining agreement after award, provided that the start of performance is within 30 days of award (see 22.1012-2); and

(ii) The contracting officer has given both the incumbent contractor and its employees' collective bargaining agent timely written notification of the applicable acquisition dates (see 22.1010).

(d)(1) If 41 U.S.C. 6707(c) applies, the contracting officer shall obtain a copy of any collective bargaining agreement between an incumbent contractor or subcontractor and its employees. Obtaining a copy of an incumbent contractor's collective bargaining agreement may involve coordination with the administrative contracting officer responsible for administering the predecessor contract. (Paragraph (m) of the clause at 52.222-41, Service Contract Labor Standards, requires the incumbent prime contractor to furnish the contracting officer a copy of each collective bargaining agreement.)

(2) If the contracting officer has timely received the collective bargaining agreement, the contracting officer may use the WDOL website to prepare a wage determination referencing the agreement and incorporate that wage determination, attached to a complete copy of the collective bargaining agreement, into the successor contract action. In using the WDOL process, it is not necessary to submit a copy of the collective bargaining agreement to the Department of Labor unless requested to do so.

(3) The contracting officer may also use the e98 process on WDOL to request that the Department of Labor prepare the cover wage determination. The Department of Labor's response to the e98 may include a request for the contracting officer to submit a complete copy of the collective bargaining agreement. Any questions regarding the applicability of the Service Contract Labor Standards statute to a collective bargaining agreement should be directed to the agency labor advisor.

(e)(1) 41 U.S.C. 6707(c) will not apply if the Secretary of Labor determines

(i) after a hearing, that the wages and fringe benefits in the predecessor contractor's collective bargaining agreement are substantially at variance with those which prevail for services of a similar character in the locality, or

(ii) that the wages and fringe benefits in the predecessor contractor's collective bargaining agreement are not the result of arm's length negotiations (see 22.1013 and 22.1021). The Department of Labor (DOL) has concluded that contingent collective bargaining agreement provisions that attempt to limit a contractor's obligations by means such as requiring issuance of a wage determination by the DOL, requiring inclusion of the wage determination in the contract, or requiring the Government to adequately reimburse the contractor, generally reflect a lack of arm's length negotiations.

(2) If the contracting officer's review (see 22.1013) indicates that monetary provisions of the collective bargaining agreement may be substantially at variance or may not have been reached as a result of arm's length bargaining, the contracting officer shall immediately contact the agency labor advisor to consider if further action is warranted.

(f) If the services are being furnished at more than one location and the collectively bargained wage rates and fringe benefits are different at different locations or do not apply to one or more locations, the contracting officer shall identify the locations to which the agreements apply.

(g) If the collective bargaining agreement does not apply to all service employees under the contract, the contracting officer shall access WDOL to obtain the prevailing wage determination for those service employee classifications that are not covered by the collective bargaining agreement. The contracting officer shall separately list in the solicitation and contract the service employee classifications—

(1) Subject to the collective bargaining agreement; and

(2) Not subject to any collective bargaining agreement.

[FAC 84-46, 54 FR 19816, 5/8/89, effective 6/7/89; FAC 90-23, 59 FR 67010, 12/28/94, effective 2/27/95; FAC 2005-10, 71 FR 36930, 6/28/2006, effective 6/28/2006; FAC 2005-16, 72 FR 13585, 3/22/2007, effective 3/22/2007; FAC 2005-21, 72 FR 63076, 11/7/2007, effective 11/7/2007; FAC 2005-30, 74 FR 2724, 1/15/2009, effective 2/17/2009; FAC 2005-73, 79 FR 24192, 4/29/2014, effective 5/29/2014]

22.1008-4 [Removed]

See 22.1009, [FAC 84-46, 54 FR 19816, 5/8/89, effective 6/7/89; FAC 2005-10, 71 FR 36930, 6/28/2006, effective 6/28/2006; FAC 2005-16, 72 FR 13585, 3/22/2007, effective 3/22/2007]

22.1008-5 [Removed]

[FAC 84-46, 54 FR 19816, 5/8/89, effective 6/7/89FAC 2005-10, 71 FR 36930, 6/28/2006, effective 6/28/2006; FAC 2005-16, 72 FR 13585, 3/22/2007, effective 3/22/2007]

22.1008-6 [Removed]

[FAC 84-46, 54 FR 19816, 5/8/89, effective 6/7/89FAC 2005-10, 71 FR 36930, 6/28/2006, effective 6/28/2006; FAC 2005-16, 72 FR 13585, 3/22/2007, effective 3/22/2007]

22.1008-7 [Removed]

[FAC 84-46, 54 FR 19816, 5/8/89, effective 6/7/89; FAC 2005-10, 71 FR 36930, 6/28/2006, effective 6/28/2006; FAC 2005-16, 72 FR 13585, 3/22/2007, effective 3/22/2007]

22.1009 Place of performance unknown. (No Text)

22.1009-1 General.

If the place of performance is unknown, the contracting officer may use the procedures in this section. The contracting officer should first attempt to identify the specific places or geographical areas where the services might be performed (see 22.1009-2) and then may follow the procedures either in 22.1009-3 or in 22.1009-4.

[FAC 84-46, 54 FR 19816, 5/8/89, effective 6/7/89]

22.1009-2 Attempt to identify possible places of performance.

The contracting officer should attempt to identify the specific places or geographical areas where the services might be performed. The following may indicate possible places of performance:

(a) Locations of previous contractors and their competitors.

(b) Databases available via the Internet for lists of prospective offerors and contractors.

(c) Responses to a presolicitation notice (see 5.204).

[FAC 84-46, 54 FR 19816, 5/8/89, effective 6/7/89; FAC 2001-15, 68 FR 43854, 7/24/2003, effective 8/25/2003]

22.1009-3 All possible places of performance identified.

(a) If the contracting officer can identify all the possible places or areas of performance (even though the actual place of performance will not be known until the successful offeror is chosen), the contracting officer shall obtain a wage determination for each locality where services may be performed (see 22.1008).

(b) If the contracting officer subsequently learns of any potential offerors in previously unidentified places before the closing date for submission of offers, the contracting officer shall—

(1) Obtain wage determinations for the additional places of performance and amend the solicitation to include all wage determinations. If necessary, the contracting officer shall extend the time for submission of final offers; and

(2) Follow the procedures in 22.1009-4.

[FAC 84-46, 54 FR 19816, 5/8/89, effective 6/7/89; FAC 2005-10, 71 FR 36930, 6/28/2006, effective 6/28/2006; FAC 2005-16, 72 FR 13585, 3/22/2007, effective 3/22/2007]

22.1009-4 All possible places of performance not identified.

If the contracting officer believes that there may be offerors interested in performing in unidentified places or areas, the contracting officer may use the following procedures:

(a) Include the following information in the synopsis and solicitation:

(1) That the place of performance is unknown.

(2) The possible places or areas of performance that the contracting officer has already identified.

(3) That the contracting officer will obtain wage determinations for additional possible places of performance if asked to do so in writing.

(4) The time and date by which offerors must notify the contracting officer of additional places of performance.

(b) Include the information required by paragraphs (a) (2) and (a) (4) of this section in the clause at 52.222-49, Service Contract Labor Standards-Place of Performance Unknown (see 22.1006(f)). The closing date for receipt of offerors' requests for wage determinations for additional possible places of performance should allow reasonable time for potential offerors to review the solicitation and determine their interest in competing. Generally, 10 to 15 days from the date of issuance of the solicitation may be considered a reasonable period of time.

(c) The procedures in 14.304 shall apply to late receipt of offerors' requests for wage determinations for additional places of performance. However, late receipt of an offeror's request for a wage determination for additional places of performance does not preclude the offeror's competing for the proposed acquisition.

(d) If the contracting officer receives any timely requests for wage determinations for additional places of performance the contracting officer shall—

(1) Obtain wage determinations for the additional places of performance; and

(2) Amend the solicitation to include all wage determinations and, if necessary, extend the time for submission of final offers.

(e) If the successful offeror did not make a timely request for a wage determination and will perform in a place of performance for which the contracting officer therefore did not request a wage determination, the contracting officer shall—

(1) Award the contract;

(2) Obtain a wage determination; and

(3) Incorporate the wage determination in the contract, retroactive to the date of contract award and with no adjustment in contract price, pursuant to the clause at 52.222-49, Service Contract Labor Standards-Place of Performance Unknown.

[FAC 84-46, 54 FR 19816, 5/8/89, effective 6/7/89; FAC 97-14, 64 FR 51828, 9/24/99, effective 11/23/99; FAC 97-26, 66 FR 27405, 5/16/2001, effective 5/16/2001; FAC 2001-16, Interim/Final rule, 68 FR 56676, 10/1/2003, effective 10/1/2003; FAC 2005-10, 71 FR 36930, 6/28/2006, effective 6/28/2006; FAC 2005-16, 72 FR 13585, 3/22/2007, effective 3/22/2007; FAC 2005-73, 79 FR 24192, 4/29/2014, effective 5/29/2014]

22.1010 Notification to interested parties under collective bargaining agreements.

(a) The contracting officer should determine whether the incumbent prime contractor's or its subcontractors' service employees performing on the current contract are represented by a collective bargaining agent. If there is a collective bargaining agent, the contracting officer shall give both the incumbent contractor and its employees' collective bargaining agent written notification of—

(1) The forthcoming successor contract and the applicable acquisition dates (issuance of solicitation, opening of bids, commencement of negotiations, award of contract, or start of performance, as the case may be); or

(2) The forthcoming contract modification and applicable acquisition dates (exercise of option, extension of contract, change in scope, or start of performance, as the case may be); or

(3) The forthcoming multiple year contract anniversary date (annual anniversary date or biennial date, as the case may be).

(b) This written notification must be given at least 30 days in advance of the earliest applicable acquisition date or the applicable annual or biennial anniversary date in order for the time-of-receipt limitations in paragraphs 22.1012-2(a) and (b) to apply. The contracting officer shall retain a copy of the notification in the contract file.

[FAC 84-46, 54 FR 19816, 5/8/89, effective 6/7/89FAC 2005-10, 71 FR 36930, 6/28/2006, effective 6/28/2006; FAC 2005-16, 72 FR 13585, 3/22/2007, effective 3/22/2007]

22.1011 [Removed and Reserved]

[FAC 2005-10, 71 FR 36930, 6/28/2006, effective 6/28/2006; FAC 2005-16, 72 FR 13585, 3/22/2007, effective 3/22/2007]

22.1011-1 [Removed and Reserved]

[FAC 84-46, 54 FR 19816, 5/8/89, effective 6/7/89; FAC 2005-10, 71 FR 36930, 6/28/2006, effective 6/28/2006; FAC 2005-16, 72 FR 13585, 3/22/2007, effective 3/22/2007]

22.1011-2 [Removed and Reserved]

[FAC 84-46, 54 FR 19816, 5/8/89, effective 6/7/89; FAC 2005-10, 71 FR 36930, 6/28/2006, effective 6/28/2006; FAC 2005-16, 72 FR 13585, 3/22/2007, effective 3/22/2007]

22.1012 Applicability of revisions to wage determinations. (No Text)

[FAC 2005-16, 72 FR 13585, 3/22/2007, effective 3/22/2007]

22.1012-1 Prevailing wage determinations.

(a) (1) The Wage and Hour Administrator may issue revisions to prevailing wage determinations periodically. The need for inclusion of a revised prevailing wage determination in a solicitation, contract or contract modification (see 22.1007) is determined by the date of receipt of the revised prevailing wage determination by the contracting agency. (Note the distinction between receipt by the agency and receipt by the contracting officer which may occur later.)

(i) For purposes of using WDOL, the time of receipt by the contracting agency shall be the first day of publication of the revised prevailing wage determination on the website.

(ii) For purposes of using the e98 process, the time of receipt by the contracting agency shall be the date the agency receives actual notice of a new or revised prevailing wage determination from the Department of Labor as an e98 response.

(2) In selecting a prevailing wage determination from the WDOL website for use in a solicitation or other contract action, the contracting officer shall monitor the WDOL website to determine whether the applicable wage determination has been revised. Revisions published on the WDOL website or otherwise communicated to the contracting officer within the timeframes prescribed at 22.1012-1(b) and (c) are effective and must be included in the resulting contract. Monitoring can be accomplished by use of the WDOL website's "Alert Service".

(b) The following shall apply when contracting by sealed bidding: a revised prevailing wage determination shall not be effective if it is received by the contracting agency less than 10 days before the opening of bids, and the contracting officer finds that there is not reasonable time to incorporate the revision in the solicitation.

(c) For contractual actions other than sealed bidding, a revised prevailing wage determination received by the contracting agency after award of a new contract or a modification as specified in 22.1007(b) shall not be effective provided that the start of performance is within 30 days of the award or the specified modification. If the contract does not specify a start of performance date which is within 30 days of the award or the specified modification, and if contract performance does not commence within 30 days of the award or the specified modification, any revision received by the contracting agency not less than 10 days before commencement of the work shall be effective.

(d) If the contracting officer has submitted an e98 to the Department of Labor requesting a prevailing wage determination and has not received a response within 10 days, the contracting officer shall contact the Wage and Hour Division by telephone to determine when the wage determination can be expected. (The telephone number is provided on the e98 website.)

[FAC 84-46, 54 FR 19816, 5/8/89, effective 6/7/89; FAC 2005-10, 71 FR 36930, 6/28/2006, effective 6/28/2006; FAC 2005-16, 72 FR 13585, 3/22/2007, effective 3/22/2007]

22.1012-2 Wage determinations based on collective bargaining agreements.

(a) In sealed bidding, a new or changed collective bargaining agreement shall not be effective under 41 U.S.C. 6707(c) if the contracting agency has received notice of the terms of the new or changed collective bargaining agreement less than 10 days before bid opening and the contracting officer determines that there is not reasonable time to incorporate the new or changed terms of the collective bargaining agreement in the solicitation.

(b) For contractual actions other than sealed bidding, a new or changed collective bargaining agreement shall not be effective under 41 U.S.C. 6707(c) if notice of the terms of the new or changed collective bargaining agreement is received by the contracting agency after award of a successor contract or a modification as specified in 22.1007(b), provided that the contract start of performance is within 30 days of the award of the contract or of the specified modification. If the contract does not specify a start of performance date which is within 30 days of the award of the contract or of the specified modification, or if contract performance does not commence within 30 days of the award of the contract or of the specified modification, any notice of the terms of a new or changed collective bargaining agreement received by the agency not less than 10 days before commencement of the work shall be effective for purposes of the successor contract under 41 U.S.C. 6707(c).

(c) The limitations in paragraphs (a) and (b) of this subsection shall apply only if timely notification required in 22.1010 has been given.

(d) If the contracting officer has submitted an e98 to Department of Labor requesting a wage determination based on a collective bargaining agreement and has not received a response from the Department of Labor within 10 days, the contracting officer shall contact the Wage and Hour Division by telephone to determine when the wage determination can be expected. (The telephone number is provided on the e98 website.) If the Department of Labor is unable to provide the wage determination by the latest date needed to maintain the acquisition schedule, the contracting officer shall incorporate the collective bargaining agreement itself in a solicitation or other contract action (e.g., exercise of option) and include a wage determination referencing that collective bargaining agreement created by use of the WDOL website (see 22.1008-2(d)(2)).

[FAC 84-46, 54 FR 19816, 5/8/89, effective 6/7/89; FAC 90-23, 59 FR 67010, 12/28/94, effective 2/27/95; FAC 2005-10, 71 FR 36930, 6/28/2006, effective 6/28/2006; FAC 2005-16, 72 FR 13585, 3/22/2007, effective 3/22/2007; FAC 2005-73, 79 FR 24192, 4/29/2014, effective 5/29/2014]

22.1012-4 [Removed]

[FAC 84-46, 54 FR 19816, 5/8/89, effective 6/7/89; FAC 2005-10, 71 FR 36930, 6/28/2006, effective 6/28/2006]

22.1012-5 [Removed]

[FAC 84-46, 54 FR 19816, 5/8/89, effective 6/7/89; FAC 90-23, 59 FR 67010, 12/28/94, effective 2/27/95; FAC 2005-10, 36930, 6/28/2006, effective 6/28/2006]

22.1013 Review of wage determination.

(a) *Based on incumbent collective bargaining agreement.* (1) If wages, fringe benefits, or periodic increases provided for in a collective bargaining agreement vary substantially from those prevailing for similar services in the locality, the contracting officer shall immediately contact the agency labor advisor to consider instituting the procedures in 22.1021.

(2) If the contracting officer believes that an incumbent or predecessor contractor's agreement was not the result of arm's length negotiations, the contracting officer shall contact the agency labor advisor to determine appropriate action.

(b) *Based on other than incumbent collective bargaining agreement.* Upon receiving a wage determination not predicated upon a collective bargaining agreement, the contracting officer shall ascertain—

(1) If the wage determination does not conform with wages and fringe benefits prevailing for similar services in the locality; or

(2) If the wage determination contains significant errors or omissions. If either subparagraph (b)(1) or (b)(2) of this section is evident, the contracting officer shall contact the agency labor advisor to determine appropriate action.

[FAC 84-46, 54 FR 19816, 5/8/89, effective 6/7/89]

22.1014 Delay over 60 days in bid opening or commencement of work.

If a wage determination was obtained through the e98 process, and bid opening, or commencement of work under a negotiated contract has been delayed, for whatever reason, more than 60 days from the date indicated on the previously submitted e98, the contracting officer shall submit a new e98. Any revision of a wage determination received by the contracting agency as a result of that communication shall supersede the earlier response as the wage determination applicable to the particular acquisition subject to the time frames in 22.1012-1(b) and (c).

[FAC 84-46, 54 FR 19816, 5/8/89, effective 6/7/89; FAC 2005-10, 71 FR 36930, 6/28/2006, effective 6/28/2006; FAC 2005-16, 72 FR 13585, 3/22/2007, effective 3/22/2007]

22.1015 Discovery of errors by the Department of Labor.

If the Department of Labor discovers and determines, whether before or after a contract award, that a contracting officer made an erroneous determination that the Service Contract Labor Standards statute did not apply to a particular acquisition or failed to include an appropriate wage determination in a covered contract, the contracting officer, within 30 days of notification by the Department of Labor, shall include in the contract the clause at 52.222-41 and any applicable wage determination issued by the Administrator. If the contract is subject to 41 U.S.C. 6070(f), the Administrator may require retroactive application of that wage determination. The contracting officer shall equitably adjust the contract price to reflect any changed cost of performance resulting from incorporating a wage determination or revision.

[FAC 84-46, 54 FR 19816, 5/8/89, effective 6/7/89; FAC 2005-73, 79 FR 24192, 4/29/2014, effective 5/29/2014]

22.1016 Statement of equivalent rates for Federal hires.

(a) The statement required under the clause at 52.222-42, Statement of Equivalent Rates for Federal Hires, (see 22.1006(b)) shall set forth those wage rates and fringe benefits that would be paid by the contracting activity to the various classes of service employees expected to be utilized under the contract if 5 U.S.C. 5332 (General Schedule—white collar) and/or 5 U.S.C. 5341 (Wage Board—blue collar) were applicable.

(b) Procedures for computation of these rates are as follows:

(1) Wages paid blue collar employees shall be the basic hourly rate for each class. The rate shall be Wage Board pay schedule step two for nonsupervisory service employees and step three for supervisory service employees.

(2) Wages paid white collar employees shall be an hourly rate for each class. The rate shall be obtained by dividing the general pay schedule step one biweekly rate by 80.

(3) Local civilian personnel offices can assist in determining and providing grade and salary data.

[FAC 84-46, 54 FR 19816, 5/8/89, effective 6/7/89]

22.1017 [Removed and Reserved]

[FAC 84-46, 54 FR 19816, 5/8/89, effective 6/7/89; FAC 2005-10, 71 FR 36930, 6/28/2006, effective 6/28/2006; FAC 2005-16, 72 FR 13585, 3/22/2007, effective 3/22/2007]

22.1018 Notification to contractors and employees.

The contracting officer shall take the following steps to ensure that service employees are notified of minimum wages and fringe benefits.

(a) As soon as possible after contract award, inform the contractor of the labor standards requirements of the contract relating to the Service Contract Labor Standards statute and of the contractor's responsibilities under these requirements, unless it is clear that the contractor is fully informed.

(b) At the time of award, furnish the contractor Department of Labor Publication WH-1313, Notice to Employees Working on Government Contracts, for posting at a prominent and accessible place at the worksite before contract performance begins. The publication advises employees of the compensation (wages and fringe benefits) required to be paid or furnished under the Service Contract Labor Standards statute and satisfies the notice requirements in paragraph (g) of the clause at 52.222-41, Service Contract Service Contract Labor Standards.

(c) Attach any applicable wage determination to Publication WH-1313.

[FAC 84-46, 54 FR 19816, 5/8/89, effective 6/7/89; FAC 2005-21, 72 FR 63076, 11/7/2007, effective 11/7/2007; FAC 2005-30, 74 FR 2724, 1/15/2009, effective 2/17/2009; FAC 2005-73, 79 FR 24192, 4/29/2014, effective 5/29/2014]

22.1019 Additional classes of service employees.

(a) If the contracting officer is aware that contract performance involves classes of service employees not included in the wage determination, the contracting officer shall require the contractor to classify the unlisted classes so as to provide a reasonable relationship (i.e., appropriate level of skill comparison) between the unlisted classifications and the classifications listed in the determination (see paragraph (c) of the clause at 52.222-41, Service Contract Labor Standards). The contractor shall initiate the conforming procedure before unlisted classes of employees perform contract work. The contractor shall submit Standard Form (SF)

1444, Request For Authorization of Additional Classification and Rate. The contracting officer shall review the proposed classification and rate and promptly submit the completed SF 1444 (which must include information regarding the agreement or disagreement of the employees' representative or the employees themselves together with the agency recommendation) and all other pertinent information to the Wage and Hour Division. Within 30 days of receipt of the request, the Wage and Hour Division will (1) approve, modify, or disapprove the request when the parties are in agreement or (2) render a final determination in the event of disagreement among the parties. If the Wage and Hour Division will require more than 30 days to take action, it will notify the contracting officer within 30 days of receipt of the request that additional time is necessary.

(b) Some wage determinations will list a series of classes within a job classification family, for example, Computer Operators, level I, II, and III, or Electronic Technicians, level I, II, and III, or Clerk Typist, level I and II. Generally, level I is the lowest level. It is the entry level, and establishment of a lower level through conformance is not permissible. Further, trainee classifications may not be conformed. Helpers in skilled maintenance trades (for example, electricians, machinists, and automobile mechanics) whose duties constitute, in fact, separate and distinct jobs may also be used if listed on the wage determination, but may not be conformed. Conformance may not be used to artificially split or subdivide classifications listed in the wage determination. However, conforming procedures may be used if the work which an employee performs under the contract is not within the scope of any classification listed on the wage determination, regardless of job title. (See 29 CFR 4.152.)

(c) Subminimum rates for apprentices, student learners, and disabled workers are permissible in accordance with paragraph (q) of the clause at 52.222-41, Service Contract Labor Standards.

[FAC 84-46, 54 FR 19816, 5/8/89, effective 6/7/89; FAC 2005-21, 72 FR 63076, 11/7/2007, effective 11/7/2007; FAC 2005-30, 74 FR 2724, 1/15/2009, effective 2/17/2009; FAC 2005-73, 79 FR 24192, 4/29/2014, effective 5/29/2014]

22.1020 Seniority lists.

If a contract is performed at a Federal facility where employees may be hired/retained by a succeeding contractor, the incumbent prime contractor is required to furnish a certified list of all service employees on the contractor's or subcontractor's payroll during the last month of the contract, together with anniversary dates of employment, to the contracting officer no later than 10 days before contract completion. (See paragraph (n) of the clause at 52.222-41, Service Contract Labor Standards.) At the commencement of the succeeding contract, the contracting officer shall provide a copy of the list to the successor contractor for determining employee eligibility for vacation or other fringe benefits which are based upon length of service, including service with predecessor contractors if such benefit is required by an applicable wage determination.

[FAC 84-46, 54 FR 19816, 5/8/89, effective 6/7/89; FAC 2005-21, 72 FR 63076, 11/7/2007, effective 11/7/2007; FAC 2005-30, 74 FR 2724, 1/15/2009, effective 2/17/2009; FAC 2005-73, 79 FR 24192, 4/29/2014, effective 5/29/2014]

22.1021 Request for hearing.

(a) A contracting agency or other interested party may request a hearing on an issue presented in 22.1013(a). To obtain a hearing for the contracting agency, the contracting officer shall submit a written request through appropriate channels (ordinarily the agency labor advisor) to: Administrator, Wage and Hour Division, U.S. Department of Labor, Washington, DC 20210.

(b) A request for a substantial variance hearing shall include sufficient data to show that the rates at issue vary substantially from those prevailing for similar services in the locality. The request shall also include—

(1) The number of the wage determinations at issue;

(2) The name of the contracting agency whose contract is involved;

(3) A brief description of the services to be performed under the contract;

(4) The status of the procurement and any estimated procurement dates, such as bid opening, contract award, and commencement date of the contract or its follow-up option period;

(5) A statement of the applicant's case, setting forth in detail the reasons why the applicant believes that a substantial variance exists with respect to some or all of the wages and/or fringe benefits;

(6) Names and addresses (to the extent known) of interested parties; and

(7) Any other data required by the Administrator.

(c) A request for an arm's length hearing shall include—

(1) A statement of the applicant's case setting forth in detail the reasons why the applicant believes that the wages and fringe benefits contained in the collective bargaining agreement were not reached as a result of arm's length negotiations;

(2) A statement regarding the status of the procurement and any estimated procurement dates, such as bid opening, contract award, and commencement date of the contract or its follow-up option period; and

(3) Names and addresses (to the extent known) of interested parties.

(d) Unless the Administrator determines that extraordinary circumstances exist, the Administrator will not consider requests for a hearing unless received as follows:

(1) For sealed bid contracts, more than 10 days before the award of the contract; or

(2) For negotiated contracts and for contracts with provisions exceeding the initial term by option, before the commencement date of the contract or the follow-up option period.

[FAC 90-23, 59 FR 67010, 12/28/94, effective 2/27/95; FAC 2005-100, 83 FR 42571, 8/22/2018, effective 8/22/2018]

22.1022 Withholding of contract payments.

Any violations of the clause at 52.222-41, Service Contract Labor Standards, as amended, renders the responsible contractor liable for the amount of any deductions, rebates, refunds, or underpayments (which includes nonpayment) of compensation due employees performing the contract. The contracting officer may withhold—or, upon written request of the Department of Labor from a level no lower than that of Deputy Regional Administrator, Wage and Hour Division, Department of Labor, shall withhold—the amount needed to pay such underpaid employees from accrued payments due the contractor on the contract, or on any other prime contract (whether subject to the Service Contract Labor Standards statute or not) with the contractor. The agency shall place the amount withheld in a deposit fund. Such withheld funds shall be transferred to the Department of Labor for disbursement to the underpaid employees on order of the Secretary (or authorized representatives), an Administrative Law Judge, or the Administrative Review Board. In addition, the Department of Labor has given blanket approval to forward withheld funds pending completion of an investigation or other administrative proceeding when disposition of withheld funds remains the final action necessary to close out a contract.

[FAC 84-46, 54 FR 19816, 5/8/89, effective 6/7/89; FAC 90-40, 61 FR 39186, 7/26/96, effective 8/26/96; FAC 2005-21, 72 FR 63076, 11/7/2007, effective 11/7/2007; FAC 2005-30, 74 FR 2724, 1/15/2009, effective 2/17/2009; FAC 2005-73, 79 FR 24192, 4/29/2014, effective 5/29/2014; FAC 2005-100, 83 FR 42571, 8/22/2018, effective 8/22/2018]

22.1023 Termination for default.

As provided by the Service Contract Labor Standards statute, any contractor failure to comply with the requirements of the contract clauses related to the Service Contract Labor Standards statute may be grounds for termination for default (see paragraph (k) of the clause at 52.222-41, Service Contract Labor Standards).

[FAC 84-46, 54 FR 19816, 5/8/89, effective 6/7/89; FAC 2005-21, 72 FR 63076, 11/7/2007, effective 11/7/2007; FAC 2005-30, 74 FR 2724, 1/15/2009, effective 2/17/2009; FAC 2005-73, 79 FR 24192, 4/29/2014, effective 5/29/2014]

22.1024 Cooperation with the Department of Labor.

The contracting officer shall cooperate with Department of Labor representatives in the examination of records, interviews with service employees, and all other aspects of investigations undertaken by the Department. When asked, agencies shall furnish the Wage and Hour Administrator or a designee, any available information on contractors, subcontactors, their contracts, and the nature of the contract services. The contracting officer shall promptly refer, in writing to the appropriate regional office of the Department, apparent violations and complaints received. Employee complaints shall not be disclosed to the employer.

[FAC 84-46, 54 FR 19816, 5/8/89, effective 6/7/89]

22.1025 Ineligibility of violators.

Persons or firms found to be in violation of the Service Contract Labor Standards statute will have an active exclusion record contained in the System for Award Management (see 9.404). No Government contract may be awarded to any violator so listed because of a violation of the Service Contract Labor Standards statute, or to any firm, corporation, partnership, or association in which the violator has a substantial interest, without the approval of the Secretary of Labor. This prohibition against award to an ineligible contractor applies to both prime and subcontracts.

[FAC 84-46, 54 FR 19816, 5/8/89, effective 6/7/89; FAC 90-28, 60 FR 33064, 6/26/95, effective 8/25/95; FAC 2001-26, 69 FR 76347, 12/20/2004, effective 1/19/2005; FAC 2005-67, 78 FR 37676, 6/21/2013, effective 7/22/2013; FAC 2005-73, 79 FR 24192, 4/29/2014, effective 5/29/2014; FAC 2005-101, 83 FR 48691, 9/26/2018, effective 10/26/2018]

22.1026 Disputes concerning labor standards.

Disputes concerning labor standards requirements of the contract are handled under paragraph (t) of the contract clause at 52.222-41, Service Contract Act Labor Standards, and not under the clause at 52.233-1, Disputes.

[FAC 84-46, 54 FR 19816, 5/8/89, effective 6/7/89; FAC 2005-21, 72 FR 63076, 11/7/2007, effective 11/7/2007; FAC 2005-30, 74 FR 2724, 1/15/2009, effective 2/17/2009; FAC 2005-73, 79 FR 24192, 4/29/2014, effective 5/29/2014]

SUBPART 22.11—PROFESSIONAL EMPLOYEE COMPENSATION

22.1101 Applicability.

The Service Contract Act of 1965, now codified at 41 U.S.C. chapter 67, Service Contract Labor Standards, was enacted to ensure that Government contractors compensate their blue-collar service workers and some white-collar service workers fairly, but it does not cover bona fide executive, administrative, or professional employees.

[FAC 84-12, 51 FR 2665, 1/17/86 effective 1/20/86; FAC 90-16, 57 FR 60582, 12/21/92, effective 2/19/93; FAC 97-18, 65 FR 36014, 6/6/2000, effective 6/6/2000; FAC 2005-73, 79 FR 24192, 4/29/2014, effective 5/29/2014]

22.1102 Definition.

Professional employee, as used in this subpart, means any person meeting the definition of *employee employed in a bona fide . . . professional capacity* given in 29 CFR 541. The term embraces members of those professions having a recognized status based upon acquiring professional knowledge through prolonged study. Examples of these professions include accountancy, actuarial computation, architecture, dentistry, engineering, law, medicine, nursing, pharmacy, the sciences (such as biology, chemistry, and physics, and teaching). To be a professional employee, a person must not only be a professional but must be involved essentially in discharging professional duties.

[FAC 97-22, 66 FR 2116, 1/10/2001, effective 3/12/2001; Delay of effective date, 66 FR 14259, 3/9/2001, effective 5/11/2001]

22.1103 Policy, procedures, and solicitation provision.

All professional employees shall be compensated fairly and properly. Accordingly, the contracting officer shall insert the provision at 52.222-46, Evaluation of Compensation for Professional Employees, in solicitations for negotiated contracts when the contract amount is expected to exceed $700,000 and services are to be provided which will require meaningful numbers of professional employees. This provision requires that offerors submit for evaluation a total compensation plan setting forth proposed salaries and fringe benefits for professional employees working on the contract. Supporting information will include data, such as recognized national and regional compensation surveys and studies of professional, public and private organizations, used in establishing the total compensation structure. Plans indicating unrealistically low professional employee compensation may be assessed adversely as one of the factors considered in making an award.

[FAC 90-16, 57 FR 60582, 12/21/92, effective 2/19/93; FAC 2005-13, 71 FR 57363, 9/28/2006, effective 9/28/2006; FAC 2005-45, 75 FR 53129, 8/30/2010, effective 10/1/2010; FAC 2005-64, 77 FR 75766, 12/21/2012, effective 1/18/2013; FAC 2005-83, 80 FR 38293, 7/2/2015, effective 10/1/2015]

SUBPART 22.12—NONDISPLACEMENT OF QUALIFIED WORKERS UNDER SERVICE CONTRACTS

22.1200 Scope of subpart.

This subpart prescribes policies and procedures for implementing Executive Order 13495 of January 30, 2009, Nondisplacement of Qualified Workers Under Service Contracts, and related Secretary of Labor regulations and instructions (see 29 CFR part 9).

[Removed and reserved, FAC 97-26, 66 FR 27405, 5/16/2001, effective 5/16/2001, finalized without change, FAC 2001-04, 67 FR 6112, 2/8/2002, effective 2/20/2002; FAC 2005-64, 77 FR 75766, 12/21/2012, effective 1/18/2013]

22.1201 Definitions.

As used in this subpart—

United States means the 50 States, the District of Columbia, Puerto Rico, the Northern Mariana Islands, American Samoa, Guam, the U.S. Virgin Islands, Johnston Island, Wake Island, and outer Continental Shelf as defined in the Outer Continental Shelf Lands Act (43 U.S.C. 1331, *et seq.*), but does not include any other place subject to United States jurisdiction or any United States base or possession in a foreign country (see 29 CFR 4.112).

[FAC 2005-64, 77 FR 75766, 12/21/2012, effective 1/18/2013]

22.1202 Policy.

(a) When a service contract succeeds a contract for performance of the same or similar services, as defined at 29 CFR 9.2, at the same location, the successor contractor and its subcontractors are required to offer those service employees that are employed under the predecessor contract, and whose employment will be terminated as a result of the award of the successor contract, a right of first refusal of employment under the contract in positions for which they are qualified. Executive Order 13495 generally prohibits employment openings under the successor contract until such right of first refusal has been provided, when consistent with applicable law.

(b) Nothing in Executive Order 13495 shall be construed to permit a contractor or subcontractor to fail to comply with any provision of any other Executive order or law. For example, the requirements of the HUBZone Program (see subpart 19.13), Executive Order 11246 (Equal Employment Opportunity), and the Vietnam Era Veterans' Readjustment Assistance Act of 1974 may, in certain circumstances, conflict with the requirements of Executive Order 13495. All applicable laws and Executive orders must be satisfied in tandem with, and if necessary prior to, the requirements of Executive Order 13495 and this subpart.

[FAC 2005-64, 77 FR 75766, 12/21/2012, effective 1/18/2013]

22.1203 Applicability. (No Text)

[FAC 2005-64, 77 FR 75766, 12/21/2012, effective 1/18/2013]

22.1203-1 General.

This subpart applies to service contracts that succeed contracts for the same or similar services (29 CFR 9.2) at the same location.

[FAC 2005-64, 77 FR 75766, 12/21/2012, effective 1/18/2013]

22.1203-2 Exemptions.

(a) This subpart does not apply to—

(1) Contracts and subcontracts under the simplified acquisition threshold;

(2) Contracts or subcontracts awarded pursuant to 41 U.S.C. chapter 85, Committee for Purchase from People Who Are Blind or Severely Disabled;

(3) Guard, elevator operator, messenger, or custodial services provided to the Government under contracts or subcontracts with sheltered workshops employing the "severely handicapped" as described in 40 U.S.C. 593;

(4) Agreements for vending facilities entered into pursuant to the preference regulations issued under the Randolph Sheppard Act, 20 U.S.C. 107; or

(5) Service employees who were hired to work under a Federal service contract and one or more nonfederal service contracts as part of a single job, provided that the service employees were not deployed in a manner that was designed to avoid the purposes of this subpart.

(b) The exemptions in paragraphs (a)(2) through (a)(4) of this subsection apply when either the predecessor or successor contract has been awarded for services produced or provided by the "severely handicapped."

[FAC 2005-64, 77 FR 75766, 12/21/2012, effective 1/18/2013]

22.1203-3 Waiver.

(a) The senior procurement executive of the procuring agency may waive some or all of the provisions of this subpart after determining in writing that the application of this subpart would not serve the purposes of Executive Order 13495 or would impair the ability of the Federal Government to procure services on an economical and efficient basis. Such waivers may be made for a contract, subcontract, or purchase order, or with respect to a class of contracts, subcontracts, or purchase orders. See 29 CFR 9.4(d)(4) for regulatory provisions addressing circumstances in which a waiver could or would not be appropriate. The waiver must be reflected in a written analysis as described in 29 CFR 9.4(d)(4)(i) and must be completed by the contract solicitation date, or the waiver is inoperative. The senior procurement executive shall not redelegate this waiver authority.

(b)(1) When an agency exercises its waiver authority with respect to any contract, subcontract, or purchase order, the contracting officer shall direct the contractor to notify affected workers and their collective bargaining representative in writing, no later than five business days after the solicitation issuance date, of the agency's determination. The notice shall include facts supporting the determination. The contracting officer's failure to direct that the contractor provide the notice as provided in this subparagraph shall render the waiver decision inoperative, and the contracting officer shall include the clause at 52.222-17 in the solicitation.

(2) Where a contracting agency waives application to a class of contracts, subcontracts, or purchase orders, the contracting officer shall, with respect to each individual solicitation, direct the contractor to notify incumbent workers and their collective bargaining representatives in writing, no later than five business days after each solicitation issuance date, of the agency's determination. The notice shall include facts supporting the determination. The contracting officer's failure to direct that the contractor provide the notice provided in this subparagraph shall render the waiver decision inoperative, and the contracting officer shall include the clause at 52.222-17 in the solicitation.

(3) In addition, the agency shall notify the Department of Labor of its waiver decision and provide the Department of Labor with a copy of its written analysis no later than five business days after the solicitation issuance date (see 29 CFR 9.4(d)(2)). Failure to comply with this notification requirement shall render the waiver decision inoperative, and the contracting officer shall include the clause at 52.222-17 in the solicitation. The waiver decision and related written analysis shall be sent to the following address: U.S. Department of Labor, Wage and Hour Division, Branch of Government Contracts Enforcement, 200 Constitution Avenue, Room S-3006, Washington, DC 20210, or email to: *Displaced@dol.gov*.

[FAC 2005-64, 77 FR 75766, 12/21/2012, effective 1/18/2013]

22.1203-4 Method of job offer.

A job offer made by a successor contractor must be a bona fide express offer of employment on the contract. Each bona fide express offer made to a qualified service employee on the predecessor contract must have a stated time limit of not less than 10 days for an employee response. Prior to the expiration of the 10-day period, the contractor is prohibited from offering employment on the contract to any other person, subject to the exceptions at 22.1203-5. Any question concerning an employee's qualifications shall be decided based upon the individual's education and employment history, with particular emphasis on the employee's experience on the predecessor contract, and a contractor may utilize employment screening processes only when such processes are provided for by the contracting agency, are conditions of the service contract, and are consistent with the Executive Order. An offer of employment will be presumed to be bona fide even if it is not for a position similar to the one the employee previously held, but is one for which the employee is qualified, and even if it is subject to different employment terms and conditions, including changes to pay or benefits. (See 29 CFR 9.12(b) for regulatory provisions addressing circumstances in which a bona fide offer of employment can occur.)

[FAC 2005-64, 77 FR 75766, 12/21/2012, effective 1/18/2013]

22.1203-5 Exceptions.

(a) A successor contractor or its subcontractors are not required to offer employment to any service employee of the predecessor contractor who—

(1) Will be retained by the predecessor contractor.

(2) The successor contractor or any of its subcontractors reasonably believes, based on the particular service employee's past performance, has failed to perform suitably on the job. (See 29 CFR 9.12(c)(4) for regulatory provisions addressing circumstances in which this exception would or would not be appropriate.)

(b) A successor contractor or its subcontractors may employ under the contract any of its current service employees who (1) have worked for the successor contractor or its subcontractors for at least three months immediately preceding the commencement of the successor contract, and (2) would otherwise face lay-off or discharge.

(c) The successor contractor bears the responsibility of demonstrating the appropriateness of claiming any of the preceding exceptions and the exemption listed at 22.1203-2(a)(5) involving nonfederal work.

[FAC 2005-64, 77 FR 75766, 12/21/2012, effective 1/18/2013]

22.1203-6 Reduced staffing.

A successor contractor and its subcontractors may employ fewer service employees than the predecessor contractor employed in connection with performance of the work. Thus, the successor contractor need not offer employment on the contract to all service employees on the predecessor contract, but must offer employment only to the number of eligible service employees the successor contractor believes necessary to meet its anticipated staffing pattern. Where a successor contractor does not initially offer employment to all the predecessor contract service employees, the obligation to offer employment shall continue for 90 days after the successor contractor's first date of performance on the contract. (See 29 CFR 9.12(d) for regulatory provisions addressing circumstances in which reduced staffing can occur.)

[FAC 2005-64, 77 FR 75766, 12/21/2012, effective 1/18/2013]

22.1204 Certified service employee lists.

(a) Not less than 30 days before completion of the contract, the predecessor contractor is required to furnish to the contracting officer a certified list of the names of all service employees working under the contract and its subcontracts at the time the list is submitted. The certified list must also contain anniversary dates of employment of each service employee under the contract and subcontracts for services. The information on this list is the same as that on the seniority list required by paragraph (n) of the clause at 52.222-41, Service Contract Labor Standards. If there are no changes to the workforce before the predecessor contract is completed, then the predecessor contractor is not required to submit a revised list 10 days prior to completion of performance and the requirements of 52.222-41(n) are met. When there are changes to the workforce after submission of the 30-day list, the predecessor contractor shall submit a revised certified list not less than 10 days prior to performance completion.

(b) Immediately upon receipt of the certified service employee list but not before contract award, the contracting officer shall provide the certified service employee list to the successor contractor, and, if requested, to employees of the predecessor contractor or subcontractors or their authorized representatives.

[FAC 2005-64, 77 FR 75766, 12/21/2012, effective 1/18/2013; FAC 2005-73, 79 FR 24192, 4/29/2014, effective 5/29/2014]

22.1205 Notification to contractors and service employees.

(a) The contracting officer shall direct that the predecessor contractor provides written notice to service employees of their possible right to an offer of employment with the successor contractor. The written notice shall be—

(1) Posted in a conspicuous place at the worksite; or

(2) Delivered to the service employees individually. If such delivery is via email, the notification must result in an electronic delivery receipt or some other reliable confirmation that the intended recipient received the notice.

(b) Contracting officers may advise contractors to provide the notice in Appendix B to 29 CFR chapter 9. Where a significant portion of the predecessor contractor's workforce is not fluent in English, the contractor shall provide the notice in English and the language(s) with which service employees are more familiar. English and Spanish versions of the notice are available on the Department of Labor Web site at *http://www.dol.gov/whd/govcontracts.*

[FAC 2005-64, 77 FR 75766, 12/21/2012, effective 1/18/2013]

22.1206 Remedies and sanctions for violations of this subpart.

(a) The Secretary of Labor has the authority to issue orders prescribing appropriate remedies, including, but not limited to, requiring the successor contractor to offer employment, in positions for which the employees are qualified, to service employees from the predecessor contract and payment of wages lost. (See 29 CFR 9.24(a)).

(b) After an investigation (see 29 CFR 9.23) and a determination by the Administrator, Wage and Hour Division, Department of Labor, that lost wages or other monetary relief is due, the Administrator may direct that so much of the accrued payments due on either the contract or any other contract between the contractor and the Government shall be withheld as are necessary to pay the monies due. Upon the final order of the Secretary of Labor that such monies are due, the Administrator may direct that such withheld funds be transferred to the Department of Labor for disbursement. (See 29 CFR 9.24(c)).

(c) If the contracting officer or the Administrator, Wage and Hour Division, Department of Labor, finds that the predecessor contractor has failed to provide the list required by 22.1204, the contracting officer may, in his or her discretion, or on request by the Administrator, suspend contract payment until such time as the contractor provides the list to the contracting officer.

(d) The Secretary of Labor may also suspend or debar a contractor or subcontractor for a period of up to three years for violations of 29 CFR part 9.

[FAC 2005-64, 77 FR 75766, 12/21/2012, effective 1/18/2013]

22.1207 Contract clause.

The contracting officer shall insert the clause at 52.222-17, Nondisplacement of Qualified Workers, in solicitations and contracts for (1) service contracts, as defined at 22.001, (2) that succeed contracts for performance of the same or similar work at the same location and (3) that are not exempted by 22.1203-2 or waived in accordance with 22.1203-3.

[FAC 2005-64, 77 FR 75766, 12/21/2012, effective 1/18/2013]

SUBPART 22.13—EQUAL OPPORTUNITY FOR VETERANS

22.1300 Scope of subpart.

This subpart prescribes policies and procedures for implementing the following:

(a) The Vietnam Era Veterans' Readjustment Assistance Act of 1972 (38 U.S.C. 4211 and 4212) (the Act).

(b) The Veterans Employment Opportunities Act of 1998, Public Law 105-339.

(c) The Jobs for Veterans Act, Public Law 107-288.

(d) Executive Order 11701, January 24, 1973 (3 CFR, 1971-1975 Comp., p. 752).

(e) The regulations of the Secretary of Labor (41 CFR parts 60-300 and 61-300).

[Removed and reserved, FAC 97-26, 66 FR 27405, 5/16/2001, effective 5/16/2001, finalized without change, FAC 2001-04, 67 FR 6112, 2/8/2002, effective 2/20/2002; FAC 2005-76, 79 FR 43575, 7/25/2014, effective 7/25/2014; FAC 2005-82, 80 FR 26423, 5/7/2015, effective 5/7/2015; FAC 2005-85, 80 FR 75908, 12/4/2015, effective 2/26/2016; FAC 2005-91, 81 FR 67731, 9/30/2016, effective 9/30/2016]

22.1301 Definitions.

As used in this subpart—

Active duty wartime or campaign badge veteran means a veteran who served on active duty in the U.S. military, ground, naval, or air service, during a war or in a campaign or expedition for which a campaign badge has been authorized under the laws administered by the Department of Defense.

Armed Forces service medal veteran means any veteran who, while serving on active duty in the U.S. military, ground, naval, or air service, participated in a United States military operation for which an Armed Forces service medal was awarded pursuant to Executive Order 12985 (61 FR 1209).

Disabled veteran means—

(1) A veteran of the U.S. military, ground, naval, or air service, who is entitled to compensation (or who, but for the receipt of military retired pay, would be entitled to compensation) under laws administered by the Secretary of Veterans Affairs; or

(2) A person who was discharged or released from active duty because of a service-connected disability.

Executive and senior management means—

(1) Any employee—

(i) Compensated on a salary basis at a rate of not less than $455 per week (or $380 per week, if employed in American Samoa by employers other than the Federal Government), exclusive of board, lodging, or other facilities;

(ii) Whose primary duty consists of the management of the enterprise in which the individual is employed or of a customarily recognized department or subdivision thereof;

(iii) Who customarily and regularly directs the work of two or more other employees; and

(iv) Who has the authority to hire or fire other employees or whose suggestions and recommendations as to the hiring or firing and as to the advancement and promotion or any other change of status of other employees will be given particular weight; or

(2) Any employee who owns at least a bona fide 20-percent equity interest in the enterprise in which the employee is employed, regardless of whether the business is a corporate or other type of organization, and who is actively engaged in its management.

Other protected veteran means a veteran who served on active duty in the U.S. military, ground, naval, or air service, during a war or in a campaign or expedition for which a campaign badge has been authorized under the laws administered by the Department of Defense.

Protected veteran means a veteran who is protected under the non-discrimination and affirmative action provisions of 38 U.S.C. 4212; specifically, a veteran who may be classified as a *disabled veteran*, *recently separated veteran*, *active duty wartime or campaign badge veteran*, or an *Armed Forces service medal veteran*, as defined by this section.

Qualified disabled veteran means a disabled veteran who has the ability to perform the essential functions of the employment positions with or without reasonable accommodation.

Recently separated veteran means any veteran during the three-year period beginning on the date of such veteran's discharge or release from active duty in the U.S. military, ground, naval, or air service.

United States, means the 50 States, the District of Columbia, Puerto Rico, the Northern Mariana Islands, American Samoa, Guam, the U.S. Virgin Islands, and Wake Island.

[FAC 2001-01, 66 FR 53478, 10/22/2001, effective 12/21/2001; FAC 2005-46, 75 FR 60249, 9/29/2010, effective 9/29/2010; FAC 2005-53, 76 FR 39233, 7/5/2011, effective 8/4/2011; FAC 2005-76, 79 FR 43575, 7/25/2014, effective 7/25/2014; FAC 2005-82, 80 FR 26423, 5/7/2015, effective 5/7/2015]

22.1302 Policy.

(a) Contractors and subcontractors, when entering into contracts and subcontracts subject to the Act, are required to—

(1) List all employment openings, with the appropriate employment service delivery system where the opening occurs, except for—

(i) Executive and senior management positions;

(ii) Positions to be filled from within the contractor's organization; and

(iii) Positions lasting three days or less;

(2) Take affirmative action to employ, advance in employment, and otherwise treat qualified individuals, including qualified disabled veterans, without discrimination based upon their status as a protected veteran, in all employment practices;

(3) Undertake appropriate outreach and positive recruitment activities that are reasonably designed to effectively recruit protected veterans; and

(4) Establish a hiring benchmark and apply it to hiring of protected veterans in each establishment, on an annual basis, in the manner prescribed in the regulations of the Secretary of Labor.

(b) Except for contracts for commercial items or contracts that do not exceed the simplified acquisition threshold, contracting officers must not obligate or expend funds appropriated for the agency for a fiscal year to enter into a contract for the procurement of personal property and nonpersonal services (including construction) with a contractor that has not submitted the required annual VETS-4212, Federal Contractor Veterans' Employment Report (VETS-4212 Report), with respect to the preceding fiscal year if the contractor was subject to the reporting requirements of 38 U.S.C. 4212(d) for that fiscal year.

[FAC 2001-01, 66 FR 53478, 10/22/2001, effective 12/21/2001; FAC 2005-46, 75 FR 60249, 9/29/2010, effective 9/29/2010; FAC 2005-53, 76 FR 39233, 7/5/2011, effective 8/4/2011; FAC 2005-76, 79 FR 43575, 7/25/2014, effective 7/25/2014; FAC 2005-82, 80 FR 26423, 5/7/2015, effective 5/7/2015; FAC 2005-85, 80 FR 75908, 12/4/2015, effective 2/26/2016; FAC 2005-91, 81 FR 67731, 9/30/2016, effective 9/30/2016]

22.1303 Applicability.

(a) The Act applies to all contracts and subcontracts for personal property and nonpersonal services (including construction) of $150,000 or more except as waived by the Secretary of Labor.

(b) The requirements of the clause at 52.222-35, Equal Opportunity for Veterans, in any contract with a State or local government (or any agency, instrumentality, or subdivision) do not apply to any agency, instrumentality, or subdivision of that government that does not participate in work on or under the contract.

(c) The Act requires submission of the VETS-4212 Report in all cases where the contractor or subcontractor has received an award of $150,000 or more, except for awards to State and local governments, and foreign organizations where the workers are recruited outside of the United States.

[FAC 2001-01, 66 FR 53478, 10/22/2001, effective 12/21/2001; FAC 2005-13, 71 FR 57363, 9/28/2006, effective 9/28/2006; FAC 2005-46, 75 FR 60249, 9/29/2010, effective 9/29/2010; FAC 2005-53, 76 FR 39233, 7/5/2011, effective 8/4/2011; FAC 2005-83, 80 FR 38293, 7/2/2015, effective 10/1/2015; FAC 2005-85, 80 FR 75908, 12/4/2015, effective 2/26/2016; FAC 2005-91, 81 FR 67731, 9/30/2016, effective 9/30/2016]

22.1304 Procedures.

To verify if a proposed contractor is current with its submission of the VETS-4212 Report, the contracting officer may—

(a) Query the Department of Labor's VETS-4212 Database via the Internet at *http://www.dol.gov/vets/vets4212.htm* under "Filing Verification"; and

(b) Contact the VETS-4212 customer support via email at *VETS4212-customersupport@dol.gov* for confirmation, if the proposed contractor represents that it has submitted the VETS-4212 Report and is not listed on the verification file.

[FAC 2001-01, 66 FR 53478, 10/22/2001, effective 12/21/2001; FAC 2005-14, 71 FR 67779, 11/22/2006, effective 11/22/2006; FAC 2005-46, 75 FR 60249, 9/29/2010, effective 9/29/2010; FAC 2005-53, 76 FR 39233, 7/5/2011, effective 8/4/2011; FAC 2005-55, 77 FR 204, 1/3/2012, effective 1/3/2012; FAC 2005-85, 80 FR 75908, 12/4/2015, effective 2/26/2016; FAC 2005-91, 81 FR 67731, 9/30/2016, effective 9/30/2016; FAC 2005-100, 83 FR 42571, 8/22/2018, effective 8/22/2018]

22.1305 Waivers.

(a) The Director, Office of Federal Contract Compliance Programs, Department of Labor, may waive any or all of the terms of the clause at 52.222-35, Equal Opportunity for Veterans, for—

(1) Any contract if a waiver is in the national interest; or

(2) Groups or categories of contracts if a waiver is in the national interest and it is—

(i) Impracticable to act on each request individually; and

(ii) Determined that the waiver will substantially contribute to convenience in administering the Act.

(b) The head of the agency may waive any requirement in this subpart when it is determined that the contract is essential to the national security, and that its award without complying with such requirements is necessary to the national security. Upon making such a determination, the head of the agency must notify the Deputy Assistant Secretary of Labor in writing within 30 days.

(c) The contracting officer must submit requests for waivers in accordance with agency procedures.

(d) The Deputy Assistant Secretary of Labor may withdraw an approved waiver for a specific contract or group of contracts to be awarded, when in the Deputy's judgment such action is necessary to achieve the purposes of the Act. The withdrawal does not apply to awarded contracts. For procurements entered into by sealed bidding, such withdrawal does not apply unless the withdrawal is made more than 10 calendar days before the date set for the opening of bids.

[FAC 2001-01, 66 FR 53478, 10/22/2001, effective 12/21/2001; FAC 2005-46, 75 FR 60249, 9/29/2010, effective 9/29/2010; FAC

2005-53, 76 FR 39233, 7/5/2011, effective 8/4/2011]

22.1306 Department of Labor notices and reports.

(a) The contracting officer must furnish to the contractor appropriate notices for posting when they are prescribed by the Deputy Assistant Secretary of Labor (see *http://www.dol.gov/ofccp/regs/compliance/posters/ofccpost.htm*).

(b) The Act requires contractors and subcontractors to submit a report at least annually to the Secretary of Labor regarding employment of protected veterans (*i.e.*, active duty wartime or campaign badge veterans, Armed Forces service medal veterans, disabled veterans, and recently separated veterans, unless all of the terms of the clause at 52.222-35, Equal Opportunity for Veterans, have been waived see 22.1305). The contractor and subcontractor must file VETS-4212, Federal Contractor Veterans' Employment Report (see "VETS-4212 Federal Contractor Reporting" and "Filing Your VETS-4212 Report" at *http://www.dol.gov/vets/vets4212.htm*).

[FAC 2001-01, 66 FR 53478, 10/22/2001, effective 12/21/2001; FAC 2005-46, 75 FR 60249, 9/29/2010, effective 9/29/2010; FAC 2005-53, 76 FR 39233, 7/5/2011, effective 8/4/2011; FAC 2005-55, 77 FR 204, 1/3/2012, effective 1/3/2012; FAC 2005-85, 80 FR 75908, 12/4/2015, effective 2/26/2016; FAC 2005-91, 81 FR 67731, 9/30/2016, effective 9/30/2016]

22.1307 Collective bargaining agreements.

If performance under the clause at 52.222-35, Equal Opportunity for Veterans, may necessitate a revision of a collective bargaining agreement, the contracting officer must advise the affected labor unions that the Department of Labor will give them appropriate opportunity to present their views. However, neither the contracting officer nor any representative of the contracting officer may discuss with the contractor or any labor representative any aspect of the collective bargaining agreement.

[FAC 2001-01, 66 FR 53478, 10/22/2001, effective 12/21/2001; FAC 2005-46, 75 FR 60249, 9/29/2010, effective 9/29/2010; FAC 2005-53, 76 FR 39233, 7/5/2011, effective 8/4/2011]

22.1308 Complaint procedures.

Following agency procedures, the contracting office must forward any complaints received about the administration of the Act to the Veterans' Employment and Training Service of the Department of Labor, or to the Director, Office of Federal Contract Compliance Programs, 200 Constitution Avenue, NW., Washington, DC 20210, or to any OFCCP regional, district, or area office or through the local Veterans' Employment Representative or designee, at the local State employment office. The Director, Office of Federal Contract Compliance Programs, is responsible for investigating complaints.

[FAC 2001-01, 66 FR 53478, 10/22/2001, effective 12/21/2001; FAC 2005-46, 75 FR 60249, 9/29/2010, effective 9/29/2010; FAC 2005-53, 76 FR 39233, 7/5/2011, effective 8/4/2011]

22.1309 Actions because of noncompliance.

The contracting officer must take necessary action as soon as possible upon notification by the appropriate agency official to implement any sanctions imposed on a contractor by the Department of Labor for violations of the clause at 52.222-35, Equal Opportunity for Veterans. These sanctions (see 41 CFR 60-300.66) may include—

(a) Withholding progress payments;

(b) Termination or suspension of the contract; or

(c) Debarment of the contractor.

[FAC 2001-01, 66 FR 53478, 10/22/2001, effective 12/21/2001; FAC 2005-46, 75 FR 60249, 9/29/2010, effective 9/29/2010; FAC 2005-53, 76 FR 39233, 7/5/2011, effective 8/4/2011]

22.1310 Solicitation provision and contract clauses.

(a) (1) Insert the clause at 52.222-35, Equal Opportunity for Veterans, in solicitations and contracts if the expected value is $150,000 or more, except when—

(i) Work is performed outside the United States by employees recruited outside the United States; or

(ii) The Director, Office of Federal Contract Compliance Programs of the U.S. Department of Labor, has waived, in accordance with 22.1305(a), or the head of the agency has waived, in accordance with 22.1305(b), all of the terms of the clause.

(2) If the Director, Office of Federal Contract Compliance Programs of the U.S. Department of Labor, or the head of the agency waives one or more (but not all) of the terms of the clause, use the basic clause with its Alternate I.

(b) Insert the clause at 52.222-37, Employment Reports on Veterans, in solicitations and contracts containing the clause at 52.222-35, Equal Opportunity for Veterans.

(c) Insert the provision at 52.222-38, Compliance with Veterans' Employment Reporting Requirements, in solicitations when it is anticipated the contract award will exceed the simplified acquisition threshold and the contract is not for acquisition of commercial items.

[FAC 2001-01, 66 FR 53478, 10/22/2001, effective 12/21/2001; FAC 2005-13, 71 FR 57363, 9/28/2006, effective 9/28/2006; FAC 2005-46, 75 FR 60249, 9/29/2010, effective 9/29/2010; FAC 2005-53, 76 FR 39233, 7/5/2011, effective 8/4/2011; FAC 2005-76, 79 FR 43575, 7/25/2014, effective 7/25/2014; FAC 2005-82, 80 FR 26423, 5/7/2015, effective 5/7/2015; FAC 2005-83, 80 FR 38293, 7/2/2015, effective 10/1/2015]

SUBPART 22.14—EMPLOYMENT OF WORKERS WITH DISABILITIES

22.1400 Scope of subpart.

This subpart prescribes policies and procedures for implementing section 503 of the Rehabilitation Act of 1973, as amended (29 U.S.C. 793) (the Act); Executive Order 11758, January 15, 1974; and the regulations of the Secretary of Labor (41 CFR Part 60-741). In this subpart, the terms *contract* and *contractor* include *subcontract* and *subcontractor*.

[FAC 2005-76, 79 FR 43575, 7/25/2014, effective 7/25/2014; FAC 2005-82, 80 FR 26423, 5/7/2015, effective 5/7/2015]

22.1401 Policy.

Contractors and subcontractors, when entering into contracts and subcontracts subject to the Act, are required to—

(a) Take affirmative action to employ, and advance in employment, qualified individuals with disabilities, and to otherwise treat qualified individuals without discrimination based on their physical or mental disability;

(b) Undertake appropriate outreach and positive recruitment activities that are reasonably designed to effectively recruit qualified individuals with disabilities; and

(c) Compare the utilization of individuals with disabilities in their workforces to the utilization goal, as prescribed in the regulations of the Secretary of Labor, on an annual basis.

[FAC 97-5, 63 FR 34058, 6/22/98, effective 6/22/98, finalized without change, FAC 97-9, 63 FR 58587, 10/30/98; FAC 2005-76, 79 FR 43575, 7/25/2014, effective 7/25/2014; FAC 2005-82, 80 FR 26423, 5/7/2015, effective 5/7/2015]

22.1402 Applicability.

(a) Section 503 of the Act applies to all Government contracts in excess of $15,000 for supplies and services (including construction) except as waived by the Secretary of Labor. The clause at 52.222-36, Equal Opportunity for Workers with Disabilities, implements the Act.

(b) The requirements of the clause at 52.222-36, Equal Opportunity for Workers with Disabilities, in any contract with a State or local government (or any agency, instrumentality, or subdivision) shall not apply to any agency, instrumentality, or subdivision of that government that does not participate in work on or under the contract.

[FAC 97-5, 63 FR 34058, 6/22/98, effective 6/22/98, finalized without change, FAC 97-9, 63 FR 58587, 10/30/98; FAC 2005-45, 75 FR 53129, 8/30/2010, effective 10/1/2010; FAC 2005-76, 79 FR 43575, 7/25/2014, effective 7/25/2014; FAC 2005-82, 80 FR 26423, 5/7/2015, effective 5/7/2015]

22.1403 Waivers.

(a) The Director of the Office of Federal Contract Compliance Programs of the U.S. Department of Labor (Director of OFCCP), may waive the application of any or all of the terms of the clause at 52.222-36, Equal Opportunity for Workers with Disabilities, for—

(1) Any contract if a waiver is deemed to be in the national interest; or

(2) Groups or categories of contracts if a waiver is in the national interest and it is—

(i) Impracticable to act on each request individually; and

(ii) Determined that the waiver will substantially contribute to convenience in administering the Act.

(b) The head of an agency may waive any requirement in this subpart when it is determined that the contract is essential to the national security, and that its award without complying with such requirements is necessary to the national security. Upon making such a determination, the head of the agency shall notify the Director of OFCCP in writing within 30 days.

(c) The contracting officer shall submit requests for waivers in accordance with agency procedures.

(d) A waiver granted for a particular class of contracts may be withdrawn for any contract within that class whenever considered necessary by the Director of OFCCP to achieve the purposes of the Act. The withdrawal shall not apply to contracts awarded before the withdrawal. The withdrawal shall not apply to solicitations under any means of sealed bidding unless it is made more than 10 days before the date set for bid opening.

[FAC 84-26, 52 FR 19803, 5/27/87, effective 7/30/87; FAC 97-5, 63 FR 34058, 6/22/98, effective 6/22/98, finalized without change, FAC 97-9, 63 FR 58587, 10/30/98; FAC 2005-76, 79 FR 43575, 7/25/2014, effective 7/25/2014; FAC 2005-82, 80 FR 26423, 5/7/2015, effective 5/7/2015]

22.1404 Department of Labor notices.

The contracting officer shall furnish to the contractor appropriate notices that state the contractor's obligations and the rights of individuals with disabilities. The contracting officer may obtain these notices from the Office of Federal Contract Compliance Programs (OFCCP) regional office.

[FAC 97-5, 63 FR 34058, 6/22/98, effective 6/22/98, finalized without change, FAC 97-9, 63 FR 58587, 10/30/98]

22.1405 Collective bargaining agreements.

If performance under the clause at 52.222-36, Equal Opportunity For Workers with Disabilities, may necessitate a revision of a collective bargaining agreement, the contracting officer shall advise the affected labor unions that the Department of Labor will give them appropriate opportunity to present their views. However, neither the contracting officer nor any representative of the contracting officer shall discuss with the contractor or any labor representative any aspect of the collective bargaining agreement.

[FAC 97-5, 63 FR 34058, 6/22/98, effective 6/22/98, finalized without change, FAC 97-9, 63 FR 58587, 10/30/98; FAC 2005-76, 79 FR 43575, 7/25/2014, effective 7/25/2014; FAC 2005-82, 80 FR 26423, 5/7/2015, effective 5/7/2015]

22.1406 Complaint procedures.

(a) Following agency procedures, the contracting office shall forward any complaints received about the administration of the Act to—

(1) Director, Office of Federal Contract Compliance Programs, U.S. Department of Labor, 200 Constitution Avenue, NW, Washington, DC 20210; or

(2) Any OFCCP regional or area office.

(b) The OFCCP shall institute investigation of each complaint and shall be responsible for developing a complete case record.

[FAC 97-5, 63 FR 34058, 6/22/98, effective 6/22/98, finalized without change, FAC 97-9, 63 FR 58587, 10/30/98; FAC 2005-76, 79 FR 43575, 7/25/2014, effective 7/25/2014; FAC 2005-82, 80 FR 26423, 5/7/2015, effective 5/7/2015]

22.1407 Actions because of noncompliance.

The contracting officer shall take necessary action, as soon as possible upon notification by the appropriate agency official, to implement any sanctions imposed on a contractor by the Department of Labor for violations of the clause at 52.222-36, Equal Opportunity for Workers with Disabilities. These sanctions (see 41 CFR 60-741.66) may include—

(a) Withholding from payments otherwise due;

(b) Termination or suspension of the contract; or

(c) Debarment of the contractor.

[FAC 97-5, 63 FR 34058, 6/22/98, effective 6/22/98, finalized without change, FAC 97-9, 63 FR 58587, 10/30/98; FAC 2005-76, 79 FR 43575, 7/25/2014, effective 7/25/2014; FAC 2005-82, 80 FR 26423, 5/7/2015, effective 5/7/2015]

22.1408 Contract clause.

(a) Insert the clause at 52.222-36, Equal Opportunity for Workers with Disabilities, in solicitations and contracts that exceed or are expected to exceed $15,000, except when—

(1) Both the performance of the work and the recruitment of workers will occur outside the United States, Puerto Rico, the Northern Mariana Islands, American Samoa, Guam, the U.S. Virgin Islands, and Wake Island; or

(2) The Director of OFCCP or agency head has waived, in accordance with 22.1403(a) or 22.1403(b) all the terms of the clause.

(b) If the Director of OFCCP or agency head waives one or more (but not all) of the terms of the clause in accordance with 22.1403(a) or 22.1403(b), use the basic clause with its Alternate I.

[FAC 97-5, 63 FR 34058, 6/22/98, effective 6/22/98, finalized without change, FAC 97-9, 63 FR 58587, 10/30/98; FAC 2001-14, 68 FR 28079, 5/22/2003, effective 6/23/2003; FAC 2005-45, 75 FR 53129, 8/30/2010, effective 10/1/2010; FAC 2005-76, 79 FR 43575, 7/25/2014, effective 7/25/2014; FAC 2005-82, 80 FR 26423, 5/7/2015, effective 5/7/2015]

SUBPART 22.15—PROHIBITION OF ACQUISITION OF PRODUCTS PRODUCED BY FORCED OR INDENTURED CHILD LABOR

22.1500 Scope.

This subpart applies to acquisitions of supplies that exceed the micro-purchase threshold.

[FAC 97-23, 66 FR 5345, 1/18/2001, effective 2/20/2001]

22.1501 Definitions.

As used in this subpart—

Forced or indentured child labor means all work or service—

(1) Exacted from any person under the age of 18 under the menace of any penalty for its nonperformance and for which the worker does not offer himself voluntarily; or

(2) Performed by any person under the age of 18 pursuant to a contract the enforcement of which can be accomplished by process or penalties.

List of Products Requiring Contractor Certification as to Forced or Indentured Child Labor means the list published by the Department of Labor in accordance with Executive Order 13126 of June 12, 1999, Prohibition of Acquisition of Products Produced by Forced or Indentured Child Labor. The list identifies products, by their country of origin, that the Departments of Labor, Treasury, and State have a reasonable basis to believe might have been mined, produced, or manufactured by forced or indentured child labor.

[FAC 97-23, 66 FR 5345, 1/18/2001, effective 2/20/2001]

22.1502 Policy.

Agencies must take appropriate action to enforce the laws prohibiting the manufacture or importation of products that have been mined, produced, or manufactured wholly or in part by forced or indentured child labor, consistent with 19 U.S.C. 1307, 29 U.S.C. 201, *et seq.*, and 41 U.S.C. chapter

65. Agencies should make every effort to avoid acquiring such products.

[FAC 97-23, 66 FR 5345, 1/18/2001, effective 2/20/2001; FAC 2005-73, 79 FR 24192, 4/29/2014, effective 5/29/2014]

22.1503 Procedures for acquiring end products on the List of Products Requiring Contractor Certification as to Forced or Indentured Child Labor.

(a) When issuing a solicitation for supplies expected to exceed the micro-purchase threshold, the contracting officer must check the List of Products Requiring Contractor Certification as to Forced or Indentured Child Labor (the List) (*www.dol.gov/ilab/*) (see 22.1505(a)). Appearance of a product on the List is not a bar to purchase of any such product mined, produced, or manufactured in the identified country, but rather is an alert that there is a reasonable basis to believe that such product may have been mined, produced, or manufactured by forced or indentured child labor.

(b) The requirements of this subpart that result from the appearance of any end product on the List do not apply to a solicitation or contract if the identified country of origin on the List is—

(1) Canada, and the anticipated value of the acquisition is $25,000 or more (see subpart 25.4);

(2) Israel, and the anticipated value of the acquisition is $50,000 or more (see 25.406);

(3) Mexico, and the anticipated value of the acquisition is $80,317 or more (see subpart 25.4); or

(4) Armenia, Aruba, Australia, Austria, Belgium, Bulgaria, Croatia, Cyprus, Czech Republic, Denmark, Estonia, Finland, France, Germany, Greece, Hong Kong, Hungary, Iceland, Ireland, Italy, Japan, Korea, Latvia, Liechtenstein, Lithuania, Luxembourg, Malta, Moldova, Montenegro, Netherlands, New Zealand, Norway, Poland, Portugal, Romania, Singapore, Slovak Republic, Slovenia, Spain, Sweden, Switzerland, Taiwan, Ukraine, or the United Kingdom and the anticipated value of the acquisition is $180,000 or more (see 25.402(b)).

(c) Except as provided in paragraph (b) of this section, before the contracting officer may make an award for an end product (regardless of country of origin) of a type identified by country of origin on the List the offeror must certify that—

(1) It will not supply any end product on the List that was mined, produced, or manufactured in a country identified on the List for that product, as specified in the solicitation by the contracting officer in the Certification Regarding Knowledge of Child Labor for Listed End Products; or

(2) (i) It has made a good faith effort to determine whether forced or indentured child labor was used to mine, produce, or manufacture any end product to be furnished under the contract that is on the List and was mined, produced, or manufactured in a country identified on the List for that product; and

(ii) On the basis of those efforts, the offeror is unaware of any such use of child labor.

(d) Absent any actual knowledge that the certification is false, the contracting officer must rely on the offerors' certifications in making award decisions.

(e) Whenever a contracting officer has reason to believe that forced or indentured child labor was used to mine, produce, or manufacture an end product furnished pursuant to a contract awarded subject to the certification required in paragraph (c) of this section, the contracting officer must refer the matter for investigation by the agency's Inspector General, the Attorney General, or the Secretary of the Treasury, whichever is determined appropriate in accordance with agency procedures, except to the extent that the end product is from the country listed in paragraph (b) of this section, under a contract exceeding the applicable threshold.

(f) Proper certification will not prevent the head of an agency from imposing remedies in accordance with section 22.1504(a)(4) if it is later discovered that the contractor has furnished an end product or component that has in fact been mined, produced, or manufactured, wholly or in part, using forced or indentured child labor.

[FAC 97-23, 66 FR 5345, 1/18/2001, effective 2/20/2001; FAC 2001-02, 66 FR 65347, 12/18/2001, effective 12/18/2001; FAC 2001-09, 67 FR 56115, 8/30/2002, effective 9/30/2002; FAC 2001-19, 69 FR 1051, 1/7/2004, effective 1/1/2004; FAC 2001-24, 69 FR 34239, 6/18/2004, effective 6/18/23004; FAC 2001-25, 69 FR 59700, 10/5/2004, effective 10/5/2004; FAC 2001-27, interim rule, 69 FR 77870, 12/28/2004, effective 1/1/2005; FAC 2005-07, 71 FR 219, 1/3/2006, effective 1/3/2006; FAC 2005-08, 71 FR 864, 1/5/2006, effective 1/5/2006; FAC 2005-13, 71 FR 57375, 9/28/2006, effective 9/28/2006; FAC 2005-19, 72 FR 46357, 8/17/2007, effective 8/17/2007; FAC 2005-24, 73 FR 10962, 10964, 2/28/2008, effective 2/28/2008; FAC 2005-30, 74 FR 2745, 1/15/2009, effective 2/17/2009; FAC 2005-36, 74 FR 40461, 8/11/2009, effective 8/11/2009; FAC 2005-42, 75 FR 34282, 6/16/2010, effective 6/16/2010; FAC 2005-43, 75 FR 38689, 7/2/2010, effective 7/2/2010; FAC 2005-50, 76 FR 14570, 3/16/2011, effective 3/16/2011; FAC 2005-56, 77 FR 12933, 12935, 3/2/2012, effective 3/2/2012; FAC 2005-71, 78 FR 70480, 11/25/2013, effective 11/25/2013; FAC 2005-72, 78 FR 80379, 12/31/2013, effective 1/1/2014; FAC 2005-86, 80 FR 81892, 12/31/2015, effective 2/1/2016; FAC 2005-86, 80 FR 81894, 12/31/2015, effective 1/1/2016; FAC 2005-91, 81 FR 67774, 9/30/2016, effective 10/31/2016; FAC 2005-97, 83 FR 3396, 1/24/2018, effective 1/24/2018; FAC 2019-06, 84 FR 47866, 9/10/2019, effective 10/10/2019]

22.1504 Violations and remedies.

(a) *Violations.* The Government may impose remedies set forth in paragraph (b) of this section for the following violations (note that the violations in paragraphs (a)(3) and (a)(4) of this section go beyond violations of the requirements relating to certification of end products) (see 22.1503):

(1) The contractor has submitted a false certification regarding knowledge of the use of forced or indentured child labor.

(2) The contractor has failed to cooperate as required in accordance with the clause at 52.222-19, Child Labor Cooperation with Authorities and Remedies, with an investigation of the use of forced or indentured child labor by an Inspector General, the Attorney General, or the Secretary of the Treasury.

(3) The contractor uses forced or indentured child labor in its mining, production, or manufacturing processes.

(4) The contractor has furnished an end product or component mined, produced, or manufactured, wholly or in part, by forced or indentured child labor. Remedies in paragraphs (b)(2) and (b)(3) of this section are inappropriate unless the contractor knew of the violation.

(b) *Remedies.*

(1) The contracting officer may terminate the contract.

(2) The suspending official may suspend the contractor in accordance with the procedures in subpart 9.4.

(3) The debarring official may debar the contractor for a period not to exceed 3 years in accordance with the procedures in subpart 9.4.

[FAC 97-23, 66 FR 5345, 1/18/2001, effective 2/20/2001]

22.1505 Solicitation provision and contract clause.

(a) Except as provided in paragraph (b) of 22.1503, insert the provision at 52.222-18, Certification Regarding Knowledge of Child Labor for Listed End Products, in all solicitations that are expected to exceed the micro-purchase threshold and are for the acquisition of end products (regardless of country of origin) of a type identified by country of origin on the List of Products Requiring Contractor Certification as to Forced or Indentured Child Labor, except solicitations for commercial items that include the provision at 52.212-3, Offeror Representations and Certifications—Commercial Items. The contracting officer must identify in paragraph (b) of the provision at 52.222-18, Certification Regarding Knowledge of Child Labor for Listed End Products, or paragraph (i)(1) of the provision at 52.212-3, any applicable end products and countries of origin from the List. For solicitations estimated to equal or exceed $25,000, the contracting officer must exclude from the List in the solicitation end products from any countries identified at 22.1503(b), in accordance with the specified thresholds.

(b) Insert the clause at 52.222-19, Child Labor—Cooperation with Authorities and Remedies, in all solicitations and contracts for the acquisition of supplies that are expected to exceed the micro-purchase threshold.

[FAC 97-23, 66 FR 5345, 1/18/2001, effective 2/20/2001]

SUBPART 22.16—NOTIFICATION OF EMPLOYEE RIGHTS UNDER THE NATIONAL LABOR RELATIONS ACT

22.1600 Scope of subpart.

This subpart prescribes policies and procedures to implement Executive Order 13496, dated January 30, 2009 (74 FR 6107, February 4, 2009).

[FAC 2001-26, 69 FR 76351, 12/20/2004, effective 12/20/2004; FAC 2005-04, 70 FR 33655, 6/8/2005, effective 6/8/2005; FAC 2005-38, 74 FR 65599, 12/10/2009, effective 12/10/2009; FAC 2005-47, 75 FR 77723, 12/13/2010, effective 12/13/2010; FAC 2005-54, 76 FR 68015, 11/2/2011, effective 11/2/2011]

22.1601 Definitions.

As used in this subpart—

Secretary means the Secretary of Labor, U.S. Department of Labor.

United States means the 50 States, the District of Columbia, Puerto Rico, the Commonwealth of the Northern Mariana Islands, American Samoa, Guam, the U.S. Virgin Islands, and Wake Island.

[FAC 2001-26, 69 FR 76351, 12/20/2004, effective 12/20/2004; FAC 2005-04, 70 FR 33655, 6/8/2005, effective 6/8/2005; FAC 2005-38, 74 FR 65599, 12/10/2009, effective 12/10/2009; FAC 2005-47, 75 FR 77723, 12/13/2010, effective 12/13/2010; FAC 2005-54, 76 FR 68015, 11/2/2011, effective 11/2/2011]

22.1602 Policy.

(a) Executive Order 13496 requires contractors to post a notice informing employees of their rights under Federal labor laws.

(b) The Secretary has determined that the notice must contain employee rights under the National Labor Relations Act (Act), 29 U.S.C. 151 *et seq.* The Act encourages collective bargaining, and protects the exercise by employees of their freedom to associate, to self-organize, and to designate representatives of their own choosing for the purpose of negotiating the terms and conditions of their employment or other mutual aid or protection.

[FAC 2001-26, 69 FR 76351, 12/20/2004, effective 12/20/2004; FAC 2005-04, 70 FR 33655, 6/8/2005, effective 6/8/2005; FAC 2005-38, 74 FR 65599, 12/10/2009, effective 12/10/2009; FAC 2005-47, 75 FR 77723, 12/13/2010, effective 12/13/2010; FAC 2005-54, 76 FR 68015, 11/2/2011, effective 11/2/2011]

22.1603 Exceptions.

(a) The requirements of this subpart do not apply to—

(1) Contracts under the simplified acquisition threshold;

(2) Subcontracts of $10,000 or less; and

(3) Contracts or subcontracts for work performed exclusively outside the United States.

(b) *Exemptions granted by the Secretary.* (1) If the Secretary finds that the requirements of the Executive Order impair the ability of the Government to procure goods and services on an economical and efficient basis or if special circumstances require an exemption in order to serve the national interest, the Secretary may exempt a contracting department or agency, or groups of departments or agencies, from the requirements of any or all of the provisions of this Executive Order with respect to a particular contract or subcontract, or any class of contracts or subcontracts, including the requirement to include the clause at 52.222-40, or parts of that clause, in contracts.

(2) Requests for exemptions may be submitted in accordance with Department of Labor regulations at 29 CFR 471.3.

[FAC 2001-26, 69 FR 76351, 12/20/2004, effective 12/20/2004; FAC 2005-04, 70 FR 33655, 6/8/2005, effective 6/8/2005; FAC 2005-38, 74 FR 65599, 12/10/2009, effective 12/10/2009; FAC 2005-47, 75 FR 77723, 12/13/2010, effective 12/13/2010; FAC 2005-54, 76 FR 68015, 11/2/2011, effective 11/2/2011]

22.1604 Compliance evaluation and complaint investigations and sanctions for violations.

(a) The Secretary may conduct compliance evaluations or investigate complaints of any contractor or subcontractor to determine if any of the requirements of the clause at 52.222-40 have been violated.

(b) Contracting departments and agencies shall cooperate with the Secretary and provide such information and assistance as the Secretary may require in the performance of the Secretary's functions.

(c) If the Secretary determines that there has been a violation, the Secretary may take such actions as set forth in 29 CFR 471.14.

(d) The Secretary may not terminate or suspend a contract or suspend or debar a contractor if the agency head has provided written objections, which must include a statement of reasons for the objection and a finding that the contractor's performance is essential to the agency's mission, and continues to object to the imposition of such sanctions and penalties. Procedures for enforcement by the Secretary are set out in 29 CFR 471.10 through 29 CFR 471.16.

[FAC 2001-26, 69 FR 76351, 12/20/2004, effective 12/20/2004; FAC 2005-04, 70 FR 33655, 6/8/2005, effective 6/8/2005; FAC 2005-38, 74 FR 65599, 12/10/2009, effective 12/10/2009; FAC 2005-47, 75 FR 77723, 12/13/2010, effective 12/13/2010; FAC 2005-54, 76 FR 68015, 11/2/2011, effective 11/2/2011]

22.1605 Contract clause.

(a) Insert the clause at 52.222-40, Notification of Employee Rights under the National Labor Relations Act, in all solicitations and contracts, including acquisitions for commercial items and commercially available off-the-shelf items, except acquisitions—

(1) *Under the simplified acquisition threshold.* For indefinite-quantity contracts, include the clause only if the value of orders in any calendar year of the contract is expected to exceed the simplified acquisition threshold;

(2) For work performed exclusively outside the United States; or

(3) Covered (in their entirety) by an exemption granted by the Secretary.

(b) A contracting agency may modify the clause at 52.222-40, if necessary, to reflect an exemption granted by the Secretary (*see* 22.1603(b)).

[FAC 2001-26, 69 FR 76351, 12/20/2004, effective 12/20/2004; FAC 2005-04, 70 FR 33655, 6/8/2005, effective 6/8/2005; FAC 2005-38, 74 FR 65599, 12/10/2009, effective 12/10/2009; FAC 2005-47, 75 FR 77723, 12/13/2010, effective 12/13/2010; FAC 2005-54, 76 FR 68015, 11/2/2011, effective 11/2/2011]

SUBPART 22.17—COMBATING TRAFFICKING IN PERSONS

22.1700 Scope of subpart.

This subpart prescribes policy for implementing 22 U.S.C. chapter 78 and Executive Order 13627, Strengthening Protections Against Trafficking in Persons in Federal Contracts, dated September 25, 2012.

[FAC 2005-09, 71 FR 20301, 4/19/2006, effective 4/19/2006; FAC 2005-19, 72 FR 46335, 8/17/2007, effective 8/17/2007; FAC 2005-30, 74 FR 2741, 1/15/2009, effective 2/17/2009; FAC 2005-80, 80 FR 4967, 1/29/2015, effective 3/2/2015]

22.1701 Applicability.

(a) This subpart applies to all acquisitions.

(b) The requirement at 22.1703(c) for a certification and compliance plan applies only to any portion of a contract or subcontract that—

(1) Is for supplies, other than commercially available off-the-shelf (COTS) items, to be acquired outside the United States, or

services to be performed outside the United States; and

(2) Has an estimated value that exceeds $500,000.

[FAC 2005-09, Interim rule, 71 FR 20301, 4/19/2006, effective 4/19/2006; FAC 2005-19, 72 FR 46335, 8/17/2007, effective 8/17/2007; FAC 2005-30, 74 FR 2741, 1/15/2009, effective 2/17/2009; FAC 2005-80, 80 FR 4967, 1/29/2015, effective 3/2/2015]

22.1702 Definitions.

As used in this subpart—

Agent means any individual, including a director, an officer, an employee, or an independent contractor, authorized to act on behalf of the organization.

Coercion means—

(1) Threats of serious harm to or physical restraint against any person;

(2) Any scheme, plan, or pattern intended to cause a person to believe that failure to perform an act would result in serious harm to or physical restraint against any person; or

(3) The abuse or threatened abuse of the legal process.

Commercial sex act means any sex act on account of which anything of value is given to or received by any person.

Debt bondage means the status or condition of a debtor arising from a pledge by the debtor of his or her personal services or of those of a person under his or her control as a security for debt, if the value of those services as reasonably assessed is not applied toward the liquidation of the debt or the length and nature of those services are not respectively limited and defined.

Employee means an employee of the Contractor directly engaged in the performance of work under the contract who has other than a minimal impact or involvement in contract performance.

Forced labor means knowingly providing or obtaining the labor or services of a person—

(1) By threats of serious harm to, or physical restraint against, that person or another person;

(2) By means of any scheme, plan, or pattern intended to cause the person to believe that, if the person did not perform such labor or services, that person or another person would suffer serious harm or physical restraint; or

(3) By means of the abuse or threatened abuse of law or the legal process.

Involuntary servitude includes a condition of servitude induced by means of—

(1) Any scheme, plan, or pattern intended to cause a person to believe that, if the person did not enter into or continue in such conditions, that person or another person would suffer serious harm or physical restraint; or

(2) The abuse or threatened abuse of the legal process.

Recruitment fees means fees of any type, including charges, costs, assessments, or other financial obligations, that are associated with the recruiting process, regardless of the time, manner, or location of imposition or collection of the fee.

(1) Recruitment fees include, but are not limited to, the following fees (when they are associated with the recruiting process) for—

(i) Soliciting, identifying, considering, interviewing, referring, retaining, transferring, selecting, training, providing orientation to, skills testing, recommending, or placing employees or potential employees;

(ii) Advertising;

(iii) Obtaining permanent or temporary labor certification, including any associated fees;

(iv) Processing applications and petitions;

(v) Acquiring visas, including any associated fees;

(vi) Acquiring photographs and identity or immigration documents, such as passports, including any associated fees;

(vii) Accessing the job opportunity, including required medical examinations and immunizations; background, reference, and security clearance checks and examinations; and additional certifications;

(viii) An employer's recruiters, agents or attorneys, or other notary or legal fees;

(ix) Language interpretation or translation, arranging for or accompanying on travel, or providing other advice to employees or potential employees;

(x) Government-mandated fees, such as border crossing fees, levies, or worker welfare funds;

(xi) Transportation and subsistence costs—

(A) While in transit, including, but not limited to, airfare or costs of other modes of transportation, terminal fees, and travel taxes associated with travel from the country of origin to the country of performance and the return journey upon the end of employment; and

(B) From the airport or disembarkation point to the worksite;

(xii) Security deposits, bonds, and insurance; and

(xiii) Equipment charges.

(2) A recruitment fee, as described in the introductory text of this definition, is a recruitment fee, regardless of whether the payment is—

(i) Paid in property or money;

(ii) Deducted from wages;

(iii) Paid back in wage or benefit concessions;

(iv) Paid back as a kickback, bribe, in-kind payment, free labor, tip, or tribute; or

(v) Collected by an employer or a third party, whether licensed or unlicensed, including, but not limited to—

(A) Agents;

(B) Labor brokers;

(C) Recruiters;

(D) Staffing firms (including private employment and placement firms);

(E) Subsidiaries/affiliates of the employer;

(F) Any agent or employee of such entities; and

(G) Subcontractors at all tiers.

Severe forms of trafficking in persons means—

(1) Sex trafficking in which a commercial sex act is induced by force, fraud, or coercion, or in which the person induced to perform such act has not attained 18 years of age; or

(2) The recruitment, harboring, transportation, provision, or obtaining of a person for labor or services, through the use of force, fraud, or coercion for the purpose of subjection to involuntary servitude, peonage, debt bondage, or slavery.

Sex trafficking means the recruitment, harboring, transportation, provision, or obtaining of a person for the purpose of a commercial sex act.

Subcontract means any contract entered into by a subcontractor to furnish supplies or services for performance of a prime contract or a subcontract.

Subcontractor means any supplier, distributor, vendor, or firm that furnishes supplies or services to or for a prime contractor or another subcontractor.

United States means the 50 States, the District of Columbia, and outlying areas.

[FAC 2005-09, Interim rule, 71 FR 20301, 4/19/2006, effective 4/19/2006; FAC 2005-19, 72 FR 46335, 8/17/2007, effective 8/17/2007; FAC 2005-30, 74 FR 2741, 1/15/2009, effective 2/17/2009; FAC 2005-80, 80 FR 4967, 1/29/2015, effective 3/2/2015; FAC 2019-01, 83 FR 65466, 12/20/2018, effective 1/22/2019]

22.1703 Policy.

The United States Government has adopted a policy prohibiting trafficking in persons, including the trafficking-related activities below. Additional information about trafficking in persons may be found at the Web site for the Department of State's Office to Monitor and Combat Trafficking in Persons at *http://www.state.gov/j/tip /*. Government solicitations and contracts shall—

(a) Prohibit contractors, contractor employees, subcontractors, subcontractor employees, and their agents from—

(1) Engaging in severe forms of trafficking in persons during the period of performance of the contract;

(2) Procuring commercial sex acts during the period of performance of the contract;

(3) Using forced labor in the performance of the contract;

(4) Destroying, concealing, confiscating, or otherwise denying access by an employee to the employee's identity or immigration documents, such as passports or drivers' licenses, regardless of issuing authority;

(5) (i) Using misleading or fraudulent practices during the recruitment of employees or offering of employment, such as failing to disclose, in a format and language understood by the employee or potential employee, basic information or making material misrepresentations during the recruitment of employees regarding the key terms and conditions of employment, including wages and fringe benefits, the location of work, the living conditions, housing and associated costs (if employer or agent provided or arranged), any significant costs to be charged to the employee or potential employee, and, if applicable, the hazardous nature of the work;

(ii) Using recruiters that do not comply with local labor laws of the country in which the recruiting takes place;

(6) Charging employees or potential employees recruitment fees;

(7) (i) (A) Failing to provide return transportation or pay for the cost of return transportation upon the end of employment, for an employee who is not a national of the country in which the work is taking place and who was brought into that country for the purpose of working on a U.S. Government contract or subcontract, for portions of contracts and subcontracts performed outside the United States; or

(B) Failing to provide return transportation or pay for the cost of return transportation upon the end of employment, for an employee who is not a United States national and who was brought into the United States for the purpose of working on a U.S. Government contract or subcontract, if the payment of such costs is required under existing temporary worker programs or pursuant to a written agreement with the employee for portions of contracts and subcontracts performed inside the United States; except that—

(ii) The requirements of paragraph (a) (7) (i) of this section do not apply to an employee who is—

(A) Legally permitted to remain in the country of employment and who chooses to do so; or

(B) Exempted by an authorized official of the contracting agency, designated by the agency head in accordance with agency procedures, from the requirement to provide return transportation or pay for the cost of return transportation;

(iii) The requirements of paragraph (a) (7) (i) of this section are modified for a victim of trafficking in persons who is seeking victim services or legal redress in the country of employment, or for a witness in an enforcement action related to trafficking in persons. The contractor shall provide the return transportation or pay the cost of return transportation in a way that does not obstruct the victim services, legal redress, or witness activity. For example, the contractor shall also offer return transportation to a witness at a time that supports the witness' need to testify. This paragraph does not apply when the exemptions at paragraph (a) (7) (ii) of this section apply.

(8) Providing or arranging housing that fails to meet the host country housing and safety standards; or

(9) If required by law or contract, failing to provide an employment contract, recruitment agreement, or other required work document in writing. Such written document shall be in a language the employee understands. If the employee must relocate to perform the work, the work document shall be provided to the employee at least five days prior to the employee relocating. The employee's work document shall include, but is not limited to, details about work description, wages, prohibition on charging recruitment fees, work location(s), living accommodations and associated costs, time off, round trip transportation arrangements,

grievance process, and the content of applicable laws and regulations that prohibit trafficking in persons. The contracting officer shall consider the risk that the contract or subcontract will involve services or supplies susceptible to trafficking in persons, and the number of non-U.S. citizens expected to be employed, when deciding whether to require work documents in the contract;

(b) Require contractors and subcontractors to notify employees of the prohibited activities described in paragraph (a) of this section and the actions that may be taken against them for violations;

(c) With regard to certification and a compliance plan—

(1) (i) Require the apparent successful offeror to provide, before contract award, a certification (see 52.222-56) that the offeror has a compliance plan if any portion of the contract or subcontract—

(A) Is for supplies, other than COTS items (see 2.101), to be acquired outside the United States, or services to be performed outside the United States; and

(B) The estimated value exceeds $500,000.

(ii) The certification must state that—

(A) The offeror has implemented the plan and has implemented procedures to prevent any prohibited activities and to monitor, detect, and terminate the contract with a subcontractor or agent engaging in prohibited activities; and

(B) After having conducted due diligence, either—

(*1*) To the best of the offeror's knowledge and belief, neither it nor any of its agents, proposed subcontractors, or their agents, has engaged in any such activities; or

(*2*) If abuses relating to any of the prohibited activities identified in 52.222-50(b) have been found, the offeror or proposed subcontractor has taken the appropriate remedial and referral actions;

(2) Require annual certifications (see 52.222-50(h)(5)) during performance of the contract, when a compliance plan was required at award;

(3) (i) Require the contractor to obtain a certification from each subcontractor, prior to award of a subcontract, if any portion of the subcontract—

(A) Is for supplies, other than COTS items (see 2.101), to be acquired outside the United States, or services to be performed outside the United States; and

(B) The estimated value exceeds $500,000.

(ii) The certification must state that—

(A) The subcontractor has implemented a compliance plan; and

(B) After having conducted due diligence, either—

(*1*) To the best of the subcontractor's knowledge and belief, neither it nor any of its agents, subcontractors, or their agents, has engaged in any such activities; or

(*2*) If abuses relating to any of the prohibited activities identified in 52.222-50(b) have been found, the subcontractor has taken the appropriate remedial and referral actions;

(4) Require the contractor to obtain annual certifications from subcontractors during performance of the contract, when a compliance plan was required at the time of subcontract award; and

(5) Require that any compliance plan or procedures shall be appropriate to the size and complexity of the contract and the nature and scope of its activities, including the number of non-U.S. citizens expected to be employed and the risk that the contract or subcontract will involve services or supplies susceptible to trafficking in persons. The minimum elements of the plan are specified at 52.222-50(h);

(d) Require the contractor and subcontractors to—

(1) Disclose to the contracting officer and the agency Inspector General information sufficient to identify the nature and extent of an offense and the individuals responsible for the conduct;

(2) Provide timely and complete responses to Government auditors' and investigators' requests for documents;

(3) Cooperate fully in providing reasonable access to their facilities and staff (both inside and outside the U.S.) to allow contracting agencies and other responsible Federal agencies to conduct audits, investigations, or other actions to ascertain compliance with the Trafficking Victims Protection Act (22 U.S.C. chapter 78), Executive Order 13627, or any other applicable law or regulation establishing restrictions on trafficking in persons, the procurement of commercial sex acts, or the use of forced labor; and

(4) Protect all employees suspected of being victims of or witnesses to prohibited activities, prior to returning to the country from which the employee was recruited, and shall not prevent or hinder the ability of these employees from cooperating fully with Government authorities; and

(e) Provide suitable remedies, including termination, to be imposed on contractors that fail to comply with the requirements of paragraphs (a) through (d) of this section.

[FAC 2005-09, Interim rule, 71 FR 20301, 4/19/2006, effective 4/19/2006; FAC 2005-19, 72 FR 46335, 8/17/2007, effective 8/17/2007; FAC 2005-30, 74 FR 2741, 1/15/2009, effective 2/17/2009; FAC 2005-80, 80 FR 4967, 1/29/2015, effective 3/2/2015; FAC 2019-01, 83 FR 65466, 12/20/2018, effective 1/22/2019]

22.1704 Violations and remedies.

(a) *Violations.* It is a violation of the Trafficking Victims Protection Act of 2000, as amended, (22 U.S.C. chapter 78), E.O. 13627, or the policies of this subpart if—

(1) The contractor, contractor employee, subcontractor, subcontractor employee, or agent engages in severe forms of trafficking in persons during the period of performance of the contract;

(2) The contractor, contractor employee, subcontractor, subcontractor employee, or agent procures a commercial sex act during the period of performance of the contract;

(3) The contractor, contractor employee, subcontractor, subcontractor employee, or agent uses forced labor in the performance of the contract; or

(4) The contractor fails to comply with the requirements of the clause at 52.222-50, Combating Trafficking in Persons.

(b) *Credible information.* Upon receipt of credible information regarding a violation listed in paragraph (a) of this section, the contracting officer—

(1) Shall promptly notify, in accordance with agency procedures, the agency Inspector General, the agency debarring and suspending official, and if appropriate, law enforcement officials with jurisdiction over the alleged offense; and

(2) May direct the contractor to take specific steps to abate the alleged violation or enforce the requirements of its compliance plan.

(c) *Receipt of agency Inspector General report.* (1) The head of an executive agency shall ensure that the contracting officer is provided a copy of the agency Inspector General report of an investigation of a violation of the trafficking in persons prohibitions in 22.1703(a) and 52.222-50(b).

(2)(i) Upon receipt of a report from the agency Inspector General that provides support for the allegations, the head of the executive agency, in accordance with agency procedures, shall delegate to an authorized agency official, such as the agency suspending or debarring official, the responsibility to—

(A) Expeditiously conduct an administrative proceeding, allowing the contractor the opportunity to respond to the report;

(B) Make a final determination as to whether the allegations are substantiated; and

(C) Notify the contracting officer of the determination.

(ii) Whether or not the official authorized to conduct the administrative proceeding is the suspending and debarring official, the suspending and debarring official has the authority, at any time before or after the final determination as to whether the allegations are substantiated, to use the suspension and debarment procedures in subpart 9.4 to suspend, propose for debarment, or debar the contractor, if appropriate, also considering the factors at 22.1704(d)(2).

(d) *Remedies.* After a final determination in accordance with paragraph (c)(2)(ii) of this section that the allegations of a trafficking in persons violation are substantiated, the contracting officer shall—

(1) Enter the violation in FAPIIS (see 42.1503(h)); and

(2) Consider taking any of the remedies specified in paragraph (e) of the clause at 52.222-50, Combating Trafficking in Persons. These remedies are in addition to any other remedies available to the United States Government. When determining the appropriate remedies, the contracting officer may consider the following factors:

(i) *Mitigating factors.* The contractor had a Trafficking in Persons compliance plan or awareness program at the time of the violation, was in compliance with the plan at the time of the violation, and has taken appropriate remedial actions for the violations, that may include reparation to victims for such violations.

(ii) *Aggravating factors.* The contractor failed to abate an alleged violation or enforce the requirements of a compliance plan, when directed by a contracting officer to do so.

[FAC 2005-09, Interim rule, 71 FR 20301, 4/19/2006, effective 4/19/2006; FAC 2005-19, 72 FR 46335, 8/17/2007, effective 8/17/2007; FAC 2005-30, 74 FR 2741, 1/15/2009, effective 2/17/2009; FAC 2005-80, 80 FR 4967, 1/29/2015, effective 3/2/2015]

22.1705 Solicitation provision and contract clause.

(a)(1) Insert the clause at 52.222-50, Combating Trafficking in Persons, in all solicitations and contracts.

(2) Use the clause with its Alternate I when the contract will be performed outside the United States (as defined at 22.1702) and the contracting officer has been notified of specific U.S. directives or notices regarding combating trafficking in persons (such as general orders or military listings of "off-limits" local establishments) that apply to contractor employees at the contract place of performance.

(b) Insert the provision at 52.222-56, Certification Regarding Trafficking in Persons Compliance Plan, in solicitations if—

(1) It is possible that at least $500,000 of the value of the contract may be performed outside the United States; and

(2) The acquisition is not entirely for commercially available off-the-shelf items.

[FAC 2005-09, Interim rule, 71 FR 20301, 04/19/2006, effective 4/19/2006; FAC 2005-19, 72 FR 46335, 8/17/2007, effective 8/17/2007; FAC 2005-30, 74 FR 2741, 1/15/2009, effective 2/17/2009; FAC 2005-80, 80 FR 4967, 1/29/2015, effective 3/2/2015]

SUBPART 22.18—EMPLOYMENT ELIGIBILITY VERIFICATION

22.1800 Scope.

This subpart prescribes policies and procedures requiring contractors to utilize the Department of Homeland Security (DHS), United States Citizenship and Immigration Service's employment eligibility verification program (E-Verify) as the means for verifying employment eligibility of certain employees.

[FAC 2005-29, 73 FR 67551, 11/14/2008, effective 1/15/2009; Amendment-1, FAC 2005-29, 74 FR 1937, 1/14/2009, effective 1/19/2009; Amendment-2, FAC 2005-29, 74 FR 5621, 1/30/2009, effective 5/21/2009; Amendment-3, FAC 2005-29, 74 FR 17793, 4/17/2009, effective 6/30/2009; Amendment-4, FAC 2005-29, 74 FR 26981, 6/5/2009, effective 9/8/2009]

22.1801 Definitions.

As used in this subpart—

Commercially available off-the-shelf (COTS) item—

(1) Means any item of supply that is—

(i) A commercial item (as defined in paragraph (1) of the definition at 2.101);

(ii) Sold in substantial quantities in the commercial marketplace; and

(iii) Offered to the Government, without modification, in the same form in which it is sold in the commercial marketplace; and

(2) Does not include bulk cargo, as defined in 46 U.S.C. 40102(4), such as agricultural products and petroleum products. Per 46 CFR 525.1 (c)(2), "bulk cargo" means cargo that is loaded and carried in bulk on board ship without mark or count, in a loose unpackaged form, having homogenous characteristics. Bulk cargo loaded into intermodal equipment, except LASH or Seabee barges, is subject to mark and count and, therefore, ceases to be bulk cargo.

Employee assigned to the contract means an employee who was hired after November 6, 1986 (after November 27, 2009, in the Commonwealth of the Northern Mariana Islands), who is directly performing work, in the United States, under a contract that is required to include the clause prescribed at 22.1803. An employee is not considered to be directly performing work under a contract if the employee—

(1) Normally performs support work, such as indirect or overhead functions; and

(2) Does not perform any substantial duties applicable to the contract.

Subcontract means any contract, as defined in 2.101, entered into by a subcontractor to furnish supplies or services for performance of a prime contract or a subcontract. It includes but is not limited to purchase orders, and changes and modifications to purchase orders.

Subcontractor means any supplier, distributor, vendor, or firm that furnishes supplies or services to or for a prime contractor or another subcontractor.

United States, as defined in 8 U.S.C. 1101(a)(38), means the 50 States, the District of Columbia, Puerto Rico, Guam, the Commonwealth of the Northern Mariana Islands and the U.S. Virgin Islands.

[FAC 2005-29, 73 FR 67551, 11/14/2008, effective 1/15/2009; Amendment-1, FAC 2005-29, 74 FR 1937, 1/14/2009, effective 1/19/2009; Amendment-2, FAC 2005-29, 74 FR 5621, 1/30/2009, effective 5/21/2009; Amendment-3, FAC 2005-29, 74 FR 17793, 4/17/2009, effective 6/30/2009; Amendment-4, FAC 2005-29, 74 FR 26981, 6/5/2009, effective 9/8/2009; FAC 2005-60, 77 FR 44065, 7/26/2012, effective 7/26/2012; FAC 2005-69, 78 FR 46795, 8/1/2013, effective 8/1/2013]

22.1802 Policy.

(a) Statutes and Executive orders require employers to abide by the immigration laws of the United States and to employ in the United States only individuals who are eligible to work in the United States. The E-Verify program provides an Internet-based means of verifying employment eligibility of workers employed in the United States, but is not a substitute for any other employment eligibility verification requirements.

(b) Contracting officers shall include in solicitations and contracts, as prescribed at 22.1803, requirements that Federal contractors must—

(1) Enroll as Federal contractors in E-Verify;

(2) Use E-Verify to verify employment eligibility of all new hires working in the United States, except that the contractor may choose to verify only new hires assigned to the contract if the contractor is—

(i) An institution of higher education (as defined at 20 U.S.C. 1001(a));

(ii) A State or local government or the government of a Federally recognized Indian tribe; or

(iii) A surety performing under a takeover agreement entered into with a Federal agency pursuant to a performance bond;

(3) Use E-Verify to verify employment eligibility of all employees assigned to the contract; and

(4) Include these requirements, as required by the clause at 52.222-54, in subcontracts for—

(i) Commercial or noncommercial services, except for commercial services that are part of the purchase of a COTS item (or an item that would be a COTS item, but for minor modifications), performed by the COTS provider, and are normally provided for that COTS item; and

(ii) Construction.

(c) Contractors may elect to verify employment eligibility of all existing employees working in the United States who were hired after November 6, 1986 (after November 27, 2009, in the Commonwealth of the Northern Mariana Islands), instead of just those employees assigned to the contract. The contractor is not required to verify employment eligibility of—

(1) Employees who hold an active security clearance of confidential, secret, or top secret; or

(2) Employees for whom background investigations have been completed and credentials issued pursuant to Homeland Security Presidential Directive (HSPD)-12.

(d) In exceptional cases, the head of the contracting activity may waive the E-Verify requirement for a contract or subcontract or a class of contracts or subcontracts, either temporarily or for the period of performance. This waiver authority may not be delegated.

(e) DHS and the Social Security Administration (SSA) may terminate a contractor's MOU and deny access to the E-Verify system in accordance with the terms of the MOU. If DHS or SSA terminates a contractor's MOU, the terminating agency must refer the contractor to a suspension or debarment official for possible suspension or debarment action. During the period between termination of the MOU and a decision by the suspension or debarment official whether to suspend or debar, the contractor is excused from its obligations under paragraph (b) of the clause at 52.222-54. If the contractor is suspended or debarred as a result of the MOU termination, the contractor is not eligible to participate in E-Verify during the period of its suspension or debarment. If the suspension or debarment official determines not to suspend or debar the contractor, then the contractor must reenroll in E-Verify.

[FAC 2005-29, 73 FR 67551, 11/14/2008, effective 1/15/2009; Amendment-1, FAC 2005-29, 74 FR 1937, 1/14/2009, effective 1/19/2009; Amendment-2, FAC 2005-29, 74 FR 5621, 1/30/2009, effective 5/21/2009; Amendment-3, FAC 2005-29, 74 FR 17793, 4/17/2009, effective 6/30/2009; Amendment-4, FAC 2005-29, 74 FR 26981, 6/5/2009, effective 9/8/2009; FAC 2005-60, 77 FR 44065, 7/26/2012, effective 7/26/2012]

22.1803 Contract clause.

Insert the clause at 52.222-54, Employment Eligibility Verification, in all solicitations and contracts that exceed the simplified acquisition threshold, except those that—

(a) Are only for work that will be performed outside the United States;

(b) Are for a period of performance of less than 120 days; or

(c) Are only for—

(1) Commercially available off-the-shelf items;

(2) Items that would be COTS items, but for minor modifications (as defined at paragraph (3) (ii) of the definition of "commercial item" at 2.101);

(3) Items that would be COTS items if they were not bulk cargo; or

(4) Commercial services that are—

(i) Part of the purchase of a COTS item (or an item that would be a COTS item, but for minor modifications);

(ii) Performed by the COTS provider; and

(iii) Are normally provided for that COTS item.

[FAC 2005-29, 73 FR 67551, 11/14/2008, effective 1/15/2009; Amendment-1, FAC 2005-29, 74 FR 1937, 1/14/2009, effective 1/19/2009; Amendment-2, FAC 2005-29, 74 FR 5621, 1/30/2009, effective 5/21/2009; Amendment-3, FAC 2005-29, 74 FR 17793, 4/17/2009, effective 6/30/2009; Amendment-4, FAC 2005-29, 74 FR 26981, 6/5/2009, effective 9/8/2009]

SUBPART 22.19—ESTABLISHING A MINIMUM WAGE FOR CONTRACTORS

22.1900 Scope of subpart.

This subpart prescribes policies and procedures to implement Executive Order (E.O.) 13658, Establishing a Minimum Wage for Contractors, dated February 12, 2014, and Department of Labor (DOL) implementing regulations at 29 CFR part 10.

[FAC 2005-79, 79 FR 74544, 12/15/2014, effective 12/15/2014; FAC 2005-85, 80 FR 75915, 12/4/2015, effective 12/4/2015]

22.1901 Definitions.

Worker, as used in this subpart, (in accordance with 29 CFR 10.2)–

(1) Means any person engaged in performing work on, or in connection with, a contract covered by Executive Order 13658, and

(i) Whose wages under such contract are governed by the Fair Labor Standards Act (29 U.S.C. chapter 8), the Service Contract Labor Standards statute (41 U.S.C. chapter 67), or the Wage Rate Requirements (Construction) statute (40 U.S.C. chapter 31, subchapter IV),

(ii) Other than individuals employed in a bona fide executive, administrative, or professional capacity, as those terms are defined in 29 CFR part 541,

(iii) Regardless of the contractual relationship alleged to exist between the individual and the employer.

(2) Includes workers performing on, or in connection with, the contract whose wages are calculated pursuant to special certificates issued under 29 U.S.C. 214(c).

(3) Also includes any person working on, or in connection with, the contract and individually registered in a bona fide apprenticeship or training program registered with the Department of Labor's Employment and Training Administration, Office of Apprenticeship, or with a State Apprenticeship Agency recognized by the Office of Apprenticeship.

[FAC 2005-79, 79 FR 74544, 12/15/2014, effective 12/15/2014; FAC 2005-85, 80 FR 75915, 12/4/2015, effective 12/4/2015]

22.1902 Policy.

(a) Pursuant to Executive Order 13658, the minimum hourly wage rate required to be paid to workers performing on, or in connection with, contracts and subcontracts subject to this subpart is at least $10.10 per hour beginning January 1, 2015, and beginning January 1, 2016, and annually thereafter, an amount determined by the Secretary of Labor. The Administrator of the Wage and Hour Division (the Administrator) will notify the public of the new E.O. minimum wage rate at least 90 days before it is to take effect. (See 22.1904.)

(b) *Relationship with other wage rates.* (1) Nothing in this subpart shall excuse noncompliance with any applicable Federal or State prevailing wage law or any applicable law or municipal ordinance establishing a minimum wage higher than the E.O. minimum wage. However, wage increases under such other laws or municipal ordinances are not subject to price adjustment under this subpart.

(2) The E.O. minimum wage rate applies whenever it is higher than any applicable collective bargaining agreement(s) wage rate.

(c) *Application to tipped workers.* Policies and procedures in DOL regulations at 29 CFR 10.24(b) and 10.28 address the relationship between the E.O. minimum wage and wages of workers engaged in an occupation in which they customarily and regularly receive more than $30 a month in tips.

[FAC 2005-79, 79 FR 74544, 12/15/2014, effective 12/15/2014; FAC 2005-85, 80 FR 75915, 12/4/2015, effective 12/4/2015]

22.1903 Applicability.

(a) This subpart applies to contracts covered by the Service Contract Labor Standards statute (41 U.S.C. chapter 67, formerly known as the Service Contract Act, subpart 22.10), or the Wage Rate Requirements (Construction) statute (40 U.S.C. chapter 31, Subchapter IV, formerly known as the Davis Bacon Act, subpart 22.4), that require performance in whole or in part within the United States (the 50 states and the District of Columbia). When performance is in part within and in part outside the United States, this subpart applies to the part of the contract that is performed within the United States.

(b)(1) This subpart applies to workers as defined at 22.1901. As provided in that definition—

(i) Workers are covered regardless of the contractual relationship alleged to exist between the contractor or subcontractor and the worker;

(ii) Workers with disabilities whose wages are calculated pursuant to special certificates issued under 29 U.S.C. 214(c) are covered; and

(iii) Workers who are registered in a bona fide apprenticeship program or training program registered with the Department of Labor's Employment and Training Administration, Office of Apprenticeship, or with a State Apprenticeship Agency recognized by the Office of Apprenticeship, are covered.

(2) This subpart does not apply to—

(i) Fair Labor Standards Act (FLSA)-covered individuals performing in connection with contracts covered by the E.O., *i.e.*, those individuals who perform duties necessary to the performance of the contract, but who are not directly engaged in performing the specific work called for by the contract, and who spend less than 20 percent of their hours worked in a particular workweek performing in connection with such contracts;

(ii) Individuals exempted from the minimum wage requirements of the FLSA under 29 U.S.C. 213(a) and 214(a) and (b), unless otherwise covered by the Service Contract Labor Standards statute or the Wage Rate Requirements (Construction) statute. These individuals include but are not limited to—

(A) Learners, apprentices, or messengers whose wages are calculated pursuant to special certificates issued under 29 U.S.C. 214(a);

(B) Students whose wages are calculated pursuant to special certificates issued under 29 U.S.C. 214(b); and

(C) Those employed in a bona fide executive, administrative, or professional capacity (29 U.S.C. 213(a)(1) and 29 CFR part 541).

(c) Agency Labor Advisors, as defined at 22.001, are listed at http://wdol.gov, and are available to provide guidance and assistance with the application of this subpart.

[FAC 2005-79, 79 FR 74544, 12/15/2014, effective 12/15/2014; FAC 2005-85, 80 FR 75915, 12/4/2015, effective 12/4/2015]

22.1904 Annual Executive Order Minimum Wage Rate.

(a) For the E.O. minimum wage rate that becomes effective on January 1, 2016, and annually thereafter, the Administrator will—

(1) Notify the public of the new E.O. minimum wage rate at least 90 days before it becomes effective by publishing a notice in the Federal Register;

(2) Publish and maintain on Wage Determinations OnLine (WDOL), *http://www.wdol.gov*, or any successor site, the E.O. minimum wage rate; and

(3) Include a general notice on wage determinations which are issued under the Service Contract Labor Standards statute or the Wage Rate Requirements (Construction) statute. The notice will provide information on the E.O. minimum wage and how to obtain annual updates.

(b) (1) The contractor may request a price adjustment only after the effective date of a new annual E.O. minimum wage determination published pursuant to paragraph (a). Prices will be adjusted only for increased labor costs (including subcontractor labor costs) as a result of the annual E.O. minimum wage, and for associated labor costs (including those for subcontractors). Associated labor costs shall include increases or decreases that result from changes in social security and unemployment taxes and workers' compensation insurance, but will not otherwise include any amount for general and administrative costs, overhead, or profit.

(2) The wage rate price adjustment under this clause is the lowest amount calculated by subtracting from the new E.O. wage rate the following: The current E.O. minimum wage rate; the current service or construction wage determination rate under the contract (if the wage rate is applicable to that worker); or the actual wage currently paid the worker. If the amount is zero or below, there will be no increase paid for this worker.

(i) Example 1—New E.O. wage rate is $11.10	
Previous E.O. wage rate is $10.70 .... The current service or construction wage determination rate applicable to this worker under the contract is $10.75. The actual wage currently paid to the worker is $10.80.	Analysis: The calculation is $11.10 - $10.80 = $.30. The price adjustment for this worker is $.30.

(ii) Example 2—New E.O. wage or rate is $10.50	
Previous E.O. wage rate is $10.10 .... The current service or construction wage determination rate applicable to this worker under the contract is $10.75. The actual wage currently paid to the worker is $10.80.	Analysis: The calculation is $10.50-$10.80 = –$.30. There is no price adjustment for this worker.

(3) The contracting officer shall not adjust the contract price for any costs other than those identified in paragraph (b)(1) of this section, and shall not provide duplicate price adjustments with any price adjustment under clauses implementing the Service Contract Labor Standards statute or the Wage Rate Requirements (Construction) statute.

[FAC 2005-79, 79 FR 74544, 12/15/2014, effective 12/15/2014; FAC 2005-85, 80 FR 75915, 12/4/2015, effective 12/4/2015; FAC 2005-87, 81 FR 11992, 3/7/2016, effective 3/7/2016]

22.1905 Enforcement of Executive Order Minimum Wage Requirements.

(a) *Authority*. (1) Section 5 of the E.O. grants the authority for investigating potential violations of, and obtaining compliance with, the E.O. to the Secretary of Labor. The Secretary of Labor, in promulgating the implementing regulations required by Section 4 of the E.O., has assigned this authority to the Administrator. Contracting agencies do not have authority to conduct compliance investigations under 29 CFR part 10 as implemented in this subpart. This does not limit the contracting officer's authority to otherwise enforce the terms and conditions of the contract.

(2) Contracting officers shall withhold payment at the direction of the Administrator.

(3) The contracting officer shall withhold payment, without a request from the Administrator, if the contractor fails to comply with the requirements in paragraph (e)(2) of 52.222-55, Minimum Wages Under Executive Order 13658 to furnish payroll records, until such time as the noncompliance is corrected.

(b) *Complaints*. (1) Complaints may be filed with the contracting officer or the Administrator by any person, entity, or organization that believes a violation of this subpart has occurred.

(2) The identity of any individual who makes a written or oral statement as a complaint or in the course of an investigation, as well as portions of the statement which would reveal the individual's identity, shall not be disclosed in any manner to anyone other than Federal officials without the prior consent of the individual, unless otherwise authorized by law.

(3) Upon receipt of a complaint, or if notified that the Administrator has received a complaint, the contracting officer shall report the following information, within 14 days, if available without conducting an investigation, to the Department of Labor, Wage and Hour Division, Office of Government Contracts, 200 Constitution Avenue N.W., Room S3006, Washington, D.C. 20210.

(i) The complaint or description of the alleged violation;

(ii) Available statements by the worker, contractor, or any other person regarding the alleged violation;

(iii) Evidence that clause 52.222-55, Minimum Wages Under Executive Order 13658, was included in the contract;

(iv) Information concerning known settlement negotiations between the parties, if applicable; and

(v) Any other relevant facts known to the contracting officer or other information requested by the Wage and Hour Division.

(c) *Investigations*. Complaints will be investigated by the Administrator, if warranted, in accordance with the procedures in 29 CFR part 10.43.

(d) *Remedies and sanctions*—(1) *Unpaid wages*. When the Administrator's investigation reveals that a contractor has failed to pay the applicable E.O. minimum wage, the Administrator will notify the contractor and the contracting agency of the unpaid wage violation, and request that the contractor remedy the violation. If the contractor does not remedy the violation, the Administrator may direct withholding of payments due on the contract or any other contract between the contractor and the Federal Government. Upon final decision and direction of the Administrator, the contracting agency shall transfer the withheld funds to the Department of Labor for disbursement in accordance with the procedures at 22.406-9(c).

(2) *Antiretaliation*. When a contractor has been found to have violated paragraph (i) of clause 52.222-55, Minimum Wages Under Executive Order 13658, the Administrator may provide for relief to the worker in accordance with 29 CFR 10.44.

(3) *Debarment*. (i) The Department of Labor may initiate debarment proceedings under 29 CFR 10.52 whenever a contractor is found to have disregarded its obligations under 29 CFR part 10.

(ii) Contracting officers shall consider notifying the agency suspending and debarring official in accordance with agency procedures when a contractor commits significant violations of contract terms and conditions related to this subpart.

(4) *Retroactive inclusion of contract clause*. If a contracting agency fails to include the contract clause in a contract to which the E.O. applies, the contracting agency, on its own initiative or within 15 calendar days of notification by an authorized representative of the Department of Labor, shall incorporate the contract clause in the contract retroactive to commencement of performance under the contract through the exercise of any and all authority that may be needed (including, where necessary, its authority to negotiate or amend, its authority to pay any necessary additional costs, and its authority under any contract provision authorizing changes, cancellation and termination).

[FAC 2005-79, 79 FR 74544, 12/15/2014, effective 12/15/2014; FAC 2005-85, 80 FR 75915, 12/4/2015, effective 12/4/2015]

22.1906 Contract clause.

Insert the clause at 52.222-55, Minimum Wages Under Executive Order 13658, in solicitations and contracts that include the clause at 52.222-6, Construction Wage Rate Requirements, or 52.222-41, Service Contract Labor Standards, where work is to be performed, in whole or in part, in the United States (the 50 States and the District of Columbia).

[FAC 2005-79, 79 FR 74544, 12/15/2014, effective 12/15/2014; FAC 2005-85, 80 FR 75915, 12/4/2015, effective 12/4/2015]

SUBPART 22.20—[REMOVED AND RESERVED]

22.2000 [Removed and Reserved]

[FAC 2005-90, 81 FR 58562, 8/25/2016, effective 10/25/2016; FAC 2005-93, 81 FR 91636, 12/16/2016, effective 12/16/2016; FAC 2005-96, 82 FR 51773, 11/8/2017, effective 11/6/2017]

22.2001 [Removed and Reserved]

[FAC 2005-90, 81 FR 58562, 8/25/2016, effective 10/25/2016; FAC 2005-96, 82 FR 51773, 11/8/2017, effective 11/6/2017]

22.2002 [Removed and Reserved]

[FAC 2005-90, 81 FR 58562, 8/25/2016, effective 10/25/2016; FAC 2005-93, 81 FR 91636, 12/16/2016, effective 12/16/2016;

FAC 2005-96, 82 FR 51773, 11/8/2017, effective 11/6/2017]

22.2003 [Removed and Reserved]

[FAC 2005-90, 81 FR 58562, 8/25/2016, effective 10/25/2016; FAC 2005-93, 81 FR 91636, 12/16/2016, effective 12/16/2016; FAC 2005-96, 82 FR 51773, 11/8/2017, effective 11/6/2017]

22.2004 [Removed and Reserved]

[FAC 2005-90, 81 FR 58562, 8/25/2016, effective 10/25/2016; FAC 2005-96, 82 FR 51773, 11/8/2017, effective 11/6/2017]

22.2004-1 [Removed and Reserved]

[FAC 2005-90, 81 FR 58562, 8/25/2016, effective 10/25/2016; FAC 2005-93, 81 FR 91636, 12/16/2016, effective 12/16/2016; FAC 2005-96, 82 FR 51773, 11/8/2017, effective 11/6/2017]

22.2004-2 [Removed and Reserved]

[FAC 2005-90, 81 FR 58562, 8/25/2016, effective 10/25/2016; FAC 2005-93, 81 FR 91636, 12/16/2016, effective 12/16/2016; FAC 2005-96, 82 FR 51773, 11/8/2017, effective 11/6/2017]

22.2004-3 [Removed and Reserved]

[FAC 2005-90, 81 FR 58562, 8/25/2016, effective 10/25/2016; FAC 2005-93, 81 FR 91636, 12/16/2016, effective 12/16/2016; FAC 2005-96, 82 FR 51773, 11/8/2017, effective 11/6/2017]

22.2004-4 [Removed and Reserved]

[FAC 2005-90, 81 FR 58562, 8/25/2016, effective 10/25/2016; FAC 2005-93, 81 FR 91636, 12/16/2016, effective 12/16/2016; FAC 2005-96, 82 FR 51773, 11/8/2017, effective 11/6/2017]

22.2005 [Removed and Reserved]

[FAC 2005-90, 81 FR 58562, 8/25/2016, effective 10/25/2016; FAC 2005-96, 82 FR 51773, 11/8/2017, effective 11/6/2017]

22.2006 [Removed and Reserved]

[FAC 2005-90, 81 FR 58562, 8/25/2016, effective 10/25/2016; FAC 2005-93, 81 FR 91636, 12/16/2016, effective 12/16/2016; FAC 2005-96, 82 FR 51773, 11/8/2017, effective 11/6/2017]

22.2007 [Removed and Reserved]

[FAC 2005-90, 81 FR 58562, 8/25/2016, effective 10/25/2016; FAC 2005-93, 81 FR 91636, 12/16/2016, effective 12/16/2016; FAC 2005-96, 82 FR 51773, 11/8/2017, effective 11/6/2017]

SUBPART 22.21—ESTABLISHING PAID SICK LEAVE FOR FEDERAL CONTRACTORS

22.2100 Scope of subpart.

This subpart prescribes policies and procedures to implement E.O. 13706, Establishing Paid Sick Leave for Federal Contractors, dated September 7, 2015, and Department of Labor implementing regulations at 29 CFR part 13.

[FAC 2005-93, 81 FR 91627, 12/16/2016, effective 1/1/2017; FAC 2005-100, 83 FR 42569, 8/22/2018, effective 8/22/2018]

22.2101 Definitions.

As used in this subpart (in accordance with 29 CFR 13.2)—

Accrual year means the 12-month period during which a contractor may limit an employee's accrual of paid sick leave to no less than 56 hours (see 29 CFR 13.5(b) (1)).

Certification issued by a health care provider has the meaning given in 29 CFR 13.2.

Employee—

(1) (i) Means any person engaged in performing work on or in connection with a contract covered by E.O. 13706; and

(A) Whose wages under such contract are governed by the Service Contract Labor Standards statute (41 U.S.C. chapter 67), the Wage Rate Requirements (Construction) statute (40 U.S.C. chapter 31, subchapter IV), or the Fair Labor Standards Act (29 U.S.C. chapter 8);

(B) Including employees who qualify for an exemption from the Fair Labor Standards Act's minimum wage and overtime provisions; and

(C) Regardless of the contractual relationship alleged to exist between the individual and the employer; and

(ii) Includes any person performing work on or in connection with the contract and individually registered in a bona fide apprenticeship or training program registered with the Department of Labor's Employment and Training Administration, Office of Apprenticeship, or with a State Apprenticeship Agency recognized by the Office of Apprenticeship.

(2) (i) An employee performs on a contract if the employee directly performs the specific services called for by the contract; and

(ii) An employee performs in connection with a contract if the employee's work activities are necessary to the performance of a contract but are not the specific services called for by the contract.

Health care provider has the meaning given in 29 CFR 13.2.

Multiemployer plan means a plan to which more than one employer is required to contribute and which is maintained pursuant to one or more collective bargaining agreements between one or more employee organizations and more than one employer.

Paid sick leave means compensated absence from employment that is required by E.O. 13706 and 29 CFR part 13.

[FAC 2005-93, 81 FR 91627, 12/16/2016, effective 1/1/2017; FAC 2005-100, 83 FR 42569, 8/22/2018, effective 8/22/2018]

22.2102 Policy.

(a) The Government shall require contractors to allow employees performing work on or in connection with a contract covered by E.O. 13706 to accrue and use paid sick leave in accordance with the E.O. and 29 CFR part 13.

(b) *Interaction with other laws.* Nothing in E.O. 13706 or 29 CFR part 13 shall excuse noncompliance with or supersede any applicable Federal or State law, any applicable law or municipal ordinance, or a collective bargaining agreement requiring greater paid sick leave or leave rights than those established under E.O. 13706 and 29 CFR part 13. For additional details regarding interaction with the Service Contract Labor Standards statute, the Wage Rate Requirements (Construction) statute, the Family and Medical Leave Act, and State and local paid sick time laws, see 29 CFR 13.5(f) (2) through (4).

(c) *Interaction with paid time off policies.* In accordance with 29 CFR 13.5(f) (5) (i), the paid sick leave requirements of E.O. 13706 and 29 CFR part 13 may be satisfied by a contractor's voluntary paid time off policy, whether provided pursuant to a collective bargaining agreement or otherwise, where the voluntary paid time off policy meets or exceeds the requirements. For additional details regarding paid time off policies, see 29 CFR 13.5(f) (5) (ii) and (iii).

(d) Unless otherwise provided in this subpart, compliance is the responsibility of the contractor, and enforcement is the responsibility of the Department of Labor.

[FAC 2005-93, 81 FR 91627, 12/16/2016, effective 1/1/2017; FAC 2005-100, 83 FR 42569, 8/22/2018, effective 8/22/2018]

22.2103 Applicability.

This subpart applies to—

(a) Contracts that—

(1) Are covered by the Service Contract Labor Standards statute (41 U.S.C. chapter 67, formerly known as the Service Contract Act, subpart 22.10), or the Wage Rate Requirements (Construction) statute (40 U.S.C. chapter 31, Subchapter IV, formerly known as the Davis-Bacon Act, subpart 22.4); and

(2) Require performance in whole or in part within the United States. When performance is in part within and in part outside the United States, this subpart applies to the part of the contract that is performed within the United States; and

(b) Employees performing on or in connection with such contracts whose wages are governed by the Service Contract Labor Standards statute, the Wage Rate Requirements (Construction) statute, or the Fair Labor Standards Act, including employees who qualify for an exemption from the Fair Labor Standards Act's minimum wage and overtime provisions.

[FAC 2005-93, 81 FR 91627, 12/16/2016, effective 1/1/2017; FAC 2005-100, 83 FR 42569, 8/22/2018, effective 8/22/2018]

22.2104 Exclusions.

The following are excluded from coverage under this subpart:

(a) Employees performing in connection with contracts covered by the E.O. for less than 20 percent of their work hours in a given workweek. This exclusion is inapplicable to employees performing on contracts covered by the E.O., *i.e.*, those employees directly engaged in performing the specific work called for by the contract, at any point during the workweek (see 29 CFR 13.4(e)).

(b) Until the earlier of the date the agreement terminates or January 1, 2020, employees whose covered work is governed by a collective bargaining agreement ratified before September 30, 2016, that—

(1) Already provides 56 hours (or 7 days, if the agreement refers to days rather than hours) of paid sick time (or paid time off that may be used for reasons related to sickness or health care) each year; or

(2) Provides less than 56 hours (or 7 days, if the agreement refers to days rather than hours) of paid sick time (or paid time off that may be used for reasons related to sickness or health care) each year, provided that each year the contractor provides covered employees with the difference between 56 hours (or 7 days) and the amount provided under the existing agreement in accordance with 29 CFR 13.4(f).

(c) The Government's unilateral exercise of a prenegotiated option to renew an existing contract that does not contain the clause at 52.222-62 will not automatically trigger the application of that clause. (See definition of "new contract" at 29 CFR 13.2).

[FAC 2005-93, 81 FR 91627, 12/16/2016, effective 1/1/2017; FAC 2005-100, 83 FR 42569, 8/22/2018, effective 8/22/2018]

22.2105 Paid sick leave for Federal contractors and subcontractors.

In accordance with 29 CFR 13.5, and by operation of the clause at 52.222-62, Paid Sick Leave Under Executive Order 13706, the following contractor requirements apply:

(a) *Accrual.* (1) Contractors are required to permit an employee to accrue not less than 1 hour of paid sick leave for every 30 hours worked on or in connection with a contract covered by the E.O. (see 29 CFR 13.5(a)(1)).

(2) Contractors are required to inform each employee, in writing, of the amount of paid sick leave the employee has accrued but not used no less than once each pay period or each month, whichever interval is shorter, as well as upon a separation from employment and upon reinstatement of paid sick leave, pursuant to 29 CFR 13.5(b)(4) (see 29 CFR 13.5(a)(2)).

(3) Contractors may choose to provide employees with at least 56 hours of paid sick leave at the beginning of each accrual year rather than allowing the employee to accrue such leave based on hours worked over time (see 29 CFR 13.5(a)(3)).

(b) *Maximum accrual, carryover, reinstatement, and payment for unused leave.* (1) Contractors may limit the amount of paid sick leave employees are permitted to accrue to not less than 56 hours in each accrual year (see 29 CFR 13.5(b)(1)).

(2) Paid sick leave shall carry over from one accrual year to the next. Paid sick leave carried over from the previous accrual year shall not count toward any limit the contractor sets on annual accrual (see 29 CFR 13.5(b)(2)).

(3) Contractors may limit the amount of paid sick leave an employee is permitted to have available for use at any point to not less than 56 hours (see 29 CFR 13.5(b)(3)).

(4) Contractors are required to reinstate paid sick leave for employees only when rehired by the same contractor within 12 months after a job separation (see 29 CFR 13.5(b)(4)).

(5) Nothing in E.O. 13706 or 29 CFR part 13 requires contractors to make a financial payment to an employee for accrued paid sick leave that has not been used upon a separation from employment. If a contractor nevertheless makes such a payment in an amount equal to or greater than the value of the pay and benefits the employee would have received pursuant to 29 CFR 13.5(c)(3) had the employee used the paid sick leave, the contractor is relieved of the obligation to reinstate an employee's accrued paid sick leave upon rehiring the employee within 12 months of the separation pursuant to 29 CFR 13.5(b)(4) (see 29 CFR 13.5(b)(5)).

(c) *Use.* Contractors are required to permit an employee to use paid sick leave in accordance with 29 CFR 13.5(c).

(d) *Request for paid sick leave.* Contractors are required to permit an employee to use any or all of the employee's available paid sick leave upon the oral or written request of an employee that includes information sufficient to inform the contractor that the employee is seeking to be absent from work for a purpose described in 29 CFR 13.5(c) and, to the extent reasonably feasible, the anticipated duration of the leave (see 29 CFR 13.5(d)).

(e) *Certification or documentation for leave of 3 or more consecutive full workdays.* Contractors may require certification issued by a health care provider to verify the need for paid sick leave used for a purpose described in 29 CFR 13.5(c)(1)(i), (ii), or (iii), or documentation from an appropriate individual or organization to verify the need for paid sick leave used for a purpose described in 29 CFR 13.5(c)(1)(iv), only if the employee is absent for 3 or more consecutive full workdays (see 29 CFR 13.5(e)).

[FAC 2005-93, 81 FR 91627, 12/16/2016, effective 1/1/2017; FAC 2005-100, 83 FR 42569, 8/22/2018, effective 8/22/2018]

22.2106 Prohibited acts.

In accordance with 29 CFR 13.6, and by operation of the clause at 52.222-62, Paid Sick Leave Under Executive Order 13706, a contractor may not—

(a) Interfere with an employee's accrual or use of paid sick leave as required by E.O. 13706 or 29 CFR part 13 (see 29 CFR 13.6(a));

(b) Discharge or in any other manner discriminate against any employee for—

(1) Using, or attempting to use, paid sick leave as provided for under E.O. 13706 and 29 CFR part 13;

(2) Filing any complaint, initiating any proceeding, or otherwise asserting any right or claim under E.O. 13706 or 29 CFR part 13;

(3) Cooperating in any investigation or testifying in any proceeding under E.O. 13706 or 29 CFR part 13; or

(4) Informing any other person about his or her rights under E.O. 13706 or 29 CFR part 13 (see 29 CFR 13.6(b)); or

(c) Fail to make and maintain or to make available to authorized representatives of the Wage and Hour Division records for inspection, copying, and transcription as required by 29 CFR 13.25, or otherwise fail to comply with the requirements of 29 CFR 13.25 (see 29 CFR 13.6(c)).

[FAC 2005-93, 81 FR 91627, 12/16/2016, effective 1/1/2017; FAC 2005-100, 83 FR 42569, 8/22/2018, effective 8/22/2018]

22.2107 Waiver of rights.

Employees cannot waive, nor may contractors induce employees to waive, their rights under E.O. 13706 or 29 CFR part 13 (see 29 CFR 13.7).

[FAC 2005-93, 81 FR 91627, 12/16/2016, effective 1/1/2017; FAC 2005-100, 83 FR 42569, 8/22/2018, effective 8/22/2018]

22.2108 Multiemployer plans or other funds, plans, or programs.

Contractors may fulfill their obligations under E.O. 13706 and 29 CFR part 13 jointly with other contractors through a multiemployer plan, or may fulfill their obligations through an individual fund, plan, or program (see 29 CFR 13.8).

[FAC 2005-93, 81 FR 91627, 12/16/2016, effective 1/1/2017; FAC 2005-100, 83 FR 42569, 8/22/2018, effective 8/22/2018]

22.2109 Enforcement of Executive Order 13706 paid sick leave requirements.

(a) *Authority.* Section 4 of the E.O. grants to the Secretary of Labor the authority for investigating potential violations of, and obtaining compliance with, the E.O. The Secretary of Labor, in promulgating the implementing regulations required by section 3 of the E.O., has assigned this authority to the Administrator of the Wage and Hour Division. Contracting agencies do not have authority to conduct compliance investigations under 29 CFR part 13 as implemented in this subpart. This does not limit the contracting officer's authority to otherwise enforce the terms and conditions of the contract.

(b) *Complaints*. (1) Complaints are filed with the Administrator of the Wage and Hour Division and may be brought by any person (including the employee), entity, or organization that believes a violation of this subpart has occurred.

(2) The identity of any individual who makes a written or oral statement as a complaint or in the course of an investigation, as well as portions of the statement which would reveal the individual's identity, shall not be disclosed in any manner to anyone other than Federal officials without the prior consent of the individual, unless otherwise authorized by law.

(3) If the contracting agency receives a complaint or is notified that the Administrator of the Wage and Hour Division has received a complaint, the contracting officer shall report, within 14 days, to the Department of Labor, Wage and Hour Division, Office of Government Contracts, 200 Constitution Avenue N.W., Room S3006, Washington, D.C. 20210, all of the following information that is available without conducting an investigation:

(i) The complaint or description of the alleged violation.

(ii) Available statements by the employee, contractor, or any other person regarding the alleged violation.

(iii) Evidence that clause 52.222-62, Paid Sick Leave Under Executive Order 13706, was included in the contract.

(iv) Information concerning known settlement negotiations between the parties, if applicable.

(v) Any other relevant facts known to the contracting officer or other information requested by the Wage and Hour Division.

(c) *Investigations*. Complaints will be investigated by the Administrator of the Wage and Hour Division, if warranted, in accordance with the procedures in 29 CFR 13.43.

(d) *Remedies and sanctions*–(1) *Withholding or suspending payment*. The contracting officer shall, upon his or her own action or upon written request of the Administrator of the Wage and Hour Division—

(i)(A) Withhold or cause to be withheld from the contractor under the contract covered by the E.O. or any other Federal contract with the same contractor, so much of the accrued payments or advances as may be considered necessary to pay employees the full amount owed to compensate for any violation of E.O. 13706 or 29 CFR part 13; and

(B) In the event of any such violation, the contracting agency may, after authorization or by direction of the Administrator of the Wage and Hour Division and written notification to the contractor, take action to cause suspension of any further payment, advance, or guarantee of funds until such violations have ceased; or

(ii) Take action to cause suspension of any further payment, advance, or guarantee of funds to a contractor that has failed to make available for inspection, copying, and transcription any of the records identified in 29 CFR 13.25.

(2) *Civil actions to recover greater underpayments than those withheld*. (i) If the payments withheld under 29 CFR 13.11(c) are insufficient to reimburse all monetary relief due, or if there are no payments to withhold, the Department of Labor, following a final order of the Secretary of Labor, may bring an action against the contractor in any court of competent jurisdiction to recover the remaining amount.

(ii) The Department of Labor shall, to the extent possible, pay any sums it recovers in this manner directly to the employees who suffered the violation(s) of 29 CFR 13.6(a) or (b).

(iii) Any sum not paid to an employee because of inability to do so within 3 years shall be transferred into the Treasury of the United States as miscellaneous receipts.

(3) *Termination*. Contracting officers may consider the failure of a contractor to comply with the requirements of E.O. 13706 or 29 CFR part 13 as grounds for termination for default or cause.

(4) *Debarment*. (i) The Department of Labor may initiate debarment proceedings

under 29 CFR 13.44(d) and 29 CFR 13.52 whenever a contractor is found to have disregarded its obligations under E.O. 13706 or 29 CFR part 13.

(ii) Contracting officers shall consider notifying the agency suspending and debarring official in accordance with agency procedures when a contractor commits significant violations of contract terms and conditions related to this subpart (see subpart 9.4).

(5) *Remedies for interference*. (i) When the Administrator of the Wage and Hour Division determines that a contractor has interfered with an employee's accrual or use of paid sick leave in violation of 29 CFR 13.6(a), the Administrator of the Wage and Hour Division will notify the contractor and the relevant contracting agency of the interference and request that the contractor remedy the violation.

(ii) If the contractor does not remedy the violation, the Administrator of the Wage and Hour Division shall direct the contractor to provide any appropriate relief to the affected employee(s) in the investigative findings letter issued pursuant to 29 CFR 13.51. Such relief may include—

(A) Any pay and/or benefits denied or lost by reason of the violation;

(B) Other actual monetary losses sustained as a direct result of the violation; or

(C) Appropriate equitable or other relief.

(iii) Payment of liquidated damages in an amount equaling any monetary relief may also be directed unless such amount is reduced by the Administrator of the Wage and Hour Division because the violation was in good faith and the contractor had reasonable grounds for believing it had not violated the E.O. or 29 CFR part 13.

(iv) The Administrator of the Wage and Hour Division may additionally direct that payments due on the contract or any other contract between the contractor and the Federal Government be withheld as may be necessary to provide any appropriate monetary relief. Upon the final order of the Secretary of Labor that monetary relief is due, the Administrator of the Wage and Hour Division may direct the relevant contracting agency to transfer the withheld funds to the Department of Labor for disbursement.

(6) *Remedies for discrimination*. (i) When the Administrator of the Wage and Hour Division determines that a contractor has discriminated against an employee in violation of 29 CFR 13.6(b), the Administrator of the Wage and Hour Division will notify the contractor and the relevant contracting agency of the discrimination and request that the contractor remedy the violation.

(ii) If the contractor does not remedy the violation, the Administrator of the Wage and Hour Division shall direct the contractor to provide appropriate relief to the affected employee(s) in the investigative findings letter issued pursuant to 29 CFR 13.51. Such relief may include, but is not limited to—

(A) Employment;

(B) Reinstatement;

(C) Promotion; and

(D) Restoration of leave, or lost pay and/or benefits.

(iii) Payment of liquidated damages in an amount equaling any monetary relief may also be directed unless such amount is reduced by the Administrator of the Wage and Hour Division because the violation was in good faith and the contractor had reasonable grounds for believing the contractor had not violated the E.O. or 29 CFR part 13.

(iv) The Administrator of the Wage and Hour Division may additionally direct that payments due on the contract or any other contract between the contractor and the Federal Government be withheld as may be necessary to provide any appropriate monetary relief. Upon the final order of the Secretary of Labor that monetary relief is due, the Administrator of the Wage and Hour Division may direct the relevant contracting agency to transfer the withheld funds to the Department of Labor for disbursement.

(7) *Recordkeeping*. When a contractor fails to make, maintain, or protect records; or produce records when requested by authorized representatives of the Administrator of the Wage and Hour Division, or otherwise comply with the requirements of 29 CFR 13.25 in violation of 29 CFR 13.6(c), the Ad-

ministrator of the Wage and Hour Division will request that the contractor remedy the violation. If the contractor fails to produce required records upon request, the contracting officer shall, upon his or her own action or upon direction of an authorized representative of the Department of Labor, take such action as may be necessary to cause suspension of any further payment, advance, or guarantee of funds on the contract until such time as the violations are discontinued.

(e) *Inclusion of contract clause.* If a contracting agency fails to include the clause at FAR 52.222-62 in a contract to which the E.O. applies, the contracting officer, on his or her own initiative or within 15 days of notification by an authorized representative of the Department of Labor, shall incorporate the contract clause in the contract retroactive to commencement of performance under the contract through the exercise of any and all authority that may be needed (including, where necessary, its authority to negotiate or amend, its authority to pay any necessary additional costs, and its authority under any contract provision authorizing changes, cancellation, and termination).

[FAC 2005-93, 81 FR 91627, 12/16/2016, effective 1/1/2017; FAC 2005-100, 83 FR 42569, 8/22/2018, effective 8/22/2018]

22.2110 Contract clause.

Insert the clause at 52.222-62, Paid Sick Leave Under Executive Order 13706, in solicitations and contracts that include the clause at 52.222-6, Construction Wage Rate Requirements, or 52.222-41, Service Contract Labor Standards, where work is to be performed, in whole or in part, in the United States (the 50 States and the District of Columbia).

[FAC 2005-93, 81 FR 91627, 12/16/2016, effective 1/1/2017; FAC 2005-100, 83 FR 42569, 8/22/2018, effective 8/22/2018]

PART 23—ENVIRONMENT, ENERGY AND WATER EFFICIENCY, RENEWABLE ENERGY TECHNOLOGIES, OCCUPATIONAL SAFETY, AND DRUG-FREE WORKPLACE

Table of Contents

Scope . . . 23.000
Definitions . . . 23.001
Policy . . . 23.002

Subpart 23.1—Sustainable Acquisition Policy

Definition . . . 23.101
Authorities . . . 23.102
Sustainable acquisitions . . . 23.103
Exceptions . . . 23.104
Exemption authority . . . 23.105

Subpart 23.2—Energy and Water Efficiency and Renewable Energy

Scope . . . 23.200
Authorities . . . 23.201
Policy . . . 23.202
Energy-efficient products . . . 23.203
Procurement exemptions . . . 23.204
Energy-savings performance contracts . . . 23.205
Contract clause . . . 23.206

Subpart 23.3—Hazardous Material Identification and Material Safety Data

Scope of subpart . . . 23.300
Definition . . . 23.301
Policy . . . 23.302
Contract clause . . . 23.303

Subpart 23.4—Use of Recovered Materials and Biobased Products

Scope of subpart . . . 23.400
Definitions . . . 23.401
Authorities . . . 23.402
Policy . . . 23.403
Agency affirmative procurement programs . . . 23.404
Procedures . . . 23.405
Solicitation provisions and contract clauses . . . 23.406

Subpart 23.5—Drug-Free Workplace

Scope of subpart . . . 23.500
Applicability . . . 23.501
Authority . . . 23.502
Definitions . . . 23.503
Policy . . . 23.504
Contract clause. . . . 23.505
Suspension of payments, termination of contract, and debarment and suspension actions . . . 23.506

Subpart 23.6—Notice of Radioactive Material

Requirements . . . 23.601
Contract clause . . . 23.602

Subpart 23.7—Contracting for Environmentally Preferable Products and Services

Scope . . . 23.700
Definitions . . . 23.701
Authorities . . . 23.702
Policy . . . 23.703

Electronic products environmental assessment tool. 23.704
Contract clauses 23.705

Subpart 23.8—Ozone-Depleting Substances and Greenhouse Gases

Scope of subpart 23.800
Authorities 23.801
Policy 23.802
Procedures 23.803
Contract provision and clauses 23.804

Subpart 23.9—Contractor Compliance with Environmental Management Systems

Scope 23.900
Authority 23.901
Policy 23.902
Contract clause 23.903

Subpart 23.10—Federal Compliance with Right-To-Know Laws and Pollution Prevention Requirements

Scope 23.1000
Authorities 23.1001
Applicability 23.1002
Definition 23.1003
Requirements 23.1004
Contract clause 23.1005

Subpart 23.11—Encouraging Contractor Policies to Ban Text Messaging While Driving

Purpose 23.1101
Applicability 23.1102
Definitions 23.1103
Policy 23.1104
Contract clause 23.1105

PART 23—ENVIRONMENT, ENERGY AND WATER EFFICIENCY, RENEWABLE ENERGY TECHNOLOGIES, OCCUPATIONAL SAFETY, AND DRUG-FREE WORKPLACE

23.000 Scope.

This part prescribes acquisition policies and procedures supporting the Government's program for ensuring a drug-free workplace, for protecting and improving the quality of the environment, and to foster markets for sustainable technologies, materials, products, and services, and for encouraging the safe operation of vehicles.

[FAC 2001-02, 66 FR 65347, 12/18/2001, effective 2/19/2002; FAC 2001-14, 68 FR 28079, 5/22/2003, effective 6/23/2003; FAC 2005-21, 72 FR 63040, 11/7/2007, effective 12/7/2007; FAC 2005-25, 73 FR 21789, 4/22/2008, effective 5/22/2008; FAC 2005-46, 75 FR 60264, 9/29/2010, effective 9/29/2010; FAC 2005-52, 76 FR 31395, 5/31/2011, effective 5/31/2011; FAC 2005-53, 76 FR 39240, 7/5/2011, effective 8/4/2011; FAC 2005-75, 79 FR 35859, 6242014, effective 6/24/2014; FAC 2005-84, 80 FR 53436 , 9/3/2015, effective 10/5/2015; FAC 2005-88, 81 FR 30429, 5/16/2016, effective 6/15/2016; FAC 2005-92, 81 FR 83092, 11/18/2016, effective 12/19/2016]

23.001 Definitions.

As used in this part—

Environmental means environmental aspects of internal agency operations and activities, including those aspects related to energy and transportation functions.

Greenhouse gases means carbon dioxide, methane, nitrous oxide, hydrofluorocarbons, perflourocarbons, nitrogen triflouride, and sulfur hexafluoride.

Toxic chemical means a chemical or chemical category listed in 40 CFR 372.65.

United States, except as used in subpart 23.10, means—

(1) The fifty States;

(2) The District of Columbia;

(3) The commonwealths of Puerto Rico and the Northern Mariana Islands;

(4) The territories of Guam, American Samoa, and the United States Virgin Islands; and

(5) Associated territorial waters and airspace.

[FAC 2001-15, 68 FR 43868, 7/24/2003, effective 8/25/2003; FAC 2005-52, 76 FR 31395, 5/31/2011, effective 5/31/2011; FAC 2005-92, 81 FR 83092, 11/18/2016, effective 12/19/2016]

23.002 Policy.

Executive Order 13423 sections 3(e) and (f) require that contracts for contractor operation of a Government-owned or -leased facility and contracts for support services at a Government-owned or -operated facility include provisions that obligate the contractor to comply with the requirements of the order to the same extent as the agency would be required to comply if the agency operated or supported the facility. Compliance includes developing programs to promote and implement cost-effective waste reduction.

[FAC 2005-52, 76 FR 31395, 5/31/2011, effective 5/31/2011]

SUBPART 23.1—SUSTAINABLE ACQUISITION POLICY

23.101 Definition.

As used in this subpart—

Contract action means any oral or written action that results in the purchase, rent, or lease of supplies or equipment, services, or construction using appropriated dollars, including purchases below the micro-purchase threshold. Contract action does not include grants, cooperative agreements, other transactions, real property leases, requisitions from Federal stock, training authorizations, or other non-FAR based transactions.

[FAC 2005-52, 76 FR 31395, 5/31/2011, effective 5/31/2011]

23.102 Authorities.

(a) Executive Order 13423 of January 24, 2007, Strengthening Federal Environmental, Energy, and Transportation Management.

(b) Executive Order 13514 of October 5, 2009, Federal Leadership in Environmental, Energy, and Economic Performance.

(c) All of the authorities specified in subparts 23.2, 23.4, 23.7, 23.8, 23.9, and 23.10.

[FAC 2005-52, 76 FR 31395, 5/31/2011, effective 5/31/2011]

23.103 Sustainable acquisitions.

(a) Federal agencies shall advance sustainable acquisition by ensuring that 95 percent of new contract actions for the supply of products and for the acquisition of services (including construction) require that the products are—

(1) Energy-efficient (ENERGY STAR[reg] or Federal Energy Management Program (FEMP)-designated);

(2) Water-efficient;

(3) Biobased;

(4) Environmentally preferable (e.g., EPEAT®-registered, or non-toxic or less toxic alternatives);

(5) Non-ozone depleting; or

(6) Made with recovered materials.

(b) The required products in the contract actions for services include products that are—

(1) Delivered to the Government during performance;

(2) Acquired by the contractor for use in performing services at a Federally-controlled facility; or

(3) Furnished by the contractor for use by the Government.

(c) The required products in the contract actions must meet agency performance requirements.

(d) For purposes of meeting the 95 percent sustainable acquisition requirement, the term "contract actions" includes new contracts (and task and delivery orders placed against them) and new task and delivery orders on existing contracts.

[FAC 2005-52, 76 FR 31395, 5/31/2011, effective 5/31/2011; FAC 2005-75, 79 FR 35859, 6/24/2014, effective 6/24/2014; FAC 2005-84, 80 FR 53436 , 9/3/2015, effective 10/5/2015]

23.104 Exceptions.

This subpart does not apply to the following acquisitions:

(a) Contracts performed outside of the United States, unless the agency head determines that such application is in the interest of the United States.

(b) Weapon systems.

[FAC 2005-52, 76 FR 31395, 5/31/2011, effective 5/31/2011]

23.105 Exemption authority.

(a) The head of an agency may exempt—

(1) Intelligence activities of the United States, and related personnel, resources, and facilities, to the extent the Director of National Intelligence or agency head determines it necessary to protect intelligence sources and methods from unauthorized disclosure;

(2) Law enforcement activities of that agency and related personnel, resources, and facilities, to the extent the head of an agency determines it necessary to protect undercover operations from unauthorized disclosure;

(3) Law enforcement, protective, emergency response, or military tactical vehicle fleets of that agency; and

(4) Agency activities and facilities in the interest of national security.

(b) If the head of the agency issues an exemption under paragraph (a) of this section, the agency must notify the Chair of the Council on Environmental Quality in writing within 30 days of the issuance of the exemption.

(c) The agency head may submit through the Chair of the Council on Environmental Quality a request for exemption of an agency activity other than those activities listed in paragraph (a) of this section and related personnel, resources, and facilities.

[FAC 2005-52, 76 FR 31395, 5/31/2011, effective 5/31/2011]

SUBPART 23.2—ENERGY AND WATER EFFICIENCY AND RENEWABLE ENERGY

23.200 Scope.

(a) This subpart prescribes policies and procedures for—

(1) Acquiring energy- and water-efficient products and services, and products that use renewable energy technology; and

(2) Using an energy-savings performance contract to obtain energy-efficient technologies at Government facilities without Government capital expense.

(b) This subpart applies to acquisitions in the United States and its outlying areas. Agencies conducting acquisitions outside of these areas must use their best efforts to comply with this subpart.

[FAC 2001-02, 66 FR 65347, 12/18/2001, effective 2/19/2002; FAC 2001-14, 68 FR 28079, 5/22/2003, effective 6/23/2003]

23.201 Authorities.

(a) Energy Policy and Conservation Act (42 U.S.C. 6361(a)(1)) and Resource Conservation and Recovery Act of 1976 (42 U.S.C. 6901, et seq.).

(b) National Energy Conservation Policy Act (42 U.S.C. 8253, 8259b, 8262g, and 8287).

(c) Section 706 of Division D, Title VII of the Omnibus Appropriations Act, 2009 (Pub. L. 111-8).

(d) Title VI of the Clean Air Act, as amended (42 U.S.C. 7671, et seq.).

(e) Executive Order 11912 of April 13, 1976, Delegations of Authority under the Energy Policy and Conservation Act.

(f) Executive Order 13221 of July 31, 2001, Energy-Efficient Standby Power Devices.

(g) Executive Order 13423 of January 24, 2007, Strengthening Federal Environmental, Energy, and Transportation Management.

(h) Executive Order 13514 of October 5, 2009, Federal Leadership in Environmental, Energy, and Economic Performance.

[FAC 2001-02, 66 FR 65347, 12/18/2001, effective 2/19/2002; FAC 2001-15, 68 FR 43857, 7/24/2003, effective 8/25/2003; FAC 2005-22, 72 FR 65868, 11/23/2007, effective 12/24/2007; FAC 2005-52, 76 FR 31395, 5/31/2011, effective 5/31/2011]

23.202 Policy.

(a) *Introduction.* The Government's policy is to acquire supplies and services that promote a clean energy economy that increases our Nation's energy security, safeguards the health of our environment, and reduces greenhouse gas emissions from direct and indirect Federal activities. To implement this policy, Federal acquisitions will foster markets for sustainable technologies, products, and services. This policy extends to all acquisitions, including those below the simplified acquisition threshold and those at or below the micro-purchase threshold (including those made with a Government purchase card).

(b) *Water-efficient.* In accordance with Executive Order 13514, dated October 5, 2009, Federal Leadership in Environmental, Energy, and Economic Performance, it is the policy and objective of the Government to use and manage water through water-efficient means by—

(1) Reducing potable water consumption intensity to include low-flow fixtures and efficient cooling towers;

(2) Reducing agency, industry, landscaping, and agricultural water consumption; and

(3) Storm water management in accordance with section 438 of the Energy Independence and Security Act of 2007 (42 U.S.C. 17094) as implemented in *https://www.epa.gov/nps/stormwater-management-federal-facilities-under-section-438-energy-independence-and-security-act.*

[FAC 2001-02, 66 FR 65347, 12/18/2001, effective 2/19/2002; FAC 2005-52, 76 FR 31395, 5/31/2011, effective 5/31/2011; FAC 2005-100, 83 FR 42571, 8/22/2018, effective 8/22/2018]

23.203 Energy-efficient products.

(a) Unless exempt as provided at 23.204—

(1) When acquiring energy-consuming products listed in the ENERGY STAR® Program or Federal Energy Management Program (FEMP)—

(i) Agencies shall purchase ENERGY STAR® or FEMP-designated products; and

(ii) For products that consume power in a standby mode and are listed on FEMP's Low Standby Power Devices product listing, agencies shall—

(A) Purchase items which meet FEMP's standby power wattage recommendation or document the reason for not purchasing such items; or

(B) If FEMP has listed a product without a corresponding wattage recommendation, purchase items which use no more than one watt in their standby power consuming mode. When it is impracticable to meet the one watt requirement, agencies shall purchase items with the lowest standby wattage practicable; and

(2) When contracting for services or construction that will include the provision of energy-consuming products, agencies shall specify products that comply with the applicable requirements in paragraph (a)(1) of this section.

(b) Information is available via the Internet about—

(1) ENERGY STAR® at *http://www.energystar.gov/products*; and

(2) FEMP at *http://energy.gov/eere/femp/energy-and-water-efficient-products*.

[FAC 2001-02, 66 FR 65347, 12/18/2001, effective 2/19/2002; FAC 2001-15, 68 FR 43857, 7/24/2003, effective 8/25/2003; FAC 2005-22, 72 FR 65868, 11/23/2007, effective 12/24/2007; FAC 2005-100, 83 FR 42571, 8/22/2018, effective 8/22/2018]

23.204 Procurement exemptions.

An agency is not required to procure an ENERGY STAR® or FEMP-designated product if the head of the agency determines in writing that—

(a) No ENERGY STAR® or FEMP-designated product is reasonably available that meets the functional requirements of the agency; or

(b) No ENERGY STAR® or FEMP-designated product is cost effective over the life of the product taking energy cost savings into account.

[FAC 2005-22, 72 FR 65868, 11/23/2007, effective 12/24/2007]

23.205 Energy-savings performance contracts.

(a) Agencies should make maximum use of the authority provided in the National Energy Conservation Policy Act (42 U.S.C. 8287) to use an energy-savings performance contract (ESPC), when life-cycle cost-effective, to reduce energy use and cost in the agency's facilities and operations.

(b) (1) Under an ESPC, an agency can contract with an energy service company for a period not to exceed 25 years to improve energy efficiency in one or more agency facilities at no direct capital cost to the United States Treasury. The energy service company finances the capital costs of implementing energy conservation measures and receives, in return, a contractually determined share of the cost savings that result.

(2) Except as provided in 10 CFR 436.34, ESPC's are subject to subpart 17.1.

(c) To solicit and award an ESPC, the contracting officer—

(1) Must use the procedures, selection method, and terms and conditions provided in 10 CFR part 436, subpart B; at; and

(2) May use the "Qualified List" of energy service companies established by the Department of Energy and other agencies.

(d) For more information see *https://energy.gov/eere/femp/energy-savings-performance-contracts-federal-agencies*.

[FAC 2001-02, 66 FR 65347, 12/18/2001, effective 2/19/2002; FAC 2005-22, 72 FR 65868, 11/23/2007, effective 12/24/2007; FAC 2005-52, 76 FR 31395, 5/31/2011, effective 5/31/2011; FAC 2005-55, 77 FR 204, 1/3/2012, effective 1/3/2012; FAC 2005-100, 83 FR 42571, 8/22/2018, effective 8/22/2018]

23.206 Contract clause.

Unless exempt pursuant to 23.204, insert the clause at 52.223-15, Energy Efficiency in Energy-Consuming Products, in solicitations and contracts when energy-consuming products listed in the ENERGY STAR® Program or FEMP will be—

(a) Delivered;

(b) Acquired by the contractor for use in performing services at a Federally-controlled facility;

(c) Furnished by the contractor for use by the Government; or

(d) Specified in the design of a building or work, or incorporated during its construction, renovation, or maintenance.

[FAC 2005-22, 72 FR 65868, 11/23/2007, effective 12/24/2007]

SUBPART 23.3—HAZARDOUS MATERIAL IDENTIFICATION AND MATERIAL SAFETY DATA

23.300 Scope of subpart.

This subpart prescribes policies and procedures for acquiring deliverable items, other than ammunition and explosives, that require the furnishing of data involving hazardous materials. Agencies may prescribe special procedures for ammunition and explosives.

23.301 Definition.

Hazardous material is defined in the latest version of Federal Standard No. 313 (Federal Standards are sold to the public and Federal agencies through: General Services Administration, Specifications Unit (3FBP-W), 7th & D Sts., SW., Washington, DC 20407).

[FAC 90-8, 56 FR 55374, 10/25/91, effective 11/25/91]

23.302 Policy.

(a) The Occupational Safety and Health Administration (OSHA) is responsible for issuing and administering regulations that require Government activities to apprise their employees of—

(1) All hazards to which they may be exposed;

(2) Relative symptoms and appropriate emergency treatment; and

(3) Proper conditions and precautions for safe use and exposure.

(b) To accomplish this objective, it is necessary to obtain certain information relative to the hazards which may be introduced into the workplace by the supplies being acquired. Accordingly, offerors and contractors are required to submit hazardous materials data whenever the supplies being acquired are identified as hazardous materials. The latest version of Federal Standard No. 313 (Material Safety Data Sheet, Preparation and Submission of) includes criteria for identification of hazardous materials.

(c) Hazardous material data (Material Safety Data Sheets (MSDS's)) are required—

(1) As specified in the latest version of Federal Standard No. 313 (including revisions adopted during the term of the contract);

(2) For any other material designated by a Government technical representative as potentially hazardous and requiring safety controls.

(d) MSDS's must be submitted—

(1) By the apparent successful offeror prior to contract award if hazardous materials are expected to be used during contract performance.

(2) For agencies other than the Department of Defense, again by the contractor with the supplies at the time of delivery.

(e) The contracting officer shall provide a copy of all MSDS's received to the safety officer or other designated individual.

[FAC 90-8, 56 FR 55374, 10/25/91, effective 11/25/91; FAC 90-45, Final rule, 62 FR 224, 1/2/97, effective 1/1/97]

23.303 Contract clause.

(a) The contracting officer shall insert the clause at 52.223-3, Hazardous Material Identification and Material Safety Data, in solicitations and contracts if the contract will require the delivery of hazardous materials as defined in 23.301.

(b) If the contract is awarded by an agency other than the Department of Defense, the contracting officer shall use the clause at 52.223-3 with its Alternate I.

[FAC 90-8, 56 FR 55374, 10/25/91, effective 11/25/91]

SUBPART 23.4—USE OF RECOVERED MATERIALS AND BIOBASED PRODUCTS

23.400 Scope of subpart.

(a) The procedures in this subpart apply to all agency acquisitions of an Environmental Protection Agency (EPA) or United States Department of Agriculture (USDA)-designated item, if—

(1) The price of the designated item exceeds $10,000; or

(2) The aggregate amount paid for designated items, or for functionally equivalent designated items, in the preceding fiscal year was $10,000 or more.

(b) While micro-purchases are included in determining the aggregate amount paid under paragraph (a)(2) of this section, it is not recommended that an agency track micro-purchases when—

(1) The agency anticipates the aggregate amount paid will exceed $10,000; or

(2) The agency intends to establish or continue an affirmative procurement program in the following fiscal year.

[FAC 97-18, 65 FR 36014, 6/6/2000, effective 8/7/2000; FAC 2005-21, 72 FR 63040, 11/7/2007, effective 12/7/2007]

23.401 Definitions.

As used in this subpart—

(a) *EPA-designated item* means a product that is or can be made with recovered material—

(1) That is listed by EPA in a procurement guideline (40 CFR part 247); and

(2) For which EPA has provided purchasing recommendations in a related Recovered Materials Advisory Notice (RMAN) (available at *https://www.epa.gov/smm/comprehensive-procurement-guideline-cpg-program*).

(b) *USDA-designated item* means a generic grouping of products that are or can be made with biobased materials—

(1) That is listed by USDA in a procurement guideline (7 CFR part 3201, subpart B); and

(2) For which USDA has provided purchasing recommendations.

[Redesignated from 23.402, FAC 97-18, 65 FR 36014, 6/6/2000, effective 8/7/2000; FAC 2005-21, 72 FR 63040, 11/7/2007, effective 12/7/2007; FAC 2005-25, 73 FR 21789, 4/22/2008, effective 5/22/2008; FAC 2005-55, 77 FR 204, 1/3/2012, effective 1/3/2012; FAC 2005-58, 77 FR 23365, 4/18/2012, effective 5/18/2012; FAC 2005-100, 83 FR 42571, 8/22/2018, effective 8/22/2018]

23.402 Authorities.

(a) The Resource Conservation and Recovery Act of 1976 (RCRA), 42 U.S.C. 6962.

(b) The Farm Security and Rural Investment Act of 2002 (FSRIA), 7 U.S.C. 8102.

(c) Executive Order 13423 of January 24, 2007, Strengthening Federal Environmental, Energy, and Transportation Management.

(d) The Energy Policy Act of 2005, Public Law 109-58.

(e) Executive Order 13514 of October 5, 2009, Federal Leadership in Environmental, Energy, and Economic Performance.

[Redesignated from 23.401, FAC 97-18, 65 FR 36014, 6/6/2000, effective 8/7/2000; FAC 2005-21, 72 FR 63040, 11/7/2007, effective 12/7/2007; FAC 2005-52, 76 FR 31395, 5/31/2011, effective 5/31/2011]

23.403 Policy.

Government policy on the use of products containing recovered materials and biobased products considers cost, availability of competition, and performance. Agencies shall purchase these products or require in the acquisition of services, the delivery, use, or furnishing (see 23.103(b)) of such products. Agency contracts should specify that these products are composed of the highest percent of recovered material or biobased content practicable, or at least meet, but may exceed, the minimum recovered materials or biobased content of an EPA- or USDA-designated product. Agencies shall purchase these products to the maximum extent practicable without jeopardizing the intended use of the product while maintaining a satisfactory level of competition at a reasonable price. Such products shall meet the reasonable performance standards of the agency and be acquired competitively, in a cost-effective manner. Except as provided at 23.404(b), virgin material shall not be required by the solicitation (see 11.302).

[FAC 97-18, 65 FR 36014, 6/6/2000, effective 8/7/2000; FAC 2005-21, 72 FR 63040, 11/7/2007, effective 12/7/2007; FAC 2005-52, 76 FR 31395, 5/31/2011, effective 5/31/2011]

23.404 Agency affirmative procurement programs.

(a) An agency must establish an affirmative procurement program for EPA and USDA-designated items if the agency's purchases of designated items exceed the threshold set forth in 23.400.

(1) Agencies have a period of 1 year to revise their procurement program(s) after the designation of any new item by EPA or USDA.

(2) Technical or requirements personnel and procurement personnel are responsible for the preparation, implementation, and monitoring of affirmative procurement programs.

(3) Agency affirmative procurement programs must include—

(i) A recovered materials and biobased products preference program;

(ii) An agency promotion program;

(iii) For EPA-designated items only, a program for requiring reasonable estimates, certification, and verification of recovered material used in the performance of contracts. Both the recovered material content and biobased programs require preaward certification that the products meet EPA or USDA recommendations. A second certification is required at contract completion for recovered material content; and

(iv) Annual review and monitoring of the effectiveness of the program.

(b) *Exemptions.* (1) Agency affirmative procurement programs must require that 100 percent of purchases of EPA or USDA-designated items contain recovered material or biobased content, respectively, unless the item cannot be acquired—

(i) Competitively within a reasonable time frame;

(ii) Meeting reasonable performance standards; or

(iii) At a reasonable price.

(2) EPA and USDA may provide categorical exemptions for items that they designate, when procured for a specific purpose. For example, all USDA-designated items (see 7 CFR 3201.3(e)) are exempt from the preferred procurement requirement for the following:

(i) Spacecraft system and launch support equipment.

(ii) Military equipment, *i.e.*, a product or system designed or procured for combat or combat-related missions.

(c) Agency affirmative procurement programs must provide guidance for purchases of EPA-designated items at or below the micro-purchase threshold.

(d) Agencies may use their own specifications or commercial product descriptions when procuring products containing recovered materials or biobased products. When using either, the contract should specify—

(1) For products containing recovered materials, that the product is composed of the—

(i) Highest percent of recovered materials practicable; or

(ii) Minimum content standards in accordance with EPA's Recovered Materials Advisory Notices; and

(2) For biobased products, that the product is composed of—

(i) The highest percentage of biobased material practicable; or

(ii) USDA's recommended minimum contents standards.

(e) Agencies shall treat as eligible for the preference for biobased products, products from *designated countries*, as defined in 25.003, provided that those products—

(1) Meet the criteria for the definition of biobased product, except that the products need not meet the requirement that renewable agricultural materials or forestry materials in such product must be domestic; and

(2) Otherwise meet all requirements for participation in the preference program.

[FAC 97-18, 65 FR 36014, 6/6/2000, effective 8/7/2000; FAC 2005-21, 72 FR 63040, 11/7/2007, effective 12/7/2007; FAC 2005-58, 77 FR 23365, 4/18/2012, effective 5/18/2012]

23.405 Procedures.

(a) *Designated items and procurement guidelines.*

(1) *Recovered Materials.* Contracting officers should refer to EPA's list of EPA-designated items (available via the Internet at *https://www.epa.gov/smm/comprehensive-procurement-guideline-cpg-program#products*) and to their agencies' affirmative procurement program when purchasing products that contain recovered material, or services that could include the use of products that contain recovered material.

(2) *Biobased products.* Contracting officers should refer to USDA's list of USDA-designated items (available through the Internet at *http://www.biopreferred.gov*) and to their agencies affirmative procurement program when purchasing supplies that contain biobased material or when purchasing services that could include supplies that contain biobased material.

(3) When acquiring recovered material or biobased products, the contracting officer may request information or data on such products, including recycled or biobased content or related standards of the products (see 11.302(c)).

(b) *Procurement exemptions.*

(1) Once an item has been designated by either EPA or USDA, agencies shall purchase conforming products unless an exemption applies (see 23.404(b)).

(2) When an exemption is used for an EPA-designated item or the procurement of a product containing recovered material does not meet or exceed the EPA recovered material content guidelines, the contracting officer shall place a written justification in the contract file.

(c) *Program priorities.* When both the USDA-designated item and the EPA-designated item will be used for the same purposes, and both meet the agency's needs, the agency shall purchase the EPA-designated item.

[Redesignated from 23.404, FAC 97-18, 65 FR 36014, 6/6/2000, effective 8/7/2000; FAC 2001-15, 68 FR 43857, 7/24/2003, effective 8/25/2003; FAC 2005-21, 72 FR 63040, 11/7/2007, effective 12/7/2007; FAC 2005-25, 73 FR 21789, 4/22/2008, effective 5/22/2008; FAC 2005-58, 77 FR 23365, 4/18/2012, effective 5/18/2012; FAC 2005-100, 83 FR 42571, 8/22/2018, effective 8/22/2018]

23.406 Solicitation provisions and contract clauses.

(a) Insert the provision at 52.223-1, Biobased Product Certification, in solicitations that—

(1) Require the delivery or specify the use of USDA-designated items; or

(2) Include the clause at 52.223-2.

(b) Insert the clause at 52.223-2, Affirmative Procurement of Biobased Products Under Service and Construction Contracts, in service or construction solicitations and contracts, unless the contract will not involve the use of USDA-designated items at *http://www.biopreferred.gov* or 7 CFR part 3201.

(c) Except for the acquisition of commercially available off-the-shelf items, insert the provision at 52.223-4, Recovered Material Certification, in solicitations that—

(1) Require the delivery or specify the use of EPA-designated items; or

(2) Include the clause at 52.223-17, Affirmative Procurement of EPA-designated Items in Service and Construction Contracts.

(d) Insert the clause at 52.223-9, Estimate of Percentage of Recovered Material Content for EPA-designated Items, in solicitations and contracts exceeding $150,000 that are for, or specify the use of, EPA-designated items containing recovered materials. If technical personnel advise that estimates can be verified, use the clause with its Alternate I.

(e) Insert the clause at 52.223-17, Affirmative Procurement of EPA-designated Items in Service and Construction Contracts, in service or construction solicitations and contracts unless the contract will not involve the use of EPA-designated items.

[Redesignated from 23.405, FAC 97-18, 65 FR 36014, 6/6/2000, effective 8/7/2000; FAC 2001-15, 68 FR 43857, 7/24/2003, effective 8/25/2003; FAC 2005-19, 72 FR 46359, 8/17/2007, effective 8/17/2007; FAC 2005-21, 72 FR 63040, 11/7/2007, effective 12/7/2007; FAC 2005-25, 73 FR 21789, 4/22/2008, effective 5/22/2008; FAC 2005-27, 73 FR 54011, 9/17/2008, effective 9/17/2008; FAC 2005-30, 74 FR 2713, 1/15/2009, effective 2/17/2009; FAC 2005-45, 75 FR 53129, 8/30/2010, effective 10/1/2010; FAC 2005-58, 77 FR 23365, 4/18/2012, effective 5/18/2012]

SUBPART 23.5—DRUG-FREE WORKPLACE

23.500 Scope of subpart.

This subpart implements 41 U.S.C. chapter 81, Drug Free Workplace.

[Interim rule, FAC 84-43, 54 FR 4968, 1/31/89, effective 3/18/89; FAC 2005-73, 79 FR 24192, 4/29/2014, effective 5/29/2014]

23.501 Applicability.

This subpart applies to contracts, including contracts with 8(a) contractors under FAR subpart 19.8 and modifications that require a justification and approval (see subpart 6.3), except contracts—

(a) At or below the simplified acquisition threshold; however, the requirements of this subpart apply to all contracts of any value awarded to an individual;

(b) For the acquisition of commercial items (see part 12);

(c) Performed outside the United States and its outlying areas or any part of a contract performed outside the United States and its outlying areas;

(d) By law enforcement agencies, if the head of the law enforcement agency or designee involved determines that application of this subpart would be inappropriate in connection with the law enforcement agency's undercover operations; or

(e) Where application would be inconsistent with the international obligations of the United States or with the laws and regulations of a foreign country.

[Interim rule, FAC 84-43, 54 FR 4968, 1/31/89, effective 3/18/89 for contracts issued on or after that date; FAC 84-57, 55 FR 21707, 5/25/90, effective 7/24/90; FAC 90-29, 60 FR 34732, 7/3/95, effective 7/3/95; FAC 90-32, 60 FR 48206, 9/18/95, effective 10/1/95; FAC 2001-14, 68 FR 28079, 5/22/2003, effective 6/23/2003]

23.502 Authority.

41 U.S.C. chapter 81, Drug Free Workplace.

[Interim rule, FAC 84-43, 54 FR 4968, 1/31/89, effective 3/18/89; FAC 2005-73, 79 FR 24192, 4/29/2014, effective 5/29/2014]

23.503 Definitions.

As used in this subpart—

Controlled substance means a controlled substance in schedules I through V of section 202 of the Controlled Substances Act (21 U.S.C. 812), and as further defined in regulation at 21 CFR 1308.11—1308.15.

Conviction means a finding of guilt (including a plea of nolo contendere) or imposition of sentence, or both, by any judicial body charged with the responsibility to determine violations of the Federal or State criminal drug statutes.

Criminal drug statute means a Federal or non-Federal criminal statute involving the manufacture, distribution, dispensing, possession, or use of any controlled substance.

Employee means an employee of a contractor directly engaged in the performance of work under a Government contract. *Directly engaged* is defined to include all direct cost employees and any other contract employee who has other than a minimal impact or involvement in contract performance.

Individual means an offeror/contractor that has no more than one employee including the offeror/contractor.

[Interim rule, FAC 84-43, 54 FR 4968, 1/31/89, effective 3/18/89 for contracts issued on or after that date; FAC 84-57, 55 FR 21707, 5/25/90, effective 7/24/90; FAC 97-22, 66 FR 2116, 1/10/2001, effective

3/12/2001; Delay of effective date, 66 FR 14259, 3/9/2001, effective 5/11/2001]

23.504 Policy.

(a) No offeror other than an individual shall be considered a responsible source (see 9.104-1(g) and 19.602-1(a)(2)(i)) for a contract that exceeds the simplified acquisition threshold, unless it agrees that it will provide a drug-free workplace by—

(1) Publishing a statement notifying its employees that the unlawful manufacture, distribution, dispensing, possession, or use of a controlled substance is prohibited in the contractor's workplace, and specifying the actions that will be taken against employees for violations of such prohibition;

(2) Establishing an ongoing drug-free awareness program to inform its employees about—

(i) The dangers of drug abuse in the workplace;

(ii) The contractor's policy of maintaining a drug-free workplace;

(iii) Any available drug counseling, rehabilitation, and employee assistance programs; and

(iv) The penalties that may be imposed upon employees for drug abuse violations occurring in the workplace;

(3) Providing all employees engaged in performance of the contract with a copy of the statement required by paragraph (a)(1) of this section;

(4) Notifying all employees in writing in the statement required by subparagraph (a)(1) of this section, that as a condition of employment on a covered contract, the employee will—

(i) Abide by the terms of the statement; and

(ii) Notify the employer in writing of the employee's conviction under a criminal drug statute for a violation occurring in the workplace no later than 5 days after such conviction;

(5) Notifying the contracting officer in writing within 10 days after receiving notice under subdivision (a)(4)(ii) of this section, from an employee or otherwise receiving actual notice of such conviction. The notice shall include the position title of the employee;

(6) Within 30 days after receiving notice under subparagraph (a)(4) of this section of a conviction, taking one of the following actions with respect to any employee who is convicted of a drug abuse violation occurring in the workplace:

(i) Taking appropriate personnel action against such employee, up to and including termination; or

(ii) Requiring such employee to satisfactorily participate in a drug abuse assistance or rehabilitation program approved for such purposes by a Federal, State, or local health, law enforcement, or other appropriate agency.

(7) Making a good faith effort to maintain a drug-free workplace through implementation of subparagraphs (a)(1) through (a)(6) of this section.

(b) No individual shall be awarded a contract of any dollar value unless that individual agrees not to engage in the unlawful manufacture, distribution, dispensing, possession, or use of a controlled substance while performing the contract.

(c) For a contract of 30 days or more performance duration, the contractor shall comply with the provisions of paragraph (a) of this section within 30 days after contract award, unless the contracting officer agrees in writing that circumstances warrant a longer period of time to comply. Before granting such an extension, the contracting officer shall consider such factors as the number of contractor employees at the worksite, whether the contractor has or must develop a drug-free workplace program, and the number of contractor worksites. For contracts of less than 30 days performance duration, the contractor shall comply with the provisions of paragraph (a) of this section as soon as possible, but in any case, by a date prior to when performance is expected to be completed.

[Interim rule, FAC 84-43, 54 FR 4968, 1/31/89, effective 3/18/89 for contracts issued on or after that date; FAC 84-57, 55 FR 21707, 5/25/90, effective 7/24/90; Final rule,

55 FR 38517, 9/18/90; FAC 90-29, 60 FR 34732, 7/3/95, effective 7/3/95; FAC 90-44, Final rule, 61 FR 69286, 12/31/96, effective 1/1/97]

23.505 Contract clause.

Except as provided in 23.501, insert the clause at 52.223-6, Drug-Free Workplace, in solicitations and contracts.

[Interim rule, FAC 84-43, 54 FR 4968, 1/31/89, effective 3/18/89 for contracts issued on or after that date; FAC 84-57, 55 FR 21707, 5/25/90, effective 7/24/90; FAC 90-29, 60 FR 34732, 7/3/95, effective 7/3/95; FAC 90-44, Final rule, 61 FR 69286, 12/31/96, effective 1/1/97; FAC 2001-14, 68 FR 28079, 5/22/2003, effective 6/23/2003]

23.506 Suspension of payments, termination of contract, and debarment and suspension actions.

(a) After determining in writing that adequate evidence to suspect any of the causes at paragraph (d) of this section exists, the contracting officer may suspend contract payments in accordance with the procedures at 32.503-6(a)(1).

(b) After determining in writing that any of the causes at paragraph (d) of this section exists, the contracting officer may terminate the contract for default.

(c) Upon initiating action under paragraph (a) or (b) of this section, the contracting officer shall refer the case to the agency suspension and debarment official, in accordance with agency procedures, pursuant to Subpart 9.4.

(d) The specific causes for suspension of contract payments, termination of a contract for default, or suspension and debarment are—

(1) The contractor has failed to comply with the requirements of the clause at 52.223-6, Drug-Free Workplace; or

(2) The number of contractor employees convicted of violations of criminal drug statutes occurring in the workplace indicates that the contractor has failed to make a good faith effort to provide a drug-free workplace.

(e) A determination under this section to suspend contract payments, terminate a contract for default, or debar or suspend a contractor may be waived by the agency head for a particular contract, in accordance with agency procedures, only if such waiver is necessary to prevent a severe disruption of the agency operation to the detriment of the Federal Government or the general public (see Subpart 9.4). The waiver authority of the agency head cannot be delegated.

[Interim rule, FAC 84-43, 54 FR 4968, 1/31/89, effective 3/18/89; FAC 84-57, 55 FR 21708, 5/25/90, effective 7/24/90; FAC 90-44, Final rule, 61 FR 69286, 12/31/96, effective 1/1/97]

SUBPART 23.6—NOTICE OF RADIOACTIVE MATERIAL

23.601 Requirements.

(a) The clause at 52.223-7, Notice of Radioactive Materials, requires the contractor to notify the contracting officer prior to delivery of radioactive material.

(b) Upon receipt of the notice, the contracting officer shall notify receiving activities so that appropriate safeguards can be taken.

(c) The clause permits the contracting officer to waive the notification if the contractor states that the notification on prior deliveries is still current. The contracting officer may waive the notice only after consultation with cognizant technical representatives.

(d) The contracting officer is required to specify in the clause at 52.223-7, the number of days in advance of delivery that the contractor will provide notification. The determination of the number of days should be done in coordination with the installation/facility radiation protection officer (RPO). The RPO is responsible for insuring the proper license, authorization or permit is obtained prior to receipt of the radioactive material.

[FAC 90-8, 56 FR 55374, 10/25/91, effective 11/25/91; FAC 90-45, Final rule, 62 FR 224, 1/2/97, effective 1/1/97]

23.602 Contract clause.

The contracting officer shall insert the clause at 52.223-7, Notice of Radioactive Materials, in solicitations and contracts for supplies which are, or which contain—(a) radioactive material requiring specific licensing under regulations issued pursuant to the Atomic Energy Act of 1954; or (b) radioactive material not requiring specific licensing in which the specific activity is greater than 0.002 microcuries per gram or the activity per item equals or exceeds 0.01 microcuries. Such supplies include, but are not limited to, aircraft, ammunition, missiles, vehicles, electronic tubes, instrument panel gauges, compasses and identification markers.

[FAC 90-8, 56 FR 55374, 10/25/91, effective 11/25/91]

SUBPART 23.7—CONTRACTING FOR ENVIRONMENTALLY PREFERABLE PRODUCTS AND SERVICES

23.700 Scope.

This subpart prescribes policies for acquiring environmentally preferable products and services.

[FAC 2001-02, 66 FR 65347, 12/18/2001, effective 2/19/2002]

23.701 Definitions.

As used in this subpart—

Computer means a device that performs logical operations and processes data. Computers are composed of, at a minimum:

(1) A central processing unit (CPU) to perform operations;

(2) User input devices such as a keyboard, mouse, digitizer, or game controller; and

(3) A computer display screen to output information. Computers include both stationary and portable units, including desktop computers, integrated desktop computers, notebook computers, thin clients, and workstations. Although computers must be capable of using input devices and computer displays, as noted in paragraphs (2) and (3) of this definition, computer systems do not need to include these devices on shipment to meet this definition. This definition does not include server computers, gaming consoles, mobile telephones, portable hand-held calculators, portable digital assistants (PDAs), MP3 players, or any other mobile computing device with displays less than 4 inches, measured diagonally.

Computer display means a display screen and its associated electronics encased in a single housing or within the computer housing (e.g., notebook or integrated desktop computer) that is capable of displaying output information from a computer via one or more inputs such as a VGA, DVI, USB, DisplayPort, and/or IEEE 1394–2008TM, Standard for High Performance Serial Bus. Examples of computer display technologies are the cathode-ray tube (CRT) and liquid crystal display (LCD).

Desktop computer means a computer where the main unit is intended to be located in a permanent location, often on a desk or on the floor. Desktops are not designed for portability and utilize an external computer display, keyboard, and mouse. Desktops are designed for a broad range of home and office applications.

Electronic products means products that are dependent on electric currents or electromagnetic fields in order to work properly.

Imaging equipment means the following products:

(1) *Copier*—A commercially available imaging product with a sole function of the production of hard copy duplicates from graphic hard-copy originals. The unit is capable of being powered from a wall outlet or from a data or network connection. This definition is intended to cover products that are marketed as copiers or upgradeable digital copiers (UDCs).

(2) *Digital duplicator*—A commercially available imaging product that is sold in the market as a fully automated duplicator system through the method of stencil duplicating with digital reproduction functionality. The unit is capable of being powered from a wall outlet or from a data or network connection. This definition is intended to cover products that are marketed as digital duplicators.

(3) *Facsimile machine (fax machine)*—A commercially available imaging product whose primary functions are scanning hard-copy originals for electronic transmission to remote units and receiving similar electronic transmissions to produce hard-copy output. Electronic transmission is primarily over a

public telephone system but also may be via computer network or the Internet. The product also may be capable of producing hard copy duplicates. The unit is capable of being powered from a wall outlet or from a data or network connection. This definition is intended to cover products that are marketed as fax machines.

(4) *Mailing machine*—A commercially available imaging product that serves to print postage onto mail pieces. The unit is capable of being powered from a wall outlet or from a data or network connection. This definition is intended to cover products that are marketed as mailing machines.

(5) *Multifunction device (MFD)*—A commercially available imaging product, which is a physically integrated device or a combination of functionally integrated components, that performs two or more of the core functions of copying, printing, scanning, or faxing. The copy functionality as addressed in this definition is considered to be distinct from singlesheet convenience copying offered by fax machines. The unit is capable of being powered from a wall outlet or from a data or network connection. This definition is intended to cover products that are marketed as MFDs or multifunction products.

(6) *Printer*—A commercially available imaging product that serves as a hardcopy output device and is capable of receiving information from single-user or networked computers, or other input devices (*e.g.*, digital cameras). The unit is capable of being powered from a wall outlet or from a data or network connection. This definition is intended to cover products that are marketed as printers, including printers that can be upgraded into MFDs in the field.

(7) *Scanner*—A commercially available imaging product that functions as an electro-optical device for converting information into electronic images that can be stored, edited, converted, or transmitted, primarily in a personal computing environment. The unit is capable of being powered from a wall outlet or from a data or network connection. This definition is intended to cover products that are marketed as scanners.

Integrated desktop computer means a desktop system in which the computer and computer display function as a single unit that receives its AC power through a single cable. Integrated desktop computers come in one of two possible forms:

(1) A system where the computer display and computer are physically combined into a single unit; or

(2) A system packaged as a single system where the computer display is separate but is connected to the main chassis by a DC power cord and both the computer and computer display are powered from a single power supply. As a subset of desktop computers, integrated desktop computers are typically designed to provide similar functionality as desktop systems.

Notebook computer means a computer designed specifically for portability and to be operated for extended periods of time either with or without a direct connection to an AC power source. Notebooks must utilize an integrated computer display and be capable of operation off of an integrated battery or other portable power source. In addition, most notebooks use an external power supply and have an integrated keyboard and pointing device. Notebook computers are typically designed to provide similar functionality to desktops, including operation of software similar in functionality to that used in desktops. Docking stations are considered accessories for notebook computers, not notebook computers. Tablet PCs, which may use touch-sensitive screens along with, or instead of, other input devices, are considered notebook computers.

Personal computer product means a computer, computer display, desktop computer, integrated desktop computer, or notebook computer.

Television, or *TV*, means a commercially available electronic product designed primarily for the reception and display of audiovisual signals received from terrestrial, cable, satellite, Internet Protocol TV (IPTV), or other digital or analog sources. A TV consists of a tuner/receiver and a display encased in a single enclosure. The product usually relies upon a cathode-ray tube (CRT), liquid crystal display (LCD), plasma display, or other display technology. Televisions with computer capability (e.g., computer input port) may be considered to be a TV as long as they are marketed and sold to consumers primarily as televisions.

[FAC 97-18, 65 FR 36014, 6/6/2000, effective 8/7/2000; FAC 2005-21, 72 FR 63040, 11/7/2007, effective 12/7/2007; FAC 2005-23, 72 FR 73215, 12/26/2007, effective 12/26/2007; FAC 2005-30, 74 FR 2740, 1/15/2009, effective 2/17/2009; FAC 2005-75, 79 FR 35859, 6/24/2014, effective 6/24/2014; FAC 2005-84, 80 FR 53436 , 9/3/2015, effective 10/5/2015]

23.702 Authorities.

(a) Resource Conservation and Recovery Act (RCRA) (42 U.S.C. 6901, et seq.).

(b) National Energy Conservation Policy Act (42 U.S.C. 8262g).

(c) Pollution Prevention Act of 1990 (42 U.S.C. 13101, et seq.).

(d) Farm Security and Rural Investment Act of 2002 (FSRIA) (7 U.S.C. 8102).

(e) Executive Order 13221 of July 31, 2001, Energy Efficient Standby Power Devices.

(f) Executive Order 13423 of January 24, 2007, Strengthening Federal Environmental, Energy, and Transportation Management.

(g) Executive Order 13514 of October 5, 2009, Federal Leadership in Environmental, Energy, and Economic Performance.

[FAC 90-27, 60 FR 28492, 5/31/95, effective 5/31/95; FAC 97-18, 65 FR 36014, 6/6/2000, effective 8/7/2000; FAC 2001-02, 66 FR 65347, 12/18/2001, effective 2/19/2002; FAC 2001-15, 68 FR 43868, 7/24/2003, effective 8/25/2003; FAC 2005-21, 72 FR 63040, 11/7/2007, effective 12/7/2007; FAC 2005-23, 72 FR 73215, 12/26/2007, effective 12/26/2007; FAC 2005-30, 74 FR 2740, 1/15/2009, effective 2/17/2009; FAC 2005-52, 76 FR 31395, 5/31/2011, effective 5/31/2011]

23.703 Policy.

Agencies must—

(a) Implement cost-effective contracting preference programs promoting energy-efficiency, water conservation, and the acquisition of environmentally preferable products and services; and

(b) Employ acquisition strategies that affirmatively implement the following environmental objectives:

(1) Maximize the utilization of environmentally preferable products and services (based on EPA-issued guidance).

(2) Promote energy-efficiency and water conservation.

(3) Eliminate or reduce the generation of hazardous waste and the need for special material processing (including special handling, storage, treatment, and disposal).

(4) Promote the use of nonhazardous and recovered materials.

(5) Realize life-cycle cost savings.

(6) Promote cost-effective waste reduction when creating plans, drawings, specifications, standards, and other product descriptions authorizing material substitutions, extensions of shelf-life, and process improvements.

(7) Promote the use of biobased products.

(8) Purchase only plastic ring carriers that are degradable (7 USC 8102(c)(1), 40 CFR part 238).

[Redesignated from 23.704, FAC 97-18, 65 FR 36014, 6/6/2000, effective 8/7/2000; FAC 2001-02, 66 FR 65347, 12/18/2001, effective 2/19/2002; FAC 2005-21, 72 FR 63040, 11/7/2007, effective 12/7/2007]

23.704 Electronic products environmental assessment tool.

(a) *General.* (1) As required by E.O.s 13423 and 13514, agencies, when acquiring an electronic product to meet their requirements, shall meet at least 95 percent of those requirements with Electronic Product Environmental Assessment Tool (EPEAT®)-registered electronic products, unless—

(i) There is no EPEAT® standard for such product;

(ii) No EPEAT®-registered product meets agency requirements; or

(iii) The agency head has provided an exemption in accordance with 23.105.

(2) Contracting officers, when acquiring an electronic product, except as specified in paragraphs (a)(1)(i), (ii), or (iii) of this sec-

tion, shall acquire an EPEAT®-registered electronic product, unless the agency determines, in accordance with agency procedures, that the EPEAT®-registered product will not be cost effective over the life of the product.

(3) This section applies to acquisitions of electronic products to be used in the United States, unless otherwise provided by agency procedures. When acquiring electronic products to be used outside the United States, agencies must use their best efforts to comply with this section.

(b) Personal computer products, imaging equipment, and televisions. These are categories of EPEAT®-registered electronic products.

(1) The IEEE 1680.1™-2009 Standard for the Environmental Assessment of Personal Computer Products, the IEEE 1680.2™-2012 Standard for the Environmental Assessment of Imaging Equipment, and the IEEE 1680.3™-2012 Standard for the Environmental Assessment of Televisions—

(i) Were issued by the Institute of Electrical and Electronics Engineers, Inc., on March 5, 2010; October 19, 2012, and October 19, 2012, respectively;

(ii) Are voluntary consensus standards consistent with section 12(d) of Pub. L. 104–113 (15 U.S.C. 272 note), the "National Technology Transfer and Advancement Act of 1995," (see 11.102);

(iii) Meet EPA-issued guidance on environmentally preferable products and services; and

(iv) Are described in more detail at *https://www.epa.gov/greenerproducts/epas-recommendations-specificationsstandards-and-ecolabels.*

(2) A list of EPEAT® product categories and EPEAT®-registered electronic products that are in conformance with these standards can be found at *https://www.epa.gov/greenerproducts/epas-recommendations-specificationsstandards-and-ecolabels.*

(3) EPEAT® electronic products are designated "bronze-," "silver-," or "gold-" registered.

(4) Agencies shall, at a minimum, acquire EPEAT® bronze-registered products.

(5) Agencies are encouraged to acquire EPEAT® silver- or gold-registered products.

[FAC 2005-23, 72 FR 73215, 12/26/2007, effective 12/26/2007; FAC 2005-30, 74 FR 2740, 1/15/2009, effective 2/17/2009; Redesignated, FAC 2005-52, 76 FR 31395, 5/31/2011, effective 5/31/2011; FAC 2005-73, 79 FR 24192, 4/29/2014, effective 5/29/2014; FAC 2005-75, 79 FR 35859, 6/24/2014, effective 6/24/2014; FAC 2005-84, 80 FR 53436, 9/3/2015, effective 10/5/2015; FAC 2005-91, 81 FR 67781, 9/30/2016, effective 9/30/2016]

23.705 Contract clauses.

(a) Insert the clause at 52.223-10, Waste Reduction Program, in all solicitations and contracts for contractor operation of Government-owned or -leased facilities and all solicitations and contracts for support services at Government-owned or -operated facilities.

(b) (1) Unless an exception applies in accordance with 23.704(a), insert the clause at 52.223-13, Acquisition of EPEAT®-Registered Imaging Equipment, in all solicitations and contracts when imaging equipment (copiers, digital duplicators, facsimile machines, mailing machines, multifunction devices, printers, and scanners) will be—

(i) Delivered;

(ii) Acquired by the contractor for use in performing services at a Federally controlled facility; or

(iii) Furnished by the contractor for use by the Government.

(2) Agencies may use the clause with its Alternate I when there are sufficient EPEAT® silver- or gold-registered products available to meet agency needs.

(c) (1) Unless an exception applies in accordance with 23.704(a), insert the clause at 52.223-14, Acquisition of EPEAT®-Registered Televisions, in all solicitations and contracts when televisions will be—

(i) Delivered;

(ii) Acquired by the contractor for use in performing services at a Federally controlled facility; or

(iii) Furnished by the contractor for use by the Government.

(2) Agencies may use the clause with its Alternate I when there are sufficient EPEAT® silver- or gold-registered products available to meet agency needs.

(d) (1) Unless an exception has been approved in accordance with 23.704(c), insert the clause at 52.223-16, IEEE 1680 Standard for the Environmental Assessment of Personal Computer Products, in all solicitations and contracts for—

(i) Personal computer products;

(ii) Services that require furnishing of personal computer products for use by the Government; or

(iii) Contractor operation of Government-owned facilities.

(2) Agencies may use the clause with its Alternate I when there are sufficient EPEAT Silver registered products available to meet agency needs.

[Redesignated from 23.706, FAC 97-18, 65 FR 36014, 6/6/2000, effective 8/7/2000; FAC 2005-23, 72 FR 73215, 12/26/2007, effective 12/26/2007; FAC 2005-30, 74 FR 2740, 1/15/2009, effective 2/17/2009; Redesignated, FAC 2005-52, 76 FR 31395, 5/31/2011, effective 5/31/2011; FAC 2005-75, 79 FR 35859, 6/24/2014, effective 6/24/2014; FAC 2005-84, 80 FR 53436 , 9/3/2015, effective 10/5/2015]

SUBPART 23.8—OZONE-DEPLETING SUBSTANCES AND GREENHOUSE GASES

23.800 Scope of subpart.

This subpart—

(a) Sets forth policies and procedures for the acquisition of items that—

(1) Contain, use, or are manufactured with ozone-depleting substances; or

(2) Contain or use high global warming potential hydrofluorocarbons; and

(b) Addresses public disclosure of greenhouse gas emissions and reduction goals.

[FAC 90-27, 60 FR 28492, 5/31/95, effective 5/31/95; FAC 90-39, 61 FR 31612, 6/20/96, effective 6/20/96; FAC 2005-88, 81 FR 30429, 5/16/2016, effective 6/15/2016; FAC 2005-92, 81 FR 83092, 11/18/2016, effective 12/19/2016]

23.801 Authorities.

(a) Title VI of the Clean Air Act (42 U.S.C. 7671, *et seq.*).

(b) Section 706 of division D, title VII of the Omnibus Appropriations Act, 2009 (Public Law 111-8).

(c) Executive Order 13693 of March 25, 2015, Planning for Federal Sustainability in the Next Decade.

(d) Environmental Protection Agency (EPA) regulations, Protection of Stratospheric Ozone (40 CFR part 82).

[FAC 90-27, 60 FR 28492, 5/31/95, effective 5/31/95, adopted as final, FAC 90-39, 61 FR 31612, 6/20/96; FAC 2001-15, 68 FR 43868, 7/24/2003, effective 8/25/2003; FAC 2005-52, 76 FR 31395, 5/31/2011, effective 5/31/2011; FAC 2005-88, 81 FR 30429, 5/16/2016, effective 6/15/2016]

23.802 Policy.

It is the policy of the Federal Government that Federal agencies—

(a) Implement cost-effective programs to minimize the procurement of materials and substances that contribute to the depletion of stratospheric ozone and/or result in the use, release or emission of high global warming potential hydrofluorocarbons;

(b) Give preference to the procurement of acceptable alternative chemicals, products, and manufacturing processes that reduce overall risks to human health and the environment by minimizing—

(1) The depletion of ozone in the upper atmosphere; and

(2) The potential use, release, or emission of high global warming potential hydrofluorocarbons;

(c) Lead efforts to reduce greenhouse gas emissions at the Federal level in accordance with Executive Order 13693; and

(d) In order to better understand both direct and indirect greenhouse gas emissions that result from Federal activities, require offerors that are registered in the

System for Award Management (SAM) and received $7.5 million or more in Federal contract awards in the prior Federal fiscal year to—

(1) Represent whether they publicly disclose greenhouse gas emissions;

(2) Represent whether they publicly disclose a quantitative greenhouse gas emissions reduction goal; and

(3) Provide the website for any such disclosures.

[FAC 90-39, 61 FR 31612, 6/20/96, effective 6/20/96; FAC 2001-15, 68 FR 43868, 7/24/2003, effective 8/25/2003; FAC 2005-52, 76 FR 31395, 5/31/2011, effective 5/31/2011; FAC 2005-88, 81 FR 30429, 5/16/2016, effective 6/15/2016; FAC 2005-92, 81 FR 83092, 11/18/2016, effective 12/19/2016; FAC 2005-100, 83 FR 42571, 8/22/2018, effective 8/22/2018; FAC 2005-101, 83 FR 48691, 9/26/2018, effective 10/26/2018]

23.803 Procedures.

In preparing specifications and purchase descriptions, and in the acquisition of products and services, agencies shall—

(a) Comply with the requirements of title VI of the Clean Air Act, section 706 of division D, title VII of Public Law 111-8, Executive Order 13693, and 40 CFR 82.84(a)(2), (3), (4), and (5);

(b) Substitute acceptable alternatives to ozone-depleting substances, as identified under 42 U.S.C. 7671k, to the maximum extent practicable, as provided in 40 CFR 82.84(a)(1), except in the case of Class I substances being used for specified essential uses, as identified under 40 CFR 82.4(n);

(c) Unless a particular contract requires otherwise, specify that, when feasible, contractors shall use another acceptable alternative in lieu of a high global warming potential hydrofluorocarbon in products and services in a particular end use for which EPA's Significant New Alternatives Policy (SNAP) program has identified other acceptable alternatives that have lower global warming potential; and

(d) Refer to EPA's SNAP program for the list of alternatives, found at 40 CFR part 82, subpart G, as well as supplemental tables of alternatives (available at *http://www.epa.gov/snap*).

[FAC 2005-88, 81 FR 30429, 5/16/2016, effective 6/15/2016]

23.804 Contract provision and clauses.

(a) Except for contracts for supplies that will be delivered outside the United States and its outlying areas, or contracts for services that will be performed outside the United States and its outlying areas, the contracting officer shall insert the following clauses:

(1) 52.223-11, Ozone-Depleting Substances and High Global Warming Potential Hydrofluorocarbons, in solicitations and contracts for—

(i) Refrigeration equipment (in product or service code (PSC) 4110);

(ii) Air conditioning equipment (PSC 4120);

(iii) Clean agent fire suppression systems/equipment (*e.g.*, installed room flooding systems, portable fire extinguishers, aircraft/tactical vehicle fire/explosion suppression systems) (in PSC 4210);

(iv) Bulk refrigerants and fire suppressants (in PSC 6830);

(v) Solvents, dusters, freezing compounds, mold release agents, and any other miscellaneous chemical specialty that may contain ozone-depleting substances or high global warming potential hydrofluorocarbons (in PSC 6850);

(vi) Corrosion prevention compounds, foam sealants, aerosol mold release agents, and any other preservative or sealing compound that may contain ozone-depleting substances or high global warming potential hydrofluorocarbons (in PSC 8030);

(vii) Fluorocarbon lubricants (primarily aerosols) (in PSC 9150); and

(viii) Any other manufactured end products that may contain or be manufactured with ozone-depleting substances.

(a)(2) 52.223-12, Maintenance, Service, Repair, or Disposal of Refrigeration Equipment and Air Conditioners, in solicitations and contracts that include the maintenance, service, repair, or disposal of—

(i) Refrigeration equipment, such as refrigerators, chillers, or freezers; or

(ii) Air conditioners, including air conditioning systems in motor vehicles.

(a)(3) 52.223-20, Aerosols, in solicitations and contracts—

(i) For products that may contain high global warming potential hydrofluorocarbons as a propellant, or as a solvent; or

(ii) That involve maintenance or repair of electronic or mechanical devices.

(a)(4) 52.223-21, Foams, in solicitations and contracts for—

(i) Products that may contain high global warming potential hydrofluorocarbons or refrigerant blends containing hydrofluorocarbons as a foam blowing agent, such as building foam insulation or appliance foam insulation; or

(ii) Construction of buildings or facilities.

(b) The provision at 52.223-22, Public Disclosure of Greenhouse Gas Emissions and Reduction Goals—Representation, is required only when 52.204-7, System for Award Management, is included in the solicitation (see 52.204-8, Annual Representations and Certifications).

[FAC 90-39, 61 FR 31612, 6/20/96, effective 6/20/96; FAC 2001-14, 68 FR 28079, 5/22/2003, effective 6/23/2003; FAC 2005-88, 81 FR 30429, 5/16/2016, effective 6/15/2016; FAC 2005-92, 81 FR 83092, 11/18/2016, effective 12/19/2016]

SUBPART 23.9—CONTRACTOR COMPLIANCE WITH ENVIRONMENTAL MANAGEMENT SYSTEMS

23.900 Scope.

This subpart implements the environmental management systems requirements for contractors.

[FAC 2005-52, 76 FR 31395, 5/31/2011, effective 5/31/2011]

23.901 Authority.

(a) Executive Order 13423 of January 24, 2007, Strengthening Federal Environmental, Energy, and Transportation Management.

(b) Executive Order 13514 of October 5, 2009, Federal Leadership in Environmental, Energy, and Economic Performance.

[FAC 90-34, 60 FR 55306, 10/30/95, effective 10/30/95; FAC 90-41, 61 FR 41466, 8/8/96, effective 10/7/96; FAC 2001-15, 68 FR 43868, 7/24/2003, effective 8/25/2003; FAC 2005-52, 76 FR 31395, 5/31/2011, effective 5/31/2011]

23.902 Policy.

(a) Agencies shall implement environmental management systems (EMS) at all appropriate organizational levels. Where contractor activities affect an agency's environmental management aspects, EMS requirements shall be included in contracts to ensure proper implementation and execution of EMS roles and responsibilities.

(b) The contracting officer shall—

(1) Specify the EMS directives with which the contractor must comply; and

(2) Ensure contractor compliance to the same extent as the agency would be required to comply, if the agency operated the facilities or vehicles.

[FAC 90-34, 60 FR 55306, 10/30/95, effective 10/30/95; FAC 90-41, 61 FR 41466, 8/8/96, effective 10/7/96; FAC 2001-15, 68 FR 43868, 7/24/2003, effective 8/25/2003; FAC 2005-52, 76 FR 31395, 5/31/2011, effective 5/31/2011]

23.903 Contract clause.

The contracting officer shall insert the clause at 52.223-19, Compliance With Environmental Management Systems, in all solicitations and contracts for contractor operation of Government-owned or -leased facilities or vehicles, located in the United States. For facilities located outside the United States, the agency head may determine that use of the clause is in the best interest of the Government.

[FAC 90-34, 60 FR 55306, 10/30/95, effective 10/30/95; FAC 90-41, 61 FR 41466, 8/8/96, effective 10/7/96; FAC 2001-14, 68

FR 28079, 5/22/2003, effective 6/23/2003; FAC 2001-15, 68 FR 43868, 7/24/2003, effective 8/25/2003; FAC 2005-52, 76 FR 31395, 5/31/2011, effective 5/31/2011]

SUBPART 23.10—FEDERAL COMPLIANCE WITH RIGHT-TO-KNOW LAWS AND POLLUTION PREVENTION REQUIREMENTS

23.1000 Scope.

This subpart prescribes policies and procedures for obtaining information needed for Government—

(a) Compliance with right-to-know laws and pollution prevention requirements;

(b) Implementation of an environmental management system (EMS) at a Federal facility; and

(c) Completion of facility compliance audits (FCAs) at a Federal facility.

[FAC 2001-15, 68 FR 43868, 7/24/2003, effective 8/25/2003]

23.1001 Authorities.

(a) Emergency Planning and Community Right-to-Know Act of 1986, 42 U.S.C. 11001-11050 (EPCRA).

(b) Pollution Prevention Act of 1990, 42 U.S.C. 13101-13109 (PPA).

(c) Executive Order 13423 of January 24, 2007, Strengthening Federal Environmental, Energy, and Transportation Management.

(d) Executive Order 13514 of October 5, 2009, Federal Leadership in Environmental, Energy, and Economic Performance.

[FAC 90-46, 62 FR 12690, 3/17/97, effective 3/17/97, finalized without change, FAC 97-4, 63 FR 9048, 2/23/98, effective 4/24/98; FAC 2001-15, 68 FR 43868, 7/24/2003, effective 8/25/2003; FAC 2005-52, 76 FR 31395, 5/31/2011, effective 5/31/2011]

23.1002 Applicability.

The requirements of this subpart apply to facilities owned or operated by an agency in the customs territory of the United States.

[FAC 90-46, 62 FR 12690, 3/17/97, effective 3/17/97, finalized without change, FAC 97-4, 63 FR 9048, 2/23/98, effective 4/24/98; FAC 2001-14, 68 FR 28079, 5/22/2003, effective 6/23/2003; FAC 2001-15, 68 FR 43868, 7/24/2003, effective 8/25/2003]

23.1003 Definitions.

As used in this subpart—

Federal agency means an executive agency (see 2.101).

[FAC 90-46, 62 FR 12690, 3/17/97, effective 3/17/97, finalized without change, FAC 97-4, 63 FR 9048, 2/23/98, effective 4/24/98; FAC 2001-15, 68 FR 43868, 7/24/2003, effective 8/25/2003; FAC 2005-52, 76 FR 31395, 5/31/2011, effective 5/31/2011]

23.1004 Requirements.

(a) Federal facilities are required to comply with—

(1) The emergency planning and toxic release reporting requirements in EPCRA and PPA; and

(2) The toxic chemical, and hazardous substance release and use reduction goals of sections 2(e) and 3(a)(vi) of Executive Order 13423.

(b) Pursuant to EPCRA, PPA, E.O. 13423, and any agency implementing procedures, every new contract that provides for performance on a Federal facility shall require the contractor to provide information necessary for the Federal agency to comply with the—

(1) Requirements in paragraph (a) of this section; and

(2) Requirements for EMSs and FCAs if the place of performance is at a Federal facility designated by the agency.

[FAC 90-46, 62 FR 12690, 3/17/97, effective 3/17/97; FAC 97-4, 63 FR 9048, 2/23/98, effective 4/24/98; FAC 2001-15, 68 FR 43868, 7/24/2003, effective 8/25/2003; FAC 2005-52, 76 FR 31395, 5/31/2011, effective 5/31/2011]

23.1005 Contract clause.

(a) Insert the clause at 52.223-5, Pollution Prevention and Right-to-Know Information, in solicitations and contracts that provide for performance, in whole or in part, on a Federal facility.

(b) Use the clause with its Alternate I if the contract provides for contractor—

(1) Operation or maintenance of a Federal facility at which the agency has implemented or plans to implement an EMS; or

(2) Activities and operations—

(i) To be performed at a Government-operated Federal facility that has implemented or plans to implement an EMS; and

(ii) That the agency has determined are covered within the EMS.

(c) Use the clause with its Alternate II if—

(1) The contract provides for contractor activities on a Federal facility; and

(2) The agency has determined that the contractor activities should be included within the FCA or an environmental management system audit.

[FAC 90-46, 62 FR 12690, 3/17/97, effective 3/17/97, finalized without change, FAC 97-4, 63 FR 9048, 2/23/98, effective 4/24/98; FAC 2001-15, 68 FR 43868, 7/24/2003, effective 8/25/2003]

SUBPART 23.11—ENCOURAGING CONTRACTOR POLICIES TO BAN TEXT MESSAGING WHILE DRIVING

23.1101 Purpose.

This subpart implements the requirements of the Executive Order (E.O.) 13513, dated October 1, 2009 (74 FR 51225, October 6, 2009), Federal Leadership on Reducing Text Messaging while Driving.

[FAC 2005-46, 75 FR 60264, 9/29/2010, effective 9/29/2010; FAC 2005-53, 76 FR 39240, 7/5/2011, effective 8/4/2011]

23.1102 Applicability.

This subpart applies to all solicitations and contracts.

[FAC 2005-46, 75 FR 60264, 9/29/2010, effective 9/29/2010; FAC 2005-53, 76 FR 39240, 7/5/2011, effective 8/4/2011]

23.1103 Definitions.

As used in this subpart—

Driving—(1) Means operating a motor vehicle on an active roadway with the motor running, including while temporarily stationary because of traffic, a traffic light, stop sign, or otherwise.

(2) Does not include operating a motor vehicle with or without the motor running when one has pulled over to the side of, or off, an active roadway and has halted in a location where one can safely remain stationary.

Text messaging means reading from or entering data into any handheld or other electronic device, including for the purpose of short message service texting, e-mailing, instant messaging, obtaining navigational information, or engaging in any other form of electronic data retrieval or electronic data communication. The term does not include glancing at or listening to a navigational device that is secured in a commercially designed holder affixed to the vehicle, provided that the destination and route are programmed into the device either before driving or while stopped in a location off the roadway where it is safe and legal to park.

[FAC 2005-46, 75 FR 60264, 9/29/2010, effective 9/29/2010; FAC 2005-53, 76 FR 39240, 7/5/2011, effective 8/4/2011]

23.1104 Policy.

Agencies shall encourage contractors and subcontractors to adopt and enforce policies that ban text messaging while driving—

(a) Company-owned or -rented vehicles or Government-owned vehicles; or

(b) Privately-owned vehicles when on official Government business or when performing any work for or on behalf of the Government.

[FAC 2005-46, 75 FR 60264, 9/29/2010, effective 9/29/2010; FAC 2005-53, 76 FR 39240, 7/5/2011, effective 8/4/2011]

23.1105 Contract clause.

The contracting officer shall insert the clause at 52.223-18, Encouraging Contractor Policies to Ban Text Messaging While Driving, in all solicitations and contracts.

[FAC 2005-46, 75 FR 60264, 9/29/2010, effective 9/29/2010; FAC 2005-53, 76 FR 39240, 7/5/2011, effective 8/4/2011]

PART 24—PROTECTION OF PRIVACY AND FREEDOM OF INFORMATION

Table of Contents

Scope of part 24.000

Subpart 24.1—Protection of Individual Privacy

Definitions 24.101
General 24.102
Procedures 24.103
Contract clauses 24.104

Subpart 24.2—Freedom of Information Act

Authority 24.201
Prohibitions 24.202
Policy 24.203

Subpart 24.3—Privacy Training

Privacy training 24.301
Contract clause 24.302

PART 24—PROTECTION OF PRIVACY AND FREEDOM OF INFORMATION

24.000 Scope of part.

This part prescribes policies and procedures that apply requirements of the Privacy Act of 1974 (5 U.S.C. 552a) (the Act) and OMB Circular No. A-130, December 12, 1985, to Government contracts and cites the Freedom of Information Act (5 U.S.C. 552, as amended.)

[Final rule, 55 FR 38517, 9/18/90]

SUBPART 24.1—PROTECTION OF INDIVIDUAL PRIVACY

24.101 Definitions.

As used in this subpart—

Agency means any executive department, military department, Government corporation, Government controlled corporation, or other establishment in the executive branch of the Government (including the Executive Office of the President), or any independent regulatory agency.

Individual means a citizen of the United States or an alien lawfully admitted for permanent residence.

Maintain means maintain, collect, use, or disseminate.

Operation of a system of records means performance of any of the activities associated with maintaining the system of records, including the collection, use, and dissemination of records.

Personally identifiable information means information that can be used to distinguish or trace an individual's identity, either alone or when combined with other information that is linked or linkable to a specific individual. (See Office of Management and Budget (OMB) Circular No. A-130, Managing Federal Information as a Strategic Resource).

Record means any item, collection, or grouping of information about an individual that is maintained by an agency, including, but not limited to, education, financial transactions, medical history, and criminal or employment history, and that contains the individual's name, or the identifying number, symbol, or other identifying particular assigned to the individual, such as a fingerprint or voiceprint or a photograph.

System of records on individuals means a group of any records under the control of any agency from which information is retrieved by the name of the individual or by some identifying number, symbol, or other identifying particular assigned to the individual.

[FAC 97-22, 66 FR 2116, 1/10/2001, 3/12/2001; Delay of effective date, 66 FR 14259, 3/9/2001, effective 5/11/2001; FAC 2005-94, 81 FR 93476, 12/20/2016, effective 1/19/2017]

24.102 General.

(a) The Act requires that when an agency contracts for the design, development, or operation of a system of records on individuals on behalf of the agency to accomplish an agency function the agency must apply the requirements of the Act to the contractor and its employees working on the contract.

(b) An agency officer or employee may be criminally liable for violations of the Act. When the contract provides for operation of a system of records on individuals, contractors and their employees are considered employees of the agency for purposes of the criminal penalties of the Act.

(c) If a contract specifically provides for the design, development, or operation of a system of records on individuals on behalf of an agency to accomplish an agency function, the agency must apply the requirements of the Act to the contractor and its employees working on the contract. The system of records operated under the contract is deemed to be maintained by the agency and is subject to the Act.

(d) Agencies, which within the limits of their authorities, fail to require that systems of records on individuals operated on their behalf under contracts be operated in conformance with the Act may be civilly liable to individuals injured as a consequence of any subsequent failure to maintain records in conformance with the Act.

24.103 Procedures.

(a) The contracting officer shall review requirements to determine whether the contract will involve the design, development, or operation of a system of records on individuals to accomplish an agency function.

(b) If one or more of those tasks will be required, the contracting officer shall—

(1) Ensure that the contract work statement specifically identifies the system of records on individuals and the design, development, or operation work to be performed; and

(2) Make available, in accordance with agency procedures, agency rules and regulation implementing the Act.

24.104 Contract clauses.

When the design, development, or operation of a system of records on individuals is required to accomplish an agency function, the contracting officer shall insert the following clauses in solicitations and contracts:

(a) The clause at 52.224-1, Privacy Act Notification.

(b) The clause at 52.224-2, Privacy Act.

SUBPART 24.2—FREEDOM OF INFORMATION ACT

24.201 Authority.

The Freedom of Information Act (5 U.S.C. 552, as amended) provides that information is to be made available to the public either by (a) publication in the Federal Register; (b) providing an opportunity to read and copy records at convenient locations; or (c) upon request, providing a copy of a reasonably described record.

24.202 Prohibitions.

(a) A proposal in the possession or control of the Government, submitted in response to a competitive solicitation, shall not be made available to any person under the Freedom of Information Act. This prohibition does not apply to a proposal, or any part of a proposal, that is set forth or incorporated by reference in a contract between the Government and the contractor that submitted the proposal. (See 10 U.S.C. 2305(g) and 41 U.S.C. 4702.)

(b) No agency shall disclose any information obtained pursuant to 15.403-3(b) that is exempt from disclosure under the Freedom of Information Act. (See 10 U.S.C. 2306a(d)(2)(C) and 41 U.S.C. 3505(b)(3).)

(c) A dispute resolution communication that is between a neutral person and a party to alternative dispute resolution proceedings, and that may not be disclosed under 5 U.S.C. 574, is exempt from disclosure under the Freedom of Information Act (5 U.S.C. 552(b)(3)).

[FAC 90-45, Final rule, 62 FR 224, 1/2/97, effective 1/1/97; FAC 97-2, 62 FR 51224, 9/30/97, effective 10/10/97; FAC 97-9, 63 FR 58587, 10/30/98, effective 12/29/98; FAC 2001-16, 68 FR 56688, 10/2/2003, effective 10/1/2003; FAC 2005-73, 79 FR 24192, 4/29/2014, effective 5/29/2014]

24.203 Policy.

(a) The Act specifies, among other things, how agencies shall make their records available upon public request, imposes strict time standards for agency responses, and exempts certain records from public disclosure. Each agency's implementation of these requirements is located in its respective title of the Code of Federal Regulations and referenced in Subpart 24.2 of its implementing acquisition regulations.

(b) Contracting officers may receive requests for records that may be exempted from mandatory public disclosure. The exemptions most often applicable are those relating to classified information, to trade secrets and confidential commercial or financial information, to interagency or intra-agency memoranda, or to personal and medical information pertaining to an individual. Other exemptions include agency personnel practices, and law enforcement. Since these requests often involve complex issues requiring an in-depth knowledge of a large and increasing body of court rulings and policy guidance, contracting officers are cautioned to comply with the implementing regulations of their agency and to obtain necessary guidance from the agency officials having Freedom of Information Act responsibility. If additional assistance is needed, authorized agency officials may contact the Department of Justice, Office of Information and Privacy. A Freedom of Information Act guide and other resources are available at the Department of Justice website under FOIA reference materials: *http://www.usdoj.gov/oip*.

[FAC 84-21, 51 FR 31426, 9/3/86, effective 8/29/86; Redesignated from 24.202, FAC 90-45, Final rule, 62 FR 224, 1/2/97, effective 1/1/97; FAC 2005-30, 74 FR 2731, 1/15/2009, effective 2/17/2009; FAC 2005-42, 75 FR 34273, 6/16/2010, effective 7/16/2010]

SUBPART 24.3—PRIVACY TRAINING

24.301 Privacy training.

(a) Contractors are responsible for ensuring that initial privacy training, and annual privacy training thereafter, is completed by contractor employees who—

(1) Have access to a system of records;

(2) Create, collect, use, process, store, maintain, disseminate, disclose, dispose, or otherwise handle personally identifiable information on behalf of the agency; or

(3) Design, develop, maintain, or operate a system of records (see FAR subpart 24.1 and 39.105).

(b) Privacy training shall address the key elements necessary for ensuring the safeguarding of personally identifiable information or a system of records. The training shall be role-based, provide foundational as well as more advanced levels of training, and have measures in place to test the knowledge level of users. At a minimum, the privacy training shall cover—

(1) The provisions of the Privacy Act of 1974 (5 U.S.C. 552a), including penalties for violations of the Act;

(2) The appropriate handling and safeguarding of personally identifiable information;

(3) The authorized and official use of a system of records or any other personally identifiable information;

(4) The restriction on the use of unauthorized equipment to create, collect, use, process, store, maintain, disseminate, disclose, dispose, or otherwise access personally identifiable information;

(5) The prohibition against the unauthorized use of a system of records or unauthorized disclosure, access, handling, or use of personally identifiable information; and

(6) Procedures to be followed in the event of a suspected or confirmed breach of a system of records or unauthorized disclosure, access, handling, or use of personally identifiable information (see Office of Management and Budget guidance for Preparing for and Responding to a Breach of Personally Identifiable Information).

(c) The contractor may provide its own training or use the training of another agency unless the contracting agency specifies that only its agency-provided training is acceptable (see 24.302(b)).

(d) The contractor is required to maintain and, upon request, to provide documentation of completion of privacy training for all applicable employees.

(e) No contractor employee shall be permitted to have or retain access to a system of records, create, collect, use, process, store, maintain, disseminate, disclose, or dispose, or otherwise handle personally identifiable information, or design, develop, maintain, or operate a system of records, unless the employee has completed privacy training that, at a minimum, addresses the elements in paragraph (b) of this section.

[Final rule, 81 FR 93476, 12/20/2016, effective 1/19/2017]

24.302 Contract clause.

(a) The contracting officer shall insert the clause at FAR 52.224-3, Privacy Training, in solicitations and contracts when, on behalf of the agency, contractor employees will—

(1) Have access to a system of records;

(2) Create, collect, use, process, store, maintain, disseminate, disclose, dispose, or otherwise handle personally identifiable information; or

(3) Design, develop, maintain, or operate a system of records.

(b) When an agency specifies that only its agency-provided training is acceptable, use the clause with its Alternate I.

[Final rule, 81 FR 93476, 12/20/2016, effective 1/19/2017]

PART 25—FOREIGN ACQUISITION

Table of Contents

Scope of part . . . 25.000
General . . . 25.001
Applicability of subparts . . . 25.002
Definitions . . . 25.003
[Removed] . . . 25.004

Subpart 25.1—Buy American—Supplies

Scope of subpart . . . 25.100
General . . . 25.101
Policy . . . 25.102
Exceptions . . . 25.103
Nonavailable articles . . . 25.104
Determining reasonableness of cost . . . 25.105

Subpart 25.2—Buy American—Construction Materials

Scope of subpart . . . 25.200
Policy . . . 25.201
Exceptions . . . 25.202
Preaward determinations . . . 25.203
Evaluating offers of foreign construction material . . . 25.204
Postaward determinations . . . 25.205
Noncompliance . . . 25.206

Subpart 25.3—Contracts Performed Outside the United States

Contractor personnel in a designated operational area or supporting a diplomatic or consular mission outside the United States . . . 25.301
Scope . . . 25.301-1
Government support . . . 25.301-2
Weapons . . . 25.301-3
Contract clause . . . 25.301-4
Contractors performing private security functions outside the United States . . . 25.302
Scope . . . 25.302-1
Definitions . . . 25.302-2
Applicability . . . 25.302-3
Policy . . . 25.302-4
Remedies . . . 25.302-5
Contract clause . . . 25.302-6

Subpart 25.4—Trade Agreements

Scope of subpart . . . 25.400
Exceptions . . . 25.401
General . . . 25.402
World Trade Organization Government Procurement Agreement and Free Trade Agreements . . . 25.403
Least developed countries . . . 25.404
Caribbean Basin Trade Initiative . . . 25.405
Israeli Trade Act . . . 25.406
Agreement on Trade in Civil Aircraft . . . 25.407
Procedures . . . 25.408

Subpart 25.5—Evaluating Foreign Offers—Supply Contracts

General . . . 25.501
Application . . . 25.502
Group offers . . . 25.503
Evaluation examples . . . 25.504
Buy American statute . . . 25.504-1
WTO GPA/Caribbean Basin Trade Initiative/FTAs . . . 25.504-2

FTA/Israeli Trade Act 25.504-3
Group award basis 25.504-4

Subpart 25.6—American Recovery and Reinvestment Act—Buy American Statute—Construction Materials

Scope of subpart 25.600
Definitions 25.601
Policy 25.602
Section 1605 of the Recovery Act 25.602-1
Buy American statute 25.602-2
Exceptions 25.603
Preaward determination concerning the inapplicability of section 1605 of the Recovery Act or the Buy American statute 25.604
Evaluating offers of foreign construction material 25.605
Postaward determinations 25.606
Noncompliance 25.607

Subpart 25.7—Prohibited Sources

Scope of subpart 25.700
Restrictions administered by the Department of the Treasury on acquisitions of supplies or services from prohibited sources 25.701
Prohibition on contracting with entities that conduct restricted business operations in Sudan 25.702
Definitions 25.702-1
Certification 25.702-2
Remedies 25.702-3
Waiver 25.702-4
Prohibition on contracting with entities that engage in certain activities or transactions relating to Iran 25.703
Definitions 25.703-1
Iran Sanctions Act 25.703-2
Prohibition on contracting with entities that export sensitive technology to Iran. 25.703-3
Waiver 25.703-4

Subpart 25.8—Other International Agreements and Coordination

General. 25.801
Procedures 25.802

Subpart 25.9—Customs and Duties

Scope of subpart 25.900
Policy 25.901
Procedures 25.902
Exempted supplies 25.903

Subpart 25.10—Additional Foreign Acquisition Regulations

Waiver of right to examination of records 25.1001
Use of foreign currency 25.1002

Subpart 25.11—Solicitation Provisions and Contract Clauses

Acquisition of supplies 25.1101
Acquisition of construction 25.1102
Other provisions and clauses 25.1103

PART 25—FOREIGN ACQUISITION

25.000 Scope of part.

(a) This part provides policies and procedures for—

(1) Acquisition of foreign supplies, services, and construction materials; and

(2) Contracts performed outside the United States.

(b) It implements 41 U.S.C. chapter 83, Buy American; trade agreements; and other laws and regulations.

[FAC 97-15, 64 FR 72414, 12/27/99, effective 2/25/2000; FAC 2001-07, FR 67 21534, 4/30/2002, effective 5/15/2002; FAC 2001-07, 67 FR 21534, 4/30/2002, effective 5/15/2002; FAC 2005-24, 73 FR 10943, 2/28/2008, effective 3/31/2008; FAC 2005-73, 79 FR 24192, 4/29/2014, effective 5/29/2014]

25.001 General.

(a) 41 U.S.C. chapter 83, Buy American—

(1) Restricts the purchase of supplies, that are not domestic end products, for use within the United States. A foreign end product may be purchased if the contracting officer determines that the price of the lowest domestic offer is unreasonable or if another exception applies (see Subpart 25.1); and

(2) Requires, with some exceptions, the use of only domestic construction materials in contracts for construction in the United States (see Subpart 25.2).

(b) The restrictions in the Buy American statute are not applicable in acquisitions subject to certain trade agreements (see Subpart 25.4). In these acquisitions, end products and construction materials from certain countries receive nondiscriminatory treatment in evaluation with domestic offers. Generally, the dollar value of the acquisition determines which of the trade agreements applies. Exceptions to the applicability of the trade agreements are described in Subpart 25.4.

(c) The test to determine the country of origin for an end product under the Buy American statute (see the various country *end product* definitions in 25.003) is different from the test to determine the country of origin for an end product under the trade agreements, or the criteria for the representation on end products manufactured outside the United States (see 52.225-18).

(1) The Buy American statute uses a two-part test to define a *domestic end product* or *domestic construction material* (manufactured in the United States and a formula based on cost of domestic components). The component test has been waived for acquisition of commercially available off-the-shelf items.

(2) Under the trade agreements, the test to determine country of origin is *substantial transformation* (i.e., transforming an article into a new and different article of commerce, with a name, character, or use distinct from the original article).

(3) For the representation at 52.225-18, the only criterion is whether the place of manufacture of an end product is in the United States or outside the United States, without regard to the origin of the components.

(4) When using funds appropriated under the American Recovery and Reinvestment Act of 2009 (Pub. L. 111-5), the definition of *domestic manufactured construction material* requires manufacture in the United States but does not include a requirement with regard to the origin of the components. If the construction material consists wholly or predominantly of iron or steel, the iron or steel must be produced in the United States.

[FAC 97-15, 64 FR 72414, 12/27/99, effective 2/25/2000; FAC 2001-07, 67 FR 21534, 4/30/2002, effective 5/15/2002; FAC 2005-09, Interim rule 71 FR 20305, 4/19/2006, effective 4/19/2006; FAC 2005-13, 71 FR 57375, 9/28/2006, effective 9/28/2006; FAC 2005-14, 71 FR 67775, 11/22/2006, effective 11/22/2006; FAC 2005-19, 72 FR 46326, 8/17/2007, effective 8/17/2007; FAC 2005-32, 74 FR 14623, 3/31/2009, effective 3/31/2009; FAC 2005-45, 75 FR 53153, 8/30/2010, effective 10/1/2010; FAC 2005-67, 78 FR 37694, 6/21/2013, effective 7/22/2013; FAC 2005-73, 79 FR 24192, 4/29/2014, effective 5/29/2014]

25.002 Applicability of subparts.

The following table shows the applicability of the subparts. Subpart 25.5 provides comprehensive procedures for offer evaluation and examples.

	Subpart	Supplies for use		Construction		Services performed	
		Inside U.S.	Outside U.S.	Inside U.S.	Outside U.S.	Inside U.S.	Outside U.S.
25.1	Buy American—Supplies	X					
25.2	Buy American—Construction Materials			X			
25.3	Contracts Performed Outside the United States		X		X		X
25.4	Trade Agreements	X	X	X	X	X	X
25.5	Evaluating Foreign Offers—Supply Contracts	X	X				
25.6	American Recovery and Reinvestment Act—Buy American statute—Construction Materials			X			
25.7	Prohibited Sources	X	X	X	X	X	X
25.8	Other International Agreements and Coordination	X	X				X
25.9	Customs and Duties	X					
25.10	Additional Foreign Acquisition Regulations	X	X	X	X	X	X
25.11	Solicitation Provisions and Contract Clauses	X	X	X	X	X	X

[FAC 97-15, 64 FR 72414, 12/27/99, effective 2/25/2000; FAC 2001-07, 67 FR 21534, 4/30/2002, effective 5/15/2002; FAC 2005-09, 71 FR 20305, 4/19/2006, effective 4/19/2006; FAC 2005-14, 71 FR 67775, 11/22/2006, effective 11/22/2006; FAC 2005-24, 73 FR 10943, 2/28/2008, effective 2/28/2008; FAC 2005-32, 74 FR 14623, 3/31/2009, effective 3/31/2009; FAC 2005-45, 75 FR 53153, 8/30/2010, effective 10/1/2010; FAC 2005-73, 79 FR 24192, 4/29/2014, effective 5/29/2014]

25.003 Definitions.

As used in this part—

Caribbean Basin country means any of the following countries: Antigua and Barbuda, Aruba, Bahamas, Barbados, Belize, Bonaire, British Virgin Islands, Curacao, Dominica, Grenada, Guyana, Haiti, Jamaica, Montserrat, Saba, St. Kitts and Nevis, St. Lucia, St. Vincent and the Grenadines, Sint Eustatius, Sint Maarten, or Trinidad and Tobago.

Caribbean Basin country end product—

(1) Means an article that—

(i) (A) Is wholly the growth, product, or manufacture of a Caribbean Basin country; or

(B) In the case of an article that consists in whole or in part of materials from another country, has been substantially transformed in a Caribbean Basin country into a new and different article of commerce with a name, character, or use distinct from that of the article or articles from which it was transformed; and

(ii) Is not excluded from duty-free treatment for Caribbean countries under 19 U.S.C. 2703(b).

(A) For this reason, the following articles are not Caribbean Basin country end products:

(1) Tuna, prepared or preserved in any manner in airtight containers.

(2) Petroleum, or any product derived from petroleum.

(3) Watches and watch parts (including cases, bracelets, and straps) of whatever type including, but not limited to, mechanical, quartz digital, or quartz analog, if such watches or watch parts contain any material that is the product of any country to which the Harmonized Tariff Schedule of the United States (HTSUS) column 2 rates of duty apply (i.e., Afghanistan, Cuba, Laos, North Korea, and Vietnam).

(4) Certain of the following: textiles and apparel articles; footwear, handbags, lug-

gage, flat goods, work gloves, and leather wearing apparel; or handloomed, handmade, and folklore articles.

(B) Access to the HTSUS to determine duty-free status of articles of the types listed in paragraph (1) (ii) (A) (4) of this definition is available via the Internet at ***https://usitc.gov/tata/hts/index.htm***. In particular, see the following:

(1) General Note 3(c), Products Eligible for Special Tariff treatment.

(2) General Note 17, Products of Countries Designated as Beneficiary Countries under the United States—Caribbean Basin Trade Partnership Act of 2000.

(3) Section XXII, Chapter 98, Subchapter II, Articles Exported and Returned, Advanced or Improved Abroad, U.S. Note 7(b).

(4) Section XXII, Chapter 98, Subchapter XX, Goods Eligible for Special Tariff Benefits under the United States-Caribbean Basin Trade Partnership Act; and

(B) Refers to a product offered for purchase under a supply contract, but for purposes of calculating the value of the acquisition, includes services (except transportation services) incidental to the article, provided that the value of those incidental services does not exceed that of the article itself.

Civil aircraft and related articles means—

(1) All aircraft other than aircraft to be purchased for use by the Department of Defense or the U.S. Coast Guard;

(2) The engines (and parts and components for incorporation into the engines) of these aircraft;

(3) Any other parts, components, and subassemblies for incorporation into the aircraft; and

(4) Any ground flight simulators, and parts and components of these simulators, for use with respect to the aircraft, whether to be used as original or replacement equipment in the manufacture, repair, maintenance, rebuilding, modification, or conversion of the aircraft and without regard to whether the aircraft or articles receive dutyfree treatment under section 601(a)(2) of the Trade Agreements Act.

Component means an article, material, or supply incorporated directly into an end product or construction material.

Construction material means an article, material, or supply brought to the construction site by a contractor or subcontractor for incorporation into the building or work. The term also includes an item brought to the site preassembled from articles, materials, or supplies. However, emergency life safety systems, such as emergency lighting, fire alarm, and audio evacuation systems, that are discrete systems incorporated into a public building or work and that are produced as complete systems, are evaluated as a single and distinct construction material regardless of when or how the individual parts or components of those systems are delivered to the construction site. Materials purchased directly by the Government are supplies, not construction material.

Cost of components means—

(1) For components purchased by the contractor, the acquisition cost, including transportation costs to the place of incorporation into the end product or construction material (whether or not such costs are paid to a domestic firm), and any applicable duty (whether or not a duty-free entry certificate is issued); or

(2) For components manufactured by the contractor, all costs associated with the manufacture of the component, including transportation costs as described in paragraph (1) of this definition, plus allocable overhead costs, but excluding profit. Cost of components does not include any costs associated with the manufacture of the end product.

Designated country means any of the following countries:

(1) A World Trade Organization Government Procurement Agreement (WTO GPA) country (Armenia, Aruba, Australia, Austria, Belgium, Bulgaria, Canada, Croatia, Cyprus, Czech Republic, Denmark, Estonia, Finland, France, Germany, Greece, Hong Kong, Hungary, Iceland, Ireland, Israel, Italy, Japan, Korea (Republic of), Latvia, Liechtenstein, Lithuania, Luxembourg, Malta, Moldova, Montenegro, Netherlands, New Zealand, Norway, Poland, Portugal, Romania, Singa-

pore, Slovak Republic, Slovenia, Spain, Sweden, Switzerland, Taiwan (known in the World Trade Organization as "the Separate Customs Territory of Taiwan, Penghu, Kinmen and Matsu (Chinese Taipei)", Ukraine, or United Kingdom);

(2) A Free Trade Agreement (FTA) country (Australia, Bahrain, Canada, Chile, Colombia, Costa Rica, Dominican Republic, El Salvador, Guatemala, Honduras, Korea (Republic of), Mexico, Morocco, Nicaragua, Oman, Panama, Peru, or Singapore);

(3) A least developed country (Afghanistan, Angola, Bangladesh, Benin, Bhutan, Burkina Faso, Burundi, Cambodia, Central African Republic, Chad, Comoros, Democratic Republic of Congo, Djibouti, Equatorial Guinea, Eritrea, Ethiopia, Gambia, Guinea, Guinea-Bissau, Haiti, Kiribati, Laos, Lesotho, Liberia, Madagascar, Malawi, Mali, Mauritania, Mozambique, Nepal, Niger, Rwanda, Samoa, Sao Tome and Principe, Senegal, Sierra Leone, Solomon Islands, Somalia, South Sudan, Tanzania, Timor-Leste, Togo, Tuvalu, Uganda, Vanuatu, Yemen, or Zambia); or

(4) A Caribbean Basin country (Antigua and Barbuda, Aruba, Bahamas, Barbados, Belize, Bonaire, British Virgin Islands, Curacao, Dominica, Grenada, Guyana, Haiti, Jamaica, Montserrat, Saba, St. Kitts and Nevis, St. Lucia, St. Vincent and the Grenadines, Sint Eustatius, Sint Maarten, or Trinidad and Tobago).

Designated country end product means a WTO GPA country end product, an FTA country end product, a least developed country end product, or a Caribbean Basin country end product.

Domestic construction material means—

(1) (i) An unmanufactured construction material mined or produced in the United States;

(ii) A construction material manufactured in the United States, if—

(A) The cost of the components mined, produced, or manufactured in the United States exceeds 50 percent of the cost of all its components. Components of foreign origin of the same class or kind for which nonavailability determinations have been made are treated as domestic; or

(B) The construction material is a COTS item;

(2) Except that for use in subpart 25.6, see the definition in 25.601.

Domestic end product means—

(1) An unmanufactured end product mined or produced in the United States;

(2) An end product manufactured in the United States, if—

(i) The cost of its components mined, produced, or manufactured in the United States exceeds 50 percent of the cost of all its components. Components of foreign origin of the same class or kind as those that the agency determines are not mined, produced, or manufactured in sufficient and reasonably available commercial quantities of a satisfactory quality are treated as domestic. Scrap generated, collected, and prepared for processing in the United States is considered domestic; or

(ii) The end product is a COTS item.

Domestic offer means an offer of a domestic end product. When the solicitation specifies that award will be made on a group of line items, a domestic offer means an offer where the proposed price of the domestic end products exceeds 50 percent of the total proposed price of the group.

Eligible offer means an offer of an eligible product. When the solicitation specifies that award will be made on a group of line items, an eligible offer means a foreign offer where the combined proposed price of the eligible products and the domestic end products exceeds 50 percent of the total proposed price of the group.

Eligible product means a foreign end product, construction material, or service that, due to applicability of a trade agreement to a particular acquisition, is not subject to discriminatory treatment.

End product means those articles, materials, and supplies to be acquired for public use.

Foreign construction material means a construction material other than a domestic construction material.

Foreign contractor means a contractor or subcontractor organized or existing under the laws of a country other than the United States.

Foreign end product means an end product other than a domestic end product.

Foreign offer means any offer other than a domestic offer.

Free Trade Agreement country means Australia, Bahrain, Canada, Chile, Colombia, Costa Rica, Dominican Republic, El Salvador, Guatemala, Honduras, Korea (Republic of), Mexico, Morocco, Nicaragua, Oman, Panama, Peru, or Singapore.

Free Trade Agreement country end product means an article that—

(1) Is wholly the growth, product, or manufacture of a Free Trade Agreement (FTA) country; or

(2) In the case of an article that consists in whole or in part of materials from another country, has been substantially transformed in an FTA country into a new and different article of commerce with a name, character, or use distinct from that of the article or articles from which it was transformed. The term refers to a product offered for purchase under a supply contract, but for purposes of calculating the value of the end product, includes services (except transportation services) incidental to the article, provided that the value of those incidental services does not exceed that of the article itself.

Israeli end product means an article that—

(1) Is wholly the growth, product, or manufacture of Israel; or

(2) In the case of an article that consists in whole or in part of materials from another country, has been substantially transformed in Israel into a new and different article of commerce with a name, character, or use distinct from that of the article or articles from which it was transformed.

Least developed country means any of the following countries: Afghanistan, Angola, Bangladesh, Benin, Bhutan, Burkina Faso, Burundi, Cambodia, Central African Republic, Chad, Comoros, Democratic Republic of Congo, Djibouti, Equatorial Guinea, Eritrea, Ethiopia, Gambia, Guinea, Guinea-Bissau, Haiti, Kiribati, Laos, Lesotho, Liberia, Madagascar, Malawi, Mali, Mauritania, Mozambique, Nepal, Niger, Rwanda, Samoa, Sao Tome and Principe, Senegal, Sierra Leone, Solomon Islands, Somalia, South Sudan, Tanzania, Timor-Leste, Togo, Tuvalu, Uganda, Vanuatu, Yemen, or Zambia.

Least developed country end product means an article that—

(1) Is wholly the growth, product, or manufacture of a least developed country; or

(2) In the case of an article that consists in whole or in part of materials from another country, has been substantially transformed in a least developed country into a new and different article of commerce with a name, character, or use distinct from that of the article or articles from which it was transformed. The term refers to a product offered for purchase under a supply contract, but for purposes of calculating the value of the end product, includes services (except transportation services) incidental to the article, provided that the value of those incidental services does not exceed that of the article itself.

Noneligible offer means an offer of a noneligible product.

Noneligible product means a foreign end product that is not an eligible product.

United States means the 50 States, the District of Columbia, and outlying areas.

U.S.-made end product means an article that is mined, produced, or manufactured in the United States or that is substantially transformed in the United States into a new and different article of commerce with a name, character, or use distinct from that of the article or articles from which it was transformed.

World Trade Organization Government Procurement Agreement (WTO GPA) country means any of the following countries: Armenia, Aruba, Australia, Austria, Belgium, Bulgaria, Canada, Croatia, Cyprus, Czech Republic, Denmark, Estonia, Finland, France, Germany, Greece, Hong Kong, Hungary, Iceland, Ireland, Israel, Italy, Japan, Korea (Republic of), Latvia, Liechtenstein, Lithuania, Luxembourg, Malta, Moldova, Montenegro, Netherlands, New Zealand,

Norway, Poland, Portugal, Romania, Singapore, Slovak Republic, Slovenia, Spain, Sweden, Switzerland, Taiwan, Ukraine, or United Kingdom.

WTO GPA country end product means an article that—

(1) Is wholly the growth, product, or manufacture of a WTO GPA country; or

(2) In the case of an article that consists in whole or in part of materials from another country, has been substantially transformed in a WTO GPA country into a new and different article of commerce with a name, character, or use distinct from that of the article or articles from which it was transformed. The term refers to a product offered for purchase under a supply contract, but for purposes of calculating the value of the end product includes services (except transportation services) incidental to the article, provided that the value of those incidental services does not exceed that of the article itself.

[FAC 97-15, 64 FR 72414, 12/27/99, effective 2/25/2000; FAC 97-17, 65 FR 24316, 4/25/2000, effective 4/25/2000; FAC 2001-02, 66 FR 65347, 12/18/2001, effective 12/18/2001; FAC 2001-02, 66 FR 65347, 12/18/2001, effective 2/19/2002; FAC 2001-04, 67 FR 6112, 2/8/2002, effective 2/20/2002; FAC 2001-07, 67 FR 21534, 4/30/2002, effective 5/15/2002; FAC 2001-10, 67 FR 70519, 11/22/2002, effective 11/22/2002; FAC 2001-14, 68 FR 28079, 5/22/2003, effective 6/23/2003; FAC 2001-16, 68 FR 56684, 10/1/2003, effective 10/31/2003; FAC 2001-19, 69 FR 1051, 1/7/2004, effective 1/1/2004; FAC 2001-24, 69 FR 34239, 6/18/2004, effective 6/18/2004; FAC 2001-25, 69 FR 59700, 10/5/2004, effective 10/5/2004; FAC 2001-27, interim rule 69 FR 77870, 12/28/2004, effective 1/1/2005; FAC 2005-07, 71 FR 219, 1/3/2006, effective 1/3/2006; FAC 2005-09, interim rule, 71 FR 20305, 4/19/2006, effective 4/19/2006; FAC 2005-09, 71 FR 20306, 4/19/2006, effective 4/19/2006; FAC 2005-10, 71 FR 36935, 6/28/2006, effective 6/28/2006; FAC 2005-14, 71 FR 67775, 71 FR 67776, 71 FR 67778, 11/22/2006, effective 11/22/2006; FAC 2005-19, 72 FR 46357, 46360, 46361, 8/17/2007, effective 8/17/2007; FAC 2005-21, 72 FR 63089, 11/7/2007, effective 11/7/2007; FAC 2005-24, 73 FR 10964, 2/28/2008, effective 2/28/2008; FAC 2005-30, 74 FR 2713, 1/15/2009, effective 2/17/2009; FAC 2005-31, 74 FR 11828, 3/19/2009, effective 3/19/2009; FAC 2005-33, Interim rule, 74 FR 28426, 6/15/2009, effective 6/15/2009; FAC 2005-36, 74 FR 40461, 8/11/2009, effective 8/11/2009; FAC 2005-39, 75 FR 13421, 3/19/2010, effective 3/19/2010; FAC 2005-42, 75 FR 34282, 6/16/2010, effective 6/16/2010; FAC 2005-45, 75 FR 53153, 8/30/2010, effective 10/1/2010; FAC 2005-54, 76 FR 68027, 68039, 11/2/2011, effective 11/2/2011; FAC 2005-56, 77 FR 12935, 3/2/2012, effective 3/2/2012; FAC 2005-57, 77 FR 13952, 3/7/2012, effective 3/15/2012; FAC 2005-59, 77 FR 27548, 5/10/2012, effective 5/15/2012; FAC 2005-61, 77 FR 56739, 9/13/2012, effective 9/13/2012; FAC 2005-62, 77 FR 69723, 11/20/2012, effective 11/20/2012; FAC 2005-65, 78 FR 6188, 1/29/2013, effective 1/29/2013; FAC 2005-67, 78 FR 37695, 6/21/2013, effective 6/21/2013; FAC 2005-69, 78 FR 46792, 8/1/2013, effective 9/3/2013; FAC 2005-71, 78 FR 70480, 11/25/2013, effective 12/26/2013; FAC 2005-86, 80 FR 81892, 12/31/2015, effective 2/1/2016; FAC 2005-91, 81 FR 67774, 9/30/2016, effective 10/31/2016; FAC 2005-100, 83 FR 42571, 8/22/2018, effective 8/22/2018; FAC 2019-06, 84 FR 47866, 9/10/2019, effective 10/10/2019]

25.004 [Removed]

[FAC 2005-13, 71 FR 57375, 9/28/2006, effective 9/28/2006; FAC 2005-19, 72 FR 46326, 8/17/2007, effective 8/17/2007; FAC 2005-65, 78 FR 6188, 1/29/2013, effective 1/29/2013; FAC 2005-67, 78 FR 37694, 6/21/2013, effective 7/22/2013]

SUBPART 25.1—BUY AMERICAN—SUPPLIES

25.100 Scope of subpart.

(a) This subpart implements—

(1) 41 U.S.C. chapter 83, Buy American;

(2) E.O. Executive Order 10582, December 17, 1954; and

(3) Waiver of the component test of the Buy American statute for acquisition of commercially available off-the-shelf (COTS) items in accordance with 41 U.S.C. 1907.

(b) It applies to supplies acquired for use in the United States, including supplies acquired under contracts set aside for small business concerns, if—

(1) The supply contract exceeds the micro-purchase threshold; or

(2) The supply portion of a contract for services that involves the furnishing of supplies (e.g., lease) exceeds the micro-purchase threshold.

[FAC 97-15, 64 FR 72414, 12/27/99, effective 2/25/2000, corrected 65 FR 4633, 1/31/2000; FAC 2005-30, 74 FR 2713, 1/15/2009, effective 2/17/2009; FAC 2005-73, 79 FR 24192, 4/29/2014, effective 5/29/2014]

25.101 General.

(a) The Buy American statute restricts the purchase of supplies that are not domestic end products. For manufactured end products, the Buy American statute uses a two-part test to define a domestic end product.

(1) The article must be manufactured in the United States; and

(2) The cost of domestic components must exceed 50 percent of the cost of all the components. In accordance with 41 U.S.C. 1907, this component test of the Buy American statute has been waived for acquisitions of COTS items (see 12.505(a)).

(b) The Buy American statute applies to small business set-asides. A manufactured product of a small business concern is a U.S.-made end product, but is not a domestic end product unless it meets the component test in paragraph (a)(2) of this section.

(c) Exceptions that allow the purchase of a foreign end product are listed at 25.103. The unreasonable cost exception is implemented through the use of an evaluation factor applied to low foreign offers that are not eligible offers. The evaluation factor is not used to provide a preference for one foreign offer over another. Evaluation procedures and examples are provided in Subpart 25.5.

[FAC 97-15, 64 FR 72414, 12/27/99, effective 2/25/2000; FAC 2005-30, 74 FR 2713, 1/15/2009, effective 2/17/2009; FAC 2005-73, 79 FR 24192, 4/29/2014, effective 5/29/2014]

25.102 Policy.

Except as provided in 25.103, acquire only domestic end products for public use inside the United States.

[FAC 97-15, 64 FR 72414, 12/27/99, effective 2/25/2000]

25.103 Exceptions.

When one of the following exceptions applies, the contracting officer may acquire a foreign end product without regard to the restrictions of the Buy American statute:

(a) *Public interest.* The head of the agency may make a determination that domestic preference would be inconsistent with the public interest. This exception applies when an agency has an agreement with a foreign government that provides a blanket exception to the Buy American statute.

(b) *Nonavailability.* The Buy American statute does not apply with respect to articles, materials, or supplies if articles, materials, or supplies of the class or kind to be acquired, either as end items or components, are not mined, produced, or manufactured in the United States in sufficient and reasonably available commercial quantities and of a satisfactory quality.

(1) *Class determinations.* (i) A nonavailability determination has been made for the articles listed in 25.104. This determination does not necessarily mean that there is no domestic source for the listed items, but that domestic sources can only meet 50 percent or less of total U.S. Government and nongovernment demand.

(ii) Before acquisition of an article on the list, the procuring agency is responsible to conduct market research appropriate to the circumstances, including seeking of domestic sources. This applies to acquisition of an article as—

(A) An end product; or

(B) A significant component (valued at more than 50 percent of the value of all the components).

(iii) The determination in paragraph (b)(1)(i) of this section does not apply if the contracting officer learns at any time before the time designated for receipt of bids in sealed bidding or final offers in negotiation that an article on the list is available domestically in sufficient and reasonably available commercial quantities of a satisfactory quality to meet the requirements of the solicitation. The contracting officer must—

(A) Ensure that the appropriate Buy American statute provision and clause are included in the solicitation (see 25.1101(a), 25.1101(b), or 25.1102);

(B) Specify in the solicitation that the article is available domestically and that offerors and contractors may not treat foreign components of the same class or kind as domestic components; and

(C) Submit a copy of supporting documentation to the appropriate council identified in 1.201-1, in accordance with agency procedures, for possible removal of the article from the list.

(2) *Individual determinations*. (i) The head of the contracting activity may make a determination that an article, material, or supply is not mined, produced, or manufactured in the United States in sufficient and reasonably available commercial quantities of a satisfactory quality.

(ii) If the contracting officer considers that the nonavailability of an article is likely to affect future acquisitions, the contracting officer may submit a copy of the determination and supporting documentation to the appropriate council identified in 1.201-1, in accordance with agency procedures, for possible addition to the list in 25.104.

(3) A written determination is not required if all of the following conditions are present:

(i) The acquisition was conducted through use of full and open competition.

(ii) The acquisition was synopsized in accordance with 5.201.

(iii) No offer for a domestic end product was received.

(c) *Unreasonable cost*. The contracting officer may determine that the cost of a domestic end product would be unreasonable, in accordance with 25.105 and Subpart 25.5.

(d) *Resale*. The contracting officer may purchase foreign end products specifically for commissary resale.

(e) *Information technology that is a commercial item*. The restriction on purchasing foreign end products does not apply to the acquisition of information technology that is a commercial item, when using fiscal year 2004 or subsequent fiscal year funds (Section 535 (a) of Division F, Title V, Consolidated Appropriations Act, 2004, and similar sections in subsequent appropriation acts).

[FAC 97-15, 64 FR 72414, 12/27/99, effective 2/25/2000; FAC 2005-01, 70 FR 11742, 3/9/2005, effective 4/8/2005; FAC 2005-07, 71 FR 223, 1/3/2006, effective 1/3/2006; FAC 2005-13, 71 FR 57378, 9/28/2006, effective 9/28/2006; FAC 2005-73, 79 FR 24192, 4/29/2014, effective 5/29/2014]

25.104 Nonavailable articles.

(a) The following articles have been determined to be nonavailable in accordance with 25.103(b)(1)(i):

Acetylene, black.

Agar, bulk.

Anise.

Antimony, as metal or oxide.

Asbestos, amosite, chrysotile, and crocidolite.

Bamboo shoots.

Bananas.

Bauxite.

Beef, corned, canned.

Beef extract.

Bephenium hydroxynapthoate.

Bismuth.

Books, trade, text, technical, or scientific; newspapers; pamphlets; magazines; periodicals; printed briefs and films; not printed in the United States and for which domestic editions are not available.

Brazil nuts, unroasted.

Cadmium, ores and flue dust.

Calcium cyanamide.

Capers.

Cashew nuts.

Castor beans and castor oil.

Chalk, English.

Chestnuts.

Chicle.

Chrome ore or chromite.

Cinchona bark.

Cobalt, in cathodes, rondelles, or other primary ore and metal forms.

Cocoa beans.

Coconut and coconut meat, unsweetened, in shredded, desiccated, or similarly prepared form.

Coffee, raw or green bean.

Colchicine alkaloid, raw.

Copra.

Cork, wood or bark and waste.

Cover glass, microscope slide.

Crane rail (85-pound per foot).

Cryolite, natural.

Dammar gum.

Diamonds, industrial, stones and abrasives.

Emetine, bulk.

Ergot, crude.

Erythrityl tetranitrate.

Fair linen, altar.

Fibers of the following types: abaca, abace, agave, coir, flax, jute, jute burlaps, palmyra, and sisal.

Goat and kidskins.

Goat hair canvas.

Grapefruit sections, canned.

Graphite, natural, crystalline, crucible grade.

Hand file sets (Swiss pattern).

Handsewing needles.

Hemp yarn.

Hog bristles for brushes.

Hyoscine, bulk.

Ipecac, root.

Iodine, crude.

Kaurigum.

Lac.

Leather, sheepskin, hair type.

Lavender oil.

Manganese.

Menthol, natural bulk.

Mica.

Microprocessor chips (brought onto a Government construction site as separate units for incorporation into building systems during construction or repair and alteration of real property).

Modacrylic fiber.

Nickel, primary, in ingots, pigs, shots, cathodes, or similar forms; nickel oxide and nickel salts.

Nitroguanidine (also known as picrite).

Nux vomica, crude.

Oiticica oil.

Olive oil.

Olives (green), pitted or unpitted, or stuffed, in bulk.

Opium, crude.

Oranges, mandarin, canned.

Petroleum, crude oil, unfinished oils, and finished products.

Pineapple, canned.

Pine needle oil.

Platinum and related group metals, refined, as sponge, powder, ingots, or cast bars.

Pyrethrum flowers.

Quartz crystals.

Quebracho.

Quinidine.

Quinine.

Rabbit fur felt.

Radium salts, source and special nuclear materials.

Rosettes.

Rubber, crude and latex.

Rutile.

Santonin, crude.

Secretin.

Shellac.

Silk, raw and unmanufactured.

Spare and replacement parts for equipment of foreign manufacture, and for which domestic parts are not available.

Spices and herbs, in bulk.

Sugars, raw.

Swords and scabbards.

Talc, block, steatite.

Tantalum.

Tapioca flour and cassava.

Tartar, crude; tartaric acid and cream of tartar in bulk.

Tea in bulk.

Thread, metallic (gold).

Thyme oil.

Tin in bars, blocks, and pigs.

Triprolidine hydrochloride.

Tungsten.

Vanilla beans.

Venom, cobra.

Water chestnuts.

Wax, carnauba.

Wire glass.

Woods; logs, veneer, and lumber of the following species: Alaskan yellow cedar, angelique, balsa, ekki, greenheart, lignum vitae, mahogany, and teak.

Yarn, 50 Denier rayon.

Yeast, active dry and instant active dry.

(b) This list will be published in the *Federal Register* for public comment no less frequently than once every five years. Unsolicited recommendations for deletions from this list may be submitted at any time and should provide sufficient data and rationale to permit evaluation (see 1.502).

[FAC 97-15, 64 FR 72414, 12/27/99, effective 2/25/2000; FAC 2001-24, 69 FR 34241, 6/18/2004, effective 7/19/2004; FAC 2005-01, 70 FR 11742, 3/9/2005, effective 4/8/2005; FAC 2005-42, 75 FR 34282, 6/16/2010, effective 6/16/2010]

25.105 Determining reasonableness of cost.

(a) The contracting officer—

(1) Must use the evaluation factors in paragraph (b) of this section unless the head of the agency makes a written determination that the use of higher factors is more appropriate. If the determination applies to all agency acquisitions, the agency evaluation factors must be published in agency regulations; and

(2) Must not apply evaluation factors to offers of eligible products if the acquisition is subject to a trade agreement under Subpart 25.4.

(b) If there is a domestic offer that is not the low offer, and the restrictions of the Buy American statute apply to the low offer, the contracting officer must determine the reasonableness of the cost of the domestic offer by adding to the price of the low offer, inclusive of duty—

(1) 6 percent, if the lowest domestic offer is from a large business concern; or

(2) 12 percent, if the lowest domestic offer is from a small business concern. The contracting officer must use this factor, or another factor established in agency regulations, in small business set-asides if the low offer is from a small business concern offering the product of a small business concern that is not a domestic end product (see Subpart 19.5).

(c) The price of the domestic offer is reasonable if it does not exceed the evaluated price of the low offer after addition of the appropriate evaluation factor in accordance with paragraph (a) or (b) of this section. (See evaluation procedures at Subpart 25.5.)

[FAC 97-15, 64 FR 72414, 12/27/99, effective 2/25/2000; FAC 2005-73, 79 FR 24192, 4/29/2014, effective 5/29/2014]

SUBPART 25.2—BUY AMERICAN—CONSTRUCTION MATERIALS

25.200 Scope of subpart.

(a) This subpart implements—

(1) 41 U.S.C. chapter 83, Buy American;

(2) Executive Order 10582, December 17, 1954; and

(3) Waiver of the component test of the Buy American statute for acquisitions of commercially available off-the-shelf (COTS) items in accordance with 41 U.S.C. 1907.

(b) It applies to contracts for the construction, alteration, or repair of any public building or public work in the United States.

(c) When using funds appropriated or otherwise provided by the American Recovery and Reinvestment Act of 2009 (Pub. L. 111-5) (Recovery Act) for construction, see Subpart 25.6.

[FAC 97-15, 64 FR 72414, 12/27/99, effective 2/25/2000; FAC 2005-30, 74 FR 2713, 1/15/2009, effective 2/17/2009; Technical amendments, 74 FR 22809, 5/14/2009, effective 5/14/2009; FAC 2005-73, 79 FR 24192, 4/29/2014, effective 5/29/2014]

25.201 Policy.

Except as provided in 25.202, use only domestic construction materials in construction contracts performed in the United States.

[FAC 97-15, 64 FR 72414, 12/27/99, effective 2/25/2000]

25.202 Exceptions.

(a) When one of the following exceptions applies, the contracting officer may allow the contractor to acquire foreign construction materials without regard to the restrictions of the Buy American statute:

(1) *Impracticable or inconsistent with public interest.* The head of the agency may determine that application of the restrictions of the Buy American statute to a particular construction material would be impracticable or would be inconsistent with the public interest. The public interest exception applies when an agency has an agreement with a foreign government that provides a blanket exception to the Buy American statute.

(2) *Nonavailability.* The head of the contracting activity may determine that a particular construction material is not mined, produced, or manufactured in the United States in sufficient and reasonably available commercial quantities of a satisfactory quality. The determinations of nonavailability of the articles listed at 25.104(a) and the procedures at 25.103(b)(1) also apply if any of those articles are acquired as construction materials.

(3) *Unreasonable cost.* The contracting officer concludes that the cost of domestic construction material is unreasonable in accordance with 25.204.

(4) *Information technology that is a commercial item.* The restriction on purchasing foreign construction material does not apply to the acquisition of information technology that is a commercial item, when using Fiscal Year 2004 or subsequent fiscal year funds (Section 535(a) of Division F, Title V, Consolidated Appropriations Act, 2004, and similar sections in subsequent appropriations acts).

(b) *Determination and findings.* When a determination is made for any of the reasons stated in this section that certain foreign construction materials may be used, the contracting officer must list the excepted materials in the contract. The agency must make the findings justifying the exception available for public inspection.

(c) *Acquisitions under trade agreements.* For construction contracts with an estimated acquisition value of $6,932,000 or more, see subpart 25.4.

[FAC 97-15, 64 FR 72414, 12/27/99, effective 2/25/2000; FAC 97-18, 65 FR 36014, 6/6/2000, effective 6/6/2000; FAC 2001-09, 67 FR 56115, 8/30/2002, effective 9/30/2002; FAC 2001-19, 69 FR 1051, 1/7/2004, effective 1/1/2004; FAC 2001-25, 69 FR 59700, 10/5/2004, effective 10/5/2004; FAC 2005-01, 70 FR 11742, 3/9/2005, effective 4/8/2005; FAC 2005-08, 71 FR 864, 1/5/2006, effective 1/5/2006; FAC 2005-13, 71 FR 57375, 9/28/2006, effective 9/28/2006; FAC 2005-24, 73 FR 10962, 2/28/2008, effective 2/28/2008; FAC 2005-30, 74 FR 2745, 1/15/2009, effective 1/15/2009; FAC 2005-43, 75 FR 38689, 7/2/2010, effective 7/2/2010; FAC 2005-46, 75 FR 60266, 9/29/2010, effective 9/29/2010; FAC 2005-50, 76 FR 14570, 3/16/2011, effective 3/16/2011; FAC 2005-52, 76 FR 31415, 5/31/2011, effective

5/31/2011; FAC 2005-56, 77 FR 12933, 3/2/2012, effective 3/2/2012; FAC 2005-72, 78 FR 80379, 12/31/2013, effective 1/1/2014; FAC 2005-73, 79 FR 24192, 4/29/2014, effective 5/29/2014; FAC 2005-86, 80 FR 81894, 12/31/2015, effective 1/1/2016; FAC 2005-97, 83 FR 3396, 1/24/2018, effective 1/24/2018]

25.203 Preaward determinations.

(a) For any acquisition, an offeror may request from the contracting officer a determination concerning the inapplicability of the Buy American statute for specifically identified construction materials. The time for submitting the request is specified in the solicitation in paragraph (b) of either 52.225-10 or 52.225-12, whichever applies. The information and supporting data that must be included in the request are also specified in the solicitation in paragraphs (c) and (d) of either 52.225-9 or 52.225-11, whichever applies.

(b) Before award, the contracting officer must evaluate all requests based on the information provided and may supplement this information with other readily available information.

[FAC 97-15, 64 FR 72414, 12/27/99, effective 2/25/2000; FAC 2005-73, 79 FR 24192, 4/29/2014, effective 5/29/2014]

25.204 Evaluating offers of foreign construction material.

(a) Offerors proposing to use foreign construction material other than that listed by the Government in the applicable clause at 52.225-9, paragraph (b)(2), or 52.225-11, paragraph (b)(3), or covered by the WTO GPA or a Free Trade Agreement (paragraph (b)(2) of 52.225-11), must provide the information required by paragraphs (c) and (d) of the respective clauses.

(b) Unless the head of the agency specifies a higher percentage, the contracting officer must add to the offered price 6 percent of the cost of any foreign construction material proposed for exception from the requirements of the Buy American statute based on the unreasonable cost of domestic construction materials. In the case of a tie, the contracting officer must give preference to an offer that does not include foreign construction material excepted at the request of the offeror on the basis of unreasonable cost.

(c) Offerors also may submit alternate offers based on use of equivalent domestic construction material to avoid possible rejection of the entire offer if the Government determines that an exception permitting use of a particular foreign construction material does not apply.

(d) If the contracting officer awards a contract to an offeror that proposed foreign construction material not listed in the applicable clause in the solicitation (paragraph (b)(2) of 52.225-9, or paragraph (b)(3) of 52.225-11), the contracting officer must add the excepted materials to the list in the contract clause.

[FAC 97-15, 64 FR 72414, 12/27/99, effective 2/25/2000; FAC 2001-19, 69 FR 1051, 1/7/2004, effective 1/7/2004; FAC 2001-25, 69 FR 59700, 10/5/2004, effective 10/5/2004; FAC 2001-27, interim rule, 69 FR 77870, 12/28/2004, effective 1/1/2005; FAC 2005-07, 71 FR 219, 1/3/2006, effective 1/3/2006; FAC 2005-73, 79 FR 24192, 4/29/2014, effective 5/29/2014]

25.205 Postaward determinations.

(a) If a contractor requests a determination regarding the inapplicability of the Buy American statute after contract award, the contractor must explain why it could not request the determination before contract award or why the need for such determination otherwise was not reasonably foreseeable. If the contracting officer concludes that the contractor should have made the request before contract award, the contracting officer may deny the request.

(b) The contracting officer must base evaluation of any request for a determination regarding the inapplicability of the Buy American statute made after contract award on information required by paragraphs (c) and (d) of the applicable clause at 52.225-9 or 52.225-11 and/or other readily available information.

(c) If a determination, under 25.202(a), is made after contract award that an exception to the Buy American statute applies, the contracting officer must negotiate adequate consideration and modify the contract to allow use of the foreign construction material. When the basis for the exception is the unreasonable price of a domestic construction material, adequate consideration is at least the differential established in 25.202(a) or in accordance with agency procedures.

[FAC 97-15, 64 FR 72414, 12/27/99, effective 2/25/2000; FAC 2005-73, 79 FR 24192, 4/29/2014, effective 5/29/2014]

25.206 Noncompliance.

The contracting officer must—

(a) Review allegations of Buy American statute violations;

(b) Unless fraud is suspected, notify the contractor of the apparent unauthorized use of foreign construction material and request a reply, to include proposed corrective action; and

(c) If the review reveals that a contractor or subcontractor has used foreign construction material without authorization, take appropriate action, including one or more of the following:

(1) Process a determination concerning the inapplicability of the Buy American statute in accordance with 25.205.

(2) Consider requiring the removal and replacement of the unauthorized foreign construction material.

(3) If removal and replacement of foreign construction material incorporated in a building or work would be impracticable, cause undue delay, or otherwise be detrimental to the interests of the Government, the contracting officer may determine in writing that the foreign construction material need not be removed and replaced. A determination to retain foreign construction material does not constitute a determination that an exception to the Buy American statute applies, and this should be stated in the determination. Further, a determination to retain foreign construction material does not affect the Government's right to suspend or debar a contractor, subcontractor, or supplier for violation of the Buy American statute, or to exercise other contractual rights and remedies, such as reducing the contract price or terminating the contract for default.

(4) If the noncompliance is sufficiently serious, consider exercising appropriate contractual remedies, such as terminating the contract for default. Also consider preparing and forwarding a report to the agency suspending or debarring official in accordance with Subpart 9.4. If the noncompliance appears to be fraudulent, refer the matter to other appropriate agency officials, such as the officer responsible for criminal investigation.

[FAC 97-15, 64 FR 72414, 12/27/99, effective 2/25/2000; FAC 2005-73, 79 FR 24192, 4/29/2014, effective 5/29/2014]

SUBPART 25.3—CONTRACTS PERFORMED OUTSIDE THE UNITED STATES

25.301 Contractor personnel in a designated operational area or supporting a diplomatic or consular mission outside the United States. (No Text)

[FAC 2005-24, 73 FR 10943, 2/28/2008, effective 3/31/2008]

25.301-1 Scope.

(a) This section applies to contracts requiring contractor personnel to perform outside the United States—

(1) In a designated operational area during—

(i) Contingency operations;

(ii) Humanitarian or peacekeeping operations; or

(iii) Other military operations or military exercises, when designated by the combatant commander; or

(2) When supporting a diplomatic or consular mission—

(i) That has been designated by the Department of State as a danger pay post (see *http://aoprals.state.gov/Web920/danger_pay_all.asp*); or

(ii) That the contracting officer determines is a post at which application of the clause at FAR 52.225-19, Contractor Personnel in a Designated Operational Area or Supporting a Diplomatic or Consular Mission outside the United States, is appropriate.

(b) Any of the types of operations listed in paragraph (a)(1) of this section may include stability operations such as—

(1) Establishment or maintenance of a safe and secure environment; or

(2) Provision of emergency infrastructure reconstruction, humanitarian relief, or essential governmental services (until feasible to transition to local government).

(c) This section does not apply to personal services contracts (see FAR 37.104), unless specified otherwise in agency procedures.

[FAC 2005-24, 73 FR 10943, 2/28/2008, effective 3/31/2008]

25.301-2 Government support.

(a) Generally, contractors are responsible for providing their own logistical and security support, including logistical and security support for their employees. The agency shall provide logistical or security support only when the appropriate agency official, in accordance with agency guidance, determines that—

(1) Such Government support is available and is needed to ensure continuation of essential contractor services; and

(2) The contractor cannot obtain adequate support from other sources at a reasonable cost.

(b) The contracting officer shall specify in the contract, and in the solicitation if possible, the exact support to be provided, and whether this support is provided on a reimbursable basis, citing the authority for the reimbursement.

[FAC 2005-24, 73 FR 10943, 2/28/2008, effective 3/31/2008]

25.301-3 Weapons.

The contracting officer shall follow agency procedures and the weapons policy established by the combatant commander or the chief of mission when authorizing contractor personnel to carry weapons (see paragraph (i) of the clause at 52.225-19, Contractor Personnel in a Designated Operational Area or Supporting a Diplomatic or Consular Mission outside the United States).

[FAC 2005-24, 73 FR 10943, 2/28/2008, effective 3/31/2008]

25.301-4 Contract clause.

Insert the clause at 52.225-19, Contractor Personnel in a Designated Operational Area or Supporting a Diplomatic or Consular Mission outside the United States, in solicitations and contracts, other than personal service contracts with individuals, that will require contractor personnel to perform outside the United States—

(a) In a designated operational area during—

(1) Contingency operations;

(2) Humanitarian or peacekeeping operations; or

(3) Other military operations or military exercises, when designated by the combatant commander; or

(b) When supporting a diplomatic or consular mission—

(1) That has been designated by the Department of State as a danger pay post (see *http://aoprals.state.gov/Web920/danger_pay_all.asp*); or

(2) That the contracting officer determines is a post at which application of the clause FAR 52.225-19, Contractor Personnel in a Designated Operational Area or Supporting a Diplomatic or Consular Mission outside the United States, is appropriate.

[FAC 2005-24, 73 FR 10943, 2/28/2008, effective 3/31/2008]

25.302 Contractors performing private security functions outside the United States. (No Text)

[FAC 2005-67, 78 FR 37670, 6/21/2013, effective 7/22/2013]

25.302-1 Scope.

This section prescribes policy for implementing section 862 of the National Defense Authorization Act (NDAA) for Fiscal Year (FY) 2008 (Pub. L. 110–181), as amended by section 853 of the NDAA for FY 2009 (Pub. L. 110–417), and sections 831 and 832 of the NDAA for FY 2011 (Pub. L. 111–383) (see 10 U.S.C. 2302 Note).

[FAC 2005-67, 78 FR 37670, 6/21/2013, effective 7/22/2013]

25.302-2 Definitions.

As used in this section—

Area of combat operations means an area of operations designated as such by the Secretary of Defense when enhanced coordination of contractors performing private security functions working for Government agencies is required.

Other significant military operations means activities, other than combat operations, as part of a contingency operation outside the United States that is carried out by United States Armed Forces in an uncontrolled or unpredictable high-threat environment where personnel performing security functions may be called upon to use deadly force (see 25.302-3(a)(2)).

Private security functions means activities engaged in by a contractor, as follows—

(1) Guarding of personnel, facilities, designated sites, or property of a Federal agency, the contractor or subcontractor, or a third party; or

(2) Any other activity for which personnel are required to carry weapons in the performance of their duties in accordance with the terms of the contract.

[FAC 2005-67, 78 FR 37670, 6/21/2013, effective 7/22/2013; FAC 2005-91, 81 FR 67776, 9/30/2016, effective 10/31/2016]

25.302-3 Applicability.

(a) This section applies to contracts that require performance outside the United States—

(1) In an area of combat operations as designated by the Secretary of Defense; or

(2) In an area of other significant military operations as designated by the Secretary of Defense, and only upon agreement of the Secretary of Defense and the Secretary of State.

(b) These designations can be found at *http://www.acq.osd.mil/dpap/pacc/cc/designated_areas_of_other_significant_ military_operations.html* and *http://www.acq.osd.mil/dpap/pacc/cc/designated_areas_of_combat_ operations.html.*

(c) When the applicability requirements of this subsection are met, contractors and subcontractors must comply with 32 CFR part 159, whether the contract is for the performance of private security functions as a primary deliverable or the provision of private security functions is ancillary to the stated deliverables.

(d) The requirements of section 25.302 shall not apply to—

(1) Contracts entered into by elements of the intelligence community in support of intelligence activities; or

(2) Temporary arrangements entered into on a non-DoD contract for the performance of private security functions by individual indigenous personnel not affiliated with a local or expatriate security company. These temporary arrangements must still comply with local law.

[FAC 2005-67, 78 FR 37670, 6/21/2013, effective 7/22/2013; FAC 2005-91, 81 FR 67776, 9/30/2016, effective 10/31/2016]

25.302-4 Policy.

(a) *General.* (1) The policy, responsibilities, procedures, accountability, training, equipping, and conduct of personnel performing private security functions in designated areas are addressed at 32 CFR part 159, entitled "Private Security Contractors Operating in Contingency Operations." Contractor responsibilities include ensuring that employees are aware of, and comply with, relevant orders, directives, and instructions; keeping appropriate personnel records; accounting for weapons; registering and identifying armored vehicles, helicopters, and other military vehicles; and reporting specified incidents in which personnel performing private security functions under a contract are involved.

(2) In addition, contractors are required to fully cooperate with any Government-authorized investigation into incidents reported pursuant to paragraph (c)(3) of the clause at 52.225–26, Contractors Performing Private Security Functions Outside the United States, by providing access to employees performing private security functions and relevant information in the possession of the contractor regarding the incident concerned.

(b) *Implementing guidance.* In accordance with 32 CFR part 159—

(1) Geographic combatant commanders will provide DoD contractors performing private security functions with guidance and procedures for the operational environment in their area of responsibility; and

(2) In a designated area of combat operations, or areas of other significant military operations, as designated by the Secretary of Defense and only upon agreement of the Secretary of Defense and the Secretary of State, the relevant Chief of Mission will provide implementing instructions for non-DoD contractors performing private security functions and their personnel consistent with the standards set forth by the geographic combatant commander. In accordance with 32 CFR 159.4(c), the Chief of Mission has the option of instructing non-DoD contractors performing private security functions and their personnel to follow the guidance and procedures of the geographic combatant commander and/or a sub-unified commander or joint force commander where specifically authorized by the combatant commander to do so and notice of that authorization is provided to non-DoD agencies.

[FAC 2005-67, 78 FR 37670, 6/21/2013, effective 7/22/2013; FAC 2005-91, 81 FR 67776, 9/30/2016, effective 10/31/2016]

25.302-5 Remedies.

(a) In addition to other remedies available to the Government—

(1) The contracting officer may direct the contractor, at its own expense, to remove and replace any contractor or subcontractor personnel performing private security functions who fail to comply with or violate applicable requirements. Such action may be taken at the Government's discretion without prejudice to its rights under any other contract provision, *e.g.*, termination for default;

(2) The contracting officer shall include the contractor's failure to comply with the requirements of this section in appropriate databases of past performance and consider any such failure in any responsibility determination or evaluation of past performance; and

(3) In the case of award-fee contracts, the contracting officer shall consider a contractor's failure to comply with the requirements of this subsection in the evaluation of the contractor's performance during the relevant evaluation period, and may treat such failure as a basis for reducing or denying award fees for such period or for recovering all or part of award fee previously paid for such period.

(b) If the performance failures are severe, prolonged, or repeated, the contracting officer shall refer the matter to the appropriate suspending and debarring official.

[FAC 2005-67, 78 FR 37670, 6/21/2013, effective 7/22/2013]

25.302-6 Contract clause.

(a) Use the clause at 52.225-26, Contractors Performing Private Security Functions Outside the United States, in solicitations and contracts for performance outside the United States in an area of—

(1) Combat operations, as designated by the Secretary of Defense; or

(2) Other significant military operations, as designated by the Secretary of Defense and only upon agreement of the Secretary of Defense and the Secretary of State.

(b) The clause is not required to be used for—

(1) Contracts entered into by elements of the intelligence community in support of intelligence activities; or

(2) Temporary arrangements entered into by non-DoD contractors for the performance of private security functions by individual indigenous personnel not affiliated with a local or expatriate security company.

[FAC 2005-67, 78 FR 37670, 6/21/2013, effective 7/22/2013; FAC 2005-91, 81 FR 67776, 9/30/2016, effective 10/31/2016]

SUBPART 25.4—TRADE AGREEMENTS

25.400 Scope of subpart.

(a) This subpart provides policies and procedures applicable to acquisitions that are covered by—

(1) The World Trade Organization Government Procurement Agreement (WTO GPA), as approved by Congress in the Uruguay Round Agreements Act (Pub. L. 103-465);

(2) Free Trade Agreements (FTA), consisting of—

(i) NAFTA (the North American Free Trade Agreement, as approved by Congress in the North American Free Trade Agreement Implementation Act of 1993 (Pub. L. 103-182) (19 U.S.C. 3301 note));

(ii) Chile FTA (the United States-Chile Free Trade Agreement, as approved by Congress in the United States-Chile Free Trade Agreement Implementation Act (Pub. L. 108-77)) (19 U.S.C. 3805 note);

(iii) Singapore FTA (the United States-Singapore Free Trade Agreement, as approved by Congress in the United States-Singapore Free Trade Agreement Implementation Act (Pub. L. 108-78) (19 U.S.C. 3805 note));

(iv) Australia FTA (the United States-Australia Free Trade Agreement, as approved by Congress in the United States-Australia Free Trade Agreement Implementation Act (Pub. L. 108-286) (19 U.S.C. 3805 note));

(v) Morocco FTA (The United States—Morocco Free Trade Agreement, as approved by Congress in the United States—Morocco Free Trade Agreement Implementation Act (Pub. L. 108-302) (19 U.S.C. 3805 note));

(vi) CAFTA-DR (The Dominican Republic-Central America-United States Free Trade Agreement, as approved by Congress in the Dominican Republic-Central America-United States Free Trade Agreement Implementation Act (Pub. L. 109-53) (19 U.S.C. 4001 note));

(vii) Bahrain FTA (the United States-Bahrain Free Trade Agreement, as approved by Congress in the United States-Bahrain Free Trade Agreement Implementation Act (Pub. L. 109-169) (19 U.S.C. 3805 note));

(viii) Oman FTA (the United States-Oman Free Trade Agreement, as approved by Congress in the United States-Oman Free Trade Agreement Implementation Act (Pub. L. 109-283) (19 U.S.C. 3805 note));

(ix) Peru FTA (the United States-Peru Trade Promotion Agreement, as approved by Congress in the United States-Peru Trade Promotion Agreement Implementation Act (Pub. L. 110-138) (19 U.S.C. 3805 note));

(x) Korea FTA (the United States-Korea Free Trade Agreement Implementation Act (Pub. L. 112-41) (19 U.S.C 3805 note));

(xi) Colombia FTA (the United States-Colombia Trade Promotion Agreement Implementation Act (Pub. L. 112-42) (19 U.S.C. 3805 note)); and

(xii) Panama FTA (the United States-Panama Trade Promotion Agreement Implementation Act (Pub. L. 112-43) (19 U.S.C. 3805 note));

(3) The least developed country designation made by the U.S. Trade Representative, pursuant to the Trade Agreements Act (19 U.S.C. 2511(b)(4)), in acquisitions covered by the WTO GPA;

(4) The Caribbean Basin Trade Initiative (CBTI) (determination of the U.S. Trade Representative that end products or construction material granted duty-free entry from countries designated as beneficiaries under the Caribbean Basin Economic Recovery Act (19 U.S.C. 2701, et seq.), with the exception of Panama, must be treated as eligible products in acquisitions covered by the WTO GPA);

(5) The Israeli Trade Act (the U.S.-Israel Free Trade Area Agreement, as approved by Congress in the United States-Israel Free Trade Area Implementation Act of 1985 (19 U.S.C. 2112 note)); or

(6) The Agreement on Trade in Civil Aircraft (U.S. Trade Representative waiver of the Buy American statute for signatories of the Agreement on Trade in Civil Aircraft, as implemented in the Trade Agreements Act of 1979 (19 U.S.C. 2513)).

(b) For application of the trade agreements that are unique to individual agencies, see agency regulations.

[FAC 97-15, 64 FR 72414, 12/27/99, effective 2/25/2000; FAC 97-17, 65 FR 24316, 4/25/2000, effective 4/25/2000; FAC

2001-04, 67 FR 6112, 2/8/2002, effective 2/20/2002; FAC 2001-10, 67 FR 70519, 11/22/2002, effective 11/22/2002; FAC 2001-16, 68 FR 56684, 10/1/2003, effective 10/31/2003; FAC 2001-19, 69 FR 1051, 1/7/2004, effective 1/1/2004; FAC 2001-25, 69 FR 59700, 10/5/2004, effective 10/5/2004; FAC 2001-27, interim rule, 69 FR 77870, 12/28/2004, effective 1/1/2005; FAC 2005-07, 71 FR 219, 1/3/2006, effective 1/3/2006; FAC 2005-09, Interim rule 71 FR 20306, 4/19/2006, effective 4/19/2006; FAC 2005-10, 71 FR 36935, 6/28/2006, effective 6/28/2006; FAC 2005-14, 71 FR 67776, 71 FR 67778, 11/22/2006, effective 11/22/2006; FAC 2005-19, 72 FR 46360, 46361, 8/17/2007, effective 8/17/2007; FAC 2005-33, Interim rule, 74 FR 28426, 6/15/2009, effective 6/15/2009; FAC 2005-39, 75 FR 13421, 3/19/2010, effective 3/19/2010; FAC 2005-57, 77 FR 13952, 3/7/2012, effective 3/15/2012; FAC 2005-59, 77 FR 27548, 5/10/2012, effective 5/15/2012; FAC 2005-61, 77 FR 56739, 9/13/2012, effective 9/13/2012; FAC 2005-62, 77 FR 69723, 11/20/2012, effective 11/20/2012; FAC 2005-65, 78 FR 6188, 1/29/2013, effective 1/29/2013; FAC 2005-67, 78 FR 37695, 6/21/2013, effective 6/21/2013; FAC 2005-73, 79 FR 24192, 4/29/2014, effective 5/29/2014]

25.401 Exceptions.

(a) This subpart does not apply to—

(1) Acquisitions set aside for small businesses;

(2) Acquisitions of arms, ammunition, or war materials, or purchases indispensable for national security or for national defense purposes;

(3) Acquisitions of end products for resale;

(4) Acquisitions from Federal Prison Industries, Inc., under Subpart 8.6, and acquisitions under Subpart 8.7, Acquisition from Nonprofit Agencies Employing People Who Are Blind or Severely Disabled; and

(5) Other acquisitions not using full and open competition, if authorized by Subpart 6.2 or 6.3, when the limitation of competition would preclude use of the procedures of this subpart or sole source acquisitions justified in accordance with 13.501(a).

(b) In the World Trade Organization Government Procurement Agreement (WTO GPA) and each FTA, there is a U.S. schedule that lists services that are excluded from that agreement in acquisitions by the United States. Acquisitions of the following services are excluded from coverage by the U.S. schedule of the WTO GPA or an FTA as indicated in this table:

	The service (Federal Service Codes from the Federal Procurement Data System Product/Service Code Manual are indicated in parentheses for some services.)	WTO GPA AND KOREA FTA	Bahrain FTA, CAFTA-DR, Chile FTA, Colombia FTA, NAFTA, Oman FTA Panama FTA, and Peru FTA	Singapore FTA	Australia and Morocco FTA
(1)	All services purchased in support of military services overseas	X	X	X	X
(2)	(i) Automatic data processing (ADP) telecommunications and transmission services (D304), except enhance (i.e., value-added) telecommunications services	X	X	....	....

The service (Federal Service Codes from the Federal Procurement Data System Product/Service Code Manual are indicated in parentheses for some services.)	WTO GPA AND KOREA FTA	Bahrain FTA, CAFTA-DR, Chile FTA, Colombia FTA, NAFTA, Oman FTA Panama FTA, and Peru FTA	Singapore FTA	Australia and Morocco FTA
(ii) ADP teleprocessing and timesharing services (D305), telecommunications network management services (D316), automated news services, data services or other information services (D317), and other ADP and telecommunications services (D399).	X	X	. . . .	. . . .
(iii) Basic telecommunications network services (i.e., voice telephone services, packet-switched data transmission services, circuit-switched data transmission services, telex services, facsimile services, and private leased circuit services, but not information services, as defined in 47 U.S.C. 153(24))	*	*	X	X
(3) Dredging	X	X	X	X
(4) (i) Operation and management contracts of certain Government or privately owned facilities used for Government purposes, including Federally Funded Research and Development Centers.	X	. . . .	X	. . . .
(ii) Operation of all Department of Defense, Department of Energy, or the National Aeronautics and Space Administration facilities; and all Government-owned research and development facilities or Government-owned environmental laboratories.	**	X	**	X
(5) Research and development	X	X	X	X
(6) Transportation services (including launching services, but not including travel agent services).	X	X	X	X
(7) Utility services	X	X	X	X
(8) Maintenance, repair, modification, rebuilding and installation of equipment related to ships (J019).	. . . . .	X	. . . .	X

The service (Federal Service Codes from the Federal Procurement Data System Product/Service Code Manual are indicated in parentheses for some services.)	WTO GPA AND KOREA FTA	Bahrain FTA, CAFTA-DR, Chile FTA, Colombia FTA, NAFTA, Oman FTA Panama FTA, and Peru FTA	Singapore FTA	Australia and Morocco FTA
(9) Nonnuclear ship repair (J998).		X		X

* Note 1. Acquisitions of the services listed at (2) (iii) of this table are a subset of the excluded services at (2) (i) and (ii), and are therefore not covered under the WTO GPA.

** Note 2. Acquisitions of the services listed at (4) (ii) of this table are a subset of the excluded services at (4) (i), and are therefore not covered under the WTO GPA.

[FAC 97-15, 64 FR 72414, 12/27/99, effective 2/25/2000; FAC 2001-19, 69 FR 1051, 1/7/2004, effective 1/1/2004; FAC 2001-25, 69 FR 59700, 10/5/2004, effective 10/5/2004; FAC 2001-27, 69 FR 77870, 12/28/2004, effective 1/1/2005; FAC 2005-03, 70 FR 18954, 4/11/2005, effective 4/11/2005; FAC 2005-07, 71 FR 219, 221, 1/3/2006, effective 1/3/2006; FAC 2005-09, Interim rule, 71 FR 20306, 4/19/2006, effective 4/19/2006; FAC 2005-10, 71 FR 36935, 6/28/2006, effective 6/28/2006; FAC 2005-14, 71 FR 67776, 71 FR 67778, 11/22/2006, effective 11/22/2006; FAC 2005-19, 72 FR 46360, 46361, 8/17/2007, effective 8/17/2007; FAC 2005-33, Interim rule, 74 FR 28426, 6/15/2009, effective 6/15/2009; FAC 2005-39, 75 FR 13421, 3/19/2010, effective 3/19/2010; FAC 2005-57, 77 FR 13952, 3/7/2012, effective 3/15/2012; FAC 2005-59, 77 FR 27548, 5/10/2012, effective 5/15/2012; FAC 2005-61, 77 FR 56739, 9/13/2012, effective 9/13/2012; FAC 2005-62, 77 FR 69723, 11/20/2012, effective 11/20/2012; FAC 2005-65, 78 FR 6188, 1/29/2013, effective 1/29/2013; FAC 2005-67, 78 FR 37695, 6/21/2013, effective 6/21/2013; FAC 2005-92, 81 FR 83097, 11/18/2016, effective 12/19/2016]

25.402 General.

(a) (1) The Trade Agreements Act (19 U.S.C. 2501, et seq.) provides the authority for the President to waive the Buy American statute and other discriminatory provisions for eligible products from countries that have signed an international trade agreement with the United States, or that meet certain other criteria, such as being a least developed country. The President has delegated this waiver authority to the U.S. Trade Representative. In acquisitions covered by the WTO GPA, Free Trade Agreements, or the Israeli Trade Act, the U.S. Trade Representative has waived the Buy American statute and other discriminatory provisions for eligible products. Offers of eligible products receive equal consideration with domestic offers.

(2) The contracting officer shall determine the origin of services by the country in which the firm providing the services is established. See Subpart 25.5 for evaluation procedures for supply contracts covered by trade agreements.

(b) The value of the acquisition is a determining factor in the applicability of trade agreements. Most of these dollar thresholds are subject to revision by the U.S. Trade Representative approximately every 2 years. The various thresholds are summarized as follows:

Trade Agreement	Supply Contract (equal to or exceeding)	Service Contract (equal to or exceeding)	Construction Contract (equal to or exceeding)
WTO GPA	$180,000	$180,000	$6,932,000
FTAs:			
Australia FTA	80,317	80,317	6,932,000
Bahrain FTA	180,000	180,000	10,441,216
CAFTA-DR (Costa Rica, Dominican Republic, El Salvador, Guatemala, Honduras, and Nicaragua)	80,317	80,317	6,932,000
Chile FTA	80,317	80,317	6,932,000
Colombia FTA	80,317	80,317	6,932,000
Korea FTA	100,000	100,000	6,932,000
Morocco FTA	180,000	180,000	6,932,000
NAFTA:			
—Canada	25,000	80,317	10,441,216
—Mexico	80,317	80,317	10,441,216
Oman FTA	180,000	180,000	10,441,216
Panama FTA	180,000	180,000	6,932,000
Peru FTA	180,000	180,000	6,932,000
Singapore FTA	80,317	80,317	6,932,000
Israeli Trade Act	50,000	—	—

[FAC 97-15, 64 FR 72414, 12/27/99, effective 2/25/2000; FAC 2001-07, 67 FR 21534, 4/30/2002, effective 5/15/2002; FAC 2001-19, 69 FR 1051, 1/7/2004, effective 1/1/2004; FAC 2001-25, 69 FR 59700, 10/5/2004, effective 10/5/2004; FAC 2001-27, interim rule, 69 FR 77870, 12/28/2004, effective 1/1/2005; FAC 2005-07, 71 FR 219, 1/3/2006, effective 1/3/2006; FAC 2005-08, 71 FR 864, 1/5/2006, effective 1/5/2006; FAC 2005-09, Interim rule, 71 FR 20306, 4/19/2006, effective 4/19/2006; FAC 2005-10, 71 FR 36935, 6/28/2006, effective 6/28/2006; FAC 2005-13, 71 FR 57375, 9/28/2006, effective 9/28/2006; FAC 2005-14, 71 FR 67776, 71 FR 67778, 11/22/2006, effective 11/22/2006; FAC 2005-19, 72 FR 46357, 46360, 46361, 8/17/2007, effective 8/17/2007; FAC 2005-24, 73 FR 10962, 10964, 2/28/2008, effective 2/28/2008; Correction, 73 FR 16747, 3/28/2008, effective 3/28/2008; FAC 2005-30, 74 FR 2745, 1/15/2009, effective 1/15/2009; FAC 2005-33, Interim rule, 74 FR 28426, 6/15/2009, effective 6/15/2009; FAC 2005-39, 75 FR 13421, 3/19/2010, effective 3/19/2010; FAC 2005-43, 75 FR 38689, 7/2/2010, effective 7/2/2010; FAC 2005-50, 76 FR 14570, 3/16/2011, effective 3/16/2011; FAC 2005-56, 77 FR 12933, 3/2/2012, effective 3/2/2012; FAC 2005-57, 77 FR 13952, 3/7/2012, effective

3/15/2012;FAC 2005-59, 77 FR 27548, 5/10/2012, effective 5/15/2012; FAC 2005-61, 77 FR 56739, 9/13/2012, effective 9/13/2012; FAC 2005-62, 77 FR 69723, 11/20/2012, effective 11/20/2012; FAC 2005-65, 78 FR 6188, 1/29/2013, effective 1/29/2013; FAC 2005-67, 78 FR 37695, 6/21/2013, effective 6/21/2013; FAC 2005-72, 78 FR 80379, 12/31/2013, effective 1/1/2014; FAC 2005-73, 79 FR 24192, 4/29/2014, effective 5/29/2014; FAC 2005-86, 80 FR 81894, 12/31/2015, effective 1/1/2016; FAC 2005-97, 83 FR 3396, 1/24/2018, effective 1/24/2018]

25.403 World Trade Organization Government Procurement Agreement and Free Trade Agreements.

(a) Eligible products from WTO GPA and FTA countries are entitled to the nondiscriminatory treatment specified in 25.402(a)(1). The WTO GPA and FTAs specify procurement procedures designed to ensure fairness (see 25.408).

(b) *Thresholds*. (1) To determine whether the acquisition of products by lease, rental, or lease-purchase contract (including lease-to-ownership, or lease-with-option-to purchase) is covered by the WTO GPA or an FTA, calculate the estimated acquisition value as follows:

(i) If a fixed-term contract of 12 months or less is contemplated, use the total estimated value of the acquisition.

(ii) If a fixed-term contract of more than 12 months is contemplated, use the total estimated value of the acquisition plus the estimated residual value of the leased equipment at the conclusion of the contemplated term of the contract.

(iii) If an indefinite-term contract is contemplated, use the estimated monthly payment multiplied by the total number of months that ordering would be possible under the proposed contract, i.e., the initial ordering period plus any optional ordering periods.

(iv) If there is any doubt as to the contemplated term of the contract, use the estimated monthly payment multiplied by 48.

(2) The estimated value includes the value of all options.

(3) If, in any 12-month period, recurring or multiple awards for the same type of product or products are anticipated, use the total estimated value of these projected awards to determine whether the WTO GPA or an FTA applies. Do not divide any acquisition with the intent of reducing the estimated value of the acquisition below the dollar threshold of the WTO GPA or an FTA.

(c) *Purchase restriction*. (1) Under the Trade Agreements Act (19 U.S.C. 2512), in acquisitions covered by the WTO GPA, acquire only U.S.-made or designated country end products or U.S. or designated country services, unless offers for such end products or services are either not received or are insufficient to fulfill the requirements. This purchase restriction does not apply below the WTO GPA threshold for supplies and services, even if the acquisition is covered by an FTA.

(2) This restriction does not apply to purchases of supplies by the Department of Defense from a country with which it has entered into a reciprocal agreement, as provided in departmental regulations.

[FAC 97-15, 64 FR 72414, 12/27/99, effective 2/25/2000; FAC 97-18, 65 FR 36014, 6/6/2000, effective 6/6/2000; FAC 2001-07, 67 FR 21534, 4/30/2002, effective 5/15/2002; FAC 2001-09, 67 FR 56115, 8/30/2002, effective 9/30/2002; FAC 2001-19, 69 FR 1051, 1/7/2004, effective 1/1/2004; FAC 2001-25, 69 FR 59700, 10/5/2004, effective 10/5/2004; FAC 2001-27, interim rule, 69 FR 77870, 12/28/2004, effective 1/1/2005; FAC 2005-07, 71 FR 219, 1/3/2006, effective 1/3/2006]

25.404 Least developed countries.

For acquisitions covered by the WTO GPA, least developed country end products, construction material, and services must be treated as eligible products.

[FAC 2001-27, interim rule, 69 FR 77870, 12/28/2004, effective 1/1/2005; FAC 2005-07, 71 FR 219, 1/3/2006, effective 1/3/2006]

25.405 Caribbean Basin Trade Initiative.

Under the Caribbean Basin Trade Initiative, the United States Trade Representative has determined that, for acquisitions covered by the WTO GPA, Caribbean Basin country end products, construction material, and services must be treated as eligible products. In accordance with Section 201 (a)(3) of the Dominican Republic—Central America—United States Free Trade Implementation Act (Pub. L. 109-53) (19 U.S.C. 4031), when the CAFTA-DR agreement enters into force with respect to a country, that country is no longer designated as a beneficiary country for purposes of the Caribbean Basin Economic Recovery Act, and is therefore no longer included in the definition of Caribbean Basin country for purposes of the Caribbean Basin Trade Initiative.

[FAC 97-17, 65 FR 24316, 4/25/2000, effective 4/25/2000; FAC 2001-04, 67 FR 6112, 2/8/2002, effective 2/20/2002; FAC 2001-10, 67 FR 70519, 11/22/2002, effective 11/22/2002; FAC 2001-19, 69 FR 1051, 1/7/2004, effective 1/1/2004; FAC 2001-25, 69 FR 59700, 10/5/2004, effective 10/5/2004; FAC 2001-27, interim rule, 69 FR 77870, 12/28/2004, effective 1/1/2005; FAC 2005-07, 71 FR 219, 1/3/2006, effective 1/3/2006; FAC 2005-10, 71 FR 36935, 6/28/2006, effective 6/28/2006; FAC 2005-19, 72 FR 46360, 8/17/2007, effective 8/17/2007; FAC 2005-73, 79 FR 24192, 4/29/2014, effective 5/29/2014]

25.406 Israeli Trade Act.

Acquisitions of supplies by most agencies are covered by the Israeli Trade Act, if the estimated value of the acquisition is $50,000 or more but does not exceed the WTO GPA threshold for supplies (see 25.402(b)). Agencies other than the Department of Defense, the Department of Energy, the Department of Transportation, the Bureau of Reclamation of the Department of the Interior, the Federal Housing Finance Board, and the Office of Thrift Supervision must evaluate offers of Israeli end products without regard to the restrictions of the Buy American statute. The Israeli Trade Act does not prohibit the purchase of other foreign end products.

[FAC 97-15, 64 FR 72414, 12/27/99, effective 2/25/2000; FAC 2001-07, 67 FR 21534, 4/30/2002, effective 5/15/2002; FAC 2001-19, 69 FR 1051, 1/7/2004, effective 1/1/2004; FAC 2001-25, 69 FR 59700, 10/5/2004, effective 10/5/2004; FAC 2001-27, interim rule, 69 FR 77870, 12/28/2004, effective 1/1/2005; FAC 2005-07, 71 FR 219, 1/3/2006, effective 1/3/2006; FAC 2005-73, 79 FR 24192, 4/29/2014, effective 5/29/2014]

25.407 Agreement on Trade in Civil Aircraft.

Under the authority of Section 303 of the Trade Agreements Act, the U.S. Trade Representative has waived the Buy American statute for civil aircraft and related articles that meet the substantial transformation test of the Trade Agreements Act, from countries that are parties to the Agreement on Trade in Civil Aircraft. Those countries are Albania, Austria, Belgium, Bulgaria, Canada, Croatia, Cyprus, Czech Republic, Denmark, Egypt, Estonia, Finland, France, Georgia, Germany, Greece, Hungary, Ireland, Italy, Japan, Latvia, Lithuania, Luxembourg, Macao China, Malta, Montenegro, the Netherlands, Norway, Poland, Portugal, Romania, Slovakia, Slovenia, Spain, Sweden, Switzerland, Taiwan (Chinese Taipei), and the United Kingdom.

[FAC 97-15, 64 FR 72414, 12/27/99, effective 2/25/2000; FAC 2005-56, 77 FR 12935, 3/2/2012, effective 3/2/2012; FAC 2005-71, 78 FR 70480, 11/25/2013, effective 12/26/2013; FAC 2005-73, 79 FR 24192, 4/29/2014, effective 5/29/2014; FAC 2005-86, 80 FR 81892, 12/31/2015, effective 2/1/2016]

25.408 Procedures.

(a) If the WTO GPA or an FTA applies (see 25.401), the contracting officer must—

(1) Comply with the requirements of 5.203, Publicizing and response time;

(2) Comply with the requirements of 5.207, Preparation and transmittal of synopses;

(3) Not include technical requirements in solicitations solely to preclude the acquisition of eligible products;

(4) Specify in solicitations that offerors must submit offers in the English language and in U.S. dollars (see 52.214-34, Submission of Offers in the English Language, and 52.214-35, Submission of Offers in U.S. Currency, or paragraph (c)(5) of 52.215-1, Instruction to Offerors—Competitive Acquisitions); and

(5) Provide unsuccessful offerors from WTO GPA or FTA countries notice in accordance with 14.409-1 or 15.503.

(b) See Subpart 25.5 for evaluation procedures and examples.

[FAC 97-15, 64 FR 72414, 12/27/99, effective 2/25/2000; FAC 2001-16, Interim/Final rule, 68 FR 56676, 10/1/2003, effective 10/1/2003; FAC 2001-19, 69 FR 1051, 1/7/2004, effective 1/7/2004; FAC 2001-25, 69 FR 59700, 10/5/2004, effective 10/5/2004; FAC 2001-27, interim rule, 69 FR 77870, 12/28/2004, effective 1/1/2005; FAC 2005-07, 71 FR 219, 1/3/2006, effective 1/3/2006; FAC 2005-24, 73 FR 10960, 2/28/2008, effective 3/31/2008]

SUBPART 25.5—EVALUATING FOREIGN OFFERS—SUPPLY CONTRACTS

25.501 General.

The contracting officer—

(a) Must apply the evaluation procedures of this subpart to each line item of an offer unless either the offer or the solicitation specifies evaluation on a group basis (see 25.503);

(b) May rely on the offeror's certification of end product origin when evaluating a foreign offer;

(c) Must identify and reject offers of end products that are prohibited in accordance with Subpart 25.7; and

(d) Must not use the Buy American statute evaluation factors prescribed in this subpart to provide a preference for one foreign offer over another foreign offer.

[FAC 97-15, 64 FR 72414, 12/27/99, effective 2/25/2000; FAC 2001-07, 67 FR 21534, 4/30/2002, effective 5/15/2002; FAC 2005-09, Interim rule, 71 FR 20305, 4/19/2006, effective 4/19/2006; FAC 2005-14, 71 FR 67775, 11/22/2006, effective 11/22/2006; FAC 2005-73, 79 FR 24192, 4/29/2014, effective 5/29/2014]

25.502 Application.

(a) Unless otherwise specified in agency regulations, perform the following steps in the order presented:

(1) Eliminate all offers or offerors that are unacceptable for reasons other than price; e.g., nonresponsive, debarred or suspended, or a prohibited source (see Subpart 25.7).

(2) Rank the remaining offers by price.

(3) If the solicitation specifies award on the basis of factors in addition to cost or price, apply the evaluation factors as specified in this section and use the evaluated cost or price in determining the offer that represents the best value to the Government.

(b) For acquisitions covered by the WTO GPA (see Subpart 25.4)—

(1) Consider only offers of U.S.-made or designated country end products, unless no offers of such end products were received;

(2) If the agency gives the same consideration given eligible offers to offers of U.S.-made end products that are not domestic end products, award on the low offer. Otherwise, evaluate in accordance with agency procedures; and

(3) If there were no offers of U.S.-made or designated country end products, make a nonavailability determination (see 25.103(b)(2)) and award on the low offer (see 25.403(c)).

(c) For acquisitions not covered by the WTO GPA, but subject to the Buy American statute (an FTA or the Israeli Trade Act also may apply), the following applies:

(1) If the low offer is a domestic offer or an eligible offer under FTA or the Israeli Trade Act, award on that offer.

(2) If the low offer is a noneligible offer and there were no domestic offers (see 25.103(b)(3)), award on the low offer.

(3) If the low offer is a noneligible offer and there is an eligible offer that is lower than the lowest domestic offer, award on the low offer. The Buy American statute pro-

vides an evaluation preference only for domestic offers.

(4) Otherwise, apply the appropriate evaluation factor provided in 25.105 to the low offer.

(i) If the evaluated price of the low offer remains less than the lowest domestic offer, award on the low offer.

(ii) If the price of the lowest domestic offer is less than the evaluated price of the low offer, award on the lowest domestic offer.

(d) Ties.

(1) If application of an evaluation factor results in a tie between a domestic offer and a foreign offer, award on the domestic offer.

(2) If no evaluation preference was applied (i.e., offers afforded nondiscriminatory treatment under the Buy American statute), resolve ties between domestic and foreign offers by a witnessed drawing of lots by an impartial individual.

(3) Resolve ties between foreign offers from small business concerns (under the Buy American statute, a small business offering a manufactured article that does not meet the definition of "domestic end product" is a foreign offer) or foreign offers from a small business concern and a large business concern in accordance with 14.408-6(a).

[FAC 97-15, 64 FR 72414, 12/27/99, effective 2/25/2000; FAC 2001-07, 67 FR 21534, 4/30/2002, effective 5/15/2002; FAC 2001-19, 69 FR 1051, 1/7/2004, effective 1/1/2004; FAC 2001-25, 69 FR 59700, 10/5/2004, effective 10/5/2004; FAC 2001-27, interim rule, 69 FR 77870, 12/28/2004, effective 1/1/2005; FAC 2005-07, 71 FR 219, 1/3/2006, effective 1/3/2006; FAC 2005-09, Interim rule, 71 FR 20305, 4/19/2006, effective 4/19/2006; FAC 2005-14, 71 FR 67775, 11/22/2006, effective 11/22/2006; FAC 2005-73, 79 FR 24192, 4/29/2014, effective 5/29/2014]

25.503 Group offers.

(a) If the solicitation or an offer specifies that award can be made only on a group of line items or on all line items contained in the solicitation or offer, reject the offer—

(1) If any part of the award would consist of prohibited end products (see Subpart 25.7); or

(2) If the acquisition is covered by the WTO GPA and any part of the offer consists of items restricted in accordance with 25.403(c).

(b) If an offer restricts award to a group of line items or to all line items contained in the offer, determine for each line item whether to apply an evaluation factor (see 25.504-4, Example 1).

(1) First, evaluate offers that do not specify an award restriction on a line item basis in accordance with 25.502, determining a tentative award pattern by selecting for each line item the offer with the lowest evaluated price.

(2) Evaluate an offer that specifies an award restriction against the offered prices of the tentative award pattern, applying the appropriate evaluation factor on a line item basis.

(3) Compute the total evaluated price for the tentative award pattern and the offer that specified an award restriction.

(4) Unless the total evaluated price of the offer that specified an award restriction is less than the total evaluated price of the tentative award pattern, award based on the tentative award pattern.

(c) If the solicitation specifies that award will be made only on a group of line items or all line items contained in the solicitation, determine the category of end products on the basis of each line item, but determine whether to apply an evaluation factor on the basis of the group of items (see 25.504-4, Example 2).

(1) If the proposed price of domestic end products exceeds 50 percent of the total proposed price of the group, evaluate the entire group as a domestic offer. Evaluate all other groups as foreign offers.

(2) For foreign offers, if the proposed price of domestic end products and eligible products exceeds 50 percent of the total proposed price of the group, evaluate the entire group as an eligible offer.

(3) Apply the evaluation factor to the entire group in accordance with 25.502.

[FAC 97-15, 64 FR 72414, 12/27/99, effective 2/25/2000; FAC 2001-27, interim rule, 69 FR 77870, 12/28/2004, effective 1/1/2005; FAC 2005-07, 71 FR 219, 1/3/2006, effective 1/3/2006; FAC 2005-09, Interim rule, 71 FR 20305, 4/19/2006, effective 4/19/2006; FAC 2005-14, 71 FR 67775, 11/22/2006, effective 11/22/2006]

25.504 Evaluation examples.

The following examples illustrate the application of the evaluation procedures in 25.502and 25.503. The examples assume that the contracting officer has eliminated all offers that are unacceptable for reasons other than price or a trade agreement (see 25.502(a)(1)). The evaluation factor may change as provided in agency regulations.

[FAC 97-15, 64 FR 72414, 12/27/99, effective 2/25/2000; FAC 2001-07, 67 FR 21534, 4/30/02, effective 5/15/2002]

25.504-1 Buy American statute.

(a)(1) Example 1.

Offer A . . .	$12,000	Domestic end product, small business.
Offer B . .	11,700	Domestic end product, small business.
Offer C . .	10,000	U.S.-made end product (not domestic), small business.

(2) Analysis: This acquisition is for end products for use in the United States and is set aside for small business concerns. The Buy American statute applies. Since the acquisition value is less than $25,000 and the acquisition is set aside, none of the trade agreements apply. Perform the steps in 25.502(a). Offer C is evaluated as a foreign end product because it is the product of a small business, but is not a domestic end product (see 25.502(c)(4)). Since Offer B is a domestic offer, apply the 12 percent factor to Offer C (see 25.105(b)(2)). The resulting evaluated price of $11,200 remains lower than Offer B. The cost of Offer B is therefore unreasonable (see 25.105(c)). Award on Offer C at $10,000 (see 25.502(c)(4)(i)).

(b)(1) Example 2.

Offer A . . .	$11,000	Domestic end product, small business.
Offer B . .	10,700	Domestic end product, small business.
Offer C . .	10,200	U.S.-made end product (not domestic), small business.

(2) Analysis: This acquisition is for end products for use in the United States and is set aside for small business concerns. The Buy American statute applies. Perform the steps in 25.502(a). Offer C is evaluated as a foreign end product because it is the product of a small business but is not a domestic end product (see 25.502(c)(4)). After applying the 12 percent factor, the evaluated price of Offer C is $11,424. Award on Offer B at $10,700 (see 25.502(c)(4)(ii)).

[FAC 97-15, 64 FR 72414, 12/27/99, effective 2/25/2000; FAC 2001-07, 67 FR 21534, 4/30/2002, effective 5/15/2002; FAC 2005-73, 79 FR 24192, 4/29/2014, effective 5/29/2014]

25.504-2 WTO GPA/Caribbean Basin Trade Initiative/FTAs.

Example 1.

Offer A	304,000 U.S.-made end product (not domestic).
Offer B	303,000 U.S.-made end product (domestic), small business.
Offer C	300,000 Eligible product.
Offer D	295,000 Noneligible product (not U.S.-made).

Analysis: Eliminate Offer D because the acquisition is covered by the WTO GPA and there is an offer of a U.S.-made or an eligible product (see 25.502(b)(1)). If the agency gives the same consideration given eligible offers to offers of U.S.-made end products that are not domestic offers, it is unnecessary to determine if U.S.-made end products are domestic (large or small business). No further analysis is necessary. Award on the low remaining offer, Offer C (see 25.502(b)(2)).

[FAC 97-15, 64 FR 72414, 12/27/99, effective 2/25/2000; FAC 2001-19, 69 FR 1051, 1/7/2004, effective 1/1/2004; FAC 2001-25, 69 FR 59700, 10/5/2004, effective 10/5/2004; FAC 2001-27, interim rule, 69 FR 77870, 12/28/2004, effective 1/1/2005; FAC 2005-07, 71 FR 219, 1/3/2006, effective 1/3/2006; FAC 2005-43, 75 FR 38689, 7/2/2010, effective 7/2/2010; FAC 2005-50, 76 FR 14570, 3/16/2011, effective 3/16/2011]

25.504-3 FTA/Israeli Trade Act.

(a) Example 1.

Offer A . . .	$105,000	Domestic end product, small business.
Offer B . .	100,000	Eligible product.

Analysis: Since the low offer is an eligible offer, award on the low offer (see 25.502(c)(1)).

(b) Example 2.

Offer A . . .	$105,000	Eligible product.
Offer B . .	103,000	Noneligible product.

Analysis: Since the acquisition is not covered by the WTO GPA, the contracting officer can consider the noneligible offer. Since no domestic offer was received, make a nonavailability determination and award on Offer B (see 25.502(c)(2)).

(c) Example 3.

Offer A . . .	$105,000	Domestic end product, large business.
Offer B . .	103,000	Eligible product.
Offer C . .	100,000	Noneligible product.

Analysis: Since the acquisition is not covered by the WTO GPA, the contracting officer can consider the noneligible offer. Because the eligible offer (Offer B) is lower than the domestic offer (Offer A), no evaluation factor applies to the low offer (Offer C). Award on the low offer (see 25.502(c)(3)).

[FAC 97-15, 64 FR 72414, 12/27/99, effective 2/25/2000; FAC 2001-19, 69 FR 1051, 1/7/2004, effective 1/1/2004; FAC 2001-25, 69 FR 59700, 10/5/2004, effective 10/5/2004; FAC 2001-27, interim rule, 69 FR 77870, 12/28/2004, effective 1/1/2005; FAC 2005-07, 71 FR 219, 1/3/2006, effective 1/3/2006]

25.504-4 Group award basis.

(a) Example 1.

	Offers								
Item	A			B			C		
1	DO	=	$55,000	EL	=	$56,000	NEL	=	$50,000
2	NEL	=	13,000	EL	=	10,000	EL	=	13,000
3	NEL	=	11,500	DO	=	12,000	DO	=	10,000
4	NEL	=	24,000	EL	=	28,000	NEL	=	22,000
5	DO	=	18,000	NEL	=	10,000	DO	=	14,000
			121,500			116,000			109,000

Key: DO = Domestic end product; EL = Eligible product; NEL = Noneligible product.

Problem: Offeror C specifies all-or-none award. Assume all offerors are large businesses. The acquisition is not covered by the WTO GPA.

Analysis: (see 25.503)

STEP 1: Evaluate Offers A & B before considering Offer C and determine which offer has the lowest evaluated cost for each line item (the tentative award pattern):

Item 1: Low offer A is domestic; select A.

Item 2: Low offer B is eligible; do not apply factor; select B.

Item 3: Low offer A is noneligible and Offer B is a domestic offer. Apply a 6 percent factor to Offer A. The evaluated price of Offer A is higher than Offer B; select B.

Item 4: Low offer A is noneligible. Since neither offer is a domestic offer, no evaluation factor applies; select A.

Item 5: Low offer B is noneligible; apply a 6 percent factor to Offer B. Offer A is still higher than Offer B; select B.

Item	Low offer	Tentative award pattern from A and B			Offers C		
1	A	DO	=	$55,000	* NEL	=	$53,000
2	B	EL	=	10,000	EL	=	13,000
3	B	DO	=	12,000	DO	=	10,000
4	A	NEL	=	24,000	NEL	=	22,000
5	B	* NEL	=	10,600	DO	=	14,000
				111,600			112,000

* Offer + 6 percent.

On a line item basis, apply a factor to any noneligible offer if the other offer for that line item is domestic.

For Item 1, apply a factor to Offer C because Offer A is domestic and the acquisition was not covered by the WTO GPA. The evaluated price of Offer C, Item 1, becomes $53,000 ($50,000 plus 6 percent). Apply a factor to Offer B, Item 5, because it is a noneligible product and Offer C is domestic. The evaluated price of Offer B is $10,600 ($10,000 plus 6 percent). Evaluate the remaining items without applying a factor.

STEP 2: Evaluate Offer C against the tentative award pattern for Offers A and B:

STEP 3: The tentative unrestricted award pattern from Offers A and B is lower than the evaluated price of Offer C. Award the combination of Offers A and B. Note that if Offer C had not specified all-or-none award, award would be made on Offer C for line items 1, 3, and 4, totaling an award of $82,000.

(b) Example 2.

Item	Offers A			B			C		
1	DO	=	$50,000	EL	=	$50,500	NEL	=	$50,000
2	NEL	=	10,300	NEL	=	10,000	EL	=	10,200
3	EL	=	20,400	EL	=	21,000	NEL	=	20,200
4	DO	=	10,500	DO	=	10,300	DO	=	10,400
			91,200			91,800			90,800

Problem: The solicitation specifies award on a group basis. Assume the Buy American statute applies and the acquisition cannot be set aside for small business concerns. All offerors are large businesses.

Analysis: (see 25.503(c))

STEP 1: Determine which of the offers are domestic (see 25.503(c)(1)):

	Domestic [percent]	*Determination*
A	60,500/91,200=66.3%	Domestic
B	10,300/91,800=11.2%	Foreign
C	10,400/90,800=11.5%	Foreign

STEP 2: Determine whether foreign offers are eligible or noneligible offers (see 25.503(c)(2)):

	Domestic + eligible [percent]	*Determination*
A	N/A	Domestic
B	81,800/91,800=89.1%	Eligible
C	20,600/90,800=22.7%	Noneligible

STEP 3: Determine whether to apply an evaluation factor (see 25.503(c)(3)). The low offer (Offer C) is a foreign offer. There is no eligible offer lower than the domestic offer. Therefore, apply the factor to the low offer. Addition of the 6 percent factor (use 12 percent if Offer A is a small business) to Offer C yields an evaluated price of $96,248 ($90,800 + 6 percent). Award on Offer A (see 25.502(c)(4)(ii)). Note that, if Offer A were greater than Offer B, an evaluation factor

would not be applied and award would be on Offer C (see 25.502(c)(3)).

[FAC 97-15, 64 FR 72414, 12/27/99, effective 2/25/2000, corrected 65 FR 4633, 1/31/2000; FAC 2001-27, interim rule, 69 FR 77870, 12/28/2004, effective 1/1/2005; FAC 2005-07, 71 FR 219, 1/3/2006, effective 1/3/2006; FAC 2005-73, 79 FR 24192, 4/29/2014, effective 5/29/2014]

SUBPART 25.6—AMERICAN RECOVERY AND REINVESTMENT ACT—BUY AMERICAN STATUTE—CONSTRUCTION MATERIALS

25.600 Scope of subpart.

This subpart implements section 1605 in Division A of the American Recovery and Reinvestment Act of 2009 (Pub. L. 111-5) (Recovery Act) with regard to manufactured construction material and the 41 U.S.C. chapter 83, Buy American (referred to in this subpart as the Buy American statute) with regard to unmanufactured construction material. It applies to construction projects that use funds appropriated or otherwise provided by the Recovery Act.

[FAC 97-15, 64 FR 72414, 12/27/99, effective 2/25/2000; Interim rule, 71 FR 864, 1/5/2006, effective 1/5/2006; Removed and Reserved, FAC 2005-09, 71 FR 20305, 4/19/2006, effective 4/19/2006; FAC 2005-13, 71 FR 57375, 9/28/2006, effective 9/28/2006; FAC 2005-14, 71 FR 67775, 11/22/2006, effective 11/22/2006; FAC 2005-32, 74 FR 14623, 3/31/2009, effective 3/31/2009; FAC 2005-45, 75 FR 53153, 8/30/2010, effective 10/1/2010; FAC 2005-73, 79 FR 24192, 4/29/2014, effective 5/29/2014]

25.601 Definitions.

As used in this subpart—

Domestic construction material means the following:

(1) An unmanufactured construction material mined or produced in the United States. (The Buy American statute applies.)

(2) A manufactured construction material that is manufactured in the United States and, if the construction material consists wholly or predominantly of iron or steel, the iron or steel was produced in the United States. (Section 1605 of the Recovery Act applies.)

Foreign construction material means a construction material other than a domestic construction material.

Manufactured construction material means any construction material that is not unmanufactured construction material.

Public building or public work means a building or work, the construction, prosecution, completion, or repair of which is carried on directly or indirectly by authority of, or with funds of, a Federal agency to serve the interest of the general public regardless of whether title thereof is in a Federal agency (see 22.401). These buildings and works may include, without limitation, bridges, dams, plants, highways, parkways, streets, subways, tunnels, sewers, mains, power lines, pumping stations, heavy generators, railways, airports, terminals, docks, piers, wharves, ways, lighthouses, buoys, jetties, breakwaters, levees, and canals, and the construction, alteration, maintenance, or repair of such buildings and works.

Recovery Act designated country means a World Trade Organization Government Procurement Agreement country, a Free Trade Agreement country, or a least developed country.

Steel means an alloy that includes at least 50 percent iron, between .02 and 2 percent carbon, and may include other elements.

Unmanufactured construction material means raw material brought to the construction site for incorporation into the building or work that has not been—

(1) Processed into a specific form and shape; or

(2) Combined with other raw material to create a material that has different properties than the properties of the individual raw materials.

[FAC 97-15, 64 FR 72414, 12/27/99, effective 2/25/2000; Interim rule, 71 FR 864, 1/5/2006, effective 1/5/2006; Removed and Reserved, FAC 2005-09, 71 FR 20305, 4/19/2006, effective 4/19/2006; FAC 2005-13, 71 FR 57375, 9/28/2006, effective

9/28/2006; FAC 2005-14, 71 FR 67775, 11/22/2006, effective 11/22/2006; FAC 2005-32, 74 FR 14623, 3/31/2009, effective 3/31/2009; FAC 2005-45, 75 FR 53153, 8/30/2010, effective 10/1/2010; FAC 2005-73, 79 FR 24192, 4/29/2014, effective 5/29/2014]

25.602 Policy.

[FAC 97-15, 64 FR 72414, 12/27/99, effective 2/25/2000; Interim rule, 71 FR 864, 1/5/2006, effective 1/5/2006; Removed and Reserved, FAC 2005-09, 71 FR 20305, 4/19/2006, effective 4/19/2006; FAC 2005-13, 71 FR 57375, 9/28/2006, effective 9/28/2006; FAC 2005-14, 71 FR 67775, 11/22/2006, effective 11/22/2006; FAC 2005-32, 74 FR 14623, 3/31/2009, effective 3/31/2009; FAC 2005-45, 75 FR 53153, 8/30/2010, effective 10/1/2010]

25.602-1 Section 1605 of the Recovery Act.

Except as provided in 25.603—

(a) None of the funds appropriated or otherwise made available by the Recovery Act may be used for a project for the construction, alteration, maintenance, or repair of a public building or public work unless the public building or public work is located in the United States and—

(1) All of the iron, steel, and manufactured goods used as construction material in the project are produced or manufactured in the United States.

(i) All manufactured construction material must be manufactured in the United States.

(ii) *Iron or steel components.* (A) Iron or steel components of construction material consisting wholly or predominantly of iron or steel must be produced in the United States. This does not restrict the origin of the elements of the iron or steel, but requires that all manufacturing processes of the iron or steel must take place in the United States, except metallurgical processes involving refinement of steel additives.

(B) The requirement in paragraph (a)(1)(ii)(A) of this section does not apply to iron or steel components or subcomponents in construction material that does not consist wholly or predominantly of iron or steel.

(iii) *All other components.* There is no restriction on the origin or place of production or manufacture of components or subcomponents that do not consist of iron or steel.

(iv) *Examples.* (A) If a steel guardrail consists predominantly of steel, even though coated with aluminum, then the steel would be subject to the section 1605 restriction requiring that all stages of production of the steel occur in the United States, in addition to the requirement to manufacture the guardrail in the United States. There would be no restrictions on the other components of the guardrail.

(B) If a wooden window frame is delivered to the site as a single construction material, there is no restriction on any of the components, including the steel lock on the window frame; or

(2) If trade agreements apply, the manufactured construction material shall either comply with the requirements of paragraph (a)(1) of this subsection, or be wholly the product of or be substantially transformed in a Recovery Act designated country;

(b) Manufactured materials purchased directly by the Government and delivered to the site for incorporation into the project shall meet the same domestic source requirements as specified for manufactured construction material in paragraphs (a)(1) and (a)(2) of this section; and

(c) A project may include several contracts, a single contract, or one or more line items on a contract.

[FAC 2005-45, 75 FR 53153, 8/30/2010, effective 10/1/2010]

25.602-2 Buy American statute.

Except as provided in 25.603, use only unmanufactured construction material mined or produced in the United States, as required by the Buy American statute or, if trade agreements apply, unmanufactured construction material mined or produced in a designated country may also be used.

[FAC 2005-45, 75 FR 53153, 8/30/2010, effective 10/1/2010; FAC 2005-73, 79 FR 24192, 4/29/2014, effective 5/29/2014]

25.603 Exceptions.

(a)(1) When one of the following exceptions applies, the contracting officer may allow the contractor to incorporate foreign manufactured construction materials without regard to the restrictions of section 1605 of the Recovery Act or foreign unmanufactured construction material without regard to the restrictions of the Buy American statute:

(i) *Nonavailability.* The head of the contracting activity may determine that a particular construction material is not mined, produced, or manufactured in the United States in sufficient and reasonably available commercial quantities of a satisfactory quality. The determinations of nonavailability of the articles listed at 25.104(a) and the procedures at 25.103(b)(1) also apply if any of those articles are acquired as construction materials.

(ii) *Unreasonable cost.* The contracting officer concludes that the cost of domestic construction material is unreasonable in accordance with 25.605.

(iii) *Inconsistent with public interest.* The head of the agency may determine that application of the restrictions of section 1605 of the Recovery Act to a particular manufactured construction material, or the restrictions of the Buy American statute to a particular unmanufactured construction material would be inconsistent with the public interest.

(2) In addition, the head of the agency may determine that application of the Buy American statute to a particular unmanufactured construction material would be impracticable.

(b) *Determinations.* When a determination is made, for any of the reasons stated in this section, that certain foreign construction materials may be used—

(1) The contracting officer shall list the excepted materials in the contract; and

(2) For determinations with regard to the inapplicability of section 1605 of the Recovery Act, unless the construction material has already been determined to be domestically nonavailable (*see* list at 25.104), the head of the agency shall provide a notice to the Federal Register within three business days after the determination is made, with a copy to the Administrator for Federal Procurement Policy and to the Recovery Accountability and Transparency Board. The notice shall include—

(i) The title "Buy American Exception under the American Recovery and Reinvestment Act of 2009";

(ii) The dollar value and brief description of the project; and

(iii) A detailed justification as to why the restriction is being waived.

(c) *Acquisitions under trade agreements.* (1) For construction contracts with an estimated acquisition value of $6,932,000 or more, also see subpart 25.4. Offers proposing the use of construction material from a designated country shall receive equal consideration with offers proposing the use of domestic construction material.

(2) For purposes of applying section 1605 of the Recovery Act to evaluation of manufactured construction material, designated countries do not include the Caribbean Basin Countries.

[FAC 97-15, 64 FR 72414, 12/27/99, effective 2/25/2000; Interim rule, 71 FR 864, 1/5/2006, effective 1/5/2006; Removed and Reserved, FAC 2005-09, 71 FR 20305, 4/19/2006, effective 4/19/2006; FAC 2005-13, 71 FR 57375, 9/28/2006, effective 9/28/2006; FAC 2005-14, 71 FR 67775, 11/22/2006, effective 11/22/2006; FAC 2005-32, 74 FR 14623, 3/31/2009, effective 3/31/2009; FAC 2005-43, 75 FR 38689, 7/2/2010, effective 7/2/2010 FAC 2005-45, 75 FR 53153, 8/30/2010, effective 10/1/2010; FAC 2005-50, 76 FR 14570, 3/16/2011, effective 3/16/2011; FAC 2005-56, 77 FR 12933, 3/2/2012, effective 3/2/2012; FAC 2005-72, 78 FR 80379, 12/31/2013, effective 1/1/2014; FAC 2005-73, 79 FR 24192, 4/29/2014, effective 5/29/2014; FAC 2005-86, 80 FR 81894, 12/31/2015, effective 1/1/2016; FAC 2005-97, 83 FR 3396, 1/24/2018, effective 1/24/2018]

25.604 Preaward determination concerning the inapplicability of

section 1605 of the Recovery Act or the Buy American statute.

(a) For any acquisition, an offeror may request from the contracting officer a determination concerning the inapplicability of section 1605 of the Recovery Act or the Buy American statute for specifically identified construction materials. The time for submitting the request is specified in the solicitation in paragraph (b) of either 52.225-22 or 52.225-24, whichever applies. The information and supporting data that must be included in the request are also specified in the solicitation in paragraphs (c) and (d) of either 52.225-21 or 52.225-23, whichever applies.

(b) Before award, the contracting officer must evaluate all requests based on the information provided and may supplement this information with other readily available information.

(c) Determination based on unreasonable cost of domestic construction material.

(1) *Manufactured construction material.* The contracting officer must compare the offered price of the contract using foreign manufactured construction material (*i.e.*, any construction material not manufactured in the United States, or construction material consisting predominantly of iron or steel and the iron or steel is not produced in the United States) to the estimated price if all domestic manufactured construction material were used. If use of domestic manufactured construction material would increase the overall offered price of the contract by more than 25 percent, then the contracting officer shall determine that the cost of the domestic manufactured construction material is unreasonable.

(2) *Unmanufactured construction material.* The contracting officer must compare the cost of each foreign unmanufactured construction material to the cost of domestic unmanufactured construction material. If the cost of the domestic unmanufactured construction material exceeds the cost of the foreign unmanufactured construction material by more than 6 percent, then the contracting officer shall determine that the cost of the domestic unmanufactured construction material is unreasonable.

[FAC 97-15, 64 FR 72414, 12/27/99, effective 2/25/2000; Interim rule, 71 FR 864, 1/5/2006, effective 1/5/2006; Removed and Reserved, FAC 2005-09, 71 FR 20305, 4/19/2006, effective 4/19/2006; FAC 2005-13, 71 FR 57375, 9/28/2006, effective 9/28/2006; FAC 2005-14, 71 FR 67775, 11/22/2006, effective 11/22/2006; FAC 2005-32, 74 FR 14623, 3/31/2009, effective 3/31/2009; FAC 2005-45, 75 FR 53153, 8/30/2010, effective 10/1/2010; FAC 2005-73, 79 FR 24192, 4/29/2014, effective 5/29/2014]

25.605 Evaluating offers of foreign construction material.

(a) If the contracting officer has determined that an exception applies because the cost of certain domestic construction material is unreasonable, in accordance with section 25.604, then the contracting officer shall apply evaluation factors to the offer incorporating the use of such foreign construction material as follows:

(1) Use an evaluation factor of 25 percent, applied to the total offered price of the contract, if foreign manufactured construction material is incorporated in the offer based on an exception for unreasonable cost of comparable domestic construction material requested by the offeror.

(2) In addition, use an evaluation factor of 6 percent applied to the cost of foreign unmanufactured construction material incorporated in the offer based on an exception for unreasonable cost of comparable domestic unmanufactured construction material requested by the offeror.

(3) Total evaluated price = offered price + (.25 × offered price, if (a) (1) applies) + (.06 × cost of foreign unmanufactured construction material, if (a) (2) applies).

(b) If the solicitation specifies award on the basis of factors in addition to cost or price, apply the evaluation factors as specified in paragraph (a) of this section and use the evaluated price in determining the offer that represents the best value to the Government.

(c) Unless paragraph (b) applies, if two or more offers are equal in price, the contracting officer must give preference to an offer that does not include foreign construction material excepted at the request of the offeror on the basis of unreasonable cost.

(d) Offerors also may submit alternate offers based on use of equivalent domestic construction material to avoid possible rejection of the entire offer if the Government determines that an exception permitting use of a particular foreign construction material does not apply.

(e) If the contracting officer awards a contract to an offeror that proposed foreign construction material not listed in the applicable clause in the solicitation (paragraph (b)(3) of 52.225-21, or paragraph (b)(3) of 52.225-23), the contracting officer must add the excepted materials to the list in the contract clause.

[FAC 97-15, 64 FR 72414, 12/27/99, effective 2/25/2000; Interim rule, 71 FR 864, 1/5/2006, effective 1/5/2006; Removed and Reserved, FAC 2005-09, 71 FR 20305, 4/19/2006, effective 4/19/2006; FAC 2005-13, 71 FR 57375, 9/28/2006, effective 9/28/2006; FAC 2005-14, 71 FR 67775, 11/22/2006, effective 11/22/2006; FAC 2005-32, 74 FR 14623, 3/31/2009, effective 3/31/2009; FAC 2005-45, 75 FR 53153, 8/30/2010, effective 10/1/2010]

25.606 Postaward determinations.

(a) If a contractor requests a determination regarding the inapplicability of section 1605 of the Recovery Act or the Buy American statute after contract award, the contractor must explain why it could not request the determination before contract award or why the need for such determination otherwise was not reasonably foreseeable. If the contracting officer concludes that the contractor should have made the request before contract award, the contracting officer may deny the request.

(b) The contracting officer must base evaluation of any request for a determination regarding the inapplicability of section 1605 of the Recovery Act or the Buy American statute made after contract award on information required by paragraphs (c) and (d) of the applicable clause at 52.225-21 or 52.225-23 and/or other readily available information.

(c) If a determination, under 25.603(a), is made after contract award that an exception to section 1605 of the Recovery Act or to the Buy American statute applies, the contracting officer must negotiate adequate consideration and modify the contract to allow use of the foreign construction material. When the basis for the exception is the unreasonable cost of a domestic construction material, adequate consideration is at least the differential established in 25.605(a).

[FAC 97-15, 64 FR 72414, 12/27/99, effective 2/25/2000; Interim rule, 71 FR 864, 1/5/2006, effective 1/5/2006; Removed and Reserved, FAC 2005-09, 71 FR 20305, 4/19/2006, effective 4/19/2006; FAC 2005-13, 71 FR 57375, 9/28/2006, effective 9/28/2006; FAC 2005-14, 71 FR 67775, 11/22/2006, effective 11/22/2006; FAC 2005-32, 74 FR 14623, 3/31/2009, effective 3/31/2009; FAC 2005-45, 75 FR 53153, 8/30/2010, effective 10/1/2010; FAC 2005-73, 79 FR 24192, 4/29/2014, effective 5/29/2014]

25.607 Noncompliance.

The contracting officer must—

(a) Review allegations of violations of section 1605 of the Recovery Act or Buy American statute;

(b) Unless fraud is suspected, notify the contractor of the apparent unauthorized use of foreign construction material and request a reply, to include proposed corrective action; and

(c) If the review reveals that a contractor or subcontractor has used foreign construction material without authorization, take appropriate action, including one or more of the following:

(1) Process a determination concerning the inapplicability of section 1605 of the Recovery Act or the Buy American statute in accordance with 25.606.

(2) Consider requiring the removal and replacement of the unauthorized foreign construction material.

(3) If removal and replacement of foreign construction material incorporated in a building or work would be impracticable, cause undue delay, or otherwise be detri-

mental to the interests of the Government, the contracting officer may determine in writing that the foreign construction material need not be removed and replaced. A determination to retain foreign construction material does not constitute a determination that an exception to section 1605 of the Recovery Act or the Buy American statute applies, and this should be stated in the determination. Further, a determination to retain foreign construction material does not affect the Government's right to suspend or debar a contractor, subcontractor, or supplier for violation of section 1605 of the Recovery Act or the Buy American statute, or to exercise other contractual rights and remedies, such as reducing the contract price or terminating the contract for default.

(4) If the noncompliance is sufficiently serious, consider exercising appropriate contractual remedies, such as terminating the contract for default. Also consider preparing and forwarding a report to the agency suspending or debarring official in accordance with subpart 9.4. If the noncompliance appears to be fraudulent, refer the matter to other appropriate agency officials, such as the agency's inspector general or the officer responsible for criminal investigation.

[FAC 97-15, 64 FR 72414, 12/27/99, effective 2/25/2000; Interim rule, 71 FR 864, 1/5/2006, effective 1/5/2006; Removed and Reserved, FAC 2005-09, 71 FR 20305, 4/19/2006, effective 4/19/2006; FAC 2005-13, 71 FR 57375, 9/28/2006, effective 9/28/2006; FAC 2005-14, 71 FR 67775, 11/22/2006, effective 11/22/2006; FAC 2005-32, 74 FR 14623, 3/31/2009, effective 3/31/2009; FAC 2005-32, 74 FR 14623, 3/31/2009, effective 3/31/2009; FAC 2005-45, 75 FR 53153, 8/30/2010, effective 10/1/2010; FAC 2005-73, 79 FR 24192, 4/29/2014, effective 5/29/2014]

SUBPART 25.7—PROHIBITED SOURCES

25.700 Scope of subpart.

This subpart implements—

(a) Economic sanctions administered by the Office of Foreign Assets Control (OFAC) in the Department of the Treasury prohibiting transactions involving certain countries, entities, and individuals;

(b) The Sudan Accountability and Divestment Act of 2007 (Pub. L. 110-174) (50 U.S.C. 1701 note);

(c) The Iran Sanctions Act of 1996 (Iran Sanctions Act) (Pub. L. 104–172; 50 U.S.C. 1701 note), including amendments by the Iran Freedom Support Act (Pub. L. 109–293), section 102 of the Comprehensive Iran Sanctions, Accountability, and Divestment Act of 2010 (Pub. L. 111–195), and Titles II and III of the Iran Threat Reduction and Syria Human Rights Act of 2012 (Pub. L. 112–158); and

(d) Prohibition against contracting with entities that export sensitive technologies to Iran (22 U.S.C. 8515).

[FAC 2005-26, 73 FR 33636, 6/12/2008, effective 6/12/2008; FAC 2005-36, 74 FR 40463, 8/11/2009, effective 8/11/2009; FAC 2005-46, 75 FR 60254, 9/29/2010, effective 9/29/2010; FAC 2005-54, 76 FR 68027, 11/2/2011, effective 11/2/2011; FAC 2005-63, 77 FR 73516, 12/10/2012, effective 12/10/2012; FAC 2005-69, 78 FR 46782, 8/1/2013, effective 8/1/2013; FAC 2005-69, 78 FR 46782, 8/1/2013, effective 8/1/2013; FAC 2005-73, 79 FR 24192, 4/29/2014, effective 5/29/2014]

25.701 Restrictions administered by the Department of the Treasury on acquisitions of supplies or services from prohibited sources.

(a) Except as authorized by OFAC, agencies and their contractors and subcontractors must not acquire any supplies or services if any proclamation, Executive order, or statute administered by OFAC, or if OFAC's implementing regulations at 31 CFR Chapter V, would prohibit such a transaction by a person subject to the jurisdiction of the United States.

(b) Except as authorized by OFAC, most transactions involving Cuba, Iran, and Sudan are prohibited, as are most imports from Burma or North Korea into the United States or its outlying areas. In addition, lists of entities and individuals subject to economic sanctions are included in OFAC's List of Specially Designated Nationals and

Blocked Persons at *http://www.treas.gov/offices/enforcement/ofac/sdn*. More information about these restrictions, as well as updates, is available in OFAC's regulations at 31 CFR Chapter V and/or on OFAC's website at *http://www.treas.gov/offices/enforcement/ofac*.

(c) Refer questions concerning the restrictions in paragraphs (a) or (b) of this section to the Department of the Treasury, Office of Foreign Assets Control, Washington, DC 20220, (Telephone (202) 622-2490).

[FAC 97-15, 64 FR 72414, 12/27/99, effective 2/25/2000; FAC 97-18, 65 FR 36014, 6/6/2000, effective 7/6/2000; FAC 2001-16, Final rule, 68 FR 56685, 10/1/2003, effective 10/31/2003; FAC 2001-18, 68 FR 69258, 12/11/2003, effective 12/11/2003; FAC 2005-07, 71 FR 224, 1/3/2006/ effective 2/2/2006; FAC 2005-26, 73 FR 33636, 6/12/2008, effective 6/12/2008; FAC 2005-36, 74 FR 40463, 8/11/2009, effective 8/11/2009; FAC 2005-46, 75 FR 60254, 9/29/2010, effective 9/29/2010; FAC 2005-54, 76 FR 68027, 11/2/2011, effective 11/2/2011]

25.702 Prohibition on contracting with entities that conduct restricted business operations in Sudan. (No Text)

[FAC 97-18, 65 FR 36014, 6/6/2000, effective 7/6/2000; FAC 2001-16, Final rule, 68 FR 56685, 10/1/2003, effective 10/31/2003; FAC 2005-26, 73 FR 33636, 6/12/2008, effective 6/12/2008; FAC 2005-36, 74 FR 40463, 8/11/2009, effective 8/11/2009]

25.702-1 Definitions.

As used in this section—

Appropriate Congressional committees means—

(1) The Committee on Banking, Housing, and Urban Affairs, The Committee on Foreign Relations, and the Select Committee on Intelligence of the Senate; and

(2) The Committee on Financial Services, the Committee on Foreign Relations, and the Permanent Select Committee on Intelligence of the House of Representatives.

Business operations means engaging in commerce in any form, including by acquiring, developing, maintaining, owning, selling, possessing, leasing, or operating equipment, facilities, personnel, products, services, personal property, real property, or any other apparatus of business or commerce.

Marginalized populations of Sudan means—

(1) Adversely affected groups in regions authorized to receive assistance under section 8(c) of the Darfur Peace and Accountability Act (Pub. L. 109- 344) (50 U.S.C. 1701 note); and

(2) Marginalized areas in Northern Sudan described in section 4(9) of such Act.

Restricted business operations—

(1) Means, except as provided in paragraph (2) of this definition, business operations in Sudan that include power production activities, mineral extraction activities, oil-related activities, or the production of military equipment, as those terms are defined in the Sudan Accountability and Divestment Act of 2007 (Pub. L. 110-174).

(2) Does not include business operations that the person (as that term is defined in Section 2 of the Sudan Accountability and Divestment Act of 2007) conducting the business can demonstrate—

(i) Are conducted under contract directly and exclusively with the regional government of southern Sudan;

(ii) Are conducted pursuant to specific authorization from the Office of Foreign Assets Control in the Department of the Treasury, or are expressly exempted under Federal law from the requirement to be conducted under such authorization;

(iii) Consist of providing goods or services to marginalized populations of Sudan;

(iv) Consist of providing goods or services to an internationally recognized peacekeeping force or humanitarian organization;

(v) Consist of providing goods or services that are used only to promote health or education; or

(vi) Have been voluntarily suspended.

[FAC 2005-26, 73 FR 33636, 6/12/2008, effective 6/12/2008; FAC 2005-36, 74 FR 40463, 8/11/2009, effective 8/11/2009]

25.702-2 Certification.

As required by the Sudan Accountability and Divestment Act of 2007 (Pub. L. 110-174), each offeror must certify that it does not conduct restricted business operations in Sudan.

[FAC 2005-26, 73 FR 33636, 6/12/2008, effective 6/12/2008; FAC 2005-36, 74 FR 40463, 8/11/2009, effective 8/11/2009]

25.702-3 Remedies.

Upon the determination of a false certification under subsection 25.702- 2—

(a) The contracting officer may terminate the contract;

(b) The suspending official may suspend the contractor in accordance with the procedures in Subpart 9.4; and

(c) The debarring official may debar the contractor for a period not to exceed 3 years in accordance with the procedures in Subpart 9.4.

[FAC 2005-26, 73 FR 33636, 6/12/2008, effective 6/12/2008; FAC 2005-36, 74 FR 40463, 8/11/2009, effective 8/11/2009]

25.702-4 Waiver.

(a) The President may waive the requirement of subsection 25.702-2 on a case-by-case basis if the President determines and certifies in writing to the appropriate congressional committees that it is in the national interest to do so.

(b) An agency seeking waiver of the requirement shall submit the request to the Administrator of the Office of Federal Procurement Policy (OFPP), allowing sufficient time for review and approval. Upon receipt of the waiver request, OFPP shall consult with the President's National Security Council, Office of African Affairs, and the Department of State Sudan Office and Sanctions Office to assess foreign policy aspects of making a national interest recommendation.

(c) Agencies may request a waiver on an individual or class basis; however, waivers are not indefinite and can be cancelled if warranted.

(1) A class waiver may be requested only when the class of supplies is not available from any other source and it is in the national interest.

(2) Prior to submitting the waiver request, the request must be reviewed and cleared by the agency head.

(3) All waiver requests must include the following information:

(i) Agency name, complete mailing address, and point of contact name, telephone number, and email address;

(ii) Offeror's name, complete mailing address, and point of contact name, telephone number, and email address;

(iii) Description/nature of product or service;

(iv) The total cost and length of the contract;

(v) Justification, with market research demonstrating that no other offeror can provide the product or service and stating why the product or service must be procured from this offeror, as well as why it is in the national interest for the President to waive the prohibition on contracting with this offeror that conducts restricted business operations in Sudan, including consideration of foreign policy aspects identified in consultation(s) pursuant to 25.702-4(b);

(vi) Documentation regarding the offeror's past performance and integrity (see the Contractor Performance Assessment Reporting System (CPARS) including the Federal Awardee Performance Information and Integrity System at *https://www.cpars.gov* and any other relevant information);

(vii) Information regarding the offeror's relationship or connection with other firms that conduct prohibited business operations in Sudan; and

(viii) Any humanitarian efforts engaged in by the offeror, the human rights impact of doing business with the offeror for which the waiver is requested, and the extent of the offeror's business operations in Sudan.

(d) The consultation in 25.702-4(b) and the information in 25.702-4(c)(3) will be considered in determining whether to recommend that the President waive the requirement of subsection 25.702-2. In accordance with section 6(c) of the Sudan Accountability and Divestment Act of 2007, OFPP will semiannually submit a report to Congress, on April 15th and October 15th, on the waivers granted.

[FAC 2005-26, 73 FR 33636, 6/12/2008, effective 6/12/2008; FAC 2005-36, 74 FR 40463, 8/11/2009, effective 8/11/2009; FAC 2005-54, 76 FR 68037, 11/2/2011, effective 12/2/2011; FAC 2019-06, 84 FR 47865, 9/10/2019, effective 10/10/2019]

25.703 Prohibition on contracting with entities that engage in certain activities or transactions relating to Iran. (No Text)

[FAC 2005-46, 75 FR 60254, 9/29/2010, effective 9/29/2010; FAC 2005-54, 76 FR 68027, 11/2/2011, effective 11/2/2011; FAC 2005-63, 77 FR 73516, 12/10/2012, effective 12/10/2012; FAC 2005-69, 78 FR 46782, 8/1/2013, effective 8/1/2013]

25.703-1 Definitions.

As used in this section—

Person—

(1) Means—

(i) A natural person;

(ii) A corporation, business association, partnership, society, trust, financial institution, insurer, underwriter, guarantor, and any other business organization, any other nongovernmental entity, organization, or group, and any governmental entity operating as a business enterprise; and

(iii) Any successor to any entity described in paragraph (1)(ii) of this definition; and

(2) Does not include a government or governmental entity that is not operating as a business enterprise.

Sensitive technology—

(1) Means hardware, software, telecommunications equipment, or any other technology that is to be used specifically—

(i) To restrict the free flow of unbiased information in Iran; or

(ii) To disrupt, monitor, or otherwise restrict speech of the people of Iran; and

(2) Does not include information or informational materials the export of which the President does not have the authority to regulate or prohibit pursuant to section 203(b)(3) of the International Emergency Economic Powers Act (50 U.S.C. 1702(b)(3)).

[FAC 2005-46, 75 FR 60254, 9/29/2010, effective 9/29/2010; FAC 2005-54, 76 FR 68027, 68028, 11/2/2011, effective 11/2/2011; FAC 2005-58, 77 FR 23368, 4/18/2012, effective 5/18/2012]

25.703-2 Iran Sanctions Act.

(a) *Certification.*

(1) *Certification relating to activities described in section 5 of the Iran Sanctions Act.* As required by section 6(b)(1)(A) of the Iran Sanctions Act (50 U.S.C. 1701 note), unless an exception applies in accordance with paragraph (c) of this subsection, or a waiver is granted in accordance with 25.703–4, each offeror must certify that the offeror, and any person owned or controlled by the offeror, does not engage in any activity for which sanctions may be imposed under section 5 of the Iran Sanctions Act. Such activities, which are described in detail in section 5 of the Iran Sanctions Act, relate to the energy sector of Iran and development by Iran of weapons of mass destruction or other military capabilities.

(2) *Certification relating to transactions with Iran's Revolutionary Guard Corps.* As required by section 6(b)(1)(B) of the Iran Sanctions Act (50 U.S.C. 1701 note), unless an exception applies in accordance with paragraph (c) of this subsection, or a waiver is granted in accordance with 25.703–4, each offeror must certify that the offeror, and any person owned or controlled by the offeror, does not knowingly engage in any significant transaction (i.e., a transaction that exceeds $3,500) with Iran's Revolutionary Guard Corps or any of its officials, agents, or affiliates, the property and interests in property of which are blocked pursuant to the International Emergency Economic Powers Act (50 U.S.C. 1701 *et seq.*) (see OFAC's Specially Designated Nationals and Blocked

Persons List at *https://www.treasury.gov/resource-center/sanctions/SDN-List/Pages/default.aspx*).

(b) *Remedies.* Upon the determination of a false certification under paragraph (a) of this subsection, the agency shall take one or more of the following actions:

(1) The contracting officer terminates the contract in accordance with procedures in part 49, or for commercial items, see 12.403.

(2) The suspending official suspends the contractor in accordance with the procedures in subpart 9.4.

(3) The debarring official debars the contractor for a period of at least two years in accordance with the procedures in subpart 9.4.

(c) *Exception for trade agreements.* The certification requirements of paragraph (a) of this subsection do not apply if the acquisition is subject to trade agreements and the offeror certifies that all the offered products are designated country end products or designated country construction material (see subpart 25.4).

[FAC 2005-46, 75 FR 60254, 9/29/2010, effective 9/29/2010; FAC 2005-54, 76 FR 68027, 68028, 11/2/2011, effective 11/2/2011; FAC 2005-58, 77 FR 23368, 4/18/2012, effective 5/18/2012; FAC 2005-63, 77 FR 73516, 12/10/2012, effective 12/10/2012; FAC 2005-69, 78 FR 46782, 8/1/2013, effective 8/1/2013; FAC 2005-83, 80 FR 38293, 7/2/2015, effective 10/1/2015; FAC 2005-100, 83 FR 42571, 8/22/2018, effective 8/22/2018]

25.703-3 Prohibition on contracting with entities that export sensitive technology to Iran.

(a) The head of an executive agency may not enter into or extend a contract for the procurement of goods or services with a person that exports certain sensitive technology to Iran, as determined by the President, and has an active exclusion in the System for Award Management at *http://www.sam.gov* (22 U.S.C. 8515).

(b) Each offeror must represent that it does not export any sensitive technology to the government of Iran or any entities or individuals owned or controlled by, or acting on behalf or at the direction of, the government of Iran.

(c) *Exception for trade agreements.* The representation requirement of paragraph (b) of this subsection does not apply if the acquisition is subject to trade agreements and the offeror certifies that all the offered products are designated country end products or designated country construction material (see subpart 25.4).

[FAC 2005-46, 75 FR 60254, 9/29/2010, effective 9/29/2010; FAC 2005-54, 76 FR 68027, 68028, 11/2/2011, effective 11/2/2011; FAC 2005-55, 77 FR 187, 1/3/2012, effective 2/2/2012; FAC 2005-58, 77 FR 23368, 4/18/2012, effective 5/18/2012; FAC 2005-63, 77 FR 73516, 12/10/2012, effective 12/10/2012; FAC 2005-67, 78 FR 37676, 6/21/2013, effective 7/22/2013; FAC 2005-69, 78 FR 46782, 8/1/2013, effective 8/1/2013; FAC 2005-101, 83 FR 48691, 9/26/2018, effective 10/26/2018]

25.703-4 Waiver.

(a) An agency or contractor seeking a waiver of the requirements of 25.703–2 or 25.703–3, consistent with section 6(b)(5) of the Iran Sanctions Act or 22 U.S.C. 8551(b), respectively, and the Presidential Memorandum of September 23, 2010 (75 FR 67025), shall submit the request to the Office of Federal Procurement Policy, allowing sufficient time for review and approval.

(b) Agencies may request a waiver on an individual or class basis; however, waivers are not indefinite and can be cancelled, if warranted.

(1) A class waiver may be requested only when the class of supplies or equipment is not available from any other source and it is in the national interest.

(2) Prior to submitting the waiver request, the request must be reviewed and cleared by the agency head.

(c) In general, all waiver requests should include the following information:

(1) Agency name, complete mailing address, and point of contact name, telephone number, and email address.

(2) Offeror's name, complete mailing address, and point of contact name, telephone number, and email address.

(3) Description/nature of product or service.

(4) The total cost and length of the contract.

(5) Justification, with market research demonstrating that no other offeror can provide the product or service and stating why the product or service must be procured from this offeror.

(i) If the offeror exports sensitive technology to the government of Iran or any entities or individuals owned or controlled by, or acting on behalf or at the direction of, the government of Iran, provide rationale why it is in the national interest for the President to waive the prohibition on contracting with this offeror, as required by 22 U.S.C. 8551(b).

(ii) If the offeror conducts activities for which sanctions may be imposed under section 5 of the Iran Sanctions Act or engages in any transaction that exceeds $3,500 with Iran's Revolutionary Guard Corps or any of its officials, agents, or affiliates, the property and interests in property of which are blocked pursuant to the International Emergency Economic Powers Act, provide rationale why it is essential to the national security interests of the United States for the President to waive the prohibition on contracting with this offeror, as required by section 6(b)(5) of the Iran Sanctions Act.

(6) Documentation regarding the offeror's past performance and integrity (see the Contractor Performance Assessment Reporting System (CPARS) and the Federal Awardee Performance Information and Integrity System at *https://www.cpars.gov*, and any other relevant information).

(7) Information regarding the offeror's relationship or connection with other firms that—

(i) Export sensitive technology to the government of Iran or any entities or individuals owned or controlled by, or acting on behalf or at the direction of, the government of Iran;

(ii) Conduct activities for which sanctions may be imposed under section 5 of the Iran Sanctions Act; or

(iii) Conduct any transaction that exceeds $3,500 with Iran's Revolutionary Guard Corps or any of its officials, agents, or affiliates, the property and interests in property of which are blocked pursuant to the International Emergency Economic Powers Act.

(8) Describe—

(i) The sensitive technology and the entity or individual to which it was exported (*i.e.*, the government of Iran or an entity or individual owned or controlled by, or acting on behalf or at the direction of, the government of Iran);

(ii) The activities in which the offeror is engaged for which sanctions may be imposed under section 5 of the Iran Sanctions Act; or

(iii) The transactions that exceed $3,500 with Iran's Revolutionary Guard Corps or any of its officials, agents, or affiliates, the property and interests in property of which are blocked pursuant to the International Emergency Economic Powers Act.

[FAC 2005-54, 76 FR 68028, 11/2/2011, effective 11/2/2011; FAC 2005-58, 77 FR 23368, 4/18/2012, effective 5/18/2012; FAC 2005-63, 77 FR 73516, 12/10/2012, effective 12/10/2012; FAC 2005-69, 78 FR 46782, 8/1/2013, effective 8/1/2013; FAC 2005-83, 80 FR 38293, 7/2/2015, effective 10/1/2015; FAC 2019-06, 84 FR 47865, 9/10/2019, effective 10/10/2019]

SUBPART 25.8—OTHER INTERNATIONAL AGREEMENTS AND COORDINATION

25.801 General.

Treaties and agreements between the United States and foreign governments affect the evaluation of offers from foreign entities and the performance of contracts in foreign countries.

[FAC 97-15, 64 FR 72414, 12/27/99, effective 2/25/2000]

25.802 Procedures.

(a) When placing contracts with contractors located outside the United States, for performance outside the United States, contracting officers must—

(1) Determine the existence and applicability of any international agreements and ensure compliance with these agreements; and

(2) Conduct the necessary advance acquisition planning and coordination between the appropriate U.S. executive agencies and foreign interests as required by these agreements.

(b) The Department of State publishes many international agreements in the "United States Treaties and Other International Agreements" series. Copies of this publication normally are available in overseas legal offices and U.S. diplomatic missions.

(c) Contracting officers must award all contracts with Taiwanese firms or organizations through the American Institute of Taiwan (AIT). AIT is under contract to the Department of State.

[FAC 97-15, 64 FR 72414, 12/27/99, effective 2/25/2000]

SUBPART 25.9—CUSTOMS AND DUTIES

25.900 Scope of subpart.

This subpart provides policies and procedures for exempting from import duties certain supplies purchased under Government contracts.

[FAC 97-15, 64 FR 72414, 12/27/99, effective 2/25/2000]

25.901 Policy.

United States laws impose duties on foreign supplies imported into the customs territory of the United States. Certain exemptions from these duties are available to Government agencies. Agencies must use these exemptions when the anticipated savings to appropriated funds will outweigh the administrative costs associated with processing required documentation.

[FAC 97-15, 64 FR 72414, 12/27/99, effective 2/25/2000]

25.902 Procedures.

For regulations governing importations and duties, see the Customs Regulations issued by the U.S. Customs Service, Department of the Treasury (19 CFR Chapter 1). Except as provided elsewhere in the Customs Regulations (see 19 CFR 10.100), all shipments of imported supplies purchased under Government contracts are subject to the usual Customs entry and examination requirements. Unless the agency obtains an exemption (see 25.903), those shipments are also subject to duty.

[FAC 97-15, 64 FR 72414, 12/27/99, effective 2/25/2000]

25.903 Exempted supplies.

(a) Subchapters VIII and X of Chapter 98 of the Harmonized Tariff Schedule of the United States (19 U.S.C. 1202) list supplies for which exemptions from duty may be obtained when imported into the customs territory of the United States under a Government contract. For certain of these supplies, the contracting agency must certify to the Commissioner of Customs that they are for the purpose stated in the Harmonized Tariff Schedule (see 19 CFR 10.102-104, 10.114, and 10.121 and 15 CFR part 301 for requirements and formats).

(b) Supplies (excluding equipment) for Government-operated vessels or aircraft may be withdrawn from any customs-bonded warehouse, from continuous customs custody elsewhere than in a bonded warehouse, or from a foreign-trade zone, free of duty and internal revenue tax as provided in 19 U.S.C. 1309 and 1317. The contracting activity must cite this authority on the appropriate customs form when making purchases (see 19 CFR 10.59—10.65).

[FAC 97-15, 64 FR 72414, 12/27/99, effective 2/25/2000]

SUBPART 25.10—ADDITIONAL FOREIGN ACQUISITION REGULATIONS

25.1001 Waiver of right to examination of records.

(a) *Policy.* The clause at 52.215-2, Audit and Records—Negotiation, prescribed at 15.209(b), and paragraph (d) of the clause at

52.212-5, Contract Terms and Conditions Required to Implement Statutes or Executive Orders—Commercial Items, prescribed at 12.301(b)(4), implement 10 U.S.C. 2313 and 41 U.S.C. 4706. The basic clauses authorize examination of records by the Comptroller General.

(1) Insert the appropriate basic clause, whenever possible, in negotiated contracts with foreign contractors.

(2) The contracting officer may use 52.215-2 with its Alternate III or 52.212-5 with its Alternate I after—

(i) Exhausting all reasonable efforts to include the basic clause;

(ii) Considering factors such as alternate sources of supply, additional cost, and time of delivery; and

(iii) The head of the agency has executed a determination and findings in accordance with paragraph (b) of this section, with the concurrence of the Comptroller General. However, concurrence of the Comptroller General is not required if the contractor is a foreign government or agency thereof or is precluded by the laws of the country involved from making its records available for examination.

(b) *Determination and findings*. The determination and findings must—

(1) Identify the contract and its purpose, and identify if the contract is with a foreign contractor or with a foreign government or an agency of a foreign government;

(2) Describe the efforts to include the basic clause;

(3) State the reasons for the contractor's refusal to include the basic clause;

(4) Describe the price and availability of the supplies or services from the United States and other sources; and

(5) Determine that it will best serve the interest of the United States to use the appropriate alternate clause in paragraph (a)(2) of this section.

[FAC 97-15, 64 FR 72414, 12/27/99, effective 2/25/2000; FAC 2005-73, 79 FR 24192, 4/29/2014, effective 5/29/2014]

25.1002 Use of foreign currency.

(a) Unless an international agreement or the WTO GPA (25.408(a)(4)) requires a specific currency, contracting officers must determine whether solicitations for contracts to be entered into and performed outside the United States will require submission of offers in U.S. currency or a specified foreign currency. In unusual circumstances, the contracting officer may permit submission of offers in other than a specified currency.

(b) To ensure a fair evaluation of offers, solicitations generally should require all offers to be priced in the same currency. However, if the solicitation permits submission of offers in other than a specified currency, the contracting officer must convert the offered prices to U.S. currency for evaluation purposes. The contracting officer must use the current market exchange rate from a commonly used source in effect as follows:

(1) For acquisitions conducted using sealed bidding procedures, on the date of bid opening.

(2) For acquisitions conducted using negotiation procedures—

(i) On the date specified for receipt of offers, if award is based on initial offers; otherwise

(ii) On the date specified for receipt of final proposal revisions.

(c) If a contract is priced in foreign currency, the agency must ensure that adequate funds are available to cover currency fluctuations to avoid a violation of the Anti-Deficiency Act (31 U.S.C. 1341, 1342, 1511-1519).

[FAC 97-15, 64 FR 72414, 12/27/99, effective 2/25/2000; FAC 2001-19, 69 FR 1051, 1/7/2004, effective 1/1/2004; FAC 2001-25, 69 FR 59700, 10/5/2004, effective 10/5/2004; FAC 2001-27, interim rule, 69 FR 77870, 12/28/2004, effective 1/1/2005; FAC 2005-07, 71 FR 219, 1/3/2006, effective 1/3/2006]

SUBPART 25.11—SOLICITATION PROVISIONS AND CONTRACT CLAUSES

25.1101 Acquisition of supplies.

The following provisions and clauses apply to the acquisition of supplies and the acquisition of services involving the furnishing of supplies.

(a) (1) Insert the clause at 52.225-1, Buy American—Supplies, in solicitations and contracts with a value exceeding the micro-purchase threshold but not exceeding $25,000; and in solicitations and contracts with a value exceeding $25,000, if none of the clauses prescribed in paragraphs (b) and (c) of this section apply, except if—

(i) The solicitation is restricted to domestic end products in accordance with Subpart 6.3;

(ii) The acquisition is for supplies for use within the United States and an exception to the Buy American statute applies (e.g., nonavailability, public interest, or information technology that is a commercial item); or

(iii) The acquisition is for supplies for use outside the United States.

(2) Insert the provision at 52.225-2, Buy American Certificate, in solicitations containing the clause at 52.225-1.

(b) (1) (i) Insert the clause at 52.225-3, Buy American-Free Trade Agreements-Israeli Trade Act, in solicitations and contracts if—

(A) The acquisition is for supplies, or for services involving the furnishing of supplies, for use within the United States, and the acquisition value is more than $25,000 or more, but is less than $180,000;

(B) The acquisition is not for information technology that is a commercial item, using fiscal year 2004 or subsequent fiscal year funds; and

(C) No exception in 25.401 applies. For acquisitions of agencies not subject to the Israeli Trade Act (see 25.406), see agency regulations.

(ii) If the acquisition value is $25,000 or more but is less than $50,000, use the clause with its Alternate I.

(iii) If the acquisition value is $50,000 or more but is less than $80,317, use the clause with its Alternate II.

(iv) If the acquisition value is $80,317 or more but is less than $100,000, use the clause with its Alternate III.

(2) (i) Insert the provision at 52.225-4, Buy American-Free Trade Agreements-Israeli Trade Act Certificate, in solicitations containing the clause at 52.225-3.

(ii) If the acquisition value is $25,000 or more but is less than $50,000, use the provision with its Alternate I.

(iii) If the acquisition value is $50,000 or more but is less than $80,317, use the provision with its Alternate II.

(iv) If the acquisition value is $80,317 or more, but is less than $100,000, use the provision with its Alternate III.

(c) (1) Insert the clause at 52.225-5, Trade Agreements, in solicitations and contracts valued at $180,000 or more, if the acquisition is covered by the WTO GPA (see subpart 25.4) and the agency has determined that the restrictions of the Buy American statute are not applicable to U.S.-made end products. If the agency has not made such a determination, the contracting officer must follow agency procedures.

(2) Insert the provision at 52.225-6, Trade Agreements Certificate, in solicitations containing the clause at 52.225-5.

(d) Insert the provision at 52.225-7, Waiver of Buy American Statute for Civil Aircraft and Related Articles, in solicitations for civil aircraft and related articles (see 25.407), if the acquisition value is less than $180,000.

(e) Insert the clause at 52.225-8, Duty-Free Entry, in solicitations and contracts for supplies that may be imported into the United States and for which duty-free entry may be obtained in accordance with 25.903(a), if the value of the acquisition—

(1) Exceeds the simplified acquisition threshold; or

(2) Does not exceed the simplified acquisition threshold, but the savings from waiving the duty is anticipated to be more than the administrative cost of waiving the duty. When used for acquisitions that do not ex-

ceed the simplified acquisition threshold, the contracting officer may modify paragraphs (c)(1) and (j)(2) of the clause to reduce the dollar figure.

(f) Insert the provision at 52.225-18, Place of Manufacture, in solicitations that are predominantly for the acquisition of manufactured end products (i.e., the estimated value of the manufactured end products exceeds the estimated value of other items to be acquired as a result of the solicitation).

[FAC 97-15, 64 FR 72414, 12/27/99, effective 2/25/2000; FAC 97-18, 65 FR 36014, 6/6/2000, effective 6/6/2000; FAC 2001-07, 67 FR 21534, 4/30/2002, effective 5/15/2002; FAC 2001-09, 67 FR 56115, 8/30/2002, effective 9/30/2002; FAC 2001-12, 1/27/2003, effective 1/24/2003; FAC 2001-19, 69 FR 1051, 1/7/2004, effective 1/1/2004; FAC 2001-20, 69 FR 8311, 2/23/2004, effective 2/23/2004; FAC 2001-26, 69 FR 76350, 12/20/2004, effective 1/19/2005; FAC 2001-27, interim rule, 69 FR 77870, 12/28/2004, effective 1/1/2005; FAC 2005-07, 71 FR 219, 1/3/2006, effective 1/3/2006; FAC 2005-08, 71 FR 864, 1/5/2006, effective 1/5/2006; FAC 2005-13, 71 FR 57363, 71 FR 57375, 71 FR 57378, 9/28/2006, effective 9/28/2006; FAC 2005-19, 72 FR 46326, 8/17/2007, effective 8/17/2007; Correction, 73 FR 3409, 1/18/2008; FAC 2005-24, 73 FR 10962, 2/28/2008, effective 2/28/2008; FAC 2005-30, 74 FR 2745, 1/15/2009, effective 1/15/2009; FAC 2005-43, 75 FR 38689, 7/2/2010, effective 7/2/2010; FAC 2005-50, 76 FR 14570, 3/16/2011, effective 3/16/2011; FAC 2005-56, 77 FR 12933, 3/2/2012, effective 3/2/2012; FAC 2005-57, 77 FR 13952, 3/7/2012, effective 3/15/2012; FAC 2005-61, 77 FR 56739, 9/13/2012, effective 9/13/2012; FAC 2005-72, 78 FR 80379, 12/31/2013, effective 1/1/2014; FAC 2005-73, 79 FR 24192, 4/29/2014, effective 5/29/2014; FAC 2005-86, 80 FR 81894, 12/31/2015, effective 1/1/2016; FAC 2005-88, 81 FR 30429, 5/16/2016, effective 6/15/2016; FAC 2005-97, 83 FR 3396, 1/24/2018, effective 1/24/2018]

25.1102 Acquisition of construction.

When using funds other than those appropriated under the American Recovery and Reinvestment Act of 2009 (Pub. L. 111-5) (Recovery Act), follow the prescriptions in paragraphs (a) through (d) of this section. Otherwise, follow the prescription in paragraph (e).

(a) Insert the clause at 52.225-9, Buy American—Construction Materials, in solicitations and contracts for construction that is performed in the United States valued at less than $6,932,000.

(1) List in paragraph (b)(2) of the clause all foreign construction material excepted from the requirements of the Buy American statute

(2) If the head of the agency determines that a higher percentage is appropriate, substitute the higher evaluation percentage in paragraph (b)(3)(i) of the clause.

(b)(1) Insert the provision at 52.225-10, Notice of Buy American Requirement—Construction Materials, in solicitations containing the clause at 52.225-9.

(2) If insufficient time is available to process a determination regarding the inapplicability of the Buy American statute before receipt of offers, use the provision with its Alternate I.

(c) Insert the clause at 52.225-11, Buy American—Construction Materials under Trade Agreements, in solicitations and contracts for construction that is performed in the United States valued at $6,932,000 or more.

(1) List in paragraph (b)(3) of the clause all foreign construction material excepted from the requirements of the Buy American statute, other than designated country construction material.

(2) If the head of the agency determines that a higher percentage is appropriate, substitute the higher evaluation percentage in paragraph (b)(4)(i) of the clause.

(3) For acquisitions valued at $6,932,000 or more, but less than $10,441,216, use the clause with its Alternate I. List in paragraph (b)(3) of the clause all foreign construction material excepted from the requirements of the Buy American statute, unless the excepted foreign construction material is from

a designated country other than Bahrain, Mexico, and Oman.

(d) (1) Insert the provision at 52.225-12, Notice of Buy American Requirement—Construction Materials under Trade Agreements, in solicitations containing the clause at 52.225-11.

(2) If insufficient time is available to process a determination regarding the inapplicability of the Buy American statute before receipt of offers, use the provision with its Alternate I.

(3) For acquisitions valued at $6,932,000 or more, but less than $10,441,216, use the provision with its Alternate II.

(e) (1) When using funds appropriated under the Recovery Act for construction, use provisions and clauses 52.225-21, 52.225-22, 52.225-23, or 52.225-24 (with appropriate Alternates) in lieu of the provisions and clauses 52.225-9, 52.225-10, 52.225-11, or 52.225-12 (with appropriate Alternates), respectively, that would be applicable as prescribed in paragraphs (a) through (d) of this section if Recovery Act funds were not used.

(2) If these Recovery Act provisions and clauses are only applicable to a project consisting of certain line items in the contract, identify in the schedule the line items to which the provisions and clauses apply.

(3) When using clause 52.225-23, list foreign construction material in paragraph (b) (3) of the clause as follows:

(i) *Basic clause.* List all foreign construction materials excepted from the Buy American statute or section 1605 of the Recovery Act, other than manufactured construction material from a Recovery Act designated country or unmanufactured construction material from a designated country.

(ii) *Alternate I.* List in paragraph (b) (3) of the clause all foreign construction material excepted from the Buy American statute or section 1605 of the Recovery Act, other than—

(A) Manufactured construction material from a Recovery Act designated country other than Bahrain, Mexico, or Oman; or

(B) Unmanufactured construction material from a designated country other than Bahrain, Mexico, or Oman.

[FAC 97-15, 64 FR 72414, 12/27/99, effective 2/25/2000; FAC 97-18, 65 FR 36014, 6/6/2000, effective 6/6/2000; FAC 2001-07, 67 FR 21534, 4/30/2002, effective 5/15/2002; FAC 2001-09, 67 FR 56115, 8/30/2002, effective 9/30/2002; FAC 2001-19, 69 FR 1051, 1/7/2004, effective 1/1/2004; FAC 2001-25, 69 FR 59700, 10/5/2004, effective 10/5/2004; FAC 2001-27, interim rule, 69 FR 77870, 12/28/2004, effective 1/1/2005; FAC 2005-07, 71 FR 219, 1/3/2006, effective 1/3/2006; FAC 2005-08, 71 FR 864, 1/5/2006, effective 1/5/2006; FAC 2005-09, 71 FR 20306, Interim rule, 4/19/2006, effective 4/19/2006; FAC 2005-13, 71 FR 57375, 9/28/2006, effective 9/28/2006; FAC 2005-14, 71 FR 67778, 11/22/2006, effective 11/22/2006; FAC 2005-24, 73 FR 10962, 2/28/2008, effective 2/28/2008; FAC 2005-30, 74 FR 2745, 1/15/2009, effective 1/15/2009; FAC 2005-32, 74 FR 14623, 3/31/2009, effective 3/31/2009; Technical amendments, 74 FR 22809, 5/14/1009, effective 5/14/2009; FAC 2005-43, 75 FR 38689, 7/2/2010, effective 7/2/2010; FAC 2005-32, 74 FR 14623, 3/31/2009, effective 3/31/2009; FAC 2005-45, 75 FR 53153, 8/30/2010, effective 10/1/2010; FAC 2005-50, 76 FR 14570, 3/16/2011, effective 3/16/2011; FAC 2005-56, 77 FR 12933, 3/2/2012, effective 3/2/2012; FAC 2005-72, 78 FR 80379, 12/31/2013, effective 1/1/2014; FAC 2005-73, 79 FR 24192, 4/29/2014, effective 5/29/2014; FAC 2005-86, 80 FR 81894, 12/31/2015, effective 1/1/2016; FAC 2005-87, 81 FR 11992, 3/7/2016, effective 3/7/2016; FAC 2005-97, 83 FR 3396, 1/24/2018, effective 1/24/2018]

25.1103 Other provisions and clauses.

(a) *Restrictions on certain foreign purchases.* Insert the clause at 52.225-13, Restrictions on Certain Foreign Purchases, in solicitations and contracts, unless an exception applies.

(b) *Translations.* Insert the clause at 52.225-14, Inconsistency Between English Version and Translation of Contract, in solicitations and contracts if anticipating translation into another language.

(c) *Foreign currency offers.* Insert the provision at 52.225-17, Evaluation of Foreign Currency Offers, in solicitations that permit the use of other than a specified currency. Insert in the provision the source of the rate to be used in the evaluation of offers.

(d) The contracting officer shall include in each solicitation for the acquisition of products or services (other than commercial items procured under Part 12) the provision at 52.225- 20, Prohibition on Conducting Restricted Business Operations in Sudan—Certification.

(e) The contracting officer shall include in all solicitations the provision at 52.225-25, Prohibition on Contracting with Entities Engaging in Certain Activities or Transactions Relating to Iran—Representation and Certification.

[FAC 97-15, 64 FR 72414, 12/27/99, effective 2/25/2000; FAC 97-18, 65 FR 36014, 6/6/2000, effective 6/6/2000; FAC 97-18, 65 FR 36014, 6/6/2000, effective 7/6/2000; FAC 2001-07, 67 FR 21538, 4/3/2002, effective 5/15/2002; FAC 2001-09, 67 FR 56115, 8/30/2002, effective 9/30/2002; FAC 2001-12, 1/27/2003, effective 1/24/2003; FAC 2001-16, 68 FR 56685, 10/1/2003, effective 10/31/2003; FAC 2001-19, 69 FR 1051, 1/7/2004, effective 1/1/2004; FAC 2001-20, 69 FR 8311, 2/23/2003, effective 2/23/2004; FAC 2001-25, 69 FR 59700, 10/5/2004, effective 10/5/2004; FAC 2001-26, 69 FR 76350, 12/20/2004, effective 1/19/2005; FAC 2005-08, 71 FR 864, 1/5/2006, effective 1/5/2006; FAC 2005-09, Interim rule, 71 FR 20305, 4/19/2006, effective 4/19/2006; FAC 2005-13, 71 FR 57363, 71 FR 57375, 9/28/2006, effective 9/28/2006; FAC 2005-14, 71 FR 67775, 11/22/2006, effective 11/22/2006; FAC 2005-26, 73 FR 33636, 6/12/2008, effective 6/12/2008; FAC 2005-36, 74 FR 40463, 8/11/2009, effective 8/11/2009; FAC 2005-46, 75 FR 60254, 9/29/2010, effective 9/29/2010; FAC 2005-54, 76 FR 68027, 68028, 11/2/2011, effective 11/2/2011; FAC 2005-58, 77 FR 23368, 4/18/2012, effective 5/18/2012; FAC 2005-63, 77 FR 73516, 12/10/2012, effective 12/10/2012; FAC 2005-69, 78 FR 46782, 8/1/2013, effective 8/1/2013]

PART 26—OTHER SOCIOECONOMIC PROGRAMS

Table of Contents

Subpart 26.1—Indian Incentive Program

Scope of subpart 26.100
Definitions 26.101
Policy 26.102
Procedures 26.103
Contract clause 26.104

Subpart 26.2—Major Disaster or Emergency Assistance Activities

Scope of subpart 26.200
Definitions 26.201
Local area preference 26.202
Local area set-aside 26.202-1
Evaluation preference 26.202-2
Transition of work 26.203
Justification for expenditures to other than local firms 26.204
Disaster Response Registry 26.205
Solicitation provision and contract clauses 26.206

Subpart 26.3—Historically Black Colleges and Universities and Minority Institutions

Scope of subpart 26.300
[Reserved] 26.301
General policy 26.302
Data collection and reporting requirements 26.303
Solicitation provision 26.304

Subpart 26.4—Food Donations to Nonprofit Organizations

Scope of subpart 26.400
Definitions 26.401
Policy 26.402
Procedures 26.403
Contract clause 26.404

PART 26—OTHER SOCIOECONOMIC PROGRAMS

Note

Note: This part has been created to facilitate promulgation of additional FAR and agency level socioeconomic coverage which properly falls under FAR Subchapter D—Socioeconomic Programs, but neither implements nor supplements existing FAR Parts 19, 22 through 25.

[Interim Rule, FAC 90-7, 56 FR 41736, 8/22/91, effective 8/22/91; FAC 90-32, 60 FR 48206, 9/18/95, effective 10/1/95]

SUBPART 26.1—INDIAN INCENTIVE PROGRAM

26.100 Scope of subpart.

This subpart implements 25 U.S.C. 1544, which provides an incentive to prime contractors that use Indian organizations and Indian-owned economic enterprises as subcontractors.

[Interim Rule, FAC 90-7, 56 FR 41736, 8/22/91, effective 8/22/91]

26.101 Definitions.

As used in this subpart—

Indian means any person who is a member of any Indian tribe, band, group, pueblo, or community that is recognized by the Federal Government as eligible for services from the Bureau of Indian Affairs (BIA) in accordance with 25 U.S.C. 1452(c) and any *Native* as defined in the Alaska Native Claims Settlement Act (43 U.S.C. 1601).

Indian organization means the governing body of any Indian tribe or entity established or recognized by the governing body of an Indian tribe for the purposes of 25 U.S.C., chapter 17.

Indian-owned economic enterprise means any Indian-owned (as determined by the Secretary of the Interior) commercial, industrial, or business activity established or organized for the purpose of profit, provided that Indian ownership constitutes not less than 51 percent of the enterprise.

Indian tribe means any Indian tribe, band, group, pueblo, or community, including native villages and native groups (including corporations organized by Kenai, Juneau, Sitka, and Kodiak) as defined in the Alaska Native Claims Settlement Act, that is recognized by the Federal Government as eligible for services from BIA in accordance with 25 U.S.C. 1452(c).

Interested party means a prime contractor or an actual or prospective offeror whose direct economic interest would be affected by the award of a subcontract or by the failure to award a subcontract.

[Interim Rule, FAC 90-7, 56 FR 41736, 8/22/91, effective 8/22/91; FAC 90-40, 61 FR 39186, 7/26/96, effective 9/24/96; FAC 97-17, 65 FR 24316, 4/25/2000, effective 6/26/2000]

26.102 Policy.

Indian organizations and Indian-owned economic enterprises shall have the maximum practicable opportunity to participate in performing contracts awarded by Federal agencies. In fulfilling this requirement, the Indian Incentive Program allows an incentive payment equal to 5 percent of the amount paid to a subcontractor in performing the contract, if the contract so authorizes and the subcontractor is an Indian organization or Indian-owned economic enterprise.

[FAC 90-40, 61 FR 39186, 7/26/96, effective 9/24/96]

26.103 Procedures.

(a) Contracting officers and prime contractors, acting in good faith, may rely on the representation of an Indian organization or Indian-owned economic enterprise as to its eligibility, unless an interested party challenges its status or the contracting officer has independent reason to question that status.

(b) In the event of a challenge to the representation of a subcontractor, the contracting officer shall refer the matter to the U.S. Department of the Interior, Bureau of Indian Affairs (BIA), Attn: Acquisition Management Director, 12220 Sunrise Valley Drive, Reston, VA 20191. The BIA will determine the eligibility and notify the contracting officer.

(c) The BIA will acknowledge receipt of the request from the contracting officer within 5 working days. Within 45 additional working days, BIA will advise the contracting officer, in writing, of its determination.

(d) The contracting officer will notify the prime contractor upon receipt of a challenge.

(1) To be considered timely, a challenge shall—

(i) Be in writing;

(ii) Identify the basis for the challenge;

(iii) Provide detailed evidence supporting the claim; and

(iv) Be filed with and received by the contracting officer prior to award of the subcontract in question.

(2) If the notification of a challenge is received by the prime contractor prior to award, it shall withhold award of the subcontract pending the determination by BIA, unless the prime contractor determines, and the contracting officer agrees, that award must be made in order to permit timely performance of the prime contract.

(3) Challenges received after award of the subcontract shall be referred to BIA, but the BIA determination shall have prospective application only.

(e) If the BIA determination is not received within the prescribed time period, the contracting officer and the prime contractor may rely on the representation of the subcontractor.

(f) Subject to the terms and conditions of the contract and the availability of funds, contracting officers shall authorize an incentive payment of 5 percent of the amount paid to the subcontractor. Contracting officers shall seek funding in accordance with agency procedures.

[Interim Rule, FAC 90-7, 56 FR 41736, 8/22/91, effective 8/22/91; FAC 90-11, 57 FR 20377, 5/12/92, effective 5/12/92; FAC 90-40, 61 FR 39186, 7/26/96, effective 9/24/96; Final rule, 62 FR 40236, 7/25/97, effective 6/30/97; FAC 97-11, 64 FR 10530, 3/4/99, effective 5/3/99; FAC 2005-91, 81 FR 67781, 9/30/2016, effective 9/30/2016]

26.104 Contract clause.

Contracting officers in civilian agencies may insert the clause at 52.226-1, Utilization of Indian Organizations and Indian-Owned Economic Enterprises, in solicitations and contracts if—

(a) In the opinion of the contracting officer, subcontracting possibilities exist for Indian organizations or Indian-owned economic enterprises; and

(b) Funds are available for any increased costs as described in paragraph (b) (2) of the clause at 52.226-1.

[FAC 97-17, 65 FR 24316, 4/25/2000, effective 6/26/2000]

SUBPART 26.2—MAJOR DISASTER OR EMERGENCY ASSISTANCE ACTIVITIES

26.200 Scope of subpart.

This subpart implements the Robert T. Stafford Disaster Relief and Emergency Assistance Act (42 U.S.C. 5150), which provides a preference for local organizations, firms, and individuals when contracting for major disaster or emergency assistance activities.

[FAC 90-40, 61 FR 39186, 7/26/96, effective 9/24/96; FAC 2005-12, 71 FR 44546, 8/4/2006, effective 8/4/2006; FAC 2005-21, 72 FR 63084, 11/7/2007, effective 11/7/2007; FAC 2005-27, 73 FR 53995, 9/17/2008, effective 10/17/2008]

26.201 Definitions.

Emergency response contract means a contract with private entities that supports assistance activities in a major disaster or emergency area, such as debris clearance, distribution of supplies, or reconstruction.

Local firm means a private organization, firm, or individual residing or doing business primarily in a major disaster or emergency area.

Major disaster or emergency area means the area included in the official Presidential declaration(s) and any additional areas identified by the Department of Homeland Security. Major disaster declarations and emergency declarations are published in the

Federal Register and are available at *http://www.fema.gov/news/disasters.fema.*

[FAC 90-40, 61 FR 39186, 7/26/96, effective 9/24/96; FAC 2005-21, 72 FR 63084, 11/7/2007, effective 11/7/2007; FAC 2005-27, 73 FR 53995, 9/17/2008, effective 10/17/2008]

26.202 Local area preference.

(a) When awarding emergency response contracts during the term of a major disaster or emergency declaration by the President of the United States under the authority of the Robert T. Stafford Disaster Relief and Emergency Assistance Act (42 U.S.C. 5121, et seq.), preference shall be given, to the extent feasible and practicable, to local firms. Preference may be given through a local area set-aside or an evaluation preference.

(b) When using the authority under the Stafford Act, see the definitions of "micro-purchase threshold" and "simplified acquisition threshold" in 2.101 for the authority to use an increased micro-purchase threshold and simplified acquisition threshold.

[FAC 2005-12, 71 FR 44546, 8/4/2006, effective 8/4/2006; FAC 2005-13, 71 FR 57380, 9/28/2006, effective 9/28/2006; FAC 2005-21, 72 FR 63084, 11/7/2007, effective 11/7/2007; FAC 2005-27, 73 FR 53995, 9/17/2008, effective 10/17/2008; FAC 2019-02, 84 FR 19835, 5/6/2019, effective 6/5/2019]

26.202-1 Local area set-aside.

The contracting officer may set aside solicitations to allow only local firms within a specific geographic area to compete (*see* 6.208).

(a) The contracting officer, in consultation with the requirements office, shall define the specific geographic area for the local set-aside.

(b) A major disaster or emergency area may span counties in several contiguous States. The set-aside area need not include all the counties in the declared disaster/emergency area(s), but cannot go outside it.

(c) The contracting officer shall also determine whether a local area set-aside should be further restricted to small business concerns in the set-aside area (see Part 19).

[FAC 2005-21, 72 FR 63084, 11/7/2007, effective 11/7/2007; FAC 2005-27, 73 FR 53995, 9/17/2008, effective 10/17/2008; FAC 2005-51, 76 FR 18304, 4/1/2011, effective 4/1/2011; FAC 2005-56, 77 FR 12913, 3/2/2012, effective 4/2/2012]

26.202-2 Evaluation preference.

The contracting officer may use an evaluation preference, when authorized in agency regulations or procedures.

[FAC 2005-21, 72 FR 63084, 11/7/2007, effective 11/7/2007; FAC 2005-27, 73 FR 53995, 9/17/2008, effective 10/17/2008]

26.203 Transition of work.

(a) In anticipation of potential emergency response requirements, agencies involved in response planning should consider awarding emergency response contracts before a major disaster or emergency occurs to ensure immediate response and relief. These contracts should be structured to respond to immediate emergency response needs, and should not be structured in any way that may inhibit the transition of emergency response work to local firms (*e.g.*, unnecessarily broad scopes of work or long periods of performance).

(b) 42 U.S.C. 5150(b)(2) requires that agencies performing response, relief, and reconstruction activities transition to local firms any work performed under contracts in effect on the date on which the President declares a major disaster or emergency, unless the head of such agency determines in writing that it is not feasible or practicable. This determination may be made on an individual contract or class basis. The written determination shall be prepared within a reasonable time given the circumstances of the emergency.

(c) In effecting the transition, agencies are not required to terminate or renegotiate existing contracts. Agencies should transition the work at the earliest practical opportunity after consideration of the following:

(1) The potential duration of the disaster or emergency.

(2) The severity of the disaster or emergency.

(3) The scope and structure of the existing contract, including its period of performance and the milestone(s) at which a transition is reasonable (*e.g.*, before exercising an option).

(4) The potential impact of a transition, including safety, national defense, and mobilization.

(5) The expected availability of qualified local offerors who can provide the products or services at a reasonable price.

(d) The agency shall transition the work to local firms using the local area set-aside identified in 26.202-1.

[FAC 2005-12, 71 FR 44546, 8/4/2006, effective 8/4/2006; FAC 2005-13, 71 FR 57380, 9/28/2006, effective 9/28/2006; FAC 2005-21, 72 FR 63084, 11/7/2007, effective 11/7/2007; FAC 2005-27, 73 FR 53995, 9/17/2008, effective 10/17/2008]

26.204 Justification for expenditures to other than local firms.

(a) 42 U.S.C. 5150(b)(1) requires that, subsequent to any Presidential declaration of a major disaster or emergency, any expenditure of Federal funds, under an emergency response contract not awarded to a local firm, must be justified in writing in the contract file. The justification should include consideration for the scope of the major disaster or emergency and the immediate requirements or needs of supplies and services to ensure life is protected, victims are cared for, and property is protected.

(b) The justification may be made on an individual or class basis. The contracting officer approves the justification.

[FAC 2005-21, 72 FR 63084, 11/7/2007, effective 11/7/2007; FAC 2005-27, 73 FR 53995, 9/17/2008, effective 10/17/2008]

26.205 Disaster Response Registry.

(a) Contracting officers shall consult the Disaster Response Registry via *https://www.sam.gov* to determine the availability of contractors for debris removal, distribution of supplies, reconstruction, and other disaster or emergency relief activities inside the United States and outlying areas.

(b) A list of prospective vendors voluntarily participating in the Disaster Response Registry can be retrieved using the System for Award Management (SAM) search tool which can accessed via *https://www.sam.gov*, Search Records, Advanced Search, Disaster Response Registry Search. These vendors may be identified by selecting the criteria for "Disaster Response Contractors". Contractors are required to register in SAM in order to gain access to the Disaster Response Registry.

[FAC 2005-37, 74 FR 52847, 10/14/2009, effective 10/14/2009; FAC 2005-43, 75 FR 38683, 7/2/2010, effective 8/2/2010; FAC 2005-55, 77 FR 187, 1/3/2012, effective 2/2/2012; FAC 2005-67, 78 FR 37676, 6/21/2013, effective 7/22/2013; FAC 2005-101, 83 FR 48691, 9/26/2018, effective 10/26/2018; FAC 2019-02, 84 FR 19839, 5/6/2019, effective 5/6/2019]

26.206 Solicitation provision and contract clauses.

(a) The contracting officer shall insert the provision at 52.226-3, Disaster or Emergency Area Representation, in solicitations involving the local area set-aside. For commercial items, see 12.301(e)(4).

(b) The contracting officer shall insert the clause at 52.226-4, Notice of Disaster or Emergency Area Set-aside in solicitations and contracts involving local area set-asides.

(c) The contracting officer shall insert the clause at 52.226-5, Restrictions on Subcontracting Outside Disaster or Emergency Area, in all solicitations and contracts that involve local area set-asides.

[FAC 2005-21, 72 FR 63084, 11/7/2007, effective 11/7/2007; FAC 2005-27, 73 FR 53995, 9/17/2008, effective 10/17/2008; Redesignated, FAC 2005-37, 74 FR 52847, 10/14/2009, effective 10/14/2009; FAC 2005-43, 75 FR 38683, 7/2/2010, effective 8/2/2010]

SUBPART 26.3—HISTORICALLY BLACK COLLEGES AND

UNIVERSITIES AND MINORITY INSTITUTIONS

26.300 Scope of subpart.

(a) This subpart implements Executive Order 12928 of September 16, 1994, which promotes participation of Historically Black Colleges and Universities (HBCUs) and Minority Institutions (MIs) in Federal procurement.

(b) This subpart does not pertain to contracts performed entirely outside the United States and its outlying areas.

[FAC 90-46, 62 FR 12690, 3/17/97, effective 5/16/97; FAC 2001-14, 68 FR 28079, 5/22/2003, effective 6/23/2003]

26.301 [Reserved]

[Removed and reserved, FAC 97-22, 66 FR 2116, 1/10/2001, effective 3/12/2001; Delay of effective date, 66 FR 14259, 3/9/2001, effective 5/11/2001]

26.302 General policy.

It is the policy of the Government to promote participation of HBCUs and MIs in Federal procurement.

[FAC 90-46, 62 FR 12690, 3/17/97, effective 5/16/97]

26.303 Data collection and reporting requirements.

Executive Order 12928 requires periodic reporting to the President on the progress of departments and agencies in complying with the laws and requirements mentioned in the Executive order.

[FAC 90-46, 62 FR 12690, 3/17/97, effective 5/16/97]

26.304 Solicitation provision.

Insert the provision at 52.226-2, Historically Black College or University and Minority Institution Representation, in solicitations exceeding the micro-purchase threshold, for research, studies, supplies, or services of the type normally acquired from higher educational institutions.

[FAC 97-13, 64 FR 36222, 7/2/99, effective 10/1/99; FAC 2005-77, 79 FR 61746, 10/14/2014, effective 10/14/2014]

SUBPART 26.4—FOOD DONATIONS TO NONPROFIT ORGANIZATIONS

26.400 Scope of subpart.

This section implements the Federal Food Donation Act of 2008 (42 U.S.C. 1792).

[FAC 2005-31, 74 FR 11829, 3/19/2009, effective 3/19/2009; FAC 2005-38, 74 FR 65607, 12/10/2009, effective 12/10/2009; FAC 2005-73, 79 FR 24192, 4/29/2014, effective 5/29/2014]

26.401 Definitions.

This section implements the Federal Food Donation Act of 2008 (Pub. L. 110-247). As used in this subpart—

Apparently wholesome food means food that meets all quality and labeling standards imposed by Federal, State, and local laws and regulations even though the food may not be readily marketable due to appearance, age, freshness, grade, size, surplus, or other conditions, in accordance with (b) (2) of the Bill Emerson Good Samaritan Food Donation Act (42 U.S.C. 1791(b)).

Excess food means food that—

(1) Is not required to meet the needs of the executive agencies; and

(2) Would otherwise be discarded.

Food-insecure means inconsistent access to sufficient, safe, and nutritious food.

Nonprofit organization means any organization that is—

(1) Described in section 501(c) of the Internal Revenue Code of 1986; and

(2) Exempt from tax under section 501(a) of that Code.

[FAC 2005-31, 74 FR 11829, 3/19/2009, effective 3/19/2009; FAC 2005-38, 74 FR 65607, 12/10/2009, effective 12/10/2009]

26.402 Policy.

The Government encourages executive agencies and their contractors, to the maximum extent practicable and safe, to donate excess apparently wholesome food to nonprofit organizations that provide assistance to food-insecure people in the United States.

[FAC 2005-31, 74 FR 11829, 3/19/2009, effective 3/19/2009; FAC 2005-38, 74 FR 65607, 12/10/2009, effective 12/10/2009]

26.403 Procedures.

(a) In accordance with the Federal Food Donation Act of 2008 an executive agency shall comply with the following:

(1) *Encourage donations.* In the applicable contracts stated at section 26.404, encourage contractors, to the maximum extent practicable and safe, to donate apparently wholesome excess food to nonprofit organizations that provide assistance to food-insecure people in the United States.

(2) *Costs.* (i) In any case in which a contractor enters into a contract with an executive agency under which apparently wholesome food is donated to food-insecure people in the United States, the head of the executive agency shall not assume responsibility for the costs and logistics of collecting, transporting, maintaining the safety of, or distributing excess, apparently wholesome food to food-insecure people in the United States under this Act.

(ii) The Government will not reimburse any costs incurred by the contractor against this contract or any other contract for the donation of Federal excess foods. Any costs incurred for Federal excess food donations are not considered allowable public relations costs in accordance with 31.205-1(f)(8).

(3) *Liability.* An executive agency (including an executive agency that enters into a contract with a contractor) and any contractor making donations pursuant to this Act shall be exempt from civil and criminal liability to the extent provided under the Bill Emerson Good Samaritan Food Donation Act (42 U.S.C. 1791).

[FAC 2005-31, 74 FR 11829, 3/19/2009, effective 3/19/2009; FAC 2005-38, 74 FR 65607, 12/10/2009, effective 12/10/2009; FAC 2005-73, 79 FR 24192, 4/29/2014, effective 5/29/2014]

26.404 Contract clause.

Insert the clause at 52.226-6, Promoting Excess Food Donation to Nonprofit Organizations, in solicitations and contracts greater than $25,000 for the provision, service, or sale of food in the United States.

[FAC 2005-31, 74 FR 11829, 3/19/2009, effective 3/19/2009; FAC 2005-38, 74 FR 65607, 12/10/2009, effective 12/10/2009]

Federal Acquisition Regulation
Parts 27—41
General Contracting Requirements
Special Categories of Contracting

Table of Contents

SUBCHAPTER E—GENERAL CONTRACTING REQUIREMENTS

Part 27—Patents, Data, and Copyrights 809

Part 28—Bonds and Insurance 841

Part 29—Taxes 865

Part 30—Cost Accounting Standards Administration 873

Part 31—Contract Cost Principles and Procedures 893

Part 32—Contract Financing 953

Part 33—Protests, Disputes, and Appeals 1031

SUBCHAPTER F—SPECIAL CATEGORIES OF CONTRACTING

Part 34—Major System Acquisition 1049

Part 35—Research and Development Contracting . . . 1057

Part 36—Construction and Architect-Engineer Contracts 1071

Part 37—Service Contracting 1093

Part 38—Federal Supply Schedule Contracting 1109

Part 39—Acquisition of Information Technology . . . 1113

Part 40—[Reserved]

Part 41—Acquisition of Utility Services 1121

PART 27—PATENTS, DATA, AND COPYRIGHTS

Table of Contents

Scope of part 27.000
Definition 27.001

Subpart 27.1—General

Applicability 27.101
General guidance 27.102

Subpart 27.2—Patents and Copyrights

Scope of subpart 27.200
Patent and copyright infringement liability. (No Text) 27.201
General 27.201-1
Contract clauses 27.201-2
Royalties. (No Text) 27.202
Reporting of royalties 27.202-1
Notice of Government as a licensee 27.202-2
Adjustment of royalties 27.202-3
Refund of royalties 27.202-4
Solicitation provisions and contract clause 27.202-5
Security requirements for patent applications containing classified subject matter. (No Text) 27.203
General 27.203-1
Contract clause 27.203-2
Patented technology under trade agreements. (No Text) 27.204
Use of patented technology under the North American Free Trade Agreement 27.204-1
Use of patented technology under the General Agreement on Tariffs and Trade (GATT) 27.204-2

Subpart 27.3—Patent Rights Under Government Contracts

Scope of subpart 27.300
Definitions 27.301
Policy 27.302
Contract clauses 27.303
Procedures. (No Text) 27.304
General 27.304-1
Contracts placed by or for other Government agencies 27.304-2
Subcontracts 27.304-3
Appeals 27.304-4
Administration of patent rights clauses. (No Text) 27.305
Goals 27.305-1
Administration by the Government 27.305-2
Securing invention rights acquired by the Government 27.305-3
Protection of invention disclosures 27.305-4
Licensing background patent rights to third parties 27.306

Subpart 27.4—Rights in Data and Copyrights

Scope of subpart 27.400
Definitions 27.401
Policy 27.402
Data rights—General 27.403
Basic rights in data clause 27.404
Unlimited rights data 27.404-1
Limited rights data and restricted computer software 27.404-2
Copyrighted works 27.404-3
Contractor's release, publication, and use of data 27.404-4
Unauthorized, omitted, or incorrect markings 27.404-5

Inspection of data at the contractor's facility 27.404-6
Other data rights provisions. (No Text) 27.405
Special works 27.405-1
Existing works 27.405-2
Commercial computer software 27.405-3
Other existing data 27.405-4
Acquisition of data. (No Text) 27.406
General 27.406-1
Additional data requirements 27.406-2
Major system acquisition 27.406-3
Rights to technical data in successful proposals 27.407
Cosponsored research and development activities 27.408
Solicitation provisions and contract clauses 27.409

Subpart 27.5—Foreign License and Technical Assistance Agreements

General 27.501

PART 27—PATENTS, DATA, AND COPYRIGHTS

27.000 Scope of part.

This part prescribes the policies, procedures, solicitation provisions, and contract clauses pertaining to patents, data, and copyrights.

[FAC 84-1, 49 FR 12974, 3/30/84, effective 4/1/84; FAC 2005-21, 72 FR 63045, 11/7/2007, effective 12/7/2007]

27.001 Definition.

United States, as used in this part, means the 50 States and the District of Columbia, U.S. territories and possessions, Puerto Rico, and the Northern Mariana Islands.

[FAC 2005-21, 72 FR 63045, 11/7/2007, effective 12/7/2007]

SUBPART 27.1—GENERAL

27.101 Applicability.

This part applies to all agencies. However, agencies are authorized to adopt alternative policies, procedures, solicitation provisions, and contract clauses to the extent necessary to meet the specific requirements of laws, executive orders, treaties, or international agreements. Any agency adopting alternative policies, procedures, solicitation provisions, and contract clauses should include them in the agency's published regulations.

[FAC 84-1, 49 FR 12974, 3/30/84, effective 4/1/84; FAC 2005-21, 72 FR 63045, 11/7/2007, effective 12/7/2007]

27.102 General guidance.

(a) The Government encourages the maximum practical commercial use of inventions made under Government contracts.

(b) Generally, the Government will not refuse to award a contract on the grounds that the prospective contractor may infringe a patent. The Government may authorize and consent to the use of inventions in the performance of certain contracts, even though the inventions may be covered by U.S. patents.

(c) Generally, contractors providing commercial items should indemnify the Government against liability for the infringement of U.S. patents.

(d) The Government recognizes rights in data developed at private expense, and limits its demands for delivery of that data. When such data is delivered, the Government will acquire only those rights essential to its needs.

(e) Generally, the Government requires that contractors obtain permission from copyright owners before including copyrighted works, owned by others, in data to be delivered to the Government.

[Reserved, FAC 90-29, 60 FR 34732, 7/3/95, effective 7/3/95; FAC 2005-21, 72 FR 63045, 11/7/2007, effective 12/7/2007]

SUBPART 27.2—PATENTS AND COPYRIGHTS

27.200 Scope of subpart.

This subpart prescribes policies and procedures with respect to—

(a) Patent and copyright infringement liability;

(b) Royalties;

(c) Security requirements for patent applications containing classified subject matter; and

(d) Patented technology under trade agreements.

[FAC 84-1, 49 FR 12974, 3/30/84, effective 4/1/84; FAC 2005-21, 72 FR 63045, 11/7/2007, effective 12/7/2007]

27.201 Patent and copyright infringement liability. (No Text)

[FAC 2005-21, 72 FR 63045, 11/7/2007, effective 12/7/2007]

27.201-1 General.

(a) Pursuant to 28 U.S.C. 1498, the exclusive remedy for patent or copyright infringement by or on behalf of the Government is a suit for monetary damages against the Government in the Court of Federal Claims. There is no injunctive relief available, and there is no direct cause of action against a contractor that is infringing a patent or copyright with the authorization or consent of the Government (e.g., while performing a contract).

(b) The Government may expressly authorize and consent to a contractor's use or manufacture of inventions covered by U.S. patents by inserting the clause at 52.227-1, Authorization and Consent.

(c) Because of the exclusive remedies granted in 28 U.S.C. 1498, the Government requires notice and assistance from its contractors regarding any claims for patent or copyright infringement by inserting the clause at 52.227-2, Notice and Assistance, Regarding Patent and Copyright Infringement.

(d) The Government may require a contractor to reimburse it for liability for patent infringement arising out of a contract for commercial items by inserting the clause at FAR 52.227-3, Patent Indemnity.

[FAC 84-1, 49 FR 12974, 3/30/84, effective 4/1/84; FAC 2005-21, 72 FR 63045, 11/7/2007, effective 12/7/2007]

27.201-2 Contract clauses.

(a) (1) Insert the clause at 52.227-1, Authorization and Consent, in solicitations and contracts except that use of the clause is—

(i) Optional when using simplified acquisition procedures; and

(ii) Prohibited when both complete performance and delivery are outside the United States.

(2) Use the clause with its Alternate I in all R&D solicitations and contracts for which the primary purpose is R&D work, except that this alternate shall not be used in construction and architect-engineer contracts unless the contract calls exclusively for R&D work.

(3) Use the clause with its Alternate II in solicitations and contracts for communication services with a common carrier and the services are unregulated and not priced by a tariff schedule set by a regulatory body.

(b) Insert the clause at 52.227-2, Notice and Assistance Regarding Patent and Copyright Infringement, in all solicitations and contracts that include the clause at 52.227-1, Authorization and Consent.

(c) (1) Insert the clause at 52.227-3, Patent Indemnity, in solicitations and contracts that may result in the delivery of commercial items, unless—

(i) Part 12 procedures are used;

(ii) The simplified acquisition procedures of Part 13 are used;

(iii) Both complete performance and delivery are outside the United States; or

(iv) The contracting officer determines after consultation with legal counsel that omission of the clause would be consistent with commercial practice.

(2) Use the clause with either its Alternate I (identification of excluded items) or II (identification of included items) if—

(i) The contract also requires delivery of items that are not commercial items; or

(ii) The contracting officer determines after consultation with legal counsel that limitation of applicability of the clause would be consistent with commercial practice.

(3) Use the clause with its Alternate III if the solicitation or contract is for communication services and facilities where performance is by a common carrier, and the services are unregulated and are not priced by a tariff schedule set by a regulatory body.

(d) (1) Insert the clause at 52.227-4, Patent Indemnity—Construction Contracts, in solicitations and contracts for construction or that are fixed-price for dismantling, demolition, or removal of improvements. Do not insert the clause in contracts solely for architect-engineer services.

(2) If the contracting officer determines that the construction will necessarily involve the use of structures, products, materials, equipment, processes, or methods that are nonstandard, noncommercial, or special, the contracting officer may expressly exclude them from the patent indemnification by using the clause with its Alternate I. Note that this exclusion is for items, as distinguished from identified patents (see paragraph (e) of this subsection).

(e) It may be in the Government's interest to exempt specific U.S. patents from the patent indemnity clause. Exclusion from indemnity of identified patents, as distinguished from items, is the prerogative of the agency head. Upon written approval of the agency head, the contracting officer may insert the clause at 52.227-5, Waiver of Indemnity, in solicitations and contracts in addition to the appropriate patent indemnity clause.

(f) If a patent indemnity clause is not prescribed, the contracting officer may include one in the solicitation and contract if it is in the Government's interest to do so.

(g) The contracting officer shall not include in any solicitation or contract any clause whereby the Government agrees to indemnify a contractor for patent infringement.

[FAC 84-1, 49 FR 12974, 3/30/84, effective 4/1/84; FAC 90-29, 60 FR 34732, 7/3/95, effective 7/3/95; FAC 2005-21, 72 FR 63045, 11/7/2007, effective 12/7/2007]

27.202 Royalties. (No Text)

[FAC 2005-21, 72 FR 63045, 11/7/2007, effective 12/7/2007]

27.202-1 Reporting of royalties.

(a) To determine whether royalties anticipated or actually paid under Government contracts are excessive, improper, or inconsistent with Government patent rights the solicitation provision at 52.227-6 requires prospective contractors to furnish royalty information. The contracting officer shall take appropriate action to reduce or eliminate excessive or improper royalties.

(b) If the response to a solicitation includes a charge for royalties, the contracting officer shall, before award of the contract, forward the information to the office having cognizance of patent matters for the contracting activity. The cognizant office shall promptly advise the contracting officer of appropriate action.

(c) The contracting officer, when considering the approval of a subcontract, shall require royalty information if it is required under the prime contract. The contracting officer shall forward the information to the office having cognizance of patent matters. However, the contracting officer need not delay consent while awaiting advice from the cognizant office.

(d) The contracting officer shall forward any royalty reports to the office having cognizance of patent matters for the contracting activity.

[FAC 84-1, 49 FR 12974, 3/30/84, effective 4/1/84; FAC 2005-21, 72 FR 63045, 11/7/2007, effective 12/7/2007]

27.202-2 Notice of Government as a licensee.

(a) When the Government is obligated to pay a royalty on a patent because of an existing license agreement and the contracting officer believes that the licensed patent will be applicable to a prospective contract, the Government should furnish the prospective offerors with—

(1) Notice of the license;

(2) The number of the patent; and

(3) The royalty rate cited in the license.

(b) When the Government is obligated to pay such a royalty, the solicitation should also require offerors to furnish information indicating whether or not each offeror is the patent owner or a licensee under the patent. This information is necessary so that the Government may either—

(1) Evaluate an offeror's price by adding an amount equal to the royalty; or

(2) Negotiate a price reduction with an offeror when the offeror is licensed under the same patent at a lower royalty rate.

[FAC 90-29, 60 FR 34732, 7/3/95, effective 7/3/95; FAC 2005-21, 72 FR 63045, 11/7/2007, effective 12/7/2007]

27.202-3 Adjustment of royalties.

(a) If at any time the contracting officer believes that any royalties paid, or to be paid, under a contract or subcontract are inconsistent with Government rights, excessive, or otherwise improper, the contracting officer shall promptly report the facts to the office having cognizance of patent matters for the contracting activity concerned.

(b) In coordination with the cognizant office, the contracting officer shall promptly act to protect the Government against payment of royalties—

(1) With respect to which the Government has a royalty-free license;

(2) At a rate in excess of the rate at which the Government is licensed; or

(3) When the royalties in whole or in part otherwise constitute an improper charge.

(c) In appropriate cases, the contracting officer in coordination with the cognizant office shall demand a refund pursuant to any refund of royalties clause in the contract (see 27.202-4) or negotiate for a reduction of royalties.

(d) For guidance in evaluating information furnished pursuant to 27.202-1, see 31.205-37. See also 31.109regarding advance understandings on particular cost items, including royalties.

[FAC 2005-21, 72 FR 63045, 11/7/2007, effective 12/7/2007]

27.202-4 Refund of royalties.

The clause at 52.227-9, Refund of Royalties, establishes procedures to pay the contractor royalties under the contract and recover royalties not paid by the contractor when the royalties were included in the contractor's fixed price.

[FAC 2005-21, 72 FR 63045, 11/7/2007, effective 12/7/2007]

27.202-5 Solicitation provisions and contract clause.

(a) (1) Insert a solicitation provision substantially the same as the provision at 52.227-6, Royalty Information, in—

(i) Any solicitation that may result in a negotiated contract for which royalty information is desired and for which certified cost or pricing data are obtained under 15.403; or

(ii) Sealed bid solicitations only if the need for such information is approved at a level above the contracting officer as being necessary for proper protection of the Government's interests.

(2) If the solicitation is for communication services and facilities by a common carrier, use the provision with its Alternate I.

(b) If the Government is obligated to pay a royalty on a patent involved in the prospective contract, insert in the solicitation a provision substantially the same as the provision at 52.227-7, Patents—Notice of Government Licensee. If the clause at 52.227-6 is not included in the solicitation, the contracting officer may require offerors to provide information sufficient to provide this notice to the other offerors.

(c) Insert the clause at 52.227-9, Refund of Royalties, in negotiated fixed-price solicitations and contracts when royalties may be paid under the contract. If a fixed-price incentive contract is contemplated, change "price" to "target cost and target profit" wherever it appears in the clause. The clause may be used in cost-reimbursement contracts where agency approval of royalties is necessary to protect the Government's interests.

[FAC 2005-21, 72 FR 63045, 11/7/2007, effective 12/7/2007; FAC 2005-45, 75 FR 53135, 8/30/2010, effective 10/1/2010]

27.203 Security requirements for patent applications containing classified subject matter. (No Text)

[FAC 2005-21, 72 FR 63045, 11/7/2007, effective 12/7/2007]

27.203-1 General.

(a) Unauthorized disclosure of classified subject matter, whether in patent applications or resulting from the issuance of a patent, may be a violation of 18 U.S.C. 792, *et seq.* (Chapter 37—Espionage and Censorship), and related statutes, and may be contrary to the interests of national security.

(b) Upon receipt of a patent application under paragraph (a) or (b) of the clause at 52.227-10, Filing of Patent Applications—Classified Subject Matter, the contracting officer shall ascertain the proper security classification of the patent application. If the application contains classified subject matter, the contracting officer shall inform the contractor how to transmit the application to the United States Patent Office in accordance with procedures provided by legal counsel. If the material is classified "Secret" or higher, the contracting officer shall make every effort to notify the contractor within 30 days of the Government's determination, pursuant to paragraph (a) of the clause.

(c) Upon receipt of information furnished by the contractor under paragraph (d) of the clause at 52.227-10, the contracting officer shall promptly submit that information to legal counsel in order that the steps necessary to ensure the security of the application will be taken.

(d) The contracting officer shall act promptly on requests for approval of foreign filing under paragraph (c) of the clause at 52.227-10 in order to avoid the loss of valuable patent rights of the Government or the contractor.

[FAC 84-1, 49 FR 12974, 3/30/84, effective 4/1/84; FAC 84-5, 50 FR 1743, 1/11/85, effective 4/1/85; FAC 90-29, 60 FR 34732, 7/3/95, effective 7/3/95; FAC 2005-21, 72 FR 63045, 11/7/2007, effective 12/7/2007]

27.203-2 Contract clause.

Insert the clause at 52.227-10, Filing of Patent Applications—Classified Subject Matter, in all classified solicitations and contracts and in all solicitations and contracts where the nature of the work reasonably might result in a patent application containing classified subject matter.

[FAC 84-1, 49 FR 12974, 3/30/84, effective 4/1/84; FAC 84-5, 50 FR 1743, 1/11/85, effective 4/1/85; 50 FR 52429, 12/23/85; FAC 2005-21, 72 FR 63045, 11/7/2007, effective 12/7/2007]

27.204 Patented technology under trade agreements. (No Text)

[FAC 2005-21, 72 FR 63045, 11/7/2007, effective 12/7/2007]

27.204-1 Use of patented technology under the North American Free Trade Agreement.

(a) The requirements of this section apply to the use of technology covered by a valid patent when the patent holder is from a country that is a party to the North American Free Trade Agreement (NAFTA).

(b) Article 1709(10) of NAFTA generally requires a user of technology covered by a valid patent to make a reasonable effort to obtain authorization prior to use of the patented technology. However, NAFTA provides that this requirement for authorization may be waived in situations of national emergency or other circumstances of extreme urgency, or for public noncommercial use.

(c) Section 6 of Executive Order 12889, "Implementation of the North American Free Trade Act," of December 27, 1993, waives the requirement to obtain advance authorization for an invention used or manufactured by or for the Federal Government. However, the patent owner shall be notified in advance whenever the agency or its contractor knows or has reasonable grounds to know, without making a patent search, that an invention described in and covered by a valid U.S. patent is or will be used or manufactured without a license. In cases of national emergency or other circumstances of extreme urgency, this notification need not be made in advance, but shall be made as soon as reasonably practicable.

(d) The contracting officer, in consultation with the office having cognizance of patent matters, shall ensure compliance with the notice requirements of NAFTA Article 1709(10) and Executive Order 12889. A contract award should not be suspended pending notification to the patent owner.

(e) Section 6(c) of Executive Order 12889 provides that the notice to the patent owner does not constitute an admission of infringement of a valid privately-owned patent.

(f) When addressing issues regarding compensation for the use of patented technology, Government personnel should be advised that NAFTA uses the term *adequate remuneration*. Executive Order 12889 equates *remuneration* to *reasonable and entire compensation* as used in 28 U.S.C. 1498, the statute that gives jurisdiction to the U.S. Court of Federal Claims to hear patent and copyright cases involving infringement by the Government.

(g) When questions arise regarding the notice requirements or other matters relating to this section, the contracting officer should consult with legal counsel.

[FAC 84-1, 49 FR 12974, 3/30/84, effective 4/1/84; FAC 84-26, 52 FR 19803, 5/27/87, effective 7/30/87; FAC 90-4, 56 FR 15152, 4/15/91, effective 5/15/91; FAC 97-2, 62 FR 51224, 9/30/97, effective 10/10/97; FAC

2005-21, 72 FR 63045, 11/7/2007, effective 12/7/2007]

27.204-2 Use of patented technology under the General Agreement on Tariffs and Trade (GATT).

Article 31 of Annex 1C, Agreement on Trade-Related Aspects of Intellectual Property Rights, to GATT (Uruguay Round) addresses situations where the law of a member country allows for use of a patent without authorization, including use by the Government.

[FAC 84-1, 49 FR 12974, 3/30/84, effective 4/1/84; FAC 90-4, 56 FR 15153, 4/15/91, effective 5/15/91; FAC 97-2, 62 FR 51224, 9/30/97, effective 10/10/97; FAC 2005-21, 72 FR 63045, 11/7/2007, effective 12/7/2007]

SUBPART 27.3—PATENT RIGHTS UNDER GOVERNMENT CONTRACTS

27.300 Scope of subpart.

This subpart prescribes policies, procedures, solicitation provisions, and contract clauses pertaining to inventions made in the performance of work under a Government contract or subcontract for experimental, developmental, or research work. Agency policies, procedures, solicitation provisions, and contract clauses may be specified in agency supplemental regulations as permitted by law, including 37 CFR 401.1.

[FAC 84-1, 49 FR 12974, 3/30/84, effective 4/1/84; FAC 84-58, 55 FR 25525, 6/21/90, effective 7/23/90; FAC 2005-21, 72 FR 63045, 11/7/2007, effective 12/7/2007]

27.301 Definitions.

As used in this subpart—

Invention means any invention or discovery that is or may be patentable or otherwise protectable under title 35 of the U.S. Code, or any variety of plant that is or may be protectable under the Plant Variety Protection Act (7 U.S.C. 2321, *et seq.*)

Made means—

(1) When used in relation to any invention other than a plant variety, means the conception or first actual reduction to practice of the invention; or

(2) When used in relation to a plant variety, means that the contractor has at least tentatively determined that the variety has been reproduced with recognized characteristics.

Nonprofit organization means a university or other institution of higher education or an organization of the type described in section 501(c)(3) of the Internal Revenue Code of 1954 (26 U.S.C. 501(c)) and exempt from taxation under section 501(a) of the Internal Revenue Code (26 U.S.C. 501(a)), or any nonprofit scientific or educational organization qualified under a State nonprofit organization statute.

Practical application means to manufacture, in the case of a composition or product; to practice, in the case of a process or method; or to operate, in the case of a machine or system; and, in each case, under such conditions as to establish that the invention is being utilized and that its benefits are, to the extent permitted by law or Government regulations, available to the public on reasonable terms.

Subject invention means any invention of the contractor made in the performance of work under a Government contract.

[FAC 84-1, 49 FR 12974, 3/30/84, effective 4/1/84; Interim Rule, FAC 84-48, 54 FR 25063, 6/12/89, effective 6/12/89; FAC 84-58, 55 FR 25525, 6/21/90, effective 7/23/90; FAC 97-22, 66 FR 2116, 1/10/2001, effective 3/12/2001; Delay of effective date, 66 FR 14259, 3/9/2001, effective 5/11/2001; FAC 2005-21, 72 FR 63045, 11/7/2007, effective 12/7/2007]

27.302 Policy.

(a) *Introduction.* In accordance with chapter 18 of title 35, U.S.C. (as implemented by 37 CFR part 401), Presidential Memorandum on Government Patent Policy to the Heads of Executive Departments and Agencies dated February 18, 1983, and Executive Order 12591, Facilitating Access to Science and Technology dated April 10, 1987, it is the policy and objective of the Government to—

(1) Use the patent system to promote the use of inventions arising from federally supported research or development;

(2) Encourage maximum participation of industry in federally supported research and development efforts;

(3) Ensure that these inventions are used in a manner to promote free competition and enterprise without unduly encumbering future research and discovery;

(4) Promote the commercialization and public availability of the inventions made in the United States by United States industry and labor;

(5) Ensure that the Government obtains sufficient rights in federally supported inventions to meet the needs of the Government and protect the public against nonuse or unreasonable use of inventions; and

(6) Minimize the costs of administering patent policies.

(b) *Contractor right to elect title.* (1) Generally, pursuant to 35 U.S.C. 202 and the Presidential Memorandum and Executive order cited in paragraph (a) of this section, each contractor may, after required disclosure to the Government, elect to retain title to any subject invention.

(2) A contract may require the contractor to assign to the Government title to any subject invention—

(i) When the contractor is not located in the United States or does not have a place of business located in the United States or is subject to the control of a foreign government (see 27.303 (e)(1)(i));

(ii) In exceptional circumstances, when an agency determines that restriction or elimination of the right to retain title in any subject invention will better promote the policy and objectives of chapter 18 of title 35, U.S.C. and the Presidential Memorandum;

(iii) When a Government authority, that is authorized by statute or executive order to conduct foreign intelligence or counterintelligence activities, determines that the restriction or elimination of the right to retain title to any subject invention is necessary to protect the security of such activities;

(iv) When the contract includes the operation of a Government-owned, contractor-operated facility of the Department of Energy (DOE) primarily dedicated to the Department's naval nuclear propulsion or weapons related programs and all funding agreement limitations under 35 U.S.C. 202(a)(iv) for agreements with small business concerns and nonprofit organizations are limited to inventions occurring under the above two programs; or

(v) Pursuant to statute or in accordance with agency regulations.

(3) When the Government has the right to acquire title to a subject invention, the contractor may, nevertheless, request greater rights to a subject invention (see 27.304-1(c)).

(4) Consistent with 37 CFR part 401, when a contract with a small business concern or nonprofit organization requires assignment of title to the Government based on the exceptional circumstances enumerated in paragraph (b)(2)(ii) or (iii) of this section for reasons of national security, the contract shall still provide the contractor with the right to elect ownership to any subject invention that—

(i) Is not classified by the agency; or

(ii) Is not limited from dissemination by the DOE within 6 months from the date it is reported to the agency.

(5) Contracts in support of DOE's naval nuclear propulsion program are exempted from this paragraph (b).

(6) When a contract involves a series of separate task orders, an agency may structure the contract to apply the exceptions at paragraph (b)(2)(ii) or (iii) of this section to individual task orders.

(c) *Government license.* The Government shall have at least a nonexclusive, nontransferable, irrevocable, paid-up license to practice, or have practiced for or on behalf of the United States, any subject invention throughout the world. The Government may require additional rights in order to comply with treaties or other international agreements. In such case, these rights shall be made a part of the contract (see 27.303).

(d) *Government right to receive title.* (1) In addition to the right to obtain title to subject inventions pursuant to paragraph (b)(2)(i) through (v) of this section, the Government has the right to receive title to an invention—

(i) If the contractor has not disclosed the invention within the time specified in the clause; or

(ii) In any country where the contractor—

(A) Does not elect to retain rights or fails to elect to retain rights to the invention within the time specified in the clause;

(B) Has not filed a patent or plant variety protection application within the time specified in the clause;

(C) Decides not to continue prosecution of a patent or plant variety protection application, pay maintenance fees, or defend in a reexamination or opposition proceeding on the patent; or

(D) No longer desires to retain title.

(2) For the purposes of this paragraph, filing in a European Patent Office Region or under the Patent Cooperation Treaty constitutes election in the countries selected in the application(s).

(e) *Utilization reports.* The Government has the right to require periodic reporting on how any subject invention is being used by the contractor or its licensees or assignees. In accordance with 35 U.S.C. 202(c)(5) and 37 CFR part 401, agencies shall not disclose such utilization reports to persons outside the Government without permission of the contractor. Contractors should mark as confidential/proprietary any utilization report to help prevent inadvertent release outside the Government.

(f) *March-in rights.* (1) Pursuant to 35 U.S.C. 203, agencies have certain march-in rights that require the contractor, an assignee, or exclusive licensee of a subject invention to grant a nonexclusive, partially exclusive, or exclusive license in any field of use to responsible applicants, upon terms that are reasonable under the circumstances. If the contractor, assignee or exclusive licensee of a subject invention refuses to grant such a license, the agency can grant the license itself. March-in rights may be exercised only if the agency determines that this action is necessary—

(i) Because the contractor or assignee has not taken, or is not expected to take within a reasonable time, effective steps to achieve practical application of the subject invention in the field(s) of use;

(ii) To alleviate health or safety needs that are not reasonably satisfied by the contractor, assignee, or their licensees;

(iii) To meet requirements for public use specified by Federal regulations and these requirements are not reasonably satisfied by the contractor, assignee, or licensees; or

(iv) Because the agreement required by paragraph (g) of this section has neither been obtained nor waived, or because a licensee of the exclusive right to use or sell any subject invention in the United States is in breach of its agreement obtained pursuant to paragraph (g) of this section.

(2) The agency shall not exercise its march-in rights unless the contractor has been provided a reasonable time to present facts and show cause why the proposed agency action should not be taken. The agency shall provide the contractor an opportunity to dispute or appeal the proposed action, in accordance with 27.304-1(g).

(g) *Preference for United States industry.* In accordance with 35 U.S.C. 204, no contractor that receives title to any subject invention and no assignee of the contractor shall grant to any person the exclusive right to use or sell any subject invention in the United States unless that person agrees that any products embodying the subject invention or produced through the use of the subject invention will be manufactured substantially in the United States. However, in individual cases, the requirement for this agreement may be waived by the agency upon a showing by the contractor or assignee that reasonable but unsuccessful efforts have been made to grant licenses on similar terms to potential licensees that would be likely to manufacture substantially in the United States or that under the circumstances domestic manufacture is not commercially feasible.

(h) *Special conditions for nonprofit organizations' preference for small business concerns.* (1) Nonprofit organization contractors are expected to use reasonable efforts to attract small business licensees (see paragraph (i)(4) of the clause at 52.227-11, Patent Rights—Ownership by the Contractor). What constitutes reasonable efforts to attract small business licensees will vary with the circumstances and the nature, duration, and expense of efforts needed to bring the invention to the market.

(2) Small business concerns that believe a nonprofit organization is not meeting its obligations under the clause may report the matter to the Secretary of Commerce. To the extent deemed appropriate, the Secretary of Commerce will undertake informal investigation of the matter, and may discuss or negotiate with the nonprofit organization ways to improve its efforts to meet its obligations under the clause. However, in no event will the Secretary of Commerce intervene in ongoing negotiations or contractor decisions concerning the licensing of a specific subject invention. These investigations, discussions, and negotiations involving the Secretary of Commerce will be in coordination with other interested agencies, including the Small Business Administration. In the case of a contract for the operation of a Government-owned, contractor-operated research or production facility, the Secretary of Commerce will coordinate with the agency responsible for the facility prior to any discussions or negotiations with the contractor.

(i) *Minimum rights to contractor.* (1) When the Government acquires title to a subject invention, the contractor is normally granted a revocable, nonexclusive, paid-up license to that subject invention throughout the world. The contractor's license extends to any of its domestic subsidiaries and affiliates within the corporate structure of which the contractor is a part and includes the right to grant sublicenses to the extent the contractor was legally obligated to do so at the time of contract award. The contracting officer shall approve or disapprove, in writing, any contractor request to transfer its licenses. No approval is necessary when the transfer is to the successor of that part of the contractor's business to which the subject invention pertains.

(2) In response to a third party's proper application for an exclusive license, the contractor's domestic license may be revoked or modified to the extent necessary to achieve expeditious practical application of the subject invention. The application shall be submitted in accordance with the applicable provisions in 37 CFR part 404 and agency licensing regulations. The contractor's license will not be revoked in that field of use or the geographical areas in which the contractor has achieved practical application and continues to make the benefits of the subject invention reasonably accessible to the public. The license in any foreign country may be revoked or modified to the extent the contractor, its licensees, or its domestic subsidiaries or affiliates have failed to achieve practical application in that country. (See the procedures at 27.304-1(f).)

(j) *Confidentiality of inventions.* Publishing information concerning an invention before a patent application is filed on a subject invention may create a bar to a valid patent. To avoid this bar, agencies may withhold information from the public that discloses any invention in which the Government owns or may own a right, title, or interest (including a nonexclusive license) (see 35 U.S.C. 205 and 37 CFR part 401). Agencies may only withhold information concerning inventions for a reasonable time in order for a patent application to be filed. Once filed in any patent office, agencies are not required to release copies of any document that is a part of a patent application for those subject inventions. (See also 27.305-4.)

[FAC 84-1, 49 FR 12974, 3/30/84, effective 4/1/84; FAC 84-5, 50 FR 1743, 1/11/85, effective 4/1/85; FAC 84-12, 51 FR 2665, 1/17/86, effective 1/20/86; Interim rule, FAC 84-48, 54 FR 25065, 6/12/89, effective 6/12/89; FAC 84-58, 55 FR 25525, 6/21/90, effective 7/23/90; Final rule, 62 FR 40236, 7/25/97, effective 6/30/97; FAC 2005-21, 72 FR 63045, 11/7/2007, effective 12/7/2007]

27.303 Contract clauses.

(a)(1) Insert a patent rights clause in all solicitations and contracts for experimental, developmental, or research work as prescribed in this section.

(2) This section also applies to solicitations or contracts for construction work or architect-engineer services that include—

(i) Experimental, developmental, or research work;

(ii) Test and evaluation studies; or

(iii) The design of a Government facility that may involve novel structures, machines, products, materials, processes, or equipment (including construction equipment).

(3) The contracting officer shall not include a patent rights clause in solicitations or contracts for construction work or architect-engineer services that call for or can be expected to involve only "standard types of construction." "Standard types of construction" are those involving previously developed equipment, methods, and processes and in which the distinctive features include only—

(i) Variations in size, shape, or capacity of conventional structures; or

(ii) Purely artistic or aesthetic (as distinguished from functionally significant) architectural configurations and designs of both structural and nonstructural members or groupings, whether or not they qualify for design patent protection.

(b) (1) Unless an alternative patent rights clause is used in accordance with paragraph (c), (d), or (e) of this section, insert the clause at 52.227-11, Patent Rights—Ownership by the Contractor.

(2) To the extent the information is not required elsewhere in the contract, and unless otherwise specified by agency supplemental regulations, the contracting officer may modify 52.227-11(e) or otherwise supplement the clause to require the contractor to do one or more of the following:

(i) Provide periodic (but not more frequently than annually) listings of all subject inventions required to be disclosed during the period covered by the report.

(ii) Provide a report prior to the closeout of the contract listing all subject inventions or stating that there were none.

(iii) Provide the filing date, serial number, title, patent number and issue date for any patent application filed on any subject invention in any country or, upon request, copies of any patent application so identified.

(iv) Furnish the Government an irrevocable power to inspect and make copies of the patent application file when a Government employee is a co-inventor.

(3) Use the clause with its Alternate I if the Government must grant a foreign government a sublicense in subject inventions pursuant to a specified treaty or executive agreement. The contracting officer may modify Alternate I, if the agency head determines, at contract award, that it would be in the national interest to sublicense foreign governments or international organizations pursuant to any existing or future treaty or agreement. When necessary to effectuate a treaty or agreement, Alternate I may be appropriately modified.

(4) Use the clause with its Alternate II in contracts that may be affected by existing or future treaties or agreements.

(5) Use the clause with its Alternate III in contracts with nonprofit organizations for the operation of a Government-owned facility.

(6) If the contract is for the operation of a Government-owned facility, the contracting officer may use the clause with its Alternate IV.

(7) If the contract is for the performance of services at a Government owned and operated laboratory or at a Government owned and contractor operated laboratory directed by the Government to fulfill the Government's obligations under a Cooperative Research and Development Agreement (CRADA) authorized by 15 U.S.C. 3710a, the contracting officer may use the clause with its Alternate V. Since this provision is considered an exercise of an agency's "exceptional circumstances" authority, the contracting officer must comply with 37 CFR 401.3(e) and 401.4.

(c) Insert a patent rights clause in accordance with the procedures at 27.304-2 if the solicitation or contract is being placed on behalf of another Government agency.

(d) Insert a patent rights clause in accordance with agency procedures if the solicitation or contract is for DoD, DOE, or NASA, and the contractor is other than a small business concern or nonprofit organization.

(e)(1) Except as provided in paragraph (e)(2) of this section, and after compliance with the applicable procedures in 27.304-1(b), the contracting officer may insert the clause at 52.227-13, Patent Rights—Ownership by the Government, or a clause prescribed by agency supplemental regulations, if—

(i) The contractor is not located in the United States or does not have a place of business located in the United States or is subject to the control of a foreign government;

(ii) There are exceptional circumstances and the agency head determines that restriction or elimination of the right to retain title to any subject invention will better promote the policy and objectives of chapter 18 of title 35 of the United States Code;

(iii) A Government authority that is authorized by statute or executive order to conduct foreign intelligence or counterintelligence activities, determines that restriction or elimination of the right to retain any subject invention is necessary to protect the security of such activities; or

(iv) The contract includes the operation of a Government-owned, contractor-operated facility of DOE primarily dedicated to that Department's naval nuclear propulsion or weapons related programs.

(2) If an agency exercises the exceptions at paragraph (e)(1)(ii) or (iii) of this section in a contract with a small business concern or a nonprofit organization, the contracting officer shall use the clause at 52.227-11 with only those modifications necessary to address the exceptional circumstances and shall include in the modified clause greater rights determinations procedures equivalent to those at 52.227-13(b)(2).

(3) When using the clause at 52.227-13, Patent Rights—Ownership by the Government, the contracting officer may supplement the clause to require the contractor to—

(i) Furnish a copy of each subcontract containing a patent rights clause (but if a copy of a subcontract is furnished under another clause, a duplicate shall not be requested under the patent rights clause);

(ii) Submit interim and final invention reports listing subject inventions and notifying the contracting officer of all subcontracts awarded for experimental, developmental, or research work;

(iii) Provide the filing date, serial number, title, patent number, and issue date for any patent application filed on any subject invention in any country or, upon specific request, copies of any patent application so identified; and

(iv) Submit periodic reports on the utilization of a subject invention.

(4) Use the clause at 52.227-13 with its Alternate I if—

(i) The Government must grant a foreign government a sublicense in subject inventions pursuant to a treaty or executive agreement; or

(ii) The agency head determines, at contract award, that it would be in the national interest to sublicense foreign governments or international organizations pursuant to any existing or future treaty or agreement. If other rights are necessary to effectuate any treaty or agreement, Alternate I may be appropriately modified.

(5) Use the clause at 52.227-13 with its Alternate II in the contract when necessary to effectuate an existing or future treaty or agreement.

[FAC 84-1, 49 FR 12974, 3/30/84, effective 4/1/84; Interim rule, FAC 84-48, 54 FR 25065 6/12/89, effective 6/12/89; FAC 84-58, 55 FR 25525, 6/21/90, effective 7/23/90; FAC 90-45, Final rule, 62 FR 224, 1/2/97, effective 1/1/97; FAC 2005-21, 72 FR 63045, 11/7/2007, effective 12/7/2007]

27.304 Procedures. (No Text)

[FAC 2005-21, 72 FR 63045, 11/7/2007, effective 12/7/2007]

27.304-1 General.

(a) *Status as small business concern or nonprofit organization.* If an agency has reason to question the size or nonprofit status of the prospective contractor, the agency may require the prospective contractor to furnish evidence of its nonprofit status or may file a size protest in accordance with FAR 19.302.

(b) *Exceptions.* (1) Before using any of the exceptions under 27.303(e)(1) in a contract with a small business concern or a nonprofit organization and before using the exception of 27.303(e)(1)(ii) for any contractor, the agency shall follow the applicable procedures at 37 CFR 401.

(2) A small business concern or nonprofit organization is entitled to an administrative review of the use of the exceptions at 27.303(e)(1)(i) through (e)(1)(iv) in accordance with agency procedures and 37 CFR part 401.

(c) *Greater rights determinations.* Whenever the contract contains the clause at 52.227-13, Patent Rights—Ownership by the Government, or a patent rights clause modified pursuant to 27.303(e)(2), the contractor (or an employee-inventor of the contractor after consultation with the contractor) may request greater rights to an identified invention within the period specified in the clause. The contracting officer may grant requests for greater rights if the contracting officer determines that the interests of the United States and the general public will be better served. In making these determinations, the contracting officer shall consider at least the following objectives (see 37 CFR 401.3(b) and 401.15):

(1) Promoting the utilization of inventions arising from federally supported research and development.

(2) Ensuring that inventions are used in a manner to promote full and open competition and free enterprise without unduly encumbering future research and discovery.

(3) Promoting public availability of inventions made in the United States by United States industry and labor.

(4) Ensuring that the Government obtains sufficient rights in federally supported inventions to meet the needs of the Government and protect the public against nonuse or unreasonable use of inventions.

(d) *Retention of rights by inventor.* If the contractor elects not to retain title to a subject invention, the agency may consider and, after consultation with the contractor, grant requests for retention of rights by the inventor. Retention of rights by the inventor will be subject to the conditions in paragraphs (d) (except paragraph (d)(1)(i)), (e)(4), (f), (g), and (h) of the clause at 52.227-11, Patent Rights—Ownership by the Contractor.

(e) *Government assignment to contractor of rights in Government employees' inventions.* When a Government employee is a co-inventor of an invention made under a contract with a small business concern or nonprofit organization, the agency employing the co-inventor may license or assign whatever rights it may acquire in the subject invention from its employee to the contractor, subject at least to the conditions of 35 U.S.C. 202-204.

(f) *Revocation or modification of contractor's minimum rights.* Before revoking or modifying the contractor's license in accordance with 27.302(i)(2), the contracting officer shall furnish the contractor a written notice of intention to revoke or modify the license. The agency shall allow the contractor at least 30 days (or another time as may be authorized for good cause by the contracting officer) after the notice to show cause why the license should not be revoked or modified. The contractor has the right to appeal, in accordance with applicable regulations in 37 CFR part 404 and agency licensing regulations, any decisions concerning the revocation or modification.

(g) *Exercise of march-in rights.* When exercising march-in rights, agencies shall follow the procedures set forth in 37 CFR 401.6.

(h) *Licenses and assignments under contracts with nonprofit organizations.* If the contractor is a nonprofit organization, paragraph (i) of the clause at 52.227-11 provides that certain contractor actions require agency approval.

[Interim Rule, FAC 84-48, 54 FR 25066, 6/12/89, effective 6/12/89; FAC 84-58, 55 FR 25525, 6/21/90, effective 7/23/90; FAC 2005-21, 72 FR 63045, 11/7/2007, effective 12/7/2007]

27.304-2 Contracts placed by or for other Government agencies.

The following procedures apply unless an interagency agreement provides otherwise:

(a) When a Government agency requests another Government agency to award a contract on its behalf, the request should explain any special circumstances surrounding the contract and specify the patent rights clause to be used. The clause should be selected and modified, if necessary, in accordance with the policies and procedures of this subpart. If, however, the request states that a clause of the requesting agency is required (*e.g.*, because of statutory requirements, a deviation, or exceptional circumstances), the awarding agency shall use that clause rather than those of this subpart.

(1) If the request states that an agency clause is required and the work to be performed under the contract is not severable and is funded wholly or in part by the requesting agency, then include the requesting agency clause and no other patent rights clause in the contract.

(2) If the request states that an agency clause is required, and the work to be performed under the contract is severable, then the contracting officer shall assure that the requesting agency clause applies only to that severable portion of the work and that the work for the awarding agency is subject to the appropriate patent rights clause.

(3) If the request states that a requesting agency clause is not required in any resulting contract, the awarding agency shall use the appropriate patent rights clause, if any.

(b) Any action requiring an agency determination, report, or deviation involved in the use of the requesting agency's clause is the responsibility of the requesting agency unless the agencies agree otherwise. However, the awarding agency may not alter the requesting agency's clause without prior approval of the requesting agency.

(c) The requesting agency may require, and provide instructions regarding, the forwarding or handling of any invention disclosures or other reporting requirements of the specified clauses. Normally, the requesting agency is responsible for the administration of any subject inventions. This responsibility shall be established in advance of awarding any contracts.

[FAC 84-1, 49 FR 12974, 3/30/84, effective 4/1/84; Interim Rule, FAC 84-48, 54 FR 25068, 6/12/89, effective 6/12/89; FAC 84-58, 55 FR 25525, 6/21/90, effective 7/23/90; FAC 2005-21, 72 FR 63045, 11/7/2007, effective 12/7/2007]

27.304-3 Subcontracts.

(a) The policies and procedures in this subpart apply to all subcontracts at any tier.

(b) Whenever a prime contractor or a subcontractor considers including a particular clause in a subcontract to be inappropriate or a subcontractor refuses to accept the clause, the contracting officer, in consultation with counsel, shall resolve the matter.

(c) It is Government policy that contractors shall not use their ability to award subcontracts as economic leverage to acquire rights for themselves in inventions resulting from subcontracts.

[FAC 84-1, 49 FR 12974, 3/30/84, effective 4/1/84; FAC 2005-21, 72 FR 63045, 11/7/2007, effective 12/7/2007]

27.304-4 Appeals.

(a) The designated agency official shall provide the contractor with a written statement of the basis, including any relevant facts, for taking any of the following actions:

(1) A refusal to grant an extension to the invention disclosure period under paragraph (c)(4) of the clause at 52.227-11;

(2) A demand for a conveyance of title to the Government under 27.302(d)(1)(i) and (ii);

(3) A refusal to grant a waiver under 27.302(g), Preference for United States industry; or

(4) A refusal to approve an assignment under 27.304-1(h).

(b) Each agency may establish and publish procedures under which any of these actions may be appealed. These appeal procedures should include administrative due process procedures and standards for fact-finding. The resolution of any appeal shall consider both the factual and legal basis for the action and its consistency with the policy and objectives of 35 U.S.C. 200-206 and 210.

(c) To the extent that any of the actions described in paragraph (a) of this section are subject to appeal under the Contract Disputes statute, the procedures under that statute will satisfy the requirements of paragraph (b).

[FAC 84-1, 49 FR 12974, 3/30/84, effective 4/1/84; Interim Rule, FAC 84-48, 54 FR 25068, 6/12/89, effective 6/12/89; FAC 84-58, 55 FR 25525, 6/21/90, effective 7/23/90; FAC 2005-21, 72 FR 63045, 11/7/2007, effective 12/7/2007; FAC 2005-73, 79 FR 24192, 4/29/2014, effective 5/29/2014]

27.305 Administration of patent rights clauses. (No Text)

[FAC 2005-21, 72 FR 63045, 11/7/2007, effective 12/7/2007]

27.305-1 Goals.

(a) Contracts having a patent rights clause should be so administered that—

(1) Inventions are identified, disclosed, and reported as required by the contract, and elections are made;

(2) The rights of the Government in subject inventions are established;

(3) When patent protection is appropriate, patent applications are timely filed and prosecuted by contractors or by the Government;

(4) The rights of the Government in filed patent applications are documented by formal instruments such as licenses or assignments; and

(5) Expeditious commercial utilization of subject inventions is achieved.

(b) If a subject invention is made under a contract funded by more than one agency, at the request of the contractor or on their own initiative, the agencies shall designate one agency as responsible for administration of the rights of the Government in the invention.

[FAC 84-1, 49 FR 12974, 3/30/84, effective 4/1/84; FAC 84-58, 55 FR 25525, 6/21/90, effective 7/23/90; FAC 2005-21, 72 FR 63045, 11/7/2007, effective 12/7/2007]

27.305-2 Administration by the Government.

(a) Agencies should establish and maintain appropriate follow-up procedures to protect the Government's interest and to check that subject inventions are identified and disclosed, and when appropriate, patent applications are filed, and that the Government's rights therein are established and protected. Follow-up activities for contracts that include a clause referenced in 27.304-2 should be coordinated with the appropriate agency.

(b) (1) The contracting officer administering the contract (or other representative specifically designated in the contract for this purpose) is responsible for receiving invention disclosures, reports, confirmatory instruments, notices, requests, and other documents and information submitted by the contractor pursuant to a patent rights clause.

(i) For other than confirmatory instruments, if the contractor fails to furnish documents or information as called for by the clause within the time required, the contracting officer shall promptly request the contractor to supply the required documents or information. If the failure persists, the contracting officer shall take appropriate action to secure compliance.

(ii) If the contractor does not furnish confirmatory instruments within 6 months after filing each patent application, or within 6 months after submitting the invention disclosure if the application has been previously filed, the contracting officer shall request the contractor to supply the required documents.

(2) The contracting officer shall promptly furnish all invention disclosures, reports, confirmatory instruments, notices, requests, and other documents and information relating to patent rights clauses to legal counsel.

(c) Contracting activities should establish appropriate procedures to detect and correct failures by the contractor to comply with its obligations under the patent rights clauses, such as failures to disclose and report subject inventions, both during and after contract performance. Government effort to review and correct contractor compliance with its patent rights obligations should be directed primarily toward contracts that are more likely to result in subject inventions significant in number or quality. These contracts include contracts of a research, developmental, or experimental nature; contracts of a large dollar amount; and any other contracts when there is reason to believe the contractor may not be complying with its contractual obligations. Other contracts may be reviewed using a spot-check method, as feasible. Appropriate follow-up procedures and activities may include the investigation or review of selected contracts or contractors by those qualified in patent and technical matters to detect failures to comply with contract obligations.

(d) Follow-up activities should include, where appropriate, use of Government patent personnel—

(1) To interview agency technical personnel to identify novel developments made in contracts;

(2) To review technical reports submitted by contractors with cognizant agency technical personnel;

(3) To check the Official Gazette of the United States Patent and Trademark Office and other sources for patents issued to the contractor in fields related to its Government contracts; and

(4) To have cognizant Government personnel interview contractor personnel regarding work under the contract involved, observe the work on site, and inspect laboratory notebooks and other records of the contractor related to work under the contract.

(e) If a contractor or subcontractor does not have a clear understanding of its obligations under the clause, or its procedures for complying with the clause are deficient, the contracting officer should explain to the contractor its obligations. The withholding of payments provision (if any) of the patent rights clause may be invoked if the contractor fails to meet the obligations required by the patents rights clause. Significant or repeated failures by a contractor to comply with the patent rights obligation in its contracts shall be documented and made a part of the general file (see 4.801(c)(3)).

[FAC 84-1, 49 FR 12974, 3/30/84, effective 4/1/84; FAC 84-58, 55 FR 25525, 6/21/90, effective 7/23/90; FAC 2005-21, 72 FR 63045, 11/7/2007, effective 12/7/2007]

27.305-3 Securing invention rights acquired by the Government.

(a) Agencies are responsible for implementing procedures necessary to protect the Government's interest in subject inventions. When the Government acquires the entire right, title, and interest in an invention by contract, the chain of title from the inventor to the Government shall be clearly established. This is normally accomplished by an assignment either from each inventor to the contractor and from the contractor to the Government, or from the inventor to the Government with the consent of the contractor. When the Government's rights are limited to a license, there should be a confirmatory instrument to that effect.

(b) Agencies may, by supplemental instructions, develop suitable assignments, licenses, and other papers evidencing any rights of the Government in patents or patents applications. These instruments should be recorded in the U.S. Patent and Trademark Office (see Executive Order 9424, Establishing in the United States Patent Office a Register of Government Interests in Patents and Applications for Patents, (February 18, 1944).

[FAC 84-1, 49 FR 12974, 3/30/84, effective 4/1/84; FAC 84-58, 55 FR 25525, 6/21/90, effective 7/23/90; FAC 2005-21, 72 FR 53045, 11/7/2007, effective 12/7/2007]

27.305-4 Protection of invention disclosures.

(a) The Government will, to the extent authorized by 35 U.S.C. 205, withhold from disclosure to the public any invention disclosures reported under the patent rights clauses of 52.227-11 or 52.227-13 for a reasonable time in order for patent applications to be filed. The Government will follow the policy in 27.302(j) regarding protection of confidentiality.

(b) The Government should also use reasonable efforts to withhold from disclosure to the public for a reasonable time other information disclosing a subject invention. This information includes any data delivered pursuant to contract requirements provided that the contractor notifies the agency as to the identity of the data and the subject invention to which it relates at the time of delivery of the data. This notification shall be provided to both the contracting officer and to any patent representative to which the invention is reported, if other than the contracting officer.

(c) For more information on protection of invention disclosures, also see 37 CFR 401.13.

[FAC 84-1, 49 FR 12974, 3/30/84, effective 4/1/84; FAC 84-58, 55 FR 25525, 6/21/90, effective 7/23/90; FAC 2005-21, 72 FR 63045, 11/7/2007, effective 12/7/2007]

27.306 Licensing background patent rights to third parties.

(a) A contract with a small business concern or nonprofit organization shall not contain a provision allowing the Government to require the licensing to third parties of inventions owned by the contractor that are not subject inventions unless the agency head has approved and signed a written justification in accordance with paragraph (b) of this section. The agency head may not delegate this authority and may exercise the authority only if it is determined that the—

(1) Use of the invention by others is necessary for the practice of a subject invention or for the use of a work object of the contract; and

(2) Action is necessary to achieve the practical application of the subject invention or work object.

(b) Any determination will be on the record after an opportunity for a hearing, and the agency shall notify the contractor of the determination by certified or registered mail. The notification shall include a statement that the contractor must bring any action for judicial review of the determination within 60 days after the notification.

[FAC 84-1, 49 FR 12974, 3/30/84, effective 4/1/84; FAC 84-58, 55 FR 25525, 6/21/90, effective 7/23/90; FAC 2005-21, 72 FR 63045, 11/7/2007, effective 12/7/2007]

SUBPART 27.4—RIGHTS IN DATA AND COPYRIGHTS

27.400 Scope of subpart.

This subpart sets forth policies and procedures regarding rights in data and copyrights, and acquisition of data. The policy statement in 27.402 applies to all executive agencies. The remainder of the subpart applies to all executive agencies except the Department of Defense.

[FAC 84-27, 52 FR 18140, 5/13/87, effective 6/1/87; FAC 84-51, 54 FR 34755, 8/21/89, effective 9/20/89; FAC 2005-21, 72 FR 63045, 11/7/2007, effective 12/7/2007]

27.401 Definitions.

As used in this subpart—

Data means recorded information, regardless of form or the media on which it may be recorded. The term includes technical data and computer software. The term does not include information incidental to contract administration, such as financial, administrative, cost or pricing, or management information.

Form, fit, and function data means data relating to items, components, or processes that are sufficient to enable physical and functional interchangeability, and data identifying source, size, configuration, mating and attachment characteristics, functional characteristics, and performance requirements. For computer software it means data identifying source, functional characteristics, and performance requirements, but specifically excludes the source code, algorithms, processes, formulas, and flow charts of the software.

Limited rights means the rights of the Government in limited rights data as set forth in a Limited Rights Notice.

Limited rights data means data, other than computer software, that embody trade secrets or are commercial or financial and confidential or privileged, to the extent that such data pertain to items, components, or processes developed at private expense, including minor modifications. (Agencies may, however, adopt the following alternate definition: Limited rights data means data (other than computer software) developed at private expense that embody trade secrets or are commercial or financial and confidential or privileged (see 27.404-2(b)).

Restricted computer software means computer software developed at private expense and that is a trade secret, is commercial or financial and confidential or privileged, or is copyrighted computer software, including minor modifications of the computer software.

Restricted rights means the rights of the Government in restricted computer software as set forth in a Restricted Rights Notice.

Unlimited rights means the rights of the Government to use, disclose, reproduce, prepare derivative works, distribute copies to the public, and perform publicly and display publicly, in any manner and for any purpose, and to have or permit others to do so.

[FAC 84-27, 52 FR 18140, 5/13/87, effective 6/1/87; FAC 97-22, 66 FR 2116, 1/10/2001, effective 3/12/2001; Delay of effective date, 66 FR 14259, 3/9/2001, effective 5/11/2001; FAC 2005-21, 72 FR 63045, 11/7/2007, effective 12/7/2007]

27.402 Policy.

(a) To carry out their missions and programs, agencies acquire or obtain access to many kinds of data produced during or used in the performance of their contracts. Agencies require data to—

(1) Obtain competition among suppliers;

(2) Fulfill certain responsibilities for disseminating and publishing the results of their activities;

(3) Ensure appropriate utilization of the results of research, development, and demonstration activities including the dissemination of technical information to foster subsequent technological developments;

(4) Meet other programmatic and statutory requirements; and

(5) Meet specialized acquisition needs and ensure logistics support.

(b) Contractors may have proprietary interests in data. In order to prevent the compromise of these interests, agencies shall protect proprietary data from unauthorized use and disclosure. The protection of such data is also necessary to encourage qualified contractors to participate in and apply innovative concepts to Government programs. In light of these considerations, agencies shall balance the Government's needs and the contractor's legitimate proprietary interests.

[FAC 84-27, 52 FR 18140, 5/13/87, effective 6/1/87; FAC 2005-21, 72 FR 63045, 11/7/2007, effective 12/7/2007]

27.403 Data rights—General.

All contracts that require data to be produced, furnished, acquired, or used in meeting contract performance requirements, must contain terms that delineate the respective rights and obligations of the Government and the contractor regarding the use, reproduction, and disclosure of that data. Data rights clauses do not specify the type, quantity or quality of data that is to be delivered, but only the respective rights of the Government and the contractor regarding the use, disclosure, or reproduction of the data. Accordingly, the contract shall specify the data to be delivered.

[FAC 84-27, 52 FR 18140, 5/13/87, effective 6/1/87; FAC 2005-21, 72 FR 63045, 11/7/2007, effective 12/7/2007]

27.404 Basic rights in data clause.

This section describes the operation of the clause at 52.227-14, Rights in Data—General, and also the use of the provision at 52.227-15, Representation of Limited Rights Data and Restricted Computer Software.

[FAC 84-27, 52 FR 18140, 5/13/87, effective 6/1/87; FAC 97-11, 64 FR 10530, 3/4/99, effective 5/3/99; FAC 2005-21, 72 FR 63045, 11/7/2007, effective 12/7/2007]

27.404-1 Unlimited rights data.

The Government acquires unlimited rights in the following data except for copyrighted works as provided in 27.404-3:

(a) Data first produced in the performance of a contract (except to the extent the data constitute minor modifications to data that are limited rights data or restricted computer software).

(b) Form, fit, and function data delivered under contract.

(c) Data (except as may be included with restricted computer software) that constitute manuals or instructional and training material for installation, operation, or routine maintenance and repair of items, components, or processes delivered or furnished for use under a contract.

(d) All other data delivered under the contract other than limited rights data or restricted computer software (see 27.404-2).

[FAC 2005-21, 72 FR 63045, 11/7/2007, effective 12/7/2007]

27.404-2 Limited rights data and restricted computer software.

(a) *General.* The basic clause at 52.227-14, Rights in Data—General, enables the contractor to protect qualifying limited rights data and restricted computer software by withholding the data from the Government and instead delivering form, fit, and function data.

(b) *Alternate definition of limited rights data.* For contracts that do not require the development, use, or delivery of items, components, or processes that are intended to be acquired by or for the Government, an agency may adopt the alternate definition of limited rights data set forth in Alternate I to the clause at 52.227-14. The alternate definition does not require that the data pertain to items, components, or processes developed at private expense; but rather that the data were developed at private expense and embody a trade secret or are commercial or financial and confidential or privileged.

(c) *Protection of limited rights data specified for delivery.* (1) The clause at 52.227-14 with its Alternate II enables the Government to require delivery of limited rights data rather than allow the contractor to withhold the data. To obtain delivery, the contract may identify and specify data to be delivered, or the contracting officer may require, by written request during contract performance, the delivery of data that has been withheld or identified to be withheld under paragraph (g)(1) of the clause. In addition, the contract may specifically identify data that are not to be delivered under Alternate II or which, if delivered, will be delivered with limited rights. The limited rights obtained by the Government are set forth in the Limited Rights Notice contained in paragraph (g)(3) of Alternate II. Agencies shall not, without permission of the contractor, use limited rights data for purposes of manufacture or disclose the data outside the Government except as set forth in the Notice. Any disclosure by the Government shall be subject to prohibition against further use and disclosure by the recipient. The following are examples of specific purposes that may be adopted by an agency in its supplement and added to the Limited Rights Notice of paragraph (g)(3) of Alternate II of the clause:

(i) Use (except for manufacture) by support service contractors.

(ii) Evaluation by nongovernment evaluators.

(iii) Use (except for manufacture) by other contractors participating in the Government's program of which the specific contract is a part.

(iv) Emergency repair or overhaul work.

(v) Release to a foreign government, or its instrumentalities, if required to serve the interests of the U.S. Government, for information or evaluation, or for emergency repair or overhaul work by the foreign government.

(2) The provision at 52.227-15, Representation of Limited Rights Data and Restricted Computer Software, helps the contracting officer to determine whether the clause at 52.227-14 should be used with its Alternate II. This provision requests that an offeror state whether limited rights data are likely to be delivered. Where limited rights data are expected to be delivered, use Alternate II. Where negotiations are based on an unsolicited proposal, the need for Alternate II of the clause at 52.227-14 should be addressed during negotiations or discussions, and if Alternate II was not included initially it may be added by modification, if needed, during contract performance.

(3) If data that would otherwise qualify as limited rights data is delivered as a computer database, the data shall be treated as limited rights data, rather than restricted

computer software, for the purposes of paragraph (g) of the clause at 52.227-14.

(d) *Protection of restricted computer software specified for delivery.* (1) Alternate III of the clause at 52.227-14, enables the Government to require delivery of restricted computer software rather than allow the contractor to withhold such restricted computer software. To obtain delivery of restricted computer software the contracting officer shall—

(i) Identify and specify the deliverable computer software in the contract; or

(ii) Require by written request during contract performance, the delivery of computer software that has been withheld or identified to be withheld under paragraph (g) (1) of the clause.

(2) In considering whether to use Alternate III, contracting officers should note that, unlike other data, computer software is also an end item in itself. Thus, the contracting officer shall use Alternate III if delivery of restricted computer software is required to meet agency needs.

(3) Unless otherwise agreed (see paragraph (d) (4) of this subsection), the restricted rights obtained by the Government are set forth in the Restricted Rights Notice contained in paragraph (g) (4) (Alternate III). Such restricted computer software will not be used or reproduced by the Government, or disclosed outside the Government, except that the computer software may be—

(i) Used or copied for use with the computers for which it was acquired, including use at any Government installation to which the computers may be transferred;

(ii) Used or copied for use with a backup computer if any computer for which it was acquired is inoperative;

(iii) Reproduced for safekeeping (archives) or backup purposes;

(iv) Modified, adapted, or combined with other computer software, *provided* that the modified, adapted, or combined portions of the derivative software incorporating any of the delivered, restricted computer software shall be subject to the same restricted rights;

(v) Disclosed to and reproduced for use by support service contractors or their subcontractors, in accordance with paragraphs (3) (i) through (iv) of this section; and

(vi) Used or copied for use with a replacement computer.

(4) The restricted rights set forth in paragraph (d) (3) of this subsection are the minimum rights the Government normally obtains with restricted computer software and will automatically apply when such software is acquired under the Restricted Rights Notice of paragraph (g) (4) of Alternate III of the clause at 52.227-14. However, the contracting officer may specify different rights in the contract, consistent with the purposes and needs for which the software is to be acquired. For example, the contracting officer should consider any networking needs or any requirements for use of the computer software from remote terminals. Also, in addressing such needs, the scope of the restricted rights may be different for the documentation accompanying the computer software than for the programs and databases. Any additions to, or limitations on, the restricted rights set forth in the Restricted Rights Notice of paragraph (g) (4) of Alternate III of the clause at 52.227-14 shall be expressly stated in the contract or in a collateral agreement incorporated in and made part of the contract, and the notice modified accordingly.

(5) The provision at 52.227-15, Representation of Limited Rights Data and Restricted Computer Software, helps the contracting officer determine whether to use the clause at 52.227-14 with its Alternate III. This provision requests that an offeror state whether restricted computer software is likely to be delivered under the contract. In addition, the need for Alternate III should be addressed during negotiations or discussions with an offeror, particularly where negotiations are based on an unsolicited proposal. However, if Alternate III is not used initially, it may be added by modification, if needed, during contract performance.

[FAC 2005-21, 72 FR 63045, 11/7/2007, effective 12/7/2007]

27.404-3 Copyrighted works.

(a) *Data first produced in the performance of a contract.* (1) Generally, the contractor must obtain permission of the contracting officer prior to asserting rights in any copyrighted work containing data first produced in the performance of a contract. However, contractors are normally authorized, without prior approval of the contracting officer, to assert copyright in technical or scientific articles based on or containing such data that is published in academic, technical or professional journals, symposia proceedings and similar works.

(2) The contractor must make a written request for permission to assert its copyright in works containing data first produced under the contract. In its request, the contractor should identify the data involved or furnish copies of the data for which permission is requested, as well as a statement as to the intended publication or dissemination media or other purpose for which the permission is requested. Generally, a contracting officer should grant the contractor's request when copyright protection will enhance the appropriate dissemination or use of the data unless the—

(i) Data consist of a report that represents the official views of the agency or that the agency is required by statute to prepare;

(ii) Data are intended primarily for internal use by the Government;

(iii) Data are of the type that the agency itself distributes to the public under an agency program;

(iv) Government determines that limitation on distribution of the data is in the national interest; or

(v) Government determines that the data should be disseminated without restriction.

(3) Alternate IV of the clause at 52.227-14 provides a substitute paragraph (c)(1) granting permission for contractors to assert copyright in any data first produced in the performance of the contract without the need for any further requests. Except for contracts for management or operation of Government facilities and contracts and subcontracts in support of programs being conducted at those facilities or where international agreements require otherwise, Alternate IV shall be used in all contracts for basic or applied research to be performed solely by colleges and universities. Alternate IV shall not be used in contracts with colleges and universities if a purpose of the contract is for development of computer software for distribution to the public (including use in solicitations) by or on behalf of the Government. In addition, Alternate IV may be used in other contracts if an agency determines that it is not necessary for a contractor to request further permission to assert copyright in data first produced in performance of the contract. The contracting officer may exclude any data, or items or categories of data, from the provisions of Alternate IV by expressly so providing in the contract or by adding a paragraph (d)(4) to the clause, consistent with 27.404-4(b).

(4) Pursuant to paragraph (c)(1) of the clause at 52.227-14, the contractor grants the Government a paid-up nonexclusive, irrevocable, worldwide license to reproduce, prepare derivative works, distribute to the public, perform publicly and display publicly by or on behalf of the Government, for all data (other than computer software) first produced in the performance of a contract. For computer software, the scope of the Government's license includes all of the above rights except the right to distribute to the public. Agencies may also obtain a license of different scope if the contracting officer determines, after consulting with legal counsel, such a license will substantially enhance the dissemination of any data first produced under the contract or if such a license is required to comply with international agreements. If an agency obtains a different license, the contractor shall clearly state the scope of that license in a conspicuous place on the medium on which the data is recorded. For example, if the data is delivered as a report, the terms of the license shall be stated on the cover, or first page, of the report.

(5) The clause requires the contractor to affix the applicable copyright notices of 17 U.S.C. 401 or 402, and acknowledgment of Government sponsorship, (including the contract number) to data when it asserts

copyright in data. Failure to do so could result in such data being treated as unlimited rights data (see 27.404-5(b)).

(b) *Data not first produced in the performance of a contract.* (1) Contractors shall not deliver any data that is not first produced under the contract without either—

(i) Acquiring for or granting to the Government a copyright license for the data; or

(ii) Obtaining permission from the contracting officer to do otherwise.

(2) The copyright license the Government acquires for such data will normally be of the same scope as discussed in paragraph (a)(4) of this subsection, and is set forth in paragraph (c)(2) of the clause at 52.227-14. However, agencies may obtain a license of different scope if the agency determines, after consultation with its legal counsel, that such different license will not be inconsistent with the purpose of acquiring the data. If a license of a different scope is acquired, it must be so stated in the contract and clearly set forth in a conspicuous place on the data when delivered to the Government. If the contractor delivers computer software not first produced under the contract, the contractor shall grant the Government the license set forth in paragraph (g)(4) of Alternate III if included in the clause at 52.227-14, or a license agreed to in a collateral agreement made part of the contract.

[FAC 2005-21, 72 FR 63045, 11/7/2007, effective 12/7/2007]

27.404-4 Contractor's release, publication, and use of data.

(a) In contracts for basic or applied research with universities or colleges, agencies shall not place any restrictions on the conduct of or reporting on the results of unclassified basic or applied research, except as provided in applicable U.S. statutes. However, agencies may restrict the release or disclosure of computer software that is or is intended to be developed to the point of practical application (including for agency distribution under established programs). This is not considered a restriction on the reporting of the results of basic or applied research. Agencies may also preclude a contractor from asserting copyright in any computer software for purposes of established agency distribution programs, or where required to accomplish the purpose for which the software is acquired.

(b) Except for the results of basic or applied research under contracts with universities or colleges, agencies may, to the extent provided in their FAR supplements, place limitations or restrictions on the contractor's exercise of its rights in data first produced in the performance of the contract, including a requirement to assign copyright to the Government or another party. Any of these restrictions shall be expressly included in the contract.

[FAC 2005-21, 72 FR 63045, 11/7/2007, effective 12/7/2007]

27.404-5 Unauthorized, omitted, or incorrect markings.

(a) *Unauthorized marking of data.* (1) The Government has, in accordance with paragraph (e) of the clause at 52.227-14, the right to either return data containing unauthorized markings or to cancel or ignore the markings.

(2) Agencies shall not cancel or ignore markings without making written inquiry of the contractor and affording the contractor at least 60 days to provide a written justification substantiating the propriety of the markings.

(i) If the contractor fails to respond or fails to provide a written justification substantiating the propriety of the markings within the time afforded, the Government may cancel or ignore the markings.

(ii) If the contractor provides a written justification substantiating the propriety of the markings, the contracting officer shall consider the justification.

(A) If the contracting officer determines that the markings are authorized, the contractor will be so notified in writing.

(B) If the contracting officer determines, with concurrence of the head of the contracting activity, that the markings are not authorized, the contractor will be furnished a written determination which becomes the final agency decision regarding the appropriateness of the markings and the markings will be cancelled or ignored and the data will no longer be made subject to disclosure prohibitions, unless the contractor files suit within 90 days in a court of competent jurisdiction. The markings will not be cancelled or ignored until final resolution of the matter, either by the contracting officer's determination becoming the final agency decision or by final disposition of the matter by court decision if suit is filed.

(3) The foregoing procedures may be modified in accordance with agency regulations implementing the Freedom of Information Act (5 U.S.C. 552) if necessary to respond to a request. In addition, the contractor may bring a claim, in accordance with the Disputes clause of the contract, that may arise as the result of the Government's action to remove or ignore any markings on data, unless the action occurs as the result of a final disposition of the matter by a court of competent jurisdiction.

(b) *Omitted or incorrect notices.* (1) Data delivered under a contract containing the clause without a limited rights notice or restricted rights notice, and without a copyright notice, will be presumed to have been delivered with unlimited rights, and the Government assumes no liability for the disclosure, use, or reproduction of the data. However, to the extent the data has not been disclosed without restriction outside the Government, the contractor may, within 6 months (or a longer period approved by the contracting officer for good cause shown), request permission of the contracting officer to have the omitted limited rights or restricted rights notices, as applicable, placed on qualifying data at the contractor's expense. The contracting officer may permit adding appropriate notices if the contractor—

(i) Identifies the data for which a notice is to be added;

(ii) Demonstrates that the omission of the proposed notice was inadvertent;

(iii) Establishes that use of the proposed notice is authorized; and

(iv) Acknowledges that the Government has no liability with respect to any disclosure or use of any such data made prior to the addition of the notice or resulting from the omission of the notice.

(2) The contracting officer may also—

(i) Permit correction, at the contractor's expense, of incorrect notices if the contractor identifies the data on which correction of the notice is to be made, and demonstrates that the correct notice is authorized; or

(ii) Correct any incorrect notices.

[FAC 2005-21, 72 FR 63045, 11/7/2007, effective 12/7/2007]

27.404-6 Inspection of data at the contractor's facility.

Contracting officers may obtain the right to inspect data at the contractor's facility by use of the clause at 52.227-14with its Alternate V, which adds paragraph (j) to provide that right. Agencies may also adopt Alternate V for general use. The data subject to inspection may be data withheld or withholdable under paragraph (g)(1) of the clause. Inspection may be made by the contracting officer or designee (including nongovernmental personnel under the same conditions as the contracting officer) for the purpose of verifying a contractor's assertion regarding the limited rights or restricted rights status of the data, or for evaluating work performance under the contract. This right may be exercised up to 3 years after acceptance of all items to be delivered under the contract. The contract may specify data items that are not subject to inspection under paragraph (j) of the Alternate. If the contractor demonstrates to the contracting officer that there would be a possible conflict of interest if inspection were made by a particular representative, the contracting officer shall designate an alternate representative.

[FAC 2005-21, 72 FR 63045, 11/7/2007, effective 12/7/2007]

27.405 Other data rights provisions. (No Text)

[FAC 84-27, 52 FR 18140, 5/13/87, effective 6/1/87; FAC 97-5, 63 FR 34058, 6/22/98, effective 8/21/98; FAC 2005-21, 72 FR 63045, 11/7/2007, effective 12/7/2007]

27.405-1 Special works.

(a) The clause at 52.227-17, Rights in Data—Special Works, is for use in contracts (or may be made applicable to portions thereof) that are primarily for the production or compilation of data (other than limited rights data or restricted computer software) for the Government's own use, or when there is a specific need to limit distribution and use of the data or to obtain indemnity for liabilities that may arise out of the content, performance, or disclosure of the data. Examples are contracts for—

(1) The production of audiovisual works, including motion pictures or television recordings with or without accompanying sound, or for the preparation of motion picture scripts, musical compositions, sound tracks, translation, adaptation, and the like;

(2) Histories of the respective agencies, departments, services, or units thereof;

(3) Surveys of Government establishments;

(4) Works pertaining to the instruction or guidance of Government officers and employees in the discharge of their official duties;

(5) The compilation of reports, books, studies, surveys, or similar documents that do not involve research, development, or experimental work;

(6) The collection of data containing personally identifiable information such that the disclosure thereof would violate the right of privacy or publicity of the individual to whom the information relates;

(7) Investigatory reports;

(8) The development, accumulation, or compilation of data (other than that resulting from research, development, or experimental work performed by the contractor), the early release of which could prejudice follow-on acquisition activities or agency regulatory or enforcement activities; or

(9) The development of computer software programs, where the program—

(i) May give a commercial advantage; or

(ii) Is agency mission sensitive, and release could prejudice agency mission, programs, or follow-on acquisitions.

(b) The contract may specify the purposes and conditions (including time limitations) under which the data may be used, released, or reproduced other than for contract performance. Contracts for the production of audiovisual works, sound recordings, etc., may include limitations in connection with talent releases, music licenses, and the like that are consistent with the purposes for which the works are acquired.

(c) Paragraph (c)(1)(ii) of the clause, which enables the Government to obtain assignment of copyright in any data first produced in the performance of the contract, may be deleted if the contracting officer determines that such assignment is not needed to further the objectives of the contract.

(d) Paragraph (e) of the clause, which requires the contractor to indemnify the Government against any liability incurred as the result of any violation of trade secrets, copyrights, right of privacy or publicity, or any libelous or other unlawful matter arising out of or contained in any production or compilation of data that are subject to the clause, may be deleted or limited in scope where the contracting officer determines that, because of the nature of the particular data involved, such liability will not arise.

(e) When the audiovisual or other special works are produced to accomplish a public purpose other than acquisition for the Government's own use (such as for production and distribution to the public of the works by other than a Federal agency) agencies are authorized to modify the clause for use in contracts, with rights in data provisions that meet agency mission needs yet protect free speech and freedom of expression, as well as the artistic license of the creator of the work.

[FAC 2005-21, 72 FR 63045, 11/7/2007, effective 12/7/2007]

27.405-2 Existing works.

The clause at 52.227-18, Rights in Data—Existing Works, is for use in contracts exclusively for the acquisition (without modification) of existing works such as, motion pictures, television recordings, and other audiovisual works; sound recordings; musical, dramatic, and literary works; pantomimes and choreographic works; pictorial, graphic, and sculptural works; and works of a similar nature. The contract may set forth limitations consistent with the purposes for which the works covered by the contract are being acquired. Examples of these limitations are means of exhibition or transmission, time, type of audience, and geographical location. However, if the contract requires that works of the type indicated in this paragraph are to be modified through editing, translation, or addition of subject matter, etc. (rather than purchased in existing form), then see 27.405-1.

[FAC 2005-21, 72 FR 63045, 11/7/2007, effective 12/7/2007]

27.405-3 Commercial computer software.

(a) When contracting other than from GSA's Multiple Award Schedule contracts for the acquisition of commercial computer software, no specific contract clause prescribed in this subpart need be used, but the contract shall specifically address the Government's rights to use, disclose, modify, distribute, and reproduce the software. Section 12.212 sets forth the guidance for the acquisition of commercial computer software and states that commercial computer software or commercial computer software documentation shall be acquired under licenses customarily provided to the public to the extent the license is consistent with Federal law and otherwise satisfies the Government's needs. The clause at 52.227-19, Commercial Computer Software License, may be used when there is any confusion as to whether the Government's needs are satisfied or whether a customary commercial license is consistent with Federal law. Additional or lesser rights may be negotiated using the guidance concerning restricted rights as set forth in 27.404-2(d), or the clause at 52.227-19. If greater rights than the minimum rights identified in the clause at 52.227-19 are needed, or lesser rights are to be acquired, they shall be negotiated and set forth in the contract. This includes any additions to, or limitations on, the rights set forth in paragraph (b) of the clause at 52.227-19 when used. Examples of greater rights may be those necessary for networking purposes or use of the software from remote terminals communicating with a host computer where the software is located. If the computer software is to be acquired with unlimited rights, the contract shall also so state. In addition, the contract shall adequately describe the computer programs and/or databases, the media on which it is recorded, and all the necessary documentation.

(b) If the contract incorporates, makes reference to, or uses a vendor's standard commercial lease, license, or purchase agreement, the contracting officer shall ensure that the agreement is consistent with paragraph (a) (1) of this subsection. The contracting officer should exercise caution in accepting a vendor's terms and conditions, since they may be directed to commercial sales and may not be appropriate for Government contracts. Any inconsistencies in a vendor's standard commercial agreement shall be addressed in the contract and the contract terms shall take precedence over the vendor's standard commercial agreement. If the clause at 52.227-19 is used, inconsistencies in the vendor's standard commercial agreement regarding the Government's right to use, reproduce or disclose the computer software are reconciled by that clause.

(c) If a prime contractor under a contract containing the clause at 52.227-14, Rights in Data—General, with paragraph (g) (4) (Alternate III) in the clause, acquires restricted computer software from a subcontractor (at any tier) as a separate acquisition for delivery to or for use on behalf of the Government, the contracting officer may approve any additions to, or limitations on the restricted rights in the Restricted Rights Notice of paragraph (g) (4) in a collateral agreement incorporated in and made part of the contract.

[FAC 2005-21, 72 FR 63045, 11/7/2007, effective 12/7/2007]

27.405-4 Other existing data.

(a) Except for existing works pursuant to 27.405-2 or commercial computer software pursuant to 27.405-3, no clause contained in this subpart is required to be included in—

(1) Contracts solely for the acquisition of books, periodicals, and other printed items

in the exact form in which these items are to be obtained unless reproduction rights are to be acquired; or

(2) Other contracts that require only existing data (other than limited rights data) to be delivered and the data are available without disclosure prohibitions, unless reproduction rights to the data are to be obtained.

(b) If the reproduction rights to the data are to be obtained in any contract of the type described in paragraph (b)(1) (i) or (ii) of this section, the rights shall be specifically set forth in the contract. No clause contained in this subpart is required to be included in contracts substantially for on-line data base services in the same form as they are normally available to the general public.

[FAC 2005-21, 72 FR 63045, 11/7/2007, effective 12/7/2007]

27.406 Acquisition of data. (No Text)

[FAC 84-27, 52 FR 18140, 5/13/87, effective 6/1/87; FAC 90-45, Final rule, 62 FR 224, 1/2/97, effective 1/1/97; FAC 2005-21, 72 FR 63045, 11/7/2007, effective 12/7/2007]

27.406-1 General.

(a) It is the Government's practice to determine, to the extent feasible, its data requirements in time for inclusion in solicitations. The data requirements may be subject to revision during contract negotiations. Since the preparation, reformatting, maintenance and updating, cataloging, and storage of data represents an expense to both the Government and the contractor, efforts should be made to keep the contract data requirements to a minimum, consistent with the purposes of the contract.

(b) The contracting officer shall specify in the contract all known data requirements, including the time and place for delivery and any limitations and restrictions to be imposed on the contractor in the handling of the data. Further, and to the extent feasible, in major system acquisitions, the contracting officer shall set out data requirements as separate line items. In establishing the contract data requirements and in specifying data items to be delivered by a contractor, agencies may, consistent with paragraph (a) of this subsection, develop their own contract schedule provisions. Agency procedures may, among other things, provide for listing, specifying, identifying source, assuring delivery, and handling any data required to be delivered, first produced, or specifically used in the performance of the contract.

(c) Data delivery requirements should normally not require that a contractor provide the Government, as a condition of the procurement, unlimited rights in data that qualify as limited rights data or restricted computer software. Rather, form, fit, and function data may be furnished with unlimited rights instead of the qualifying data, or the qualifying data may be furnished with limited rights or restricted rights if needed (see 27.404-2(c) and (d)). If greater rights are needed, they should be clearly set forth in the solicitation and the contractor fairly compensated for the greater rights.

[FAC 2005-21, 72 FR 63045, 11/7/2007, effective 12/7/2007; FAC 2005-95, 82 FR 4709, 1/13/2017, effective 1/13/2017]

27.406-2 Additional data requirements.

(a) In some contracting situations, such as experimental, developmental, research, or demonstration contracts, it may not be feasible to ascertain all the data requirements at contract award. The clause at 52.227-16, Additional Data Requirements, may be used to enable the subsequent ordering by the contracting officer of additional data first produced or specifically used in the performance of these contracts as the actual requirements become known. The clause shall normally be used in solicitations and contracts involving experimental, developmental, research or demonstration work (other than basic or applied research to be performed under a contract solely by a university or college when the contract amount will be $500,000 or less) unless all the requirements for data are believed to be known at the time of contracting and specified in the contract. If the contract is for basic or applied research to be performed by a university or college, and the contracting officer believes the contract effort will in the future exceed $500,000, even though the initial award does not, the contracting officer may include the clause in the initial award.

(b) Data may be ordered under the clause at 52.227-16 at any time during contract performance or within a period of 3 years after acceptance of all items to be delivered under the contract. The contractor is to be compensated for converting the data into the prescribed form, for reproduction, and for delivery. In order to minimize storage costs for the retention of data, the contracting officer may relieve the contractor of the retention requirements for specified data items at any time during the retention period required by the clause. The contracting officer may permit the contractor to identify and specify in the contract data not to be ordered for delivery under the clause if the data is not necessary to meet the Government's requirements for data. Also, the contracting officer may alter the clause by deleting the term "or specifically used" in paragraph (a) of the clause if delivery of the data is not necessary to meet the Government's requirements for data. Any data ordered under this clause will be subject to the clause at 52.227-14, Rights in Data—General, (or other equivalent clause setting forth the respective rights of the Government and the contractor) in the contract. Data authorized to be withheld under such clause will not be required to be delivered under the clause at 52.227-16, except as provided in Alternate II or Alternate III, if included (see 27.404-2(c) and (d)).

(c) Absent an established program for dissemination of computer software, agencies should not order additional computer software under the clause at 52.227-16, for the sole purpose of disseminating or marketing the software to the public. In ordering software for internal purposes, the contracting officer shall consider, consistent with the Government's needs, not ordering particular source codes, algorithms, processes, formulas, or flow charts of the software if the contractor shows that this aids its efforts to disseminate or market the software.

[FAC 2005-21, 72 FR 63045, 11/7/2007, effective 12/7/2007]

27.406-3 Major system acquisition.

(a) The clause at 52.227-21, Technical Data Declaration, Revision, and Withholding of Payment—Major Systems, implements 41 U.S.C. 2302(e). When using the clause at 52.227-21, the section of the contract specifying data delivery requirements (see 27.406-1(b)) shall expressly identify those line items of technical data to which the clause applies. Upon delivery of the technical data, the contracting officer shall review the technical data and the contractor's declaration relating to it to assure that the data are complete, accurate, and comply with contract requirements. If the data are not complete, accurate, or compliant, the contracting officer should request the contractor to correct the deficiencies, and may withhold payment. Final payment shall not be made under the contract until it has been determined that the delivery requirements of those line items of data to which the clause applies have been satisfactorily met.

(b) In a contract for, or in support of, a major system awarded by a civilian agency other than NASA or the U.S. Coast Guard, the following applies:

(1) The contracting officer shall require the delivery of any technical data relating to the major system or supplies for the major system, that are to be developed exclusively with Federal funds if the delivery of the technical data is needed to ensure the competitive acquisition of supplies or services that will be required in substantial quantities in the future. The clause at 52.227-22, Major System—Minimum Rights, is used in addition to the clause at 52.227-14, Rights in Data—General, and other required clauses, to ensure that the Government acquires at least those rights required by Pub. L. 98-577 in technical data developed exclusively with Federal funds.

(2) Technical data, relating to a major system or supplies for a major system, procured or to be procured by the Government and also relating to the design, development, or manufacture of products or processes offered or to be offered for sale to the public (except for such data as may be necessary for the Government to operate or maintain the product, or use the process if obtained

by the Government as an element of performance under the contract), shall not be required to be provided to the Government from persons who have developed such products or processes as a condition for the procurement of such products or processes by the Government.

[FAC 2005-21, 72 FR 63045, 11/7/2007, effective 12/7/2007; FAC 2005-73, 79 FR 24192, 4/29/2014, effective 5/29/2014]

27.407 Rights to technical data in successful proposals.

The clause at 52.227-23, Rights to Proposal Data (Technical), allows the Government to acquire unlimited rights to technical data in successful proposals. Pursuant to the clause, the prospective contractor is afforded the opportunity to specifically identify pages containing technical data to be excluded from the grant of unlimited rights. This exclusion is not dispositive of the protective status of the data, but any excluded technical data, as well as any commercial and financial information contained in the proposal, will remain subject to the policies in Subpart 15.2 or 15.6 (or agency supplements) relating to proposal information (*e.g.*, will be used for evaluation purposes only). If there is a need to have access to any of the excluded technical data during contract performance, consideration should be given to acquiring the data with limited rights, if they so qualify, in accordance with 27.404-2(c).

[FAC 84-27, 52 FR 18140, 5/13/87, effective 6/1/87; FAC 97-2, 62 FR 51224, 9/30/97, effective 10/10/97; FAC 2005-21, 72 FR 63045, 11/7/2007, effective 12/7/2007]

27.408 Cosponsored research and development activities.

(a) In contracts involving cosponsored research and development that require the contractor to make substantial contributions of funds or resources (*e.g.*, by cost-sharing or by repayment of nonrecurring costs), and the contractor's and the Government's respective contributions to any item, component, process, or computer software, developed or produced under the contract are not readily segregable, the contracting officer may limit the acquisition of, or acquire less than unlimited rights to, any data developed and delivered under the contract. Agencies may regulate the use of this authority in their supplements. Lesser rights shall, at a minimum, assure use of the data for agreed-to Governmental purposes (including reprocurement rights as appropriate), and address any disclosure limitations or restrictions to be imposed on the data. Also, consideration may be given to requiring the contractor to directly license others if needed to carry out the objectives of the contract. Since the purpose of the cosponsored research and development, the legitimate proprietary interests of the contractor, the needs of the Government, and the respective contributions of both parties may vary, no specific clauses are prescribed, but a clause providing less than unlimited rights in the Government for data developed and delivered under the contract (such as license rights) may be tailored to the circumstances consistent with the foregoing and the policy set forth in 27.402. As a guide, a clause may be appropriate when the contractor contributes money or resources, or agrees to make repayment of nonrecurring costs, of a value of approximately 50 percent of the total cost of the contract (*i.e.*, Government, contractor, and/or third party paid costs), and the respective contributions are not readily segregable for any work element to be performed under the contract. A clause may be used for all or for only specifically identified tasks or work elements under the contract. In the latter instance, its use will be in addition to whatever other data rights clause is prescribed under this subpart, with the contract specifically identifying which clause is to apply to which tasks or work elements. Further, this type of clause may not be appropriate where the purpose of the contract is to produce data for dissemination to the public, or to develop or demonstrate technologies that will be available, in any event, to the public for its direct use.

(b) Where the contractor's contributions are readily segregable (by performance requirements and the funding for the contract) and so identified in the contract, any resulting data may be treated under this clause as limited rights data or restricted computer software in accordance with 27.404-2(c) or (d), as applicable; or if this treatment is inconsistent with the purpose of the contract, rights to the data may, if so negotiated and stated in the contract, be treated in a manner consistent with paragraph (a) of this section.

[FAC 84-27, 52 FR 18140, 5/13/87, effective 6/1/87; FAC 2005-21, 72 FR 63045, 11/7/2007, effective 12/7/2007]

27.409 Solicitation provisions and contract clauses.

(a) Generally, a contract should contain only one data rights clause. However, where more than one is needed, the contract should distinguish the portion of contract performance to which each pertains.

(b) (1) Insert the clause at 52.227-14, Rights in Data—General, in solicitations and contracts if it is contemplated that data will be produced, furnished, or acquired under the contract, unless the contract is—

(i) For the production of special works of the type set forth in 27.405-1, although in these cases insert the clause at 52.227-14, Rights in Data—General, and make it applicable to data other than special works, as appropriate (see paragraph (e) of this section);

(ii) For the acquisition of existing data, commercial computer software, or other existing data, as described in 27.405-2 through 27.405-4 (see paragraphs (f) and (g) of this section);

(iii) A small business innovation research contract (see paragraph (h) of this section);

(iv) To be performed outside the United States (see paragraph (i) (1) of this section);

(v) For architect-engineer services or construction work (see paragraph (i) (2) of this section);

(vi) For the management, operation, design, or construction of a Government-owned facility to perform research, development, or production work (see paragraph (i) (3) of this section); or

(vii) A contract involving cosponsored research and development in which a clause providing for less than unlimited right has been authorized (see 27.408).

(2) If an agency determines, in accordance with 27.404-2(b), to adopt the alternate definition of "Limited Rights Data" in paragraph (a) of the clause, use the clause with its Alternate I.

(3) If a contracting officer determines, in accordance with 27.404-2(c) that it is necessary to obtain limited rights data, use the clause with its Alternate II. The contracting officer shall complete paragraph (g) (3) to include the purposes, if any, for which limited rights data are to be disclosed outside the Government.

(4) In accordance with 27.404-2(d), if a contracting officer determines it is necessary to obtain restricted computer software, use the clause with its Alternate III. Any greater or lesser rights regarding the use, reproduction, or disclosure of restricted computer software than those set forth in the Restricted Rights Notice of paragraph (g) (4) of the clause shall be specified in the contract and the notice modified accordingly.

(5) Use the clause with its Alternate IV in contracts for basic or applied research (other than those for the management or operation of Government facilities, and contracts and subcontracts in support of programs being conducted at those facilities or where international agreements require otherwise) to be performed solely by universities and colleges. The clause may be used with its Alternate IV in other contracts if in accordance with 27.404-3(a), an agency determines to grant permission for the contractor to assert claim to copyright subsisting in all data first produced without further request being made by the contractor. When Alternate IV is used, the contract may exclude items or categories of data from the permission granted, either by express provisions in the contract or by the addition of a paragraph (d) (4) to the clause (see 27.404-4).

(6) In accordance with 27.404-6, if the Government needs the right to inspect certain data at a contractor's facility, use the clause with its Alternate V.

(c) In accordance with 27.404-2(c) (2) and 27.404-2(d) (5), if the contracting officer desires to have an offeror state in response to a solicitation whether limited rights data or restricted computer software are likely to be used in meeting the data delivery requirements set forth in the solicitation, insert the provision at 52.227-15, Representation of Limited Rights Data and Restricted Computer Software, in any solicitation containing the clause at 52.227-14, Rights in Data—General. The contractor's response may provide an aid in determining whether the clause should be used with Alternate II and/or Alternate III.

(d) Insert the clause at 52.227-16, Additional Data Requirements, in solicitations and contracts involving experimental, developmental, research, or demonstration work (other than basic or applied research to be performed solely by a university or college where the contract amount will be $500,000 or less) unless all the requirements for data are believed to be known at the time of contracting and specified in the contract (see 27.406-2). This clause may also be used in other contracts when considered appropriate. For example, if the contract is for basic or applied research to be performed by a university or college, and the contracting officer believes the contract effort will in the future exceed $500,000, even though the initial award does not, the contracting officer may include the clause in the initial award.

(e) In accordance with 27.405-1, insert the clause at 52.227-17, Rights in Data—Special Works, in solicitations and contracts primarily for the production or compilation of data (other than limited rights data or restricted computer software) for the Government's internal use, or when there is a specific need to limit distribution and use of the data or to obtain indemnity for liabilities that may arise out of the content, performance, or disclosure of the data. Examples of such contracts are set forth in 27.405-1.

(1) Insert the clause if existing works are to be modified, as by editing, translation, addition of subject matter, etc.

(2) The contract may specify the purposes and conditions (including time limitations) under which the data may be used, released, or reproduced by the contractor for other than contract performance.

(3) Contracts for the production of audiovisual works, sound recordings, etc. may include limitations in connection with talent releases, music licenses, and the like that are consistent with the purposes for which the data is acquired.

(4) The clause may be modified in accordance with paragraphs (c) through (e) of 27.405-1.

(f) Insert the clause at 52.227-18, Rights in Data—Existing Works, in solicitations and contracts exclusively for the acquisition, without modification, of existing audiovisual and similar works of the type set forth in 27.405-2. The contract may set forth limitations consistent with the purposes for which the work is being acquired. While no specific clause of this subpart is required to be included in contracts solely for the acquisition, without disclosure prohibitions, of books, publications, and similar items in the exact form in which the items exist prior to the request for purchase (*i.e.*, the off-the-shelf purchase of such items), or in other contracts where only existing data available without disclosure prohibitions is to be furnished, if reproduction rights are to be acquired, the contract shall include terms addressing such rights. (See 27.405-4.)

(g) In accordance with 27.405-3, when contracting (other than from GSA's Multiple Award Schedule contracts) for the acquisition of commercial computer software, the contracting officer may insert the clause at 52.227-19, Commercial Computer Software License, in the solicitation and contract. In any event, the contracting officer shall assure that the contract contains terms to obtain sufficient rights for the Government to fulfill the need for which the software is being acquired and is otherwise consistent with 27.405-3).

(h) If the contract is a Small Business Innovation Research (SBIR) contract, insert the clause at 52.227-20, Rights in Data—SBIR Program in all Phase I, Phase II, and Phase III contracts awarded under the Small Business Innovation Research Program established pursuant to 15 U.S.C. 638. The SBIR protection period may be extended in accordance with the Small Business Administration's "Small Business Innovation Research Program Policy Directive" (September 24, 2002).

(i) Agencies may prescribe in their procedures, as appropriate, a clause consistent with the policy of 27.402in contracts—

(1) To be performed outside the United States;

(2) For architect-engineer services and construction work, *e.g.*, the clause at 52.227-17, Rights in Data—Special Works); or

(3) For management, operation, design, or construction of Government-owned research, development, or production facilities, and in contracts and subcontracts in support of programs being conducted at such facilities.

(j) In accordance with 27.406-3(a), insert the clause at 52.227-21, Technical Data Declaration, Revision, and Withholding of Payment—Major Systems, in contracts for major systems acquisitions or for support of major systems acquisitions. This requirement includes contracts for detailed design, development, or production of a major system and contracts for any individual part, component, subassembly, assembly, or subsystem integral to the major system, and other property that may be replaced during the service life of the system, including spare parts. When used, this clause requires that the technical data to which it applies be specified in the contract (see 27.406-3(a)).

(k) In accordance with 27.406-3(b), in the case of civilian agencies other than NASA and the U.S. Coast Guard, insert the clause at 52.227-22, Major System—Minimum Rights, in contracts for major systems or contracts in support of major systems.

(l) In accordance with 27.407, if a contracting officer desires to acquire unlimited rights in technical data contained in a successful proposal upon which a contract award is based, insert the clause at 52.227-23, Rights to Proposal Data (Technical). Rights to technical data in a proposal are not acquired by mere incorporation by reference of the proposal in the contract, and if a proposal is incorporated by reference, the contracting officer shall follow 27.404 to assure that the rights are appropriately addressed.

[FAC 84-27, 52 FR 18140, 5/13/87, effective 6/1/87; Final rule, 55 FR 38517, 9/18/90; FAC 90-45, Final rule, 62 FR 224, 1/2/97, effective 1/1/97; FAC 97-11, 64 FR 10530, 3/4/99, effective 5/3/99; FAC 2005-21, 72 FR 63045, 11/7/2007, effective 12/7/2007]

SUBPART 27.5—FOREIGN LICENSE AND TECHNICAL ASSISTANCE AGREEMENTS

27.501 General.

Agencies shall provide necessary policy and procedures regarding foreign technical assistance agreements and license agreements involving intellectual property, including avoiding unnecessary royalty charges.

[FAC 2005-21, 72 FR 63045, 11/7/2007, effective 12/7/2007]

PART 28—BONDS AND INSURANCE

Table of Contents

Scope of part 28.000
Definitions 28.001

Subpart 28.1—Bonds and Other Financial Protections

Scope of subpart 28.100
Bid guarantees 28.101
Policy on use 28.101-1
Solicitation provision or contract clause 28.101-2
Authority of an attorney-in-fact for a bid bond 28.101-3
Noncompliance with bid guarantee requirements 28.101-4
Performance and payment bonds and alternative payment protections for construction contracts 28.102
General 28.102-1
Amount required 28.102-2
Contract clauses 28.102-3
Performance and payment bonds for other than construction contracts 28.103
General 28.103-1
Performance bonds 28.103-2
Payment bonds 28.103-3
Contract clause 28.103-4
Annual performance bonds 28.104
Other types of bonds 28.105
Advance payment bonds 28.105-1
Patent infringement bonds 28.105-2
Administration 28.106
Bonds and bond-related forms 28.106-1
Substitution of surety bonds 28.106-2
Additional bond and security 28.106-3
Contract clause 28.106-4
Consent of surety 28.106-5
Furnishing information 28.106-6
Withholding contract payments 28.106-7
Payment to subcontractors or suppliers 28.106-8

Subpart 28.2—Sureties and Other Security for Bonds

Scope of subpart 28.200
Requirements for security 28.201
Acceptability of corporate sureties 28.202
Acceptability of individual sureties 28.203
Security interests by an individual surety 28.203-1
Acceptability of assets 28.203-2
Acceptance of real property 28.203-3
Substitution of assets 28.203-4
Release of lien 28.203-5
Contract clause 28.203-6
Exclusion of individual sureties 28.203-7
Alternatives in lieu of corporate or individual sureties 28.204
United States bonds or notes 28.204-1
Certified or cashier's checks, bank drafts, money orders, or currency 28.204-2
Irrevocable letter of credit 28.204-3
Contract clause 28.204-4

Subpart 28.3—Insurance

Policy 28.301
Notice of cancellation or change 28.302

Insurance against loss of or damage to Government property 28.303
Risk-pooling arrangements 28.304
Overseas workers' compensation and war-hazard insurance 28.305
Insurance under fixed-price contracts 28.306
Insurance under cost-reimbursement contracts 28.307
Group insurance plans 28.307-1
Liability 28.307-2
Self-insurance 28.308
Contract clauses for workers' compensation insurance 28.309
Contract clause for work on a Government installation 28.310
Solicitation provision and contract clause on liability insurance under cost-reimbursement contracts 28.311
Contract clause 28.311-1
Agency solicitation provisions and contract clauses 28.311-2
Contract clause for insurance of leased motor vehicles 28.312
Contract clauses for insurance of transportation or transportation-related services 28.313

PART 28—BONDS AND INSURANCE

28.000 Scope of part.

This part prescribes requirements for obtaining financial protection against losses under contracts that result from the use of the sealed bid or negotiated methods. It covers bid guarantees, bonds, alternative payment protections, security for bonds, and insurance.

[FAC 2001-06, 67 FR 13048, 3/20/2002, effective 4/4/2002]

28.001 Definitions.

As used in this part—

Attorney-in-fact means an agent, independent agent, underwriter, or any other company or individual holding a power of attorney granted by a surety (see also *power of attorney* at 2.101).

Bid means any response to a solicitation, including a proposal under a negotiated acquisition. See the definition of *offer* at 2.101.

Bid guarantee means a form of security assuring that the bidder—

(1) Will not withdraw a bid within the period specified for acceptance; and

(2) Will execute a written contract and furnish required bonds, including any necessary coinsurance or reinsurance agreements, within the time specified in the bid, unless a longer time is allowed, after receipt of the specified forms.

Bidder means any entity that is responding or has responded to a solicitation, including an offeror under a negotiated acquisition.

Bond means a written instrument executed by a bidder or contractor (the "principal"), and a second party ("the surety" or "sureties") (except as provided in 28.204), to assure fulfillment of the principal's obligations to a third party (the "obligee" or "Government"), identified in the bond. If the principal's obligations are not met, the bond assures payment, to the extent stipulated, of any loss sustained by the obligee. The types of bonds and related documents are as follows:

(1) An advance payment bond secures fulfillment of the contractor's obligations under an advance payment provision.

(2) An annual bid bond is a single bond furnished by a bidder, in lieu of separate bonds, which secure all bids (on other than construction contracts) requiring bonds submitted during a specific Government fiscal year.

(3) An annual performance bond is a single bond furnished by a contractor, in lieu of separate performance bonds, to secure fulfillment of the contractor's obligations under contracts (other than construction contracts) requiring bonds entered into during a specific Government fiscal year.

(4) A patent infringement bond secures fulfillment of the contractor's obligations under a patent provision.

(5) A payment bond assures payments as required by law to all persons supplying labor or material in the prosecution of the work provided for in the contract.

(6) A performance bond secures performance and fulfillment of the contractor's obligations under the contract.

Consent of surety means an acknowledgment by a surety that its bond given in connection with a contract continues to apply to the contract as modified.

Penal sum or *penal amount* means the amount of money specified in a bond (or a percentage of the bid price in a bid bond) as the maximum payment for which the surety is obligated or the amount of security required to be pledged to the Government in lieu of a corporate or individual surety for the bond.

Reinsurance means a transaction which provides that a surety, for a consideration, agrees to indemnify another surety against loss which the latter may sustain under a bond which it has issued.

[FAC 90-39, 61 FR 31612, 6/20/96, effective 6/20/96; FAC 97-1, 62 FR 44802, 8/22/97, effective 10/21/97; FAC 97-22, 66 FR 2116, 1/10/2001, effective 3/12/2001; Delay of effective date, 66 FR 14259, 3/9/2001, effective 5/11/2001; FAC 2001-06, 67 FR 13048, 3/20/2002, effective 4/4/2002]

SUBPART 28.1—BONDS AND OTHER FINANCIAL PROTECTIONS

28.100 Scope of subpart.

This subpart prescribes requirements and procedures for the use of bonds, alternative payment protections, and all types of bid guarantees.

[FAC 97-1, 62 FR 44802, 8/22/97, effective 10/21/97]

28.101 Bid guarantees. (No Text)

28.101-1 Policy on use.

(a) A contracting officer shall not require a bid guarantee unless a performance bond or a performance and payment bond is also required (see 28.102 and 28.103). Except as provided in paragraph (c) of this subsection, bid guarantees shall be required whenever a performance bond or a performance and payment bond is required.

(b) All types of bid guarantees are acceptable for supply or service contracts (see annual bid bonds and annual performance bonds coverage in 28.001). Only separate bid guarantees are acceptable in connection with construction contracts. Agencies may specify that only separate bid bonds are acceptable in connection with construction contracts.

(c) The chief of the contracting office may waive the requirement to obtain a bid guarantee when a performance bond or a performance and payment bond is required if it is determined that a bid guarantee is not in the best interest of the Government for a specific acquisition (*e.g.*, overseas construction, emergency acquisitions, sole-source contracts). Class waivers may be authorized by the agency head or designee.

[FAC 84-12, 51 FR 2665, 1/17/86, effective 1/20/86; FAC 84-26, 52 FR 19803, 5/27/87, effective 7/30/87; FAC 84-29, 52 FR 30076, 8/12/87, effective 8/24/87; FAC 84-51, 54 FR 34755, 8/21/89, effective 9/20/89; FAC 90-40, 61 FR 39186, 7/26/96, effective 9/24/96]

28.101-2 Solicitation provision or contract clause.

(a) The contracting officer shall insert a provision or clause substantially the same as the provision at 52.228-1, Bid Guarantee, in solicitations or contracts that require a bid guarantee or similar guarantee. For example, the contracting officer may modify this provision—

(1) To set a period of time that is other than 10 days for the return of executed bonds;

(2) For use in connection with construction solicitations when the agency has specified that only separate bid bonds are acceptable in accordance with 28.101-1(b);

(3) For use in solicitations for negotiated contracts; or

(4) For use in service contracts containing options for extended performance.

(b) The contracting officer shall determine the amount of the bid guarantee for insertion in the provision at 52.228-1(see 28.102-2(a)). The amount shall be adequate to protect the Government from loss should the successful bidder fail to execute further contractual documents and bonds as required. The bid guarantee amount shall be at least 20 percent of the bid price but shall not exceed $3 million. When the penal sum is expressed as a percentage, a maximum dollar limitation may be stated.

[FAC 90-40, 61 FR 39186, 7/26/96, effective 9/24/96; FAC 97-19, 65 FR 46052, 7/26/2000, effective 7/26/2000]

28.101-3 Authority of an attorney-in-fact for a bid bond.

(a) Any person signing a bid bond as an attorney-in-fact shall include with the bid bond evidence of authority to bind the surety.

(b) An original, or a photocopy or facsimile of an original, power of attorney is sufficient evidence of such authority.

(c) For purposes of this section, electronic, mechanically-applied and printed signatures, seals and dates on the power of attorney shall be considered original signatures, seals and dates, without regard to the order in which they were affixed.

(d) The contracting officer shall—

(1) Treat the failure to provide a signed and dated power of attorney at the time of bid opening as a matter of responsiveness; and

(2) Treat questions regarding the authenticity and enforceability of the power of attorney at the time of bid opening as a matter of responsibility. These questions are handled after bid opening.

(e)(1) If the contracting officer contacts the surety to validate the power of attorney, the contracting officer shall document the file providing, at a minimum, the following information:

(i) Name of person contacted.

(ii) Date and time of contact.

(iii) Response of the surety.

(2) If, upon investigation, the surety declares the power of attorney to have been valid at the time of bid opening, the contracting officer may require correction of any technical error.

(3) If the surety declares the power of attorney to have been invalid, the contracting officer shall not allow the bidder to substitute a replacement power of attorney or a replacement surety.

(f) Determinations of non-responsibility based on the unacceptability of a power of attorney are not subject to the Certificate of Competency process of subpart 19.6 if the surety has disavowed the validity of the power of attorney.

[FAC 90-40, 61 FR 39186, 7/26/96, effective 9/24/96; FAC 2005-06, 70 FR 57459, 9/30/2005, effective 9/30/2005]

28.101-4 Noncompliance with bid guarantee requirements.

(a) In sealed bidding, noncompliance with a solicitation requirement for a bid guarantee requires rejection of the bid, except in the situations described in paragraph (c) of this subsection when the noncompliance shall be waived.

(b) In negotiation, noncompliance with a solicitation requirement for a bid guarantee requires rejection of an initial proposal as unacceptable, if a determination is made to award the contract based on initial proposals without discussion, except in the situations described in paragraph (c) of this subsection when noncompliance shall be waived. (See 15.306(a)(2) for conditions regarding making awards based on initial proposals.) If the conditions for awarding based on initial proposals are not met, deficiencies in bid guarantees submitted by offerors determined to be in the competitive range shall be addressed during discussions and the offeror shall be given an opportunity to correct the deficiency.

(c) Noncompliance with a solicitation requirement for a bid guarantee shall be waived in the following circumstances unless the contracting officer determines in writing that acceptance of the bid would be detrimental to the Government's interest when—

(1) Only one offer is received. In this case, the contracting officer may require the furnishing of the bid guarantee before award;

(2) The amount of the bid guarantee submitted is less than required, but is equal to or greater than the difference between the offer price and the next higher acceptable offer;

(3) The amount of the bid guarantee submitted, although less than that required by the solicitation for the maximum quantity offered, is sufficient for a quantity for which the offeror is otherwise eligible for award. Any award to the offeror shall not exceed the quantity covered by the bid guarantee;

(4) The bid guarantee is received late, and late receipt is waived under 14.304;

(5) A bid guarantee becomes inadequate as a result of the correction of a mistake under 14.407(but only if the bidder will increase the bid guarantee to the level required for the corrected bid);

(6) An otherwise acceptable bid bond was submitted with a signed offer, but the bid bond was not signed by the offeror;

(7) An otherwise acceptable bid bond is erroneously dated or bears no date at all; or

(8) A bid bond does not list the United States as obligee, but correctly identifies the offeror, the solicitation number, and the

name and location of the project involved, so long as it is acceptable in all other respects.

[FAC 84-53, 54 FR 48986, 11/28/89, effective 2/26/90; FAC 90-29, 60 FR 34732, 7/3/95, effective 7/3/95; FAC 97-2, 62 FR 51224, 9/30/97, effective 10/10/97; FAC 2005-92, 81 FR 83097, 11/18/2016, effective 12/19/2016]

28.102 Performance and payment bonds and alternative payment protections for construction contracts. (No Text)

28.102-1 General.

(a) 40 U.S.C. chapter 31, subchapter III, Bonds (formerly known as the Miller Act), requires performance and payment bonds for any construction contract exceeding $150,000, except that this requirement may be waived—

(1) By the contracting officer for as much of the work as is to be performed in a foreign country upon finding that it is impracticable for the contractor to furnish such bond; or

(2) As otherwise authorized by the Bonds statute or other law.

(b) (1) Pursuant to 40 U.S.C. 3132, for construction contracts greater than $35,000, but not greater than $150,000, the contracting officer shall select two or more of the following payment protections, giving particular consideration to inclusion of an irrevocable letter of credit as one of the selected alternatives:

(i) A payment bond.

(ii) An irrevocable letter of credit (ILC).

(iii) *A tripartite escrow agreement.* The prime contractor establishes an escrow account in a federally insured financial institution and enters into a tripartite escrow agreement with the financial institution, as escrow agent, and all of the suppliers of labor and material. The escrow agreement shall establish the terms of payment under the contract and of resolution of disputes among the parties. The Government makes payments to the contractor's escrow account, and the escrow agent distributes the payments in accordance with the agreement, or triggers the disputes resolution procedures if required.

(iv) *Certificates of deposit.* The contractor deposits certificates of deposit from a federally insured financial institution with the contracting officer, in an acceptable form, executable by the contracting officer.

(v) A deposit of the types of security listed in 28.204-1 and 28.204-2.

(2) The contractor shall submit to the Government one of the payment protections selected by the contracting officer.

(c) The contractor shall furnish all bonds or alternative payment protections, including any necessary reinsurance agreements, before receiving a notice to proceed with the work or being allowed to start work.

[FAC 90-39, 61 FR 31612, 6/20/96, effective 6/20/96; FAC 2005-06, 70 FR 57453, 9/30/2005, effective 9/30/2005; FAC 2005-13, 71 FR 57363, 9/28/2006, effective 9/28/2006; FAC 2005-45, 75 FR 53129, 8/30/2010, effective 10/1/2010; FAC 2005-73, 79 FR 24192, 4/29/2014, effective 5/29/2014; FAC 2005-83, 80 FR 38293, 7/2/2015, effective 10/1/2015]

28.102-2 Amount required.

(a) *Definition.* As used in this subsection—

Original contract price means the award price of the contract; or, for requirements contracts, the price payable for the estimated total quantity; or, for indefinite-quantity contracts, the price payable for the specified minimum quantity. Original contract price does not include the price of any options, except those options exercised at the time of contract award.

(b) *Contracts exceeding $150,000.*

(1) *Performance bonds.* Unless the contracting officer determines that a lesser amount is adequate for the protection of the Government, the penal amount of performance bonds must equal—

(i) 100 percent of the original contract price; and

(ii) If the contract price increases, an additional amount equal to 100 percent of the increase.

(2) *Payment bonds.* (i) Unless the contracting officer makes a written determination supported by specific findings that a payment bond in this amount is impractical, the amount of the payment bond must equal—

(A) 100 percent of the original contract price; and

(B) If the contract price increases, an additional amount equal to 100 percent of the increase.

(ii) The amount of the payment bond must be no less than the amount of the performance bond.

(c) *Contracts exceeding $35,000 but not exceeding $150,000.* Unless the contracting officer determines that a lesser amount is adequate for the protection of the Government, the penal amount of the payment bond or the amount of alternative payment protection must equal—

(1) 100 percent of the original contract price; and

(2) If the contract price increases, an additional amount equal to 100 percent of the increase.

(d) *Securing additional payment protection.* If the contract price increases, the Government must secure any needed additional protection by directing the contractor to—

(1) Increase the penal sum of the existing bond;

(2) Obtain an additional bond; or

(3) Furnish additional alternative payment protection.

(e) *Reducing amounts.* The contracting officer may reduce the amount of security to support a bond, subject to the conditions of 28.203-5(c) or 28.204(b).

[FAC 97-19, 65 FR 46052, 7/26/2000, effective 7/26/2000; FAC 2005-13, 71 FR 57363, 9/28/2006, effective 9/28/2006; FAC 2005-45, 75 FR 53129, 8/30/2010, effective 10/1/2010; FAC 2005-73, 79 FR 24192, 4/29/2014, effective 5/29/2014; FAC 2005-83, 80 FR 38293, 7/2/2015, effective 10/1/2015]

28.102-3 Contract clauses.

(a) Insert a clause substantially the same as the clause at 52.228-15, Performance and Payment Bonds—Construction, in solicitations and contracts for construction that contain a requirement for performance and payment bonds if the resultant contract is expected to exceed $150,000. The contracting officer may revise paragraphs (b)(1) and/or (b)(2) of the clause to establish a lower percentage in accordance with 28.102-2(b). If the provision at 52.228-1 is not included in the solicitation, the contracting officer must set a period of time for return of executed bonds.

(b) Insert the clause at 52.228-13, Alternative Payment Protections, in solicitations and contracts for construction, when the estimated or actual value exceeds $35,000 but does not exceed $150,000. Complete the clause by specifying the payment protections selected (see 28.102-1(b)(1)) and the deadline for submission. The contracting officer may revise paragraph (b) of the clause to establish a lower percentage in accordance with 28.102-2(c).

[FAC 90-39, 61 FR 31612, 6/20/96, effective 6/20/96; FAC 90-40, 61 FR 39186, 7/26/96, effective 9/24/96; FAC 97-1, 62 FR 44802, 8/22/97, effective 10/21/97; FAC 97-19, 65 FR 46052, 7/26/2000, effective 7/26/2000; FAC 2005-13, 71 FR 57363, 9/28/2006, effective 9/28/2006; FAC 2005-45, 75 FR 53129, 8/30/2010, effective 10/1/2010; FAC 2005-83, 80 FR 38293, 7/2/2015, effective 10/1/2015]

28.103 Performance and payment bonds for other than construction contracts. (No Text)

28.103-1 General.

(a) Generally, agencies shall not require performance and payment bonds for other than construction contracts. However, performance and payment bonds may be used as permitted in 28.103-2 and 28.103-3.

(b) The contractor shall furnish all bonds before receiving a notice to proceed with the work.

(c) No bond shall be required after the contract has been awarded if it was not specifically required in the contract, except as may be determined necessary for a contract modification.

28.103-2 Performance bonds.

(a) Performance bonds may be required for contracts exceeding the simplified acquisition threshold when necessary to protect the Government's interest. The following situations may warrant a performance bond:

(1) Government property or funds are to be provided to the contractor for use in performing the contract or as partial compensation (as in retention of salvaged material).

(2) A contractor sells assets to or merges with another concern, and the Government, after recognizing the latter concern as the successor in interest, desires assurance that it is financially capable.

(3) Substantial progress payments are made before delivery of end items starts.

(4) Contracts are for dismantling, demolition, or removal of improvements.

(b) The Government may require additional performance bond protection when a contract price is increased.

(c) The contracting officer must determine the contractor's responsibility (see Subpart 9.1) even though a bond has been or can be obtained.

[FAC 90-29, 60 FR 34732, 7/3/95, effective 7/3/95; FAC 90-40, 61 FR 39186, 7/26/96, effective 9/24/96]

28.103-3 Payment bonds.

(a) A payment bond is required only when a performance bond is required, and if the use of payment bond is in the Government's interest.

(b) When a contract price is increased, the Government may require additional bond protection in an amount adequate to protect suppliers of labor and material.

[FAC 90-40, 61 FR 39186, 7/26/96, effective 9/24/96]

28.103-4 Contract clause.

The contracting officer shall insert a clause substantially the same as the clause at 52.228-16, Performance and Payment Bonds—Other than Construction, in solicitations and contracts that contain a requirement for both payment and performance bonds. The contracting officer shall determine the amount of each bond for insertion in the clause. The amount shall be adequate to protect the interest of the Government. The contracting officer shall also set a period of time (normally 10 days) for return of executed bonds. Alternate I shall be used when only performance bonds are required.

[FAC 90-40, 61 FR 39186, 7/26/96, effective 9/24/96]

28.104 Annual performance bonds.

(a) Annual performance bonds only apply to non-construction contracts. They shall provide a gross penal sum applicable to the total amount of all covered contracts.

(b) When the penal sums obligated by contracts are approximately equal to or exceed the penal sum of the annual performance bond, an additional bond will be required to cover additional contracts.

28.105 Other types of bonds.

The head of the contracting activity may approve using other types of bonds in connection with acquiring particular supplies or services. These types include advance payment bonds and patent infringement bonds.

28.105-1 Advance payment bonds.

Advance payment bonds may be required only when the contract contains an advance payment provision and a performance bond is not furnished. The contracting officer shall determine the amount of the advance payment bond necessary to protect the Government.

28.105-2 Patent infringement bonds.

(a) Contracts providing for patent indemnity may require these bonds only if—

(1) A performance bond is not furnished; and

(2) The financial responsibility of the contractor is unknown or doubtful.

(b) The contracting officer shall determine the penal sum.

28.106 Administration. (No Text)

28.106-1 Bonds and bond-related forms.

The following Standard Forms (SF's) and Optional Forms (OF's), shall be used, except in foreign countries, when a bid bond, performance or payment bond, or an individual surety is required. The bond forms shall be used as indicated in the instruction portion of each form:

(a) SF 24, Bid Bond (see 28.101).

(b) SF 25, Performance Bond (see 28.102-1 and 28.106-3(b)).

(c) SF 25-A, Payment Bond (see 28.102-1and 28.106-3(b)).

(d) SF 25-B, Continuation Sheet (for SF's 24, 25, and 25-A).

(e) SF 28, Affidavit of Individual Surety (see 28.203).

(f) SF 34, Annual Bid Bond (see 28.001).

(g) SF 35, Annual Performance Bond (see 28.104).

(h) SF 273, Reinsurance Agreement for a Bonds Statute Performance Bond (see 28.202(a)(4)).

(i) SF 274, Reinsurance Agreement for a Bonds Statute Payment Bond (see 28.202(a)(4)).

(j) SF 275, Reinsurance Agreement in Favor of the United States (see 28.202(a)(4)).

(k) SF 1414, Consent of Surety (see 28.106-5).

(l) SF 1415, Consent of Surety and Increase of Penalty (see 28.106-3).

(m) SF 1416, Payment Bond for Other Than Construction Contracts (see 28.103-3 and 28.106-3(b)).

(n) SF 1418, Performance Bond for Other Than Construction Contracts (see 28.103-2 and 28.106-3(b)).

(o) OF 90, Release of Lien on Real Property (see 28.203-5).

(p) OF 91, Release of Personal Property from Escrow (see 28.203-5).

[FAC 84-53, 54 FR 48986, 11/28/89, effective 2/26/90; FAC 90-40, 61 FR 39186, 7/26/96, effective 9/24/96; FAC 2005-73, 79 FR 24192, 4/29/2014, effective 5/29/2014; FAC 2005-100, 83 FR 42571, 8/22/2018, effective 8/22/2018]

28.106-2 Substitution of surety bonds.

(a) A new surety bond covering all or part of the obligations on a bond previously approved may be substituted for the original bond if approved by the head of the contracting activity, or as otherwise specified in agency regulation.

(b) When a new surety bond is approved, the contracting officer shall notify the principal and surety of the original bond of the effective date of the new bond.

[FAC 90-40, 61 FR 39186, 7/26/96, effective 9/24/96]

28.106-3 Additional bond and security.

(a) When additional bond coverage is required and is secured in whole or in part by the original surety or sureties, agencies shall use Standard Form 1415, Consent of Surety and Increase of Penalty. Standard Form 1415 is authorized for local reproduction.

(b) When additional bond coverage is required and is secured in whole or in part by a new surety or by one of the alternatives described in 28.204 in lieu of corporate or individual surety, agencies shall use Standard Form 25, Performance Bond; Standard Form 1418, Performance Bond for Other Than Construction Contracts; Standard Form 25-A, Payment Bond; or Standard Form 1416, Payment Bond for Other Than Construction Contracts.

[FAC 97-1, 62 FR 44802, 8/22/97, effective 10/21/97; FAC 2005-100, 83 FR 42571, 8/22/2018, effective 8/22/2018]

28.106-4 Contract clause.

(a) The contracting officer shall insert the clause at 52.228-2, Additional Bond Security, in solicitations and contracts when bonds are required.

(b) In accordance with Section 806(a)(3) of Pub. L. 102-190, as amended by Sections 2091 and 8105 of Pub. L. 103-355 (10 U.S.C. 2302 note), the contracting officer shall insert the clause at 52.228-12, Prospective Subcontractor Requests for Bonds, in solicitations and contracts with respect to which a payment bond will be furnished pursuant to 40 U.S.C. chapter 31, subchapter III, Bonds (see 28.102-1), except for contracts for the acquisition of commercial items as defined in Subpart 2.1.

[FAC 90-32, 60 FR 48206, 9/18/95, effective 10/1/95; FAC 2005-73, 79 FR 24192, 4/29/2014, effective 5/29/2014]

28.106-5 Consent of surety.

(a) When any contract is modified, the contracting officer shall obtain the consent of surety if—

(1) An additional bond is obtained from other than the original surety;

(2) No additional bond is required and—

(i) The modification is for new work beyond the scope of the original contract; or

(ii) The modification does not change the contract scope but changes the contract price (upward or downward) by more than 25 percent or $50,000; or

(3) Consent of surety is required for a novation agreement (see Subpart 42.12).

(b) When a contract for which performance or payment is secured by any of the types of security listed in 28.204 is modified as described in paragraph (a) of this subsection, no consent of surety is required.

(c) Agencies shall use Standard Form 1414, Consent of Surety, for all types of contracts.

[FAC 90-39, 61 FR 31612, 6/20/96, effective 6/20/96]

28.106-6 Furnishing information.

(a) The surety on the bond, upon its written request, may be furnished information on the progress of the work, payments, and the estimated percentage of completion, concerning the contract for which the bond was furnished.

(b) When a payment bond has been provided, the contracting officer shall, upon request, furnish the name and address of the surety or sureties to any subcontractor or supplier who has furnished or been requested to furnish labor or material for the contract. In addition, general information concerning the work progress, payments, and the estimated percentage of completion may be furnished to persons who have provided labor or materials and have not been paid.

(c) When a payment bond has been provided for a contract, the head of the agency or designee shall furnish a certified copy of the bond and the contract for which it was given to any person who makes a request therefor and who furnishes an affidavit that the requestor has supplied labor or materials for such work and payment therefor has not been made or that the requestor is being sued on such bond. The person who makes the request shall be required to pay such costs of preparation as determined by the head of the agency or designee to be reasonable and appropriate (see 40 U.S.C. 3133).

(d) Section 806(a)(2) of Pub. L. 102-190, as amended by Sections 2091 and 8105 of Pub. L. 103-355 (10 U.S.C. 2302 note), requires that the Federal Government provide information to subcontractors on payment bonds under contracts for other than commercial items as defined in Subpart 2.1. Upon the written or oral request of a subcontractor/supplier, or prospective subcontractor/supplier, under a contract with respect to which a payment bond has been furnished pursuant to the Bonds statute, the contracting officer shall promptly provide to the requester, either orally or in writing, as appropriate, any of the following:

(1) Name and address of the surety or sureties on the payment bond.

(2) Penal amount of the payment bond.

(3) Copy of the payment bond. The contracting officer may impose reasonable fees to cover the cost of copying and providing a copy of the payment bond.

[FAC 84-8, 50 FR 26903, 6/28/85, effective 7/1/85; FAC 90-32, 60 FR 48206, 9/18/95, effective 10/1/95; FAC 2005-06, 70 FR 57453, 9/30/2005, effective 9/30/2005; FAC 2005-73, 79 FR 24192, 4/29/2014, effective 5/29/2014]

28.106-7 Withholding contract payments.

(a) During contract performance, agencies shall not withhold payments due contractors or assignees because subcontractors or suppliers have not been paid.

(b) If, after completion of the contract work, the Government receives written notice from the surety regarding the contractor's failure to meet its obligation to its subcontractors or suppliers, the contracting officer shall withhold final payment. However, the surety must agree to hold the Government harmless from any liability resulting from withholding the final payment. The contracting officer will authorize final payment upon agreement between the contractor and surety or upon a judicial determination of the rights of the parties.

(c) For any withholding incident to the labor standards provisions of the contract, see Part 22.

28.106-8 Payment to subcontractors or suppliers.

The contracting officer will only authorize payment to subcontractors or suppliers from an ILC (or any other cash equivalent security) upon a judicial determination of the rights of the parties, a signed notarized statement by the contractor that the payment is due and owed, or a signed agreement between the parties as to amount due and owed.

[FAC 97-1, 62 FR 44802, 8/22/97, effective 10/21/97]

SUBPART 28.2—SURETIES AND OTHER SECURITY FOR BONDS

28.200 Scope of subpart.

This subpart prescribes procedures for the use of sureties and other security to protect the Government from financial losses.

[FAC 97-1, 62 FR 44802, 8/22/97, effective 10/21/97]

28.201 Requirements for security.

(a) Agencies shall obtain adequate security for bonds (including coinsurance and reinsurance agreements) required or used with a contract for supplies or services (including construction). Acceptable forms of security include—

(1) Corporate or individual sureties; or

(2) Any of the types of security authorized in lieu of sureties by 28.204.

(b) Solicitations shall not preclude offerors from using the types of surety or other security permitted by this subpart, unless prohibited by law or regulation.

[FAC 84-58, 55 FR 25522, 6/21/90, effective 7/23/90; FAC 97-1, 62 FR 44802, 8/22/97, effective 10/21/97]

28.202 Acceptability of corporate sureties.

(a) (1) Corporate sureties offered for bonds furnished with contracts performed in the United States or its outlying areas must appear on the list contained in the Department of Treasury Circular 570, "Companies Holding Certificates of Authority as Acceptable Sureties on Federal Bonds and Acceptable Reinsuring Companies."

(2) The penal amount of the bond should not exceed the surety's underwriting limit stated in the Department of the Treasury circular. If the penal amount exceeds the underwriting limit, the bond will be acceptable only if—

(i) The amount which exceeds the specified limit is coinsured or reinsured; and

(ii) The amount of coinsurance or reinsurance does not exceed the underwriting limit of each coinsurer or reinsurer.

(3) Coinsurance or reinsurance agreements shall conform to the Department of the Treasury regulations in 31 CFR 223.10 and 223.11. When reinsurance is contemplated, the contracting office generally shall require reinsurance agreements to be executed and submitted with the bonds before making a final determination on the bonds.

(4) When specified in the solicitation, the contracting officer may accept a bond from the direct writing company in satisfaction of the total bond requirement of the contract. This is permissible until necessary reinsurance agreements are executed, even though the total bond requirement may exceed the

insurer's underwriting limitation. The contractor shall execute and submit necessary reinsurance agreements to the contracting officer within the time specified on the bid form, which may not exceed 45 calendar days after the execution of the bond. The contractor shall use Standard Form 273, Reinsurance Agreement for a Bonds Statute Performance Bond, and Standard Form 274, Reinsurance Agreement for a Bonds Statute Payment Bond, when reinsurance is furnished with the required performance or payment bonds. Standard Form 275, Reinsurance Agreement in Favor of the United States, is used when reinsurance is furnished with bonds for other purposes.

(b) For contracts performed in a foreign country, sureties not appearing on Treasury Department Circular 570 are acceptable if the contracting officer determines that it is impracticable for the contractor to use Treasury listed sureties.

(c) The Department of the Treasury issues supplements to Circular 570, notifying all Federal agencies of (1) new approved corporate surety companies and (2) the termination of the authority of any specific corporate surety to qualify as a surety on Federal bonds. Upon receipt of notification of termination of a company's authority to qualify as a surety on Federal bonds, the contracting officer shall review the outstanding contracts and take action necessary to protect the Government, including, where appropriate, securing new bonds with acceptable sureties in lieu of outstanding bonds with the named company.

(d) The Department of the Treasury Circular 570 may be obtained from the U.S. Department of the Treasury, Financial Management Service, Surety Bond Branch, 3700 East West Highway, Room 6F01, Hyattsville, MD 20782. Or via the internet at *http://www.fms.treas.gov/c570/*.

[FAC 84-53, 54 FR 48986, 11/28/89, effective 2/26/90; FAC 2001-14, 68 FR 28079, 5/22/2003, effective 6/23/2003; FAC 2005-14, 71 FR 67779, 11/22/2006, effective 11/22/2006; FAC 2005-73, 79 FR 24192, 4/29/2014, effective 5/29/2014]

28.203 Acceptability of individual sureties.

(a) An individual surety is acceptable for all types of bonds except position schedule bonds. The contracting officer shall determine the acceptability of individuals proposed as sureties, and shall ensure that the surety's pledged assets are sufficient to cover the bond obligation. (See 28.203-7 for information on excluded individual sureties.)

(b) An individual surety must execute the bond, and the unencumbered value of the assets (exclusive of all outstanding pledges for other bond obligations) pledged by the individual surety, must equal or exceed the penal amount of each bond. The individual surety shall execute the Standard Form 28 and provide a security interest in accordance with 28.203-1. One individual surety is adequate support for a bond, provided the unencumbered value of the assets pledged by that individual surety equal or exceed the amount of the bond. An offeror may submit up to three individual sureties for each bond, in which case the pledged assets, when combined, must equal or exceed the penal amount of the bond. Each individual surety must accept both joint and several liability to the extent of the penal amount of the bond.

(c) If the contracting officer determines that no individual surety in support of a bid guarantee is acceptable, the offeror utilizing the individual surety shall be rejected as nonresponsible, except as provided in 28.101-4. A finding of nonresponsibility based on unacceptability of an individual surety, need not be referred to the Small Business Administration for a competency review. (See 19.602-1(a)(2)(i) and 61 Comp. Gen. 456 (1982).)

(d) A contractor submitting an unacceptable individual surety in satisfaction of a performance or payment bond requirement may be permitted a reasonable time, as determined by the contracting officer, to substitute an acceptable surety for a surety previously determined to be unacceptable.

(e) When evaluating individual sureties, contracting officers may obtain assistance from the office identified in 28.202(d).

(f) Contracting officers shall obtain the opinion of legal counsel as to the adequacy of the documents pledging the assets prior to accepting the bid guarantee and payment and performance bonds.

(g) Evidence of possible criminal or fraudulent activities by an individual surety shall be referred to the appropriate agency official in accordance with agency procedures.

[FAC 84-53, 54 FR 48986, 11/28/89, effective 2/26/90]

28.203-1 Security interests by an individual surety.

(a) An individual surety may be accepted only if a security interest in assets acceptable under 28.203-2 is provided to the Government by the individual surety. The security interest shall be furnished with the bond.

(b) The value at which the contracting officer accepts the assets pledged must be equal to or greater than the aggregate penal amounts of the bonds required by the solicitation and may be provided by one or a combination of the following methods:

(1) An escrow account with a federally insured financial institution in the name of the contracting agency. (See 28.203-2(b)(2) with respect to Government securities in book entry form.) Acceptable securities for deposit in escrow are discussed in 28.203-2. While the offeror is responsible for establishing the escrow account, the terms and conditions must be acceptable to the contracting officer. At a minimum, the escrow account shall provide for the following:

(i) The account must provide the contracting officer the sole and unrestricted right to draw upon all or any part of the funds deposited in the account. A written demand for withdrawal shall be sent to the financial institution, after obtaining the concurrence of legal counsel, by the contracting officer with a copy to the offeror/contractor and to the surety. Within the time period specified in the demand, the financial institution would pay the Government the amount demanded up to the amount on deposit. If any dispute should arise between the Government and the offeror/contractor, the surety, or the subcontractors or suppliers with respect to the offer or contract, the financial institution would be required, unless precluded by order of a court of competent jurisdiction, to disburse monies to the Government as directed by the contracting officer.

(ii) The financial institution would be authorized to release to the individual surety all or part of the balance of the escrow account, including any accrued interest, upon receipt of written authorization from the contracting officer.

(iii) The Government would not be responsible for any cost attributable to the establishment, maintenance, administration, or any other aspect of the account.

(iv) The financial institution would not be liable or responsible for the interpretation of any provisions or terms and conditions of the solicitation or contract.

(v) The financial institution would provide periodic account statements to the contracting officer.

(vi) The terms of the escrow account could not be amended without the consent of the contracting officer.

(2) A lien on real property, subject to the restrictions in 28.203-2 and 28.203-3.

[FAC 84-53, 54 FR 48987, 11/28/89, effective 2/26/90]

28.203-2 Acceptability of assets.

(a) The Government will accept only cash, readily marketable assets, or irrevocable letters of credit from a federally insured financial institution from individual sureties to satisfy the underlying bond obligations.

(b) Acceptable assets include—

(1) Cash, or certificates of deposit, or other cash equivalents with a federally insured financial institution;

(2) United States Government securities at market value. (An escrow account is not required if an individual surety offers Government securities held in book entry form at a depository institution. In lieu thereof, the individual shall provide evidence that the depository institution has—

(i) placed a notation against the individual's book entry account indicating that the security has been pledged in favor of the respective agency;

(ii) agreed to notify the agency prior to maturity of the security; and—

(iii) agreed to hold the proceeds of the security subject to the pledge in favor of the agency until a substitution of securities is made or the security interest is formally released by the agency);

(3) Stocks and bonds actively traded on a national U.S. security exchange with certificates issued in the name of the individual surety. National security exchanges are—

(i) the New York Stock Exchange;

(ii) the American Stock Exchange;

(iii) the Boston Stock Exchange;

(iv) the Cincinnati Stock Exchange;

(v) the Midwest Stock Exchange;

(vi) the Philadelphia Stock Exchange;

(vii) the Pacific Stock Exchange; and—

(viii) the Spokane Stock Exchange.

These assets will be accepted at 90 percent of their 52-week low, as reflected at the time of submission of the bond. Stock options and stocks on the over-the-counter (OTC) market or NASDQ Exchanges will not be accepted. Assistance in evaluating the acceptability of securities may be obtained from the Securities and Exchange Commission, Division of Enforcement, 450 Fifth Street NW, Washington, DC 20549.

(4) Real property owned in fee simple by the surety without any form of concurrent ownership, except as provided in paragraph (c)(3)(iii) of this subsection, and located in the United States or its outlying areas. These assets will be accepted at 100 percent of the most current tax assessment value (exclusive of encumbrances) or 75 percent of the properties' unencumbered market value provided a current appraisal is furnished (see 28.203-3).

(5) Irrevocable letters of credit (ILC) issued by a federally insured financial institution in the name of the contracting agency and which identify the agency and solicitation or contract number for which the ILC is provided.

(c) Unacceptable assets include but are not limited to—

(1) Notes or accounts receivable;

(2) Foreign securities;

(3) Real property as follows:

(i) Real property located outside the United States and its outlying areas.

(ii) Real property which is a principal residence of the surety.

(iii) Real property owned concurrently regardless of the form of co-tenancy (including joint tenancy, tenancy by the entirety, and tenancy in common) except where all cotenants agree to act jointly.

(iv) Life estates, leasehold estates, or future interests in real property.

(4) Personal property other than that listed in paragraph (b) of this subsection (*e.g.*, jewelry, furs, antiques);

(5) Stocks and bonds of the individual surety in a controlled, affiliated, or closely held concern of the offeror/contractor;

(6) Corporate assets (*e.g.*, plant and equipment);

(7) Speculative assets (*e.g.*, mineral rights);

(8) Letters of credit, except as provided in 28.203-2(b)(5).

[FAC 84-53, 54 FR 48986, 11/28/89, effective 2/26/90; FAC 2001-14, 68 FR 28079, 5/22/2003, effective 6/23/2003]

28.203-3 Acceptance of real property.

(a) Whenever a bond with a security interest in real property is submitted, the individual surety shall provide—

(1) A mortgagee title insurance policy, in an insurance amount equal to the amount of the lien, or other evidence of title that is consistent with the requirements of Section 2 of the United States Department of Justice Title Standards at *https://www.justice.gov/enrd/page/file/922431/download*. This title evidence must show fee simple title vested in the surety along with any concurrent owners; whether any real estate taxes are due and payable; and any recorded encumbrances against the property, including the

lien filed in favor of the Government under paragraph (d) of this subsection. Agency contracting officers should request the assistance of their designated agency legal counsel in determining if the title evidence is consistent with the Department of Justice standards;

(2) Evidence of the amount due under any encumbrance shown in the evidence of title;

(3) A copy of the current real estate tax assessment of the property or a current appraisal dated no earlier than 6 months prior to the date of the bond, prepared by a professional appraiser who certifies that the appraisal has been conducted in accordance with the generally accepted appraisal standards as reflected in the Uniform Standards of Professional Appraisal Practice as promulgated by the Appraisal Foundation, 1029 Vermont Avenue, NW, Washington, DC 20005.

(b) Failure to provide evidence that the lien has been properly recorded will render the offeror nonresponsible.

(c) The individual surety is liable for the payment of all administrative costs of the Government, including legal fees, associated with the liquidation of pledged real estate.

(d) The following format, or any document substantially the same, shall be signed by all owners of the property and used by the surety and recorded in the local recorder's office when a surety pledges real estate on Standard Form 28, Affidavit of Individual Surety.

Lien on Real Estate

I/we agree that this instrument constitutes a lien in the amount of $___ on the property described in this lien. The rights of the United States Government shall take precedence over any subsequent lien or encumbrance until the lien is formally released by a duly authorized representative of the United States. I/we hereby grant the United States the power of sale of subject property, including the right to satisfy its reasonable administrative costs, including legal fees associated with any sale of subject property, in the event of contractor default if I/we otherwise fail to satisfy the underlying ( ) bid guarantee, ( ) performance bond, ( ) or payment bond obligations as an individual surety on solicitation/contract number ___. The lien is upon the real estate now owned by me/us described as follows: (legal description, street address and other identifying description)

IN WITNESS HEREOF, I/we have hereunto affixed my/our hand(s) and seal(s) this ___ DAY OF ___ 20___.

WITNESS:

(SEAL)

I, ___, a Notary Public in and for the (CITY) ___, (STATE) ___, do hereby certify that ___, a party or parties to a certain Agreement bearing the date ___ day of ___ 20___, and hereunto annexed, personally appeared before me, the said ___ being personally known to me as the person(s) who executed said lien, and acknowledged the same to be his/her/their act and deed. GIVEN under my hand and seal this ___ day of ___ 20___.

NOTARY PUBLIC, STATE

My Commission expires:

[FAC 84-53, 54 FR 48987, 11/28/89, effective 2/26/90; FAC 2005-01, 70 FR 11763, 3/9/2005, effective 3/9/2005; FAC 2005-36, 74 FR 40466, 8/11/2009, effective 9/10/2009; FAC 2005-55, 77 FR 204, 1/3/2012, effective 1/3/2012; FAC 2005-100, 83 FR 42571, 8/22/2018, effective 8/22/2018]

28.203-4 Substitution of assets.

An individual surety may request the Government to accept a substitute asset for that currently pledged by submitting a written request to the responsible contracting officer. The contracting officer may agree to the substitution of assets upon determining, after consultation with legal counsel, that the substitute assets to be pledged are adequate to protect the outstanding bond or guarantee obligations. If acceptable, the substitute assets shall be pledged as provided for in Subpart 28.2.

[FAC 84-53, 54 FR 48988, 11/28/89, effective 2/26/90]

28.203-5 Release of lien.

(a) After consultation with legal counsel, the contracting officer shall release the security interest on the individual surety's assets using the Optional Form 90, Release of Lien on Real Property, or Optional Form 91, Release of Personal Property from Escrow, or a similar release as soon as possible consistent with the conditions in subparagraphs (a)(1) and (2) of this subsection. A surety's assets pledged in support of a payment bond may be released to a subcontractor or supplier upon Government receipt of a Federal district court judgment, or a sworn statement by the subcontractor or supplier that the claim is correct along with a notarized authorization of the release by the surety stating that it approves of such release.

(1) *Contracts subject to the Bonds statute.* The security interest shall be maintained for the later of—

(i) 1 year following final payment;

(ii) Until completion of any warranty period (applicable only to performance bonds); or

(iii) Pending resolution of all claims filed against the payment bond during the 1-year period following final payment.

(2) *Contracts subject to alternative payment protection (28.102-1(b)(1)).* The security interest shall be maintained for the full contract performance period plus one year.

(3) *Other contracts not subject to the Bonds statute.* The security interest shall be maintained for 90 days following final payment or until completion of any warranty period (applicable only to performance bonds), whichever is later.

(b) Upon written request, the contracting officer may release the security interest on the individual surety's assets in support of a bid guarantee based upon evidence that the offer supported by the individual surety will not result in contract award.

(c) Upon written request by the individual surety, the contracting officer may release a portion of the security interest on the individual surety's assets based upon substantial performance of the contractor's obligations under its performance bond. Release of the security interest in support of a payment bond must comply with the subparagraphs (a)(1) through (3) of this subsection. In making this determination, the contracting officer will give consideration as to whether the unreleased portion of the lien is sufficient to cover the remaining contract obligations, including payments to subcontractors and other potential liabilities. The individual surety shall, as a condition of the partial release, furnish an affidavit agreeing that the release of such assets does not relieve the individual surety of its obligations under the bond(s).

[FAC 84-53, 54 FR 48988, 11/28/89, effective 2/26/90; FAC 90-39, 61 FR 31612, 6/20/96, effective 6/20/96; FAC 2005-73, 79 FR 24192, 4/29/2014, effective 5/29/2014]

28.203-6 Contract clause.

Insert the clause at 52.228-11 in solicitations and contracts which require the submission of bid guarantees, performance, or payment bonds.

[FAC 84-53, 54 FR 48988, 11/28/89, effective 2/26/90]

28.203-7 Exclusion of individual sureties.

(a) An individual may be excluded from acting as a surety on bonds submitted by offerors on procurement by the executive branch of the Federal Government, by the acquiring agency's head or designee utilizing the procedures in Subpart 9.4. The exclusion shall be for the purpose of protecting the Government.

(b) An individual may be excluded for any of the following causes:

(1) Failure to fulfill the obligations under any bond.

(2) Failure to disclose all bond obligations.

(3) Misrepresentation of the value of available assets or outstanding liabilities.

(4) Any false or misleading statement, signature or representation on a bond or affidavit of individual suretyship.

(5) Any other cause affecting responsibility as a surety of such serious and compelling nature as may be determined to warrant exclusion.

(c) An individual surety excluded pursuant to this subsection shall be entered as an exclusion in the System for Award Management (see 9.404).

(d) Contracting officers shall not accept the bonds of individual sureties whose names appear in an active exclusion record in the System for Award Management (see 9.404), unless the acquiring agency's head or a designee states in writing the compelling reasons justifying acceptance.

(e) An exclusion of an individual surety under this subsection will also preclude such party from acting as a contractor in accordance with Subpart 9.4.

[FAC 90-28, 60 FR 33064, 6/26/95, effective 8/25/95; FAC 2001-26, 69 FR 76347, 12/20/2004, effective 1/19/2005; FAC 2005-67, 78 FR 37676, 6/21/2013, effective 7/22/2013; FAC 2005-101, 83 FR 48691, 9/26/2018, effective 10/26/2018]

28.204 Alternatives in lieu of corporate or individual sureties.

(a) Any person required to furnish a bond to the Government may furnish any of the types of security listed in 28.204-1 through 28.204-3 instead of a corporate or individual surety for the bond. When any of those types of security are deposited, a statement shall be incorporated in the bond form pledging the security in lieu of execution of the bond form by corporate or individual sureties. The contractor shall execute the bond forms as the principal. Agencies shall establish safeguards to protect against loss of the security and shall return the security or its equivalent to the contractor when the bond obligation has ceased.

(b) Upon written request by any contractor securing a performance or payment bond by any of the types of security listed in 28.204-1 through 28.204-3, the contracting officer may release a portion of the security only when the conditions allowing the partial release of lien in 28.203-5(c) are met. The contractor shall, as a condition of the partial release, furnish an affidavit agreeing that the release of such security does not relieve the contractor of its obligations under the bond(s).

(c) The contractor may satisfy a requirement for bond security by furnishing a combination of the types of security listed in 28.204-1 through 28.204-3 or a combination of bonds supported by these types of security and additional surety bonds under 28.202 or 28.203. During the period for which a bond supported by security is required, the contractor may substitute one type of security listed in 28.204-1 through 28.204-3 for another, or may substitute, in whole or combination, additional surety bonds under 28.202 or 28.203.

[FAC 90-39, 61 FR 31612, 6/20/96, effective 6/20/96; FAC 97-1, 62 FR 44802, 8/22/97, effective 10/21/97]

28.204-1 United States bonds or notes.

Any person required to furnish a bond to the Government has the option, instead of furnishing a surety or sureties on the bond, of depositing certain United States bonds or notes in an amount equal at their par value to the penal sum of the bond (the Act of February 24, 1919 (31 U.S.C. 9303) and Treasury Department Circular No. 154 dated July 1, 1978 (31 CFR Part 225)). In addition, a duly executed power of attorney and agreement authorizing the collection or sale of such United States bonds or notes in the event of default of the principal on the bond shall accompany the deposited bonds or notes. The contracting officer may—

(a) Turn securities over to the finance or other authorized agency official; or

(b) Deposit them with the Treasurer of the United States, a Federal Reserve Bank (or branch with requisite facilities), or other depository designated for that purpose by the Secretary of the Treasury, under procedures prescribed by the agency concerned and Treasury Department Circular No. 154 (exception: The contracting officer shall deposit all bonds and notes received in the District of Columbia with the Treasurer of the United States).

[FAC 84-53, 54 FR 48986, 11/28/89, effective 2/26/90]

28.204-2 Certified or cashier's checks, bank drafts, money orders, or currency.

Any person required to furnish a bond has an option to furnish a certified or cashier's check, bank draft, Post Office money order, or currency, in an amount equal to the penal sum of the bond, instead of furnishing surety or sureties on the bonds. Those furnishing checks, drafts, or money orders shall draw them to the order of the appropriate Federal agency.

[FAC 84-53, 54 FR 48986, 11/28/89, effective 2/26/90]

28.204-3 Irrevocable letter of credit.

(a) Any person required to furnish a bond has the option to furnish a bond secured by an irrevocable letter of credit (ILC) in an amount equal to the penal sum required to be secured (see 28.204). A separate ILC is required for each bond.

(b) The ILC shall be irrevocable, require presentation of no document other than a written demand and the ILC (and letter of confirmation, if any), expire only as provided in paragraph (f) of this subsection, and be issued/confirmed by an acceptable federally insured financial institution as provided in paragraph (g) of this subsection.

(c) To draw on the ILC, the contracting officer shall use the sight draft set forth in the clause at 52.228-14, and present it with the ILC (including letter of confirmation, if any) to the issuing financial institution or the confirming financial institution (if any).

(d) If the contractor does not furnish an acceptable replacement ILC, or other acceptable substitute, at least 30 days before an ILC's scheduled expiration, the contracting officer shall immediately draw on the ILC.

(e) If, after the period of performance of a contract where ILCs are used to support payment bonds, there are outstanding claims against the payment bond, the contracting officer shall draw on the ILC prior to the expiration date of the ILC to cover these claims.

(f) The period for which financial security is required shall be as follows:

(1) If used as a bid guarantee, the ILC should expire no earlier than 60 days after the close of the bid acceptance period.

(2) If used as an alternative to corporate or individual sureties as security for a performance or payment bond, the offeror/contractor may submit an ILC with an initial expiration date estimated to cover the entire period for which financial security is required or an ILC with an initial expiration date that is a minimum period of one year from the date of issuance. The ILC shall provide that, unless the issuer provides the beneficiary written notice of non-renewal at least 60 days in advance of the current expiration date, the ILC is automatically extended without amendment for one year from the expiration date, or any future expiration date, until the period of required coverage is completed and the contracting officer provides the financial institution with a written statement waiving the right to payment. The period of required coverage shall be:

(i) For contracts subject to the Bonds statute, the later of—

(A) One year following the expected date of final payment;

(B) For performance bonds only, until completion of any warranty period; or

(C) For payment bonds only, until resolution of all claims filed against the payment bond during the one-year period following final payment.

(ii) For contracts not subject to the Bonds statute, the later of—

(A) 90 days following final payment; or

(B) For performance bonds only, until completion of any warranty period.

(g) Only federally insured financial institutions rated investment grade shall issue or confirm the ILC. Unless the financial institution issuing the ILC had letter of credit business of at least $25 million in the past year, ILCs over $5 million must be confirmed by another acceptable financial institution that had letter of credit business of at least $25 million in the past year.

(1) The offeror/contractor is required by paragraph (d) of the clause at 52.228-14, Ir-

revocable Letter of Credit, to provide the contracting officer a credit rating from a recognized commercial rating service that indicates the financial institution has the required rating(s) as of the date of issuance of the ILC.

(2) To support the credit rating of the financial institution(s) issuing or confirming the ILC, the contracting officer shall verify the following information:

(i) *Federal insurance:* Each financial institution is federally insured. Verification of federal insurance is available through the Federal Deposit Insurance Corporation (FDIC) institution directory at the Web site *http://www2.fdic.gov/idasp/index.asp*.

(ii) *Current credit rating.* The current credit rating for each financial institution is investment grade and that the credit rating is from a Nationally Recognized Statistical Rating Organization (NRSRO). NRSROs can be located at the Web site *http://www.sec.gov/answers/nrsro.htm* maintained by the SEC.

(3) The rating services listed in the Web site *http://www.sec.gov/answers/nrsro.htm* use different rating scales (*e.g.*, AAA, AA, A, BBB, BB, B, CCC, CC, C, and D; or Aaa, Aa, A, Baa, Ba, B, Caa, Ca, and C) to provide evaluations of institutional credit risk; however, all such systems specify the range of investment grade ratings (*e.g.*, BBB-AAA or Baa-Aaa in the examples in this section) and permit evaluation of the relative risk associated with a specific institution. If the contracting officer learns that a financial institution's rating has dropped below investment grade level, the contracting officer shall give the contractor 30 days to substitute an acceptable ILC or shall draw on the ILC using the sight draft in paragraph (g) of the clause at 52.228-14.

(h) A copy of the Uniform Customs and Practice (UCP) for Documentary Credits, 2007 Edition, International Chamber of Commerce Publication No. 600, is available from: ICC Books USA, 1212 Avenue of the Americas, 21st Floor, New York, NY 10036; Phone: 212-703-5078; Fax: 212-391-6568; *E-Mail: iccbooks@uscib.org;* Via the Internet at: *http://www.uscib.org/ucp-600-ud-4465/*.

[FAC 90-39, 61 FR 31612, 6/20/96, effective 6/20/96; FAC 97-1, 62 FR 44802, 8/22/97, effective 10/21/97; FAC 2005-73, 79 FR 24192, 4/29/2014, effective 5/29/2014; FAC 2005-77, 79 FR 61743, 10/14/2014, effective 11/13/2014; FAC 2005-100, 83 FR 42571, 8/22/2018, effective 8/22/2018]

28.204-4 Contract clause.

Insert the clause at 52.228-14, Irrevocable Letter of Credit, in solicitations and contracts for services, supplies, or construction, when a bid guarantee, or performance bonds, or performance and payment bonds are required.

[FAC 90-39, 61 FR 31612, 6/20/96, effective 6/20/96]

SUBPART 28.3—INSURANCE

28.301 Policy.

Contractors shall carry insurance under the following circumstances:

(a) (1) The Government requires any contractor subject to Cost Accounting Standard (CAS) 416 (48 CFR 9004.416 (Appendix B, FAR looseleaf edition)) to obtain insurance, by purchase or self-coverage, for the perils to which the contractor is exposed, except when:

(i) The Government, by providing in the contract in accordance with law, agrees to indemnify the contractor under specified circumstances; or

(ii) The contract specifically relieves the contractor of liability for loss of or damage to Government property.

(2) The Government reserves the right to disapprove the purchase of any insurance coverage not in the Government's interest.

(3) Allowability of the insurance program's cost shall be determined in accordance with the criteria in 31.205-19.

(b) Contractors, whether or not their contracts are subject to CAS 416, are required by law and this regulation to provide insurance for certain types of perils (*e.g.*, workers' compensation). Insurance is mandatory also when commingling of property, type of operation, circumstances of ownership, or condition of the contract make it necessary for the protection of the Government. The minimum amounts of insurance required by this regulation (see 28.307-2) may be reduced when a contract is to be performed outside the United States and its outlying areas. When more than one agency is involved, the agency responsible for review and approval of a contractor's insurance program shall coordinate with other interested agencies before acting on significant insurance matters.

(c) Contractors awarded nonpersonal services contracts for health care services are required to maintain medical liability insurance and indemnify the Government for liability producing acts or omissions by the contractor, its employees and agents (see 37.400).

[FAC 84-42, 54 FR 5056, 1/31/89, effective 3/2/89; FAC 90-23, 59 FR 67010, 12/28/94, effective 2/27/95; corrected 60 FR 14377, 3/17/95; FAC 2001-14, 68 FR 28079, 5/22/2003, effective 6/23/2003]

28.302 Notice of cancellation or change.

When the Government requires the contractor to provide insurance coverage, the policies shall contain an endorsement that any cancellation or material change in the coverage adversely affecting the Government's interest shall not be effective unless the insurer or the contractor gives written notice of cancellation or change as required by the contracting officer. When the coverage is provided by self-insurance, the contractor shall not change or decrease the coverage without the administrative contracting officer's prior approval (see 28.308(c)).

28.303 Insurance against loss of or damage to Government property.

When the Government requires or approves insurance to cover loss of or damage to Government property (see 45.104, Responsibility and liability for Government property), it may be provided by specific insurance policies or by inclusion of the risks in the contractor's existing policies. The policies shall disclose the Government's interest in the property.

[FAC 2005-17, 72 FR 27364, 5/15/2007, effective 6/14/2007]

28.304 Risk-pooling arrangements.

Agencies may establish risk-pooling arrangements. These arrangements are designed to use the services of the insurance industry for safety engineering and the handling of claims at minimum cost to the Government. The agency responsible shall appoint a single manager or point of contact for each arrangement.

28.305 Overseas workers' compensation and war-hazard insurance.

(a) *Public-work contract,* as used in this subpart, means any contract for a fixed improvement or for any other project, fixed or not, for the public use of the United States or its allies, involving construction, alteration, removal, or repair, including projects or operations under service contracts and projects in connection with the national defense or with war activities, dredging, harbor improvements, dams, roadways, and housing, as well as preparatory and ancillary work in connection therewith at the site or on the project.

(b) The Defense Base Act (42 U.S.C. 1651 *et seq.*) extends the Longshoremen's and Harbor Workers' Compensation Act (33 U.S.C. 901) to various classes of employees working outside the United States, including those engaged in performing—

(1) Public-work contracts; or

(2) Contracts approved or financed under the Foreign Assistance Act of 1961 (Pub. L. 87-195) other than—

(i) Contracts approved or financed by the Development Loan Fund (unless the Secretary of Labor, acting upon the recommendation of a department or agency, determines that such contracts should be covered); or

(ii) Contracts exclusively for materials or supplies.

(c) When the Defense Base Act applies (see 42 U.S.C. 1651 *et seq.*) to these employees, the benefits of the Longshoremen's and Harbor Workers' Compensation Act are extended through operation of the War Hazards Compensation Act (42 U.S.C. 1701 *et seq.*) to protect the employees against the risk of war hazards (injury, death, capture, or detention). When, by means of an insurance policy or a self-insurance program, the contractor provides the workers' compensation coverage required by the Defense Base Act, the contractor's employees automatically receive war-hazard risk protection.

(d) When the agency head recommends a waiver to the Secretary of Labor, the Secretary may waive the applicability of the Defense Base Act to any contract, subcontract, work location, or classification of employees.

(e) If the Defense Base Act is waived for some or all of the contractor's employees, the benefits of the War Hazards Compensation Act are automatically waived with respect to those employees for whom the Defense Base Act is waived. For those employees, the contractor shall provide workers' compensation coverage against the risk of work injury or death and assume liability toward the employees and their beneficiaries for war-hazard injury, death, capture, or detention. The contract shall provide either that the costs of this liability or the reasonable costs of insurance against this liability shall be allowed as a cost under the contract.

28.306 Insurance under fixed-price contracts.

(a) *General.* Although the Government is not ordinarily concerned with the contractor's insurance coverage if the contract is a fixed-price contract, in special circumstances agencies may specify insurance requirements under fixed-price contracts. Examples of such circumstances include the following:

(1) The contractor is, or has a separate operation, engaged principally in Government work.

(2) Government property is involved.

(3) The work is to be performed on a Government installation.

(4) The Government elects to assume risks for which the contractor ordinarily obtains commercial insurance.

(b) *Work on a Government installation.* (1) When the clause at 52.228-5, Insurance—Work on a Government Installation, is required to be included in a fixed-price contract by 28.310, the coverage specified in 28.307 is the minimum insurance required and shall be included in the contract Schedule or elsewhere in the contract. The contracting officer may require additional coverage and higher limits.

(2) When the clause at 52.228-5, Insurance—Work on a Government Installation, is not required by 28.310 but is included because the contracting officer considers it to be in the Government's interest to do so, any of the types of insurance specified in 28.307 may be omitted or the limits may be lowered, if appropriate.

28.307 Insurance under cost-reimbursement contracts.

Cost-reimbursement contracts (and subcontracts, if the terms of the prime contract are extended to the subcontract) ordinarily require the types of insurance listed in 28.307-2, with the minimum amounts of liability indicated. (See 28.308 for self-insurance.)

28.307-1 Group insurance plans.

(a) *Prior approval requirement.* Under cost-reimbursement contracts, before buying insurance under a group insurance plan, the contractor must submit the plan for approval, in accordance with agency regulations. Any change in benefits provided under an approved plan that can reasonably be expected to increase significantly the cost to the Government requires similar approval.

(b) *Premium refunds or credits.* The plan shall provide for the Government to share in any premium refunds or credits paid or otherwise allowed to the contractor. In determining the extent of the Government's share in any premium refunds or credits, any special reserves and other refunds to which the contractor may be entitled in the future shall be taken into account.

28.307-2 Liability.

(a) *Workers' compensation and employer's liability.* Contractors are required to comply with applicable Federal and State workers' compensation and occupational disease statutes. If occupational diseases are not compensable under those statutes, they shall be covered under the employer's liability section of the insurance policy, except when contract operations are so commingled with a contractor's commercial operations that it would not be practical to require this coverage. Employer's liability coverage of at least $100,000 shall be required, except in States with exclusive or monopolistic funds that do not permit workers' compensation to be written by private carriers. (See 28.305(c) for treatment of contracts subject to the Defense Base Act.)

(b) *General liability.* (1) The contracting officer shall require bodily injury liability insurance coverage written on the comprehensive form of policy of at least $500,000 per occurrence.

(2) Property damage liability insurance shall be required only in special circumstances as determined by the agency.

(c) *Automobile liability.* The contracting officer shall require automobile liability insurance written on the comprehensive form of policy. The policy shall provide for bodily injury and property damage liability covering the operation of all automobiles used in connection with performing the contract. Policies covering automobiles operated in the United States shall provide coverage of at least $200,000 per person and $500,000 per occurrence for bodily injury and $20,000 per occurrence for property damage. The amount of liability coverage on other policies shall be commensurate with any legal requirements of the locality and sufficient to meet normal and customary claims.

(d) *Aircraft public and passenger liability.* When aircraft are used in connection with performing the contract, the contracting officer shall require aircraft public and passenger liability insurance. Coverage shall be at least $200,000 per person and $500,000 per occurrence for bodily injury, other than passenger liability, and $200,000 per occurrence for property damage. Coverage for passenger liability bodily injury shall be at least $200,000 multiplied by the number of seats or passengers, whichever is greater.

(e) *Vessel liability.* When contract performance involves use of vessels, the contracting officer shall require, as determined by the agency, vessel collision liability and protection and indemnity liability insurance.

28.308 Self-insurance.

(a) When it is anticipated that 50 percent or more of the self-insurance costs to be incurred at a segment of a contractor's business will be allocable to negotiated Government contracts, and the self-insurance costs at the segment for the contractor's fiscal year are expected to be $200,000 or more, the contractor shall submit, in writing, information on its proposed self-insurance program to the administrative contracting officer and obtain that official's approval of the program. The submission shall be by segment or segments of the contractor's business to which the program applies and shall include—

(1) A complete description of the program, including any resolution of the board of directors authorizing and adopting coverage, including types of risks, limits of coverage, assignments of safety and loss control, and legal service responsibilities;

(2) If available, the corporate insurance manual and organization chart detailing fiscal responsibilities for insurance;

(3) The terms regarding insurance coverage for any Government property;

(4) The contractor's latest financial statements;

(5) Any self-insurance feasibility studies or insurance market surveys reporting comparative alternatives;

(6) Loss history, premiums history, and industry ratios;

(7) A formula for establishing reserves, including percentage variations between losses paid and losses reserved;

(8) Claims administration policy, practices, and procedures;

(9) The method of calculating the projected average loss; and

(10) A disclosure of all captive insurance company and reinsurance agreements, including methods of computing cost.

(b) Programs of self-insurance covering a contractor's insurable risks, including the deductible portion of purchased insurance, may be approved when examination of a program indicates that its application is in the Government's interest. Agencies shall not approve a program of self-insurance for workers' compensation in a jurisdiction where workers' compensation does not completely cover the employer's liability to employees, unless the contractor—

(1) Maintains an approved program of self-insurance for any employer's liability not so covered; or

(2) Shows that the combined cost to the Government of self-insurance for workers' compensation and commercial insurance for employer's liability will not exceed the cost of covering both kinds of risk by commercial insurance.

(c) Once the administrative contracting officer has approved a program, the contractor must submit to that official for approval any major proposed changes to the program. Any program approval may be withdrawn if a contracting officer finds that either—

(1) Any part of a program does not comply with the requirements of this subpart and/or the criteria at 31.205-19; or

(2) Conditions or situations existing at the time of approval that were a basis for original approval of the program have changed to the extent that a program change is necessary.

(d) To qualify for a self-insurance program, a contractor must demonstrate ability to sustain the potential losses involved. In making the determination, the contracting officer shall consider the following factors:

(1) The soundness of the contractor's financial condition, including available lines of credit.

(2) The geographic dispersion of assets, so that the potential of a single loss depleting all the assets is unlikely.

(3) The history of previous losses, including frequency of occurrence and the financial impact of each loss.

(4) The type and magnitude of risk, such as minor coverage for the deductible portion of purchased insurance or major coverage for hazardous risks.

(5) The contractor's compliance with Federal and State laws and regulations.

(e) Agencies shall not approve a program of self-insurance for catastrophic risks (*e.g.*, see 50.104-3, Special procedures for unusually hazardous or nuclear risks). Should performance of Government contracts create the risk of catastrophic losses, the Government may, to the extent authorized by law, agree to indemnify the contractor or recognize an appropriate share of premiums for purchased insurance, or both.

(f) Self-insurance programs to protect a contractor against the costs of correcting its own defects in materials or workmanship shall not be approved. For these purposes, normal rework estimates and warranty costs will not be considered self-insurance.

[FAC 84-56, 55 FR 3883, 2/5/90, effective 3/7/90; FAC 97-22, 66 FR 2116, 1/10/2001, effective 3/12/2001; Delay of effective date, 66 FR 14259, 3/9/2001, effective 5/11/2001; FAC 2005-21, 72 FR 63027, 11/7/2007, effective 11/7/2007; FAC 2005-30, 74 FR 2733, 1/15/2009, effective 2/17/2009]

28.309 Contract clauses for workers' compensation insurance.

(a) The contracting officer shall insert the clause at 52.228-3, Workers' Compensation Insurance (Defense Base Act), in solicitations and contracts when the Defense Base Act applies (see 28.305) and—

(1) The contract will be a public-work contract performed outside the United States; or

(2) The contract will be approved or financed under the Foreign Assistance Act of 1961 (Pub. L. 87-195) and is not excluded by 28.305(b)(2).

(b) The contracting officer shall insert the clause at 52.228-4, Workers' Compensation and War-Hazard Insurance Overseas, in solicitations and contracts when the contract will be a public-work contract performed outside the United States and the Secretary of Labor waives the applicability of the Defense Base Act (see 28.305(d)).

28.310 Contract clause for work on a Government installation.

(a) Insert the clause at 52.228-5, Insurance—Work on a Government Installation, in solicitations and contracts if a fixed-price contract is contemplated, the contract amount is expected to exceed the simplified acquisition threshold, and the contract will require work on a Government installation, unless—

(1) Only a small amount of work is required on the Government installation (*e.g.*, a few brief visits per month); or

(2) All work on the Government installation will be performed outside the United States and its outlying areas.

(b) The contracting officer may insert the clause at 52.228-5 in solicitations and contracts described in paragraphs (a)(1) and (2) of this section if it is in the Government's interest to do so.

[FAC 90-29, 60 FR 34732, 7/3/95, effective 7/3/95; FAC 90-40, 61 FR 39186, 7/26/96, effective 8/26/96; FAC 2001-14, 68 FR 28079, 5/22/2003, effective 6/23/2003]

28.311 Solicitation provision and contract clause on liability insurance under cost-reimbursement contracts. (No Text)

28.311-1 Contract clause.

In accordance with agency acquisition regulations, the contracting officer shall insert the clause at 52.228-7, Insurance—Liability to Third Persons, in solicitations and contracts, other than those for construction contracts and those for architect-engineer services, when a cost-reimbursement contract is contemplated.

[FAC 90-3, 55 FR 52793, 12/21/90, effective 1/22/91; Redesignated from 28.311-2, FAC 90-37, 61 FR 2626, 1/26/96, effective 3/26/96]

28.311-2 Agency solicitation provisions and contract clauses.

Agencies may prescribe their own solicitation provisions and contract clauses to implement the basic policies contained in this Subpart 28.3.

[FAC 90-3, 55 FR 52793, 12/21/90, effective 1/22/91; Redesignated from 28.311-3, FAC 90-37, 61 FR 2626, 1/26/96, effective 3/26/96]

28.312 Contract clause for insurance of leased motor vehicles.

The contracting officer shall insert the clause at 52.228-8, Liability and Insurance—Leased Motor Vehicles, in solicitations and contracts for the leasing of motor vehicles (see Subpart 8.11).

28.313 Contract clauses for insurance of transportation or transportation-related services.

(a) The contracting officer shall insert the clause at 52.228-9, Cargo Insurance, in solicitations and contracts for transportation or for transportation-related services, except when freight is shipped under rates subject to released or declared value.

(b) The contracting officer shall insert a clause substantially the same as that at 52.228-10, Vehicular and General Public Liability Insurance, in solicitations and contracts for transportation or for transportation-related services when the contracting officer determines that vehicular liability or general public liability insurance required by law is not sufficient.

PART 29—TAXES

Table of Contents

Scope of part 29.000

Subpart 29.1—General

Resolving tax problems 29.101

Subpart 29.2—Federal Excise Taxes

General 29.201
General exemptions 29.202
Other federal tax exemptions 29.203

Subpart 29.3—State and Local Taxes

Scope of subpart 29.300
[Reserved] 29.301
Application of State and local taxes to the Government 29.302
Application of State and local taxes to Government contractors and subcontractors 29.303
Matters requiring special consideration 29.304
State and local tax exemptions 29.305

Subpart 29.4—Contract Clauses

Domestic contracts 29.401
Indefinite-delivery contracts for leased equipment 29.401-1
Construction contracts performed in North Carolina 29.401-2
Federal, State, and local taxes 29.401-3
New Mexico gross receipts and compensating tax 29.401-4
Foreign contracts 29.402
Foreign fixed-price contracts 29.402-1
Foreign cost-reimbursement contracts 29.402-2

PART 29—TAXES

29.000 Scope of part.

This part prescribes policies and procedures for (a) using tax clauses in contracts (including foreign contracts), (b) asserting immunity or exemption from taxes, and (c) obtaining tax refunds. It explains Federal, State, and local taxes on certain supplies and services acquired by executive agencies and the applicability of such taxes to the Federal Government. It is for the general information of Government personnel and does not present the full scope of the tax laws and regulations.

SUBPART 29.1—GENERAL

29.101 Resolving tax problems.

(a) Contract tax problems are essentially legal in nature and vary widely. Specific tax questions must be resolved by reference to the applicable contract terms and to the pertinent tax laws and regulations. Therefore, when tax questions arise, contracting officers should request assistance from the agency-designated legal counsel.

(b) To keep treatment within an agency consistent, contracting officers or other authorized personnel shall consult the agency-designated counsel before negotiating with any taxing authority for the purpose of—

(1) Determining whether or not a tax is valid or applicable; or

(2) Obtaining exemption from, or refund of, a tax.

(c) When the constitutional immunity of the Government from State or local taxation may reasonably be at issue, contractors should be discouraged from negotiating independently with taxing authorities if the contract involved is either—

(1) A cost-reimbursement contract; or

(2) A fixed-price contract containing a tax escalation clause.

(d) Before purchasing goods or services from a foreign source, the contracting officer should consult the agency-designated counsel—

(1) For information on foreign tax treaties and agreements in force and on the implementation of any foreign-tax-relief programs; and—

(2) To resolve any other tax questions affecting the prospective contract.

SUBPART 29.2—FEDERAL EXCISE TAXES

29.201 General.

(a) Federal excise taxes are levied on the sale or use of particular supplies or services. Subtitle D of the Internal Revenue Code of 1954, Miscellaneous Excise Taxes, 26 U.S.C. 4041 *et seq.*, and its implementing regulations, 26 CFR 40 through 299, cover miscellaneous federal excise tax requirements. Questions arising in this area should be directed to the agency-designated counsel. The most common excise taxes are—

(1) Manufacturers' excise taxes imposed on certain motor-vehicle articles, tires and inner tubes, gasoline, lubricating oils, coal, fishing equipment, firearms, shells, and cartridges sold by manufacturers, producers, or importers; and

(2) Special-fuels excise taxes imposed at the retail level on diesel fuel and special motor fuels.

(b) Sometimes the law exempts the Federal Government from these taxes. Contracting officers should solicit prices on a tax-exclusive basis when it is known that the Government is exempt from these taxes, and on a tax-inclusive basis when no exemption exists.

(c) Executive agencies shall take maximum advantage of available Federal excise tax exemptions.

[FAC 90-3, 55 FR 52793, 12/21/90, effective 1/22/91]

29.202 General exemptions.

No Federal manufacturers' or special-fuels excise taxes are imposed in many contracting situations as, for example, when the supplies are for any of the following:

(a) The exclusive use of any State or political subdivision, including the District of Columbia (26 U.S.C. 4041 and 4221).

(b) Shipment for export to a foreign country or an outlying area of the United States. Shipment must occur within 6 months of the time title passes to the Government. When the exemption is claimed, the words "for export" must appear on the contract or purchase document, and the contracting officer must furnish the seller proof of export (see 26 CFR 48.4221-3).

(c) Further manufacture, or resale for further manufacture (this exemption does not include tires and inner tubes) (26 CFR 48.4221-2).

(d) Use as fuel supplies, ships or sea stores, or legitimate equipment on vessels of war, including (1) aircraft owned by the United States and constituting a part of the armed forces and (2) guided missiles and pilotless aircraft owned or chartered by the United States. When this exemption is to be claimed, the purchase should be made on a tax-exclusive basis. The contracting officer shall furnish the seller an exemption certificate for Supplies for Vessels of War (an example is given in 26 CFR 48.4221-4(d)(2); the IRS will accept one certificate covering all orders under a single contract for a specified period of up to 12 calendar quarters) (26 U.S.C. 4041 and 4221).

(e) A nonprofit educational organization (26 U.S.C. 4041 and 4221).

(f) Emergency vehicles (26 U.S.C. 4053 and 4064(b)(1)(c)).

[FAC 84-32, 53 FR 662, 1/11/88, effective 1/29/88; FAC 2001-14, 68 FR 28079, 5/22/2003, effective 6/23/2003]

29.203 Other Federal tax exemptions.

(a) Pursuant to 26 U.S.C. 4293, the Secretary of the Treasury has exempted the United States from the communications excise tax imposed in 26 U.S.C. 4251, when the supplies and services are for the exclusive use of the United States. (Secretarial Authorization, June 20, 1947, Internal Revenue Cumulative Bulletin, 1947-1, 205.)

(b) Pursuant to 26 U.S.C. 4483(b), the Secretary of the Treasury has exempted the United States from the federal highway vehicle users tax imposed in 26 U.S.C. 4481. The exemption applies whether the vehicle is owned or leased by the United States. (Secretarial Authorization, Internal Revenue Cumulative Bulletin, 1956-2, 1369.)

[FAC 84-32, 53 FR 662, 1/11/88, effective 1/29/88]

SUBPART 29.3—STATE AND LOCAL TAXES

29.300 Scope of subpart.

This subpart prescribes the policies and procedures regarding the exemption or immunity of Federal Government purchases and property from State and local taxation.

29.301 [Reserved]

[Removed and reserved, FAC 97-22, 66 FR 2116, 1/10/2001, effective 3/12/2001; Delay of effective date, 66 FR 14259, 3/9/2001, effective 5/11/2001]

29.302 Application of State and local taxes to the Government.

(a) Generally, purchases and leases made by the Federal Government are immune from State and local taxation. Whether any specific purchase or lease is immune, however, is a legal question requiring advice and assistance of the agency-designated counsel.

(b) When it is economically feasible to do so, executive agencies shall take maximum advantage of all exemptions from State and local taxation that may be available. If appropriate, the contracting officer shall provide a Standard Form 1094, U.S. Tax Exemption Form (see Part 53), or other evidence listed in 29.305(a) to establish that the purchase is being made by the Government.

[FAC 90-45, Final rule, 62 FR 224, 1/2/97, effective 1/1/97]

29.303 Application of State and local taxes to Government contractors and subcontractors.

(a) Prime contractors and subcontractors shall not normally be designated as agents of the Government for the purpose of claiming immunity from State or local sales or use taxes. Before any activity contends that a contractor is an agent of the Government, the matter shall be referred to the agency head for review. The referral shall include all pertinent data on which the contention is based, together with a thorough analysis of all relevant legal precedents.

(b) When purchases are not made by the Government itself, but by a prime contractor or by a subcontractor under a prime contract, the right to an exemption of the transaction from a sales or use tax may not rest on the Government's immunity from direct taxation by States and localities. It may rest instead on provisions of the particular State or local law involved, or, in some cases, the transaction may not in fact be expressly exempt from the tax. The Government's interest shall be protected by using the procedures in 29.101.

(c) Frequently, property (including property acquired under the progress payments clause of fixed-price contracts or the Government property clause of cost-reimbursement contracts) owned by the Government is in the possession of a contractor or subcontractor. Situations may arise in which States or localities assert the right to tax Government property directly or to tax the contractor's or subcontractor's possession of, interest in, or use of that property. In such cases, the contracting officer shall seek review and advice from the agency-designated counsel on the appropriate course of action.

29.304 Matters requiring special consideration.

The imposition of State and local taxes may result in special contract considerations including the following:

(a) With coordination of the agency-designated counsel, a contract may—

(1) state that the contract price includes or excludes a specified tax or—

(2) require that the contractor take certain actions with regard to payment, nonpayment, refund, protest, or other treatment of a specified tax. Such special treatment may be appropriate when there is doubt as to the applicability or allocability of the tax, or when the applicability of the tax is being litigated.

(b) The applicability of State and local taxes to purchases by the Federal Government may depend on the place and terms of delivery. When the contract price will be substantial, alternative places and terms of delivery should be considered in light of possible tax consequences.

(c) Indefinite-delivery contracts for equipment rental may require the contractor to furnish equipment in any of the States. Since leased equipment remains the contractor's property, States and local governments impose a wide variety of property, use, or other taxes on equipment leased to the Government. The amount of these taxes can vary considerably from jurisdiction to jurisdiction. See 29.401-1 for the prescription of the contract clause to be included in contracts when delivery points are not known at time of contracting.

(d) *The North Carolina State and local sales and use tax.*

(1) The North Carolina Sales and Use Tax Act authorizes counties and incorporated cities and towns to obtain each year from the Commissioner of Revenue of the State of North Carolina a refund of sales and use taxes indirectly paid on building materials, supplies, fixtures, and equipment that become a part of or are annexed to any building or structure erected, altered, or repaired for such counties and incorporated cities and towns in North Carolina. In United States v. Clayton, 250 F. Supp. 827 (1965), it was held that the United States is entitled to the benefit of the refund, but must follow the refund procedure of the Act and the regulations to recover what it is due.

(2) The Act provides that, to receive the refund, claimants must file, within 6 months after the claimant's fiscal year closes, a written request substantiated by such records, receipts, and information as the Commissioner of Revenue may require. No refund will be made on an application not filed within the time allowed and in such manner as the Commissioner may require. The requirements of the Commissioner are set forth in regulations that provide that, to substantiate a refund claim for sales or use taxes paid on purchases of building materials, supplies, fixtures, or equipment by a contractor, the Government must secure from the contractor certified statements setting forth the cost of the property purchased from each

vendor and the amount of sales or use taxes paid. In the event the contractor makes several purchases from the same vendor, the certified statement must indicate the invoice numbers, the inclusive dates of the invoices, the total amount of the invoices, and the sales and use taxes paid. The statement must also include the cost of any tangible personal property withdrawn from the contractor's warehouse stock and the amount of sales or use tax paid by the contractor. Similar certified statements by subcontractors must be obtained by the general contractor and furnished to the claimant. Any local sales or use taxes included in the contractor's statement must be shown separately from the State sales or use taxes.

(3) The clause prescribed at 29.401-2 requires contractors to submit to contracting officers by November 30 of each year a certified statement disclosing North Carolina State and local sales and use taxes paid during the 12-month period that ended the preceding September 30. The contracting officer shall ensure that contractors comply with this requirement and shall obtain the annual refund to which the Government may be entitled. The application for refund must be filed each year before March 31 and in the manner and form required by the Commissioner of Revenue. Copies of the form may be obtained from the State of North Carolina Department of Revenue, P.O. Box 25000, Raleigh, North Carolina 27640.

[Final rule, 62 FR 40236, 7/25/97, effective 6/30/97]

29.305 State and local tax exemptions.

(a) *Evidence of exemption*. Evidence needed to establish exemption from State or local taxes depends on the grounds for the exemption claimed, the parties to the transaction, and the requirements of the taxing jurisdiction. Such evidence may include the following:

(1) A copy of the contract or relevant portion.

(2) Copies of purchase orders, shipping documents, credit-card-imprinted sales slips, paid or acknowledged invoices, or similar documents that identify an agency or instrumentality of the United States as the buyer.

(3) A U.S. Tax Exemption Form (SF 1094).

(4) A State or local form indicating that the supplies or services are for the exclusive use of the United States.

(5) Any other State or locally required document for establishing general or specific exemption.

(6) Shipping documents indicating that shipments are in interstate or foreign commerce.

(b) *Furnishing proof of exemption*. If a reasonable basis to sustain a claimed exemption exists, the seller will be furnished evidence of exemption, as follows:

(1) Under a contract containing the clause at 52.229-3, Federal, State, and Local Taxes, or at 52.229-4, Federal, State, and Local Taxes (State and Local Adjustments), in accordance with the terms of those clauses.

(2) Under a cost-reimbursement contract, if requested by the contractor and approved by the contracting officer or at the discretion of the contracting officer.

(3) Under a contract or purchase order that contains no tax provision, if—

(i) Requested by the contractor and approved by the contracting officer or at the discretion of the contracting officer; and

(ii) Either the contract price does not include the tax or, if the transaction or property is tax exempt, the contractor consents to a reduction in the contract price.

[FAC 90-45, Final rule, 62 FR 224, 1/2/97, effective 1/1/97; FAC 2001-13, 68 FR 13204, 3/18/2003, 4/17/2003]

SUBPART 29.4—CONTRACT CLAUSES

29.401 Domestic contracts. (No Text)

29.401-1 Indefinite-delivery contracts for leased equipment.

Insert the clause at 52.229-1, State and Local Taxes, in solicitations and contracts for leased equipment when—

(a) A fixed-price indefinite-delivery contract is contemplated;

(b) The contract will be performed wholly or partly in the United States or its outlying areas; and

(c) The place or places of delivery are not known at the time of contracting.

[FAC 2001-14, 68 FR 28079, 5/22/2003, effective 6/23/2003]

29.401-2 Construction contracts performed in North Carolina.

The contracting officer shall insert the clause at 52.229-2, North Carolina State and Local Sales and Use Tax, in solicitations and contracts for construction to be performed in North Carolina. If the requirement is for vessel repair to be performed in North Carolina, the clause shall be used with its Alternate I.

29.401-3 Federal, State, and local taxes.

(a) Except as provided in paragraph (b) of this section, insert the clause at 52.229-3, Federal, State, and Local Taxes, in solicitations and contracts if—

(1) The contract is to be performed wholly or partly in the United States or its outlying areas;

(2) A fixed-price contract is contemplated; and

(3) The contract is expected to exceed the simplified acquisition threshold.

(b) In a noncompetitive contract that meets all the conditions in paragraph (a) of this section, the contracting officer may insert the clause at 52.229-4, Federal, State, and Local Taxes (State and Local Adjustments), instead of the clause at 52.229-3, if the price would otherwise include an inappropriate contingency for potential postaward change(s) in State or local taxes.

[FAC 90-29, 60 FR 34732, 7/3/95, effective 7/3/95; FAC 90-40, 61 FR 39186, 7/26/96, effective 8/26/96; FAC 2001-13, 68 FR 13204, 3/18/2003, 4/17/2003; FAC 2001-14, 68 FR 28079, 5/22/2003, effective 6/23/2003]

29.401-4 New Mexico gross receipts and compensating tax.

(a) *Definition. Services,* as used in this subsection, is as defined in the Gross Receipts and Compensating Tax Act of the State of New Mexico, Sec. 7-9-3(k) NM SA 1978, and means all activities engaged in for other persons for a consideration, which activities involve predominately the performance of a service as distinguished from selling or leasing property. *Services* includes activities performed by a person for its members or shareholders. In determining what is a service, the intended use, principal objective or ultimate objective of the contracting parties shall not be controlling. *Services* also includes construction activities and all tangible personal property that will become an ingredient or component part of a construction project. Such tangible personal property retains its character as tangible personal property until it is installed as an ingredient or component part of a construction project in New Mexico. However, sales of tangible personal property that will become an ingredient or component part of a construction project to persons engaged in the construction business are sales of tangible personal property.

(b) *Contract clause.* The contracting officer shall insert the clause at 52.229-10, State of New Mexico Gross Receipts and Compensating Tax, in solicitations and contracts issued by the agencies identified in paragraph (c) of this subsection when all three of the following conditions exist:

(1) The contractor will be performing a cost-reimbursement contract.

(2) The contract directs or authorizes the contractor to acquire tangible personal property as a direct cost under a contract and title to such property passes directly to and vests in the United States upon delivery of the property by the vendor.

(3) The contract will be for services to be performed in whole or in part within the State of New Mexico.

(c) *Participating agencies.* (1) The agencies listed below have entered into an agreement with the State of New Mexico to eliminate the double taxation of Government cost-reimbursement contracts when contractors and their subcontractors purchase tangible personal property to be used in performing services in whole or in part in the State of New Mexico and for which title to such property will pass to the United States upon delivery of the property to the contractor and its subcontractors by the vendor. Therefore, the clause applies only to solicitations and contracts issued by the—

United States Defense Advanced Research Projects Agency;

United States Defense Threat Reduction Agency;

United States Department of Agriculture;

United States Department of the Air Force;

United States Department of the Army;

United States Department of Energy;

United States Department of Health and Human Services;

United States Department of the Interior;

United States Department of Labor;

United States Department of the Navy;

United States Department of Transportation;

United States General Services Administration;

United States Missile Defense Agency; and

United States National Aeronautics and Space Administration.

(2) Any other Federal agency which expects to award cost-reimbursement contracts to be performed in New Mexico should contact the New Mexico Taxation and Revenue Department to execute a similar agreement.

[FAC 84-39, 53 FR 34228, 9/2/88, effective 10/3/88; FAC 84-56, 55 FR 3883, 2/5/90, effective 3/7/90; Final rule, 55 FR 38517, 9/18/90; FAC 97-3, 62 FR 64912, 12/9/97, effective 12/9/97; FAC 2001-13, 68 FR 13204, 3/18/2003, effective 4/17/2003; FAC 2001-22, 69 FR 17769, 4/5/2004, effective 4/5/2004; FAC 2005-60, 77 FR 44063, 7/26/2012, effective 8/27/2012]

29.402 Foreign contracts. (No Text)

29.402-1 Foreign fixed-price contracts.

(a) The contracting officer shall insert the clause at 52.229-6, Taxes—Foreign Fixed-Price Contracts, in solicitations and contracts expected to exceed the simplified acquisition threshold when a fixed-price contract is contemplated and the contract is to be performed wholly or partly in a foreign country, unless it is contemplated that the contract will be with a foreign government.

(b) The contracting officer shall insert the clause at 52.229-7, Taxes—Fixed-Price Contracts With Foreign Governments, in solicitations and contracts that exceed the simplified acquisition threshold when a fixed-price contract with a foreign government is contemplated.

[FAC 90-3, 55 FR 52793, 12/21/90, effective 1/22/91; FAC 90-40, 61 FR 39186, 7/26/96, effective 8/26/96]

29.402-2 Foreign cost-reimbursement contracts.

(a) The contracting officer shall insert the clause at 52.229-8, Taxes—Foreign Cost-Reimbursement Contracts, in solicitations and contracts when a cost-reimbursement contract is contemplated and the contract is to be performed wholly or partly in a foreign country, unless it is contemplated that the contract will be with a foreign government.

(b) The contracting officer shall insert the clause at 52.229-9, Taxes—Cost-Reimbursement Contracts with Foreign Governments, in solicitations and contracts when a cost-reimbursement contract with a foreign government is contemplated.

PART 30—COST ACCOUNTING STANDARDS ADMINISTRATION

Table of Contents

Scope of part 30.000
Definitions 30.001

Subpart 30.1—General

Cost Accounting Standards 30.101
Cost Accounting Standards Board Publication 30.102

Subpart 30.2—CAS Program Requirements

Contract requirements 30.201
CAS applicability 30.201-1
Types of CAS coverage 30.201-2
Solicitation provisions 30.201-3
Contract clauses 30.201-4
Waiver 30.201-5
Findings 30.201-6
Cognizant Federal agency responsibilities 30.201-7
Disclosure requirements 30.202
General requirements 30.202-1
Impracticality of submission 30.202-2
Amendments and revisions 30.202-3
Privileged and confidential information 30.202-4
Filing Disclosure Statements 30.202-5
Responsibilities 30.202-6
Determinations 30.202-7
Subcontractor disclosure statements 30.202-8

Subpart 30.3—CAS Rules and Regulations [Reserved]

Subpart 30.4—Cost Accounting Standards [Reserved]

Subpart 30.5—Cost Accounting Standards for Educational Institutions [Reserved]

Subpart 30.6—CAS Administration

Responsibility 30.601
Materiality 30.602
Changes to disclosed or established cost accounting practices 30.603
Required changes 30.603-1
Unilateral and desirable changes 30.603-2
Processing changes to disclosed or established cost accounting practices 30.604
Processing noncompliances 30.605
Receiving cost impacts 30.606
Subcontract administration 30.607

PART 30—COST ACCOUNTING STANDARDS ADMINISTRATION

30.000 Scope of part.

This part describes policies and procedures for applying the Cost Accounting Standards Board (CASB) rules and regulations (48 CFR Chapter 99 (FAR Appendix)) to negotiated contracts and subcontracts. This part does not apply to sealed bid contracts or to any contract with a small business concern (see 48 CFR 9903.201-1(b) (FAR Appendix), for these and other exemptions).

[FAC 90-12, 57 FR 39587, 8/31/92, effective 8/31/92; FAC 90-38, 61 FR 18914, 4/29/96, effective 4/29/96; Final rule, 62 FR 40236, 7/25/97, effective 6/30/97]

30.001 Definitions.

As used in this part—

Affected CAS-covered contract or subcontract means a contract or subcontract subject to Cost Accounting Standards (CAS) rules and regulations for which a contractor or subcontractor—

(1) Used one cost accounting practice to estimate costs and a changed cost accounting practice to accumulate and report costs under the contract or subcontract; or

(2) Used a noncompliant practice for purposes of estimating or accumulating and reporting costs under the contract or subcontract.

Cognizant Federal agency official (CFAO) means the contracting officer assigned by the cognizant Federal agency to administer the CAS.

Desirable change means a compliant change to a contractor's established or disclosed cost accounting practices that the CFAO finds is desirable and not detrimental to the Government and is, therefore, not subject to the no increased cost prohibition provisions of CAS covered contracts and subcontracts affected by the change.

Fixed-price contracts and subcontracts means—

(1) Fixed-price contracts and subcontracts described at 16.202, 16.203 (except when price adjustments are based on actual costs of labor or material, described at 16.203-1(a)(2)), and 16.207;

(2) Fixed-price incentive contracts and subcontracts where the price is not adjusted based on actual costs incurred (Subpart 16.4);

(3) Orders issued under indefinite delivery contracts and subcontracts where final payment is not based on actual costs incurred (Subpart 16.5); and

(4) The fixed-hourly rate portion of time-and-materials and labor-hours contracts and subcontracts (Subpart 16.6).

Flexibly-priced contracts and subcontracts means—

(1) Fixed-price contracts and subcontracts described at 16.203- 1(a)(2), 16.204, 16.205, and 16.206;

(2) Cost-reimbursement contracts and subcontracts (Subpart 16.3);

(3) Incentive contracts and subcontracts where the price may be adjusted based on actual costs incurred (Subpart 16.4);

(4) Orders issued under indefinite-delivery contracts and subcontracts where final payment is based on actual costs incurred (Subpart 16.5); and

(5) The materials portion of time-and-materials contracts and subcontracts (Subpart 16.6).

Noncompliance means a failure in estimating, accumulating, or reporting costs to—

(1) Comply with applicable CAS; or

(2) Consistently follow disclosed or established cost accounting practices.

Required change means—

(1) A change in cost accounting practice that a contractor is required to make in order to comply with applicable Standards, modifications or interpretations thereto, that subsequently becomes applicable to an existing CAS-covered contract or subcontract due to the receipt of another CAS-covered contract or subcontract; or

(2) A prospective change to a disclosed or established cost accounting practice when the CFAO determines that the former practice was in compliance with applicable CAS

and the change is necessary for the contractor to remain in compliance.

Unilateral change means a change in cost accounting practice from one compliant practice to another compliant practice that a contractor with a CAS covered contract(s) or subcontract(s) elects to make that has not been deemed a desirable change by the CFAO and for which the Government will pay no aggregate increased costs.

[FAC 2005-01, 70 FR 11743, 3/9/2005, effective 4/8/2005; FAC 2005-24, 73 FR 10965, 2/28/2008, effective 3/31/2008]

SUBPART 30.1—GENERAL

30.101 Cost Accounting Standards.

(a) 41 U.S.C. chapter 15, Cost Accounting Standards, requires certain contractors and subcontractors to comply with Cost Accounting Standards (CAS) and to disclose in writing and follow consistently their cost accounting practices.

(b) Contracts that refer to this Part 30 for the purpose of applying the policies, procedures, standards and regulations promulgated by the CASB pursuant to 41 U.S.C. chapter 15, shall be deemed to refer to the CAS, and any other regulations promulgated by the CASB (see 48 CFR Chapter 99), all of which are hereby incorporated in this Part 30.

(c) The appendix to the FAR loose-leaf edition contains—

(1) Cost Accounting Standards and Cost Accounting Standards Board Rules and Regulations Recodified by the Cost Accounting Standards Board at 48 CFR Chapter 99; and

(2) The following preambles:

(i) Part I—Preambles to the Cost Accounting Standards Published by the Cost Accounting Standards Board.

(ii) Part II—Preambles to the Related Rules and Regulations Published by the Cost Accounting Standards Board.

(iii) Part III—Preambles Published under the FAR System.

(d) The preambles are not regulatory but are intended to explain why the Standards and related Rules and Regulations were written, and to provide rationale for positions taken relative to issues raised in the public comments. The preambles are printed in chronological order to provide an administrative history.

[FAC 90-12, 57 FR 39587, 8/31/92, effective 8/31/92; Final rule, 62 FR 40236, 7/25/97, effective 6/30/97; FAC 97-4, 63 FR 9048, 2/23/98, effective 4/24/98; FAC 2005-73, 79 FR 24192, 4/29/2014, effective 5/29/2014]

30.102 Cost Accounting Standards Board Publication.

Copies of the CASB Standards and Regulations are printed in title 48 of the *Code of Federal Regulations*, Chapter 99, and may be obtained by writing the Superintendent of Documents, U.S. Government Publishing Office, Washington, DC 20402, or by calling the Washington, DC, ordering desk at (202) 512-1800.

[FAC 90-12, 57 FR 39587, 8/31/92, effective 8/31/92; Final rule, 62 FR 40236, 7/25/97, effective 6/30/97; FAC 2019-02, 84 FR 19839, 5/6/2019, effective 5/6/2019]

SUBPART 30.2—CAS PROGRAM REQUIREMENTS

30.201 Contract requirements.

Title 48 CFR 9903.201-1 (FAR Appendix), describes the rules for determining whether a proposed contract or subcontract is exempt from CAS. Negotiated contracts not exempt in accordance with 48 CFR 9903.201-1(b) shall be subject to CAS. A CAS-covered contract may be subject to either full or modified coverage. The rules for determining whether full or modified coverage applies are in 48 CFR 9903.201-2 (FAR Appendix).

[FAC 90-12, 57 FR 39587, 8/31/92, effective 8/31/92; FAC 90-38, 61 FR 18914, 4/29/96, effective 4/29/96; Final rule, 62 FR 40236, 7/25/97, effective 6/30/97]

30.201-1 CAS applicability.

See 48 CFR 9903.201-1 (FAR Appendix).

[FAC 90-38, 61 FR 18914, 4/29/96, effective 4/29/96; Final rule, 62 FR 40236, 7/25/97, effective 6/30/97]

30.201-2 Types of CAS coverage.

See 48 CFR 9903.201-2 (FAR Appendix).

[FAC 90-38, 61 FR 18914, 4/29/96, effective 4/29/96; Final rule, 62 FR 40236, 7/25/97, effective 6/30/97]

30.201-3 Solicitation provisions.

(a) The contracting officer shall insert the provision at 52.230-1, Cost Accounting Standards Notices and Certification, in solicitations for proposed contracts subject to CAS as specified in 48 CFR 9903.201 (FAR Appendix).

(b) If an award to an educational institution is contemplated prior to July 1, 1997, the contracting officer shall insert the basic provision set forth at 52.230-1 with its Alternate I, unless the contract is to be performed by a Federally Funded Research and Development Center (FFRDC) (see 48 CFR 9903.201-2(c)(5) (FAR Appendix)), or the provision at 48 CFR 9903.201-2(c)(6) (FAR Appendix) applies.

(c) Insert the provision at 52.230-7, Proposal Disclosure—Cost Accounting Practice Changes, in solicitations for contracts subject to CAS as specified in 48 CFR 9903.201 (FAR Appendix).

[FAC 90-38, 61 FR 18914, 4/29/96, effective 4/29/96; Final rule, 62 FR 40236, 7/25/97, effective 6/30/97; FAC 2005-01, 70 FR 11743, 3/9/2005, effective 4/8/2005]

30.201-4 Contract clauses.

(a) *Cost Accounting Standards.*

(1) The contracting officer shall insert the clause at FAR 52.230-2, Cost Accounting Standards, in negotiated contracts, unless the contract is exempted (see 48 CFR 9903.201-1 (FAR Appendix)), the contract is subject to modified coverage (see 48 CFR 9903.201-2 (FAR Appendix)), or the clause prescribed in paragraph (c) of this subsection is used.

(2) The clause at FAR 52.230-2 requires the contractor to comply with all CAS specified in 48 CFR 9904 (FAR Appendix), to disclose actual cost accounting practices (applicable to CAS-covered contracts only), and to follow disclosed and established cost accounting practices consistently.

(b) *Disclosure and consistency of cost accounting practices.*

(1) Insert the clause at FAR 52.230-3, Disclosure and Consistency of Cost Accounting Practices, in negotiated contracts when the contract amount is over $750,000, but less than $50 million, and the offeror certifies it is eligible for and elects to use modified CAS coverage (see 48 CFR 9903.201-2 (FAR Appendix)), unless the clause prescribed in paragraph (c) of this subsection is used.

(2) The clause at FAR 52.230-3 requires the contractor to comply with 48 CFR 9904.401, 9904.402, 9904.405, and 9904.406 (FAR Appendix) to disclose (if it meets certain requirements) actual cost accounting practices, and to follow consistently its established cost accounting practices.

(c) *Disclosure and Consistency of Cost Accounting Practices—Foreign Concerns.*

(1) The contracting officer shall insert the clause at 52.230-4, Disclosure and Consistency of Cost Accounting Practices—Foreign Concerns, in negotiated contracts with foreign concerns, unless the contract is otherwise exempt from CAS (see 48 CFR 9903.201-1). Foreign concerns do not include foreign governments or their agents or instrumentalities.

(2) The clause at 52.230-4 requires the contractor to comply with 48 CFR 9904.401 and 48 CFR 9904.402 to disclose (if it meets certain requirements) actual cost accounting practices, and to follow consistently its disclosed and established cost accounting practices.

(d) *Administration of Cost Accounting Standards.*

(1) The contracting officer shall insert the clause at FAR 52.230-6, Administration of Cost Accounting Standards, in contracts containing any of the clauses prescribed in paragraphs (a), (b), (c), or (e) of this subsection.

(2) The clause at FAR 52.230-6 specifies rules for administering CAS requirements and procedures to be followed in cases of failure to comply.

(e) *Cost Accounting Standards—Educational Institutions.*

(1) The contracting officer shall insert the clause at FAR 52.230-5, Cost Accounting Standards—Educational Institution, in negotiated contracts awarded to educational institutions, unless the contract is exempted (see 48 CFR 9903.201-1 (FAR Appendix)), the contract is to be performed by an FFRDC (see 48 CFR 9903.201-2(c)(5) (FAR Appendix)), or the provision at 48 CFR 9903.201-2(c)(6) (FAR Appendix) applies.

(2) The clause at 52.230-5 requires the educational institution to comply with all CAS specified in 48 CFR 9905 (FAR Appendix), to disclose actual cost accounting practices as required by 48 CFR 9903.202-1(f) (FAR Appendix), and to follow disclosed and established cost accounting practices consistently.

[FAC 90-38, 61 FR 18914, 4/29/96, effective 4/29/96; Final rule, 62 FR 40236, 7/25/97, effective 6/30/97; FAC 97-18, 65 FR 36014, 6/6/2000, effective 6/6/2000, finalized without change, FAC 97-22, 66 FR 2135, 1/10/2001; FAC 2005-27, 73 FR 54011, 54013, 9/17/2008, effective 10/17/2008; FAC 2005-36, 74 FR 40467, 8/11/2009, effective 8/11/2009; FAC 2005-42, 75 FR 34283, 6/16/2010, effective 6/16/2010; FAC 2005-50, 76 FR 14570, 3/16/2011, effective 3/16/2011; FAC 2005-59, 77 FR 27550, 5/10/2012, effective 5/10/2012; FAC 2005-83, 80 FR 38293, 7/2/2015, effective 10/1/2015]

30.201-5 Waiver.

(a) The head of the agency—

(1) May waive the applicability of CAS for a particular contract or subcontract under the conditions listed in paragraph (b) of this subsection; and

(2) Must not delegate this waiver authority to any official in the agency below the senior contract policymaking level.

(b) The head of the agency may grant a waiver when one of the following conditions exists:

(1) The contract or subcontract value is less than $15,000,000, and the head of the agency determines, in writing, that the segment of the contractor or subcontractor that will perform the contract or subcontract—

(i) Is primarily engaged in the sale of commercial items; and

(ii) Has no contracts or subcontracts that are subject to CAS.

(2) The head of the agency determines that exceptional circumstances exist whereby a waiver of CAS is necessary to meet the needs of the agency. Exceptional circumstances exist only when the benefits to be derived from waiving the CAS outweigh the risk associated with the waiver. The determination that exceptional circumstances exist must—

(i) Be set forth in writing; and

(ii) Include a statement of the specific circumstances that justify granting the waiver.

(c) When one of the conditions in paragraph (b) of this subsection exists, the request for waiver should include the following:

(1) The amount of the proposed award.

(2) A description of the contract or subcontract type (*e.g.*, firm-fixed-price, cost-reimbursement).

(3) Whether the segment(s) that will perform the contract or subcontract has CAS-covered contracts or subcontracts.

(4) A description of the item(s) being procured.

(5) When the contractor or subcontractor will not accept the contract or subcontract if CAS applies, a statement to that effect.

(6) Whether certified cost or pricing data will be obtained, and if so, a discussion of how the data will be used in negotiating the contract or subcontract price.

(7) The benefits to the Government of waiving CAS.

(8) The potential risk to the Government of waiving CAS.

(9) The date by which the waiver is needed.

(10) Any other information that may be useful in evaluating the request.

(d) When neither of the conditions in paragraph (b) of this subsection exists, the waiver request must be prepared in accordance with 48 CFR 9903.201-5(e) (FAR Appendix) and submitted to the CAS Board.

(e) Each agency must report any waivers granted under paragraph (a) of this subsection to the CAS Board, on a fiscal year basis, not later than 90 days after the close of the Government's fiscal year.

[FAC 97-18, 65 FR 36014, 6/6/2000, effective 6/6/2000, finalized without change, FAC 97-22, 66 FR 2135, 1/10/2001; FAC 2005-45, 75 FR 53135, 8/30/2010, effective 10/1/2010]

30.201-6 Findings.

See 48 CFR 9903.201-6 (FAR Appendix).

[FAC 90-38, 61 FR 18914, 4/29/96, effective 4/29/96; Final rule, 62 FR 40236, 7/25/97, effective 6/30/97]

30.201-7 Cognizant Federal agency responsibilities.

See 48 CFR 9903.201-7 (FAR Appendix).

[FAC 90-38, 61 FR 18914, 4/29/96, effective 4/29/96; Final rule, 62 FR 40236, 7/25/97, effective 6/30/97]

30.202 Disclosure requirements. (No Text)

30.202-1 General requirements.

See 48 CFR 9903.202-1 (FAR Appendix).

[FAC 90-38, 61 FR 18914, 4/29/96, effective 4/29/96; Final rule, 62 FR 40236, 7/25/97, effective 6/30/97]

30.202-2 Impracticality of submission.

See 48 CFR 9903.202-2 (FAR Appendix).

[FAC 90-38, 61 FR 18914, 4/29/96, effective 4/29/96; Final rule, 62 FR 40236, 7/25/97, effective 6/30/97]

30.202-3 Amendments and revisions.

See 48 CFR 9903.202-3 (FAR Appendix).

[FAC 90-38, 61 FR 18914, 4/29/96, effective 4/29/96; Final rule, 62 FR 40236, 7/25/97, effective 6/30/97]

30.202-4 Privileged and confidential information.

See 48 CFR 9903.202-4 (FAR Appendix).

[FAC 90-38, 61 FR 18914, 4/29/96, effective 4/29/96; Final rule, 62 FR 40236, 7/25/97, effective 6/30/97]

30.202-5 Filing Disclosure Statements.

See 48 CFR 9903.202-5 (FAR Appendix).

[FAC 90-38, 61 FR 18914, 4/29/96, effective 4/29/96; Final rule, 62 FR 40236, 7/25/97, effective 6/30/97]

30.202-6 Responsibilities.

(a) The contracting officer is responsible for determining when a proposed contract may require CAS coverage and for including the appropriate notice in the solicitation. The contracting officer must then ensure that the offeror has made the required solicitation certifications and that required Disclosure Statements are submitted. (Also see 48 CFR 9903.201-3 and 9903.202 (FAR Appendix).)

(b) The contracting officer shall not award a CAS-covered contract until the cognizant Federal agency official (CFAO) has made a written determination that a required Disclosure Statement is adequate unless, in order to protect the Government's interest, the agency head, on a nondelegable basis, authorizes award without obtaining submission of the required Disclosure Statement (see 48 CFR 9903.202-2). In this event, the contractor shall submit the required Disclosure Statement and the CFAO shall make a determination of adequacy as soon as possible after the award.

(c) The cognizant auditor is responsible for conducting reviews of Disclosure Statements for adequacy and compliance.

(d) The CFAO is responsible for issuing determinations of adequacy and compliance of the Disclosure Statement.

[FAC 90-12, 57 FR 39587, 8/31/92, effective 8/31/92; FAC 90-38, 61 FR 18914, 4/29/96, effective 4/29/96; Final rule, 62 FR 40236, 7/25/97, effective 6/30/97; FAC 2005-01, Final rule, 70 FR 11743, 3/9/2005, effective 4/8/2005]

30.202-7 Determinations.

(a) *Adequacy determination.* (1) As prescribed by 48 CFR 9903.202-6 (FAR Appendix), the auditor shall—

(i) Conduct a review of the Disclosure Statement to ascertain whether it is current, accurate, and complete; and

(ii) Report the results to the CFAO.

(2) The CFAO shall determine if the Disclosure Statement adequately describes the contractor's cost accounting practices. Also, the CFAO shall—

(i) If the Disclosure Statement is adequate, notify the contractor in writing, and provide a copy to the auditor with a copy to the contracting officer if the proposal triggers submission of a Disclosure Statement. The notice of adequacy shall state that—

(A) The disclosed practices are adequately described and the CFAO currently is not aware of any additional practices that should be disclosed;

(B) The notice is not a determination that all cost accounting practices were disclosed; and

(C) The contractor shall not consider a disclosed practice, by virtue of such disclosure, an approved practice for estimating proposals or accumulating and reporting contract and subcontract cost data; or

(ii) If the Disclosure Statement is inadequate, notify the contractor of the inadequacies and request a revised Disclosure Statement.

(3) Generally, the CFAO should furnish the contractor notification of adequacy or inadequacy within 30 days after the CFAO receives the Disclosure Statement.

(b) *Compliance determination.* (1) After the notification of adequacy, the auditor shall—

(i) Conduct a detailed compliance review to ascertain whether or not the disclosed practices comply with CAS and Part 31, as applicable; and

(ii) Advise the CFAO of the results.

(2) The CFAO shall make a determination of compliance or take action regarding a report of alleged noncompliance in accordance with FAR 30.605(b). Such action should include requesting a revised Disclosure Statement that corrects the CAS noncompliance. Noncompliances with Part 31 shall be processed separately.

[FAC 90-12, 57 FR 39587, 8/31/92, effective 8/31/92; FAC 90-38, 61 FR 18914, 4/29/96, effective 4/29/96; Final rule, 62 FR 40236, 7/25/97, effective 6/30/97; FAC 2005-01, 70 FR 11743, 3/9/2005, effective 4/8/2005]

30.202-8 Subcontractor disclosure statements.

(a) When the Government requires determinations of adequacy of subcontractor disclosure statements, the CFAO for the subcontractor shall provide this determination to the CFAO for the contractor or next higher-tier subcontractor. The higher-tier CFAO shall not change the determination of the lower-tier CFAO.

(b) Any determination that it is impractical to secure a subcontractor's Disclosure Statement must be made in accordance with 48 CFR 9903.202-2 (FAR Appendix).

[FAC 90-12, 57 FR 39587, 8/31/92, effective 8/31/92; FAC 90-38, 61 FR 18914, 4/29/96, effective 4/29/96; Final rule, 62 FR 40236, 7/25/97, effective 6/30/97; FAC 2005-01, 70 FR 11743, 3/9/2005, effective 4/8/2005]

SUBPART 30.3—CAS RULES AND REGULATIONS [RESERVED]

Note: See 48 CFR 9903.3 (FAR Appendix B).

[FAC 90-38, 61 FR 18914, 4/29/96, effective 4/29/96; Final rule, 62 FR 40236, 7/25/97, effective 6/30/97]

SUBPART 30.4—COST ACCOUNTING STANDARDS [RESERVED]

Note: See 48 CFR 9904 (FAR Appendix B).

[FAC 90-38, 61 FR 18914, 4/29/96, effective 4/29/96; Final rule, 62 FR 40236, 7/25/97, effective 6/30/97]

SUBPART 30.5—COST ACCOUNTING STANDARDS FOR EDUCATIONAL INSTITUTIONS [RESERVED]

Note: See 48 CFR 9905 (FAR Appendix B).

[FAC 90-38, 61 FR 18914, 4/29/96, effective 4/29/96; Final rule, 62 FR 40236, 7/25/97, effective 6/30/97]

SUBPART 30.6—CAS ADMINISTRATION

30.601 Responsibility.

(a) The CFAO shall perform CAS administration for all contracts and subcontracts in a business unit, even when the contracting officer retains other administration functions. The CFAO shall make all CAS-related required determinations and findings (*see* Subpart 1.7) for all CAS-covered contracts and subcontracts, including—

(1) Whether a change in cost accounting practice or noncompliance has occurred; and

(2) If a change in cost accounting practice or noncompliance has occurred, how any resulting cost impacts are resolved.

(b) Within 30 days after the award of any new contract subject to CAS, the contracting officer making the award shall request the CFAO to perform administration for CAS matters (see Subpart 42.2). For subcontract awards, the contractor awarding the subcontract must follow the procedures at 52.230-6(l), (m), and (n).

(c) In performing CAS administration, the CFAO shall request and consider the advise of the auditor as appropriate (see 1.602-2).

[FAC 90-12, 57 FR 39587, 8/31/92, effective 8/31/92; FAC 90-23, 59 FR 67010, 12/28/94, effective 11/4/93; FAC 2005-01, 70 FR 11743, 3/9/2005, effective 4/8/2005; FAC 2005-24, 73 FR 10965, 2/28/2008, effective 3/31/2008]

30.602 Materiality.

(a) In determining materiality, the CFAO shall use the criteria in 48 CFR 9903.305 (FAR Appendix).

(b) A CFAO determination of materiality—

(1) May be made before or after a general dollar magnitude proposal has been submitted, depending on the particular facts and circumstances; and

(2) Shall be based on adequate documentation.

(c) When the CFAO determines the cost impact is immaterial, the CFAO shall—

(1) Make no contract adjustments and conclude the cost impact process;

(2) Document the rationale for the determination; and

(3) In the case of noncompliance issues, inform the contractor that—

(i) The noncompliance should be corrected; and

(ii) If the noncompliance is not corrected, the Government reserves the right to make appropriate contract adjustments should the cost impact become material in the future.

(d) For required, unilateral, and desirable changes, and CAS noncompliances, when the amount involved is material, the CFAO shall follow the applicable provisions in 30.603, 30.604, 30.605, and 30.606.

[FAC 2005-01, 70 FR 11743, 3/9/2005, effective 4/8/2005; FAC 2005-24, 73 FR 10965, 2/28/2008, effective 3/31/2008]

30.603 Changes to disclosed or established cost accounting practices. (No Text)

30.603-1 Required changes.

(a) *General.* Offerors shall state whether or not the award of a contract would require a change to an established cost accounting practice affecting existing contracts and subcontracts (*see* 52.230-1). The contracting officer shall notify the CFAO if the offeror states that a change in cost accounting practice would be required.

(b) *CFAO responsibilities.* Prior to making an equitable adjustment under the applicable paragraph(s) that address a required change at 52.230-2, Cost Accounting Standards; 52.230-3, Disclosure and Consistency of Cost Accounting Practices; or 52.230-5, Cost Accounting Standards—Educational Institution, the CFAO shall determine that—

(1) The cost accounting practice change is required to comply with a CAS, or a modification or interpretation thereof, that subsequently became applicable to one or more contracts or subcontracts; or

(2) The former cost accounting practice was in compliance with applicable CAS and the change is necessary to remain in compliance.

(c) *Notice and proposal preparation.*

(1) When the award of a contract would require a change to an established cost accounting practice, the provision at 52.230-7, Proposal Disclosure—Cost Accounting Practice Changes, requires the offeror to—

(i) Prepare the contract pricing proposal in response to the solicitation using the changed cost accounting practice for the period of performance for which the practice will be used; and

(ii) Submit a description of the changed cost accounting practice to the contracting officer and the CFAO as pricing support for the proposal.

(2) When a change is required to remain in compliance (for reasons other than a contract award) or to comply with a new or modified standard, the clause at 52.230-6, Administration of Cost Accounting Standards, requires the contractor to—

(i) Submit a description of the change to the CFAO not less than 60 days (or other mutually agreeable date) before implementation of the change; and

(ii) Submit rationale to support any contractor written statement that the cost impact of the change is immaterial.

(d) *Equitable adjustments for new or modified standards.* (1) Required changes made to comply with new or modified standards may require equitable adjustments, but only to those contracts awarded before the effective date of the new or modified standard (*see* 52.230-2, 52.230-3, or 52.230-5).

(2) When a contractor elects to implement a required change to comply with a new or modified standard prior to the applicability date of the standard, the CFAO shall administer the change as a unilateral change (*see* 30.603-2). Contractors shall not receive an equitable adjustment that will result in increased costs in the aggregate to the Government prior to the applicability date unless the CFAO determines that the unilateral change is a desirable change.

[FAC 2005-01, 70 FR 11743, 3/9/2005, effective 4/8/2005]

30.603-2 Unilateral and desirable changes.

(a) *Unilateral changes.* (1) The contractor may unilaterally change its disclosed or established cost accounting practices, but the Government shall not pay any increased cost, in the aggregate, as a result of the unilateral change.

(2) Prior to making any contract price or cost adjustments under the applicable paragraph(s) addressing a unilateral change at 52.230-2, 52.230-3, or 52.230-5, the CFAO shall determine that—

(i) The contemplated contract price or cost adjustments will protect the Government from the payment of the estimated increased costs, in the aggregate; and

(ii) The net effect of the contemplated adjustments will not result in the recovery of more than the increased costs to the Government, in the aggregate.

(b) *Desirable changes.* (1) Prior to taking action under the applicable paragraph(s) addressing a desirable change at 52.230-2, 52.230-3, or 52.230-5, the CFAO shall determine the change is a desirable change and not detrimental to the interests of the Government.

(2) Until the CFAO has determined a change to a cost accounting practice is a desirable change, the change is a unilateral change.

(3) Some factors to consider in determining if a change is desirable include, but are not limited to, whether—

(i) The contractor must change the cost accounting practices it uses for Government contract and subcontract costing purposes to remain in compliance with the provisions of Part 31;

(ii) The contractor is initiating management actions directly associated with the change that will result in cost savings for segments with CAS-covered contracts and subcontracts over a period for which forward pricing rates are developed or 5 years, whichever is shorter, and the cost savings are reflected in the forward pricing rates; and

(iii) Funds are available if the determination would necessitate an upward adjustment of contract cost or price.

(c) *Notice and proposal preparation.*

(1) When a contractor makes a unilateral change, the clause at 52.230-6, Administration of Cost Accounting Standards, requires the contractor to—

(i) Submit a description of the change to the CFAO not less than 60 days (or other mutually agreeable date) before implementation of the change; and

(ii) Submit rationale to support any contractor written statement that the cost impact of the change is immaterial.

(2) If a contractor implements the change in cost accounting practice without submitting the notice as required in paragraph (c)(1) of this subsection, the CFAO may determine the change a failure to follow a cost accounting practice consistently and process it as a noncompliance in accordance with 30.605.

(d) *Retroactive changes.* (1) If a contractor requests that a unilateral change be retroactive, the contractor shall submit supporting rationale.

(2) The CFAO shall promptly evaluate the contractor's request and shall, as soon as practical, notify the contractor in writing whether the request is or is not approved.

(3) The CFAO shall not approve a date for the retroactive change that is before the beginning of the contractor's fiscal year in which the request is made.

(e) *Contractor accounting changes due to external restructuring activities.* The requirements for contract price and cost adjustments do not apply to compliant cost accounting practice changes that are directly associated with external restructuring activities that are subject to and meet the requirements of 10 U.S.C. 2325. However, the disclosure requirements in 52.230-6(b) shall be followed.

[FAC 2005-01, 70 FR 11743, 3/9/2005, effective 4/8/2005]

30.604 Processing changes to disclosed or established cost accounting practices.

(a) *Scope.* This section applies to required, unilateral, and desirable changes in cost accounting practices.

(b) *Procedures.* Upon receipt of the contractor's notification and description of the change in cost accounting practice, the CFAO should review the proposed change concurrently for adequacy and compliance. The CFAO shall—

(1) If the description of the change is both adequate and compliant, notify the contractor in writing and—

(i) For required or unilateral changes (except those requested to be determined desirable changes), request the contractor submit a general dollar magnitude (GDM) proposal by a specified date, unless the CFAO determines the cost impact is immaterial; or

(ii) For unilateral changes that the contractor requests to be determined desirable changes, inform the contractor that the request shall include supporting rationale and—

(A) For any request based on the criteria in 30.603-2(b)(3)(ii), the data necessary to demonstrate the required cost savings; or

(B) For any request other than those based on the criteria in 30.603- 2(b)(3)(ii), a GDM proposal and any other data necessary for the CFAO to determine if the change is a desirable change;

(2) If the description of the change is inadequate, request a revised description of the new cost accounting practice; and

(3) If the disclosed practice is noncompliant, notify the contractor in writing that, if implemented, the CFAO will determine the cost accounting practice to be noncompliant and process it accordingly.

(c) *Evaluating requests for desirable changes.* (1) When a contractor requests a unilateral change be determined a desirable change, the CFAO shall promptly evaluate the contractor's request and, as soon as practical, notify the contractor in writing whether the change is a desirable change or the request is denied.

(2) If the CFAO determines the change is a desirable change, the CFAO shall negotiate any cost or price adjustments that may be needed to resolve the cost impact (see 30.606).

(3) If the request is denied, the change is a unilateral change and shall be processed accordingly.

(d) *General dollar magnitude proposal.* The GDM proposal—

(1) Provides information to the CFAO on the estimated overall impact of a change in cost accounting practice on affected CAS-covered contracts and subcontracts that were awarded based on the previous cost accounting practice;

(2) Assists the CFAO in determining whether individual contract price or cost adjustments are required; and

(3) The contractor may submit a detailed cost-impact (DCI) proposal in lieu of a GDM proposal provided the DCI proposal is in accordance with paragraph (g) of this section.

(e) *General dollar magnitude proposal content.* The GDM proposal—

(1) Shall calculate the cost impact in accordance with paragraph (h) of this section;

(2) May use one or more of the following methods to determine the increase or decrease in cost accumulations:

(i) A representative sample of affected CAS-covered contracts and subcontracts.

(ii) The change in indirect rates multiplied by the total estimated base computed for each of the following groups:

(A) Fixed-price contracts and subcontracts.

(B) Flexibly-priced contracts and subcontracts.

(iii) Any other method that provides a reasonable approximation of the total increase or decrease in cost accumulations for all affected fixed-price and flexibly-priced contracts and subcontracts.

(3) May be in any format acceptable to the CFAO but, as a minimum, shall include the following data:

(i) A general dollar magnitude estimate of the total increase or decrease in cost accumulations by Executive agency, including any impact the change may have on contract and subcontract incentives, fees, and profits, for each of the following groups:

(A) Fixed-price contracts and subcontracts.

(B) Flexibly-priced contracts and subcontracts.

(ii) For unilateral changes, the increased or decreased costs to the Government for each of the following groups:

(A) Fixed-price contracts and subcontracts.

(B) Flexibly-priced contracts and subcontracts; and

(4) When requested by the CFAO, shall identify all affected CAS-covered contracts and subcontracts.

(f) *General dollar magnitude proposal evaluation.* The CFAO shall promptly evaluate the GDM proposal. If the cost impact is immaterial, the CFAO shall notify the contractor in writing and conclude the cost-impact process with no contract adjustments. Otherwise, the CFAO shall—

(1) Negotiate and resolve the cost impact (see 30.606). If necessary, the CFAO may request that the contractor submit a revised GDM proposal by a specified date with specific additional data needed to resolve the cost impact (*e.g.,* an expanded sample of affected CAS-covered contracts and subcontracts or a revised method of computing the increase or decrease in cost accumulations); or

(2) Request that the contractor submit a DCI proposal by a specified date if the CFAO determines that the GDM proposal is not sufficient to resolve the cost impact.

(g) *Detailed cost-impact proposal.* If the contractor is required to submit a DCI proposal, the CFAO shall promptly evaluate the DCI proposal and follow the procedures at 30.606 to negotiate and resolve the cost impact. The DCI proposal—

(1) Shall calculate the cost impact in accordance with paragraph (h) of this section;

(2) Shall show the estimated increase or decrease in cost accumulations for each affected CAS-covered contract and subcontract unless the CFAO and contractor agree to—

(i) Include only those affected CAS covered contracts and subcontracts exceeding a specified amount; and

(ii) Estimate the total increase or decrease in cost accumulations for all affected CAS-covered contracts and subcontracts, using the results in paragraph (g)(2)(i) of this section;

(3) May be in any format acceptable to the CFAO but, as a minimum, shall include the requirements at paragraphs (e)(3)(i) and (ii) of this section; and

(4) When requested by the CFAO, shall identify all affected contracts and subcontracts.

(h) *Calculating cost impacts.* The cost impact calculation shall—

(1) Include all affected CAS-covered contracts and subcontracts regardless of their status (*i.e.,* open or closed) or the fiscal year(s) in which the costs are incurred (*i.e.,* whether or not the final indirect rates have been established);

(2) Combine the cost impact for all affected CAS-covered contracts and subcontracts for all segments if the effect of a change results in costs flowing between those segments;

(3) For unilateral changes—

(i) Determine the increased or decreased cost to the Government for flexibly-priced contracts and subcontracts as follows:

(A) When the estimated cost to complete using the changed practice exceeds the estimated cost to complete using the current practice, the difference is increased cost to the Government.

(B) When the estimated costs to complete using the changed practice is less than the estimated cost to complete using the current practice, the difference is decreased cost to the Government.

(ii) Determine the increased or decreased cost to the Government for fixed-price contracts and subcontracts as follows:

(A) When the estimated cost to complete using the changed practice is less than the estimated cost to complete using the current practice, the difference is increased cost to the Government.

(B) When the estimated cost to complete using the changed practice exceeds the estimated cost to complete using the current practice, the difference is decreased cost to the Government.

(iii) Calculate the total increase or decrease in contract and subcontract incentives, fees, and profits associated with the increased or decreased cost to the Government in accordance with 48 CFR 9903.306(c). The associated increase or decrease is based on the difference between the negotiated incentives, fees and profits and the amounts that would have been negotiated had the cost impact been known at the time the contracts and subcontracts were negotiated.

(iv) Calculate the increased cost to the Government in the aggregate.

(4) For required or desirable changes, negotiate an equitable adjustment as provided in the Changes clause of the contract.

(i) *Remedies.* If the contractor does not submit the accounting change description or the proposals required in paragraph (d) or (g) of this section within the specified time, or any extension granted by the CFAO, the CFAO shall—

(1) Estimate the general dollar magnitude of the cost impact on affected CAS-covered contracts and subcontracts; and

(2) Take one or both of the following actions:

(i) Withhold an amount not to exceed 10 percent of each subsequent payment related to the contractor's CAS-covered contracts (up to the estimated general dollar magnitude of the cost impact), until the contractor furnishes the required information.

(ii) Issue a final decision in accordance with 33.211 and unilaterally adjust the contract(s) by the estimated amount of the cost impact.

[FAC 2005-01, 70 FR 11743, 3/9/2005, effective 4/8/2005; FAC 2005-24, 73 FR 10965, 2/28/2008, effective 3/31/2008]

30.605 Processing noncompliances.

(a) *General.* Prior to making any contract price or cost adjustments under the applicable paragraph(s) addressing noncompliance at 52.230-2, 52.230-3, or 52.230-5, the CFAO shall determine that—

(1) The contemplated contract price or cost adjustments will protect the Government from the payment of increased costs, in the aggregate;

(2) The net effect of the contemplated contract price or cost adjustments will not result in the recovery of more than the increased costs to the Government, in the aggregate;

(3) The net effect of any invoice adjustments made to correct an estimating noncompliance will not result in the recovery of more than the increased costs paid by the Government, in the aggregate; and

(4) The net effect of any interim and final voucher billing adjustments made to correct a cost accumulation noncompliance will not result in the recovery of more than the increased cost paid by the Government, in the aggregate.

(b) *Notice and determination.* (1) Within 15 days of receiving a report of alleged noncompliance from the auditor, the CFAO shall—

(i) Notify the auditor that the CFAO disagrees with the alleged noncompliance; or

(ii) Issue a notice of potential noncompliance to the contractor and provide a copy to the auditor.

(2) The notice of potential noncompliance shall—

(i) Notify the contractor in writing of the exact nature of the noncompliance; and

(ii) Allow the contractor 60 days or other mutually agreeable date to—

(A) Agree or submit reasons why the contractor considers the existing practices to be in compliance; and

(B) Submit rationale to support any written statement that the cost impact of the noncompliance is immaterial.

(3) The CFAO shall—

(i) If applicable, review the reasons why the contractor considers the existing practices to be compliant or the cost impact to be immaterial;

(ii) Make a determination of compliance or noncompliance consistent with 1.704; and

(iii) Notify the contractor and the auditor in writing of the determination of compliance or noncompliance and the basis for the determination.

(4) If the CFAO makes a determination of noncompliance, the CFAO shall follow the procedures in paragraphs (c) through (h) of this section, as appropriate, unless the CFAO also determines the cost impact is immaterial. If immaterial, the CFAO shall—

(i) Inform the contractor in writing that—

(A) The noncompliance should be corrected; and

(B) If the noncompliance is not corrected, the Government reserves the right to make appropriate contract adjustments should the noncompliance become material in the future; and

(ii) Conclude the cost-impact process with no contract adjustments.

(c) *Correcting noncompliances.* (1) The clause at 52.230-6 requires the contractor to submit a description of any cost accounting practice change needed to correct a noncompliance within 60 days after the earlier of—

(i) Agreement with the CFAO that there is a noncompliance; or

(ii) Notification by the CFAO of a determination of noncompliance.

(2) The CFAO should review the proposed change to correct the noncompliance concurrently for adequacy and compliance (see 30.202-7). The CFAO shall—

(i) When the description of the change is both adequate and compliant—

(A) Notify the contractor in writing;

(B) Request that the contractor submit by a specified date a general dollar magnitude

(GDM) proposal, unless the CFAO determines the cost impact is immaterial; and

(C) Follow the procedures at paragraph (b)(4) of this section if the CFAO determines the cost impact is immaterial.

(ii) If the description of the change is inadequate, request a revised description of the new cost accounting practice; or

(iii) If the disclosed practice is noncompliant, notify the contractor in writing that, if implemented, the CFAO will determine the cost accounting practice to be noncompliant and process it accordingly.

(d) *General dollar magnitude proposal content.* The GDM proposal—

(1) Shall calculate the cost impact in accordance with paragraph (h) of this section;

(2) May use one or more of the following methods to determine the increase or decrease in contract and subcontract price or cost accumulations, as applicable:

(i) A representative sample of affected CAS-covered contracts and subcontracts affected by the noncompliance.

(ii) When the noncompliance involves cost accumulation, the change in indirect rates multiplied by the applicable base for flexibly-priced contracts and subcontracts.

(iii) Any other method that provides a reasonable approximation of the total increase or decrease in contract and subcontract prices and cost accumulations;

(3) The contractor may submit a DCI proposal in lieu of a GDM proposal provided the DCI proposal is in accordance with paragraph (f) of this section.

(4) May be in any format acceptable to the CFAO but, as a minimum, shall include the following data:

(i) The total increase or decrease in contract and subcontract prices and cost accumulations, as applicable, by Executive agency, including any impact the noncompliance may have on contract and subcontract incentives, fees, and profits, for each of the following groups:

(A) Fixed-price contracts and subcontracts.

(B) Flexibly-priced contracts and subcontracts.

(ii) The increased or decreased costs to the Government for each of the following groups:

(A) Fixed-price contracts and subcontracts.

(B) Flexibly-priced contracts and subcontracts.

(iii) The total overpayments and underpayments for fixed-price and flexibly-priced contracts made by the Government during the period of noncompliance; and

(5) When requested by the CFAO, shall identify all affected CAS-covered contracts and subcontracts.

(e) *General dollar magnitude proposal evaluation.* The CFAO shall promptly evaluate the GDM proposal. If the cost impact is immaterial, the CFAO shall follow the requirements in paragraph (b)(4) of this section. Otherwise, the CFAO shall—

(1) Negotiate and resolve the cost impact (see 30.606). If necessary, the CFAO may request the contractor submit a revised GDM proposal by a specified date, with specific additional data needed to resolve the cost impact (*e.g.*, an expanded sample of affected CAS-covered contracts and subcontracts or a revised method of computing the increase or decrease in contract and subcontract price and cost accumulations); or

(2) Request that the contractor submit a DCI proposal by a specified date if the CFAO determines that the GDM proposal is not sufficient to resolve the cost impact.

(f) *Detailed cost-impact proposal.* If the contractor is required to submit a DCI proposal, the CFAO shall promptly evaluate the DCI proposal and follow the procedures at 30.606 to negotiate and resolve the cost impact. The DCI proposal—

(1) Shall calculate the cost impact in accordance with paragraph (h) of this section.

(2) Shall show the increase or decrease in price and cost accumulations, as applicable for each affected CAS-covered contract and subcontract unless the CFAO and contractor agree to—

(i) Include only those affected CAS-covered contracts and subcontracts having—

(A) Contract and subcontract values exceeding a specified amount when the noncompliance involves estimating costs; and

(B) Incurred costs exceeding a specified amount when the noncompliance involves accumulating costs; and

(ii) Estimate the total increase or decrease in price and cost accumulations for all affected CAS covered contracts and subcontracts using the results in paragraph (f) (2) (i) of this section;

(3) May be in any format acceptable to the CFAO but, as a minimum, shall include the information in paragraph (d) (4) of this section; and

(4) When requested by the CFAO, shall identify all affected CAS-covered contracts and subcontracts.

(g) *Interest.* The CFAO shall—

(1) Separately identify interest on any increased cost paid, in the aggregate, as a result of the noncompliance;

(2) Compute interest from the date of overpayment to the date of repayment using the rate specified in 26 U.S.C. 6621(a) (2).

(h) *Calculating cost impacts.* The cost impact calculation shall—

(1) Include all affected CAS-covered contracts and subcontracts regardless of their status (*i.e.*, open or closed) or the fiscal year in which the costs are incurred (*i.e.*, whether or not the final indirect cost rates have been established);

(2) Combine the cost impact for all affected CAS-covered contracts and subcontracts for all segments if the effect of a change results in costs flowing between those segments;

(3) For noncompliances that involve estimating costs, determine the increased or decreased cost to the Government for fixed-price contracts and subcontracts as follows:

(i) When the negotiated contract or subcontract price exceeds what the negotiated price would have been had the contractor used a compliant practice, the difference is increased cost to the Government.

(ii) When the negotiated contract or subcontract price is less than what the negotiated price would have been had the contractor used a compliant practice, the difference is decreased cost to the Government;

(4) For noncompliances that involve accumulating costs, determine the increased or decreased cost to the Government for flexibly-priced contracts and subcontracts as follows:

(i) When the costs that were accumulated under the noncompliant practice exceed the costs that would have been accumulated using a compliant practice (from the time the noncompliant practice was first implemented until the date the noncompliant practice was replaced with a compliant practice), the difference is increased cost to the Government.

(ii) When the costs that were accumulated under the noncompliant practice are less than the costs that would have been accumulated using a compliant practice (from the time the noncompliant practice was first implemented until the date the noncompliant practice was replaced with a compliant practice) the difference is decreased cost to the Government;

(5) Calculate the total increase or decrease in contract and subcontract incentives, fees, and profits associated with the increased or decreased costs to the Government in accordance with 48 CFR 9903.306(c). The associated increase or decrease is based on the difference between the negotiated incentives, fees, and profits and the amounts that would have been negotiated had the contractor used a compliant practice;

(6) Determine the cost impact of each noncompliance that affects both cost estimating and cost accumulation by combining the cost impacts in paragraphs (h) (3), (h) (4), and (h) (5) of this section; and

(7) Calculate the increased cost to the Government in the aggregate.

(i) *Remedies.* If the contractor does not correct the noncompliance or submit the proposal required in paragraph (d) or (f) of this section within the specified time, or any extension granted by the CFAO, the CFAO shall follow the procedures at 30.604(i).

[FAC 2005-01, 70 FR 11743, 3/9/2005, effective 4/8/2005; FAC 2005-24, 73 FR 10965, 2/28/2008, effective 3/31/2008]

30.606 Resolving cost impacts.

(a) *General.* (1) The CFAO shall coordinate with the affected contracting officers before negotiating and resolving the cost impact when the estimated cost impact on any of their contracts is at least $100,000. However, the CFAO has the sole authority for negotiating and resolving the cost impact.

(2) The CFAO may resolve a cost impact attributed to a change in cost accounting practice or a noncompliance by adjusting a single contract, several but not all contracts, all contracts, or any other suitable method.

(3) In resolving the cost impact, the CFAO—

(i) Shall not combine the cost impacts of any of the following:

(A) A required change and a unilateral change.

(B) A required change and a noncompliance.

(C) A desirable change and a unilateral change.

(D) A desirable change and a noncompliance.

(ii) Shall not combine the cost impacts of any of the following unless all of the cost impacts are increased costs to Government:

(A) One or more unilateral changes.

(B) One or more noncompliances.

(C) Unilateral changes and noncompliances; and

(iii) May consider the cost impacts of a unilateral change affecting two or more segments to be a single change if—

(A) The change affects the flow of costs between segments; or

(B) Implements a common cost accounting practice for two or more segments.

(4) For desirable changes, the CFAO should consider the estimated cost impact of associated management actions on contract costs in resolving the cost impact.

(b) *Negotiations.* The CFAO shall—

(1) Negotiate and resolve the cost impact on behalf of all Government agencies; and

(2) At the conclusion of negotiations, prepare a negotiation memorandum and send copies to the auditor and affected contracting officers.

(c) *Contract adjustments.* (1) The CFAO may adjust some or all contracts with a material cost impact, subject to the provisions in paragraphs (c)(2) through (c)(6) of this section.

(2) In selecting the contract or contracts to be adjusted, the CFAO should assure, to the maximum extent practical and subject to the provisions in paragraphs (c)(3) through (c)(6) of this section, that the adjustments reflect a *pro rata* share of the cost impact based on the ratio of the cost impact of each Executive agency to the total cost impact.

(3) For unilateral changes and noncompliances, the CFAO shall—

(i) To the maximum extent practical, not adjust the price upward for fixed-price contracts;

(ii) If contract adjustments are made, preclude payment of aggregate increased costs by taking one or both of the following actions:

(A) Reduce the contract price on fixed-price contracts.

(B) Disallow costs on flexibly-priced contracts; and

(iii) The CFAO may, in consultation with the affected contracting officers, increase or decrease individual contract prices, including contract cost ceilings or target costs on flexibly-priced contracts. In such cases, the CFAO shall limit any upward contract price adjustments on affected contracts to the amount of downward price adjustments to other affected contracts, *i.e.*, the aggregate price of all contracts affected by a unilateral change shall not be increased (48 CFR 9903.201-6(b)).

(4) For noncompliances that involve estimating costs, the CFAO—

(i) Shall, to the extent practical, not adjust the price upward for fixed-price contracts;

(ii) Shall, if contract adjustments are made, preclude payment of aggregate increased costs by reducing the contract price on fixed-price contracts;

(iii) May, in consultation with the affected contracting officers, increase or decrease individual contract prices, including costs ceilings or target costs on flexibly-priced contracts. In such cases, the CFAO shall limit any upward contract price adjustments to affected contracts to the amount of downward price adjustments to other affected contracts, *i.e.*, the aggregate price of all contracts affected by a noncompliance that involves estimating costs shall not be increased (48 CFR 9903.201-6(d));

(iv) Shall require the contractor to correct the noncompliance, *i.e.*, ensure that compliant cost accounting practices will now be utilized to estimate proposed contract costs; and

(v) Shall require the contractor to adjust any invoices that were paid based on noncompliant contract prices to reflect the adjusted contract prices, after any contract price adjustments are made to resolve the noncompliance.

(5) For noncompliances that involve cost accumulation, the CFAO—

(i) Shall require the contractor to—

(A) Correct noncompliant contract cost accumulations in the contractor's cost accounting records for affected contracts to reflect compliant contract cost accumulations; and

(B) Adjust interim payment requests (public vouchers and/or progress payments) and final vouchers to reflect the difference between the costs paid using the noncompliant practice and the costs that should have been paid using the compliant practice; or

(ii) Shall adjust contract prices. In adjusting contract prices, the CFAO shall preclude payment of aggregate increased costs by disallowing costs on flexibly-priced contracts.

(A) The CFAO may, in consultation with the affected contracting officers, increase or decrease individual contract prices, including costs ceilings or target costs on flexibly-priced contracts. In such cases, the CFAO shall limit any upward contract price adjustments to affected contracts to the amount of downward price adjustments to other affected contracts, *i.e.*, the aggregate price of all contracts affected by a noncompliance that involves cost accumulation shall not be increased (48 CFR 9903.201-6(d)).

(B) Shall require the contractor to—

(*1*) Correct contract cost accumulations in the contractor's cost accounting records to reflect the contract price adjustments; and

(*2*) Adjust interim payment requests (public vouchers and/or progress payments) and final vouchers to reflect the contract price adjustments.

(6) When contract adjustments are made, the CFAO shall—

(i) Execute the bilateral modifications if the CFAO and contractor agree on the amount of the cost impact and the adjustments (see 42.302(a)(11)(iv)); or

(ii) When the CFAO and contractor do not agree on the amount of the cost impact or the contract adjustments, issue a final decision in accordance with 33.211 and unilaterally adjust the contract(s).

(d) *Alternate methods.* (1) The CFAO may use an alternate method instead of adjusting contracts to resolve the cost impact, provided the Government will not pay more, in the aggregate, than would be paid if the CFAO did not use the alternate method and the contracting parties agree on the use of that alternate method.

(2) The CFAO may not use an alternate method for contracts when application of the alternate method to contracts would result in—

(i) An under recovery of monies by the Government (*e.g.*, due to cost overruns); or

(ii) Distortions of incentive provisions and relationships between target costs, ceiling costs, and actual costs for incentive type contracts.

(3) When using an alternate method that excludes the costs from an indirect cost pool, the CFAO shall—

(i) Apply such exclusion only to the determination of final indirect cost rates (*see* 42.705); and

(ii) Adjust the exclusion to reflect the Government participation rate for flexibly-priced contracts and subcontracts. For example, if there are aggregate increased costs to the Government of $100,000, and the indirect cost pool where the adjustment is to be effected has a Government participation rate of 50 percent for flexibly-priced contracts and subcontracts, the contractor shall exclude $200,000 from the indirect cost pool ($100,000/50% = $200,000).

[FAC 2005-01, 70 FR 11743, 3/9/2005, effective 4/8/2005]

30.607 Subcontract administration.

When a negotiated CAS price adjustment or a determination of noncompliance is required at the subcontract level, the CFAO for the subcontractor shall furnish a copy of the negotiation memorandum or the determination to the CFAO for the contractor of the next higher-tier subcontractor. The CFAO of the contractor or the next higher-tier subcontractor shall not change the determination of the CFAO for the lower-tier subcontractor. If the subcontractor refuses to submit a GDM or DCI proposal, remedies are made at the prime contractor level.

[FAC 90-12, 57 FR 39587, 8/31/92, effective 8/31/92; FAC 90-38, 61 FR 18914, 4/29/96, effective 4/29/96; FAC 2005-01, 70 FR 11743, 3/9/2005, effective 4/8/2005]

PART 31—CONTRACT COST PRINCIPLES AND PROCEDURES

Table of Contents

Scope of part 31.000
Definitions 31.001
Availability of accounting guide 31.002

Subpart 31.1—Applicability

Scope of subpart 31.100
Objectives 31.101
Fixed-price contracts 31.102
Contracts with commercial organizations 31.103
Contracts with educational institutions 31.104
Construction and architect-engineer contracts 31.105
[Removed and Reserved] 31.106
Contracts with state, local, and federally recognized Indian tribal governments 31.107
Contracts with nonprofit organizations 31.108
Advance agreements 31.109
Indirect cost rate certification and penalties on unallowable costs 31.110

Subpart 31.2—Contracts with Commercial Organizations

General 31.201
Composition of total cost 31.201-1
Determining allowability 31.201-2
Determining reasonableness 31.201-3
Determining allocability 31.201-4
Credits 31.201-5
Accounting for unallowable costs 31.201-6
Construction and architect-engineer contracts 31.201-7
Direct costs 31.202
Indirect costs 31.203
Application of principles and procedures 31.204
Selected costs 31.205
Public relations and advertising costs 31.205-1
[Removed and Reserved] 31.205-2
Bad debts 31.205-3
Bonding costs 31.205-4
[Removed and Reserved] 31.205-5
Compensation for personal services 31.205-6
Contingencies 31.205-7
Contributions or donations 31.205-8
[Reserved] 31.205-9
Cost of money 31.205-10
Depreciation 31.205-11
Economic planning costs 31.205-12
Employee morale, health, welfare, food service, and dormitory costs and credits 31.205-13
Entertainment costs 31.205-14
Fines, penalties, and mischarging costs 31.205-15
Gains and losses on disposition or impairment of depreciable property or other capital assets 31.205-16
Idle facilities and idle capacity costs 31.205-17
Independent research and development and bid and proposal costs 31.205-18
Insurance and indemnification 31.205-19
Interest and other financial costs 31.205-20
Labor relations costs 31.205-21

Lobbying and political activity costs 31.205-22
Losses on other contracts 31.205-23
[Reserved] 31.205-24
Manufacturing and production engineering costs 31.205-25
Material costs 31.205-26
Organization costs 31.205-27
Other business expenses 31.205-28
Plant protection costs 31.205-29
Patent costs 31.205-30
Plant reconversion costs 31.205-31
Precontract costs 31.205-32
Professional and consultant service costs 31.205-33
Recruitment costs 31.205-34
Relocation costs 31.205-35
Rental costs 31.205-36
Royalties and other costs for use of patents 31.205-37
Selling costs 31.205-38
Service and warranty costs 31.205-39
Special tooling and special test equipment costs 31.205-40
Taxes 31.205-41
Termination costs 31.205-42
Trade, business, technical, and professional activity costs 31.205-43
Training and education costs 31.205-44
[Reserved] 31.205-45
Travel costs 31.205-46
Costs related to legal and other proceedings 31.205-47
Research and development costs 31.205-48
Goodwill 31.205-49
[Reserved] 31.205-50
Costs of alcoholic beverages 31.205-51
Asset valuations resulting from business combinations 31.205-52

Subpart 31.3—Contracts with Educational Institutions

Purpose 31.301
General 31.302
Requirements 31.303

Subpart 31.4—[Reserved]

Subpart 31.5—[Reserved]

Subpart 31.6—Contracts with State, Local, and Federally Recognized Indian Tribal Governments

Purpose 31.601
General 31.602
Requirements 31.603

Subpart 31.7—Contracts with Nonprofit Organizations

Purpose 31.701
General 31.702
Requirements 31.703

PART 31—CONTRACT COST PRINCIPLES AND PROCEDURES

31.000 Scope of part.

This part contains cost principles and procedures for

(a) the pricing of contracts, subcontracts, and modifications to contracts and subcontracts whenever cost analysis is performed (see 15.404-1(c))

(b) the determination, negotiation, or allowance of costs when required by a contract clause.

[FAC 97-2, 62 FR 51224, 9/30/97, effective 10/10/97]

31.001 Definitions.

As used in this part—

Accrued benefit cost method means an actuarial cost method under which units of benefits are assigned to each cost accounting period and are valued as they accrue; i.e., based on the services performed by each employee in the period involved. The measure of normal cost under this method for each cost accounting period is the present value of the units of benefit deemed to be credited to employees for service in that period. The measure of the actuarial accrued liability at a plan's inception date is the present value of the units of benefit credited to employees for service prior to that date. (This method is also known as the unit credit cost method without salary projection.)

Accumulating costs means collecting cost data in an organized manner, such as through a system of accounts.

Actual cash value means the cost of replacing damaged property with other property of like kind and quality in the physical condition of the property immediately before the damage.

Actual costs means (except for subpart 31.6) amounts determined on the basis of costs incurred, as distinguished from forecasted costs. Actual costs include standard costs properly adjusted for applicable variances.

Actuarial accrued liability means pension cost attributable, under the actuarial cost method in use, to years prior to the current period considered by a particular actuarial valuation. As of such date, the actuarial accrued liability represents the excess of the present value of future benefits and administrative expenses over the present value of future normal costs for all plan participants and beneficiaries. The excess of the actuarial accrued liability over the actuarial value of the assets of a pension plan is the unfunded actuarial liability. The excess of the actuarial value of the assets of a pension plan over the actuarial accrued liability is an actuarial surplus and is treated as a negative unfunded actuarial liability.

Actuarial assumption means an estimate of future conditions affecting pension cost; e.g., mortality rate, employee turnover, compensation levels, earnings on pension plan assets, and changes in values of pension plan assets.

Actuarial cost method means a technique which uses actuarial assumptions to measure the present value of future pension benefits and pension plan administrative expenses, and that assigns the cost of such benefits and expenses to cost accounting periods. The actuarial cost method includes the asset valuation method used to determine the actuarial value of the assets of a pension plan.

Actuarial gain and loss means the effect on pension cost resulting from differences between actuarial assumptions and actual experience.

Actuarial valuation means the determination, as of a specified date, of the normal cost, actuarial accrued liability, actuarial value of the assets of a pension plan, and other relevant values for the pension plan.

Allocate means to assign an item of cost, or a group of items of cost, to one or more cost objectives. This term includes both direct assignment of cost and the reassignment of a share from an indirect cost pool.

Compensated personal absence means any absence from work for reasons such as illness, vacation, holidays, jury duty, military training, or personal activities for which an employer pays compensation directly to an employee in accordance with a plan or custom of the employer.

Compensation for personal services means all remuneration paid currently or accrued, in whatever form and whether paid immediately or deferred, for services rendered by employees to the contractor.

Cost input means the cost, except general and administrative (G&A) expenses, which for contract costing purposes is allocable to the production of goods and services during a cost accounting period.

Cost objective means (except for subpart 31.6) a function, organizational subdivision, contract, or other work unit for which cost data are desired and for which provision is made to accumulate and measure the cost of processes, products, jobs, capitalized projects, etc.

Deferred compensation means an award made by an employer to compensate an employee in a future cost accounting period or periods for services rendered in one or more cost accounting periods before the date of the receipt of compensation by the employee. This definition shall not include the amount of year end accruals for salaries, wages, or bonuses that are to be paid within a reasonable period of time after the end of a cost accounting period.

Defined-benefit pension plan means a pension plan in which the benefits to be paid, or the basis for determining such benefits, are established in advance and the contributions are intended to provide the stated benefits.

Defined-contribution pension plan means a pension plan in which the contributions to be made are established in advance and the benefits are determined thereby.

Directly associated cost means any cost which is generated solely as a result of the incurrence of another cost, and which would not have been incurred had the other cost not been incurred.

Estimating costs means the process of forecasting a future result in terms of cost, based upon information available at the time.

Expressly unallowable cost means a particular item or type of cost which, under the express provisions of an applicable law, regulation, or contract, is specifically named and stated to be unallowable.

Final cost objective means (except for subparts 31.3 and 31.6) a cost objective that has allocated to it both direct and indirect costs and, in the contractors accumulation system, is one of the final accumulation points.

Fiscal year means the accounting period for which annual financial statements are regularly prepared, generally a period of 12 months, 52 weeks, or 53 weeks.

Funded pension cost means the portion of pension cost for a current or prior cost accounting period that has been paid to a funding agency.

Home office means an office responsible for directing or managing two or more, but not necessarily all, segments of an organization. It typically establishes policy for, and provides guidance to, the segments in their operations. It usually performs management, supervisory, or administrative functions, and may also perform service functions in support of the operations of the various segments. An organization which has intermediate levels, such as groups, may have several home offices which report to a common home office. An intermediate organization may be both a segment and a home office.

Immediate-gain actuarial cost method means any of the several actuarial cost methods under which actuarial gains and losses are included as part of the unfunded actuarial liability of the pension plan, rather than as part of the normal cost of the plan.

Independent research and development (IR&D) cost means the cost of effort which is neither sponsored by a grant, nor required in performing a contract, and which falls within any of the following four areas: (a) basic research, (b) applied research, (c) development, and (d) systems and other concept formulation studies.

Indirect cost pools means (except for subparts 31.3 and 31.6) groupings of incurred costs identified with two or more cost objectives but not identified specifically with any final cost objective.

Insurance administration expenses means the contractor's costs of administering an

(d) Except as otherwise provided in this paragraph (d), the allowability of costs for construction and architect-engineer contracts shall be determined in accordance with Subpart 31.2.

(1) Because of widely varying factors such as the nature, size, duration, and location of the construction project, advance agreements as set forth in 31.109, for such items as home office overhead, partners' compensation, employment of consultants, and equipment usage costs, are particularly important in construction and architect-engineer contracts. When appropriate, they serve to express the parties' understanding and avoid possible subsequent disputes or disallowances.

(2) *Construction equipment,* as used in this section, means equipment (including marine equipment) in sound workable condition, either owned or controlled by the contractor or the subcontractor at any tier, or obtained from a commercial rental source, and furnished for use under Government contracts.

(i) Allowable ownership and operating costs shall be determined as follows:

(A) Actual cost data shall be used when such data can be determined for both ownership and operations costs for each piece of equipment, or groups of similar serial or series equipment, from the contractor's accounting records. When such costs cannot be so determined, the contracting agency may specify the use of a particular schedule of predetermined rates or any part thereof to determine ownership and operating costs of construction equipment (see subdivisions (d)(2)(i)(B) and (C) of this section). However, costs otherwise unallowable under this part shall not become allowable through the use of any schedule (see 31.109(c)). For example, schedules need to be adjusted for Government contract costing purposes if they are based on replacement cost, include unallowable interest costs, or use improper cost of money rates or computations. Contracting officers should review the computations and factors included within the specified schedule and ensure that unallowable or unacceptably computed factors are not allowed in cost submissions.

(B) Predetermined schedules of construction equipment use rates (*e.g.*, the Construction Equipment Ownership and Operating Expense Schedule, published by the U.S. Army Corps of Engineers, industry sponsored construction equipment cost guides, or commercially published schedules of construction equipment use cost) provide average ownership and operating rates for construction equipment. The allowance for operating costs may include costs for such items as fuel, filters, oil, and grease; servicing, repairs, and maintenance; and tire wear and repair. Costs of labor, mobilization, demobilization, overhead, and profit are generally not reflected in schedules, and separate consideration may be necessary.

(C) When a schedule of predetermined use rates for construction equipment is used to determine direct costs, all costs of equipment that are included in the cost allowances provided by the schedule shall be identified and eliminated from the contractor's other direct and indirect costs charged to the contract. If the contractor's accounting system provides for site or home office overhead allocations, all costs which are included in the equipment allowances may need to be included in any cost input base before computing the contractor's overhead rate. In periods of suspension of work pursuant to a contract clause, the allowance for equipment ownership shall not exceed an amount for standby cost as determined by the schedule or contract provision.

(ii) Reasonable costs of renting construction equipment are allowable (but see paragraph (C) of this subsection).

(A) Costs, such as maintenance and minor or running repairs incident to operating such rented equipment, that are not included in the rental rate are allowable.

(B) Costs incident to major repair and overhaul of rental equipment are unallowable.

(C) The allowability of charges for construction equipment rented from any division, subsidiary, or organization under common control, will be determined in accordance with 31.205-36(b)(3).

(3) Costs incurred at the job site incident to performing the work, such as the cost of superintendence, timekeeping and clerical work, engineering, utility costs, supplies, material handling, restoration and cleanup, etc., are allowable as direct or indirect costs, provided the accounting practice used is in accordance with the contractor's established and consistently followed cost accounting practices for all work.

(4) Rental and any other costs, less any applicable credits incurred in acquiring the temporary use of land, structures, and facilities are allowable. Costs, less any applicable credits, incurred in constructing or fabricating structures and facilities of a temporary nature are allowable.

[FAC 84-7, 50 FR 23607, 6/4/85, effective 4/30/85; FAC 84-26, 52 FR 19804, 5/27/87, effective 7/30/87; FAC 97-2, 62 FR 51224, 9/30/97, effective 10/10/97; FAC 2005-89, 81 FR 45852, 7/14/2016, effective 8/15/2016]

31.106 [Removed and Reserved]

[FAC 2005-17, 72 FR 27364, 5/15/2007, effective 6/14/2007]

31.107 Contracts with state, local, and federally recognized Indian tribal governments.

(a) Subpart 31.6 provides principles and standards for determining costs applicable to contracts with State, local, and federally recognized Indian tribal governments. They provide the basis for a uniform approach to the problem of determining costs and to promote efficiency and better relationships between State, local, and federally recognized Indian tribal governments, and Federal Government entities. They apply to all programs that involve contracts with State, local, and federally recognized Indian tribal governments, except contracts with—

(1) Publicly financed educational institutions subject to Subpart 31.3; or

(2) Publicly owned hospitals and other providers of medical care subject to requirements promulgated by the sponsoring Government agencies.

(b) The Office of Management and Budget will approve any other exceptions in particular cases when adequate justification is presented.

[FAC 84-29, 52 FR 30076, 8/12/87, effective 8/24/87]

31.108 Contracts with nonprofit organizations.

Subpart 31.7 provides principles and standards for determining costs applicable to contracts with nonprofit organizations other than educational institutions (see subpart 31.3), State and local governments (see subpart 31.6), and those nonprofit organizations exempted under the OMB Uniform Guidance at 2 CFR part 200, appendix VIII (see subpart 31.2 for the cost principles applicable to nonprofit organizations exempt from the cost principles in the OMB Uniform Guidance at 2 CFR part 200).

[FAC 2005-89, 81 FR 45852, 7/14/2016, effective 8/15/2016]

31.109 Advance agreements.

(a) The extent of allowability of the costs covered in this part applies broadly to many accounting systems in varying contract situations. Thus, the reasonableness, the allocability and the allowability under the specific cost principles at Subparts 31.2, 31.3, 31.6, and 31.7 of certain costs may be difficult to determine. To avoid possible subsequent disallowance or dispute based on unreasonableness, unallocability, or unallowability under the specific cost principles at Subparts 31.2, 31.3, 31.6, and 31.7, contracting officers and contractors should seek advance agreement on the treatment of special or unusual costs and on statistical sampling methodologies at 31.201-6(c). However, an advance agreement is not an absolute requirement and the absence of an advance agreement on any cost will not, in itself, affect the reasonableness, allocability or the allowability under the specific cost principles at subparts 31.2, 31.3, 31.6, and 31.7 of that cost.

(b) Advance agreements may be negotiated either before or during a contract but should be negotiated before incurrence of the costs involved. The agreements must be in writing, executed by both contracting parties, and incorporated into applicable current and future contracts. An advance agreement shall contain a statement of its applicability and duration.

(c) The contracting officer is not authorized by this 31.109 to agree to a treatment of costs inconsistent with this part. For example, an advance agreement may not provide that, notwithstanding 31.205-20, interest is allowable.

(d) Advance agreements may be negotiated with a particular contractor for a single contract, a group of contracts, or all the contracts of a contracting office, an agency, or several agencies.

(e) The cognizant administrative contracting officer (ACO), or other contracting officer established in Part 42, shall negotiate advance agreements except that an advance agreement affecting only one contract, or class of contracts from a single contracting office, shall be negotiated by a contracting officer in the contracting office, or an ACO when delegated by the contracting officer. When the negotiation authority is delegated, the ACO shall coordinate the proposed agreement with the contracting officer before executing the advance agreement.

(f) Before negotiating an advance agreement, the Government negotiator shall—

(1) Determine if other contracting offices inside the agency or in other agencies have a significant unliquidated dollar balance in contracts with the same contractor;

(2) Inform any such office or agency of the matters under consideration for negotiation; and—

(3) As appropriate, invite the office or agency and the responsible audit agency to participate in prenegotiation discussions and/or in the subsequent negotiations.

(g) Upon completion of the negotiation, the sponsor shall prepare and distribute to other interested agencies and offices, including the audit agency, copies of the executed agreement and a memorandum providing the information specified in 15.406-3, Price negotiation memorandum, as applicable.

(h) Examples for which advance agreements may be particularly important are—

(1) Compensation for personal services, including but not limited to allowances for off-site pay, incentive pay, location allowances, hardship pay, cost of living differential, and termination of defined benefit pension plans;

(2) Use charges for fully depreciated assets;

(3) Deferred maintenance costs;

(4) Precontract costs;

(5) Independent research and development and bid and proposal costs;

(6) Royalties and other costs for use of patents;

(7) Selling and distribution costs;

(8) Travel and relocation costs, as related to special or mass personnel movements, as related to travel via contractor-owned, -leased, or -chartered aircraft, or as related to maximum per diem rates;

(9) Costs of idle facilities and idle capacity;

(10) Severance pay to employees on support service contracts;

(11) Plant reconversion;

(12) Professional services (*e.g.*, legal, accounting, and engineering);

(13) General and administrative costs (*e.g.*, corporate, division, or branch allocations) attributable to the general management, supervision, and conduct of the contractor's business as a whole. These costs are particularly significant in construction, job-site, architect-engineer, facilities, and Government-owned contractor operated (GOCO) plant contracts (see 31.203(h));

(14) Costs of construction plant and equipment (see 31.105(d));

(15) Costs of public relations and advertising; and

(16) Statistical sampling methods (see 31.201-6(c)(4)).

[FAC 84-15, 51 FR 12298, 4/9/86, effective 4/7/86; FAC 84-19, 51 FR 27489, 7/31/86, effective 7/31/86; FAC 84-25, 52 FR 9038, 3/20/87, effective 7/1/87; Corrected 52 FR 27806, 7/24/87; FAC 84-51, 54 FR 34755, 8/21/89, effective 9/20/89; FAC 90-23, 59 FR 67010, 12/28/94, effective 2/27/95; FAC

90-44, Interim rule, 61 FR 69286, 12/31/96, effective 12/31/96, finalized without change, FAC 97-1, 62 FR 44802, 8/22/97, effective 10/21/97; FAC 97-2, 62 FR 51224, 9/30/97, effective 10/10/97; FAC 97-4, 63 FR 9048, 2/23/98, effective 4/24/98; FAC 2001-22, 69 FR 17764, 4/5/2004, effective 5/5/2004; FAC 2005-06, 70 FR 57463, 9/30/2005, effective 10/31/2005; FAC 2005-78, 79 FR 70348, 11/25/2014, effective 11/25/2014]

31.110 Indirect cost rate certification and penalties on unallowable costs.

(a) Certain contracts require certification of the indirect cost rates proposed for final payment purposes. See 42.703-2 for administrative procedures regarding the certification provisions and the related contract clause prescription.

(b) If unallowable costs are included in final indirect cost settlement proposals, penalties may be assessed. See 42.709 for administrative procedures regarding the penalty assessment provisions and the related contract clause prescription.

[FAC 90-31, 60 FR 42648, 8/16/95, effective 10/1/95; FAC 90-45, Final rule, 62 FR 224, 1/2/97, effective 1/1/97]

SUBPART 31.2—CONTRACTS WITH COMMERCIAL ORGANIZATIONS

31.201 General. (No Text)

31.201-1 Composition of total cost.

(a) The total cost, including standard costs properly adjusted for applicable variances, of a contract is the sum of the direct and indirect costs allocable to the contract, incurred or to be incurred, plus any allocable cost of money pursuant to 31.205-10, less any allocable credits. In ascertaining what constitutes a cost, any generally accepted method of determining or estimating costs that is equitable and is consistently applied may be used.

(b) While the total cost of a contract includes all costs properly allocable to the contract, the allowable costs to the Government are limited to those allocable costs which are allowable pursuant to Part 31 and applicable agency supplements.

[FAC 90-23, 59 FR 67010, 12/28/94, effective 2/27/95; FAC 2001-22, 69 FR 17764, 4/5/2004, effective 5/5/2004]

31.201-2 Determining allowability.

(a) A cost is allowable only when the cost complies with all of the following requirements:

(1) Reasonableness.

(2) Allocability.

(3) Standards promulgated by the CAS Board, if applicable, generally accepted accounting principles and practices appropriate to the circumstances.

(4) Terms of the contract.

(5) Any limitations set forth in this subpart.

(b) Certain cost principles in this subpart incorporate the measurement, assignment, and allocability rules of selected CAS and limit the allowability of costs to the amounts determined using the criteria in those selected standards. Only those CAS or portions of standards specifically made applicable by the cost principles in this subpart are mandatory unless the contract is CAS-covered (see Part 30). Business units that are not otherwise subject to these standards under a CAS clause are subject to the selected standards only for the purpose of determining allowability of costs on Government contracts. Including the selected standards in the cost principles does not subject the business unit to any other CAS rules and regulations. The applicability of the CAS rules and regulations is determined by the CAS clause, if any, in the contract and the requirements of the standards themselves.

(c) When contractor accounting practices are inconsistent with this Subpart 31.2, costs resulting from such inconsistent practices in excess of the amount that would have resulted from using practices consistent with this subpart are unallowable.

(d) A contractor is responsible for accounting for costs appropriately and for maintaining records, including supporting documentation, adequate to demonstrate that costs claimed have been incurred, are allocable to the contract, and comply with applicable cost principles in this subpart and agency supplements. The contracting officer may disallow all or part of a claimed cost that is inadequately supported.

[FAC 90-12, 57 FR 39590, 8/31/92, effective 8/31/92; FAC 90-39, 61 FR 31612, 6/20/96, effective 8/19/96; FAC 2001-22, 69 FR 17764, 4/5/2004, effective 5/5/2004]

31.201-3 Determining reasonableness.

(a) A cost is reasonable if, in its nature and amount, it does not exceed that which would be incurred by a prudent person in the conduct of competitive business. Reasonableness of specific costs must be examined with particular care in connection with firms or their separate divisions that may not be subject to effective competitive restraints. No presumption of reasonableness shall be attached to the incurrence of costs by a contractor. If an initial review of the facts results in a challenge of a specific cost by the contracting officer or the contracting officer's representative, the burden of proof shall be upon the contractor to establish that such cost is reasonable.

(b) What is reasonable depends upon a variety of considerations and circumstances, including—

(1) Whether it is the type of cost generally recognized as ordinary and necessary for the conduct of the contractor's business or the contract performance;

(2) Generally accepted sound business practices, arm's-length bargaining, and Federal and State laws and regulations;

(3) The contractor's responsibilities to the Government, other customers, the owners of the business, employees, and the public at large; and—

(4) Any significant deviations from the contractor's established practices.

[FAC 84-26, 52 FR 19804, 5/27/87, effective 7/30/87]

31.201-4 Determining allocability.

A cost is allocable if it is assignable or chargeable to one or more cost objectives on the basis of relative benefits received or other equitable relationship. Subject to the foregoing, a cost is allocable to a Government contract if it—

(a) Is incurred specifically for the contract;

(b) Benefits both the contract and other work, and can be distributed to them in reasonable proportion to the benefits received; or

(c) Is necessary to the overall operation of the business, although a direct relationship to any particular cost objective cannot be shown.

31.201-5 Credits.

The applicable portion of any income, rebate, allowance, or other credit relating to any allowable cost and received by or accruing to the contractor shall be credited to the Government either as a cost reduction or by cash refund. See 31.205-6(j) (3) for rules governing refund or credit to the Government associated with pension adjustments and asset reversions.

[FAC 84-51, 54 FR 34755, 8/21/89, effective 9/20/89; FAC 97-2, 62 FR 51224, 9/30/97, effective 10/10/97; FAC 97-9, 63 FR 58587, 10/30/98, effective 12/29/98; FAC 2005-19, 72 FR 46363, 8/17/2007, effective 8/17/2007]

31.201-6 Accounting for unallowable costs.

(a) Costs that are expressly unallowable or mutually agreed to be unallowable, including mutually agreed to be unallowable directly associated costs, shall be identified and excluded from any billing, claim, or proposal applicable to a Government contract. A directly associated cost is any cost that is generated solely as a result of incurring another cost, and that would not have been incurred had the other cost not been incurred. When an unallowable cost is incurred, its directly associated costs are also unallowable.

(b) Costs that specifically become designated as unallowable or as unallowable directly associated costs of unallowable costs as a result of a written decision furnished by a contracting officer shall be identified if included in or used in computing any billing, claim, or proposal applicable to a Government contract. This identification requirement applies also to any costs incurred for the same purpose under like circumstances as the costs specifically identified as unallowable under either this paragraph or paragraph (a) above.

(c) (1) The practices for accounting for and presentation of unallowable costs must be those described in 48 CFR 9904.405, Accounting for Unallowable Costs.

(2) Statistical sampling is an acceptable practice for contractors to follow in accounting for and presenting unallowable costs provided the following criteria in paragraphs (c) (2) (i), (c) (2) (ii), and (c) (2) (iii) of this subsection are met:

(i) The statistical sampling results in an unbiased sample that is a reasonable representation of the sampling universe.

(ii) Any large dollar value or high risk transaction is separately reviewed for unallowable costs and excluded from the sampling process.

(iii) The statistical sampling permits audit verification.

(3) For any indirect cost in the selected sample that is subject to the penalty provisions at 42.709, the amount projected to the sampling universe from that sampled cost is also subject to the same penalty provisions.

(4) Use of statistical sampling methods for identifying and segregating unallowable costs should be the subject of an advance agreement under the provisions of 31.109 between the contractor and the cognizant administrative contracting officer or Federal official. The advance agreement should specify the basic characteristics of the sampling process. The cognizant administrative contracting officer or Federal official shall request input from the cognizant auditor before entering into any such agreements.

(5) In the absence of an advance agreement, if an initial review of the facts results in a challenge of the statistical sampling methods by the contracting officer or the contracting officer's representative, the burden of proof shall be on the contractor to establish that such a method meets the criteria in paragraph (c) (2) of this subsection.

(d) If a directly associated cost is included in a cost pool that is allocated over a base that includes the unallowable cost with which it is associated, the directly associated cost shall remain in the cost pool. Since the unallowable costs will attract their allocable share of costs from the cost pool, no further action is required to assure disallowance of the directly associated costs. In all other cases, the directly associated costs, if material in amount, must be purged from the cost pool as unallowable costs.

(e) (1) In determining the materiality of a directly associated cost, consideration should be given to the significance of

(i) the actual dollar amount,

(ii) the cumulative effect of all directly associated costs in a cost pool, and

(iii) the ultimate effect on the cost of Government contracts.

(2) Salary expenses of employees who participate in activities that generate unallowable costs shall be treated as directly associated costs to the extent of the time spent on the proscribed activity, provided the costs are material in accordance with subparagraph (e) (1) above (except when such salary expenses are, themselves, unallowable). The time spent in proscribed activities should be compared to total time spent on company activities to determine if the costs are material. Time spent by employees outside the normal working hours should not be considered except when it is evident that an employee engages so frequently in company activities during periods outside normal working hours as to indicate that such activities are a part of the employee's regular duties.

(3) When a selected item of cost under 31.205 provides that directly associated costs be unallowable, such directly associated costs are unallowable only if determined to be material in amount in accordance with the criteria provided in paragraphs (e) (1) and (e) (2) of this subsection, except in those situations where allowance of any of the directly associated costs involved would be considered to be contrary to public policy.

[FAC 90-23, 59 FR 67010, 12/28/94, effective 2/27/95; FAC 2005-06, 70 FR 57463,

9/30/2005, effective 10/31/2005; correction, 70 FR 69100, 11/14/2005, effective 11/14/2005]

31.201-7 Construction and architect-engineer contracts.

Specific principles and procedures for evaluating and determining costs in connection with contracts and subcontracts for construction, and architect-engineer contracts related to construction projects, are in 31.105. The applicability of these principles and procedures is set forth in 31.000 and 31.100.

31.202 Direct costs.

(a) No final cost objective shall have allocated to it as a direct cost any cost, if other costs incurred for the same purpose in like circumstances have been included in any indirect cost pool to be allocated to that or any other final cost objective. Direct costs of the contract shall be charged directly to the contract. All costs specifically identified with other final cost objectives of the contractor are direct costs of those cost objectives and are not to be charged to the contract directly or indirectly.

(b) For reasons of practicality, the contractor may treat any direct cost of a minor dollar amount as an indirect cost if the accounting treatment—

(1) Is consistently applied to all final cost objectives; and

(2) Produces substantially the same results as treating the cost as a direct cost.

[FAC 2001-22, 69 FR 17764, 4/5/2004, effective 5/5/2004]

31.203 Indirect costs.

(a) For contracts subject to full CAS coverage, allocation of indirect costs shall be based on the applicable provisions. For all other contracts, the applicable CAS provisions in paragraphs (b) through (h) of this section apply.

(b) After direct costs have been determined and charged directly to the contract or other work, indirect costs are those remaining to be allocated to intermediate or two or more final cost objectives. No final cost objective shall have allocated to it as an indirect cost any cost, if other costs incurred for the same purpose, in like circumstances, have been included as a direct cost of that or any other final cost objective.

(c) The contractor shall accumulate indirect costs by logical cost groupings with due consideration of the reasons for incurring such costs. The contractor shall determine each grouping so as to permit use of an allocation base that is common to all cost objectives to which the grouping is to be allocated. The base selected shall allocate the grouping on the basis of the benefits accruing to intermediate and final cost objectives. When substantially the same results can be achieved through less precise methods, the number and composition of cost groupings should be governed by practical considerations and should not unduly complicate the allocation.

(d) Once an appropriate base for allocating indirect costs has been accepted, the contractor shall not fragment the base by removing individual elements. All items properly includable in an indirect cost base shall bear a pro rata share of indirect costs irrespective of their acceptance as Government contract costs. For example, when a cost input base is used for the allocation of G&A costs, the contractor shall include in the base all items that would properly be part of the cost input base, whether allowable or unallowable, and these items shall bear their pro rata share of G&A costs.

(e) The method of allocating indirect costs may require revision when there is a significant change in the nature of the business, the extent of subcontracting, fixed-asset improvement programs, inventories, the volume of sales and production, manufacturing processes, the contractor's products, or other relevant circumstances.

(f) Separate cost groupings for costs allocable to offsite locations may be necessary to permit equitable distribution of costs on the basis of the benefits accruing to the several cost objectives.

(g) A base period for allocating indirect costs is the cost accounting period during which such costs are incurred and accumulated for allocation to work performed in that period.

(1) For contracts subject to full or modified CAS coverage, the contractor shall follow the criteria and guidance in 48 CFR 9904.406 for selecting the cost accounting periods to be used in allocating indirect costs.

(2) For contracts other than those subject to paragraph (g) (1) of this section, the base period for allocating indirect costs shall be the contractor's fiscal year used for financial reporting purposes in accordance with generally accepted accounting principles. The fiscal year will normally be 12 months, but a different period may be appropriate (e.g., when a change in fiscal year occurs due to a business combination or other circumstances).

(h) Special care should be exercised in applying the principles of paragraphs (c), (d), and (e) of this section when Government-owned contractor-operated (GOCO) plants are involved. The distribution of corporate, division or branch office G&A expenses to such plants operating with little or no dependence on corporate administrative activities may require more precise cost groupings, detailed accounts screening, and carefully developed distribution bases.

(i) Indirect costs that meet the definition of *excessive pass-through charge* in 52.215-23, are unallowable.

[FAC 84-30, 9/30/87, effective 9/30/87; FAC 90-12, 57 FR 39590, 8/31/92, effective 8/31/92; FAC 2001-22, 69 FR 17764, 4/5/2004, effective 5/5/2004; FAC 2005-37, 74 FR 52853, 10/14/2009, effective 10/14/2009; FAC 2005-47, 75 FR 77741, 12/13/2010, effective 1/12/2011]

31.204 Application of principles and procedures.

(a) Costs are allowable to the extent they are reasonable, allocable, and determined to be allowable under 31.201, 31.202, 31.203, and 31.205. These criteria apply to all of the selected items that follow, even if particular guidance is provided for certain items for emphasis or clarity.

(b) (1) For the following subcontract types, costs incurred as reimbursements or payments to a subcontractor are allowable to the extent the reimbursements or payments are for costs incurred by the subcontractor that are consistent with this part:

(i) Cost-reimbursement.

(ii) Fixed-price incentive.

(iii) Price redeterminable (i.e., fixed-price contracts with prospective price redetermination and fixed-ceiling-price contracts with retroactive price redetermination).

(2) The requirements of paragraph (b) (1) of this section apply to any tier above the first firm-fixed-price subcontract or fixed-price subcontract with economic price adjustment provisions.

(c) Costs incurred as payments under firm-fixed-price subcontracts or fixed-price subcontracts with economic price adjustment provisions or modifications thereto, for which subcontract cost analysis was performed are allowable if the price was negotiated in accordance with 31.102.

(d) Section 31.205 does not cover every element of cost. Failure to include any item of cost does not imply that it is either allowable or unallowable. The determination of allowability shall be based on the principles and standards in this subpart and the treatment of similar or related selected items. When more than one subsection in 31.205 is relevant to a contractor cost, the cost shall be apportioned among the applicable subsections, and the determination of allowability of each portion shall be based on the guidance contained in the applicable subsection. When a cost, to which more than one subsection in 31.205 is relevant, cannot be apportioned, the determination of allowability shall be based on the guidance contained in the subsection that most specifically deals with, or best captures the essential nature of, the cost at issue.

[FAC 84-37, 53 FR 17858, 5/18/88, effective 6/17/88; FAC 97-2, 62 FR 51224, 9/30/97, effective 10/10/97; FAC 2001-24, 69 FR 34241, 6/18/2004, effective 7/19/2004]

31.205 Selected costs. (No Text)

31.205-1 Public relations and advertising costs.

(a) *Public relations* means all functions and activities dedicated to—

(1) Maintaining, protecting, and enhancing the image of a concern or its products; or

(2) Maintaining or promoting reciprocal understanding and favorable relations with the public at large, or any segment of the public. The term public relations includes activities associated with areas such as advertising, customer relations, etc.

(b) *Advertising* means the use of media to promote the sale of products or services and to accomplish the activities referred to in paragraph (d) of this subsection, regardless of the medium employed, when the advertiser has control over the form and content of what will appear, the media in which it will appear, and when it will appear. Advertising media include but are not limited to conventions, exhibits, free goods, samples, magazines, newspapers, trade papers, direct mail, dealer cards, window displays, outdoor advertising, radio, and television.

(c) Public relations and advertising costs include the costs of media time and space, purchased services performed by outside organizations, as well as the applicable portion of salaries, travel, and fringe benefits of employees engaged in the functions and activities identified in paragraphs (a) and (b) of this subsection.

(d) The only allowable advertising costs are those that are—

(1) Specifically required by contract, or that arise from requirements of Government contracts, and that are exclusively for—

(i) Acquiring scarce items for contract performance; or

(ii) Disposing of scrap or surplus materials acquired for contract performance;

(2) Costs of activities to promote sales of products normally sold to the U.S. Government, including trade shows, which contain a significant effort to promote exports from the United States. Such costs are allowable, notwithstanding paragraphs (f) (1), (f) (3), (f) (4) (ii), and (f) (5) of this subsection. However, such costs do not include the costs of memorabilia (e.g., models, gifts, and souvenirs), alcoholic beverages, entertainment, and physical facilities that are used primarily for entertainment rather than product promotion; or

(3) Allowable in accordance with 31.205-34.

(e) Allowable public relations costs include the following:

(1) Costs specifically required by contract.

(2) Costs of—

(i) Responding to inquiries on company policies and activities;

(ii) Communicating with the public, press, stockholders, creditors, and customers; and

(iii) Conducting general liaison with news media and Government public relations officers, to the extent that such activities are limited to communication and liaison necessary to keep the public informed on matters of public concern such as notice of contract awards, plant closings or openings, employee layoffs or rehires, financial information, etc.

(3) Costs of participation in community service activities (*e.g.*, blood bank drives, charity drives, savings bond drives, disaster assistance, etc.) (But see paragraph (f) (8) of this section.).

(4) Costs of plant tours and open houses (but see subparagraph (f) (5) of this subsection).

(5) Costs of keel laying, ship launching, commissioning, and roll-out ceremonies, to the extent specifically provided for by contract.

(f) Unallowable public relations and advertising costs include the following:

(1) All public relations and advertising costs, other than those specified in paragraphs (d) and (e) of this subsection, whose primary purpose is to promote the sale of products or services by stimulating interest in a product or product line (except for those costs made allowable under 31.205-38(b) (5)), or by disseminating messages calling favorable attention to the contractor for purposes of enhancing the

company image to sell the company's products or services.

(2) All costs of trade shows and other special events which do not contain a significant effort to promote the export sales of products normally sold to the U.S. Government.

(3) Costs of sponsoring meetings, conventions, symposia, seminars, and other special events when the principal purpose of the event is other than dissemination of technical information or stimulation of production.

(4) Costs of ceremonies such as—

(i) Corporate celebrations and—

(ii) New product announcements.

(5) Costs of promotional material, motion pictures, videotapes, brochures, handouts, magazines, and other media that are designed to call favorable attention to the contractor and its activities.

(6) Costs of souvenirs, models, imprinted clothing, buttons, and other mementos provided to customers or the public.

(7) Costs of memberships in civic and community organizations.

(8) Costs associated with the donation of excess food to nonprofit organizations in accordance with the Federal Food Donation Act of 2008 (42 U.S.C. 1792, see subpart 26.4).

[FAC 84-15, 51 FR 12298, 4/9/86, effective 4/7/86; FAC 84-36, 53 FR 12130, 4/12/88, effective 4/12/88, corrected 53 FR 13274, 4/22/88; FAC 84-51, 54 FR 34755, 8/21/89, effective 9/20/89; FAC 90-4, 56 FR 15153, 4/15/91, effective 5/15/91; FAC 90-31, 60 FR 42648, 8/16/95, effective 10/1/95; FAC 90-43, Final rule, 61 FR 67408, 12/20/96, effective 2/18/97; FAC 90-46, 62 FR 12690, 3/17/97, effective 5/16/97; FAC 97-11, 64 FR 10530, 3/4/99, effective 5/3/99; FAC 2001-15, 68 FR 43871, 7/24/2003, effective 8/25/2003; FAR 2005-31, 74 FR 11829, 3/19/2009, effective 3/19/2009; FAC 2005-38, 74 FR 65607, 12/10/2009, effective 12/10/2009; FAC 2005-73, 79 FR 24192, 4/29/2014, effective 5/29/2014]

31.205-2 [Removed and Reserved]

[Removed and Reserved, FAC 90-44, Interim rule, 61 FR 69286, 12/31/96, effective 12/31/96, finalized without change, FAC 97-1, 62 FR 44802, 8/22/97, effective 10/21/97]

31.205-3 Bad debts.

Bad debts, including actual or estimated losses arising from uncollectible accounts receivable due from customers and other claims, and any directly associated costs such as collection costs, and legal costs are unallowable.

31.205-4 Bonding costs.

(a) Bonding costs arise when the Government requires assurance against financial loss to itself or others by reason of the act or default of the contractor. They arise also in instances where the contractor requires similar assurance. Included are such bonds as bid, performance, payment, advance payment, infringement, and fidelity bonds.

(b) Costs of bonding required pursuant to the terms of the contract are allowable.

(c) Costs of bonding required by the contractor in the general conduct of its business are allowable to the extent that such bonding is in accordance with sound business practice and the rates and premiums are reasonable under the circumstances.

31.205-5 [Removed and Reserved]

[Removed and Reserved, FAC 97-9, 63 FR 58587, 10/30/98, effective 12/29/98]

31.205-6 Compensation for personal services.

(a) *General.* Compensation for personal services is allowable subject to the following general criteria and additional requirements contained in other parts of this cost principle:

(1) Compensation for personal services must be for work performed by the employee in the current year and must not represent a retroactive adjustment of prior years' salaries or wages (but see paragraphs (g), (h), (j), (k), (m), and (o) of this subsection).

(2) The total compensation for individual employees or job classes of employees must be reasonable for the work performed; however, specific restrictions on individual compensation elements apply when prescribed.

(3) The compensation must be based upon and conform to the terms and conditions of the contractor's established compensation plan or practice followed so consistently as to imply, in effect, an agreement to make the payment.

(4) No presumption of allowability will exist where the contractor introduces major revisions of existing compensation plans or new plans and the contractor has not provided the cognizant ACO, either before implementation or within a reasonable period after it, an opportunity to review the allowability of the changes.

(5) Costs that are unallowable under other paragraphs of this Subpart 31.2 are not allowable under this subsection 31.205-6 solely on the basis that they constitute compensation for personal services.

(6) (i) Compensation costs for certain individuals give rise to the need for special consideration. Such individuals include:

(A) Owners of closely held corporations, members of limited liability companies, partners, sole proprietors, or members of their immediate families; and

(B) Persons who are contractually committed to acquire a substantial financial interest in the contractor's enterprise.

(ii) For these individuals, compensation must—

(A) Be reasonable for the personal services rendered; and

(B) Not be a distribution of profits (which is not an allowable contract cost).

(iii) For owners of closely held companies, compensation in excess of the costs that are deductible as compensation under the Internal Revenue Code (26 U.S.C.) and regulations under it is unallowable.

(b) *Reasonableness.* (1) Compensation pursuant to labor-management agreements. If costs of compensation established under "arm's length" labor-management agreements negotiated under the terms of the Federal Labor Relations Act or similar state statutes are otherwise allowable, the costs are reasonable unless, as applied to work in performing Government contracts, the costs are unwarranted by the character and circumstances of the work or discriminatory against the Government. The application of the provisions of a labor-management agreement designed to apply to a given set or circumstances and conditions of employment (e.g., work involving extremely hazardous activities or work not requiring recurrent use of overtime) is unwarranted when applied to a Government contract involving significantly different circumstances and conditions of employment (e.g., work involving less hazardous activities or work continually requiring use of overtime). It is discriminatory against the Government if it results in employee compensation (in whatever form or name) in excess of that being paid for similar non-Government work under comparable circumstances.

(2) Compensation not covered by labor-management agreements. Compensation for each employee or job class of employees must be reasonable for the work performed. Compensation is reasonable if the aggregate of each measurable and allowable element sums to a reasonable total. In determining the reasonableness of total compensation, consider only allowable individual elements of compensation. In addition to the provision of 31.201-3, in testing the reasonableness of compensation for particular employees or job classes of employees, consider factors determined to be relevant by the contracting officer. Factors that may be relevant include, but are not limited to, conformity with compensation practices of other firms—

(i) Of the same size;

(ii) In the same industry;

(iii) In the same geographic area; and

(iv) Engaged in similar non-Government work under comparable circumstances.

(c) [Reserved]

(d) *Form of payment.* (1) Compensation for personal services includes compensation paid or to be paid in the future to employees in the form of—

(i) Cash;

(ii) Corporate securities, such as stocks, bonds, and other financial instruments (see paragraph (d)(2) of this subsection regarding valuation); or

(iii) Other assets, products, or services.

(2) When compensation is paid with securities of the contractor or of an affiliate, the following additional restrictions apply:

(i) Valuation placed on the securities is the fair market value on the first date the number of shares awarded is known, determined upon the most objective basis available.

(ii) Accruals for the cost of securities before issuing the securities to the employees are subject to adjustment according to the possibilities that the employees will not receive the securities and that their interest in the accruals will be forfeited.

(e) *Income tax differential pay.* (1) Differential allowances for additional income taxes resulting from foreign assignments are allowable.

(2) Differential allowances for additional income taxes resulting from domestic assignments are unallowable. (However, payments for increased employee income or Federal Insurance Contributions Act taxes incident to allowable reimbursed relocation costs are allowable under 31.205-35(a)(10).)

(f) *Bonuses and incentive compensation.* (1) Bonuses and incentive compensation are allowable provided the—

(i) Awards are paid or accrued under an agreement entered into in good faith between the contractor and the employees before the services are rendered or pursuant to an established plan or policy followed by the contractor so consistently as to imply, in effect, an agreement to make such payment; and

(ii) Basis for the award is supported.

(2) When the bonus and incentive compensation payments are deferred, the costs are subject to the requirements of paragraphs (f)(1) and (k) of this subsection.

(g) *Severance pay.* (1) Severance pay is a payment in addition to regular salaries and wages by contractors to workers whose employment is being involuntarily terminated. Payments for early retirement incentive plans are covered in paragraph (j)(6) of this subsection.

(2) Severance pay is allowable only to the extent that, in each case, it is required by—

(i) Law;

(ii) Employer-employee agreement;

(iii) Established policy that constitutes, in effect, an implied agreement on the contractor's part; or

(iv) Circumstances of the particular employment.

(3) Payments made in the event of employment with a replacement contractor where continuity of employment with credit for prior length of service is preserved under substantially equal conditions of employment, or continued employment by the contractor at another facility, subsidiary, affiliate, or parent company of the contractor are not severance pay and are unallowable.

(4) Actual normal turnover severance payments shall be allocated to all work performed in the contractor's plant. However, if the contractor uses the accrual method to account for normal turnover severance payments, that method will be acceptable if the amount of the accrual is—

(i) Reasonable in light of payments actually made for normal severances over a representative past period; and

(ii) Allocated to all work performed in the contractor's plant.

(5) Abnormal or mass severance pay is of such a conjectural nature that accruals for this purpose are not allowable. However, the Government recognizes its obligation to participate, to the extent of its fair share, in any specific payment. Thus, the Government will consider allowability on a case-by-case basis.

(6) Under 10 U.S.C. 2324(e)(1)(M) and 41 U.S.C. 4304(a)(13), the costs of severance payments to foreign nationals employed under a service contract performed outside the United States are unallowable to the extent that such payments exceed amounts typically paid to employees providing similar services in the same industry in the United States. Further, under 10 U.S.C. 2324(e)(1)(N) and 41 U.S.C. 4304(a)(14), all

such costs of severance payments that are otherwise allowable are unallowable if the termination of employment of the foreign national is the result of the closing of, or the curtailment of activities at, a United States facility in that country at the request of the government of that country; this does not apply if the closing of a facility or curtailment of activities is made pursuant to a status-of-forces or other country-to-country agreement entered into with the government of that country before November 29, 1989. 10 U.S.C. 2324(e)(3) and 41 U.S.C. 4304(b) permit the head of the agency to waive these cost allowability limitations under certain circumstances (see 37.113 and the solicitation provision at 52.237-8).

(h) *Backpay.* Backpay is a retroactive adjustment of prior years' salaries or wages. Backpay is unallowable except as follows:

(1) Payments to employees resulting from underpaid work actually performed are allowable, if required by a negotiated settlement, order, or court decree.

(2) Payments to union employees for the difference in their past and current wage rates for working without a contract or labor agreement during labor management negotiation are allowable.

(3) Payments to nonunion employees based upon results of union agreement negotiation are allowable only if—

(i) A formal agreement or understanding exists between management and the employees concerning these payments; or

(ii) An established policy or practice exists and is followed by the contractor so consistently as to imply, in effect, and agreement to make such payments.

(i) *Compensation based on changes in the prices of corporate securities or corporate security ownership, such as stock options, stock appreciation rights, phantom stock plans, and junior stock conversions.*

(1) Any compensation which is calculated, or valued, based on changes in the price of corporate securities is unallowable.

(2) Any compensation represented by dividend payments or which is calculated based on dividend payments is unallowable.

(3) If a contractor pays an employee in lieu of the employee receiving or exercising a right, option, or benefit which would have been unallowable under this paragraph (i), such payments are also unallowable.

(j) *Pension costs.* (1) Pension plans are normally segregated into two types of plans: defined-benefit and defined-contribution pension plans. The contractor shall measure, assign, and allocate the costs of all defined-benefit pension plans and the costs of all defined-contribution pension plans in compliance with 48 CFR 9904.412—Cost Accounting Standard for Composition and Measurement of Pension Cost, and 48 CFR 9904.413—Adjustment and Allocation of Pension Cost. Pension costs are allowable subject to the referenced standards and the cost limitations and exclusions set forth in paragraph (j)(1)(i) and in paragraphs (j)(2) through (j)(6) of this subsection.

(i) Except for nonqualified pension plans using the pay-as-you-go cost method, to be allowable in the current year, the contractor shall fund pension costs by the time set for filing of the Federal income tax return or any extension. Pension costs assigned to the current year, but not funded by the tax return time, are not allowable in any subsequent year. For nonqualified pension plans using the pay-as-you-go method, to be allowable in the current year, the contractor shall allocate pension costs in the cost accounting period that the pension costs are assigned.

(ii) Pension payments must be paid pursuant to an agreement entered into in good faith between the contractor and employees before the work or services are performed and to the terms and conditions of the established plan. The cost of changes in pension plans are not allowable if the changes are discriminatory to the Government or are not intended to be applied consistently for all employees under similar circumstances in the future.

(iii) Except as provided for early retirement benefits in paragraph (j)(6) of this subsection, one-time-only pension supplements not available to all participants of the basic plan are not allowable as pension costs, unless the supplemental benefits represent a separate pension plan and the benefits are payable for life at the option of the employee.

(iv) Increases in payments to previously retired plan participants covering cost-of-living adjustments are allowable if paid in accordance with a policy or practice consistently followed.

(2) *Defined-benefit pension plans.* The cost limitations and exclusions pertaining to defined-benefit plans are as follows:

(i) (A) Except for nonqualified pension plans, pension costs (see 48 CFR 9904.412-40(a)(1)) assigned to the current accounting period, but not funded during it, are not allowable in subsequent years (except that a payment made to a fund by the time set for filing the Federal income tax return or any extension thereof is considered to have been made during such taxable year). However, any portion of pension cost computed for a cost accounting period, that exceeds the amount required to be funded pursuant to a waiver granted under the provisions of the Employee Retirement Income Security Act of 1974 (ERISA), will be allowable in those future accounting periods in which the funding of such excess amounts occurs (see 48 CFR 9904.412-50(c)(5)).

(B) For nonqualified pension plans, except those using the pay-as-you-go cost method, allowable costs are limited to the amount allocable in accordance with 48 CFR 9904.412-50(d)(2).

(C) For nonqualified pension plans using the pay-as-you-go cost method, allowable costs are limited to the amounts allocable in accordance with 48 CFR 9904.412-50(d)(3).

(ii) Any amount funded in excess of the pension cost assigned to a cost accounting period is not allowable in that period and shall be accounted for as set forth at 48 CFR 9904.412-50(a)(4). The excess amount is allowable in the future period to which it is assigned, to the extent it is not otherwise unallowable.

(iii) Increased pension costs are unallowable if the increase is caused by a delay in funding beyond 30 days after each quarter of the year to which they are assignable. If a composite rate is used for allocating pension costs between the segments of a company and if, because of differences in the timing of the funding by the segments, an inequity exists, allowable pension costs for each segment will be limited to that particular segment's calculation of pension costs as provided for in 48 CFR 9904.413-50(c). The contractor shall make determinations of unallowable costs in accordance with the actuarial method used in calculating pension costs.

(iv) The contracting officer will consider the allowability of the cost of indemnifying the Pension Benefit Guaranty Corporation (PBGC) under ERISA section 4062 or 4064 arising from terminating an employee deferred compensation plan on a case-by-case basis, provided that if insurance was required by the PBGC under ERISA section 4023, it was so obtained and the indemnification payment is not recoverable under the insurance. Consideration under the foregoing circumstances will be primarily for the purpose of appraising the extent to which the indemnification payment is allocable to Government work. If a beneficial or other equitable relationship exists, the Government will participate, despite the requirements of 31.205-19(c)(3) and (d)(3), in the indemnification payment to the extent of its fair share.

(v) Increased pension costs resulting from the withdrawal of assets from a pension fund and transfer to another employee benefit plan fund, or transfer of assets to another account within the same fund, are unallowable except to the extent authorized by an advance agreement. If the withdrawal of assets from a pension fund is a plan termination under ERISA, the provisions of paragraph (j)(3) of this subsection apply. The advance agreement shall—

(A) State the amount of the Government's equitable share in the gross amount withdrawn or transferred; and

(B) Provide that the Government receives a credit equal to the amount of the Government's equitable share of the gross withdrawal or transfer.

(3) *Pension adjustments and asset reversions.* (i) For segment closings, pension plan terminations, or curtailment of benefits, the amount of the adjustment shall be—

(A) For contracts and subcontracts that are subject to full coverage under the Cost Accounting Standards (CAS) Board rules and regulations, the amount measured, assigned, and allocated in accordance with 48 CFR 9904.413-50(c)(12); and

(B) For contracts and subcontracts that are not subject to full coverage under the CAS, the amount measured, assigned, and allocated in accordance with 48 CFR 9904.413-50(c)(12), except the numerator of the fraction at 48 CFR 9904.413-50(c)(12)(vi) is the sum of the pension plan costs allocated to all non-CAS-covered contracts and subcontracts that are subject to Subpart 31.2 or for which certified cost or pricing data were submitted.

(ii) For all other situations where assets revert to the contractor, or such assets are constructively received by it for any reason, the contractor shall, at the Government's option, make a refund or give a credit to the Government for its equitable share of the gross amount withdrawn. The Government's equitable share shall reflect the Government's participation in pension costs through those contracts for which certified cost or pricing data were submitted or that are subject to Subpart 31.2. Excise taxes on pension plan asset reversions or withdrawals under this paragraph (j)(3)(ii) are unallowable in accordance with 31.205-41(b)(6).

(4) *Defined-contribution pension plans.* In addition to defined-contribution pension plans, this paragraph also covers profit sharing, savings plans, and other such plans, provided the plans fall within the definition of a pension plan at 31.001.

(i) Allowable pension cost is limited to the net contribution required to be made for a cost accounting period after taking into account dividends and other credits, where applicable. However, any portion of pension cost computed for a cost accounting period that exceeds the amount required to be funded pursuant to a waiver granted under the provisions of ERISA will be allowable in those future accounting periods in which the funding of such excess amounts occurs (see 48 CFR 9904.412-50(c)(5)).

(ii) The provisions of paragraphs (j)(2)(ii) and (iv) of this subsection apply to defined-contribution plans.

(5) *Pension plans using the pay-as-you-go cost method.* When using the pay-as-you-go cost method, the contractor shall measure, assign, and allocate the cost of pension plans in accordance with 48 CFR 9904.412 and 9904.413. Pension costs for a pension plan using the pay-as-you-go cost method are allowable to the extent they are not otherwise unallowable.

(6) *Early retirement incentives.* An early retirement incentive is an incentive given to an employee to retire early. For contract costing purposes, costs of early retirement incentives are allowable subject to the pension cost criteria contained in paragraphs (j)(2)(i) through (iv) of this subsection provided—

(i) The contractor measures, assigns, and allocates the costs in accordance with the contractor's accounting practices for pension costs;

(ii) The incentives are in accordance with the terms and conditions of an early retirement incentive plan;

(iii) The contractor applies the plan only to active employees. The cost of extending the plan to employees who retired or were terminated before the adoption of the plan is unallowable; and

(iv) The present value of the total incentives given to any employee in excess of the amount of the employee's annual salary for the previous fiscal year before the employee's retirement is unallowable. The contractor shall compute the present value in accordance with its accounting practices for pension costs. The contractor shall account for any unallowable costs in accordance with 48 CFR 9904.412-50(a)(2).

(k) *Deferred compensation other than pensions.* The costs of deferred compensation awards are allowable subject to the following limitations:

(1) The costs shall be measured, assigned, and allocated in accordance with 48 CFR 9904.415, Accounting for the Cost of Deferred Compensation.

(2) The costs of deferred compensation awards are unallowable if the awards are made in periods subsequent to the period when the work being remunerated was performed.

(l) *Compensation incidental to business acquisitions.* The following costs are unallowable:

(1) Payments to employees under agreements in which they receive special compensation, in excess of the contractor's normal severance pay practice, if their employment terminates following a change in the management control over, or ownership of, the contractor or a substantial portion of its assets.

(2) Payments to employees under plans introduced in connection with a change (whether actual or prospective) in the management control over, or ownership of, the contractor or a substantial portion of its assets in which those employees receive special compensation, which is contingent upon the employee remaining with the contractor for a specified period of time.

(m) *Fringe benefits.* (1) Fringe benefits are allowances and services provided by the contractor to its employees as compensation in addition to regular wages and salaries. Fringe benefits include, but are not limited to, the cost of vacations, sick leave, holidays, military leave, employee insurance, and supplemental unemployment benefit plans. Except as provided otherwise in Subpart 31.2, the costs of fringe benefits are allowable to the extent that they are reasonable and are required by law, employer-employee agreement, or an established policy of the contractor.

(2) That portion of the cost of company-furnished automobiles that relates to personal use by employees (including transportation to and from work) is unallowable regardless of whether the cost is reported as taxable income to the employees (see 31.205-46(d)).

(n) *Employee rebate and purchase discount plans.* Rebates and purchase discounts, in whatever form, granted to employees on products or services produced by the contractor or affiliates are unallowable.

(o) *Postretirement benefits other than pensions (PRB).* (1) PRB covers all benefits, other than cash benefits and life insurance benefits paid by pension plans, provided to employees, their beneficiaries, and covered dependents during the period following the employees' retirement. Benefits encompassed include, but are not limited to, postretirement health care; life insurance provided outside a pension plan; and other welfare benefits such as tuition assistance, day care, legal services, and housing subsidies provided after retirement.

(2) To be allowable, PRB costs shall be incurred pursuant to law, employer-employee agreement, or an established policy of the contractor, and shall comply with paragraphs (o)(2)(i), (ii), or (iii) of this subsection.

(i) Pay-as-you-go. PRB costs are not accrued during the working lives of employees. Costs are assigned to the period in which—

(A) Benefits are actually provided; or

(B) The costs are paid to an insurer, provider, or other recipient for current year benefits or premiums.

(ii) Terminal funding. PRB costs are not accrued during the working lives of the employees.

(A) Terminal funding occurs when the entire PRB liability is paid in a lump sum upon the termination of employees (or upon conversion to such a terminal-funded plan) to an insurer or trustee to establish and maintain a fund or reserve for the sole purpose of providing PRB to retirees.

(B) Terminal funded costs shall be amortized over a period of 15 years.

(iii) *Accrual basis.* PRB costs are accrued during the working lives of employees. Accrued PRB costs shall comply with the following:

(A) Be measured and assigned in accordance with one of the following two methods described under paragraphs (o)(2)(iii)(A)(*1*) or (o)(2)(iii)(A)(*2*) of this subsection:

(*1*) Generally accepted accounting principles. However, transitions from the pay-as-you-go method to the accrual accounting method must be handled according to paragraphs (o)(2)(iii)(A)(*1*)(*i*) through (*iii*) of this subsection.

(*i*) In the year of transition from the pay-as-you-go method to accrual accounting for purposes of Government contract cost accounting, the transition obligation shall be the excess of the accumulated PRB obligation over the fair value of plan assets determined in accordance with subparagraph (o)(2)(iii)(E) of this section; the fair value must be reduced by the prepayment credit as determined in accordance with subparagraph (o)(2)(iii)(F) of this subsection.

(*ii*) PRB cost attributable to the transition obligation assigned to the current year that is in excess of the amount assignable to accounting periods on the basis of a straight line amortization of the transition obligation over the average remaining working lives of active employees covered by the PRB plan or a 20-year period, whichever period is longer, is unallowable. However, if the plan is comprised of inactive participants only, the PRB cost attributable to the transition obligation assigned to the current year that is in excess of the amount assignable to accounting periods on a straight line amortization of the transition obligation over the average future life expectancy of the participants is unallowable.

(*iii*) For a plan that transitioned from pay-as-you-go to accrual accounting for Government contract cost accounting prior to July 22, 2013, the unallowable amount of PRB cost attributable to the transition obligation amortization shall continue to be based on the cost principle in effect at the time of the transition until the original transition obligation schedule is fully amortized.

(*2*) Contributions to a welfare benefit fund determined in accordance with applicable Internal Revenue Code. Allowable PRB costs based on such contributions shall—

(*i*) Be measured using reasonable actuarial assumptions, which shall include a health care inflation assumption unless prohibited by the Internal Revenue Code provisions governing welfare benefit funds;

(*ii*) Be assigned to accounting periods on the basis of the average working lives of active employees covered by the PRB plan or a 15 year period, whichever period is longer. However, if the plan is comprised of inactive participants only, the cost shall be spread over the average future life expectancy of the participants; and

(*iii*) Exclude Federal income taxes, whether incurred by the fund or the contractor (including any increase in PRB costs associated with such taxes), unless the fund holding the plan assets is tax-exempt under the provisions of 26 U.S.C 501(c).

(B) Be paid to an insurer or trustee to establish and maintain a fund or reserve for the sole purpose of providing PRB to retirees. The assets shall be segregated in the trust, or otherwise effectively restricted, so that they cannot be used by the employer for other purposes.

(C) Be calculated in accordance with generally accepted actuarial principles and practices as promulgated by the Actuarial Standards Board.

(D) Eliminate from costs of current and future periods the accumulated value of any prior period costs that were unallowable in accordance with paragraph (o)(3) of this section, adjusted for interest under paragraph (o)(4) of this section.

(E) Calculate the unfunded actuarial liability (unfunded accumulated postretirement benefit obligation) using the market (fair) value of assets that have been accumulated by funding costs assigned to prior periods for contract accounting purposes.

(F) Recognize as a prepayment credit the market (fair) value of assets that were accumulated by deposits or contributions that were not used to fund costs assigned to previous periods for contract accounting purposes.

(G) Comply with the following when changing from one accrual accounting method to another: the contractor shall—

(1) Treat the change in the unfunded actuarial liability (unfunded accumulated postretirement benefit obligation) as a gain or loss; and

(2) Present an analysis demonstrating that all costs assigned to prior periods have been accounted for in accordance with paragraphs (o)(2)(iii)(D), (E), and (F) of this section to ensure that no duplicate recovery of costs exists. Any duplicate recovery of costs due to the change from one method to another is unallowable. The analysis and new accrual accounting method may be a subject appropriate for an advance agreement in accordance with 31.109.

(3) To be allowable, PRB costs must be funded by the time set for filing the Federal income tax return or any extension thereof, or paid to an insurer, provider, or other recipient by the time set for filing the Federal income tax return or extension thereof. PRB costs assigned to the current year, but not funded, paid or otherwise liquidated by the tax return due date as extended are not allowable in any subsequent year.

(4) Increased PRB costs caused by delay in funding beyond 30 days after each quarter of the year to which they are assignable are unallowable.

(5) The Government shall receive an equitable share of any amount of previously funded PRB costs which revert or inure to the contractor. Such equitable share shall reflect the Government's previous participation in PRB costs through those contracts for which certified cost or pricing data were required or which were subject to Subpart 31.2.

(p) *Limitation on allowability of compensation.*

TABLE 31-1-EMPLOYEE COMPENSATION LIMITS

Contract award date	Applicable agencies	Covered employees	31.205-6
Before June 24, 2014 . . .	Executive Agencies Other than DoD, NASA and Coast Guard.	Senior Executive	(p)(2).
Before December 31, 2011	DoD, NASA and Coast Guard	Senior Executive	(p)(2).
On/after December 31, 2011, and before June 24, 2014.	DoD, NASA, and Coast Guard	All Employees	(p)(3).
On/after June 24, 2014 . . .	All Executive Agencies . . .	All Employees	(p)(4).

(1) *Definitions.* As used in this paragraph (p)—

(i) *Compensation* means the total amount of wages, salary, bonuses, deferred compensation (see paragraph (k) of this subsection), and employer contributions to defined contribution pension plans (see paragraphs (j)(4) and (q) of this subsection), for the fiscal year, whether paid, earned, or otherwise accruing, as recorded in the contractor's cost accounting records for the fiscal year.

(ii) *Senior executive* means—

(A) Prior to January 2, 1999—

(*1*) The Chief Executive Officer (CEO) or any individual acting in a similar capacity at the contractor's headquarters;

(*2*) The four most highly compensated employees in management positions at the contractor's headquarters, other than the CEO; and

(*3*) If the contractor has intermediate home offices or segments that report directly to the contractor's headquarters, the five most highly compensated employees in management positions at each such intermediate home office or segment.

(B) Effective January 2, 1999, the five most highly compensated employees in management positions at each home office and each segment of the contractor, whether or not the home office or segment reports directly to the contractor's headquarters.

(iii) *Fiscal year* means the fiscal year established by the contractor for accounting purposes.

(iv) *Contractor's headquarters* means the highest organizational level from which executive compensation costs are allocated to Government contracts.

(2) *Senior executive compensation limit for contracts awarded before June 24, 2014*—(i) Applicability. This paragraph (p)(2) applies to the following:

(A) To all executive agencies, other than DoD, NASA and the Coast Guard, for contracts awarded before June 24, 2014;

(B) To DoD, NASA, and the Coast Guard for contracts awarded before December 31, 2011;

(ii) Costs incurred after January 1, 1998, for the compensation of a senior executive in excess of the benchmark compensation amount determined applicable for the contractor fiscal year by the Administrator, Office of Federal Procurement Policy (OFPP), under 41 U.S.C. 1127 as in effect prior to June 24, 2014, are unallowable (10 U.S.C. 2324(e)(1)(P) and 41 U.S.C. 4304(a)(16), as in effect prior to June 24, 2014). This limitation is the sole statutory limitation on allowable senior executive compensation costs incurred after January 1, 1998, under contracts awarded before June 24, 2014, and applies whether or not the affected contracts were previously subject to a statutory limitation on such costs. (Note that pursuant to section 804 of Pub. L. 105–261, the definition of "senior executive" in paragraph (p)(1) of this section has been changed for compensation costs incurred after January 1, 1999.) See *https://www.whitehouse.gov/wp-content/uploads/2017/11/ContractorCompensationCapContractsAwardedBeforeJune24.pdf*.

(3) All employee compensation limit for contracts awarded before June 24, 2014.

(i) *Applicability.* This paragraph (p)(3) applies to DOD, NASA, and the Coast Guard for contracts awarded on or after December 31, 2011, and before June 24, 2014.

(ii) Costs incurred after January 1, 2012, for the compensation of any contractor employee in excess of the benchmark compensation amount, determined applicable for the contractor fiscal year by the Administrator, Office of Federal Procurement Policy (OFPP) under 41 U.S.C. 1127 as in effect prior to June 24, 2014 are unallowable (10 U.S.C. 2324(e)(1)(P) as in effect prior to June 24, 2014.) This limitation is the sole statutory limitation on allowable employee compensation costs incurred after January 1, 2012, under contracts awarded on or after December 31, 2011 and before June 24, 2014. (Note that pursuant to section 803 of Pub. L. 112-81, 10 U.S.C. 2324, Allowable costs under defense contracts, was amended by striking "senior executives" and inserting "any contractor employee," making unallowable the excess compensation costs incurred after January 1, 2012, under affected contracts.) See *https://www.whitehouse.gov/wp-content/uploads/2017/11/ContractorCompensationCapContractsAwardedBeforeJune24.pdf*.

(4) All employee compensation limit for contracts awarded on or after June 24, 2014.

(i) *Applicability.* This paragraph (p)(4) applies to all executive agency contracts awarded on or after June 24, 2014, and any subcontracts thereunder.

(ii) Costs incurred on or after June 24, 2014, for the compensation of all employees in excess of the benchmark compensation amount determined applicable for the contractor fiscal year by the Administrator, Office of Federal Procurement Policy (OFPP) are unallowable under 10 U.S.C. 2324(e)(1)(P) and 41 U.S.C. 4304(a)(16), as in effect on or after June 24, 2014, pursuant to section 702 of Public Law 113–67. This limitation is the sole statutory limitation on allowable employee compensation costs incurred on or after June 24, 2014, under contracts awarded on or after June 24, 2014. See *https://www.whitehouse.gov/*

wp-content/uploads/2017/11/ContractorCompensationCapContractsAwardedafterJune24.pdf.

(iii) *Exceptions.* An agency head may establish one or more narrowly targeted exceptions for scientists, engineers, or other specialists upon a determination that such exceptions are needed to ensure that the executive agency has continued access to needed skills and capabilities. In making such a determination, the agency shall consider, at a minimum, for each contractor employee in a narrowly targeted excepted position—

(A) The amount of taxpayer funded compensation to be received by each employee; and

(B) The duties and services performed by each employee.

(q) *Employee stock ownership plans (ESOP).* (1) An ESOP is a stock bonus plan designed to invest primarily in the stock of the employer corporation. The contractor's contributions to an Employee Stock Ownership Trust (ESOT) may be in the form of cash, stock, or property.

(2) Costs of ESOPs are allowable subject to the following conditions:

(i) The contractor measures, assigns, and allocates costs in accordance with 48 CFR 9904.415.

(ii) Contributions by the contractor in any one year that exceed the deductibility limits of the Internal Revenue Code for that year are unallowable.

(iii) When the contribution is in the form of stock, the value of the stock contribution is limited to the fair market value of the stock on the date that title is effectively transferred to the trust.

(iv) When the contribution is in the form of cash—

(A) Stock purchases by the ESOT in excess of fair market value are unallowable; and

(B) When stock purchases are in excess of fair market value, the contractor shall credit the amount of the excess to the same indirect cost pools that were charged for the ESOP contributions in the year in which the stock purchase occurs. However, when the trust purchases the stock with borrowed funds which will be repaid over a period of years by cash contributions from the contractor to the trust, the contractor shall credit the excess price over fair market value to the indirect cost pools pro rata over the period of years during which the contractor contributes the cash used by the trust to repay the loan.

(v) When the fair market value of unissued stock or stock of a closely held corporation is not readily determinable, the valuation will be made on a case-by-case basis taking into consideration the guidelines for valuation used by the IRS.

[FAC 84-15, 51 FR 12299, 4/9/86, effective 4/7/86; FAC 84-21, 51 FR 31426, 9/3/86, effective 8/29/86; FAC 84-26, 52 FR 19804, 5/27/87, effective 7/30/87; FAC 84-30, 9/30/87, effective 9/30/87; FAC 84-35, 53 FR 10830, 4/1/88, effective 4/4/88; FAC 84-39, 53 FR 34228, 9/2/88, effective 10/3/88; FAC 84-44, 54 FR 13024, 3/29/89, 31.205-6(j)(2), (3), (6), effective 3/29/89, 31.205-6(g), effective 3/28/89; corrected 54 FR 18507, 5/1/89; FAC 84-51, 54 FR 34755, 8/21/89, effective 9/20/89; corrected 54 FR 51401, 12/15/89; FAC 90-5, 56 FR 29127, 6/25/91, effective 7/25/91; Interim rule, FAC 90-7, 56 FR 41739, 8/22/91, effective 8/22/91; FAC 90-12, 57 FR 39591, 8/31/92, effective 8/31/92; FAC 90-16, 57 FR 60584, 12/21/92, effective 2/19/93; FAC 90-23, 59 FR 67010, 12/28/94, effective 2/27/95; FAC 90-31, 60 FR 42648, 8/16/95, effective 10/1/95; FAC 90-40, 61 FR 39186, 7/26/96, effective 9/24/96; FAC 90-43, 61 FR 6748, 12/20/96, effective 12/20/96; FAC 90-44, Interim rule, 61 FR 69286, 12/31/96, effective 12/31/96, finalized without change, FAC 97-1, 62 FR 44802, 8/22/97, effective 10/21/97; FAC 90-45, Interim rule, 62 FR 224, 1/2/97, effective 1/1/97; FAC 97-2, 62 FR 51224, 9/30/97, effective 10/10/97; FAC 97-3, 62 FR 64912, 12/9/97, effective 2/9/98; FAC 97-4, 63 FR 9048, 2/23/98, effective 2/23/98; FAC 97-9, 63 FR 58587, 10/30/98 effective 12/29/98; FAC 97-10, 63 FR 70264, 12/18/98, effective 2/16/99; FAC 97-11, 64 FR 10530, 3/4/99, effective 3/4/99, finalized without change, FAC 97-14, 64 FR 51828,

9/24/99; FAC 97-12, 64 FR 32740, 6/17/99, effective 6/17/99; FAC 2001-08, 67 FR 43513, 6/27/2002, effective 7/29/2002; FAC 2001-15, 68 FR 43863, 7/24/2003, effective 8/25/2003; FAC 2001-16, 68 FR 56686, 10/1/2003, effective 10/31/2003; FAC 2001-18, 68 FR 69251, 12/11/2003, effective 1/12/2004; FAC 2005-04, 70 FR 33671, 6/8/2005, effective 7/8/2005; FAC 2005-38, 74 FR 65608, 12/10/2009, effective 1/11/2010; FAC 2005-42, 75 FR 34285, 75 FR 34291, 6/16/2010, effective 6/16/2010; FAC 2005-45, 75 FR 53135, 8/30/2010, effective 10/1/2010; FAC 2005-50, 76 FR 14571, 3/16/2011, effective 3/16/2011; FAC 2005-65, 78 FR 6191, 1/29/2013, effective 1/29/2013; FAC 2005-67, 78 FR 37696, 6/21/2013, effective 7/22/2013; FAC 2005-68, 78 FR 38535, 6/26/2013, effective 6/26/2013; FAC 2005-71, 78 FR 70481, 11/25/2013, effective 11/25/2013; FAC 2005-73, 79 FR 24192, 4/29/2014, effective 5/29/2014; FAC 2005-74, 79 FR 31195, 5/30/2014, effective 5/30/2014; FAC 2005-75, 79 FR 35865, 6/24/2014, effective 6/24/2014; FAC 2005-84, FAC 2005-84, 80 FR 53439, 9/3/2015, effective 9/3/2015; FAC 2005-91, 81 FR 67778, 9/30/2016, effective 9/30/2016; FAC 2005-100, 83 FR 42571, 8/22/2018, effective 8/22/2018]

31.205-7 Contingencies.

(a) *Contingency,* as used in this subpart, means a possible future event or condition arising from presently known or unknown causes, the outcome of which is indeterminable at the present time.

(b) Costs for contingencies are generally unallowable for historical costing purposes because such costing deals with costs incurred and recorded on the contractor's books. However, in some cases, as for example, terminations, a contingency factor may be recognized when it is applicable to a past period to give recognition to minor unsettled factors in the interest of expediting settlement.

(c) In connection with estimates of future costs, contingencies fall into two categories:

(1) Those that may arise from presently known and existing conditions, the effects of which are foreseeable within reasonable limits of accuracy; e.g., anticipated costs of rejects and defective work. Contingencies of this category are to be included in the estimates of future costs so as to provide the best estimate of performance cost.

(2) Those that may arise from presently known or unknown conditions, the effect of which cannot be measured so precisely as to provide equitable results to the contractor and to the Government; e.g., results of pending litigation. Contingencies of this category are to be excluded from cost estimates under the several items of cost, but should be disclosed separately (including the basis upon which the contingency is computed) to facilitate the negotiation of appropriate contractual coverage. (See, for example, 31.205-6(g) and 31.205-19.)

[FAC 2001-24, 69 FR 34242, 6/18/2004, effective 7/19/2004]

31.205-8 Contributions or donations.

Contributions or donations, including cash, property and services, regardless of recipient, are unallowable, except as provided in 31.205-1(e)(3).

[FAC 84-15, 51 FR 12300, 4/9/86, effective 4/7/86]

31.205-9 [Reserved]

31.205-10 Cost of money.

(a) *General. Cost of money*—

(1) Is an imputed cost that is not a form of interest on borrowings (see 31.205-20);

(2) Is an *incurred cost* for cost-reimbursement purposes under applicable cost-reimbursement contracts and for progress payment purposes under fixed-price contracts; and

(3) Refers to—

(i) Facilities capital cost of money (48 CFR 9904.414); and

(ii) Cost of money as an element of the cost of capital assets under construction (48 CFR 9904.417).

(b) Cost of money is allowable, provided—

(1) It is measured, assigned, and allocated to contracts in accordance with 48 CFR 9904.414 or measured and added to the cost

of capital assets under construction in accordance with 48 CFR 9904.417, as applicable;

(2) The requirements of 31.205-52, which limit the allowability of cost of money, are followed; and

(3) The estimated facilities capital cost of money is specifically identified and proposed in cost proposals relating to the contract under which the cost is to be claimed.

(c) Actual interest cost in lieu of the calculated imputed cost of money is unallowable.

[FAC 84-3, 49 FR 26743, 6/29/84, effective 10/1/84; FAC 84-30, 9/30/87, effective 9/30/87; FAC 84-58, 55 FR 25530, 6/21/90, effective 7/23/90; FAC 90-5, 56 FR 29128, 6/25/91, effective 7/25/91; FAC 90-12, 57 FR 39591, 8/31/92, effective 8/31/92; FAC 97-4, 63 FR 9048, 2/23/98, effective 4/24/98; FAC 2001-14, 68 FR 28091, 5/22/2003, effective 6/23/2003]

31.205-11 Depreciation.

(a) Depreciation on a contractor's plant, equipment, and other capital facilities is an allowable contract cost, subject to the limitations contained in this cost principle. For tangible personal property, only estimated residual values that exceed 10 percent of the capitalized cost of the asset need be used in establishing depreciable costs. Where either the declining balance method of depreciation or the class life asset depreciation range system is used, the residual value need not be deducted from capitalized cost to determine depreciable costs. Depreciation cost that would significantly reduce the book value of a tangible capital asset below its residual value is unallowable.

(b) Contractors having contracts subject to 48 CFR 9904.409, Depreciation of Tangible Capital Assets, shall adhere to the requirement of that standard for all fully CAS-covered contracts and may elect to adopt the standard for all other contracts. All requirements of 48 CFR 9904.409 are applicable if the election is made, and contractors must continue to follow it until notification of final acceptance of all deliverable items on all open negotiated Government contracts.

(c) For contracts to which 48 CFR 9904.409 is not applied, except as indicated in paragraphs (g) and (h) of this subsection, allowable depreciation shall not exceed the amount used for financial accounting purposes, and shall be determined in a manner consistent with the depreciation policies and procedures followed in the same segment on non-Government business.

(d) Depreciation, rental, or use charges are unallowable on property acquired from the Government at no cost by the contractor or by any division, subsidiary, or affiliate of the contractor under common control.

(e) The depreciation on any item which meets the criteria for allowance at price under 31.205-26(e) may be based on that price, provided the same policies and procedures are used for costing all business of the using division, subsidiary, or organization under common control.

(f) No depreciation or rental is allowed on property fully depreciated by the contractor or by any division, subsidiary, or affiliate of the contractor under common control. However, a reasonable charge for using fully depreciated property may be agreed upon and allowed (but, see 31.109(h)(2)). In determining the charge, consideration shall be given to cost, total estimated useful life at the time of negotiations, effect of any increased maintenance charges or decreased efficiency due to age, and the amount of depreciation previously charged to Government contracts or subcontracts.

(g) Whether or not the contract is otherwise subject to CAS the following apply:

(1) The requirements of 31.205-52 shall be observed.

(2) In the event of a write-down from carrying value to fair value as a result of impairments caused by events or changes in circumstances, allowable depreciation of the impaired assets is limited to the amounts that would have been allowed had the assets not been written down (see 31.205-16(g)). However, this does not preclude a change in depreciation resulting from other causes such as permissible changes in estimates of service life, consumption of services, or residual value.

(3)(i) In the event the contractor reacquires property involved in a sale and leaseback arrangement, allowable depreciation of reacquired property shall be based on the net book value of the asset as of the date the contractor originally became a lessee of the property in the sale and leaseback arrangement—

(A) Adjusted for any allowable gain or loss determined in accordance with 31.205-16(b); and

(B) Less any amount of depreciation expense included in the calculation of the amount that would have been allowed had the contractor retained title under 31.205-11(h)(1) and 31.205-36(b)(2).

(ii) As used in this paragraph (g)(3), reacquired property is property that generated either any depreciation expense or any cost of money considered in the calculation of the limitations under 31.205-11(h)(1) and 31.205-36(b)(2) during the most recent accounting period prior to the date of reacquisition.

(h) A *capital lease*, as defined in Financial Accounting Standards Board's Accounting Standards Codification (FASB ASC) 840, Leases, is subject to the requirements of this cost principle. (See 31.205-36 for Operating Leases.) FASB ASC 840 requires that capital leases be treated as purchased assets, *i.e.*, be capitalized, and the capitalized value of such assets be distributed over their useful lives as depreciation charges or over the leased life as amortization charges, as appropriate, except that—

(1) Lease costs under a sale and leaseback arrangement are allowable only up to the amount that would be allowed if the contractor retained title, computed based on the net book value of the asset on the date the contractor becomes a lessee of the property adjusted for any gain or loss recognized in accordance with 31.205-16(b); and

(2) If it is determined that the terms of the capital lease have been significantly affected by the fact that the lessee and lessor are related, depreciation charges are not allowable in excess of those that would have occurred if the lease contained terms consistent with those found in a lease between unrelated parties.

[FAC 84-30, 9/30/87, effective 9/30/87; FAC 84-58, 55 FR 25530, 6/21/90, effective 7/23/90; FAC 90-12, 57 FR 39591, 8/31/92, effective 8/31/92; FAC 90-35, 60 FR 64254, 12/14/95, effective 12/14/95; FAC 90-43, Interim rule, 61 FR 67408, 12/20/96, effective 2/18/97; FAC 2001-18, 68 FR 69246, 12/11/2003, effective 1/12/2004; FAC 2005-04, 70 FR 33673, 6/8/2005, effective 7/8/2005; FAC 2005-10, 71 FR 36939, 6/28/2006, effective 7/28/2006; FAC 2005-55, 77 FR 202, 1/3/2012, effective 2/2/2012]

31.205-12 Economic planning costs.

Economic planning costs are the costs of general long-range management planning that is concerned with the future overall development of the contractor's business and that may take into account the eventual possibility of economic dislocations or fundamental alterations in those markets in which the contractor currently does business. Economic planning costs are allowable. Economic planning costs do not include organization or reorganization costs covered by 31.205-27. See 31.205-38 for market planning costs other than economic planning costs.

[FAC 2001-15, 68 FR 43871, 7/24/2003, effective 8/25/2003; FAC 2001-16, 68 FR 56686, 10/1/2003, effective 10/31/2003]

31.205-13 Employee morale, health, welfare, food service, and dormitory costs and credits.

(a) Aggregate costs incurred on activities designed to improve working conditions, employer-employee relations, employee morale, and employee performance (less income generated by these activities) are allowable, subject to the limitations contained in this subsection. Some examples of allowable activities are—

(1) House publications;

(2) Health clinics;

(3) Wellness/fitness centers;

(4) Employee counseling services; and

(5) Food and dormitory services for the contractor's employees at or near the contractor's facilities. These services include—

(i) Operating or furnishing facilities for cafeterias, dining rooms, canteens, lunch wagons, vending machines, living accommodations; and

(ii) Similar types of services.

(b) Costs of gifts are unallowable. (Gifts do not include awards for performance made pursuant to 31.205-6(f) or awards made in recognition of employee achievements pursuant to an established contractor plan or policy.)

(c) Costs of recreation are unallowable, except for the costs of employees' participation in company sponsored sports teams or employee organizations designed to improve company loyalty, team work, or physical fitness.

(d) (1) The allowability of food and dormitory losses are determined by the following factors:

(i) Losses from operating food and dormitory services are allowable only if the contractor's objective is to operate such services on a break-even basis.

(ii) Losses sustained because food services or lodging accommodations are furnished without charge or at prices or rates which obviously would not be conducive to the accomplishment of the objective in paragraph (d) (1) (i) of this subsection are not allowable, except as described in paragraph (d) (1) (iii) of this subsection.

(iii) A loss may be allowed to the extent that the contractor can demonstrate that unusual circumstances exist such that even with efficient management, operating the services on a break-even basis would require charging inordinately high prices, or prices or rates higher than those charged by commercial establishments offering the same services in the same geographical areas. The following are examples of unusual circumstances:

(A) The contractor must provide food or dormitory services at remote locations where adequate commercial facilities are not reasonably available.

(B) The contractor's charged (but unproductive) labor costs would be excessive if the services were not available.

(C) If cessation or reduction of food or dormitory operations will not otherwise yield net cost savings.

(2) Costs of food and dormitory services shall include an allocable share of indirect expenses pertaining to these activities.

(e) When the contractor has an arrangement authorizing an employee association to provide or operate a service, such as vending machines in the contractor's plant, and retain the profits, such profits shall be treated in the same manner as if the contractor were providing the service (but see paragraph (f) of this subsection).

(f) Contributions by the contractor to an employee organization, including funds from vending machine receipts or similar sources, are allowable only to the extent that the contractor demonstrates that an equivalent amount of the costs incurred by the employee organization would be allowable if directly incurred by the contractor.

[FAC 90-31, 60 FR 42648, 8/16/95, effective 10/1/95; FAC 2001-16, 68 FR 56686, 10/1/2003, effective 10/31/2003]

31.205-14 Entertainment costs.

Costs of amusement, diversions, social activities, and any directly associated costs such as tickets to shows or sports events, meals, lodging, rentals, transportation, and gratuities are unallowable. Costs made specifically unallowable under this cost principle are not allowable under any other cost principle. Costs of membership in social, dining, or country clubs or other organizations having the same purposes are also unallowable, regardless of whether the cost is reported as taxable income to the employees.

[FAC 90-31, 60 FR 42648, 8/16/95, effective 10/1/95]

31.205-15 Fines, penalties, and mischarging costs.

(a) Costs of fines and penalties resulting from violations of, or failure of the contractor to comply with, Federal, State, local, or foreign laws and regulations, are unallowable except when incurred as a result of compliance with specific terms and conditions of the contract or written instructions from the contracting officer.

(b) Costs incurred in connection with, or related to, the mischarging of costs on Government contracts are unallowable when the costs are caused by, or result from, alteration or destruction of records, or other false or improper charging or recording of costs. Such costs include those incurred to measure or otherwise determine the magnitude of the improper charging, and costs incurred to remedy or correct the mischarging, such as costs to rescreen and reconstruct records.

[FAC 84-15, 51 FR 12301, 4/9/86, effective 4/7/86; FAC 84-44, 54 FR 13024, 3/29/89, effective 4/17/89; FAC 90-3, 55 FR 52793, 12/21/90, effective 1/22/91]

31.205-16 Gains and losses on disposition or impairment of depreciable property or other capital assets.

(a) Gains and losses from the sale, retirement, or other disposition (but see 31.205-19) of depreciable property shall be included in the year in which they occur as credits or charges to the cost grouping(s) in which the depreciation or amortization applicable to those assets was included (but see paragraph (f) of this subsection). However, no gain or loss shall be recognized as a result of the transfer of assets in a business combination (see 31.205-52).

(b) Notwithstanding the provisions in paragraph (c) of this subsection, when costs of depreciable property are subject to the sale and leaseback limitations in 31.205-11(h)(1) or 31.205-36(b)(2)—

(1) The gain or loss is the difference between the net amount realized and the undepreciated balance of the asset on the date the contractor becomes a lessee; and

(2) When the application of (b)(1) of this subsection results in a loss—

(i) The allowable portion of the loss is zero if the fair market value exceeds the undepreciated balance of the asset on the date the contractor becomes a lessee; and

(ii) The allowable portion of the loss is limited to the difference between the fair market value and the undepreciated balance of the asset on the date the contractor becomes a lessee if the fair market value is less than the undepreciated balance of the asset on the date the contractor becomes a lessee.

(c) Gains and losses on disposition of tangible capital assets, including those acquired under capital leases (see 31.205-11(h)), shall be considered as adjustments of depreciation costs previously recognized. The gain or loss for each asset disposed of is the difference between the net amount realized, including insurance proceeds from involuntary conversions, and its undepreciated balance.

(d) The gain recognized for contract costing purposes shall be limited to the difference between the acquisition cost (or for assets acquired under a capital lease, the value at which the leased asset is capitalized) of the asset and its undepreciated balance (except see paragraphs (e)(2)(i) or (ii) of this subsection).

(e) Special considerations apply to an involuntary conversion which occurs when a contractor's property is destroyed by events over which the owner has no control, such as fire, windstorm, flood, accident, theft, etc., and an insurance award is recovered. The following govern involuntary conversions:

(1) When there is a cash award and the converted asset is not replaced, gain or loss shall be recognized in the period of disposition. The gain recognized for contract costing purposes shall be limited to the difference between the acquisition cost of the asset and its undepreciated balance.

(2) When the converted asset is replaced, the contractor shall either—

(i) Adjust the depreciable basis of the new asset by the amount of the total realized gain or loss; or

(ii) Recognize the gain or loss in the period of disposition, in which case the Government shall participate to the same extent as outlined in subparagraph (e)(1) of this subsection.

(f) Gains and losses on the disposition of depreciable property shall not be recognized as a separate charge or credit when—

(1) Gains and losses are processed through the depreciation reserve account and reflected in the depreciation allowable under 31.205-11; or

(2) The property is exchanged as part of the purchase price of a similar item, and the gain or loss is taken into consideration in the depreciation cost basis of the new item.

(g) Gains and losses arising from mass or extraordinary sales, retirements, or other disposition other than through business combinations shall be considered on a case-by-case basis.

(h) Gains and losses of any nature arising from the sale or exchange of capital assets other than depreciable property shall be excluded in computing contract costs.

(i) With respect to long-lived tangible and identifiable intangible assets held for use, no loss shall be allowed for a write-down from carrying value to fair value as a result of impairments caused by events or changes in circumstances (*e.g.*, environmental damage, idle facilities arising from a declining business base, etc.). If depreciable property or other capital assets have been written down from carrying value to fair value due to impairments, gains or losses upon disposition shall be the amounts that would have been allowed had the assets not been written down.

[FAC 84-58, 55 FR 25530, 6/21/90, effective 7/23/90; FAC 90-35, 60 FR 64254, 12/14/95, effective 12/14/95; FAC 90-43, Interim rule, 61 FR 67408, 12/20/96, effective 2/18/97; FAC 2001-18, 68 FR 69246, 12/11/2003, effective 1/12/2004; FAC 2005-04, 70 FR 33673, 6/8/2005, effective 7/8/2005; FAC 2005-10, 71 FR 36939, 6/28/2006, effective 7/28/2006; FAC 2005-42, 75 FR 34291, 6/16/2010, effective 6/16/2010]

31.205-17 Idle facilities and idle capacity costs.

(a) *Definitions*. As used in this subsection—

Costs of idle facilities or idle capacity means costs such as maintenance, repair, housing, rent, and other related costs; *e.g.*, property taxes, insurance, and depreciation.

Facilities means plant or any portion thereof (including land integral to the operation), equipment, individually or collectively, or any other tangible capital asset, wherever located, and whether owned or leased by the contractor.

Idle capacity means the unused capacity of partially used facilities. It is the difference between that which a facility could achieve under 100 percent operating time on a one-shift basis, less operating interruptions resulting from time lost for repairs, setups, unsatisfactory materials, and other normal delays, and the extent to which the facility was actually used to meet demands during the accounting period. A multiple-shift basis may be used in the calculation instead of a one-shift basis if it can be shown that this amount of usage could normally be expected for the type of facility involved.

Idle facilities means completely unused facilities that are excess to the contractor's current needs.

(b) The costs of idle facilities are unallowable unless the facilities—

(1) Are necessary to meet fluctuations in workload; or

(2) Were necessary when acquired and are now idle because of changes in requirements, production economies, reorganization, termination, or other causes which could not have been reasonably foreseen. (Costs of idle facilities are allowable for a reasonable period, ordinarily not to exceed 1 year, depending upon the initiative taken to use, lease, or dispose of the idle facilities (but see 31.205-42)).

(c) Costs of idle capacity are costs of doing business and are a factor in the normal fluctuations of usage or overhead rates from period to period. Such costs are allowable provided the capacity is necessary or was originally reasonable and is not subject to reduction or elimination by subletting, renting, or sale, in accordance with sound business, economics, or security practices. Widespread idle capacity throughout an entire plant or among a group of assets having substantially the same function may be idle facilities.

(d) Any costs to be paid directly by the Government for idle facilities or idle capacity reserved for defense mobilization production shall be the subject of a separate agreement.

[FAC 97-22, 66 FR 2116, 1/10/2001, effective 3/12/2001; Delay of effective date, 66 FR 14259, 3/9/2001, effective 5/11/2001; FAC 2001-04, 67 FR 6112, 2/8/2002, effective 2/8/2002]

31.205-18 Independent research and development and bid and proposal costs.

(a) *Definitions.* As used in this subsection—

Applied research means that effort which—

(1) normally follows basic research, but may not be severable from the related basic research,

(2) attempts to determine and exploit the potential of scientific discoveries or improvements in technology, materials, processes, methods, devices, or techniques, and

(3) attempts to advance the state of the art. Applied research does not include efforts whose principal aim is design, development, or test of specific items or services to be considered for sale; these efforts are within the definition of the "term development", defined in this subsection.

Basic research (see 2.101).

Bid and proposal (B&P) costs means the costs incurred in preparing, submitting, and supporting bids and proposals (whether or not solicited) on potential Government or non-Government contracts. The term does not include the costs of effort sponsored by a grant or cooperative agreement, or required in the performance of a contract.

Company means all divisions, subsidiaries, and affiliates of the contractor under common control.

Development means the systematic use, under whatever name, of scientific and technical knowledge in the design, development, test, or evaluation of a potential new product or service (or of an improvement in an existing product or service) for the purpose of meeting specific performance requirements or objectives. Development includes the functions of design engineering, prototyping, and engineering testing. Development excludes—

(1) Subcontracted technical effort which is for the sole purpose of developing an additional source for an existing product; or

(2) Development effort for manufacturing or production materials, systems, processes, methods, equipment, tools, and techniques not intended for sale.

Independent research and development (IR&D) means a contractor's IR&D cost that consists of projects falling within the four following areas:

(1) basic research,

(2) applied research,

(3) development, and

(4) systems and other concept formulation studies. The term does not include the costs of effort sponsored by a grant or required in the performance of a contract. IR&D effort shall not include technical effort expended in developing and preparing technical data specifically to support submitting a bid or proposal.

Systems and other concept formulation studies means analyses and study efforts either related to specific IR&D efforts or directed toward identifying desirable new systems, equipment or components, or modifications and improvements to existing systems, equipment, or components.

(b) *Composition and allocation of costs.* The requirements of 48 CFR 9904.420, Accounting for independent research and development costs and bid and proposal costs, are incorporated in their entirety and shall apply as follows—

(1) *Fully-CAS-covered contracts.* Contracts that are fully-CAS-covered shall be subject to all requirements of 48 CFR 9904.420.

(2) *Modified-CAS-covered and non-CAS-covered contracts.* Contracts that are not CAS-covered or that contain terms or conditions requiring modified CAS coverage shall be subject to all requirements of 48 CFR 9904.420 except 48 CFR 9904.420-50(e) (2) and 48 CFR 9904.420-50(f) (2), which are not then applicable. However, non-CAS-covered or modified CAS-covered contracts awarded at a time the contractor has CAS-covered contracts requiring compliance with 48 CFR 9904.420, shall be subject to all the require-

ments of 48 CFR 9904.420. When the requirements of 48 CFR 9904.420-50(e)(2) and 48 CFR 9904.420-50(f)(2) are not applicable, the following apply:

(i) IR&D and B&P costs shall be allocated to final cost objectives on the same basis of allocation used for the G&A expense grouping of the profit center (see 31.001) in which the costs are incurred. However, when IR&D and B&P costs clearly benefit other profit centers or benefit the entire company, those costs shall be allocated through the G&A of the other profit centers or through the corporate G&A, as appropriate.

(ii) If allocations of IR&D or B&P through the G&A base do not provide equitable cost allocation, the contracting officer may approve use of a different base.

(c) *Allowability.* Except as provided in paragraphs (d) and (e) of this subsection, or as provided in agency regulations, costs for IR&D and B&P are allowable as indirect expenses on contracts to the extent that those costs are allocable and reasonable.

(d) *Deferred IR&D costs.* (1) IR&D costs that were incurred in previous accounting periods are unallowable, except when a contractor has developed a specific product at its own risk in anticipation of recovering the development costs in the sale price of the product provided that—

(i) The total amount of IR&D costs applicable to the product can be identified;

(ii) The proration of such costs to sales of the product is reasonable;

(iii) The contractor had no Government business during the time that the costs were incurred or did not allocate IR&D costs to Government contracts except to prorate the cost of developing a specific product to the sales of that product; and

(iv) No costs of current IR&D programs are allocated to Government work except to prorate the costs of developing a specific product to the sales of that product.

(2) When deferred costs are recognized, the contract (except firm-fixed-price and fixed-price with economic price adjustment) will include a specific provision setting forth the amount of deferred IR&D costs that are allocable to the contract. The negotiation memorandum will state the circumstances pertaining to the case and the reason for accepting the deferred costs.

(e) *Cooperative arrangements.*

(1) IR&D costs may be incurred by contractors working jointly with one or more non-Federal entities pursuant to a cooperative arrangement (for example, joint ventures, limited partnerships, teaming arrangements, and collaboration and consortium arrangements). IR&D costs also may include costs contributed by contractors in performing cooperative research and development agreements, or similar arrangements, entered into under—

(i) Section 12 of the Stevenson-Wydler Technology Transfer Act of 1980 (15 U.S.C. 3710(a));

(ii) Sections 203(c)(5) and (6) of the National Aeronautics and Space Act of 1958, as amended (42 U.S.C. 2473(c)(5) and (6));

(iii) 10 U.S.C. 2371 for the Defense Advanced Research Projects Agency; or

(iv) Other equivalent authority.

(2) IR&D costs incurred by a contractor pursuant to these types of cooperative arrangements should be considered as allowable IR&D costs if the work performed would have been allowed as contractor IR&D had there been no cooperative arrangement.

(3) Costs incurred in preparing, submitting, and supporting offers on potential cooperative arrangements are allowable to the extent they are allocable, reasonable, and not otherwise unallowable.

[FAC 90-13, 57 FR 44265, 9/24/92, effective 9/24/92, except 31.205-18, which was effective 11/5/90; Final rule, FAC 90-20, 59 FR 11368, 3/10/94, effective 5/9/94; FAC 90-46, 62 FR 12690, 3/17/97, effective 5/16/97; FAC 97-2, 62 FR 51224, 9/30/97, effective 10/10/97; FAC 97-3, 62 FR 64912, 12/9/97, effective 2/9/98; FAC 97-22, 66 FR 2116, 1/10/2001, effective 3/12/2001; Delay of effective date, 66 FR 14259, 3/9/2001, effective 5/11/2001]

31.205-19 Insurance and indemnification.

(a) Insurance by purchase or by self-insuring includes—

(1) Coverage the contractor is required to carry or to have approved, under the terms of the contract; and

(2) Any other coverage the contractor maintains in connection with the general conduct of its business.

(b) For purposes of applying the provisions of this subsection, the Government considers insurance provided by captive insurers (insurers owned by or under control of the contractor) as self-insurance, and charges for it shall comply with the provisions applicable to self-insurance costs in this subsection. However, if the captive insurer also sells insurance to the general public in substantial quantities and it can be demonstrated that the charge to the contractor is based on competitive market forces, the Government will consider the insurance as purchased insurance.

(c) Whether or not the contract is subject to CAS, self-insurance charges are allowable subject to paragraph (e) of this subsection and the following limitations:

(1) The contractor shall measure, assign, and allocate costs in accordance with 48 CFR 9904.416, Accounting for Insurance Costs.

(2) The contractor shall comply with (48 CFR) part 28. However, approval of a contractor's insurance program in accordance with part 28 does not constitute a determination as to the allowability of the program's cost.

(3) If purchased insurance is available, any self-insurance charge plus insurance administration expenses in excess of the cost of comparable purchased insurance plus associated insurance administration expenses is unallowable.

(4) Self-insurance charges for risks of catastrophic losses are unallowable (see 28.308(e)).

(d) Purchased insurance costs are allowable, subject to paragraph (e) of this subsection and the following limitations:

(1) For contracts subject to full CAS coverage, the contractor shall measure, assign, and allocate costs in accordance with 48 CFR 9904.416.

(2) For all contracts, premiums for insurance purchased from fronting insurance companies (insurance companies not related to the contractor but who reinsure with a captive insurer of the contractor) are unallowable to the extent they exceed the sum of—

(i) The amount that would have been allowed had the contractor insured directly with the captive insurer; and

(ii) Reasonable fronting company charges for services rendered.

(3) Actual losses are unallowable unless expressly provided for in the contract, except—

(i) Losses incurred under the nominal deductible provisions of purchased insurance, in keeping with sound business practice, are allowable; and

(ii) Minor losses, such as spoilage, breakage, and disappearance of small hand tools that occur in the ordinary course of business and that are not covered by insurance, are allowable.

(e) Self-insurance and purchased insurance costs are subject to the cost limitations in the following paragraphs:

(1) Costs of insurance required or approved pursuant to the contract are allowable.

(2) Costs of insurance maintained by the contractor in connection with the general conduct of its business are allowable subject to the following limitations:

(i) Types and extent of coverage shall follow sound business practice, and the rates and premiums shall be reasonable.

(ii) Costs allowed for business interruption or other similar insurance shall be limited to exclude coverage of profit.

(iii) The cost of property insurance premiums for insurance coverage in excess of the acquisition cost of the insured assets is allowable only when the contractor has a formal written policy assuring that in the event the insured property is involuntarily converted, the new asset shall be valued at the book value of the replaced asset plus or minus adjustments for differences between insurance proceeds and actual replacement cost. If the contractor does not have such a formal written policy, the cost of premiums for insurance coverage in excess of the acquisition cost of the insured asset is unallowable.

(iv) Costs of insurance for the risk of loss of Government property are allowable to the extent that—

(A) The contractor is liable for such loss;

(B) The contracting officer has not revoked the Government's assumption of risk (see 45.104(b)); and

(C) Such insurance does not cover loss of Government property that results from willful misconduct or lack of good faith on the part of any of the contractor's managerial personnel (as described in FAR 52.245-1 (h) (1) (ii)).

(v) Costs of insurance on the lives of officers, partners, proprietors, or employees are allowable only to the extent that the insurance represents additional compensation (see 31.205-6).

(3) The cost of insurance to protect the contractor against the costs of correcting its own defects in materials and workmanship is unallowable. However, insurance costs to cover fortuitous or casualty losses resulting from defects in materials or workmanship are allowable as a normal business expense.

(4) Premiums for retroactive or backdated insurance written to cover losses that have occurred and are known are unallowable.

(5) The Government is obligated to indemnify the contractor only to the extent authorized by law, as expressly provided for in the contract, except as provided in paragraph (d) (3) of this subsection.

(6) Late premium payment charges related to employee deferred compensation plan insurance incurred pursuant to section 4007 (29 U.S.C. 1307) or section 4023 (29 U.S.C. 1323) of the Employee Retirement Income Security Act of 1974 are unallowable.

[FAC 84-7, 50 FR 23607, 6/4/85, effective 4/30/85; FAC 84-21, 51 FR 31427, 9/3/86, effective 8/29/86; FAC 84-30, 9/30/87, effective 9/30/87; FAC 90-12, 57 FR 39591, 8/31/92, effective 8/31/92; FAC 2001-18, 68 FR 69251, 12/11/2003, effective 1/12/2004; FAC 2005-17, 72 FR 27364, 5/15/2007, effective 6/14/2007; FAC 2005-43, 75 FR 38675, 7/2/2010, effective 8/2/2010; FAC 2005-56, 77 FR 12937, 3/2/2012, effective 4/2/2012]

31.205-20 Interest and other financial costs.

Interest on borrowings (however represented), bond discounts, costs of financing and refinancing capital (net worth plus long-term liabilities), legal and professional fees paid in connection with preparing prospectuses, and costs of preparing and issuing stock rights are unallowable (but see 31.205-28). However, interest assessed by State or local taxing authorities under the conditions specified in 31.205-41(a) (3) is allowable.

[FAC 97-14, 64 FR 51828, 9/24/99, effective 11/23/99]

31.205-21 Labor relations costs.

(a) Costs incurred in maintaining satisfactory relations between the contractor and its employees (other than those made unallowable in paragraph (b) of this section), including costs of shop stewards, labor management committees, employee publications, and other related activities, are allowable.

(b) As required by Executive Order 13494, Economy in Government Contracting, costs of any activities undertaken to persuade employees, of any entity, to exercise or not to exercise, or concerning the manner of exercising, the right to organize and bargain collectively through representatives of the employees' own choosing are unallowable. Examples of unallowable costs under this paragraph include, but are not limited to, the costs of—

(1) Preparing and distributing materials;

(2) Hiring or consulting legal counsel or consultants;

(3) Meetings (including paying the salaries of the attendees at meetings held for this purpose); and

(4) Planning or conducting activities by managers, supervisors, or union representatives during work hours.

[FAC 97-21, 65 FR 80255, 12/20/2000, effective 1/19/2001, class deviation 1/31/2001, stayed FAC 97-24, 66 FR 17754, 4/3/2001, effective 4/3/2001, finalized with changes FAC 2001-03, 66 FR 66984, 12/27/2001, effective 12/27/2001; FAC 2005-54, 76 FR 68040, 11/2/2011, effective 12/2/2011]

31.205-22 Lobbying and political activity costs.

(a) Costs associated with the following activities are unallowable:

(1) Attempts to influence the outcomes of any Federal, State, or local election, referendum, initiative, or similar procedure, through in kind or cash contributions, endorsements, publicity, or similar activities;

(2) Establishing, administering, contributing to, or paying the expenses of a political party, campaign, political action committee, or other organization established for the purpose of influencing the outcomes of elections;

(3) Any attempt to influence—

(i) The introduction of Federal, state, or local legislation; or

(ii) The enactment or modification of any pending Federal, state, or local legislation through communication with any member or employee of the Congress or state legislature (including efforts to influence state or local officials to engage in similar lobbying activity), or with any government official or employee in connection with a decision to sign or veto enrolled legislation;

(4) Any attempt to influence—

(i) The introduction of Federal, state, or local legislation; or

(ii) The enactment or modification of any pending Federal, state, or local legislation by preparing, distributing or using publicity or propaganda, or by urging members of the general public or any segment thereof to contribute to or participate in any mass demonstration, march, rally, fund raising drive, lobbying campaign or letter writing or telephone campaign;

(5) Legislative liaison activities, including attendance at legislative sessions or committee hearings, gathering information regarding legislation, and analyzing the effect of legislation, when such activities are carried on in support of or in knowing preparation for an effort to engage in unallowable activities; or

(6) Costs incurred in attempting to improperly influence (see 3.401), either directly or indirectly, an employee or officer of the Executive branch of the Federal Government to give consideration to or act regarding a regulatory or contract matter.

(b) The following activities are excepted from the coverage of (a) of this section:

(1) Providing a technical and factual presentation of information on a topic directly related to the performance of a contract through hearing testimony, statements or letters to the Congress or a state legislature, or subdivision, member, or cognizant staff member thereof, in response to a documented request (including a Congressional Record notice requesting testimony or statements for the record at a regularly scheduled hearing) made by the recipient member, legislative body or subdivision, or a cognizant staff member thereof; provided such information is readily obtainable and can be readily put in deliverable form; and further provided that costs under this section for transportation, lodging or meals are unallowable unless incurred for the purpose of offering testimony at a regularly scheduled Congressional hearing pursuant to a written request for such presentation made by the Chairman or Ranking Minority Member of the Committee or Subcommittee conducting such hearing.

(2) Any lobbying made unallowable by paragraph (a)(3) of this subsection to influence state or local legislation in order to directly reduce contract cost, or to avoid material impairment of the contractor's authority to perform the contract.

(3) Any activity specifically authorized by statute to be undertaken with funds from the contract.

(c) When a contractor seeks reimbursement for indirect costs, total lobbying costs shall be separately identified in the indirect cost rate proposal, and thereafter treated as other unallowable activity costs.

(d) Contractors shall maintain adequate records to demonstrate that the certification of costs as being allowable or unallowable (see 42.703-2) pursuant to this subsection complies with the requirements of this subsection.

(e) Existing procedures should be utilized to resolve in advance any significant questions or disagreements concerning the interpretation or application of this subsection.

[FAC 84-2, 49 FR 18278, 4/27/84, effective 7/1/84; FAC 84-15, 51 FR 12301, 4/9/86, effective 4/7/86; FAC 84-26, 52 FR 19804, 5/27/87, effective 7/30/87; FAC 90-31, 60 FR 42648, 8/16/95, effective 10/1/95; FAC 90-39, 61 FR 31612, 6/20/96, effective 8/19/96; FAC 90-43, Interim rule, 61 FR 67408, 12/20/96, effective 12/20/96, finalized without change, FAC 97-1, 62 FR 44802, 8/22/97, effective 10/21/97; FAC 90-45, Final rule, 62 FR 224, 1/2/97, effective 1/1/97]

31.205-23 Losses on other contracts.

An excess of costs over income under any other contract (including the contractor's contributed portion under cost-sharing contracts) is unallowable.

31.205-24 [Removed and Reserved]

[FAC 84-30, 9/30/87, effective 9/30/87; FAC 90-12, 57 FR 39591, 8/31/92, effective 8/31/92; FAC 2001-24, 69 FR 34242, 6/18/2004, effective 7/19/2004]

31.205-25 Manufacturing and production engineering costs.

(a) The costs of manufacturing and production engineering effort as described in (1) through (4) of this paragraph are all allowable:

(1) Developing and deploying new or improved materials, systems, processes, methods, equipment, tools and techniques that are or are expected to be used in producing products or services;

(2) Developing and deploying pilot production lines;

(3) Improving current production functions, such as plant layout, production scheduling and control, methods and job analysis, equipment capabilities and capacities, inspection techniques, and tooling analysis (including tooling design and application improvements); and

(4) Material and manufacturing producibility analysis for production suitability and to optimize manufacturing processes, methods, and techniques.

(b) This cost principle does not cover—

(1) Basic and applied research effort (as defined in 31.205-18(a)) related to new technology, materials, systems, processes, methods, equipment, tools and techniques. Such technical effort is governed by 31.205-18, Independent research and development and bid and proposal costs; and

(2) Development effort for manufacturing or production materials, systems, processes, methods, equipment, tools, and techniques that are intended for sale is also governed by 31.205-18.

(c) Where manufacturing or production development costs are capitalized or required to be capitalized under the contractor's capitalization policies, allowable cost will be determined in accordance with the requirements of 31.205-11, Depreciation.

31.205-26 Material costs.

(a) Material costs include the costs of such items as raw materials, parts, subassemblies, components, and manufacturing supplies, whether purchased or manufactured by the contractor, and may include such collateral items as inbound transportation and in-transit insurance. In computing material costs, the contractor shall consider reasonable overruns, spoilage, or defective work (unless otherwise provided in any contract provision relating to inspecting and correcting defective work).

(b) The contractor shall—

(1) Adjust the costs of material for income and other credits, including available trade discounts, refunds, rebates, allowances, and cash discounts, and credits for scrap, salvage, and material returned to vendors; and

(2) Credit such income and other credits either directly to the cost of the material or allocate such income and other credits as a credit to indirect costs. When the contractor can demonstrate that failure to take cash discounts was reasonable, the contractor does not need to credit lost discounts.

(c) Reasonable adjustments arising from differences between periodic physical inventories and book inventories may be included in arriving at costs; provided such adjustments relate to the period of contract performance.

(d) When materials are purchased specifically for and are identifiable solely with performance under a contract, the actual purchase cost of those materials should be charged to the contract. If material is issued from stores, any generally recognized method of pricing such material is acceptable if that method is consistently applied and the results are equitable.

(e) Allowance for all materials, supplies and services that are sold or transferred between any divisions, subdivisions, subsidiaries, or affiliates of the contractor under a common control shall be on the basis of cost incurred in accordance with this subpart. However, allowance may be at price when—

(1) It is the established practice of the transferring organization to price interorganizational transfers at other than cost for commercial work of the contractor or any division, subsidiary or affiliate of the contractor under a common control; and

(2) The item being transferred qualifies for an exception under 15.403-1(b) and the contracting officer has not determined the price to be unreasonable.

(f) When a commercial item under paragraph (e) of this subsection is transferred at a price based on a catalog or market price, the contractor—

(1) Should adjust the price to reflect the quantities being acquired; and

(2) May adjust the price to reflect the actual cost of any modifications necessary because of contract requirements.

[FAC 90-27, 60 FR 28492, 5/31/95, effective 5/31/95; FAC 90-32, 60 FR 48206, 9/18/95, effective 10/1/95; FAC 90-45, Final rule, 62 FR 224, 1/2/97, effective 1/1/97; FAC 97-2, 62 FR 51224, 9/30/97, effective 10/10/97; FAC 2001-24, 69 FR 34242, 6/18/2004, effective 7/19/2004]

31.205-27 Organization costs.

(a) Except as provided in paragraph (b) of this subsection, expenditures in connection with—

(1) planning or executing the organization or reorganization of the corporate structure of a business, including mergers and acquisitions,

(2) resisting or planning to resist the reorganization of the corporate structure of a business or a change in the controlling interest in the ownership of a business, and

(3) raising capital (net worth plus long-term liabilities), are unallowable. Such expenditures include but are not limited to incorporation fees and costs of attorneys, accountants, brokers, promoters and organizers, management consultants and investment counselors, whether or not employees of the contractor. Unallowable "reorganization" costs include the cost of any change in the contractor's financial structure, excluding administrative costs of short-term borrowings for working capital, resulting in alterations in the rights and interests of security holders, whether or not additional capital is raised.

(b) The cost of activities primarily intended to provide compensation will not be considered organizational costs subject to this subsection, but will be governed by 31.205-6. These activities include acquiring stock for—

(1) executive bonuses;

(2) Employee savings plans, and

(3) employee stock ownership plans.

[FAC 84-35, 53 FR 10830, 4/1/88, effective 4/4/88]

31.205-28 Other business expenses.

The following types of recurring costs are allowable:

(a) Registry and transfer charges resulting from changes in ownership of securities issued by the contractor.

(b) Cost of shareholders' meetings.

(c) Normal proxy solicitations.

(d) Preparing and publishing reports to shareholders.

(e) Preparing and submitting required reports and forms to taxing and other regulatory bodies.

(f) Incidental costs of directors' and committee meetings.

(g) Other similar costs.

[FAC 2001-14, 68 FR 28091, 5/22/2003, effective 6/23/2003]

31.205-29 Plant protection costs.

Costs of items such as—

(a) Wages, uniforms, and equipment of personnel engaged in plant protection,

(b) Depreciation on plant protection capital assets; and

(c) Necessary expenses to comply with military requirements, are allowable.

31.205-30 Patent costs.

(a) The following patent costs are allowable to the extent that they are incurred as requirements of a Government contract (but see 31.205-33):

(1) Costs of preparing invention disclosures, reports, and other documents.

(2) Costs for searching the art to the extent necessary to make the invention disclosures.

(3) Other costs in connection with the filing and prosecution of a United States patent application where title or royalty-free license is to be conveyed to the Government.

(b) General counseling services relating to patent matters, such as advice on patent laws, regulations, clauses, and employee agreements, are allowable (but see 31.205-33).

(c) Other than those for general counseling services, patent costs not required by the contract are unallowable. (See also 31.205-37.)

31.205-31 Plant reconversion costs.

Plant reconversion costs are those incurred in restoring or rehabilitating the contractor's facilities to approximately the same condition existing immediately before the start of the Government contract, fair wear and tear excepted. Reconversion costs are unallowable except for the cost of removing Government property and the restoration or rehabilitation costs caused by such removal. However, in special circumstances where equity so dictates, additional costs may be allowed to the extent agreed upon before costs are incurred. Care should be exercised to avoid duplication through allowance as contingencies, additional profit or fee, or in other contracts.

31.205-32 Precontract costs.

Precontract costs means costs incurred before the effective date of the contract directly pursuant to the negotiation and in anticipation of the contract award when such incurrence is necessary to comply with the proposed contract delivery schedule. These costs are allowable to the extent that they would have been allowable if incurred after the date of the contract (see 31.109).

[FAC 97-22, 66 FR 2116, 1/10/2001, effective 3/12/2001; Delay of effective date, 66 FR 14259, 3/9/2001, effective 5/11/2001]

31.205-33 Professional and consultant service costs.

(a) *Definition. Professional and consultant services,* as used in this subsection, means those services rendered by persons who are members of a particular profession or possess a special skill and who are not officers or employees of the contractor. Examples include those services acquired by contractors or subcontractors in order to enhance their legal, economic, financial, or technical positions. Professional and consultant services are generally acquired to obtain information, advice, opinions, alternatives, conclusions, recommendations, training or direct assistance, such as studies, analyses, evaluations, liaison with Government officials, or other forms of representation.

(b) Costs of professional and consultant services are allowable subject to this paragraph and paragraphs (c) through (f) of this subsection when reasonable in relation to the services rendered and when not contingent upon recovery of the costs from the

Government (but see 31.205-30 and 31.205-47).

(c) Costs of professional and consultant services performed under any of the following circumstances are unallowable:

(1) Services to improperly obtain, distribute, or use information or data protected by law or regulation (*e.g.*, 52.215-1(e), Restriction on Disclosure and Use of Data).

(2) Services that are intended to improperly influence the contents of solicitations, the evaluation of proposals or quotations, or the selection of sources for contract award, whether award is by the Government, or by a prime contractor or subcontractor.

(3) Any other service obtained, performed, or otherwise resulting in violation of any statute or regulation prohibiting improper business practices or conflicts of interest.

(4) Services performed which are not consistent with the purpose and scope of the services contracted for or otherwise agreed to.

(d) In determining the allowability of costs (including retainer fees) in a particular case, no single factor or any special combination of factors is necessarily determinative. However, the contracting officer shall consider the following factors, among others:

(1) The nature and scope of the service rendered in relation to the service required.

(2) The necessity of contracting for the service, considering the contractor's capability in the particular area.

(3) The past pattern of acquiring such services and their costs, particularly in the years prior to the award of Government contracts.

(4) The impact of Government contracts on the contractor's business.

(5) Whether the proportion of Government work to the contractor's total business is such as to influence the contractor in favor of incurring the cost, particularly when the services rendered are not of a continuing nature and have little relationship to work under Government contracts.

(6) Whether the service can be performed more economically by employment rather than by contracting.

(7) The qualifications of the individual or concern rendering the service and the customary fee charged, especially on non-Government contracts.

(8) Adequacy of the contractual agreement for the service (*e.g.*, description of the service, estimate of time required, rate of compensation, termination provisions).

(e) Retainer fees, to be allowable, must be supported by evidence that—

(1) The services covered by the retainer agreement are necessary and customary;

(2) The level of past services justifies the amount of the retainer fees (if no services were rendered, fees are not automatically unallowable);

(3) The retainer fee is reasonable in comparison with maintaining an in-house capability to perform the covered services, when factors such as cost and level of expertise are considered; and

(4) The actual services performed are documented in accordance with paragraph (f) of this subsection.

(f) Fees for services rendered are allowable only when supported by evidence of the nature and scope of the service furnished (see also 31.205-38(c)). However, retainer agreements generally are not based on specific statements of work. Evidence necessary to determine that work performed is proper and does not violate law or regulation shall include—

(1) Details of all agreements (*e.g.*, work requirements, rate of compensation, and nature and amount of other expenses, if any) with the individuals or organizations providing the services and details of actual services performed;

(2) Invoices or billings submitted by consultants, including sufficient detail as to the time expended and nature of the actual services provided; and

(3) Consultants' work products and related documents, such as trip reports indicating persons visited and subjects discussed,

minutes of meetings, and collateral memoranda and reports.

[FAC 90-3, 55 FR 52793, 12/21/90, effective 1/22/91; FAC 90-16, 57 FR 60610, 12/21/92, effective 12/21/92; FAC 97-2, 62 FR 51224, 9/30/97, effective 10/10/97; FAC 97-22, 66 FR 2116, 1/10/2001, effective 3/12/2001; Delay of effective date, 66 FR 14259, 3/9/2001, effective 5/11/2001; FAC 2001-15, 68 FR 43871, 7/24/2003, effective 8/25/2003]

31.205-34 Recruitment costs.

(a) Subject to paragraph (b) of this subsection, the following costs are allowable:

(1) Costs of help-wanted advertising.

(2) Costs of operating an employment office needed to secure and maintain an adequate labor force.

(3) Costs of operating an aptitude and educational testing program.

(4) Travel costs of employees engaged in recruiting personnel.

(5) Travel costs of applicants for interviews.

(6) Costs for employment agencies, not in excess of standard commercial rates.

(b) Help-wanted advertising costs are unallowable if the advertising—

(1) Does not describe specific positions or classes of positions; or

(2) Includes material that is not relevant for recruitment purposes, such as extensive illustrations or descriptions of the company's products or capabilities.

[FAC 97-11, 64 FR 10530, 3/4/99, effective 5/3/99]

31.205-35 Relocation costs.

(a) Relocation costs are costs incident to the permanent change of assigned work location (for a period of 12 months or more) of an existing employee or upon recruitment of a new employee. The following types of relocation costs are allowable as noted, subject to the limitations in paragraphs (b) and (f) of this subsection:

(1) Costs of travel of the employee and members of the employee's immediate family (see 31.205-46) and transportation of the household and personal effects to the new location.

(2) Costs of finding a new home, such as advance trips by the employee or the spouse, or both, to locate living quarters, and temporary lodging during the transition period for the employee and members of the employee's immediate family.

(3) Closing costs incident to the disposition of the actual residence owned by the employee when notified of the transfer (e.g., brokerage fees, legal fees, appraisal fees, points, and finance charges), except that these costs, when added to the costs described in paragraph (a)(4) of this subsection, shall not exceed 14 percent of the sales price of the property sold.

(4) Continuing costs of ownership of the vacant former actual residence being sold, such as maintenance of building and grounds (exclusive of fixing up expenses), utilities, taxes, property insurance, and mortgage interest, after the settlement date or lease date of a new permanent residence, except that these costs, when added to the costs described in paragraph (a)(3) of this subsection, shall not exceed 14 percent of the sales price of the property sold.

(5) Other necessary and reasonable expenses normally incident to relocation, such as disconnecting and connecting household appliances; automobile registration; driver's license and use taxes; cutting and fitting rugs, draperies, and curtains; forfeited utility fees and deposits; and purchase of insurance against damage to or loss of personal property while in transit.

(6) Costs incident to acquiring a home in the new work location, except that—

(i) These costs are not allowable for existing employees or newly recruited employees who were not homeowners before the relocation; and

(ii) The total costs shall not exceed 5 percent of the purchase price of the new home.

(7) Mortgage interest differential payments, except that these costs are not allowable for existing or newly recruited employees who, before the relocation, were not homeowners and the total payments are limited to an amount determined as follows:

(i) The difference between the mortgage interest rates of the old and new residences times the current balance of the old mortgage times 3 years.

(ii) When mortgage differential payments are made on a lump-sum basis and the employee leaves or is transferred again in less than 3 years, the amount initially recognized shall be proportionately adjusted to reflect payments only for the actual time of the relocation.

(8) Rental differential payments covering situations where relocated employees retain ownership of a vacated home in the old location and rent at the new location. The rented quarters at the new location must be comparable to those vacated, and the allowable differential payments may not exceed the actual rental costs for the new home, less the fair market rent for the vacated home times 3 years.

(9) Costs of canceling an unexpired lease.

(10) Payments for increased employee income or Federal Insurance Contributions Act (26 U.S.C. chapter 21) taxes incident to allowable reimbursed relocation costs.

(11) Payments for spouse employment assistance.

(b) The costs described in paragraph (a) of this subsection must also meet the following criteria to be considered allowable:

(1) The move must be for the benefit of the employer.

(2) Reimbursement must be in accordance with an established policy or practice that is consistently followed by the employer and is designed to motivate employees to relocate promptly and economically.

(3) The costs must not be otherwise unallowable under subpart 31.2.

(4) Amounts to be reimbursed shall not exceed the employee's actual expenses, except as provided for in paragraphs (b)(5) and (b)(6) of this subsection.

(5) For miscellaneous costs of the type discussed in paragraph (a)(5) of this subsection, a lump-sum amount, not to exceed $5,000, may be allowed in lieu of actual costs.

(6)(i) Reimbursement on a lump-sum basis may be allowed for any of the following relocation costs when adequately supported by data on the individual elements (e.g., transportation, lodging, and meals) comprising the build-up of the lump-sum amount to be paid based on the circumstances of the particular employee's relocation:

(A) Costs of finding a new home, as discussed in paragraph (a)(2) of this subsection.

(B) Costs of travel to the new location, as discussed in paragraph (a)(1) of this subsection (but not costs for the transportation of household goods).

(C) Costs of temporary lodging, as discussed in paragraph (a)(2) of this subsection.

(ii) When reimbursement on a lump-sum basis is used, any adjustments to reflect actual costs are unallowable.

(c) The following types of costs are unallowable:

(1) Loss on the sale of a home.

(2) Costs incident to acquiring a home in the new location as follows:

(i) Real estate brokers' fees and commissions.

(ii) Costs of litigation.

(iii) Real and personal property insurance against damage or loss of property.

(iv) Mortgage life insurance.

(v) Owner's title policy insurance when such insurance was not previously carried by the employee on the old residence. (However, the cost of a mortgage title policy is allowable.)

(vi) Property taxes and operating or maintenance costs.

(3) Continuing mortgage principal payments on a residence being sold.

(4) Costs incident to furnishing equity or nonequity loans to employees or making arrangements with lenders for employees to obtain lower-than-market rate mortgage loans.

(d) If relocation costs for an employee have been allowed either as an allocable indirect or direct cost, and the employee resigns within 12 months for reasons within the employee's control, the contractor shall refund or credit the relocation costs to the Government.

(e) Subject to the requirements of paragraphs (a) through (d) of this section, the costs of family movements and of personnel movements of a special or mass nature are allowable. The cost, however, should be assigned on the basis of work (contracts) or time period benefited.

(f) Relocation costs (both outgoing and return) of employees who are hired for performance on specific contracts or long-term field projects are allowable if—

(1) The term of employment is 12 months or more;

(2) The employment agreement specifically limits the duration of employment to the time spent on the contract or field project for which the employee is hired;

(3) The employment agreement provides for return relocation to the employee's permanent and principal home immediately prior to the outgoing relocation, or other location of equal or lesser cost; and

(4) The relocation costs are determined under the rules of paragraphs (a) through (d) of this section. However, the costs to return employees, who are released from employment upon completion of field assignments pursuant to their employment agreements, are not subject to the refund or credit requirement of paragraph (d).

[FAC 84-25, 52 FR 9038, 3/20/87, effective 7/1/87; FAC 2001-08, 67 FR 43513, 6/27/2002, effective 7/29/2002; FAC 2005-06, 70 FR 57467, 9/30/2005, effective 10/31/2005]

31.205-36 Rental costs.

(a) This subsection is applicable to the cost of renting or leasing real or personal property acquired under "operating leases" as defined in Financial Accounting Standards Board's Accounting Standards Codification (FASB ASC) 840, Leases. (See 31.205-11 for Capital Leases.)

(b) The following costs are allowable:

(1) Rental costs under operating leases, to the extent that the rates are reasonable at the time of the lease decision, after consideration of—

(i) Rental costs of comparable property, if any;

(ii) Market conditions in the area;

(iii) The type, life expectancy, condition, and value of the property leased;

(iv) Alternatives available; and

(v) Other provisions of the agreement.

(2) Rental costs under a sale and leaseback arrangement only up to the amount the contractor would be allowed if the contractor retained title, computed based on the net book value of the asset on the date the contractor becomes a lessee of the property adjusted for any gain of loss recognized in accordance with 31.205-16(b).

(3) Charges in the nature of rent for property between any divisions, subsidiaries, or organizations under common control, to the extent that they do not exceed the normal costs of ownership, such as depreciation, taxes, insurance, facilities capital cost of money, and maintenance (excluding interest or other unallowable costs pursuant to Part 31), provided that no part of such costs shall duplicate any other allowed cost. Rental cost of personal property leased from any division, subsidiary, or affiliate of the contractor under common control, that has an established practice of leasing the same or similar property to unaffiliated lessees shall be allowed in accordance with subparagraph (b)(1) of this section.

(c) The allowability of rental costs under unexpired leases in connection with terminations is treated in 31.205-42(e).

[FAC 84-12, 51 FR 2665, 1/17/86, effective 1/20/86; FAC 90-44, Interim rule, 61 FR 69286, 12/31/96, effective 12/31/96, finalized without change, FAC 97-1, 62 FR 44802, 8/22/97, effective 10/21/97; FAC 2001-18, 68 FR 69246, 12/11/2003, effective 1/12/2004; FAC 2005-04, 70 FR 33673, 6/8/2005, effective 7/8/2005; FAC 2005-55, 77 FR 202, 1/3/2012, effective 2/2/2012]

31.205-37 Royalties and other costs for use of patents.

(a) Royalties on a patent or amortization of the cost of purchasing a patent or patent rights necessary for the proper performance of the contract and applicable to contract products or processes are allowable unless—

(1) The Government has a license or the right to a free use of the patent;

(2) The patent has been adjudicated to be invalid, or has been administratively determined to be invalid;

(3) The patent is considered to be unenforceable; or

(4) The patent is expired.

(b) Care should be exercised in determining reasonableness when the royalties may have been arrived at as a result of less-than-arm's-length bargaining; *e.g.*, royalties—

(1) Paid to persons, including corporations, affiliated with the contractor;

(2) Paid to unaffiliated parties, including corporations, under an agreement entered into in contemplation that a Government contract would be awarded; or

(3) Paid under an agreement entered into after the contract award.

(c) In any case involving a patent formerly owned by the contractor, the royalty amount allowed should not exceed the cost which would have been allowed had the contractor retained title.

(d) See 31.109 regarding advance agreements.

31.205-38 Selling costs.

(a) *Selling* is a generic term encompassing all efforts to market the contractor's products or services, some of which are covered specifically in other subsections of 31.205. The costs of any selling efforts other than those addressed in this cost principle are unallowable.

(b) Selling activity includes the following broad categories:

(1) *Advertising*. Advertising is defined at 31.205-1(b), and advertising costs are subject to the allowability provisions of 31.205-1(d) and (f).

(2) *Corporate image enhancement*. Corporate image enhancement activities, including broadly targeted sales efforts, other than advertising, are included within the definition of public relations at 31.205-1(a), and the costs of such efforts are subject to the allowability provisions at 31.205-1(e) and (f).

(3) *Bid and proposal costs*. Bid and proposal costs are defined at 31.205-18 and are subject to the allowability provisions of that subsection.

(4) *Market planning*. Market planning involves market research and analysis and general management planning concerned with development of the contractor's business. Long-range market planning costs are subject to the allowability provisions of 31.205-12. Other market planning costs are allowable.

(5) *Direct selling*. Direct selling efforts are those acts or actions to induce particular customers to purchase particular products or services of the contractor. Direct selling is characterized by person-to-person contact and includes such efforts as familiarizing a potential customer with the contractor's products or services, conditions of sale, service capabilities, etc. It also includes negotiation, liaison between customer and contractor personnel, technical and consulting efforts, individual demonstrations, and any other efforts having as their purpose the application or adaptation of the contractor's products or services for a particular customer's use. The cost of direct selling efforts is allowable.

(c) Notwithstanding any other provision of this subsection, sellers' or agents' compensation, fees, commissions, percentages, retainer or brokerage fees, whether or not contingent upon the award of contracts, are allowable only when paid to bona fide employees or established commercial or selling agencies maintained by the contractor for the purpose of securing business.

[FAC 84-15, 51 FR 12296, 4/9/86, effective 4/7/86; FAC 84-26, 52 FR 19805, 5/27/87, effective 7/30/87; FAC 84-30, 9/30/87, effective 9/30/87; Final rule, 55 FR 38517,

9/18/90; FAC 90-4, 56 FR 15153, 4/15/91, effective 5/15/91; FAC 90-12, 57 FR 39591, 8/31/92, effective 8/31/92; Interim rule, FAC 90-20, 59 FR 11368, 3/10/94, effective 3/10/94; FAC 90-40, 61 FR 39186, 7/26/96, effective 9/24/96; FAC 90-46, 12690, 3/17/97, effective 5/16/97; FAC 2001-15, 68 FR 43871, 7/24/2003, effective 8/25/2003]

31.205-39 Service and warranty costs.

Service and warranty costs include those arising from fulfillment of any contractual obligation of a contractor to provide services such as installation, training, correcting defects in the products, replacing defective parts, and making refunds in the case of inadequate performance. When not inconsistent with the terms of the contract, service and warranty costs are allowable. However, care should be exercised to avoid duplication of the allowance as an element of both estimated product cost and risk.

[FAC 97-22, 66 FR 2116, 1/10/2001, effective 3/12/2001; Delay of effective date, 66 FR 14259, 3/9/2001, effective 5/11/2001]

31.205-40 Special tooling and special test equipment costs.

(a) The terms *special tooling* and *special test equipment* are defined in 2.101(b).

(b) The cost of special tooling and special test equipment used in performing one or more Government contracts is allowable and shall be allocated to the specific Government contract or contracts for which acquired, except that the cost of (1) Items acquired by the contractor before the effective date of the contract (or replacement of such items), whether or not altered or adapted for use in performing the contract; and (2) Items which the contract schedule specifically excludes, shall be allowable only as depreciation or amortization.

(c) When items are disqualified as special tooling or special test equipment because with relatively minor expense they can be made suitable for general purpose use and have a value as such commensurate with their value as special tooling or special test equipment, the cost of adapting the items for use under the contract and the cost of returning them to their prior configuration are allowable.

[FAC 2005-17, 72 FR 27364, 5/15/2007, effective 6/14/2007]

31.205-41 Taxes.

(a) The following types of costs are allowable:

(1) Federal, State, and local taxes (see Part 29), except as otherwise provided in paragraph (b) of this section that are required to be and are paid or accrued in accordance with generally accepted accounting principles. Fines and penalties are not considered taxes.

(2) Taxes otherwise allowable under subparagraph (a)(1) of this section, but upon which a claim of illegality or erroneous assessment exists; provided the contractor, before paying such taxes—

(i) Promptly requests instructions from the contracting officer concerning such taxes; and

(ii) Takes all action directed by the contracting officer arising out of subparagraph (2)(i) of this section or an independent decision of the Government as to the existence of a claim of illegality or erroneous assessment, to—

(A) Determine the legality of the assessment; or

(B) Secure a refund of such taxes.

(3) Pursuant to subparagraph (a) (2) of this section, the reasonable costs of any action taken by the contractor at the direction or with the concurrence of the contracting officer. Interest or penalties incurred by the contractor for non-payment of any tax at the direction of the contracting officer or by reason of the failure of the contracting officer to ensure timely direction after a prompt request.

(4) The Environmental Tax found at section 59A of the Internal Revenue Code, also called the "Superfund Tax."

(b) The following types of costs are not allowable:

(1) Federal income and excess profits taxes.

(2) Taxes in connection with financing, refinancing, refunding operations, or reorganizations (see 31.205-20 and 31.205-27).

(3) Taxes from which exemptions are available to the contractor directly, or available to the contractor based on an exemption afforded the Government, except when the contracting officer determines that the administrative burden incident to obtaining the exemption outweighs the corresponding benefits accruing to the Government. When partial exemption from a tax is attributable to Government contract activity, taxes charged to such work in excess of that amount resulting from application of the preferential treatment are unallowable. These provisions intend that tax preference attributable to Government contract activity be realized by the Government. The term *exemption* means freedom from taxation in whole or in part and includes a tax abatement or reduction resulting from mode of assessment, method of calculation, or otherwise.

(4) Special assessments on land that represent capital improvements.

(5) Taxes (including excises) on real or personal property, or on the value, use, possession or sale thereof, which is used solely in connection with work other than on Government contracts (see paragraph (c) of this section).

(6) Any excise tax in subtitle D, chapter 43 of the Internal Revenue Code of 1986, as amended. That chapter includes excise taxes imposed in connection with qualified pension plans, welfare plans, deferred compensation plans, or other similar types of plans.

(7) Income tax accruals designed to account for the tax effects of differences between taxable income and pretax income as reflected by the books of account and financial statements.

(8) Any tax imposed under 26 U.S.C. 5000C.

(c) Taxes on property (see subparagraph (b)(5) of this section) used solely in connection with either non-Government or Government work should be considered directly applicable to the respective category of work unless the amounts involved are insignificant or comparable results would otherwise be obtained; *e.g.*, taxes on contractor-owned work-in-process which is used solely in connection with non-Government work should be allocated to such work; taxes on contractor-owned work-in-process inventory (and Government-owned work-in-process inventory when taxed) used solely in connection with Government work should be charged to such work. The cost of taxes incurred on property used in both Government and non-Government work shall be apportioned to all such work based upon the use of such property on the respective final cost objectives.

(d) Any taxes, interest, or penalties that were allowed as contract costs and are refunded to the contractor shall be credited or paid to the Government in the manner it directs. If a contractor or subcontractor obtains a foreign tax credit that reduces its U.S. Federal income tax because of the payment of any tax or duty allowed as contract costs, and if those costs were reimbursed by a foreign government, the amount of the reduction shall be paid to the Treasurer of the United States at the time the Federal income tax return is filed. However, any interest actually paid or credited to a contractor incident to a refund of tax, interest, or penalty shall be paid or credited to the Government only to the extent that such interest accrued over the period during which the contractor had been reimbursed by the Government for the taxes, interest, or penalties.

[FAC 84-56, 55 FR 3884, 2/5/90, effective 3/7/90; FAC 90-3, 55 FR 52794, 12/21/90, effective 1/22/91; FAC 90-37, 61 FR 2626, 1/26/96, effective 3/26/96; FAC 2005-65, 78 FR 6189, 1/29/2013, effective 2/28/2013]

31.205-42 Termination costs.

Contract terminations generally give rise to the incurrence of costs or the need for special treatment of costs that would not have arisen had the contract not been terminated. The following cost principles peculiar to termination situations are to be used in conjunction with the other cost principles in Subpart 31.2:

(a) *Common items*. The costs of items reasonably usable on the contractor's other work shall not be allowable unless the contractor submits evidence that the items could not be retained at cost without sustaining a loss. The contracting officer should consider the contractor's plans and orders for current and planned production when determining if items can reasonably be used on other work of the contractor. Contemporaneous purchases of common items by the contractor shall be regarded as evidence that such items are reasonably usable on the contractor's other work. Any acceptance of common items as allocable to the terminated portion of the contract should be limited to the extent that the quantities of such items on hand, in transit, and on order are in excess of the reasonable quantitative requirements of other work.

(b) *Costs continuing after termination*. Despite all reasonable efforts by the contractor, costs which cannot be discontinued immediately after the effective date of termination are generally allowable. However, any costs continuing after the effective date of the termination due to the negligent or willful failure of the contractor to discontinue the costs shall be unallowable.

(c) *Initial costs*. Initial costs, including starting load and preparatory costs, are allowable as follows:

(1) Starting load costs not fully absorbed because of termination are nonrecurring labor, material, and related overhead costs incurred in the early part of production and result from factors such as—

(i) Excessive spoilage due to inexperienced labor;

(ii) Idle time and subnormal production due to testing and changing production methods;

(iii) Training; and

(iv) Lack of familiarity or experience with the product, materials, or manufacturing processes.

(2) Preparatory costs incurred in preparing to perform the terminated contract include such costs as those incurred for initial plant rearrangement and alterations, management and personnel organization, and production planning. They do not include special machinery and equipment and starting load costs.

(3) When initial costs are included in the settlement proposal as a direct charge, such costs shall not also be included in overhead. Initial costs attributable to only one contract shall not be allocated to other contracts.

(4) If initial costs are claimed and have not been segregated on the contractor's books, they shall be segregated for settlement purposes from cost reports and schedules reflecting that high unit cost incurred during the early stages of the contract.

(5) If the settlement proposal is on the inventory basis, initial costs should normally be allocated on the basis of total end items called for by the contract immediately before termination; however, if the contract includes end items of a diverse nature, some other equitable basis may be used, such as machine or labor hours.

(d) *Loss of useful value*. Loss of useful value of special tooling, and special machinery and equipment is generally allowable, provided—

(1) The special tooling, or special machinery and equipment is not reasonably capable of use in the other work of the contractor;

(2) The Government's interest is protected by transfer of title or by other means deemed appropriate by the contracting officer; and

(3) The loss of useful value for any one terminated contract is limited to that portion of the acquisition cost which bears the same ratio to the total acquisition cost as the terminated portion of the contract bears to the entire terminated contract and other Government contracts for which the special tooling, or special machinery and equipment was acquired.

(e) *Rental under unexpired leases*. Rental costs under unexpired leases, less the residual value of such leases, are generally allowable when shown to have been reasonably necessary for the performance of the terminated contract, if—

(1) The amount of rental claimed does not exceed the reasonable use value of the property leased for the period of the contract and such further period as may be reasonable; and

(2) The contractor makes all reasonable efforts to terminate, assign, settle, or otherwise reduce the cost of such lease.

(f) *Alterations of leased property*. The cost of alterations and reasonable restorations required by the lease may be allowed when the alterations were necessary for performing the contract.

(g) *Settlement expenses*. (1) Settlement expenses, including the following, are generally allowable:

(i) Accounting, legal, clerical, and similar costs reasonably necessary for—

(A) The preparation and presentation, including supporting data, of settlement claims to the contracting officer; and

(B) The termination and settlement of subcontracts.

(ii) Reasonable costs for the storage, transportation, protection, and disposition of property acquired or produced for the contract.

(iii) Indirect costs related to salary and wages incurred as settlement expenses in (i) and (ii); normally, such indirect costs shall be limited to payroll taxes, fringe benefits, occupancy costs, and immediate supervision costs.

(2) If settlement expenses are significant, a cost account or work order shall be established to separately identify and accumulate them.

(h) *Subcontractor claims*. Subcontractor claims, including the allocable portion of the claims common to the contract and to other work of the contractor, are generally allowable. An appropriate share of the contractor's indirect expense may be allocated to the amount of settlements with subcontractors; provided, that the amount allocated is reasonably proportionate to the relative benefits received and is otherwise consistent with 31.201-4 and 31.203(d). The indirect expense so allocated shall exclude the same and similar costs claimed directly or indirectly as settlement expenses.

[FAC 97-2, 62 FR 51224, 9/30/97, effective 10/10/97; FAC 2001-22, 69 FR 17764, 4/5/2004, effective 5/5/2004]

31.205-43 Trade, business, technical and professional activity costs.

The following types of costs are allowable:

(a) Memberships in trade, business, technical, and professional organizations.

(b) Subscriptions to trade, business, professional, or other technical periodicals.

(c) When the principal purpose of a meeting, convention, conference, symposium, or seminar is the dissemination of trade, business, technical or professional information or the stimulation of production or improved productivity—

(1) Costs of organizing, setting up, and sponsoring the meetings, conventions, symposia, etc., including rental of meeting facilities, transportation, subsistence, and incidental costs;

(2) Costs of attendance by contractor employees, including travel costs (see 31.205-46); and

(3) Costs of attendance by individuals who are not employees of the contractor, provided—

(i) Such costs are not also reimbursed to the individual by the employing company or organization; and

(ii) The individual's attendance is essential to achieve the purpose of the conference, meeting, convention, symposium, etc.

[FAC 84-38, 53 FR 27467, 7/20/88, effective 8/19/88; FAC 90-31, 60 FR 42648, 8/16/95, effective 10/1/95]

31.205-44 Training and education costs.

Costs of training and education that are related to the field in which the employee is working or may reasonably be expected to work are allowable, except as follows:

(a) Overtime compensation for training and education is unallowable.

(b) The cost of salaries for attending undergraduate level classes or part-time graduate level classes during working hours is unallowable, except when unusual circumstances do not permit attendance at such classes outside of regular working hours.

(c) Costs of tuition, fees, training materials and textbooks, subsistence, salary, and any other payments in connection with full-time graduate level education are unallowable for any portion of the program that exceeds two school years or the length of the degree program, whichever is less.

(d) Grants to educational or training institutions, including the donation of facilities or other properties, scholarships, and fellowships are considered contributions and are unallowable.

(e) Training or education costs for other than bona fide employees are unallowable, except that the costs incurred for educating employee dependents (primary and secondary level studies) when the employee is working in a foreign country where suitable public education is not available may be included in overseas differential pay.

(f) Contractor contributions to college savings plans for employee dependents are unallowable.

[FAC 84-25, 52 FR 9038, 3/20/87, effective 7/1/87; Corrected by 52 FR 27806, 7/24/87; FAC 84-29, 52 FR 30077, 8/12/87, effective 8/24/87; FAC 2001-24, 69 FR 34242, 6/18/2004, effective 7/19/2004; FAC 2005-06, 70 FR 57470, 9/30/2005, effective 10/31/2005]

31.205-45 [Removed and Reserved]

[FAC 2001-14, 68 FR 28091, 5/22/2003, effective 6/23/2003]

31.205-46 Travel costs.

(a) Costs for transportation, lodging, meals, and incidental expenses.

(1) Costs incurred by contractor personnel on official company business are allowable, subject to the limitations contained in this subsection. Costs for transportation may be based on mileage rates, actual costs incurred, or on a combination thereof, provided the method used results in a reasonable charge. Costs for lodging, meals, and incidental expenses may be based on per diem, actual expenses, or a combination thereof, provided the method used results in a reasonable charge.

(2) Except as provided in subparagraph (a)(3) of this subsection, costs incurred for lodging, meals, and incidental expenses (as defined in the regulations cited in paragraphs (a)(2)(i) through (iii) of this section) shall be considered to be reasonable and allowable only to the extent that they do not exceed on a daily basis the maximum per diem rates in effect at the time of travel as set forth in the—

(i) Federal Travel Regulation, prescribed by the General Services Administration, for travel in the contiguous United States, available on a subscription basis from the Superintendent of Documents, U.S. Government Publishing Office, Washington, DC 20402, Stock No. 922-002-00000-2;

(ii) Joint Travel Regulations, DoD Civilian Personnel, Appendix A, prescribed by the Department of Defense, for travel in Alaska, Hawaii, and outlying areas of the United States, available on a subscription basis from the Superintendent of Documents, U.S. Government Publishing Office, Washington, DC 20402, Stock No. 908-010-00000-1; or

(iii) Standardized Regulations (Government Civilians, Foreign Areas), section 925, "Maximum Travel Per Diem Allowances for Foreign Areas," prescribed by the Department of State, for travel in areas not covered in paragraphs (a)(2)(i) and (ii) of this section, available on a subscription basis from the Superintendent of Documents, U.S. Government Publishing Office, Washington, DC 20402, Stock No. 744-008-00000-0.

(3) In special or unusual situations, actual costs in excess of the above-referenced maximum per diem rates are allowable provided that such amounts do not exceed the higher amounts authorized for Federal civilian employees as permitted in the regulations referenced in paragraph (a)(2)(i), (ii), or (iii) of this section. For such higher amounts to be allowable, all of the following conditions must be met:

(i) One of the conditions warranting approval of the actual expense method, as set forth in the regulations referred in paragraph (a)(2)(i), (ii), or (iii) of this subsection, must exist.

(ii) A written justification for use of the higher amounts must be approved by an officer of the contractor's organization or proceeding does not involve an allegation of fraud or similar misconduct;

(3) A final decision by an appropriate official of an executive agency to—

(i) Debar or suspend the contractor;

(ii) Rescind or void a contract; or

(iii) Terminate a contract for default by reason of a violation or failure to comply with a law or regulation.

(4) Disposition of the matter by consent or compromise if the proceeding could have led to any of the outcomes listed in paragraphs (b)(1) through (3) of this subsection (but see paragraphs (c) and (d) of this subsection); or

(5) Not covered by paragraphs (b)(1) through (4) of this subsection, but where the underlying alleged contractor misconduct was the same as that which led to a different proceeding whose costs are unallowable by reason of paragraphs (b)(1) through (4) of this subsection.

(c)(1) To the extent they are not otherwise unallowable, costs incurred in connection with any proceeding under paragraph (b) of this subsection commenced by the United States that is resolved by consent or compromise pursuant to an agreement entered into between the contractor and the United States, and which are unallowable solely because of paragraph (b) of this subsection, may be allowed to the extent specifically provided in such agreement.

(2)(i) In the event of a settlement of any proceeding brought by a third party under the False Claims Act in which the United States did not intervene, reasonable costs incurred by the contractor in connection with such a proceeding that are not otherwise unallowable by regulation or by separate agreement with the United States may be allowed if the contracting officer, in consultation with his or her legal advisor, determines that there was very little likelihood that the third party would have been successful on the merits.

(ii) In the event of disposition by consent or compromise of a proceeding brought by a whistleblower for alleged reprisal in accordance with 41 U.S.C. 4712 or 10 U.S.C. 2409, reasonable costs incurred by a contractor or subcontractor in connection with such a proceeding that are not otherwise unallowable by regulation or by agreement with the United States may be allowed if the contracting officer, in consultation with his or her legal advisor, determined that there was very little likelihood that the claimant would have been successful on the merits.

(d) To the extent that they are not otherwise unallowable, costs incurred in connection with any proceeding under paragraph (b) of this subsection commenced by a State, local, or foreign government may be allowable when the contracting officer (or other official specified in agency procedures) determines, that the costs were incurred either:

(1) As a direct result of a specific term or condition of a Federal contract; or

(2) As a result of compliance with specific written direction of the cognizant contracting officer.

(e) Costs incurred in connection with proceedings described in paragraph (b) of this subsection, but which are not made unallowable by that paragraph, may be allowable to the extent that:

(1) The costs are reasonable in relation to the activities required to deal with the proceeding and the underlying cause of action;

(2) The costs are not otherwise recovered from the Federal Government or a third party, either directly as a result of the proceeding or otherwise; and

(3) The percentage of costs allowed does not exceed the percentage determined to be appropriate considering the complexity of procurement litigation, generally accepted principles governing the award of legal fees in civil actions involving the United States as a party, and such other factors as may be appropriate. Such percentage shall not exceed 80 percent. Agreements reached under paragraph (c) of this subsection shall be subject to this limitation. If, however, an agreement described in paragraph (c)(1) of this subsection explicitly states the amount of otherwise allowable incurred legal fees and limits the allowable recovery to 80 percent or less of the stated legal fees, no addi-

tional limitation need be applied. The amount of reimbursement allowed for legal costs in connection with any proceeding described in paragraph (c)(2) of this subsection shall be determined by the cognizant contracting officer, but shall not exceed 80 percent of otherwise allowable legal costs incurred.

(f) Costs not covered elsewhere in this subsection are unallowable if incurred in connection with:

(1) Defense against Federal Government claims or appeals or the prosecution of claims or appeals against the Federal Government (see 2.101).

(2) Organization, reorganization, (including mergers and acquisitions) or resisting mergers and acquisitions (see also 31.205-27).

(3) Defense of antitrust suits.

(4) Defense of suits brought by employees or ex-employees of the contractor under section 2 of the Major Fraud Act of 1988 where the contractor was found liable or settled.

(5) Costs of legal, accounting, and consultant services and directly associated costs incurred in connection with the defense or prosecution of lawsuits or appeals between contractors arising from either—

(i) An agreement or contract concerning a teaming arrangement, a joint venture, or similar arrangement of shared interest; or

(ii) Dual sourcing, coproduction, or similar programs, are unallowable, except when—

(A) Incurred as a result of compliance with specific terms and conditions of the contract or written instructions from the contracting officer, or

(B) When agreed to in writing by the contracting officer.

(6) Patent infringement litigation, unless otherwise provided for in the contract.

(7) Representation of, or assistance to, individuals, groups, or legal entities which the contractor is not legally bound to provide, arising from an action where the participant was convicted of violation of a law or regulation or was found liable in a civil or administrative proceeding.

(8) Protests of Federal Government solicitations or contract awards, or the defense against protests of such solicitations or contract awards, unless the costs of defending against a protest are incurred pursuant to a written request from the cognizant contracting officer.

(9) A Congressional investigation or inquiry into an issue that is the subject matter of a proceeding resulting in a disposition as described in paragraphs (b)(1) through (5) of this section (see 10 U.S.C. 2324(e)(1)(Q)).

(g) Costs which may be unallowable under 31.205-47, including directly associated costs, shall be segregated and accounted for by the contractor separately. During the pendency of any proceeding covered by paragraph (b) and paragraphs (f)(4) and (f)(7) of this subsection, the contracting officer shall generally withhold payment of such costs. However, if in the best interests of the Government, the contracting officer may provide for conditional payment upon provision of adequate security, or other adequate assurance, and agreement by the contractor to repay all unallowable costs, plus interest, if the costs are subsequently determined to be unallowable.

[FAC 84-12, 51 FR 2665, 1/17/86, effective 1/20/86; FAC 84-15, 51 FR 12302, 4/9/86, effective 4/7/86; FAC 84-44, 54 FR 13024, 3/29/89, effective 4/17/89; FAC 90-3, 55 FR 52794, 12/21/90, effective 1/22/91; FAC 90-41, 61 FR 41466, 8/8/96, effective 10/7/96; FAC 97-9, 63 FR 58587, 10/30/98, effective 12/29/98; FAC 97-21, 65 FR 80255, 12/20/2000, effective 1/19/2001; FAC 97-22, 66 FR 2116, 1/10/2001, effective 3/12/2001, class deviation 1/31/2001; Delay of effective date, 66 FR 14259, 3/9/2001, effective 5/11/2001, stayed FAC 97-24, 66 FR 17753, 4/3/2001, effective 4/3/2001, finalized with changes FAC 2001-03, 66 FR 66984, 12/27/2001, effective 12/27/2001; FAC 2001-08, 67 FR 43513, 6/27/2002, effective 7/29/2002; FAC 2005-70, 78 FR 60173, 9/30/2013, effective 9/30/2013; FAC 2005-73, 79 FR 24192, 4/29/2014, effective 5/29/2014; FAC 2005-76, 79 FR 43589, 7/25/2014, effective 7/25/2014; FAC

2005-95, 82 FR 4732, 1/13/2017, effective 1/13/2017]

31.205-48 Research and development costs.

Research and development, as used in this subsection, means the type of technical effort described in 31.205-18 but sponsored by a grant or required in the performance of a contract. When costs are incurred in excess of either the price of a contract or amount of a grant for research and development effort, the excess is unallowable under any other Government contract.

[FAC 97-19, 65 FR 46052, 7/26/2000, effective 9/25/2000; FAC 2001-14, 68 FR 28091, 5/22/2003, effective 6/23/2003]

31.205-49 Goodwill.

Goodwill, an unidentifiable intangible asset, originates under the purchase method of accounting for a business combination when the price paid by the acquiring company exceeds the sum of the identifiable individual assets acquired less liabilities assumed, based upon their fair values. The excess is commonly referred to as goodwill. Goodwill may arise from the acquisition of a company as a whole or a portion thereof. Any costs for amortization, expensing, write-off, or write-down of goodwill (however represented) are unallowable.

[FAC 84-3, 49 FR 26743, 6/29/84, effective 10/1/84]

31.205-50 [Reserved]

[Reserved, FAC 90-39, 61 FR 31612, 6/20/96, effective 8/19/96]

31.205-51 Costs of alcoholic beverages.

Costs of alcoholic beverages are unallowable.

[FAC 84-15, 51 FR 12302, 4/9/86, effective 4/7/86]

31.205-52 Asset valuations resulting from business combinations.

(a) For tangible capital assets, when the purchase method of accounting for a business combination is used, whether or not the contract or subcontract is subject to CAS, the allowable depreciation and cost of money shall be based on the capitalized asset values measured and assigned in accordance with 48 CFR 9904.404-50(d), if allocable, reasonable, and not otherwise unallowable.

(b) For intangible capital assets, when the purchase method of accounting for a business combination is used, allowable amortization and cost of money shall be limited to the total of the amounts that would have been allowed had the combination not taken place.

[FAC 97-4, 63 FR 9048, 2/23/98, effective 4/24/98]

SUBPART 31.3—CONTRACTS WITH EDUCATIONAL INSTITUTIONS

31.301 Purpose.

This subpart provides the principles for determining the cost of research and development, training, and other work performed by educational institutions under contracts with the Government.

31.302 General.

The OMB Uniform Guidance at 2 CFR part 200, subpart E and appendix III, provides principles for determining the costs applicable to research and development, training, and other work performed by educational institutions (defined as institutions of higher education in the OMB Uniform Guidance at 2 CFR part 200, subpart A, and 20 U.S.C. 1001) under contracts with the Government.

[FAC 2005-89, 81 FR 45852, 7/14/2016, effective 8/15/2016]

31.303 Requirements.

(a) Contracts that refer to this subpart 31.3 for determining allowable costs under contracts with educational institutions (defined as institutions of higher education in the OMB Uniform Guidance at 2 CFR part 200, subpart A, and 20 U.S.C. 1001) shall be deemed to refer to, and shall have the allowability of costs determined by the contracting officer in accordance with, the OMB Uniform Guidance at 2 CFR part 200, subpart E and appendix III, in effect on the date of the contract.

(b) Agencies are not expected to place additional restrictions on individual items of cost.

[FAC 2005-89, 81 FR 45852, 7/14/2016, effective 8/15/2016]

SUBPART 31.4—[RESERVED]

SUBPART 31.5—[RESERVED]

SUBPART 31.6—CONTRACTS WITH STATE, LOCAL, AND FEDERALLY RECOGNIZED INDIAN TRIBAL GOVERNMENTS

31.601 Purpose.

This subpart provides the principles for determining allowable cost of contracts and subcontracts with State, local, and federally recognized Indian tribal governments.

31.602 General.

The OMB Uniform Guidance at 2 CFR part 200, subpart E and appendices V and VII sets forth the principles for determining the allowable costs of contracts and subcontracts with State, local, and federally recognized Indian tribal governments. These principles are for cost determination and are not intended to identify the circumstances or dictate the extent of Federal and State or local participation in financing a particular contract.

[FAC 2005-89, 81 FR 45852, 7/14/2016, effective 8/15/2016]

31.603 Requirements.

(a) Contracts that refer to this Subpart 31.6 for determining allowable costs under contracts with State, local and Indian tribal governments shall be deemed to refer to, and shall have the allowability of costs determined by the contracting officer in accordance with, the OMB Uniform Guidance at 2 CFR part 200, subpart E and appendices V and VII, in effect on the date of the contract.

(b) Agencies are not expected to place additional restrictions on individual items of cost. However, under 10 U.S.C. 2324, 41 U.S.C. 4304, 31 U.S.C. 3730, and 41 U.S.C. 4310, the following costs are unallowable:

(1) Costs of entertainment, including amusement, diversion, and social activities, and any costs directly associated with such costs (such as tickets to shows or sports events, meals, lodging, rentals, transportation, and gratuities).

(2) Costs incurred to influence (directly or indirectly) legislative action on any matter pending before Congress, a State legislature, or a legislative body of a political subdivision of a State.

(3) Costs incurred in defense of any civil or criminal fraud proceeding or similar proceeding (including filing of any false certification) brought by the United States where the contractor is found liable or has pleaded nolo contendere to a charge of fraud or similar proceeding (including filing of a false certification).

(4) Payments of fines and penalties resulting from violations of, or failure to comply with, Federal, state, local, or foreign laws and regulations, except when incurred as a result of compliance with specific terms and conditions of the contract or specific written instructions from the contracting officer authorizing in advance such payments in accordance with applicable regulations in the FAR or an executive agency supplement to the FAR.

(5) Costs of any membership in any social, dining, or country club or organization.

(6) Costs of alcoholic beverages.

(7) Contributions or donations, regardless of the recipient.

(8) Costs of advertising designed to promote the contractor or its products.

(9) Costs of promotional items and memorabilia, including models, gifts, and souvenirs.

(10) Costs for travel by commercial aircraft which exceed the amount of the standard commercial fare.

(11) Costs incurred in making any payment (commonly known as a "golden parachute payment") which is—

(i) In an amount in excess of the normal severance pay paid by the contractor to an employee upon termination of employment; and

(ii) Is paid to the employee contingent upon, and following, a change in management control over, or ownership of, the contractor or a substantial portion of the contractor's assets.

(12) Costs of commercial insurance that protects against the costs of the contractor for correction of the contractor's own defects in materials or workmanship.

(13) Costs of severance pay paid by the contractor to foreign nationals employed by the contractor under a service contract performed outside the United States, to the extent that the amount of the severance pay paid in any case exceeds the amount paid in the industry involved under the customary or prevailing practice for firms in that industry providing similar services in the United States, as determined by regulations in the FAR or in an executive agency supplement to the FAR.

(14) Costs of severance pay paid by the contractor to a foreign national employed by the contractor under a service contract performed in a foreign country if the termination of the employment of the foreign national is the result of the closing of, or curtailment of activities at, a United States facility in that country at the request of the government of that country.

(15) Unless any of the exceptions at 31.205-47(c) or (d) apply, costs incurred by a contractor in connection with any criminal, civil, or administrative proceedings that result in dispositions described at 31.205-47(b)(1) through (5) commenced by: a Federal, State, local, or foreign government, for a violation of, or failure to comply with, law or regulation by the contractor (including its agents or employees); a contractor or subcontractor employee submitting a whistleblower complaint of reprisal in accordance with 41 U.S.C. 4712 or 10 U.S.C. 2409; or a third party in the name of the United States under the False Claims Act, 31 U.S.C. 3730. For any such proceeding that does not result in a disposition described at 31.205- 47(b)(1) through (5), or to which 31.205-47(c) exceptions apply, the cost of that proceeding shall be subject to the limitations in 31.205-47(e).

(16) Costs incurred in connection with a Congressional investigation or inquiry into an issue that is the subject matter of a proceeding resulting in a disposition as described at 31.205-47(b)(1) through (5).

[FAC 90-31, 60 FR 42648, 8/16/95, effective 10/1/95; FAC 2005-73, 79 FR 24192, 4/29/2014, effective 5/29/2014; FAC 2005-89, 81 FR 45852, 7/14/2016, effective 8/15/2016; FAC 2005-95, 82 FR 4732, 1/13/2017, effective 1/13/2017]

SUBPART 31.7—CONTRACTS WITH NONPROFIT ORGANIZATIONS

31.701 Purpose.

This subpart provides the principles for determining the cost applicable to work performed by nonprofit organizations under contracts with the Government. A nonprofit organization, for purpose of identification, is defined as a business entity organized and operated exclusively for charitable, scientific, or educational purposes, of which no part of the net earnings inure to the benefit of any private shareholder or individual, of which no substantial part of the activities is carrying on propaganda or otherwise attempting to influence legislation or participating in any political campaign on behalf of any candidate for public office, and which are exempt from federal income taxation under section 501 of the Internal Revenue Code.

31.702 General.

The OMB Uniform Guidance at 2 CFR part 200, subpart E and appendix IV, sets forth principles for determining the costs applicable to work performed by nonprofit organizations (as defined in the OMB Uniform Guidance at 2 CFR part 200) under contracts (as well as grants and other agreements) with the Government. See 31.108 for exceptions to the cost principles for nonprofit organizations.

[FAC 2005-89, 81 FR 45852, 7/14/2016, effective 8/15/2016]

31.703 Requirements.

(a) Contracts which refer to this Subpart 31.7 for determining allowable costs shall be deemed to refer to, and shall have the allowability of costs determined by the contracting officer in accordance with, the OMB Uniform Guidance at 2 CFR part 200, subpart E and appendix IV in effect on the date of the contract.

(b) Agencies are not expected to place additional restrictions on individual items of cost. However, under 10 U.S.C. 2324(e) and 41 U.S.C. 4304, the costs cited in 31.603(b) are unallowable.

[FAC 90-31, 60 FR 42648, 8/16/95, effective 10/1/95; FAC 2005-73, 79 FR 24192, 4/29/2014, effective 5/29/2014; FAC 2005-89, 81 FR 45852, 7/14/2016, effective 8/15/2016]

PART 32—CONTRACT FINANCING

Table of Contents

Scope of part 32.000
Definitions 32.001
Applicability of subparts 32.002
Simplified acquisition procedures financing 32.003
Contract performance in foreign countries 32.004
Consideration for contract financing 32.005
Reduction or suspension of contract payments upon finding of fraud 32.006
General 32.006-1
Definition 32.006-2
Responsibilities 32.006-3
Procedures 32.006-4
Reporting 32.006-5
Contract financing payments 32.007
Notification of overpayment 32.008
Providing accelerated payments to small business subcontractors 32.009
General 32.009-1
Contract clause 32.009-2

Subpart 32.1—Non-Commercial Item Purchase Financing

Scope of subpart 32.100
Authority 32.101
Description of contract financing methods 32.102
Progress payments under construction contracts 32.103
Providing contract financing 32.104
Uses of contract financing 32.105
Order of preference 32.106
Need for contract financing not a deterrent 32.107
Financial consultation 32.108
Termination financing 32.109
Payment of subcontracts under cost-reimbursement prime contracts 32.110
Contract clauses for non-commercial purchases 32.111
Non-payment of subcontractors under contracts for non-commercial items 32.112
Subcontractor assertions of nonpayment 32.112-1
Subcontractor requests for information 32.112-2
Customary contract financing 32.113
Unusual contract financing 32.114

Subpart 32.2—Commercial Item Purchase Financing

Scope of subpart 32.200
Statutory authority 32.201
General 32.202
Policy 32.202-1
Types of payments for commercial item purchases 32.202-2
Conducting market research about financing terms 32.202-3
Security for Government financing 32.202-4
Determining contract financing terms 32.203
Procedures for contracting officer-specified commercial contract financing 32.204
Procedures for offeror-proposed commercial contract financing 32.205
Solicitation provisions and contract clauses 32.206
Administration and payment of commercial financing payments 32.207

Subpart 32.3—Loan Guarantees for Defense Production

Scope of subpart 32.300
Definitions 32.301
Authority 32.302

General 32.303
Procedures 32.304
Application for guarantee 32.304-1
Certificate of eligibility 32.304-2
Asset formula 32.304-3
Guarantee amount and maturity 32.304-4
Assignment of claims under contracts 32.304-5
Other collateral security 32.304-6
Contract surety bonds and loan guarantees 32.304-7
Other borrowing 32.304-8
Loan guarantees for terminated contracts 32.305
Loan guarantees for subcontracts 32.306

Subpart 32.4—Advance Payments for Non-Commercial Items

Scope of subpart 32.400
Statutory authority 32.401
General 32.402
Applicability 32.403
Exclusions 32.404
Applying Pub. L. 85-804 to advance payments under sealed bid contracts 32.405
Letters of credit 32.406
Interest 32.407
Application for advance payments 32.408
Contracting officer action 32.409
Recommendation for approval 32.409-1
Recommendation for disapproval 32.409-2
Security, supervision, and covenants 32.409-3
Findings, determination, and authorization 32.410
Agreement for special account at a financial institution 32.411
Contract clause 32.412

Subpart 32.5—Progress Payments Based on Costs

Scope of subpart 32.500
General 32.501
Customary progress payment rates 32.501-1
Unusual progress payments 32.501-2
Contract price 32.501-3
[Reserved] 32.501-4
Other protective terms 32.501-5
Preaward matters 32.502
Use of customary progress payments 32.502-1
Contract finance office clearance 32.502-2
Solicitation provisions 32.502-3
Contract clauses 32.502-4
Postaward matters 32.503
[Reserved] 32.503-1
Supervision of progress payments 32.503-2
Initiation of progress payments and review of accounting system 32.503-3
Approval of progress payment requests 32.503-4
Administration of progress payments 32.503-5
Suspension or reduction of payments 32.503-6
[Removed and Reserved] 32.503-7
Liquidation rates—ordinary method 32.503-8
Liquidation rates—alternate method 32.503-9
Establishing alternate liquidation rates 32.503-10
Adjustments for price reduction 32.503-11
Maximum unliquidated amount 32.503-12

[Removed and Reserved] . . . 32.503-13
Protection of Government title . . . 32.503-14
Application of Government title terms . . . 32.503-15
Risk of loss . . . 32.503-16
Subcontracts under prime contracts providing progress payments . . . 32.504

Subpart 32.6—Contract Debts

Scope of subpart . . . 32.600
General . . . 32.601
Responsibilities . . . 32.602
Debt determination . . . 32.603
Demand for payment . . . 32.604
Final decisions . . . 32.605
Debt collection . . . 32.606
Installment payments and deferment of collection . . . 32.607
Installment payments . . . 32.607-1
Deferment of collection . . . 32.607-2
Interest . . . 32.608
Interest charges . . . 32.608-1
Interest credits . . . 32.608-2
Delays in receipt of notices or demands . . . 32.609
Compromising debts . . . 32.610
Contract clause . . . 32.611
[Removed] . . . 32.612
[Removed] . . . 32.613
[Removed] . . . 32.614
[Removed] . . . 32.614-1
[Removed] . . . 32.614-2
[Removed] . . . 32.615
[Removed] . . . 32.616
[Removed] . . . 32.617

Subpart 32.7—Contract Funding

Scope of subpart . . . 32.700
[Reserved] . . . 32.701
Policy . . . 32.702
Contract funding requirements . . . 32.703
General . . . 32.703-1
Contracts conditioned upon availability of funds . . . 32.703-2
Contracts crossing fiscal years . . . 32.703-3
Limitation of cost or funds . . . 32.704
Unenforceability of unauthorized obligations . . . 32.705
Contract clauses . . . 32.706
Clauses for contracting in advance of funds . . . 32.706-1
Clauses for limitation of cost or funds . . . 32.706-2
Clause for unenforceability of unauthorized obligations . . . 32.706-3

Subpart 32.8—Assignment of Claims

Scope of subpart . . . 32.800
Definitions . . . 32.801
Conditions . . . 32.802
Policies . . . 32.803
Extent of assignee's protection . . . 32.804
Procedure . . . 32.805
Contract clauses . . . 32.806

Subpart 32.9—Prompt Payment

Scope of subpart . . . 32.900

Applicability 32.901
Definitions 32.902
Responsibilities 32.903
Determining payment due dates 32.904
Payment documentation and process 32.905
Making payments 32.906
Interest penalties 32.907
Contract clauses 32.908
Contractor inquiries 32.909

Subpart 32.10—Performance-Based Payments

Scope of subpart 32.1000
Policy 32.1001
Bases for performance-based payments 32.1002
Criteria for use 32.1003
Procedures 32.1004
Solicitation provision and contract clause 32.1005
[Removed and Reserved] 32.1006
Administration and payment of performance-based payments 32.1007
Suspension or reduction of performance-based payments 32.1008
Title 32.1009
Risk of loss 32.1010

Subpart 32.11—Electronic Funds Transfer

Scope of subpart 32.1100
Statutory requirements 32.1101
Definitions 32.1102
Applicability 32.1103
Protection of EFT information 32.1104
Assignment of claims 32.1105
EFT Mechanisms 32.1106
Payment information 32.1107
Payment by Governmentwide commercial purchase card 32.1108
EFT information submitted by offerors 32.1109
Solicitation provision and contract clauses 32.1110

PART 32—CONTRACT FINANCING

32.000 Scope of part.

This part prescribes policies and procedures for contract financing and other payment matters. This part addresses—

(a) Payment methods, including partial payments and progress payments based on percentage or stage of completion;

(b) Loan guarantees, advance payments, and progress payments based on costs;

(c) Administration of debts to the Government arising out of contracts;

(d) Contract funding, including the use of contract clauses limiting costs or funds;

(e) Assignment of claims to aid in private financing;

(f) Selected payment clauses;

(g) Financing of purchases of commercial items;

(h) Performance-based payments; and

(i) Electronic funds transfer payments.

[FAC 90-33, 60 FR 49706, 9/26/95, effective 10/1/95; FAC 90-42, 61 FR 45769, 8/29/96, effective 8/29/96; FAC 2001-06, 67 FR 13048, 3/20/2002, effective 4/4/2002]

32.001 Definitions.

As used in this part—

Commercial interim payment means any payment that is not a commercial advance payment or a delivery payment. These payments are contract financing payments for prompt payment purposes (i.e., not subject to the interest penalty provisions of the Prompt Payment Act in accordance with subpart 32.9). A commercial interim payment is given to the contractor after some work has been done, whereas a commercial advance payment is given to the contractor when no work has been done.

Contract action means an action resulting in a contract, as defined in subpart 2.1, including actions for additional supplies or services outside the existing contract scope, but not including actions that are within the scope and under the terms of the existing contract, such as contract modifications issued pursuant to the Changes clause, or funding and other administrative changes.

Contract financing payment means an authorized Government disbursement of monies to a contractor prior to acceptance of supplies or services by the Government.

(1) Contract financing payments include—

(i) Advance payments;

(ii) Performance-based payments;

(iii) Commercial advance and interim payments;

(iv) Progress payments based on cost under the clause at 52.232-16, Progress Payments;

(v) Progress payments based on a percentage or stage of completion (see 32.102(e)), except those made under the clause at 52.232-5, Payments Under Fixed-Price Construction Contracts, or the clause at 52.232-10, Payments Under Fixed-Price Architect-Engineer Contracts; and

(vi) Interim payments under a cost reimbursement contract, except for a cost reimbursement contract for services when Alternate I of the clause at 52.232-25, Prompt Payment, is used.

(2) Contract financing payments do not include—

(i) Invoice payments;

(ii) Payments for partial deliveries; or

(iii) Lease and rental payments.

Customary contract financing means that financing deemed by an agency to be available for routine use by contracting officers. Most customary contract financing arrangements should be usable by contracting officers without specific reviews or approvals by higher management.

Delivery payment means a payment for accepted supplies or services, including payments for accepted partial deliveries. Commercial financing payments are liquidated by deduction from these payments. Delivery payments are invoice payments for prompt payment purposes.

Designated billing office means the office or person (governmental or nongovernmental) designated in the contract where the contractor first submits invoices and contract financing requests. The contract might designate different offices to receive invoices and contract financing requests. The designated billing office might be—

(1) The Government disbursing office;

(2) The contract administration office;

(3) The office accepting the supplies delivered or services performed by the contractor;

(4) The contract audit office; or

(5) A nongovernmental agent.

Designated payment office means the office designated in the contract to make invoice payments or contract financing payments. Normally, this will be the Government disbursing office.

Due date means the date on which payment should be made.

Invoice payment means a Government disbursement of monies to a contractor under a contract or other authorization for supplies or services accepted by the Government.

(1) Invoice payments include—

(i) Payments for partial deliveries that have been accepted by the Government;

(ii) Final cost or fee payments where amounts owed have been settled between the Government and the contractor;

(iii) For purposes of subpart 32.9 only, all payments made under the clause at 52.232-5, Payments Under Fixed-Price Construction Contracts, and the clause at 52.232-10, Payments Under Fixed-Price Architect-Engineer Contracts; and

(iv) Interim payments under a cost-reimbursement contract for services when Alternate I of the clause at 52.232-25, Prompt Payment, is used.

(2) Invoice payments do not include contract financing payments.

Liquidate means to decrease a payment for an accepted supply item or service under a contract for the purpose of recouping financing payments previously paid to the contractor.

Unusual contract financing means any financing not deemed customary contract financing by the agency. Unusual contract financing is financing that is legal and proper under applicable laws, but that the agency has not authorized contracting officers to use without specific reviews or approvals by higher management.

[FAC 84-29, 52 FR 30077, 8/12/87, effective 8/24/87; FAC 90-33, 60 FR 49706, 9/26/95, effective 10/1/95; FAC 97-22, 66 FR 2116, 1/10/2001, effective 3/12/2001; Delay of effective date, 66 FR 14259, 3/9/2001, effective 5/11/2001; FAC 2001-02, 66 FR 65347, 12/18/2001, effective 2/19/2002; FAC 2001-06, 67 FR 13048, 3/20/2002, effective 4/4/2002; FAC 2005-33, 74 FR 28430, 6/15/2009, effective 7/15/2009]

32.002 Applicability of subparts.

(a) The following sections and subparts of this part are applicable to all purchases subject to Part 32:

(1) Sections 32.000 through 32.009.

(2) Subpart 32.3, Loan Guarantees for Defense Production.

(3) Subpart 32.6, Contract Debts.

(4) Subpart 32.7, Contract Funding.

(5) Subpart 32.8, Assignment of Claims.

(6) Subpart 32.9, Prompt Payment.

(7) Subpart 32.11, Electronic Funds Transfer.

(b) Subpart 32.2, Commercial Item Purchase Financing, is applicable only to purchases of commercial items under authority of Part 12.

(c) The following subparts of this part are applicable to all purchases made under any authority other than Part 12:

(1) Subpart 32.1, Non-Commercial Item Purchase Financing.

(2) Subpart 32.4, Advance Payments For Non-Commercial Items.

(3) Subpart 32.5, Progress Payments Based on Costs.

(4) Subpart 32.10, Performance-Based Payments.

[FAC 90-33, 60 FR 49706, 9/26/95, effective 10/1/95; FAC 90-42, 61 FR 45769, 8/29/96, effective 8/29/96; FAC 2005-71, 78

FR 70477, 11/25/2013, effective 12/26/2013]

32.003 Simplified acquisition procedures financing.

Unless agency regulations otherwise permit, contract financing shall not be provided for purchases made under the authority of Part 13.

[FAC 90-33, 60 FR 49706, 9/26/95, effective 10/1/95]

32.004 Contract performance in foreign countries.

The enforceability of contract provisions for security of Government financing in a foreign jurisdiction is dependent upon local law and procedure. Prior to providing contract financing where foreign jurisdictions may become involved, the contracting officer shall ensure the Government's security is enforceable. This may require the provision of additional or different security than that normally provided for in the standard contract clauses.

[FAC 90-33, 60 FR 49706, 9/26/95, effective 10/1/95]

32.005 Consideration for contract financing.

(a) *Requirement.* When a contract financing clause is included at the inception of a contract, there shall be no separate consideration for the contract financing clause. The value of the contract financing to the contractor is expected to be reflected in either

(1) A bid or negotiated price that will be lower than such price would have been in the absence of the contract financing, or—

(2) Contract terms and conditions, other than price, that are more beneficial to the Government than they would have been in the absence of the contract financing. Adequate new consideration is required for changes to, or the addition of, contract financing after award.

(b) *Amount of new consideration*. The contractor may provide new consideration by monetary or nonmonetary means, provided the value is adequate. The fair and reasonable consideration should approximate the amount by which the price would have been less had the contract financing terms been contained in the initial contract. In the absence of definite information on this point, the contracting officer should apply the following criteria in evaluating whether the proposed new consideration is adequate:

(1) The value to the contractor of the anticipated amount and duration of the contract financing at the imputed financial costs of the equivalent working capital.

(2) The estimated profit rate to be earned through contract performance.

(c) *Interest.* Except as provided in Subpart 32.4, Advance Payments for Non-Commercial Items, the contract shall not provide for any other type of specific charges, such as interest, for contract financing.

[FAC 90-33, 60 FR 49706, 9/26/95, effective 10/1/95]

32.006 Reduction or suspension of contract payments upon finding of fraud. (No Text)

32.006-1 General.

(a) Under 10 U.S.C. 2307(i)(8), the statutory authority implemented by this section is available to the Department of Defense and the National Aeronautics and Space Administration; this statutory authority is not available to the United States Coast Guard. Under 41 U.S.C. 4506, this statutory authority is available to all agencies subject to Division C of subtitle I of title 41.

(b) 10 U.S.C. 2307(i)(2) and 41 U.S.C. 4506 provide for a reduction or suspension of further payments to a contractor when the agency head determines there is substantial evidence that the contractor's request for advance, partial, or progress payments is based on fraud. This authority does not apply to commercial interim payments under Subpart 32.2, or performance-based payments under Subpart 32.10.

(c) The agency head may not delegate his or her responsibilities under these statutes below Level IV of the Executive Schedule.

(d) Authority to reduce or suspend payments under these statutes is in addition to other Government rights, remedies, and procedures.

(e) In accordance with these statutes, agency head determinations and decisions under this section may be made for an individual contract or any group of contracts affected by the fraud.

[FAC 90-33, 60 FR 49706, 9/26/95, effective 10/1/95; FAC 2005-19, 72 FR 46363, 8/17/2007, effective 8/17/2007; FAC 2005-73, 79 FR 24192, 4/29/2014, effective 5/29/2014]

32.006-2 Definition.

Remedy coordination official, as used in this section means the person or entity in the agency who coordinates within that agency the administration of criminal, civil, administrative, and contractual remedies resulting from investigations of fraud or corruption related to procurement activities. (See 10 U.S.C. 2307(i)(10) and 41 U.S.C. 4506(a).)

[FAC 90-33, 60 FR 49706, 9/26/95, effective 10/1/95; FAC 97-22, 66 FR 2116, 1/10/2001, effective 3/12/2001; Delay of effective date, 66 FR 14259, 3/9/2001, effective 5/11/2001; FAC 2005-19, 72 FR 46363, 8/17/2007, effective 8/17/2007; FAC 2005-73, 79 FR 24192, 4/29/2014, effective 5/29/2014]

32.006-3 Responsibilities.

(a) Agencies shall establish appropriate procedures to implement the policies and procedures of this section.

(b) Government personnel shall report suspected fraud related to advance, partial, or progress payments in accordance with agency regulations.

[FAC 90-33, 60 FR 49706, 9/26/95, effective 10/1/95]

32.006-4 Procedures.

(a) In any case in which an agency's remedy coordination official finds substantial evidence that a contractor's request for advance, partial, or progress payments under a contract awarded by that agency is based on fraud, the remedy coordination official shall recommend that the agency head reduce or suspend further payments to the contractor. The remedy coordination official shall submit to the agency head a written report setting forth the remedy coordination official's findings that support each recommendation.

(b) Upon receiving a recommendation from the remedy coordination official under paragraph (a) of this subsection, the agency head shall determine whether substantial evidence exists that the request for payment under a contract is based on fraud.

(c) If the agency head determines that substantial evidence exists, the agency head may reduce or suspend further payments to the contractor under the affected contract(s). Such reduction or suspension shall be reasonably commensurate with the anticipated loss to the Government resulting from the fraud.

(d) In determining whether to reduce or suspend further payment(s), as a minimum, the agency head shall consider—

(1) A recommendation from investigating officers that disclosure of the allegations of fraud to the contractor may compromise an ongoing investigation;

(2) The anticipated loss to the Government as a result of the fraud;

(3) The contractor's overall financial condition and ability to continue performance if payments are reduced or suspended;

(4) The contractor's essentiality to the national defense, or to the execution of the agency's official business; and

(5) Assessment of all documentation concerning the alleged fraud, including documentation submitted by the contractor in its response to the notice required by paragraph (e) of this subsection.

(e) Before making a decision to reduce or suspend further payments, the agency head shall, in accordance with agency procedures—

(1) Notify the contractor in writing of the action proposed by the remedy coordination official and the reasons therefor (such notice must be sufficiently specific to permit the contractor to collect and present evidence addressing the aforesaid reasons); and

(2) Provide the contractor an opportunity to submit information within a reasonable

time, in response to the action proposed by the remedy coordination official.

(f) When more than one agency has contracts affected by the fraud, the agencies shall consider designating one agency as the lead agency for making the determination and decision.

(g) The agency shall retain in its files the written justification for each—

(1) Decision of the agency head whether to reduce or suspend further payments; and

(2) Recommendation received by an agency head in connection with such decision.

(h) Not later than 180 calendar days after the date of the reduction or suspension action, the remedy coordination official shall—

(1) Review the agency head's determination on which the reduction or suspension decision is based; and

(2) Transmit a recommendation to the agency head as to whether the reduction or suspension should continue.

[FAC 90-33, 60 FR 49706, 9/26/95, effective 10/1/95]

32.006-5 Reporting.

(a) In accordance with 41 U.S.C. 4506(h), the head of an agency, other than the Department of Defense, shall prepare a report for each fiscal year in which a recommendation has been received pursuant to 32.006-4(a). Reports within the Department of Defense shall be prepared in accordance with 10 U.S.C. 2307(i)(7).

(b) In accordance with 41 U.S.C. 4506(h) and 10 U.S.C. 2307(i)(7), each report shall contain—

(1) Each recommendation made by the remedy coordination official;

(2) The actions taken on the recommendation(s), with reasons for such actions; and

(3) An assessment of the effects of each action on the Government.

[FAC 90-33, 60 FR 49706, 9/26/95, effective 10/1/95; FAC 2005-73, 79 FR 24192, 4/29/2014, effective 5/29/2014]

32.007 Contract financing payments.

(a)(1) Unless otherwise prescribed in agency policies and procedures or otherwise specified in paragraph (b) of this section, the due date for making contract financing payments by the designated payment office is the 30th day after the designated billing office receives a proper contract financing request.

(2) If an audit or other review of a specific financing request is required to ensure compliance with the terms and conditions of the contract, the designated payment office is not compelled to make payment by the specified due date.

(3) Agency heads may prescribe shorter periods for payment based on contract pricing or administrative considerations. For example, a shorter period may be justified by an agency if the nature and extent of contract financing arrangements are integrated with agency contract pricing policies.

(4) Agency heads must not prescribe a period shorter than 7 days or longer than 30 days.

(b) For advance payments, loans, or other arrangements that do not involve recurrent submission of contract financing requests, the designated payment office will make payment in accordance with the applicable contract financing terms or as directed by the contracting officer.

(c) A proper contract financing request must comply with the terms and conditions specified by the contract. The contractor must correct any defects in requests submitted in the manner specified in the contract or as directed by the contracting officer.

(d) The designated billing office and designated payment office must annotate each contract financing request with the date their respective offices received the request.

(e) The Government will not pay an interest penalty to the contractor as a result of delayed contract financing payments.

[FAC 2001-02, 66 FR 65347, 12/18/2001, effective 2/19/2002]

32.008 Notification of overpayment.

[66 FR 65355, 12/18/2001, effective 12/18/2001; FAC 2001-16, 68 FR 56682, 10/1/2003, effective 10/31/2003; FAC 2005-27, 73 FR 53997, 9/17/2008, effective 10/17/2008]

32.009 Providing accelerated payments to small business subcontractors.

[FAC 2005-71, 78 FR 70477, 11/25/2013, effective 12/26/2013]

32.009-1 General.

Pursuant to the policy provided by OMB Memorandum M-12-16, Providing Prompt Payment to Small Business Subcontractors (and as extended by OMB Memorandum M-13-15 and M-14-10, both titled, Extension of Policy to Provide Accelerated Payment to Small Business Subcontractors), agencies shall take measures to ensure that prime contractors pay small business subcontractors on an accelerated timetable to the maximum extent practicable, and upon receipt of accelerated payments from the Government. This acceleration does not provide any new rights under the Prompt Payment Act and does not affect the application of the Prompt Payment Act late payment interest provisions.

[FAC 2005-71, 78 FR 70477, 11/25/2013, effective 12/26/2013; FAC 2005-76, 79 FR 4360, 7/25/2014, effective 7/25/2014]

32.009-2 Contract clause.

Insert clause 52.232-40, Providing Accelerated Payments to Small Business Subcontractors, in all solicitations and contracts.

[FAC 2005-71, 78 FR 70477, 11/25/2013, effective 12/26/2013]

SUBPART 32.1—NON-COMMERCIAL ITEM PURCHASE FINANCING

32.100 Scope of subpart.

This subpart provides policies and procedures applicable to contract financing and payment for any purchases other than purchases of commercial items in accordance with Part 12.

[FAC 90-33, 60 FR 49706, 9/26/95, effective 10/1/95]

32.101 Authority.

The basic authority for the contract financing described in this part is contained in 41 U.S.C. chapter 45, Contract Financing, 10 U.S.C. 2307, and Title III of the Defense Production Act of 1950 (50 U.S.C. App. 2091).

[FAC 90-33, 60 FR 49706, 9/26/95, effective 10/1/95; FAC 2005-73, 79 FR 24192, 4/29/2014, effective 5/29/2014]

32.102 Description of contract financing methods.

(a) Advance payments are advances of money by the Government to a prime contractor before, in anticipation of, and for the purpose of complete performance under one or more contracts. They are expected to be liquidated from payments due to the contractor incident to performance of the contracts. Since they are not measured by performance, they differ from partial, progress, or other payments based on the performance or partial performance of a contract. Advance payments may be made to prime contractors for the purpose of making advances to subcontractors.

(b) Progress payments based on costs are made on the basis of costs incurred by the contractor as work progresses under the contract. This form of contract financing does not include—

(1) Payments based on the percentage or stage of completion accomplished;

(2) Payments for partial deliveries accepted by the Government;

(3) Partial payments for a contract termination proposal; or

(4) Performance-based payments.

(c) Loan guarantees are made by Federal Reserve banks, on behalf of designated guaranteeing agencies, to enable contractors to obtain financing from private sources under contracts for the acquisition of supplies or services for the national defense.

(d) Payments for accepted supplies and services that are only a part of the contract requirements (i.e., partial deliveries) are authorized under 41 U.S.C. chapter 45 and 10 U.S.C. 2307. In accordance with 5 CFR 1315.4(k), agencies must pay for partial delivery of supplies or partial performance of services unless specifically prohibited by the contract. Although payments for partial deliveries generally are treated as a method of payment and not as a method of contract financing, using partial delivery payments can assist contractors to participate in contracts without, or with minimal, contract financing. When appropriate, contract statements of work and pricing arrangements must permit acceptance and payment for discrete portions of the work, as soon as accepted (see 32.906(c)).

(e) (1) Progress payments based on a percentage or stage of completion are authorized by the statutes cited in 32.101.

(2) This type of progress payment may be used as a payment method under agency procedures. Agency procedures must ensure that payments are commensurate with work accomplished, which meets the quality standards established under the contract. Furthermore, progress payments may not exceed 80 percent of the eligible costs of work accomplished on undefinitized contract actions.

(f) Performance-based payments are contract financing payments made on the basis of—

(1) Performance measured by objective, quantifiable methods;

(2) Accomplishment of defined events; or

(3) Other quantifiable measures of results.

[FAC 84-29, 52 FR 30077, 8/12/87, effective 8/24/87; FAC 90-33, 60 FR 49706, 9/26/95, effective 10/1/95; FAC 90-46, 62 FR 12690, 3/17/97, effective 5/16/97; FAC 2001-02, 66 FR 65347, 12/18/2001, effective 2/19/2002; FAC 2005-73, 79 FR 24192, 4/29/2014, effective 5/29/2014]

32.103 Progress payments under construction contracts.

When satisfactory progress has not been achieved by a contractor during any period for which a progress payment is to be made, a percentage of the progress payment may be retained. Retainage should not be used as a substitute for good contract management, and the contracting officer should not withhold funds without cause. Determinations to retain and the specific amount to be withheld shall be made by the contracting officers on a case-by-case basis. Such decisions will be based on the contracting officer's assessment of past performance and the likelihood that such performance will continue. The amount of retainage withheld shall not exceed 10 percent of the approved estimated amount in accordance with the terms of the contract and may be adjusted as the contract approaches completion to recognize better than expected performance, the ability to rely on alternative safeguards, and other factors. Upon completion of all contract requirements, retained amounts shall be paid promptly.

[FAC 84-16, 51 FR 19716, 5/30/86, effective 5/30/86; FAC 84-30, 9/30/87, effective 9/30/87; FAC 90-33, 60 FR 49706, 9/26/95, effective 10/1/95]

32.104 Providing contract financing.

(a) Prudent contract financing can be a useful working tool in Government acquisition by expediting the performance of essential contracts. Contracting officers must consider the criteria in this part in determining whether to include contract financing in solicitations and contracts. Resolve reasonable doubts by including contract financing in the solicitation. The contracting officer must—

(1) Provide Government financing only to the extent actually needed for prompt and efficient performance, considering the availability of private financing and the probable impact on working capital of the predelivery expenditures and production lead-times associated with the contract, or groups of contracts or orders (e.g., issued under indefinite-delivery contracts, basic ordering agreements, or their equivalent);

(2) Administer contract financing so as to aid, not impede, the acquisition;

(3) Avoid any undue risk of monetary loss to the Government through the financing;

(4) Include the form of contract financing deemed to be in the Government's best interest in the solicitation (see 32.106 and 32.113); and

(5) Monitor the contractor's use of the contract financing provided and the contractor's financial status.

(b) If the contractor is a small business concern, the contracting officer must give special attention to meeting the contractor's contract financing need. However, a contractor's receipt of a certificate of competency from the Small Business Administration has no bearing on the contractor's need for or entitlement to contract financing.

(c) Subject to specific agency regulations and paragraph (d) of this section, the contracting officer—

(1) May provide customary contract financing in accordance with 32.113; and

(2) Must not provide unusual contract financing except as authorized in 32.114.

(d) Unless otherwise authorized by agency procedures, the contracting officer may provide contract financing in the form of performance-based payments (see subpart 32.10) or customary progress payments (see subpart 32.5) if the following conditions are met:

(1) The contractor—

(i) Will not be able to bill for the first delivery of products for a substantial time after work must begin (normally 4 months or more for small business concerns, and 6 months or more for others), and will make expenditures for contract performance during the predelivery period that have a significant impact on the contractor's working capital; or

(ii) Demonstrates actual financial need or the unavailability of private financing.

(2) If the contractor is not a small business concern—

(i) For an individual contract, the contract price is $2.5 million or more; or

(ii) For an indefinite-delivery contract, a basic ordering agreement or a similar ordering instrument, the contracting officer expects the aggregate value of orders or contracts that individually exceed the simplified acquisition threshold to have a total value of $2.5 million or more. The contracting officer must limit financing to those orders or contracts that exceed the simplified acquisition threshold.

(3) If the contractor is a small business concern—

(i) For an individual contract, the contract price exceeds the simplified acquisition threshold; or

(ii) For an indefinite-delivery contract, a basic ordering agreement or a similar ordering instrument, the contracting officer expects the aggregate value of orders or contracts to exceed the simplified acquisition threshold.

[FAC 97-16, 65 FR 16274, 3/27/2000, effective 3/27/2000; FAC 2005-13, 71 FR 57363, 9/28/2006, effective 9/28/2006]

32.105 Uses of contract financing.

(a) Contract financing methods covered in this part are intended to be self-liquidating through contract performance. Consequently, agencies shall only use the methods for financing of contractor working capital, not for the expansion of contractor-owned facilities or the acquisition of fixed assets. However, under loan guarantees, exceptions may be made for—

(1) Facilities expansion of a minor or incidental nature, if a relatively small part of the guaranteed loan is used for the expansion and the contractor's repayment would not be delayed or impaired; or

(2) Other instances of facilities expansion for which contract financing is appropriate under agency procedures.

(b) The limitations in this section do not apply to contracts under which facilities are being acquired for Government ownership.

32.106 Order of preference.

The contracting officer must consider the following order of preference when a contractor requests contract financing, unless an exception would be in the Government's best interest in a specific case:

(a) Private financing without Government guarantee. It is not intended, however, that the contracting officer require the contractor to obtain private financing—

(1) At unreasonable terms; or

(2) From other agencies.

(b) Customary contract financing other than loan guarantees and certain advance payments (see 32.113).

(c) Loan guarantees.

(d) Unusual contract financing (see 32.114).

(e) Advance payments (see exceptions in 32.402(b)).

[FAC 90-33, 60 FR 49706, 9/26/95, effective 10/1/95; FAC 97-16, 65 FR 16274, 3/27/2000, effective 3/27/2000]

32.107 Need for contract financing not a deterrent.

(a) If the contractor or offeror meets the standards prescribed for responsible prospective contractors at 9.104, the contracting officer shall not treat the contractor's need for contract financing as a handicap for a contract award; *e.g.*, as a responsibility factor or evaluation criterion.

(b) The contractor should not be disqualified from contract financing solely because the contractor failed to indicate a need for contract financing before the contract was awarded.

32.108 Financial consultation.

Each contracting office should have available and use the services of contract financing personnel competent to evaluate credit and financial problems. In resolving any questions concerning—

(a) the financial capability of an offeror or contractor to perform a contract, or—

(b) what form of contract financing is appropriate in a given case, the contracting officer should consult the appropriate contract financing office.

32.109 Termination financing.

To encourage contractors to invest their own funds in performance despite the susceptibility of the contract to termination for the convenience of the Government, the contract financing procedures under this part may be applied to the financing of terminations either in connection with or independently of financing for contract performance (see 49.112-1).

32.110 Payment of subcontractors under cost-reimbursement prime contracts.

If the contractor makes financing payments to a subcontractor under a cost-reimbursement prime contract, the contracting officer should accept the financing payments as reimbursable costs of the prime contract only under the following conditions:

(a) The payments are made under the criteria in subpart 32.5 for customary progress payments based on costs, 32.202-1 for commercial item purchase financing, or 32.1003 for performance-based payments, as applicable.

(b) If customary progress payments are made, the payments do not exceed the progress payment rate in 32.501-1, unless unusual progress payments to the subcontractor have been approved in accordance with 32.501-2.

(c) If customary progress payments are made, the subcontractor complies with the liquidation principles of 32.503-8, 32.503-9, and 32.503-10.

(d) If performance-based payments are made, the subcontractor complies with the liquidation principles of 32.1004(d).

(e) The subcontract contains financing payments terms as prescribed in this part.

[FAC 97-16, 65 FR 16274, 3/27/2000, effective 3/27/2000]

32.111 Contract clauses for non-commercial purchases.

(a) The contracting officer shall insert the following clauses, appropriately modified with respect to payment due dates, in accordance with agency regulations—

(1) The clause at 52.232-1, Payments, in solicitations and contracts when a fixed-price supply contract, a fixed-price service contract, or a contract for nonregulated communication services is contemplated;

(2) The clause at 52.232-2, Payment under Fixed-Price Research and Development Contracts, in solicitations and contracts when a fixed-price research and development contract is contemplated;

(3) The clause at 52.232-3, Payments under Personal Services Contracts, in solicitations and contracts for personal services;

(4) The clause at 52.232-4, Payments under Transportation Contracts and Transportation-Related Services Contracts, in solicitations and contracts for transportation or transportation-related services;

(5) The clause at 52.232-5, Payments under Fixed-Price Construction Contracts, in solicitations and contracts for construction when a fixed-price contract is contemplated;

(6) The clause at 52.232-6, Payments under Communication Service Contracts with Common Carriers, in solicitations and contracts for regulated communication services by common carriers; and

(7) The clause at 52.232-7, Payments under Time-and-Materials and Labor-Hour Contracts, in solicitations and contracts when a time-and-materials or labor-hour contract is contemplated. If the contracting officer determines that it is necessary to withhold payment to protect the Government's interests, paragraph (a)(7) of the clause permits the contracting officer to unilaterally issue a modification requiring the contractor to withhold 5 percent of amounts due, up to a maximum of $50,000 under the contract. The contracting officer shall ensure that the modification specifies the percentage and total amount of the withheld payment. Normally, there should be no need to withhold payment for a contractor with a record of timely submittal of the release discharging the Government from all liabilities, obligations, and claims, as required by paragraph (g) of the clause.

(i) If a labor-hour contract is contemplated, the contracting officer shall use the clause with its Alternate I.

(ii) If the contracting officer determines that it is necessary to withhold payment to protect the Government's interests, paragraph (a)(7) of the clause permits the contracting officer to unilaterally issue a modification requiring the contractor to withhold 5 percent of amounts due, up to a maximum of $50,000 under the contract. The contracting officer shall ensure that the modification specifies the percentage and total amount of the withhold payment. Normally, there should be no need to withhold payment for a contractor with a record of timely submittal of the release discharging the Government from all liabilities, obligations, and claims, as required by paragraph (g) of the clause.

(b) The contracting officer shall insert the following clauses, appropriately modified with respect to payment due dates in accordance with agency regulations:

(1) The clause at 52.232-8, Discounts for Prompt Payment, in solicitations and contracts when a fixed-price supply contract or fixed-price service contract is contemplated.

(2) A clause, substantially the same as the clause at 52.232-9, Limitation on Withholding of Payments, in solicitations and contracts when a supply contract, research and development contract, service contract, time-and-materials contract, or labor-hour contract is contemplated that includes two or more terms authorizing the temporary withholding of amounts otherwise payable to the contractor for supplies delivered or services performed.

(c) The contracting officer shall insert the following clauses, appropriately modified with respect to payments due dates in accordance with agency regulations:

(1) The clause at 52.232-10, Payments under Fixed-Price Architect-Engineer Contracts, in fixed-price architect-engineer contracts.

(2) The clause at 52.232-11, Extras, in solicitations and contracts when a fixed-price supply contract, fixed-price service contract, or a transportation contract is contemplated.

[FAC 84-12, 51 FR 2665, 1/17/86, effective 1/20/86; FAC 90-33, 60 FR 49706, 9/26/95, effective 10/1/95; FAC 2005-05, 70 FR 43580, 7/27/2005, effective 8/26/2005; FAC 2005-15, 71 FR 74656, 12/12/2006, effective 2/12/2007; Final rule, 72 FR 6881, 2/13/2007, effective 2/12/2007; FAC 2005-60, 77 FR 44059, 7/26/2012, effective 8/27/2012]

32.112 Nonpayment of subcontractors under contracts for noncommercial items. (No Text)

32.112-1 Subcontractor assertions of nonpayment.

(a) In accordance with Section 806(a)(4) of Pub. L. 102-190, as amended by Sections 2091 and 8105 of Pub. L. 103-355 (10 U.S.C. 2302 note), upon the assertion by a subcontractor or supplier of a Federal contractor that the subcontractor or supplier has not been paid in accordance with the payment terms of the subcontract, purchase order, or other agreement with the prime contractor, the contracting officer may determine—

(1) For a construction contract, whether the contractor has made—

(i) Progress payments to the subcontractor or supplier in compliance with Chapter 39 of Title 31, United States Code (Prompt Payment Act); or

(ii) Final payment to the subcontractor or supplier in compliance with the terms of the subcontract, purchase order, or other agreement with the prime contractor;

(2) For a contract other than construction, whether the contractor has made progress payments, final payments, or other payments to the subcontractor or supplier in compliance with the terms of the subcontract, purchase order, or other agreement with the prime contractor; or

(3) For any contract, whether the contractor's certification of payment of a subcontractor or supplier accompanying its payment request to the Government is accurate.

(b) If, in making the determination in paragraphs (a)(1) and (2) of this subsection, the contracting officer finds the prime contractor is not in compliance, the contracting officer may—

(1) Encourage the contractor to make timely payment to the subcontractor or supplier; or

(2) If authorized by the applicable payment clauses, reduce or suspend progress payments to the contractor.

(c) If the contracting officer determines that a certification referred to in paragraph (a)(3) of this subsection is inaccurate in any material respect, the contracting officer shall initiate administrative or other remedial action.

[FAC 90-32, 60 FR 48206, 9/18/95, effective 10/1/95; FAC 2005-73, 79 FR 24192, 4/29/2014, effective 5/29/2014]

32.112-2 Subcontractor requests for information.

(a) In accordance with Section 806(a)(1) of Pub. L. 102-190, as amended by Sections 2091 and 8105 of Pub. L. 103-355 (10 U.S.C. 2302 note), upon the request of a subcontractor or supplier under a Federal contract for a noncommercial item, the contracting officer shall promptly advise the subcontractor or supplier as to—

(1) Whether the prime contractor has submitted requests for progress payments or other payments to the Federal Government under the contract; and

(2) Whether final payment under the contract has been made by the Federal Government to the prime contractor.

(b) In accordance with 5 U.S.C. 552(b)(1), this subsection does not apply to matters that are—

(1) Specifically authorized under criteria established by an Executive order to be kept classified in the interest of national defense or foreign policy; and

(2) Properly classified pursuant to such Executive order.

[FAC 90-32, 60 FR 48206, 9/18/95, effective 10/1/95; FAC 2005-73, 79 FR 24192, 4/29/2014, effective 5/29/2014]

32.113 Customary contract financing.

The solicitation must specify the customary contract financing offerors may propose. The following are customary contract financing when provided in accordance with this part and agency regulations:

(a) Financing of shipbuilding, or ship conversion, alteration, or repair, when agency regulations provide for progress payments based on a percentage or stage of completion.

(b) Financing of construction or architect-engineer services purchased under the authority of part 36.

(c) Financing of contracts for supplies or services awarded under the sealed bid method of procurement in accordance with part 14 through progress payments based on costs in accordance with subpart 32.5.

(d) Financing of contracts for supplies or services awarded under the competitive negotiation method of procurement in accordance with part 15, through either progress payments based on costs in accordance with subpart 32.5, or performance-based payments in accordance with subpart 32.10 (but not both).

(e) Financing of contracts for supplies or services awarded under a sole-source acquisition as defined in 2.101 and using the procedures of part 15, through either progress payments based on costs in accordance with subpart 32.5, or performance-based payments in accordance with subpart 32.10 (but not both).

(f) Financing of contracts for supplies or services through advance payments in accordance with subpart 32.4.

(g) Financing of contracts for supplies or services through guaranteed loans in accordance with subpart 32.3.

(h) Financing of contracts for supplies or services through any appropriate combination of advance payments, guaranteed loans, and either performance-based payments or progress payments (but not both) in accordance with their respective subparts.

[FAC 97-16, 65 FR 16274, 3/27/2000, effective 3/27/2000; FAC 97-22, 66 FR 2116, 1/10/2001, effective 3/12/2001; Delay of effective date, 66 FR 14259, 3/9/2001, effective 5/11/2001]

32.114 Unusual contract financing.

Any contract financing arrangement that deviates from this part is unusual contract financing. Unusual contract financing shall be authorized only after approval by the head of the agency or as provided for in agency regulations.

[FAC 90-33, 60 FR 49706, 9/26/95, effective 10/1/95]

SUBPART 32.2—COMMERCIAL ITEM PURCHASE FINANCING

32.200 Scope of subpart.

This subpart provides policies and procedures for commercial financing arrangements under commercial purchases pursuant to Part 12.

[FAC 90-33, 60 FR 49706, 9/26/95, effective 10/1/95]

32.201 Statutory authority.

10 U.S.C. 2307(f) and 41 U.S.C. 4505 provide that payment for commercial items may be made under such terms and conditions as the head of the agency determines are appropriate or customary in the commercial marketplace and are in the best interest of the United States.

[FAC 90-33, 60 FR 49706, 9/26/95, effective 10/1/95; FAC 2005-73, 79 FR 24192, 4/29/2014, effective 5/29/2014]

32.202 General. (No Text)

32.202-1 Policy.

(a) *Use of financing in contracts.* It is the responsibility of the contractor to provide all resources needed for performance of the contract. Thus, for purchases of commercial items, financing of the contract is normally the contractor's responsibility. However, in some markets the provision of financing by the buyer is a commercial practice. In these circumstances, the contracting officer may include appropriate financing terms in contracts for commercial purchases when doing so will be in the best interest of the Government.

(b) *Authorization.* Commercial interim payments and commercial advance payments may be made under the following circumstances—

(1) The contract item financed is a commercial supply or service;

(2) The contract price exceeds the simplified acquisition threshold;

(3) The contracting officer determines that it is appropriate or customary in the commercial marketplace to make financing payments for the item;

(4) Authorizing this form of contract financing is in the best interest of the Government (see paragraph (e) of this subsection);

(5) Adequate security is obtained (see 32.202-4);

(6) Prior to any performance of work under the contract, the aggregate of commercial advance payments shall not exceed 15 percent of the contract price;

(7) The contract is awarded on the basis of competitive procedures or, if only one offer is solicited, adequate consideration is obtained (based on the time value of the additional financing to be provided) if the financing is expected to be substantially more advantageous to the offeror than the offeror's normal method of customer financing; and

(8) The contracting officer obtains concurrence from the payment office concerning liquidation provisions when required by 32.206(e).

(c) *Difference from non-commercial financing.* Government financing of commercial purchases under this subpart is expected to be different from that used for non-commercial purchases under Subpart 32.1 and its related subparts. While the contracting officer may adapt techniques and procedures from the non-commercial subparts for use in implementing commercial contract financing arrangements, the contracting officer must have a full understanding of effects of the differing contract environments and of what is needed to protect the interests of the Government in commercial contract financing.

(d) *Unusual contract financing.* Any contract financing arrangement not in accord with the requirements of agency regulations or this part is unusual contract financing and requires advance approval in accordance with agency procedures. If not otherwise specified, such unusual contract financing shall be approved by the head of the contracting activity.

(e) *Best interest of the Government.* The statutes cited in 32.201 do not allow contract financing by the Government unless it is in the best interest of the United States. Agencies may establish standards to determine whether contract financing is in the best interest of the Government. These standards may be for certain types of procurements, certain types of items, or certain dollar levels of procurements.

[FAC 90-33, 60 FR 49706, 9/26/95, effective 10/1/95; FAC 90-40, 61 FR 39186, 7/26/96, effective 8/26/96]

32.202-2 Types of payments for commercial item purchases.

These definitions incorporate the requirements of the statutory commercial financing authority and the implementation of the Prompt Payment Act.

Commercial advance payment, as used in this subsection, means a payment made before any performance of work under the contract. The aggregate of these payments shall not exceed 15 percent of the contract price. These payments are contract financing payments for prompt payment purposes (*i.e.*, not subject to the interest penalty provisions of the Prompt Payment Act in accordance with Subpart 32.9). These payments are not subject to Subpart 32.4, Advance Payments for Non-Commercial Items.

Commercial interim payment (see 32.001).

Delivery payment (see 32.001).

[FAC 90-33, 60 FR 49706, 9/26/95, effective 10/1/95; FAC 97-22, 66 FR 2116, 1/10/2001, effective 3/12/2001; Delay of effective date, 66 FR 14259, 3/9/2001, effective 5/11/2001]

32.202-3 Conducting market research about financing terms.

Contract financing may be a subject included in the market research conducted in accordance with Part 10. If market research for contract financing is conducted, the contracting officer should consider—

(a) The extent to which other buyers provide contract financing for purchases in that market;

(b) The overall level of financing normally provided;

(c) The amount or percentages of any payments equivalent to commercial advance payments (see 32.202-2);

(d) The basis for any payments equivalent to commercial interim payments (see

32.001), as well as the frequency, and amounts or percentages; and

(e) Methods of liquidation of contract financing payments and any special or unusual payment terms applicable to delivery payments (see 32.001).

[FAC 90-33, 60 FR 49706, 9/26/95, effective 10/1/95; FAC 97-22, 66 FR 2116, 1/10/2001, effective 3/12/2001; Delay of effective date, 66 FR 14259, 3/9/2001, effective 5/11/2001]

32.202-4 Security for Government financing.

(a) *Policy.* (1) 10 U.S.C. 2307(f) and 41 U.S.C. 4505 require the Government to obtain adequate security for Government financing. The contracting officer shall specify in the solicitation the type of security the Government will accept. If the Government is willing to accept more than one form of security, the offeror shall be required to specify the form of security it will provide. If acceptable to the contracting officer, the resulting contract shall specify the security (see 32.206(b) (1) (iv)).

(2) Subject to agency regulations, the contracting officer may determine the offeror's financial condition to be adequate security, provided the offeror agrees to provide additional security should that financial condition become inadequate as security (see paragraph (c) of the clause at 52.232-29, Terms for Financing of Purchases of Commercial Items). Assessment of the contractor's financial condition shall consider both net worth and liquidity. If the contracting officer finds the offeror's financial condition is not adequate security, the contracting officer shall require other adequate security. Paragraphs (b), (c), and (d) of this subsection list other (but not all) forms of security that the contracting officer may find acceptable.

(3) The value of the security must be at least equal to the maximum unliquidated amount of contract financing payments to be made to the contractor. The value of security may be adjusted periodically during contract performance, as long as it is always equal to or greater than the amount of unliquidated financing.

(b) *Paramount lien.* (1) The statutes cited in 32.201 provide that if the Government's security is in the form of a lien, such lien is paramount to all other liens and is effective immediately upon the first payment, without filing, notice, or other action by the United States.

(2) When the Government's security is in the form of a lien, the contract shall specify what the lien is upon, *e.g.*, the work in process, the contractor's plant, or the contractor's inventory. Contracting officers may be flexible in the choice of assets. The contract must also give the Government a right to verify the existence and value of the assets.

(3) Provision of Government financing shall be conditioned upon a contractor certification that the assets subject to the lien are free from any prior encumbrances. Prior liens may result from such things as capital equipment loans, installment purchases, working capital loans, various lines of credit, and revolving credit arrangements.

(c) *Other assets as security.* Contracting officers may consider the guidance at 28.203-2, 28.203-3, and 28.204 in determining which types of assets may be acceptable as security. For the purpose of applying the guidance in Part 28 to this subsection, the term *surety* and/or *individual surety* should be interpreted to mean *offeror* and/or *contractor*.

(d) *Other forms of security.* Other acceptable forms of security include—

(1) An irrevocable letter of credit from a federally insured financial institution;

(2) A bond from a surety, acceptable in accordance with Part 28 (note that the bond must guarantee repayment of the unliquidated contract financing);

(3) A guarantee of repayment from a person or corporation of demonstrated liquid net worth, connected by significant ownership to the contractor; or

(4) Title to identified contractor assets of adequate worth.

(e) *Management of risk and security.* In establishing contract financing terms, the contracting officer must be aware of certain risks. For example, very high amounts of financing early in the contract (front-end loading) may unduly increase the risk to the Government. The security and the amounts and timing of financing payments must be analyzed as a whole to determine whether the arrangement will be in the best interest of the Government.

[FAC 90-33, 60 FR 49706, 9/26/95, effective 10/1/95; FAC 2005-73, 79 FR 24192, 4/29/2014, effective 5/29/2014]

32.203 Determining contract financing terms.

When the criteria in 32.202-1(b) are met, the contracting officer may either specify the financing terms in the solicitation (see 32.204) or permit each offeror to propose its own customary financing terms (see 32.205). When the contracting officer has sufficient information on financing terms that are customary in the commercial marketplace for the item, those terms may be specified in the solicitation.

[FAC 90-33, 60 FR 49706, 9/26/95, effective 10/1/95]

32.204 Procedures for contracting officer-specified commercial contract financing.

The financing terms shall be included in the solicitation. Contract financing shall not be a factor in the evaluation of resulting proposals, and proposals of alternative financing terms shall not be accepted (but see 14.208 and 15.206 concerning amendments of solicitations). However, an offer stating that the contracting officer-specified contract financing terms will not be used by the offeror does not alter the evaluation of the offer, nor does it render the offer nonresponsive or otherwise unacceptable. In the event of award to an offeror who declined the proposed contract financing, the contract financing provisions shall not be included in the resulting contract. Contract financing shall not be a basis for adjusting offerors' proposed prices, because the effect of contract financing is reflected in each offeror's proposed prices.

[FAC 90-33, 60 FR 49706, 9/26/95, effective 10/1/95; FAC 97-2, 62 FR 51224, 9/30/97, effective 10/10/97]

32.205 Procedures for offeror-proposed commercial contract financing.

(a) Under this procedure, each offeror may propose financing terms. The contracting officer must then determine which offer is in the best interests of the United States.

(b) *Solicitations.* The contracting officer must include in the solicitation the provision at 52.232-31, Invitation to Propose Financing Terms. The contracting officer must also—

(1) Specify the delivery payment (invoice) dates that will be used in the evaluation of financing proposals; and

(2) Specify the interest rate to be used in the evaluation of financing proposals (see paragraph (c)(4) of this section).

(c) *Evaluation of proposals.* (1) When contract financing terms vary among offerors, the contracting officer must adjust each proposed price for evaluation purposes to reflect the cost of providing the proposed financing in order to determine the total cost to the Government of that particular combination of price and financing.

(2) Contract financing results in the Government making payments earlier than it otherwise would. In order to determine the cost to the Government of making payments earlier, the contracting officer must compute the imputed cost of those financing payments and add it to the proposed price to determine the evaluated price for each offeror.

(3) The imputed cost of a single financing payment is the amount of the payment multiplied by the annual interest rate, multiplied by the number of years, or fraction thereof, between the date of the financing payment and the date the amount would have been paid as a delivery payment. The imputed cost of financing is the sum of the imputed costs of each of the financing payments.

(4) The contracting officer must calculate the time value of proposal-specified contract financing arrangements using as the interest rate the nominal discount rate specified in Appendix C of the Office of Management and Budget (OMB) Circular A-94, "Guidelines and Discount Rates for Benefit-Cost

Analysis of Federal Programs", appropriate to the period of contract financing. Where the period of proposed financing does not match the periods in the OMB Circular, the interest rate for the period closest to the finance period shall be used. Appendix C is updated yearly, and is available from the Office of Economic Policy in the Office of Management and Budget (OMB).

[FAC 90-33, 60 FR 49706, 9/26/95, effective 10/1/95; FAC 97-16, 65 FR 16274, 3/27/2000, effective 3/27/2000]

32.206 Solicitation provisions and contract clauses.

(a) The contract shall contain the paragraph entitled "Payment" of the clause at 52.212-4, Contract Terms and Conditions—Commercial Items. If the contract will provide for contract financing, the contracting officer shall construct a solicitation provision and contract clause. This solicitation provision shall be constructed in accordance with 32.204 or 32.205. If the procedure at 32.205 is used, the solicitation provision at 52.232-31, Invitation to Propose Financing Terms, shall be included. The contract clause shall be constructed in accordance with the requirements of this subpart and any agency regulations.

(b) Each contract financing clause shall include:

(1) A description of the—

(i) Computation of the financing payment amounts (see paragraph (c) of this section);

(ii) Specific conditions of contractor entitlement to those financing payments (see paragraph (c) of this section);

(iii) Liquidation of those financing payments by delivery payments (see paragraph (e) of this section);

(iv) Security the contractor will provide for financing payments and any terms or conditions specifically applicable thereto (see 32.202-4); and

(v) Frequency, form, and any additional content of the contractor's request for financing payment (in addition to the requirements of the clause at 52.232-29, Terms for Financing of Purchases of Commercial Items; and

(2) Unless agency regulations authorize alterations, the unaltered text of the clause at 52.232-29, Terms for Financing of Purchases of Commercial Items.

(c) *Computation of amounts, and contractor entitlement provisions.* (1) Contracts shall provide that delivery payments shall be made only for completed supplies and services accepted by the Government in accordance with the terms of the contract. Contracts may provide for commercial advance and commercial interim payments based upon a wide variety of bases, including (but not limited to) achievement or occurrence of specified events, the passage of time, or specified times prior to the delivery date(s). The basis for payment must be objectively determinable. The clause written by the contracting officer shall specify, to the extent access is necessary, the information and/or facilities to which the Government shall have access for the purpose of verifying the contractor's entitlement to payment of contract financing.

(2) If the contract is awarded using the offeror-proposed procedure at 32.205, the clause constructed by the contracting officer under paragraph (b)(1) of this section shall contain the following:

(i) A statement that the offeror's proposed listing of earliest times and greatest amounts of projected financing payments submitted in accordance with paragraph (d)(2) of the provision at 52.232-31, Invitation to Propose Financing Terms, is incorporated into the contract, and

(ii) A statement that financing payments shall be made in the lesser amount and on the later of the date due in accordance with the financing terms of the contract, or in the amount and on the date projected in the listing of earliest times and greatest amounts incorporated in the contract.

(3) If the security accepted by the contracting officer is the contractor's financial condition, the contracting officer shall incorporate in the clause constructed under paragraph (b)(1) of this section the following—

(i) A statement that the contractor's financial condition has been accepted as adequate security for commercial financing payments; and

(ii) A statement that the contracting officer may exercise the Government's rights to require other security under paragraph (c), Security for Government Financing, of the clause at 52.232-29, Terms for Financing of Purchases of Commercial Items, in the event the contractor's financial condition changes and is found not to be adequate security.

(d) *Instructions for multiple appropriations.* If contract financing is to be computed for the contract as a whole, and if there is more than one appropriation account (or subaccount) funding payments under the contract, the contracting officer shall include, in the contract, instructions for distribution of financing payments to the respective funds accounts. Distribution instructions and contract liquidation instructions must be mutually consistent.

(e) *Liquidation.* Liquidation of contract financing payments shall be on the same basis as the computation of contract financing payments; that is, financing payments computed on a whole contract basis shall be liquidated on a whole contract basis; and a payment computed on a line item basis shall be liquidated against that line item. If liquidation is on a whole contract basis, the contracting officer shall use a uniform liquidation percentage as the liquidation method, unless the contracting officer obtains the concurrence of the cognizant payment office that the proposed liquidation provisions can be executed by that office, or unless agency regulations provide alternative liquidation methods.

(f) *Prompt payment for commercial purchase payments.* The provisions of subpart 32.9, Prompt Payment, apply to contract financing and invoice payments for commercial purchases in the same manner they apply to non-commercial purchases. The contracting officer is responsible for including in the contract all the information necessary to implement prompt payment. In particular, contracting officers must be careful to clearly differentiate in the contract between contract financing and invoice payments and between items having different prompt payment times.

(g) *Installment payment financing for commercial items.* Contracting officers may insert the clause at 52.232-30, Installment Payments for Commercial Items, in solicitations and contracts in lieu of constructing a specific clause in accordance with paragraphs (b) through (e) of this section, if the contract action qualifies under the criteria at 32.202-1(b) and installment payments for the item are either customary or are authorized in accordance with agency procedures.

(1) *Description.* Installment payment financing is payment by the Government to a contractor of a fixed number of equal interim financing payments prior to delivery and acceptance of a contract item. The installment payment arrangement is designed to reduce administrative costs. However, if a contract will have a large number of deliveries, the administrative costs may increase to the point where installment payments are not in the best interests of the Government.

(2) *Authorized types of installment payment financing and rates.* Installment payments may be made using the clause at 52.232-30, Installment Payments for Commercial Items, either at the 70 percent financing rate cited in the clause or at a lower rate in accordance with agency procedures.

(3) *Calculating the amount of installment financing payments.* The contracting officer shall identify in the contract schedule those items for which installment payment financing is authorized. Monthly installment payment amounts are to be calculated by the contractor pursuant to the instructions in the contract clause only for items authorized to receive installment payment financing.

(4) *Liquidating installment payments.* If installment payments have been made for an item, the amount paid to the contractor upon acceptance of the item by the Government shall be reduced by the amount of installment payments made for the item. The contractor's request for final payment for each item is required to show this calculation.

[FAC 90-33, 60 FR 49706, 9/26/95, effective 10/1/95]

32.207 Administration and payment of commercial financing payments.

(a) *Responsibility.* The contracting officer responsible for administration of the contract shall be responsible for review and approval of contract financing requests.

(b) *Approval of financing requests.* Unless otherwise provided in agency regulations, or by agreement with the appropriate payment official—

(1) The contracting officer shall be responsible for receiving, approving, and transmitting all contract financing requests to the appropriate payment office; and

(2) Each approval shall specify the amount to be paid, necessary contractual information, and the account(s) (see 32.206(d)) to be charged for the payment.

(c) *Management of security.* After contract award, the contracting officer responsible for approving requests for financing payments shall be responsible for determining that the security continues to be adequate. If the contractor's financial condition is the Government's security, this contracting officer is also responsible for monitoring the contractor's financial condition.

[FAC 90-33, 60 FR 49706, 9/26/95, effective 10/1/95]

SUBPART 32.3—LOAN GUARANTEES FOR DEFENSE PRODUCTION

32.300 Scope of subpart.

This subpart prescribes policies and procedures for designated agencies' guarantees of loans made by private financial institutions to borrowers performing contracts related to national defense (see 30.102).

32.301 Definitions.

As used in this subpart—

Borrower means a contractor, subcontractor (at any tier), or other supplier who receives a guaranteed loan.

Federal Reserve Board means the Board of Governors of the Federal Reserve System.

Guaranteed loan or *V loan* means a loan, revolving credit fund, or other financial arrangement made pursuant to Regulation V of the Federal Reserve Board, under which the guaranteeing agency is obligated, on demand of the lender, to purchase a stated percentage of the loan and to share any losses in the amount of the guaranteed percentage.

Guaranteeing agency means any agency that the President has authorized to guarantee loans, through Federal Reserve Banks, for expediting national defense production.

[FAC 97-22, 66 FR 2116, 1/10/2001, effective 3/12/2001; Delay of effective date, 66 FR 14259, 3/9/2001, effective 5/11/2001]

32.302 Authority.

Congress has authorized Federal Reserve Banks to act, on behalf of guaranteeing agencies, as fiscal agents of the United States in the making of loan guarantees for defense production (Section 301, Defense Production Act of 1950 (50 U.S.C. App. 2091)). By Executive Order 10480, August 14, 1953 (3 CFR 1949-53), as amended, the President has designated the following agencies as guaranteeing agencies:

(a) Department of Defense.

(b) Department of Energy.

(c) Department of Commerce.

(d) Department of the Interior.

(e) Department of Agriculture.

(f) General Services Administration.

(g) National Aeronautics and Space Administration.

32.303 General.

(a) Section 301 of the Defense Production Act authorizes loan guarantees for contract performance or other operations related to national defense, subject to amounts annually authorized by Congress on the maximum obligation of any guaranteeing agency under any loan, discount, advance, or commitment in connection therewith, entered into under section 301. (See 50 U.S.C. App. 2091 for statutory limitations and exceptions concerning the authorization of loan guarantee amounts and the use of loan guarantees for the prevention of insolvency or bankruptcy.)

(b) The guarantee shall be for less than 100 percent of the loan unless the agency determines that—

(1) The circumstances are exceptional;

(2) The operations of the contractor are vital to the national defense; and

(3) No other suitable means of financing are available.

(c) Loan guarantees are not issued to other agencies of the Government.

(d) Guaranteed loans are essentially the same as conventional loans made by private financial institutions, except that the guaranteeing agency is obligated, on demand of the lender, to purchase a stated percentage of the loan and to share any losses in the amount of the guaranteed percentage. It is the responsibility of the private financial institution to disburse and collect funds and to administer the loan. Under Regulation V of the Federal Reserve Board (12 CFR 245), any private financing institution may submit an application to the Federal Reserve Bank of its district for guarantee of a loan or credit.

(e) Federal Reserve Banks will make the loan guarantee agreements on behalf of the guaranteeing agencies.

(f) Under Section 302(c) of Executive Order 10480, August 14, 1953 (3 CFR 1949-53), as amended, all actions and operations of Federal Reserve Banks, as fiscal agents, are subject to the supervision of the Federal Reserve Board. The Federal Reserve Board is authorized to prescribe the following, after consultation with the heads of guaranteeing agencies:

(1) Regulations governing the actions and operations of fiscal agents.

(2) Rates of interest, guarantee and commitment fees, and other charges that may be made for loans, discounts, advances, or commitments guaranteed by the guaranteeing agencies through the Federal Reserve Banks. These prescriptions may be in the form of specific rates or limits, or in other forms.

(3) Uniform forms and procedures to be used in connection with the guarantees.

(g) The guaranteeing agency is responsible for certifying eligibility for the guarantee and fixing the maximum dollar amount and maturity date of the guaranteed loan to meet the contractor's requirement for financing performance of the defense production contract on hand at the time the guarantee application is submitted.

32.304 Procedures. (No Text)

32.304-1 Application for guarantee.

(a) A contractor, subcontractor, or supplier that needs operating funds to perform a contract related to national defense may apply to a financing institution for a loan. If the financing institution is willing to extend credit, but considers a Government guarantee necessary, the institution may apply to the Federal Reserve Bank of its district for the guarantee. Application forms and guidance are available at all Federal Reserve Banks.

(b) The Federal Reserve Bank will promptly send a copy of the application, including a list of the relevant defense contracts held by the contractor, to the Federal Reserve Board. The Board will transmit the application and the list of contracts to the interested guaranteeing agency, so that the agency can determine the eligibility of the contractor.

(c) To expedite the process, the Federal Reserve Bank may, pursuant to instructions of a guaranteeing agency, submit lists of the defense contracts to the interested contracting officers.

(d) While eligibility is being determined, the Federal Reserve Bank will make any necessary credit investigations to supplement the information furnished by the applicant financing institution in order to—

(1) Expedite necessary defense financing; and

(2) Protect the Government against monetary loss.

(e) The Federal Reserve Bank will send its report and recommendation to the Federal Reserve Board. The Board will transmit them to the interested guaranteeing agency.

32.304-2 Certificate of eligibility.

(a) The contracting officer shall prepare the certificate of eligibility for a contract that the contracting officer deems to be of material consequence, when—

(1) The contract financing office requests it;

(2) Another interested agency requests it; or

(3) The application for a loan guarantee relates to a contract or subcontract within the cognizance of the contracting officer.

(b) The agency shall evaluate the relevant data, including the certificate of eligibility, the accompanying data, and any other relevant information on the contractor's financial status and performance, to determine whether authorization of a loan guarantee would be in the Government's interest.

(c) If the contractor has several major national defense contracts, it is normally not necessary to evaluate the eligibility of relatively minor contracts. The determination of eligibility should be processed, without delay, based on the preponderance of the amount of the contracts.

(d) The certificate of eligibility shall include the following determinations:

(1) The supplies or services to be acquired are essential to the national defense.

(2) The contractor has the facilities and the technical and management ability required for contract performance.

(3) There is no practicable alternate source for the acquisition without prejudice to the national defense. (This statement shall not be included if the contractor is a small business concern.)

(e) The contracting officer shall consider the following factors in determining if a practicable alternate source exists:

(1) Prejudice to the national defense, because reletting of a contract with another source would conflict with a major policy on defense acquisition; *e.g.*, policies relating to the mobilization base.

(2) The urgency of contract performance schedules.

(3) The technical ability and facilities of other potential sources.

(4) The extent to which other sources would need contract financing to perform.

(5) The willingness of other sources to enter into contracts.

(6) The time and expense involved in repurchasing for contracts or parts of contracts. This may include potential claims under a termination for convenience or delays incident to default at a later date.

(7) The comparative prices available from other sources.

(8) The disruption of established subcontracting arrangements.

(9) Other pertinent factors.

(f) The contracting officer shall attach sufficient data to the certificate of eligibility to support the determinations made. Available pertinent information shall be included on—

(1) The contractor's past performance;

(2) The relationship of the contractor's operations to performance schedules; and

(3) Other factors listed in paragraph (e) of this section, if relevant to the case under consideration.

(g) If the contracting officer determines that a certificate of eligibility is not justified, the facts and reasons supporting that conclusion shall be documented and furnished to the agency contract finance office.

(h) The guaranteeing agency shall review the proposed guarantee terms and conditions. If they are considered appropriate, the guaranteeing agency shall complete a standard form of authorization as prescribed by the Federal Reserve Board. The agency shall transmit the authorization through the Federal Reserve Board to the Federal Reserve Bank. The Bank is authorized to execute and deliver to the financing institution a standard form of guarantee agreement, with the terms and conditions approved for the particular case. The financing institution will then make the loan.

(i) Substantially the same procedure may be followed for the application of an offeror who is actively negotiating or bidding for a defense contract, except that the guarantee shall not be authorized until the contract has been executed.

(j) The contracting officer shall report to the agency contract finance office any information about the contractor that would have a potentially adverse impact on a pending guarantee application. The contracting officer is not required, however, to initiate any special investigation for this purpose.

(k) With regard to existing contracts, the agency shall not consider the percentage of guarantee requested by the financing institution in determining the contractor's eligibility.

32.304-3 Asset formula.

(a) Under guaranteed loans made primarily for working capital purposes, the agency shall normally limit the guarantee, by use of an asset formula, to an amount that does not exceed a specified percentage (90 percent or less) of the contractor's investment (*e.g.*, payrolls and inventories) in defense production contracts. The asset formula may include all items under defense contracts for which the contractor would be entitled to payment on performance or termination. The formula shall exclude—

(1) Amounts for which the contractor has not done any work or made any expenditure;

(2) Amounts that would become due as the result of later performance under the contracts; and

(3) Cash collateral or bank deposit balances.

(b) Progress payments are deducted from the asset formula.

(c) The agency may relax the asset formula to an appropriate extent for the time actually necessary for contract performance, if the contractor's working capital and credit are inadequate.

32.304-4 Guarantee amount and maturity.

The agency may change the guarantee amount or maturity date, within the limitations at 32.304-3, as follows:

(a) If the contractor enters into additional defense production contracts after the application for, but before authorization of, a guarantee, the agency may adjust the loan guarantee amount or maturity date to meet any significant increase in financing need.

(b) If the contractor enters into defense production contracts during the term of the guaranteed loan, the parties may adjust the existing guarantee agreement to provide for financing the new contracts. Pertinent information and the Federal Reserve Bank reports will be submitted to the guaranteeing agency under the procedures for the original guarantee application, described in 32.304-1. Normally, a new certificate of eligibility is required.

32.304-5 Assignment of claims under contracts.

(a) The agency shall generally require a contractor that is provided a guaranteed loan to execute an assignment of claims under defense production contracts (including any contracts entered into during the term of the guaranteed loan that are eligible for financing under the loan); however, the agency need not require assignment if any of the following conditions are present:

(1) The contractor's financial condition is so strong that the protection to the Government provided by an assignment of claims is unnecessary.

(2) In connection with the assignment of claims under a major contract, the increased protection of the loan that would be provided by the assignments under additional, relatively smaller contracts is not considered necessary by the agency.

(3) The assignment of claims would create an administrative burden disproportionate to the protection required; *e.g.*, if the contractor has a large number of contracts with individually small dollar amounts.

(b) The contractor shall also execute an assignment of claims if requested to do so by the guarantor or the financing institution.

(c) A subcontract or purchase order issued to a subcontractor shall not be considered eligible for financing under guaranteed loans when the issuer of the subcontract or purchase order reserves

(1) the privilege of making payments directly to the assignor or to the assignor and

assignee jointly, after notice of the assignment, or

(2) the right to reduce or set off assigned proceeds under defense production contracts by reason of claims against the borrower arising after notice of assignment and independently of defense production contracts under which the borrower is the seller.

32.304-6 Other collateral security.

The following are examples of other forms of security that, although seldom invoked under guaranteed loans, may be required when considered necessary for protection of the Government interest:

(a) Mortgages on fixed assets.

(b) Liens against inventories.

(c) Endorsements.

(d) Guarantees.

(e) Subordinations or standbys of other indebtedness.

32.304-7 Contract surety bonds and loan guarantees.

(a) Contract surety bonds are incompatible with the Government's interests under guaranteed loans, unless the interests of the surety are subordinated to the guaranteed loan.

(b) If a substantial share of the contractor's defense contracts are covered by surety bonds, or the amount of the bond is substantial in relation to the contractor's net worth, the agency shall not authorize the guarantee of a loan on a bonded contract unless the surety enters into an agreement with the financing institution to subordinate the surety's rights and claims in favor of the guaranteed loan.

(c) The agency approval of a guarantee for a loan involving relatively substantial subcontracts covered by surety bonds shall also depend on the establishment of a reasonable allocation agreement between the sureties and the financing institution. The agreement should give the financing institution the benefit, with regard to payments to be made on the contract, of the portion of its loans fairly attributable to expenditures made under the bonded subcontracts before notice of default.

32.304-8 Other borrowing.

(a) Because of the limitations under guaranteed loans, some contractors seek to supplement the loan by other borrowing (outside the guarantee) from the financing institution or other sources. It has been recognized in practice that, while prohibition of borrowings outside the guaranteed loan is preferable when practicable in a given V-loan case, such other borrowings should be permitted when necessary.

(b) If the agency consents to the contractor obtaining other borrowing during the guaranteed loan period, the agency shall apply the following restrictions:

(1) A reasonable limit on the amount of other borrowing.

(2) If guaranteed and unguaranteed loans are made by the same financing institution, a requirement that any collateral security requested by the institution under the unguaranteed loan is also to be secondary collateral for the guaranteed loan.

(3) A requirement that the contractor provide appropriate documentation to the guaranteeing agency, at intervals not longer than 30 days, to disclose outstanding unguaranteed borrowings.

[FAC 90-45, Final rule, 62 FR 224, 1/2/97, effective 1/1/97]

32.305 Loan guarantees for terminated contracts.

(a) The purpose of guaranteed loans; *i.e.*, to provide for financing based on the borrower's recoverable investment in defense production contracts, may also apply to contracts that have been terminated (partially or totally) for the convenience of the Government. Guaranteed loans also may be made before such termination if it is known that termination of particular contracts for the convenience of the Government is about to occur. These loans are expected to provide necessary financing pending termination settlements and payments. They may also finance continuing performance of defense production contracts that are eligible for guaranteed loans.

(b) The procedure for such guarantees is substantially the same as that outlined in 32.304, except that certificates of eligibility are not required for (1) contracts that have been totally terminated or (2) the terminated portion of contracts that have been partially terminated. The agency shall take precautions necessary to avoid Government losses and to ensure the loans will be self-liquidating from the proceeds of defense production contracts.

(c) Loan guarantees for contract termination financing shall not be provided before specific contract terminations are certain.

32.306 Loan guarantees for subcontracts.

If the request for a loan guarantee concerns a subcontractor that is financially weak in comparison with its contractor, the Government's interests may be fostered by the contractor making progress payments to the subcontractor. If so, the agency shall try to arrange for the contractor to provide the progress payments. As a result, the need for the loan guarantee may be reduced or eliminated and the contractor would bear part or all of the risk of loss arising from the selection of the subcontractor.

SUBPART 32.4—ADVANCE PAYMENTS FOR NON-COMMERCIAL ITEMS

32.400 Scope of subpart.

This subpart provides policies and procedures for advance payments on prime contracts and subcontracts. It does not include policies and procedures for advance payments for the types of transactions listed in 32.404. This subpart does not apply to commercial advance payments, which are subject to Subpart 32.2.

[FAC 90-33, 60 FR 49706, 9/26/95, effective 10/1/95]

32.401 Statutory authority.

The agency may authorize advance payments in negotiated and sealed bid contracts if the action is appropriate under—

(a) 41 U.S.C. chapter 45;

(b) 10 U.S.C. 2307; or

(c) Pub. L. 85-804 (50 U.S.C. 1431-1435) and Executive Order 10789, November 14, 1958 (3 CFR 1958 Supp. pp. 72-74) (see Subpart 50.1 for other applications of this statute).

[FAC 84-5, 50 FR 1744, 1/11/85, effective 4/1/85; FAC 2005-21, 72 FR 63027, 11/7/2007, effective 11/7/2007; FAC 2005-30, 74 FR 2733, 1/15/2009, effective 2/17/2009; FAC 2005-73, 79 FR 24192, 4/29/2014, effective 5/29/2014]

32.402 General.

(a) A limitation on authority to grant advance payments under Pub. L. 85-804 (50 U.S.C. 1431-1435) is described at FAR 50.102-3(b)(4).

(b) Advance payments may be provided on any type of contract; however, the agency shall authorize advance payments sparingly. Except for the contracts described in 32.403(a) and (b), advance payment is the least preferred method of contract financing (see 32.106) and generally they should not be authorized if other types of financing are reasonably available to the contractor in adequate amounts. Loans and credit at excessive interest rates or other exorbitant charges, or loans from other Government agencies, are not considered reasonably available financing.

(c) If statutory requirements and standards for advance payment determinations are met, the contracting officer shall generally recommend that the agency authorize advance payments.

(1) The statutory requirements are that—

(i) The contractor gives adequate security;

(ii) The advance payments will not exceed the unpaid contract price (see 32.410(b), subparagraph (a)(2)); and

(iii) The agency head or designee determines, based on written findings, that the advance payment—

(A) Is in the public interest (under 32.401(a) or (b)); or

(B) Facilitates the national defense (under 32.401(c)).

(2) The standards for advance payment determinations are that—

(i) The advance payments will not exceed the contractor's interim cash needs based on—

(A) Analysis of the cash flow required for contract performance;

(B) Consideration of the reimbursement or other payment cycle; and

(C) To the extent possible, employment of the contractor's own working capital;

(ii) The advance payments are necessary to supplement other funds or credit available to a contractor;

(iii) The recipient is otherwise qualified as a responsible contractor;

(iv) The Government will benefit from performance prospects or there are other practical advantages; and

(v) The case fits one or more of the categories described in 32.403.

(d) If necessary, the agency may authorize advance payments in addition to progress or partial payments on the same contract (see 32.501-1(c)).

(e) Each agency that provides advance payments shall—

(1) Place the responsibility for making findings and determinations, and for approval of contract terms concerning advance payments (see 32.410), at an organizational level high enough to ensure uniform application of this subpart (see the limitation at 50.102-1(b) which also applies to advance payments authorized under Pub. L. 85-804 (50 U.S.C. 1431-1435)); and

(2) Establish procedures for coordination, before advance payment authorization, with the activity that provides contract financing support.

(f) If the contract provides for advance payments under Pub. L. 85-804, the contracting officer shall ensure conformance with the requirements of FAR 50.103-7.

[FAC 90-23, 59 FR 67010, 12/28/94, effective 2/27/95; FAC 2005-21, 72 FR 63027, 11/7/2007, effective 11/7/2007; FAC 2005-30, 1/15/2009, effective 2/17/2009]

32.403 Applicability.

Advance payments may be considered useful and appropriate for the following:

(a) Contracts for experimental, research, or development work with nonprofit educational or research institutions.

(b) Contracts solely for the management and operation of Government-owned plants.

(c) Contracts for acquisition, at cost, of property for Government ownership.

(d) Contracts of such a highly classified nature that the agency considers it undesirable for national security to permit assignment of claims under the contract.

(e) Contracts entered into with financially weak contractors whose technical ability is considered essential to the agency. In these cases, the agency shall closely monitor the contractor's performance and financial controls to reduce the Government's financial risk.

(f) Contracts for which a loan by a private financial institution is not practicable, whether or not a loan guarantee under this part is issued; for example, if—

(1) Financing institutions will not assume a reasonable portion of the risk under a guaranteed loan;

(2) Loans with reasonable interest rates or finance charges are not available to the contractor; or

(3) Contracts involve operations so remote from a financial institution that the institution could not be expected to suitably administer a guaranteed loan.

(g) Contracts with small business concerns, under which circumstances that make advance payments appropriate often occur (but see 32.104(b)).

(h) Contracts under which exceptional circumstances make advance payments the most advantageous contract financing method for both the Government and the contractor.

[FAC 2005-17, 72 FR 27364, 5/15/2007, effective 6/14/2007]

32.404 Exclusions.

(a) This subpart does not apply to advance payments authorized by law for—

(1) Rent;

(2) Tuition;

(3) Insurance premiums;

(4) Expenses of investigations in foreign countries;

(5) Extension or connection of public utilities for Government buildings or installations;

(6) Subscriptions to publications;

(7) Purchases of supplies or services in foreign countries, if—

(i) The purchase price does not exceed $15,000 (or equivalent amount of the applicable foreign currency); and

(ii) The advance payment is required by the laws or government regulations of the foreign country concerned;

(8) Enforcement of the customs or narcotics laws; or

(9) Other types of transactions excluded by agency procedures under statutory authority.

(b) Agencies may issue their own instructions to deal with advance payment items in paragraph (a) of this section authorized under statutes relevant to their agencies.

[FAC 2005-45, 75 FR 53129, 8/30/2010, effective 10/1/2010]

32.405 Applying Pub. L. 85-804 to advance payments under sealed bid contracts.

(a) Actions that designated agencies may take to facilitate the national defense without regard to other provisions of law relating to contracts, as explained in 50.101-1(a), also include making advance payments. These advance payments may be made at or after award of sealed bid contracts, as well as negotiated contracts.

(b) Bidders may request advance payments before or after award, even if the invitation for bids does not contain an advance payment provision. However, the contracting officer shall reject any bid requiring that advance payments be provided as a basis for acceptance.

(c) When advance payments are requested, the agency may—

(1) Enter into the contract and provide for advance payments conforming to this Part 32;

(2) Enter into the contract without providing for advance payments if the contractor does not actually need advance payments; or

(3) Deny award of the contract if the request for advance payments has been disapproved under 32.409-2 and funds adequate for performance are not otherwise available to the offeror.

[FAC 84-5, 50 FR 1744, 1/11/85, effective 4/1/85; FAC 2005-21, 72 FR 63027, 11/7/2007, effective 11/7/2007; FAC 2005-30, 1/15/2009, effective 2/17/2009]

32.406 Letters of credit.

(a) The Department of the Treasury (Treasury) prescribes regulations and instructions covering the use of letters of credit for advance payments under contracts. See Treasury Department Circular 1075 (31 CFR 205), and the implementing instructions in the Treasury Financial Manual, available in offices providing financial advice and assistance.

(b) If agencies provide advance payments to contractors, use of the following methods is required unless the agency has obtained a waiver from the Treasury Department:

(1) By letter of credit if the contracting agency expects to have a continuing relationship with the contractor for a year or more, with advances totaling at least $120,000 a year.

(2) By direct Treasury check if the circumstances do not meet the criteria in subparagraph (b)(1) of this section.

(c) If the agency has entered into multiple contracts (or a combination of contract(s) and assistance agreement(s)) involving eligibility of a contractor for more than one letter of credit, the agency shall follow arrangements made under Treasury procedures for—

(1) Consolidating funding to the same contractor under one letter of credit or

(2) Replacing multiple letters of credit with a single letter of credit.

(d) The letter of credit enables the contractor to withdraw Government funds in amounts needed to cover its own disbursements of cash for contract performance. Whenever feasible, the agency shall, under the direction and approval of the Department of the Treasury, use a letter of credit method that requires the contractor not to withdraw the Government funds until the contractor's checks have been—

(1) Forwarded to the payees (delay of drawdown technique), or

(2) Presented to the contractor's bank for payment (checks paid technique) (see 31 CFR 205.3 and 205.4(d)).

(e) The Treasury regulations provide for terminating the advance financing arrangement if the contractor is unwilling or unable to minimize the elapsed time between receipt of the advance and disbursement of the funds. In such cases, if reversion to normal payment methods is not feasible, the Treasury regulation provides for use of a working capital method of advance; *i.e.*, for limiting advances to—

(1) Only the estimated disbursements for a given initial period and

(2) Subsequently, for only actual cash disbursements (31 CFR 205.3(k) and 205.7).

[FAC 84-26, 52 FR 19805, 5/27/87, effective 7/30/87]

32.407 Interest.

(a) Except as provided in paragraph (d) of this section, the contracting officer shall charge interest on the daily unliquidated balance of all advance payments at the higher of—

(1) The published prime rate of the financial institution (depository) in which the special account (see 32.409-3) is established; or

(2) The rate established by the Secretary of the Treasury under 50 U.S.C. App. 1215(b)(2).

(b) The interest rate for advance payments shall be adjusted for changes in the prime rate of the depository and the semiannual determination by the Secretary of the Treasury under 50 U.S.C. App. 1215(b)(2). The contracting officer shall obtain data from the depository on changes in the interest rate during the month. Interest shall be computed at the end of each month on the daily unliquidated balance of advance payments at the applicable daily interest rate.

(c) Interest shall be required on contracts that are for acquisition, at cost, of property for Government ownership, if the contracts are awarded in combination with, or in contemplation of, supply contracts or subcontracts.

(d) The agency head or designee may authorize advance payments without interest under the following types of contracts, if in the Government's interest:

(1) Contracts for experimental, research, or development work (including studies, surveys, and demonstrations in socio-economic areas) with nonprofit education or research institutions.

(2) Contracts solely for the management and operation of Government-owned plants.

(3) Cost-reimbursement contracts with governments, including State or local governments, or their instrumentalities.

(4) Other classes of contracts, or unusual cases, for which the exclusion of interest on advances is specifically authorized by agency procedures.

(e) If a contract provides for interest-free advance payments, the contracting officer may require the contractor to charge interest on advances or down payments to subcontractors and credit the Government for the proceeds from the interest charges. Interest rates shall be determined as described in paragraphs (a) and (b) of this section. The contracting officer need not require the contractor to charge interest on an advance to a subcontractor that is an institution of the kind described in subparagraph (d)(1) of this section.

(f) The contracting officer shall not allow interest charges, required by this 32.407, as reimbursable costs under cost-reimbursement contracts, whether the interest charge was incurred by the prime contractor or a subcontractor.

[FAC 97-22, 66 FR 2117, 1/10/2001, effective 3/12/2001; Delay of effective date, 66 FR 14259, 3/9/2001, effective 5/11/2001; FAC 2005-17, 72 FR 27364, 5/15/2007, effective 6/14/2007]

32.408 Application for advance payments.

(a) A contractor may apply for advance payments before or after the award of a contract.

(b) The contractor shall submit any advance payment request in writing to the contracting officer and provide the following information:

(1) A reference to the contract if the request concerns an existing contract, or a reference to the solicitation if the request concerns a proposed contract.

(2) A cash flow forecast showing estimated disbursements and receipts for the period of contract performance. If the application pertains to a type of contract described in 32.403(a) or (b), the contractor shall limit the forecast to the contract to be financed by advance payments.

(3) The proposed total amount of advance payments.

(4) The name and address of the financial institution at which the contractor expects to establish a special account as depository for the advance payments. If advance payments in the form of a letter of credit are anticipated, the contractor shall identify the specific account at the financial institution to be used. This subparagraph (b)(4) is not applicable if an alternate method is used under agency procedures.

(5) A description of the contractor's efforts to obtain unguaranteed private financing or a V-loan (see 32.301) under eligible contracts. This requirement is not applicable to the contract types described in 32.403(a) or (b).

(6) Other information appropriate to an understanding of—

(i) the contractor's financial condition and need,

(ii) the contractor's ability to perform the contract without loss to the Government, and—

(iii) financial safeguards needed to protect the Government's interest. Ordinarily, if the contract is a type described in 32.403(a) or (b), the contractor may limit the response to this subparagraph (b)(6) to information on the contractor's reliability, technical ability, and accounting system and controls.

[FAC 97-22, 66 FR 2117, 1/10/2001, effective 3/12/2001; Delay of effective date, 66 FR 14259, 3/9/2001, effective 5/11/2001]

32.409 Contracting officer action.

After analysis of the contractor's application and any appropriate investigation, the contracting officer shall recommend approval or disapproval and transmit the request and recommendation to the approving authority designated under 32.402(e).

32.409-1 Recommendation for approval.

If recommending approval, the contracting officer shall transmit the following, under agency procedures, to the approving authority:

(a) Contract data, including—

(1) Identification and date of the award;

(2) Citation of the appropriation;

(3) Type and dollar amount of the contract;

(4) Items to be supplied, schedule of deliveries or performance, and status of any deliveries or performance;

(5) The contract fee or profit contemplated; and

(6) A copy of the contract, if available.

(b) The contractor's request and supporting information.

(c) A report on the contractor's past performance, responsibility, technical ability, and plant capacity.

(d) Comments on—

(1) The contractor's need for advance payments and;

(2) Potential Government benefits from the contract performance.

(e) Proposed advance payment contract terms, including proposed security requirements.

(f) The findings, determination, and authorization (see 32.410).

(g) The recommendation for approval of the advance payment request.

(h) Justification of any proposal for waiver of interest charges (see 32.407).

32.409-2 Recommendation for disapproval.

If recommending disapproval, the contracting officer shall, under agency procedures, transmit—

(a) The items prescribed in 32.409-1(a), (b), and (c); and

(b) The recommendation for disapproval and the reasons.

32.409-3 Security, supervision, and covenants.

(a) If advance payments are approved, the contracting officer shall enter into an agreement with the contractor covering special accounts and suitable covenants protecting the Government's interest (see 32.411). This requirement generally applies under all statutory authorities, but modified requirements applicable to certain specific cases are prescribed in paragraphs (e) through (g) of this section.

(b) The agency shall—

(1) Ensure that the amount of advance payments does not exceed the contractor's financial needs, and

(2) Closely supervise the contractor's withdrawal of funds from special accounts in which the advance payments are deposited.

(c) In the terms of the agreement, the contracting officer should provide for a paramount lien in favor of the Government. This lien may supplement or replace other security requirements. The lien should cover—

(1) Supplies being acquired;

(2) Any credit balance in the special account in which advance payments are deposited; and

(3) All property that the contractor acquires for performing the contract, except to the extent to which the Government otherwise has valid title to the property.

(d) Security requirements vary to fit the circumstances of different cases. Minimum security requirements are covered by the clauses prescribed in the contract. The contracting officer may supplement these as necessary in each case for protection of the Government's interest. Examples of additional security terms are—

(1) Personal or corporate endorsements or guarantees;

(2) Pledges of collateral;

(3) Subordination or standby of other indebtedness;

(4) Controls or limitations on profit distributions, salaries, bonuses or commissions, rentals and royalties, capital expenditures, creation of liens, retirement of stock or debt, and creation of additional obligations; and

(5) Advance payment bonds (rarely required).

(e) In an advance payment agreement with an instrumentality of the Government, a State, a local government, or an agency or instrumentality of a State or local government, the contracting officer may omit the requirement for deposit of the advances in a special account, if the official approving the advance determines that other adequate security exists to protect the Government's interest.

(f) The requirements of this 32.409-3 do not apply when using letters of credit if an agency's procedures provide for—

(1) The use under a cost-reimbursement contract of Federal funds deposited in the contractor's account at a financial institution (without the contractor acquiring title to the funds); and

(2) The security of such deposit of public moneys in accordance with governing regulations of the Treasury Department.

(g) If a separate special account is not required; *e.g.*, advance payment by a letter of credit, an agency may require a special account for an individual case, or classes of cases, if the circumstances warrant.

[FAC 97-22, 66 FR 2117, 1/10/2001, effective 3/12/2001; Delay of effective date, 66 FR 14259, 3/9/2001, effective 5/11/2001]

32.410 Findings, determination, and authorization.

(a) Each determination concerning advance payments shall be supported by written findings (see 32.402(c)(1)(iii)).

(b) The following is an example of the format and text of findings, determination, and authorization with alternative words, phrases, and paragraphs to be selected to conform to the circumstances involved:

FINDINGS, DETERMINATION, AND AUTHORIZATION FOR ADVANCE PAYMENTS

FINDINGS

(a) The undersigned hereby finds that:

(1) The ____ [*insert the name of the contracting activity*]and ____ [*insert the name of the contractor*] (have entered) (propose to enter) into (negotiated) (sealed bid) Contract No. ____, dated ____.

[*Summarize the specific facts and significant circumstances concerning the contract and the contractor, that, together with the other findings, will clearly support the determination below.*]

(2) Advance payments (in an amount not to exceed $____ at any time outstanding) (in an aggregate amount not exceeding $____, less the aggregate amounts repaid, or withdrawn by the Government) are required by the Contractor to perform under the contract. The amount does not exceed the unpaid contract price or the estimated interim cash needs arising during the reimbursement cycle.

(3) The advance payments are necessary for prompt, efficient contract performance that will benefit the Government.

(4) The proposed advance payment clause provides for security for the protection of the Government. The clause requires that all payments will be deposited in a special account at the Contractor's financial institution and that the Government will have a paramount lien on—

(i) the credit balance in the special account,

(ii) any supplies contracted for, and—

(iii) any material or other property acquired for performance of the contract. [*Insert the following, if applicable* (The Contractor's financial management system provides for effective control over and accountability for all Federal funds under governing regulations of the Treasury Department.) (An advance payment bond is required.)] This security is considered adequate.

(5) Advance payments are the only adequate means of financing available to the Contractor, and the amount designated in (2) of this section is based, to the extent possible, on the use of the Contractor's own working capital in performing the contract.

[*Insert paragraph (6), (7), or (8), as applicable.*]

(6) The Contractor is a nonprofit (educational) (and) (research) institution, and the contract is for (experimental) (,) (research and development) work.

(7) The contract is solely for the management and operation of a Government-owned plant.

(8) The following unusual facts and circumstances favor making advance payments to the Contractor without interest:

[*List the pertinent facts and circumstances.*]

DETERMINATION

(b) Based on the findings in (a) of this section, the undersigned determined that the making of the proposed advance payments, (with interest at the rate of ____ [*Insert the interest rate computed in accordance with 32.407*] percent on the daily unliquidated balance of the advance payments,) (without interest, except as provided by the proposed advance payment clause,) (is in the public interest) (will facilitate the national defense).

AUTHORIZATION

(c) The advance payments, of which (the amount at any time outstanding) (the aggregate amount, less the aggregate amounts repaid, or withdrawn by the Government), shall not exceed $____, are hereby authorized under (41 U.S.C. chapter 45, Contract Financing) (10 U.S.C. 2307) (the Extraordinary Contracting Authority of Government Agencies in Connection with National Defense Functions (50 U.S.C. 1431-1435) and Executive Order No. 10789 of November 14, 1958 (3 CFR 1958 Supp. pp. 72-74)) [*or, if other, cite appropriate authority*] on (terms substantially as contained in the proposed advance payment clause, a copy (an outline) of which is annexed to this authorization) (the following terms:) [*Insert the appropriate terms.*]

(All prior authorizations for advance payments under Contract No. ____ are superseded.)

[*Signature*]

[*Name typed*]

[*Title of authorized official*]

[*Each Findings, Determination, and Authorization shall be individually prepared to fit the particular circumstances at hand. Subparagraphs (a)(1), (2), (3) and (4) and paragraphs (b) and (c) shall be used in each case. If the contract is (a) for experimental, developmental, or research work and with a nonprofit educational or research institution, or (b) only for management and operation of a Government-owned plant, subparagraph (a)(5) should not be included. If the advance payment is to be made without interest to the contractor, include subparagraph (a)(6), (7), or (8). If any advance payments have previously been authorized for the contract, include the final sentence of paragraph (c). The alternate parenthetical wording or other modifications may be used as appropriate. The paragraphs actually used shall be renumbered sequentially.*]

[FAC 84-5, 50 FR 1744, 1/11/85, effective 4/1/85; FAC 97-22, 66 FR 2117, 1/10/2001, effective 3/12/2001; Delay of effective date, 66 FR 14259, 3/9/2001, effective 5/11/2001; FAC 2005-73, 79 FR 24192, 4/29/2014, effective 5/29/2014]

32.411 Agreement for special account at a financial institution.

The contracting officer must use substantially the following form of agreement for a special account for advance payments:

Agreement for Special Account

This agreement is entered into this ____ day of ____, 20____, between the United States of America (the Government), represented by the Contracting Officer executing this agreement, ____ [*Insert the name of the Contractor*], a ____ [*Insert the name of the State of incorporation*] corporation (the Contractor), and ____, a financial institution operating under the laws of ____, located at ____ (the financial institution).

Recitals

(a) Under date of ____, 20____, the Government and the Contractor entered into Contract No. ____, or a related supplemental agreement, providing for advance payments to the Contractor. A copy of the advance payment terms was furnished to the financial institution.

(b) The contract or supplemental agreement requires that amounts advanced to the Contractor be deposited separate from the Contractor's general or other funds, in a Special Account at a member bank of the Federal Reserve System, any "insured" bank within the meaning of the Act creating the Federal Deposit Insurance Corporation (12 U.S.C. 1811), or a credit union insured by the National Credit Union Administration. The parties agree to deposit the amounts with the financial institution, which meets the requirement.

(c) This Special Account is designated "____ [*Insert the Contractor's name*], ____ [*Insert the name of the Government agency*] Special Account."

Covenants

In consideration of the foregoing, and for other good and valuable considerations, the parties agree to the following conditions:

(a) The Government shall have a lien on the credit balance in the account to secure the repayment of all advance payments made to the Contractor. The lien is paramount to any lien or claim of the financial institution regarding the account.

(b) The financial institution is bound by the terms of the contract relating to the deposit and withdrawal of funds in the Special Account, but is not responsible for the application of funds withdrawn from the account. The financial institution shall act on written directions from the Contracting Officer, the administering office, or a duly authorized representative of either. The financial institution is not liable to any party to this agreement for any action that complies with the written directions. Any written directions received by the financial institution through the Contracting Officer on _____ [*Insert the name of the agency*] stationery and purporting to be signed by, or by the direction of _____ or duly authorized representative, shall be, as far as the rights, duties, and liabilities of the financial institution are concerned, considered as being properly issued and filed with the financial institution by the _____ [*Insert the name of the agency*].

(c) The Government, or its authorized representatives, shall have access to the books and records maintained by the financial institution regarding the Special Account at all reasonable times and for all reasonable purposes, including (but not limited to), the inspection or copying of the books and records and any and all pertinent memoranda, checks, correspondence, or documents. The financial institution shall preserve the books and records for a period of 6 years after the closing of this Special Account.

(d) In the event of the service of any writ of attachment, levy of execution, or commencement of garnishment proceedings regarding the Special Account, the financial institution will promptly notify _____ [*Insert the name of the administering office*].

(e) While this Special Account exists, the financial institution shall inform the Government each month of the financial institution's published prime interest rate and changes to the rate during the month. The financial institution shall give this information to the Contracting Officer on the last business day of the month. [This covenant will not be included in the Special Account Agreements covering interest-free advance payments.]

Each of the parties to this agreement has executed the agreement on _____, 20_____.

_____

_____

[*Signatures and Official Titles*]

[FAC 97-22, 66 FR 2117, 1/10/2001, effective 3/12/2001; Delay of effective date, 66 FR 14259, 3/9/2001, effective 5/11/2001]

32.412 Contract clause.

(a) The contracting officer shall insert the clause at 52.232-12, Advance Payments, in solicitations and contracts under which the Government will provide advance payments, except as provided in 32.412(b).

(b) If the agency desires to waive the countersignature requirement because of the contractor's financial strength, good performance record, and favorable experience concerning cost disallowances, the contracting officer shall use the clause with its Alternate I.

(c) If a cost-reimbursement contract is contemplated, the contracting officer shall use the clause with its Alternate II.

(d) If the agency considers a more rapid liquidation appropriate, the contracting officer shall use the clause with its Alternate III.

(e) If the agency provides advance payments under the contract at no interest to the prime contractor, the contracting officer shall use the clause with its Alternate IV.

(f) If the requirement for a special account is eliminated in accordance with 32.409-3(e) or (g), the contracting officer shall insert in the solicitation or contract the clause set forth in Alternate V of 52.232-12, Advance Payments, instead of the basic clause.

[FAC 84-58, 55 FR 25530, 6/21/90, effective 7/23/90; FAC 97-22, 66 FR 2117, 1/10/2001, effective 3/12/2001; Delay of effective date, 66 FR 14259, 3/9/2001, effective 5/11/2001]

SUBPART 32.5—PROGRESS PAYMENTS BASED ON COSTS

32.500 Scope of subpart.

This subpart prescribes policies, procedures, forms, solicitation provisions, and contract clauses for providing contract financing through progress payments based on costs. This subpart does not apply to—

(a) Payments under cost-reimbursement contracts, but see 32.110 for progress payments made to subcontractors under cost-reimbursement prime contracts; or

(b) Contracts for construction or for shipbuilding or ship conversion, alteration, or repair, when the contracts provide for progress payments based on a percentage or stage of completion.

[FAC 97-16, 65 FR 16274, 3/27/2000, effective 3/27/2000]

32.501 General.

Progress payments may be customary or unusual. Customary progress payments are those made under the general guidance in this subpart, using the customary progress payment rate, the cost base, and frequency of payment established in the Progress Payments clause, and either the ordinary liquidation method or the alternate method as provided in subsections 32.503-8 and 32.503-9. Any other progress payments are considered unusual, and may be used only in exceptional cases when authorized in accordance with subsection 32.501-2.

32.501-1 Customary progress payment rates.

(a) The customary progress payment rate is 80 percent, applicable to the total costs of performing the contract. The customary rate for contracts with small business concerns is 85 percent.

(b) The contracting officer must—

(1) Consider any rate higher than those permitted in paragraph (a) of this section an unusual progress payment; and

(2) Not include a higher rate in a contract unless advance agency approval is obtained as prescribed in 32.501-2.

(c) When advance payments and progress payments are authorized under the same contract, the contracting officer must not authorize a progress payment rate higher than the customary rate.

(d) In accordance with 10 U.S.C. 2307(e)(2) and 41 U.S.C. 4504(b), the limit for progress payments is 80 percent on work accomplished under undefinitized contract actions. The contracting officer must not authorize a higher rate under unusual progress payments or other customary progress payments for the undefinitized actions.

[FAC 97-16, 65 FR 16274, 3/27/2000, effective 3/27/2000; FAC 2005-73, 79 FR 24192, 4/29/2014, effective 5/29/2014]

32.501-2 Unusual progress payments.

(a) The contracting officer may provide unusual progress payments only if—

(1) The contract necessitates predelivery expenditures that are large in relation to contract price and in relation to the contractor's working capital and credit;

(2) The contractor fully documents an actual need to supplement any private financing available, including guaranteed loans; and

(3) The contractor's request is approved by the head of the contracting activity or a designee. In addition, see 32.502-2.

(b) The excess of the unusual progress payment rate approved over the customary progress payment rate should be the lowest amount possible under the circumstances.

(c) Progress payments will not be considered unusual merely because they are on letter contracts or the definitive contracts that supersede letter contracts.

32.501-3 Contract price.

(a) For the purpose of making progress payments and determining the limitation on progress payments, the contract price shall be as follows:

(1) Under firm-fixed price contracts, the contract price is the current amount fixed by the contract plus the not-to-exceed amount for any unpriced modifications.

(2) If the contract is redeterminable or subject to economic price adjustment, the contract price is the initial price until modified.

(3) Under a fixed-price incentive contract, the contract price is the target price plus the not-to-exceed amount of unpriced modifications. However, if the contractor's properly incurred costs exceed the target price, the contracting officer may provisionally increase the price up to the ceiling or maximum price.

(4) Under a letter contract, the contract price is the maximum amount obligated by the contract as modified.

(5) Under an unpriced order issued against a basic ordering agreement, the contract price is the maximum amount obligated by the order, as modified.

(6) Any portion of the contract specifically providing for reimbursement of costs only shall be excluded from the contract price.

(b) The contracting officer shall not make progress payments or increase the contract price beyond the funds obligated under the contract, as amended.

[FAC 2005-33, 74 FR 28430, 6/15/2009, effective 7/15/2009]

32.501-4 [Reserved]

[Reserved, FAC 90-33, 60 FR 49706, 9/26/95, effective 10/1/95]

32.501-5 Other protective terms.

If the contracting officer considers it necessary for protection of the Government's interest, protective terms such as the following may be used in addition to the Progress Payments clause of the contract:

(a) Personal or corporate guarantees.

(b) Subordinations or standbys of indebtedness.

(c) Special bank accounts.

(d) Protective covenants of the kinds in paragraph (p) of the clause at 52.232-12, Advance Payments.

(e) A provision, included in the solicitation and resultant contract when first article testing is required (see Subpart 9.3), limiting progress payments on first article work by a stated amount or percentage.

[FAC 90-3, 55 FR 52794, 12/21/90, effective 1/22/91]

32.502 Preaward matters.

This section covers matters that generally are relevant only before contract award. This does not preclude taking actions discussed here after award, if appropriate; *e.g.*, postaward addition of a Progress Payments clause for consideration.

32.502-1 Use of customary progress payments.

The contracting officer may use a Progress Payments clause in solicitations and contracts, in accordance with this subpart. The contracting officer must reject as nonresponsive bids conditioned on progress payments when the solicitation did not provide for progress payments.

[FAC 97-16, 65 FR 16274, 3/27/2000, effective 3/27/2000]

32.502-2 Contract finance office clearance.

The contracting officer shall obtain the approval of the contract finance office or other offices designated under agency procedures before taking any of the following actions:

(a) Providing a progress payment rate higher than the customary rate (see 32.501-1).

(b) Deviating from the progress payments terms prescribed in this part.

(c) Providing progress payments to a contractor—

(1) Whose financial condition is in doubt;

(2) Who has had an advance payment request or loan guarantee denied for financial reasons (or approved but withdrawn or lapsed) within the previous 12 months; or

(3) Who is named in the consolidated list of contractors indebted to the United States (known commonly as the "Hold-up List").

32.502-3 Solicitation provisions.

(a) The contracting officer shall insert the provision at 52.232-13, Notice of Progress

Payments, in invitations for bids and requests for proposals that include a Progress Payments clause.

(b) (1) Under the authority of the statutes cited in 32.101, an invitation for bids may restrict the availability of progress payments to small business concerns only.

(2) The contracting officer shall insert the provision at 52.232-14, Notice of Availability of Progress Payments Exclusively for Small Business Concerns, in invitations for bids if it is anticipated that—

(i) Both small business concerns and others may submit bids in response to the same invitation and

(ii) Only the small business bidders would need progress payments.

(c) The contracting officer shall insert the provision at 52.232-15, Progress Payments Not Included, in invitations for bids if the solicitation will not contain one of the provisions prescribed in paragraphs (a) and (b) of this section.

32.502-4 Contract clauses.

(a) (1) Insert the clause at 52.232-16, Progress Payments, in—

(i) Solicitations that may result in contracts providing for progress payments based on costs; and

(ii) Fixed-price contracts under which the Government will provide progress payments based on costs.

(2) If advance agency approval has been given in accordance with 32.501-1, the contracting officer may substitute a different customary rate for other than small business concerns for the progress payment and liquidation rate indicated.

(3) If an unusual progress payment rate is approved for the prime contractor (see 32.501-2), substitute the approved rate for the customary rate in paragraphs (a) (1), (a) (6), and (b) of the clause.

(4) If the liquidation rate is changed from the customary progress payment rate (see 32.503-8 and 32.503-9), substitute the new rate for the rate in paragraphs (a) (1), (a) (6), and (b) of the clause.

(5) If an unusual progress payment rate is approved for a subcontract (see 32.504(c) and 32.501-2), modify paragraph (j) (6) of the clause to specify the new rate, the name of the subcontractor, and that the new rate shall be used for that subcontractor in lieu of the customary rate.

(b) If the contractor is a small business concern, use the clause with its Alternate I.

(c) If the contract is a letter contract, use the clause with its Alternate II.

(d) If the contractor is not a small business concern, and progress payments are authorized under an indefinite-delivery contract, basic ordering agreement, or their equivalent, use the clause with its Alternate III.

(e) If the nature of the contract necessitates separate progress payment rates for portions of work that are clearly severable and accounting segregation would be maintained (e.g., annual production requirements), describe the application of separate progress payment rates in a supplementary special provision within the contract. The contractor must submit separate progress payment requests and subsequent invoices for the severable portions of work in order to maintain accounting integrity.

[FAC 97-16, 65 FR 16274, 3/27/2000, effective 3/27/2000; FAC 97-17, 65 FR 24316, 4/25/2000, effective 4/25/2000]

32.503 Postaward matters.

This section covers matters that are generally relevant only after award of a contract. This does not preclude taking actions discussed here before award, if appropriate; *e.g.*, preaward review of accounting systems and controls.

32.503-1 [Reserved]

[FAC 97-16, 65 FR 16274, 3/27/2000, effective 3/27/2000; FAC 2005-33, 74 FR 28430, 6/15/2009, effective 7/15/2009]

32.503-2 Supervision of progress payments.

(a) The extent of progress payments supervision, by prepayment review or periodic review, should vary inversely with the contractor's experience, performance record, reliability, quality of management, and financial strength, and with the adequacy of the contractor's accounting system and controls. Supervision shall be of a kind and degree sufficient to provide timely knowledge of the need for, and timely opportunity for, any actions necessary to protect Government interests.

(b) The administering office must keep itself informed of the contractor's overall operations and financial condition, since difficulties encountered and losses suffered in operations outside the particular progress payment contract may affect adversely the performance of that contract and the liquidation of the progress payments.

(c) For contracts with contractors—

(1) Whose financial condition is doubtful or not strong in relation to progress payments outstanding or to be outstanding;

(2) With management of doubtful capacity;

(3) Whose accounting controls are found by experience to be weak; or

(4) Experiencing substantial difficulties in performance, full information on progress under the contract involved (including the status of subcontracts) and on the contractor's other operations and overall financial condition should be obtained and analyzed frequently, with a view to protecting the Government's interests better and taking such action as may be proper to make contract performance more certain.

(d) So far as practicable, all cost problems, particularly those involving indirect costs, that are likely to create disagreements in future administration of the contract should be identified and resolved at the inception of the contract (see 31.109).

32.503-3 Initiation of progress payments and review of accounting system.

(a) For contractors that the administrative contracting officer (ACO) has found by previous experience or recent audit review (within the last 12 months) to be—

(1) Reliable, competent, and capable of satisfactory performance;

(2) Possessed of an adequate accounting system and controls; and

(3) In sound financial condition, progress payments in amounts requested by the contractor should be approved as a matter of course.

(b) For all other contractors, the ACO shall not approve progress payments before determining

(1) that (i) the contractor will be capable of liquidating any progress payments or

(ii) the Government is otherwise protected against loss by additional protective provisions, and

(2) that the contractor's accounting system and controls are adequate for proper administration of progress payments. The services of the responsible audit agency or office should be used to the greatest extent practicable. However, if the auditor so advises, a complete audit may not be necessary.

[FAC 97-4, 63 FR 9048, 2/23/98, effective 4/24/98]

32.503-4 Approval of progress payment requests.

(a) When the reliability of the contractor and the adequacy of the contractor's accounting system and controls have been established (see 32.503-3 of this section) the ACO may, in approving any particular progress payment request (including initial requests on new contracts), rely upon that accounting system and upon the contractor's certification, without requiring audit or review of the request before payment.

(b) The ACO should not routinely ask for audits of progress payment requests. However, when there is reason to—

(1) Question the reliability or accuracy of the contractor's certification; or

(2) Believe that the contract will involve a loss, the ACO should ask for a review or audit of the request before payment is approved or the request is otherwise disposed of.

(c) When there is reason to doubt the amount of a progress payment request, only the doubtful amount should be withheld, subject to later adjustment after review or audit; any clearly proper and due amounts should be paid without awaiting resolution of the differences.

32.503-5 Administration of progress payments.

(a) While the ACO may, in approving progress payment requests under 32.503-3 of this section, rely on the contractor's accounting system and certification without prepayment review, postpayment reviews (including audits when considered necessary) shall be made periodically, or when considered desirable by the ACO to determine the validity of progress payments already made and expected to be made.

(b) These postpayment reviews or audits shall, as a minimum, include a determination of whether or not—

(1) The unliquidated progress payments are fairly supported by the value of the work accomplished on the undelivered portion of the contract;

(2) The applicable limitation on progress payments in the Progress Payments clause has been exceeded;

(3) (i) The unpaid balance of the contract price will be adequate to cover the anticipated cost of completion; or

(ii) The contractor has adequate resources to complete the contract; and

(4) There is reason to doubt the adequacy and reliability of the contractor's accounting system and controls and certification.

(c) Under indefinite-delivery contracts, the contracting officer should administer progress payments made under each individual order as if the order constituted a separate contract, unless agency procedures provide otherwise. When the contract will be administered by an agency other than the awarding agency, the contracting officer shall coordinate with the contract administration office if the awarding agency wants the administration of progress payments to be on a basis other than order—by—order.

[FAC 97-16, 65 FR 16274, 3/27/2000, effective 3/27/2000; FAC 2001-13, 68 FR 13205, 3/18/2003, effective 4/17/2003]

32.503-6 Suspension or reduction of payments.

(a) *General.* The Progress Payments clause provides a Government right to reduce or suspend progress payments, or to increase the liquidation rate, under specified conditions. These conditions and actions are discussed in paragraphs (b) through (g) below.

(1) The contracting officer shall take these actions only in accordance with the contract terms and never precipitately or arbitrarily. These actions should be taken only after—

(i) Notifying the contractor of the intended action and providing an opportunity for discussion;

(ii) Evaluating the effect of the action on the contractor's operations, based on the contractor's financial condition, projected cash requirements, and the existing or available credit arrangements; and

(iii) Considering the general equities of the particular situation.

(2) The contracting officer shall take immediate unilateral action only if warranted by circumstances such as overpayments or unsatisfactory contract performance.

(3) In all cases, the contracting officer shall—

(i) Act fairly and reasonably;

(ii) Base decisions on substantial evidence; and

(iii) Document the contract file. Findings made under paragraph (c) of the Progress Payments clause shall be in writing.

(b) *Contractor noncompliance.*

(1) The contractor must comply with all material requirements of the contract. This includes the requirement to maintain an efficient and reliable accounting system and controls, adequate for the proper administration of progress payments. If the system or controls are deemed inadequate, progress payments shall be suspended (or the portion of progress payments associated with the unacceptable portion of the contractor's accounting system shall be suspended) until the necessary changes have been made.

(2) If the contractor fails to comply with the contract without fault or negligence, the contracting officer will not take action permitted by paragraph (c)(1) of the Progress Payments clause, other than to correct overpayments and collect amounts due from the contractor.

(c) *Unsatisfactory financial condition.*

(1) If the contracting officer finds that contract performance (including full liquidation of progress payments) is endangered by the contractor's financial condition, or by a failure to make progress, the contracting officer shall require the contractor to make additional operating or financial arrangements adequate for completing the contract without loss to the Government.

(2) If the contracting officer concludes that further progress payments would increase the probable loss to the Government, the contracting officer shall suspend progress payments and all other payments until the unliquidated balance of progress payments is eliminated.

(d) *Excessive inventory.* If the inventory allocated to the contract exceeds reasonable requirements (including a reasonable accumulation of inventory for continuity of operations), the contracting officer should, in addition to requiring the transfer of excessive inventory from the contract, take one or more of the following actions, as necessary, to avoid or correct overpayment:

(1) Eliminate the costs of the excessive inventory from the costs eligible for progress payments, with appropriate reduction in progress payments outstanding.

(2) Apply additional deductions to billings for deliveries (increase liquidation).

(e) *Delinquency in payment of costs of performance.*

(1) If the contractor is delinquent in paying the costs of contract performance in the ordinary course of business, the contracting officer shall evaluate whether the delinquency is caused by an unsatisfactory financial condition and, if so, shall apply the guidance in paragraph (c) of this section. If the contractor's financial condition is satisfactory, the contracting officer shall not deny progress payments if the contractor agrees to—

(i) Cure the payment delinquencies;

(ii) Avoid further delinquencies; and

(iii) Make additional arrangements adequate for completing the contract without loss to the Government.

(2) If the contractor has, in good faith, disputed amounts claimed by subcontractors, suppliers, or others, the contracting officer shall not consider the payments delinquent until the amounts due are established by the parties through litigation or arbitration. However, the amounts shall be excluded from costs eligible for progress payments so long as they are disputed.

(3) Determinations of delinquency in making contributions under employee pension, profit sharing, or stock ownership plans, and exclusion of costs for such contributions from progress payment requests, shall be in accordance with paragraph (a)(3) of the clause at 52.232-16, Progress Payments, without regard to the provisions of 32.503-6.

(f) *Fair value of undelivered work.* Progress payments must be commensurate with the fair value of work accomplished in accordance with contract requirements. The contracting officer must adjust progress payments when necessary to ensure that the fair value of undelivered work equals or exceeds the amount of unliquidated progress payments. On loss contracts, the application of a loss ratio as provided at paragraph (g) of this subsection constitutes this adjustment.

(g) *Loss contracts.* (1) If the sum of the total costs incurred under a contract plus the estimated costs to complete the performance are likely to exceed the contract price, the contracting officer shall compute a loss ratio factor and adjust future progress payments to exclude the element of loss. The loss ratio factor is computed as follows:

(i) Revise the current contract price used in progress payment computations (the current ceiling price under fixed-price incentive contracts) to include the not-to-exceed amount for any pending change orders and unpriced orders.

(ii) Divide the revised contract price by the sum of the total costs incurred to date plus the estimated additional costs of completing the contract performance.

(2) If the contracting officer believes a loss is probable, future progress payment requests shall be modified as follows:

(i) The contract price shall be the revised amount computed under subparagraph (g) (1) (i) of this section.

(ii) The total costs eligible for progress payments shall be the product of—

(A) The sum of paid costs eligible for progress payments times

(B) The loss ratio factor computed under subparagraph (g) (1) (ii) of this section.

(iii) The costs applicable to items delivered, invoiced, and accepted shall not include costs in excess of the contract price of the items.

(3) The contracting officer may use audit assistance, technical services, management reports, and other sources of pertinent data to evaluate progress payment requests. If the contracting officer concludes that the contractor's figures in the contractor's progress payment request are not correct, the contracting officer shall—

(i) In the manner prescribed in paragraph (g) (4) in this section, prepare a supplementary analysis to be attached to the contractor's request;

(ii) Advise the contractor in writing of the differences; and

(iii) Adjust all further progress payments in accordance with paragraph (g) (1) of this section, using the contracting officer's figures, until the difference is resolved.

(4) The following is an example of the supplementary analysis required in paragraph (g) (3) of this subsection:

Section I	
Contract price	$2,850,000
Change orders and unpriced orders (to extent funds have been obligated)	150,000
Revised contract price	3,000,000
Section II	
Total costs incurred to date	2,700,000
Estimated additional costs to complete	900,000
Total costs to complete	3,600,000
Loss ratio factor $3,000,000 / $3,600,000 =	83.3%
Total costs eligible for progress payments	2,700,000
Loss ratio factor	× 83.3%
Recognized costs for progress payments	2,249,100
Progress payment rate	× 80.0%
Alternate amount to be used	1,799,280
Section III	
Factored costs of items delivered*	750,000
Recognized costs applicable to undelivered items ($2,249,100-750,000)	1,499,100

* This amount must be the same as the contract price of the items delivered.

[FAC 84-29, 52 FR 30077, 8/12/87, effective 8/24/87; FAC 84-42, 54 FR 5056, 1/31/89, effective 3/2/89; FAC 84-53, 54 FR 48989, 11/28/89, effective 12/28/89; FAC 97-15, 64 FR 72414, 12/27/99, effective 12/27/99; FAC 97-16, 65 FR 16274, 3/27/2000, effective 3/27/2000; FAC 2005-33, 74 FR 28430, 6/15/2009, effective 7/15/2009]

32.503-7 [Removed and Reserved]

[Removed and Reserved, FAC 97-16, 65 FR 16274, 3/27/2000, effective 3/27/2000]

32.503-8 Liquidation rates—ordinary method.

The Government recoups progress payments through the deduction of liquidations from payments that would otherwise be due to the contractor for completed contract items. To determine the amount of the liquidation, the contracting officer applies a liquidation rate to the contract price of contract items delivered and accepted. The ordinary method is that the liquidation rate is the same as the progress payment rate. At the beginning of a contract, the contracting officer must use this method.

[FAC 97-16, 65 FR 16274, 3/27/2000, effective 3/27/2000]

32.503-9 Liquidation rates—alternate method.

(a) The liquidation rate determined under 32.503-8 shall apply throughout the period of contract performance unless the contracting officer adjusts the liquidation rate under the alternate method in this 32.503-9. The objective of the alternate liquidation rate method is to permit the contractor to retain the earned profit element of the contract prices for completed items in the liquidation process. The contracting officer may reduce the liquidation rate if—

(1) The contractor requests a reduction in the rate;

(2) The rate has not been reduced in the preceding 12 months;

(3) The contract delivery schedule extends at least 18 months from the contract award date;

(4) Data on actual costs are available—

(i) For the products delivered, or

(ii) If no deliveries have been made, for a performance period of at least 12 months;

(5) The reduced liquidation rate would result in the Government recouping under each invoice the full extent of the progress payments applicable to the costs allocable to that invoice;

(6) The contractor would not be paid for more than the costs of items delivered and accepted (less allocable progress payments) and the earned profit on those items;

(7) The unliquidated progress payments would not exceed the limit prescribed in paragraph (a)(5) of the Progress Payments clause;

(8) The parties agree on an appropriate rate; and

(9) The contractor agrees to certify annually, or more often if requested by the contracting officer, that the alternate rate continues to meet the conditions of subsections 5, 6, and 7 of this section. The certificate must be accompanied by adequate supporting information.

(b) The contracting officer shall change the liquidation rate in the following circumstances:

(1) The rate shall be increased for both previous and subsequent transactions, if the contractor experiences a lower profit rate than the rate anticipated at the time the liquidation rate was established. Accordingly, the contracting officer shall adjust the progress payments associated with contract items already delivered, as well as subsequent progress payments.

(2) The rate shall be increased or decreased in keeping with the successive changes to the contract price or target profit when—

(i) The target profit is changed under a fixed-price incentive contract with successive targets; or

(ii) A redetermined price involves a change in the profit element under a contract with prospective price redetermination at stated intervals.

(c) Whenever the liquidation rate is changed, the contracting officer shall issue a contract modification to specify the new rate in the Progress Payments clause. Adequate consideration for these contract modifications is provided by the consideration included in the initial contract. The parties shall promptly make the payment or liquidation required in the circumstances.

[FAC 2005-36, 74 FR 40468, 8/11/2009, effective 8/11/2009]

32.503-10 Establishing alternate liquidation rates.

(a) The contracting officer must ensure that the liquidation rate is—

(1) High enough to result in Government recoupment of the applicable progress payments on each billing; and

(2) Supported by documentation included in the administration office contract file.

(b) The minimum liquidation rate is the expected progress payments divided by the contract price. Each of these factors is discussed below:

(1) The contracting officer must compute the expected progress payments by multiplying the estimated cost of performing the contract by the progress payment rate.

(2) For purposes of computing the liquidation rate, the contracting officer may adjust the estimated cost and the contract price to include the estimated value of any work authorized but not yet priced and any projected economic adjustments; however, the contracting officer's adjustment must not exceed the Government's estimate of the price

of all authorized work or the funds obligated for the contract.

(3) The following are examples of the computation. Assuming an estimated price of $2,200,000 and total estimated costs eligible for progress payments of $2,000,000:

(i) If the progress payment rate is 80 percent, the minimum liquidation rate should be 72.7 percent, computed as follows:

$$\frac{\$2{,}000{,}000 \times 80\%}{\$2{,}200{,}000} = 72.7\%$$

(ii) If the progress payment rate is 85 percent, the minimum liquidation rate should be 77.3 percent, computed as follows:

$$\frac{\$2{,}000{,}000 \times 85\%}{\$2{,}200{,}000} = 77.3\%$$

(4) Minimum liquidation rates will generally be expressed to tenths of a percent. Decimals between tenths will be rounded up to the next highest tenth (not necessarily the nearest tenth), since rounding down would produce a rate below the minimum rate calculated.

[FAC 84-29, 52 FR 30077, 8/12/87, effective 8/24/87; FAC 97-16, 65 FR 16274, 3/27/2000, effective 3/27/2000]

32.503-11 Adjustments for price reduction.

(a) If a retroactive downward price reduction occurs under a redeterminable contract that provides for progress payments, the contracting officer shall—

(1) Determine the refund due and obtain repayment from the contractor for the excess of payments made for delivered items over amounts due as recomputed at the reduced prices; and

(2) Increase the unliquidated progress payments amount for overdeductions made from the contractor's billings for items delivered.

(b) The contracting officer shall also increase the unliquidated progress payments amount if the contractor makes an interim or voluntary price reduction under a redeterminable or incentive contract.

32.503-12 Maximum unliquidated amount.

(a) The contracting officer shall ensure that any excess of the unliquidated progress payments over the contractual limitation in paragraph (a) of the Progress Payments clause in the contract is promptly corrected through one or more of the following actions:

(1) Increasing the liquidation rate.

(2) Reducing the progress payment rate.

(3) Suspending progress payments.

(b) The excess described in paragraph (a) of this section is most likely to arise under the following circumstances:

(1) The costs of performance exceed the contract price.

(2) The alternate method of liquidation (see 32.503-9) is used and the actual costs of performance exceed the cost estimates used to establish the liquidation rate.

(3) The rate of progress or the quality of contract performance is unsatisfactory.

(4) The rate of rejections, waste, or spoilage is excessive.

(c) As required, the services of the responsible audit agency or office should be fully utilized, along with the services of qualified cost analysis and engineering personnel.

[FAC 97-4, 63 FR 9048, 2/23/98, effective 4/24/98]

32.503-13 [Removed and Reserved]

[Removed and reserved, FAC 97-16, 65 FR 16274, 3/27/2000, effective 3/27/2000]

32.503-14 Protection of Government title.

(a) Since the Progress Payments clause gives the Government title to all of the materials, work-in-process, finished goods, and other items of property described in paragraph (d) of the Progress Payments clause, under the contract under which progress payments have been made, the ACO must ensure that the Government title to these inventories is not compromised by other encumbrances. Ordinarily, the ACO, in the absence of reason to believe otherwise, may rely upon the contractor's certification contained in the progress payment request.

(b) If the ACO becomes aware of any arrangement or condition that would impair the Government's title to the property affected by progress payment, the ACO shall require additional protective provisions (see 32.501-5) to establish and protect the Government's title.

(c) The existence of any such encumbrance is a violation of the contractor's obligations under the contract, and the ACO may, if necessary, suspend or reduce progress payments under the terms of the Progress Payments clause covering failure to comply with any material requirement of the contract. In addition, if the contractor fails to disclose an existing encumbrance in the progress payments certification, the ACO should consult with legal counsel concerning possible violation of 31 U.S.C. 3729, the False Claims Act.

[FAC 84-12, 51 FR 2665, 1/17/86, effective 1/20/86]

32.503-15 Application of Government title terms.

(a) Property to which the Government obtains title by operation of the Progress Payments clause solely is not, as a consequence, Government-furnished property.

(b) Although property title is vested in the Government under the Progress Payments clause, the acquisition, handling, and disposition of certain types of property are governed by—

(1) The clause at 52.245-1, Government Property; and

(2) The termination clauses at 52.249, for termination inventory.

(c) The contractor may sell or otherwise dispose of current production scrap in the ordinary course of business on its own volition, even if title has vested in the Government under the Progress Payments clause. The contracting officer shall require the contractor to credit the costs of the contract performance with the proceeds of the scrap disposition.

(d) When the title to materials or other inventories is vested in the Government under the Progress Payments clause, the contractor may transfer the inventory items from the contract for its own use or other disposition only if, and on terms, approved by the contracting officer. The contractor shall—

(1) Eliminate the costs allocable to the transferred property from the costs of contract performance, and

(2) Repay or credit to the Government an amount equal to the unliquidated progress payments, allocable to the transferred property.

(e) If excess property remains after the contract performance is complete and all contractor obligations under the contract are satisfied, including full liquidation of progress payments, the excess property is outside the scope of the Progress Payments clause. Therefore, the contractor holds title to it.

[FAC 2005-17, 72 FR 27364, 5/15/2007, effective 6/14/2007]

32.503-16 Risk of loss.

(a) Under the Progress Payments clause, and except for normal spoilage, the contractor bears the risk of loss for Government property under the clause, even though title is vested in the Government, unless the Government has expressly assumed this risk. The clauses prescribed in this regulation related to progress payments, default, and terminations do not constitute a Government assumption of this risk.

(b) If a loss occurs in connection with property for which the contractor bears the risk, the contractor is obligated to repay to the Government the amount of unliquidated progress payments based on costs allocable to the property.

(c) The contractor is not obligated to pay for the loss of property for which the Government has assumed the risk of loss. However, a serious loss may impede the satisfactory progress of contract performance, so that the contracting officer may need to act under paragraph (c)(5) of the Progress Payments clause.

[FAC 2005-43, 75 FR 38675, 7/2/2010, effective 8/2/2010; FAC 2005-56, 77 FR 12937, 3/2/2012, effective 4/2/2012]

32.504 Subcontracts under prime contracts providing progress payments.

(a) Subcontracts may include either performance-based payments, provided they meet the criteria in 32.1003, or progress payments, provided they meet the criteria in subpart 32.5 for customary progress payments, but not both. Subcontracts for commercial purchases may include commercial item purchase financing terms, provided they meet the criteria in 32.202-1.

(b) The contractor's requests for progress payments may include the full amount of commercial item purchase financing payments, performance-based payments, or progress payments to a subcontractor, whether paid or unpaid, provided that unpaid amounts are limited to amounts determined due and that the contractor will pay—

(1) In accordance with the terms and conditions of a subcontract or invoice; and

(2) Ordinarily within 30 days of the submission of the contractor's progress payment request to the Government.

(c) If the contractor is considering making unusual progress payments to a subcontractor, the parties will be guided by the policies in 32.501-2. If the Government approves unusual progress payments for the subcontract, the contracting officer must issue a contract modification to specify the new rate in paragraph (j)(6) of the clause at 52.232-16, Progress Payments, in the prime contract. This will allow the contractor to include the progress payments to the subcontractor in the cost basis for progress payments by the Government. This modification is not a deviation and does not require the clearance prescribed in 32.502-2(b).

(d) The contractor has a duty to ensure that financing payments to subcontractors conform to the standards and principles prescribed in paragraph (j) of the Progress Payments clause in the prime contract. Although the contracting officer should, to the extent appropriate, review the subcontract as part of the overall administration of progress payments in the prime contract, there is no special requirement for contracting officer review or consent merely because the subcontract includes financing payments, except as provided in paragraph (c) of this section. However, the contracting officer must ensure that the contractor has installed the necessary management control systems, including internal audit procedures.

(e) When financing payments are in the form of progress payments, the Progress Payments clause at 52.232-16 requires that the subcontract include the substance of the Progress Payments clause in the prime contract, modified to indicate that the contractor, not the Government, awards the subcontract and administers the progress payments. The following exceptions apply to wording modifications:

(1) The subcontract terms on title to property under progress payments shall provide for vesting of title in the Government, not the contractor, as in paragraph (d) of the Progress Payments clause in the prime contract. A reference to the contractor may, however, be substituted for *Government* in paragraph (d)(2)(iv) of the clause.

(2) In the subcontract terms on reports and access to records, the contractor shall not delete the references to *Contracting Officer* and *Government* in adapting paragraph (g) of the Progress Payments clause in the contract, but may expand the terms as follows:

(i) The term *Contracting Officer* may be changed to *Contracting Officer or Prime Contractor*.

(ii) The term *the Government* may be changed to *the Government or Prime Contractor*.

(3) The subcontract special terms regarding default shall include paragraph (h) of the Progress Payments clause in the contract through its subdivision (i). The rest of paragraph (h) is optional.

(f) When financing payments are in the form of performance-based payments, the Performance-Based Payments clause at 52.232-32 requires that the subcontract terms include the substance of the Performance-Based Payments clause, modified to indicate that the contractor, not the Government, awards the subcontract and administers the performance-based payments, and include appropriately worded modifications similar to those noted in paragraph (e) of this section.

(g) When financing payments are in the form of commercial item purchase financing, the subcontract must include a contract financing clause structured in accordance with 32.206.

[FAC 97-16, 65 FR 16274, 3/27/2000, effective 3/27/2000; FAC 2001-10, 67 FR 70520, 11/22/2002, effective 12/23/2002]

SUBPART 32.6—CONTRACT DEBTS

32.600 Scope of subpart.

This subpart prescribes policies and procedures for identifying, collecting, and deferring collection of contract debts (including interest, if applicable). Sections 32.607, 32.608, and 32.610of this subpart do not apply to claims against common carriers for transportation overcharges and freight and cargo losses (31 U.S.C. 3726).

[FAC 2005-27, 73 FR 53997, 9/17/2008, effective 10/17/2008]

32.601 General.

(a) Contract debts are amounts that—

(1) Have been paid to a contractor to which the contractor is not currently entitled under the terms and conditions of the contract; or

(2) Are otherwise due from the contractor under the terms and conditions of the contract.

(b) Contract debts include, but are not limited to, the following:

(1) Billing and price reductions resulting from contract terms for price redetermination or for determination of prices under incentive type contracts.

(2) Price or cost reductions for defective certified cost or pricing data.

(3) Financing payments determined to be in excess of the contract limitations at 52.232-16(a)(7), Progress Payments, or 52.232-32(d)(2), Performance—Based Payments, or any contract clause for commercial item financing.

(4) Increases to financing payment liquidation rates.

(5) Overpayments disclosed by quarterly statements required under price redetermination or incentive contracts.

(6) Price adjustments resulting from Cost Accounting Standards (CAS) noncompliances or changes in cost accounting practice.

(7) Reinspection costs for nonconforming supplies or services.

(8) Duplicate or erroneous payments.

(9) Damages or excess costs related to defaults in performance.

(10) Breach of contract obligations concerning progress payments, performance-based payments, advance payments, commercial item financing, or Government-furnished property.

(11) Government expense of correcting defects.

(12) Overpayments related to errors in quantity or billing or deficiencies in quality.

(13) Delinquency in contractor payments due under agreements or arrangements for deferral or postponement of collections.

(14) Reimbursement of amounts due under 33.102(b)(3) and 33.104(h)(8).

[FAC 2005-27, 73 FR 53997, 9/17/2008, effective 10/17/2008; FAC 2005-45, 75 FR 53135, 8/30/2010, effective 10/1/2010]

32.602 Responsibilities.

(a) The contracting officer has primary responsibility for identifying and demanding payment of contract debts except those resulting from errors made by the payment office. The contracting officer shall not collect contract debts or otherwise agree to liquidate contract debts (e.g., offset the amount of the debt against existing unpaid bills due the contractor, or allow contractors to retain contract debts to cover amounts that may become payable in future periods).

(b) The payment office has primary responsibility for—

(1) Collecting contract debts identified by contracting officers;

(2) Identifying and collecting duplicate and erroneous payments; and

(3) Authorizing the liquidation of contract debts in accordance with agency procedures.

[FAC 2005-27, 73 FR 53997, 9/17/2008, effective 10/17/2008]

32.603 Debt determination.

(a) If the contracting officer has any indication that a contractor owes money to the Government under a contract, the contracting officer shall determine promptly whether an actual debt is due and the amount. Any unnecessary delay may contribute to—

(1) Loss of timely availability of the funds to the program for which the funds were initially provided;

(2) Increased difficulty in collecting the debt; or

(3) Actual monetary loss to the Government.

(b) The amount of indebtedness determined by the contracting officer shall be an amount that—

(1) Is based on the merits of the case; and

(2) Is consistent with the contract terms.

[FAC 2005-27, 73 FR 53997, 9/17/2008, effective 10/17/2008]

32.604 Demand for payment.

(a) Except as provided in paragraph (c) of this section, the contracting officer shall take the following actions:

(1) Issue the demand for payment as soon as the contracting officer has determined that an actual debt is due the Government and the amount.

(2) Issue the demand for payment even if—

(i) The debt is or will be the subject of a bilateral modification;

(ii) The contractor is otherwise obligated to pay the money under the existing contract terms; or

(iii) The contractor has agreed to repay the debt.

(3) Issue the demand for payment as a part of the final decision, if a final decision is required by 32.605(a).

(b) The demand for payment shall include the following:

(1) A description of the debt, including the debt amount.

(2) A distribution of the principal amount of the debt by line(s) of accounting subject to the following:

(i) If the debt affects multiple lines of accounting, the contracting officer shall, to the maximum extent practicable, identify all affected lines of accounting. If it is not practicable to identify all affected lines of accounting, the contracting officer may select representative lines of accounting in accordance with paragraph (b)(2)(ii) of this section.

(ii) In selecting representative lines of accounting, the contracting officer shall—

(A) Consider the affected departments or agencies, years of appropriations, and the predominant types of appropriations; and

(B) Not distribute to any line of accounting an amount of the principal in excess of the total obligation for the line of accounting; and

(iii) Include the lines of accounting even if the associated funds are expired or cancelled. While cancelled funds will be deposited in a miscellaneous receipt account of the Treasury if collected, the funds are tracked under the closed year appropriation(s) to comply with the Anti-Deficiency Act.

(iv) If the debt affects multiple contracts and the lines of accounting are not readily available, the contracting officer shall—

(A) Issue the demand for payment without the distribution of the principal amount to the affected lines of accounting;

(B) Include a statement in the demand for payment advising when the distribution will be provided; and

(C) Provide the distribution by the date identified in the demand for payment.

(3) The basis for and amount of any accrued interest or penalty.

(4) (i) For debts resulting from specific contract terms (e.g., debts resulting from incentive clause provisions, Quarterly Limitation on Payments Statement, Cost Accounting Standards, price reduction for defective pricing), a notification stating that payment should be made promptly, and that interest is due in accordance with the terms of the contract. Interest shall be computed from the date specified in the applicable contract clause until repayment by the contractor. The interest rate shall be the rate specified in the applicable contract clause. In the case of a debt arising from a price reduction for defective pricing, or as specifically set forth in a Cost Accounting Standards (CAS) clause in the contract, interest is computed from the date of overpayment by the Government until repayment by the contractor at the underpayment rate established by the Secretary of the Treasury, for the periods affected, under 26 U.S.C. 6621 (a) (2).

(ii) For all other contract debts, a notification stating that any amounts not paid within 30 days from the date of the demand for payment will bear interest. Interest shall be computed from the date of the demand for payment until repayment by the contractor. The interest rate shall be the interest rate established by the Secretary of the Treasury, as provided in 41 U.S.C. 7109, which is applicable to the period in which the amount becomes due, and then at the rate applicable for each six-month period as established by the Secretary until the amount is paid.

(5) A statement advising the contractor—

(i) To contact the contracting officer if the contractor believes the debt is invalid or the amount is incorrect; and

(ii) If the contractor agrees, to remit a check payable to the agency's payment office annotated with the contract number along with a copy of the demand for payment to the payment office identified in the contract or as otherwise specified in the demand letter in accordance with agency procedures.

(6) Notification that the payment office may initiate procedures, in accordance with the applicable statutory and regulatory requirements, to offset the debt against any payments otherwise due the contractor.

(7) Notification that the debt may be subject to administrative charges in accordance with the requirements of 31 U.S.C. 3717(e) and the Debt Collection Improvement Act of 1996.

(8) Notification that the contractor may submit a request for installment payments or deferment of collection if immediate payment is not practicable or if the amount is disputed.

(c) Except as provided in paragraph (d) of this section, the contracting officer should not issue a demand for payment if the contracting officer only becomes aware of the debt when the contractor—

(1) Provides a lump sum payment or submits a credit invoice. (A credit invoice is a contractor's request to liquidate the debt against existing unpaid bills due the contractor); or

(2) Notifies the contracting officer that the payment office overpaid on an invoice payment. When the contractor provides the notification, the contracting officer shall notify the payment office of the overpayment.

(d) If a demand for payment was not issued as provided for in paragraph (c) of this section, the contracting officer shall issue a demand for payment no sooner than 30 days after the contracting officer becomes aware of the debt unless—

(1) The contractor has liquidated the debt;

(2) The contractor has requested an installment payment agreement; or

(3) The payment office has issued a demand for payment.

(e) The contracting officer shall—

(1) Furnish a copy of the demand for payment to the contractor by certified mail, return receipt requested, or by any other method that provides evidence of receipt; and

(2) Forward a copy of the demand to the payment office.

[FAC 2005-27, 73 FR 53997, 9/17/2008, effective 10/17/2008; FAC 2005-73, 79 FR 24192, 4/29/2014, effective 5/29/2014]

32.605 Final decisions.

(a) The contracting officer shall issue a final decision as required by 33.211 if—

(1) The contracting officer and the contractor are unable to reach agreement on the existence or amount of a debt in a timely manner;

(2) The contractor fails to liquidate a debt previously demanded by the contracting officer within the timeline specified in the demand for payment unless the amounts were not repaid because the contractor has requested an installment payment agreement; or

(3) The contractor requests a deferment of collection on a debt previously demanded by the contracting officer (see 32.607-2).

(b) If a demand for payment was previously issued for the debt, the demand for payment included in the final decision shall identify the same due date as the original demand for payment.

(c) The contracting officer shall—

(1) Furnish the decision to the contractor by certified mail, return receipt requested, or by any other method that provides evidence of receipt; and

(2) Forward a copy to the payment office identified in the contract.

[FAC 90-32, 60 FR 48206, 9/18/95, effective 10/1/95; FAC 2005-27, 73 FR 53997, 9/17/2008, effective 10/17/2008]

32.606 Debt collection.

(a) If the contractor has not liquidated the debt within 30 days of the date due or requested installment payments or deferment of collection, the payment office shall initiate withholding of principal, interest, penalties, and administrative charges. In the event the contract is assigned under the Assignment of Claims Act of 1940 (31 U.S.C. 3727 and 41 U.S.C. 6305), the rights of the assignee will be scrupulously respected and withholding of payments shall be consistent with those rights. For additional information on assignment of claims, see Subpart 32.8.

(b) As provided for in the Debt Collection Improvement Act of 1996 (31 U.S.C. 3711(g)(1)), payment offices are required to transfer any debt that is delinquent more than 180 days to the Department of Treasury for collection.

(c) The contracting officer shall periodically follow up with the payment office to determine whether the debt has been collected and credited to the correct appropriation(s).

[Final rule, 55 FR 38517, 9/18/90; FAC 2005-27, 73 FR 53997, 9/17/2008, effective 10/17/2008; FAC 2005-73, 79 FR 24192, 4/29/2014, effective 5/29/2014]

32.607 Installment payments and deferment of collection.

(a) The contracting officer shall not approve or deny a contractor's request for installment payments or deferment of collections. The office designated in agency procedures is responsible for approving or denying requests for installment payments or deferment of collections.

(b) If a contractor has not appealed the debt or filed an action under the Disputes clause of the contract and the contractor has submitted a proposal for debt deferment or installment payments—

(1) The office designated in agency procedures may arrange for deferment/installment payments if the contractor is unable to pay at once in full or the contractor's operations under national defense contracts would be seriously impaired. The arrangement shall include appropriate covenants and securities and should be limited to the shortest practicable maturity; and

(2) The deferment/installment agreement shall include a specific schedule or plan for payment. It should permit the Government to make periodic financial reviews of the contractor and to require payments earlier than required by the agreement if the Government considers the contractor's ability to pay improved. It should also provide for required stated or measurable payments on the occurrence of specific events or contingencies that improve the contractor's ability to pay.

(c) If not already applicable under the contract terms, interest on contract debt shall be made an element of any agreement entered into for installment payments or deferment of collection.

[FAC 2005-27, 73 FR 53997, 9/17/2008, effective 10/17/2008]

32.607-1 Installment payments.

If a contractor requests an installment payment agreement, the contracting officer shall notify the contractor to send a written request for installment payments to the office designated in agency procedures.

[FAC 2005-27, 73 FR 53997, 9/17/2008, effective 10/17/2008]

32.607-2 Deferment of collection.

(a) All requests for deferment of collection must be submitted in writing to the contracting officer.

(1) If the contractor has appealed the debt under the procedures of the Disputes clause of the contract, the information with the request for deferment may be limited to an explanation of the contractor's financial condition.

(2) Actions filed by contractors under the Disputes Clause shall not suspend or delay collection.

(3) If there is no appeal pending or action filed under the Disputes clause of the contract, the following information about the contractor should be submitted with the request:

(i) Financial condition.

(ii) Contract backlog.

(iii) Projected cash receipts and requirements.

(iv) The feasibility of immediate payment of the debt.

(v) The probable effect on operations of immediate payment in full.

(b) Upon receipt of the contractor's written request, the contracting officer shall promptly provide a notification to the payment office and advise the payment office that the contractor's request is under consideration.

(c) (1) The contracting officer should consider any information necessary to develop a recommendation on the deferment request.

(2) The contracting officer shall forward the following to the office designated in agency procedures for a decision:

(i) A copy of the contractor's request for a deferment of collection.

(ii) A written recommendation on the request and the basis for the recommendation including the advisability of deferment to avoid possible overcollections.

(iii) A statement as to whether the contractor has an appeal pending or action filed under the Disputes clause of the contract and the docket number if the appeal has been filed.

(iv) A copy of the contracting officer's final decision (see 32.605).

(d) The office designated in agency procedures may authorize a deferment pending the resolution of appeal to avoid possible overcollections. The agency is required to use unexpired funds to pay interest on overcollections.

(e) Deferments pending disposition of appeal may be granted to small business concerns and financially weak contractors, balancing the need for Government security against loss and undue hardship on the contractor.

(f) The deferment agreement shall not provide that a claim of the Government will not become due and payable pending mutual agreement on the amount of the claim or, in the case of a dispute, until the decision is reached.

(g) At a minimum, the deferment agreement shall contain the following:

(1) A description of the debt.

(2) The date of first demand for payment.

(3) Notice of an interest charge, in conformity with 32.608 and the FAR clause at 52.232-17, Interest; or, in the case of a debt arising from a defective pricing or a CAS noncompliance overpayment, interest, as prescribed by the applicable Price Reduction for Defective Certified Cost or Pricing Data or CAS clause (see 32.607(c)).

(4) Identification of the office to which the contractor is to send debt payments.

(5) A requirement for the contractor to submit financial information requested by the Government and for reasonable access to the contractor's records and property by Government representatives.

(6) Provision for the Government to terminate the deferment agreement and accelerate the maturity of the debt if the contractor defaults or if bankruptcy or insolvency proceedings are instituted by or against the contractor.

(7) Protective requirements that are considered by the Government to be prudent and feasible in the specific circumstances. The coverage of protective terms at 32.409 and 32.501-5 may be used as a guide.

(h) If a contractor appeal of the debt determination is pending, the deferment agreement shall also include a requirement that the contractor shall—

(1) Diligently prosecute the appeal; and

(2) Pay the debt in full when the appeal is decided, or when the parties reach agreement on the debt amount.

(i) The deferment agreement may provide for the right to make early payments without prejudice, for refund of overpayments, and for crediting of interest.

[FAC 2005-27, 73 FR 53997, 9/17/2008, effective 10/17/2008; FAC 2005-45, 75 FR 35135, 8/30/2010, effective 10/1/2010]

32.608 Interest. (No Text)

[FAC 84-51, 54 FR 34755, 8/21/89, effective 9/20/89; FAC 2005-27, 73 FR 53997, 9/17/2008, effective 10/17/2008]

32.608-1 Interest charges.

Unless specified otherwise in the clause at 52.232-17, Interest, interest charges shall apply to any contract debt unpaid after 30 days from the issuance of a demand unless—

(a) The contract is a kind excluded under 32.611; or

(b) The contract or debt has been exempted from interest charges under agency procedures.

[FAC 2005-27, 73 FR 53997, 9/17/2008, effective 10/17/2008]

32.608-2 Interest credits.

(a) An equitable interest credit shall be applied under the following circumstances:

(1) When the amount of debt initially determined is subsequently reduced; e.g., through a successful appeal.

(2) When any amount collected by the Government is in excess of the amount found to be due on appeal under the Disputes Clause of the contract.

(3) When the collection procedures followed in a given case result in an overcollection of the debt due.

(4) When the responsible official determines that the Government has unduly delayed payments to the contractor on the same contract at some time during the period to which the interest charge applied, provided an interest penalty was not paid for such late payment.

(b) Any appropriate interest credits shall be computed under the following procedures:

(1) Interest at the rate under 52.232-17 shall be charged on the reduced debt from the date of collection by the Government until the date the monies are remitted to the contractor.

(2) Interest may not be reduced for any time between the due date under the demand and the period covered by a deferment of collection, unless the contract includes an interest clause; e.g., the clause prescribed in 32.611.

(3) Interest shall not be credited in an amount that, when added to other amounts refunded or released to the contractor, exceeds the total amount that has been collected, or withheld for the purpose of collecting the debt. This limitation shall be further reduced by the amount of any limitation applicable under paragraph (b)(2) of this subsection.

[FAC 2005-27, 73 FR 53997, 9/17/2008, effective 10/17/2008]

32.609 Delays in receipt of notices or demands.

If interest is accrued based on the date of the demand letter and delivery of the demand letter is delayed by the Government (e.g., undue delay after dating at the originating office or delays in the mail), the date of the debt and accrual of interest shall be extended to a time that is fair and reasonable under the particular circumstances.

[FAC 2005-27, 73 FR 53997, 9/17/2008, effective 10/17/2008]

32.610 Compromising debts.

For debts under $100,000, excluding interest, the designated agency official may compromise the debt pursuant to the Federal Claims Collection Standards (31 CFR part 902) and agency regulations. Unless specifically authorized by agency procedures, contracting officers cannot compromise debts.

[FAC 84-51, 54 FR 34755, 8/21/89, effective 9/20/89; FAC 90-3, 55 FR 52794, 12/21/90, effective 1/22/91; FAC 90-5, 56 FR 29128, effective 7/25/91; FAC 90-38, 61 FR 18914, 4/29/96, effective 6/28/96; FAC 2005-27, 73 FR 53997, 9/17/2008, effective 10/17/2008]

32.611 Contract clause.

(a) The contracting officer shall insert the clause at 52.232–17, Interest, in solicitations and contracts unless it is contemplated that the contract will be in one or more of the following categories:

(1) Contracts at or below the simplified acquisition threshold.

(2) Contracts with Government agencies.

(3) Contracts with a State or local government or instrumentality.

(4) Contracts with a foreign government or instrumentality.

(5) Contracts without any provision for profit or fee with a nonprofit organization.

(6) Contracts described in Subpart 5.5, Paid Advertisements.

(7) Any other exceptions authorized under agency procedures.

(b) The contracting officer may insert the FAR clause at 52.232–17, Interest, in solicitations and contracts when it is contemplated that the contract will be in any of the categories specified in 32.611(a).

[FAC 2005-27, 73 FR 53997, 9/17/2008, effective 10/17/2008]

32.612 [Removed]

[FAC 84-12, 51 FR 2665, 1/17/86, effective 1/20/86; FAC 2005-27, 73 FR 53997, 9/17/2008, effective 10/17/2008]

32.613 [Removed]

[FAC 90-3, 55 FR 52795, 12/21/90, effective 1/22/91; FAC 90-5, 56 FR 29128, 6/25/91, effective 7/25/91; FAC 90-38, 61 FR 18914, 4/29/96, effective 6/28/96; FAC 2005-27, 73 FR 53997, 9/17/2008, effective 10/17/2008]

32.614 [Removed]

[FAC 2005-27, 73 FR 53997, 9/17/2008, effective 10/17/2008]

32.614-1 [Removed]

[FAC 90-5, 56 FR 29128, 6/25/91, effective 7/25/91; FAC 90-38, 61 FR 18914, 4/29/96, effective 6/28/96; FAC 2005-27, 73 FR 53997, 9/17/2008, effective 10/17/2008]

32.614-2 [Removed]

[FAC 2005-27, 73 FR 53997, 9/17/2008, effective 10/17/2008]

32.615 [Removed]

[FAC 2005-27, 73 FR 53997, 9/17/2008, effective 10/17/2008]

32.616 [Removed]

[FAC 84-12, 51 FR 2665, 1/17/86, effective 1/20/86; FAC 90-5, 56 FR 29128, 6/25/91, effective 7/25/91; FAC 2005-27, 73 FR 53997, 9/17/2008, effective 10/17/2008]

32.617 [Removed]

[FAC 90-29, 60 FR 34732, 7/3/95, effective 7/3/95; FAC 2005-27, 73 FR 53997, 9/17/2008, effective 10/17/2008]

SUBPART 32.7—CONTRACT FUNDING

32.700 Scope of subpart.

This subpart (a) describes basic requirements for contract funding and (b) prescribes procedures for using limitation of cost or limitation of funds clauses. Detailed acquisition funding requirements are contained in agency fiscal regulations.

[Final rule, 55 FR 38517, 9/18/90]

32.701 [Reserved]

32.702 Policy.

No officer or employee of the Government may create or authorize an obligation in excess of the funds available, or in advance of appropriations (Anti-Deficiency Act, 31 U.S.C. 1341), unless otherwise authorized by law. Before executing any contract, the contracting officer shall

(a) obtain written assurance from responsible fiscal authority that adequate funds are available or

(b) expressly condition the contract upon availability of funds in accordance with 32.703-2.

[FAC 84-12, 51 FR 2665, 1/17/86, effective 1/20/86]

32.703 Contract funding requirements. (No Text)

32.703-1 General.

(a) If the contract is fully funded, funds are obligated to cover the price or target price of a fixed-price contract or the estimated cost and any fee of a cost-reimbursement contract.

(b) If the contract is incrementally funded, funds are obligated to cover the amount allotted and any corresponding increment of fee.

32.703-2 Contracts conditioned upon availability of funds.

(a) *Fiscal year contracts.* The contracting officer may initiate a contract action properly chargeable to funds of the new fiscal year before these funds are available, *provided* that the contract includes the clause at 52.232-18, Availability of Funds (see 32.706-1(a)). This authority may be used only for operation and maintenance and continuing services (e.g., rentals, utilities, and supply items not financed by stock funds)

(1) necessary for normal operations and

(2) for which Congress previously had consistently appropriated funds, unless specific statutory authority exists permitting applicability to other requirements.

(b) *Indefinite-quantity or requirements contracts.* A one-year indefinite-quantity or requirements contract for services that is funded by annual appropriations may extend beyond the fiscal year in which it begins; *provided,* that

(1) any specified minimum quantities are certain to be ordered in the initial fiscal year (see 37.106) and

(2) the contract includes the clause at 52.232-19, Availability of Funds for the Next Fiscal Year (see 32.706-1(b)).

(c) *Acceptance of supplies or services.* The Government shall not accept supplies or services under a contract conditioned upon the availability of funds until the contracting officer has given the contractor notice, to be confirmed in writing, that funds are available.

[FAC 2001-06, 67 FR 13048, 3/20/2002, effective 4/4/2002; FAC 2005-67, 78 FR 37686, 6/21/2013, effective 6/21/2013; FAC 2005-72, 78 FR 80382,12/31/2013, effective 12/31/2013]

32.703-3 Contracts crossing fiscal years.

(a) A contract that is funded by annual appropriations may not cross fiscal years, except in accordance with statutory authorization (*e.g.*, 41 U.S.C. 6302, 31 U.S.C. 1308, 42 U.S.C. 2459a, 42 U.S.C. 3515, and paragraph (b) of this subsection), or when the contract calls for an end product that cannot feasibly be subdivided for separate performance in each fiscal year (*e.g.*, contracts for expert or consultant services).

(b) The head of an executive agency, except NASA, may enter into a contract, exercise an option, or place an order under a contract for severable services for a period that begins in one fiscal year and ends in the next fiscal year if the period of the contract awarded, option exercised, or order placed does not exceed one year (10 U.S.C. 2410a and 41 U.S.C. 3902). Funds made available for a fiscal year may be obligated for the total amount of an action entered into under this authority.

[FAC 97-9, 63 FR 58587, 10/30/98, effective 12/29/98; FAC 2005-73, 79 FR 24192, 4/29/2014, effective 5/29/2014]

32.704 Limitation of cost or funds.

(a) (1) When a contract contains the clause at 52.232-20, Limitation of Cost; or 52.232-22, Limitation of Funds, the contracting officer, upon learning that the contractor is approaching the estimated cost of the contract or the limit of the funds allotted, shall promptly obtain funding and programming information pertinent to the contract's continuation and notify the contractor in writing that—

(i) Additional funds have been allotted, or the estimated cost has been increased, in a specified amount;

(ii) The contract is not to be further funded and that the contractor should submit a proposal for an adjustment of fee, if any, based on the percentage of work completed in relation to the total work called for under the contract;

(iii) The contract is to be terminated; or

(iv) (A) The Government is considering whether to allot additional funds or increase the estimated cost,

(B) the contractor is entitled by the contract terms to stop work when the funding or cost limit is reached, and

(C) any work beyond the funding or cost limit will be at the contractor's risk.

(2) Upon learning that a partially funded contract containing any of the clauses referenced in subparagraph (1) above will receive no further funds, the contracting officer shall promptly give the contractor written notice of the decision not to provide funds.

(b) Under a cost-reimbursement contract, the contracting officer may issue a change order, a direction to replace or repair defective items or work, or a termination notice without immediately increasing the funds available. Since a contractor is not obligated to incur costs in excess of the estimated cost in the contract, the contracting officer shall ensure availability of funds for directed actions. The contracting officer may direct that any increase in the estimated cost or amount allotted to a contract be used for the sole purpose of funding termination or other specified expenses.

(c) Government personnel encouraging a contractor to continue work in the absence of funds will incur a violation of Revised Statutes Section 3679 (31 U.S.C. 1341) that may subject the violator to civil or criminal penalties.

[48 FR 42328, 8/19/83, as amended at 51 FR 2665, 1/17/86; FAC 2005-17, 72 FR 27364, 5/15/2007, effective 6/14/2007]

32.705 Unenforceability of unauthorized obligations.

Many supplies or services are acquired subject to supplier license agreements. These are particularly common in information technology acquisitions, but they may apply to any supply or service. For example, computer software and services delivered through the internet (web services) are often subject to license agreements, referred to as End User License Agreements (EULA), Terms of Service (TOS), or other similar legal instruments or agreements. Many of these agreements contain indemnification clauses that are inconsistent with Federal law and unenforceable, but which could create a violation of the Anti-Deficiency Act (31 U.S.C. 1341) if agreed by the Government.

[FAC 2005-67, 78 FR 37686, 6/21/2013, effective 6/21/2013; FAC 2005-72, 78 FR 80382,12/31/2013, effective 12/31/2013]

32.706 Contract clauses. (No Text)

32.706-1 Clauses for contracting in advance of funds.

(a) Insert the clause at 52.232-18, Availability of Funds, in solicitations and contracts if the contract will be chargeable to funds of the new fiscal year and the contract action will be initiated before the funds are available.

(b) The contracting officer shall insert the clause at 52.232-19, Availability of Funds for the Next Fiscal Year, in solicitations and contracts if a one-year indefinite-quantity or requirements contract for services is contemplated and the contract—

Is funded by annual appropriations; and—

Is to extend beyond the initial fiscal year (see 32.703-2(b)).

[48 FR 42328, 8/19/83, as amended at 63 FR 58602, 10/30/98; FAC 2001-06, 67 FR 13048, 3/20/2002, effective 4/4/2002; Redesignated, FAC 2005-67, 78 FR 37686, 6/21/2013, effective 6/21/2013]

32.706-2 Clauses for limitation of cost or funds.

(a) The contracting officer shall insert the clause at 52.232-20, Limitation of Cost, in solicitation and contracts if a fully funded cost-reimbursement contract is contemplated, whether or not the contract provides for payment of a fee.

(b) The contracting officer shall insert the clause at 52.232-22, Limitation of Funds, in solicitations and contracts if an incrementally funded cost-reimbursement contract is contemplated.

[FAC 2005-17, 72 FR 27364, 5/15/2007, effective 6/14/2007; Redesignated, FAC 2005-67, 78 FR 37686, 6/21/2013, effective 6/21/2013; FAC 2005-72, 78 FR 80382,12/31/2013, effective 12/31/2013]

32.706-3 Clause for unenforceability of unauthorized obligations.

The contracting officer shall insert the clause at 52.232–39, Unenforceability of Unauthorized Obligations in all solicitations and contracts.

[FAC 2005-67, 78 FR 37686, 6/21/2013, effective 6/21/2013; FAC 2005-72, 78 FR 80382,12/31/2013, effective 12/31/2013]

SUBPART 32.8—ASSIGNMENT OF CLAIMS

32.800 Scope of subpart.

This subpart prescribes policies and procedures for the assignment of claims under the Assignment of Claims Act of 1940, as amended, (31 U.S.C. 3727, 41 U.S.C. 6305) (hereafter referred to as "the Act").

[FAC 84-12, 51 FR 2665, 1/17/86, effective 1/20/86; FAC 2005-73, 79 FR 24192, 4/29/2014, effective 5/29/2014]

32.801 Definitions.

Designated agency, as used in this subpart, means any department or agency of the executive branch of the United States Government (see 32.803(d)).

No-setoff commitment, as used in this subpart, means a contractual undertaking that, to the extent permitted by the Act, payments by the designated agency to the assignee under an assignment of claims will not be reduced to liquidate the indebtedness of the contractor to the Government.

[FAC 90-33, 60 FR 49706, 9/26/95, effective 10/1/95; FAC 97-22, 66 FR 2116, 1/10/2001, effective 3/12/2001; Delay of effective date, 66 FR 14259, 3/9/2001, effective 5/11/2001]

32.802 Conditions.

Under the Assignment of Claims Act, a contractor may assign moneys due or to become due under a contract if all the following conditions are met:

(a) The contract specifies payments aggregating $1,000 or more.

(b) The assignment is made to a bank, trust company, or other financing institution, including any Federal lending agency.

(c) The contract does not prohibit the assignment.

(d) Unless otherwise expressly permitted in the contract, the assignment—

(1) Covers all unpaid amounts payable under the contract;

(2) Is made only to one party, except that any assignment may be made to one party as agent or trustee for two or more parties participating in the financing of the contract; and

(3) Is not subject to further assignment.

(e) The assignee sends a written notice of assignment together with a true copy of the assignment instrument to the—

(1) Contracting officer or the agency head;

(2) Surety on any bond applicable to the contract; and

(3) Disbursing officer designated in the contract to make payment.

32.803 Policies.

(a) Any assignment of claims that has been made under the Act to any type of financing institution listed in 32.802(b) may thereafter be further assigned and reassigned to any such institution if the conditions in 32.802(d) and (e) continue to be met.

(b) A contract may prohibit the assignment of claims if the agency determines the prohibition to be in the Government's interest.

(c) Under a requirements or indefinite quantity type contract that authorizes ordering and payment by multiple Government activities, amounts due for individual orders for $1,000 or more may be assigned.

(d) Any contract of a designated agency (see FAR 32.801), except a contract under which full payment has been made, may include a no-setoff commitment only when a determination of need is made by the head of the agency, in accordance with the Presidential delegation of authority dated October 3, 1995, and after such determination has been published in the Federal Register. The Presidential delegation makes such determinations of need subject to further guidance issued by the Office of Federal Procurement Policy. The following guidance has been provided: Use of the no-setoff provision may be appropriate to facilitate the national defense; in the event of a national emergency or natural disaster; or when the use of the no-setoff provision may facilitate private financing of contract performance. However, in the event an offeror is significantly indebted to the United States, the contracting officer should consider whether the inclusion of the no-setoff commitment in a particular contract is in the best interests of the United States. In such an event, the contracting officer should consult with the Government officer(s) responsible for collecting the debt(s).

(e) When an assigned contract does not include a no-setoff commitment, the Government may apply against payments to the assignee any liability of the contractor to the Government arising independently of the assigned contract if the liability existed at the time notice of the assignment was received even though that liability had not yet matured so as to be due and payable.

[FAC 90-33, 60 FR 49706, 9/26/95, effective 10/1/95; FAC 90-38, 61 FR 18914, 4/29/96, effective 6/28/96]

32.804 Extent of assignee's protection.

(a) No payments made by the Government to the assignee under any contract assigned in accordance with the Act may be recovered on account of any liability of the contractor to the Government. This immunity of the assignee is effective whether the contractor's liability arises from or independently of the assigned contract.

(b) Except as provided in paragraph (c) of this section, the inclusion of a no-setoff commitment in an assigned contract entitles the assignee to receive contract payments free of reduction or setoff for—

(1) Any liability of the contractor to the Government arising independently of the contract; and

(2) Any of the following liabilities of the contractor to the Government arising from the assigned contract:

(i) Renegotiation under any statute or contract clause.

(ii) Fines.

(iii) Penalties, exclusive of amounts that may be collected or withheld from the contractor under, or for failure to comply with, the terms of the contract.

(iv) Taxes or social security contributions.

(v) Withholding or nonwithholding of taxes or social security contributions.

(c) In some circumstances, a setoff may be appropriate even though the assigned contract includes a no-setoff commitment; *e.g.*—

(1) When the assignee has neither made a loan under the assignment nor made a commitment to do so; or

(2) To the extent that the amount due on the contract exceeds the amount of any loans made or expected to be made under a firm commitment for financing.

32.805 Procedure.

(a) *Assignments.* (1) Assignments by corporations shall be—

(i) Executed by an authorized representative;

(ii) Attested by the secretary or the assistant secretary of the corporation; and

(iii) Impressed with the corporate seal or accompanied by a true copy of the resolution of the corporation's board of directors authorizing the signing representative to execute the assignment.

(2) Assignments by a partnership may be signed by one partner, if the assignment is accompanied by adequate evidence that the signer is a general partner of the partnership and is authorized to execute assignments on behalf of the partnership.

(3) Assignments by an individual shall be signed by that individual and the signature acknowledged before a notary public or other person authorized to administer oaths.

(b) *Filing*. The assignee shall forward to each party specified in 32.802(e) an original and three copies of the notice of assignment, together with one true copy of the instrument of assignment. The true copy shall be a certified duplicate or photostat copy of the original assignment.

(c) *Format for notice of assignment*. The following is a suggested format for use by an assignee in providing the notice of assignment required by 32.802(e).

NOTICE OF ASSIGNMENT

TO: ________ [*address to one of the parties specified in 32.802(e)*].

This has reference to Contract No. ____ dated ____, entered into between ____ [*contractor's name and address*]and ____ [*government agency, name of office, and address*], for ____ [*describe nature of the contract*].

Moneys due or to become due under the contract described above have been assigned to the undersigned under the provisions of the Assignment of Claims Act of 1940, as amended, (31 U.S.C. 3727, 41 U.S.C. 6305).

A true copy of the instrument of assignment executed by the Contractor on ____ [*date*], is attached to the original notice.

Payments due or to become due under this contract should be made to the undersigned assignee.

Please return to the undersigned the three enclosed copies of this notice with appropriate notations showing the date and hour of receipt, and signed by the person acknowledging receipt on behalf of the addressee.

Very truly yours,

____

[*name of assignee*]

By________

[*signature of signing officer*]

Title________

[*title of signing officer*]

____

____

[*address of assignee*]

ACKNOWLEDGMENT

Receipt is acknowledged of the above notice and of a copy of the instrument of assignment. They were received at __ (a.m.) (p.m.) on ____, 20____.

____

[*signature*]

____

[*title*]

____

On behalf of

____

[*name of addressee of this notice*]

(d) *Examination by the Government*. In examining and processing notices of assignment and before acknowledging their receipt, contracting officers should assure that the following conditions and any additional conditions specified in agency regulations, have been met:

(1) The contract has been properly approved and executed.

(2) The contract is one under which claims may be assigned.

(3) The assignment covers only money due or to become due under the contract.

(4) The assignee is registered separately in the System for Award Management unless one of the exceptions in 4.1102 applies.

(e) *Release of assignment.* (1) A release of an assignment is required whenever—

(i) There has been a further assignment or reassignment under the Act; or

(ii) The contractor wishes to reestablish its right to receive further payments after the contractor's obligations to the assignee have been satisfied and a balance remains due under the contract.

(2) The assignee, under a further assignment or reassignment, in order to establish a right to receive payment from the Government, must file with the addressees listed in 32.802(e) a—

(i) Written notice of release of the contractor by the assigning financing institution;

(ii) Copy of the release instrument;

(iii) Written notice of the further assignment or reassignment; and

(iv) Copy of the further assignment or reassignment instrument.

(3) If the assignee releases the contractor from an assignment of claims under a contract, the contractor, in order to establish a right to receive payment of the balance due under the contract, must file a written notice of release together with a true copy of the release of assignment instrument with the addressees noted in 32.802(e).

(4) The addressee of a notice of release of assignment or the official acting on behalf of that addressee shall acknowledge receipt of the notice.

[FAC 84-12, 51 FR 2666, 1/17/86, effective 1/20/86; FAC 84-25, 52 FR 9039, 3/20/87, effective 7/1/87; FAC 90-45, Final rule, 62 FR 224, 1/2/97, effective 1/1/97; FAC 97-11, 64 FR 10530, 3/4/99, effective 5/3/99; FAC 97-17, 65 FR 24316, 4/25/2000, effective 4/25/2000; FAC 2001-16, Final rule, 68 FR 56669, 10/1/2003, effective 10/1/2003; FAC 2005-67, 78 FR 37676, 6/21/2013, effective 7/22/2013; FAC 2005-73, 79 FR 24192, 4/29/2014, effective 5/29/2014]

32.806 Contract clauses.

(a) (1) The contracting officer shall insert the clause at 52.232-23, Assignment of Claims, in solicitations and contracts expected to exceed the micro-purchase threshold, unless the contract will prohibit the assignment of claims (see 32.803(b)). The use of the clause is not required for purchase orders. However, the clause may be used in purchase orders expected to exceed the micro-purchase threshold, that are accepted in writing by the contractor, if such use is consistent with agency policies and regulations.

(2) If a no-setoff commitment has been authorized (see FAR 32.803(d)), the contracting officer shall use the clause with its Alternate I.

(b) The contracting officer shall insert the clause at 52.232-24, Prohibition of Assignment of Claims, in solicitations and contracts for which a determination has been made under agency regulations that the prohibition of assignment of claims is in the Government's interest.

[FAC 84-12, 51 FR 2666, 1/17/86, effective 1/20/86; FAC 90-33, 60 FR 49706, 9/26/95, effective 10/1/95; FAC 90-38, 61 FR 18914, 4/29/96, effective 6/28/96]

SUBPART 32.9—PROMPT PAYMENT

32.900 Scope of subpart.

This subpart prescribes policies, procedures, and clauses for implementing Office of Management and Budget (OMB) prompt payment regulations at 5 CFR part 1315.

[FAC 2001-02, 66 FR 65347, 12/18/2001, effective 2/19/2002]

32.901 Applicability.

(a) This subpart applies to invoice payments on all contracts, except contracts with payment terms and late payment penalties established by other governmental authority (e.g., tariffs).

(b) This subpart does not apply to contract financing payments (see definition at 32.001).

[FAC 2001-02, 66 FR 65347, 12/18/2001, effective 2/19/2002]

32.902 Definitions.

As used in this subpart—

Discount for prompt payment means an invoice payment reduction offered by the contractor for payment prior to the due date.

Mixed invoice means an invoice that contains items with different payment due dates.

Payment date means the date on which a check for payment is dated or, for an electronic funds transfer (EFT), the settlement date.

Settlement date, as it applies to electronic funds transfer, means the date on which an electronic funds transfer payment is credited to the contractor's financial institution.

[FAC 2001-02, 66 FR 65347, 12/18/2001, effective 2/19/2002; FAC 2001-14, 68 FR 28092, 5/22/2002, effective 5/22/2003]

32.903 Responsibilities.

(a) Agency heads—

(1) Must establish the policies and procedures necessary to implement this subpart;

(2) May prescribe additional standards for establishing invoice payment due dates (see 32.904) necessary to support agency programs and foster prompt payment to contractors;

(3) May adopt different payment procedures in order to accommodate unique circumstances, provided that such procedures are consistent with the policies in this subpart;

(4) Must inform contractors of points of contact within their cognizant payment offices to enable contractors to obtain status of invoices; and

(5) May authorize the use of the accelerated payment methods specified at 5 CFR 1315.5.

(b) When drafting solicitations and contracts, contracting officers must identify for each line item number, subline item number, or exhibit line item number—

(1) The applicable Prompt Payment clauses that apply to each item when the solicitation or contract contains items that will be subject to different payment terms; and

(2) The applicable Prompt Payment food category (e.g., which item numbers are meat or meat food products, which are perishable agricultural commodities), when the solicitation or contract contains multiple payment terms for various classes of foods and edible products.

[FAC 2001-02, 66 FR 65347, 12/18/2001, effective 2/19/2002; FAC 2005-95, 82 FR 4709, 1/13/2017, effective 1/13/2017]

32.904 Determining payment due dates.

(a) *General*. Agency procedures must ensure that, when specifying due dates, contracting officers give full consideration to the time reasonably required by Government officials to fulfill their administrative responsibilities under the contract.

(b) *Payment due dates*. Except as prescribed in paragraphs (c) through (f) of this section, or as authorized in 32.908(a)(2) or (c)(2), the due date for making an invoice payment is as follows:

(1) The later of the following two events:

(i) The 30th day after the designated billing office receives a proper invoice from the contractor (except as provided in paragraph (b)(3) of this section).

(ii) The 30th day after Government acceptance of supplies delivered or services performed.

(A) For a final invoice, when the payment amount is subject to contract settlement actions, acceptance is deemed to occur on the effective date of the contract settlement.

(B) For the sole purpose of computing an interest penalty that might be due the contractor—

(1) Government acceptance is deemed to occur constructively on the 7th day after the contractor delivers supplies or performs services in accordance with the terms and conditions of the contract, unless there is a disagreement over quantity, quality, or contractor compliance with a contract requirement;

(2) If actual acceptance occurs within the constructive acceptance period, the Government must base the determination of an interest penalty on the actual date of acceptance;

(3) The constructive acceptance requirement does not compel Government officials to accept supplies or services, perform contract administration functions, or make payment prior to fulfilling their responsibilities; and

(4) Except for a contract for the purchase of a commercial item, including a brand-name commercial item for authorized resale (e.g., commissary items), the contracting officer may specify a longer period for constructive acceptance in the solicitation and resulting contract, if required to afford the Government a reasonable opportunity to inspect and test the supplies furnished or to evaluate the services performed. The contracting officer must document in the contract file the justification for extending the constructive acceptance period beyond 7 days. Extended acceptance periods must not be a routine agency practice and must be used only when necessary to permit proper Government inspection and testing of the supplies delivered or services performed.

(2) If the contract does not require submission of an invoice for payment (e.g., periodic lease payments), the contracting officer must specify the due date in the contract.

(3) If the designated billing office fails to annotate the invoice with the actual date of receipt at the time of receipt, the invoice payment due date is the 30th day after the date of the contractor's invoice, provided the designated billing office receives a proper invoice and there is no disagreement over quantity, quality, or contractor compliance with contract requirements.

(c) *Architect-engineer contracts.* (1) The due date for making payments on contracts that contain the clause at 52.232-10, Payments Under Fixed-Price Architect-Engineer Contracts, is as follows:

(i) The due date for work or services completed by the contractor is the later of the following two events:

(A) The 30th day after the designated billing office receives a proper invoice from the contractor.

(B) The 30th day after Government acceptance of the work or services completed by the contractor.

(1) For a final invoice, when the payment amount is subject to contract settlement actions (e.g., release of claims), acceptance is deemed to occur on the effective date of the settlement.

(2) For the sole purpose of computing an interest penalty that might be due the contractor, Government acceptance is deemed to occur constructively on the 7th day after the contractor completes the work or services in accordance with the terms and conditions of the contract (see also paragraph (c)(2) of this section). If actual acceptance occurs within the constructive acceptance period, the Government must base the determination of an interest penalty on the actual date of acceptance.

(ii) The due date for progress payments is the 30th day after Government approval of contractor estimates of work or services accomplished. For the sole purpose of computing an interest penalty that might be due the contractor—

(A) Government approval is deemed to occur constructively on the 7th day after the designated billing office receives the contractor estimates (see also paragraph (c)(2) of this section).

(B) If actual approval occurs within the constructive approval period, the Government must base the determination of an interest penalty on the actual date of approval.

(iii) If the designated billing office fails to annotate the invoice or payment request with the actual date of receipt at the time of receipt, the payment due date is the 30th day after the date of the contractor's invoice or payment request, provided the designated billing office receives a proper invoice or payment request and there is no disagreement over quantity, quality, or contractor compliance with contract requirements.

(2) The constructive acceptance and constructive approval requirements described in paragraphs (c)(1)(i) and (ii) of this section

are conditioned upon receipt of a proper payment request and no disagreement over quantity, quality, contractor compliance with contract requirements, or the requested progress payment amount. These requirements do not compel Government officials to accept work or services, approve contractor estimates, perform contract administration functions, or make payment prior to fulfilling their responsibilities. The contracting officer may specify a longer period for constructive acceptance or constructive approval, if required to afford the Government a reasonable opportunity to inspect and test the supplies furnished or to evaluate the services performed. The contracting officer must document in the contract file the justification for extending the constructive acceptance or approval period beyond 7 days.

(d) *Construction contracts.* (1) The due date for making payments on construction contracts is as follows:

(i) The due date for making progress payments based on contracting officer approval of the estimated amount and value of work or services performed, including payments for reaching milestones in any project, is 14 days after the designated billing office receives a proper payment request.

(A) If the designated billing office fails to annotate the payment request with the actual date of receipt at the time of receipt, the payment due date is the 14th day after the date of the contractor's payment request, provided the designated billing office receives a proper payment request and there is no disagreement over quantity, quality, or contractor compliance with contract requirements.

(B) The contracting officer may specify a longer period in the solicitation and resulting contract if required to afford the Government a reasonable opportunity to adequately inspect the work and to determine the adequacy of the contractor's performance under the contract. The contracting officer must document in the contract file the justification for extending the due date beyond 14 days.

(C) The contracting officer must not approve progress payment requests unless the certification and substantiation of amounts requested are provided as required by the clause at 52.232-5, Payments Under Fixed-Price Construction Contracts.

(ii) The due date for payment of any amounts retained by the contracting officer in accordance with the clause at 52.232-5, Payments Under Fixed-Price Construction Contracts, will be as specified in the contract or, if not specified, 30 days after approval by the contracting officer for release to the contractor. The contracting officer must base the release of retained amounts on the contracting officer's determination that satisfactory progress has been made.

(iii) The due date for final payments based on completion and acceptance of all work (including any retained amounts), and payments for partial deliveries that have been accepted by the Government (e.g., each separate building, public work, or other division of the contract for which the price is stated separately in the contract) is as follows:

(A) The later of the following two events:

(*1*) The 30th day after the designated billing office receives a proper invoice from the contractor.

(*2*) The 30th day after Government acceptance of the work or services completed by the contractor. For a final invoice, when the payment amount is subject to contract settlement actions (e.g., release of contractor claims), acceptance is deemed to occur on the effective date of the contract settlement.

(B) If the designated billing office fails to annotate the invoice with the actual date of receipt at the time of receipt, the invoice payment due date is the 30th day after the date of the contractor's invoice, provided the designated billing office receives a proper invoice and there is no disagreement over quantity, quality, or contractor compliance with contract requirements.

(2) For the sole purpose of computing an interest penalty that might be due the contractor for payments described in paragraph (d)(1)(iii) of this section—

(i) Government acceptance or approval is deemed to occur constructively on the 7th day after the contractor completes the work or services in accordance with the terms and conditions of the contract, unless there is a disagreement over quantity, quality, contractor compliance with a contract requirement, or the requested amount;

(ii) If actual acceptance occurs within the constructive acceptance period, the Government must base the determination of an interest penalty on the actual date of acceptance;

(iii) The constructive acceptance requirement does not compel Government officials to accept work or services, approve contractor estimates, perform contract administration functions, or make payment prior to fulfilling their responsibilities; and

(iv) The contracting officer may specify a longer period for constructive acceptance or constructive approval in the solicitation and resulting contract, if required to afford the Government a reasonable opportunity to adequately inspect the work and to determine the adequacy of the contractor's performance under the contract. The contracting officer must document in the contract file the justification for extending the constructive acceptance or approval beyond 7 days.

(3) Construction contracts contain special provisions concerning contractor payments to subcontractors, along with special contractor certification requirements. The Office of Management and Budget has determined that these certifications must not be construed as final acceptance of the subcontractor's performance. The certification in 52.232-5(c) implements this determination; however, certificates are still acceptable if the contractor deletes paragraph (c)(4) of 52.232-5 from the certificate.

(4)(i) Paragraph (d) of the clause at 52.232-5, Payments under Fixed-Price Construction Contracts, and paragraph (e)(6) of the clause at 52.232-27, Prompt Payment for Construction Contracts, provide for the contractor to pay interest on unearned amounts in certain circumstances. The Government must recover this interest from subsequent payments to the contractor. Therefore, contracting officers normally must make no demand for payment. Contracting officers must—

(A) Compute the amount in accordance with the clause;

(B) Provide the contractor with a final decision; and

(C) Notify the payment office of the amount to be withheld.

(ii) The payment office is responsible for making the deduction of interest. Amounts collected in accordance with these provisions revert to the United States Treasury.

(e) *Cost-reimbursement contracts for services.* For purposes of computing late payment interest penalties that may apply, the due date for making interim payments on cost-reimbursement contracts for services is 30 days after the date of receipt of a proper invoice.

(f) *Food and specified items.*

If the items delivered are:	*Payment must be made as close as possible to, but not later than:*
(1) Meat or meat food products. As defined in section 2(a)(3) of the Packers and Stockyard Act of 1921 (7 U.S.C. 182(3)), and as further defined in Public Law 98-181, including any edible fresh or frozen poultry meat, any perishable poultry meat food product, fresh eggs, and any perishable egg product.	7th day after product delivery.
(2) Fresh or frozen fish. As defined in section 204(3) of the Fish and Seafood Promotion Act of 1986 (16 U.S.C. 4003(3)).	7th day after product delivery.

If the items delivered are:	*Payment must be made as close as possible to, but not later than:*
(3) Perishable agricultural commodities. As defined in section 1(4) of the Perishable Agricultural Commodities Act of 1930 (7 U.S.C. 499a(4)).	10th day after product delivery, unless another date is specified in the contract.
(4) Dairy products. As defined in section 111(e) of the Dairy Production Stabilization Act of 1983 (7 U.S.C. 4502(e)), edible fats or oils, and food products prepared from edible fats or oils. Liquid milk, cheese, certain processed cheese products, butter, yogurt, ice cream, mayonnaise, salad dressings, and other similar products fall within this classification. Nothing in the Act limits this classification to refrigerated products. If questions arise regarding the proper classification of a specific product, the contracting officer must follow prevailing industry practices in specifying a contract payment due date. The burden of proof that a classification of a specific product is, in fact, prevailing industry practice is upon the contractor making the representation.	10th day after a proper invoice has been received.

(g) *Multiple payment due dates.* Contracting officers may encourage, but not require, contractors to submit separate invoices for products with different payment due dates under the same contract or order. When an invoice contains items with different payment due dates (i.e., a mixed invoice), the payment office will, subject to agency policy—

(1) Pay the entire invoice on the earliest due date; or

(2) Split invoice payments, making payments by the applicable due dates.

[FAC 2001-02, 66 FR 65347, 12/18/2001, effective 2/19/2002]

32.905 Payment documentation and process.

(a) *General.* Payment will be based on receipt of a proper invoice and satisfactory contract performance.

(b) *Content of invoices.* (1) A proper invoice must include the following items (except for interim payments on cost reimbursement contracts for services):

(i) Name and address of the contractor.

(ii) Invoice date and invoice number. (Contractors should date invoices as close as possible to the date of mailing or transmission.)

(iii) Contract number or other authorization for supplies delivered or services performed (including order number and line item number).

(iv) Description, quantity, unit of measure, unit price, and extended price of supplies delivered or services performed.

(v) Shipping and payment terms (e.g., shipment number and date of shipment, discount for prompt payment terms). Bill of lading number and weight of shipment will be shown for shipments on Government bills of lading.

(vi) Name and address of contractor official to whom payment is to be sent (must be the same as that in the contract or in a proper notice of assignment).

(vii) Name (where practicable), title, phone number, and mailing address of person to notify in the event of a defective invoice.

(viii) Taxpayer Identification Number (TIN). The contractor must include its TIN on the invoice only if required by agency procedures. (See 4.9 TIN requirements.)

(ix) Electronic funds transfer (EFT) banking information.

(A) The contractor must include EFT banking information on the invoice only if required by agency procedures.

(B) If EFT banking information is not required to be on the invoice, in order for the invoice to be a proper invoice, the contractor must have submitted correct EFT banking information in accordance with the applicable solicitation provision (e.g., 52.232-38, Submission of Electronic Funds Transfer Information with Offer), contract clause (e.g., 52.232-33, Payment by Electronic Funds Transfer—System for Award Management, or 52.232-34, Payment by Electronic Funds Transfer—Other Than System for Award Management), or applicable agency procedures.

(C) EFT banking information is not required if the Government waived the requirement to pay by EFT.

(x) Any other information or documentation required by the contract (e.g., evidence of shipment).

(2) An interim payment request under a cost-reimbursement contract for services constitutes a proper invoice for purposes of this subsection if it includes all of the information required by the contract.

(3) If the invoice does not comply with these requirements, the designated billing office must return it within 7 days after receipt (3 days on contracts for meat, meat food products, or fish; 5 days on contracts for perishable agricultural commodities, dairy products, edible fats or oils, and food products prepared from edible fats or oils), with the reasons why it is not a proper invoice. If such notice is not timely, then the designated billing office must adjust the due date for the purpose of determining an interest penalty, if any.

(c) *Authorization to pay*. All invoice payments, with the exception of interim payments on cost-reimbursement contracts for services, must be supported by a receiving report or other Government documentation authorizing payment (e.g., Government certified voucher). The agency receiving official should forward the receiving report or other Government documentation to the designated payment office by the 5th working day after Government acceptance or approval, unless other arrangements have been made. This period of time does not extend the due dates prescribed in this section. Acceptance should be completed as expeditiously as possible. The receiving report or other Government documentation authorizing payment must, as a minimum, include the following:

(1) Contract number or other authorization for supplies delivered or services performed.

(2) Description of supplies delivered or services performed.

(3) Quantities of supplies received and accepted or services performed, if applicable.

(4) Date supplies delivered or services performed.

(5) Date that the designated Government official—

(i) Accepted the supplies or services; or

(ii) Approved the progress payment request, if the request is being made under the clause at 52.232-5, Payments Under Fixed-Price Construction Contracts, or the clause at 52.232-10, Payments Under Fixed-Price Architect-Engineer Contracts.

(6) Signature, printed name, title, mailing address, and telephone number of the designated Government official responsible for acceptance or approval functions.

(d) *Billing office*. The designated billing office must immediately annotate each invoice with the actual date it receives the invoice.

(e) *Payment office*. The designated payment office will annotate each invoice and receiving report with the actual date it receives the invoice.

[FAC 2001-01, 66 FR 53485, 10/22/2001, effective 10/22/2001; FAC 2001-02, 66 FR 65347, 12/18/2001, effective 2/19/2002; FAC 2001-14, 68 FR 28092, 5/22/2003, effective 5/22/2003; FAC 2005-67, 78 FR 37676, 6/21/2013, effective 7/22/2013; FAC 2005-95, 82 FR 4709, 1/13/2017, effective 1/13/2017]

32.906 Making payments.

(a) *General*. The Government will not make invoice payments earlier than 7 days prior to the due dates specified in the contract unless the agency head determines—

(1) To make earlier payment on a case-by-case basis; or

(2) That the use of accelerated payment methods are necessary (see 32.903(a)(5)).

(b) *Payment office*. The designated payment office—

(1) Will mail checks on the same day they are dated;

(2) For payments made by EFT, will specify a date on or before the established due date for settlement of the payment at a Federal Reserve Bank;

(3) When the due date falls on a Saturday, Sunday, or legal holiday when Government offices are closed, may make payment on the following working day without incurring a late payment interest penalty.

(4) When it is determined that the designated billing office erroneously rejected a proper invoice and upon resubmission of the invoice, will enter in the payment system the original date the invoice was received by the designated billing office for the purpose of calculating the correct payment due date and any interest penalties that may be due.

(c) *Partial deliveries*. (1) Contracting officers must, where the nature of the work permits, write contract statements of work and pricing arrangements that allow contractors to deliver and receive invoice payments for discrete portions of the work as soon as completed and found acceptable by the Government (see 32.102(d)).

(2) Unless specifically prohibited by the contract, the clause at 52.232-1, Payments, provides that the contractor is entitled to payment for accepted partial deliveries of supplies or partial performance of services that comply with all applicable contract requirements and for which prices can be calculated from the contract terms.

(d) *Contractor identifier*. Each payment or remittance advice will use the contractor invoice number in addition to any Government or contract information in describing any payment made.

(e) *Discounts*. When a discount for prompt payment is taken, the designated payment office will make payment to the contractor as close as possible to, but not later than, the end of the discount period. The discount period is specified by the contractor and is calculated from the date of the contractor's proper invoice. If the contractor has not placed a date on the invoice, the due date is calculated from the date the designated billing office receives a proper invoice, provided the agency annotates such invoice with the date of receipt at the time of receipt. When the discount date falls on a Saturday, Sunday, or legal holiday when Government offices are closed, the designated payment office may make payment on the following working day and take a discount. Payment terms are specified in the clause at 52.232-8, Discounts for Prompt Payment.

[FAC 2001-02, 66 FR 65347, 12/18/2001, effective 2/19/2002]

32.907 Interest penalties.

(a) *Late payment*. The designated payment office will pay an interest penalty automatically, without request from the contractor, when all of the following conditions, if applicable, have been met:

(1) The designated billing office received a proper invoice.

(2) The Government processed a receiving report or other Government documentation authorizing payment, and there was no disagreement over quantity, quality, or contractor compliance with any contract requirement.

(3) In the case of a final invoice, the payment amount is not subject to further contract settlement actions between the Government and the contractor.

(4) The designated payment office paid the contractor after the due date.

(5) In the case of interim payments on cost-reimbursement contracts for services, when payment is made more than 30 days after the designated billing office receives a proper invoice.

(b) *Improperly taken discount*. The designated payment office will pay an interest penalty automatically, without request from the contractor, if the Government takes a discount for prompt payment improperly.

The interest penalty is calculated on the amount of discount taken for the period beginning with the first day after the end of the discount period through the date when the contractor is paid.

(c) *Failure to pay interest.* (1) The designated payment office will pay a penalty amount, in addition to the interest penalty amount, only if—

(i) The Government owes an interest penalty of $1 or more;

(ii) The designated payment office does not pay the interest penalty within 10 days after the date the invoice amount is paid; and

(iii) The contractor makes a written demand to the designated payment office for additional penalty payment in accordance with paragraph (c)(2) of this section, postmarked not later than 40 days after the date the invoice amount is paid.

(2)(i) Contractors must support written demands for additional penalty payments with the following data. The Government must not request additional data. Contractors must—

(A) Specifically assert that late payment interest is due under a specific invoice, and request payment of all overdue late payment interest penalty and such additional penalty as may be required;

(B) Attach a copy of the invoice on which the unpaid late payment interest is due; and

(C) State that payment of the principal has been received, including the date of receipt.

(ii) If there is no postmark or the postmark is illegible—

(A) The designated payment office that receives the demand will annotate it with the date of receipt, provided the demand is received on or before the 40th day after payment was made; or

(B) If the designated payment office fails to make the required annotation, the Government will determine the demand's validity based on the date the contractor has placed on the demand; provided such date is no later than the 40th day after payment was made.

(d) *Disagreements.* (1) The payment office will not pay interest penalties if payment delays are due to disagreement between the Government and contractor concerning—

(i) The payment amount;

(ii) Contract compliance; or

(iii) Amounts temporarily withheld or retained in accordance with the terms of the contract.

(2) The Government and the contractor must resolve claims involving disputes, and any interest that may be payable in accordance with the Disputes clause.

(e) *Computation of interest penalties.* The Government will compute interest penalties in accordance with OMB prompt payment regulations at 5 CFR part 1315. These regulations are available via the Internet at *http://www.fms.treas.gov/prompt/*.

(f) *Unavailability of funds.* The temporary unavailability of funds to make a timely payment does not relieve an agency from the obligation to pay interest penalties.

[FAC 2001-02, 66 FR 65347, 12/18/2001, effective 2/19/2002]

32.908 Contract clauses.

(a) Insert the clause at 52.232-26, Prompt Payment for Fixed-Price Architect-Engineer Contracts, in solicitations and contracts that contain the clause at 52.232-10, Payments Under Fixed-Price Architect- Engineer Contracts.

(1) As authorized in 32.904(c)(2), the contracting officer may modify the date in paragraph (a)(4)(i) of the clause to specify a period longer than 7 days for constructive acceptance or constructive approval, if required to afford the Government a practicable opportunity to inspect and test the supplies furnished or evaluate the services performed.

(2) As provided in 32.903, agency policies and procedures may authorize amendment of paragraphs (a)(1)(i) and (ii) of the clause to insert a period shorter than 30 days (but not less than 7 days) for making contract invoice payments.

(b) Insert the clause at 52.232-27, Prompt Payment for Construction Contracts, in all solicitations and contracts for construction (see part 36).

(1) As authorized in 32.904(d)(1)(i)(B), the contracting officer may modify the date in paragraph (a)(1)(i)(A) of the clause to specify a period longer than 14 days if required to afford the Government a reasonable opportunity to adequately inspect the work and to determine the adequacy of the Contractor's performance under the contract.

(2) As authorized in 32.904(d)(2)(iv), the contracting officer may modify the date in paragraph (a)(4)(i) of the clause to specify a period longer than 7 days for constructive acceptance or constructive approval if required to afford the Government a reasonable opportunity to inspect and test the supplies furnished or evaluate the services performed.

(c) Insert the clause at 52.232-25, Prompt Payment, in all other solicitations and contracts, except when the clause at 52.212-4, Contract Terms and Conditions—Commercial Items, applies, or when payment terms and late payment penalties are established by other governmental authority (e.g., tariffs).

(1) As authorized in 32.904(b)(1)(ii)(B)(4), the contracting officer may modify the date in paragraph (a)(5)(i) of the clause to specify a period longer than 7 days for constructive acceptance, if required to afford the Government a reasonable opportunity to inspect and test the supplies furnished or to evaluate the services performed, except in the case of a contract for the purchase of a commercial item, including a brand-name commercial item for authorized resale (e.g., commissary items).

(2) As provided in 32.903, agency policies and procedures may authorize amendment of paragraphs (a)(1)(i) and (ii) of the clause to insert a period shorter than 30 days (but not less than 7 days) for making contract invoice payments.

(3) If the contract is a cost-reimbursement contract for services, use the clause with its Alternate I.

[FAC 2001-01, 66 FR 53485, 10/22/2001, effective 10/22/2001; FAC 2001-02, 66 FR 65347, 12/18/2001, effective 2/19/2002; FAC 2001-14, 68 FR 28092, 5/22/2003, effective 5/22/2003]

32.909 Contractor inquiries.

(a) Direct questions involving—

(1) Delinquent payments to the designated billing office or designated payment office; and

(2) Disagreements in payment amount or timing to the contracting officer for resolution. The contracting officer must coordinate within appropriate contracting channels and seek the advice of other offices as necessary to resolve disagreements.

(b) Small business concerns may contact the agency's local small business specialist or representative from the Office of Small and Disadvantaged Business Utilization to obtain additional assistance related to payment issues, late payment interest penalties, and information on the Prompt Payment Act.

[FAC 2001-02, 66 FR 65347, 12/18/2001, effective 2/19/2002]

SUBPART 32.10—PERFORMANCE-BASED PAYMENTS

32.1000 Scope of subpart.

This subpart provides policy and procedures for performance-based payments under noncommercial purchases pursuant to subpart 32.1.

[FAC 90-33, 60 FR 49706, 9/26/95, effective 10/1/95; FAC 97-16, 65 FR 16274, 3/27/2000, effective 3/27/2000; FAC 2005-23, 72 FR 73219, 12/26/2007, effective 1/25/2008]

32.1001 Policy.

(a) Performance-based payments are the preferred Government financing method when the contracting officer finds them practical, and the contractor agrees to their use.

(b) Performance-based payments are contract financing payments that are not payment for accepted items.

(c) Performance-based payments are fully recoverable, in the same manner as progress payments, in the event of default.

(d) Performance-based payments are contract financing payments and, therefore, are not subject to the interest-penalty provisions of prompt payment (see subpart 32.9). These payments shall be made in accordance with the agency policy.

(e) Performance-based payments shall not be used for—

(1) Payments under cost-reimbursement line items;

(2) Contracts for architect-engineer services or construction, or for shipbuilding or ship conversion, alteration, or repair, when the contracts provide for progress payments based upon a percentage or stage of completion; or

(3) Contracts awarded through sealed bid procedures.

[FAC 97-16, 65 FR 16274, 3/27/2000, effective 3/27/2000; FAC 2005-23, 72 FR 73219, 12/26/2007, effective 1/25/2008]

32.1002 Bases for performance-based payments.

Performance-based payments may be made on any of the following bases:

(a) Performance measured by objective, quantifiable methods.

(b) Accomplishment of defined events.

(c) Other quantifiable measures of results.

[FAC 90-33, 60 FR 49706, 9/26/95, effective 10/1/95; FAC 2005-23, 72 FR 73219, 12/26/2007, effective 1/25/2008]

32.1003 Criteria for use.

The contracting officer may use performance-based payments for individual orders and contracts provided–

(a) The contracting officer and offeror agree on the performance-based payment terms;

(b) The contract, individual order, or line item is a fixed-price type;

(c) For indefinite delivery contracts, the individual order does not provide for progress payments; and

(d) For other than indefinite delivery contracts, the contract does not provide for progress payments.

[FAC 90-33, 60 FR 49706, 9/26/95, effective 10/1/95; FAC 97-16, 65 FR 16274, 3/27/2000, effective 3/27/2000; FAC 2001-10, 67 FR 70520, 11/22/2002, effective 12/23/2002; FAC 2005-23, 72 FR 73219, 12/26/2007, effective 1/25/2008]

32.1004 Procedures.

Performance-based payments may be made either on a whole contract or on a deliverable item basis, unless otherwise prescribed by agency regulations. Financing payments to be made on a whole contract basis are applicable to the entire contract, and not to specific deliverable items. Financing payments to be made on a deliverable item basis are applicable to a specific individual deliverable item. (A deliverable item for these purposes is a separate item with a distinct unit price. Thus, a contract line item for 10 airplanes, with a unit price of $1,000,000 each, has 10 deliverable items-the separate planes. A contract line item for 1 lot of 10 airplanes, with a lot price of $10,000,000, has only one deliverable item-the lot.)

(a) *Establishing performance bases.* (1) The basis for performance-based payments may be either specifically described events (e.g., milestones) or some measurable criterion of performance. Each event or performance criterion that will trigger a finance payment shall be an integral and necessary part of contract performance and shall be identified in the contract, along with a description of what constitutes successful performance of the event or attainment of the performance criterion. The signing of contracts or modifications, the exercise of options, the passage of time, or other such occurrences do not represent meaningful efforts or actions and shall not be identified as events or criteria for performance-based payments. An event need not be a critical event in order to trigger a payment, but the Government must be able to readily verify successful performance of each such event or performance criterion.

(2) Events or criteria may be either severable or cumulative. The successful completion of a severable event or criterion is independent of the accomplishment of any other event or criterion. Conversely, the successful accomplishment of a cumulative event or criterion is dependent upon the previous accomplishment of another event. A contract may provide for more than one

series of severable and/or cumulative performance events or criteria performed in parallel. The contracting officer shall include the following in the contract:

(i) The contract shall not permit payment for a cumulative event or criterion until the dependent event or criterion has been successfully completed.

(ii) The contract shall specifically identify severable events or criteria.

(iii) The contract shall specifically identify cumulative events or criteria and identify which events or criteria are preconditions for the successful achievement of each event or criterion.

(iv) Because performance-based payments are contract financing, events or criteria shall not serve as a vehicle to reward the contractor for completion of performance levels over and above what is required for successful completion of the contract.

(v) If payment of performance-based finance amounts is on a deliverable item basis, each event or performance criterion shall be part of the performance necessary for that deliverable item and shall be identified to a specific line item or subline item.

(b) *Establishing performance-based finance payment amounts.*

(1) The contracting officer shall establish a complete, fully defined schedule of events or performance criteria and payment amounts when negotiating contract terms. If a contract action significantly affects the price, or event or performance criterion, the contracting officer responsible for pricing the contract modification shall adjust the performance-based payment schedule appropriately.

(2) Total performance-based payments shall—

(i) Reflect prudent contract financing provided only to the extent needed for contract performance (see 32.104(a)); and

(ii) Not exceed 90 percent of the contract price if on a whole contract basis, or 90 percent of the delivery item price if on a delivery item basis.

(3) The contract shall specifically state the amount of each performance-based payment either as a dollar amount or as a percentage of a specifically identified price (e.g., contract price or unit price of the deliverable item). The payment of contract financing has a cost to the Government in terms of interest paid by the Treasury to borrow funds to make the payment. Because the contracting officer has wide discretion as to the timing and amount of the performance-based payments, the contracting officer shall ensure that—

(i) The total contract price is fair and reasonable, all factors considered; and

(ii) Performance-based payment amounts are commensurate with the value of the performance event or performance criterion and are not expected to result in an unreasonably low or negative level of contractor investment in the contract. To confirm sufficient investment, the contracting officer may request expenditure profile information from offerors, but only if other information in the proposal, or information otherwise available to the contracting officer, is expected to be insufficient.

(4) Unless agency procedures prescribe the bases for establishing performance-based payment amounts, contracting officers may establish them on any rational basis, including (but not limited to)—

(i) Engineering estimates of stages of completion;

(ii) Engineering estimates of hours or other measures of effort to be expended in performance of an event or achievement of a performance criterion; or

(iii) The estimated projected cost of performance of particular events.

(5) When subsequent contract modifications are issued, the contracting officer shall adjust the performance-based payment schedule as necessary to reflect the actions required by those contract modifications.

(c) *Instructions for multiple appropriations.* If there is more than one appropriation account (or subaccount) funding payments on the contract, the contracting officer shall provide instructions to the Government payment office for distribution of financing payments to the respective funds accounts.

Distribution instructions shall be consistent with the contract's liquidation provisions.

(d) *Liquidating performance-based finance payments.* Performance-based amounts shall be liquidated by deducting a percentage or a designated dollar amount from the delivery payments. The contracting officer shall specify the liquidation rate or designated dollar amount in the contract. The method of liquidation shall ensure complete liquidation no later than final payment.

(1) If the contracting officer establishes the performance-based payments on a delivery item basis, the liquidation amount for each line item is the percent of that delivery item price that was previously paid under performance-based finance payments or the designated dollar amount.

(2) If the performance-based finance payments are on a whole contract basis, liquidation is by predesignated liquidation amounts or liquidation percentages.

(e) *Competitive negotiated solicitations.* (1) If a solicitation requests offerors to propose performance-based payments, the solicitation shall specify—

(i) What, if any, terms shall be included in all offers; and

(ii) The extent to which and how offeror-proposed performance-based payment terms will be evaluated. Unless agencies prescribe other evaluation procedures, if the contracting officer anticipates that the cost of providing performance-based payments would have a significant impact on determining the best value offer, the solicitation should state that the evaluation of the offeror's proposed prices will include an adjustment to reflect the estimated cost to the Government of providing each offeror's proposed performance-based payments (see Alternate I to the provision at 52.232-28).

(2) The contracting officer shall—

(i) Review the proposed terms to ensure they comply with this section; and

(ii) Use the adjustment method at 32.205(c) if the price is to be adjusted for evaluation purposes in accordance with paragraph (e)(1)(ii) of this section.

[FAC 2005-23, 72 FR 73219, 12/26/2007, effective 1/25/2008; FAC 2005-95, 82 FR 4709, 1/13/2017, effective 1/13/2017]

32.1005 Solicitation provision and contract clause.

(a) Insert the clause at 52.232-32, Performance-Based Payments, in—

(1) Solicitatations that may result in contracts providing for performance-based payments; and—

(2) Fixed-price contracts under which the Government will provide performance-based payments.

(b)(1) Insert the solicitation provision at 52.232-28, Invitation to Propose Performance-Based Payments, in negotiated solicitations that invite offerors to propose performance-based payments.

(2) Use the provision with its Alternate I in competitive negotiated solicitations if the Government intends to adjust proposed prices for proposal evaluation purposes (see 32.1004(e)).

[FAC 97-16, 65 FR 16274, 3/27/2000, effective 3/27/2000; FAC 2005-23, 72 FR 73219, 12/26/2007, effective 1/25/2008]

32.1006 [Removed and Reserved]

[Removed and Reserved, FAC 97-16, 65 FR 16274, 3/27/2000, effective 3/27/2000]

32.1007 Administration and payment of performance-based payments.

(a) *Responsibility.* The contracting officer responsible for administering performance-based payments (see 42.302(a)(13)) for the contract shall review and approve all performance-based payments for that contract.

(b) *Approval of financing requests.* Unless otherwise provided in agency regulations, or by agreement with the appropriate payment official—

(1) The contracting officer shall be responsible for receiving, approving, and transmitting all performance-based payment requests to the appropriate payment office; and

(2) Each approval shall specify the amount to be paid, necessary contractual informa-

tion, and the appropriation account(s) (see 32.1004(c)) to be charged for the payment.

(c) *Reviews.* The contracting officer is responsible for determining what reviews are required for protection of the Government's interests. The contracting officer should consider the contractor's experience, performance record, reliability, financial strength, and the adequacy of controls established by the contractor for the administration of performance-based payments. Based upon the risk to the Government, post-payment reviews and verifications should normally be arranged as considered appropriate by the contracting officer. If considered necessary by the contracting officer, pre-payment reviews may be required.

(d) *Incomplete performance.* The contracting officer shall not approve a performance-based payment until the specified event or performance criterion has been successfully accomplished in accordance with the contract. If an event is cumulative, the contracting officer shall not approve the performance-based payment unless all identified preceding events or criteria are accomplished.

(e) *Government-caused delay.* Entitlement to a performance-based payment is solely on the basis of successful performance of the specified events or performance criteria. However, if there is a Government-caused delay, the contracting officer may renegotiate the performance-based payment schedule to facilitate contractor billings for any successfully accomplished portions of the delayed event or criterion.

[FAC 90-33, 60 FR 49706, 9/26/95, effective 10/1/95; FAC 2005-23, 72 FR 73219, 12/26/2007, effective 1/25/2008; FAC 2005-50, 76 FR 14543, 3/16/2011, effective 3/16/2011; FAC 2005-56, 77 FR 12925, 3/2/2012, effective 4/2/2012]

32.1008 Suspension or reduction of performance-based payments.

The contracting officer shall apply the policy and procedures in paragraphs (a), (b), (c), and (e) of 32.503-6, Suspension or reduction of payments, whenever exercising the Government's rights to suspend or reduce performance-based payments in accordance with paragraph (e) of the clause at 52.232-32, Performance-Based Payments.

[FAC 90-33, 60 FR 49706, 9/26/95, effective 10/1/95]

32.1009 Title.

(a) Since the clause at 52.232-32, Performance-Based Payments, gives the Government title to the property described in paragraph (f) of the clause, the contracting officer shall ensure that the Government title is not compromised by other encumbrances. Ordinarily, the contracting officer, in the absence of reason to believe otherwise, may rely upon the contractor's certification contained in the payment request.

(b) If the contracting officer becomes aware of any arrangement or condition that would impair the Government's title to the property affected by the Performance-Based Payments clause, the contracting officer shall require additional protective provisions.

(c) The existence of any such encumbrance is a violation of the contractor's obligations under the contract, and the contracting officer may, if necessary, suspend or reduce payments under the terms of the Performance-Based Payments clause covering failure to comply with a material requirement of the contract. In addition, if the contractor fails to disclose an existing encumbrance in the certification, the contracting officer should consult with legal counsel concerning possible violation of 31 U.S.C. 3729, the False Claims Act.

[FAC 90-33, 60 FR 49706, 9/26/95, effective 10/1/95; FAC 2005-23, 72 FR 73215, 12/26/2007, effective 1/25/2008]

32.1010 Risk of loss.

(a) Under the clause at 52.232-32, Performance-Based Payments, and except for normal spoilage, the contractor bears the risk of loss for Government property, even though title is vested in the Government, unless the Government has expressly assumed this risk. The clauses prescribed in this regulation related to performance-based payments, default, and terminations do not constitute a Government assumption of risk.

(b) If a loss occurs in connection with property for which the contractor bears the risk, and the property is needed for performance, the contractor is obligated to repay the Government the performance-based payments related to the property.

(c) The contractor is not obligated to pay for the loss of property for which the Government has assumed the risk of loss. However, a serious loss may impede the satisfactory progress of contract performance, so that the contracting officer may need to act under paragraph (e)(2) of the Performance-Based Payments clause. In addition, while the contractor is not required to repay previous performance-based payments in the event of a loss for which the Government has assumed the risk, such a loss may prevent the contractor from making the certification required by the Performance-Based Payments clause.

[FAC 90-33, 60 FR 49706, 9/26/95, effective 10/1/95; FAC 2005-43, 75 FR 38675, 7/2/2010, effective 8/2/2010; FAC 2005-56, 77 FR 12937, 3/2/2012, effective 4/2/2012]

SUBPART 32.11—ELECTRONIC FUNDS TRANSFER

32.1100 Scope of subpart.

This subpart provides policy and procedures for contract financing and delivery payments to contractors by electronic funds transfer (EFT).

[FAC 97-11, 64 FR 10530, 3/4/99, effective 5/3/99]

32.1101 Statutory requirements.

31 U.S.C. 3332 requires, subject to implementing regulations of the Secretary of the Treasury at 31 CFR part 208, that EFT be used to make all contract payments.

[FAC 97-11, 64 FR 10530, 3/4/99, effective 5/3/99]

32.1102 Definitions.

As used in this subpart—

Electronic funds transfer information (EFT) means information necessary for making a payment by EFT through specified EFT mechanisms.

Governmentwide commercial purchase card means a card that is similar in nature to a commercial credit card that is used to make financing and delivery payments for supplies and services. The purchase card is an EFT method and it may be used as a means to meet the requirement to pay by EFT, to the extent that purchase card limits do not preclude such payments.

Payment information means the payment advice provided by the Government to the contractor that identifies what the payment is for, any computations or adjustments made by the Government, and any information required by the Prompt Payment Act.

[FAC 97-11, 64 FR 10530, 3/4/99, effective 5/3/99; FAC 97-22, 66 FR 2116, 1/10/2001, effective 3/12/2001, delay of effective date, 66 FR 14259, 3/9/2001, effective 5/11/2001]

32.1103 Applicability.

The Government shall provide all contract payments through EFT except if—

(a) The office making payment under a contract that requires payment by EFT, loses the ability to release payment by EFT. To the extent authorized by 31 CFR part 208, the payment office shall make necessary payments pursuant to paragraph (a)(2) of the clause at either 52.232-33 or 52.232-34 until such time as it can make EFT payments;

(b) The payment is to be received by or on behalf of the contractor outside the United States and Puerto Rico (but see 32.1106(b));

(c) A contract is paid in other than United States currency (but see 32.1106(b));

(d) Payment by EFT under a classified contract could compromise the safeguarding of classified information or national security , or where arrangements for appropriate EFT payments would be impractical due to security considerations;

(e) A contract is awarded by a deployed contracting officer in the course of military operations, including, but not limited to, contingency operations as defined in 2.101, or a contract is awarded by any contracting officer in the conduct of emergency operations, such as responses to natural disasters or national or civil emergencies, if—

(1) EFT is not known to be possible; or—

(2) EFT payment would not support the objectives of the operation;

(f) The agency does not expect to make more than one payment to the same recipient within a one-year period;

(g) An agency's need for supplies and services is of such unusual and compelling urgency that the Government would be seriously injured unless payment is made by a method other than EFT;

(h) There is only one source for supplies and services and the Government would be seriously injured unless payment is made by a method other than EFT; or—

(i) Otherwise authorized by Department of the Treasury Regulations at 31 CFR part 208.

[FAC 97-11, 64 FR 10530, 3/4/99, effective 5/3/99; FAC 2001-04, 67 FR 6112, 2/8/2002, effective 2/20/2002; FAC 2001-13, 68 FR 13202, 3/18/2003, effective 4/17/2003]

32.1104 Protection of EFT information.

The Government shall protect against improper disclosure of contractors' EFT information.

[FAC 97-11, 64 FR 10530, 3/4/99, effective 5/3/99]

32.1105 Assignment of claims.

The use of EFT payment methods is not a substitute for a properly executed assignment of claims in accordance with Subpart 32.8. EFT information that shows the ultimate recipient of the transfer to be other than the contractor, in the absence of a proper assignment of claims, is considered to be incorrect EFT information within the meaning of the "Suspension of Payment" paragraphs of the EFT clauses at 52.232-33 and 52.232-34.

[FAC 97-11, 64 FR 10530, 3/4/99, effective 5/3/99]

32.1106 EFT mechanisms.

(a) *Domestic EFT mechanisms.* The EFT clauses at 52.232-33 and 52.232-34are designed for use with the domestic United States banking system, using United States currency, and only the specified mechanisms (U.S. Automated Clearing House, and Fedwire Transfer System) of EFT. However, the head of an agency may authorize the use of any other EFT mechanism for domestic EFT with the concurrence of the office or agency responsible for making payments.

(b) *Nondomestic EFT mechanisms and other than United States currency.* The Government shall provide payment by other than EFT for payments received by or on behalf of the contractor outside the United States and Puerto Rico or for contracts paid in other than United States currency. However, the head of an agency may authorize appropriate use of EFT with the concurrence of the office or agency responsible for making payments if—

(1) The political, financial, and communications infrastructure in a foreign country supports payment by EFT; or

(2) Payments of other than United States currency may be made safely.

[FAC 97-11, 64 FR 10530, 3/4/99, effective 5/3/99]

32.1107 Payment information.

The payment or disbursing office shall forward to the contractor available payment information that is suitable for transmission as of the date of release of the EFT instruction to the Federal Reserve System.

[FAC 97-11, 64 FR 10530, 3/4/99, effective 5/3/99]

32.1108 Payment by Governmentwide commercial purchase card.

A Governmentwide commercial purchase card charge authorizes the third party (e.g., financial institution) that issued the purchase card to make immediate payment to the contractor. The Government reimburses the third party at a later date for the third party's payment to the contractor.

(a) The clause at 52.232-36, Payment by Third Party, governs when a contractor submits a charge against the purchase card for contract payment. The clause provides that the contractor shall make such payment requests by a charge to a Government account with the third party at the time the payment clause(s) of the contract authorizes the contractor to submit a request for payment, and for the amount due in accordance with the terms of the contract. To the extent that such a payment would otherwise be approved, the charge against the purchase card should not be disputed when the charge is reported to the Government by the third party. To the extent that such payment would otherwise not have been approved, an authorized individual (see 1.603-3) shall take action to remove the charge, such as by disputing the charge with the third party or by requesting that the contractor credit the charge back to the Government under the contract.

(b)(1) Written contracts to be paid by purchase card should include the clause at 52.232-36, Payment by Third Party, as prescribed by 32.1110(d). However, payment by a purchase card also may be made under a contract that does not contain the clause to the extent the contractor agrees to accept that method of payment.

(2)(i) When it is contemplated that the Governmentwide commercial purchase card will be used as the method of payment, and the contract or order is above the micro-purchase threshold, contracting officers are required to verify by looking in the System for Award Management (SAM) whether the contractor has any delinquent debt subject to collection under the Treasury Offset Program (TOP) at contract award and order placement. Information on TOP is available at *http://fms.treas.gov/debt/index.html*.

(ii) The contracting officer shall not authorize the Governmentwide commercial purchase card as a method of payment during any period the SAM indicates that the contractor has delinquent debt subject to collection under the TOP. In such cases, payments under the contract shall be made in accordance with the clause at 52.232-33, Payment by Electronic Funds Transfer—System for Award Management, or 52.232-34, Payment by Electronic Funds Transfer—Other Than System for Award Management, as appropriate (see FAR 32.1110(d)).

(iii) Contracting officers shall not use the presence of the SAM debt flag indicator to exclude a contractor from receipt of the contract award or issuance or placement of an order.

(iv) The contracting officer may take steps to authorize payment by Governmentwide commercial purchase card when a contractor alerts the contracting officer that the SAM debt flag indicator has been changed to no longer show a delinquent debt.

(c) The clause at 52.232-36, Payment by Third Party, requires that the contract—

(1) Identify the third party and the particular purchase card to be used; and

(2) Not include the purchase card account number. The purchase card account number should be provided separately to the contractor.

[FAC 97-11, 64 FR 10530, 3/4/99, effective 5/3/99; FAC 2005-38, 74 FR 65600, 12/10/2009, effective 2/1/2010; FAC 2005-67, 78 FR 37676, 6/21/2013, effective 7/22/2013; FAC 2005-101, 83 FR 48691, 9/26/2018, effective 10/26/2018]

32.1109 EFT information submitted by offerors.

If offerors are required to submit EFT information prior to award, the successful offeror is not responsible for resubmitting this information after award of the contract except to make changes, or to place the information on invoices if required by agency procedures. Therefore, contracting officers shall forward EFT information provided by the successful offeror to the appropriate office.

[FAC 97-11, 64 FR 10530, 3/4/99, effective 5/3/99]

32.1110 Solicitations provision and contract clauses.

(a) The contracting officer shall insert the clause at—

(1) 52.232-33, Payment by Electronic Funds Transfer—System for Award Management, in solicitations and contracts that include the provision at 52.204-7, System for Award Management, or an agency clause that requires a contractor to be registered in SAM and maintain registration until final payment, unless—

(i) Payment will be made through a third party arrangement (see 13.301 and paragraph (d) of this section); or

(ii) An exception listed in 32.1103(a) through (i) applies.

(2)(i) 52.232-34, Payment by Electronic Funds Transfer--Other than System for Award Management, in solicitations and contracts that require EFT as the method for payment but do not include the provision at 52.204-7, System for Award Management, or a similar agency clause that requires the contractor to be registered in SAM.

(ii)(A) If permitted by agency procedures, the contracting officer may insert in paragraph (b)(1) of the clause, a particular time after award, such as a fixed number of days, or event such as the submission of the first request for payment.

(B) If no agency procedures are prescribed, the time period inserted in paragraph (b)(1) of the clause shall be "no later than 15 days prior to submission of the first request for payment."

(b) If the head of the agency has authorized, in accordance with 32.1106, to use a nondomestic EFT mechanism, the contracting officer shall insert in solicitations and contracts a clause substantially the same as 52.232-33 or 52.232-34 that clearly addresses the nondomestic EFT mechanism.

(c) If EFT information is to be submitted to other than the payment office in accordance with agency procedures, the contracting officer shall insert in solicitations and contracts the clause at 52.232-35, Designation of Office for Government Receipt of Electronic Funds Transfer Information, or a clause substantially the same as 52.232-35 that clearly informs the contractor where to send the EFT information.

(d) If payment under a written contract will be made by a charge to a Government account with a third party such as a Government wide commercial purchase card, then the contracting officer shall insert the clause at 52.232-36, Payment by Third Party, in solicitations and contracts. Payment by a purchase card may also be made under a contract that does not contain the clause at 52.232-36, to the extent the contractor agrees to accept that method of payment. When the clause at 52.232-36 is included in a solicitation or contract, the contracting officer shall also insert the clause at 52.232-33, Payment by Electronic Funds Transfer—System for Award Management, or 52.232-34, Payment by Electronic Funds Transfer—Other Than System for Award Management, as appropriate.

(e) If the contract or agreement provides for the use of delivery orders, and provides that the ordering office designate the method of payment for individual orders, the contracting officer shall insert, in the solicitation and contract or agreement, the clause at 52.232-37, Multiple Payment Arrangements, and, to the extent they are applicable, the clauses at—

(1) 52.232-33, Payment by Electronic Funds Transfer--System for Award Management;

(2) 52.232-34, Payment by Electronic Funds Transfer--Other than System for Award Management; and

(3) 52.232-36, Payment by Third Party.

(f) If more than one disbursing office will make payment under a contract or agreement, the contracting officer, or ordering office (if the contract provides for choices between EFT clauses on individual orders or classes of orders), shall include or identify the EFT clause appropriate for each office and shall identify the applicability by disbursing office and line item.

(g) If the solicitation contains the clause at 52.232-34, Payment by Electronic Funds Transfer–Other than System for Award Management, and an offeror is required to submit EFT information prior to award—

(1) The contracting officer shall insert in the solicitation the provision at 52.232-38, Submission of Electronic Funds Transfer Information with Offer, or a provision substantially the same; and

(2) For sealed bid solicitations, the contracting officer shall amend 52.232-38 to ensure that a bidder's EFT information—

(i) Is not a part of the bid to be opened at the public opening; and

(ii) May not be released to members of the general public who request a copy of the bid.

[FAC 97-11, 64 FR 10530, 3/4/99, effective 5/3/99; 2001-16, Final rule, 68 FR 56669, 10/1/2003, effective 10/1/2003; Correction, 68 FR 61866, 10/30/2003, effective 10/30/2003; FAC 2005-38, 74 FR 65600, 12/10/2009, effective 2/1/2010; FAC 2005-62, 77 FR 69715, 11/20/2012, effective 12/20/2012; FAC 2005-67, 78 FR 37676, 6/21/2013, effective 7/22/2013; FAC 2005-95, 82 FR 4709, 1/13/2017, effective 1/13/2017; FAC 2005-101, 83 FR 48691, 9/26/2018, effective 10/26/2018]

PART 33—PROTESTS, DISPUTES, AND APPEALS

Table of Contents

Scope of part 33.000
General 33.001

Subpart 33.1—Protests

Definitions 33.101
General 33.102
Protests to the agency 33.103
Protests to GAO 33.104
Protests at the U.S. Court of Federal Claims 33.105
Solicitation provision and contract clause 33.106

Subpart 33.2—Disputes and Appeals

Definitions 33.201
Disputes 33.202
Applicability 33.203
Policy 33.204
Relationship of the Disputes statute to Pub. L. 85-804 . . . . . 33.205
Initiation of a claim 33.206
Contractor certification 33.207
Interest on claims 33.208
Suspected fraudulent claims 33.209
Contracting officer's authority 33.210
Contracting officer's decision 33.211
Contracting officer's duties upon appeal 33.212
Obligation to continue performance 33.213
Alternative dispute resolution (ADR) 33.214
Contract clauses 33.215

PART 33—PROTESTS, DISPUTES, AND APPEALS

33.000 Scope of part.

This part prescribes policies and procedures for filing protests and for processing contract disputes and appeals.

[FAC 84-6, 50 FR 2270, 1/15/85, effective 1/15/85; FAC 84-6, 50 FR 2270, 1/15/85, effective 1/15/85]

33.001 General.

There are other Federal court-related protest authorities and dispute-appeal authorities that are not covered by this part of the FAR, e.g., 28 U.S.C. 1491 for Court of Federal Claims jurisdiction. Contracting officers should contact their designated legal advisor for additional information whenever they become aware of any litigation related to their contracts.

[FAC 2005-61, 77 FR 56742, 9/13/2012, effective 9/13/2012]

SUBPART 33.1—PROTESTS

33.101 Definitions.

As used in this subpart—

Day means a calendar day, unless otherwise specified. In the computation of any period—

(1) The day of the act, event, or default from which the designated period of time begins to run is not included; and

(2) The last day after the act, event, or default is included unless—

(i) The last day is a Saturday, Sunday, or Federal holiday; or

(ii) In the case of a filing of a paper at any appropriate administrative forum, the last day is a day on which weather or other conditions cause the closing of the forum for all or part of the day, in which event the next day on which the appropriate administrative forum is open is included.

Filed means the complete receipt of any document by an agency before its close of business. Documents received after close of business are considered filed as of the next day. Unless otherwise stated, the agency close of business is presumed to be 4:30 p.m., local time.

Interested Party for the purpose of filing a protest means an actual or prospective offeror whose direct economic interest would be affected by the award of a contract or by the failure to award a contract.

Protest means a written objection by an interested party to any of the following:

(1) A solicitation or other request by an agency for offers for a contract for the procurement of property or services.

(2) The cancellation of the solicitation or other request.

(3) An award or proposed award of the contract.

(4) A termination or cancellation of an award of the contract, if the written objection contains an allegation that the termination or cancellation is based in whole or in part on improprieties concerning the award of the contract.

Protest venue means protests filed with the agency, the Government Accountability Office, or the U.S. Court of Federal Claims. U.S. District Courts do not have any bid protest jurisdiction.

[FAC 84-6, 50 FR 2270, 1/15/85, effective 1/15/85; FAC 84-40, 53 FR 43391, 10/26/88, effective 11/25/88; FAC 84-46, 54 FR 19827, 5/8/89, effective 6/7/89; FAC 90-32, 60 FR 48206, 9/18/95, effective 10/1/95; FAC 97-3, 62 FR 64912, 12/9/97, effective 2/9/98; FAC 97-22, 66 FR 2116, 1/10/2001, effective 3/12/2001; Delay of effective date, 66 FR 14259, 3/9/2001, effective 5/11/2001; FAC 2005-61, 77 FR 56742, 9/13/2012, effective 9/13/2012]

33.102 General.

(a) Without regard to the protest venue, contracting officers shall consider all protests and seek legal advice, whether protests are submitted before or after award and whether filed directly with the agency, the Government Accountability Office (GAO), or the U.S. Court of Federal Claims. (*See* 19.302 for protests of small business status, 19.305 for protests of disadvantaged business status, 19.306 for protests of HUBZone small business status, and 19.307 for protests of service-disabled veteran-owned small business status, and 19.308 for protests of the status of an economically disadvantaged women-owned small business concern or of a women-owned small business concern eligible under the Women-Owned Small Business Program.)

(b) If, in connection with a protest, the head of an agency determines that a solicitation, proposed award, or award does not comply with the requirements of law or regulation, the head of the agency may—

(1) Take any action that could have been recommended by the Comptroller General had the protest been filed with the Government Accountability Office;

(2) Pay appropriate costs as stated in 33.104(h); and

(3) Require the awardee to reimburse the Government's costs, as provided in this paragraph, where a postaward protest is sustained as the result of an awardee's intentional or negligent misstatement, misrepresentation, or miscertification. In addition to any other remedy available, and pursuant to the requirements of Subpart 32.6, the Government may collect this debt by offsetting the amount against any payment due the awardee under any contract between the awardee and the Government.

(i) When a protest is sustained by GAO under circumstances that may allow the Government to seek reimbursement for protest costs, the contracting officer will determine whether the protest was sustained based on the awardee's negligent or intentional misrepresentation. If the protest was sustained on several issues, protest costs shall be apportioned according to the costs attributable to the awardee's actions.

(ii) The contracting officer shall review the amount of the debt, degree of the awardee's fault, and costs of collection, to determine whether a demand for reimbursement ought to be made. If it is in the best interests of the Government to seek reimbursement, the contracting officer shall notify the contractor in writing of the nature and amount of the debt, and the intention to collect by offset if necessary. Prior to issuing a final decision, the contracting officer shall afford the contractor an opportunity to inspect and copy agency records pertaining to the debt to the extent permitted by statute and regulation, and to request review of the matter by the head of the contracting activity.

(iii) When appropriate, the contracting officer shall also refer the matter to the agency debarment official for consideration under Subpart 9.4.

(c) In accordance with 31 U.S.C. 1558, with respect to any protest filed with the GAO, if the funds available to the agency for a contract at the time a protest is filed in connection with a solicitation for, proposed award of, or award of such a contract would otherwise expire, such funds shall remain available for obligation for 100 days after the date on which the final ruling is made on the protest. A ruling is considered final on the date on which the time allowed for filing an appeal or request for reconsideration has expired, or the date on which a decision is rendered on such appeal or request, whichever is later.

(d) *Protest likely after award.* The contracting officer may stay performance of a contract within the time period contained in subparagraph 33.104(c)(1) if the contracting officer makes a written determination that—

(1) A protest is likely to be filed; and

(2) Delay of performance is, under the circumstances, in the best interests of the United States.

(e) An interested party wishing to protest is encouraged to seek resolution within the agency (see 33.103) before filing a protest with the GAO, but may protest to the GAO in accordance with GAO regulations (4 CFR Part 21).

(f) No person may file a protest at GAO for a procurement integrity violation unless that person reported to the contracting officer the information constituting evidence of the violation within 14 days after the person first discovered the possible violation (41 U.S.C. 2106).

[FAC 84-6, 50 FR 2270, 1/15/85, effective 1/15/85; Final rule, 55 FR 38517, 9/18/90; FAC 90-3, 55 FR 52795, 12/21/90, effective 1/22/91; FAC 90-32, 60 FR 48206, 9/18/95, effective 10/1/95; FAC 90-41, 61 FR 41466,

8/8/96, effective 8/8/96, finalized without change, FAC 97-3, 62 FR 64912, 12/9/97, effective 2/9/98; FAC 90-43, Interim rule, 61 FR 67408, 12/20/96, effective 12/20/96, finalized without change, FAC 97-1, 62 FR 44802, 8/22/97, effective 10/21/97; FAC 90-45, Final rule, 62 FR 224, 1/2/97, effective 1/1/97; FAC 97-6, 63 FR 35719, 6/30/98, effective 10/1/98, finalized without change, FAC 97-13, 7/2/99; FAC 2001-23, 69 FR 25273, 5/5/2004, effective 5/5/2004; FAC 2005-02, 70 FR 14950, 3/23/2005, effective 3/23/2005; FAC 2005-10, 71 FR 36941, 6/28/2006, effective 6/28/2006; FAC 2005-13, 71 FR 57380, 9/28/2006, effective 9/28/2006; FAC 2005-47, 75 77727, 12/13/2010, effective 1/12/2011; FAC 2005-51, 76 FR 18304, 4/1/2011, effective 4/1/2011; FAC 2005-56, 77 FR 12913, 3/2/2012, effective 4/2/2012; FAC 2005-61, 77 FR 56742, 9/13/2012, effective 9/13/2012; FAC 2005-73, 79 FR 24192, 4/29/2014, effective 5/29/2014]

33.103 Protests to the agency.

(a) *Reference*. Executive Order 12979, Agency Procurement Protests, establishes policy on agency procurement protests.

(b) Prior to submission of an agency protest, all parties shall use their best efforts to resolve concerns raised by an interested party at the contracting officer level through open and frank discussions.

(c) The agency should provide for inexpensive, informal, procedurally simple, and expeditious resolution of protests. Where appropriate, the use of alternative dispute resolution techniques, third party neutrals, and another agency's personnel are acceptable protest resolution methods.

(d) The following procedures are established to resolve agency protests effectively, to build confidence in the Government's acquisition system, and to reduce protests outside of the agency:

(1) Protests shall be concise and logically presented to facilitate review by the agency. Failure to substantially comply with any of the requirements of subparagraph (d)(2) of this section may be grounds for dismissal of the protest.

(2) Protests shall include the following information:

(i) Name, address, and fax and telephone numbers of the protester.

(ii) Solicitation or contract number.

(iii) Detailed statement of the legal and factual grounds for the protest, to include a description of resulting prejudice to the protester.

(iv) Copies of relevant documents.

(v) Request for a ruling by the agency.

(vi) Statement as to the form of relief requested.

(vii) All information establishing that the protester is an interested party for the purpose of filing a protest.

(viii) All information establishing the timeliness of the protest.

(3) All protests filed directly with the agency will be addressed to the contracting officer or other official designated to receive protests.

(4) In accordance with agency procedures, interested parties may request an independent review of their protest at a level above the contracting officer; solicitations should advise potential bidders and offerors that this review is available. Agency procedures and/or solicitations shall notify potential bidders and offerors whether this independent review is available as an alternative to consideration by the contracting officer of a protest or is available as an appeal of a contracting officer decision on a protest. Agencies shall designate the official(s) who are to conduct this independent review, but the official(s) need not be within the contracting officer's supervisory chain. When practicable, officials designated to conduct the independent review should not have had previous personal involvement in the procurement. If there is an agency appellate review of the contracting officer's decision on the protest, it will not extend GAO's timeliness requirements. Therefore, any subsequent protest to the GAO must be filed within 10 days of knowledge of initial adverse agency action (4 CFR 21.2(a)(3)).

(e) Protests based on alleged apparent improprieties in a solicitation shall be filed before bid opening or the closing date for receipt of proposals. In all other cases, protests shall be filed no later than 10 days after the basis of protest is known or should have been known, whichever is earlier. The agency, for good cause shown, or where it determines that a protest raises issues significant to the agency's acquisition system, may consider the merits of any protest which is not timely filed.

(f) *Action upon receipt of protest.* (1) Upon receipt of a protest before award, a contract may not be awarded, pending agency resolution of the protest, unless contract award is justified, in writing, for urgent and compelling reasons or is determined, in writing, to be in the best interest of the Government. Such justification or determination shall be approved at a level above the contracting officer, or by another official pursuant to agency procedures.

(2) If award is withheld pending agency resolution of the protest, the contracting officer will inform the offerors whose offers might become eligible for award of the contract. If appropriate, the offerors should be requested, before expiration of the time for acceptance of their offers, to extend the time for acceptance to avoid the need for resolicitation. In the event of failure to obtain such extension of offers, consideration should be given to proceeding with award pursuant to subparagraph (f)(1) of this section.

(3) Upon receipt of a protest within 10 days after contract award or within 5 days after a debriefing date offered to the protester under a timely debriefing request in accordance with 15.505 or 15.506, whichever is later, the contracting officer shall immediately suspend performance, pending resolution of the protest within the agency, including any review by an independent higher level official, unless continued performance is justified, in writing, for urgent and compelling reasons or is determined, in writing, to be in the best interest of the Government. Such justification or determination shall be approved at a level above the contracting officer, or by another official pursuant to agency procedures.

(4) Pursuing an agency protest does not extend the time for obtaining a stay at GAO. Agencies may include, as part of the agency protest process, a voluntary suspension period when agency protests are denied and the protester subsequently files at GAO.

(g) Agencies shall make their best efforts to resolve agency protests within 35 days after the protest is filed. To the extent permitted by law and regulation, the parties may exchange relevant information.

(h) Agency protest decisions shall be well-reasoned, and explain the agency position. The protest decision shall be provided to the protester using a method that provides evidence of receipt.

[FAC 90-40, 61 FR 39186, 7/26/96, effective 7/26/96; FAC 90-44, Final rule, 61 FR 69286, 12/31/96, effective 1/1/97; FAC 90-45, Final rule, 62 FR 224, 1/2/97, effective 3/3/97, corrected 62 FR 10709, 3/10/97; FAC 97-2, 62 FR 51224, 9/30/97, effective 10/10/97]

33.104 Protests to GAO.

Procedures for protests to GAO are found at 4 CFR Part 21 (GAO Bid Protest Regulations). In the event guidance concerning GAO procedure in this section conflicts with 4 CFR Part 21, 4 CFR Part 21 governs.

(a) *General procedures.* (1) A protester is required to furnish a copy of its complete protest to the official and location designated in the solicitation or, in the absence of such a designation, to the contracting officer, so it is received no later than 1 day after the protest is filed with the GAO. The GAO may dismiss the protest if the protester fails to furnish a complete copy of the protest within 1 day.

(2) Immediately after receipt of the GAO's written notice that a protest has been filed, the agency shall give notice of the protest to the contractor if the award has been made, or, if no award has been made, to all parties who appear to have a reasonable prospect of receiving award if the protest is denied. The agency shall furnish copies of the protest submissions to such parties with instructions to (i) communicate directly with the GAO, and (ii) provide copies of any such communication to the agency and to other participating parties when they become known. However, if the protester has identi-

fied sensitive information and requests a protective order, then the contracting officer shall obtain a redacted version from the protester to furnish to other interested parties, if one has not already been provided.

(3) (i) Upon notice that a protest has been filed with the GAO, the contracting officer shall immediately begin compiling the information necessary for a report to the GAO. The agency shall submit a complete report to the GAO within 30 days after the GAO notifies the agency by telephone that a protest has been filed, or within 20 days after receipt from the GAO of a determination to use the express option, unless the GAO—

(A) Advises the agency that the protest has been dismissed; or

(B) Authorizes a longer period in response to an agency's request for an extension. Any new date is documented in the agency's file.

(ii) When a protest is filed with the GAO, and an actual or prospective offeror so requests, the procuring agency shall, in accordance with any applicable protective orders, provide actual or prospective offerors reasonable access to the protest file. However, if the GAO dismisses the protest before the documents are submitted to the GAO, then no protest file need be made available. Information exempt from disclosure under 5 U.S.C. 552 may be redacted from the protest file. The protest file shall be made available to non-intervening actual or prospective offerors within a reasonable time after submittal of an agency report to the GAO. The protest file shall include an index and as appropriate—

(A) The protest;

(B) The offer submitted by the protester;

(C) The offer being considered for award or being protested;

(D) All relevant evaluation documents;

(E) The solicitation, including the specifications or portions relevant to the protest;

(F) The abstract of offers or relevant portions; and

(G) Any other documents that the agency determines are relevant to the protest, including documents specifically requested by the protester.

(iii) At least 5 days prior to the filing of the report, in cases in which the protester has filed a request for specific documents, the agency shall provide to all parties and the GAO a list of those documents, or portions of documents, that the agency has released to the protester or intends to produce in its report, and those documents that the agency intends to withhold from the protester and the reasons for the proposed withholding. Any objection to the scope of the agency's proposed disclosure or nondisclosure of the documents must be filed with the GAO and the other parties within 2 days after receipt of this list.

(iv) The agency report to the GAO shall include—

(A) A copy of the documents described in 33.104(a)(3)(ii);

(B) The contracting officer's signed statement of relevant facts, including a best estimate of the contract value, and a memorandum of law. The contracting officer's statement shall set forth findings, actions, and recommendations, and any additional evidence or information not provided in the protest file that may be necessary to determine the merits of the protest; and

(C) A list of parties being provided the documents.

(4) (i) At the same time the agency submits its report to the GAO, the agency shall furnish copies of its report to the protester and any intervenors. A party shall receive all relevant documents, except—

(A) Those that the agency has decided to withhold from that party for any reason, including those covered by a protective order issued by the GAO. Documents covered by a protective order shall be released only in accordance with the terms of the order. Examples of documents the agency may decide to exclude from a copy of the report include documents previously furnished to or prepared by a party; classified information; and information that would give the party a competitive advantage; and

(B) Protester's documents which the agency determines, pursuant to law or regulation, to withhold from any interested party.

(ii) (A) If the protester requests additional documents within 2 days after the protester knew the existence or relevance of additional documents, or should have known, the agency shall provide the requested documents to the GAO within 2 days of receipt of the request.

(B) The additional documents shall also be provided to the protester and other interested parties within this 2-day period unless the agency has decided to withhold them for any reason (see subdivision (a) (4) (i) of this section). This includes any documents covered by a protective order issued by the GAO. Documents covered by a protective order shall be provided only in accordance with the terms of the order.

(C) The agency shall notify the GAO of any documents withheld from the protester and other interested parties and shall state the reasons for withholding them.

(5) The GAO may issue protective orders which establish terms, conditions, and restrictions for the provision of any document to an interested party. Protective orders prohibit or restrict the disclosure by the party of procurement sensitive information, trade secrets or other proprietary or confidential research, development or commercial information that is contained in such document. Protective orders do not authorize withholding any documents or information from the United States Congress or an executive agency.

(i) *Requests for protective orders.* Any party seeking issuance of a protective order shall file its request with the GAO as soon as practicable after the protest is filed, with copies furnished simultaneously to all parties.

(ii) *Exclusions and rebuttals.* Within 2 days after receipt of a copy of the protective order request, any party may file with the GAO a request that particular documents be excluded from the coverage of the protective order, or that particular parties or individuals be included in or excluded from the protective order. Copies of the request shall be furnished simultaneously to all parties.

(iii) *Additional documents.* If the existence or relevance of additional documents first becomes evident after a protective order has been issued, any party may request that these additional documents be covered by the protective order. Any party to the protective order also may request that individuals not already covered by the protective order be included in the order. Requests shall be filed with the GAO, with copies furnished simultaneously to all parties.

(iv) *Sanctions and remedies.* The GAO may impose appropriate sanctions for any violation of the terms of the protective order. Improper disclosure of protected information will entitle the aggrieved party to all appropriate remedies under law or equity. The GAO may also take appropriate action against an agency which fails to provide documents designated in a protective order.

(6) The protester and other interested parties are required to furnish a copy of any comments on the agency report directly to the GAO within 10 days, or 5 days if express option is used, after receipt of the report, with copies provided to the contracting officer and to other participating interested parties. If a hearing is held, these comments are due within 5 days after the hearing.

(7) Agencies shall furnish the GAO with the name, title, and telephone number of one or more officials (in both field and headquarters offices, if desired) whom the GAO may contact who are knowledgeable about the subject matter of the protest. Each agency shall be responsible for promptly advising the GAO of any change in the designated officials.

(b) *Protests before award.* (1) When the agency has received notice from the GAO of a protest filed directly with the GAO, a contract may not be awarded unless authorized, in accordance with agency procedures, by the head of the contracting activity, on a nondelegable basis, upon a written finding that—

(i) Urgent and compelling circumstances which significantly affect the interest of the

United States will not permit awaiting the decision of the GAO; and

(ii) Award is likely to occur within 30 days of the written finding.

(2) A contract award shall not be authorized until the agency has notified the GAO of the finding in subparagraph (b)(1) of this section.

(3) When a protest against the making of an award is received and award will be withheld pending disposition of the protest, the contracting officer should inform the offerors whose offers might become eligible for award of the protest. If appropriate, those offerors should be requested, before expiration of the time for acceptance of their offer, to extend the time for acceptance to avoid the need for resolicitation. In the event of failure to obtain such extensions of offers, consideration should be given to proceeding under subparagraph (b)(1) of this section.

(c) *Protests after award.* (1) When the agency receives notice of a protest from the GAO within 10 days after contract award or within 5 days after a debriefing date offered to the protester for any debriefing that is required by 15.505 or 15.506, whichever is later, the contracting officer shall immediately suspend performance or terminate the awarded contract, except as provided in paragraphs (c) (2) and (3) of this section.

(2) In accordance with agency procedures, the head of the contracting activity may, on a nondelegable basis, authorize contract performance, notwithstanding the protest, upon a written finding that—

(i) Contract performance will be in the best interests of the United States; or

(ii) Urgent and compelling circumstances that significantly affect the interests of the United States will not permit waiting for the GAO's decision.

(3) Contract performance shall not be authorized until the agency has notified the GAO of the finding in subparagraph (c)(2) of this section.

(4) When it is decided to suspend performance or terminate the awarded contract, the contracting officer should attempt to negotiate a mutual agreement on a no-cost basis.

(5) When the agency receives notice of a protest filed with the GAO after the dates contained in subparagraph (c)(1), the contracting officer need not suspend contract performance or terminate the awarded contract unless the contracting officer believes that an award may be invalidated and a delay in receiving the supplies or services is not prejudicial to the Government's interest.

(d) *Findings and notice.* If the decision is to proceed with contract award, or continue contract performance under paragraphs (b) or (c) of this section, the contracting officer shall include the written findings or other required documentation in the file. The contracting officer also shall give written notice of the decision to the protester and other interested parties.

(e) *Hearings.* The GAO may hold a hearing at the request of the agency, a protester, or other interested party who has responded to the notice in paragraph (a)(2) of this section. A recording or transcription of the hearing will normally be made, and copies may be obtained from the GAO. All parties may file comments on the hearing and agency report within 5 days of the hearing.

(f) *GAO decision time.* GAO issues its recommendation on a protest within 100 days from the date of filing of the protest with the GAO, or within 65 days under the express option. The GAO attempts to issue its recommendation on an amended protest that adds a new ground of protest within the time limit of the initial protest. If an amended protest cannot be resolved within the initial time limit, the GAO may resolve the amended protest through an express option.

(g) *Notice to GAO.* If the agency has not fully implemented the GAO recommendations with respect to a solicitation for a contract or an award or a proposed award of a contract within 60 days of receiving the GAO recommendations, the head of the contracting activity responsible for that contract shall report the failure to the GAO not later than 5 days after the expiration of the 60-day period. The report shall explain the reasons why the GAO's recommendation, exclusive of costs, has not been followed by the agency.

(h) *Award of costs.*

(1) If the GAO determines that a solicitation for a contract, a proposed award, or an award of a contract does not comply with a statute or regulation, the GAO may recommend that the agency pay to an appropriate protester the cost, exclusive of profit, of filing and pursuing the protest, including reasonable attorney, consultant, and expert witness fees, and bid and proposal preparation costs. The agency shall use funds available for the procurement to pay the costs awarded.

(2) The protester shall file its claim for costs with the contracting agency within 60 days after receipt of the GAO's recommendation that the agency pay the protester its costs. Failure to file the claim within that time may result in forfeiture of the protester's right to recover its costs.

(3) The agency shall attempt to reach an agreement on the amount of costs to be paid. If the agency and the protester are unable to agree on the amount to be paid, the GAO may, upon request of the protester, recommend to the agency the amount of costs that the agency should pay.

(4) Within 60 days after the GAO recommends the amount of costs the agency should pay the protester, the agency shall notify the GAO of the action taken by the agency in response to the recommendation.

(5) No agency shall pay a party, other than a small business concern within the meaning of section 3(a) of the Small Business Act (see 2.101, "Small business concern"), costs under paragraph (h)(2) of this section—

(i) For consultant and expert witness fees that exceed the highest rate of compensation for expert witnesses paid by the Government pursuant to 5 U.S.C. 3109 and 5 CFR 304.105; or

(ii) For attorney's fees that exceed $150 per hour, unless the agency determines, based on the recommendation of the Comptroller General on a case-by-case basis, that an increase in the cost of living or a special factor, such as the limited availability of qualified attorneys for the proceedings involved, justifies a higher fee. The cap placed on attorneys' fees for businesses, other than small businesses, constitutes a benchmark as to a "reasonable" level for attorney's fees for small businesses.

(6) Before paying a recommended award of costs, agency personnel should consult legal counsel. Section 33.104(h) applies to all recommended awards of costs that have not yet been paid.

(7) Any costs the contractor receives under this section shall not be the subject of subsequent proposals, billings, or claims against the Government, and those exclusions should be reflected in the cost agreement.

(8) If the Government pays costs, as provided in paragraph (h)(1) of this section, where a postaward protest is sustained as the result of an awardee's intentional or negligent misstatement, misrepresentation, or miscertification, the Government may require the awardee to reimburse the Government the amount of such costs. In addition to any other remedy available, and pursuant to the requirements of subpart 32.6, the Government may collect this debt by offsetting the amount against any payment due the awardee under any contract between the awardee and the Government.

[FAC 90-16, 57 FR 60585, 12/21/92, effective 4/1/91; FAC 90-32, 60 FR 48206, 9/18/95, effective 10/1/95; FAC 90-41, 61 FR 41466, 8/8/96, effective 8/8/96, finalized without change, FAC 97-3, 62 FR 64912, 12/9/97, effective 2/9/98; FAC 90-44, Final rule, 61 FR 69286, 12/31/96, effective 1/1/97; FAC 90-46, 62 FR 12690, 3/17/97, effective 5/16/97; FAC 97-2, 62 FR 51224, 9/30/97, effective 10/10/97; FAC 97-3, 62 FR 64912, 12/9/97, effective 2/9/98; corrected, 63 FR 1532, 1/9/98; FAC 97-9, 63 FR 58587, 10/30/98, effective 10/30/98; FAC 2005-21, 72 FR 63045, 11/7/2007, effective 12/7/2007]

33.105 Protests at the U.S. Court of Federal Claims.

Procedures for protests at the U.S. Court of Federal Claims are set forth in the rules of the U.S. Court of Federal Claims. The rules may be found at *http://www.uscfc.uscourts.gov/rules-and-forms.*

[Reserved, FAC 90-41, 61 FR 41466, 8/8/96, effective 8/8/96, finalized without change, FAC 97-3, 62 FR 64912, 12/9/97, effective 2/9/98; FAC 2005-61, 77 FR 56742, 9/13/2012, effective 9/13/2012]

33.106 Solicitation provision and contract clause.

(a) The contracting officer shall insert the provision at 52.233-2, Service of Protest, in solicitations for contracts expected to exceed the simplified acquisition threshold.

(b) The contracting officer shall insert the clause at 52.233-3, Protest After Award, in all solicitations and contracts. If a cost reimbursement contract is contemplated, the contracting officer shall use the clause with its Alternate I.

[FAC 84-6, 50 FR 2270, 1/15/85, effective 1/15/85; FAC 84-9, 50 FR 25681, 6/20/85, effective 6/20/85; FAC 90-29, 60 FR 34732, 7/3/95, effective 7/3/95]

SUBPART 33.2—DISPUTES AND APPEALS

33.201 Definitions.

As used in this subpart—

Accrual of a claim means the date when all events, that fix the alleged liability of either the Government or the contractor and permit assertion of the claim, were known or should have been known. For liability to be fixed, some injury must have occurred. However, monetary damages need not have been incurred.

Alternative dispute resolution (ADR), means any type of procedure or combination of procedures voluntarily used to resolve issues in controversy. These procedures may include, but are not limited to, conciliation, facilitation, mediation, fact-finding, minitrials, arbitration, and use of ombudsmen.

Defective certification means a certificate which alters or otherwise deviates from the language in 33.207(c) or which is not executed by a person authorized to bind the contractor with respect to the claim. Failure to certify shall not be deemed to be a defective certification.

Issue in controversy means a material disagreement between the Government and the contractor that

(1) may result in a claim or

(2) is all or part of an existing claim.

Misrepresentation of fact means a false statement of substantive fact, or any conduct which leads to the belief of a substantive fact material to proper understanding of the matter in hand, made with intent to deceive or mislead.

[FAC 84-6, 50 FR 2270, 1/15/85, effective 1/15/85; Interim rule, FAC 90-10, 56 FR 67417, 12/30/91, effective 12/30/91; Interim rule, FAC 90-20, 59 FR 11368, 3/10/94, effective 10/29/92, finalized without change, FAC 90-39, 61 FR 31612, 6/20/96, effective 6/20/96; FAC 90-32, 60 FR 48206, 9/18/95, effective 10/1/95; FAC 97-9, 63 FR 58587, 10/30/98, effective 12/29/98; FAC 97-22, 66 FR 2116, 1/10/2001, effective 3/12/2001; Delay of effective date, 66 FR 14259, 3/9/2001, effective 5/11/2001; FAC 2001-08, 67 FR 43513, 6/27/2002, effective 7/29/2002; FAC 2005-73, 79 FR 24192, 4/29/2014, effective 5/29/2014]

33.202 Disputes.

41 U.S.C. chapter 71, Disputes, establishes procedures and requirements for asserting and resolving claims subject to the Disputes statute. In addition, the Disputes statute provides for—

(a) the payment of interest on contractor claims;

(b) certification of contractor claims; and

(c) a civil penalty for contractor claims that are fraudulent or based on a misrepresentation of fact.

[FAC 84-6, 50 FR 2270, 1/15/85, effective 1/15/85; Interim rule, FAC 90-10, 56 FR 67417, 12/30/91, effective 12/30/91; Interim rule, FAC 90-20, 59 FR 11368, 3/10/94, effective 3/10/94, finalized without change, FAC 90-39, 61 FR 31612, 6/20/96, effective 6/20/96; FAC 2005-73, 79 FR 24192, 4/29/2014, effective 5/29/2014]

33.203 Applicability.

(a) Except as specified in paragraph (b) below, this part applies to any express or implied contract covered by the Federal Acquisition Regulation.

(b) This subpart does not apply to any contract with

(1) A foreign government or agency of that government; or

(2) an international organization or a subsidiary body of that organization, if the agency head determines that the application of the Disputes statute to the contract would not be in the public interest.

(c) This part applies to all disputes with respect to contracting officer decisions on matters "arising under" or "relating to" a contract. Agency Boards of Contract Appeals (BCAs) authorized under the Disputes statute continue to have all of the authority they possessed before the Disputes statute with respect to disputes arising under a contract, as well as authority to decide disputes relating to a contract. The clause at 52.233-1, Disputes, recognizes the "all disputes" authority established by the Disputes statute and states certain requirements and limitations of the Disputes statute for the guidance of contractors and contracting agencies. The clause is not intended to affect the rights and obligations of the parties as provided by the Disputes statute or to constrain the authority of the statutory agency BCAs in the handling and deciding of contractor appeals under the Disputes statute.

[FAC 84-6, 50 FR 2270, 1/15/85, effective 1/15/85; FAC 2005-73, 79 FR 24192, 4/29/2014, effective 5/29/2014]

33.204 Policy.

The Government's policy is to try to resolve all contractual issues in controversy by mutual agreement at the contracting officer's level. Reasonable efforts should be made to resolve controversies prior to the submission of a claim. Agencies are encouraged to use ADR procedures to the maximum extent practicable. Certain factors, however, may make the use of ADR inappropriate (see 5 U.S.C. 572(b)). Except for arbitration conducted pursuant to the Administrative Dispute Resolution Act (ADRA) (5 U.S.C. 571, *et seq.*), agencies have authority which is separate from that provided by the ADRA to use ADR procedures to resolve issues in controversy. Agencies may also elect to proceed under the authority and requirements of the ADRA.

[FAC 84-6, 50 FR 2270, 1/15/85, effective 1/15/85; Interim rule, FAC 90-10, 56 FR 67417, 12/30/91, effective 12/30/91; Interim rule, FAC 90-20, 59 FR 11368, 3/10/94, effective 3/10/94, finalized without change, FAC 90-39, 61 FR 31612, 6/20/96, effective 6/20/96; FAC 97-9, 63 FR 58587, 10/30/98, effective 12/29/98]

33.205 Relationship of the Disputes statute to Pub. L. 85-804.

(a) Requests for relief under Public Law 85-804 (50 U.S.C. 1431-1435) are not claims within the Disputes statute or the Disputes clause at 52.233-1, Disputes, and shall be processed under Subpart 50.1, Extraordinary Contractual Actions. However, relief formerly available only under Public Law 85-804; i.e., legal entitlement to rescission or reformation for mutual mistake, is now available within the authority of the contracting officer under the Disputes statute and the Disputes clause. In case of a question whether the contracting officer has authority to settle or decide specific types of claims, the contracting officer should seek legal advice.

(b) A contractor's allegation that it is entitled to rescission or reformation of its contract in order to correct or mitigate the effect of a mistake shall be treated as a claim under the Disputes statute. A contract may be reformed or rescinded by the contracting officer if the contractor would be entitled to such remedy or relief under the law of Federal contracts. Due to the complex legal issues likely to be associated with allegations of legal entitlement, contracting officers shall make written decisions, prepared with the advice and assistance of legal counsel, either granting or denying relief in whole or in part.

(c) A claim that is either denied or not approved in its entirety under paragraph (b) above may be cognizable as a request for relief under Public Law 85-804 as implemented by subpart 50.1. However, the claim must first be submitted to the contracting officer for consideration under the Disputes statute because the claim is not cognizable under Public Law 85-804, as implemented by subpart 50.1, unless other legal authority in the agency concerned is determined to be lacking or inadequate.

[FAC 84-6, 50 FR 2270, 1/15/85, effective 1/15/85; FAC 2005-21, 72 FR 63027, 11/7/2007, effective 11/7/2007; FAC 2005-30, 74 FR 2733, 1/15/2009, effective 2/17/2009; FAC 2005-73, 79 FR 24192, 4/29/2014, effective 5/29/2014]

33.206 Initiation of a claim.

(a) Contractor claims shall be submitted, in writing, to the contracting officer for a decision within 6 years after accrual of a claim, unless the contracting parties agreed to a shorter time period. This 6-year time period does not apply to contracts awarded prior to October 1, 1995. The contracting officer shall document the contract file with evidence of the date of receipt of any submission from the contractor deemed to be a claim by the contracting officer.

(b) The contracting officer shall issue a written decision on any Government claim initiated against a contractor within 6 years after accrual of the claim, unless the contracting parties agreed to a shorter time period. The 6-year period shall not apply to contracts awarded prior to October 1, 1995, or to a Government claim based on a contractor claim involving fraud.

[FAC 90-32, 60 FR 48206, 9/18/95, effective 10/1/95]

33.207 Contractor certification.

(a) Contractors shall provide the certification specified in paragraph (c) of this section when submitting any claim exceeding $100,000.

(b) The certification requirements does not apply to issues in controversy that have not been submitted as all or part of a claim.

(c) The certification shall state as follows:

I certify that the claim is made in good faith; that the supporting data are accurate and complete to the best of my knowledge and belief; that the amount requested accurately reflects the contract adjustment for which the contractor believes the Government is liable; and that I am duly authorized to certify the claim on behalf of the contractor.

(d) The aggregate amount of both increased and decreased costs shall be used in determining when the dollar thresholds requiring certification are met (see example in 15.403-4(a)(1)(iii) regarding certified cost or pricing data).

(e) The certification may be executed by any person authorized to bind the contractor with respect to the claim.

(f) A defective certification shall not deprive a court or an agency BCA of jurisdiction over that claim. Prior to the entry of a final judgment by a court or a decision by an agency BCA, however, the court or agency BCA shall require a defective certification to be corrected.

[FAC 84-6, 50 FR 2270, 1/15/85, effective 1/15/85; Interim rule, FAC 90-10, 56 FR 67417, 12/30/91, effective 12/30/91; Interim rule, FAC 90-20, 59 FR 11368, 3/10/94, effective 10/29/92, finalized without change, FAC 90-39, 61 FR 31612, 6/20/96, effective 6/20/96; FAC 90-32, 60 FR 48206, 9/18/95, effective 10/1/95; FAC 97-2, 62 FR 51224, 9/30/97, effective 10/10/97; FAC 97-9, 63 FR 58587, 10/30/98, effective 12/29/98; FAC 2005-45, 75 FR 53135, 8/30/2010, effective 10/1/2010; FAC 2005-73, 79 FR 24192, 4/29/2014, effective 5/29/2014]

33.208 Interest on claims.

(a) The Government shall pay interest on a contractor's claim on the amount found due and unpaid from the date that—

(1) The contracting officer receives the claim (certified if required by 33.207(a)); or

(2) Payment otherwise would be due, if that date is later, until the date of payment.

(b) Simple interest on claims shall be paid at the rate, fixed by the Secretary of the Treasury as provided in the Disputes statute, which is applicable to the period during which the contracting officer receives the claim and then at the rate applicable for each 6-month period as fixed by the Treasury Secretary during the pendency of the claim. (See the clause at 52.232-17 for the right of the Government to collect interest on its claims against a contractor.)

(c) With regard to claims having defective certifications, interest shall be paid from either the date that the contracting officer initially receives the claim or October 29, 1992, whichever is later. However, if a contractor has provided a proper certificate prior to October 29, 1992, after submission of a defective certificate, interest shall be paid from the date of receipt by the Government of a proper certificate.

[FAC 84-6, 50 FR 2270, 1/15/85, effective 1/15/85; Interim rule, FAC 90-20, 59 FR 11368, 3/10/94, effective 10/29/92, finalized without change, FAC 90-39, 61 FR 31612, 6/20/96; FAC 90-32, 60 FR 48206, 9/18/95, effective 10/1/95; FAC 2005-27, 73 FR 53997, 9/17/2008, effective 10/17/2008; FAC 2005-73, 79 FR 24192, 4/29/2014, effective 5/29/2014]

33.209 Suspected fraudulent claims.

If the contractor is unable to support any part of the claim and there is evidence that the inability is attributable to misrepresentation of fact or to fraud on the part of the contractor, the contracting officer shall refer the matter to the agency official responsible for investigating fraud.

[FAC 84-6, 50 FR 2270, 1/15/85, effective 1/15/85]

33.210 Contracting officer's authority.

Except as provided in this section, contracting officers are authorized, within any specific limitations of their warrants, to decide or resolve all claims arising under or relating to a contract subject to the Disputes statute. In accordance with agency policies and 33.214, contracting officers are authorized to use ADR procedures to resolve claims. The authority to decide or resolve claims does not extend to—

(a) A claim or dispute for penalties or forfeitures prescribed by statute or regulation that another Federal agency is specifically authorized to administer, settle, or determine; or

(b) The settlement, compromise, payment or adjustment of any claim involving fraud.

[FAC 84-6, 50 FR 2270, 1/15/85, effective 1/15/85; FAC 84-23, 51 FR 36972, 10/16/86, effective 9/30/86; Interim rule, FAC 90-20, 59 FR 11368, 3/10/94, effective 3/10/94, finalized without change, FAC 90-39, 61 FR 31612, 6/20/96; FAC 2005-73, 79 FR 24192, 4/29/2014, effective 5/29/2014]

33.211 Contracting officer's decision.

(a) When a claim by or against a contractor cannot be satisfied or settled by mutual agreement and a decision on the claim is necessary, the contracting officer shall—

(1) Review the facts pertinent to the claim;

(2) Secure assistance from legal and other advisors;

(3) Coordinate with the contract administration officer or contracting office, as appropriate; and

(4) Prepare a written decision that shall include—

(i) A description of the claim or dispute;

(ii) A reference to the pertinent contract terms;

(iii) A statement of the factual areas of agreement and disagreement;

(iv) A statement of the contracting officer's decision, with supporting rationale;

(v) Paragraphs substantially as follows:

"This is the final decision of the Contracting Officer. You may appeal this decision to the agency board of contract appeals. If you decide to appeal, you must, within 90 days from the date you receive this decision, mail or otherwise furnish written notice to the agency board of contract appeals and provide a copy to the Contracting Officer from whose decision this appeal is taken. The notice shall indicate that an appeal is intended, reference this decision, and identify the contract by number.

With regard to appeals to the agency board of contract appeals, you may, solely at your election, proceed under the board's—

(1) Small claim procedure for claims of $50,000 or less or, in the case of a small business concern (as defined in the Small Business Act and regulations under that Act), $150,000 or less; or

(2) Accelerated procedure for claims of $100,000 or less.

Instead of appealing to the agency board of contract appeals, you may bring an action directly in the United States Court of Federal Claims (except as provided in 41 U.S.C. 7102(d), regarding Maritime Contracts) within 12 months of the date you receive this decision" ; and

(vi) Demand for payment prepared in accordance with 32.604 and 32.605 in all cases where the decision results in a finding that the contractor is indebted to the Government.

(b) The contracting officer shall furnish a copy of the decision to the contractor by certified mail, return receipt requested, or by any other method that provides evidence of receipt. This requirement shall apply to decisions on claims initiated by or against the contractor.

(c) The contracting officer shall issue the decision within the following statutory time limitations:

(1) For claims of $100,000 or less, 60 days after receiving a written request from the contractor that a decision be rendered within that period, or within a reasonable time after receipt of the claim if the contractor does not make such a request.

(2) For claims over $100,000, 60 days after receiving a certified claim; provided, however, that if a decision will not be issued within 60 days, the contracting officer shall notify the contractor, within that period, of the time within which a decision will be issued.

(d) The contracting officer shall issue a decision within a reasonable time, taking into account—

(1) The size and complexity of the claim;

(2) The adequacy of the contractor's supporting data; and

(3) Any other relevant factors.

(e) The contracting officer shall have no obligation to render a final decision on any claim exceeding $100,000 which contains a defective certification, if within 60 days after receipt of the claim, the contracting officer notifies the contractor, in writing, or the reasons why any attempted certification was found to be defective.

(f) In the event of undue delay by the contracting officer in rendering a decision on a claim, the contractor may request the tribunal concerned to direct the contracting officer to issue a decision in a specified time period determined by the tribunal.

(g) Any failure of the contracting officer to issue a decision within the required time periods will be deemed a decision by the contracting officer denying the claim and will authorize the contractor to file an appeal or suit on the claim.

(h) The amount determined payable under the decision, less any portion already paid, should be paid, if otherwise proper, without awaiting contractor action concerning appeal. Such payment shall be without prejudice to the rights of either party.

[FAC 84-6, 50 FR 2270, 1/15/85, effective 1/15/85; FAC 84-51, 54 FR 34755, 8/21/89, effective 9/20/89; Interim rule, FAC 90-20, 59 FR 11368, 3/10/94, effective 10/29/92, finalized without change, FAC 90-39, 61 FR 31612, 6/20/96; FAC 90-32, 60 FR 48206, 9/18/95, effective 10/1/95; FAC 2005-25, 73 FR 21799, 4/22/2008, effective 5/22/2008; FAC 2005-27, 73 FR 53997, 9/17/2007, effective 10/17/2008; FAC 2005-73, 79 FR 24192, 4/29/2014, effective 5/29/2014]

33.212 Contracting officer's duties upon appeal.

To the extent permitted by any agency procedures controlling contacts with agency BCA personnel, the contracting officer shall provide data, documentation, information, and support as may be required by the agency BCA for use on a pending appeal from the contracting officer's decision.

[FAC 84-6, 50 FR 2270, 1/15/85, effective 1/15/85]

33.213 Obligation to continue performance.

(a) In general, before passage of the Disputes statute, the obligation to continue performance applied only to claims arising under a contract. However, the Disputes statute, at 41 U.S.C. 7103(g), authorizes agencies to require a contractor to continue contract performance in accordance with the contracting officer's decision pending a final resolution of any claim arising under, or relating to, the contract. (A claim arising under a contract is a claim that can be resolved under a contract clause, other than the clause at 52.233-1, Disputes, that provides for the relief sought by the claimant; however, relief for such claim can also be sought under the clause at 52.233-1. A claim relating to a contract is a claim that cannot be resolved under a contract clause other than the clause at 52.233-1.) This distinction is recognized by the clause with its Alternate I (see 33.215).

(b) In all contracts that include the clause at 52.233-1, Disputes, with its Alternate I, in the event of a dispute not arising under, but relating to, the contract, the contracting officer shall consider providing, through appropriate agency procedures, financing of the continued performance; provided, that the Government's interest is properly secured.

[FAC 84-6, 50 FR 2270, 1/15/85, effective 1/15/85; FAC 97-15, 64 FR 72414, 12/27/99, effective 12/27/99; FAC 2001-08, 67 FR 43513, 6/27/2002, effective 7/29/2002; FAC 2005-73, 79 FR 24192, 4/29/2014, effective 5/29/2014]

33.214 Alternative dispute resolution (ADR).

(a) The objective of using ADR procedures is to increase the opportunity for relatively inexpensive and expeditious resolution of issues in controversy. Essential elements of ADR include—

(1) Existence of an issue in controversy;

(2) A voluntary election by both parties to participate in the ADR process;

(3) An agreement on alternative procedures and terms to be used in lieu of formal litigation; and

(4) Participation in the process by officials of both parties who have the authority to resolve the issue in controversy.

(b) If the contracting officer rejects a contractor's request for ADR proceedings, the contracting officer shall provide the contractor a written explanation citing one or more of the conditions in 5 U.S.C. 572(b) or such other specific reasons that ADR procedures are inappropriate for the resolution of the dispute. In any case where a contractor rejects a request of an agency for ADR proceedings, the contractor shall inform the agency in writing of the contractor's specific reasons for rejecting the request.

(c) ADR procedures may be used at any time that the contracting officer has authority to resolve the issue in controversy. If a claim has been submitted, ADR procedures may be applied to all or a portion of the claim. When ADR procedures are used subsequent to issuance of a contracting officer's final decision, their use does not alter any of the time limitations or procedural requirements for filing an appeal of the contracting officer's final decision and does not constitute a reconsideration of the final decision.

(d) When appropriate, a neutral person may be used to facilitate resolution of the issue in controversy using the procedures chosen by the parties.

(e) The confidentiality of ADR proceedings shall be protected consistent with 5 U.S.C. 574.

(f)(1) A solicitation shall not require arbitration as a condition of award, unless arbitration is otherwise required by law. Contracting officers should have flexibility to select the appropriate ADR procedure to resolve the issues in controversy as they arise.

(2) An agreement to use arbitration shall be in writing and shall specify a maximum award that may be issued by the arbitrator, as well as any other conditions limiting the range of possible outcomes.

(g) Binding arbitration, as an ADR procedure, may be agreed to only as specified in agency guidelines. Such guidelines shall provide advice on the appropriate use of binding arbitration and when an agency has authority to settle an issue in controversy through binding arbitration.

[FAC 84-6, 50 FR 2270, 1/15/85, effective 1/15/85; Interim rule, FAC 90-10, 56 FR 67417, 12/30/91, effective 12/30/91; Interim rule, FAC 90-20, 59 FR 11368, 3/10/94, effective 3/10/94, finalized without change, FAC 90-39, 61 FR 31612, 6/20/96, effective

6/20/96; FAC 90-32, 60 FR 48206, 9/18/95, effective 10/1/95; FAC 97-9, 63 FR 58587, 10/30/98, effective 12/29/98]

33.215 Contract clauses.

(a) Insert the clause at 52.233-1, Disputes, in solicitations and contracts, unless the conditions in 33.203(b) apply. If it is determined under agency procedures that continued performance is necessary pending resolution of any claim arising under or relating to the contract, the contracting officer shall use the clause with its Alternate I.

(b) Insert the clause at 52.233-4 in all solicitations and contracts.

[FAC 84-6, 50 FR 2270, 1/15/85, effective 1/15/85; Redesignated as 33,215, Interim rule, FAC 90-10, 12/30/91, effective 12/30/91, finalized without change, FAC 90-39, 61 FR 31612, 6/20/96, effective 6/20/96; FAC 90-16, 57 FR 60610, 12/21/92, effective 12/21/92; FAC 2001-25, 69 FR 59700, 10/5/2004, effective 10/5/2004]

PART 34—MAJOR SYSTEM ACQUISITION

Table of Contents

Scope of part 34.000
Definition 34.001
Policy 34.002
Responsibilities 34.003
Acquisition strategy 34.004
General requirements 34.005
Competition 34.005-1
Mission-oriented solicitation 34.005-2
Concept exploration contracts 34.005-3
Demonstration contracts 34.005-4
Full-scale development contracts 34.005-5
Full production 34.005-6

Subpart 34.1—Testing, Qualification and Use of Industrial Resources Developed Under Title III, Defense Production Act

Scope of subpart 34.100
Definitions 34.101
Policy 34.102
Testing and qualification 34.103
Contract clause 34.104

Subpart 34.2—Earned Value Management System

Policy 34.201
Integrated Baseline Reviews 34.202
Solicitation provisions and contract clause 34.203

SUBCHAPTER F—SPECIAL CATEGORIES OF CONTRACTING (Parts 34-41)

PART 34—MAJOR SYSTEM ACQUISITION

34.000 Scope of part.

This part describes acquisition policies and procedures for use in acquiring major systems consistent with OMB Circular No. A-109; and the use of an Earned Value Management System in acquisitions designated as major acquisitions consistent with OMB Circular A-11, Part 7.

[FAC 2005-11, 71 FR 38238, 7/5/2006, effective 7/5/2006]

34.001 Definition.

Effective competition, as used in this part, is a market condition that exists when two or more contractors, acting independently, actively contend for the Government's business in a manner that ensures that the Government will be offered the lowest cost or price alternative or best technical design meeting its minimum needs.

[FAC 84-10, 50 FR 27562, 7/3/85, effective 7/3/85; FAC 84-13, 50 FR 52434, 12/23/85, effective 2/3/86; FAC 90-41, 61 FR 41466, 8/8/96, effective 8/8/96, finalized without change, FAC 97-3, 62 FR 64912, 12/9/97, effective 2/9/98; FAC 97-22, 66 FR 2116, 1/10/2001, effective 3/12/2001; Delay of effective date, 66 FR 14259, 3/9/2001, effective 5/11/2001]

34.002 Policy.

The policies of this part are designed to ensure that agencies acquire major systems in the most effective, economical, and timely manner. Agencies acquiring major systems shall—

(a) Promote innovation and full and open competition as required by Part 6 in the development of major system concepts by—

(1) Expressing agency needs and major system acquisition program objectives in terms of the agency's mission and not in terms of specified systems to satisfy needs; and

(2) Focusing agency resources and special management attention on activities conducted in the initial stage of major programs; and

(b) Sustain effective competition between alternative system concepts and sources for as long as it is beneficial.

[FAC 84-5, 50 FR 1744, 1/11/85, effective 4/1/85; FAC 84-13, 50 FR 52434, 12/23/85, effective 2/3/86]

34.003 Responsibilities.

(a) As required by A-109, the agency head or designee shall establish written procedures for its implementation.

(b) The agency procedures shall identify the key decision points of each major system acquisition and the agency official(s) for making those decisions.

(c) Systems acquisitions normally designated as major are those programs that, as determined by the agency head,

(1) are directed at and critical to fulfilling an agency mission need,

(2) entail allocating relatively large resources for the particular agency, and

(3) warrant special management attention, including specific agency-head decisions. The agency procedures may establish additional criteria, as specified in A-109, for designating major programs system acquisitions.

34.004 Acquisition strategy.

The program manager, as specified in agency procedures, shall develop an acquisition strategy tailored to the particular major system acquisition program. This strategy is the program manager's overall plan for satisfying the mission need in the most effective, economical, and timely manner. The strategy shall be in writing and prepared in accordance with the requirements of Subpart 7.1, except where inconsistent with this part, and shall qualify as the acquisition plan for the major system acquisition, as required by that subpart.

34.005 General requirements. (No Text)

34.005-1 Competition.

(a) The program manager shall, throughout the acquisition process, promote full and open competition and sustain effective competition between alternative major system concepts and sources, as long as it is economically beneficial and practicable to do so. Notice of the proposed acquisition shall be given the broadest and most effective circulation practicable throughout the business, academic, and Government communities. Foreign contractors, technology, and equipment may be considered when it is feasible and permissible to do so.

(b) The contracting officer should time solicitation issuance and contract award to maintain continuity of concept development during the transition from withdrawing concept proposer to new contractor.

[FAC 84-5, 50 FR 1744, 1/11/85, effective 4/1/85]

34.005-2 Mission-oriented solicitation.

(a) Before issuing the solicitation, whenever practicable and consistent with agency procedures, the contracting officer should take the actions outlined in subparagraphs (a) (1) and (2):

(1) Advance notification of the acquisition should be given the widest practicable dissemination, including publicizing through the Governmentwide point of entry (see Subpart 5.2) and should be sent to as wide a selection of potential sources as practicable, including smaller and newer firms, Government laboratories, federally funded research and development centers, educational institutions and other not-for-profit organizations, and, if it would be beneficial and is not prohibited, foreign sources.

(2) If appropriate, hold a presolicitation conference (see 15.201) and/or send copies of the proposed solicitation to all prospective offerors for their comments. After evaluation of these comments, the solicitation should be revised, if appropriate.

(b) The contracting officer shall send the final solicitation to all prospective offerors. It shall—

(1) Describe the nature of the need in terms of mission capabilities required, without reference to any specific systems to satisfy the need;

(2) Indicate, and explain when appropriate, the schedule, capability, and cost objectives and any known constraints in the acquisition;

(3) Provide, or indicate how access can be obtained to, all Government data related to the acquisition;

(4) Include selection requirements consistent with the acquisition strategy; and

(5) Clearly state that each offeror is free to propose its own technical approach, main design features, subsystems, and alternatives to schedule, cost, and capability goals.

(6) Require the use of an Earned Value Management System that complies with the guidelines of Electronic Industries Alliance Standard 748 (EIA-748) (current version at time of solicitation). See 34.201 for earned value management systems and reporting requirements.

(c) To the extent practicable, the solicitation shall not reference or mandate Government specifications or standards, unless the agency is mandating a subsystem or other component as approved under agency procedure.

[FAC 84-5, 50 FR 1744, 1/11/85, effective 4/1/85; FAC 97-2, 62 FR 51224, 9/30/97, effective 10/10/97; FAC 97-26, 66 FR 27405, 5/16/2001, effective 5/16/2001; FAC 2005-11, 71 FR 38238, 7/5/2006, effective 7/5/2006; FAC 2005-92 81 FR 83103, 11/18/2016, effective 11/18/2016]

34.005-3 Concept exploration contracts.

Whenever practicable, contracts to be performed during the concept exploration phase shall be for relatively short periods, at planned dollar levels. These contracts are to refine the proposed concept and to reduce the concept's technical uncertainties. The scope of work for this phase of the program shall be consistent with the Government's planned budget for the phase. Follow-on contracts for such tasks in the exploration phase shall be awarded as long as the concept approach remains promising, the contractor's progress is acceptable, and it is economically practicable to do so.

34.005-4 Demonstration contracts.

Whenever practicable, contracts for the demonstration phase should provide for contractors to submit, by the end of the phase, priced proposals, totally funded by the Government, for full-scale development. The contracting officer should provide contractors with operational test conditions, performance criteria, life cycle cost factors, and any other selection criteria necessary for the contractors to prepare their proposals.

34.005-5 Full-scale development contracts.

Whenever practicable, the full-scale development contracts should provide for the contractors to submit priced proposals for production that are based on the latest quantity, schedule, and logistics requirements and other considerations that will be used in making the production decision.

34.005-6 Full production.

Contracts for full production of successfully tested major systems selected from the full-scale development phase may be awarded if the agency head—

(a) Reaffirms the mission need and program objectives; and

(b) Grants approval to proceed with production.

SUBPART 34.1—TESTING, QUALIFICATION AND USE OF INDUSTRIAL RESOURCES DEVELOPED UNDER TITLE III, DEFENSE PRODUCTION ACT

34.100 Scope of subpart.

This subpart prescribes policies and procedures for the testing, qualification, and use of industrial resources manufactured or developed with assistance provided under section 301, 302, or 303 of the Defense Production Act (50 U.S.C. App. 2091-2093). Title III of the Defense Production Act authorizes various forms of Government assistance to encourage expansion of production capacity and supply of industrial resources essential to national defense.

[FAC 90-23, 59 FR 67010, 12/28/94, effective 12/28/94, finalized without change, FAC 90-39, 61 FR 31612, 6/20/96, effective 6/20/96]

34.101 Definitions.

Item of supply, as used in this subpart, means any individual part, component, subassembly, assembly, or subsystem integral to a major system, and other property which may be replaced during the service life of the system. The term includes spare parts and replenishment parts, but does not include packaging or labeling associated with shipment or identification of an *item*.

[FAC 90-23, 59 FR 67010, 12/28/94, effective 12/28/94, finalized without change, FAC 90-39, 61 FR 31612, 6/20/96, effective 6/20/96; FAC 97-22, 66 FR 2116, 1/10/2001, effective 3/12/2001; Delay of effective date, 66 FR 14259, 3/9/2001, effective 5/11/2001]

34.102 Policy.

It is the policy of the Government, as required by section 126 of Public Law 102-558, to pay for any testing and qualification required for the use or incorporation of the industrial resources manufactured or developed with assistance provided under Title III of the Defense Production Act of 1950.

[FAC 90-23, 59 FR 67010, 12/28/94, effective 12/28/94, finalized without change, FAC 90-39, 61 FR 31612, 6/20/96, effective 6/20/96]

34.103 Testing and qualification.

(a) Contractors receiving requests from a Title III project contractor for testing and qualification of a Title III industrial resource shall refer such requests to the contracting officer. The contracting officer shall evaluate the request in accordance with agency procedures to determine whether: (1) the Title III industrial resource is being or potentially may be used in the development or manufacture of a major system or item of supply; and (2) for major systems in production, remaining quantities to be acquired are sufficient to justify incurring the cost of testing and qualification. In evaluating this request, the contracting officer shall consult with the Defense Production Act Office, Title III Program, located at Wright Patterson Air Force Base, OH 45433-7739.

(b) If the determination at 34.103(a) is affirmative, the contracting officer shall modify the contract to require the contractor to test the Title III industrial resource for qualification.

(c) The Defense Production Act Office, Title III Program, shall provide to the contractor the industrial resource produced by the Title III project contractor in sufficient amounts to meet testing needs.

[FAC 90-23, 59 FR 67010, 12/28/94, effective 12/28/94, finalized without change, FAC 90-39, 61 FR 31612, 6/20/96, effective 6/20/96]

34.104 Contract clause.

Insert the clause at 52.234-1, Industrial Resources Developed under Title III, Defense Production Act, in all contracts for major systems and items of supply.

[FAC 90-23, 59 FR 67010, 12/28/94, effective 12/28/94, finalized without change, FAC 90-39, 61 FR 31612, 6/20/96, effective 6/20/96]

SUBPART 34.2—EARNED VALUE MANAGEMENT SYSTEM

34.201 Policy.

(a) An Earned Value Management System (EVMS) is required for major acquisitions for development, in accordance with OMB Circular A-11. The Government may also require an EVMS for other acquisitions, in accordance with agency procedures.

(b) If the offeror proposes to use a system that has not been determined to be in compliance with the Electronic Industries Alliance Standard 748 (EIA-748), the offeror shall submit a comprehensive plan for compliance with these EVMS standards. Offerors shall not be eliminated from consideration for contract award because they do not have an EVMS that complies with these standards.

(c) As a minimum, contracting officers shall require contractors to submit EVMS monthly reports for those contracts for which an EVMS applies.

(d) EVMS requirements will be applied to subcontractors using the same rules as applied to the prime contractor.

(e) When an offeror is required to provide an EVMS plan as part of its proposal, the contracting officer will determine the adequacy of the proposed EVMS plan prior to contract award.

[FAC 2005-11, 71 FR 38238, 7/5/2006, effective 7/5/2006; FAC 2005-92 81 FR 83103, 11/18/2016, effective 11/18/2016]

34.202 Integrated Baseline Reviews.

(a) When an EVMS is required, the Government will conduct an Integrated Baseline Review (IBR).

(b) The purpose of the IBR is to verify the technical content and the realism of the related performance budgets, resources, and schedules. It should provide a mutual understanding of the inherent risks in offerors'/contractors' performance plans and the underlying management control systems, and it should formulate a plan to handle these risks.

(c) The IBR is a joint assessment by the offeror or contractor, and the Government, of the—

(1) Ability of the project's technical plan to achieve the objectives of the scope of work;

(2) Adequacy of the time allocated for performing the defined tasks to successfully achieve the project schedule objectives;

(3) Ability of the Performance Measurement Baseline (PMB) to successfully execute the project and attain cost objectives, recognizing the relationship between budget resources, funding, schedule, and scope of work;

(4) Availability of personnel, facilities, and equipment when required, to perform the defined tasks needed to execute the program successfully; and

(5) The degree to which the management process provides effective and integrated technical/schedule/cost planning and baseline control.

(d) The timing and conduct of the IBR shall be in accordance with agency procedures. If a pre-award IBR will be conducted, the solicitation must include the procedures for conducting the IBR and address whether offerors will be reimbursed for the associated costs. If permitted, reimbursement of offerors' pre-award IBR costs is governed by the provisions of FAR Part 31.

[FAC 2005-11, 71 FR 38238, 7/5/2006, effective 7/5/2006]

34.203 Solicitation provisions and contract clause.

(a) The contracting officer shall insert a provision that is substantially the same as the provision at FAR 52.234-2, Notice of Earned Value Management System—Preaward Integrated Baseline Review, in solicitations for contracts that require the contractor to use an Earned Value Management System (EVMS) and for which the Government requires an Integrated Baseline Review (IBR) prior to award.

(b) The contracting officer shall insert a provision that is substantially the same as the provision at 52.234-3, Notice of Earned Value Management System—Postaward Integrated Baseline Review, in solicitations for contracts that require the contractor to use an Earned Value Management System (EVMS) and for which the Government requires an Integrated Baseline Review (IBR) after contract award.

(c) The contracting officer shall insert a clause that is substantially the same as the clause at FAR 52.234-4, Earned Value Management System, in solicitations and contracts that require a contractor to use an EVMS.

[FAC 2005-11, 71 FR 38238, 7/5/2006, effective 7/5/2006; FAC 2005-92 81 FR 83103, 11/18/2016, effective 11/18/2016]

PART 35—RESEARCH AND DEVELOPMENT CONTRACTING

Table of Contents

Scope of part 35.000
Definitions 35.001
General 35.002
Policy 35.003
Publicizing requirements and expanding research and development sources . . 35.004
Work statement 35.005
Contracting methods and contract type 35.006
Solicitations 35.007
Evaluation for award 35.008
Subcontracting research and development effort 35.009
Scientific and technical reports 35.010
Data 35.011
Patent rights 35.012
Insurance 35.013
Government property and title 35.014
Contracts for research with educational institutions and nonprofit organizations 35.015
Broad agency announcement 35.016
Federally Funded Research and Development Centers 35.017
Sponsoring agreements 35.017-1
Establishing or changing an FFRDC 35.017-2
Using an FFRDC 35.017-3
Reviewing FFRDC's 35.017-4
Terminating an FFRDC 35.017-5
Master list of FFRDC's 35.017-6
Limitation on the creation of new FFRDC'S 35.017-7

PART 35—RESEARCH AND DEVELOPMENT CONTRACTING

35.000 Scope of part.

(a) This part prescribes policies and procedures of special application to research and development (R&D) contracting.

(b) R&D integral to acquisition of major systems is covered in Part 34. Independent research and development (IR&D) is covered at 31.205-18.

[FAC 84-56, 55 FR 3884, 2/5/90, effective 3/7/90; FAC 97-18, 65 FR 36014, 6/6/2000, effective 6/6/2000]

35.001 Definitions.

Applied research means the effort that

(a) normally follows basic research, but may not be severable from the related basic research;

(b) attempts to determine and exploit the potential of scientific discoveries or improvements in technology, materials, processes, methods, devices, or techniques; and

(c) attempts to advance the state of the art. When being used by contractors in cost principle applications, this term does not include efforts whose principal aim is the design, development, or testing of specific items or services to be considered for sale; these efforts are within the definition of *development*, given below.

Development, as used in this part, means the systematic use of scientific and technical knowledge in the design, development, testing, or evaluation of a potential new product or service (or of an improvement in an existing product or service) to meet specific performance requirements or objectives. It includes the functions of design engineering, prototyping, and engineering testing; it excludes subcontracted technical effort that is for the sole purpose of developing an additional source for an existing product.

Recoupment, as used in this part, means the recovery by the Government of Government-funded nonrecurring costs from contractors that sell, lease, or license the resulting products or technology to buyers other than the Federal Government.

[FAC 84-38, 53 FR 27467, 7/20/88, effective 8/19/88; FAC 84-56, 55 FR 3884, 2/5/90, effective 3/7/90; FAC 97-22, 66 FR 2116, 1/10/2001, effective 3/12/2001; Delay of effective date, 66 FR 14259, 3/9/2001, effective 5/11/2001]

35.002 General.

The primary purpose of contracted R&D programs is to advance scientific and technical knowledge and apply that knowledge to the extent necessary to achieve agency and national goals. Unlike contracts for supplies and services, most R&D contracts are directed toward objectives for which the work or methods cannot be precisely described in advance. It is difficult to judge the probabilities of success or required effort for technical approaches, some of which offer little or no early assurance of full success. The contracting process shall be used to encourage the best sources from the scientific and industrial community to become involved in the program and must provide an environment in which the work can be pursued with reasonable flexibility and minimum administrative burden.

35.003 Policy.

(a) *Use of contracts.* Contracts shall be used only when the principal purpose is the acquisition of supplies or services for the direct benefit or use of the Federal Government. Grants or cooperative agreements should be used when the principal purpose of the transaction is to stimulate or support research and development for another public purpose.

(b) *Cost sharing.* Cost sharing policies (which are not otherwise required by law) under Government contracts shall be in accordance with 16.303, 42.707(a) and agency procedures.

(c) *Recoupment.* Recoupment not otherwise required by law shall be in accordance with agency procedures.

35.004 Publicizing requirements and expanding research and development sources.

(a) In order to obtain a broad base of the best contractor sources from the scientific and industrial community, agencies must, in addition to following the requirements of Part 5, continually search for and develop information on sources (including small business concerns) competent to perform R&D work. These efforts should include—

(1) Early identification and publication of agency R&D needs and requirements, including publicizing through the Governmentwide point of entry (GPE) (see part 5);

(2) Cooperation among technical personnel, contracting officers, and Government small business personnel early in the acquisition process; and

(3) Providing agency R&D points of contact for potential sources.

(b) See Subpart 9.7 for information regarding R&D pools and Subpart 9.6 for teaming arrangements.

[FAC 97-26, 66 FR 27405, 5/16/2001, effective 5/16/2001]

35.005 Work statement.

(a) A clear and complete work statement concerning the area of exploration (for basic research) or the end objectives (for development and applied research) is essential. The work statement should allow contractors freedom to exercise innovation and creativity. Work statements must be individually tailored by technical and contracting personnel to attain the desired degree of flexibility for contractor creativity and the objectives of the R&D.

(b) In basic research the emphasis is on achieving specified objectives and knowledge rather than on achieving predetermined end results prescribed in a statement of specific performance characteristics. This emphasis applies particularly during the early or conceptual phases of the R&D effort.

(c) In reviewing work statements, contracting officers should ensure that language suitable for a level-of-effort approach, which requires the furnishing of technical effort and a report on the results, is not intermingled with language suitable for a task-completion approach, which often requires the development of a tangible end item designed to achieve specific performance characteristics. The wording of the work statement should also be consistent with the type and form of contract to be negotiated (see 16.207 and 16.306(d)). For example, the work statement for a cost-reimbursement contract promising the contractor's best efforts for a fixed term would be phrased differently than a work statement for a cost-reimbursement completion contract promising the contractor's best efforts for a defined task. Differences between work statements for fixed-price contracts and cost-reimbursement contracts should be even clearer.

(d) In preparing work statements, technical and contracting personnel shall consider and, as appropriate, provide in the solicitation—

(1) A statement of the area of exploration, tasks to be performed, and objectives of the research or development effort;

(2) Background information helpful to a clear understanding of the objective or requirement (*e.g.*, any known phenomena, techniques, methodology, or results of related work);

(3) Information on factors such as personnel, environment, and interfaces that may constrain the results of the effort;

(4) Reporting requirements and information on any additional items that the contractor is required to furnish (at specified intervals) as the work progresses;

(5) The type and form of contract contemplated by the Government and, for level-of-effort work statements, an estimate of applicable professional and technical effort involved; and

(6) Any other considerations peculiar to the work to be performed; for example, any design-to-cost requirements.

35.006 Contracting methods and contract type.

(a) In R&D acquisitions, the precise specifications necessary for sealed bidding are generally not available, thus making negotiation necessary. However, the use of negotiation in R&D contracting does not change the obligation to comply with Part 6.

(b) Selecting the appropriate contract type is the responsibility of the contracting officer. However, because of the importance of technical considerations in R&D, the choice of contract type should be made after obtaining the recommendations of technical personnel. Although the Government ordinarily prefers fixed-price arrangements in contracting, this preference applies in R&D contracting only to the extent that goals, objectives, specifications, and cost estimates are sufficient to permit such a preference. The precision with which the goals, performance objectives, and specifications for the work can be defined will largely determine the type of contract employed. The contract type must be selected to fit the work required.

(c) Because the absence of precise specifications and difficulties in estimating costs with accuracy (resulting in a lack of confidence in cost estimates) normally precludes using fixed-price contracting for R&D, the use of cost-reimbursement contracts is usually appropriate (see Subpart 16.3). The nature of development work often requires a cost-reimbursement completion arrangement (see 16.306(d)). When the use of cost and performance incentives is desirable and practicable, fixed-price incentive and cost-plus-incentive-fee contracts should be considered in that order of preference.

(d) When levels of effort can be specified in advance, a short-duration fixed-price contract may be useful for developing system design concepts, resolving potential problems, and reducing Government risks. Fixed-price contracting may also be used in minor projects when the objectives of the research are well defined and there is sufficient confidence in the cost estimate for price negotiations. (See 16.207.)

(e) Projects having production requirements as a follow-on to R&D efforts normally should progress from cost-reimbursement contracts to fixed-price contracts as designs become more firmly established, risks are reduced, and production tooling, equipment, and processes are developed and proven. When possible, a final commitment to undertake specific product development and testing should be avoided until—

(1) Preliminary exploration and studies have indicated a high degree of probability that development is feasible and

(2) The Government has determined both its minimum requirements and desired objectives for product performance and schedule completion.

[FAC 84-5, 50 FR 1744, 1/11/85, effective 4/1/85]

35.007 Solicitations.

(a) The submission and subsequent evaluation of an inordinate number of R&D proposals from sources lacking appropriate qualifications is costly and time-consuming to both industry and the Government. Therefore, contracting officers should initially distribute solicitations only to sources technically qualified to perform research or development in the specific field of science or technology involved. Cognizant technical personnel should recommend potential sources that appear qualified, as a result of—

(1) Present and past performance of similar work;

(2) Professional stature and reputation;

(3) Relative position in a particular field of endeavor;

(4) Ability to acquire and retain the professional and technical capability, including facilities, required to perform the work; and

(5) Other relevant factors.

(b) Proposals generally shall be solicited from technically qualified sources, including sources that become known as a result of synopses or other means of publicizing requirements. If it is not practicable to initially solicit all apparently qualified sources, only a reasonable number need be solicited. In the interest of competition, contracting officers shall furnish copies of the solicitation to other apparently qualified sources.

(c) Solicitations shall require offerors to describe their technical and management approach, identify technical uncertainties, and make specific proposals for the resolution of any uncertainties. The solicitation should require offerors to include in the proposal any planned subcontracting of scientific or technical work (see 35.009).

(d) Solicitations may require that proposals be organized so that the technical portions can be efficiently evaluated by technical personnel (see 15.204-5(b)). Solicitation and evaluation of proposals should be planned to minimize offerors' and Government expense.

(e) R&D solicitations should contain evaluation factors to be used to determine the most technically competent (see 15.304), such as—

(1) The offeror's understanding of the scope of the work;

(2) The approach proposed to accomplish the scientific and technical objectives of the contract or the merit of the ideas or concepts proposed;

(3) The availability and competence of experienced engineering, scientific, or other technical personnel;

(4) The offeror's experience;

(5) Pertinent novel ideas in the specific branch of science and technology involved; and

(6) The availability, from any source, of necessary research, test, laboratory, or shop facilities.

(f) In addition to evaluation factors for technical competence, the contracting officer shall consider, as appropriate, management capability (including cost management techniques), experience and past performance, subcontracting practices, and any other significant evaluation criteria (*e.g.*, unrealistically low cost estimates in proposals for cost-reimbursement or fixed-price incentive contracts). Although cost or price is not normally the controlling factor in selecting a contractor to perform R&D, it should not be disregarded in arriving at a selection that best satisfies the Government's requirement at a fair and reasonable cost.

(g) The contracting officer should ensure that potential offerors fully understand the details of the work, especially the Government interpretation of the work statement. If the effort is complex, the contracting officer should provide potential offerors an opportunity to comment on the details of the requirements as contained in the work statement, the contract Schedule, and any related specifications. This may be done at a preproposal conference (see 15.201).

(h) If it is appropriate to do so, solicitations should permit offerors to propose an alternative contract type (see 16.103).

(i) In circumstances when a concern has a new idea or product to discuss that incorporates the results of independent R&D work funded by the concern in the private sector and is of interest to the Government, there should be no hesitancy to discuss it; however, the concern should be warned that the Government will not be obligated by the discussion. Under such circumstances, it may be appropriate to negotiate directly with the concern without competition. Also, see Subpart 15.6 concerning unsolicited proposals.

(j) The Government may issue an exploratory request to determine the existence of ideas or prior work in a specific field of research. Any such request shall clearly state that it does not impose any obligation on the Government or signify a firm intention to enter into a contract.

[FAC 97-2, 62 FR 51224, 9/30/97, effective 10/10/97; FAC 2001-06, 67 FR 13048, 3/20/2002, effective 4/4/2002]

35.008 Evaluation for award.

(a) Generally, an R&D contract should be awarded to that organization, including any educational institution, that proposes the best ideas or concepts and has the highest competence in the specific field of science or technology involved. However, an award should not be made to obtain capabilities that exceed those needed for successful performance of the work.

(b) In R&D contracting, precise specifications are ordinarily not available. The contracting officer should therefore take special care in reviewing the solicitation evaluation factors to assure that they are properly presented and consistent with the solicitation.

(c) When a small business concern would otherwise be selected for award but is considered not responsible, the SBA Certificate of Competency procedure shall be followed (see Subpart 19.6).

(d) The contracting officer should use the procedures in Subpart 15.5 to notify and debrief offerors.

(e) It is important to evaluate a proposed contractor's cost or price estimate, not only to determine whether the estimate is reasonable but also to provide valuable insight into the offeror's understanding of the project, perception of risks, and ability to organize and perform the work. Cost or price analysis, as appropriate (see 15.404-1(c)), is a useful tool.

[FAC 97-2, 62 FR 51224, 9/30/97, effective 10/10/97]

35.009 Subcontracting research and development effort.

Since the selection of R&D contractors is substantially based on the best scientific and technological sources, it is important that the contractor not subcontract technical or scientific work without the contracting officer's advance knowledge. During the negotiation of a cost-reimbursement R&D contract, the contracting officer shall obtain complete information concerning the contractor's plans for subcontracting any portion of the experimental, research, or development effort (see also 35.007(c)). Also, when negotiating a fixed-price contract, the contracting officer should evaluate this information and may obtain an agreement that protects the Government's interests. The clause at 52.244-2, Subcontracts, prescribed for certain types of contracts at 44.204(a), requires the contracting officer's prior approval for the placement of certain subcontracts.

[FAC 97-5, 63 FR 34058, 6/22/98, effective 8/21/98]

35.010 Scientific and technical reports.

(a) R&D contracts shall require contractors to furnish scientific and technical reports, consistent with the objectives of the effort involved, as a permanent record of the work accomplished under the contract.

(b) Agencies should make R&D contract results available to other Government activities and the private sector. Contracting officers shall follow agency regulations regarding such matters as national security, protection of data, and new-technology dissemination policy. Reports should be sent to the National Technical Information Service (NTIS), 5285 Port Royal Road, Springfield, VA 22161. When agencies require that completed reports be covered by a report documentation page, Standard Form (SF) 298, Report Documentation Page, the contractor should submit a copy with the report.

[FAC 84-56, 55 FR 3884, 2/5/90, effective 3/7/90; FAC 90-23, 59 FR 67010, 12/28/94, effective 2/27/95]

35.011 Data.

(a) R&D contracts shall specify the technical data to be delivered under the contract, since the data clauses required by Part 27 do not require the delivery of any such data.

(b) In planning a developmental program when subsequent production contracts are contemplated, consideration should be given to the need and time required to obtain a technical package (plans, drawings, specifications, and other descriptive information) that can be used to achieve competition in production contracts. In some situations, the developmental contractor may be in the best position to produce such a technical package.

35.012 Patent rights.

For a discussion of patent rights, see agency regulations and Part 27.

35.013 Insurance.

Nonprofit, educational, or State institutions performing cost-reimbursement contracts often do not carry insurance. They may claim immunity from liability for torts, or, as State institutions, they may be prohibited by State law from expending funds for insurance. When this is the case, see 28.311 for appropriate clause coverage.

35.014 Government property and title.

(a) The requirements in Part 45 for establishing and maintaining control over Government property apply to all R&D contracts.

(b) In implementing 31 U.S.C. 6306, and unless an agency head provides otherwise, the policies in subparagraphs (1) through

(4) following, regarding title to equipment (and other tangible personal property) purchased by the contractor using Government funds provided for the conduct of basic or applied scientific research, apply to contracts with nonprofit institutions of higher education and nonprofit organizations whose primary purpose is the conduct of scientific research:

(1) If the contractor obtains the contracting officer's advance approval, the contractor shall automatically acquire and retain title to any item of equipment costing less than $5,000 (or a lesser amount established by agency regulations) acquired on a reimbursable basis.

(2) If purchased equipment costs $5,000 (or a lesser amount established by agency regulations) or more, and as the parties specifically agree in the contract, title may—

(i) Vest in the contractor upon acquisition without further obligation to the Government;

(ii) Vest in the contractor, subject to the Government's right to direct transfer of the title to the Government or to a third party within 12 months after the contract's completion or termination (transfer of title to the Government or third party shall not be the basis for any claim by the contractor); or

(iii) Vest in the Government, if the contracting officer determines that vesting of title in the contractor would not further the objectives of the agency's research program.

(3) If title to equipment is vested in the contractor, depreciation, amortization, or use charges are not allowable with respect to that equipment under any existing or future Government contract or subcontract.

(4) If the contract is performed at a Government installation and there is a continuing need for the equipment following contract completion, title need not be transferred to the contractor.

(c) The absence of an agreement covering title to equipment acquired by the contractor with Government funds that cost $1,000 or more does not limit an agency's right to act to vest title in a contractor as authorized by 31 U.S.C. 6306.

(d) (1) Vesting title under paragraph (b) of this section is subject to civil rights legislation, 42 U.S.C. 2000d. Before title is vested, the contractor must agree that—

"No person in the United States or its outlying areas shall, on the ground of race, color, or national origin, be excluded from participation in, be denied the benefits of, or be otherwise subjected to discrimination under this contemplated financial assistance (title to equipment)."

(2) By signing the contract, the contractor accepts and agrees to comply with this requirement.

(e) The policies in paragraphs (b)(1) through (b)(3) and paragraph (d) of this section are implemented in the Government Property clauses.

[FAC 84-8, 50 FR 26903, 6/28/85, effective 7/1/85; FAC 2001-14, 68 FR 28079, 5/22/2003, effective 6/23/2003; FAC 2005-17, 72 FR 27364, 5/15/2007, effective 6/14/2007]

35.015 Contracts for research with educational institutions and nonprofit organizations.

(a) *General.* (1) When the R&D work is not defined precisely and the contract states only a period during which work is conducted (that is, a specific time for achievement of results is not required), research contracts with educational institutions and nonprofit organizations shall—

(i) State that the contractor bears primary responsibility for the research;

(ii) Give—

(A) The name of the principal investigator (or project leader), if the decision to contract is based on that particular individual's research effort and management capabilities; and

(B) The contractor's estimate of the amount of time that individual will devote to the work;

(iii) Provide that the named individual shall be closely involved and continuously responsible for the conduct of the work;

(iv) Provide that the contractor must obtain the contracting officer's approval to change the principal investigator (or project leader);

(v) Require that the contractor advise the contracting officer if the principal investigator (or project leader) will, or plans to, devote substantially less effort to the work than anticipated; and

(vi) Require that the contractor obtain the contracting officer's approval to change the phenomenon under study, the stated objectives of the research, or the methodology.

(2) If a research contract does provide precise objectives or a specific date for achievement of results, the contracting officer may include in the contract the requirements set forth in subparagraph (a)(1) of this section, if it is necessary for the Government to exercise oversight and approval over the avenues of approach, methods, or schedule of work.

(b) *Basic agreements.* (1) A basic agreement should be negotiated if the number of contracts warrants such an agreement (see 16.702). Basic agreements should be reviewed and updated at least annually.

(2) To promote uniformity and consistency in dealing with educational institutions and nonprofit organizations, agencies are encouraged to use basic agreements of other agencies.

[FAC 90-4, 56 FR 15153, 4/15/91, effective 5/15/91]

35.016 Broad agency announcement.

(a) *General.* This paragraph prescribes procedures for the use of the broad agency announcement (BAA) with Peer or Scientific Review (see 6.102(d)(2)) for the acquisition of basic and applied research and that part of development not related to the development of a specific system or hardware procurement. BAA's may be used by agencies to fulfill their requirements for scientific study and experimentation directed toward advancing the state-of-the-art or increasing knowledge or understanding rather than focusing on a specific system or hardware solution. The BAA technique shall only be used when meaningful proposals with varying technical/scientific approaches can be reasonably anticipated.

(b) The BAA, together with any supporting documents, shall—

(1) Describe the agency's research interest, either for an individual program requirement or for broadly defined areas of interest covering the full range of the agency's requirements;

(2) Describe the criteria for selecting the proposals, their relative importance, and the method of evaluation;

(3) Specify the period of time during which proposals submitted in response to the BAA will be accepted; and

(4) Contain instructions for the preparation and submission of proposals.

(c) The availability of the BAA must be publicized through the Governmentwide point of entry (GPE) and, if authorized pursuant to subpart 5.5, may also be published in noted scientific, technical, or engineering periodicals. The notice must be published no less frequently than annually.

(d) Proposals received as a result of the BAA shall be evaluated in accordance with evaluation criteria specified therein through a peer or scientific review process. Written evaluation reports on individual proposals will be necessary but proposals need not be evaluated against each other since they are not submitted in accordance with a common work statement.

(e) The primary basis for selecting proposals for acceptance shall be technical, importance to agency programs, and fund availability. Cost realism and reasonableness shall also be considered to the extent appropriate.

(f) Synopsis under Subpart 5.2, Synopses of Proposed Contract Actions, of individual contract actions based upon proposals received under the BAA is not required. The notice published pursuant to paragraph (c) of this section fulfills the synopsis requirement.

[FAC 84-38, 53 FR 27467, 7/20/88, effective 8/19/88; FAC 97-26, 66 FR 27405, 5/16/2001, effective 5/16/2001; FAC

2001-16, Interim rule, 68 FR 56676, 10/1/2003, effective 10/1/2003]

35.017 Federally Funded Research and Development Centers.

(a) *Policy.* (1) This section sets forth Federal policy regarding the establishment, use, review, and termination of Federally Funded Research and Development Centers (FFRDC's) and related sponsoring agreements.

(2) An FFRDC meets some special long-term research or development need which cannot be met as effectively by existing in-house or contractor resources. FFRDC's enable agencies to use private sector resources to accomplish tasks that are integral to the mission and operation of the sponsoring agency. An FFRDC, in order to discharge its responsibilities to the sponsoring agency, has access, beyond that which is common to the normal contractual relationship, to Government and supplier data, including sensitive and proprietary data, and to employees and installations equipment and real property. The FFRDC is required to conduct its business in a manner befitting its special relationship with the Government, to operate in the public interest with objectivity and independence, to be free from organizational conflicts of interest, and to have full disclosure of its affairs to the sponsoring agency. It is not the Government's intent that an FFRDC use its privileged information or access to installations equipment and real property to compete with the private sector. However, an FFRDC may perform work for other than the sponsoring agency under the Economy Act, or other applicable legislation, when the work is not otherwise available from the private sector.

(3) FFRDC's are operated, managed, and/or administered by either a university or consortium of universities, other not-for-profit or nonprofit organization, or an industrial firm, as an autonomous organization or as an identifiable separate operating unit of a parent organization.

(4) Long-term relationships between the Government and FFRDC's are encouraged in order to provide the continuity that will attract high-quality personnel to the FFRDC. This relationship should be of a type to encourage the FFRDC to maintain currency in its field(s) of expertise, maintain its objectivity and independence, preserve its familiarity with the needs of its sponsor(s), and provide a quick response capability.

(b) *Definitions.* As used in this section—

Nonsponsor means any other organization, in or outside of the Federal Government, which funds specific work to be performed by the FFRDC and is not a party to the sponsoring agreement.

Primary sponsor means the lead agency responsible for managing, administering, or monitoring overall use of the FFRDC under a multiple sponsorship agreement.

Sponsor means the executive agency which manages, administers, monitors, funds, and is responsible for the overall use of an FFRDC. Multiple agency sponsorship is possible as long as one agency agrees to act as the "primary sponsor." In the event of multiple sponsors, "sponsor" refers to the primary sponsor.

[FAC 84-56, 55 FR 3885, 2/5/90, effective 3/7/90; FAC 97-22, 66 FR 2116, 1/10/2001, effective 3/12/2001; Delay of effective date, 66 FR 14259, 3/9/2001, effective 5/11/2001; FAC 2005-17, 72 FR 27364, 5/15/2007, effective 6/14/2007]

35.017-1 Sponsoring agreements.

(a) In order to facilitate a long-term relationship between the Government and an FFRDC, establish the FFRDC's mission, and ensure a periodic reevaluation of the FFRDC, a written agreement of sponsorship between the Government and the FFRDC shall be prepared when the FFRDC is established. The sponsoring agreement may take various forms; it may be included in a contract between the Government and the FFRDC, or in another legal instrument under which an FFRDC accomplishes effort, or it may be in a separate written agreement. Notwithstanding its form, the sponsoring agreement shall be clearly designated as such by the sponsor.

(b) While the specific content of any sponsoring agreement will vary depending on the situation, the agreement shall contain, as a minimum, the requirements of paragraph (c) of this subsection. The requirements for, and the contents of, sponsoring agreements may be as further specified in sponsoring agencies' policies and procedures.

(c) As a minimum, the following requirements must be addressed in either a sponsoring agreement or sponsoring agencies' policies and procedures:

(1) A statement of the purpose and mission of the FFRDC.

(2) Provisions for the orderly termination or nonrenewal of the agreement, disposal of assets, and settlement of liabilities. The responsibility for capitalization of an FFRDC must be defined in such a manner that ownership of assets may be readily and equitably determined upon termination of the FFRDC's relationship with its sponsor(s).

(3) A provision for the identification of retained earnings (reserves) and the development of a plan for their use and disposition.

(4) A prohibition against the FFRDC competing with any non-FFRDC concern in response to a Federal agency request for proposal for other than the operation of an FFRDC. This prohibition is not required to be applied to any parent organization or other subsidiary of the parent organization in its non-FFRDC operations. Requests for information, qualifications or capabilities can be answered unless otherwise restricted by the sponsor.

(5) A delineation of whether or not the FFRDC may accept work from other than the sponsor(s). If nonsponsor work can be accepted, a delineation of the procedures to be followed, along with any limitations as to the nonsponsors from which work can be accepted (other Federal agencies, State or local governments, nonprofit or profit organizations, etc.).

(d) The sponsoring agreement or sponsoring agencies' policies and procedures may also contain, as appropriate, other provisions, such as identification of—

(1) Any cost elements which will require advance agreement if cost-type contracts are used; and

(2) Considerations which will affect negotiation of fees where payment of fees is determined by the sponsor(s) to be appropriate.

(e) The term of the agreement will not exceed 5 years, but can be renewed, as a result of periodic review, in increments not to exceed 5 years.

[FAC 84-56, 55 FR 3885, 2/5/90, effective 3/7/90]

35.017-2 Establishing or changing an FFRDC.

To establish an FFRDC, or change its basic purpose and mission, the sponsor shall ensure the following:

(a) Existing alternative sources for satisfying agency requirements cannot effectively meet the special research or development needs.

(b) The notices required for publication (see 5.205(b)) are placed as required.

(c) There is sufficient Government expertise available to adequately and objectively evaluate the work to be performed by the FFRDC.

(d) The Executive Office of the President, Office of Science and Technology Policy, Washington, DC 20506, is notified.

(e) Controls are established to ensure that the costs of the services being provided to the Government are reasonable.

(f) The basic purpose and mission of the FFRDC is stated clearly enough to enable differentiation between work which should be performed by the FFRDC and that which should be performed by non-FFRDC's.

(g) A reasonable continuity in the level of support to the FFRDC is maintained, consistent with the agency's need for the FFRDC and the terms of the sponsoring agreement.

(h) The FFRDC is operated, managed, or administered by an autonomous organization or as an identifiably separate operating unit of a parent organization, and is required to operate in the public interest, free from organizational conflict of interest, and to disclose its affairs (as an FFRDC) to the primary sponsor.

(i) Quantity production or manufacturing is not performed unless authorized by legislation.

(j) Approval is received from the head of the sponsoring agency.

[FAC 84-56, 55 FR 3885, 2/5/90, effective 3/7/90; FAC 90-46, 62 FR 12690, 3/17/97, effective 5/16/97]

35.017-3 Using an FFRDC.

(a) All work placed with the FFRDC must be within the purpose, mission, general scope of effort, or special competency of the FFRDC.

(b) Where the use of the FFRDC by a nonsponsor is permitted by the sponsor, the sponsor shall be responsible for compliance with paragraph (a) of this subsection.

(1) The nonsponsoring agency shall provide the documentation required by 17.503(e) to the sponsoring agency.

(2) When a D&F is required pursuant to 17.502-2(c), the nonsponsoring agency shall prepare the D&F and provide the documentation required by 17.503(e) to the sponsoring agency.

(3) When permitted by the sponsor, a Federal agency may contract directly with the FFRDC, in which case that Federal agency is responsible for compliance with part 6.

[FAC 84-56, 55 FR 3886, 2/5/90, effective 3/7/90; FAC 2005-47, 75 FR 77733, 12/13/2010, effective 12/13/2010; FAC 2005-55, 77 FR 183, 1/3/2012, 2/2/2012; FAC 2019-02, 84 FR 19837, 5/6/2019, effective 6/5/2019]

35.017-4 Reviewing FFRDC's.

(a) The sponsor, prior to extending the contract or agreement with an FFRDC, shall conduct a comprehensive review of the use and need for the FFRDC. The review will be coordinated with any co-sponsors and may be performed in conjunction with the budget process. If the sponsor determines that its sponsorship is no longer appropriate, it shall apprise other agencies which use the FFRDC of the determination and afford them an opportunity to assume sponsorship.

(b) Approval to continue or terminate the sponsorship shall rest with the head of the sponsoring agency. This determination shall be based upon the results of the review conducted in accordance with paragraph (c) of this subsection.

(c) An FFRDC review should include the following:

(1) An examination of the sponsor's special technical needs and mission requirements that are performed by the FFRDC to determine if and at what level they continue to exist.

(2) Consideration of alternative sources to meet the sponsor's needs.

(3) An assessment of the efficiency and effectiveness of the FFRDC in meeting the sponsor's needs, including the FFRDC's ability to maintain its objectivity, independence, quick response capability, currency in its field(s) of expertise, and familiarity with the needs of its sponsor.

(4) An assessment of the adequacy of the FFRDC management in ensuring a cost-effective operation.

(5) A determination that the criteria for establishing the FFRDC continue to be satisfied and that the sponsoring agreement is in compliance with 35.017-1.

[FAC 84-56, 55 FR 3886, 2/5/90, effective 3/7/90]

35.017-5 Terminating an FFRDC.

When a sponsor's need for the FFRDC no longer exists, the sponsorship may be transferred to one or more Government agencies, if appropriately justified. If the FFRDC is not transferred to another Government agency, it shall be phased out.

[FAC 84-56, 55 FR 3886, 2/5/90, effective 3/7/90]

35.017-6 Master list of FFRDC's.

The National Science Foundation (NSF) maintains a master Government list of FFRDC's. Primary sponsors will provide information on each FFRDC, including sponsoring agreements, mission statements, funding data, and type of R&D being performed, to the NSF upon its request for such information.

[FAC 84-56, 55 FR 3886, 2/5/90, effective 3/7/90]

35.017-7 Limitation on the creation of new FFRDC's.

Pursuant to 10 U.S.C. 2367, the Secretary of Defense, the Secretary of the Army, the Secretary of the Navy, the Secretary of the Air Force, the Secretary of Homeland Security, and the Administrator of the National Aeronautics and Space Administration may not obligate or expend amounts appropriated to the Department of Defense for purposes of operating an FFRDC that was not in existence before June 2, 1986, until—

(a) The head of the agency submits to Congress a report with respect to such center that describes the purpose, mission, and general scope of effort of the center; and

(b) A period of 60 days, beginning on the date such report is received by Congress, has elapsed.

[FAC 84-56, 55 FR 3886, 2/5/90, effective 3/7/90; FAC 2005-84, 80 FR 53439, 9/3/2015, effective 9/3/2015]

PART 36—CONSTRUCTION AND ARCHITECT-ENGINEER CONTRACTS

Table of Contents

Scope of part 36.000
Definitions 36.001

Subpart 36.1—General

Applicability 36.101
Definitions 36.102
Methods of contracting 36.103
Policy 36.104

Subpart 36.2—Special Aspects of Contracting for Construction

Evaluation of contractor performance 36.201
Specifications 36.202
Government estimate of construction costs 36.203
Disclosure of the magnitude of construction projects 36.204
Statutory cost limitations 36.205
Liquidated damages 36.206
Pricing fixed-price construction contracts 36.207
Concurrent performance of firm-fixed-price and other types of construction contracts 36.208
Construction contracts with architect-engineer firms 36.209
Inspection of site and examination of data 36.210
Distribution of advance notices and solicitations 36.211
Preconstruction orientation 36.212
Special procedures for sealed bidding in construction contracting 36.213
General 36.213-1
Presolicitation notices 36.213-2
Invitations for bids 36.213-3
Notice of award 36.213-4
Special procedures for price negotiation in construction contracting 36.214
Special procedure for cost-reimbursement contracts for construction 36.215

Subpart 36.3—Two-Phase Design-Build Selection Procedures

Scope of subpart 36.300
Use of two-phase design-build selection procedures 36.301
Scope of work 36.302
Procedures 36.303
Phase One 36.303-1
Phase Two 36.303-2

Subpart 36.4—[Reserved]

Subpart 36.5—Contract Clauses

Scope of subpart 36.500
Performance of work by the contractor 36.501
Differing site conditions 36.502
Site investigation and conditions affecting the work 36.503
Physical data 36.504
Material and workmanship 36.505
Superintendence by the contractor 36.506
Permits and responsibilities 36.507
Other contracts 36.508
Protection of existing vegetation, structures, equipment, utilities, and improvements 36.509
Operations and storage areas 36.510
Use and possession prior to completion 36.511

Cleaning up . . . 36.512
Accident prevention . . . 36.513
Availability and use of utility services . . . 36.514
Schedules for construction contracts . . . 36.515
Quantity surveys . . . 36.516
Layout of work . . . 36.517
Work oversight in cost-reimbursement construction contracts . . . 36.518
Organization and direction of the work . . . 36.519
Contracting by negotiation . . . 36.520
Specifications and drawings for construction . . . 36.521
Preconstruction conference . . . 36.522
Site visit . . . 36.523

Subpart 36.6—Architect-Engineer Services

Scope of subpart . . . 36.600
Policy . . . 36.601
Public announcement . . . 36.601-1
Competition . . . 36.601-2
Applicable contracting procedures . . . 36.601-3
Implementation . . . 36.601-4
Selection of firms for architect-engineer contracts . . . 36.602
Selection criteria . . . 36.602-1
Evaluation boards . . . 36.602-2
Evaluation board functions . . . 36.602-3
Selection authority . . . 36.602-4
Short selection process for contracts not to exceed the simplified acquisition threshold . . . 36.602-5
Collecting data on and appraising firms' qualifications . . . 36.603
Performance evaluation . . . 36.604
Government cost estimate for architect-engineer work . . . 36.605
Negotiations . . . 36.606
Release of information on firm selection . . . 36.607
Liability for Government costs resulting from design errors or deficiencies . . . 36.608
Contract clauses . . . 36.609
Design within funding limitations . . . 36.609-1
Redesign responsibility for design errors or deficiencies . . . 36.609-2
Work oversight in architect-engineer contracts . . . 36.609-3
Requirements for registration of designers . . . 36.609-4

Subpart 36.7—Standard and Optional Forms for Contracting for Construction, Architect-Engineer Services, and Dismantling, Demolition, or Removal of Improvements

Scope of subpart . . . 36.700
Standard and optional forms for use in contracting for construction or dismantling, demolition, or removal of improvements . . . 36.701
Forms for use in contracting for architect-engineer services . . . 36.702

PART 36—CONSTRUCTION AND ARCHITECT-ENGINEER CONTRACTS

36.000 Scope of part.

This part prescribes policies and procedures peculiar to contracting for construction and architect-engineer services. It includes requirements for using certain clauses and standard forms that apply also to contracts for dismantling, demolition, or removal of improvements.

36.001 Definitions.

As used in this part—

Construction and demolition materials and debris means materials and debris generated during construction, renovation, demolition, or dismantling of all structures and buildings and associated infrastructure.

Diverting means redirecting materials that might otherwise be placed in the waste stream to recycling or recovery, excluding diversion to waste-to-energy facilities.

[FAC 2005-52, 76 FR 31395, 5/31/2011, effective 5/31/2011]

SUBPART 36.1—GENERAL

36.101 Applicability.

(a) Construction and architect-engineer contracts are subject to the requirements in other parts of this regulation, which shall be followed when applicable.

(b) When a requirement in this part is inconsistent with a requirement in another part of this regulation, this Part 36 shall take precedence if the acquisition of construction or architect-engineer services is involved.

(c) A contract for both construction and supplies or services shall include—

(1) Clauses applicable to the predominant part of the work (see Subpart 22.4), or

(2) If the contract is divided into parts, the clauses applicable to each portion.

[Interim rule, FAC 90-15, 57 FR 55471, 11/25/92, effective 11/23/92; FAC 90-17, 58 FR 12140, 3/2/93, effective 3/2/93]

36.102 Definitions.

As used in this part—

Contract is intended to refer to a contract for construction or a contract for architect-engineer services, unless another meaning is clearly intended.

Design means defining the construction requirement (including the functional relationships and technical systems to be used, such as architectural, environmental, structural, electrical, mechanical, and fire protection), producing the technical specifications and drawings, and preparing the construction cost estimate.

Design-bid-build means the traditional delivery method where design and construction are sequential and contracted for separately with two contracts and two contractors.

Design-build means combining design and construction in a single contract with one contractor.

Firm, in conjunction with architect-engineer services, means any individual, partnership, corporation, association, or other legal entity permitted by law to practice the professions of architecture or engineering.

Plans and specifications means drawings, specifications, and other data for and preliminary to the construction.

Record drawings means drawings submitted by a contractor or subcontractor at any tier to show the construction of a particular structure or work as actually completed under the contract.

Two-phase design-build selection procedures is a selection method in which a limited number of offerors (normally five or fewer) is selected during Phase One to submit detailed proposals for Phase Two (see subpart 36.3).

[FAC 84-23, 51 FR 36972, 10/16/86, effective 9/30/86; FAC 84-45, 54 FR 13336, 3/31/89, effective 3/31/89; FAC 84-46, 54 FR 19827, 5/8/89, effective 6/7/89; FAC 90-5, 56 FR 29128, 6/25/91, effective 7/25/91; FAC 90-45, Final rule, 62 FR 224, 1/2/97, effective 1/1/97; FAC 97-15, 64 FR 72414, 12/27/99, effective 2/25/2000; FAC 97-22, 66 FR 2116, 1/10/2001, effective 3/12/2001; Delay of effective date, 66 FR 14259, 3/9/2001, effective 5/11/2001]

36.103 Methods of contracting.

(a) The contracting officer shall use sealed bid procedures for a construction contract if the conditions in 6.401(a) apply, unless the contract will be performed outside the United States and its outlying areas. (See 6.401(b)(2).)

(b) Contracting officers shall acquire architect-engineer services by negotiation, and select sources in accordance with applicable law, Subpart 36.6, and agency regulations.

[FAC 84-5, 50 FR 1744, 1/11/85, effective 4/1/85; FAC 2001-14, 68 FR 28079, 5/22/2003, effective 6/23/2003]

36.104 Policy.

(a) Unless the traditional acquisition approach of design-bid-build established under 40 U.S.C. chapter 11, Selection of Architects and Engineers or another acquisition procedure authorized by law is used, the contracting officer shall use the two-phase selection procedures authorized by 10 U.S.C. 2305a or 41 U.S.C. 3309 when entering into a contract for the design and construction of a public building, facility, or work, if the contracting officer makes a determination that the procedures are appropriate for use (see subpart 36.3). Other acquisition procedures authorized by law include the procedures established in this part and other parts of this chapter and, for DoD, the design-build process described in 10 U.S.C. 2862.

(b) Agencies shall implement high-performance sustainable building design, construction, renovation, repair, commissioning, operation and maintenance, management, and deconstruction practices so as to—

(1) Ensure that all new construction, major renovation, or repair and alteration of Federal buildings complies with the Guiding Principles for Federal Leadership in High-Performance and Sustainable Buildings (available at *https://www.epa.gov/greeningepa/guiding-principles-federal-leadership-high-performance-and-sustainable-buildings*);

(2) Pursue cost-effective, innovative strategies, such as highly reflective and vegetated roofs, to minimize consumption of energy, water, and materials;

(3) Identify alternatives to renovation that reduce existing assets' deferred maintenance costs;

(4) Ensure that rehabilitation of Federally-owned historic buildings utilizes best practices and technologies in retrofitting to promote long-term viability of the buildings; and

(5) Ensure pollution prevention and eliminate waste by diverting at least 50 percent of construction and demolition materials and debris by the end of Fiscal Year 2015.

[FAC 90-45, Final rule, 62 FR 224, 1/2/97, effective 1/1/97; FAC 97-15, 64 FR 72414, 12/27/99, effective 12/27/99; FAC 2005-06, 70 FR 57453, 9/30/2005, effective 9/30/2005; FAC 2005-52, 76 FR 31395, 5/31/2011, effective 5/31/2011; FAC 2005-73, 79 FR 24192, 4/29/2014, effective 5/29/2014; FAC 2005-100, 83 FR 42571, 8/22/2018, effective 8/22/2018]

SUBPART 36.2—SPECIAL ASPECTS OF CONTRACTING FOR CONSTRUCTION

36.201 Evaluation of contractor performance.

See 42.1502(e) for the requirements for preparing past performance evaluations for construction contracts.

[FAC 84-12, 51 FR 2666, 1/17/86, effective 1/20/86; FAC 84-53, 54 FR 48989, 11/28/89, effective 12/28/89; FAC 2005-13, 71 FR 57363, 9/28/2006, effective 9/28/2006; FAC 2005-34, 74 FR 31557, 7/1/2009, effective 7/1/2009; FAC 2005-35, 74 FR 34206, 7/14/2009, effective 7/14/2009]

36.202 Specifications.

(a) Construction specifications shall conform to the requirements in Part 11 of this regulation.

(b) Whenever possible, contracting officers shall ensure that references in specifications are to widely recognized standards or specifications promulgated by governments, industries, or technical societies.

(c) When "brand name or equal" descriptions are necessary, specifications must clearly identify and describe the particular physical, functional, or other characteristics of the brand-name items which are considered essential to satisfying the requirement.

[FAC 90-32, 60 FR 48206, 9/18/95, effective 10/1/95; FAC 97-26, 66 FR 27405, 5/16/2001, effective 5/16/2001; FAC 2001-10, 67 FR 70518, 11/22/2002, effective 11/22/2002; FAC 2005-35, 74 FR 34206, 7/14/2009, effective 7/14/2009]

36.203 Government estimate of construction costs.

(a) An independent Government estimate of construction costs shall be prepared and furnished to the contracting officer at the earliest practicable time for each proposed contract and for each contract modification anticipated to exceed the simplified acquisition threshold. The contracting officer may require an estimate when the cost of required work is not anticipated to exceed the simplified acquisition threshold. The estimate shall be prepared in as much detail as though the Government were competing for award.

(b) When two-step sealed bidding is used, the independent Government estimate shall be prepared when the contract requirements are definitized.

(c) Access to information concerning the Government estimate shall be limited to Government personnel whose official duties require knowledge of the estimate. An exception to this rule may be made during contract negotiations to allow the contracting officer to identify a specialized task and disclose the associated cost breakdown figures in the Government estimate, but only to the extent deemed necessary to arrive at a fair and reasonable price. The overall amount of the Government's estimate shall not be disclosed except as permitted by agency regulations.

[FAC 84-5, 50 FR 1744, 1/11/85, effective 4/1/85; FAC 97-1, 62 FR 44802, 8/22/97, effective 10/21/97; FAC 2005-13, 71 FR 57363, 9/28/2006, effective 9/28/2006]

36.204 Disclosure of the magnitude of construction projects.

Advance notices and solicitations shall state the magnitude of the requirement in terms of physical characteristics and estimated price range. In no event shall the statement of magnitude disclose the Government's estimate. Therefore, the estimated price should be described in terms of one of the following price ranges:

(a) Less than $25,000.

(b) Between $25,000 and $100,000.

(c) Between $100,000 and $250,000.

(d) Between $250,000 and $500,000.

(e) Between $500,000 and $1,000,000.

(f) Between $1,000,000 and $5,000,000.

(g) Between $5,000,000 and $10,000,000.

(h) More than $10,000,000.

36.205 Statutory cost limitations.

(a) Contracts for construction shall not be awarded at a cost to the Government—

(1) In excess of statutory cost limitations, unless applicable limitations can be and are waived in writing for the particular contract; or

(2) Which, with allowances for Government-imposed contingencies and overhead, exceeds the statutory authorization.

(b) Solicitations containing one or more items subject to statutory cost limitations shall state—

(1) The applicable cost limitation for each affected item in a separate schedule;

(2) That an offer which does not contain separately-priced schedules will not be considered; and

(3) That the price on each schedule shall include an approximate apportionment of all estimated direct costs, allocable indirect costs, and profit.

(c) The Government shall reject an offer if its prices exceed applicable statutory limitations, unless laws or agency procedures provide pertinent exemptions. However, if it is in the Government's interest, the contracting officer may include a provision in the solicitation which permits the award of separate contracts for individual items whose prices are within or subject to applicable statutory limitations.

(d) The Government shall also reject an offer if its prices are within statutory limitations only because it is materially unbalanced. An offer is unbalanced if its prices are significantly less than cost for some work, and overstated for other work.

[FAC 84-5, 50 FR 1744, 1/11/85, effective 4/1/85; FAC 90-45, Final rule, 62 FR 224, 1/2/97, effective 1/1/97]

36.206 Liquidated damages.

The contracting officer must evaluate the need for liquidated damages in a construction contract in accordance with 11.502 and agency regulations.

[FAC 90-32, 60 FR 48206, 9/18/95, effective 10/1/95; FAC 97-19, 65 FR 46052, 7/26/2000, effective 9/25/2000]

36.207 Pricing fixed-price construction contracts.

(a) Generally, firm-fixed-price contracts shall be used to acquire construction. They may be priced—

(1) On a lump-sum basis (when a lump sum is paid for the total work or defined parts of the work),

(2) On a unit-price basis (when a unit price is paid for a specified quantity of work units), or

(3) Using a combination of the two methods.

(b) Lump-sum pricing shall be used in preference to unit pricing except when—

(1) Large quantities of work such as grading, paving, building outside utilities, or site preparation are involved;

(2) Quantities of work, such as excavation, cannot be estimated with sufficient confidence to permit a lump-sum offer without a substantial contingency;

(3) Estimated quantities of work required may change significantly during construction; or

(4) Offerors would have to expend unusual effort to develop adequate estimates.

(c) Fixed-price contracts with economic price adjustment may be used if such a provision is customary in contracts for the type of work being acquired, or when omission of an adjustment provision would preclude a significant number of firms from submitting offers or would result in offerors including unwarranted contingencies in proposed prices.

36.208 Concurrent performance of firm-fixed-price and other types of construction contracts.

In view of potential labor and administrative problems, cost-plus-fixed-fee, price-incentive, or other types of contracts with cost variation or cost adjustment features shall not be permitted concurrently, at the same work site, with firm-fixed-price, lump sum, or unit price contracts except with the prior approval of the head of the contracting activity.

36.209 Construction contracts with architect-engineer firms.

No contract for the construction of a project shall be awarded to the firm that designed the project or its subsidiaries or affiliates, except with the approval of the head of the agency or authorized representative.

36.210 Inspection of site and examination of data.

The contracting officer should make appropriate arrangements for prospective offerors to inspect the work site and to have the opportunity to examine data available to the Government which may provide information concerning the performance of the work, such as boring samples, original boring logs, and records and plans of previous construction. The data should be assembled in one place and made available for examination. The solicitation should notify offerors of the time and place for the site inspection and data examination. If it is not feasible for offerors to inspect the site or examine the data on their own, the solicitation should also designate an individual who will show the site or data to the offerors. Significant site information and the data should be made available to all offerors in the same manner, including information regarding any utilities to be furnished during construction. A record should be kept of the identity and affiliation of all offerors' representatives who inspect the site or examine the data.

36.211 Distribution of advance notices and solicitations.

Advance notices and solicitations should be distributed to reach as many prospective offerors as practicable. Contracting officers may send notices and solicitations to organizations that maintain, without charge to the public, display rooms for the benefit of prospective offerors, subcontractors, and material suppliers. If requested by such organizations, this may be done for all or a stated class of construction projects on an annual or semiannual basis. Contracting officers may determine the geographical extent of distribution of advance notices and solicitations on a case-by-case basis.

36.212 Preconstruction orientation.

(a) The contracting officer will inform the successful offeror of significant matters of interest, including—

(1) Statutory matters such as labor standards (Subpart 22.4), and subcontracting plan requirements (Subpart 19.7); and

(2) Other matters of significant interest, including who has authority to decide matters such as contractual, administrative (*e.g.*, security, safety, and fire and environmental protection), and construction responsibilities.

(b) As appropriate, the contracting officer may issue an explanatory letter or conduct a preconstruction conference.

(c) If a preconstruction conference is to be held, the contracting officer shall—

(1) Conduct the conference prior to the start of construction at the work site;

(2) Notify the successful offeror of the date, time, and location of the conference (see 36.522); and

(3) Inform the successful offeror of the proposed agenda and any need for attendance by subcontractors.

[FAC 90-23, 59 FR 67010, 12/28/94, effective 2/27/95]

36.213 Special procedures for sealed bidding in construction contracting. (No Text)

36.213-1 General.

Contracting officers shall follow the procedures for sealed bidding in Part 14, as modified and supplemented by the requirements in this subpart.

[Redesignated from 36.301, FAC 90-45, Final rule, 62 FR 224, 1/2/97, effective 1/1/97]

36.213-2 Presolicitation notices.

(a) Unless the requirement is waived by the head of the contracting activity or a designee, the contracting officer shall issue presolicitation notices on any construction requirement when the proposed contract is expected to exceed the simplified acquisition threshold. Presolicitation notices may also be used when the proposed contract is not expected to exceed the simplified acquisition threshold. These notices shall be issued sufficiently in advance of the invitation for bids to stimulate the interest of the greatest number of prospective bidders.

(b) Presolicitation notices must—

(1) Describe the proposed work in sufficient detail to disclose the nature and volume of work (in terms of physical characteristics and estimated price range) (see 36.204);

(2) State the location of the work;

(3) Include tentative dates for issuing invitations, opening bids, and completing contract performance;

(4) State where plans will be available for inspection without charge;

(5) Specify a date by which requests for the invitation for bids should be submitted;

(6) State whether award is restricted to small businesses;

(7) Specify any amount to be charged for solicitation documents; and

(8) Be publicized through the Governmentwide point of entry in accordance with 5.204.

[Redesignated from 36.302, FAC 90-45, Final rule, 62 FR 224, 1/2/97, effective 1/1/97;

FAC 97-26, 66 FR 27405, 5/16/2001, effective 5/16/2001; FAC 2001-25, 69 FR 59699, 10/5/2004, effective 11/4/2004; FAC 2005-13, 71 FR 57363, 9/28/2006, effective 9/28/2006]

36.213-3 Invitations for bids.

(a) Invitations for bids for construction shall allow sufficient time for bid preparation (*i.e.*, the period of time between the date invitations are distributed and the date set for opening of bids) (but see 5.203 and 14.202-1) to allow bidders an adequate opportunity to prepare and submit their bids, giving due regard to the construction season and the time necessary for bidders to inspect the site, obtain subcontract bids, examine data concerning the work, and prepare estimates based on plans and specifications.

(b) Invitations for bids shall be prepared in accordance with Subpart 14.2 and this section using the forms prescribed in Part 53.

(c) Contracting officers should assure that each invitation for bids includes the following information, when applicable:

(1) The appropriate wage determination of the Secretary of Labor (see Subpart 22.4), or, if the invitation for bids must be issued before the wage determination is received, a notice that the schedule of minimum wage rates to be paid under the contract will be issued as an amendment to the invitation for bids before the opening date for bids (see 14.208 and Subpart 22.4).

(2) The Performance of Work by the Contractor clause (see 36.501 and 52.236-1).

(3) The magnitude of the proposed construction project (see 36.204).

(4) The period of performance (see Subpart 11.4).

(5) Arrangements made for bidders to inspect the site and examine the data concerning performance of the work (see 36.210).

(6) Information concerning any facilities, such as utilities, office space, and warehouse space, to be furnished during construction.

(7) Information concerning the prebid conference (see 14.207).

(8) Any special qualifications or experience requirements that will be considered in determining the responsibility of bidders (see Subpart 9.1).

(9) Any special instructions concerning bids, alternate bids, and award.

(10) Any instructions concerning reporting requirements.

(d) The contracting officer shall send invitations for bids to prospective bidders who requested them in response to the presolicitation notice, and should send them to other prospective bidders upon their specific request (see 5.102(a)).

[Redesignated from 36.303, FAC 90-45, Final rule, 62 FR 224, 1/2/97, effective 1/1/97; FAC 2001-15, 68 FR 43854, 7/24/2003, effective 8/25/2003]

36.213-4 Notice of award.

When a notice of award is issued, it shall be done in writing or electronically, shall contain information required by 14.408, and shall—

(a) Identify the invitation for bids;

(b) Identify the contractor's bid;

(c) State the award price;

(d) Advise the contractor that any required payment and performance bonds must be promptly executed and returned to the contracting officer;

(e) Specify the date of commencement of work, or advise that a notice to proceed will be issued.

[Redesignated from 36.304, FAC 90-45, Final rule, 62 FR 224, 1/2/97, effective 1/1/97]

36.214 Special procedures for price negotiation in construction contracting.

(a) Agencies shall follow the policies and procedures in Part 15 when negotiating prices for construction.

(b) The contracting officer shall evaluate proposals and associated certified cost or pricing data and data other than certified cost or pricing data and shall compare them to the Government estimate.

(1) When submission of certified cost or pricing data is not required (see 15.403-1 and 15.403-2), and any element of proposed cost differs significantly from the Government estimate, the contracting officer should request the offeror to submit cost information concerning that element (*e.g.*, wage rates or fringe benefits, significant materials, equipment allowances, and subcontractor costs).

(2) When a proposed price is significantly lower than the Government estimate, the contracting officer shall make sure both the offeror and the Government estimator completely understand the scope of the work. If negotiations reveal errors in the Government estimate, the estimate shall be corrected and the changes shall be documented in the contract file.

(c) When appropriate, additional pricing tools may be used. For example, proposed prices may be compared to current prices for similar types of work, adjusted for differences in the work site and the specifications. Also, rough yardsticks may be developed and used, such as cost per cubic foot for structures, cost per linear foot for utilities, and cost per cubic yard for excavation or concrete.

[Redesignated from 36.402, FAC 90-45, Final rule, 62 FR 224, 1/2/97, effective 1/1/97; FAC 97-2, 62 FR 51224, 9/30/97, effective 10/10/97; FAC 2005-45; 75 FR 53135, 8/30/2010, effective 10/1/2010]

36.215 Special procedure for cost-reimbursement contracts for construction.

Contracting officers may use a cost-reimbursement contract to acquire construction only when its use is consistent with Subpart 16.3 and Part 15 (see 15.404-4(c) (4) (i) for fee limitation on cost-reimbursement contracts).

[Redesignated from 36.403, FAC 90-45, Final rule, 62 FR 224, 1/2/97, effective 1/1/97; FAC 97-2, 62 FR 51224, 9/30/97, effective 10/10/97]

SUBPART 36.3—TWO-PHASE DESIGN-BUILD SELECTION PROCEDURES

36.300 Scope of subpart.

This subpart prescribes policies and procedures for the use of the two-phase design-build selection procedures authorized by 10 U.S.C. 2305a and 41 U.S.C. 3309.

[FAC 90-45, Final rule, 62 FR 224, 1/2/97, effective 1/1/97; FAC 2005-73, 79 FR 24192, 4/29/2014, effective 5/29/2014]

36.301 Use of two-phase design-build selection procedures.

(a) During formal or informal acquisition planning (see Part 7), if considering the use of two-phase design-build selection procedures, the contracting officer shall conduct the evaluation in paragraph (b) of this section.

(b) The two-phase design-build selection procedures shall be used when the contracting officer determines that this method is appropriate, based on the following:

(1) Three or more offers are anticipated.

(2) Design work must be performed by offerors before developing price or cost proposals, and offerors will incur a substantial amount of expense in preparing offers.

(3) The following criteria have been considered:

(i) The extent to which the project requirements have been adequately defined.

(ii) The time constraints for delivery of the project.

(iii) The capability and experience of potential contractors.

(iv) The suitability of the project for use of the two-phase selection method.

(v) The capability of the agency to manage the two-phase selection process.

(vi) Other criteria established by the head of the contracting activity.

[FAC 90-45, Final rule, 62 FR 224, 1/2/97, effective 1/1/97]

36.302 Scope of work.

The agency shall develop, either in-house or by contract, a scope of work that defines the project and states the Government's requirements. The scope of work may include criteria and preliminary design, budget parameters, and schedule or delivery requirements. If the agency contracts for development of the scope of work, the procedures in Subpart 36.6 shall be used.

[FAC 90-45, Final rule, 62 FR 224, 1/2/97, effective 1/1/97]

36.303 Procedures.

One solicitation may be issued covering both phases, or two solicitations may be issued in sequence. Proposals will be evaluated in Phase One to determine which offerors will submit proposals for Phase Two. One contract will be awarded using competitive negotiation.

[FAC 90-45, Final rule, 62 FR 224, 1/2/97, effective 1/1/97]

36.303-1 Phase One.

(a) Phase One of the solicitation(s) shall include—

(1) The scope of work;

(2) The phase-one evaluation factors, including—

(i) Technical approach (but not detailed design or technical information);

(ii) Technical qualifications, such as—

(A) Specialized experience and technical competence;

(B) Capability to perform;

(C) Past performance of the offeror's team (including the architect-engineer and construction members); and

(iii) Other appropriate factors (excluding cost or price related factors, which are not permitted in Phase One);

(3) Phase-two evaluation factors (see 36.303-2); and

(4) A statement of the maximum number of offerors that will be selected to submit phase-two proposals. The maximum number specified in the solicitation shall not exceed five unless the contracting officer determines, for that particular solicitation, that a number greater than five is in the Government's interest and is consistent with the purposes and objectives of the two-phase design-build selection procedures. The contracting officer shall document this determination in the contract file. For acquisitions greater than $4 million, the determination shall be approved by the head of the contracting activity, delegable to a level no lower than the senior contracting official within the contracting activity. In civilian agencies, for this paragraph (a)(4), the senior contracting official is the advocate for competition for the procuring activity, unless the agency designates a different position in agency procedures. The approval shall be documented in the contract file.

(b) After evaluating phase-one proposals, the contracting officer shall select the most highly qualified offerors (not to exceed the maximum number specified in the solicitation in accordance with 36.303-1(a)(4)) and request that only those offerors submit phase-two proposals.

[FAC 90-45, Final rule, 62 FR 224, 1/2/97, effective 1/1/97, corrected 62 FR 10709, 3/10/97; FAC 2005-88, 81 FR 30447, 5/16/2016, effective 6/15/2016]

36.303-2 Phase Two.

(a) Phase Two of the solicitation(s) shall be prepared in accordance with Part 15, and include phase-two evaluation factors, developed in accordance with 15.304. Examples of potential phase-two technical evaluation factors include design concepts, management approach, key personnel, and proposed technical solutions.

(b) Phase Two of the solicitation(s) shall require submission of technical and price proposals, which shall be evaluated separately, in accordance with Part 15.

[FAC 90-45, Final rule, 62 FR 224, 1/2/97, effective 1/1/97; FAC 97-2, 62 FR 51224, 9/30/97, effective 10/10/97]

SUBPART 36.4—[RESERVED]

SUBPART 36.5—CONTRACT CLAUSES

36.500 Scope of subpart.

This subpart prescribes clauses for insertion in solicitations and contracts for (a) construction and (b) dismantling, demolition, or removal of improvements contracts. Provisions and clauses prescribed elsewhere in the Federal Acquisition Regulation (FAR) shall also be used in such solicitations and contracts when the conditions specified in the prescriptions for the provisions and clauses are applicable.

36.501 Performance of work by the contractor.

(a) To assure adequate interest in and supervision of all work involved in larger projects, the contractor shall be required to perform a significant part of the contract work with its own forces. The contract shall express this requirement in terms of a percentage that reflects the minimum amount of work the contractor must perform with its own forces. This percentage is (1) as high as the contracting officer considers appropriate for the project, consistent with customary or necessary specialty subcontracting and the complexity and magnitude of the work, and (2) ordinarily not less than 12 percent unless a greater percentage is required by law or agency regulation. Specialties such as plumbing, heating, and electrical work are usually subcontracted, and should not normally be considered in establishing the amount of work required to be performed by the contractor.

(b) The contracting officer shall insert the clause at 52.236-1, Performance of Work by the Contractor, in solicitations and contracts, except those awarded pursuant to Subparts 19.5, 19.8, 19.13, 19.14, or 1915 when a fixed-price construction contract is contemplated and the contract amount is expected to exceed $1.5 million. The contracting officer may insert the clause in solicitations and contracts when a fixed-price construction contract is contemplated and the contract amount is expected to be $1.5 million or less.

[FAC 84-40, 53 FR 43392, 10/26/88, effective 11/25/88; FAC 2001-23, 69 FR 25273, 5/5/2004, effective 5/5/2004; FAC 2005-02, 70 FR 14950, 3/23/2005, effective 3/23/2005; FAC 2005-45, 75 FR 53129, 8/30/2010, effective 10/1/2010; FAC 2005-51, 76 FR 18304, 4/1/2011, effective 4/1/2011; FAC 2005-56, 77 FR 12913, 3/2/2012, effective 4/2/2012; FAC 2005-77, 79 FR 61746, 10/14/2014, effective 10/14/2014]

36.502 Differing site conditions.

The contracting officer shall insert the clause at 52.236-2, Differing Site Conditions, in solicitations and contracts when a fixed-price construction contract or a fixed-price dismantling, demolition, or removal of improvements contract is contemplated and the contract amount is expected to exceed the simplified acquisition threshold. The contracting officer may insert the clause in solicitations and contracts when a fixed-price construction or a fixed-price contract for dismantling, demolition, or removal of improvements is contemplated and the contract amount is expected to be at or below the simplified acquisition threshold.

[FAC 90-29, 60 FR 34732, 7/3/95, effective 7/3/95]

36.503 Site investigation and conditions affecting the work.

The contracting officer shall insert the clause at 52.236-3, Site Investigation and Conditions Affecting the Work, in solicitations and contracts when a fixed-price construction contract or a fixed-price dismantling, demolition, or removal of improvements contract is contemplated and the contract amount is expected to exceed the simplified acquisition threshold. The contracting officer may insert the clause in solicitations and contracts when a fixed-price construction or a fixed-price contract for dismantling, demolition, or removal of improvements is contemplated and the contract amount is expected to be at or below the simplified acquisition threshold.

[FAC 90-29, 60 FR 34732, 7/3/95, effective 7/3/95]

36.504 Physical data.

The contracting officer shall insert the clause at 52.236-4, Physical Data, in solicitations and contracts when a fixed-price construction contract is contemplated and physical data (*e.g.*, test borings, hydrographic data, weather conditions data) will be furnished or made available to offerors.

36.505 Material and workmanship.

The contracting officer shall insert the clause at 52.236-5, Material and Workmanship, in solicitations and contracts for construction contracts.

[FAC 84-53, 54 FR 48989, 11/28/89, effective 12/28/89]

36.506 Superintendence by the contractor.

The contracting officer shall insert the clause at 52.236-6, Superintendence by the Contractor, in solicitations and contracts when a fixed-price construction contract or a fixed-price dismantling, demolition, or removal of improvements contract is contemplated and the contract amount is expected to exceed the simplified acquisition threshold. The contracting officer may insert the clause in solicitations and contracts when a fixed-price construction or a fixed-price contract for dismantling, demolition, or removal of improvements is contemplated and the contract amount is expected to be at or below the simplified acquisition threshold.

[FAC 90-29, 60 FR 34732, 7/3/95, effective 7/3/95]

36.507 Permits and responsibilities.

The contracting officer shall insert the clause at 52.236-7, Permits and Responsibilities, in solicitations and contracts when a fixed-price or cost-reimbursement construction contract or a fixed-price dismantling, demolition, or removal of improvements contract is contemplated.

[FAC 84-53, 54 FR 48989, 11/28/89, effective 12/28/89]

36.508 Other contracts.

The contracting officer shall insert the clause at 52.236-8, Other Contracts, in solicitations and contracts when a fixed-price construction contract or a fixed-price dismantling, demolition, or removal of improvements contract is contemplated and the contract amount is expected to exceed the simplified acquisition threshold. The contracting officer may insert the clause in solicitations and contracts when a fixed-price construction or a fixed-price contract for dismantling, demolition, or removal of improvements is contemplated and the contract amount is expected to be at or below the simplified acquisition threshold.

[FAC 90-29, 60 FR 34732, 7/3/95, effective 7/3/95]

36.509 Protection of existing vegetation, structures, equipment, utilities, and improvements.

The contracting officer shall insert the clause at 52.236-9, Protection of Existing Vegetation, Structures, Equipment, Utilities, and Improvements, in solicitations and contracts when a fixed-price construction contract or a fixed-price dismantling, demolition, or removal of improvements contract is contemplated and the contract amount is expected to exceed the simplified acquisition threshold. The contracting officer may insert the clause in solicitations and contracts when a fixed-price construction or a fixed-price contract for dismantling, demolition, or removal of improvements is contemplated and the contract amount is expected to be at or below the simplified acquisition threshold.

[FAC 90-29, 60 FR 34732, 7/3/95, effective 7/3/95]

36.510 Operations and storage areas.

The contracting officer shall insert the clause at 52.236-10, Operations and Storage Areas, in solicitations and contracts when a fixed-price construction contract or a fixed-price dismantling, demolition, or removal of improvements contract is contemplated and the contract amount is expected to exceed the simplified acquisition threshold. The contracting officer may insert the clause in solicitations and contracts when a fixed-price construction or a fixed-price contract for dismantling, demolition, or removal of improvements is contemplated and the contract amount is expected to be at or below the simplified acquisition threshold.

[FAC 90-29, 60 FR 34732, 7/3/95, effective 7/3/95]

36.511 Use and possession prior to completion.

The contracting officer shall insert the clause at 52.236-11, Use and Possession Prior to Completion, in solicitations and contracts when a fixed-price construction contract is contemplated and the contract award amount is expected to exceed the simplified acquisition threshold. This clause may be inserted in solicitations and contracts when the contract amount is expected to be at or below the simplified acquisition threshold.

[FAC 90-29, 60 FR 34732, 7/3/95, effective 7/3/95]

36.512 Cleaning up.

The contracting officer shall insert the clause at 52.236-12, Cleaning Up, in solicitations and contracts when a fixed-price construction contract or a fixed-price dismantling, demolition, or removal of improvements contract is contemplated and the contract amount is expected to exceed the simplified acquisition threshold. The contracting officer may insert the clause in solicitations and contracts when a fixed-price construction or a fixed-price contract for dismantling, demolition, or removal of improvements is contemplated and the contract amount is expected to be at or below the simplified acquisition threshold.

[FAC 90-29, 60 FR 34732, 7/3/95, effective 7/3/95]

36.513 Accident prevention.

(a) The contracting officer shall insert the clause at 52.236-13, Accident Prevention, in solicitations and contracts when a fixed-price construction contract or a fixed-price dismantling, demolition, or removal of improvements contract is contemplated and the contract amount is expected to exceed the simplified acquisition threshold. The contracting officer may insert the clause in solicitations and contracts when a fixed-price construction or a fixed-price contract for dismantling, demolition, or removal of improvements is contemplated and the contract amount is expected to be at or below the simplified acquisition threshold. If the contract will involve work of a long duration or hazardous nature, the contracting officer shall use the clause with its Alternate I.

(b) The contracting officer shall insert the clause or the clause with its Alternate I in solicitations and contracts when a contract for services to be performed at Government facilities (see 48 CFR Part 37) is contemplated, and technical representatives advise that special precautions are appropriate.

(c) The contracting officer should inform the Occupational Safety and Health Administration (OSHA), or other cognizant Federal, State, or local officials, of instances where the contractor has been notified to take immediate action to correct serious or imminent dangers.

[FAC 90-8, 56 FR 18279, 10/25/91, effective 11/25/91; FAC 90-29, 60 FR 34732, 7/3/95, effective 7/3/95]

36.514 Availability and use of utility services.

The contracting officer shall insert the clause at 52.236-14, Availability and Use of Utility Services, in solicitations and contracts when a fixed-price construction contract or a fixed-price dismantling, demolition, or removal of improvements contract is contemplated, the contract is to be performed on Government sites, and the contracting officer decides (a) that the existing utility system(s) is adequate for the needs of both the Government and the contractor, and (b) furnishing it is in the Government's interest. When this clause is used, the contracting officer shall list the available utilities in the contract.

36.515 Schedules for construction contracts.

The contracting officer may insert the clause at 52.236-15, Schedules for Construction Contracts, in solicitations and contracts when a fixed-price construction contract is contemplated, the contract amount is expected to exceed the simplified acquisition threshold, and the period of actual work performance exceeds 60 days. This clause may also be inserted in such solicitations and contracts when work performance is expected to last less than 60 days and an unusual situation exists that warrants imposition of the requirements. This clause should not be used in the same contract with clauses covering other management approaches for ensuring that a contractor makes adequate progress.

[FAC 90-29, 60 FR 34732, 7/3/95, effective 7/3/95]

36.516 Quantity surveys.

The contracting officer may insert the clause at 52.236-16, Quantity Surveys, in solicitations and contracts when a fixed-price construction contract providing for unit pricing of items and for payment based on quantity surveys is contemplated. If it is determined at a level above that of the contracting officer that it is impracticable for Government personnel to perform the original and final surveys, and the Government wishes the contractor to perform these surveys, the clause shall be used with its Alternate.

36.517 Layout of work.

The contracting officer shall insert the clause at 52.236-17, Layout of Work, in solicitations and contracts when a fixed-price construction contract is contemplated and use of this clause is appropriate due to a need for accurate work layout and for siting verification during work performance.

36.518 Work oversight in cost-reimbursement construction contracts.

The contracting officer shall insert the clause at 52.236-18, Work Oversight in Cost-Reimbursement Construction Contracts, in solicitations and contracts when a cost-reimbursement construction contract is contemplated.

36.519 Organization and direction of the work.

The contracting officer shall insert the clause at 52.236-19, Organization and Direction of the Work, in solicitations and contracts when a cost-reimbursement construction contract is contemplated.

36.520 Contracting by negotiation.

The contracting officer shall insert in solicitations for construction the provision at 52.236-28, Preparation of Proposals—Construction, when contracting by negotiation.

[FAC 97-2, 62 FR 51224, 9/30/97, effective 10/10/97]

36.521 Specifications and drawings for construction.

The contracting officer shall insert the clause at 52.236-21, Specifications and Drawings for Construction, in solicitations and contracts when a fixed-price construction contract or a fixed-price dismantling, demolition, or removal of improvements contract is contemplated and the contract amount is expected to exceed the simplified acquisition threshold. The contracting officer may insert the clause in solicitations and contracts when a fixed-price construction or a fixed-price contract for dismantling, demolition, or removal of improvements is contemplated and the contract amount is expected to be at or below the simplified acquisition threshold. When the Government needs record drawings, the contracting officer shall—

(a) Use the clause with its Alternate I, if reproducible shop drawings are needed; or

(b) Use the clause with its Alternate II, if reproducible shop drawings are not needed.

[FAC 84-12, 51 FR 2666, 1/17/86, effective 1/20/86; FAC 84-53, 54 FR 48989, 11/28/89, effective 12/28/89; FAC 84-58, 55 FR 25530, 6/21/90, effective 7/23/90; FAC 90-29, 60 FR 34732, 7/3/95, effective 7/3/95]

36.522 Preconstruction conference.

If the contracting officer determines it may be desirable to hold a preconstruction conference, the contracting officer shall insert a clause substantially the same as the clause at 52.236-26, Preconstruction Conference, in solicitations and fixed price contracts for construction or for dismantling, demolition or removal of improvements.

[FAC 90-23, 59 FR 67010, 12/28/94, effective 2/27/95]

36.523 Site visit.

The contracting officer shall insert a provision substantially the same as the provision at 52.236-27, Site Visit (Construction), in solicitations which include the clauses at 52.236-2, Differing Site Conditions, and 52.236-3, Site Investigations and Conditions Affecting the Work. Alternate I may be used when an organized site visit will be conducted.

[FAC 90-23, 59 FR 67010, 12/28/94, effective 2/27/95]

SUBPART 36.6—ARCHITECT-ENGINEER SERVICES

36.600 Scope of subpart.

This subpart prescribes policies and procedures applicable to the acquisition of architect-engineer services, including orders for architect-engineer services under multi-agency contracts (see 16.505(a)(9)).

[FAC 2005-01, 70 FR 11737, 3/9/2005, effective 3/9/2005; FAC 2005-06, 70 FR 57452, 9/30/2005, effective 9/30/2005; FAC 2005-55, 77 FR 189, 1/3/2012, effective 2/2/2012]

36.601 Policy. (No Text)

36.601-1 Public announcement.

The Government shall publicly announce all requirements for architect-engineer services and negotiate contracts for these services based on the demonstrated competence and qualifications of prospective contractors to perform the services at fair and reasonable prices. (See 40 U.S.C. 1101, *et seq.*)

[FAC 90-5, 56 FR 29128, 6/25/91, effective 7/25/91; FAC 2005-06, 70 FR 57453, 9/30/2005, effective 9/30/2005]

36.601-2 Competition.

Acquisition of architect-engineer services in accordance with the procedures in this subpart will constitute a competitive procedure. (See 6.102(d)(1).)

[FAC 90-5, 56 FR 29128, 6/25/91, effective 7/25/91]

36.601-3 Applicable contracting procedures.

(a)(1) For facility design contracts, the statement of work shall require that the architect-engineer specify, in the construction design specifications, use of the maximum practicable amount of recovered materials consistent with the performance requirements, availability, price reasonableness, and cost-effectiveness. Where appropriate, the statement of work also shall require the architect-engineer to consider energy conservation, pollution prevention, and waste reduction to the maximum extent practicable in developing the construction design specifications.

(2) Facility design solicitations and contracts that include the specification of energy-consuming products must comply with the requirements at subpart 23.2.

(b) Sources for contracts for architect-engineer services shall be selected in accordance with the procedures in this subpart rather than the solicitation or source selection procedures prescribed in parts 13, 14, and 15 of this regulation.

(c) When the contract statement of work includes both architect-engineer services and other services, the contracting officer shall follow the procedures in this subpart if the statement of work, substantially or to a dominant extent, specifies performance or approval by a registered or licensed architect or engineer. If the statement of work does not specify such performance or approval, the contracting officer shall follow the procedures in parts 13, 14 or 15.

(d) Other than *incidental services* as specified in the definition of *architect-engineer services* in Section 2.101 and in Section 36.601-4(a)(3), services that do not require performance by a registered or licensed architect or engineer, notwithstanding the fact that architect-engineers also may perform those services, should be acquired pursuant to parts 13, 14, and 15.

[FAC 90-5, 56 FR 29128, 6/25/91, effective 7/25/91; FAC 90-27, 60 FR 28492, 5/31/95, effective 5/31/95; FAC 97-1, 62 FR 44802, 8/22/97, effective 10/21/97; FAC 97-22, 66 FR 2116, 1/10/2001, effective 3/12/2001; Delay of effective date, 66 FR 14259, 3/9/2001, effective 5/11/2001; FAC 2005-22, 72 FR 65868, 11/23/2007, effective 12/24/2007]

36.601-4 Implementation.

(a) Contracting officers should consider the following services to be *architect-engineer services* subject to the procedures of this subpart:

(1) Professional services of an architectural or engineering nature, as defined by

applicable State law, which the State law requires to be performed or approved by a registered architect or engineer.

(2) Professional services of an architectural or engineering nature associated with design or construction of real property.

(3) Other professional services of an architectural or engineering nature or services incidental thereto (including studies, investigations, surveying and mapping, tests, evaluations, consultations, comprehensive planning, program management, conceptual designs, plans and specifications, value engineering, construction phase services, soils engineering drawing reviews, preparation of operating and maintenance manuals and other related services) that logically or justifiably require performance by registered architects or engineers or their employees.

(4) Professional surveying and mapping services of an architectural or engineering nature. Surveying is considered to be an architectural and engineering service and shall be procured pursuant to 36.601 from registered surveyors or architects and engineers. Mapping associated with the research, planning, development, design, construction, or alteration of real property is considered to be an architectural and engineering service and is to be procured pursuant to 36.601. However, mapping services that are not connected to traditionally understood or accepted architectural and engineering activities, are not incidental to such architectural and engineering activities or have not in themselves traditionally been considered architectural and engineering services shall be procured pursuant to provisions in parts 13, 14, and 15.

(b) Contracting officers may award contracts for architect-engineer services to any firm permitted by law to practice the professions of architecture or engineering.

[FAC 90-5, 56 FR 29128, 6/25/91, effective 7/25/91; FAC 97-9, 63 FR 58587, 10/30/98, effective 10/30/98; FAC 97-12, 64 FR 32740, 6/17/99, effective 8/16/99]

36.602 Selection of firms for architect-engineer contracts. (No Text)

36.602-1 Selection criteria.

(a) Agencies shall evaluate each potential contractor in terms of its—

(1) Professional qualifications necessary for satisfactory performance of required services;

(2) Specialized experience and technical competence in the type of work required, including, where appropriate, experience in energy conservation, pollution prevention, waste reduction, and the use of recovered materials;

(3) Capacity to accomplish the work in the required time;

(4) Past performance on contracts with Government agencies and private industry in terms of cost control, quality of work, and compliance with performance schedules;

(5) Location in the general geographical area of the project and knowledge of the locality of the project; *provided,* that application of this criterion leaves an appropriate number of qualified firms, given the nature and size of the project; and

(6) Acceptability under other appropriate evaluation criteria.

(b) When the use of design competition is approved by the agency head or a designee, agencies may evaluate firms on the basis of their conceptual design of the project. Design competition may be used when—

(1) Unique situations exist involving prestige projects, such as the design of memorials and structures of unusual national significance;

(2) Sufficient time is available for the production and evaluation of conceptual designs; and

(3) The design competition, with its costs, will substantially benefit the project.

[FAC 90-27, 60 FR 28492, 5/31/95, effective 5/31/95; FAC 97-1, 62 FR 44802, 8/22/97, effective 10/21/97; Technical amendments, 62 FR 51379, 10/1/97, effective 10/1/97]

36.602-2 Evaluation boards.

(a) When acquiring architect-engineer services, an agency shall provide for one or more permanent or ad hoc architect-engineer evaluation boards (which may include preselection boards when authorized by agency regulations) to be composed of members who, collectively, have experience in architecture, engineering, construction, and Government and related acquisition matters. Members shall be appointed from among highly qualified professional employees of the agency or other agencies, and if authorized by agency procedure, private practitioners of architecture, engineering, or related professions. One Government member of each board shall be designated as the chairperson.

(b) No firm shall be eligible for award of an architect-engineer contract during the period in which any of its principals or associates are participating as members of the awarding agency's evaluation board.

36.602-3 Evaluation board functions.

Under the general direction of the head of the contracting activity, an evaluation board shall perform the following functions:

(a) Review the current data files on eligible firms and responses to a public notice concerning the particular project (see 36.603).

(b) Evaluate the firms in accordance with the criteria in 36.602-1.

(c) Hold discussions with at least three of the most highly qualified firms regarding concepts and the relative utility of alternative methods of furnishing the required services.

(d) Prepare a selection report for the agency head or other designated selection authority recommending, in order of preference, at least three firms that are considered to be the most highly qualified to perform the required services. The report shall include a description of the discussions and evaluation conducted by the board to allow the selection authority to review the considerations upon which the recommendations are based.

[FAC 84-53, 54 FR 48989, 11/28/89, effective 12/28/89; FAC 90-27, 60 FR 28492, 5/31/95, effective 5/31/95; FAC 97-1, 62 FR 44802, 8/22/97, effective 10/21/97; FAC 2005-34, 74 FR 31557, 7/1/2009, effective 7/1/2009]

36.602-4 Selection authority.

(a) The final selection decision shall be made by the agency head or a designated selection authority.

(b) The selection authority shall review the recommendations of the evaluation board and shall, with the advice of appropriate technical and staff representatives, make the final selection. This final selection shall be a listing, in order of preference, of the firms considered most highly qualified to perform the work. If the firm listed as the most preferred is not the firm recommended as the most highly qualified by the evaluation board, the selection authority shall provide for the contract file a written explanation of the reason for the preference. All firms on the final selection list are considered "selected firms" with which the contracting officer may negotiate in accordance with 36.606.

(c) The selection authority shall not add firms to the selection report. If the firms recommended in the report are not deemed to be qualified or the report is considered inadequate for any reason, the selection authority shall record the reasons and return the report through channels to the evaluation board for appropriate revision.

(d) The board shall be promptly informed of the final selection.

36.602-5 Short selection process for contracts not to exceed the simplified acquisition threshold.

When authorized by the agency, either or both of the short processes described in this subsection may be used to select firms for contracts not expected to exceed the simplified acquisition threshold. Otherwise, the procedures prescribed in 36.602-3 and 36.602-4 shall be followed.

(a) *Selection by the board.* The board shall review and evaluate architect-engineer firms in accordance with 36.602-3, except that the selection report shall serve as the final selection list and shall be provided directly to the contracting officer. The report shall serve as an authorization for the contracting officer to commence negotiations in accordance with 36.606.

(b) *Selection by the chairperson of the board.* When the board decides that formal action by the board is not necessary in connection with a particular selection, the following procedures shall be followed:

(1) The chairperson of the board shall perform the functions required in 36.602-3.

(2) The agency head or designated selection authority shall review the report and approve it or return it to the chairperson for appropriate revision.

(3) Upon receipt of an approved report, the chairperson of the board shall furnish the contracting officer a copy of the report which will serve as an authorization for the contracting officer to commence negotiations in accordance with 36.606.

[FAC 84-53, 54 FR 48989, 11/28/89, effective 12/28/89; FAC 90-29, 60 FR 34732, 7/3/95, effective 7/3/95]

36.603 Collecting data on and appraising firms' qualifications.

(a) *Establishing offices.* Agencies shall maintain offices or permanent evaluation boards, or arrange to use the offices or boards of other agencies, to receive and maintain data on firms wishing to be considered for Government contracts. Each office or board shall be assigned a jurisdiction by its parent agency, making it responsible for a geographical region or area, or a specialized type of construction.

(b) *Qualifications data.* To be considered for architect-engineer contracts, a firm must file with the appropriate office or board the Standard Form 330, "Architect-Engineer Qualifications," Part II, and when applicable, SF 330, Part I.

(c) *Data files and the classification of firms.* Under the direction of the parent agency, offices or permanent evaluation boards shall maintain an architect-engineer qualifications data file. These offices or boards shall review the SF's 330filed, and shall classify each firm with respect to—

(1) Location;

(2) Specialized experience;

(3) Professional capabilities; and

(4) Capacity, with respect to the scope of work that can be undertaken. A firm's ability and experience in computer-assisted design should be considered, when appropriate.

(d) *Currency of files.* Any office or board maintaining qualifications data files shall review and update each file at least once a year. This process should include:

(1) Encouraging firms to submit annually an updated statement of qualifications and performance data on a SF 330.

(2) Reviewing the SF 330Part, and, if necessary, updating the firm's classification (see 36.603(c)).

(3) Recording any contract awards made to the firm in the past year.

(4) Assuring that the file contains a copy of each pertinent performance evaluation (see 42.1502(f)).

(5) Discarding any material that has not been updated within the past three years, if it is no longer pertinent, see 42.1502(f).

(6) Posting the date of the review in the file.

(e) *Use of data files.* Evaluation boards and other appropriate Government employees, including contracting officers, shall use data files on firms.

[FAC 2001-18, 68 FR 69227, 12/11/2003, effective 1/12/2004, delay of effective date 6/8/2004; FAC 2001-19, 69 FR 1050, 1/7/2004, effective 1/7/2004; FAC 2005-34, 74 FR 31557, 7/1/2009, effective 7/1/2009]

36.604 Performance evaluation.

See 42.1502(f) for the requirements for preparing past performance evaluations for architect-engineer contracts.

[FAC 90-4, 56 FR 15153, 5/15/91, effective 5/15/91; FAC 2005-13, 71 FR 57363, 9/28/2006, effective 9/28/2006; FAC 2005-34, 74 FR 31557, 7/1/2009, effective 7/1/2009]

36.605 Government cost estimate for architect-engineer work.

(a) An independent Government estimate of the cost of architect-engineer services shall be prepared and furnished to the contracting officer before commencing negotiations for each proposed contract or contract modification expected to exceed the simplified acquisition threshold. The estimate shall be prepared on the basis of a detailed analysis of the required work as though the Government were submitting a proposal.

(b) Access to information concerning the Government estimate shall be limited to Government personnel whose official duties require knowledge of the estimate. An exception to this rule may be made during contract negotiations to allow the contracting officer to identify a specialized task and disclose the associated cost breakdown figures in the Government estimate, but only to the extent deemed necessary to arrive at a fair and reasonable price. The overall amount of the Government's estimate shall not be disclosed except as permitted by agency regulations.

[FAC 97-1, 62 FR 44802, 8/22/97, effective 10/21/97; FAC 2005-13, 71 FR 57363, 9/28/2006, effective 9/28/2006]

36.606 Negotiations.

(a) Unless otherwise specified by the selection authority, the final selection authorizes the contracting officer to begin negotiations. Negotiations shall be conducted in accordance with Part 15 of this chapter, beginning with the most preferred firm in the final selection (see 15.404-4(c) (4) (i) on fee limitation).

(b) The contracting officer should ordinarily request a proposal from the firm, ensuring that the solicitation does not inadvertently preclude the firm from proposing the use of modern design methods.

(c) The contracting officer shall inform the firm that no construction contract may be awarded to the firm that designed the project, except as provided in 36.209.

(d) During negotiations, the contracting officer should seek advance agreement (see 31.109) on any charges for computer-assisted design. When the firm's proposal does not cover appropriate modern and cost-effective design methods (*e.g.*, computer-assisted design), the contracting officer should discuss this topic with the firm.

(e) Because selection of firms is based upon qualifications, the extent of any subcontracting is an important negotiation topic. The clause prescribed at 44.204(b), Subcontractors and Outside Associates and Consultants (Architect-Engineer Services) (see 52.244-4), limits a firm's subcontracting to firms agreed upon during negotiations.

(f) If a mutually satisfactory contract cannot be negotiated, the contracting officer shall obtain a written final proposal revision from the firm, and notify the firm that negotiations have been terminated. The contracting officer shall then initiate negotiations with the next firm on the final selection list. This procedure shall be continued until a mutually satisfactory contract has been negotiated. If negotiations fail with all selected firms, the contracting officer shall refer the matter to the selection authority who, after consulting with the contracting officer as to why a contract cannot be negotiated, may direct the evaluation board to recommend additional firms in accordance with 36.602.

[FAC 90-30, 60 FR 37772, 7/21/95, effective 9/19/95; FAC 97-2, 62 FR 51224, 9/30/97, effective 10/10/97; FAC 97-5, 63 FR 34058, 6/22/98, effective 8/21/98; FAC 2001-04, 67 FR 6112, 2/8/2002, effective 2/8/2002; FAC 2001-09, 67 FR 56115, 8/30/2002, effective 9/30/2002]

36.607 Release of information on firm selection.

(a) After final selection has taken place, the contracting officer may release information identifying only the architect-engineer firm with which a contract will be negotiated for certain work. The work should be described in any release only in general terms, unless information relating to the work is classified. If negotiations are terminated without awarding a contract to the highest rated firm, the contracting officer may release that information and state that negotiations will be undertaken with another (named) architect-engineer firm. When an award has been made, the contracting officer may release award information (see 5.401).

(b) Debriefings of successful and unsuccessful firms will be held after final selection has taken place and will be conducted, to the extent practicable, in accordance with 15.503, 15.506(b) through (f), and 15.507(c), and 15.506(d)(2) through (d)(5). Note that 15.506(d)(2) through (d)(5) do not apply to architect-engineer contracts.

[FAC 90-31, 60 FR 42648, 8/16/95, effective 10/1/95; FAC 90-44, Final rule, 61 FR 69286, 12/31/96, effective 1/1/97; FAC 97-2, 62 FR 51224, 9/30/97, effective 10/10/97; FAC 2005-87, 81 FR 11992, 3/7/2016, effective 3/7/2016]

36.608 Liability for Government costs resulting from design errors or deficiencies.

Architect-engineer contractors shall be responsible for the professional quality, technical accuracy, and coordination of all services required under their contracts. A firm may be liable for Government costs resulting from errors or deficiencies in designs furnished under its contract. Therefore, when a modification to a construction contract is required because of an error or deficiency in the services provided under an architect-engineer contract, the contracting officer (with the advice of technical personnel and legal counsel) shall consider the extent to which the architect-engineer contractor may be reasonably liable. The contracting officer shall enforce the liability and issue a demand for payment of the amount due, if the recoverable cost will exceed the administrative cost involved or is otherwise in the Government's interest. The contracting officer shall include in the contract file a written statement of the reasons for the decision to recover or not to recover the costs from the firm.

[FAC 2005-27, 73 FR 53997, 9/17/2008, effective 10/17/2008]

36.609 Contract clauses. (No Text)

36.609-1 Design within funding limitations.

(a) The Government may require the architect-engineer contractor to design the project so that construction costs will not exceed a contractually specified dollar limit (funding limitation). If the price of construction proposed in response to a Government solicitation exceeds the construction funding limitation in the architect-engineer contract, the firm shall be solely responsible for redesigning the project within the funding limitation. These additional services shall be performed at no increase in the price of this contract. However, if the cost of proposed construction is affected by events beyond the firm's reasonable control (*e.g.*, if there is an increase in material costs which could not have been anticipated, or an undue delay by the Government in issuing a construction solicitation), the firm shall not be obligated to redesign at no cost to the Government. If a firm's design fails to meet the contractual limitation on construction cost and the Government determines that the firm should not redesign the project, a written statement of the reasons for that determination shall be placed in the contract file.

(b) The amount of the construction funding limitation (to be inserted in paragraph (c) of the clause at 52.236-22) is to be established during negotiations between the contractor and the Government. This estimated construction contract price shall take into account any statutory or other limitations and exclude any allowances for Government supervision and overhead and any amounts set aside by the Government for contingencies. In negotiating the amount, the contracting officer should make available to the contractor the information upon which the Government has based its initial construction estimate and any subsequently acquired information that may affect the construction costs.

(c) The contracting officer shall insert the clause at 52.236-22, Design Within Funding Limitations, in fixed-price architect-engineer contracts except when—

(1) The head of the contracting activity or a designee determines in writing that cost limitations are secondary to performance considerations and additional project funding can be expected, if necessary,

(2) The design is for a standard structure and is not intended for a specific location, or

(3) There is little or no design effort involved.

[FAC 84-8, 50 FR 26903, 6/28/85, effective 7/1/85]

36.609-2 Redesign responsibility for design errors or deficiencies.

(a) Under architect-engineer contracts, contractors shall be required to make necessary corrections at no cost to the Government when the designs, drawings, specifications, or other items or services furnished contain any errors, deficiencies, or inadequacies. If, in a given situation, the Government does not require a firm to correct such errors, the contracting officer shall include a written statement of the reasons for that decision in the contract file.

(b) The contracting officer shall insert the clause at 52.236-23, Responsibility of the Architect-Engineer Contractor, in fixed-price architect-engineer contracts.

[FAC 84-8, 50 FR 26903, 6/28/85, effective 7/1/85]

36.609-3 Work oversight in architect-engineer contracts.

The contracting officer shall insert the clause at 52.236-24, Work Oversight in Architect-Engineer Contracts, in all architect-engineer contracts.

[FAC 84-8, 50 FR 26903, 6/28/85, effective 7/1/85; FAC 97-14, 64 FR 51828, 9/24/99, effective 11/23/99]

36.609-4 Requirements for registration of designers.

Insert the clause at 52.236-25, Requirements for Registration of Designers, in architect-engineer contracts, except that it may be omitted when the design will be performed—

(a) Outside the United States and its outlying areas; or

(b) In a State or outlying area of the United States that does not have registration requirements for the particular field involved.

[FAC 97-14, 64 FR 51828, 9/24/99, effective 11/23/99; FAC 2001-14, 68 FR 28079, 5/22/2003, effective 6/23/2003]

SUBPART 36.7—STANDARD AND OPTIONAL FORMS FOR CONTRACTING FOR CONSTRUCTION, ARCHITECT-ENGINEER SERVICES, AND DISMANTLING, DEMOLITION, OR REMOVAL OF IMPROVEMENTS

36.700 Scope of subpart.

This subpart sets forth requirements for the use of standard and optional forms, prescribed in Part 53, for contracting for construction, architect-engineer services, or dismantling, demolition, or removal of improvements. A listing of the Standard forms is located in subpart 53.3.

[FAC 84-49, 54 FR 29282, 7/11/89, effective 8/10/89; FAC 2005-100, 83 FR 42571, 8/22/2018, effective 8/22/2018]

36.701 Standard and optional forms for use in contracting for construction or dismantling, demolition, or removal of improvements.

(a) Standard Form 1442, Solicitation, Offer, and Award (Construction, Alteration, or Repair), shall be used to solicit and submit offers, and award construction or dismantling, demolition, or removal of improvements contracts expected to exceed the simplified acquisition threshold, and may be used for contracts at or below the simplified acquisition threshold. In all sealed bid solicitations, or when the Government otherwise requires a noncancellable offer acceptance period, the contracting officer shall insert in the blank provided in Block 13D the number of calendar days that the offer must be available for acceptance after the date offers are due.

(b) Optional Form 347, Order for Supplies or Services, may be used for construction or dismantling, demolition, or removal of improvements contracts that are at or below the simplified acquisition threshold; provided, that the contracting officer includes the clauses required (see Subpart 36.5) in the simplified acquisitions (see Part 13).

(c) Contracting officers may use Optional Form 1419, Abstract of Offers—Construction, and Optional Form 1419A, Abstract of Offers—Construction, Continuation Sheet, or the automated equivalent, to record offers submitted in response to a sealed bid solicitation (see 14.403) and may also use it to record offers submitted in response to negotiated solicitations.

[FAC 84-26, 52 FR 19805, 5/27/87, effective 7/30/87; FAC 84-49, 54 FR 29282, 7/11/89, effective 8/10/89; FAC 90-29, 60 FR 34732, 7/3/95, effective 7/3/95; FAC 90-40, 61 FR 39186, 7/26/96, effective 8/26/96; FAC 2001-25, 69 FR 59699, 10/5/2004, effective 11/4/2004; FAC 2005-34, 74 FR 31557, 7/1/2009, effective 7/1/2009]

36.702 Forms for use in contracting for architect-engineer services.

(a) Contracting officers must use Standard Form 252, Architect-Engineer Contract, to award fixed-price contracts for architect-engineer services when the services will be performed in the United States or its outlying areas.

(b) The SF 330, Architect-Engineer Qualifications, shall be used to evaluate firms before awarding a contract for architect-engineer services:

(1) Use the SF 330, Part I—Contract-Specific Qualifications, to obtain information from an architect-engineer firm about its qualifications for a specific contract when the contract amount is expected to exceed the simplified acquisition threshold. Part I may be used when the contract amount is expected to be at or below the simplified acquisition threshold, if the contracting officer determines that its use is appropriate.

(2) Use the SF 330Part II—General Qualifications, to obtain information from an architect-engineer firm about its general professional qualifications.

[FAC 90-29, 60 FR 34732, 7/3/95, effective 7/3/95; FAC 2001-14, 68 FR 28079, 5/22/2003, effective 6/23/2003; FAC 2001-18, 68 FR 69227, 12/11/2003, effective 1/12/2004, delay of effective date, 6/8/2004; FAC 2001-19, 69 FR 1050, 1/7/2004, effective 1/7/2004; FAC 2005-34, 74 FR 31557, 7/1/2009, effective 7/1/2009]

PART 37—SERVICE CONTRACTING

Table of Contents

Scope of part . . . 37.000

Subpart 37.1—Service Contracts—General

Definitions . . . 37.101
Policy . . . 37.102
Contracting officer responsibility . . . 37.103
Personal services contracts . . . 37.104
Competition in service contracting . . . 37.105
Funding and term of service contracts . . . 37.106
Service Contract Labor Standards . . . 37.107
Small business Certificate of Competency . . . 37.108
Services of quasi-military armed forces . . . 37.109
Solicitation provisions and contract clauses . . . 37.110
Extension of services . . . 37.111
Government use of private sector temporaries . . . 37.112
Severance payments to foreign nationals . . . 37.113
Waiver of cost allowability limitations . . . 37.113-1
Solicitation provision and contract clause . . . 37.113-2
Special acquisition requirements . . . 37.114
Uncompensated overtime . . . 37.115
Scope . . . 37.115-1
General policy . . . 37.115-2
Solicitation provision . . . 37.115-3
[Removed] . . . 37.116
[Removed] . . . 37.116-1
[Removed] . . . 37.116-2

Subpart 37.2—Advisory and Assistance Services

Scope of subpart . . . 37.200
Definition . . . 37.201
Exclusions . . . 37.202
Policy . . . 37.203
Guidelines for determining availability of personnel . . . 37.204
Contracting officer responsibilities . . . 37.205

Subpart 37.3—Dismantling, Demolition, or Removal of Improvements

Scope of subpart . . . 37.300
Labor standards . . . 37.301
Bonds or other security . . . 37.302
Payments . . . 37.303
Contract clauses . . . 37.304

Subpart 37.4—Nonpersonal Health Care Services

Scope of subpart . . . 37.400
Policy . . . 37.401
Contracting officer responsibilities . . . 37.402
Contract clause . . . 37.403

Subpart 37.5—Management Oversight of Service Contracts

Scope of subpart . . . 37.500
Definition . . . 37.501
Exclusions . . . 37.502
Agency-head responsibilities . . . 37.503
Contracting officials' responsibilities . . . 37.504

Subpart 37.6—Performance-Based Acquisition

Scope of subpart . . . 37.600

General 37.601
Performance work statement 37.602
Performance standards 37.603
Quality assurance surveillance plans 37.604

PART 37—SERVICE CONTRACTING

37.000 Scope of part.

This part prescribes policy and procedures that are specific to the acquisition and management of services by contract. This part applies to all contracts and orders for services regardless of the contract type or kind of service being acquired. This part requires the use of performance-based acquisitions for services to the maximum extent practicable and prescribes policies and procedures for use of performance-based acquisition methods (see Subpart 37.6). Additional guidance for research and development services is in Part 35; architect-engineering services is in Part 36; information technology is in Part 39; and transportation services is in Part 47. Parts 35, 36, 39, and 47 take precedence over this part in the event of inconsistencies. This part includes, but is not limited to, contracts for services to which the Service Contract Act of 1965, as amended, applies (see Subpart 22.10). This part includes, but is not limited to, contracts for services to which 41 U.S.C. chapter 67, Service Contract Labor Standards, applies (see subpart 22.10).

[FAC 90-46, 62 FR 12690, 3/17/97, effective 5/16/97; FAC 97-1, 62 FR 44802, 8/22/97, effective 10/21/97; FAC 2005-07, 71 FR 211, 1/3/2006, effective 2/2/2006; FAC 2005-73, 79 FR 24192, 4/29/2014, effective 5/29/2014]

SUBPART 37.1—SERVICE CONTRACTS—GENERAL

37.101 Definitions.

As used in this part—

Adjusted hourly rate (including uncompensated overtime) is the rate that results from multiplying the hourly rate for a 40-hour work week by 40, and then dividing by the proposed hours per week which includes uncompensated overtime hours over and above the standard 40-hour work week. For example, 45 hours proposed on a 40-hour work week basis at $20 per hour would be converted to an uncompensated overtime rate of $17.78 per hour ($20.00 × 40/45 = $17.78).

Child care services means child protective services (including the investigation of child abuse and neglect reports), social services, health and mental health care, child (day) care, education (whether or not directly involved in teaching), foster care, residential care, recreational or rehabilitative programs, and detention, correctional, or treatment services.

Nonpersonal services contract means a contract under which the personnel rendering the services are not subject, either by the contract's terms or by the manner of its administration, to the supervision and control usually prevailing in relationships between the Government and its employees.

Performance-base contracting means structuring all aspects of an acquisition around the purpose of the work to be performed as opposed to either the manner by which the work is to be performed or broad and imprecise statements of work.

Service contract means a contract that directly engages the time and effort of a contractor whose primary purpose is to perform an identifiable task rather than to furnish an end item of supply. A service contract may be either a nonpersonal or personal contract. It can also cover services performed by either professional or nonprofessional personnel whether on an individual or organizational basis. Some of the areas in which service contracts are found include the following:

(1) Maintenance, overhaul, repair, servicing, rehabilitation, salvage, modernization, or modification of supplies, systems, or equipment.

(2) Routine recurring maintenance of real property.

(3) Housekeeping and base services.

(4) Advisory and assistance services.

(5) Operation of Government-owned equipment, real property, and systems.

(6) Communications services.

(7) Architect—Engineering (see Subpart 36.6).

(8) Transportation and related services (see Part 47).

(9) Research and development (see Part 35).

Uncompensated overtime means the hours worked without additional compensation in excess of an average of 40 hours per week by direct charge employees who are exempt from the Fair Labor Standards Act. Compensated personal absences such as holidays, vacations, and sick leave shall be included in the normal work week for purposes of computing uncompensated overtime hours.

[FAC 84-40, 53 FR 43392, 10/26/88, effective 11/25/88; FAC 90-23, 59 FR 67010, 12/28/94, effective 12/28/94, finalized without change, FAC 90-39, 61 FR 31612, 6/20/96, effective 6/20/96; FAC 97-1, 62 FR 44802, 8/22/97, effective 10/21/97; FAC 97-22, 66 FR 2116, 1/10/2001, effective 3/12/2001; Delay of effective date, 66 FR 14259, 3/9/2001, effective 5/11/2001; FAC 97-25, 66 FR 22081, 5/2/2001, effective 5/2/200; FAC 2005-17, 72 FR 27364, 5/15/2007, effective 6/14/2007; FAC 2005-80, 80 FR 4992, 1/29/2015, effective 3/2/2015]

37.102 Policy.

(a) Performance-based acquisition (see Subpart 37.6) is the preferred method for acquiring services (Public Law 106-398, section 821). When acquiring services, including those acquired under supply contracts or orders, agencies must—

(1) Use performance-based acquisition methods to the maximum extent practicable, except for—

(i) Architect-engineer services acquired in accordance with 40 U.S.C. 1101 *et seq.* (see part 36);

(ii) Construction (see part 36);

(iii) Utility services (see part 41); or

(iv) Services that are incidental to supply purchases; and

(2) Use the following order of precedence (Public Law 106-398, section 821(a));

(i) A firm-fixed price performance-based contract or task order.

(ii) A performance-based contract or task order that is not firm-fixed price.

(iii) A contract or task order that is not performance-based.

(b) Agencies shall generally rely on the private sector for commercial services (see OMB Circular No. A-76, Performance of Commercial Activities and Subpart 7.3).

(c) Agencies shall not award a contract for the performance of an inherently governmental function (see Subpart 7.5).

(d) Non-personal service contracts are proper under general contracting authority.

(e) Agency program officials are responsible for accurately describing the need to be filled, or problem to be resolved, through service contracting in a manner that ensures full understanding and responsive performance by contractors and, in so doing, should obtain assistance from contracting officials, as needed. To the maximum extent practicable, the program officials shall describe the need to be filled using performance-based acquisition methods.

(f) Agencies shall establish effective management practices in accordance with Office of Federal Procurement Policy (OFPP) Policy Letter 93-1, Management Oversight of Service Contracting, to prevent fraud, waste, and abuse in service contracting.

(g) Services are to be obtained in the most cost-effective manner, without barriers to full and open competition, and free of any potential conflicts of interest.

(h) Agencies shall ensure that sufficiently trained and experienced officials are available within the agency to manage and oversee the contract administration function.

(i) Agencies shall ensure that service contracts that require the delivery, use, or furnishing of products are consistent with part 23.

[FAC 90-37, 61 FR 2626, 1/26/96, effective 3/26/96; FAC 90-46, 62 FR 12690, 3/17/97 effective 5/16/97; FAC 97-1, 62 FR 44802, 8/22/97, effective 10/21/97; FAC 97-25, 66 FR 22081, 5/2/2001, effective 5/2/2001; FAC 2005-06, 70 FR 57453, 9/30/2005, effective 9/30/2005; FAC 2005-07, 71 FR 211, 1/3/2006, effective 2/2/2006; FAC 2005-52,

76 FR 31395, 5/31/2011, effective 5/31/2011]

37.103 Contracting officer responsibility.

(a) The contracting officer is responsible for ensuring that a proposed contract for services is proper. For this purpose the contracting officer shall—

(1) Determine whether the proposed service is for a personal or nonpersonal services contract using the definitions at 2.101 and 37.101 and the guidelines in 37.104;

(2) In doubtful cases, obtain the review of legal counsel; and

(3) Document the file (except as provided in paragraph (b) of this section) with—

(i) The opinion of legal counsel, if any,

(ii) A memorandum of the facts and rationale supporting the conclusion that the contract does not violate the provisions in 37.104(b), and

(iii) Any further documentation that the contracting agency may require.

(b) Nonpersonal services contracts are exempt from the requirements of subparagraph (a)(3) of this section.

(c) Ensure that performance-based acquisition methods are used to the maximum extent practicable when acquiring services.

(d) Ensure that contracts for child care services include requirements for criminal history background checks on employees who will perform child care services under the contract in accordance with 42 U.S.C. 13041, as amended, and agency procedures.

(e) Ensure that service contractor reporting requirements are met in accordance with subpart 4.17, Service Contracts Inventory.

[FAC 84-60, 55 FR 36796, 9/6/90, effective 9/6/90; FAC 90-23, 59 FR 67010, 12/28/94, effective 12/28/94, finalized without change, FAC 90-39, 61 FR 31612, 6/20/96, effective 6/20/96; FAC 90-45, Final rule, 62 FR 224, 1/2/97, effective 1/1/97; FAC 90-46, GPO version, 62 FR 12690, 3/17/97, effective 5/16/97; FAC 97-1, 62 FR 44802, 8/22/97, effective 10/21/97, corrected, 62 FR 51379, 10/1/97, effective 10/1/97; FAC 97-22, 66 FR 2116, 1/10/2001, effective 3/12/2001; Delay of effective date, 66 FR 14259, 3/9/2001, effective 5/11/2001; FAC 2005-07, 71 FR 211, 1/3/2006, effective 2/2/2006; FAC 2005-72, 78 FR 80369, 12/31/2013, effective 1/30/2014]

37.104 Personal services contracts.

(a) A personal services contract is characterized by the employer-employee relationship it creates between the Government and the contractor's personnel. The Government is normally required to obtain its employees by direct hire under competitive appointment or other procedures required by the civil service laws. Obtaining personal services by contract, rather than by direct hire, circumvents those laws unless Congress has specifically authorized acquisition of the services by contract.

(b) Agencies shall not award personal services contracts unless specifically authorized by statute (e.g., 5 U.S.C. 3109) to do so.

(c) (1) An employer-employee relationship under a service contract occurs when, as a result of—

(i) the contract's terms or—

(ii) the manner of its administration during performance, contractor personnel are subject to the relatively continuous supervision and control of a Government officer or employee. However, giving an order for a specific article or service, with the right to reject the finished product or result, is not the type of supervision or control that converts an individual who is an independent contractor (such as a contractor employee) into a Government employee.

(2) Each contract arrangement must be judged in the light of its own facts and circumstances, the key question always being: Will the Government exercise relatively continuous supervision and control over the contractor personnel performing the contract? The sporadic, unauthorized supervision of only one of a large number of contractor employees might reasonably be considered not relevant, while relatively continuous Government supervision of a substantial number of contractor employees would have to be taken strongly into account (see (d) below).

(d) The following descriptive elements should be used as a guide in assessing whether or not a proposed contract is personal in nature:

(1) Performance on site.

(2) Principal tools and equipment furnished by the Government.

(3) Services are applied directly to the integral effort of agencies or an organizational subpart in furtherance of assigned function or mission.

(4) Comparable services, meeting comparable needs, are performed in the same or similar agencies using civil service personnel.

(5) The need for the type of service provided can reasonably be expected to last beyond 1 year.

(6) The inherent nature of the service, or the manner in which it is provided, reasonably requires directly or indirectly, Government direction or supervision of contractor employees in order to—

(i) Adequately protect the Government's interest;

(ii) Retain control of the function involved; or

(iii) Retain full personal responsibility for the function supported in a duly authorized Federal officer or employee.

(e) When specific statutory authority for a personal service contract is cited, obtain the review and opinion of legal counsel.

(f) Personal services contracts for the services of individual experts or consultants are limited by the Classification Act. In addition, the Office of Personnel Management has established requirements which apply in acquiring the personal services of experts or consultants in this manner (e.g., benefits, taxes, conflicts of interest). Therefore, the contracting officer shall effect necessary coordination with the cognizant civilian personnel office.

[FAC 97-22, 66 FR 2116, 1/10/2001, effective 3/12/2001; Delay of effective date, 66 FR 14259, 3/9/2001, effective 5/11/2001]

37.105 Competition in service contracting.

(a) Unless otherwise provided by statute, contracts for services shall be awarded through sealed bidding whenever the conditions in 6.401(a) are met, (except see 6.401(b)).

(b) The provisions of statute and Part 6 in this regulation requiring competition apply fully to service contracts. The method of contracting used to provide for competition may vary with the type of service being acquired and may not necessarily be limited to price competition.

[FAC 84-5, 50 FR 1744, 1/11/85, effective 4/1/85]

37.106 Funding and term of service contracts.

(a) When contracts for services are funded by annual appropriations, the term of contracts so funded shall not extend beyond the end of the fiscal year of the appropriation except when authorized by law (see paragraph (b) of this section for certain service contracts, 32.703-2 for contracts conditioned upon availability of funds, and 32.703-3 for contracts crossing fiscal years).

(b) The head of an executive agency, except NASA, may enter into a contract, exercise an option, or place an order under a contract for severable services for a period that begins in one fiscal year and ends in the next fiscal year if the period of the contract awarded, option exercised, or order placed does not exceed one year (10 U.S.C. 2410a and 41 U.S.C. 3902). Funds made available for a fiscal year may be obligated for the total amount of an action entered into under this authority.

(c) Agencies with statutory multiyear authority shall consider the use of this authority to encourage and promote economical business operations when acquiring services.

[FAC 90-30, 60 FR 37772, 7/21/95, effective 8/21/95; FAC 97-1, 62 FR 44802, 8/22/97, effective 10/21/97; FAC 97-9, 63 FR 58587, 10/30/98, effective 12/29/98;FAC 2005-73, 79 FR 24192, 4/29/2014, effective 5/29/2014]

37.107 Service Contract Labor Standards.

41 U.S.C. chapter 67, Service Contract Labor Standards, provides for minimum wages and fringe benefits as well as other conditions of work under certain types of service contracts. Whether or not the Service Contract Labor Standards statute applies to a specific service contract will be determined by the definitions and exceptions given in the Service Contract Labor Standards statute, or implementing regulations.

[FAC 2005-73, 79 FR 24192, 4/29/2014, effective 5/29/2014]

37.108 Small business Certificate of Competency.

In those service contracts for which the Government requires the highest competence obtainable, as evidenced in a solicitation by a request for a technical/management proposal and a resultant technical evaluation and source selection, the small business Certificate of Competency procedures may not apply (see Subpart 19.6).

37.109 Services of quasi-military armed forces.

Contracts with "Pinkerton Detective Agencies or similar organizations" are prohibited by 5 U.S.C. 3108. This prohibition applies only to contracts with organizations that offer quasi-military armed forces for hire, or with their employees, regardless of the contract's character. An organization providing guard or protective services does not thereby become a "quasi-military armed force," even though the guards are armed or the organization provides general investigative or detective services. (See 57 Comp. Gen. 524).

37.110 Solicitation provisions and contract clauses.

(a) The contracting officer shall insert the provision at 52.237-1, Site Visit, in solicitations for services to be performed on Government installations, unless the solicitation is for construction.

(b) The contracting officer shall insert the clause at 52.237-2, Protection of Government Buildings, Equipment, and Vegetation, in solicitations and contracts for services to be performed on Government installations, unless a construction contract is contemplated.

(c) The contracting officer may insert the clause at 52.237-3, Continuity of Services, in solicitations and contracts for services, when—

(1) The services under the contract are considered vital to the Government and must be continued without interruption and when, upon contract expiration, a successor, either the Government or another contractor, may continue them; and

(2) The Government anticipates difficulties during the transition from one contractor to another or to the Government. Examples of instances where use of the clause may be appropriate are services in remote locations or services requiring personnel with special security clearances.

(d) See 9.508 regarding the use of an appropriate provision and clause concerning the subject of conflict-of-interest, which may at times be significant in solicitations and contracts for services.

(e) The contracting officer shall also insert in solicitations and contracts for services the provisions and clauses prescribed elsewhere in the 48 CFR Chapter 1, as appropriate for each acquisition, depending on the conditions that are applicable.

[FAC 84-44, 54 FR 13025, 3/29/89, effective 4/28/89; FAC 90-3, 55 FR 52795, 12/21/90, effective 12/21/90 and 1/22/91; FAC 90-16, 57 FR 60584, 12/21/92, effective 2/19/93]

37.111 Extension of services.

Award of contracts for recurring and continuing service requirements are often delayed due to circumstances beyond the control of contracting offices. Examples of circumstances causing such delays are bid protests and alleged mistakes in bid. In order to avoid negotiation of short extensions to existing contracts, the contracting officer may include an option clause (see 17.208(f)) in solicitations and contracts which will enable the Government to require continued performance of any services within the limits and at the rates specified in the contract.

However, these rates may be adjusted only as a result of revisions to prevailing labor rates provided by the Secretary of Labor. The option provision may be exercised more than once, but the total extension of performance thereunder shall not exceed 6 months.

[FAC 84-49, 54 FR 29282, 7/11/89, effective 8/10/89]

37.112 Government use of private sector temporaries.

Contracting officers may enter into contracts with temporary help service firms for the brief or intermittent use of the skills of private sector temporaries. Services furnished by temporary help firms shall not be regarded or treated as personal services. These services shall not be used in lieu of regular recruitment under civil service laws or to displace a Federal employee. Acquisition of these services shall comply with the authority, criteria, and conditions of 5 CFR Part 300, Subpart E, Use of Private Sector Temporaries, and agency procedures.

[FAC 90-8, 56 FR 55380, 10/25/91, effective 11/25/91]

37.113 Severance payments to foreign nationals. (No Text)

37.113-1 Waiver of cost allowability limitations.

(a) The head of the agency may waive the 31.205-6(g)(6) cost allowability limitations on severance payments to foreign nationals for contracts that—

(1) Provide significant support services for—

(i) Members of the armed forces stationed or deployed outside the United States; or

(ii) Employees of an executive agency posted outside the United States; and

(2) Will be performed in whole or in part outside the United States.

(b) Waivers can be granted only before contract award.

(c) Waivers cannot be granted for—

(1) Military banking contracts, which are covered by 10 U.S.C. 2324(e)(2); or

(2) Severance payments made by a contractor to a foreign national employed by the contractor under a DOD service contract in the Republic of the Philippines, if the discontinuation of the foreign national is the result of the termination of basing rights of the United States military in the Republic of the Philippines (section 1351(b) of Public Law 102-484, 10 U.S.C. 1592, note).

[FAC 90-31, 60 FR 42648, 8/16/95, effective 10/1/95; FAC 2001-15, 68 FR 43863, 7/24/2003, effective 8/25/2003]

37.113-2 Solicitation provision and contract clause.

(a) Use the provision at 52.237-8, Restriction on Severance Payments to Foreign Nationals, in all solicitations that meet the criteria in 37.113-1(a), except for those excluded by 37.113-1(c).

(b) When the head of an agency, has granted a waiver pursuant to 37.113-1, use the clause at 52.237-9, Waiver of Limitation on Severance Payments to Foreign Nationals.

[FAC 90-31, 60 FR 42648, 8/16/95, effective 10/1/95; FAC 2001-15, 68 FR 43863, 7/24/2003, effective 8/25/2003]

37.114 Special acquisition requirements.

Contracts for services which require the contractor to provide advice, opinions, recommendations, ideas, reports, analyses, or other work products have the potential for influencing the authority, accountability, and responsibilities of Government officials. These contracts require special management attention to ensure that they do not result in performance of inherently governmental functions by the contractor and that Government officials properly exercise their authority. Agencies must ensure that—

(a) A sufficient number of qualified Government employees are assigned to oversee contractor activities, especially those that involve support of government policy or decision making. During performance of service contracts, the functions being performed shall not be changed or expanded to become inherently governmental.

(b) A greater scrutiny and an appropriate enhanced degree of management oversight is exercised when contracting for functions that are not inherently governmental but closely support the performance of inherently governmental functions (see 7.503(c)).

(c) All contractor personnel attending meetings, answering Government telephones, and working in other situations where their contractor status is not obvious to third parties are required to identify themselves as such to avoid creating an impression in the minds of members of the public or Congress that they are Government officials, unless, in the judgment of the agency, no harm can come from failing to identify themselves. They must also ensure that all documents or reports produced by contractors are suitably marked as contractor products or that contractor participation is appropriately disclosed.

[FAC 90-37, 61 FR 2626, 1/26/96, effective 3/26/96]

37.115 Uncompensated overtime. (No Text)

37.115-1 Scope.

The policies in this section are based on Section 834 of Public Law 101-510 (10 U.S.C. 2331).

[FAC 97-1, 62 FR 44802, 8/22/97, effective 10/21/97]

37.115-2 General policy.

(a) Use of uncompensated overtime is not encouraged.

(b) When professional or technical services are acquired on the basis of the number of hours to be provided, rather than on the task to be performed, the solicitation shall require offerors to identify uncompensated overtime hours and the uncompensated overtime rate for direct charge Fair Labor Standards Act—exempt personnel included in their proposals and subcontractor proposals. This includes uncompensated overtime hours that are in indirect cost pools for personnel whose regular hours are normally charged direct.

(c) Contracting officers must ensure that the use of uncompensated overtime in contracts to acquire services on the basis of the number of hours provided will not degrade the level of technical expertise required to fulfill the Government's requirements (see 15.305 for competitive negotiations and 15.404-1(d) for cost realism analysis). When acquiring these services, contracting officers must conduct a risk assessment and evaluate, for award on that basis, any proposals received that reflect factors such as:

(1) Unrealistically low labor rates or other costs that may result in quality or service shortfalls; and

(2) Unbalanced distribution of uncompensated overtime among skill levels and its use in key technical positions.

(d) Whenever there is uncompensated overtime, the adjusted hourly rate (including uncompensated overtime) (see definition at 37.101), rather than the hourly rate, shall be applied to all proposed hours, whether regular or overtime hours.

[FAC 97-1, 62 FR 44802, 8/22/97, effective 10/21/97; FAC 97-14, 64 FR 51828, 9/24/99, effective 11/23/99; FAC 2005-80, 80 FR 4992, 1/29/2015, effective 3/2/2015]

37.115-3 Solicitation provision.

The contracting officer shall insert the provision at 52.237-10, Identification of Uncompensated Overtime, in all solicitations valued above the simplified acquisition threshold, for professional or technical services to be acquired on the basis of the number of hours to be provided.

[FAC 97-1, 62 FR 44802, 8/22/97, effective 10/21/97]

37.116 [Removed]

[FAC 2005-19, 72 FR 46363, 8/17/2007, effective 8/17/2007; FAC 2005-27, 73 FR 53997, 9/17/2007, effective 10/17/2007; FAC 2005-101, 83 FR 48700, 9/26/2018, effective 10/26/2018]

37.116-1 [Removed]

[FAC 2005-19, 72 FR 46363, 8/17/2007, effective 8/17/2007; FAC 2005-27, 73 FR 53997, 9/17/2007, effective 10/17/2007; FAC 2005-101, 83 FR 48700, 9/26/2018, effective 10/26/2018]

37.116-2 [Removed]

[FAC 2005-19, 72 FR 46363, 8/17/2007, effective 8/17/2007; FAC 2005-27, 73 FR 54014, 9/17/2008, effective 9/17/2008; FAC 2005-101, 83 FR 48700, 9/26/2018, effective 10/26/2018]

SUBPART 37.2—ADVISORY AND ASSISTANCE SERVICES

37.200 Scope of subpart.

This subpart prescribes policies and procedures for acquiring advisory and assistance services by contract. The subpart applies to contracts, whether made with individuals or organizations, that involve either personal or nonpersonal services.

[FAC 90-33, 60 FR 49706, 9/26/95, effective 10/1/95]

37.201 Definition.

Covered personnel means—

(1) An officer or an individual who is appointed in the civil service by one of the following acting in an official capacity—

(i) The President;

(ii) A Member of Congress;

(iii) A member of the uniformed services;

(iv) An individual who is an employee under 5 U.S.C. 2105;

(v) The head of a Government-controlled corporation; or

(vi) An adjutant general appointed by the Secretary concerned under 32 U.S.C. 709(c).

(2) A member of the Armed Services of the United States.

(3) A person assigned to a Federal agency who has been transferred to another position in the competitive service in another agency.

[FAC 90-33, 60 FR 49706, 9/26/95, effective 10/1/95; FAC 97-17, 65 FR 24316, 4/25/2000, effective 4/25/2000; FAC 97-22, 66 FR 2116, 1/10/2001, effective 3/12/2001; Delay of effective date, 66 FR 14259, 3/9/2001, effective 5/11/2001]

37.202 Exclusions.

The following activities and programs are excluded or exempted from the definition of advisory or assistance services:

(a) Routine information technology services unless they are an integral part of a contract for the acquisition of advisory and assistance services.

(b) Architectural and engineering services as defined in 40 U.S.C. 1102.

(c) Research on theoretical mathematics and basic research involving medical, biological, physical, social, psychological, or other phenomena.

[FAC 90-33, 60 FR 49706, 9/26/95, effective 10/1/95; FAC 90-41, 61 FR 41466, 8/8/96, effective 8/8/96, finalized without change, FAC 97-3, 62 FR 64912, 12/9/97, effective 2/9/98; FAC 2005-06, 70 FR 57453, 9/30/2005, effective 9/30/2005; FAC 2005-73, 79 FR 24192, 4/29/2014, effective 5/29/2014]

37.203 Policy.

(a) The acquisition of advisory and assistance services is a legitimate way to improve Government services and operations. Accordingly, advisory and assistance services may be used at all organizational levels to help managers achieve maximum effectiveness or economy in their operations.

(b) Subject to 37.205, agencies may contract for advisory and assistance services, when essential to the agency's mission, to—

(1) Obtain outside points of view to avoid too limited judgment on critical issues;

(2) Obtain advice regarding developments in industry, university, or foundation research;

(3) Obtain the opinions, special knowledge, or skills of noted experts;

(4) Enhance the understanding of, and develop alternative solutions to, complex issues;

(5) Support and improve the operation of organizations; or

(6) Ensure the more efficient or effective operation of managerial or hardware systems.

(c) Advisory and assistance services shall not be—

(1) Used in performing work of a policy, decision-making, or managerial nature

which is the direct responsibility of agency officials;

(2) Used to bypass or undermine personnel ceilings, pay limitations, or competitive employment procedures;

(3) Contracted for on a preferential basis to former Government employees;

(4) Used under any circumstances specifically to aid in influencing or enacting legislation; or

(5) Used to obtain professional or technical advice which is readily available within the agency or another Federal agency.

(d) *Limitation on payment for advisory and assistance services*. Contractors may not be paid for services to conduct evaluations or analyses of any aspect of a proposal submitted for an initial contract award unless—

(1) Neither covered personnel from the requesting agency, nor from another agency, with adequate training and capabilities to perform the required proposal evaluation, are readily available and a written determination is made in accordance with 37.204;

(2) The contractor is a Federally-Funded Research and Development Center (FFRDC) as authorized in 41 U.S.C. 1709(c) and the work placed under the FFRDC's contract meets the criteria of 35.017-3; or

(3) Such functions are otherwise authorized by law.

[FAC 90-33, 60 FR 49706, 9/26/95, effective 10/1/95;FAC 2005-73, 79 FR 24192, 4/29/2014, effective 5/29/2014]

37.204 Guidelines for determining availability of personnel.

(a) The head of an agency shall determine, for each evaluation or analysis of proposals, if sufficient personnel with the requisite training and capabilities are available within the agency to perform the evaluation or analysis of proposals submitted for the acquisition.

(b) If, for a specific evaluation or analysis, such personnel are not available within the agency, the head of the agency shall—

(1) Determine which Federal agencies may have personnel with the required training and capabilities; and

(2) Consider the administrative cost and time associated with conducting the search, the dollar value of the procurement, other costs, such as travel costs involved in the use of such personnel, and the needs of the Federal agencies to make management decisions on the best use of available personnel in performing the agency's mission.

(c) If the supporting agency agrees to make the required personnel available, the agencies shall execute an agreement for the detail of the supporting agency's personnel to the requesting agency.

(d) If the requesting agency, after reasonable attempts to obtain personnel with the required training and capabilities, is unable to identify such personnel, the head of the agency may make the determination required by 37.203.

(e) An agency may make a determination regarding the availability of covered personnel for a class of proposals for which evaluation and analysis would require expertise so unique or specialized that it is not reasonable to expect such personnel to be available.

[FAC 90-33, 60 FR 49706, 9/26/95, effective 10/1/95]

37.205 Contracting officer responsibilities.

The contracting officer shall ensure that the determination required in accordance with the guidelines at 37.204 has been made prior to issuing a solicitation.

[FAC 90-33, 60 FR 49706, 9/26/95, effective 10/1/95]

SUBPART 37.3—DISMANTLING, DEMOLITION, OR REMOVAL OF IMPROVEMENTS

37.300 Scope of subpart.

This subpart prescribes procedures for contracting for dismantling or demolition of buildings, ground improvements and other real property structures and for the removal of such structures or portions of them (hereafter referred to as "dismantling, demolition, or removal of improvements").

37.301 Labor standards.

Contracts for dismantling, demolition, or removal of improvements are subject to either 41 U.S.C. chapter 67, Service Contract Labor Standards, or 40 U.S.C. chapter 31, subchapter IV, Wage Rate Requirements (Construction). If the contract is solely for dismantling, demolition, or removal of improvements, the Service Contract Labor Standards statute applies unless further work which will result in the construction, alteration, or repair of a public building or public work at that location is contemplated. If such further construction work is intended, even though by separate contract, then the Construction Wage Rate Requirements statute applies to the contract for dismantling, demolition, or removal.

[FAC 2005-06, 70 FR 57453, 9/30/2005, effective 9/30/2005; FAC 2005-73, 79 FR 24192, 4/29/2014, effective 5/29/2014]

37.302 Bonds or other security.

When a contract is solely for dismantling, demolition, or removal of improvements, 40 U.S.C. 31, subchapter III, Bonds, (see 28.102) does not apply. However, the contracting officer may require the contractor to furnish a performance bond or other security (see 28.103) in an amount that the contracting officer considers adequate to—

(a) Ensure completion of the work;

(b) Protect property to be retained by the Government;

(c) Protect property to be provided as compensation to the contractor; and

(d) Protect the Government against damage to adjoining property.

[FAC 2005-06, 70 FR 57453, 9/30/2005, effective 9/30/2005; FAC 2005-73, 79 FR 24192, 4/29/2014, effective 5/29/2014]

37.303 Payments.

(a) The contract may provide that the—

(1) Government pay the contractor for the dismantling or demolition of structures or

(2) Contractor pay the Government for the right to salvage and remove the materials resulting from the dismantling or demolition operation.

(b) The contracting officer shall consider the usefulness to the Government of all salvageable property. Any of the property that is more useful to the Government than its value as salvage to the contractor should be expressly designated in the contract for retention by the Government. The contracting officer shall determine the fair market value of any property not so designated, since the contractor will get title to this property, and its value will therefore be important in determining what payment, if any, shall be made to the contractor and whether additional compensation will be made if the contract is terminated.

37.304 Contract clauses.

(a) The contracting officer shall insert the clause at 52.237-4, Payment by Government to Contractor, in solicitations and contracts solely for dismantling, demolition, or removal of improvements whenever the contracting officer determines that the Government shall make payment to the contractor in addition to any title to property that the contractor may receive under the contract. If the contracting officer determines that all material resulting from the dismantling or demolition work is to be retained by the Government, use the basic clause with its Alternate I.

(b) The contracting officer shall insert the clause at 52.237-1, Payment by Contractor to Government, in solicitations and contracts for dismantling, demolition, or removal of improvements whenever the contractor is to receive title to dismantled or demolished property and a net amount of compensation is due to the Government, except if the contracting officer determines that it would be advantageous to the Government for the contractor to pay in increments and the government to transfer title to the contractor for increments of property only upon receipt of those payments.

(c) The contracting officer shall insert the clause at 52.237-6, Incremental Payment by Contractor to Government, in solicitations and contracts for dismantling, demolition, or removal of improvements if (1) the contractor is to receive title to dismantled or demolished property and a net amount of compensation is due the Government, and

(2) the contracting officer determines that it would be advantageous to the Government for the contractor to pay in increments, and for the Government to transfer title to the contractor for increments of property only upon receipt of those payments. This determination may be appropriate, for example, if it encourages greater competition or participation of small business concerns.

SUBPART 37.4—NONPERSONAL HEALTH CARE SERVICES

37.400 Scope of subpart.

This subpart prescribes policies and procedures for obtaining health care services of physicians, dentists and other health care providers by nonpersonal services contracts, as defined in 37.101.

[FAC 84-42, 54 FR 5056, 1/31/89, effective 3/2/89]

37.401 Policy.

Agencies may enter into nonpersonal health care services contracts with physicians, dentists and other health care providers under authority of 10 U.S.C. 2304 and 41 U.S.C. chapter 33, Planning and Solicitation. Each contract shall—

(a) State that the contract is a nonpersonal health care services contract, as defined in 37.101, under which the contractor is an independent contractor;

(b) State that the Government may evaluate the quality of professional and administrative services provided, but retains no control over the medical, professional aspects of services rendered (*e.g.*, professional judgments, diagnosis for specific medical treatment);

(c) Require that the contractor indemnify the Government for any liability producing act or omission by the contractor, its employees and agents occurring during contract performance;

(d) Require that the contractor maintain medical liability insurance, in a coverage amount acceptable to the contracting officer, which is not less than the amount normally prevailing within the local community for the medical specialty concerned; and

(e) State that the contractor is required to ensure that its subcontracts for provisions of health care services, contain the requirements of the clause at 52.237-7, including the maintenance of medical liability insurance.

[FAC 84-42, 54 FR 5056, 1/31/89, effective 3/2/89; FAC 2005-73, 79 FR 24192, 4/29/2014, effective 5/29/2014]

37.402 Contracting officer responsibilities.

Contracting officers shall obtain evidence of insurability concerning medical liability insurance from the apparent successful offeror prior to contract award and shall obtain evidence of insurance demonstrating the required coverage prior to commencement of performance.

[FAC 90-45, Final rule, 62 FR 224, 1/2/97, effective 1/1/97]

37.403 Contract clause.

The contracting officer shall insert the clause at 52.237-7, Indemnification and Medical Liability Insurance, in solicitations and contracts for nonpersonal health care services. The contracting officer may include the clause in bilateral purchase orders for nonpersonal health care services awarded under the procedures in Part 13.

[FAC 84-42, 54 FR 5056, 1/31/89, effective 3/2/89]

SUBPART 37.5—MANAGEMENT OVERSIGHT OF SERVICE CONTRACTS

37.500 Scope of subpart.

This subpart establishes responsibilities for implementing Office of Federal Procurement Policy (OFPP) Policy Letter 93-1, Management Oversight of Service Contracting.

[FAC 90-46, 62 FR 12690, 3/17/97, effective 5/16/97]

37.501 Definition.

Best practices, as used in this subpart, means techniques that agencies may use to help detect problems in the acquisition, management, and administration of service contracts. Best practices are practical techniques gained from experience that agencies may use to improve the procurement process.

[FAC 90-46, 62 FR 12690, 3/17/97, effective 5/16/97]

37.502 Exclusions.

(a) This subpart does not apply to services that are—

(1) Obtained through personnel appointments and advisory committees;

(2) Obtained through personal service contracts authorized by statute;

(3) For construction as defined in 2.101; or

(4) Obtained through interagency agreements where the work is being performed by in-house Federal employees.

(b) Services obtained under contracts below the simplified acquisition threshold and services incidental to supply contracts also are excluded from the requirements of this subpart. However, good management practices and contract administration techniques should be used regardless of the contracting method.

[FAC 90-46, 62 FR 12690, 3/17/97, effective 5/16/97; FAC 97-22, 66 FR 2116, 1/10/2001, effective 3/12/2001; Delay of effective date, 66 FR 14259, 3/9/2001, effective 5/11/2001]

37.503 Agency-head responsibilities.

The agency head or designee should ensure that—

(a) Requirements for services are clearly defined and appropriate performance standards are developed so that the agency's requirements can be understood by potential offerors and that performance in accordance with contract terms and conditions will meet the agency's requirements;

(b) Service contracts are awarded and administered in a manner that will provide the customer its supplies and services within budget and in a timely manner;

(c) Specific procedures are in place before contracting for services to ensure that inherently governmental functions are performed by Government personnel; and

(d) Strategies are developed and necessary staff training is initiated to ensure effective implementation of the policies in 37.102.

[FAC 90-46, 62 FR 12690, 3/17/97, effective 5/16/97; FAC 97-18, 65 FR 36014, 6/6/2000, effective 6/6/2000; FAC 2005-09, Final rule, 71 FR 20299, 4/19/2006, effective 5/19/2006]

37.504 Contracting officials' responsibilities.

Contracting officials should ensure that *best practices* techniques are used when contracting for services and in contract management and administration (see OFPP Policy Letter 93-1).

[FAC 90-46, 62 FR 12690, 3/17/97, effective 5/16/97]

SUBPART 37.6—PERFORMANCE-BASED ACQUISITION

37.600 Scope of subpart.

This subpart prescribes policies and procedures for use of performance-based acquisition methods.

[FAC 97-1, 62 FR 44802, 8/22/97, effective 10/21/97; FAC 97-18, 65 FR 36014, 6/6/2000, effective 6/6/2000; FAC 2005-07, 71 FR 211, 1/3/2006, effective 2/2/2006]

37.601 General.

(a) Solicitations may use either a performance work statement or a statement of objectives (see 37.602).

(b) Performance-based contracts for services shall include—

(1) A performance work statement (PWS);

(2) Measurable performance standards (i.e., in terms of quality, timeliness, quantity, etc.) and the method of assessing contractor performance against performance standards; and

(3) Performance incentives where appropriate. When used, the performance incentives shall correspond to the performance standards set forth in the contract (see 16.402-2).

(c) See 12.102(g) for the use of Part 12 procedures for performance-based acquisitions.

[FAC 97-1, 62 FR 44802, 8/22/97, effective 10/21/97; FAC 2001-24, 69 FR 34225, 6/18/2004, effective 6/18/2004; FAC 2005-04, 70 FR 33657, 6/8/2005, effective

6/8/2005; FAC 2005-07, 71 FR 211, 1/3/2006, effective 2/2/2006]

37.602 Performance work statement.

(a) A Performance work statement (PWS) may be prepared by the Government or result from a Statement of objectives (SOO) prepared by the Government where the offeror proposes the PWS.

(b) Agencies shall, to the maximum extent practicable—

(1) Describe the work in terms of the required results rather than either "how" the work is to be accomplished or the number of hours to be provided (see 11.002(a)(2) and 11.101);

(2) Enable assessment of work performance against measurable performance standards;

(3) Rely on the use of measurable performance standards and financial incentives in a competitive environment to encourage competitors to develop and institute innovative and cost-effective methods of performing the work.

(c) Offerors use the SOO to develop the PWS; however, the SOO does not become part of the contract. The SOO shall, at a minimum, include—

(1) Purpose;

(2) Scope or mission;

(3) Period and place of performance;

(4) Background;

(5) Performance objectives, i.e., required results; and

(6) Any operating constraints.

[FAC 2005-07, 71 FR 211, 1/3/2006, effective 2/2/2006]

37.603 Performance standards.

(a) Performance standards establish the performance level required by the Government to meet the contract requirements. The standards shall be measurable and structured to permit an assessment of the contractor's performance.

(b) When offerors propose performance standards in response to a SOO, agencies shall evaluate the proposed standards to determine if they meet agency needs.

[FAC 2005-07, 71 FR 211, 1/3/2006, effective 2/2/2006]

37.604 Quality assurance surveillance plans.

Requirements for quality assurance and quality assurance surveillance plans are in Subpart 46.4. The Government may either prepare the quality assurance surveillance plan or require the offerors to submit a proposed quality assurance surveillance plan for the Government's consideration in development of the Government's plan.

[FAC 2005-07, 71 FR 211, 1/3/2006, effective 2/2/2006]

PART 38—FEDERAL SUPPLY SCHEDULE CONTRACTING

Table of Contents

Scope of part 38.000

Subpart 38.1—Federal Supply Schedule Program

General 38.101

Subpart 38.2—Establishing and Administering Federal Supply Schedules

Coordination requirements 38.201

PART 38—FEDERAL SUPPLY SCHEDULE CONTRACTING

38.000 Scope of part.

This part prescribes policies and procedures for contracting for supplies and services under the Federal Supply Schedule program, which is directed and managed by the General Services Administration (see Subpart 8.4, Federal Supply Schedules, for additional information). GSA may delegate certain responsibilities to other agencies (e.g., GSA has delegated authority to the Department of Veterans Affairs (VA) to procure medical supplies under the VA Federal Supply Schedules Program). The VA Federal Supply Schedules Program is covered by this subpart. Additionally, the Department of Defense manages a similar system of schedule contracting for military items; however, the Department of Defense systems are not a part of the Federal Supply Schedule program.

[FAC 2001-24, 69 FR 34231, 6/18/2004, effective 7/19/2004]

SUBPART 38.1—FEDERAL SUPPLY SCHEDULE PROGRAM

38.101 General.

(a) The Federal Supply Schedule program, pursuant to 41 U.S.C. 152(3), provides Federal agencies with a simplified process of acquiring commercial supplies and services in varying quantities while obtaining volume discounts. Indefinite-delivery contracts are awarded using competitive procedures to firms. The firms provide supplies and services at stated prices for given periods of time, for delivery within a stated geographic area such as the 48 contiguous states, the District of Columbia, Alaska, Hawaii, and overseas. The schedule contracting office issues Federal Supply Schedule publications that contain a general overview of the Federal Supply Schedule (FSS) program and address pertinent topics.

(b) Each schedule identifies agencies that are required to use the contracts as primary sources of supply.

(c) Federal agencies not identified in the schedules as mandatory users may issue orders under the schedules. Contractors are encouraged to accept the orders.

(d) Although GSA awards most Federal Supply Schedule contracts, it may authorize other agencies to award schedule contracts and publish schedules. For example, the Department of Veterans Affairs awards schedule contracts for certain medical and nonperishable subsistence items.

(e) When establishing Federal Supply Schedules, GSA, or an agency delegated that authority, is responsible for complying with all applicable statutory and regulatory requirements (e.g., Parts 5, 6, and 19). The requirements of parts 5, 6, and 19 apply at the acquisition planning stage prior to issuing the schedule solicitation and, generally, do not apply to orders and BPAs placed under resulting schedule contracts (except see 8.404 and 8.405-5).

[FAC 97-18, 65 FR 36014, 6/6/2000, effective 8/7/2000; FAC 2001-24, 69 FR 34231, 6/18/2004, effective 7/19/2004; FAC 2005-50, 76 FR 14548, 3/16/2011, effective 5/16/2011; FAC 2005-54, 76 FR 68032, 11/2/2011, effective 11/2/2011; Interim rule, 77 FR 1889, 1/12/2012, effective 2/13/2012; FAC 2005-56, 77 FR 12927, 3/2/2012, effective 4/2/2012; FAC 2005-73, 79 FR 24192, 4/29/2014, effective 5/29/2014]

SUBPART 38.2—ESTABLISHING AND ADMINISTERING FEDERAL SUPPLY SCHEDULES

38.201 Coordination requirements.

(a) Subject to interagency agreements, contracting officers having responsibility for awarding Federal Supply Schedule contracts shall coordinate and obtain approval of the General Services Administration's Federal Supply Service (FSS) before—

(1) Establishing new schedules;

(2) Discontinuing existing schedules;

(3) Changing the scope of agency or geographical coverage of existing schedules; or

(4) Adding or deleting special item numbers, national stock numbers, or revising their description.

(b) Requests should be forwarded to the General Services Administration, Federal

Supply Service, Office of Acquisition (FC), Washington, DC 20406.

[FAC 84-49, 54 FR 29282, 7/11/89, effective 8/10/89; FAC 90-8, 56 FR 55372, 10/25/91, effective 11/25/91; FAC 90-21, 59 FR 53716, 10/25/94, effective 10/25/94; Final rule, 62 FR 40236, 7/25/97, effective 6/30/97]

PART 39—ACQUISITION OF INFORMATION TECHNOLOGY

Table of Contents

Scope of part 39.000
Applicability 39.001
Definitions 39.002

Subpart 39.1—General

Policy 39.101
Management of risk 39.102
Modular contracting 39.103
Information technology services 39.104
Privacy 39.105
Contract clause 39.106

Subpart 39.2—Electronic and Information Technology

Scope of subpart 39.201
Definition 39.202
Applicability 39.203
Exceptions 39.204

PART 39—ACQUISITION OF INFORMATION TECHNOLOGY

39.000 Scope of part.

This part prescribes acquisition policies and procedures for use in acquiring—

(a) Information technology, including financial management systems, consistent with other parts of this regulation, OMB Circular No. A-127, Financial Management Systems, and OMB Circular No. A-130, Management of Federal Information Resources; and

(b) Electronic and information technology.

[FAC 97-27, 66 FR 20894, 4/25/2001, effective 6/25/2001]

39.001 Applicability.

This part applies to the acquisition of information technology by or for the use of agencies except for acquisitions of information technology for national security systems. However, acquisitions of information technology for national security systems shall be conducted in accordance with 40 U.S.C. 11302 with regard to requirements for performance and results-based management; the role of the agency Chief Information Officer in acquisitions; and accountability. These requirements are addressed in OMB Circular No. A-130.

[FAC 90-41, 61 FR 41466, 8/8/96, effective 8/8/96, finalized without change, FAC 97-3, 62 FR 64912, 12/9/97, effective 2/9/98; FAC 2005-06, 70 FR 57453, 9/30/2005, effective 9/30/2005]

39.002 Definitions.

As used in this part—

Modular contracting means use of one or more contracts to acquire information technology systems in successive, interoperable increments.

National security system means any telecommunications or information system operated by the United States Government, the function, operation, or use of which—

(1) Involves intelligence activities;

(2) Involves cryptologic activities related to national security;

(3) Involves command and control of military forces;

(4) Involves equipment that is an integral part of a weapon or weapons system; or

(5) Is critical to the direct fulfillment of military or intelligence missions. This does not include a system that is to be used for routine administrative and business applications, such as payroll, finance, logistics, and personnel management applications.

[FAC 90-41, 61 FR 41466, 8/8/96, effective 8/8/96, finalized without change, FAC 97-3, 62 FR 64912, 12/9/97, effective 2/9/98; FAC 90-45, Final rule, 62 FR 224, 1/2/97, effective 1/1/97; FAC 97-1, 62 FR 44802, 8/22/97, effective 10/21/97; FAC 97-4, 63 FR 9048, 2/23/98, effective 4/24/98; FAC 97-22, 66 FR 2116, 1/10/2001, effective 3/12/2001; Delay of effective date, 66 FR 14259, 3/9/2001, effective 5/11/2001; FAC 2005-78, 79 FR 70343, 11/25/2014, effective 12/26/2014]

SUBPART 39.1—GENERAL

39.101 Policy.

(a)(1) In acquiring information technology, agencies shall identify their requirements pursuant to—

(i) OMB Circular A-130, including consideration of security of resources, protection of privacy, national security and emergency preparedness, accommodations for individuals with disabilities, and energy efficiency;

(ii) Electronic Product Environmental Assessment Tool (EPEAT®) standards (see 23.704);

(iii) Policies to enable power management, double-sided printing, and other energy-efficient or environmentally preferable features on all agency electronic products; and

(iv) Best management practices for energy-efficient management of servers and Federal data centers.

(b) Agencies must follow OMB Circular A-127, Financial Management Systems, when acquiring financial management systems. Agencies may acquire only core financial management software certified by the

Joint Financial Management Improvement Program.

(c) In acquiring information technology, agencies shall include the appropriate information technology security policies and requirements, including use of common security configurations available from the National Institute of Standards and Technology's Web site at *http://checklists.nist.gov*. Agency contracting officers should consult with the requiring official to ensure the appropriate standards are incorporated.

(d) When acquiring information technology using Internet Protocol, agencies must include the appropriate Internet Protocol compliance requirements in accordance with 11.002(g).

(e) Contracting officers shall not purchase any hardware, software, or services developed or provided by Kaspersky Lab that the Government will use on or after October 1, 2018. (See 4.2002.)

(f) On or after August 13, 2019, contracting officers shall not procure or obtain, or extend or renew a contract to procure or obtain, any equipment, system, or service that uses covered telecommunications equipment or services as a substantial or essential component of any system, or as critical technology as part of any system on or after August 13, 2019, unless an exception applies or a waiver is granted. (See subpart 4.21.)

[FAC 97-15, 64 FR 72414, 12/27/99, effective 2/25/2000; FAC 2005-06, 70 FR 57449, 9/30/2005, effective 9/30/2005; FAC 2005-13, 71 FR 57360, 9/28/2006, effective 9/28/2006; FAC 2005-23, 72 FR 73215, 12/26/2007, effective 12/26/2007; FAC 2005-24, 73 FR 10967, 2/28/2008, effective 3/31/2008; FAC 2005-30, 74 FR 2740, 1/15/2009, effective 2/17/2009; FAC 2005-38, 74 FR 65605, 12/10/2009, effective 12/10/2009; FAC 2005-52, 76 FR 31395, 5/31/2011, effective 5/31/2011; FAC 2005-75, 79 FR 35859, 6/24/2014, effective 6/24/2014; FAC 2005-78, 79 FR 70343, 11/25/2014, effective 12/26/2014; FAC 2005-82, 80 FR 26427, 5/7/2015, effective 5/7/2015; FAC 2005-84, 80 FR 53436, 9/3/2015, effective 10/5/2015; FAC 2005-99, 83 FR 28141, 6/15/2018, effective 7/16/2018; FAC 2019-05, 84 FR 40216, 8/13/2019, effective 8/13/2019; FAC 2019-06, 84 FR 47861, 9/10/2019, effective 9/10/2019]

39.102 Management of risk.

(a) Prior to entering into a contract for information technology, an agency should analyze risks, benefits, and costs. (See Part 7 for additional information regarding requirements definition.) Reasonable risk taking is appropriate as long as risks are controlled and mitigated. Contracting and program office officials are jointly responsible for assessing, monitoring and controlling risk when selecting projects for investment and during program implementation.

(b) Types of risk may include schedule risk, risk of technical obsolescence, cost risk, risk implicit in a particular contract type, technical feasibility, dependencies between a new project and other projects or systems, the number of simultaneous high risk projects to be monitored, funding availability, and program management risk.

(c) Appropriate techniques should be applied to manage and mitigate risk during the acquisition of information technology. Techniques include, but are not limited to: prudent project management; use of modular contracting; thorough acquisition planning tied to budget planning by the program, finance and contracting offices; continuous collection and evaluation of risk-based assessment data; prototyping prior to implementation; post implementation reviews to determine actual project cost, benefits and returns; and focusing on risks and returns using quantifiable measures.

[FAC 90-41, 61 FR 41466, 8/8/96, effective 8/8/96, finalized without change, FAC 97-3, 62 FR 64912, 12/9/97, effective 2/9/98]

39.103 Modular contracting.

(a) This section implements 41 U.S.C. 2308. Modular contracting is intended to reduce program risk and to incentivize contractor performance while meeting the Government's need for timely access to rapidly changing technology. Consistent with the agency's information technology architecture, agencies should, to the maximum extent practicable, use modular contracting to acquire major systems (see 2.101) of information technology. Agencies may also use modular contracting to acquire non-major systems of information technology.

(b) When using modular contracting, an acquisition of a system of information technology may be divided into several smaller acquisition increments that—

(1) Are easier to manage individually than would be possible in one comprehensive acquisition;

(2) Address complex information technology objectives incrementally in order to enhance the likelihood of achieving workable systems or solutions for attainment of those objectives;

(3) Provide for delivery, implementation, and testing of workable systems or solutions in discrete increments, each of which comprises a system or solution that is not dependent on any subsequent increment in order to perform its principal functions;

(4) Provide an opportunity for subsequent increments to take advantage of any evolution in technology or needs that occur during implementation and use of the earlier increments; and

(5) Reduce risk of potential adverse consequences on the overall project by isolating and avoiding custom-designed components of the system.

(c) The characteristics of an increment may vary depending upon the type of information technology being acquired and the nature of the system being developed. The following factors may be considered:

(1) To promote compatibility, the information technology acquired through modular contracting for each increment should comply with common or commercially acceptable information technology standards when available and appropriate, and shall conform to the agency's master information technology architecture.

(2) The performance requirements of each increment should be consistent with the performance requirements of the completed, overall system within which the information technology will function and should address interface requirements with succeeding increments.

(d) For each increment, contracting officers shall choose an appropriate contracting technique that facilitates the acquisition of subsequent increments. Pursuant to Parts 16 and 17 of the Federal Acquisition Regulations, contracting officers shall select the contract type and method appropriate to the circumstances (*e.g.*, indefinite delivery, indefinite quantity contracts, single contract with options, successive contracts, multiple awards, task order contracts). Contract(s) shall be structured to ensure that the Government is not required to procure additional increments.

(e) To avoid obsolescence, a modular contract for information technology should, to the maximum extent practicable, be awarded within 180 days after the date on which the solicitation is issued. If award cannot be made within 180 days, agencies should consider cancellation of the solicitation in accordance with 14.209 or 15.206(e). To the maximum extent practicable, deliveries under the contract should be scheduled to occur within 18 months after issuance of the solicitation.

[FAC 97-4, 63 FR 9048, 2/23/98, effective 4/24/98; FAC 2005-73, 79 FR 24192, 4/29/2014, effective 5/29/2014]

39.104 Information technology services.

When acquiring information technology services, solicitations must not describe any minimum experience or educational requirement for proposed contractor personnel unless the contracting officer determines that the needs of the agency—

(a) Cannot be met without that requirement; or

(b) Require the use of other than a performance-based acquisition (see subpart 37.6).

[FAC 97-25, 66 FR 22084, 5/2/2001, effective 5/2/2001; finalized without change, FAC 2001-02, 66 FR 65347, 12/18/2001, effective 12/18/2001, FAC 2005-07, 71 FR 211, 1/3/2006, effective 2/2/2006]

39.105 Privacy.

Agencies shall ensure that contracts for information technology address protection of privacy in accordance with the Privacy Act (5 U.S.C. 552a) and Part 24. In addition, each agency shall ensure that contracts for the design, development, or operation of a system of records using commercial information technology services or information technology support services include the following:

(a) Agency rules of conduct that the contractor and the contractor's employees shall be required to follow.

(b) A list of the anticipated threats and hazards that the contractor must guard against.

(c) A description of the safeguards that the contractor must specifically provide.

(d) Requirements for a program of Government inspection during performance of the contract that will ensure the continued efficacy and efficiency of safeguards and the discovery and countering of new threats and hazards.

[FAC 90-41, 61 FR 41466, 8/8/96, effective 8/8/96, finalized without change, FAC 97-3, 62 FR 64912, 12/9/97, effective 2/9/98]

39.106 Contract clause.

The contracting officer shall insert a clause substantially the same as the clause at 52.239-1, Privacy or Security Safeguards, in solicitations and contracts for information technology which require security of information technology, and/or are for the design, development, or operation of a system of records using commercial information technology services or support services.

[Redesignated from 39.106, FAC 90-45, Final rule, 62 FR 224, 1/2/97, effective 1/1/97; Redesignated from 39.107, FAC 2005-78, 79 FR 70343, 11/25/2014, effective 12/26/2014]

SUBPART 39.2—ELECTRONIC AND INFORMATION TECHNOLOGY

39.201 Scope of subpart.

(a) This subpart implements section 508 of the Rehabilitation Act of 1973 (29 U.S.C. 794d), and the Architectural and Transportation Barriers Compliance Board Electronic and Information Technology (EIT) Accessibility Standards (36 CFR part 1194).

(b) Further information on section 508 is available via the Internet at *http://www.section508.gov*.

(c) When acquiring EIT, agencies must ensure that—

(1) Federal employees with disabilities have access to and use of information and data that is comparable to the access and use by Federal employees who are not individuals with disabilities; and

(2) Members of the public with disabilities seeking information or services from an agency have access to and use of information and data that is comparable to the access to and use of information and data by members of the public who are not individuals with disabilities.

[FAC 97-27, 66 FR 20894, 4/25/2001, effective 6/25/2001; FAC 2005-30, 74 FR 2740, 1/15/2009, effective 2/17/2009]

39.202 Definition.

Undue burden, as used in this subpart, means a significant difficulty or expense.

[FAC 97-27, 66 FR 20894, 4/25/2001, effective 6/25/2001]

39.203 Applicability.

(a) Unless an exception at 39.204 applies, acquisitions of EIT supplies and services must meet the applicable accessibility standards at 36 CFR part 1194.

(b) (1) Exception determinations are required prior to contract award, except for indefinite-quantity contracts (see paragraph (b) (2) of this section).

(2) Exception determinations are not required prior to award of indefinite-quantity contracts, except for requirements that are to be satisfied by initial award. Contracting offices that award indefinite-quantity contracts must indicate to requiring and ordering activities which supplies and services the contractor indicates as compliant, and show where full details of compliance can be found (e.g., vendor's or other exact website location).

(3) Requiring and ordering activities must ensure supplies or services meet the applicable accessibility standards at 36 CFR part 1194, unless an exception applies, at the time of issuance of task or delivery orders. Accordingly, indefinite-quantity contracts may include noncompliant items; however, any task or delivery order issued for noncompliant items must meet an applicable exception.

(c) (1) When acquiring commercial items, an agency must comply with those accessibility standards that can be met with supplies or services that are available in the commercial marketplace in time to meet the agency's delivery requirements.

(2) The requiring official must document in writing the nonavailability, including a description of market research performed and which standards cannot be met, and provide documentation to the contracting officer for inclusion in the contract file.

[FAC 97-27, 66 FR 20894, 4/25/2001, effective 6/25/2001]

39.204 Exceptions.

The requirements in 39.203 do not apply to EIT that—

(a) Is purchased in accordance with Subpart 13.2 (micro-purchases) prior to April 1, 2005. However, for micro-purchases, contracting officers and other individuals designated in accordance with 1.603-3 are strongly encouraged to comply with the applicable accessibility standards to the maximum extent practicable;

(b) Is for a national security system;

(c) Is acquired by a contractor incidental to a contract;

(d) Is located in spaces frequented only by service personnel for maintenance, repair or occasional monitoring of equipment; or

(e) Would impose an undue burden on the agency.

(1) Basis. In determining whether compliance with all or part of the applicable accessibility standards in 36 CFR part 1194 would be an undue burden, an agency must consider—

(i) The difficulty or expense of compliance; and

(ii) Agency resources available to its program or component for which the supply or service is being acquired.

(2) Documentation.

(i) The requiring official must document in writing the basis for an undue burden decision and provide the documentation to the contracting officer for inclusion in the contract file.

(ii) When acquiring commercial items, an undue burden determination is not required to address individual standards that cannot be met with supplies or service available in the commercial marketplace in time to meet the agency delivery requirements (see 39.203(c)(2) regarding documentation of nonavailability).

[FAC 97-27, 66 FR 20894, 4/25/2001, effective 6/25/2001; FAC 2001-11, 67 FR 80321, 12/31/2002, effective 1/1/2003; FAC 2001-15, 68 FR 43872, 7/24/2003, effective 7/24/2003; FAC 2001-25, 69 FR 59702, 10/5/2004, effective 10/5/2004, finalized without change, FAC 2005-03, 70 FR 18958, 4/11/2005, effective 4/11/2005]

PART 40—[RESERVED]

PART 41—ACQUISITION OF UTILITY SERVICES

Table of Contents

Subpart 41.1—General

Scope of part . . . 41.100
Definitions . . . 41.101
Applicability . . . 41.102
Statutory and delegated authority . . . 41.103

Subpart 41.2—Acquiring Utility Services

Policy . . . 41.201
Procedures . . . 41.202
GSA assistance . . . 41.203
GSA areawide contracts . . . 41.204
Separate contracts . . . 41.205
Interagency agreements . . . 41.206

Subpart 41.3—Requests for Assistance

Requirements . . . 41.301

Subpart 41.4—Administration

Monthly and annual review . . . 41.401
Rate changes and regulatory intervention . . . 41.402

Subpart 41.5—Solicitation Provision and Contract Clauses

Solicitation provision and contract clauses . . . 41.501

Subpart 41.6—Forms

Utility services forms . . . 41.601

Subpart 41.7—Formats

Formats for utility service specifications . . . 41.701
Formats for annual utility service review . . . 41.702

PART 41—ACQUISITION OF UTILITY SERVICES

41.100 Scope of part.

This part prescribes policies, procedures, and contract format for the acquisition of utility services. (See 41.102(b) for services that are excluded from this part.)

[FAC 90-23, 59 FR 67010, 12/28/94, effective 2/27/95]

41.101 Definitions.

As used in this part,

Areawide contract means a contract entered into between the General Services Administration (GSA) and a utility service supplier to cover utility service needs of Federal agencies within the franchise territory of the supplier. Each areawide contract includes an *Authorization* form for requesting service, connection, disconnection, or change in service.

Authorization means the document executed by the ordering agency and the utility supplier to order service under an areawide contract.

Connection charge means all nonrecurring costs, whether refundable or nonrefundable, to be paid by the Government to the utility supplier for the required connecting facilities, which are installed, owned, operated, and maintained by the utility supplier (see Termination liability).

Delegated agency means an agency that has received a written delegation of authority from GSA to contract for utility services for periods not exceeding ten years (see 41.103(b)).

Federal Power and Water Marketing Agency means a Government entity that produces, manages, transports, controls, and sells electrical and water supply service to customers.

Franchise territory means a geographical area that a utility supplier has a right to serve based upon a franchise, a certificate of public convenience and necessity, or other legal means.

Intervention means action by GSA or a delegated agency to formally participate in a utility regulatory proceeding on behalf of all Federal executive agencies.

Multiple service locations means the various locations or delivery points in the utility supplier's service area to which it provides service under a single contract.

Rates may include rate schedules, riders, rules, terms and conditions of service, and other tariff and service charges, e.g., facilities use charges.

Separate contract means a utility services contract (other than a GSA areawide contract, an Authorization under an areawide contract, or an interagency agreement) to cover the acquisition of utility services.

Termination liability means a contingent Government obligation to pay a utility supplier the unamortized portion of a connection charge and any other applicable nonrefundable service charge as defined in the contract in the event the Government terminates the contract before the cost of connection facilities has been recovered by the utility supplier (see *Connection charge*).

Utility service means a service such as furnishing electricity, natural or manufactured gas, water, sewerage, thermal energy, chilled water, steam, hot water, or high temperature hot water. The application of part 41 to other services (e.g., rubbish removal, snow removal) may be appropriate when the acquisition is not subject to the 41 U.S.C. chapter 67, Service Contract Labor Standards (see 37.107).

[FAC 90-23, 59 FR 67010, 12/28/94, effective 2/27/95; FAC 2005-73, 79 FR 24192, 4/29/2014, effective 5/29/2014]

41.102 Applicability.

(a) Except as provided in paragraph (b) of this section, this part applies to the acquisition of utility services for the Government, including connection charges and termination liabilities.

(b) This part does not apply to—

(1) Utility services produced, distributed, or sold by another Federal agency. In those cases, agencies shall use interagency agreements (see 41.206);

(2) Utility services obtained by purchase, exchange, or otherwise by a Federal power

or water marketing agency incident to that agency's marketing or distribution program;

(3) Cable television (CATV) and telecommunications services;

(4) Acquisition of natural or manufactured gas when purchased as a commodity;

(5) Acquisition of utilities services in foreign countries;

(6) Acquisition of rights in real property, acquisition of public utility facilities, and on-site equipment needed for the facility's own distribution system, or construction/maintenance of Government-owned equipment and real property; or

(7) Third party financed shared-savings projects authorized by 42 U.S.C. 8287. However, agencies may utilize part 41 for any energy savings or purchased utility service directly resulting from implementation of a third party financed shared-savings project under 42 U.S.C. 8287 for periods not to exceed 25 years.

[FAC 90-23, 59 FR 67010, 12/28/94, effective 2/27/95; FAC 2005-17, 72 FR 27364, 5/15/2007, effective 6/14/2007]

41.103 Statutory and delegated authority.

(a) *Statutory authority*. (1) The General Services Administration (GSA) is authorized by 40 U.S.C. 501 to prescribe policies and methods governing the acquisition and supply of utility services for Federal agencies. This authority includes related functions such as managing public utility services and representing Federal agencies in proceedings before Federal and state regulatory bodies. GSA is authorized by 40 U.S.C. 501 to contract for utility services for periods not exceeding ten years.

(2) The Department of Defense (DOD) is authorized by 10 U.S.C. 2304 and 40 U.S.C. 113(e)(3) to acquire utility services for military facilities.

(3) The Department of Energy (DOE) is authorized by the Department of Energy Organization Act (42 U.S.C. 7251, et seq.) to acquire utility services. DOE is authorized by the Atomic Energy Act of 1954, as amended (42 U.S.C. 2204), to enter into new contracts or modify existing contracts for electric services for periods not exceeding 25 years for uranium enrichment installations.

(b) *Delegated authority*. GSA has delegated its authority to enter into utility service contracts for periods not exceeding ten years to DOD and DOE, and for connection charges only to the Department of Veteran Affairs. Contracting pursuant to this delegated authority shall be consistent with the requirements of this part. Other agencies requiring utility service contracts for periods over one year, but not exceeding ten years, may request a delegation of authority from GSA at the address specified in 41.301(a). In keeping with its statutory authority, GSA will, as necessary, conduct reviews of delegated agencies' acquisitions of utility services to ensure compliance with the terms of the delegation and applicable laws and regulations.

(c) Requests for delegations of contracting authority from GSA shall include a certification from the acquiring agency's Senior Procurement Executive that the agency has—

(1) An established acquisition program;

(2) Personnel technically qualified to deal with specialized utilities problems; and

(3) The ability to accomplish its own pre-award contract review.

[FAC 90-23, 59 FR 67010, 12/28/94, effective 2/27/95; FAC 90-30, 60 FR 37772, 7/21/95, effective 9/19/95; FAC 97-9, 63 FR 58587, 10/30/98, effective 10/30/98; FAC 2005-06, 70 FR 57453, 9/30/2005, effective 9/30/2005]

SUBPART 41.2—ACQUIRING UTILITY SERVICES

41.201 Policy.

(a) Subject to paragraph (d) of this section, it is the policy of the Federal Government that agencies obtain required utility services from sources of supply which are most advantageous to the Government in terms of economy, efficiency, reliability, or service.

(b) Except for acquisitions at or below the simplified acquisition threshold, agencies shall acquire utility services by a bilateral written contract, which must include the clauses required by 41.501, regardless of whether rates or terms and conditions of service are fixed or adjusted by a regulatory body. Agencies may not use the utility supplier's forms and clauses to avoid the inclusion of provisions and clauses required by 41.501 or by statute. (See 41.202(c) for procedures to be used when the supplier refuses to execute a written contract.)

(c) Specific operating and management details, such as procedures for internal agency contract assistance and review, delegations of authority, and approval thresholds, may be prescribed by an individual agency subject to compliance with applicable statutes and regulations.

(d) (1) Section 8093 of the Department of Defense Appropriations Act of 1988, Pub. L. 100-202, provides that none of the funds appropriated by that Act or any other Act with respect to any fiscal year by any department, agency, or instrumentality of the United States, may be used for the purchase of electricity by the Government in any manner that is inconsistent with state law governing the providing of electric utility service, including state utility commission rulings and electric utility franchises or service territories established pursuant to state statute, state regulation, or state-approved territorial agreements.

(2) The Act does not preclude—

(i) The head of a Federal agency from entering into a contract pursuant to 42 U.S.C. 8287 (which pertains to the subject of shared energy savings including cogeneration);

(ii) The Secretary of a military department from entering into a contract pursuant to 10 U.S.C. 2394 (which pertains to contracts for energy or fuel for military installations including the provision and operation of energy production facilities); or

(iii) The Secretary of a military department from purchasing electricity from any provider when the utility or utilities having applicable state-approved franchise or other service authorizations are found by the Secretary to be unwilling or unable to meet unusual standards for service reliability that are necessary for purposes of national defense.

(3) Additionally, the head of a Federal agency may—

(i) Consistent with applicable state law, enter into contracts for the purchase or transfer of electricity to the agency by a non-utility, including a qualifying facility under the Public Utility Regulatory Policies Act of 1978;

(ii) Enter into an interagency agreement, pursuant to 41.206 and 17.5, with a Federal power marketing agency or the Tennessee Valley Authority for the transfer of electric power to the agency; and

(iii) Enter into a contract with an electric utility under the authority or tariffs of the Federal Energy Regulatory Commission.

(e) Prior to acquiring electric utility services on a competitive basis, the contracting officer shall determine, with the advice of legal counsel, by a market survey or any other appropriate means, *e.g.* consultation with the state agency responsible for regulating public utilities, that such competition would not be inconsistent with state law governing the provision of electric utility service, including state utility commission rulings and electric utility franchises or service territories established pursuant to state statute, state regulation, or state-approved territorial agreements. Proposals from alternative electric suppliers shall provide a representation that service can be provided in a manner consistent with section 8093 of Public Law 100-202 (see 41.201(d)).

[FAC 90-23, 59 FR 67010, 12/28/94, effective 2/27/95; FAC 90-29, 60 FR 34732, 7/3/95, effective 7/3/95; FAC 90-40, 61 FR 39186, 7/26/96, effective 8/26/96; FAC 97-11, 64 FR 10530, 3/4/99, effective 5/3/99]

41.202 Procedures.

(a) Prior to executing a utility service contract, the contracting officer shall comply with Parts 6 and 7 and Subsections 41.201(d) and (e). In accordance with Parts 6 and 7, agencies shall conduct market surveys and perform acquisition planning in order to promote and provide for full and open competition provided that the contracting officer determines that any resultant contract would not be inconsistent with applicable state law governing the provision of electric utility services. If competition for an entire utility service is not available, the market survey may be used to determine the availability of competitive sources for certain portions of the requirement. The scope of the term "entire utility service" includes the provision of the utility service capacity, energy, water, sewage, transportation, standby or back-up service, transmission and/or distribution service, quality assurance, system reliability, system operation and maintenance, metering, and billing.

(b) In performing a market survey (see 7.101), the contracting officer shall consider, in addition to alternative competitive sources, use of the following:

(1) GSA areawide contracts (see 41.204).

(2) Separate contracts (see 41.205).

(3) Interagency agreements (see 41.206).

(c) When a utility supplier refuses to execute a tendered contract as outlined in 41.201(b), the agency shall obtain a written definite and final refusal signed by a corporate officer or other responsible official of the supplier (or if unobtainable, document any unwritten refusal), and transmit this document, along with statements of the reasons for the refusal and the record of negotiations, to GSA at the address specified at 41.301(a). Unless urgent and compelling circumstances exist, the contracting officer shall notify GSA prior to acquiring utility services without executing a tendered contract. After such notification, the agency may proceed with the acquisition and pay for the utility service under the provisions of 31 U.S.C. 1501(a)(8)—

(1) By issuing a purchase order in accordance with 13.302; or

(2) By ordering the necessary utility service and paying for it upon the presentation of an invoice, provided that a determination is approved by the head of the contracting activity that a written contract cannot be obtained and that the issuance of a purchase order is not feasible.

(d) When obtaining service without a bilateral written contract, the contracting officer shall establish a utility history file on each acquisition of utility service provided by a contractor. This utility history file shall contain, in addition to applicable documents in 4.803, the following information:

(1) The unsigned, tendered contract and any related letter of transmittal.

(2) The reasons stated by the utility supplier for not executing the tendered contract, the record of negotiations, and a written definite and final refusal by a corporate officer or other responsible official of the supplier (or if unobtainable, documentation of unwritten refusal).

(3) Services to be furnished and the estimated annual cost.

(4) Historical record of any applicable connection charges.

(5) Historical record of any applicable ongoing capital credits.

(6) A copy of the applicable rate schedule.

(e) If the Government obtains utility service pursuant to paragraph (c) of this section, the contracting officer shall, on an annual basis beginning from the date of final refusal, take action to execute a bilateral written contract. The contracting officer shall document the utility history file with the efforts made and the agency shall notify GSA, in writing, if the utility continues to refuse to execute a bilateral contract.

[FAC 90-23, 59 FR 67010, 12/28/94, effective 2/27/95; FAC 97-3, 62 FR 64912, 12/9/97, effective 2/9/98]

41.203 GSA assistance.

(a) GSA will, upon request, provide technical and acquisition assistance, or will delegate its contracting authority for the furnishing of the services described in this part for any Federal agency, mixed-ownership Government corporation, the District of Columbia, the Senate, the House of Representatives, or the Architect of the Capitol and any activity under the Architect's direction.

(b) Agencies seeking assistance shall provide, upon request by GSA, the information listed in 41.301.

[FAC 90-23, 59 FR 67010, 12/28/94, effective 2/27/95]

41.204 GSA areawide contracts.

(a) *Purpose*. GSA enters into areawide contracts (see 41.101) for use by Federal agencies. Areawide contracts provide a pre-established contractual vehicle for ordering utility services under the conditions in paragraph (c)(1) of this section.

(b) *Features*. (1) Areawide contracts generally provide for ordering utility service at rates approved and/or established by a regulatory body and published in a tariff or rate schedule. However, agencies are permitted to negotiate other rates and terms and conditions of service with the supplier (see paragraph (c) of this section). Rates other than those published may require the approval of the regulatory body.

(2) Areawide contracts are negotiated with utility service suppliers for the provision of service within the supplier's franchise territory or service area.

(3) Due to the regulated nature of the utility industry, as well as statutory restrictions associated with the procurement of electricity (see 41.201(d)), competition is typically not available within the entire geographical area covered by an areawide contract, although it may be available at specific locations within the utility's service area. When competing suppliers are available, the provisions of Subparagraph (c)(1) of this section apply.

(c) *Procedures for obtaining service*. (1) Any Federal agency having a requirement for utility services within an area covered by an areawide contract shall acquire services under that areawide contract unless—

(i) Service is available from more than one supplier, or

(ii) The head of the contracting activity or designee otherwise determines that use of the areawide contract is not advantageous to the Government. If service is available from more than one supplier, service shall be acquired using competitive acquisition procedures (see 41.202(a)). The determination required by Subparagraph (c)(1)(ii) of this section shall be documented in the contract file with an information copy furnished to GSA at the address in 41.301(a).

(2) Each areawide contract includes an authorization form for ordering service, connection, disconnection, or change in service. Upon execution of an authorization by the contracting officer and utility supplier, the utility supplier is required to furnish services, without further negotiation, at the current, applicable published or unpublished rates, unless other rates, and/or terms and conditions are separately negotiated by the Federal agency with the supplier.

(3) The contracting officer shall execute the Authorization, and attach it to a Standard Form (SF) 26, Award/Contract, along with any modifications such as connection charges, special facilities, or service arrangements. The contracting officer shall also attach any specific fiscal, operational, and administrative requirements of the agency, applicable rate schedules, technical information and detailed maps or drawings of delivery points, details on Government ownership, maintenance, or repair of facilities, and other information deemed necessary to fully define the service conditions in the Authorization/contract.

(d) *List of areawide contracts*. A list of current GSA areawide contracts is available from the GSA office specified at 41.301(a). The list identifies the types of services and the geographic area served. A copy of the contract may also be obtained from this office.

(e) *Notification*. Agencies shall provide GSA at the address specified at 41.301(a) a copy of each SF 26 and executed Authorization issued under an areawide contract within 30 days after execution.

[FAC 90-23, 59 FR 67010, 12/28/94, effective 2/27/95]

41.205 Separate contracts.

(a) In the absence of an areawide contract or interagency agreement (see 41.206), agencies shall acquire utility services by separate contract subject to this part, and subject to agency contracting authority.

(b) If an agency enters into a separate contract, the contracting officer shall document the contract file with the following information:

(1) The number of available suppliers.

(2) Any special equipment, service reliability, or facility requirements and related costs.

(3) The utility supplier's rates, connection charges, and termination liability.

(4) Total estimated contract value (including costs in subparagraphs (b) (2) and (3) of this subsection).

(5) Any technical or special contract terms required.

(6) Any unusual characteristics of services required.

(7) The utility's wheeling or transportation policy for utility service.

(c) If requesting GSA assistance with a separate contract, the requesting agency shall furnish the technical and acquisition data specified in 41.205(b), 41.301, and such other data as GSA may deem necessary.

(d) A contract exceeding a 1-year period, but not exceeding ten years (except pursuant to 41.103), may be justified, and is usually required, where any of the following circumstances exist:

(1) The Government will obtain lower rates, larger discounts, or more favorable terms and conditions of service;

(2) A proposed connection charge, termination liability, or any other facilities charge to be paid by the Federal Government will be reduced or eliminated; or

(3) The utility service supplier refuses to render the desired service except under a contract exceeding a 1-year period.

[FAC 90-23, 59 FR 67010, 12/28/94, effective 2/27/95]

41.206 Interagency agreements.

Agencies shall use interagency agreements (*e.g.*, consolidated purchase, joint use, or cross-service agreements) when acquiring utility service or facilities from other Government agencies and shall comply with the policies and procedures at 17.502-2, The Economy Act.

[FAC 90-23, 59 FR 67010, 12/28/94, effective 2/27/95; FAC 2005-47, 75 FR 77733, 12/13/2010, effective 12/13/2010; FAC 2005-55, 77 FR 183, 1/3/2012, effective 2/2/2012]

SUBPART 41.3—REQUESTS FOR ASSISTANCE

41.301 Requirements.

(a) Requests for delegations of GSA contracting authority, assistance with a proposed contract as provided in 41.203, and the submission of other information required by this part, shall be sent or submitted to the General Services Administration (GSA) region in which service is required. The names and locations of GSA regional offices are available from the General Services Administration, Energy Division—PMA, 1800 F St, NW, Washington, DC 20405; Website: *www.gsa.gov/energy*; Email: *energy@gsa.gov*.

(b) Requests for contracting assistance for utility services shall be sent not later than 120 days prior to the date new services are required to commence or existing contract will expire. Requests for assistance shall contain the following information:

(1) A technical description or specification of the type, quantity, and quality of service required, and a delivery schedule.

(2) A copy of any service proposal or proposed contract.

(3) Copies of all current published or unpublished rates of the utility supplier.

(4) Identification of any unusual factors affecting the acquisition.

(5) Identification of all available sources or methods of supply, an analysis of the cost-effectiveness of each, and a statement of the ability of each source to provide the required services, including the location and a description of each available supplier's facilities at the nearest point of service, and the cost of providing or obtaining necessary backup and other ancillary services.

(c) For new utility service requirements, the agency shall furnish the information in paragraph (a) of this section and the following as applicable:

(1) The date initial service is required.

(2) For the first 12 months of full service, estimated maximum demand, monthly consumption, other pertinent information (*e.g.*, demand side management, load or energy management, peak shaving, on site generation, load shaping), and annual cost of the service.

(3) Known or estimated time schedule for growth to ultimate requirements.

(4) Estimated ultimate maximum demand and ultimate monthly consumption.

(5) A simple schematic diagram or line drawing showing the meter locations, the location of the new utility facilities to be constructed on Federal property by the Federal agency, and any required new connection facilities on either side of the delivery point to be constructed by the utility supplier to provide the new services.

(6) Accounting and appropriation data to cover the required utility services and any connection charges required to be paid by the agency receiving such utility services.

(7) The following data concerning proposed facilities and related charges or costs:

(i) Proposed refundable or nonrefundable connection charge, termination liability, or other facilities charge to be paid by the agency, together with a description of the supplier's proposed facilities and estimated construction costs, and its rationale for the charge (*e.g.*, tariff provisions or policies).

(ii) A copy of the acquiring agency's estimate to make its own connection to the supplier's facilities through use of its own resources or by separate contract. When feasible, the acquiring agency shall provide its estimates to construct and operate its own utility facilities in lieu of participating in a cost-sharing construction program with the proposed utility supplier.

(d) For existing utility service, the agency shall furnish GSA the information in paragraph (b) of this section and the following, as applicable:

(1) A copy of the most recent 12-months' service invoices.

(2) A tabulation, by month, for the most recent 12 months, showing the actual utility demands, consumption, connection charges, fuel adjustment charges, and the average monthly cost per unit of consumption.

(3) An estimate, by month, for the next 12 months, showing the estimated maximum demands, monthly consumption, other pertinent information (*e.g.*, demand side management, load or energy management, peak shaving, on site generation, load shaping), and annual cost of the service.

(4) Accounting and appropriation data to cover the costs for the continuation of utility services.

(5) A statement noting whether the transformer, or other system components, on either side of the delivery point are owned by the Federal agency or the utility supplier, and if the metering is on the primary or secondary side of the transformer.

[FAC 90-23, 59 FR 67010, 12/28/94, effective 2/27/95; FAC 2001-26, 69 FR 76358, 12/20/2004, effective 12/20/2004; FAC 2005-100, 83 FR 42571, 8/22/2018, effective 8/22/2018]

SUBPART 41.4—ADMINISTRATION

41.401 Monthly and annual review.

Agencies shall review utility service invoices on a monthly basis and all utility accounts, with annual values exceeding the simplified acquisition threshold, on an annual basis. Annual reviews of accounts with annual values at or below the simplified acquisition threshold shall be conducted when deemed advantageous to the Government. The purpose of the monthly review is to ensure the accuracy of utility service invoices. The purpose of the annual review is to ensure that the utility supplier is furnishing the services to each facility under the utility's most economical, applicable rate and to examine competitive markets for more advantageous service offerings. The annual review shall be based upon the facility's usage, conditions and characteristics of service at each individual delivery point for the most recent 12 months. If a more advantageous rate is appropriate, the Federal agency shall request the supplier to make such rate change immediately.

[FAC 90-23, 59 FR 67010, 12/28/94, effective 2/27/95; FAC 90-29, 60 FR 34732, 7/3/95, effective 7/3/95]

41.402 Rate changes and regulatory intervention.

(a) When a change is proposed to rates or terms and conditions of service to the Government, the agency shall promptly determine whether the proposed change is reasonable, justified, and not discriminatory.

(b) If a change is proposed to rates or terms and conditions of service that may be of interest to other Federal agencies, and intervention before a regulatory body is considered justified, the matter shall be referred to GSA. The agency may request from GSA a delegation of authority for the agency to intervene on behalf of the consumer interests of the Federal executive agencies (see 41.301).

(c) Pursuant to 52.241-7, Change in Rates or Terms and Conditions of Service for Regulated Services, if a regulatory body approves a rate change, any rate change shall be made a part of the contract by unilateral contract modification or otherwise documented in accordance with agency procedures. The approved applicable rate shall be effective on the date determined by the regulatory body and resulting rates and charges shall be paid promptly to avoid late payment provisions. Copies of the modification containing the approved rate change shall be sent to the agency's paying office or office responsible for verifying billed amounts (see 41.401).

(d) If the utility supplier is not regulated and the rates, terms, and conditions of service are subject to negotiation pursuant to the clause at 52.241-8, Change in Rates or Terms and Conditions of Service for Unregulated Services, any rate change shall be made a part of the contract by contract modification, with copies sent to the agency's paying office or office responsible for verifying billed amounts.

[FAC 90-23, 59 FR 67010, 12/28/94, effective 2/27/95]

SUBPART 41.5—SOLICITATION PROVISION AND CONTRACT CLAUSES

41.501 Solicitation provision and contract clauses.

(a) Because the terms and conditions under which utility suppliers furnish service may vary from area to area, the differences may influence the terms and conditions appropriate to a particular utility's contracting situation. To accommodate requirements that are peculiar to the contracting situation, this section prescribes provisions and clauses on a "substantially the same as" basis (see 52.101) which permits the contracting officer to prepare and utilize variations of the prescribed provision and clauses in accordance with agency procedures.

(b) The contracting officer shall insert in solicitations for utility services a provision substantially the same as the provision at 52.241-1, Electric Service Territory Compliance Representation, when proposals from alternative electric suppliers are sought.

(c) The contracting officer shall insert in solicitations and contracts for utility services clauses substantially the same as the clauses at—

(1) 52.241-2, Order of Precedence—Utilities;

(2) 52.241-3, Scope and Duration of Contract;

(3) 52.241-4, Change in Class of Service;

(4) 52.241-5, Contractor's Facilities; and

(5) 52.241-6, Service Provisions.

(d) The contracting officer shall insert clauses substantially the same as the clauses listed below in solicitations and contracts under the prescribed conditions—

(1) 52.241-7, Change in Rates or Terms and Conditions of Service for Regulated Services, when the utility services are subject to a regulatory body. (Except for GSA areawide contracts, the contracting officer shall insert in the blank space provided in the clause the name of the contracting officer. For GSA areawide contracts, the contracting officer shall insert the following: "GSA and each

areawide customer with annual billings that exceed $250,000.")

(2) 52.241-8, Change in Rates or Terms and Conditions of Service for Unregulated Services, when the utility services are not subject to a regulatory body.

(3) 52.241-9, Connection Charge, when a refundable connection charge is required to be paid by the Government to compensate the contractor for furnishing additional facilities necessary to supply service. (Use Alternate I to the clause if a nonrefundable charge is to be paid. When conditions require the incorporation of a nonrecurring, nonrefundable service charge or a termination liability, see paragraphs (f) and (i) of this section.)

(4) 52.241-10, Termination Liability, when payment is to be made to the contractor upon termination of service in conjunction with or in lieu of a connection charge upon completion of the facilities.

(5) 52.241-11, Multiple Service Locations (as defined in 41.101), when providing for possible alternative service locations, except under areawide contracts, is required.

(6) 52.241-12, Nonrefundable, Nonrecurring Service Charge, when the Government is required to pay a nonrefundable, nonrecurring membership fee, a charge for initiation of service, or a contribution for the cost of facilities construction. The Government may provide for inclusion of such agreed amount or fee as a part of the connection charge, a part of the initial payment for services, or as periodic payments to fulfill the Government's obligation.

(7) 52.241-13, Capital Credits, when the Federal Government is a member of a cooperative and is entitled to capital credits, consistent with the bylaws and governing documents of the cooperative.

(e) Depending on the conditions that are appropriate for each acquisition, the contracting officer shall also insert in solicitations and contracts for utility services the provisions and clauses prescribed elsewhere in the FAR.

[FAC 90-23, 59 FR 67010, 12/28/94, effective 2/27/95; corrected 60 FR 14377, 3/17/95]

SUBPART 41.6—FORMS

41.601 Utility services forms.

(a) If acquiring utility services under other than an areawide contract, a purchase order or an interagency agreement, the Standard Form (SF) 33, Solicitation, Offer and Award; SF 26, Award/Contract; or SF 1447, Solicitation/Contract, shall be used.

(b) The contracting officer shall incorporate the applicable rate schedule in each contract, purchase order or modification.

[FAC 90-23, 59 FR 67010, 12/28/94, effective 2/27/95]

SUBPART 41.7—FORMATS

41.701 Formats for utility service specifications.

(a) The following specification formats for use in acquiring utility services are available from the address specified at 41.301(a) and may be used and modified at the agency's discretion:

(1) Electric service.

(2) Water service.

(3) Steam service.

(4) Sewage service.

(5) Natural gas service.

(b) Contracting officers may modify the specification format referenced in paragraph (a) of this section and attach technical items, details on Government ownership of equipment and real property and maintenance or repair obligations, maps or drawings of delivery points, and other information deemed necessary to fully define the service conditions.

(c) The specifications and attachments (see paragraph (b) of this section) shall be inserted in Section C of the utility service solicitation and contract.

[FAC 90-23, 59 FR 67010, 12/28/94, effective 2/27/95; FAC 2005-17, 72 FR 27364, 5/15/2007, effective 6/14/2007]

41.702 Formats for annual utility service review.

(a) Formats for use in conducting annual reviews of the following utility services are available from the address specified at

41.301(a) and may be used at the agency's discretion:

(1) Electric service.

(2) Gas service.

(3) Water and sewage service.

(b) Contracting officers may modify the annual utility service review format as necessary to fully cover the service used.

[FAC 90-23, 59 FR 67010, 12/28/94, effective 2/27/95]

Federal Acquisition Regulation Parts 42—51 Contract Management

Table of Contents

SUBCHAPTER G—CONTRACT MANAGEMENT

Part 42—Contract Administration and Audit Services 1135
Part 43—Contract Modifications 1181
Part 44—Subcontracting Policies and Procedures . . . 1189
Part 45—Government Property 1199
Part 46—Quality Assurance 1215
Part 47—Transportation 1237
Part 48—Value Engineering 1279
Part 49—Termination of Contracts 1291
Part 50—Extraordinary Contractual Actions and the SAFETY ACT 1341
Part 51—Use of Government Sources by Contractors 1357

PART 42—CONTRACT ADMINISTRATION AND AUDIT SERVICES

Table of Contents

Scope of part . . . 42.000
[Removed and Reserved] . . . 42.001
Interagency agreements . . . 42.002
Cognizant Federal agency . . . 42.003

Subpart 42.1—Contract Audit Services

Contract audit responsibilities . . . 42.101
Assignment of contract audit services . . . 42.102
Contract audit services directory . . . 42.103

Subpart 42.2—Contract Administration Services

Contract administration responsibilities . . . 42.201
Assignment of contract administration . . . 42.202
Contract administration services directory . . . 42.203

Subpart 42.3—Contract Administration Office Functions

General . . . 42.301
Contract administration functions . . . 42.302

Subpart 42.4—Correspondence and Visits

Contract correspondence . . . 42.401
Visits to contractors' facilities . . . 42.402
Evaluation of contract administration offices . . . 42.403

Subpart 42.5—Postaward Orientation

Scope of subpart . . . 42.500
General . . . 42.501
Selecting contracts for postaward orientation . . . 42.502
Postaward conferences. (No Text) . . . 42.503
Postaward conference procedure . . . 42.503-2
Postaward conference report . . . 42.503-3
Postaward letters . . . 42.504
Postaward subcontractor conferences . . . 42.505

Subpart 42.6—Corporate Administrative Contracting Officer

General . . . 42.601
Assignment and location . . . 42.602
Responsibilities . . . 42.603

Subpart 42.7—Indirect Cost Rates

Scope of subpart . . . 42.700
Definition . . . 42.701
Purpose . . . 42.702
General. (No Text) . . . 42.703
Certificate of indirect costs . . . 42.703-2
Billing rates . . . 42.704
Final indirect cost rates . . . 42.705
Contracting officer determination procedure . . . 42.705-1
Auditor determination procedure . . . 42.705-2
Educational institutions . . . 42.705-3
State and local governments . . . 42.705-4
Nonprofit organizations other than educational and state and local governments . . . 42.705-5
Distribution of documents . . . 42.706
Cost-sharing rates and limitations on indirect cost rates . . . 42.707
Quick-closeout procedure . . . 42.708
Penalties for Unallowable Costs. (No Text) . . . 42.709
Scope . . . 42.709-0

General 42.709-1
Responsibilities 42.709-2
Assessing the penalty 42.709-3
Computing interest 42.709-4
Waiver of the penalty 42.709-5
Contract clause 42.709-6

Subpart 42.8—Disallowance of Costs

Scope of subpart 42.800
Notice of intent to disallow costs 42.801
Contract clause 42.802
Disallowing costs after incurrence 42.803

Subpart 42.9—Bankruptcy

Scope of subpart 42.900
General 42.901
Procedures 42.902
Solicitation provision and contract clause 42.903

Subpart 42.10—[Reserved]

Subpart 42.11—Production Surveillance and Reporting

General 42.1101
Applicability 42.1102
Policy 42.1103
Surveillance requirements 42.1104
Assignment of criticality designator 42.1105
Reporting requirements 42.1106
Contract clause 42.1107

Subpart 42.12—Novation and Change-of-Name Agreements

Scope of subpart 42.1200
[Removed and Reserved] 42.1201
Responsibility for executing agreements 42.1202
Processing agreements 42.1203
Applicability of novation agreements 42.1204
Agreement to recognize contractor's change of name 42.1205

Subpart 42.13—Suspension of Work, Stop-Work Orders, and Government Delay of Work

General 42.1301
Suspension of work 42.1302
Stop-work orders 42.1303
Government delay of work 42.1304
Contract clauses 42.1305

Subpart 42.14—[Removed and Reserved]

Subpart 42.15—Contractor Performance Information

Scope of subpart 42.1500
General 42.1501
Policy 42.1502
Procedures 42.1503
Contract clause 42.1504

Subpart 42.16—Small Business Contract Administration

General 42.1601

Subpart 42.17—Forward Pricing Rate Agreements

Procedures 42.1701

SUBCHAPTER G—CONTRACT MANAGEMENT (Parts 42-51)

PART 42—CONTRACT ADMINISTRATION AND AUDIT SERVICES

42.000 Scope of part.

This part prescribes policies and procedures for assigning and performing contract administration and contract audit services.

[FAC 97-4, 63 FR 9048, 2/23/98, effective 4/24/98]

42.001 [Removed and Reserved]

[Removed and Reserved, FAC 97-22, 66 FR 2117, 1/10/2001, effective 3/12/2001; Delay of effective date, 66 FR 14259, 3/9/2001, effective 5/11/2001]

42.002 Interagency agreements.

(a) Agencies shall avoid duplicate audits, reviews, inspections, and examinations of contractors or subcontractors, by more than one agency, through the use of interagency agreements.

(b) Subject to the fiscal regulations of the agencies and applicable interagency agreements, the requesting agency shall reimburse the servicing agency for rendered services in accordance with the Economy Act (31 U.S.C. 1535).

(c) When an interagency agreement is established, the agencies are encouraged to consider establishing procedures for the resolution of issues that may arise under the agreement.

[FAC 97-4, 63 FR 9048, 2/23/98, effective 4/24/98; FAC 97-18, 65 FR 36014, 6/6/2000, effective 6/6/2000]

42.003 Cognizant Federal agency.

(a) For contractors other than educational institutions and nonprofit organizations, the cognizant Federal agency normally will be the agency with the largest dollar amount of negotiated contracts, including options. For educational institutions (defined as institutions of higher education in the OMB Uniform Guidance at 2 CFR part 200, subpart A, and 20 U.S.C. 1001) and nonprofit organizations (as defined in the OMB Uniform Guidance at 2 CFR part 200), the cognizant Federal agency for indirect costs is established according to the OMB Uniform Guidance at 2 CFR part 200, appendices III and IV, respectively.

(b) Once a Federal agency assumes cognizance for a contractor, it should remain cognizant for at least 5 years to ensure continuity and ease of administration. If, at the end of the 5-year period, another agency has the largest dollar amount of negotiated contracts, including options, the two agencies shall coordinate and determine which will assume cognizance. However, if circumstances warrant it and the affected agencies agree, cognizance may transfer prior to the expiration of the 5-year period.

[FAC 97-4, 63 FR 9048, 2/23/98, effective 4/24/98; FAC 2005-89, 81 FR 45852, 7/14/2016, effective 8/15/2016]

SUBPART 42.1—CONTRACT AUDIT SERVICES

42.101 Contract audit responsibilities.

(a) The auditor is responsible for—

(1) Submitting information and advice to the requesting activity, based on the auditor's analysis of the contractor's financial and accounting records or other related data as to the acceptability of the contractor's incurred and estimated costs;

(2) Reviewing the financial and accounting aspects of the contractor's cost control systems; and

(3) Performing other analyses and reviews that require access to the contractor's financial and accounting records supporting proposed and incurred costs.

(b) Normally, for contractors other than educational institutions and nonprofit organizations, the Defense Contract Audit Agency (DCAA) is the responsible Government audit agency. However, there may be instances where an agency other than DCAA desires cognizance of a particular contractor. In those instances, the two agencies shall agree on the most efficient and economical approach to meet contract audit requirements. For educational institutions (defined as institutions of higher education in the OMB Uniform Guidance at 2 CFR part 200, subpart A, and 20 U.S.C. 1001) and nonprofit organizations (as defined in the OMB Uniform Guidance at 2 CFR part 200), audit cognizance will be determined according to the provisions of the OMB Uniform Guidance at 2 CFR part 200, subpart F.

[FAC 97-4, 63 FR 9048, 2/23/98, effective 4/24/98; FAC 2005-89, 81 FR 45852, 7/14/2016, effective 8/15/2016]

42.102 Assignment of contract audit services.

(a) As provided in agency procedures or interagency agreements, contracting officers may request audit services directly from the responsible audit agency cited in the Directory of Federal Contract Audit Offices. The audit request should include a suspense date and should identify any information needed by the contracting officer.

(b) The responsible audit agency may decline requests for services on a case-by-case basis, if resources of the audit agency are inadequate to accomplish the tasks. Declinations shall be in writing.

[FAC 97-4, 63 FR 9048, 2/23/98, effective 4/24/98]

42.103 Contract audit services directory.

(a) DCAA maintains and distributes the Directory of Federal Contract Audit Offices. The directory identifies cognizant audit offices and the contractors over which they have cognizance. Changes to audit cognizance shall be provided to DCAA so that the directory can be updated.

(b) Agencies may obtain a copy of the directory or information concerning cognizant audit offices by contacting the—Defense Contract Audit Agency, ATTN: CMO, Publications Officer, 8725 John J. Kingman Road, Suite 2135, Fort Belvoir, VA 22060-6219.

[FAC 97-4, 63 FR 9048, 2/23/98, effective 4/24/98]

SUBPART 42.2—CONTRACT ADMINISTRATION SERVICES

42.201 Contract administration responsibilities.

(a) For each contract assigned for administration, the contract administration office (CAO) (see 2.101) shall—

(1) Perform the functions listed in 42.302(a) to the extent that they apply to the contract, except for the functions specifically withheld;

(2) Perform the functions listed in 42.302(b) only when and to the extent specifically authorized by the contracting officer; and

(3) Request supporting contract administration under 42.202(e) and (f) when it is required.

(b) The Defense Contract Management Agency and other agencies offer a wide variety of contract administration and support services.

[FAC 97-4, 63 FR 9048, 2/23/98, effective 4/24/98; FAC 97-22, 66 FR 2117, 1/10/2001, effective 1/10/2001]

42.202 Assignment of contract administration.

(a) *Delegating functions.* As provided in agency procedures, contracting officers may delegate contract administration or specialized support services, either through interagency agreements or by direct request to the cognizant CAO listed in the Federal Directory of Contract Administration Services Components. The delegation should include—

(1) The name and address of the CAO designated to perform the administration (this information also shall be entered in the contract);

(2) Any special instructions, including any functions withheld or any specific authorization to perform functions listed in 42.302(b);

(3) A copy of the contract to be administered; and

(4) Copies of all contracting agency regulations or directives that are—

(i) Incorporated into the contract by reference; or

(ii) Otherwise necessary to administer the contract, unless copies have been provided previously.

(b) *Special instructions.* As necessary, the contracting officer also shall advise the contractor (and other activities as appropriate) of any functions withheld from or additional functions delegated to the CAO.

(c) *Delegating additional functions.* For individual contracts or groups of contracts, the contracting office may delegate to the CAO functions not listed in 42.302: *Provided* that—

(1) Prior coordination with the CAO ensures the availability of required resources;

(2) In the case of authority to issue orders under provisioning procedures in existing contracts and under basic ordering agreements for items and services identified in the schedule, the head of the contracting activity or designee approves the delegation; and

(3) The delegation does not require the CAO to undertake new or follow-on acquisitions.

(d) *Rescinding functions.* The contracting officer at the requesting agency may rescind or recall a delegation to administer a contract or perform a contract administration function, except for functions pertaining to cost accounting standards and negotiation of forward pricing rates and indirect cost rates (also see 42.003). The requesting agency must coordinate with the CAO to establish a reasonable transition period prior to rescinding or recalling the delegation.

(e) *Secondary delegations of contract administration.* (1) A CAO that has been delegated administration of a contract under paragraph (a) or (c) of this section, or a contracting office retaining contract administration, may request supporting contract administration from the CAO cognizant of the contractor location where performance of specific contract administration functions is required. The request shall—

(i) Be in writing;

(ii) Clearly state the specific functions to be performed; and

(iii) Be accompanied by a copy of pertinent contractual and other necessary documents.

(2) The prime contractor is responsible for managing its subcontracts. The CAO's review of subcontracts is normally limited to evaluating the prime contractor's management of the subcontracts (see Part 44). Therefore, supporting contract administration shall not be used for subcontracts unless—

(i) The Government otherwise would incur undue cost;

(ii) Successful completion of the prime contract is threatened; or

(iii) It is authorized under paragraph (f) of this section or elsewhere in this regulation.

(f) *Special surveillance.* For major system acquisitions (see Part 34), the contracting officer may designate certain high risk or critical subsystems or components for special surveillance in addition to requesting supporting contract administration. This surveillance shall be conducted in a manner consistent with the policy of requesting that the cognizant CAO perform contract administration functions at a contractor's facility (see 42.002).

(g) *Refusing delegation of contract administration.* An agency may decline a request for contract administration services on a case-by-case basis if resources of the agency are inadequate to accomplish the tasks. Declinations shall be in writing.

[FAC 97-4, 63 FR 9048, 2/23/98, effective 4/24/98]

42.203 Contract administration services directory.

The Defense Contract Management Agency (DCMA) maintains the Federal Directory of Contract Administration Services Components. The directory lists the names and telephone numbers of those DCMA and other agency offices that offer contract administration services within designated geographic areas and at specified contractor plants. Federal agencies may access it on the Internet at ***https://pubapp.dcma.mil/CASD/main.jsp***. For additional information contact—Defense Contract Management

Agency, 3901 A Avenue, Building 10500, Ft. Lee, VA 22801-1809.

[FAC 97-22, 66 FR 2117, 1/10/2001, effective 1/10/2001; FAC 2005-01, 70 FR 11763, 3/9/2005, effective 3/9/2005; FAC 2005-55, 77 FR 204, 1/3/2012, effective 1/3/2012; FAC 2005-56, 77 FR 12948, 3/2/2012, effective 3/2/2012]

SUBPART 42.3—CONTRACT ADMINISTRATION OFFICE FUNCTIONS

42.301 General.

When a contract is assigned for administration under Subpart 42.2, the contract administration office (CAO) shall perform contract administration functions in accordance with 48 CFR Chapter I, the contract terms, and, unless otherwise agreed to in an interagency agreement (see 42.002), the applicable regulations of the servicing agency.

[FAC 97-4, 63 FR 9048, 2/23/98, effective 4/24/98]

42.302 Contract administration functions.

(a) The contracting officer normally delegates the following contract administration functions to a CAO. The contracting officer may retain any of these functions, except those in paragraphs (a)(5), (a)(9), (a)(11), and (a)(12) of this section, unless the cognizant Federal agency (see 2.101) has designated the contracting officer to perform these functions.

(1) Review the contractor's compensation structure.

(2) Review the contractor's insurance plans.

(3) Conduct post-award orientation conferences.

(4) Review and evaluate contractors' proposals under Subpart 15.4 and, when negotiation will be accomplished by the contracting officer, furnish comments and recommendations to that officer.

(5) Negotiate forward pricing rate agreements (see 15.407-3).

(6) Negotiate advance agreements applicable to treatment of costs under contracts currently assigned for administration (see 31.109).

(7) Determine the allowability of costs suspended or disapproved as required (see Subpart 42.8), direct the suspension or disapproval of costs when there is reason to believe they should be suspended or disapproved, and approve final vouchers.

(8) Issue Notices of Intent to Disallow or not Recognize Costs (see Subpart 42.8).

(9) Establish final indirect cost rates and billing rates for those contractors meeting the criteria for contracting officer determination in Subpart 42.7.

(10) Attempt to resolve issues in controversy, using ADR procedures when appropriate (see subpart 33.2); prepare findings of fact and issue decisions under the Disputes clause on matters in which the administrative contracting officer (ACO) has the authority to take definitive action.

(11) In connection with Cost Accounting Standards (see 48 CFR 30.601 and 48 CFR Chapter 99 (FAR Appendix))—

(i) Determine the adequacy of the contractor's disclosure statements;

(ii) Determine whether disclosure statements are in compliance with Cost Accounting Standards and Part 31;

(iii) Determine the contractor's compliance with Cost Accounting Standards and disclosure statements, if applicable; and

(iv) Negotiate price adjustments and execute supplemental agreements under the Cost Accounting Standards clauses at 48 CFR 52.230-2, 52.230-3, 52.230-4, 52.230-5, and 52.230-6.

(12) Determine the adequacy of the contractor's accounting system. The contractor's accounting system should be adequate during the entire period of contract performance. The adequacy of the contractor's accounting system and its associated internal control system, as well as contractor compliance with the Cost Accounting Standards (CAS), affect the quality and validity of the contractor data upon which the Government must rely for its management oversight of the contractor and contract performance.

(13) Review and approve or disapprove the contractor's requests for payments under the progress payments or performance-based payments clauses.

(14) Make payments on assigned contracts when prescribed in agency acquisition regulations.

(15) Manage special bank accounts.

(16) Ensure timely notification by the contractor of any anticipated overrun or underrun of the estimated cost under cost-reimbursement contracts.

(17) Monitor the contractor's financial condition and advise the contracting officer when it jeopardizes contract performance.

(18) Analyze quarterly limitation on payments statements and take action in accordance with Subpart 32.6 to recover overpayments from the contractor.

(19) Issue tax exemption forms.

(20) Ensure processing and execution of duty-free entry certificates.

(21) For classified contracts, administer those portions of the applicable industrial security program delegated to the CAO (see Subpart 4.4).

(22) Issue work requests under maintenance, overhaul, and modification contracts.

(23) Negotiate prices and execute supplemental agreements for spare parts and other items selected through provisioning procedures when prescribed by agency acquisition regulations.

(24) Negotiate and execute contractual documents for settlement of partial and complete contract terminations for convenience, except as otherwise prescribed by Part 49.

(25) Negotiate and execute contractual documents settling cancellation charges under multi-year contracts.

(26) Process and execute novation and change of name agreements under Subpart 42.12.

(27) Perform property administration (see Part 45).

(28) Perform necessary screening, redistribution, and disposal of contractor inventory.

(29) Issue contract modifications requiring the contractor to provide packing, crating, and handling services on excess Government property. When the ACO determines it to be in the Government's interests, the services may be secured from a contractor other than the contractor in possession of the property.

(30) When contractors request Government property—

(i) Evaluate the contractor's requests for Government property and for changes to existing Government property and provide appropriate recommendations to the contracting officer;

(ii) Ensure required screening of Government property before acquisition by the contractor;

(iii) Evaluate the use of Government property on a non-interference basis in accordance with the clause at 52.245-9, Use and Charges;

(iv) Ensure payment by the contractor of any rental due; and

(v) Modify contracts to reflect the addition of Government-furnished property and ensure appropriate consideration.

(31) Perform production support, surveillance, and status reporting, including timely reporting of potential and actual slippages in contract delivery schedules.

(32) Perform preaward surveys (see Subpart 9.1).

(33) Advise and assist contractors regarding their priorities and allocations responsibilities and assist contracting offices in processing requests for special assistance and for priority ratings for privately owned capital equipment.

(34) Monitor contractor industrial labor relations matters under the contract; apprise the contracting officer and, if designated by the agency, the cognizant labor relations advisor, of actual or potential labor disputes; and coordinate the removal of urgently required material from the strikebound contractor's plant upon instruction from, and authorization of, the contracting officer.

(35) Perform traffic management services, including issuance and control of Govern-

ment bills of lading and other transportation documents.

(36) Review the adequacy of the contractor's traffic operations.

(37) Review and evaluate preservation, packaging, and packing.

(38) Ensure contractor compliance with contractual quality assurance requirements (see Part 46).

(39) Ensure contractor compliance with contractual safety requirements.

(40) Perform engineering surveillance to assess compliance with contractual terms for schedule, cost, and technical performance in the areas of design, development, and production.

(41) Evaluate for adequacy and perform surveillance of contractor engineering efforts and management systems that relate to design, development, production, engineering changes, subcontractors, tests, management of engineering resources, reliability and maintainability, data control systems, configuration management, and independent research and development.

(42) Review and evaluate for technical adequacy the contractor's logistics support, maintenance, and modification programs.

(43) Report to the contracting office any inadequacies noted in specifications.

(44) Perform engineering analyses of contractor cost proposals.

(45) Review and analyze contractor-proposed engineering and design studies and submit comments and recommendations to the contracting office, as required.

(46) Review engineering change proposals for proper classification, and when required, for need, technical adequacy of design, producibility, and impact on quality, reliability, schedule, and cost; submit comments to the contracting office.

(47) Assist in evaluating and make recommendations for acceptance or rejection of waivers and deviations.

(48) Evaluate and monitor the contractor's procedures for complying with procedures regarding restrictive markings on data.

(49) Monitor the contractor's value engineering program.

(50) Review, approve or disapprove, and maintain surveillance of the contractor's purchasing system (see Part 44).

(51) Consent to the placement of subcontracts.

(52) Review, evaluate, and approve plant or division-wide small, small disadvantaged, women-owned, veteran-owned, HUBZone, and service-disabled veteran-owned small business master subcontracting plans.

(53) Obtain the contractor's currently approved company- or division-wide plans for small, small disadvantaged, women-owned, veteran-owned, HUBZone, and service-disabled veteran-owned small business subcontracting for its commercial products, or, if there is no currently approved plan, assist the contracting officer in evaluating the plans for those products.

(54) Assist the contracting officer, upon request, in evaluating an offeror's proposed small, small disadvantaged women-owned, veteran-owned, HUBZone, and service-disabled veteran-owned small business subcontracting plans, including documentation of compliance with similar plans under prior contracts.

(55) By periodic surveillance, ensure the contractor's compliance with small, small disadvantaged, women-owned, veteran-owned, HUBZone, and service-disabled veteran-owned small business subcontracting plans and any labor surplus area contractual requirements; maintain documentation of the contractor's performance under and compliance with these plans and requirements; and provide advice and assistance to the firms involved, as appropriate.

(56) Maintain surveillance of flight operations.

(57) Assign and perform supporting contract administration.

(58) Ensure timely submission of required reports.

(59) Issue administrative changes, correcting errors or omissions in typing, contractor address, facility or activity code, remittance address, computations, which do

not require additional contract funds, and other such changes (see 43.101).

(60) Cause release of shipments from contractor's plants according to the shipping instructions. When applicable, the order of assigned priority shall be followed; shipments within the same priority shall be determined by date of the instruction.

(61) Obtain contractor proposals for any contract price adjustments resulting from amended shipping instructions. Review all amended shipping instructions on a periodic, consolidated basis to ensure that adjustments are timely made. Except when the ACO has settlement authority, the ACO shall forward the proposal to the contracting officer for contract modification. The ACO shall not delay shipments pending completion and formalization of negotiations of revised shipping instructions.

(62) Negotiate and/or execute supplemental agreements, as required, making changes in packaging subcontractors or contract shipping points.

(63) Cancel unilateral purchase orders when notified of nonacceptance by the contractor. The CAO shall notify the contracting officer when the purchase order is canceled.

(64) Negotiate and execute one-time supplemental agreements providing for the extension of contract delivery schedules up to 90 days on contracts with an assigned Criticality Designator of C (see 42.1105). Notification that the contract delivery schedule is being extended shall be provided to the contracting office. Subsequent extensions on any individual contract shall be authorized only upon concurrence of the contracting office.

(65) Accomplish administrative closeout procedures (see 4.804-5).

(66) Determine that the contractor has a drug-free workplace program and drug-free awareness program (see Subpart 23.5)

(67) Support the program, product, and project offices regarding program reviews, program status, program performance and actual or anticipated program problems.

(68) Monitor the contractor's environmental practices for adverse impact on contract performance or contract cost, and for compliance with environmental requirements specified in the contract. ACO responsibilities include—

(i) Requesting environmental technical assistance, if needed;

(ii) Monitoring contractor compliance with specifications or other contractual requirements requiring the delivery or use of environmentally preferable products, energy-efficient products, products containing recovered materials, and biobased products. This must occur as part of the quality assurance procedures set forth in Part 46; and

(iii) As required in the contract, ensuring that the contractor complies with the reporting requirements relating to recovered material content utilized in contract performance (see subpart 23.4).

(69) Administer commercial financing provisions and monitor contractor security to ensure its continued adequacy to cover outstanding payments, when on-site review is required.

(70) Deobligate excess funds after final price determination.

(71) Ensure that the contractor has implemented the requirements of 52.203-13, Contractor Code of Business Ethics and Conduct.

(b) The CAO shall perform the following functions only when and to the extent specifically authorized by the contracting office:

(1) Negotiate or negotiate and execute supplemental agreements incorporating contractor proposals resulting from change orders issued under the Changes clause. Before completing negotiations, coordinate any delivery schedule change with the contracting office.

(2) Negotiate prices and execute priced exhibits for unpriced orders issued by the contracting officer under basic ordering agreements.

(3) Negotiate or negotiate and execute supplemental agreements changing contract delivery schedules.

(4) Negotiate or negotiate and execute supplemental agreements providing for the deobligation of unexpended dollar balances

considered excess to known contract requirements.

(5) Issue amended shipping instructions and, when necessary, negotiate and execute supplemental agreements incorporating contractor proposals resulting from these instructions.

(6) Negotiate changes to interim billing prices.

(7) Negotiate and definitize adjustments to contract prices resulting from exercise of an economic price adjustment clause (see Subpart 16.2).

(8) Issue change orders and negotiate and execute resulting supplemental agreements under contracts for ship construction, conversion, and repair.

(9) Execute supplemental agreements on firm-fixed-price supply contracts to reduce required line item quantities and deobligate excess funds when notified by the contractor of an inconsequential delivery shortage, and it is determined that such action is in the best interests of the Government, notwithstanding the default provisions of the contract. Such action will be taken only upon the written request of the contractor and, in no event, shall the total downward contract price adjustment resulting from an inconsequential delivery shortage exceed $250.00 or 5 percent of the contract price, whichever is less.

(10) Execute supplemental agreements to permit a change in place of inspection at origin specified in firm-fixed-price supply contracts awarded to nonmanufacturers, as deemed necessary to protect the Government's interests.

(11) Prepare evaluations of contractor performance in accordance with Subpart 42.15.

(c) Any additional contract administration functions not listed in 42.302(a) and (b), or not otherwise delegated, remain the responsibility of the contracting office.

[FAC 84-51, 54 FR 34756, 8/21/89, effective 9/20/89; FAC 84-53, 54 FR 48989, 11/28/89, effective 12/28/89; FAC 84-56, 55 FR 3886, 2/5/90, effective 3/7/90; FAC 84-57, 55 FR 21708, 5/25/90, effective 7/24/90; Final rule, 55 FR 38517, 9/18/90; FAC 90-4, 56 FR 15154, 4/15/91, effective 5/15/91; Interim rule, FAC 90-20, 59 FR 11368, 3/10/94, effective 3/10/94, finalized without change, FAC 90-39, 61 FR 31612, 6/20/96, effective 6/20/96; FAC 90-23, 59 FR 67010, 12/28/94, effective 2/27/95; corrected 60 FR 14377, 3/17/95; FAC 90-26, 60 FR 16718, 3/31/95, effective 5/30/95; FAC 90-27, 60 FR 28492, 5/31/95, effective 5/31/95; FAC 90-32, 60 FR 48206, 9/18/95, effective 10/1/95; FAC 90-33, 60 FR 49706, 9/26/95, effective 10/1/95; FAC 90-38, 61 FR 18914, 4/29/96, effective 4/29/96; FAC 90-45, 62 FR 224, 1/2/97, effective 1/1/97; Final rule, 62 FR 40236, 7/25/97, effective 6/30/97; FAC 97-1, 62 FR 44802, 8/22/97, effective 10/21/97; FAC 97-2, 62 FR 51224, 9/30/97, effective 10/10/97; FAC 97-4, 63 FR 9048, 2/23/98, effective 4/24/98; FAC 97-15, 64 FR 12/27/99, effective 2/25/2000; FAC 97-22, 66 FR 2117, 1/10/2001, effective 3/12/2001; Delay of effective date, 66 FR 14259, 3/9/2001, effective 5/11/2001; FAC 2001-02, 66 FR 65347, 12/18/2001, effective 2/19/2002; FAC 2005-02, 70 FR 14950, 3/23/2005, effective 3/23/2005; FAC 2005-17, 72 FR 27364, 5/15/2007, effective 6/14/2007; FAC 2005-21, Final rule, 72 FR 63040, 11/7/2007, effective 12/7/2007; FAC 2005-27, 73 FR 53997, 9/17/2008, effective 10/17/2008; FAC 2005-43, 75 FR 38675, 7/2/2010, effective 8/2/2010; FAC 2005-50, 76 FR 14543, 3/16/2011, effective 3/16/2011; FAC 2005-52, 76 FR 31416, 5/31/2011, effective 6/30/2011; FAC 2005-56, 77 FR 12925, 3/2/2012, effective 4/2/2012; FAC 2005-95, 82 FR 4709, 1/13/2017, effective 1/13/2017]

SUBPART 42.4—CORRESPONDENCE AND VISITS

42.401 Contract correspondence.

(a) The contracting officer (or other contracting agency personnel) normally shall (1) forward correspondence relating to assigned contract administration functions through the cognizant contract administration office (CAO) to the contractor, and (2) provide a copy for the CAO's file. When urgency requires sending such correspondence directly to the contractor, a copy shall be sent concurrently to the CAO.

(b) The CAO shall send the contracting office a copy of pertinent correspondence conducted between the CAO and the contractor.

42.402 Visits to contractors' facilities.

(a) Government personnel planning to visit a contractor's facility in connection with one or more Government contracts shall provide the cognizant CAO with the following information, sufficiently in advance to permit the CAO to make necessary arrangements. Such notification is for the purpose of eliminating duplicative reviews, requests, investigations, and audits relating to the contract administration functions in Subpart 42.3 delegated to CAO's and shall, as a minimum, include the following (see also paragraph (b) of this section):

(1) Visitors' names, official positions, and security clearances.

(2) Date and duration of visit.

(3) Name and address of contractor and personnel to be contacted.

(4) Contract number, program involved, and purpose of visit.

(5) If desired, visitors to a contractor's plant may request that a representative of the CAO accompany them. In any event, the CAO has final authority to decide whether a representative shall accompany a visitor.

(b) If the visit will result in reviewing, auditing, or obtaining any information from the contractor relating to contract administration functions, the prospective visitor shall identify the information in sufficient detail so as to permit the CAO, after consultation with the contractor and the cognizant audit office, to determine whether such information, adequate to fulfill the requirement, has recently been reviewed by or is available within the Government. If so, the CAO will discourage the visit and refer the prospective visitor to the Government office where such information is located. Where the office is the CAO, such information will be immediately forwarded or otherwise made available to the requestor.

(c) Visitors shall fully inform the CAO of any agreements reached with the contractor or other results of the visit that may affect the CAO.

[FAC 84-32, 53 FR 662, 1/11/88, effective 1/29/88; FAC 84-37, 53 FR 17859, 5/18/88, effective 6/17/88]

42.403 Evaluation of contract administration offices.

Onsite inspections or evaluations of the performance of the assigned functions of a contract administration office shall be accomplished only by or under the direction of the agency of which that office is a part.

SUBPART 42.5—POSTAWARD ORIENTATION

42.500 Scope of subpart.

This subpart prescribes policies and procedures for the postaward orientation of contractors and subcontractors through—

(a) A conference or

(b) A letter or other form of written communication.

42.501 General.

(a) A postaward orientation aids both Government and contractor personnel to (1) achieve a clear and mutual understanding of all contract requirements, and (2) identify and resolve potential problems. However, it is not a substitute for the contractor's fully understanding the work requirements at the time offers are submitted, nor is it to be used to alter the final agreement arrived at in any negotiations leading to contract award.

(b) Postaward orientation is encouraged to assist (see part 19)—

(1) Small business concerns;

(2) Small disadvantaged business concerns;

(3) Veteran-owned small business concerns;

(4) Service-disabled veteran-owned small business concerns;

(5) HUBZone small business concerns; and

(6) Women-owned small business concerns (including economically disadvantaged women-owned small business concerns and women-owned small business

concerns eligible under the Women-Owned Small Business Program).

(c) While cognizant Government or contractor personnel may request the contracting officer to arrange for orientation, it is up to the contracting officer to decide whether a postaward orientation in any form is necessary.

(d) Maximum benefits will be realized when orientation is conducted promptly after award.

[FAC 90-32, 60 FR 48206, 9/18/95, effective 10/1/95; FAC 2005-02, 70 FR 14950, 3/23/2005, effective 3/23/2005; FAC 2005-51, 76 FR 18304, 4/1/2011, effective 4/1/2011; FAC 2005-56, 77 FR 12925, 3/2/2012, effective 4/2/2012]

42.502 Selecting contracts for postaward orientation.

When deciding whether postaward orientation is necessary and, if so, what form it shall take, the contracting officer shall consider, as a minimum, the—

(a) Nature and extent of the preaward survey and any other prior discussions with the contractor;

(b) Type, value, and complexity of the contract;

(c) Complexity and acquisition history of the product or service;

(d) Requirements for spare parts and related equipment;

(e) Urgency of the delivery schedule and relationship of the product or service to critical programs;

(f) Length of the planned production cycle;

(g) Extent of subcontracting;

(h) Contractor's performance history and experience with the product or service;

(i) Contractor's status, if any, as a small business, small disadvantaged, women-owned, veteran-owned, HUBZone, or service-disabled veteran-owned, small business concern;

(j) Contractor's performance history with small, small disadvantaged, women-owned, veteran-owned, HUBZone, or service-disabled veteran-owned, small business subcontracting programs;

(k) Safety precautions required for hazardous materials or operations; and

(l) Complex financing arrangements, such as progress payments, advance payments, or guaranteed loans.

[FAC 90-32, 60 FR 48206, 9/18/95, effective 10/1/95; FAC 2005-02, 70 FR 14950, 3/23/2005, effective 3/23/2005]

42.503 Postaward conferences. (No Text)

42.503-1 Postaward conference arrangements.

(a) The contracting officer who decides that a conference is needed is responsible for—

(1) Establishing the time and place of the conference;

(2) Preparing the agenda, when necessary;

(3) Notifying appropriate Government representatives (*e.g.*, contracting/contract administration office) and the contractor;

(4) Designating or acting as the chairperson;

(5) Conducting a preliminary meeting of Government personnel; and

(6) Preparing a summary report of the conference.

(b) When the contracting office initiates a conference, the arrangements may be made by that office or, at its request, by the contract administration office.

42.503-2 Postaward conference procedure.

The chairperson of the conference shall conduct the meeting. Unless a contract change is contemplated, the chairperson shall emphasize that it is not the purpose of the meeting to change the contract. The contracting officer may make commitments or give directions within the scope of the contracting officer's authority and shall put in writing and sign any commitment or direction, whether or not it changes the contract. Any change to the contract that results from the postaward conference shall be made only by a contract modification referencing the applicable terms of the contract. Participants without authority to bind the Government shall not take action that in any way alters the contract. The chairperson shall include in the summary report (see 42.503-3 below) all information and guidance provided to the contractor.

[FAC 97-22, 66 FR 2117, 1/10/2001, effective 3/12/2001; Delay of effective date, 66 FR 14259, 3/9/2001, effective 5/11/2001]

42.503-3 Postaward conference report.

The chairperson shall prepare and sign a report of the postaward conference. The report shall cover all items discussed, including areas requiring resolution, controversial matters, the names of the participants assigned responsibility for further actions, and the due dates for the actions. The chairperson shall furnish copies of the report to the contracting office, the contract administration office, the contractor, and others who require the information.

42.504 Postaward letters.

In some circumstances, a letter or other written form of communication to the contractor may be adequate postaward orientation (in lieu of a conference). The letter should identify the Government representative responsible for administering the contract and cite any unusual or significant contract requirements. The rules on changes to the contract in 42.503-2 also apply here.

42.505 Postaward subcontractor conferences.

(a) The prime contractor is generally responsible for conducting postaward conferences with subcontractors. However, the prime contractor may invite Government representatives to a conference with subcontractors, or the Government may request that the prime contractor initiate a conference with subcontractors. The prime contractor should ensure that representatives from involved contract administration offices are invited.

(b) Government representatives—

(1) Must recognize the lack of privity of contract between the Government and subcontractors;

(2) Shall not take action that is inconsistent with or alters subcontracts; and

(3) Shall ensure that any changes in direction or commitment affecting the prime contract or contractor resulting from a subcontractor conference are made by written direction of the contracting officer to the prime contractor in the same manner as described in 42.503-2.

SUBPART 42.6—CORPORATE ADMINISTRATIVE CONTRACTING OFFICER

42.601 General.

Contractors with more than one operational location (*e.g.*, division, plant, or subsidiary) often have corporate-wide policies, procedures, and activities requiring Government review and approval and affecting the work of more than one administrative contracting officer (ACO). In these circumstances, effective and consistent contract administration may require the assignment of a corporate administrative contracting officer (CACO) to deal with corporate management and to perform selected contract administration functions on a corporate-wide basis.

42.602 Assignment and location.

(a) A CACO may be assigned only when (1) the contractor has at least two locations with resident ACO's or (2) the need for a CACO is approved by the agency head or designee (for this purpose, a nonresident ACO will be considered as resident if at least 75 percent of the ACO's effort is devoted to a single contractor). One of the resident ACO's may be designated to perform the CACO functions, or a full-time CACO may be assigned. In determining the location of the CACO, the responsible agency shall take into account such factors as the location(s) of the corporate records, corporate office, major plant, cognizant government auditor, and overall cost effectiveness.

(b) A decision to initiate or discontinue a CACO assignment should be based on such factors as—

(1) The benefits of coordination and liaison at the corporate level;

(2) The volume of Government sales;

(3) The degree of control exercised by the contractor's corporate office over Government-oriented lower-tier operating elements; and

(4) The impact of corporate policies and procedures on those elements.

(c) Responsibility for assigning a CACO shall be determined as follows:

(1) When all locations of a corporate entity are under the contract administration cognizance of a single agency, that agency is responsible.

(2) When the locations are under the contract administration cognizance of more than one agency, the agencies concerned shall agree on the responsible agency (normally on the basis of the agency with the largest dollar balance, including options, of affected contracts). In such cases, agencies may also consider geographic location.

(d) The directory of contract administration services components referenced in 42.203 includes a listing of CACO's and the contractors for which they are assigned responsibility.

[FAC 97-4, 63 FR 9048, 2/23/98, effective 4/24/98]

42.603 Responsibilities.

(a) The CACO shall perform, on a corporate-wide basis, the contract administration functions as designated by the responsible agency. Typical CACO functions include—

(1) The determination of final indirect cost rates for cost-reimbursement contracts;

(2) Establishment of advance agreements or recommendations on corporate/home office expense allocations; and

(3) Administration of Cost Accounting Standards (CAS) applicable to corporate-level and corporate-directed accounting practices.

(b) The CACO shall—

(1) Fully utilize the responsible contract audit agency financial and advisory accounting services, including—

(i) Advice regarding the acceptability of corporate-wide policies; and

(ii) Advisory audit reports;

(2) Keep cognizant ACO's and auditors informed of important matters under consideration and determinations made; and

(3) Solicit their advice and participation as appropriate.

[FAC 97-4, 63 FR 9048, 2/23/98, effective 4/24/98]

SUBPART 42.7—INDIRECT COST RATES

42.700 Scope of subpart.

This subpart prescribes policies and procedures for establishing—

(a) Billing rates; and

(b) Final indirect cost rates.

42.701 Definition.

Billing rate as used in this subpart means an indirect cost rate—

(1) Established temporarily for interim reimbursement of incurred indirect costs; and

(2) Adjusted as necessary pending establishment of final indirect cost rates.

[Final rule, FAC 90-20, 59 FR 11368, 3/10/94, effective 3/10/94; FAC 97-4, 63 FR 9048, 2/23/98, effective 4/24/98; FAC 97-22, 66 FR 2117, 1/10/2001, effective 3/12/2001; Delay of effective date, 66 FR 14259, 3/9/2001, effective 5/11/2001]

42.702 Purpose.

(a) Establishing final indirect cost rates under this subpart provides—

(1) Uniformity of approach with a contractor when more than one contract or agency is involved;

(2) Economy of administration; and

(3) Timely settlement under cost-reimbursement contracts.

(b) Establishing billing rates provides a method for interim reimbursement of indirect costs at estimated rates subject to adjustment during contract performance and at the time the final indirect cost rates are established.

42.703 General. (No Text)

42.703-1 Policy.

(a) A single agency (see 42.705-1) shall be responsible for establishing final indirect cost rates for each business unit. These rates shall be binding on all agencies and their contracting offices, unless otherwise specifically prohibited by statute. An agency shall not perform an audit of indirect cost rates when the contracting officer determines that the objectives of the audit can reasonably be met by accepting the results of an audit that was conducted by any other department or agency of the Federal Government (10 U.S.C. 2313(d) and 41 U.S.C. 4706(e)).

(b) Billing rates and final indirect cost rates shall be used in reimbursing indirect costs under cost-reimbursement contracts and in determining progress payments under fixed-price contracts.

(c) To ensure compliance with 10 U.S.C. 2324(a) and 41 U.S.C. 4303(a)—

(1) Final indirect cost rates shall be used for contract closeout for a business unit, unless the quick-closeout procedure in 42.708 is used. These final rates shall be binding for all cost-reimbursement contracts at the business unit, subject to any specific limitation in a contract or advance agreement; and

(2) Established final indirect cost rates shall be used in negotiating the final price of fixed-price incentive and fixed-price redeterminable contracts and in other situations requiring that indirect costs be settled before contract prices are established, unless the quick-closeout procedure in 42.708 is used.

[FAC 90-31, 60 FR 42648, 8/16/95, effective 10/1/95; FAC 90-45, Final rule, 62 FR 224, 1/2/97, effective 1/1/97; FAC 97-4, 63 FR 9048, 2/23/98, effective 4/24/98; FAC 2005-73, 79 FR 24192, 4/29/2014, effective 5/29/2014]

42.703-2 Certificate of indirect costs.

(a) *General.* In accordance with 10 U.S.C. 2324(h) and 41 U.S.C. 4307, a proposal shall not be accepted and no agreement shall be made to establish final indirect cost rates unless the costs have been certified by the contractor.

(b) *Waiver of certification.* (1) The agency head, or designee, may waive the certification requirement when—

(i) It is determined to be in the interest of the United States; and

(ii) The reasons for the determination are put in writing and made available to the public.

(2) A waiver may be appropriate for a contract with—

(i) A foreign government or international organization, such as a subsidiary body of the North Atlantic Treaty Organization;

(ii) A State or local government subject to the OMB Uniform Guidance at 2 CFR part 200, subpart E and appendices V and VII;

(iii) An educational institution (defined as an institution of higher education in the OMB Uniform Guidance at 2 CFR part 200, subpart A, and 20 U.S.C. 1001) subject to the OMB Uniform Guidance at 2 CFR part 200, subpart E and appendix III; and

(iv) A nonprofit organization (as defined in the OMB Uniform Guidance at 2 CFR part 200) subject to the OMB Uniform Guidance at 2 CFR part 200, subpart E and appendix IV.

(c) *Failure to certify.* (1) If the contractor has not certified its proposal for final indirect cost rates and a waiver is not appropriate, the contracting officer may unilaterally establish the rates.

(2) Rates established unilaterally should be—

(i) Based on audited historical data or other available data as long as unallowable costs are excluded; and

(ii) Set low enough to ensure that unallowable costs will not be reimbursed.

(d) *False certification.* The contracting officer should consult with legal counsel to determine appropriate action when a contractor's certificate of final indirect costs is thought to be false.

(e) *Penalties for unallowable costs.* 10 U.S.C. 2324(a) through (d) and 41 U.S.C. 4303 prescribe penalties for submission of unallowable costs in final indirect cost rate proposals (see 42.709 for penalties and contracting officer responsibilities).

(f) *Contract clause.* (1) Except as provided in paragraph (f)(2) of this subsection, the clause at 52.242-4, Certification of Final Indirect Costs, shall be incorporated into all solicitations and contracts which provide for establishment of final indirect cost rates.

(2) The Department of Energy may provide an alternate clause in its agency supplement for its Management and Operating contracts.

[FAC 90-31, 60 FR 42648, 8/16/95, effective 10/1/95; FAC 90-45, Final rule, 62 FR 224, 1/2/97, effective 1/1/97, corrected 62 FR 10709, 3/10/97; FAC 97-4, 63 FR 9048, 2/23/98, effective 4/24/98; FAC 2005-73, 79 FR 24192, 4/29/2014, effective 5/29/2014; FAC 2005-89, 81 FR 45852, 7/14/2016, effective 8/15/2016]

42.704 Billing rates.

(a) The contracting officer (or cognizant Federal agency official) or auditor responsible under 42.705 for establishing the final indirect cost rates also shall be responsible for determining the billing rates.

(b) The contracting officer (or cognizant Federal agency official) or auditor shall establish billing rates on the basis of information resulting from recent review, previous rate audits or experience, or similar reliable data or experience of other contracting activities. In establishing billing rates, the contracting officer (or cognizant Federal agency official) or auditor should ensure that the billing rates are as close as possible to the final indirect cost rates anticipated for the contractor's fiscal period, as adjusted for any unallowable costs. When the contracting officer (or cognizant Federal agency official) or auditor determines that the dollar value of contracts requiring use of billing rates does not warrant submission of a detailed billing rate proposal, the billing rates may be established by making appropriate adjustments from the prior year's indirect cost experience to eliminate unallowable and nonrecurring costs and to reflect new or changed conditions.

(c) Once established, billing rates may be prospectively or retroactively revised by mutual agreement of the contracting officer (or cognizant Federal agency official) or auditor and the contractor at either party's request, to prevent substantial overpayment or underpayment. When agreement cannot be reached, the billing rates may be unilaterally determined by the contracting officer (or cognizant Federal agency official).

(d) The elements of indirect cost and the base or bases used in computing billing rates shall not be construed as determinative of the indirect costs to be distributed or of the bases of distribution to be used in the final settlement.

(e) When the contractor provides to the cognizant contracting officer the certified final indirect cost rate proposal in accordance with 42.705-1(b) or 42.705-2(b), the contractor and the Government may mutually agree to revise billing rates to reflect the proposed indirect cost rates, as approved by the Government to reflect historically disallowed amounts from prior years' audits, until the proposal has been audited and settled. The historical decrement will be determined by either the cognizant contracting officer (42.705-1(b)) or the cognizant auditor (42.705-2(b)).

[FAC 90-44, Final rule, 61 FR 69286, 12/31/96, effective 3/3/97; FAC 97-4, 63 FR 9048, 2/23/98, effective 4/24/98]

42.705 Final indirect cost rates.

(a) Final indirect cost rates shall be established on the basis of—

(1) Contracting officer determination procedure (see 42.705-1), or

(2) Auditor determination procedure (see 42.705-2).

(b) Within 120 days (or longer period, if approved in writing by the contracting officer,) after settlement of the final annual indirect cost rates for all years of a physically complete contract, the contractor must submit a completion invoice or voucher reflecting the settled amounts and rates. To determine whether a period longer than 120 days is appropriate, the contracting officer should consider whether there are extenuating circumstances, such as the following:

(1) Pending closeout of subcontracts awaiting Government audit.

(2) Pending contractor, subcontractor, or Government claims.

(3) Delays in the disposition of Government property.

(4) Delays in contract reconciliation.

(5) Any other pertinent factors.

(c)(1) If the contractor fails to submit a completion invoice or voucher within the time specified in paragraph (b) of this section, the contracting officer may—

(i) Determine the amounts due to the contractor under the contract; and

(ii) Record this determination in a unilateral modification to the contract.

(2) This contracting officer determination must be issued as a final decision in accordance with 33.211.

[FAC 90-44, Final rule, 61 FR 69286, 12/31/96, effective 3/3/97; FAC 2001-04, 67 FR 6112, 2/8/2002, effective 2/20/2002]

42.705-1 Contracting officer determination procedure.

(a) *Applicability and responsibility.* Contracting officer determination shall be used for the following, with the indicated cognizant contracting officer (or cognizant Federal agency official) responsible for establishing the final indirect cost rates:

(1) Business units of a multidivisional corporation under the cognizance of a corporate administrative contracting officer (see Subpart 42.6), with that officer responsible for the determination, assisted, as required, by the administrative contracting officers assigned to the individual business units. Negotiations may be conducted on a coordinated or centralized basis, depending upon the degree of centralization within the contractor's organization.

(2) Business units not under the cognizance of a corporate administrative contracting officer, but having a resident administrative contracting officer (see 42.602), with that officer responsible for the determination. For this purpose, a nonresident administrative contracting officer is considered as resident if at least 75 percent of the administrative contracting officer's time is devoted to a single contractor.

(3) For business units not included in paragraph (a)(1) or (a)(2) of this subsection, the contracting officer (or cognizant Federal agency official) will determine whether the rates will be contracting officer or auditor determined.

(4) Educational institutions (see 42.705-3).

(5) State and local governments (see 42.705-4).

(6) Nonprofit organizations other than educational and state and local governments (see 42.705-5).

(b) *Procedures.* (1) In accordance with the Allowable Cost and Payment clause at 52.216-7, the contractor is required to submit an adequate final indirect cost rate proposal to the contracting officer (or cognizant Federal agency official) and to the cognizant auditor.

(i) The required content of the proposal and supporting data will vary depending on such factors as business type, size, and accounting system capabilities. The contractor, contracting officer, and auditor must work together to make the proposal, audit, and negotiation process as efficient as possible.

(ii) Each contractor is required to submit the final indirect cost rate proposal within the six-month period following the expiration of each of its fiscal years. The contracting officer may grant, in writing, reasonable extensions, for exceptional circumstances only, when requested in writing by the contractor.

(iii) Upon receipt of the proposal—

(A) The cognizant auditor will review the adequacy of the contractor's proposal for audit in support of negotiating final indirect cost rates and will provide a written description of any inadequacies to the contractor and contracting officer.

(B) If the auditor and contractor are unable to resolve the proposal's inadequacies identified by the auditor, the auditor will elevate the issue to the contracting office to resolve the inadequacies.

(iv) The proposal must be supported with adequate supporting data, some of which may be required subsequent to finding that the proposal is adequate for audit in support of negotiating final indirect cost rates (e.g., during the course of the performance of the advisory audit). See the clause at 52.216-7(d)(2) for the description of an adequate final indirect cost rate proposal and supporting data.

(2) Once a proposal has been determined to be adequate for audit in support of negotiating final indirect cost rates, the auditor will audit the proposal and prepare an advisory audit report to the contracting officer (or cognizant Federal agency official), including a listing of any relevant advance agreements or restrictive terms of specific contracts.

(3) The contracting officer (or cognizant Federal agency official) shall head the Government negotiating team, which includes the cognizant auditor and technical or functional personnel as required. Contracting offices having significant dollar interest shall be invited to participate in the negotiation and in the preliminary discussion of critical issues. Individuals or offices that have provided a significant input to the Government position should be invited to attend.

(4) The Government negotiating team shall develop a negotiation position. Pursuant to 10 U.S.C. 2324(f) and 41 U.S.C. 4305, the contracting officer shall—

(i) Not resolve any questioned costs until obtaining—

(A) Adequate documentation on the costs; and

(B) The contract auditor's opinion on the allowability of the costs.

(ii) Whenever possible, invite the contract auditor to serve as an advisor at any negotiation or meeting with the contractor on the determination of the contractor's final indirect cost rates.

(5) The cognizant contracting officer shall—

(i) Conduct negotiations;

(ii) Prepare a written indirect cost rate agreement conforming to the requirements of the contracts;

(iii) Prepare, sign, and place in the contractor general file (see 4.801(c)(3)) a negotiation memorandum covering—

(A) The disposition of significant matters in the advisory audit report;

(B) Reconciliation of all costs questioned, with identification of items and amounts allowed or disallowed in the final settlement as well as the disposition of period costing or allocability issues;

(C) Reasons why any recommendations of the auditor or other Government advisors were not followed; and

(D) Identification of certified cost or pricing data submitted during the negotiations and relied upon in reaching a settlement; and

(iv) Distribute resulting documents in accordance with 42.706.

(v) Notify the contractor of the individual costs which were considered unallowable and the respective amounts of the disallowance.

[FAC 90-31, 60 FR 42648, 8/16/95, effective 10/1/95; FAC 97-2, 62 FR 51224, 9/30/97, effective 10/10/97; FAC 97-3, 62 FR 64912, 12/9/97, effective 2/9/98; FAC 97-4, 63 FR 9048, 2/23/98, effective 4/24/98; FAC 2001-04, 67 FR 6112, 2/8/2002, effective 2/8/2002; FAC 2005-17, 72 FR 27364, 5/15/2007, effective 6/14/2007; FAC 2005-45, 75 FR 53135, 8/30/2010, effective 10/1/2010; FAC 2005-52, 76 FR 31402, 5/31/2011, effective 6/30/2011; FAC 2005-73, 79 FR 24192, 4/29/2014, effective 5/29/2014]

42.705-2 Auditor determination procedure.

(a) *Applicability and responsibility.* (1) The cognizant Government auditor shall establish final indirect cost rates for business units not covered in 42.705-1(a).

(2) In addition, auditor determination may be used for business units that are covered in 42.705-1(a) when the contracting officer (or cognizant Federal agency official) and auditor agree that the indirect costs can be settled with little difficulty and any of the following circumstances apply:

(i) The business unit has primarily fixed-price contracts, with only minor involvement in cost-reimbursement contracts.

(ii) The administrative cost of contracting officer determination would exceed the expected benefits.

(iii) The business unit does not have a history of disputes and there are few cost problems.

(iv) The contracting officer (or cognizant Federal agency official) and auditor agree that special circumstances require auditor determination.

(b) *Procedures.* (1) The contractor shall submit to the cognizant contracting officer (or cognizant Federal agency official) and auditor a final indirect cost rate proposal in accordance with 42.705-1(b)(1).

(2) Once a proposal has been determined to be adequate for audit in support of negotiating final indirect cost rates, the auditor shall—

(i) Audit the proposal and prepare an advisory audit report, including a listing of any relevant advance agreements or restrictive terms of specific contracts;

(ii) Seek agreement on indirect costs with the contractor;

(iii) Prepare an indirect cost rate agreement conforming to the requirements of the contracts. The agreement shall be signed by the contractor and the auditor;

(iv) If agreement with the contractor is not reached, forward the audit report to the contracting officer (or cognizant Federal agency official) identified in the Directory of Contract Administration Services Components (see 42.203), who will then resolve the disagreement; and

(v) Distribute resulting documents in accordance with 42.706.

[FAC 90-23, 59 FR 67010, 12/28/94, effective 2/27/95; FAC 97-2, 62 FR 51224, 9/30/97, effective 10/10/97; FAC 97-3, 62 FR 64912, 12/9/97, effective 2/9/98; FAC 97-4, 63 FR 9048, 2/23/98, effective 4/24/98; Final rule, FAC 2005-52, 76 FR 31402, 5/31/2011, effective 6/30/2011]

42.705-3 Educational institutions.

(a) *General.* (1) Postdetermined final indirect cost rates shall be used in the settlement of indirect costs for all cost-reimbursement contracts with educational institutions, unless predetermined final indirect cost rates are authorized and used (see paragraph (b) below).

(2) The OMB Uniform Guidance at 2 CFR part 200, appendix III assigns each educational institution (defined as an institution of higher education in the OMB Uniform Guidance at 2 CFR part 200, subpart A, and 20 U.S.C. 1001) to a single Government agency for the negotiation of indirect cost rates and provides that those rates shall be accepted by all Federal agencies. Cognizant Government agencies and educational institutions are listed in the Directory of Federal Contract Audit Offices (see 42.103).

(3) The cognizant agency for indirect costs shall establish the billing rates and final indirect cost rates at the educational institution (defined as an institution of higher education in 2 CFR 200, subpart A, and 20 U.S.C. 1001) consistent with the requirements of this subpart, Subpart 31.3, and the OMB Uniform Guidance at 2 CFR part 200, subpart E and appendix III. The agency shall follow the procedures outlined in 42.705-1(b).

(4) If the cognizant agency is unable to reach agreement with an institution, the appeals system of the cognizant agency shall be followed for resolution of the dispute.

(b) *Predetermined final indirect cost rates.* (1) Under cost-reimbursement research and development contracts with universities, colleges, or other educational institutions (41 U.S.C. 4708), payment for reimbursable indirect costs may be made on the basis of predetermined final indirect cost rates. The cognizant agency is not required to establish predetermined rates, but if they are established, their use must be extended to all the institution's Government contracts.

(2) In deciding whether the use of predetermined rates would be appropriate for the educational institution concerned, the agency should consider both the stability of the institution's indirect costs and bases over

a period of years and any anticipated changes in the amount of the direct and indirect costs.

(3) Unless their use is approved at a level in the agency (see subparagraph (a)(2) above) higher than the contracting officer, predetermined rates shall not be used when—

(i) There has been no recent audit of the indirect costs;

(ii) There have been frequent or wide fluctuations in the indirect cost rates and the bases over a period of years; or

(iii) The estimated reimbursable costs for any individual contract are expected to exceed $1 million annually.

(4)(i) If predetermined rates are to be used and no rates have been previously established for the institution's current fiscal year, the agency shall obtain from the institution a proposal for predetermined rates.

(ii) If the proposal is found to be generally acceptable, the agency shall negotiate the predetermined rates with the institution. The rates should be based on an audit of the institution's costs for the year immediately preceding the year in which the rates are being negotiated. If this is not possible, an earlier audit may be used, but appropriate steps should be taken to identify and evaluate significant variations in costs incurred or in bases used that may have a bearing on the reasonableness of the proposed rates. However, in the case of smaller contracts (i.e., contracts that do not exceed the simplified acquisition threshold), an audit made at an earlier date is acceptable if—

(A) There have been no significant changes in the contractor's organization; and

(B) It is reasonably apparent that another audit would have little effect on the rates finally agreed upon and the potential for overpayment of indirect cost is relatively insignificant.

(5) If predetermined rates are used—

(i) The contracting officer shall include the negotiated rates and bases in the contract Schedule; and

(ii) See 16.307(g), which prescribes the clause at 52.216-15, Predetermined Indirect Cost Rates.

(6) Predetermined indirect cost rates shall be applicable for a period of not more than four years. The agency shall obtain the contractor's proposal for new predetermined rates sufficiently in advance so that the new rates, based on current data, may be promptly negotiated near the beginning of the new fiscal year or other period agreed to by the parties (see paragraphs (b) and (d) of the clause at 52.216-15, Predetermined Indirect Cost Rates).

(7) Contracting officers shall use billing rates established by the agency to reimburse the contractor for work performed during a period not covered by predetermined rates.

(8) The OMB Uniform Guidance at 2 CFR part 200, subpart E and appendix III, provides additional guidance on how long predetermined rates may be used.

[FAC 90-39, 61 FR 31612, 6/20/96, effective 8/19/96; FAC 97-4, 63 FR 9048, 2/23/98, effective 4/24/98; FAC 2005-13, 71 FR 57363, 9/28/2006, effective 9/28/2006; FAC 2005-17, 72 FR 27364, 5/15/2007, effective 6/14/2007; FAC 2005-73, 79 FR 24192, 4/29/2014, effective 5/29/2014; FAC 2005-89, 81 FR 45852, 7/14/2016, effective 8/15/2016]

42.705-4 State and local governments.

The OMB Uniform Guidance at 2 CFR part 200, subpart E and appendix V, concerning cost principles for state and local governments (see Subpart 31.6) establishes the cognizant agency concept and the procedures for determining a cognizant agency for approving State and local government indirect costs associated with federally-funded programs and activities. The indirect cost rates negotiated and approved by the cognizant agency for indirect costs will be used by all Federal agencies that also award contracts to these same State and local governments.

[FAC 2005-89, 81 FR 45852, 7/14/2016, effective 8/15/2016]

42.705-5 Nonprofit organizations other than educational and state and local governments.

See the OMB Uniform Guidance at 2 CFR part 200, subpart E and appendix IV; but see appendix VIII for nonprofit organizations exempt from subpart E.

[FAC 2005-89, 81 FR 45852, 7/14/2016, effective 8/15/2016]

42.706 Distribution of documents.

(a) The contracting officer or auditor shall promptly distribute executed copies of the indirect cost rate agreement to the contractor and to each affected contracting agency and shall provide copies of the agreement for the contract files, in accordance with the guidance for contract modifications in Subpart 4.2, Contract Distribution.

(b) Copies of the negotiation memorandum prepared under contracting officer determination or audit report prepared under auditor determination shall be furnished, as appropriate, to the contracting offices and Government audit offices.

42.707 Cost-sharing rates and limitations on indirect cost rates.

(a) Cost-sharing arrangements, when authorized, may call for the contractor to participate in the costs of the contract by accepting indirect cost rates lower than the anticipated actual rates. In such cases, a negotiated indirect cost rate ceiling may be incorporated into the contract for prospective application. For cost sharing under research and development contracts, see 35.003(b).

(b) (1) Other situations may make it prudent to provide a final indirect cost rate ceiling in a contract. Examples of such circumstances are when the proposed contractor—

(i) Is a new or recently reorganized company, and there is no past or recent record of incurred indirect costs;

(ii) Has a recent record of a rapidly increasing indirect cost rate due to a declining volume of sales without a commensurate decline in indirect expenses; or

(iii) Seeks to enhance its competitive position in a particular circumstance by basing its proposal on indirect cost rates lower than those that may reasonably be expected to occur during contract performance, thereby causing a cost overrun.

(2) In such cases, an equitable ceiling covering the final indirect cost rates may be negotiated and specified in the contract.

(c) When ceiling provisions are utilized, the contract shall also provide that—

(1) The Government will not be obligated to pay any additional amount should the final indirect cost rates exceed the negotiated ceiling rates, and

(2) In the event the final indirect cost rates are less than the negotiated ceiling rates, the negotiated rates will be reduced to conform with the lower rates.

42.708 Quick-closeout procedure.

(a) The contracting officer responsible for contract closeout shall negotiate the settlement of direct and indirect costs for a specific contract, task order, or delivery order to be closed, in advance of the determination of final direct costs and indirect rates set forth in 42.705, if—

(1) The contract, task order, or delivery order is physically complete;

(2) The amount of unsettled direct costs and indirect costs to be allocated to the contract, task order, or delivery order is relatively insignificant. Cost amounts will be considered relatively insignificant when the total unsettled direct costs and indirect costs to be allocated to any one contract, task order, or delivery order does not exceed the lesser of—

(i) $1,000,000; or

(ii) 10 percent of the total contract, task order, or delivery order amount;

(3) The contracting officer performs a risk assessment and determines that the use of the quick-closeout procedure is appropriate. The risk assessment shall include—

(i) Consideration of the contractor's accounting, estimating, and purchasing systems;

(ii) Other concerns of the cognizant contract auditors; and

(iii) Any other pertinent information, such as, documented history of Federal Government approved indirect cost rate agreements, changes to contractor's rate structure, volatility of rate fluctuations during affected periods, mergers or acquisitions, special contract provisions limiting contractor's recovery of otherwise allowable indirect costs under cost reimbursement or time-and-materials contracts; and

(4) Agreement can be reached on a reasonable estimate of allocable dollars.

(b) Determinations of final indirect costs under the quick-closeout procedure provided for by the Allowable Cost and Payment clause at 52.216-7 shall be final for the contract it covers and no adjustment shall be made to other contracts for over- or under-recoveries of costs allocated or allocable to the contract covered by the agreement.

(c) Indirect cost rates used in the quick closeout of a contract shall not be considered a binding precedent when establishing the final indirect cost rates for other contracts.

[FAC 90-3, 55 FR 52796, 12/21/90, effective 1/22/91; FAC 90-39, 61 FR 31612, 6/20/96, effective 8/19/96; FAC 2005-17, 72 FR 27364, 5/15/2007, effective 6/14/2007; FAC 2005-52, 76 FR 31402, 5/31/2011, effective 6/30/2011]

42.709 Penalties for Unallowable Costs. (No Text)

[FAC 2005-92 81 FR 83103, 11/18/2016, effective 11/18/2016]

42.709-0 Scope.

(a) This section implements 10 U.S.C. 2324(a) through (d) and 41 U.S.C. 4303. It covers the assessment of penalties against contractors which include unallowable indirect costs in—

(1) Final indirect cost rate proposals; or

(2) The final statement of costs incurred or estimated to be incurred under a fixed-price incentive contract.

(b) This section applies to all contracts in excess of $750,000, except fixed-price contracts without cost incentives or any firm-fixed-price contracts for the purchase of commercial items.

[FAC 90-31, 60 FR 42648, 8/16/95, effective 10/1/95; FAC 2001-26, 69 FR 76356, 12/20/2004, effective 1/19/2005; FAC 2005-13, 71 FR 57363, 9/28/2006, effective 9/28/2006; FAC 2005-45, 75 FR 53129, 8/30/2010, effective 10/1/2010; FAC 2005-73, 79 FR 24192, 4/29/2014, effective 5/29/2014; FAC 2005-83, 80 FR 38293, 7/2/2015, effective 10/1/2015; FAC 2005-92 81 FR 83103, 11/18/2016, effective 11/18/2016]

42.709-1 General.

(a) The following penalties apply to contracts covered by this section:

(1) If the indirect cost is expressly unallowable under a cost principle in the FAR, or an executive agency supplement to the FAR, that defines the allowability of specific selected costs, the penalty is equal to—

(i) The amount of the disallowed costs allocated to contracts that are subject to this section for which an indirect cost proposal has been submitted; plus

(ii) Interest on the paid portion, if any, of the disallowance.

(2) If the indirect cost was determined to be unallowable for that contractor before proposal submission, the penalty is two times the amount in paragraph (a)(1)(i) of this section.

(b) These penalties are in addition to other administrative, civil, and criminal penalties provided by law.

(c) It is not necessary for unallowable costs to have been paid to the contractor in order to assess a penalty.

[FAC 90-31, 60 FR 42648, 8/16/95, effective 10/1/95]

42.709-2 Responsibilities.

(a) The cognizant contracting officer is responsible for—

(1) Determining whether the penalties in 42.709-1(a) should be assessed;

(2) Determining whether such penalties should be waived pursuant to 42.709-5; and

(3) Referring the matter to the appropriate criminal investigative organization for review and for appropriate coordination of remedies, if there is evidence that the contractor knowingly submitted unallowable costs.

(b) The contract auditor, in the review and/or the determination of final indirect cost proposals for contracts subject to this section, is responsible for—

(1) Recommending to the contracting officer which costs may be unallowable and subject to the penalties in 42.709-1(a);

(2) Providing rationale and supporting documentation for any recommendation; and

(3) Referring the matter to the appropriate criminal investigative organization for review and for appropriate coordination of remedies, if there is evidence that the contractor knowingly submitted unallowable costs.

[FAC 90-31, 60 FR 42648, 8/16/95, effective 10/1/95]

42.709-3 Assessing the penalty.

Unless a waiver is granted pursuant to 42.709-5, the cognizant contracting officer shall—

(a) Assess the penalty in 42.709-1(a)(1), when the submitted cost is expressly unallowable under a cost principle in the FAR or an executive agency supplement that defines the allowability of specific selected costs; or

(b) Assess the penalty in 42.709-1(a)(2), when the submitted cost was determined to be unallowable for that contractor prior to submission of the proposal. Prior determinations of unallowability may be evidenced by—

(1) A DCAA Form 1, Notice of Contract Costs Suspended and/or Disapproved (see 48 CFR 242.705-2), or any similar notice which the contractor elected not to appeal and was not withdrawn by the cognizant Government agency;

(2) A contracting officer final decision which was not appealed;

(3) A prior executive agency Board of Contract Appeals or court decision involving the contractor, which upheld the cost disallowance; or

(4) A determination or agreement of unallowability under 31.201-6.

(c) Issue a final decision (see 33.211) which includes a demand for payment of any penalty assessed under paragraph (a) or (b) of this section. The letter shall state that the determination is a final decision under the Disputes clause of the contract. (Demanding payment of the penalty is separate from demanding repayment of any paid portion of the disallowed cost.)

[FAC 90-31, 60 FR 42648, 8/16/95, effective 10/1/95]

42.709-4 Computing interest.

For 42.709-1(a)(1)(ii), compute interest on any paid portion of the disallowed cost as follows:

(a) Consider the overpayment to have occurred, and interest to have begun accumulating, from the midpoint of the contractor's fiscal year. Use an alternate equitable method if the cost was not paid evenly over the fiscal year.

(b) Use the interest rate specified by the Secretary of the Treasury pursuant to Pub. L. 92-41 (85 Stat. 97).

(c) Compute interest from the date of overpayment to the date of the demand letter for payment of the penalty.

(d) Determine the paid portion of the disallowed costs in consultation with the contract auditor.

[FAC 90-31, 60 FR 42648, 8/16/95, effective 10/1/95]

42.709-5 Waiver of the penalty.

The cognizant contracting officer shall waive the penalties at 42.709-1(a) when—

(a) The contractor withdraws the proposal before the Government formally initiates an audit of the proposal and the contractor submits a revised proposal (an audit will be deemed to be formally initiated when the Government provides the contractor with written notice, or holds an entrance conference, indicating that audit work on a specific final indirect cost proposal has begun);

(b) The amount of the unallowable costs under the proposal which are subject to the penalty is $10,000 or less (*i.e.*, if the amount of expressly or previously determined unallowable costs which would be allocated to the contracts specified in 42.709(b) is $10,000 or less); or

(c) The contractor demonstrates, to the cognizant contracting officer's satisfaction, that—

(1) It has established policies and personnel training and an internal control and review system that provide assurance that unallowable costs subject to penalties are precluded from being included in the contractor's final indirect cost rate proposals (*e.g.*, the types of controls required for satisfactory participation in the Department of Defense sponsored self-governance programs, specific accounting controls over indirect costs, compliance tests which demonstrate that the controls are effective, and Government audits which have not disclosed recurring instances of expressly unallowable costs); and

(2) The unallowable costs subject to the penalty were inadvertently incorporated into the proposal; *i.e.*, their inclusion resulted from an unintentional error, notwithstanding the exercise of due care.

[FAC 90-31, 60 FR 42648, 8/16/95, effective 10/1/95]

42.709-6 Contract clause.

Use the clause at 52.242-3, Penalties for Unallowable Costs, in all solicitations and contracts over $750,000 except fixed-price contracts without cost incentives or any firm-fixed-price contract for the purchase of commercial items. Generally, covered contracts are those which contain one of the clauses at 52.216-7, 52.216-16, or 52.216-17, or a similar clause from an executive agency's supplement to the FAR.

[FAC 90-31, 60 FR 42648, 8/16/95, effective 10/1/95; FAC 2001-26, 69 FR 76356, 12/20/2004, effective 1/19/2005; FAC 2005-13, 71 FR 57363, 9/28/2006, effective 9/28/2006; FAC 2005-17, 72 FR 27364, 5/15/2007, effective 6/14/2007; FAC 2005-45, 75 FR 53129, 8/30/2010, effective 10/1/2010; FAC 2005-83, 80 FR 38293, 7/2/2015, effective 10/1/2015]

SUBPART 42.8—DISALLOWANCE OF COSTS

42.800 Scope of subpart.

This subpart prescribes policies and procedures for—

(a) Issuing notices of intent to disallow costs; and

(b) Disallowing costs already incurred during the course of performance.

42.801 Notice of intent to disallow costs.

(a) At any time during the performance of a contract of a type referred to in 42.802, the cognizant contracting officer responsible for administering the contract may issue the contractor a written notice of intent to disallow specified costs incurred or planned for incurrence. However, before issuing the notice, the contracting officer responsible for administering the contract shall make every reasonable effort to reach a satisfactory settlement through discussions with the contractor.

(b) A notice of intent to disallow such costs usually results from monitoring contractor costs. The purpose of the notice is to notify the contractor as early as practicable during contract performance that the cost is considered unallowable under the contract terms and to provide for timely resolution of any resulting disagreement. In the event of disagreement, the contractor may submit to the contracting officer a written response. Any such response shall be answered by withdrawal of the notice or by making a written decision within 60 days.

(c) As a minimum, the notice shall—

(1) Refer to the contract's Notice of Intent to Disallow Costs clause;

(2) State the contractor's name and list the numbers of the affected contracts;

(3) Describe the costs to be disallowed, including estimated dollar value by item and applicable time periods, and state the reasons for the intended disallowance;

(4) Describe the potential impact on billing rates and forward pricing rate agreements;

(5) State the notice's effective date and the date by which written response must be received;

(6) List the recipients of copies of the notice; and

(7) Request the contractor to acknowledge receipt of the notice.

(d) The contracting officer issuing the notice shall furnish copies to all contracting officers cognizant of any segment of the contractor's organization.

(e) If the notice involves elements of indirect cost, it shall not be issued without coordination with the contracting officer or auditor having authority for final indirect cost settlement (see 42.705).

(f) In the event the contractor submits a response that disagrees with the notice (see paragraph (b) above), the contracting officer who issued the notice shall either withdraw the notice or issue the written decision, except when elements of indirect cost are involved, in which case the contracting officer responsible under 42.705 for determining final indirect cost rates shall issue the decision.

42.802 Contract clause.

The contracting officer shall insert the clause at 52.242-1, Notice of Intent to Disallow Costs, in solicitations and contracts when a cost-reimbursement contract, a fixed-price incentive contract, or a contract providing for price redetermination is contemplated.

42.803 Disallowing costs after incurrence.

Cost-reimbursement contracts, the cost-reimbursement portion of fixed-price contracts, letter contracts that provide for reimbursement of costs, and time-and-material and labor-hour contracts provide for disallowing costs during the course of performance after the costs have been incurred. The following procedures shall apply:

(a) *Contracting officer receipt of vouchers.* When contracting officers receive vouchers directly from the contractor and, with or without auditor assistance, approve or disapprove them, the process shall be conducted in accordance with the normal procedures of the individual agency.

(b) *Auditor receipt of vouchers.* (1) When authorized by agency regulations, the contract auditor may be authorized to (i) receive reimbursement vouchers directly from contractors, (ii) approve for payment those vouchers found acceptable, and (iii) suspend payment of questionable costs. The auditor shall forward approved vouchers for payment to the cognizant contracting, finance, or disbursing officer, as appropriate under the agency's procedures.

(2) If the examination of a voucher raises a question regarding the allowability of a cost under the contract terms, the auditor, after informal discussion as appropriate, may, where authorized by agency regulations, issue a notice of contract costs suspended and/or disapproved simultaneously to the contractor and the disbursing officer, with a copy to the cognizant contracting officer, for deduction from current payments with respect to costs claimed but not considered reimbursable.

(3) If the contractor disagrees with the deduction from current payments, the contractor may—

(i) Submit a written request to the cognizant contracting officer to consider whether the unreimbursed costs should be paid and to discuss the findings with the contractor;

(ii) File a claim under the Disputes clause, which the cognizant contracting officer will process in accordance with agency procedures; or

(iii) Do both of the above.

SUBPART 42.9—BANKRUPTCY

42.900 Scope of subpart.

This subpart prescribes policies and procedures regarding actions to be taken when a contractor enters into proceedings relating to bankruptcy. It establishes a requirement for the contractor to notify the contracting officer upon filing a petition for bankruptcy. It further establishes minimum requirements for agencies to follow in the event of a contractor bankruptcy.

[FAC 90-4, 56 FR 15154, 4/15/91, effective 5/15/91]

42.901 General.

The contract administration office shall take prompt action to determine the potential impact of a contractor bankruptcy on the Government in order to protect the interests of the Government.

[FAC 90-4, 56 FR 15154, 4/15/91, effective 5/15/91]

42.902 Procedures.

(a) When notified of bankruptcy proceedings, agencies shall, as a minimum—

(1) Furnish the notice of bankruptcy to legal counsel and other appropriate agency offices (*e.g.,* contracting, financial, property) and affected buying activities;

(2) Determine the amount of the Government's potential claim against the contractor (in assessing this impact, identify and review any contracts that have not been closed out, including those physically completed or terminated);

(3) Take actions necessary to protect the Government's financial interests and safeguard Government property; and

(4) Furnish pertinent contract information to the legal counsel representing the Government.

(b) The contracting officer shall consult with legal counsel, whenever possible, prior to taking any action regarding the contractor's bankruptcy proceedings.

[FAC 90-4, 56 FR 15154, 4/15/91, effective 5/15/91]

42.903 Solicitation provision and contract clause.

The contracting officer shall insert the clause at 52.242-13, Bankruptcy, in all solicitations and contracts exceeding the simplified acquisition threshold.

[FAC 90-4, 56 FR 15154, 4/15/91, effective 5/15/91; FAC 90-29, 60 FR 34732, 7/3/95, effective 7/3/95; FAC 90-40, 61 FR 39186, 7/26/96, effective 8/26/96]

SUBPART 42.10—[RESERVED]

SUBPART 42.11—PRODUCTION SURVEILLANCE AND REPORTING

42.1101 General.

Production surveillance is a function of contract administration used to determine contractor progress and to identify any factors that may delay performance. Production surveillance involves Government review and analysis of—

(a) Contractor performance plans, schedules, controls, and industrial processes; and

(b) The contractor's actual performance under them.

42.1102 Applicability.

This subpart applies to all contracts for supplies or services other than construction contracts, and Federal Supply Schedule contracts. See Part 37, especially Subpart 37.6, regarding surveillance of contracts for services.

[FAC 97-1, 62 FR 44802, 8/22/97, effective 10/21/97; FAC 2005-17, 72 FR 27364, 5/15/2007, effective 6/14/2007]

42.1103 Policy.

The contractor is responsible for timely contract performance. The Government will maintain surveillance of contractor performance as necessary to protect its interests. When the contracting office retains a contract for administration, the contracting officer administering the contract shall determine the extent of surveillance.

42.1104 Surveillance requirements.

(a) The contract administration office determines the extent of production surveillance on the basis of—

(1) The criticality (degree of importance to the Government) assigned by the contracting officer (see 42.1105) to the supplies or services; and

(2) Consideration of the following factors:

(i) Contract requirements for reporting production progress and performance.

(ii) The contract performance schedule.

(iii) The contractor's production plan.

(iv) The contractor's history of contract performance.

(v) The contractor's experience with the contract supplies or services.

(vi) The contractor's financial capability.

(vii) Any supplementary written instructions from the contracting office.

(b) Contracts at or below the simplified acquisition threshold should not normally require production surveillance.

(c) In planning and conducting surveillance, contract administration offices shall make maximum use of any reliable contractor production control or data management systems.

(d) In performing surveillance, contract administration office personnel shall avoid any action that may—

(1) Be inconsistent with any contract requirement; or

(2) Result in claims of waivers, of changes, or of other contract modifications.

[FAC 90-29, 60 FR 34732, 7/3/95, effective 7/3/95]

42.1105 Assignment of criticality designator.

Contracting officers shall assign a criticality designator to each contract in the space for designating the contract administration office, as follows:

Criticality Designator	*Criterion*
A	Critical contracts, including DX-rated contracts (see Subpart 11.6), contracts citing the authority in 6.302-2 (unusual and compelling urgency), and contracts for major systems.
B	Contracts (other than those designated "A") for items needed to maintain a Government or contractor production or repair line, to preclude out-of-stock conditions or to meet user needs for nonstock items.
C	All contracts other than those designated "A" or "B."

[FAC 84-5, 50 FR 1745, 1/11/85, effective 4/1/85; FAC 90-32, 60 FR 48206, 9/18/95, effective 10/1/95]

42.1106 Reporting requirements.

(a) When information on contract performance status is needed, contracting officers may require contractors to submit production progress reports (see 42.1107(a)). Reporting requirements shall be limited to that information essential to Government needs and shall take maximum advantage of data output generated by contractor management systems.

(b) Contract administration offices shall review and verify the accuracy of contractor reports and advise the contracting officer of any required action. The accuracy of contractor-prepared reports shall be verified either by a program of continuous surveillance of the contractor's report-preparation system or by individual review of each report.

(c) The contract administration office may at any time initiate a report to advise the contracting officer (and the inventory manager, if one is designated in the contract) of any potential or actual delay in performance. This advice shall—

(1) Be in writing,

(2) Be provided in sufficient time for the contracting officer to take necessary action, and

(3) Provide a definite recommendation, if action is appropriate.

42.1107 Contract clause.

(a) The contracting officer shall insert the clause at 52.242-2, Production Progress Reports, in solicitations and contracts when production progress reporting is required; unless a construction contract, or a Federal Supply Schedule contract is contemplated.

(b) When the clause at 52.242-2 is used, the contracting officer shall specify appropriate reporting instructions in the Schedule (see 42.1106(a)).

[FAC 2005-17, 72 FR 27364, 5/15/2007, effective 6/14/2007]

SUBPART 42.12—NOVATION AND CHANGE-OF-NAME AGREEMENTS

42.1200 Scope of subpart.

This subpart prescribes policies and procedures for—

(a) Recognition of a successor in interest to Government contracts when contractor assets are transferred;

(b) Recognition of a change in a contractor's name; and

(c) Execution of novation agreements and change-of-name agreements by the responsible contracting officer.

42.1201 [Removed and Reserved]

[Removed and Reserved, FAC 97-22, 66 FR 2117, 1/10/2001, effective 3/12/2001; Delay of effective date, 66 FR 14259, 3/9/2001, effective 5/11/2001]

42.1202 Responsibility for executing agreements.

The contracting officer responsible for processing and executing novation and change-of-name agreements shall be determined as follows:

(a) If any of the affected contracts held by the transferor have been assigned to an administrative contracting officer (ACO) (see 2.1 and 42.202), the responsible contracting officer shall be—

(1) This ACO; or

(2) The ACO responsible for the corporate office, if affected contracts are in more than one plant or division of the transferor.

(b) If none of the affected contracts held by the transferor have been assigned to an ACO, the contracting officer responsible for the largest unsettled (unbilled plus billed but unpaid) dollar balance of contracts shall be the responsible contracting officer.

(c) If several transferors are involved, the responsible contracting officer shall be—

(1) The ACO administering the largest unsettled dollar balance; or

(2) The contracting officer (or ACO) designated by the agency having the largest unsettled dollar balance, if none of the affected contracts have been assigned to an ACO.

42.1203 Processing agreements.

(a) If a contractor wishes the Government to recognize a successor in interest to its contracts or a name change, the contractor must submit a written request to the responsible contracting officer (see 42.1202). If the contractor received its contract under subpart 8.7 under 41 U.S.C. chapter 85, Committee for Purchase from People Who Are Blind or Severely Disabled, use the procedures at 8.716 instead.

(b) The responsible contracting officer shall—

(1) Identify and request that the contractor submit the information necessary to evaluate the proposed agreement for recognizing a successor in interest or a name change. This information should include the items identified in 42.1204 (e) and (f) or 42.1205(a), as applicable;

(2) Notify each contract administration office and contracting office affected by a proposed agreement for recognizing a successor in interest, and provide those offices with a list of all affected contracts; and

(3) Request submission of any comments or objections to the proposed transfer within 30 days after notification. Any submission should be accompanied by supporting documentation.

(c) Upon receipt of the necessary information, the responsible contracting officer shall determine whether or not it is in the Government's interest to recognize the proposed successor in interest on the basis of—

(1) The comments received from the affected contract administration offices and contracting offices;

(2) The proposed successor's responsibility under Subpart 9.1, Responsible Prospective Contractors; and

(3) Any factor relating to the proposed successor's performance of contracts with the Government that the Government determines would impair the proposed successor's ability to perform the contract satisfactorily.

(d) The execution of a novation agreement does not preclude the use of any other method available to the contracting officer to resolve any other issues related to a transfer of contractor assets, including the treatment of costs.

(e) Any separate agreement between the transferor and transferee regarding the assumption of liabilities (*e.g.*, long-term incentive compensation plans, cost accounting standards noncompliances, environmental cleanup costs, and final overhead costs) should be referenced specifically in the novation agreement.

(f) Before novation and change-of-name agreements are executed, the responsible contracting officer shall ensure that Government counsel has reviewed them for legal sufficiency.

(g) The responsible contracting officer shall—

(1) Forward a signed copy of the executed novation or change-of-name agreement to the transferor and to the transferee; and

(2) Retain a signed copy in the case file.

(h) Following distribution of the agreement, the responsible contracting officer shall—

(1) Prepare a Standard Form 30, Amendment of Solicitation/Modification of Contract, incorporating a summary of the agreement and attaching a complete list of contracts affected;

(2) Retain the original Standard Form 30 with the attached list in the case file;

(3) Send a signed copy of the Standard Form 30, with attached list to the transferor and to the transferee; and

(4) Send a copy of this Standard Form 30 with attached list to each contract administration office or contracting office involved, which shall be responsible for further appropriate distribution.

[FAC 97-3, 62 FR 64912, 12/9/97, effective 2/9/98, corrected, 63 FR 1533, 1/9/98; FAC 97-14, 64 FR 51828, 9/24/99, effective 11/23/99; FAC 2005-73, 79 FR 24192, 4/29/2014, effective 5/29/2014]

42.1204 Applicability of novation agreements.

(a) 41 U.S.C. 6305 prohibits transfer of Government contracts from the contractor to a third party. The Government may, when in its interest, recognize a third party as the successor in interest to a Government contract when the third party's interest in the contract arises out of the transfer of—

(1) All the contractor's assets; or

(2) The entire portion of the assets involved in performing the contract. (See 14.404-2(l) for the effect of novation agreements after bid opening but before award.) Examples of such transactions include, but are not limited to—

(i) Sale of these assets with a provision for assuming liabilities;

(ii) Transfer of these assets incident to a merger or corporate consolidation; and

(iii) Incorporation of a proprietorship or partnership, or formation of a partnership.

(b) A novation agreement is unnecessary when there is a change in the ownership of a contractor as a result of a stock purchase, with no legal change in the contracting party, and when that contracting party remains in control of the assets and is the party performing the contract. However, whether there is a purchase of assets or a stock purchase, there may be issues related to the change in ownership that appropriately should be addressed in a formal agreement between the contractor and the Government (see 42.1203(e)).

(c) When it is in the Government's interest not to concur in the transfer of a contract from one company to another company, the original contractor remains under contractual obligation to the Government, and the contract may be terminated for reasons of default, should the original contractor not perform.

(d) When considering whether to recognize a third party as a successor in interest to Government contracts, the responsible contracting officer shall identify and evaluate any significant organizational conflicts of interest in accordance with Subpart 9.5. If the responsible contracting officer determines that a conflict of interest cannot be resolved, but that it is in the best interest of the Government to approve the novation request, a request for a waiver may be submitted in accordance with the procedures at 9.503.

(e) When a contractor asks the Government to recognize a successor in interest, the contractor shall submit to the responsible contracting officer three signed copies of the proposed novation agreement and one copy each, as applicable, of the following:

(1) The document describing the proposed transaction, *e.g.*, purchase/sale agreement or memorandum of understanding.

(2) A list of all affected contracts between the transferor and the Government, as of the date of sale or transfer of assets, showing for each, as of that date, the—

(i) Contract number and type;

(ii) Name and address of the contracting office;

(iii) Total dollar value, as amended; and

(iv) Approximate remaining unpaid balance.

(3) Evidence of the transferee's capability to perform.

(4) Any other relevant information requested by the responsible contracting officer.

(f) Except as provided in paragraph (g) of this section, the contractor shall submit to the responsible contracting officer one copy of each of the following documents, as applicable, as the documents become available:

(1) An authenticated copy of the instrument effecting the transfer of assets; *e.g.*, bill of sale, certificate of merger, contract, deed, agreement, or court decree.

(2) A certified copy of each resolution of the corporate parties' boards of directors authorizing the transfer of assets.

(3) A certified copy of the minutes of each corporate party's stockholder meeting necessary to approve the transfer of assets.

(4) An authenticated copy of the transferee's certificate and articles of incorporation, if a corporation was formed for the purpose of receiving the assets involved in performing the Government contracts.

(5) The opinion of legal counsel for the transferor and transferee stating that the transfer was properly effected under applicable law and the effective date of transfer.

(6) Balance sheets of the transferor and transferee as of the dates immediately before and after the transfer of assets, audited by independent accountants.

(7) Evidence that any security clearance requirements have been met.

(8) The consent of sureties on all contracts listed under paragraph (e)(2) of this section if bonds are required, or a statement from the transferor that none are required.

(g) If the Government has acquired the documents during its participation in the pre-merger or pre-acquisition review process, or the Government's interests are adequately protected with an alternative formulation of the information, the responsible contracting officer may modify the list of documents to be submitted by the contractor.

(h) When recognizing a successor in interest to a Government contract is consistent with the Government's interest, the responsible contracting officer shall execute a novation agreement with the transferor and the transferee. It shall ordinarily provide in part that—

(1) The transferee assumes all the transferor's obligations under the contract;

(2) The transferor waives all rights under the contract against the Government;

(3) The transferor guarantees performance of the contract by the transferee (a satisfactory performance bond may be accepted instead of the guarantee); and

(4) Nothing in the agreement shall relieve the transferor or transferee from compliance with any Federal law.

(i) The responsible contracting officer shall use the following format for agreements when the transferor and transferee are corporations and all the transferor's assets are transferred. This format may be adapted to fit specific cases and may be used as a guide in preparing similar agreements for other situations.

NOVATION AGREEMENT

The ABC CORPORATION (Transferor), a corporation duly organized and existing under the laws of ____[*insert State*] with its principal office in ____[*insert city*]; the XYZ

CORPORATION (Transferee), [*if appropriate add "formerly known as the EFG Corporation"*] a corporation duly organized and existing under the laws of ____[*insert State*] with its principal office in ____[*insert city*]; and the UNITED STATES OF AMERICA (Government) enter into this Agreement as of ____[*insert the date transfer of assets became effective under applicable State law*].

(a) THE PARTIES AGREE TO THE FOLLOWING FACTS:

(1) The Government, represented by various Contracting Officers of the ____[*insert name(s) of agency(ies)*], has entered into certain contracts with the Transferor, namely: ____[*insert contract or purchase order identifications*]; [*or delete "namely" and insert "as shown in the attached list marked 'Exhibit A' and incorporated in this Agreement by reference."*]. The term "the contracts," as used in this Agreement, means the above contracts and purchase orders and all other contracts and purchase orders, including all modifications, made between the Government and the Transferor before the effective date of this Agreement (whether or not performance and payment have been completed and releases executed if the Government or the Transferor has any remaining rights, duties, or obligations under these contracts and purchase orders). Included in the term "the contracts" are also all modifications made under the terms and conditions of these contracts and purchase orders between the Government and the Transferee, on or after the effective date of this Agreement.

(2) As of ____, 20____, the Transferor has transferred to the Transferee all the assets of the Transferor by virtue of a ____[*insert term descriptive of the legal transaction involved*] between the Transferor and the Transferee.

(3) The Transferee has acquired all the assets of the Transferor by virtue of the above transfer.

(4) The Transferee has assumed all obligations and liabilities of the Transferor under the contracts by virtue of the above transfer.

(5) The Transferee is in a position to fully perform all obligations that may exist under the contracts.

(6) It is consistent with the Government's interest to recognize the Transferee as the successor party to the contracts.

(7) Evidence of the above transfer has been filed with the Government.

[*When a change of name is also involved; e.g., a prior or concurrent change of the Transferee's name, an appropriate statement shall be inserted (see example in paragraph (8) below)*].

(8) A certificate dated____, 20____, signed by the Secretary of State of ____[*insert State*], to the effect that the corporate name of EFG CORPORATION was changed to XYZ CORPORATION on ____, 20____, has been filed with the Government.

(b) IN CONSIDERATION OF THESE FACTS, THE PARTIES AGREE THAT BY THIS AGREEMENT—

(1) The Transferor confirms the transfer to the Transferee, and waives any claims and rights against the Government that it now has or may have in the future in connection with the contracts.

(2) The Transferee agrees to be bound by and to perform each contract in accordance with the conditions contained in the contracts. The Transferee also assumes all obligations and liabilities of, and all claims against, the Transferor under the contracts as if the Transferee were the original party to the contracts.

(3) The Transferee ratifies all previous actions taken by the Transferor with respect to the contracts, with the same force and effect as if the action had been taken by the Transferee.

(4) The Government recognizes the Transferee as the Transferor's successor in interest in and to the contracts. The Transferee by this Agreement becomes entitled to all rights, titles, and interests of the Transferor in and to the contracts as if the Transferee were the original party to the contracts. Following the effective date of this Agreement, the term "Contractor," as used

in the contracts, shall refer to the Transferee.

(5) Except as expressly provided in this Agreement, nothing in it shall be construed as a waiver of any rights of the Government against the Transferor.

(6) All payments and reimbursements previously made by the Government to the Transferor, and all other previous actions taken by the Government under the contracts, shall be considered to have discharged those parts of the Government's obligations under the contracts. All payments and reimbursements made by the Government after the date of this Agreement in the name of or to the Transferor shall have the same force and effect as if made to the Transferee, and shall constitute a complete discharge of the Government's obligations under the contracts, to the extent of the amounts paid or reimbursed.

(7) The Transferor and the Transferee agree that the Government is not obligated to pay or reimburse either of them for, or otherwise give effect to, any costs, taxes, or other expenses, or any related increases, directly or indirectly arising out of or resulting from the transfer or this Agreement, other than those that the Government in the absence of this transfer or Agreement would have been obligated to pay or reimburse under the terms of the contracts.

(8) The Transferor guarantees payment of all liabilities and the performance of all obligations that the Transferee—

(i) Assumes under this Agreement or

(ii) May undertake in the future should these contracts be modified under their terms and conditions. The Transferor waives notice of, and consents to, any such future modifications.

(9) The contracts shall remain in full force and effect, except as modified by this Agreement. Each party has executed this Agreement as of the day and year first above written.

UNITED STATES OF AMERICA,

By_____

Title_____

ABC CORPORATION,

By_____

Title_____

[CORPORATE SEAL]

XYZ CORPORATION,

By_____

Title_____

[CORPORATE SEAL]

CERTIFICATE

I, ____, certify that I am the Secretary of ABC CORPORATION, that ____, who signed this Agreement for this corporation, was then ____ of this corporation; and that this Agreement was duly signed for and on behalf of this corporation by authority of its governing body and within the scope of its corporate powers.

Witness my hand and the seal of this corporation this ____ day of ____ 20____.

By_____

[CORPORATE SEAL]

CERTIFICATE

I, ____, certify that I am the Secretary of XYZ CORPORATION, that ____, who signed this Agreement for this corporation, was then ____ of this corporation; and that this Agreement was duly signed for and on behalf of this corporation by authority of its governing body and within the scope of its corporate powers. Witness my hand and the seal of this corporation this ____ day of ____ 20_

By_____

[CORPORATE SEAL]

[FAC 97-3, 62 FR 64912, 12/9/97, effective 2/9/98, corrected, 63 FR 1533, 1/9/98; FAC 97-17, 65 FR 24316, 4/25/2000, effective 4/25/2000; FAC 2005-73, 79 FR 24192, 4/29/2014, effective 5/29/2014]

42.1205 Agreement to recognize contractor's change of name.

(a) If only a change of the contractor's name is involved and the Government's and contractor's rights and obligations remain unaffected, the parties shall execute an agreement to reflect the name change. The contractor shall forward to the responsible contracting officer three signed copies of the Change-of-Name Agreement, and one copy each of the following:

(1) The document effecting the name change, authenticated by a proper official of the State having jurisdiction.

(2) The opinion of the contractor's legal counsel stating that the change of name was properly effected under applicable law and showing the effective date.

(3) A list of all affected contracts and purchase orders remaining unsettled between the contractor and the Government, showing for each the contract number and type, and name and address of the contracting office. The contracting officer may request the total dollar value as amended and the remaining unpaid balance for each contract.

(b) The following suggested format for an agreement may be adapted for specific cases:

CHANGE-OF-NAME AGREEMENT

The ABC CORPORATION (Contractor), a corporation duly organized and existing under the laws of ____ [*insert State*], and the UNITED STATES OF AMERICA (Government), enter into this Agreement as of ____ [*insert date when the change of name became effective under applicable State law*].

(a) THE PARTIES AGREE TO THE FOLLOWING FACTS:

(1) The Government, represented by various Contracting Officers of the ____ [*insert name(s) of agency(ies)*], has entered into certain contracts and purchase orders with the XYZ CORPORATION, namely: ____[*insert contract or purchase order identifications*]; [*or delete "namely" and insert "as shown in the attached list marked 'Exhibit A' and incorporated in this Agreement by reference."*]. The term "the contracts," as used in this Agreement, means the above contracts and purchase orders and all other contracts and purchase orders, including all modifications, made by the Government and the Contractor before the effective date of this Agreement (whether or not performance and payment have been completed and releases executed if the Government or the Contractor has any remaining rights, duties, or obligations under these contracts and purchase orders).

(2) The XYZ CORPORATION, by an amendment to its certificate of incorporation, dated ___, 20_, has changed its corporate name to ABC CORPORATION.

(3) This amendment accomplishes a change of corporate name only and all rights and obligations of the Government and of the Contractor under the contracts are unaffected by this change.

(4) Documentary evidence of this change of corporate name has been filed with the Government.

(b) IN CONSIDERATION OF THESE FACTS, THE PARTIES AGREE THAT—

(1) The contracts covered by this Agreement are amended by substituting the name "ABC CORPORATION" for the name "XYZ CORPORATION" wherever it appears in the contracts; and

(2) Each party has executed this Agreement as of the day and year first above written.

UNITED STATES OF AMERICA,

By ______

Title ______

ABC CORPORATION,

By ______

Title ______

[CORPORATE SEAL]

CERTIFICATE

I, ______ certify that I am the Secretary of ABC CORPORATION; that ______, who signed this Agreement for this corporation, was then ___ of this corporation; and that this Agreement was duly signed for and on behalf of this corporation by authority of its governing body and within the scope of its corporate powers. Witness my hand and the seal of this corporation this ___ day of ___ 20_.

By ______

[CORPORATE SEAL]

[FAC 90-9, 56 FR 67134, 12/27/91, effective 2/25/92; FAC 97-17, 65 FR 24316, 4/25/2000, effective 4/25/2000]

SUBPART 42.13—SUSPENSION OF WORK, STOP-WORK ORDERS, AND GOVERNMENT DELAY OF WORK

42.1301 General.

Situations may occur during contract performance that cause the Government to order a suspension of work, or a work stoppage. This subpart provides clauses to meet these situations and a clause for settling contractor claims for unordered Government caused delays that are not otherwise covered in the contract.

[Redesignated from 12.501, FAC 90-32, 60 FR 48206, 9/18/95, effective 10/1/95]

42.1302 Suspension of work.

A suspension of work under a construction or architect-engineer contract may be ordered by the contracting officer for a reasonable period of time. If the suspension is unreasonable, the contractor may submit a written claim for increases in the cost of performance, excluding profit.

[Redesignated from 12.502, FAC 90-32, 60 FR 48206, 9/18/95, effective 10/1/95]

42.1303 Stop-work orders.

(a) Stop-work orders may be used, when appropriate, in any negotiated fixed-price or cost-reimbursement supply, research and development, or service contract if work stoppage may be required for reasons such as advancement in the state-of-the-art, production or engineering breakthroughs, or realignment of programs.

(b) Generally, a stop-work order will be issued only if it is advisable to suspend work pending a decision by the Government and a supplemental agreement providing for the suspension is not feasible. Issuance of a stop-work order shall be approved at a level higher than the contracting officer. Stop-work orders shall not be used in place of a termination notice after a decision to terminate has been made.

(c) Stop-work orders should include—

(1) A description of the work to be suspended;

(2) Instructions concerning the contractor's issuance of further orders for materials or services;

(3) Guidance to the contractor on action to be taken on any subcontracts; and

(4) Other suggestions to the contractor for minimizing costs.

(d) Promptly after issuing the stop-work order, the contracting officer should discuss the stop-work order with the contractor and modify the order, if necessary, in light of the discussion.

(e) As soon as feasible after a stop-work order is issued, but before its expiration, the contracting officer shall take appropriate action to—

(1) Terminate the contract;

(2) Cancel the stop-work order (any cancellation of a stop-work order shall be subject to the same approvals as were required for its issuance); or

(3) Extend the period of the stop-work order if it is necessary and if the contractor agrees (any extension of the stop-work order shall be by a supplemental agreement).

[Redesignated from 12.503, FAC 90-32, 60 FR 48206, 9/18/95, effective 10/1/95]

42.1304 Government delay of work.

(a) The clause at 52.242-17, Government Delay of Work, provides for the administrative settlement of contractor claims that arise from delays and interruptions in the contract work caused by the acts, or failures to act, of the contracting officer. This clause is not applicable if the contract otherwise specifically provides for an equitable adjustment because of the delay or interruption; *e.g.*, when the Changes clause is applicable.

(b) The clause does not authorize the contracting officer to order a suspension, delay, or interruption of the contract work and it shall not be used as the basis or justification of such an order.

(c) If the contracting officer has notice of an unordered delay or interruption covered by the clause, the contracting officer shall act to end the delay or take other appropriate action as soon as practicable.

(d) The contracting officer shall retain in the file a record of all negotiations leading to any adjustment made under the clause, and related certified cost or pricing data, or data other than certified cost or pricing data.

[Redesignated from 12.504, FAC 90-32, 60 FR 48206, 9/18/95, effective 10/1/95; FAC 2005-45, 75 FR 53135, 8/30/2010, effective 10/1/2010]

42.1305 Contract clauses.

(a) The contracting officer shall insert the clause at 52.242-14, Suspension of Work, in solicitations and contracts when a fixed-price construction or architect-engineer contract is contemplated.

(b) (1) The contracting officer may, when contracting by negotiation, insert the clause at 52.242-15, Stop-Work Order, in solicitations and contracts for supplies, services, or research and development.

(2) If a cost-reimbursement contract is contemplated, the contracting officer shall use the clause with its Alternate I.

(c) The contracting officer shall insert the clause at 52.242-17, Government Delay of Work, in solicitations and contracts when a fixed-price contract is contemplated for supplies other than commercial or modified-commercial items. The clause use is optional when a fixed-price contract is contemplated for services, or for supplies that are commercial or modified-commercial items.

[Redesignated from 12.505, FAC 90-32, 60 FR 48206, 9/18/95, effective 10/1/95; FAC 2005-17, 72 FR 27364, 5/15/2007, effective 6/14/2007]

SUBPART 42.14—[REMOVED AND RESERVED]

SUBPART 42.15—CONTRACTOR PERFORMANCE INFORMATION

42.1500 Scope of subpart.

This subpart provides policies and establishes responsibilities for recording and maintaining contractor performance information. This subpart does not apply to procedures used by agencies in determining fees under award or incentive fee contracts. See subpart 16.4. However, the fee amount paid to contractors should be reflective of the contractor's performance and the past performance evaluation should closely parallel and be consistent with the fee determinations.

[FAC 90-26, 60 FR 16718, 3/31/95, effective 5/30/95; FAC 97-18, 65 FR 36014, 6/6/2000, effective 6/6/2000; FAC 2005-69, 78 FR 46783, 8/1/2013, effective 9/3/2013]

42.1501 General.

(a) Past performance information (including the ratings and supporting narratives) is relevant information, for future source selection purposes, regarding a contractor's actions under previously awarded contracts or orders. It includes, for example, the contractor's record of—

(1) Conforming to requirements and to standards of good workmanship;

(2) Forecasting and controlling costs;

(3) Adherence to schedules, including the administrative aspects of performance;

(4) Reasonable and cooperative behavior and commitment to customer satisfaction;

(5) Reporting into databases (see subpart 4.14, and reporting requirements in the solicitation provisions and clauses referenced in 9.104-7);

(6) Integrity and business ethics; and

(7) Business-like concern for the interest of the customer.

(b) Agencies shall monitor their compliance with the past performance evaluation requirements (see 42.1502), and use the Contractor Performance Assessment Reporting System (CPARS) metric tools to measure the quality and timely reporting of past performance information. CPARS is the official source for past performance information.

[FAC 90-26, 60 FR 16718, 3/31/95, effective 5/30/95; FAC 2005-28, 73 FR 67064, 11/12/2008, effective 12/12/2008; FAC 2005-44, 75 FR 39414, 7/8/2010, effective 7/8/2010; FAC 2005-60, 77 FR 44047, 7/26/2012, effective 8/27/2012; FAC 2005-69, 78 FR 46783, 8/1/2013, effective 9/3/2013; FAC 2005-74, 79 FR 31193,

5/30/2014, effective 5/30/2014; FAC 2019-06, 84 FR 47865, 9/10/2019, effective 10/10/2019]

42.1502 Policy.

(a) *General.* Past performance evaluations shall be prepared at least annually and at the time the work under a contract or order is completed. Past performance evaluations are required for contracts and orders as specified in paragraphs (b) through (f) of this section, including contracts and orders performed outside the United States. These evaluations are generally for the entity, division, or unit that performed the contract or order. Past performance information shall be entered into CPARS, the Governmentwide evaluation reporting tool for all past performance reports on contracts and orders. Instructions for submitting evaluations into CPARS are available at *http://www.cpars.gov/*.

(b) *Contracts.* Except as provided in paragraphs (e), (f), and (h) of this section, agencies shall prepare evaluations of contractor performance for each contract (as defined in FAR part 2) that exceeds the simplified acquisition threshold and for each order that exceeds the simplified acquisition threshold. Agencies are required to prepare an evaluation if a modification to the contract causes the dollar amount to exceed the simplified acquisition threshold.

(c) *Orders under multiple-agency contracts.* Agencies shall prepare an evaluation of contractor performance for each order that exceeds the simplified acquisition threshold that is placed under a Federal Supply Schedule contract or placed under a task-order contract or a delivery-order contract awarded by another agency (*i.e.,* Governmentwide acquisition contract or multi-agency contract). Agencies placing orders under their own multiple-agency contract shall also prepare evaluations for their own orders. This evaluation shall not consider the requirements under paragraph (g) of this section. Agencies are required to prepare an evaluation if a modification to the order causes the dollar amount to exceed the simplified acquisition threshold.

(d) *Orders under single-agency contracts.* For single-agency task-order and delivery-order contracts, the contracting officer may require performance evaluations for each order in excess of the simplified acquisition threshold when such evaluations would produce more useful past performance information for source selection officials than that contained in the overall contract evaluation (*e.g.,* when the scope of the basic contract is very broad and the nature of individual orders could be significantly different). This evaluation need not consider the requirements under paragraph (g) of this section unless the contracting officer deems it appropriate.

(e) Past performance evaluations shall be prepared for each construction contract of $700,000 or more, and for each construction contract terminated for default regardless of contract value. Past performance evaluations may also be prepared for construction contracts below $700,000.

(f) Past performance evaluations shall be prepared for each architect-engineer services contract of $35,000 or more, and for each architect-engineer services contract that is terminated for default regardless of contract value. Past performance evaluations may also be prepared for architect-engineer services contracts below $35,000.

(g) Past performance evaluations shall include an assessment of the contractor's—

(1) Performance against, and efforts to achieve, the goals identified in the small business subcontracting plan when the contract includes the clause at 52.219-9, Small Business Subcontracting Plan; and

(2) Reduced or untimely payments (as defined in 19.701), made to small business subcontractors, determined by the contracting officer to be unjustified. The contracting officer shall—

(i) Consider and evaluate a contractor's written explanation for a reduced or an untimely payment when determining whether the reduced or untimely payment is justified; and

(ii) Determine that a history of unjustified reduced or untimely payments has occurred when the contractor has reported three or more occasions of unjustified reduced or untimely payments under a single contract within a 12-month period (see 42.1503(h)(1)(vi) and the evaluation ratings in Table 42-2). The following payment or nonpayment situations are not considered to be unjustified:

(A) There is a contract dispute on performance.

(B) A partial payment is made for amounts not in dispute.

(C) A payment is reduced due to past overpayments.

(D) There is an administrative mistake.

(E) Late performance by the subcontractor leads to later payment by the prime contractor.

(h) Agencies shall not evaluate performance for contracts awarded under Subpart 8.7.

(i) Agencies shall promptly report other contractor information in accordance with 42.1503(h).

[FAC 90-26, 60 FR 16718, 3/31/95, effective 5/30/95; FAC 97-2, 62 FR 51224, 9/30/97, effective 10/10/97; FAC 2001-14, 68 FR 28095, 5/22/2003, effective 6/23/2003; FAC 2001-17, 68 FR 59999, 10/20/2003, effective 10/20/2003; FAC 2005-13, 71 FR 57363, 9/28/2006, effective 9/28/2006; FAC 2005-34, 74 FR 31557, 7/1/2009, effective 7/1/2009; FAC 2005-45, 75 FR 53129, 8/30/2010, effective 10/1/2010; FAC 2005-46, 75 FR 60258, 9/29/2010, effective 10/29/2010; FAC 2005-69, 78 FR 46783, 8/1/2013, effective 9/3/2013; FAC 2005-74, 79 FR 31193, 5/30/2014, effective 5/30/2014; FAC 2005-82, 80 FR 26426, 5/7/2015, effective 6/8/2015; FAC 2005-83, 80 FR 38293, 7/2/2015, effective 10/1/2015; FAC 2005-90, 81 FR 58562, 8/25/2016, effective 10/25/2016; FAC 2005-93, 81 FR 91636, 12/16/2016, effective 12/16/2016; FAC 2005-94, 81 FR 93481, 12/20/2016, effective 1/19/2017; FAC 2005-96, 82 FR 51773, 11/8/2017, effective 11/6/2017]

42.1503 Procedures.

(a)(1) Agencies shall assign responsibility and management accountability for the completeness of past performance submissions. Agency procedures for the past performance evaluation system shall—

(i) Generally provide for input to the evaluations from the technical office, contracting office, program management office, and, where appropriate, quality assurance and end users of the product or service;

(ii) Identify and assign past performance evaluation roles and responsibilities to those individuals responsible for preparing and reviewing interim evaluations, if prepared, and final evaluations (*e.g.*, contracting officers, contracting officer representatives, project managers, and program managers). Those individuals identified may obtain information for the evaluation of performance from the program office, administrative contracting office, audit office, end users of the product or service, and any other technical or business advisor, as appropriate; and

(iii) Address management controls and appropriate management reviews of past performance evaluations, to include accountability for documenting past performance on CPARS.

(2) If agency procedures do not specify the individuals responsible for past performance evaluation duties, the contracting officer is responsible for this function.

(3) Interim evaluations may be prepared as required, in accordance with agency procedures.

(b)(1) The evaluation should include a clear, non-technical description of the principal purpose of the contract or order. The evaluation should reflect how the contractor performed. The evaluation should include clear relevant information that accurately depicts the contractor's performance, and be based on objective facts supported by program and contract or order performance data. The evaluations should be tailored to the contract type, size, content, and complexity of the contractual requirements.

(2) Evaluation factors for each assessment shall include, at a minimum, the following:

(i) Technical (quality of product or service).

(ii) Cost control (not applicable for firm-fixed-price or fixed-price with economic price adjustment arrangements).

(iii) Schedule/timeliness.

(iv) Management or business relations.

(v) Small business subcontracting, including reduced or untimely payments to small business subcontractors when 19.702(a) requires a subcontracting plan (as applicable, see Table 42-2).

(vi) Other (as applicable) (*e.g.*, trafficking violations, tax delinquency, failure to report in accordance with contract terms and conditions, defective cost or pricing data, terminations, suspension and debarments).

(3) Evaluation factors may include subfactors.

(4) Each factor and subfactor used shall be evaluated and a supporting narrative provided. Each evaluation factor, as listed in paragraph (b)(2) of this section, shall be rated in accordance with a five scale rating system (*i.e.*, exceptional, very good, satisfactory, marginal, and unsatisfactory). The ratings and narratives must reflect the definitions in the tables 42-1 or 42-2 of this section.

(c)(1) When the contract provides for incentive fees, the incentive-fee contract performance evaluation shall be entered into CPARS.

(2) When the contract provides for award fee, the award fee-contract performance adjectival rating as described in 16.401(e)(3) shall be entered into CPARS.

(d) Agency evaluations of contractor performance, including both negative and positive evaluations, prepared under this subpart shall be provided to the contractor as soon as practicable after completion of the evaluation. The contractor will receive a CPARS-system generated notification when an evaluation is ready for comment. Contractors shall be afforded up to 14 calendar days from the date of notification of availability of the past performance evaluation to submit comments, rebutting statements, or additional information. Agencies shall provide for review at a level above the contracting officer to consider disagreements between the parties regarding the evaluation. The ultimate conclusion on the performance evaluation is a decision of the contracting agency. Copies of the evaluation, contractor response, and review comments, if any, shall be retained as part of the evaluation. These evaluations may be used to support future award decisions, and should therefore be marked "Source Selection Information". Evaluation of Federal Prison Industries (FPI) performance may be used to support a waiver request (see 8.604) when FPI is a mandatory source in accordance with subpart 8.6. The completed evaluation shall not be released to other than Government personnel and the contractor whose performance is being evaluated during the period the information may be used to provide source selection information. Disclosure of such information could cause harm both to the commercial interest of the Government and to the competitive position of the contractor being evaluated as well as impede the efficiency of Government operations. Evaluations used in determining award or incentive fee payments may also be used to satisfy the requirements of this subpart. A copy of the annual or final past performance evaluation shall be provided to the contractor as soon as it is finalized.

(e) Agencies shall require frequent evaluation (*e.g.*, monthly, quarterly) of agency compliance with the reporting requirements in 42.1502, so agencies can readily identify delinquent past performance reports and monitor their reports for quality control.

(f) Agencies shall prepare and submit all past performance evaluations electronically in CPARS at *https://www.cpars.gov*. These evaluations, including any contractor-submitted information (with indication whether agency review is pending), become available for source selection officials not later than 14 days after the date on which the contractor is notified of the evaluation's availability for comment. The Government shall update CPARS with any contractor comments provided after 14 days, as well as any subsequent agency review of comments received. Past performance evaluations for classified contracts and special access programs shall not be reported in CPARS, but will be reported as stated in this subpart and in accordance with agency procedures. Agencies shall ensure that appropriate management and technical controls are in place to ensure that only authorized personnel have access to the data and the information safeguarded in accordance with 42.1503(d).

(g) Agencies shall use the past performance information in CPARS that is within three years (six for construction and architect-engineer contracts) of the completion of performance of the evaluated contract or order, and information contained in the Federal Awardee Performance and Integrity Information System (FAPIIS), *e.g.*, terminations for default or cause.

(h) *Other contractor performance information.*

(1) Agencies shall ensure information is accurately reported in the FAPIIS module of CPARS within 3 calendar days after a contracting officer—

(i) Issues a final determination that a contractor has submitted defective cost or pricing data;

(ii) Makes a subsequent change to the final determination concerning defective cost or pricing data pursuant to 15.407-1(d);

(iii) Issues a final termination for cause or default notice;

(iv) Makes a subsequent withdrawal or a conversion of a termination for default to a termination for convenience;

(v) Receives a final determination after an administrative proceeding, in accordance with 22.1704(d)(1), that substantiates an allegation of a violation of the trafficking in persons prohibitions in 22.1703(a) and 52.222-50(b); or

(vi) Determines that a contractor has a history of three or more unjustified reduced or untimely payments to small business subcontractors under a single contract within a 12-month period (see 42.1502(g)(2)).

(2) The information to be posted in accordance with this paragraph (h) is information relating to contractor performance, but does not constitute a "past performance review," which would be exempted from public availability in accordance with section 3010 of the Supplemental Appropriations Act, 2010 (Pub. L. 111-212). Therefore, all such information posted in FAPIIS will be publicly available, unless covered by a disclosure exemption under the Freedom of Information Act (see 9.105-2(b)(2)).

(3) Agencies shall establish CPARS focal points who will register users to report data into the FAPIIS module of CPARS (available at *https://www.cpars.gov*).

(4) With regard to information that may be covered by a disclosure exemption under the Freedom of Information Act, the contracting officer shall follow the procedures at 9.105-2(b)(2)(iv).

TABLE 42-1—EVALUATION RATINGS DEFINITIONS

Rating	Definition	Note
(a) Exceptional	Performance meets contractual requirements and exceeds many to the Government's benefit. The contractual performance of the element or sub-element being evaluated was accomplished with few minor problems for which corrective actions taken by the contractor were highly effective.	To justify an Exceptional rating, identify multiple significant events and state how they were of benefit to the Government. A singular benefit, however, could be of such magnitude that it alone constitutes an Exceptional rating. Also, there should have been NO significant weaknesses identified.
(b) Very Good	Performance meets and exceeds some to the Government's benefit. The contractual performance of the element or sub-element being evaluated was accomplished with some minor problems for which corrective actions taken by the contractor were effective.	To justify a Very Good rating, identify a significant event and state how it was a benefit to the Government. There should have been no significant weaknesses identified.
(c) Satisfactory	Performance meets contractual requirements. The contractual performance of the element or sub-element contains some minor problems for which corrective actions taken by the contractor appear or were satisfactory.	To justify a Satisfactory rating, there should have been only minor problems, or major problems the contractor recovered from without impact to the contract/order. There should have been NO significant weaknesses identified. A fundamental principle of assigning ratings is that contractors will not be evaluated with a rating lower than Satisfactory solely for not performing beyond the requirements of the contract/order.
(d) Marginal	Performance does not meet some contractual requirements. The contractual performance of the element or sub-element being evaluated reflects a serious problem for which the contractor has not yet identified corrective actions. The contractor's proposed actions appear only marginally effective or were not fully implemented.	To justify Marginal performance, identify a significant event in each category that the contractor had trouble overcoming and state how it impacted the Government. A Marginal rating should be supported by referencing the management tool that notified the contractor of the contractual deficiency (*e.g.,* management, quality, safety, or environmental deficiency report or letter).

Rating	Definition	Note
(e) Unsatisfactory	Performance does not meet most contractual requirements and recovery is not likely in a timely manner. The contractual performance of the element or sub-element contains a serious problem(s) for which the contractor's corrective actions appear or were ineffective.	To justify an Unsatisfactory rating, identify multiple significant events in each category that the contractor had trouble overcoming and state how it impacted the Government. A singular problem, however, could be of such serious magnitude that it alone constitutes an unsatisfactory rating. An Unsatisfactory rating should be supported by referencing the management tools used to notify the contractor of the contractual deficiencies (*e.g.*, management, quality, safety, or environmental deficiency reports, or letters).

Note 1: Plus or minus signs may be used to indicate an improving (+) or worsening (-) trend insufficient to change the evaluation status.

Note 2: N/A (not applicable) should be used if the ratings are not going to be applied to a particular area for evaluation.

TABLE 42-2—EVALUATION RATINGS DEFINITIONS
[For the small business subcontracting evaluation factor, when 52.219-9 is used]

Rating	Definition	Note
(a) Exceptional	Exceeded all statutory goals or goals as negotiated. Had exceptional success with initiatives to assist, promote, and utilize small business (SB), small disadvantaged business (SDB), women-owned small business (WOSB), HUBZone small business, veteran-owned small business (VOSB) and service disabled veteran owned small business (SDVOSB). Complied with FAR 52.219-8, Utilization of Small Business Concerns. Exceeded any other small business participation requirements incorporated in the contract/order, including the use of small businesses in mission critical aspects of the program. Went above and beyond the required elements of the subcontracting plan and other small business requirements of the contract/order. Completed and submitted Individual Subcontract Reports and/or Summary Subcontract Reports in an accurate and timely manner. Did not have a history of three or more unjustified reduced or untimely payments to small business subcontractors within a 12-month period.	To justify an Exceptional rating, identify multiple significant events and state how they were a benefit to small business utilization. A singular benefit, however, could be of such magnitude that it constitutes an Exceptional rating. Small businesses should be given meaningful and innovative work directly related to the contract, and opportunities should not be limited to indirect work such as cleaning offices, supplies, landscaping, etc. Also, there should have been no significant weaknesses identified
(b) Very Good .	Met all of the statutory goals or goals as negotiated. Had significant success with initiatives to assist, promote and utilize SB, SDB, WOSB, HUBZone, VOSB, and SDVOSB. Complied with FAR 52.219-8, Utilization of Small Business Concerns. Met or exceeded any other small business participation requirements incorporated in the contract/order, including the use of small businesses in mission critical aspects of the program. Endeavored to go above and beyond the required elements of the subcontracting plan. Completed and submitted Individual Subcontract	To justify a Very Good rating, identify a significant event and state how it was a benefit to small business utilization. Small businesses should be given meaningful and innovative opportunities to participate as subcontractors for work directly related to the contract, and opportunities should not be limited to indirect work such as cleaning offices, supplies, landscaping, etc. There should be no significant weaknesses identified

Rating	Definition	Note
	Reports and/or Summary Subcontract Reports in an accurate and timely manner. Did not have a history of three or more unjustified reduced or untimely payments to small business subcontractors within a 12-month period.	
(c) Satisfactory	Demonstrated a good faith effort to meet all of the negotiated subcontracting goals in the various socio-economic categories for the current period. Complied with FAR 52.219-8, Utilization of Small Business Concerns. Met any other small business participation requirements included in the contract/order. Fulfilled the requirements of the subcontracting plan included in the contract/order. Completed and submitted Individual Subcontract Reports and/or Summary Subcontract Reports in an accurate and timely manner. Did not have a history of three or more unjustified reduced or untimely payments to small business subcontractors within a 12-month period.	To justify a Satisfactory rating, there should have been only minor problems, or major problems the contractor has addressed or taken corrective action. There should have been no significant weaknesses identified. A fundamental principle of assigning ratings is that contractors will not be assessed a rating lower than Satisfactory solely for not performing beyond the requirements of the contract/order

Rating	Definition	Note
(d) Marginal . .	Deficient in meeting key subcontracting plan elements. Deficient in complying with FAR 52.219-8, Utilization of Small Business Concerns, and any other small business participation requirements in the contract/order. Did not submit Individual Subcontract Reports and/or Summary Subcontract Reports in an accurate or timely manner. Failed to satisfy one or more requirements of a corrective action plan currently in place; however, does show an interest in bringing performance to a satisfactory level and has demonstrated a commitment to apply the necessary resources to do so. Required a corrective action plan. Did not have a history of three or more unjustified reduced or untimely payments to small business subcontractors within a 12-month period.	To justify a Marginal rating, identify a significant event that the contractor had trouble overcoming and how it impacted small business utilization. A Marginal rating should be supported by referencing the actions taken by the Government that notified the contractor of the contractual deficiency.
(e) Unsatisfactory	Noncompliant with FAR 52.219-8 and 52.219-9, and any other small business participation requirements in the contract/order. Did not submit Individual Subcontract Reports and/or Summary Subcontract Reports in an accurate or timely manner. Showed little interest in bringing performance to a satisfactory level or is generally uncooperative. Required a corrective action plan. Had a history of three or more unjustified reduced or untimely payments to small business subcontractors within a 12-month period.	To justify an Unsatisfactory rating, identify multiple significant events that the contractor had trouble overcoming and state how it impacted small business utilization. A singular problem, however, could be of such serious magnitude that it alone constitutes an Unsatisfactory rating. An Unsatisfactory rating should be supported by referencing the actions taken by the Government to notify the contractor of the deficiencies. When an Unsatisfactory rating is justified, the contracting officer must consider whether the contractor made a good faith effort to comply with the requirements of the subcontracting plan required by FAR 52.219-9 and follow the procedures outlined in FAR 52.219-16, Liquidated Damages-Subcontracting Plan.

[FAC 90-26, 60 FR 16718, 3/31/95, effective 5/30/95; FAC 97-2, 62 FR 51224, 9/30/97, effective 10/10/97; FAC 2001-14, 68 FR 28095, 5/22/2003, effective 6/23/2003; FAC 2001-21, 69 FR 16147, 3/26/2004, effective 3/26/2004; FAC 2005-07, 71 FR 221, 1/3/2006, effective 1/3/2006; FAC 2005-34, 74 FR 31557,

7/1/2009, effective 7/1/2009; FAC 2005-40, 75 FR 14059, 3/23/2010, effective 4/22/2010; FAC 2005-46, 75 FR 60258, 9/29/2010, effective 10/29/2010; FAC 2005-55, 77 FR 197, 1/3/2012, effective 1/3/2012; FAC 2005-69, 78 FR 46783, 8/1/2013, effective 9/3/2013; FAC 2005-74, 79 FR 31197, 5/30/2014, effective 7/1/2014; FAC 2005-80, 80 FR 4967, 1/29/2015, effective 3/2/2015; FAC 2005-90, 81 FR 58562, 8/25/2016, effective 10/25/2016; FAC 2005-93, 81 FR 91636, 12/16/2016, effective 12/16/2016; FAC 2005-94, 81 FR 93481, 12/20/2016, effective 1/19/2017; FAC 2005-96, 82 FR 51773, 11/8/2017, effective 11/6/2017; FAC 2019-06, 84 FR 47865, 9/10/2019, effective 10/10/2019]

42.1504 Contract clause.

Insert the clause at 52.242-5, Payments to Small Business Subcontractors, in all solicitations and contracts containing the clause at 52.219-9, Small Business Subcontracting Plan.

[Final rule, 81 FR 93481, 12/20/2016, effective 1/19/2017]

SUBPART 42.16—SMALL BUSINESS CONTRACT ADMINISTRATION

42.1601 General.

The contracting officer shall make every reasonable effort to respond in writing within 30 days to any written request to the contracting officer from a small business concern with respect to a contract administration matter. In the event the contracting officer cannot respond to the request within the 30-day period, the contracting officer shall, within the period, transmit to the contractor a written notification of the specific date the contracting officer expects to respond. This provision shall not apply to a request for a contracting officer decision under 41 U.S.C. chapter 71, Contract Disputes.

[FAC 90-32, 60 FR 48206, 9/18/95, effective 10/1/95; FAC 2005-73, 79 FR 24192, 4/29/2014, effective 5/29/2014]

SUBPART 42.17—FORWARD PRICING RATE AGREEMENTS

42.1701 Procedures.

(a) Negotiation of forward pricing rate agreements (FPRAs) may be requested by the contracting officer or the contractor or initiated by the administrative contracting officer (ACO). In determining whether or not to establish such an agreement, the ACO should consider whether the benefits to be derived from the agreement are commensurate with the effort of establishing and monitoring it. Normally, FPRAs should be negotiated only with contractors having a significant volume of Government contract proposals. The cognizant contract administration agency shall determine whether an FPRA will be established.

(b) The ACO shall obtain the contractor's forward pricing rate proposal and require that it include cost or pricing data that are accurate, complete, and current as of the date of submission (but see 15.407-3(c)). The ACO shall invite the cognizant contract auditor and contracting offices having a significant interest to participate in developing a Government objective and in the negotiations. Upon completing negotiations, the ACO shall prepare a price negotiation memorandum (PNM) (see 15.406-3) and forward copies of the PNM and FPRA to the cognizant auditor and to all contracting offices that are known to be affected by the FPRA.

(c) The FPRA shall provide specific terms and conditions covering expiration, application, and data requirements for systematic monitoring to ensure the validity of the rates. The agreement shall provide for cancellation at the option of either party and shall require the contractor to submit to the ACO and to the cognizant contract auditor any significant change in cost or pricing data used to support the FPRA.

(d) When an FPRA is invalid, the contractor should submit and negotiate a new proposal to reflect the changed conditions. If an FPRA has not been established or has been invalidated, the ACO will issue a forward pricing rate recommendation (FPRR) to buying activities with documentation to assist negotiators. In the absence of an FPRA or

FPRR, the ACO shall include support for rates utilized.

(e) The ACO may negotiate continuous updates to the FPRA. The FPRA will provide specific terms and conditions covering notification, application, and data requirements for systematic monitoring to ensure the validity of the rates.

[FAC 97-2, 62 FR 51224, 9/30/97, effective 10/10/97; FAC 2005-45, 75 FR 53135, 8/30/2010, effective 10/1/2010]

PART 43—CONTRACT MODIFICATIONS

Table of Contents

Scope of part 43.000

Subpart 43.1—General

Definitions 43.101
Policy 43.102
Types of contract modifications 43.103
Notification of contract changes 43.104
Availability of funds 43.105
[Removed and Reserved] 43.106
Contract clause 43.107

Subpart 43.2—Change Orders

General 43.201
Authority to issue change orders 43.202
Change order accounting procedures 43.203
Administration 43.204
Contract clauses 43.205

Subpart 43.3—Forms

Use of forms 43.301

PART 43—CONTRACT MODIFICATIONS

43.000 Scope of part.

This part prescribes policies and procedures for preparing and processing contract modifications for all types of contracts including construction and architect-engineer contracts. It does not apply to—

(a) Orders for supplies or services not otherwise changing the terms of contracts or agreements (*e.g.*, delivery orders under indefinite-delivery contracts); or

(b) Modifications for extraordinary contractual relief (see Subpart 50.1).

[FAC 2005-21, 72 FR 63027, 11/7/2007, effective 11/7/2007; FAC 2005-30, 74 FR 2733, 1/15/2009, effective 2/17/2009]

SUBPART 43.1—GENERAL

43.101 Definitions.

As used in this part—

Administrative change means a unilateral (see 43.103(b)) contract change, in writing, that does not affect the substantive rights of the parties (*e.g.*, a change in the paying office or the appropriation data).

Effective date—

(1) For a solicitation amendment, change order, or administrative change, the effective date shall be the issue date of the amendment, change order, or administrative change.

(2) For a supplemental agreement, the effective date shall be the date agreed upon by the contracting parties.

(3) For a modification issued as a confirming notice of termination for the convenience of the Government, the effective date of the confirming notice shall be the same as the effective date of the initial notice.

(4) For a modification converting a termination for default to a termination for the convenience of the Government, the effective date shall be the same as the effective date of the termination for default.

(5) For a modification confirming the termination contracting officer's previous letter determination of the amount due in settlement of a contract termination for convenience, the effective date shall be the same as the effective date of the previous letter determination.

[FAC 97-22, 66 FR 2116, 1/10/2001, effective 3/12/2001; Delay of effective date, 66 FR 14259, 3/9/2001, effective 5/11/2001]

43.102 Policy.

(a) Only contracting officers acting within the scope of their authority are empowered to execute contract modifications on behalf of the Government. Other Government personnel shall not—

(1) Execute contract modifications;

(2) Act in such a manner as to cause the contractor to believe that they have authority to bind the Government; or

(3) Direct or encourage the contractor to perform work that should be the subject of a contract modification.

(b) Contract modifications, including changes that could be issued unilaterally, shall be priced before their execution if this can be done without adversely affecting the interest of the Government. If a significant cost increase could result from a contract modification and time does not permit negotiation of a price, at least a ceiling price shall be negotiated unless impractical.

[FAC 90-38, 61 FR 18914, 4/29/96, effective 4/29/96; FAC 90-44, Interim rule, 61 FR 69286, 12/31/96, effective 1/1/97, finalized without change, FAC 97-1, 62 FR 44802, 8/22/97, effective 10/21/97; FAC 2005-33, 74 FR 28430, 6/15/2009, effective 7/15/2009; FAC 2005-73, 79 FR 24192, 4/29/2014, effective 5/29/2014]

43.103 Types of contract modifications.

Contract modifications are of the following types:

(a) *Bilateral*. A bilateral modification (supplemental agreement) is a contract modification that is signed by the contractor and the contracting officer. Bilateral modifications are used to—

(1) Make negotiated equitable adjustments resulting from the issuance of a change order;

(2) Definitize letter contracts; and

(3) Reflect other agreements of the parties modifying the terms of contracts.

(b) *Unilateral.* A unilateral modification is a contract modification that is signed only by the contracting officer. Unilateral modifications are used, for example, to—

(1) Make administrative changes;

(2) Issue change orders;

(3) Make changes authorized by clauses other than a changes clause (e.g., Property clause, Options clause, or Suspension of Work clause); and

(4) Issue termination notices.

[FAC 97-22, 66 FR 2116, 1/10/2001, effective 3/12/2001; Delay of effective date, 66 FR 14259, 3/9/2001, effective 5/11/2001]

43.104 Notification of contract changes.

(a) When a contractor considers that the Government has effected or may effect a change in the contract that has not been identified as such in writing and signed by the contracting officer, it is necessary that the contractor notify the Government in writing as soon as possible. This will permit the Government to evaluate the alleged change and—

(1) Confirm that it is a change, direct the mode of further performance, and plan for its funding;

(2) Countermand the alleged change; or

(3) Notify the contractor that no change is considered to have occurred.

(b) The clause at 52.243-7, Notification of Changes, which is prescribed in 43.107—

(1) Incorporates the policy expressed in paragraph (a) of this section;

(2) Requires the contractor to notify the Government promptly of any Government conduct that the contractor considers a change to the contract, and

(3) Specifies the responsibilities of the contractor and the Government with respect to such notifications.

[FAC 90-7, 56 FR 41744, 8/22/91, effective 9/23/91]

43.105 Availability of funds.

(a) The contracting officer shall not execute a contract modification that causes or will cause an increase in funds without having first obtained a certification of fund availability, except for modifications to contracts that—

(1) Are conditioned on availability of funds (see 32.703-2); or

(2) Contain a limitation of cost or funds clause (see 32.704).

(b) The certification required by paragraph (a) of this section shall be based on the negotiated price, except that modifications executed before agreement on price may be based on the best available estimate of cost.

43.106 [Removed and Reserved]

[Removed and Reserved, FAC 90-45, Final rule, 62 FR 224, 1/2/97, effective 1/1/97]

43.107 Contract clause.

The contracting officer may insert a clause substantially the same as the clause at 52.243-7, Notification of Changes, in solicitations and contracts. The clause is available for use primarily in negotiated research and development or supply contracts for the acquisition of major weapon systems or principal subsystems. If the contract amount is expected to be less than $1,000,000, the clause shall not be used, unless the contracting officer anticipates that situations will arise that may result in a contractor alleging that the Government has effected changes other than those identified as such in writing and signed by the contracting officer.

[Redesignated from 43.106, FAC 84-47, 54 FR 20497, 5/11/89, effective date delayed to 7/16/89, 54 FR 22282, 5/23/89]

SUBPART 43.2—CHANGE ORDERS

43.201 General.

(a) Generally, Government contracts contain a changes clause that permits the contracting officer to make unilateral changes, in designated areas, within the general scope of the contract. These are accomplished by issuing written change orders on Standard Form 30, Amendment of Solicitation/Modification of Contract (SF 30), unless otherwise provided (see 43.301).

(b) The contractor must continue performance of the contract as changed, except that in cost-reimbursement or incrementally funded contracts the contractor is not obligated to continue performance or incur costs beyond the limits established in the Limitation of Cost or Limitation of Funds clause (see 32.706-2).

(c) The contracting officer may issue a change order by electronic means without a SF 30 under unusual or urgent circumstances, *provided* that the message contains substantially the information required by the SF 30 and immediate action is taken to issue the SF 30.

(1) Copies of the message are furnished promptly to the same addressees that received the basic contract;

(2) Immediate action is taken to confirm the change by issuance of an SF 30;

(3) The message contains substantially the information required by the SF 30(except that the estimated change in price shall not be indicated), including in the body of the message the statement, "Signed by (Name), Contracting Officer"; and

(4) The contracting officer manually signs the original copy of the message.

[FAC 2005-67, 78 FR 37686, 6/21/2013, effective 6/21/2013; FAC 2005-72, 78 FR 80382,12/31/2013, effective 12/31/2013; FAC 2005-92, 81 FR 83097, 11/18/2016, effective 12/19/2016]

43.202 Authority to issue change orders.

Change orders shall be issued by the contracting officer except when authority is delegated to an administrative contracting officer (see 42.202(c)).

43.203 Change order accounting procedures.

(a) Contractors' accounting systems are seldom designed to segregate the costs of performing changed work. Therefore, before prospective contractors submit offers, the contracting officer should advise them of the possible need to revise their accounting procedures to comply with the cost segregation requirements of the Change Order Accounting clause at 52.243-6.

(b) The following categories of direct costs normally are segregable and accountable under the terms of the Change Order Accounting clause:

(1) Nonrecurring costs (*e.g.*, engineering costs and costs of obsolete or reperformed work).

(2) Costs of added distinct work caused by the change order (*e.g.*, new subcontract work, new prototypes, or new retrofit or backfit kits).

(3) Costs of recurring work (*e.g.*, labor and material costs).

43.204 Administration.

(a) *Change order documentation.* When change orders are not forward priced, they require two documents: the change order and a supplemental agreement reflecting the resulting equitable adjustment in contract terms. If an equitable adjustment in the contract price or delivery terms or both can be agreed upon in advance, only a supplemental agreement need be issued, but administrative changes and changes issued pursuant to a clause giving the Government a unilateral right to make a change (*e.g.*, an option clause) initially require only one document.

(b) *Definitization.*

(1) Contracting officers shall negotiate equitable adjustments resulting from change orders in the shortest practicable time.

(2) Administrative contracting officers negotiating equitable adjustments by delegation under 42.302(b)(1), shall obtain the contracting officer's concurrence before adjusting the contract delivery schedule.

(3) Contracting offices and contract administration offices, as appropriate, shall establish suspense systems adequate to ensure accurate identification and prompt definitization of unpriced change orders.

(4) The contracting officer shall ensure that a cost analysis is made, if appropriate, under 15.404-1(c) and shall consider the contractor's segregable costs of the change, if available. If additional funds are required as a result of the change, the contracting officer

shall secure the funds before making any adjustment to the contract.

(5) When the contracting officer requires a field pricing review of requests for equitable adjustment, the contracting officer shall provide a list of any significant contract events which may aid in the analysis of the request. This list should include—

(i) Date and dollar amount of contract award and/or modification;

(ii) Date of submission of initial contract proposal and dollar amount;

(iii) Date of alleged delays or disruptions;

(iv) Performance dates as scheduled at date of award and/or modification;

(v) Actual performance dates;

(vi) Date entitlement to an equitable adjustment was determined or contracting officer decision was rendered, if applicable;

(vii) Date of certification of the request for adjustment if certification is required; and

(viii) Dates of any pertinent Government actions or other key events during contract performance which may have an impact on the contractor's request for equitable adjustment.

(c) *Complete and final equitable adjustments.* To avoid subsequent controversies that may result from a supplemental agreement containing an equitable adjustment as the result of a change order, the contracting officer should—

(1) Ensure that all elements of the equitable adjustment have been presented and resolved; and

(2) Include, in the supplemental agreement, a release similar to the following:

CONTRACTOR'S STATEMENT OF RELEASE

In consideration of the modification(s) agreed to herein as complete equitable adjustments for the Contractor's ____ (*describe*) ____"proposal(s) for adjustment," the Contractor hereby releases the Government from any and all liability under this contract for further equitable adjustments attributable to such facts or circumstances giving rise to the "proposal(s) for adjustment" (except for ____).

[FAC 90-4, 56 FR 15154, 4/15/91, effective 5/15/91; FAC 97-2, 62 FR 51224, 9/30/97, effective 10/10/97]

43.205 Contract clauses.

(a) (1) The contracting officer shall insert the clause at 52.243-1, Changes—Fixed-Price, in solicitations and contracts when a fixed-price contract for supplies is contemplated.

(2) If the requirement is for services, other than architect-engineer or other professional services, and no supplies are to be furnished, the contracting officer shall use the clause with its Alternate I.

(3) If the requirement is for services (other than architect-engineer services, transportation, or research and development) and supplies are to be furnished, the contracting officer shall use the clause with its Alternate II.

(4) If the requirement is for architect-engineer or other professional services, the contracting officer shall use the clause with its Alternate III.

(5) If the requirement is for transportation services, the contracting officer shall use the clause with its Alternate IV.

(6) If it is desired to include the clause in solicitations and contracts when a research and development contract is contemplated, the contracting officer shall use the clause with its Alternate V.

(b) (1) The contracting officer shall insert the clause at 52.243-2, Changes—Cost-Reimbursement, in solicitations and contracts when a cost-reimbursement contract for supplies is contemplated.

(2) If the requirement is for services and no supplies are to be furnished, the contracting officer shall use the clause with its Alternate I.

(3) If the requirement is for services and supplies are to be furnished, the contracting officer shall use the clause with its Alternate II.

(4) If the requirement is for construction, the contracting officer shall use the clause with its Alternate III.

(5) [Reserved]

(6) If it is desired to include the clause in solicitations and contracts when a research and development contract is contemplated, the contracting officer shall use the clause with its Alternate V.

(c) Insert the clause at 52.243-3, Changes—Time-and-Materials or Labor-Hours, in solicitations and contracts when a time-and-materials or labor-hour contract is contemplated. The contracting officer may vary the 30-day period in paragraph (c) of the clause according to agency procedures.

(d) The contracting officer shall insert the clause at 52.243-4, Changes, in solicitations and contracts for —

(1) Dismantling, demolition, or removal of improvements; and

(2) Construction, when a fixed-price contract is contemplated and the contract amount is expected to exceed the simplified acquisition threshold.

(e) The contracting officer shall insert the clause at 52.243-5, Changes and Changed Conditions, in solicitations and contracts for construction, when the contract amount is not expected to exceed the simplified acquisition threshold.

(f) The contracting officer may insert a clause, substantially the same as the clause at 52.243-6, Change Order Accounting, in solicitations and contracts for supply and research and development contracts of significant technical complexity, if numerous changes are anticipated. The clause may be included in solicitations and contracts for construction if deemed appropriate by the contracting officer.

[FAC 90-4, 56 FR 15154, 4/15/91, effective 5/15/91; FAC 90-29, 60 FR 34732, 7/3/95, effective 7/3/95; FAC 90-40, 61 FR 39186, 7/26/96, effective 8/26/96; FAC 97-19, 65 FR 46052, 7/26/2000, effective 9/25/2000; FAC 2005-17, 72 FR 27364, 5/15/2007, effective 6/14/2007]

SUBPART 43.3—FORMS

43.301 Use of forms.

(a) (1) The Standard Form 30(SF 30), Amendment of Solicitation/Modification of Contract, shall (except for the options stated in 43.301(a)(2) or actions processed under Part 15) be used for—

(i) Any amendment to a solicitation;

(ii) Change orders issued under the Changes clause of the contract;

(iii) Any other unilateral contract modification issued under a contract clause authorizing such modification without the consent of the contractor;

(iv) Administrative changes such as the correction of typographical mistakes, changes in the paying office, and changes in accounting and appropriation data;

(v) Supplemental agreements (see 43.103); and

(vi) Removal, reinstatement, or addition of funds to a contract.

(2) The SF 30 may be used for—

(i) Modifications that change the price of contracts for the acquisition of petroleum as a result of economic price adjustment;

(ii) Termination notices; and

(iii) Purchase order modifications as specified in 13.302-3.

(3) If it is anticipated that a change will result in a price change, the estimated amount of the price change shall not be shown on copies of SF 30 furnished to the contractor.

(b) The Optional Form 336 (OF 336), Continuation Sheet, or a blank sheet of paper, may be used as a continuation sheet for a contract modification.

[FAC 84-8, 50 FR 26903, 6/28/85, effective 7/1/85; FAC 84-18, 51 FR 27120, 7/29/86, effective 7/30/86; FAC 97-2, 62 FR 51224, 9/30/97, effective 10/10/97; FAC 97-3, 62 FR 64912, 12/9/97, effective 2/9/98]

PART 44—SUBCONTRACTING POLICIES AND PROCEDURES

Table of Contents

Scope of part 44.000

Subpart 44.1—General

Definitions 44.101

Subpart 44.2—Consent to Subcontracts

Consent and advance notification requirements 44.201
Consent requirements 44.201-1
Advance notification requirements 44.201-2
Contracting officer's evaluation 44.202
Responsibilities 44.202-1
Considerations 44.202-2
Consent limitations 44.203
Contract clauses 44.204

Subpart 44.3—Contractors' Purchasing Systems Reviews

Objective 44.301
Requirements 44.302
Extent of review 44.303
Surveillance 44.304
Granting, withholding, or withdrawing approval 44.305
Responsibilities 44.305-1
Notification 44.305-2
Withholding or withdrawing approval 44.305-3
Disclosure of approval status 44.306
Reports 44.307

Subpart 44.4—Subcontracts for Commercial Items and Commercial Components

Scope of subpart 44.400
Applicability 44.401
Policy requirements 44.402
Contract clause 44.403

PART 44—SUBCONTRACTING POLICIES AND PROCEDURES

44.000 Scope of part.

(a) This part prescribes policies and procedures for consent to subcontracts or advance notification of subcontracts, and for review, evaluation, and approval of contractors' purchasing systems.

(b) The consent and advance notification requirements of subpart 44.2 are not applicable to prime contracts for commercial items acquired pursuant to part 12.

[FAC 97-5, 63 FR 34058, 6/22/98, effective 8/21/98]

SUBPART 44.1—GENERAL

44.101 Definitions.

As used in this part—

Approved purchasing system means a contractor's purchasing system that has been reviewed and approved in accordance with this part.

Contractor means the total contractor organization or a separate entity of it, such as an affiliate, division, or plant, that performs its own purchasing.

Contractor purchasing system review (CPSR) means the complete evaluation of a contractor's purchasing of material and services, subcontracting, and subcontract management from development of the requirement through completion of subcontract performance.

Subcontract means any contract as defined in Subpart 2.1 entered into by a subcontractor to furnish supplies or services for performance of a prime contract or a subcontract. It includes but is not limited to purchase orders, and changes and modifications to purchase orders.

Subcontractor means any supplier, distributor, vendor, or firm that furnishes supplies or services to or for a prime contractor or another subcontractor.

[FAC 84-8, 50 FR 26903, 6/28/85, effective 7/1/85; FAC 97-22, 66 FR 2116, 1/10/2001, effective 3/12/2001; Delay of effective date, 66 FR 14259, 3/9/2001, effective 5/11/2001; FAC 2005-17, 72 FR 27364, 5/15/2007, effective 6/14/2007]

SUBPART 44.2—CONSENT TO SUBCONTRACTS

44.201 Consent and advance notification requirements. (No Text)

44.201-1 Consent requirements.

(a) If the contractor has an approved purchasing system, consent is required for subcontracts specifically identified by the contracting officer in the subcontracts clause of the contract. The contracting officer may require consent to subcontract if the contracting officer has determined that an individual consent action is required to protect the Government adequately because of the subcontract type, complexity, or value, or because the subcontract needs special surveillance. These can be subcontracts for critical systems, subsystems, components, or services. Subcontracts may be identified by subcontract number or by class of items (*e.g.*, subcontracts for engines on a prime contract for airframes).

(b) If the contractor does not have an approved purchasing system, consent to subcontract is required for cost-reimbursement, time-and-materials, labor-hour, or letter contracts, and also for unpriced actions (including unpriced modifications and unpriced delivery orders) under fixed-price contracts that exceed the simplified acquisition threshold, for—

(1) Cost-reimbursement, time-and-materials, or labor-hour subcontracts; and

(2) Fixed-price subcontracts that exceed—

(i) For the Department of Defense, the Coast Guard, and the National Aeronautics and Space Administration, the greater of the simplified acquisition threshold or 5 percent of the total estimated cost of the contract; or

(ii) For civilian agencies other than the Coast Guard and the National Aeronautics and Space Administration, either the simplified acquisition threshold or 5 percent of the total estimated cost of the contract.

(c) Consent may be required for subcontracts under prime contracts for architect-engineer services.

(d) The contracting officer's written authorization for the contractor to purchase from Government sources (see part 51) constitutes consent.

[FAC 90-3, 55 FR 52796, 12/21/90, effective 1/22/91; FAC 97-5, 63 FR 34058, 6/22/98, effective 8/21/98]

44.201-2 Advance notification requirements.

Under cost-reimbursement contracts, the contractor is required by statute to notify the contracting officer as follows:

(a) For the Department of Defense, the Coast Guard, and the National Aeronautics and Space Administration, unless the contractor maintains an approved purchasing system, 10 U.S.C. 2306 requires notification before the award of any cost-plus-fixed-fee subcontract, or any fixed-price subcontract that exceeds the greater of the simplified acquisition threshold or 5 percent of the total estimated cost of the contract.

(b) For civilian agencies other than the Coast Guard and the National Aeronautics and Space Administration, even if the contractor has an approved purchasing system, 41 U.S.C. 3905 requires notification before the award of any cost-plus-fixed-fee subcontract, or any fixed-price subcontract that exceeds either the simplified acquisition threshold or 5 percent of the total estimated cost of the contract.

[FAC 97-5, 63 FR 34058, 6/22/98, effective 8/21/98; FAC 2005-01, 70 FR 11761, 3/9/2005, effective 3/9/2005; FAC 2005-07, 71 FR 225, 1/3/2006, effective 1/3/2005; FAC 2005-73, 79 FR 24192, 4/29/2014, effective 5/29/2014]

44.202 Contracting officer's evaluation. (No Text)

44.202-1 Responsibilities.

(a) The cognizant administrative contracting officer (ACO) is responsible for consent to subcontracts, except when the contracting officer retains the contract for administration or withholds the consent responsibility from delegation to the ACO. In such cases, the contract administration office should assist the contracting office in its evaluation as requested.

(b) The contracting officer responsible for consent shall review the contractor's notification and supporting data to ensure that the proposed subcontract is appropriate for the risks involved and consistent with current policy and sound business judgment.

(c) Designation of specific subcontractors during contract negotiations does not in itself satisfy the requirements for advance notification or consent pursuant to the clause at 52.244-2. However, if, in the opinion of the contracting officer, the advance notification or consent requirements were satisfied for certain subcontracts evaluated during negotiations, the contracting officer shall identify those subcontracts in paragraph (j) of the clause at 52.244-2.

[FAC 90-3, 55 FR 52796, 12/21/90, effective 1/22/91; FAC 97-5, 63 FR 34058, 6/22/98, effective 8/21/98; FAC 2005-17, 72 FR 27364, 5/15/2007, effective 6/14/2007]

44.202-2 Considerations.

(a) The contracting officer responsible for consent must, at a minimum, review the request and supporting data and consider the following:

(1) Is the decision to subcontract consistent with the contractor's approved make-or-buy program, if any (see 15.407-2)?

(2) Is the subcontract for special test equipment, equipment or real property that are available from Government sources?

(3) Is the selection of the particular supplies, equipment, or services technically justified?

(4) Has the contractor complied with the prime contract requirements regarding—

(i) Small business subcontracting, including, if applicable, its plan for subcontracting with small, veteran-owned, service-disabled veteran-owned, HUBZone, small disadvantaged and women-owned small business concerns (see part 19); and

(ii) Purchase from nonprofit agencies designated by the Committee for Purchase From People Who Are Blind or Severely Disabled (41 U.S.C. 8504) (see part 8)

(5) Was adequate price competition obtained or its absence properly justified?

(6) Did the contractor adequately assess and dispose of subcontractors' alternate proposals, if offered?

(7) Does the contractor have a sound basis for selecting and determining the responsibility of the particular subcontractor?

(8) Has the contractor performed adequate cost or price analysis or price comparisons and obtained certified cost or pricing data and data other than certified cost or pricing data?

(9) Is the proposed subcontract type appropriate for the risks involved and consistent with current policy?

(10) Has adequate consideration been obtained for any proposed subcontract that will involve the use of Government-provided equipment and real property?

(11) Has the contractor adequately and reasonably translated prime contract technical requirements into subcontract requirements?

(12) Does the prime contractor comply with applicable cost accounting standards for awarding the subcontract?

(13) Is the proposed subcontractor listed as excluded in the System for Award Management (see subpart 9.4)?

(b) Particularly careful and thorough consideration under paragraph (a) of this section is necessary when—

(1) The prime contractor's purchasing system or performance is inadequate;

(2) Close working relationships or ownership affiliations between the prime and subcontractor may preclude free competition or result in higher prices;

(3) Subcontracts are proposed for award on a noncompetitive basis, at prices that appear unreasonable, or at prices higher than those offered to the Government in comparable circumstances; or

(4) Subcontracts are proposed on a cost-reimbursement, time-and-materials, or labor-hour basis.

[FAC 90-28, 60 FR 33064, 6/26/95, effective 8/25/95; FAC 90-32, 60 FR 48206, 9/18/95, effective 10/1/95; FAC 97-2, 62 FR 51224, 9/30/97, effective 10/10/97; FAC 97-5, 63 FR 34058, 6/22/98, effective 8/21/98; FAC 2001-02, 66 FR 65347, 12/18/2001, effective 2/19/2002; FAC 2001-26, 69 FR 76347, 12/20/2004, effective 1/19/2005; FAC 2005-17, 72 FR 27364, 5/15/2007, effective 6/14/2007; FAC 2005-27, 73 FR 53994, 9/17/2008, effective 10/17/2008; FAC 2005-45, 75 FR 53135, 8/30/2010, effective 10/1/2010; FAC 2005-67, 78 FR 37676, 6/21/2013, effective 7/22/2013; FAC 2005-73, 79 FR 24192, 4/29/2014, effective 5/29/2014; FAC 2005-101, 83 FR 48691, 9/26/2018, effective 10/26/2018]

44.203 Consent limitations.

(a) The contracting officer's consent to a subcontract or approval of the contractor's purchasing system does not constitute a determination of the acceptability of the subcontract terms or price, or of the allowability of costs, unless the consent or approval specifies otherwise.

(b) Contracting officers shall not consent to—

(1) Cost-reimbursement subcontracts if the fee exceeds the fee limitations of 15.404-4(c)(4)(i);

(2) Subcontracts providing for payment on a cost-plus-a-percentage-of-cost basis;

(3) Subcontracts obligating the contracting officer to deal directly with the subcontractor;

(4) Subcontracts that make the results of arbitration, judicial determination, or voluntary settlement between the prime contractor and subcontractor binding on the Government; or

(5) Repetitive or unduly protracted use of cost-reimbursement, time-and-materials, or labor-hour subcontracts (contracting officers should follow the principles of 16.103(c)).

(c) Contracting officers should not refuse consent to a subcontract merely because it contains a clause giving the subcontractor the right of indirect appeal to an agency board of contract appeals if the subcontractor is affected by a dispute between the Government and the prime contractor. Indirect appeal means assertion by the subcontractor of the prime contractor's right to appeal or the prosecution of an appeal by the prime contractor on the subcontractor's behalf. The clause may also provide that the prime contractor and subcontractor shall be equally bound by the contracting officer's or board's decision. The clause may not attempt to obligate the contracting officer or the appeals board to decide questions that do not arise between the Government and the prime contractor or that are not cognizable under the clause at 52.233-1, Disputes.

[FAC 2001-26, 69 FR 76358, 12/20/2004, effective 12/20/2004]

44.204 Contract clauses.

(a) (1) The contracting officer shall insert the clause at 52.244-2, Subcontracts, in solicitations and contracts when contemplating—

(i) A cost-reimbursement contract;

(ii) A letter contract that exceeds the simplified acquisition threshold;

(iii) A fixed-price contract that exceeds the simplified acquisition threshold under which unpriced contract actions (including unpriced modifications or unpriced delivery orders) are anticipated;

(iv) A time-and-materials contract that exceeds the simplified acquisition threshold; or

(v) A labor-hour contract that exceeds the simplified acquisition threshold.

(2) If a cost-reimbursement contract is contemplated, for civilian agencies other than the Coast Guard and the National Aeronautics and Space Administration, the contracting officer shall use the clause with its Alternate I.

(3) Use of this clause is not required in—

(i) Fixed-price architect-engineer contracts; or

(ii) Contracts for mortuary services, refuse services, or shipment and storage of personal property, when an agency-prescribed clause on approval of subcontractors' facilities is required.

(b) The contracting officer may insert the clause at 52.244-4, Subcontractors and Outside Associates and Consultants (Architect-Engineer Services), in architect-engineer contracts.

(c) The contracting officer shall, when contracting by negotiation, insert the clause at 52.244-5, Competition in Subcontracting, in solicitations and contracts when the contract amount is expected to exceed the simplified acquisition threshold, unless—

(1) A firm-fixed-price contract, awarded on the basis of adequate price competition or whose prices are set by law or regulation, is contemplated; or

(2) A time-and-materials, labor-hour, or architect-engineer contract is contemplated.

[FAC 97-5, 63 FR 34058, 6/22/98, effective 8/21/98; FAC 97-14, 64 FR 51828, 9/24/99, effective 11/23/99; FAC 2005-07, 71 FR 225, 1/3/2006, effective 1/3/2006]

SUBPART 44.3—CONTRACTORS' PURCHASING SYSTEMS REVIEWS

44.301 Objective.

The objective of a contractor purchasing system review (CPSR) is to evaluate the efficiency and effectiveness with which the contractor spends Government funds and complies with Government policy when subcontracting. The review provides the administrative contracting officer (ACO) a basis for granting, withholding, or withdrawing approval of the contractor's purchasing system.

44.302 Requirements.

(a) The ACO shall determine the need for a CPSR based on, but not limited to, the past performance of the contractor, and the volume, complexity and dollar value of subcontracts. If a contractor's sales to the Government (excluding competitively awarded firm-fixed-price and competitively awarded fixed-price with economic price adjustment contracts and sales of commercial items pursuant to Part 12) are expected to exceed $25 million during the next 12 months, perform a review to determine if a CPSR is needed. Sales include those represented by prime contracts, subcontracts under Government prime contracts, and modifications. Generally, a CPSR is not performed for a specific contract. The head of the agency responsible for contract administration may raise or lower the $25 million review level if it is considered to be in the Government's best interest.

(b) Once an initial determination has been made under paragraph (a) of this section, at least every three years the ACO shall determine whether a purchasing system review is necessary. If necessary, the cognizant contract administration office will conduct a purchasing system review.

[FAC 97-10, 63 FR 70264, 12/18/98, effective 2/16/99]

44.303 Extent of review.

A CPSR requires an evaluation of the contractor's purchasing system. Unless segregation of subcontracts is impracticable, this evaluation shall not include subcontracts awarded by the contractor exclusively in support of Government contracts that are competitively awarded firm-fixed-price, competitively awarded fixed-price with economic price adjustment, or awarded for commercial items pursuant to part 12. The considerations listed in 44.202-2 for consent evaluation of particular subcontracts also shall be used to evaluate the contractor's purchasing system, including the contractor's policies, procedures, and performance under that system. Special attention shall be given to—

(a) The results of market research accomplished;

(b) The degree of price competition obtained;

(c) Pricing policies and techniques, including methods of obtaining certified cost or pricing data, and data other than certified cost or pricing data;

(d) Methods of evaluating subcontractor responsibility, including the contractor's use of the System for Award Management (see 9.404) and, if the contractor has subcontracts with parties on the Exclusions list, the documentation, systems, and procedures the contractor has established to protect the Government's interests (see 9.405-2);

(e) Treatment accorded affiliates and other concerns having close working arrangements with the contractor;

(f) Policies and procedures pertaining to small business concerns, including small disadvantaged, women-owned, veteran-owned, HUBZone, and service-disabled veteran-owned small business concerns;

(g) Planning, award, and postaward management of major subcontract programs;

(h) Compliance with Cost Accounting Standards in awarding subcontracts;

(i) Appropriateness of types of contracts used (see 16.103);

(j) Management control systems, including internal audit procedures, to administer progress payments to subcontractors; and

(k) Implementation of higher-level quality standards.

[FAC 84-25, 52 FR 9039, 3/20/87, effective 7/1/87; FAC 84-46, 54 FR 19827, 5/8/89, effective 6/7/89; FAC 90-28, 60 FR 33064, 6/26/95, effective 8/25/95; FAC 90-32, 60 FR 48206, 9/18/95, effective 10/1/95; FAC 90-46, 62 FR 12690, 3/17/97, effective 5/16/97; FAC 97-10, 63 FR 70264, 12/18/98, effective 2/16/99; FAC 2001-26, 69 FR 76347, 12/20/2004, effective 1/19/2005; FAC 2005-02, 70 FR 14950, 3/23/2005, effective 3/23/2005; FAC 2005-42, 75 FR 34277, 6/16/2010, effective 6/16/2010; FAC 2005-45, 75 FR 53135, 8/30/2010, effective 10/1/2010; FAC 2005-50, 76 FR 14562, 3/16/2011, effective 4/15/2011; FAC 2005-67, 78 FR 37676, 6/21/2013, effective 7/22/2013; FAC 2005-78, 79 FR 70344, 11/25/2014, effective 12/26/2014]

44.304 Surveillance.

(a) The ACO shall maintain a sufficient level of surveillance to ensure that the contractor is effectively managing its purchasing program.

(b) Surveillance shall be accomplished in accordance with a plan developed by the ACO with the assistance of subcontracting, audit, pricing, technical, or other specialists as necessary. The plan should cover pertinent phases of a contractor's purchasing system (preaward, postaward, performance, and contract completion) and pertinent operations that affect the contractor's purchasing and subcontracting. The plan should also provide for reviewing the effectiveness of the contractor's corrective actions taken as a result of previous Government recommendations. Duplicative reviews of the same areas by CPSR and other surveillance monitors should be avoided.

[FAC 90-23, 59 FR 67010, 12/28/94, effective 2/27/95; FAC 90-46, 62 FR 12690, 3/17/97, effective 5/16/97]

44.305 Granting, withholding, or withdrawing approval. (No Text)

44.305-1 Responsibilities.

The cognizant ACO is responsible for granting, withholding, or withdrawing approval of a contractor's purchasing system. The ACO shall—

(a) Approve a purchasing system only after determining that the contractor's purchasing policies and practices are efficient and provide adequate protection of the Government's interests; and

(b) Promptly notify the contractor in writing of the granting, withholding, or withdrawal of approval.

[FAC 90-46, 62 FR 12690, 3/17/97, effective 5/16/97]

44.305-2 Notification.

(a) The notification granting system approval shall include—

(1) Identification of the plant or plants covered by the approval;

(2) The effective date of approval; and

(3) A statement that system approval—

(i) Applies to all Federal Government contracts at that plant to the extent that cross-servicing arrangements exist;

(ii) Waives the contractual requirement for advance notification in fixed-price contracts, but not for cost-reimbursement contracts;

(iii) Waives the contractual requirement for consent to subcontracts in fixed-price contracts and for specified subcontracts in cost-reimbursement contracts but not for those subcontracts, if any, selected for special surveillance and identified in the contract Schedule; and

(iv) May be withdrawn at any time at the ACO's discretion.

(b) In exceptional circumstances, consent to certain subcontracts or classes of subcontracts may be required even though the contractor's purchasing system has been approved. The system approval notification shall identify the class or classes of subcontracts requiring consent. Reasons for selecting the subcontracts include the fact that a CPSR or continuing surveillance has revealed sufficient weaknesses in a particular area of subcontracting to warrant special attention by the ACO.

(c) When recommendations are made for improvement of an approved system, the contractor shall be requested to reply within 15 days with a position regarding the recommendations.

[FAC 90-46, 62 FR 12690, 3/17/97, effective 5/16/97]

44.305-3 Withholding or withdrawing approval.

(a) The ACO shall withhold or withdraw approval of a contractor's purchasing system when there are major weaknesses or when the contractor is unable to provide sufficient information upon which to make an affirmative determination. The ACO may withdraw approval at any time on the basis of a determination that there has been a deterioration of the contractor's purchasing system or to protect the Government's interest. Approval shall be withheld or withdrawn when there is a recurring noncompliance with requirements, including but not limited to—

(1) Certified cost or pricing data (see 15.403);

(2) Implementation of cost accounting standards (see 48 CFR Chapter 99 (FAR Appendix, loose-leaf edition));

(3) Advance notification as required by the clauses prescribed in 44.204; or

(4) Small business subcontracting (see Subpart 19.7).

(b) When approval of the contractor's purchasing system is withheld or withdrawn, the ACO shall within 10 days after completing the in-plant review

(1) inform the contractor in writing,

(2) specify the deficiencies that must be corrected to qualify the system for approval, and—

(3) request the contractor to furnish within 15 days a plan for accomplishing the necessary actions. If the plan is accepted, the ACO shall make a follow-up review as soon as the contractor notifies the ACO that the deficiencies have been corrected.

[FAC 90-23, 59 FR 67010, 12/28/94, effective 2/27/95; corrected 60 FR 14377, 3/17/95; FAC 97-2, 62 FR 51224, 9/30/97, effective 10/10/97; FAC 2005-45, 75 FR 53135, 8/30/2010, effective 10/1/2010]

44.306 Disclosure of approval status.

Upon request, the ACO may inform a contractor that the purchasing system of a proposed subcontractor has been approved or disapproved, but shall caution that the Government will not keep the contractor advised of any changes in the approval status. If the proposed subcontractor's purchasing system has not been reviewed, the contractor shall be so advised.

[FAC 90-46, 62 FR 12690, 3/17/97, effective 5/16/97]

44.307 Reports.

The ACO shall distribute copies of CPSR reports; notifications granting, withholding, or withdrawing system approval; and Government recommendations for improvement of an approved system, including the contractor's response, to at least—

(a) The cognizant contract audit office;

(b) Activities prescribed by the cognizant agency; and

(c) The contractor (except that furnishing copies of the contractor's response is optional).

[FAC 90-46, 62 FR 12690, 3/17/97, effective 5/16/97]

SUBPART 44.4—SUBCONTRACTS FOR COMMERCIAL ITEMS AND COMMERCIAL COMPONENTS

44.400 Scope of subpart.

This subpart prescribes the policies limiting the contract clauses a contractor may be required to apply to any subcontractors that are furnishing commercial items or commercial components in accordance with 41 U.S.C 3307.

[FAC 90-32, 60 FR 48206, 9/18/95, effective 10/1/95; FAC 2005-42, 75 FR 34277, 6/16/2010, effective 6/16/2010; FAC 2005-50, 76 FR 14562, 3/16/2011, effective 4/15/2011; FAC 2005-73, 79 FR 24192, 4/29/2014, effective 5/29/2014]

44.401 Applicability.

This subpart applies to all contracts and subcontracts. For the purpose of this subpart, the term *subcontract* has the same meaning as defined in Part 12.

[FAC 90-32, 60 FR 48206, 9/18/95, effective 10/1/95]

44.402 Policy requirements.

(a) Contractors and subcontractors at all tiers shall, to the maximum extent practicable:

(1) Be required to incorporate commercial items or nondevelopmental items as components of items delivered to the Government; and

(2) Not be required to apply to any of its divisions, subsidiaries, affiliates, subcontractors or suppliers that are furnishing commercial items or commercial components any clause, except those—

(i) Required to implement provisions of law or executive orders applicable to subcontractors furnishing commercial items or commercial components; or

(ii) Determined to be consistent with customary commercial practice for the item being acquired.

(b) The clause at 52.244-6, Subcontracts for Commercial Items, implements the policy in paragraph (a) of this section. Notwithstanding any other clause in the prime contract, only those clauses identified in the clause at 52.244-6 are required to be in subcontracts for commercial items or commercial components.

(c) Agencies may supplement the clause at 52.244-6 only as necessary to reflect agency unique statutes applicable to the acquisition of commercial items.

[FAC 90-32, 60 FR 48206, 9/18/95, effective 10/1/95; FAC 2005-42, 75 FR 34277,

6/16/2010, effective 6/16/2010; FAC 2005-50, 76 FR 14562, 3/16/2011, effective 4/15/2011; FAC 2005-73, 79 FR 24192, 4/29/2014, effective 5/29/2014]

44.403 Contract clause.

The contracting officer shall insert the clause at 52.244-6, Subcontracts for Commercial Items, in solicitations and contracts other than those for commercial items.

[FAC 90-32, 60 FR 48206, 9/18/95, effective 10/1/95; FAC 2005-01, 70 FR 11762, 3/9/2005, effective 3/9/2005; FAC 2005-42, 75 FR 34277, 6/16/2010, effective 6/16/2010; FAC 2005-50, 76 FR 14562, 3/16/2011, effective 4/15/2011]

PART 45—GOVERNMENT PROPERTY

Table of Contents

Scope of part . . . 45.000

Subpart 45.1—General

Definitions . . . 45.101
Policy . . . 45.102
General . . . 45.103
Responsibility and liability for Government property . . . 45.104
Contractors' property management system compliance . . . 45.105
Transferring accountability . . . 45.106
Contract clauses . . . 45.107

Subpart 45.2—Solicitation and Evaluation Procedures

Solicitation . . . 45.201
Evaluation procedures . . . 45.202

Subpart 45.3—Authorizing the Use and Rental of Government Property

Use and rental . . . 45.301
Contracts with foreign governments or international organizations . . . 45.302
Use of Government property on independent research and development programs . . . 45.303

Subpart 45.4—Title to Government Property

Title to Government-furnished property . . . 45.401
Title to contractor-acquired property . . . 45.402

Subpart 45.5—Support Government Property Administration

Prime contractor alternate locations . . . 45.501
Subcontractor and alternate prime contractor locations . . . 45.502
Support property administrator findings . . . 45.503

Subpart 45.6—Reporting, Reutilization, and Disposal

Scope of subpart . . . 45.600
[Removed and Reserved] . . . 45.601
Reutilization of Government property . . . 45.602
Inventory disposal schedules . . . 45.602-1
Reutilization priorities . . . 45.602-2
Screening . . . 45.602-3
Interagency property transfer costs . . . 45.602-4
Abandonment or destruction of personal property . . . 45.603
Sale of surplus personal property . . . 45.604
Sales procedures . . . 45.604-1
Use of GSA sponsored sales centers . . . 45.604-2
Proceeds from sales of surplus property . . . 45.604-3
Sale of property pursuant to the exchange/sale authority . . . 45.604-4
Inventory disposal reports . . . 45.605
Contractor scrap procedures . . . 45.606
[Removed] . . . 45.606-1
[Removed] . . . 45.606-2
[Removed] . . . 45.606-3

PART 45—GOVERNMENT PROPERTY

45.000 Scope of part.

(a) This part prescribes policies and procedures for providing Government property to contractors; contractors' management and use of Government property; and reporting, redistributing, and disposing of contractor inventory.

(b) It does not apply to—

(1) Government property provided under any statutory leasing authority, except as to non-Government use of property under 45.301(f);

(2) Property to which the Government has acquired a lien or title solely because of partial, advance, progress, or performance based payments;

(3) Disposal of real property;

(4) Software and intellectual property; or

(5) Government property that is incidental to the place of performance, when the contract requires contractor personnel to be located on a Government site or installation, and when the property used by the contractor within the location remains accountable to the Government. Items considered to be incidental to the place of performance include, for example, office space, desks, chairs, telephones, computers, and fax machines.

[FAC 2005-17, 72 FR 27364, 5/15/2007, effective 6/14/2007; FAC 2005-56, 77 FR 12937, 3/2/2012, effective 4/2/2012]

SUBPART 45.1—GENERAL

45.101 Definitions.

As used in this part—

Cannibalize means to remove parts from Government property for use or for installation on other Government property.

Contractor-acquired property means property acquired, fabricated, or otherwise provided by the contractor for performing a contract and to which the Government has title.

Contractor inventory means—

(1) Any property acquired by and in the possession of a contractor or subcontractor under a contract for which title is vested in the Government and which exceeds the amounts needed to complete full performance under the entire contract;

(2) Any property that the Government is obligated or has the option to take over under any type of contract, e.g., as a result either of any changes in the specifications or plans thereunder or of the termination of the contract (or subcontract thereunder), before completion of the work, for the convenience or at the option of the Government; and

(3) Government-furnished property that exceeds the amounts needed to complete full performance under the entire contract.

Contractor's managerial personnel means the contractor's directors, officers, managers, superintendents, or equivalent representatives who have supervision or direction of—

(1) All or substantially all of the contractor's business;

(2) All or substantially all of the contractor's operation at any one plant or separate location; or

(3) A separate and complete major industrial operation.

Demilitarization means rendering a product unusable for, and not restorable to, the purpose for which it was designed or is customarily used.

Discrepancies incident to shipment means any differences (e.g., count or condition) between the items documented to have been shipped and items actually received.

Equipment means a tangible item that is functionally complete for its intended purpose, durable, nonexpendable, and needed for the performance of a contract. Equipment is not intended for sale, and does not ordinarily lose its identity or become a component part of another article when put into use. Equipment does not include material, real property, special test equipment or special tooling.

Government-furnished property means property in the possession of, or directly acquired by, the Government and subsequently furnished to the contractor for performance of a contract. Government-furnished property includes, but is not limited to, spares and property furnished for repair, maintenance, overhaul, or modification. Government-furnished property also includes contractor-acquired property if the contractor-acquired property is a deliverable under a cost contract when accepted by the Government for continued use under the contract.

Government property means all property owned or leased by the Government. Government property includes both Government-furnished property and contractor-acquired property. Government property includes material, equipment, special tooling, special test equipment, and real property. Government property does not include intellectual property and software.

Loss of Government property means unintended, unforeseen or accidental loss, damage, or destruction of Government property that reduces the Government's expected economic benefits of the property. Loss of Government property does not include occurrences such as purposeful destructive testing, obsolescence, normal wear and tear, or manufacturing defects. Loss of Government property includes, but is not limited to—

(1) Items that cannot be found after a reasonable search;

(2) Theft;

(3) Damage resulting in unexpected harm to property requiring repair to restore the item to usable condition; or

(4) Destruction resulting from incidents that render the item useless for its intended purpose or beyond economical repair.

Material means property that may be consumed or expended during the performance of a contract, component parts of a higher assembly, or items that lose their individual identity through incorporation into an end-item. Material does not include equipment, special tooling, special test equipment or real property.

Nonseverable means property that cannot be removed after construction or installation without substantial loss of value or damage to the installed property or to the premises where installed.

Precious metals means silver, gold, platinum, palladium, iridium, osmium, rhodium, and ruthenium.

Production scrap means unusable material resulting from production, engineering, operations and maintenance, repair, and research and development contract activities. Production scrap may have value when remelted or reprocessed, *e.g.*, textile and metal clippings, borings, and faulty castings and forgings.

Property means all tangible property, both real and personal.

Property Administrator means an authorized representative of the contracting officer appointed in accordance with agency procedures, responsible for administering the contract requirements and obligations relating to Government property in the possession of a contractor.

Property records means the records created and maintained by the contractor in support of its stewardship responsibilities for the management of Government property.

Provide means to furnish, as in Government-furnished property, or to acquire, as in contractor-acquired property.

Real property. See Federal Management Regulation 102-71.20 (41 CFR 102-71.20).

Sensitive property means property potentially dangerous to the public safety or security if stolen, lost, or misplaced, or that shall be subject to exceptional physical security, protection, control, and accountability. Examples include weapons, ammunition, explosives, controlled substances, radioactive materials, hazardous materials or wastes, or precious metals.

Unit acquisition cost means—

(1) For Government-furnished property, the dollar value assigned by the Government and identified in the contract; and

(2) For contractor-acquired property, the cost derived from the contractor's records that reflect consistently applied generally accepted accounting principles.

[FAC 84-16, 51 FR 19716, 5/30/86, effective 5/30/86, corrected 51 FR 33270, 9/19/86; FAC 84-38, 53 FR 27468, 7/20/88, effective 8/19/88; FAC 2005-17, 72 FR 27364,

5/15/2007, effective 6/14/2007; FAC 2005-43, 75 FR 38675, 7/2/2010, effective 8/2/2010; FAC 2005-56, 77 FR 12937, 3/2/2012, effective 4/2/2012]

45.102 Policy.

(a) Contractors are ordinarily required to furnish all property necessary to perform Government contracts.

(b) Contracting officers shall provide property to contractors only when it is clearly demonstrated—

(1) To be in the Government's best interest;

(2) That the overall benefit to the acquisition significantly outweighs the increased cost of administration, including ultimate property disposal;

(3) That providing the property does not substantially increase the Government's assumption of risk; and

(4) That Government requirements cannot otherwise be met.

(c) The contractor's inability or unwillingness to supply its own resources is not sufficient reason for the furnishing or acquisition of property.

(d) *Exception.* Property provided under contracts for repair, maintenance, overhaul, or modification is not subject to the requirements of paragraph (b) of this section.

(e) Government property, other than foundations and similar improvements necessary for installing special tooling, special test equipment, or equipment, shall not be installed or constructed on contractor-owned real property in such fashion as to become nonseverable, unless the head of the contracting activity determines that such installation or construction is necessary and in the Government's interest.

[Final rule, FAC 2001-22, 69 FR 17741, 4/5/2004, effective 5/5/2004; FAC 2005-17, 72 FR 27364, 5/15/2007, effective 6/14/2007; FAC 2005-43, 75 FR 38675, 7/2/2010, effective 8/2/2010; FAC 2005-56, 77 FR 12937, 3/2/2012, effective 4/2/2012]

45.103 General.

(a) Agencies shall—

(1) Allow and encourage contractors to use voluntary consensus standards (see FAR 11.101(b)) and industry-leading practices and standards to manage Government property in their possession;

(2) Eliminate to the maximum practical extent any competitive advantage a prospective contractor may have by using Government property;

(3) Ensure maximum practical reutilization of contractor inventory for government purposes;

(4) Require contractors to use Government property already in their possession to the maximum extent practical in performing Government contracts;

(5) Charge appropriate rentals when the property is authorized for use on other than a rent-free basis; and

(6) Require contractors to justify retaining Government property not needed for contract performance and to declare property as excess when no longer needed for contract performance.

(b) Agencies will not generally require contractors to establish property management systems that are separate from a contractor's established procedures, practices, and systems used to account for and manage contractor-owned property.

[FAC 84-32, 53 FR 663, 1/11/88, effective 1/29/88; FAC 90-32, 60 FR 48206, 9/18/95, effective 10/1/95; FAC 97-2, 62 FR 51224, 9/30/97, effective 10/10/97; FAC 2005-17, 72 FR 27364, 5/15/2007, effective 6/14/2007; FAC 2005-21, Final rule, 72 FR 63040, 11/7/2007, effective 12/7/2007]

45.104 Responsibility and liability for Government property.

(a) Generally, contractors are not held liable for loss of Government property under the following types of contracts:

(1) Cost-reimbursement contracts.

(2) Time-and-material contracts.

(3) Labor-hour contracts.

(4) Fixed-price contracts awarded on the basis of submission of certified cost or pricing data.

(b) The contracting officer may revoke the Government's assumption of risk when the property administrator determines that the contractor's property management practices are noncompliant with contract requirements.

(c) A prime contractor that provides Government property to a subcontractor shall not be relieved of any responsibility to the Government that the prime contractor may have under the terms of the prime contract.

(d) With respect to loss of Government property, the contracting officer, in consultation with the property administrator, shall determine—

(1) The extent, if any, of contractor liability based upon the amount of damages corresponding to the associated property loss; and

(2) The appropriate form and method of Government recovery (may include repair, replacement, or other restitution).

(e) Any monies received as financial restitution shall be credited to the Treasury of the United States as miscellaneous receipts, unless otherwise authorized by statute (31 U.S.C. 3302(b)).

[FAC 2005-17, 72 FR 27364, 5/15/2007, effective 6/14/2007; FAC 2005-43, 75 FR 38675, 7/2/2010, effective 8/2/2010; FAC 2005-45, 75 FR 53135, 8/30/2010, effective 10/1/2010; FAC 2005-56, 77 FR 12937, 3/2/2012, effective 4/2/2012]

45.105 Contractors' property management system compliance.

(a) The agency responsible for contract administration shall conduct an analysis of the contractor's property management policies, procedures, practices, and systems. This analysis shall be accomplished as frequently as conditions warrant, in accordance with agency procedures.

(b) The property administrator shall notify the contractor in writing when the contractor's property management system does not comply with contractual requirements, shall request prompt correction of deficiencies, and shall request from the contractor a corrective action plan, including a schedule for correction of the deficiencies. If the contractor does not correct the deficiencies in accordance with the schedule, the contracting officer shall notify the contractor, in writing, that failure to take the required corrective action(s) may result in—

(1) Revocation of the Government's assumption of risk for loss of Government property; and/or

(2) The exercise of other rights or remedies available to the contracting officer.

(c) If the contractor fails to take the required corrective action(s) in response to the notification provided by the contracting officer in accordance with paragraph (b) of this section, the contracting officer shall notify the contractor in writing of any Government decision to apply the remedies described in paragraphs (b)(1) and (b)(2) of this section.

(d) When the property administrator determines that a reported case of loss of Government property is a risk assumed by the Government, the property administrator shall notify the contractor in writing that it is granted relief of stewardship responsibility and liability in accordance with 52.245-1(f)(1)(vii). Where the property administrator determines that the risk of loss of Government property is not assumed by the Government, the property administrator shall request that the contracting officer hold the contractor responsible and liable.

[FAC 84-12, 51 FR 2666, 1/17/86, effective 1/20/86; FAC 90-16, 57 FR 60588, 12/21/92, effective 2/19/93; FAC 2005-17, 72 FR 27364, 5/15/2007, effective 6/14/2007; FAC 2005-43, 75 FR 38675, 7/2/2010, effective 8/2/2010; FAC 2005-56, 77 FR 12937, 3/2/2012, effective 4/2/2012]

45.106 Transferring accountability.

Government property shall be transferred from one contract to another only when firm requirements exist under the gaining contract (see 45.102). Such transfers shall be documented by modifications to both gaining and losing contracts. Once transferred, all property shall be considered Government-furnished property to the gaining contract. The warranties of suitability of use and timely delivery of Government-furnished property do not apply to property acquired or fabricated by the contractor as contractor-acquired property that is subsequently transferred to another contract with the same contractor.

[FAC 84-32, 53 FR 663, 1/11/88, effective 1/29/88; FAC 90-16, 57 FR 60588, 12/21/92, effective 2/19/93; FAC 90-29, 60 FR 34732, 7/3/95, effective 7/3/95; FAC 90-32, 60 FR 48206, 9/18/95, effective 10/1/95; FAC 90-40, 61 FR 39186, 7/26/96, effective 8/26/96; FAC 97-2, 62 FR 51224, 9/30/97, effective 10/10/97; FAC 2005-05, 70 FR 43583, 7/27/2005, effective 8/26/2005; FAC 2005-17, 72 FR 27364, 5/15/2007, effective 6/14/2007]

45.107 Contract clauses.

(a) (1) Except as provided in paragraph (d) of this section, the contracting officer shall insert the clause at 52.245-1, Government Property, in—

(i) All cost-reimbursement and time-and-material type solicitations and contracts, and labor-hour solicitations when property is expected to be furnished for the labor-hour contracts.

(ii) Fixed-price solicitations and contracts when the Government will provide Government property.

(iii) Contracts or modifications awarded under FAR Part 12 procedures where Government property that exceeds the simplified acquisition threshold, as defined in FAR 2.101, is furnished or where the contractor is directed to acquire property for use under the contract that is titled in the Government.

(2) The contracting officer shall use the clause with its Alternate I in contracts other than those identified in FAR 45.104(a), Responsibility and Liability for Government Property.

(3) The contracting officer shall use the clause with its Alternate II when a contract for the conduct of basic or applied research at nonprofit institutions of higher education or at nonprofit organizations whose primary purpose is the conduct of scientific research (see 35.014) is contemplated.

(b) The contracting officer shall also insert the clause at 52.245-2, Government Property (Installation Operation Services), in fixed-price service contracts to be performed on a Government installation when Government-furnished property will be provided for initial provisioning only and the Government is not responsible for repair or replacement.

(c) The contracting officer shall insert the clause at 52.245-9, Use and Charges, in solicitations and contracts when the clause at 52.245-1 is included.

(d) Purchase orders for property repair need not include a Government property clause when the unit acquisition cost of Government property to be repaired does not exceed the simplified acquisition threshold, unless other Government property (not for repair) is provided.

[FAC 2005-17, 72 FR 27364, 5/15/2007, effective 6/14/2007; FAC 2005-56, 77 FR 12937, 3/2/2012, effective 4/2/2012]

SUBPART 45.2—SOLICITATION AND EVALUATION PROCEDURES

45.201 Solicitation.

(a) The contracting officer shall insert a listing of the Government property to be offered in all solicitations where Government-furnished property is anticipated (see 45.102). The listing shall include at a minimum—

(1) The name, part number and description, manufacturer, model number, and National Stock Number (if needed for additional item identification tracking and management, and disposition);

(2) Quantity/unit of measure;

(3) Unit acquisition cost;

(4) Unique-item identifier or equivalent (if available and necessary for individual item tracking and management); and

(5) A statement as to whether the property is to be furnished in an "as-is" condition and instructions for physical inspection.

(b) When Government property is offered for use in a competitive acquisition, solicitations should specify that the contractor is responsible for all costs related to making the property available for use, such as payment of all transportation, installation or rehabilitation costs.

(c) The solicitation shall describe the evaluation procedures to be followed, including rental charges or equivalents and other costs or savings to be evaluated, and shall require all offerors to submit the following information with their offers—

(1) A list or description of all Government property that the offeror or its subcontractors propose to use on a rent-free basis. The list shall identify the accountable contract under which the property is held and the authorization for its use (from the contracting officer having cognizance of the property);

(2) The dates during which the property will be available for use (including the first, last, and all intervening months) and, for any property that will be used concurrently in performing two or more contracts, the amounts of the respective uses in sufficient detail to support prorating the rent;

(3) The amount of rent that would otherwise be charged in accordance with FAR 52.245-9, Use and Charges; and

(4) A description of the offeror's property management system, plan, and any customary commercial practices, voluntary consensus standards, or industry-leading practices and standards to be used by the offeror in managing Government property.

(d) Any additional instructions to the contractor regarding property management, accountability, and use, not addressed in FAR clause 52.245-1, Government Property, should be specifically addressed in the statement of work on the contract providing property or in a special provision.

[FAC 2005-17, 72 FR 27364, 5/15/2007, effective 6/14/2007; FAC 2005-43, 75 FR 38675, 7/2/2010, effective 8/2/2010; FAC 2005-56, 77 FR 12937, 3/2/2012, effective 4/2/2012]

45.202 Evaluation procedures.

(a) The contracting officer shall consider any potentially unfair competitive advantage that may result from an offeror or contractor possessing Government property. This shall be done by adjusting the offers by applying, for evaluation purposes only, a rental equivalent evaluation factor as specified in FAR 52.245-9.

(b) The contracting officer shall ensure the offeror's property management plans, methods, practices, or procedures for accounting for property are consistent with the requirements of the solicitation.

[FAC 2005-17, 72 FR 27364, 5/15/2007, effective 6/14/2007; FAC 2005-56, 77 FR 12937, 3/2/2012, effective 4/2/2012]

SUBPART 45.3—AUTHORIZING THE USE AND RENTAL OF GOVERNMENT PROPERTY

45.301 Use and rental.

This subpart prescribes policies and procedures for contractor use and rental of Government property.

(a) Government property shall normally be provided on a rent-free basis in performance of the contract under which it is accountable or otherwise authorized.

(b) Rental charges, to the extent authorized do not apply to Government property that is left in place or installed on contractor-owned property for mobilization or future Government production purposes; however, rental charges shall apply to that portion of property or its capacity used for non-government commercial purposes or otherwise authorized for use.

(c) The contracting officer cognizant of the Government property may authorize the rent-free use of property in the possession of nonprofit organizations when used for research, development, or educational work and—

(1) The use of the property is in the national interest;

(2) The property will not be used for the direct benefit of a profit-making organization; and

(3) The Government receives some direct benefit, such as rights to use the results of the work without charge, from its use.

(d) In exchange for consideration as determined by the cognizant contracting officer(s), the contractor may use Government property under fixed-price contracts other than the contract to which it is accountable.

When, after contract award, a contractor requests the use of Government property, the contracting officer shall obtain a fair rental or other adequate consideration if use is authorized.

(e) The cognizant contracting officer(s) may authorize the use of Government property on a rent-free basis on a cost type Government contract other than the contract to which it is accountable.

(f) In exchange for consideration as determined by the cognizant contracting officer, the contractor may use Government property for commercial use. Prior approval of the Head of the Contracting Activity is required where non-Government use is expected to exceed 25 percent of the total use of Government and commercial work performed.

[FAC 2005-17, 72 FR 27364, 5/15/2007, effective 6/14/2007]

45.302 Contracts with foreign governments or international organizations.

Requests by, or for the benefit of, foreign Governments or international organizations to use Government property shall be processed in accordance with agency procedures.

[FAC 2005-17, 72 FR 27364, 5/15/2007, effective 6/14/2007]

45.303 Use of Government property on independent research and development programs.

The contracting officer may authorize a contractor to use the property on an independent research and development (IR&D) program, if—

(a) Such use will not conflict with the primary use of the property or enable the contractor to retain property that could otherwise be released;

(b) The contractor agrees not to claim reimbursement against any Government contract for the rental value of the property; and

(c) A rental charge for the portion of the contractor's IR&D program cost allocated to commercial work is deducted from the claim for reimbursement of any agreed-upon Government share of the contractor's IR&D costs.

[FAC 2005-17, 72 FR 27364, 5/15/2007, effective 6/14/2007]

SUBPART 45.4—TITLE TO GOVERNMENT PROPERTY

45.401 Title to Government-furnished property.

The Government retains title to all Government-furnished property until properly disposed of, as authorized by law or regulation. Property that is leased by the Government and subsequently furnished to the contractor for use shall be considered Government-furnished property under the clause 52.245-1, Government Property.

[FAC 84-16, 51 FR 19717, 5/30/86, effective 5/30/86; FAC 2005-17, 72 FR 27364, 5/15/2007, effective 6/14/2007]

45.402 Title to contractor-acquired property.

(a) Title vests in the Government for all property acquired or fabricated by the contractor in accordance with the financing provisions or other specific requirements for passage of title in the contract. Under fixed-price type contracts, in the absence of financing provisions or other specific requirements for passage of title in the contract, the contractor retains title to all property acquired by the contractor for use on the contract, except for property identified as a deliverable end item. If a deliverable item is to be retained by the contractor for use after inspection and acceptance by the Government, it shall be made accountable to the contract through a contract modification listing the item as Government-furnished property.

(b) Under cost type and time-and-material contracts, the Government acquires title to all property to which the contractor is entitled to reimbursement, in accordance with paragraph (e)(3) of clause 52.245-1.

[FAC 2005-17, 72 FR 27364, 5/15/2007, effective 6/14/2007; FAC 2005-43, 75 FR 38675, 7/2/2010, effective 8/2/2010]

SUBPART 45.5—SUPPORT GOVERNMENT PROPERTY ADMINISTRATION

45.501 Prime contractor alternate locations.

The property administrator assigned to the prime contract may request support property administration from another contract administration office, for purposes of evaluating prime contractor management of property located at subcontractors and alternate locations.

[Final rule, FAC 90-20, 59 FR 11368, 3/10/94, effective 5/9/94; Final rule, FAC 2001-22, 69 FR 17741, 4/5/2004, effective 5/5/2004; FAC 2005-17, 72 FR 27364, 5/15/2007, effective 6/14/2007]

45.502 Subcontractor and alternate prime contractor locations.

(a) To ensure subcontractor compliance with Government property administration requirements, and with prime contractor consent, the property administrator assigned to the prime contract may request support property administration from another contract administration office. If the prime contractor does not provide consent to support property administration at subcontractor locations, the property administrator shall refer the matter to the contracting officer for resolution.

(b) The prime property administrator shall accept the findings of the delegated support property administrator and advise the prime contractor of the results of property management reviews, including deficiencies found with the subcontractor's property management system.

(c) Prime contractor consent is not required for support delegations involving prime contractor alternate locations.

[FAC 84-12, 51 FR 2666, 1/17/86, effective 1/20/86; FAC 2005-17, 72 FR 27364, 5/15/2007, effective 6/14/2007; FAC 2005-43, 75 FR 38675, 7/2/2010, effective 8/2/2010]

45.503 Support property administrator findings.

In instances where the prime contractor does not concur with the findings of the support Property Administrator, the prime property administrator shall immediately refer the matter to the contracting officer.

[FAC 2005-17, 72 FR 27364, 5/15/2005, effective 6/14/2007]

SUBPART 45.6—REPORTING, REUTILIZATION, AND DISPOSAL

45.600 Scope of subpart.

This subpart establishes policies and procedures for the reporting, reutilization, and disposal of contractor inventory excess to contracts and of property that forms the basis of a claim against the Government (e.g., termination inventory under fixed-price contracts). This subpart does not apply to the disposal of real property or to property for which the Government has a lien or title solely as a result of advance, progress, or performance-based payments that have been liquidated.

[FAC 2001-22, 69 FR 17741, 4/5/2004, effective 5/5/2004; FAC 2005-17, 72 FR 27364, 5/15/2007, effective 6/14/2007]

45.601 [Removed and Reserved]

[FAC 2001-22, 69 FR 17741, 4/5/2004, effective 5/5/2004; FAC 2005-17, 72 FR 27364, 5/15/2007, effective 6/14/2007]

45.602 Reutilization of Government property.

This section is applicable to the reutilization, including transfer and donation, of Government property that is not required for continued performance of a Government contract. Except for 45.602-1, this section does not apply to scrap other than scrap aircraft parts.

[FAC 2001-22, 69 FR 17741, 4/5/2004, effective 5/5/2004]

45.602-1 Inventory disposal schedules.

(a) Plant clearance officers should review and accept, or return for correction, inventory disposal schedules within 10 days following receipt from a contractor. Schedules that are completed in accordance with the instructions for Standard Form 1428 should be accepted.

(b) Plant clearance officers shall—

(1) Use Standard Form 1423 to verify, in accordance with agency procedures, accepted schedules within 20 days following acceptance;

(2) Require the contractor to correct any discrepancies found during verification;

(3) Require the contractor to correct any failure to complete predisposal requirements of the contract; and

(4) Provide the contractor disposition instructions for property identified on an acceptable inventory disposal schedule within 120 days. A failure to provide timely disposition instructions may entitle the contractor to an equitable adjustment.

(c) The contractor may request the plant clearance officer's approval to remove the Government property from an inventory schedule.

(1) Plant clearance officers should approve removal of Government property from an inventory schedule when—

(i) The contractor wishes to purchase a contractor-acquired or contractor-produced item at unit acquisition cost and credit the contract;

(ii) The contractor is able to return unused property to the supplier at fair market value and credit the contract (less, if applicable, a reasonable restocking fee that is consistent with the supplier's customary practices);

(iii) The Government has authorized the contractor to use the property on another Government contract; or

(iv) The contractor has requested continued use of the Government property, and the contracting officer has authorized its retention and further use.

(2) If the screening process (see 45.602-3) has not begun, the plant clearance officer shall adjust the schedule or return the schedule to the contractor for correction. If screening has begun, the plant clearance officer shall promptly notify the activity performing the screening that the items should be removed from the screening process.

[FAC 2001-22, 69 FR 17741, 4/5/2004, effective 5/5/2004; FAC 2005-56, 77 FR 12937, 3/2/2012, effective 4/2/2012]

45.602-2 Reutilization priorities.

Plant clearance officers shall initiate reutilization actions for all property not meeting the abandonment or destruction criteria of 45.603(b). Authorized methods, listed in descending order from highest to lowest priority, are—

(a) Reuse within the owning agency;

(b) Transfer of educationally useful equipment to schools and nonprofit organizations (see Executive Order 12999, Educational Technology: Ensuring Opportunity For All Children In The Next Century, April 17, 1996, and 15 U.S.C. 3710(i));

(c) Report to GSA for reuse within the Federal Government or donation as surplus property;

(d) Dispose of the following property in accordance with agency procedures without reporting to GSA:

(1) Property determined appropriate for abandonment or destruction (see Federal Management Regulation (FMR) 102-36.305, 41 CFR 102-36.305).

(2) Property furnished to nonappropriated fund activities (see FMR 102-36.165, 41 CFR 102-36.165).

(3) Foreign excess personal property (see FMR 102-36.380, 41 CFR 102-36.380).

(4) Scrap, except aircraft in scrap condition.

(5) Perishables, defined for the purposes of this section as any personal property subject to spoilage or decay.

(6) Trading stamps and bonus goods.

(7) Hazardous waste or toxic and hazardous materials.

(8) Controlled substances.

(9) Property dangerous to public health and safety.

(10) Classified items or property determined to be sensitive for reasons of national security; and

(e) Dispose of nuclear materials (see 45.603-3(b)(5)) in accordance with the Nuclear Regulatory Commission, applicable state licenses, applicable Federal regulations, and agency regulations.

[FAC 2001-22, 69 FR 17741, 4/5/2004, effective 5/5/2004; FAC 2005-56, 77 FR 12937, 3/2/2012, effective 4/2/2012]

45.602-3 Screening.

The screening period begins upon the plant clearance officer's acceptance of an inventory disposal schedule. The plant clearance officer shall determine whether standard or special screening is appropriate and initiate screening actions.

(a) *Standard screening*. The standard screening period is 46 days.

(1) *First through twentieth day—Screening by the contracting agency*. The contracting agency has 20 days to screen property reported on the inventory disposal schedule for: Other use within the agency; transfer of educationally useful equipment to other Federal agencies that have expressed a need for the property; and transfer of educationally useful equipment to schools and nonprofit organizations if a Federal agency has not expressed a need for the property. Excess personal property, meeting the conditions of 45.603, may be abandoned, destroyed, or donated to public bodies. No later than the 21st day, the plant clearance officer shall submit four copies of the revised schedules and Standard Form (SF) 120, Report of Excess Personal Property, or an electronic equivalent to GSA (see 41 CFR 102-36.215).

(2) *Twenty-first through forty-sixth day (21 days concurrent screening plus 5 days donation processing)*.—(i) Screening by other Federal agencies. GSA will normally honor requests for transfers of property on a first-come-first-served basis through the 41st day. When a request is honored, the GSA regional office shall promptly transmit to the plant clearance officer an approved transfer order that includes shipping instructions.

(ii) Screening for possible donation. Screening for donation is also completed during days 21 through 41. Property is not available for allocation to donees until after the completion of screening. Days 42 through 46 are reserved for GSA to make such allocation.

(3) *Screening period transfer request*. If an agency receives an intra-agency transfer request during the screening periods described in paragraph (a)(2) of this section, the plant clearance officer shall request GSA approval to withdraw the item from the inventory disposal schedule.

(b) *Special screening requirements*.—(1) Special tooling and special test equipment without commercial components. Agencies shall follow the procedures in paragraph (a) of this section. This property owned by the Department of Defense (DoD) or the National Aeronautics and Space Administration (NASA) may be screened for reutilization only within these agencies.

(2) *Special test equipment with commercial components*.—(i) Agencies shall complete the screening required by paragraph (a) of this section. If an agency has no further need for the property and the contractor has not expressed an interest in using or acquiring the property by annotating the inventory disposal schedule, the plant clearance officer shall forward the inventory disposal schedule to the GSA regional office that serves the region in which the property is located.

(ii) If the contractor has expressed an interest in using the property on another Government contract, the plant clearance officer shall contact the contracting officer for that contract. If the contracting officer concurs with the proposed use, the contracting officer for the contract under which the property is accountable shall transfer the property's accountability to that contract. If the contracting officer does not concur with the proposed use, the plant clearance officer shall deny the contractor's request and shall continue the screening process.

(iii) If the property is contractor-acquired or -produced, and the contractor or subcontractor has expressed an interest in acquiring the property, and no other party expresses an interest during agency or GSA screening, the property may be sold to the contractor or subcontractor at acquisition cost.

(3) *Printing equipment*. Agencies shall report all excess printing equipment to the Public Printer, Government Publishing Office, 732 North Capitol Street, NW., Washington, DC 20401, after screening within the agency (see 44 U.S.C. 312). If the Public Printer does not express a need for the equipment within 21 days, the agency shall submit the report to GSA for further use and donation screening as described in paragraph (a) of this section.

(4) *Non-nuclear hazardous materials, hazardous wastes, and classified items*. These items shall be screened in accordance with agency procedures. Report non-nuclear hazardous materials to GSA if the agency has no requirement for them.

(5) *Nuclear materials*. The possession, use, and transfer of certain nuclear materials are subject to the regulatory controls of the Nuclear Regulatory Commission (NRC). Contracting activities shall screen excess nuclear materials in the following categories:

(i) *By-product material*. Any radioactive material (except special nuclear material) yielded in or made radioactive by exposure to the radiation incident to producing or using special nuclear material.

(ii) *Source material*. Uranium or thorium, or any combination thereof, in any physical or chemical form; or ores that contain by weight one-twentieth of 1 percent (0.05 percent) or more of uranium, thorium, or any combination thereof. Source material does not include special nuclear material.

(iii) *Special nuclear material*. Plutonium, Uranium 233, Uranium enriched in the isotope 233 or in the isotope 235, any other material that the NRC determines to be special nuclear material (but not including source material); or any material artificially enriched by any nuclear material.

[FAC 2001-22, 69 FR 17741, 4/5/2004, effective 5/5/2004; FAC 2005-43, 75 FR 38675, 7/2/2010, effective 8/2/2010; FAC 2019-02, 84 FR 19839, 5/6/2019, effective 5/6/2019]

45.602-4 Interagency property transfer costs.

Agencies whose property is transferred to other agencies shall not be reimbursed for the property in any manner unless the circumstances of FMR 102-36.285 (41 CFR 102-36.285) apply. The agency receiving the property shall pay any transportation costs that are not the contractor's responsibility and any costs to pack, crate, or otherwise prepare the property for shipment. The contract administration office shall process appropriate contract modifications. To accelerate plant clearance, the receiving agency shall promptly furnish funding data, and transfer or shipping documents to the contract administration office.

[FAC 2001-22, 69 FR 17741, 4/5/2004, effective 5/5/2004]

45.603 Abandonment or destruction of personal property.

(a) When contractor inventory is processed through the reutilization screening process prescribed in 45.602-2 without success, and provided the property has no commercial value, does not require demilitarization, and does not constitute a danger to public health or welfare, plant clearance officers or other authorized officials may without further approval—

(1) Direct the contractor to destroy the property;

(2) Abandon non-sensitive property at the contractor's or subcontractor's premises; or

(3) Abandon sensitive property at the contractor's or subcontractor's premises, with contractor consent.

(b) Provided a Government reviewing official at least one level higher than the plant clearance officer or other agency authorized official approves, plant clearance officers or other agency authorized officials may authorize the abandonment, or order the destruction of other contractor inventory at the contractor's or subcontractor's premises, in accordance with FMR 102-36.305 through 325 (41 CFR 102-36.305-325) and consistent with the following:

(1) The property is not considered sensitive, does not require demilitarization, has no commercial value or reutilization, transfer or donation potential, and does not constitute a danger to public health or welfare.

(2) The estimated cost of continued care and handling of the property (including advertising, storage and other costs associated with making the sale), exceed the estimated proceeds from its sale.

(c) In lieu of abandonment or its authorized destruction, the plant clearance officer or authorized official may authorize the donation of property including unsold surplus property to public bodies, provided that the property is not sensitive property, does not require demilitarization, and it does not constitute a danger to public health or welfare. The Government will not bear any of the costs incident to such donations.

(d) Unless the property qualifies for one of the exceptions under FMR 102-36.330 (41 CFR 102-36.330), the plant clearance officer or requesting official will ensure prior public notice of such actions of abandonment or destruction consistent with FMR 102-36.325 (41 CFR 102-36.325).

[FAC 2001-22, 69 FR 17741, 4/5/2004, effective 5/5/2004; FAC 2005-56, 77 FR 12937, 3/2/2012, effective 4/2/2012]

45.604 Sale of surplus personal property.

[FAC 2005-56, 77 FR 12937, 3/2/2012, effective 4/2/2012]

45.604-1 Sales procedures.

Surplus personal property that has completed screening in accordance with 45.602-3(a) shall be sold in accordance with the policy for the sale of surplus personal property contained in the Federal Management Regulation, at part 102-38 (41 CFR part 102-38). Agencies may specify implementing procedures.

[FAC 2001-22, 69 FR 17741, 4/5/2004, effective 5/5/2004; FAC 2005-56, 77 FR 12937, 3/2/2012, effective 4/2/2012]

45.604-2 Use of GSA sponsored sales centers.

Agencies may use sales center services. Use of such centers for sale of surplus property is authorized when in the best interest of the Government, consistent with contract terms and conditions.

[FAC 2001-22, 69 FR 17741, 4/5/2004, effective 5/5/2004; FAC 2005-43, 75 FR 38675, 7/2/2010, effective 8/2/2010; FAC 2005-56, 77 FR 12937, 3/2/2012, effective 4/2/2012]

45.604-3 Proceeds from sales of surplus property.

Proceeds of any sale are to be credited to the Treasury of the United States as miscellaneous receipts, unless otherwise authorized by statute or the contract or any subcontract thereunder authorizes the proceeds to be credited to the price or cost of the work (40 U.S.C. 571 and 574).

[FAC 2001-22, 69 FR 17741, 4/5/2004, effective 5/5/2004; FAC 2005-56, 77 FR 12937, 3/2/2012, effective 4/2/2012]

45.604-4 Sale of property pursuant to the exchange/sale authority.

Agencies should consider the sale of property pursuant to the exchange/sale authority in FMR 102-39 (41 CFR part 102-39) when agencies are acquiring or plan to acquire similar products and other requirements of the authority are satisfied.

[FAC 2005-56, 77 FR 12937, 3/2/2012, effective 4/2/2012]

45.605 Inventory disposal reports.

The plant clearance officer shall promptly prepare an SF 1424, Inventory Disposal Report, following disposition of the property identified on an inventory disposal schedule and the crediting of any related proceeds. The report shall identify any lost or otherwise unaccounted for property and any changes in quantity or value of the property made by the contractor after submission of the initial inventory disposal schedule. The report shall be provided to the administrative contracting officer or, for termination inventory, to the termination contracting officer, with a copy to the property administrator.

[FAC 2001-22, 69 FR 17741, 4/5/2004, effective 5/5/2004; FAC 2005-56, 77 FR 12937, 3/2/2012, effective 4/2/2012]

45.606 Contractor scrap procedures.

(a) The property administrator should, in coordination with the plant clearance officer, ensure that contractor scrap disposal processes, methods, and practices allow for effective, efficient, and proper disposition and are properly documented in the contractor's property management procedures.

(b) The property administrator should determine the extent to which separate disposal processing or physical segregation for different scrap types is or may be required. Such scrap may require physical segregation, unique disposal processing, or separate plant clearance reporting. For example, the scope of work may create scrap—

(1) Consisting of sensitive items;

(2) Containing hazardous materials or wastes;

(3) Contaminated with hazardous materials or wastes;

(4) That is classified or otherwise controlled;

(5) Containing precious or strategic metals; or

(6) That is dangerous to public health or safety.

(c) Absent contract terms and conditions to the contrary, the Government may abandon parts removed and replaced from property as a result of normal maintenance actions or removed from property as a result of the repair, maintenance, overhaul, or modification process.

[FAC 2001-22, 69 FR 17741, 4/5/2004, effective 5/5/2004; FAC 2005-43, 75 FR 38675, 7/2/2010, effective 8/2/2010; FAC 2005-56, 77 FR 12937, 3/2/2012, effective 4/2/2012]

45.606-2 [Removed]

[FAC 2001-22, 69 FR 17741, 4/5/2004, effective 5/5/2004; FAC 2005-56, 77 FR 12937, 3/2/2012, effective 4/2/2012]

45.606-3 [Removed]

[FAC 2001-22, 69 FR 17741, 4/5/2004, effective 5/5/2004; FAC 2005-56, 77 FR 12937, 3/2/2012, effective 4/2/2012]

PART 46—QUALITY ASSURANCE

Table of Contents

Scope of part . . . 46.000

Subpart 46.1—General

Definitions . . . 46.101
Policy . . . 46.102
Contracting office responsibilities . . . 46.103
Contract administration office responsibilities . . . 46.104
Contractor responsibilities . . . 46.105

Subpart 46.2—Contract Quality Requirements

General . . . 46.201
Types of contract quality requirements . . . 46.202
Contracts for commercial items . . . 46.202-1
Government reliance on inspection by contractor . . . 46.202-2
Standard inspection requirements . . . 46.202-3
Higher-level contract quality requirements . . . 46.202-4
Criteria for use of contract quality requirements . . . 46.203

Subpart 46.3—Contract Clauses

Contractor inspection requirements . . . 46.301
Fixed-price supply contracts . . . 46.302
Cost-reimbursement supply contracts . . . 46.303
Fixed-price service contracts . . . 46.304
Cost-reimbursement service contracts . . . 46.305
Time-and-material and labor-hour contracts . . . 46.306
Fixed-price research and development contracts . . . 46.307
Cost-reimbursement research and development contracts . . . 46.308
Research and development contracts (short form) . . . 46.309
[Removed and Reserved] . . . 46.310
Higher-level contract quality requirement . . . 46.311
Construction contracts . . . 46.312
Contracts for dismantling, demolition, or removal of improvements . . . 46.313
Transportation contracts . . . 46.314
Certificate of conformance . . . 46.315
Responsibility for supplies . . . 46.316
Reporting Nonconforming Items . . . 46.317

Subpart 46.4—Government Contract Quality Assurance

General . . . 46.401
Government contract quality assurance at source . . . 46.402
Government contract quality assurance at destination . . . 46.403
Government contract quality assurance for acquisitions at or below the simplified acquisition threshold . . . 46.404
Subcontracts . . . 46.405
Foreign governments . . . 46.406
Nonconforming supplies or services . . . 46.407
Single agency assignments of Government contract quality assurance . . . 46.408

Subpart 46.5—Acceptance

General . . . 46.501
Responsibility for acceptance . . . 46.502
Place of acceptance . . . 46.503
Certificate of conformance . . . 46.504
Transfer of title and risk of loss . . . 46.505

Subpart 46.6—Material Inspection and Receiving Reports

General . . . 46.601

Subpart 46.7—Warranties

[Removed and Reserved] 46.701
General 46.702
Criteria for use of warranties 46.703
Authority for use of warranties 46.704
Limitations 46.705
Warranty terms and conditions 46.706
Pricing aspects of fixed-price incentive contract warranties 46.707
Warranties of data 46.708
Warranties of commercial items 46.709
Contract clauses 46.710

Subpart 46.8—Contractor Liability for Loss of or Damage to Property of the Government

Scope of subpart 46.800
Applicability 46.801
Definition 46.802
Policy 46.803
[Removed and Reserved] 46.804
Contract clauses 46.805
[Removed] 46.806

PART 46—QUALITY ASSURANCE

46.000 Scope of part.

This part prescribes policies and procedures to ensure that supplies and services acquired under Government contract conform to the contract's quality and quantity requirements. Included are inspection, acceptance, warranty, and other measures associated with quality requirements.

SUBPART 46.1—GENERAL

46.101 Definitions.

As used in this part—

Acceptance means the act of an authorized representative of the Government by which the Government, for itself or as agent of another, assumes ownership of existing identified supplies tendered or approves specific services rendered as partial or complete performance of the contract.

Conditional acceptance means acceptance of supplies or services that do not conform to contract quality requirements, or are otherwise incomplete, that the contractor is required to correct or otherwise complete by a specified date.

Contract quality requirements means the technical requirements in the contract relating to the quality of the product or service and those contract clauses prescribing inspection, and other quality controls incumbent on the contractor, to assure that the product or service conforms to the contractual requirements.

Counterfeit item means an unlawful or unauthorized reproduction, substitution, or alteration that has been knowingly mismarked, misidentified, or otherwise misrepresented to be an authentic, unmodified item from the original manufacturer, or a source with the express written authority of the original manufacturer or current design activity, including an authorized aftermarket manufacturer. Unlawful or unauthorized substitution includes used items represented as new, or the false identification of grade, serial number, lot number, date code, or performance characteristics.

Critical item means an item, the failure of which is likely to result in hazardous or unsafe conditions for individuals using, maintaining, or depending upon the item; or is likely to prevent performance of a vital agency mission.

Critical nonconformance means a nonconformance that is likely to result in hazardous or unsafe conditions for individuals using, maintaining, or depending upon the supplies or services; or is likely to prevent performance of a vital agency mission.

Design activity means an organization, Government or contractor, that has responsibility for the design and configuration of an item, including the preparation or maintenance of design documents. Design activity could be the original organization, or an organization to which design responsibility has been transferred.

Government contract quality assurance means the various functions, including inspection, performed by the Government to determine whether a contractor has fulfilled the contract obligations pertaining to quality and quantity.

Major nonconformance means a nonconformance, other than critical, that is likely to result in failure of the supplies or services, or to materially reduce the usability of the supplies or services for their intended purpose.

Minor nonconformance means a nonconformance that is not likely to materially reduce the usability of the supplies or services for their intended purpose, or is a departure from established standards having little bearing on the effective use or operation of the supplies or services.

Off-the-shelf item means an item produced and placed in stock by a contractor, or stocked by a distributor, before receiving orders or contracts for its sale. The item may be commercial or produced to military or Federal specifications or description.

Patent defect means any defect which exists at the time of acceptance and is not a latent defect.

Subcontractor (see 44.101).

Suspect counterfeit item means an item for which credible evidence (including but not limited to, visual inspection or testing) provides reasonable doubt that the item is authentic.

Testing means that element of inspection that determines the properties or elements, including functional operation of supplies or their components, by the application of established scientific principles and procedures.

[FAC 90-32, 60 FR 48206, 9/18/95, effective 10/1/95; FAC 90-39, 61 FR 31612, 6/20/96, effective 8/19/96; FAC 97-14, 64 FR 51828, 9/24/99, effective 11/23/99; FAC 97-22, 66 FR 2116, 1/10/2001, effective 3/12/2001; Delay of effective date, 66 FR 14259, 3/9/2001, effective 5/11/2001; FAC 2020-02, 84 FR 64680, 11/22/2019, effective 12/23/2019]

46.102 Policy.

Agencies shall ensure that—

(a) Contracts include inspection and other quality requirements, including warranty clauses when appropriate, that are determined necessary to protect the Government's interest;

(b) Supplies or services tendered by contractors meet contract requirements;

(c) Government contract quality assurance is conducted before acceptance (except as otherwise provided in this part), by or under the direction of Government personnel;

(d) No contract precludes the Government from performing inspection;

(e) Nonconforming supplies or services are rejected, except as otherwise provided in 46.407;

(f) Contracts for commercial items shall rely on a contractor's existing quality assurance system as a substitute for compliance with Government inspection and testing before tender for acceptance unless customary market practices for the commercial item being acquired permit in-process inspection (41 U.S.C. 3307). Any in-process inspection by the Government shall be conducted in a manner consistent with commercial practice; and

(g) The quality assurance and acceptance services of other agencies are used when this will be effective, economical, or otherwise in the Government's interest (see Subpart 42.1).

[FAC 90-32, 60 FR 48206, 9/18/95, effective 10/1/95; FAC 2005-73, 79 FR 24192, 4/29/2014, effective 5/29/2014]

46.103 Contracting office responsibilities.

Contracting offices are responsible for—

(a) Receiving from the activity responsible for technical requirements any specifications for inspection, testing, and other contract quality requirements essential to ensure the integrity of the supplies or services (the activity responsible for technical requirements is responsible for prescribing contract quality requirements, such as inspection and testing requirements or, for service contracts, a quality assurance surveillance plan);

(b) Including in solicitations and contracts the appropriate requirements for the contractor's control of quality for the supplies or services to be acquired;

(c) Issuing any necessary instructions to the cognizant contract administration office and acting on recommendations submitted by that office (see 42.301 and 46.104(f));

(d) When contract administration is retained (see 42.201), verifying that the contractor fulfills the contract quality requirements; and

(e) Ensuring that nonconformances are identified, and establishing the significance of a nonconformance when considering the acceptability of supplies or services which do not meet contract requirements.

[FAC 90-39, 61 FR 31612, 6/20/96, effective 8/19/96; FAC 97-1, 62 FR 44802, 8/22/97, effective 10/21/97; FAC 97-4, 63 FR 9048, 2/23/98, effective 4/24/98]

46.104 Contract administration office responsibilities.

When a contract is assigned for administration to the contract administration office cognizant of the contractor's plant, that office, unless specified otherwise, shall—

(a) Develop and apply efficient procedures for performing Government contract quality assurance actions under the contract in accordance with the written direction of the contracting office;

(b) Perform all actions necessary to verify whether the supplies or services conform to contract quality requirements;

(c) Maintain, as part of the performance records of the contract, suitable records reflecting—

(1) The nature of Government contract quality assurance actions, including, when appropriate, the number of observations made and the number and type of defects; and

(2) Decisions regarding the acceptability of the products, the processes, and the requirements, as well as action to correct defects.

(d) Implement any specific written instructions from the contracting office;

(e) Report to the contracting office any defects observed in design or technical requirements, including contract quality requirements; and

(f) Recommend any changes necessary to the contract, specifications, instructions, or other requirements that will provide more effective operations or eliminate unnecessary costs (see 46.103(c)).

[FAC 97-4, 63 FR 9048, 2/23/98, effective 4/24/98]

46.105 Contractor responsibilities.

(a) The contractor is responsible for carrying out its obligations under the contract by—

(1) Controlling the quality of supplies or services;

(2) Tendering to the Government for acceptance only those supplies or services that conform to contract requirements;

(3) Ensuring that vendors or suppliers of raw materials, parts, components, subassemblies, etc., have an acceptable quality control system; and

(4) Maintaining substantiating evidence, when required by the contract, that the supplies or services conform to contract quality requirements, and furnishing such information to the Government as required.

(b) The contractor may be required to provide and maintain an inspection system or program for the control of quality that is acceptable to the Government (see 46.202).

(c) The control of quality by the contractor may relate to, but is not limited to—

(1) Manufacturing processes, to ensure that the product is produced to, and meets, the contract's technical requirements;

(2) Drawings, specifications, and engineering changes, to ensure that manufacturing methods and operations meet the contract's technical requirements;

(3) Testing and examination, to ensure that practices and equipment provide the means for optimum evaluation of the characteristics subject to inspection;

(4) Reliability and maintainability assessment (life, endurance, and continued readiness);

(5) Fabrication and delivery of products, to ensure that only conforming products are tendered to the Government;

(6) Technical documentation, including drawings, specifications, handbooks, manuals, and other technical publications;

(7) Preservation, packaging, packing, and marking; and

(8) Procedures and processes for services to ensure that services meet contract performance requirements.

(d) The contractor is responsible for performing all inspections and tests required by the contract except those specifically reserved for performance by the Government (see 46.201(c)).

[Final rule, 55 FR 38517, 9/18/90]

SUBPART 46.2—CONTRACT QUALITY REQUIREMENTS

46.201 General.

(a) The contracting officer shall include in the solicitation and contract the appropriate quality requirements. The type and extent of contract quality requirements needed depends on the particular acquisition and may range from inspection at time of acceptance to a requirement for the contractor's implementation of a comprehensive program for controlling quality.

(b) As feasible, solicitations and contracts may provide for alternative, but substantially equivalent, inspection methods to obtain wide competition and low cost. The contracting officer may also authorize contractor-recommended alternatives when in the Government's interest and approved by the activity responsible for technical requirements.

(c) Although contracts generally make contractors responsible for performing inspection before tendering supplies to the Government, there are situations in which contracts will provide for specialized inspections to be performed solely by the Government. Among situations of this kind are—

(1) Tests that require use of specialized test equipment or facilities not ordinarily available in suppliers' plants or commercial laboratories (*e.g.*, ballistic testing of ammunition, unusual environmental tests, and simulated service tests); and

(2) Contracts that require Government testing for first article approval (see Subpart 9.3).

(d) Except as otherwise specified by the contract, required contractor testing may be performed in the contractor's or subcontractor's laboratory or testing facility, or in any other laboratory or testing facility acceptable to the Government.

46.202 Types of contract quality requirements.

Contract quality requirements fall into four general categories, depending on the extent of quality assurance needed by the Government for the acquisition involved.

[FAC 90-32, 60 FR 48206, 9/18/95, effective 10/1/95]

46.202-1 Contracts for commercial items.

When acquiring commercial items (see part 12), the Government shall rely on contractors' existing quality assurance systems as a substitute for Government inspection and testing before tender for acceptance unless customary market practices for the commercial item being acquired include in-process inspection. Any in-process inspection by the Government shall be conducted in a manner consistent with commercial practice.

[FAC 90-32, 60 FR 48206, 9/18/95, effective 10/1/95]

46.202-2 Government reliance on inspection by contractor.

(a) Except as specified in (b) below, the Government shall rely on the contractor to accomplish all inspection and testing needed to ensure that supplies or services acquired at or below the simplified acquisition threshold conform to contract quality requirements before they are tendered to the Government (see 46.301).

(b) The Government shall not rely on inspection by the contractor if the contracting officer determines that the Government has a need to test the supplies or services in advance of their tender for acceptance, or to pass judgment upon the adequacy of the contractor's internal work processes. In making the determination, the contracting officer shall consider—

(1) The nature of the supplies and services being purchased and their intended use;

(2) The potential losses in the event of defects;

(3) The likelihood of uncontested replacement or correction of defective work; and

(4) The cost of detailed Government inspection.

[FAC 84-12, 51 FR 2666, 1/17/86, effective 1/20/86; FAC 90-29, 60 FR 34732, 7/3/95, effective 7/3/95; Redesignated from 46.202-1, FAC 90-32, 60 FR 48206, 9/18/95, effective 10/1/95]

46.202-3 Standard inspection requirements.

(a) Standard inspection requirements are contained in the clauses prescribed in 46.302 through 46.308, and in the product and service specifications that are included in solicitations and contracts.

(b) The clauses referred to in (a) above—

(1) Require the contractor to provide and maintain an inspection system that is acceptable to the Government;

(2) Give the Government the right to make inspections and tests while work is in process; and

(3) Require the contractor to keep complete, and make available to the Government, records of its inspection work.

[Redesignated from 46.202-2, FAC 90-32, 60 FR 48206, 9/18/95, effective 10/1/95; FAC 2005-17, 72 FR 27364, 5/15/2007, effective 6/14/2007]

46.202-4 Higher-level contract quality requirements.

(a) Agencies shall establish procedures for determining when higher-level contract quality requirements are necessary, for determining the risk (both the likelihood and the impact) of nonconformance, and for advising the contracting officer about which higher-level standards should be applied and included in the solicitation and contract. Requiring compliance with higher-level quality standards is necessary in solicitations and contracts for complex or critical items (see 46.203) or when the technical requirements of the contract require—

(1) Control of such things as design, work operations, in-process controls, testing, and inspection; or

(2) Attention to such factors as organization, planning, work instructions, documentation control, and advanced metrology.

(b) Examples of higher-level quality standards include overarching quality management system standards such as ISO 9001, ASQ/ANSI E4, ASME NQA-1, SAE AS9100, SAE AS9003, and ISO/TS 16949, and product or process specific quality standards such as SAE AS5553.

[FAC 97-10, 63 FR 70264, 12/18/98, effective 2/16/99; FAC 2001-04, 67 FR 6112, 2/8/2002, effective 2/8/2002; FAC 2005-78, 79 FR 70344, 11/25/2014, effective 12/26/2014; FAC 2005-80, 80 FR 4994, 1/29/2015, effective 3/2/2015]

46.203 Criteria for use of contract quality requirements.

The extent of contract quality requirements, including contractor inspection, required under a contract shall usually be based upon the classification of the contract item (supply or service) as determined by its technical description, its complexity, and the criticality of its application.

(a) *Technical description.* Contract items may be technically classified as—

(1) Commercial (described in commercial catalogs, drawings, or industrial standards; see part 2); or

(2) Military-Federal (described in Government drawings and specifications).

(b) *Complexity.* (1) Complex items have quality characteristics, not wholly visible in the end item, for which contractual conformance must be established progressively through precise measurements, tests, and controls applied during purchasing, manufacturing, performance, assembly, and functional operation either as an individual item or in conjunction with other items.

(2) Noncomplex items have quality characteristics for which simple measurement and test of the end item are sufficient to determine conformance to contract requirements.

(c) *Criticality.* (1) A critical application of an item is one in which the failure of the item could injure personnel or jeopardize a vital agency mission. A critical item may be either peculiar, meaning it has only one application, or common, meaning it has multiple applications.

(2) A noncritical application is any other application. Noncritical items may also be either peculiar or common.

[FAC 90-32, 60 FR 48206, 9/18/95, effective 10/1/95]

SUBPART 46.3—CONTRACT CLAUSES

46.301 Contractor inspection requirements.

The contracting officer shall insert the clause at 52.246-1, Contractor Inspection Requirements, in solicitations and contracts for supplies or services when the contract amount is expected to be at or below the simplified acquisition threshold and (a) inclusion of the clause is necessary to ensure an explicit understanding of the contractor's inspection responsibilities, or (b) inclusion of the clause is required under agency procedures. The clause shall not be used if the contracting officer has made the determination specified in 46.202-2(b).

[FAC 90-29, 60 FR 34732, 7/3/95, effective 7/3/95; FAC 90-32, 60 FR 48206, 9/18/95, effective 10/1/95]

46.302 Fixed-price supply contracts.

The contracting officer shall insert the clause at 52.246-2, Inspection of Supplies—Fixed-Price, in solicitations and contracts for supplies, or services that involve the furnishing of supplies, when a fixed-price contract is contemplated and the contract amount is expected to exceed the simplified acquisition threshold. The contracting officer may insert the clause in such solicitations and contracts when the contract amount is expected to be at or below the simplified acquisition threshold and inclusion of the clause is in the Government's interest. If a fixed-price incentive contract is contemplated, the contracting officer shall use the clause with its Alternate I. If a fixed-ceiling-price contract with retroactive price redetermination is contemplated, the contracting officer shall use the clause with its Alternate II.

[FAC 90-29, 60 FR 34732, 7/3/95, effective 7/3/95]

46.303 Cost-reimbursement supply contracts.

The contracting officer shall insert the clause at 52.246-3, Inspection of Supplies—Cost-Reimbursement, in solicitations and contracts for supplies, or services that involve the furnishing of supplies, when a cost-reimbursement contract is contemplated.

46.304 Fixed-price service contracts.

The contracting officer shall insert the clause at 52.246-4, Inspection of Services—Fixed-Price, in solicitations and contracts for services, or supplies that involve the furnishing of services, when a fixed-price contract is contemplated and the contract amount is expected to exceed the simplified acquisition threshold. The contracting officer may insert the clause in such solicitations and contracts when the contract amount is expected to be at or below the simplified acquisition threshold and inclusion is in the Government's interest.

[FAC 90-29, 60 FR 34732, 7/3/95, effective 7/3/95]

46.305 Cost-reimbursement service contracts.

The contracting officer shall insert the clause at 52.246-5, Inspection of Services—Cost Reimbursement, in solicitations and contracts for services, or supplies that involve the furnishing of services, when a cost-reimbursement contract is contemplated.

46.306 Time-and-material and labor-hour contracts.

The contracting officer shall insert the clause at 52.246-6, Inspection—Time-and-Material and Labor-Hour, in solicitations and contracts when a time-and-material contract or a labor-hour contract is contemplated. If Government inspection and acceptance are to be performed at the contractor's plant, the contracting officer shall use the clause with its Alternate I.

[FAC 84-12, 51 FR 2666, 1/17/86, effective 1/20/86]

46.307 Fixed-price research and development contracts.

(a) The contracting officer shall insert the clause at 52.246-7, Inspection of Research and Development—Fixed-Price, in solicitations and contracts for research and development when—

(1) the primary objective of the contract is the delivery of end items other than designs, drawings, or reports,

(2) a fixed-price contract is contemplated, and

(3) the contract amount is expected to exceed the simplified acquisition threshold; unless use of the clause is impractical and the clause prescribed in 46.309 is considered to be more appropriate.

(b) The contracting officer may insert the clause in such solicitations and contracts when the contract amount is expected to be at or below the simplified acquisition threshold, and its use is in the Government's interest.

[FAC 90-29, 60 FR 34732, 7/3/95, effective 7/3/95]

46.308 Cost-reimbursement research and development contracts.

The contracting officer shall insert the clause at 52.246-8, Inspection of Research and Development—Cost-Reimbursement, in solicitations and contracts for research and development when (a) the primary objective of the contract is the delivery of end items other than designs, drawings, or reports, and (b) a cost-reimbursement contract is contemplated; unless use of the clause is impractical and the clause prescribed in 46.309 is considered to be more appropriate. If it is contemplated that the contract will be on a no-fee basis, the contracting officer shall use the clause with its Alternate I.

46.309 Research and development contracts (short form).

The contracting officer shall insert the clause at 52.246-9, Inspection of Research and Development (Short Form), in solicitations and contracts for research and development when the clause prescribed in 46.307 or the clause prescribed in 46.308 is not used.

[FAC 84-18, 51 FR 27120, 7/29/86, effective 7/30/86]

46.310 [Removed and Reserved]

[FAC 2005-17, 72 FR 27364, 5/15/2007, effective 6/14/2007]

46.311 Higher-level contract quality requirement.

(a) The contracting officer shall insert the clause at 52.246-11, Higher-Level Contract Quality Requirement, in solicitations and contracts when the inclusion of a higher-level contract quality requirement is necessary (see 46.202-4).

(b) For each higher-level quality standard, the contracting officer shall fill in the title, number, date, and tailoring (if any).

[FAC 97-10, 63 FR 70264, 12/18/98, effective 2/16/99; FAC 2005-78, 79 FR 70344, 11/25/2014, effective 12/26/2014]

46.312 Construction contracts.

The contracting officer shall insert the clause at 52.246-12, Inspection of Construction, in solicitations and contracts for construction when a fixed-price contract is contemplated and the contract amount is expected to exceed the simplified acquisition threshold. The contracting officer may insert the clause in such solicitations and contracts when the contract amount is expected to be at or below the simplified acquisition threshold, and its use is in the Government's interest.

[FAC 90-29, 60 FR 34732, 7/3/95, effective 7/3/95]

46.313 Contracts for dismantling, demolition, or removal of improvements.

The contracting officer shall insert the clause at 52.246-13, Inspection—Dismantling, Demolition, or Removal of Improvements, in solicitations and contracts for dismantling, demolition, or removal of improvements.

46.314 Transportation contracts.

The contracting officer shall insert the clause at 52.246-14, Inspection of Transportation, in solicitations and contracts for freight transportation services (including local drayage) by rail, motor (including bus), domestic freight forwarder, and domestic water carriers (including inland, coastwise, and intercoastal). The contracting officer shall not use the clause for the acquisition of transportation services by domestic or international air carriers or by international ocean carriers, or to freight services provided under bills of lading or to those negotiated for reduced rates under 49 U.S.C. 10721 or 13712. (See Part 47, Transportation.)

[FAC 2005-07, 71 FR 200, 1/3/2006, effective 2/2/2006]

46.315 Certificate of conformance.

The contracting officer shall insert the clause at 52.246-15, Certificate of Conformance, in solicitations and contracts for supplies or services when the conditions in 46.504 apply.

46.316 Responsibility for supplies.

The contracting officer shall insert the clause at 52.246-16, Responsibility for Supplies, in solicitations and contracts for (a) supplies, (b) services involving the furnishing of supplies, or (c) research and development, when a fixed-price contract is contemplated and the contract amount is expected to exceed the simplified acquisition threshold. The contracting officer may insert the clause in such solicitations and contracts when the contract amount is not expected to exceed the simplified acquisition threshold and inclusion of the clause is authorized under agency procedures.

[FAC 90-29, 60 FR 34732, 7/3/95, effective 7/3/95]

46.317 Reporting Nonconforming Items.

(a) Except as provided in paragraph (b) of this section, the contracting officer shall insert the clause at 52.246-26, Reporting Nonconforming Items, in solicitations and contracts—as follows:

(1) For an acquisition by any agency, including the Department of Defense, of—

(i) Any items that are subject to higher-level quality standards in accordance with the clause at 52.246-11, Higher-Level Contract Quality Requirement;

(ii) Any items that the contracting officer, in consultation with the requiring activity determines to be critical items for which use of the clause is appropriate;

(2) In addition (as required by paragraph (c)(4) of section 818 of the National Defense Authorization Act for Fiscal Year 2012 (Pub. L. 112-81)), for an acquisition that exceeds the simplified acquisition threshold and is by, or for, the Department of Defense of electronic parts or end items, components, parts, or materials containing electronic parts, whether or not covered in paragraph (a)(1) of this section; or

(3) For the acquisition of services, if the contractor will furnish, as part of the service, any items that meet the criteria specified in paragraphs (a)(1) through (a)(2) of this section.

(b) The contracting officer shall not insert the clause at 52.246-26, Reporting Nonconforming Items, in solicitations and contracts when acquiring—

(1) Commercial items using part 12 procedures; or

(2) Medical devices that are subject to the Food and Drug Administration reporting requirements at 21 CFR 803.

(c) If required by agency policy, the contracting officer may modify paragraph (b)(4) of the clause at 52.246-26, but only to change the responsibility for the contractor to submit reports to the agency rather than to Government-Industry Data Exchange Program (GIDEP), so that the agency instead of the contractor submits reports to GIDEP within the mandatory 60 days.

[FAC 2020-02, 84 FR 64680, 11/22/2019, effective 12/23/2019]

SUBPART 46.4—GOVERNMENT CONTRACT QUALITY ASSURANCE

46.401 General.

(a) Government contract quality assurance shall be performed at such times (including any stage of manufacture or performance of services) and places (including subcontractors' plants) as may be necessary to determine that the supplies or services conform to contract requirements. Quality assurance surveillance plans should be prepared in conjunction with the preparation of the statement of work. The plans should specify—

(1) All work requiring surveillance; and

(2) The method of surveillance.

(b) Each contract shall designate the place or places where the Government reserves the right to perform quality assurance.

(c) If the contract provides for performance of Government quality assurance at source, the place or places of performance may not be changed without the authorization of the contracting officer.

(d) If a contract provides for delivery and acceptance at destination and the Government inspects the supplies at a place other than destination, the supplies shall not ordinarily be reinspected at destination, but should be examined for quantity, damage in transit, and possible substitution or fraud.

(e) Government inspection shall be performed by or under the direction or supervision of Government personnel.

(f) Government inspection shall be documented on an inspection or receiving report form or commercial shipping document/packing list, under agency procedures (see Subpart 46.6).

(g) Agencies may prescribe the use of inspection approval or disapproval stamps to identify and control supplies and materials that have been inspected for conformance with contract quality requirements.

[FAC 97-1, 62 FR 44802, 8/22/97, effective 10/21/97]

46.402 Government contract quality assurance at source.

Agencies shall perform contract quality assurance, including inspection, at source if—

(a) Performance at any other place would require uneconomical disassembly or destructive testing;

(b) Considerable loss would result from the manufacture and shipment of unacceptable supplies, or from the delay in making necessary corrections;

(c) Special required instruments, gauges, or facilities are available only at source;

(d) Performance at any other place would destroy or require the replacement of costly special packing and packaging;

(e) Government inspection during contract performance is essential; or

(f) It is determined for other reasons to be in the Government's interest.

[FAC 90-32, 60 FR 48206, 9/18/95, effective 10/1/95; FAC 97-10, 63 FR 70264, 12/18/98, effective 2/16/99]

46.403 Government contract quality assurance at destination.

(a) Government contract quality assurance that can be performed at destination is normally limited to inspection of the supplies or services. Inspection shall be performed at destination under the following circumstances—

(1) Supplies are purchased off-the-shelf and require no technical inspection;

(2) Necessary testing equipment is located only at destination;

(3) Perishable subsistence supplies purchased within the United States, except that those supplies destined for overseas shipment will normally be inspected for condition and quantity at points of embarkation;

(4) Brand name products purchased for authorized resale through commissaries or similar facilities (however, supplies destined for direct overseas shipment may be accepted by the contracting officer or an authorized representative on the basis of a tally sheet evidencing receipt of shipment signed by the port transportation officer or other designated official at the transshipment point);

(5) The products being purchased are processed under direct control of the National Institutes of Health or the Food and Drug Administration of the Department of Health and Human Services;

(6) The contract is for services performed at destination; or

(7) It is determined for other reasons to be in the Government's interest.

(b) Overseas inspection of supplies shipped from the United States shall not be required except in unusual circumstances, and then only when the contracting officer determines in advance that inspection can be performed or makes necessary arrangements for its performance.

46.404 Government contract quality assurance for acquisitions at or below the simplified acquisition threshold.

(a) In determining the type and extent of Government contract quality assurance to be required for contracts at or below the simplified acquisition threshold, the contracting officer shall consider the criticality of application of the supplies or services, the amount of possible losses, and the likelihood of uncontested replacement of defective work (see 46.202-2).

(b) When the conditions in 46.202-2(b) apply, the following policies shall govern:

(1) Unless a special situation exists, the Government shall inspect contracts at or below the simplified acquisition threshold at destination and only for type and kind; quantity; damage; operability (if readily determinable); and preservation, packaging, packing, and marking, if applicable.

(2) Special situations may require more detailed quality assurance and the use of a standard inspection or higher-level contract quality requirement. These situations include those listed in 46.402 and contracts for items having critical applications.

(3) Detailed Government inspection may be limited to those characteristics that are special or likely to cause harm to personnel or property. When repetitive purchases of the same item are made from the same manufacturer with a history of defect-free work, Government inspection may be reduced to a periodic check of occasional purchases.

[FAC 90-29, 60 FR 34732, 7/3/95, effective 7/3/95; FAC 90-32, 60 FR 48206, 9/18/95, effective 10/1/95]

46.405 Subcontracts.

(a) Government contract quality assurance on subcontracted supplies or services shall be performed only when required in the Government's interest. The primary purpose is to assist the contract administration office cognizant of the prime contractor's plant in determining the conformance of subcontracted supplies or services with contract requirements or to satisfy one or more of the factors included in (b) of this section. It does not relieve the prime contractor of any responsibilities under the contract. When appropriate, the prime contractor shall be requested to arrange for timely Government access to the subcontractor facility.

(b) The Government shall perform quality assurance at the subcontract level when—

(1) The item is to be shipped from the subcontractor's plant to the using activity and inspection at source is required;

(2) The conditions for quality assurance at source are applicable (see 46.402);

(3) The contract specifies that certain quality assurance functions, which can be performed only at the subcontractor's plant, are to be performed by the Government; or

(4) It is otherwise required by the contract or determined to be in the Government's interest.

(c) Supplies or services for which certificates, records, reports, or similar evidence of quality are available at the prime contractor's plant shall not be inspected at the subcontractor's plant, except occasionally to verify this evidence or when required under (b) of this section.

(d) All oral and written statements and contract terms and conditions relating to Government quality assurance actions at the subcontract level shall be worded so as not to—

(1) Affect the contractual relationship between the prime contractor and the Government, or between the prime contractor and the subcontractor;

(2) Establish a contractual relationship between the Government and the subcontractor; or

(3) Constitute a waiver of the Government's right to accept or reject the supplies or services.

46.406 Foreign governments.

Government contract quality assurance performed for foreign governments or international agencies shall be administered according to the foreign policy and security objectives of the United States. Such support shall be furnished only when consistent with or required by legislation, executive orders, or agency policies concerning mutual international programs.

46.407 Nonconforming supplies or services.

(a) The contracting officer should reject supplies or services not conforming in all respects to contract requirements (see 46.102). In those instances where deviation from this policy is found to be in the Government's interest, such supplies or services may be accepted only as authorized in this section.

(b) The contracting officer ordinarily must give the contractor an opportunity to correct or replace nonconforming supplies or services when this can be accomplished within the required delivery schedule. Unless the contract specifies otherwise (as may be the case in some cost-reimbursement contracts), correction or replacement must be without additional cost to the Government. Subparagraph (e)(2) of the clause at 52.246-2, Inspection of Supplies—Fixed-Price, reserves to the Government the right to charge the contractor the cost of Government reinspection and retests because of prior rejection.

(c)(1) In situations not covered by paragraph (b) of this section, the contracting officer ordinarily must reject supplies or services when the nonconformance is critical or major or the supplies or services are otherwise incomplete. However, there may be circumstances (e.g., reasons of economy or urgency) when the contracting officer determines acceptance or conditional acceptance of supplies or services is in the best interest of the Government. The contracting officer must make this determination based upon—

(i) Advice of the technical activity that the item is safe to use and will perform its intended purpose;

(ii) Information regarding the nature and extent of the nonconformance or otherwise incomplete supplies or services;

(iii) A request from the contractor for acceptance of the nonconforming or otherwise incomplete supplies or services (if feasible);

(iv) A recommendation for acceptance, conditional acceptance, or rejection, with supporting rationale; and

(v) The contract adjustment considered appropriate, including any adjustment offered by the contractor.

(2) The cognizant contract administration office, or other Government activity directly involved, must furnish this data to the contracting officer in writing, except that in urgent cases it may be furnished orally and later confirmed in writing. Before making a decision to accept, the contracting officer must obtain the concurrence of the activity responsible for the technical requirements of the contract and, where health factors are involved, of the responsible health official of the agency concerned.

(d) If the nonconformance is minor, the cognizant contract administration office may make the determination to accept or reject, except where this authority is withheld by the contracting office of the contracting activity. To assist in making this determination, the contract administration office may establish a joint contractor-contract administrative office review group. Acceptance of supplies and services with critical or major nonconformances is outside the scope of the review group.

(e) The contracting officer must discourage the repeated tender of nonconforming supplies or services, including those with only minor nonconformances, by appropriate action, such as rejection and documenting the contractor's performance record.

(f) When supplies or services are accepted with critical or major nonconformances as authorized in paragraph (c) of this section, the contracting officer must modify the contract to provide for an equitable price reduction or other consideration. In the case of conditional acceptance, amounts withheld from payments generally should be at least sufficient to cover the estimated cost and related profit to correct deficiencies and complete unfinished work. The contracting officer must document in the contract file the basis for the amounts withheld. For services, the contracting officer can consider identifying the value of the individual work requirements or tasks (subdivisions) that may be subject to price or fee reduction. This value may be used to determine an equitable adjustment for nonconforming services. However, when supplies or services involving minor nonconformances are accepted, the contract need not be modified unless it appears that the savings to the contractor in fabricating the nonconforming supplies or performing the nonconforming services will exceed the cost to the Government of processing the modification.

(g) Notices of rejection must include the reasons for rejection and be furnished promptly to the contractor. Promptness in giving this notice is essential because, if timely nature of rejection is not furnished, acceptance may in certain cases be implied as a matter of law. The notice must be in writing if—

(1) The supplies or services have been rejected at a place other than the contractor's plant;

(2) The contractor persists in offering nonconforming supplies or services for acceptance; or

(3) Delivery or performance was late without excusable cause.

(h) The contracting officer shall provide disposition instructions for counterfeit or suspect counterfeit items in accordance with agency policy. Agency policy may require the contracting officer to direct the contractor to retain such items for investigative or evidentiary purposes.

[FAC 90-39, 61 FR 31612, 6/20/96, effective 8/19/96; FAC 97-1, 62 FR 44802, 8/22/97, effective 10/21/97; FAC 97-14, 64 FR 51828, 9/24/99, effective 11/23/99; FAC 2020-02, 84 FR 64680, 11/22/2019, effective 12/23/2019]

46.408 Single-agency assignments of Government contract quality assurance.

(a) Government-wide responsibility for quality assurance support for acquisitions of certain commodities is assigned as follows:

(1) For drugs, biologics, and other medical supplies—the Food and Drug Administration;

(2) For food, except seafood—the Department of Agriculture;

(3) For seafood—the National Marine Fisheries Service of the Department of Commerce.

(b) Agencies requiring quality assurance support for acquiring these supplies should request the support directly from the cognizant office.

SUBPART 46.5—ACCEPTANCE

46.501 General.

Acceptance constitutes acknowledgment that the supplies or services conform with applicable contract quality and quantity requirements, except as provided in this subpart and subject to other terms and conditions of the contract. Acceptance may take place before delivery, at the time of delivery, or after delivery, depending on the provisions of the terms and conditions of the contract. Supplies or services shall ordinarily not be accepted before completion of Government contract quality assurance actions (however, see 46.504). Acceptance shall ordinarily be evidenced by execution of an acceptance certificate on an inspection or receiving report form or commercial shipping document/packing list.

46.502 Responsibility for acceptance.

Acceptance of supplies or services is the responsibility of the contracting officer. When this responsibility is assigned to a cognizant contract administration office or to another agency (see 42.202(g)), acceptance by that office or agency is binding on the Government.

[FAC 97-4, 63 FR 9048, 2/23/98, effective 4/24/98]

46.503 Place of acceptance.

Each contract shall specify the place of acceptance. Contracts that provide for Government contract quality assurance at source shall ordinarily provide for acceptance at source. Contracts that provide for Government contract quality assurance at destination shall ordinarily provide for acceptance at destination. (For transportation terms, see Subpart 47.3). Supplies accepted at a place other than destination shall not be reinspected at destination for acceptance purposes, but should be examined at destination for quantity, damage in transit, and possible substitution or fraud.

46.504 Certificate of conformance.

A certificate of conformance (see 46.315) may be used in certain instances instead of source inspection (whether the contract calls for acceptance at source or destination) at the discretion of the contracting officer if the following conditions apply:

(a) Acceptance on the basis of a contractor's certificate of conformance is in the Government's interest.

(b) (1) Small losses would be incurred in the event of a defect; or

(2) Because of the contractor's reputation or past performance, it is likely that the supplies or services furnished will be acceptable and any defective work would be replaced, corrected, or repaired without contest. In no case shall the Government's right to inspect supplies under the inspection provisions of the contract be prejudiced.

46.505 Transfer of title and risk of loss.

(a) Title to supplies shall pass to the Government upon formal acceptance, regardless of when or where the Government takes physical possession, unless the contract specifically provides for earlier passage of title.

(b) Unless the contract specifically provides otherwise, risk of loss of or damage to supplies shall remain with the contractor until, and shall pass to the Government upon—

(1) Delivery of the supplies to a carrier if transportation is f.o.b. origin; or

(2) Acceptance by the Government or delivery of the supplies to the Government at the destination specified in the contract, whichever is later, if transportation is f.o.b. destination.

(c) Paragraph (b) of this section shall not apply to supplies that so fail to conform to contract requirements as to give a right of rejection. The risk of loss of or damage to such nonconforming supplies remains with the contractor until cure or acceptance. After cure or acceptance, paragraph (b) of this section shall apply.

(d) Under paragraph (b) of this section, the contractor shall not be liable for loss of or damage to supplies caused by the negligence of officers, agents, or employees of the Government acting within the scope of their employment.

(e) The policy expressed in (a) through (d) of this section is specified in the clause at 52.246-16, Responsibility for Supplies, which is prescribed in 46.316.

SUBPART 46.6—MATERIAL INSPECTION AND RECEIVING REPORTS

46.601 General.

Agencies shall prescribe procedures and instructions for the use, preparation, and distribution of material inspection and receiving reports and commercial shipping document/packing lists to evidence Government inspection (see 46.401) and acceptance (see 46.501).

[Final rule, 62 FR 40236, 7/25/97, effective 6/30/97]

SUBPART 46.7—WARRANTIES

46.701 [Removed and Reserved]

[Removed and Reserved, FAC 97-22, 66 FR 2116, 1/10/2001, effective 3/12/2001; Delay of effective date, 66 FR 14259, 3/9/2001, effective 5/11/2001]

46.702 General.

(a) The principal purposes of a warranty in a Government contract are—

(1) To delineate the rights and obligations of the contractor and the Government for defective items and services and

(2) To foster quality performance.

(b) Generally, a warranty should provide—

(1) A contractual right for the correction of defects notwithstanding any other requirement of the contract pertaining to acceptance of the supplies or services by the Government; and

(2) A stated period of time or use, or the occurrence of a specified event, after acceptance by the Government to assert a contractual right for the correction of defects.

(c) The benefits to be derived from a warranty must be commensurate with the cost of the warranty to the Government.

46.703 Criteria for use of warranties.

The use of warranties is not mandatory. In determining whether a warranty is appropriate for a specific acquisition, the contracting officer shall consider the following factors:

(a) *Nature and use of the supplies or services.* This includes such factors as—

(1) Complexity and function;

(2) Degree of development;

(3) State of the art;

(4) End use;

(5) Difficulty in detecting defects before acceptance; and

(6) Potential harm to the Government if the item is defective.

(b) *Cost.* Warranty costs arise from—

(1) The contractor's charge for accepting the deferred liability created by the warranty; and

(2) Government administration and enforcement of the warranty (see paragraph (c) of this section).

(c) *Administration and enforcement.* The Government's ability to enforce the warranty is essential to the effectiveness of any warranty. There must be some assurance that an adequate administrative system for reporting defects exists or can be established. The adequacy of a reporting system may depend upon such factors as the—

(1) Nature and complexity of the item;

(2) Location and proposed use of the item;

(3) Storage time for the item;

(4) Distance of the using activity from the source of the item;

(5) Difficulty in establishing existence of defects; and

(6) Difficulty in tracing responsibility for defects.

(d) *Trade practice.* In many instances an item is customarily warranted in the trade, and, as a result of that practice, the cost of an item to the Government will be the same whether or not a warranty is included. In those instances, it would be in the Government's interest to include such a warranty.

(e) *Reduced requirements.* The contractor's charge for assumption of added liability may be partially or completely offset by reducing the Government's contract quality assurance requirements where the warranty provides adequate assurance of a satisfactory product.

46.704 Authority for use of warranties.

The use of a warranty in an acquisition shall be approved in accordance with agency procedures.

46.705 Limitations.

(a) Except for the warranties in the clauses at 52.246-3, Inspection of Supplies—Cost-Reimbursement, and 52.246-8, Inspection of Research and Development—Cost-Reimbursement, the contracting officer shall not include warranties in cost-reimbursement contracts, unless authorized in accordance with agency regulations (see 46.708).

(b) Warranty clauses shall not limit the Government's rights under an inspection clause (see Subpart 46.3) in relation to latent defects, fraud, or gross mistakes that amount to fraud.

(c) Except for warranty clauses in construction contracts, warranty clauses shall provide that the warranty applies notwithstanding inspection and acceptance or other clauses or terms of the contract.

46.706 Warranty terms and conditions.

(a) To facilitate the pricing and enforcement of warranties, the contracting officer shall ensure that warranties clearly state the—

(1) Exact nature of the item and its components and characteristics that the contractor warrants;

(2) Extent of the contractor's warranty including all of the contractor's obligations to the Government for breach of warranty;

(3) Specific remedies available to the Government; and

(4) Scope and duration of the warranty.

(b) The contracting officer shall consider the following guidelines when preparing warranty terms and conditions:

(1) *Extent of contractor obligations.* (i) Generally, the contractor's obligations under warranties extend to all defects discovered during the warranty period, but do not include damage caused by the Government. When a warranty for the entire item is not advisable, a warranty may be required for a

particular aspect of the item that may require special protection (*e.g.*, installation, components, accessories, subassemblies, preservation, packaging, and packing, etc.).

(ii) If the Government specifies the design of the end item and its measurements, tolerances, materials, tests, or inspection requirements, the contractor's obligations for correction of defects shall usually be limited to defects in material and workmanship or failure to conform to specifications. If the Government does not specify the design, the warranty extends also to the usefulness of the design.

(iii) If express warranties are included in a contract (except contracts for commercial items), all implied warranties of merchantability and fitness for a particular purpose shall be negated by the use of specific language in the clause (see clauses 52.246-17, Warranty of Supplies of a Noncomplex Nature; 52.246-18, Warranty of Supplies of a Complex Nature; and 52.246-19, Warranty of Systems and Equipment under Performance Specifications or Design Criteria).

(2) *Remedies.* (i) Normally, a warranty shall provide as a minimum that the Government may—

(A) Obtain an equitable adjustment of the contract, or

(B) Direct the contractor to repair or replace the defective items at the contractor's expense.

(ii) If it is not practical to direct the contractor to make the repair or replacement, or, because of the nature of the item, the repair or replacement does not afford an appropriate remedy to the Government, the warranty should provide alternate remedies, such as authorizing the Government to—

(A) Retain the defective item and reduce the contract price by an amount equitable under the circumstances; or

(B) Arrange for the repair or replacement of the defective item, by the Government or by another source, at the contractor's expense.

(iii) If it can be foreseen that it will not be practical to return an item to the contractor for repair, to remove it to an alternate source for repair, or to replace the defective item, the warranty should provide that the Government may repair, or require the contractor to repair, the item in place at the contractor's expense. The contract shall provide that in the circumstance where the Government is to accomplish the repair, the contractor will furnish at the place of delivery the material or parts, and the installation instructions required to successfully accomplish the repair.

(iv) Unless provided otherwise in the warranty, the contractor's obligation to repair or replace the defective item, or to agree to an equitable adjustment of the contract, shall include responsibility for the costs of furnishing all labor and material to—

(A) Reinspect items that the Government reasonably expected to be defective,

(B) Accomplish the required repair or replacement of defective items, and

(C) Test, inspect, package, pack, and mark repaired or replaced items.

(v) If repair or replacement of defective items is required, the contractor shall generally be required by the warranty to bear the expense of transportation for returning the defective item from the place of delivery specified in the contract (irrespective of the f.o.b. point or the point of acceptance) to the contractor's plant and subsequent return. When defective items are returned to the contractor from other than the place of delivery specified in the contract, or when the Government exercises alternate remedies, the contractor's liability for transportation charges incurred shall not exceed an amount equal to the cost of transportation by the usual commercial method of shipment between the place of delivery specified in the contract and the contractor's plant and subsequent return.

(3) *Duration of the warranty.* The time period or duration of the warranty must be clearly specified and shall be established after consideration of such factors as (i) the estimated useful life of the item, (ii) the nature of the item including storage or shelf-life, and (iii) trade practice. The period specified shall not extend the contractor's liability

for patent defects beyond a reasonable time after acceptance by the Government.

(4) *Notice*. The warranty shall specify a reasonable time for furnishing notice to the contractor regarding the discovery of defects. This notice period, which shall apply to all defects discovered during the warranty period, shall be long enough to assure that the Government has adequate time to give notice to the contractor. The contracting officer shall consider the following factors when establishing the notice period:

(i) The time necessary for the Government to discover the defects.

(ii) The time reasonably required for the Government to take necessary administrative steps and make a timely report of discovery of the defects to the contractor.

(iii) The time required to discover and report defective replacements.

(5) *Markings*. The packaging and preservation requirements of the contract shall require the contractor to stamp or mark the supplies delivered or otherwise furnish notice with the supplies of the existence of the warranty. The purpose of the markings or notice is to inform Government personnel who store, stock, or use the supplies that the supplies are under warranty. Markings may be brief but should include (i) a brief statement that a warranty exists, (ii) the substance of the warranty, (iii) its duration, and (iv) who to notify if the supplies are found to be defective. For commercial items (see 46.709), the contractor's trade practice in warranty marking is acceptable if sufficient information is presented for supply personnel and users to identify warranted supplies.

(6) *Consistency*. Contracting officers shall ensure that the warranty clause and any other warranty conditions in the contract (*e.g.*, in the specifications or an inspection clause) are consistent. To the extent practicable, all of the warranties to be contained in the contract should be expressed in the warranty clause.

46.707 Pricing aspects of fixed-price incentive contract warranties.

If a fixed-price incentive contract contains a warranty (see 46.708), the estimated cost of the warranty to the contractor should be considered in establishing the incentive target price and the ceiling price of the contract. All costs incurred, or estimated to be incurred, by the contractor in complying with the warranty shall be considered when establishing the total final price. Contractor compliance with the warranty after the establishment of the total final price shall be at no additional cost to the Government.

46.708 Warranties of data.

Warranties of data shall be developed and used in accordance with agency regulations.

46.709 Warranties of commercial items.

The contracting officer should take advantage of commercial warranties, including extended warranties, where appropriate and in the Government's best interests, offered by the contractor for the repair and replacement of commercial items (see Part 12).

[FAC 90-32, 60 FR 48206, 9/18/95, effective 10/1/95]

46.710 Contract clauses.

The clauses and alternates prescribed in this section may be used in solicitations and contracts in which inclusion of a warranty is appropriate (see 46.709 for warranties for commercial items). However, because of the many situations that may influence the warranty terms and conditions appropriate to a particular acquisition, the contracting officer may vary the terms and conditions of the clauses and alternates to the extent necessary. The alternates prescribed in this section address the clauses; however, the conditions pertaining to each alternate must be considered if the terms and conditions are varied to meet a particular need.

(a) (1) The contracting officer may insert a clause substantially the same as the clause at 52.246-17, Warranty of Supplies of a Noncomplex Nature, in solicitations and contracts for noncomplex items when a fixed-price supply contract is contemplated and the use of a warranty clause has been approved under agency procedures. If the contractor's design rather than the Government's design will be used, insert the word "design" before "material" in paragraph (b)(1)(i).

(2) If it is desirable to specify that necessary transportation incident to correction or replacement will be at the Government's expense (as might be the case if, for example, the cost of a warranty would otherwise be prohibitive), the contracting officer may use the clause with its Alternate II.

(3) If the supplies cannot be obtained from another source, the contracting officer may use the clause with its Alternate III.

(4) If a fixed-price incentive contract is contemplated, the contracting officer may use the clause with its Alternate IV.

(5) If it is anticipated that recovery of the warranted item will involve considerable Government expense for disassembly and/ or reassembly of larger items, the contracting officer may use the clause with its Alternate V.

(b) (1) The contracting officer may insert a clause substantially the same as the clause at 52.246-18, Warranty of Supplies of a Complex Nature, in solicitations and contracts for deliverable complex items when a fixed-price supply or research and development contract is contemplated and the use of a warranty clause has been approved under agency procedures. If the contractor's design rather than the Government's design will be used, insert the word "design" before "material" in paragraph (b)(1).

(2) If it is desirable to specify that necessary transportation incident to correction or replacement will be at the Government's expense (as might be the case if, for example, the cost of a warranty would otherwise be prohibitive), the contracting officer may use the clause with its Alternate II.

(3) If a fixed-price incentive contract is contemplated, the contracting officer may use the clause with its Alternate III.

(4) If it is anticipated that recovery of the warranted item will involve considerable Government expense for disassembly and/ or reassembly of larger items, the contracting officer may use the clause with its Alternate IV.

(c) (1) The contracting officer may insert a clause substantially the same as the clause at 52.246-19, Warranty of Systems and Equipment under Performance Specifications or Design Criteria, in solicitations and contracts when performance specifications or design are of major importance; a fixed-price supply, service, or research and development contract for systems and equipment is contemplated; and the use of a warranty clause has been approved under agency procedures.

(2) If it is desirable to specify that necessary transportation incident to correction or replacement will be at the Government's expense (as might be the case if, for example, the cost of a warranty would otherwise be prohibitive), the contracting officer may use the clause with its Alternate I.

(3) If a fixed-price incentive contract is contemplated, the contracting officer may use the clause with its Alternate II.

(4) If it is anticipated that recovery of the warranted item will involve considerable Government expense for disassembly and/ or reassembly of larger items, the contracting officer may use the clause with its Alternate III.

(d) The contracting officer may insert a clause substantially the same as the clause at 52.246-20, Warranty of Services, in solicitations and contracts for services when a fixed-price contract for services is contemplated and the use of a warranty clause has been approved under agency procedures; unless a clause substantially the same as the clause at 52.246-19, Warranty of Systems and Equipment under Performance Specifications or Design Criteria, has been used.

(e) (1) The contracting officer may insert a clause substantially the same as the clause at 52.246-21, Warranty of Construction, in solicitations and contracts when a fixed-price construction contract (see 46.705(c)) is contemplated and the use of a warranty clause has been approved under agency procedures.

(2) If the Government specifies in the contract the use of any equipment by "brand name and model," the contracting officer may use the clause with its Alternate I.

[FAC 90-32, 60 FR 48206, 9/18/95, effective 10/1/95; FAC 97-22, 66 FR 2116, 1/10/2001, effective 3/12/2001; Delay of effective date, 66 FR 14259, 3/9/2001, effective 5/11/2001]

SUBPART 46.8—CONTRACTOR LIABILITY FOR LOSS OF OR DAMAGE TO PROPERTY OF THE GOVERNMENT

46.800 Scope of subpart.

This subpart prescribes policies and procedures for limiting contractor liability for loss of or damage to property of the Government that—

(a) Occurs after acceptance and

(b) Results from defects or deficiencies in the supplies delivered or services performed.

46.801 Applicability.

(a) This subpart applies to contracts other than those for (1) information technology, including telecommunications, (2) construction, (3) architect-engineer services, and (4) maintenance and rehabilitation of real property. This subpart does not apply to commercial items.

(b) See Subpart 46.7, Warranties, for policies and procedures concerning contractor liability caused by nonconforming technical data.

[FAC 90-41, 61 FR 41466, 8/8/96, effective 8/8/96, finalized without change, FAC 97-3, 62 FR 64912, 12/9/97, effective 2/9/98; FAC 2001-01, 66 FR 53478, 10/22/2001, effective 12/21/2001]

46.802 Definition.

High-value item as used in this subpart, means a contract end item that—

(a) Has a high unit cost (normally exceeding $100,000 per unit), such as an aircraft, an aircraft engine, a communication system, a computer system, a missile, or a ship, and

(b) Is designated by the contracting officer as a high-value item.

46.803 Policy.

(a) *General*. The Government will generally act as a self-insurer by relieving contractors, as specified in this subpart, of liability for loss of or damage to property of the Government that (1) occurs after acceptance of supplies delivered or services performed under a contract and (2) results from defects or deficiencies in the supplies or services. However, the Government will not relieve the contractor of liability for loss of or damage to the contract end item itself, except for high-value items.

(b) *High-value items*. In contracts requiring delivery of high-value items, the Government will relieve contractors of contractual liability for loss of or damage to those items. However, this relief shall not limit the Government's rights arising under the contract to—

(1) Have any defective item or its components corrected, repaired, or replaced when the defect or deficiency is discovered before the loss of or damage to a high-value item occurs; or

(2) Obtain equitable relief when the defect or deficiency is discovered after such loss or damage occurs.

(c) *Exception*. The Government will not provide contractual relief under paragraphs (a) and (b) of this section when contractor liability can be preserved without increasing the contract price.

(d) *Limitations*. Subject to the specific terms of the limitation of liability clause included in the contract, the relief provided under paragraphs (a) and (b) of this section does not apply—

(1) To the extent that contractor liability is expressly provided under a contract clause authorized by this regulation;

(2) When a defect or deficiency in, or Government's acceptance of, the supplies or services results from willful misconduct or lack of good faith on the part of the contractor's managerial personnel; or

(3) To the extent that any contractor insurance, or self-insurance reserve, covers liability for loss or damage suffered by the Government through purchase or use of the supplies delivered or services performed under the contract.

46.804 [Removed and Reserved]

[Removed and Reserved by FAC 2001-01, 66 FR 53478, 10/22/2001, effective 12/21/2001]

46.805 Contract clauses.

(a) *Contracts that exceed the simplified acquisition threshold.* The contracting officer shall insert the appropriate clause or combination of clauses specified in subparagraphs (a)(1) through (a)(5) of this section in solicitations and contracts when the contract amount is expected to be in excess of the simplified acquisition threshold and the contract is subject to the requirements of this subpart as indicated in 46.801:

(1) In contracts requiring delivery of end items that are not high-value items, insert the clause at 52.246-23, Limitation of Liability.

(2) In contracts requiring delivery of high-value items, insert the clause at 52.246-24, Limitation of Liability—High-Value Items.

(3) In contracts requiring delivery of both high-value items and other end items, insert both clauses prescribed in (a)(1) and (a)(2) of this section, Alternate I of the clause at 52.246-24, and identify clearly in the contract schedule the line items designated as high-value items.

(4) In contracts requiring the performance of services, insert the clause at 52.246-25, Limitation of Liability—Services.

(5) In contracts requiring both the performance of services and the delivery of end items, insert the clause prescribed in subparagraph (a)(4) of this section and the appropriate clause or clauses prescribed in subparagraph (a)(1), (2), or (3) of this section, and identify clearly in the contract schedule any high-value line items.

(b) *Acquisitions at or below the simplified acquisition threshold.* The clauses prescribed by paragraph (a) of this section are not required for contracts at or below the simplified acquisition threshold. However, in response to a contractor's specific request, the contracting officer may insert the clauses prescribed in paragraph (a)(1) or (a)(4) of this section in a contract at or below the simplified acquisition threshold and may obtain any price reduction that is appropriate.

[FAC 84-56, 55 FR 3886, 2/5/90, effective 3/7/90; FAC 90-29, 60 FR 34732, 7/3/95, effective 7/3/95; FAC 90-40, 61 FR 39186, 7/26/96, effective 8/26/96; FAC 90-43, GPO Version, effective 12/20/96]

46.806 [Removed]

[Removed by FAC 90-43, 12/20/96, effective 2/18/97, 61 FR 67408]

PART 47—TRANSPORTATION

Table of Contents

Scope of part 47.000
Definitions 47.001
Applicability 47.002

Subpart 47.1—General

Policies 47.101
Transportation insurance 47.102
Transportation Payment and Audit Regulation 47.103
General 47.103-1
Contract clause 47.103-2
Government rate tenders under sections 10721 and 13712 of the Interstate Commerce Act (49 U.S.C. 10721 and 13712) 47.104
Government rate tender procedures 47.104-1
Fixed-price contracts 47.104-2
Cost-reimbursement contracts 47.104-3
Contract clause 47.104-4
Citation of Government rate tenders 47.104-5
Transportation assistance 47.105

Subpart 47.2—Contracts for Transportation or for Transportation-Related Services

Scope of subpart 47.200
Definitions 47.201
Presolicitation planning 47.202
[Removed and Reserved] 47.203
Single-movement contracts 47.204
Availability of term contracts and basic ordering agreements for transportation or for transportation-related services 47.205
Preparation of solicitations and contracts 47.206
Solicitation provisions, contract clauses, and special requirements 47.207
Qualifications of offerors 47.207-1
Duration of contract and time of performance 47.207-2
Description of shipment, origin, and destination 47.207-3
Determination of weights 47.207-4
Contractor responsibilities 47.207-5
Rates and charges 47.207-6
Liability and insurance 47.207-7
Government responsibilities 47.207-8
Annotation and distribution of shipping and billing documents 47.207-9
Discrepancies incident to shipments 47.207-10
Volume movements within the contiguous United States 47.207-11
Report of shipment (REPSHIP) 47.208
Advance notice 47.208-1
Contract clause 47.208-2

Subpart 47.3—Transportation in Supply Contracts

Scope of subpart 47.300
General 47.301
Responsibilities of contracting officers 47.301-1
Participation of transportation officers 47.301-2
Using the Defense Transportation System (DTS) 47.301-3
Place of delivery—f.o.b. point 47.302
Standard delivery terms and contract clauses 47.303
F.o.b. origin 47.303-1
F.o.b. origin, contractor's facility 47.303-2

F.o.b. origin, freight allowed 47.303-3
F.o.b. origin, freight prepaid 47.303-4
F.o.b. origin, with differentials 47.303-5
F.o.b. destination 47.303-6
F.o.b. destination, within consignee's premises 47.303-7
F.a.s. vessel, port of shipment 47.303-8
F.o.b. vessel, port of shipment 47.303-9
F.o.b. inland carrier, point of exportation 47.303-10
F.o.b. inland point, country of importation 47.303-11
Ex dock, pier, or warehouse, port of importation 47.303-12
C.&f. destination 47.303-13
C.i.f. destination 47.303-14
F.o.b. designated air carrier's terminal, point of exportation 47.303-15
F.o.b. designated air carrier's terminal, point of importation 47.303-16
Contractor-prepaid commercial bills of lading, small package shipments 47.303-17
Determination of delivery terms 47.304
General 47.304-1
Shipments within CONUS 47.304-2
Shipments from CONUS for overseas delivery 47.304-3
Shipments originating outside CONUS 47.304-4
Exceptions 47.304-5
Solicitation provisions, contract clauses, and transportation factors 47.305
Solicitation requirements 47.305-1
Solicitations f.o.b. origin and f.o.b. destination—lowest overall cost 47.305-2
F.o.b. origin solicitations 47.305-3
F.o.b. destination solicitations 47.305-4
Destination unknown 47.305-5
Shipments to ports and air terminals 47.305-6
Quantity analysis, direct delivery, and reduction of crosshauling and backhauling 47.305-7
Consolidation of small shipments and the use of stopoff privileges 47.305-8
Commodity description and freight classification 47.305-9
Packing, marking, and consignment instructions 47.305-10
Options in shipment and delivery 47.305-11
Delivery of Government-furnished property 47.305-12
Transit arrangements 47.305-13
Mode of transportation 47.305-14
Loading responsibilities of contractors 47.305-15
Shipping characteristics 47.305-16
Returnable cylinders 47.305-17
Transportation factors in the evaluation of offers 47.306
Transportation cost determinations 47.306-1
Lowest overall transportation costs 47.306-2
Adequacy of loading and unloading facilities 47.306-3

Subpart 47.4—Air Transportation by U.S.-Flag Carriers

Definitions 47.401
Policy 47.402
Guidelines for implementation of the Fly America Act 47.403
Availability and unavailability of U.S.-flag air carrier service 47.403-1
Air transport agreements between the United States and foreign governments 47.403-2
Disallowance of expenditures 47.403-3
Air freight forwarders 47.404
Contract clause 47.405

Subpart 47.5—Ocean Transportation by U.S.-Flag Vessels

Scope of subpart 47.500
Definitions 47.501
Policy 47.502
Applicability 47.503
Exceptions 47.504
Construction contracts 47.505
Procedures 47.506
Contract clauses 47.507

PART 47—TRANSPORTATION

47.000 Scope of part.

(a) This part prescribes policies and procedures for—

(1) Applying transportation and traffic management considerations in the acquisition of supplies; and

(2) Acquiring transportation or transportation-related services by contract methods other than bills of lading, transportation requests, transportation warrants, and similar transportation forms. Transportation and transportation services can be obtained by acquisition subject to the FAR or by acquisition under 49 U.S.C. 10721 or 49 U.S.C. 13712. Even though the FAR does not regulate the acquisition of transportation or transportation-related services when the bill of lading is the contract, this contract method is widely used and, therefore, relevant guidance on the use of the bill of lading is provided in this part (see 47.104).

(b) The definitions in this part have been condensed from statutory definitions. In case of inconsistency between the language of this part and the statutory requirements, the statute shall prevail.

[FAC 2005-07, 71 FR 200, 1/3/2006, effective 2/2/2006]

47.001 Definitions.

As used in this part—

Bill of lading means a transportation document, used as a receipt of goods, as documentary evidence of title, for clearing customs, and generally used as a contract of carriage.

(1) Commercial bill of lading (CBL), unlike the Government bill of lading, is not an accountable transportation document.

(2) Government bill of lading (GBL) is an accountable transportation document, authorized and prepared by a Government official.

Carrier or *commercial carrier* means a common carrier or a contract carrier.

Common carrier means a person holding itself out to the general public to provide transportation for compensation.

Contract carrier means a person providing transportation for compensation under continuing agreements with one person or a limited number of persons.

Government rate tender under 49 U.S.C. 10721 and 13712 means an offer by a common carrier to the United States at a rate below the regulated rate offered to the general public.

Household goods in accordance with 49 U.S.C. 13102 means personal effects and property used or to be used in a dwelling, when a part of the equipment or supply of such dwelling, and similar property if the transportation of such effects or property is arranged and paid for by—

(1) The householder, except such term does not include property moving from a factory or store, other than property that the householder has purchased with the intent to use in his or her dwelling and is transported at the request of, and the transportation charges are paid to the carrier by, the householder; or

(2) Another party.

Noncontiguous domestic trade means transportation (except with regard to bulk cargo, forest products, recycled metal scrap, waste paper, and paper waste) subject to regulation by the Surface Transportation Board involving traffic originating in or destined to Alaska, Hawaii, or a territory or possession of the United States (see 49 U.S.C. 13102(15) and 13702).

Released or declared value means the assigned value of the cargo for reimbursement purposes, not necessarily the actual value of the cargo. Released value may be more or less than the actual value of the cargo. The released value is the maximum amount that could be recovered by the agency in the event of loss or damage for the shipments of freight and household goods.

[FAC 97-22, 66 FR 2116, 1/10/2001, effective 3/12/2001; Delay of effective date, 66 FR 14259, 3/9/2001, effective 5/11/2001; FAC 2001-14, 68 FR 28079, 5/22/2003, effective 6/23/2003; FAC 2005-07, 71 FR 200, 1/3/2006, effective 2/2/2006]

47.002 Applicability.

All Government personnel concerned with the following activities shall follow the regulations in Part 47 as applicable:

(a) Acquisition of supplies.

(b) Acquisition of transportation and transportation-related services.

(c) Transportation assistance and traffic management.

(d) Administration of transportation contracts, transportation-related services, and other contracts that involve transportation.

(e) The making and administration of contracts under which payments are made from Government funds for—

(1) The transportation of supplies;

(2) Transportation-related services; or

(3) Transportation of contractor personnel and their personal belongings.

[FAC 2005-07, 71 FR 200, 1/3/2006, effective 2/2/2006]

SUBPART 47.1—GENERAL

47.101 Policies.

(a) For domestic shipments, the contracting officer shall authorize shipments on commercial bills of lading (CBL's). Government bills of lading (GBL's) may be used for international or noncontiguous domestic trade shipments or when otherwise authorized.

(b) The contract administration office (CAO) shall ensure that instructions to contractors result in the most efficient and economical use of transportation services and equipment. Transportation personnel will assist and provide transportation management expertise to the CAO. Specific responsibilities and details on transportation management are located in the Federal Management Regulation at 41 CFR parts 102-117 and 102-118. (For the Department of Defense, DoD 4500.9-R, Defense Transportation Regulation.)

(c) The contracting officer shall obtain traffic management advice and assistance (see 47.105) in the consideration of transportation factors required for—

(1) Solicitations and awards;

(2) Contract administration, modification, and termination; and

(3) Transportation of property by the Government to and from contractors' plants.

(d) (1) The preferred method of transporting supplies for the Government is by commercial carriers. However, Government-owned, leased, or chartered vehicles, aircraft, and vessels may be used if—

(i) They are available and not fully utilized;

(ii) Their use will result in substantial economies; and

(iii) Their use is in accordance with all applicable statutes, agency policies and regulations.

(2) If the three circumstances listed in subparagraph (d) (1) above apply, Government vehicles may be used for purposes such as—

(i) Local transportation of supplies between Government installations;

(ii) Pickup and delivery services that commercial carriers do not perform in connection with line-haul transportation;

(iii) Transportation of supplies to meet emergencies; and

(iv) Accomplishment of program objectives that cannot be attained by using commercial carriers.

(e) Agencies shall not accord preferential treatment to any mode of transportation or to any particular carrier either in awarding or administering contracts for the acquisition of supplies or in awarding contracts for the acquisition of transportation. (See Subparts 47.2 and 47.3 for situations in which the contracting officer is permitted to use specific modes of transportation.)

(f) Agencies shall place with small business concerns purchases and contracts for transportation and transportation-related services as prescribed in Part 19.

(g) Agencies shall comply with the Fly America Act, the Cargo Preference Act, and related statutes as prescribed in Subparts 47.4, Air Transportation by U.S.-Flag Carriers, and 47.5, Ocean Transportation by U.S.-Flag Vessels.

(h) When a contract specifies delivery of supplies f.o.b. origin with transportation costs to be paid by the Government, the contractor shall make shipments on bills of lading, or on other shipping documents prescribed by Military Surface Deployment and Distribution Command (SDDC) in the case of seavan containers, either at the direction of or furnished by the CAO or the appropriate agency transportation office.

[FAC 2005-07, 71 FR 200, 1/3/2006, effective 2/2/2006]

47.102 Transportation insurance.

(a) The Government generally—

(1) Retains the risk of loss of and/or damage to its property that is not the legal liability of commercial carriers and

(2) Does not buy insurance coverage for its property in the possession of commercial carriers (40 U.S.C. 17307). (See Part 28, Bonds and Insurance.)

(b) Under special circumstances the Government may, if such action is considered necessary and in the Government's interest,

(1) buy insurance coverage for Government property or—

(2) require the carrier to—

(i) assume full responsibility for loss of or damage to the Government property in its possession and—

(ii) buy insurance to cover the carrier's assumed responsibility. The cost of this insurance to the carrier shall be part of the transportation cost. (The Secretary of the Treasury prescribes regulations regarding shipments of valuables in 31 CFR 361 and 362.)

(c) (1) If special circumstances dictate the need for the Government to buy insurance coverage, the contracting officer shall ascertain that

(i) There is no statutory prohibition and

(ii) Funds for insurance are available.

(2) The contracting officer shall document the need and authorization for insurance coverage in the contract file.

[FAC 2005-06, 70 FR 57453, 9/30/2005, effective 9/30/2005; FAC 2005-07, 71 FR 200, 1/3/2006, effective 2/2/2006]

47.103 Transportation Payment and Audit Regulation.

[FAC 2005-07, 71 FR 200, 1/3/2006, effective 2/2/2006]

47.103-1 General.

(a) (1) Regulations and procedures governing the bill of lading, documentation, payment, and audit of transportation services acquired by the United States Government are prescribed in 41 CFR part 102-118, Transportation Payment and Audit.

(2) For DoD shipments, corresponding guidance is in DoD 4500.9-R, Defense Transportation Regulation, Part II.

(b) Under 31 U.S.C. 3726, all agencies are required to establish a prepayment audit program. For details on the establishment of a prepayment audit, see 41 CFR part 102-118.

(c) The agency designated in paragraph (a) (3) of the clause at 52.247-67 shall forward original copies of paid freight bills/invoices, bills of lading, passenger coupons, and supporting documents as soon as possible following the end of the month, in one package for postpayment audit to the General Services Administration, Transportation Audit Division (QMCA), Crystal Plaza 4, Room 300, 2200 Crystal Drive, Arlington, VA 22202. The specified agency shall include the paid freight bills/invoices, bills of lading, passenger coupons, and supporting documents for first-tier subcontractors under a cost-reimbursement contract. If the inclusion of the paid freight bills/invoices, bills of lading, passenger coupons, and supporting documents for any subcontractor in the shipment is not practicable, the documents may be forwarded to GSA in a separate package.

(d) Any original transportation bills or other documents requested by GSA shall be forwarded promptly. The specified agency shall ensure that the name of the contracting agency is stamped or written on the face of the bill before sending it to GSA.

(e) A statement prepared in duplicate by the specified agency shall accompany each shipment of transportation documents. GSA will acknowledge receipt of the shipment by signing and returning the copy of the statement. The statement shall show—

(1) The name and address of the specified agency;

(2) The contract number, including any alpha-numeric prefix identifying the contracting office;

(3) The name and address of the contracting office;

(4) The total number of bills submitted with the statement; and

(5) A listing of the respective amounts paid or, in lieu of such listing, an adding machine tape of the amounts paid showing the Contractor's voucher or check numbers.

[FAC 2005-07, 71 FR 200, 1/3/2006, effective 2/2/2006; FAC 2005-31, 74 FR 11832, 3/19/2009, effective 3/19/2009]

47.103-2 Contract clause.

Complete and insert the clause at 52.247-67, Submission of Transportation Documents for Audit, in solicitations and contracts when a cost-reimbursement contract is contemplated and the contract or a first-tier cost-reimbursement subcontract thereunder will authorize reimbursement of transportation as a direct charge to the contract or subcontract.

[FAC 2005-07, 71 FR 200, 1/3/2006, effective 2/2/2006]

47.104 Government rate tenders under sections 10721 and 13712 of the Interstate Commerce Act (49 U.S.C. 10721 and 13712).

(a) This section explains statutory authority for common carriers subject to the jurisdiction of the Surface Transportation Board (motor carrier, water carrier, freight forwarder, rail carrier) to offer to transport persons or property for the account of the United States without charge or at "a rate reduced from the applicable commercial rate." Reduced rates are offered in a Government rate tender. Additional information for civilian agencies is available in the Federal Management Regulation (41 CFR parts 102-117 and 102-118) and for DoD in the Defense Transportation Regulation (DoD 4500.9-R).

(b) Reduced rates offered in a Government rate tender are authorized for transportation provided by a rail carrier, for the movement of household goods, and for movement by or with a water carrier in noncontiguous domestic trade.

(1) For Government rate tenders submitted by a rail carrier, a rate reduced from the applicable commercial rate is a rate reduced from a rate regulated by the Surface Transportation Board.

(2) For Government rate tenders submitted for the movement of household goods, "a rate reduced from the applicable commercial rate" is a rate reduced from a rate contained in a published tariff subject to regulation by the Surface Transportation Board.

(3) For Government rate tenders submitted for movement by or with a water carrier in noncontiguous domestic trade, "a rate reduced from the applicable commercial rate" is a rate reduced from a rate contained in a published tariff required to be filed with the Surface Transportation Board.

[FAC 2005-07, 71 FR 200, 1/3/2006, effective 2/2/2006]

47.104-1 Government rate tender procedures.

(a) 49 U.S.C. 10721 and 13712 rates are published in Government rate tenders and apply to shipments moving for the account of the Government on—

(1) Commercial bills of lading endorsed to show that total transportation charges are assignable to, and will be reimbursed by, the Government (see the clause at 52.247-1, Commercial Bill of Lading Notations); and

(2) Government bills of lading.

(b) Agencies may negotiate with carriers for additional or revised 49 U.S.C. 10721 and 13712 rates in appropriate situations. Only personnel authorized in agency procedures may carry out these negotiations. The following are examples of situations in which negotiations for additional or revised 49 U.S.C. 10721 and 13712 rates may be appropriate:

(1) Volume movements are expected.

(2) Shipments will be made on a recurring basis between designated places, and substantial savings in transportation costs appear possible even though a volume movement is not involved.

(3) Transit arrangements are feasible and advantageous to the Government.

[FAC 2005-07, 71 FR 200, 1/3/2006, effective 2/2/2006]

47.104-2 Fixed-price contracts.

(a) F.o.b. destination. 49 U.S.C. 10721 and 13712 rates do not apply to shipments under fixed-price f.o.b. destination contracts (delivered price).

(b) F.o.b. origin. If it is advantageous to the Government, the contracting officer may occasionally require the contractor to prepay the freight charges to a specific destination. In such cases, the contractor shall use a commercial bill of lading and be reimbursed for the direct and actual transportation cost as a separate item in the invoice. The clause at 52.247-1, Commercial Bill of Lading Notations, will ensure that the Government in this type of arrangement obtains the benefit of 49 U.S.C. 10721 and 13712 rates.

[FAC 2005-07, 71 FR 200, 1/3/2006, effective 2/2/2006]

47.104-3 Cost-reimbursement contracts.

(a) 49 U.S.C. 10721 and 13712 rates may be applied to shipments other than those made by the Government if the total benefit accrues to the Government, i.e., the Government shall pay the charges or directly and completely reimburse the party that initially bears the freight charges. Therefore, 49 U.S.C. 10721 and 13712 rates may be used for shipments moving on commercial bills of lading in cost reimbursement contracts under which the transportation costs are direct and allowable costs under the cost principles of Part 31.

(b) 49 U.S.C. 10721 and 13712 rates may be applied to the movement of household goods and personal effects of contractor employees who are relocated for the convenience and at the direction of the Government and whose total transportation costs are reimbursed by the Government.

(c) The clause at 52.247-1, Commercial Bill of Lading Notations, will ensure that the Government receives the benefit of lower 49 U.S.C. 10721 and 13712 rates in cost-reimbursement contracts as described in paragraphs (a) and (b) of this section.

(d) Contracting officers shall—

(1) Include in contracts a statement requiring the contractor to use carriers that offer acceptable service at reduced rates if available; and

(2) Ensure that contractors receive the name and location of the transportation officer designated to furnish support and guidance when using Government rate tenders.

(e) The transportation office shall—

(1) Advise and assist contracting officers and contractors; and

(2) Make available to contractors the names of carriers that provide service under 49 U.S.C. 10721 and 13712 rates, cite applicable rate tenders, and advise contractors of the statement that must be shown on the carrier's commercial bill of lading (see the clause at 52.247-1, Commercial Bill of Lading Notations).

[FAC 2005-07, 71 FR 200, 1/3/2006, effective 2/2/2006]

47.104-4 Contract clause.

(a) In order to ensure the application of 49 U.S.C. 10721 and 13712 rates, where authorized (see 47.104(b)), insert the clause at 52.247-1, Commercial Bill of Lading Notations, in solicitations and contracts when the contracts will be—

(1) Cost-reimbursement contracts, including those that may involve the movement of household goods (see 47.104-3(b)); or

(2) Fixed-price f.o.b. origin contracts (other than contracts at or below the simplified acquisition threshold) (see 47.104-2(b) and 47.104-3).

(b) The contracting officer may insert the clause at 52.247-1, Commercial Bill of Lading Notations, in solicitations and contracts made at or below the simplified acquisition threshold when it is contemplated that the delivery terms will be f.o.b. origin.

[FAC 2005-07, 71 FR 200, 1/3/2006, effective 2/2/2006]

47.104-5 Citation of Government rate tenders.

When 49 U.S.C. 10721 and 13712 rates apply, transportation offices or contractors, as appropriate, shall identify the applicable Government rate tender by endorsement on bills of lading.

[FAC 90-23, 59 FR 67010, 12/28/94, effective 2/27/95; FAC 90-29, 60 FR 34732, 7/3/95, effective 7/3/95; FAC 90-40, 61 FR 39186, 7/26/96, effective 8/26/96; FAC 2005-07, 71 FR 200, 1/3/2006, effective 2/2/2006]

47.105 Transportation assistance.

(a) Civilian Government activities that do not have transportation officers, or otherwise need assistance on transportation matters, shall obtain assistance from—

(1) The GSA Regional Federal Supply Service Bureau that provides support to the activity or

(2) The transportation element of the contract administration office designated in the contract.

(b) Military installations shall obtain transportation assistance from the transportation office of the contracting activity, unless another military activity has been designated as responsible for furnishing assistance, guidance, or data. Military transportation offices shall request needed additional aid from the Military Surface Deployment and Distribution Command (SDDC).

[FAC 84-49, 54 FR 29282, 7/11/89, effective 8/10/89; FAC 2005-07, 71 FR 200, 1/3/2006, effective 2/2/2006]

SUBPART 47.2—CONTRACTS FOR TRANSPORTATION OR FOR TRANSPORTATION-RELATED SERVICES

47.200 Scope of subpart.

(a) This subpart prescribes procedures for the acquisition by sealed bid or negotiated contracts of—

(1) Freight transportation (including local drayage) from rail, motor (including bus), domestic water (including inland, coastwise, and intercoastal) carriers, and from freight forwarders; and

(2) Transportation-related services including but not limited to stevedoring, storage, packing, marking, and ocean freight forwarding.

(b) Except as provided in paragraph (c) of this section, this subpart does not apply to—

(1) The acquisition of freight transportation from—

(i) Domestic or international air carriers; and

(ii) International ocean carriers (see Subparts 47.4 and 47.5);

(2) Freight transportation acquired by bills of lading;

(3) Household goods for which rates are negotiated under 49 U.S.C. 10721 and 13712. (These statutes do not apply in intrastate moves); or

(4) Contracts at or below the simplified acquisition threshold.

(c) With appropriate modifications, the procedures in this subpart may be applied to the acquisition of freight transportation from the carriers listed in subparagraph (b) (1) of this section and passenger transportation from any carrier or mode.

(d) The procedures in this subpart are applicable to the transportation of household goods of persons being relocated at Government expense except when acquired—

(1) Under the commuted rate schedules as required in the Federal Travel Regulation (41 CFR Chapter 302);

(2) By DoD under the DoD 4500.9-R, Defense Transportation Regulation; or

(3) Under 49 U.S.C. 10721 and 13712 rates. (These statutes do not apply in intrastate moves.)

(e) Additional guidance for DoD acquisition of freight and passenger transportation is in the Defense Transportation Regulation.

[FAC 84-5, 50 FR 1745, 1/11/85, effective 4/1/85; Final rule, FAC 90-20, 59 FR 11368, 3/10/94, effective 5/9/94; FAC 90-29, 60 FR 34732, 7/3/95, effective 7/3/95; FAC 90-40, 61 FR 39186, 7/26/96, effective 8/26/96;

FAC 2005-07, 71 FR 200, 1/3/2006, effective 2/2/2006]

47.201 Definitions.

As used in this subpart—

General freight means supplies, goods, and transportable property not encompassed in the definitions of *household goods* or *office furniture*.

Office furniture means furniture, equipment, fixtures, records, and other equipment and materials used in Government offices, hospitals, and similar establishments.

[FAC 97-22, 66 FR 2116, 1/10/2001, effective 3/12/2001; Delay of effective date, 66 FR 14259, 3/9/2001, effective 5/11/2001; FAC 2005-07, 71 FR 200, 1/3/2006, effective 2/2/2006]

47.202 Presolicitation planning.

Contracting officers shall inform activities that plan to acquire transportation or transportation-related services of the applicable lead-time requirements, that is—

(a) The Service Contract Labor Standards statute requirement to obtain a wage determination by accessing the Wage Determination OnLine Web site (*http://www.wdol.gov)* using the WDOL process or by submitting a request directly to the Department of Labor on this Web site using the e98 process before the issuance of an invitation for bid, request for proposal, or commencement of negotiations for any contract exceeding $2,500 that may be subject to the Service Contract Labor Standards statute (see subpart 22.10);

(b) The possible requirement to provide, during the solicitation period, time for prospective offerors or contractors to inspect origin and destination locations; or

(c) The possible requirement for inspection by agency personnel of prospective contractor facilities and equipment.

[FAC 2005-10, 71 FR 36930, 6/28/2006, effective 6/28/2006; FAC 2005-16, 72 FR 13585, 3/22/2007, effective 3/22/2007; FAC 2005-73, 79 FR 24192, 4/29/2014, effective 5/29/2014]

47.203 [Removed and Reserved]

[FAC 2005-07, 71 FR 200, 1/3/2006, effective 2/2/2006]

47.204 Single-movement contracts.

Single-movement contracts may be awarded for unique transportation services that are not otherwise available under carrier tariffs or covered by DOD or GSA contracts; *e.g.*, special requirements at origin and/or destination.

47.205 Availability of term contracts and basic ordering agreements for transportation or for transportation-related services.

(a) All Government agencies may contract for transportation or for transportation-related services and execute basic ordering agreements (BOA's) (see Subpart 16.7) unless agency regulations prescribe otherwise. However, it is generally more economical and efficient for most agencies to make use of term contracts and basic ordering agreements that have been executed by agencies that employ personnel experienced in contracting for transportation or for transportation-related services. The Department of Defense (DOD) and the General Services Administration (GSA) contract for transportation or for transportation-related services on behalf of other activities and agencies. For instance, GSA awards term contracts for services such as local drayage, office moves, and ocean-freight forwarding (see 47.105 for assistance).

(b) Agencies may obtain transportation or transportation-related services for which the cost does not exceed the simplified acquisition threshold, if term contracts or basic ordering agreements are not available.

[FAC 90-29, 60 FR 34732, 7/3/95, effective 7/3/95; FAC 90-40, 61 FR 39186, 7/26/96, effective 8/26/96]

47.206 Preparation of solicitations and contracts.

(a) Contracting officers shall prepare solicitations and contracts for transportation or for transportation-related services as prescribed elsewhere in the FAR for fixed-price service contracts to the extent that those requirements are applicable and not inconsistent with the requirements in Subpart 47.2.

(b) In addition, the contracting officer shall include in solicitations and contracts for transportation or for transportation-related services provisions, clauses, and instructions as prescribed in section 47.207.

[FAC 84-5, 50 FR 1745, 1/11/85, effective 4/1/85]

47.207 Solicitation provisions, contract clauses, and special requirements.

The contracting officer shall include provisions, clauses, and special requirements in solicitations and contracts for transportation or for transportation-related services as prescribed in 47.207-1 through 47.207-9.

[FAC 2005-07, 71 FR 200, 1/3/2006, effective 2/2/2006]

47.207-1 Qualifications of offerors.

(a) *Operating authorities.* The contracting officer shall insert the clause at 52.247-2, Permits, Authorities, or Franchises, when regulated transportation is involved. The clause need not be used when a Federal office move is intrastate and the contracting officer determines that it is in the Government's interest not to apply the requirement for holding or obtaining State authority to operate within the State.

(b) *Performance capability for Federal office moving contracts.* (1) The contracting officer shall insert the clause at 52.247-3, Capability to Perform a Contract for the Relocation of a Federal Office, when a Federal office is relocated, to ensure that offerors are capable to perform interstate or intrastate moving contracts involving the relocation of Federal offices.

(2) If a Federal office move is intrastate and the contracting officer determines that it is in the Government's interest not to apply the requirements for holding or obtaining State authority to operate within the State, and to maintain a facility within the State or commercial zone, the contracting officer shall use the clause with its Alternate I.

(c) *Inspection of shipping and receiving facilities.* The contracting officer shall insert the provision at 52.247-4, Inspection of Shipping and Receiving Facilities, when it is desired for offerors to inspect the shipping, receiving, or other sites to ensure realistic bids.

(d) *Familiarization with conditions.* The contracting officer shall insert the clause at 52.247-5, Familiarization with Conditions, to ensure that offerors become familiar with conditions under which and where the services will be performed.

(e) *Financial statement.* The contracting officer shall insert the provision at 52.247-6, Financial Statement, to ensure that offerors are prepared to furnish financial statements.

47.207-2 Duration of contract and time of performance.

The contracting officer shall—

(a) Establish a specific expiration date (month, day, and year) for the contract or state the length of time that the contract will remain in effect; *e.g.*, 6 months commencing from the date of award; and

(b) Include the following items as appropriate:

(1) A statement of the time period during which the service is required when the service is a one-time job; *e.g.*, a routine office relocation.

(2) A time schedule for the performance of segments of a major job; *e.g.*, an office relocation for which the work phases must be coordinated to meet other needs of the agency.

(3) Statements of performance times for particular services; *e.g.*, pickup and delivery services. Specify—

(i) On which days of the week and during which hours of the day pickup and delivery services may be required;

(ii) The maximum time allowable to the contractor for accomplishing delivery under regular or priority service; and

(iii) How much advance notice the contractor will be given for regular pickup services and, if applicable, priority pickup services.

47.207-3 Description of shipment, origin, and destination.

(a) *Origin of shipments.* The contracting officer shall include in solicitations full details regarding the location from which the freight is to be shipped. For example, if a single location is shown, furnish the shipper's name, street address, city, State, and ZIP code. If several or indefinite locations are involved, as in the case of multiple shippers or drayage contracts, describe the area of origin including boundaries and ZIP codes.

(b) *Destination of shipments.* The contracting officer shall include full details regarding delivery points. For example, if a single delivery point is shown, furnish the consignee's name, street address, city, State, and ZIP code. If several or indefinite delivery points are involved, describe the delivery area, including boundaries and ZIP codes.

(c) *Description of the freight.* The contracting officer shall include in solicitations—

(1) An inventory if the freight consists of nonbulk items; and

(2) The freight classification description, which should be obtained from the transportation office. If a freight classification description is not available, use a clear nontechnical description. Include additional details necessary to ensure that the prospective offerors have complete information about the freight; *e.g.*, size, weight, hazardous material, whether packed for export, or unusual value.

(d) *Exclusion of freight.* The contracting officer shall—

(1) Clearly identify any freight or types of shipments that are subject to exclusion; *e.g.*, bulk freight, hazardous commodities, or shipments under or over specified weights; and

(2) Insert a clause substantially the same as the clause at 52.247-7, Freight Excluded, when any commodities or types of shipments have been identified for exclusion.

(e) *Quantity.* (1) The contracting officer shall state the actual weight of the freight or a reasonably accurate estimate. The following are examples:

(i) If the contract covers transportation services required over an extended period of time, include a schedule of actual or estimated tonnage or number of items to be transported per week, month, or other time period.

(ii) If the contract covers a group movement of household goods, give an estimate of the aggregate weights and the basis for determining the aggregate weight.

(2) The contracting officer shall insert the clause at 52.247-8, Estimated Weights or Quantities Not Guaranteed, when weights or quantities are estimates.

47.207-4 Determination of weights.

The contracting officer shall specify in the contract the method of determining the weights of shipments as appropriate for the kind of freight involved and the type of service required.

(a) *Shipments of freight other than household goods and office furniture.* (1) The contracting officer shall insert the clause at 52.247-9, Agreed Weight—General Freight, when the shipping activity determines the weight of shipments of freight other than household goods or office furniture.

(2) The contracting officer shall insert the clause at 52.247-10, Net Weight—General Freight, when the weight of shipments of freight other than household goods or office furniture is not known at the time of shipment and the contractor is responsible for determining the net weight of the shipments.

(b) *Shipments of household goods or office furniture.* The contracting officer shall insert the clause at 52.247-11, Net Weight—Household Goods or Office Furniture, when movements of Government employees' household goods or relocations of Government offices are involved.

47.207-5 Contractor responsibilities.

Contractor responsibilities vary with the kinds of freight to be shipped and services required. The contracting officer shall specify clearly those service requirements that are not considered normal transportation or transportation-related requirements.

(a) *Type of equipment*. If appropriate, the contracting officer shall specify the type and size of equipment to be furnished by the contractor. Otherwise, state that the contractor shall furnish clean and sound closed-type equipment of sufficient size to accommodate the shipment.

(b) *Supervision, labor, or materials*. The contracting officer shall insert a clause substantially the same as the clause at 52.247-12, Supervision, Labor, or Materials, when the contractor is required to furnish supervision, labor, or materials.

(c) *Accessorial services—moving contracts*. The contracting officer shall insert a clause substantially the same as the clause at 52.247-13, Accessorial Services—Moving Contracts, in contracts for the transportation of household goods or office furniture.

(d) *Receipt of shipment*. The contracting officer shall insert the clause at 52.247-14, Contractor Responsibility for Receipt of Shipment.

(e) *Loading and unloading*. The contracting officer shall insert the clause at 52.247-15, Contractor Responsibility for Loading and Unloading, when the contractor is responsible for loading and unloading shipments.

(f) *Return of undelivered freight*. The contracting officer shall insert the clause at 52.247-16, Contractor Responsibility for Returning Undelivered Freight, when the contractor is responsible for returning undelivered freight.

47.207-6 Rates and charges.

(a) (1) The contracting officer shall include in the solicitation a statement that the charges in the contract shall not exceed the contractor's charges for the same service that is—

(i) Available to the general public; or

(ii) Otherwise tendered to the Government.

(2) The contracting officer shall insert the clause at 52.247-17, Charges.

(b) The contracting officer shall include in the solicitation a tabulation listing each required service and the basis for the rate (price); *e.g.*, "unit of weight" or "per work-hour," leaving sufficient space for offerors to insert the rates offered for each service.

(c) The following guidelines apply to the composition of a tabulation of transportation or of transportation-related services and their rate (price) bases:

(1) *Combination of pricing bases*. If various types of services with different bases for assessing charges are required under the same contract, show each service separately and the applicable basis for that service.

(2) *Hourly rate basis*. If charges are based on an hourly rate, state the method for charging for fractions of an hour; *e.g.*,—

(i) A period of 30 minutes or less is charged at one-half the hourly rate; and

(ii) The hourly rate applies to any portion of an hour that exceeds 30 minutes.

(3) *Shipments of varying weights*. If charges are based on weight and shipments will vary in weight, request rates on a graduated weight basis. Include a table of graduated weights for offerors to insert rates.

(4) *Multiple origins and/or destinations*. Specify whether rates are requested for each origin and/or each destination or for specific groups of origins and/or destinations.

(5) *Multiple shipments from one origin*. If multiple shipments will be tendered at one time to the contractor for delivery to two or more consignees at the same destination, request the rate applicable to the aggregate weight. If such shipments are for delivery to various destinations along the route between origin and last destination, request the rate applicable to the aggregate weight and a stopoff charge for each intermediate destination.

(i) The contracting officer shall insert the clause at 52.247-18, Multiple Shipments, when multiple shipments are tendered at one time to the contractor for transportation from one origin to two or more consignees at the same destination.

(ii) The contracting officer shall insert the clause at 52.247-19, Stopping in Transit for

Partial Unloading, when multiple shipments are tendered at one time to the contractor for transportation from one origin to two or more consignees along the route between origin and last destination.

(6) *Estimated quantities or weights.* The contracting officer shall insert in solicitations the provision at 52.247-20, Estimated Quantities or Weights for Evaluation of Offers, when quantities or weights of shipments between each origin and destination are not known, stating estimated quantity or weight for each origin/destination pair.

(7) *Additional services.* If services in addition to those covered in the basic rate are anticipated; *e.g.*, inside delivery, state the conditions under which payment will be made for those services.

47.207-7 Liability and insurance.

(a) The contracting officer shall specify—

(1) The contractor's liability for injury to persons or damage to property other than the freight being transported;

(2) The contractor's liability for loss of and/or damage to the freight being transported; and

(3) The amount of insurance the contractor is required to maintain.

(b) When the contractor's liability for loss of and/or damage to the freight being transported is not specified, the usual measure of liability as prescribed in section 11706 of the Interstate Commerce Act (49 U.S.C. 11706) applies.

(c) The contracting officer shall insert the clause at 52.247-21, Contractor Liability for Personal Injury and/or Property Damage.

(d) The contracting officer shall insert the clause at 52.247-22, Contractor Liability for Loss of and/or Damage to Freight other than Household Goods, in solicitations and contracts for the transportation of freight other than household goods.

(e) The contracting officer shall insert the clause at 52.247-23, Contractor Liability for Loss of and/or Damage to Household Goods, in solicitations and contracts for the transportation of household goods, including the rate per pound appropriate to the situation.

(f) When freight is not shipped under rates subject to released or declared value, see 28.313(a) and the clause at 52.228-9, Cargo Insurance.

(g) When the contracting officer determines that vehicular liability and/or general public liability insurance required by law are not sufficient for a contract, see 28.313(b) and the clause at 52.228-10, Vehicular and General Public Liability Insurance.

[FAC 2005-07, 71 FR 200, 1/3/2006, effective 2/2/2006]

47.207-8 Government responsibilities.

(a) The contracting officer shall state clearly the Government's responsibilities that have a direct bearing on the contractor's performance under the contract; *e.g.*, the Government's responsibility to notify the contractor in advance when hazardous materials are included in a shipment.

(1) *Advance notification.* The contracting officer shall insert the clause at 52.247-24, Advance Notification by the Government, when the Government is responsible for notifying the contractor of specific service times or unusual shipments.

(2) *Government equipment with or without operators.* (i) The contracting officer shall insert the clause at 52.247-25, Government-Furnished Equipment with or without Operators, when the Government furnishes equipment with or without operators.

(ii) Insert the kind of equipment and the locations where the equipment will be furnished.

(3) *Direction and marking.* The contracting officer shall insert the clause at 52.247-26, Government Direction and Marking, when office relocations are involved.

(b) The contracting officer shall insert the clause at 52.247-27, Contract Not Affected by Oral Agreement.

47.207-9 Annotation and distribution of shipping and billing documents.

(a) The contracting officer shall state in detail the responsibilities of the contractor, the contracting agency, and, if appropriate, the consignee for the annotation and distribution of shipping and billing documents. See 41 CFR part 102-118, Transportation Payment and Audit.

(b) In instances of mass movements of freight made available to the contractor at one time, it is particularly important that the contracting officer specifies that bills of lading be cross-referenced so that the Government benefits from applicable volume rates.

(c) The contracting officer shall insert the clause at 52.247-28, Contractor's Invoices, in drayage or other term contracts.

[FAC 2005-07, 71 FR 200, 1/3/2006, effective 2/2/2006]

47.207-10 Discrepancies incident to shipments.

Discrepancies incident to shipment include overage, shortage, loss, damage, and other discrepancies between the quantity and/or condition of supplies received from commercial carrier and the quantity and/or condition of these supplies as shown on the covering bill of lading or other transportation document. Regulations and procedures for reporting and adjusting discrepancies in Government shipments are in 41 CFR parts 102-117 and 118. (For the Department of Defense (DoD), see DoD 4500.9-R, Defense Transportation Regulation, Part II, Chapter 210).

[FAC 2005-07, 71 FR 200, 1/3/2006, effective 2/2/2006]

47.207-11 Volume movements within the contiguous United States.

(a) For purposes of contract administration, a volume movement is—

(1) In DoD, the aggregate of freight shipments amounting to or exceeding 25 carloads, 25 truckloads, or 500,000 pounds, to move during the contract period from one origin point for delivery to one destination point or area; and

(2) In civilian agencies, 50 short tons (100,000 pounds) in the aggregate to move during the contract period from one origin point for delivery to one destination point or area.

(b) Transportation personnel assigned to or supporting the CAO, or appropriate agency personnel, shall report planned and actual volume movements in accordance with agency regulations. DoD activities report to the Military Surface Deployment and Distribution Command (SDDC) under DoD 4500.9-R, Defense Transportation Regulation. Civilian agencies report to the local office of GSA's Office of Transportation (see *http://www.gsa.gov/transportation* (click on Transportation Management

Zone Offices in left-hand column, then click on Transportation Management Zones under Contacts on right-hand column).

[FAC 2005-07, 71 FR 200, 1/3/2006, effective 2/2/2006]

47.208 Report of shipment (REPSHIP). (No Text)

[FAC 2005-07, 71 FR 200, 1/3/2006, effective 2/2/2006]

47.208-1 Advance notice.

Military (and as required, civilian agency) storage and distribution points, depots, and other receiving activities require advance notice of shipments en route from contractors' plants. Generally, this notification is required only for classified material; sensitive, controlled, and certain other protected material; explosives, and some other hazardous materials; selected shipments requiring movement control; or minimum carload or truckload shipments. It facilitates arrangements for transportation control, labor, space, and use of materials handling equipment at destination. Also, timely receipt of notices by the consignee transportation office precludes the incurring of demurrage and vehicle detention charges.

[FAC 2005-07, 71 FR 200, 1/3/2006, effective 2/2/2006]

47.208-2 Contract clause.

The contracting officer shall insert the clause at 52.247-68, Report of Shipment (REPSHIP), in solicitations and contracts when advance notice of shipment is required for safety or security reasons, or where carload or truckload shipments will be made to DoD installations or, as required, to civilian agency facilities.

[FAC 2005-07, 71 FR 200, 1/3/2006, effective 2/2/2006]

SUBPART 47.3—TRANSPORTATION IN SUPPLY CONTRACTS

47.300 Scope of subpart.

(a) This subpart prescribes policies and procedures for the application of transportation and traffic management considerations in the acquisition of supplies. The terms and conditions contained in this subpart are applicable to fixed-price contracts.

(b) If a special requirement exists for application of any of these terms and conditions to other types of contracts; *e.g.*, cost-reimbursement contracts, for which transportation arrangements are normally the responsibility of the contractor and transportation costs are allowable, the contracting officer shall use the terms and conditions prescribed in this subpart as a guide for—

(1) Contract coverage of transportation; and

(2) Instructions to the contractor to minimize the ultimate transportation costs to the Government.

[FAC 2001-14, 68 FR 28091, 5/22/2003, effective 6/23/2003]

47.301 General.

(a) Transportation and traffic management factors are important in awarding and administering contracts to ensure that (1) acquisitions are made on the basis most advantageous to the Government and (2) supplies arrive in good order and condition and on time at the required place. (See 47.104 for possible reduced transportation rates for Government shipments.)

(b) The requiring activity shall—

(1) Consider all transportation factors including present and future requirements, positioning of supplies, and subsequent distribution to the extent known or ascertainable; and

(2) Provide the contracting office with information and instructions reflecting transportation factors applicable to the particular acquisition.

47.301-1 Responsibilities of contracting officers.

(a) Contracting officers shall obtain from traffic management offices transportation factors required for—

(1) Solicitations and awards and

(2) Contract administration, modification, and termination, including the movement of property by the Government to and from contractors' plants.

(b) Contracting officers shall request transportation office participation especially before making an initial acquisition of supplies that are unusually large, heavy, high, wide, or long; have sensitive or dangerous characteristics; or lend themselves to containerized movements from the source. In determining total transportation charges, contracting officers shall also consider additional costs arising from factors such as the use of special equipment, excess blocking and bracing material, or circuitous routing.

47.301-2 Participation of transportation officers.

Agencies' transportation officers shall participate in the solicitation and evaluation of offers to ensure that all necessary transportation factors, such as transportation costs, transit arrangements, time in transit, and port capabilities, are considered and result in solicitations and contracts advantageous to the Government. Transportation officers shall provide traffic management assistance throughout the acquisition cycle (see 47.105, Transportation assistance).

[FAC 84-5, 50 FR 1745, 1/11/85, effective 4/1/85; 59 FR 52729, 12/23/85]

47.301-3 Using the Defense Transportation System (DTS).

(a) All military and civilian agencies shipping, or arranging for the acquisition and shipment by Government contractors, through the use of military-controlled transport or through military transshipment facilities shall follow Department of Defense (DoD) Regulation DoD 4500.9-R, Defense Transportation Regulation Part II. This establishes uniform procedures and documents for the generation, documentation, communication, and use of transportation information, thus providing the capability for control of shipments moving in the DTS. DoD 4500.9-R, Defense Transportation Regulation Part II has been implemented on a world-wide basis.

(b) Contracting activities are responsible for—

(1) ensuring that the requirements of the DoD 4500.9-R, Defense Transportation Regulation Part II regulation are included in appropriate contracts for all applicable shipments and—

(2) enforcing these requirements with regard to shipments under their control. This includes requirements relating to documentation, marking, advance notification of shipment dates, and terminal clearances.

(c) Contractual documents shall designate a contract administration office (see 42.202(a)) as the contact point to which the contractor will provide necessary information to—

(1) Effect DoD 4500.9-R, Defense Transportation Regulation Part II documentation and movement control, including air or water terminal shipment clearances; and

(2) Obtain data necessary for shipment marking and freight routing. Contractual documents shall specify that the contractor shall not ship directly to a military air or water port terminal without authorization from the designated contract administration office (see 47.305-6(f)).

[FAC 84-12, 51 FR 2666, 1/17/86, effective 1/20/86; Final rule, 55 FR 38517, 9/18/90; FAC 97-4, 63 FR 9048, 2/23/98, effective 4/24/98; FAC 2005-07, 71 FR 200, 1/3/2006, effective 2/2/2006]

47.302 Place of delivery—f.o.b. point.

(a) The policies and procedures in 47.304-1, -2, and -3 govern the transportation of supplies from sources in the Contiguous United States (CONUS), except when identifiable costs, nature of the supplies (security, safety, or value), delivery requirements (premium modes of transport, escorts, transit arrangements, and tentative conditions), or other advantages, limitations, or requirements dictate otherwise. The policies and procedures in 47.304-4 govern the transportation of supplies from sources outside CONUS.

(b) Generally, the contracting officer shall solicit offers, and award contracts, with delivery terms on the basis prescribed in 47.304. The contracting officer shall document the contract file (see 4.801) with justifications for solicitations that do not specify delivery on the basis prescribed in 47.304.

(c) (1) The place of performance of Government acquisition quality assurance actions and the place of acceptance shall not control the delivery term, except that if acceptance is at destination, transportation shall be f.o.b. destination (see 47.304-1(f)).

(2) The fact that transportation is f.o.b. destination does not alone necessitate changing the place of acceptance from origin to destination; and the fact that acceptance is at origin does not necessitate an f.o.b. origin delivery term. Providing for inspection and acceptance at origin (if appropriate under 46.402), in conjunction with an f.o.b. destination term, may be advantageous to both the Government and the contractor. Acceptance of title at origin by the Government permits payment of the contractor, provided the invoice is supported either by a copy of the signed commercial bill of lading (indicating the carrier's receipt of the supplies covered by the invoice for transportation to the particular destination specified in the contract) or by other appropriate evidence of shipment to the particular destination for the contractor's account.

47.303 Standard delivery terms and contract clauses.

Standard delivery terms are listed in 47.303-1 through 47.303-16 (but see 47.300 regarding applicability to cost reimbursement contracts).

[FAC 84-39, 53 FR 34228, 9/2/88, effective 10/3/88; FAC 2001-14, 68 FR 28079, 5/22/2003, effective 6/23/2003]

47.303-1 F.o.b. origin.

(a) *Explanation of delivery term. F.o.b. origin* means free of expense to the Government delivered—

(1) On board the indicated type of conveyance of the carrier (or of the Government, if specified) at a designated point in the city, county, and State from which the shipment will be made and from which line-haul transportation service (as distinguished from switching, local drayage, or other terminal service) will begin;

(2) To, and placed on, the carrier's wharf (at shipside, within reach of the ship's loading tackle, when the shipping point is within a port area having water transportation service) or the carrier's freight station;

(3) To a U.S. Postal Service facility; or

(4) If stated in the solicitation, to any Government-designated point located within the same city or commercial zone as the f.o.b. origin point specified in the contract (the Federal Motor Carrier Safety Administration prescribes commercial zones at Subpart B of 49 CFR part 372).

(b) *Contractor responsibilities*. The contractor shall—

(1) (i) Pack and mark the shipment to comply with contract specifications; or

(ii) In the absence of specifications, prepare the shipment in conformance with carrier requirements to protect the goods and to ensure assessment of the lowest applicable transportation charge;

(2) (i) Order specified carrier equipment when requested by the Government; or

(ii) If not specified, order appropriate carrier equipment not in excess of capacity to accommodate shipment;

(3) Deliver the shipment in good order and condition to the carrier, and load, stow, trim, block, and/or brace carload or truckload shipment (when loaded by the contractor) on or in the carrier's conveyance as required by carrier rules and regulations;

(4) Be responsible for any loss of and/or damage to the goods—

(i) Occurring before delivery to the carrier;

(ii) Resulting from improper packing and marking; or

(iii) Resulting from improper loading, stowing, trimming, blocking, and/or bracing of the shipment, if loaded by the contractor on or in the carrier's conveyance;

(5) Complete the Government bill of lading supplied by the ordering agency or, when a Government bill of lading is not supplied, prepare a commercial bill of lading or other transportation receipt. The bill of lading shall show—

(i) A description of the shipment in terms of the governing freight classification or tariff (or Government rate tender) under which lowest freight rates are applicable;

(ii) The seals affixed to the conveyance with their serial numbers or other identification;

(iii) Lengths and capacities of cars or trucks ordered and furnished;

(iv) Other pertinent information required to effect prompt delivery to the consignee, including name, delivery address, postal address and ZIP code of consignee, routing, etc.;

(v) Special instructions or annotations requested by the ordering agency for commercial bills of lading; e.g., "This shipment is the property of, and the freight charges paid to the carrier(s) will be reimbursed by, the Government"; and

(vi) The signature of the carrier's agent and the date the shipment is received by the carrier; and

(6) Distribute the copies of the bill of lading, or other transportation receipts, as directed by the ordering agency.

(c) *Contract clause*. The contracting officer shall insert in solicitations and contracts the clause at 52.247-29, F.o.b. Origin, when the delivery term is f.o.b. origin.

[FAC 84-37, 53 FR 17859, 5/18/88, effective 6/17/88; FAC 2005-07, 71 FR 200, 1/3/2006, effective 2/2/2006]

47.303-2 F.o.b. origin, contractor's facility.

(a) *Explanation of delivery term. F.o.b. origin, contractor's facility* means free of expense to the Government delivered on board the indicated type of conveyance of the carrier (or of the Government if specified) at the designated facility, on the named street or highway, in the city, county, and State from which the shipment will be made.

(b) *Contractor responsibilities.* The contractor's responsibilities are the same as those listed in 47.303-1(b).

(c) *Contract clause.* The contracting officer shall insert in solicitations and contracts the clause at 52.247-30, F.o.b. Origin, Contractor's Facility, when the delivery term is f.o.b. origin, contractor's facility.

47.303-3 F.o.b. origin, freight allowed.

(a) *Explanation of delivery term. F.o.b. origin, freight allowed* means—

(1) Free of expense to the Government delivered—

(i) On board the indicated type or conveyance of the carrier (or of the Government, if specified) at a designated point in the city, county, and State from which the shipments will be made and from which line-haul transportation service (as distinguished from switching, local drayage, or other terminal service) will begin;

(ii) To, and placed on, the carrier's wharf (at shipside, within reach of the ship's loading tackle, when the shipping point is within a port area having water transportation service) or the carrier's freight station;

(iii) To a U.S. Postal Service facility; or

(iv) If stated in the solicitation, to any Government-designated point located within the same city or commercial zone as the f.o.b. origin point specified in the contract (the Federal Motor Carrier Safety Administration prescribes commercial zones at Subpart B of 49 CFR part 372); and

(2) An allowance for freight, based on applicable published tariff rates (or Government rate tenders) between the points specified in the contract, is deducted from the contract price.

(b) *Contractor responsibilities.* The contractor's responsibilities are the same as those listed in 47.303-1(b).

(c) *Contract clause.* The contracting officer shall insert in solicitations and contracts the clause at 52.247-31, F.o.b. Origin, Freight Allowed, when the delivery term is f.o.b. origin, freight allowed.

[FAC 84-37, 53 FR 17859, 5/18/88, effective 6/17/88; FAC 2005-07, 71 FR 200, 1/3/2006, effective 2/2/2006]

47.303-4 F.o.b. origin, freight prepaid.

(a) *Explanation of delivery term. F.o.b. origin, freight prepaid* means—

(1) Free of expense to the Government delivered—

(i) On board the indicated type of conveyance of the carrier (or of the Government, if specified) at a designated point in the city, county, and State from which the shipments will be made and from which line-haul transportation service (as distinguished from switching, local drayage, or other terminal service) will begin;

(ii) To, and placed on, the carrier's wharf (at shipside, within reach of the ship's loading tackle, when the shipping point is within a port area having water transportation service) or the carrier's freight station;

(iii) To a U.S. Postal Service facility; or

(iv) If stated in the solicitation, to any Government-designated point located within the same city or commercial zone as the f.o.b. origin point specified in the contract (the Federal Motor Carrier Safety Administration prescribes commercial zones at Subpart B of 49 CFR part 372); and

(2) The cost of transportation, ultimately the Government's obligation, is prepaid by the contractor to the point specified in the contract.

(b) *Contractor responsibilities.* The contractor's responsibilities are the same as those listed in 47.303-1(b), except that the contractor shall prepare commercial bills of lading or other transportation receipts and shall prepay all freight charges to the extent specified in the contract.

(c) *Contract clause.* The contracting officer shall insert in solicitations and contracts the clause at 52.247-32, F.o.b. Origin, Freight Prepaid, when the delivery term is f.o.b. origin, freight prepaid.

[FAC 84-37, 53 FR 17859, 5/18/88, effective 6/17/88; FAC 2005-07, 71 FR 200, 1/3/2006, effective 2/2/2006]

47.303-5 F.o.b. origin, with differentials.

(a) *Explanation of delivery term. F.o.b. origin, with differentials* means—

(1) Free of expense to the Government delivered—

(i) On board the indicated type of conveyance of the carrier (or of the Government, if specified) at a designated point in the city, county, and State from which the shipments will be made and from which line-haul transportation service (as distinguished from switching, local drayage, or other terminal service) will begin;

(ii) To, and placed on, the carrier's wharf (at shipside, within reach of the ship's loading tackle, when the shipping point is within a port area having water transportation service) or the carrier's freight station;

(iii) To a U.S. Postal Service facility; or

(iv) If stated in the solicitation, to any Government-designated point located within the same city or commercial zone as the f.o.b. origin point specified in the contract (the Federal Motor Carrier Safety Administration prescribes commercial zones at Subpart B of 49 CFR part 372); and

(2) Differentials for mode of transportation, type of vehicle, or place of delivery as indicated in contractor's offer may be added to the contract price.

(b) *Contractor responsibilities*. The contractor's responsibilities are the same as those listed in 47.303-1(b).

(c) *Contract clause*. Insert in solicitations and contracts the clause at 52.247-33, F.o.b. Origin, with Differentials, when it is likely that offerors may include in f.o.b. origin offers a contingency to compensate for unfavorable routing conditions by the Government at the time of shipment.

[FAC 84-37, 53 FR 17859, 5/18/88, effective 6/17/88; FAC 2005-07, 71 FR 200, 1/3/2006, effective 2/2/2006]

47.303-6 F.o.b. destination.

(a) *Explanation of delivery term. F.o.b. destination* means—

(1) Free of expense to the Government delivered, on board the carrier's conveyance, at a specified delivery point where the consignee's facility (plant, warehouse, store, lot, or other location to which shipment can be made) is located; and

(2) Supplies shall be delivered to the destination consignee's wharf (if destination is a port city and supplies are for export), warehouse unloading platform, or receiving dock, at the expense of the contractor. The Government shall not be liable for any delivery, storage, demurrage, accessorial, or other charges involved before the actual delivery (or "constructive placement" as defined in carrier tariffs) of the supplies to the destination, unless such charges are caused by an act or order of the Government acting in its contractual capacity. If rail carrier is used, supplies shall be delivered to the specified unloading platform of the consignee. If motor carrier (including "piggyback") is used, supplies shall be delivered to truck tailgate at the unloading platform of the consignee, except when the supplies delivered meet the requirements of Item 568 of the National Motor Freight Classification for "heavy or bulky freight." When supplies meeting the requirements of the referenced Item 568 are delivered, unloading (including movement to the tailgate) shall be performed by the consignee, with assistance from the truck driver, if requested. If the contractor uses rail carrier or freight forwarder for less than carload shipments, the contractor shall ensure that the carrier will furnish tailgate delivery when required, if transfer to truck is required to complete delivery to consignee.

(b) *Contractor responsibilities*. The contractor shall—

(1) (i) Pack and mark the shipment to comply with contract specifications; or

(ii) In the absence of specifications, prepare the shipment in conformance with carrier requirements;

(2) Prepare and distribute commercial bills of lading;

(3) Deliver the shipment in good order and condition to the point of delivery specified in the contract;

(4) Be responsible for any loss of and/or damage to the goods occurring before receipt of the shipment by the consignee at the delivery point specified in the contract;

(5) Furnish a delivery schedule and designate the mode of delivering carrier; and

(6) Pay and bear all charges to the specified point of delivery.

(c) *Contract clause.* The contracting officer shall insert in solicitations and contracts the clause at 52.247-34, F.o.b. Destination, when the delivery term is f.o.b. destination.

[FAC 90-3, 55 FR 52796, 12/21/90, effective 1/22/91]

47.303-7 F.o.b. destination, within consignee's premises.

(a) *Explanation of delivery term. F.o.b. destination, within consignee's premises* means free of expense to the Government delivered and laid down within the doors of the consignee's premises, including delivery to specific rooms within a building if so specified.

(b) *Contractor responsibilities.* The contractor's responsibilities are the same as those listed in 47.303-6(b).

(c) *Contract clause.* The contracting officer shall insert in solicitations and contracts the clause at 52.247-35, F.o.b. Destination, within Consignee's Premises, when the delivery term is f.o.b. destination, within consignee's premises.

47.303-8 F.a.s. vessel, port of shipment.

(a) *Explanation of delivery term. F.a.s. vessel, port of shipment* means free of expense to the Government delivered alongside the ocean vessel and within reach of its loading tackle at the specified port of shipment.

(b) *Contractor responsibilities.* The contractor shall—

(1) (i) Pack and mark the shipment to comply with contract specifications; or

(ii) In the absence of specifications, prepare the shipment for ocean transportation in conformance with carrier requirements to protect the goods and to ensure assessment of the lowest applicable transportation charge;

(2) (i) Deliver the shipment in good order and condition alongside the ocean vessel and within reach of its loading tackle, at the point of delivery and on the date or within the period specified in the contract; and

(ii) Pay and bear all applicable charges, including transportation costs, wharfage, handling, and heavy lift charges, if necessary, up to this point;

(3) Provide a clean dock or ship's receipt;

(4) Be responsible for any loss of and/or damage to the goods occurring before delivery of the shipment to the point specified in the contract; and

(5) At the Government's request and expense, assist in obtaining the documents required for—

(i) Exportation; or

(ii) Importation at destination.

(c) *Contract clause.* The contracting officer shall insert in solicitations and contracts the clause at 52.247-36, F.a.s. Vessel, Port of Shipment, when the delivery term is f.a.s. vessel, port of shipment.

47.303-9 F.o.b. vessel, port of shipment.

(a) *Explanation of delivery term. F.o.b. vessel, port of shipment* means free of expense to the Government loaded, stowed, and trimmed on board the ocean vessel at the specified port of shipment.

(b) *Contractor responsibilities.* The contractor shall—

(1) (i) Pack and mark the shipment to comply with contract specifications; or

(ii) In the absence of specifications, prepare the shipment for ocean transportation in conformance with carrier requirements to protect the goods and to ensure assessment of the lowest applicable transportation charge;

(2) (i) Deliver the shipment on board the ocean vessel in good order and condition on the date or within the period fixed; and

(ii) Pay and bear all charges incurred in placing the shipment actually on board;

(3) Provide a clean ship's receipt or on-board ocean bill of lading;

(4) Be responsible for any loss of and/or damage to the goods occurring before delivery of the shipment on board the ocean vessel; and

(5) At the Government's request and expense, assist in obtaining the documents required for—

(i) Exportation; or

(ii) Importation at destination.

(c) *Contract clause.* The contracting officer shall insert in solicitations and contracts the clause at 52.247-37, F.o.b. Vessel, Port of Shipment, when the delivery term is f.o.b. vessel, port of shipment.

47.303-10 F.o.b. inland carrier, point of exportation.

(a) *Explanation of delivery term. F.o.b. inland carrier, point of exportation* means free of expense to the Government, on board the conveyance of the inland carrier, delivered to the specified point of exportation.

(b) *Contractor responsibilities.* The contractor shall—

(1) (i) Pack and mark the shipment to comply with contract specifications; or

(ii) In the absence of specifications, prepare the shipment for ocean transportation in conformance with carrier requirements to protect the goods and to ensure assessment of the lowest applicable transportation charge;

(2) Prepare and distribute commercial bills of lading;

(3) (i) Deliver the shipment in good order and condition in or on the conveyance of the carrier on the date or within the period specified; and

(ii) Pay and bear all applicable charges, including transportation costs, to the point of delivery specified in the contract;

(4) Be responsible for any loss of and/or damage to the goods occurring before delivery of the shipment to the point of delivery specified in the contract; and

(5) At the Government's request and expense, assist in obtaining the documents required for—

(i) Exportation; or

(ii) Importation at destination.

(c) *Contract clause.* The contracting officer shall insert in solicitations and contracts the clause at 52.247-38, F.o.b. Inland Carrier, Point of Exportation, when the delivery term is f.o.b. inland carrier, point of exportation.

47.303-11 F.o.b. inland point, country of importation.

(a) *Explanation of delivery term. F.o.b. inland point, country of importation* means free of expense to the Government, on board the indicated type of conveyance of the carrier, delivered to the specified inland point where the consignee's facility is located.

(b) *Contractor responsibilities.* The contractor shall—

(1) (i) Pack and mark the shipment to comply with contract specifications; or

(ii) In the absence of specifications, prepare the shipment for ocean transportation in conformance with carrier requirements to protect the goods;

(2) (i) Deliver, in or on the inland carrier's conveyance, the shipment in good order and condition to the specified inland point where the consignee's facility is located;

(ii) Pay and bear all applicable charges incurred up to the point of delivery, including transportation costs; export, import, or other fees or taxes; costs of landing; wharfage costs; customs duties and costs of certificates of origin; consular invoices; and other documents that may be required for importation; and

(3) Be responsible for any loss of and/or damage to the goods until their arrival on or in the carrier's conveyance at the specified inland point.

(c) *Contract clause.* The contracting officer shall insert in solicitations and contracts the clause at 52.247-39, F.o.b. Inland Point, Country of Importation, when the delivery term is f.o.b. inland point, country of importation.

47.303-12 Ex dock, pier, or warehouse, port of importation.

(a) *Explanation of delivery term. Ex dock, pier, or warehouse, port of importation* means free of expense to the Government delivered on the designated dock or pier or in the warehouse at the specified port of importation.

(b) *Contractor responsibilities.* The contractor shall—

(1) (i) Pack and mark the shipment to comply with contract specifications; or

(ii) In the absence of specifications, prepare the shipment for ocean transportation in conformance with carrier requirements to protect the goods;

(2) (i) Deliver shipment in good order and condition; and

(ii) Pay and bear all charges up to the point of delivery specified in the contract, including transportation costs; export, import, or other fees or taxes; costs of wharfage and landing, if any; customs duties; and costs of certificates of origin, consular invoices, or other documents that may be required for exportation or importation; and

(3) Be responsible for any loss of and/or damage to the goods occurring before delivery of the shipment to the point of delivery specified in the contract.

(c) *Contract clause.* The contracting officer shall insert in solicitations and contracts the clause at 52.247-40, Ex Dock, Pier, or Warehouse, Port of Importation, when the delivery term is ex dock, pier, or warehouse, port of importation.

47.303-13 C.& f. destination.

(a) *Explanation of delivery term. C.&f. (cost & freight) destination* means free of expense to the Government delivered on board the ocean vessel to the specified point of destination, with the cost of transportation paid by the contractor.

(b) *Contractor responsibilities.* The contractor shall—

(1) (i) Pack and mark the shipment to comply with contract specifications; or

(ii) In the absence of specifications, prepare the shipment for ocean transportation in conformance with carrier requirements;

(2) (i) Deliver the shipment in good order and condition; and

(ii) Pay and bear all applicable charges to the point of destination specified in the contract, including transportation costs and export taxes or other fees or charges levied because of exportation;

(3) Obtain and dispatch promptly to the Government clean on-board ocean bills of lading to the specified point of destination;

(4) Be responsible for any loss of and/or damage to the goods occurring before delivery; and

(5) At the Government's request and expense, provide certificates of origin, consular invoices, or any other documents issued in the country of origin or of shipment, or both, that may be required for importation into the country of destination.

(c) *Contract clause.* The contracting officer shall insert in solicitations and contracts the clause at 52.247-41, C.&f. Destination, when the delivery term is c.&f. (Cost & freight) destination.

[FAC 2005-07, 71 FR 200, 1/3/2006, effective 2/2/2006]

47.303-14 C.i.f. destination.

(a) *Explanation of delivery term. C.i.f. (Cost, insurance, freight) destination* means free of expense to the Government delivered on board the ocean vessel to the specified point of destination, with the cost of transportation and marine insurance paid by the contractor.

(b) *Contractor responsibilities.* The contractor's responsibilities are the same as those listed in 47.303-13(b), except that, in addition, the contractor shall obtain and dispatch to the Government an insurance policy or certificate providing the amount and extent of marine insurance coverage specified in the contract or agreed upon by the Government contracting officer.

(c) *Contract clause.* The contracting officer shall insert in solicitations and contracts the clause at 52.247-42, C.i.f. (Cost, insurance, freight) Destination, when the delivery term is c.i.f. destination.

[FAC 2005-07, 71 FR 200, 1/3/2006, effective 2/2/2006]

47.303-15 F.o.b. designated air carrier's terminal, point of exportation.

(a) *Explanation of delivery term. F.o.b. designated air carrier's terminal, point of exportation* means free of expense to the Government loaded aboard the aircraft, or delivered to the custody of the air carrier (if only the air carrier performs the loading), at the air carrier's terminal specified in the contract.

(b) *Contractor responsibilities.* The contractor shall—

(1) (i) Pack and mark the shipment to comply with contract specifications; or

(ii) In the absence of specifications, prepare the shipment for air transportation in conformance with carrier requirements to protect the goods and to ensure assessment of the lowest applicable transportation charge;

(2) (i) Deliver the shipment in good order and condition into the conveyance of the carrier, or to the custody of the carrier (if only the carrier performs the loading), at the point of delivery and on the date or within the period specified in the contract; and

(ii) Pay and bear all applicable charges up to this point;

(3) Provide a clean bill of lading and/or air waybill;

(4) Be responsible for any loss of and/or damage to the goods occurring before delivery of the goods to the point specified in the contract; and

(5) At the Government's request and expense, assist in obtaining the documents required for the purpose of exportation.

(c) *Contract clause.* The contracting officer shall insert in solicitations and contracts the clause at 52.247-43, F.o.b. Designated Air Carrier's Terminal, Point of Exportation, when the delivery term is f.o.b. designated air carrier's terminal, point of exportation.

[FAC 2005-07, 71 FR 200, 1/3/2006, effective 2/2/2006]

47.303-16 F.o.b. designated air carrier's terminal, point of importation.

(a) *Explanation of delivery term. F.o.b. designated air carrier's terminal, point of importation* means free of expense to the Government delivered to the air carrier's terminal at the point of importation specified in the contract.

(b) *Contractor responsibilities.* The contractor shall—

(1) (i) Pack and mark the shipment to comply with contract specifications; or

(ii) In the absence of specifications, prepare the shipment for air transportation in conformance with carrier requirements to protect the goods;

(2) Prepare and distribute bills of lading or air waybills;

(3) (i) Deliver the shipment in good order and condition to the point of delivery specified in the contract; and

(ii) Pay and bear all charges incurred up to the point of delivery specified in the contract, including transportation costs; export, import, or other fees or taxes; cost of landing, if any; customs duties; and costs of certificates of origin, consular invoices, or other documents that may be required for exportation or importation; and

(4) Be responsible for any loss of and/or damage to the goods until delivery of the goods to the Government at the designated air carrier's terminal.

(c) *Contract clause.* The contracting officer shall insert in solicitations and contracts the clause at 52.247-44, F.o.b. Designated Air Carrier's Terminal, Point of Importation, when the delivery term is f.o.b. designated air carrier's terminal, point of importation.

47.303-17 Contractor-prepaid commercial bills of lading, small package shipments.

(a) If it is advantageous to the Government, the contracting officer may authorize the contractor to ship supplies, which have been acquired f.o.b. origin, to domestic destinations, including DoD air and water terminals, by common carriers on commercial bills of lading. Such shipments shall not exceed 150 pounds by commercial air or 1,000 pounds by other commercial carriers and shall not have a security classification.

(b) The contracting officer may authorize the shipments under paragraph (a) of this subsection to be consolidated with the contractor's own prepaid shipments for delivery to one or more destinations, if all appropriate f.o.b. origin shipments under one or more Government contracts have been consolidated initially. The contractor may be authorized to consolidate less-than-carload or less-than-truckload Government shipments with its own shipments so that the Government can take advantage of lower carload or truckload freight costs. The Government shall assume its pro rata share of the combined shipment cost. Agency transportation personnel shall evaluate overall transportation costs before authorizing any movement to ensure savings to the Government consistent with other contract and traffic management considerations. When consolidation is authorized, a copy of the commercial bill of lading shall be mailed promptly to each consignee.

(c) Shipments under prepaid commercial bills of lading, as authorized in paragraph (a) of this subsection, do not require a contract modification. Unless otherwise provided in the contract, the supplies move for the account of, and at the risk of, the Government. The supplies become Government property when loaded on the carrier's equipment and the contractor has obtained the carrier's receipt. The contractor pays the transportation charges and is reimbursed by the Government. Loss or damage claims shall be processed in accordance with agency regulations.

(d) The contractor's invoice for reimbursement by the Government shall show the prepaid transportation charges as agreed (see paragraph (b) of this subsection), as a separate item for each individual shipment. The contractor shall support the transportation charges with a copy of the carrier's receipted freight bill or other evidence of receipt, except as follows:

(1) A Government agency may determine that receipted freight bills or other evidence of receipt are not required for transportation charges of $100 or less.

(2) A Government agency may pay an invoiced but unsupported transportation charge of $250 or less per transaction (*i.e.*, purchase, invoice, or aggregate billing or payment for multiple purchases), if—

(i) The contractor cannot reasonably provide a receipted freight bill; and

(ii) The agency has determined that the charges are reasonable. Determination of reasonableness may be based on—

(A) Past experience (authenticated transportation charges for similar shipments);

(B) Rate checks;

(C) Copies of previous freight bills submitted by the contractor; or

(D) Other information submitted by the contractor to substantiate the amount claimed.

(3) Receipted freight bills in support of invoiced transportation charges of $100 or less are not required for reimbursement by the Government, if—

(i) The underlying contract specifies retention by the contractor of all records for at least 3 years after final payment under the contract; and

(ii) The contractor agrees to furnish evidence of payment when requested by the Government.

(e) Shipments and invoices shall not be split to reduce transportation charges to $100 or less per transaction as a means of avoiding the required documented support for the charges. See paragraph (d)(2) of this subsection for unsupported transportation charges of $250 or less.

(f) The contracting officer shall insert the clause at 52.247-65, F.o.b. Origin, Prepaid Freight-Small Package Shipments, in solicitations and contracts when f.o.b. origin shipments are to be made.

[FAC 90-3, 55 FR 52796, 12/21/90, effective 1/22/91; FAC 90-45, Final rule, 62 FR 224, 1/2/97, effective 1/1/97; FAC 97-3, 62 FR 64912, 12/9/97, effective 2/9/98]

47.304 Determination of delivery terms. (No Text)

47.304-1 General.

(a) The contracting officer shall determine f.o.b. terms generally on the basis of overall costs, giving due consideration to the criteria given in 47.304.

(b) Solicitations shall specify whether offerors must submit offers f.o.b. origin, f.o.b. destination, or both; or whether offerors may choose the basis on which they make an offer. The contracting officer shall consider the most advantageous delivery point, such as—

(1) F.o.b. origin, carrier's equipment, wharf, or specified freight station near contractor's plant; or

(2) F.o.b. destination.

(c) In determining whether f.o.b. origin or f.o.b. destination is more advantageous to the Government, the contracting officer shall consider the availability of lower freight rates (Government rate tenders) to the Government for f.o.b. origin acquisitions. F.o.b. origin contracts also present other desirable traffic management features, in that they—

(1) Permit use of transit privileges (see 47.305-13);

(2) Permit diversions to new destinations without price adjustment for transportation (see 47.305-11);

(3) Facilitate use of special routings or types of equipment (*e.g.*, circuitous routing or oversize shipments) (see 47.305-14);

(4) Facilitate, if necessary, use of premium cost transportation and permit Government-controlled transportation;

(5) Permit negotiations for reduced freight rates (see 47.104-1(b)); and

(6) Permit use of small shipment consolidation stations.

(d) When destinations are tentative or unknown, the solicitation shall be f.o.b. origin only (see 47.305-5).

(e) When the size or quantity of supplies with confidential or higher security classification requires commercial transportation services, the contracting officer shall generally specify f.o.b. origin acquisitions.

(f) When acceptance must be at destination, solicitation shall be on an f.o.b. destination only basis.

(g) Following are examples of situations when solicitations shall normally be on an f.o.b. destination only basis because it is advantageous to the Government (see 47.305-4):

(1) Bulk supplies, such as coal, that require other than Government-owned or operated handling, storage, and loading facilities, are destined for shipment outside CONUS.

(2) Steel or other bulk construction products are destined for shipment outside CONUS.

(3) Supplies consist of forest products such as lumber.

(4) Perishable or medical supplies are subject to in-transit deterioration.

(5) Evaluation of f.o.b. origin offers is anticipated to result in increased administrative lead time or administrative cost that would outweigh the potential advantages of an f.o.b. origin determination.

[FAC 2001-14, 68 FR 28079, 5/22/2003, effective 6/23/2003]

47.304-2 Shipments within CONUS.

(a) Solicitations shall provide that offers may be submitted on the basis of either or both f.o.b origin and f.o.b. destination and that they will be evaluated on the basis of the lowest overall cost to the Government.

(b) When sufficient reasons exist not to follow this policy, the contract file shall be documented to include the reasons.

47.304-3 Shipments from CONUS for overseas delivery.

(a) When Government acquisitions involve shipments from CONUS to overseas destinations, delivery f.o.b. origin may afford not only the economies of lower freight rates available to the Government within CONUS, but also flexibility for selection of—

(1) The port of export; and

(2) The ocean transportation providing the lowest overall cost to the Government.

(b) (1) Unless there are valid reasons to the contrary (see 47.304-5), acquisition of supplies originating within CONUS for ultimate delivery to destinations outside CONUS shall be made on the basis of f.o.b. origin. This policy applies to supplies and equipment to be shipped either directly to a port area for export or to a storage or holding area for subsequent forwarding to a port area for export.

(2) Justification for the solicitation of offers on other than an f.o.b. origin basis shall be recorded and the contract file documented accordingly.

(c) Export cargo involves considerations of operational and cost factors from the point of origin within CONUS to the overseas port destination. The lowest cost of shipping can be determined only by evaluating and comparing the various prospective landed costs (including inland, terminal, and ocean costs). Also, agencies may have export licensing privileges for shipments to foreign destinations. The contracting officer shall obtain advice from the transportation officer to ensure full use of these privileges.

[FAC 2001-14, 68 FR 28079, 5/22/2003, effective 6/23/2003]

47.304-4 Shipments originating outside CONUS.

(a) Unless there are valid reasons to the contrary (see 47.304-5), acquisition of supplies originating outside CONUS for ultimate delivery to destinations within CONUS or elsewhere, regardless of the quantity of the shipments, shall be on the basis of f.o.b. origin or f.o.b. destination, whichever is more advantageous to the Government.

(b) The contracting officer shall request the advice of the transportation officer to determine the most appropriate place of delivery to be specified in acquisition documents, giving full consideration to the possible use of Government transportation facilities, reduced rates available, special licensing or custom requirements, and availability of U.S. flag shipping services between the points involved (see Subpart 47.5).

47.304-5 Exceptions.

(a) Unusual conditions or circumstances may require the use of terms other than f.o.b. origin or f.o.b. destination. Such conditions or circumstances include, but are not limited to—

(1) Transportation disabilities at origin or destination;

(2) Mode of transportation required;

(3) Availability of Government or commercial loading, unloading, or transshipment facilities;

(4) Characteristics of the supplies;

(5) Trade customs related to certain supplies;

(6) Origins or destinations in Alaska and Hawaii; and

(7) Program requirements.

(b) Contracting officers shall obtain assistance from transportation officers before issuing solicitations when unusual conditions or circumstances exist that relate to f.o.b. terms.

47.305 Solicitation provisions, contract clauses, and transportation factors.

(a) The contracting officer shall coordinate transportation factors with the transportation office during the planning, solicitation, and award phases of the acquisition process (see 47.105).

(b) To the extent feasible, activities shall schedule deliveries to effect savings in transportation costs, and concomitant reductions in energy consumption by carriers (see 47.305-7 and 47.305-8 for specific possibilities).

47.305-1 Solicitation requirements.

When the acquisition of supplies is on f.o.b. origin or f.o.b. destination delivery terms, the contracting officer shall include in solicitations a requirement that the offeror furnish the Government as much of the following data as is applicable to the particular acquisition:

(a) Modes of transportation and, if rail transportation is used, names of rail carriers serving the offeror's facility.

(b) The number of railroad cars, motor trucks, or other conveyances that can be loaded per day.

(c) Type of packaging; *e.g.*, box, carton, crate, drum, bundle, skids, and when applicable, package number from the governing freight classification.

(d) Number of units packed in one container.

(e) Guaranteed maximum shipping weight; cubic measurement; and length, width, and height of each container.

(f) Minimum size of each shipment.

(g) Number of containers or units that can be loaded in a car, truck, or other conveyance of the size normally used (specify type and size) for the commodity.

(h) Description of material in terms of the governing freight classification or tariff (or Government rate tender) under which lowest freight rates are applicable.

(i) Benefits available to the Government under transit arrangements made by the offeror.

(j) Other requirements as stated under specific section headings.

47.305-2 Solicitations f.o.b. origin and f.o.b. destination—lowest overall cost.

(a) Solicitations, when appropriate, shall specify that offers may be f.o.b. origin, f.o.b. destination, or both; and that they will be evaluated on the basis of the lowest overall cost to the Government.

(b) When offers are solicited on the basis of both f.o.b. origin and f.o.b. destination, the contracting officer shall insert in solicitations the provision at 52.247-45, F.o.b. Origin and/or F.o.b. Destination Evaluation.

47.305-3 F.o.b. origin solicitations.

When preparing f.o.b. origin solicitations, the contracting officer shall refer to 47.303, where f.o.b. origin clauses relating to standard delivery terms are prescribed. Supply solicitations that will or may result in f.o.b. origin contracts shall also contain requirements, information, provisions, and clauses concerning the following items:

(a) Delivery in carload or truckload lots f.o.b. carrier's equipment, wharf, or freight station.

(b) The requirement that the offeror furnish the following information with the offer:

(1) Location of the offeror's actual shipping point(s) (street address, city, State, and ZIP code) from which supplies will be delivered to the Government.

(2) Whether the offeror's shipping point has a private railroad siding, and the name of the rail carrier serving it.

(3) When the offeror's shipping point does not have a private siding, the names and addresses of the nearest public rail siding and of the carrier serving it. (This will enable transportation officers, when issuing routing instructions, to select the mode of transportation that will provide the required service at the lowest possible overall cost.)

(4) (i) The quantity of supplies to be shipped from each shipping point.

(ii) The contracting officer shall insert in f.o.b. origin solicitations the provision at 52.247-46, Shipping Point(s) Used in Evaluation of F.o.b. Origin Offers, when price evaluation for shipments from various shipping points is contemplated.

(c) When delivery is "f.o.b. origin, contractor's facility," and the designated facility is not covered by the line-haul transportation rate, the charges required to deliver the shipment to the point where the line-haul rate is applicable.

(d) When delivery is "f.o.b. origin, freight allowed," the basis on which transportation charges will be allowed, including the origin and destination from and to which transportation charges will be allowed.

(e) If f.o.b. origin offers only are desired, a statement that offers submitted on any other basis will be rejected as nonresponsive.

(f) (1) *The methods of transportation used in evaluating offers.* The Government normally uses land transportation by regulated common carriers between points in the 48 contiguous United States and the District of Columbia.

(2) The contracting officer shall insert the provision at 52.247-47, Evaluation—F.o.b.

Origin, in solicitations that require prices f.o.b. origin for the purpose of establishing the basis on which offers will be evaluated.

(g) (1) When it is believed that prospective contractors are likely to include in f.o.b. origin offers a contingency to compensate for what may be an unfavorable routing condition by the Government at the time of shipment, the contracting officer may permit prospective contractors to state in offers a reimbursable differential that represents the cost of bringing the supplies to any f.o.b. origin place of delivery specified by the Government at the time of shipment (see the clause at 52.247-33, F.o.b. Origin, with Differentials).

(2) Following are situations that might impose on the contractor a substantial cost above "at plant" or "commercial shipping point" prices because of Government-required routings:

(i) The loading nature of the supplies; *e.g.*, wheeled vehicles.

(ii) The different methods of shipment specified by the Government; *e.g.*, towaway, driveaway, tri-level vehicle, or rail car, that may increase the contractor's cost in varying amounts for bringing the supplies to, or loading and bracing the supplies at, the specified place of delivery.

(iii) The contractor's f.o.b. origin shipping point is a port city served by United States inland, coastwise, or intercoastal water transportation, and the contractor would incur additional costs to make delivery f.o.b. a wharf in that city to accommodate water routing specified by the Government.

(iv) The contractor's plant does not have a private rail siding and in order to ship by Government-specified rail routing, the contractor would be required to deliver the supplies to a public siding or freight terminal and to load, brace, and install dunnage in rail cars.

[FAC 84-21, 51 FR 31426, 9/3/86, effective 8/29/86; FAC 2005-07, 71 FR 200, 1/3/2006, effective 2/2/2006]

47.305-4 F.o.b. destination solicitations.

(a) When preparing f.o.b destination solicitations, the contracting officer shall refer to 47.303 for the prescription of f.o.b. destination clauses relating to standard delivery terms.

(b) If f.o.b. destination only offers are desired, the solicitation shall state that offers submitted on a basis other than f.o.b. destination will be rejected as nonresponsive.

(c) When supplies will or may be purchased f.o.b. destination but inspection and acceptance will be at origin, the contracting officer shall insert in solicitations and contracts the clause at 52.247-48, F.o.b. Destination—Evidence of Shipment.

47.305-5 Destination unknown.

(a) (1) When destinations are unknown, solicitations shall be f.o.b. origin only.

(2) The contracting officer shall include in the contract file justifications for such solicitations.

(b) (1) When the exact destination of the supplies to be acquired is not known, but the general location of the users can be reasonably established, the acquiring activity shall designate tentative destinations for the purpose of computing transportation costs, showing estimated quantities for each tentative destination.

(2) The contracting officer shall insert in solicitations the provision at 52.247-49, Destination Unknown, when destinations are tentative and only for the purpose of evaluating offers.

(3) If it is necessary to control subsequent shipping weights, the solicitation shall state that subsequent shipments shall be made in carloads or truckloads (see the clause at 52.247-59, F.o.b. Origin—Carload and Truckload Shipments).

(c) (1) When exact destinations are not known and it is impracticable to establish tentative or general delivery places for the purpose of evaluating transportation costs, the contracting officer shall insert in solicitations the provision at 52.247-50, No Evaluation of Transportation Costs.

(2) The solicitation shall also state that the transportation costs of subsequent shipments must be controlled (see, for example, the clause at 52.247-61, F.o.b. Origin—Minimum Size of Shipments).

47.305-6 Shipments to ports and air terminals.

(a) When supplies are acquired on the basis of the delivery terms in 47.303-8 through 47.303-16, the solicitation shall include a requirement that the offeror furnish the Government the following information:

(1) When the delivery term is "f.a.s. vessel, port of shipment," "f.o.b. vessel, port of shipment," or "f.o.b. inland carrier, point of exportation," the required data shall include—

(i) A delivery schedule in number of units and/or long or short tons;

(ii) Maximum quantities available per shipment;

(iii) The quantity that can be made available for loading to vessel per running day of 24 hours (if acquisition involves a commodity to be shipped in bulk);

(iv) The minimum leadtime required to make supplies available for loading to vessel; and

(v) The port and pier or other designation and, when applicable, the maximum draft of vessel (in feet) that can be accommodated.

(2) When the delivery term is "f.o.b. inland point, country of importation" or "f.o.b. designated air carrier's terminal, point of importation," the required data shall include—

(i) A delivery schedule in number of units and/or long or short tons;

(ii) Maximum quantities available per shipment; and

(iii) Other data appropriate to shipment by air carrier.

(3) When the delivery term is "ex dock, pier, or warehouse, port of importation" or "c.&f. (cost & freight) destination," the required data shall include—

(i) A delivery schedule in number of units and/or long or short tons;

(ii) Maximum quantities available per shipment; and

(iii) The number of containers or units that can be loaded in a car, truck, or other conveyance of the size normally used (specify type and size) for the commodity.

(4) When the delivery term is "c.i.f. (cost, insurance, freight) destination," the required data shall include—

(i) The same as specified in 47.305-6(a)(3); and

(ii) The amount and type of marine insurance coverage; *e.g.*, whether the coverage is "With Average" or "Free of Particular Average" and whether it covers any special risks or excludes any of the usual risks associated with the specific commodity involved.

(5) When the delivery term is "f.o.b. designated air carrier's terminal, point of exportation," the required data shall include—

(i) A delivery schedule in number of units, type of package, and individual weight and dimensions of each package;

(ii) Minimum leadtime required to make supplies available for loading into aircraft;

(iii) Name of airport and location to which shipment will be delivered; and

(iv) Other data appropriate to shipment by air carrier.

(b) When supplies are acquired for known destinations outside CONUS and originate within CONUS, the contracting officer shall, for transportation evaluation purposes, note in the solicitation the CONUS port of loading or point of exit (aerial or water) and the water port of debarkation that serves the overseas destination.

(c) The contracting officer may also, for evaluation purposes, list in the solicitation other CONUS ports that meet the eligibility criteria compatible with the nature and quantity of the supplies, their destination, type of carrier required, and specified overseas delivery dates. This permits offerors that are geographically remote from the port that normally serves the overseas destination to be competitive as far as transportation costs are concerned.

(d) Unless logistics requirements limit the ports of loading to the ports listed in the solicitation, the solicitation shall state that—

(1) Offerors may nominate additional ports (including ports in Alaska and Hawaii) more favorably located to their shipping points; and

(2) These ports will be considered in the evaluation of offers if they possess all requisite capabilities of the listed ports in relation to the supplies being acquired.

(e) When supplies are to be exported through CONUS ports and offers are solicited on an f.o.b. origin or f.o.b. destination basis, the contracting officer shall insert in solicitations the provision at 52.247-51, Evaluation of Export Offers. The contracting officer shall use the provision with its—

(1) Alternate I, when the CONUS ports of export are DOD water terminals;

(2) Alternate II, when offers are solicited on an f.o.b. origin only basis; or

(3) Alternate III, when offers are solicited on an f.o.b. destination only basis.

(f) (1) When the supplies are to move in the Defense Transportation System (DTS) (see 47.301-3), the contract shall specify that—

(i) A Transportation Control Movement Document (TCMD) must be dispatched to the appropriate DOD air or water clearance authority in accordance with DoD 4500.9-R, Defense Transportation Regulation, Part II, procedures for all shipments consigned to DOD air or water terminal transshipment points; and

(ii) An Export Release must be obtained for supplies to be transshipped via a water port of loading to overseas destinations, except for shipments for which an Export Release is not required, generally shipments of less than 10,000 pounds, (see DoD 4500.9-R, Defense Transportation Regulation, Part II).

(2) When shipments will be consigned to DOD air or water terminal transshipment points, the contracting officer shall insert in solicitations and contracts the clause at 52.247-52, Clearance and Documentation Requirements—Shipments to DOD Air or Water Terminal Transshipment Points.

(g) When a contract will not generate any shipments that require an Export Release, only the DOD CONUS ports that serve the overseas destination shall be listed in the solicitation, except that the responsible contracting officer may limit the water ports listed when such limitation is considered necessary to meet delivery or other requirements.

(h) The award shall specify the United States ports of loading that afford the lowest overall cost to the overseas destination.

(i) When supplies will be from origins outside CONUS to destinations either within or outside CONUS, the contracting officer shall use the appropriate f.o.b. term and include evaluation-of-offers information.

(j) In furtherance of the Cargo Preference Act of 1954 (46 U.S.C. 1241(b)), to encourage and foster the American Merchant Marine, the port of delivery of supplies originating outside the United States and shipped by ocean vessel shall be based on the availability of United States-flag vessels between the ports involved, unless the acquiring activity has given other specific instructions. (See Subpart 47.5—Ocean Transportation by U.S.-Flag Vessels.)

(k) For application of the Fly America Act to the transportation of supplies and personnel when the Government is responsible for the transportation costs, see Subpart 47.4—Air Transportation by U.S.-Flag Carriers.

(l) Military and civilian agencies shall obtain assistance from transportation offices in connection with all export shipments (see 47.105).

[Final rule, FAC 90-20, 59 FR 11368, 3/10/94, effective 5/9/94; FAC 2005-07, 71 FR 200, 1/3/2006, effective 2/2/2006]

47.305-7 Quantity analysis, direct delivery, and reduction of crosshauling and backhauling.

(a) *Quantity analysis.* (1) The requiring activity shall consider the acquisition of carload or truckload quantities.

(2) When additional quantities of the supplies being acquired can be transported at lower unit transportation costs or with a relatively small increase in total transportation

costs, with no impairment to the program schedule, the contracting officer shall ascertain from the requiring activity whether there is a known requirement for additional quantities. This may be the case, for example, when the additional quantity could profitably be stored by the activity for future use, or could be distributed advantageously to several using activities on the same transportation route or in the same geographical area.

(b) *Direct delivery.* When it is the usual practice of a requiring activity to acquire supplies in large quantities for shipment to a central point and subsequent distribution to using activities, as needed, consideration shall be given, if sufficient quantities are involved to warrant scheduling direct delivery, to the feasibility of providing for direct delivery from the contractor to the using activity, thereby reducing the cost of transportation and handling.

(c) *Crosshauling and backhauling.* The contracting officer shall select distribution and transshipment facilities intermediate to origins and ultimate destinations to reduce crosshauling and backhauling; i.e., to the transportation of personal property of the same kind in opposite directions or the return of the property to or through areas previously traversed in shipment.

47.305-8 Consolidation of small shipments and the use of stopoff privileges.

(a) *Consolidation of small shipments.* Consolidation of small shipments into larger lots frequently results in lower transportation costs. Therefore, the contracting officer, after consultation with the transportation office and the activity requiring the supplies, may revise the delivery schedules to provide for deliveries in larger quantities.

(b) *Stopping for partial unloading.* When feasible, schedules for delivery of supplies to multiple destinations shall be consolidated and the stopoff privileges permitted under carrier tariffs shall be used for partial unloading at one or more points directly en route between the point of origin and the last destination.

47.305-9 Commodity description and freight classification.

(a) Generally, the freight rate for supplies is based on the rating applicable to the freight classification description published in the National Motor Freight Classification (NMFC) (for carriers) and the Uniform Freight Classification (UFC) (for rail) filed with Federal and State regulatory bodies. Therefore, the contracting officer shall show in the solicitation a complete description of the commodity to be acquired and of packing requirements to determine proper transportation charges for the evaluation of offers. If supplies cannot be properly classified through reference to freight classification tariffs or if doubt exists, the contracting officer shall obtain the applicable freight classification from the transportation office. In some situations prospective contractors have established an official freight classification description that can be applied.

(b) (1) When the supplies being acquired are new to the supply system, nonstandard, or modifications of previously shipped items, and different freight classifications may apply, the contracting officer shall insert in solicitations the provision at 52.247-53, Freight Classification Description.

(2) The contracting officer shall alert the transportation officer to the possibility of negotiations for appropriate freight classification ratings and reasonable transportation rates.

(c) The solicitation shall contain adequate descriptions of explosives and other dangerous supplies according to—

(1) The regular freight classification; and

(2) The hazardous material description and hazard class as shown in 49 CFR 172.101.

(d) The contracting officer shall furnish the freight classification information developed in 47.305-9(a), (b), and (c) of this section to the contract administration office.

[FAC 2005-07, 71 FR 200, 1/3/2006, effective 2/2/2006]

47.305-10 Packing, marking, and consignment instructions.

(a) Acquisition documents shall include packing and marking requirements necessary to prevent deterioration of supplies and damages due to the hazards of shipping, handling, and storage, and, when appropriate, marking in accordance with the requirements of 49 CFR 172.300.

(b) Contracts shall include complete consignment and marking instructions at the time the contract is awarded to ensure that supplies are delivered to proper destinations without delay. If complete consignment information is not initially known, the contracting officer shall issue amended delivery instructions under the Changes clause of the contract (see 43.205) as soon as the information becomes known.

(c) If necessary to meet required delivery schedules, the contracting officer may issue instructions by telephone or electronic means. The contracting officer shall confirm telephonic instructions in writing, and confirm electronic instructions if the contracting officer did not receive confirmation of receipt.

(d) Marking and consignment instructions for military shipments shall conform to the current issue of MIL-STD-129 (Military Standard Marking for Shipment and Storage) and other applicable DOD regulations. Shipments for civilian agencies shall be marked as specified in Federal Standard 123, Marking for Domestic Shipment (Civil Agencies).

[FAC 2005-92, 81 FR 83097, 11/18/2016, effective 12/19/2016]

47.305-11 Options in shipment and delivery.

Although the clauses prescribed in Subpart 43.2 allow certain changes to be made in regard to shipment and delivery, it may be desirable to provide specifically for certain options in the solicitation. The Government may reserve the right to—

(a) Direct deliveries of all or part of the contract quantity to destinations or to consignees other than those specified in the solicitation and in the contract;

(b) Direct shipments in quantities that may require transportation rates different from those on which the contract price is based; and

(c) Direct shipments by a mode of transportation other than that stipulated in the solicitation and in the contract.

[FAC 90-45, Final rule, 62 FR 224, 1/2/97, effective 1/1/97]

47.305-12 Delivery of Government-furnished property.

(a) (1) When Government property is furnished to a contractor and transportation costs to the Government are a factor in the evaluation of offers, the contracting officer shall include in the solicitation a clear description of the property, its location, and other information necessary for the preparation of cost estimates.

(2) The contracting officer shall insert in solicitations and contracts the clause at 52.247-55, F.o.b. Point for Delivery of Government-Furnished Property, when Government property is to be furnished under a contract and the Government will be responsible for transportation arrangements and costs.

(b) The contracting officer shall describe explosive and dangerous material according to—

(1) The regular freight classification and

(2) The hazardous material description and hazard class as shown in 49 CFR 172.101.

47.305-13 Transit arrangements.

(a) *Transit privileges*. (1) Transit arrangements permit the stopping of a carload or truckload shipment at a specific intermediate point en route to the final destination for storage, processing, or other purposes, as specified in carrier tariffs or rate tenders. A single through rate is charged from origin to final destination plus a transit or other related charge, rather than a more expensive combination of rates to and from the transit point.

(2) The contracting officer shall consider possible benefits available to the Government through the use of existing transit ar-

rangements or through efforts to obtain additional transit privileges from the carriers. Solicitations incorporating transit arrangements shall be restricted to f.o.b. origin offers, as f.o.b. destination offers can only quote fixed overall delivered prices at first destination.

(3) (i) Traffic management personnel shall furnish information and analyses of situations in which transit arrangements may be beneficial. The quantity to be awarded must be of sufficient tonnage to ensure that carload/truckload shipments can be made by the contractor, and there should be reasonable certainty that shipments out of the transit point will be requested in carload/truckload quantities.

(ii) The contracting officer shall insert in solicitations the provision at 52.247-56, Transit Arrangements, when benefits may accrue to the Government because transit arrangements may apply.

(b) *Transit credits*. (1) In evaluations of f.o.b. origin offers for large quantities of supplies that contractors normally have in process or storage at intermediate points, contracting officers shall make use of contractors' earned commercial transit credits, which are recorded with the carriers. A transit credit represents the transportation costs for a recorded tonnage from the initial point to an intermediate point. The remaining transportation charges from the intermediate point to the Government destination, because they are based on through rates, are frequently lower than the transportation charges that would apply for the same tonnage if the intermediate point were the initial origin point.

(2) If transit credits apply, the contract shall state that the contractor shall ship the goods on prepaid commercial bills of lading, subject to reimbursement by the Government. The contracting officer shall ensure that this does not preclude a proper change in delivery terms under the Changes clause. The shipments move for the account and at the risk of the Government, as they become Government property at origin.

(3) The contractor shall show the transportation and transit charges as separate amounts on the invoice for each individual shipment. The amount to be reimbursed by the Government shall not exceed the amount quoted in the offer.

(4) The contracting officer shall insert in solicitations and contracts the clause at 52.247-57, Transportation Transit Privilege Credits, when supplies are of such a nature, or when it is the custom of the trade, that offerors may have potential transit credits available and the Government may reduce transportation costs through the use of transit credits.

[FAC 2005-07, 71 FR 200, 1/3/2006, effective 2/2/2006]

47.305-14 Mode of transportation.

Generally, solicitations shall not specify a particular mode of transportation or a particular carrier. If the use of particular types of carriers is necessary to meet program requirements, the solicitation shall provide that only offers involving the specified types of carriers will be considered. The contracting officer shall obtain all specifications for mode, route, delivery, etc., from the transportation office.

47.305-15 Loading responsibilities of contractors.

(a) (1) Contractors are responsible for loading, blocking, and bracing carload shipments as specified in standards published by the Association of American Railroads.

(2) The contracting officer shall insert in solicitations and contracts the clause at 52.247-58, Loading, Blocking, and Bracing of Freight Car Shipments, when supplies may be shipped in carload lots by rail.

(b) If the nature of the supplies or safety, environmental, or transportability factors require special methods for securing the supplies on the carrier's equipment, or if only a special mode of transportation or type vehicle is appropriate, the contracting officer shall include in solicitations detailed specifications that have been coordinated with the transportation office.

47.305-16 Shipping characteristics.

(a) *Required shipping weights*. The contracting officer shall insert in solicitations and contracts the clause at 52.247-59, F.o.b.

Origin—Carload and Truckload Shipments, when it is contemplated that they may result in f.o.b. origin contracts with shipments in carloads or truckloads. This will facilitate realistic freight cost evaluations of offers and ensure that contractors produce economical shipments of agreed size.

(b) *Guaranteed shipping characteristics.* (1) The contracting officer shall insert in solicitations and contracts, excluding those at or below the simplified acquisition threshold, the clause at 52.247-60, Guaranteed Shipping Characteristics, when shipping and other characteristics are required to evaluate offers as to transportation costs. When all of the shipping characteristics listed in paragraph (a) of the clause at 52.247-60 are not required to evaluate offers as to transportation costs, the contracting officer shall delete the characteristics not required from the clause.

(2) The award document shall show the shipping characteristics used in the evaluation.

(c) *Minimum size of shipments.* When volume rates may apply, the contracting officer shall insert in solicitations and contracts the clause at 52.247-61, F.o.b. Origin—Minimum Size of Shipments.

(d) *Specific quantities unknown.* (1) When total requirements and destinations to which shipments will be made are known, but the specific quantity to be shipped to each destination cannot be predetermined, solicitations shall state that offers are to be submitted on the basis of delivery "f.o.b. origin" and/or "f.o.b. destination" and that offers will be evaluated on both bases.

(2) The contracting officer shall insert in solicitations and contracts the clause at 52.247-62, Specific Quantities Unknown, when total requirements and destinations to which shipments will be made are known, but the specific quantity to be shipped to each destination cannot be predetermined. This clause protects the interests of both the Government and the contractor during the course of the performance of the contract.

[FAC 84-53, 54 FR 48990, 11/28/89, effective 12/28/89; FAC 90-29, 60 FR 34732, 7/3/95, effective 7/3/95; FAC 90-40, 61 FR 39186, 7/26/96, effective 8/26/96]

47.305-17 Returnable cylinders.

The contracting officer shall insert the clause at 52.247-66, Returnable Cylinders, in a solicitation and contract whenever the contract involves the purchase of gas in contractor-furnished returnable cylinders and the contractor retains title to the cylinders.

[Final rule, FAC 90-20, 59 FR 11368, 3/10/94, effective 5/9/94]

47.306 Transportation factors in the evaluation of offers.

When evaluating offers, contracting officers shall consider transportation and transportation-related costs as well as the offerors' shipping and receiving facilities.

47.306-1 Transportation cost determinations.

When requesting the transportation officer to assist in evaluating offers, the contracting officer shall give the transportation officer all pertinent data, including the following information:

(a) A complete description of the commodity being acquired including packaging instructions.

(b) Planned date of award.

(c) Date of initial shipment.

(d) Total quantity to be shipped (including weight and cubic content, when appropriate).

(e) Delivery schedule.

(f) Contract period.

(g) Possible use of transit privileges, including stopoffs for partial loading or unloading, or both.

47.306-2 Lowest overall transportation costs.

(a) For the evaluation of offers, the transportation officer shall give to the contracting officer, and the contracting officer shall use, the lowest available freight rates and related accessorial and incidental charges that—

(1) Are in effect on, or become effective before, the expected date of the initial shipment; and

(2) Are on file or published on the date of the bid opening.

(b) If rates or related charges become available after the bid opening or the due date of offers, they shall not be used in the evaluation unless they cover transportation for which no applicable rates or accessorial or incidental costs were in existence at the time of bid opening or due date of the offers.

47.306-3 Adequacy of loading and unloading facilities.

(a) When determining the transportation capabilities of an offeror, the contracting officer shall consider the type and adequacy of the offeror's shipping facilities, including the ability to consolidate and ship in carload or truckload lots.

(b) The contracting officer shall consider the type and adequacy of the consignee's receiving facilities to avoid shipping schedules that cannot be properly accommodated.

SUBPART 47.4—AIR TRANSPORTATION BY U.S.-FLAG CARRIERS

47.401 Definitions.

As used in this subpart—

Air freight forwarder means an indirect air carrier that is responsible for the transportation of property from the point of receipt to the point of destination, and utilizes for the whole or any part of such transportation the services of a direct air carrier or its agent, or of another air freight forwarder.

Gateway airport abroad means the airport from which the traveler last embarks en route to the United States or at which the traveler first debarks incident to travel from the United States.

Gateway airport in the United States means the last U.S. airport from which the traveler's flight departs or the first U.S. airport at which the traveler's flight arrives.

International air transportation means transportation by air between a place in the United States and a place outside the United States or between two places both of which are outside the United States.

United States means the 50 States, the District of Columbia, and outlying areas of the United States.

U.S.-flag air carrier means an air carrier holding a certificate under section 401 of the Federal Aviation Act of 1958 (49 U.S.C. 41102).

[FAC 97-22, 66 FR 2116, 1/10/2001, effective 3/12/2001; Delay of effective date, 66 FR 14259, 3/9/2001, effective 5/11/2001; FAC 2001-14, 68 FR 28079, 5/22/2003, effective 6/23/2003]

47.402 Policy.

Federal employees and their dependents, consultants, contractors, grantees, and others must use U.S.-flag air carriers for U.S. Government-financed international air travel and transportation of their personal effects or property, if available (section 5 of the International Air Transportation Fair Competitive Practices Act of 1974 (49 U.S.C. 40118) (Fly America Act)).

[FAC 2001-14, 68 FR 28079, 5/22/2003, effective 6/23/2003]

47.403 Guidelines for implementation of the Fly America Act.

This section 47.403 is based on the Guidelines for Implementation of the Fly America Act (case number B-138942), issued by the Comptroller General of the United States on March 31, 1981.

47.403-1 Availability and unavailability of U.S.-flag air carrier service.

(a) If a U.S.-flag air carrier cannot provide the international air transportation needed or if the use of U.S.-flag air carrier service would not accomplish an agency's mission, foreign-flag air carrier service may be deemed necessary.

(b) U.S.-flag air carrier service is considered available even though—

(1) Comparable or a different kind of service can be provided at less cost by a foreign-flag air carrier;

(2) Foreign-flag air carrier service is preferred by, or is more convenient for, the agency or traveler; or

(3) Service by a foreign-flag air carrier can be paid for in excess foreign currency (unless U.S.-flag air carriers decline to accept excess or near excess foreign currencies for transportation payable only out of such monies).

(c) Except as provided in paragraph 47.403-1(a), U.S.-flag air carrier service shall be used for U.S. Government-financed commercial foreign air travel if service provided by U.S.-flag air carriers is available. In determining availability of a U.S.-flag air carrier, the following scheduling principles shall be followed unless their application would result in the last or first leg of travel to or from the United States being performed by a foreign-flag air carrier:

(1) U.S.-flag air carrier service available at point of origin shall be used to destination or, in the absence of direct or through service, to the farthest interchange point on a usually traveled route.

(2) When an origin or interchange point is not served by a U.S.-flag air carrier, foreign-flag air carrier service shall be used only to the nearest interchange point on a usually traveled route to connect with U.S.-flag air carrier service.

(3) When a U.S.-flag air carrier involuntarily reroutes the traveler via a foreign-flag air carrier, the foreign-flag air carrier may be used notwithstanding the availability of alternative U.S.-flag air carrier service.

(d) For travel between a gateway airport in the United States and a gateway airport abroad, passenger service by U.S.-flag air carrier shall not be considered available if—

(1) The gateway airport abroad is the traveler's origin or destination airport and the use of U.S.-flag air carrier service would extend the time in a travel status, including delay at origin and accelerated arrival at destination, by at least 24 hours more than travel by a foreign-flag air carrier; or

(2) The gateway airport abroad is an interchange point and the use of U.S.-flag air carrier service would require the traveler to wait 6 hours or more to make connections at that point, or if delayed departure from, or accelerated arrival at, the gateway airport in the United States would extend time in a travel status by at least 6 hours more than travel by a foreign-flag air carrier.

(e) For travel between two points outside the United States, the rules in paragraphs 47.403-1(a), (b), and (c) shall be applicable, but passenger service by a U.S.-flag air carrier shall not be considered to be reasonably available if—

(1) Travel by a foreign-flag air carrier would eliminate two or more aircraft changes en route;

(2) One of the two points abroad is the gateway airport en route to or from the United States and the use of a U.S.-flag air carrier would extend the time in a travel status by at least 6 hours more than travel by a foreign-flag air carrier, including accelerated arrival at the overseas destination or delayed departure from the overseas origin, as well as delay at the gateway airport or other interchange point abroad; or

(3) The travel is not part of the trip to or from the United States and the use of a U.S.-flag air carrier would extend the time in a travel status by at least 6 hours more than travel by a foreign-flag air carrier including delay at origin, delay en route, and accelerated arrival at destination.

(f) For all short-distance travel under either paragraph (d) or paragraph (e) of 47.403-1, U.S. air carrier service shall not be considered available when the elapsed travel time on a scheduled flight from origin to destination airport by foreign-flag air carrier is 3 hours or less and service by a U.S.-flag air carrier would involve twice such travel time.

47.403-2 Air transport agreements between the United States and foreign governments.

Nothing in the guidelines of the Comptroller General (see 47.403) shall preclude, and no penalty shall attend, the use of a foreign-flag air carrier that provides transportation under an air transport agreement between the United States and a foreign government, the terms of which are consistent with the international aviation policy goals at 49 U.S.C. 1502(b) and provide reciprocal rights and benefits.

47.403-3 Disallowance of expenditures.

(a) Agencies shall disallow expenditures for U.S. Government-financed commercial international air transportation on foreign-flag air carriers unless there is attached to the appropriate voucher a memorandum adequately explaining why service by U.S.-flag air carriers was not available, or why it was necessary to use foreign-flag air carriers.

(b) When the travel is by indirect route or the traveler otherwise fails to use available U.S.-flag air carrier service, the amount to be disallowed against the traveler is based on the loss of revenues suffered by U.S.-flag air carriers as determined under the following formula, which is prescribed and more fully explained in 56 Comp. Gen. 209 (1977):

$$\frac{\text{Sum of U.S.-flag carrier segment mileage, authorized}}{\text{Sum of all segment mileage, authorized}} \times \text{Fare payable by Government}$$

MINUS

$$\frac{\text{Sum of U.S.-flag carrier segment mileage, traveled}}{\text{Sum of all segment mileage, traveled}} \times \text{Through fare paid}$$

(c) The justification requirement is satisfied by the contractor's use of a statement similar to the one contained in the clause at 52.247-63, Preference for U.S.-Flag Air Carriers. (See 47.405.)

[FAC 90-45, Final rule, 62 FR 224, 1/2/97, effective 1/1/97]

47.404 Air freight forwarders.

(a) Agencies may use air freight forwarders that are engaged in international air transportation (49 U.S.C. 1301(24)(c)) for U.S. Government-financed movements of property. The rule on disallowance of expenditures in 47.403-3(a) applies also to the air carriers used by these international air freight forwarders.

(b) Agency personnel shall inform international air freight forwarders that to facilitate prompt payments of their bills, they shall submit with their bills—

(1) A copy of the airway bill or manifest showing the air carriers used; and

(2) Justification for the use of foreign-flag air carriers similar to the one shown in the clause at 52.247-63, Preference for U.S.-Flag Air Carriers.

[FAC 90-45, Final rule, 62 FR 224, 1/2/97, effective 1/1/97]

47.405 Contract clause.

The contracting officer shall insert the clause at 52.247-63, Preference for U.S.-Flag Air Carriers, in solicitations and contracts whenever it is possible that U.S. Government-financed international air transportation of personnel (and their personal effects) or property will occur in the performance of the contract. This clause does not apply to contracts awarded using the simplified acquisition procedures in Part 13 or contracts for commercial items (see Part 12).

[FAC 84-38, 53 FR 27468, 7/20/88, effective 8/19/88; FAC 90-29, 60 FR 34732, 7/3/95, effective 7/3/95; FAC 90-32, 60 FR 48206, 9/18/95, effective 10/1/95]

SUBPART 47.5—OCEAN TRANSPORTATION BY U.S.-FLAG VESSELS

47.500 Scope of subpart.

This subpart prescribes policy and procedures for giving preference to U.S.-flag vessels when transportation of supplies by ocean vessel is required. This subpart does not apply to the Department of Defense (DoD). Policy and procedures applicable to DoD appear in DFARS Subpart 247.5.

[FAC 84-56, 55 FR 3886, 2/5/90, effective 3/7/90]

47.501 Definitions.

As used in this subpart—

Dry bulk carrier means a vessel used primarily for the carriage of shipload lots of homogeneous unmarked nonliquid cargoes such as grain, coal, cement, and lumber.

Dry cargo liner means a vessel used for the carriage of heterogeneous marked cargoes in parcel lots. However, any cargo may be carried in these vessels, including part cargoes of dry bulk items or, when carried in deep tanks, bulk liquids such as petroleum and vegetable oils.

Foreign-flag vessel means any vessel of foreign registry including vessels owned by U.S. citizens but registered in a nation other than the United States.

Government vessel means a vessel owned by the U.S. Government and operated directly by the Government or for the Government by an agent or contractor, including a privately owned U.S.-flag vessel under bareboat charter to the Government.

Privately owned U.S.-flag commercial vessel means a vessel—

(1) Registered and operated under the laws of the United States,

(2) Used in commercial trade of the United States,

(3) Owned and operated by U.S. citizens, including a vessel under voyage or time charter to the Government, and

(4) A Government-owned vessel under bareboat charter to, and operated by, U.S. citizens.

Tanker means a vessel used primarily for the carriage of bulk liquid cargoes such as liquid petroleum products, vegetable oils, and molasses.

U.S.-flag vessel when used independently means either a Government vessel or a privately owned U.S.-flag commercial vessel.

[FAC 97-22, 66 FR 2116, 1/10/2001, effective 3/12/2001; Delay of effective date, 66 FR 14259, 3/9/2001, effective 5/11/2001]

47.502 Policy.

(a) The policy of the United States regarding the use of U.S.-flag vessels is stated in the following acts:

(1) The Cargo Preference Act of 1904 (10 U.S.C. 2631), which requires the Department of Defense to use only U.S.-flag vessels for ocean transportation of supplies for the Army, Navy, Air Force, or Marine Corps unless those vessels are not available at fair and reasonable rates.

(2) The Merchant Marine Act of 1936 (46 U.S.C. 1101), which declares it is the policy of the United States to foster the development and encourage the maintenance of its merchant marine.

(3) The Cargo Preference Act of 1954 (46 U.S.C. 1241(b), which is Section 901(b) of the Merchant Marine Act). Under this Act, Government agencies acquiring, either within or outside the United States, supplies that may require ocean transportation shall ensure that at least 50 percent of the gross tonnage of these supplies (computed separately for dry bulk carriers, dry cargo liners, and tankers) is transported on privately owned U.S.-flag commercial vessels to the extent that such vessels are available at rates that are fair and reasonable for U.S.-flag commercial vessels. This applies when the supplies are—

(i) Acquired for the account of the United States;

(ii) Furnished to, or for the account of, a foreign nation without provision for reimbursement;

(iii) Furnished for the account of a foreign nation in connection with which the United States advances funds or credits, or guarantees the convertibility of foreign currencies; or

(iv) Acquired with advance of funds, loans, or guaranties made by or on behalf of the United States.

(b) Additional policies providing preference for the use of U.S.-flag vessels are contained in—

(1) 10 U.S.C. 2634 for the transportation of privately-owned vehicles belonging to service members when making permanent change of station moves;

(2) 46 U.S.C. 1241(a) for official business travel by officers and employees of the United States and for the transportation of their personal effects; and

(3) 46 U.S.C. 1241(e) for the transportation of motor vehicles owned by Government personnel when transportation is at Government expense or otherwise authorized by law.

(c) The provisions of the Cargo Preference Act of 1954 may be temporarily waived when the Congress, the President, or the Secretary of Defense declares that an emergency justifying a temporary waiver exists and so notifies the appropriate agency or agencies.

47.503 Applicability.

(a) Except as stated in paragraph (b) of this section and in 47.504, the Cargo Preference Acts of 1904 and 1954 described in 47.502(a) apply to the following cargoes:

(1) Supplies owned by the Government and in the possession of—

(i) The Government;

(ii) A contractor; or

(iii) A subcontractor at any tier.

(2) Supplies for use of the Government that are contracted for and require subsequent delivery to a Government activity but are not owned by the Government at the time of shipment.

(3) Supplies not owned by the Government at the time of shipment that are to be transported for distribution to foreign assistance programs, but only if these supplies are not acquired or contracted for with local currency funds (see 47.504(b)).

(b) Government-owned supplies to be shipped commercially that are—

(1) In the possession of a department, a contractor, or a subcontractor at any tier and

(2) For use of military departments shall be transported exclusively in privately owned U.S.-flag commercial vessels if such vessels are available at rates that are fair and reasonable for U.S.-flag commercial vessels.

(c) The 50-percent requirement shall not prevent the use of privately owned U.S.-flag commercial vessels for transportation of up to 100 percent of the cargo subject to the Cargo Preference Act of 1954.

47.504 Exceptions.

The policy and procedures in this subpart do not apply to the following:

(a) Shipments aboard vessels as required or authorized by law or treaty.

(b) Ocean transportation between foreign countries of supplies purchased with foreign currencies made available, or derived from funds that are made available, under the Foreign Assistance Act of 1961 (22 U.S.C. 2353).

(c) Shipments of classified supplies when the classification prohibits the use of non-Government vessels.

(d) Subcontracts for the acquisition of commercial items or commercial components (see 12.504(a)(1) and (a)(11)). This exception does not apply to—

(1) Grants-in-aid shipments, such as agricultural and food-aid shipments;

(2) Shipments covered under 46 U.S.C. Appx 1241-1, such as those generated by Export-Import Bank loans or guarantees;

(3) Subcontracts under—

(i) Government contracts or agreements for ocean transportation services; or

(ii) Construction contracts; or

(4) Shipments of commercial items that are—

(i) Items the contractor is reselling or distributing to the Government without adding value (see FAR 12.501(b)). Generally, the contractor does not add value to the items when it subcontracts items for f.o.b. destination shipment; or

(ii) Shipped in direct support of U.S. military—

(A) Contingency operations;

(B) Exercises; or

(C) Forces deployed in connection with United Nations or North Atlantic Treaty Organization humanitarian or peacekeeping operations.

[FAC 90-29, 60 FR 34732, 7/3/95, effective 7/3/95; FAC 90-32, 60 FR 48206, 9/18/95, effective 10/1/95; FAC 97-17, 65 FR 24316, 4/25/2000, effective 6/26/2000; FAC 97-18, 65 FR 36014, 6/6/2000, effective 6/6/2000; FAC 2001-13, 68 FR 13202, 3/18/2003, effective 4/17/2003; FAC 2005-07, 71 FR 200, 1/3/2006, effective 2/2/2006]

47.505 Construction contracts.

(a) Except as stated in paragraph (b) of this section, construction contractors, including subcontractors and suppliers, engaged in overseas work shall comply with the policies and regulations in this subpart.

(b) These requirements shall not apply to military assistance, foreign aid, or similar projects under the auspices of the U.S. Government when the recipient nation furnishes, or pays for, at least 50 percent of the transportation, in which event foreign-flag vessels may be used for a portion not to exceed 50 percent of the gross tonnage for the project.

47.506 Procedures.

(a) The contracting officer shall obtain assistance from the transportation activity (see 47.105) in developing appropriate shipping instructions and delivery terms for inclusion in solicitations and contracts that may involve ocean transportation of supplies subject to the requirements of the Cargo Preference Act of 1954 (see 47.502(a)(3)).

(b) When the contractor notifies the contracting officer that a privately owned U.S.-flag commercial vessel is not available, the contracting officer shall seek assistance from the transportation activity.

(c) For purposes of determining the availability of privately owned U.S.-flag commercial vessels at fair and reasonable rates, rates filed and published in accordance with the requirements of the Federal Maritime Commission may be accepted as fair and reasonable. When applicable rates for charter cargoes are not in published tariffs, a determination as to whether the rates are fair and reasonable shall be obtained from the Maritime Administration.

(d) The Maritime Administration has issued regulations (46 CFR 381) that require agencies to submit reports regarding ocean shipments. Contracting officers shall follow agency regulations when preparing, or furnishing information for, these reports.

47.507 Contract clauses.

(a)(1) Insert the clause at 52.247-64, Preference for Privately Owned U.S.-Flag Commercial Vessels, in solicitations and contracts that may involve ocean transportation of supplies subject to the Cargo Preference Act of 1954. (For application of the Cargo Preference Act of 1954, see 47.502(a)(3), 47.503(a), and 47.504.)

(2) If an applicable statute requires, or if it has been determined under agency procedures, that the supplies to be furnished under the contracts must be transported exclusively in privately owned U.S.-flag commercial vessels (see 47.502(a)(1) and 47.503(b)), use the clause with its Alternate I.

(3) Except for contracts or agreements for ocean transportation services or construction contracts, use the clause with its Alternate II if any of the supplies to be transported are commercial items that are shipped in direct support of U.S. military—

(i) Contingency operations;

(ii) Exercises; or

(iii) Forces deployed in connection with United Nations or North Atlantic Treaty Organization humanitarian or peacekeeping operations.

(b) The contracting officer may insert in solicitations and contracts, under agency procedures, additional appropriate clauses concerning the vessels to be used.

[FAC 2001-13, 68 FR 13202, 3/18/2003, effective 4/17/2003]

PART 48—VALUE ENGINEERING

Table of Contents

Scope of part 48.000
Definitions 48.001

Subpart 48.1—Policies and Procedures

General 48.101
Policies 48.102
Processing value engineering change proposals 48.103
Sharing arrangements 48.104
Determining sharing period 48.104-1
Sharing acquisition savings 48.104-2
Sharing collateral savings 48.104-3
Sharing alternative—no-cost settlement method 48.104-4
Relationship to other incentives 48.105

Subpart 48.2—Contract Clauses

Clauses for supply or service contracts 48.201
Clause for construction contracts 48.202

PART 48—VALUE ENGINEERING

48.000 Scope of part.

This part prescribes policies and procedures for using and administering value engineering techniques in contracts.

48.001 Definitions.

As used in this part—

Acquisition savings means savings resulting from the application of a value engineering change proposal (VECP) to contracts awarded by the same contracting office or its successor for essentially the same unit. Acquisition savings include—

(1) Instant contract savings, that are the net cost reductions on the contract under which the VECP is submitted and accepted, and that are equal to the instant unit cost reduction multiplied by the number of instant contract units affected by the VECP, less the contractor's allowable development and implementation costs;

(2) Concurrent contract savings, that are net reductions in the prices of other contracts that are definitized and ongoing at the time the VECP is accepted; and

(3) Future contract savings, that are the product of the future unit cost reduction multiplied by the number of future contract units in the sharing base. On an instant contract, future contract savings include savings on increases in quantities after VECP acceptance that are due to contract modifications, exercise of options, additional orders, and funding of subsequent year requirements on a multiyear contract.

Collateral costs means agency costs of operation, maintenance, logistic support, or Government-furnished property.

Collateral savings means those measurable net reductions resulting from a VECP in the agency's overall projected collateral costs, exclusive of acquisition savings, whether or not the acquisition cost changes.

Contracting office includes any contracting office that the acquisition is transferred to, such as another branch of the agency or another agency's office that is performing a joint acquisition action.

Contractor's development and implementation costs means those costs the contractor incurs on a VECP specifically in developing, testing, preparing, and submitting the VECP, as well as those costs the contractor incurs to make the contractual changes required by Government acceptance of a VECP.

Future unit cost reduction means the instant unit cost reduction adjusted as the contracting officer considers necessary for projected learning or changes in quantity during the sharing period. It is calculated at the time the VECP is accepted and applies either—

(1) Throughout the sharing period, unless the contracting officer decides that recalculation is necessary because conditions are significantly different from those previously anticipated, or

(2) To the calculation of a lump-sum payment, that cannot later be revised.

Government costs means those agency costs that result directly from developing and implementing the VECP, such as any net increases in the cost of testing, operations, maintenance, and logistics support. The term does not include the normal administrative costs of processing the VECP or any increase in instant contract cost or price resulting from negative instant contract savings, except that for use in 52.248-3, see the definition at 52.248-3(b).

Instant contract means the contract under which the VECP is submitted. It does not include increases in quantities after acceptance of the VECP that are due to contract modifications, exercise of options, or additional orders. If the contract is a multiyear contract, the term does not include quantities funded after VECP acceptance. In a fixed-price contract with prospective price redetermination, the term refers to the period for which firm prices have been established.

Instant unit cost reduction means the amount of the decrease in unit cost of performance (without deducting any contractor's development or implementation costs) resulting from using the VECP on the instant contract. In service contracts, the instant unit cost reduction is normally equal to the number of hours per line-item task saved by using the VECP on the instant contract, multiplied by the appropriate contract labor rate.

Negative instant contract savings means the increase in the instant contract cost or price when the acceptance of a VECP results in an excess of the contractor's allowable development and implementation costs over the product of the instant unit cost reduction multiplied by the number of instant contract units affected.

Net acquisition savings means total acquisition savings, including instant, concurrent, and future contract savings, less Government costs.

Sharing base means the number of affected end items on contracts of the contracting office accepting the VECP.

Sharing period means the period beginning with acceptance of the first unit incorporating the VECP and ending at a calendar date or event determined by the contracting officer for each VECP.

Unit means the item or task to which the contracting officer and the contractor agree the VECP applies.

Value engineering proposal means, in connection with an A-E contract, a change proposal developed by employees of the Federal Government or contractor value engineering personnel under contract to an agency to provide value engineering services for the contract or program.

[FAC 84-42, 54 FR 5056, 1/31/89, effective 3/2/89; FAC 84-56, 55 FR 3887, 2/5/90, effective 3/7/90; FAC 90-40, 61 FR 39186, 7/26/96, effective 8/26/96; FAC 97-14, 64 FR 51828, 9/24/99, effective 11/23/99; FAC 97-22, 66 FR 2116, 1/10/2001, effective 3/12/2001; Delay of effective date, 66 FR 14259, 3/9/2001, effective 5/11/2001]

SUBPART 48.1—POLICIES AND PROCEDURES

48.101 General.

(a) Value engineering is the formal technique by which contractors may (1) voluntarily suggest methods for performing more economically and share in any resulting savings or (2) be required to establish a program to identify and submit to the Government methods for performing more economically. Value engineering attempts to eliminate, without impairing essential functions or characteristics, anything that increases acquisition, operation, or support costs.

(b) There are two value engineering approaches:

(1) The first is an incentive approach in which contractor participation is voluntary and the contractor uses its own resources to develop and submit any value engineering change proposals (VECP's). The contract provides for sharing of savings and for payment of the contractor's allowable development and implementation costs only if a VECP is accepted. This voluntary approach should not in itself increase costs to the Government.

(2) The second approach is a mandatory program in which the Government requires and pays for a specific value engineering program effort. The contractor must perform value engineering of the scope and level of effort required by the Government's program plan and included as a separately priced item of work in the contract Schedule. No value engineering sharing is permitted in architect-engineer contracts. All other contracts with a program clause share in savings on accepted VECP's, but at a lower percentage rate than under the voluntary approach. The objective of this value engineering program requirement is to ensure that the contractor's value engineering effort is applied to areas of the contract that offer opportunities for considerable savings consistent with the functional requirements of the end item of the contract.

[FAC 84-42, 54 FR 5056, 1/31/89, effective 3/2/89]

48.102 Policies.

(a) As required by 41 U.S.C. 1711, agencies shall establish and maintain cost-effective value engineering procedures and processes. Agencies shall provide contractors a substantial financial incentive to develop and submit VECP's. Contracting activities will include value engineering provisions in appropriate supply, service, architect-engineer and construction contracts as prescribed by 48.201 and 48.202 except where exemptions are granted on a case-by-case basis, or for specific classes of contracts, by the agency head.

(b) Agencies shall—

(1) Establish guidelines for processing VECP's;

(2) Process VECP's objectively and expeditiously; and

(3) Provide contractors a fair share of the savings on accepted VECP's.

(c) Agencies shall consider requiring incorporation of value engineering clauses in appropriate subcontracts.

(d) (1) Agencies other than the Department of Defense shall use the value engineering program requirement clause (52.248-1, Alternates I or II) in initial production contracts for major systems programs (see definition of major system in 34.001) and for contracts for major systems research and development except where the contracting officer determines and documents the file to reflect that such use is not appropriate.

(2) In Department of Defense contracts, the VE program requirement clause (52.248-1, Alternates I or II), shall be placed in initial production solicitations and contracts (first and second production buys) for major system acquisition programs as defined in DoD Directive 5000.1, except as specified in subdivisions (d) (2) (i) and (ii) of this section. A program requirement clause may be included in initial production contracts for less than major systems acquisition programs if there is a potential for savings. The contracting officer is not required to include a program requirement clause in initial production contracts—

(i) Where, in the judgment of the contracting officer, the prime contractor has demonstrated an effective VE program during either earlier program phases, or during other recent comparable production contracts.

(ii) Which are awarded on the basis of competition.

(e) Value engineering incentive payments do not constitute profit or fee within the limitations imposed by 10 U.S.C. 2306(d) and 41 U.S.C. 3905 (see 15.404-4(c) (4) (i)).

(f) Generally, profit or fee on the instant contract should not be adjusted downward as a result of acceptance of a VECP. Profit or fee shall be excluded when calculating instant or future contract savings.

(g) The contracting officer determines the sharing periods and sharing rates on a case-by-case basis using the guidelines in 48.104-1 and 48.104-2, respectively. In establishing a sharing period and sharing rate, the contracting officer must consider the following, as appropriate, and must insert supporting rationale in the contract file:

(1) Extent of the change.

(2) Complexity of the change.

(3) Development risk (e.g., contractor's financial risk).

(4) Development cost.

(5) Performance and/or reliability impact.

(6) Production period remaining at the time of VECP acceptance.

(7) Number of units affected.

(h) Contracts for architect-engineer services must require a mandatory value engineering program to reduce total ownership cost in accordance with 48.101(b) (2). However, there must be no sharing of value engineering savings in contracts for architect-engineer services.

(i) Agencies shall establish procedures for funding and payment of the contractor's share of collateral savings and future contract savings.

[FAC 84-12, 51 FR 2666, 1/17/86, effective 1/20/86; FAC 84-42, 54 FR 5057, 1/31/89, effective 3/2/89; FAC 84-56, 55 FR 3887, 2/5/90, effective 3/7/90; FAC 90-40, 61 FR 39186, 7/26/96, effective 8/26/96; FAC 97-2, 62 FR 51224, 9/30/97, effective 10/10/97; FAC 97-14, 64 FR 51828, 9/24/99, effective 11/23/99; FAC 2005-73, 79 FR 24192, 4/29/2014, effective 5/29/2014]

48.103 Processing value engineering change proposals.

(a) Instructions to the contractor for preparing a VECP and submitting it to the Government are included in paragraphs (c) and (d) of the value engineering clauses prescribed in Subpart 48.2. Upon receiving a VECP, the contracting officer or other designated official shall promptly process and objectively evaluate the VECP in accordance with agency procedures and shall document the contract file with the rationale for accepting or rejecting the VECP.

(b) The contracting officer is responsible for accepting or rejecting the VECP within 45 days from its receipt by the Government. If the Government will need more time to evaluate the VECP, the contracting officer shall notify the contractor promptly in writing, giving the reasons and the anticipated decision date. The contractor may withdraw, in whole or in part, any VECP not accepted by the Government within the period specified in the VECP. Any VECP may be approved, in whole or in part, by a contract modification incorporating the VECP. Until the effective date of the contract modification, the contractor shall perform in accordance with the existing contract. If the Government accepts the VECP, but properly rejects units subsequently delivered or does not receive units on which a savings share was paid, the contractor shall reimburse the Government for the proportionate share of these payments. If the VECP is not accepted, the contracting officer shall provide the contractor with prompt written notification, explaining the reasons for rejection.

(c) The following Government decisions are unilateral decisions made solely at the discretion of the Government:

(1) The decision to accept or reject a VECP.

(2) The determination of collateral costs or collateral savings.

(3) The decision as to which of the sharing rates applies when Alternate II of the clause at 52.248-1, Value Engineering, is used.

(4) The contracting officer's determination of the duration of the sharing period and the contractor's sharing rate.

[FAC 84-42, 54 FR 5057, 1/31/89, effective 3/2/89; FAC 97-15, 64 FR 72414, 12/27/99, effective 2/25/2000]

48.104 Sharing arrangements. (No Text)

48.104-1 Determining sharing period.

(a) Contracting officers must determine discrete sharing periods for each VECP. If more than one VECP is incorporated into a contract, the sharing period for each VECP need not be identical.

(b) The sharing period begins with acceptance of the first unit incorporating the VECP. Except as provided in paragraph (c) of this section, the end of the sharing period is a specific calendar date that is the later of—

(1) 36 to 60 consecutive months (set at the discretion of the contracting officer for each VECP) after the first unit affected by the VECP is accepted; or

(2) The last scheduled delivery date of an item affected by the VECP under the instant contract delivery schedule in effect at the time the VECP is accepted.

(c) For engineering-development contracts and contracts containing low-rate-initial-production or early production units, the end of the sharing period is based not on a calendar date, but on acceptance of a specified quantity of future contract units. This quantity is the number of units affected by the VECP that are scheduled to be delivered over a period of between 36 and 60 consecutive months (set at the discretion of the contracting officer for each VECP) that spans the highest planned production, based on planning and programming or production documentation at the time the VECP is accepted. The specified quantity begins with the first future contract unit affected by the VECP and continues over consecutive deliveries until the sharing period ends at acceptance of the last of the specified quantity of units.

(d) For contracts (other than those in paragraph (c) of this subsection) for items requiring a prolonged production schedule (e.g., ship construction, major system acquisition), the end of the sharing period is determined according to paragraph (b) of this subsection. Agencies may prescribe sharing of future contract savings on all future contract units to be delivered under contracts awarded within the sharing period for essentially the same item, even if the scheduled delivery date is outside the sharing period.

[FAC 97-14, 64 FR 51828, 9/24/99, effective 11/23/99]

48.104-2 Sharing acquisition savings.

(a) *Supply or service contracts.* (1) The sharing base for acquisition savings is the number of affected end items on contracts of the contracting office accepting the VECP. The sharing rates (Government/contractor) for net acquisition savings for supplies and services are based on the type of contract, the value engineering clause or alternate used, and the type of savings, as follows:

Government/Contractor Shares of Net Acquisition Savings
[Figures in percent]

Contract type	Sharing arrangement: Incentive (voluntary): Instant contract rate	Incentive (voluntary): Concurrent and future contract rate	Program requirement (mandatory): Instant contract rate	Program requirement (mandatory): Concurrent and future contract rate
Fixed-price (includes fixed-price-award-fee; excludes other fixed-price incentive contracts)	[1] 50/50	[1] 50/50	75/25	75/25
Incentive (fixed-price or cost) (other than award fee)	(2)	[1] 50/50	(2)	75/25
Cost-reimbursement (includes cost-plus-award-fee; excludes other cost-type incentive contracts)	[3] 75/25	[3] 75/25	85/15	85/15

[1] The contracting officer may increase the contractor's sharing rate to as high as 75 percent for each VECP. (See 48.102(g)(1) through (7).)

[2] Same sharing arrangement as the contract's profit or fee adjustment formula.

[3] The contracting officer may increase the contractor's sharing rate to as high as 50 percent for each VECP. (See 48.102(g)(1) through (7).)

(2) Acquisition savings may be realized on the instant contract, concurrent contracts, and future contracts. The contractor is entitled to a percentage share (see paragraph (a)(1) of this section) of any net acquisition savings. Net acquisition savings result when the total of acquisition savings becomes greater than the total of Government costs and any negative instant contract savings. This may occur on the instant contract or it may not occur until reductions have been negotiated on concurrent contracts or until future contract savings are calculated, either through lump-sum payment or as each future contract is awarded.

(i) When the instant contract is not an incentive contract, the contractor's share of net acquisition savings is calculated and paid each time such savings are realized. This may occur once, several times, or, in rare cases, not at all.

(ii) When the instant contract is an incentive contract, the contractor shares in instant contract savings through the contract's incentive structure. In calculating acquisition savings under incentive contracts, the contracting officer shall add any negative instant contract savings to the target cost or to the target price and ceiling price and then offset these negative instant contract savings and any Government costs against concurrent and future contract savings.

(3) The contractor shares in the savings on all affected units scheduled for delivery during the sharing period. The contractor is responsible for maintaining, for 3 years after final payment on the contract under which the VECP was accepted, records adequate to identify the first delivered unit incorporating the applicable VECP.

(4) Contractor shares of savings are paid through the contract under which the VECP was accepted. On incentive contracts, the

contractor's share of concurrent and future contract savings and of collateral savings shall be paid as a separate firm-fixed-price line item on the instant contract.

(5) Within 3 months after concurrent contracts have been modified to reflect price reductions attributable to use of the VECP, the contracting officer shall modify the instant contract to provide the contractor's share of savings.

(6) The contractor's share of future contract savings may be paid as subsequent contracts are awarded or in a lump-sum payment at the time the VECP is accepted. The lump-sum method may be used only if the contracting officer has established that this is the best way to proceed and the contractor agrees. The contracting officer ordinarily shall make calculations as future contracts are awarded and, within 3 months after award, modify the instant contract to provide the contractor's share of savings. For future contract savings calculated under the optional lump-sum method, the sharing base is an estimate of the number of items that the contracting office will purchase for delivery during the sharing period. In deciding whether or not to use the more convenient lump-sum method for an individual VECP, the contracting officer shall consider—

(i) The accuracy with which the number of items to be delivered during the sharing period can be estimated and the probability of actual production of the projected quantity;

(ii) The availability of funds for a lump-sum payment; and

(iii) The administrative expense of amending the instant contract as future contracts are awarded.

(b) *Construction contracts*. Sharing on construction contracts applies only to savings on the instant contract and to collateral savings. The Government's share of savings is determined by subtracting Government costs from instant contract savings and multiplying the result by (1) 45 percent for fixed-price contracts; or (2) 75 percent for cost-reimbursement contracts. Value engineering sharing does not apply to incentive construction contracts.

[FAC 84-42, 54 FR 5057, 1/31/89, effective 3/2/89; FAC 84-56, 55 FR 3887, 2/5/90, effective 3/7/90; Final rule, FAC 90-20, 59 FR 11368, 3/10/94, effective 3/10/94; Redesignated from 48.104-1, FAC 97-14, 64 FR 51828, 9/24/99, effective 11/23/99; FAC 2005-95, 82 FR 4709, 1/13/2017, effective 1/13/2017]

48.104-3 Sharing collateral savings.

(a) The Government shares collateral savings with the contractor, unless the head of the contracting activity has determined that the cost of calculating and tracking collateral savings will exceed the benefits to be derived (see 48.201(e)).

(b) The contractor's share of collateral savings may range from 20 to 100 percent of the estimated savings to be realized during a typical year of use but must not exceed the greater of—

(1) The contract's firm-fixed-price, target price, target cost, or estimated cost, at the time the VECP is accepted; or

(2) $100,000.

(c) The contracting officer must determine the sharing rate for each VECP.

(d) In determining collateral savings, the contracting officer must consider any degradation of performance, service life, or capability.

[Redesignated from 48.104-2, FAC 97-14, 64 FR 51828, 9/24/99, effective 11/23/99]

48.104-4 Sharing alternative—no-cost settlement method.

In selecting an appropriate mechanism for incorporating a VECP into a contract, the contracting officer shall analyze the different approaches available to determine which one would be in the Government's best interest. Contracting officers should balance the administrative costs of negotiating a settlement against the anticipated savings. A no-cost settlement may be used if, in the contracting officer's judgment, reliance on other VECP approaches likely would not be more cost-effective, and the no-cost settlement would provide adequate consideration to the Government. Under this method of settlement, the contractor would keep all of the savings on the instant contract, and all savings on its concurrent contracts only. The Government would keep all savings resulting from concurrent contracts placed with other sources, savings from all future contracts, and all collateral savings. Use of this method must be by mutual agreement of both parties for individual VECPs.

[FAC 97-5, 63 FR 34058, 6/22/98, effective 6/22/98, finalized without change, FAC 97-10, 63 FR 70264, 12/18/98; Redesignated from 48.104-3, FAC 97-14, 64 FR 51828, 9/24/99, effective 11/23/99]

48.105 Relationship to other incentives.

Contractors should be offered the fullest possible range of motivation, yet the benefits of an accepted VECP should not be rewarded both as value engineering shares and under performance, design-to-cost, or similar incentives of the contract. To that end, when performance, design-to-cost, or similar targets are set and incentivized, the targets of such incentives affected by the VECP are not to be adjusted because of the acceptance of the VECP. Only those benefits of an accepted VECP not rewardable under other incentives are rewarded under a value engineering clause.

[FAC 84-42, 54 FR 5057, 1/31/89, effective 3/2/89]

SUBPART 48.2—CONTRACT CLAUSES

48.201 Clauses for supply or service contracts.

(a) *General*. The contracting officer shall insert a value engineering clause in solicitations and contracts when the contract amount is expected to exceed the simplified acquisition threshold, except as specified in subparagraphs (1) through (5) and in paragraph (f) below. A value engineering clause may be included in contracts of lesser value if the contracting officer sees a potential for significant savings. Unless the chief of the contracting office authorizes its inclusion, the contracting officer shall *not* include a value engineering clause in solicitations and contracts—

(1) For research and development other than full-scale development;

(2) For engineering services from not-for-profit or nonprofit organizations;

(3) For personal services (see Subpart 37.1);

(4) Providing for product or component improvement, unless the value engineering incentive application is restricted to areas not covered by provisions for product or component improvement;

(5) For commercial products (see Part 11) that do not involve packaging specifications or other special requirements or specifications; or

(6) When the agency head has exempted the contract (or a class of contracts) from the requirements of this Part 48.

(b) *Value engineering incentive*. To provide a value engineering incentive, the contracting officer shall insert the clause at 52.248-1, Value Engineering, in solicitations and contracts except as provided in paragraph (a) above (but see subparagraph (e) (1) below).

(c) *Value engineering program requirement*. (1) If a mandatory value engineering effort is appropriate (i.e., if the contracting officer considers that substantial savings to the Government may result from a sustained value engineering effort of a specified level), the contracting officer shall use the clause with its Alternate I (but see subparagraph (e) (2) below).

(2) The value engineering program requirement may be specified by the Government in the solicitation or, in the case of negotiated contracting, proposed by the contractor as part of its offer and included as a subject for negotiation. The program requirement shall be shown as a separately priced line item in the contract Schedule.

(d) *Value engineering incentive and program requirement*. (1) If both a value engineering incentive and a mandatory program requirement are appropriate, the contracting officer shall use the clause with its Alternate II (but see subparagraph (e) (3) below).

(2) The contract shall restrict the value engineering program requirement to well-defined areas of performance designated by line item in the contract Schedule. Alternate

II applies a value engineering program to the specified areas and a value engineering incentive to the remaining areas of the contract.

(e) *Collateral savings computation not cost-effective.* If the head of the contracting activity determines for a contract or class of contracts that the cost of computing and tracking collateral savings will exceed the benefits to be derived, the contracting officer shall use the clause with its—

(1) Alternate III if a value engineering incentive is involved;

(2) Alternate III and Alternate I if a value engineering program requirement is involved; or

(3) Alternate III and Alternate II if *both* an incentive and a program requirement are involved.

(f) *Architect-engineering contracts.* The contracting officer shall insert the clause at 52.248-2, Value Engineering—Architect-Engineer, in solicitations and contracts whenever the Government requires and pays for a specific value engineering effort in architect-engineer contracts. The clause at 52.248-1, Value Engineering, shall not be used in solicitations and contracts for architect-engineer services.

(g) *Engineering-development solicitations and contracts.* For engineering-development solicitations and contracts, and solicitations and contracts containing low-rate-initial-production or early production units, the contracting officer must modify the clause at 52.248-1, Value Engineering, by—

(1) Revising paragraph (i)(3)(i) of the clause by substituting "a number equal to the quantity required to be delivered over a period of between 36 and 60 consecutive months (set at the discretion of the Contracting Officer for each VECP) that spans the highest planned production, based on planning and programming or production documentation at the time the VECP is accepted;" for "the number of future contract units scheduled for delivery during the sharing period;" and

(2) Revising the first sentence under paragraph (3) of the definition of "acquisition savings" by substituting "a number equal to the quantity to be delivered over a period of between 36 and 60 consecutive months (set at the discretion of the Contracting Officer for each VECP) that spans the highest planned production, based on planning and programming or production documentation at the time the VECP is accepted." for "the number of future contract units in the sharing base."

(h) *Extended production period solicitations and contracts.* In solicitations and contracts for items requiring an extended period for production (e.g., ship construction, major system acquisition), if agency procedures prescribe sharing of future contract savings on all units to be delivered under contracts awarded during the sharing period (see 48.104-1(c)), the contracting officer must modify the clause at 52.248-1, Value Engineering, by revising paragraph (i)(3)(i) of the clause and the first sentence under paragraph (3) of the definition of "acquisition savings" by substituting "under contracts awarded during the sharing period" for "during the sharing period."

[FAC 84-42, 54 FR 5057, 1/31/89, effective 3/2/89; FAC 84-56, 55 FR 3887, 2/5/90, effective 3/7/90; FAC 97-14, 64 FR 51828, 9/24/99, effective 11/23/99; FAC 2005-13, 71 FR 57363, 9/28/2006, effective 9/28/2006]

48.202 Clause for construction contracts.

The contracting officer shall insert the clause at 52.248-3, Value Engineering—Construction, in construction solicitations and contracts when the contract amount is estimated to exceed the simplified acquisition threshold, unless an incentive contract is contemplated. The contracting officer may include the clause in contracts of lesser value if the contracting officer sees a potential for significant savings. The contracting officer shall not include the clause in incentive-type construction contracts. If the head of the contracting activity determines that the cost of computing and tracking collateral savings for a contract will exceed the benefits to be derived, the contracting officer shall use the clause with its Alternate I.

[FAC 2005-13, 71 FR 57363, 9/28/2006, effective 9/28/2006]

PART 49—TERMINATION OF CONTRACTS

Table of Contents

Scope of part . . . 49.000
Definitions . . . 49.001
Applicability . . . 49.002

Subpart 49.1—General Principles

Scope of subpart . . . 49.100
Authorities and responsibilities . . . 49.101
Notice of termination . . . 49.102
Methods of settlement . . . 49.103
Duties of prime contractor after receipt of notice of termination . . . 49.104
Duties of termination contracting officer after issuance of notice of termination . . . 49.105
Termination status reports . . . 49.105-1
Release of excess funds . . . 49.105-2
Termination case file . . . 49.105-3
Cleanup of construction site . . . 49.105-4
Fraud or other criminal conduct . . . 49.106
Audit of prime contract settlement proposals and subcontract settlements . . . 49.107
Settlement of subcontract settlement proposals . . . 49.108
Subcontractor's rights . . . 49.108-1
Prime contractor's rights and obligations . . . 49.108-2
Settlement procedure . . . 49.108-3
Authorization for subcontract settlements without approval or ratification . . . 49.108-4
Recognition of judgments and arbitration awards . . . 49.108-5
Delay in settling subcontractor settlement proposals . . . 49.108-6
Government assistance in settling subcontracts . . . 49.108-7
Assignment of rights under subcontracts . . . 49.108-8
Settlement agreements . . . 49.109
General . . . 49.109-1
Reservations . . . 49.109-2
Government property . . . 49.109-3
No-cost settlement . . . 49.109-4
Partial settlements . . . 49.109-5
Joint settlement of two or more settlement proposals . . . 49.109-6
Settlement by determination . . . 49.109-7
Settlement negotiation memorandum . . . 49.110
Review of proposed settlements . . . 49.111
Payment . . . 49.112
Partial payments . . . 49.112-1
Final payment . . . 49.112-2
Cost principles . . . 49.113
Unsettled contract changes . . . 49.114
Settlement of terminated incentive contracts . . . 49.115

Subpart 49.2—Additional Principles for Fixed-Price Contracts Terminated for Convenience

General . . . 49.201
Profit . . . 49.202
Adjustment for loss . . . 49.203
Deductions . . . 49.204
Completed end items . . . 49.205
Settlement proposals . . . 49.206
Submission of settlement proposals . . . 49.206-1
Bases for settlement proposals . . . 49.206-2

Submission of inventory schedules 49.206-3
Limitation on settlements 49.207
Equitable adjustment after partial termination 49.208

Subpart 49.3—Additional Principles for Cost-Reimbursement Contracts Terminated for Convenience

General 49.301
Discontinuance of vouchers 49.302
Procedure after discontinuing vouchers 49.303
Submission of settlement proposal 49.303-1
Submission of inventory disposal schedules 49.303-2
Audit of settlement proposal 49.303-3
Adjustment of indirect costs 49.303-4
Final settlement 49.303-5
Procedure for partial termination 49.304
General 49.304-1
Submission of settlement proposal (fee only) 49.304-2
Submission of vouchers 49.304-3
Adjustment of fee 49.305
General 49.305-1
Construction contracts 49.305-2

Subpart 49.4—Termination for Default

General 49.401
Termination of fixed-price contracts for default 49.402
The Government's right 49.402-1
Effect of termination for default 49.402-2
Procedure for default 49.402-3
Procedure in lieu of termination for default 49.402-4
Memorandum by the contracting officer 49.402-5
Repurchase against contractor's account 49.402-6
Other damages 49.402-7
Reporting information 49.402-8
Termination of cost-reimbursement contracts for default 49.403
Surety-takeover agreements 49.404
Completion by another contractor 49.405
Liquidation of liability 49.406

Subpart 49.5—Contract Termination Clauses

General 49.501
Termination for convenience of the Government 49.502
Termination for convenience of the Government and default 49.503
Termination of fixed-price contracts for default 49.504
Other termination clauses 49.505

Subpart 49.6—Contract Termination Forms and Formats

Notice of termination for convenience 49.601
Electronic notice 49.601-1
Letter notice 49.601-2
Forms for settlement of terminated contracts 49.602
Termination settlement proposal forms 49.602-1
Inventory forms 49.602-2
Schedule of accounting information 49.602-3
Partial payments 49.602-4
Settlement agreement 49.602-5
Formats for termination for convenience settlement agreements 49.603
Fixed-price contracts—complete termination 49.603-1
Fixed-price contracts—partial termination 49.603-2

Cost-reimbursement contracts—complete termination, if settlement includes cost 49.603-3
Cost-reimbursement contracts—complete termination, with settlement limited to fee 49.603-4
Cost-reimbursement contracts—partial termination 49.603-5
No-cost settlement agreement—complete termination 49.603-6
No-cost settlement agreement—partial termination 49.603-7
Fixed-price contracts—settlements with subcontractors only 49.603-8
Settlement of reservations 49.603-9
Release of excess funds under terminated contracts 49.604
Request to settle subcontractor settlement proposals 49.605
Granting subcontract settlement authorization 49.606
Delinquency notices 49.607

PART 49—TERMINATION OF CONTRACTS

49.000 Scope of part.

This part establishes policies and procedures relating to the complete or partial termination of contracts for the convenience of the Government or for default. It prescribes contract clauses relating to termination and excusable delay and includes instructions for using termination and settlement forms.

49.001 Definitions.

As used in this part—

Other work means any current or scheduled work of the contractor, whether Government or commercial, other than work related to the terminated contract.

Plant clearance period, as used in this subpart, means the period beginning on the effective date of contract completion or termination and ending 90 days (or such longer period as may be agreed to) after receipt by the contracting officer of acceptable inventory schedules for each property classification. The final phase of the plant clearance period means that period after receipt of acceptable inventory schedules.

Settlement agreement means a written agreement in the form of a contract modification settling all or a severable portion of a settlement proposal.

Settlement proposal means a proposal for effecting settlement of a contract terminated in whole or in part, submitted by a contractor or subcontractor in the form, and supported by the data, required by this part. A settlement proposal is included within the generic meaning of the word "claim" under false claims acts (see 18 U.S.C. 287 and 31 U.S.C. 3729).

Unsettled contract change means any contract change or contract term for which a definitive modification is required but has not been executed.

[FAC 84-12, 51 FR 2666, 1/17/86, effective 1/20/86; FAC 97-22, 66 FR 2116, 1/10/2001, effective 3/12/2001; Delay of effective date, 66 FR 14259, 3/9/2001, effective 5/11/2001; FAC 2002-08, 67 FR 43513, 6/27/2002, effective 7/29/2002; FAC 2001-22, 69 FR 17741, 4/5/2004, effective 5/5/2004]

49.002 Applicability.

(a) (1) This part applies to contracts that provide for termination for the convenience of the Government or for the default of the contractor (see also 12.403 and 13.302-4).

(2) This part does not apply to commercial item contracts awarded using part 12 procedures. See 12.403 for termination policies for contracts for the acquisition of commercial items. However, for contracts for the acquisition of commercial items, this part provides administrative guidance which may be followed unless it is inconsistent with the requirements and procedures in 12.403, Termination, and the clause at 52.212-4, Contract Terms and Conditions—Commercial Items.

(b) Contractors shall use this part, unless inappropriate, to settle subcontracts terminated as a result of modification of prime contracts. The contracting officer shall use this part as a guide in evaluating settlements of subcontracts terminated for the convenience of a contractor whenever the settlement will be the basis of a proposal for reimbursement from the Government under a cost-reimbursement contract.

(c) The contracting officer may use this part in determining an equitable adjustment resulting from a modification under the Changes clause of any contract, except cost-reimbursement contracts.

(d) When action to be taken or authority to be exercised under this part depends upon the "amount" of the settlement proposal, that amount shall be determined by deducting from the gross settlement proposed the amounts payable for completed articles or work at the contract price and amounts for the settlement of subcontractor settlement proposals. Credits for retention or other disposal of termination inventory and amounts for advance or partial payments shall not be deducted.

[FAC 97-3, 62 FR 64912, 12/9/97, effective 2/9/98; FAC 2005-48, 75 FR 82576, 12/30/2010, effective 1/31/2011]

SUBPART 49.1—GENERAL PRINCIPLES

49.100 Scope of subpart.

(a) This subpart deals with—

(1) The authority and responsibility of contracting officers to terminate contracts in whole or in part for the convenience of the Government or for default;

(2) Duties of the contractor and the contracting officer after issuance of the notice of termination;

(3) General procedures for the settlement of terminated contracts; and

(4) Settlement agreements.

(b) Additional principles applicable to the termination for convenience and settlement of fixed-price and cost-reimbursement contracts are included in Subparts 49.2 and 49.3. Additional principles applicable to the termination of contracts for default are included in Subpart 49.4.

49.101 Authorities and responsibilities.

(a) The termination clauses or other contract clauses authorize contracting officers to terminate contracts for convenience, or for default, and to enter into settlement agreements under this regulation.

(b) The contracting officer shall terminate contracts, whether for default or convenience, only when it is in the Government's interest. The contracting officer shall effect a no-cost settlement instead of issuing a termination notice when—

(1) It is known that the contractor will accept one,

(2) Government property was not furnished, and

(3) There are no outstanding payments, debts due the Government, or other contractor obligations.

(c) When the price of the undelivered balance of the contract is less than $5,000, the contract should not normally be terminated for convenience but should be permitted to run to completion.

(d) After the contracting officer issues a notice of termination, the termination contracting officer (TCO) is responsible for negotiating any settlement with the contractor, including a no-cost settlement if appropriate. Auditors and TCO's shall promptly schedule and complete audit reviews and negotiations, giving particular attention to the need for timely action on all settlements involving small business concerns.

(e) If the same item is under contract with both large and small business concerns and it is necessary to terminate for convenience part of the units still to be delivered, preference shall be given to the continuing performance of small business contracts over large business contracts unless the chief of the contracting office determines that this is not in the Government's interest.

(f) The contracting officer is responsible for the release of excess funds resulting from the termination unless this responsibility is specifically delegated to the TCO.

[FAC 90-3, 55 FR 52797, 12/21/90, effective 1/22/91; FAC 90-9, 56 FR 67134, 12/27/91, effective 2/25/92]

49.102 Notice of termination.

(a) *General.* The contracting officer shall terminate contracts for convenience or default only by a written notice to the contractor (see 49.601). The notice of termination may be expedited by means of electronic communication capable of providing confirmation of receipt by the contractor. When the notice is mailed, it shall be sent by certified mail, return receipt requested. When the contracting office arranges for hand delivery of the notice, a written acknowledgment shall be obtained from the contractor. The notice shall state—

(1) That the contract is being terminated for the convenience of the Government (or for default) under the contract clause authorizing the termination;

(2) The effective date of termination;

(3) The extent of termination;

(4) Any special instructions; and

(5) The steps the contractor should take to minimize the impact on personnel if the termination, together with all other outstanding terminations, will result in a significant reduction in the contractor's work force (see

paragraph (g) of the notice in 49.601-2). If the termination notice is by telegram, include these "steps" in the confirming letter or modification.

(b) *Distribution of copies*. The contracting officer shall simultaneously send the termination notice to the contractor, and a copy to the contract administration office and to any known assignee, guarantor, or surety of the contractor.

(c) *Amendment of termination notice*. The contracting officer may amend a termination notice to—

(1) Correct nonsubstantive mistakes in the notice;

(2) Add supplemental data or instructions; or

(3) Rescind the notice if it is determined that items terminated had been completed or shipped before the contractor's receipt of the notice.

(d) *Reinstatement of terminated contracts*. Upon written consent of the contractor, the contracting office may reinstate the terminated portion of a contract in whole or in part by amending the notice of termination if it has been determined in writing that—

(1) Circumstances clearly indicate a requirement for the terminated items; and

(2) Reinstatement is advantageous to the Government.

[FAC 2005-92, 81 FR 83097, 11/18/2016, effective 12/19/2016]

49.103 Methods of settlement.

Settlement of terminated cost-reimbursement contracts and fixed-price contracts terminated for convenience may be effected by (a) negotiated agreement, (b) determination by the TCO, (c) costing-out under vouchers using SF 1034, Public Voucher for Purchases and Services Other Than Personal, for cost-reimbursement contracts (as prescribed in Subpart 49.3), or (d) a combination of these methods. When possible, the TCO should negotiate a fair and prompt settlement with the contractor. The TCO shall settle a settlement proposal by determination only when it cannot be settled by agreement.

49.104 Duties of prime contractor after receipt of notice of termination.

After receipt of the notice of termination, the contractor shall comply with the notice and the termination clause of the contract, except as otherwise directed by the TCO. The notice and clause applicable to convenience terminations generally require that the contractor—

(a) Stop work immediately on the terminated portion of the contract and stop placing subcontracts thereunder;

(b) Terminate all subcontracts related to the terminated portion of the prime contract;

(c) Immediately advise the TCO of any special circumstances precluding the stoppage of work;

(d) Perform the continued portion of the contract and submit promptly any request for an equitable adjustment of price for the continued portion, supported by evidence of any increase in the cost, if the termination is partial;

(e) Take necessary or directed action to protect and preserve property in the contractor's possession in which the Government has or may acquire an interest and, as directed by the TCO, deliver the property to the Government;

(f) Promptly notify the TCO in writing of any legal proceedings growing out of any subcontract or other commitment related to the terminated portion of the contract;

(g) Settle outstanding liabilities and proposals arising out of termination of subcontracts, obtaining any approvals or ratifications required by the TCO;

(h) Promptly submit the contractor's own settlement proposal, supported by appropriate schedules; and

(i) Dispose of termination inventory, as directed or authorized by the TCO.

49.105 Duties of termination contracting officer after issuance of notice of termination.

(a) Consistent with the termination clause and the notice of termination, the TCO shall—

(1) Direct the action required of the prime contractor;

(2) Examine the settlement proposal of the prime contractor and, when appropriate, the settlement proposals of subcontractors;

(3) Promptly negotiate settlement with the contractor and enter into a settlement agreement; and

(4) Promptly settle the contractor's settlement proposal by determination for the elements that cannot be agreed on, if unable to negotiate a complete settlement.

(b) To expedite settlement, the TCO may request specially qualified personnel to—

(1) Assist in dealings with the contractor;

(2) Advise on legal and contractual matters;

(3) Conduct accounting reviews and advise and assist on accounting matters; and

(4) Perform the following functions regarding termination inventory (see Subpart 45.6):

(i) Verify its existence.

(ii) Determine qualitative and quantitative allocability.

(iii) Make recommendations concerning serviceability.

(iv) Undertake necessary screening and redistribution.

(v) Assist the contractor in accomplishing other disposition.

(c) The TCO should promptly hold a conference with the contractor to develop a definite program for effecting the settlement. When appropriate in the judgment of the TCO, after consulting with the contractor, principal subcontractors should be requested to attend. Topics that should be discussed at the conference and documented include—

(1) General principles relating to the settlement of any settlement proposal, including obligations of the contractor under the termination clause of the contract;

(2) Extent of the termination, point at which work is stopped, and status of any plans, drawings, and information that would have been delivered had the contract been completed;

(3) Status of any continuing work;

(4) Obligation of the contractor to terminate subcontracts and general principles to be followed in settling subcontractor settlement proposals;

(5) Names of subcontractors involved and the dates termination notices were issued to them;

(6) Contractor personnel handling review and settlement of subcontractor settlement proposals and the methods being used;

(7) Arrangements for transfer of title and delivery to the Government of any material required by the Government;

(8) General principles and procedures to be followed in the protection, preservation, and disposition of the contractor's and subcontractors' termination inventories, including the preparation of termination inventory schedules;

(9) Contractor accounting practices and preparation of SF 1439 (Schedule of Accounting Information (49.602-3));

(10) Form in which to submit settlement proposals;

(11) Accounting review of settlement proposals;

(12) Any requirement for interim financing in the nature of partial payments;

(13) Tentative time schedule for negotiation of the settlement, including submission by the contractor and subcontractors of settlement proposals, termination inventory schedules, and accounting information schedules (see 49.206-3 and 49.303-2);

(14) Actions taken by the contractor to minimize impact upon employees affected adversely by the termination (see paragraph (g) of the letter notice in 49.601-2); and

(15) Obligation of the contractor to furnish accurate, complete, and current cost or pricing data, and to certify to that effect in accordance with 15.403-4(a)(1) when the amount of a termination settlement agreement, or a partial termination settlement agreement plus the estimate to complete the

continued portion of the contract exceeds the threshold in 15.403-4.

[FAC 90-40, 61 FR 39186, 7/26/96, effective 9/24/96; FAC 97-2, 62 FR 51224, 9/30/97, effective 10/10/97]

49.105-1 Termination status reports.

When the TCO and contracting officer are in different activities, the TCO will furnish periodic status reports on termination actions to the contracting office upon request. The contracting office shall specify the information required.

49.105-2 Release of excess funds.

(a) The TCO shall estimate the funds required to settle the termination, and within 30 days after the receipt of the termination notice, recommend the release of excess funds to the contracting officer. The initial deobligation of excess funds should be accomplished in a timely manner by the contracting officer, or the TCO, if delegated the responsibility. The TCO shall not recommend the release of amounts under $1,000, unless requested by the contracting officer.

(b) The TCO shall maintain continuous surveillance of required funds to permit timely release of any additional excess funds (a recommended format for release of excess funds is in 49.604). If previous releases of excess funds result in a shortage of the amount required for settlement, the TCO shall promptly inform the contracting officer, who shall reinstate the funds within 30 days.

[FAC 90-9, 56 FR 67134, 12/27/91, effective 2/25/92]

49.105-3 Termination case file.

The TCO responsible for negotiating the final settlement shall establish a separate case file for each termination. This file will include memoranda and records of all actions relative to the settlement (see 4.801).

49.105-4 Cleanup of construction site.

In the case of terminated construction contracts, the contracting officer shall direct action to ensure the cleanup of the site, protection of serviceable materials, removal of hazards, and other action necessary to leave a safe and healthful site.

49.106 Fraud or other criminal conduct.

If the TCO suspects fraud or other criminal conduct related to the settlement of a terminated contract, the TCO shall discontinue negotiations and report the facts under agency procedures.

49.107 Audit of prime contract settlement proposals and subcontract settlements.

(a) The TCO shall refer each prime contractor settlement proposal valued at or above the threshold for obtaining certified cost or pricing data set forth in FAR 15.403-4(a)(1) to the appropriate audit agency for review and recommendations. The TCO may submit settlement proposals of less than the threshold for obtaining certified cost or pricing data to the audit agency. Referrals shall indicate any specific information or data that the TCO considers relevant and shall include facts and circumstances that will assist the audit agency in performing its function. The audit agency shall develop requested information and may make any further accounting reviews it considers appropriate. After its review, the audit agency shall submit written comments and recommendations to the TCO. When a formal examination of settlement proposals valued under the threshold for obtaining certified cost or pricing data is not warranted, the TCO will perform or have performed a desk review and include a written summary of the review in the termination case file.

(b) The TCO shall refer subcontract settlements received for approval or ratification to the appropriate audit agency for review and recommendations when—

(1) The amount exceeds the threshold for obtaining certified cost or pricing data; or

(2) The TCO determines that a complete or partial accounting review is advisable. The audit agency shall submit written comments and recommendations to the TCO. The review by the audit agency does not relieve the prime contractor or higher tier subcontractor of the responsibility for performing an accounting review.

(c) (1) The responsibility of the prime contractor and of each subcontractor (see 49.108) includes performance of accounting reviews and any necessary field audits. However, the TCO should request the Government audit agency to perform the accounting review of a subcontractor's settlement proposal when—

(i) A subcontractor objects, for competitive reasons, to an accounting review of its records by an upper tier contractor;

(ii) The Government audit agency is currently performing audit work at the subcontractor's plant, or can perform the audit more economically or efficiently;

(iii) Audit by the Government is necessary for consistent audit treatment and orderly administration; or

(iv) The contractor has a substantial or controlling financial interest in the subcontractor.

(2) The audit agency should avoid duplication of accounting reviews performed by the upper tier contractor on subcontractor settlement proposals. However, this should not preclude the Government from making additional reviews when appropriate. When the contractor is performing accounting reviews according to this section, the TCO should request the audit agency to periodically examine the contractor's accounting review procedures and performance, and to make appropriate comments and recommendations to the TCO.

(d) The audit report is advisory only, and is for the TCO to use in negotiating a settlement or issuing a unilateral determination. Government personnel handling audit reports must be careful not to reveal privileged information or information that will jeopardize the negotiation position of the Government, the prime contractor, or a higher tier subcontractor. Consistent with this, and when in the Government's interest, the TCO may furnish audit reports under paragraph (c) of this section to prime and higher tier subcontractors for their use in settling subcontract settlement proposals.

[FAC 90-3, 55 FR 52797, 12/21/90, effective 1/22/91; FAC 2005-98, 83 FR 19149, 5/1/2018, effective 5/31/2018]

49.108 Settlement of subcontract settlement proposals. (No Text)

49.108-1 Subcontractor's rights.

A subcontractor has no contractual rights against the Government upon the termination of a prime contract. A subcontractor may have rights against the prime contractor or intermediate subcontractor with whom it has contracted. Upon termination of a prime contract, the prime contractor and each subcontractor are responsible for the prompt settlement of the settlement proposals of their immediate subcontractors.

49.108-2 Prime contractor's rights and obligations.

(a) Termination for convenience clauses provide that after receipt of a termination notice the prime contractor shall, unless directed otherwise by the TCO, terminate all subcontracts to the extent that they relate to the performance of prime work terminated. Therefore, prime contractors should include a termination clause in their subcontracts for their own protection. Suggestions regarding use of subcontract termination clauses are in Subpart 49.5.

(b) The failure of a prime contractor to include an appropriate termination clause in any subcontract, or to exercise the clause rights, shall not—

(1) Affect the Government's right to require the termination of the subcontract; or

(2) Increase the obligation of the Government beyond what it would have been if the subcontract had contained an appropriate clause.

(c) In any case, the reasonableness of the prime contractor's settlement with the subcontractor should normally be measured by the aggregate amount due under paragraph (f) of the subcontract termination clause suggested in 49.502(e). The TCO shall allow reimbursement in excess of that amount only in unusual cases and then only to the extent that the terms of the subcontract did not unreasonably increase the rights of the subcontractor.

49.108-3 Settlement procedure.

(a) Contractors shall settle with subcontractors in general conformity with the policies and principles relating to settlement of prime contracts in this subpart and Subparts 49.2 or 49.3. However, the basis and form of the subcontractor's settlement proposal must be acceptable to the prime contractor or the next higher tier subcontractor. Each settlement must be supported by accounting data and other information sufficient for adequate review by the Government. In no event will the Government pay the prime contractor any amount for loss of anticipatory profits or consequential damages resulting from the termination of any subcontract (but see 49.108-5).

(b) Except as provided in 49.108-4, the TCO shall require that—

(1) All subcontractor termination inventory be disposed of and accounted for in accordance with the procedures contained in paragraph (j) of the clause at 52.245-1, Government Property; and

(2) The prime contractor submit, for approval or ratification, all termination settlements with subcontractors.

(c) The TCO shall promptly examine each subcontract settlement received to determine that the subcontract termination was made necessary by the termination of the prime contract (or by issuance of a change order—see 49.002(b)). The TCO will also determine if the settlement was arrived at in good faith, is reasonable in amount, and is allocable to the terminated portion of the contract (or, if allocable only in part, that the proposed allocation is reasonable). In considering the reasonableness of any subcontract settlement, the TCO shall generally be guided by the provisions of this part relating to the settlement of prime contracts, and shall comply with any applicable requirements of 49.107 and 49.111 relating to accounting and other reviews. After the examination, the TCO shall notify the contractor in writing of—

(1) Approval or ratification, or

(2) The reasons for disapproval.

[FAC 90-45, Final rule, 62 FR 224, 1/2/97, effective 1/1/97; FAC 2001-22, Final rule, 69 FR 17741, 4/5/2004, effective 5/5/2004; FAC 2005-17, 72 FR 27364, 5/15/2007, effective 6/14/2007]

49.108-4 Authorization for subcontract settlements without approval or ratification.

(a) (1) The TCO may, upon written request, give written authorization to the prime contractor to conclude settlements of subcontracts terminated in whole or in part without approval or ratification when the amount of settlement (see 49.002(d)) is $100,000 or less, if—

(i) The TCO is satisfied with the adequacy of the procedures used by the contractor in settling settlement proposals, including proposals for retention, sale, or other disposal of termination inventory of the immediate and lower tier subcontractors (the TCO shall obtain the advice and recommendations of—

(A) The appropriate audit agency relating to the adequacy of the contractor's audit administration, including personnel, and

(B) The cognizant plant clearance officer relating to the adequacy of the contractor's procedures and personnel for the administration of property disposal matters);

(ii) Any termination inventory included in determining the amount of the settlement will be disposed of as directed by the prime contractor, except that the disposition of the inventory shall not be subject to—

(A) Review by the TCO under 49.108-3(c); or

(B) The screening requirements in 45.602-3; and

(iii) A certificate similar to the certificate in the settlement proposal form in 49.602-1(a) will accompany the settlement.

(2) Except as provided in subparagraph (a)(4) of this section, authority granted to a prime contractor under subparagraph (a)(1) of this section by any TCO shall apply to all Executive agencies' prime contracts that are terminated, or modified by change orders.

(3) Except as provided in subparagraph (a)(4) of this section, the TCO shall accept, as part of the prime contractor's settlement proposal, settlements of terminated lower tier subcontracts concluded by any of the

prime contractor's immediate or lower tier subcontractors who have been granted authority as prime contractors to settle subcontracts; provided, that the settlement is within the limit of the authority. Authorization to settle proposals of lower tier subcontractors shall not be granted directly to subcontractors. However, a prime contractor authorized to approve subcontractor settlements may also exercise this authority in its capacity as a subcontractor, with respect to its terminated subcontracts and orders. When exercising this authority as a subcontractor, the contractor shall notify the purchaser.

(4) The provisions of subparagraphs (a)(1), (2), and (3) of this section shall not apply to contracts under the administration of any contracting officer if the contracting officer so notifies the prime contractor concerned. This notice shall (i) be in writing, and (ii) if subparagraph (a)(3) of this section is involved, specify any subcontractor affected.

(b) Section 45.602 shall apply to disposal of completed end items allocable to the terminated subcontract. However, these items may be disposed of without review by the TCO under 49.108-3 and without screening under 45.602-3, if the items do not require demilitarization and the total amount (at the subcontract price) when added to the amount of the settlement does not exceed the amount authorized under this subsection.

(c) A TCO granting the authorization in subparagraph (a)(1) of this section shall periodically (at least annually) make a selective review of settlements and settlement procedures to determine if the contractor is making adequate reviews and fair settlements, and whether the authorization should remain in effect. The TCO shall obtain the advice and recommendations of the appropriate audit agency and the cognizant plant clearance officer. When it is determined that the contractor's procedures are not adequate, or that improper settlements are being made, or when the authority has not been used in the preceding 2 years, the TCO shall revoke the authorization by written notice to the contractor, effective on the date of receipt.

(d) The contractor may make any number of separate settlements with a single subcontractor but shall not divide settlement proposals solely to bring them under an authorization limit. Separate settlement proposals that would normally be included in a single proposal, such as those based on a series of separate orders for the same item under one contract, shall be consolidated whenever possible.

(e) Upon written request of the contractor, the TCO may increase an authorization granted under subparagraph (a)(1) of this subsection to authorize the contractor to conclude settlements under a particular prime contract. The TCO may limit the increased authorization to specific subcontracts or classes of subcontracts.

(f) Authorizations granted under this 49.108-4 shall not authorize the settlement of requisitions or orders placed with any unit within the contractor's corporate entity.

(g) Recommended formats for a request to settle subcontractor settlement proposals and the TCO's letter of authorization to the contractor are in 49.605 and 49.606, respectively.

[FAC 90-3, 55 FR 52797, 12/21/90, effective 1/22/91; FAC 2001-22, 69 FR 17741, 4/5/2004, effective 5/5/2004]

49.108-5 Recognition of judgments and arbitration awards.

(a) When a subcontractor obtains a final judgment against a prime contractor, the TCO shall, for the purposes of settling the prime contract, treat the amount of the judgment as a cost of settling with the contractor, to the extent the judgment is properly allocable to the terminated portion of the prime contract, if—

(1) The prime contractor has made reasonable efforts to include in the subcontract a termination clause described in 49.502(e), 49.503(c), or a similar clause excluding payment of anticipatory profits or consequential damages;

(2) The provisions of the subcontract relating to the rights of the parties upon its termination are fair and reasonable and do

not unreasonably increase the common law rights of the subcontractor;

(3) The contractor made reasonable efforts to settle the settlement proposal of the subcontractor;

(4) The contractor gave prompt notice to the contracting officer of the initiation of the proceedings in which the judgment was rendered and did not refuse to give the Government control of the defense of the proceedings; and

(5) The contractor diligently defended the suit or, if the Government assumed control of the defense of the proceedings, rendered reasonable assistance requested by the Government.

(b) If the conditions in subparagraphs (a)(1) through (5) of this section are not all met, the TCO may allow the contractor the part of the judgment considered fair for settling the subcontract settlement proposal, giving due regard to the policies in this part for settlement of proposals.

(c) When a contractor and a subcontractor submit the subcontractor's settlement proposal to arbitration under any applicable law or contract provision, the TCO shall recognize the arbitration award as the cost of settling the proposal of the contractor to the same extent and under the same conditions as in paragraphs (a) and (b) of this section.

49.108-6 Delay in settling subcontractor settlement proposals.

When a prime contractor's inability to settle with a subcontractor delays the settlement of the prime contract, the TCO may settle with the prime contractor. The TCO shall except the subcontractor settlement proposal from the settlement in whole or part and reserve the rights of the Government and the prime contractor with respect to the subcontractor proposal.

49.108-7 Government assistance in settling subcontracts.

In unusual cases the TCO may determine, with the consent of the prime contractor, that it is in the Government's interest to provide assistance to the prime contractor in the settlement of a particular subcontract. In these situations, the Government, the prime contractor, and a subcontractor may enter into an agreement covering the settlement of one or more subcontracts. In these settlements, the subcontractor shall be paid through the prime contractor as part of the overall settlement with the prime contractor.

49.108-8 Assignment of rights under subcontracts.

(a) The termination for convenience clauses in 52.249, except the short-form clauses, obligate the prime contractor to assign to the Government, as directed by the TCO, all rights, titles, and interest under any subcontract terminated because of termination of the prime contract. The TCO shall not require the assignment unless it is in the Government's interest.

(b) The termination for convenience clauses (except the short-form clauses) also provide the Government the right, in its discretion, to settle and pay any settlement proposal arising out of the termination of subcontracts. This right does not obligate the Government to settle and pay settlement proposals of subcontractors. As a general rule, the prime contractor is obligated to settle and pay these proposals. However, when the TCO determines that it is in the Government's interest, the TCO shall, after notifying the contractor, settle the subcontractor's proposal using the procedures for settlement of prime contracts. An example in which the Government's interest would be served is when a subcontractor is a sole source and it appears that a delay by the prime contractor in settlement or payment of the subcontractor's proposal will jeopardize the financial position of the subcontractor. Direct settlements with subcontractors are not encouraged.

49.109 Settlement agreements. (No Text)

49.109-1 General.

When a termination settlement has been negotiated and all required reviews have been obtained, the contractor and the TCO shall execute a settlement agreement on Standard Form 30 (Amendment of Solicitation/Modification of Contract) (see 49.603). The settlement shall cover—

(a) Any setoffs that the Government has against the contractor that may be applied against the terminated contract and

(b) All settlement proposals of subcontractors, except proposals that are specifically excepted from the agreement and reserved for separate settlement.

49.109-2 Reservations.

(a) The TCO shall—

(1) Reserve in the settlement agreement any rights or demands of the parties that are excepted from the settlement;

(2) Ensure that the wording of the reservation does not create any rights for the parties beyond those in existence before execution of the settlement agreement;

(3) Mark each applicable settlement agreement with "This settlement agreement contains a reservation" and retain the contract file until the reservation is removed;

(4) Ensure that sufficient funds are retained to cover complete settlement of the reserved items; and

(5) At the appropriate time, prepare a separate settlement of reserved items and include it in a separate settlement agreement.

(b) A recommended format for settlement of reservations appears in 49.603-9.

49.109-3 Government property.

Before execution of a settlement agreement, the TCO shall determine the accuracy of the Government property account for the terminated contract. If an audit discloses property for which the contractor cannot account, the TCO shall reserve in the settlement agreement the rights of the Government regarding that property or make an appropriate deduction from the amount otherwise due the contractor.

49.109-4 No-cost settlement.

The TCO shall execute a no-cost settlement agreement (see 49.603-6 or 49.603-7, as applicable) if—

(a) The contractor has not incurred costs for the terminated portion of the contract or

(b) The contractor is willing to waive the costs incurred and

(c) No amounts are due the Government under the contract.

49.109-5 Partial settlements.

The TCO should attempt to settle in one agreement all rights and liabilities of the parties under the contract except those arising from any continued portion of the contract. Generally, the TCO shall not attempt to make partial settlements covering particular items of the prime contractor's settlement proposal. However, when a TCO cannot promptly complete settlement under the terminated contract, a partial settlement may be entered into if—

(a) The issues on which agreement has been reached are clearly severable from other issues and

(b) The partial settlement will not prejudice the Government's or contractor's interests in disposing of the unsettled part of the settlement proposal.

49.109-6 Joint settlement of two or more settlement proposals.

(a) With the consent of the contractor, the TCO or TCO's concerned may negotiate jointly two or more termination settlement proposals of the same contractor under different contracts, even though the contracts are with different contracting offices or agencies. In such cases, accounting work shall be consolidated to the greatest extent practical. The resulting settlement may be evidenced by one settlement agreement covering all contracts involved or by a separate agreement for each contract involved.

(b) When the settlement agreement covers more than one contract, it shall—

(1) Clearly identify the contracts involved,

(2) Assign an amendment modification number to each contract,

(3) Apportion the total amount of the settlement among the several contracts on some reasonable basis,

(4) Have attached or incorporated a schedule showing the apportionment, and

(5) Be distributed and attached to each contract involved in the same manner as other contract modifications.

49.109-7 Settlement by determination.

(a) *General.* If the contractor and TCO cannot agree on a termination settlement, or if a settlement proposal is not submitted within the period required by the termination clause, the TCO shall issue a determination of the amount due consistent with the termination clause, including any cost principles incorporated by reference. The TCO shall comply with 49.109-1 through 49.109-6 in making a settlement by determination and with 49.203 in making an adjustment for loss, if any. Copies of determinations shall receive the same distribution as other contract modifications.

(b) *Notice to contractor.* Before issuing a determination of the amount due the contractor, the TCO shall give the contractor at least 15 days notice by certified mail (return receipt requested) to submit written evidence, so as to reach the TCO on or before a stated date, substantiating the amount previously proposed.

(c) *Justification of settlement proposal.* (1) The contractor has the burden of establishing, by proof satisfactory to the TCO, the amount proposed.

(2) The contractor may submit vouchers, verified transcripts of books of account, affidavits, audit reports, and other documents as desired. The TCO may request the contractor to submit additional documents and data, and may request appropriate accountings, investigations, and audits.

(3) The TCO may accept copies of documents and records without requiring original documents unless there is a question of authenticity.

(4) The TCO may hold any conferences considered appropriate—

(i) To confer with the contractor,

(ii) To obtain additional information from Government personnel or from independent experts, or

(iii) To consult persons who have submitted affidavits or reports.

(d) *Determinations.* After reviewing the information available, the TCO shall determine the amount due and shall transmit a copy of the determination to the contractor by certified mail (return receipt requested), or by any other method that provides evidence of receipt. The transmittal letter shall advise the contractor that the determination is a final decision from which the contractor may appeal under the Disputes clause, except as shown in paragraph (f) of this section. The determination shall specify the amount due the contractor and will be supported by detailed schedules conforming generally to the forms for settlement proposals prescribed in 49.602-1 and by additional information, schedules, and analyses as appropriate. The TCO shall explain each major item of disallowance. The TCO need not reconsider any other action relating to the terminated portion of the contract that was ratified or approved by the TCO or another contracting officer.

(e) *Preservation of evidence.* The TCO shall retain all written evidence and other data relied upon in making a determination, except that copies of original books of account need not be made. The TCO shall return books of account, together with other original papers and documents, to the contractor within a reasonable time.

(f) *Appeals.* The contractor may appeal, under the Disputes clause, any settlement by determination, except when the contractor has failed to submit the settlement proposal within the time provided in the contract and failed to request an extension of time. The pendency of an appeal shall not affect the authority of the TCO to settle the settlement proposal or any part by negotiation with the contractor at any time before the appeal is decided.

(g) *Decision on the contractor's appeal.* The TCO shall give effect to a decision of the Claims Court or a board of contract appeals, when necessary, by an appropriate modification to the contract. When appropriate, the TCO should obtain a release from the contractor. TCO's are authorized to modify the formats of settlement agreements in 49.603 to agree with this provision.

[FAC 84-26, 52 FR 19805, 5/27/87, effective 7/30/87]

49.110 Settlement negotiation memorandum.

(a) The TCO shall, at the conclusion of negotiations, prepare a settlement negotiation memorandum describing the principal elements of the settlement for inclusion in the termination case file and for use by reviewing authorities. Pricing aspects of the settlement shall be documented in accordance with 15.406-3. The memorandum shall be distributed in accordance with 15.406-3.

(b) If the settlement was negotiated on the basis of individual items, the TCO shall specify the factors considered for each item. If the settlement was negotiated on an overall lump-sum basis, the TCO need not evaluate each item or group of items individually, but shall support the total amount of the recommended settlement in reasonable detail. The memorandum shall include explanations of matters involving differences and doubtful questions settled by agreement, and the factors considered. The TCO should include any other matters that will assist reviewing authorities in understanding the basis for the settlement.

[FAC 90-9, 56 FR 67135, 12/27/91, effective 2/25/92; FAC 97-2, 62 FR 51224, 9/30/97, effective 10/10/97]

49.111 Review of proposed settlements.

Each agency shall establish procedures, when necessary, for the administrative review of proposed termination settlements. When one agency provides termination settlement services for another agency, the agency providing the services shall also perform the settlement review function.

49.112 Payment. (No Text)

49.112-1 Partial payments.

(a) *General.* If the contract authorizes partial payments on settlement proposals before settlement, a prime contractor may request them on the form prescribed in 49.602-4 at any time after submission of interim or final settlement proposals. The Government will process applications for partial payments promptly. A subcontractor shall submit its application through the prime contractor which shall attach its own invoice and recommendations to the subcontractor's application. Partial payments to a subcontractor shall be made only through the prime contractor and only after the prime contractor has submitted its interim or final settlement proposal. Except for undelivered acceptable finished products, partial payments shall not be made for profit or fee claimed under the terminated portion of the contract. In exercising discretion on the extent of partial payments to be made, the TCO shall consider the diligence of the contractor in settling with subcontractors and in preparing its own settlement proposal.

(b) *Amount of partial payment.* Before approving any partial payment, the TCO shall obtain any desired accounting, engineering, or other specialized reviews of the data submitted in support of the contractor's settlement proposal. If the reviews and the TCO's examination of the data indicate that the requested partial payment is proper, reasonable payments may be authorized in the discretion of the TCO up to—

(1) 100 percent of the contract price, adjusted for undelivered acceptable items completed before the termination date, or later completed with the approval of the TCO (see 49.205);

(2) 100 percent of the amount of any subcontract settlement paid by the prime contractor if the settlement was approved or ratified by the TCO under 49.108-3(c) or was authorized under 49.108-4;

(3) 90 percent of the direct cost of termination inventory, including costs of raw materials, purchased parts, supplies, and direct labor;

(4) 90 percent of other allowable costs (including settlement expense and manufacturing and administrative indirect costs) allocable to the terminated portion of the contract and not included in subparagraphs (b)(1), (2), or (3) of this section; and

(5) 100 percent of partial payments made to subcontractors under this section.

(c) *Recognition of assignments.* When an assignment of claims has been made under the contract, the Government shall not make partial payments to other than the assignee unless the parties to the assignment consent in writing (see 32.805(e)).

(d) *Security for partial payments.* If any partial payment is made for completed end items or for costs of termination inventory, the TCO shall protect the Government's interest. This shall be done by obtaining title to the completed end items or termination inventory, or by the creation of a lien in favor of the Government, paramount to all other liens, on the completed end items or termination inventory, or by other appropriate means.

(e) *Deductions in computing amount of partial payments.* The TCO shall deduct from the gross amount of any partial payment otherwise payable under 49.112-1(b)—

(1) All unliquidated balances of progress and advance payments (including interest) made to the contractor, which are allocable to the terminated portion of the contract; and

(2) The amounts of all credits arising from the purchase, retention, or sale of property, the costs of which are included in the application for payment.

(f) *Limitation on total amount.* The total amount of all partial payments shall not exceed the amount that will, in the opinion of the TCO, become due to the contractor because of the termination.

(g) *Effect of overpayment.* If the total of partial payments exceeds the amount finally determined due on the settlement proposal, the contractor shall repay the excess to the Government on demand, together with interest. The interest shall be computed at the rate established by the Secretary of the Treasury under 50 U.S.C. App. 1215(b)(2) from the date the excess payment was received by the contractor to the date of repayment. However, interest will not be charged for any—

(1) excess payment attributable to a reduction in the settlement proposal because of retention or other disposition of termination inventory, until 10 days after the date of the retention or disposition, or a later date determined by the TCO, or

(2) Overpayment under cost-reimbursement research and development contracts without profit or fee if the overpayments are repaid to the Government within 30 days after demand.

(h) *Certification and approval of partial payments.* (1) The contractor shall place the following certification on vouchers or invoices for partial payments:

The payment covered by this voucher is a partial payment on the Contractor's settlement proposal under contract No. ____ made under Part 49 of the Federal Acquisition Regulation.

(2) The TCO shall approve the invoice or voucher by noting on it the following:

Payment of $____ is approved.

49.112-2 Final payment.

(a) *Negotiated settlement.* After execution of a settlement agreement, the contractor shall submit a voucher or invoice showing the amount agreed upon, less any portion previously paid. The TCO shall attach a copy of the settlement agreement to the voucher or invoice and forward the documents to the disbursing officer for payment.

(b) *Settlement by determination.* If the settlement is by determination and—

(1) There is no appeal within the allowed time, the contractor shall submit a voucher or invoice showing the amount determined due, less any portion previously paid; or

(2) There is an appeal, the contractor shall submit a voucher or invoice showing the amount finally determined due on the appeal, less any portion previously paid. Pending determination of any appeal, the contractor may submit vouchers or invoices for charges that are not directly involved with the portion being appealed, without prejudice to the rights of either party on the appeal.

(c) *Construction contracts.* In the case of construction contracts, before forwarding the final payment voucher, the contracting officer shall ascertain whether there are any outstanding labor violations. If so, the contracting officer shall determine the amount to be withheld from the final payment (see Subpart 22.4).

(d) *Interest.* The Government shall not pay interest on the amount due under a settlement agreement or a settlement by determination. The Government may, however, pay interest on a successful contractor appeal from a contracting officer's determination under the Disputes clause at 52.233-1.

49.113 Cost principles.

The cost principles and procedures in the applicable subpart of Part 31 shall, subject to the general principles in 49.201—

(a) Be used in asserting, negotiating, or determining costs relevant to termination settlements under contracts with other than educational institutions, and

(b) Be a guide for the negotiation of settlements under contracts for experimental, developmental, or research work with educational institutions (but see 31.104).

49.114 Unsettled contract changes.

(a) Before settlement of a completely terminated contract, the TCO shall obtain from the contracting office a list of all related unsettled contract changes. The TCO shall settle, as part of final settlement, all unsettled contract changes after obtaining the recommendations of the contracting office concerning the changes.

(b) When the contract has been partially terminated, any outstanding unsettled contract changes will usually be handled by the contracting officer. However, the contracting officer may delegate this function to the TCO.

49.115 Settlement of terminated incentive contracts.

(a) *Fixed-price incentive contracts*. The TCO shall settle terminated fixed-price incentive (FPI) contracts under the provisions of paragraph (j) of the clause at 52.216-16, Incentive Price Revision—Firm Target, and 52.249-2, Termination for Convenience of the Government (Fixed-Price).

(1) *Partial termination*. Under a partially terminated contract, the TCO shall negotiate a settlement as provided in the termination clause of the contract, and paragraph (j) of the clause at 52.216-16, Incentive Price Revision—Firm Target, or paragraph (1) of the clause at 52.216-17, Incentive Price Revision—Successive Targets. The contracting officer shall apply the incentive price revision provisions to completed items accepted by the Government, including any for which the contractor may request reimbursement in the settlement proposal. The TCO shall reimburse the contractor at target price for completed articles included in the settlement proposal for which a final price has not been established. The TCO shall incorporate in the settlement agreement an appropriate reservation as to final price for these completed articles.

(2) *Complete termination*. If any items were delivered and accepted by the Government, the contracting officer shall establish prices under the incentive provisions of the contract. On the terminated portion of the contract, the provisions of the termination clause (see 52.249-2, Termination for Convenience of the Government (Fixed-Price)) shall govern and the provisions of the incentive clause shall not apply. The TCO responsible for the termination settlement will ensure, on the basis of evidence considered proper (including coordination with the contracting officer), that no portion of the costs considered in the negotiations under the incentive provisions are included in the termination settlement.

(b) *Cost-plus-incentive-fee contracts*. The TCO shall settle terminated cost-plus-incentive-fee contracts under the clause at 52.249-6, Termination (Cost-Reimbursement).

(1) *Partial termination*. Under a partial termination, the TCO shall limit the settlement to an adjustment of target fee as provided in paragraph (e) of the clause at 52.216-10, Incentive Fee. The settlement agreement shall include a reservation regarding any adjustment of target cost resulting from the partial termination. The contracting officer shall adjust the target cost, if required.

(2) *Complete termination*. The parties shall negotiate the settlement under the provisions of Subpart 49.3 and the clause at 52.249-6, Termination (Cost-Reimbursement). The fee shall be adjusted on the basis of the target fee, and the incentive provisions shall not be applied or considered.

SUBPART 49.2—ADDITIONAL PRINCIPLES FOR FIXED-PRICE CONTRACTS TERMINATED FOR CONVENIENCE

49.201 General.

(a) A settlement should compensate the contractor fairly for the work done and the preparations made for the terminated portions of the contract, including a reasonable allowance for profit. Fair compensation is a matter of judgment and cannot be measured exactly. In a given case, various methods may be equally appropriate for arriving at fair compensation. The use of business judgment, as distinguished from strict accounting principles, is the heart of a settlement.

(b) The primary objective is to negotiate a settlement by agreement. The parties may agree upon a total amount to be paid the contractor without agreeing on or segregating the particular elements of costs or profit comprising this amount.

(c) Cost and accounting data may provide guides, but are not rigid measures, for ascertaining fair compensation. In appropriate cases, costs may be estimated, differences compromised, and doubtful questions settled by agreement. Other types of data, criteria, or standards may furnish equally reliable guides to fair compensation. The amount of recordkeeping, reporting, and accounting related to the settlement of terminated contracts should be kept to a minimum compatible with the reasonable protection of the public interest.

49.202 Profit.

(a) The TCO shall allow profit on preparations made and work done by the contractor for the terminated portion of the contract but not on the settlement expenses. Anticipatory profits and consequential damages shall not be allowed (but see 49.108-5). Profit for the contractor's efforts in settling subcontractor proposals shall not be based on the dollar amount of the subcontract settlement agreements but the contractor's efforts will be considered in determining the overall rate of profit allowed the contractor. Profit shall not be allowed the contractor for material or services that, as of the effective date of termination, have not been delivered by a subcontractor, regardless of the percentage of completion. The TCO may use any reasonable method to arrive at a fair profit.

(b) In negotiating or determining profit, factors to be considered include—

(1) Extent and difficulty of the work done by the contractor as compared with the total work required by the contract (engineering estimates of the percentage of completion ordinarily should not be required, but if available should be considered);

(2) Engineering work, production scheduling, planning, technical study and supervision, and other necessary services;

(3) Efficiency of the contractor, with particular regard to—

(i) Attainment of quantity and quality production;

(ii) Reduction of costs;

(iii) Economic use of materials, facilities, and manpower; and

(iv) Disposition of termination inventory;

(4) Amount and source of capital and extent of risk assumed;

(5) Inventive and developmental contributions, and cooperation with the Government and other contractors in supplying technical assistance;

(6) Character of the business, including the source and nature of materials and the complexity of manufacturing techniques;

(7) The rate of profit that the contractor would have earned had the contract been completed;

(8) The rate of profit both parties contemplated at the time the contract was negotiated; and

(9) Character and difficulty of subcontracting, including selection, placement, and management of subcontracts, and effort in negotiating settlements of terminated subcontracts.

(c) When computing profit on the terminated portion of a construction contract, the contracting officer shall—

(1) Comply with paragraphs (a) and (b) of this section;

(2) Allow profit on the prime contractor's settlements with construction subcontractors for actual work in place at the job site; and

(3) Exclude profit on the prime contractor's settlements with construction subcontractors for materials on hand and for preparations made to complete the work.

49.203 Adjustment for loss.

(a) In the negotiation or determination of any settlement, the TCO shall not allow profit if it appears that the contractor would have incurred a loss had the entire contract been completed. The TCO shall negotiate or determine the amount of loss and make an adjustment in the amount of settlement as specified in paragraph (b) or (c) of this section. In estimating the cost to complete, the TCO shall consider expected production efficiencies and other factors affecting the cost to complete.

(b) If the settlement is on an inventory basis (see 49.206-2(a)), the contractor shall not be paid more than the total of the amounts in subparagraphs (b)(1), (2), and (3) of this section, less all disposal credits and all unliquidated advance and progress payments previously made under the contract:

(1) The amount negotiated or determined for settlement expenses.

(2) The contract price, as adjusted, for acceptable completed end items (see 49.205).

(3) The remainder of the settlement amount otherwise agreed upon or determined (including the allocable portion of initial costs (see 31.205-42(c))), reduced by multiplying the remainder by the ratio of—

(i) The total contract price to

(ii) The total cost incurred before termination plus the estimated cost to complete the entire contract.

(c) If the settlement is on a total cost basis (see 49.206-2(b)), the contractor shall not be paid more than the total of the amounts in subparagraphs (c)(1) and (2) of this section, less all disposal and other credits, all advance and progress payments, and all other amounts previously paid under the contract:

(1) The amount negotiated or determined for settlement expenses.

(2) The remainder of the total settlement amount otherwise agreed upon or determined (lines 7 and 14 of SF 1436, Settlement Proposal (Total Cost Basis)) reduced by multiplying the remainder by the ratio of—

(i) The total contract price to

(ii) The remainder plus the estimated cost to complete the entire contract.

49.204 Deductions.

From the amount payable to the contractor under a settlement, the TCO shall deduct—

(a) The agreed price for any part of the termination inventory purchased or retained by the contractor, and the proceeds from any materials sold that have not been paid or credited to the Government;

(b) The fair value, as determined by the TCO, of any part of the termination inventory that, before transfer of title to the Government or to a buyer under Part 45, is lost or so damaged as to become undeliverable (normal spoilage is excepted, as is inventory for which the Government has expressly assumed the risk of loss); and

(c) Any other amounts as appropriate in the particular case.

[FAC 2005–56, 77 FR 12937, 3/2/2012, effective 4/2/2012]

49.205 Completed end items.

(a) Promptly after the effective date of termination, the TCO shall (1) have all undelivered completed end items inspected and accepted if they comply with the contract requirements, and (2) determine which accepted end items are to be delivered under the contract. The contractor shall invoice accepted and delivered end items at the contract price in the usual manner and shall not include them in the settlement proposal. When completed end items, though accepted, are not to be delivered under the contract, the contractor shall include them in the settlement proposal at the contract price, adjusted for any saving of freight or other charges, together with any credits for their purchase, retention, or sale.

(b) Work in place accepted by the Government under a construction contract is not considered a completed item even though that work may have been paid for at unit prices specified in the contract.

49.206 Settlement proposals. (No Text)

49.206-1 Submission of settlement proposals.

(a) Subject to the provisions of the termination clause, the contractor should promptly submit to the TCO a settlement proposal for the amount claimed because of the termination. The final settlement proposal must be submitted within one year from the effective date of the termination, unless the period is extended by the TCO. Termination charges under a single prime contract involving two or more divisions or units of the prime contractor may be consolidated and included in a single settlement proposal.

(b) The settlement proposal must cover all cost elements including settlements with subcontractors and any proposed profit. With the consent of the TCO, proposals may be filed in successive steps covering separate portions of the contractor's costs. Such interim proposals shall include all costs of a particular type, except as the TCO may authorize otherwise.

(c) Settlement proposals must be on the forms prescribed in 49.602 unless the forms are inadequate for a particular contract. Settlement proposals must be in reasonable detail supported by adequate accounting data. Actual, standard (appropriately adjusted), or average costs may be used in preparing settlement proposals if they are determined under generally recognized accounting principles consistently followed by the contractor. When actual, standard, or average costs are not reasonably available, estimated costs may be used if the method of arriving at the estimates is approved by the TCO. Contractors shall not be required to maintain unduly elaborate cost accounting systems merely because their contracts may subsequently be terminated.

(d) The contractor may use the Settlement Proposal (Short Form), SF 1438 (see 49.602-1(d) and 53.249), when the total proposal is less than $10,000, unless otherwise instructed by the TCO. Settlement proposals that would normally be included in a single settlement proposal; *e.g.*, those based on a series of separate orders for the same item under one contract, should be consolidated whenever possible and not divided to bring them below $10,000.

(e) The Schedule of Accounting Information, SF 1439, must be submitted for each termination under a contract for which a settlement proposal is submitted, except when the Standard Form 1438 is used. Although several interim proposals may be submitted, SF 1439 need be submitted only once unless, subsequent to filing the original form, major changes occur in the information submitted.

49.206-2 Bases for settlement proposals.

(a) *Inventory basis*. (1) Use of the inventory basis for settlement proposals is preferred. Under this basis, the contractor may propose only costs allocable to the terminated portion of the contract, and the settlement proposal must itemize separately—

(i) Metals, raw materials, purchased parts, work in process, finished parts, components, dies, jigs, fixtures, and tooling, at purchase or manufacturing cost;

(ii) Charges such as engineering costs, initial costs, and general administrative costs;

(iii) Costs of settlements with subcontractors;

(iv) Settlement expenses; and

(v) Other proper charges.

(2) An allowance for profit (49.202) or adjustment for loss (49.203(b)) must be made to complete the gross settlement proposal. All unliquidated advance and progress payments and all disposal and other credits known when the proposal is submitted must then be deducted.

(3) This inventory basis is also appropriate for use under the following circumstances:

(i) The partial termination of a construction or related professional services contract.

(ii) The partial or complete termination of supply orders under any terminated construction contract.

(iii) The complete termination of a unit-price (as distinguished from a lump-sum) professional services contract.

(b) *Total cost basis.* (1) When use of the inventory basis is not practicable or will unduly delay settlement, the total-cost basis (SF 1436) may be used if approved in advance by the TCO as in the following examples:

(i) If production has not commenced and the accumulated costs represent planning and preproduction or "get ready" expenses.

(ii) If, under the contractor's accounting system, unit costs for work in process and finished products cannot readily be established.

(iii) If the contract does not specify unit prices.

(iv) If the termination is complete and involves a letter contract.

(2) When the total-cost basis is used under a complete termination, the contractor must itemize all costs incurred under the contract up to the effective date of termination. The costs of settlements with subcontractors and applicable settlement expenses must also be added. An allowance for profit (49.202) or adjustment for loss (49.203(c)) must be made. The contract price for all end items delivered or to be delivered and accepted must be deducted. All unliquidated advance and progress payments and disposal and other credits known when the proposal is submitted must also be deducted.

(3) When the total-cost basis is used under a partial termination, the settlement proposal shall not be submitted until completion of the continued portion of the contract. The settlement proposal must be prepared as in subparagraph (b)(2) of this section, except that all costs incurred to the date of completion of the continued portion of the contract must be included.

(4) If a construction contract or a lump-sum professional services contract is completely terminated, the contractor shall—

(i) Use the total cost basis of settlement;

(ii) Omit Line 10 "Deduct-Finished Product Invoiced or to be Invoiced" from Section II of SF 1436 Settlement Proposal (Total Cost Basis); and

(iii) Reduce the gross amount of the settlement by the total of all progress and other payments.

(c) *Other basis.* Settlement proposals may not be submitted on any basis other than paragraph (a) or (b) of this section without the prior approval of the chief of the contracting or contract administration office.

49.206-3 Submission of inventory schedules.

Subject to the terms of the termination clause, and whenever termination inventory is involved, the contractor shall submit complete inventory disposal schedules to the TCO reflecting inventory that is allocable to the terminated portion of the contract. The inventory disposal schedules shall be submitted within 120 days from the effective date of termination unless otherwise extended by the TCO based on a written justification to support the extension. The inventory schedules shall be prepared on Standard Form 1428, Inventory Disposal Schedule.

[FAC 90-40, 61 FR 39186, 7/26/96, effective 9/24/96; FAC 2001-22, 69 FR 17741, 4/5/2004, effective 5/5/2004]

49.207 Limitation on settlements.

The total amount payable to the contractor for a settlement, before deducting disposal or other credits and exclusive of settlement costs, must not exceed the contract price less payments otherwise made or to be made under the contract.

49.208 Equitable adjustment after partial termination.

Under the termination clause, after partial termination, a contractor may request an equitable adjustment in the price or prices of the continued portion of a fixed-price contract. The TCO shall forward the proposal to the contracting officer except when negotiation authority is delegated to the TCO. The contractor shall submit the proposal in the format of Table 15-2 of 15.408.

(a) When the contracting officer retains responsibility for negotiating the equitable adjustment and executing a supplemental agreement, the contracting officer shall ensure that no portion of an increase in price is included in a termination settlement made or in process.

(b) The TCO shall also ensure that no portion of the costs included in the equitable adjustment are included in the termination settlement.

[FAC 90-32, 60 FR 48206, 9/18/95, effective 10/1/95; FAC 97-2, 62 FR 51224, 9/30/97, effective 10/10/97]

SUBPART 49.3—ADDITIONAL PRINCIPLES FOR COST-REIMBURSEMENT CONTRACTS TERMINATED FOR CONVENIENCE

49.301 General.

Termination clauses for cost-reimbursement contracts (see 49.503(a)) provide for the settlement of costs and fee, if any. The contract clauses governing costs shall determine what costs are allowable.

49.302 Discontinuance of vouchers.

(a) When the contract has been completely terminated, the contractor shall not use Standard Form 1034 (Public Voucher for Purchases and Services Other than Personal) after the last day of the sixth month following the month in which the termination is effective. The contractor may elect to stop using vouchers at any time during the 6-month period. When the contractor has vouchered out all costs within the 6-month period, a proposal for fee, if any, may be submitted on SF 1437 (see 49.602-1) or by letter appropriately certified. The contractor must submit a substantiated proposal for fee to the TCO within 1 year from the effective date of termination, unless the period is extended by the TCO. When the use of vouchers is discontinued, the contractor shall submit all unvouchered costs and the proposed fee, if any, as specified in 49.303.

(b) When the contract is partially terminated, 49.304 shall apply.

49.303 Procedure after discontinuing vouchers. (No Text)

49.303-1 Submission of settlement proposal.

The contractor shall submit a final settlement proposal covering unvouchered costs and any proposed fee to within 1 year from the effective date of termination, unless the period is extended by the TCO. The contractor shall use the form prescribed in 49.602-1, unless the TCO authorizes otherwise. The proposal shall not include costs that have been—

(a) Finally disallowed by the contracting officer; or

(b) Previously vouchered and formally questioned by the Government but not yet decided as to allowability.

49.303-2 Submission of inventory disposal schedules.

Subject to the terms of the termination clause, and whenever termination inventory is involved, the contractor shall submit complete inventory disposal schedules to the TCO reflecting inventory that is allocable to the terminated portion of the contract. The inventory disposal schedules shall be submitted within 120 days from the effective date of termination unless otherwise extended by the TCO based on a written justification to support the extension. The inventory disposal schedules shall be prepared on Standard Form 1428, Inventory Disposal Schedule.

[FAC 90-40, 61 FR 39186, 7/26/96, effective 9/24/96; FAC 2001-22, 69 FR 17741, 4/5/2004, effective 5/5/2004]

49.303-3 Audit of settlement proposal.

The TCO shall submit the settlement proposal to the appropriate audit agency for review (see 49.107). However, if the settlement proposal is limited to an adjustment of fee, no referral to the audit agency is required.

[Redesignated from 49.303-2, FAC 90-40, 61 FR 39186, 7/26/96, effective 9/24/96]

49.303-4 Adjustment of indirect costs.

(a) If the contract contains the clause at 52.216-7, Allowable Cost and Payment, and it appears that adjustment of indirect costs will unduly delay final settlement, the TCO, after obtaining information from the appropriate audit agency, may agree with the contractor to—

(1) Negotiate the amount of indirect costs for the contract period for which final indirect cost rates have not been negotiated, or to use billing rates as final rates for this period if the billing rates appear reasonable; or

(2) Reserve any indirect cost adjustment in the final settlement agreement, pending establishment of negotiated rates under Subpart 42.7.

(b) When an amount of indirect cost is negotiated under subparagraph (a)(1) of this section, the contractor shall eliminate the indirect cost and the related direct costs on which it was based from the total pool and base used to compute indirect costs for other contracts performed during the applicable accounting period.

[Redesignated from 49.303-3, FAC 90-40, 61 FR 39186, 7/26/96, effective 9/24/96]

49.303-5 Final settlement.

(a) The TCO shall proceed with the settlement and execution of a settlement agreement upon receipt of the audit report, if applicable, and the contract audit closing statement covering vouchered costs.

(b) The TCO shall adjust the fee as provided in 49.305.

(c) The final settlement agreement may include all demands of the Government and proposals of the contractor under the terminated contract. However, no amount shall be allowed for any item of cost disallowed by the Government, nor for any other item of cost of the same nature.

(d) If an overall settlement of costs is agreed upon, agreement on each element of cost is not necessary. If appropriate, differences may be compromised and doubtful questions settled by agreement. An overall settlement shall not include costs that are clearly not allowable under the terms of the contract.

[Redesignated from 49.303-4, FAC 90-40, 61 FR 39186, 7/26/96, effective 9/24/96]

49.304 Procedure for partial termination. (No Text)

49.304-1 General.

(a) In a partial termination, the TCO shall limit the settlement to an adjustment of the fee, if any, and with the concurrence of the contracting office to a reduction in the estimated cost. The TCO shall adjust the fee as provided in 49.304-2 and 49.305, unless—

(1) The terminated portion is clearly severable from the balance of the contract; or

(2) Performance of the contract is virtually complete, or performance of any continued portion is only on subsidiary items or spare parts, or is otherwise not substantial.

(b) In the case of the exceptions in paragraph (a), the procedures in 49.302 and 49.303 apply.

49.304-2 Submission of settlement proposal (fee only).

The contractor shall limit the settlement proposal to a proposed reduction in the amount of fee. The final settlement proposal shall be submitted to the TCO within one year from the effective date of termination, unless the period is extended by the TCO. The proposal may be submitted in the form prescribed in 49.602-1 or by letter appropriately certified. The contractor shall substantiate the amount of fee claimed (see 49.305).

49.304-3 Submission of vouchers.

When a partial termination settlement is limited to adjustment of fee, the contractor shall continue to submit the SF 1034, Public Voucher for Purchases and Services Other than Personal, for costs reimbursable under the contract. The contractor shall not be reimbursed for costs of settlements with subcontractors unless required approvals or ratifications have been obtained (see 49.108).

49.305 Adjustment of fee. (No Text)

49.305-1 General.

(a) The TCO shall determine the adjusted fee to be paid, if any, in the manner provided by the contract. The determination is generally based on a percentage of completion of the contract or of the terminated portion. When this basis is used, factors such as the extent and difficulty of the work performed by the contractor (*e.g.*, planning, scheduling, technical study, engineering work, production and supervision, placing and supervising subcontracts, and work performed by the contractor in (1) stopping performance, (2) settling terminated subcontracts, and (3) disposing of termination inventory) shall be compared with the total work required by the contract or by the terminated portion. The contractor's adjusted fee shall not include an allowance for fee for subcontract effort included in subcontractors' settlement proposals.

(b) The ratio of costs incurred to the total estimated cost of performing the contract or the terminated portion is only one factor in computing the percentage of completion. This percentage may be either greater or less than that indicated by the ratio of costs incurred, depending upon the evaluation by the TCO of other pertinent factors.

49.305-2 Construction contracts.

(a) The percentage of completion basis refers to the contractor's total effort and not solely to the actual construction work. Generally, the effort of a contractor under a cost-reimbursement construction or professional services contract can be segregated into factors such as—

(1) Mobilization including organization,

(2) Use of finances,

(3) Contracting for and receipt of materials,

(4) Placement of subcontracts,

(5) Preparation of shop drawings,

(6) Work in place performed by own forces,

(7) Supervision of subcontractors' work,

(8) Job administration, and

(9) Demobilization.

(b) Each of the applicable factors in paragraph (a) of this section shall be assigned a weighted value depending on its importance and difficulty. The total weight value of all factors should be easily divisible (*e.g.*, by 100) to determine percentages. The percentage of completion of each factor must be established based upon the specific facts of each contract. When totaled, the percentage of completion of each factor applied to the weighted value of each factor results in the overall percentage of contract completion. The percentage of completion is then applied to the total contract fee or to the fee applicable to the terminated portion of the contract to arrive at an equitable adjustment.

SUBPART 49.4—TERMINATION FOR DEFAULT

49.401 General.

(a) Termination for default is generally the exercise of the Government's contractual right to completely or partially terminate a contract because of the contractor's actual or anticipated failure to perform its contractual obligations.

(b) If the contractor can establish, or it is otherwise determined that the contractor was not in default or that the failure to perform is excusable; *i.e.*, arose out of causes beyond the control and without the fault or negligence of the contractor, the default clauses prescribed in 49.503 and located at 52.249 provide that a termination for default will be considered to have been a termination for the convenience of the Government, and the rights and obligations of the parties governed accordingly.

(c) The Government may, in appropriate cases, exercise termination or cancellation rights in addition to those in the contract clauses (see for example, paragraph (h) of the Default clause at 52.249-8).

(d) For default terminations of orders under Federal Supply Schedule contracts, see Subpart 8.4.

(e) Notwithstanding the provisions of this 49.401, the contracting officer may, with the written consent of the contractor, reinstate the terminated contract by amending the notice of termination, after a written determination is made that the supplies or services are still required and reinstatement is advantageous to the Government.

49.402 Termination of fixed-price contracts for default. (No Text)

49.402-1 The Government's right.

Under contracts containing the Default clause at 52.249-8, the Government has the right, subject to the notice requirements of the clause, to terminate the contract completely or partially for default if the contractor fails to—

(a) Make delivery of the supplies or perform the services within the time specified in the contract,

(b) Perform any other provision of the contract, or

(c) Make progress and that failure endangers performance of the contract.

49.402-2 Effect of termination for default.

(a) Under a termination for default, the Government is not liable for the contractor's costs on undelivered work and is entitled to the repayment of advance and progress payments, if any, applicable to that work. The Government may elect, under the Default clause, to require the contractor to transfer title and deliver to the Government completed supplies and manufacturing materials, as directed by the contracting officer.

(b) The contracting officer shall not use the Default clause as authority to acquire any completed supplies or manufacturing materials unless it has been ascertained that the Government does not already have title under some other provision of the contract. The contracting officer shall acquire manufacturing materials under the Default clause for furnishing to another contractor only after considering the difficulties the other contractor may have in using the materials.

(c) Subject to paragraph (d) of this section, the Government shall pay the contractor the contract price for any completed supplies, and the amount agreed upon by the contracting officer and the contractor for any manufacturing materials, acquired by the Government under the Default clause.

(d) The Government must be protected from overpayment that might result from failure to provide for the Government's potential liability to laborers and material suppliers for lien rights outstanding against the completed supplies or materials after the Government has paid the contractor for them. To accomplish this, before paying for supplies or materials, the contracting officer shall take one or more of the following measures:

(1) Ascertain whether the payment bonds, if any, furnished by the contractor are adequate to satisfy all lienors' claims or whether it is feasible to obtain similar bonds to cover outstanding liens.

(2) Require the contractor to furnish appropriate statements from laborers and material suppliers disclaiming any lien rights they may have to the supplies and materials.

(3) Obtain appropriate agreement by the Government, the contractor, and lienors ensuring release of the Government from any potential liability to the contractor or lienors.

(4) Withhold from the amount due for the supplies or materials any amount the contracting officer determines necessary to protect the Government's interest, but only if the measures in subparagraphs (d) (1), (2), and (3) of this section cannot be accomplished or are considered inadequate.

(5) Take other appropriate action considering the circumstances and the degree of the contractor's solvency.

(e) The contractor is liable to the Government for any excess costs incurred in acquiring supplies and services similar to those terminated for default (see 49.402-6), and for any other damages, whether or not repurchase is effected (see 49.402-7).

49.402-3 Procedure for default.

(a) When a default termination is being considered, the Government shall decide which type of termination action to take (*i.e.*, default, convenience, or no-cost cancellation) only after review by contracting and technical personnel, and by counsel, to ensure the propriety of the proposed action.

(b) The administrative contracting officer shall not issue a show cause notice or cure notice without the prior approval of the contracting office, which should be obtained by the most expeditious means.

(c) Subdivision (a)(1)(i) of the Default clause covers situations when the contractor has defaulted by failure to make delivery of the supplies or to perform the services within the specified time. In these situations, no notice of failure or of the possibility of termination for default is required to be sent to the contractor before the actual notice of termination (but see paragraph (e) of this section). However, if the Government has taken any action that might be construed as a waiver of the contract delivery or performance date, the contracting officer shall send a notice to the contractor setting a new date for the contractor to make delivery or complete performance. The notice shall reserve the Government's rights under the Default clause.

(d) Subdivisions (a)(1)(ii) and (a)(1)(iii) of the Default clause cover situations when the contractor fails to perform some of the other provisions of the contract (such as not furnishing a required performance bond) or so fails to make progress as to endanger performance of the contract. If the termination is predicated upon this type of failure, the contracting officer shall give the contractor written notice specifying the failure and providing a period of 10 days (or longer period as necessary) in which to cure the failure. When appropriate, this notice may be made a part of the notice described in subparagraph (e)(1) of this section. Upon expiration of the 10 days (or longer period), the contracting officer may issue a notice of termination for default unless it is determined that the failure to perform has been cured. A format for a cure notice is in 49.607.

(e)(1) If termination for default appears appropriate, the contracting officer should, if practicable, notify the contractor in writing of the possibility of the termination. This notice shall call the contractor's attention to the contractual liabilities if the contract is terminated for default, and request the contractor to show cause why the contract should not be terminated for default. The notice may further state that failure of the contractor to present an explanation may be taken as an admission that no valid explanation exists. When appropriate, the notice may invite the contractor to discuss the matter at a conference. A format for a show cause notice is in 49.607.

(2) When a termination for default appears imminent, the contracting officer shall provide a written notification to the surety. If the contractor is subsequently terminated for default, a copy of the notice of default shall be sent to the surety.

(3) If requested by the surety, and agreed to by the contractor and any assignees, arrangements may be made to have future checks mailed to the contractor in care of the surety. In this case, the contractor must forward a written request to the designated disbursing officer specifically directing a change in address for mailing checks.

(4) If the contractor is a small business firm, the contracting officer shall immediately provide a copy of any cure notice or show cause notice to the contracting office's small business specialist and the Small Business Administration Regional Office nearest the contractor. The contracting officer should, whenever practicable, consult with the small business specialist before proceeding with a default termination (see also 49.402-4).

(f) The contracting officer shall consider the following factors in determining whether to terminate a contract for default:

(1) The terms of the contract and applicable laws and regulations.

(2) The specific failure of the contractor and the excuses for the failure.

(3) The availability of the supplies or services from other sources.

(4) The urgency of the need for the supplies or services and the period of time required to obtain them from other sources, as compared with the time delivery could be obtained from the delinquent contractor.

(5) The degree of essentiality of the contractor in the Government acquisition program and the effect of a termination for

default upon the contractor's capability as a supplier under other contracts.

(6) The effect of a termination for default on the ability of the contractor to liquidate guaranteed loans, progress payments, or advance payments.

(7) Any other pertinent facts and circumstances.

(g) If, after compliance with the procedures in paragraphs (a) through (f) of this 49.402-3, the contracting officer determines that a termination for default is proper, the contracting officer shall issue a notice of termination stating—

(1) The contract number and date;

(2) The acts or omissions constituting the default;

(3) That the contractor's right to proceed further under the contract (or a specified portion of the contract) is terminated;

(4) That the supplies or services terminated may be purchased against the contractor's account, and that the contractor will be held liable for any excess costs;

(5) If the contracting officer has determined that the failure to perform is not excusable, that the notice of termination constitutes such decision, and that the contractor has the right to appeal such decision under the Disputes clause;

(6) That the Government reserves all rights and remedies provided by law or under the contract, in addition to charging excess costs; and

(7) That the notice constitutes a decision that the contractor is in default as specified and that the contractor has the right to appeal under the Disputes clause.

(h) The contracting officer shall make the same distribution of the termination notice as was made of the contract. A copy shall also be furnished to the contractor's surety, if any, when the notice is furnished to the contractor. The surety should be requested to advise if it desires to arrange for completion of the work. In addition, the contracting officer shall notify the disbursing officer to withhold further payments under the terminated contract, pending further advice, which should be furnished at the earliest practicable time.

(i) In the case of a construction contract, promptly after issuance of the termination notice, the contracting officer shall determine the manner in which the work is to be completed and whether the materials, appliances, and plant that are on the site will be needed.

(j) If the contracting officer determines before issuing the termination notice that the failure to perform is excusable, the contract shall not be terminated for default. If termination is in the Government's interest, the contracting officer may terminate the contract for the convenience of the Government.

(k) If the contracting officer has not been able to determine, before issuance of the notice of termination whether the contractor's failure to perform is excusable, the contracting officer shall make a written decision on that point as soon as practicable after issuance of the notice of termination. The decision shall be delivered promptly to the contractor with a notification that the contractor has the right to appeal as specified in the Disputes clause.

[FAC 84-53, 54 FR 48990, 11/28/89, effective 2/26/90]

49.402-4 Procedure in lieu of termination for default.

The following courses of action, among others, are available to the contracting officer in lieu of termination for default when in the Government's interest:

(a) Permit the contractor, the surety, or the guarantor, to continue performance of the contract under a revised delivery schedule.

(b) Permit the contractor to continue performance of the contract by means of a subcontract or other business arrangement with an acceptable third party, provided the rights of the Government are adequately preserved.

(c) If the requirement for the supplies and services in the contract no longer exists, and the contractor is not liable to the Government for damages as provided in 49.402-7, execute a no-cost termination settlement agreement using the formats in 49.603-6 and 49.603-7 as a guide.

49.402-5 Memorandum by the contracting officer.

When a contract is terminated for default or a procedure authorized by 49.402-4 is followed, the contracting officer shall prepare a memorandum for the contract file explaining the reasons for the action taken.

49.402-6 Repurchase against contractor's account.

(a) When the supplies or services are still required after termination, the contracting officer shall repurchase the same or similar supplies or services against the contractor's account as soon as practicable. The contracting officer shall repurchase at as reasonable a price as practicable, considering the quality and delivery requirements. The contracting officer may repurchase a quantity in excess of the undelivered quantity terminated for default when the excess quantity is needed, but excess cost may not be charged against the defaulting contractor for more than the undelivered quantity terminated for default (including variations in quantity permitted by the terminated contract). Generally, the contracting officer will make a decision whether or not to repurchase before issuing the termination notice.

(b) If the repurchase is for a quantity not over the undelivered quantity terminated for default, the Default clause authorizes the contracting officer to use any terms and acquisition method deemed appropriate for the repurchase. However, the contracting officer shall obtain competition to the maximum extent practicable for the repurchase. The contracting officer shall cite the Default clause as the authority. If the repurchase is for a quantity over the undelivered quantity terminated for default, the contracting officer shall treat the entire quantity as a new acquisition.

(c) If repurchase is made at a price over the price of the supplies or services terminated, the contracting officer shall, after completion and final payment of the repurchase contract, make written demand on the contractor for the total amount of the excess, giving consideration to any increases or decreases in other costs such as transportation, discounts, etc. If the contractor fails to make payment, the contracting officer shall follow the procedures in Subpart 32.6 for collecting contract debts due the Government.

[FAC 84-5, 50 FR 1745, 1/11/85, effective 4/1/85]

49.402-7 Other damages.

(a) If the contracting officer terminates a contract for default or follows a course of action instead of termination for default (see 49.402-4), the contracting officer promptly must assess and demand any liquidated damages to which the Government is entitled under the contract. Under the contract clause at 52.211-11, these damages are in addition to any excess repurchase costs.

(b) If the Government has suffered any other ascertainable damages, including administrative costs, as a result of the contractor's default, the contracting officer must, on the basis of legal advice, take appropriate action as prescribed in Subpart 32.6 to assert the Government's demand for the damages.

[FAC 90-4, 56 FR 15154, 4/15/91, effective 5/15/91; FAC 90-32, 60 FR 48206, 9/18/95, effective 10/1/95; FAC 97-19, 65 FR 46052, 7/26/2000, effective 9/25/2000]

49.402-8 Reporting information.

The contracting officer, in accordance with agency procedures, shall ensure that information relating to the termination for default notice and a subsequent withdrawal or a conversion to a termination for convenience is reported in accordance with 42.1503(h).

[FAC 2005-46, 75 FR 60258, 9/29/2010, effective 10/29/2010; FAC 2005-69, 78 FR 46783, 8/1/2013, effective 9/3/2013]

49.403 Termination of cost-reimbursement contracts for default.

(a) The right to terminate a cost-reimbursement contract for default is provided for in the Termination for Default or for Convenience of the Government clause at 52.249-6. A 10-day notice to the contractor before termination for default is required in every case by the clause.

(b) Settlement of a cost-reimbursement contract terminated for default is subject to the principles in Subparts 49.1 and 49.3 the same as when a contract is terminated for convenience, except that—

(1) The costs of preparing the contractor's settlement proposal are not allowable (see subparagraph (h)(3) of the clause); and

(2) The contractor is reimbursed the allowable costs, and an appropriate reduction is made in the total fee, if any, (see subparagraph (h)(4) of the clause).

(c) The contracting officer shall use the procedures in 49.402 to the extent appropriate in considering the termination for default of a cost-reimbursement contract. However, a cost-reimbursement contract does not contain any provision for recovery of excess repurchase costs after termination for default (but see paragraph (g) of the clause at 52.246-3 with respect to failure of the contractor to replace or correct defective supplies).

[FAC 90-40, 61 FR 39186, 7/26/96, effective 9/24/96]

49.404 Surety-takeover agreements.

(a) The procedures in this section apply primarily, but not solely, to fixed-price construction contracts terminated for default.

(b) Since the surety is liable for damages resulting from the contractor's default, the surety has certain rights and interests in the completion of the contract work and application of any undisbursed funds. Therefore, the contracting officer must consider carefully the surety's proposals for completing the contract. The contracting officer must take action on the basis of the Government's interest, including the possible effect upon the Government's rights against the surety.

(c) The contracting officer should permit surety offers to complete the contract, unless the contracting officer believes that the persons or firms proposed by the surety to complete the work are not competent and qualified or the proposal is not in the best interest of the Government.

(d) There may be conflicting demands for the defaulting contractor's assets, including unpaid prior earnings (retained percentages and unpaid progress estimates). Therefore, the surety may include a "takeover" agreement in its proposal, fixing the surety's rights to payment from those funds. The contracting officer may (but not before the effective date of termination) enter into a written agreement with the surety. The contracting officer should consider using a tripartite agreement among the Government, the surety, and the defaulting contractor to resolve the defaulting contractor's residual rights, including assertions to unpaid prior earnings.

(e) Any takeover agreement must require the surety to complete the contract and the Government to pay the surety's costs and expenses up to the balance of the contract price unpaid at the time of default, subject to the following conditions:

(1) Any unpaid earnings of the defaulting contractor, including retained percentages and progress estimates for work accomplished before termination, must be subject to debts due the Government by the contractor, except to the extent that the unpaid earnings may be used to pay the completing surety its actual costs and expenses incurred in the completion of the work, but not including its payments and obligations under the payment bond given in connection with the contract.

(2) The surety is bound by contract terms governing liquidated damages for delays in completion of the work, unless the delays are excusable under the contract.

(3) If the contract proceeds have been assigned to a financing institution, the surety must not be paid from unpaid earnings, unless the assignee provides written consent.

(4) The contracting officer must not pay the surety more than the amount it expended completing the work and discharging its liabilities under the defaulting contractor's payment bond. Payments to the surety to reimburse it for discharging its liabilities under the payment bond of the defaulting contractor must be only on authority of—

(i) Mutual agreement among the Government, the defaulting contractor, and the surety;

(ii) Determination of the Comptroller General as to payee and amount; or

(iii) Order of a court of competent jurisdiction.

[FAC 97-19, 65 FR 46052, 7/26/2000, effective 9/25/2000]

49.405 Completion by another contractor.

If the surety does not arrange for completion of the contract, the contracting officer normally will arrange for completion of the work by awarding a new contract based on the same plans and specifications. The new contract may be the result of sealed bidding or any other appropriate contracting method or procedure. The contracting officer shall exercise reasonable diligence to obtain the lowest price available for completion.

[FAC 84-5, 50 FR 1746, 1/11/85, effective 4/1/85]

49.406 Liquidation of liability.

The contract provides that the contractor and the surety are liable to the Government for resultant damages. The contracting officer shall use all retained percentages of progress payments previously made to the contractor and any progress payments due for work completed before the termination to liquidate the contractor's and the surety's liability to the Government. If the retained and unpaid amounts are insufficient, the contracting officer shall take steps to recover the additional sum from the contractor and the surety.

SUBPART 49.5—CONTRACT TERMINATION CLAUSES

49.501 General.

This subpart prescribes the principal contract termination clauses. This subpart does not apply to contracts that use the clause at 52.213-4, Terms and Conditions—Simplified Acquisitions (Other Than Commercial Items). In appropriate cases, agencies may authorize the use of special purpose clauses, if consistent with this chapter.

[FAC 90-32, 60 FR 48206, 9/18/95, effective 10/1/95; FAC 97-3, 62 FR 64912, 12/9/97, effective 2/9/98; FAC 2005-48, 75 FR 82576, 12/30/2010, effective 1/31/2011]

49.502 Termination for convenience of the Government.

(a) *Fixed-price contracts that do not exceed the simplified acquisition threshold (short form)*—(1) *General use.* The contracting officer shall insert the clause at 52.249-1, Termination for Convenience of the Government (Fixed-Price) (Short Form), in solicitations and contracts when a fixed-price contract is contemplated and the contract amount is not expected to exceed the simplified acquisition threshold, except—

(i) If use of the clause at 52.249-4, Termination for Convenience of the Government (Services) (Short Form) is appropriate,

(ii) In contracts for research and development work with an educational or nonprofit institution on a no-profit basis,

(iii) In contracts for architect-engineer services, or

(iv) if one of the clauses prescribed or cited at 49.505(a), or (c), is appropriate.

(2) *Dismantling and demolition.* If the contract is for dismantling, demolition, or removal of improvements, the contracting officer shall use the clause with its Alternate I.

(b) *Fixed-price contracts that exceed the simplified acquisition threshold*— (1)(i) *General use.* The contracting officer shall insert the clause at 52.249-2, Termination for Convenience of the Government (Fixed-Price), in solicitations and contracts when a fixed-price contract is contemplated and the contract amount is expected to exceed the simplified acquisition threshold, except in contracts for (A) dismantling and demolition, (B) research and development work with an educational or nonprofit institution on a no-profit basis, or (C) architect-engineer services; it shall not be used if the clause at 52.249-4, Termination for Convenience of the Government (Services) (Short Form), is appropriate (see 49.502(c)), or one of the clauses prescribed or cited at 49.505(a), (b), or (e), is appropriate.

(ii) *Construction*. If the contract is for construction, the contracting officer shall use the clause with its Alternate I.

(iii) *Partial payments*. If the contract is with an agency of the U.S. Government or with State, local, or foreign governments or their agencies, and if the contracting officer determines that the requirement to pay interest on excess partial payments is inappropriate, the contracting officer shall use the clause with its Alternate II. In such contracts for construction, the contracting officer shall use the clause with its Alternate III.

(2) *Dismantling and demolition*. The contracting officer shall insert the clause at 52.249-3, Termination for Convenience of the Government (Dismantling, Demolition, or Removal of Improvements), in solicitations and contracts for dismantling, demolition, or removal of improvements, when a fixed-price contract is contemplated and the contract amount is expected to exceed the simplified acquisition threshold. If the contract is with an agency of the U.S. Government or with State, local, or foreign governments or their agencies, and if the contracting officer determines that the requirement to pay interest on excess partial payments is inappropriate, the contracting officer shall use the clause with its Alternate I.

(c) *Service contracts (short form)*. The contracting officer shall insert the clause at 52.249-4, Termination for Convenience of the Government (Services) (Short Form), in solicitations and contracts for services, regardless of value, when a fixed-price contract is contemplated and the contracting officer determines that because of the kind of services required, the successful offeror will not incur substantial charges in preparation for and in carrying out the contract, and would, if terminated for the convenience of the Government, limit termination settlement charges to services rendered before the date of termination. Examples of services where this clause may be appropriate are contracts for rental of unreserved parking space, laundry and dry cleaning, etc.

(d) *Research and development contracts*. The contracting officer shall insert the clause at 52.249-5, Termination for the Convenience of the Government (Educational and Other Nonprofit Institutions), in solicitations and contracts when either a fixed-price or cost-reimbursement contract is contemplated for research and development work with an educational or nonprofit institution on a no-profit or no-fee basis.

(e) *Subcontracts*. (1) *General use*. The prime contractor may find the clause at 52.249-1, Termination for Convenience of the Government (Fixed-Price) (Short Form), or at 52.249-2, Termination for Convenience of the Government (Fixed-Price), as appropriate, suitable for use in fixed-price subcontracts, except as noted in subparagraph (e)(2) of this section; provided, that the relationship between the contractor and subcontractor is clearly indicated. Inapplicable conditions (*e.g.*, paragraph (d)) in 52.249-2 should be deleted and the periods reduced for submitting the subcontractor's termination settlement proposal (*e.g.*, 6 months), and for requesting an equitable price adjustment (*e.g.*, 45 days).

(2) *Research and development*. The prime contractor may find the clause at 52.249-5, Termination for the Convenience of the Government (Educational and Other Nonprofit Institutions), suitable for use in subcontracts placed with educational or nonprofit institutions on a no-profit or no-fee basis; provided, that the relationship between the contractor and subcontractor is clearly indicated. Inapplicable conditions (*e.g.*, paragraph (h)) should be deleted, the period for submitting the subcontractor's termination settlement proposal should be reduced (*e.g.*, 6 months), the subcontract should be placed on a no-profit or no-fee basis, and the subcontract should incorporate or be negotiated on the basis of the cost principles in Part 31 of the Federal Acquisition Regulation.

[FAC 90-40, 61 FR 39186, 7/26/96, effective 9/24/96; FAC 2005-13, 71 FR 57363, 9/28/2006, effective 9/28/2006; FAC 2005-17, 72 FR 27364, 5/15/2007, effective 6/14/2007]

49.503 Termination for convenience of the Government and default.

(a) *Cost-reimbursement contracts*—(1) *General use*. Insert the clause at 52.249-6, Termination (Cost-Reimbursement), in solicitations and contracts when a cost-reimbursement contract is contemplated, except contracts for research and development with an educational or nonprofit institution on a no-fee basis.

(2) *Construction*. If the contract is for construction, the contracting officer shall use the clause with its Alternate I.

(3) *Partial payments*. If the contract is with an agency of the U.S. Government or with State, local, or foreign governments or their agencies, and if the contracting officer determines that the requirement to pay interest on excess partial payments is inappropriate, the contracting officer shall use the clause with its Alternate II. In such contracts for construction, the contracting officer shall use the clause with its Alternate III.

(4) *Time-and-material and labor-hour contracts*. If the contract is a time-and-material or labor-hour contract, the contracting officer shall use the clause with its Alternate IV. If the contract is with an agency of the U.S. Government or with State, local, or foreign governments or their agencies, and if the contracting officer determines that the requirement to pay interest on excess partial payments is inappropriate, the contracting officer shall use the clause with its Alternate V.

(b) Insert the clause at 52.249-7, Termination (Fixed-Price Architect-Engineer), in solicitations and contracts for architect-engineer services, when a fixed-price contract is contemplated.

(c) *Subcontracts*. The prime contractor may find the clause at 52.249-6, Termination (Cost-Reimbursement), suitable for use in cost-reimbursement subcontracts; provided, that the relationship between the contractor and subcontractor is clearly indicated. Inapplicable conditions (*e.g.*, paragraphs (e), (j) and (n)) should be deleted and the period for submitting the subcontractor's termination settlement proposal should be reduced (*e.g.*, 6 months).

[FAC 90-40, 61 FR 39186, 7/26/96, effective 9/24/96; FAC 97-14, 64 FR 51828, 9/24/99, effective 11/23/99]

49.504 Termination of fixed-price contracts for default.

(a) (1) *Supplies and services*. The contracting officer shall insert the clause at 52.249-8, Default (Fixed-Price Supply and Service), in solicitations and contracts when a fixed-price contract is contemplated and the contract amount is expected to exceed the simplified acquisition threshold. The contracting officer may use the clause when the contract amount is at or below the simplified acquisition threshold, if appropriate (*e.g.*, if the acquisition involves items with a history of unsatisfactory quality).

(2) *Transportation*. If the contract is for transportation or transportation-related services, the contracting officer shall use the clause with its Alternate I.

(b) *Research and development*. The contracting officer shall insert the clause at 52.249-9, Default (Fixed-Price Research and Development), in solicitations and contracts for research and development when a fixed-price contract is contemplated and the contract amount is expected to exceed the simplified acquisition threshold, except those with educational or nonprofit institutions on a no-profit basis. The contracting officer may use the clause when the contract amount is at or below the simplified acquisition threshold, if appropriate (*e.g.*, if the contracting officer believes that key personnel essential to the work may be devoted to other programs).

(c) (1) *Construction*. The contracting officer shall insert the clause at 52.249-10, Default (Fixed-Price Construction), in solicitations and contracts for construction, when a fixed-price contract is contemplated and the contract amount is expected to exceed the simplified acquisition threshold. The contracting officer may use the clause when the contract amount is at or below the simplified acquisition threshold, if appropriate (*e.g.*, if completion dates are essential).

(2) *Dismantling and demolition*. If the contract is for dismantling, demolition, or removal of improvements, the contracting officer shall use the clause with its Alternate I.

(3) *National emergencies.* If the contract is to be awarded during a period of national emergency, the contracting officer may use the clause—

(i) With its Alternate II when a fixed-price contract for construction is contemplated, or

(ii) With its Alternate III when a contract for dismantling, demolition, or removal of improvements is contemplated.

[FAC 90-29, 60 FR 34732, 7/3/95, effective 7/3/95]

49.505 Other termination clauses.

(a) *Personal service contracts.* The contracting officer shall insert the clause at 52.249-12, Termination (Personal Services), in solicitations and contracts for personal services (see Part 37).

(b) *Excusable delays.* The contracting officer shall insert the clause at 52.249-14, Excusable Delays, in solicitations and contracts for supplies, services, construction, and research and development on a fee basis, when a cost-reimbursement contract is contemplated. The contracting officer shall also insert the clause in time-and-material contracts, and labor-hour contracts.

(c) *Communication service contracts.* This regulation does not prescribe a clause for the cancellation or termination of orders under communication service contracts with common carriers because of special agency requirements that apply to these services. An appropriate clause, however, shall be prescribed at agency level, within those agencies contracting for these services.

[FAC 2005-17, 72 FR 27364, 5/15/2007, effective 6/14/2007; FAC 2005-42, 75 FR 34291, 6/16/2010, effective 6/16/2010]

SUBPART 49.6—CONTRACT TERMINATION FORMS AND FORMATS

49.601 Notice of termination for convenience.

(See 49.402-3(g) for notice of termination for default.)

49.601-1 Electronic notice.

The contracting officer may provide expedited notice of termination by electronic means that includes a requirement for the contractor to confirm receipt. If the contractor does not confirm receipt promptly, the contracting officer shall resend the notice electronically, and expedite the letter notice described in 49.601-2. If confirmation of the electronic notice is received, and the electronic notice includes all content in 49.601-2, the contracting officer need not send the letter notice described in 49.601-2.

(a) *Complete termination.* The following electronic notice is suggested for use if a supply contract is being completely terminated for convenience. If appropriately modified, the notice may be used for other than supply contracts.

DATE

XYZ Corporation

New York, NY 12345

Contract No. __ is completely terminated under clause ____, effective ____ [*insert* "immediately, (*today's date*)" *or* "on ____, 20__," *or* "as soon as you have delivered, including prior deliveries, the following items:" (*list*)]. Immediately stop all work, terminate subcontracts, and place no further orders except to the extent [*insert if applicable* "necessary to complete items not terminated or"] that you or a subcontractor wish to retain and continue for your own account any work-in-process or other materials. Provide by electronic means similar instructions to all subcontractors and suppliers. Detailed instructions follow.

(Contracting Officer)

(b) *Partial termination.* The following electronic notice is suggested for use if a supply contract is being partially terminated for convenience. If appropriately modified, the notice may be used for other than supply contracts.

DATE

XYZ Corporation

New York, NY 12345

Contract No. __ is partially terminated under clause ______, effective ____ [*insert* "immediately, (*today's date*)" *or* "on ______, 20__"]. Reduce items to be delivered as follows: [*insert instructions*]. Immediately stop all work, terminate subcontracts, and place no further orders except as necessary to perform the portion not terminated or that you or a subcontractor wish to retain and continue for your account any work-in-process or other materials. Provide by electronic means similar instructions to all subcontractors and suppliers. Detailed instructions follow.

(Contracting Officer)

[FAC 97-18, 65 FR 36014, 6/6/2000, effective 6/6/2000; FAC 2005-92, 81 FR 83097, 11/18/2016, effective 12/19/2016]

49.601-2 Letter notice.

The following letter notice of termination is suggested for use if a contract for supplies is being terminated for convenience. With appropriate modifications, it may be used in terminating contracts for other than supplies and in terminating subcontracts. This notice shall be sent by certified mail, return receipt requested, or electronically, provided evidence of receipt is received by the contracting officer. If no prior electronic notice was issued, or if no confirmation of an electronic notice was received, use the alternate notice that follows this notice.

NOTICE OF TERMINATION TO PRIME CONTRACTORS

[*At the top of the notice, set out all special details relating to the particular termination; e.g., name and address of company, contract number of terminated contract, line items, etc.*]

(a) *Effective date of termination.* This confirms the Government's electronic notice to you dated ____, 20__, terminating ___ [*insert* "completely" *or* "in part"] Contract No. __ (referred to as "the contract") for the Government's convenience under the clause entitled ____ [*insert title of appropriate termination clause*]. The termination is effective on the date and in the manner stated in the electronic notice.

(b) *Cessation of work and notification to immediate subcontractors.* You shall take the following steps:

(1) Stop all work, make no further shipments, and place no further orders relating to the contract, except for—

(i) The continued portion of the contract, if any;

(ii) Work-in-process or other materials that you may wish to retain for your own account; or

(iii) Work-in-process that the Contracting Officer authorizes you to continue (A) for safety precautions, (B) to clear or avoid damage to equipment, (C) to avoid immediate complete spoilage of work-in-process having a definite commercial value, or (D) to prevent any other undue loss to the Government. (If you believe this authorization is necessary or advisable, immediately notify the Contracting Officer by telephone or personal conference and obtain instructions.)

(2) Keep adequate records of your compliance with subparagraph (1) of this section showing the—

(i) Date you received the Notice of Termination;

(ii) Effective date of the termination; and

(iii) Extent of completion of performance on the effective date.

(3) Furnish notice of termination to each immediate subcontractor and supplier that will be affected by this termination. In the notice—

(i) Specify your Government contract number;

(ii) State whether the contract has been terminated completely or partially;

(iii) Provide instructions to stop all work, make no further shipments, place no further orders, and terminate all subcontracts under the contract, subject to the exceptions in subparagraph (b) (1) of this section;

(iv) Provide instructions to submit any settlement proposal promptly; and

(v) Request that similar notices and instructions be given to its immediate subcontractors.

(4) Notify the Contracting Officer of all pending legal proceedings that are based on subcontracts or purchase orders under the contract, or in which a lien has been or may be placed against termination inventory to be reported to the Government. Also,

promptly notify the Contracting Officer of any such proceedings that are filed after receipt of this Notice.

(5) Take any other action required by the Contracting Officer or under the Termination clause in the contract.

(c) *Termination inventory.* (1) As instructed by the Contracting Officer, transfer title and deliver to the Government all termination inventory of the following types or classes, including subcontractor termination inventory that you have the right to take: [*Contracting Officer insert proper identification or* "None"].

(2) To settle your proposal, it will be necessary to establish that all prime and subcontractor termination inventory has been properly accounted for. For detailed information, see Part 45.

(d) *Settlements with subcontractors.* You remain liable to your subcontractors and suppliers for proposals arising because of the termination of their subcontracts or orders. You are requested to settle these settlement proposals as promptly as possible. For purposes of reimbursement by the Government, settlements will be governed by the provisions of Part 49.

(e) *Completed end items.* (1) Notify the Contracting Officer of the number of items completed under the contract and still on hand and arrange for their delivery or other disposal (see 49.205).

(2) Invoice acceptable completed end items under the contract in the usual way and do not include them in the settlement proposal.

(f) *Patents.* If required by the contract, promptly forward the following to the Contracting Officer:

(1) Disclosure of all inventions, discoveries, and patent applications made in the performance of the contract.

(2) Instruments of license or assignment on all inventions, discoveries, and patent applications made in the performance of the contract.

(g) *Employees affected.* (1) If this termination, together with other outstanding terminations, will necessitate a significant reduction in your work force, you are urged to—

(i) Promptly inform the local State Employment Service of your reduction-in-force schedule in numbers and occupations, so that the Service can take timely action in assisting displaced workers;

(ii) Give affected employees maximum practical advance notice of the employment reduction and inform them of the facilities and services available to them through the local State Employment Service offices;

(iii) Advise affected employees to file applications with the State Employment Service to qualify for unemployment insurance, if necessary;

(iv) Inform officials of local unions having agreements with you of the impending reduction-in-force; and

(v) Inform the local Chamber of Commerce and other appropriate organizations which are prepared to offer practical assistance in finding employment for displaced workers of the impending reduction-in-force.

(2) If practicable, urge subcontractors to take similar actions to those described in subparagraph (1) of this section.

(h) *Administrative.* The contract administration office named in the contract will identify the Contracting Officer who will be in charge of the settlement of this termination and who will, upon request, provide the necessary settlement forms. Matters not covered by this notice should be brought to the attention of the undersigned.

(i) Please acknowledge receipt of this notice as provided below.

(Contracting Officer)

(Name of Office)

(Address)

Acknowledgment of Notice

The undersigned acknowledges receipt of a signed copy of this notice on ____, 20__. Two signed copies of this notice are returned.

(Name of Contractor)

By

(Name)

(Title)

(End of notice)

Alternate notice. Substitute the following paragraph (a) for paragraph (a) of 49.601-2, Notice of Termination to Prime Contractors, if no prior electronic notice was issued, or if no confirmation of an electronic notice was received:

(a) *Effective date of termination*. You are notified that Contract No. __ (referred to as "the contract") is terminated ____ [*insert* "completely" *or* "in part"] for the Government's convenience under the clause entitled ____ [*insert title of appropriate termination clause*]. The termination is effective ____ [*insert either* "immediately upon receipt of this Notice" *or* "on __, 20 __," *or* "as soon as you have delivered, including prior deliveries, the following items:" (*list*)]. Reduce items to be delivered as follows: [*insert instructions*].

[FAC 97-18, 65 FR 36014, 6/6/2000, effective 6/6/2000; FAC 2005-92, 81 FR 83097, 11/18/2016, effective 12/19/2016; FAC 2005-95, 82 FR 4709, 1/13/2017, effective 1/13/2017]

49.602 Forms for settlement of terminated contracts.

The standard forms listed below shall be used for settling terminated prime contracts. The forms at 49.602-1 and 49.602-2 may also be used for settling terminated subcontracts. A listing of the Standard forms is located in subpart 53.3.

[FAC 2005-100, 83 FR 42571, 8/22/2018, effective 8/22/2018]

49.602-1 Termination settlement proposal forms.

(a) Standard Form 1435, Settlement Proposal (Inventory Basis), shall be used to submit settlement proposals resulting from the termination of fixed-price contracts if the proposals are computed on an inventory basis (see 49.206-2(a)).

(b) Standard Form 1436, Settlement Proposal (Total Cost Basis), shall be used to submit settlement proposals resulting from the termination of fixed-price contracts if the proposals are computed on a total cost basis (see 49.206-2(b)).

(c) Standard Form 1437, Settlement Proposal for Cost-Reimbursement Type Contracts, shall be used to submit settlement proposals resulting from the termination of cost-reimbursement contracts (see 49.302).

(d) Standard Form 1438, Settlement Proposal (Short Form), shall be used to submit settlement proposals resulting from the termination of fixed-price contracts if the total proposal is less than $10,000 (see 49.206-1(d)).

49.602-2 Inventory forms.

Standard Form (SF) 1428, Inventory Disposal Schedule, and SF 1429, Inventory Disposal Schedule — Continuation Sheet, shall be used to support settlement proposals submitted on the forms specified in 49.602-1 (b) and (d).

[FAC 2001-22, 69 FR 17741, 4/5/2004, effective 5/5/2004]

49.602-3 Schedule of accounting information.

Standard Form 1439, Schedule of Accounting Information, shall be filed in support of a settlement proposal unless the proposal is filed on Standard Form 1438, Settlement Proposal (Short Form) (see 49.206-1(e)).

49.602-4 Partial payments.

Standard Form 1440, Application for Partial Payment, shall be used to apply for partial payments (see 49.112-1).

49.602-5 Settlement agreement.

Standard Form 30 (SF 30), Amendment of Solicitation/Modification of Contract, shall be used to execute a settlement agreement (see 49.109-1).

49.603 Formats for termination for convenience settlement agreements.

The formats to be used for termination for convenience settlement agreements should be substantially as shown in this section (see 49.109). Termination contracting officers

(TCO's) may, however, modify the contents of these agreements to conform with special termination clauses prescribed or authorized by their agencies (*e.g.*, see 49.501 and 49.505(c)).

[FAC 2005-17, 72 FR 27364, 5/15/2007, effective 6/14/2007]

49.603-1 Fixed-price contracts—complete termination.

[*Insert the following in Block 14 of SF 30 for settlements of fixed-price contracts completely terminated.*]

(a) This supplemental agreement settles the settlement proposal resulting from the Notice of Termination dated ____.

(b) The parties agree to the following:

(1) The Contractor certifies that all contract termination inventory (including scrap) has been retained or acquired by the Contractor, sold to third parties, returned to suppliers, delivered to or stored for the Government, or otherwise properly accounted for, and that all proceeds and retention credits have been used in arriving at this agreement.

(2) The Contractor certifies that each immediate subcontractor, whose settlement proposal is included in the proposal settled by this agreement, has furnished the Contractor a certificate stating—

(i) That all subcontract termination inventory (including scrap) has been retained or acquired by the subcontractor, sold to third parties, returned to suppliers, delivered to or stored for the Government, or otherwise properly accounted for, and that all proceeds and retention credits were used in arriving at the settlement of the subcontract, and

(ii) That the subcontractor has received a similar certificate from each immediate subcontractor whose proposal was included in its proposal.

(3) The Contractor certifies that all items of termination inventory, the costs of which were used in arriving at the amount of this settlement or the settlement of any subcontract settlement proposal included in this settlement,

(i) are properly allocable to the terminated portion of the contract,

(ii) do not exceed the reasonable quantitative requirements of the terminated portion of the contract, and

(iii) do not include any items reasonably usable without loss to the Contractor on its other work. The Contractor further certifies that the Contracting Officer has been informed of any substantial change in the status of the items between the dates of the termination inventory schedules and the date of this agreement.

(4) The Contractor transfers, conveys, and assigns to the Government all the right, title, and interest, if any, that the Contractor has received, or is entitled to receive, in and to subcontract termination inventory not otherwise properly accounted for.

(5) The Contractor shall, within 10 days after receipt of the payment specified in this agreement, pay to each of its immediate subcontractors (or their respective assignees) the amounts to which they are entitled, after deducting any prior payments and, if the Contractor so elects, any amounts due and payable to the Contractor by those subcontractors.

(6) (i) The Contractor has received $____ for work and services performed, or items delivered, under the completed portion of the contract. The Government confirms the right of the Contractor, subject to paragraph (7) below, to retain this sum and agrees that it constitutes a portion of the total amount to which the Contractor is entitled in settlement of the contract.

(ii) Further, the Government agrees to pay to the Contractor or its assignee, upon presentation of a proper invoice or voucher, the sum of $____ [*insert net amount of settlement*], arrived at by deducting from the sum of $____ [*for proposals on an inventory basis insert gross amount of settlement; for proposals on a total cost basis, insert gross amount of settlement less amount shown in subdivision (6) (i) of this section*—

(A) The amount of $____ for all unliquidated partial or progress payments previously made to the Contractor or its assignee and all unliquidated advance payments (with any interest) and

(B) The amount of $___ for all applicable property disposal credits [*insert if appropriate*, "and

(C) the amount of $___ for all other amounts due the Government under this contract, except as provided in paragraph (7) of this section"].

(iii) The net settlement of $___ in subdivision (ii) of this section, together with sums previously paid, constitutes payment in full and complete settlement of the amount due the Contractor for the complete termination of the contract and of all other demands and liabilities of the Contractor and the Government under the contract, except as provided in paragraph (7) of this section.

(7) Regardless of any other provision of this agreement, the following rights and liabilities of the parties under the contract are reserved:

[*The following list of reserved or excepted rights and liabilities is intended to cover those that should most frequently be reserved and that should be scrutinized at the time a settlement agreement is negotiated (see 49.109-2). The suggested language of the excepted items on the list may be varied at the discretion of the contracting officer. If accuracy or completeness can be achieved by referencing the number of a contract clause or provision covering the matter in question, then follow that method of enumerating reserved rights and liabilities. Omit any of the following that are not applicable and add any additional exceptions or reservations required.*]

(i) All rights and liabilities, if any, of the parties, as to matters covered by any renegotiation authority.

(ii) All rights of the Government to take the benefit of agreements or judgments affecting royalties paid or payable in connection with the performance of the contract.

(iii) All rights and liabilities, if any, of the parties under those clauses inserted in the contract because of the requirements of Acts of Congress and Executive Orders, including, without limitation, any applicable clauses relating to: labor law, contingent fees, domestic articles, and employment of aliens. [*If the contract contains clauses of this character inserted for reasons other than requirements of Acts of Congress or Executive orders, the suggested language should be appropriately modified.*]

(iv) All rights and liabilities of the parties arising under the contract and relating to reproduction rights, patent infringements, inventions, or applications for patents, including rights to assignments, invention reports, licenses, covenants of indemnity against patent risks, and bonds for patent indemnity obligations, together with all rights and liabilities under the bonds.

(v) All rights and liabilities of the parties, arising under the contract or otherwise, and concerning defects, guarantees, or warranties relating to any articles or component parts furnished to the Government by the Contractor under the contract or this agreement.

(vi) All rights and liabilities of the parties under the contract relating to any contract termination inventory stored for the Government.

(vii) All rights and liabilities of the parties under agreements relating to the future care and disposition by the Contractor of Government-owned property remaining in the Contractor's custody.

(viii) All rights and liabilities of the parties relating to Government property furnished to the Contractor for the performance of this contract.

(ix) All rights and liabilities of the parties under the contract relating to options (except options to continue or increase the work under the contract), covenants not to compete, and covenants of indemnity.

(x) All rights and liabilities, if any, of the parties under those clauses of the contract relating to price reductions for defective certified cost or pricing data.

(End of agreement)

[FAC 90-30, 60 FR 37772, 7/21/95, effective 9/19/95; FAC 90-33, 60 FR 49706, 9/26/95, effective 10/1/95; FAC 2005-45, 75 FR 53135, 8/30/2010, effective 10/1/2010]

49.603-2 Fixed-price contracts—partial termination.

[*Insert the following in Block 14 of SF 30 for settlements of fixed-price contracts partially terminated.*]

(a) This supplemental agreement settles the settlement proposal resulting from the Notice of Termination dated ____.

(b) The parties agree to the following:

(1) The terminated portion of the contract is as follows: [*specify the terminated portion clearly as to—*

(i) Line item numbers,

(ii) Descriptions,

(iii) Quantity terminated,

(iv) Unit price of items,

(v) Total price of terminated items, and

(vi) Any other explanation necessary to avoid uncertainty or misunderstanding].

(2) The Contractor certifies that all contract termination inventory (including scrap) has been retained or acquired by the Contractor, sold to third parties, returned to suppliers, delivered to or stored for the Government, or otherwise properly accounted for, and that all proceeds and retention credits have been used in arriving at this agreement.

(3) The Contractor certifies that each immediate subcontractor, whose settlement proposal is included in the proposal settled by this agreement, has furnished the Contractor a certificate stating—

(i) That all subcontract termination inventory (including scrap) has been retained or acquired by the subcontractor, sold to third parties, returned to suppliers, delivered to or stored for the Government, or otherwise properly accounted for, and that all proceeds and retention credits were used in arriving at the settlement of the subcontract, and

(ii) That the subcontractor has received a similar certificate from each immediate subcontractor whose proposal was included in its proposal.

(4) The Contractor certifies that all items of termination inventory, the costs of which were used in arriving at the amount of this settlement or the settlement of any subcontract settlement proposal included in this settlement,

(i) are properly allocable to the terminated portion of the contract,

(ii) do not exceed the reasonable quantitative requirements of the terminated portion of the contract, and—

(iii) do not include any items reasonably usable without loss to the Contractor on its other work. The Contractor further certifies that the Contracting Officer has been informed of any substantial change in the status of the items between the dates of the termination inventory schedules and the date of this agreement.

(5) The Contractor transfers, conveys, and assigns to the Government all the right, title, and interest, if any, that the Contractor has received, or is entitled to receive, in and to subcontract termination inventory not otherwise properly accounted for.

(6) The Contractor shall, within 10 days after receipt of the payment specified in this agreement, pay to each of its immediate subcontractors (or their respective assignees) the amounts to which they are entitled, after deducting any prior payments and, if the Contractor so elects, any amounts due and payable to the Contractor by those subcontractors.

(7) (i) The Government agrees to pay to the Contractor or its assignee, upon presentation of a proper invoice or voucher, the sum of $___ [*insert net amount of settlement*], arrived at by deducting from $___ [*insert gross amount of settlement*],—

(A) the amount of $___ for all unliquidated partial or progress payments previously made to the Contractor or its assignee and all unliquidated advance payments (with any interest) applicable to the terminated portion of the contract and

(B) the amount of $___ for all applicable property disposal credits.

(ii) The net settlement of $___ in subdivision (b) (7) (i) of this section, together with sums previously paid, constitutes payment in full and complete settlement of the amount due the Contractor for the terminated portion of the contract, except as provided in subparagraph (b)(8) of this section.

(iii) Upon payment of the net settlement of $___, all obligations of the Contractor to perform further work or services or to make further deliveries under the terminated portion of the contract and all obligations of the Government to make further payments or carry out other undertakings concerning the terminated portion of the contract shall cease; provided, that nothing in this agreement shall impair or affect any covenants, terms, or conditions of the contract relating to the completed or continued portion of this contract.

(8) Regardless of any other provision of this agreement, the following rights and liabilities of the parties under the contract are reserved:

[*The following list of reserved or excepted rights and liabilities is intended to cover those that should most frequently be reserved and that should be scrutinized at the time a settlement agreement is negotiated (see 49.109-2). The suggested language of the excepted items on the list may be varied at the discretion of the contracting officer. If accuracy or completeness can be achieved by referencing the number of a contract clause or provision covering the matter in question, then follow that method of enumerating reserved rights and liabilities. Omit any of the following that are not applicable and add any additional exceptions or reservations required.*]

(i) All rights and liabilities, if any, of the parties, as to matters covered by any renegotiation authority.

(ii) All rights of the Government to take the benefit of agreements or judgments affecting royalties paid or payable in connection with the performance of the contract.

(iii) All rights and liabilities, if any, of the parties under those clauses inserted in the contract because of the requirements of Acts of Congress and Executive orders, including, without limitation, any applicable clauses relating to: labor law, contingent fees, domestic articles, and employment of aliens. [*If the contract contains clauses of this character inserted for reasons other than requirements of Acts of Congress or Executive orders, the suggested language should be appropriately modified.*]

(iv) All rights and liabilities of the parties arising under the contract and relating to reproduction rights, patent infringements, inventions, or applications for patents, including rights to assignments, invention reports, licenses, covenants of indemnity against patent risks, and bonds for patent indemnity obligations, together with all rights and liabilities under the bonds.

(v) All rights and liabilities of the parties, arising under the contract or otherwise, and concerning defects, guarantees, or warranties relating to any articles or component parts furnished to the Government by the Contractor under the contract or this agreement.

(vi) All rights and liabilities of the parties under the contract relating to any contract termination inventory stored for the Government.

(vii) All rights and liabilities, if any, of the parties under those clauses of the contract relating to price reductions for defective certified cost or pricing data.

(End of agreement)

[FAC 90-30, 60 FR 37772, 7/21/95, effective 9/19/95; FAC 90-33, 60 FR 49706, 9/26/95, effective 10/1/95; FAC 2005-45, 75 FR 53135, 8/30/2010, effective 10/1/2010; FAC 2005-95, 82 FR 4709, 1/13/2017, effective 1/13/2017]

49.603-3 Cost-reimbursement contracts—complete termination, if settlement includes cost.

[*Insert the following in Block 14 of SF 30 for settlement of cost-reimbursement contracts that are completely terminated, if settlement includes costs.*]

(a) This supplemental agreement settles the settlement proposal resulting from the Notice of Termination dated ___.

(b) The parties agree to the following:

(1) The Contractor certifies that all contract termination inventory (including scrap) has been retained or acquired by the Contractor, sold to third parties, returned to suppliers, delivered to or stored for the

Government, or otherwise properly accounted for, and that all proceeds and retention credits have been used in arriving at this agreement.

(2) The Contractor certifies that each immediate subcontractor, whose settlement proposal is included in the proposal settled by this agreement, has furnished the Contractor a certificate stating—

(i) That all subcontract termination inventory (including scrap) has been retained or acquired by the subcontractor, sold to third parties, returned to suppliers, delivered to or stored for the Government, or otherwise properly accounted for, and that all proceeds and retention credits were used in arriving at the settlement of the subcontract; and

(ii) That the subcontractor has received a similar certificate from each immediate subcontractor whose proposal was included in its proposal.

(3) The Contractor certifies that all items of termination inventory, the costs of which were used in arriving at the amount of this settlement or the settlement of any subcontract settlement proposal included in this settlement,

(i) are properly allocable to the terminated portion of the contract,

(ii) do not exceed the reasonable quantitative requirements of the terminated portion of the contract, and

(iii) do not include any items reasonably usable without loss to the Contractor on its other work. The Contractor further certifies that the Contracting Officer has been informed of any substantial change in the status of the items between the dates of the termination inventory schedules and the date of this agreement.

(4) The Contractor transfers, conveys, and assigns to the Government all the right, title and interest, if any, that the Contractor has received, or is entitled to receive, in and to subcontract termination inventory not otherwise properly accounted for.

(5) The Contractor shall, within 10 days after receipt of the payment specified in this agreement, pay to each of its immediate subcontractors (or their respective assignees) the amounts to which they are entitled, after deducting any prior payments and, if the Contractor so elects, any amounts due and payable to the Contractor by those subcontractors.

(6) (i) The Contractor has received $___ for work and services performed, or articles delivered, under the contract before the effective date of termination. The Government confirms the right of the Contractor, subject to subparagraph (b)(7) of this section, to retain this sum and agrees that it constitutes a portion of the total amount to which the Contractor is entitled in complete and final settlement of the contract.

(ii) Further, the Government agrees to pay to the Contractor or its assignee, upon presentation of a proper invoice or voucher, the sum of $___ [*insert net amount of settlement*], arrived at by deducting from the sum of $___ [*insert gross amount of settlement less amount shown in subdivision (6)(i) of this section*]—

(A) The amount of $___ for all unliquidated partial or progress payments previously made to the Contractor or its assignee and all unliquidated advance payments (with any interest),

(B) The amount of $___ for all applicable property disposal credits [*insert if appropriate*, "and

(C) The amount of $___ for all other amounts due the Government under this contract, except as provided in paragraph (b)(7) of this section."]

(iii) The net settlement of $___ in subdivision (b)(6)(ii) of this section, together with sums previously paid, constitutes payment in full and complete settlement of the amount due the Contractor for the complete termination of the contract and of all other demands and liabilities of the Contractor and the Government under the contract, except as provided in subparagraph (b)(7) in this section.

(7) Regardless of any other provision of this agreement, the following rights and liabilities of the parties under the contract are reserved:

[*The following list of reserved or excepted rights and liabilities is intended to cover those that should most frequently be reserved and that should be scrutinized at the time a settlement agreement is negotiated (see 49.109-2). The suggested language of the excepted items on the list may be varied at the discretion of the contracting officer. If accuracy or completeness can be achieved by referencing the number of a contract clause or provision covering the matter in question, then follow that method of enumerating reserved rights and liabilities. Omit any of the following that are not applicable and add any additional exceptions or reservations required.*]

(i) All rights and liabilities, if any, of the parties, as to matters covered by any renegotiation authority.

(ii) All rights of the Government to take the benefit of agreements or judgments affecting royalties paid or payable in connection with the performance of the contract.

(iii) All rights and liabilities, if any, of the parties under those clauses inserted in the contract because of the requirements of Acts of Congress and Executive orders, including, without limitation, any applicable clauses relating to: labor law, contingent fees, domestic articles, and employment of aliens. [*If the contract contains clauses of this character inserted for reasons other than requirements of Acts of Congress or Executive orders, the suggested language should be appropriately modified.*]

(iv) All rights and liabilities of the parties arising under the contract and relating to reproduction rights, patent infringements, inventions, or applications for patents, including rights to assignments, invention reports, licenses, covenants of indemnity against patent risks, and bonds for patent indemnity obligations, together with all rights and liabilities under the bonds.

(v) All rights and liabilities of the parties, arising under the contract or otherwise, and concerning defects, guarantees, or warranties relating to any articles or component parts furnished to the Government by the Contractor under the contract or this agreement.

(vi) All rights and liabilities of the parties under the contract relating to any contract termination inventory stored for the Government.

(vii) All rights and liabilities of the parties under agreements relating to the future care and disposition by the Contractor of Government-owned property remaining in the Contractor's custody.

(viii) All rights and liabilities of the parties relating to Government property furnished to the Contractor for the performance of this contract.

(ix) All rights and liabilities of the parties under the contract relating to options (except options to continue or increase the work under the contract), covenants not to compete, and covenants of indemnity.

(x) Unresolved demands or assertions by the Contractor against the Government for costs under Government Accountability Office exceptions or other costs of the same nature that are excluded from the settlement without prejudice to the rights of either party, as follows: [*Insert amount and describe charges not waived.*]

(xi) Claims by the Contractor against the Government, when the Contractor's rights of reimbursement are disputed, that are excluded without prejudice to the rights of either party are as follows: [*Insert the amounts and describe the claims on which the Contracting Officer has made findings and has disallowed and on which the Contractor has taken, or intends to take, timely appeal.*]

(xii) Unresolved demands or assertions by the Contractor against the Government that are unknown in amount and involve costs alleged to be reimbursable under the contract are as follows: [*Insert the estimated amounts and describe the charges.*]

(xiii) Unknown amounts alleged by the Contractor against the Government, based upon responsibility of the Contractor to third parties that involve costs reimbursable under the contract.

(xiv) Debts due the Government by the Contractor that are based on refunds, rebates, credits, or other amounts not now known to the Government, with interest, now due or that may become due the Contractor from third parties, if the amounts arise out of transactions for which reimbursement has been made to the Contractor under the contract. The Contractor shall pay to the Government, within 30 days after receipt, any of these amounts that become due from any third party or any other source. Interest at the rate established by the Secretary of the Treasury under 50 U.S.C. (App.) 1215(b)(2) shall accrue and shall be paid to the Government on any amounts that remain unpaid after the 30-day period.

(xv) All rights and liabilities, if any, of the parties under those clauses of the contract relating to price reductions for defective certified cost or pricing data.

(End of agreement)

[FAC 90-30, 60 FR 37772, 7/21/95, effective 9/19/95; FAC 90-33, 60 FR 49706, 9/26/95, effective 10/1/95; FAC 2005-13, 71 FR 57380, 9/28/2006, effective 9/28/2006; FAC 2005-45, 75 FR 53135, 8/30/2010, effective 10/1/2010]

49.603-4 Cost-reimbursement contracts—complete termination, with settlement limited to fee.

[*Insert the following in Block 14 of SF 30 for settlement of cost-reimbursement contracts that are completely terminated, if settlement is limited to fee.*]

(a) This supplemental agreement settles the amount of fee due under the contract, terminated in its entirety by Notice of Termination dated ____.

(b) The parties agree to the following:

(1) The Contractor has received $____ on account of its fee under the contract before the effective date of termination.

(2) The Government agrees to pay to the Contractor or its assignee, upon presentation of a proper invoice or voucher, $____ [*insert net amount to be paid on account of fee*]. This sum, with sums previously paid, constitutes payment in full and complete settlement of the amount due the Contractor on account of its fee under the contract.

(3) The Contractor's allowable costs under the contract will be paid under the terms and conditions of the contract and Parts 31 and 49 of the Federal Acquisition Regulation.

[*Insert subparagraph (a)(3) only if there are costs to be vouchered out (see 49.302) or if there are costs to be covered later by a separate settlement agreement.*]

(4) Regardless of any other provision of this agreement, the following rights and liabilities of the parties under the contract are reserved:

[*The following list of reserved or excepted rights and liabilities is intended to cover those that should most frequently be reserved and that should be scrutinized at the time a settlement agreement is negotiated (see 49.109-2). The suggested language of the excepted items on the list may be varied at the discretion of the contracting officer. If accuracy or completeness can be achieved by referencing the number of a contract clause or provision covering the matter in question, then follow that method of enumerating reserved rights and liabilities. Omit any of the following that are not applicable and add any additional exceptions or reservations required.*]

(i) All rights and liabilities, if any, of the parties, as to matters covered by any renegotiation authority.

(ii) All rights and liabilities, if any, of the parties under those clauses inserted in the contract because of the requirements of Acts of Congress and Executive orders, including, without limitation, any applicable clauses relating to: labor law, contingent fees, domestic articles, and employment of aliens. [*If the contract contains clauses of this character inserted for reasons other than requirements of Acts of Congress or Executive orders, the suggested language should be appropriately modified.*]

(iii) All rights and liabilities of the parties arising under the contract and relating to reproduction rights, patent infringements, inventions, or applications for patents, including rights to assignments, invention reports, licenses, covenants of indemnity against patent risks, and bonds for patent indemnity obligations, together with all rights and liabilities under the bonds.

(iv) All rights and liabilities of the parties, arising under the contract or otherwise, and concerning defects, guarantees, or warranties relating to any articles or component parts furnished to the Government by the Contractor under the contract or this agreement.

(v) All rights and liabilities of the parties under agreements relating to the future care and disposition by the Contractor of Government-owned property remaining in the Contractor's custody.

(vi) All rights and liabilities of the parties relating to Government property furnished to, or acquired by, the Contractor for the performance of the contract.

(vii) All rights and liabilities of the parties under the contract relating to options (except options to continue or increase the work under the contract), covenants not to compete, and covenants of indemnity.

(viii) All rights and liabilities, if any, of the parties under those clauses of the contract relating to price reductions for defective certified cost or pricing data.

(End of agreement)

[FAC 90-30, 60 FR 37772, 7/21/95, effective 9/19/95; FAC 90-33, 60 FR 49706, 9/26/95, effective 10/1/95; FAC 2005-45, 75 FR 53135, 8/30/2010, effective 10/1/2010]

49.603-5 Cost-reimbursement contracts—partial termination.

[*Insert the following in Block 14 of SF 30, Amendment of Solicitation/Modification of Contract, for settlement agreements for cost-reimbursement contracts as a result of partial termination.*]

(a) This supplemental agreement settles the termination settlement proposal resulting from the Notice of Termination dated ___.

(b) The parties agree as follows:

(1) The contract is amended by deleting the terminated portion as follows: [*specify the terminated portion clearly as to—*

(i) Line Item numbers,

(ii) Descriptions,

(iii) Quantity terminated,

(iv) Unit and total price of terminated items, and

(v) Any other explanation necessary to avoid uncertainty or misunderstanding].

(2) The fee stated in the contract is decreased by $___, from $___ to $___[*Insert, if appropriate,* "(3) The estimated cost of the contract is decreased by $___, from $___ to $___"].

(c) The Contractor's allowable costs and earned fee, if any, for the terminated portion of the contract will continue to be reimbursed on SF 1034, Public Voucher for Purchase and Services Other Than Personal, under the applicable provisions of the contract and Part 31 of the Federal Acquisition Regulation.

(End of agreement)

[FAC 2005-95, 82 FR 4709, 1/13/2017, effective 1/13/2017]

49.603-6 No-cost settlement agreement—complete termination.

[*Insert the following in Block 14 of SF 30 if a no-cost settlement agreement, under a complete termination, is to be executed.*]

(a) This supplemental agreement [*insert* "modifies the contract to reflect a no-cost settlement agreement with respect to the Notice of Termination dated ___" *or, if not previously terminated,* "terminates the contract in its entirety"].

(b) The parties agree as follows:

The Contractor unconditionally waives any charges against the Government because of the termination of the contract and, except as set forth below, releases it from all obligations under the contract or due to its termination. The Government agrees that all obligations under the contract are concluded, except as follows:

[*List reserved or excepted rights and liabilities. See 49.109-2 and 49.603-1(b)(7).*]

(End of agreement)

49.603-7 No-cost settlement agreement—partial termination.

[*Insert the following in Block 14 of SF 30 if a no-cost settlement agreement, under a partial termination, is to be executed.*]

(a) This supplemental agreement modifies the contract to reflect a no-cost settlement agreement with respect to the Notice of Termination dated ___.

(b) The parties agree as follows:

(1) The terminated portion of the contract is as follows: [*Specify—*

(i) line item numbers,

(ii) descriptions,

(iii) quantity terminated,

(iv) unit and total price of terminated items, and

(v) any other explanation necessary to avoid uncertainty or misunderstanding.]

(2) The Contractor unconditionally waives any charges against the Government arising under the terminated portion of the contract or by reason of its termination, including, without limitation, all obligations of the Government to make further payments or to carry out any further undertakings under the terminated portion of the contract. The Government acknowledges that the Contractor has no obligation to perform further work or services or to make further deliveries under the terminated portion of the contract. Nothing in this paragraph affects any other covenants, terms, or conditions of the contract. Under the terminated portion of the contract, the following rights and liabilities of the parties are reserved: [*List reserved or excepted rights and liabilities. See 49.109-2 and 49.603-1(b)(7).*]

(End of agreement)

[FAC 2005-95, 82 FR 4709, 1/13/2017, effective 1/13/2017]

49.603-8 Fixed-price contracts—settlements with subcontractors only.

[*Insert the following in Block 14 of SF 30 for settlements of fixed-price contracts covering only settlements with subcontractors.*]

(a) This agreement settles that portion of the settlement proposal of the contractor that is based upon termination of the following subcontracts entered into in performing this contract:

[*Insert a list of the terminated subcontracts included in this settlement.*]

(b) The parties agree to the following:

(1) The Contractor certifies that each immediate subcontractor, whose settlement proposal is included in the proposal settled by the agreement, has furnished the Contractor a certificate stating—

(i) That all subcontract termination inventory (including scrap) has been retained or acquired by the subcontractor, sold to third parties, returned to suppliers, delivered to or stored for the Government, or otherwise properly accounted for, and that all proceeds and retention credits were used in arriving at the settlement of the subcontract, and

(ii) That the subcontractor has received a similar certificate from each immediate subcontractor whose proposal was included in its proposal.

(2) The Contractor certifies that all items of termination inventory, the costs of which were used in arriving at the amount of this settlement or the settlement of any subcontract settlement proposal included in this settlement—

(i) Are properly allocable to the terminated portion of the contract,

(ii) Do not exceed the reasonable quantitative requirements of the terminated portion of the contract, and

(iii) Do not include any items reasonably usable without loss to the Contractor on its other work. The Contractor further certifies that the Contracting Officer has been informed of any substantial change in the status of the items between the dates of the termination inventory schedules and the date of this agreement.

(3) The Contractor transfers, conveys, and assigns to the Government all the right, title, and interest, if any, that the Contractor has received or is entitled to receive, in and to subcontract termination inventory not otherwise properly accounted for.

(4) The Contractor shall, within 10 days after receipt of the payment specified in this agreement, pay to each of its immediate subcontractors (or their respective assignees) the amounts to which they are entitled, after deducting any prior payments and, if the Contractor so elects, any amounts due and payable to the Contractor by those subcontractors.

(5) The Government agrees to pay the Contractor or its assignee, upon presenta-

tion of a proper invoice or voucher, $___ [*insert net amount of settlement*], which, together with the amount of $___ previously paid the Contractor as partial, progress, or advance payments, constitutes payment in full and complete settlement, except as provided in subparagraph (b) (6) of this section, of the amount due the Contractor for that portion of its settlement proposal that is based upon termination of the subcontracts listed above.

(6) Regardless of any other provision of this agreement, the following rights and liabilities of the parties under the contract are reserved: [*List reserved or excepted rights and liabilities. See 49.109-2 and 49.603-1(b) (7).*]

(End of agreement)

49.603-9 Settlement of reservations.

[*Insert the following in Block 14 of SF 30 for settlement of reservations.*]

(a) Supplemental Agreement No. ___, dated ___, was executed to reflect the settlement of the termination of this contract. The supplemental agreement excepted from the settlement certain items described in the agreement including the items described in paragraph (b) of this section. This supplemental agreement settles those items listed in paragraph (b) of this section.

(b) The parties agree to the following:

(1) The Government agrees to pay the Contractor $___ for the following reserved or excepted items:* [*List items.*]

(2) The Contractor releases and forever discharges the Government from all liability and from all existing and future claims and demands that it may have under this contract, insofar as it pertains to the contract, for the items described in subparagraph (1) of this section.*

**When payment is due the Government, reverse the words "Government" and "Contractor" in subparagraphs (b) (1) and (b) (2).*

(End of agreement)

49.604 Release of excess funds under terminated contracts.

The following format shall be used to recommend the release of excess funds under terminated contracts, except if the contracting office retains responsibility for settlement of the termination:

FROM: Termination Contracting Officer ___ [*address*]

TO: Contracting office ___ [*address*]

SUBJ: Terminated Contract No. ___ with ___ [*Contractor*]

Refs:

(a) [*Cite termination notice and effective date.*]

(b) [*Cite prior letters releasing excess funds, if any.*]

1. Referenced termination notice, ___ [*insert* "completely" *or* "partially"]terminated contract ___

2. Based on the best information available, it is estimated that the gross settlement cost will be $___. The amount available for release as excess to the contract is $___. Any payments previously made to the Contractor for terminated items have been considered in arriving at the above amounts.

[*If prior letters recommending release of excess funds are cited, use the following as paragraph 2*:

The estimated settlement costs previously reported by reference (b) in the amount of $___ are revised. On the best evidence now available, it is estimated that the settlement costs will be $___. The additional amount available for release is $___.]

3. The related appropriations and amounts involved are:

Appropriations	Allocated Amounts

Copies to:

Paying Office

Accounting and Finance Office

Other

49.605 Request to settle subcontractor settlement proposals.

Contractors requesting authority to settle subcontractor settlement proposals shall furnish applicable information from the list below and any additional information required by the contracting officer:

(a) Name of contractor and address of principal office.

(b) Name and location of divisions of the applicant's plant for which authorization is requested.

(c) An explanation of the necessity and justification for the authorization requested.

(d) A full description of the applicant's organization for handling terminations, including the names of the officials in charge of processing and settling proposals.

(e) The number and dollar amount (estimated if necessary) of uncompleted contracts with Government agencies and the percentage applicable to each agency.

(f) The number and dollar amount (estimated if necessary) of uncompleted subcontracts under Government contracts and the percentage applicable to each agency.

(g) The extent of the applicant's experience in termination matters, including the handling of proposals of subcontractors.

(h) The approximate amount and general nature of terminations of the applicant currently in process.

(i) A statement that no other application has been made for any division of the applicant's plant covered by the application or, if one has been made, a full statement of the facts.

(j) The limit of authorization requested.

49.606 Granting subcontract settlement authorization.

Contracting officers shall use the following format when granting subcontract settlement authorization:

LETTER OF AUTHORIZATION

(a) Your request of ___ (*date*) is approved, and you are authorized, subject to the limitations of subsection 49.108-4 and those stated below, to settle, without further approval of the Government, all subcontracts and purchase orders terminated by you as a result of a Government contract being terminated or modified—

(1) For the convenience of the Government; or

(2) Under any other circumstances that may require the Government to bear the cost of their settlement.

(b) This authorization does not extend to the disposition of Government-furnished material or articles completed but undelivered under the subcontract or purchase order, as these require screening and approval of disposal actions by the Government, except that allocable completed articles may be disposed of without Government approval or screening if the total amount (at subcontract price) when added to the amount of settlement (as computed below) does not exceed $___ [*insert limit of authorization being granted*].

(c) This authorization is subject to the following conditions and requirements:

(1) The amount of the subcontract termination settlement does not exceed $___ [*insert limit of authorization being granted*], computed as follows:

(i) Do not deduct advance or partial payments or credits for retention or other disposal of termination inventory allocated to the settlement proposal.

(ii) Deduct amounts payable for completed articles or work at the contract price or for the settlement of termination proposals of subcontractors (except those settlements that have not been approved by the Government).

(2) Any termination inventory involved has been disposed of under subsection 49.108-4, except that screening and Government approval of scrap and salvage determinations are not required.

(3) The Contracting Officer may incorporate into each Notice of Termination specific instructions about the disposition of specific items of termination inventory, or the Contracting Officer may, at any time before final settlement, issue specific instructions. These instructions will not affect any disposal action taken by you or your subcontractors before their receipt.

(4) The settlements made by you with your subcontractors and suppliers under this

authorization, including sales, retention, or other dispositions of property involved in making these settlements, are reimbursable under Part 49 and the Termination clause of the contract, and do not require approval of the Contracting Officer.

(5) Any number of separate settlements of $___ [*insert limit of authorization granted*] or less may be made with a single subcontractor. Settlement proposals that would normally be included in a single proposal; *e.g.*, those based on a series of separate orders for the same item under one contract, should be consolidated whenever possible and shall not be divided to bring them within the authorization.

(6) This authorization does not apply if a subcontractor or supplier is affiliated with you. For this purpose, you should consider a contractor to be affiliated with you if you are under common control or if there is any common interest between you by reason of stock ownership, or otherwise, that is sufficient to create a reasonable doubt that the bargaining between you is completely at arm's length.

(7) A representative of this office will, from time to time, review the methods used in negotiating settlements with your subcontractors and will make a selective examination of the settlements made by you. If the review indicates that you are not adequately protecting the Government's interest, this delegation will be revoked.

(End of letter)

49.607 Delinquency notices.

The formats of the delinquency notices in this section may be used to satisfy the requirements of 49.402-3. All notices will be sent with proof of delivery requested. (See Subpart 42.13 for stop-work orders.)

(a) *Cure notice*. If a contract is to be terminated for default before the delivery date, a "Cure Notice" is required by the Default clause. Before using this notice, it must be ascertained that an amount of time equal to or greater than the period of "cure" remains in the contract delivery schedule or any extension to it. If the time remaining in the contract delivery schedule is not sufficient to permit a realistic "cure" period of 10 days or more, the "Cure Notice" should not be issued. The "Cure Notice" may be in the following format:

CURE NOTICE

You are notified that the Government considers your ___ [*specify the contractor's failure or failures*] a condition that is endangering performance of the contract. Therefore, unless this condition is cured within 10 days after receipt of this notice [*or insert any longer time that the Contracting Officer may consider reasonably necessary*], the Government may terminate for default under the terms and conditions of the ___ [*insert clause title*] clause of this contract.

(End of notice)

(b) *Show cause notice*. If the time remaining in the contract delivery schedule is not sufficient to permit a realistic "cure" period of 10 days or more, the following "Show Cause Notice" may be used. It should be sent immediately upon expiration of the delivery period.

SHOW CAUSE NOTICE

Since you have failed to ___ [*insert* "perform Contract No. ___ within the time required by its terms", *or* "cure the conditions endangering performance under Contract No. ___ as described to you in the Government's letter of ____ (*date*)"], the Government is considering terminating the contract under the provisions for default of this contract. Pending a final decision in this matter, it will be necessary to determine whether your failure to perform arose from causes beyond your control and without fault or negligence on your part. Accordingly, you are given the opportunity to present, in writing, any facts bearing on the question to ___ [*insert the name and complete address of the contracting officer*], within 10 days after receipt of this notice. Your failure to present any excuses within this time may be considered as an admission that none exist. Your attention is invited to the respective rights of the Contractor and the Government and the liabilities that may be invoked if a decision is made to terminate for default.

Any assistance given to you on this contract or any acceptance by the Government of delinquent goods or services will be solely for the purpose of mitigating damages, and it is not the intention of the Government to condone any delinquency or to waive any rights the Government has under the contract.

(End of notice)

[FAC 90-32, 60 FR 48206, 9/18/95, effective 10/1/95]

PART 50—EXTRAORDINARY CONTRACTUAL ACTIONS AND THE SAFETY ACT

Table of Contents

Scope of part . . . 50.000

Subpart 50.1—Extraordinary Contractual Actions

Definitions . . . 50.100
General . . . 50.101
Authority . . . 50.101-1
Policy . . . 50.101-2
Records . . . 50.101-3
Delegation of and limitations on exercise of authority . . . 50.102
Delegation of authority . . . 50.102-1
Contract adjustment boards . . . 50.102-2
Limitations on exercise of authority . . . 50.102-3
Contract adjustments . . . 50.103
General . . . 50.103-1
Types of contract adjustment . . . 50.103-2
Contract adjustment . . . 50.103-3
Facts and evidence . . . 50.103-4
Processing cases . . . 50.103-5
Disposition . . . 50.103-6
Contract requirements . . . 50.103-7
Residual powers . . . 50.104
Standards of use . . . 50.104-1
General . . . 50.104-2
Special procedures for unusually hazardous or nuclear risks . . . 50.104-3
Contract clause . . . 50.104-4

Subpart 50.2—Support Anti-terrorism by Fostering Effective Technologies Act of 2002

Scope of subpart . . . 50.200
Definitions . . . 50.201
Authorities . . . 50.202
General . . . 50.203
Policy . . . 50.204
Procedures . . . 50.205
SAFETY Act considerations . . . 50.205-1
Pre-qualification designation notice . . . 50.205-2
Authorization of offers contingent upon SAFETY Act designation or certification before contract award . . . 50.205-3
Authorization of awards made presuming SAFETY Act designation or certification after contract award . . . 50.205-4
Solicitation provisions and contract clause . . . 50.206

PART 50—EXTRAORDINARY CONTRACTUAL ACTIONS AND THE SAFETY ACT

50.000 Scope of part.

This part—

(a) (1) Prescribes policies and procedures for entering into, amending, or modifying contracts in order to facilitate the national defense under the extraordinary emergency authority granted by Public Law 85-804 (50 U.S.C. 1431—1434) and Executive Order 10789, dated November 14, 1958. It does not cover advance payments (see Subpart 32.4); and

(2) Implements indemnification authority granted by Pub. L. 85-804 and paragraph 1A of E.O. 10789 with respect to any matter that has been, or could be, designated by the Secretary of Homeland Security as a qualified anti-terrorism technology as defined in the Support Anti-terrorism by Fostering Effective Technologies Act of 2002 (SAFETY Act); and

(b) Implements SAFETY Act liability protections to promote development and use of anti-terrorism technologies.

[FAC 97-19, 65 FR 46052, 7/26/2000, effective 9/25/2000; FAC 2005-21, 72 FR 63027, 11/7/2007, effective 11/7/2007; FAC 2005-30, 74 FR 2733, 1/15/2009, effective 2/17/2009]

SUBPART 50.1—EXTRAORDINARY CONTRACTUAL ACTIONS

50.100 Definitions.

As used in this part—

Approving authority means an agency official or contract adjustment board authorized to approve actions under Pub. L. 85-804 and E.O. 10789.

Secretarial level means a level at or above the level of a deputy assistant agency head, or a contract adjustment board.

[FAC 2005-21, 72 FR 63027, 11/7/2007, effective 11/7/2007; FAC 2005-30, 74 FR 2733, 1/15/2009, effective 2/17/2009]

50.101 General. (No Text)

[FAC 2005-21, 72 FR 63027, 11/7/2007, effective 11/7/2007; FAC 2005-30, 74 FR 2733, 1/15/2009, effective 2/17/2009]

50.101-1 Authority.

(a) Pub. L. 85-804 empowers the President to authorize agencies exercising functions in connection with the national defense to enter into, amend, and modify contracts, without regard to other provisions of law related to making, performing, amending, or modifying contracts, whenever the President considers that such action would facilitate the national defense.

(b) E.O. 10789 authorizes the heads of the following agencies to exercise the authority conferred by Pub. L. 85-804 and to delegate it to other officials within the agency: the Government Publishing Office; the Department of Homeland Security; the Tennessee Valley Authority; the National Aeronautics and Space Administration; the General Services Administration; the Defense, Army, Navy, Air Force, Treasury, Interior, Agriculture, Commerce, and Transportation Departments; the Department of Energy for functions transferred to that Department from other authorized agencies; and any other agency that may be authorized by the President.

[FAC 2005-21, 72 FR 63027, 11/7/2007, effective 11/7/2007; FAC 2005-30, 74 FR 2733, 1/15/2009, effective 2/17/2009; FAC 2019-02, 84 FR 19839, 5/6/2019, effective 5/6/2019]

50.101-2 Policy.

(a) The authority conferred by Pub. L. 85-804 may not—

(1) Be used in a manner that encourages carelessness and laxity on the part of persons engaged in the defense effort; or

(2) Be relied upon when other adequate legal authority exists within the agency.

(b) Actions authorized under Pub. L. 85-804 shall be accomplished as expeditiously as practicable, consistent with the care, restraint, and exercise of sound judgment appropriate to the use of such extraordinary authority.

(c) Certain kinds of relief previously available only under Pub. L. 85-804; *e.g.*, rescission or reformation for mutual mistake, are now available under the authority of 41

U.S.C. chapter 71, Contract Disputes. In accordance with paragraph (a)(2) of this subsection, part 33 must be followed in preference to subpart 50.1 for such relief. In case of doubt as to whether part 33 applies, the contracting officer should seek legal advice.

[FAC 2005-21, 72 FR 63027, 11/7/2007, effective 11/7/2007; FAC 2005-30, 74 FR 2733, 1/15/2009, effective 2/17/2009; FAC 2005-73, 79 FR 24192, 4/29/2014, effective 5/29/2014]

50.101-3 Records.

Agencies shall maintain complete records of all actions taken under this Subpart 50.1. For each request for relief processed, these records shall include, as a minimum—

(a) The contractor's request;

(b) All relevant memorandums, correspondence, affidavits, and other pertinent documents;

(c) The Memorandum of Decision (see 50.103-6 and 50.104-2); and

(d) A copy of the contractual document implementing an approved request.

[FAC 2005-21, 72 FR 63027, 11/7/2007, effective 11/7/2007; FAC 2005-30, 74 FR 2733, 1/15/2009, effective 2/17/2009]

50.102 Delegation of and limitations on exercise of authority. (No Text)

[FAC 2005-21, 72 FR 63027, 11/7/2007, effective 11/7/2007; FAC 2005-30, 74 FR 2733, 1/15/2009, effective 2/17/2009]

50.102-1 Delegation of authority.

An agency head may delegate in writing authority under Pub. L. 85-804 and E.O. 10789, subject to the following limitations:

(a) Authority delegated shall be to a level high enough to ensure uniformity of action.

(b) Authority to approve requests to obligate the Government in excess of $70,000 may not be delegated below the secretarial level.

(c) Regardless of dollar amount, authority to approve any amendment without consideration that increases the contract price or unit price may not be delegated below the secretarial level, except in extraordinary cases or classes of cases when the agency head finds that special circumstances clearly justify such delegation.

(d) Regardless of dollar amount, authority to indemnify against unusually hazardous or nuclear risks, including extension of such indemnification to subcontracts, shall be exercised only by the Secretary or Administrator of the agency concerned, the Public Printer, or the Chairman of the Board of Directors of the Tennessee Valley Authority (see 50.104-3).

[FAC 2005-21, 72 FR 63027, 11/7/2007, effective 11/7/2007; FAC 2005-30, 74 FR 2733, 1/15/2009, effective 2/17/2009; FAC 2005-45, 75 FR 53129, 8/30/2010, effective 10/1/2010; FAC 2005-83, 80 FR 38293, 7/2/2015, effective 10/1/2015]

50.102-2 Contract adjustment boards.

An agency head may establish a contract adjustment board with authority to approve, authorize, and direct appropriate action under this Subpart 50.1 and to make all appropriate determinations and findings. The decisions of the board shall not be subject to appeal; however, the board may reconsider and modify, correct, or reverse its previous decisions. The board shall determine its own procedures and have authority to take all action necessary or appropriate to conduct its functions.

[FAC 2005-21, 72 FR 63027, 11/7/2007, effective 11/7/2007; FAC 2005-30, 74 FR 2733, 1/15/2009, effective 2/17/2009]

50.102-3 Limitations on exercise of authority.

(a) Pub. L. 85-804 is not authority for—

(1) Using a cost-plus-a-percentage-of-cost system of contracting;

(2) Making any contract that violates existing law limiting profit or fees;

(3) Providing for other than full and open competition for award of contracts for supplies or services; or

(4) Waiving any bid bond, payment bond, performance bond, or other bond required by law.

(b) No contract, amendment, or modification shall be made under Pub. L. 85-804's authority—

(1) Unless the approving authority finds that the action will facilitate the national defense;

(2) Unless other legal authority within the agency concerned is deemed to be lacking or inadequate;

(3) Except within the limits of the amounts appropriated and the statutory contract authorization (however, indemnification agreements authorized by an agency head (50.104-3) are not limited to amounts appropriated or to contract authorization); and

(4) That will obligate the Government for any amount over $34 million, unless the Senate and House Committees on Armed Services are notified in writing of the proposed obligation and 60 days of continuous session of Congress have passed since the transmittal of such notification. However, this paragraph (b)(4) does not apply to indemnification agreements authorized under 50.104-3.

(c) No contract shall be amended or modified unless the contractor submits a request before all obligations (including final payment) under the contract have been discharged. No amendment or modification shall increase the contract price to an amount higher than the lowest rejected bid of any responsible bidder, if the contract was negotiated under 14.404-1(f).

(d) No informal commitment shall be formalized unless—

(1) The contractor submits a written request for payment within 6 months after furnishing, or arranging to furnish, supplies or services in reliance upon the commitment; and

(2) The approving authority finds that, at the time the commitment was made, it was impracticable to use normal contracting procedures.

(e) The exercise of authority by officials below the secretarial level is subject to the following additional limitations:

(1) The action shall not—

(i) Release a contractor from performance of an obligation over $70,000;

(ii) Result in an increase in cost to the Government over $70,000;

(iii) Deal with, or directly affect, any matter that has been submitted to the Government Accountability Office; or

(iv) Involve disposal of Government surplus property.

(2) Mistakes shall not be corrected by an action obligating the Government for over $1,000, unless the contracting officer receives notice of the mistake before final payment.

(3) The correction of a contract because of a mistake in its making shall not increase the original contract price to an amount higher than the next lowest responsive offer of a responsible offeror.

(f) No executive department or agency shall exercise the indemnification authority granted under paragraph 1A of E.O. 10789 with respect to any supply or service that has been, or could be, designated by the Secretary of Homeland Security as a qualified anti-terrorism technology unless—

(1) For the Department of Defense, the Secretary of Defense has determined that the exercise of authority under E.O. 10789 is necessary for the timely and effective conduct of the United States military or intelligence activities, after consideration of the authority provided under the SAFETY Act (Subtitle G of title VIII of the Homeland Security Act of 2002, 6 U.S.C. 441-444); or

(2) For other departments and agencies that have authority under E.O. 10789—

(i) The Secretary of Homeland Security has advised whether the use of the authority under the SAFETY Act would be appropriate; and

(ii) The Director of the Office of Management and Budget has approved the exercise of authority under the Executive order.

[FAC 2005-21, 72 FR 63027, 11/7/2007, effective 11/7/2007; FAC 2005-30, 74 FR 2733, 1/15/2009, effective 2/17/2009; FAC 2005-45, 75 FR 53129, 8/30/2010, effective 10/1/2010; FAC 2005-73, 79 FR 24192, 4/29/2014, effective 5/29/2014; FAC

2005-83, 80 FR 38293, 7/2/2015, effective 10/1/2015]

50.103 Contract adjustments.

This section prescribes standards and procedures for processing contractors' requests for contract adjustment under Pub. L. 85-804 and E.O. 10789.

[FAC 2005-21, 72 FR 63027, 11/7/2007, effective 11/7/2007; FAC 2005-30, 74 FR 2733, 1/15/2009, effective 2/17/2009]

50.103-1 General.

The fact that losses occur under a contract is not sufficient basis for exercising the authority conferred by Pub. L. 85-804. Whether appropriate action will facilitate the national defense is a judgment to be made on the basis of all of the facts of the case. Although it is impossible to predict or enumerate all the types of cases in which action may be appropriate, examples are included in 50.103-2. Even if all of the factors in any of the examples are present, other considerations may warrant denying a contractor's request for contract adjustment. The examples are not intended to exclude other cases in which the approving authority determines that the circumstances warrant action.

[FAC 2005-21, 72 FR 63027, 11/7/2007, effective 11/7/2007; FAC 2005-30, 74 FR 2733, 1/15/2009, effective 2/17/2009]

50.103-2 Types of contract adjustment.

(a) *Amendments without consideration.* (1) When an actual or threatened loss under a defense contract, however caused, will impair the productive ability of a contractor whose continued performance on any defense contract or whose continued operation as a source of supply is found to be essential to the national defense, the contract may be amended without consideration, but only to the extent necessary to avoid such impairment to the contractor's productive ability.

(2) When a contractor suffers a loss (not merely a decrease in anticipated profits) under a defense contract because of Government action, the character of the action will generally determine whether any adjustment in the contract will be made, and its extent. When the Government directs its action primarily at the contractor and acts in its capacity as the other contracting party, the contract may be adjusted in the interest of fairness. Thus, when Government action, while not creating any liability on the Government's part, increases performance cost and results in a loss to the contractor, fairness may make some adjustment appropriate.

(b) *Correcting mistakes.* (1) A contract may be amended or modified to correct or mitigate the effect of a mistake. The following are examples of mistakes that may make such action appropriate:

(i) A mistake or ambiguity consisting of the failure to express, or express clearly, in a written contract, the agreement as both parties understood it.

(ii) A contractor's mistake so obvious that it was or should have been apparent to the contracting officer.

(iii) A mutual mistake as to a material fact.

(2) Amending contracts to correct mistakes with the least possible delay normally will facilitate the national defense by expediting the contracting program and assuring contractors that mistakes will be corrected expeditiously and fairly.

(c) *Formalizing informal commitments.* Under certain circumstances, informal commitments may be formalized to permit payment to persons who have taken action without a formal contract; for example, when a person, responding to an agency official's written or oral instructions and relying in good faith upon the official's apparent authority to issue them, has furnished or arranged to furnish supplies or services to the agency, or to a defense contractor or subcontractor, without formal contractual coverage. Formalizing commitments under such circumstances normally will facilitate the national defense by assuring such persons that they will be treated fairly and paid expeditiously.

[FAC 2005-21, 72 FR 63027, 11/7/2007, effective 11/7/2007; FAC 2005-30, 74 FR 2733, 1/15/2009, effective 2/17/2009]

50.103-3 Contract adjustments.

(a) *Contractor requests.* A contractor seeking a contract adjustment shall submit a request in duplicate to the contracting officer or an authorized representative. The request, normally a letter, shall state as a minimum—

(1) The precise adjustment requested;

(2) The essential facts, summarized chronologically in narrative form;

(3) The contractor's conclusions based on these facts, showing, in terms of the considerations set forth in 50.103-1 and 50.103-2, when the contractor considers itself entitled to the adjustment; and

(4) Whether or not—

(i) All obligations under the contracts involved have been discharged;

(ii) Final payment under the contracts involved has been made;

(iii) Any proceeds from the request will be subject to assignment or other transfer, and to whom; and

(iv) The contractor has sought the same, or a similar or related, adjustment from the Government Accountability Office or any other part of the Government, or anticipates doing so.

(b) *Contractor certification.* A contractor seeking a contract adjustment that exceeds the simplified acquisition threshold shall, at the time the request is submitted, submit a certification by a person authorized to certify the request on behalf of the contractor that—

(1) The request is made in good faith; and

(2) The supporting data are accurate and complete to the best of that person's knowledge and belief.

[FAC 2005-21, 72 FR 63027, 11/7/2007, effective 11/7/2007; FAC 2005-30, 74 FR 2733, 1/15/2009, effective 2/17/2009]

50.103-4 Facts and evidence.

(a) *General.* When it is appropriate, the contracting officer or other agency official shall request the contractor to support any request made under 50.103-3(a) with any of the following information:

(1) A brief description of the contracts involved, the dates of execution and amendments, the items being acquired, the price or prices, the delivery schedules, and any special contract provisions relevant to the request.

(2) A history of performance indicating when work under the contracts or commitments began, the progress made to date, an exact statement of the contractor's remaining obligations, and the contractor's expectations regarding completion.

(3) A statement of payments received, due, and yet to be received or to become due, including advance and progress payments; amounts withheld by the Government; and information as to any obligations of the Government yet to be performed under the contracts.

(4) A detailed analysis of the request's monetary elements, including precisely how the actual or estimated dollar amount was determined and the effect of approval or denial on the contractor's profits before Federal income taxes.

(5) A statement of the contractor's understanding of why the request's subject matter cannot now, and could not at the time it arose, be disposed of under the contract terms.

(6) The best supporting evidence available to the contractor, including contemporaneous memorandums, correspondence, and affidavits.

(7) Relevant financial statements, cost analyses, or other such data, preferably certified by a certified public accountant, as necessary to support the request's monetary elements.

(8) A list of persons connected with the contracts who have factual knowledge of the subject matter, including, when possible, their names, offices or titles, addresses, and telephone numbers.

(9) A statement and evidence of steps taken to reduce losses and claims to a minimum.

(10) Any other relevant statements or evidence that may be required.

(b) *Amendments without consideration—essentiality a factor.* When a request involves possible amendment without consideration, and essentiality to the national defense is a factor (50.103-2(a)(1)), the contractor may be asked to furnish, in addition to the facts and evidence listed in paragraph (a) of this subsection, any of the following information:

(1) A statement and evidence of the contractor's original breakdown of estimated costs, including contingency allowances, and profit.

(2) A statement and evidence of the contractor's present estimate of total costs under the contracts involved if it is enabled to complete them, broken down between costs accrued to date and completion costs, and between costs paid and those owed.

(3) A statement and evidence of the contractor's estimate of the final price of the contracts, taking into account all known or contemplated escalation, changes, extras, and the like.

(4) A statement of any claims known or contemplated by the contractor against the Government involving the contracts, other than those stated in response to paragraph (b)(3) of this subsection.

(5) An estimate of the contractor's total profit or loss under the contracts if it is enabled to complete them at the estimated final contract price, broken down between profit or loss to date and completion profit or loss.

(6) An estimate of the contractor's total profit or loss from other Government business and all other sources, from the date of the first contract involved to the estimated completion date of the last contract involved.

(7) A statement of the amount of any tax refunds to date, and an estimate of those anticipated, for the period from the date of the first contract involved to the estimated completion date of the last contract involved.

(8) A detailed statement of efforts the contractor has made to obtain funds from commercial sources to enable contract completion.

(9) A statement of the minimum amount the contractor needs as an amendment without consideration to enable contract completion, and the detailed basis for that amount.

(10) A estimate of the time required to complete each contract if the request is granted.

(11) A statement of the factors causing the loss under the contracts involved.

(12) A statement of the course of events anticipated if the request is denied.

(13) Balance sheets, preferably certified by a certified public accountant, (i) for the contractor's fiscal year immediately preceding the date of the first contract, (ii) for each subsequent fiscal year, (iii) as of the request date, and (iv) projected as of the completion date of all the contracts involved (assuming the contractor is enabled to complete them at the estimated final prices), together with income statements for annual periods subsequent to the date of the first balance sheet. Balance sheets and income statements should be both consolidated and broken down by affiliates. They should show all transactions between the contractor and its affiliates, stockholders, and partners, including loans to the contractor guaranteed by any stockholder or partner.

(14) A list of all salaries, bonuses, and other compensation paid or furnished to the principal officers or partners, and of all dividends and other withdrawals, and of all payments to stockholders in any form since the date of the first contract involved.

(c) *Amendments without consideration—essentiality not a factor.* When a request involves possible amendment without consideration because of Government action, and essentiality to the national defense is not a factor (50.103-2(a)(2)), the contractor may be asked to furnish, in addition to the facts and evidence listed in paragraph (a) of this subsection, any of the following information:

(1) A clear statement of the precise Government action that the contractor considers to have caused a loss under the contract, with evidence to support each essential fact.

(2) A statement and evidence of the contractor's original breakdown of estimated costs, including contingency allowances, and profit.

(3) The estimated total loss under the contract, with detailed supporting analysis.

(4) The estimated loss resulting specifically from the Government action, with detailed supporting analysis.

(d) *Correcting mistakes.* When a request involves possible correction of a mistake (50.103-2(b)), the contractor may be asked to furnish, in addition to the facts and evidence listed in paragraph (a) of this subsection, any of the following information:

(1) A statement and evidence of the precise error made, ambiguity existing, or misunderstanding arising, showing what it consists of, how it occurred, and the intention of the parties.

(2) A statement explaining when the mistake was discovered, when the contracting officer was given notice of it, and whether this notice was given before completion of work under, or the effective termination date of, the contract.

(3) An estimate of profit or loss under the contract, with detailed supporting analysis.

(4) An estimate of the increase in cost to the Government resulting from the adjustment requested, with detailed supporting analysis.

(e) *Formalizing informal commitments.* When a request involves possible formalizing of an informal commitment (50.103-2(c)), the contractor may be asked to furnish, in addition to the facts and evidence listed in paragraph (a) of this subsection, any of the following information:

(1) Copies of any written instructions or assurances (or a sworn statement of any oral instructions or assurances) given the contractor, and identification of the Government official who gave them.

(2) A statement as to when the contractor furnished or arranged to furnish the supplies or services involved, and to whom.

(3) Evidence that the contractor relied upon the instructions or assurances, with a full description of the circumstances that led to this reliance.

(4) Evidence that, when performing the work, the contractor expected to be compensated directly for it by the Government and did not anticipate recovering the costs in some other way.

(5) A cost breakdown supporting the amount claimed as fair compensation for the work performed.

(6) A statement and evidence of the impracticability of providing, in an appropriate contractual instrument, for the work performed.

[FAC 2005-21, 72 FR 63027, 11/7/2007, effective 11/7/2007; FAC 2005-30, 74 FR 2733, 1/15/2009, effective 2/17/2009]

50.103-5 Processing cases.

(a) In response to a contractor request made in accordance with 50.103-3(a), the contracting officer or an authorized representative shall make a thorough investigation to establish the facts necessary to decide a given case. Facts and evidence, including signed statements of material facts within the knowledge of individuals when documentary evidence is lacking, and audits if considered necessary to establish financial or cost facts, shall be obtained from contractor and Government personnel.

(b) When a case involves matters of interest to more than one Government agency, the interested agencies should maintain liaison with each other to determine whether joint action should be taken.

(c) When additional funds are required from another agency, the contracting agency may not approve adjustment requests before receiving advice that the funds will be available. The request for this advice shall give the contractor's name, the contract number, the amount of proposed relief, a brief description of the contract, and the accounting classification or fund citation. If the other agency makes additional funds available, the agency considering the adjustment request shall be solely responsible for any action taken on the request.

(d) When essentiality to the national defense is an issue (50.103-2(a)(1)), agencies considering requests for amendment without consideration involving another agency shall obtain advice on the issue from the other agency before making the final decision. When this advice is received, the agency considering the request for amendment without consideration shall be responsible for taking whatever action is appropriate.

[FAC 2005-21, 72 FR 63027, 11/7/2007, effective 11/7/2007; FAC 2005-30, 74 FR 2733, 1/15/2009, effective 2/17/2009]

50.103-6 Disposition.

When approving or denying a contractor's request made in accordance with 50.103-3(a), the approving authority shall sign and date a Memorandum of Decision containing—

(a) The contractor's name and address, the contract identification, and the nature of the request;

(b) A concise description of the supplies or services involved;

(c) The decision reached and the actual cost or estimated potential cost involved, if any;

(d) A statement of the circumstances justifying the decision;

(e) Identification of any of the foregoing information classified "Confidential" or higher (instead of being included in the memorandum, such information may be set forth in a separate classified document referenced in the memorandum); and

(f) If some adjustment is approved, a statement in substantially the following form: "I find that the action authorized herein will facilitate the national defense." The case files supporting this statement will show the derivation and rationale for the dollar amount of the award. When the dollar amount exceeds the amounts supported by audit or other independent reviews, the approving authority will further document the rationale for deviating from the recommendation.

[FAC 2005-21, 72 FR 63027, 11/7/2007, effective 11/7/2007; FAC 2005-30, 74 FR 2733, 1/15/2009, effective 2/17/2009]

50.103-7 Contract requirements.

(a) Pub. L. 85-804 and E.O. 10789require that every contract entered into, amended, or modified under this Subpart 50.1 shall contain—

(1) A citation of Pub. L. 85-804 and E.O. 10789;

(2) A brief statement of the circumstances justifying the action; and

(3) A recital of the finding that the action will facilitate the national defense.

(b) The authority in 50.101-1(a) shall not be used to omit from contracts, when otherwise required, the clauses at 52.203-5, Covenant Against Contingent Fees; 52.215-2, Audit and Records—Negotiation; 52.222-4, Contract Work Hours and Safety Standards—Overtime Compensation; 52.222-6, Construction Wage Rate Requirements; 52.222-10, Compliance With Copeland Act Requirements; 52.222-20, Contracts for Materials, Supplies, Articles, and Equipment Exceeding $15,000; 52.222-26, Equal Opportunity; and 52.232-23, Assignment of Claims.

[FAC 2005-21, 72 FR 63027, 11/7/2007, effective 11/7/2007; FAC 2005-30, 74 FR 2733, 1/15/2009, effective 2/17/2009; FAC 2005-73, 79 FR 24192, 4/29/2014, effective 5/29/2014]

50.104 Residual powers.

This section prescribes standards and procedures for exercising residual powers under Pub. L. 85-804. The term *residual powers* includes all authority under Pub. L. 85-804 except—

(a) That covered by section 50.103; and

(b) The authority to make advance payments (see Subpart 32.4).

[FAC 2005-21, 72 FR 63027, 11/7/2007, effective 11/7/2007; FAC 2005-30, 74 FR 2733, 1/15/2009, effective 2/17/2009]

50.104-1 Standards for use.

Subject to the limitations in 50.102-3, residual powers may be used in accordance with the policies in 50.101-2 when necessary and appropriate, all circumstances considered. In authorizing the inclusion of the clause at 52.250-1, Indemnification Under Public Law 85-804, in a contract or subcontract, an agency head may require the indemnified contractor to provide and maintain financial protection of the type and amount determined appropriate. In deciding whether to approve use of the indemnification clause, and in determining the type and amount of financial protection the indemnified contractor is to provide and maintain, an agency head shall consider such factors as self-insurance, other proof of financial responsibility, workers' compensation insurance, and the availability, cost, and terms of private insurance. The approval and determination shall be final.

[FAC 2005-21, 72 FR 63027, 11/7/2007, effective 11/7/2007; FAC 2005-30, 74 FR 2733, 1/15/2009, effective 2/17/2009]

50.104-2 General.

(a) When approving or denying a proposal for the exercise of residual powers, the approving authority shall sign and date a Memorandum of Decision containing substantially the same information called for by 50.103-6.

(b) Every contract entered into, amended, or modified under residual powers shall comply with the requirements of 50.103-7.

[FAC 2005-21, 72 FR 63027, 11/7/2007, effective 11/7/2007; FAC 2005-30, 74 FR 2733, 1/15/2009, effective 2/17/2009]

50.104-3 Special procedures for unusually hazardous or nuclear risks.

(a) *Indemnification requests.* (1) Contractor requests for the indemnification clause to cover unusually hazardous or nuclear risks should be submitted to the contracting officer and shall include the following information:

(i) Identification of the contract for which the indemnification clause is requested.

(ii) Identification and definition of the unusually hazardous or nuclear risks for which indemnification is requested, with a statement indicating how the contractor would be exposed to them.

(iii) A statement, executed by a corporate official with binding contractual authority, of all insurance coverage applicable to the risks to be defined in the contract as unusually hazardous or nuclear, including—

(A) Names of insurance companies, policy numbers, and expiration dates;

(B) A description of the types of insurance provided (including the extent to which the contractor is self-insured or intends to self-insure), with emphasis on identifying the risks insured against and the coverage extended to persons or property, or both;

(C) Dollar limits per occurrence and annually, and any other limitation, for relevant segments of the total insurance coverage;

(D) Deductibles, if any, applicable to losses under the policies;

(E) Any exclusions from coverage under such policies for unusually hazardous or nuclear risks; and

(F) Applicable workers' compensation insurance coverage.

(iv) The controlling or limiting factors for determining the amount of financial protection the contractor is to provide and maintain, with information regarding the availability, cost, and terms of additional insurance or other forms of financial protection.

(v) Whether the contractor's insurance program has been approved or accepted by any Government agency; and whether the contractor has an indemnification agreement covering similar risks under any other Government program, and, if so, a brief description of any limitations.

(vi) If the contractor is a division or subsidiary of a parent corporation—

(A) A statement of any insurance coverage of the parent corporation that bears on the risks for which the contractor seeks indemnification; and

(B) A description of the precise legal relationship between parent and subsidiary or division.

(2) If the dollar value of the contractor's insurance coverage varies by 10 percent or more from that stated in an indemnification request submitted in accordance with paragraph (a)(1) of this subsection, or if other significant changes in insurance coverage occur after submission and before approval, the contractor shall immediately submit to the contracting officer a brief description of the changes.

(b) *Action on indemnification requests.* (1) The contracting officer, with assistance from legal counsel and cognizant program office personnel, shall review the indemnification request and ascertain whether it contains all required information. If the contracting officer, after considering the facts and evidence, denies the request, the contracting officer shall notify the contractor promptly of the denial and of the reasons for it. If recommending approval, the contracting officer shall forward the request (as modified, if necessary, by negotiation) through channels to the appropriate official specified in 50.102-1(d). The contracting officer's submission shall include all information submitted by the contractor and—

(i) All pertinent information regarding the proposed contract or program, including the period of performance, locations, and facilities involved;

(ii) A definition of the unusually hazardous or nuclear risks involved in the proposed contract or program, with a statement that the parties have agreed to it;

(iii) A statement by responsible authority that the indemnification action would facilitate the national defense;

(iv) A statement that the contract will involve unusually hazardous or nuclear risks that could impose liability upon the contractor in excess of financial protection reasonably available;

(v) A statement that the contractor is complying with applicable Government safety requirements;

(vi) A statement of whether the indemnification should be extended to subcontractors; and

(vii) A description of any significant changes in the contractor's insurance coverage (see 50.104-3(a)(2)) occurring since submission of the indemnification request.

(2) Approval of a request to include the indemnification clause in a contract shall be by a Memorandum of Decision executed by the appropriate official specified in 50.102-1(d).

(3) When use of the indemnification clause is approved under paragraph (b)(2) of this subsection, the definition of unusually hazardous or nuclear risks (see paragraph (b)(1)(ii) of this subsection) shall be incorporated into the contract, along with the clause.

(4) When approval is—

(i) Authorized in the Memorandum of Decision; and

(ii) Justified by the circumstances, the contracting officer may approve the contractor's written request to provide for indemnification of subcontractors, using the same procedures as those required for contractors.

[FAC 2005-21, 72 FR 63027, 11/7/2007, effective 11/7/2007; FAC 2005-30, 74 FR 2733, 1/15/2009, effective 2/17/2009]

50.104-4 Contract clause.

The contracting officer shall insert the clause at 52.250-1, Indemnification Under Public Law 85-804, in contracts whenever the approving official determines that the contractor shall be indemnified against unusually hazardous or nuclear risks (also see 50.104-3(b)(3)). In cost-reimbursement contracts, the contracting officer shall use the clause with its Alternate I.

[FAC 2005-21, 72 FR 63027, 11/7/2007, effective 11/7/2007; FAC 2005-30, 74 FR 2733, 1/15/2009, effective 2/17/2009]

SUBPART 50.2—SUPPORT ANTI-TERRORISM BY FOSTERING TECHNOLOGIES ACT OF 2002

50.200 Scope of subpart.

This subpart implements the Support Anti-terrorism by Fostering Effective Technologies Act of 2002 (SAFETY Act) liability protections to promote development and use of anti-terrorism technologies.

[FAC 2005-21, 72 FR 63027, 11/7/2007, effective 11/7/2007; FAC 2005-30, 74 FR 2733, 1/15/2009, effective 2/17/2009]

50.201 Definitions.

Act of terrorism means any act determined to have met the following requirements or such other requirements as defined and specified by the Secretary of Homeland Security:

(1) Is unlawful.

(2) Causes harm, including financial harm, to a person, property, or entity, in the United States, or in the case of a domestic United States air carrier or a United States-flag vessel (or a vessel based principally in the United States on which United States income tax is paid and whose insurance coverage is subject to regulation in the United States), in or outside the United States.

(3) Uses or attempts to use instrumentalities, weapons or other methods designed or intended to cause mass destruction, injury or other loss to citizens or institutions of the United States.

Block certification means SAFETY Act certification of a technology class that the Department of Homeland Security (DHS) has determined to be an approved class of approved products for homeland security.

Block designation means SAFETY Act designation of a technology class that the DHS has determined to be a Qualified Anti-Terrorism Technology (QATT).

Pre-qualification designation notice means a notice in a procurement solicitation or other publication by the Government stating that the technology to be procured either affirmatively or presumptively satisfies the technical criteria necessary to be deemed a qualified anti-terrorism technology. A pre-qualification designation notice authorizes offeror(s) to submit streamlined SAFETY Act applications for SAFETY Act designation and receive expedited processing of those applications.

Qualified Anti-Terrorism Technology (QATT) means any technology designed, developed, modified, procured, or sold for the purpose of preventing, detecting, identifying, or deterring acts of terrorism or limiting the harm such acts might otherwise cause, for which a SAFETY Act designation has been issued. For purposes of defining a QATT, technology means any product, equipment, service (including support services), device, or technology (including information technology) or any combination of the foregoing. Design services, consulting services, engineering services, software development services, software integration services, threat assessments, vulnerability studies, and other analyses relevant to homeland security may be deemed a technology.

SAFETY Act certification means a determination by DHS pursuant to 6 U.S.C. 442(d), as further delineated in 6 CFR 25.8 and 25.9, that a QATT for which a SAFETY Act designation has been issued is an approved product for homeland security, i.e., it will perform as intended, conforms to the seller's specifications, and is safe for use as intended.

SAFETY Act designation means a determination by DHS pursuant to 6 U.S.C. 441(b) and 6 U.S.C. 443(a), as further delineated in 6 CFR 25.4, that a particular Anti-Terrorism Technology constitutes a QATT under the SAFETY Act.

[FAC 2005-21, 72 FR 63027, 11/7/2007, effective 11/7/2007; FAC 2005-30, 74 FR 2733, 1/15/2009, effective 2/17/2009]

50.202 Authorities.

The following authorities apply:

(a) Support Anti-terrorism by Fostering Effective Technologies Act of 2002 (SAFETY Act), 6 U.S.C. 441-444.

(b) Executive Order 13286 of February 28, 2003, Amendment of Executive Orders, and Other Actions, in Connection With the Transfer of Certain Functions to the Secretary of Homeland Security.

(c) Executive Order 10789 of November 14, 1958, Contracting Authority of Government Agencies in Connection with National Defense Functions.

(d) 6 CFR Part 25.

[FAC 2005-21, 72 FR 63027, 11/7/2007, effective 11/7/2007; FAC 2005-30, 74 FR 2733, 1/15/2009, effective 2/17/2009]

50.203 General.

(a) As part of the Homeland Security Act of 2002, Pub. L. 107-296, Congress enacted the SAFETY Act to—

(1) Encourage the development and use of anti-terrorism technologies that will enhance the protection of the nation; and

(2) Provide risk management and litigation management protections for sellers of QATTs and others in the supply and distribution chain.

(b) The SAFETY Act's liability protections are complementary to the Terrorism Risk Insurance Act of 2002.

(c) Questions concerning the SAFETY Act may be directed to DHS Office of SAFETY Act Implementation (OSAI). Additional information about the SAFETY Act may be found at *http://www.SAFETYAct.gov.* Included on this website are block designations and block certifications granted by DHS.

[FAC 2005-21, 72 FR 63027, 11/7/2007, effective 11/7/2007; FAC 2005-30, 74 FR 2733, 1/15/2009, effective 2/17/2009]

50.204 Policy.

(a) Agencies should—

(1) Determine whether the technology to be procured is appropriate for SAFETY Act protections and, if appropriate, formally relay this determination to DHS for purposes of supporting contractor application(s) for SAFETY Act protections in relation to criteria (b)(viii) of 6 CFR 25.4, Designation of Qualified Anti-Terrorism Technologies;

(2) Encourage offerors to seek SAFETY Act protections for their offered technologies, even in advance of the issuance of a solicitation; and

(3) Not mandate SAFETY Act protections for acquisitions because applying for SAFETY Act protections for a particular technology is the choice of the offeror.

(b) Agencies shall not solicit offers contingent upon SAFETY Act designation or certification occurring before contract award unless authorized in accordance with 50.205-3.

(c) Agencies shall not solicit offers or award contracts presuming DHS will issue a SAFETY Act designation or certification after contract award unless authorized in accordance with 50.205-4.

(d) The DHS determination to extend SAFETY Act protections for a particular technology is not a determination that the technology meets, or fails to meet, the requirements of a solicitation.

[FAC 2005-21, 72 FR 63027, 11/7/2007, effective 11/7/2007; FAC 2005-30, 74 FR 2733, 1/15/2009, effective 2/17/2009]

50.205 Procedures. (No Text)

[FAC 2005-21, 72 FR 63027, 11/7/2007, effective 11/7/2007; FAC 2005-30, 74 FR 2733, 1/15/2009, effective 2/17/2009]

50.205-1 SAFETY Act Considerations.

(a) *SAFETY Act applicability.* Requiring activities should review requirements to identify potential technologies that prevent, detect, identify, or deter acts of terrorism or limit the harm such acts might cause, and may be appropriate for SAFETY Act protections. In questionable cases, the agency shall consult with DHS. For acquisitions involving such technologies, the requiring activity should ascertain through discussions with DHS whether a block designation or block certification exists for the technology being acquired.

(1) If one does exist, the requiring activity should request that the contracting officer notify offerors.

(2) If one does not exist, see 50.205-2, Prequalification designation notice.

(b) *Early consideration of the SAFETY Act.* Acquisition officials shall consider SAFETY Act issues as early in the acquisition cycle as possible (see FAR 7.105(b)(20)(v)). Normally, this would be at the point where the required capabilities or performance characteristics are addressed. This is important because the processing times for issuing determinations on all types of SAFETY Act applications vary depending on many factors, including the influx of applications to DHS and the technical complexity of individual applications.

(c) *Industry outreach.* When applicable, acquisition officials should include SAFETY Act considerations in all industry outreach efforts including, but not limited to, requests for information, draft requests for proposal, and industry conferences.

(d) *Reciprocal waiver of claims.* For purposes of 6 CFR 25.5(e), the Government is not a customer from which a contractor must request a reciprocal waiver of claims.

[FAC 2005-21, 72 FR 63027, 11/7/2007, effective 11/7/2007; FAC 2005-30, 74 FR 2733, 1/15/2009, effective 2/17/2009; FAC 2005-50, 76 FR 14543, 3/16/2011, effective 3/16/2011; FAC 2005-56, 77 FR 12925, 3/2/2012, effective 4/2/2012]

50.205-2 Pre-qualification designation notice.

(a) *Requiring activity responsibilities.* (1) If the requiring activity determines that the technology to be acquired may qualify for SAFETY Act protection, the requiring activity is responsible for requesting a pre-qualification designation notice from DHS. Such a request for a pre-qualification designation notice should be made once the requiring activity has determined that the technology specifications or statement of work are established and are unlikely to undergo substantive modification. DHS will then determine whether the technology identified in the request either affirmatively or presumptively satisfies the technical criteria for SAFETY Act designation. An affirmative determination means the technology described in the pre-qualification designation notice satisfies the technical criteria for SAFETY Act designation as a QATT. A presumptive determination means that the technology is a good candidate for SAFETY Act designation as a QATT. In either case, the notice will authorize offerors to—

(i) Submit a streamlined application for SAFETY Act designation; and

(ii) Receive expedited review of their application for SAFETY Act designation.

(2) The requiring activity shall make requests using the procurement pre-qualification request form available at *http://www.SAFETYAct.gov.* The website includes instructions for completing and submitting the form.

(3) The requiring activity shall provide a copy of the request, as well as a copy of the resulting pre-qualification designation notice or DHS denial, to the contracting officer.

(b) *Contracting officer responsibilities.* Upon receipt of the documentation specified in paragraph (a)(3) of this subsection, the contracting officer shall—

(1) Include in any pre-solicitation notice (Subpart 5.2) that a pre-qualification designation notice has been—

(i) Requested and is under review by DHS;

(ii) Denied by DHS; or

(iii) Issued and a copy will be included with the solicitation; and

(2) Incorporate the pre-qualification designation notice into the solicitation.

[FAC 2005-21, 72 FR 63027, 11/7/2007, effective 11/7/2007; FAC 2005-30, 74 FR 2733, 1/15/2009, effective 2/17/2009]

50.205-3 Authorization of offers contingent upon SAFETY Act designation or certification before contract award.

(a) Contracting officers may authorize such contingent offers, only if—

(1) DHS has issued—

(i) For offers contingent upon SAFETY Act designation, a pre-qualification designation notice or a block designation; or

(ii) For offers contingent upon SAFETY Act certification, a block certification;

(2) To the contracting officer's knowledge, the Government has not provided advance notice so that potential offerors could have obtained SAFETY Act designations/certifications for their offered technologies before release of any solicitation; and

(3) Market research shows that there will be insufficient competition without SAFETY Act protections or the subject technology would be sold to the Government only with SAFETY Act protections.

(b) Contracting officers shall not authorize offers contingent upon obtaining a SAFETY Act certification (as opposed to a SAFETY Act designation), unless a block certification applies to the class of technology to be acquired under the solicitation.

[FAC 2005-21, 72 FR 63027, 11/7/2007, effective 11/7/2007; FAC 2005-30, 74 FR 2733, 1/15/2009, effective 2/17/2009]

50.205-4 Authorization of awards made presuming SAFETY Act

designation or certification after contract award.

(a) When necessary to award a contract prior to DHS issuing SAFETY Act protections, contracting officers may award contracts presuming that DHS will issue a SAFETY Act designation/certification to the contractor after contract award only if—

(1) The criteria of 50.205-3(a) are met;

(2) The chief of the contracting office (or other official designated in agency procedures) approves the action; and

(3) The contracting officer advises DHS of the timelines for potential award and consults DHS as to when DHS could reasonably complete evaluations of offerors' applications for SAFETY Act designations or certifications.

(b) Contracting officers shall not authorize offers contingent upon obtaining a SAFETY Act certification (as opposed to a SAFETY Act designation), unless a block certification applies to the class of technology to be acquired under the solicitation.

[FAC 2005-21, 72 FR 63027, 11/7/2007, effective 11/7/2007; FAC 2005-30, 74 FR 2733, 1/15/2009, effective 2/17/2009]

50.206 Solicitation provisions and contract clause.

(a) Insert the provision at 52.250-2, SAFETY Act Coverage Not Applicable, in solicitations if—

(1) The agency consulted with DHS on a questionable case of SAFETY Act applicability to an acquisition in accordance with 50.205-1(a), and after the consultation, the agency has determined that SAFETY Act protection is not applicable for the acquisition; or

(2) DHS has denied approval of a prequalification designation notice.

(b)(1) Insert the provision at 52.250-3, SAFETY Act Block Designation/Certification, in a solicitation when DHS has issued a block designation/certification for the solicited technologies.

(2) Use the provision at 52.250-3 with its Alternate I when contingent offers are authorized in accordance with 50.205-3.

(3) Use the provision at 52.250-3 with its Alternate II when offers presuming SAFETY Act designation or certification are authorized in accordance with 50.205-4. If this alternate is used, the contracting officer may increase the number of days within which offerors must submit their SAFETY Act designation or certification application.

(c)(1) Insert the provision at 52.250-4, SAFETY Act Pre-qualification Designation Notice, in a solicitation for which DHS has issued a pre-qualification designation notice.

(2) Use the provision at 52.250-4 with its Alternate I when contingent offers are authorized in accordance with 50.205-3.

(3) Use the provision at 52.250-4 with its Alternate II when offers presuming SAFETY Act designation or certification are authorized in accordance with 50.205-4. If this alternate is used, the contracting officer may increase the number of days within which offerors must submit their SAFETY Act designation or certification application.

(d) Insert the clause at 52.250-5, SAFETY Act—Equitable Adjustment—

(1) In the solicitation, if the provision at 52.250-3 or 52.250-4 is used with its Alternate II; and

(2) In any resultant contract, if DHS has not issued SAFETY Act designation or certification to the successful offeror before contract award.

[FAC 2005-21, 72 FR 63027, 11/7/2007, effective 11/7/2007; FAC 2005-30, 74 FR 2733, 1/15/2009, effective 2/17/2009]

PART 51—USE OF GOVERNMENT SOURCES BY CONTRACTORS

Table of Contents

Scope of part 51.000

Subpart 51.1—Contractor Use of Government Supply Sources

Scope of subpart 51.100
Policy 51.101
Authorization to use Government supply sources 51.102
Ordering from Government supply sources 51.103
Furnishing assistance to contractors 51.104
Payment for shipments 51.105
Title 51.106
Contract clause 51.107

Subpart 51.2—Contractor Use of Interagency Fleet Management System (IFMS) Vehicles

Scope of subpart 51.200
Policy 51.201
Authorization 51.202
Means of obtaining service 51.203
Use of interagency fleet management system (IFMS) vehicles and related services 51.204
Contract clause 51.205

PART 51—USE OF GOVERNMENT SOURCES BY CONTRACTORS

51.000 Scope of part.

This part prescribes policies and procedures for the use by contractors of Government supply sources and interagency fleet management system (IFMS) vehicles and related services.

SUBPART 51.1—CONTRACTOR USE OF GOVERNMENT SUPPLY SOURCES

51.100 Scope of subpart.

This subpart prescribes policies and procedures for the use of Government supply sources (see 51.102(c)) by contractors. In this subpart, the terms *contractors* and *contracts* include *subcontractors* and *subcontracts*.

51.101 Policy.

(a) If it is in the Government's interest, and if supplies or services required in the performance of a Government contract are available from Government supply sources, contracting officers may authorize contractors to use these sources in performing—

(1) Government cost-reimbursement contracts;

(2) Other types of negotiated contracts when the agency determines that a substantial dollar portion of the contractor's contracts are of a Government cost-reimbursement nature; or

(3) A contract under 41 U.S.C. chapter 85, Committee for Purchase from People Who Are Blind or Severely Disabled, if—

(i) The nonprofit agency requesting use of the supplies and services is providing a commodity or service to the Federal Government; and

(ii) The supplies or services received are directly used in making or providing a commodity or service, approved by the Committee for Purchase From People Who Are Blind or Severely Disabled, to the Federal Government (see Subpart 8.7).

(b) Contractors with fixed-price Government contracts that require protection of security classified information may acquire security equipment through GSA sources (see 41 CFR 101-26.507).

(c) Contracting officers shall authorize contractors purchasing supply items for Government use that are available from the Committee for Purchase from People Who Are Blind or Severely Disabled (see Subpart 8.7) to purchase such items from the Defense Logistics Agency (DLA), the General Services Administration (GSA), and the Department of Veterans Affairs (VA) if they are available from these agencies through their distribution facilities. Mandatory supplies that are not available from DLA/GSA/VA shall be ordered through the appropriate central nonprofit agency (see 52.208-9(c)).

[FAC 90-31, 60 FR 42648, 8/16/95, effective 10/1/95; FAC 90-37, 61 FR 2626, 1/26/96, effective 3/26/96; FAC 2001-04, 67 FR 6112, 2/8/2002, effective 2/8/2002; FAC 2005-73, 79 FR 24192, 4/29/2014, effective 5/29/2014]

51.102 Authorization to use Government supply sources.

(a) Before issuing an authorization to a contractor to use Government supply sources in accordance with 51.101(a) or (b), the contracting officer shall place in the contract file a written finding supporting issuance of the authorization. A written finding is not required when authorizing use of the Government supply sources in accordance with 51.101(c). Except for findings under 51.101(a)(3), the determination shall be based on, but not limited to, considerations of the following factors:

(1) The administrative cost of placing orders with Government supply sources and the program impact of delay factors, if any.

(2) The lower cost of items available through Government supply sources.

(3) Suitability of items available through Government supply sources.

(4) Delivery factors such as cost and time.

(5) Recommendations of the contractor.

(b) Authorizations to subcontractors shall be issued through, and with the approval of, the contractor.

(c) Upon deciding to authorize a contractor to use Government supply sources, the contracting officer shall request, in writing, as applicable—

(1) A FEDSTRIP activity address code, through the agency's central contact point for matters involving activity address codes, from the General Services Administration, FXS, Washington, DC 20406;

(2) A MILSTRIP activity address code from the appropriate Department of Defense (DOD) service point listed in Section 1 of the Introduction to the DOD Activity Address Directory;

(3) Approval for the contractor to use Department of Veterans Affairs (VA) supply sources from the Deputy Assistant Secretary for Acquisition and Materiel Management (Code 90), Office of Acquisition and Materiel Management, Department of Veterans Affairs, 810 Vermont Avenue, NW., Washington, DC 20420;

(4) Approval for the contractor to acquire helium from the Department of the Interior, Bureau of Land Management, Helium Field Operations, 801 S. Fillmore Street, Amarillo, TX 79101-3545; or

(5) Approval from the appropriate agency for the contractor to use a Government supply source other than those identified in (c)(1) through (c)(4) of this section.

(d) Each request made under paragraph (c) of this section shall contain—

(1) The complete address(es) to which the contractor's mail, freight, and billing documents are to be directed;

(2) A copy of the contracting officer's letter of authorization to the contractor;

(3) The prime contract number(s); and

(4) The effective date and duration of each contract.

(e) In each authorization to the contractor, the contracting officer—

(1) Shall cite the contract number(s) involved;

(2) Shall, when practicable, limit the period of the authorization;

(3) Shall specify, as appropriate, that—

(i) When requisitioning from GSA or DOD, the contractor shall use FEDSTRIP or MILSTRIP, as appropriate, and include the activity address code assigned by GSA or DOD;

(ii) When requisitioning from the VA, the contractor should use FEDSTRIP or MILSTRIP, as appropriate, Optional Form 347, Order for Supplies or Services (see 53.302-347), or an agency-approved form; and

(iii) When placing orders for helium with the Bureau of Land Management, the contractor shall reference the Federal contract number on the purchase order;

(4) May include any other limitations or conditions deemed necessary. For example, the contracting officer may—

(i) Authorize purchases from Government supply sources of any overhead supplies, but no production supplies;

(ii) Limit any authorization requirement to use Government sources to a specific dollar amount, thereby leaving the contractor free to make smaller purchases from other sources if so desired;

(iii) Restrict the authorization to certain facilities or to specific contracts; or

(iv) Provide specifically if vesting of title is to differ from other property acquired or otherwise furnished by the contractor for use under the contract; and

(5) Shall instruct the contractor to comply with the applicable policies and procedures prescribed in this subpart.

(f) After issuing the authorization, the authorizing agency shall be responsible for—

(1) Ensuring that contractors comply with the terms of their authorizations and that supplies and services obtained from Government supply sources are properly accounted for and properly used;

(2) Any indebtedness incurred for supplies or services and not satisfied by the contractor; and

(3) Submitting, in writing, to the appropriate Government sources, address changes of the contractor and deletions when contracts are completed or terminated.

[FAC 84-49, 54 FR 29282, 7/11/89, effective 8/10/89; FAC 90-31, 60 FR 42648, 8/16/95, effective 10/1/95; FAC 90-37, 61

FR 2626, 1/26/96, effective 3/26/96; Final rule, 62 FR 40236, 7/25/97, effective 6/30/97; FAC 2001-26, 69 FR 76358, 12/20/2004, effective 12/20/2004]

51.103 Ordering from Government supply sources.

(a) Contractors placing orders under Federal Supply Schedules shall follow the terms of the applicable schedule and authorization and include with each order—

(1) A copy of the authorization (unless a copy was previously furnished to the Federal Supply Schedule contractor); and

(2) The following statement: This order is placed under written authorization from ____ dated ____. In the event of any inconsistency between the terms and conditions of this order and those of your Federal Supply Schedule contract, the latter will govern.

(b) Contractors placing orders for Government stock shall—

(1) Comply with the requirements of the contracting officer's authorization, using FEDSTRIP or MILSTRIP procedures, as appropriate;

(2) Use only the Government activity address code obtained by the contracting officer in accordance with 51.102(e) along with the contractor's assigned access code, when ordering from GSA Customer Supply Centers.

(3) Order only those items required in the performance of their contracts.

[FAC 84-49, 54 FR 29282, 7/11/89, effective 8/10/89; FAC 90-3, 55 FR 52797, 12/21/90, effective 1/22/91; FAC 90-8, 56 FR 55372, 10/25/91, effective 11/25/91; FAC 90-41, 61 FR 41466, 8/8/96, effective 8/8/96, finalized without change, FAC 97-3, 62 FR 64912, 12/9/97, effective 2/9/98; FAC 97-1, 62 FR 44802, 8/22/97, effective 10/21/97; FAC 2001-08, 67 FR 43514, 6/27/2002, effective 7/29/2002]

51.104 Furnishing assistance to contractors.

After receiving an activity address code, the contracting officer will notify the appropriate GSA regional office or military activity, which will contact the contractor and—

(a) Provide initial copies of ordering information and instructions; and

(b) When necessary, assist the contractor in preparing and submitting, as appropriate—

(1) The initial FEDSTRIP or MILSTRIP requisitions, the Optional Form 347, or the agency-approved forms;

(2) A completed GSA Form 457, FSS Publications Mailing List Application, so that the contractor will automatically receive current copies of required publications; or

(3) A completed GSA Form 3525, Application for Customer Supply Center Services and (Address Change).

[FAC 84-49, 54 FR 29282, 7/11/89, effective 8/10/89]

51.105 Payment for shipments.

GSA, DOD, and VA will not forward bills to contractors for supplies ordered from Government stock until after the supplies have been shipped. Receipt of billing is sufficient evidence to establish contractor liability and to provide a basis for payment. Contracting officers should direct their contractors to make payment promptly upon receipt of billings.

51.106 Title.

(a) Title to all property acquired by the contractor under the contracting officer's authorization shall vest in the parties as provided in the contract, unless specifically provided for otherwise.

(b) If contracts are with educational institutions and the Government Property clause at 52.245-1, Alternate II, is used, title to property having a unit acquisition cost of less than $5,000 shall vest in the contractor as provided in the clause. Agencies may provide higher thresholds, if appropriate.

[FAC 90-16, 57 FR 60590, 12/21/92, effective 2/19/93; FAC 2005-17, 72 FR 27364, 5/15/2007, effective 6/14/2007; FAC 2005-56, 77 FR 12937, 3/2/2012, effective 4/2/2012]

51.107 Contract clause.

The contracting officer shall insert the clause at 52.251-1, Government Supply

Sources, in solicitations and contracts when the contracting officer authorizes the contractor to acquire supplies or services from a Government supply source.

[FAC 2005-17, 72 FR 27364, 5/15/2007, effective 6/14/2007; Correction, 73 FR 55450, 9/25/2008, effective 9/25/2008]

SUBPART 51.2—CONTRACTOR USE OF INTERAGENCY FLEET MANAGEMENT SYSTEM (IFMS) VEHICLES

51.200 Scope of subpart.

This subpart prescribes policies and procedures for the use by contractors of interagency fleet management system (IFMS) vehicles and related services. In this subpart, the terms *contractors* and *contracts* include *subcontractors* and *subcontracts* (see 45.102).

[FAC 84-49, 54 FR 29282, 7/11/89, effective 8/10/89; FAC 90-3, 55 FR 52797, 12/21/90, effective 1/22/91; FAC 2005-17, 72 FR 27364, 5/15/2007, effective 6/14/2007]

51.201 Policy.

(a) If it is in the Government's interest, the contracting officer may authorize cost-reimbursement contractors to obtain, for official purposes only, interagency fleet management system (IFMS) vehicles and related services, including—

(1) Fuel and lubricants,

(2) Vehicle inspection, maintenance, and repair,

(3) Vehicle storage, and

(4) Commercially rented vehicles for short-term use.

(b) Complete rebuilding of major components of contractor-owned or -leased equipment requires the approval of the contracting officer in each instance.

(c) Government contractors shall not be authorized to obtain interagency fleet management system (IFMS) vehicles and related services for use in performance of any contract other than a cost-reimbursement contract, except as otherwise specifically approved by the Administrator of the General Services Administration at the request of the agency involved.

[FAC 84-49, 54 FR 29282, 7/11/89, effective 8/10/89]

51.202 Authorization.

(a) The contracting officer may authorize a cost-reimbursement contractor to obtain interagency fleet management system (IFMS) vehicles and related services, if the contracting officer has—

(1) Determined that the authorization will accomplish the agency's contractual objectives and effect demonstrable economies;

(2) Received evidence that the contractor has obtained motor vehicle liability insurance covering bodily injury and property damage, with limits of liability as required or approved by the agency, protecting the contractor and the Government against third-party claims arising from the ownership, maintenance, or use of an interagency fleet management system (IFMS) vehicle;

(3) Arranged for periodic checks to ensure that authorized contractors are using vehicles and related services exclusively under cost-reimbursement contracts;

(4) Ensured that contractors shall establish and enforce suitable penalties for their employees who use or authorize the use of Government vehicles for other than performance of Government contracts (see 41 CFR 101-38.301-1);

(5) Received a written statement that the contractor will assume, without the right of reimbursement from the Government, the cost or expense of any use of interagency fleet management system (IFMS) vehicles and services not related to the performance of the contract; and

(6) Considered any recommendations of the contractor.

(b) The authorization shall—

(1) Be in writing;

(2) Cite the contract number;

(3) Specify any limitations on the authority, including its duration, and any other pertinent information; and

(4) Instruct the contractor to comply with the applicable policies and procedures provided in this subpart.

(c) Authorizations to subcontractors shall be issued through, and with the approval of, the contractor.

(d) Contracting officers authorizing contractor use of interagency fleet management system (IFMS) vehicles and related services subject their agencies to the responsibilities and liabilities provided in 41 CFR 101-39.4 regarding accidents and claims.

[FAC 84-49, 54 FR 29283, 7/11/89, effective 8/10/89]

51.203 Means of obtaining service.

(a) Authorized contractors shall submit requests for interagency fleet management system (IFMS) vehicles and related services in writing to the appropriate GSA regional Federal Supply Service Bureau, Attention: Regional fleet manager, except that requests for more than five vehicles shall be submitted to General Services Administration, FBF, Washington, DC 20406, and not to the regions. Each request shall include the following:

(1) Two copies of the agency authorization to obtain vehicles and related services from GSA.

(2) The number of vehicles and related services required and period of use.

(3) A list of the contractor's employees who are authorized to request vehicles and related services.

(4) A listing of the make, model, and serial numbers of contractor-owned or -leased equipment authorized to be serviced.

(5) Billing instructions and address.

(b) Contractors requesting unusual quantities of vehicles should do so as far in advance as possible to facilitate availability.

[FAC 84-49, 54 FR 29283, 7/11/89, effective 8/10/89]

51.204 Use of interagency fleet management system (IFMS) vehicles and related services.

Contractors authorized to use interagency fleet management system (IFMS) vehicles and related services shall comply with the requirements of 41 CFR 101-39 and 41 CFR 101-38.301-1 and the operator's packet furnished with each vehicle. See 41 CFR 101-6.4 for additional guidance for home-to-work use of Government vehicles.

[FAC 90-3, 55 FR 52782, 12/21/90, effective 1/22/91]

51.205 Contract clause.

The contracting officer shall insert the clause at 52.251-2, Interagency Fleet Management System (IFMS) Vehicles and Related Services, in solicitations and contracts when a cost-reimbursement contract is contemplated and the contracting officer may authorize the contractor to use interagency fleet management system (IFMS) vehicles and related services.

[FAC 84-49, 54 FR 29283, 7/11/89, effective 8/10/89]

Federal Acquisition Regulation
Part 52
Solicitation Provisions and Contract Clauses

Table of Contents

SUBCHAPTER H—CLAUSES AND FORMS

Part 52—Solicitation Provisions and Contract Clauses 1367

PART 52—SOLICITATION PROVISIONS AND CONTRACT CLAUSES

Table of Contents

Scope of part . . . 52.000

Subpart 52.1—Instructions for Using Provisions and Clauses

Scope of subpart . . . 52.100
Using Part 52 . . . 52.101
Incorporating provisions and clauses . . . 52.102
Identification of provisions and clauses . . . 52.103
Procedures for modifying and completing provisions and clauses . . . 52.104
Procedures for using alternates . . . 52.105
[Reserved] . . . 52.106
Provisions and clauses prescribed in Subpart 52.1 . . . 52.107

Subpart 52.2—Texts of Provisions and Clauses

Scope of subpart . . . 52.200
[Reserved] . . . 52.201
Definitions . . . 52.202-1
[Reserved] . . . 52.203-1
Certificate of Independent Price Determination . . . 52.203-2
Gratuities . . . 52.203-3
[Reserved] . . . 52.203-4
Covenant Against Contingent Fees . . . 52.203-5
Restrictions on Subcontractor Sales to the Government . . . 52.203-6
Anti-Kickback Procedures . . . 52.203-7
Cancellation, Rescission, and Recovery of Funds for Illegal or Improper Activity . . . 52.203-8
[Reserved] . . . 52.203-9
Price or Fee Adjustment for Illegal or Improper Activity . . . 52.203-10
Certification and Disclosure Regarding Payments to Influence Certain Federal Transactions . . . 52.203-11
Limitation on Payments to Influence Certain Federal Transactions . . . 52.203-12
Contractor Code of Business Ethics and Conduct . . . 52.203-13
Display of Hotline Poster(s) . . . 52.203-14
Whistleblower Protections Under the American Recovery and Reinvestment Act of 2009 . . . 52.203-15
Preventing Personal Conflicts of Interest . . . 52.203-16
Contractor Employee Whistleblower Rights and Requirement to Inform Employees of Whistleblower Rights . . . 52.203-17
Prohibition on Contracting with Entities that Require Certain Internal Confidentiality Agreements or Statements—Representation . . . 52.203-18
Prohibition on Requiring Certain Internal Confidentiality Agreements or Statements . . . 52.203-19
Approval of Contract . . . 52.204-1
Security Requirements . . . 52.204-2
Taxpayer Identification . . . 52.204-3
Printed or Copied Double-Sided on Postconsumer Fiber Content Paper . . . 52.204-4
Women-Owned Business other than Small Business . . . 52.204-5
Unique Entity Identifier . . . 52.204-6
System for Award Management . . . 52.204-7
Annual Representations and Certifications . . . 52.204-8
Personal Identity Verification of Contractor Personnel . . . 52.204-9
Reporting Executive Compensation and First-Tier Subcontract Awards . . . 52.204-10
[Removed and Reserved] . . . 52.204-11
Unique Entity Identifier Maintenance . . . 52.204-12
System for Award Management Maintenance . . . 52.204-13

Service Contract Reporting Requirements 52.204-14
Service Contract Reporting Requirements for Indefinite-Delivery Contracts 52.204-15
Commercial and Government Entity Code Reporting 52.204-16
Ownership or Control of Offeror 52.204-17
Commercial and Government Entity Code Maintenance 52.204-18
Incorporation by Reference of Representations and Certifications 52.204-19
Predecessor of Offeror 52.204-20
Basic Safeguarding of Covered Contractor Information Systems 52.204-21
Alternative Line Item Proposal 52.204-22
Prohibition on Contracting for Hardware, Software, and Services Developed or Provided by Kaspersky Lab and Other Covered Entities 52.204-23
Representation Regarding Certain Telecommunications and Video Surveillance Services or Equipment 52.204-24
Prohibition on Contracting for Certain Telecommunications and Video Surveillance Services or Equipment 52.204-25
Covered Telecommunications Equipment or Services —Representation 52.204-26
[Reserved] 52.205
[Reserved] 52.206
Notice of Cost Comparison (Sealed Bid) 52.207-1
Notice of Cost Comparison (Negotiated) 52.207-2
Right of First Refusal of Employment 52.207-3
Economic Purchase Quantity—Supplies 52.207-4
Option to Purchase Equipment 52.207-5
Solicitation of Offers from Small Business Concerns and Small Business Teaming Arrangements or Joint Ventures (Multiple-Award Contracts) 52.207-6
[Reserved] 52.208-1
[Reserved] 52.208-2
[Reserved] 52.208-3
Vehicle Lease Payments 52.208-4
Condition of Leased Vehicles 52.208-5
Marking of Leased Vehicles 52.208-6
Tagging of Leased Vehicles 52.208-7
Required Sources for Helium and Helium Usage Data 52.208-8
Contractor Use of Mandatory Sources of Supply or Services 52.208-9
Qualification Requirements 52.209-1
Prohibition on Contracting with Inverted Domestic Corporations—Representation 52.209-2
First Article Approval—Contractor Testing 52.209-3
First Article Approval—Government Testing 52.209-4
Certification Regarding Responsibility Matters 52.209-5
Protecting the Government's Interest When Subcontracting with Contractors Debarred, Suspended, or Proposed for Debarment 52.209-6
Information Regarding Responsibility Matters 52.209-7
[Removed and Reserved] 52.209-8
Updates of Publicly Available Information Regarding Responsibility Matters 52.209-9
Prohibition on Contracting With Inverted Domestic Corporations 52.209-10
Representation by Corporations Regarding Delinquent Tax Liability or a Felony Conviction under any Federal Law 52.209-11
Certification Regarding Tax Matters 52.209-12
Violation of Arms Control Treaties or Agreements—Certification 52.209-13
[Reserved] 52.210
Market Research 52.210-1

Availability of Specifications Listed in the GSA Index of Federal Specifications, Standards and Commercial Item Descriptions, FPMR Part 101-29 .... 52.211-1
Availability of Specifications, Standards, and Data Item Descriptions Listed in the Acquisition Streamlining and Standardization Information System (ASSIST) 52.211-2
Availability of Specifications Not Listed in the GSA Index of Federal Specifications, Standards and Commercial Item Descriptions 52.211-3
Availability for Examination of Specifications Not Listed in the GSA Index of Federal Specifications, Standards and Commercial Item Descriptions 52.211-4
Material Requirements 52.211-5
Brand Name or Equal 52.211-6
Alternatives to Government-unique Standards 52.211-7
Time of Delivery 52.211-8
Desired and Required Time of Delivery 52.211-9
Commencement, Prosecution, and Completion of Work 52.211-10
Liquidated Damages—Supplies, Services, or Research and Development 52.211-11
Liquidated Damages—Construction 52.211-12
Time Extensions 52.211-13
Notice of Priority Rating for National Defense, Emergency Preparedness, and Energy Program Use 52.211-14
Defense Priority and Allocation Requirements 52.211-15
Variation in Quantity 52.211-16
Delivery of Excess Quantities 52.211-17
Variation in Estimated Quantity 52.211-18
Instructions to Offerors—Commercial Items 52.212-1
Evaluation—Commercial Items 52.212-2
Offeror Representations and Certifications—Commercial Items 52.212-3
Contract Terms and Conditions—Commercial Items 52.212-4
Contract Terms and Conditions Required to Implement Statutes or Executive Orders—Commercial Items 52.212-5
Fast Payment Procedure 52.213-1
Invoices 52.213-2
Notice to Supplier 52.213-3
Terms and Conditions—Simplified Acquisitions (Other Than Commercial Items) 52.213-4
[Reserved] 52.214-1
[Reserved] 52.214-2
Amendments to Invitations for Bids 52.214-3
False Statements in Bids 52.214-4
Submission of Bids 52.214-5
Explanation to Prospective Bidders 52.214-6
Late Submissions, Modifications, and Withdrawals of Bids 52.214-7
[Removed and Reserved] 52.214-8
[Removed and Reserved] 52.214-9
Contract Award—Sealed Bidding 52.214-10
[Reserved] 52.214-11
Preparation of Bids 52.214-12
[Removed and Reserved] 52.214-13
Place of Performance—Sealed Bidding 52.214-14
Period for Acceptance of Bids 52.214-15
Minimum Bid Acceptance Period 52.214-16
[Reserved] 52.214-17
Preparation of Bids—Construction 52.214-18

Contract Award—Sealed Bidding—Construction . . . 52.214-19
Bid Samples . . . 52.214-20
Descriptive Literature . . . 52.214-21
Evaluation of Bids for Multiple Awards . . . 52.214-22
Late Submissions, Modifications, and Withdrawals of Technical Proposals under Two-Step Sealed Bidding . . . 52.214-23
Multiple Technical Proposals . . . 52.214-24
Step Two of Two-Step Sealed Bidding . . . 52.214-25
Audit and Records—Sealed Bidding . . . 52.214-26
Price Reduction for Defective Certified Cost or Pricing Data—Modifications—Sealed Bidding . . . 52.214-27
Subcontractor Certified Cost or Pricing Data—Modifications—Sealed Bidding . . . 52.214-28
Order of Precedence—Sealed Bidding . . . 52.214-29
[Reserved] . . . 52.214-30
Facsimile Bids . . . 52.214-31
[Reserved] . . . 52.214-32
[Reserved] . . . 52.214-33
Submission of Offers in the English Language . . . 52.214-34
Submission of Offers in U.S. Currency . . . 52.214-35
Instructions to Offerors—Competitive Acquisition . . . 52.215-1
Audit and Records—Negotiation . . . 52.215-2
Request for Information or Solicitation for Planning Purposes . . . 52.215-3
[Reserved] . . . 52.215-4
Facsimile Proposals . . . 52.215-5
Place of Performance . . . 52.215-6
[Reserved] . . . 52.215-7
Order of Precedence—Uniform Contract Format . . . 52.215-8
Changes or Additions to Make-or-Buy Program . . . 52.215-9
Price Reduction for Defective Certified Cost or Pricing Data . . . 52.215-10
Price Reduction for Defective Certified Cost or Pricing Data—Modifications . . . 52.215-11
Subcontractor Certified Cost or Pricing Data . . . 52.215-12
Subcontractor Certified Cost or Pricing Data—Modifications . . . 52.215-13
Integrity of Unit Prices . . . 52.215-14
Pension Adjustments and Asset Reversions . . . 52.215-15
Facilities Capital Cost of Money . . . 52.215-16
Waiver of Facilities Capital Cost of Money . . . 52.215-17
Reversion or Adjustment of Plans for Postretirement Benefits (PRB) Other Than Pensions . . . 52.215-18
Notification of Ownership Changes . . . 52.215-19
Requirement for Certified Cost or Pricing Data and Data Other Than Cost or Pricing Data . . . 52.215-20
Requirements for Certified Cost or Pricing Data and Data Other Than Cost or Pricing Data—Modifications . . . 52.215-21
Limitations on Pass-Through Charges—Identification of Subcontract Effort . . . 52.215-22
Limitations on Pass-Through Charges . . . 52.215-23
Type of Contract . . . 52.216-1
Economic Price Adjustment—Standard Supplies . . . 52.216-2
Economic Price Adjustment—Semistandard Supplies . . . 52.216-3
Economic Price Adjustment—Labor and Material . . . 52.216-4
Price Redetermination—Prospective . . . 52.216-5
Price Redetermination—Retroactive . . . 52.216-6
Allowable Cost and Payment . . . 52.216-7
Fixed Fee . . . 52.216-8

Fixed Fee—Construction 52.216-9
Incentive Fee 52.216-10
Cost Contract—No Fee 52.216-11
Cost-Sharing Contract—No Fee 52.216-12
[Removed and Reserved] 52.216-13
[Removed and Reserved] 52.216-14
Predetermined Indirect Cost Rates 52.216-15
Incentive Price Revision—Firm Target 52.216-16
Incentive Price Revision—Successive Targets 52.216-17
Ordering 52.216-18
Order Limitations 52.216-19
Definite Quantity 52.216-20
Requirements 52.216-21
Indefinite Quantity 52.216-22
Execution and Commencement of Work 52.216-23
Limitation of Government Liability 52.216-24
Contract Definitization 52.216-25
Payments of Allowable Costs Before Definitization 52.216-26
Single or Multiple Awards 52.216-27
Multiple Awards for Advisory and Assistance Services 52.216-28
Time-and-Materials/Labor-Hour Proposal Requirements—Non-Commercial Item Acquisition with Adequate Price Competition 52.216-29
Time-and-Materials/Labor-Hour Proposal Requirements—Non-Commercial Item Acquisition without Adequate Price Competition 52.216-30
Time-and-Materials/Labor-Hour Proposal Requirements—Commercial Item Acquisition 52.216-31
Task-Order and Delivery-Order Ombudsman 52.216-32
[Reserved] 52.217-1
Cancellation Under Multiyear Contracts 52.217-2
Evaluation Exclusive of Options 52.217-3
Evaluation of Options Exercised at Time of Contract Award 52.217-4
Evaluation of Options 52.217-5
Option for Increased Quantity 52.217-6
Option for Increased Quantity—Separately Priced Line Item 52.217-7
Option to Extend Services 52.217-8
Option to Extend the Term of the Contract 52.217-9
[Reserved] 52.218
Small Business Program Representations 52.219-1
Equal Low Bids 52.219-2
Notice of HUBZone Set-Aside or Sole Source Award 52.219-3
Notice of Price Evaluation Preference for HUBZone Small Business Concerns 52.219-4
[Removed and Reserved] 52.219-5
Notice of Total Small Business Set-Aside 52.219-6
Notice of Partial Small Business Set-Aside 52.219-7
Utilization of Small Business Concerns 52.219-8
Small Business Subcontracting Plan 52.219-9
Incentive Subcontracting Program 52.219-10
Special 8(a) Contract Conditions 52.219-11
Special 8(a) Subcontract Conditions 52.219-12
Notice of Set-Aside of Orders 52.219-13
Limitations on Subcontracting 52.219-14
[Reserved] 52.219-15
Liquidated Damages—Subcontracting Plan 52.219-16
Section 8(a) Award 52.219-17

Notification of Competition Limited to Eligible 8(a) Participants 52.219-18
[Removed and Reserved] 52.219-19
[Removed and Reserved] 52.219-20
[Removed and Reserved] 52.219-21
[Removed and Reserved] 52.219-22
[Removed and Reserved] 52.219-23
[Removed and Reserved] 52.219-24
[Removed and Reserved] 52.219-25
[Removed and Reserved] 52.219-26
Notice of Service-Disabled Veteran-Owned Small Business Set-Aside. 52.219-27
Post-Award Small Business Program Rerepresentation 52.219-28
Notice of Set-Aside for, or Sole Source Award to, Economically Disadvantaged Women-Owned Small Business Concerns 52.219-29
Notice of Set-Aside for, or Sole Source Award to, Women-Owned Small Business Concerns Eligible Under the Women-Owned Small Business Program 52.219-30
[Reserved] 52.220
[Reserved] 52.221
Notice to the Government of Labor Disputes 52.222-1
Payment for Overtime Premiums 52.222-2
Convict Labor 52.222-3
Contract Work Hours and Safety Standards—Overtime Compensation 52.222-4
Construction Wage Rate Requirements—Secondary Site of the Work 52.222-5
Construction Wage Rate Requirements 52.222-6
Withholding of Funds 52.222-7
Payrolls and Basic Records 52.222-8
Apprentices and Trainees 52.222-9
Compliance with Copeland Act Requirements 52.222-10
Subcontracts (Labor Standards) 52.222-11
Contract Termination—Debarment 52.222-12
Compliance with Construction Wage Rate Requirements and Related Regulations 52.222-13
Disputes Concerning Labor Standards 52.222-14
Certification of Eligibility 52.222-15
Approval of Wage Rates 52.222-16
Nondisplacement of Qualified Workers 52.222-17
Certification Regarding Knowledge of Child Labor for Listed End Products 52.222-18
Child Labor—Cooperation with Authorities and Remedies 52.222-19
Contracts for Materials, Supplies, Articles, and Equipment Exceeding $15,000 . . . . 52.222-20
Prohibition of Segregated Facilities 52.222-21
Previous Contracts and Compliance Reports 52.222-22
Notice of Requirement for Affirmative Action to Ensure Equal Employment Opportunity for Construction 52.222-23
Preaward On-Site Equal Opportunity Compliance Evaluation 52.222-24
Affirmative Action Compliance 52.222-25
Equal Opportunity 52.222-26
Affirmative Action Compliance Requirements for Construction 52.222-27
[Reserved] 52.222-28
Notification of Visa Denial 52.222-29
Construction Wage Rate Requirements—Price Adjustment (None or Separately Specified Method) 52.222-30

Construction Wage Rate Requirements—Price Adjustment (Percentage Method) . . . 52.222-31
Construction Wage Rate Requirements—Price Adjustment (Actual Method) . . . 52.222-32
Notice of Requirement for Project Labor Agreement . . . 52.222-33
Project Labor Agreement . . . 52.222-34
Equal Opportunity for Veterans . . . 52.222-35
Equal Opportunity for Workers With Disabilities . . . 52.222-36
Employment Reports on Veterans . . . 52.222-37
Compliance With Veterans' Employment Reporting Requirements . . . 52.222-38
[Removed and Reserved] . . . 52.222-39
Notification of Employee Rights Under the National Labor Relations Act . . . 52.222-40
Service Contract Labor Standards . . . 52.222-41
Statement of Equivalent Rates for Federal Hires . . . 52.222-42
Fair Labor Standards Act and Service Contract Act and Service Contract Labor Standards—Price Adjustment (Multiple Year and Option Contracts) . . . 52.222-43
Fair Labor Standards Act and Service Contract Labor Standards—Price Adjustment . . . 52.222-44
[Reserved] . . . 52.222-45
Evaluation of Compensation for Professional Employees . . . 52.222-46
[Removed and Reserved] . . . 52.222-47
Exemption from Application of the Service Contract Labor Standards to Contracts for Maintenance, Calibration, or Repair of Certain Equipment—Certification . . . 52.222-48
Service Contract Labor Standards—Place of Performance Unknown . . . 52.222-49
Combating Trafficking in Persons . . . 52.222-50
Exemption from Application of the Service Contract Labor Standards to Contracts for Maintenance, Calibration, or Repair of Certain Equipment—Requirements . . . 52.222-51
Exemption from Application of the Service Contract Labor Standards to Contracts for Certain Services—Certification . . . 52.222-52
Exemption from Application of the Service Contract Labor Standards to Contracts for Certain Services—Requirements . . . 52.222-53
Employment Eligibility Verification . . . 52.222-54
Minimum Wages Under Executive Order 13658 . . . 52.222-55
Certification Regarding Trafficking in Persons Compliance Plan . . . 52.222-56
[Removed and Reserved] . . . 52.222-57
[Removed and Reserved] . . . 52.222-58
[Removed and Reserved] . . . 52.222-59
[Removed and Reserved] . . . 52.222-60
[Removed and Reserved] . . . 52.222-61
Paid Sick Leave Under Executive Order 13706 . . . 52.222-62
Biobased Product Certification . . . 52.223-1
Affirmative Procurement of Biobased Products Under Service and Construction Contracts . . . 52.223-2
Hazardous Material Identification and Material Safety Data . . . 52.223-3
Recovered Material Certification . . . 52.223-4
Pollution Prevention and Right-to-Know Information . . . 52.223-5
Drug-Free Workplace . . . 52.223-6
Notice of Radioactive Materials . . . 52.223-7
[Reserved] . . . 52.223-8
Estimate of Percentage of Recovered Material Content for EPA-Designated Items . . . 52.223-9
Waste Reduction Program . . . 52.223-10

Ozone-Depleting Substances and High Global Warming Potential Hydrofluorocarbons . . . 52.223-11
Maintenance, Service, Repair, or Disposal of Refrigeration Equipment and Air Conditioners . . . 52.223-12
Acquisition of EPEAT®-Registered Imaging Equipment. . . . 52.223-13
Acquisition of EPEAT®-Registered Televisions. . . . 52.223-14
Energy Efficiency in Energy-Consuming Products . . . 52.223-15
Acquisition of EPEAT®-Registered Personal Computer Products. . . . 52.223-16
Affirmative Procurement of EPA-Designated Items in Service and Construction Contracts . . . 52.223-17
Encouraging Contractor Policies to Ban Text Messaging While Driving . . 52.223-18
Compliance with Environmental Management Systems . . . 52.223-19
Aerosols . . . 52.223-20
Foams . . . 52.223-21
Public Disclosure of Greenhouse Gas Emissions and Reduction Goals—Representation . . . 52.223-22
Privacy Act Notification . . . 52.224-1
Privacy Act . . . 52.224-2
Privacy Training . . . 52.224-3
Buy American—Supplies . . . 52.225-1
Buy American—Certificate . . . 52.225-2
Buy American—Free Trade Agreements—Israeli Trade Act . . . 52.225-3
Buy American—Free Trade Agreements—Israeli Trade Act Certificate . . . 52.225-4
Trade Agreements . . . 52.225-5
Trade Agreements Certificate . . . 52.225-6
Waiver of Buy American Statute for Civil Aircraft and Related Articles . . . 52.225-7
Duty-Free Entry . . . 52.225-8
Buy American—Construction Materials . . . 52.225-9
Notice of Buy American Requirement—Construction Materials . . . 52.225-10
Buy American Act—Construction Materials under Trade Agreements . . . 52.225-11
Notice of Buy American Requirement—Construction Materials under Trade Agreements . . . 52.225-12
Restrictions on Certain Foreign Purchases . . . 52.225-13
Inconsistency between English Version and Translation of Contract . . . 52.225-14
[Reserved] . . . 52.225-15
[Reserved] . . . 52.225-16
Evaluation of Foreign Currency Offers . . . 52.225-17
Place of Manufacture . . . 52.225-18
Contractor Personnel in a Designated Operational Area or Supporting a Diplomatic or Consular Mission Outside the United States . . . 52.225-19
Prohibition on Conducting Restricted Business Operations in Sudan—Certification . . . 52.225-20
Required Use of American Iron, Steel, and Manufactured Goods—Buy American Statute—Construction Materials . . . 52.225-21
Notice of Required Use of American Iron, Steel, and Manufactured Goods—Buy American Statute—Construction Materials . . . 52.225-22
Required Use of American Iron, Steel, and Manufactured Goods—Buy American Statute—Construction Materials Under Trade Agreements . . . 52.225-23
Notice of Required Use of American Iron, Steel, and Manufactured Goods—Buy American Statute—Construction Materials under Trade Agreements . . . 52.225-24
Prohibition on Contracting with Entities Engaging in Certain Activities or Transactions Relating to Iran—Representation and Certifications . . . 52.225-25

Contractors Performing Private Security Functions Outside the United States 52.225-26
Utilization of Indian Organizations and Indian-Owned Economic Enterprises 52.226-1
Historically Black College or University and Minority Institution Representation 52.226-2
Disaster or Emergency Area Representation 52.226-3
Notice of Disaster or Emergency Area Set-Aside 52.226-4
Restrictions on Subcontracting Outside Disaster or Emergency Area 52.226-5
Promoting Excess Food Donation to Nonprofit Organizations 52.226-6
Authorization and Consent 52.227-1
Notice and Assistance Regarding Patent and Copyright Infringement 52.227-2
Patent Indemnity 52.227-3
Patent Indemnity—Construction Contracts 52.227-4
Waiver of Indemnity 52.227-5
Royalty Information 52.227-6
Patents—Notice of Government Licensee 52.227-7
[Reserved] 52.227-8
Refund of Royalties 52.227-9
Filing of Patent Applications—Classified Subject Matter 52.227-10
Patent Rights—Ownership by the Contractor 52.227-11
[Reserved] 52.227-12
Patent Rights—Ownership by the Government 52.227-13
Rights in Data—General 52.227-14
Representation of Limited Rights Data and Restricted Computer Software 52.227-15
Additional Data Requirements 52.227-16
Rights in Data—Special Works 52.227-17
Rights in Data—Existing Works 52.227-18
Commercial Computer Software License 52.227-19
Rights in Data—SBIR Program 52.227-20
Technical Data Declaration, Revision, and Withholding of Payment—Major Systems 52.227-21
Major System—Minimum Rights 52.227-22
Rights to Proposal Data (Technical) 52.227-23
Bid Guarantee 52.228-1
Additional Bond Security 52.228-2
Workers' Compensation Insurance (Defense Base Act) 52.228-3
Workers' Compensation and War-Hazard Insurance Overseas 52.228-4
Insurance—Work on a Government Installation 52.228-5
[Reserved] 52.228-6
Insurance—Liability to Third Persons 52.228-7
Liability and Insurance—Leased Motor Vehicles 52.228-8
Cargo Insurance 52.228-9
Vehicular and General Public Liability Insurance 52.228-10
Pledges of Assets 52.228-11
Prospective Subcontractor Requests for Bonds 52.228-12
Alternative Payment Protections 52.228-13
Irrevocable Letter of Credit 52.228-14
Performance and Payment Bonds—Construction 52.228-15
Performance and Payment Bonds—Other Than Construction 52.228-16
State and Local Taxes 52.229-1
North Carolina State and Local Sales and Use Tax 52.229-2
Federal, State, and Local Taxes 52.229-3
Federal, State, and Local Taxes (State and Local Adjustments) 52.229-4
[Reserved] 52.229-5

Taxes—Foreign Fixed-Price Contracts 52.229-6
Taxes—Fixed-Price Contracts with Foreign Governments 52.229-7
Taxes—Foreign Cost-Reimbursement Contracts 52.229-8
Taxes—Cost-Reimbursement Contracts with Foreign Governments 52.229-9
State of New Mexico Gross Receipts and Compensating Tax 52.229-10
Cost Accounting Standards Notices and Certification 52.230-1
Cost Accounting Standards 52.230-2
Disclosure and Consistency of Cost Accounting Practices 52.230-3
Disclosure and Consistency of Cost Accounting Practices—Foreign Concerns 52.230-4
Cost Accounting Standards—Educational Institution 52.230-5
Administration of Cost Accounting Standards 52.230-6
Proposal Disclosure—Cost Accounting Practice Changes 52.230-7
[Reserved] 52.231
Payments 52.232-1
Payments under Fixed-Price Research and Development Contracts 52.232-2
Payments under Personal Services Contracts 52.232-3
Payments under Transportation Contracts and Transportation-Related Services Contracts 52.232-4
Payments under Fixed-Price Construction Contracts 52.232-5
Payment under Communication Service Contracts with Common Carriers 52.232-6
Payments under Time-and-Materials and Labor-Hour Contracts 52.232-7
Discounts for Prompt Payment 52.232-8
Limitation on Withholding of Payments 52.232-9
Payments under Fixed-Price Architect-Engineer Contracts 52.232-10
Extras 52.232-11
Advance Payments 52.232-12
Notice of Progress Payments 52.232-13
Notice of Availability of Progress Payments Exclusively for Small Business Concerns 52.232-14
Progress Payments Not Included 52.232-15
Progress Payments 52.232-16
Interest 52.232-17
Availability of Funds 52.232-18
Availability of Funds for the Next Fiscal Year 52.232-19
Limitation of Cost 52.232-20
[Removed and Reserved] 52.232-21
Limitation of Funds 52.232-22
Assignment of Claims 52.232-23
Prohibition of Assignment of Claims 52.232-24
Prompt payment 52.232-25
Prompt Payment for Fixed-Price Architect-Engineer Contracts 52.232-26
Prompt Payment for Construction Contracts 52.232-27
Invitation to Propose Performance-Based Payments 52.232-28
Terms for Financing of Purchases of Commercial Items 52.232-29
Installment Payments for Commercial Items 52.232-30
Invitation to Propose Financing Terms 52.232-31
Performance-Based Payments 52.232-32
Payment by Electronic Funds Transfer—System for Award Management . 52.232-33
Payment by Electronic Funds Transfer—Other than System for Award Management 52.232-34
Designation of Office for Government Receipt of Electronic Funds Transfer Information 52.232-35
Payment by Third Party 52.232-36
Multiple Payment Arrangements 52.232-37

Submission of Electronic Funds Transfer Information with Offer 52.232-38
Unenforceability of Unauthorized Obligations 52.232-39
Providing Accelerated Payments to Small Business Subcontractors 52.232-40
Disputes 52.233-1
Service of Protest 52.233-2
Protest After Award 52.233-3
Applicable Law for Breach of Contract Claim 52.233-4
Industrial Resources Developed Under Title III,
Defense Production Act. 52.234-1
Notice of Earned Value Management System—Preaward Integrated
Baseline Review 52.234-2
Notice of Earned Value Management System—Postward Integrated
Baseline Review 52.234-3
Earned Value Management System 52.234-4
[Reserved] 52.235
Performance of Work by the Contractor 52.236-1
Differing Site Conditions 52.236-2
Site Investigation and Conditions Affecting the Work 52.236-3
Physical Data 52.236-4
Material and Workmanship 52.236-5
Superintendence by the Contractor 52.236-6
Permits and Responsibilities 52.236-7
Other Contracts 52.236-8
Protection of Existing Vegetation, Structures, Equipment, Utilities, and
Improvements 52.236-9
Operations and Storage Areas 52.236-10
Use and Possession Prior to Completion 52.236-11
Cleaning Up 52.236-12
Accident Prevention 52.236-13
Availability and Use of Utility Services 52.236-14
Schedules for Construction Contracts 52.236-15
Quantity Surveys 52.236-16
Layout of Work 52.236-17
Work Oversight in Cost-Reimbursement Construction Contracts 52.236-18
Organization and Direction of the Work 52.236-19
[Reserved] 52.236-20
Specifications and Drawings for Construction 52.236-21
Design within Funding Limitations 52.236-22
Responsibility of the Architect-Engineer Contractor 52.236-23
Work Oversight in Architect-Engineer Contracts 52.236-24
Requirements for Registration of Designers 52.236-25
Preconstruction Conference 52.236-26
Site Visit (Construction) 52.236-27
Preparation of Proposals—Construction 52.236-28
Site Visit 52.237-1
Protection of Government Buildings, Equipment, and Vegetation 52.237-2
Continuity of Services 52.237-3
Payment by Government to Contractor 52.237-4
Payment by Contractor to Government 52.237-5
Incremental Payment by Contractor to Government 52.237-6
Indemnification and Medical Liability Insurance 52.237-7
Restriction on Severance Payments to Foreign Nationals 52.237-8
Waiver of Limitation on Severance Payments to Foreign Nationals 52.237-9
Identification of Uncompensated Overtime 52.237-10
[Removed] 52.237-11
[Reserved] 52.238

Privacy or Security Safeguards 52.239-1
[Reserved] 52.240
Electric Service Territory Compliance Representation 52.241-1
Order of Precedence—Utilities 52.241-2
Scope and Duration of Contract 52.241-3
Change in Class of Service 52.241-4
Contractor's Facilities 52.241-5
Service Provisions 52.241-6
Change in Rates or Terms and Conditions of Service for Regulated Services 52.241-7
Change in Rates or Terms and Conditions of Service for Unregulated Services 52.241-8
Connection Charge 52.241-9
Termination Liability 52.241-10
Multiple Service Locations 52.241-11
Nonrefundable, Nonrecurring Service Charge 52.241-12
Capital Credits 52.241-13
Notice of Intent to Disallow Costs 52.242-1
Production Progress Reports 52.242-2
Penalties for Unallowable Costs 52.242-3
Certification of Final Indirect Costs 52.242-4
Payments to Small Business Subcontractors 52.242-5
[Reserved] 52.242-6
[Reserved] 52.242-7
[Reserved] 52.242-8
[Reserved] 52.242-9
[Removed and Reserved] 52.242-10
[Removed and Reserved] 52.242-11
[Removed and Reserved] 52.242-12
Bankruptcy 52.242-13
Suspension of Work 52.242-14
Stop-Work Order 52.242-15
[Removed and Reserved] 52.242-16
Government Delay of Work 52.242-17
Changes—Fixed-Price 52.243-1
Changes—Cost-Reimbursement 52.243-2
Changes—Time-and-Materials or Labor-Hours 52.243-3
Changes 52.243-4
Changes and Changed Conditions 52.243-5
Change Order Accounting 52.243-6
Notification of Changes 52.243-7
[Reserved] 52.244-1
Subcontracts 52.244-2
[Reserved] 52.244-3
Subcontractors and Outside Associates and Consultants (Architect-Engineer Services) 52.244-4
Competition in Subcontracting 52.244-5
Subcontracts for Commercial Items 52.244-6
Government Property 52.245-1
Government Property Installation Operation Services 52.245-2
[Removed and Reserved] 52.245-3
[Removed and Reserved] 52.245-4
[Removed and Reserved] 52.245-5
[Removed and Reserved] 52.245-6
[Removed and Reserved] 52.245-7
[Removed and Reserved] 52.245-8

Use and Charges 52.245-9
[Removed] 52.245-10
[Removed] 52.245-11
[Removed] 52.245-12
[Removed] 52.245-13
[Removed] 52.245-14
[Removed] 52.245-15
[Removed] 52.245-16
[Removed] 52.245-17
[Removed] 52.245-18
[Removed] 52.245-19
Contractor Inspection Requirements 52.246-1
Inspection of Supplies—Fixed-Price 52.246-2
Inspection of Supplies—Cost-Reimbursement 52.246-3
Inspection of Services—Fixed-Price 52.246-4
Inspection of Services—Cost-Reimbursement 52.246-5
Inspection—Time-and-Material and Labor-Hour 52.246-6
Inspection of Research and Development—Fixed-Price 52.246-7
Inspection of Research and Development—Cost-Reimbursement 52.246-8
Inspection of Research and Development (Short Form) 52.246-9
[Removed and Reserved] 52.246-10
Higher-Level Contract Quality Requirement 52.246-11
Inspection of Construction 52.246-12
Inspection—Dismantling, Demolition, or Removal of Improvements 52.246-13
Inspection of Transportation 52.246-14
Certificate of Conformance 52.246-15
Responsibility for Supplies 52.246-16
Warranty of Supplies of a Noncomplex Nature 52.246-17
Warranty of Supplies of a Complex Nature 52.246-18
Warranty of Systems and Equipment under Performance Specifications or Design Criteria 52.246-19
Warranty of Services 52.246-20
Warranty of Construction 52.246-21
[Reserved] 52.246-22
Limitation of Liability 52.246-23
Limitation of Liability—High-Value Items 52.246-24
Limitation of Liability—Services 52.246-25
Reporting Nonconforming Items 52.246-26
Commercial Bill of Lading Notations 52.247-1
Permits, Authorities, or Franchises 52.247-2
Capability to Perform a Contract for the Relocation of a Federal Office 52.247-3
Inspection of Shipping and Receiving Facilities 52.247-4
Familiarization With Conditions 52.247-5
Financial Statement 52.247-6
Freight Excluded 52.247-7
Estimated Weights or Quantities Not Guaranteed 52.247-8
Agreed Weight—General Freight 52.247-9
Net Weight—General Freight 52.247-10
Net Weight—Household Goods or Office Furniture 52.247-11
Supervision, Labor, or Materials 52.247-12
Accessorial Services—Moving Contracts 52.247-13
Contractor Responsibility for Receipt of Shipment 52.247-14
Contractor Responsibility for Loading and Unloading 52.247-15
Contractor Responsibility for Returning Undelivered Freight 52.247-16
Charges 52.247-17
Multiple Shipments 52.247-18

Stopping in Transit for Partial Unloading 52.247-19
Estimated Quantities or Weights for Evaluation of Offers 52.247-20
Contractor Liability for Personal Injury and/or Property Damage 52.247-21
Contractor Liability for Loss of and/or Damage to Freight other than Household Goods 52.247-22
Contractor Liability for Loss of and/or Damage to Household Goods 52.247-23
Advance Notification by the Government 52.247-24
Government-Furnished Equipment with or without Operators 52.247-25
Government Direction and Marking 52.247-26
Contract Not Affected by Oral Agreement 52.247-27
Contractor's Invoices 52.247-28
F.o.b. Origin 52.247-29
F.o.b. Origin, Contractor's Facility 52.247-30
F.o.b. Origin, Freight Allowed 52.247-31
F.o.b. Origin, Freight Prepaid 52.247-32
F.o.b. Origin, with Differentials 52.247-33
F.o.b. Destination 52.247-34
F.o.b. Destination, within Consignee's Premises 52.247-35
F.a.s. Vessel, Port of Shipment 52.247-36
F.o.b. Vessel, Port of Shipment 52.247-37
F.o.b. Inland Carrier, Point of Exportation 52.247-38
F.o.b. Inland Point, Country of Importation 52.247-39
Ex Dock, Pier, or Warehouse, Port of Importation 52.247-40
C. & f. Destination 52.247-41
C.i.f. Destination 52.247-42
F.o.b. Designated Air Carrier's Terminal, Point of Exportation 52.247-43
F.o.b. Designated Air Carrier's Terminal, Point of Importation 52.247-44
F.o.b. Origin and/or F.o.b. Destination Evaluation 52.247-45
Shipping Point(s) Used in Evaluation of F.o.b. Origin Offers 52.247-46
Evaluation—F.o.b. Origin 52.247-47
F.o.b. Destination—Evidence of Shipment 52.247-48
Destination Unknown 52.247-49
No Evaluation of Transportation Costs 52.247-50
Evaluation of Export Offers 52.247-51
Clearance and Documentation Requirements—Shipments to DOD Air or Water Terminal Transshipment Points 52.247-52
Freight Classification Description 52.247-53
[Reserved] 52.247-54
F.o.b. Point for Delivery of Government-Furnished Property 52.247-55
Transit Arrangements 52.247-56
Transportation Transit Privilege Credits 52.247-57
Loading, Blocking, and Bracing of Freight Car Shipments 52.247-58
F.o.b. Origin—Carload and Truckload Shipments 52.247-59
Guaranteed Shipping Characteristics 52.247-60
F.o.b. Origin—Minimum Size of Shipments 52.247-61
Specific Quantities Unknown 52.247-62
Preference for U.S.-Flag Air Carriers 52.247-63
Preference for Privately Owned U.S.-Flag Commercial Vessels 52.247-64
F.o.b. Origin, Prepaid Freight—Small Package Shipments 52.247-65
Returnable Cylinders 52.247-66
Submission of Transportation Documents for Audit 52.247-67
Report of Shipment (RESHIP) 52.247-68
Value Engineering 52.248-1
Value Engineering—Architect-Engineer 52.248-2
Value Engineering—Construction 52.248-3

Termination for Convenience of the Government (Fixed-Price) (Short Form) 52.249-1
Termination for Convenience of the Government (Fixed-Price) 52.249-2
Termination for Convenience of the Government (Dismantling, Demolition, or Removal of Improvements) 52.249-3
Termination for Convenience of the Government (Services) (Short Form) 52.249-4
Termination for Convenience of the Government (Educational and Other Nonprofit Institutions) 52.249-5
Termination (Cost-Reimbursement) 52.249-6
Termination (Fixed-Price Architect-Engineer) 52.249-7
Default (Fixed-Price Supply and Service) 52.249-8
Default (Fixed-Price Research and Development) 52.249-9
Default (Fixed-Price Construction) 52.249-10
[Removed and Reserved] 52.249-11
Termination (Personal Services) 52.249-12
[Removed and Reserved] 52.249-13
Excusable Delays 52.249-14
Indemnification under Public Law 85-804 . . . . . 52.250-1
SAFETY Act Coverage Not Applicable 52.250-2
SAFETY Act Block Designation/Certification 52.250-3
SAFETY Act Pre-qualification Designation Notice 52.250-4
SAFETY Act—Equitable Adjustment 52.250-5
Government Supply Sources 52.251-1
Interagency Fleet Management System Vehicles and Related Services . . . 52.251-2
Solicitation Provisions Incorporated by Reference 52.252-1
Clauses Incorporated by Reference 52.252-2
Alterations in Solicitation 52.252-3
Alterations in Contract 52.252-4
Authorized Deviations in Provisions 52.252-5
Authorized Deviations in Clauses 52.252-6
Computer Generated Forms 52.253-1

Subpart 52.3—Provision and Clause Matrix

Scope of subpart 52.300
Solicitation provisions and contract clauses (Matrix) 52.301

SUBCHAPTER H—CLAUSES AND FORMS (Parts 52-53)

PART 52—SOLICITATION PROVISIONS AND CONTRACT CLAUSES

52.000 Scope of part.

This part—

(a) Gives instructions for using provisions and clauses in solicitations and/or contracts;

(b) Sets forth the solicitation provisions and contract clauses prescribed by this regulation; and

(c) Presents a matrix listing the FAR provisions and clauses applicable to each principal contract type and/or purpose (*e.g.*, fixed-price supply, cost-reimbursement research and development).

[FAC 84-56, 55 FR 3887, 2/5/90, effective 3/7/90]

SUBPART 52.1—INSTRUCTIONS FOR USING PROVISIONS AND CLAUSES

52.100 Scope of subpart.

This subpart (a) gives instructions for using Part 52, including the explanation and use of provision and clause numbers, prescriptions, prefaces, and the matrix; (b) prescribes procedures for incorporating, identifying, and modifying provisions and clauses in solicitations and contracts, and for using alternates; and (c) describes the derivation of FAR provisions and clauses.

[FAC 84-56, 55 FR 3887, 2/5/90, effective 3/7/90]

52.101 Using Part 52.

(a) *Definition.*

Modification, as used in this subpart, means a minor change in the details of a provision or clause that is specifically authorized by the FAR and does not alter the substance of the provision or clause (see 52.104).

(b) *Numbering*—(1) *FAR provisions and clauses.* Subpart 52.2 sets forth the texts of all FAR provisions and clauses, each in its own separate subsection. The subpart is arranged by subject matter, in the same order as, and keyed to, the parts of the FAR. Each FAR provision or clause is uniquely identified. All FAR provision and clause numbers begin with "52.2," since the text of all FAR provisions and clauses appear in Subpart 52.2. The next two digits of the provision or clause number correspond to the number of the FAR subject part in which the provision or clause is prescribed. The FAR provision or clause number is then completed by a hyphen and a sequential number assigned within each section of Subpart 52.2. The following example illustrates the makeup of the FAR provision or clause number:

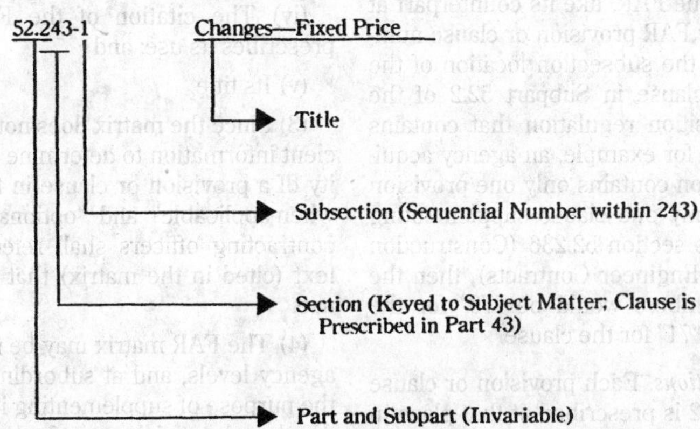

(2) (i) *Provisions or clauses that supplement the FAR.* Provisions or clauses that supplement the FAR are—

(A) Prescribed and included in authorized agency acquisition regulations issued within an agency to satisfy the specific needs of the agency as a whole;

(B) Prescribed and included in a regulation issued by a suborganization of an agency to satisfy the needs of that particular suborganization; or

(C) Developed for use at a suborganizational level of an agency, not meant for repetitive use, but intended to meet the needs of an individual acquisition and, thus, impractical to include in either an agency or suborganization acquisition regulation. (See 1.301(c).)

(ii) Supplemental provisions or clauses published in agency acquisition regulations shall be in full text and the prescription for the use of each shall be included. Supplemental provisions or clauses published in agency acquisition regulations shall be numbered in the same manner in which FAR provisions and clauses are numbered except that—

(A) If it is included in an agency acquisition regulation that is published in the *Federal Register* and is codified in Title 48, *Code of Federal Regulations* (48 CFR), the number shall be preceded by the chapter number within 48 CFR assigned by the CFR staff; and

(B) The sequential number shall be "70" or a higher number (see 1.303).

(iii) The sequential number at the end of the number of a provision or clause that supplements the FAR, like its counterpart at the end of any FAR provision or clause number, indicates the subsection location of the provision or clause in Subpart 52.2 of the agency acquisition regulation that contains its full text. If, for example, an agency acquisition regulation contains only one provision followed by only one clause supplementing the FAR in its section 52.236 (Construction and Architect-Engineer Contracts), then the sequential numbers would be "70" for the provision and "71" for the clause.

(c) *Prescriptions.* Each provision or clause in Subpart 52.2 is prescribed at that place in the FAR text where the subject matter of the provision or clause receives its primary treatment. The prescription includes all conditions, requirements, and instructions for using the provision or clause and its alternates, if any. The provision or clause may be referred to in other FAR locations.

(d) *Introductory text.* Within Subpart 52.2, the introductory text of each provision or clause includes a cross-reference to the location in the FAR subject text that prescribes its use.

(e) *Matrix.*

(1) The matrix in subpart 52.3 contains a column for each principal type and/or purpose of contract (*e.g.*, fixed-price supply, cost reimbursement research and development). The matrix lists the—

(i) Required solicitation provisions;

(ii) Required-when-applicable solicitation provisions;

(iii) Optional solicitation provisions;

(iv) Required contract clauses;

(v) Required-when-applicable contract clauses; and

(vi) Optional contract clauses.

(2) For each provision or clause listed, the matrix provides information on—

(i) Whether incorporation by reference is or is not authorized (see 52.102);

(ii) The section of the Uniform Contract Format (UCF) in which it is to be located, if it is used in an acquisition that is subject to the UCF;

(iii) Its number;

(iv) The citation of the FAR text that prescribes its use; and

(v) Its title.

(3) Since the matrix does not provide sufficient information to determine the applicability of a provision or clause in the "required-when-applicable" and "optional" categories, contracting officers shall refer to the FAR text (cited in the matrix) that prescribes its use.

(4) The FAR matrix may be reproduced at agency levels, and at subordinate levels, for the purpose of supplementing it with agency-developed provisions and clauses. The resulting consolidated matrices may be included in agency acquisition regulations.

(f) *Dates.* Since they are subject to revision from time to time, all provisions, clauses, and alternates are dated; *e.g.*, (DEC 1983). To avoid questions concerning which version of any provision, clause, or alternate is operative in any given solicitation or contract, its date shall be included whether it is incorporated by reference or in full text.

[FAC 84-56, 55 FR 3887, 2/5/90, effective 3/7/90; FAC 90-20, GPO Version, 3/10/94, effective 3/10/94, finalized without change, FAC 90-39, 61 FR 31612, 6/20/96; Final rule, 62 FR 40236, 7/25/97, effective 6/30/97; FAC 97-3, 62 FR 64912, 12/9/97, effective 2/9/98; FAC 97-18, 65 FR 36014, 6/6/2000, effective 8/7/2000; FAC 97-22, 66 FR 2116, 1/10/2001, effective 3/12/2001; Delay of effective date, 66 FR 14259, 3/9/2001, effective 5/11/2001]

52.102 Incorporating provisions and clauses.

(a) Provisions and clauses should be incorporated by reference to the maximum practical extent, rather than being incorporated in full text, even if they—

(1) Are used with one or more alternates or on an optional basis;

(2) Are prescribed on a "substantially as follows" or "substantially the same as" basis, provided they are used verbatim;

(3) Require modification or the insertion by the Government of fill-in material (see 52.104); or

(4) Require completion by the offeror or prospective contractor. This instruction also applies to provisions completed as annual representations and certifications.

(b) Except for provisions and clauses prescribed in 52.107, any provision or clause that can be accessed electronically by the offeror or prospective contractor may be incorporated by reference in solicitations and/ or contracts. However, the contracting officer, upon request, shall provide the full text of any provision or clause incorporated by reference.

(c) Agency approved provisions and clauses prescribed in agency acquisition regulations, and provisions and clauses not authorized by Subpart 52.3 to be incorporated by reference, need not be incorporated in full text, provided the contracting officer includes in the solicitation and contract a statement that—

(1) Identifies all provisions and clauses that require completion by the offeror or prospective contractor;

(2) Specifies that the provisions and clauses must be completed by the offeror or prospective contractor and must be submitted with the quotation or offer; and

(3) Identifies to the offeror or prospective contractor at least one electronic address where the full text may be accessed.

(d) An agency may develop a group listing of provisions and clauses that apply to a specific category of contracts. An agency group listing may be incorporated by reference in solicitations and/or contracts in lieu of citing the provisions and clauses individually, provided the group listing is made available electronically to offerors and prospective contractors.

(e) A provision or clause that is not available electronically to offerors and prospective contractors shall be incorporated in solicitations and/or contracts in full text if it is–

(1) A FAR provision or clause that otherwise is not authorized to be incorporated by reference (see Subpart 52.3); or

(2) A provision or clause prescribed for use in an agency acquisition regulation.

(f) Provisions or clauses may not be incorporated by reference by being listed in the—

(1) Provision at 52.252-3, Alterations in Solicitations; or

(2) Clause at 52.252-4, Alterations in Contract.

[FAC 97-3, 62 FR 64912, 12/9/97, effective 2/9/98]

52.103 Identification of provisions and clauses.

(a) Whenever any FAR provision or clause is used without deviation in a solicitation or contract, whether it is incorporated by reference or in full text, it shall be identified by number, title, and date. This identification shall also be used if the FAR provision or clause is used with an authorized deviation, except that the contracting officer shall then insert "(DEVIATION)" after the date. Solicited firms and contractors will be advised of the meaning of this insertion through the use of the (1) provision at 52.252-5, Authorized Deviations in Provisions, or (2) clause at 52.252-6, Authorized Deviations in Clauses. The above mentioned provision and clause are prescribed in 52.107(e) and (f).

(b) Any provision or clause that supplements the FAR whether it is incorporated by reference or in full text shall be clearly identified by number, title, date, and name of the regulation. When a supplemental provision or clause is used with an authorized deviation, insert "(DEVIATION)" after the name of the regulation.

(c) A provision or clause of the type described in 52.101(b)(2)(i)(C) shall be identified by the title, date, and the name of the agency or suborganization within the agency that developed it.

(d) Except for provisions or clauses covered by 52.103(c), the following hypothetical examples illustrate how a provision or clause that supplements the FAR shall be identified when it is incorporated in solicitations and/or contracts by reference or in full text:

(1) If Part 14 (Sealed Bidding) of the X Agency Acquisition Regulation, published in the *Federal Register* and codified as Chapter 99 in 48 CFR, prescribes the use of a provision entitled "Bid Envelopes," dated October 1983, and that provision is sequentially the first provision or clause appearing in Section 52.214 of the X Agency Acquisition Regulation, then the identification of that provision shall be "9952.214-70—Bid Envelopes (OCT 1983)."

(2) Assume that Y, a major organizational element of the X Agency, is authorized to issue the Y Acquisition Regulation, which is not published in the *Federal Register* and codified in 48 CFR. If Part 36 (Construction and Architect-Engineer Contracts) of the Y Acquisition Regulation prescribes the use of a clause entitled "Refrigerated Display Cases," dated March 1983, pertaining to a specialized type of construction work, and that clause is sequentially the second provision or clause appearing in Section 52.236 of the Y Acquisition Regulation, then the identification of that clause shall be "52.236-71—Refrigerated Display Cases (MAR 1983)—Y Acquisition Regulation".

[FAC 84-25, 52 FR 9039, 3/20/87, effective 7/1/87]

52.104 Procedures for modifying and completing provisions and clauses.

(a) The contracting officer must not modify provisions and clauses unless the FAR authorizes their modification. For example—

(1) "The contracting officer may use a period shorter than 60 days (but not less than 30 days) in paragraph (x) of the clause"; or

(2) "The contracting officer may substitute the words 'task order' for the word 'Schedule' wherever that word appears in the clause."

(b) When modifying provisions or clauses incorporated by reference, insert the changed wording directly below the title of the provision or clause identifying to the lowest level necessary (*e.g.*, paragraph, sentence, word), to clearly indicate what is being modified.

(c) When modifying provisions or clauses incorporated in full text, modify the language directly by substituting the changed wording as permitted.

(d) When completing blanks in provisions or clauses incorporated by reference, insert the fill-in information directly below the title of the provision or clause identifying to the lowest level necessary to clearly indicate the blanks being filled in.

(e) When completing blanks in provisions or clauses incorporated in full text, insert the fill-in information in the blanks of the provision or clause.

[FAC 97-18, 65 FR 36014, 6/6/2000, effective 8/7/2000]

52.105 Procedures for using alternates.

(a) The FAR accommodates a major variation in a provision or clause by use of an alternate. The FAR prescribes alternates to a given provision or clause in the FAR subject text where the provision or clause is prescribed. The alternates to each provision or clause are titled "Alternate I," "Alternate II," "Alternate III," etc.

(b) When an alternate is used, its date shall be cited along with the date of the basic provision or clause; *e.g.*, 52.209-3FIRST ARTICLE APPROVAL—CONTRACTOR TESTING (OCT 1983)—ALTERNATE I (DEC 1983).

(c) Under certain circumstances, a provision or clause may be used with two or more alternates. In these circumstances, each of the applicable alternates shall be cited, whether incorporated by reference or in full text; *e.g.*, 52.209-3 FIRST ARTICLE APPROVAL—CONTRACTOR TESTING (OCT 1983)—ALTERNATE I (DEC 1983) AND ALTERNATE II (FEB 1984). However, under no circumstances may an alternate to a specific provision or clause be applied to any other provision or clause.

[FAC 97-18, 65 FR 36014, 6/6/2000, effective 8/7/2000]

52.106 [Reserved]

[Removed and reserved, Final rule, 62 FR 40236, 7/25/97, effective 6/30/97]

52.107 Provisions and clauses prescribed in Subpart 52.1.

(a) The contracting officer shall insert the provision at 52.252-1, Solicitation Provisions Incorporated by Reference, in solicitations in order to incorporate provisions by reference.

(b) The contracting officer shall insert the clause at 52.252-2, Clauses Incorporated by Reference, in solicitations and contracts in order to incorporate clauses by reference.

(c) The contracting officer shall insert the provision at 52.252-3, Alterations in Solicitation, in solicitations in order to revise or supplement, as necessary, other parts of the solicitation that apply to the solicitation phase only, except for any provision authorized for use with a deviation.

(d) The contracting officer shall insert the clause at 52.252-4, Alterations in Contract, in solicitations and contracts in order to revise or supplement, as necessary, other parts of the contract, or parts of the solicitations that apply to the contract phase, except for any clause authorized for use with a deviation.

(e) The contracting officer shall insert the provision at 52.252-5, Authorized Deviations in Provisions, in solicitations that include any FAR or supplemental provision with an authorized deviation. Whenever any FAR or supplemental provision is used with an authorized deviation, the contracting officer shall identify it by the same number, title, and date assigned to the provision when it is used without deviation, include regulation name for any supplemental provision, except that the contracting officer shall insert "(DEVIATION)" after the date of the provision.

(f) The contracting officer shall insert the clause at 52.252-6, Authorized Deviations in Clauses, in solicitations and contracts that include any FAR or supplemental clause with an authorized deviation. Whenever any FAR or supplemental clause is used with an authorized deviation, the contracting officer shall identify it by the same number, title, and date assigned to the clause when it is used without deviation, include regulation name for any supplemental clause, except that the contracting officer shall insert "(DEVIATION)" after the date of the clause.

[FAC 84-37, 53 FR 17859, 5/18/88, effective 6/17/88; FAC 84-53, 54 FR 48990, 11/28/89, effective 12/28/89]

SUBPART 52.2—TEXTS OF PROVISIONS AND CLAUSES

52.200 Scope of subpart.

This subpart sets forth the text of all FAR provisions and clauses (see 52.101(b)(1)) and gives a cross-reference to the location in the FAR that prescribes the provision or clause.

[FAC 97-18, 65 FR 36014, 6/6/2000, effective 8/7/2000]

52.201 [Reserved]

52.202-1 Definitions.

As prescribed in 2.201, insert the following clause:

DEFINITIONS (NOV 2013)

When a solicitation provision or contract clause uses a word or term that is defined in the Federal Acquisition Regulation (FAR), the word or term has the same meaning as the definition inFAR 2.101 in effect at the time the solicitation was issued, unless—

(a) The solicitation, or amended solicitation, provides a different definition;

(b) The contracting parties agree to a different definition;

(c) The part, subpart, or section of the FAR where the provision or clause is prescribed provides a different meaning; or

(d) The word or term is defined in FAR Part 31, for use in the cost principles and procedures.

(End of clause)

[FAC 90-7, 56 FR 41744, 8/22/91, effective 9/23/91; FAC 90-9, 56 FR 67137, 12/27/91, effective 2/25/92; FAC 90-32, 60 FR 48206, 9/18/95, effective 10/1/95; FAC 97-22, 66 FR 2116, 1/10/2001, effective 3/12/2001; Delay of effective date, 66 FR 14259, 3/9/2001, effective 5/11/2001; FAC 2001-01, 66 FR 53478, 10/22/2001, effective 12/21/2001; FAC 2001-08, 67 FR 43513, 6/27/2002, effective 7/29/2002; FAC 2001-24, 69 FR 34225, 6/18/2004, effective 6/18/2004; 69 FR 34228, 6/18/2004, effective 7/19/2004; FAC 2005-04, 70 FR 33657, 6/8/2005, effective 6/8/2005; FAC 2005-55, 77 FR 204, 1/3/2012, effective 1/3/2012; FAC 2005-71, 78 FR 70481, 11/25/2013, effective 11/25/2013]

52.203-1 [Reserved]

[Reserved, FAC 90-30, 60 FR 37772, 7/21/95, effective 9/19/95]

52.203-2 Certificate of Independent Price Determination.

As prescribed in 3.103-1, insert the following provision. If the solicitation is a Request for Quotations, the terms *Quotation* and *Quoter* may be substituted for *Offer* and *Offeror*.

CERTIFICATE OF INDEPENDENT PRICE DETERMINATION (APR 1985)

(a) The offeror certifies that—

(1) The prices in this offer have been arrived at independently, without, for the purpose of restricting competition, any consultation, communication, or agreement with any other offeror or competitor relating to—

(i) Those prices;

(ii) The intention to submit an offer; or

(iii) The methods or factors used to calculate the prices offered;

(2) The prices in this offer have not been and will not be knowingly disclosed by the offeror, directly or indirectly, to any other offeror or competitor before bid opening (in the case of a sealed bid solicitation) or contract award (in the case of a negotiated solicitation) unless otherwise required by law; and

(3) No attempt has been made or will be made by the offeror to induce any other concern to submit or not to submit an offer for the purpose of restricting competition.

(b) Each signature on the offer is considered to be a certification by the signatory that the signatory—

(1) Is the person in the offeror's organization responsible for determining the prices being offered in this bid or proposal, and that the signatory has not participated and will not participate in any action contrary to subparagraphs (a)(1) through (a)(3) of this provision; or

(2) (i) Has been authorized, in writing, to act as agent for the following principals in certifying that those principals have not participated, and will not participate in any action contrary to subparagraphs (a)(1) through (a)(3) of this provision ____________________ [*insert full name of person(s) in the offeror's organization responsible for determining the prices offered in this bid or proposal, and the title of his or her position in the offeror's organization*];

(ii) As an authorized agent, does certify that the principals named in subdivision (b)(2)(i) of this provision have not participated, and will not participate, in any action contrary to subparagraphs (a)(1) through (a)(3) of this provision; and

(iii) As an agent, has not personally participated, and will not participate, in any action contrary to subparagraphs (a)(1) through (a)(3) of this provision.

(c) If the offeror deletes or modifies subparagraph (a)(2) of this provision, the offeror must furnish with its offer a signed statement setting forth in detail the circumstances of the disclosure.

(End of provision)

[FAC 84-5, 50 FR 1746, 1/11/85, effective 4/1/85]

52.203-3 Gratuities.

As prescribed in 3.202, insert the following clause:

GRATUITIES (APR 1984)

(a) The right of the Contractor to proceed may be terminated by written notice if, after notice and hearing, the agency head or a designee determines that the Contractor, its agent, or another representative—

(1) Offered or gave a gratuity (*e.g.*, an entertainment or gift) to an officer, official, or employee of the Government; and

(2) Intended, by the gratuity, to obtain a contract or favorable treatment under a contract.

(b) The facts supporting this determination may be reviewed by any court having lawful jurisdiction.

(c) If this contract is terminated under paragraph (a) of this clause, the Government is entitled—

(1) To pursue the same remedies as in a breach of the contract; and

(2) In addition to any other damages provided by law, to exemplary damages of not less than 3 nor more than 10 times the cost incurred by the Contractor in giving gratuities to the person concerned, as determined by the agency head or a designee. (This subparagraph (c)(2) is applicable only if this contract uses money appropriated to the Department of Defense.)

(d) The rights and remedies of the Government provided in this clause shall not be exclusive and are in addition to any other rights and remedies provided by law or under this contract.

(End of clause)

[FAC 90-32, 60 FR 48206, 9/18/95, effective 10/1/95; FAC 90-40, 61 FR 39186, 7/26/96, effective 7/26/96, finalized without change, FAC 90-46, 62 FR 12690, 3/17/97, effective 5/16/97]

52.203-4 [Reserved]

[Removed and reserved, FAC 90-40, 61 FR 39186, 7/26/96, effective 9/24/96]

52.203-5 Covenant Against Contingent Fees.

As prescribed in 3.404, insert the following clause:

COVENANT AGAINST CONTINGENT FEES (MAY 2014)

(a) The Contractor warrants that no person or agency has been employed or retained to solicit or obtain this contract upon an agreement or understanding for a contingent fee, except a bona fide employee or agency. For breach or violation of this warranty, the Government shall have the right to annul this contract without liability or, to deduct from the contract price or consideration, or otherwise recover, the full amount of the contingent fee.

(b) *Bona fide agency,* as used in this clause, means an established commercial or selling agency, maintained by a contractor for the purpose of securing business, that neither exerts nor proposes to exert improper influence to solicit or obtain Government contracts nor holds itself out as being able to obtain any Government contract or contracts through improper influence.

Bona fide employee, as used in this clause, means a person, employed by a contractor and subject to the contractor's supervision and control as to time, place, and manner of performance, who neither exerts nor proposes to exert improper influence to solicit or obtain Government contracts nor holds out as being able to obtain any Government contract or contracts through improper influence.

Contingent fee, as used in this clause, means any commission, percentage, brokerage, or other fee that is contingent upon the success that a person or concern has in securing a Government contract.

Improper influence, as used in this clause, means any influence that induces or tends to induce a Government employee or officer to give consideration or to act regarding a Government contract on any basis other than the merits of the matter.

(End of clause)

[FAC 90-7, 56 FR 41730, 8/22/91, effective 9/23/91; FAC 90-32, 60 FR 48206, 9/18/95, effective 10/1/95; FAC 90-40, 61 FR 39186, 7/26/96, effective 9/24/96; FAC 2005-73, 79 FR 24192, 4/29/2014, effective 5/29/2014]

52.203-6 Restrictions on Subcontractor Sales to the Government.

As prescribed in 3.503-2, insert the following clause:

RESTRICTIONS ON SUBCONTRACTOR SALES TO THE GOVERNMENT (SEP 2006)

(a) Except as provided in (b) of this clause, the Contractor shall not enter into any agreement with an actual or prospective subcontractor, nor otherwise act in any manner, which has or may have the effect of restricting sales by such subcontractors directly to the Government of any item or process (including computer software) made or furnished by the subcontractor under this contract or under any follow-on production contract.

(b) The prohibition in (a) of this clause does not preclude the Contractor from asserting rights that are otherwise authorized by law or regulation.

(c) The Contractor agrees to incorporate the substance of this clause, including this paragraph (c), in all subcontracts under this contract which exceed the simplified acquisition threshold.

(End of clause)

Alternate I (OCT 1995) As prescribed in 3.503-2, substitute the following paragraph in place of paragraph (b) of the basic clause:

(b) The prohibition in paragraph (a) of this clause does not preclude the Contractor from asserting rights that are otherwise authorized by law or regulation. For acquisitions of commercial items, the prohibition in paragraph (a) applies only to the extent that any agreement restricting sales by subcontractors results in the Federal Government being treated differently from any other prospective purchaser for the sale of the commercial item(s).

[FAC 84-11, 50 FR 35479, 8/30/85, effective 8/30/85; FAC 90-29, 60 FR 34732, 7/3/95, effective 7/3/95; FAC 90-32, 60 FR 48206, 9/18/95, effective 10/1/95; FAC 90-40, 61 FR 39186, 7/26/96, effective 8/26/96; FAC 2005-13, 71 FR 57363, 9/28/2006, effective 9/28/2006]

52.203-7 Anti-Kickback Procedures.

As prescribed in 3.502-3, insert the following clause:

ANTI-KICKBACK PROCEDURES (MAY 2014)

(a) *Definitions.*

Kickback as used in this clause, means any money, fee, commission, credit, gift, gratuity, thing of value, or compensation of any kind which is provided to any prime Contractor, prime Contractor employee, subcontractor, or subcontractor employee for the purpose of improperly obtaining or rewarding favorable treatment in connection with a prime contract or in connection with a subcontract relating to a prime contract.

Person as used in this clause, means a corporation, partnership, business association of any kind, trust, joint-stock company, or individual.

Prime contract as used in this clause, means a contract or contractual action entered into by the United States for the purpose of obtaining supplies, materials, equipment, or services of any kind.

Prime Contractor as used in this clause, means a person who has entered into a prime contract with the United States.

Prime Contractor employee as used in this clause, means any officer, partner, employee, or agent of a prime Contractor.

Subcontract as used in this clause, means a contract or contractual action entered into by a prime Contractor or subcontractor for the purpose of obtaining supplies, materials, equipment, or services of any kind under a prime contract.

Subcontractor as used in this clause, (1) means any person, other than the prime

Contractor, who offers to furnish or furnishes any supplies, materials, equipment, or services of any kind under a prime contract or a subcontract entered into in connection with such prime contract, and (2) includes any person who offers to furnish or furnishes general supplies to the prime Contractor or a higher tier subcontractor.

Subcontractor employee as used in this clause, means any officer, partner, employee, or agent of a subcontractor.

(b) 41 U.S.C. chapter 87, Kickbacks, prohibits any person from—

(1) Providing or attempting to provide or offering to provide any kickback;

(2) Soliciting, accepting, or attempting to accept any kickback; or

(3) Including, directly or indirectly, the amount of any kickback in the contract price charged by a prime Contractor to the United States or in the contract price charged by a subcontractor to a prime Contractor or higher tier subcontractor.

(c)(1) The Contractor shall have in place and follow reasonable procedures designed to prevent and detect possible violations described in paragraph (b) of this clause in its own operations and direct business relationships.

(2) When the Contractor has reasonable grounds to believe that a violation described in paragraph (b) of this clause may have occurred, the Contractor shall promptly report in writing the possible violation. Such reports shall be made to the inspector general of the contracting agency, the head of the contracting agency if the agency does not have an inspector general, or the Attorney General.

(3) The Contractor shall cooperate fully with any Federal agency investigating a possible violation described in paragraph (b) of this clause.

(4) The Contracting Officer may (i) offset the amount of the kickback against any monies owed by the United States under the prime contract and/or (ii) direct that the Prime Contractor withhold, from sums owed a subcontractor under the prime contract, the amount of any kickback. The Contracting Officer may order that monies withheld under subdivision (c)(4)(ii) of this clause be paid over to the Government unless the Government has already offset those monies under subdivision (c)(4)(i) of this clause. In either case, the Prime Contractor shall notify the Contracting Officer when the monies are withheld.

(5) The Contractor agrees to incorporate the substance of this clause, including this subparagraph (c)(5) but excepting subparagraph (c)(1), in all subcontracts under this contract which exceed $150,000.

(End of clause)

[FAC 84-24, 52 FR 6122, 2/27/87, effective 2/6/87; FAC 84-39, 53 FR 34229, 9/2/88, effective 10/3/88; corrected 53 FR 36028, 9/16/88; FAC 90-29, 60 FR 34732, 7/3/95, effective 7/3/95; FAC 2005-45, 75 FR 53129, 8/30/2010, effective 10/1/2010; FAC 2005-73, 79 FR 24192, 4/29/2014, effective 5/29/2014]

52.203-8 Cancellation, Rescission, and Recovery of Funds for Illegal or Improper Activity.

As prescribed in 3.104-9(a), insert the following clause:

CANCELLATION, RESCISSION, AND RECOVERY OF FUNDS FOR ILLEGAL OR IMPROPER ACTIVITY (MAY 2014)

(a) If the Government receives information that a contractor or a person has violated 41 U.S.C. 2102-2104, Restrictions on Obtaining and Disclosing Certain Information, the Government may—

(1) Cancel the solicitation, if the contract has not yet been awarded or issued; or

(2) Rescind the contract with respect to which—

(i) The Contractor or someone acting for the Contractor has been convicted for an offense where the conduct violates 41 U.S.C. 2102 for the purpose of either—

(A) Exchanging the information covered by such subsections for anything of value; or

(B) Obtaining or giving anyone a competitive advantage in the award of a Federal agency procurement contract; or

(ii) The head of the contracting activity has determined, based upon a preponderance of the evidence, that the Contractor or someone acting for the Contractor has engaged in conduct punishable under 41 U.S.C. 2105(a).

(b) If the Government rescinds the contract under paragraph (a) of this clause, the Government is entitled to recover, in addition to any penalty prescribed by law, the amount expended under the contract.

(c) The rights and remedies of the Government specified herein are not exclusive, and are in addition to any other rights and remedies provided by law, regulation, or under this contract.

(End of clause)

[FAC 90-45, Final rule, 62 FR 224, 1/2/97, effective 1/1/97, corrected 62 FR 10709, 3/10/97; FAC 2001-06, 67 FR 13048, 3/20/2002, effective 4/4/2002; FAC 2005-73, 79 FR 24192, 4/29/2014, effective 5/29/2014]

52.203-9 [Reserved]

[Removed and reserved, FAC 90-45, Final rule, 62 FR 224, 1/2/97, effective 1/1/97]

52.203-10 Price or Fee Adjustment for Illegal or Improper Activity.

As prescribed in 3.104-9(b), insert the following clause:

PRICE OR FEE ADJUSTMENT FOR ILLEGAL OR IMPROPER ACTIVITY (MAY 2014)

(a) The Government, at its election, may reduce the price of a fixed-price type contract and the total cost and fee under a cost-type contract by the amount of profit or fee determined as set forth in paragraph (b) of this clause if the head of the contracting activity or designee determines that there was a violation of 41 U.S.C. 2102 or 2103, as implemented in section 3.104 of the Federal Acquisition Regulation.

(b) The price or fee reduction referred to in paragraph (a) of this clause shall be—

(1) For cost-plus-fixed-fee contracts, the amount of the fee specified in the contract at the time of award;

(2) For cost-plus-incentive-fee contracts, the target fee specified in the contract at the time of award, notwithstanding any minimum fee or "fee floor" specified in the contract;

(3) For cost-plus-award-fee contracts—

(i) The base fee established in the contract at the time of contract award;

(ii) If no base fee is specified in the contract, 30 percent of the amount of each award fee otherwise payable to the Contractor for each award fee evaluation period or at each award fee determination point.

(4) For fixed-price-incentive contracts, the Government may—

(i) Reduce the contract target price and contract target profit both by an amount equal to the initial target profit specified in the contract at the time of contract award; or

(ii) If an immediate adjustment to the contract target price and contract target profit would have a significant adverse impact on the incentive price revision relationship under the contract, or adversely affect the contract financing provisions, the Contracting Officer may defer such adjustment until establishment of the total final price of the contract. The total final price established in accordance with the incentive price revision provisions of the contract shall be reduced by an amount equal to the initial target profit specified in the contract at the time of contract award and such reduced price shall be the total final contract price.

(5) For firm-fixed-price contracts, by 10 percent of the initial contract price or a profit amount determined by the Contracting Officer from records or documents in existence prior to the date of the contract award.

(c) The Government may, at its election, reduce a prime contractor's price or fee in accordance with the procedures of paragraph (b) of this clause for violations of the statute by its subcontractors by an amount not to exceed the amount of profit or fee reflected in the subcontract at the time the subcontract was first definitively priced.

(d) In addition to the remedies in paragraphs (a) and (c) of this clause, the Government may terminate this contract for default. The rights and remedies of the Government specified herein are not exclusive and are in addition to any other rights and remedies provided by law or under this contract.

(End of clause)

[FAC 84-60, 55 FR 36782, 9/6/90, effective 9/6/90; FAC 90-45, Final rule, 62 FR 224, 1/2/97, effective 1/1/97; FAC 2005-73, 79 FR 24192, 4/29/2014, effective 5/29/2014]

52.203-11 Certification and Disclosure Regarding Payments to Influence Certain Federal Transactions.

As prescribed in 3.808(a), insert the following provision:

CERTIFICATION AND DISCLOSURE REGARDING PAYMENTS TO INFLUENCE CERTAIN FEDERAL TRANSACTIONS (SEP 2007)

(a) *Definitions*. As used in this provision—

Lobbying contact has the meaning provided at 2 U.S.C. 1602(8). The terms *agency, influencing or attempting to influence, officer or employee of an agency, person, reasonable compensation,* and *regularly employed* are defined in the FAR clause of this solicitation entitled "Limitation on Payments to Influence Certain Federal Transactions" (52.203-12).

(b) *Prohibition*. The prohibition and exceptions contained in the FAR clause of this solicitation entitled "Limitation on Payments to Influence Certain Federal Transactions" (52.203-12) are hereby incorporated by reference in this provision.

(c) *Certification*. The offeror, by signing its offer, hereby certifies to the best of its knowledge and belief that no Federal appropriated funds have been paid or will be paid to any person for influencing or attempting to influence an officer or employee of any agency, a Member of Congress, an officer or employee of Congress, or an employee of a Member of Congress on its behalf in connection with the awarding of this contract.

(d) *Disclosure*. If any registrants under the Lobbying Disclosure Act of 1995 have made a lobbying contact on behalf of the offeror with respect to this contract, the offeror shall complete and submit, with its offer, OMB Standard Form LLL, Disclosure of Lobbying Activities, to provide the name of the registrants. The offeror need not report regularly employed officers or employees of the offeror to whom payments of reasonable compensation were made.

(e) *Penalty*. Submission of this certification and disclosure is a prerequisite for making or entering into this contract imposed by 31 U.S.C. 1352. Any person who makes an expenditure prohibited under this provision or who fails to file or amend the disclosure required to be filed or amended by this provision, shall be subject to a civil penalty of not less than $10,000, and not more than $100,000, for each such failure.

(End of provision)

[FAC 84-55, 55 FR 3193, 1/30/90, effective 1/30/90; FAC 90-4, 56 FR 15155, 4/15/91, effective 5/15/91; Final rule, 62 FR 40236, 7/25/97, effective 6/30/97; FAC 2005-06, 70 FR 57455, 9/30/2005, effective 9/30/2005; FAC 2005-19, 72 FR 46327, 8/17/2007, effective 9/17/2007]

52.203-12 Limitation on Payments to Influence Certain Federal Transactions.

As prescribed in 3.808(b), insert the following clause:

LIMITATION ON PAYMENTS TO INFLUENCE CERTAIN FEDERAL TRANSACTIONS (OCT 2010)

(a) *Definitions*. As used in this clause—

Agency means executive agency as defined in Federal Acquisition Regulation (FAR) 2.101.

Covered Federal action means any of the following actions:

(1) Awarding any Federal contract.

(2) Making any Federal grant.

(3) Making any Federal loan.

(4) Entering into any cooperative agreement.

(5) Extending, continuing, renewing, amending, or modifying any Federal contract, grant, loan, or cooperative agreement.

Indian tribe and *tribal organization* have the meaning provided in section 4 of the Indian Self-Determination and Education Assistance Act (25 U.S.C. 450b) and include Alaskan Natives.

Influencing or attempting to influence means making, with the intent to influence, any communication to or appearance before an officer or employee of any agency, a Member of Congress, an officer or employee of Congress, or an employee of a Member of Congress in connection with any covered Federal action.

Local government means a unit of government in a State and, if chartered, established, or otherwise recognized by a State for the performance of a governmental duty, including a local public authority, a special district, an intrastate district, a council of governments, a sponsor group representative organization, and any other instrumentality of a local government.

Officer or employee of an agency includes the following individuals who are employed by an agency:

(1) An individual who is appointed to a position in the Government under Title 5, United States Code, including a position under a temporary appointment.

(2) A member of the uniformed services, as defined in subsection 101(3), Title 37, United States Code.

(3) A special Government employee, as defined in section 202, Title 18, United States Code.

(4) An individual who is a member of a Federal advisory committee, as defined by the Federal Advisory Committee Act, Title 5, United States Code, appendix 2.

Person means an individual, corporation, company, association, authority, firm, partnership, society, State, and local government, regardless of whether such entity is operated for profit, or not for profit. This term excludes an Indian tribe, tribal organization, or any other Indian organization eligible to receive Federal contracts, grants, cooperative agreements, or loans from an agency, but only with respect to expenditures by such tribe or organization that are made for purposes specified in paragraph (b) of this clause and are permitted by other Federal law.

Reasonable compensation means, with respect to a regularly employed officer or employee of any person, compensation that is consistent with the normal compensation for such officer or employee for work that is not furnished to, not funded by, or not furnished in cooperation with the Federal Government.

Reasonable payment means, with respect to professional and other technical services, a payment in an amount that is consistent with the amount normally paid for such services in the private sector.

Recipient includes the Contractor and all subcontractors. This term excludes an Indian tribe, tribal organization, or any other Indian organization eligible to receive Federal contracts, grants, cooperative agreements, or loans from an agency, but only with respect to expenditures by such tribe or organization that are made for purposes specified in paragraph (b) of this clause and are permitted by other Federal law.

Regularly employed means, with respect to an officer or employee of a person requesting or receiving a Federal contract, an officer or employee who is employed by such person for at least 130 working days within 1 year immediately preceding the date of the submission that initiates agency consideration of such person for receipt of such contract. An officer or employee who is employed by such person for less than 130 working days within 1 year immediately preceding the date of the submission that initiates agency consideration of such person shall be considered to be regularly employed as soon as he or she is employed by such person for 130 working days.

State means a State of the United States, the District of Columbia, or an outlying area of the United States, an agency or instrumentality of a State, and multi-State, regional, or interstate entity having governmental duties and powers.

(b) *Prohibition*. 31 U.S.C. 1352 prohibits a recipient of a Federal contract, grant, loan, or cooperative agreement from using appropriated funds to pay any person for influencing or attempting to influence an officer or employee of any agency, a Member of Congress, an officer or employee of Congress, or an employee of a Member of Congress in connection with any covered Federal actions. In accordance with 31 U.S.C. 1352, the Contractor shall not use appropriated funds to pay any person for influencing or attempting to influence an officer or employee of any agency, a Member of Congress, an officer or employee of Congress, or an employee of a Member of Congress in connection with the award of this contractor the extension, continuation, renewal, amendment, or modification of this contract.

(1) The term appropriated funds does not include profit or fee from a covered Federal action.

(2) To the extent the Contractor can demonstrate that the Contractor has sufficient monies, other than Federal appropriated funds, the Government will assume that these other monies were spent for any influencing activities that would be unallowable if paid for with Federal appropriated funds.

(c) *Exceptions.* The prohibition in paragraph (b) of this clause does not apply under the following conditions:

(1) *Agency and legislative liaison by Contractor employees.* (i) Payment of reasonable compensation made to an officer or employee of the Contractor if the payment is for agency and legislative liaison activities not directly related to this contract. For purposes of this paragraph, providing any information specifically requested by an agency or Congress is permitted at any time.

(ii) Participating with an agency in discussions that are not related to a specific solicitation for any covered Federal action, but that concern—

(A) The qualities and characteristics (including individual demonstrations) of the person's products or services, conditions or terms of sale, and service capabilities; or

(B) The application or adaptation of the person's products or services for an agency's use.

(iii) Providing prior to formal solicitation of any covered Federal action any information not specifically requested but necessary for an agency to make an informed decision about initiation of a covered Federal action;

(iv) Participating in technical discussions regarding the preparation of an unsolicited proposal prior to its official submission; and

(v) Making capability presentations prior to formal solicitation of any covered Federal action by persons seeking awards from an agency pursuant to the provisions of the Small Business Act, as amended by Pub.L. 95-507, and subsequent amendments.

(2) *Professional and technical services.* (i) A payment of reasonable compensation made to an officer or employee of a person requesting or receiving a covered Federal action or an extension, continuation, renewal, amendment, or modification of a covered Federal action, if payment is for professional or technical services rendered directly in the preparation, submission, or negotiation of any bid, proposal, or application for that Federal action or for meeting requirements imposed by or pursuant to law as a condition for receiving that Federal action.

(ii) Any reasonable payment to a person, other than an officer or employee of a person requesting or receiving a covered Federal action or an extension, continuation, renewal, amendment, or modification of a covered Federal action if the payment is for professional or technical services rendered directly in the preparation, submission, or negotiation of any bid, proposal, or application for that Federal action or for meeting requirements imposed by or pursuant to law as a condition for receiving that Federal action. Persons other than officers or employees of a person requesting or receiving a covered Federal action include consultants and trade associations.

(iii) As used in paragraph (c)(2) of this clause, "professional and technical services" are limited to advice and analysis directly applying any professional or technical discipline (for examples, see FAR 3.803(a)(2)(iii)).

(iv) Requirements imposed by or pursuant to law as a condition for receiving a covered Federal award include those required by law or regulation and any other requirements in the actual award documents.

(3) Only those communications and services expressly authorized by paragraphs (c)(1) and (2) of this clause are permitted.

(d) *Disclosure.* (1) If the Contractor did not submit OMB Standard Form LLL, Disclosure of Lobbying Activities, with its offer, but registrants under the Lobbying Disclosure Act of 1995 have subsequently made a lobbying contact on behalf of the Contractor with respect to this contract, the Contractor shall complete and submit OMB Standard Form LLL to provide the name of the lobbying registrants, including the individuals performing the services.

(2) If the Contractor did submit OMB Standard Form LLL disclosure pursuant to paragraph (d) of the provision at FAR 52.203-11, Certification and Disclosure Regarding Payments to Influence Certain Federal Transactions, and a change occurs that affects Block 10 of the OMB Standard Form LLL (name and address of lobbying registrant or individuals performing services), the Contractor shall, at the end of the calendar quarter in which the change occurs, submit to the Contracting Officer within 30 days an updated disclosure using OMB Standard Form LLL.

(e) *Penalties.* (1) Any person who makes an expenditure prohibited under paragraph (b) of this clause or who fails to file or amend the disclosure to be filed or amended by paragraph (d) of this clause shall be subject to civil penalties as provided for by 31 U.S.C. 1352. An imposition of a civil penalty does not prevent the Government from seeking any other remedy that may be applicable.

(2) Contractors may rely without liability on the representation made by their subcontractors in the certification and disclosure form.

(f) *Cost allowability.* Nothing in this clause makes allowable or reasonable any costs which would otherwise be unallowable or unreasonable. Conversely, costs made specifically unallowable by the requirements in this clause will not be made allowable under any other provision.

(g) *Subcontracts.* (1) The Contractor shall obtain a declaration, including the certification and disclosure in paragraphs (c) and (d) of the provision at FAR 52.203-11, Certification and Disclosure Regarding Payments to Influence Certain Federal Transactions, from each person requesting or receiving a subcontract exceeding $150,000 under this contract. The Contractor or subcontractor that awards the subcontract shall retain the declaration.

(2) A copy of each subcontractor disclosure form (but not certifications) shall be forwarded from tier to tier until received by the prime Contractor. The prime Contractor shall, at the end of the calendar quarter in which the disclosure form is submitted by the subcontractor, submit to the Contracting Officer within 30 days a copy of all disclosures. Each subcontractor certification shall be retained in the subcontract file of the awarding Contractor.

(3) The Contractor shall include the substance of this clause, including this paragraph (g), in any subcontract exceeding $150,000.

(End of clause)

[FAC 84-55, 55 FR 3193, 1/30/90, effective 1/30/90; Final rule, 55 FR 38517, 9/18/90; Final rule, 62 FR 40236, 7/25/97, effective 6/30/97; FAC 2001-14, 68 FR 28079, 5/22/2003, effective 6/23/2003; FAC 2005-06, 70 FR 57455, 9/30/2005, effective 9/30/2005; FAC 2005-19, 72 FR 46327, 8/17/2007, effective 9/17/2007; FAC 2005-45, 75 FR 53129, 8/30/2010, effective 10/1/2010]

52.203-13 Contractor Code of Business Ethics and Conduct.

As prescribed in 3.1004(a), insert the following clause:

CONTRACTOR CODE OF BUSINESS ETHICS AND CONDUCT (OCT 2015)

(a) *Definitions.* As used in this clause—

Agent means any individual, including a director, an officer, an employee, or an independent Contractor, authorized to act on behalf of the organization.

Full cooperation—(1) Means disclosure to the Government of the information sufficient for law enforcement to identify the nature and extent of the offense and the individuals responsible for the conduct. It includes providing timely and complete response to Government auditors' and investigators' request for documents and access to employees with information;

(2) Does not foreclose any Contractor rights arising in law, the FAR, or the terms of the contract. It does not require—

(i) A Contractor to waive its attorney-client privilege or the protections afforded by the attorney work product doctrine; or

(ii) Any officer, director, owner, or employee of the Contractor, including a sole proprietor, to waive his or her attorney client privilege or Fifth Amendment rights; and

(3) Does not restrict a Contractor from—

(i) Conducting an internal investigation; or

(ii) Defending a proceeding or dispute arising under the contract or related to a potential or disclosed violation.

Principal means an officer, director, owner, partner, or a person having primary management or supervisory responsibilities within a business entity (e.g., general manager; plant manager; head of a division or business segment; and similar positions).

Subcontract means any contract entered into by a subcontractor to furnish supplies or services for performance of a prime contract or a subcontract.

Subcontractor means any supplier, distributor, vendor, or firm that furnished supplies or services to or for a prime contractor or another subcontractor.

United States means the 50 States, the District of Columbia, and outlying areas.

(b) *Code of business ethics and conduct.* (1) Within 30 days after contract award, unless the Contracting Officer establishes a longer time period, the Contractor shall—

(i) Have a written code of business ethics and conduct;

(ii) Make a copy of the code available to each employee engaged in performance of the contract.

(2) The Contractor shall—

(i) Exercise due diligence to prevent and detect criminal conduct; and

(ii) Otherwise promote an organizational culture that encourages ethical conduct and a commitment to compliance with the law.

(3) (i) The Contractor shall timely disclose, in writing, to the agency Office of the Inspector General (OIG), with a copy to the Contracting Officer, whenever, in connection with the award, performance, or closeout of this contract or any subcontract thereunder, the Contractor has credible evidence that a principal, employee, agent, or subcontractor of the Contractor has committed—

(A) A violation of Federal criminal law involving fraud, conflict of interest, bribery, or gratuity violations found in Title 18 of the United States Code; or

(B) A violation of the civil False Claims Act (31 U.S.C. 3729-3733).

(ii) The Government, to the extent permitted by law and regulation, will safeguard and treat information obtained pursuant to the Contractor's disclosure as confidential where the information has been marked "confidential" or "proprietary" by the company. To the extent permitted by law and regulation, such information will not be released by the Government to the public pursuant to a Freedom of Information Act request, 5 U.S.C. Section 552, without prior notification to the Contractor. The Government may transfer documents provided by the Contractor to any department or agency within the Executive Branch if the information relates to matters within the organization's jurisdiction.

(iii) If the violation relates to an order against a Governmentwide acquisition contract, a multi-agency contract, a multiple-award schedule contract such as the Federal Supply Schedule, or any other procurement instrument intended for use by multiple agencies, the Contractor shall notify the OIG of the ordering agency and the IG of the agency responsible for the basic contract.

(c) *Business ethics awareness and compliance program and internal control system.* This paragraph (c) does not apply if the Contractor has represented itself as a small business concern pursuant to the award of this contract or if this contract is for the acquisition of a commercial item as defined at FAR 2.101. The Contractor shall establish the following within 90 days after contract award, unless the Contracting Officer establishes a longer time period:

(1) An ongoing business ethics awareness and compliance program.

(i) This program shall include reasonable steps to communicate periodically and in a practical manner the Contractor's standards and procedures and other aspects of the Contractor's business ethics awareness and compliance program and internal control system, by conducting effective training programs and otherwise disseminating information appropriate to an individual's respective roles and responsibilities.

(ii) The training conducted under this program shall be provided to the Contractor's principals and employees, and as appropriate, the Contractor's agents and subcontractors.

(2) An internal control system.

(i) The Contractor's internal control system shall—

(A) Establish standards and procedures to facilitate timely discovery of improper conduct in connection with Government contracts; and

(B) Ensure corrective measures are promptly instituted and carried out.

(ii) At a minimum, the Contractor's internal control system shall provide for the following:

(A) Assignment of responsibility at a sufficiently high level and adequate resources to ensure effectiveness of the business ethics awareness and compliance program and internal control system.

(B) Reasonable efforts not to include an individual as a principal, whom due diligence would have exposed as having engaged in conduct that is in conflict with the Contractor's code of business ethics and conduct.

(C) Periodic reviews of company business practices, procedures, policies, and internal controls for compliance with the Contractor's code of business ethics and conduct and the special requirements of Government contracting, including—

(1) Monitoring and auditing to detect criminal conduct;

(2) Periodic evaluation of the effectiveness of the business ethics awareness and compliance program and internal control system, especially if criminal conduct has been detected; and

(3) Periodic assessment of the risk of criminal conduct, with appropriate steps to design, implement, or modify the business ethics awareness and compliance program and the internal control system as necessary to reduce the risk of criminal conduct identified through this process.

(D) An internal reporting mechanism, such as a hotline, which allows for anonymity or confidentiality, by which employees may report suspected instances of improper conduct, and instructions that encourage employees to make such reports.

(E) Disciplinary action for improper conduct or for failing to take reasonable steps to prevent or detect improper conduct.

(F) Timely disclosure, in writing, to the agency OIG, with a copy to the Contracting Officer, whenever, in connection with the award, performance, or closeout of any Government contract performed by the Contractor or a subcontractor thereunder, the Contractor has credible evidence that a principal, employee, agent, or subcontractor of the Contractor has committed a violation of Federal criminal law involving fraud, conflict of interest, bribery, or gratuity violations found in Title 18 U.S.C. or a violation of the civil False Claims Act (31 U.S.C. 3729-3733).

(1) If a violation relates to more than one Government contract, the Contractor may make the disclosure to the agency OIG and Contracting Officer responsible for the largest dollar value contract impacted by the violation.

(2) If the violation relates to an order against a Governmentwide acquisition contract, a multi-agency contract, a multiple-award schedule contract such as the Federal Supply Schedule, or any other procurement instrument intended for use by multiple agencies, the contractor shall notify the OIG of the ordering agency and the IG of the agency responsible for the basic contract, and the respective agencies' contracting officers.

(3) The disclosure requirement for an individual contract continues until at least 3 years after final payment on the contract.

(4) The Government will safeguard such disclosures in accordance with paragraph (b) (3) (ii) of this clause.

(G) Full cooperation with any Government agencies responsible for audits, investigations, or corrective actions.

(d) *Subcontracts.* (1) The Contractor shall include the substance of this clause, including this paragraph (d), in subcontracts that have a value in excess of $5.5 million and a performance period of more than 120 days.

(2) In altering this clause to identify the appropriate parties, all disclosures of violation of the civil False Claims Act or of Federal criminal law shall be directed to the agency Office of the Inspector General, with a copy to the Contracting Officer.

(End of clause)

[FAC 2005-22, 72 FR 65873, 11/23/2007, effective 12/24/2007; FAC 2005-28, 73 FR 67064, 11/12/2008, effective 12/12/2008; FAC 2005-40, 75 FR 14059, 3/23/2010, effective 4/22/2010; FAC 2005-83, 80 FR 38293, 7/2/2015, effective 10/1/2015]

52.203-14 Display of Hotline Poster(s).

As prescribed in 3.1004(b), insert the following clause:

DISPLAY OF HOTLINE POSTER(S) (OCT 2015)

(a) *Definition.*

United States, as used in this clause, means the 50 States, the District of Columbia, and outlying areas.

(b) *Display of fraud hotline poster(s).* Except as provided in paragraph (c)—

(1) During contract performance in the United States, the Contractor shall prominently display in common work areas within business segments performing work under this contract and at contract work sites—

(i) Any agency fraud hotline poster or Department of Homeland Security (DHS) fraud hotline poster identified in paragraph (b) (3) of this clause; and

(ii) Any DHS fraud hotline poster subsequently identified by the Contracting Officer.

(2) Additionally, if the Contractor maintains a company website as a method of providing information to employees, the Contractor shall display an electronic version of the poster(s) at the website.

(3) Any required posters may be obtained as follows:

Poster(s)

Obtain from

(*Contracting Officer shall insert*—

(i) Appropriate agency name(s) and/or title of applicable Department of Homeland Security fraud hotline poster); and

(ii) The website(s) or other contact information for obtaining the poster(s).)

(c) If the Contractor has implemented a business ethics and conduct awareness program, including a reporting mechanism, such as a hotline poster, then the Contractor need not display any agency fraud hotline posters as required in paragraph (b) of this clause, other than any required DHS posters.

(d) *Subcontracts.* The Contractor shall include the substance of this clause, including this paragraph (d), in all subcontracts that exceed $5.5 million, except when the subcontract—

(1) Is for the acquisition of a commercial item; or

(2) Is performed entirely outside the United States.

(End of clause)

[FAC 2005-22, 72 FR 65873, 11/23/2007, effective 12/24/2007; FAC 2005-83, 80 FR 38293, 7/2/2015, effective 10/1/2015]

52.203-15 Whistleblower Protections Under the American Recovery and Reinvestment Act of 2009.

As prescribed in 3.907-7, use the following clause:

WHISTLEBLOWER PROTECTIONS UNDER THE AMERICAN RECOVERY AND REINVESTMENT ACT OF 2009 (JUN 2010)

(a) The Contractor shall post notice of employees rights and remedies for whistleblower protections provided under section 1553 of the American Recovery and Reinvestment Act of 2009 (Pub. L. 111–5) (Recovery Act).

(b) The Contractor shall include the substance of this clause, including this paragraph (b), in all subcontracts that are funded in whole or in part with Recovery Act funds.

(End of clause)

[FAC 2005-32, 74 FR 14633, 3/31/2009, effective 3/31/2009; FAC 2005-42, 75 FR 34258, 6/16/2010, effective 6/16/2010]

52.203-16 Preventing Personal Conflicts of Interest.

As prescribed in 3.1106, use the following clause:

PREVENTING PERSONAL CONFLICTS OF INTEREST (DEC 2011)

(a) *Definitions.* As used in this clause—

Acquisition function closely associated with inherently governmental functions means supporting or providing advice or recommendations with regard to the following activities of a Federal agency:

(1) Planning acquisitions.

(2) Determining what supplies or services are to be acquired by the Government, including developing statements of work.

(3) Developing or approving any contractual documents, to include documents defining requirements, incentive plans, and evaluation criteria.

(4) Evaluating contract proposals.

(5) Awarding Government contracts.

(6) Administering contracts (including ordering changes or giving technical direction in contract performance or contract quantities, evaluating contractor performance, and accepting or rejecting contractor products or services).

(7) Terminating contracts.

(8) Determining whether contract costs are reasonable, allocable, and allowable.

Covered employee means an individual who performs an acquisition function closely associated with inherently governmental functions and is—

(1) An employee of the contractor; or

(2) A subcontractor that is a self-employed individual treated as a covered employee of the contractor because there is no employer to whom such an individual could submit the required disclosures.

Non-public information means any Government or third-party information that—

(1) Is exempt from disclosure under the Freedom of Information Act (5 U.S.C. 552) or otherwise protected from disclosure by statute, Executive order, or regulation; or

(2) Has not been disseminated to the general public and the Government has not yet determined whether the information can or will be made available to the public.

Personal conflict of interest means a situation in which a covered employee has a financial interest, personal activity, or relationship that could impair the employee's ability to act impartially and in the best interest of the Government when performing under the contract. (A *de minimis* interest that would not "impair the employee's ability to act impartially and in the best interest of the Government" is not covered under this definition.)

(1) Among the sources of personal conflicts of interest are—

(i) Financial interests of the covered employee, of close family members, or of other members of the covered employee's household;

(ii) Other employment or financial relationships (including seeking or negotiating for prospective employment or business); and

(iii) Gifts, including travel.

(2) For example, financial interests referred to in paragraph (1) of this definition may arise from—

(i) Compensation, including wages, salaries, commissions, professional fees, or fees for business referrals;

(ii) Consulting relationships (including commercial and professional consulting and service arrangements, scientific and technical advisory board memberships, or serving as an expert witness in litigation);

(iii) Services provided in exchange for honorariums or travel expense reimbursements;

(iv) Research funding or other forms of research support;

(v) Investment in the form of stock or bond ownership or partnership interest (excluding diversified mutual fund investments);

(vi) Real estate investments;

(vii) Patents, copyrights, and other intellectual property interests; or

(viii) Business ownership and investment interests.

(b) *Requirements*. The Contractor shall—

(1) Have procedures in place to screen covered employees for potential personal conflicts of interest, by—

(i) Obtaining and maintaining from each covered employee, when the employee is initially assigned to the task under the contract, a disclosure of interests that might be affected by the task to which the employee has been assigned, as follows:

(A) Financial interests of the covered employee, of close family members, or of other members of the covered employee's household.

(B) Other employment or financial relationships of the covered employee (including seeking or negotiating for prospective employment or business).

(C) Gifts, including travel; and

(ii) Requiring each covered employee to update the disclosure statement whenever the employee's personal or financial circumstances change in such a way that a new personal conflict of interest might occur because of the task the covered employee is performing.

(2) For each covered employee—

(i) Prevent personal conflicts of interest, including not assigning or allowing a covered employee to perform any task under the contract for which the Contractor has identified a personal conflict of interest for the employee that the Contractor or employee cannot satisfactorily prevent or mitigate in consultation with the contracting agency;

(ii) Prohibit use of non-public information accessed through performance of a Government contract for personal gain; and

(iii) Obtain a signed non-disclosure agreement to prohibit disclosure of non-public information accessed through performance of a Government contract.

(3) Inform covered employees of their obligation—

(i) To disclose and prevent personal conflicts of interest;

(ii) Not to use non-public information accessed through performance of a Government contract for personal gain; and

(iii) To avoid even the appearance of personal conflicts of interest;

(4) Maintain effective oversight to verify compliance with personal conflict-of-interest safeguards;

(5) Take appropriate disciplinary action in the case of covered employees who fail to comply with policies established pursuant to this clause; and

(6) Report to the Contracting Officer any personal conflict-of-interest violation by a covered employee as soon as it is identified. This report shall include a description of the violation and the proposed actions to be

taken by the Contractor in response to the violation. Provide follow-up reports of corrective actions taken, as necessary. Personal conflict-of-interest violations include—

(i) Failure by a covered employee to disclose a personal conflict of interest;

(ii) Use by a covered employee of nonpublic information accessed through performance of a Government contract for personal gain; and

(iii) Failure of a covered employee to comply with the terms of a non-disclosure agreement.

(c) *Mitigation or waiver.* (1) In exceptional circumstances, if the Contractor cannot satisfactorily prevent a personal conflict of interest as required by paragraph (b)(2)(i) of this clause, the Contractor may submit a request through the Contracting Officer to the Head of the Contracting Activity for—

(i) Agreement to a plan to mitigate the personal conflict of interest; or

(ii) A waiver of the requirement.

(2) The Contractor shall include in the request any proposed mitigation of the personal conflict of interest.

(3) The Contractor shall—

(i) Comply, and require compliance by the covered employee, with any conditions imposed by the Government as necessary to mitigate the personal conflict of interest; or

(ii) Remove the Contractor employee or subcontractor employee from performance of the contract or terminate the applicable subcontract.

(d) *Subcontract flowdown.* The Contractor shall include the substance of this clause, including this paragraph (d), in subcontracts—

(1) That exceed $150,000; and

(2) In which subcontractor employees will perform acquisition functions closely associated with inherently governmental functions (i.e., instead of performance only by a self-employed individual).

(End of clause)

[FAC 2005-54, 76 FR 68017, 11/2/2011, effective 12/2/2011]

52.203-17 Contractor Employee Whistleblower Rights and Requirement to Inform Employees of Whistleblower Rights.

As prescribed in 3.908-9, insert the following clause:

CONTRACTOR EMPLOYEE WHISTLEBLOWER RIGHTS AND REQUIREMENT TO INFORM EMPLOYEES OF WHISTLEBLOWER RIGHTS (APR 2014)

(a) This contract and employees working on this contract will be subject to the whistleblower rights and remedies in the pilot program on Contractor employee whistleblower protections established at 41 U.S.C. 4712 by section 828 of the National Defense Authorization Act for Fiscal Year 2013 (Pub. L. 112-239) and FAR 3.908.

(b) The Contractor shall inform its employees in writing, in the predominant language of the workforce, of employee whistleblower rights and protections under 41 U.S.C. 4712, as described in section 3.908 of the Federal Acquisition Regulation.

(c) The Contractor shall insert the substance of this clause, including this paragraph (c), in all subcontracts over the simplified acquisition threshold.

(End of clause)

[FAC 2005-70, 78 FR 60169, 9/30/2013, effective 9/30/2013; FAC 2005-73, 79 FR 24253, 4/29/2014, effective 4/29/2014; FAC 2005-85, 80 FR 75911, 12/4/2015, effective 12/4/2015]

52.203-18 Prohibition on Contracting with Entities that Require Certain Internal Confidentiality Agreements or Statements—Representation.

As prescribed in 3.909-3(a), insert the following provision:

PROHIBITION ON CONTRACTING WITH ENTITIES THAT REQUIRE CERTAIN INTERNAL CONFIDENTIALITY AGREEMENTS OR STATEMENTS—REPRESENTATION (JAN 2017)

(a) *Definition.* As used in this provision—

Internal confidentiality agreement or statement, subcontract, and *subcontractor*, are defined in the clause at 52.203-19, Prohibition on Requiring Certain Internal Confidentiality Agreements or Statements.

(b) In accordance with section 743 of Division E, Title VII, of the Consolidated and Further Continuing Appropriations Act, 2015 (Pub. L. 113-235) and its successor provisions in subsequent appropriations acts (and as extended in continuing resolutions), Government agencies are not permitted to use funds appropriated (or otherwise made available) for contracts with an entity that requires employees or subcontractors of such entity seeking to report waste, fraud, or abuse to sign internal confidentiality agreements or statements prohibiting or otherwise restricting such employees or subcontractors from lawfully reporting such waste, fraud, or abuse to a designated investigative or law enforcement representative of a Federal department or agency authorized to receive such information.

(c) The prohibition in paragraph (b) of this provision does not contravene requirements applicable to Standard Form 312, (Classified Information Nondisclosure Agreement), Form 4414 (Sensitive Compartmented Information Nondisclosure Agreement), or any other form issued by a Federal department or agency governing the nondisclosure of classified information.

(d) Representation. By submission of its offer, the Offeror represents that it will not require its employees or subcontractors to sign or comply with internal confidentiality agreements or statements prohibiting or otherwise restricting such employees or subcontractors from lawfully reporting waste, fraud, or abuse related to the performance of a Government contract to a designated investigative or law enforcement representative of a Federal department or agency authorized to receive such information (e.g., agency Office of the Inspector General).

(End of provision)

[FAC 2005-95, 82 FR 4717, 1/13/2017, effective 1/19/2017]

52.203-19 Prohibition on Requiring Certain Internal Confidentiality Agreements or Statements.

As prescribed in 3.909-3(b), insert the following clause:

PROHIBITION ON REQUIRING CERTAIN INTERNAL CONFIDENTIALITY AGREEMENTS OR STATEMENTS (JAN 2017)

(a) *Definitions*. As used in this clause—

Internal confidentiality agreement or statement means a confidentiality agreement or any other written statement that the contractor requires any of its employees or subcontractors to sign regarding nondisclosure of contractor information, except that it does not include confidentiality agreements arising out of civil litigation or confidentiality agreements that contractor employees or subcontractors sign at the behest of a Federal agency.

Subcontract means any contract as defined in subpart 2.1 entered into by a subcontractor to furnish supplies or services for performance of a prime contract or a subcontract. It includes but is not limited to purchase orders, and changes and modifications to purchase orders.

Subcontractor means any supplier, distributor, vendor, or firm (including a consultant) that furnishes supplies or services to or for a prime contractor or another subcontractor.

(b) The Contractor shall not require its employees or subcontractors to sign or comply with internal confidentiality agreements or statements prohibiting or otherwise restricting such employees or subcontractors from lawfully reporting waste, fraud, or abuse related to the performance of a Government contract to a designated investigative or law enforcement representative of a Federal department or agency authorized to receive such information (e.g., agency Office of the Inspector General).

(c) The Contractor shall notify current employees and subcontractors that prohibitions and restrictions of any preexisting internal confidentiality agreements or statements covered by this clause, to the extent that such prohibitions and restrictions are inconsistent with the prohibitions of this clause, are no longer in effect.

(d) The prohibition in paragraph (b) of this clause does not contravene requirements applicable to Standard Form 312 (Classified Information Nondisclosure Agreement), Form 4414 (Sensitive Compartmented Information Nondisclosure Agreement), or any other form issued by a Federal department or agency governing the nondisclosure of classified information.

(e) In accordance with section 743 of Division E, Title VII, of the Consolidated and Further Continuing Appropriations Act, 2015, (Pub. L. 113-235), and its successor provisions in subsequent appropriations acts (and as extended in continuing resolutions) use of funds appropriated (or otherwise made available) is prohibited, if the Government determines that the Contractor is not in compliance with the provisions of this clause.

(f) The Contractor shall include the substance of this clause, including this paragraph (f), in subcontracts under such contracts.

(End of clause)

[FAC 2005-95, 82 FR 4717, 1/13/2017, effective 1/19/2017]

52.204-1 Approval of Contract.

As prescribed in 4.103, insert the following clause:

APPROVAL OF CONTRACT (DEC 1989)

This contract is subject to the written approval of ______ [*identify title of designated agency official here*] and shall not be binding until so approved.

(End of clause)

[FAC 84-42, 54 FR 5058, 1/31/89, effective 3/2/89; FAC 84-53, 54 FR 48990, 11/28/89, effective 12/28/89]

52.204-2 Security Requirements.

As prescribed in 4.404(a), insert the following clauses:

SECURITY REQUIREMENTS (AUG 1996)

(a) This clause applies to the extent that this contract involves access to information classified "Confidential," "Secret," or "Top Secret."

(b) The Contractor shall comply with—

(1) The Security Agreement (DD Form 441), including the *National Industrial Security Program Operating Manual* (DoD 5220.22-M); and

(2) Any revisions to that manual, notice of which has been furnished to the Contractor.

(c) If, subsequent to the date of this contract, the security classification or security requirements under this contract are changed by the Government and if the changes cause an increase or decrease in security costs or otherwise affect any other term or condition of this contract, the contract shall be subject to an equitable adjustment as if the changes were directed under the Changes clause of this contract.

(d) The Contractor agrees to insert terms that conform substantially to the language of this clause, including this paragraph (d) but excluding any reference to the Changes clause of this contract, in all subcontracts under this contract that involve access to classified information.

(End of clause)

Alternate I (APR 1984). If a cost contract for research and development with an educational institution is contemplated, add the following paragraphs (e), (f), and (g) to the basic clause:

(e) If a change in security requirements, as provided in paragraphs (b) and (c), results (1) in a change in the security classification of this contract or any of its elements from an unclassified status or a lower classification to a higher classification, or (2) in more restrictive area controls than previously required, the Contractor shall exert every reasonable effort compatible with the Contractor's established policies to continue the performance of work under the contract in compliance with the change in security classification or requirements. If, despite reasonable efforts, the Contractor determines that the continuation of work under this contract is not practicable because of the change in security classification or requirements, the Contractor shall notify the

Contracting Officer in writing. Until resolution of the problem is made by the Contracting Officer, the Contractor shall continue safeguarding all classified material as required by this contract.

(f) After receiving the written notification, the Contracting Officer shall explore the circumstances surrounding the proposed change in security classification or requirements, and shall endeavor to work out a mutually satisfactory method whereby the Contractor can continue performance of the work under this contract.

(g) If, 15 days after receipt by the Contracting Officer of the notification of the Contractor's stated inability to proceed, (1) the application to this contract of the change in security classification or requirements has not been withdrawn or (2) a mutually satisfactory method for continuing performance of work under this contract has not been agreed upon, the Contractor may request the Contracting Officer to terminate the contract in whole or in part. The Contracting Officer shall terminate the contract in whole or in part, as may be appropriate, and the termination shall be deemed a termination under the terms of the Termination for the Convenience of the Government clause.

Alternate II (APR 1984). If employee identification is required for security or other reasons in a construction contract or architect-engineer contract, add the following paragraph (e) to the basic clause:

(e) The Contractor shall be responsible for furnishing to each employee and for requiring each employee engaged on the work to display such identification as may be approved and directed by the Contracting Officer. All prescribed identification shall immediately be delivered to the Contracting Officer, for cancellation upon the release of any employee. When required by the Contracting Officer, the Contractor shall obtain and submit fingerprints of all persons employed or to be employed on the project.

[FAC 90-32, 60 FR 48206, 9/18/95, effective 10/1/95; FAC 90-39, 61 FR 31612, 6/20/96, effective 8/19/96]

52.204-3 Taxpayer Identification.

As prescribed in 4.905, insert the following provision:

TAXPAYER IDENTIFICATION (OCT 1998)

(a) *Definitions.*

Common parent, as used in this provision, means that corporate entity that owns or controls an affiliated group of corporations that files its Federal income tax returns on a consolidated basis, and of which the offeror is a member.

Taxpayer Identification Number (TIN), as used in this solicitation provision, means the number required by the Internal Revenue Service (IRS) to be used by the offeror in reporting income tax and other returns. The TIN may be either a Social Security Number or an Employer Identification Number.

(b) All offerors must submit the information required in paragraphs (d) through (f) of this provision to comply with debt collection requirements of 31 U.S.C. 7701(c) and 3325(d), reporting requirements of 26 U.S.C. 6041, 6041A, and 6050M, and implementing regulations issued by the IRS. If the resulting contract is subject to the payment reporting requirements described in Federal Acquisition Regulation (FAR) 4.904, the failure or refusal by the offeror to furnish the information may result in a 31 percent reduction of payments otherwise due under the contract.

(c) The TIN may be used by the Government to collect and report on any delinquent amounts arising out of the offeror's relationship with the Government (31 U.S.C. 7701(c)(3)). If the resulting contract is subject to the payment reporting requirements described in FAR 4.904, the TIN provided hereunder may be matched with IRS records to verify the accuracy of the offeror's TIN.

(d) *Taxpayer Identification Number (TIN).*

☐ TIN: ____________.

☐ TIN has been applied for.

☐ TIN is not required because:

☐ Offeror is a nonresident alien, foreign corporation, or foreign partnership that does not have income effectively connected with the conduct of a trade or business in the United States and does not have an office or place of business or a fiscal paying agent in the United States;

☐ Offeror is an agency or instrumentality of a foreign government;

☐ Offeror is an agency or instrumentality of the Federal Government.

(e) *Type of organization.*

☐ Sole proprietorship;

☐ Partnership;

☐ Corporate entity (not tax-exempt);

☐ Corporate entity (tax-exempt);

☐ Government entity (Federal, State, or local);

☐ Foreign government;

☐ International organization per 26 CFR 1.6049-4;

☐ Other __________

(f) *Common parent.*

☐ Offeror is not owned or controlled by a common parent as defined in paragraph (a) of this provision.

☐ Name and TIN of common parent:

Name __________

TIN __________

(End of provision)

[FAC 97-9, 63 FR 58587, 10/30/98, effective 10/30/98, finalized without change, FAC 97-12, 64 FR 32740, 6/17/99]

52.204-4 Printed or Copied Double-Sided on Postconsumer Fiber Content Paper.

As prescribed in 4.303, insert the following clause:

PRINTED OR COPIED DOUBLE-SIDED ON POSTCONSUMER FIBER CONTENT PAPER (MAY 2011)

(a) *Definitions.* As used in this clause—

Postconsumer fiber means—(1) Paper, paperboard, and fibrous materials from retail stores, office buildings, homes, and so forth, after they have passed through their end-usage as a consumer item, including: used corrugated boxes; old newspapers; old magazines; mixed waste paper; tabulating cards; and used cordage; or

(2) All paper, paperboard, and fibrous materials that enter and are collected from municipal solid waste; but not

(3) Fiber derived from printers' over-runs, converters' scrap, and over-issue publications.

(b) The Contractor is required to submit paper documents, such as offers, letters, or reports that are printed or copied double-sided on paper containing at least 30 percent postconsumer fiber, whenever practicable, when not using electronic commerce methods to submit information or data to the Government.

(End of clause)

[FAC 97-18, 65 FR 36014, 6/6/2000, effective 8/7/2000; FAC 2005-52, 76 FR 31395, 5/31/2011, effective 5/31/2011]

52.204-5 Women-Owned Business (Other Than Small Business).

As prescribed in 4.607(a), insert the following provision:

WOMEN-OWNED BUSINESS (OTHER THAN SMALL BUSINESS) (OCT 2014)

(a) *Definition. Women-owned business concern*, as used in this provision, means a concern that is at least 51 percent owned by one or more women; or in the case of any publicly owned business, at least 51 percent of its stock is owned by one or more women; and whose management and daily business operations are controlled by one or more women.

(b) *Representation.* [*Complete only if the offeror is a women-owned business concern and has not represented itself as a small business concern in paragraph (c)(1) of FAR 52.219-1, Small Business Program Representations, of this solicitation.*] The offeror represents that it ______ is a women-owned business concern.

(End of provision)

[FAC 97-11, 64 FR 10530, 3/4/99, effective 5/3/99, corrected 64 FR 30103, 6/4/99; FAC 2005-25, 73 FR 21773, 4/22/2008, effective

4/22/2008; FAC 2005-30, 74 FR 2712, 1/15/2009, effective 2/17/2009; FAC 2005-62, 77 FR 69715, 11/20/2012, effective 12/20/2012; FAC 2005-77, 79 FR 61746, 10/14/2014, effective 10/14/2014]

52.204-6 Unique Entity Identifier.

As prescribed in 4.607(b), insert the following provision:

UNIQUE ENTITY IDENTIFIER (OCT 2016)

(a) *Definitions.* As used in this provision—

Electronic Funds Transfer (EFT) indicator means a four-character suffix to the unique entity identifier. The suffix is assigned at the discretion of the commercial, nonprofit, or Government entity to establish additional System for Award Management records for identifying alternative EFT accounts (see subpart 32.11) for the same entity.

Unique entity identifier means a number or other identifier used to identify a specific commercial, nonprofit, or Government entity. See *www.sam.gov* for the designated entity for establishing unique entity identifiers.

(b) The Offeror shall enter, in the block with its name and address on the cover page of its offer, the annotation "Unique Entity Identifier" followed by the unique entity identifier that identifies the Offeror's name and address exactly as stated in the offer. The Offeror also shall enter its EFT indicator, if applicable.

(c) If the Offeror does not have a unique entity identifier, it should contact the entity designated at *www.sam.gov* for establishment of the unique entity identifier directly to obtain one. The Offeror should be prepared to provide the following information:

(1) Company legal business name.

(2) Tradestyle, doing business, or other name by which your entity is commonly recognized.

(3) Company physical street address, city, state and Zip Code.

(4) Company mailing address, city, state and Zip Code (if separate from physical).

(5) Company telephone number.

(6) Date the company was started.

(7) Number of employees at your location.

(8) Chief executive officer/key manager.

(9) Line of business (industry).

(10) Company headquarters name and address (reporting relationship within your entity).

(End of provision)

[FAC 90-43, Interim rule, 61 FR 67408, 12/20/96, effective 12/20/96; FAC 97-4, 63 FR 9048, 2/23/98, effective 4/24/98; FAC 97-12, 64 FR 32740, 6/17/99, effective 6/17/99; FAC 2001-16, Final rule, 68 FR 56669, 10/1/2003, effective 10/1/2003; FAC 2005-25, 73 FR 21773, 4/22/2008, effective 4/22/2008; FAC 2005-30, 74 FR 2712, 1/15/2009, effective 2/17/2009; FAC 2005-62, 77 FR 69715, 11/20/2012, effective 12/20/2012; FAC 2005-67, 78 FR 37676, 6/21/2013, effective 7/22/2013; FAC 2005-91, 81 FR 67736, 9/30/2016, effective 10/31/2016]

52.204-7 System for Award Management.

As prescribed in 4.1105(a)(1), use the following provision:

SYSTEM FOR AWARD MANAGEMENT (OCT 2018)

(a) *Definitions.* As used in this provision—

Electronic Funds Transfer (EFT) indicator means a four-character suffix to the unique entity identifier. The suffix is assigned at the discretion of the commercial, nonprofit, or Government entity to establish additional System for Award Management records for identifying alternative EFT accounts (see subpart 32.11) for the same entity.

Registered in the System for Award Management (SAM) means that—

(1) The Offeror has entered all mandatory information, including the unique entity identifier and the EFT indicator, if applicable, the Commercial and Government Entity (CAGE) code, as well as data required by the Federal Funding Accountability and Transparency Act of 2006 (see subpart 4.14) into SAM;

(2) The Contractor has completed the Core, Assertions, Representations and Certi-

fications, and Points of Contact sections of the registration in SAM;

(3) The Government has validated all mandatory data fields, to include validation of the Taxpayer Identification Number (TIN) with the Internal Revenue Service (IRS). The contractor will be required to provide consent for TIN validation to the Government as a part of the SAM registration process; and

(4) The Government has marked the record "Active".

Unique entity identifier means a number or other identifier used to identify a specific commercial, nonprofit, or Government entity. See *www.sam.gov* for the designated entity for establishing unique entity identifiers.

(b)(1) An Offeror is required to be registered in SAM when submitting an offer or quotation, and shall continue to be registered until time of award, during performance, and through final payment of any contract, basic agreement, basic ordering agreement, or blanket purchasing agreement resulting from this solicitation.

(2) The Offeror shall enter, in the block with its name and address on the cover page of its offer, the annotation "Unique Entity Identifier" followed by the unique entity identifier that identifies the Offeror's name and address exactly as stated in the offer. The Offeror also shall enter its EFT indicator, if applicable. The unique entity identifier will be used by the Contracting Officer to verify that the Offeror is registered in SAM.

(c) If the Offeror does not have a unique entity identifier, it should contact the entity designated at *www.sam.gov* for establishment of the unique entity identifier directly to obtain one. The Offeror should be prepared to provide the following information:

(1) Company legal business name.

(2) Tradestyle, doing business, or other name by which your entity is commonly recognized.

(3) Company physical street address, city, state, and Zip Code.

(4) Company mailing address, city, state and Zip Code (if separate from physical).

(5) Company telephone number.

(6) Date the company was started.

(7) Number of employees at your location.

(8) Chief executive officer/key manager.

(9) Line of business (industry).

(10) Company headquarters name and address (reporting relationship within your entity).

(d) Processing time should be taken into consideration when registering. Offerors who are not registered in SAM should consider applying for registration immediately upon receipt of this solicitation. See *https://www.sam.gov* for information on registration.

(End of provision)

Alternate I (OCT 2018). As prescribed in 4.1105(a)(2), substitute the following paragraph (b)(1) for paragraph (b)(1) of the basic provision:

(b)(1) An Offeror is required to be registered in SAM as soon as possible. If registration is not possible when submitting an offer or quotation, the awardee shall be registered in SAM in accordance with the requirements of clause 52.204-13, System for Award Management Maintenance.

[FAC 2001-16, Final rule, 68 FR 56669, 10/1/2003, effective 10/1/2003; Correction, 68 FR 61866, 10/30/2003, effective 10/30/2003; FAC 2001-18, FR 69258, 12/11/2003, effective 12/11/2003; FAC 2005-10, 71 FR 36923, 6/28/2006, effective 7/28/2006; FAC 2005-25, 73 FR 21773, 4/22/2008, effective 4/22/2008; FAC 2005-30, 74 FR 2712, 1/15/2009, effective 2/17/2009; FAC 2005-37, 74 FR 52860, 10/14/2009, effective 10/14/2009; FAC 2005-43, 75 FR 38683, 7/2/2010, effective 8/2/2010; FAC 2005-55, 77 FR 187, 1/3/2012, effective 2/2/2012; FAC 2005-60, 77 FR 44047, 7/26/2012, effective 8/27/2012; FAC 2005-62, 77 FR 69715, 11/20/2012, effective 12/20/2012; FAC 2005-67, 78 FR 37676, 6/21/2013, effective 7/22/2013; FAC 2005-91, 81 FR 67736, 9/30/2016, effective 10/31/2016; Final rule, 81 FR 71384, 10/17/2016, effective 10/17/2016; FAC 2005-101, 83 FR 48691, 9/26/2018, effective 10/26/2018]

52.204-8 Annual Representations and Certifications.

As prescribed in 4.1202(a), insert the following provision:

ANNUAL REPRESENTATIONS AND CERTIFICATIONS (DEC 2019)

(a) (1) The North American Industry Classification System (NAICS) code for this acquisition is ____ [*insert NAICS code*].

(2) The small business size standard is ____ [*insert size standard*].

(3) The small business size standard for a concern which submits an offer in its own name, other than on a construction or service contract, but which proposes to furnish a product which it did not itself manufacture, is 500 employees.

(b) (1) If the provision at 52.204-7, System for Award Management, is included in this solicitation, paragraph (d) of this provision applies.

(2) If the provision at 52.204-7, System for Award Management, is not included in this solicitation, and the Offeror has an active registration in the System for Award Management (SAM), the Offeror may choose to use paragraph (d) of this provision instead of completing the corresponding individual representations and certifications in the solicitation. The Offeror shall indicate which option applies by checking one of the following boxes:

[ ] (i) Paragraph (c) applies.

[ ] (ii) Paragraph (c) does not apply and the offeror has completed the individual representations and certifications in the solicitation.

(c) (1) The following representations or certifications in SAM are applicable to this solicitation as indicated:

(i) 52.203-2, Certificate of Independent Price Determination. This provision applies to solicitations when a firmed-fixed-price contract or fixed-price contract with economic price adjustment is contemplated, unless—

(A) The acquisition is to be made under the simplified acquisition procedures in Part 13;

(B) The solicitation is a request for technical proposals under two-step sealed bidding procedures; or

(C) The solicitation is for utility services for which rates are set by law or regulation.

(ii) 52.203-11, Certification and Disclosure Regarding Payments to Influence Certain Federal Transactions. This provision applies to solicitations expected to exceed $150,000.

(iii) 52.203-18, Prohibition on Contracting with Entities that Require Certain Internal Confidentiality Agreements or Statements-Representation. This provision applies to all solicitations.

(iv) 52.204-3, Taxpayer Identification. This provision applies to solicitations that do not include the provision at 52.204-7, System for Award Management.

(v) 52.204-5, Women-Owned Business (Other Than Small Business). This provision applies to solicitations that—

(A) Are not set aside for small business concerns;

(B) Exceed the simplified acquisition threshold; and

(C) Are for contracts that will be performed in the United States or its outlying areas.

(vi) 52.204-26, Covered Telecommunications Equipment or Services—Representation. This provision applies to all solicitations.

(vii) 52.209-2, Prohibition on Contracting with Inverted Domestic Corporations—Representation.

(viii) 52.209-5, Certification Regarding Responsibility Matters. This provision applies to solicitations where the contract value is expected to exceed the simplified acquisition threshold.

(ix) 52.209–11, Representation by Corporations Regarding Delinquent Tax Liability or a Felony Conviction under any Federal Law. This provision applies to all solicitations.

(x) 52.214-14, Place of Performance—Sealed Bidding. This provision applies to invitations for bids except those in which the place of performance is specified by the Government.

(xi) 52.215-6, Place of Performance. This provision applies to solicitations unless the place of performance is specified by the Government.

(xii) 52.219-1, Small Business Program Representations (Basic & Alternate I). This provision applies to solicitations when the contract will be performed in the United States or its outlying areas.

(A) The basic provision applies when the solicitations are issued by other than DoD, NASA, and the Coast Guard.

(B) The provision with its Alternate I applies to solicitations issued by DoD, NASA, or the Coast Guard.

(xiii) 52.219-2, Equal Low Bids. This provision applies to solicitations when contracting by sealed bidding and the contract will be performed in the United States or its outlying areas.

(xiv) 52.222-22, Previous Contracts and Compliance Reports. This provision applies to solicitations that include the clause at 52.222-26, Equal Opportunity.

(xv) 52.222-25, Affirmative Action Compliance. This provision applies to solicitations, other than those for construction, when the solicitation includes the clause at 52.222-26, Equal Opportunity.

(xvi) 52.222-38, Compliance with Veterans' Employment Reporting Requirements. This provision applies to solicitations when it is anticipated the contract award will exceed the simplified acquisition threshold and the contract is not for acquisition of commercial items.

(xvii) 52.223-1, Biobased Product Certification. This provision applies to solicitations that require the delivery or specify the use of USDA-designated items; or include the clause at 52.223-2, Affirmative Procurement of Biobased Products Under Service and Construction Contracts.

(xviii) 52.223-4, Recovered Material Certification. This provision applies to solicitations that are for, or specify the use of, EPA-designated items.

(xvix) 52.223-22, Public Disclosure of Greenhouse Gas Emissions and Reduction Goals—Representation. This provision applies to solicitations that include the clause at 52.204-7.

(xx) 52.225-2, Buy American Certificate. This provision applies to solicitations containing the clause at 52.225-1.

(xxi) 52.225-4, Buy American—Free Trade Agreements—Israeli Trade Act Certificate. (Basic, Alternates I, II, and III.) This provision applies to solicitations containing the clause at 52.225-3.

(A) If the acquisition value is less than $25,000, the basic provision applies.

(B) If the acquisition value is $25,000 or more but is less than $50,000, the provision with its Alternate I applies.

(C) If the acquisition value is $50,000 or more but is less than $80,317, the provision with its Alternate II applies.

(D) If the acquisition value is $80,317 or more but is less than $100,000, the provision with its Alternate III applies.

(xxii) 52.225-6, Trade Agreements Certificate. This provision applies to solicitations containing the clause at 52.225-5.

(xxiii) 52.225-20, Prohibition on Conducting Restricted Business Operations in Sudan—Certification. This provision applies to all solicitations.

(xxiv) 52.225-25, Prohibition on Contracting with Entities Engaging in Certain Activities or Transactions Relating to Iran—Representation and Certification. This provision applies to all solicitations.

(xxiv) 52.226-2, Historically Black College or University and Minority Institution Representation. This provision applies to solicitations for research, studies, supplies, or services of the type normally acquired from higher educational institutions.

(2) The following representations or certifications are applicable as indicated by the Contracting Officer:

[*Contracting Officer check as appropriate.*]

____(i) 52.204–17, Ownership or Control of Offeror.

____(ii) 52.204–20, Predecessor of Offeror.

____(iii) 52.222–18, Certification Regarding Knowledge of Child Labor for Listed End Products.

____(iv) 52.222–48, Exemption from Application of the Service Contract Labor Standards to Contracts for Maintenance, Calibration, or Repair of Certain Equipment—Certification.

____(v) 52.222–52, Exemption from Application of the Service Contract Labor Standards to Contracts for Certain Services—Certification.

____(vi) 52.223–9, with its Alternate I, Estimate of Percentage of Recovered Material Content for EPA-Designated Products (Alternate I only).

____(vii) 52.227–6, Royalty Information.

____(A) Basic.

____(B) Alternate I.

____(viii) 52.227–15, Representation of Limited Rights Data and Restricted Computer Software.

(d) The Offeror has completed the annual representations and certifications electronically in SAM accessed through *https://www.sam.gov*. After reviewing the SAM information, the Offeror verifies by submission of the offer that the representations and certifications currently posted electronically that apply to this solicitation as indicated in paragraph (c) of this provision have been entered or updated within the last 12 months, are current, accurate, complete, and applicable to this solicitation (including the business size standard applicable to the NAICS code referenced for this solicitation), as of the date of this offer and are incorporated in this offer by reference (see FAR 4.1201); except for the changes identified below [*offeror to insert changes, identifying change by clause number, title, date*]. These amended representation(s) and/or certification(s) are also incorporated in this offer and are current, accurate, and complete as of the date of this offer.

FAR Clause No.	Title	Date	Change

Any changes provided by the offeror are applicable to this solicitation only, and do not result in an update to the representations and certifications posted on SAM.

(End of Provision)

[FAC 2001-26, 69 FR 76341, 12/20/2004, effective 1/1/2005; FAC 2005-07, 71 FR 226, 1/3/2006, effective 1/3/2006; FAC 2005-30, 74 FR 2724, 1/15/2009, effective 2/17/2009; FAC 2005-45, 75 FR 53129, 8/30/2010, effective 10/1/2010; FAC 2005-46, 75 FR 60254, 9/29/2010, effective 9/29/2010; FAC 2005-48, 75 FR 82567, 12/30/2010, effective 1/31/2011; FAC 2005-52, 76 FR 31395, 31410, 5/31/2011, effective 5/31/2011; FAC 2005-54, 76 FR 68027, 68028, 11/2/2011, effective 11/2/2011; FAC 2005-55, 77 FR 187, 1/3/2012, effective 2/2/2012; FAC 2005-56, 77 FR 12933, 3/2/2012, effective 3/2/2012; FAC 2005-57, 77 FR 13952, 3/7/2012, effective 3/15/2012; FAC 2005-58, 77 FR 23368, 4/18/2012, effective 5/18/2012; FAC 2005-59, 77 FR 27547, 5/10/2012, effective 5/10/2012; FAC 2005-61, 77 FR 56739, 9/13/2012, effective 9/13/2012; FAC 2005-63, 77 FR 73516, 12/10/2012, effective 12/10/2012; FAC 2005-65, 78 FR 6185, 1/29/2013, effective 1/29/2013; FAC 2005-67, 78 FR 37697, 6/21/2013, effective 6/21/2013; FAC 2005-67, 78 FR 37676, 6/21/2013, effective 7/22/2013; FAC 2005-69, 78 FR 46782, 8/1/2013, effective 8/1/2013; FAC 2005-72, 78 FR 80379, 12/31/2013, effective 1/1/14; Final rule, 79 FR 4630, 1/29/2014, effective 1/29/2014; FAC 2005-73, 79 FR 24192, 4/29/2014, effective 5/29/2014; FAC 2005-74, 79 FR 31187,

5/30/2014, effective 11/1/2014; FAC 2005-77, 79 FR 61746, 10/14/2014, effective 10/14/2014; FAC 2005-78, 79 FR 70348, 11/25/2014, effective 11/25/2014; FAC 2005-78, 79 FR 70341, 11/25/2014, effective 12/26/2014; FAC 2005-79, 79 FR 74554, 12/15/2014, effective 12/15/2014; FAC 2005-83, 80 FR 38309, 7/2/2015, effective 7/2/2015; FAC 2005-85, 80 FR 75903, 12/4/15, effective 2/26/2016; FAC 2005-86, 80 FR 81894, 12/31/2015, effective 1/1/2016; FAC 2005-87, 81 FR 11988, 3/7/2016, effective 4/6/2016; FAC 2005-90, 81 FR 58562, 8/25/2016, effective 10/25/2016; FAC 2005-91, 81 FR 67728, 9/30/2016, effective 9/30/2016; FAC 2005-92, 81 FR 83092, 11/18/2016, effective 12/19/2016; FAC 2005-93, 81 FR 91636, 12/16/2016, effective 12/16/2016; FAC 2005-95, 82 FR 4717, 1/13/2017, effective 1/19/2017; FAC 2005-96, 82 FR 51773, 11/8/2017, effective 11/6/2017; FAC 2005-97, 83 FR 3396, 1/24/2018, effective 1/24/2018; FAC 2005-101, 83 FR 48691, 9/26/2018, effective 10/26/2018; FAC 2020-03, 84 FR 68314, 12/13/2019, effective 12/13/2019]

52.204-9 Personal Identity Verification of Contractor Personnel.

As prescribed in 4.1303, insert the following clause:

PERSONAL IDENTITY VERIFICATION OF CONTRACTOR PERSONNEL (JAN 2011)

(a) The Contractor shall comply with agency personal identity verification procedures identified in the contract that implement Homeland Security Presidential Directive-12 (HSPD-12), Office of Management and Budget (OMB) guidance M-05-24, and Federal Information Processing Standards Publication (FIPS PUB) Number 201.

(b) The Contractor shall account for all forms of Government-provided identification issued to the Contractor employees in connection with performance under this contract. The Contractor shall return such identification to the issuing agency at the earliest of any of the following, unless otherwise determined by the Government:

(1) When no longer needed for contract performance.

(2) Upon completion of the Contractor employee's employment.

(3) Upon contract completion or termination.

(c) The Contracting Officer may delay final payment under a contract if the Contractor fails to comply with these requirements.

(d) The Contractor shall insert the substance of this clause, including this paragraph (d), in all subcontracts when the subcontractor's employees are required to have routine physical access to a Federally-controlled facility and/or routine access to a Federally-controlled information system. It shall be the responsibility of the prime Contractor to return such identification to the issuing agency in accordance with the terms set forth in paragraph (b) of this section, unless otherwise approved in writing by the Contracting Officer.

(End of clause)

[FAC 2005-07, 71 FR 208, 1/3/2006, effective 1/3/2006; FAC 2005-14, 71 FR 67771, 11/22/2006, effective 11/22/2006; FAC 2005-19, 72 FR 46333, 8/17/2007, effective 9/17/2007; FAC 2005-48, 75 FR 82575, 12/30/2010, effective 1/31/2011]

52.204-10 Reporting Executive Compensation and First-Tier Subcontract Awards.

As prescribed in 4.1403(a), insert the following clause:

REPORTING EXECUTIVE COMPENSATION AND FIRST-TIER SUBCONTRACT AWARDS (OCT 2018)

(a) *Definitions.* As used in this clause:

Executive means officers, managing partners, or any other employees in management positions.

First-tier subcontract means a subcontract awarded directly by the Contractor for the purpose of acquiring supplies or services (including construction) for performance of a prime contract. It does not include the Contractor's supplier agreements with vendors, such as long-term arrangements for materials or supplies that benefit multiple contracts and/or the costs of which are normally applied to a Contractor's general and administrative expenses or indirect costs.

Month of award means the month in which a contract is signed by the Contracting Officer or the month in which a first-tier subcontract is signed by the Contractor.

Total compensation means the cash and noncash dollar value earned by the executive during the Contractor's preceding fiscal year and includes the following (for more information see 17 CFR 229.402(c)(2)):

(1) *Salary and bonus.*

(2) *Awards of stock, stock options, and stock appreciation rights.* Use the dollar amount recognized for financial statement reporting purposes with respect to the fiscal year in accordance with the Financial Accounting Standards Board's Accounting Standards Codification (FASB ASC) 718, Compensation-Stock Compensation.

(3) *Earnings for services under non-equity incentive plans.* This does not include group life, health, hospitalization or medical reimbursement plans that do not discriminate in favor of executives, and are available generally to all salaried employees.

(4) *Change in pension value.* This is the change in present value of defined benefit and actuarial pension plans.

(5) *Above-market earnings on deferred compensation which is not tax-qualified.*

(6) Other compensation, if the aggregate value of all such other compensation (*e.g.,* severance, termination payments, value of life insurance paid on behalf of the employee, perquisites or property) for the executive exceeds $10,000.

(b) Section 2(d)(2) of the Federal Funding Accountability and Transparency Act of 2006 (Pub. L. 109-282), as amended by section 6202 of the Government Funding Transparency Act of 2008 (Pub. L. 110-252), requires the Contractor to report information on subcontract awards. The law requires all reported information be made public, therefore, the Contractor is responsible for notifying its subcontractors that the required information will be made public.

(c) Nothing in this clause requires the disclosure of classified information.

(d)(1) *Executive compensation of the prime contractor.* As a part of its annual registration requirement in the System for Award Management (SAM) (FAR provision 52.204-7), the Contractor shall report the names and total compensation of each of the five most highly compensated executives for its preceding completed fiscal year, if—

(i) In the Contractor's preceding fiscal year, the Contractor received—

(A) 80 percent or more of its annual gross revenues from Federal contracts (and subcontracts), loans, grants (and subgrants), cooperative agreements, and other forms of Federal financial assistance; and

(B) $25,000,000 or more in annual gross revenues from Federal contracts (and subcontracts), loans, grants (and subgrants), cooperative agreements, and other forms of Federal financial assistance; and

(ii) The public does not have access to information about the compensation of the executives through periodic reports filed under section 13(a) or 15(d) of the Securities Exchange Act of 1934 (15 U.S.C. 78m(a), 78o(d)) or section 6104 of the Internal Revenue Code of 1986. (To determine if the public has access to the compensation information, see the U.S. Security and Exchange Commission total compensation filings at *http://www.sec.gov/answers/execomp.htm.*).

(2) *First-tier subcontract information.* Unless otherwise directed by the contracting officer, or as provided in paragraph (g) of this clause, by the end of the month following the month of award of a first-tier subcontract with a value of $30,000 or more, the Contractor shall report the following information at *http://www.fsrs.gov* for that first-tier subcontract. (The Contractor shall follow the instructions at *http://www.fsrs.gov* to report the data.)

(i) Unique entity identifier for the subcontractor receiving the award and for the subcontractor's parent company, if the subcontractor has a parent company.

(ii) Name of the subcontractor.

(iii) Amount of the subcontract award.

(iv) Date of the subcontract award.

(v) A description of the products or services (including construction) being provided under the subcontract, including the overall purpose and expected outcomes or results of the subcontract.

(vi) Subcontract number (the subcontract number assigned by the Contractor).

(vii) Subcontractor's physical address including street address, city, state, and country. Also include the nine-digit zip code and congressional district.

(viii) Subcontractor's primary performance location including street address, city, state, and country. Also include the nine-digit zip code and congressional district.

(ix) The prime contract number, and order number if applicable.

(x) Awarding agency name and code.

(xi) Funding agency name and code.

(xii) Government contracting office code.

(xiii) Treasury account symbol (TAS) as reported in FPDS.

(xiv) The applicable North American Industry Classification System code (NAICS).

(3) *Executive compensation of the first-tier subcontractor.* Unless otherwise directed by the Contracting Officer, by the end of the month following the month of award of a first-tier subcontract with a value of $30,000 or more, and annually thereafter (calculated from the prime contract award date), the Contractor shall report the names and total compensation of each of the five most highly compensated executives for that first-tier subcontractor for the first-tier subcontractor's preceding completed fiscal year at *http://www.fsrs.gov*, if—

(i) In the subcontractor's preceding fiscal year, the subcontractor received—

(A) 80 percent or more of its annual gross revenues from Federal contracts (and subcontracts), loans, grants (and subgrants), cooperative agreements, and other forms of Federal financial assistance; and

(B) $25,000,000 or more in annual gross revenues from Federal contracts (and subcontracts), loans, grants (and subgrants), cooperative agreements, and other forms of Federal financial assistance; and

(ii) The public does not have access to information about the compensation of the executives through periodic reports filed under section 13(a) or 15(d) of the Securities Exchange Act of 1934 (15 U.S.C. 78m(a), 78o(d)) or section 6104 of the Internal Revenue Code of 1986. (To determine if the public has access to the compensation information, see the U.S. Security and Exchange Commission total compensation filings at *http://www.sec.gov/answers/execomp.htm.*)

(e) The Contractor shall not split or break down first-tier subcontract awards to a value less than $30,000 to avoid the reporting requirements in paragraph (d) of this clause.

(f) The Contractor is required to report information on a first-tier subcontract covered by paragraph (d) when the subcontract is awarded. Continued reporting on the same subcontract is not required unless one of the reported data elements changes during the performance of the subcontract. The Contractor is not required to make further reports after the first-tier subcontract expires.

(g) (1) If the Contractor in the previous tax year had gross income, from all sources, under $300,000, the Contractor is exempt from the requirement to report subcontractor awards.

(2) If a subcontractor in the previous tax year had gross income from all sources under $300,000, the Contractor does not need to report awards for that subcontractor.

(h) The FSRS database at *http://www.fsrs.gov* will be prepopulated with some information from SAM and the FPDS database. If FPDS information is incorrect, the contractor should notify the contracting officer. If the SAM information is incorrect, the contractor is responsible for correcting this information.

(End of clause)

[FAC 2005-20, 72 FR 51306, 9/6/2007, effective 9/6/2007; FAC 2005-44, 75 FR 39414, 7/8/2010, effective 7/8/2010; FAC 2005-55, 77 FR 187, 202, 1/3/2012, effective 2/2/2012; FAC 2005-60, 77 FR 44047, 7/26/2012, effective 8/27/2012; FAC 2005-60, 77 FR 44047, 7/26/2012, effective 8/27/2012; FAC 2005-67, 78 FR 37676, 6/21/2013, effective 7/22/2013; 78 FR 37697, 6/21/2013, effective 6/21/2013; FAC 2005-83, 80 FR 38293, 7/2/2015, effective 10/1/2015; FAC 2005-91, 81 FR 67736, 9/30/2016, effective 10/31/2016; FAC 2005-101, 83 FR 48691, 9/26/2018, effective 10/26/2018]

52.204-11 [Removed and Reserved]

[FAC 2005-32, 74 FR 14639, 3/31/2009, effective 3/31/2009; Technical amendment, 74 FR 22809, 5/14/2009, effective 5/14/2009; Technical Amendment, 74 FR 22809, 5/14/2009, effective 5/14/2009; FAC 2005-43, 75 FR 38684, 7/2/2010, effective 7/2/2010; Correction, 75 FR 43090, 7/23/2010, effective 7/23/2010; FAC 2005-74, 79 FR 31193, 5/30/2014, effective 5/30/2014]

52.204-12 Unique Entity Identifier Maintenance.

As prescribed in 4.607(c), insert the following clause:

UNIQUE ENTITY IDENTIFIER MAINTENANCE (OCT 2016)

(a) *Definition. Unique entity identifier*, as used in this clause, means a number or other identifier used to identify a specific commercial, nonprofit, or Government entity. See *www.sam.gov* for the designated entity for establishing unique entity identifiers.

(b) The Contractor shall ensure that the unique entity identifier is maintained with the entity designated at the System for Award Management (SAM) for establishment of the unique entity identifier throughout the life of the contract. The Contractor shall communicate any change to the unique entity identifier to the Contracting Officer within 30 days after the change, so an appropriate modification can be issued to update the data on the contract. A change in the unique entity identifier does not necessarily require a novation be accomplished.

(End of clause)

[FAC 2005-62, 77 FR 69715, 11/20/2012, effective 12/20/2012; FAC 2005-91, 81 FR 67736, 9/30/2016, effective 10/31/2016]

52.204-13 System for Award Management Maintenance.

As prescribed in 4.1105(b), use the following clause:

SYSTEM FOR AWARD MANAGEMENT MAINTENANCE (OCT 2018)

(a) *Definitions.* As used in this clause—

Electronic Funds Transfer (EFT) indicator means a four-character suffix to the unique entity identifier. The suffix is assigned at the discretion of the commercial, nonprofit, or Government entity to establish additional System for Award Management (SAM) records for identifying alternative EFT accounts (see subpart 32.11) for the same entity.

Registered in the System for Award Management (SAM) means that—

(1) The Contractor has entered all mandatory information, including the unique entity identifier and the EFT indicator (if applicable), the Commercial and Government Entity (CAGE) code, as well as data required by the Federal Funding Accountability and Transparency Act of 2006 (see subpart 4.14), into SAM;

(2) The Contractor has completed the Core, Assertions, Representations and Certifications, and Points of Contact sections of the registration in SAM;

(3) The Government has validated all mandatory data fields, to include validation of the Taxpayer Identification Number (TIN) with the Internal Revenue Service (IRS). The Contractor will be required to provide consent for TIN validation to the Government as a part of the SAM registration process; and

(4) The Government has marked the record "Active".

System for Award Management (SAM) means the primary Government repository for prospective Federal awardee and Federal awardee information and the centralized Government system for certain contracting, grants, and other assistance-related processes. It includes—

(1) Data collected from prospective Federal awardees required for the conduct of business with the Government;

(2) Prospective contractor-submitted annual representations and certifications in accordance with FAR subpart 4.12; and

(3) Identification of those parties excluded from receiving Federal contracts, certain subcontracts, and certain types of Federal financial and non-financial assistance and benefits.

Unique entity identifier means a number or other identifier used to identify a specific commercial, nonprofit, or Government entity. See *www.sam.gov* for the designated entity for establishing unique entity identifiers.

(b) If the solicitation for this contract contained the provision 52.204-7 with its Alternate I, and the Contractor was unable to register prior to award, the Contractor shall be registered in SAM within 30 days after award or before three days prior to submission of the first invoice, whichever occurs first.

(c) The Contractor shall maintain registration in SAM during contract performance and through final payment of any contract, basic agreement, basic ordering agreement, or blanket purchasing agreement. The Contractor is responsible for the currency, accuracy and completeness of the data within SAM, and for any liability resulting from the Government's reliance on inaccurate or incomplete data. To remain registered in SAM after the initial registration, the Contractor is required to review and update on an annual basis, from the date of initial registration or subsequent updates, its information in SAM to ensure it is current, accurate and complete. Updating information in SAM does not alter the terms and conditions of this contract and is not a substitute for a properly executed contractual document.

(d) (1) (i) If a Contractor has legally changed its business name or "doing business as" name (whichever is shown on the contract), or has transferred the assets used in performing the contract, but has not completed the necessary requirements regarding novation and change-of-name agreements in subpart 42.12, the Contractor shall provide the responsible Contracting Officer a minimum of one business day's written notification of its intention to—

(A) Change the name in SAM;

(B) Comply with the requirements of subpart 42.12 of the FAR; and

(C) Agree in writing to the timeline and procedures specified by the responsible Contracting Officer. The Contractor shall provide with the notification sufficient documentation to support the legally changed name.

(ii) If the Contractor fails to comply with the requirements of paragraph (d) (1) (i) of this clause, or fails to perform the agreement at paragraph (d) (1) (i) (C) of this clause, and, in the absence of a properly executed novation or change-of-name agreement, the SAM information that shows the Contractor to be other than the Contractor indicated in the contract will be considered to be incorrect information within the meaning of the "Suspension of Payment" paragraph of the electronic funds transfer (EFT) clause of this contract.

(2) The Contractor shall not change the name or address for EFT payments or manual payments, as appropriate, in SAM record to reflect an assignee for the purpose of assignment of claims (see FAR subpart 32.8, Assignment of Claims). Assignees shall be separately registered in the SAM. Information provided to the Contractor's SAM record that indicates payments, including those made by EFT, to an ultimate recipient other than that Contractor will be considered to be incorrect information within the meaning of the "Suspension of Payment" paragraph of the EFT clause of this contract.

(3) The Contractor shall ensure that the unique entity identifier is maintained with the entity designated at *www.sam.gov* for establishment of the unique entity identifier throughout the life of the contract. The Contractor shall communicate any change to the unique entity identifier to the Contracting

Officer within 30 days after the change, so an appropriate modification can be issued to update the data on the contract. A change in the unique entity identifier does not necessarily require a novation be accomplished.

(e) Contractors may obtain additional information on registration and annual confirmation requirements at *https://www.sam.gov*

(End of clause)

[FAC 2005-62, 77 FR 69715, 11/20/2012, effective 12/20/2012; FAC 2005-67, 78 FR 37676, 6/21/2013, effective 7/22/2013; FAC 2005-91, 81 FR 67736, 9/30/2016, effective 10/31/2016; FAC 2005-101, 83 FR 48691, 9/26/2018, effective 10/26/2018]

52.204-14 Service Contract Reporting Requirements.

As prescribed in 4.1705(a), insert the following clause:

SERVICE CONTRACT REPORTING REQUIREMENTS (OCT 2016)

(a) *Definition.*

First-tier subcontract means a subcontract awarded directly by the Contractor for the purpose of acquiring supplies or services (including construction) for performance of a prime contract. It does not include the Contractor's supplier agreements with vendors, such as long-term arrangements for materials or supplies that benefit multiple contracts and/or the costs of which are normally applied to a Contractor's general and administrative expenses or indirect costs.

(b) The Contractor shall report, in accordance with paragraphs (c) and (d) of this clause, annually by October 31, for services performed under this contract during the preceding Government fiscal year (October 1–September 30).

(c) The Contractor shall report the following information:

(1) Contract number and, as applicable, order number.

(2) The total dollar amount invoiced for services performed during the previous Government fiscal year under the contract.

(3) The number of Contractor direct labor hours expended on the services performed during the previous Government fiscal year.

(4) Data reported by subcontractors under paragraph (f) of this clause.

(d) The information required in paragraph (c) of this clause shall be submitted via the internet at *www.sam.gov.* (See SAM User Guide). If the Contractor fails to submit the report in a timely manner, the contracting officer will exercise appropriate contractual remedies. In addition, the Contracting Officer will make the Contractor's failure to comply with the reporting requirements a part of the Contractor's performance information under FAR subpart 42.15.

(e) Agencies will review Contractor reported information for reasonableness and consistency with available contract information. In the event the agency believes that revisions to the Contractor reported information are warranted, the agency will notify the Contractor no later than November 15. By November 30, the Contractor shall revise the report, or document its rationale for the agency.

(f) (1) The Contractor shall require each first-tier subcontractor providing services under this contract, with subcontract(s) each valued at or above the thresholds set forth in 4.1703(a)(2), to provide the following detailed information to the Contractor in sufficient time to submit the report:

(i) Subcontract number (including subcontractor name and unique entity identifier); and

(ii) The number of first-tier subcontractor direct-labor hours expended on the services performed during the previous Government fiscal year.

(2) The Contractor shall advise the subcontractor that the information will be made available to the public as required by section 743 of Division C of the Consolidated Appropriations Act, 2010.

(End of clause)

[FAC 2005-72, 78 FR 80369, 12/31/2013, effective 1/30/2014; FAC 2005-91, 81 FR 67736, 9/30/2016, effective 10/31/2016]

52.204-15 Service Contract Reporting Requirements for Indefinite-Delivery Contracts.

As prescribed in 4.1705(b), insert the following clause:

SERVICE CONTRACT REPORTING REQUIREMENTS FOR INDEFINITE-DELIVERY CONTRACTS (OCT 2016)

(a) *Definition.*

First-tier subcontract means a subcontract awarded directly by the Contractor for the purpose of acquiring supplies or services (including construction) for performance of a prime contract. It does not include the Contractor's supplier agreements with vendors, such as long-term arrangements for materials or supplies that benefit multiple contracts and/or the costs of which are normally applied to a Contractor's general and administrative expenses or indirect costs.

(b) The Contractor shall report, in accordance with paragraphs (c) and (d) of this clause, annually by October 31, for services performed during the preceding Government fiscal year (October 1–September 30) under this contract for orders that exceed the thresholds established in 4.1703(a)(2).

(c) The Contractor shall report the following information:

(1) Contract number and order number.

(2) The total dollar amount invoiced for services performed during the previous Government fiscal year under the order.

(3) The number of Contractor direct labor hours expended on the services performed during the previous Government fiscal year.

(4) Data reported by subcontractors under paragraph (f) of this clause.

(d) The information required in paragraph (c) of this clause shall be submitted via the internet at *www.sam.gov.* (See SAM User Guide). If the Contractor fails to submit the report in a timely manner, the Contracting Officer will exercise appropriate contractual remedies. In addition, the Contracting Officer will make the Contractor's failure to comply with the reporting requirements a part of the Contractor's performance information under FAR subpart 42.15.

(e) Agencies will review Contractor reported information for reasonableness and consistency with available contract information. In the event the agency believes that revisions to the Contractor reported information are warranted, the agency will notify the Contractor no later than November 15. By November 30, the Contractor shall revise the report, or document its rationale for the agency.

(f)(1) The Contractor shall require each first-tier subcontractor providing services under this contract, with subcontract(s) each valued at or above the thresholds set forth in 4.1703(a)(2), to provide the following detailed information to the Contractor in sufficient time to submit the report:

(i) Subcontract number (including subcontractor name and unique entity identifier), and

(ii) The number of first-tier subcontractor direct-labor hours expended on the services performed during the previous Government fiscal year.

(2) The Contractor shall advise the subcontractor that the information will be made available to the public as required by section 743 of Division C of the Consolidated Appropriations Act, 2010.

(End of clause)

[FAC 2005-72, 78 FR 80369, 12/31/2013, effective 1/30/2014; Final rule, 79 FR 4630, 1/29/2014, effective 1/30/2014; FAC 2005-91, 81 FR 67736, 9/30/2016, effective 10/31/2016]

52.204-16 Commercial and Government Entity Code Reporting.

As prescribed in 4.1804(a), use the following provision:

COMMERCIAL AND GOVERNMENT ENTITY CODE REPORTING (JUL 2016)

(a) *Definition.* As used in this provision—

Commercial and Government Entity (CAGE) code means—

(1) An identifier assigned to entities located in the United States or its outlying areas by the Defense Logistics Agency (DLA) Commercial and Government Entity

(CAGE) Branch to identify a commercial or government entity; or

(2) An identifier assigned by a member of the North Atlantic Treaty Organization (NATO) or by the NATO Support and Procurement Agency (NSPA) to entities located outside the United States and its outlying areas that the DLA Commercial and Government Entity (CAGE) Branch records and maintains in the CAGE master file. This type of code is known as a NATO CAGE (NCAGE) code.

(b) The Offeror shall enter its CAGE code in its offer with its name and address or otherwise include it prominently in its proposal. The CAGE code entered must be for that name and address. Enter "CAGE" before the number. The CAGE code is required prior to award.

(c) CAGE codes may be obtained via—

(1) Registration in the System for Award Management (SAM) at *www.sam.gov*. If the Offeror is located in the United States or its outlying areas and does not already have a CAGE code assigned, the DLA Commercial and Government Entity (CAGE) Branch will assign a CAGE code as a part of the SAM registration process. SAM registrants located outside the United States and its outlying areas shall obtain a NCAGE code prior to registration in SAM (see paragraph (c)(3) of this provision).

(2) The DLA Commercial and Government Entity (CAGE) Branch. If registration in SAM is not required for the subject procurement, and the offeror does not otherwise register in SAM, an offeror located in the United States or its outlying areas may request that a CAGE code be assigned by submitting a request at *https://cage.dla.mil*.

(3) The appropriate country codification bureau. Entities located outside the United States and its outlying areas may obtain an NCAGE code by contacting the Codification Bureau in the foreign entity's country if that country is a member of NATO or a sponsored nation. NCAGE codes may be obtained from the NSPA at *https://eportal.nspa.nato.int/AC135Public/scage/CageList.aspx* if the foreign entity's country is not a member of NATO or a sponsored nation. Points of contact for codification bureaus, as well as additional information on obtaining NCAGE codes, are available at *http://www.nato.int/structur/AC/135/main/links/contacts.htm*.

(d) Additional guidance for establishing and maintaining CAGE codes is available at *https://cage.dla.mil*.

(e) When a CAGE Code is required for the immediate owner and/or the highest-level owner by 52.204-17 or 52.212-3(p), the Offeror shall obtain the respective CAGE Code from that entity to supply the CAGE Code to the Government.

(f) Do not delay submission of the offer pending receipt of a CAGE code.

(End of provision)

[FAC 2005-74, 79 FR 31187, 5/30/2014, effective 11/1/2014; FAC 2005-83, 80 FR 38312, 7/2/2015, effective 7/2/2015; FAC 2005-89, 81 FR 45832, 7/14/2016, effective 7/14/2016; FAC 2005-89, 81 FR 45866, 7/14/2016, effective 7/14/2016]

52.204-17 Ownership or Control of Offeror.

As prescribed in 4.1804(b), use the following provision:

OWNERSHIP OR CONTROL OF OFFEROR (JUL 2016)

(a) *Definitions.* As used in this provision—

Commercial and Government Entity (CAGE) code means—

(1) An identifier assigned to entities located in the United States or its outlying areas by the Defense Logistics Agency (DLA) Commercial and Government Entity (CAGE) Branch to identify a commercial or government entity; or

(2) An identifier assigned by a member of the North Atlantic Treaty Organization (NATO) or by the NATO Support and Procurement Agency (NSPA) to entities located outside the United States and its outlying areas that the DLA Commercial and Government Entity (CAGE) Branch records and maintains in the CAGE master file. This type of code is known as a NATO CAGE (NCAGE) code.

Highest-level owner means the entity that owns or controls an immediate owner of the offeror, or that owns or controls one or more entities that control an immediate owner of the offeror. No entity owns or exercises control of the highest level owner.

Immediate owner means an entity, other than the offeror, that has direct control of the offeror. Indicators of control include, but are not limited to, one or more of the following: Ownership or interlocking management, identity of interests among family members, shared facilities and equipment, and the common use of employees.

(b) The Offeror represents that it [__] has or [__] does not have an immediate owner. If the Offeror has more than one immediate owner (such as a joint venture), then the Offeror shall respond to paragraph (c) and if applicable, paragraph (d) of this provision for each participant in the joint venture.

(c) If the Offeror indicates "has" in paragraph (b) of this provision, enter the following information:

Immediate owner CAGE code:

____

Immediate owner legal name:

____

(*Do not use a "doing business as" name*)

Is the immediate owner owned or controlled by another entity?: [__] Yes or [__] No.

(d) If the Offeror indicates "yes" in paragraph (c) of this provision, indicating that the immediate owner is owned or controlled by another entity, then enter the following information:

Highest-level owner CAGE code:

____

Highest-level owner legal name:

____

(Do not use a "doing business as" name)

(End of provision)

[FAC 2005-74, 79 FR 31187, 5/30/2014, effective 11/1/2014; FAC 2005-89, 81 FR 45832, 7/14/2016, effective 7/14/2016; FAC 2005-89, 81 FR 45866, 7/14/2016, effective 7/14/2016]

52.204-18 Commercial and Government Entity Code Maintenance.

As prescribed in 4.1804(c), use the following clause:

COMMERCIAL AND GOVERNMENT ENTITY CODE MAINTENANCE (JUL 2016)

(a) *Definition.* As used in this clause—

Commercial and Government Entity (CAGE) code means—

(1) An identifier assigned to entities located in the United States or its outlying areas by the Defense Logistics Agency (DLA) Commercial and Government Entity (CAGE) Branch to identify a commercial or government entity; or

(2) An identifier assigned by a member of the North Atlantic Treaty Organization (NATO) or by the NATO Support and Procurement Agency (NSPA) to entities located outside the United States and its outlying areas that the DLA Commercial and Government Entity (CAGE) Branch records and maintains in the CAGE master file. This type of code is known as a NATO CAGE (NCAGE) code.

(b) Contractors shall ensure that the CAGE code is maintained throughout the life of the contract. For contractors registered in the System for Award Management (SAM), the DLA Commercial and Government Entity (CAGE) Branch shall only modify data received from SAM in the CAGE master file if the contractor initiates those changes via update of its SAM registration. Contractors undergoing a novation or change-of-name agreement shall notify the contracting officer in accordance with subpart 42.12. The contractor shall communicate any change to the CAGE code to the contracting officer within 30 days after the change, so that a modification can be issued to update the CAGE code on the contract.

(c) Contractors located in the United States or its outlying areas that are not registered in SAM shall submit written change requests to the DLA Commercial and Government Entity (CAGE) Branch. Requests for changes shall be provided at *https://cage.dla.mil.* Change requests to the CAGE master file are accepted from the entity identified by the code.

(d) Contractors located outside the United States and its outlying areas that are not registered in SAM shall contact the appropriate National Codification Bureau (points of contact available at *http://www.nato.int/structur/AC/135/main/links/contacts.htm*) or NSPA at *https://eportal.nspa.nato.int/AC135Public/scage/CageList.aspx* to request CAGE changes.

(e) Additional guidance for maintaining CAGE codes is available at *https://cage.dla.mil.*

(End of clause)

[FAC 2005-74, 79 FR 31187, 5/30/2014, effective 11/1/2014; FAC 2005-83, 80 FR 38312, 7/2/2015, effective 7/2/2015; FAC 2005-89, 81 FR 45832, 7/14/2016, effective 7/14/2016; FAC 2005-89, 81 FR 45866, 7/14/2016, effective 7/14/2016]

52.204-19 Incorporation by Reference of Representations and Certifications.

As prescribed in 4.1202(b), use the following clause:

INCORPORATION BY REFERENCE OF REPRESENTATIONS AND CERTIFICATIONS (DEC 2014)

The Contractor's representations and certifications, including those completed electronically via the System for Award Management (SAM), are incorporated by reference into the contract.

(End of clause)

[FAC 2005-78, 79 FR 70341, 11/25/2014, effective 12/26/2014]

52.204-20 Predecessor of Offeror.

As prescribed in 4.1804(d), insert the following provision:

PREDECESSOR OF OFFEROR (JUL 2016)

(a) *Definitions.* As used in this provision—

Commercial and Government Entity (CAGE) code means—

(1) An identifier assigned to entities located in the United States or its outlying areas by the Defense Logistics Agency (DLA) Commercial and Government Entity (CAGE) Branch to identify a commercial or government entity; or

(2) An identifier assigned by a member of the North Atlantic Treaty Organization (NATO) or by the NATO Support and Procurement Agency (NSPA) to entities located outside the United States and its outlying areas that the DLA Commercial and Government Entity (CAGE) Branch records and maintains in the CAGE master file. This type of code is known as a NATO CAGE (NCAGE) code.

Predecessor means an entity that is replaced by a successor and includes any predecessors of the predecessor.

Successor means an entity that has replaced a predecessor by acquiring the assets and carrying out the affairs of the predecessor under a new name (often through acquisition or merger). The term *successor* does not include new offices/divisions of the same company or a company that only changes its name. The extent of the responsibility of the successor for the liabilities of the predecessor may vary, depending on State law and specific circumstances.

(b) The Offeror represents that it b is or b is not a successor to a predecessor that held a Federal contract or grant within the last three years.

(c) If the Offeror has indicated "is" in paragraph (b) of this provision, enter the following information for all predecessors that held a Federal contract or grant within the last three years (if more than one predecessor, list in reverse chronological order):

Predecessor CAGE code:

___ (or mark "Unknown").

Predecessor CAGE code:

___ (or mark "Unknown").

(*Do not use a doing business as name*).

(End of provision)

[FAC 2005-87, 81 FR 11988, 3/7/2016, effective 4/6/2016; FAC 2005-89, 81 FR 45866, 7/14/2016, effective 7/14/2016]

52.204-21 Basic Safeguarding of Covered Contractor Information Systems.

As prescribed in 4.1903, insert the following clause:

BASIC SAFEGUARDING OF COVERED CONTRACTOR INFORMATION SYSTEMS (JUN 2016)

(a) *Definitions.* As used in this clause—

Covered contractor information system means an information system that is owned or operated by a contractor that processes, stores, or transmits Federal contract information.

Federal contract information means information, not intended for public release, that is provided by or generated for the Government under a contract to develop or deliver a product or service to the Government, but not including information provided by the Government to the public (such as on public Web sites) or simple transactional information, such as necessary to process payments.

Information means any communication or representation of knowledge such as facts, data, or opinions, in any medium or form, including textual, numerical, graphic, cartographic, narrative, or audiovisual (Committee on National Security Systems Instruction (CNSSI) 4009).

Information system means a discrete set of information resources organized for the collection, processing, maintenance, use, sharing, dissemination, or disposition of information (44 U.S.C. 3502).

Safeguarding means measures or controls that are prescribed to protect information systems.

(b) *Safeguarding requirements and procedures.* (1) The Contractor shall apply the following basic safeguarding requirements and procedures to protect covered contractor information systems. Requirements and procedures for basic safeguarding of covered contractor information systems shall include, at a minimum, the following security controls:

(i) Limit information system access to authorized users, processes acting on behalf of authorized users, or devices (including other information systems).

(ii) Limit information system access to the types of transactions and functions that authorized users are permitted to execute.

(iii) Verify and control/limit connections to and use of external information systems.

(iv) Control information posted or processed on publicly accessible information systems.

(v) Identify information system users, processes acting on behalf of users, or devices.

(vi) Authenticate (or verify) the identities of those users, processes, or devices, as a prerequisite to allowing access to organizational information systems.

(vii) Sanitize or destroy information system media containing Federal Contract Information before disposal or release for reuse.

(viii) Limit physical access to organizational information systems, equipment, and the respective operating environments to authorized individuals.

(ix) Escort visitors and monitor visitor activity; maintain audit logs of physical access; and control and manage physical access devices.

(x) Monitor, control, and protect organizational communications (*i.e.*, information transmitted or received by organizational information systems) at the external boundaries and key internal boundaries of the information systems.

(xi) Implement subnetworks for publicly accessible system components that are physically or logically separated from internal networks.

(xii) Identify, report, and correct information and information system flaws in a timely manner.

(xiii) Provide protection from malicious code at appropriate locations within organizational information systems.

(xiv) Update malicious code protection mechanisms when new releases are available.

(xv) Perform periodic scans of the information system and real-time scans of files from external sources as files are downloaded, opened, or executed.

(2) *Other requirements.* This clause does not relieve the Contractor of any other specific safeguarding requirements specified by Federal agencies and departments relating to covered contractor information systems generally or other Federal safeguarding requirements for controlled unclassified information (CUI) as established by Executive Order 13556.

(c) *Subcontracts.* The Contractor shall include the substance of this clause, including this paragraph (c), in subcontracts under this contract (including subcontracts for the acquisition of commercial items, other than commercially available off-the-shelf items), in which the subcontractor may have Federal contract information residing in or transiting through its information system.

(End of clause)

[FAC 2005-88, 81 FR 30439, 5/16/2016, effective 6/15/2016]

52.204-22 Alternative Line Item Proposal.

As prescribed in 4.1008, insert the following provision:

ALTERNATIVE LINE ITEM PROPOSAL (JAN 2017)

(a) The Government recognizes that the line items established in this solicitation may not conform to the Offeror's practices. Failure to correct these issues can result in difficulties in acceptance of deliverables and processing payments. Therefore, the Offeror is invited to propose alternative line items for which bids, proposals, or quotes are requested in this solicitation to ensure that the resulting contract is economically and administratively advantageous to the Government and the Offeror.

(b) The Offeror may submit one or more additional proposals with alternative line items, provided that alternative line items are consistent with subpart 4.10 of the Federal Acquisition Regulation. However, acceptance of an alternative proposal is a unilateral decision made solely at the discretion of the Government. Offers that do not comply with the line items specified in this solicitation may be determined to be nonresponsive or unacceptable.

(End of provision)

[FAC 2005-95, 82 FR 4709, 1/13/2017, effective 1/13/2017]

52.204-23 Prohibition on Contracting for Hardware, Software, and Services Developed or Provided by Kaspersky Lab and Other Covered Entities.

As prescribed in 4.2004, insert the following clause:

PROHIBITION ON CONTRACTING FOR HARDWARE, SOFTWARE, AND SERVICES DEVELOPED OR PROVIDED BY KASPERSKY LAB AND OTHER COVERED ENTITIES (JUL 2018)

(a) *Definitions.* As used in this clause—

Covered article means any hardware, software, or service that—

(1) Is developed or provided by a covered entity;

(2) Includes any hardware, software, or service developed or provided in whole or in part by a covered entity; or

(3) Contains components using any hardware or software developed in whole or in part by a covered entity.

Covered entity means—

(1) Kaspersky Lab;

(2) Any successor entity to Kaspersky Lab;

(3) Any entity that controls, is controlled by, or is under common control with Kaspersky Lab; or

(4) Any entity of which Kaspersky Lab has a majority ownership.

(b) *Prohibition*. Section 1634 of Division A of the National Defense Authorization Act for Fiscal Year 2018 (Pub. L. 115-91) prohibits Government use of any covered article. The Contractor is prohibited from—

(1) Providing any covered article that the Government will use on or after October 1, 2018; and

(2) Using any covered article on or after October 1, 2018, in the development of data or deliverables first produced in the performance of the contract.

(c) *Reporting requirement*. (1) In the event the Contractor identifies a covered article provided to the Government during contract performance, or the Contractor is notified of such by a subcontractor at any tier or any other source, the Contractor shall report, in writing, to the Contracting Officer or, in the case of the Department of Defense, to the website at *https://dibnet.dod.mil*. For indefinite delivery contracts, the Contractor shall report to the Contracting Officer for the indefinite delivery contract and the Contracting Officer(s) for any affected order or, in the case of the Department of Defense, identify both the indefinite delivery contract and any affected orders in the report provided at *https://dibnet.dod.mil*.

(2) The Contractor shall report the following information pursuant to paragraph (c)(1) of this clause:

(i) Within 1 business day from the date of such identification or notification: The contract number; the order number(s), if applicable; supplier name; brand; model number (Original Equipment Manufacturer (OEM) number, manufacturer part number, or wholesaler number); item description; and any readily available information about mitigation actions undertaken or recommended.

(ii) Within 10 business days of submitting the report pursuant to paragraph (c)(1) of this clause: Any further available information about mitigation actions undertaken or recommended. In addition, the Contractor shall describe the efforts it undertook to prevent use or submission of a covered article, any reasons that led to the use or submission of the covered article, and any additional efforts that will be incorporated to prevent future use or submission of covered articles.

(d) *Subcontracts*. The Contractor shall insert the substance of this clause, including this paragraph (d), in all subcontracts, including subcontracts for the acquisition of commercial items.

(End of clause)

[FAC 2005-99, 83 FR 28141, 6/15/2018, effective 7/16/2018; FAC 2019-06, 84 FR 47861, 9/10/2019, effective 9/10/2019]

52.204-24 Representation Regarding Certain Telecommunications and Video Surveillance Services or Equipment.

As prescribed in 4.2105(a), insert the following provision:

REPRESENTATION REGARDING CERTAIN TELECOMMUNICATIONS AND VIDEO SURVEILLANCE SERVICES OR EQUIPMENT (DEC 2019)

The Offeror shall not complete the representation in this provision if the Offeror has represented that it "does not provide covered telecommunications equipment or services as a part of its offered products or services to the Government in the performance of any contract, subcontract, or other contractual instrument" in the provision at 52.204-26, Covered Telecommunications Equipment or Services—Representation, or in paragraph (v) of the provision at 52.212-3, Offeror Representations and Certifications—Commercial Items.

(a) *Definitions*. As used in this provision—

Covered telecommunications equipment or services, critical technology, and *substantial or essential component* have the meanings provided in clause 52.204-25, Prohibition on Contracting for Certain Telecommunications and Video Surveillance Services or Equipment.

(b) *Prohibition*. Section 889(a)(1)(A) of the John S. McCain National Defense Authorization Act for Fiscal Year 2019 (Pub. L. 115-232) prohibits the head of an executive agency on or after August 13, 2019, from procuring or obtaining, or extending or renewing a contract to procure or obtain, any equipment, system, or service that uses covered telecommunications equipment or services as a substantial or essential component of any system, or as critical technology as part of any system. Contractors are not prohibited from providing—

(1) A service that connects to the facilities of a third-party, such as backhaul, roaming, or interconnection arrangements; or

(2) Telecommunications equipment that cannot route or redirect user data traffic or permit visibility into any user data or packets that such equipment transmits or otherwise handles.

(c) *Procedures.* The Offeror shall review the list of excluded parties in the System for Award Management (SAM) (https://www.sam.gov) for entities excluded from receiving federal awards for "covered telecommunications equipment or services".

(d) *Representation.* The Offeror represents that it [ ] will, [ ] will not provide covered telecommunications equipment or services to the Government in the performance of any contract, subcontract or other contractual instrument resulting from this solicitation.

(e) *Disclosures.* If the Offeror has represented in paragraph (d) of this provision that it "will" provide covered telecommunications equipment or services", the Offeror shall provide the following information as part of the offer—

(1) A description of all covered telecommunications equipment and services offered (include brand; model number, such as original equipment manufacturer (OEM) number, manufacturer part number, or wholesaler number; and item description, as applicable);

(2) Explanation of the proposed use of covered telecommunications equipment and services and any factors relevant to determining if such use would be permissible under the prohibition in paragraph (b) of this provision;

(3) For services, the entity providing the covered telecommunications services (include entity name, unique entity identifier, and Commercial and Government Entity (CAGE) code, if known); and

(4) For equipment, the entity that produced the covered telecommunications equipment (include entity name, unique entity identifier, CAGE code, and whether the entity was the OEM or a distributor, if known).

(End of provision)

[FAC 2019-05, 84 FR 40216, 8/13/2019, effective 8/13/2019; FAC 2020-03, 84 FR 68314, 12/13/2019, effective 12/13/2019]

52.204-25 Prohibition on Contracting for Certain Telecommunications and Video Surveillance Services or Equipment.

As prescribed in 4.2105(b), insert the following clause:

PROHIBITION ON CONTRACTING FOR CERTAIN TELECOMMUNICATIONS AND VIDEO SURVEILLANCE SERVICES OR EQUIPMENT (AUG 2019)

(a) *Definitions.* As used in this clause—

Covered foreign country means The People's Republic of China.

Covered telecommunications equipment or services means—

(1) Telecommunications equipment produced by Huawei Technologies Company or ZTE Corporation (or any subsidiary or affiliate of such entities);

(2) For the purpose of public safety, security of Government facilities, physical security surveillance of critical infrastructure, and other national security purposes, video surveillance and telecommunications equipment produced by Hytera Communications Corporation, Hangzhou Hikvision Digital Technology Company, or Dahua Technology Company (or any subsidiary or affiliate of such entities);

(3) Telecommunications or video surveillance services provided by such entities or using such equipment; or

(4) Telecommunications or video surveillance equipment or services produced or provided by an entity that the Secretary of Defense, in consultation with the Director of

National Intelligence or the Director of the Federal Bureau of Investigation, reasonably believes to be an entity owned or controlled by, or otherwise connected to, the government of a covered foreign country.

Critical technology means—

(1) Defense articles or defense services included on the United States Munitions List set forth in the International Traffic in Arms Regulations under subchapter M of chapter I of title 22, Code of Federal Regulations;

(2) Items included on the Commerce Control List set forth in Supplement No. 1 to part 774 of the Export Administration Regulations under subchapter C of chapter VII of title 15, Code of Federal Regulations, and controlled—

(i) Pursuant to multilateral regimes, including for reasons relating to national security, chemical and biological weapons proliferation, nuclear nonproliferation, or missile technology; or

(ii) For reasons relating to regional stability or surreptitious listening;

(3) Specially designed and prepared nuclear equipment, parts and components, materials, software, and technology covered by part 810 of title 10, Code of Federal Regulations (relating to assistance to foreign atomic energy activities);

(4) Nuclear facilities, equipment, and material covered by part 110 of title 10, Code of Federal Regulations (relating to export and import of nuclear equipment and material);

(5) Select agents and toxins covered by part 331 of title 7, Code of Federal Regulations, part 121 of title 9 of such Code, or part 73 of title 42 of such Code; or

(6) Emerging and foundational technologies controlled pursuant to section 1758 of the Export Control Reform Act of 2018 (50 U.S.C. 4817).

Substantial or essential component means any component necessary for the proper function or performance of a piece of equipment, system, or service.

(b) *Prohibition*. Section 889(a)(1)(A) of the John S. McCain National Defense Authorization Act for Fiscal Year 2019 (Pub. L. 115-232) prohibits the head of an executive agency on or after August 13, 2019, from procuring or obtaining, or extending or renewing a contract to procure or obtain, any equipment, system, or service that uses covered telecommunications equipment or services as a substantial or essential component of any system, or as critical technology as part of any system. The Contractor is prohibited from providing to the Government any equipment, system, or service that uses covered telecommunications equipment or services as a substantial or essential component of any system, or as critical technology as part of any system, unless an exception at paragraph (c) of this clause applies or the covered telecommunication equipment or services are covered by a waiver described in Federal Acquisition Regulation 4.2104.

(c) *Exceptions*. This clause does not prohibit contractors from providing—

(1) A service that connects to the facilities of a third-party, such as backhaul, roaming, or interconnection arrangements; or

(2) Telecommunications equipment that cannot route or redirect user data traffic or permit visibility into any user data or packets that such equipment transmits or otherwise handles.

(d) *Reporting requirement*. (1) In the event the Contractor identifies covered telecommunications equipment or services used as a substantial or essential component of any system, or as critical technology as part of any system, during contract performance, or the Contractor is notified of such by a subcontractor at any tier or by any other source, the Contractor shall report the information in paragraph (d)(2) of this clause to the Contracting Officer, unless elsewhere in this contract are established procedures for reporting the information; in the case of the Department of Defense, the Contractor shall report to the website at *https://dibnet.dod.mil*. For indefinite delivery contracts, the Contractor shall report to the Contracting Officer for the indefinite delivery contract and the Contracting Officer(s) for any affected order or, in the case of the Department of Defense, identify both the indefinite delivery contract and any affected orders in the report provided at *https://dibnet.dod.mil*.

(2) The Contractor shall report the following information pursuant to paragraph (d) (1) of this clause:

(i) Within one business day from the date of such identification or notification: The contract number; the order number(s), if applicable; supplier name; supplier unique entity identifier (if known); supplier Commercial and Government Entity (CAGE) code (if known); brand; model number (original equipment manufacturer number, manufacturer part number, or wholesaler number); item description; and any readily available information about mitigation actions undertaken or recommended.

(ii) Within 10 business days of submitting the information in paragraph (d) (2) (i) of this clause: Any further available information about mitigation actions undertaken or recommended. In addition, the Contractor shall describe the efforts it undertook to prevent use or submission of covered telecommunications equipment or services, and any additional efforts that will be incorporated to prevent future use or submission of covered telecommunications equipment or services.

(e) *Subcontracts.* The Contractor shall insert the substance of this clause, including this paragraph (e), in all subcontracts and other contractual instruments, including subcontracts for the acquisition of commercial items.

(End of clause)

[FAC 2019-05, 84 FR 40216, 8/13/2019, effective 8/13/2019]

52.204-26 Covered Telecommunications Equipment or Services—Representation.

As prescribed in 4.2105(c), insert the following provision:

COVERED TELECOMMUNICATIONS EQUIPMENT OR SERVICES—REPRESENTATION (DEC 2019)

(a) *Definitions.* As used in this provision, covered telecommunications equipment or services has the meaning provided in the clause 52.204-25, Prohibition on Contracting for Certain Telecommunications and Video Surveillance Services or Equipment.

(b) *Procedures.* The Offeror shall review the list of excluded parties in the System for Award Management (SAM) (*https://www.sam.gov*) for entities excluded from receiving federal awards for *covered telecommunications equipment or services.*

(c) *Representation.* The Offeror represents that it [ ] does, [ ] does not provide covered telecommunications equipment or services as a part of its offered products or services to the Government in the performance of any contract, subcontract, or other contractual instrument.

(End of provision)

[FAC 2020-03, 84 FR 68314, 12/13/2019, effective 12/13/2019]

52.205 [Reserved]

52.206 [Reserved]

52.207-1 Notice of Standard Competition.

NOTICE OF STANDARD COMPETITION (MAY 2006)

(a) This solicitation is part of a standard competition under Office of Management and Budget Circular No. A-76 (Revised), Performance of Commercial Activities, dated May 29, 2003 (hereafter "the Circular"), to determine whether to accomplish the specified work under contract or by Government performance.

(b) The Government will evaluate private sector offers, the agency tender, and public reimbursable tenders, as provided in this solicitation and the Circular.

(c) A performance decision resulting from this standard competition will be publicly announced in accordance with the Circular. If the performance decision favors a private sector offeror, a contract will be awarded. If the performance decision favors an agency or a public reimbursable tender, the Contracting Officer shall establish, respectively, either a Most Efficient Organization letter of obligation or a fee-for-service agreement, as those terms are defined in the Circular.

(d) As provided in the Circular, directly interested parties may file contests, which are governed by the procedures in Federal Acquisition Regulation 33.103. Until resolution of any contest, or the expiration of the time for filing a contest, only legal agents for directly interested parties shall have access to the certified standard competition form, the agency tender, and public reimbursable tenders.

(End of provision)

[FAC 84-5, 50 FR 1746, 1/11/85 effective 4/1/85; FAC 84-58, 55 FR 25530, 6/21/90, effective 7/23/90; FAC 90-16, 57 FR 60575, 12/21/92, effective 2/19/93; FAC 2005-09, Final rule, 71 FR 20299, 4/19/2006, effective 5/19/2006]

52.207-2 Notice of Streamlined Competition.

As prescribed in 7.305(b), insert the following provision:

NOTICE OF STREAMLINED COMPETITION (MAY 2006)

(a) This solicitation is part of a streamlined competition under Office of Management and Budget Circular No. A-76 (Revised), Performance of Commercial Activities, dated May 29, 2003 (hereafter "the Circular"), to determine whether to accomplish the specified work under contract or by Government performance.

(b) The Government will evaluate the cost of private sector and Agency or public reimbursable performance, as provided in this solicitation and the Circular.

(c) A performance decision resulting from this streamlined competition will be publicly announced in accordance with the Circular. If the performance decision favors private sector performance, the Contracting Officer shall either award a contract or issue a competitive solicitation for private sector offers. If the performance decision favors Agency or public reimbursable performance, the Agency shall establish, respectively, either a letter of obligation or a fee-for-service agreement, as those terms are defined in the Circular.

(End of provision)

[FAC 84-58, 55 FR 25530, 6/21/90, effective 7/23/90; FAC 90-16, 57 FR 60575, 12/21/92, effective 2/19/93; FAC 2005-09, final rule, 71 FR 20299, 4/19/2006, effective 5/19/2006]

52.207-3 Right of First Refusal of Employment.

As prescribed in 7.305(c), insert the following clause:

RIGHT OF FIRST REFUSAL OF EMPLOYMENT (MAY 2006)

(a) The Contractor shall give Government personnel who have been or will be adversely affected or separated as a result of award of this contract the right of first refusal for employment openings under the contract in positions for which they are qualified, if that employment is consistent with post-Government employment conflict of interest standards.

(b) Within 10 days after contract award, the Contracting Officer will provide to the Contractor a list of all Government personnel who have been or will be adversely affected or separated as a result of award of this contract.

(c) The Contractor shall report to the Contracting Officer the names of individuals identified on the list who are hired within 90 days after contract performance begins. This report shall be forwarded within 120 days after contract performance begins.

(End of clause)

[FAC 84-25, 52 FR 9039, 3/20/87, effective 7/1/87; FAC 90-8, 56 FR 55372, 10/25/91, effective 11/25/91; FAC 90-32, 60 FR 48206, 9/18/95, effective 10/1/95; FAC 2005-09, Final rule, 71 FR 20299, 4/19/2006, effective 5/19/2006]

52.207-4 Economic Purchase Quantity—Supplies.

As prescribed in 7.203, insert the following provision:

ECONOMIC PURCHASE QUANTITY—SUPPLIES (AUG 1987)

(a) Offerors are invited to state an opinion on whether the quantity(ies) of supplies on which bids, proposals or quotes are requested in this solicitation is (are) economically advantageous to the government.

(b) Each offeror who believes that acquisitions in different quantities would be more advantageous is invited to recommend an economic purchase quantity. If different quantities are recommended, a total and a unit price must be quoted for applicable items. An economic purchase quantity is that quantity at which a significant price break occurs. If there are significant price breaks at different quantity points, this information is desired as well.

OFFEROR RECOMMENDATIONS

Item	Quantity	Price quotation	Total

(c) The information requested in this provision is being solicited to avoid acquisitions in disadvantageous quantities and to assist the Government in developing a data base for future acquisitions of these items. However, the Government reserves the right to amend or cancel the solicitation and resolicit with respect to any individual item in the event quotations received and the Government's requirements indicate that different quantities should be acquired.

(End of provision)

[FAC 84-11, 50 FR 35480, 8/30/85, effective 8/30/85; FAC 84-29, 52 FR 30078, 8/12/87, effective 8/24/87]

52.207-5 Option to Purchase Equipment.

As prescribed in 7.404, insert a clause substantially the same as the following:

OPTION TO PURCHASE EQUIPMENT (FEB 1995)

(a) The Government may purchase the equipment provided on a lease or rental basis under this contract. The Contracting Officer may exercise this option only by providing a unilateral modification to the Contractor. The effective date of the purchase will be specified in the unilateral modification and may be any time during the period of the contract, including any extensions thereto.

(b) Except for final payment and transfer of title to the Government, the lease or rental portion of the contract becomes complete and lease or rental charges shall be discontinued on the day immediately preceding the effective date of purchase specified in the unilateral modification required in paragraph (a) of this clause.

(c) The purchase conversion cost of the equipment shall be computed as of the effective date specified in the unilateral modification required in paragraph (a) of this clause, on the basis of the purchase price set forth in the contract, minus the total purchase option credits accumulated during the period of lease or rental, calculated by the formula contained elsewhere in this contract.

(d) The accumulated purchase option credits available to determine the purchase conversion cost will also include any credits accrued during a period of lease or rental of the equipment under any previous Government contract if the equipment has been on continuous lease or rental. The movement of equipment from one site to another site shall be "continuous rental."

[FAC 90-23, 59 FR 67010, 12/28/94, effective 2/27/95]

52.207-6 Solicitation of Offers from Small Business Concerns and Small Business Teaming Arrangements or Joint Ventures (Multiple-Award Contracts).

As prescribed in 7.107-6, insert the following provision:

SOLICITATION OF OFFERS FROM SMALL BUSINESS CONCERNS AND SMALL BUSINESS TEAMING ARRANGEMENTS OR JOINT VENTURES (MULTIPLE-AWARD CONTRACTS) (OCT 2016)

(a) *Definition. Small Business Teaming Arrangement,* as used in this provision—

(1) Means an arrangement where—

(i) Two or more small business concerns have formed a joint venture; or

(ii) A small business offeror agrees with one or more other small business concerns to have them act as its subcontractors under a specified Government contract. A Small Business Teaming Arrangement between the offeror and its small business subcontractor(s) exists through a written agreement between the parties that—

(A) Is specifically referred to as a "Small Business Teaming Arrangement"; and

(B) Sets forth the different responsibilities, roles, and percentages (or other allocations) of work as it relates to the acquisition;

(2) (i) For civilian agencies, may include two business concerns in a mentor-protégé relationship when both the mentor and the protégé are small or the protégé is small and the concerns have received an exception to affiliation pursuant to 13 CFR 121.103(h)(3)(ii) or (iii).

(ii) For DoD, may include two business concerns in a mentor-protégé relationship in the Department of Defense Pilot Mentor-Protégé Program (see section 831 of the National Defense Authorization Act for Fiscal Year 1991 (Pub. L. 101-510; 10 U.S.C. 2302 note)) when both the mentor and the protégé are small. There is no exception to joint venture size affiliation for offers received from teaming arrangements under the Department of Defense Pilot Mentor-Protégé Program; and

(3) See 13 CFR 121.103(b)(9) regarding the exception to affiliation for offers received from Small Business Teaming Arrangements in the case of a solicitation of offers for a bundled contract with a reserve.

(b) The Government is soliciting and will consider offers from any responsible source, including responsible small business concerns and offers from Small Business Teaming Arrangements or joint ventures of small business concerns.

(End of provision)

[FAC 2005-91, 81 FR 67763, 9/30/2016, effective 10/31/2016]

52.208-1 [Reserved]

[Removed and reserved, FAC 90-45, Final rule, 62 FR 224, 1/2/97, effective 1/1/97]

52.208-2 [Reserved]

[Removed and reserved, FAC 90-45, Final rule, 62 FR 224, 1/2/97, effective 1/1/97]

52.208-3 [Reserved]

[Removed and reserved, FAC 90-23, 59 FR 67010, 12/28/94, effective 2/27/95]

52.208-4 Vehicle Lease Payments.

As prescribed in 8.1104(a), insert the following clause in solicitations and contracts for leasing motor vehicles, unless the motor vehicles are leased in foreign countries:

VEHICLE LEASE PAYMENTS (APR 1984)

(a) Upon the submission of proper invoices or vouchers, the Government shall pay rent for each vehicle at the rate(s) specified in this contract.

(b) Rent shall accrue from the beginning of this contract, or from the date each vehicle is delivered to the Government, whichever is later, and shall continue until the expiration of the contract term or the termination of this contract. However, rent shall accrue only for the period that each vehicle is in the possession of the Government.

(c) Rent shall not accrue for any vehicle that the Contracting Officer determines does not comply with the Condition of Leased Vehicles clause of this contract or otherwise does not comply with the requirements of this contract, until the vehicle is replaced or the defects are corrected.

(d) Rent shall not accrue for any vehicle during any period when the vehicle is unavailable or unusable as a result of the Contractor's failure to render services for the operation and maintenance of the vehicle as prescribed by this contract.

(e) Rent stated in monthly terms shall be prorated on the basis of 1/30th of the monthly rate for each day the vehicle is in the Government's possession. If this contract contains a mileage provision, the Government shall pay rent as provided in the Schedule.

(End of clause)

[FAC 90-32, 60 FR 48206, 9/18/95, effective 10/1/95]

52.208-5 Condition of Leased Vehicles.

As prescribed in 8.1104(b), insert the following clause in solicitations and contracts for leasing motor vehicles, unless the motor vehicles are leased in foreign countries:

CONDITION OF LEASED VEHICLES (APR 1984)

Each vehicle furnished under this contract shall be of good quality and in safe operating condition, and shall comply with the Federal Motor Vehicle Safety Standards (49 CFR 571) and State safety regulations applicable to the vehicle. The Government shall accept or reject the vehicles promptly after receipt. If the Contracting Officer determines that any vehicle furnished is not in compliance with this contract, the Contracting Officer shall promptly inform the Contractor in writing. If the Contractor fails to replace the vehicle or correct the defects as required by the Contracting Officer, the Government may—

(a) By contract or otherwise, correct the defect or arrange for the lease of a similar vehicle and shall charge or set off against the Contractor any excess costs occasioned thereby; or

(b) Terminate the contract under the Default clause of this contract.

(End of clause)

[FAC 90-32, 60 FR 48206, 9/18/95, effective 10/1/95]

52.208-6 Marking of Leased Vehicles.

As prescribed in 8.1104(c), insert the following clause in solicitations and contracts for leasing motor vehicles, unless the motor vehicles are leased in foreign countries:

MARKING OF LEASED VEHICLES (APR 1984)

(a) The Government may place nonpermanent markings or decals, identifying the using agency, on each side, and on the front and rear bumpers, of any motor vehicle leased under this contract. The Government shall use markings or decals that are removable without damage to the vehicle.

(b) The Contractor may use placards for temporary identification of vehicles except that the placards may not contain any references to the Contractor that may be construed as advertising or endorsement by the Government of the Contractor.

(End of clause)

[FAC 90-32, 60 FR 48206, 9/18/95, effective 10/1/95]

52.208-7 Tagging of Leased Vehicles.

As prescribed in 8.1104(d), insert a clause substantially as follows:

TAGGING OF LEASED VEHICLES (MAY 1986)

While it is the intent that vehicles leased under this contract will operate on Federal tags, the Government reserves the right to utilize State tags if necessary to accomplish its mission. Should State tags be required, the Contractor shall furnish the Government documentation necessary to allow acquisition of such tags. Federal tags are the responsibility of the Government.

(End of clause)

[FAC 84-16, 51 FR 19717, 5/30/86, effective 5/30/86]

52.208-8 Required Sources for Helium and Helium Usage Data.

As prescribed in 8.505, insert the following clause:

REQUIRED SOURCES FOR HELIUM AND HELIUM USAGE DATA (AUG 2018)

(a) *Definitions.*

Bureau of Land Management, as used in this clause, means the Department of the Interior, Bureau of Land Management, Amarillo Field Office, Helium Operations, located at 801 South Fillmore Street, Suite 500, Amarillo, TX 79101-3545.

Federal helium supplier means a private helium vendor that has an in-kind crude helium sales contract with the Bureau of Land Management (BLM) and that is on the BLM

Amarillo Field Office's Authorized List of Federal Helium Suppliers available via the Internet at *https://www.blm.gov/programs/energy-and-minerals/helium/partners*.

Major helium requirement means an estimated refined helium requirement greater than 200,000 standard cubic feet (scf) (measured at 14.7 pounds per square inch absolute pressure and 70 degrees Fahrenheit temperature) of gaseous helium or 7510 liters of liquid helium delivered to a helium use location per year.

(b) *Requirements*—(1) Contractors must purchase major helium requirements from Federal helium suppliers, to the extent that supplies are available.

(2) The Contractor shall provide to the Contracting Officer the following data within 10 days after the Contractor or subcontractor receives a delivery of helium from a Federal helium supplier—

(i) The name of the supplier;

(ii) The amount of helium purchased;

(iii) The delivery date(s); and

(iv) The location where the helium was used.

(c) *Subcontracts.* The Contractor shall insert this clause, including this paragraph (c), in any subcontract or order that involves a major helium requirement.

(End of clause)

[FAC 2001-06, 67 FR 13048, 3/20/2002, effective 4/4/2002; FAC 2005-73, 79 FR 24253, 4/29/2014, effective 4/29/2014; FAC 2005-100, 83 FR 42571, 8/22/2018, effective 8/22/2018]

52.208-9 Contractor Use of Mandatory Sources of Supply or Services.

As prescribed in 8.005, insert the following clause:

CONTRACTOR USE OF MANDATORY SOURCES OF SUPPLY OR SERVICES (MAY 2014)

(a) Certain supplies or services to be provided under this contract for use by the Government are required by law to be obtained from nonprofit agencies participating in the program operated by the Committee for Purchase From People Who Are Blind or Severely Disabled (the Committee) under 41 U.S.C. 8504. Additionally, certain of these supplies are available from the Defense Logistics Agency (DLA), the General Services Administration (GSA), or the Department of Veterans Affairs (VA). The contractor shall obtain mandatory supplies or services to be provided for Government use under this contract from the specific sources indicated in the contract schedule.

(b) The Contractor shall immediately notify the Contracting Officer if a mandatory source is unable to provide the supplies or services by the time required, or if the quality of supplies or services provided by the mandatory source is unsatisfactory. The Contractor shall not purchase the supplies or services from other sources until the Contracting Officer has notified the Contractor that the Committee or an AbilityOne central nonprofit agency has authorized purchase from other sources.

(c) Price and delivery information for the mandatory supplies is available from the Contracting Officer for the supplies obtained through the DLA/GSA/VA distribution facilities. For mandatory supplies or services that are not available from DLA/GSA/VA, price and delivery information is available from the appropriate central nonprofit agency. Payments shall be made directly to the source making delivery. Points of contact for AbilityOne central nonprofit agencies are:

(1) National Industries for the Blind (NIB), 1901 North Beauregard Street, Suite 200, Alexandria, VA 22311-1705, (703) 998-0770.

(2) NISH, 2235 Cedar Lane, Vienna, VA 22182-5200, (703) 560-6800.

(End of clause)

[FAC 90-37, 61 FR 2626, 1/26/96, effective 3/26/96; FAC 90-43, 61 FR 67408, 12/20/96, effective 12/20/96; FAC 2001-02, 66 FR 65347, 12/18/2001, effective 2/19/2002; FAC 2001-09, 67 FR 56115, 8/30/2002, effective 9/30/2002; FAC 2001-24, 69 FR 34229, 6/18/2004, effective 7/19/2004; FAC 2005-10, 71 FR 36941, 6/28/2006, effective 6/28/2006; Correction, 71 FR 50862,

8/28/2006, effective 8/28/2006; FAC 2005-27, 73 FR 53994, 9/17/2008, effective 10/17/2008; FAC 2005-72, 78 FR 80376, 12/31/203, effective 1/30/2014; FAC 2005-73, 79 FR 24192, 4/29/2014, effective 5/29/2014]

52.209-1 Qualification Requirements.

As prescribed in 9.206-2, insert the following clause:

QUALIFICATION REQUIREMENTS (FEB 1995)

(a) *Definition*: *Qualification requirement* as used in this clause, means a Government requirement for testing or other quality assurance demonstration that must be completed before award.

(b) One or more qualification requirements apply to the supplies or services covered by this contract. For those supplies or services requiring qualification, whether the covered product or service is an end item under this contract or simply a component of an end item, the product, manufacturer, or source must have demonstrated that it meets the standards prescribed for qualification before award of this contract. The product, manufacturer, or source must be qualified at the time of award whether or not the name of the product, manufacturer, or source is actually included on a qualified products list, qualified manufacturers list, or qualified bidders list. Offerors should contact the agency activity designated below to obtain all requirements that they or their products or services, or their subcontractors or their products or services, must satisfy to become qualified and to arrange for an opportunity to demonstrate their abilities to meet the standards specified for qualification.

(Name)____________________

(Address)____________________

(c) If an offeror, manufacturer, source, product or service covered by a qualification requirement has already met the standards specified, the relevant information noted below should be provided.

Offeror's Name____________________

Manufacturer's Name____________________

Source's Name____________________

Item Name____________________

Service Identification____________________

Test Number____________________

(to the extent known)

(d) Even though a product or service subject to a qualification requirement is not itself an end item under this contract, the product, manufacturer, or source must nevertheless be qualified at the time of award of this contract. This is necessary whether the Contractor or a subcontractor will ultimately provide the product or service in question. If, after award, the Contracting Officer discovers that an applicable qualification requirement was not in fact met at the time of award, the Contracting Officer may either terminate his contract for default or allow performance to continue if adequate consideration is offered and the action is determined to be otherwise in the Government's best interests.

(e) If an offeror, manufacturer, source, product or service has met the qualification requirement but is not yet on a qualified products list, qualified manufacturers list, or qualified bidders list, the offeror must submit evidence of qualification prior to award of this contract. Unless determined to be in the Government's interest, award of this contract shall not be delayed to permit an offeror to submit evidence of qualification.

(f) Any change in location or ownership of the plant where a previously qualified product or service was manufactured or performed requires reevaluation of the qualification. Similarly, any change in location or ownership of a previously qualified manufacturer or source requires reevaluation of the qualification. The reevaluation must be accomplished before the date of award.

(End of clause)

[FAC 84-39, 53 FR 34229, 9/2/88, effective 10/3/88; corrected 53 FR 36028, 9/16/88; FAC 90-23, 59 FR 67010, 12/28/94, effective 2/27/95]

52.209-2 Prohibition on Contracting with Inverted Domestic Corporations—Representation.

As prescribed in 9.108-5(a), insert the following provision:

PROHIBITION ON CONTRACTING WITH INVERTED DOMESTIC CORPORATIONS—REPRESENTATION (NOV 2015)

(a) *Definitions. Inverted domestic corporation* and *subsidiary* have the meaning given in the clause of this contract entitled Prohibition on Contracting with Inverted Domestic Corporations (52.209-10).

(b) Government agencies are not permitted to use appropriated (or otherwise made available) funds for contracts with either an inverted domestic corporation, or a subsidiary of an inverted domestic corporation, unless the exception at 9.108-2(b) applies or the requirement is waived in accordance with the procedures at 9.108-4.

(c) *Representation.* The Offeror represents that—

(1) It ☐ is, ☐ is not an inverted domestic corporation; and

(2) It ☐ is, ☐ is not a subsidiary of an inverted domestic corporation.

(End of provision)

[Reserved, FAC 84-39, 53 FR 34229, 9/2/88, effective 10/3/88; FAC 2005-34, Interim rule, 74 FR 31561, 7/1/2009, effective 7/1/2009; FAC 2005-52, 76 FR 31410, 5/31/2011, effective 5/31/2011; FAC 2005-79, 79 FR 74554, 12/15/2014, effective 12/15/2014; FAC 2005-83, 80 FR 38306, 7/2/2015, effective 11/1/2015, 80 FR 38309, 7/2/2015, effective 7/2/2015]

52.209-3 First Article Approval—Contractor Testing.

As prescribed in 9.308-1(a) and (b), insert the following clause:

FIRST ARTICLE APPROVAL—CONTRACTOR TESTING (SEP 1989)

[*Contracting Officer shall insert details*]

(a) The Contractor shall test ________ unit(s) of Lot/Item ________ as specified in this contract. At least ________ calendar days before the beginning of first article tests, the Contractor shall notify the Contracting Officer, in writing, of the time and location of the testing so that the Government may witness the tests.

(b) The Contractor shall submit the first article test report within ________ calendar days from the date of this contract to ________ [*insert address of the Government activity to receive the report*] marked "FIRST ARTICLE TEST REPORT: Contract No. ________, Lot/Item No. ________." Within ________ calendar days after the Government receives the test report, the Contracting Officer shall notify the Contractor, in writing, of the conditional approval, approval, or disapproval of the first article. The notice of conditional approval or approval shall not relieve the Contractor from complying with all requirements of the specifications and all other terms and conditions of this contract. A notice of conditional approval shall state any further action required of the Contractor. A notice of disapproval shall cite reasons for the disapproval.

(c) If the first article is disapproved, the Contractor, upon Government request, shall repeat any or all first article tests. After each request for additional tests, the Contractor shall make any necessary changes, modifications, or repairs to the first article or select another first article for testing. All costs related to these tests are to be borne by the Contractor, including any and all costs for additional tests following a disapproval. The Contractor shall then conduct the tests and deliver another report to the Government under the terms and conditions and within the time specified by the Government. The Government shall take action on this report within the time specified in paragraph (b) above. The Government reserves the right to require an equitable adjustment of the contract price for any extension of the delivery schedule, or for any additional costs to the Government related to these tests.

(d) If the Contractor fails to deliver any first article report on time, or the Contracting Officer disapproves any first article, the Contractor shall be deemed to have failed to make delivery within the meaning of the Default clause of this contract.

(e) Unless otherwise provided in the contract, and if the approved first article is not consumed or destroyed in testing, the Contractor may deliver the approved first article as part of the contract quantity if it meets all contract requirements for acceptance.

(f) If the Government does not act within the time specified in paragraph (b) or (c) above, the Contracting Officer shall, upon timely written request from the Contractor, equitably adjust under the Changes clause of this contract the delivery or performance dates and/or the contract price, and any other contractual term affected by the delay.

(g) Before first article approval, the acquisition of materials or components for, or the commencement of production of, the balance of the contract quantity is at the sole risk of the Contractor. Before first article approval, the costs thereof shall not be allocable to this contract for (1) progress payments, or (2) termination settlements if the contract is terminated for the convenience of the Government.

(h) The Government may waive the requirement for first article approval test where supplies identical or similar to those called for in the schedule have been previously furnished by the offeror/contractor and have been accepted by the Government. The offeror/contractor may request a waiver.

(End of clause)

Alternate I (JAN 1997). As prescribed in 9.308-1(a)(2) and (b)(2), add the following paragraph (i) to the basic clause:

(i) The Contractor shall produce both the first article and the production quantity at the same facility.

Alternate II (SEP 1989). As prescribed in 9.308-1(a)(3) and (b)(3), substitute the following paragraph (g) for paragraph (g) of the basic clause:

(g) Before first article approval, the Contracting Officer may, by written authorization, authorize the Contractor to acquire specific materials or components or to commence production to the extent essential to meet the delivery schedules. Until first article approval is granted, only costs for the first article and costs incurred under this authorization are allocable to this contract for (1) progress payments, or (2) termination settlements if the contract is terminated for the convenience of the Government. If first article tests reveal deviations from contract requirements, the Contractor shall, at the location designated by the Government, make the required changes or replace all items produced under this contract at no change in the contract price.

[FAC 84-58, 55 FR 25531, 6/21/90, effective 7/23/90; FAC 90-45, Final rule, 62 FR 224, 1/2/97, effective 1/1/97]

52.209-4 First Article Approval—Government Testing.

As prescribed in 9.308-2(a) and (b), insert the following clause:

FIRST ARTICLE APPROVAL—GOVERNMENT TESTING (SEP 1989)

[*Contracting Officer shall insert details*]

(a) The Contractor shall deliver ____ unit(s) of Lot/Item ____ within ____ calendar days from the date of this contract to the Government at ____ [*insert name and address of the testing facility*] for first article tests. The shipping documentation shall contain this contract number and the Lot/Item identification. The characteristics that the first article must meet and the testing requirements are specified elsewhere in this contract.

(b) Within ____ calendar days after the Government receives the first article, the Contracting Officer shall notify the Contractor, in writing, of the conditional approval, approval, or disapproval of the first article. The notice of conditional approval or approval shall not relieve the Contractor from complying with all requirements of the specifications and all other terms and conditions of this contract. A notice of conditional approval shall state any further action required of the Contractor. A notice of disapproval shall cite reasons for the disapproval.

(c) If the first article is disapproved, the Contractor, upon Government request, shall submit an additional first article for testing. After each request, the Contractor shall make any necessary changes, modifications, or repairs to the first article or select another first article for testing. All costs related to these tests are to be borne by the Contractor, including any and all costs for additional tests following a disapproval. The Contractor shall furnish any additional first article to the Government under the terms and conditions and within the time specified by the Government. The Government shall act on this first article within the time limit specified in paragraph (b) of this clause. The Government reserves the right to require an equitable adjustment of the contract price for any extension of the delivery schedule or for any additional costs to the Government related to these tests.

(d) If the Contractor fails to deliver any first article on time, or the Contracting Officer disapproves any first article, the Contractor shall be deemed to have failed to make delivery within the meaning of the Default clause of this contract.

(e) Unless otherwise provided in the contract, the Contractor—

(1) May deliver the approved first article as a part of the contract quantity, provided it meets all contract requirements for acceptance and was not consumed or destroyed in testing; and

(2) Shall remove and dispose of any first article from the Government test facility at the Contractor's expense.

(f) If the Government does not act within the time specified in paragraph (b) or (c) of this clause, the Contracting Officer shall, upon timely written request from the Contractor, equitably adjust under the Changes clause of this contract the delivery or performance dates and/or the contract price, and any other contractual term affected by the delay.

(g) The Contractor is responsible for providing operating and maintenance instructions, spare parts support, and repair of the first article during any first article test.

(h) Before first article approval, the acquisition of materials or components for, or the commencement of production of, the balance of the contract quantity is at the sole risk of the Contractor. Before first article approval, the costs thereof shall not be allocable to this contract for (1) progress payments, or (2) termination settlements if the contract is terminated for the convenience of the Government.

(i) The Government may waive the requirement for first article approval test where supplies identical or similar to those called for in the schedule have been previously furnished by the Offeror/Contractor and have been accepted by the Government. The Offeror/Contractor may request a waiver.

(End of clause)

Alternate I (JAN 1997). As prescribed in 9.308-2(a)(2) and (b)(2), add the following paragraph (j) to the basic clause:

(j) The Contractor shall produce both the first article and the production quantity at the same facility.

Alternate II (SEP 1989). As prescribed in 9.308-2(a)(3) and (b)(3), substitute the following paragraph (h) for paragraph (h) of the basic clause:

(h) Before first article approval, the Contracting Officer may, by written authorization, authorize the Contractor to acquire specific materials or components or to commence production to the extent essential to meet the delivery schedules. Until first article approval is granted, only costs for the first article and costs incurred under this authorization are allocable to this contract for (1) progress payments, or (2) termination settlements if the contract is terminated for the convenience of the Government. If first article tests reveal deviations from contract requirements, the Contractor shall, at the location designated by the Government, make the required changes or replace all items produced under this contract at no change in the contract price.

[FAC 84-51, 54 FR 34757, 8/21/89, effective 9/20/89; FAC 90-45, Final rule, 62 FR 224, 1/2/97, effective 1/1/97]

52.209-5 Certification Regarding Responsibility Matters.

As prescribed in 9.104-7(a), insert the following provision:

CERTIFICATION REGARDING RESPONSIBILITY MATTERS (OCT 2015)

(a) (1) The Offeror certifies, to the best of its knowledge and belief, that—

(i) The Offeror and/or any of its Principals—

(A) Are ( ) are not ( ) presently debarred, suspended, proposed for debarment, or declared ineligible for the award of contracts by any Federal agency;

(B) Have ( ) have not ( ), within a three-year period preceding this offer, been convicted of or had a civil judgment rendered against them for: commission of fraud or a criminal offense in connection with obtaining, attempting to obtain, or performing a public (Federal, State, or local) contract or subcontract; violation of Federal or State antitrust statutes relating to the submission of offers; or commission of embezzlement, theft, forgery, bribery, falsification or destruction of records, making false statements, tax evasion, violating Federal criminal tax laws, or receiving stolen property (if offeror checks "have", the offeror shall see 52.209-7, if included in this solicitation); and

(C) Are ( ) are not ( ) presently indicted for, or otherwise criminally or civilly charged by a governmental entity with, commission of any of the offenses enumerated in paragraph (a) (1) (i) (B) of this provision; and

(D) Have [ballot], have not [ballot], within a three-year period preceding this offer, been notified of any delinquent Federal taxes in an amount that exceeds $3,500 for which the liability remains unsatisfied.

(1) Federal taxes are considered delinquent if both of the following criteria apply:

(i) The tax liability is finally determined. The liability is finally determined if it has been assessed. A liability is not finally determined if there is a pending administrative or judicial challenge. In the case of a judicial challenge to the liability, the liability is not finally determined until all judicial appeal rights have been exhausted.

(ii) The taxpayer is delinquent in making payment. A taxpayer is delinquent if the taxpayer has failed to pay the tax liability when full payment was due and required. A taxpayer is not delinquent in cases where enforced collection action is precluded.

(2) Examples. (i) The taxpayer has received a statutory notice of deficiency, under I.R.C. Sec. 6212, which entitles the taxpayer to seek Tax Court review of a proposed tax deficiency. This is not a delinquent tax because it is not a final tax liability. Should the taxpayer seek Tax Court review, this will not be a final tax liability until the taxpayer has exercised all judicial appeal rights.

(ii) The IRS has filed a notice of Federal tax lien with respect to an assessed tax liability, and the taxpayer has been issued a notice under I.R.C. Sec. 6320 entitling the taxpayer to request a hearing with the IRS Office of Appeals contesting the lien filing, and to further appeal to the Tax Court if the IRS determines to sustain the lien filing. In the course of the hearing, the taxpayer is entitled to contest the underlying tax liability because the taxpayer has had no prior opportunity to contest the liability. This is not a delinquent tax because it is not a final tax liability. Should the taxpayer seek tax court review, this will not be a final tax liability until the taxpayer has exercised all judicial appeal rights.

(iii) The taxpayer has entered into an installment agreement pursuant to I.R.C. Sec. 6159. The taxpayer is making timely payments and is in full compliance with the agreement terms. The taxpayer is not delinquent because the taxpayer is not currently required to make full payment.

(iv) The taxpayer has filed for bankruptcy protection. The taxpayer is not delinquent because enforced collection action is stayed under 11 U.S.C. 362 (the Bankruptcy Code).

(ii) The Offeror has ( ) has not ( ), within a three-year period preceding this offer, had one or more contracts terminated for default by any Federal agency.

(2) *Principal*, for the purposes of this certification, means an officer, director, owner, partner, or a person having primary management or supervisory responsibilities within a business entity (e.g., general manager; plant manager; head of a division or business segment; and similar positions).

This Certification Concerns a Matter Within the Jurisdiction of an Agency of the United States and the Making of a False, Fictitious, or Fraudulent Certification May Render the Maker Subject to Prosecution Under Section 1001, Title 18, United States Code.

(b) The Offeror shall provide immediate written notice to the Contracting Officer if, at any time prior to contract award, the Offeror learns that its certification was erroneous when submitted or has become erroneous by reason of changed circumstances.

(c) A certification that any of the items in paragraph (a) of this provision exists will not necessarily result in withholding of an award under this solicitation. However, the certification will be considered in connection with a determination of the Offeror's responsibility. Failure of the Offeror to furnish a certification or provide such additional information as requested by the Contracting Officer may render the Offeror nonresponsible.

(d) Nothing contained in the foregoing shall be construed to require establishment of a system of records in order to render, in good faith, the certification required by paragraph (a) of this provision. The knowledge and information of an Offeror is not required to exceed that which is normally possessed by a prudent person in the ordinary course of business dealings.

(e) The certification in paragraph (a) of this provision is a material representation of fact upon which reliance was placed when making award. If it is later determined that the Offeror knowingly rendered an erroneous certification, in addition to other remedies available to the Government, the Contracting Officer may terminate the contract resulting from this solicitation for default.

(End of provision)

[FAC 84-46, 54 FR 19827, 5/8/89, effective 6/7/89; FAC 90-37, 61 FR 2626, 1/26/96, effective 3/26/96; FAC 97-21, 65 FR 80255, 12/20/2000, effective 1/19/2001, stayed FAC 97-24, 66 FR 17753, 4/3/2001, effective 4/3/2001, corrected 66 FR 18735, 4/11/2001, finalized with changes FAC 2001-03, 66 FR 66984, 12/27/2001, effective 12/27/2001; FAC 2005-25, 73 FR 21791, 4/22/2008, effective 5/22/2008; FAC 2005-28, 73 FR 67064, 11/12/2008, effective 12/12/2008; FAC 2005-40, 75 FR 14059, 3/23/2010, effective 4/22/2010; FAC 2005-83, 80 FR 38293, 7/2/2015, effective 10/1/2015]

52.209-6 Protecting the Government's Interest When Subcontracting with Contractors Debarred, Suspended, or Proposed for Debarment.

As prescribed in 9.409, insert the following clause:

PROTECTING THE GOVERNMENT'S INTEREST WHEN SUBCONTRACTING WITH CONTRACTORS DEBARRED, SUSPENDED, OR PROPOSED FOR DEBARMENT (OCT 2015)

(a) *Definition. Commercially available off-the-shelf (COTS) item*, as used in this clause—

(1) Means any item of supply (including construction material) that is—

(i) A commercial item (as defined in paragraph (1) of the definition in FAR 2.101);

(ii) Sold in substantial quantities in the commercial marketplace; and

(iii) Offered to the Government, under a contract or subcontract at any tier, without modification, in the same form in which it is sold in the commercial marketplace; and

(2) Does not include bulk cargo, as defined in 46 U.S.C. 40102(4), such as agricultural products and petroleum products.

(b) The Government suspends or debars Contractors to protect the Government's interests. Other than a subcontract for a commercially available off-the-shelf item, the Contractor shall not enter into any subcontract, in excess of $35,000 with a Contractor that is debarred, suspended, or proposed for debarment by any executive agency unless there is a compelling reason to do so.

(c) The Contractor shall require each proposed subcontractor whose subcontract will exceed $35,000, other than a subcontractor providing a commercially available off-the-shelf item, to disclose to the Contractor, in writing, whether as of the time of award of the subcontract, the subcontractor, or its principals, is or is not debarred, suspended, or proposed for debarment by the Federal Government.

(d) A corporate officer or a designee of the Contractor shall notify the Contracting Officer, in writing, before entering into a subcontract with a party (other than a subcontractor providing a commercially available off-the-shelf item) that is debarred, suspended, or proposed for debarment (see FAR 9.404 for information on the System for Award Management (SAM) Exclusions). The notice must include the following:

(1) The name of the subcontractor.

(2) The Contractor's knowledge of the reasons for the subcontractor being listed with an exclusion in SAM.

(3) The compelling reason(s) for doing business with the subcontractor notwithstanding its being listed with an exclusion in SAM.

(4) The systems and procedures the Contractor has established to ensure that it is fully protecting the Government's interests when dealing with such subcontractor in view of the specific basis for the party's debarment, suspension, or proposed debarment.

(e) *Subcontracts.* Unless this is a contract for the acquisition of commercial items, the Contractor shall include the requirements of this clause, including this paragraph (e) (appropriately modified for the identification of the parties), in each subcontract that—

(1) Exceeds $35,000 in value; and

(2) Is not a subcontract for commercially available off-the-shelf items.

(End of clause)

[FAC 90-5, 56 FR 29138, 6/25/91, effective 6/25/91; FAC 90-13, 57 FR 44269, 9/24/92, effective 11/23/92; FAC 90-28, 60 FR 33064, 6/26/95, effective 8/25/95; FAC 90-29, 60 FR 34732, 7/3/95, effective 7/3/95; FAC 2001-26, 69 FR 76347, 12/20/2004, effective 1/19/2005; FAC 2005-13, 71 FR 57363, 9/28/2006, effective 9/28/2006; FAC 2005-38, 74 FR 65614, 12/10/2009, effective 12/10/2009; FAC 2005-47, 75 FR 77739, 12/13/2010, effective 12/13/2010; FAC 2005-53, 76 FR 39236, 7/5/2011, effective 8/4/2011; FAC 2005-67, 78 FR 37676, 6/21/2013, effective 7/22/2013; FAC 2005-69, 78 FR 46795, 8/1/2013, effective 8/1/2013; FAC 2005-83, 80 FR 38293, 7/2/2015, effective 10/1/2015]

52.209-7 Information Regarding Responsibility Matters.

As prescribed at 9.104-7(c), insert the following provision:

INFORMATION REGARDING RESPONSIBILITY MATTERS (OCT 2018)

(a) *Definitions.* As used in this provision—

Administrative proceeding means a non-judicial process that is adjudicatory in nature in order to make a determination of fault or liability (*e.g.*, Securities and Exchange Commission Administrative Proceedings, Civilian Board of Contract Appeals Proceedings, and Armed Services Board of Contract Appeals Proceedings). This includes administrative proceedings at the Federal and State level but only in connection with performance of a Federal contract or grant. It does not include agency actions such as contract audits, site visits, corrective plans, or inspection of deliverables.

Federal contracts and grants with total value greater than $10,000,000 means—

(1) The total value of all current, active contracts and grants, including all priced options; and

(2) The total value of all current, active orders including all priced options under indefinite-delivery, indefinite-quantity, 8(a), or requirements contracts (including task and delivery and multiple-award Schedules).

Principal means an officer, director, owner, partner, or a person having primary management or supervisory responsibilities within a business entity (e.g., general manager; plant manager; head of a division or business segment; and similar positions).

(b) The offeror [ ] has [ ] does not have current active Federal contracts and grants with total value greater than $10,000,000.

(c) If the offeror checked "has" in paragraph (b) of this provision, the offeror represents, by submission of this offer, that the information it has entered in the Federal Awardee Performance and Integrity Information System (FAPIIS) is current, accurate, and complete as of the date of submission of this offer with regard to the following information:

(1) Whether the offeror, and/or any of its principals, has or has not, within the last five years, in connection with the award to or performance by the offeror of a Federal contract or grant, been the subject of a proceeding, at the Federal or State level that resulted in any of the following dispositions:

(i) In a criminal proceeding, a conviction.

(ii) In a civil proceeding, a finding of fault and liability that results in the payment of a monetary fine, penalty, reimbursement, restitution, or damages of $5,000 or more.

(iii) In an administrative proceeding, a finding of fault and liability that results in—

(A) The payment of a monetary fine or penalty of $5,000 or more; or

(B) The payment of a reimbursement, restitution, or damages in excess of $100,000.

(iv) In a criminal, civil, or administrative proceeding, a disposition of the matter by consent or compromise with an acknowledgment of fault by the Contractor if the proceeding could have led to any of the outcomes specified in paragraphs (c)(1)(i), (c)(1)(ii), or (c)(1)(iii) of this provision.

(2) If the offeror has been involved in the last five years in any of the occurrences listed in (c)(1) of this provision, whether the offeror has provided the requested information with regard to each occurrence.

(d) The offeror shall post the information in paragraphs (c)(1)(i) through (c)(1)(iv) of this provision in FAPIIS as required through maintaining an active registration in the System for Award Management, which can be accessed via *https://www.sam.gov* (see 52.204-7).

(End of clause)

[FAC 2005-40, 75 FR 14059, 3/23/2010, effective 4/22/2010; FAC 2005-49, 76 FR 4188, 1/24/2011, effective 1/24/2011; FAC 2005-55, 77 FR 187, 1/3/2012, effective 2/2/2012; 77 FR 197, 1/3/2012, effective 1/3/2012; FAC 2005-67, 78 FR 37676, 6/21/2013, effective 7/22/2013; FAC 2005-101, 83 FR 48691, 9/26/2018, effective 10/26/2018]

52.209-8 [Removed and Reserved]

[FAC 2005-40, 75 FR 14059, 3/23/2010, effective 4/22/2010; FAC 2005-49, 76 FR 4188, 1/24/2011, effective 1/24/2011; FAC 2005-55, 77 FR 197, 1/3/2012, effective 1/3/2012]

52.209-9 Updates of Publicly Available Information Regarding Responsibility Matters.

As prescribed at 9.104-7(c), insert the following clause:

UPDATES OF PUBLICLY AVAILABLE INFORMATION REGARDING RESPONSIBILITY MATTERS (OCT 2018)

(a) The Contractor shall update the information in the Federal Awardee Performance and Integrity Information System (FAPIIS) on a semi-annual basis, throughout the life of the contract, by posting the required information in the System for Award Management via *https://www.sam.gov*.

(b) As required by section 3010 of the Supplemental Appropriations Act, 2010 (Pub. L. 111-212), all information posted in FAPIIS on or after April 15, 2011, except past performance reviews, will be publicly available. FAPIIS consists of two segments—

(1) The non-public segment, into which Government officials and the Contractor post information, which can only be viewed by—

(i) Government personnel and authorized users performing business on behalf of the Government; or

(ii) The Contractor, when viewing data on itself; and

(2) The publicly-available segment, to which all data in the non-public segment of FAPIIS is automatically transferred after a waiting period of 14 calendar days, except for—

(i) Past performance reviews required by subpart 42.15;

(ii) Information that was entered prior to April 15, 2011; or

(iii) Information that is withdrawn during the 14-calendar-day waiting period by the Government official who posted it in accordance with paragraph (c) (1) of this clause.

(c) The Contractor will receive notification when the Government posts new information to the Contractor's record.

(1) If the Contractor asserts in writing within 7 calendar days, to the Government official who posted the information, that some of the information posted to the nonpublic segment of FAPIIS is covered by a disclosure exemption under the Freedom of Information Act, the Government official who posted the information must within 7 calendar days remove the posting from FAPIIS and resolve the issue in accordance with agency Freedom of Information procedures, prior to reposting the releasable information. The contractor must cite 52.209-9 and request removal within 7 calendar days of the posting to FAPIIS.

(2) The Contractor will also have an opportunity to post comments regarding information that has been posted by the Government. The comments will be retained as long as the associated information is retained, *i.e.,* for a total period of 6 years. Contractor comments will remain a part of the record unless the Contractor revises them.

(3) As required by section 3010 of Pub. L. 111-212, all information posted in FAPIIS on or after April 15, 2011, except past performance reviews, will be publicly available.

(d) Public requests for system information posted prior to April 15, 2011, will be handled under Freedom of Information Act procedures, including, where appropriate, procedures promulgated under E.O. 12600.

(End of clause)

[FAC 2005-40, 75 FR 14059, 3/23/2010, effective 4/22/2010; FAC 2005-49, 76 FR 4188, 1/24/2011, effective 1/24/2011; FAC 2005-55, 77 FR 187, 1/3/2012, effective 2/2/2012; 77 FR 197, 1/3/2012, effective 1/3/2012; FAC 2005-56, 77 FR 12948, 3/2/2012, effective 3/2/2012; FAC 2005-67, 78 FR 37676, 6/21/2013, effective 7/22/2013; FAC 2005-101, 83 FR 48691, 9/26/2018, effective 10/26/2018]

52.209-10 Prohibition on Contracting with Inverted Domestic Corporations.

As prescribed at 9.108-5(b), insert the following clause:

PROHIBITION ON CONTRACTING WITH INVERTED DOMESTIC CORPORATIONS (NOV 2015)

(a) *Definitions.* As used in this clause—

Inverted domestic corporation means a foreign incorporated entity that meets the definition of an inverted domestic corporation under 6 U.S.C. 395(b), applied in accordance with the rules and definitions of 6 U.S.C. 395(c).

Subsidiary means an entity in which more than 50 percent of the entity is owned—

(1) Directly by a parent corporation; or

(2) Through another subsidiary of a parent corporation.

(b) If the contractor reorganizes as an inverted domestic corporation or becomes a subsidiary of an inverted domestic corporation at any time during the period of performance of this contract, the Government may be prohibited from paying for Contractor activities performed after the date when it becomes an inverted domestic corporation or subsidiary. The Government may seek any available remedies in the event the Contractor fails to perform in accordance with the terms and conditions of the contract as a result of Government action under this clause.

(c) Exceptions to this prohibition are located at 9.108-2.

(d) In the event the Contractor becomes either an inverted domestic corporation, or a subsidiary of an inverted domestic corporation during contract performance, the Contractor shall give written notice to the Contracting Officer within five business days from the date of the inversion event.

(End of clause)

[FAC 2005-52, 76 FR 31410, 5/31/2011, effective 5/31/2011; FAC 2005-59, 77 FR 27547, 5/10/2012, effective 5/10/2012; FAC 2005-65, 78 FR 6185, 1/29/2013, effective 1/29/2013; FAC 2005-79, 79 FR 74554, 12/15/2014, effective 12/15/2014; FAC 2005-83, Final rule, 80 FR 38306, 7/2/2015, effective 11/1/2015, 80 FR 38309, 7/2/2015, effective 7/2/2015]

52.209-11 Representation by Corporations Regarding Delinquent Tax Liability or a Felony Conviction under any Federal Law.

As prescribed in 9.104–7(d), insert the following provision:

REPRESENTATION BY CORPORATIONS REGARDING DELINQUENT TAX LIABILITY OR A FELONY CONVICTION UNDER ANY FEDERAL LAW (FEB 2016)

(a) As required by sections 744 and 745 of Division E of the Consolidated and Further Continuing Appropriations Act, 2015 (Pub. L. 113–235), and similar provisions, if contained in subsequent appropriations acts, the Government will not enter into a contract with any corporation that—

(1) Has any unpaid Federal tax liability that has been assessed, for which all judicial and administrative remedies have been exhausted or have lapsed, and that is not being paid in a timely manner pursuant to an agreement with the authority responsible for collecting the tax liability, where the awarding agency is aware of the unpaid tax liability, unless an agency has considered suspension or debarment of the corporation and made a determination that suspension or debarment is not necessary to protect the interests of the Government; or

(2) Was convicted of a felony criminal violation under any Federal law within the preceding 24 months, where the awarding agency is aware of the conviction, unless an agency has considered suspension or debarment of the corporation and made a determination that this action is not necessary to protect the interests of the Government.

(b) The Offeror represents that—

(1) It is [ ] is not [ ] a corporation that has any unpaid Federal tax liability that has been assessed, for which all judicial and administrative remedies have been exhausted or have lapsed, and that is not being paid in a timely manner pursuant to an agreement with the authority responsible for collecting the tax liability; and

(2) It is [ ] is not [ ] a corporation that was convicted of a felony criminal violation under a Federal law within the preceding 24 months.

(End of provision)

[FAC 2005-85, 80 FR 75903, 12/4/2015, effective 2/26/2015; FAC 2005-91, 81 FR 67728, 9/30/2016, effective 9/30/2016]

52.209-12 Certification Regarding Tax Matters.

As prescribed in 9.104–7(e), insert the following provision:

CERTIFICATION REGARDING TAX MATTERS (FEB 2016)

(a) This provision implements section 523 of Division B of the Consolidated and Further Continuing Appropriations Act, 2015 (Pub. L. 113–235), and similar provisions, if contained in subsequent appropriations acts.

(b) If the Offeror is proposing a total contract price that will exceed $5,000,000 (including options), the Offeror shall certify that, to the best of its knowledge and belief, it—

(1) Has [ ] filed all Federal tax returns required during the three years preceding the certification;

(2) Has not [ ] been convicted of a criminal offense under the Internal Revenue Code of 1986; and

(3) Has not [ ], more than 90 days prior to certification, been notified of any unpaid Federal tax assessment for which the liability remains unsatisfied, unless the assessment is the subject of an installment agreement or offer in compromise that has been approved by the Internal Revenue Service and is not in default, or the assessment is the subject of a non-frivolous administrative or judicial proceeding.

(End of provision)

[FAC 2005-85, 80 FR 75903, 12/4/2015, effective 2/26/2015; FAC 2005-91, 81 FR 67728, 9/30/2016, effective 9/30/2016]

52.209-13 Violation of Arms Control Treaties or Agreements—Certification.

As prescribed in 9.109-5, insert the following provision:

VIOLATION OF ARMS CONTROL TREATIES OR AGREEMENTS—CERTIFICATION (JUN 2018)

(a) This provision does not apply to acquisitions below the simplified acquisition threshold or to acquisitions of commercial items as defined at FAR 2.101.

(b) *Certification. [Offeror shall check either (1) or (2).]*

(1) The Offeror certifies that—

(i) It does not engage and has not engaged in any activity that contributed to or was a significant factor in the President's or Secretary of State's determination that a foreign country is in violation of its obligations undertaken in any arms control, nonproliferation, or disarmament agreement to which the United States is a party, or is not adhering to its arms control, nonproliferation, or disarmament commitments in which the United States is a participating state. The determinations are described in the most recent unclassified annual report provided to Congress pursuant to section 403 of the Arms Control and Disarmament Act (22 U.S.C. 2593a). The report is available via the Internet at *https://www.state.gov/t/avc/rls/rpt/*; and

(ii) No entity owned or controlled by the Offeror has engaged in any activity that contributed to or was a significant factor in the President's or Secretary of State's determination that a foreign country is in violation of its obligations undertaken in any arms control, nonproliferation, or disarmament agreement to which the United States is a party, or is not adhering to its arms control, nonproliferation, or disarmament commitments in which the United States is a participating state. The determinations are described in the most recent unclassified annual report provided to Congress pursuant to section 403 of the Arms Control and Disarmament Act (22 U.S.C. 2593a). The report is available via the Internet at *https://www.state.gov/t/avc/rls/rpt/*; or

(2) The Offeror is providing separate information with its offer in accordance with paragraph (d)(2) of this provision.

(c) Procedures for reviewing the annual unclassified report (see paragraph (b)(1) of this provision). For clarity, references to the report in this section refer to the entirety of the annual unclassified report, including any separate reports that are incorporated by reference into the annual unclassified report.

(1) Check the table of contents of the annual unclassified report and the country section headings of the reports incorporated by reference to identify the foreign countries listed there. Determine whether the Offeror or any person owned or controlled by the Offeror may have engaged in any activity related to one or more of such foreign countries.

(2) If there may have been such activity, review all findings in the report associated with those foreign countries to determine whether or not each such foreign country was determined to be in violation of its obligations undertaken in an arms control, nonproliferation, or disarmament agreement to which the United States is a party, or to be not adhering to its arms control, nonproliferation, or disarmament commitments in which the United States is a participating state. For clarity, in the annual report an explicit certification of non-compliance is equivalent to a determination of violation. However, the following statements in the annual report are not equivalent to a determination of violation:

(i) An inability to certify compliance.

(ii) An inability to conclude compliance.

(iii) A statement about compliance concerns.

(3) If so, determine whether the Offeror or any person owned or controlled by the Offeror has engaged in any activity that contributed to or is a significant factor in the determination in the report that one or more

of these foreign countries is in violation of its obligations undertaken in an arms control, nonproliferation, or disarmament agreement to which the United States is a party, or is not adhering to its arms control, nonproliferation, or disarmament commitments in which the United States is a participating state. Review the narrative for any such findings reflecting a determination of violation or non-adherence related to those foreign countries in the report, including the finding itself, and to the extent necessary, the conduct giving rise to the compliance or adherence concerns, the analysis of compliance or adherence concerns, and efforts to resolve compliance or adherence concerns.

(4) The Offeror may submit any questions with regard to this report by email to *NDAA1290Cert@state.gov.* To the extent feasible, the Department of State will respond to such email inquiries within 3 business days.

(d) Do not submit an offer unless—

(1) A certification is provided in paragraph (b) (1) of this provision and submitted with the offer; or

(2) In accordance with paragraph (b) (2) of this provision, the Offeror provides with its offer information that the President of the United States has—

(i) Waived application under U.S.C. 2593e(d) or (e); or

(ii) Determined under 22 U.S.C. 2593e(g)(2) that the entity has ceased all activities for which measures were imposed under 22 U.S.C.2593e(b).

(e) *Remedies.* The certification in paragraph (b)(1) of this provision is a material representation of fact upon which reliance was placed when making award. If it is later determined that the Offeror knowingly submitted a false certification, in addition to other remedies available to the Government, such as suspension or debarment, the Contracting Officer may terminate any contract resulting from the false certification.

(End of provision)

[FAC 2005-99, 83 FR 28145, 6/15/2018, effective 6/15/2018]

52.210 [Reserved]

[Reserved, FAC 90-32, 60 FR 48206, 9/18/95, effective 10/1/95]

52.210-1 Market Research.

As prescribed in 10.003, insert the following clause:

MARKET RESEARCH (APR 2011)

(a) *Definition.* As used in this clause—

Commercial item and *nondevelopmental item* have the meaning contained in Federal Acquisition Regulation 2.101.

(b) Before awarding subcontracts over the simplified acquisition threshold for items other than commercial items, the Contractor shall conduct market research to—

(1) Determine if commercial items or, to the extent commercial items suitable to meet the agency's needs are not available, nondevelopmental items are available that—

(i) Meet the agency's requirements;

(ii) Could be modified to meet the agency's requirements; or

(iii) Could meet the agency's requirements if those requirements were modified to a reasonable extent; and

(2) Determine the extent to which commercial items or nondevelopmental items could be incorporated at the component level.

(End of clause)

[FAC 2005-50, 76 FR 14562, 3/16/2011, effective 4/15/2011]

52.211-1 Availability of Specifications Listed in the GSA Index of Federal Specifications, Standards and Commercial Item Descriptions, FPMR Part 101-29.

As prescribed in 11.204(a), insert the following provision:

AVAILABILITY OF SPECIFICATIONS LISTED IN THE GSA INDEX OF FEDERAL SPECIFICATIONS, STANDARDS AND COMMERCIAL ITEM DESCRIPTIONS, FPMR PART 101-29 (AUG 1998)

(a) The GSA Index of Federal Specifications, Standards and Commercial Item Descriptions, FPMR Part 101-29, and copies of specifications, standards, and commercial item descriptions cited in this solicitation may be obtained for a fee by submitting a request to—GSA Federal Supply Service, Specifications Section, Suite 8100, 470 East L'Enfant Plaza, SW, Washington, DC 20407, Telephone (202) 619-8925, Facsimile (202) 619-8978.

(b) If the General Services Administration, Department of Agriculture, or Department of Veterans Affairs issued this solicitation, a single copy of specifications, standards, and commercial item descriptions cited in this solicitation may be obtained free of charge by submitting a request to the addressee in paragraph (a) of this provision. Additional copies will be issued for a fee.

(End of provision)

[FAC 97-5, 63 FR 34058, 6/22/98, effective 8/21/98]

52.211-2 Availability of Specifications, Standards, and Data Item Descriptions Listed in the Acquisition Streamlining and Standardization Information System (ASSIST).

As prescribed in 11.204(b), insert the following provision:

AVAILABILITY OF SPECIFICATIONS, STANDARDS, AND DATA ITEM DESCRIPTIONS LISTED IN THE ACQUISITION STREAMLINING AND STANDARDIZATION INFORMATION SYSTEM (ASSIST) (APR 2014)

(a) Most unclassified Defense specifications and standards may be downloaded from the following ASSIST websites:

(1) ASSIST (*https://assist.dla.mil/online/start/*);

(2) Quick Search (*http://quicksearch.dla.mil/*);

(3) ASSISTdocs.com (*http://assistdocs.com*).

(b) Documents not available from ASSIST may be ordered from the Department of Defense Single Stock Point (DoDSSP) by—

(1) Using the ASSIST Shopping Wizrard (*http://assist.dla.mil/wizard/index.cfm*);

(2) Phoning the DoDSSP Customer Service Desk (215) 697-2179, Mon-Fri, 0730 to 1600 EST; or

(3) Ordering from DoDSSP, Building 4, Section D, 700 Robbins Avenue, Philadelphia, PA 19111-5094, Telephone (215) 697-2667/2179, Facsimile (215) 697-1462.

(End of provision)

[FAC 97-15, 64 FR 72414, 12/27/99, effective 12/27/99; FAC 2001-18, 68 FR 69258, 12/11/2003, effective 12/11/2003; FAC 2005-07, 71 FR 227, 1/3/2006, effective 1/3/2006; FAC 2005-73, 79 FR 24253, 4/29/2014, effective 4/29/2014]

52.211-3 Availability of Specifications Not Listed in the GSA Index of Federal Specifications, Standards and Commercial Item Descriptions.

As prescribed in 11.204(c), insert a provision substantially the same as the following:

AVAILABILITY OF SPECIFICATIONS NOT LISTED IN THE GSA INDEX OF FEDERAL SPECIFICATIONS, STANDARDS AND COMMERCIAL ITEM DESCRIPTIONS (JUN 1988)

The specifications cited in this solicitation may be obtained from:

(Activity)________________

(Complete address)________________

(Telephone number)________________

(Person to be contacted)________________

The request should identify the solicitation number and the specification requested by date, title, and number, as cited in the solicitation.

(End of provision)

[FAC 84-37, 53 FR 17860, 5/18/88, effective 6/17/88; Redesignated from 52.210-3, FAC 90-32, 60 FR 48206, 9/18/95, effective 10/1/95; FAC 90-39, 61 FR 31612, 6/20/96, effective 8/20/96]

52.211-4 Availability for Examination of Specifications Not Listed in the GSA Index of Federal

Specifications, Standards and Commercial Item Descriptions.

As prescribed in 11.204(d), insert a provision substantially the same as the following:

AVAILABILITY FOR EXAMINATION OF SPECIFICATIONS NOT LISTED IN THE GSA INDEX OF FEDERAL SPECIFICATIONS, STANDARDS AND COMMERCIAL ITEM DESCRIPTIONS (JUN 1988)

(Activity)____________________

(Complete address)________________

____

____

(Telephone number)________________

(Person to be contacted)________________

(Time(s) for viewing)________________

(End of provision)

[FAC 84-37, 53 FR 17860, 5/18/88, effective 6/17/88; Redesignated from 52.210-4, FAC 90-32, 60 FR 48206, 9/18/95, effective 10/1/95; FAC 90-43, 61 FR 67408, 12/20/96, effective 12/20/96]

52.211-5 Material Requirements.

As prescribed in 11.304, insert the following clause:

MATERIAL REQUIREMENTS (AUG 2000)

(a) *Definitions.*

As used in this clause—

New means composed of previously unused components, whether manufactured from virgin material, recovered material in the form of raw material, or materials and by-products generated from, and reused within, an original manufacturing process; *provided* that the supplies meet contract requirements, including but not limited to, performance, reliability, and life expectancy.

Reconditioned means restored to the original normal operating condition by readjustments and material replacement.

Recovered material means waste materials and by-products recovered or diverted from solid waste, but the term does not include those materials and by-products generated from, and commonly reused within, an original manufacturing process.

Remanufactured means factory rebuilt to original specifications.

Virgin material means—

(1) Previously unused raw material, including previously unused copper, aluminum, lead, zinc, iron, other metal or metal ore; or

(2) Any undeveloped resource that is, or with new technology will become, a source of raw materials.

(b) Unless this contract otherwise requires virgin material or supplies composed of or manufactured from virgin material, the Contractor shall provide supplies that are new, reconditioned, or remanufactured, as defined in this clause.

(c) A proposal to provide unused former Government surplus property shall include a complete description of the material, the quantity, the name of the Government agency from which acquired, and the date of acquisition.

(d) A proposal to provide used, reconditioned, or remanufactured supplies shall include a detailed description of such supplies and shall be submitted to the Contracting Officer for approval.

(e) Used, reconditioned, or remanufactured supplies, or unused former Government surplus property, may be used in contract performance if the Contractor has proposed the use of such supplies, and the Contracting Officer has authorized their use.

(End of clause)

[FAC 97-1, 62 FR 44802, 8/22/97, effective 10/21/97; FAC 97-18, 65 FR 36014, 6/6/2000, effective 8/7/2000]

52.211-6 Brand Name or Equal.

As prescribed in 11.107(a), insert the following provision:

BRAND NAME OR EQUAL (AUG 1999)

(a) If an item in this solicitation is identified as "brand name or equal," the purchase description reflects the characteristics and level of quality that will satisfy the Government's needs. The salient physical, functional, or performance characteristics that "equal" products must meet are specified in the solicitation.

(b) To be considered for award, offers of "equal" products, including "equal" products of the brand name manufacturer, must—

(1) Meet the salient physical, functional, or performance characteristic specified in this solicitation;

(2) Clearly identify the item by—

(i) Brand name, if any; and

(ii) Make or model number;

(3) Include descriptive literature such as illustrations, drawings, or a clear reference to previously furnished descriptive data or in formation available to the Contracting Officer; and

(4) Clearly describe any modifications the offeror plans to make in a product to make it conform to the solicitation requirements. Mark any descriptive material to clearly show the modifications.

(c) The Contracting Officer will evaluate "equal" products on the basis of information furnished by the offeror or identified in the offer and reasonably available to the Contracting Officer. The Contracting Officer is not responsible for locating or obtaining any information not identified in the offer.

(d) Unless the offeror clearly indicates in its offer that the product being offered is an "equal" product, the offeror shall provide the brand name product referenced in the solicitation.

(End of provision)

[FAC 97-12, 64 FR 32740, 6/17/99, effective 8/16/99; FAC 97-14, 64 FR 51828, 9/24/99, effective 11/23/99, corrected, 64 FR 53264, 10/7/99]

52.211-7 Alternatives to Government-unique Standards.

As prescribed in 11.107(b), insert the following provision:

ALTERNATIVES TO GOVERNMENT-UNIQUE STANDARDS (NOV 1999)

(a) This solicitation includes Government-unique standards. The offeror may propose voluntary consensus standards that meet the Government's requirements as alternatives to the Government-unique standards. The Government will accept use of the voluntary consensus standard instead of the Government-unique standard if it meets the Government's requirements unless inconsistent with law or otherwise impractical.

(b) If an alternative standard is proposed, the offeror must furnish data and/or information regarding the alternative in sufficient detail for the Government to determine if it meets the Government's requirements. Acceptance of the alternative standard is a unilateral decision made solely at the discretion of the Government.

(c) Offers that do not comply with the Government-unique standards specified in this solicitation may be determined to be nonresponsive or unacceptable. The offeror may submit an offer that complies with the Government-unique standards specified in this solicitation, in addition to any proposed alternative standard(s).

(End of provision)

[FAC 97-14, 64 FR 51828, 9/24/99, effective 11/23/99]

52.211-8 Time of Delivery.

As prescribed in 11.404(a)(2), insert the following clause:

TIME OF DELIVERY (JUN 1997)

(a) The Government requires delivery to be made according to the following schedule:

REQUIRED DELIVERY SCHEDULE
[*Contracting Officer insert specific details*]

ITEM NO.	QUANTITY	WITHIN DAYS AFTER DATE OF CONTRACT

The Government will evaluate equally, as regards time of delivery, offers that propose delivery of each quantity within the applicable delivery period specified above. Offers that propose delivery that will not clearly fall within the applicable required delivery period specified above, will be considered nonresponsive and rejected. The Government reserves the right to award under either the required delivery schedule or the proposed delivery schedule, when an offeror offers an earlier delivery schedule than required above. If the offeror proposes no other delivery schedule, the required delivery schedule above will apply.

OFFEROR'S PROPOSED DELIVERY SCHEDULE

ITEM NO.	QUANTITY	WITHIN DAYS AFTER DATE OF CONTRACT

(b) Attention is directed to the Contract Award provision of the solicitation that provides that a written award or acceptance of offer mailed, or otherwise furnished to the successful offeror, results in a binding contract. The Government will mail or otherwise furnish to the offeror an award or notice of award not later than the day award is dated. Therefore, the offeror should compute the time available for performance beginning with the actual date of award, rather than the date the written notice of award is received from the Contracting Officer through the ordinary mails. However, the Government will evaluate an offer that proposes delivery based on the Contractor's date of receipt of the contract or notice of award by adding (1) five calendar days for delivery of the award through the ordinary mails, or (2) one working day if the solicitation states that the contract or notice of award will be transmitted electronically. (The term "working day" excludes weekends and U.S. Federal holidays.) If, as so computed, the offered delivery date is later than the required delivery date, the offer will be considered nonresponsive and rejected.

(End of clause)

Alternate I (APR 1984). If the delivery schedule is expressed in terms of specific calendar dates or specific periods and is based on an assumed date of award, the contracting officer may substitute the following paragraph (b) for paragraph (b) of the basic clause. The time may be expressed by substituting "on or before"; "during the months _______"; or "not sooner than ______ or later than ______" as headings for the third column of paragraph (a) the basic clause.

(b) The delivery dates or specific periods above are based on the assumption that the Government will make award by ______ [*Contracting Officer insert date*]. Each delivery date in the delivery schedule above will be extended by the number of calendar days after the above date that the contract is in fact awarded. Attention is directed to the Contract Award provision of the solicitation that provides that a written award or acceptance of offer mailed or otherwise furnished to the successful offeror results in a binding contract. Therefore, the offeror should compute the time available for performance beginning with the actual date of award, rather than the date the written notice of award is received from the Contracting Officer through the ordinary mails.

Alternate II (APR 1984). If the delivery schedule is expressed in terms of specific calendar dates or specific periods and is based on an assumed date the contractor will receive notice of award, the contracting officer may substitute the following paragraph (b) for paragraph (b) of the basic clause. The time may be expressed by substituting "within days after the date of receipt of a written notice of award" as the heading for the third column of paragraph (a) of the basic clause.

(b) The delivery dates or specific periods above are based on the assumption that the successful offeror will receive notice of award by ______ [*Contracting Officer insert date*]. Each delivery date in the delivery schedule above will be extended by the number of calendar days after the above date that the Contractor receives notice of award; provided, that the Contractor promptly acknowledges receipt of notice of award.

Alternate III (APR 1984). If the delivery schedule is to be based on the actual date the contractor receives a written notice of award, the contracting officer may delete paragraph (b) of the basic clause. The time may be expressed by substituting "within days after the date of receipt of a written notice of award" as the heading for the third column of paragraph (a) of the basic clause.

[FAC 90-7, 56 FR 41732, 8/22/91, effective 9/23/91; FAC 90-29, 60 FR 34732, 7/3/95, effective 7/3/95; Redesignated from 52.212-1, FAC 90-32, 60 FR 48206, 9/18/95, effective 10/1/95; Final rule, 62 FR 40236, 7/25/97, effective 6/30/97]

52.211-9 Desired and Required Time of Delivery.

As prescribed in 11.404(a)(3), insert the following clause:

DESIRED AND REQUIRED TIME OF DELIVERY (JUN 1997)

(a) The Government desires delivery to be made according to the following schedule:

DESIRED DELIVERY SCHEDULE
[*Contracting Officer insert specific details*]

ITEM NO.	QUANTITY	WITHIN DAYS AFTER DATE OF CONTRACT

If the offeror is unable to meet the desired delivery schedule, it may, without prejudicing evaluation of its offer, propose a delivery schedule below. However, the offeror's proposed delivery schedule must not extend the delivery period beyond the time for delivery in the Government's required delivery schedule as follows:

REQUIRED DELIVERY SCHEDULE
[*Contracting Officer insert specific details*]

ITEM NO.	QUANTITY	WITHIN DAYS AFTER DATE OF CONTRACT

Offers that propose delivery of a quantity under such terms or conditions that delivery will not clearly fall within the applicable required delivery period specified above, will be considered nonresponsive and rejected. If the offeror proposes no other delivery schedule, the desired delivery schedule above will apply.

OFFEROR'S PROPOSED DELIVERY SCHEDULE
[*Contracting Officer insert specific details*]

ITEM NO.	QUANTITY	WITHIN DAYS AFTER DATE OF CONTRACT

(b) Attention is directed to the Contract Award provision of the solicitation that provides that a written award or acceptance of offer mailed or otherwise furnished to the successful offeror results in a binding contract. The Government will mail or otherwise furnish to the offeror an award or notice of award not later than the day the award is dated. Therefore, the offeror shall compute the time available for performance beginning with the actual date of award, rather than the date the written notice of award is received from the Contracting Officer through the ordinary mails. However, the Government will evaluate an offer that proposes delivery based on the Contractor's date of receipt of the contract or notice of award by adding (1) five calendar days for delivery of the award through the ordinary mails, or (2) one working day if the solicitation states that the contract or notice of award will be transmitted electronically. (The term "working day" excludes weekends and U.S. Federal holidays.) If, as so computed, the offered delivery date is later than the required delivery date, the offer will be considered nonresponsive and rejected.

(End of clause)

Alternate I (APR 1984). If the delivery schedule is expressed in terms of specific calendar dates or specific periods and is based on an assumed date of award, the contracting officer may substitute the following paragraph (b) for paragraph (b) of the basic clause. The time may be expressed by substituting "on or before"; "during the months _______"; or "not sooner than _______, or later than _______" as headings for the third column of paragraph (a) of the basic clause.

(b) The delivery dates or specific periods above are based on the assumption that the Government will make award by _______

[*Contracting Officer insert date*]. Each delivery date in the delivery schedule above will be extended by the number of calendar days after the above date that the contract is in fact awarded. Attention is directed to the Contract Award provision of the solicitation that provides that a written award or acceptance of offer mailed or otherwise furnished to the successful offeror results in a binding contract. Therefore, the offeror shall compute the time available for performance beginning with the actual date of award, rather than the date the written notice of award is received from the Contracting Officer through the ordinary mails.

Alternate II (APR 1984). If the delivery schedule is expressed in terms of specific calendar dates or specific periods and is based on an assumed date the contractor receives notice of award, the contracting officer may substitute the following paragraph (b) for paragraph (b) of the basic clause. The time may be expressed by substituting "within days after the date of receipt of a written notice of award" as the heading of the third column of paragraph (a) of the basic clause.

(b) The delivery dates or specific periods above are based on the assumption that the successful offeror will receive notice of award by ______ [*Contracting Officer insert date*]. Each delivery date in the delivery schedule above will be extended by the number of calendar days after the above date that the Contractor receives notice of award; provided, that the Contractor promptly acknowledges receipt of notice of award.

Alternate III (APR 1984). If the delivery schedule is to be based on the actual date the contractor receives a written notice of award, the contracting officer may delete paragraph (b) of the basic clause. The time may be expressed by substituting "within days after the date of receipt of a written notice of award" as the heading of the third column of paragraph (a) of the basic clause.

[FAC 90-7, 56 FR 41732, 8/22/91, effective 9/23/91; FAC 90-29, 60 FR 34732, 7/3/95, effective 7/3/95; Redesignated from 52.212-2, FAC 90-32, 60 FR 48206, 9/18/95, effective 10/1/95; Final rule, 62 FR 40236, 7/25/97, effective 6/30/97]

52.211-10 Commencement, Prosecution, and Completion of Work.

As prescribed in 11.404(b), insert the following clause in solicitations and contracts when a fixed-price construction contract is contemplated. The clause may be changed to accommodate the issuance of orders under indefinite-delivery contracts for construction.

COMMENCEMENT, PROSECUTION, AND COMPLETION OF WORK (APR 1984)

The Contractor shall be required to (a) commence work under this contract within ______ [*Contracting Officer insert number*] calendar days after the date the Contractor receives the notice to proceed, (b) prosecute the work diligently, and (c) complete the entire work ready for use not later than ______ The time stated for completion shall include final cleanup of the premises.

(End of clause)

*The Contracting Officer shall specify either a number of days after the date the contractor receives the notice to proceed, or a calendar date.

Alternate I (APR 1984). If the completion date is expressed as a specific calendar date, computed on the basis of the contractor receiving the notice to proceed by a certain day, add the following paragraph to the basic clause:

The completion date is based on the assumption that the successful offeror will receive the notice to proceed by ______ [*Contracting Officer insert date*]. The completion date will be extended by the number of calendar days after the above date that the Contractor receives the notice to proceed, except to the extent that the delay in issuance of the notice to proceed results from the failure of the Contractor to execute the contract and give the required performance and payment bonds within the time specified in the offer.

[Redesignated from 52.212-3, FAC 90-32, 60 FR 48206, 9/18/95, effective 10/1/95]

52.211-11 Liquidated Damages—Supplies, Services, or Research and Development.

As prescribed in 11.503(a), insert the following clause in solicitations and contracts:

LIQUIDATED DAMAGES—SUPPLIES, SERVICES, OR RESEARCH AND DEVELOPMENT (SEP 2000)

(a) If the Contractor fails to deliver the supplies or perform the services within the time specified in this contract, the Contractor shall, in place of actual damages, pay to the Government liquidated damages of $____ per calendar day of delay [*Contracting Officer insert amount*].

(b) If the Government terminates this contract in whole or in part under the Default—Fixed-Price Supply and Service clause, the Contractor is liable for liquidated damages accruing until the Government reasonably obtains delivery or performance of similar supplies or services. These liquidated damages are in addition to excess costs of repurchase under the Termination clause.

(c) The Contractor will not be charged with liquidated damages when the delay in delivery or performance is beyond the control and without the fault or negligence of the Contractor as defined in the Default—Fixed-Price Supply and Service clause in this contract.

(End of clause)

[FAC 97-19, 65 FR 46052, 7/26/2000, effective 9/25/2000]

52.211-12 Liquidated Damages—Construction.

As prescribed in 11.503(b), insert the following clause in solicitations and contracts:

LIQUIDATED DAMAGES—CONSTRUCTION (SEP 2000)

(a) If the Contractor fails to complete the work within the time specified in the contract, the Contractor shall pay liquidated damages to the Government in the amount of $____ [*Contracting Officer insert amount*] for each calendar day of delay until the work is completed or accepted.

(b) If the Government terminates the Contractor's right to proceed, liquidated damages will continue to accrue until the work is completed. These liquidated damages are in addition to excess costs of repurchase under the Termination clause.

(End of clause)

[FAC 97-19, 65 FR 46052, 7/26/2000, effective 9/25/2000]

52.211-13 Time Extensions.

As prescribed in 11.503(c), insert the following clause:

TIME EXTENSIONS (SEP 2000)

Time extensions for contract changes will depend upon the extent, if any, by which the changes cause delay in the completion of the various elements of construction. The change order granting the time extension may provide that the contract completion date will be extended only for those specific elements related to the changed work and that the remaining contract completion dates for all other portions of the work will not be altered. The change order also may provide an equitable readjustment of liquidated damages under the new completion schedule.

(End of clause)

[FAC 97-19, 65 FR 46052, 7/26/2000, effective 9/25/2000]

52.211-14 Notice of Priority Rating for National Defense Use, Emergency Preparedness, and Energy Use Program.

As prescribed in 11.604(a), insert the following provision:

NOTICE OF PRIORITY RATING FOR NATIONAL DEFENSE USE, EMERGENCY PREPAREDNESS, AND ENERGY USE PROGRAM (APR 2008)

Any contract awarded as a result of this solicitation will be [] DX rated order; [] DO rated order certified for national defense, emergency preparedness, and energy program use under the Defense Priorities and Allocations System (DPAS) (15 CFR 700), and the Contractor will be required to follow all of the requirements of this regulation. [*Contracting Officer check appropriate box.*]

(End of provision)

[FAC 84-16, 51 FR 19717, 5/30/86, effective 5/30/86; Final rule, 55 FR 38518, 9/18/90; Redesignated from 52.212-7, FAC 90-32, 60 FR 48206, 9/18/95, effective 10/1/95; FAC 2005-25, 73 FR 21783, 4/22/2008, effective 4/22/2008]

52.211-15 Defense Priority and Allocation Requirements.

As prescribed in 11.604(b), insert the following clause:

DEFENSE PRIORITY AND ALLOCATION REQUIREMENTS (APR 2008)

This is a rated order certified for national defense, emergency preparedness, and energy program use, and the Contractor shall follow all the requirements of the Defense Priorities and Allocations System regulation (15 CFR 700).

(End of clause)

[FAC 84-16, 51 FR 19717, 5/30/86, effective 5/30/86; Final rule, 55 FR 38518, 9/18/90; Redesignated from 52.212-8, FAC 90-32, 60 FR 48206, 9/18/95, effective 10/1/95; FAC 2005-25, 73 FR 21783, 4/22/2008, effective 4/22/2008]

52.211-16 Variation in Quantity.

As prescribed in 11.703(a), insert the following clause:

VARIATION IN QUANTITY (APR 1984)

(a) A variation in the quantity of any item called for by this contract will not be accepted unless the variation has been caused by conditions of loading, shipping, or packing, or allowances in manufacturing processes, and then only to the extent, if any, specified in paragraph (b) below.

(b) The permissible variation shall be limited to:

________ Percent increase [*Contracting Officer insert percentage*]

________ Percent decrease [*Contracting Officer insert percentage*]

This increase or decrease shall apply to ________*.

(End of clause)

* Contracting Officer shall insert in the blank the designation(s) to which the percentages apply, such as—

(1) The total contract quantity;

(2) Item 1 only;

(3) Each quantity specified in the delivery schedule;

(4) The total item quantity for each destination; or

(5) The total quantity of each item without regard to destination.

[Redesignated from 52.212-9, FAC 90-32, 60 FR 48206, 9/18/95, effective 10/1/95; FAC 97-11, 64 FR 10530, 3/4/99, effective 5/3/99]

52.211-17 Delivery of Excess Quantities.

As prescribed in 11.703(b), insert the following clause:

DELIVERY OF EXCESS QUANTITIES (SEP 1989)

The Contractor is responsible for the delivery of each item quantity within allowable variations, if any. If the Contractor delivers and the Government receives quantities of any item in excess of the quantity called for (after considering any allowable variation in quantity), such excess quantities will be treated as being delivered for the convenience of the Contractor. The Government may retain such excess quantities up to $250 in value without compensating the Contractor therefor, and the Contractor waives all right, title, or interests therein. Quantities in excess of $250 will, at the option of the Government, either be returned at the Contractor's expense or retained and paid for by the Government at the contract unit price.

(End of clause)

[FAC 84-51, 54 FR 34757, 8/21/89, effective 9/20/89; Redesignated from 52.212-10, FAC 90-32, 60 FR 48206, 9/18/95, effective 10/1/95]

52.211-18 Variation in Estimated Quantity.

As prescribed in 11.703(c), insert the following clause in solicitations and contracts when a fixed-price construction contract is contemplated that authorizes a variation in the estimated quantity of unit-priced items:

VARIATION IN ESTIMATED QUANTITY (APR 1984)

If the quantity of a unit-priced item in this contract is an estimated quantity and the actual quantity of the unit-priced item varies more than 15 percent above or below the estimated quantity, an equitable adjustment in the contract price shall be made upon demand of either party. The equitable adjustment shall be based upon any increase or decrease in costs due solely to the variation above 115 percent or below 85 percent of the estimated quantity. If the quantity variation is such as to cause an increase in the time necessary for completion, the Contractor may request, in writing, an extension of time, to be received by the Contracting Officer within 10 days from the beginning of the delay, or within such further period as may be granted by the Contracting Officer before the date of final settlement of the contract. Upon the receipt of a written request for an extension, the Contracting Officer shall ascertain the facts and make an adjustment for extending the completion date as, in the judgment of the Contracting Officer, is justified.

(End of clause)

[Redesignated from 52.212-11, FAC 90-32, 60 FR 48206, 9/18/95, effective 10/1/95]

52.212-1 Instructions to Offerors—Commercial Items.

As prescribed in 12.301(b)(1), insert the following provision:

INSTRUCTIONS TO OFFERORS—COMMERCIAL ITEMS (OCT 2018)

(a) *North American Industry Classification System (NAICS) code and small business size standard.* The NAICS code and small business size standard for this acquisition appear in Block 10 of the solicitation cover sheet (SF 1449). However, the small business size standard for a concern which submits an offer in its own name, but which proposes to furnish an item which it did not itself manufacture, is 500 employees.

(b) *Submission of offers.* Submit signed and dated offers to the office specified in this solicitation at or before the exact time specified in this solicitation. Offers may be submitted on the SF 1449, letterhead stationery, or as otherwise specified in the solicitation. As a minimum, offers must show—

(1) The solicitation number;

(2) The time specified in the solicitation for receipt of offers;

(3) The name, address, and telephone number of the offeror;

(4) A technical description of the items being offered in sufficient detail to evaluate compliance with the requirements in the solicitation. This may include product literature, or other documents, if necessary;

(5) Terms of any express warranty;

(6) Price and any discount terms;

(7) "Remit to" address, if different than mailing address;

(8) A completed copy of the representations and certifications at FAR 52.212-3 (see FAR 52.212-3(b) for those representations and certifications that the offeror shall complete electronically);

(9) Acknowledgment of Solicitation Amendments;

(10) Past performance information, when included as an evaluation factor, to include recent and relevant contracts for the same or similar items and other references (including contract numbers, points of contact with telephone numbers and other relevant information); and

(11) If the offer is not submitted on the SF 1449, include a statement specifying the extent of agreement with all terms, conditions, and provisions included in the solicitation. Offers that fail to furnish required representations or information, or reject the terms and conditions of the solicitation may be excluded from consideration.

(c) *Period for acceptance of offers.* The offeror agrees to hold the prices in its offer firm for 30 calendar days from the date specified for receipt of offers, unless another time period is specified in an addendum to the solicitation.

(d) *Product samples.* When required by the solicitation, product samples shall be submitted at or prior to the time specified for receipt of offers. Unless otherwise specified in this solicitation, these samples shall be submitted at no expense to the Government, and returned at the sender's request and expense, unless they are destroyed during preaward testing.

(e) *Multiple offers.* Offerors are encouraged to submit multiple offers presenting alternative terms and conditions, including alternative line items (provided that the alternative line items are consistent with subpart 4.10 of the Federal Acquisition Regulation), or alternative commercial items for satisfying the requirements of this solicitation. Each offer submitted will be evaluated separately.

(f) *Late submissions, modifications, revisions, and withdrawals of offers.* (1) Offerors are responsible for submitting offers, and any modifications, revisions, or withdrawals, so as to reach the Government office designated in the solicitation by the time specified in the solicitation. If no time is specified in the solicitation, the time for receipt is 4:30 p.m., local time, for the designated Government office on the date that offers or revisions are due.

(2) (i) Any offer, modification, revision, or withdrawal of an offer received at the Government office designated in the solicitation after the exact time specified for receipt of offers is "late" and will not be considered unless it is received before award is made, the Contracting Officer determines that accepting the late offer would not unduly delay the acquisition; and—

(A) If it was transmitted through an electronic commerce method authorized by the solicitation, it was received at the initial point of entry to the Government infrastructure not later than 5:00 p.m. one working day prior to the date specified for receipt of offers; or

(B) There is acceptable evidence to establish that it was received at the Government installation designated for receipt of offers and was under the Government's control prior to the time set for receipt of offers; or

(C) If this solicitation is a request for proposals, it was the only proposal received.

(ii) However, a late modification of an otherwise successful offer, that makes its terms more favorable to the Government, will be considered at any time it is received and may be accepted.

(3) Acceptable evidence to establish the time of receipt at the Government installation includes the time/date stamp of that installation on the offer wrapper, other documentary evidence of receipt maintained by the installation, or oral testimony or statements of Government personnel.

(4) If an emergency or unanticipated event interrupts normal Government processes so that offers cannot be received at the Government office designated for receipt of offers by the exact time specified in the solicitation, and urgent Government requirements preclude amendment of the solicitation or other notice of an extension of the closing date, the time specified for receipt of offers will be deemed to be extended to the same time of day specified in the solicitation on the first work day on which normal Government processes resume.

(5) Offers may be withdrawn by written notice received at any time before the exact time set for receipt of offers. Oral offers in response to oral solicitations may be withdrawn orally. If the solicitation authorizes facsimile offers, offers may be withdrawn via facsimile received at any time before the exact time set for receipt of offers, subject to the conditions specified in the solicitation concerning facsimile offers. An offer may be withdrawn in person by an offeror or its authorized representative if, before the exact time set for receipt of offers, the identity of the person requesting withdrawal is established and the person signs a receipt for the offer.

(g) *Contract award (not applicable to Invitation for Bids).* The Government intends to evaluate offers and award a contract without discussions with offerors. Therefore, the offeror's initial offer should contain the offeror's best terms from a price and technical standpoint. However, the Government reserves the right to conduct discussions if later determined by the Contracting Officer to be necessary. The Government may reject any or all offers if such action is in the public interest; accept other than the lowest offer; and waive informalities and minor irregularities in offers received.

(h) *Multiple awards.* The Government may accept any item or group of items of an offer, unless the offeror qualifies the offer by specific limitations. Unless otherwise provided in the Schedule, offers may not be submitted for quantities less than those specified. The Government reserves the right to make an award on any item for a quantity less than the quantity offered, at the unit prices offered, unless the offeror specifies otherwise in the offer.

(i) *Availability of requirements documents cited in the solicitation.* (1) (i) The GSA Index of Federal Specifications, Standards and Commercial Item Descriptions, FPMR Part 101-29, and copies of specifications, standards, and commercial item descriptions cited in this solicitation may be obtained for a fee by submitting a request to—GSA Federal Supply Service Specifications Section, Suite 8100, 470 East L'Enfant Plaza, SW, Washington, DC 20407, Telephone (202) 619-8925, Facsimile (202) 619-8978.

(ii) If the General Services Administration, Department of Agriculture, or Department of Veterans Affairs issued this solicitation, a single copy of specifications, standards, and commercial item descriptions cited in this solicitation may be obtained free of charge by submitting a request to the addressee in paragraph (i) (1) (i) of this provision. Additional copies will be issued for a fee.

(2) Most unclassified Defense specifications and standards may be downloaded from the following ASSIST websites:

(i) ASSIST (*http://assist.dla.mil/online/start/*).

(ii) Quick Search (*http://quicksearch.dla.mil/*).

(iii) ASSISTdocs.com (*http://assistdocs.com*).

(3) Documents not available from ASSIST may be ordered from the Department of Defense Single Stock Point (DoDSSP) by—

(i) Using the ASSIST Shopping Wizard (*http://assist.dla.mil/wizard/index.cfm*);

(ii) Phoning the DoDSSP Customer Service Desk (215) 697-2179, Mon-Fri, 0730 to 1600 EST; or

(iii) Ordering from DoDSSP, Building 4, Section D, 700 Robbins Avenue, Philadelphia, PA 19111-5094, Telephone (215) 697-2667/2179, Facsimile (215) 697-1462.

(4) Nongovernment (voluntary) standards must be obtained from the organization responsible for their preparation, publication, or maintenance.

(j) *Unique entity identifier.* (Applies to all offers exceeding $3,500, and offers of $3,500 or less if the solicitation requires the Contractor to be registered in the System for Award Management (SAM).) The Offeror shall enter, in the block with its name and address on the cover page of its offer, the annotation "Unique Entity Identifier" followed by the unique entity identifier that identifies the Offeror's name and address. The Offeror also shall enter its Electronic Funds Transfer (EFT) indicator, if applicable. The EFT indicator is a four-character suffix to the unique entity identifier. The suffix is assigned at the discretion of the Offeror to establish additional SAM records for identifying alternative EFT accounts (see subpart 32.11) for the same entity. If the Offeror does not have a unique entity identifier, it should contact the entity designated at *www.sam.gov* for unique entity identifier establishment directly to obtain one. The Offeror should indicate that it is an offeror for a Government contract when contacting the entity designated at *www.sam.gov* for establishing the unique entity identifier.

(k) [Removed and Reserved]

(l) *Debriefing.* If a post-award debriefing is given to requesting offerors, the Government shall disclose the following information, if applicable:

(1) The agency's evaluation of the significant weak or deficient factors in the debriefed offeror's offer.

(2) The overall evaluated cost or price and technical rating of the successful and the debriefed offeror and past performance information on the debriefed offeror.

(3) The overall ranking of all offerors, when any ranking was developed by the agency during source selection.

(4) A summary of the rationale for award;

(5) For acquisitions of commercial items, the make and model of the item to be delivered by the successful offeror.

(6) Reasonable responses to relevant questions posed by the debriefed offeror as to whether source-selection procedures set forth in the solicitation, applicable regulations, and other applicable authorities were followed by the agency.

(End of provision)

[FAC 90-32, 60 FR 48206, 9/18/95, effective 10/1/95; Final rule, 62 FR 40236, 7/25/97, effective 6/30/97; FAC 97-4, 63 FR 9048, 2/23/98, effective 4/24/98, FAC 97-5, 63 FR 34058, 6/22/98, effective 8/21/98; FAC 97-12, 64 FR 32740, 6/17/99, effective 6/17/99; FAC 97-14, 64 FR 51828, 9/24/99, effective 11/23/99; FAC 97-16, 65 FR 16274, 3/27/2000, effective 3/27/2000; FAC 97-19, 65 FR 46052, 7/26/2000, effective 10/1/2000, finalized without change by FAC 2001-02, 66 FR 65347, 12/18/2001, effective 12/18/2001; FAC 2001-15, 68 FR 43873, 7/24/2003, effective 7/24/2003; FAC 2001-16, Final rule, 68 FR 56669, 10/1/2003, effective 10/1/2003; FAC 2001-18, 68 FR 69257, 12/11/2003; effective 1/12/2004; FAC 2001-26, 69 FR 76341, 12/20/2004, effective 1/1/2005; FAC 2005-07, 71 FR 227, 1/3/2006, effective 1/3/2006; FAC 2005-13, 71 FR 57363, 71 FR 57380, 9/28/2006, effective 9/28/2006; FAC 2005-21, 72 FR 63076, 11/7/2007, effective 11/7/2007; FAC 2005-25, 73 FR 21773, 4/22/2008, effective 4/22/2008; FAC 2005-26, 73 FR 33636, 5/12/2008, effective 6/12/2008; FAC 2005-30, 74 FR 2712, 2724, 1/15/2009, effective 2/17/2009; FAC 2005-36, 74 FR 40463, 8/11/2009, effective 8/11/2009; FAC 2005-55, 77 FR 187, 1/3/2012, effective 2/2/2012; FAC 2005-67, 78 FR 37676, 6/21/2013, effective 7/22/2013; FAC 2005-73, 79 FR 24253, 4/29/2014, effective 4/29/2014; FAC 2005-83, 80 FR 38293, 7/2/2015, effective 10/1/2015; FAC 2005-91, 81 FR 67736, 9/30/2016, effective 10/31/2016; FAC 2005-95, 82 FR 4709, 1/13/2017, effective 1/13/2017; FAC 2005-100, 83 FR 42571, 8/22/2018, effective 8/22/2018; FAC 2005-101, 83 FR 48691, 9/26/2018, effective 10/26/2018]

52.212-2 Evaluation—Commercial Items.

As prescribed in 12.301(c), the Contracting Officer may insert a provision substantially as follows:

EVALUATION—COMMERCIAL ITEMS (OCT 2014)

(a) The Government will award a contract resulting from this solicitation to the responsible offeror whose offer conforming to the solicitation will be most advantageous to the Government, price and other factors considered. The following factors shall be used to evaluate offers:

____

____

____

[*Contracting Officer shall insert the significant evaluation factors, such as (i) technical capability of the item offered to meet the Government requirement; (ii) price; (iii) past performance (see FAR 15.304); and include them in the relative order of importance of the evaluation factors, such as in descending order of importance.*]

Technical and past performance, when combined, are __ [*Contracting Officer state, in accordance with FAR 15.304, the relative importance of all other evaluation factors, when combined, when compared to price.*]

(b) *Options.* The Government will evaluate offers for award purposes by adding the total price for all options to the total price for the basic requirement. The Government may determine that an offer is unacceptable if the option prices are significantly unbalanced. Evaluation of options shall not obligate the Government to exercise the option(s).

(c) A written notice of award or acceptance of an offer, mailed or otherwise furnished to the successful offeror within the time for acceptance specified in the offer, shall result in a binding contract without further action by either party. Before the offer's specified expiration time, the Government may accept an offer (or part of an offer), whether or not there are negotiations after its receipt, unless a written notice of withdrawal is received before award.

(End of provision)

[FAC 90-32, 60 FR 48206, 9/18/95, effective 10/1/95; FAC 97-2, 62 FR 51224, 9/30/97, effective 10/10/97; FAC 97-7, 63 FR 36120, 7/1/98, effective 1/1/99, finalized without change, FAC 97-13, 7/2/99; FAC 2005-77, 79 FR 61746, 10/14/2014, effective 10/14/2014]

52.212-3 Offeror Representations and Certifications—Commercial Items.

As prescribed in 12.301(c) through (u), insert the following provision:

OFFEROR REPRESENTATIONS AND CERTIFICATIONS—COMMERCIAL ITEMS (DEC 2019)

The Offeror shall complete only paragraph (b) of this provision if the Offeror has completed the annual representations and certification electronically in the System for Award Management (SAM) accessed through *https://www.sam.gov*. If the Offeror has not completed the annual representations and certifications electronically, the Offeror shall complete only paragraphs (c) through (v)) of this provision.

(a) *Definitions.* As used in this provision—

Covered telecommunications equipment or services has the meaning provided in the clause 52.204-25, Prohibition on Contracting for Certain Telecommunications and Video Surveillance Services or Equipment.

Economically disadvantaged women-owned small business (EDWOSB) concern means a small business concern that is at least 51 percent directly and unconditionally owned by, and the management and daily business operations of which are controlled by, one or more women who are citizens of the United States and who are economically disadvantaged in accordance with 13 CFR part 127. It automatically qualifies as a women-owned small business eligible under the WOSB Program.

Forced or indentured child labor means all work or service—

(1) Exacted from any person under the age of 18 under the menace of any penalty for its nonperformance and for which the worker does not offer himself voluntarily; or

(2) Performed by any person under the age of 18 pursuant to a contract the enforcement of which can be accomplished by process or penalties.

Highest-level owner means the entity that owns or controls an immediate owner of the offeror, or that owns or controls one or more entities that control an immediate owner of the offeror. No entity owns or exercises control of the highest level owner.

Immediate owner means an entity, other than the offeror, that has direct control of the offeror. Indicators of control include, but are not limited to, one or more of the following: Ownership or interlocking management, identity of interests among family members, shared facilities and equipment, and the common use of employees.

Inverted domestic corporation means a foreign incorporated entity that meets the definition of an inverted domestic corporation under 6 U.S.C. 395(b), applied in accordance with the rules and definitions of 6 U.S.C. 395(c).

Manufactured end product means any end product in product and service codes (PSCs) 1000-9999, except—

(1) PSC 5510, Lumber and Related Basic Wood Materials;

(2) Product or Service Group (PSG) 87, Agricultural Supplies;

(3) PSG 88, Live Animals;

(4) PSG 89, Subsistence;

(5) PSC 9410, Crude Grades of Plant Materials;

(6) PSC 9430, Miscellaneous Crude Animal Products, Inedible;

(7) PSC 9440, Miscellaneous Crude Agricultural and Forestry Products;

(8) PSC 9610, Ores;

(9) PSC 9620, Minerals, Natural and Synthetic; and

(10) PSC 9630, Additive Metal Materials.

Place of manufacture means the place where an end product is assembled out of components, or otherwise made or processed from raw materials into the finished product that is to be provided to the Government. If a product is disassembled and reassembled, the place of reassembly is not the place of manufacture.

Predecessor means an entity that is replaced by a successor and includes any predecessors of the predecessor.

Restricted business operations means business operations in Sudan that include power production activities, mineral extraction activities, oil-related activities, or the production of military equipment, as those terms are defined in the Sudan Accountability and Divestment Act of 2007 (Pub. L. 110-174). Restricted business operations do not include business operations that the person (as that term is defined in Section 2 of the Sudan Accountability and Divestment Act of 2007) conducting the business can demonstrate—

(1) Are conducted under contract directly and exclusively with the regional government of southern Sudan;

(2) Are conducted pursuant to specific authorization from the Office of Foreign Assets Control in the Department of the Treasury, or are expressly exempted under Federal law from the requirement to be conducted under such authorization;

(3) Consist of providing goods or services to marginalized populations of Sudan;

(4) Consist of providing goods or services to an internationally recognized peacekeeping force or humanitarian organization;

(5) Consist of providing goods or services that are used only to promote health or education; or

(6) Have been voluntarily suspended.

Sensitive technology—

(1) Means hardware, software, telecommunications equipment, or any other technology that is to be used specifically—

(i) To restrict the free flow of unbiased information in Iran; or

(ii) To disrupt, monitor, or otherwise restrict speech of the people of Iran; and

(2) Does not include information or informational materials the export of which the President does not have the authority to regulate or prohibit pursuant to section 203(b)(3) of the International Emergency Economic Powers Act (50 U.S.C. 1702(b)(3)).

Service-disabled veteran-owned small business concern—

(1) Means a small business concern—

(i) Not less than 51 percent of which is owned by one or more service—disabled veterans or, in the case of any publicly owned business, not less than 51 percent of the stock of which is owned by one or more service-disabled veterans; and

(ii) The management and daily business operations of which are controlled by one or more service-disabled veterans or, in the case of a service-disabled veteran with permanent and severe disability, the spouse or permanent caregiver of such veteran.

(2) *Service-disabled veteran* means a veteran, as defined in 38 U.S.C. 101(2), with a disability that is service-connected, as defined in 38 U.S.C. 101(16).

Small business concern means a concern, including its affiliates, that is independently owned and operated, not dominant in the field of operation in which it is bidding on Government contracts, and qualified as a small business under the criteria in 13 CFR Part 121 and size standards in this solicitation.

Small disadvantaged business concern, consistent with 13 CFR 124.1002, means a small business concern under the size standard applicable to the acquisition, that—

(1) Is at least 51 percent unconditionally and directly owned (as defined at 13 CFR 124.105) by—

(i) One or more socially disadvantaged (as defined at 13 CFR 124.103) and economically disadvantaged (as defined at 13 CFR 124.104) individuals who are citizens of the United States; and

(ii) Each individual claiming economic disadvantage has a net worth not exceeding $750,000 after taking into account the applicable exclusions set forth at 13 CFR 124.104(c)(2); and

(2) The management and daily business operations of which are controlled (as defined at 13 CFR 124.106) by individuals, who meet the criteria in paragraphs (1)(i) and (ii) of this definition.

Subsidiary means an entity in which more than 50 percent of the entity is owned—

(1) Directly by a parent corporation; or

(2) Through another subsidiary of a parent corporation.

Successor means an entity that has replaced a predecessor by acquiring the assets and carrying out the affairs of the predecessor under a new name (often through acquisition or merger). The term *successor* does not include new offices/divisions of the same company or a company that only changes its name. The extent of the responsibility of the successor for the liabilities of the predecessor may vary, depending on State law and specific circumstances.

Veteran-owned small business concern means a small business concern—

(1) Not less than 51 percent of which is owned by one or more veterans (as defined at 38 U.S.C. 101(2)) or, in the case of any publicly owned business, not less than 51 percent of the stock of which is owned by one or more veterans; and

(2) The management and daily business operations of which are controlled by one or more veterans.

Women-owned business concern means a concern which is at least 51 percent owned by one or more women; or in the case of any publicly owned business, at least 51 percent of its stock is owned by one or more women; and whose management and daily business operations are controlled by one or more women.

Women-owned small business concern means a small business concern—

(1) That is at least 51 percent owned by one or more women; or, in the case of any publicly owned business, at least 51 percent of its stock is owned by one or more women; and

(2) Whose management and daily business operations are controlled by one or more women.

Women-owned small business (WOSB) concern eligible under the WOSB Program (in accordance with 13 CFR part 127), means a small business concern that is at least 51 percent directly and unconditionally owned by, and the management and daily business operations of which are controlled by, one or more women who are citizens of the United States.

(b)(1) *Annual Representations and Certifications.* Any changes provided by the Offeror in paragraph (b)(2) of this provision do not automatically change the representations and certifications in SAM.

(2) The offeror has completed the annual representations and certifications electronically in SAM accessed through *http://www.sam.gov*. After reviewing SAM information, the Offeror verifies by submission of this offer that the representations and certifications currently posted electronically at FAR 52.212-3, Offeror Representations and Certifications—Commercial Items, have been entered or updated in the last 12 months, are current, accurate, complete, and applicable to this solicitation (including the business size standard applicable to the NAICS code referenced for this solicitation), at the time this offer is submitted and are incorporated in this offer by reference (see FAR 4.1201), except for paragraphs __.

[*Offeror to identify the applicable paragraphs at (c) through (v) of this provision that the offeror has completed for the purposes of this solicitation only, if any.*

These amended representation(s) and/or certification(s) are also incorporated in this offer and are current, accurate, and complete as of the date of this offer.

Any changes provided by the offeror are applicable to this solicitation only, and do not result in an update to the representations and certifications posted electronically on SAM.]

(c) Offerors must complete the following representations when the resulting contract will be performed in the United States or its outlying areas. Check all that apply.

(1) *Small business concern.* The offeror represents as part of its offer that it [] is, [] is not a small business concern.

(2) *Veteran-owned small business concern.* [*Complete only if the offeror represented itself as a small business concern in paragraph (c)(1) of this provision.*] The offeror represents as part of its offer that it []is, [] is not a veteran-owned small business concern.

(3) *Service-disabled veteran-owned small business concern.* [*Complete only if the offeror represented itself as a veteran-owned small business concern in paragraph (c)(2) of this provision.*] The offeror represents as part of its offer that it []is, [] is not a service-disabled veteran-owned small business concern.

(4) *Small disadvantaged business concern.* [*Complete only if the offeror represented itself as a small business concern in paragraph (c)(1) of this provision.*] The offeror represents, that it []is [] is not a small disadvantaged business concern as defined in 13 CFR 124.1002.

(5) *Women-owned small business concern.* [*Complete only if the offeror represented itself as a small business concern in paragraph (c)(1) of this provision.*] The offeror represents that it [] is, [] is not a women-owned small business concern.

(6) *WOSB concern eligible under the WOSB Program.* [*Complete only if the offeror represented itself as a women-owned small business concern in paragraph (c)(5) of this provision.*] The offeror represents that—

(i) It ☐ is, ☐ is not a WOSB concern eligible under the WOSB Program, has provided all the required documents to the WOSB Repository, and no change in circumstances or adverse decisions have been issued that affects its eligibility; and

(ii) It ☐ is, ☐ is not a joint venture that complies with the requirements of 13 CFR part 127, and the representation in paragraph (c)(6)(i) of this provision is accurate for each WOSB concern eligible under the WOSB Program participating in the joint venture. [*The offeror shall enter the name or names of the WOSB concern eligible under the WOSB Program and other small businesses that are participating in the joint venture:* ______.] Each WOSB concern eligible under the WOSB Program participating in the joint venture shall submit a separate signed copy of the WOSB representation.

(7) *Economically disadvantaged women-owned small business (EDWOSB) concern.* [*Complete only if the offeror represented itself as a WOSB concern eligible under the WOSB Program in (c)(6) of this provision.*] The offeror represents that—

(i) It ☐ is, ☐ is not an EDWOSB concern, has provided all the required documents to the WOSB Repository, and no change in circumstances or adverse decisions have been issued that affects its eligibility; and

(ii) It ☐ is, ☐ is not a joint venture that complies with the requirements of 13 CFR part 127, and the representation in paragraph (c)(7)(i) of this provision is accurate for each EDWOSB concern participating in the joint venture. [*The offeror shall enter the name or names of the EDWOSB concern and other small businesses that are participating in the joint venture:* ______.] Each EDWOSB concern participating in the joint venture shall submit a separate signed copy of the EDWOSB representation.

Note to paragraphs (c)(8) and (9): Complete paragraphs (c)(8) and (c)(9) only if this solicitation is expected to exceed the simplified acquisition threshold.

(8) *Women-owned business concern (other than small business concern).* [*Complete only if the offeror is a women-owned business concern and did not represent itself as a small business concern in paragraph (c)(1) of this provision.*] The offeror represents that it []

is, [] is not a women-owned business concern.

(9) *Tie bid priority for labor surplus area concerns.* If this is an invitation for bid, small business offerors may identify the labor surplus areas in which costs to be incurred on account of manufacturing or production (by offeror or first-tier subcontractors) amount to more than 50 percent of the contract price: ______

(10) *HUBZone small business concern.* [*Complete only if the offeror represented itself as a small business concern in paragraph (c)(1) of this provision.*] The offeror represents, as part of its offer, that—

(i) It [] is, [] is not a HUBZone small business concern listed, on the date of this representation, on the List of Qualified HUBZone Small Business Concerns maintained by the Small Business Administration, and no material changes in ownership and control, principal office, or HUBZone employee percentage have occurred since it was certified in accordance with 13 CFR Part 126; and

(ii) It [] is, [] is not a HUBZone joint venture that complies with the requirements of 13 CFR Part 126, and the representation in paragraph (c)(10)(i) of this provision is accurate for each HUBZone small business concern participating in the HUBZone joint venture. [*The offeror shall enter the names of each of the HUBZone small business concerns participating in the HUBZone joint venture:* ________] Each HUBZone small business concern participating in the HUBZone joint venture shall submit a separate signed copy of the HUBZone representation.

(d) Representations required to implement provisions of Executive Order 11246—

(1) Previous contracts and compliance. The offeror represents that—

(i) It [] has, [] has not participated in a previous contract or subcontract subject to the Equal Opportunity clause of this solicitation; and

(ii) It [] has, [] has not filed all required compliance reports.

(2) *Affirmative Action Compliance.* The offeror represents that—

(i) It [] has developed and has on file, [] has not developed and does not have on file, at each establishment, affirmative action programs required by rules and regulations of the Secretary of Labor (41 CFR parts 60-1 and 60-2, or

(ii) It [] has not previously had contracts subject to the written affirmative action programs requirement of the rules and regulations of the Secretary of Labor.

(e) Certification Regarding Payments to Influence Federal Transactions (31 U.S.C. 1352). (Applies only if the contract is expected to exceed $150,000.) By submission of its offer, the offeror certifies to the best of its knowledge and belief that no Federal appropriated funds have been paid or will be paid to any person for influencing or attempting to influence an officer or employee of any agency, a Member of Congress, an officer or employee of Congress or an employee of a Member of Congress on his or her behalf in connection with the award of any resultant contract. If any registrants under the Lobbying Disclosure Act of 1995 have made a lobbying contact on behalf of the offeror with respect to this contract, the offeror shall complete and submit, with its offer, OMB Standard Form LLL, Disclosure of Lobbying Activities, to provide the name of the registrants. The offeror need not report regularly employed officers or employees of the offeror to whom payments of reasonable compensation were made.

(f) *Buy American Certificate.* (Applies only if the clause at Federal Acquisition Regulation (FAR) 52.225-1, Buy American—Supplies, is included in this solicitation.)

(1) The offeror certifies that each end product, except those listed in paragraph (f)(2) of this provision, is a domestic end product and that for other than COTS items, the offeror has considered components of unknown origin to have been mined, produced, or manufactured outside the United States. The offeror shall list as foreign end products those end products manufactured in the United States that do not qualify as domestic end products, i.e., an end product that is not a COTS item and does not meet the component test in paragraph (2) of the definition of *domestic end product.* The terms

commercially available off-the-shelf (COTS) item, component, domestic end product, end product, foreign end product, and *United States* are defined in the clause of this solicitation entitled "Buy American—Supplies."

(2) Foreign End Products:

Line Item No.: ______

Country of Origin: ______

[*List as necessary*]

(3) The Government will evaluate offers in accordance with the policies and procedures of FAR Part 25.

(g)(1) *Buy American—Free Trade Agreements—Israeli Trade Act Certificate.* (Applies only if the clause at FAR 52.225-3, Buy American—Free Trade Agreements—Israeli Trade Act, is included in this solicitation.)

(i) The offeror certifies that each end product, except those listed in paragraph (g)(1)(ii) or (g)(1)(iii) of this provision, is a domestic end product and that for other than COTS items, the offeror has considered components of unknown origin to have been mined, produced, or manufactured outside the United States. The terms *Bahrainian, Moroccan, Omani, Panamanian, or Peruvian end product, commercially available off-the-shelf (COTS) item, component, domestic end product, end product, foreign end product, Free Trade Agreement country, Free Trade Agreement country end product, Israeli end product*, and *United States* are defined in the clause of this solicitation entitled "Buy American-Free Trade Agreements-Israeli Trade Act."

(ii) The offeror certifies that the following supplies are Free Trade Agreement country end products (other than Bahrainian, Moroccan, Omani, Panamanian, or Peruvian end products) or Israeli end products as defined in the clause of this solicitation entitled "Buy American—Free Trade Agreements—Israeli Trade Act":

Free Trade Agreement Country End Products (Other than Bahrainian, Moroccan, Omani, or Peruvian End Products) or Israeli End Products:

Line Item No.: ______

Country of Origin: ______

[*List as necessary*]

(iii) The offeror shall list those supplies that are foreign end products (other than those listed in paragraph (g)(1)(ii) of this provision) as defined in the clause of this solicitation entitled "Buy American—Free Trade Agreements—Israeli Trade Act." The offeror shall list as other foreign end products those end products manufactured in the United States that do not qualify as domestic end products, i.e., an end product that is not a COTS item and does not meet the component test in paragraph (2) of the definition of "domestic end product."

Other Foreign End Products

Line Item No.: ______

Country of Origin: ______

[*List as necessary*]

(iv) The Government will evaluate offers in accordance with the policies and procedures of FAR Part 25.

(2) Buy American—Free Trade Agreements—Israeli Trade Act Certificate, Alternate I. If Alternate I to the clause at FAR 52.225-3 is included in this solicitation, substitute the following paragraph (g)(1)(ii) for paragraph (g)(1)(ii) of the basic provision:

(g)(1)(ii) The offeror certifies that the following supplies are Canadian end products as defined in the clause of this solicitation entitled "Buy American—Free Trade Agreements—Israeli Trade Act":

Canadian End Products

Line Item No.: ______

[*List as necessary*]

(3) Buy American—Free Trade Agreements—Israeli Trade Act Certificate, Alternate II. If Alternate II to the clause at FAR 52.225-3 is included in this solicitation, substitute the following paragraph (g)(1)(ii) for paragraph (g)(1)(ii) of the basic provision:

(g)(1)(ii) The offeror certifies that the following supplies are Canadian end products or Israeli end products as defined in the clause of this solicitation entitled "Buy American—Free Trade Agreements—Israeli Trade Act":

Canadian or Israeli End Products

Line Item No.: ____________

Country of Origin: ____________

[*List as necessary*]

(4) *Buy American—Free Trade Agreements—Israeli Trade Act Certificate, Alternate III.* If Alternate III to the clause at FAR 52.225-3 is included in this solicitation, substitute the following paragraph (g) (1) (ii) for paragraph (g) (1) (ii) of the basic provision:

(g) (1) (ii) The offeror certifies that the following supplies are Free Trade Agreement country end products (other than Bahrainian, Korean, Moroccan, Omani, Panamanian, or Peruvian end products) or Israeli end products as defined in the clause of this solicitation entitled "Buy American Act—Free Trade Agreements—Israeli Trade Act":

Free Trade Agreement Country End Products (Other than Bahrainian, Korean, Moroccan, Omani, Panamanian, or Peruvian End Products) or Israeli End Products:

Line Item No.: ____________

Country of Origin: ____________

[*List as necessary*]

(5) *Trade Agreements Certificate*. (Applies only if the clause at FAR 52.225-5, Trade Agreements, is included in this solicitation.)

(i) The offeror certifies that each end product, except those listed in paragraph (g) (5) (ii) of this provision, is a U.S.-made or designated country end product, as defined in the clause of this solicitation entitled "Trade Agreements."

(ii) The offeror shall list as other end products those end products that are not U.S.-made or designated country end products.

Other End Products

Line Item No.: ____________

Country of Origin: ____________

[*List as necessary*]

(iii) The Government will evaluate offers in accordance with the policies and procedures of FAR Part 25. For line items covered by the WTO GPA, the Government will evaluate offers of U.S.-made or designated country end products without regard to the restrictions of the Buy American statute. The Government will consider for award only offers of U.S.-made or designated country end products unless the Contracting Officer determines that there are no offers for such products or that the offers for such products are insufficient to fulfill the requirements of the solicitation.

(h) Certification Regarding Responsibility Matters (Executive Order 12689). (Applies only if the contract value is expected to exceed the simplified acquisition threshold.) The offeror certifies, to the best of its knowledge and belief, that the offeror and/or any of its principals—

(1) []Are, [] are not presently debarred, suspended, proposed for debarment, or declared ineligible for the award of contracts by any Federal agency;

(2) [] Have, [] have not, within a three-year period preceding this offer, been convicted of or had a civil judgment rendered against them for: Commission of fraud or a criminal offense in connection with obtaining, attempting to obtain, or performing a Federal, state or local government contract or subcontract; violation of Federal or state antitrust statutes relating to the submission of offers; or Commission of embezzlement, theft, forgery, bribery, falsification or destruction of records, making false statements, tax evasion, violating Federal criminal tax laws, or receiving stolen property;

(3) [] Are, [] are not presently indicted for, or otherwise criminally or civilly charged by a Government entity with, commission of any of these offenses enumerated in paragraph (h) (2) of this clause; and

(4) [] Have, [] have not, within a three-year period preceding this offer, been notified of any delinquent Federal taxes in an amount that exceeds $3,500 for which the liability remains unsatisfied.

(i) Taxes are considered delinquent if both of the following criteria apply:

(A) The tax liability is finally determined. The liability is finally determined if it has been assessed. A liability is not finally determined if there is a pending administrative or judicial challenge. In the case of a judicial challenge to the liability, the liability is not finally determined until all judicial appeal rights have been exhausted.

(B) The taxpayer is delinquent in making payment. A taxpayer is delinquent if the taxpayer has failed to pay the tax liability when full payment was due and required. A taxpayer is not delinquent in cases where enforced collection action is precluded.

(ii) *Examples.* (A) The taxpayer has received a statutory notice of deficiency, under I.R.C. Sec. 6212, which entitles the taxpayer to seek Tax Court review of a proposed tax deficiency. This is not a delinquent tax because it is not a final tax liability. Should the taxpayer seek Tax Court review, this will not be a final tax liability until the taxpayer has exercised all judicial appeal rights.

(B) The IRS has filed a notice of Federal tax lien with respect to an assessed tax liability, and the taxpayer has been issued a notice under I.R.C. Sec. 6320 entitling the taxpayer to request a hearing with the IRS Office of Appeals contesting the lien filing, and to further appeal to the Tax Court if the IRS determines to sustain the lien filing. In the course of the hearing, the taxpayer is entitled to contest the underlying tax liability because the taxpayer has had no prior opportunity to contest the liability. This is not a delinquent tax because it is not a final tax liability. Should the taxpayer seek tax court review, this will not be a final tax liability until the taxpayer has exercised all judicial appeal rights.

(C) The taxpayer has entered into an installment agreement pursuant to I.R.C. Sec. 6159. The taxpayer is making timely payments and is in full compliance with the agreement terms. The taxpayer is not delinquent because the taxpayer is not currently required to make full payment.

(D) The taxpayer has filed for bankruptcy protection. The taxpayer is not delinquent because enforced collection action is stayed under 11 U.S.C. 362 (the Bankruptcy Code).

(i) Certification Regarding Knowledge of Child Labor for Listed End Products (Executive Order 13126). [The Contracting Officer must list in paragraph (i)(1) any end products being acquired under this solicitation that are included in the List of Products Requiring Contractor Certification as to Forced or Indentured Child Labor, unless excluded at 22.1503(b).]

(1) Listed end products.

Listed End Product

____

____

Listed Countries of Origin

____

____

(2) *Certification.* [If the Contracting Officer has identified end products and countries of origin in paragraph (i)(1) of this provision, then the offeror must certify to either (i)(2)(i) or (i)(2)(ii) by checking the appropriate block.]

(i) The offeror will not supply any end product listed in paragraph (i)(1) of this provision that was mined, produced, or manufactured in the corresponding country as listed for that product.

(ii) The offeror may supply an end product listed in paragraph (i)(1) of this provision that was mined, produced, or manufactured in the corresponding country as listed for that product. The offeror certifies that it has made a good faith effort to determine whether forced or indentured child labor was used to mine, produce, or manufacture any such end product furnished under this contract. On the basis of those efforts, the offeror certifies that it is not aware of any such use of child labor.

(j) *Place of manufacture.* (Does not apply unless the solicitation is predominantly for the acquisition of manufactured end products.) For statistical purposes only, the offeror shall indicate whether the place of manufacture of the end products it expects to provide in response to this solicitation is predominantly—

(1) [] In the United States (Check this box if the total anticipated price of offered end products manufactured in the United States exceeds the total anticipated price of offered

end products manufactured outside the United States); or

(2) [ ]Outside the United States.

(k) *Certificates regarding exemptions from the application of the Service Contract Labor Standards.* (Certification by the offeror as to its compliance with respect to the contract also constitutes its certification as to compliance by its subcontractor if it subcontracts out the exempt services.) [*The contracting officer is to check a box to indicate if paragraph (k)(1) or (k)(2) applies.*]

(1) Maintenance, calibration, or repair of certain equipment as described in FAR 22.1003-4(c)(1). The offeror ☐ does ☐ does not certify that—

(i) The items of equipment to be serviced under this contract are used regularly for other than Governmental purposes and are sold or traded by the offeror (or subcontractor in the case of an exempt subcontract) in substantial quantities to the general public in the course of normal business operations;

(ii) The services will be furnished at prices which are, or are based on, established catalog or market prices (see FAR 22.1003-4(c)(2)(ii)) for the maintenance, calibration, or repair of such equipment; and

(iii) The compensation (wage and fringe benefits) plan for all service employees performing work under the contract will be the same as that used for these employees and equivalent employees servicing the same equipment of commercial customers.

(2) Certain services as described in FAR 22.1003-4(d)(1). The offeror ☐ does ☐ does not certify that—

(i) The services under the contract are offered and sold regularly to non-Governmental customers, and are provided by the offeror (or subcontractor in the case of an exempt subcontract) to the general public in substantial quantities in the course of normal business operations;

(ii) The contract services will be furnished at prices that are, or are based on, established catalog or market prices (see FAR 22.1003-4(d)(2)(iii));

(iii) Each service employee who will perform the services under the contract will spend only a small portion of his or her time (a monthly average of less than 20 percent of the available hours on an annualized basis, or less than 20 percent of available hours during the contract period if the contract period is less than a month) servicing the Government contract; and

(iv) The compensation (wage and fringe benefits) plan for all service employees performing work under the contract is the same as that used for these employees and equivalent employees servicing commercial customers.

(3) If paragraph (k)(1) or (k)(2) of this clause applies—

(i) If the offeror does not certify to the conditions in paragraph (k)(1) or (k)(2) and the Contracting Officer did not attach a Service Contract Labor Standards wage determination to the solicitation, the offeror shall notify the Contracting Officer as soon as possible; and

(ii) The Contracting Officer may not make an award to the offeror if the offeror fails to execute the certification in paragraph (k)(1) or (k)(2) of this clause or to contact the Contracting Officer as required in paragraph (k)(3)(i) of this clause.

(l) *Taxpayer Identification Number (TIN) (26 U.S.C. 6109, 31 U.S.C. 7701).* (Not applicable if the offeror is required to provide this information to SAM to be eligible for award.)

(1) All offerors must submit the information required in paragraphs (l)(3) through (l)(5) of this provision to comply with debt collection requirements of 31 U.S.C. 7701(c) and 3325(d), reporting requirements of 26 U.S.C. 6041, 6041A, and 6050M, and implementing regulations issued by the Internal Revenue Service (IRS).

(2) The TIN may be used by the Government to collect and report on any delinquent amounts arising out of the offeror's relationship with the Government (31 U.S.C. 7701(c)(3)). If the resulting contract is subject to the payment reporting requirements described in FAR 4.904, the TIN provided

hereunder may be matched with IRS records to verify the accuracy of the offeror's TIN.

(3) *Taxpayer Identification Number (TIN).*

TIN: ________.

TIN has been applied for. ________

TIN is not required because: ________

Offeror is a nonresident alien, foreign corporation, or foreign partnership that does not have income effectively connected with the conduct of a trade or business in the United States and does not have an office or place of business or a fiscal paying agent in the United States;

Offeror is an agency or instrumentality of a foreign government;

Offeror is an agency or instrumentality of the Federal Government.

(4) *Type of organization.*

Sole proprietorship;

Partnership;

Corporate entity (not tax-exempt);

Corporate entity (tax-exempt);

Government entity (Federal, State, or local);

Foreign government;

International organization per 26 CFR 1.6049-4;

Other ______.

(5) *Common parent.*

Offeror is not owned or controlled by a common parent;

Name and TIN of common parent:

Name ________.

TIN ________.

(m) *Restricted business operations in Sudan.* By submission of its offer, the offeror certifies that the offeror does not conduct any restricted business operations in Sudan.

(n) *Prohibition on Contracting with Inverted Domestic Corporations.* (1) Government agencies are not permitted to use appropriated (or otherwise made available) funds for contracts with either an inverted domestic corporation, or a subsidiary of an inverted domestic corporation, unless the exception at 9.108-2(b) applies or the requirement is waived in accordance with the procedures at 9.108-4.

(2) *Representation.* The Offeror represents that—

(i) It ☐ is, ☐ is not an inverted domestic corporation; and

(ii) It ☐ is, ☐ is not a subsidiary of an inverted domestic corporation.

(2) *Representation.* By submission of its offer, the offeror represents that it is not an inverted domestic corporation and is not a subsidiary of one.

(o) *Prohibition on contracting with entities engaging in certain activities or transactions relating to Iran.* (1) The offeror shall email questions concerning sensitive technology to the Department of State at *CISADA106@state.gov.*

(2) *Representation and certifications.* Unless a waiver is granted or an exception applies as provided in paragraph (o)(3) of this provision, by submission of its offer, the offeror—

(i) Represents, to the best of its knowledge and belief, that the offeror does not export any sensitive technology to the government of Iran or any entities or individuals owned or controlled by, or acting on behalf or at the direction of, the government of Iran;

(ii) Certifies that the offeror, or any person owned or controlled by the offeror, does not engage in any activities for which sanctions may be imposed under section 5 of the Iran Sanctions Act; and

(iii) Certifies that the offeror, and any person owned or controlled by the offeror, does not knowingly engage in any transaction that exceeds $3,500 with Iran's Revolutionary Guard Corps or any of its officials, agents, or affiliates, the property and interests in property of which are blocked pursuant to the International Emergency Economic Powers Act (50 U.S.C. 1701 et seq.) (see OFAC's Specially Designated Nationals and Blocked Persons List at *https://www.treasury.gov/resource-center/sanctions/SDN-List/Pages/default.aspx*).

(3) The representation and certification requirements of paragraph (o)(2) of this provision do not apply if—

(i) This solicitation includes a trade agreements certification (*e.g.*, 52.212-3(g) or a comparable agency provision); and

(ii) The offeror has certified that all the offered products to be supplied are designated country end products.

(p) *Ownership or Control of Offeror.* (Applies in all solicitations when there is a requirement to be registered in SAM or a requirement to have a unique entity identifier in the solicitation).

(1) The Offeror represents that it [__] has or [__] does not have an immediate owner. If the Offeror has more than one immediate owner (such as a joint venture), then the Offeror shall respond to paragraph (2) and if applicable, paragraph (3) of this provision for each participant in the joint venture.

(2) If the Offeror indicates "has" in paragraph (p)(1) of this provision, enter the following information:

Immediate owner CAGE code: ____________

Immediate owner legal name: ____________

(*Do not use a "doing business as" name*)

Is the immediate owner owned or controlled by another entity: [__] Yes or [__] No.

(3) If the Offeror indicates "yes" in paragraph (p)(2) of this provision, indicating that the immediate owner is owned or controlled by another entity, then enter the following information:

Highest-level owner CAGE code: ____________

Highest-level owner legal name: ____________

(*Do not use a "doing business as" name*)

(q) *Representation by Corporations Regarding Delinquent Tax Liability or a Felony Conviction under any Federal Law.* (1) As required by sections 744 and 745 of Division E of the Consolidated and Further Continuing Appropriations Act, 2015 (Pub. L. 113–235), and similar provisions, if contained in subsequent appropriations acts, The Government will not enter into a contract with any corporation that—

(i) Has any unpaid Federal tax liability that has been assessed, for which all judicial and administrative remedies have been exhausted or have lapsed, and that is not being paid in a timely manner pursuant to an agreement with the authority responsible for collecting the tax liability, where the awarding agency is aware of the unpaid tax liability, unless an agency has considered suspension or debarment of the corporation and made a determination that suspension or debarment is not necessary to protect the interests of the Government; or

(ii) Was convicted of a felony criminal violation under any Federal law within the preceding 24 months, where the awarding agency is aware of the conviction, unless an agency has considered suspension or debarment of the corporation and made a determination that this action is not necessary to protect the interests of the Government.

(2) The Offeror represents that—

(i) It is [] is not [] a corporation that has any unpaid Federal tax liability that has been assessed, for which all judicial and administrative remedies have been exhausted or have lapsed, and that is not being paid in a timely manner pursuant to an agreement with the authority responsible for collecting the tax liability; and

(ii) It is [] is not [] a corporation that was convicted of a felony criminal violation under a Federal law within the preceding 24 months.

(r) *Predecessor of Offeror.* (Applies in all solicitations that include the provision at 52.204–16, Commercial and Government Entity Code Reporting.)

(1) The Offeror represents that it b is or b is not a successor to a predecessor that held a Federal contract or grant within the last three years.

(2) If the Offeror has indicated "is" in paragraph (r)(1) of this provision, enter the

following information for all predecessors that held a Federal contract or grant within the last three years (if more than one predecessor, list in reverse chronological order):

Predecessor CAGE code: ___ (or mark "Unknown").

Predecessor legal name: ___.

(*Do not use a doing business as name*).

(s) [Removed and Reserved]

(t) *Public Disclosure of Greenhouse Gas Emissions and Reduction Goals.* Applies in all solicitations that require offerors to register in SAM (12.301(d)(1)).

(1) This representation shall be completed if the Offeror received $7.5 million or more in contract awards in the prior Federal fiscal year. The representation is optional if the Offeror received less than $7.5 million in Federal contract awards in the prior Federal fiscal year.

(2) *Representation.* [*Offeror to check applicable block(s) in paragraph (t)(2)(i) and (ii)*]. (i) The Offeror (itself or through its immediate owner or highest-level owner) [ ] does, [ ] does not publicly disclose greenhouse gas emissions, *i.e.*, makes available on a publicly accessible Web site the results of a greenhouse gas inventory, performed in accordance with an accounting standard with publicly available and consistently applied criteria, such as the Greenhouse Gas Protocol Corporate Standard.

(ii) The Offeror (itself or through its immediate owner or highest-level owner) [ ] does, [ ] does not publicly disclose a quantitative greenhouse gas emissions reduction goal, *i.e.*, make available on a publicly accessible Web site a target to reduce absolute emissions or emissions intensity by a specific quantity or percentage.

(iii) A publicly accessible Web site includes the Offeror's own Web site or a recognized, third-party greenhouse gas emissions reporting program.

(3) If the Offeror checked "does" in paragraphs (t)(2)(i) or (t)(2)(ii) of this provision, respectively, the Offeror shall provide the publicly accessible Web site(s) where greenhouse gas emissions and/or reduction goals are reported:___.

(u)(1) In accordance with section 743 of Division E, Title VII, of the Consolidated and Further Continuing Appropriations Act, 2015 (Pub. L. 113-235) and its successor provisions in subsequent appropriations acts (and as extended in continuing resolutions), Government agencies are not permitted to use appropriated (or otherwise made available) funds for contracts with an entity that requires employees or subcontractors of such entity seeking to report waste, fraud, or abuse to sign internal confidentiality agreements or statements prohibiting or otherwise restricting such employees or subcontractors from lawfully reporting such waste, fraud, or abuse to a designated investigative or law enforcement representative of a Federal department or agency authorized to receive such information.

(2) The prohibition in paragraph (u)(1) of this provision does not contravene requirements applicable to Standard Form 312 (Classified Information Nondisclosure Agreement), Form 4414 (Sensitive Compartmented Information Nondisclosure Agreement), or any other form issued by a Federal department or agency governing the nondisclosure of classified information.

(3) *Representation.* By submission of its offer, the Offeror represents that it will not require its employees or subcontractors to sign or comply with internal confidentiality agreements or statements prohibiting or otherwise restricting such employees or subcontractors from lawfully reporting waste, fraud, or abuse related to the performance of a Government contract to a designated investigative or law enforcement representative of a Federal department or agency authorized to receive such information (e.g., agency Office of the Inspector General).

(v) *Covered Telecommunications Equipment or Services—Representation.* Section 889(a)(1)(A) of Public Law 115-232.

(1) The Offeror shall review the list of excluded parties in the System for Award Management (SAM) (https://www.sam.gov) for entities excluded from re-

ceiving federal awards for "covered telecommunications equipment or services".

(2) The Offeror represents that it []does, [] does not provide covered telecommunications equipment or services as a part of its offered products or services to the Government in the performance of any contract, subcontract, or other contractual instrument.

(End of provision)

Alternate I (OCT 2014).

As prescribed in 12.301(b)(2), add the following paragraph (c)(11) to the basic provision:

(11) (Complete if the offeror has represented itself as disadvantaged in paragraph (c)(4) of this provision.)

___ Black American.

___ Hispanic American.

___ Native American (American Indians, Eskimos, Aleuts, or Native Hawaiians).

___ Asian-Pacific American (persons with origins from Burma, Thailand, Malaysia, Indonesia, Singapore, Brunei, Japan, China, Taiwan, Laos, Cambodia (Kampuchea), Vietnam, Korea, The Philippines, Republic of Palau, Republic of the Marshall Islands, Federated States of Micronesia, the Commonwealth of the Northern Mariana Islands, Guam, Samoa, Macao, Hong Kong, Fiji, Tonga, Kiribati, Tuvalu, or Nauru).

___ Subcontinent Asian (Asian-Indian) American (persons with origins from India, Pakistan, Bangladesh, Sri Lanka, Bhutan, the Maldives Islands, or Nepal).

___ Individual/concern, other than one of the preceding.

[FAC 90-32, 60 FR 48206, 91895, effective 10/1/95, corrected 60 FR 54817, 10/26/95; FAC 90-37, 61 FR 2626, 1/26/96, effective 32696; FAC 90-39, 61 FR 31612, 6/20/96, effective 6/20/96; FAC 90-45, Final rule, 62 FR 224, 1297, effective 11/97; FAC 97-6, 63 FR 35719, 6/30/98, effective 10/1/98; FAC 97-7, 63 FR 36120, 7198, effective 11/99; FAC 97-8, 63 FR 52425, 9/30/98, effective 10/1/98; FAC 97-9, 63 FR 58587, 10/30/98, effective 10/30/98, finalized without change, FAC 97-12, 64 FR 32740, 6/17/99; FAC 97-10, 63 FR 70264, 12/18/98, Alternate III effective 1/4/99, (d)(1) and (2) effective 2/16/99; FAC 97-11, 64 FR 10530, 3/4/99, effective 5/3/99; FAC 97-12, 64 FR 32740, 6/17/99, effective 6/17/99; FAC 97-13, 64 FR 36222, 7/2/99, effective 10/1/99; FAC 97-15, 64 FR 72414, 12/27/99, effective 2/25/2000; FAC 97-19, 65 FR 46052, 7/26/2000, effective 10/1/2000; FAC 97-20, 65 FR 60542, 10/11/2000, effective 10/11/2000, finalized without change by FAC 2002-02, 66 FR 65347, 12/18/2001, effective 12/18/2001; FAC 97-21, 65 FR 80255, 12/20/2000, effective 1/19/2001; FAC 97-22, 66 FR 2116, 1/10/2001, effective 3/12/2001; FAC 97-23, 66 FR 5345, 1/18/2001, effective 2/20/2001, delay of effective date, 66 FR 14259, 3/9/2001, effective 5/11/2001, stayed FAC 97-24, 66 FR 17753, 4/3/2001, effective 4/3/2001, corrected 66 FR 18735, 4/11/2001; FAC 2001-02, 66 FR 65347, 12/18/2001, effective 2/19/2002; FAC 2001-03, 66 FR 66984, 12/27/2001, effective 12/27/2001; FAC 2001-04, 67 FR 6112, 2/8/2002, effective 2/8/2002; FAC 2001-06, 67 FR 13048, 3/20/2002, effective 4/4/2002; FAC 2001-07, 67 FR 21534, 4/30/2002, effective 5/15/2002; FAC 2001-08, 67 FR 43520, 6/27/2002, effective 7/29/2002; FAC 2001-14, 68 FR 28079, 5/22/2003, effective 6/23/2003; FAC 2001-19, 69 FR 1051, 1/7/2004, effective 1/1/2004; FAC 2001-23, 69 FR 25273, 5/5/2004, effective 5/5/2004; FAC 2001-25, 69 FR 59700, 10/5/2004, effective 10/5/2004; FAC 2001-26, 69 FR 76341, 12/20/2004, effective 1/1/2005; FAC 2001-27, 69 FR 77870, 12/28/2004, effective 1/1/2005; FAC 2005-01, 70 FR 11740, 3/9/2005, effective 3/9/2005; FAC 2005-02, 70 FR 14950, 3/23/2005, effective 3/23/2005; FAC 2005-06, 70 FR 57458, 9/30/2004, effective 9/30/2005; FAC 2005-07, 71 FR 219, 1/3/2006, effective 1/3/2006; FAC 2005-10, 71 FR 36935, 6/28/2006, effective 6/28/2006; FAC 2005-10, 71 FR 36941, 6/28/2006, effective 6/28/2006; FAC 2005-13, 71 FR 57375, 9/28/2006, effective 9/28/2006; FAC 2005-14, 71 FR 67776, 11/22/2006, effective 11/22/2006; FAC 2005-19, 72 FR 46326, 46327, 46357, 46360, 46361, 8/17/2007, effective 8/17/2007; FAC 2005-21, 72 FR 63076, 11/7/2007, effective 11/7/2007; FAC

2005-24, 73 FR 10964, 2/28/2008, effective 2/28/2008; FAC 2005-25, 73 FR 21791, 4/22/2008, effective 5/22/2008; FAC 2005-26, 73 FR 33636, 6/12/2008, effective 6/12/2008; FAC 2005-30, 74 FR 2713, 2724, 1/15/2009, effective 2/17/2009; FAC 2005-33, Interim rule, 74 FR 28426, 6/15/2009, effective 6/15/2009; FAC 2005-34, Interim rule, 74 FR 31561, 7/1/2009, effective 7/1/2009; FAC 2005-36, 74 FR 40463, 8/11/2009, effective 8/11/2009; FAC 2005-39, 75 FR 13421, 3/19/2010, effective 3/19/2010; FAC 2005-45, 75 FR 53129, 8/30/2010, effective 10/1/2010; FAC 2005-46, 75 FR 60254, 9/29/2010, effective 9/29/2010; FAC 2005-47, 75 FR 77727, 12/13/2010, effective 1/12/2011; FAC 2005-48, 75 FR 82567, 12/30/2010, effective 1/31/2011; FAC 2005-50, 76 FR 14572, 3/16/2011, effective 3/16/2011; FAC 2005-51, 76 FR 18304, 4/1/2011, effective 4/1/2011; FAC 2005-52, 76 FR 31410, 31416, 5/31/2011, effective 5/31/2011; FAC 2005-54, 76 FR 68027, 68028, 11/2/2011, effective 11/2/2011; FAC 2005-55, 77 FR 187, 1/3/2012, effective 2/2/2012; 77 FR 204, 1/3/2012, effective 1/3/2012; FAC 2005-56, 77 FR 12913, 3/2/2012, effective 4/2/2012; FAC 2005-57, 77 FR 13952, 3/7/2012, effective 3/15/2012; Correction, 77 FR 14303, 3/9/2012, effective 3/9/2012; Correction, 77 FR 17352, 3/26/2012; FAC 2005-58, 77 FR 23368, 4/18/2012, effective 5/18/2012; FAC 2005-61, 77 FR 56739, 9/13/2012, effective 9/13/2012; FAC 2005-62, 77 FR 69723, 11/20/2012, effective 11/20/2012; FAC 2005-63, 77 FR 73516, 12/10/2012, effective 12/10/2012; FAC 2005-67, 78 FR 37676, 6/21/2013, effective 7/22/2013; 78 FR 37695, 6/21/2013, effective 6/21/2013; FAC 2005-69, 78 FR 46782, 8/1/2013, effective 8/1/2013; FAC 2005-71, 78 FR 70481, 11/25/2013, effective 11/25/2013; FAC 2005-73, 79 FR 24192, 4/29/2014, effective 5/29/2014; FAC 2005-74, 79 FR 31187, 5/30/2014, effective 11/1/2014; FAC 2005-77, 79 FR 61746, 10/14/2014, effective 10/14/2014; FAC 2005-79, 79 FR 74554, 12/15/2014, effective 12/15/2014; FAC 2005-80, 80 FR 4994, 1/29/2015, effective 3/2/2015; Correction, 80 FR 6909, 2/9/2015, effective 3/2/2015; FAC 2005-83, 80 FR 38293, 7/2/2015, effective 10/1/2015, 80 FR 38306, 7/2/2015, effective 11/1/2015; 80 FR 38309, 7/2/2015, effective 7/2/2015; FAC 2005-85, 80 FR 75903, 12/4/2015, effective 2/26/2016; FAC 2005-87, 81 FR 11988, 3/7/2016, effective 4/6/2016; FAC 2005-87, 81 FR 11992, 3/7/2016, effective 3/7/2016; FAC 2005-89, 81 FR 45832, 7/14/2016, effective 7/14/2016; FAC 2005-89, 81 FR 45866, 7/14/2016, effective 7/14/2016; FAC 2005-90, 81 FR 58562, 8/25/2016, effective 10/25/2016; FAC 2005-91, 81 FR 67728, 9/30/2016, effective 9/30/2016; FAC 2005-91, 81 FR 67736, 9/30/2016, effective 10/31/2016; FAC 2005-92, 81 FR 83092, 11/18/2016, effective 12/19/2016; FAC 2005-93, 81 FR 91636, 12/16/2016, effective 12/16/2016; FAC 2005-95, 82 FR 4717, 1/13/2017, effective 1/19/2017; FAC 2005-96, 82 FR 51773, 11/8/2017, effective 11/6/2017; FAC 2005-100, 83 FR 42571, 8/22/2018, effective 8/22/2018; FAC 2005-101, 83 FR 48691, 9/26/2018, effective 10/26/2018; FAC 2020-03, 84 FR 68314, 12/13/2019, effective 12/13/2019]

52.212-4 Contract Terms and Conditions—Commercial Items.

As prescribed in 12.301(b)(3), insert the following clause:

CONTRACT TERMS AND CONDITIONS—COMMERCIAL ITEMS (OCT 2018)

(a) *Inspection/Acceptance.* The Contractor shall only tender for acceptance those items that conform to the requirements of this contract. The Government reserves the right to inspect or test any supplies or services that have been tendered for acceptance. The Government may require repair or replacement of nonconforming supplies or reperformance of nonconforming services at no increase in contract price. If repair/replacement or reperformance will not correct the defects or is not possible, the Government may seek an equitable price reduction or adequate consideration for acceptance of nonconforming supplies or services. The Government must exercise its post-acceptance rights (1) within a reasonable time after the defect was discovered or should have been discovered; and (2) before any substantial change occurs in the condition of the item, unless the change is due to the defect in the item.

(b) *Assignment.* The Contractor or its assignee may assign its rights to receive payment due as a result of performance of this contract to a bank, trust company, or other financing institution, including any Federal lending agency in accordance with the Assignment of Claims Act (31 U.S.C. 3727). However, when a third party makes payment (e.g., use of the Governmentwide commercial purchase card), the Contractor may not assign its rights to receive payment under this contract.

(c) *Changes.* Changes in the terms and conditions of this contract may be made only by written agreement of the parties.

(d) *Disputes.* This contract is subject to 41 U.S.C. chapter 71, Contract Disputes. Failure of the parties to this contract to reach agreement on any request for equitable adjustment, claim, appeal or action arising under or relating to this contract shall be a dispute to be resolved in accordance with the clause at FAR 52.233-1, Disputes, which is incorporated herein by reference. The Contractor shall proceed diligently with performance of this contract, pending final resolution of any dispute arising under the contract.

(e) *Definitions.* The clause at FAR 52.202-1, Definitions, is incorporated herein by reference.

(f) *Excusable delays.* The Contractor shall be liable for default unless nonperformance is caused by an occurrence beyond the reasonable control of the Contractor and without its fault or negligence such as, acts of God or the public enemy, acts of the Government in either its sovereign or contractual capacity, fires, floods, epidemics, quarantine restrictions, strikes, unusually severe weather, and delays of common carriers. The Contractor shall notify the Contracting Officer in writing as soon as it is reasonably possible after the commencement of any excusable delay, setting forth the full particulars in connection therewith, shall remedy such occurrence with all reasonable dispatch, and shall promptly give written notice to the Contracting Officer of the cessation of such occurrence.

(g) *Invoice.*

(1) The Contractor shall submit an original invoice and three copies (or electronic invoice, if authorized) to the address designated in the contract to receive invoices. An invoice must include—

(i) Name and address of the Contractor;

(ii) Invoice date and number;

(iii) Contract number, line item number and, if applicable, the order number;

(iv) Description, quantity, unit of measure, unit price and extended price of the items delivered;

(v) Shipping number and date of shipment, including the bill of lading number and weight of shipment if shipped on Government bill of lading;

(vi) Terms of any discount for prompt payment offered;

(vii) Name and address of official to whom payment is to be sent;

(viii) Name, title, and phone number of person to notify in event of defective invoice; and

(ix) Taxpayer Identification Number (TIN). The Contractor shall include its TIN on the invoice only if required elsewhere in this contract.

(x) Electronic funds transfer (EFT) banking information.

(A) The Contractor shall include EFT banking information on the invoice only if required elsewhere in this contract.

(B) If EFT banking information is not required to be on the invoice, in order for the invoice to be a proper invoice, the Contractor shall have submitted correct EFT banking information in accordance with the applicable solicitation provision, contract clause (e.g., 52.232-33, Payment by Electronic Funds Transfer—System for Award Management, or 52.232-34, Payment by Electronic Funds Transfer—Other Than System for Award Management), or applicable agency procedures.

(C) EFT banking information is not required if the Government waived the requirement to pay by EFT.

(2) Invoices will be handled in accordance with the Prompt Payment Act (31 U.S.C. 3903) and Office of Management and Budget (OMB) prompt payment regulations at 5 CFR part 1315.

(h) *Patent indemnity.* The Contractor shall indemnify the Government and its officers, employees and agents against liability, including costs, for actual or alleged direct or contributory infringement of, or inducement to infringe, any United States or foreign patent, trademark or copyright, arising out of the performance of this contract, provided the Contractor is reasonably notified of such claims and proceedings.

(i) *Payment.*—(1) *Items accepted.* Payment shall be made for items accepted by the Government that have been delivered to the delivery destinations set forth in this contract.

(2) *Prompt payment.* The Government will make payment in accordance with the Prompt Payment Act (31 U.S.C. 3903) and prompt payment regulations at 5 CFR part 1315.

(3) *Electronic Funds Transfer (EFT).* If the Government makes payment by EFT, see 52.212-5(b) for the appropriate EFT clause.

(4) *Discount.* In connection with any discount offered for early payment, time shall be computed from the date of the invoice. For the purpose of computing the discount earned, payment shall be considered to have been made on the date which appears on the payment check or the specified payment date if an electronic funds transfer payment is made.

(5) *Overpayments.* If the Contractor becomes aware of a duplicate contract financing or invoice payment or that the Government has otherwise overpaid on a contract financing or invoice payment, the Contractor shall—

(i) Remit the overpayment amount to the payment office cited in the contract along with a description of the overpayment including the—

(A) Circumstances of the overpayment (e.g., duplicate payment, erroneous payment, liquidation errors, date(s) of overpayment);

(B) Affected contract number and delivery order number, if applicable;

(C) Affected line item or subline item, if applicable; and

(D) Contractor point of contact.

(ii) Provide a copy of the remittance and supporting documentation to the Contracting Officer.

(6) *Interest.* (i) All amounts that become payable by the Contractor to the Government under this contract shall bear simple interest from the date due until paid unless paid within 30 days of becoming due. The interest rate shall be the interest rate established by the Secretary of the Treasury as provided in 41 U.S.C. 7109, which is applicable to the period in which the amount becomes due, as provided in (i)(6)(v) of this clause, and then at the rate applicable for each six-month period as fixed by the Secretary until the amount is paid.

(ii) The Government may issue a demand for payment to the Contractor upon finding a debt is due under the contract.

(iii) Final decisions. The Contracting Officer will issue a final decision as required by 33.211 if—

(A) The Contracting Officer and the Contractor are unable to reach agreement on the existence or amount of a debt within 30 days;

(B) The Contractor fails to liquidate a debt previously demanded by the Contracting Officer within the timeline specified in the demand for payment unless the amounts were not repaid because the Contractor has requested an installment payment agreement; or

(C) The Contractor requests a deferment of collection on a debt previously demanded by the Contracting Officer (see 32.607-2).

(iv) If a demand for payment was previously issued for the debt, the demand for payment included in the final decision shall identify the same due date as the original demand for payment.

(v) Amounts shall be due at the earliest of the following dates:

(A) The date fixed under this contract.

(B) The date of the first written demand for payment, including any demand for payment resulting from a default termination.

(vi) The interest charge shall be computed for the actual number of calendar days involved beginning on the due date and ending on—

(A) The date on which the designated office receives payment from the Contractor;

(B) The date of issuance of a Government check to the Contractor from which an amount otherwise payable has been withheld as a credit against the contract debt; or

(C) The date on which an amount withheld and applied to the contract debt would otherwise have become payable to the Contractor.

(vii) The interest charge made under this clause may be reduced under the procedures prescribed in 32.608-2 of the Federal Acquisition Regulation in effect on the date of this contract.

(j) *Risk of loss.* Unless the contract specifically provides otherwise, risk of loss or damage to the supplies provided under this contract shall remain with the Contractor until, and shall pass to the Government upon:

(1) Delivery of the supplies to a carrier, if transportation is f.o.b. origin; or

(2) Delivery of the supplies to the Government at the destination specified in the contract, if transportation is f.o.b. destination.

(k) *Taxes.* The contract price includes all applicable Federal, State, and local taxes and duties.

(l) *Termination for the Government's convenience.* The Government reserves the right to terminate this contract, or any part hereof, for its sole convenience. In the event of such termination, the Contractor shall immediately stop all work hereunder and shall immediately cause any and all of its suppliers and subcontractors to cease work. Subject to the terms of this contract, the Contractor shall be paid a percentage of the contract price reflecting the percentage of the work performed prior to the notice of termination, plus reasonable charges the Contractor can demonstrate to the satisfaction of the Government using its standard record keeping system, have resulted from the termination. The Contractor shall not be required to comply with the cost accounting standards or contract cost principles for this purpose. This paragraph does not give the Government any right to audit the Contractor's records. The Contractor shall not be paid for any work performed or costs incurred which reasonably could have been avoided.

(m) *Termination for cause.* The Government may terminate this contract, or any part hereof, for cause in the event of any default by the Contractor, or if the Contractor fails to comply with any contract terms and conditions, or fails to provide the Government, upon request, with adequate assurances of future performance. In the event of termination for cause, the Government shall not be liable to the Contractor for any amount for supplies or services not accepted, and the Contractor shall be liable to the Government for any and all rights and remedies provided by law. If it is determined that the Government improperly terminated this contract for default, such termination shall be deemed a termination for convenience.

(n) *Title.* Unless specified elsewhere in this contract, title to items furnished under this contract shall pass to the Government upon acceptance, regardless of when or where the Government takes physical possession.

(o) *Warranty.* The Contractor warrants and implies that the items delivered hereunder are merchantable and fit for use for the particular purpose described in this contract.

(p) *Limitation of liability.* Except as otherwise provided by an express warranty, the Contractor will not be liable to the Government for consequential damages resulting from any defect or deficiencies in accepted items.

(q) *Other compliances.* The Contractor shall comply with all applicable Federal,

State and local laws, executive orders, rules and regulations applicable to its performance under this contract.

(r) *Compliance with laws unique to Government contracts.* The Contractor agrees to comply with 31 U.S.C. 1352 relating to limitations on the use of appropriated funds to influence certain Federal contracts; 18 U.S.C. 431 relating to officials not to benefit; 40 U.S.C. chapter 37, Contract Work Hours and Safety Standards; 41 U.S.C. chapter 87, Kickbacks; 41 U.S.C. 4712 and 10 U.S.C. 2409 relating to whistleblower protections; 49 U.S.C. 40118, Fly American; and 41 U.S.C. chapter 21 relating to procurement integrity.

(s) *Order of precedence.* Any inconsistencies in this solicitation or contract shall be resolved by giving precedence in the following order:

(1) the schedule of supplies/services;

(2) the Assignments, Disputes, Payments, Invoice, Other Compliances, Compliance with Laws Unique to Government Contracts, and Unauthorized Obligations paragraphs of this clause;

(3) the clause at 52.212-5;

(4) addenda to this solicitation or contract, including any license agreements for computer software;

(5) solicitation provisions if this is a solicitation;

(6) other paragraphs of this clause;

(7) the Standard Form 1449;

(8) other documents, exhibits, and attachments; and (9) the specification.

(t) [Removed and Reserved]

(u) *Unauthorized Obligations.* (1) Except as stated in paragraph (u)(2) of this clause, when any supply or service acquired under this contract is subject to any End User License Agreement (EULA), Terms of Service (TOS), or similar legal instrument or agreement, that includes any clause requiring the Government to indemnify the Contractor or any person or entity for damages, costs, fees, or any other loss or liability that would create an Anti-Deficiency Act violation (31 U.S.C. 1341), the following shall govern:

(i) Any such clause is unenforceable against the Government.

(ii) Neither the Government nor any Government authorized end user shall be deemed to have agreed to such clause by virtue of it appearing in the EULA, TOS, or similar legal instrument or agreement. If the EULA, TOS, or similar legal instrument or agreement is invoked through an "I agree" click box or other comparable mechanism (e.g., "click-wrap" or "browse-wrap" agreements), execution does not bind the Government or any Government authorized end user to such clause.

(iii) Any such clause is deemed to be stricken from the EULA, TOS, or similar legal instrument or agreement.

(2) Paragraph (u)(1) of this clause does not apply to indemnification by the Government that is expressly authorized by statute and specifically authorized under applicable agency regulations and procedures.

(v) *Incorporation by reference.* The Contractor's representations and certifications, including those completed electronically via the System for Award Management (SAM), are incorporated by reference into the contract.

(End of clause)

Alternate I (JAN 2017). When a time-and-materials or labor-hour contract is contemplated, substitute the following paragraphs (a), (e), (i), (l), and (m) for those in the basic clause.

(a) *Inspection/Acceptance.* (1) The Government has the right to inspect and test all materials furnished and services performed under this contract, to the extent practicable at all places and times, including the period of performance, and in any event before acceptance. The Government may also inspect the plant or plants of the Contractor or any subcontractor engaged in contract performance. The Government will perform inspections and tests in a manner that will not unduly delay the work.

(2) If the Government performs inspection or tests on the premises of the Contractor or a subcontractor, the Contractor shall furnish and shall require subcontractors to furnish

all reasonable facilities and assistance for the safe and convenient performance of these duties.

(3) Unless otherwise specified in the contract, the Government will accept or reject services and materials at the place of delivery as promptly as practicable after delivery, and they will be presumed accepted 60 days after the date of delivery, unless accepted earlier.

(4) At any time during contract performance, but not later than 6 months (or such other time as may be specified in the contract) after acceptance of the services or materials last delivered under this contract, the Government may require the Contractor to replace or correct services or materials that at time of delivery failed to meet contract requirements. Except as otherwise specified in paragraph (a)(6) of this clause, the cost of replacement or correction shall be determined under paragraph (i) of this clause, but the "hourly rate" for labor hours incurred in the replacement or correction shall be reduced to exclude that portion of the rate attributable to profit. Unless otherwise specified below, the portion of the "hourly rate" attributable to profit shall be 10 percent. The Contractor shall not tender for acceptance materials and services required to be replaced or corrected without disclosing the former requirement for replacement or correction, and, when required, shall disclose the corrective action taken. [Insert portion of labor rate attributable to profit.]

(5)(i) If the Contractor fails to proceed with reasonable promptness to perform required replacement or correction, and if the replacement or correction can be performed within the ceiling price (or the ceiling price as increased by the Government), the Government may—

(A) By contract or otherwise, perform the replacement or correction, charge to the Contractor any increased cost, or deduct such increased cost from any amounts paid or due under this contract; or

(B) Terminate this contract for cause.

(ii) Failure to agree to the amount of increased cost to be charged to the Contractor shall be a dispute under the Disputes clause of the contract.

(6) Notwithstanding paragraphs (a)(4) and (5) above, the Government may at any time require the Contractor to remedy by correction or replacement, without cost to the Government, any failure by the Contractor to comply with the requirements of this contract, if the failure is due to—

(i) Fraud, lack of good faith, or willful misconduct on the part of the Contractor's managerial personnel; or

(ii) The conduct of one or more of the Contractor's employees selected or retained by the Contractor after any of the Contractor's managerial personnel has reasonable grounds to believe that the employee is habitually careless or unqualified.

(7) This clause applies in the same manner and to the same extent to corrected or replacement materials or services as to materials and services originally delivered under this contract.

(8) The Contractor has no obligation or liability under this contract to correct or replace materials and services that at time of delivery do not meet contract requirements, except as provided in this clause or as may be otherwise specified in the contract.

(9) Unless otherwise specified in the contract, the Contractor's obligation to correct or replace Government-furnished property shall be governed by the clause pertaining to Government property.

(e) *Definitions.* (1) The clause at FAR 52.202-1, Definitions, is incorporated herein by reference. As used in this clause—

(i) *Direct materials* means those materials that enter directly into the end product, or that are used or consumed directly in connection with the furnishing of the end product or service.

(ii) *Hourly rate* means the rate(s) prescribed in the contract for payment for labor that meets the labor category qualifications of a labor category specified in the contract that are—

(A) Performed by the contractor;

(B) Performed by the subcontractors; or

(C) Transferred between divisions, subsidiaries, or affiliates of the contractor under a common control.

(iii) *Materials* means—

(A) Direct materials, including supplies transferred between divisions, subsidiaries, or affiliates of the contractor under a common control;

(B) Subcontracts for supplies and incidental services for which there is not a labor category specified in the contract;

(C) Other direct costs (e.g., incidental services for which there is not a labor category specified in the contract, travel, computer usage charges, etc.);

(D) The following subcontracts for services which are specifically excluded from the hourly rate: [Insert any subcontracts for services to be excluded from the hourly rates prescribed in the schedule.]; and

(E) Indirect costs specifically provided for in this clause.

(iv) *Subcontract* means any contract, as defined in FAR Subpart 2.1, entered into with a subcontractor to furnish supplies or services for performance of the prime contract or a subcontract including transfers between divisions, subsidiaries, or affiliates of a contractor or subcontractor. It includes, but is not limited to, purchase orders, and changes and modifications to purchase orders.

(i) *Payments.* (1) *Work performed.* The Government will pay the Contractor as follows upon the submission of commercial invoices approved by the Contracting Officer:

(i) Hourly rate.

(A) The amounts shall be computed by multiplying the appropriate hourly rates prescribed in the contract by the number of direct labor hours performed. Fractional parts of an hour shall be payable on a prorated basis.

(B) The rates shall be paid for all labor performed on the contract that meets the labor qualifications specified in the contract. Labor hours incurred to perform tasks for which labor qualifications were specified in the contract will not be paid to the extent the work is performed by individuals that do not meet the qualifications specified in the contract, unless specifically authorized by the Contracting Officer.

(C) Invoices may be submitted once each month (or at more frequent intervals, if approved by the Contracting Officer) to the Contracting Officer or the authorized representative.

(D) When requested by the Contracting Officer or the authorized representative, the Contractor shall substantiate invoices (including any subcontractor hours reimbursed at the hourly rate in the schedule) by evidence of actual payment, individual daily job timecards, records that verify the employees meet the qualifications for the labor categories specified in the contract, or other substantiation specified in the contract.

(E) Unless the Schedule prescribes otherwise, the hourly rates in the Schedule shall not be varied by virtue of the Contractor having performed work on an overtime basis.

(1) If no overtime rates are provided in the Schedule and the Contracting Officer approves overtime work in advance, overtime rates shall be negotiated.

(2) Failure to agree upon these overtime rates shall be treated as a dispute under the Disputes clause of this contract.

(3) If the Schedule provides rates for overtime, the premium portion of those rates will be reimbursable only to the extent the overtime is approved by the Contracting Officer.

(ii) Materials.

(A) If the Contractor furnishes materials that meet the definition of a commercial item at 2.101, the price to be paid for such materials shall not exceed the Contractor's established catalog or market price, adjusted to reflect the—

(1) Quantities being acquired; and

(2) Any modifications necessary because of contract requirements.

(B) Except as provided for in paragraph (i)(1)(ii)(A) and (D)(2) of this clause, the Government will reimburse the Contractor the actual cost of materials (less any rebates, refunds, or discounts received by the contractor that are identifiable to the contract) provided the Contractor—

(1) Has made payments for materials in accordance with the terms and conditions of the agreement or invoice; or

(2) Makes these payments within 30 days of the submission of the Contractor's payment request to the Government and such payment is in accordance with the terms and conditions of the agreement or invoice.

(C) To the extent able, the Contractor shall—

(1) Obtain materials at the most advantageous prices available with due regard to securing prompt delivery of satisfactory materials; and

(2) Give credit to the Government for cash and trade discounts, rebates, scrap, commissions, and other amounts that are identifiable to the contract.

(D) *Other Costs.* Unless listed below, other direct and indirect costs will not be reimbursed.

(1) *Other Direct Costs.* The Government will reimburse the Contractor on the basis of actual cost for the following, provided such costs comply with the requirements in paragraph (i) (1) (ii) (B) of this clause: [*Insert each element of other direct costs (e.g., travel, computer usage charges, etc. Insert "None" if no reimbursement for other direct costs will be provided. If this is an indefinite delivery contract, the Contracting Officer may insert "Each order must list separately the elements of other direct charge(s) for that order or, if no reimbursement for other direct costs will be provided, insert 'None".'*]

(2) *Indirect Costs (Material Handling, Subcontract Administration, etc.).* The Government will reimburse the Contractor for indirect costs on a pro-rata basis over the period of contract performance at the following fixed price: [*Insert a fixed amount for the indirect costs and payment schedule. Insert "$0" if no fixed price reimbursement for indirect costs will be provided. (If this is an indefinite delivery contract, the Contracting Officer may insert "Each order must list separately the fixed amount for the indirect costs and payment schedule or, if no reimbursement for indirect costs, insert 'None.')"*]

(2) *Total cost.* It is estimated that the total cost to the Government for the performance of this contract shall not exceed the ceiling price set forth in the Schedule and the Contractor agrees to use its best efforts to perform the work specified in the Schedule and all obligations under this contract within such ceiling price. If at any time the Contractor has reason to believe that the hourly rate payments and material costs that will accrue in performing this contract in the next succeeding 30 days, if added to all other payments and costs previously accrued, will exceed 85 percent of the ceiling price in the Schedule, the Contractor shall notify the Contracting Officer giving a revised estimate of the total price to the Government for performing this contract with supporting reasons and documentation. If at any time during the performance of this contract, the Contractor has reason to believe that the total price to the Government for performing this contract will be substantially greater or less than the then stated ceiling price, the Contractor shall so notify the Contracting Officer, giving a revised estimate of the total price for performing this contract, with supporting reasons and documentation. If at any time during performance of this contract, the Government has reason to believe that the work to be required in performing this contract will be substantially greater or less than the stated ceiling price, the Contracting Officer will so advise the Contractor, giving the then revised estimate of the total amount of effort to be required under the contract.

(3) *Ceiling price.* The Government will not be obligated to pay the Contractor any amount in excess of the ceiling price in the Schedule, and the Contractor shall not be obligated to continue performance if to do so would exceed the ceiling price set forth in the Schedule, unless and until the Contracting Officer notifies the Contractor in writing that the ceiling price has been increased and specifies in the notice a revised ceiling that shall constitute the ceiling price for performance under this contract. When and to the extent that the ceiling price set forth in the Schedule has been increased,

any hours expended and material costs incurred by the Contractor in excess of the ceiling price before the increase shall be allowable to the same extent as if the hours expended and material costs had been incurred after the increase in the ceiling price.

(4) *Access to records.* At any time before final payment under this contract, the Contracting Officer (or authorized representative) will have access to the following (access shall be limited to the listing below unless otherwise agreed to by the Contractor and the Contracting Officer):

(i) Records that verify that the employees whose time has been included in any invoice meet the qualifications for the labor categories specified in the contract;

(ii) For labor hours (including any subcontractor hours reimbursed at the hourly rate in the schedule), when timecards are required as substantiation for payment—

(A) The original timecards (paper-based or electronic);

(B) The Contractor's timekeeping procedures;

(C) Contractor records that show the distribution of labor between jobs or contracts; and

(D) Employees whose time has been included in any invoice for the purpose of verifying that these employees have worked the hours shown on the invoices.

(iii) For material and subcontract costs that are reimbursed on the basis of actual cost—

(A) Any invoices or subcontract agreements substantiating material costs; and

(B) Any documents supporting payment of those invoices.

(5) *Overpayments/Underpayments.* Each payment previously made shall be subject to reduction to the extent of amounts, on preceding invoices, that are found by the Contracting Officer not to have been properly payable and shall also be subject to reduction for overpayments or to increase for underpayments. The Contractor shall promptly pay any such reduction within 30 days unless the parties agree otherwise. The Government within 30 days will pay any such increases, unless the parties agree otherwise. The Contractor's payment will be made by check. If the Contractor becomes aware of a duplicate invoice payment or that the Government has otherwise overpaid on an invoice payment, the Contractor shall—

(i) Remit the overpayment amount to the payment office cited in the contract along with a description of the overpayment including the—

(A) Circumstances of the overpayment (e.g., duplicate payment, erroneous payment, liquidation errors, date(s) of overpayment);

(B) Affected contract number and delivery order number, if applicable;

(C) Affected contract line item or subline item, if applicable; and

(D) Contractor point of contact.

(ii) Provide a copy of the remittance and supporting documentation to the Contracting Officer.

(6) (i) All amounts that become payable by the Contractor to the Government under this contract shall bear simple interest from the date due until paid unless paid within 30 days of becoming due. The interest rate shall be the interest rate established by the Secretary of the Treasury, as provided in 41 U.S.C. 7109, which is applicable to the period in which the amount becomes due, and then at the rate applicable for each six month period as established by the Secretary until the amount is paid.

(ii) The Government may issue a demand for payment to the Contractor upon finding a debt is due under the contract.

(iii) *Final Decisions.* The Contracting Officer will issue a final decision as required by 33.211 if—

(A) The Contracting Officer and the Contractor are unable to reach agreement on the existence or amount of a debt in a timely manner;

(B) The Contractor fails to liquidate a debt previously demanded by the Contracting Officer within the timeline specified in the demand for payment unless the amounts were not repaid because the Contractor has requested an installment payment agreement; or

(C) The Contractor requests a deferment of collection on a debt previously demanded by the Contracting Officer (see FAR 32.607-2).

(iv) If a demand for payment was previously issued for the debt, the demand for payment included in the final decision shall identify the same due date as the original demand for payment.

(v) Amounts shall be due at the earliest of the following dates:

(A) The date fixed under this contract.

(B) The date of the first written demand for payment, including any demand for payment resulting from a default termination.

(vi) The interest charge shall be computed for the actual number of calendar days involved beginning on the due date and ending on—

(A) The date on which the designated office receives payment from the Contractor;

(B) The date of issuance of a Government check to the Contractor from which an amount otherwise payable has been withheld as a credit against the contract debt; or

(C) The date on which an amount withheld and applied to the contract debt would otherwise have become payable to the Contractor.

(vii) The interest charge made under this clause may be reduced under the procedures prescribed in 32.608-2 of the Federal Acquisition Regulation in effect on the date of this contract.

(viii) Upon receipt and approval of the invoice designated by the Contractor as the "completion invoice" and supporting documentation, and upon compliance by the Contractor with all terms of this contract, any outstanding balances will be paid within 30 days unless the parties agree otherwise. The completion invoice, and supporting documentation, shall be submitted by the Contractor as promptly as practicable following completion of the work under this contract, but in no event later than 1 year (or such longer period as the Contracting Officer may approve in writing) from the date of completion.

(7) *Release of claims*. The Contractor, and each assignee under an assignment entered into under this contract and in effect at the time of final payment under this contract, shall execute and deliver, at the time of and as a condition precedent to final payment under this contract, a release discharging the Government, its officers, agents, and employees of and from all liabilities, obligations, and claims arising out of or under this contract, subject only to the following exceptions.

(i) Specified claims in stated amounts, or in estimated amounts if the amounts are not susceptible to exact statement by the Contractor.

(ii) Claims, together with reasonable incidental expenses, based upon the liabilities of the Contractor to third parties arising out of performing this contract, that are not known to the Contractor on the date of the execution of the release, and of which the Contractor gives notice in writing to the Contracting Officer not more than 6 years after the date of the release or the date of any notice to the Contractor that the Government is prepared to make final payment, whichever is earlier.

(iii) Claims for reimbursement of costs (other than expenses of the Contractor by reason of its indemnification of the Government against patent liability), including reasonable incidental expenses, incurred by the Contractor under the terms of this contract relating to patents.

(8) *Prompt payment*. The Government will make payment in accordance with the Prompt Payment Act (31 U.S.C. 3903) and prompt payment regulations at 5 CFR part 1315.

(9) *Electronic Funds Transfer (EFT)*. If the Government makes payment by EFT, see 52.212-5(b) for the appropriate EFT clause.

(10) *Discount*. In connection with any discount offered for early payment, time shall be computed from the date of the invoice. For the purpose of computing the discount earned, payment shall be considered to have

been made on the date that appears on the payment check or the specified payment date if an electronic funds transfer payment is made.

(l) *Termination for the Government's convenience*. The Government reserves the right to terminate this contract, or any part hereof, for its sole convenience. In the event of such termination, the Contractor shall immediately stop all work hereunder and shall immediately cause any and all of its suppliers and subcontractors to cease work. Subject to the terms of this contract, the Contractor shall be paid an amount for direct labor hours (as defined in the Schedule of the contract) determined by multiplying the number of direct labor hours expended before the effective date of termination by the hourly rate(s) in the contract, less any hourly rate payments already made to the Contractor plus reasonable charges the Contractor can demonstrate to the satisfaction of the Government using its standard record keeping system that have resulted from the termination. The Contractor shall not be required to comply with the cost accounting standards or contract cost principles for this purpose. This paragraph does not give the Government any right to audit the Contractor's records. The Contractor shall not be paid for any work performed or costs incurred that reasonably could have been avoided.

(m) *Termination for cause*. The Government may terminate this contract, or any part hereof, for cause in the event of any default by the Contractor, or if the Contractor fails to comply with any contract terms and conditions, or fails to provide the Government, upon written request, with adequate assurances of future performance. Subject to the terms of this contract, the Contractor shall be paid an amount computed under paragraph (i) Payments of this clause, but the "hourly rate" for labor hours expended in furnishing work not delivered to or accepted by the Government shall be reduced to exclude that portion of the rate attributable to profit. Unless otherwise specified in paragraph (a)(4) of this clause, the portion of the "hourly rate" attributable to profit shall be 10 percent. In the event of termination for cause, the Contractor shall be liable to the Government for any and all rights and remedies provided by law. If it is determined that the Government improperly terminated this contract for default, such termination shall be deemed a termination for convenience.

[FAC 90-32, 60 FR 48206, 9/18/95, effective 10/1/95; FAC 90-42, 61 FR 45769, 8/29/96, effective 8/29/96; FAC 90-46, 62 FR 12690, 3/17/97, effective 5/16/97; FAC 97-4, 63 FR 9048, 2/23/98, effective 4/24/98; FAC 97-11, 64 FR 10530, 3/4/99, (b)(21) through (b)(26) effective 5/3/99, (b)(2) through (b)(10) effective 3/4/99; FAC 97-22, 66 FR 2117, 1/10/2001, effective 3/12/2001; Delay of effective date, 66 FR 14259, 3/9/2001, effective 5/11/2001; FAC 2001-01, 66 FR 53478, 10/22/2001, effective 12/21/2001; FAC 2001-02, 66 FR 65347, 12/18/2001, effective 2/19/2002; FAC 2001-16, Final rule, 68 FR 56669, 10/1/2003, effective 10/1/2003; FAC 2001-16, 68 FR 56682, 10/1/2003, effective 10/31/2003; FAC 2005-06, 70 FR 57453, 9/30/2005, effective 9/30/2005; FAC 2005-15, 71 FR 74667, 12/12/2006, effective 2/12/2007; FAC 2005-27, 73 FR 53997, 9/17/2008, effective 10/17/2008; FAC 2005-32, 74 FR 14633, 3/31/2009, effective 3/31/2009; FAC 2005-42, 75 FR 34258, 6/16/2010, effective 6/16/2010; FAC 2005-55, 77 FR 187, 1/3/2012, effective 2/2/2012; FAC 2005-60, 77 FR 44059, 7/26/2012, effective 8/27/2012; FAC 2005-67, 78 FR 37676, 6/21/2013, effective 7/22/2013; 78 FR 37686, 6/21/2013, effective 6/21/2013; FAC 2005-70, 78 FR 60169, 9/30/2013, effective 9/30/2013; FAC 2005-72, 78 FR 80382, 12/31/2013, effective 12/31/2013; FAC 2005-73, 79 FR 24192, 4/29/2014, effective 5/29/2014; FAC 2005-78, 79 FR 70341, 11/25/2014, effective 12/26/2014; FAC 2005-82, 80 FR 26427, 5/7/2015, effective 5/7/2015; FAC 2005-85, 80 FR 75911, 12/4/2015, effective 12/4/2015; FAC 2005-95, 82 FR 4709, 1/13/2017, effective 1/13/2017; FAC 2005-101, 83 FR 48691, 9/26/2018, effective 10/26/2018]

52.212-5 Contract Terms and Conditions Required to Implement Statutes or Executive Orders—Commercial Items.

As prescribed in 12.301(b)(4), insert the following clause:

CONTRACT TERMS AND CONDITIONS REQUIRED TO IMPLEMENT STATUTES OR EXECUTIVE ORDERS—COMMERCIAL ITEMS (OCT 2019)

(a) The Contractor shall comply with the following Federal Acquisition Regulation (FAR) clauses, which are incorporated in this contract by reference, to implement provisions of law or Executive orders applicable to acquisitions of commercial items:

(1) 52.203-19, Prohibition on Requiring Certain Internal Confidentiality Agreements or Statements (JAN 2017) (section 743 of Division E, Title VII, of the Consolidated and Further Continuing Appropriations Act, 2015 (Pub. L. 113-235) and its successor provisions in subsequent appropriations acts (and as extended in continuing resolutions)).

(2) 52.204-23, Prohibition on Contracting for Hardware, Software, and Services Developed or Provided by Kaspersky Lab and Other Covered Entities (JUL 2018) (Section 1634 of Pub. L. 115-91).

(3) 52.204-25, Prohibition on Contracting for Certain Telecommunications and Video Surveillance Services or Equipment. (AUG 2019) (Section 889(a)(1)(A) of Pub. L. 115-232).

(4) 52.209-10, Prohibition on Contracting with Inverted Domestic Corporations (NOV 2015).

(5) 52.233-3, Protest after Award (AUG 1996) (31 U.S.C. 3553).

(6) 52.233-4, Applicable Law for Breach of Contract Claim (OCT 2004) (Pub. Laws 108-77 and 108-78 (19 U.S.C. 3805 note)).

(b) The Contractor shall comply with the FAR clauses in this paragraph (b) that the Contracting Officer has indicated as being incorporated in this contract by reference to implement provisions of law or Executive orders applicable to acquisitions of commercial items: [*Contracting Officer check as appropriate.*]

____(1) 52.203-6, Restrictions on Subcontractor Sales to the Government (SEP 2006), with Alternate I (OCT 1995) (41 U.S.C. 4704 and 10 U.S.C. 2402).

____(2) 52.203-13, Contractor Code of Business Ethics and Conduct (OCT 2015) (41 U.S.C. 3509).

____(3) 52.203-15, Whistleblower Protections under the American Recovery and Reinvestment Act of 2009 (JUN 2010) (Section 1553 of Pub. L. 111-5). (Applies to contracts funded by the American Recovery and Reinvestment Act of 2009).

____(4) 52.204-10, Reporting Executive Compensation and First-Tier Subcontract Awards (OCT 2018) (Pub. L. 109-282) (31 U.S.C. 6101 note).

(5) [Removed and Reserved].

____(6) 52.204-14, Service Contract Reporting Requirements (OCT 2016) (Pub. L. 111-117, section 743 of Div. C).

____(7) 52.204-15, Service Contract Reporting Requirements for Indefinite-Delivery Contracts (OCT 2016) (Pub. L. 111-117, section 743 of Div. C).

____(8) 52.209-6, Protecting the Government's Interest When Subcontracting with Contractors Debarred, Suspended, or Proposed for Debarment. (OCT 2015) (31 U.S.C. 6101 note).

____(9) 52.209-9, Updates of Publicly Available Information Regarding Responsibility Matters (OCT 2018) (41 U.S.C. 2313).

(10) [Removed and Reserved]

____(11)(i) 52.219-3, Notice of HUBZone Set-Aside or Sole-Source Award (NOV 2011) (15 U.S.C. 657a).

____(ii) *Alternate I* (NOV 2011) of 52.219-3.

____(12)(i) 52.219-4, Notice of Price Evaluation Preference for HUBZone Small Business Concerns (OCT 2014) (if the offeror elects to waive the preference, it shall so indicate in its offer) (15 U.S.C. 657a).

____(ii) *Alternate I* (JAN 2011) of 52.219-4,.

(13) [Reserved]

____(14) (i) 52.219-6, Notice of Total Small Business Set-Aside (NOV 2011) (15 U.S.C. 644).

____(ii) *Alternate I* (NOV 2011) of 52.219-6.

____(iii) *Alternate II* (MAR 2016) of 52.219-6.

____(15) (i) 52.219-7, Notice of Partial Small Business Set-Aside (JUN 2003) (15 U.S.C. 644).

____(ii) *Alternate I* (OCT 1995) of 52.219-7.

____(iii) *Alternate II* (MAR 2016) of 52.219-7.

____(16) 52.219-8, Utilization of Small Business Concerns (OCT 2018) (15 U.S.C. 637(d)(2) and (3)).

____(17) (i) 52.219-9, Small Business Subcontracting Plan (AUG 2018) (15 U.S.C. 637(d)(4)).

____(ii) *Alternate I* (NOV 2016) of 52.219-9.

____(iii) *Alternate II* (NOV 2016) of 52.219-9.

____(iv) *Alternate III* (NOV 2016) of 52.219-9.

____(v) *Alternate IV* (AUG 2018) of 52.219-9.

____(18) 52.219.13, Notice of Set-Aside of Orders (NOV 2011) (15 U.S.C. 644(r)).

____(19) 52.219-14, Limitations on Subcontracting (JAN 2017) (15 U.S.C. 637(a)(14)).

____(20) 52.219-16, Liquidated Damages—Subcontracting Plan (JAN 1999) (15 U.S.C. 637 (d)(4)(F)(i)).

____(21) 52.219-27, Notice of Service-Disabled Veteran-Owned Small Business Set-Aside (OCT 2019) (15 U.S.C. 657f).

____(22) 52.219-28, Post Award Small Business Program Rerepresentation (JUL 2013) (15 U.S.C. 632(a)(2)).

____(23) 52.219-29, Notice of Set-Aside for, or Sole Source Award to, Economically Disadvantaged Women-Owned Small Business Concerns (DEC 2015) (15 U.S.C. 637(m)).

____(24) 52.219-30, Notice of Set-Aside for, or Sole Source Award to, Women-Owned Small Business Concerns Eligible Under the Women-Owned Small Business Program (DEC 2015) (15 U.S.C. 637(m)).

____(25) 52.222-3, Convict Labor (JUN 2003) (E.O. 11755).

____(26) 52.222-19, Child Labor—Cooperation with Authorities and Remedies (OCT 2019) (E.O. 13126).

____(27) 52.222-21, Prohibition of Segregated Facilities (APR 2015).

____(28) (i) 52.222-26, Equal Opportunity (SEPT 2016) (E.O. 11246).

____(ii) Alternate I (FEB 1999) of 52.222-26.

____(29) (i) 52.222-35, Equal Opportunity for Veterans (OCT 2015) (38 U.S.C. 4212).

____(ii) Alternate I (JUL 2014) of 52.222-35.

____(30) (i) 52.222-36, Equal Opportunity for Workers with Disabilities (JUL 2014) (29 U.S.C. 793).

____(ii) Alternate I (July 2014) of 52.222-36.

____(31) 52.222-37, Employment Reports on Veterans (FEB 2016) (38 U.S.C. 4212).

____(32) 52.222-40, Notification of Employee Rights Under the National Labor Relations Act (DEC 2010) (E.O. 13496).

____(33) (i) 52.222-50, Combating Trafficking in Persons (JAN 2019) (22 U.S.C. chapter 78 and E.O. 13627).

____(ii) *Alternate I* (MAR 2015) of 52.222-50 (22 U.S.C. chapter 78 and E.O. 13627).

____(34) 52.222-54, Employment Eligibility Verification (OCT 2015). (E. O. 12989). (Not applicable to the acquisition of commercially available off-the-shelf items or certain other types of commercial items as prescribed in 22.1803.)

____(35) (i) 52.223-9, Estimate of Percentage of Recovered Material Content for EPA—Designated Items (MAY 2008) (42 U.S.C. 6962(c)(3)(A)(ii)). (Not applicable to the acquisition of commercially available off-the-shelf items.)

____(ii) *Alternate I* (MAY 2008) of 52.223-9(42 U.S.C. 6962(i)(2)(C)). (Not applicable to the acquisition of commercially available off-the-shelf items.)

____(36) 52.223-11, Ozone-Depleting Substances and High Global Warming Potential Hydrofluorocarbons (JUN 2016) (E.O. 13693).

____(37) 52.223-12, Maintenance, Service, Repair, or Disposal of Refrigeration Equipment and Air Conditioners (JUN 2016) (E.O. 13693).

____(38) (i) 52.223-13, Acquisition of EPEAT®-Registered Imaging Equipment (JUN 2014) (E.O.s 13423 and 13514).

____(ii) *Alternate I* (OCT 2015) of 52.223-13.

____(39) (i) 52.223-14, Acquisition of EPEAT®-Registered Televisions (JUN 2014) (E.O.s 13423 and 13514).

(ii) *Alternate I* (JUN 2014) of 52.223-14.

____(40) 52.223-15, Energy Efficiency in Energy-Consuming Products (DEC 2007) (42 U.S.C. 8259b).

____(41) (i) 52.223-16, Acquisition of EPEAT®-Registered Personal Computer Products (OCT 2015) (E.O.s 13423 and 13514).

____(ii) *Alternate I* (JUN 2014) of 52.223-16.

____(42) 52.223-18, Encouraging Contractor Policies to Ban Text Messaging while Driving (AUG 2011) (E.O. 13513).

____(43) 52.223-20, Aerosols (JUN 2016) (E.O. 13693).

____(44) 52.223-21, Foams (JUN 2016) (E.O. 13693).

____(45) (i) 52.224-3, Privacy Training (JAN 2017) (5 U.S.C. 552a).

____(ii) Alternate I (JAN 2017) of 52.224-3.

____(46) 52.225-1, Buy American—Supplies (MAY 2014) (41 U.S.C. chapter 83).

____(47) (i) 52.225-3, Buy American—Free Trade Agreements—Israeli Trade Act (MAY 2014) (41 U.S.C. chapter 83, 19 U.S.C. 3301 note, 19 U.S.C. 2112 note, 19 U.S.C. 3805 note, 19 U.S.C. 4001 note, Pub. L. 103-182, 108-77, 108-78, 108-286, 108-302, 109-53, 109-169, 109-283, 110-138, 112-41, 112-42, and 112-43.

____(ii) *Alternate I* (MAY 2014) of 52.225-3.

____(iii) *Alternate II* (MAR 2016) of 52.225-3.

____(iv) *Alternate III* (MAR 2016) of 52.225-3.

____(48) 52.225-5, Trade Agreements (OCT 2019) (19 U.S.C. 2501, *et seq.*, 19 U.S.C. 3301 note).

____(49) 52.225-13, Restrictions on Certain Foreign Purchases (JUN 2008) (E.O.'s, proclamations, and statutes administered by the Office of Foreign Assets Control of the Department of the Treasury).

____(50) 52.225-26, Contractors Performing Private Security Functions Outside the United States (OCT 2016) (Section 862, as amended, of the National Defense Authorization Act for Fiscal Year 2008; 10 U.S.C. 2302 Note).

____(51) 52.226-4, Notice of Disaster or Emergency Area Set-Aside (NOV 2007) (42 U.S.C. 5150).

____(52) 52.226-5, Restrictions on Subcontracting Outside Disaster or Emergency Area (NOV 2007) (42 U.S.C. 5150).

____(53) 52.232-30, Installment Payments for Commercial Items (JAN 2017) (41 U.S.C. 4505, 10 U.S.C. 2307(f)).

____(54)52.232-30, Installment Payments for Commercial Items (OCT 1995) (41 U.S.C. 4505, 10 U.S.C. 2307(f)).

____(55) 52.232-33, Payment by Electronic Funds Transfer—System for Award Management (OCT 2018) (31 U.S.C. 3332).

____(56)52.232-34, Payment by Electronic Funds Transfer—Other than System for

Award Management (JUL 2013) (31 U.S.C. 3332).

____(57) 52.232-36, Payment by Third Party (MAY 2014) (31 U.S.C. 3332).

____(58) 52.239-1, Privacy or Security Safeguards (AUG 1996) (5 U.S.C. 552a).

____(59) 52.239-1, Privacy or Security Safeguards (AUG 1996) (5 U.S.C. 332).

____(60) (i) 52.247-64, Preference for Privately Owned U.S.-Flag Commercial Vessels (FEB 2006) (46 U.S.C. Appx. 1241(b) and 10 U.S.C. 2631).

____(ii) Alternate I (APR 2003) of 52.247-64.

____(iii) Alternate II (FEB 2006) of 52.247-64.

____(61) (i) 52.247-64, Preference for Privately Owned U.S.-Flag Commercial Vessels (FEB 2006) (46 U.S.C. Appx. 1241(b) and 10 U.S.C2 2631).

____(ii) *Alternate I* (APR 2003) of 52.247-64.

(c) The Contractor shall comply with the FAR clauses in this paragraph (c), applicable to commercial services, that the Contracting Officer has indicated as being incorporated in this contract by reference to implement provisions of law or Executive orders applicable to acquisitions of commercial items: [*Contracting Officer check as appropriate.*]

____(1) 52.222-17, Nondisplacement of Qualified Workers (MAY 2014) (E.O. 13495).

____(2) 52.222-41, Service Contract Labor Standards (AUG 2018) (41 U.S.C. chapter 67).

____(3) 52.222-42, Statement of Equivalent Rates for Federal Hires (MAY 2014) (29 U.S.C. 206 and 41 U.S.C. chapter 67).

____(4) 52.222-43, Fair Labor Standards Act and Service Contract Labor Standards-Price Adjustment (Multiple Year and Option Contracts) (AUG 2018) (29 U.S.C. 206 and 41 U.S.C. chapter 67).

____(5) 52.222-44, Fair Labor Standards Act and Service Contract Labor Standards—Price Adjustment (MAY 2014) (29 U.S.C 206 and 41 U.S.C. chapter 67).

____(6) 52.222-51, Exemption from Application of the Service Contract Labor Standards to Contracts for Maintenance, Calibration, or Repair of Certain Equipment—Requirements (MAY 2014) (41 U.S.C. chapter 67).

____(7) 52.222-53, Exemption from Application of the Service Contract Labor Standards to Contracts for Certain Services—Requirements (MAY 2014) (41 U.S.C. chapter 67).

____(8) 52.222-55, Minimum Wages Under Executive Order 13658 (DEC 2015).

____(9) 52.222-62, Paid Sick Leave Under Executive Order 13706 (JAN 2017) (E.O. 13706).

____(10) 52.226-6, Promoting Excess Food Donation to Nonprofit Organizations (MAY 2014) (42 U.S.C. 1792).

(d) *Comptroller General Examination of Record.* The Contractor shall comply with the provisions of this paragraph (d) if this contract was awarded using other than sealed bid, is in excess of the simplified acquisition threshold, and does not contain the clause at 52.215-2, Audit and Records—Negotiation.

(1) The Comptroller General of the United States, or an authorized representative of the Comptroller General, shall have access to and right to examine any of the Contractor's directly pertinent records involving transactions related to this contract.

(2) The Contractor shall make available at its offices at all reasonable times the records, materials, and other evidence for examination, audit, or reproduction, until 3 years after final payment under this contract or for any shorter period specified in FAR Subpart 4.7, Contractor Records Retention, of the other clauses of this contract. If this contract is completely or partially terminated, the records relating to the work terminated shall be made available for 3 years after any resulting final termination settlement. Records relating to appeals under the disputes clause or to litigation or the settlement of claims arising under or relating to this contract

shall be made available until such appeals, litigation, or claims are finally resolved.

(3) As used in this clause, records include books, documents, accounting procedures and practices, and other data, regardless of type and regardless of form. This does not require the Contractor to create or maintain any record that the Contractor does not maintain in the ordinary course of business or pursuant to a provision of law.

(e)(1) Notwithstanding the requirements of the clauses in paragraphs (a), (b), (c), and (d) of this clause, the Contractor is not required to flow down any FAR clause, other than those in paragraphs (e) (1) of this paragraph in a subcontract for commercial items. Unless otherwise indicated below, the extent of the flow down shall be as required by the clause—

(i) 52.203-13, Contractor Code of Business Ethics and Conduct (OCT 2015) (41 U.S.C. 3509).

(ii) 52.203-19, Prohibition on Requiring Certain Internal Confidentiality Agreements or Statements (Jan 2017) (section 743 of Division E, Title VII, of the Consolidated and Further Continuing Appropriations Act, 2015 (Pub. L. 113-235) and its successor provisions in subsequent appropriations acts (and as extended in continuing resolutions)).

(iii) 52.204-23, Prohibition on Contracting for Hardware, Software, and Services Developed or Provided by Kaspersky Lab and Other Covered Entities (Jul 2018) (Section 1634 of Pub. L. 115-91).

(iv) 52.204-25, Prohibition on Contracting for Certain Telecommunications and Video Surveillance Services or Equipment. (AUG 2019) (Section 889(a)(1)(A) of Pub. L. 115-232).

(v) 52.219-8, Utilization of Small Business Concerns (OCT 2018) (15 U.S.C. 637(d)(2) and (3)), in all subcontracts that offer further subcontracting opportunities. If the subcontract (except subcontracts to small business concerns) exceeds $700,000 ($1.5 million for construction of any public facility), the subcontractor must include 52.219-8 in lower tier subcontracts that offer subcontracting opportunities.

(vi) 52.222-17, Nondisplacement of Qualified Workers (MAY 2014) (E.O. 13495). Flow down required in accordance with paragraph (l) of FAR clause 52.222-17.

(vii) 52.222-21, Prohibition of Segregated Facilities (APR 2015).

(viii) 52.222-26, Equal Opportunity (SEP 2016) (E.O. 11246).

(ix) 52.222-35, Equal Opportunity for Veterans (OCT 2015) (38 U.S.C. 4212).

(x) 52.222-36, Equal Opportunity for Workers with Disabilities (JUL 2014) (29 U.S.C. 793).

(xi) 52.222-37, Employment Reports on Veterans (FEB 2016) (38 U.S.C. 4212).

(xii) 52.222-40, Notification of Employee Rights Under the National Labor Relations Act (DEC 2010) (E.O. 13496). Flow down required in accordance with paragraph (f) of FAR clause 52.222-40.

(xiii) 52.222-41, Service Contract Labor Standards (AUG 2018) (41 U.S.C. chapter 67).

(xiv)(A) 52.222-50, Combating Trafficking in Persons (JAN 2019) (22 U.S.C. chapter 78 and E.O. 13627).

(B) *Alternate I* (MAR 2015) of 52.222-50 (11 U.S.C. 7104(g)).

(xv) 52.222-51, Exemption from Application of the Service Contract Labor Standards to Contracts for Maintenance, Calibration, or Repair of Certain Equipment—Requirements (MAY 2014) (41 U.S.C. chapter 67).

(xvi) 52.222-53, Exemption from Application of the Service Contract Labor Standards to Contracts for Certain Services—Requirements (MAY 2014) (41 U.S.C. chapter 67).

(xvii) 52.222-54, Employment Eligibility Verification (OCT 2015) (E. O. 12989).

(xviii) 52.222-55, Minimum Wages Under Executive Order 13658 (DEC 2015).

(xix) 52.222-62 Paid Sick Leave Under Executive Order 13706 (JAN 2017) (E.O. 13706).

(xx)(A) 52.224-3, Privacy Training (JAN 2017) (5 U.S.C. 552a).

(B) Alternate I (JAN 2017) of 52.224-3.

(xxi) 52.225-26, Contractors Performing Private Security Functions Outside the United States (OCT 2016) (Section 862, as amended, of the National Defense Authorization Act for Fiscal Year 2008; 10 U.S.C. 2302 Note).

(xxii) 52.226-6, Promoting Excess Food Donation to Nonprofit Organizations (MAY 2014) (42 U.S.C. 1792). Flow down required in accordance with paragraph (e) of FAR clause 52.226-6.

(xxiii) 52.247-64, Preference for Privately Owned U.S.-Flag Commercial Vessels (FEB 2006) (46 U.S.C. Appx. 1241(b) and 10 U.S.C. 2631). Flow down required in accordance with paragraph (d) of FAR clause 52.247-64.

(2) While not required, the Contractor may include in its subcontracts for commercial items a minimal number of additional clauses necessary to satisfy its contractual obligations.

(End of clause)

Alternate I (APR 2015). As prescribed in 12.301(b)(4)(i), delete paragraph (d) from the basic clause, redesignate paragraph (e) as paragraph (d), and revise the reference to "paragraphs (a), (b), (c), or (d) of this clause" in the redesignated paragraph (d) to read "paragraphs (a), (b), and (c) of this clause."

Alternate II (AUG 2019). As prescribed in 12.301(b)(4)(ii), substitute the following paragraphs (d)(1) and (e)(1) for paragraphs (d)(1) and (e)(1) of the basic clause as follows:

(d)(1) The Comptroller General of the United States, an appropriate Inspector General appointed under section 3 or 8G of the Inspector General Act of 1978 (5 U.S.C. App.), or an authorized representative of either of the foregoing officials shall have access to and right to—

(i) Examine any of the Contractor's or any subcontractors' records that pertain to, and involve transactions relating to, this contract; and

(ii) Interview any officer or employee regarding such transactions.

(e)(1) Notwithstanding the requirements of the clauses in paragraphs (a), (b), and (c), of this clause, the Contractor is not required to flow down any FAR clause in a subcontract for commercial items, other than—

(i) *Paragraph (d) of this clause.* This paragraph flows down to all subcontracts, except the authority of the Inspector General under paragraph (d)(1)(ii) does not flow down; and

(ii) *Those clauses listed in this paragraph (e)(1).* Unless otherwise indicated below, the extent of the flow down shall be as required by the clause—

(A) 52.203-13, Contractor Code of Business Ethics and Conduct (OCT 2015) (41 U.S.C. 3509).

(B) 52.203-15, Whistleblower Protections Under the American Recovery and Reinvestment Act of 2009 (JUN 2010) (Section 1553 of Pub. L. 111-5).

(C) 52.204-23, Prohibition on Contracting for Hardware, Software, and Services Developed or Provided by Kaspersky Lab and Other Covered Entities (Jul 2018) (Section 1634 of Pub. L. 115-91).

(D) 52.204-25, Prohibition on Contracting for Certain Telecommunications and Video Surveillance Services or Equipment. (AUG 2019) (Section 889(a)(1)(A) of Pub. L. 115-232).

(E) 52.219-8, Utilization of Small Business Concerns (OCT 2018) (15 U.S.C. 637(d)(2) and (3)), in all subcontracts that offer further subcontracting opportunities. If the subcontract (except subcontracts to small business concerns) exceeds $700,000 ($1.5 million for construction of any public facility), the subcontractor must include 52.219-8 in lower tier subcontracts that offer subcontracting opportunities.

(F) 52.222-21, Prohibition of Segregated Facilities (APR 2015).

(G) 52.222-26, Equal Opportunity (SEP 2016) (E.O. 11246).

(H) 52.222-35, Equal Opportunity for Veterans (OCT 2015) (38 U.S.C. 4212).

(I) 52.222-36, Equal Opportunity for Workers with Disabilities (JUL 2014) (29 U.S.C. 793).

(J) 52.222-40, Notification of Employee Rights Under the National Labor Relations Act (DEC 2010) (E.O. 13496). Flow down required in accordance with paragraph (f) of FAR clause 52.222-40.

(K) 52.222-41, Service Contract Labor Standards (AUG 2018) (41 U.S.C. chapter 67).

(L) (*1*) 52.222-50, Combating Trafficking in Persons (JAN 2019) (22 U.S.C. chapter 78 and E.O. 13627).

(*2*) *Alternate I* (MAR 2015) of 52.222-50 (22 U.S.C. chapter 78 and E.O. 13627).

(M) 52.222-51, Exemption from Application of the Service Contract Labor Standards to Contracts for Maintenance, Calibration, or Repair of Certain Equipment—Requirements (MAY 2014) (41 U.S.C. chapter 67).

(N) 52.222-53, Exemption from Application of the Service Contract Labor Standards to Contracts for Certain Services—Requirements (MAY 2014) (41 U.S.C. chapter 67).

(O) 52.222-54, Employment Eligibility Verification (OCT 2015) (Executive Order 12989).

(P) 52.222-55, Minimum Wages Under Executive Order 13658 (DEC 2015).

(Q) 52.222-62, Paid Sick Leave Under Executive Order 13706 (JAN 2017) (E.O. 13706).

(R) (1) 52.224-3, Privacy Training (JAN 2017) (5 U.S.C. 552a).

(2) Alternate I (JAN 2017) of 52.224-3.

(S) 52.225-26, Contractors Performing Private Security Functions Outside the United States (OCT 2016) (Section 862, as amended, of the National Defense Authorization Act for Fiscal Year 2008; 10 U.S.C. 2302 Note).

(T) 52.226-6, Promoting Excess Food Donation to Nonprofit Organizations. (MAY 2014) (42 U.S.C. 1792). Flow down required in accordance with paragraph (e) of FAR clause 52.226-6.

(U) 52.247-64, Preference for Privately Owned U.S.-Flag Commercial Vessels (FEB 2006) (46 U.S.C. Appx. 1241(b) and 10 U.S.C. 2631). Flow down required in accordance with paragraph (d) of FAR clause 52.247-64.

[FAC 90-32, 60 FR 48206, 91895, effective 10195; FAC 90-36, Interim rule, 60 FR 67514, 12/29/95, effective 1/1/96; FAC 90-39, Interim rule, 61 FR 31612, 6/20/96, effective 6/20/96, finalized without change, FAC 90-45, 62 FR 224, 1/2/97, effective 1/1/97; FAC 90-41, Interim rule, 61 FR 41466, 8/8/96, effective 8/8/96, finalized without change, FAC 97-3, 62 FR 64912, 12/9/97, effective 2/9/98; FAC 97-4, 63 FR 9048, 2/23/98, effective 4/24/98; FAC 97-5, 63 FR 34058, 6/22/98, effective 6/22/98, finalized without change, FAC 97-9, 63 FR 58587, 10/30/98; FAC 97-6, 63 FR 35719, 6/30/98, effective 10/1/98, finalized without change, FAC 97-13, 7299; FAC 97-7, 63 FR 36120, 7198, effective 1199, finalized without change, FAC 97-13, 7299; FAC 97-9, 63 FR 58587, 10/30/98, effective 10/30/98; FAC 97-10, 63 FR 70264, 12/18/98, effective 1/4/99; FAC 97-11, 64 FR 10530, 3/4/99, effective 5/3/99; FAC 97-15, 64 FR 72414, 12/27/99, effective 2/25/2000; FAC 97-17, 65 FR 24316, 4/25/2000, effective 6/26/2000; FAC 97-18, 65 FR 36014, 6/6/2000, effective 8/7/2000; FAC 97-18, 65 FR 36014, 6/6/2000, effective 7/6/2000; FAC 97-19, 65 FR 46052, 7/26/2000, effective 8/25/2000; FAC 97-23, 66 FR 5345, 1/18/2001, effective 2/20/2001; FAC 97-26, 66 FR 27405, 5/16/2001, effective 5/16/2001, finalized without change, FAC 2001-04, 67 FR 6112, 2/8/2002, effective 2/20/2002; FAC 2001-01, 66 FR 53478, 10/22/2001, effective 12/21/2001; FAC 2001-07, 67 FR 21534, 4/30/2002, effective 5//15/2002; FAC 2001-13, 68 FR 13202, 3/18/2003, effective 4/17/2003; FAC 2001-14, 68 FR 28096, 5/22/2003, effective 6/23/2003; FAC 2001-16, 68 FR 56669, 10/1/2003, effective 10/1/2003; FAC 2001-16, 68 FR 56685, 10/1/2003, effective 10/31/2003; FAC 2001-16, 68 FR 56684, 10/1/2003, effective 10/31/2003; FAC 2001-19, Interim rule, 69 FR 1051, 1/7/2004, effective 1/1/2004; FAC 2001-21, 69 FR 16147, 3/26/2004, effective 3/26/2004; FAC 2001-22, 69 FR 17770, 4/5/2004, effective 4/5/2004; FAC 2001-23, 69 FR 25273, 5/5/2004, effective 5/5/2004; FAC 2001-24, 69 FR 34239, 6/18/2004, effective

6/18/2004; FAC 2001-25, 69 FR 59700, 10/5/2004, effective 10/5/2004, Final rule, 69 FR 59703, 10/5/2004, effective 10/5/2004; FAC 2001-26, 69 FR 76351, 12/20/2004, effective 12/29/02004; FAC 2001-27, 69 FR 77870, 12/28/2004, effective 1/1/2005; FAC 2005-02, 70 FR 14950, 3/23/2005, effective 3/23/2005; FAC 2005-03, 70 FR 18959, 4/11/2005, effective 4/11/2005; FAC 2005-04, 70 FR 33655, 6/8/2005, effective 6/8/2005; 70 FR 33661, 6/8/2005, effective 6/8/2005; 70 FR 33662, 6/8/2005, effective 7/8/2005; FAC 2005-05, 70 FR 43581, 7/27/2005, effective 7/2/72005; FAC 2005-06, 70 FR 57462, 9/30/2005, effective 9/30/2005; FAC 2005-07, 71 FR 208, 1/3/2006, effective 1/3/2006; FAC 2005-07, 71 FR 200, 1/3/2006, effective 2/2/2006; FAC 2005-08, 71 FR 864, 1/5/2006, effective 1/5/2006; FAC 2005-09, 71 FR 20303, 71 FR 20304, 71 FR 20305, 71 FR 20306, 4/19/2006, effective 4/19/2006; FAC 2005-10, 71 FR 36930, 6/28/2006, effective 6/28/2006; FAC 2005-10, 71 FR 36935, 6/28/2006, effective 6/28/2006; FAC 2005-12, 71 FR 44546, 8/4/2006, effective 8/4/2006; FAC 2005-13, 71 FR 57363, 71 FR 57375, 9/28/2006, effective 9/28/2006; FAC 2005-14, 71 FR 67775, 71 FR 67776, 71 FR 67778, 71 FR 67779, 11/22/2006, effective 11/22/2006; FAC 2005-16, 72 FR 13585, 13586, 13588, 3/22/2007, effective 3/22/2007; FAC 2005-18, Interim rule, 72 FR 36852, 7/5/2007, effective 6/30/2007; FAC 2005-19, 72 FR 46335, 46345, 46357, 46360, 46361, 46363, 8/17/2007, effective 8/17/2007; FAC 2005-21, 72 FR 63076, 63084, 63089, 11/7/2007, effective 11/7/2007; FAC 2005-22, 72 FR 65868, 11/23/2007, effective 12/24/2007; FAC 2005-23, 72 FR 73215, 73218, 12/26/2007, effective 12/26/2007; FAC 2005-24, 73 FR 10962, 10964, 2/28/2008, effective 2/28/2008; FAC 2005-25, 73 FR 21779, 21789, 4/22/2008, effective 4/22/2008, 5/22/2008; FAC 2005-26, 73 FR 33636, 6/12/2008, effective 6/12/2008; FAC 2005-27, 73 FR 53992, 53995, 54014, 54016, 9/17/2008, effective 9/17/2008, 10/17/2008; FAC 2005-28, 73 FR 67064, 11/12/2008, effective 12/12/2008; FAC 2005-29, 73 FR 67651, 11/14/2008, effective 1/15/2009; Amendment-1, FAC 2005-29, 74 FR 1937, 1/14/2009, effective 1/19/2009; FAC 2005-30, 74 FR 2713, 2724, 2740, 2741, 1/15/2009, effective 2/17/2009; 74 FR 2745, 1/15/2009, effective 1/15/2009; Amendment-2, FAC 2005-29, 74 FR 5621, 1/30/2009, effective 5/21/2009; FAC 2005-31, 74 FR 11821, 11838, 3/19/2009, effective 4/20/2009; 74 FR 11828, 11829, 3/19/2009, effective 3/19/2009; FAC 2005-32, 74 FR 14633, 14639, 14646, 3/31/2009, effective 3/31/2009; Correction, 74 FR 14492, 3/31/2009, effective 3/31/2009; Amendment-3, FAC 2005-29, 74 FR 17793, 4/17/2009, effective 6/30/2009; Technical amendment, 74 FR 22809, 5/14/2009, effective 5/14/2009; Amendment-4, FAC 2005-29, 74 FR 26981, 6/5/2009, effective 9/8/2009; FAC 2005-33, Interim rule, 74 FR 28426, 6/15/2009, effective 6/15/2009; FAC 2005-36, 74 FR 40460, 8/11/2009, effective 9/10/2009, 74 FR 40461, 8/11/2009, effective 8/11/2009; FAC 2005-38, 74 FR 65599, 12/10/2009, effective 12/10/2009, 74 FR 65600, 12/10/2009, effective 2/1/2010, 74 FR 65607, 12/10/2009, effective 12/10/2009, 74 FR 65614, 12/10/2009, effective 12/10/2009; FAC 2005-39, 75 FR 13421, 3/19/2010, effective 3/19/2010; FAC 2005-40, 75 FR 14059, 3/23/2010, effective 4/22/2010; FAC 2005-42, 75 FR 34258, 34282, 6/16/2010, effective 6/16/2010; 75 FR 34260, 34279, 6/16/2010, effective 7/16/2010; FAC 2005-43, 75 FR 38684, 38689, 7/2/2010, effective 7/2/2010; FAC 2005-44, 75 FR 39414, 7/8/2010, effective 7/8/2010; FAC 2005-45, 75 FR 53129, 8/30/2010, effective 10/1/2010; FAC 2005-46, 75 FR 60249, 60264, 9/29/2010, effective 9/29/2010; FAC 2005-47, 75 FR 77723, 12/13/2010, effective 12/13/2010; 75 FR 77727, 12/13/2010, effective 1/12/2011; 75 FR 77737, 77739, 12/13/2010, effective 12/13/2010; FAC 2005-50, 76 FR 14570, 76 FR 14572, 3/16/2011, effective 3/16/2011; FAC 2005-51, 76 FR 18304, 4/1/2011, effective 4/1/2011; FAC 2005-52, 76 FR 31410, 5/31/2011, effective 5/31/2011; FAC 2005-53, 76 FR 39233, 39236, 39240, 7/5/2011, effective 8/4/2011; FAC 2005-54, 76 FR 68015, 68026, 68032, 68039, 11/2/2011, effective 11/2/2011; Correction, 76 FR 76899, 12/9/2011, effective

12/9/2011; FAC 2005-55, 77 FR 197, 1/3/2012, effective 1/3/2012; 77 FR 202, 1/3/2012, effective 2/2/2012; Interim rule, 77 FR 1889, 1/12/2012, effective 2/13/2012; FAC 2005-56, 77 FR 12913, 12933, 12935, 3/2/2012, effective 3/2/2012, 4/2/2012; FAC 2005-57, 77 FR 13952, 3/7/2012, effective 3/15/2012; Correction, 77 FR 14303, 3/9/2012, effective 3/9/2012; Correction, 77 FR 17352, 3/26/2012, effective 3/26/2012; Correction, 77 FR 17353, 3/26/2012, effective 3/26/2012; FAC 2005-58, 77 FR 23370, 4/18/2012, effective 4/18/2012; FAC 2005-59, 77 FR 27547, 5/10/2012, effective 5/10/2012; 77 FR 27548, 5/10/2012, effective 5/15/2012; FAC 2005-60, 77 FR 44047, 7/26/2012, effective 8/27/2012, 77 FR 44065, 7/26/2012, effective 7/26/2012; FAC 2005-61, 77 FR 56739, 9/13/2012, effective 9/13/2012; FAC 2005-62, 77 FR 69723, 11/20/2012, effective 11/20/2012; FAC 2005-64, 77 FR 75766, 12/21/2012, effective 1/18/2013; FAC 2005-65, 78 FR 6185, 1/29/2013, effective 1/29/2013; FAC 2005-65, 78 FR 6188, 1/29/2013, effective 1/29/2013; FAC 2005-67, 78 FR 37670, 37676, 6/21/2013, effective 7/22/2013; 78 FR 37695, 6/21/2013, effective 6/21/2013; FAC 2005-69, 78 FR 46795, 8/1/2013, effective 8/1/2013; 78 FR 46792, 8/1/2013, effective 9/3/2013; FAC 2005-71, 78 FR 70480, 70481, 11/25/2013, effective 11/25/2013; FAC 2005-72, 78 FR 80369, 12/31/2013, effective 1/30/2014; FAC 2005-72, 78 FR 80379, 12/31/2013, effective 1/1/2014; Final rule, 79 FR 4630, 1/29/2014, effective 1/30/2014; Final rule, 79 FR 4630, 1/29/2014, effective 1/29/2014; FAC 2005-73, 79 FR 24192, 4/29/2014, effective 5/29/2014; FAC 2005-74, 79 FR 31193, 5/30/2014, effective 5/30/2014; FAC 2005-75, 79 FR 35859, 6/24/2014, effective 6/24/2014; FAC 2005-76, 79 FR 43575, 7/25/2014, effective 7/25/2014; FAC 2005-77, 79 FR 61746, 10/14/2014, effective 10/14/2014; FAC 2005-79, 79 FR 74544, 79 FR 74554, 12/15/2014, effective 12/15/2014; FAC 2005-80, 80 FR 4967, 1/29/2015, effective 3/2/2015; Correction, 80 FR 6908, 2/9/2015, effective 3/2/2015; FAC 2005-81,80 FR 19504, 4/10/2015, effective 4/10/2015; FAC 2005-82, 80 FR 26423, 80 FR 26427, 5/7/2015, effective 5/7/2015; FAC 2005-83, 80 FR 38293, 7/2/2015, effective 10/1/2015; FAC 2005-83, 80 FR 38306, 7/2/2015, effective 11/1/2015, 80 FR 38312, 7/2/2015, effective 7/2/2015; FAC 2005-84, 80 FR 53436, 9/3/2015, effective 10/5/2015; Final rule, 80 FR 53753, 9/8/2015, effective 10/1/2015; FAC 2005-85, 80 FR 75907, 80 FR 75908, 12/4/2015, effective 12/4/2015; FAC 2005-85, 80 FR 75908, 12/4/2015, effective 12/4/2015 and 2/26/2016; FAC 2005-86, 80 FR 81888, 12/31/2015, effective 12/31/2015; FAC 2005-86, 80 FR 81892, 12/31/2015, effective 2/1/2016; FAC 2005-86, 80 FR 81894, 12/31/2015, effective 1/1/2016; FAC 2005-87, 81 FR 11992, 3/7/2016, effective 3/7/2016; Correction, 81 FR 13998, 3/16/2016, effective 3/16/2016; FAC 2005-88, 81 FR 30429, 5/16/2016, effective 6/15/2016; FAC 2005-89, 81 FR 45833, 7/14/2016, effective 11/1/2016; FAC 2005-90, 81 FR 58562, 8/25/2016, effective 10/25/2016; FAC 2005-91, 81 FR 67731, 9/30/2016, effective 9/30/2016; FAC 2005-91, 81 FR 67732, 9/30/2016, effective 9/30/2016; FAC 2005-91, 81 FR 67735, 9/30/2016, effective 9/30/2016; FAC 2005-91, 81 FR 67736, 9/30/2016, effective 10/31/2016; FAC 2005-91, 81 FR 67774, 9/30/2016, effective 10/31/2016; FAC 2005-91, 81 FR 67776, 9/30/2016, effective 10/31/2016; Correction, 81 FR 72738, 10/21/2016, effective 10/31/2016; FAC 2005-93, 81 FR 91636, 12/16/2016, effective 12/16/2016; FAC 2005-93, 81 FR 91627, 12/16/2016, effective 1/1/2017; FAC 2005-94, 81 FR 93476, 12/20/2016, effective 1/19/2017; FAC 2005-94, 81 FR 93481, 12/20/2016, effective 1/19/2017; FAC 2005-95, 82 FR 4709, 1/13/2017, effective 1/13/2017; FAC 2005-95, 82 FR 4717, 1/13/2017, effective 1/19/2017; FAC 2005-95, 82 FR 4724, 1/13/2017, effective 1/13/2017; FAC 2005-96, 82 FR 51773, 11/8/2017, effective 11/6/2017; FAC 2005-97, 83 FR 3396, 1/24/2018, effective 1/24/2018; FAC 2005-99, 83 FR 28141, 6/15/2018, effective 7/16/2018; FAC 2005-100, 83 FR 42569, 8/22/2018, effective 8/22/2018; FAC 2005-100, 83 FR 42570, 8/22/2018, effective 8/22/2018; FAC 2005-100, 83 FR 42571, 8/22/2018, effective 8/22/2018; FAC 2005-101, 83 FR 48691, 9/26/2018, effective 10/26/2018; FAC

2005-101, 83 FR 48700, 9/26/2018, effective 10/26/2018; FAC 2019-01, 83 FR 65466, 12/20/2018, effective 1/22/2019; FAC 2019-02, 84 FR 19839, 5/6/2019, effective 5/6/2019; FAC 2019-05, 84 FR 40216, 8/13/2019, effective 8/13/2019; FAC 2019-06, 84 FR 47861, 9/10/2019, effective 9/10/2019; FAC 2019-06, 84 FR 47862, 9/10/2019, effective 10/10/2019; FAC 2019-06, 84 FR 47866, 9/10/2019, effective 10/10/2019]

52.213-1 Fast Payment Procedure.

As prescribed in 13.404, insert the following clause:

FAST PAYMENT PROCEDURE (MAY 2006)

(a) *General.* The Government will pay invoices based on the Contractor's delivery to a post office or common carrier (or, if shipped by other means, to the point of first receipt by the Government).

(b) *Responsibility for supplies.* (1) Title to the supplies passes to the Government upon delivery to—

(i) A post office or common carrier for shipment to the specific destination; or

(ii) The point of first receipt by the Government, if shipment is by means other than Postal Service or common carrier.

(2) Notwithstanding any other provision of the contract, order, or blanket purchase agreement, the Contractor shall—

(i) Assume all responsibility and risk of loss for supplies not received at destination, damaged in transit, or not conforming to purchase requirements; and

(ii) Replace, repair, or correct those supplies promptly at the Contractor's expense, if instructed to do so by the Contracting Officer within 180 days from the date title to the supplies vests in the Government.

(c) *Preparation of invoice.* (1) Upon delivery to a post office or common carrier (or, if shipped by other means, the point of first receipt by the Government), the Contractor shall—

(i) Prepare an invoice as provided in this contract, order, or blanket purchase agreement; and

(ii) Display prominently on the invoice "FAST PAY." Invoices not prominently marked "FAST PAY" via manual or electronic means may be accepted by the payment office for fast payment. If the payment office declines to make fast payment, the Contractor shall be paid in accordance with procedures applicable to invoices to which the Fast Payment clause does not apply.

(2) If the purchase price excludes the cost of transportation, the Contractor shall enter the prepaid shipping cost on the invoice as a separate item. The Contractor shall not include the cost of parcel post insurance. If transportation charges are stated separately on the invoice, the Contractor shall retain related paid freight bills or other transportation billings paid separately for a period of 3 years and shall furnish the bills to the Government upon request.

(3) If this contract, order, or blanket purchase agreement requires the preparation of a receiving report, the Contractor shall either—

(i) Submit the receiving report on the prescribed form with the invoice; or

(ii) Include the following information on the invoice:

(A) Shipment number.

(B) Mode of shipment.

(C) At line item level—

(1) National stock number and/or manufacturer's part number;

(2) Unit of measure;

(3) Ship-To Point;

(4) Mark-For Point, if in the contract; and

(5) FEDSTRIP/MILSTRIP document number, if in the contract.

(4) If this contract, order, or blanket purchase agreement does not require preparation of a receiving report on a prescribed form, the Contractor shall include on the invoice the following information at the line item level, in addition to that required in paragraph (c)(1) of this clause:

(i) Ship-To Point.

(ii) Mark-For Point.

(iii) FEDSTRIP/MILSTRIP document number, if in the contract.

(5) Where a receiving report is not required, the Contractor shall include a copy of the invoice in each shipment.

(d) *Certification of invoice*. The Contractor certifies by submitting an invoice to the Government that the supplies being billed to the Government have been shipped or delivered in accordance with shipping instructions issued by the ordering officer, in the quantities shown on the invoice, and that the supplies are in the quantity and of the quality designated by the contract, order, or blanket purchase agreement.

(e) *FAST PAY container identification*. The Contractor shall mark all outer shipping containers "FAST PAY." When outer shipping containers are not marked "FAST PAY," the payment office may make fast payment. If the payment office declines to make fast payment, the Contractor shall be paid in accordance with procedures applicable to invoices to which the Fast Payment clause does not apply.

(End of clause)

[FAC 97-3, 62 FR 64912, 12/9/97, effective 2/9/98; FAC 2005-09, Final rule, 71 FR 20308, 4/19/2006, effective 5/19/2006; Correction 71 FR 25507, 5/1/2006, effective 5/1/2006]

52.213-2 Invoices.

As prescribed in 13.302-5(b), insert the following clause:

INVOICES (APR 1984)

The Contractor's invoices must be submitted before payment can be made. The Contractor will be paid on the basis of the invoice, which must state—

(a) The starting and ending dates of the subscription delivery; and

(b) Either that orders have been placed in effect for the addressees required, or that the orders will be placed in effect upon receipt of payment.

(End of clause)

[FAC 84-12, 51 FR 2666, 1/17/86, effective 1/20/86; FAC 90-29, 60 FR 34732, 7/3/95, effective 7/3/95; FAC 90-40, 61 FR 39186, 7/26/96, effective 8/26/96; FAC 97-3, 62 FR 64912, 12/9/97, effective 2/9/98]

52.213-3 Notice to Supplier.

As prescribed in 13.302-5(c), insert the following clause:

NOTICE TO SUPPLIER (APR 1984)

This is a firm order ONLY if your price does not exceed the maximum line item or total price in the Schedule. Submit invoices to the Contracting Officer. If you cannot perform in exact accordance with this order, WITHHOLD PERFORMANCE, and notify the Contracting Officer immediately, giving your quotation.

(End of clause)

[FAC 90-29, 60 FR 34732, 7/3/95, effective 7/3/95; FAC 90-40, 61 FR 39186, 7/26/96, effective 8/26/96; FAC 97-3, 62 FR 64912, 12/9/97, effective 2/9/98]

52.213-4 Terms and Conditions—Simplified Acquisitions (Other than Commercial Items).

As prescribed in 13.302-5(d), insert the following clause:

TERMS AND CONDITIONS-SIMPLIFIED ACQUISITIONS (OTHER THAN COMMERCIAL ITEMS) (OCT 2019)

(a) The Contractor shall comply with the following Federal Acquisition Regulation (FAR) clauses that are incorporated by reference:

(1) The clauses listed below implement provisions of law or Executive order:

(i) 52.203-19, Prohibition on Requiring Certain Internal Confidentiality Agreements or Statements (JAN 2017) (section 743 of Division E, Title VII, of the Consolidated and Further Continuing Appropriations Act, 2015 (Pub. L. 113-235) and its successor provisions in subsequent appropriations acts (and as extended in continuing resolutions)).

(ii) 52.204-23, Prohibition on Contracting for Hardware, Software, and Services Developed or Provided by Kaspersky Lab and Other Covered Entities (JUL 2018) (Section 1634 of Pub. L. 115-91).

(iii) 52.204-25, Prohibition on Contracting for Certain Telecommunications and Video Surveillance Services or Equipment. (AUG 2019) (Section 889(a)(1)(A) of Pub. L. 115-232).

(iv) 52.222-3, Convict Labor (JUN 2003) (E.O. 11755).

(v) 52.222-21, Prohibition of Segregated Facilities (JAN 2016).

(vi) 52.222-26, Equal Opportunity (SEP 2016) (E.O. 11246).

(vii) 52.225-13, Restrictions on Certain Foreign Purchases (JUN 2008) (E.O.s, proclamations, and statutes administered by the Office of Foreign Assets Control of the Department of Treasury).

(viii) 52.233-3, Protest After Award (AUG 1996) (31 U.S.C. 3553).

(vix) 52.233-4, Applicable Law for Breach of Contract Claim (OCT 2004) (Pub. L. 108-77, 108-78 (19 U.S.C. 3805 note).

(2) Listed below are additional clauses that apply:

(i) 52.232-1, Payments (APR 1984).

(ii) 52.232-8, Discounts for Prompt Payment (FEB 2002).

(iii) 52.232-11, Extras (APR 1984).

(iv) 52.232-25, Prompt Payment (JAN 2017).

(v) 52.232-39, Unenforceability of Unauthorized Obligations (JUN 2013).

(vi) 52.232-40, Providing Accelerated Payments to Small Business Subcontractors (DEC 2013).

(vii) 52.233-1, Disputes (MAY 2014).

(viii) 52.244-6, Subcontracts for Commercial Items (AUG 2019).

(ix) 52.253-1, Computer Generated Forms (JAN 1991).

(b) The Contractor shall comply with the following FAR clauses, incorporated by reference, unless the circumstances do not apply:

(1) The clauses listed below implement provisions of law or Executive order:

(i) 52.204-10, Reporting Executive Compensation and First-Tier Subcontract Awards (OCT 2018) (Pub. L. 109-282) (31 U.S.C. 6101 note) (Applies to contracts valued at $30,000 or more).

(ii) 52.222-19, Child Labor-Cooperation with Authorities and Remedies (OCT 2019) (E.O. 13126). (Applies to contracts for supplies exceeding the micro-purchase threshold).

(iii) 52.222-20, Contracts for Materials, Supplies, Articles, and Equipment Exceeding $15,000 (MAY 2014) (41 U.S.C. chapter 65) (Applies to supply contracts over $15,000 in the United States, Puerto Rico, or the U.S. Virgin Islands).

(iv) 52.204–21, Basic Safeguarding of Covered Contractor Information Systems (JUN 2016) (Applies to contracts when the contractor or a subcontractor at any tier may have Federal contract information residing in or transiting through its information system.

(v) 52.222-35, Equal Opportunity for Veterans (OCT 2015) (38 U.S.C. 4212) (applies to contracts of $150,000 or more).

(vi) 52.222-36, Equal Employment for Workers with Disabilities (JUL 2014) (29 U.S.C. 793) (Applies to contracts over $15,000, unless the work is to be performed outside the United States by employees recruited outside the United States). (For purposes of this clause, "United States" includes the 50 States, the District of Columbia, Puerto Rico, the Northern Mariana Islands, American Samoa, Guam, the U.S. Virgin Islands, and Wake Island.)

(vii) 52.222-41, Service Contract Labor Standards (AUG 2018) (41 U.S.C. chapter 67) (Applies to service contracts over $2,500 that are subject to the Service Contract Labor Standards statute and will be performed in the United States, District of Columbia, Puerto Rico, the Northern Mariana Islands, American Samoa, Guam, the U.S. Virgin Islands, Johnston Island, Wake Island, or the outer Continental Shelf).

(viii) 52.222-41, Service Contract Labor Standards (MAY 2014) (41 U.S.C. chapter 67) (Applies to service contracts over $2,500 that are subject to the Service Contract Labor Standards statute and will be performed in the United States, District of Columbia, Puerto Rico, the Northern Mariana Islands, American Samoa, Guam, the U.S. Virgin Islands, Johnston Island, Wake Island, or the outer Continental Shelf).

(A) 52.222-50, Combating Trafficking in Persons (JAN 2019) (22 U.S.C. chapter 78 and E.O. 13627) (Applies to all solicitations and contracts).

(B) *Alternate I* (MAR 2015) (Applies if the Contracting Officer has filled in the following information with regard to applicable directives or notices: Document title(s), source for obtaining document(s), and contract performance location outside the United States to which the document applies).

(ix) 52.222-55, Minimum Wages Under Executive Order 13658 (DEC 2015) (Applies when 52.222-6 or 52.222-41 are in the contract and performance in whole or in part is in the United States (the 50 states and the District of Columbia)).

(x) 52.222-62, Paid Sick Leave Under Executive Order 13706 (JAN 2017) (E.O. 13706) (Applies when 52.222-6 or 52.222-41 are in the contract and performance in whole or in part is in the United States (the 50 States and the District of Columbia.))

(xi) 52.213-4, Terms and Conditions – Simplified Acquisitions (Other than Commercial Items).

(xii) 52.223-5, Pollution Prevention and Right-to-Know Information (May 2011) (E.O. 13423) (Applies to services performed on Federal facilities).

(xiii) 52.223-12, Maintenance, Service, Repair, or Disposal of Refrigeration Equipment and Air Conditioners (JUN 2016) (E.O. 13693) (Applies to maintenance, service, repair, or disposal of refrigeration equipment and air conditioners).

(xiv) 52.223-5, Pollution Prevention and Right-to- Know Information (MAY 2011) (E.O. 13423) (Applies to services performed on Federal facilities).

(xv) 52.223-20, Aerosols (JUN 2016) (E.O. 13693) (Applies to contracts for products that may contain high global warming potential hydrofluorocarbons as a propellant or as a solvent; or contracts for maintenance or repair of electronic or mechanical devices).

(xvi) 52.223-21, Foams (JUN 2016) (E.O. 13693) (Applies to contracts for products that may contain high global warming potential hydrofluorocarbons or refrigerant blends containing hydrofluorocarbons as a foam blowing agent; or contracts for construction of buildings or facilities.

(xvii) 52.223-15, Energy Efficiency in Energy- Consuming Products (DEC 2007) (42 U.S.C. 8259b) (Unless exempt pursuant to 23.204, applies to contracts when energy-consuming products listed in the ENERGY STAR® Program or Federal Energy Management Program (FEMP) will be—

(A) Delivered;

(B) Acquired by the Contractor for use in performing services at a Federally-controlled facility;

(C) Furnished by the Contractor for use by the Government; or

(D) Specified in the design of a building or work, or incorporated during its construction, renovation, or maintenance).

(xviii) 52.225-1, Buy American—Supplies (MAY 2014) (41 U.S.C. chapter 67) (Applies to contracts for supplies, and to contracts for services involving the furnishing of supplies, for use in the United States or its outlying areas, if the value of the supply contract or supply portion of a service contract exceeds the micro-purchase threshold and the acquisition—

(A) Is set aside for small business concerns; or

(B) Cannot be set aside for small business concerns (see 19.502-2), and does not exceed $25,000).

(xix) 52.232-33, Payment by Electronic Funds Transfer—System for Award Management (OCT 2018) (Applies when the payment will be made by electronic funds transfer (EFT) and the payment office uses the System for Award Management (SAM) as its source of EFT information).

(xx) 52.232-33, Payment by Electronic Funds Transfer—System for Award Management (JUL 2013) (Applies when the payment will be made by electronic funds transfer (EFT) and the payment office uses the System for Award Management (SAM) database as its source of EFT information.)

(xxi) 52.247-64, Preference for Privately Owned U.S.-Flag Commercial Vessels (FEB 2006) (46 U.S.C. App. 1241) (Applies to supplies transported by ocean vessels (except for the types of subcontracts listed at 47.504(d).)

(2) Listed below are additional clauses that may apply:

(i) 52.204-21, Basic Safeguarding of Covered Contractor Information Systems (JUN 2016) (Applies to contracts when the contractor or a subcontractor at any tier may have Federal contract information residing in or transiting through its information system.

(ii) 52.209-6, Protecting the Government's Interest When Subcontracting with Contractors Debarred, Suspended, or Proposed for Debarment (OCT 2015) (Applies to contracts over $35,000).

(iii) 52.211-17, Delivery of Excess Quantities (SEP 1989) (Applies to fixed-price supplies).

(vi) 52.247-29, F.o.b. Origin (FEB 2006) (Applies to supplies if delivery is f.o.b. origin).

(v) 52.247-34, F.o.b. Destination (NOV 1991) (Applies to supplies if delivery is f.o.b. destination).

(c) *FAR 52.252-2, Clauses Incorporated by Reference* (FEB 1998). This contract incorporates one or more clauses by reference, with the same force and effect as if they were given in full text. Upon request, the Contracting Officer will make their full text available. Also, the full text of a clause may be accessed electronically at this/these address(es):

____

____

[*Insert one or more Internet addresses*]

(d) *Inspection/Acceptance*. The Contractor shall tender for acceptance only those items that conform to the requirements of this contract. The Government reserves the right to inspect or test any supplies or services that have been tendered for acceptance. The Government may require repair or replacement of nonconforming supplies or reperformance of nonconforming services at no increase in contract price. The Government must exercise its post-acceptance rights—

(1) Within a reasonable period of time after the defect was discovered or should have been discovered; and

(2) Before any substantial change occurs in the condition of the item, unless the change is due to the defect in the item.

(e) *Excusable delays*. The Contractor shall be liable for default unless nonperformance is caused by an occurrence beyond the reasonable control of the Contractor and without its fault or negligence, such as acts of God or the public enemy, acts of the Government in either its sovereign or contractual capacity, fires, floods, epidemics, quarantine restrictions, strikes, unusually severe weather, and delays of common carriers. The Contractor shall notify the Contracting Officer in writing as soon as it is reasonably possible after the commencement of any excusable delay, setting forth the full particulars in connection therewith, shall remedy such occurrence with all reasonable dispatch, and shall promptly give written notice to the Contracting Officer of the cessation of such occurrence.

(f) *Termination for the Government's convenience*. The Government reserves the right to terminate this contract, or any part hereof, for its sole convenience. In the event of such termination, the Contractor shall immediately stop all work hereunder and shall immediately cause any and all of its suppliers and subcontractors to cease work. Subject to the terms of this contract, the Contractor shall be paid a percentage of the contract price reflecting the percentage of the work performed prior to the notice of termination, plus reasonable charges that the Contractor can demonstrate to the satisfaction of the Government, using its standard record keeping system, have resulted from the termination. The Contractor shall not be required to comply with the cost accounting standards or contract cost principles for this purpose. This paragraph does not give the Government any right to audit the Contractor's records. The Contractor shall not be paid for any work performed or costs incurred that reasonably could have been avoided.

(g) *Termination for cause.* The Government may terminate this contract, or any part hereof, for cause in the event of any default by the Contractor, or if the Contractor fails to comply with any contract terms and conditions, or fails to provide the Government, upon request, with adequate assurances of future performance. In the event of termination for cause, the Government shall not be liable to the Contractor for any amount for supplies or services not accepted, and the Contractor shall be liable to the Government for any and all rights and remedies provided by law. If it is determined that the Government improperly terminated this contract for default, such termination shall be deemed a termination for convenience.

(h) *Warranty.* The Contractor warrants and implies that the items delivered hereunder are merchantable and fit for use for the particular purpose described in this contract.

(End of clause)

[FAC 97-3, 62 FR 64912, 12/9/97, effective 2/9/98; FAC 97-4, 63 FR 9048, 2/23/98, effective 4/24/98; FAC 97-5, 63 FR 34058, 6/22/98, effective 6/22/98, finalized without change, FAC 97-9, 63 FR 58587, 10/30/98; FAC 97-11, 64 FR 10530, 3/4/99, effective 5/3/99; FAC 97-12, 64 FR 32740, 6/17/99, effective 6/17/99; FAC 97-15, 64 FR 72414, 12/27/99, effective 2/25/2000; FAC 97-17, 65 FR 24316, 4/25/2000, effective 6/26/2000; FAC 97-18, 65 FR 36014, 6/6/2000, effective 7/6/2000; FAC 97-22, 66 FR 2117, 1/10/2001, effective 3/12/2001; FAC 97-23, 66 FR 5345, 11/8/2001, effective 2/20/2001; Delay of effective date, 66 FR 14259, 3/9/2001, effective 5/11/2001; FAC 2001-01, 66 FR 53478, 10/22/2001, effective 12/21/2001; FAC 2001-02, 66 FR 6/5/347, 12/18/2001, effective 2/19/2002; FAC 2001-04, 67 FR 6112, 2/8/2002, effective 2/8/2002; FAC 2001-06, 67 FR 13048, 3/20/2002, effective 4/4/2002; FAC 2001-07, 67 FR 21534, 4/30/2002, effective 5/15/2002; FAC 2001-08, 67 FR 43513, 6/27/2002, effective 7/29/2002; FAC 2001-09, 67 FR 56115, 8/30/2002, effective 9/30/2002; FAC 2001-13, 68 FR 13202, 3/18/2003, effective 4/17/2003; FAC 2001-14, 68 FR 28079, 5/22/2003, effective 6/23/2003; FAC 2001-15, 68 FR 43868, 7/24/2003, effective 8/25/2003; FAC 2001-16, Final rule, 68 FR 56669, 10/1/2003, effective 10/1/2003; FAC 2001-16, Final rule, 68 FR 56685, 10/12/003, effective 10/31/2003; FAC 2001-16, 68 FR 56682, 10/1/2003, effective 10/31/2003; FAC 2001-19, Interim rule, 69 FR 1051, 1/7/2004, effective 1/1/2004;FAC 2001-22, 69 FR 17770, 4/5/2004, effective 4/5/2004; FAC 2001-23, 69 FR 25273, 5/5/2004, effective 5/5/2004; FAC 2001-24, 69 FR 34239, 6/18/2004, effective 6/18/2004; 69 FR 34228, 6/18/2004, effective 7/19/2004; FAC 2001-25, 69 FR 59700, 10/5/2004, effective 10/5/2004; FAC 2001-26, 69 FR 76347, 12/20/2004, effective 1/19/2005, 69 FR 76351, 12/20/2004, effective 12/20/2004; FAC 2005-03, 70 FR 18959, 4/11/2005, effective 4/11/2005; FAC 2005-04, 70 FR 33655, 6/8/2005, effective 6/8/2005; 70 FR 33662, 6/8/2005, effective 7/8/2005; Final Rule correction, 70 FR 46776, 8/11/2005; FAC 2005-07, 71 FR 200, 1/3/2006, effective 2/22/006; FAC 2005-08, 71 FR 864, 1/5/2006, effective 1/5/2006; FAC 2005-13, 71 FR 57363, 71 FR 57375, 9/28/2006, effective 9/28/2006; FAC 2005-16, 72 FR 13586, 3/22/2007, effective 3/22/2007; FAC 2005-19, 72 FR 46335, 8/17/2007, effective 8/17/2007; FAC 2005-21, 72 FR 63076, 11/7/2007, effective 11/7/2007; FAC 2005-22, 72 FR 65868, 11/23/2007, effective 12/24/2007; FAC 2005-23, 72 FR 73218, 12/26/2007, effective 12/26/2007; FAC 2005-24, 73 FR 10962, 2/28/2008, effective 2/28/2008; FAC 2005-27, 73 FR 53997, 9/17/2008, effective 10/17/2008; FAC 2005-28, 73 FR 67064, 11/12/2008, effective 12/12/2008; FAC 2005-30, 74 FR 2713, 2724, 2741, 1/15/2009, effective 2/17/2009; 74 FR 2745, 1/15/2009, effective 1/15/2009; FAC 2005-31, 74 FR 11829, 3/19/2009, effective

3/19/2009; FAC 2005-32, 74 FR 14633, 3/31/2009, effective 3/31/2009; FAC 2005-36, 74 FR 40461, 40468, 8/11/2009, effective 8/11/2009; FAC 2005-37, 74 FR 52860, 10/14/2009, effective 10/14/2009; FAC 2005-38, 74 FR 65599, 12/10/2009, effective 12/10/2009, 74 FR 65607, 12/10/2009, effective 12/10/2009; FAC 2005-40, 75 FR 14059, 3/23/2010, effective 4/22/2010; FAC 2005-42, 75 FR 34258, 34282, 6/16/2010, effective 6/16/2010; FAC 2005-43, 75 FR 38689, 7/2/2010, effective 7/2/2010; FAC 2005-44, 75 FR 39414, 7/8/2010, effective 7/8/2010; FAC 2005-45, 75 FR 53129, 8/30/2010, effective 10/1/2010; FAC 2005-46, 75 FR 60264, 9/29/2010, effective 9/29/2010; FAC 2005-47, 75 FR 77723, 12/13/2010, effective 12/13/2010; 75 FR 77727, 12/13/2010, effective 1/12/2011; 75 FR 77737, 77739, 12/13/2010, effective 12/13/2010; FAC 2005-50, 76 FR 14570, 3/16/2011, effective 3/16/2011; FAC 2005-52, 76 FR 31395, 5/31/2011, effective 5/31/2011; FAC 2005-53, 76 FR 39233, 39236, 7/5/2011, effective 8/4/2011; FAC 2005-54, 76 FR 68015, 68026, 11/2/2011, effective 11/2/2011; FAC 2005-55, 77 FR 202, 1/3/2012, effective 2/2/2012; FAC 2005-56, 77 FR 12933, 12935, 3/2/2012, effective 3/2/2012; Correction, 77 FR 14303, 3/9/2012, effective 3/9/2012; Correction, 77 FR 17353, 3/26/2012, effective 3/26/2012; FAC 2005-60, 77 FR 44047, 7/26/2012, effective 8/27/2012; FAC 2005-67, 78 FR 37676, 6/21/2013, effective 7/22/2013; 78 FR 37686, 6/21/2013, effective 6/21/2013; FAC 2005-71, 78 FR 70480, 70481, 11/25/2013, effective 11/25/2013; FAC 2005-72, 78 FR 80379, 12/31/2013, effective 1/1/2014; FAC 2005-72, 78 FR 80382, 12/31/2013, effective 12/31/2013; Final rule, 79 FR 4630, 1/29/2014, effective 1/29/2014; FAC 2005-73, 79 FR 24192, 4/29/2014, effective 5/29/2014; FAC 2005-76, 79 FR 43575, 7/25/2014, effective 7/25/2014; FAC 2005-77, 79 FR 61746, 10/14/2014, effective 10/14/2014; FAC 2005-79, 79 FR 74544, 79 FR 74554, 12/15/2014, effective 12/15/2014; FAC 2005-80, 80 FR 4967, 1/29/2015, effective 3/2/2015; Correction, 80 FR 6908, 2/9/2015, effective 3/2/2015; FAC 2005-81, 80 FR 19504, 4/10/2015, effective 4/10/2015; FAC 2005-82, 80 FR 26423, 80 FR 26427, 5/7/2015, effective 5/7/2015; FAC 2005-84, 80 FR 53439, 9/3/2015, effective 9/3/2015; FAC 2005-85, 80 FR 75915, 12/4/2015, effective 12/4/2015; FAC 2005-85, 80 FR 75907, 12/4/2015, effective 2/26/2016; FAC 2005-85, 80 FR 75907, 80 FR 75908, 12/4/2015, effective 12/4/2015 and 2/26/2016; FAC 2005-86, 80 FR 81892, 12/31/2015, effective 2/1/2016; FAC 2005-86, 80 FR 81894, 12/31/2015, effective 1/1/2016; FAC 2005-87, 81 FR 11992, 3/7/2016, effective 3/7/2016; Correction, 81 FR 13998, 3/16/2016, effective 3/16/2016; FAC 2005-88, 81 FR 30429, 5/16/2016, effective 6/15/2016; FAC 2005-88, 81 FR 30439, 5/16/2016, effective 6/15/2016; FAC 2005-89, 81 FR 45833, 7/14/2016, effective 11/1/2016; FAC 2005-90, 81 FR 58562, 8/25/2016, effective 10/25/2016; FAC 2005-91, 81 FR 67731, 9/30/2016, effective 9/30/2016; FAC 2005-91, 81 FR 67732, 9/30/2016, effective 9/30/2016; FAC 2005-91, 81 FR 67736, 9/30/2016, effective 10/31/2016; FAC 2005-91, 81 FR 67774, 9/30/2016, effective 10/31/2016; FAC 2005-91, 81 FR 67776, 9/30/2016, effective 10/31/2016; FAC 2005-92, 81 FR 83092, 11/18/2016, effective 12/19/2016; FAC 2005-93, 81 FR 91627, 12/16/2016, effective 1/1/2017; FAC 2005-94, 81 FR 93476, 12/20/2016, effective 1/19/2017; FAC 2005-95, 82 FR 4709, 1/13/2017, effective 1/13/2017; FAC 2005-95, 82 FR 4717, 1/13/2017, effective 1/19/2017; FAC 2005-96, 82 FR 51773, 11/8/2017, effective 11/6/2017; FAC 2005-97, 83 FR 3396, 1/24/2018, effective 1/24/2018; FAC 2005-99, 83 FR 28141, 6/15/2018, effective 7/16/2018; FAC 2005-100, 83 FR 42569, 8/22/2018, effective 8/22/2018; FAC 2005-100, 83 FR 42570, 8/22/2018, effective 8/22/2018; FAC 2005-100, 83 FR 42571, 8/22/2018, effective 8/22/2018; FAC 2005-101, 83 FR 48691, 9/26/2018, effective 10/26/2018; FAC 2019-01, 83 FR 65466, 12/20/2018, effective 1/22/2019; FAC 2019-05, 84 FR 40216, 8/13/2019, effective 8/13/2019; FAC 2019-06, 84 FR 47861, 9/10/2019, effective 9/10/2019; FAC 2019-06, 84 FR 47866, 9/10/2019, effective 10/10/2019]

52.214-1 [Reserved]

[Removed and reserved by FAC 2001-06, 67 FR 13048, 3/20/2002, effective 4/4/2002]

52.214-2 [Reserved]

[Removed and reserved, FAC 97-9, 63 FR 58587, 10/30/98, effective 10/30/98, finalized without change, FAC 97-12, 64 FR 32740, 6/17/99]

52.214-3 Amendments to Invitations for Bids.

As prescribed in 14.201-6(b) (1), insert the following provision:

AMENDMENTS TO INVITATIONS FOR BIDS (DEC 2016)

(a) If this solicitation is amended, then all terms and conditions which are not modified remain unchanged.

(b) (1) Bidders shall acknowledge receipt of any amendment to this solicitation—

(i) By signing and returning the amendment;

(ii) By identifying the amendment number and date in space provided for this purpose on the form for submitting a bid;

(iii) By letter;

(iv) By facsimile, if facsimile bids are authorized in the solicitation; or

(v) By email, if email bids are authorized in the solicitation.

(2) The Government must receive the acknowledgment by the time and at the place specified for receipt of bids.

(End of provision)

[FAC 84-40, 53 FR 43394, 10/26/88, effective 11/25/88; FAC 84-53, 54 FR 48990, 11/28/89, effective 12/28/89; FAC 2001-06, 67 FR 13048, 3/20/2002, effective 4/4/2002; FAC 2005-92, 81 FR 83097, 11/18/2016, effective 12/19/2016]

52.214-4 False Statements in Bids.

As prescribed in 14.201-6(b) (2), insert the following provision in all invitations for bids:

FALSE STATEMENTS IN BIDS (APR 1984)

Bidders must provide full, accurate, and complete information as required by this solicitation and its attachments. The penalty for making false statements in bids is prescribed in 18 U.S.C. 1001.

(End of provision)

[FAC 90-32, 60 FR 48206, 9/18/95, effective 10/1/95; FAC 2001-06, 67 FR 13048, 3/20/2002, effective 4/4/2002]

52.214-5 Submission of Bids.

As prescribed in 14.201-6(c) (1), insert the following provision:

SUBMISSION OF BIDS (DEC 2016)

(a) Bids and bid modifications shall be submitted in sealed envelopes or packages (unless submitted by electronic means)—

(1) Addressed to the office specified in the solicitation; and

(2) Showing the time and date specified for receipt, the solicitation number, and the name and address of the bidder.

(b) Bidders using commercial carrier services shall ensure that the bid is addressed and marked on the outermost envelope or wrapper as prescribed in subparagraphs (a) (1) and (2) of this provision when delivered to the office specified in the solicitation.

(c) Facsimile bids, modifications, or withdrawals, will not be considered unless authorized by the solicitation.

(d) Bids submitted by electronic commerce shall be considered only if the electronic commerce method was specifically stipulated or permitted by the solicitation.

(End of provision)

[FAC 84-53, 54 FR 48991, 11/28/89, effective 12/28/89; FAC 84-56, 55 FR 3887, 2/5/90, effective 3/7/90; FAC 90-29, 60 FR 34732, 7/3/95, effective 7/3/95; FAC 90-44, Final rule, 61 FR 69286, 12/31/96, effective 3/3/97; FAC 90-46, 62 FR 12690, 3/17/97, effective 5/16/97; FAC 2005-92, 81 FR 83097, 11/18/2016, effective 12/19/2016]

52.214-6 Explanation to Prospective Bidders.

As prescribed in 14.201-6(c) (2), insert the following provision:

EXPLANATION TO PROSPECTIVE BIDDERS (APR 1984)

Any prospective bidder desiring an explanation or interpretation of the solicitation, drawings, specifications, etc., must request it in writing soon enough to allow a reply to reach all prospective bidders before the submission of their bids. Oral explanations or instructions given before the award of a contract will not be binding. Any information given a prospective bidder concerning a solicitation will be furnished promptly to all other prospective bidders as an amendment to the solicitation, if that information is necessary in submitting bids or if the lack of it would be prejudicial to other prospective bidders.

(End of provision)

[FAC 84-58, 55 FR 25531, 6/21/90, effective 7/23/90; FAC 90-32, 60 FR 48206, 9/18/95, effective 10/1/95]

52.214-7 Late Submissions, Modifications, and Withdrawals of Bids.

As prescribed in 14.201-6(c) (3), insert the following provision:

LATE SUBMISSIONS, MODIFICATIONS, AND WITHDRAWALS OF BIDS (NOV 1999)

(a) Bidders are responsible for submitting bids, and any modifications or withdrawals, so as to reach the Government office designated in the invitation for bids (IFB) by the time specified in the IFB. If no time is specified in the IFB, the time for receipt is 4:30 p.m., local time, for the designated Government office on the date that bids are due.

(b) (1) Any bid, modification, or withdrawal received at the Government office designated in the IFB after the exact time specified for receipt of bids is "late" and will not be considered unless it is received before award is made, the Contracting Officer determines that accepting the late bid would not unduly delay the acquisition; and—

(i) If it was transmitted through an electronic commerce method authorized by the IFB, it was received at the initial point of entry to the Government infrastructure not later than 5:00 p.m. one working day prior to the date specified for receipt of bids; or

(ii) There is acceptable evidence to establish that it was received at the Government installation designated for receipt of bids and was under the Government's control prior to the time set for receipt of bids.

(2) However, a late modification of an otherwise successful bid that makes its terms more favorable to the Government, will be considered at any time it is received and may be accepted.

(c) Acceptable evidence to establish the time of receipt at the Government installation includes the time/date stamp of that installation on the bid wrapper, other documentary evidence of receipt maintained by the installation, or oral testimony or statements of Government personnel.

(d) If an emergency or unanticipated event interrupts normal Government processes so that bids cannot be received at the Government office designated for receipt of bids by the exact time specified in the IFB and urgent Government requirements preclude amendment of the IFB, the time specified for receipt of bids will be deemed to be extended to the same time of day specified in the solicitation on the first work day on which normal Government processes resume.

(e) Bids may be withdrawn by written notice received at any time before the exact time set for receipt of bids. If the IFB authorizes facsimile bids, bids may be withdrawn via facsimile received at any time before the exact time set for receipt of bids, subject to the conditions specified in the provision at 52.214-31, Facsimile Bids. A bid may be withdrawn in person by a bidder or its authorized representative if, before the exact time set for receipt of bids, the identity of the person requesting withdrawal is established and the person signs a receipt for the bid.

(End of provision)

[FAC 97-14, 64 FR 51828, 9/24/99, effective 11/23/99]

52.214-8 [Removed and Reserved]

[Removed and Reserved, FAC 84-58, 55 FR 25531, 6/21/90, effective 7/23/90]

52.214-9 [Removed and Reserved]

[FAC 90-29, 60 FR 34732, 7/3/95, effective 7/3/95; FAC 2001-15, 68 FR 43854, 7/24/2003, effective 8/25/2003]

52.214-10 Contract Award—Sealed Bidding.

As prescribed in 14.201-6(e), insert the following provision:

CONTRACT AWARD—SEALED BIDDING (JUL 1990)

(a) The Government will evaluate bids in response to this solicitation without discussions and will award a contract to the responsible bidder whose bid, conforming to the solicitation, will be most advantageous to the Government considering only price and the price-related factors specified elsewhere in the solicitation.

(b) The Government may—

(1) Reject any or all bids;

(2) Accept other than the lowest bid; and

(3) Waive informalities or minor irregularities in bids received.

(c) The Government may accept any item or group of items of a bid, unless the bidder qualifies the bid by specific limitations. Unless otherwise provided in the Schedule, bids may be submitted for quantities less than those specified. The Government reserves the right to make an award on any item for a quantity less than the quantity offered, at the unit prices offered, unless the bidder specifies otherwise in the bid.

(d) A written award or acceptance of a bid mailed or otherwise furnished to the successful bidder within the time for acceptance specified in the bid shall result in a binding contract without further action by either party.

(e) The Government may reject a bid as nonresponsive if the prices bid are materially unbalanced between line items or subline items. A bid is materially unbalanced when it is based on prices significantly less than cost for some work and prices which are significantly overstated in relation to cost for other work, and if there is a reasonable doubt that the bid will result in the lowest overall cost to the Government even though it may be the low evaluated bid, or if it is so unbalanced as to be tantamount to allowing an advance payment.

(End of provision)

[FAC 84-5, 50 FR 1746, 1/11/85, effective 4/1/85; FAC 84-58, 55 FR 25531, 6/21/90, effective 7/23/90; FAC 2001-15, 68 FR 43854, 7/24/2003, effective 8/25/2003]

52.214-11 [Reserved]

[Removed and reserved, FAC 84-12, 51 FR 2648, 1/17/86, effective 1/20/86]

52.214-12 Preparation of Bids.

As prescribed in 14.201-6(f), insert the following provision:

PREPARATION OF BIDS (APR 1984)

(a) Bidders are expected to examine the drawings, specifications, Schedule, and all instructions. Failure to do so will be at the bidder's risk.

(b) Each bidder shall furnish the information required by the solicitation. The bidder shall sign the bid and print or type its name on the Schedule and each continuation sheet on which it makes an entry. Erasures or other changes must be initialed by the person signing the bid. Bids signed by an agent shall be accompanied by evidence of that agent's authority, unless that evidence has been previously furnished to the issuing office.

(c) For each item offered, bidders shall (1) show the unit price, including, unless otherwise specified, packaging, packing, and preservation and (2) enter the extended price for the quantity of each item offered in the "Amount" column of the Schedule. In case of discrepancy between a unit price and an extended price, the unit price will be presumed to be correct, subject, however, to correction to the same extent and in the same manner as any other mistake.

(d) Bids for supplies or services other than those specified will not be considered unless authorized by the solicitation.

(e) Bidders must state a definite time for delivery of supplies or for performance of services, unless otherwise specified in the solicitation.

(f) Time, if stated as a number of days, will include Saturdays, Sundays, and holidays.

(End of provision)

[FAC 84-12, 51 FR 2666, 1/17/86, effective 1/20/86; FAC 90-32, 60 FR 48206, 9/18/95, effective 10/1/95]

52.214-13 [Removed and Reserved]

[FAC 84-40, 53 FR 43394, 10/26/88, effective 11/25/88; FAC 90-32, 60 FR 48206, 9/18/95, effective 10/1/95; FAC 2005-92, 81 FR 83097, 11/18/2016, effective 12/19/2016]

52.214-14 Place of Performance—Sealed Bidding.

As prescribed in 14.201-6(h), insert the following provision:

PLACE OF PERFORMANCE—SEALED BIDDING (APR 1985)

(a) The bidder, in the performance of any contract resulting from this solicitation, [ ] intends, [ ] does not intend [*check applicable box*] to use one or more plants or facilities located at a different address from the address of the bidder as indicated in this bid.

(b) If the bidder checks "intends" in paragraph (a) above, it shall insert in the spaces provided below the required information:

Place of Performance (Street, Address, City, County, State, Zip Code)	Name and Address of Owner and Operator of the Plant or Facility if Other than Bidder
____	____
____	____

(End of provision)

[FAC 84-5, 50 FR 1746, 1/11/85, effective 4/1/85]

52.214-15 Period for Acceptance of Bids.

As prescribed in 14.201-6(i), insert the following provision:

PERIOD FOR ACCEPTANCE OF BIDS (APR 1984)

In compliance with the solicitation, the bidder agrees, if this bid is accepted within ____ calendar days (60 calendar days unless a different period is inserted by the bidder) from the date specified in the solicitation for receipt of bids, to furnish any or all items upon which prices are bid at the price set opposite each item, delivered at the designated point(s), within the time specified in the Schedule.

(End of provision)

[FAC 84-53, 54 FR 48991, 11/28/89, effective 12/28/89; FAC 90-32, 60 FR 48206, 9/18/95, effective 10/1/95]

52.214-16 Minimum Bid Acceptance Period.

As prescribed in 14.201-6(j), insert the following provision in invitations for bids, except for construction, if the contracting officer determines that a minimum acceptance period must be specified:

MINIMUM BID ACCEPTANCE PERIOD (APR 1984)

(a) *Acceptance period,* as used in this provision, means the number of calendar days available to the Government for awarding a contract from the date specified in this solicitation for receipt of bids.

(b) This provision supersedes any language pertaining to the acceptance period that may appear elsewhere in this solicitation.

(c) The Government requires a minimum acceptance period of ____ calendar days [*the Contracting Officer shall insert the number of days*].

(d) In the space provided immediately below, bidders may specify a longer acceptance period than the Government's minimum requirement.

The bidder allows the following acceptance period:

_______ calendar days.

(e) A bid allowing less than the Government's minimum acceptance period will be rejected.

(f) The bidder agrees to execute all that it has undertaken to do, in compliance with its bid, if that bid is accepted in writing within—(1) the acceptance period stated in paragraph (c) of this clause; or (2) Any longer acceptance period stated in paragraph (d) of this clause.

(End of provision)

[FAC 90-32, 60 FR 48206, 9/18/95, effective 10/1/95]

52.214-17 [Reserved]

[Removed and reserved, FAC 97-11, 64 FR 10530, 3/4/99, effective 5/3/99]

52.214-18 Preparation of Bids—Construction.

As prescribed in 14.201-6(l), insert the following provision:

PREPARATION OF BIDS—CONSTRUCTION (APR 1984)

(a) Bids must be—(1) Submitted on the forms furnished by the Government or on copies of those forms, and

(2) *Manually signed.* The person signing a bid must initial each erasure or change appearing on any bid form.

(b) The bid form may require bidders to submit bid prices for one or more items on various bases, including—

(1) Lump sum bidding;

(2) Alternate prices;

(3) Units of construction; or

(4) Any combination of subparagraphs (1) through (3) above.

(c) If the solicitation requires bidding on all items, failure to do so will disqualify the bid. If bidding on all items is not required, bidders should insert the words "no bid" in the space provided for any item on which no price is submitted.

(d) Alternate bids will not be considered unless this solicitation authorizes their submission.

(End of provision)

[FAC 84-58, 55 FR 25531, 6/21/90, effective 7/23/90; FAC 90-32, 60 FR 48206, 9/18/95, effective 10/1/95]

52.214-19 Contract Award—Sealed Bidding—Construction.

As prescribed in 14.201-6(m), insert the following provision:

CONTRACT AWARD—SEALED BIDDING—CONSTRUCTION (AUG 1996)

(a) The Government will evaluate bids in response to this solicitation without discussions and will award a contract to the responsible bidder whose bid, conforming to the solicitation, will be most advantageous to the Government, considering only price and the price-related factors specified elsewhere in the solicitation.

(b) The Government may reject any or all bids, and waive informalities or minor irregularities in bids received.

(c) The Government may accept any item or combination of items, unless doing so is precluded by a restrictive limitation in the solicitation or the bid.

(d) The Government may reject a bid as nonresponsive if the prices bid are materially unbalanced between line items or subline items. A bid is materially unbalanced when it is based on prices significantly less than cost for some work and prices which are significantly overstated in relation to cost for other work, and if there is a reasonable doubt that the bid will result in the lowest overall cost to the Government even though it may be the low evaluated bid, or if it is so unbalanced as to be tantamount to allowing an advance payment.

(End of provision)

[FAC 84-5, 50 FR 1746, 1/11/85, effective 4/1/85; FAC 84-13, 50 FR 52434, 12/23/85, effective 2/3/86; FAC 90-39, 61 FR 31612, 6/20/96, effective 8/19/96]

52.214-20 Bid Samples.

As prescribed in 14.201-6(o)(1), insert the following provision:

BID SAMPLES (APR 2002)

(a) *Bid sample* means a product sample required to be submitted by a bidder to show those characteristics of the offered products that cannot adequately be described by specifications, purchase descriptions, or the invitation for bid (e.g., balance, facility of use, or pattern).

(b) Bidders must furnish bid samples as part of the bid. The Government must receive the bid samples by the time specified in the invitation for bids. If the bidder fails to submit samples on time, the Government will reject the bid, except that the Contracting Officer will consider a late sample sent by mail under the Late Submissions, Modifications, and Withdrawals of Bids provision of this solicitation.

(c) The Government will test or evaluate bid samples to determine compliance with all the characteristics listed for examination in this solicitation. The Government will reject the bid when the sample fails to conform to the required characteristics. Products delivered under any resulting contract must conform to—

(1) the approved sample for the characteristics listed for test or evaluation; and

(2) the specifications for all other characteristics.

(d) Unless otherwise specified in the solicitation, bid samples shall be

(1) submitted at no expense to the Government, and

(2) returned at the bidder's request and expense, unless they are destroyed during preaward testing.

(End of provision)

Alternate I (MAY 2002). As prescribed in 14.201-6(o)(2)(i), insert the following Alternate I:

(e) At the discretion of the Contracting Officer, the requirement for furnishing bid samples may be waived for a bidder if

(1) the bid states that the offered product is the same as a product offered by the bidder to the ________ [*as appropriate, the Contracting Officer shall designate the contracting office or an alternate activity or office*]; and

(2) The Contracting Officer determines that the previously offered product was accepted or tested and found to comply with specification and other requirements for technical acceptability conforming in every material respect with those in this solicitation.

Alternate II (MAY 2002). As prescribed in 14.201-6(o)(2)(ii), insert the following Alternate II:

(e) At the discretion of the Contracting Officer, the requirements for furnishing bid samples may be waived for a bidder if—(1) the bid states that the offered product is the same as a product offered by the bidder to the ________ [*as appropriate, the Contracting Officer shall designate the contracting office or an alternate activity or office*] on a previous acquisition;

(2) The Contracting Officer determines that the previously offered product was accepted or tested and found to comply with specification and other requirements for technical acceptability conforming in every material respect with those of this solicitation; and

(3) The product offered under this solicitation will be produced under a resulting contract at the same plant in which the previously acquired or tested product was produced.

[FAC 90-32, 60 FR 48206, 9/18/95, effective 10/1/95; FAC 2001-06, 67 FR 13048, 3/20/2002, effective 4/4/2002; FAC 2001-07,67 FR 21538, 4/30/2002, effective 5/15/2002]

52.214-21 Descriptive Literature.

As prescribed in 14.201-6(p)(1), insert the following provision:

DESCRIPTIVE LITERATURE (APR 2002)

(a) *Descriptive literature*, as used in this provision, means information furnished by a bidder, such as cuts, illustrations, drawings, and brochures, that shows a product's characteristics or construction or explains its operation. The term includes only that information required to evaluate the acceptability of the product and excludes other information for operating or maintaining the product.

(b) Descriptive literature is required to establish, for the purpose of evaluation and award, details of the product offered that are specified elsewhere in the solicitation and pertain to significant elements such as—

(1) Design;

(2) Materials;

(3) Components;

(4) Performance characteristics; and

(5) Methods of manufacture, assembly, construction, or operation.

(c) Descriptive literature, required elsewhere in this solicitation, shall be—

(1) Identified to show the item(s) of the offer to which it applies; and

(2) Received by the time specified in this solicitation.

(d) If the bidder fails to submit descriptive literature on time, the Government will reject the bid, except that late descriptive literature sent by mail may be considered under the Late Submissions, Modifications, and Withdrawals of Bids provision of this solicitation.

(e) If the descriptive literature fails to show that the product offered conforms to the requirements of the solicitation, the Government will reject the bid.

(End of provision)

Alternate I (JAN 2017). As prescribed in 14.201-6(p)(2), add the following paragraphs (f) and (g) to the basic provision:

(f) The Contracting Officer may waive the requirement for furnishing descriptive literature if the offeror has supplied a product that is the same as that required by this solicitation under a prior contract. A bidder that requests a waiver of this requirement shall provide the following information:

Prior contract number ______

Date of prior contract ______

Contract line item number of product supplied ______

Name and address of Government activity to which delivery was made ______

Date of final delivery product supplied ______

(g) Bidders shall submit bids on the basis of required descriptive literature or on the basis of a previously supplied product under paragraph (f) of this provision. A bidder submitting a bid on one of these two bases may not elect to have its bid considered on the alternative basis after the time specified for receipt of bids. The Government will disregard a bidder's request for a waiver under paragraph (f) if that bidder has submitted the descriptive literature requested under this solicitation.

[FAC 90-32, 60 FR 48206, 9/18/95, effective 10/1/95; FAC 97-11, 64 FR 10530, 3/4/99, effective 5/3/99; FAC 97-22, 66 FR 2116, 1/10/2001, effective 3/12/2001; Delay of effective date, 66 FR 14259, 3/9/2001, effective 5/11/2001; FAC 2001-06, 67 FR 13048, 3/20/2002, effective 4/4/2002; FAC 2005-95, 82 FR 4709, 1/13/2017, effective 1/13/2017]

52.214-22 Evaluation of Bids for Multiple Awards.

As prescribed in 14.201-6(q), insert the following provision:

EVALUATION OF BIDS FOR MULTIPLE AWARDS (MAR 1990)

In addition to other factors, bids will be evaluated on the basis of advantages and disadvantages to the Government that might result from making more than one award (multiple awards). It is assumed, for the purpose of evaluating bids, that $500 would be the administrative cost to the Government for issuing and administering each contract awarded under this solicitation, and individual awards will be for the items or combinations of items that result in the lowest aggregate cost to the Government, including the assumed administrative costs.

(End of provision)

[FAC 84-56, 55 FR 3887, 2/5/90, effective 3/7/90]

52.214-23 Late Submissions, Modifications, Revisions, and Withdrawals of Technical Proposals Under Two-Step Sealed Bidding.

As prescribed in 14.201-6(r), insert the following provision:

LATE SUBMISSIONS, MODIFICATIONS, REVISIONS, AND WITHDRAWALS OF TECHNICAL PROPOSALS UNDER TWO-STEP SEALED BIDDING (NOV 1999)

(a) Bidders are responsible for submitting technical proposals, and any modifications or revisions, so as to reach the Government office designated in the request for technical proposals by the time specified in the invitation for bids (IFB). If no time is specified in the IFB, the time for receipt is 4:30 p.m., local time, for the designated Government office on the date that bids or revisions are due.

(b) (1) Any technical proposal under step one of two-step sealed bidding or modification, revision, or withdrawal of such proposal received at the Government office designated in the request for technical proposals after the exact time specified for receipt will not be considered unless the Contracting Officer determines that accepting the late technical proposal would not unduly delay the acquisition; and—

(i) If it was transmitted through an electronic commerce method authorized by the request for technical proposals, it was received at the initial point of entry to the Government infrastructure not later than 5:00 p.m. one working day prior to the date specified for receipt of proposals; or

(ii) There is acceptable evidence to establish that it was received at the Government installation designated for receipt of offers and was under the Government's control prior to the time set for receipt; or

(iii) It is the only proposal received and it is negotiated under part 15 of the Federal Acquisition Regulation.

(2) However, a late modification of an otherwise successful proposal that makes its terms more favorable to the Government will be considered at any time it is received and may be accepted.

(c) Acceptable evidence to establish the time of receipt at the Government installation includes the time/date stamp of that installation on the technical proposal wrapper, other documentary evidence of receipt maintained by the installation, or oral testimony or statements of Government personnel.

(d) If an emergency or unanticipated event interrupts normal Government processes so that technical proposals cannot be received at the Government office designated for receipt of technical proposals by the exact time specified in the request for technical proposals, and urgent Government requirements preclude amendment of the request for technical proposals, the time specified for receipt of technical proposals will be deemed to be extended to the same time of day specified in the request for technical proposals on the first work day on which normal Government processes resume.

(e) Technical proposals may be withdrawn by written notice received at any time before the exact time set for receipt of technical proposals. If the request for technical proposals authorizes facsimile technical proposals, they may be withdrawn via facsimile received at any time before the exact time set for receipt of proposals, subject to the conditions specified in the provision at 52.214-31, Facsimile Bids. A technical proposal may be withdrawn in person by a bidder or its authorized representative if, before the exact time set for receipt of technical proposals, the identity of the person requesting withdrawal is established and the person signs a receipt for the technical proposal.

(End of provision)

[FAC 97-14, 64 FR 51828, 9/24/99, effective 11/23/99]

52.214-24 Multiple Technical Proposals.

As prescribed in 14.201-6(s), insert the following provision:

MULTIPLE TECHNICAL PROPOSALS (APR 1984)

In the first step of this two-step acquisition, solicited sources are encouraged to submit multiple technical proposals presenting different basic approaches. Each technical proposal submitted will be separately evaluated and the submitter will be notified as to its acceptability.

(End of provision)

[FAC 84-5, 50 FR 1747, 1/11/85, effective 4/1/85; FAC 90-32, 60 FR 48206, 9/18/95, effective 10/1/95]

52.214-25 Step Two of Two-Step Sealed Bidding.

As prescribed in 14.201-6(t), insert the following provision:

STEP TWO OF TWO-STEP SEALED BIDDING (APR 1985)

(a) This invitation for bids is issued to initiate step two of two-step sealed bidding under Subpart 14.5 of the Federal Acquisition Regulation.

(b) The only bids that the Contracting Officer may consider for award of a contract are those received from bidders that have submitted acceptable technical proposals in step one of this acquisition under ____ [*the Contracting Officer shall insert the identification of the step-one request for technical proposals*].

(c) Any bidder that has submitted multiple technical proposals in step one of this acquisition may submit a separate bid on each technical proposal that was determined to be acceptable to the Government.

(End of provision)

[FAC 84-5, 50 FR 1747, 1/11/85, effective 4/1/85]

52.214-26 Audit and Records—Sealed Bidding.

As prescribed in 14.201-7(a)(1), insert the following clause:

AUDIT AND RECORDS—SEALED BIDDING (OCT 2010)

(a) As used in this clause, *records* includes books, documents, accounting procedures and practices, and other data, regardless of type and regardless of whether such items are in written form, in the form of computer data, or in any other form.

(b) *Certified cost or pricing data.* If the Contractor has been required to submit certified cost or pricing data in connection with the pricing of any modification to this contract, the Contracting Officer, or an authorized representative of the Contracting Officer, in order to evaluate the accuracy, completeness, and currency of the certified cost or pricing data, shall have the right to examine and audit all of the Contractor's records, including computations and projections, related to—

(1) The proposal for the modification;

(2) The discussions conducted on the proposal(s), including those related to negotiating;

(3) Pricing of the modification; or

(4) Performance of the modification.

(c) *Comptroller General.* In the case of pricing any modification, the Comptroller General of the United States, or an authorized representative, shall have the same rights as specified in paragraph (b) of this clause and also the right to interview any current employee regarding such transactions.

(d) *Availability.* The Contractor shall make available at its office at all reasonable times the materials described in paragraph (b) of this clause, for examination, audit, or reproduction, until 3 years after final payment under this contract, or for any other period specified in Subpart 4.7 of the Federal Acquisition Regulation (FAR). FAR Subpart 4.7, Contractor Records Retention, in effect on the date of this contract, is incorporated by reference in its entirety and made a part of this contract.

(1) If this contract is completely or partially terminated, the records relating to the work terminated shall be made available for 3 years after any resulting final termination settlement.

(2) Records pertaining to appeals under the Disputes clause or to litigation or the settlement of claims arising under or relating to the performance of this contract shall be made available until disposition of such appeals, litigation, or claims.

(e) The Contractor shall insert a clause containing all the provisions of this clause, including this paragraph (e), in all subcontracts expected to exceed the threshold in FAR 15.403-4(a)(1) for submission of certified cost or pricing data.

(End of clause)

Alternate I (MAR 2009). As prescribed in 14.201-7 (a) (2), substitute the following paragraphs (c) and (e) for paragraphs (c) and (e) of the basic clause:

(c) The Comptroller General of the United States, an appropriate Inspector General appointed under section 3 or 8G of the Inspector General Act of 1978 (5 U.S.C. App.), or an authorized representative of either of the foregoing officials, shall have access to and the right to—

(1) Examine any of the Contractor's or any subcontractors' records that pertain to, and involve transactions relating to, this contract or a subcontract hereunder; and

(2) Interview any officer or employee regarding such transactions.

(e)(1) Except as provided in paragraph (e)(2), the Contractor shall insert a clause containing the provisions of this clause, including this paragraph (e), in all subcontracts.

(2) The authority of the Inspector General under paragraph (c)(2) of this clause does not flow down to subcontracts.

[FAC 90-31, 60 FR 42648, 8/16/95, effective 10/1/95, corrected 60 FR 44548, 8/28/95; FAC 97-2, 62 FR 51224, 9/30/97, effective 10/10/97; FAC 2005-32, 74 FR 14646, 14649, 3/31/2009, effective 3/31/2009; FAC 2005-37, 74 FR 52851, 10/14/2009, effective 10/14/2009; FAC 2005-42, 75 FR 34279, 6/16/2010, effective 7/16/2010; FAC 2005-45, 75 FR 53135, 8/30/2010, effective 10/1/2010]

52.214-27 Price Reduction for Defective Certified Cost or Pricing Data—Modifications—Sealed Bidding.

As prescribed in 14.201-7(b), insert the following clause:

PRICE REDUCTION FOR DEFECTIVE CERTIFIED COST OR PRICING DATA—MODIFICATIONS—SEALED BIDDING (AUG 2011)

(a) This clause shall become operative only for any modification to this contract involving aggregate increases and/or decreases in costs, plus applicable profits, expected to exceed the threshold for the submission of certified cost or pricing data at FAR 15.403-4(a)(1), except that this clause does not apply to a modification if an exception under FAR 15.403-1(b) applies.

(b) If any price, including profit, negotiated in connection with any modification under this clause, was increased by any significant amount because (1) the Contractor or a subcontractor furnished certified cost or pricing data that were not complete, accurate, and current as certified in its Certificate of Current Cost or Pricing Data, (2) a subcontractor or prospective subcontractor furnished the Contractor certified cost or pricing data that were not complete, accurate, and current as certified in the Contractor's Certificate of Current Cost or Pricing Data, or (3) any of these parties furnished data of any description that were not accurate, the price shall be reduced accordingly and the contract shall be modified to reflect the reduction. This right to a price reduction is limited to that resulting from defects in data relating to modifications for which this clause becomes operative under paragraph (a) of this clause.

(c) Any reduction in the contract price under paragraph (b) of this clause due to defective data from a prospective subcontractor that was not subsequently awarded the subcontract shall be limited to the amount, plus applicable overhead and profit markup, by which (1) the actual subcontract or (2) the actual cost to the Contractor, if there was no subcontract, was less than the prospective subcontract cost estimate submitted by the Contractor; provided, that the actual subcontract price was not itself affected by defective certified cost or pricing data.

(d)(1) If the Contracting Officer determines under paragraph (b) of this clause that a price or cost reduction should be made, the Contractor agrees not to raise the following matters as a defense:

(i) The Contractor or subcontractor was a sole source supplier or otherwise was in a superior bargaining position and thus the price of the contract would not have been modified even if accurate, complete, and current certified cost or pricing data had been submitted.

(ii) The Contracting Officer should have known that the certified cost or pricing data in issue were defective even though the Contractor or subcontractor took no affirmative action to bring the character of the data to the attention of the Contracting Officer.

(iii) The contract was based on an agreement about the total cost of the contract and there was no agreement about the cost of each item procured under the contract.

(iv) The Contractor or subcontractor did not submit a Certificate of Current Cost or Pricing Data.

(2) (i) Except as prohibited by subdivision (d) (2) (ii) of this clause, an offset in an amount determined appropriate by the Contracting Officer based upon the facts shall be allowed against the amount of a contract price reduction if—

(A) The Contractor certifies to the Contracting Officer that, to the best of the Contractor's knowledge and belief, the Contractor is entitled to the offset in the amount requested; and

(B) The Contractor proves that the certified cost or pricing data were available before the date of agreement on the price of the contract (or price of the modification) and that the data were not submitted before such date.

(ii) An offset shall not be allowed if—

(A) The understated data was known by the Contractor to be understated when the Certificate of Current Cost or Pricing Data was signed; or

(B) The Government proves that the facts demonstrate that the contract price would not have increased in the amount to be offset even if the available data had been submitted before the date of agreement on price.

(e) If any reduction in the contract price under this clause reduces the price of items for which payment was made prior to the date of the modification reflecting the price reduction, the Contractor shall be liable to and shall pay the United States at the time such overpayment is repaid—

(1) Interest compounded daily, as required by 26 U.S.C. 6622, on the amount of such overpayment to be computed from the date(s) of overpayment to the Contractor to the date the Government is repaid by the Contractor at the applicable underpayment rate effective for each quarter prescribed by the Secretary of the Treasury under 26 U.S.C. 6621 (a) (2); and

(2) A penalty equal to the amount of the overpayment, if the Contractor or subcontractor knowingly submitted certified cost or pricing data which were incomplete, inaccurate, or noncurrent.

(End of clause)

[FAC 84-5, 50 FR 1747, 1/11/85, effective 4/1/85; FAC 84-35, 53 FR 10830, 4/1/88, effective 4/4/88 for DoD, NASA, Coast Guard, effective 5/2/88 for all other agencies; FAC 90-3, 55 FR 52797, 12/21/90, effective 1/22/91; Interim rule, FAC 90-10, 56 FR 67415, 12/30/91, effective 12/30/91; Final rule, FAC 90-20, 59 FR 11368, 3/10/94, effective 3/10/94; FAC 90-22, 59 FR 62498, 12/5/94, effective 12/5/94; FAC 90-32, 60 FR 48206, 9/18/95, effective 10/1/95; FAC 97-2, 62 FR 51224, 9/30/97, effective 10/10/97; FAC 2005-45, 75 FR 53135, 8/30/2010, effective 10/1/2010; FAC 2005-53, 76 FR 39242, 7/5/2011, effective 8/4/2011]

52.214-28 Subcontractor Certified Cost or Pricing Data—Modifications—Sealed Bidding.

As prescribed in 14.201-7(c), insert the following clause in solicitations and contracts:

SUBCONTRACTOR CERTIFIED COST OR PRICING DATA—MODIFICATIONS—SEALED BIDDING (OCT 2010)

(a) The requirements of paragraphs (b) and (c) of this clause shall—

(1) Become operative only for any modification to this contract involving aggregate increases and/or decreases in costs, plus applicable profits, expected to exceed the threshold for submission of certified cost or pricing data at 48 CFR 15.403-4(a)(1); and

(2) Be limited to such modifications.

(b) Before awarding any subcontract expected to exceed the threshold for submission of certified cost or pricing data at FAR 15.403-4(a)(1), on the date of agreement on price or the date of award, whichever is later, or before pricing any subcontract modifications involving aggregate increases and/or decreases in costs, plus applicable profits, expected to exceed the threshold for submission of certified cost or pricing data at FAR 15.403-4(a)(1), the Contractor shall require the subcontractor to submit certified cost or pricing data (actually or by specific identification in writing), as part of the subcontractor's proposal in accordance with FAR 15.408, Table 15-2 (to include any information reasonably required to explain the subcontractor's estimating process such as the judgmental factors applied and the mathematical or other methods used in the estimate, including those used in projecting from known data, and the nature and amount of any contingencies included in the price), unless an exception under FAR 15.403-1(b) applies.

(c) The Contractor shall require the subcontractor to certify in substantially the form prescribed in subsection 15.406-2 of the Federal Acquisition Regulation that, to the best of its knowledge and belief, the data submitted under paragraph (b) above were accurate, complete, and current as of the date of agreement on the negotiated price of the subcontract or subcontract modification.

(d) The Contractor shall insert the substance of this clause, including this paragraph (d), in each subcontract that, when entered into, exceeds the threshold for submission of certified cost or pricing data at FAR 15.403-4(a)(1).

(End of clause)

[FAC 84-5, 50 FR 1747, 1/11/85, effective 4/1/85; Interim rule, FAC 90-10, 56 FR 67415, 12/30/91, effective 12/30/91; Final rule, FAC 90-20, 59 FR 11368, 3/10/94, effective 3/10/94; FAC 90-22, 59 FR 62498, 12/5/94, effective 12/5/94; FAC 90-32, 60 FR 48206, 9/18/95, effective 10/1/95; FAC 97-2, 62 FR 51224, 9/30/97, effective 10/10/97; FAC 2005-45, 75 FR 53135, 8/30/2010, effective 10/1/2010]

52.214-29 Order of Precedence—Sealed Bidding.

As prescribed in 14.201-7(d), insert the following clause:

ORDER OF PRECEDENCE—SEALED BIDDING (JAN 1986)

Any inconsistency in this solicitation or contract shall be resolved by giving precedence in the following order:

(a) The Schedule (excluding the specifications);

(b) Representations and other instructions;

(c) Contract clauses;

(d) Other documents, exhibits, and attachments; and

(e) The specifications.

(End of clause)

[FAC 84-12, 51 FR 2666, 1/17/86, effective 1/20/86; FAC 90-22, 59 FR 62498, 12/5/94, effective 12/5/94; FAC 90-32, 60 FR 48206, 9/18/95, effective 10/1/95]

52.214-30 [Reserved]

[FAC 90-45, Final rule, 62 FR 224, 1/2/97, effective 1/1/97; FAC 2001-26, 69 FR 76341, 12/20/2004, effective 1/1/2005]

52.214-31 Facsimile Bids.

As prescribed in 14.201-6(v), insert the following provision:

FACSIMILE BIDS (DEC 1989)

(a) *Definition. Facsimile bid,* as used in this solicitation, means a bid, modification of a bid, or withdrawal of a bid, that is transmitted to and received by the Government via electronic equipment that communicates and reproduces both printed and handwritten material.

(b) Bidders may submit facsimile bids as responses to this solicitation. These responses must arrive at the place and by the time, specified in the solicitation.

(c) Facsimile bids that fail to furnish required representations or information or that reject any of the terms, conditions, and provisions of the solicitation may be excluded from consideration.

(d) Facsimile bids must contain the required signatures.

(e) The Government reserves the right to make award solely on the facsimile bid. However, if requested to do so by the Contracting Officer, the apparently successful bidder agrees to promptly submit the complete original signed bid.

(f) Facsimile receiving data and compatibility characteristics are as follows:

(1) Telephone number of receiving facsimile equipment:

____

(2) Compatibility characteristics of receiving facsimile equipment (*e.g.*, make and model number, receiving speed, communications protocol):

____

(g) If the bidder chooses to transmit a facsimile bid, the Government will not be responsible for any failure attributable to the transmission or receipt of the facsimile bid including, but not limited to, the following:

(1) Receipt of garbled or incomplete bid.

(2) Availability or condition of the receiving facsimile equipment.

(3) Incompatibility between the sending and receiving equipment.

(4) Delay in transmission or receipt of bid.

(5) Failure of the bidder to properly identify the bid.

(6) Illegibility of bid.

(7) Security of bid data.

(End of provision)

[FAC 84-53, 54 FR 48992, 11/28/89, effective 12/28/89; FAC 97-14, 64 FR 51828, 9/24/99, effective 11/23/99]

52.214-32 [Reserved]

[Removed and reserved, FAC 97-14, 64 FR 51828, 9/24/99, effective 11/23/99; CFR Correction, 74 FR 49826, 9/29/2009]

52.214-33 [Reserved]

[Removed and reserved, FAC 97-14, 64 FR 51828, 9/24/99, effective 11/23/99; CFR Correction, 74 FR 49826, 9/29/2009]

52.214-34 Submission of Offers in the English Language.

As prescribed in 14.201-6(w), insert the following provision:

SUBMISSION OF OFFERS IN THE ENGLISH LANGUAGE (APR 1991)

Offers submitted in response to this solicitation shall be in the English language. Offers received in other than English shall be rejected.

(End of provision)

[FAC 90-4, 56 FR 15155, 4/15/91, effective 5/15/91; corrected, 56 FR 33487, 7/22/91; interim rule, FAC 90-18, 58 FR 31140, 5/28/93, effective 5/28/93; interim rule adopted as final, FAC 90-39, 61 FR 31612, 6/20/96, effective 6/20/96; FAC, 97-2, 62 FR 51224, 9/30/97, effective 10/10/97; FAC 97-14, 64 FR 51828, 9/24/99, effective 11/23/99; FAC 97-15, 64 FR 72414, 12/27/99, effective 2/25/2000]

52.214-35 Submission of Offers in U.S. Currency.

As prescribed in 14.201-6(x), insert the following provision:

SUBMISSION OF OFFERS IN U.S. CURRENCY (APR 1991)

Offers submitted in response to this solicitation shall be in terms of U.S. dollars. Offers received in other than U.S. dollars shall be rejected.

(End of provision)

[FAC 90-4, 56 FR 15155, 4/15/91, effective 5/15/91; interim rule, FAC 90-18, 58 FR 31140, 5/28/93, effective 5/28/93; interim rule adopted as final, FAC 90-39, 61 FR 31612, 6/20/96, effective 6/20/96; FAC 97-2, 62 FR 51224, 9/30/97, effective 10/10/97; FAC 97-14, 64 FR 51828, 9/24/99, effective

11/23/99; FAC 97-15, 64 FR 72414, 12/27/99, effective 2/25/2000]

52.215-1 Instructions to Offerors—Competitive Acquisition.

As prescribed in 15.209(a), insert the following provision:

INSTRUCTIONS TO OFFERORS—COMPETITIVE ACQUISITION (JAN 2017)

(a) *Definitions*. As used in this provision—

Discussions are negotiations that occur after establishment of the competitive range that may, at the Contracting Officer's discretion, result in the offeror being allowed to revise its proposal.

In writing, writing, or *written* means any worded or numbered expression that can be read, reproduced, and later communicated, and includes electronically transmitted and stored information.

Proposal modification is a change made to a proposal before the solicitation's closing date and time, or made in response to an amendment, or made to correct a mistake at any time before award.

Proposal revision is a change to a proposal made after the solicitation closing date, at the request of or as allowed by a Contracting Officer as the result of negotiations.

Time, if stated as a number of days, is calculated using calendar days, unless otherwise specified, and will include Saturdays, Sundays, and legal holidays. However, if the last day falls on a Saturday, Sunday, or legal holiday, then the period shall include the next working day.

(b) *Amendments to solicitations*. If this solicitation is amended, all terms and conditions that are not amended remain unchanged. Offerors shall acknowledge receipt of any amendment to this solicitation by the date and time specified in the amendment(s).

(c) *Submission, modification, revision, and withdrawal of proposals*. (1) Unless other methods (*e.g.*, electronic commerce or facsimile) are permitted in the solicitation, proposals and modifications to proposals shall be submitted in paper media in sealed envelopes or packages (i) addressed to the office specified in the solicitation, and (ii) showing the time and date specified for receipt, the solicitation number, and the name and address of the offeror. Offerors using commercial carriers should ensure that the proposal is marked on the outermost wrapper with the information in paragraphs (c)(1)(i) and (c)(1)(ii) of this provision.

(2) The first page of the proposal must show—

(i) The solicitation number;

(ii) The name, address, and telephone and facsimile numbers of the offeror (and electronic address if available);

(iii) A statement specifying the extent of agreement with all terms, conditions, and provisions included in the solicitation and agreement to furnish any or all items upon which prices are offered at the price set opposite each item;

(iv) Names, titles, and telephone and facsimile numbers (and electronic addresses if available) of persons authorized to negotiate on the offeror's behalf with the Government in connection with this solicitation; and

(v) Name, title, and signature of person authorized to sign the proposal. Proposals signed by an agent shall be accompanied by evidence of that agent's authority, unless that evidence has been previously furnished to the issuing office.

(3) *Submission, modification, revision, and withdrawal of proposals*. (i) Offerors are responsible for submitting proposals, and any modifications or revisions, so as to reach the Government office designated in the solicitation by the time specified in the solicitation. If no time is specified in the solicitation, the time for receipt is 4:30 p.m., local time, for the designated Government office on the date that proposal or revision is due.

(ii)(A) Any proposal, modification, or revision, received at the Government office designated in the solicitation after the exact time specified for receipt of offers is "late" and will not be considered unless it is received before award is made, the Contracting Officer determines that accepting the late offer would not unduly delay the acquisition; and—

(1) If it was transmitted through an electronic commerce method authorized by the solicitation, it was received at the initial point of entry to the Government infrastructure not later than 5:00 p.m. one working day prior to the date specified for receipt of proposals; or

(2) There is acceptable evidence to establish that it was received at the Government installation designated for receipt of offers and was under the Government's control prior to the time set for receipt of offers; or

(3) It is the only proposal received.

(B) However, a late modification of an otherwise successful proposal that makes its terms more favorable to the Government, will be considered at any time it is received and may be accepted.

(iii) Acceptable evidence to establish the time of receipt at the Government installation includes the time/date stamp of that installation on the proposal wrapper, other documentary evidence of receipt maintained by the installation, or oral testimony or statements of Government personnel.

(iv) If an emergency or unanticipated event interrupts normal Government processes so that proposals cannot be received at the office designated for receipt of proposals by the exact time specified in the solicitation, and urgent Government requirements preclude amendment of the solicitation, the time specified for receipt of proposals will be deemed to be extended to the same time of day specified in the solicitation on the first work day on which normal Government processes resume.

(v) Proposals may be withdrawn by written notice received at any time before award. Oral proposals in response to oral solicitations may be withdrawn orally. If the solicitation authorizes facsimile proposals, proposals may be withdrawn via facsimile received at any time before award, subject to the conditions specified in the provision at 52.215-5, Facsimile Proposals. Proposals may be withdrawn in person by an offeror or an authorized representative, if the identity of the person requesting withdrawal is established and the person signs a receipt for the proposal before award.

(4) Unless otherwise specified in the solicitation, the offeror may propose to provide any item or combination of items.

(5) Offerors shall submit proposals in response to this solicitation in English, unless otherwise permitted by the solicitation, and in U.S. dollars, unless the provision at FAR 52.225-17, Evaluation of Foreign Currency Offers, is included in the solicitation.

(6) Offerors may submit modifications to their proposals at any time before the solicitation closing date and time, and may submit modifications in response to an amendment, or to correct a mistake at any time before award.

(7) Offerors may submit revised proposals only if requested or allowed by the Contracting Officer.

(8) Proposals may be withdrawn at any time before award. Withdrawals are effective upon receipt of notice by the Contracting Officer.

(d) *Offer expiration date.* Proposals in response to this solicitation will be valid for the number of days specified on the solicitation cover sheet (unless a different period is proposed by the offeror).

(e) *Restriction on disclosure and use of data.* Offerors that include in their proposals data that they do not want disclosed to the public for any purpose, or used by the Government except for evaluation purposes, shall—

(1) Mark the title page with the following legend:

This proposal includes data that shall not be disclosed outside the Government and shall not be duplicated, used, or disclosed—in whole or in part—for any purpose other than to evaluate this proposal. If, however, a contract is awarded to this offeror as a result of—or in connection with—the submission of this data, the Government shall have the right to duplicate, use, or disclose the data to the extent provided in the resulting contract. This restriction does not limit the Government's right to use information contained in this data if it is obtained from another source without restriction. The data subject to this restriction are contained in sheets [*insert numbers or other identification of sheets*]; and

(2) Mark each sheet of data it wishes to restrict with the following legend:

Use or disclosure of data contained on this sheet is subject to the restriction on the title page of this proposal.

(f) *Contract award.* (1) The Government intends to award a contract or contracts resulting from this solicitation to the responsible offeror(s) whose proposal(s) represents the best value after evaluation in accordance with the factors and subfactors in the solicitation.

(2) The Government may reject any or all proposals if such action is in the Government's interest.

(3) The Government may waive informalities and minor irregularities in proposals received.

(4) The Government intends to evaluate proposals and award a contract without discussions with offerors (except clarifications as described in FAR 15.306(a)). Therefore, the offeror's initial proposal should contain the offeror's best terms from a cost or price and technical standpoint. The Government reserves the right to conduct discussions if the Contracting Officer later determines them to be necessary. If the Contracting Officer determines that the number of proposals that would otherwise be in the competitive range exceeds the number at which an efficient competition can be conducted, the Contracting Officer may limit the number of proposals in the competitive range to the greatest number that will permit an efficient competition among the most highly rated proposals.

(5) The Government reserves the right to make an award on any item for a quantity less than the quantity offered, at the unit cost or prices offered, unless the offeror specifies otherwise in the proposal.

(6) The Government reserves the right to make multiple awards if, after considering the additional administrative costs, it is in the Government's best interest to do so.

(7) Exchanges with offerors after receipt of a proposal do not constitute a rejection or counteroffer by the Government.

(8) The Government may determine that a proposal is unacceptable if the prices proposed are materially unbalanced between line items or subline items. Unbalanced pricing exists when, despite an acceptable total evaluated price, the price of one or more contract line items is significantly overstated or understated as indicated by the application of cost or price analysis techniques. A proposal may be rejected if the Contracting Officer determines that the lack of balance poses an unacceptable risk to the Government.

(9) If a cost realism analysis is performed, cost realism may be considered by the source selection authority in evaluating performance or schedule risk.

(10) A written award or acceptance of proposal mailed or otherwise furnished to the successful offeror within the time specified in the proposal shall result in a binding contract without further action by either party.

(11) If a post-award debriefing is given to requesting offerors, the Government shall disclose the following information, if applicable:

(i) The agency's evaluation of the significant weak or deficient factors in the debriefed offeror's offer.

(ii) The overall evaluated cost or price and technical rating of the successful and the debriefed offeror and past performance information on the debriefed offeror.

(iii) The overall ranking of all offerors, when any ranking was developed by the agency during source selection.

(iv) A summary of the rationale for award.

(v) For acquisitions of commercial items, the make and model of the item to be delivered by the successful offeror.

(vi) Reasonable responses to relevant questions posed by the debriefed offeror as to whether source-selection procedures set forth in the solicitation, applicable regulations, and other applicable authorities were followed by the agency.

(End of provision)

Alternate I (OCT 1997). As prescribed in 15.209(a)(1), substitute the following paragraph (f)(4) for paragraph (f)(4) of the basic provision:

(f)(4) The Government intends to evaluate proposals and award a contract after conducting discussions with offerors whose proposals have been determined to be within the competitive range. If the Contracting Officer determines that the number of proposals that would otherwise be in the competitive range exceeds the number at which an efficient competition can be conducted, the Contracting Officer may limit the number of proposals in the competitive range to the greatest number that will permit an efficient competition among the most highly rated proposals. Therefore, the offeror's initial proposal should contain the offeror's best terms from a price and technical standpoint.

Alternate II (OCT 1997). As prescribed in 15.209(a)(2), add a paragraph (c)(9) substantially the same as the following to the basic clause:

(9) Offerors may submit proposals that depart from stated requirements. Such proposals shall clearly identify why the acceptance of the proposal would be advantageous to the Government. Any deviations from the terms and conditions of the solicitation, as well as the comparative advantage to the Government, shall be clearly identified and explicitly defined. The Government reserves the right to amend the solicitation to allow all offerors an opportunity to submit revised proposals based on the revised requirements.

[FAC 97-2, 62 FR 51224, 9/30/97, effective 10/10/97; FAC 97-14, 64 FR 51828, 9/24/99, effective 11/23/99; FAC 97-15, 64 FR 72414, 12/27/99, effective 12/27/99; FAC 97-15, 64 FR 72414, 12/27/99, effective 2/25/2000; FAC 97-22, 66 FR 2116, 1/10/2001, effective 3/12/2001; Delay of effective date, 66 FR 14259, 3/9/2001, effective 5/11/2001; FAC 2001-18, 68 FR 69257, 12/11/2003, effective 1/12/2004; FAC 2005-95, 82 FR 4709, 1/13/2017, effective 1/13/2017]

52.215-2 Audit and Records—Negotiation.

As prescribed in 15.209(b), insert the following clause:

AUDIT AND RECORDS—NEGOTIATION (OCT 2010)

(a) As used in this clause, records includes books, documents, accounting procedures and practices, and other data, regardless of type and regardless of whether such items are in written form, in the form of computer data, or in any other form.

(b) *Examination of costs.* If this is a cost-reimbursement, incentive, time-and-materials, labor-hour, or price redeterminable contract, or any combination of these, the Contractor shall maintain and the Contracting Officer, or an authorized representative of the Contracting Officer, shall have the right to examine and audit all records and other evidence sufficient to reflect properly all costs claimed to have been incurred or anticipated to be incurred directly or indirectly in performance of this contract. This right of examination shall include inspection at all reasonable times of the Contractor's plants, or parts of them, engaged in performing the contract.

(c) *Certified cost or pricing data.* If the Contractor has been required to submit certified cost or pricing data in connection with any pricing action relating to this contract, the Contracting Officer, or an authorized representative of the Contracting Officer, in order to evaluate the accuracy, completeness, and currency of the certified cost or pricing data, shall have the right to examine and audit all of the Contractor's records, including computations and projections, related to—

(1) The proposal for the contract, subcontract, or modification;

(2) The discussions conducted on the proposal(s), including those related to negotiating;

(3) Pricing of the contract, subcontract, or modification; or

(4) Performance of the contract, subcontract or modification.

(d) *Comptroller General*—(1) The Comptroller General of the United States, or an authorized representative, shall have access to and the right to examine any of the Contractor's directly pertinent records involving transactions related to this contract or a subcontract hereunder and to interview any current employee regarding such transactions.

(2) This paragraph may not be construed to require the Contractor or subcontractor to create or maintain any record that the Contractor or subcontractor does not maintain in the ordinary course of business or pursuant to a provision of law.

(e) *Reports.* If the Contractor is required to furnish cost, funding, or performance reports, the Contracting Officer or an authorized representative of the Contracting Officer shall have the right to examine and audit the supporting records and materials, for the purpose of evaluating (1) the effectiveness of the Contractor's policies and procedures to produce data compatible with the objectives of these reports and (2) the data reported.

(f) *Availability.* The Contractor shall make available at its office at all reasonable times the records, materials, and other evidence described in paragraphs (a), (b), (c), (d), and (e) of this clause, for examination, audit, or reproduction, until 3 years after final payment under this contract or for any shorter period specified in Subpart 4.7, Contractor Records Retention, of the Federal Acquisition Regulation (FAR), or for any longer period required by statute or by other clauses of this contract. In addition—

(1) If this contract is completely or partially terminated, the Contractor shall make available the records relating to the work terminated until 3 years after any resulting final termination settlement; and

(2) The Contractor shall make available records relating to appeals under the Disputes clause or to litigation or the settlement of claims arising under or relating to this contract until such appeals, litigation, or claims are finally resolved.

(g) The Contractor shall insert a clause containing all the terms of this clause, including this paragraph (g), in all subcontracts under this contract that exceed the simplified acquisition threshold, and—

(1) That are cost-reimbursement, incentive, time-and-materials, labor-hour, or price-redeterminable type or any combination of these;

(2) For which certified cost or pricing data are required; or

(3) That require the subcontractor to furnish reports as discussed in paragraph (e) of this clause.

The clause may be altered only as necessary to identify properly the contracting parties and the Contracting Officer under the Government prime contract.

(End of clause)

Alternate I (MAR 2009). As prescribed in 15.209(b)(2), substitute the following paragraphs (d)(1) and (g) for paragraphs (d)(1) and (g) of the basic clause:

(d) *Comptroller General or Inspector General.* (1) The Comptroller General of the United States, an appropriate Inspector General appointed under section 3 or 8G of the Inspector General Act of 1978 (5 U.S.C. App.), or an authorized representative of either of the foregoing officials, shall have access to and the right to—

(i) Examine any of the Contractor's or any subcontractor's records that pertain to and involve transactions relating to this contract or a subcontract hereunder; and

(ii) Interview any officer or employee regarding such transactions.

(g)(1) Except as provided in paragraph (g)(2) of this clause, the Contractor shall insert a clause containing all the terms of this clause, including this paragraph (g), in all subcontracts under this contract. The clause may be altered only as necessary to identify properly the contracting parties and the Contracting Officer under the Government prime contract.

(2) The authority of the Inspector General under paragraph (d)(1)(ii) of this clause does not flow down to subcontracts.

Alternate II (AUG 2016). As prescribed in 15.209(b)(3), add the following paragraph (h) to the basic clause:

(h) The provisions of the OMB Uniform Guidance at 2 CFR part 200, subpart F apply to this contract.

Alternate III (JUN 1999). As prescribed in 15.209(b)(4), delete paragraph (d) of the basic clause and redesignate the remaining paragraphs accordingly, and substitute the following paragraph (e) for the redesignated paragraph (e) of the basic clause:

(e) *Availability.* The Contractor shall make available at its office at all reasonable times the records, materials, and other evidence described in paragraphs (a), (b), (c), and (d) of this clause, for examination, audit, or reproduction, until 3 years after final payment under this contract or for any shorter period specified in Subpart 4.7, Contractor Records Retention, of the Federal Acquisition Regulation (FAR), or for any longer period required by statute or by other clauses of this contract. In addition—

(1) If this contract is completely or partially terminated, the Contractor shall make available the records relating to the work terminated until 3 years after any resulting final termination settlement; and

(2) The Contractor shall make available records relating to appeals under the Disputes clause or to litigation or the settlement of claims arising under or relating to this contract until such appeals, litigation, or claims are finally resolved.

[FAC 90-31, 60 FR 42648, 8/16/95, effective 10/1/95; FAC 90-40, 61 FR 39186, 7/26/96, effective 8/26/96; FAC 90-45, Final rule, 62 FR 224, 1/2/97, effective 1/1/97; FAC 97-2, 62 FR 51224, 9/30/97, effective 10/10/97; FAC 97-4, 63 FR 9048, 2/23/98, effective 4/24/98; FAC 97-12, 64 FR 32740, 6/17/99, effective 6/17/99; FAC 2005-17, 72 FR 27364, 5/15/2007, effective 6/14/2007; FAC 2005-32, 74 FR 14646, 14649, 3/31/2009, effective 3/31/2009; FAC 2005-37, 74 FR 52851, 10/14/2009, effective 10/14/2009; FAC 2005-42, 75 FR 34279, 6/16/2010, effective 7/16/2010; FAC 2005-45, 75 FR 53135, 8/30/2010, effective 10/1/2010; FAC 2005-89, 81 FR 45852, 7/14/2016, effective 8/15/2016]

52.215-3 Request for Information or Solicitation for Planning Purposes.

As prescribed in 15.209(c), insert the following provision:

REQUEST FOR INFORMATION OR SOLICITATION FOR PLANNING PURPOSES (OCT 1997)

(a) The Government does not intend to award a contract on the basis of this solicitation or to otherwise pay for the information solicited except as an allowable cost under other contracts as provided in subsection 31.205-18, Bid and proposal costs, of the Federal Acquisition Regulation.

(b) Although "proposal" and "offeror" are used in this Request for Information, your response will be treated as information only. It shall not be used as a proposal.

(c) This solicitation is issued for the purpose of: [*state purpose*].

(End of provision)

[FAC 97-2, 62 FR 51224, 9/30/97, effective 10/10/97]

52.215-4 [Reserved]

[Removed and reserved, FAC 97-9, 63 FR 58587, 10/30/98, effective 10/30/98, finalized without change, FAC 97-12, 64 FR 32740, 6/17/99]

52.215-5 Facsimile Proposals.

As prescribed in 15.209(e), insert the following provision:

FACSIMILE PROPOSALS (OCT 1997)

(a) *Definition. Facsimile proposal*, as used in this provision, means a proposal, revision or modification of a proposal, or withdrawal of a proposal that is transmitted to and received by the Government via facsimile machine.

(b) Offerors may submit facsimile proposals as responses to this solicitation. Facsimile proposals are subject to the same rules as paper proposals.

(c) The telephone number of receiving facsimile equipment is: [*insert telephone number*].

(d) If any portion of a facsimile proposal received by the Contracting Officer is unreadable to the degree that conformance to the essential requirements of the solicitation cannot be ascertained from the document—

(1) The Contracting Officer immediately shall notify the offeror and permit the offeror to resubmit the proposal;

(2) The method and time for resubmission shall be prescribed by the Contracting Officer after consultation with the offeror; and

(3) The resubmission shall be considered as if it were received at the date and time of the original unreadable submission for the purpose of determining timeliness, provided the offeror complies with the time and format requirements for resubmission prescribed by the Contracting Officer.

(e) The Government reserves the right to make award solely on the facsimile proposal. However, if requested to do so by the Contracting Officer, the apparently successful offeror promptly shall submit the complete original signed proposal.

(End of provision)

[FAC 97-2, 62 FR 51224, 9/30/97, effective 10/10/97]

52.215-6 Place of Performance.

As prescribed in 15.209(f), insert the following provision:

PLACE OF PERFORMANCE (OCT 1997)

(a) The offeror or respondent, in the performance of any contract resulting from this solicitation, [] intends, [] does not intend [check applicable block] to use one or more plants or facilities located at a different address from the address of the offeror or respondent as indicated in this proposal or response to request for information.

(b) If the offeror or respondent checks "intends" in paragraph (a) of this provision, it shall insert in the following spaces the required information:

Place of performance (street address, city, state, county, zip code)	Name and address of owner and operator of the plant or facility if other than offeror or respondent

(End of Provision)

[FAC 97-2, 62 FR 51224, 9/30/97, effective 10/10/97]

52.215-7 [Reserved]

[FAC 97-2, 62 FR 51224, 9/30/97, effective 10/10/97; FAC 2001-26, 69 FR 76341, 12/20/2004, effective 1/1/2005]

52.215-8 Order of Precedence—Uniform Contract Format.

As prescribed in 15.209(h), insert the following clause:

ORDER OF PRECEDENCE—UNIFORM CONTRACT FORMAT (OCT 1997)

Any inconsistency in this solicitation or contract shall be resolved by giving precedence in the following order:

(a) The Schedule (excluding the specifications).

(b) Representations and other instructions.

(c) Contract clauses.

(d) Other documents, exhibits, and attachments.

(e) The specifications.

(End of clause)

[FAC 97-2, 62 FR 51224, 9/30/97, effective 10/10/97]

52.215-9 Changes or Additions to Make-or-Buy Program.

As prescribed in 15.408(a), insert the following clause:

CHANGES OR ADDITIONS TO MAKE-OR-BUY PROGRAM (OCT 1997)

(a) The Contractor shall perform in accordance with the make-or-buy program incorporated in this contract. If the Contractor proposes to change the program, the Contractor shall, reasonably in advance of the proposed change, (1) notify the Contracting Officer in writing, and (2) submit justification in sufficient detail to permit evaluation. Changes in the place of performance of any "make" items in the program are subject to this requirement.

(b) For items deferred at the time of negotiation of this contract for later addition to the program, the Contractor shall, at the earliest possible time—

(1) Notify the Contracting Officer of each proposed addition; and

(2) Provide justification in sufficient detail to permit evaluation.

(c) Modification of the make-or-buy program to incorporate proposed changes or additions shall be effective upon the Contractor's receipt of the Contracting Officer's written approval.

(End of clause)

Alternate I (OCT 2010). As prescribed in 15.408(a)(1) add the following paragraph (d) to the basic clause:

(d) If the Contractor desires to reverse the categorization of "make" or "buy" for any item or items designated in the contract as subject to this paragraph, it shall—

(1) Support its proposal with certified cost or pricing data in accordance with FAR 15.408, Table 15-2 when required by FAR 15.403, and data other than certified cost or pricing data, to permit evaluation; and

(2) After approval is granted, promptly negotiate with the Contracting Officer an equitable reduction in the contract price in accordance with paragraph (k) of the Incentive Price Revision—Firm Target clause or paragraph (m) of the Incentive Price Revision—Successive Targets clause of this contract.

Alternate II (OCT 2010). As prescribed in 15.408(a)(2), add the following paragraph (d) to the basic clause:

(d) If the Contractor desires to reverse the categorization of "make" or "buy" for any item or items designated in the contract as subject to this paragraph, it shall—

(1) Support its proposal with certified cost or pricing data in accordance with FAR 15.408, Table 15-2, when required by FAR 15.403, and data other than certified cost or pricing data, to permit evaluation; and

(2) After approval is granted, promptly negotiate with the Contracting Officer an equitable reduction in the contract's total estimated cost and fee in accordance with paragraph (e) of the Incentive Fee clause of this contract.

[FAC 97-2, 62 FR 51224, 9/30/97, effective 10/10/97; FAC 2005-45, 75 FR 53135, 8/30/2010, effective 10/1/2010]

52.215-10 Price Reduction for Defective Certified Cost or Pricing Data.

As prescribed in 15.408(b), insert the following clause:

PRICE REDUCTION FOR DEFECTIVE CERTIFIED COST OR PRICING DATA (AUG 2011)

(a) If any price, including profit or fee, negotiated in connection with this contract, or any cost reimbursable under this contract, was increased by any significant amount because—

(1) The Contractor or a subcontractor furnished certified cost or pricing data that were not complete, accurate, and current as certified in its Certificate of Current Cost or Pricing Data;

(2) A subcontractor or prospective subcontractor furnished the Contractor certified

cost or pricing data that were not complete, accurate, and current as certified in the Contractor's Certificate of Current Cost or Pricing Data; or

(3) Any of these parties furnished data of any description that were not accurate, the price or cost shall be reduced accordingly and the contract shall be modified to reflect the reduction.

(b) Any reduction in the contract price under paragraph (a) of this clause due to defective data from a prospective subcontractor that was not subsequently awarded the subcontract shall be limited to the amount, plus applicable overhead and profit markup, by which (1) the actual subcontract or (2) the actual cost to the Contractor, if there was no subcontract, was less than the prospective subcontract cost estimate submitted by the Contractor; provided, that the actual subcontract price was not itself affected by defective certified cost or pricing data.

(c)(1) If the Contracting Officer determines under paragraph (a) of this clause that a price or cost reduction should be made, the Contractor agrees not to raise the following matters as a defense:

(i) The Contractor or subcontractor was a sole source supplier or otherwise was in a superior bargaining position and thus the price of the contract would not have been modified even if accurate, complete, and current certified cost or pricing data had been submitted.

(ii) The Contracting Officer should have known that the certified cost or pricing data in issue were defective even though the Contractor or subcontractor took no affirmative action to bring the character of the data to the attention of the Contracting Officer.

(iii) The contract was based on an agreement about the total cost of the contract and there was no agreement about the cost of each item procured under the contract.

(iv) The Contractor or subcontractor did not submit a Certificate of Current Cost or Pricing Data.

(2)(i) Except as prohibited by subdivision (c)(2)(ii) of this clause, an offset in an amount determined appropriate by the Contracting Officer based upon the facts shall be allowed against the amount of a contract price reduction if—

(A) The Contractor certifies to the Contracting Officer that, to the best of the Contractor's knowledge and belief, the Contractor is entitled to the offset in the amount requested; and

(B) The Contractor proves that the certified cost or pricing data were available before the "as of" date specified on its Certificate of Current Cost or Pricing Data, and that the data were not submitted before such date.

(ii) An offset shall not be allowed if—

(A) The understated data were known by the Contractor to be understated before the "as of" date specified on its Certificate of Current Cost or Pricing Data; or

(B) The Government proves that the facts demonstrate that the contract price would not have increased in the amount to be offset even if the available data had been submitted before the "as of" date specified on its Certificate of Current Cost or Pricing Data.

(d) If any reduction in the contract price under this clause reduces the price of items for which payment was made prior to the date of the modification reflecting the price reduction, the Contractor shall be liable to and shall pay the United States at the time such overpayment is repaid—

(1) Interest compounded daily, as required by 26 U.S.C. 6622, on the amount of such overpayment to be computed from the date(s) of overpayment to the Contractor to the date the Government is repaid by the Contractor at the applicable underpayment rate effective for each quarter prescribed by the Secretary of the Treasury under 26 U.S.C. 6621(a)(2); and

(2) A penalty equal to the amount of the overpayment, if the Contractor or subcontractor knowingly submitted certified cost or pricing data that were incomplete, inaccurate, or noncurrent.

(End of clause)

[FAC 97-2, 62 FR 51224, 9/30/97, effective 10/10/97; FAC 2005-45, 75 FR 53135, 8/30/2010, effective 10/1/2010; FAC 2005-53, 76 FR 39242, 7/5/2011, effective 8/4/2011]

52.215-11 Price Reduction for Defective Certified Cost or Pricing Data—Modifications.

As prescribed in 15.408(c), insert the following clause:

PRICE REDUCTION FOR DEFECTIVE CERTIFIED COST OR PRICING DATA—MODIFICATIONS (AUG 2011)

(a) This clause shall become operative only for any modification to this contract involving a pricing adjustment expected to exceed the threshold for submission of certified cost or pricing data at FAR 15.403-4, except that this clause does not apply to any modification if an exception under FAR 15.403-1 applies.

(b) If any price, including profit or fee, negotiated in connection with any modification under this clause, or any cost reimbursable under this contract, was increased by any significant amount because (1) the Contractor or a subcontractor furnished certified cost or pricing data that were not complete, accurate, and current as certified in its Certificate of Current Cost or Pricing Data, (2) a subcontractor or prospective subcontractor furnished the Contractor certified cost or pricing data that were not complete, accurate, and current as certified in the Contractor's Certificate of Current Cost or Pricing Data, or (3) any of these parties furnished data of any description that were not accurate, the price or cost shall be reduced accordingly and the contract shall be modified to reflect the reduction. This right to a price reduction is limited to that resulting from defects in data relating to modifications for which this clause becomes operative under paragraph (a) of this clause.

(c) Any reduction in the contract price under paragraph (b) of this clause due to defective data from a prospective subcontractor that was not subsequently awarded the subcontract shall be limited to the amount, plus applicable overhead and profit markup, by which (1) the actual subcontract or (2) the actual cost to the Contractor, if there was no subcontract, was less than the prospective subcontract cost estimate submitted by the Contractor; provided, that the actual subcontract price was not itself affected by defective certified cost or pricing data.

(d) (1) If the Contracting Officer determines under paragraph (b) of this clause that a price or cost reduction should be made, the Contractor agrees not to raise the following matters as a defense:

(i) The Contractor or subcontractor was a sole source supplier or otherwise was in a superior bargaining position and thus the price of the contract would not have been modified even if accurate, complete, and current certified cost or pricing data had been submitted.

(ii) The Contracting Officer should have known that the certified cost or pricing data in issue were defective even though the Contractor or subcontractor took no affirmative action to bring the character of the data to the attention of the Contracting Officer.

(iii) The contract was based on an agreement about the total cost of the contract and there was no agreement about the cost of each item procured under the contract.

(iv) The Contractor or subcontractor did not submit a Certificate of Current Cost or Pricing Data.

(2) (i) Except as prohibited by subdivision (d) (2) (ii) of this clause, an offset in an amount determined appropriate by the Contracting Officer based upon the facts shall be allowed against the amount of a contract price reduction if—

(A) The Contractor certifies to the Contracting Officer that, to the best of the Contractor's knowledge and belief, the Contractor is entitled to the offset in the amount requested; and

(B) The Contractor proves that the certified cost or pricing data were available before the "as of" date specified on its Certificate of Current Cost or Pricing Data, and that the data were not submitted before such date.

(ii) An offset shall not be allowed if—

(A) The understated data were known by the Contractor to be understated before the "as of" date specified on its Certificate of Current Cost or Pricing Data; or

(B) The Government proves that the facts demonstrate that the contract price would not have increased in the amount to be offset even if the available data had been submitted before the "as of" date specified on its Certificate of Current Cost or Pricing Data.

(e) If any reduction in the contract price under this clause reduces the price of items for which payment was made prior to the date of the modification reflecting the price reduction, the Contractor shall be liable to and shall pay the United States at the time such overpayment is repaid—

(1) Interest compounded daily, as required by 26 U.S.C. 6622, on the amount of such overpayment to be computed from the date(s) of overpayment to the Contractor to the date the Government is repaid by the Contractor at the applicable underpayment rate effective for each quarter prescribed by the Secretary of the Treasury under 26 U.S.C. 6621(a)(2); and

(2) A penalty equal to the amount of the overpayment, if the Contractor or subcontractor knowingly submitted certified cost or pricing data that were incomplete, inaccurate, or noncurrent.

(End of clause)

[FAC 97-2, 62 FR 51224, 9/30/97, effective 10/10/97; FAC 2005-45, 75 FR 53135, 8/30/2010, effective 10/1/2010; FAC 2005-53, 76 FR 39242, 7/5/2011, effective 8/4/2011]

52.215-12 Subcontractor Certified Cost or Pricing Data.

As prescribed in 15.408(d), insert the following clause:

SUBCONTRACTOR CERTIFIED COST OR PRICING DATA (OCT 2010)

(a) Before awarding any subcontract expected to exceed the threshold for submission of certified cost or pricing data at FAR 15.403-4, on the date of agreement on price or the date of award, whichever is later; or before pricing any subcontract modification involving a pricing adjustment expected to exceed the threshold for submission of certified cost or pricing data at FAR 15.403-4, the Contractor shall require the subcontractor to submit certified cost or pricing data (actually or by specific identification in writing), in accordance with FAR 15.408, Table 15-2 (to include any information reasonably required to explain the subcontractor's estimating process such as the judgmental factors applied and the mathematical or other methods used in the estimate, including those used in projecting from known data, and the nature and amount of any contingencies included in the price), unless an exception under FAR 15.403-1 applies.

(b) The Contractor shall require the subcontractor to certify in substantially the form prescribed in FAR 15.406-2 that, to the best of its knowledge and belief, the data submitted under paragraph (a) of this clause were accurate, complete, and current as of the date of agreement on the negotiated price of the subcontract or subcontract modification.

(c) In each subcontract that exceeds the threshold for submission of certified cost or pricing data at FAR 15.403-4, when entered into, the Contractor shall insert either—

(1) The substance of this clause, including this paragraph (c), if paragraph (a) of this clause requires submission of certified cost or pricing data for the subcontract; or

(2) The substance of the clause at FAR 52.215-13, Subcontractor Certified Cost or Pricing Data—Modifications.

(End of clause)

[FAC 97-2, 62 FR 51224, 9/30/97, effective 10/10/97; FAC 2005-45, 75 FR 53135, 8/30/2010, effective 10/1/2010]

52.215-13 Subcontractor Certified Cost or Pricing Data—Modifications.

As prescribed in 15.408(e), insert the following clause:

SUBCONTRACTOR CERTIFIED COST OR PRICING DATA—MODIFICATIONS (OCT 2010)

(a) The requirements of paragraphs (b) and (c) of this clause shall—

(1) Become operative only for any modification to this contract involving a pricing adjustment expected to exceed the threshold for submission of certified cost or pricing data at FAR 15.403-4; and

(2) Be limited to such modifications.

(b) Before awarding any subcontract expected to exceed the threshold for submission of certified cost or pricing data at FAR 15.403-4, on the date of agreement on price or the date of award, whichever is later; or before pricing any subcontract modification involving a pricing adjustment expected to exceed the threshold for submission of certified cost or pricing data at FAR 15.403-4, the Contractor shall require the subcontractor to submit certified cost or pricing data (actually or by specific identification in writing), in accordance with FAR 15.408, Table 15-2 (to include any information reasonably required to explain the subcontractor's estimating process such as the judgmental factors applied and the mathematical or other methods used in the estimate, including those used in projecting from known data, and the nature and amount of any contingencies included in the price), unless an exception under FAR 15.403-1 applies.

(c) The Contractor shall require the subcontractor to certify in substantially the form prescribed in FAR 15.406-2 that, to the best of its knowledge and belief, the data submitted under paragraph (b) of this clause were accurate, complete, and current as of the date of agreement on the negotiated price of the subcontract or subcontract modification.

(d) The Contractor shall insert the substance of this clause, including this paragraph (d), in each subcontract that exceeds the threshold for submission of certified cost or pricing data at FAR 15.403-4 on the date of agreement on price or the date of award, whichever is later.

(End of clause)

[FAC 97-2, 62 FR 51224, 9/30/97, effective 10/10/97; FAC 2005-45, 75 FR 53135, 8/30/2010, effective 10/1/2010]

52.215-14 Integrity of Unit Prices.

As prescribed in 15.408(f)(1), insert the following clause:

INTEGRITY OF UNIT PRICES (OCT 2010)

(a) Any proposal submitted for the negotiation of prices for items of supplies shall distribute costs within contracts on a basis that ensures that unit prices are in proportion to the items' base cost (e.g., manufacturing or acquisition costs). Any method of distributing costs to line items that distorts unit prices shall not be used. For example, distributing costs equally among line items is not acceptable except when there is little or no variation in base cost. Nothing in this paragraph requires submission of certified cost or pricing data not otherwise required by law or regulation.

(b) When requested by the Contracting Officer, the Offeror/Contractor shall also identify those supplies that it will not manufacture or to which it will not contribute significant value.

(c) The Contractor shall insert the substance of this clause, less paragraph (b), in all subcontracts for other than: acquisitions at or below the simplified acquisition threshold in FAR Part 2; construction or architect-engineer services under FAR Part 36; utility services under FAR Part 41; services where supplies are not required; commercial items; and petroleum products.

(End of clause)

Alternate I (OCT 1997). As prescribed in 15.408(f)(2), substitute the following paragraph (b) for paragraph (b) of the basic clause:

(b) The Offeror/Contractor shall also identify those supplies that it will not manufacture or to which it will not contribute significant value.

[FAC 97-2, 62 FR 51224, 9/30/97, effective 10/10/97; FAC 2005-45, 75 FR 53135, 8/30/2010, effective 10/1/2010]

52.215-15 Pension Adjustments and Asset Reversions.

As prescribed in 15.408(g), insert the following clause:

PENSION ADJUSTMENTS AND ASSET REVERSIONS (OCT 2010)

(a) The Contractor shall promptly notify the Contracting Officer in writing when it determines that it will terminate a defined-benefit pension plan or otherwise recapture such pension fund assets.

(b) For segment closings, pension plan terminations, or curtailment of benefits, the amount of the adjustment shall be—

(1) For contracts and subcontracts that are subject to full coverage under the Cost Accounting Standards (CAS) Board rules and regulations (48 CFR Chapter 99), the amount measured, assigned, and allocated in accordance with 48 CFR 9904.413-50(c)(12); and

(2) For contracts and subcontracts that are not subject to full coverage under the CAS, the amount measured, assigned, and allocated in accordance with 48 CFR 9904.413-50(c)(12), except the numerator of the fraction at 48 CFR 9904.413-50(c)(12)(vi) shall be the sum of the pension plan costs allocated to all non-CAS covered contracts and subcontracts that are subject to Federal Acquisition Regulation (FAR) Subpart 31.2 or for which certified cost or pricing data were submitted.

(c) For all other situations where assets revert to the Contractor, or such assets are constructively received by it for any reason, the Contractor shall, at the Government's option, make a refund or give a credit to the Government for its equitable share of the gross amount withdrawn. The Government's equitable share shall reflect the Government's participation in pension costs through those contracts for which certified cost or pricing data were submitted or that are subject to FAR Subpart 31.2.

(d) The Contractor shall include the substance of this clause in all subcontracts under this contract that meet the applicability requirement of FAR 15.408(g).

(End of clause)

[FAC 97-9, 63 FR 58598, 10/30/98, effective 12/29/98; FAC 2001-18, as amended 68 FR 69257, 12/11/2003, effective 1/12/2004; FAC 2001-25, 69 FR 59704, 10/5/2004, effective 10/5/2004; Correction, 69 FR 60967, 10/14/2004, effective 10/14/2004; Correction, 72 FR 55089, 9/28/2007, effective 9/28/2007; FAC 2005-45, 75 FR 53135, 8/30/2010, effective 10/1/2010]

52.215-16 Facilities Capital Cost of Money.

As prescribed in 15.408(h), insert the following provision:

FACILITIES CAPITAL COST OF MONEY (JUN 2003)

(a) Facilities capital cost of money will be an allowable cost under the contemplated contract, if the criteria for allowability in FAR 31.205-10(b) are met. One of the allowability criteria requires the prospective Contractor to propose facilities capital cost of money in its offer.

(b) If the prospective Contractor does not propose this cost, the resulting contract will include the clause Waiver of Facilities Capital Cost of Money.

(End of provision)

[Redesignated from 52.215-30, FAC 97-2, 62 FR 51224, 9/30/97, effective 10/10/97; FAC 2001-14, 68 FR 28091, 5/22/2003, effective 6/23/2003]

52.215-17 Waiver of Facilities Capital Cost of Money.

As prescribed in 15.408(i), insert the following clause:

WAIVER OF FACILITIES CAPITAL COST OF MONEY (OCT 1997)

The Contractor did not include facilities capital cost of money as a proposed cost of this contract. Therefore, it is an unallowable cost under this contract.

(End of clause)

[Redesignated from 52.215-31, FAC 97-2, 62 FR 51224, 9/30/97, effective 10/10/97]

52.215-18 Reversion or Adjustment of Plans for Postretirement Benefits (PRB) Other Than Pensions.

As prescribed in 15.408(j), insert the following clause:

REVERSION OR ADJUSTMENT OF PLANS FOR POSTRETIREMENT BENEFITS (PRB) OTHER THAN PENSIONS (JUL 2005)

(a) The Contractor shall promptly notify the Contracting Officer in writing when the Contractor determines that it will terminate or reduce the benefits of a PRB plan.

(b) If PRB fund assets revert or inure to the Contractor or are constructively received by it under a plan termination or otherwise, the Contractor shall make a refund or give a credit to the Government for its equitable share as required by FAR 31.205-6(o)(6) of the Federal Acquisition Regulation (FAR). When determining or agreeing on the method for recovery of the Government's equitable share, the contracting parties should consider the following methods: cost reduction, amortizing the credit over a number of years (with appropriate interest), cash refund, or some other agreed upon method. Should the parties be unable to agree on the method for recovery of the Government's equitable share, through good faith negotiations, the Contractor Officer shall designate the method of recovery.

(c) The Contractor shall insert the substance of this clause in all subcontracts that meet the applicability requirements of FAR 15.408(j).

(End of clause)

[FAC 97-2, 62 FR 51224, 9/30/97, effective 10/10/97; FAC 2005-04, 70 FR 33671, 6/8/2005, effective 7/8/2005]

52.215-19 Notification of Ownership Changes.

As prescribed in 15.408(k), insert the following clause:

NOTIFICATION OF OWNERSHIP CHANGES (OCT 1997)

(a) The Contractor shall make the following notifications in writing:

(1) When the Contractor becomes aware that a change in its ownership has occurred, or is certain to occur, that could result in changes in the valuation of its capitalized assets in the accounting records, the Contractor shall notify the Administrative Contracting Officer (ACO) within 30 days.

(2) The Contractor shall also notify the ACO within 30 days whenever changes to asset valuations or any other cost changes have occurred or are certain to occur as a result of a change in ownership.

(b) The Contractor shall—

(1) Maintain current, accurate, and complete inventory records of assets and their costs;

(2) Provide the ACO or designated representative ready access to the records upon request;

(3) Ensure that all individual and grouped assets, their capitalized values, accumulated depreciation or amortization, and remaining useful lives are identified accurately before and after each of the Contractor's ownership changes; and

(4) Retain and continue to maintain depreciation and amortization schedules based on the asset records maintained before each Contractor ownership change.

(c) The Contractor shall include the substance of this clause in all subcontracts under this contract that meet the applicability requirement of FAR 15.408(k).

(End of clause)

[FAC 97-2, 62 FR 51224, 9/30/97, effective 10/10/97]

52.215-20 Requirements for Certified Cost or Pricing Data and Data Other Than Certified Cost or Pricing Data.

As prescribed in 15.408(l), insert the following provision:

REQUIREMENTS FOR CERTIFIED COST OR PRICING DATA AND DATA OTHER THAN CERTIFIED COST OR PRICING DATA (OCT 2010)

(a) *Exceptions from certified cost or pricing data*. (1) In lieu of submitting certified cost or pricing data, offerors may submit a written request for exception by submitting the information described in the following subparagraphs. The Contracting Officer may require additional supporting information, but only to the extent necessary to determine whether an exception should be granted, and whether the price is fair and reasonable.

(i) Identification of the law or regulation establishing the price offered. If the price is controlled under law by periodic rulings, reviews, or similar actions of a governmental body, attach a copy of the controlling document, unless it was previously submitted to the contracting office.

(ii) Commercial item exception. For a commercial item exception, the offeror shall submit, at a minimum, information on prices at which the same item or similar items have previously been sold in the commercial market that is adequate for evaluating the reasonableness of the price for this acquisition. Such information may include—

(A) For catalog items, a copy of or identification of the catalog and its date, or the appropriate pages for the offered items, or a statement that the catalog is on file in the buying office to which the proposal is being submitted. Provide a copy or describe current discount policies and price lists (published or unpublished), e.g., wholesale, original equipment manufacturer, or reseller. Also explain the basis of each offered price and its relationship to the established catalog price, including how the proposed price relates to the price of recent sales in quantities similar to the proposed quantities;

(B) For market-priced items, the source and date or period of the market quotation or other basis for market price, the base amount, and applicable discounts. In addition, describe the nature of the market;

(C) For items included on an active Federal Supply Service Multiple Award Schedule contract, proof that an exception has been granted for the schedule item.

(2) The offeror grants the Contracting Officer or an authorized representative the right to examine, at any time before award, books, records, documents, or other directly pertinent records to verify any request for an exception under this provision, and the reasonableness of price. For items priced using catalog or market prices, or law or regulation, access does not extend to cost or profit information or other data relevant solely to the offeror's determination of the prices to be offered in the catalog or marketplace.

(b) *Requirements for certified cost or pricing data.* If the offeror is not granted an exception from the requirement to submit certified cost or pricing data, the following applies:

(1) The offeror shall prepare and submit certified cost or pricing data, data other than certified cost or pricing data, and supporting attachments in accordance with the instructions contained in Table 15-2 of FAR 15.408, which is incorporated by reference with the same force and effect as though it were inserted here in full text. The instructions in Table 15-2 are incorporated as a mandatory format to be used in this contract, unless the Contracting Officer and the Contractor agree to a different format and change this clause to use Alternate I.

(2) As soon as practicable after agreement on price, but before contract award (except for unpriced actions such as letter contracts), the offeror shall submit a Certificate of Current Cost or Pricing Data, as prescribed by FAR 15.406-2.

(End of provision)

Alternate I (OCT 2010). As prescribed in 15.408(l) (and see 15.403-5(b)(1)), substitute the following paragraph (b)(1) for paragraph (b)(1) of the basic provision:

(b)(1) The offeror shall submit certified cost or pricing data, data other than certified cost or pricing data, and supporting attachments in the following format: [*Insert description of the data and format that are required, and include access to records necessary to permit an adequate evaluation of the proposed price in accordance with FAR 15.408, Table 15-2, Note 2. The description may be inserted at the time of issuing the solicitation, or the Contracting Officer may specify that the offeror's format will be acceptable, or the description may be inserted as the result of negotiations.*]

Alternate II (OCT 1997). As prescribed in 15.408(l), add the following paragraph (c) to the basic provision:

(c) When the proposal is submitted, also submit one copy each to: (1) the Administrative Contracting Officer, and (2) the Contract Auditor.

Alternate III (OCT 1997). As prescribed in 15.408(l), add the following paragraph (c) to the basic provision (if Alternate II is also used, redesignate the following paragraph as paragraph (d)).

(c) Submit the cost portion of the proposal via the following electronic media: [*Insert media format, e.g., electronic spreadsheet format, electronic mail, etc.*]

Alternate IV (OCT 2010).

(a) Submission of certified cost or pricing data is not required.

(b) Provide data described below: [*Insert description of the data and the format that are required, including the access to records necessary to permit an adequate evaluation of the proposed price in accordance with FAR 15.403-3.*]

[FAC 97-2, 62 FR 51224, 9/30/97, effective 10/10/97; FAC 2005-45, 75 FR 53135, 8/30/2010, effective 10/1/2010; FAC 2005-60, 77 FR 44065, 7/26/2012, effective 7/26/2012]

52.215-21 Requirements for Certified Cost or Pricing Data and Data Other Than Certified Cost or Pricing Data—Modifications.

As prescribed in 15.408(m), insert the following clause:

REQUIREMENTS FOR CERTIFIED COST OR PRICING DATA AND DATA OTHER THAN CERTIFIED COST OR PRICING DATA—MODIFICATIONS (OCT 2010)

(a) *Exceptions from certified cost or pricing data.* (1) In lieu of submitting certified cost or pricing data for modifications under this contract, for price adjustments expected to exceed the threshold set forth at FAR 15.403-4 on the date of the agreement on price or the date of the award, whichever is later, the Contractor may submit a written request for exception by submitting the information described in the following subparagraphs. The Contracting Officer may require additional supporting information, but only to the extent necessary to determine whether an exception should be granted, and whether the price is fair and reasonable—

(i) *Identification of the law or regulation establishing the price offered.* If the price is controlled under law by periodic rulings, reviews, or similar actions of a governmental body, attach a copy of the controlling document, unless it was previously submitted to the contracting office.

(ii) *Information on modifications of contracts or subcontracts for commercial items.* (A) If—

(1) The original contract or subcontract was granted an exception from certified cost or pricing data requirements because the price agreed upon was based on adequate price competition or prices set by law or regulation, or was a contract or subcontract for the acquisition of a commercial item; and

(2) The modification (to the contract or subcontract) is not exempted based on one of these exceptions, then the Contractor may provide information to establish that the modification would not change the contract or subcontract from a contract or subcontract for the acquisition of a commercial item to a contract or subcontract for the acquisition of an item other than a commercial item.

(B) For a commercial item exception, the Contractor shall provide, at a minimum, information on prices at which the same item or similar items have previously been sold that is adequate for evaluating the reasonableness of the price of the modification. Such information may include—

(1) For catalog items, a copy of or identification of the catalog and its date, or the appropriate pages for the offered items, or a statement that the catalog is on file in the buying office to which the proposal is being submitted. Provide a copy or describe current discount policies and price lists (published or unpublished), *e.g.*, wholesale, original equipment manufacturer, or reseller. Also explain the basis of each offered price and its relationship to the established

catalog price, including how the proposed price relates to the price of recent sales in quantities similar to the proposed quantities.

(2) For market-priced items, the source and date or period of the market quotation or other basis for market price, the base amount, and applicable discounts. In addition, describe the nature of the market.

(3) For items included on an active Federal Supply Service Multiple Award Schedule contract, proof that an exception has been granted for the schedule item.

(2) The Contractor grants the Contracting Officer or an authorized representative the right to examine, at any time before award, books, records, documents, or other directly pertinent records to verify any request for an exception under this clause, and the reasonableness of price. For items priced using catalog or market prices, or law or regulation, access does not extend to cost or profit information or other data relevant solely to the Contractor's determination of the prices to be offered in the catalog or marketplace.

(b) *Requirements for certified cost or pricing data.* If the Contractor is not granted an exception from the requirement to submit certified cost or pricing data, the following applies:

(1) The Contractor shall submit certified cost or pricing data, data other than certified cost or pricing data, and supporting attachments in accordance with the instructions contained in Table 15-2 of FAR 15.408, which is incorporated by reference with the same force and effect as though it were inserted here in full text. The instructions in Table 15-2 are incorporated as a mandatory format to be used in this contract, unless the Contracting Officer and the Contractor agree to a different format and change this clause to use Alternate I.

(2) As soon as practicable after agreement on price, but before award (except for unpriced actions), the Contractor shall submit a Certificate of Current Cost or Pricing Data, as prescribed by FAR 15.406-2.

(End of clause)

Alternate I (OCT 2010). As prescribed in 15.408(m) and 15.403-5(b)(1), substitute the following paragraph (b)(1) for paragraph (b)(1) of the basic clause.

(b)(1) The Contractor shall submit certified cost or pricing data, data other than certified cost or pricing data, and supporting attachments prepared in the following format: *[Insert description of the data and format that are required and include access to records necessary to permit an adequate evaluation of the proposed price in accordance with FAR 15.408, Table 15-2, Note 2. The description may be inserted at the time of issuing the solicitation, or the Contracting Officer may specify that the offeror's format will be acceptable, or the description may be inserted as the result of negotiations.]*

Alternate II (OCT 1997). As prescribed in 15.408(m), add the following paragraph (c) to the basic clause:

(c) When the proposal is submitted, also submit one copy each to: (1) the Administrative Contracting Officer, and (2) the Contract Auditor.

Alternate III (OCT 1997). As prescribed in 15.408(m), add the following paragraph (c) to the basic clause (if Alternate II is also used, redesignate the following paragraph as paragraph (d)):

(c) Submit the cost portion of the proposal via the following electronic media: [*Insert media format*]

Alternate IV (OCT 2010). As prescribed in 15.408(m), replace the text of the basic clause with the following:

(a) Submission of certified cost or pricing data is not required.

(b) Provide data described below: [*Insert description of the data and the format that are required, including the access to records necessary to permit an adequate evaluation of the proposed price in accordance with FAR 15.403-3.*]

[FAC 97-2, 62 FR 51224, 9/30/97, effective 10/10/97; FAC 2005-45, 75 FR 53135, 8/30/2010, effective 10/1/2010]

52.215-22 Limitations on Pass-Through Charges—Identification of Subcontract Effort.

As prescribed in 15.408(n)(1), use the following provision:

LIMITATIONS ON PASS-THROUGH CHARGES—IDENTIFICATION OF SUBCONTRACT EFFORT (OCT 2009)

(a) *Definitions. Added value, excessive pass-through charge, subcontract*, and *subcontractor*, as used in this provision, are defined in the clause of this solicitation entitled "Limitations on Pass-Through Charges" (FAR 52.215-23).

(b) *General.* The offeror's proposal shall exclude excessive pass-through charges.

(c) *Performance of work by the Contractor or a subcontractor.* (1) The offeror shall identify in its proposal the total cost of the work to be performed by the offeror, and the total cost of the work to be performed by each subcontractor, under the contract, task order, or delivery order.

(2) If the offeror intends to subcontract more than 70 percent of the total cost of work to be performed under the contract, task order, or delivery order, the offeror shall identify in its proposal—

(i) The amount of the offeror's indirect costs and profit/fee applicable to the work to be performed by the subcontractor(s); and

(ii) A description of the added value provided by the offeror as related to the work to be performed by the subcontractor(s).

(3) If any subcontractor proposed under the contract, task order, or delivery order intends to subcontract to a lower-tier subcontractor more than 70 percent of the total cost of work to be performed under its subcontract, the offeror shall identify in its proposal—

(i) The amount of the subcontractor's indirect costs and profit/fee applicable to the work to be performed by the lower-tier subcontractor(s); and

(ii) A description of the added value provided by the subcontractor as related to the work to be performed by the lower-tier subcontractor(s).

(End of provision)

[FAC 2005-37, 74 FR 52853, 10/14/2009, effective 10/14/2009; FAC 2005-47, 75 FR 77741, 12/13/2010, effective 1/12/2011]

52.215-23 Limitations on Pass-Through Charges.

As prescribed in 15.408(n)(2), use the following clause:

LIMITATIONS ON PASS-THROUGH CHARGES (OCT 2009)

(a) *Definitions.* As used in this clause—

Added value means that the Contractor performs subcontract management functions that the Contracting Officer determines are a benefit to the Government (*e.g.*, processing orders of parts or services, maintaining inventory, reducing delivery lead times, managing multiple sources for contract requirements, coordinating deliveries, performing quality assurance functions).

Excessive pass-through charge, with respect to a Contractor or subcontractor that adds no or negligible value to a contract or subcontract, means a charge to the Government by the Contractor or subcontractor that is for indirect costs or profit/fee on work performed by a subcontractor (other than charges for the costs of managing subcontracts and any applicable indirect costs and associated profit/fee based on such costs).

No or negligible value means the Contractor or subcontractor cannot demonstrate to the Contracting Officer that its effort added value to the contract or subcontract in accomplishing the work performed under the contract (including task or delivery orders).

Subcontract means any contract, as defined in FAR 2.101, entered into by a subcontractor to furnish supplies or services for performance of the contract or a subcontract. It includes but is not limited to purchase orders, and changes and modifications to purchase orders.

Subcontractor, as defined in FAR 44.101, means any supplier, distributor, vendor, or firm that furnishes supplies or services to or for a prime Contractor or another subcontractor.

(b) *General*. The Government will not pay excessive pass-through charges. The Contracting Officer shall determine if excessive pass-through charges exist.

(c) *Reporting*. Required reporting of performance of work by the Contractor or a subcontractor. The Contractor shall notify the Contracting Officer in writing if—

(1) The Contractor changes the amount of subcontract effort after award such that it exceeds 70 percent of the total cost of work to be performed under the contract, task order, or delivery order. The notification shall identify the revised cost of the subcontract effort and shall include verification that the Contractor will provide added value; or

(2) Any subcontractor changes the amount of lower-tier subcontractor effort after award such that it exceeds 70 percent of the total cost of the work to be performed under its subcontract. The notification shall identify the revised cost of the subcontract effort and shall include verification that the subcontractor will provide added value as related to the work to be performed by the lower-tier subcontractor(s).

(d) *Recovery of excessive pass-through charges*. If the Contracting Officer determines that excessive pass-through charges exist;

(1) For other than fixed-price contracts, the excessive pass-through charges are unallowable in accordance with the provisions in FAR subpart 31.2; and

(2) For applicable DoD fixed-price contracts, as identified in 15.408(n)(2)(i)(B), the Government shall be entitled to a price reduction for the amount of excessive pass-through charges included in the contract price.

(e) *Access to records*. (1) The Contracting Officer, or authorized representative, shall have the right to examine and audit all the Contractor's records (as defined at FAR 52.215-2(a)) necessary to determine whether the Contractor proposed, billed, or claimed excessive pass-through charges.

(2) For those subcontracts to which paragraph (f) of this clause applies, the Contracting Officer, or authorized representative, shall have the right to examine and audit all the subcontractor's records (as defined at FAR 52.215-2(a)) necessary to determine whether the subcontractor proposed, billed, or claimed excessive pass-through charges.

(f) *Flowdown*. The Contractor shall insert the substance of this clause, including this paragraph (f), in all cost-reimbursement subcontracts under this contract that exceed the simplified acquisition threshold, except if the contract is with DoD, then insert in all cost-reimbursement subcontracts and fixed-price subcontracts, except those identified in 15.408(n)(2)(i)(B)(*2*), that exceed the threshold for obtaining cost or pricing data in accordance with FAR 15.403-4.

(End of clause)

Alternate I (OCT 2009). As prescribed in 15.408(n)(2)(iii), substitute the following paragraph (b) for paragraph (b) of the basic clause:

(b) *General*. The Government will not pay excessive pass-through charges. The Contracting Officer has determined that there will be no excessive pass-through charges, provided the Contractor performs the disclosed value-added functions.

[FAC 2005-37, 74 FR 52853, 10/14/2009, effective 10/14/2009; FAC 2005-47, 75 FR 77741, 12/13/2010, effective 1/12/2011]

52.216-1 Type of Contract.

As prescribed in 16.105, complete and insert the following provision:

TYPE OF CONTRACT (APR 1984)

The Government contemplates award of a ____________ [*Contracting Officer insert specific type of contract*] contract resulting from this solicitation.

(End of provision)

[FAC 90-29, 60 FR 34732, 7/3/95, effective 7/3/95]

52.216-2 Economic Price Adjustment—Standard Supplies.

As prescribed in 16.203-4(a), insert the following clause. The clause may be modified by increasing the 10 percent limit on aggregate increases specified in subparagraph (c)(1), upon approval by the chief of the contracting office.

ECONOMIC PRICE ADJUSTMENT—STANDARD SUPPLIES (JAN 1997)

(a) The Contractor warrants that the unit price stated in the Schedule for ______________ [*offeror insert Schedule line item number*] is not in excess of the Contractor's applicable established price in effect on the contract date for like quantities of the same item. The term *unit price* excludes any part of the price directly resulting from requirements for preservation, packaging, or packing beyond standard commercial practice. The term *established price* means a price that—

(1) Is an established catalog or market price for a commercial item sold in substantial quantities to the general public; and

(2) Is the net price after applying any standard trade discounts offered by the Contractor.

(b) The Contractor shall promptly notify the Contracting Officer of the amount and effective date of each decrease in any applicable established price. Each corresponding contract unit price shall be decreased by the same percentage that the established price is decreased. The decrease shall apply to those items delivered on and after the effective date of the decrease in the Contractor's established price, and this contract shall be modified accordingly.

(c) If the Contractor's applicable established price is increased after the contract date, the corresponding contract unit price shall be increased, upon the Contractor's written request to the Contracting Officer, by the same percentage that the established price is increased, and the contract shall be modified accordingly, subject to the following limitations:

(1) The aggregate of the increases in any contract unit price under this clause shall not exceed 10 percent of the original contract unit price.

(2) The increased contract unit price shall be effective—

(i) On the effective date of the increase in the applicable established price if the Contracting Officer receives the Contractor's written request within 10 days thereafter; or

(ii) If the written request is received later, on the date the Contracting Officer receives the request.

(3) The increased contract unit price shall not apply to quantities scheduled under the contract for delivery before the effective date of the increased contract unit price, unless failure to deliver before that date results from causes beyond the control and without the fault or negligence of the Contractor, within the meaning of the Default clause.

(4) No modification increasing a contract unit price shall be executed under this paragraph (c) until the Contracting Officer verifies the increase in the applicable established price.

(5) Within 30 days after receipt of the Contractor's written request, the Contracting Officer may cancel, without liability to either party, any undelivered portion of the contract items affected by the requested increase.

(d) During the time allowed for the cancellation provided for in subparagraph (c)(5) of this clause, and thereafter if there is no cancellation, the Contractor shall continue deliveries according to the contract delivery schedule, and the Government shall pay for such deliveries at the contract unit price, increased to the extent provided by paragraph (c) of this clause.

(End of clause)

[FAC 90-32, 60 FR 48206, 9/18/95, effective 10/1/95; FAC 90-45, Final rule, 62 FR 224, 1/2/97, effective 1/1/97]

52.216-3 Economic Price Adjustment—Semistandard Supplies.

As prescribed in 16.203-4(b), insert the following clause. The clause may be modified by increasing the 10 percent limit on aggregate increases specified in subparagraph (c)(1), upon approval by the chief of the contracting office.

ECONOMIC PRICE ADJUSTMENT—SEMISTANDARD SUPPLIES (JAN 1997)

(a) The Contractor warrants that the supplies identified as line items

______________ [*offeror insert Schedule line item number*] in the Schedule are, except for modifications required by the contract specifications, supplies for which it has an established price. The term *established price* means a price that (1) is an established catalog or market price for a commercial item sold in substantial quantities to the general public, and (2) is the net price after applying any standard trade discounts offered by the Contractor. The Contractor further warrants that, as of the date of this contract, any difference between the unit prices stated in the contract for these line items and the Contractor's established prices for like quantities of the nearest commercial equivalents are due to compliance with contract specifications and with any contract requirements for preservation, packaging, and packing beyond standard commercial practice.

(b) The Contractor shall promptly notify the Contracting Officer of the amount and effective date of each decrease in any applicable established price. Each corresponding contract unit price (exclusive of any part of the unit price that reflects modifications resulting from compliance with specifications or with requirements for preservation, packaging, and packing beyond standard commercial practice) shall be decreased by the same percentage that the established price is decreased. The decrease shall apply to those items delivered on and after the effective date of the decrease in the Contractor's established price, and this contract shall be modified accordingly.

(c) If the Contractor's applicable established price is increased after the contract date, the corresponding contract unit price (exclusive of any part of the unit price resulting from compliance with specifications or with requirements for preservation, packaging, and packing beyond standard commercial practice) shall be increased, upon the Contractor's written request to the Contracting Officer, by the same percentage that the established price is increased, and the contract shall be modified accordingly, subject to the following limitations:

(1) The aggregate of the increases in any contract unit price under this clause shall not exceed 10 percent of the original contract unit price.

(2) The increased contract unit price shall be effective—

(i) On the effective date of the increase in the applicable established price if the Contracting Officer receives the Contractor's written request within 10 days thereafter; or

(ii) if the written request is received later, on the date the Contracting Officer receives the request.

(3) The increased contract unit price shall not apply to quantities scheduled under the contract for delivery before the effective date of the increased contract unit price, unless failure to deliver before that date results from causes beyond the control and without the fault or negligence of the Contractor, within the meaning of the Default clause.

(4) No modification increasing a contract unit price shall be executed under this paragraph (c) until the Contracting Officer verifies the increase in the applicable established price.

(5) Within 30 days after receipt of the Contractor's written request, the Contracting Officer may cancel, without liability to either party, any undelivered portion of the contract items affected by the requested increase.

(d) During the time allowed for the cancellation provided for in subparagraph (c)(5) of this clause, and thereafter if there is no cancellation, the Contractor shall continue deliveries according to the contract delivery schedule, and the Government shall pay for such deliveries at the contract unit price, increased to the extent provided by paragraph (c) of this clause.

(End of clause)

[FAC 90-32, 60 FR 48206, 9/18/95, effective 10/1/95; FAC 90-45, Final rule, 62 FR 224, 1/2/97, effective 1/1/97, corrected 62 FR 10709, 3/10/97]

52.216-4 Economic Price Adjustment—Labor and Material.

As prescribed in 16.203-4(c), when contracting by negotiation, insert a clause that is substantially the same as the following clause in solicitations and contracts when the conditions specified in 16.203-4(c)(1)(i) through (iv) apply (but see 16.203-4(c)(2)). The clause may be modified by increasing the 10-percent limit on aggregate increases specified in subparagraph (c)(4), upon approval by the chief of the contracting office.

ECONOMIC PRICE ADJUSTMENT—LABOR AND MATERIAL (JAN 2017)

(a) The Contractor shall notify the Contracting Officer if, at any time during contract performance, the rates of pay for labor (including fringe benefits) or the unit prices for material shown in the Schedule either increase or decrease. The Contractor shall furnish this notice within 60 days after the increase or decrease, or within any additional period that the Contracting Officer may approve in writing, but not later than the date of final payment under this contract. The notice shall include the Contractor's proposal for an adjustment in the contract unit prices to be negotiated under paragraph (b) of this clause, and shall include, in the form required by the Contracting Officer, supporting data explaining the cause, effective date, and amount of the increase or decrease and the amount of the Contractor's adjustment proposal.

(b) Promptly after the Contracting Officer receives the notice and data under paragraph (a) of this clause, the Contracting Officer and the Contractor shall negotiate a price adjustment in the contract unit prices and its effective date. However, the Contracting Officer may postpone the negotiations until an accumulation of increases and decreases in the labor rates (including fringe benefits) and unit prices of material shown in the Schedule results in an adjustment allowable under subparagraph (c)(3) of this clause. The Contracting Officer shall modify this contract (1) to include the price adjustment and its effective date and (2) to revise the labor rates (including fringe benefits) or unit prices of material as shown in the Schedule to reflect the increases or decreases resulting from the adjustment. The Contractor shall continue performance pending agreement on, or determination of, any adjustment and its effective date.

(c) Any price adjustment under this clause is subject to the following limitations:

(1) Any adjustment shall be limited to the effect on unit prices of the increases or decreases in the rates of pay for labor (including fringe benefits) or unit prices for material shown in the Schedule. There shall be no adjustment for—

(i) Supplies or services for which the production cost is not affected by such changes;

(ii) Changes in rates or unit prices other than those shown in the Schedule; or

(iii) Changes in the quantities of labor or material used from those shown in the Schedule for each item.

(2) No upward adjustment shall apply to supplies or services that are required to be delivered or performed before the effective date of the adjustment, unless the Contractor's failure to deliver or perform according to the delivery schedule results from causes beyond the Contractor's control and without its fault or negligence, within the meaning of the Default clause.

(3) There shall be no adjustment for any change in rates of pay for labor (including fringe benefits) or unit prices for material which would not result in a net change of at least 3 percent of the then-current total contract price. This limitation shall not apply, however, if, after final delivery of all line items, either party requests an adjustment under paragraph (b) of this clause.

(4) The aggregate of the increases in any contract unit price made under this clause shall not exceed 10 percent of the original unit price. There is no percentage limitation on the amount of decreases that may be made under this clause.

(d) The Contracting Officer may examine the Contractor's books, records, and other supporting data relevant to the cost of labor (including fringe benefits) and material during all reasonable times until the end of 3 years after the date of final payment under this contract or the time periods specified in Subpart 4.7 of the Federal Acquisition Regulation (FAR), whichever is earlier.

(End of clause)

[FAC 90-32, 60 FR 48206, 9/18/95, effective 10/1/95; FAC 90-45, Final rule, 62 FR 224, 1/2/97, effective 1/1/97; FAC 2005-95, 82 FR 4709, 1/13/2017, effective 1/13/2017]

52.216-5 Price Redetermination—Prospective.

As prescribed in 16.205-4, insert the following clause:

PRICE REDETERMINATION—PROSPECTIVE (OCT 1997)

(a) *General.* The unit prices and the total price stated in this contract shall be periodically redetermined in accordance with this clause, except that—

(1) The prices for supplies delivered and services performed before the first effective date of price redetermination (see paragraph (c) of this clause) shall remain fixed and

(2) In no event shall the total amount paid under this contract exceed any ceiling price included in the contract.

(b) *Definition. Costs,* as used in this clause, means allowable costs in accordance with Part 31 of the Federal Acquisition Regulation (FAR) in effect on the date of this contract.

(c) *Price redetermination periods.* For the purpose of price redetermination, performance of this contract is divided into successive periods. The first period shall extend from the date of the contract to ______________, (see Note (1)) and the second and each succeeding period shall extend for ____________ [*insert appropriate number*] months from the end of the last preceding period, except that the parties may agree to vary the length of the final period. The first day of the second and each succeeding period shall be the effective date of price redetermination for that period.

(d) *Data submission.* (1) Not more than ________ nor less than ____ (see Note (2)) days before the end of each redetermination period, except the last, the Contractor shall submit—

(i) Proposed prices for supplies that may be delivered or services that may be performed in the next succeeding period, and—

(A) An estimate and breakdown of the costs of these supplies or services in the format of Table 15-2, FAR 15.408, or in any other form on which the parties may agree;

(B) Sufficient data to support the accuracy and reliability of this estimate; and

(C) An explanation of the differences between this estimate and the original (or last preceding) estimate for the same supplies or services; and

(ii) A statement of all costs incurred in performing this contract through the end of the ____ month (see Note (3)) before the submission of proposed prices in the format of Table 15-2, FAR 15.408 (or in any other form on which the parties may agree), with sufficient supporting data to disclose unit costs and cost trends for—

(A) Supplies delivered and services performed; and

(B) Inventories of work in process and undelivered contract supplies on hand (estimated to the extent necessary).

(2) The Contractor shall also submit, to the extent that it becomes available before negotiations on redetermined prices are concluded—

(i) Supplemental statements of costs incurred after the date stated in subdivision (d) (1) (ii) of this section for—

(A) Supplies delivered and services performed; and

(B) Inventories of work in process and undelivered contract supplies on hand (estimated to the extent necessary); and

(ii) Any other relevant data that the Contracting Officer may reasonably require.

(3) If the Contractor fails to submit the data required by subparagraphs (d) (1) and (2) of this section, within the time specified, the Contracting Officer may suspend payments under this contract until the data are furnished. If it is later determined that the Government has overpaid the Contractor, the Contractor shall repay the excess to the Government immediately. Unless repaid within 30 days after the end of the data submittal period, the amount of the excess shall bear interest, computed from the date

the data were due to the date of repayment, at the rate established in accordance with the Interest clause.

(e) *Price redetermination.* Upon the Contracting Officer's receipt of the data required by paragraph (d) of this section, the Contracting Officer and the Contractor shall promptly negotiate to redetermine fair and reasonable prices for supplies that may be delivered or services that may be performed in the period following the effective date of price redetermination.

(f) *Contract modifications.* Each negotiated redetermination of prices shall be evidenced by a modification to this contract, signed by the Contractor and the Contracting Officer, stating the redetermined prices that apply during the redetermination period.

(g) *Adjusting billing prices.* Pending execution of the contract modification (see paragraph (f) of this section), the Contractor shall submit invoices or vouchers in accordance with the billing prices stated in this contract. If at any time it appears that the then-current billing prices will be substantially greater than the estimated final prices, or if the Contractor submits data showing that the redetermined price will be substantially greater than the current billing prices, the parties shall negotiate an appropriate decrease or increase in billing prices. Any billing price adjustment shall be reflected in a contract modification and shall not affect the redetermination of prices under this clause. After the contract modification for price redetermination is executed, the total amount paid or to be paid on all invoices or vouchers shall be adjusted to reflect the agreed-upon prices, and any requested additional payments, refunds, or credits shall be made promptly.

(h) *Quarterly limitation on payments statement.* This paragraph (h) applies only during periods for which firm prices have not been established.

(1) Within 45 days after the end of the quarter of the Contractor's fiscal year in which a delivery is first made (or services are first performed) and accepted by the Government under this contract, and for each quarter thereafter, the Contractor shall submit to the contract administration office (with a copy to the contracting office and the cognizant contract auditor) a statement, cumulative from the beginning of the contract, showing—

(i) The total contract price of all supplies delivered (or services performed) and accepted by the Government and for which final prices have been established;

(ii) The total costs (estimated to the extent necessary) reasonably incurred for, and properly allocable solely to, the supplies delivered (or services performed) and accepted by the Government and for which final prices have not been established;

(iii) The portion of the total interim profit (used in establishing the initial contract price or agreed to for the purpose of this paragraph (h)) that is in direct proportion to the supplies delivered (or services performed) and accepted by the Government and for which final prices have not been established; and

(iv) The total amount of all invoices or vouchers for supplies delivered (or services performed) and accepted by the Government (including amounts applied or to be applied to liquidate progress payments).

(2) The statement required by subparagraph (1) above need not be submitted for any quarter for which either no costs are to be reported under subdivision (h)(1)(ii) of this section, or revised billing prices have been established in accordance with paragraph (g) of this section, and do not exceed the existing contract price, the Contractor's price-redetermination proposal, or a price based on the most recent quarterly statement, whichever is least.

(3) Notwithstanding any provision of this contract authorizing greater payments, if on any quarterly statement the amount under subdivision (1)(iv) of this section exceeds the sum due the Contractor, as computed in accordance with subdivisions (1)(i), (ii), and (iii) of this section, the Contractor shall immediately refund or credit to the Government the amount of this excess. The Contractor may, when appropriate, reduce this refund or credit by the amount of any applicable tax credits due the Contractor

under 26 U.S.C. 1481 and by the amount of previous refunds or credits effected under this clause. If any portion of the excess has been applied to the liquidation of progress payments, then that portion may, instead of being refunded, be added to the unliquidated progress payment account, consistent with the Progress Payments clause. The Contractor shall provide complete details to support any claimed reductions in refunds.

(4) If the Contractor fails to submit the quarterly statement within 45 days after the end of each quarter and it is later determined that the Government has overpaid the Contractor, the Contractor shall repay the excess to the Government immediately. Unless repaid within 30 days after the end of the statement submittal period, the amount of the excess shall bear interest, computed from the date the quarterly statement was due to the date of repayment, at the rate established in accordance with the Interest clause.

(i) *Subcontracts*. No subcontract placed under this contract may provide for payment on a cost-plus-a-percentage-of-cost basis.

(j) *Disagreements*. If the Contractor and the Contracting Officer fail to agree upon redetermined prices for any price redetermination period within 60 days (or within such other period as the parties agree) after the date on which the data required by paragraph (d) of this section are to be submitted, the Contracting Officer shall promptly issue a decision in accordance with the Disputes clause. For the purpose of paragraphs (f), (g), and (h) of this section, and pending final settlement of the disagreement on appeal, by failure to appeal, or by agreement, this decision shall be treated as an executed contract modification. Pending final settlement, price redetermination for subsequent periods, if any, shall continue to be negotiated as provided in this clause.

(k) *Termination*. If this contract is terminated, prices shall continue to be established in accordance with this clause for (1) completed supplies and services accepted by the Government and (2) those supplies and services not terminated under a partial termination. All other elements of the termination shall be resolved in accordance with other applicable clauses of this contract.

(End of clause)

NOTES:

(1) Express in terms of units delivered, or as a date; but in either case the period should end on the last day of a month.

(2) Insert the numbers of days chosen so that the Contractor's submission will be late enough to reflect recent cost experience (taking into account the Contractor's accounting system), but early enough to permit review, audit (if necessary), and negotiation before the start of the prospective period.

(3) Insert "first," except that "second" may be inserted if necessary to achieve compatibility with the Contractor's accounting system.

[FAC 90-32, 60 FR 48206, 9/18/95, effective 10/1/95; FAC 90-43, Final rule, 61 FR 67408, 12/20/96, effective 2/18/97; FAC 97-2, 62 FR 51224, 9/30/97, effective 10/10/97]

52.216-6 Price Redetermination—Retroactive.

As prescribed in 16.206-4, insert the following clause:

PRICE REDETERMINATION—RETROACTIVE (OCT 1997)

(a) *General*. The unit price and the total price stated in this contract shall be redetermined in accordance with this clause, but in no event shall the total amount paid under this contract exceed ___ [*insert dollar amount of ceiling price*].

(b) *Definition*. *Costs,* as used in this clause, means allowable costs in accordance with Part 31 of the Federal Acquisition Regulation (FAR) in effect on the date of this contract.

(c) *Data submission*. (1) Within ___ [*Contracting Officer insert number of days*] days after delivery of all supplies to be delivered and completion of all services to be performed under this contract, the Contractor shall submit—

(i) Proposed prices;

(ii) A statement in the format of Table 15-2, FAR 15.408, or in any other form on which the parties may agree, of all costs incurred in performing the contract; and

(iii) Any other relevant data that the Contracting Officer may reasonably require.

(2) If the Contractor fails to submit the data required by subparagraph (c)(1) of this section within the time specified, the Contracting Officer may suspend payments under this contract until the data are furnished. If it is later determined that the Government has overpaid the Contractor, the excess shall be repaid to the Government immediately. Unless repaid within 30 days after the end of the data submittal period, the amount of the excess shall bear interest, computed from the date the data were due to the date of repayment, at the rate established in accordance with the Interest clause.

(d) *Price determination*. Upon the Contracting Officer's receipt of the data required by paragraph (c) of this section, the Contracting Officer and the Contractor shall promptly negotiate to redetermine fair and reasonable prices for supplies delivered and services performed by the Contractor under this contract.

(e) *Contract modification*. The negotiated redetermination of price shall be evidenced by a modification to this contract, signed by the Contractor and the Contracting Officer.

(f) *Adjusting billing prices*. Pending execution of the contract modification (see paragraph (e) of this section), the Contractor shall submit invoices or vouchers in accordance with billing prices stated in this contract. If at any time it appears that the then-current billing prices will be substantially greater than the estimated final prices, or if the Contractor submits data showing that the redetermined prices will be substantially greater than the current billing prices, the parties shall negotiate an appropriate decrease or increase in billing prices. Any billing price adjustment shall be reflected in a contract modification and shall not affect the redetermination of prices under this clause. After the contract modification for price redetermination is executed, the total amount paid or to be paid on all invoices or vouchers shall be adjusted to reflect the agreed-upon prices, and any resulting additional payments, refunds, or credits shall be made promptly.

(g) *Quarterly limitation on payments statement*. This paragraph (g) shall apply until final price redetermination under this contract has been completed.

(1) Within 45 days after the end of the quarter of the Contractor's fiscal year in which a delivery is first made (or services are first performed) and accepted by the Government under this contract, and for each quarter thereafter, the Contractor shall submit to the contract administration office (with a copy to the contracting office and the cognizant contract auditor), a statement, cumulative from the beginning of the contract, showing—

(i) The total contract price of all supplies delivered (or services performed) and accepted by the Government and for which final prices have been established;

(ii) The total costs (estimated to the extent necessary) reasonably incurred for, and properly allocable solely to, the supplies delivered (or services performed) and accepted by the Government and for which final prices have not been established;

(iii) The portion of the total interim profit (used in establishing the initial contract price or agreed to for the purpose of this paragraph (g)) that is in direct proportion to the supplies delivered (or services performed) and accepted by the Government and for which final prices have not been established; and

(iv) The total amount of all invoices or vouchers for supplies delivered (or services performed) and accepted by the Government (including amounts applied or to be applied to liquidate progress payments).

(2) Notwithstanding any provision of this contract authorizing greater payments, if on any quarterly statement the amount under subdivision (g)(1)(iv) of this section exceeds the sum due the Contractor, as computed in accordance with subdivisions (g)(1)(i), (ii), and (iii) of this section, the Contractor shall

immediately refund or credit to the Government the amount of this excess. The Contractor may, when appropriate, reduce this refund or credit by the amount of any applicable tax credits due the contractor under 26 U.S.C. 1481 and by the amount of previous refunds or credits effected under this clause. If any portion of the excess has been applied to the liquidation of progress payments, then that portion may, instead of being refunded, be added to the unliquidated progress payment account, consistent with the Progress Payments clause. The Contractor shall provide complete details to support any claimed reduction in refunds.

(3) If the Contractor fails to submit the quarterly statement within 45 days after the end of each quarter and it is later determined that the Government has overpaid the Contractor, the Contractor shall repay the excess to the Government immediately. Unless repaid within 30 days after the end of the statement submittal period, the amount of the excess shall bear interest, computed from the date the quarterly statement was due to the date of repayment, at the rate established in accordance with the Interest clause.

(h) *Subcontracts.* No subcontract placed under this contract may provide for payment on a cost-plus-a-percentage-of-cost basis.

(i) *Disagreements.* If the Contractor and the Contracting Officer fail to agree upon redetermined prices within 60 days (or within such other period as the parties agree) after the date on which the data required by paragraph (c) of this section are to be submitted, the Contracting Officer shall promptly issue a decision in accordance with the Disputes clause. For the purpose of paragraphs (e), (f), and (g) of this section, and pending final settlement of the disagreement on appeal, by failure to appeal, or by agreement, this decision shall be treated as an executed contract modification.

(j) *Termination.* If this contract is terminated before price redetermination, prices shall be established in accordance with this clause for completed supplies and services not terminated. All other elements of the termination shall be resolved in accordance with other applicable clauses of this contract.

(End of clause)

[FAC 90-32, 60 FR 48206, 9/18/95, effective 10/1/95; FAC 90-43, Final rule, 61 FR 67408, 12/20/96, effective 2/18/97; FAC 97-2, 62 FR 51224, 9/30/97, effective 10/10/97]

52.216-7 Allowable Cost and Payment.

As prescribed in 16.307(a), insert the following clause:

ALLOWABLE COST AND PAYMENT (AUG 2018)

(a) *Invoicing.* (1) The Government will make payments to the Contractor when requested as work progresses, but (except for small business concerns) not more often than once every 2 weeks, in amounts determined to be allowable by the Contracting Officer in accordance with Federal Acquisition Regulation (FAR) subpart 31.2 in effect on the date of this contract and the terms of this contract. The Contractor may submit to an authorized representative of the Contracting Officer, in such form and reasonable detail as the representative may require, an invoice or voucher supported by a statement of the claimed allowable cost for performing this contract.

(2) Contract financing payments are not subject to the interest penalty provisions of the Prompt Payment Act. Interim payments made prior to the final payment under the contract are contract financing payments, except interim payments if this contract contains Alternate I to the clause at 52.232-25.

(3) The designated payment office will make interim payments for contract financing on the ________ [*Contracting Officer insert day as prescribed by agency head; if not prescribed, insert "30th"*] day after the designated billing office receives a proper payment request.

In the event that the Government requires an audit or other review of a specific payment request to ensure compliance with the terms and conditions of the contract, the designated payment office is not compelled to make payment by the specified due date.

(b) *Reimbursing costs.* (1) For the purpose of reimbursing allowable costs (except as provided in paragraph (b)(2) of the clause, with respect to pension, deferred profit sharing, and employee stock ownership plan contributions), the term "costs" includes only—

(i) Those recorded costs that, at the time of the request for reimbursement, the Contractor has paid by cash, check, or other form of actual payment for items or services purchased directly for the contract;

(ii) When the Contractor is not delinquent in paying costs of contract performance in the ordinary course of business, costs incurred, but not necessarily paid, for—

(A) Supplies and services purchased directly for the contract and associated financing payments to subcontractors, provided payments determined due will be made—

(1) In accordance with the terms and conditions of a subcontract or invoice; and

(2) Ordinarily within 30 days of the submission of the Contractor's payment request to the Government;

(B) Materials issued from the Contractor's inventory and placed in the production process for use on the contract;

(C) Direct labor;

(D) Direct travel;

(E) Other direct in-house costs; and

(F) Properly allocable and allowable indirect costs, as shown in the records maintained by the Contractor for purposes of obtaining reimbursement under Government contracts; and

(iii) The amount of financing payments that have been paid by cash, check, or other forms of payment to subcontractors.

(2) Accrued costs of Contractor contributions under employee pension plans shall be excluded until actually paid unless—

(i) The Contractor's practice is to make contributions to the retirement fund quarterly or more frequently; and

(ii) The contribution does not remain unpaid 30 days after the end of the applicable quarter or shorter payment period (any contribution remaining unpaid shall be excluded from the Contractor's indirect costs for payment purposes).

(3) Notwithstanding the audit and adjustment of invoices or vouchers under paragraph (g) of this section, allowable indirect costs under this contract shall be obtained by applying indirect cost rates established in accordance with paragraph (d) of this section.

(4) Any statements in specifications or other documents incorporated in this contract by reference designating performance of services or furnishing of materials at the Contractor's expense or at no cost to the Government shall be disregarded for purposes of cost-reimbursement under this clause.

(c) *Small business concerns.* A small business concern may receive more frequent payments than every 2 weeks.

(d) *Final indirect cost rates.* (1) Final annual indirect cost rates and the appropriate bases shall be established in accordance with Subpart 42.7 of the Federal Acquisition Regulation (FAR) in effect for the period covered by the indirect cost rate proposal.

(2)(i) The Contractor shall submit an adequate final indirect cost rate proposal to the Contracting Officer (or cognizant Federal agency official) and auditor within the 6-month period following the expiration of each of its fiscal years. Reasonable extensions, for exceptional circumstances only, may be requested in writing by the Contractor and granted in writing by the Contracting Officer. The Contractor shall support its proposal with adequate supporting data.

(ii) The proposed rates shall be based on the Contractor's actual cost experience for that period. The appropriate Government representative and the Contractor shall establish the final indirect cost rates as promptly as practical after receipt of the Contractor's proposal.

(iii) An adequate indirect cost rate proposal shall include the following data unless otherwise specified by the cognizant Federal agency official:

(A) Summary of all claimed indirect expense rates, including pool, base, and calculated indirect rate.

(B) *General and Administrative expenses (final indirect cost pool)*. Schedule of claimed expenses by element of cost as identified in accounting records (Chart of Accounts).

(C) *Overhead expenses (final indirect cost pool)*. Schedule of claimed expenses by element of cost as identified in accounting records (Chart of Accounts) for each final indirect cost pool.

(D) *Occupancy expenses (intermediate indirect cost pool)*. Schedule of claimed expenses by element of cost as identified in accounting records (Chart of Accounts) and expense reallocation to final indirect cost pools.

(E) Claimed allocation bases, by element of cost, used to distribute indirect costs.

(F) Facilities capital cost of money factors computation.

(G) Reconciliation of books of account (i.e., General Ledger) and claimed direct costs by major cost element.

(H) Schedule of direct costs by contract and subcontract and indirect expense applied at claimed rates, as well as a subsidiary schedule of Government participation percentages in each of the allocation base amounts.

(I) Schedule of cumulative direct and indirect costs claimed and billed by contract and subcontract.

(J) *Subcontract information.* Listing of subcontracts awarded to companies for which the contractor is the prime or upper-tier contractor (include prime and subcontract numbers; subcontract value and award type; amount claimed during the fiscal year; and the subcontractor name, address, and point of contact information).

(K) Summary of each time-and-materials and labor-hour contract information, including labor categories, labor rates, hours, and amounts; direct materials; other direct costs; and, indirect expense applied at claimed rates.

(L) Reconciliation of total payroll per IRS form 941 to total labor costs distribution.

(M) Listing of decisions/agreements/approvals and description of accounting/organizational changes.

(N) Certificate of final indirect costs (see 52.242-4, Certification of Final Indirect Costs).

(O) Contract closing information for contracts physically completed in this fiscal year (include contract number, period of performance, contract ceiling amounts, contract fee computations, level of effort, and indicate if the contract is ready to close).

(iv) The following supplemental information is not required to determine if a proposal is adequate, but may be required during the audit process:

(A) Comparative analysis of indirect expense pools detailed by account to prior fiscal year and budgetary data.

(B) General organizational information and limitation on allowability of compensation for certain contractor personnel. See 31.205–6(p). Additional salary reference information is available at *https://www.whitehouse.gov/wp-content/uploads/2017/11/ContractorCompensationCapContractsAwardedBeforeJune24.pdf* and *https://www.whitehouse.gov/wp-content/uploads/2017/11/ContractorCompensationCapContractsAwardedafterJune24.pdf*.

(C) Identification of prime contracts under which the contractor performs as a subcontractor.

(D) Description of accounting system (excludes contractors required to submit a CAS Disclosure Statement or contractors where the description of the accounting system has not changed from the previous year's submission).

(E) Procedures for identifying and excluding unallowable costs from the costs claimed and billed (excludes contractors where the procedures have not changed from the previous year's submission).

(F) Certified financial statements and other financial data (e.g., trial balance, compilation, review, etc.).

(G) Management letter from outside CPAs concerning any internal control weaknesses.

(H) Actions that have been and/or will be implemented to correct the weaknesses described in the management letter from subparagraph (G) of this section.

(I) List of all internal audit reports issued since the last disclosure of internal audit reports to the Government.

(J) Annual internal audit plan of scheduled audits to be performed in the fiscal year when the final indirect cost rate submission is made.

(K) Federal and State income tax returns.

(L) Securities and Exchange Commission 10-K annual report.

(M) Minutes from board of directors meetings.

(N) Listing of delay claims and termination claims submitted which contain costs relating to the subject fiscal year.

(O) Contract briefings, which generally include a synopsis of all pertinent contract provisions, such as: Contract type, contract amount, product or service(s) to be provided, contract performance period, rate ceilings, advance approval requirements, precontract cost allowability limitations, and billing limitations.

(v) The Contractor shall update the billings on all contracts to reflect the final settled rates and update the schedule of cumulative direct and indirect costs claimed and billed, as required in paragraph (d)(2)(iii)(I) of this section, within 60 days after settlement of final indirect cost rates.

(3) The Contractor and the appropriate Government representative shall execute a written understanding setting forth the final indirect cost rates. The understanding shall specify (i) the agreed-upon final annual indirect cost rates, (ii) the bases to which the rates apply, (iii) the periods for which the rates apply, (iv) any specific indirect cost items treated as direct costs in the settlement, and (v) the affected contract and/or subcontract, identifying any with advance agreements or special terms and the applicable rates. The understanding shall not change any monetary ceiling, contract obligation, or specific cost allowance or disallowance provided for in this contract. The understanding is incorporated into this contract upon execution.

(4) Failure by the parties to agree on a final annual indirect cost rate shall be a dispute within the meaning of the Disputes clause.

(5) Within 120 days (or longer period if approved in writing by the Contracting Officer) after settlement of the final annual indirect cost rates for all years of a physically complete contract, the Contractor shall submit a completion invoice or voucher to reflect the settled amounts and rates. The completion invoice or voucher shall include settled subcontract amounts and rates. The prime contractor is responsible for settling subcontractor amounts and rates included in the completion invoice or voucher and providing status of subcontractor audits to the contracting officer upon request.

(6)(i) If the Contractor fails to submit a completion invoice or voucher within the time specified in paragraph (d)(5) of this clause, the Contracting Officer may—

(A) Determine the amounts due to the Contractor under the contract; and

(B) Record this determination in a unilateral modification to the contract.

(ii) This determination constitutes the final decision of the Contracting Officer in accordance with the Disputes clause.

(e) *Billing rates*. Until final annual indirect cost rates are established for any period, the Government shall reimburse the Contractor at billing rates established by the Contracting Officer or by an authorized representative (the cognizant auditor), subject to adjustment when the final rates are established. These billing rates—

(1) Shall be the anticipated final rates; and

(2) May be prospectively or retroactively revised by mutual agreement, at either party's request, to prevent substantial overpayment or underpayment.

(f) *Quick-closeout procedures.* Quick-closeout procedures are applicable when the conditions in FAR 42.708(a) are satisfied.

(g) *Audit.* At any time or times before final payment, the Contracting Officer may have the Contractor's invoices or vouchers and statements of cost audited. Any payment may be—

(1) Reduced by amounts found by the Contracting Officer not to constitute allowable costs; or

(2) Adjusted for prior overpayments or underpayments.

(h) *Final payment.* (1) Upon approval of a completion invoice or voucher submitted by the Contractor in accordance with paragraph (d)(5) of this clause, and upon the Contractor's compliance with all terms of this contract, the Government shall promptly pay any balance of allowable costs and that part of the fee (if any) not previously paid.

(2) The Contractor shall pay to the Government any refunds, rebates, credits, or other amounts (including interest, if any) accruing to or received by the Contractor or any assignee under this contract, to the extent that those amounts are properly allocable to costs for which the Contractor has been reimbursed by the Government. Reasonable expenses incurred by the Contractor for securing refunds, rebates, credits, or other amounts shall be allowable costs if approved by the Contracting Officer. Before final payment under this contract, the Contractor and each assignee whose assignment is in effect at the time of final payment shall execute and deliver—

(i) An assignment to the Government, in form and substance satisfactory to the Contracting Officer, of refunds, rebates, credits, or other amounts (including interest, if any) properly allocable to costs for which the Contractor has been reimbursed by the Government under this contract; and

(ii) A release discharging the Government, its officers, agents, and employees from all liabilities, obligations, and claims arising out of or under this contract, except—

(A) Specified claims stated in exact amounts, or in estimated amounts when the exact amounts are not known;

(B) Claims (including reasonable incidental expenses) based upon liabilities of the Contractor to third parties arising out of the performance of this contract; provided, that the claims are not known to the Contractor on the date of the execution of the release, and that the Contractor gives notice of the claims in writing to the Contracting Officer within 6 years following the release date or notice of final payment date, whichever is earlier; and

(C) Claims for reimbursement of costs, including reasonable incidental expenses, incurred by the Contractor under the patent clauses of this contract, excluding, however, any expenses arising from the Contractor's indemnification of the Government against patent liability.

(End of clause)

Alternate I (FEB 1997). As prescribed in 16.307(a)(2), substitute the following paragraph (b)(1)(iii) for paragraph (b)(1)(iii) of the basic clause:

(iii) The amount of progress and other payments to the Contractor's subcontractors that either have been paid, or that the Contractor is required to pay pursuant to the clause of this contract entitled "Prompt Payment for Construction Contracts." Payments shall be made by cash, check, or other form of payment to the Contractor's subcontractors under similar cost standards.

Alternate II (AUG 2012). As prescribed in 16.307(a)(3), substitute the following paragraph (a)(1) for paragraph (a)(1) of the basic clause:

(a)(1) The Government will make payments to the Contractor when requested as work progresses, but not more often than once every two weeks, in amounts determined to be allowable by the Contracting Officer in accordance with FAR subpart 31.3 in effect on the date of this contract and the terms of this contract. The Contractor may submit to an authorized representative of the Contracting Officer, in such form and reasonable detail as the representative may require, an invoice or voucher supported by a statement of the claimed allowable cost for performing this contract.

Alternate III (AUG 2012). As prescribed in 16.307(a)(4), substitute the following paragraph (a)(1) for paragraph (a)(1) of the basic clause:

(a)(1) The Government will make payments to the Contractor when requested as work progresses, but not more often than once every two weeks, in amounts determined to be allowable by the Contracting Officer in accordance with FAR subpart 31.6 in effect on the date of this contract and the terms of this contract. The Contractor may submit to an authorized representative of the Contracting Officer, in such form and reasonable detail as the representative may require, an invoice or voucher supported by a statement of the claimed allowable cost for performing this contract.

Alternate IV (AUG 2012). As prescribed in 16.307(a)(5), substitute the following paragraph (a)(1) for paragraph (a)(1) of the basic clause:

(a)(1) The Government will make payments to the Contractor when requested as work progresses, but not more often than once every two weeks, in amounts determined to be allowable by the Contracting Officer in accordance with FAR subpart 31.7 in effect on the date of this contract and the terms of this contract. The Contractor may submit to an authorized representative of the Contracting Officer, in such form and reasonable detail as the representative may require, an invoice or voucher supported by a statement of the claimed allowable cost for performing this contract.

[FAC 84-7, 50 FR 23607, 6/4/85, effective 4/30/85; FAC 90-5, 56 FR 29138, 6/25/91, effective 7/25/91; FAC 90-32, 60 FR 48206, 9/18/95, effective 10/1/95; FAC 90-39, 61 FR 31612, 6/20/96, effective 8/19/96; FAC 90-43, Final rule, 61 FR 67408, 12/20/96, effective 2/18/97; FAC 90-44, Final rule, 61 FR 69286, 12/31/96, effective 3/3/97; FAC 90-46, 62 FR 12690, 3/17/97, effective 5/16/97; FAC 97-3, 62 FR 64912, 12/9/97, effective 2/9/98; FAC 97-4, 63 FR 9048, 2/23/98, effective 4/24/98; FAC 97-16, 65 FR 16274, 3/27/2000, effective 3/27/2000; FAC 2001-02, 66 FR 65347, 12/18/2001, effective 2/19/2002; FAC 2001-04, 67 FR 6112, 2/8/2002, effective 2/20/2002; FAC 2001-10, 67 FR 70520, 11/22/2002, effective 12/23/2002; FAC 2005-52, 76 FR 31402, 5/31/2011, effective 6/30/2011; FAC 2005-60, 77 FR 44059, 7/26/2012, effective 8/27/2012; FAC 2005-68, 78 FR 38535, 6/26/2013, effective 6/26/2013; FAC 2005-74, 79 FR 31195, 5/30/2014, effective 5/30/2014; FAC 2005-100, 83 FR 42571, 8/22/2018, effective 8/22/2018]

52.216-8 Fixed Fee.

As prescribed in 16.307(b), insert the following clause:

FIXED FEE (JUN 2011)

(a) The Government shall pay the Contractor for performing this contract the fixed fee specified in the Schedule.

(b) Payment of the fixed fee shall be made as specified in the Schedule; provided that the Contracting Officer withholds a reserve not to exceed 15 percent of the total fixed fee or $100,000, whichever is less, to protect the Government's interest. The Contracting Officer shall release 75 percent of all fee withholds under this contract after receipt of an adequate certified final indirect cost rate proposal covering the year of physical completion of this contract, provided the Contractor has satisfied all other contract terms and conditions, including the submission of the final patent and royalty reports, and is not delinquent in submitting final vouchers on prior years' settlements. The Contracting Officer may release up to 90 percent of the fee withholds under this contract based on the Contractor's past performance related to the submission and settlement of final indirect cost rate proposals.

(End of clause)

[FAC 90-32, 60 FR 48206, 9/18/95, effective 10/1/95; FAC 90-44, Final rule, 61 FR 69286, 12/31/96, effective 3/3/97; FAC 90-46, 62 FR 12690, 3/17/97, effective 5/16/97; FAC 2005-52, 76 FR 31402, 5/31/2011, effective 6/30/2011]

52.216-9 Fixed Fee—Construction.

As prescribed in 16.307(c), insert the following clause:

FIXED FEE—CONSTRUCTION (JUN 2011)

(a) The Government shall pay to the Contractor for performing this contract the fixed fee specified in the Schedule.

(b) Payment of the fixed fee shall be made in installments based upon the percentage of completion of the work as determined from estimates submitted to and approved by the Contracting Officer, but subject to the withholding provisions of paragraph (c) of this section.

(c) The Contracting Officer shall withhold a reserve not to exceed 15 percent of the total fixed fee or $100,000, whichever is less, to protect the Government's interest. The Contracting Officer shall release 75 percent of all fee withholds under this contract after receipt of an adequate certified final indirect cost rate proposal covering the year of physical completion of this contract, provided the Contractor has satisfied all other contract terms and conditions, including the submission of the final patent and royalty reports, and is not delinquent in submitting final vouchers on prior years' settlements. The Contracting Officer may release up to 90 percent of the fee withholds under this contract based on the Contractor's past performance related to the submission and settlement of final indirect cost rate proposals.

(End of clause)

[FAC 90-32, 60 FR 48206, 9/18/95, effective 10/1/95; FAC 90-44, Final rule, 61 FR 69286, 12/31/96, effective 3/3/97; FAC 90-46, 62 FR 12690, 3/17/97, effective 5/16/97; FAC 2005-52, 76 FR 31402, 5/31/2011, effective 6/30/2011]

52.216-10 Incentive Fee.

As prescribed in 16.307(d), insert the following clause:

INCENTIVE FEE (JUN 2011)

(a) *General*. The Government shall pay the Contractor for performing this contract a fee determined as provided in this contract.

(b) *Target cost and target fee*. The target cost and target fee specified in the Schedule are subject to adjustment if the contract is modified in accordance with paragraph (d) of this clause.

(1) *Target cost,* as used in this contract, means the estimated cost of this contract as initially negotiated, adjusted in accordance with paragraph (d) of this clause.

(2) *Target fee,* as used in this contract, means the fee initially negotiated on the assumption that this contract would be performed for a cost equal to the estimated cost initially negotiated, adjusted in accordance with paragraph (d) below.

(c) *Withholding of payment*. (1) Normally, the Government shall pay the fee to the Contractor as specified in the Schedule. However, when the Contracting Officer considers that performance or cost indicates that the Contractor will not achieve target, the Government shall pay on the basis of an appropriate lesser fee. When the Contractor demonstrates that performance or cost clearly indicates that the Contractor will earn a fee significantly above the target fee, the Government may, at the sole discretion of the Contracting Officer, pay on the basis of an appropriate higher fee.

(2) Payment of the incentive fee shall be made as specified in the Schedule; provided that the Contracting Officer withholds a reserve not to exceed 15 percent of the total incentive fee or $100,000, whichever is less, to protect the Government's interest. The Contracting Officer shall release 75 percent of all fee withholds under this contract after receipt of an adequate certified final indirect cost rate proposal covering the year of physical completion of this contract, provided the Contractor has satisfied all other contract terms and conditions, including the submission of the final patent and royalty reports, and is not delinquent in submitting final vouchers on prior years' settlements. The Contracting Officer may release up to 90 percent of the fee withholds under this contract based on the Contractor's past performance related to the submission and settlement of final indirect cost rate proposals.

(d) *Equitable adjustments.* When the work under this contract is increased or decreased by a modification to this contract or when any equitable adjustment in the target cost is authorized under any other clause, equitable adjustments in the target cost, target fee, minimum fee, and maximum fee, as appropriate, shall be stated in a supplemental agreement to this contract.

(e) *Fee payable.* (1) The fee payable under this contract shall be the target fee increased by ____ [*Contracting Officer insert Contractor's participation*] cents for every dollar that the total allowable cost is less than the target cost or decreased by ____ [*Contracting Officer insert Contractor's participation*] cents for every dollar that the total allowable cost exceeds the target cost. In no event shall the fee be greater than ____ [*Contracting Officer insert percentage* percent or less than ____ [*Contracting Officer insert percentage*] percent of the target cost.

(2) The fee shall be subject to adjustment, to the extent provided in paragraph (d) of this clause, and within the minimum and maximum fee limitations in paragraph (e) (1) of this clause, when the total allowable cost is increased or decreased as a consequence of—

(i) Payments made under assignments; or

(ii) Claims excepted from the release as required by paragraph (h) (2) of the Allowable Cost and Payment clause.

(3) If this contract is terminated in its entirety, the portion of the target fee payable shall not be subject to an increase or decrease as provided in this paragraph. The termination shall be accomplished in accordance with other applicable clauses of this contract.

(4) For the purpose of fee adjustment, "total allowable cost" shall not include allowable costs arising out of—

(i) Any of the causes covered by the Excusable Delays clause to the extent that they are beyond the control and without the fault or negligence of the Contractor or any subcontractor;

(ii) The taking effect, after negotiating the target cost, of a statute, court decision, written ruling, or regulation that results in the Contractor's being required to pay or bear the burden of any tax or duty or rate increase in a tax or duty;

(iii) Any direct cost attributed to the Contractor's involvement in litigation as required by the Contracting Officer pursuant to a clause of this contract, including furnishing evidence and information requested pursuant to the Notice and Assistance Regarding Patent and Copyright Infringement clause;

(iv) The purchase and maintenance of additional insurance not in the target cost and required by the Contracting Officer, or claims for reimbursement for liabilities to third persons pursuant to the Insurance Liability to Third Persons clause;

(v) Any claim, loss, or damage resulting from a risk for which the Contractor has been relieved of liability by the Government Property clause; or

(vi) Any claim, loss, or damage resulting from a risk defined in the contract as unusually hazardous or as a nuclear risk and against which the Government has expressly agreed to indemnify the Contractor.

(5) All other allowable costs are included in "total allowable cost" for fee adjustment in accordance with this paragraph (e), unless otherwise specifically provided in this contract.

(f) *Contract modification.* The total allowable cost and the adjusted fee determined as provided in this clause shall be evidenced by a modification to this contract signed by the Contractor and Contracting Officer.

(g) *Inconsistencies.* In the event of any language inconsistencies between this clause and provisioning documents or Government options under this contract, compensation for spare parts or other supplies and services ordered under such documents shall be determined in accordance with this clause.

(End of clause)

[FAC 90-32, 60 FR 48206, 9/18/95, effective 10/1/95; FAC 90-44, Final rule, 61 FR 69286, 12/31/96, effective 3/3/97; FAC 90-46, 62 FR 12690, 3/17/97, effective 5/16/97; FAC 2005-52, 76 FR 31402, 5/31/2011, effective 6/30/2011]

52.216-11 Cost Contract—No Fee.

As prescribed in 16.307(e), insert the clause in solicitations and contracts when a cost-reimbursement contract is contemplated that provides no fee and is not a cost-sharing contract. This clause may be modified by substituting "$10,000" in lieu of "$100,000" as the maximum reserve in paragraph (b) if the Contractor is a nonprofit organization.

COST CONTRACT—NO FEE (APR 1984)

(a) The Government shall not pay the Contractor a fee for performing this contract.

(b) After payment of 80 percent of the total estimated cost shown in the Schedule, the Contracting Officer may withhold further payment of allowable cost until a reserve is set aside in an amount that the Contracting Officer considers necessary to protect the Government's interest. This reserve shall not exceed one percent of the total estimated cost shown in the Schedule or $100,000, whichever is less.

(End of clause)

Alternate I (APR 1984). In a contract for research and development with an educational institution or a nonprofit organization, for which the contracting officer has determined that withholding of a portion of allowable costs is not required, delete paragraph (b) of the basic clause.

[FAC 90-32, 60 FR 48206, 9/18/95, effective 10/1/95; FAC 2005-17, 72 FR 27364, 5/15/2007, effective 6/14/2007]

52.216-12 Cost-Sharing Contract—No Fee.

As prescribed in 16.307(f), insert the following clause in solicitations and contracts when a cost-sharing contract is contemplated. This clause may be modified by substituting "$10,000" in lieu of "$100,000" as the maximum reserve in paragraph (b) if the contract is with a nonprofit organization.

COST-SHARING CONTRACT—NO FEE (APR 1984)

(a) The Government shall not pay to the Contractor a fee for performing this contract.

(b) After paying 80 percent of the Government's share of the total estimated cost of performance shown in the Schedule, the Contracting Officer may withhold further payment of allowable cost until a reserve is set aside in an amount that the Contracting Officer considers necessary to protect the Government's interest. This reserve shall not exceed one percent of the Government's share of the total estimated cost shown in the Schedule or $100,000, whichever is less.

(End of clause)

Alternate I (APR 1984). In a contract for research and development with an educational institution, for which the contracting officer has determined that withholding of a portion of allowable cost is not required, delete paragraph (b) of the basic clause.

[FAC 90-32, 60 FR 48206, 9/18/95, effective 10/1/95; FAC 2005-17, 72 FR 27364, 5/15/2007, effective 6/14/2007]

52.216-13 [Removed and Reserved]

[FAC 90-23, 59 FR 67010, 12/28/94, effective 2/27/95; FAC 90-32, 60 FR 48206, 9/18/95, effective 10/1/95; FAC 90-39, 61 FR 31612, 6/20/96, effective 8/19/96; FAC 90-44, Final rule, 61 FR 69286, 12/31/96, effective 3/3/97; FAC 90-46, 62 FR 12690, 3/17/97, effective 5/16/97; FAC 97-3, 62 FR 64912, 12/9/97, effective 2/9/98, corrected, 63 FR 1533, 1/9/98; FAC 97-4, 63 FR 9048, 2/23/98, effective 4/24/98; FAC 2001-02, 66 FR 65347, 12/18/2001, effective 2/19/2002; FAC 2005-17, 72 FR 27364, 5/15/2007, effective 6/14/2007]

52.216-14 [Removed and Reserved]

[FAC 90-32, 60 FR 48206, 9/18/95, effective 10/1/95; FAC 2005-17, 72 FR 27364, 5/15/2007, effective 6/14/2007]

52.216-15 Predetermined Indirect Cost Rates.

As prescribed in 16.307(g), insert the following clause:

PREDETERMINED INDIRECT COST RATES (APR 1998)

(a) Notwithstanding the Allowable Cost and Payment clause of this contract, the allowable indirect costs under this contract shall be obtained by applying predetermined indirect cost rates to bases agreed upon by the parties, as specified below.

(b) (1) The Contractor shall submit an adequate final indirect cost rate proposal to the Contracting Officer (or cognizant Federal agency official) and auditor within the 6-month period following the expiration of each of its fiscal years. Reasonable extensions, for exceptional circumstances only, may be requested in writing by the Contractor and granted in writing by the Contracting Officer. The Contractor shall support its proposal with adequate supporting data.

(2) The proposed rates shall be based on the Contractor's actual cost experience for that period. The appropriate Government representative and the Contractor shall establish the final indirect cost rates as promptly as practical after receipt of the Contractor's proposal.

(c) Allowability of costs and acceptability of cost allocation methods shall be determined in accordance with FAR Subpart 31.3 in effect on the date of this contract.

(d) Predetermined rate agreements in effect on the date of this contract shall be incorporated into the contract Schedule. The Contracting Officer (or cognizant Federal agency official) and Contractor shall negotiate rates for subsequent periods and execute a written indirect cost rate agreement setting forth the results. The agreement shall specify (1) the agreed-upon predetermined indirect cost rates, (2) the bases to which the rates apply, (3) the period for which the rates apply, and (4) the specific items treated as direct costs or any changes in the items previously agreed to be direct costs. The indirect cost rate agreement shall not change any monetary ceiling, contract obligation, or specific cost allowance or disallowance provided for in this contract. The agreement is incorporated into this contract upon execution.

(e) Pending establishment of predetermined indirect cost rates for any fiscal year (or other period agreed to by the parties), the Contractor shall be reimbursed either at the rates fixed for the previous fiscal year (or other period) or at billing rates acceptable to the Contracting Officer (or cognizant Federal agency official), subject to appropriate adjustment when the final rates for that period are established.

(f) Any failure by the parties to agree on any predetermined indirect cost rates under this clause shall not be considered a dispute within the meaning of the Disputes clause. If for any fiscal year (or other period specified in the Schedule) the parties fail to agree to predetermined indirect cost rates, the allowable indirect costs shall be obtained by applying final indirect cost rates established in accordance with the Allowable Cost and Payment clause.

(g) Allowable indirect costs for the period from the beginning of performance until the end of the Contractor's fiscal year (or other period specified in the Schedule) shall be obtained using the predetermined indirect cost rates and the bases shown in the Schedule.

(End of clause)

[FAC 90-32, 60 FR 48206, 9/18/95, effective 10/1/95; FAC 90-39, 61 FR 31621, 6/20/96, effective 8/19/96; FAC 97-3, 62 FR 64912, 12/9/97, effective 2/9/98; FAC 97-4, 63 FR 9048, 2/23/98, effective 4/24/98; FAC 2005-17, 72 FR 27364, 5/15/2007, effective 6/14/2007]

52.216-16 Incentive Price Revision—Firm Target.

As prescribed in 16.406(a), insert the following clause:

INCENTIVE PRICE REVISION—FIRM TARGET (OCT 1997)

(a) *General.* The supplies or services identified in the Schedule as Items ____ [*Contracting Officer insert Schedule line item numbers*] are subject to price revision in accordance with this clause; provided, that in no event shall the total final price of these items exceed the ceiling price of ____ dollars ($ ____). Any supplies or services that are to be (1) ordered separately under, or otherwise added to, this contract and (2) subject to price revision in accordance with the terms of this clause shall be identified as such in a modification to this contract.

(b) *Definition. Costs*, as used in this clause, means allowable costs in accordance with Part 31 of the Federal Acquisition Regulation (FAR) in effect on the date of this contract.

(c) *Data submission*. (1) Within _____ [*Contracting Officer insert number of days*] days after the end of the month in which the Contractor has delivered the last unit of supplies and completed the services specified by item number in paragraph (a) of this clause, the Contractor shall submit in the format of Table 15-2, FAR 15.408, or in any other form on which the parties agree—

(i) A detailed statement of all costs incurred up to the end of that month in performing all work under the items;

(ii) An estimate of costs of further performance, if any, that may be necessary to complete performance of all work under the items;

(iii) A list of all residual inventory and an estimate of its value; and

(iv) Any other relevant data that the Contracting Officer may reasonably require.

(2) If the Contractor fails to submit the data required by subparagraph (c)(1) of this clause within the time specified and it is later determined that the Government has overpaid the Contractor, the Contractor shall repay the excess to the Government immediately. Unless repaid within 30 days after the end of the data submittal period, the amount of the excess shall bear interest, computed from the date the data were due to the date of repayment, at the rate established in accordance with the Interest clause.

(d) *Price revision*. Upon the Contracting Officer's receipt of the data required by paragraph (c) of this clause, the Contracting Officer and the Contractor shall promptly establish the total final price of the items specified in (a) of this clause by applying to final negotiated cost an adjustment for profit or loss, as follows:

(1) On the basis of the information required by paragraph (c) of this clause, together with any other pertinent information, the parties shall negotiate the total final cost incurred or to be incurred for supplies delivered (or services performed) and accepted by the Government and which are subject to price revision under this clause.

(2) The total final price shall be established by applying to the total final negotiated cost an adjustment for profit or loss, as follows:

(i) If the total final negotiated cost is equal to the total target cost, the adjustment is the total target profit.

(ii) If the total final negotiated cost is greater than the total target cost, the adjustment is the total target profit, less ____ [*Contracting Officer insert percent*] percent of the amount by which the total final negotiated cost exceeds the total target cost.

(iii) If the final negotiated cost is less than the total target cost, the adjustment is the total target profit plus ____ [*Contracting Officer insert percent*] percent of the amount by which the total final negotiated cost is less than the total target cost.

(e) *Contract modification*. The total final price of the items specified in paragraph (a) of this clause shall be evidenced by a modification to this contract, signed by the Contractor and the Contracting Officer. This price shall not be subject to revision, notwithstanding any changes in the cost of performing the contract, except to the extent that—

(1) The parties may agree in writing, before the determination of total final price, to exclude specific elements of cost from this price and to a procedure for subsequent disposition of those elements; and

(2) Adjustments or credits are explicitly permitted or required by this or any other clause in this contract.

(f) *Adjusting billing prices*. (1) Pending execution of the contract modification (see paragraph (e) of this clause), the Contractor shall submit invoices or vouchers in accordance with billing prices as provided in this paragraph. The billing prices shall be the target prices shown in this contract.

(2) If at any time it appears from information provided by the contractor under subparagraph (g)(2) of this clause that the then-current billing prices will be substantially

greater than the estimated final prices, the parties shall negotiate a reduction in the billing prices. Similarly, the parties may negotiate an increase in billing prices by any or all of the difference between the target prices and the ceiling price, upon the Contractor's submission of factual data showing that final cost under this contract will be substantially greater than the target cost.

(3) Any billing price adjustment shall be reflected in a contract modification and shall not affect the determination of the total final price under paragraph (d) of this clause. After the contract modification establishing the total final price is executed, the total amount paid or to be paid on all invoices or vouchers shall be adjusted to reflect the total final price, and any resulting additional payments, refunds, or credits shall be made promptly.

(g) *Quarterly limitation on payments statement.* This paragraph (g) shall apply until final price revision under this contract has been completed.

(1) Within 45 days after the end of each quarter of the Contractor's fiscal year in which a delivery is first made (or services are first performed) and accepted by the Government under this contract, and for each quarter thereafter, the Contractor shall submit to the contract administration office (with a copy to the contracting office and the cognizant contract auditor) a statement, cumulative from the beginning of the contract, showing—

(i) The total contract price of all supplies delivered (or services performed) and accepted by the Government and for which final prices have been established;

(ii) The total costs (estimated to the extent necessary) reasonably incurred for, and properly allocable solely to, the supplies delivered (or services performed) and accepted by the Government and for which final prices have not been established;

(iii) The portion of the total target profit (used in establishing the initial contract price or agreed to for the purpose of this paragraph (g)) that is in direct proportion to the supplies delivered (or services performed) and accepted by the Government and for which final prices have not been established—increased or decreased in accordance with subparagraph (d)(2) of this clause, when the amount stated under subdivision (g)(7)(ii), of this clause, differs from the aggregate target costs of the supplies or services; and

(iv) The total amount of all invoices or vouchers for supplies delivered (or services performed) and accepted by the Government (including amounts applied or to be applied to liquidate progress payments).

(2) Notwithstanding any provision of this contract authorizing greater payments, if on any quarterly statement the amount under subdivision (g)(1)(iv) of this clause exceeds the sum due the Contractor, as computed in accordance with subdivisions (1)(i), (ii), and (iii) of this clause, the Contractor shall immediately refund or credit to the Government the amount of this excess. The Contractor may, when appropriate, reduce this refund or credit by the amount of any applicable tax credits due the Contractor under 26 U.S.C. 1481 and by the amount of previous refunds or credits effected under this clause. If any portion of the excess has been applied to the liquidation of progress payments, then that portion may, instead of being refunded, be added to the unliquidated progress payment account consistent with the Progress Payments clause. The Contractor shall provide complete details to support any claimed reductions in refunds.

(3) If the Contractor fails to submit the quarterly statement within 45 days after the end of each quarter and it is later determined that the Government has overpaid the Contractor, the Contractor shall repay the excess to the Government immediately. Unless repaid within 30 days after the end of the statement submittal period, the amount of the excess shall bear interest, computed from the date the quarterly statement was due to the date of repayment, at the rate established in accordance with the Interest clause.

(h) *Subcontracts.* No subcontract placed under this contract may provide for payment on a cost-plus-a-percentage-of-cost basis.

(i) *Disagreements.* If the Contractor and the Contracting Officer fail to agree upon the total final price within 60 days (or within such other period as the Contracting Officer may specify) after the date on which the data required by paragraph (c) of this clause are to be submitted, the Contracting Officer shall promptly issue a decision in accordance with the Disputes clause.

(j) *Termination.* If this contract is terminated before the total final price is established, prices of supplies or services subject to price revision shall be established in accordance with this clause for (1) completed supplies and services accepted by the Government and (2) those supplies and services not terminated under a partial termination. All other elements of the termination shall be resolved in accordance with other applicable clauses of this contract.

(k) *Equitable adjustment under other clauses.* If an equitable adjustment in the contract price is made under any other clause of this contract before the total final price is established, the adjustment shall be made in the total target cost and may be made in the maximum dollar limit on the total final price, the total target profit, or both. If the adjustment is made after the total final price is established, only the total final price shall be adjusted.

(l) *Exclusion from target price and total final price.* If any clause of this contract provides that the contract price does not or will not include an amount for a specific purpose, then neither any target price nor the total final price includes or will include any amount for that purpose.

(m) *Separate reimbursement.* If any clause of this contract expressly provides that the cost of performance of an obligation shall be at Government expense, that expense shall not be included in any target price or in the total final price, but shall be reimbursed separately.

(n) *Taxes.* As used in the Federal, State, and Local Taxes clause or in any other clause that provides for certain taxes or duties to be included in, or excluded from, the contract price, the term "contract price" includes the total target price or, if it has been established, the total final price. When any of these clauses requires that the contract price be increased or decreased as a result of changes in the obligation of the Contractor to pay or bear the burden of certain taxes or duties, the increase or decrease shall be made in the total target price or, if it has been established, in the total final price, so that it will not affect the Contractor's profit or loss on this contract.

(End of clause)

Alternate I (APR 1984). As prescribed in 16.406(a), add the following paragraph (o) to the basic clause:

(o) *Provisioning and options.* Parts, other supplies, or services that are to be furnished under this contract on the basis of a provisioning document or Government option shall be subject to price revision in accordance with this clause. Any prices established for these parts, other supplies, or services under a provisioning document or Government option shall be treated as target prices. Target cost and profit covering these parts, other supplies, or services may be established separately, in the aggregate, or in any combination, as the parties may agree.

[FAC 90-32, 60 FR 48206, 9/18/95, effective 10/1/95; FAC 90-39, 61 FR 31612, 6/20/96, effective 8/19/96; FAC 90-43, Final rule, 61 FR 67408, 12/20/96, effective 2/18/97; FAC 90-46, 62 FR 12689, 3/17/97, effective 5/16/97; FAC 97-2, 62 FR 51224, 9/30/97, effective 10/10/97]

52.216-17 Incentive Price Revision—Successive Targets.

As prescribed in 16.406(b), insert the following clause:

INCENTIVE PRICE REVISION—SUCCESSIVE TARGETS (OCT 1997)

(a) *General.* The supplies or services identified in the Schedule as Items ___ [*Contracting Officer insert line item numbers*] are subject to price revision in accordance with this clause; *provided,* that in no event shall the total final price of these items exceed the ceiling price of ___ dollars ($___). The prices of these items shown in the Schedule are the initial target prices, which include an initial target profit of ____ [*Contracting Officer insert percent*] percent of the initial target cost. Any supplies or services that are to be—

(1) Ordered separately under, or otherwise added to, this contract; and

(2) Subject to price revision in accordance with this clause shall be identified as such in a modification to this contract.

(b) *Definition. Costs,* as used in this clause, means allowable costs in accordance with Part 31 of the Federal Acquisition Regulation (FAR) in effect on the date of this contract.

(c) *Submitting data for establishing the firm fixed price or a final profit adjustment formula.* (1) Within ____ [*Contracting Officer insert number of days*] days after the end of the month in which the Contractor has completed ____ (see Note 1), the Contractor shall submit the following data:

(i) A proposed firm fixed price or total firm target price for supplies delivered and to be delivered and services performed and to be performed.

(ii) A detailed statement of all costs incurred in the performance of this contract through the end of the month specified above, in the format of Table 15-2, FAR 15.408 (or in any other form on which the parties may agree), with sufficient supporting data to disclose unit costs and cost trends for—

(A) Supplies delivered and services performed; and

(B) Inventories of work in process and undelivered contract supplies on hand (estimated to the extent necessary).

(iii) An estimate of costs of all supplies delivered and to be delivered and all services performed and to be performed under this contract, using the statement of costs incurred plus an estimate of costs to complete performance, in the format of Table 15-2, FAR 15.408 (or in any other form on which the parties may agree), together with—

(A) Sufficient data to support the accuracy and reliability of the estimate; and

(B) An explanation of the differences between this estimate and the original estimate used to establish the initial target prices.

(2) The Contractor shall also submit, to the extent that it becomes available before negotiations establishing the total firm price are concluded—

(i) Supplemental statements of costs incurred after the end of the month specified in subparagraph (1) of this section for—

(A) Supplies delivered and services performed; and

(B) Inventories of work in process and undelivered contract supplies on hand (estimated to the extent necessary); and

(ii) Any other relevant data that the Contracting Officer may reasonably require.

(3) If the Contractor fails to submit the data required by subparagraphs (c)(1) and (2) of this section within the time specified and it is later determined that the Government has overpaid the Contractor, the Contractor shall repay the excess to the Government immediately. Unless repaid within 30 days after the end of the data submittal period, the amount of the excess shall bear interest, computed from the date the data were due to the date of repayment, at the rate established in accordance with the Interest clause.

(d) *Establishing firm fixed price or final profit adjustment formula.* Upon the Contracting Officer's receipt of the data required by paragraph (c) of this section, the Contracting Officer and the Contractor shall promptly establish either a firm fixed price or a profit adjustment formula for determining final profit, as follows:

(1) The parties shall negotiate a total firm target cost, based upon the data submitted under paragraph (c) of this section.

(2) If the total firm target cost is more than the total initial target cost, the total initial target profit shall be decreased. If the total firm target cost is less than the total initial target cost, the total initial target profit shall be increased. The initial target profit shall be increased or decreased by ____ percent (see Note 2) of the difference between the total initial target cost and the total firm

target cost. The resulting amount shall be the total firm target profit; *provided*, that in no event shall the total firm target profit be less than ___ percent or more than ___ percent [*Contracting Officer insert percents*] of the total initial target cost.

(3) If the total firm target cost plus the total firm target profit represent a reasonable price for performing that part of the contract subject to price revision under this clause, the parties may agree on a firm fixed price, which shall be evidenced by a contract modification signed by the Contractor and the Contracting Officer.

(4) Failure of the parties to agree to a firm fixed price shall not constitute a dispute under the Disputes clause. If agreement is not reached, or if establishment of a firm fixed price is inappropriate, the Contractor and the Contracting Officer shall establish a profit adjustment formula under which the total final price shall be established by applying to the total final negotiated cost an adjustment for profit or loss, determined as follows:

(i) If the total final negotiated cost is equal to the total firm target cost, the adjustment is the total firm target profit.

(ii) If the total final negotiated cost is greater than the total firm target cost, the adjustment is the total firm target profit, less ___ percent of the amount by which the total final negotiated cost exceeds the total firm target cost.

(iii) If the total final negotiated cost is less than the total firm target cost, the adjustment is the total firm target profit, plus ___ percent of the amount by which the total final negotiated cost is less than the total firm target cost.

(iv) The total firm target cost, total firm target profit, and the profit adjustment formula for determining final profit shall be evidenced by a modification to this contract signed by the Contractor and the Contracting Officer.

(e) *Submitting data for final price revision.* Unless a firm fixed price has been established in accordance with paragraph (d) of this section within ___ [*Contracting Officer insert number of days*] days after the end of the month in which the Contractor has delivered the last unit of supplies and completed the services specified by item number in paragraph (a) of this section, the Contractor shall submit in the format of Table 15-2, FAR 15.408 (or in any other form on which the parties agree)—

(1) A detailed statement of all costs incurred up to the end of that month in performing all work under the items;

(2) An estimate of costs of further performance, if any, that may be necessary to complete performance of all work under the items;

(3) A list of all residual inventory and an estimate of its value; and

(4) Any other relevant data that the Contracting Officer may reasonably require.

(f) *Final price revision.* Unless a firm fixed price has been agreed to in accordance with paragraph (d) of this section, the Contractor and the Contracting Officer shall, promptly after submission of the data required by paragraph (e) of this section, establish the total final price, as follows:

(1) On the basis of the information required by paragraph (e) of this section, together with any other pertinent information, the parties shall negotiate the total final cost incurred or to be incurred for the supplies delivered (or services performed) and accepted by the Government and which are subject to price revision under this clause.

(2) The total final price shall be established by applying to the total final negotiated cost an adjustment for final profit or loss determined as agreed upon under subparagraph (d)(4) of this section.

(g) *Contract modification.* The total final price of the items specified in paragraph (a) of this section shall be evidenced by a modification to this contract, signed by the Contractor and the Contracting Officer. This price shall not be subject to revision, notwithstanding any changes in the cost of performing the contract, except to the extent that—

(1) The parties may agree in writing, before the determination of total final price,

to exclude specific elements of cost from this price and to a procedure for subsequent disposition of these elements; and

(2) Adjustments or credits are explicitly permitted or required by this or any other clause in this contract.

(h) *Adjustment of billing prices.* (1) Pending execution of the contract modification (see paragraph (e) of this section), the Contractor shall submit invoices or vouchers in accordance with billing prices as provided in this paragraph. The billing prices shall be the initial target prices shown in this contract until firm target prices are established under paragraph (d) of this section. When established, the firm target prices shall be used as the billing prices.

(2) If at any time it appears from information provided by the Contractor under subparagraph (i) (1) of this section that the then-current billing prices will be substantially greater than the estimated final prices, the parties shall negotiate a reduction in the billing prices. Similarly, the parties may negotiate an increase in billing prices by any or all of the difference between the target prices and the ceiling price, upon the Contractor's submission of factual data showing that the final cost under this contract will be substantially greater than the target cost.

(3) Any adjustment of billing prices shall be reflected in a contract modification and shall not affect the determination of any price under paragraph (d) or (f) above. After the contract modification establishing the total final price is executed, the total amount paid or to be paid on all invoices or vouchers shall be adjusted to reflect the total final price, and any resulting additional payments, refunds, or credits shall be made promptly.

(i) *Quarterly limitation on payments statement.* This paragraph (i) shall apply until a firm fixed price or a total final price is established under subparagraph (d) (3) or (f) (2).

(1) Within 45 days after the end of each quarter of the Contractor's fiscal year in which a delivery is first made (or services are first performed) and accepted by the Government under this contract, and for each quarter thereafter, the Contractor shall submit to the contract administration office (with a copy to the contracting office and the cognizant contract auditor) a statement, cumulative from the beginning of the contract, showing—

(i) The total contract price of all supplies delivered (or services performed) and accepted by the Government and for which final prices have been established;

(ii) The total cost (estimated to the extent necessary) reasonably incurred for, and properly allocable solely to, the supplies delivered (or services performed) and accepted by the Government and for which final prices have not been established;

(iii) The portion of the total interim profit (used in establishing the initial contract price or agreed to for the purpose of this paragraph (i)) that is in direct proportion to the supplies delivered (or services performed) and accepted by the Government and for which final prices have not been established, increased or decreased in accordance with subparagraph (d) (4) of this section when the amount stated under subdivision (ii), of this section, differs from the aggregate firm target costs of the supplies or services; and

(iv) The total amount of all invoices or vouchers for supplies delivered (or services performed) and accepted by the Government (including amounts applied or to be applied to liquidate progress payments).

(2) Notwithstanding any provision of this contract authorizing greater payments, if on any quarterly statement the amount under subdivision; (1) (iv) of this section exceeds the sum due the Contractor, as computed in accordance with subdivisions; (1) (i), (ii), and (iii) of this section, the Contractor shall immediately refund or credit to the Government the amount of this excess. The Contractor may, when appropriate, reduce this refund or credit by the amount of any applicable tax credits due the Contractor under 26 U.S.C. 1481 and by the amount of previous refunds or credits effected under this clause. If any portion of the excess has been applied to the liquidation of progress payments, then that portion may, instead of being refunded, be added to the unliquidated progress payment account consistent with

the Progress Payments clause. The Contractor shall provide complete details to support any claimed reductions in refunds.

(3) If the Contractor fails to submit the quarterly statement within 45 days after the end of each quarter and it is later determined that the Government has overpaid the Contractor, the Contractor shall repay the excess to the Government immediately. Unless repaid within 30 days after the end of the statement submittal period, the amount of the excess shall bear interest, computed from the date the quarterly statement was due to the date of repayment, at the rate established in accordance with the Interest clause.

(j) *Subcontracts.* No subcontract placed under this contract may provide for payment on a cost-plus-a-percentage-of-cost basis.

(k) *Disagreements.* If the Contractor and the Contracting Officer fail to agree upon (1) a total firm target cost and a final profit adjustment formula or (2) a total final price, within 60 days (or within such other period as the Contracting Officer may specify) after the date on which the data required in paragraphs (c) and (e) of this section are to be submitted, the Contracting Officer shall promptly issue a decision in accordance with the Disputes clause.

(*l*) *Termination.* If this contract is terminated before the total final price is established, prices of supplies or services subject to price revision shall be established in accordance with this clause for (1) completed supplies and services accepted by the Government and (2) those supplies or services not terminated under a partial termination. All other elements of the termination shall be resolved in accordance with other applicable clauses of this contract.

(m) *Equitable adjustments under other clauses.* If an equitable adjustment in the contract price is made under any other clause of this contract before the total final price is established, the adjustment shall be made in the total target cost and may be made in the maximum dollar limit on the total final price, the total target profit, or both. If the adjustment is made after the total final price is established, only the total final price shall be adjusted.

(n) *Exclusion from target price and total final price.* If any clause of this contract provides that the contract price does not or will not include an amount for a specific purpose, then neither any target price nor the total final price includes or will include any amount for that purpose.

(o) *Separate reimbursement.* If any clause of this contract expressly provides that the cost of performance of an obligation shall be at Government expense, that expense shall not be included in any target price or in the total final price, but shall be reimbursed separately.

(p) *Taxes.* As used in the Federal, State, and Local Taxes clause or in any other clause that provides for certain taxes or duties to be included in, or excluded from, the contract price, the term "contract price" includes the total target price or, if it has been established, the total final price. When any of these clauses requires that the contract price be increased or decreased as a result of changes in the obligation of the Contractor to pay or bear the burden of certain taxes or duties, the increase or decrease shall be made in the total target price or, if it has been established, in the total final price, so that it will not affect the Contractor's profit or loss on this contract.

(End of clause)

NOTES:

(1) The degree of completion may be based on a percentage of contract performance or any other reasonable basis.

(2) The language may be changed to describe a negotiated adjustment pattern under which the extent of adjustment is not the same for all levels of cost variation.

Alternate I (APR 1984). As prescribed in 16.406(b), add the following paragraph (q) to the basic clause:

(q) *Provisioning and options.* Parts, other supplies, or services that are to be furnished under this contract on the basis of a provisioning document or Government option shall be subject to price revision in accordance with this clause. Any prices established for these parts, other supplies, or services under a provisioning document or Government option shall be treated as initial target prices, or target prices as agreed upon and stipulated in the pricing document supporting the provisioning or added items. Initial or firm target costs and profits and final prices covering these parts, other supplies, or services may be established separately, in the aggregate, or in any combination, as the parties may agree.

[FAC 90-32, 60 FR 48206, 9/18/95, effective 10/1/95; FAC 90-43, Final rule, 61 FR 67408, 12/20/96, effective 2/18/97; FAC 90-46, 62 FR 12689, 3/17/97, effective 5/16/97; FAC 97-2, 62 FR 51224, 9/30/97, effective 10/10/97]

52.216-18 Ordering.

As prescribed in 16.506(a), insert the following clause:

ORDERING (OCT 1995)

(a) Any supplies and services to be furnished under this contract shall be ordered by issuance of delivery orders or task orders by the individuals or activities designated in the Schedule. Such orders may be issued from __ through __ [*insert dates*].

(b) All delivery orders or task orders are subject to the terms and conditions of this contract. In the event of conflict between a delivery order or task order and this contract, the contract shall control.

(c) If mailed, a delivery order or task order is considered "issued" when the Government deposits the order in the mail. Orders may be issued orally, by facsimile, or by electronic commerce methods only if authorized in the Schedule.

(End of clause)

[FAC 90-33, 60 FR 49706, 9/26/95, effective 10/1/95]

52.216-19 Order Limitations.

As prescribed in 16.506(b), insert a clause substantially the same as follows:

ORDER LIMITATIONS (OCT 1995)

(a) *Minimum order*. When the Government requires supplies or services covered by this contract in an amount of less than ___ [*insert dollar figure or quantity*], the Government is not obligated to purchase, nor is the Contractor obligated to furnish, those supplies or services under the contract.

(b) *Maximum order*. The Contractor is not obligated to honor—

(1) Any order for a single item in excess of ___ [*insert dollar figure or quantity*];

(2) Any order for a combination of items in excess of ___ [*insert dollar figure or quantity*]; or

(3) A series of orders from the same ordering office within ___ days that together call for quantities exceeding the limitation in subparagraph (b)(1) or (2) of this section.

(c) If this is a requirements contract (*i.e.*, includes the Requirements clause at subsection 52.216-21 of the Federal Acquisition Regulation (FAR)), the Government is not required to order a part of any one requirement from the Contractor if that requirement exceeds the maximum-order limitations in paragraph (b) of this section.

(d) Notwithstanding paragraphs (b) and (c) of this section, the Contractor shall honor any order exceeding the maximum order limitations in paragraph (b), unless that order (or orders) is returned to the ordering office within ___ days after issuance, with written notice stating the Contractor's intent not to ship the item (or items) called for and the reasons. Upon receiving this notice, the Government may acquire the supplies or services from another source.

(End of clause)

[FAC 90-32, 60 FR 48206, 9/18/95, effective 10/1/95; FAC 90-33, 60 FR 49706, 9/26/95, effective 10/1/95]

52.216-20 Definite Quantity.

As prescribed in 16.506(c), insert the following clause:

DEFINITE QUANTITY (OCT 1995)

(a) This is a definite-quantity, indefinite-delivery contract for the supplies or services specified, and effective for the period stated, in the Schedule.

(b) The Government shall order the quantity of supplies or services specified in the Schedule, and the Contractor shall furnish them when ordered. Delivery or performance shall be at locations designated in orders issued in accordance with the Ordering clause and the Schedule.

(c) Except for any limitations on quantities in the Order Limitations clause or in the Schedule, there is no limit on the number of orders that may be issued. The Government may issue orders requiring delivery to multiple destinations or performance at multiple locations.

(d) Any order issued during the effective period of this contract and not completed within that time shall be completed by the Contractor within the time specified in the order. The contract shall govern the Contractor's and Government's rights and obligations with respect to that order to the same extent as if the order were completed during the contract's effective period; provided, that the Contractor shall not be required to make any deliveries under this contract after ____ [*insert date*].

(End of clause)

[FAC 90-32, 60 FR 48206, 9/18/95, effective 10/1/95; FAC 90-33, 60 FR 49706, 9/26/95, effective 10/1/95]

52.216-21 Requirements.

As prescribed in 16.506(d), insert the following clause:

REQUIREMENTS (OCT 1995)

(a) This is a requirements contract for the supplies or services specified, and effective for the period stated, in the Schedule. The quantities of supplies or services specified in the Schedule are estimates only and are not purchased by this contract. Except as this contract may otherwise provide, if the Government's requirements do not result in orders in the quantities described as "estimated" or "maximum" in the Schedule, that fact shall not constitute the basis for an equitable price adjustment.

(b) Delivery or performance shall be made only as authorized by orders issued in accordance with the Ordering clause. Subject to any limitations in the Order Limitations clause or elsewhere in this contract, the Contractor shall furnish to the Government all supplies or services specified in the Schedule and called for by orders issued in accordance with the Ordering clause. The Government may issue orders requiring delivery to multiple destinations or performance at multiple locations.

(c) Except as this contract otherwise provides, the Government shall order from the Contractor all the supplies or services specified in the Schedule that are required to be purchased by the Government activity or activities specified in the Schedule.

(d) The Government is not required to purchase from the Contractor requirements in excess of any limit on total orders under this contract.

(e) If the Government urgently requires delivery of any quantity of an item before the earliest date that delivery may be specified under this contract, and if the Contractor will not accept an order providing for the accelerated delivery, the Government may acquire the urgently required goods or services from another source.

(f) Any order issued during the effective period of this contract and not completed within that period shall be completed by the Contractor within the time specified in the order. The contract shall govern the Contractor's and Government's rights and obligations with respect to that order to the same extent as if the order were completed during the contract's effective period; *provided*, that the Contractor shall not be required to make any deliveries under this contract after ____ [*insert date*].

(End of clause)

Alternate I (APR 1984). If the requirements contract is for nonpersonal services and related supplies and covers estimated requirements that exceed a specific Government activity's internal capability to produce or perform, substitute the following paragraph (c) for paragraph (c) of the basic clause:

(c) The estimated quantities are not the total requirements of the Government activity specified in the Schedule, but are estimates of requirements in excess of the quantities that the activity may itself furnish within its own capabilities. Except as this contract otherwise provides, the Government shall order from the Contractor all of that activity's requirements for supplies and services specified in the Schedule that exceed the quantities that the activity may furnish within its own capabilities.

Alternate II (APR 1984). If the requirements contract includes subsistence for both Government use and resale in the same Schedule, and similar products may be acquired on a brand-name basis, add the following paragraph (g) to the basic clause:

(g) The requirements referred to in this contract are for items to be manufactured according to Government specifications. Notwithstanding anything to the contrary stated in the contract, the Government may acquire similar products by brand name from other sources for resale.

Alternate III (OCT 1995). If the requirements contract involves a partial small business set-aside, substitute the following paragraph (c) for paragraph (c) of the basic clause:

(c) The Government's requirements for each item or subitem of supplies or services described in the Schedule are being purchased through one non-set-aside contract and one set-aside contract. Therefore, the Government shall order from each Contractor approximately one-half of the total supplies or services specified in the Schedule that are required to be purchased by the specified Government activity or activities. The Government may choose between the set-aside Contractor and the non-set-aside Contractor in placing any particular order. However, the Government shall allocate successive orders, in accordance with its delivery requirements, to maintain as close a ratio as is reasonably practicable between the total quantities ordered from the two Contractors.

Alternate IV (OCT 1995). If the contract includes subsistence for both Government use and resale in the same Schedule and similar products may be acquired on a brand-name basis and the contract also involves a partial small business set-aside, substitute the following paragraph (c) for paragraph (c) of the basic clause and add the following paragraph (g) to the basic clause:

(c) The Government's requirements for each item or subitem of supplies or services described in the Schedule are being purchased through one non-set-aside contract and one set-aside contract. Therefore, the Government shall order from each Contractor approximately one-half of the total supplies or services specified in the Schedule that are required to be purchased by the specified Government activity or activities. The Government may choose between the set-aside Contractor and the non-set-aside Contractor in placing any particular order. However, the Government shall allocate successive orders, in accordance with its delivery requirements, to maintain as close a ratio as is reasonably practicable between the total quantities ordered from the two Contractors.

(g) The requirements referred to in this contract are for items to be manufactured according to the Government specifications. Notwithstanding anything to the contrary stated in the contract, the Government may acquire similar products by brand name from other sources for resale.

[FAC 90-32, 60 FR 48206, 9/18/95, effective 10/1/95; FAC 90-33, 60 FR 49706, 9/26/95, effective 10/1/95]

52.216-22 Indefinite Quantity.

As prescribed in 16.506(e), insert the following clause:

INDEFINITE QUANTITY (OCT 1995)

(a) This is an indefinite-quantity contract for the supplies or services specified, and effective for the period stated, in the Schedule. The quantities of supplies and services specified in the Schedule are estimates only and are not purchased by this contract.

(b) Delivery or performance shall be made only as authorized by orders issued in accordance with the Ordering clause. The Contractor shall furnish to the Government, when and if ordered, the supplies or services specified in the Schedule up to and including the quantity designated in the Schedule as the "maximum." The Government shall order at least the quantity of supplies or services designated in the Schedule as the "minimum."

(c) Except for any limitations on quantities in the Order Limitations clause or in the Schedule, there is no limit on the number of orders that may be issued. The Government may issue orders requiring delivery to multiple destinations or performance at multiple locations.

(d) Any order issued during the effective period of this contract and not completed within that period shall be completed by the Contractor within the time specified in the order. The contract shall govern the Contractor's and Government's rights and obligations with respect to that order to the same extent as if the order were completed during the contract's effective period; *provided*, that the Contractor shall not be required to make any deliveries under this contract after ____ [*insert date*].

(End of clause)

[Final rule, 55 FR 38518, 9/18/90; FAC 90-32, 60 FR 48206, 9/18/95, effective 10/1/95; FAC 90-33, 60 FR 49706, 9/26/95, effective 10/1/95]

52.216-23 Execution and Commencement of Work.

As prescribed in 16.603-4(b)(1), insert the following clause in solicitations and contracts when a letter contract is contemplated, except that it may be omitted from letter contracts awarded on SF 26:

EXECUTION AND COMMENCEMENT OF WORK (APR 1984)

The Contractor shall indicate acceptance of this letter contract by signing three copies of the contract and returning them to the Contracting Officer not later than ____ [*insert date*]. Upon acceptance by both parties, the Contractor shall proceed with performance of the work, including purchase of necessary materials.

(End of clause)

[FAC 90-32, 60 FR 48206, 9/18/95, effective 10/1/95]

52.216-24 Limitation of Government Liability.

As prescribed in 16.603-4(b)(2), insert the following clause in solicitations and contracts when a letter contract is contemplated:

LIMITATION OF GOVERNMENT LIABILITY (APR 1984)

(a) In performing this contract, the Contractor is not authorized to make expenditures or incur obligations exceeding ____ dollars.

(b) The maximum amount for which the Government shall be liable if this contract is terminated is ____ dollars.

(End of clause)

[FAC 90-32, 60 FR 48206, 9/18/95, effective 10/1/95]

52.216-25 Contract Definitization.

As prescribed in 16.603-4(b)(3), insert the following clause:

CONTRACT DEFINITIZATION (OCT 2010)

(a) A ____ *[insert specific type of contract]* definitive contract is contemplated. The Contractor agrees to begin promptly negotiating with the Contracting Officer the terms of a definitive contract that will include (1) all clauses required by the Federal Acquisition Regulation (FAR) on the date of execution of the letter contract, (2) all clauses required by law on the date of execution of the definitive contract, and (3) any other mutually agreeable clauses, terms, and conditions. The Contractor agrees to submit a ____ *[insert specific type of proposal (e.g., fixed-price or cost-and-fee)]* proposal, including data other than certified cost or pricing data, and certified cost or pricing data, in accordance with FAR 15.408, Table 15-2, supporting its proposal.

(b) The schedule for definitizing this contract is *[insert target date for definitization of the contract and dates for submission of proposal, beginning of negotiations, and, if appropriate, submission of make-or-buy and subcontracting plans and certified cost or pricing data]*:

____

____

____

____

(c) If agreement on a definitive contract to supersede this letter contract is not reached by the target date in paragraph (b) of this section, or within any extension of it granted by the Contracting Officer, the Contracting Officer may, with the approval of the head of the contracting activity, determine a reasonable price or fee in accordance with Subpart 15.4 and Part 31 of the FAR, subject to Contractor appeal as provided in the Disputes clause. In any event, the Contractor shall proceed with completion of the contract, subject only to the Limitation of Government Liability clause.

(1) After the Contracting Officer's determination of price or fee, the contract shall be governed by—

(i) All clauses required by the FAR on the date of execution of this letter contract for either fixed-price or cost-reimbursement contracts, as determined by the Contracting Officer under this paragraph (c);

(ii) All clauses required by law as of the date of the Contracting Officer's determination; and

(iii) Any other clauses, terms, and conditions mutually agreed upon.

(2) To the extent consistent with subparagraph (c)(1) of this section, all clauses, terms, and conditions included in this letter contract shall continue in effect, except those that by their nature apply only to a letter contract.

(End of clause)

Alternate I (APR 1984). In letter contracts awarded on the basis of price competition, add the following paragraph (d) to the basic clause:

(d) The definitive contract resulting from this letter contract will include a negotiated ____*[insert "price ceiling" or "firm fixed price"]* in no event to exceed ____*[insert the proposed price upon which the award was based]*.

[FAC 90-32, 60 FR 48206, 9/18/95, effective 10/1/95; FAC 97-2, 62 FR 51224, 9/30/97, effective 10/10/97; FAC 2005-45, 75 FR 53135, 8/30/2010, effective 10/1/2010]

52.216-26 Payments of Allowable Costs Before Definitization.

As prescribed in 16.603-4(c), insert the following clause:

PAYMENTS OF ALLOWABLE COSTS BEFORE DEFINITIZATION (DEC 2002)

(a) *Reimbursement rate.* Pending the placing of the definitive contract referred to in this letter contract, the Government will promptly reimburse the Contractor for all allowable costs under this contract at the following rates:

(1) One hundred percent of approved costs representing financing payments to subcontractors under fixed-price subcontracts, provided that the Government's payments to the Contractor will not exceed 80 percent of the allowable costs of those subcontractors.

(2) One hundred percent of approved costs representing cost-reimbursement subcontracts; *provided*, that the Government's payments to the Contractor shall not exceed 85 percent of the allowable costs of those subcontractors.

(3) Eighty-five percent of all other approved costs.

(b) *Limitation of reimbursement.* To determine the amounts payable to the Contractor under this letter contract, the Contracting Officer shall determine allowable costs in accordance with the applicable cost principles in Part 31 of the Federal Acquisition Regulation (FAR). The total reimbursement made under this paragraph shall not exceed 85 percent of the maximum amount of the Government's liability, as stated in this contract.

(c) *Invoicing.* Payments shall be made promptly to the Contractor when requested as work progresses, but (except for small business concerns) not more often than every 2 weeks, in amounts approved by the Contracting Officer. The Contractor may submit to an authorized representative of the Contracting Officer, in such form and reasonable detail as the representative may require, an invoice or voucher supported by a statement of the claimed allowable cost incurred by the Contractor in the performance of this contract.

(d) *Allowable costs.* For the purpose of determining allowable costs, the term *costs* includes—

(1) Those recorded costs that result, at the time of the request for reimbursement, from payment by cash, check, or other form of actual payment for items or services purchased directly for the contract;

(2) When the Contractor is not delinquent in payment of costs of contract performance in the ordinary course of business, costs incurred, but not necessarily paid, for—

(i) Supplies and services purchased directly for the contract and associated financing payments to subcontractors, provided payments determined due will be made—

(A) In accordance with the terms and conditions of a subcontract or invoice; and

(B) Ordinarily within 30 days of the submission of the Contractor's payment request to the Government;

(ii) Materials issued from the Contractor's stores inventory and placed in the production process for use on the contract;

(iii) Direct labor;

(iv) Direct travel;

(v) Other direct in-house costs; and

(vi) Properly allocable and allowable indirect costs as shown on the records maintained by the Contractor for purposes of obtaining reimbursement under Government contracts; and

(3) The amount of financing payments that the Contractor has paid by cash, check, or other forms of payment to subcontractors.

(e) *Small business concerns.* A small business concern may receive more frequent payments than every 2 weeks.

(f) *Audit.* At any time before final payment, the Contracting Officer may have the Contractor's invoices or vouchers and statements of costs audited. Any payment may be—

(1) Reduced by any amounts found by the Contracting Officer not to constitute allowable costs; or

(2) Adjusted for overpayments or underpayments made on preceding invoices or vouchers.

(End of clause)

[FAC 90-32, 60 FR 48206, 9/18/95, effective 10/1/95; FAC 97-16, 65 FR 16274, 3/27/2000, effective 3/27/2000; FAC 2001-10, 67 FR 70520, 11/22/2002, effective 12/23/2002]

52.216-27 Single or Multiple Awards.

As prescribed in 16.506(f), insert the following provision:

SINGLE OR MULTIPLE AWARDS (OCT 1995)

The Government may elect to award a single delivery order contract or task order contract or to award multiple delivery order contracts or task order contracts for the same or similar supplies or services to two or more sources under this solicitation.

(End of provision)

[FAC 90-33, 60 FR 49706, 9/26/95, effective 10/1/95]

52.216-28 Multiple Awards for Advisory and Assistance Services.

As prescribed in 16.506(g), insert the following provision:

MULTIPLE AWARDS FOR ADVISORY AND ASSISTANCE SERVICES (OCT 1995)

The Government intends to award multiple contracts for the same or similar advisory and assistance services to two or more sources under this solicitation unless the Government determines, after evaluation of offers, that only one offeror is capable of providing the services at the level of quality required.

(End of provision)

[FAC 90-33, 60 FR 49706, 9/26/95, effective 10/1/95]

52.216-29 Time-and-Materials/Labor-Hour Proposal Requirements—Non-Commercial Item Acquisition With Adequate Price Competition.

As prescribed in 16.601(f)(1), insert the following provision:

TIME-AND-MATERIALS/LABOR-HOUR PROPOSAL REQUIREMENTS—NON-COMMERCIAL ITEM ACQUISITION WITH ADEQUATE PRICE COMPETITION (FEB 2007)

(a) The Government contemplates award of a Time-and-Materials or Labor-Hour type of contract resulting from this solicitation.

(b) The offeror must specify fixed hourly rates in its offer that include wages, overhead, general and administrative expenses, and profit. The offeror must specify whether the fixed hourly rate for each labor category applies to labor performed by—

(1) The offeror;

(2) Subcontractors; and/or

(3) Divisions, subsidiaries, or affiliates of the offeror under a common control;

(c) The offeror must establish fixed hourly rates using—

(1) Separate rates for each category of labor to be performed by each subcontractor and for each category of labor to be performed by the offeror, and for each category of labor to be transferred between divisions, subsidiaries, or affiliates of the offeror under a common control;

(2) Blended rates for each category of labor to be performed by the offeror, including labor transferred between divisions, subsidiaries, or affiliates of the offeror under a common control, and all subcontractors; or

(3) Any combination of separate and blended rates for each category of labor to be performed by the offeror, affiliates of the offeror under a common control, and subcontractors.

(End of provision)

[FAC 90-33, 60 FR 49706, 9/26/95, effective 10/1/95; FAC 2005-15, 12/12/2006, effective 2/12/2007; FAC 2005-66, 78 FR 13766, 2/28/2013, effective 4/1/2013]

52.216-30 Time-and-Materials/Labor-Hour Proposal Requirements—Non-Commercial Item Acquisition without Adequate Price Competition.

As prescribed in 16.601(f)(2), insert the following provision:

TIME-AND-MATERIALS/LABOR-HOUR PROPOSAL REQUIREMENTS—NON-COMMERCIAL ITEM ACQUISITION WITHOUT ADEQUATE PRICE COMPETITION (FEB 2007)

(a) The Government contemplates award of a Time-and-Materials or Labor-Hour type of contract resulting from this solicitation.

(b) The offeror must specify separate fixed hourly rates in its offer that include wages, overhead, general and administrative expenses, and profit for each category of labor to be performed by—

(1) The offeror;

(2) Each subcontractor; and

(3) Each division, subsidiary, or affiliate of the offeror under a common control.

(c) Unless exempt under paragraph (d) of this provision, the fixed hourly rates for services transferred between divisions, subsidiaries, or affiliates of the offeror under a common control—

(1) Shall not include profit for the transferring organization; but

(2) May include profit for the prime Contractor.

(d) The fixed hourly rates for services that meet the definition of commercial item at 2.101 that are transferred between divisions, subsidiaries, or affiliates of the offeror under a common control may be the established catalog or market rate when it is the established practice of the transferring organization to price interorganizational transfers at other than cost for commercial work of the offeror or any division, subsidiary or affiliate of the offeror under a common control.

(End of provision)

[FAC 90-33, 60 FR 49706, 9/26/95, effective 10/1/95; FAC 2005-15, 71 FR 74656, 12/12/2006, effective 2/12/2007; FAC 2005-66, 78 FR 13766, 2/28/2013, effective 4/1/2013]

52.216-31 Time-and-Materials/Labor-Hour Proposal Requirements—Commercial Item Acquisition.

As prescribed in 16.601(f)(3), insert the following provision:

TIME-AND-MATERIALS/LABOR-HOUR PROPOSAL REQUIREMENTS—COMMERCIAL ITEM ACQUISITION (FEB 2007)

(a) The Government contemplates award of a Time-and-Materials or Labor-Hour type of contract resulting from this solicitation.

(b) The offeror must specify fixed hourly rates in its offer that include wages, overhead, general and administrative expenses, and profit. The offeror must specify whether the fixed hourly rate for each labor category applies to labor performed by—

(1) The offeror;

(2) Subcontractors; and/or

(3) Divisions, subsidiaries, or affiliates of the offeror under a common control.

(End of provision)

[FAC 90-33, 60 FR 49706, 9/26/95, effective 10/1/95; FAC 2005-15, 71 FR 74656, 12/12/2006, effective 2/12/2007; Final rule, 72 FR 6881, 2/13/2007, effective 2/12/2007; FAC 2005-66, 78 FR 13766, 2/28/2013, effective 4/1/2013]

52.216-32 Task-Order and Delivery-Order Ombudsman.

As prescribed in 16.506(j), use the following clause:

TASK-ORDER AND DELIVERY-ORDER OMBUDSMAN (SEP 2019)

(a) In accordance with 41 U.S.C. 4106(g), the Agency has designated the following task-order and delivery-order Ombudsman for this contract. The Ombudsman must review complaints from the Contractor concerning all task-order and delivery-order actions for this contract and ensure the Contractor is afforded a fair opportunity for consideration in the award of orders, consistent with the procedures in the contract.

[*Contracting Officer to insert name, address, telephone number, and email address for the Agency Ombudsman or provide the URL address where this information may be found.*]

(b) Consulting an ombudsman does not alter or postpone the timeline for any other process (*e.g.*, protests).

(c) Before consulting with the Ombudsman, the Contractor is encouraged to first address complaints with the Contracting Officer for resolution. When requested by the Contractor, the Ombudsman may keep the identity of the concerned party or entity confidential, unless prohibited by law or agency procedure.

(End of clause)

Alternate I. As prescribed in 16.506(j), add the following paragraph (d) to the basic clause.

(d) *Contracts used by multiple agencies.*

(1) This is a contract that is used by multiple agencies. Complaints from Contractors concerning orders placed under contracts used by multiple agencies are primarily reviewed by the task-order and delivery-order Ombudsman for the ordering activity.

(2) The ordering activity has designated the following task-order and delivery-order Ombudsman for this order:

[*The ordering activity's contracting officer to insert the name, address, telephone number, and email address for the ordering activity's Ombudsman or provide the URL address where this information may be found.*]

(3) Before consulting with the task-order and delivery-order Ombudsman for the ordering activity, the Contractor is encouraged to first address complaints with the ordering activity's Contracting Officer for resolution. When requested by the Contractor, the task-order and delivery-order Ombudsman for the ordering activity may keep the identity of the concerned party or entity confidential,

unless prohibited by law or agency procedure.

(End of clause)

[FAC 2019-04, 84 FR 38836, 8/7/2019, effective 9/6/2019]

52.217-1 [Reserved]

[Reserved, FAC 90-40, 61 FR 39186, 7/26/96, effective 7/26/96]

52.217-2 Cancellation Under Multiyear Contracts.

As prescribed in 17.109(a), insert the following clause:

CANCELLATION UNDER MULTIYEAR CONTRACTS (OCT 1997)

(a) *Cancellation,* as used in this clause, means that the Government is canceling its requirements for all supplies or services in program years subsequent to that in which notice of cancellation is provided. Cancellation shall occur by the date or within the time period specified in the Schedule, unless a later date is agreed to, if the Contracting Officer—

(1) Notifies the Contractor that funds are not available for contract performance for any subsequent program year, or

(2) Fails to notify the Contractor that funds are available for performance of the succeeding program year requirement.

(b) Except for cancellation under this clause or termination under the Default clause, any reduction by the Contracting Officer in the requirements of this contract shall be considered a termination under the Termination for Convenience of the Government clause.

(c) If cancellation under this clause occurs, the Contractor will be paid a cancellation charge not over the cancellation ceiling specified in the Schedule as applicable at the time of cancellation.

(d) The cancellation charge will cover only

(1) Costs—

(i) Incurred by the Contractor and/or subcontractor,

(ii) Reasonably necessary for performance of the contract; and

(iii) That would have been equitably amortized over the entire multiyear contract period but, because of the cancellation, are not so amortized; and

(2) A reasonable profit or fee on the costs.

(e) The cancellation charge shall be computed and the claim made for it as if the claim were being made under the Termination for Convenience of the Government clause of this contract. The Contractor shall submit the claim promptly but no later than 1 year from the date—

(1) Of notification of the nonavailability of funds; or

(2) Specified in the Schedule by which notification of the availability of additional funds for the next succeeding program year is required to be issued, whichever is earlier, unless extensions in writing are granted by the Contracting Officer.

(f) The Contractor's claim may include—

(1) Reasonable nonrecurring costs (see Subpart 15.4 of the Federal Acquisition Regulation) which are applicable to and normally would have been amortized in all supplies or services which are multiyear requirements;

(2) Allocable portions of the costs of facilities acquired or established for the conduct of the work, to the extent that it is impracticable for the Contractor to use the facilities in its commercial work, and if the costs are not charged to the contract through overhead or otherwise depreciated;

(3) Costs incurred for the assembly, training, and transportation to and from the job site of a specialized work force; and

(4) Costs not amortized solely because the cancellation had precluded anticipated benefits of Contractor or subcontractor learning.

(g) The claim shall not include—

(1) Labor, material, or other expenses incurred by the Contractor or subcontractors for performance of the canceled work;

(2) Any cost already paid to the Contractor;

(3) Anticipated profit or unearned fee on the canceled work; or

(4) For service contracts, the remaining useful commercial life of facilities. "Useful commercial life" means the commercial utility of the facilities rather than their physical life with due consideration given to such factors as location of facilities, their specialized nature, and obsolescence.

(h) This contract may include an Option clause with the period for exercising the option limited to the date in the contract for notification that funds are available for the next succeeding program year. If so, the Contractor agrees not to include in option quantities any costs of a startup or nonrecurring nature that have been fully set forth in the contract. The Contractor further agrees that the option quantities will reflect only those recurring costs and a reasonable profit or fee necessary to furnish the additional option quantities.

(i) Quantities added to the original contract through the Option clause of this contract shall be included in the quantity canceled for the purpose of computing allowable cancellation charges.

(End of clause)

[FAC 90-40, 61 FR 39186, 7/26/96, effective 7/26/96; FAC 97-2, 62 FR 51224, 9/30/97, effective 10/10/97]

52.217-3 Evaluation Exclusive of Options.

As prescribed in 17.208(a), insert a provision substantially the same as the following in solicitations when the solicitation includes an option clause and does not include one of the provisions prescribed in 17.208(b) or (c):

EVALUATION EXCLUSIVE OF OPTIONS (APR 1984)

The Government will evaluate offers for award purposes by including only the price for the basic requirement; *i.e.*, options will not be included in the evaluation for award purposes.

(End of provision)

[FAC 90-32, 60 FR 48206, 9/18/95, effective 10/1/95]

52.217-4 Evaluation of Options Exercised at Time of Contract Award.

As prescribed in 17.208(b), insert a provision substantially the same as the following:

EVALUATION OF OPTIONS EXERCISED AT TIME OF CONTRACT AWARD (JUN 1988)

Except when it is determined in accordance with FAR 17.206(b) not to be in the Government's best interests, the Government will evaluate the total price for the basic requirement together with any option(s) exercised at the time of award.

(End of provision)

[FAC 84-37, 53 FR 17860, 5/18/88, effective 6/17/88]

52.217-5 Evaluation of Options.

As prescribed in 17.208(c), insert a provision substantially the same as the following:

EVALUATION OF OPTIONS (JUL 1990)

Except when it is determined in accordance with FAR 17.206(b) not to be in the Government's best interests, the Government will evaluate offers for award purposes by adding the total price for all options to the total price for the basic requirement. Evaluation of options will not obligate the Government to exercise the option(s).

(End of provision)

[FAC 84-37, 53 FR 17860, 5/18/88, effective 6/17/88; FAC 84-58, 55 FR 25532, 6/21/90, effective 7/23/90; FAC 2001-25, 69 FR 59703, 10/5/2004, effective 10/5/2004]

52.217-6 Option for Increased Quantity.

As prescribed in 17.208(d), insert a clause substantially the same as the following:

OPTION FOR INCREASED QUANTITY (MAR 1989)

The Government may increase the quantity of supplies called for in the Schedule at the unit price specified. The Contracting Officer may exercise the option by written notice to the Contractor within ____ [*insert in the clause the period of time in which the Contracting Officer has to exercise the option*]. Delivery of the added items shall continue at the same rate as the like items called for under the contract, unless the parties otherwise agree.

(End of clause)

[FAC 84-42, 54 FR 5058, 1/31/89, effective 3/2/89]

52.217-7 Option for Increased Quantity—Separately Priced Line Item.

As prescribed in 17.208(e), insert a clause substantially the same as the following:

OPTION FOR INCREASED QUANTITY—SEPARATELY PRICED LINE ITEM (MAR 1989)

The Government may require the delivery of the numbered line item, identified in the Schedule as an option item, in the quantity and at the price stated in the Schedule. The Contracting Officer may exercise the option by written notice to the Contractor within ___ [*insert in the clause the period of time in which the Contracting Officer has to exercise the option*]. Delivery of added items shall continue at the same rate that like items are called for under the contract, unless the parties otherwise agree.

(End of clause)

[FAC 84-42, 54 FR 5058, 1/31/89, effective 3/2/89]

52.217-8 Option to Extend Services.

As prescribed in 17.208(f), insert a clause substantially the same as the following:

OPTION TO EXTEND SERVICES (NOV 1999)

The Government may require continued performance of any services within the limits and at the rates specified in the contract. These rates may be adjusted only as a result of revisions to prevailing labor rates provided by the Secretary of Labor. The option provision may be exercised more than once, but the total extension of performance hereunder shall not exceed 6 months. The Contracting Officer may exercise the option by written notice to the Contractor within ___ [*insert the period of time within which the Contracting Officer may exercise the option*].

(End of clause)

[FAC 84-49, 54 FR 29283, 7/11/89, effective 8/10/89; FAC 97-14 64 FR 51828, 9/24/99, effective 11/23/99]

52.217-9 Option to Extend the Term of the Contract.

As prescribed in 17.208(g), insert a clause substantially the same as the following:

OPTION TO EXTEND THE TERM OF THE CONTRACT (MAR 2000)

(a) The Government may extend the term of this contract by written notice to the Contractor within ___ [*insert the period of time within which the Contracting Officer may exercise the option*]; provided that the Government gives the Contractor a preliminary written notice of its intent to extend at least ___ days [*60 days unless a different number of days is inserted*] before the contract expires. The preliminary notice does not commit the Government to an extension.

(b) If the Government exercises this option, the extended contract shall be considered to include this option clause.

(c) The total duration of this contract, including the exercise of any options under this clause, shall not exceed ___ (months) (years).

(End of clause)

[FAC 84-42, 54 FR 5058, 1/31/89, effective 3/2/89; FAC 97-14, 64 FR 51828, 9/24/99, effective 11/23/99; FAC 97-16, 65 FR 16274, 3/27/2000, effective 3/27/2000]

52.218 [Reserved]

52.219-1 Small Business Program Representations.

As prescribed in 19.309(a)(1), insert the following provision:

SMALL BUSINESS PROGRAM REPRESENTATIONS (OCT 2014)

(a) *Definitions*. As used in this provision—

Economically disadvantaged women-owned small business (EDWOSB) concern means a small business concern that is at least 51 percent directly and unconditionally owned by, and the management and daily business operations of which are controlled by, one or more women who are citizens of the United States and who are economically disadvantaged in accordance with 13 CFR part 127. It automatically qualifies as a women-owned small business concern eligible under the WOSB Program.

Service-disabled veteran-owned small business concern—

(1) Means a small business concern—

(i) Not less than 51 percent of which is owned by one or more service-disabled veterans or, in the case of any publicly owned business, not less than 51 percent of the stock of which is owned by one or more service-disabled veterans; and

(ii) The management and daily business operations of which are controlled by one or more service-disabled veterans or, in the case of a service-disabled veteran with permanent and severe disability, the spouse or permanent caregiver of such veteran.

(2) *Service-disabled veteran* means a veteran, as defined in 38 U.S.C. 101(2), with a disability that is service-connected, as defined in 38 U.S.C. 101(16).

Small business concern means a concern, including its affiliates, that is independently owned and operated, not dominant in the field of operation in which it is bidding on Government contracts, and qualified as a small business under the criteria in 13 CFR Part 121 and the size standard in paragraph (b) of this provision.

Small disadvantaged business concern, consistent with 13 CFR 124.1002, means a small business concern under the size standard applicable to the acquisition, that—

(1) Is at least 51 percent unconditionally and directly owned (as defined at 13 CFR 124.105) by—

(i) One or more socially disadvantaged (as defined at 13 CFR 124.103) and economically disadvantaged (as defined at 13 CFR 124.104) individuals who are citizens of the United States, and

(ii) Each individual claiming economic disadvantage has a net worth not exceeding $750,000 after taking into account the applicable exclusions set forth at 13 CFR 124.104(c)(2); and

(2) The management and daily business operations of which are controlled (as defined at 13 CFR 124.106) by individuals who meet the criteria in paragraphs (1)(i) and (ii) of this definition.

Veteran-owned small business concern means a small business concern—

(1) Not less than 51 percent of which is owned by one or more veterans (as defined at 38 U.S.C. 101(2)) or, in the case of any publicly owned business, not less than 51 percent of the stock of which is owned by one or more veterans; and

(2) The management and daily business operations of which are controlled by one or more veterans.

Women-owned small business concern means a small business concern—

(1) That is at least 51 percent owned by one or more women; or, in the case of any publicly owned business, at least 51 percent of the stock of which is owned by one or more women; and

(2) Whose management and daily business operations are controlled by one or more women.

Women-owned small business (WOSB) concern eligible under the WOSB Program (in accordance with 13 CFR part 127), means a small business concern that is at least 51 percent directly and unconditionally owned by, and the management and daily business operations of which are controlled by, one or more women who are citizens of the United States.

(b)(1) The North American Industry Classification System (NAICS) code for this acquisition is ______ [*insert NAICS code*].

(2) The small business size standard is ______ [*insert size standard*].

(3) The small business size standard for a concern which submits an offer in its own name, other than on a construction or service contract, but which proposes to furnish a product which it did not itself manufacture, is 500 employees.

(c) *Representations.* (1) The offeror represents as part of its offer that it ☐ is, ☐ is not a small business concern.

(2) [*Complete only if the offeror represented itself as a small business concern in paragraph (c)(1) of this provision.*] The offeror represents that it ☐ is, ☐ is not, a small disadvantaged business concern as defined in 13 CFR 124.1002.

(3) [*Complete only if the offeror represented itself as a small business concern in paragraph (c)(1) of this provision.*] The offeror represents as part of its offer that it ☐ is, ☐ is not a women-owned small business concern.

(4) Women-owned small business (WOSB) concern eligible under the WOSB Program. [*Complete only if the offeror represented itself as a women-owned small business concern in paragraph (c)(3) of this provision.*] The offeror represents as part of its offer that—

(i) It ☐ is, ☐ is not a WOSB concern eligible under the WOSB Program, has provided all the required documents to the WOSB Repository, and no change in circumstances or adverse decisions have been issued that affects its eligibility; and

(ii) It. is,.is not a joint venture that complies with the requirements of 13 CFR part 127, and the representation in paragraph (c)(4)(i) of this provision is accurate for each WOSB concern eligible under the WOSB Program participating in the joint venture. [*The offeror shall enter the name or names of the WOSB concern eligible under the WOSB Program and other small businesses that are participating in the joint venture:* ________.] Each WOSB concern eligible under the WOSB Program participating in the joint venture shall submit a separate signed copy of the WOSB representation.

(5) Economically disadvantaged women-owned small business (EDWOSB) concern. [*Complete only if the offeror represented itself as a women-owned small business concern eligible under the WOSB Program in (c)(4) of this provision.*] The offeror represents as part of its offer that—

(i) It ☐ is, ☐ is not an EDWOSB concern eligible under the WOSB Program, has provided all the required documents to the WOSB Repository, and no change in circumstances or adverse decisions have been issued that affects its eligibility; and

(ii) It ☐ is, ☐ is not a joint venture that complies with the requirements of 13 CFR part 127, and the representation in paragraph (c)(5)(i) of this provision is accurate for each EDWOSB concern participating in the joint venture. [*The offeror shall enter the name or names of the EDWOSB concern and other small businesses that are participating in the joint venture:* ________.]Each EDWOSB concern participating in the joint venture shall submit a separate signed copy of the EDWOSB representation.

(6) [*Complete only if the offeror represented itself as a small business concern in paragraph (c)(1) of this provision.*] The offeror represents as part of its offer that it ☐ is, ☐ is not a veteran-owned small business concern.

(7) [*Complete only if the offeror represented itself as a veteran-owned small business concern in paragraph (c)(6) of this provision.*] The offeror represents as part of its offer that it ☐ is, ☐ is not a service-disabled veteran-owned small business concern.

(8) [*Complete only if the offeror represented itself as a small business concern in paragraph (c)(1) of this provision.*] The offeror represents, as part of its offer, that—

(i) It ☐ is, ☐ is not a HUBZone small business concern listed, on the date of this representation, on the List of Qualified HUBZone Small Business Concerns maintained by the Small Business Administration, and no material changes in ownership and control, principal office, or HUBZone employee percentage have occurred since it was certified in accordance with 13 CFR Part 126; and

(ii) It ☐ is, ☐ is not a HUBZone joint venture that complies with the requirements of 13 CFR Part 126, and the representation in paragraph (c)(8)(i) of this provision is accurate for each HUBZone small business concern participating in the HUBZone joint venture. [*The offeror shall enter the names of each of the HUBZone small business concerns participating in the HUBZone joint venture:* ____.] Each HUBZone small business concern participating in the HUBZone joint venture shall submit a separate signed copy of the HUBZone representation.

(d) *Notice.* (1) If this solicitation is for supplies and has been set aside, in whole or in part, for small business concerns, then the clause in this solicitation providing notice of the set-aside contains restrictions on the source of the end items to be furnished.

(2) Under 15 U.S.C. 645(d), any person who misrepresents a firm's status as a business concern that is small, HUBZone small, small disadvantaged, service-disabled veteran-owned small, economically disadvantaged women-owned small, or women-owned small eligible under the WOSB Program in order to obtain a contract to be awarded under the preference programs established pursuant to section 8, 9, 15, 31, and 36 of the Small Business Act or any other provision of Federal law that specifically references section 8(d) for a definition of program eligibility, shall—

(i) Be punished by imposition of fine, imprisonment, or both;

(ii) Be subject to administrative remedies, including suspension and debarment; and

(iii) Be ineligible for participation in programs conducted under the authority of the Act.

(End of provision)

Alternate I (SEP 2015). As prescribed in 19.309(a)(2), add the following paragraph (c)(9) to the basic provision:

(9) [*Complete if offeror represented itself as disadvantaged in paragraph (c)(2) of this provision.*] The offeror shall check the category in which its ownership falls:

____ Black American.

____ Hispanic American.

____ Native American (American Indians, Eskimos, Aleuts, or Native Hawaiians).

____ Asian-Pacific American (persons with origins from Burma, Thailand, Malaysia, Indonesia, Singapore, Brunei, Japan, China, Taiwan, Laos, Cambodia (Kampuchea), Vietnam, Korea, The Philippines, Republic of Palau, Republic of the Marshall Islands, Federated States of Micronesia, the Commonwealth of the Northern Mariana Islands, Guam, Samoa, Macao, Hong Kong, Fiji, Tonga, Kiribati, Tuvalu, or Nauru).

____ Subcontinent Asian (Asian-Indian) American (persons with origins from India, Pakistan, Bangladesh, Sri Lanka, Bhutan, the Maldives Islands, or Nepal).

____ Individual/Concerns, other than one of the preceding.

[FAC 90-32, 60 FR 48206, 9/18/95, effective 10/1/95; FAC 90-43, Interim rule, 61 FR 67408, 12/20/96, effective 12/20/96; FAC 90-45, Final rule, 62 FR 224, 1/2/97, effective 1/1/97; FAC 97-4, 63 FR 9048, 2/23/98, effective 2/23/98; FAC 97-6, 63 FR 35719, 6/30/98, effective 10/1/98, finalized without change, FAC 97-13, 7/2/99; FAC 97-10, 63 FR 70264, 12/18/98, effective 1/4/99; FAC 97-11, 64 FR 10530, 3/4/99, effective 5/3/99; FAC 97-12, 64 FR 32740, 6/17/99, effective 6/17/99; FAC 97-14, 64 FR 51828, 9/24/99, effective 11/23/99; FAC 97-19, 65 FR 46052, 7/26/2000, effective 10/1/2000; FAC 97-20, 65 FR 60542, 7/26/2000, effective 10/11/2000, finalized without change by FAC 2001-02, 66 FR 65347, 12/18/2001, effective 12/18/2001; FAC 97-22, 66 FR 2116, 1/10/2001, effective 3/12/2001; Delay of effective date, 66 FR 14259, 3/9/2001, effective 5/11/2001; FAC 2001-06, 67 FR 13048, 3/20/2002, effective 4/4/2002; FAC 2001-23, 69 FR 25273, 5/5/2004, effective 5/5/2004; FAC 2001-26, 69 FR 76358, 12/20/2004, effective 12/20/2004; FAC 2005-02, 70 FR 14950, 3/23/2005, effective 3/23/2005; FAC 2005-47, 75 FR 77727, 12/13/2010, effective 1/12/2011; FAC 2005-51, 76 FR 18304, 4/1/2011, effective 4/1/2011; FAC 2005-56, 77 FR 12913, 3/2/2012, effective 4/2/2012; Correction, 77 FR 14303, 3/9/2012, effective 3/9/2012; Correction, 77 FR 17352, 3/26/2012, effective 3/26/2012; FAC 2005-73, 79 FR 24192, 4/29/2014, effective 5/29/2014; FAC 2005-77, 79 FR 61746, 10/14/2014, effective 10/14/2014; FAC 2005-84, 80 FR 53439, 9/3/2015, effective 9/3/2015]

52.219-2 Equal Low Bids.

As prescribed in 19.309(b), insert the following provision:

EQUAL LOW BIDS (OCT 1995)

(a) This provision applies to small business concerns only.

(b) The bidder's status as a labor surplus area (LSA) concern may affect entitlement to award in case of tie bids. If the bidder wishes to be considered for this priority, the bidder must identify, in the following space, the LSA in which the costs to be incurred on account of manufacturing or production (by the bidder or the first-tier subcontractors) amount to more than 50 percent of the contract price.

___

___

(c) Failure to identify the labor surplus areas as specified in paragraph (b) of this provision will preclude the bidder from receiving priority consideration. If the bidder is awarded a contract as a result of receiving priority consideration under this provision and would not have otherwise received award, the bidder shall perform the contract or cause the contract to be performed in accordance with the obligations of an LSA concern.

(End of provision)

[FAC 90-32, 60 FR 48206, 9/18/95, effective 10/1/95; FAC 97-6, 63 FR 35719, 6/30/98, effective 10/1/98, finalized without change, FAC 97-13, 7/2/99; FAC 97-10, 63 FR 70264, 12/18/98, effective 1/4/99; FAC 2001-23, 69 FR 25273, 5/5/2004, effective 5/5/2004; FAC 2005-02, 70 FR 14950, 3/23/2005, effective 3/23/2005; FAC 2005-51, 76 FR 18304, 4/1/2011, effective 4/1/2011; FAC 2005-56, 77 FR 12913, 3/2/2012, effective 4/2/2012; FAC 2005-77, 79 FR 61746, 10/14/2014, effective 10/14/2014]

52.219-3 Notice of HUBZone Set-Aside or Sole Source Award.

As prescribed in 19.1309(a), insert the following clause:

NOTICE OF HUBZONE SET-ASIDE OR SOLE SOURCE AWARD (NOV 2011)

(a) *Definitions. See* 13 CFR 125.6(e) for definitions of terms used in paragraph (c).

(b) *Applicability.* This clause applies only to—

(1) Contracts that have been set aside or reserved for, or awarded on a sole source basis to, HUBZone small business concerns;

(2) Part or parts of a multiple-award contract that have been set aside for HUBZONE small business concerns; and

(3) Orders set-aside for HUBZone small business concerns under multiple-award contracts as described in 8.405-5 and 16.505(b)(2)(i)(F).

(c) *General.* (1) Offers are solicited only from HUBZone small business concerns. Offers received from concerns that are not HUBZone small business concerns will not be considered.

(2) Any award resulting from this solicitation will be made to a HUBZone small business concern.

(d) *Agreement.* A HUBZone small business concern agrees that in the performance of the contract, in the case of a contract for—

(1) Services (except construction), at least 50 percent of the cost of personnel for contract performance will be spent for employees of the concern or employees of other HUBZone small business concerns;

(2) Supplies (other than acquisition from a nonmanufacturer of the supplies), at least 50 percent of the cost of manufacturing, excluding the cost of materials, will be performed by the concern or other HUBZone small business concerns;

(3) *General construction.* (i) At least 15 percent of the cost of contract performance to be incurred for personnel will be spent on the HUBZone prime contractor's employees;

(ii) At least 50 percent of the cost of the contract performance to be incurred for personnel will be spent on the HUBZone prime contractor's employees or on a combination of the HUBZone prime contractor's employees and employees of HUBZone small business concern subcontractors; and

(iii) No more than 50 percent of the cost of contract performance to be incurred for personnel will be subcontracted to concerns that are not HUBZone small business concerns; or

(4) *Construction by special trade contractors.* (i) At least 25 percent of the cost of contract performance to be incurred for personnel will be spent on the HUBZone prime contractor's employees;

(ii) At least 50 percent of the cost of the contract performance to be incurred for personnel will be spent on the HUBZone prime contractor's employees or on a combination of the HUBZone prime contractor's employees and employees of HUBZone small business concern subcontractors;

(iii) No more than 50 percent of the cost of contract performance to be incurred for personnel will be subcontracted to concerns that are not HUBZone small business concerns.

(e) A HUBZone joint venture agrees that, in the performance of the contract, the applicable percentage specified in paragraph (d) of this clause will be performed by the aggregate of the HUBZone small business participants.

(f) (1) When the total value of the contract exceeds $25,000, a HUBZone small business concern nonmanufacturer agrees to furnish in performing this contract only end items manufactured or produced by HUBZone small business concern manufacturers.

(2) When the total value of the contract is equal to or less than $25,000, a HUBZone small business concern nonmanufacturer may provide end items manufactured by other than a HUBZone small business concern manufacturer provided the end items are produced or manufactured in the United States.

(3) Paragraphs (f) (1) and (f) (2) of this section do not apply in connection with construction or service contracts.

(g) *Notice.* The HUBZone small business offeror acknowledges that a prospective HUBZone awardee must be a HUBZone small business concern at the time of award of this contract. The HUBZone offeror shall provide the Contracting Officer a copy of the notice required by 13 CFR 126.501 if material changes occur before contract award that could affect its HUBZone eligibility. If the apparently successful HUBZone offeror is not a HUBZone small business concern at the time of award of this contract, the Contracting Officer will proceed to award to the next otherwise successful HUBZone small business concern or other offeror.

(End of clause)

Alternate I (NOV 2011). As prescribed in 19.1309(a)(1), substitute the following paragraphs (d)(3) and (d)(4) for paragraphs (d)(3) and (d)(4) of the basic clause:

(d)(3) General construction, at least 15 percent of the cost of the contract performance to be incurred for personnel will be spent on the concern's employees; or

(d)(4) Construction by special trade contractors, at least 25 percent of the cost of the contract performance to be incurred for personnel will be spent on the concern's employees.

[FAC 97-10, 63 FR 70264, 12/18/98, effective 1/4/99; FAC 2005-47, 75 FR 77727, 12/13/2010, effective 1/12/2011; FAC 2005-54, 76 FR 68032, 11/2/2011, effective 11/2/2011; Interim rule, 77 FR 1889, 1/12/2012, effective 2/13/2012]

52.219-4 Notice of Price Evaluation Preference for HUBZone Small Business Concerns.

As prescribed in 19.1309(b), insert the following clause:

NOTICE OF PRICE EVALUATION PREFERENCE FOR HUBZONE SMALL BUSINESS CONCERNS (OCT 2014)

(a) *Definitions. See* 13 CFR 125.6(e) for definitions of terms used in paragraph (d).

(b) *Evaluation preference.* (1) Offers will be evaluated by adding a factor of 10 percent to the price of all offers, except—

(i) Offers from HUBZone small business concerns that have not waived the evaluation preference; and

(ii) Otherwise successful offers from small business concerns.

(2) The factor of 10 percent shall be applied on a line item basis or to any group of items on which award may be made. Other

evaluation factors described in the solicitation shall be applied before application of the factor.

(3) When the two highest rated offerors are a HUBZone small business concern and a large business, and the evaluated offer of the HUBZone small business concern is equal to the evaluated offer of the large business after considering the price evaluation preference, award will be made to the HUBZone small business concern.

(c) *Waiver of evaluation preference.* A HUBZone small business concern may elect to waive the evaluation preference, in which case the factor will be added to its offer for evaluation purposes. The agreements in paragraphs (d) and (e) of this clause do not apply if the offeror has waived the evaluation preference.

☐ Offeror elects to waive the evaluation preference.

(d) *Agreement.* A HUBZone small business concern agrees that in the performance of the contract, in the case of a contract for

(1) Services (except construction), at least 50 percent of the cost of personnel for contract performance will be spent for employees of the concern or employees of other HUBZone small business concerns;

(2) Supplies (other than procurement from a nonmanufacturer of such supplies), at least 50 percent of the cost of manufacturing, excluding the cost of materials, will be performed by the concern or other HUBZone small business concerns;

(3) *General construction.* (i) At least 15 percent of the cost of contract performance to be incurred for personnel will be spent on the prime contractor's employees;

(ii) At least 50 percent of the cost of the contract performance to be incurred for personnel will be spent on the prime contractor's employees or on a combination of the prime contractor's employees and employees of HUBZone small business concern subcontractors;

(iii) No more than 50 percent of the cost of contract performance to be incurred for personnel will be subcontracted to concerns that are not HUBZone small business concerns; or

(4) *Construction by special trade contractors.* (i) At least 25 percent of the cost of contract performance to be incurred for personnel will be spent on the prime contractor's employees;

(ii) At least 50 percent of the cost of the contract performance to be incurred for personnel will be spent on the prime contractor's employees or on a combination of the prime contractor's employees and employees of HUBZone small business concern subcontractors;

(iii) No more than 50 percent of the cost of contract performance to be incurred for personnel will be subcontracted to concerns that are not HUBZone small business concerns.

(e) A HUBZone joint venture agrees that the aggregate of the HUBZone small business concerns to the joint venture, not each concern separately, will perform the applicable percentage of work requirements.

(f) (1) When the total value of the contract exceeds $25,000, a HUBZone small business concern nonmanufacturer agrees to furnish in performing this contract only end items manufactured or produced by HUBZone small business concern manufacturers.

(2) When the total value of the contract is equal to or less than $25,000, a HUBZone small business concern nonmanufacturer may provide end items manufactured by other than a HUBZone small business concern manufacturer provided the end items are produced or manufactured in the United States.

(3) Paragraphs (f) (1) and (f) (2) of this section do not apply in connection with construction or service contracts.

(g) *Notice.* The HUBZone small business offeror acknowledges that a prospective HUBZone awardee must be a HUBZone small business concern at the time of award of this contract. The HUBZone offeror shall provide the Contracting Officer a copy of the notice required by 13 CFR 126.501 if material changes occur before contract award that could affect its HUBZone eligibility. If the apparently successful HUBZone offeror is not a HUBZone small business concern at the time of award of this contract, the Contracting Officer will proceed to award to the next otherwise successful HUBZone small business concern or other offeror.

(End of clause)

Alternate I (JAN 2011). As prescribed in 19.1309(b)(1), substitute the following paragraphs (d)(3) and (d)(4) for paragraphs (d)(3) and (d)(4) of the basic clause:

(3) General construction, at least 15 percent of the cost of the contract performance to be incurred for personnel will be spent on the concern's employees; or

(4) Construction by special trade contractors, at least 25 percent of the cost of the contract performance to be incurred for personnel will be spent on the concern's employees.

(End of clause)

[FAC 97-10, 63 FR 70264, 12/18/98, effective 1/4/99; FAC 2001-25, 69 FR 59703, 10/5/2004, effective 10/5/2004; FAC 2005-04, 70 FR 33661, 6/8/2005, effective 7/8/2005; FAC 2005-47, 75 FR 77727, 12/13/2010, effective 1/12/2011; FAC 2005-77, 79 FR 61746, 10/14/2014, effective 10/14/2014]

52.219-5 [Removed and Reserved]

[FAC 97-11, 64 FR 10530, 3/4/99, effective 3/4/99; FAC 2001-14, 68 FR 28079, 5/22/2003, effective 6/23/2003;FAC 2005-07, 71 FR 220, 1/3/2006, effective 1/3/2006]

52.219-6 Notice of Total Small Business Set-Aside.

As prescribed in 19.508(c), insert the following clause:

NOTICE OF TOTAL SMALL BUSINESS SET-ASIDE (NOV 2011)

(a) *Definition. Small business concern,* as used in this clause, means a concern, including its affiliates, that is independently owned and operated, not dominant in the field of operation in which it is bidding on Government contracts, and qualified as a small business under the size standards in this solicitation.

(b) *Applicability.* This clause applies only to—

(1) Contracts that have been totally set aside or reserved for small business concerns; and

(2) Orders set aside for small business concerns under multiple-award contracts as described in 8.405–5 and 16.505(b)(2)(i)(F).

(c) *General.* (1) Offers are solicited only from small business concerns. Offers received from concerns that are not small business concerns shall be considered nonresponsive and will be rejected.

(2) Any award resulting from this solicitation will be made to a small business concern.

(d) *Agreement.* A small business concern submitting an offer in its own name shall furnish, in performing the contract, only end items manufactured or produced by small business concerns in the United States or its outlying areas. If this procurement is processed under simplified acquisition procedures and the total amount of this contract does not exceed $25,000, a small business concern may furnish the product of any domestic firm. This paragraph does not apply to construction or service contracts.

(End of clause)

Alternate I (NOV 2011). When the acquisition is for a product in a class for which the Small Business Administration has determined that there are no small business manufacturers or processors in the Federal market in accordance with 19.502-2(c), delete paragraph (d).

Alternate II (NOV 2011). As prescribed in 19.508(c), substitute the following paragraph (c) of the basic clause:

(c) *General.* (1) Offers are solicited only from small business concerns and Federal Prison Industries, Inc. (FPI). Offers received from concerns that are not small business concerns or FPI shall be considered nonresponsive and will be rejected.

(2) Any award resulting from this solicitation will be made to either a small business concern or FPI.

[Interim rule, FAC 84-48, 54 FR 25069, 6/12/89, effective 6/12/89; FAC 84-58, 55 FR 25525, 6/21/90, effective 7/23/90; FAC 90-32, 60 FR 48206, 9/18/95, effective 10/1/95; FAC 90-40, 61 FR 39186, 7/26/96, effective 7/26/96; FAC 2001-14, 68 FR 28079, 5/22/2003, effective 6/23/2003; FAC 2001-21, 69 FR 16147, 3/26/2004, effective 3/26/2004; FAC 2005-07, 71 FR 221, 1/3/2006, effective 1/3/2006; FAC 2005-54, 76 FR 68032, 11/2/2011, effective 11/2/2011; Interim rule, 77 FR 1889, 1/12/2012, effective 2/13/2012]

52.219-7 Notice of Partial Small Business Set-Aside.

As prescribed in 19.508(d), insert the following clause:

NOTICE OF PARTIAL SMALL BUSINESS SET-ASIDE (JUN 2003)

(a) *Definitions. Small business concern,* as used in this clause, means a concern, including its affiliates, that is independently owned and operated, not dominant in the field of operation in which it is bidding on Government contracts, and qualified as a small business under the size standards in this solicitation.

(b) *General.* (1) A portion of this requirement, identified elsewhere in this solicitation, has been set aside for award to one or more small business concerns.

(2) Offers on the non-set-aside portion will be evaluated first and award will be made on that portion in accordance with the provisions of this solicitation.

(3) The set-aside portion will be awarded at the highest unit price(s) in the contract(s) for the non-set-aside portion, adjusted to reflect transportation and other costs appropriate for the selected contractor(s).

(4) The contractor(s) for the set-aside portion will be selected from among the small business concerns that submitted responsive offers on the non-set-aside portion. Negotiations will be conducted with the concern that submitted the lowest responsive offer on the non-set-aside portion. If the negotiations are not successful or if only part of the set-aside portion is awarded to that concern, negotiations will be conducted with the concern that submitted the second-lowest responsive offer on the non-set-aside portion. This process will continue until a contract or contracts are awarded for the entire set-aside portion.

(5) The Government reserves the right to not consider token offers or offers designed to secure an unfair advantage over other offerors eligible for the set-aside portion.

(c) *Agreement.* For the set-aside portion of the acquisition, a small business concern submitting an offer in its own name shall furnish, in performing the contract, only end items manufactured or produced by small business concerns in the United States or its outlying areas. If this procurement is processed under simplified acquisition procedures and the total amount of this contract does not exceed $25,000, a small business concern may furnish the product of any domestic firm. This paragraph does not apply to construction or service contracts.

(End of clause)

Alternate I (OCT 1995). When the acquisition is for a product in a class for which the Small Business Administration has determined that there are no small business manufacturers or processors in the Federal market in accordance with 19.502-2(c), delete paragraph (c).

Alternate II (MAR 2004). As prescribed in 19.508(d), add the following paragraph (d) to the basic clause:

(d) Notwithstanding paragraph (b) of this clause, offers from Federal Prison Industries, Inc., will be solicited and considered for both set-aside and non-set-aside portion of this requirement.

[Interim rule, FAC 84-48, 54 FR 25069, 6/12/89, effective 6/12/89; FAC 90-3, 55 FR 52798, 12/21/90, effective 1/22/91; FAC 90-29, 60 FR 34732, 7/3/95, effective 7/3/95; FAC 90-32, 60 FR 48206, 9/18/95, effective 10/1/95; FAC 90-40, 61 FR 39186, 7/26/96, effective 7/26/96; FAC 2001-14, 68 FR 28079, 5/22/2003, effective 6/23/2003; FAC

2001-21, 69 FR 16147, 3/26/2004, effective 3/26/2004]

52.219-8 Utilization of Small Business Concerns.

As prescribed in 19.708(a), insert the following clause:

UTILIZATION OF SMALL BUSINESS CONCERNS (OCT 2018)

(a) *Definitions*. As used in this contract—

HUBZone small business concern means a small business concern, certified by the Small Business Administration, that appears on the List of Qualified HUBZone Small Business Concerns maintained by the Small Business Administration.

Service-disabled veteran-owned small business concern—

(1) Means a *small business concern*—

(i) Not less than 51 percent of which is owned by one or more service-disabled veterans or, in the case of any publicly owned business, not less than 51 percent of the stock of which is owned by one or more service-disabled veterans; and

(ii) The management and daily business operations of which are controlled by one or more service-disabled veterans or, in the case of a service-disabled veteran with permanent and severe disability, the spouse or permanent caregiver of such veteran.

(2) *Service-disabled veteran* means a veteran, as defined in 38 U.S.C. 101(2), with a disability that is service-connected, as defined in 38 U.S.C. 101(16).

Small business concern means a small business as defined pursuant to Section 3 of the Small Business Act and relevant regulations promulgated pursuant thereto.

Small disadvantaged business concern, consistent with 13 CFR 124.1002, means a *small business concern* under the size standard applicable to the acquisition, that—

(1) Is at least 51 percent unconditionally and directly owned (as defined at 13 CFR 124.105) by—

(i) One or more socially disadvantaged (as defined at 13 CFR 124.103) and economically disadvantaged (as defined at 13 CFR 124.104) individuals who are citizens of the United States; and

(ii) Each individual claiming economic disadvantage has a net worth not exceeding $750,000 after taking into account the applicable exclusions set forth at 13 CFR 124.104(c)(2); and

(2) The management and daily business operations of which are controlled (as defined at 13 CFR 124.106) by individuals, who meet the criteria in paragraphs (1)(i) and (ii) of this definition.

Veteran-owned small business concern means a *small business concern*—

(1) Not less than 51 percent of which is owned by one or more veterans (as defined at 38 U.S.C. 101(2)) or, in the case of any publicly owned business, not less than 51 percent of the stock of which is owned by one or more veterans; and

(2) The management and daily business operations of which are controlled by one or more veterans.

Women-owned small business concern means a *small business concern*—

(1) That is at least 51 percent owned by one or more women, or, in the case of any publicly owned business, at least 51 percent of the stock of which is owned by one or more women; and

(2) Whose management and daily business operations are controlled by one or more women.

(b) It is the policy of the United States that small business concerns, veteran-owned small business concerns, service-disabled veteran-owned small business concerns, HUBZone small business concerns, small disadvantaged business concerns, and women-owned small business concerns shall have the maximum practicable opportunity to participate in performing contracts let by any Federal agency, including contracts and subcontracts for subsystems, assemblies, components, and related services for major States that its prime contractors establish procedures to ensure the timely payment of amounts due pursuant to the terms of their subcontracts with small business concerns, veteran-owned small business concerns, service-disabled veteran-owned small business concerns, HUBZone small business concerns, small disadvantaged business concerns, and women-owned small business concerns.

(c) The Contractor hereby agrees to carry out this policy in the awarding of subcontracts to the fullest extent consistent with efficient contract performance. The Contractor further agrees to cooperate in any studies or surveys as may be conducted by the United States Small Business Administration or the awarding agency of the United States as may be necessary to determine the extent of the Contractor's compliance with this clause.

(d) (1) The Contractor may accept a subcontractor's written representations of its size and socioeconomic status as a small business, small disadvantaged business, veteran-owned small business, service-disabled veteran-owned small business, or a women-owned small business if the subcontractor represents that the size and socioeconomic status representations with its offer are current, accurate, and complete as of the date of the offer for the subcontract.

(2) The Contractor may accept a subcontractor's representations of its size and socioeconomic status as a small business, small disadvantaged business, veteran-owned small business, service-disabled veteran-owned small business, or a women-owned small business in the System for Award Management (SAM) if—

(i) The subcontractor is registered in SAM; and

(ii) The subcontractor represents that the size and socioeconomic status representations made in SAM are current, accurate and complete as of the date of the offer for the subcontract.

(3) The Contractor may not require the use of SAM for the purposes of representing size or socioeconomic status in connection with a subcontract.

(4) In accordance with 13 CFR 121.411, 124.1015, 125.29, 126.900, and 127.700, a contractor acting in good faith is not liable for misrepresentations made by its subcontractors regarding the subcontractor's size or socioeconomic status.

(5) The Contractor shall confirm that a subcontractor representing itself as a HUBZone small business concern is certified by SBA as a HUBZone small business concern by accessing the System for Award Management or by contacting the SBA. Options for contacting the SBA include—

(i) HUBZone small business database search application Web page at *http://dsbs.sba.gov/dsbs/search/dsp_searchhubzone.cfm;* or *http://www.sba.gov/hubzone;*

(ii) In writing to the Director/HUB, U.S. Small Business Administration, 409 3rd Street, SW., Washington DC 20416; or

(iii) The SBA HUBZone Help Desk at *hubzone@sba.gov*.

(End of clause)

[FAC 97-10, 63 FR 70264, 12/18/98, effective 1/4/99, corrected 64 FR 3196, 1/20/99; FAC 97-11, 64 FR 10530, 3/4/99, effective 3/4/99; FAC 97-12, 64 FR 32740, 6/17/99, effective 6/17/99; FAC 97-13, 64 FR 36222, 7/2/99, effective 10/1/99; FAC 97-20, 65 FR 60542, 10/11/2000, effective 10/11/2000; FAC 2001-23, 69 FR 25273, 5/5/2004, effective 5/5/2004; FAC 2005-02, 70 FR 14950, 3/23/2005, effective 3/23/2005; FAC 2005-47, 75 FR 77727, 12/13/2010, effective 1/12/2011; 75 FR 77737, 12/13/2010, effective 12/13/2010; FAC 2005-54, 76 FR 68026, 11/2/2011, effective 11/2/2011; FAC 2005-67, 78 FR 37676, 6/21/2013, effective 7/22/2013; FAC 2005-73, 79 FR 24192, 4/29/2014, effective 5/29/2014; FAC 2005-77, 79 FR 61746, 10/14/2014, effective 10/14/2014; FAC 2005-89, 81 FR 45833, 7/14/2016, effective 11/1/2016; FAC 2005-101, 83 FR 48691, 9/26/2018, effective 10/26/2018]

52.219-9 Small Business Subcontracting Plan.

As prescribed in 19.708(b), insert the following clause:

SMALL BUSINESS SUBCONTRACTING PLAN (AUG 2018)

(a) This clause does not apply to small business concerns.

(b) *Definitions.* As used in this clause—

Alaska Native Corporation (ANC) means any Regional Corporation, Village Corporation, Urban Corporation, or Group Corporation organized under the laws of the State of Alaska in accordance with the Alaska Native Claims Settlement Act, as amended (43 U.S.C. 1601, et seq.) and which is considered a minority and economically disadvantaged concern under the criteria at 43 U.S.C. 1626(e)(1). This definition also includes ANC direct and indirect subsidiary corporations, joint ventures, and partnerships that meet the requirements of 43 U.S.C. 1626(e)(2).

Commercial item means a product or service that satisfies the definition of commercial item insection 2.101 of the Federal Acquisition Regulation.

Commercial plan means a subcontracting plan (including goals) that covers the offeror's fiscal year and that applies to the entire production of commercial items sold by either the entire company or a portion thereof (*e.g.,* division, plant, or product line).

Electronic Subcontracting Reporting System (eSRS) means the Governmentwide, electronic, web-based system for small business subcontracting program reporting. The eSRS is located at *http://www.esrs.gov*.

Indian tribe means any Indian tribe, band, group, pueblo, or community, including native villages and native groups (including corporations organized by Kenai, Juneau, Sitka, and Kodiak) as defined in the Alaska Native Claims Settlement Act (43 U.S.C.A. 1601 et seq.), that is recognized by the Federal Government as eligible for services from the Bureau of Indian Affairs in accordance with 25 U.S.C. 1452(c). This definition also includes Indian-owned economic enterprises that meet the requirements of 25 U.S.C. 1452(e).

Individual subcontracting plan means a subcontracting plan that covers the entire contract period (including option periods), applies to a specific contract, and has goals that are based on the offeror's planned subcontracting in support of the specific contract, except that indirect costs incurred for common or joint purposes may be allocated on a prorated basis to the contract.

Master subcontracting plan means a subcontracting plan that contains all the required elements of an individual subcontracting plan, except goals, and may be incorporated into individual subcontracting plans, provided the master subcontracting plan has been approved.

Reduced payment means a payment that is for less than the amount agreed upon in a subcontract in accordance with its terms and conditions, for supplies and services for which the Government has paid the prime contractor.

Subcontract means any agreement (other than one involving an employer-employee relationship) entered into by a Federal Government prime Contractor or subcontractor calling for supplies or services required for performance of the contract or subcontract.

Total contract dollars means the final anticipated dollar value, including the dollar value of all options.

Untimely payment means a payment to a subcontractor that is more than 90 days past due under the terms and conditions of a subcontract for supplies and services for which the Government has paid the prime contractor.

(c)(1) The Offeror, upon request by the Contracting Officer, shall submit and negotiate a subcontracting plan, where applicable, that separately addresses subcontracting with small business, veteran-owned small business, service-disabled veteran-owned small business, HUBZone small business, small disadvantaged business, and women-owned small business concerns. If the Offeror is submitting an individual subcontracting plan, the plan must separately address subcontracting with small business, veteran-owned small business, service-disabled veteran-owned small business, HUBZone small business, small disadvantaged business, and women-owned small business concerns, with a separate part for the basic contract and separate parts for each option (if any). The subcontracting plan shall be included in and made a part of the resultant contract. The subcontracting plan shall be negotiated within the time specified by the Contracting Officer. Failure to submit and negotiate the subcontracting plan shall make the Offeror ineligible for award of a contract.

(2) (i) The Contractor may accept a subcontractor's written representations of its size and socioeconomic status as a small business, small disadvantaged business, veteran-owned small business, service-disabled veteran-owned small business, or a women-owned small business if the subcontractor represents that the size and socioeconomic status representations with its offer are current, accurate, and complete as of the date of the offer for the subcontract.

(ii) The Contractor may accept a subcontractor's representations of its size and socioeconomic status as a small business, small disadvantaged business, veteran-owned small business, service-disabled veteran-owned small business, or a women-owned small business in the System for Award Management (SAM) if—

(A) The subcontractor is registered in SAM; and

(B) The subcontractor represents that the size and socioeconomic status representations made in SAM are current, accurate and complete as of the date of the offer for the subcontract.

(iii) The Contractor may not require the use of SAM for the purposes of representing size or socioeconomic status in connection with a subcontract.

(iv) In accordance with 13 CFR 121.411, 124.1015, 125.29, 126.900, and 127.700, a contractor acting in good faith is not liable for misrepresentations made by its subcontractors regarding the subcontractor's size or socioeconomic status.

(d) (1) Separate goals, expressed in terms of total dollars subcontracted, and as a percentage of total planned subcontracting dollars, for the use of small business, veteran-owned small business, service-disabled veteran-owned small business, HUBZone small business, small disadvantaged business, and women-owned small business concerns as subcontractors. For individual subcontracting plans, and if required by the Contracting Officer, goals shall also be expressed in terms of percentage of total contract dollars, in addition to the goals expressed as a percentage of total subcontract dollars. The Offeror shall include all subcontracts that contribute to contract performance, and may include a proportionate share of products and services that are normally allocated as indirect costs. In accordance with 43 U.S.C. 1626—

(i) Subcontracts awarded to an ANC or Indian tribe shall be counted towards the subcontracting goals for small business and small disadvantaged business concerns, regardless of the size or Small Business Administration certification status of the ANC or Indian tribe; and

(ii) Where one or more subcontractors are in the subcontract tier between the prime Contractor and the ANC or Indian tribe, the ANC or Indian tribe shall designate the appropriate Contractor(s) to count the subcontract towards its small business and small disadvantaged business subcontracting goals.

(A) In most cases, the appropriate Contractor is the Contractor that awarded the subcontract to the ANC or Indian tribe.

(B) If the ANC or Indian tribe designates more than one Contractor to count the subcontract toward its goals, the ANC or Indian tribe shall designate only a portion of the total subcontract award to each Contractor. The sum of the amounts designated to various Contractors cannot exceed the total value of the subcontract.

(C) The ANC or Indian tribe shall give a copy of the written designation to the Contracting Officer, the prime Contractor, and the subcontractors in between the prime Contractor and the ANC or Indian tribe within 30 days of the date of the subcontract award.

(D) If the Contracting Officer does not receive a copy of the ANC's or the Indian tribe's written designation within 30 days of the subcontract award, the Contractor that awarded the subcontract to the ANC or Indian tribe will be considered the designated Contractor.

(2) A statement of—

(i) Total dollars planned to be subcontracted for an individual subcontracting plan; or the Offeror's total projected sales, expressed in dollars, and the total value of projected subcontracts to support the sales for a commercial plan;

(ii) Total dollars planned to be subcontracted to small business concerns (including ANC and Indian tribes);

(iii) Total dollars planned to be subcontracted to veteran-owned small business concerns;

(iv) Total dollars planned to be subcontracted to service-disabled veteran-owned small business;

(v) Total dollars planned to be subcontracted to HUBZone small business concerns;

(vi) Total dollars planned to be subcontracted to small disadvantaged business concerns (including ANC and Indian tribes); and

(vii) Total dollars planned to be subcontracted to women-owned small business concerns.

(3) A description of the principal types of supplies and services to be subcontracted, and an identification of the types planned for subcontracting to—

(i) Small business concerns;

(ii) Veteran-owned small business concerns;

(iii) Service-disabled veteran-owned small business concerns;

(iv) HUBZone small business concerns;

(v) Small disadvantaged business concerns; and

(vi) Women-owned small business concerns.

(4) A description of the method used to develop the subcontracting goals in paragraph (d)(1) of this clause.

(5) A description of the method used to identify potential sources for solicitation purposes (*e.g.*, existing company source lists, SAM, veterans service organizations, the National Minority Purchasing Council Vendor Information Service, the Research and Information Division of the Minority Business Development Agency in the Department of Commerce, or small, HUBZone, small disadvantaged, and women-owned small business trade associations). A firm may rely on the information contained in SAM as an accurate representation of a concern's size and ownership characteristics for the purposes of maintaining a small, veteran-owned small, service-disabled veteran-owned small, HUBZone small, small disadvantaged, and women-owned small business source list. Use of SAM as its source list does not relieve a firm of its responsibilities (*e.g.*, outreach, assistance, counseling, or publicizing subcontracting opportunities) in this clause.

(6) A statement as to whether or not the Offeror included indirect costs in establishing subcontracting goals, and a description of the method used to determine the proportionate share of indirect costs to be incurred with—

(i) Small business concerns (including ANC and Indian tribes);

(ii) Veteran-owned small business concerns;

(iii) Service-disabled veteran-owned small business concerns;

(iv) HUBZone small business concerns;

(v) Small disadvantaged business concerns (including ANC and Indian tribes); and

(vi) Women-owned small business concerns.

(7) The name of the individual employed by the Offeror who will administer the Offeror's subcontracting program, and a description of the duties of the individual.

(8) A description of the efforts the Offeror will make to assure that small business, veteran-owned small business, service-disabled veteran-owned small business, HUBZone small business, small disadvantaged business, and women-owned small business con-

cerns have an equitable opportunity to compete for subcontracts.

(9) Assurances that the Offeror will include the clause of this contract entitled "Utilization of Small Business Concerns" in all subcontracts that offer further subcontracting opportunities, and that the Offeror will require all subcontractors (except small business concerns) that receive subcontracts in excess of $700,000 ($1.5 million for construction of any public facility) with further subcontracting possibilities to adopt a subcontracting plan that complies with the requirements of this clause.

(10) Assurances that the Offeror will—

(i) Cooperate in any studies or surveys as may be required;

(ii) Submit periodic reports so that the Government can determine the extent of compliance by the Offeror with the subcontracting plan;

(iii) After November 30, 2017, include subcontracting data for each order when reporting subcontracting achievements for indefinite-delivery, indefinite-quantity contracts with individual subcontracting plans where the contract is intended for use by multiple agencies;

(iv) Submit the Individual Subcontract Report (ISR) and/or the Summary Subcontract Report (SSR), in accordance with paragraph (l) of this clause using the Electronic Subcontracting Reporting System (eSRS) at *http://www.esrs.gov*. The reports shall provide information on subcontract awards to small business concerns (including ANCs and Indian tribes that are not small businesses), veteran-owned small business concerns, service-disabled veteran-owned small business concerns, HUBZone small business concerns, small disadvantaged business concerns (including ANCs and Indian tribes that have not been certified by SBA as small disadvantaged businesses), women-owned small business concerns, and for NASA only, Historically Black Colleges and Universities and Minority Institutions. Reporting shall be in accordance with this clause, or as provided in agency regulations;

(v) Ensure that its subcontractors with subcontracting plans agree to submit the ISR and/or the SSR using eSRS;

(vi) Provide its prime contract number, its unique entity identifier, and the email address of the Offeror's official responsible for acknowledging receipt of or rejecting the ISRs, to all first-tier subcontractors with subcontracting plans so they can enter this information into the eSRS when submitting their ISRs; and

(vii) Require that each subcontractor with a subcontracting plan provide the prime contract number, its own unique entity identifier, and the email address of the subcontractor's official responsible for acknowledging receipt of or rejecting the ISRs, to its subcontractors with subcontracting plans.

(11) A description of the types of records that will be maintained concerning procedures that have been adopted to comply with the requirements and goals in the plan, including establishing source lists; and a description of the offeror's efforts to locate small business, veteran-owned small business, service-disabled veteran-owned small business, HUBZone small business, small disadvantaged business, and women-owned small business concerns and award subcontracts to them. The records shall include at least the following (on a plant-wide or company-wide basis, unless otherwise indicated):

(i) Source lists (e.g., SAM), guides, and other data that identify small business, veteran-owned small business, service-disabled veteran-owned small business, HUBZone small business, small disadvantaged business, and women-owned small business concerns.

(ii) Organizations contacted in an attempt to locate sources that are small business, veteran-owned small business, service-disabled veteran-owned small business, HUBZone small business, small disadvantaged business, or women-owned small business concerns.

(iii) Records on each subcontract solicitation resulting in an award of more than $150,000, indicating—

(A) Whether small business concerns were solicited and, if not, why not;

(B) Whether veteran-owned small business concerns were solicited and, if not, why not;

(C) Whether service-disabled veteran-owned small business concerns were solicited and, if not, why not;

(D) Whether HUBZone small business concerns were solicited and, if not, why not;

(E) Whether small disadvantaged business concerns were solicited and, if not, why not;

(F) Whether women-owned small business concerns were solicited and, if not, why not; and

(G) If applicable, the reason award was not made to a small business concern.

(iv) Records of any outreach efforts to contact—

(A) Trade associations;

(B) Business development organizations;

(C) Conferences and trade fairs to locate small, HUBZone small, small disadvantaged, service-disabled veteran-owned, and women-owned small business sources; and

(D) Veterans service organizations.

(v) Records of internal guidance and encouragement provided to buyers through—

(A) Workshops, seminars, training, etc.; and

(B) Monitoring performance to evaluate compliance with the program's requirements.

(vi) On a contract-by-contract basis, records to support award data submitted by the offeror to the Government, including the name, address, and business size of each subcontractor. Contractors having commercial plans need not comply with this requirement.

(12) Assurances that the Offeror will make a good faith effort to acquire articles, equipment, supplies, services, or materials, or obtain the performance of construction work from the small business concerns that it used in preparing the bid or proposal, in the same or greater scope, amount, and quality used in preparing and submitting the bid or proposal. Responding to a request for a quote does not constitute use in preparing a bid or proposal. The Offeror used a small business concern in preparing the bid or proposal if—

(i) The Offeror identifies the small business concern as a subcontractor in the bid or proposal or associated small business subcontracting plan, to furnish certain supplies or perform a portion of the subcontract; or

(ii) The Offeror used the small business concern's pricing or cost information or technical expertise in preparing the bid or proposal, where there is written evidence of an intent or understanding that the small business concern will be awarded a subcontract for the related work if the Offeror is awarded the contract.

(13) Assurances that the Contractor will provide the Contracting Officer with a written explanation if the Contractor fails to acquire articles, equipment, supplies, services or materials or obtain the performance of construction work as described in (d)(12) of this clause. This written explanation must be submitted to the Contracting Officer within 30 days of contract completion.

(14) Assurances that the Contractor will not prohibit a subcontractor from discussing with the Contracting Officer any material matter pertaining to payment to or utilization of a subcontractor.

(15) Assurances that the offeror will pay its small business subcontractors on time and in accordance with the terms and conditions of the underlying subcontract, and notify the contracting officer when the prime contractor makes either a reduced or an untimely payment to a small business subcontractor (see 52.242-5).

(e) In order to effectively implement this plan to the extent consistent with efficient contract performance, the Contractor shall perform the following functions:

(1) Assist small business, veteran-owned small business, service-disabled veteran-owned small business, HUBZone small business, small disadvantaged business, and wo-

men-owned small business concerns by arranging solicitations, time for the preparation of bids, quantities, specifications, and delivery schedules so as to facilitate the participation by such concerns. Where the Contractor's lists of potential small business, veteran-owned small business, service-disabled veteran-owned small business, HUBZone small business, small disadvantaged business, and women-owned small business subcontractors are excessively long, reasonable effort shall be made to give all such small business concerns an opportunity to compete over a period of time.

(2) Provide adequate and timely consideration of the potentialities of small business, veteran-owned small business, service-disabled veteran-owned small business, HUBZone small business, small disadvantaged business, and women-owned small business concerns in all "make-or-buy" decisions.

(3) Counsel and discuss subcontracting opportunities with representatives of small business, veteran-owned small business, service-disabled veteran-owned small business, HUBZone small business, small disadvantaged business, and women-owned small business firms.

(4) Confirm that a subcontractor representing itself as a HUBZone small business concern is certified by SBA as a HUBZone small business concern in accordance with 52.219-8(d)(2).

(5) Provide notice to subcontractors concerning penalties and remedies for misrepresentations of business status as small, veteran-owned small business, HUBZone small, small disadvantaged, or women-owned small business for the purpose of obtaining a subcontract that is to be included as part or all of a goal contained in the Contractor's subcontracting plan.

(6) For all competitive subcontracts over the simplified acquisition threshold in which a small business concern received a small business preference, upon determination of the successful subcontract offeror, prior to award of the subcontract the Contractor must inform each unsuccessful small business subcontract offeror in writing of the name and location of the apparent successful offeror and if the successful subcontract offeror is a small business, veteran-owned small business, service-disabled veteran-owned small business, HUBZone small business, small disadvantaged business, or women-owned small business concern.

(7) Assign each subcontract the NAICS code and corresponding size standard that best describes the principal purpose of the subcontract.

(f) A master subcontracting plan on a plant or division-wide basis that contains all the elements required by paragraph (d) of this clause, except goals, may be incorporated by reference as a part of the subcontracting plan required of the Offeror by this clause; provided—

(1) The master subcontracting plan has been approved;

(2) The Offeror ensures that the master subcontracting plan is updated as necessary and provides copies of the approved master subcontracting plan, including evidence of its approval, to the Contracting Officer; and

(3) Goals and any deviations from the master subcontracting plan deemed necessary by the Contracting Officer to satisfy the requirements of this contract are set forth in the individual subcontracting plan.

(g) A commercial plan is the preferred type of subcontracting plan for contractors furnishing commercial items. The commercial plan shall relate to the offeror's planned subcontracting generally, for both commercial and Government business, rather than solely to the Government contract. Once the Contractor's commercial plan has been approved, the Government will not require another subcontracting plan from the same Contractor while the plan remains in effect, as long as the product or service being provided by the Contractor continues to meet the definition of a commercial item. A Contractor with a commercial plan shall comply with the reporting requirements stated in paragraph (d)(10) of this clause by submitting one SSR in eSRS for all contracts covered by its commercial plan. This report shall be acknowledged or rejected in eSRS by the Contracting Officer who approved the plan. This report shall be submitted within 30 days after the end of the Government's fiscal year.

(h) Prior compliance of the offeror with other such subcontracting plans under previous contracts will be considered by the Contracting Officer in determining the responsibility of the offeror for award of the contract.

(i) A contract may have no more than one subcontracting plan. When a contract modification exceeds the subcontracting plan threshold in 19.702(a), or an option is exercised, the goals of the existing subcontracting plan shall be amended to reflect any new subcontracting opportunities. When the goals in a subcontracting plan are amended, these goal changes do not apply retroactively.

(j) Subcontracting plans are not required from subcontractors when the prime contract contains the clause at 52.212-5, Contract Terms and Conditions Required to Implement Statutes or Executive Orders—Commercial Items, or when the subcontractor provides a commercial item subject to the clause at 52.244-6, Subcontracts for Commercial Items, under a prime contract.

(k) The failure of the Contractor or subcontractor to comply in good faith with (1) the clause of this contract entitled "Utilization Of Small Business Concerns," or (2) an approved plan required by this clause, shall be a material breach of the contract and may be considered in any past performance evaluation of the Contractor.

(l) The Contractor shall submit ISRs and SSRs using the web-based eSRS at *http://www.esrs.gov*. Purchases from a corporation, company, or subdivision that is an affiliate of the Contractor or subcontractor are not included in these reports. Subcontract awards by affiliates shall be treated as subcontract awards by the Contractor. Subcontract award data reported by the Contractor and subcontractors shall be limited to awards made to their immediate next-tier subcontractors. Credit cannot be taken for awards made to lower tier subcontractors, unless the Contractor or subcontractor has been designated to receive a small business or small disadvantaged business credit from an ANC or Indian tribe. Only subcontracts involving performance in the United States or its outlying areas should be included in these reports with the exception of subcontracts under a contract awarded by the State Department or any other agency that has statutory or regulatory authority to require subcontracting plans for subcontracts performed outside the United States and its outlying areas.

(1) *ISR*. This report is not required for commercial plans. The report is required for each contract containing an individual subcontracting plan.

(i) The report shall be submitted semi-annually during contract performance for the periods ending March 31 and September 30. A report is also required for each contract within 30 days of contract completion. Reports are due 30 days after the close of each reporting period, unless otherwise directed by the Contracting Officer. Reports are required when due, regardless of whether there has been any subcontracting activity since the inception of the contract or the previous reporting period. When the Contracting Officer rejects an ISR, the Contractor shall submit a corrected report within 30 days of receiving the notice of ISR rejection.

(ii) (A) When a subcontracting plan contains separate goals for the basic contract and each option, as prescribed by FAR 19.704(c), the dollar goal inserted on this report shall be the sum of the base period through the current option; for example, for a report submitted after the second option is exercised, the dollar goal would be the sum of the goals for the basic contract, the first option, and the second option.

(B) If a subcontracting plan has been added to the contract pursuant to 19.702(a)(3) or 19.301-2(e), the Contractor's achievements must be reported in the ISR on a cumulative basis from the date of incorporation of the subcontracting plan into the contract.

(iii) When a subcontracting plan includes indirect costs in the goals, these costs must be included in this report.

(iv) The authority to acknowledge receipt or reject the ISR resides—

(A) In the case of the prime Contractor, with the Contracting Officer; and

(B) In the case of a subcontract with a subcontracting plan, with the entity that awarded the subcontract.

(2) *SSR*. (i) *Reports submitted under individual subcontracting plans.*

(A) This report encompasses all subcontracting under prime contracts and subcontracts with an executive agency, regardless of the dollar value of the subcontracts. This report also includes indirect costs on a prorated basis when the indirect costs are excluded from the subcontracting goals.

(B) The report may be submitted on a corporate, company or subdivision (*e.g.* plant or division operating as a separate profit center) basis, unless otherwise directed by the agency.

(C) If the Contractor or a subcontractor is performing work for more than one executive agency, a separate report shall be submitted to each executive agency covering only that agency's contracts, provided at least one of that agency's contracts is over $700,000 (over $1.5 million for construction of a public facility) and contains a subcontracting plan. For DoD, a consolidated report shall be submitted for all contracts awarded by military departments/agencies and/or subcontracts awarded by DoD prime contractors.

(D) The report shall be submitted annually by October 30 for the twelve month period ending September 30. When a Contracting Officer rejects an SSR, the Contractor shall submit a revised report within 30 days of receiving the notice of SSR rejection.

(E) Subcontract awards that are related to work for more than one executive agency shall be appropriately allocated.

(F) The authority to acknowledge or reject SSRs in eSRS, including SSRs submitted by subcontractors with subcontracting plans, resides with the Government agency awarding the prime contracts unless stated otherwise in the contract.

(ii) *Reports submitted under a commercial plan.*

(A) The report shall include all subcontract awards under the commercial plan in effect during the Government's fiscal year and all indirect costs.

(B) The report shall be submitted annually, within thirty days after the end of the Government's fiscal year.

(C) If a Contractor has a commercial plan and is performing work for more than one executive agency, the Contractor shall specify the percentage of dollars attributable to each agency.

(D) The authority to acknowledge or reject SSRs for commercial plans resides with the Contracting Officer who approved the commercial plan.

(End of clause)

Alternate I (NOV 2016). As prescribed in 19.708(b)(1)(i), substitute the following paragraph (c)(1) for paragraph (c)(1) of the basic clause:

(c)(1) The apparent low bidder, upon request by the Contracting Officer, shall submit a subcontracting plan, where applicable, that separately addresses subcontracting with small business, veteran-owned small business, service-disabled veteran-owned small business, HUBZone small business, small disadvantaged business, and women-owned small business concerns. If the bidder is submitting an individual subcontracting plan, the plan must separately address subcontracting with small business, veteran-owned small business, service-disabled veteran-owned small business, HUBZone small business, small disadvantaged business, and women-owned small business concerns, with a separate part for the basic contract and separate parts for each option (if any). The plan shall be included in and made a part of the resultant contract. The subcontracting plan shall be submitted within the time specified by the Contracting Officer. Failure to submit the subcontracting plan shall make the bidder ineligible for the award of a contract.

Alternate II (NOV 2016). As prescribed in 19.708(b)(1)(ii), substitute the following paragraph (c)(1) for paragraph (c)(1) of the basic clause:

(c)(1) Proposals submitted in response to this solicitation shall include a subcontracting plan that separately addresses subcontracting with small business, veteran-owned small business, service-disabled veteran-owned small business, HUBZone small business, small disadvantaged business, and women-owned small business concerns. If the Offeror is submitting an individual subcontracting plan, the plan must separately address subcontracting with small business, veteran-owned small business, service-disabled veteran-owned small business, HUBZone small business, small disadvantaged business, and women-owned small business concerns, with a separate part for the basic contract and separate parts for each option (if any). The plan shall be included in and made a part of the resultant contract. The subcontracting plan shall be negotiated within the time specified by the Contracting Officer. Failure to submit and negotiate a subcontracting plan shall make the Offeror ineligible for award of a contract.

Alternate III (JAN 2017). As prescribed in 19.708(b)(1)(iii), substitute the following paragraphs (d)(10) and (l) for paragraphs (d)(10) and (l) in the basic clause:

(d)(10) Assurances that the Offeror will—

(i) Cooperate in any studies or surveys as may be required;

(ii) Submit periodic reports so that the Government can determine the extent of compliance by the Offeror with the subcontracting plan;

(iii) Submit Standard Form (SF) 294 Subcontracting Report for Individual Contract in accordance with paragraph (l) of this clause. Submit the Summary Subcontract Report (SSR), in accordance with paragraph (l) of this clause using the Electronic Subcontracting Reporting System (eSRS) at *http://www.esrs.gov*. The reports shall provide information on subcontract awards to small business concerns (including ANCs and Indian tribes that are not small businesses), veteran-owned small business concerns, service-disabled veteran-owned small business concerns, HUBZone small business concerns, small disadvantaged business concerns (including ANCs and Indian tribes that have not been certified by the Small Business Administration as small disadvantaged businesses), women-owned small business concerns, and for NASA only, Historically Black Colleges and Universities and Minority Institutions. Reporting shall be in accordance with this clause, or as provided in agency regulations; and

(iv) Ensure that its subcontractors with subcontracting plans agree to submit the SF 294 in accordance with paragraph (l) of this clause. Ensure that its subcontractors with subcontracting plans agree to submit the SSR in accordance with paragraph (l) of this clause using the eSRS.

(l) The Contractor shall submit a SF 294. The Contractor shall submit SSRs using the web-based eSRS at *http://www.esrs.gov*. Purchases from a corporation, company, or subdivision that is an affiliate of the Contractor or subcontractor are not included in these reports. Subcontract awards by affiliates shall be treated as subcontract awards by the Contractor. Subcontract award data reported by the Contractor and subcontractors shall be limited to awards made to their immediate next-tier subcontractors. Credit cannot be taken for awards made to lower tier subcontractors, unless the Contractor or subcontractor has been designated to receive a small business or small disadvantaged business credit from an ANC or Indian tribe. Only subcontracts involving performance in the U.S. or its outlying areas should be included in these reports with the exception of subcontracts under a contract awarded by the State Department or any other agency that has statutory or regulatory authority to require subcontracting plans for subcontracts performed outside the United States and its outlying areas.

(1) *SF 294*. This report is not required for commercial plans. The report is required for each contract containing an individual subcontracting plan. For Contractors the report shall be submitted to the Contracting Officer, or as specified elsewhere in this contract. In the case of a subcontract with a subcontracting plan, the report shall be sub-

mitted to the entity that awarded the subcontract.

(i) The report shall be submitted semi-annually during contract performance for the periods ending March 31 and September 30. A report is also required for each contract within 30 days of contract completion. Reports are due 30 days after the close of each reporting period, unless otherwise directed by the Contracting Officer. Reports are required when due, regardless of whether there has been any subcontracting activity since the inception of the contract or the previous reporting period. When a Contracting Officer rejects a report, the Contractor shall submit a revised report within 30 days of receiving the notice of report rejection.

(ii) (A) When a subcontracting plan contains separate goals for the basic contract and each option, as prescribed by FAR 19.704(c), the dollar goal inserted on this report shall be the sum of the base period through the current option; for example, for a report submitted after the second option is exercised, the dollar goal would be the sum of the goals for the basic contract, the first option, and the second option.

(B) If a subcontracting plan has been added to the contract pursuant to 19.702(a)(3) or 19.301-2(e), the Contractor's achievements must be reported in the report on a cumulative basis from the date of incorporation of the subcontracting plan into the contract.

(iii) When a subcontracting plan includes indirect costs in the goals, these costs must be included in this report.

(2) *SSR*. (i) *Reports submitted under individual subcontracting plans*.

(A) This report encompasses all subcontracting under prime contracts and subcontracts with an executive agency, regardless of the dollar value of the subcontracts. This report also includes indirect costs on a prorated basis when the indirect costs are excluded from the subcontracting goals.

(B) The report may be submitted on a corporate, company or subdivision (*e.g.*, plant or division operating as a separate profit center) basis, unless otherwise directed by the agency.

(C) If the Contractor and/or a subcontractor is performing work for more than one executive agency, a separate report shall be submitted to each executive agency covering only that agency's contracts, provided at least one of that agency's contracts is over $700,000 (over $1.5 million for construction of a public facility) and contains a subcontracting plan. For DoD, a consolidated report shall be submitted for all contracts awarded by military departments/agencies and/or subcontracts awarded by DoD prime contractors.

(D) The report shall be submitted annually by October 30, for the twelve month period ending September 30. When a Contracting Officer rejects an SSR, the Contractor is required to submit a revised SSR within 30 days of receiving the notice of report rejection.

(E) Subcontract awards that are related to work for more than one executive agency shall be appropriately allocated.

(F) The authority to acknowledge or reject SSRs in the eSRS, including SSRs submitted by subcontractors with subcontracting plans, resides with the Government agency awarding the prime contracts unless stated otherwise in the contract.

(ii) *Reports submitted under a commercial plan*.

(A) The report shall include all subcontract awards under the commercial plan in effect during the Government's fiscal year and all indirect costs.

(B) The report shall be submitted annually, within 30 days after the end of the Government's fiscal year.

(C) If a Contractor has a commercial plan and is performing work for more than one executive agency, the Contractor shall specify the percentage of dollars attributable to each agency.

(D) The authority to acknowledge or reject SSRs for commercial plans resides with the Contracting Officer who approved the commercial plan.

Alternate IV (AUG 2018). As prescribed in 19.708(b)(1)(iv), substitute the following paragraphs (c) and (d) for paragraphs (c) and (d) of the basic clause:

(c)(1) The Contractor, upon request by the Contracting Officer, shall submit and negotiate a subcontracting plan, where applicable, that separately addresses subcontracting with small business, veteran-owned small business, service-disabled veteran-owned small business, HUBZone small business, small disadvantaged business, and women-owned small business concerns. If the Contractor is submitting an individual subcontracting plan, the plan shall separately address subcontracting with small business, veteran-owned small business, service-disabled veteran-owned small business, HUBZone small business, small disadvantaged business, and women-owned small business concerns, with a separate part for the basic contract and separate parts for each option (if any). The subcontracting plan shall be incorporated into the contract. The subcontracting plan shall be negotiated within the time specified by the Contracting Officer. The subcontracting plan does not apply retroactively.

(2)(i) The prime Contractor may accept a subcontractor's written representations of its size and socioeconomic status as a small business, small disadvantaged business, veteran-owned small business, service-disabled veteran-owned small business, or a women-owned small business if the subcontractor represents that the size and socioeconomic status representations with its offer are current, accurate, and complete as of the date of the offer for the subcontract.

(ii) The Contractor may accept a subcontractor's representations of its size and socioeconomic status as a small business, small disadvantaged business, veteran-owned small business, service-disabled veteran-owned small business, or a women-owned small business in the System for Award Management (SAM) if—

(A) The subcontractor is registered in SAM; and

(B) The subcontractor represents that the size and socioeconomic status representations made in SAM are current, accurate and complete as of the date of the offer for the subcontract.

(iii) The Contractor may not require the use of SAM for the purposes of representing size or socioeconomic status in connection with a subcontract.

(iv) In accordance with 13 CFR 121.411, 124.1015, 125.29, 126.900, and 127.700, a contractor acting in good faith is not liable for misrepresentations made by its subcontractors regarding the subcontractor's size or socioeconomic status.

(d) The Contractor's subcontracting plan shall include the following:

(1) Separate goals, expressed in terms of total dollars subcontracted and as a percentage of total planned subcontracting dollars, for the use of small business, veteran-owned small business, service-disabled veteran-owned small business, HUBZone small business, small disadvantaged business, and women-owned small business concerns as subcontractors. For individual subcontracting plans, and if required by the Contracting Officer, goals shall also be expressed in terms of percentage of total contract dollars, in addition to the goals expressed as a percentage of total subcontract dollars. The Contractor shall include all subcontracts that contribute to contract performance, and may include a proportionate share of products and services that are normally allocated as indirect costs. In accordance with 43 U.S.C. 1626—

(i) Subcontracts awarded to an ANC or Indian tribe shall be counted towards the subcontracting goals for small business and small disadvantaged business concerns, regardless of the size or Small Business Administration certification status of the ANC or Indian tribe; and

(ii) Where one or more subcontractors are in the subcontract tier between the prime Contractor and the ANC or Indian tribe, the ANC or Indian tribe shall designate the appropriate Contractor(s) to count the subcontract towards its small business and small disadvantaged business subcontracting goals.

(A) In most cases, the appropriate Contractor is the Contractor that awarded the subcontract to the ANC or Indian tribe.

(B) If the ANC or Indian tribe designates more than one Contractor to count the subcontract toward its goals, the ANC or Indian tribe shall designate only a portion of the total subcontract award to each Contractor. The sum of the amounts designated to various Contractors cannot exceed the total value of the subcontract.

(C) The ANC or Indian tribe shall give a copy of the written designation to the Contracting Officer, the Contractor, and the subcontractors in between the prime Contractor and the ANC or Indian tribe within 30 days of the date of the subcontract award.

(D) If the Contracting Officer does not receive a copy of the ANC's or the Indian tribe's written designation within 30 days of the subcontract award, the Contractor that awarded the subcontract to the ANC or Indian tribe will be considered the designated Contractor.

(2) A statement of—

(i) Total dollars planned to be subcontracted for an individual subcontracting plan; or the Contractor's total projected sales, expressed in dollars, and the total value of projected subcontracts to support the sales for a commercial plan;

(ii) Total dollars planned to be subcontracted to small business concerns (including ANC and Indian tribes);

(iii) Total dollars planned to be subcontracted to veteran-owned small business concerns;

(iv) Total dollars planned to be subcontracted to service-disabled veteran-owned small business;

(v) Total dollars planned to be subcontracted to HUBZone small business concerns;

(vi) Total dollars planned to be subcontracted to small disadvantaged business concerns (including ANCs and Indian tribes); and

(vii) Total dollars planned to be subcontracted to women-owned small business concerns.

(3) A description of the principal types of supplies and services to be subcontracted, and an identification of the types planned for subcontracting to—

(i) Small business concerns;

(ii) Veteran-owned small business concerns;

(iii) Service-disabled veteran-owned small business concerns;

(iv) HUBZone small business concerns;

(v) Small disadvantaged business concerns; and

(vi) Women-owned small business concerns.

(4) A description of the method used to develop the subcontracting goals in paragraph (d)(1) of this clause.

(5) A description of the method used to identify potential sources for solicitation purposes (*e.g.*, existing company source lists, SAM, veterans service organizations, the National Minority Purchasing Council Vendor Information Service, the Research and Information Division of the Minority Business Development Agency in the Department of Commerce, or small, HUBZone, small disadvantaged, and women-owned small business trade associations). The Contractor may rely on the information contained in SAM as an accurate representation of a concern's size and ownership characteristics for the purposes of maintaining a small, veteran-owned small, service-disabled veteran-owned small, HUBZone small, small disadvantaged, and women-owned small business source list. Use of SAM as its source list does not relieve a firm of its responsibilities (*e.g.*, outreach, assistance, counseling, or publicizing subcontracting opportunities) in this clause.

(6) A statement as to whether or not the Contractor included indirect costs in establishing subcontracting goals, and a description of the method used to determine the proportionate share of indirect costs to be incurred with—

(i) Small business concerns (including ANC and Indian tribes);

(ii) Veteran-owned small business concerns;

(iii) Service-disabled veteran-owned small business concerns;

(iv) HUBZone small business concerns;

(v) Small disadvantaged business concerns (including ANC and Indian tribes); and

(vi) Women-owned small business concerns.

(7) The name of the individual employed by the Contractor who will administer the Contractor's subcontracting program, and a description of the duties of the individual.

(8) A description of the efforts the Contractor will make to assure that small business, veteran-owned small business, service-disabled veteran-owned small business, HUBZone small business, small disadvantaged business, and women-owned small business concerns have an equitable opportunity to compete for subcontracts.

(9) Assurances that the Contractor will include the clause of this contract entitled "Utilization of Small Business Concerns" in all subcontracts that offer further subcontracting opportunities, and that the Contractor will require all subcontractors (except small business concerns) that receive subcontracts in excess of $700,000 ($1.5 million for construction of any public facility) with further subcontracting possibilities to adopt a subcontracting plan that complies with the requirements of this clause.

(10) Assurances that the Contractor will—

(i) Cooperate in any studies or surveys as may be required;

(ii) Submit periodic reports so that the Government can determine the extent of compliance by the Contractor with the subcontracting plan;

(iii) After November 30, 2017, include subcontracting data for each order when reporting subcontracting achievements for an indefinite-delivery, indefinite-quantity contract with an individual subcontracting plan where the contract is intended for use by multiple agencies;

(iv) Submit the Individual Subcontract Report (ISR) and/or the Summary Subcontract Report (SSR), in accordance with paragraph (l) of this clause using the Electronic Subcontracting Reporting System (eSRS) at *http://www.esrs.gov*. The reports shall provide information on subcontract awards to small business concerns (including ANCs and Indian tribes that are not small businesses), veteran-owned small business concerns, service-disabled veteran-owned small business concerns, HUBZone small business concerns, small disadvantaged business concerns (including ANCs and Indian tribes that have not been certified by SBA as small disadvantaged businesses), women-owned small business concerns, and for NASA only, Historically Black Colleges and Universities and Minority Institutions. Reporting shall be in accordance with this clause, or as provided in agency regulations;

(v) Ensure that its subcontractors with subcontracting plans agree to submit the ISR and/or the SSR using eSRS;

(vi) Provide its prime contract number, its unique entity identifier, and the email address of the Contractor's official responsible for acknowledging receipt of or rejecting the ISRs, to all first-tier subcontractors with subcontracting plans so they can enter this information into the eSRS when submitting their ISRs; and

(vii) Require that each subcontractor with a subcontracting plan provide the prime contract number, its own unique entity identifier, and the email address of the subcontractor's official responsible for acknowledging receipt of or rejecting the ISRs, to its subcontractors with subcontracting plans.

(11) A description of the types of records that will be maintained concerning procedures that have been adopted to comply with the requirements and goals in the plan, including establishing source lists; and a description of the Contractor's efforts to locate small business, veteran-owned small business, service-disabled veteran-owned small business, HUBZone small business,

small disadvantaged business, and women-owned small business concerns and award subcontracts to them. The records shall include at least the following (on a plant-wide or company-wide basis, unless otherwise indicated):

(i) Source lists (*e.g.*, SAM), guides, and other data that identify small business, veteran-owned small business, service-disabled veteran-owned small business, HUBZone small business, small disadvantaged business, and women-owned small business concerns.

(ii) Organizations contacted in an attempt to locate sources that are small business, veteran-owned small business, service-disabled veteran-owned small business, HUBZone small business, small disadvantaged business, or women-owned small business concerns.

(iii) Records on each subcontract solicitation resulting in an award of more than $150,000, indicating—

(A) Whether small business concerns were solicited and, if not, why not;

(B) Whether veteran-owned small business concerns were solicited and, if not, why not;

(C) Whether service-disabled veteran-owned small business concerns were solicited and, if not, why not;

(D) Whether HUBZone small business concerns were solicited and, if not, why not;

(E) Whether small disadvantaged business concerns were solicited and, if not, why not;

(F) Whether women-owned small business concerns were solicited and, if not, why not; and

(G) If applicable, the reason award was not made to a small business concern.

(iv) Records of any outreach efforts to contact—

(A) Trade associations;

(B) Business development organizations;

(C) Conferences and trade fairs to locate small, HUBZone small, small disadvantaged, service-disabled veteran-owned, and women-owned small business sources; and

(D) Veterans service organizations.

(v) Records of internal guidance and encouragement provided to buyers through—

(A) Workshops, seminars, training, *etc.;* and

(B) Monitoring performance to evaluate compliance with the program's requirements.

(vi) On a contract-by-contract basis, records to support award data submitted by the Contractor to the Government, including the name, address, and business size of each subcontractor. Contractors having commercial plans need not comply with this requirement.

(12) Assurances that the Contractor will make a good faith effort to acquire articles, equipment, supplies, services, or materials, or obtain the performance of construction work from the small business concerns that it used in preparing the proposal for the modification, in the same or greater scope, amount, and quality used in preparing and submitting the modification proposal. Responding to a request for a quote does not constitute use in preparing a proposal. The Contractor used a small business concern in preparing the proposal for a modification if—

(i) The Contractor identifies the small business concern as a subcontractor in the proposal or associated small business subcontracting plan, to furnish certain supplies or perform a portion of the subcontract; or

(ii) The Contractor used the small business concern's pricing or cost information or technical expertise in preparing the proposal, where there is written evidence of an intent or understanding that the small business concern will be awarded a subcontract for the related work when the modification is executed.

(13) Assurances that the Contractor will provide the Contracting Officer with a written explanation if the Contractor fails to acquire articles, equipment, supplies, services or materials or obtain the performance of

construction work as described in (d)(12) of this clause. This written explanation must be submitted to the Contracting Officer within 30 days of contract completion.

(14) Assurances that the Contractor will not prohibit a subcontractor from discussing with the contracting officer any material matter pertaining to the payment to or utilization of a subcontractor.

(15) Assurances that the offeror will pay its small business subcontractors on time and in accordance with the terms and conditions of the underlying subcontract, and notify the contracting officer when the prime contractor makes either a reduced or an untimely payment to a small business subcontractor (see 52.242-5).

[FAC 84-26, 52 FR 19805, 5/27/87, effective 7/30/87; FAC 84-49, 54 FR 29283, 7/11/89, effective 8/10/89; FAC 84-56, 55 FR 3888, 2/5/90, effective 2/5/90; FAC 90-3, 55 FR 52798, 12/21/90, effective 1/22/91; FAC 90-23, 59 FR 67010, 12/28/94, effective 2/27/95; FAC 90-32, 60 FR 48206, 9/18/95, effective 10/1/95; FAC 90-37, 61 FR 2626, 1/26/96, effective 3/26/96; FAC 90-39, 61 FR 31612, 6/20/96, effective 8/19/96; FAC 97-5, 63 FR 34058, 6/22/98, effective 8/21/98; FAC 97-7, 63 FR 36120, 7/1/98, effective 1/1/99; FAC 97-10, 63 FR 70264, 12/18/98, effective 1/4/99; FAC 97-13, 64 FR 36222, 7/2/99, effective 10/1/99; FAC 97-19, 65 FR 46052, 7/26/2000, effective 10/1/2000; FAC 97-20, 65 FR 60542, 7/26/2000, effective 10/11/2000, finalized without change by FAC 2001-02, 66 FR 65347, 12/18/2001, effective 12/18/2001; FAC 2001-01, 66 FR 53478, 10/22/2001, effective 10/22/2001, corrected 67 FR 1858, 1/14/2002, effective 1/14/2002; FAC 2001-09, 67 FR 56115, 8/30/2002, effective 8/30/2002; FAC 2005-05, 70 FR 43581, 7/27/2005, effective 7/27/2005; FAC 2005-09, Final rule, 71 FR 20303, 4/19/2006, effective 4/19/2006; FAC 2005-13, 71 FR 57363, 9/28/2006, effective 9/28/2006; FAC 2005-19, 72 FR 46345, 8/17/2007, effective 9/17/2007; FAC 2005-21, 72 FR 63089, 11/7/2007, effective 11/7/2007; FAC 2005-25, 73 FR 21779, 4/22/2008, effective 4/22/2008; CFR Correction, 74 FR 48421, 9/23/2009; FAC 2005-42, 75 FR 34260, 6/16/2010, effective 7/16/2010; FAC 2005-45, 75 FR 53129, 8/30/2010, effective 10/1/2010; FAC 2005-47, 75 FR 77727, 12/13/2010, effective 1/12/2011; FAC 2005-67, 78 FR 37676, 6/21/2013, effective 7/22/2013; FAC 2005-77, 79 FR 61746, 10/14/2014, effective 10/14/2014; FAC 2005-83, 80 FR 38293, 7/2/2015, effective 10/1/2015; FAC 2005-89, 81 FR 45833, 7/14/2016, effective 11/1/2016; FAC 2005-91, 81 FR 67736, 9/30/2016, effective 10/31/2016; FAC 2005-94, 81 FR 93481, 12/20/2016, effective 1/19/2017; FAC 2005-100, 83 FR 42571, 8/22/2018, effective 8/22/2018]

52.219-10 Incentive Subcontracting Program.

As prescribed in 19.708(c)(1), insert the following clause:

INCENTIVE SUBCONTRACTING PROGRAM (OCT 2014)

(a) Of the total dollars it plans to spend under subcontracts, the Contractor has committed itself in its subcontracting plan to try to award certain percentages to small business, veteran-owned small business, service-disabled veteran-owned small business, HUBZone small business, small disadvantaged business, and women-owned small business concerns, respectively.

(b) If the Contractor exceeds its subcontracting goals for small business, veteran-owned small business, service-disabled veteran-owned small business, HUBZone small business, small disadvantaged business, and women-owned small business concerns in performing this contract, it will receive ___ [*Contracting Officer to insert the appropriate number between 0 and 10*] percent of the dollars in excess of each goal in the plan, unless the Contracting Officer determines that the excess was not due to the Contractor's efforts (*e.g.*, a subcontractor cost overrun caused the actual subcontract amount to exceed that estimated in the subcontracting plan, or the award of subcontracts that had been planned but had not been disclosed in the subcontracting plan during contract negotiations). Determinations under this paragraph are unilateral decisions made solely at the discretion of the Government.

(c) If this is a cost-plus-fixed-fee contract, the sum of the fixed fee and the incentive fee earned under this contract may not exceed the limitations in 15.404-4 of the Federal Acquisition Regulation.

(End of clause)

[FAC 90-32, 60 FR 48206, 9/18/95, effective 10/1/95; FAC 97-2, 62 FR 51224, 9/30/97, effective 10/10/97; FAC 97-7, 63 FR 36120, 7/1/98, effective 1/1/99, finalized without change, FAC 97-13, 7/2/99; FAC 97-10, 63 FR 70264, 12/18/98, effective 1/4/99; FAC 97-15, 64 FR 72414, 12/27/99, effective 2/25/2000; FAC 97-20, 65 FR 60542, 10/11/2000, effective 10/11/2000; FAC 2001-01, 66 FR 53478, 10/22/2001, effective 10/22/2001; FAC 2005-77, 79 FR 61746, 10/14/2014, effective 10/14/2014]

52.219-11 Special 8(a) Contract Conditions.

As prescribed in 19.811-3(a), insert the following clause:

SPECIAL 8(A) CONTRACT CONDITIONS (JAN 2017)

The Small Business Administration (SBA) agrees to the following:

(a) To furnish the supplies or services set forth in this contract according to the specifications and the terms and conditions hereof by subcontracting with an eligible concern pursuant to the provisions of section 8(a) of the Small Business Act, as amended (15 U.S.C. 637(a)).

(b) That in the event SBA does not award a subcontract for all or a part of the work hereunder, this contract may be terminated either in whole or in part without cost to either party.

(c) Except for novation agreements, delegate to the ____ [*insert name of contracting agency*] the responsibility for administering the subcontract to be awarded hereunder with complete authority to take any action on behalf of the Government under the terms and conditions of the subcontract; provided, however, that the ____ [*insert name of contracting agency*] shall give advance notice to the SBA before it issues a final notice terminating the right of a subcontractor to proceed with further performance, either in whole or in part, under the subcontract for default or for the convenience of the Government.

(d) That payments to be made under any subcontract awarded under this contract will be made directly to the subcontractor by the ____ [*insert name of contracting agency*].

(e) That the subcontractor awarded a subcontract hereunder shall have the right of appeal from decisions of the Contracting Officer cognizable under the "Disputes" clause of said subcontract.

(f) To notify the ____ [*insert name of contracting agency*] Contracting Officer immediately upon notification by the subcontractor that the owner or owners upon whom 8(a) eligibility was based plan to relinquish ownership or control of the concern.

(End of clause)

[FAC 84-52, 54 FR 46009, 10/31/89, effective 11/30/89; corrected, 54 FR 48105, 11/21/89; FAC 84-56, 55 FR 3888, 2/5/90, effective 2/5/90; FAC 90-43, Interim rule, 61 FR 67408, 12/20/96, effective 12/20/96; FAC 2005-95, 82 FR 4724, 1/13/2017, effective 1/13/2017]

52.219-12 Special 8(a) Subcontract Conditions.

As prescribed in 19.811-3(b), insert the following clause:

SPECIAL 8(A) SUBCONTRACT CONDITIONS (OCT 2019)

(a) The Small Business Administration (SBA) has entered into Contract No. ____ [*insert number of contract*] with the ____ [*insert name of contracting agency*] to furnish the supplies or services as described therein. A copy of the contract is attached hereto and made a part hereof.

(b) The ____ [*insert name of subcontractor*], hereafter referred to as the subcontractor, agrees and acknowledges as follows:

(1) That it will, for and on behalf of the SBA, fulfill and perform all of the requirements of Contract No. ____ [*insert number of contract*] for the consideration stated therein

and that it has read and is familiar with each and every part of the contract.

(2) That the SBA has delegated responsibility, except for novation agreements, for the administration of this subcontract to the ___ [*insert name of contracting agency*] with complete authority to take any action on behalf of the Government under the terms and conditions of this subcontract.

(3) That it will notify the ___ [*insert name of contracting agency*] Contracting Officer in writing immediately upon entering an agreement (either oral or written) to transfer all or part of its stock or other ownership interest to any other party.

(c) Payments, including any progress payments under this subcontract, will be made directly to the subcontractor by the ___ [*insert name of contracting agency*].

(End of clause)

[FAC 84-51, 54 FR 34757, 8/21/89, effective 9/20/89; FAC 84-52, 54 FR 46009, 10/31/89, effective 11/30/89; corrected, 54 FR 48105, 11/21/89; FAC 84-56, 55 FR 3889, 2/5/90, effective 2/5/90; Final rule, 55 FR 38518, 9/18/90; FAC 90-43, Interim rule, 61 FR 67408, 12/20/96, effective 12/20/96; FAC 2005-95, 82 FR 4724, 1/13/2017, effective 1/13/2017; FAC 2019-06, 84 FR 47862, 9/10/2019, effective 10/10/2019]

52.219-13 Notice of Set-Aside of Orders.

As prescribed in 19.508(f), insert the following clause:

NOTICE OF SET-ASIDE OF ORDERS (NOV 2011)

The Contracting Officer will give notice of the order or orders, if any, to be set aside for small business concerns identified in 19.000(a)(3) and the applicable small business program. This notice, and its restrictions, will apply only to the specific orders that have been set aside for any of the small business concerns identified in 19.000(a)(3).

(End of clause)

[Reserved, FAC 90-32, 60 FR 48206, 9/18/95, effective 10/1/95; FAC 2005-54, 76 FR 68032, 11/2/2011, effective 11/2/2011; Interim rule, 77 FR 1889, 1/12/2012, effective 2/13/2012]

52.219-14 Limitations on Subcontracting.

As prescribed in 19.508(e) or 19.811-3(e), insert the following clause:

LIMITATIONS ON SUBCONTRACTING (JAN 2017)

(a) This clause does not apply to the unrestricted portion of a partial set-aside.

(b) *Applicability.* This clause applies only to—

(1) Contracts that have been set aside or reserved for small business concerns or 8(a) participants;

(2) Part or parts of a multiple-award contract that have been set aside for small business concerns or 8(a) participants; and

(3) Orders set aside for small business or 8(a) participants under multiple-award contracts as described in FAR 8.405–5 and 16.505(b)(2)(i)(F).

(c) By submission of an offer and execution of a contract, the Offeror/Contractor agrees that in performance of the contract in the case of a contract for—

(1) *Services (except construction).* At least 50 percent of the cost of contract performance incurred for personnel shall be expended for employees of the concern.

(2) *Supplies (other than procurement from a nonmanufacturer of such supplies).* The concern shall perform work for at least 50 percent of the cost of manufacturing the supplies, not including the cost of materials.

(3) *General construction.* The concern will perform at least 15 percent of the cost of the contract, not including the cost of materials, with its own employees.

(4) *Construction by special trade contractors.* The concern will perform at least 25 percent of the cost of the contract, not including the cost of materials, with its own employees.

(End of clause)

[FAC 84-31, 52 FR 38190, 10/14/87, effective 10/1/87; FAC 90-3, 55 FR 52798,

12/21/90, effective 1/22/91; FAC 90-43, Interim rule, 61 FR 67408, 12/20/96, effective 12/20/96, finalized without change, FAC 97-1, 62 FR 44802, 8/22/97, effective 10/21/97; FAC 97-12, 64 FR 32740, 6/17/99, effective 6/17/99; FAC 2005-54, 76 FR 68032, 11/2/2011, effective 11/2/2011; Interim rule, 77 FR 1889, 1/12/2012, effective 2/13/2012; FAC 2005-95, 82 FR 4724, 1/13/2017, effective 1/13/2017]

52.219-15 [Reserved]

[Removed and reserved, FAC 90-45, Final rule, 62 FR 224, 1/2/97, effective 1/1/97]

52.219-16 Liquidated Damages—Subcontracting Plan.

As prescribed in 19.708(b)(2), insert the following clause:

LIQUIDATED DAMAGES—SUBCONTRACTING PLAN (JAN 1999)

(a) *Failure to make a good faith effort to comply with the subcontracting plan,* as used in this clause, means a willful or intentional failure to perform in accordance with the requirements of the subcontracting plan approved under the clause in this contract entitled "Small Business Subcontracting Plan," or willful or intentional action to frustrate the plan.

(b) Performance shall be measured by applying the percentage goals to the total actual subcontracting dollars or, if a commercial plan is involved, to the pro rata share of actual subcontracting dollars attributable to Government contracts covered by the commercial plan. If, at contract completion or, in the case of a commercial plan, at the close of the fiscal year for which the plan is applicable, the Contractor has failed to meet its subcontracting goals and the Contracting Officer decides in accordance with paragraph (c) of this clause that the Contractor failed to make a good faith effort to comply with its subcontracting plan, established in accordance with the clause in this contract entitled "Small Business Subcontracting Plan," the Contractor shall pay the Government liquidated damages in an amount stated. The amount of probable damages attributable to the Contractor's failure to comply shall be an amount equal to the actual dollar amount by which the Contractor failed to achieve each subcontract goal.

(c) Before the Contracting Officer makes a final decision that the Contractor has failed to make such good faith effort, the Contracting Officer shall give the Contractor written notice specifying the failure and permitting the Contractor to demonstrate what good faith efforts have been made and to discuss the matter. Failure to respond to the notice may be taken as an admission that no valid explanation exists. If, after consideration of all the pertinent data, the Contracting Officer finds that the Contractor failed to make a good faith effort to comply with the subcontracting plan, the Contracting Officer shall issue a final decision to that effect and require that the Contractor pay the Government liquidated damages as provided in paragraph (b) of this clause.

(d) With respect to commercial plans, the Contracting Officer who approved the plan will perform the functions of the Contracting Officer under this clause on behalf of all agencies with contracts covered by the commercial plan.

(e) The contractor shall have the right of appeal, under the clause in this contract entitled Disputes, from any final decision of the Contracting Officer.

(f) Liquidated damages shall be in addition to any other remedies that the Government may have.

(End of clause)

[Interim rule, FAC 84-50, 54 FR 30710, 7/21/89, effective 8/15/89; FAC 90-32, 60 FR 48206, 9/18/95, effective 10/1/95; FAC 97-5, 63 FR 34058, 6/22/98, effective 8/21/98; FAC 97-10, 63 FR 70264, 12/18/98, effective 1/4/99]

52.219-17 Section 8(a) Award.

As prescribed in 19.811-3(c), insert the following clause:

SECTION 8(A) AWARD (OCT 2019)

(a) By execution of a contract, the Small Business Administration (SBA) agrees to the following:

(1) To furnish the supplies or services set forth in the contract according to the specifi-

cations and the terms and conditions by subcontracting with the Offeror who has been determined an eligible concern pursuant to the provisions of section 8(a) of the Small Business Act, as amended (15 U.S.C. 637(a)).

(2) Except for novation agreements, delegates to the __________ [*insert name of contracting activity*] the responsibility for administering the contract with complete authority to take any action on behalf of the Government under the terms and conditions of the contract; provided, however that the contracting agency shall give advance notice to the SBA before it issues a final notice terminating the right of the subcontractor to proceed with further performance, either in whole or in part, under the contract.

(3) That payments to be made under the contract will be made directly to the subcontractor by the contracting activity.

(4) To notify the ____ [*insert name of contracting agency*] Contracting Officer immediately upon notification by the subcontractor that the owner or owners upon whom 8(a) eligibility was based plan to relinquish ownership or control of the concern.

(5) That the subcontractor awarded a subcontract hereunder shall have the right of appeal from decisions of the cognizant Contracting Officer under the "Disputes" clause of the subcontract.

(b) The offeror/subcontractor agrees and acknowledges that it will, for and on behalf of the SBA, fulfill and perform all of the requirements of the contract.

(End of clause)

[FAC 84-52, 54 FR 46009, 10/31/89, effective 11/30/89; corrected, 54 FR 48105, 11/21/89; FAC 84-56, 55 FR 3889, 2/5/90, effective 2/5/90; FAC 90-43, Interim rule, 61 FR 67408, 12/20/96, effective 12/20/96; FAC 2005-95, 82 FR 4724, 1/13/2017, effective 1/13/2017; FAC 2019-06, 84 FR 47862, 9/10/2019, effective 10/10/2019]

52.219-18 Notification of Competition Limited to Eligible 8(a) Participants.

As prescribed in 19.811-3(d), insert the following clause:

NOTIFICATION OF COMPETITION LIMITED TO ELIGIBLE 8(A) PARTICIPANTS (JAN 2017)

(a) Offers are solicited only from small business concerns expressly certified by the Small Business Administration (SBA) for participation in the SBA's 8(a) Program and which meet the following criteria at the time of submission of offer—

(1) The Offeror is in conformance with the 8(a) support limitation set forth in its approved business plan; and

(2) The Offeror is in conformance with the Business Activity Targets set forth in its approved business plan or any remedial action directed by the SBA.

(b) By submission of its offer, the Offeror represents that it meets all of the criteria set forth in paragraph (a) of this clause.

(c) Any award resulting from this solicitation will be made to the Small Business Administration, which will subcontract performance to the successful 8(a) offeror selected through the evaluation criteria set forth in this solicitation.

(d) (1) *Agreement.* A small business concern submitting an offer in its own name shall furnish, in performing the contract, only end items manufactured or produced by small business concerns in the United States or its outlying areas. If this procurement is processed under simplified acquisition procedures and the total amount of this contract does not exceed $25,000, a small business concern may furnish the product of any domestic firm. This paragraph does not apply to construction or service contracts.

(2) The ____ [*insert name of SBA's contractor*] will notify the ____ [*insert name of contracting agency*] Contracting Officer in writing immediately upon entering an agreement to transfer all or part of its stock or other ownership interest to any other party.

(End of clause)

[* *Insert SIC code assigned to the acquisition by the contracting activity.*]

Alternate I (JAN 2017). If the competition is to be limited to 8(a) participants within one or more specific SBA regions or districts, add the following subparagraph (a)(3) to paragraph (a) of the clause:

(3) The offeror's approved business plan is on the file and serviced by __, * __, [* *Contracting Officer completes by inserting the appropriate SBA District and/or Regional Office(s) as identified by the SBA*].

Alternate II (DEC 1996). When the acquisition is for a product in a class for which the Small Business Administration has determined that there are no small business manufacturers or processors in the Federal market in accordance with 19.502-2(c), delete subparagraph (d)(1).

[FAC 84-52, 54 FR 46009, 10/31/89, effective 11/30/89; corrected 54 FR 48105, 11/21/89; FAC 84-56, 55 FR 3889, 2/5/90, effective 2/5/90; FAC 84-58, 55 FR 25532, 6/21/90, effective 7/23/90; Final rule, 55 FR 38518, 9/18/90; FAC 90-32, 60 FR 48206, 9/18/95, effective 10/1/95; FAC 90-40, 61 FR 39186, 7/26/96, effective 7/26/96; FAC 90-43, Interim rule, 61 FR 67408, 12/20/96, effective 12/20/96; FAC 90-45, Final rule, 62 FR 224, 1/2/97, effective 1/1/97; FAC 90-46, 62 FR 12690, 3/17/97, effective 5/16/97; FAC 97-12, 64 FR 32740, 6/17/99, effective 6/17/99, finalized without change, FAC 97-15, 64 FR 72414, 12/27/99; FAC 97-14, 64 FR 51828, 9/24/99, effective 11/23/99, corrected, 64 FR 53264, 10/7/99; FAC 2001-14, 68 FR 28079, 5/22/2003, effective 6/23/2003; FAC 2005-03, 70 FR 18959, 4/11/2005, effective 4/11/2005; FAC 2005-07, 71 FR 221, 1/3/2006, effective 1/3/2006; FAC 2005-95, 82 FR 4724, 1/13/2017, effective 1/13/2017]

52.219-19 [Removed and Reserved]

[FAC 90-3, 55 FR 52798, 12/21/90, effective 1/22/91; FAC 90-5, 56 FR 29138, 6/25/91, effective 7/25/91; FAC 90-45, Final rule, 62 FR 224, 1/2/97, effective 1/1/97; FAC 97-19, 65 FR 46052, 7/26/2000, effective 10/1/2000, finalized without change by FAC 2001-02, 66 FR 65347, 12/18/2001, effective 12/18/2001; FAC 2001-06, 67 FR 13048, 3/20/2002, effective 4/4/2002; FAC 2005-48, 75 FR 82567, 12/30/2010, effective 1/31/2011]

52.219-20 [Removed and Reserved]

[FAC 90-3, 55 FR 52799, 12/21/90, effective 1/22/91; FAC 2001-06, 67 FR 13048, 3/20/2002, effective 4/4/2002; FAC 2005-48, 75 FR 82567, 12/30/2010, effective 1/31/2011]

52.219-21 [Removed and Reserved]

[FAC 90-3, 55 FR 52799, 12/21/90, effective 1/22/91; FAC 90-5, 56 FR 29138, 6/25/91, effective 7/25/91; FAC 90-45, Final rule, 62 FR 224, 1/2/97, effective 1/1/97; FAC 97-11, 64 FR 10530, 3/4/99, effective 5/3/99; FAC 2001-04, 67 FR 6112, 2/8/2002, effective 2/8/2002; FAC 2005-48, 75 FR 82567, 12/30/2010, effective 1/31/2011]

52.219-22 [Removed and Reserved]

[FAC 97-6, 63 FR 35719, 6/30/98, effective 10/1/98; FAC 97-8, 63 FR 52425, 9/30/98, effective 10/1/98; FAC 97-10, 63 FR 70264, 12/18/98, effective 1/4/99; FAC 97-12, 64 FR 32740, 6/17/99, effective 6/17/99; FAC 97-13, 64 FR 36222, 7/2/99, effective 10/1/99; FAC 2001-23, 69 FR 25273, 5/5/2004, effective 5/5/2004; FAC 2005-02, 70 FR 14950, 3/23/2005, effective 3/23/2005; FAC 2005-51, 76 FR 18304, 4/1/2011, effective 4/1/2011; FAC 2005-55, 77 FR 204, 1/3/2012, effective 1/3/2012; FAC 2005-56, 77 FR 12913, 3/2/2012, effective 4/2/2012; FAC 2005-77, 79 FR 61746, 10/14/2014, effective 10/14/2014]

52.219-23 [Removed and Reserved]

[FAC 97-6, 63 FR 35719, 6/30/98, effective 10/1/98; FAC 97-8, 63 FR 52425, 9/30/98, effective 10/1/98; FAC 97-13, 64 FR 36222, 7/2/99, effective 10/1/99; FAC 97-16, 65 FR 16274, 3/27/2000, effective 3/27/2000; FAC 97-22, 66 FR 2116, 1/10/2001, effective 3/12/2001; Delay of effective date, 66 FR 14259, 3/9/2001, effective 5/11/2001; FAC 2001-14, 68 FR 28079, 5/22/2003, effective 6/23/2003; FAC 2005-04, 70 FR 33661, 6/8/2005, effective 7/8/2005; FAC 2005-06, 70 FR 57462, 9/30/2005, effective

9/30/2005; FAC 2005-09, Final rule, 71 FR 20304, 4/19/2006, effective 4/19/2006; FAC 2005-27, 73 FR 53992, 9/17/2008, effective 10/17/2008; FAC 2005-77, 79 FR 61746, 10/14/2014, effective 10/14/2014]

52.219-24 [Removed and Reserved]

[FAC 97-7, 63 FR 36120, 7/1/98, effective 1/1/99, finalized without change, FAC 97-13, 7/2/99; FAC 97-19, 65 FR 46052, 7/26/2000, effective 10/1/2000, finalized without change by FAC 2001-02, 66 FR 65347, 12/18/2001, effective 12/18/2001; FAC 2005-77, 79 FR 61746, 10/14/2014, effective 10/14/2014]

52.219-25 [Removed and Reserved]

[FAC 97-7, 63 FR 36120, 7/1/98, corrected, Interim Final Rule, 63 FR 71721, 12/29/98, effective 1/1/99; FAC 97-13, 64 FR 36222, 7/2/99, effective 10/1/99; FAC 2005-25, 73 FR 21779, 4/22/2008, effective 4/22/2008; FAC 2005-42, 75 FR 34260, 6/16/2010, effective 7/16/2010; FAC 2005-47, 75 FR 77737, 12/13/2010, effective 12/13/2010; FAC 2005-54, 76 FR 68026, 11/2/2011, effective 11/2/2011; FAC 2005-67, 78 FR 37676, 6/21/2013, effective 7/22/2013; FAC 2005-77, 79 FR 61746, 10/14/2014, effective 10/14/2014]

52.219-26 [Removed and Reserved]

[FAC 97-7, 63 FR 36120, 7/1/98, effective 1/1/99, finalized without change, FAC 97-13, 7/2/99; FAC 97-15, 64 FR 72414, 12/27/99, effective 2/25/2000; FAC 97-19, 65 FR 46052, 7/26/2000, effective 10/1/2000, finalized without change by FAC 2001-02, 66 FR 65347, 12/18/2001, effective 12/18/2001; FAC 2005-77, 79 FR 61746, 10/14/2014, effective 10/14/2014]

52.219-27 Notice of Service-Disabled Veteran-Owned Small Business Set-Aside.

As prescribed in 19.1407, insert the following clause:

NOTICE OF SERVICE-DISABLED VETERAN-OWNED SMALL BUSINESS SET-ASIDE (OCT 2019)

(a) *Definition. Service-disabled veteran-owned small business concern*—

(1) Means a small business concern—

(i) Not less than 51 percent of which is owned by one or more service-disabled veterans or, in the case of any publicly owned business, not less than 51 percent of the stock of which is owned by one or more service-disabled veterans; and

(ii) The management and daily business operations of which are controlled by one or more service-disabled veterans or, in the case of a service-disabled veteran with permanent and severe disability, the spouse or permanent caregiver of such veteran.

(2) *Service-disabled veteran* means a veteran, as defined in 38 U.S.C. 101(2), with a disability that is service-connected, as defined in 38 U.S.C. 101(16).

(b) *Applicability.* This clause applies only to—

(1) Contracts that have been set aside or reserved for service-disabled veteran-owned small business concerns;

(2) Part or parts of a multiple-award contract that have been set aside for service-disabled veteran-owned small business concerns; and

(3) Orders set aside for service-disabled veteran-owned small business concerns under multiple-award contracts as described in 8.405-5 and 16.505(b)(2)(i)(F).

(c) *General.* (1) Offers are solicited only from service-disabled veteran-owned small business concerns. Offers received from concerns that are not service-disabled veteran-owned small business concerns shall not be considered.

(2) Any award resulting from this solicitation will be made to a service-disabled veteran-owned small business concern.

(d) *Agreement.* A service-disabled veteran-owned small business concern agrees that in the performance of the contract, in the case of a contract for—

(1) Services (except construction), at least 50 percent of the cost of personnel for contract performance will be spent for employees of the concern or employees of other service-disabled veteran-owned small business concerns;

(2) Supplies (other than acquisition from a nonmanufacturer of the supplies), at least 50 percent of the cost of manufacturing, excluding the cost of materials, will be performed by the concern or other service-disabled veteran-owned small business concerns;

(3) General construction, at least 15 percent of the cost of the contract performance incurred for personnel will be spent on the concern's employees or the employees of other service-disabled veteran-owned small business concerns; or

(4) Construction by special trade contractors, at least 25 percent of the cost of the contract performance incurred for personnel will be spent on the concern's employees or the employees of other service-disabled veteran-owned small business concerns.

(e) A joint venture may be considered a service-disabled veteran owned small business concern if—

(1) At least one member of the joint venture is a service-disabled veteran-owned small business concern, and makes the following representations: That it is a service-disabled veteran-owned small business concern, and that it is a small business concern under the North American Industry Classification Systems (NAICS) code assigned to the procurement;

(2) Each other concern is small under the size standard corresponding to the NAICS code assigned to the procurement; and

(3) The joint venture meets the requirements of 13 CFR 121.103(h).

(4) The joint venture meets the requirements of 13 CFR 125.15(b)

(f) Any service-disabled veteran-owned small business concern (nonmanufacturer) must meet the requirements in 19.102(f) of the Federal Acquisition Regulation to receive a benefit under this program.

(End of clause)

[FAC 2001-23, 69 FR 25273, 5/5/2004, effective 5/5/2004; FAC 2005-54, 76 FR 68032, 11/2/2011, effective 11/2/2011; Interim rule, 77 FR 1889, 1/12/2012, effective 2/13/2012; FAC 2019-06, 84 FR 47862, 9/10/2019, effective 10/10/2019]

52.219-28 Post-Award Small Business Program Rerepresentation.

As prescribed in 19.309(c), insert the following clause:

POST-AWARD SMALL BUSINESS PROGRAM REREPRESENTATION (JUL 2013)

(a) *Definitions.* As used in this clause—

Long-term contract means a contract of more than five years in duration, including options. However, the term does not include contracts that exceed five years in duration because the period of performance has been extended for a cumulative period not to exceed six months under the clause at 52.217-8, Option to Extend Services, or other appropriate authority.

Small business concern means a concern, including its affiliates, that is independently owned and operated, not dominant in the field of operation in which it is bidding on Government contracts, and qualified as a small business under the criteria in 13 CFR part 121 and the size standard in paragraph (c) of this clause. Such a concern is "not dominant in its field of operation" when it does not exercise a controlling or major influence on a national basis in a kind of business activity in which a number of business concerns are primarily engaged. In determining whether dominance exists, consideration shall be given to all appropriate factors, including volume of business, number of employees, financial resources, competitive status or position, ownership or control of materials, processes, patents, license agreements, facilities, sales territory, and nature of business activity.

(b) If the Contractor represented that it was a small business concern prior to award of this contract, the Contractor shall rerepresent its size status according to paragraph (e) of this clause or, if applicable, paragraph (g) of this clause, upon the occurrence of any of the following:

(1) Within 30 days after execution of a novation agreement or within 30 days after modification of the contract to include this clause, if the novation agreement was executed prior to inclusion of this clause in the contract.

(2) Within 30 days after a merger or acquisition that does not require a novation or within 30 days after modification of the contract to include this clause, if the merger or acquisition occurred prior to inclusion of this clause in the contract.

(3) For long-term contracts—

(i) Within 60 to 120 days prior to the end of the fifth year of the contract; and

(ii) Within 60 to 120 days prior to the date specified in the contract for exercising any option thereafter.

(c) The Contractor shall rerepresent its size status in accordance with the size standard in effect at the time of this rerepresentation that corresponds to the North American Industry Classification System (NAICS) code assigned to this contract. The small business size standard corresponding to this NAICS code can be found at *http://www.sba.gov/content/table-small-business-size-standards.*

(d) The small business size standard for a Contractor providing a product which it does not manufacture itself, for a contract other than a construction or service contract, is 500 employees.

(e) Except as provided in paragraph (g) of this clause, the Contractor shall make the representation required by paragraph (b) of this clause by validating or updating all its representations in the Representations and Certifications section of the System for Award Management (SAM) and its other data in SAM, as necessary, to ensure that they reflect the Contractor's current status. The Contractor shall notify the contracting office in writing within the timeframes specified in paragraph (b) of this clause that the data have been validated or updated, and provide the date of the validation or update.

(f) If the Contractor represented that it was other than a small business concern prior to award of this contract, the Contractor may, but is not required to, take the actions required by paragraphs (e) or (g) of this clause.

(g) If the Contractor does not have representations and certifications in SAM, or does not have a representation in SAM for the NAICS code applicable to this contract, the Contractor is required to complete the following rerepresentation and submit it to the contracting office, along with the contract number and the date on which the rerepresentation was completed:

The Contractor represents that it ☐ is, ☐ is not a small business concern under NAICS Code ____ assigned to contract number ____.

[*Contractor to sign and date and insert authorized signer's name and title*].

(End of clause)

[FAC 2005-18, Interim rule, 72 FR 36852, 7/5/2007, effective 6/30/2007; FAC 2005-31, 74 FR 11821, 3/19/2009, effective 4/20/2009; Correction, 74 FR 14492, 3/31/2009, effective 3/31/2009; FAC 2005-51, 76 FR 18304, 4/1/2011, effective 4/1/2011; FAC 2005-56, 77 FR 12913, 3/2/2012, effective 4/2/2012; FAC 2005-58, 77 FR 23370, 4/18/2012, effective 4/18/2012; FAC 2005-67, 78 FR 37676, 6/21/2013, effective 7/22/2013; FAC 2005-77, 79 FR 61746, 10/14/2014, effective 10/14/2014]

52.219-29 Notice of Set-Aside for, or Sole Source Award to, Economically Disadvantaged Women-Owned Small Business Concerns.

As prescribed in 19.1507, insert the following clause:

NOTICE OF SET-ASIDE FOR, OR SOLE SOURCE AWARD TO, ECONOMICALLY DISADVANTAGED WOMEN-OWNED SMALL BUSINESS CONCERNS (DEC 2015)

(a) *Definitions. Economically disadvantaged women-owned small business (EDWOSB) concern* means—

A small business concern that is at least 51 percent directly and unconditionally owned by, and the management and daily business operations of which are controlled by, one or more women who are citizens of the United States and who are economically disadvantaged in accordance with 13 CFR part 127. It automatically qualifies as a women-owned small business (WOSB) concern eligible under the WOSB Program.

WOSB Program Repository means a secure, Web-based application that collects, stores, and disseminates documents to the contracting community and SBA, which verify the eligibility of a business concern for a contract to be awarded under the WOSB Program.

(b) *Applicability.* This clause applies only to—

(1) Contracts that have been set aside or reserved for, or awarded on a sole source basis to, EDWOSB concerns;

(2) Part or parts or a multiple-award contract that have been set aside for EDWOSB concerns; and

(3) Orders set aside for apparent successful offeror under multiple-award contracts as described in 8.405–5 and 16.505(b)(2)(i)(F).

(c) *General.* (1) Offers are solicited only from EDWOSB concerns. Offers received from concerns that are not EDWOSB concerns will not be considered.

(2) Any award resulting from this solicitation will be made to an EDWOSB concern.

(3) The contracting officer will ensure that the apparent successful offeror has provided all required documents to the WOSB Program Repository. The contract will not be awarded until all required documents are received.

(d) *Agreement.* An EDWOSB concern agrees that in the performance of the contract for—

(1) Services (except construction), the concern will perform at least 50 percent of the cost of the contract incurred for personnel with its own employees;

(2) Supplies or products (other than procurement from a non-manufacturer in such supplies or products), the concern will perform at least 50 percent of the cost of manufacturing the supplies or products (not including the costs of materials);

(3) General construction, the concern will perform at least 15 percent of the cost of the contract with its own employees (not including the costs of materials); and

(4) Construction by special trade contractors, the concern will perform at least 25 percent of the cost of the contract with its own employees (not including the cost of materials).

(e) *Joint Venture.* A joint venture may be considered an EDWOSB concern if—

(1) It meets the applicable size standard corresponding to the NAICS code assigned to the contract, unless an exception to affiliation applies pursuant to 13 CFR 121.103(h)(3);

(2) The EDWOSB participant of the joint venture is designated in the System for Award Management as an EDWOSB concern;

(3) The parties to the joint venture have entered into a written joint venture agreement that contains provisions—

(i) Setting forth the purpose of the joint venture;

(ii) Designating an EDWOSB concern as the managing venturer of the joint venture, and an employee of the managing venturer as the project manager responsible for the performance of the contract;

(iii) Stating that not less than 51 percent of the net profits earned by the joint venture will be distributed to the EDWOSB;

(iv) Specifying the responsibilities of the parties with regard to contract performance, sources of labor, and negotiation of the EDWOSB contract; and

(v) Requiring the final original records be retained by the managing venturer upon completion of the EDWOSB contract performed by the joint venture.

(4) The joint venture performs the applicable percentage of work required in accordance with paragraph (d) above; and

(5) The procuring activity executes the contract in the name of the EDWOSB or joint venture.

(f) *Nonmanufacturer.* An EDWOSB concern that is a non-manufacturer, as defined in 13 CFR 121.406(b) or FAR 19.102(f), may submit an offer on an EDWOSB requirement with a NAICS code for supplies, if it meets the requirements under the non-manufacturer rule set forth in those regulations.

(End of clause)

[FAC 2005-51, 76 FR 18304, 4/1/2011, effective 4/1/2011; FAC 2005-54, 76 FR 68032, 11/2/2011, effective 11/2/2011; Interim rule, 77 FR 1889, 1/12/2012, effective 2/13/2012; FAC 2005-56, 77 FR 12913, 3/2/2012, effective 4/2/2012; Correction, 77 FR 14303, 3/9/2012, effective 3/9/2012; Correction, 77 FR 17352, 3/26/2012, effective 3/26/2012; FAC 2005-67, 78 FR 37676, 6/21/2013, effective 7/22/2013; FAC 2005-86, 80 FR 81888, 12/31/2015, effective 12/31/2015; FAC 2005-91, 81 FR 67735, 9/30/2016, effective 9/30/2016]

52.219-30 Notice of Set-Aside for, or Sole Source Award to, Women-Owned Small Business Concerns Eligible Under the Women-Owned Small Business Program.

As prescribed in 19.1507, insert the following clause:

NOTICE OF SET-ASIDE FOR, OR SOLE SOURCE AWARD TO, WOMEN-OWNED SMALL BUSINESS CONCERNS ELIGIBLE UNDER THE WOMEN-OWNED SMALL BUSINESS PROGRAM (DEC 2015)

(a) *Definitions. Women-owned small business (WOSB) concern eligible under the WOSB Program* (in accordance with 13 CFR part 127), means a small business concern that is at least 51 percent directly and unconditionally owned by, and the management and daily business operations of which are controlled by, one or more women who are citizens of the United States.

WOSB Program Repository means a secure, Web-based application that collects, stores, and disseminates documents to the contracting community and SBA, which verify the eligibility of a business concern for a contract to be awarded under the WOSB Program.

(b) *Applicability.* This clause applies only to—

(1) Contracts that have been set aside or reserved for, or awarded on a sole source basis to, WOSB concerns eligible under the WOSB Program;

(2) Part or parts of a multiple-award contract that have been set aside for WOSB concerns eligible under the WOSB Program; and

(3) Orders set aside for WOSB concerns eligible under the WOSB Program, under multiple-award contracts as described in 8.405-5 and 16.505(b)(2)(i)(F).

(c) *General.* (1) Offers are solicited only from WOSB concerns eligible under the WOSB Program. Offers received from concerns that are not WOSB concerns eligible under the WOSB program shall not be considered.

(2) Any award resulting from this solicitation will be made to a WOSB concern eligible under the WOSB Program.

(3) The Contracting Officer will ensure that the apparent successful offeror has provided the required documents to the WOSB Program Repository. The contract shall not be awarded until all required documents are received.

(d) *Agreement.* A WOSB concern eligible under the WOSB Program agrees that in the performance of the contract for—

(1) Services (except construction), the concern will perform at least 50 percent of the cost of the contract incurred for personnel with its own employees;

(2) Supplies or products (other than procurement from a non-manufacturer in such supplies or products), the concern will perform at least 50 percent of the cost of manufacturing the supplies or products (not including the costs of materials);

(3) General construction, the concern will perform at least 15 percent of the cost of the contract with its own employees (not including the costs of materials); and

(4) Construction by special trade contractors, the concern will perform at least 25 percent of the cost of the contract with its own employees (not including cost of materials).

(e) *Joint Venture.* A joint venture may be considered a WOSB concern eligible under the WOSB Program if—

(1) It meets the applicable size standard corresponding to the NAICS code assigned to the contract, unless an exception to affiliation applies pursuant to 13 CFR 121.103(h)(3);

(2) The WOSB participant of the joint venture is designated in the System for Award Management as a WOSB concern eligible under the WOSB Program;

(3) The parties to the joint venture have entered into a written joint venture agreement that contains provisions—

(i) Setting forth the purpose of the joint venture;

(ii) Designating a WOSB concern eligible under the WOSB Program as the managing venturer of the joint venture, and an employee of the managing venturer as the project manager responsible for the performance of the contract;

(iii) Stating that not less than 51 percent of the net profits earned by the joint venture will be distributed to the WOSB;

(iv) Specifying the responsibilities of the parties with regard to contract performance, sources of labor, and negotiation of the WOSB contract; and

(v) Requiring the final original records be retained by the managing venturer upon completion of the WOSB contract performed by the joint venture.

(4) The joint venture must perform the applicable percentage of work required in accordance with paragraph (d) above; and

(5) The procuring activity executes the contract in the name of the WOSB concern eligible under the WOSB Program or joint venture.

(f) *Nonmanufacturer*. A WOSB concern eligible under WOSB Program that is a nonmanufacturer, as defined in 13 CFR 121.406(b) or FAR 19.102(f), may submit an offer on a WOSB requirement with a NAICS code for supplies, if it meets the requirements under the non-manufacturer rule set forth in those regulations.

(End of clause)

[FAC 2005-51, 76 FR 18304, 4/1/2011, effective 4/1/2011; FAC 2005-54, 76 FR 68032, 11/2/2011, effective 11/2/2011; Interim rule, 77 FR 1889, 1/12/2012, effective 2/13/2012; FAC 2005-56, 77 FR 12913, 3/2/2012, effective 4/2/2012; Correction, 77 FR 14303, 3/9/2012, effective 3/9/2012; Correction, 77 FR 17352, 3/26/2012, effective 3/26/2012; FAC 2005-67, 78 FR 37676, 6/21/2013, effective 7/22/2013; FAC 2005-86, 80 FR 81888, 12/31/2015, effective 12/31/2015; FAC 2005-91, 81 FR 67735, 9/30/2016, effective 9/30/2016]

52.220 [Reserved]

52.221 [Reserved]

52.222-1 Notice to the Government of Labor Disputes.

As prescribed in 22.103-5(a), insert the following clause:

NOTICE TO THE GOVERNMENT OF LABOR DISPUTES (FEB 1997)

If the Contractor has knowledge that any actual or potential labor dispute is delaying or threatens to delay the timely performance of this contract, the Contractor shall immediately give notice, including all relevant information, to the Contracting Officer.

(End of clause)

[FAC 90-32, 60 FR 48206, 9/18/95, effective 10/1/95; FAC 90-43, Final rule, 61 FR 67408, 12/20/96, effective 2/18/97]

52.222-2 Payment for Overtime Premiums

As prescribed in 22.103-5(b), insert the following clause:

PAYMENT FOR OVERTIME PREMIUMS (JUL 1990)

(a) The use of overtime is authorized under this contract if the overtime premium cost does not exceed *—— or the overtime premium is paid for work—

(1) Necessary to cope with emergencies such as those resulting from accidents, natural disasters, breakdowns of production equipment, or occasional production bottlenecks of a sporadic nature;

(2) By indirect-labor employees such as those performing duties in connection with administration, protection, transportation, maintenance, standby plant protection, operation of utilities, or accounting;

(3) To perform tests, industrial processes, laboratory procedures, loading or unloading of transportation conveyances, and operations in flight or afloat that are continuous in nature and cannot reasonably be interrupted or completed otherwise; or

(4) That will result in lower overall costs to the Government.

(b) Any request for estimated overtime premiums that exceeds the amount specified above shall include all estimated overtime for contract completion and shall—

(1) Identify the work unit; *e.g.*, department or section in which the requested overtime will be used, together with present workload, staffing, and other data of the affected unit sufficient to permit the Contracting Officer to evaluate the necessity for the overtime;

(2) Demonstrate the effect that denial of the request will have on the contract delivery or performance schedule;

(3) Identify the extent to which approval of overtime would affect the performance or payments in connection with other Government contracts, together with identification of each affected contract; and

(4) Provide reasons why the required work cannot be performed by using multishift operations or by employing additional personnel.

*Insert either "zero" or the dollar amount agreed to during negotiations.

(End of clause)

[FAC 84-58, 55 FR 25532, 6/21/90, effective 7/23/90; Final rule, 55 FR 38518, 9/18/90]

52.222-3 Convict Labor.

As prescribed in 22.202, insert the following clause:

CONVICT LABOR (JUN 2003)

(a) Except as provided in paragraph (b) of this clause, the Contractor shall not employ in the performance of this contract any person undergoing a sentence of imprisonment imposed by any court of a State, the District of Columbia, Puerto Rico, the Northern Mariana Islands, American Samoa, Guam, or the U.S. Virgin Islands.

(b) The Contractor is not prohibited from employing persons—

(1) On parole or probation to work at paid employment during the term of their sentence;

(2) Who have been pardoned or who have served their terms; or

(3) Confined for violation of the laws of any of the States, the District of Columbia, Puerto Rico, the Northern Mariana Islands, American Samoa, Guam, or the U.S. Virgin Islands who are authorized to work at paid employment in the community under the laws of such jurisdiction, if—

(i) The worker is paid or is in an approved work training program on a voluntary basis;

(ii) Representatives of local union central bodies or similar labor union organizations have been consulted;

(iii) Such paid employment will not result in the displacement of employed workers, or be applied in skills, crafts, or trades in which there is a surplus of available gainful labor in the locality, or impair existing contracts for services;

(iv) The rates of pay and other conditions of employment will not be less than those paid or provided for work of a similar nature in the locality in which the work is being performed; and

(v) The Attorney General of the United States has certified that the work-release laws or regulations of the jurisdiction involved are in conformity with the requirements of Executive Order 11755, as amended by Executive Orders 12608 and 12943.

(End of clause)

[FAC 90-39, 61 FR 31612, 6/20/96, effective 8/19/96; FAC 2001-14, 68 FR 28079, 5/23/2003, effective 6/23/2003]

52.222-4 Contract Work Hours and Safety Standards—Overtime Compensation.

As prescribed in 22.305, insert the following clause:

CONTRACT WORK HOURS AND SAFETY STANDARDS—OVERTIME COMPENSATION (MAY 2018)

(a) *Overtime requirements.* No Contractor or subcontractor employing laborers or mechanics (see Federal Acquisition Regulation 22.300) shall require or permit them to work over 40 hours in any workweek unless they are paid at least 1 and 1/2 times the basic rate of pay for each hour worked over 40 hours.

(b) *Violation; liability for unpaid wages; liquidated damages.* The responsible Contractor and subcontractor are liable for unpaid wages if they violate the terms in paragraph (a) of this clause. In addition, the Contractor and subcontractor are liable for liquidated damages payable to the Government. The Contracting Officer will assess liquidated damages at the rate specified at 29 CFR 5.5(b)(2) per affected employee for each calendar day on which the employer required or permitted the employee to work in excess of the standard workweek of 40 hours without paying overtime wages required by the Contract Work Hours and Safety Standards statute (found at 40 U.S.C. chapter 37). In accordance with the Federal Civil Penalties Inflation Adjustment Act of 1990 (28 U.S.C. 2461 Note), the Department of Labor adjusts this civil monetary penalty for inflation no later than January 15 each year.

(c) *Withholding for unpaid wages and liquidated damages.* The Contracting Officer will withhold from payments due under the contract sufficient funds required to satisfy any Contractor or subcontractor liabilities for unpaid wages and liquidated damages. If amounts withheld under the contract are insufficient to satisfy Contractor or subcontractor liabilities, the Contracting Officer will withhold payments from other Federal or Federally assisted contracts held by the same Contractor that are subject to the Contract Work Hours and Safety Standards statute.

(d) *Payrolls and basic records.* (1) The Contractor and its subcontractors shall maintain payrolls and basic payroll records for all laborers and mechanics working on the contract during the contract and shall make them available to the Government until 3 years after contract completion. The records shall contain the name and address of each employee, social security number, labor classifications, hourly rates of wages paid, daily and weekly number of hours worked, deductions made, and actual wages paid. The records need not duplicate those required for construction work by Department of Labor regulations at 29 CFR 5.5(a)(3) implementing the Construction Wage Rate Requirements statute.

(2) The Contractor and its subcontractors shall allow authorized representatives of the Contracting Officer or the Department of Labor to inspect, copy, or transcribe records maintained under paragraph (d)(1) of this clause. The Contractor or subcontractor also shall allow authorized representatives of the Contracting Officer or Department of Labor to interview employees in the workplace during working hours.

(e) *Subcontracts.* The Contractor shall insert the provisions set forth in paragraphs (a) through (d) of this clause in subcontracts that may require or involve the employment of laborers and mechanics and require subcontractors to include these provisions in any such lower tier subcontracts. The Contractor shall be responsible for compliance by any subcontractor or lower-tier subcontractor with the provisions set forth in paragraphs (a) through (d) of this clause.

(End of clause)

[FAC 97-19, 65 FR 46052, 7/26/2000, effective 9/25/2000; FAC 2005-04, 70 FR 33662, 6/8/2005, effective 7/8/2005; FAC 2005-73, 79 FR 24192, 4/29/2014, effective 5/29/2014; FAC 2005-98, 83 FR 19148, 5/1/2018, effective 5/31/2018]

52.222-5 Construction Wage Rate Requirements—Secondary Site of the Work.

As prescribed in 22.407(h), insert the following provision:

CONSTRUCTION WAGE RATE REQUIREMENTS—SECONDARY SITE OF THE WORK (MAY 2014)

(a)(1) The offeror shall notify the Government if the offeror intends to perform work at any secondary site of the work, as defined in paragraph (a)(1)(ii) of the FAR clause at 52.222-6, Construction Wage Rate Requirements, of this solicitation.

(2) If the offeror is unsure if a planned work site satisfies the criteria for a secondary site of the work, the offeror shall request a determination from the Contracting Officer.

(b)(1) If the wage determination provided by the Government for work at the primary site of the work is not applicable to the secondary site of the work, the offeror shall request a wage determination from the Contracting Officer.

(2) The due date for receipt of offers will not be extended as a result of an offeror's request for a wage determination for a secondary site of the work.

(End of provision)

[FAC 90-17, 58 FR 12140, 3/2/93, effective 3/2/93; FAC 2005-04, 70 FR 33662, 6/8/2005, effective 7/8/2005; FAC 2005-73, 79 FR 24192, 4/29/2014, effective 5/29/2014]

52.222-6 Construction Wage Rate Requirements.

As prescribed in 22.407(a), insert the following clause:

CONSTRUCTION WAGE RATE REQUIREMENTS (AUG 2018)

(a) *Definition.—Site of the work*—(1) Means—

(i) The primary site of the work. The physical place or places where the construction called for in the contract will remain when work on it is completed; and

(ii) The secondary site of the work, if any. Any other site where a significant portion of the building or work is constructed, provided that such site is—

(A) Located in the United States; and

(B) Established specifically for the performance of the contract or project;

(2) Except as provided in paragraph (3) of this definition, includes any fabrication plants, mobile factories, batch plants, borrow pits, job headquarters, tool yards, etc., provided—

(i) They are dedicated exclusively, or nearly so, to performance of the contract or project; and

(ii) They are adjacent or virtually adjacent to the *primary site of the work* as defined in paragraph (a)(1)(i), or the *secondary site of the work* as defined in paragraph (a)(1)(ii) of this definition;

(3) Does not include permanent home offices, branch plant establishments, fabrication plants, or tool yards of a Contractor or subcontractor whose locations and continuance in operation are determined wholly without regard to a particular Federal contract or project. In addition, fabrication plants, batch plants, borrow pits, job headquarters, yards, etc., of a commercial or material supplier which are established by a supplier of materials for the project before opening of bids and not on the Project site, are not included in the "site of the work." Such permanent, previously established facilities are not a part of the "site of the work" even if the operations for a period of time may be dedicated exclusively or nearly so, to the performance of a contract.

(b)(1) All laborers and mechanics employed or working upon the site of the work will be paid unconditionally and not less often than once a week, and without subsequent deduction or rebate on any account (except such payroll deductions as are permitted by regulations issued by the Secretary of Labor under the Copeland Act (29 CFR part 3)), the full amount of wages and bona fide fringe benefits (or cash equivalents thereof) due at time of payment computed at rates not less than those contained in the wage determination of the Secretary of Labor which is attached hereto and made a part hereof, or as may be incorporated for a secondary site of the work, regardless of any contractual relationship which may be alleged to exist between the Contractor and such laborers and mechanics. Any wage determination incorporated for a secondary site of the work shall be effective from the first day on which work under the contract was performed at that site and shall be incorporated without any adjustment in contract price or estimated cost. Laborers employed by the construction Contractor or construction subcontractor that are transporting portions of the building or work between the secondary site of the work and the primary site of the work shall be paid in accordance with the wage determination applicable to the primary site of the work.

(2) Contributions made or costs reasonably anticipated for bona fide fringe benefits under section 1(b)(2) of the Construction Wage Rate Requirements statute on behalf of laborers or mechanics are considered wages paid to such laborers or mechanics, subject to the provisions of paragraph (e) of this clause; also, regular contributions made or costs incurred for more than a weekly period (but not less often than quarterly) under plans, funds, or programs which cover the particular weekly period, are deemed to be constructively made or incurred during such period.

(3) Such laborers and mechanics shall be paid not less than the appropriate wage rate and fringe benefits in the wage determination for the classification of work actually performed, without regard to skill, except as provided in the clause entitled Apprentices and Trainees. Laborers or mechanics performing work in more than one classification may be compensated at the rate specified for each classification for the time actually worked therein; provided that the employer's payroll records accurately set forth the time spent in each classification in which work is performed.

(4) The wage determination (including any additional classifications and wage rates conformed under paragraph (c) of this clause) and the Construction Wage Rate Requirements (Davis-Bacon Act) poster (WH-1321) shall be posted at all times by the Contractor and its subcontractors at the primary site of the work and the secondary site of the work, if any, in a prominent and accessible place where it can be easily seen by the workers.

(c)(1) The Contracting Officer shall require that any class of laborers or mechanics, which is not listed in the wage determination and which is to be employed under the contract shall be classified in conformance with the wage determination. The Contracting Officer shall approve an additional classification and wage rate and fringe benefits therefor only when all the following criteria have been met:

(i) The work to be performed by the classification requested is not performed by a classification in the wage determination.

(ii) The classification is utilized in the area by the construction industry.

(iii) The proposed wage rate, including any bona fide fringe benefits, bears a reasonable relationship to the wage rates contained in the wage determination.

(iv) With respect to helpers, such a classification prevails in the area in which the work is performed.

(2) If the Contractor and the laborers and mechanics to be employed in the classification (if known), or their representatives, and the Contracting Officer agree on the classification and wage rate (including the amount designated for fringe benefits, where appropriate), a report of the action taken shall be sent by the Contracting Officer to the Administrator of the Wage and Hour Division, U.S. Department of Labor, Washington, DC 20210. The Administrator or an authorized representative will approve, modify, or disapprove every additional classification action within 30 days of receipt and so advise the Contracting Officer or will notify the Contracting Officer within the 30-day period that additional time is necessary.

(3) In the event the Contractor, the laborers or mechanics to be employed in the classification, or their representatives, and

the Contracting Officer do not agree on the proposed classification and wage rate (including the amount designated for fringe benefits, where appropriate), the Contracting Officer shall refer the questions, including the views of all interested parties and the recommendation of the Contracting Officer, to the Administrator of the Wage and Hour Division for determination. The Administrator, or an authorized representative, will issue a determination within 30 days of receipt and so advise the Contracting Officer or will notify the Contracting Officer within the 30-day period that additional time is necessary.

(4) The wage rate (including fringe benefits, where appropriate) determined pursuant to subparagraphs (c)(2) and (c)(3) of this clause shall be paid to all workers performing work in the classification under this contract from the first day on which work is performed in the classification.

(d) Whenever the minimum wage rate prescribed in the contract for a class of laborers or mechanics includes a fringe benefit which is not expressed as an hourly rate, the Contractor shall either pay the benefit as stated in the wage determination or shall pay another bona fide fringe benefit or an hourly cash equivalent thereof.

(e) If the Contractor does not make payments to a trustee or other third person, the Contractor may consider as part of the wages of any laborer or mechanic the amount of any costs reasonably anticipated in providing bona fide fringe benefits under a plan or program; *provided,* that the Secretary of Labor has found, upon the written request of the Contractor, that the applicable standards of the Construction Wage Rate Requirements statute have been met. The Secretary of Labor may require the Contractor to set aside in a separate account assets for the meeting of obligations under the plan or program.

(End of clause)

[FAC 84-34, 52 FR 4945, 2/18/88, effective 2/29/88; FAC 90-13, 57 FR 44263, 9/24/92, effective 11/23/92; FAC 90-23, 59 FR 67010, 12/28/94, effective 2/27/95; FAC 2005-04, 70 FR 33662, 6/8/2005, effective 7/8/2005; FAC 2005-73, 79 FR 24192, 4/29/2014, effective 5/29/2014; FAC 2005-100, 83 FR 42571, 8/22/2018, effective 8/22/2018]

52.222-7 Withholding of Funds.

As prescribed in 22.407(a), insert the following clause:

WITHHOLDING OF FUNDS (MAY 2014)

The Contracting Officer shall, upon his or her own action or upon written request of an authorized representative of the Department of Labor, withhold or cause to be withheld from the Contractor under this contract or any other Federal contract with the same Prime Contractor, or any other Federally assisted contract subject to prevailing wage requirements, which is held by the same Prime Contractor, so much of the accrued payments or advances as may be considered necessary to pay laborers and mechanics, including apprentices, trainees, and helpers, employed by the Contractor or any subcontractor the full amount of wages required by the contract. In the event of failure to pay any laborer or mechanic, including any apprentice, trainee, or helper, employed or working on the site of the work, all or part of the wages required by the contract, the Contracting Officer may, after written notice to the Contractor, take such action as may be necessary to cause the suspension of any further payment, advance, or guarantee of funds until such violations have ceased.

(End of clause)

[FAC 84-34, 52 FR 4945, 2/18/88, effective 2/29/88; FAC 2005-73, 79 FR 24192, 4/29/2014, effective 5/29/2014]

52.222-8 Payrolls and Basic Records.

As prescribed in 22.407(a), insert the following clause:

PAYROLLS AND BASIC RECORDS (AUG 2018)

(a) Payrolls and basic records relating thereto shall be maintained by the Contractor during the course of the work and preserved for a period of 3 years thereafter for all laborers and mechanics working at the site of the work. Such records shall contain the name, address, and social security number of each such worker, his or her correct classification, hourly rates of wages paid (including rates of contributions or costs anticipated for bona fide fringe benefits or cash equivalents thereof of the types described in 40 U.S.C. 3141(2)(B) (Construction Wage Rate Requirement statute)), daily and weekly number of hours worked, deductions made, and actual wages paid. Whenever the Secretary of Labor has found, under paragraph (d) of the clause entitled Construction Wage Rate Requirements, that the wages of any laborer or mechanic include the amount of any costs reasonably anticipated in providing benefits under a plan or program described in 40 U.S.C. 3141(2)(B), the Contractor shall maintain records which show that the commitment to provide such benefits is enforceable, that the plan or program is financially responsible, and that the plan or program has been communicated in writing to the laborers or mechanics affected, and records which show the costs anticipated or the actual cost incurred in providing such benefits. Contractors employing apprentices or trainees under approved programs shall maintain written evidence of the registration of apprenticeship programs and certification of trainee programs, the registration of the apprentices and trainees, and the ratios and wage rates prescribed in the applicable programs.

(b)(1) The Contractor shall submit weekly for each week in which any contract work is performed a copy of all payrolls to the Contracting Officer. The payrolls submitted shall set out accurately and completely all of the information required to be maintained under paragraph(a) of this clause, except that full social security numbers and home addresses shall not be included on weekly transmittals. Instead the payrolls shall only need to include an individually identifying number for each employee (*e.g.*, the last four digits of the employee's social security number). The required weekly payroll information may be submitted in any form desired. Optional Form WH-347 is available for this purpose and may be obtained from the U.S. Department of Labor Wage and Hour Division website at ***http://www.dol.gov/whd/forms/wh347.pdf***. The Prime Contractor is responsible for the submission of copies of payrolls by all subcontractors. Contractors and subcontractors shall maintain the full social security number and current address of each covered worker, and shall provide them upon request to the Contracting Officer, the Contractor, or the Wage and Hour Division of the Department of Labor for purposes of an investigation or audit of compliance with prevailing wage requirements. It is not a violation of this section for a Prime Contractor to require a subcontractor to provide addresses and social security numbers to the Prime Contractor for its own records, without weekly submission to the Contracting Officer.

(2) Each payroll submitted shall be accompanied by a "Statement of Compliance," signed by the Contractor or subcontractor or his or her agent who pays or supervises the payment of the persons employed under the contract and shall certify—

(i) That the payroll for the payroll period contains the information required to be maintained under paragraph (a) of this clause and that such information is correct and complete;

(ii) That each laborer or mechanic (including each helper, apprentice, and trainee) employed on the contract during the payroll period has been paid the full weekly wages earned, without rebate, either directly or indirectly, and that no deductions have been made either directly or indirectly from the full wages earned, other than permissible deductions as set forth in the Regulations, 29 CFR Part 3; and

(iii) That each laborer or mechanic has been paid not less than the applicable wage rates and fringe benefits or cash equivalents for the classification of work performed, as specified in the applicable wage determination incorporated into the contract.

(3) The weekly submission of a properly executed certification set forth on the reverse side of Optional Form WH-347 shall satisfy the requirement for submission of the "Statement of Compliance" required by subparagraph (b)(2) of this clause.

(4) The falsification of any of the certifications in this clause may subject the Contractor or subcontractor to civil or criminal

prosecution under Section 1001 of Title 18 and Section 3729 of Title 31 of the United States Code.

(c) The Contractor or subcontractor shall make the records required under paragraph (a) of this clause available for inspection, copying, or transcription by the Contracting Officer or authorized representatives of the Contracting Officer or the Department of Labor. The Contractor or subcontractor shall permit the Contracting Officer or representatives of the Contracting Officer or the Department of Labor to interview employees during working hours on the job. If the Contractor or subcontractor fails to submit required records or to make them available, the Contracting Officer may, after written notice to the Contractor, take such action as may be necessary to cause the suspension of any further payment. Furthermore, failure to submit the required records upon request or to make such records available may be grounds for debarment action pursuant to 29 CFR 5.12.

(End of clause)

[FAC 84-34, 52 FR 4945, 2/18/88, effective 2/29/88; FAC 2005-42, 75 FR 34286, 6/16/2010, effective 6/16/2010; FAC 2005-48, 75 FR 82577, 12/30/2010, effective 12/30/2010; FAC 2005-73, 79 FR 24192, 4/29/2014, effective 5/29/2014; FAC 2005-100, 83 FR 42571, 8/22/2018, effective 8/22/2018]

52.222-9 Apprentices and Trainees.

As prescribed in 22.407(a), insert the following clause:

APPRENTICES AND TRAINEES (JUL 2005)

(a) *Apprentices.* (1) An apprentice will be permitted to work at less than the predetermined rate for the work performed when employed—

(i) Pursuant to and individually registered in a bona fide apprenticeship program registered with the U.S. Department of Labor, Employment and Training Administration, Office of Apprenticeship Training, Employer, and Labor Services (OATELS) or with a State Apprenticeship Agency recognized by the OATELS; or

(ii) In the first 90 days of probationary employment as an apprentice in such an apprenticeship program, even though not individually registered in the program, if certified by the OATELS or a State Apprenticeship Agency (where appropriate) to be eligible for probationary employment as an apprentice.

(2) The allowable ratio of apprentices to journeymen on the job site in any craft classification shall not be greater than the ratio permitted to the Contractor as to the entire work force under the registered program.

(3) Any worker listed on a payroll at an apprentice wage rate, who is not registered or otherwise employed as stated in paragraph (a)(1) of this clause, shall be paid not less than the applicable wage determination for the classification of work actually performed. In addition, any apprentice performing work on the job site in excess of the ratio permitted under the registered program shall be paid not less than the applicable wage rate on the wage determination for the work actually performed.

(4) Where a Contractor is performing construction on a project in a locality other than that in which its program is registered, the ratios and wage rates (expressed in percentages of the journeyman's hourly rate) specified in the Contractor's or subcontractor's registered program shall be observed. Every apprentice must be paid at not less than the rate specified in the registered program for the apprentice's level of progress, expressed as a percentage of the journeyman hourly rate specified in the applicable wage determination.

(5) Apprentices shall be paid fringe benefits in accordance with the provisions of the apprenticeship program. If the apprenticeship program does not specify fringe benefits, apprentices must be paid the full amount of fringe benefits listed on the wage determination for the applicable classification. If the Administrator determines that a different practice prevails for the applicable apprentice classification, fringes shall be paid in accordance with that determination.

(6) In the event OATELS, or a State Apprenticeship Agency recognized by

OATELS, withdraws approval of an apprenticeship program, the Contractor will no longer be permitted to utilize apprentices at less than the applicable predetermined rate for the work performed until an acceptable program is approved.

(b) *Trainees.* (1) Except as provided in 29 CFR 5.16, trainees will not be permitted to work at less than the predetermined rate for the work performed unless they are employed pursuant to and individually registered in a program which has received prior approval, evidenced by formal certification by the U.S. Department of Labor, Employment and Training Administration, Office of Apprenticeship Training, Employer, and Labor Services (OATELS). The ratio of trainees to journeymen on the job site shall not be greater than permitted under the plan approved by OATELS.

(2) Every trainee must be paid at not less than the rate specified in the approved program for the trainee's level of progress, expressed as a percentage of the journeyman hourly rate specified in the applicable wage determination. Trainees shall be paid fringe benefits in accordance with the provisions of the trainee program. If the trainee program does not mention fringe benefits, trainees shall be paid the full amount of fringe benefits listed in the wage determination unless the Administrator of the Wage and Hour Division determines that there is an apprenticeship program associated with the corresponding journeyman wage rate in the wage determination which provides for less than full fringe benefits for apprentices. Any employee listed on the payroll at a trainee rate who is not registered and participating in a training plan approved by the OATELS shall be paid not less than the applicable wage rate in the wage determination for the classification of work actually performed. In addition, any trainee performing work on the job site in excess of the ratio permitted under the registered program shall be paid not less than the applicable wage rate in the wage determination for the work actually performed.

(3) In the event OATELS withdraws approval of a training program, the Contractor will no longer be permitted to utilize trainees at less than the applicable predetermined rate for the work performed until an acceptable program is approved.

(c) *Equal employment opportunity.* The utilization of apprentices, trainees, and journeymen under this clause shall be in conformity with the equal employment opportunity requirements of Executive Order 11246, as amended, and 29 CFR Part 30.

(End of clause)

[FAC 84-34, 53 FR 4946, 2/18/88, effective 2/29/88; FAC 2005-04, 70 FR 33662, 6/8/2005, effective 7/8/2005]

52.222-10 Compliance with Copeland Act Requirements.

As prescribed in 22.407(a), insert the following clause:

COMPLIANCE WITH COPELAND ACT REQUIREMENTS (FEB 1988)

The Contractor shall comply with the requirements of 29 CFR Part 3, which are hereby incorporated by reference in this contract.

(End of clause)

[FAC 84-34, 53 FR 4947, 2/18/88, effective 2/29/88]

52.222-11 Subcontracts (Labor Standards).

As prescribed in 22.407(a), insert the following clause:

SUBCONTRACTS (LABOR STANDARDS) (MAY 2014)

(a) *Definition. Construction, alteration* or *repair*, as used in this clause, means all types of work done by laborers and mechanics employed by the construction Contractor or construction subcontractor on a particular building or work at the site thereof, including without limitation—

(1) Altering, remodeling, installation (if appropriate) on the site of the work of items fabricated off-site;

(2) Painting and decorating;

(3) Manufacturing or furnishing of materials, articles, supplies, or equipment on the site of the building or work;

(4) Transportation of materials and supplies between the site of the work within the meaning of paragraphs (a)(1)(i) and (ii) of the *site of the work* as defined in the FAR clause at 52.222-6, Construction Wage Rate Requirements of this contract, and a facility which is dedicated to the construction of the building or work and is deemed part of the site of the work within the meaning of paragraph (2) of the *site of the work* definition; and

(5) Transportation of portions of the building or work between a secondary site where a significant portion of the building or work is constructed, which is part of the *site of the work* definition in paragraph (a)(1)(ii) of the FAR clause at 52.222-6, Construction Wage Rate Requirements, and the physical place or places where the building or work will remain (paragraph (a)(1)(i) of the FAR clause at 52.222-6, in the *site of the work* definition).

(b) The Contractor shall insert in any subcontracts for construction, alterations and repairs within the United States the clauses entitled—

(1) Construction Wage Rate Requirements;

(2) Contract Work Hours and Safety Standards—Overtime Compensation (if the clause is included in this contract);

(3) Apprentices and Trainees;

(4) Payrolls and Basic Records;

(5) Compliance with Copeland Act Requirements;

(6) Withholding of Funds;

(7) Subcontracts (Labor Standards);

(8) Contract Termination—Debarment;

(9) Disputes Concerning Labor Standards;

(10) Compliance with Construction Wage Rate Requirements and Related Regulations; and

(11) Certification of Eligibility.

(c) The prime Contractor shall be responsible for compliance by any subcontractor or lower tier subcontractor performing construction within the United States with all the contract clauses cited in paragraph (b).

(d)(1) Within 14 days after award of the contract, the Contractor shall deliver to the Contracting Officer a completed Standard Form (SF) 1413, Statement and Acknowledgment, for each subcontract for construction within the United States, including the subcontractor's signed and dated acknowledgment that the clauses set forth in paragraph (b) of this clause have been included in the subcontract.

(2) Within 14 days after the award of any subsequently awarded subcontract the Contractor shall deliver to the Contracting Officer an updated completed SF 1413 for such additional subcontract.

(e) The Contractor shall insert the substance of this clause, including this paragraph (e) in all subcontracts for construction within the United States.

(End of clause)

[FAC 84-34, 53 FR 4947, 2/18/88, effective 2/29/88; FAC 2005-04, 70 FR 33662, 6/8/2005, effective 7/8/2005; FAC 2005-73, 79 FR 24192, 4/29/2014, effective 5/29/2014]

52.222-12 Contract Termination—Debarment.

As prescribed in 22.407(a), insert the following clause:

CONTRACT TERMINATION—DEBARMENT (MAY 2014)

A breach of the contract clauses entitled Construction Wage Rate Requirements, Contract Work Hours and Safety Standards—Overtime Compensation, Apprentices and Trainees, Payrolls and Basic Records, Compliance with Copeland Act Requirements, Subcontracts (Labor Standards), Compliance with Construction Wage Rate Requirements and Related Regulations, or Certification of Eligibility may be grounds for termination of the contract, and for debarment as a Contractor and subcontractor as provided in 29 CFR 5.12.

(End of clause)

[FAC 84-34, 53 FR 4947, 2/18/88, effective 2/29/88; FAC 2005-73, 79 FR 24192, 4/29/2014, effective 5/29/2014]

52.222-13 Compliance With Construction Wage Rate Requirements and Related Regulations.

As prescribed in 22.407(a), insert the following clause:

COMPLIANCE WITH CONSTRUCTION WAGE RATE REQUIREMENTS AND RELATED REGULATIONS (MAY 2014)

All rulings and interpretations of the Construction Wage Rate Requirements and related statutes contained in 29 CFR parts 1, 3, and 5 are hereby incorporated by reference in this contract.

(End of clause)

[FAC 84-34, 53 FR 4947, 2/18/88, effective 2/29/88; FAC 2005-73, 79 FR 24192, 4/29/2014, effective 5/29/2014]

52.222-14 Disputes Concerning Labor Standards.

As prescribed in 22.407(a), insert the following clause:

DISPUTES CONCERNING LABOR STANDARDS (FEB 1988)

All rulings and interpretations of the Construction Wage Rate Requirements and related statutes contained in 29 CFR parts 1, 3, and 5 are hereby incorporated by reference in this contract.

(End of clause)

[FAC 84-34, 53 FR 4947, 2/18/88, effective 2/29/88]

52.222-15 Certification of Eligibility.

As prescribed in 22.407(a), insert the following clause:

CERTIFICATION OF ELIGIBILITY (MAY 2014)

(a) By entering into this contract, the Contractor certifies that neither it nor any person or firm who has an interest in the Contractor's firm is a person or firm ineligible to be awarded Government contracts by virtue of 40 U.S.C. 3144(b)(2) or 29 CFR 5.12(a)(1).

(b) No part of this contract shall be subcontracted to any person or firm ineligible for award of a Government contract by virtue of 40 U.S.C. 3144(b)(2) or 29 CFR 5.12(a)(1).

(c) The penalty for making false statements is prescribed in the U.S. Criminal Code, 18 U.S.C. 1001.

(End of clause)

[FAC 84-34, 53 FR 4947, 2/18/88, effective 2/29/88; FAC 2005-73, 79 FR 24192, 4/29/2014, effective 5/29/2014]

52.222-16 Approval of Wage Rates.

As prescribed in 22.407(b), insert the following clause:

APPROVAL OF WAGE RATES (MAY 2014)

All straight time wage rates, and overtime rates based thereon, for laborers and mechanics engaged in work under this contract must be submitted for approval in writing by the head of the contracting activity or a representative expressly designated for this purpose, if the straight time wages exceed the rates for corresponding classifications contained in the applicable Construction Wage Rate Requirements minimum wage determination included in the contract. Any amount paid by the Contractor to any laborer or mechanic in excess of the agency approved wage rate shall be at the expense of the Contractor and shall not be reimbursed by the Government. If the Government refuses to authorize the use of the overtime, the Contractor is not released from the obligation to pay employees at the required overtime rates for any overtime actually worked.

(End of clause)

[FAC 84-34, 53 FR 4947, 2/18/88, effective 2/29/88; FAC 2005-73, 79 FR 24192, 4/29/2014, effective 5/29/2014]

52.222-17 Nondisplacement of Qualified Workers.

As prescribed in 22.1207, insert the following clause:

NONDISPLACEMENT OF QUALIFIED WORKERS (MAY 2014)

(a) *Service employee*, as used in this clause, means any person engaged in the performance of a service contract other than any person employed in a bona fide executive, administrative, or professional capacity, as those terms are defined in 29 CFR part 541. The term *service employee* includes all such persons regardless of any contractual relationship that may be alleged to exist between a contractor or subcontractor and such persons.

(b) The Contractor and its subcontractors shall, except as otherwise provided herein, in good faith offer those service employees employed under the predecessor contract whose employment will be terminated as a result of award of this contract or the expiration of the contract under which the service employees were hired, a right of first refusal of employment under this contract in positions for which the service employees are qualified.

(1) The Contractor and its subcontractors shall determine the number of service employees necessary for efficient performance of this contract and may elect to employ fewer employees than the predecessor Contractor employed in connection with performance of the work.

(2) Except as provided in paragraph (c) of this clause, there shall be no employment opening under this contract, and the Contractor and any subcontractors shall not offer employment under this contract, to any person prior to having complied fully with this obligation.

(i) The successor Contractor and its subcontractors shall make a bona fide express offer of employment to each service employee as provided herein and shall state the time within which the service employee must accept such offer, but in no case shall the period within which the service employee must accept the offer of employment be less than 10 days.

(ii) The successor Contractor and its subcontractors shall decide any question concerning a service employee's qualifications based upon the individual's education and employment history, with particular emphasis on the employee's experience on the predecessor contract, and the Contractor may utilize employment screening processes only when such processes are provided for by the contracting agency, are conditions of the service contract, and are consistent with Executive Order 13495.

(iii) Where the successor Contractor does not initially offer employment to all the predecessor contract service employees, the obligation to offer employment shall continue for 90 days after the successor contractor's first date of performance on the contract.

(iv) An offer of employment will be presumed to be bona fide even if it is not for a position similar to the one the employee previously held, but is one for which the employee is qualified, and even if it is subject to different employment terms and conditions, including changes to pay or benefits. (See 29 CFR 9.12 for a detailed description of a bona fide offer of employment).

(c)(1) Notwithstanding the obligation under paragraph (b) of this clause, the successor Contractor and any subcontractors (i) may employ under this contract any service employee who has worked for the contractor or subcontractor for at least three months immediately preceding the commencement of this contract and who would otherwise face lay-off or discharge, (ii) are not required to offer a right of first refusal to any service employee(s) of the predecessor contractor who are not service employees within the meaning of the Service Contract Labor Standards statute, 41 U.S.C. 6701(3), and (iii) are not required to offer a right of first refusal to any service employee(s) of the predecessor contractor whom the Contractor or any of its subcontractors reasonably believes, based on the particular service employee's past performance, has failed to perform suitably on the job (see 29 CFR 9.12(c)(4) for additional information). The successor Contractor bears the responsibility of demonstrating the appropriateness of claiming any of these exceptions.

(2) In addition, any Contractor or subcontractor that has been certified by the U.S. Small Business Administration as a HUBZone small business concern must ensure that it complies with the statutory and regulatory requirements of the HUBZone Program (*e.g.,* it must ensure that at least 35 percent of all of its employees reside within a HUBZone). The HUBZone small business Contractor or subcontractor must consider

whether it can meet the requirements of this clause and Executive Order 13495 while also ensuring it meets the HUBZone Program's requirements.

(3) Nothing in this clause shall be construed to permit a Contractor or subcontractor to fail to comply with any provision of any other Executive order or law. For example, the requirements of the HUBZone Program (see FAR subpart 19.13), Executive Order 11246 (Equal Employment Opportunity), and the Vietnam Era Veterans' Readjustment Assistance Act of 1974 may conflict, in certain circumstances, with the requirements of Executive Order 13495. All applicable laws and Executive orders must be satisfied in tandem with, and if necessary prior to, the requirements of Executive Order 13495, 29 CFR part 9, and this clause.

(d)(1) The Contractor shall, not less than 30 days before completion of the Contractor's performance of services on the contract, furnish the Contracting Officer with a certified list of the names of all service employees working under this contract and its subcontracts at the time the list is submitted. The list shall also contain anniversary dates of employment of each service employee under this contract and its predecessor contracts with either the current or predecessor contractors or their subcontractors. Where changes to the workforce are made after the submission of the certified list described in this paragraph, the Contractor shall, in accordance with paragraph (e) of this clause, not less than 10 days before completion of the services on this contract, furnish the Contracting Officer with an updated certified list of the names of all service employees employed within the last month of contract performance. The updated list shall also contain anniversary dates of employment, and, where applicable, dates of separation of each service employee under the contract and its predecessor contracts with either the current or predecessor Contractors or their subcontractors.

(2) Immediately upon receipt of the certified service employee list but not before contract award, the contracting officer shall provide the certified service employee list to the successor contractor, and, if requested, to employees of the predecessor contractor or subcontractors or their authorized representatives.

(3) The Contracting Officer will direct the predecessor Contractor to provide written notice (Appendix B to 29 CFR chapter 9) to service employees of their possible right to an offer of employment with the successor contractor. Where a significant portion of the predecessor Contractor's workforce is not fluent in English, the notice shall be provided in English and the language(s) with which service employees are more familiar. The written notice shall be—

(i) Posted in a conspicuous place at the worksite; or

(ii) Delivered to the service employees individually. If such delivery is via email, the notification must result in an electronic delivery receipt or some other reliable confirmation that the intended recipient received the notice.

(e)(1) If required in accordance with 52.222-41(n), the predecessor Contractor shall, not less than 10 days before completion of this contract, furnish the Contracting Officer a certified list of the names of all service employees working under this contract and its subcontracts during the last month of contract performance. The list shall also contain anniversary dates of employment of each service employee under this contract and its predecessor contracts either with the current or predecessor Contractors or their subcontractors. If there are no changes to the workforce before the predecessor contract is completed, then the predecessor Contractor is not required to submit a revised list 10 days prior to completion of performance and the requirements of 52.222-41(n) are met. When there are changes to the workforce after submission of the 30-day list, the predecessor Contractor shall submit a revised certified list not less than 10 days prior to performance completion.

(2) Immediately upon receipt of the certified service employee list but not before contract award, the contracting officer shall provide the certified service employee list to the successor contractor, and, if requested,

to employees of the predecessor contractor or subcontractors or their authorized representatives.

(f) The Contractor and subcontractor shall maintain the following records (regardless of format, *e.g.,* paper or electronic) of its compliance with this clause for not less than a period of three years from the date the records were created.

(1) Copies of any written offers of employment or a contemporaneous written record of any oral offers of employment, including the date, location, and attendance roster of any service employee meeting(s) at which the offers were extended, a summary of each meeting, a copy of any written notice that may have been distributed, and the names of the service employees from the predecessor contract to whom an offer was made.

(2) A copy of any record that forms the basis for any exemption claimed under this part.

(3) A copy of the service employee list provided to or received from the contracting agency.

(4) An entry on the pay records of the amount of any retroactive payment of wages or compensation under the supervision of the Administrator of the Wage and Hour Division to each service employee, the period covered by such payment, and the date of payment, and a copy of any receipt form provided by or authorized by the Wage and Hour Division. The Contractor shall also deliver a copy of the receipt to the service employee and file the original, as evidence of payment by the Contractor and receipt by the service employee, with the Administrator or an authorized representative within 10 days after payment is made.

(g) Disputes concerning the requirements of this clause shall not be subject to the general disputes clause (52.233-1) of this contract. Such disputes shall be resolved in accordance with the procedures of the Department of Labor set forth in 29 CFR part 9. Disputes within the meaning of this clause include disputes between or among any of the following: The Contractor, the contracting agency, the U.S. Department of Labor, and the service employees under the contract or its predecessor contract. The Contracting Officer will refer any service employee who wishes to file a complaint, or ask questions concerning this contract clause, to the: Branch of Government Contracts Enforcement, Wage and Hour Division, U.S. Department of Labor, 200 Constitution Avenue NW., Washington, DC 20210. Contact email: *displaced@dol.gov*.

(h) The Contractor shall cooperate in any review or investigation by the Department of Labor into possible violations of the provisions of this clause and shall make such records requested by such official(s) available for inspection, copying, or transcription upon request.

(i) If it is determined, pursuant to regulations issued by the Secretary of Labor (Secretary), that the Contractor or its subcontractors are not in compliance with the requirements of this clause or any regulation or order of the Secretary, appropriate sanctions may be imposed and remedies invoked against the Contractor or its subcontractors, as provided in Executive Order 13495, the regulations, and relevant orders of the Secretary, or as otherwise provided by law.

(j) The Contractor shall take such action with respect to any such subcontract as may be directed by the Secretary of Labor as a means of enforcing such provisions, including the imposition of sanctions for noncompliance. However, if the Contractor, as a result of such direction, becomes involved in litigation with a subcontractor, or is threatened with such involvement, the Contractor may request that the United States, through the Secretary, enter into such litigation to protect the interests of the United States.

(k) The Contracting Officer will withhold, or cause to be withheld, from the prime Contractor under this or any other Government contract with the same prime Contractor, such sums as an authorized official of the Department of Labor requests, upon a determination by the Administrator, the Administrative Law Judge, or the Administrative Review Board, that there has been a failure to comply with the terms of this clause and that wages lost as a result of the violations are due to service employees or that other monetary relief is appropriate. If the Contracting Officer or the Administrator, upon final order of the Secretary, finds that the Contractor has failed to provide a list of the names of service employees working under the contract, the Contracting Officer may, in his or her discretion, or upon request by the Administrator, take such action as may be necessary to cause the suspension of the payment of contract funds until such time as the list is provided to the Contracting Officer.

(l) *Subcontracts.* In every subcontract over the simplified acquisition threshold entered into in order to perform services under this contract, the Contractor shall include a provision that ensures—

(1) That each subcontractor will honor the requirements of paragraphs (b) through (c) of this clause with respect to the service employees of a predecessor subcontractor or subcontractors working under this contract, as well as of a predecessor Contractor and its subcontractors;

(2) That the subcontractor will provide the Contractor with the information about the service employees of the subcontractor needed by the Contractor to comply with paragraphs (d) and (e) of this clause; and

(3) The recordkeeping requirements of paragraph (f) of this clause.

(End of clause)

[FAC 84-34, 53 FR 4947, 2/18/88, effective 2/29/88; FAC 2005-17, 72 FR 27364, 5/15/2007, effective 6/14/2007; FAC 2005-64, 77 FR 75766, 12/21/2012, effective 1/18/2013; FAC 2005-73, 79 FR 24192, 4/29/2014, effective 5/29/2014]

52.222-18 Certification Regarding Knowledge of Child Labor for Listed End Products.

As prescribed in 22.1505(a), insert the following provision:

CERTIFICATION REGARDING KNOWLEDGE OF CHILD LABOR FOR LISTED END PRODUCTS (FEB 2001)

(a) *Definition. Forced or indentured child labor* means all work or service—

(1) Exacted from any person under the age of 18 under the menace of any penalty for its nonperformance and for which the worker does not offer himself voluntarily; or

(2) Performed by any person under the age of 18 pursuant to a contract the enforcement of which can be accomplished by process or penalties.

(b) *Listed end products.* The following end product(s) being acquired under this solicitation is (are) included in the List of Products Requiring Contractor Certification as to Forced or Indentured Child Labor, identified by their country of origin. There is a reasonable basis to believe that listed end products from the listed countries of origin may have been mined, produced, or manufactured by forced or indentured child labor.

Listed End Product

____

Listed Countries of Origin

____

(c) *Certification.* The Government will not make award to an offeror unless the offeror, by checking the appropriate block, certifies to either paragraph (c)(1) or paragraph (c)(2) of this provision.

[ ] (1) The offeror will not supply any end product listed in paragraph (b) of this provision that was mined, produced, or manufactured in a corresponding country as listed for that end product.

[ ] (2) The offeror may supply an end product listed in paragraph (b) of this provision that was mined, produced, or manufactured in the corresponding country as listed for that product. The offeror certifies that it has made a good faith effort to determine whether forced or indentured child labor was used to mine, produce, or manufacture such end product. On the basis of those efforts, the offeror certifies that it is not aware of any such use of child labor.

(End of provision)

[FAC 97-23, 66 FR 5345, 1/18/2001, effective 2/20/2001]

52.222-19 Child Labor—Cooperation with Authorities and Remedies.

As prescribed in 22.1505(b), insert the following clause:

CHILD LABOR—COOPERATION WITH AUTHORITIES AND REMEDIES (OCT 2019)

(a) *Applicability*. This clause does not apply to the extent that the Contractor is supplying end products mined, produced, or manufactured in—

(1) Canada, and the anticipated value of the acquisition is $25,000 or more;

(2) Israel, and the anticipated value of the acquisition is $50,000 or more;

(3) Mexico, and the anticipated value of the acquisition is $80,317 or more; or

(4) Armenia, Aruba, Australia, Austria, Belgium, Bulgaria, Croatia, Cyprus, Czech Republic, Denmark, Estonia, Finland, France, Germany, Greece, Hong Kong, Hungary, Iceland, Ireland, Italy, Japan, Korea, Latvia, Liechtenstein, Lithuania, Luxembourg, Malta, Moldova, Montenegro, Netherlands, New Zealand, Norway, Poland, Portugal, Romania, Singapore, Slovak Republic, Slovenia, Spain, Sweden, Switzerland, Taiwan, Ukraine, or the United Kingdom and the anticipated value of the acquisition is $180,000 or more.

(b) *Cooperation with Authorities*. To enforce the laws prohibiting the manufacture or importation of products mined, produced, or manufactured by forced or indentured child labor, authorized officials may need to conduct investigations to determine whether forced or indentured child labor was used to mine, produce, or manufacture any product furnished under this contract. If the solicitation includes the provision 52.222-18, Certification Regarding Knowledge of Child Labor for Listed End Products, or the equivalent at 52.212-3(i), the Contractor agrees to cooperate fully with authorized officials of the contracting agency, the Department of the Treasury, or the Department of Justice by providing reasonable access to records, documents, persons, or premises upon reasonable request by the authorized officials.

(c) *Violations*. The Government may impose remedies set forth in paragraph (d) for the following violations:

(1) The Contractor has submitted a false certification regarding knowledge of the use of forced or indentured child labor for listed end products.

(2) The Contractor has failed to cooperate, if required, in accordance with paragraph (b) of this clause, with an investigation of the use of forced or indentured child labor by an Inspector General, Attorney General, or the Secretary of the Treasury.

(3) The Contractor uses forced or indentured child labor in its mining, production, or manufacturing processes.

(4) The Contractor has furnished under the contract end products or components that have been mined, produced, or manufactured wholly or in part by forced or indentured child labor. (The Government will not pursue remedies at paragraph (d)(2) or paragraph (d)(3) of this clause unless sufficient evidence indicates that the Contractor knew of the violation.)

(d) *Remedies*. (1) The Contracting Officer may terminate the contract.

(2) The suspending official may suspend the Contractor in accordance with procedures in FAR Subpart 9.4.

(3) The debarring official may debar the Contractor for a period not to exceed 3 years in accordance with the procedures in FAR Subpart 9.4.

(End of clause)

[FAC 97-23, 66 FR 5345, 1/18/2001, effective 2/20/2001; FAC 2001-02, 66 FR 65347, 12/18/2001, effective 12/18/2001; FAC 2001-09, 67 FR 56115, 8/30/2002, effective 8/30/2002; FAC 2001-19, 69 FR 1051, 1/7/2004, effective 1/12/004; FAC 2001-24, 69 FR 34239, 6/18/2004, effective 6/18/2004; FAC 2001-25, 69 FR 59700, 10/5/2004, effective 10/5/2004; FAC 2005-08, 71 FR 864, 1/5/2006, effective 1/5/2006; FAC 2005-13, 71 FR 57375, 9/28/2006, effective 9/28/2006; FAC 2005-19, 72 FR 46357, 8/17/2007, effective 8/17/2007; FAC 2005-24, 73 FR 10962, 10964, 2/28/2008, effective 2/28/2008; FAC

2005-30, 74 FR 2745, 1/15/2009, effective 1/15/2009; FAC 2005-36, 74 FR 40461, 8/11/2009, effective 8/11/2009; FAC 2005-42, 75 FR 34282, 6/16/2010, effective 6/16/2010; FAC 2005-43, 75 FR 38689, 7/2/2010, effective 7/2/2010; FAC 2005-50, 76 FR 14570, 3/16/2011, effective 3/16/2011; FAC 2005-56, 77 FR 12933, 12935, 3/2/2012, effective 3/2/2012; Correction, 77 FR 14303, 3/9/2012, effective 3/9/2012; Correction, 77 FR 17353, 3/26/2012, effective 3/26/2012; FAC 2005-71, 78 FR 70480, 11/25/2013, effective 11/25/2013; FAC 2005-72, 78 FR 80379, 12/31/2013, effective 1/1/2014; Final rule, 79 FR 4630, 1/29/2014, effective 1/29/2014; FAC 2005-86, 80 FR 81892, 12/31/2015, effective 2/1/2016; FAC 2005-86, 80 FR 81894, 12/31/2015, effective 1/1/2016; FAC 2005-91, 81 FR 67774, 9/30/2016, effective 10/31/2016; FAC 2005-97, 83 FR 3396, 1/24/2018, effective 1/24/2018; FAC 2019-06, 84 FR 47866, 9/10/2019, effective 10/10/2019]

52.222-20 Contracts for Materials, Supplies, Articles, and Equipment Exceeding $15,000.

As prescribed in 22.610, insert the following clause in solicitations and contracts:

CONTRACTS FOR MATERIALS, SUPPLIES, ARTICLES, AND EQUIPMENT EXCEEDING $15,000 (MAY 2014)

If this contract is for the manufacture or furnishing of materials, supplies, articles or equipment in an amount that exceeds or may exceed $15,000, and is subject to 41 U.S.C. chapter 65, the following terms and conditions apply:

(a) All stipulations required by 41 U.S.C. chapter 65 and regulations issued by the Secretary of Labor (41 CFR Chapter 50) are incorporated by reference. These stipulations are subject to all applicable rulings and interpretations of the Secretary of Labor that are now, or may hereafter, be in effect.

(b) All employees whose work relates to this contract shall be paid not less than the minimum wage prescribed by regulations issued by the Secretary of Labor (41 CFR 50-202.2). Learners, student learners, apprentices, and workers with disabilities may be employed at less than the prescribed minimum wage (see 41 CFR 50-202.3) to the same extent that such employment is permitted under section 14 of the Fair Labor Standards Act (41 U.S.C. 6508).

(End of clause)

[FAC 90-32, 60 FR 48206, 9/18/95, effective 10/1/95; FAC 90-43, Interim rule, 61 FR 67408, 12/20/96, effective 12/20/96, finalized without change, FAC 97-1, 62 FR 44802, 8/22/97, effective 10/21/97; FAC 2005-45, 75 FR 53129, 8/30/2010, effective 10/1/2010; FAC 2005-73, 79 FR 24192, 4/29/2014, effective 5/29/2014]

52.222-21 Prohibition of Segregated Facilities.

As prescribed in 22.810(a)(1), insert the following clause:

PROHIBITION OF SEGREGATED FACILITIES (APR 2015)

(a) *Definitions.* As used in this clause—Gender identity has the meaning given by the Department of Labor's Office of Federal Contract Compliance Programs, and is found at*www.dol.gov/ofccp/LGBT/LGBT_FAQs.html.*

Segregated facilities means any waiting rooms, work areas, rest rooms and wash rooms, restaurants and other eating areas, time clocks, locker rooms and other storage or dressing areas, parking lots, drinking fountains, recreation or entertainment areas, transportation, and housing facilities provided for employees, that are segregated by explicit directive or are in fact segregated on the basis of race, color, religion, sex, sexual orientation, gender identity, or national origin because of written or oral policies or employee custom. The term does not include separate or single-user rest rooms or necessary dressing or sleeping areas provided to assure privacy between the sexes.

Sexual orientation has the meaning given by the Department of Labor's Office of Federal Contract Compliance Programs, and is found at *www.dol.gov/ofccp/LGBT/LGBT_FAQs.html.*

(b) The Contractor agrees that it does not and will not maintain or provide for its employees any segregated facilities at any of its establishments, and that it does not and will not permit its employees to perform their services at any location under its control where segregated facilities are maintained. The Contractor agrees that a breach of this clause is a violation of the Equal Opportunity clause in this contract.

(c) The Contractor shall include this clause in every subcontract and purchase order that is subject to the Equal Opportunity clause of this contract.

(End of clause)

[FAC 97-10, 63 FR 70264, 12/18/98, effective 2/16/99; FAC 2005-81, 80 FR 19504, 4/10/2015, effective 4/10/2015; FAC 2005-81, 80 FR 19504, 04/10/2015, effective 04/10/2015; FAC 2005-85, 80 FR 75907, 12/4/2015, effective 2/26/2016]

52.222-22 Previous Contracts and Compliance Reports.

As prescribed in 22.810(a)(2), insert the following provision:

PREVIOUS CONTRACTS AND COMPLIANCE REPORTS (FEB 1999)

The offeror represents that—

(a) It ☐ has, ☐ has not participated in a previous contract or subcontract subject to the Equal Opportunity clause of this solicitation;

(b) It ☐ has, ☐ has not, filed all required compliance reports; and

(c) Representations indicating submission of required compliance reports, signed by proposed subcontractors, will be obtained before subcontract awards.

(End of provision)

[FAC 90-32, 60 FR 48206, 9/18/95, effective 10/1/95; FAC 97-10, 63 FR 70264, 12/18/98, effective 2/16/99]

52.222-23 Notice of Requirement for Affirmative Action To Ensure Equal Employment Opportunity for Construction.

As prescribed in 22.810(b), insert the following provision:

NOTICE OF REQUIREMENT FOR AFFIRMATIVE ACTION TO ENSURE EQUAL EMPLOYMENT OPPORTUNITY FOR CONSTRUCTION (FEB 1999)

(a) The offeror's attention is called to the Equal Opportunity clause and the Affirmative Action Compliance Requirements for Construction clause of this solicitation.

(b) The goals for minority and female participation, expressed in percentage terms for the Contractor's aggregate workforce in each trade on all construction work in the covered area, are as follows:

Goals for minority participation for each trade	Goals for female participation for each trade
[Contracting Officer shall insert goals]	*[Contracting Officer shall insert goals]*

These goals are applicable to all the Contractor's construction work performed in the covered area. If the Contractor performs construction work in a geographical area located outside of the covered area, the Contractor shall apply the goals established for the geographical area where the work is actually performed. Goals are published periodically in the Federal Register in notice form, and these notices may be obtained from any Office of Federal Contract Compliance Programs office.

(c) The Contractor's compliance with Executive Order 11246, as amended, and the regulations in 41 CFR 60-4 shall be based on (1) its implementation of the Equal Opportunity clause, (2) specific affirmative action obligations required by the clause entitled "Affirmative Action Compliance Requirements for Construction," and (3) its efforts to meet the goals. The hours of minority and female employment and training must be substantially uniform throughout the length of the contract, and in each trade. The Contractor shall make a good faith effort to employ minorities and women evenly on each of its projects. The transfer of minority or female employees or trainees from Contractor to Contractor, or from project to project, for the sole purpose of meeting the Contractor's goals shall be a violation of the contract, Executive Order 11246, as amended, and the regulations in 41 CFR 60-4. Compliance with the goals will be measured against the total work hours performed.

(d) The Contractor shall provide written notification to the Deputy Assistant Secretary for Federal Contract Compliance, U.S. Department of Labor, within 10 working days following award of any construction subcontract in excess of $10,000 at any tier for construction work under the contract resulting from this solicitation. The notification shall list the—

(1) Name, address, and telephone number of the subcontractor;

(2) Employer's identification number of the subcontractor;

(3) Estimated dollar amount of the subcontract;

(4) Estimated starting and completion dates of the subcontract; and

(5) Geographical area in which the subcontract is to be performed.

(e) As used in this Notice, and in any contract resulting from this solicitation, the "covered area" is ____ [*Contracting Officer shall insert description of the geographical areas where the contract is to be performed, giving the State, county, and city*].

(End of provision)

[Final rule, 55 FR 38518, 9/18/90; FAC 90-32, 60 FR 48206, 9/18/95, effective 10/1/95; FAC 97-10, 63 FR 70264, 12/18/98, effective 2/16/99]

52.222-24 Preaward On-Site Equal Opportunity Compliance Evaluation.

As prescribed in 22.810(c), insert the following provision:

PREAWARD ON-SITE EQUAL OPPORTUNITY COMPLIANCE EVALUATION (FEB 1999)

If a contract in the amount of $10 million or more will result from this solicitation, the prospective Contractor and its known first-tier subcontractors with anticipated subcontracts of $10 million or more shall be subject to a preaward compliance evaluation by the Office of Federal Contract Compliance Programs (OFCCP), unless, within the preceding 24 months, OFCCP has conducted an evaluation and found the prospective Contractor and subcontractors to be in compliance with Executive Order 11246.

(End of provision)

[FAC 97-10, 63 FR 70264, 12/18/98, effective 2/16/99]

52.222-25 Affirmative Action Compliance.

As prescribed in 22.810(d), insert the following provision:

AFFIRMATIVE ACTION COMPLIANCE (APR 1984)

The offeror represents that (a) it ☐ has developed and has on file, ☐ has not developed and does not have on file, at each establishment, affirmative action programs required by the rules and regulations of the Secretary of Labor (41 CFR 60-1 and 60-2), or (b) it ☐ has not previously had contracts subject to the written affirmative action programs requirement of the rules and regulations of the Secretary of Labor.

(End of provision)

[FAC 90-32, 60 FR 48206, 9/18/95, effective 10/1/95; FAC 97-10, 63 FR 70264, 12/18/98, effective 2/16/99]

52.222-26 Equal Opportunity.

As prescribed in 22.810(e), insert the following clause:

EQUAL OPPORTUNITY (SEP 2016)

(a) *Compensation* means any payments made to, or on behalf of, an employee or offered to an applicant as remuneration for employment, including but not limited to salary, wages, overtime pay, shift differentials, bonuses, commissions, vacation and holiday pay, allowances, insurance and other benefits, stock options and awards, profit sharing, and retirement.

Definitions. As used in this clause- Gender identity has the meaning given by the Department of Labor's Office of Federal Contract Compliance Programs, and is found at *www.dol.gov/ofccp/LGBT/LGBT_FAQs.html.*

Compensation information means the amount and type of compensation provided to employees or offered to applicants, including, but not limited to, the desire of the Contractor to attract and retain a particular employee for the value the employee is perceived to add to the Contractor's profit or productivity; the availability of employees with like skills in the marketplace; market research about the worth of similar jobs in the relevant marketplace; job analysis, descriptions, and evaluations; salary and pay structures; salary surveys; labor union agreements; and Contractor decisions, statements and policies related to setting or altering employee compensation.

Essential job functions means the fundamental job duties of the employment position an individual holds. A job function may be considered essential if—

(1) The access to compensation information is necessary in order to perform that function or another routinely assigned business task; or

(2) The function or duties of the position include protecting and maintaining the privacy of employee personnel records, including compensation information.

Sexual orientation has the meaning given by the Department of Labor's Office of Federal Contract Compliance Programs, and is found at *www.dol.gov/ofccp/LGBT/LGBT_FAQs.html.*

United States means the 50 States, the District of Columbia, Puerto Rico, the Northern Mariana Islands, American Samoa, Guam, the U.S. Virgin Islands, and Wake Island.

(b) (1) If, during any 12-month period (including the 12 months preceding the award of this contract), the Contractor has been or is awarded nonexempt Federal contracts and/or subcontracts that have an aggregate value in excess of $10,000, the Contractor shall comply with this clause, except for work performed outside the United States by employees who were not recruited within the United States. Upon request, the Contractor shall provide information necessary to determine the applicability of this clause.

(2) If the Contractor is a religious corporation, association, educational institution, or society, the requirements of this clause do not apply with respect to the employment of individuals of a particular religion to perform work connected with the carrying on of the Contractor's activities (41 CFR 60-1.5).

(c) (1) The Contractor shall not discriminate against any employee or applicant for employment because of race, color, religion, sex, sexual orientation, gender identity, or national origin. However, it shall not be a violation of this clause for the Contractor to extend a publicly announced preference in employment to Indians living on or near an Indian reservation, in connection with employment opportunities on or near an Indian reservation, as permitted by 41 CFR 60-1.5.

(2) The Contractor shall take affirmative action to ensure that applicants are employed, and that employees are treated during employment, without regard to their race, color, religion, sex, sexual orientation, gender identity, or national origin. This shall include, but not be limited to (i) Employment, (ii) Upgrading, (iii) Demotion, (iv) Transfer, (v) Recruitment or recruitment advertising, (vi) Layoff or termination, (vii) Rates of pay or other forms of compensation, and (viii) Selection for training, including apprenticeship.

(3) The Contractor shall post in conspicuous places available to employees and applicants for employment the notices to be provided by the Contracting Officer that explain this clause.

(4) The Contractor shall, in all solicitations or advertisements for employees placed by or on behalf of the Contractor, state that all qualified applicants will receive consideration for employment without regard to race, color, religion, sex, sexual orientation, gender identity, or national origin.

(5) (i) The Contractor shall not discharge or in any other manner discriminate against any employee or applicant for employment because such employee or applicant has inquired about, discussed, or disclosed the compensation of the employee or applicant or another employee or applicant. This prohibition against discrimination does not apply to 18 instances in which an employee who has access to the compensation information of other employees or applicants as a

part of such employee's essential job functions discloses the compensation of such other employees or applicants to individuals who do not otherwise have access to such information, unless such disclosure is in response to a formal complaint or charge, in furtherance of an investigation, proceeding, hearing, or action, including an investigation conducted by the employer, or is consistent with the Contractor's legal duty to furnish information.

(ii) The Contractor shall disseminate the prohibition on discrimination in paragraph (c)(5)(i) of this clause, using language prescribed by the Director of the Office of Federal Contract Compliance Programs (OFCCP), to employees and applicants by—

(A) Incorporation into existing employee manuals or handbooks; and

(B) Electronic posting or by posting a copy of the provision in conspicuous places available to employees and applicants for employment.

(6) The Contractor shall send, to each labor union or representative of workers with which it has a collective bargaining agreement or other contract or understanding, the notice to be provided by the Contracting Officer advising the labor union or workers' representative of the Contractor's commitments under this clause, and post copies of the notice in conspicuous places available to employees and applicants for employment.

(7) The Contractor shall comply with Executive Order 11246, as amended, and the rules, regulations, and orders of the Secretary of Labor.

(8) The Contractor shall furnish to the contracting agency all information required by Executive Order 11246, as amended, and by the rules, regulations, and orders of the Secretary of Labor. The Contractor shall also file Standard Form 100 (EEO-1), or any successor form, as prescribed in 41 CFR part 60-1. Unless the Contractor has filed within the 12 months preceding the date of contract award, the Contractor shall, within 30 days after contract award, apply to either the regional Office of Federal Contract Compliance Programs (OFCCP) or the local office of the Equal Employment Opportunity Commission for the necessary forms.

(9) The Contractor shall permit access to its premises, during normal business hours, by the contracting agency or the OFCCP for the purpose of conducting on-site compliance evaluations and complaint investigations. The Contractor shall permit the Government to inspect and copy any books, accounts, records (including computerized records), and other material that may be relevant to the matter under investigation and pertinent to compliance with Executive Order 11246, as amended, and rules and regulations that implement the Executive Order.

(10) If the OFCCP determines that the Contractor is not in compliance with this clause or any rule, regulation, or order of the Secretary of Labor, this contract may be canceled, terminated, or suspended in whole or in part and the Contractor may be declared ineligible for further Government contracts, under the procedures authorized in Executive Order 11246, as amended. In addition, sanctions may be imposed and remedies invoked against the Contractor as provided in Executive Order 11246, as amended; in the rules, regulations, and orders of the Secretary of Labor; or as otherwise provided by law.

(11) The Contractor shall include the terms and conditions of this clause in every subcontract or purchase order that is not exempted by the rules, regulations, or orders of the Secretary of Labor issued under Executive Order 11246, as amended, so that these terms and conditions will be binding upon each subcontractor or vendor.

(12) The Contractor shall take such action with respect to any subcontract or purchase order as the Director of OFCCP may direct as a means of enforcing these terms and conditions, including sanctions for noncompliance; *provided*, that if the Contractor becomes involved in, or is threatened with, litigation with a subcontractor or vendor as a result of any direction, the Contractor may request the United States to enter into the litigation to protect the interests of the United States.

(d) Notwithstanding any other clause in this contract, disputes relative to this clause will be governed by the procedures in 41 CFR part 60-1.

(End of clause)

Alternate I (FEB 1999). As prescribed in 22.810(e), add the following as a preamble to the clause:

Notice. The following terms of this clause are waived for this contract: ____ [*Contracting Officer shall list terms*].

[FAC 90-32, 60 FR 48206, 9/18/95, effective 10/1/95; FAC 97-10, 63 FR 70264, 12/18/98, effective 2/16/99; FAC 2001-06, 67 FR 13048, 3/20/2002, effective 4/4/2002; FAC 2005-16, 72 FR 13586, 3/22/2007, effective 3/22/2007; FAC 2005-23, 72 FR 73218, 12/26/2007, effective 12/26/2007; FAC 2005-81, 80 FR 19504, 4/10/2015, effective 4/10/2015; FAC 2005-85, 80 FR 19504, 4/10/2015, effective 4/10/2015; FAC 2005-85, 80 FR 75907, 12/4/2015, effective 12/4/2015; FAC 2005-91, 81 FR 67732, 9/30/2016, effective 9/30/2016; FAC 2005-100, 83 FR 42570, 8/22/2018, effective 8/22/2018]

52.222-27 Affirmative Action Compliance Requirements for Construction.

As prescribed in 22.810(f), insert the following clause:

AFFIRMATIVE ACTION COMPLIANCE REQUIREMENTS FOR CONSTRUCTION (APR 2015)

(a) *Definitions.* As used in this clause—

Covered area means the geographical area described in the solicitation for this contract.

Deputy Assistant Secretary means the Deputy Assistant Secretary for the Office of Federal Contract Compliance Programs, U.S. Department of Labor, or a designee.

Employer identification number means the Federal Social Security number used on the employer's quarterly Federal tax return, U.S. Treasury Department Form 941.

Gender identity has the meaning given by the Department of Labor's Office of Federal Contract Compliance Programs, and is found at *www.dol.gov/ofccp/LGBT/LGBT_FAQs.html.*

Minority means—

(1) American Indian or Alaskan Native (all persons having origins in any of the original peoples of North America and maintaining identifiable tribal affiliations through membership and participation or community identification).

(2) Asian and Pacific Islander (all persons having origins in any of the original peoples of the Far East, Southeast Asia, the Indian Subcontinent, or the Pacific Islands); and

(3) Black (all persons having origins in any of the black African racial groups not of Hispanic origin);

(4) Hispanic (all persons of Mexican, Puerto Rican, Cuban, Central or South American, or other Spanish culture or origin, regardless of race);

Sexual orientation has the meaning given by the Department of Labor's Office of Federal Contract Compliance Programs, and is found at *www.dol.gov/ofccp/LGBT/LGBT_FAQs.html.*

(b) If the Contractor, or a subcontractor at any tier, subcontracts a portion of the work involving any construction trade, each such subcontract in excess of $10,000 shall include this clause and the Notice containing the goals for minority and female participation stated in the solicitation for this contract.

(c) If the Contractor is participating in a Hometown Plan (41 CFR 60-4) approved by the U.S. Department of Labor in a covered area, either individually or through an association, its affirmative action obligations on all work in the plan area (including goals) shall comply with the plan for those trades that have unions participating in the plan. Contractors must be able to demonstrate participation in, and compliance with, the provisions of the plan. Each Contractor or subcontractor participating in an approved plan is also required to comply with its obligations under the Equal Opportunity clause, and to make a good faith effort to achieve each goal under the plan in each trade in which it has employees. The overall good-faith performance by other Contractors or subcontractors toward a goal in an approved plan does not excuse any Contractor's or subcontractor's failure to make good-faith efforts to achieve the plan's goals.

(d) The Contractor shall implement the affirmative action procedures in subparagraphs (g)(1) through (16) of this clause. The goals stated in the solicitation for this contract are expressed as percentages of the total hours of employment and training of minority and female utilization that the Contractor should reasonably be able to achieve in each construction trade in which it has employees in the covered area. If the Contractor performs construction work in a geographical area located outside of the covered area, it shall apply the goals established for the geographical area where that work is actually performed. The Contractor is expected to make substantially uniform progress toward its goals in each craft.

(e) Neither the terms and conditions of any collective bargaining agreement, nor the failure by a union with which the Contractor has a collective bargaining agreement, to refer minorities or women shall excuse the Contractor's obligations under this clause, Executive Order 11246, as amended, or the regulations thereunder.

(f) In order for the nonworking training hours of apprentices and trainees to be counted in meeting the goals, apprentices and trainees must be employed by the Contractor during the training period, and the Contractor must have made a commitment to employ the apprentices and trainees at the completion of their training, subject to the availability of employment opportunities. Trainees must be trained pursuant to training programs approved by the U.S. Department of Labor.

(g) The Contractor shall take affirmative action to ensure equal employment opportunity. The evaluation of the Contractor's compliance with this clause shall be based upon its effort to achieve maximum results from its actions. The Contractor shall document these efforts fully and implement affirmative action steps at least as extensive as the following:

(1) Ensure a working environment free of harassment, intimidation, and coercion at all sites and in all facilities where the Contractor's employees are assigned to work. The Contractor, if possible, will assign two or more women to each construction project. The Contractor shall ensure that foremen, superintendents, and other on-site supervisory personnel are aware of and carry out the Contractor's obligation to maintain such a working environment, with specific attention to minority or female individuals working at these sites or facilities.

(2) Establish and maintain a current list of sources for minority and female recruitment. Provide written notification to minority and female recruitment sources and community organizations when the Contractor or its unions have employment opportunities available, and maintain a record of the organizations' responses.

(3) Establish and maintain a current file of the names, addresses, and telephone numbers of each minority and female off-the-street applicant, referrals of minorities or females from unions, recruitment sources, or community organizations, and the action taken with respect to each individual. If an individual was sent to the union hiring hall for referral and not referred back to the Contractor by the union or, if referred back, not employed by the Contractor, this shall be documented in the file, along with whatever additional actions the Contractor may have taken.

(4) Immediately notify the Deputy Assistant Secretary when the union or unions with which the Contractor has a collective bargaining agreement has not referred back to the Contractor a minority or woman sent by the Contractor, or when the Contractor has other information that the union referral process has impeded the Contractor's efforts to meet its obligations.

(5) Develop on-the-job training opportunities and/or participate in training programs for the area that expressly include minorities and women, including upgrading programs and apprenticeship and trainee programs relevant to the Contractor's employment needs, especially those programs funded or approved by the Department of Labor. The

Contractor shall provide notice of these programs to the sources compiled under subparagraph (g)(2) of this clause.

(6) Disseminate the Contractor's equal employment policy by—

(i) Providing notice of the policy to unions and to training, recruitment, and outreach programs, and requesting their cooperation in assisting the Contractor in meeting its contract obligations;

(ii) Including the policy in any policy manual and in collective bargaining agreements;

(iii) Publicizing the policy in the company newspaper, annual report, etc.;

(iv) Reviewing the policy with all management personnel and with all minority and female employees at least once a year; and

(v) Posting the policy on bulletin boards accessible to employees at each location where construction work is performed.

(7) Review, at least annually, the Contractor's equal employment policy and affirmative action obligations with all employees having responsibility for hiring, assignment, layoff, termination, or other employment decisions. Conduct review of this policy with all on-site supervisory personnel before initiating construction work at a job site. A written record shall be made and maintained identifying the time and place of these meetings, persons attending, subject matter discussed, and disposition of the subject matter.

(8) Disseminate the Contractor's equal employment policy externally by including it in any advertising in the news media, specifically including minority and female news media. Provide written notification to, and discuss this policy with, other Contractors and subcontractors with which the Contractor does or anticipates doing business.

(9) Direct recruitment efforts, both oral and written, to minority, female, and community organizations, to schools with minority and female students, and to minority and female recruitment and training organizations serving the Contractor's recruitment area and employment needs. Not later than 1 month before the date for acceptance of applications for apprenticeship or training by any recruitment source, send written notification to organizations such as the above, describing the openings, screening procedures, and tests to be used in the selection process.

(10) Encourage present minority and female employees to recruit minority persons and women. Where reasonable, provide after-school, summer, and vacation employment to minority and female youth both on the site and in other areas of the Contractor's workforce.

(11) Validate all tests and other selection requirements where required under 41 CFR 60-3.

(12) Conduct, at least annually, an inventory and evaluation at least of all minority and female personnel for promotional opportunities. Encourage these employees to seek or to prepare for, through appropriate training, etc., opportunities for promotion.

(13) Ensure that seniority practices, job classifications, work assignments, and other personnel practices do not have a discriminatory effect by continually monitoring all personnel and employment-related activities to ensure that the Contractor's obligations under this contract are being carried out.

(14) Ensure that all facilities and company activities are nonsegregated except that separate or single-user rest rooms and necessary dressing or sleeping areas shall be provided to assure privacy between the sexes.

(15) Maintain a record of solicitations for subcontracts for minority and female construction contractors and suppliers, including circulation of solicitations to minority and female contractor associations and other business associations.

(16) Conduct a review, at least annually, of all supervisors' adherence to and performance under the Contractor's equal employment policy and affirmative action obligations.

(h) The Contractor is encouraged to participate in voluntary associations that may assist in fulfilling one or more of the affirmative action obligations contained in subparagraphs (g)(1) through (16) of this clause. The efforts of a contractor association, joint contractor-union, contractor-community, or similar group of which the contractor is a member and participant may be asserted as fulfilling one or more of its obligations under subparagraphs (g)(1) through (16) of this clause, provided the Contractor—

(1) Actively participates in the group;

(2) Makes every effort to ensure that the group has a positive impact on the employment of minorities and women in the industry;

(3) Ensures that concrete benefits of the program are reflected in the Contractor's minority and female workforce participation;

(4) Makes a good-faith effort to meet its individual goals and timetables; and

(5) Can provide access to documentation that demonstrates the effectiveness of actions taken on behalf of the Contractor. The obligation to comply is the Contractor's, and failure of such a group to fulfill an obligation shall not be a defense for the Contractor's noncompliance.

(i) A single goal for minorities and a separate single goal for women shall be established. The Contractor is required to provide equal employment opportunity and to take affirmative action for all minority groups, both male and female, and all women, both minority and nonminority. Consequently, the Contractor may be in violation of Executive Order 11246, as amended, if a particular group is employed in a substantially disparate manner.

(j) The Contractor shall not use goals or affirmative action standards to discriminate against any person because of race, color, religion, sex, sexual orientation, gender identity, or national origin.

(k) The Contractor shall not enter into any subcontract with any person or firm debarred from Government contracts under Executive Order 11246, as amended.

(l) The Contractor shall carry out such sanctions and penalties for violation of this clause and of the Equal Opportunity clause, including suspension, termination, and cancellation of existing subcontracts, as may be imposed or ordered under Executive Order 11246, as amended, and its implementing regulations, by the OFCCP. Any failure to carry out these sanctions and penalties as ordered shall be a violation of this clause and Executive Order 11246, as amended.

(m) The Contractor in fulfilling its obligations under this clause shall implement affirmative action procedures at least as extensive as those prescribed in paragraph (g) of this clause, so as to achieve maximum results from its efforts to ensure equal employment opportunity. If the Contractor fails to comply with the requirements of Executive Order 11246, as amended, the implementing regulations, or this clause, the Deputy Assistant Secretary shall take action as prescribed in 41 CFR 60-4.8.

(n) The Contractor shall designate a responsible official to—

(1) Monitor all employment-related activity to ensure that the Contractor's equal employment policy is being carried out;

(2) Submit reports as may be required by the Government; and

(3) Keep records that shall at least include for each employee the name, address, telephone number, construction trade, union affiliation (if any), employee identification number, social security number, race, sex, status (e.g., mechanic, apprentice, trainee, helper, or laborer), dates of changes in status, hours worked per week in the indicated trade, rate of pay, and locations at which the work was performed. Records shall be maintained in an easily understandable and retrievable form; *however*, to the degree that existing records satisfy this requirement, separate records are not required to be maintained.

(o) Nothing contained herein shall be construed as a limitation upon the application of other laws that establish different standards of compliance or upon the requirements for the hiring of local or other area residents (e.g., those under the Public Works Employment Act of 1977 and the Community Development Block Grant Program).

(End of clause)

[Final rule, 55 FR 38518, 9/18/90; FAC 90-32, 60 FR 48206, 9/18/95, effective 10/1/95; FAC 97-10, 63 FR 70264, 12/18/98, effective 2/16/99; FAC 2005-81, 80 FR 19504, 4/10/2015, effective 4/10/2015; FAC 2005-81, 80 FR 19504, 4/10/2015, effective 4/10/2015; FAC 2005-85, 80 FR 75907, 12/4/2015, effective 12/4/2015]

52.222-28 [Reserved]

[Removed and reserved, FAC 97-10, 63 FR 70264, 12/18/98, effective 2/16/99]

52.222-29 Notification of Visa Denial.

As prescribed in 22.810(g), insert the following clause:

NOTIFICATION OF VISA DENIAL (APR 2015)

(a) *Definitions.* As used in this clause-Gender identity has the meaning given by the Department of Labor's Office of Federal Contract Compliance Programs, and is found at *www.dol.gov/ofccp/LGBT/LGBT_FAQs.html.*

Sexual orientation has the meaning given by the Department of Labor's Office of Federal Contract Compliance Programs, and is found at *www.dol.gov/ofccp/LGBT/LGBT_FAQs.html.*

(b) *Requirement to notify.* (1) It is a violation of Executive Order 11246 for a Contractor to refuse to employ any applicant or not to assign any person hired in the United States, Puerto Rico, the Northern Mariana Islands, American Samoa, Guam, the U.S. Virgin Islands, or Wake Island, on the basis that the individual's race, color, religion, sex, sexual orientation, gender identity, or national origin is not compatible with the policies of the country where or for whom the work will be performed (41 CFR 60-1.10).

(2) The Contractor shall notify the U.S. Department of State, Assistant Secretary, Bureau of Political-Military Affairs (PM), 2201 C Street NW., Room 6212, Washington, DC 20520, and the U.S. Department of Labor, Deputy Assistant Secretary for Federal Contract Compliance, when it has knowledge of any employee or potential employee being denied an entry visa to a country where this contract will be performed, and it believes the denial is attributable to the race, color, religion, sex, sexual orientation, gender identity, or national origin of the employee or potential employee.

(End of clause)

[FAC 97-10, 63 FR 70264, 12/18/98, effective 2/16/99; FAC 2001-14, 68 FR 28079, 5/22/2003, effective 6/23/2003; FAC 2005-81, 80 FR 19504, 4/10/2015, effective 4/10/2015; FAC 2005-85, 80 FR 19504, 4/10/2015, effective 4/10/2015; FAC 2005-85, 80 FR 75907, 12/4/2015, effective 12/4/2015]

52.222-30 Construction Wage Rate Requirements—Price Adjustment (None or Separately Specified Method).

As prescribed in 22.407(e), insert the following clause:

CONSTRUCTION WAGE RATE REQUIREMENTS—PRICE ADJUSTMENT (NONE OR SEPARATELY SPECIFIED METHOD) (AUG 2018)

(a) The wage determination issued under the Construction Wage Rate Requirements statute by the Administrator, Wage and Hour Division, U.S. Department of Labor, that is effective for an option to extend the term of the contract, will apply to that option period.

(b) The Contracting Officer will make no adjustment in contract price, other than provided for elsewhere in this contract, to cover any increases or decreases in wages and benefits as a result of—

(1) Incorporation of the Department of Labor's wage determination applicable at the exercise of the option to extend the term of the contract;

(2) Incorporation of a wage determination otherwise applied to the contract by operation of law; or

(3) An increase in wages and benefits resulting from any other requirement applicable to workers subject to the Construction Wage Rate Requirements statute.

(End of clause)

[FAC 2001-01, 66 FR 53478, 10/22/2001, effective 12/21/2001; FAC 2005-73, 79 FR 24192, 4/29/2014, effective 5/29/2014; FAC

2005-100, 83 FR 42571, 8/22/2018, effective 8/22/2018]

52.222-31 Construction Wage Rate Requirements—Price Adjustment (Percentage Method).

As prescribed in 22.407(f), insert the following clause:

CONSTRUCTION WAGE RATE REQUIREMENTS—PRICE ADJUSTMENT (PERCENTAGE METHOD) (AUG 2018)

(a) The wage determination issued under the Construction Wage Rate Requirements statute by the Administrator, Wage and Hour Division, U.S. Department of Labor, that is effective for an option to extend the term of the contract, will apply to that option period.

(b) The Contracting Officer will adjust the portion of the contract price or contract unit price(s) containing the labor costs subject to the Construction Wage Rate Requirements statute to provide for an increase in wages and fringe benefits at the exercise of each option to extend the term of the contract in accordance with the following procedures:

(1) The Contracting Officer has determined that the portion of the contract price or contract unit price(s) containing labor costs subject to the Construction Wage Rate Requirements statute is ____ [*Contracting Officer insert percentage rate*] percent.

(2) The Contracting Officer will increase the portion of the contract price or contract unit price(s) containing the labor costs subject to the Construction Wage Rate Requirements statute by the percentage rate published in ____ [*Contracting Officer insert publication*].

(c) The Contracting Officer will make the price adjustment at the exercise of each option to extend the term of the contract. This adjustment is the only adjustment that the Contracting Officer will make to cover any increases in wages and benefits as a result of—

(1) Incorporation of the Department of Labor's wage determination applicable at the exercise of the option to extend the term of the contract;

(2) Incorporation of a wage determination otherwise applied to the contract by operation of law; or

(3) An increase in wages and benefits resulting from any other requirement applicable to workers subject to the Construction Wage Rate Requirements statute.

(End of clause)

[FAC 2001-01, 66 FR 53478, 10/22/2001, effective 12/21/2001; FAC 2005-73, 79 FR 24192, 4/29/2014, effective 5/29/2014; FAC 2005-100, 83 FR 42571, 8/22/2018, effective 8/22/2018]

52.222-32 Construction Wage Rate Requirements—Price Adjustment (Actual Method).

As prescribed in 22.407(g), insert the following clause:

CONSTRUCTION WAGE RATE REQUIREMENTS—PRICE ADJUSTMENT (ACTUAL METHOD) (AUG 2018)

(a) The wage determination issued under the Construction Wage Rate Requirements statute by the Administrator, Wage and Hour Division, U.S. Department of Labor, that is effective for an option to extend the term of the contract, will apply to that option period.

(b)(1) The Contractor states that if the prices in this contract contain an allowance for wage or benefit increases, such allowance will not be included in any request for contract price adjustment submitted under this clause.

(2) The Contractor shall provide with each request for contract price adjustment under this clause a statement that the prices in the contract do not include any allowance for any increased cost for which adjustment is being requested.

(c) The Contracting Officer will adjust the contract price or contract unit price labor rates to reflect the Contractor's actual increase or decrease in wages and fringe benefits to the extent that the increase is made to comply with, or the decrease is voluntarily made by the Contractor as a result of—

(1) Incorporation of the Department of Labor's Construction Wage Rate Require-

ments wage determination applicable at the exercise of an option to extend the term of the contract; or

(2) Incorporation of a Construction Wage Rate Requirements wage determination otherwise applied to the contract by operation of law.

(d) Any adjustment will be limited to increases or decreases in wages and fringe benefits as described in paragraph (c) of this clause, and the accompanying increases or decreases in social security and unemployment taxes and workers' compensation insurance, but will not otherwise include any amount for general and administrative costs, overhead, or profit.

(e) The Contractor shall notify the Contracting Officer of any increase claimed under this clause within 30 days after receiving a revised wage determination unless this notification period is extended in writing by the Contracting Officer. The Contractor shall notify the Contracting Officer promptly of any decrease under this clause, but nothing in this clause precludes the Government from asserting a claim within the period permitted by law. The notice shall contain a statement of the amount claimed and any relevant supporting data, including payroll records that the Contracting Officer may reasonably require. Upon agreement of the parties, the Contracting Officer will modify the contract price or contract unit price in writing. The Contractor shall continue performance pending agreement on or determination of any such adjustment and its effective date.

(f) Contract price adjustment computations shall be computed as follows:

(1) Computation for contract unit price per single craft hour for schedule of indefinite-quantity work. For each labor classification, the difference between the actual wage and benefit rates (combined) paid and the wage and benefit rates (combined) required by the new wage determination shall be added to the original contract unit price if the difference results in a combined increase. If the difference computed results in a combined decrease, the contract unit price shall be decreased by that amount if the Contractor provides notification as provided in paragraph (e) of this clause.

(2) Computation for contract unit price containing multiple craft hours for schedule of indefinite-quantity work. For each labor classification, the difference between the actual wage and benefit rates (combined) paid and the wage and benefit rates (combined) required by the new wage determination shall be multiplied by the actual number of hours expended for each craft involved in accomplishing the unit-priced work item. The product of this computation will then be divided by the actual number of units ordered in the preceding contract period. The total of these computations for each craft will be added to the current contract unit price to obtain the new contract unit price. The extended amount for the line item in its place will be obtained by multiplying the new unit price by the estimated quantity. If actual hours are not available from the preceding contract period for computation of the adjustment for a specific contract unit of work, the Contractor, in agreement with the Contracting Officer, shall estimate the total hours per craft per contract unit of work.

EXAMPLE: ASPHALT PAVING—CURRENT PRICE $3.38 PER SQUARE YARD

DBA craft	*New WD*		*Hourly rate paid*		*Diff.*		*Actual hrs.*	*Actual units (sq. yard)*		*Increase/ sq. yard*
Equip. Opr.	$18.50	–	$18.00	=	$.50	×	600 hrs./	3,000 sq. yrd.	=	$.10
Truck Driver	$19.00	–	$18.25	=	$.75	×	525 hrs./	3,000 sq. yrd.	=	$.13
Laborer	$11.50	–	$11.25	=	$.25	×	750 hrs./	3,000 sq. yrd.	=	$.06

DBA craft	New WD	Hourly rate paid	Diff.	Actual hrs.	Actual units (sq. yard)	Increase/ sq. yard
Total increase per square yard						*$.29

* Note: Adjustment for labor rate increases or decreases may be accompanied by social security and unemployment taxes and workers' compensation insurance.

Current unit price (per square yard) $3.38
Add DBA price adj. . . . . + .29
New unit price (per square yard) $3.67

[FAC 2001-01, 66 FR 53478, 10/22/2001, effective 12/21/2001; FAC 2005-73, 79 FR 24192, 4/29/2014, effective 5/29/2014; FAC 2005-95, 82 FR 4709, 1/13/2017, effective 1/13/2017; FAC 2005-100, 83 FR 42571, 8/22/2018, effective 8/22/2018]

52.222-33 Notice of Requirement for Project Labor Agreement.

As prescribed in 22.505(a)(1), insert the following provision:

NOTICE OF REQUIREMENT FOR PROJECT LABOR AGREEMENT (MAY 2010)

(a) *Definitions. Labor organization* and *project labor agreement*, as used in this provision, are defined in the clause of this solicitation entitled Project Labor Agreement.

(b) Consistent with applicable law, the offeror shall negotiate a project labor agreement with one or more labor organizations for the term of the resulting construction contract.

(c) Consistent with applicable law, the project labor agreement reached pursuant to this provision shall—

(1) Bind the offeror and all subcontractors engaged in construction on the construction project to comply with the project labor agreement;

(2) Allow the offeror and all subcontractors to compete for contracts and subcontracts without regard to whether they are otherwise parties to collective bargaining agreements;

(3) Contain guarantees against strikes, lockouts, and similar job disruptions;

(4) Set forth effective, prompt, and mutually binding procedures for resolving labor disputes arising during the term of the project labor agreement;

(5) Provide other mechanisms for labor-management cooperation on matters of mutual interest and concern, including productivity, quality of work, safety, and health; and

(6) Fully conform to all statutes, regulations, Executive orders, and agency requirements.

(d) Any project labor agreement reached pursuant to this provision does not change the terms of this contract or provide for any price adjustment by the Government.

(e) The offeror shall submit to the Contracting Officer a copy of the project labor agreement with its offer.

(End of provision)

Alternate I (MAY 2010). As prescribed in 22.505(a)(1), substitute the following paragraphs (b) and (e) for paragraphs (b) and (e) of the basic clause.

(b) The apparent successful offeror shall negotiate a project labor agreement with one or more labor organizations for the term of the resulting construction contract.

(e) The apparent successful offeror shall submit to the Contracting Officer a copy of the project labor agreement prior to contract award.

Alternate II (MAY 2010). As prescribed in 22.505(a)(2), substitute the following paragraph (b) in lieu of paragraphs (b) through (e) of the basic clause:

(b) Consistent with applicable law, if awarded the contract, the offeror shall negotiate a project labor agreement with one or more labor organizations for the term of the resulting construction contract.

[FAC 2005-41, 75 FR 19168, 4/13/2010, effective 5/13/2010]

52.222-34 Project Labor Agreement.

As prescribed in 22.505(b)(1), insert the following clause:

PROJECT LABOR AGREEMENT (MAY 2010)

(a) *Definitions*. As used in this clause—

Labor organization means a labor organization as defined in 29 U.S.C. 152(5).

Project labor agreement means a pre-hire collective bargaining agreement with one or more labor organizations that establishes the terms and conditions of employment for a specific construction project and is an agreement described in 29 U.S.C. 158(f).

(b) The Contractor shall maintain in a current status throughout the life of the contract the project labor agreement entered into prior to the award of this contract in accordance with solicitation provision 52.222-33, Notice of Requirement for Project Labor Agreement.

(c) *Subcontracts*. The Contractor shall include the substance of this clause, including this paragraph (c), in all subcontracts with subcontractors engaged in construction on the construction project.

(End of clause)

Alternate I (MAY 2010). As prescribed in 22.505(b)(2), substitute the following paragraphs (b) through (f) for paragraphs (b) and (c) of the basic clause:

(b) Consistent with applicable law, the Contractor shall negotiate a project labor agreement with one or more labor organizations for the term of this construction contract. The Contractor shall submit an executed copy of the project labor agreement to the Contracting Officer.

(c) Consistent with applicable law, the project labor agreement reached pursuant to this clause shall—

(1) Bind the Contractor and all subcontractors engaged in construction on the construction project to comply with the project labor agreement;

(2) Allow the Contractor and all subcontractors to compete for contracts and subcontracts without regard to whether they are otherwise parties to collective bargaining agreements;

(3) Contain guarantees against strikes, lockouts, and similar job disruptions;

(4) Set forth effective, prompt, and mutually binding procedures for resolving labor disputes arising during the project labor agreement;

(5) Provide other mechanisms for labor-management cooperation on matters of mutual interest and concern, including productivity, quality of work, safety, and health; and

(6) Fully conform to all statutes, regulations, Executive orders, and agency requirements.

(d) Any project labor agreement reached pursuant to this clause does not change the terms of this contract or provide for any price adjustment by the Government.

(e) The Contractor shall maintain in a current status throughout the life of the contract the project labor agreement entered into pursuant to this clause.

(f) *Subcontracts*. The Contractor shall require subcontractors engaged in construction on the construction project to agree to any project labor agreement negotiated by the prime contractor pursuant to this clause, and shall include the substance of paragraphs (d) through (f) of this clause in all subcontracts with subcontractors engaged in construction on the construction project.

[FAC 2005-41, 75 FR 19168, 4/13/2010, effective 5/13/2010; FAC 2005-42, 75 FR 34291, 6/16/2010, effective 6/16/2010]

52.222-35 Equal Opportunity for Veterans.

As prescribed in 22.1310(a)(1), insert the following clause:

EQUAL OPPORTUNITY FOR VETERANS (OCT 2015)

(a) *Definitions*. As used in this clause—

Active duty wartime or campaign badge veteran, *Armed Forces service medal veteran*, *disabled veteran*, *protected veteran*, *qualified disabled veteran*, and *recently separated vet-*

eran have the meanings given at FAR 22.1301.

(b) *Equal opportunity clause.* The Contractor shall abide by the requirements of the equal opportunity clause at 41 CFR 60-300.5(a), as of March 24, 2014. This clause prohibits discrimination against qualified protected veterans, and requires affirmative action by the Contractor to employ and advance in employment qualified protected veterans.

(c) *Subcontracts.* The Contractor shall insert the terms of this clause in subcontracts of $150,000 or more unless exempted by rules, regulations, or orders of the Secretary of Labor. The Contractor shall act as specified by the Director, Office of Federal Contract Compliance Programs, to enforce the terms, including action for noncompliance. Such necessary changes in language may be made as shall be appropriate to identify properly the parties and their undertakings.

(End of clause)

Alternate I (JUL 2014). As prescribed in 22.1310(a)(2), add the following as a preamble to the clause:

Notice: The following term(s) of this clause are waived for this contract: ___ [*List term(s)*].

[FAC 2001-01, 66 FR 53478, 10/22/2001, effective 12/21/2001; FAC 2005-13, 71 FR 57363, 9/28/2006, effective 9/28/2006; FAC 2005-46, 75 FR 60249, 9/29/2010, effective 9/29/2010; FAC 2005-53, 76 FR 39233, 7/5/2011, effective 8/4/2011; FAC 2005-76, 79 FR 43575, 7/25/2014, effective 7/25/2014; FAC 2005-82, 80 FR 26423, 5/7/2015, effective 5/7/2015; FAC 2005-83, 80 FR 38293, 7/2/2015, effective 10/1/2015]

52.222-36 Equal Opportunity for Workers with Disabilities.

As prescribed in 22.1408(a), insert the following clause:

EQUAL OPPORTUNITY FOR WORKERS WITH DISABILITIES (JUL 2014)

(a) *Equal opportunity clause.* The Contractor shall abide by the requirements of the equal opportunity clause at 41 CFR 60-741.5(a), as of March 24, 2014. This clause prohibits discrimination against qualified individuals on the basis of disability, and requires affirmative action by the Contractor to employ and advance in employment qualified individuals with disabilities.

(b) *Subcontracts.* The Contractor shall include the terms of this clause in every subcontract or purchase order in excess of $15,000 unless exempted by rules, regulations, or orders of the Secretary, so that such provisions will be binding upon each subcontractor or vendor. The Contractor shall act as specified by the Director, Office of Federal Contract Compliance Programs of the U.S. Department of Labor, to enforce the terms, including action for noncompliance. Such necessary changes in language may be made as shall be appropriate to identify properly the parties and their undertakings.

(End of clause)

Alternate I (JUL 2014). As prescribed in 22.1408(b), add the following as a preamble to the clause:

Notice: The following term(s) of this clause are waived for this contract: ___ [*List term(s)*].

[FAC 97-5, 63 FR 34058, 6/22/98, effective 6/22/98, finalized without change, FAC 97-9, 63 FR 58587, 10/30/98; FAC 2005-45, 75 FR 53129, 8/30/2010, effective 10/1/2010; FAC 2005-76, 79 FR 43575, 7/25/2014, effective 7/25/2014 FAC 2005-82, 80 FR 26423, 5/7/2015, effective 5/7/2015]

52.222-37 Employment Reports on Veterans.

As prescribed in 22.1310(b), insert the following clause:

EMPLOYMENT REPORTS ON VETERANS (FEB 2016)

(a) *Definitions.* As used in this clause, *active duty wartime or campaign badge veteran, Armed Forces service medal veteran, disabled veteran, protected veteran,* and *recently separated veteran,* have the meanings given in FAR 22.1301.

(b) Unless the Contractor is a State or local government agency, the Contractor shall report at least annually, as required by the Secretary of Labor, on—

(1) The total number of employees in the contractor's workforce, by job category and hiring location, who are protected veterans (*i.e.*, active duty wartime or campaign badge veterans, Armed Forces service medal veterans, disabled veterans, and recently separated veterans);

(2) The total number of new employees hired during the period covered by the report, and of the total, the number of protected veterans (*i.e.*, active duty wartime or campaign badge veterans, Armed Forces service medal veterans, disabled veterans, and recently separated veterans); and

(3) The maximum number and minimum number of employees of the Contractor or subcontractor at each hiring location during the period covered by the report.

(c) The Contractor shall report the above items by filing the VETS-4212 "Federal Contractor Veterans' Employment Report" (see "VETS-4212 Federal Contractor Reporting" and "Filing Your VETS-4212 Report" at *http://www.dol.gov/vets/vets4212.htm*).

(d) The Contractor shall file VETS-4212 Reports no later than September 30 of each year.

(e) The employment activity report required by paragraphs (b)(2) and (b)(3) of this clause shall reflect total new hires, and maximum and minimum number of employees, during the most recent 12-month period preceding the ending date selected for the report. Contractors may select an ending date—

(1) As of the end of any pay period between July 1 and August 31 of the year the report is due; or

(2) As of December 31, if the Contractor has prior written approval from the Equal Employment Opportunity Commission to do so for purposes of submitting the Employer Information Report EEO-1 (Standard Form 100).

(f) The number of veterans reported must be based on data known to the contractor when completing the VETS-4212. The contractor's knowledge of veterans status may be obtained in a variety of ways, including an invitation to applicants to self-identify (in accordance with 41 CFR 60-300.42), voluntary self-disclosure by employees, or actual knowledge of veteran status by the contractor. This paragraph does not relieve an employer of liability for discrimination under 38 U.S.C. 4212.

(g) The Contractor shall insert the terms of this clause in subcontracts of $150,000 or more unless exempted by rules, regulations, or orders of the Secretary of Labor.

(End of clause)

[FAC 2001-01, 66 FR 53478, 10/22/2001, effective 12/21/2001; FAC 2005-13, 71 FR 57363, 9/28/2006, effective 9/28/2006; FAC 2005-46, 75 FR 60249, 9/29/2010, effective 9/29/2010; FAC 2005-53, 76 FR 39233, 7/5/2011, effective 8/4/2011; FAC 2005-76, 79 FR 43575, 7/25/2014, effective 7/25/2014 FAC 2005-82, 80 FR 26423, 5/7/2015, effective 5/7/2015; FAC 2005-83, 80 FR 38293, 7/2/2015, effective 10/1/2015; FAC 2005-85, 80 FR 75908, 12/4/15, effective 2/26/2016; FAC 2005-91, 81 FR 67731, 9/30/2016, effective 9/30/2016]

52.222-38 Compliance with Veterans' Employment Reporting Requirements.

As prescribed in 22.1310(c), insert the following provision:

COMPLIANCE WITH VETERANS' EMPLOYMENT REPORTING REQUIREMENTS (FEB 2016)

By submission of its offer, the offeror represents that, if it is subject to the reporting requirements of 38 U.S.C. 4212(d) (*i.e.*, if it has any contract containing Federal Acquisition Regulation clause 52.222-37, Employment Reports on Veterans), it has filed the most recent VETS-4212 Report required by that clause.

(End of provision)

[FAC 2001-01, 66 FR 53478, 10/22/2001, effective 12/21/2001; FAC 2005-46, 75 FR 60249, 9/29/2010, effective 9/29/2010; FAC 2005-53, 76 FR 39233, 7/5/2011, effective 8/4/2011; FAC 2005-85, 80 FR 75908, 12/4/15, effective 2/26/2016; FAC 2005-91, 81 FR 67731, 9/30/2016, effective 9/30/2016]

52.222-39 [Removed and Reserved]

[FAC 2001-26, 69 FR 76351, 12/20/2004, effective 12/20/2004; FAC 2005-04, 70 FR 33655, 6/8/2005, effective 6/8/2005; FAC 2005-38, 74 FR 65599, 12/10/2009, effective 12/10/2009]

52.222-40 Notification of Employee Rights Under the National Labor Relations Act.

As prescribed in 22.1605, insert the following clause:

NOTIFICATION OF EMPLOYEE RIGHTS UNDER THE NATIONAL LABOR RELATIONS ACT (DEC 2010)

(a) During the term of this contract, the Contractor shall post an employee notice, of such size and in such form, and containing such content as prescribed by the Secretary of Labor, in conspicuous places in and about its plants and offices where employees covered by the National Labor Relations Act engage in activities relating to the performance of the contract, including all places where notices to employees are customarily posted both physically and electronically, in the languages employees speak, in accordance with 29 CFR 471.2(d) and (f).

(1) Physical posting of the employee notice shall be in conspicuous places in and about the Contractor's plants and offices so that the notice is prominent and readily seen by employees who are covered by the National Labor Relations Act and engage in activities related to the performance of the contract.

(2) If the Contractor customarily posts notices to employees electronically, then the Contractor shall also post the required notice electronically by displaying prominently, on any Web site that is maintained by the Contractor and is customarily used for notices to employees about terms and conditions of employment, a link to the Department of Labor's Web site that contains the full text of the poster. The link to the Department's Web site, as referenced in (b)(3) of this section, must read, "Important Notice about Employee Rights to Organize and Bargain Collectively with Their Employers."

(b) This required employee notice, printed by the Department of Labor, may be—

(1) Obtained from the Division of Interpretations and Standards, Office of Labor-Management Standards, U.S. Department of Labor, 200 Constitution Avenue, NW., Room N-5609, Washington, DC 20210, (202) 693-0123, or from any field office of the Office of Labor-Management Standards or Office of Federal Contract Compliance Programs;

(2) Provided by the Federal contracting agency if requested;

(3) Downloaded from the Office of Labor-Management Standards Web site at *http://www.dol.gov/olms/regs/compliance/EO13496.htm;* or

(4) Reproduced and used as exact duplicate copies of the Department of Labor's official poster.

(c) The required text of the employee notice referred to in this clause is located at Appendix A, Subpart A, 29 CFR Part 471.

(d) The Contractor shall comply with all provisions of the employee notice and related rules, regulations, and orders of the Secretary of Labor.

(e) In the event that the Contractor does not comply with the requirements set forth in paragraphs (a) through (d) of this clause, this contract may be terminated or suspended in whole or in part, and the Contractor may be suspended or debarred in accordance with 29 CFR 471.14 and subpart 9.4. Such other sanctions or remedies may be imposed as are provided by 29 CFR part 471, which implements Executive Order 13496 or as otherwise provided by law.

(f) *Subcontracts.* (1) The Contractor shall include the substance of this clause, including this paragraph (f), in every subcontract that exceeds $10,000 and will be performed wholly or partially in the United States, unless exempted by the rules, regulations, or orders of the Secretary of Labor issued pursuant to section 3 of Executive Order 13496 of January 30, 2009, so that such provisions will be binding upon each subcontractor.

(2) The Contractor shall not procure supplies or services in a way designed to avoid the applicability of Executive Order 13496 or this clause.

(3) The Contractor shall take such action with respect to any such subcontract as may be directed by the Secretary of Labor as a means of enforcing such provisions, including the imposition of sanctions for noncompliance.

(4) However, if the Contractor becomes involved in litigation with a subcontractor, or is threatened with such involvement, as a result of such direction, the Contractor may request the United States, through the Secretary of Labor, to enter into such litigation to protect the interests of the United States.

(End of clause)

[FAC 90-40, 61 FR 39186, 7/26/96, effective 8/26/96; FAC 2005-47, 75 FR 77723, 12/13/2010, effective 12/13/2010; FAC 2005-54, 76 FR 68015, 11/2/2011, effective 11/2/2011]

52.222-41 Service Contract Labor Standards.

As prescribed in 22.1006(a), insert the following clause:

SERVICE CONTRACT LABOR STANDARDS (AUG 2018)

(a) *Definitions.* As used in this clause—

Contractor when this clause is used or in any subcontract, shall be deemed to refer to the subcontractor, except in the term *Government Prime Contractor.*

Service employee, means any person engaged in the performance of this contract other than any person employed in a bona fide executive, administrative, or professional capacity, as these terms are defined in Part 541 of Title 29, Code of Federal Regulations, as revised. It includes all such persons regardless of any contractual relationship that may be alleged to exist between a Contractor or subcontractor and such persons.

(b) *Applicability.* This contract is subject to the following provisions and to all other applicable provisions of 41 U.S.C. chapter 37, Service Contract Labor Standards and regulations of the Secretary of Labor (29 CFR Part 4). This clause does not apply to contracts or subcontracts administratively exempted by the Secretary of Labor or exempted by 41 U.S.C. 6702 as interpreted in Subpart C of 29 CFR Part 4.

(c) *Compensation.* (1) Each service employee employed in the performance of this contract by the Contractor or any subcontractor shall be paid not less than the minimum monetary wages and shall be furnished fringe benefits in accordance with the wages and fringe benefits determined by the Secretary of Labor, or authorized representative, as specified in any wage determination attached to this contract.

(2) (i) If a wage determination is attached to this contract, the Contractor shall classify any class of service employee which is not listed therein and which is to be employed under the contract (i.e., the work to be performed is not performed by any classification listed in the wage determination) so as to provide a reasonable relationship (i.e., appropriate level of skill comparison) between such unlisted classifications and the classifications listed in the wage determination. Such conformed class of employees shall be paid the monetary wages and furnished the fringe benefits as are determined pursuant to the procedures in this paragraph (c).

(ii) This conforming procedure shall be initiated by the contractor prior to the performance of contract work by the unlisted class of employee. The Contractor shall submit Standard Form (SF) 1444, Request for Authorization of Additional Classification and Rate, to the Contracting Officer no later than 30 days after the unlisted class of employee performs any contract work. The Contracting Officer shall review the proposed classification and rate and promptly submit the completed SF 1444 (which must include information regarding the agreement or disagreement of the employees' authorized representatives or the employees themselves together with the agency recommendation), and all pertinent information to the Wage and Hour Division, U.S. Department of Labor. The Wage and Hour Division will approve, modify, or disapprove the action or render a final determination in the event of disagreement within 30 days of receipt or will notify the Contracting Officer within 30 days of receipt that additional time is necessary.

(iii) The final determination of the conformance action by the Wage and Hour Division shall be transmitted to the Contracting Officer who shall promptly notify the Contractor of the action taken. Each affected employee shall be furnished by the Contractor with a written copy of such determination or it shall be posted as a part of the wage determination.

(iv) (A) The process of establishing wage and fringe benefit rates that bear a reasonable relationship to those listed in a wage determination cannot be reduced to any single formula. The approach used may vary from wage determination to wage determination depending on the circumstances. Standard wage and salary administration practices which rank various job classifications by pay grade pursuant to point schemes or other job factors may, for example, be relied upon. Guidance may also be obtained from the way different jobs are rated under Federal pay systems (Federal Wage Board Pay System and the General Schedule) or from other wage determinations issued in the same locality. Basic to the establishment of any conformable wage rate(s) is the concept that a pay relationship should be maintained between job classifications based on the skill required and the duties performed.

(B) In the case of a contract modification, an exercise of an option, or extension of an existing contract, or in any other case where a Contractor succeeds a contract under which the classification in question was previously conformed pursuant to paragraph (c) of this clause, a new conformed wage rate and fringe benefits may be assigned to the conformed classification by indexing (*i.e.*, adjusting) the previous conformed rate and fringe benefits by an amount equal to the average (mean) percentage increase (or decrease, where appropriate) between the wages and fringe benefits specified for all classifications to be used on the contract which are listed in the current wage determination, and those specified for the corresponding classifications in the previously applicable wage determination. Where conforming actions are accomplished in accordance with this paragraph prior to the performance of contract work by the unlisted class of employees, the Contractor shall advise the Contracting Officer of the action taken but the other procedures in subdivision (c)(2)(ii) of this clause need not be followed.

(C) No employee engaged in performing work on this contract shall in any event be paid less than the currently applicable minimum wage specified under section 6(a)(1) of the Fair Labor Standards Act of 1938, as amended.

(v) The wage rate and fringe benefits finally determined under this subparagraph (c)(2) of this clause shall be paid to all employees performing in the classification from the first day on which contract work is performed by them in the classification. Failure to pay the unlisted employees the compensation agreed upon by the interested parties and/or finally determined by the Wage and Hour Division retroactive to the date such class of employees commenced contract work shall be a violation of the Service Contract Labor Standards statute and this contract.

(vi) Upon discovery of failure to comply with subparagraph (c)(2) of this clause, the Wage and Hour Division shall make a final determination of conformed classification, wage rate, and/or fringe benefits which shall be retroactive to the date such class or classes of employees commenced contract work.

(3) *Adjustment of Compensation.* If the term of this contract is more than 1 year, the minimum monetary wages and fringe benefits required to be paid or furnished thereunder to service employees under this contract shall be subject to adjustment after 1 year and not less often than once every 2 years, under wage determinations issued by the Wage and Hour Division.

(d) *Obligation to Furnish Fringe Benefits.* The Contractor or subcontractor may discharge the obligation to furnish fringe benefits specified in the attachment or determined under subparagraph (c)(2) of this clause by furnishing equivalent combinations of bona fide fringe benefits, or by making equivalent or differential cash payments, only in accordance with Subpart D of 29 CFR Part 4.

(e) *Minimum Wage.* In the absence of a minimum wage attachment for this contract, neither the Contractor nor any subcontractor under this contract shall pay any person performing work under this contract (regardless of whether the person is a service employee) less than the minimum wage specified by section 6(a)(1) of the Fair Labor Standards Act of 1938. Nothing in this clause shall relieve the Contractor or any subcontractor of any other obligation under law or contract for payment of a higher wage to any employee.

(f) *Successor Contracts.* If this contract succeeds a contract subject to the Service Contract Labor Standards statute under which substantially the same services were furnished in the same locality and service employees were paid wages and fringe benefits provided for in a collective bargaining agreement, in the absence of the minimum wage attachment for this contract setting forth such collectively bargained wage rates and fringe benefits, neither the Contractor nor any subcontractor under this contract shall pay any service employee performing any of the contract work (regardless of whether or not such employee was employed under the predecessor contract), less than the wages and fringe benefits provided for in such collective bargaining agreement, to which such employee would have been entitled if employed under the predecessor contract, including accrued wages and fringe benefits and any prospective increases in wages and fringe benefits provided for under such agreement. No Contractor or subcontractor under this contract may be relieved of the foregoing obligation unless the limitations of 29 CFR 4.1b(b) apply or unless the Secretary of Labor or the Secretary's authorized representative finds, after a hearing as provided in 29 CFR 4.10 that the wages and/or fringe benefits provided for in such agreement are substantially at variance with those which prevail for services of a character similar in the locality, or determines, as provided in 29 CFR 4.11, that the collective bargaining agreement applicable to service employees employed under the predecessor contract was not entered into as a result of arm's length negotiations. Where it is found in accordance with the review procedures provided in 29 CFR 4.10 and/or 4.11 and Parts 6 and 8 that some or all of the wages and/or fringe benefits contained in a predecessor Contractor's collective bargaining agreement are substantially at variance with those which prevail for services of a character similar in the locality, and/or that the collective bargaining agreement applicable to service employees employed under the predecessor contract was not entered into as a result of arm's length negotiations, the Department will issue a new or revised wage determination setting forth the applicable wage rates and fringe benefits. Such determination shall be made part of the contract or subcontract, in accordance with the decision of the Administrator, the Administrative Law Judge, or the Administrative Review Board, as the case may be, irrespective of whether such issuance occurs prior to or after the award of a contract or subcontract (53 Comp. Gen. 401 (1973)). In the case of a wage determination issued solely as a result of a finding of substantial variance, such determination shall be effective as of the date of the final administrative decision.

(g) *Notification to Employees.* The Contractor and any subcontractor under this contract shall notify each service employee commencing work on this contract of the minimum monetary wage and any fringe benefits required to be paid pursuant to this contract, or shall post the wage determination attached to this contract. The poster provided by the Department of Labor (Publication WH 1313) shall be posted in a prominent and accessible place at the worksite. Failure to comply with this requirement is a violation of 41 U.S.C. 6703 and of this contract.

(h) *Safe and Sanitary Working Conditions.* The Contractor or subcontractor shall not permit any part of the services called for by this contract to be performed in buildings or surroundings or under working conditions provided by or under the control or supervision of the Contractor or subcontractor which are unsanitary, hazardous, or dangerous to the health or safety of the service employees. The Contractor or subcontractor shall comply with the safety and health standards applied under 29 CFR Part 1925.

(i) *Records.* (1) The Contractor and each subcontractor performing work subject to the Service Contract Labor Standards statute shall make and maintain for 3 years from the completion of the work, and make them available for inspection and transcription by authorized representatives of the Wage and Hour Division, a record of the following:

(i) For each employee subject to the Service Contract Labor Standards statute—

(A) Name and address and social security number;

(B) Correct work classification or classifications, rate or rates of monetary wages paid and fringe benefits provided, rate or rates of payments in lieu of fringe benefits, and total daily and weekly compensation;

(C) Daily and weekly hours worked by each employee; and

(D) Any deductions, rebates, or refunds from the total daily or weekly compensation of each employee.

(ii) For those classes of service employees not included in any wage determination attached to this contract, wage rates or fringe benefits determined by the interested parties or by the Administrator or authorized representative under the terms of paragraph (c) of this clause. A copy of the report required by subdivision (c) (2) (ii) of this clause will fulfill this requirement.

(iii) Any list of the predecessor Contractor's employees which had been furnished to the Contractor as prescribed by paragraph (n) of this clause.

(2) The Contractor shall also make available a copy of this contract for inspection or transcription by authorized representatives of the Wage and Hour Division.

(3) Failure to make and maintain or to make available these records for inspection and transcription shall be a violation of the regulations and this contract, and in the case of failure to produce these records, the Contracting Officer, upon direction of the Department of Labor and notification to the Contractor, shall take action to cause suspension of any further payment or advance of funds until the violation ceases.

(4) The Contractor shall permit authorized representatives of the Wage and Hour Division to conduct interviews with employees at the worksite during normal working hours.

(j) *Pay Periods.* The Contractor shall unconditionally pay to each employee subject to the Service Contract Labor Standards statute all wages due free and clear and without subsequent deduction (except as otherwise provided by law or regulations, 29 CFR Part 4), rebate, or kickback on any account. These payments shall be made no later than one pay period following the end of the regular pay period in which the wages were earned or accrued. A pay period under this statute may not be of any duration longer than semi-monthly.

(k) *Withholding of Payments and Termination of Contract.* The Contracting Officer shall withhold or cause to be withheld from the Government Prime Contractor under this or any other Government contract with the Prime Contractor such sums as an appropriate official of the Department of Labor requests or such sums as the Contracting Officer decides may be necessary to pay underpaid employees employed by the Contractor or subcontractor. In the event of failure to pay any employees subject to the Service Contract Labor Standards statute all or part of the wages or fringe benefits due under the Service Contract Labor statute, the Contracting Officer may, after authorization or by direction of the Department of Labor and written notification to the Contractor, take action to cause suspension of any further payment or advance of funds until such violations have ceased. Additionally, any failure to comply with the requirements of this clause may be grounds for termination of the right to proceed with the contract work. In such event, the Government may enter into other contracts or arrangements for completion of the work, charging the Contractor in default with any additional cost.

(l) *Subcontracts.* The Contractor agrees to insert this clause in all subcontracts subject to the Service Contract Labor Standards statute.

(m) *Collective Bargaining Agreements Applicable to Service Employees.* If wages to be paid or fringe benefits to be furnished any service employees employed by the Government Prime Contractor or any subcontractor under the contract are provided for in a collective bargaining agreement which is or will be effective during any period in which the contract is being performed, the Government Prime Contractor shall report such fact to the Contracting Officer, together with full information as to the application and accrual of such wages and fringe benefits, including any prospective increase, to service employees engaged in work on the contract, and a copy of the collective bargaining agreement. Such report shall be made upon commencing performance of the contract, in the case of collective bargaining agreements effective at such time, and in the case of such agreements or provisions or amendments thereof effective at a later time during the period of contract performance such agreements shall be reported promptly after negotiation thereof.

(n) *Seniority List.* Not less than 10 days prior to completion of any contract being performed at a Federal facility where service employees may be retained in the performance of the succeeding contract and subject to a wage determination which contains vacation or other benefit provisions based upon length of service with a Contractor (predecessor) or successor (29 CFR 4.173), the incumbent Prime Contractor shall furnish the Contracting Officer a certified list of the names of all service employees on the Contractor's or subcontractor's payroll during the last month of contract performance. Such list shall also contain anniversary dates of employment on the contract either with the current or predecessor Contractors of each such service employee. The Contracting Officer shall turn over such list to the successor Contractor at the commencement of the succeeding contract.

(o) *Rulings and Interpretations.* Rulings and interpretations of the Service Contract Labor Standards statute are contained in Regulations, 29 CFR Part 4.

(p) *Contractor's Certification.* (1) By entering into this contract, the Contractor (and officials thereof) certifies that neither it nor any person or firm who has a substantial interest in the Contractor's firm is a person or firm ineligible to be awarded Government contracts by virtue of the sanctions imposed under 41 U.S.C. 6706.

(2) No part of this contract shall be subcontracted to any person or firm ineligible for award of a Government contract under 41 U.S.C. 6706.

(3) The penalty for making false statements is prescribed in the U.S. Criminal Code, 18 U.S.C. 1001.

(q) *Variations, Tolerances, and Exemptions Involving Employment.* Notwithstanding any of the provisions in paragraphs (b) through (o) of this clause, the following employees may be employed in accordance with the following variations, tolerances, and exemptions, which the Secretary of Labor, pursuant to 41 U.S.C. 6707 prior to its amendment by Pub. L. 92-473, found to be necessary and proper in the public interest or to avoid serious impairment of the conduct of Government business:

(1) Apprentices, student-learners, and workers whose earning capacity is impaired by age, physical or mental deficiency, or injury may be employed at wages lower than the minimum wages otherwise required by 41 U.S.C. 6703(1) without diminishing any fringe benefits or cash payments in lieu thereof required under 41 U.S.C. 6703(2), in accordance with the conditions and procedures prescribed for the employment of apprentices, student-learners, persons with disabilities, and disabled clients of work centers under section 14 of the Fair Labor Standards Act of 1938, in the regulations issued by the Administrator (29 CFR parts 520, 521, 524, and 525).

(2) The Administrator will issue certificates under the statute for the employment of apprentices, student-learners, persons with disabilities, or disabled clients of work centers not subject to the Fair Labor Standards Act of 1938, or subject to different

minimum rates of pay under the two statutes, authorizing appropriate rates of minimum wages (but without changing requirements concerning fringe benefits or supplementary cash payments in lieu thereof), applying procedures prescribed by the applicable regulations issued under the Fair Labor Standards Act of 1938 (29 CFR parts 520, 521, 524, and 525).

(3) The Administrator will also withdraw, annul, or cancel such certificates in accordance with the regulations in 29 CFR Parts 525 and 528.

(r) *Apprentices.* Apprentices will be permitted to work at less than the predetermined rate for the work they perform when they are employed and individually registered in a bona fide apprenticeship program registered with a State Apprenticeship Agency which is recognized by the U.S. Department of Labor, or if no such recognized agency exists in a State, under a program registered with the Office of Apprenticeship Training, Employer, and Labor Services (OATELS), U.S. Department of Labor. Any employee who is not registered as an apprentice in an approved program shall be paid the wage rate and fringe benefits contained in the applicable wage determination for the journeyman classification of work actually performed. The wage rates paid apprentices shall not be less than the wage rate for their level of progress set forth in the registered program, expressed as the appropriate percentage of the journeyman's rate contained in the applicable wage determination. The allowable ratio of apprentices to journeymen employed on the contract work in any craft classification shall not be greater than the ratio permitted to the Contractor as to his entire work force under the registered program.

(s) *Tips.* An employee engaged in an occupation in which the employee customarily and regularly receives more than $30 a month in tips may have the amount of these tips credited by the employer against the minimum wage required by 41 U.S.C. 6703(1), in accordance with section 3(m) of the Fair Labor Standards Act and Regulations 29 CFR Part 531. However, the amount of credit shall not exceed $1.34 per hour beginning January 1, 1981. To use this provision—

(1) The employer must inform tipped employees about this tip credit allowance before the credit is utilized;

(2) The employees must be allowed to retain all tips (individually or through a pooling arrangement and regardless of whether the employer elects to take a credit for tips received);

(3) The employer must be able to show by records that the employee receives at least the applicable Service Contract Labor Standards minimum wage through the combination of direct wages and tip credit; and

(4) The use of such tip credit must have been permitted under any predecessor collective bargaining agreement applicable by virtue of 41 U.S.C. 6707(c).

(t) *Disputes Concerning Labor Standards.* The U.S. Department of Labor has set forth in 29 CFR Parts 4, 6, and 8 procedures for resolving disputes concerning labor standards requirements. Such disputes shall be resolved in accordance with those procedures and not the Disputes clause of this contract. Disputes within the meaning of this clause include disputes between the Contractor (or any of its subcontractors) and the contracting agency, the U.S. Department of Labor, or the employees or their representatives.

(End of clause)

[FAC 84-46, 54 FR 19828, 5/8/89, effective 6/7/89; FAC 2005-04, 70 FR 33662, 6/8/2005, effective 7/8/2005; FAC 2005-21, 72 FR 63076, 11/7/2007, effective 11/7/2007; FAC 2005-30, 74 FR 2724, 1/15/2009, effective 2/17/2009; FAC 2005-73, 79 FR 24192, 4/29/2014, effective 5/29/2014; FAC 2005-100, 83 FR 42571, 8/22/2018, effective 8/22/2018]

52.222-42 Statement of Equivalent Rates for Federal Hires.

As prescribed in 22.1006(b), insert the following clause:

STATEMENT OF EQUIVALENT RATES FOR FEDERAL HIRES (MAY 2014)

In compliance with the Service Contract Labor Standards statute and the regulations of the Secretary of Labor (29 CFR part 4), this clause identifies the classes of service employees expected to be employed under the contract and states the wages and fringe benefits payable to each if they were employed by the contracting agency subject to the provisions of 5 U.S.C. 5341 or 5332.

This Statement is for Information Only: *It is not a Wage Determination*

Employee class	Monetary wage— Fringe benefits
________	________
________	________
________	________
________	________

(End of clause)

[FAC 84-46, 54 FR 19831, 5/8/89, effective 6/7/89; FAC 2005-73, 79 FR 24192, 4/29/2014, effective 5/29/2014]

52.222-43 Fair Labor Standards Act and Service Contract Labor Standards—Price Adjustment (Multiple Year and Option Contracts).

As prescribed in 22.1006(c)(1), insert the following clause:

FAIR LABOR STANDARDS ACT AND SERVICE CONTRACT LABOR STANDARDS—PRICE ADJUSTMENT (MULTIPLE YEAR AND OPTION CONTRACTS) (AUG 2018)

(a) This clause applies to both contracts subject to area prevailing wage determinations and contracts subject to collective bargaining agreements.

(b) The Contractor warrants that the prices in this contract do not include any allowance for any contingency to cover increased costs for which adjustment is provided under this clause.

(c) The wage determination, issued under the Service Contract Act of 1965, as amended, (41 U.S.C. 351, *et seq.*), by the Administrator, Wage and Hour Division, U.S. Department of Labor, current on the anniversary date of a multiple year contract or the beginning of each renewal option period, shall apply to this contract. If no such determination has been made applicable to this contract, then the Federal minimum wage as established by section 6(a)(1) of the Fair Labor Standards Act of 1938, as amended, (29 U.S.C. 206) current on the anniversary date of a multiple year contract or the beginning of each renewal option period, shall apply to this contract.

(d) The contract price, contract unit price labor rates, or fixed hourly labor rates will be adjusted to reflect the Contractor's actual increase or decrease in applicable wages and fringe benefits to the extent that the increase is made to comply with or the decrease is voluntarily made by the Contractor as a result of:

(1) The Department of Labor wage determination applicable on the anniversary date of the multiple year contract, or at the beginning of the renewal option period. For example, the prior year wage determination required a minimum wage rate of $4.00 per hour. The Contractor chose to pay $4.10. The new wage determination increases the minimum rate to $4.50 per hour. Even if the Contractor voluntarily increases the rate to $4.75 per hour, the allowable price adjustment is $.40 per hour;

(2) An increased or decreased wage determination otherwise applied to the contract by operation of law; or

(3) An amendment to the Fair Labor Standards Act of 1938 that is enacted after award of this contract, affects the minimum wage, and becomes applicable to this contract under law.

(e) Any adjustment will be limited to increases or decreases in wages and fringe benefits as described in paragraph (d) of this clause, and the accompanying increases or decreases in social security and unemployment taxes and workers' compensation insurance, but shall not otherwise include any amount for general and administrative costs, overhead, or profit.

(f) The Contractor shall notify the Contracting Officer of any increase claimed under this clause within 30 days after receiving a new wage determination unless this notification period is extended in writing by the Contracting Officer. The Contractor shall promptly notify the Contracting Officer of any decrease under this clause, but nothing in the clause shall preclude the Government from asserting a claim within the period permitted by law. The notice shall contain a statement of the amount claimed and the change in fixed hourly rates (if this is a time-and-materials or labor-hour contract), and any relevant supporting data, including payroll records, that the Contracting Officer may reasonably require. Upon agreement of the parties, the contract price, contract unit price labor rates, or fixed hourly rates shall be modified in writing. The Contractor shall continue performance pending agreement on or determination of any such adjustment and its effective date.

(g) The Contracting Officer or an authorized representative shall have access to and the right to examine any directly pertinent books, documents, papers and records of the Contractor until the expiration of 3 years after final payment under the contract.

(End of clause)

[FAC 84-46, 54 FR 19831, 5/8/89, effective 6/7/89; FAC 2005-14, 71 FR 67779, 11/22/2006, effective 11/22/2006; FAC 2005-36, 74 FR 40460, 8/11/2009, effective 9/10/2009; FAC 2005-73, 79 FR 24192, 4/29/2014, effective 5/29/2014; FAC 2005-100, 83 FR 42571, 8/22/2018, effective 8/22/2018]

52.222-44 Fair Labor Standards Act and Service Contract Labor Standards—Price Adjustment.

As prescribed in 22.1006(c)(2), insert the following clause:

FAIR LABOR STANDARDS ACT AND SERVICE CONTRACT LABOR STANDARDS—PRICE ADJUSTMENT (MAY 2014)

(a) This clause applies to both contracts subject to area prevailing wage determinations and contracts subject to Contractor collective bargaining agreements.

(b) The Contractor warrants that the prices in this contract do not include any allowance for any contingency to cover increased costs for which adjustment is provided under this clause.

(c) The contract price, contract unit price labor rates, or fixed hourly labor rates will be adjusted to reflect increases or decreases by the Contractor in wages and fringe benefits to the extent that these increases or decreases are made to comply with—

(1) An increased or decreased wage determination applied to this contract by operation of law; or

(2) An amendment to the Fair Labor Standards Act of 1938 that is enacted subsequent to award of this contract, affects the minimum wage, and becomes applicable to this contract under law.

(d) Any such adjustment will be limited to increases or decreases in wages and fringe benefits as described in paragraph (c) of this clause, and to the accompanying increases or decreases in social security and unemployment taxes and workers' compensation insurance; it shall not otherwise include any amount for general and administrative costs, overhead, or profit.

(e) The Contractor shall notify the Contracting Officer of any increase claimed under this clause within 30 days after the effective date of the wage change, unless this period is extended by the Contracting Officer in writing. The Contractor shall promptly notify the Contracting Officer of any decrease under this clause, but nothing in the clause shall preclude the Government from asserting a claim within the period permitted by law. The notice shall contain a statement of the amount and the change in fixed hourly rates (if this is a time-and-materials or labor-hour contract) claimed and any relevant supporting data that the Contracting Officer may reasonably require. Upon agreement of the parties, the contract price, contract unit price labor rates, or fixed hourly rates shall be modified in writing. The Contractor shall continue performance pending agreement on or determination of any such adjustment and its effective date.

(f) The Contracting Officer or an authorized representative shall, until the expiration of 3 years after final payment under the contract, have access to and the right to examine any directly pertinent books, documents, papers, and records of the Contractor.

(End of clause)

[FAC 84-46, 54 FR 19831, 5/8/89, effective 6/7/89; FAC 2001-04, 67 FR 6112, 2/8/2002, effective 2/8/2002; FAC 2005-36, 74 FR 40460, 8/11/2009, effective 9/10/2009; FAC 2005-73, 79 FR 24192, 4/29/2014, effective 5/29/2014]

52.222-45 [Reserved]

52.222-46 Evaluation of Compensation for Professional Employees.

As prescribed in 22.1103, insert the following provision:

EVALUATION OF COMPENSATION FOR PROFESSIONAL EMPLOYEES (FEB 1993)

(a) Recompetition of service contracts may in some cases result in lowering the compensation (salaries and fringe benefits) paid or furnished professional employees. This lowering can be detrimental in obtaining the quality of professional services needed for adequate contract performance. It is therefore in the Government's best interest that professional employees, as defined in 29 CFR 541, be properly and fairly compensated. As a part of their proposals, offerors will submit a total compensation plan setting forth salaries and fringe benefits proposed for the professional employees who will work under the contract. The Government will evaluate the plan to assure that it reflects a sound management approach and understanding of the contract requirements. This evaluation will include an assessment of the offeror's ability to provide uninterrupted high-quality work. The professional compensation proposed will be considered in terms of its impact upon recruiting and retention, its realism, and its consistency with a total plan for compensation. Supporting information will include data, such as recognized national and regional compensation surveys and studies of professional, public and private organizations, used in establishing the total compensation structure.

(b) The compensation levels proposed should reflect a clear understanding of work to be performed and should indicate the capability of the proposed compensation structure to obtain and keep suitably qualified personnel to meet mission objectives. The salary rates or ranges must take into account differences in skills, the complexity of various disciplines, and professional job difficulty. Additionally, proposals envisioning compensation levels lower than those of predecessor contractors for the same work will be evaluated on the basis of maintaining program continuity, uninterrupted high-quality work, and availability of required competent professional service employees. Offerors are cautioned that lowered compensation for essentially the same professional work may indicate lack of sound management judgment and lack of understanding of the requirement.

(c) The Government is concerned with the quality and stability of the work force to be employed on this contract. Professional compensation that is unrealistically low or not in reasonable relationship to the various job categories, since it may impair the Contractor's ability to attract and retain competent professional service employees, may be viewed as evidence of failure to comprehend the complexity of the contract requirements.

(d) Failure to comply with these provisions may constitute sufficient cause to justify rejection of a proposal.

(End of provision)

[FAC 90-16, 57 FR 60582, 12/21/92, effective 2/19/93]

52.222-47 [Removed and Reserved]

[FAC 84-46, 54 FR 19831, 5/8/89, effective 6/7/89; FAC 2005-10, 71 FR 36930, 6/28/2006, effective 6/28/2006; FAC 2005-16, 72 FR 13585, 3/22/2007, effective 3/22/2007]

52.222-48 Exemption from Application of the Service Contract Labor Standards to Contracts for Maintenance, Calibration, or Repair of Certain Equipment—Certification.

As prescribed in 22.1006(e)(1), insert the following provision:

EXEMPTION FROM APPLICATION OF THE SERVICE CONTRACT LABOR STANDARDS TO CONTRACTS FOR MAINTENANCE, CALIBRATION, OR REPAIR OF CERTAIN EQUIPMENT—CERTIFICATION (MAY 2014)

(a) The offeror shall check the following certification:

CERTIFICATION

The offeror ☐ does ☐ does not certify that—

(1) The items of equipment to be serviced under this contract are used regularly for other than Government purposes, and are sold or traded by the offeror (or subcontractor in the case of an exempt subcontractor) in substantial quantities to the general public in the course of normal business operations;

(2) The services will be furnished at prices which are, or are based on, established catalog or market prices for the maintenance, calibration, or repair of equipment.

(i) An *established catalog price* is a price included in a catalog, price list, schedule, or other form that is regularly maintained by the manufacturer or the offeror, is either published or otherwise available for inspection by customers, and states prices at which sales currently, or were last, made to a significant number of buyers constituting the general public.

(ii) An *established market price* is a current price, established in the usual course of trade between buyers and sellers free to bargain, which can be substantiated from sources independent of the manufacturer or offeror; and

(3) The compensation (wage and fringe benefits) plan for all service employees performing work under the contract are the same as that used for these employees and equivalent employees servicing the same equipment of commercial customers.

(b) Certification by the offeror as to its compliance with respect to the contract also constitutes its certification as to compliance by its subcontractor if it subcontracts out the exempt services. If the offeror certifies to the conditions in paragraph (a) of this provision, and the Contracting Officer determines in accordance with FAR 22.1003-4(c)(3) that the Service Contract Labor Standards statute—

(1) Will not apply to this offeror, then the Service Contract Labor Standards clause in this solicitation will not be included in any resultant contract to this offeror; or

(2) Will apply to this offeror, then the clause at 52.222-51, Exemption from Application of the Service Contract Labor Standards to Contracts for Maintenance, Calibration, or Repair of Certain Equipment—Requirements, in this solicitation will not be included in any resultant contract awarded to this offeror, and the offeror may be provided an opportunity to submit a new offer on that basis.

(c) If the offeror does not certify to the conditions in paragraph (a) of this provision—

(1) The clause in this solicitation at 52.222-51, Exemption from Application of the Service Contract Labor Standards to Contracts for Maintenance, Calibration, or Repair of Certain Equipment—Requirements, will not be included in any resultant contract awarded to this offeror; and

(2) The offeror shall notify the Contracting Officer as soon as possible, if the Contracting Officer did not attach a Service Contract Act wage determination to the solicitation.

(d) The Contracting Officer may not make an award to the offeror, if the offeror fails to execute the certification in paragraph (a) of this provision or to contact the Contracting Officer as required in paragraph (c) of this provision.

(End of provision)

[FAC 84-46, 54 FR 19832, 5/8/89, effective 6/7/89; FAC 90-32, 60 FR 48206, 9/18/95, effective 10/1/95; FAC 90-41, 61 FR 41466, 8/8/96, effective 8/8/96, finalized without change, FAC 97-3, 62 FR 64912, 12/9/97, effective 2/9/98; FAC 2005-10, 71 FR 36930, 6/28/2006, effective 6/28/2006; FAC 2005-16, 72 FR 13585, 3/22/2007, effective 3/22/2007; FAC 2005-21, 72 FR 63076, 11/7/2007, effective 11/7/2007; FAC 2005-30, 74 FR 2724, 1/15/2009, effective

2/17/2009; FAC 2005-73, 79 FR 24192, 4/29/2014, effective 5/29/2014]

52.222-49 Service Contract Labor Standards—Place of Performance Unknown.

As prescribed in 22.1006(f), insert the following clause:

SERVICE CONTRACT LABOR STANDARDS—PLACE OF PERFORMANCE UNKNOWN (MAY 2014)

(a) This contract is subject to the Service Contract Labor Standards, and the place of performance was unknown when the solicitation was issued. In addition to places or areas identified in wage determinations, if any, attached to the solicitation, wage determinations have also been requested for the following: ____ [*insert places or areas*]. The Contracting Officer will request wage determinations for additional places or areas of performance if asked to do so in writing by ____ [*insert time and date*].

(b) Offerors who intend to perform in a place or area of performance for which a wage determination has not been attached or requested may nevertheless submit bids or proposals. However, a wage determination shall be requested and incorporated in the resultant contract retroactive to the date of contract award, and there shall be no adjustment in the contract price.

(End of clause)

[FAC 84-46, 54 FR 19832, 5/8/89, effective 6/7/89; FAC 2005-10, 71 FR 36930, 6/28/2006, effective 6/28/2006; FAC 2005-16, 72 FR 13585, 3/22/2007, effective 3/22/2007; FAC 2005-73, 79 FR 24192, 4/29/2014, effective 5/29/2014]

52.222-50 Combating Trafficking in Persons.

As prescribed in 22.1705 (a)(1), insert the following clause:

COMBATING TRAFFICKING IN PERSONS (JAN 2019)

(a) *Definitions*. As used in this clause—

Agent means any individual, including a director, an officer, an employee, or an independent contractor, authorized to act on behalf of the organization.

Coercion means—

(1) Threats of serious harm to or physical restraint against any person;

(2) Any scheme, plan, or pattern intended to cause a person to believe that failure to perform an act would result in serious harm to or physical restraint against any person; or

(3) The abuse or threatened abuse of the legal process.

Commercially available off-the-shelf (COTS) item means—

(1) Any item of supply (including construction material) that is—

(i) A commercial item (as defined in paragraph (1) of the definition at FAR 2.101);

(ii) Sold in substantial quantities in the commercial marketplace; and

(iii) Offered to the Government, under a contract or subcontract at any tier, without modification, in the same form in which it is sold in the commercial marketplace; and

(2) Does not include bulk cargo, as defined in 46 U.S.C. 40102(4), such as agricultural products and petroleum products.

Commercial sex act means any sex act on account of which anything of value is given to or received by any person.

Debt bondage means the status or condition of a debtor arising from a pledge by the debtor of his or her personal services or of those of a person under his or her control as a security for debt, if the value of those services as reasonably assessed is not applied toward the liquidation of the debt or the length and nature of those services are not respectively limited and defined.

Employee means an employee of the Contractor directly engaged in the performance of work under the contract who has other than a minimal impact or involvement in contract performance.

Forced labor means knowingly providing or obtaining the labor or services of a person—

(1) By threats of serious harm to, or physical restraint against, that person or another person;

(2) By means of any scheme, plan, or pattern intended to cause the person to believe that, if the person did not perform such labor or services, that person or another person would suffer serious harm or physical restraint; or

(3) By means of the abuse or threatened abuse of law or the legal process.

Involuntary servitude includes a condition of servitude induced by means of—

(1) Any scheme, plan, or pattern intended to cause a person to believe that, if the person did not enter into or continue in such conditions, that person or another person would suffer serious harm or physical restraint; or

(2) The abuse or threatened abuse of the legal process.

Recruitment fees means fees of any type, including charges, costs, assessments, or other financial obligations, that are associated with the recruiting process, regardless of the time, manner, or location of imposition or collection of the fee.

(1) Recruitment fees include, but are not limited to, the following fees (when they are associated with the recruiting process) for—

(i) Soliciting, identifying, considering, interviewing, referring, retaining, transferring, selecting, training, providing orientation to, skills testing, recommending, or placing employees or potential employees;

(ii) Advertising;

(iii) Obtaining permanent or temporary labor certification, including any associated fees;

(iv) Processing applications and petitions;

(v) Acquiring visas, including any associated fees;

(vi) Acquiring photographs and identity or immigration documents, such as passports, including any associated fees;

(vii) Accessing the job opportunity, including required medical examinations and immunizations; background, reference, and security clearance checks and examinations; and additional certifications;

(viii) An employer's recruiters, agents or attorneys, or other notary or legal fees;

(ix) Language interpretation or translation, arranging for or accompanying on travel, or providing other advice to employees or potential employees;

(x) Government-mandated fees, such as border crossing fees, levies, or worker welfare funds;

(xi) Transportation and subsistence costs—

(A) While in transit, including, but not limited to, airfare or costs of other modes of transportation, terminal fees, and travel taxes associated with travel from the country of origin to the country of performance and the return journey upon the end of employment; and

(B) From the airport or disembarkation point to the worksite;

(xii) Security deposits, bonds, and insurance; and

(xiii) Equipment charges.

(2) A recruitment fee, as described in the introductory text of this definition, is a recruitment fee, regardless of whether the payment is—

(i) Paid in property or money;

(ii) Deducted from wages;

(iii) Paid back in wage or benefit concessions;

(iv) Paid back as a kickback, bribe, in-kind payment, free labor, tip, or tribute; or

(v) Collected by an employer or a third party, whether licensed or unlicensed, including, but not limited to—

(A) Agents;

(B) Labor brokers;

(C) Recruiters;

(D) Staffing firms (including private employment and placement firms);

(E) Subsidiaries/affiliates of the employer;

(F) Any agent or employee of such entities; and

(G) Subcontractors at all tiers.

Severe forms of trafficking in persons means—

(1) Sex trafficking in which a commercial sex act is induced by force, fraud, or coercion, or in which the person induced to perform such act has not attained 18 years of age; or

(2) The recruitment, harboring, transportation, provision, or obtaining of a person for labor or services, through the use of force, fraud, or coercion for the purpose of subjection to involuntary servitude, peonage, debt bondage, or slavery.

Subcontract means any contract entered into by a subcontractor to furnish supplies or services for performance of a prime contract or a subcontract.

Subcontractor means any supplier, distributor, vendor, or firm that furnishes supplies or services to or for a prime contractor or another subcontractor.

United States means the 50 States, the District of Columbia, and outlying areas.

(b) *Policy.* The United States Government has adopted a policy prohibiting trafficking in persons including the trafficking-related activities of this clause. Contractors, contractor employees, and their agents shall not—

(1) Engage in severe forms of trafficking in persons during the period of performance of the contract;

(2) Procure commercial sex acts during the period of performance of the contract;

(3) Use forced labor in the performance of the contract;

(4) Destroy, conceal, confiscate, or otherwise deny access by an employee to the employee's identity or immigration documents, such as passports or drivers' licenses, regardless of issuing authority;

(5) (i) Use misleading or fraudulent practices during the recruitment of employees or offering of employment, such as failing to disclose, in a format and language understood by the employee or potential employee, basic information or making material misrepresentations during the recruitment of employees regarding the key terms and conditions of employment, including wages and fringe benefits, the location of work, the living conditions, housing and associated costs (if employer or agent provided or arranged), any significant costs to be charged to the employee or potential employee, and, if applicable, the hazardous nature of the work;

(ii) Use recruiters that do not comply with local labor laws of the country in which the recruiting takes place;

(6) Charge employees or potential employees recruitment fees;

(7) (i) Fail to provide return transportation or pay for the cost of return transportation upon the end of employment—

(A) For an employee who is not a national of the country in which the work is taking place and who was brought into that country for the purpose of working on a U.S. Government contract or subcontract (for portions of contracts performed outside the United States); or

(B) For an employee who is not a United States national and who was brought into the United States for the purpose of working on a U.S. Government contract or subcontract, if the payment of such costs is required under existing temporary worker programs or pursuant to a written agreement with the employee (for portions of contracts performed inside the United States); except that—

(ii) The requirements of paragraphs (b) (7) (i) of this clause shall not apply to an employee who is—

(A) Legally permitted to remain in the country of employment and who chooses to do so; or

(B) Exempted by an authorized official of the contracting agency from the requirement to provide return transportation or pay for the cost of return transportation;

(iii) The requirements of paragraph (b) (7) (i) of this clause are modified for a victim of trafficking in persons who is seeking victim services or legal redress in the country of employment, or for a witness in an enforcement action related to trafficking in persons. The contractor shall provide the return transportation or pay the cost of return transportation in a way that does not obstruct the victim services, legal redress, or witness activity. For example, the contractor shall not only offer return transportation to a witness at a time when the witness is still needed to testify. This paragraph does not apply when the exemptions at paragraph (b) (7) (ii) of this clause apply.

(8) Provide or arrange housing that fails to meet the host country housing and safety standards; or

(9) If required by law or contract, fail to provide an employment contract, recruitment agreement, or other required work document in writing. Such written work document shall be in a language the employee understands. If the employee must relocate to perform the work, the work document shall be provided to the employee at least five days prior to the employee relocating. The employee's work document shall include, but is not limited to, details about work description, wages, prohibition on charging recruitment fees, work location(s), living accommodations and associated costs, time off, round trip transportation arrangements, grievance process, and the content of applicable laws and regulations that prohibit trafficking in persons.

(c) *Contractor requirements.* The Contractor shall—

(1) Notify its employees and agents of—

(i) The United States Government's policy prohibiting trafficking in persons, described in paragraph (b) of this clause; and

(ii) The actions that will be taken against employees or agents for violations of this policy. Such actions for employees may include, but are not limited to, removal from the contract, reduction in benefits, or termination of employment; and

(2) Take appropriate action, up to and including termination, against employees, agents, or subcontractors that violate the policy in paragraph (b) of this clause.

(d) *Notification.* (1) The Contractor shall inform the Contracting Officer and the agency Inspector General immediately of—

(i) Any credible information it receives from any source (including host country law enforcement) that alleges a Contractor employee, subcontractor, subcontractor employee, or their agent has engaged in conduct that violates the policy in paragraph (b) of this clause (see also 18 U.S.C. 1351, Fraud in Foreign Labor Contracting, and 52.203-13(b) (3) (i) (A), if that clause is included in the solicitation or contract, which requires disclosure to the agency Office of the Inspector General when the Contractor has credible evidence of fraud); and

(ii) Any actions taken against a Contractor employee, subcontractor, subcontractor employee, or their agent pursuant to this clause.

(2) If the allegation may be associated with more than one contract, the Contractor shall inform the contracting officer for the contract with the highest dollar value.

(e) *Remedies.* In addition to other remedies available to the Government, the Contractor's failure to comply with the requirements of paragraphs (c), (d), (g), (h), or (i) of this clause may result in—

(1) Requiring the Contractor to remove a Contractor employee or employees from the performance of the contract;

(2) Requiring the Contractor to terminate a subcontract;

(3) Suspension of contract payments until the Contractor has taken appropriate remedial action;

(4) Loss of award fee, consistent with the award fee plan, for the performance period in which the Government determined Contractor noncompliance;

(5) Declining to exercise available options under the contract;

(6) Termination of the contract for default or cause, in accordance with the termination clause of this contract; or

(7) Suspension or debarment.

(f) *Mitigating and aggravating factors.* When determining remedies, the Contracting Officer may consider the following:

(1) *Mitigating factors.* The Contractor had a Trafficking in Persons compliance plan or an awareness program at the time of the violation, was in compliance with the plan, and has taken appropriate remedial actions for the violation, that may include reparation to victims for such violations.

(2) *Aggravating factors.* The Contractor failed to abate an alleged violation or enforce the requirements of a compliance plan, when directed by the Contracting Officer to do so.

(g) *Full cooperation.* (1) The Contractor shall, at a minimum—

(i) Disclose to the agency Inspector General information sufficient to identify the nature and extent of an offense and the individuals responsible for the conduct;

(ii) Provide timely and complete responses to Government auditors' and investigators' requests for documents;

(iii) Cooperate fully in providing reasonable access to its facilities and staff (both inside and outside the U.S.) to allow contracting agencies and other responsible Federal agencies to conduct audits, investigations, or other actions to ascertain compliance with the Trafficking Victims Protection Act of 2000 (22 U.S.C. chapter 78), E.O. 13627, or any other applicable law or regulation establishing restrictions on trafficking in persons, the procurement of commercial sex acts, or the use of forced labor; and

(iv) Protect all employees suspected of being victims of or witnesses to prohibited activities, prior to returning to the country from which the employee was recruited, and shall not prevent or hinder the ability of these employees from cooperating fully with Government authorities.

(2) The requirement for full cooperation does not foreclose any Contractor rights arising in law, the FAR, or the terms of the contract. It does not—

(i) Require the Contractor to waive its attorney-client privilege or the protections afforded by the attorney work product doctrine;

(ii) Require any officer, director, owner, employee, or agent of the Contractor, including a sole proprietor, to waive his or her attorney client privilege or Fifth Amendment rights; or

(iii) Restrict the Contractor from—

(A) Conducting an internal investigation; or

(B) Defending a proceeding or dispute arising under the contract or related to a potential or disclosed violation.

(h) *Compliance plan.* (1) This paragraph (h) applies to any portion of the contract that—

(i) Is for supplies, other than commercially available off-the-shelf items, acquired outside the United States, or services to be performed outside the United States; and

(ii) Has an estimated value that exceeds $500,000.

(2) The Contractor shall maintain a compliance plan during the performance of the contract that is appropriate—

(i) To the size and complexity of the contract; and

(ii) To the nature and scope of the activities to be performed for the Government, including the number of non-United States citizens expected to be employed and the risk that the contract or subcontract will involve services or supplies susceptible to trafficking in persons.

(3) *Minimum requirements.* The compliance plan must include, at a minimum, the following:

(i) An awareness program to inform contractor employees about the Government's policy prohibiting trafficking-related activities described in paragraph (b) of this clause, the activities prohibited, and the actions that will be taken against the employee for violations. Additional information about Trafficking in Persons and examples of awareness programs can be found at the Web site for the Department of State's Office to Monitor and Combat Trafficking in Persons at *http://www.state.gov/j/tip/*.

(ii) A process for employees to report, without fear of retaliation, activity inconsistent with the policy prohibiting trafficking in persons, including a means to make available to all employees the hotline phone number of the Global Human Trafficking Hotline at 1-844-888-FREE and its email address at *help@befree.org*.

(iii) A recruitment and wage plan that only permits the use of recruitment companies with trained employees, prohibits charging recruitment fees to the employee or potential employee, and ensures that wages meet applicable host-country legal requirements or explains any variance.

(iv) A housing plan, if the Contractor or subcontractor intends to provide or arrange housing, that ensures that the housing meets host-country housing and safety standards.

(v) Procedures to prevent agents and subcontractors at any tier and at any dollar value from engaging in trafficking in persons (including activities in paragraph (b) of this clause) and to monitor, detect, and terminate any agents, subcontracts, or subcontractor employees that have engaged in such activities.

(4) *Posting.* (i) The Contractor shall post the relevant contents of the compliance plan, no later than the initiation of contract performance, at the workplace (unless the work is to be performed in the field or not in a fixed location) and on the Contractor's Web site (if one is maintained). If posting at the workplace or on the Web site is impracticable, the Contractor shall provide the relevant contents of the compliance plan to each worker in writing.

(ii) The Contractor shall provide the compliance plan to the Contracting Officer upon request.

(5) *Certification.* Annually after receiving an award, the Contractor shall submit a certification to the Contracting Officer that—

(i) It has implemented a compliance plan to prevent any prohibited activities identified at paragraph (b) of this clause and to monitor, detect, and terminate any agent, subcontract or subcontractor employee engaging in prohibited activities; and

(ii) After having conducted due diligence, either—

(A) To the best of the Contractor's knowledge and belief, neither it nor any of its agents, subcontractors, or their agents is engaged in any such activities; or

(B) If abuses relating to any of the prohibited activities identified in paragraph (b) of this clause have been found, the Contractor or subcontractor has taken the appropriate remedial and referral actions.

(i) *Subcontracts.* (1) The Contractor shall include the substance of this clause, including this paragraph (i), in all subcontracts and in all contracts with agents. The requirements in paragraph (h) of this clause apply only to any portion of the subcontract that—

(A) Is for supplies, other than commercially available off-the-shelf items, acquired outside the United States, or services to be performed outside the United States; and

(B) Has an estimated value that exceeds $500,000.

(2) If any subcontractor is required by this clause to submit a certification, the Contractor shall require submission prior to the award of the subcontract and annually thereafter. The certification shall cover the items in paragraph (h)(5) of this clause.

(End of clause)

Alternate I (MAR 2015). As prescribed in 22.1705(a)(2), substitute the following paragraph in place of paragraph (c)(1)(i) of the basic clause:

(i)(A) The United States Government's policy prohibiting trafficking in persons described in paragraph (b) of this clause; and

(B) The following directive(s) or notice(s) applicable to employees performing work at the contract place(s) of performance as indicated below:

Document Title	Document may be obtained from:	Applies to performance to in/ at:
______	______	______
______	______	______

[*Contracting Officer shall insert title of directive/notice; indicate the document is attached or provide source (such as website link) for obtaining document; and, indicate the contract performance location outside the United States to which the document applies.*]

[FAC 97-26, 66 FR 27305, 5/16/2001, effective 5/16/2001, finalized without change, FAC 2001-04, 67 FR 6112, 2/8/2002, effective 2/20/2002; FAC 2005-09, Interim rule, 71 FR 20301, 4/19/2006, effective 4/19/2006; FAC 2005-19, 72 FR 46335, 8/17/2007, effective 8/17/2007; FAC 2005-30, 74 FR 2741, 1/15/2009, effective 2/17/2009; FAC 2005-80, 80 FR 4967, 1/29/2015, effective 3/2/2015; FAC 2019-01, 83 FR 65466, 12/20/2018, effective 1/22/2019]

52.222-51 Exemption from Application of the Service Contract Labor Standards to Contracts for Maintenance, Calibration, or Repair of Certain Equipment—Requirements.

As prescribed in 22.1006 (e) (2), insert the following clause:

EXEMPTION FROM APPLICATION OF THE SERVICE CONTRACT LABOR STANDARDS TO CONTRACTS FOR MAINTENANCE, CALIBRATION, OR REPAIR OF CERTAIN EQUIPMENT—REQUIREMENTS (MAY 2014)

(a) The items of equipment to be serviced under this contract are used regularly for other than Government purposes, and are sold or traded by the Contractor in substantial quantities to the general public in the course of normal business operations.

(b) The services shall be furnished at prices which are, or are based on, established catalog or market prices for the maintenance, calibration, or repair of equipment.

(1) An *established catalog price* is a price included in a catalog, price list, schedule, or other form that is regularly maintained by the manufacturer or the Contractor, is either published or otherwise available for inspection by customers, and states prices at which sales currently, or were last, made to a significant number of buyers constituting the general public.

(2) An *established market price* is a current price, established in the usual course of trade between buyers and sellers free to bargain, which can be substantiated from sources independent of the manufacturer or Contractor.

(c) The compensation (wage and fringe benefits) plan for all service employees performing work under the contract shall be the same as that used for these employees and for equivalent employees servicing the same equipment of commercial customers.

(d) The Contractor is responsible for compliance with all the conditions of this exemption by its subcontractors. The Contractor shall determine the applicability of this exemption to any subcontract on or before subcontract award. In making a judgment that the exemption applies, the Contractor shall consider all factors and make an affirmative determination that all of the conditions in paragraphs (a) through (c) of this clause will be met.

(e) If the Department of Labor determines that any conditions for exemption in paragraphs (a) through (c) of this clause have not been met, the exemption shall be deemed inapplicable, and the contract shall become subject to the Service Contract Labor Standards statute. In such case, the procedures at 29 CFR 4.123(e)(1)(iv) and 29 CFR 4.5(c) will be followed.

(f) The Contractor shall include the substance of this clause, including this paragraph (f), in subcontracts for exempt services under this contract.

(End of clause)

[FAC 2005-21, 72 FR 63076, 11/7/2007, effective 11/7/2007; FAC 2005-30, 74 FR 2724, 1/15/2009, effective 2/17/2009; FAC 2005-73, 79 FR 24192, 4/29/2014, effective 5/29/2014]

52.222-52 Exemption from Application of the Service Contract Labor Standards to Contracts for Certain Services—Certification.

As prescribed in 22.1006(e)(3), insert the following provision:

EXEMPTION FROM APPLICATION OF THE SERVICE CONTRACT LABOR STANDARDS TO CONTRACTS FOR CERTAIN SERVICES—CERTIFICATION (MAY 2014)

(a) The offeror shall check the following certification:

CERTIFICATION

The offeror ___ does ___ does not certify that—

(1) The services under the contract are offered and sold regularly to non-Governmental customers, and are provided by the offeror (or subcontractor in the case of an exempt subcontract) to the general public in substantial quantities in the course of normal business operations;

(2) The contract services are furnished at prices that are, or are based on, established catalog or market prices. An *established catalog price* is a price included in a catalog, price list, schedule, or other form that is regularly maintained by the manufacturer or the offeror, is either published or otherwise available for inspection by customers, and states prices at which sales currently, or were last, made to a significant number of buyers constituting the general public. An *established market price* is a current price, established in the usual course of ordinary and usual trade between buyers and sellers free to bargain, which can be substantiated from sources independent of the manufacturer or offeror;

(3) Each service employee who will perform the services under the contract will spend only a small portion of his or her time (a monthly average of less than 20 percent of the available hours on an annualized basis, or less than 20 percent of available hours during the contract period if the contract period is less than a month) servicing the Government contract; and

(4) The offeror uses the same compensation (wage and fringe benefits) plan for all service employees performing work under the contract as the offeror uses for these employees and for equivalent employees servicing commercial customers.

(b) Certification by the offeror as to its compliance with respect to the contract also constitutes its certification as to compliance by its subcontractor if it subcontracts out the exempt services. If the offeror certifies to the conditions in paragraph (a) of this provision, and the Contracting Officer determines in accordance with FAR 22.1003-4 (d)(3) that the Service Contract Labor Standards statute—

(1) Will not apply to this offeror, then the Service Contract Labor Standards clause in this solicitation will not be included in any resultant contract to this offeror; or

(2) Will apply to this offeror, then the clause at FAR 52.222-53, Exemption from Application of the Service Contract Labor Standards to Contracts for Certain Services—Requirements, in this solicitation will not be included in any resultant contract awarded to this offer, and the offeror may be provided an opportunity to submit a new offer on that basis.

(c) If the offeror does not certify to the conditions in paragraph (a) of this provision—

(1) The clause of this solicitation at 52.222-53, Exemption from Application of the Service Contract Labor Standards to Contracts for Certain Services—Requirements, will not be included in any resultant contract to this offeror; and

(2) The offeror shall notify the Contracting Officer as soon as possible if the Contracting Officer did not attach a Service Contract Labor Standards wage determination to the solicitation.

(d) The Contracting Officer may not make an award to the offeror, if the offeror fails to execute the certification in paragraph (a) of this provision or to contact the Contracting Officer as required in paragraph (c) of this provision.

(End of provision)

[FAC 2005-21, 72 FR 63076, 11/7/2007, effective 11/7/2007; FAC 2005-30, 74 FR 2724, 1/15/2009, effective 2/17/2009; FAC 2005-73, 79 FR 24192, 4/29/2014, effective 5/29/2014]

52.222-53 Exemption from Application of the Service Contract Labor Standards to Contracts for Certain Services—Requirements.

As prescribed in 22.1006(e)(4), insert the following clause:

EXEMPTION FROM APPLICATION OF THE SERVICE CONTRACT LABOR STANDARDS TO CONTRACTS FOR CERTAIN SERVICES—REQUIREMENTS (MAY 2014)

(a) The services under this contract are offered and sold regularly to non-Governmental customers, and are provided by the Contractor to the general public in substantial quantities in the course of normal business operations.

(b) The contract services are furnished at prices that are, or are based on, established catalog or market prices. An *established catalog price* is a price included in a catalog, price list, schedule, or other form that is regularly maintained by the manufacturer or the Contractor, is either published or otherwise available for inspection by customers, and states prices at which sales currently, or were last, made to a significant number of buyers constituting the general public. An *established market price* is a current price, established in the usual course of ordinary and usual trade between buyers and sellers free to bargain, which can be substantiated from sources independent of the manufacturer or Contractor.

(c) Each service employee who will perform the services under the contract will spend only a small portion of his or her time (a monthly average of less than 20 percent of the available hours on an annualized basis, or less than 20 percent of available hours during the contract period if the contract period is less than a month) servicing the Government contract.

(d) The Contractor uses the same compensation (wage and fringe benefits) plan for all service employees performing work under the contract as the Contractor uses for these employees and for equivalent employees servicing commercial customers.

(e) (1) Except for services identified in FAR 22.1003-4 (d)(1)(iv), the subcontractor shall be selected for award based on other factors in addition to price or cost with the combination of other factors at least as important as price or cost; or

(2) A subcontract for exempt services shall be awarded on a sole source basis.

(f) The Contractor is responsible for compliance with all the conditions of this exemption by its subcontractors. The Contractor shall determine in advance, based on the nature of the subcontract requirements and knowledge of the practices of likely subcontractors, that all or nearly all likely subcontractors will meet the conditions in paragraphs (a) through (d) of this clause. If the services are currently being performed under a subcontract, the Contractor shall consider the practices of the existing subcontractor in making a determination regarding the conditions in paragraphs (a) through (d) of this clause. If the Contractor has reason to doubt the validity of the certification, the requirements of the Service Contract Labor Standards statute shall be included in the subcontract.

(g) If the Department of Labor determines that any conditions for exemption at paragraphs (a) through (e) of this clause have not been met, the exemption shall be deemed inapplicable, and the contract shall become subject to the Service Contract Labor Standards statute. In such case, the procedures in at 29 CFR 4.123(e)(2)(iii) and 29 CFR 4.5(c) will be followed.

(h) The Contractor shall include the substance of this clause, including this paragraph (h), in subcontracts for exempt services under this contract.

(End of clause)

[FAC 2005-21, 72 FR 63076, 11/7/2007, effective 11/7/2007; FAC 2005-30, 74 FR 2724, 1/15/2009, effective 2/17/2009; FAC 2005-73, 79 FR 24192, 4/29/2014, effective 5/29/2014]

52.222-54 Employment Eligibility Verification.

As prescribed in 22.1803, insert the following clause:

EMPLOYMENT ELIGIBILITY VERIFICATION (OCT 2015)

(a) *Definitions.* As used in this clause—*Commercially available off-the-shelf (COTS) item*—

(1) Means any item of supply that is—

(i) A commercial item (as defined in paragraph (1) of the definition at 2.101);

(ii) Sold in substantial quantities in the commercial marketplace; and

(iii) Offered to the Government, without modification, in the same form in which it is sold in the commercial marketplace; and

(2) Does not include bulk cargo, as defined in 46 U.S.C. 40102(4), such as agricultural products and petroleum products. Per 46 CFR 525.1(c)(2), *bulk cargo* means cargo that is loaded and carried in bulk onboard ship without mark or count, in a loose unpackaged form, having homogenous characteristics. Bulk cargo loaded into intermodal equipment, except LASH or Seabee barges, is subject to mark and count and, therefore, ceases to be bulk cargo.

Employee assigned to the contract means an employee who was hired after November 6, 1986 (after November 27, 2009, in the Commonwealth of the Northern Mariana Islands), who is directly performing work, in the United States, under a contract that is required to include the clause prescribed at 22.1803. An employee is not considered to be directly performing work under a contract if the employee—

(1) Normally performs support work, such as indirect or overhead functions; and

(2) Does not perform any substantial duties applicable to the contract.

Subcontract means any contract, as defined in 2.101, entered into by a subcontractor to furnish supplies or services for performance of a prime contract or a subcontract. It includes but is not limited to purchase orders, and changes and modifications to purchase orders.

Subcontractor means any supplier, distributor, vendor, or firm that furnishes supplies or services to or for a prime Contractor or another subcontractor.

United States, as defined in 8 U.S.C. 1101(a)(38), means the 50 States, the District of Columbia, Puerto Rico, Guam, the Commonwealth of the Northern Mariana Islands, and the U.S. Virgin Islands.

(b) *Enrollment and verification requirements.* (1) If the Contractor is not enrolled as a Federal Contractor in E-Verify at time of contract award, the Contractor shall—

(i) *Enroll.* Enroll as a Federal Contractor in the E-Verify program within 30 calendar days of contract award;

(ii) *Verify all new employees.* Within 90 calendar days of enrollment in the E-Verify program, begin to use E-Verify to initiate verification of employment eligibility of all new hires of the Contractor, who are working in the United States, whether or not assigned to the contract, within 3 business days after the date of hire (but see paragraph (b)(3) of this section); and

(iii) *Verify employees assigned to the contract.* For each employee assigned to the contract, initiate verification within 90 calendar days after date of enrollment or within 30 calendar days of the employee's assignment to the contract, whichever date is later (but see paragraph (b)(4) of this section).

(2) If the Contractor is enrolled as a Federal Contractor in E-Verify at time of contract award, the Contractor shall use E-Verify to initiate verification of employment eligibility of—

(i) *All new employees.* (A) *Enrolled 90 calendar days or more.* The Contractor shall initiate verification of all new hires of the Contractor, who are working in the United States, whether or not assigned to the contract, within 3 business days after the date of hire (but see paragraph (b)(3) of this section); or

(B) *Enrolled less than 90 calendar days.* Within 90 calendar days after enrollment as a Federal Contractor in E-Verify, the Contractor shall initiate verification of all new hires of the Contractor, who are working in the United States, whether or not assigned to the contract, within 3 business days after the date of hire (but see paragraph (b)(3) of this section); or

(ii) *Employees assigned to the contract.* For each employee assigned to the contract, the Contractor shall initiate verification within 90 calendar days after date of contract award or within 30 days after assignment to the contract, whichever date is later (but see paragraph (b)(4) of this section).

(3) If the Contractor is an institution of higher education (as defined at 20 U.S.C. 1001(a)); a State or local government or the government of a Federally recognized Indian tribe; or a surety performing under a takeover agreement entered into with a Federal agency pursuant to a performance bond, the Contractor may choose to verify only employees assigned to the contract, whether existing employees or new hires. The Contractor shall follow the applicable verification requirements at (b)(1) or (b)(2), respectively, except that any requirement for verification of new employees applies only to new employees assigned to the contract.

(4) *Option to verify employment eligibility of all employees.* The Contractor may elect to verify all existing employees hired after November 6, 1986 (after November 27, 2009, in the Commonwealth of the Northern Mariana Islands), rather than just those employees assigned to the contract. The Contractor shall initiate verification for each existing employee working in the United States who was hired after November 6, 1986 (after November 27, 2009, in the Commonwealth of the Northern Mariana Islands), within 180 calendar days of—

(i) Enrollment in the E-Verify program; or

(ii) Notification to E-Verify Operations of the Contractor's decision to exercise this option, using the contact information provided in the E-Verify program Memorandum of Understanding (MOU).

(5) The Contractor shall comply, for the period of performance of this contract, with the requirements of the E-Verify program MOU.

(i) The Department of Homeland Security (DHS) or the Social Security Administration (SSA) may terminate the Contractor's MOU and deny access to the E-Verify system in accordance with the terms of the MOU. In such case, the Contractor will be referred to a suspension or debarment official.

(ii) During the period between termination of the MOU and a decision by the suspension or debarment official whether to suspend or debar, the Contractor is excused from its obligations under paragraph (b) of this clause. If the suspension or debarment official determines not to suspend or debar the Contractor, then the Contractor must reenroll in E-Verify.

(c) *Web site.* Information on registration for and use of the E-Verify program can be obtained via the Internet at the Department of Homeland Security Web site: *http://www.dhs.gov/E-Verify.*

(d) *Individuals previously verified.* The Contractor is not required by this clause to perform additional employment verification using E-Verify for any employee—

(1) Whose employment eligibility was previously verified by the Contractor through the E-Verify program;

(2) Who has been granted and holds an active U.S. Government security clearance for access to confidential, secret, or top secret information in accordance with the National Industrial Security Program Operating Manual; or

(3) Who has undergone a completed background investigation and been issued credentials pursuant to Homeland Security Presidential Directive (HSPD)-12, Policy for a Common Identification Standard for Federal Employees and Contractors.

(e) *Subcontracts.* The Contractor shall include the requirements of this clause, including this paragraph (e) (appropriately modified for identification of the parties), in each subcontract that—

(1) *Is for*—(i) Commercial or noncommercial services (except for commercial services that are part of the purchase of a COTS item (or an item that would be a COTS item, but for minor modifications), performed by the COTS provider, and are normally provided for that COTS item); or

(ii) Construction;

(2) Has a value of more than $3,500 and

(3) Includes work performed in the United States.

(End of clause)

[FAC 2005-29, 73 FR 67651, 11/14/2008, effective 1/15/2009; Correction, 73 FR 72241, 11/26/2008, effective 1/15/2009; Amendment-1, FAC 2005-29, 74 FR 1937, 1/14/2009, effective 1/19/2009; Amendment-2, FAC 2005-29, 74 FR 5621, 1/30/2009, effective 5/21/2009; Amendment-3, FAC 2005-29, 74 FR 17793, 4/17/2009, effective 6/30/2009; Amendment-4, FAC 2005-29, 74 FR 26981, 6/5/2009, effective 9/8/2009; FAC 2005-60, 77 FR 44065, 7/26/2012, effective 7/26/2012; FAC 2005-69, 78 FR 46795, 8/1/2013, effective 8/1/2013; FAC 2005-83, 80 FR 38293, 7/2/2015, effective 10/1/2015]

52.222-55 Minimum Wages Under Executive Order 13658.

As prescribed in 22.1906, insert the following clause:

MINIMUM WAGES UNDER EXECUTIVE ORDER 13658 (DEC 2015)

(a) *Definitions.* As used in this clause —

United States means the 50 states and the District of Columbia.

Worker—

(1) Means any person engaged in performing work on, or in connection with, a contract covered by Executive Order 13658, and—

(i) Whose wages under such contract are governed by the Fair Labor Standards Act (29 U.S.C. chapter 8), the Service Contract Labor Standards statute (41 U.S.C. chapter 67), or the Wage Rate Requirements (Construction) statute (40 U.S.C. chapter 31, subchapter IV);

(ii) Other than individuals employed in a bona fide executive, administrative, or professional capacity, as those terms are defined in 29 CFR part 541; and

(iii) Regardless of the contractual relationship alleged to exist between the individual and the employer.

(2) Includes workers performing on, or in connection with, the contract whose wages are calculated pursuant to special certificates issued under 29 U.S.C. 214(c).

(3) Also includes any person working on, or in connection with, the contract and individually registered in a bona fide apprenticeship or training program registered with the Department of Labor's Employment and Training Administration, Office of Apprenticeship, or with a State Apprenticeship Agency recognized by the Office of Apprenticeship.

(b) *Executive Order Minimum Wage rate.* (1) The Contractor shall pay to workers, while performing in the United States, and performing on, or in connection with, this contract, a minimum hourly wage rate of $10.10 per hour beginning January 1, 2015.

(2) The Contractor shall adjust the minimum wage paid, if necessary, beginning January 1, 2016, and annually thereafter, to meet the applicable annual E.O. minimum wage. The Administrator of the Department of Labor's Wage and Hour Division (the Administrator) will publish annual determinations in the Federal Register no later than 90 days before the effective date of the new E.O. minimum wage rate. The Administrator will also publish the applicable E.O. minimum wage on *www.wdol.gov* (or any successor Web site), and a general notice on all wage determinations issued under the Service Contract Labor Standards statute or the Wage Rate Requirements (Construction) statute, that will provide information on the E.O. minimum wage and how to obtain annual updates. The applicable published E.O. minimum wage is incorporated by reference into this contract.

(3)(i) The Contractor may request a price adjustment only after the effective date of the new annual E.O. minimum wage determination. Prices will be adjusted only for increased labor costs (including subcontractor labor costs) as a result of an increase in the annual E.O. minimum wage, and for associated labor costs (including those for subcontractors). Associated labor costs shall include increases or decreases that result from changes in social security and unemployment taxes and workers' compensation insurance, but will not otherwise include any amount for general and administrative costs, overhead, or profit.

(ii) Subcontractors may be entitled to adjustments due to the new minimum wage, pursuant to paragraph (b)(2). Contractors shall consider any subcontractor requests for such price adjustment.

(iii) The Contracting Officer will not adjust the contract price under this clause for any costs other than those identified in paragraph (b)(3)(i) of this clause, and will not provide duplicate price adjustments with any price adjustment under clauses implementing the Service Contract Labor Standards statute or the Wage Rate Requirements (Construction) statute.

(4) The Contractor warrants that the prices in this contract do not include allowance for any contingency to cover increased costs for which adjustment is provided under this clause.

(5) A pay period under this clause may not be longer than semi-monthly, but may be shorter to comply with any applicable law or other requirement under this contract establishing a shorter pay period. Workers shall be paid no later than one pay period following the end of the regular pay period in which such wages were earned or accrued.

(6) The Contractor shall pay, unconditionally to each worker, all wages due free and clear without subsequent rebate or kickback. The Contractor may make deductions that reduce a worker's wages below the E.O. minimum wage rate only if done in accordance with 29 CFR 10.23, Deductions.

(7) The Contractor shall not discharge any part of its minimum wage obligation under this clause by furnishing fringe benefits or, with respect to workers whose wages are governed by the Service Contract Labor Standards statute, the cash equivalent thereof.

(8) Nothing in this clause shall excuse the Contractor from compliance with any applicable Federal or State prevailing wage law or any applicable law or municipal ordinance establishing a minimum wage higher than the E.O. minimum wage. However, wage increases under such other laws or municipal ordinances are not subject to price adjustment under this subpart.

(9) The Contractor shall pay the E.O. minimum wage rate whenever it is higher than any applicable collective bargaining agreement(s) wage rate.

(10) The Contractor shall follow the policies and procedures in 29 CFR 10.24(b) and 10.28 for treatment of workers engaged in an occupation in which they customarily and regularly receive more than $30 a month in tips.

(c)(1) This clause applies to workers as defined in paragraph (a). As provided in that definition—

(i) Workers are covered regardless of the contractual relationship alleged to exist between the contractor or subcontractor and the worker;

(ii) Workers with disabilities whose wages are calculated pursuant to special certificates issued under 29 U.S.C. 214(c) are covered; and

(iii) Workers who are registered in a bona fide apprenticeship program or training program registered with the Department of Labor's Employment and Training Administration, Office of Apprenticeship, or with a State Apprenticeship Agency recognized by the Office of Apprenticeship, are covered.

(2) This clause does not apply to—

(i) Fair Labor Standards Act (FLSA)-covered individuals performing in connection with contracts covered by the E.O., i.e. those individuals who perform duties necessary to the performance of the contract, but who are not directly engaged in performing the specific work called for by the contract, and who spend less than 20 percent of their hours worked in a particular workweek performing in connection with such contracts;

(ii) Individuals exempted from the minimum wage requirements of the FLSA under 29 U.S.C. 213(a) and 214(a) and (b), unless otherwise covered by the Service Contract Labor Standards statute, or the Wage Rate Requirements (Construction) statute. These individuals include but are not limited to—

(A) Learners, apprentices, or messengers whose wages are calculated pursuant to special certificates issued under 29 U.S.C. 214(a).

(B) Students whose wages are calculated pursuant to special certificates issued under 29 U.S.C. 214(b).

(C) Those employed in a bona fide executive, administrative, or professional capacity (29 U.S.C. 213(a)(1) and 29 CFR part 541).

(d) *Notice*. The Contractor shall notify all workers performing work on, or in connection with, this contract of the applicable E.O. minimum wage rate under this clause. With respect to workers covered by the Service Contract Labor Standards statute or the Wage Rate Requirements (Construction) statute, the Contractor may meet this requirement by posting, in a prominent and accessible place at the worksite, the applicable wage determination under those statutes. With respect to workers whose wages are governed by the FLSA, the Contractor shall post notice, utilizing the poster provided by the Administrator, which can be obtained at *www.dol.gov/whd/govcontracts*, in a prominent and accessible place at the worksite. Contractors that customarily post notices to workers electronically may post the notice electronically provided the electronic posting is displayed prominently on any Web site that is maintained by the contractor, whether external or internal, and customarily used for notices to workers about terms and conditions of employment.

(e) *Payroll Records*. (1) The Contractor shall make and maintain records, for three years after completion of the work, containing the following information for each worker:

(i) Name, address, and social security number;

(ii) The worker's occupation(s) or classification(s);

(iii) The rate or rates of wages paid;

(iv) The number of daily and weekly hours worked by each worker;

(v) Any deductions made; and

(vi) Total wages paid.

(2) The Contractor shall make records pursuant to paragraph (e)(1) of this clause available for inspection and transcription by authorized representatives of the Administrator. The Contractor shall also make such records available upon request of the Contracting Officer.

(3) The Contractor shall make a copy of the contract available, as applicable, for inspection or transcription by authorized representatives of the Administrator.

(4) Failure to comply with this paragraph (e) shall be a violation of 29 CFR 10.26 and this contract. Upon direction of the Administrator or upon the Contracting Officer's own action, payment shall be withheld until such time as the noncompliance is corrected.

(5) Nothing in this clause limits or otherwise modifies the Contractor's payroll and recordkeeping obligations, if any, under the Service Contract Labor Standards statute, the Wage Rate Requirements (Construction) statute, the Fair Labor Standards Act, or any other applicable law.

(f) *Access*. The Contractor shall permit authorized representatives of the Administrator to conduct investigations, including interviewing workers at the worksite during normal working hours.

(g) *Withholding*. The Contracting Officer, upon his or her own action or upon written request of the Administrator, will withhold funds or cause funds to be withheld, from the Contractor under this or any other Federal contract with the same Contractor, sufficient to pay workers the full amount of wages required by this clause.

(h) *Disputes*. Department of Labor has set forth in 29 CFR 10.51, Disputes concerning contractor compliance, the procedures for resolving disputes concerning a contractor's compliance with Department of Labor regulations at 29 CFR part 10. Such disputes shall be resolved in accordance with those procedures and not the Disputes clause of this contract. These disputes include disputes between the Contractor (or any of its subcontractors) and the contracting agency, the Department of Labor, or the workers or their representatives.

(i) *Antiretaliation*. The Contractor shall not discharge or in any other manner discriminate against any worker because such worker has filed any complaint or instituted or caused to be instituted any proceeding under or related to compliance with the E.O. or this clause, or has testified or is about to testify in any such proceeding.

(j) *Subcontractor compliance*. The Contractor is responsible for subcontractor compliance with the requirements of this clause and may be held liable for unpaid wages due subcontractor workers.

(k) *Subcontracts*. The Contractor shall include the substance of this clause, including this paragraph (k) in all subcontracts, regardless of dollar value, that are subject to the Service Contract Labor Standards statute or the Wage Rate Requirements (Construction) statute, and are to be performed in whole or in part in the United States.

(End of clause)

[FAC 2005-79, 79 FR 74544, 12/15/2014, effective 12/15/2014; FAC 2005-85, 80 FR 75915, 12/4/2015, effective 12/4/2015]

52.222-56 Certification Regarding Trafficking in Persons Compliance Plan.

As prescribed in 22.1705(b), insert the following provision:

CERTIFICATION REGARDING TRAFFICKING IN PERSONS COMPLIANCE PLAN (MAR 2015)

(a) The term *commercially available off-the-shelf (COTS) item*, is defined in the clause of this solicitation entitled *Combating Trafficking in Persons* (FAR clause 52.222-50).

(b) The apparent successful Offeror shall submit, prior to award, a certification, as specified in paragraph (c) of this provision, for the portion (if any) of the contract that—

(1) Is for supplies, other than commercially available off-the-shelf items, to be acquired outside the United States, or services to be performed outside the United States; and

(2) Has an estimated value that exceeds $500,000.

(c) The certification shall state that—

(1) It has implemented a compliance plan to prevent any prohibited activities identified in paragraph (b) of the clause at 52.222-50, Combating Trafficking in Persons, and to monitor, detect, and terminate the contract with a subcontractor engaging in prohibited activities identified at paragraph (b) of the clause at 52.222-50, Combating Trafficking in Persons; and

(2) After having conducted due diligence, either—

(i) To the best of the Offeror's knowledge and belief, neither it nor any of its proposed agents, subcontractors, or their agents is engaged in any such activities; or

(ii) If abuses relating to any of the prohibited activities identified in 52.222-50(b) have been found, the Offeror or proposed subcontractor has taken the appropriate remedial and referral actions.

(End of provision)

[FAC 2005-80, 80 FR 4967, 1/29/2015, effective 3/2/2015; Correction, 80 FR 6908, 2/9/2015, effective 3/2/2015]

52.222-57 [Removed and Reserved]

[FAC 2005-90, 81 FR 58562, 8/25/2016, effective 10/25/2016; FAC 2005-93, 81 FR 91636, 12/16/2016, effective 12/16/2016; FAC 2005-96, 82 FR 51773, 11/8/2017, effective 11/6/2017]

52.222-58 [Removed and Reserved]

[FAC 2005-90, 81 FR 58562, 8/25/2016, effective 10/25/2016; FAC 2005-93, 81 FR 91636, 12/16/2016, effective 12/16/2016; FAC 2005-96, 82 FR 51773, 11/8/2017, effective 11/6/2017]

52.222-59 [Removed and Reserved]

[FAC 2005-90, 81 FR 58562, 8/25/2016, effective 10/25/2016; FAC 2005-93, 81 FR 91636, 12/16/2016, effective 12/16/2016; FAC 2005-96, 82 FR 51773, 11/8/2017, effective 11/6/2017]

52.222-60 [Removed and Reserved]

[FAC 2005-90, 81 FR 58562, 8/25/2016, effective 10/25/2016; FAC 2005-96, 82 FR 51773, 11/8/2017, effective 11/6/2017]

52.222-61 [Removed and Reserved]

[FAC 2005-90, 81 FR 58562, 8/25/2016, effective 10/25/2016; FAC 2005-93, 81 FR 91636, 12/16/2016, effective 12/16/2016; FAC 2005-96, 82 FR 51773, 11/8/2017, effective 11/6/2017]

52.222-62 Paid Sick Leave Under Executive Order 13706.

As prescribed at 22.2110, insert the following clause:

PAID SICK LEAVE UNDER EXECUTIVE ORDER 13706 (JAN 2017)

(a) *Definitions*. As used in this clause (in accordance with 29 CFR 13.2)—

Child, *domestic partner*, and *domestic violence* have the meaning given in 29 CFR 13.2.

Employee—(1) (i) Means any person engaged in performing work on or in connection with a contract covered by Executive Order (E.O.) 13706; and

(A) Whose wages under such contract are governed by the Service Contract Labor Standards statute (41 U.S.C. chapter 67), the Wage Rate Requirements (Construction) statute (40 U.S.C. chapter 31, subchapter IV), or the Fair Labor Standards Act (29 U.S.C. chapter 8);

(B) Including employees who qualify for an exemption from the Fair Labor Standards Act's minimum wage and overtime provisions;

(C) Regardless of the contractual relationship alleged to exist between the individual and the employer; and

(ii) Includes any person performing work on or in connection with the contract and individually registered in a bona fide apprenticeship or training program registered with the Department of Labor's Employment and Training Administration, Office of Apprenticeship, or with a State Apprenticeship Agency recognized by the Office of Apprenticeship.

(2) (i) An employee performs "on" a contract if the employee directly performs the specific services called for by the contract; and

(ii) An employee performs "in connection with" a contract if the employee's work activities are necessary to the performance of a contract but are not the specific services called for by the contract.

Individual related by blood or affinity whose close association with the employee is the equivalent of a family relationship has the meaning given in 29 CFR 13.2.

Multiemployer plan means a plan to which more than one employer is required to contribute and which is maintained pursuant to one or more collective bargaining agreements between one or more employee organizations and more than one employer.

Paid sick leave means compensated absence from employment that is required by E.O. 13706 and 29 CFR part 13.

Parent, *sexual assault*, *spouse*, and *stalking* have the meaning given in 29 CFR 13.2.

United States means the 50 States and the District of Columbia.

(b) *Executive Order 13706*. (1) This contract is subject to E.O. 13706 and the regulations issued by the Secretary of Labor in 29 CFR part 13 pursuant to the E.O.

(2) If this contract is not performed wholly within the United States, this clause only applies with respect to that part of the contract that is performed within the United States.

(c) *Paid sick leave*. The Contractor shall—

(1) Permit each employee engaged in performing work on or in connection with this contract to earn not less than 1 hour of paid sick leave for every 30 hours worked;

(2) Allow accrual and use of paid sick leave as required by E.O. 13706 and 29 CFR part 13;

(3) Comply with the accrual, use, and other requirements set forth in 29 CFR 13.5 and 13.6, which are incorporated by reference in this contract;

(4) Provide paid sick leave to all employees when due free and clear and without subsequent deduction (except as otherwise provided by 29 CFR 13.24), rebate, or kickback on any account;

(5) Provide pay and benefits for paid sick leave used no later than one pay period following the end of the regular pay period in which the paid sick leave was taken; and

(6) Be responsible for the compliance by any subcontractor with the requirements of E.O. 13706, 29 CFR part 13, and this clause.

(d) Contractors may fulfill their obligations under E.O. 13706 and 29 CFR part 13 jointly with other contractors through a multiemployer plan, or may fulfill their obligations through an individual fund, plan, or program (see 29 CFR 13.8).

(e) *Withholding*. The Contracting Officer will, upon his or her own action or upon written request of an authorized representative of the Department of Labor, withhold or cause to be withheld from the Contractor under this or any other Federal contract with the same Contractor, so much of the accrued payments or advances as may be considered necessary to pay employees the full amount owed to compensate for any violation of the requirements of E.O. 13706, 29 CFR part 13, or this clause, including—

(1) Any pay and/or benefits denied or lost by reason of the violation;

(2) Other actual monetary losses sustained as a direct result of the violation; and

(3) Liquidated damages.

(f) *Payment suspension/contract termination/contractor debarment*. (1) In the event of a failure to comply with E.O. 13706, 29 CFR part 13, or this clause, the contracting agency may, on its own action or after authorization or by direction of the Department of Labor and written notification to the Contractor take action to cause suspension of any further payment, advance, or guarantee of funds until such violations have ceased.

(2) Any failure to comply with the requirements of this clause may be grounds for termination for default or cause.

(3) A breach of the contract clause may be grounds for debarment as a contractor and subcontractor as provided in 29 CFR 13.52.

(g) The paid sick leave required by E.O. 13706, 29 CFR part 13, and this clause is in addition to the Contractor's obligations under the Service Contract Labor Standards statute and Wage Rate Requirements (Construction) statute, and the Contractor may not receive credit toward its prevailing wage or fringe benefit obligations under those Acts for any paid sick leave provided in satisfaction of the requirements of E.O. 13706 and 29 CFR part 13.

(h) Nothing in E.O. 13706 or 29 CFR part 13 shall excuse noncompliance with or supersede any applicable Federal or State law, any applicable law or municipal ordinance, or a collective bargaining agreement requiring greater paid sick leave or leave rights than those established under E.O. 13706 and 29 CFR part 13.

(i) *Recordkeeping*. (1) The Contractor shall make and maintain, for no less than three (3) years from the completion of the work on the contract, records containing the following information for each employee, which the Contractor shall make available upon request for inspection, copying, and transcription by authorized representatives of the Administrator of the Wage and Hour Division of the Department of Labor:

(i) Name, address, and social security number of each employee.

(ii) The employee's occupation(s) or classification(s).

(iii) The rate or rates of wages paid (including all pay and benefits provided).

(iv) The number of daily and weekly hours worked.

(v) Any deductions made.

(vi) The total wages paid (including all pay and benefits provided) each pay period.

(vii) A copy of notifications to employees of the amount of paid sick leave the employee has accrued, as required under 29 CFR 13.5(a)(2).

(viii) A copy of employees' requests to use paid sick leave, if in writing, or, if not in writing, any other records reflecting such employee requests.

(ix) Dates and amounts of paid sick leave taken by employees (unless the Contractor's paid time off policy satisfies the requirements of E.O. 13706 and 29 CFR part 13 as described in 29 CFR 13.5(f)(5), leave shall be designated in records as paid sick leave pursuant to E.O. 13706).

(x) A copy of any written responses to employees' requests to use paid sick leave, including explanations for any denials of such requests, as required under 29 CFR 13.5(d)(3).

(xi) Any records reflecting the certification and documentation the Contractor may require an employee to provide under 29 CFR 13.5(e), including copies of any certification or documentation provided by an employee.

(xii) Any other records showing any tracking of or calculations related to an employee's accrual or use of paid sick leave.

(xiii) The relevant contract.

(xiv) The regular pay and benefits provided to an employee for each use of paid sick leave.

(xv) Any financial payment made for unused paid sick leave upon a separation from employment intended, pursuant to 29 CFR 13.5(b)(5), to relieve the Contractor from the obligation to reinstate such paid sick leave as otherwise required by 29 CFR 13.5(b)(4).

(2)(i) If the Contractor wishes to distinguish between an employee's covered and noncovered work, the Contractor shall keep records or other proof reflecting such distinctions. Only if the Contractor adequately segregates the employee's time will time spent on noncovered work be excluded from hours worked counted toward the accrual of paid sick leave. Similarly, only if the Contractor adequately segregates the employee's time may the Contractor properly refuse an employee's request to use paid sick leave on the ground that the employee was scheduled to perform noncovered work during the time he or she asked to use paid sick leave.

(ii) If the Contractor estimates covered hours worked by an employee who performs work in connection with contracts covered by the E.O. pursuant to 29 CFR 13.5(a)(1)(i) or (iii), the Contractor shall keep records or other proof of the verifiable information on which such estimates are reasonably based. Only if the Contractor relies on an estimate that is reasonable and based on verifiable information will an employee's time spent in connection with noncovered work be excluded from hours worked counted toward the accrual of paid sick leave. If the Contractor estimates the amount of time an employee spends performing in connection with contracts covered by the E.O., the Contractor shall permit the employee to use his or her paid sick leave during any work time for the Contractor.

(3) In the event the Contractor is not obligated by the Service Contract Labor Standards statute, the Wage Rate Requirements (Construction) statute, or the Fair Labor Standards Act to keep records of an employee's hours worked, such as because the employee is exempt from the Fair Labor Standards Act's minimum wage and overtime requirements, and the Contractor chooses to use the assumption permitted by 29 CFR 13.5(a)(1)(iii), the Contractor is excused from the requirement in paragraph (i)(1)(iv) of this clause and 29 CFR 13.25(a)(4) to keep records of the employee's number of daily and weekly hours worked.

(4)(i) Records relating to medical histories or domestic violence, sexual assault, or stalking, created for purposes of E.O. 13706, whether of an employee or an employee's child, parent, spouse, domestic partner, or other individual related by blood or affinity whose close association with the employee is the equivalent of a family relationship, shall be maintained as confidential records in separate files/records from the usual personnel files.

(ii) If the confidentiality requirements of the Genetic Information Nondiscrimination Act of 2008 (GINA), section 503 of the Rehabilitation Act of 1973, and/or the Americans with Disabilities Act (ADA) apply to records or documents created to comply with the recordkeeping requirements in this contract clause, the records and documents shall also be maintained in compliance with the confidentiality requirements of the GINA, section 503 of the Rehabilitation Act of 1973, and/or ADA as described in 29 CFR 1635.9, 41 CFR 60-741.23(d), and 29 CFR 1630.14(c)(1), respectively.

(iii) The Contractor shall not disclose any documentation used to verify the need to use 3 or more consecutive days of paid sick leave for the purposes listed in 29 CFR 13.5(c)(1)(iv) (as described in 29 CFR 13.5(e)(1)(ii)) and shall maintain confidentiality about any domestic abuse, sexual assault, or stalking, unless the employee consents or when disclosure is required by law.

(5) The Contractor shall permit authorized representatives of the Wage and Hour Division to conduct interviews with employees at the worksite during normal working hours.

(6) Nothing in this contract clause limits or otherwise modifies the Contractor's recordkeeping obligations, if any, under the Service Contract Labor Standards statute, the Wage Rate Requirements (Construction) statute, the Fair Labor Standards Act, the Family and Medical Leave Act, E.O. 13658, their respective implementing regulations, or any other applicable law.

(j) *Interference/discrimination.* (1) The Contractor shall not in any manner interfere with an employee's accrual or use of paid sick leave as required by E.O. 13706 or 29 CFR part 13. Interference includes, but is not limited to—

(i) Miscalculating the amount of paid sick leave an employee has accrued;

(ii) Denying or unreasonably delaying a response to a proper request to use paid sick leave;

(iii) Discouraging an employee from using paid sick leave;

(iv) Reducing an employee's accrued paid sick leave by more than the amount of such leave used;

(v) Transferring an employee to work on contracts not covered by the E.O. to prevent the accrual or use of paid sick leave;

(vi) Disclosing confidential information contained in certification or other documentation provided to verify the need to use paid sick leave; or

(vii) Making the use of paid sick leave contingent on the employee's finding a replacement worker or the fulfillment of the Contractor's operational needs.

(2) The Contractor shall not discharge or in any other manner discriminate against any employee for—

(i) Using, or attempting to use, paid sick leave as provided for under E.O. 13706 and 29 CFR part 13;

(ii) Filing any complaint, initiating any proceeding, or otherwise asserting any right or claim under E.O. 13706 and 29 CFR part 13;

(iii) Cooperating in any investigation or testifying in any proceeding under E.O. 13706 and 29 CFR part 13; or

(iv) Informing any other person about his or her rights under E.O. 13706 and 29 CFR part 13.

(k) *Notice.* The Contractor shall notify all employees performing work on or in connection with a contract covered by the E.O. of the paid sick leave requirements of E.O. 13706, 29 CFR part 13, and this clause by posting a notice provided by the Department of Labor in a prominent and accessible place at the worksite so it may be readily seen by employees. Contractors that customarily post notices to employees electronically may post the notice electronically, provided such electronic posting is displayed prominently on any website that is maintained by the Contractor, whether external or internal, and customarily used for notices to employees about terms and conditions of employment.

(l) *Disputes concerning labor standards.* Disputes related to the application of E.O. 13706 to this contract shall not be subject to the general disputes clause of the contract. Such disputes shall be resolved in accordance with the procedures of the Department of Labor set forth in 29 CFR part 13. Disputes within the meaning of this contract clause include disputes between the Contractor (or any of its subcontractors) and the contracting agency, the Department of Labor, or the employees or their representatives.

(m) *Subcontracts.* The Contractor shall insert the substance of this clause, including this paragraph (m), in all subcontracts, regardless of dollar value, that are subject to the Service Contract Labor Standards statute or the Wage Rate Requirements (Construction) statute, and are to be performed in whole or in part in the United States.

(End of clause)

Note to 52.222-61: By a court order issued on October 24, 2016, 52.222-61 is enjoined indefinitely as of the date of the order. The enjoined section will become effective immediately if the court terminates the injunction. At that time, DoD, GSA, and NASA will publish a document in the Federal Register advising the public of the termination of the injunction.

[FAC 2005-93, 81 FR 91627, 12/16/2016, effective 1/1/2017; FAC 2005-100, 83 FR 42569, 8/22/2018, effective 8/22/2018]

52.223-1 Biobased Product Certification.

As prescribed in 23.406(a), insert the following provision:

BIOBASED PRODUCT CERTIFICATION (MAY 2012)

As required by the Farm Security and Rural Investment Act of 2002 and the Energy Policy Act of 2005 (7 U.S.C. 8102(c)(3)), the offeror certifies, by signing this offer, that biobased products (within categories of products listed by the United States Department of Agriculture in 7 CFR part 3201, subpart B) to be used or delivered in the performance of the contract, other than biobased products that are not purchased by the offeror as a direct result of this contract, will comply with the applicable specifications or other contractual requirements.

(End of provision)

[Removed and reserved, FAC 97-15, 64 FR 72414, 12/27/99, effective 2/25/2000; FAC 2005-21, 72 FR 63040, 11/7/2007, effective 12/7/2007; FAC 2005-58, 77 FR 23365, 4/18/2012, effective 5/18/2012]

52.223-2 Affirmative Procurement of Biobased Products Under Service and Construction Contracts.

As prescribed in 23.406(b), insert the following clause:

AFFIRMATIVE PROCUREMENT OF BIOBASED PRODUCTS UNDER SERVICE AND CONSTRUCTION CONTRACTS (SEP 2013)

(a) In the performance of this contract, the contractor shall make maximum use of biobased products that are United States Department of Agriculture (USDA)-designated items unless—

(1) The product cannot be acquired—

(i) Competitively within a time frame providing for compliance with the contract performance schedule;

(ii) Meeting contract performance requirements; or

(iii) At a reasonable price.

(2) The product is to be used in an application covered by a USDA categorical exemption (see 7 CFR 3201.3(e)). For example, all USDA-designated items are exempt from the preferred procurement requirement for the following:

(i) Spacecraft system and launch support equipment.

(ii) Military equipment, *i.e.*, a product or system designed or procured for combat or combat-related missions.

(b) Information about this requirement and these products is available at *http://www.biopreferred.gov.*

(c) In the performance of this contract, the Contractor shall—

(1) Report to *http://www.sam.gov*, with a copy to the Contracting Officer, on the product types and dollar value of any USDA-designated biobased products purchased by the Contractor during the previous Government fiscal year, between October 1 and September 30; and

(2) Submit this report no later than—

(i) October 31 of each year during contract performance; and

(ii) At the end of contract performance.

(End of clause)

[Removed and reserved, FAC 97-15, 64 FR 72414, 12/27/99, effective 2/25/2000; FAC 2005-21, 72 FR 63040, 11/7/2007, effective 12/7/2007; FAC 2005-58, 77 FR 23365, 4/18/2012, effective 5/18/2012; FAC 2005-60, 77 FR 44065, 7/26/2012, effective 7/26/2012; FAC 2005-69, 78 FR 46794, 8/1/2013, effective 9/3/2013]

52.223-3 Hazardous Material Identification and Material Safety Data.

As prescribed in 23.303, insert the following clause:

HAZARDOUS MATERIAL IDENTIFICATION AND MATERIAL SAFETY DATA (JAN 1997)

(a) *Hazardous material,* as used in this clause, includes any material defined as hazardous under the latest version of Federal Standard No. 313 (including revisions adopted during the term of the contract).

(b) The offeror must list any hazardous material, as defined in paragraph (a) of this clause, to be delivered under this contract. The hazardous material shall be properly identified and include any applicable identification number, such as National Stock Number or Special Item Number. This information shall also be included on the Material Safety Data Sheet submitted under this contract.

Material (If none, insert "None")

______

______

______

Identification No.

______

______

______

(c) This list must be updated during performance of the contract whenever the Contractor determines that any other material to be delivered under this contract is hazardous.

(d) The apparently successful offeror agrees to submit, for each item as required prior to award, a Material Safety Data Sheet, meeting the requirements of 29 CFR 1910.1200(g) and the latest version of Federal Standard No. 313, for all hazardous material identified in paragraph (b) of this clause. Data shall be submitted in accordance with Federal Standard No. 313, whether or not the apparently successful offeror is the actual manufacturer of these items. Failure to submit the Material Safety Data Sheet prior to award may result in the apparently successful offeror being considered nonresponsible and ineligible for award.

(e) If, after award, there is a change in the composition of the item(s) or a revision to Federal Standard No. 313, which renders incomplete or inaccurate the data submitted under paragraph (d) of this clause, the Contractor shall promptly notify the Contracting Officer and resubmit the data.

(f) Neither the requirements of this clause nor any act or failure to act by the Government shall relieve the Contractor of any responsibility or liability for the safety of Government, Contractor, or subcontractor personnel or property.

(g) Nothing contained in this clause shall relieve the Contractor from complying with applicable Federal, State, and local laws, codes, ordinances, and regulations (including the obtaining of licenses and permits) in connection with hazardous material.

(h) The Government's rights in data furnished under this contract with respect to hazardous material are as follows:

(1) To use, duplicate and disclose any data to which this clause is applicable. The purposes of this right are to—

(i) Apprise personnel of the hazards to which they may be exposed in using, handling, packaging, transporting, or disposing of hazardous materials;

(ii) Obtain medical treatment for those affected by the material; and

(iii) Have others use, duplicate, and disclose the data for the Government for these purposes.

(2) To use, duplicate, and disclose data furnished under this clause, in accordance with subparagraph (h)(1) of this clause, in precedence over any other clause of this contract providing for rights in data.

(3) The Government is not precluded from using similar or identical data acquired from other sources.

(End of clause)

Alternate I (JUL 1995). If the contract is awarded by an agency other than the Department of Defense, add the following paragraph (i) to the basic clause:

(i) Except as provided in paragraph (i)(2), the Contractor shall prepare and submit a sufficient number of Material Safety Data Sheets (MSDS's), meeting the requirements of 29 CFR 1910.1200(g) and the latest version of Federal Standard No. 313, for all hazardous materials identified in paragraph (b) of this clause.

(1) For items shipped to consignees, the Contractor shall include a copy of the MSDS's with the packing list or other suitable shipping document which accompanies each shipment. Alternatively, the Contractor is permitted to transmit MSDS's to consignees in advance of receipt of shipments by consignees, if authorized in writing by the Contracting Officer.

(2) For items shipped to consignees identified by mailing address as agency depots, distribution centers or customer supply centers, the Contractor shall provide one copy of the MSDS's in or on each shipping container. If affixed to the outside of each container, the MSDS's must be placed in a weather resistant envelope.

[FAC 90-8, 56 FR 55375, 10/25/91, effective 11/25/91; FAC 90-29, 60 FR 34732, 7/3/95, effective 7/3/95; FAC 90-45, Final rule, 62 FR 224, 1/2/97, effective 1/1/97]

52.223-4 Recovered Material Certification.

As prescribed in 23.406(c), insert the following provision:

RECOVERED MATERIAL CERTIFICATION (MAY 2008)

As required by the Resource Conservation and Recovery Act of 1976 (42 U.S.C. 6962(c)(3)(A)(i)), the offeror certifies, by signing this offer, that the percentage of recovered materials content for EPA-designated items to be delivered or used in the performance of the contract will be at least the amount required by the applicable contract specifications or other contractual requirements.

(End of provision)

[FAC 97-1, 62 FR 44802, 8/22/97, effective 10/21/97; FAC 97-18, 65 FR 36014, 6/6/2000, effective 8/7/2000; FAC 2005-21, 72 FR 63040, 11/7/2007, effective 12/7/2007; FAC 2005-25, 73 FR 21789, 4/22/2008, effective 5/22/2008]

52.223-5 Pollution Prevention and Right-to-Know Information.

As prescribed in 23.1005, insert the following clause:

POLLUTION PREVENTION AND RIGHT-TO-KNOW INFORMATION (MAY 2011)

(a) *Definitions*. As used in this clause—

Toxic chemical means a chemical or chemical category listed in 40 CFR 372.65.

(b) Federal facilities are required to comply with the provisions of the Emergency Planning and Community Right-to-Know Act of 1986 (EPCRA) (42 U.S.C. 11001-11050), and the Pollution Prevention Act of 1990 (PPA) (42 U.S.C. 13101-13109).

(c) The Contractor shall provide all information needed by the Federal facility to comply with the following:

(1) The emergency planning reporting requirements of section 302 of EPCRA.

(2) The emergency notice requirements of section 304 of EPCRA.

(3) The list of Material Safety Data Sheets, required by section 311 of EPCRA.

(4) The emergency and hazardous chemical inventory forms of section 312 of EPCRA.

(5) The toxic chemical release inventory of section 313 of EPCRA, which includes the reduction and recycling information required by section 6607 of PPA.

(6) The toxic chemical and hazardous substance release and use reduction goals of section 2(e) of Executive Order 13423 and of Executive Order 13514.

(End of clause)

Alternate I (MAY 2011). As prescribed in 23.1005(b), add the following paragraph (c)(7) to the basic clause:

(c)(7) The environmental management system as described in section 3(b) of E.O. 13423 and 2(j) of E.O. 13514.

Alternate II (MAY 2011). As prescribed in 23.1005(c), add the following paragraph (c)(7) to the basic clause. If Alternate I is also prescribed, renumber paragraph (c)(7) as paragraph (c)(8).

(c)(7) The facility compliance audits as described in section 3(c) of E.O. 13423.

[FAC 90-46, 62 FR 12690, 3/17/97, effective 3/16/97; FAC 97-4, 63 FR 9048, 2/23/98, effective 4/24/98; FAC 2001-15, 68 FR 43868, 7/24/2003, effective 8/25/2003; FAC 2005-52, 76 FR 31395, 5/31/2011, effective 5/31/2011]

52.223-6 Drug-Free Workplace.

As prescribed in 23.505, insert the following clause:

DRUG-FREE WORKPLACE (MAY 2001)

(a) *Definitions.* As used in this clause—

Controlled substance means a controlled substance in schedules I through V of section 202 of the Controlled Substances Act (21 U.S.C. 812) and as further defined in regulation at 21 CFR 1308.11—1308.15.

Conviction means a finding of guilt (including a plea of nolo contendere) or imposition of sentence, or both, by any judicial body charged with the responsibility to determine violations of the Federal or State criminal drug statutes.

Criminal drug statute means a Federal or non-Federal criminal statute involving the manufacture, distribution, dispensing, possession or use of any controlled substance.

Drug-free workplace means the site(s) for the performance of work done by the Contractor in connection with a specific contract where employees of the Contractor are prohibited from engaging in the unlawful manufacture, distribution, dispensing, possession, or use of a controlled substance.

Employee means an employee of a Contractor directly engaged in the performance of work under a Government contract. "Directly engaged" is defined to include all direct cost employees and any other Contractor employee who has other than a minimal impact or involvement in contract performance.

Individual means an offeror/contractor that has no more than one employee including the offeror/contractor.

(b) The Contractor, if other than an individual, shall—within 30 days after award (unless a longer period is agreed to in writing for contracts of 30 days or more performance duration), or as soon as possible for contracts of less than 30 days performance duration—

(1) Publish a statement notifying its employees that the unlawful manufacture, distribution, dispensing, possession, or use of a controlled substance is prohibited in the Contractor's workplace and specifying the actions that will be taken against employees for violations of such prohibition;

(2) Establish an ongoing drug-free awareness program to inform such employees about—

(i) The dangers of drug abuse in the workplace;

(ii) The Contractor's policy of maintaining a drug-free workplace;

(iii) Any available drug counseling, rehabilitation, and employee assistance programs; and

(iv) The penalties that may be imposed upon employees for drug abuse violations occurring in the workplace.

(3) Provide all employees engaged in performance of the contract with a copy of the statement required by subparagraph (b)(1) of this clause;

(4) Notify such employees in writing in the statement required by subparagraph (b)(1) of this clause that, as a condition of continued employment on this contract, the employee will—

(i) Abide by the terms of the statement; and

(ii) Notify the employer in writing of the employee's conviction under a criminal drug statute for a violation occurring in the workplace no later than 5 days after such conviction.

(5) Notify the Contracting Officer in writing within 10 days after receiving notice under subdivision (b)(4)(ii) of this clause, from an employee or otherwise receiving actual notice of such conviction. The notice shall include the position title of the employee;

(6) Within 30 days after receiving notice under subdivision (b)(4)(ii) of this clause of a conviction, take one of the following actions with respect to any employee who is convicted of a drug abuse violation occurring in the workplace:

(i) Taking appropriate personnel action against such employee, up to and including termination; or

(ii) Require such employee to satisfactorily participate in a drug abuse assistance or rehabilitation program approved for such purposes by a Federal, State, or local health, law enforcement, or other appropriate agency; and

(7) Make a good faith effort to maintain a drug-free workplace through implementation of subparagraphs (b)(1) through (b)(6) of this clause.

(c) The Contractor, if an individual, agrees by award of the contract or acceptance of a purchase order, not to engage in the unlawful manufacture, distribution, dispensing, possession, or use of a controlled substance while performing this contract.

(d) In addition to other remedies available to the Government, the Contractor's failure to comply with the requirements of paragraph (b) or (c) of this clause may, pursuant to FAR 23.506, render the Contractor subject to suspension of contract payments, termination of the contract for default, and suspension or debarment.

(End of clause)

[Interim rule, FAC 84-43, 54 FR 4970, 1/31/89, effective 3/18/89 for contracts issued on or after that date; corrected, 54 FR 6931, 2/15/89; FAC 84-57, 55 FR 21708, 5/25/90, effective 7/24/90; corrected, 55 FR 30465, 7/26/90; FAC 90-44, Final rule, 61 FR 69286, 12/31/96, effective 1/1/97; FAC 97-22, 66 FR 2116, 1/10/2001, effective 3/12/2001; Delay of effective date, 66 FR 14259, 3/9/2001, effective 5/11/2001]

52.223-7 Notice of Radioactive Materials.

As prescribed in 23.602, insert the following clause:

NOTICE OF RADIOACTIVE MATERIALS (JAN 1997)

(a) The Contractor shall notify the Contracting Officer or designee, in writing, ___*days prior to the delivery of, or prior to completion of any servicing required by this contract of, items containing either (1) radioactive material requiring specific licensing under the regulations issued pursuant to the Atomic Energy Act of 1954, as amended, as set forth in Title 10 of the Code of Federal Regulations, in effect on the date of this contract, or (2) other radioactive material not requiring specific licensing in which the specific activity is greater than 0.002 microcuries per gram or the activity per item equals or exceeds 0.01 microcuries. Such notice shall specify the part or parts of the items which contain radioactive materials, a description of the materials, the name and activity of the isotope, the manufacturer of the materials, and any other information known to the Contractor which will put users of the items on notice as to the hazards involved (OMB No. 9000-0107).

* The Contracting Officer shall insert the number of days required in advance of delivery of the item or completion of the servicing to assure that required licenses are obtained and appropriate personnel are notified to institute any necessary safety and health precautions. See FAR 23.601(d).

(b) If there has been no change affecting the quantity of activity, or the characteristics and composition of the radioactive material from deliveries under this contract or prior contracts, the Contractor may request that the Contracting Officer or designee waive the notice requirement in paragraph (a) of this clause. Any such request shall—

(1) Be submitted in writing;

(2) State that the quantity of activity, characteristics, and composition of the radioactive material have not changed; and

(3) Cite the contract number on which the prior notification was submitted and the contracting office to which it was submitted.

(c) All items, parts, or subassemblies which contain radioactive materials in which the specific activity is greater than 0.002 microcuries per gram or activity per item equals or exceeds 0.01 microcuries, and all containers in which such items, parts or subassemblies are delivered to the Government shall be clearly marked and labeled as required by the latest revision of MIL-STD 129 in effect on the date of the contract.

(d) This clause, including this paragraph (d), shall be inserted in all subcontracts for radioactive materials meeting the criteria in paragraph (a) of this clause.

(End of clause)

[FAC 90-8, 56 FR 55375, 10/25/91, effective 11/25/91; FAC 90-45, Final rule, 62 FR 224, 1/2/97, effective 1/1/97]

52.223-8 [Reserved]

[Removed and reserved, FAC 97-1, 62 FR 44802, 8/22/97, effective 10/21/97]

52.223-9 Estimate of Percentage of Recovered Material Content for EPA-Designated Items.

As prescribed in 23.406(d), insert the following clause:

ESTIMATE OF PERCENTAGE OF RECOVERED MATERIAL CONTENT FOR EPA-DESIGNATED ITEMS (MAY 2008)

(a) *Definitions.* As used in this clause—

Postconsumer material means a material or finished product that has served its intended use and has been discarded for disposal or recovery, having completed its life as a consumer item. Postconsumer material is a part of the broader category of recovered material. Recovered material means waste materials and by-products recovered or diverted from solid waste, but the term does not include those materials and by-products generated from, and commonly reused within, an original manufacturing process.

(b) The Contractor, on completion of this contract, shall—

(1) Estimate the percentage of the total recovered material content for EPA-designated item(s) delivered and/or used in contract performance, including, if applicable, the percentage of post-consumer material content; and

(2) Submit this estimate to ____________________ [*Contracting Officer complete in accordance with agency procedures*].

(End of clause)

Alternate I (MAY 2008). As prescribed in 23.406(d), redesignate paragraph (b) of the basic clause as paragraph (c) and add the following paragraph (b) to the basic clause:

(b) The Contractor shall execute the following certification required by the Resource Conservation and Recovery Act of 1976 (42 U.S.C. 6962(i)(2)(C)):

Certification

I, ____________________ (name of certifier), am an officer or employee responsible for the performance of this contract and hereby certify that the percentage of recovered material content for EPA-designated items met the applicable contract specifications or other contractual requirements.

(End of certification)

[FAC 97-18, 65 FR 36014, 6/6/2000, effective 8/7/2000; FAC 2005-21, 72 FR 63040, 11/7/2007, effective 12/7/2007; FAC 2005-25, 73 FR 21789, 4/22/2008, effective 5/22/2008]

52.223-10 Waste Reduction Program.

As prescribed in 23.705(a), insert the following clause:

WASTE REDUCTION PROGRAM (MAY 2011)

(a) *Definitions.* As used in this clause—

Recycling means the series of activities, including collection, separation, and processing, by which products or other materials are recovered from the solid waste stream for use in the form of raw materials in the manufacture of products other than fuel for producing heat or power by combustion.

Waste prevention means any change in the design, manufacturing, purchase, or use of materials or products (including packaging) to reduce their amount or toxicity before they are discarded. Waste prevention also refers to the reuse of products or materials

Waste reduction means preventing or decreasing the amount of waste being generated through waste prevention, recycling, or purchasing recycled and environmentally preferable products.

(b) Consistent with the requirements of section 3(e) of Executive Order 13423, the Contractor shall establish a program to promote cost-effective waste reduction in all operations and facilities covered by this contract. The Contractor's programs shall comply with applicable Federal, State, and local requirements, specifically including Section 6002 of the Resource Conservation and Recovery Act (42 U.S.C. 6962, et seq.) and implementing regulations (40 CFR part 247).

(End of clause)

[FAC 97-18, 65 FR 36014, 6/6/2000, effective 8/7/2000; FAC 2005-23, 72 FR 73215, 12/26/2007, effective 12/26/2007; FAC 2005-30, 74 FR 2740, 1/15/2009, effective 2/17/2009; FAC 2005-52, 76 FR 31395, 5/31/2011, effective 5/31/2011]

52.223-11 Ozone-Depleting Substances and High Global Warming Potential Hydrofluorocarbons.

As prescribed in 23.804(a)(1), insert the following clause:

OZONE-DEPLETING SUBSTANCES AND HIGH GLOBAL WARMING POTENTIAL HYDROFLUOROCARBONS (JUN 2016)

(a) *Definitions.* As used in this clause—

Global warming potential means how much a given mass of a chemical contributes to global warming over a given time period compared to the same mass of carbon dioxide. Carbon dioxide's global warming potential is defined as 1.0.

High global warming potential hydrofluorocarbons means any hydrofluorocarbons in a particular end use for which EPA's Significant New Alternatives Policy (SNAP) program has identified other acceptable alternatives that have lower global warming potential. The SNAP list of alternatives is found at 40 CFR part 82, subpart G, with supplemental tables of alternatives available at (*http://www.epa.gov/snap/*).

Hydrofluorocarbons means compounds that only contain hydrogen, fluorine, and carbon.

Ozone-depleting substance means any substance the Environmental Protection Agency designates in 40 CFR part 82 as—

(1) Class I, including, but not limited to, chlorofluorocarbons, halons, carbon tetrachloride, and methyl chloroform; or

(2) Class II, including, but not limited to, hydrochlorofluorocarbons.

(b) The Contractor shall label products that contain or are manufactured with ozone-depleting substances in the manner and to the extent required by 42 U.S.C. 7671j (b), (c), (d), and (e) and 40 CFR part 82, subpart E, as follows:

Warning: Contains (or manufactured with, if applicable) *_____, a substance(s) which harm(s) public health and environment by destroying ozone in the upper atmosphere.

* The Contractor shall insert the name of the substance(s).

(c) *Reporting.* For equipment and appliances that normally each contain 50 or more pounds of hydrofluorocarbons or refrigerant blends containing hydrofluorocarbons, the Contractor shall—

(1) Track on an annual basis, between October 1 and September 30, the amount in pounds of hydrofluorocarbons or refrigerant blends containing hydrofluorocarbons contained in the equipment and appliances delivered to the Government under this contract by—

(i) Type of hydrofluorocarbon (*e.g.*, HFC-134a, HFC-125, R-410A, R-404A, etc.);

(ii) Contract number; and

(iii) Equipment/appliance;

(2) Report that information to the Contracting Officer for FY16 and to *www.sam.gov*, for FY17 and after—

(i) Annually by November 30 of each year during contract performance; and

(ii) At the end of contract performance.

(d) The Contractor shall refer to EPA's SNAP program (available at *http://www.epa.gov/snap*) to identify alternatives. The SNAP list of alternatives is found at 40 CFR part 82, subpart G, with supplemental tables available at *http://www.epa.gov/snap*.

(End of clause)

[FAC 90-39, 61 FR 31612, 6/20/96, effective 6/20/96; FAC 97-22, 66 FR 2116, 1/10/2001, effective 3/12/2001; Delay of effective date, 66 FR 14259, 3/9/2001, effective 5/11/2001; FAC 2005-88, 81 FR 30429, 5/16/2016, effective 6/15/2016; FAC 2005-92, 81 FR 83092, 11/18/2016, effective 12/19/2016]

52.223-12 Maintenance, Service, Repair, or Disposal of Refrigeration Equipment and Air Conditioners.

As prescribed in 23.804(a)(2), insert the following clause:

MAINTENANCE, SERVICE, REPAIR, OR DISPOSAL OF REFRIGERATION EQUIPMENT AND AIR CONDITIONERS (JUN 2016)

(a) *Definitions.* As used in this clause—

Global warming potential means how much a given mass of a chemical contributes to global warming over a given time period compared to the same mass of carbon dioxide. Carbon dioxide's global warming potential is defined as 1.0.

High global warming potential hydrofluorocarbons means any hydrofluorocarbons in a particular end use for which EPA's Significant New Alternatives Policy (SNAP) program has identified other acceptable alternatives that have lower global warming potential. The SNAP list of alternatives is found at 40 CFR part 82, subpart G, with supplemental tables of alternatives available at (*http://www.epa.gov/snap/*).

Hydrofluorocarbons means compounds that contain only hydrogen, fluorine, and carbon.

(b) The Contractor shall comply with the applicable requirements of sections 608 and 609 of the Clean Air Act (42 U.S.C. 7671g and 7671h) as each or both apply to this contract.

(c) Unless otherwise specified in the contract, the Contractor shall reduce the use, release, or emissions of high global warming potential hydrofluorocarbons under this contract by—

(1) Transitioning over time to the use of another acceptable alternative in lieu of high global warming potential hydrofluorocarbons in a particular end use for which EPA's SNAP program has identified other acceptable alternatives that have lower global warming potential.

(2) Preventing and repairing refrigerant leaks through service and maintenance during contract performance;

(3) Implementing recovery, recycling, and responsible disposal programs that avoid release or emissions during equipment service and as the equipment reaches the end of its useful life; and

(4) Using reclaimed hydrofluorocarbons, where feasible.

(d) For equipment and appliances that normally each contain 50 or more pounds of hydrofluorocarbons or refrigerant blends containing hydrofluorocarbons, that will be maintained, serviced, repaired, or disposed under this contract, the Contractor shall—

(1) Track on an annual basis, between October 1 and September 30, the amount in pounds of hydrofluorocarbons or refrigerant blends containing hydrofluorocarbons added or taken out of equipment or appliances under this contract by—

(i) Type of hydrofluorocarbon (*e.g.*, HFC-134a, HFC-125, R-410A, R-404A, *etc.*);

(ii) Contract number;

(iii) Equipment/appliance; and

(2) Report that information to the Contracting Officer for FY16 and to *www.sam.gov*, for FY17 and after—

(i) No later than November 30 of each year during contract performance; and

(ii) At the end of contract performance.

(e) The Contractor shall refer to EPA's SNAP program to identify alternatives. The SNAP list of alternatives is found at 40 CFR part 82, subpart G, with supplemental tables available at *http://www.epa.gov/snap/*.

(End of clause)

[FAC 90-27, 60 FR 28492, 5/31/95, effective 5/31/95, finalized without change, FAC 90-39, 61 FR 31612, 6/20/96; FAC 2005-88, 81 FR 30429, 5/16/2016, effective 6/15/2016; FAC 2005-92, 81 FR 83092, 11/18/2016, effective 12/19/2016]

52.223-13 Acquisition of EPEAT®-Registered Imaging Equipment.

As prescribed in 23.705(b)(1), insert the following clause:

ACQUISITION OF EPEAT®-REGISTERED IMAGING EQUIPMENT (JUN 2014)

(a) *Definitions.* As used in this clause—*Imaging equipment* means the following products:

(1) *Copier*—A commercially available imaging product with a sole function of the production of hard copy duplicates from graphic hard-copy originals. The unit is capable of being powered from a wall outlet or from a data or network connection. This definition is intended to cover products that are marketed as copiers or upgradeable digital copiers (UDCs).

(2) *Digital duplicator*—A commercially available imaging product that is sold in the market as a fully automated duplicator system through the method of stencil duplicating with digital reproduction functionality. The unit is capable of being powered from a wall outlet or from a data or network connection. This definition is intended to cover products that are marketed as digital duplicators.

(3) *Facsimile machine (fax machine)*—A commercially available imaging product whose primary functions are scanning hard-copy originals for electronic transmission to remote units and receiving similar electronic transmissions to produce hard-copy output. Electronic transmission is primarily over a public telephone system but also may be via computer network or the Internet. The product also may be capable of producing hard copy duplicates. The unit is capable of being powered from a wall outlet or from a data or network connection. This definition is intended to cover products that are marketed as fax machines.

(4) *Mailing machine*—A commercially available imaging product that serves to print postage onto mail pieces. The unit is capable of being powered from a wall outlet or from a data or network connection. This definition is intended to cover products that are marketed as mailing machines.

(5) *Multifunction device (MFD)*—A commercially available imaging product, which is a physically integrated device or a combination of functionally integrated components, that performs two or more of the core functions of copying, printing, scanning, or faxing. The copy functionality as addressed in this definition is considered to be distinct from single-sheet convenience copying offered by fax machines. The unit is capable of being powered from a wall outlet or from a data or network connection. This definition

is intended to cover products that are marketed as MFDs or multifunction products.

(6) *Printer*—A commercially available imaging product that serves as a hard-copy output device and is capable of receiving information from single-user or networked computers, or other input devices (e.g., digital cameras). The unit is capable of being powered from a wall outlet or from a data or network connection. This definition is intended to cover products that are marketed as printers, including printers that can be upgraded into MFDs in the field.

(7) *Scanner*—A commercially available imaging product that functions as an electro-optical device for converting information into electronic images that can be stored, edited, converted, or transmitted, primarily in a personal computing environment. The unit is capable of being powered from a wall outlet or from a data or network connection. This definition is intended to cover products that are marketed as scanners.

(b) Under this contract, the Contractor shall deliver, furnish for Government use, or furnish for Contractor use at a Federally controlled facility, only imaging equipment that, at the time of submission of proposals and at the time of award, was EPEAT® bronze-registered or higher.

(c) For information about EPEAT®, see *www.epa.gov/epeat.*

(End of clause)

Alternate I (OCT 2015). As prescribed in 23.705(b)(2), substitute the following paragraph (b) for paragraph (b) of the basic clause:

(b) Under this contract, the Contractor shall deliver, furnish for Government use, or furnish for contractor use at a Federally controlled facility, only imaging equipment that, at the time of submission of proposals and at the time of award, was EPEAT® silver-registered or gold-registered.

[FAC 90-41, 61 FR 41466, 8/8/96, effective 10/7/96; FAC 97-19, 65 FR 46052, 7/26/2000, effective 10/1/2000; FAC 2001-02, 66 FR 65347, 12/18/2001, effective 2/19/2002; FAC 2001-14, 68 FR 28079, 5/22/2003, effective 6/23/2003; FAC 2001-15, 68 FR 43868, 7/24/2003, effective 8/25/2003; FAC 2005-52, 76 FR 31395, 5/31/2011, effective 5/31/2011; FAC 2005-75, 79 FR 35859, 6/24/2014, effective 6/24/2014;FAC 2005-84, 80 FR 53436, 9/3/2015, effective 10/5/2015]

52.223-14 Acquisition of EPEAT®-Registered Televisions.

As prescribed in 23.705(c)(1), insert the following clause:

ACQUISITION OF EPEAT®-REGISTERED TELEVISIONS (JUN 2014)

(a) *Definitions.* As used in this clause—

Television or *TV* means a commercially available electronic product designed primarily for the reception and display of audiovisual signals received from terrestrial, cable, satellite, Internet Protocol TV (IPTV), or other digital or analog sources. A TV consists of a tuner/receiver and a display encased in a single enclosure. The product usually relies upon a cathode-ray tube (CRT), liquid crystal display (LCD), plasma display, or other display technology. Televisions with computer capability (*e.g.*, computer input port) may be considered to be a TV as long as they are marketed and sold to consumers primarily as televisions.

(b) Under this contract, the Contractor shall deliver, furnish for Government use, or furnish for Contractor use at a Federally controlled facility, only televisions that, at the time of submission of proposals and at the time of award, were EPEAT® bronze-registered or higher.

(c) For information about EPEAT®, see *www.epa.gov/epeat.*

(End of clause)

Alternate I (JUN 2014). As prescribed in 23.705(c)(2), substitute the following paragraph (b) for paragraph (b) of the basic clause:

(b) Under this contract, the Contractor shall deliver, furnish for Government use, or furnish for Contractor use at a Federally controlled facility, only televisions that, at the time of submission of proposals and at the time of award, were EPEAT® silver-registered or gold-registered.

[FAC 90-41, 61 FR 41466, 8/8/96, effective 10/7/96; FAC 97-19, 65 FR 46052, 7/26/2000, effective 10/1/2000; FAC 2001-02, 66 FR 65347, 12/18/2001, effective 2/19/2002; FAC 2001-14, 68 FR 28079, 5/22/2003, effective 6/23/2003; FAC 2001-15, 68 FR 43868, 7/24/2003, effective 8/25/2003; FAC 2005-52, 76 FR 31395, 5/31/2011, effective 5/31/2011; FAC 2005-75, 79 FR 35859, 6/24/2014, effective 6/24/2014; FAC 2005-84, 80 FR 53436, 9/3/2015, effective 10/5/2015]

52.223-15 Energy Efficiency in Energy-Consuming Products.

As prescribed in 23.206, insert the following clause:

ENERGY EFFICIENCY IN ENERGY-CONSUMING PRODUCTS (DEC 2007)

(a) *Definition.* As used in this clause—

Energy-efficient product—(1) Means a product that—

(i) Meets Department of Energy and Environmental Protection Agency criteria for use of the Energy Star trademark label; or

(ii) Is in the upper 25 percent of efficiency for all similar products as designated by the Department of Energy's Federal Energy Management Program.

(2) The term *product* does not include any energy-consuming product or system designed or procured for combat or combat-related missions (42 U.S.C. 8259b).

(b) The Contractor shall ensure that energy-consuming products are energy efficient products (i.e., ENERGY STAR® products or FEMP-designated products) at the time of contract award, for products that are—

(1) Delivered;

(2) Acquired by the Contractor for use in performing services at a Federally-controlled facility;

(3) Furnished by the Contractor for use by the Government; or

(4) Specified in the design of a building or work, or incorporated during its construction, renovation, or maintenance.

(c) The requirements of paragraph (b) apply to the Contractor (including any subcontractor) unless—

(1) The energy-consuming product is not listed in the ENERGY STAR® Program or FEMP; or

(2) Otherwise approved in writing by the Contracting Officer.

(d) Information about these products is available for—

(1) ENERGY STAR® at *http://www.energystar.gov/products*; and

(2) FEMP at *http://www1.eere.energy.gov/femp/procurement/eep_requirements.html.*

(End of clause)

[FAC 2005-22, 72 FR 65868, 11/23/2007, effective 12/24/2007]

52.223-16 Acquisition of EPEAT®-Registered Personal Computer Products.

As prescribed in 23.705(d)(1), insert the following clause:

ACQUISITION OF EPEAT®-REGISTERED PERSONAL COMPUTER PRODUCTS (OCT 2015)

(a) *Definitions.* As used in this clause—

Computer means a device that performs logical operations and processes data. Computers are composed of, at a minimum:

(1) A central processing unit (CPU) to perform operations;

(2) User input devices such as a keyboard, mouse, digitizer, or game controller; and

(3) A computer display screen to output information. Computers include both stationary and portable units, including desktop computers, integrated desktop computers, notebook computers, thin clients, and workstations. Although computers must be capable of using input devices and computer displays, as noted in (2) and (3) above, computer systems do not need to include these devices on shipment to meet this definition. This definition does not include server computers, gaming consoles, mobile telephones, portable hand-held calculators, portable digital assistants (PDAs), MP3 players, or any

other mobile computing device with displays less than 4 inches, measured diagonally.

Computer display means a display screen and its associated electronics encased in a single housing or within the computer housing (e.g., notebook or integrated desktop computer) that is capable of displaying output information from a computer via one or more inputs such as a VGA, DVI, USB, DisplayPort, and/or IEEE 1394-2008™, Standard for High Performance Serial Bus. Examples of computer display technologies are the cathode-ray tube (CRT) and liquid crystal display (LCD).

Desktop computer means a computer where the main unit is intended to be located in a permanent location, often on a desk or on the floor. Desktops are not designed for portability and utilize an external computer display, keyboard, and mouse. Desktops are designed for a broad range of home and office applications.

Integrated desktop computer means a desktop system in which the computer and computer display function as a single unit that receives its AC power through a single cable. Integrated desktop computers come in one of two possible forms:

(1) A system where the computer display and computer are physically combined into a single unit; or

(2) A system packaged as a single system where the computer display is separate but is connected to the main chassis by a DC power cord and both the computer and computer display are powered from a single power supply. As a subset of desktop computers, integrated desktop computers are typically designed to provide similar functionality as desktop systems.

Notebook computer means a computer designed specifically for portability and to be operated for extended periods of time either with or without a direct connection to an AC power source. Notebooks must utilize an integrated computer display and be capable of operation off of an integrated battery or other portable power source. In addition, most notebooks use an external power supply and have an integrated keyboard and pointing device. Notebook computers are typically designed to provide similar functionality to desktops, including operation of software similar in functionality to that used in desktops. Docking stations are considered accessories for notebook computers, not notebook computers. Tablet PCs, which may use touch-sensitive screens along with, or instead of, other input devices, are considered notebook computers.

Personal computer product means a computer, computer display, desktop computer, integrated desktop computer, or notebook computer.

(b) Under this contract, the Contractor shall deliver, furnish for Government use, or furnish for Contractor use at a Federally controlled facility, only personal computer products that, at the time of submission of proposals and at the time of award, were EPEAT® bronze-registered or higher.

(c) For information about EPEAT®, see *www.epa.gov/epeat.*

(End of clause)

Alternate I (JUN 2014) As prescribed in 23.705(d)(2), substitute the following paragraph (b) for paragraph (b) of the basic clause:

(b) Under this contract, the Contractor shall deliver, furnish for Government use, or furnish for Contractor use at a Federally controlled facility, only personal computer products that, at the time of submission of proposals and at the time of award, were EPEAT® silver-registered or gold-registered.

[FAC 2005-23, 72 FR 73215, 12/26/2007, effective 12/26/2007; FAC 2005-30, 74 FR 2740, 1/15/2009, effective 2/17/2009; FAC 2005-52, 76 FR 31395, 5/31/2011, effective 5/31/2011; FAC 2005-75, 79 FR 35859, 6/24/2014, effective 6/24/2014; FAC 2005-82, 80 FR 26427, 5/7/2015, effective 5/7/2015; FAC 2005-84, 80 FR 53436, 9/3/2015, effective 10/5/2015]

52.223-17 Affirmative Procurement of EPA-designated Items in Service and Construction Contracts.

As prescribed in 23.406(e), insert the following clause:

AFFIRMATIVE PROCUREMENT OF EPA-DESIGNATED ITEMS IN SERVICE AND CONSTRUCTION CONTRACTS (AUG 2018)

(a) In the performance of this contract, the Contractor shall make maximum use of products containing recovered materials that are EPA-designated items unless the product cannot be acquired—

(1) Competitively within a time frame providing for compliance with the contract performance schedule;

(2) Meeting contract performance requirements; or

(3) At a reasonable price.

(b) Information about this requirement is available at EPA's Comprehensive Procurement Guidelines web site, *https://www.epa.gov/smm/comprehensive-procurement-guideline-cpg-program*. The list of EPA-designated items is available at *https://www.epa.gov/smm/comprehensive-procurement-guideline-cpg-program*.

(End of clause)

[FAC 2005-25, 73 FR 21789, 4/22/2008, effective 5/22/2008; FAC 2005-100, 83 FR 42571, 8/22/2018, effective 8/22/2018]

52.223-18 Encouraging Contractor Policies to Ban Text Messaging While Driving.

As prescribed in 23.1105, insert the following clause:

ENCOURAGING CONTRACTOR POLICIES TO BAN TEXT MESSAGING WHILE DRIVING (AUG 2011)

(a) *Definitions.* As used in this clause—

Driving—(1) Means operating a motor vehicle on an active roadway with the motor running, including while temporarily stationary because of traffic, a traffic light, stop sign, or otherwise.

(2) Does not include operating a motor vehicle with or without the motor running when one has pulled over to the side of, or off, an active roadway and has halted in a location where one can safely remain stationary.

Text messaging means reading from or entering data into any handheld or other electronic device, including for the purpose of short message service texting, e-mailing, instant messaging, obtaining navigational information, or engaging in any other form of electronic data retrieval or electronic data communication. The term does not include glancing at or listening to a navigational device that is secured in a commercially designed holder affixed to the vehicle, provided that the destination and route are programmed into the device either before driving or while stopped in a location off the roadway where it is safe and legal to park.

(b) This clause implements Executive Order 13513, Federal Leadership on Reducing Text Messaging while Driving, dated October 1, 2009.

(c) The Contractor is encouraged to—

(1) Adopt and enforce policies that ban text messaging while driving—

(i) Company-owned or -rented vehicles or Government-owned vehicles; or

(ii) Privately-owned vehicles when on official Government business or when performing any work for or on behalf of the Government.

(2) Conduct initiatives in a manner commensurate with the size of the business, such as—

(i) Establishment of new rules and programs or re-evaluation of existing programs to prohibit text messaging while driving; and

(ii) Education, awareness, and other outreach to employees about the safety risks associated with texting while driving.

(d) *Subcontracts.* The Contractor shall insert the substance of this clause, including this paragraph (d), in all subcontracts that exceed the micro-purchase threshold.

(End of clause)

[FAC 2005-46, 75 FR 60264, 9/29/2010, effective 9/29/2010; FAC 2005-53, 76 FR 39240, 7/5/2011, effective 8/4/2011]

52.223-19 Compliance with Environmental Management Systems.

As prescribed in 23.903, insert the following clause:

COMPLIANCE WITH ENVIRONMENTAL MANAGEMENT SYSTEMS (MAY 2011)

The Contractor's work under this contract shall conform with all operational controls identified in the applicable agency or facility Environmental Management Systems and provide monitoring and measurement information necessary for the Government to address environmental performance relative to the goals of the Environmental Management Systems.

[FAC 2005-52, 76 FR 31395, 5/31/2011, effective 5/31/2011]

52.223-20 Aerosols.

As prescribed in 23.804(a)(3), insert the following clause:

AEROSOLS (JUN 2016)

(a) *Definitions.* As used in this clause—

Global warming potential means how much a given mass of a chemical contributes to global warming over a given time period compared to the same mass of carbon dioxide. Carbon dioxide's global warming potential is defined as 1.0.

High global warming potential hydrofluorocarbons means any hydrofluorocarbons in a particular end use for which EPA's Significant New Alternatives Policy (SNAP) program has identified other acceptable alternatives that have lower global warming potential. The SNAP list of alternatives is found at 40 CFR part 82, subpart G, with supplemental tables of alternatives available at *http://www.epa.gov/snap/*).

Hydrofluorocarbons means compounds that contain only hydrogen, fluorine, and carbon.

(b) Unless otherwise specified in the contract, the Contractor shall reduce its use, release, or emissions of high global warming potential hydrofluorocarbons, when feasible, from aerosol propellants or solvents under this contract. When determining feasibility of using a particular alternative, the Contractor shall consider environmental, technical, and economic factors such as—

(1) In-use emission rates, energy efficiency;

(2) Safety, such as flammability or toxicity;

(3) Ability to meet technical performance requirements; and

(4) Commercial availability at a reasonable cost.

(c) The Contractor shall refer to EPA's SNAP program to identify alternatives. The SNAP list of alternatives is found at 40 CFR part 82, subpart G, with supplemental tables available at *http://www.epa.gov/snap/*.

(End of clause)

[FAC 2005-88, 81 FR 30429, 5/16/2016, effective 6/15/2016; FAC 2005-92, 81 FR 83092, 11/18/2016, effective 12/19/2016]

52.223-21 Foams.

As prescribed in 23.804(a)(4), insert the following clause:

FOAMS (JUN 2016)

(a) *Definitions.* As used in this clause—

Global warming potential means how much a given mass of a chemical contributes to global warming over a given time period compared to the same mass of carbon dioxide. Carbon dioxide's global warming potential is defined as 1.0.

High global warming potential hydrofluorocarbons means any hydrofluorocarbons in a particular end use for which EPA's Significant New Alternatives Policy (SNAP) program has identified other acceptable alternatives that have lower global warming potential. The SNAP list of alternatives is found at 40 CFR part 82, subpart G, with supplemental tables of alternatives available at *http://www.epa.gov/snap/*.

Hydrofluorocarbons means compounds that contain only hydrogen, fluorine, and carbon.

(b) Unless otherwise specified in the contract, the Contractor shall reduce its use, release, and emissions of high global warming potential hydrofluorocarbons and refrigerant blends containing hydrofluorocarbons, when feasible, from foam blowing agents, under this contract. When determining feasibility of using a particular alternative, the Contractor shall consider environmental, technical, and economic factors such as—

(1) In-use emission rates, energy efficiency, and safety;

(2) Ability to meet performance requirements; and

(3) Commercial availability at a reasonable cost.

(c) The Contractor shall refer to EPA's SNAP program to identify alternatives. The SNAP list of alternatives is found at 40 CFR part 82, subpart G, with supplemental tables available at *http://www.epa.gov/snap/*.

(End of clause)

[FAC 2005-88, 81 FR 30429, 5/16/2016, effective 6/15/2016; FAC 2005-92, 81 FR 83092, 11/18/2016, effective 12/19/2016]

52.223-22 Public Disclosure of Greenhouse Gas Emissions and Reduction Goals—Representation.

As prescribed in 23.804(b), insert the following provision:

PUBLIC DISCLOSURE OF GREENHOUSE GAS EMISSIONS AND REDUCTION GOALS—REPRESENTATION (DEC 2016)

(a) This representation shall be completed if the Offeror received $7.5 million or more in Federal contract awards in the prior Federal fiscal year. The representation is optional if the Offeror received less than $7.5 million in Federal contract awards in the prior Federal fiscal year.

(b) *Representation. [Offeror is to check applicable blocks in paragraphs (b)(1) and (2).]*

(1) The Offeror (itself or through its immediate owner or highest-level owner) [ ] does, [ ] does not publicly disclose greenhouse gas emissions, *i.e.*, make available on a publicly accessible Web site the results of a greenhouse gas inventory, performed in accordance with an accounting standard with publicly available and consistently applied criteria, such as the Greenhouse Gas Protocol Corporate Standard.

(2) The Offeror (itself or through its immediate owner or highest-level owner) [ ] does, [ ] does not publicly disclose a quantitative greenhouse gas emissions reduction goal, *i.e.*, make available on a publicly accessible Web site a target to reduce absolute emissions or emissions intensity by a specific quantity or percentage.

(3) A publicly accessible Web site includes the Offeror's own Web site or a recognized, third-party greenhouse gas emissions reporting program.

(c) If the Offeror checked "does" in paragraphs (b)(1) or (b)(2) of this provision, respectively, the Offeror shall provide the publicly accessible Web site(s) where greenhouse gas emissions and/or reduction goals are reported:______.

(End of provision)

[FAC 2005-92, 81 FR 83092, 11/18/2016, effective 12/19/2016]

52.224-1 Privacy Act Notification.

As prescribed in 24.104, insert the following clause in solicitations and contracts, when the design, development, or operation of a system of records on individuals is required to accomplish an agency function:

PRIVACY ACT NOTIFICATION (APR 1984)

The Contractor will be required to design, develop, or operate a system of records on individuals, to accomplish an agency function subject to the Privacy Act of 1974, Public Law 93-579, December 31, 1974 (5 U.S.C. 552a) and applicable agency regulations. Violation of the Act may involve the imposition of criminal penalties.

(End of clause)

[FAC 90-32, 60 FR 48206, 9/18/95, effective 10/1/95]

52.224-2 Privacy Act.

As prescribed in 24.104, insert the following clause in solicitations and contracts, when the design, development, or operation of a system of records on individuals is required to accomplish an agency function:

PRIVACY ACT (APR 1984)

(a) The Contractor agrees to—

(1) Comply with the Privacy Act of 1974 (the Act) and the agency rules and regulations issued under the Act in the design, development, or operation of any system of records on individuals to accomplish an

agency function when the contract specifically identifies—

(i) The systems of records; and

(ii) The design, development, or operation work that the contractor is to perform;

(2) Include the Privacy Act notification contained in this contract in every solicitation and resulting subcontract and in every subcontract awarded without a solicitation, when the work statement in the proposed subcontract requires the design, development, or operation of a system of records on individuals that is subject to the Act; and

(3) Include this clause, including this subparagraph (3), in all subcontracts awarded under this contract which requires the design, development, or operation of such a system of records.

(b) In the event of violations of the Act, a civil action may be brought against the agency involved when the violation concerns the design, development, or operation of a system of records on individuals to accomplish an agency function, and criminal penalties may be imposed upon the officers or employees of the agency when the violation concerns the operation of a system of records on individuals to accomplish an agency function. For purposes of the Act, when the contract is for the operation of a system of records on individuals to accomplish an agency function, the Contractor is considered to be an employee of the agency.

(c) (1) *Operation of a system of records,* as used in this clause, means performance of any of the activities associated with maintaining the system of records, including the collection, use, and dissemination of records.

(2) *Record,* as used in this clause, means any item, collection, or grouping of information about an individual that is maintained by an agency, including, but not limited to, education, financial transactions, medical history, and criminal or employment history and that contains the person's name, or the identifying number, symbol, or other identifying particular assigned to the individual, such as a fingerprint or voiceprint or a photograph.

(3) *System of records on individuals,* as used in this clause, means a group of any records under the control of any agency from which information is retrieved by the name of the individual or by some identifying number, symbol, or other identifying particular assigned to the individual.

(End of clause)

[FAC 90-32, 60 FR 48206, 9/18/95, effective 10/1/95]

52.224-3 Privacy Training.

As prescribed in 24.302(a), insert the following clause:

PRIVACY TRAINING (JAN 2017)

(a) *Definition*. As used in this clause, *personally identifiable information* means information that can be used to distinguish or trace an individual's identity, either alone or when combined with other information that is linked or linkable to a specific individual. (See Office of Management and Budget (OMB) Circular A-130, Managing Federal Information as a Strategic Resource).

(b) The Contractor shall ensure that initial privacy training, and annual privacy training thereafter, is completed by contractor employees who—

(1) Have access to a system of records;

(2) Create, collect, use, process, store, maintain, disseminate, disclose, dispose, or otherwise handle personally identifiable information on behalf of an agency; or

(3) Design, develop, maintain, or operate a system of records (see also FAR subpart 24.1 and 39.105).

(c) (1) Privacy training shall address the key elements necessary for ensuring the safeguarding of personally identifiable information or a system of records. The training shall be role-based, provide foundational as well as more advanced levels of training, and have measures in place to test the knowledge level of users. At a minimum, the privacy training shall cover—

(i) The provisions of the Privacy Act of 1974 (5 U.S.C. 552a), including penalties for violations of the Act;

(ii) The appropriate handling and safeguarding of personally identifiable information;

(iii) The authorized and official use of a system of records or any other personally identifiable information;

(iv) The restriction on the use of unauthorized equipment to create, collect, use, process, store, maintain, disseminate, disclose, dispose or otherwise access personally identifiable information;

(v) The prohibition against the unauthorized use of a system of records or unauthorized disclosure, access, handling, or use of personally identifiable information; and

(vi) The procedures to be followed in the event of a suspected or confirmed breach of a system of records or the unauthorized disclosure, access, handling, or use of personally identifiable information (see OMB guidance for Preparing for and Responding to a Breach of Personally Identifiable Information).

(2) Completion of an agency-developed or agency-conducted training course shall be deemed to satisfy these elements.

(d) The Contractor shall maintain and, upon request, provide documentation of completion of privacy training to the Contracting Officer.

(e) The Contractor shall not allow any employee access to a system of records, or permit any employee to create, collect, use, process, store, maintain, disseminate, disclose, dispose or otherwise handle personally identifiable information, or to design, develop, maintain, or operate a system of records unless the employee has completed privacy training, as required by this clause.

(f) The substance of this clause, including this paragraph (f), shall be included in all subcontracts under this contract, when subcontractor employees will—

(1) Have access to a system of records;

(2) Create, collect, use, process, store, maintain, disseminate, disclose, dispose, or otherwise handle personally identifiable information; or

(3) Design, develop, maintain, or operate a system of records.

(End of clause)

Alternate I (JAN 2017). As prescribed in 24.302(b), if the agency specifies that only its agency-provided training is acceptable, substitute the following paragraph (c) for paragraph (c) of the basic clause:

(c) The contracting agency will provide initial privacy training, and annual privacy training thereafter, to Contractor employees for the duration of this contract.

(End of clause)

[Final rule, 81 FR 93476, 12/20/2016, effective 1/19/2017]

52.225-1 Buy American—Supplies.

As prescribed in 25.1101(a)(1), insert the following clause:

BUY AMERICAN—SUPPLIES (MAY 2014)

(a) *Definitions*. As used in this clause—

Commercially available off-the-shelf (COTS) item— (1) Means any item of supply (including construction material) that is—

(i) A commercial item (as defined in paragraph (1) of the definition at FAR 2.101);

(ii) Sold in substantial quantities in the commercial marketplace; and

(iii) Offered to the Government, under a contract or subcontract at any tier, without modification, in the same form in which it is sold in the commercial marketplace; and

(2) Does not include bulk cargo, as defined in 46 U.S.C. 40102(4), such as agricultural products and petroleum products.

Component means any article, material, or supply incorporated directly into an end product.

Cost of components means—

(1) For components purchased by the Contractor, the acquisition cost, including transportation costs to the place of incorporation into the end product (whether or not such costs are paid to a domestic firm), and any applicable duty (whether or not a duty-free entry certificate is issued); or

(2) For components manufactured by the Contractor, all costs associated with the manufacture of the component, including transportation costs as described in paragraph (1) of this definition, plus allocable overhead costs, but excluding profit. Cost of components does not include any costs associated with the manufacture of the end product.

Domestic end product means—

(1) An unmanufactured end product mined or produced in the United States;

(2) An end product manufactured in the United States, if—

(i) The cost of its components mined, produced, or manufactured in the United States exceeds 50 percent of the cost of all its components. Components of foreign origin of the same class or kind as those that the agency determines are not mined, produced, or manufactured in sufficient and reasonably available commercial quantities of a satisfactory quality are treated as domestic. Scrap generated, collected, and prepared for processing in the United States is considered domestic; or

(ii) The end product is a COTS item.

End product means those articles, materials, and supplies to be acquired under the contract for public use.

Foreign end product means an end product other than a domestic end product.

United States means the 50 States, the District of Columbia, and outlying areas.

(b) 41 U.S.C. chapter 83, Buy American, provides a preference for domestic end products for supplies acquired for use in the United States. In accordance with 41 U.S.C. 1907, the component test of the Buy American statute is waived for an end product that is a COTS item (See 12.505(a)(1)).

(c) Offerors may obtain from the Contracting Officer a list of foreign articles that the Contracting Officer will treat as domestic for this contract.

(d) The Contractor shall deliver only domestic end products except to the extent that it specified delivery of foreign end products in the provision of the solicitation entitled "Buy American Certificate."

(End of clause)

[FAC 97-15, 64 FR 72414, 12/27/99, effective 2/25/2000; FAC 2001-02, 66 FR 65347, 12/18/2001, effective 2/19/2002; FAC 2001-07, 67 FR 21534, 4/30/2002, 5/15/2002; FAC 2001-14, 68 FR 28079, 5/22/2003, effective 6/23/2003; FAC 2005-30, 74 FR 2713, 1/15/2009, effective 2/17/2009; FAC 2005-73, 79 FR 24192, 4/29/2014, effective 5/29/2014]

52.225-2 Buy American Certificate.

As prescribed in 25.1101(a)(2), insert the following provision:

BUY AMERICAN CERTIFICATE (MAY 2014)

(a) The offeror certifies that each end product, except those listed in paragraph (b) of this provision, is a domestic end product and that for other than COTS items, the offeror has considered components of unknown origin to have been mined, produced, or manufactured outside the United States. The offeror shall list as foreign end products those end products manufactured in the United States that do not qualify as domestic end products, i.e., an end product that is not a COTS item and does not meet the component test in paragraph (2) of the definition of *domestic end product*. The terms *commercially available off-the-shelf (COTS) item*, *component*, *domestic end product*, *end product*, *foreign end product*, and *United States* are defined in the clause of this solicitation entitled "Buy American—Supplies."

(b) Foreign End Products:

Line Item No.: ______________

Country of Origin: ______________

[*List as necessary*]

(c) The Government will evaluate offers in accordance with the policies and procedures of Part 25 of the Federal Acquisition Regulation.

(End of provision)

[FAC 97-15, 64 FR 72414, 12/27/99, effective 2/25/2000, corrected 65 FR 4633, 1/31/2000; FAC 2001-07, 67 FR 21534, 4/30/2002, 5/15/2002; FAC 2001-14, 68 FR

28079, 5/22/2003, effective 6/23/2003; FAC 2005-30, 74 FR 2713, 1/15/2009, effective 2/17/2009; FAC 2005-73, 79 FR 24192, 4/29/2014, effective 5/29/2014]

52.225-3 Buy American—Free Trade Agreements—Israeli Trade Act.

As prescribed in 25.1101(b)(1)(i), insert the following clause:

BUY AMERICAN—FREE TRADE AGREEMENTS—ISRAELI TRADE ACT (NOV 2012)

(a) *Definitions*. As used in this clause—

Bahrainian, Moroccan, Omani, Panamanian, or Peruvian end product means an article that—

(1) Is wholly the growth, product, or manufacture of Bahrain, Morocco, Oman, Panama, or Peru; or

(2) In the case of an article that consists in whole or in part of materials from another country, has been substantially transformed in Bahrain, Morocco, Oman, Panama, or Peru into a new and different article of commerce with a name, character, or use distinct from that of the article or articles from which it was transformed. The term refers to a product offered for purchase under a supply contract, but for purposes of calculating the value of the end product includes services (except transportation services) incidental to the article, provided that the value of those incidental services does not exceed that of the article itself.

Commercially available off-the-shelf (COTS) item— (1) Means any item of supply (including construction material) that is—

(i) A commercial item (as defined in paragraph (1) of the definition at FAR 2.101);

(ii) Sold in substantial quantities in the commercial marketplace; and

(iii) Offered to the Government, under a contract or subcontract at any tier, without modification, in the same form in which it is sold in the commercial marketplace; and

(2) Does not include bulk cargo, as defined in 46 U.S.C. 40102(4), such as agricultural products and petroleum products.

Component means any article, material, or supply incorporated directly into an end product.

Cost of components means—

(1) For components purchased by the Contractor, the acquisition cost, including transportation costs to the place of incorporation into the end product (whether or not such costs are paid to a domestic firm), and any applicable duty (whether or not a duty-free entry certificate is issued); or

(2) For components manufactured by the Contractor, all costs associated with the manufacture of the component, including transportation costs as described in paragraph (1) of this definition, plus allocable overhead costs, but excluding profit. Cost of components does not include any costs associated with the manufacture of the end product.

Domestic end product means—

(1) An unmanufactured end product mined or produced in the United States;

(2) An end product manufactured in the United States, if—

(i) The cost of its components mined, produced, or manufactured in the United States exceeds 50 percent of the cost of all its components. Components of foreign origin of the same class or kind as those that the agency determines are not mined, produced, or manufactured in sufficient and reasonably available commercial quantities of a satisfactory quality are treated as domestic. Scrap generated, collected, and prepared for processing in the United States is considered domestic; or

(ii) The end product is a COTS item.

End product means those articles, materials, and supplies to be acquired under the control for public use.

Free Trade Agreement country means Australia, Bahrain, Canada, Chile, Columbia, Costa Rica, Dominican Republic, El Salvador, Guatemala, Honduras, Korea (Republic of), Mexico, Morocco, Nicaragua, Oman, Panama, Peru, or Singapore.

Free Trade Agreement country end product means an article that—

(1) Is wholly the growth, product, or manufacture of a Free Trade Agreement country; or

(2) In the case of an article that consists in whole or in part of materials from another country, has been substantially transformed in a Free Trade Agreement country into a new and different article of commerce with a name, character, or use distinct from that of the article or articles from which it was transformed. The term refers to a product offered for purchase under a supply contract, but for purposes of calculating the value of the end product includes services (except transportation services) incidental to the article, provided that the value of those incidental services does not exceed that of the article itself.

Foreign end product means an end product other than a domestic end product.

Israeli end product means an article that—

(1) Is wholly the growth, product, or manufacture of Israel; or

(2) In the case of an article that consists in whole or in part of materials from another country, has been substantially transformed in Israel into a new and different article of commerce with a name, character, or use distinct from that of the article or articles from which it was transformed.

(b) *Components of foreign origin*. Offerors may obtain from the Contracting Officer a list of foreign articles that the Contracting Officer will treat as domestic for this contract.

(c) *Delivery of end products*. 41 U.S.C. chapter 83, Buy American statute, provides a preference for domestic end products for supplies acquired for use in the United States. In accordance with 41 U.S.C. 1907, the component test of the Buy American statute is waived for an end product that is a COTS item (See 12.505(a)(1)). In addition, the Contracting Officer has determined that FTAs (except the Bahrain, Morocco, Oman, Panama, and Peru FTAs) and the Israeli Trade Act apply to this acquisition. Unless otherwise specified, these trade agreements apply to all items in the Schedule. The Contractor shall deliver under this contract only domestic end products except to the extent that, in its offer, it specified delivery of foreign end products in the provision entitled "Buy American—Free Trade Agreements—Israeli Trade Act Certificate." If the Contractor specified in its offer that the Contractor would supply a Free Trade Agreement country end product (other than a Bahrainian, Moroccan, Omani, Panamanian, or Peruvian end product) or an Israeli end product, then the Contractor shall supply a Free Trade Agreement country end product (other than a Bahrainian, Moroccan, Omani, Panamanian, or Peruvian end product), an Israeli end product or, at the Contractor's option, a domestic end product.

(End of clause)

Alternate I (MAY 2014). As prescribed in 25.1101(b)(1)(ii), add the following definition to paragraph (a) of the basic clause, and substitute the following paragraph (c) for paragraph (c) of the basic clause:

Canadian end product means an article that—

(1) Is wholly the growth, product, or manufacture of Canada; or

(2) In the case of an article that consists in whole or in part of materials from another country, has been substantially transformed in Canada into a new and different article of commerce with a name, character, or use distinct from that of the article or articles from which it was transformed. The term refers to a product offered for purchase under a supply contract, but for purposes of calculating the value of the end product includes services (except transportation services) incidental to the article, provided that the value of those incidental services does not exceed that of the article itself.

(c) *Delivery of end products*. 41 U.S.C. chapter 83 provides a preference for domestic end products for supplies acquired for use in the United States. In accordance with 41 U.S.C. 1907, the component test of the Buy American statute is waived for an end product that is a COTS item (See 12.505(a)(1)). In addition, the Contracting Officer has determined that NAFTA applies to this acquisition. Unless otherwise specified, NAFTA applies to all items in the

Schedule. The Contractor shall deliver under this contract only domestic end products except to the extent that, in its offer, it specified delivery of foreign end products in the provision entitled "Buy American—Free Trade Agreements—Israeli Trade Act Certificate." If the Contractor specified in its offer that the Contractor would supply a Canadian end product, then the Contractor shall supply a Canadian end product or, at the Contractor's option, a domestic end product.

Alternate II (MAY 2014). As prescribed in 25.1101(b)(1)(iii), add the following definition to paragraph (a) of the basic clause, and substitute the following paragraph (c) for paragraph (c) of the basic clause:

Canadian end product means an article that—

(1) Is wholly the growth, product, or manufacture of Canada; or

(2) In the case of an article that consists in whole or in part of materials from another country, has been substantially transformed in Canada into a new and different article of commerce with a name, character, or use distinct from that of the article or articles from which it was transformed. The term refers to a product offered for purchase under a supply contract, but for purposes of calculating the value of the end product includes services (except transportation services) incidental to the article, provided that the value of those incidental services does not exceed that of the article itself.

(c) *Delivery of end products.* 41 U.S.C. chapter 83 provides a preference for domestic end products for supplies acquired for use in the United States. In accordance with 41 U.S.C. 1907, the component test of the Buy American statute is waived for an end product that is a COTS item (See 12.505(a)(1)). In addition, the Contracting Officer has determined that NAFTA and the Israeli Trade Act apply to this acquisition. Unless otherwise specified, these trade agreements apply to all items in the Schedule. The Contractor shall deliver under this contract only domestic end products except to the extent that, in its offer, it specified delivery of foreign end products in the provision entitled "Buy American—Free Trade Agreements—Israeli Trade Act Certificate." If the Contractor specified in its offer that the Contractor would supply a Canadian end product or an Israeli end product, then the Contractor shall supply a Canadian end product, an Israeli end product or, at the Contractor's option, a domestic end product.

Alternate III (MAY 2014). As prescribed in 25.1101(b)(1)(iv), delete the definition of *Bahrainian, Moroccan, Omani, Panamanian, or Peruvian end product* and add in its place the following definition of *Bahrainian, Korean, Moroccan, Omani, Panamanian, or Peruvian end product* in paragraph (a) of the basic clause; and substitute the following paragraph (c) for paragraph (c) of the basic clause:

Bahrainian, Korean, Moroccan, Omani, Panamanian, or Peruvian end product means an article that—

(1) Is wholly the growth, product, or manufacture of Bahrain, Korea (Republic of), Morocco, Oman, Panama, or Peru; or

(2) In the case of an article that consists in whole or in part of materials from another country, has been substantially transformed in Bahrain, Korea (Republic of), Morocco, Oman, Panama, or Peru into a new and different article of commerce with a name, character, or use distinct from that of the article or articles from which it was transformed. The term refers to a product offered for purchase under a supply contract, but for purposes of calculating the value of the end product includes services (except transportation services) incidental to the article, provided that the value of those incidental services does not exceed that of the article itself.

(c) *Delivery of end products.* 41 U.S.C. chapter 83 provides a preference for domestic end products for supplies acquired for use in the United States. In accordance with 41 U.S.C. 1907, the component test of the Buy American statute is waived for an end product that is a COTS item (See 12.505(a)(1)). In addition, the Contracting Officer has determined that FTAs (except the Bahrain, Korea (Republic of), Morocco, Oman, Panama, and Peru FTAs) and the Israeli Trade Act apply to this acquisition.

Unless otherwise specified, these trade agreements apply to all items in the Schedule. The Contractor shall deliver under this contract only domestic end products except to the extent that, in its offer, it specified delivery of foreign end products in the provision entitled "Buy American—Free Trade Agreements—Israeli Trade Act Certificate." If the Contractor specified in its offer that the Contractor would supply a Free Trade Agreement country end product (other than a Bahrainian, Korean, Moroccan, Omani, Panamanian, or Peruvian end product) or an Israeli end product, then the Contractor shall supply a Free Trade Agreement country end product (other than a Bahrainian, Korean, Moroccan, Omani, Panamanian, or Peruvian end product), an Israeli end product or, at the Contractor's option, a domestic end product.

[FAC 97-15, 64 FR 72414, 12/27/99, effective 2/25/2000; FAC 2001-02, 66 FR 65347, 12/18/2001, effective 2/19/2002; FAC 2001-07, 67 FR 21534, 4/30/2002, effective 5/15/2002; FAC 2001-14, 68 FR 28079, 5/22/2003, effective 6/23/2003; FAC 2001-19, Interim rule, 69 FR 1051, 1/7/2004, effective 1/1/2004; FAC 2001-25, 69 FR 59700, 10/5/2004, effective 10/5/2004; FAC 2001-27, interim rule, 69 FR 77870, 12/28/2004, effective 1/1/2005; FAC 2005-07, 71 FR 219, 1/3/2006, effective 1/3/2006; FAC 2005-09, Interim rule, 71 FR 20306, 4/19/2006, effective 4/19/2006; FAC 2005-10, 71 FR 36935, 6/28/2006, effective 6/28/2006; FAC 2005-14, 71 FR 67776, 71 FR 67778, 11/22/2006, effective 11/22/2006; FAC 2005-19, 72 FR 46357, 46360, 46361, 8/17/2007, effective 8/17/2007; FAC 2005-24, 73 FR 10964, 2/28/2008, effective 2/28/2008; FAC 2005-30, 74 FR 2713, 1/15/2009, effective 2/17/2009; FAC 2005-33, Interim rule, 74 FR 28426, 6/15/2009, effective 6/15/2009; FAC 2005-39, 75 FR 13421, 3/19/2010, effective 3/19/2010; FAC 2005-57, 77 FR 13952, 3/7/2012, effective 3/15/2012; FAC 2005-59, 77 FR 27548, 5/10/2012, effective 5/15/2012; FAC 2005-61, 77 FR 56739, 9/13/2012, effective 9/13/2012; FAC 2005-62, 77 FR 69723, 11/20/2012, effective 11/20/2012; FAC 2005-65, 78 FR 6188, 1/29/2013, effective 1/29/2013; FAC 2005-67, 78 FR 37695, 6/21/2013, effective 6/21/2013; FAC 2005-73, 79 FR 24192, 4/29/2014, effective 5/29/2014]

52.225-4 Buy American—Free Trade Agreements—Israeli Trade Act Certificate.

As prescribed in 25.1101(b)(2)(i), insert the following provision:

BUY AMERICAN—FREE TRADE AGREEMENT—ISRAELI TRADE ACT CERTIFICATE (MAY 2014)

(a) The offeror certifies that each end product, except those listed in paragraph (b) or (c) of this provision, is a domestic end product and that the offeror has considered components of unknown origin to have been mined, produced, or manufactured outside the United States. The terms *Bahrainian, Moroccan, Omani, Panamanian, or Peruvian end product, component, domestic end product, end product, foreign end product, Free Trade Agreement country, Free Trade Agreement country end product, Israeli end product,* and *United States* are defined in the clause of this solicitation entitled "Buy American—Free Trade Agreements—Israeli Trade Act."

(b) The offeror certifies that the following supplies are Free Trade Agreement country end products (other than Bahrainian, Moroccan, Omani, Panamanian, or Peruvian end products) or Israeli end products as defined in the clause of this solicitation entitled "Buy American—Free Trade Agreements—Israeli Trade Act":

Free Trade Agreement Country End Products (Other than Bahrainian, Moroccan, Omani, Panamanian, or Peruvian End Products) or Israeli End Products:

Line Item No.

____

____

____

[*List as necessary*]

(c) The offeror shall list those supplies that are foreign end products (other than those listed in paragraph (b) of this provision) as defined in the clause of this solicitation entitled "Buy American—Free Trade Agreements—Israeli Trade Act." The offeror shall list as other foreign end products those end products manufactured in the United States that do not qualify as domestic end products, i.e., an end product that is not a COTS item and does not meet the component test in paragraph (2) of the definition of *domestic end product*.

Other Foreign End Products

Line Item No.: ______

Country of Origin: ______

[*List as necessary*]

(d) The Government will evaluate offers in accordance with the policies and procedures of Part 25 of the Federal Acquisition Regulation.

(End of provision)

Alternate I (MAY 2014). As prescribed in 25.1101(b)(2)(ii), substitute the following paragraph (b) for paragraph (b) of the basic provision:

(b) The offeror certifies that the following supplies are Canadian end products as defined in the clause of this solicitation entitled "Buy American—Free Trade Agreements—Israeli Trade Act":

Canadian End Products:

Line Item No.: ______

Country of Origin: ______

[*List as necessary*]

Alternate II (MAY 2014). As prescribed in 25.1101(b)(2)(iii), substitute the following paragraph (b) for paragraph (b) of the basic provision:

(b) The offeror certifies that the following supplies are Canadian end products or Israeli end products as defined in the clause of this solicitation entitled "Buy American—Free Trade Agreements—Israeli Trade Act":

Canadian or Israeli End Products

Line Item No.: ______

Country of Origin: ______

[*List as necessary*]

Alternate III (MAY 2014). As prescribed in 25.1101(b)(2)(iv), substitute the following paragraph (b) for paragraph (b) of the basic provision:

(b) The offeror certifies that the following supplies are Free Trade Agreement country end products (other than Bahrainian, Korean, Moroccan, Omani, Panamanian, or Peruvian end products) or Israeli end products as defined in the clause of this solicitation entitled "Buy American—Free Trade Agreements—Israeli Trade Act":

Free Trade Agreement Country End Products (Other than Bahrainian, Korean, Moroccan, Omani, Panamanian, or Peruvian End Products) or Israeli End Products:

Line Item No.: ______

Country of Origin: ______

[*List as necessary*]

[FAC 97-15, 64 FR 72414, 12/27/99, effective 2/25/2000, corrected 65 FR 4633, 1/31/2000; FAC 2001-07, 67 FR 21534, 4/30/2002, effective 5/15/2002; FAC 2001-14, 68 FR 28079, 5/22/2003, effective 6/23/2003; FAC 2001-19, Interim rule, 69 FR 1051, 1/7/2004, effective 1/7/2004; FAC 2001-25, 69 FR 59700, 10/5/2004, effective 10/5/2004; FAC 2001-27, interim rule, 69 FR 77870, 12/28/2004, effective 1/1/2005; FAC 2005-07, 71 FR 219, 1/3/2006, effective 1/3/2006; FAC 2005-10, 71 FR 36935, 6/28/2006, effective 6/28/2006; FAC 2005-14, 71 FR 67776, 11/22/2006, effective 11/22/2006; FAC 2005-19, 72 FR 46357, 46360, 46361, 8/17/2007, effective 8/17/2007; FAC 2005-24, 73 FR 10964, 2/28/2008, effective 2/28/2008; FAC 2005-30, 74 FR 2713, 1/15/2009, effective 2/17/2009; FAC 2005-33, Interim rule, 74 FR 28426, 6/15/2009, effective 6/15/2009; FAC 2005-39, 75 FR 13421, 3/19/2010, effective 3/19/2010; FAC 2005-54, 76 FR 68027, 11/2/2011, effective 11/2/2011; FAC 2005-57, 77 FR 13952, 3/7/2012, effective 3/15/2012; FAC 2005-61, 77 FR 56739, 9/13/2012, effective 9/13/2012; FAC 2005-62, 77 FR 69723, 11/20/2012, effective 11/20/2012; FAC 2005-67, 78 FR 37695, 6/21/2013, effective 6/21/2013; FAC 2005-73, 79 FR 24192, 4/29/2014, effective 5/29/2014]

52.225-5 Trade Agreements.

As prescribed in 25.1101(c)(1), insert the following clause:

TRADE AGREEMENTS (OCT 2019)

(a) *Definitions*. As used in this clause—

Caribbean Basin country end product—

(1) Means an article that—

(i)(A) Is wholly the growth, product, or manufacture of a Caribbean Basin country; or

(B) In the case of an article that consists in whole or in part of materials from another country, has been substantially transformed in a Caribbean Basin country into a new and different article of commerce with a name, character, or use distinct from that of the article or articles from which it was transformed; and

(ii) Is not excluded from duty-free treatment for Caribbean countries under 19 U.S.C. 2703(b).

(A) For this reason, the following articles are not Caribbean Basin country end products:

(1) Tuna, prepared or preserved in any manner in airtight containers;

(2) Petroleum, or any product derived from petroleum;

(3) Watches and watch parts (including cases, bracelets, and straps) of whatever type including, but not limited to, mechanical, quartz digital, or quartz analog, if such watches or watch parts contain any material that is the product of any country to which the Harmonized Tariff Schedule of the United States (HTSUS) column 2 rates of duty apply (*i.e.*, Afghanistan, Cuba, Laos, North Korea, and Vietnam); and

(4) Certain of the following: textiles and apparel articles; footwear, handbags, luggage, flat goods, work gloves, and leather wearing apparel; or handloomed, handmade, and folklore articles;

(B) Access to the HTSUS to determine duty-free status of articles of these types is available at *https://usitc.gov/tata/hts/index.htm*. In particular, see the following:

(1) General Note 3(c), Products Eligible for Special Tariff treatment.

(2) General Note 17, Products of Countries Designated as Beneficiary Countries under the United States–Caribbean Basin Trade Partnership Act of 2000.

(3) Section XXII, Chapter 98, Subchapter II, Articles Exported and Returned, Advanced or Improved Abroad, U.S. Note 7(b).

(4) Section XXII, Chapter 98, Subchapter XX, Goods Eligible for Special Tariff Benefits under the United States Caribbean Basin Trade Partnership Act; and

(2) Refers to a product offered for purchase under a supply contract, but for purposes of calculating the value of the acquisition, includes services (except transportation services) incidental to the article, provided that the value of those incidental services does not exceed that of the article itself.

Designated country means any of the following countries:

(1) A World Trade Organization Government Procurement Agreement (WTO GPA) country (Armenia, Aruba, Australia, Austria, Belgium, Bulgaria, Canada, Croatia, Cyprus, Czech Republic, Denmark, Estonia, Finland, France, Germany, Greece, Hong Kong, Hungary, Iceland, Ireland, Israel, Italy, Japan, Korea (Republic of), Latvia, Liechtenstein, Lithuania, Luxembourg, Malta, Moldova, Montenegro, Netherlands, New Zealand, Norway, Poland, Portugal, Romania, Singapore, Slovak Republic, Slovenia, Spain, Sweden, Switzerland, Taipei, Taiwan (known in the World Trade Organization as "the Separate Customs Territory of Taiwan, Penghu, Kinmen and Matsu (Chinese Taipei)"), Ukraine, or United Kingdom);

(2) A Free Trade Agreement (FTA) country (Australia, Bahrain, Canada, Chile, Colombia, Costa Rica, Dominican Republic, El Salvador, Guatemala, Honduras, Korea (Republic of), Mexico, Morocco, Nicaragua, Oman, Panama, Peru, or Singapore);

(3) A least developed country (Afghanistan, Angola, Bangladesh, Benin, Bhutan, Burkina Faso, Burundi, Cambodia, Central African Republic, Chad, Comoros, Demo-

cratic Republic of Congo, Djibouti, Equatorial Guinea, Eritrea, Ethiopia, Gambia, Guinea, Guinea-Bissau, Haiti, Kiribati, Laos, Lesotho, Liberia, Madagascar, Malawi, Mali, Mauritania, Mozambique, Nepal, Niger, Rwanda, Samoa, Sao Tome and Principe, Senegal, Sierra Leone, Solomon Islands, Somalia, South Sudan, Tanzania, Timor-Leste, Togo, Tuvalu, Uganda, Vanuatu, Yemen, or Zambia); or

(4) A Caribbean Basin country (Antigua and Barbuda, Aruba, Bahamas, Barbados, Belize, Bonaire, British Virgin Islands, Curacao, Dominica, Grenada, Guyana, Haiti, Jamaica, Montserrat, Saba, St. Kitts and Nevis, St. Lucia, St. Vincent and the Grenadines, Sint Eustatius, Sint Maarten, or Trinidad and Tobago).

Designated country end product means a WTO GPA country end product, an FTA country end product, a least developed country end product, or a Caribbean Basin country end product.

End product means those articles, materials, and supplies to be acquired under the contract for public use.

Free Trade Agreement country end product means an article that—

(1) Is wholly the growth, product, or manufacture of a Free Trade Agreement (FTA) country; or

(2) In the case of an article that consists in whole or in part of materials from another country, has been substantially transformed in an FTA country into a new and different article of commerce with a name, character, or use distinct from that of the article or articles from which it was transformed. The term refers to a product offered for purchase under a supply contract, but for purposes of calculating the value of the end product includes services (except transportation services) incidental to the article, provided that the value of those incidental services does not exceed that of the article itself.

Least developed country end product means an article that—

(1) Is wholly the growth, product, or manufacture of a least developed country; or

(2) In the case of an article that consists in whole or in part of materials from another country, has been substantially transformed in a least developed country into a new and different article of commerce with a name, character, or use distinct from that of the article or articles from which it was transformed. The term refers to a product offered for purchase under a supply contract, but for purposes of calculating the value of the end product, includes services (except transportation services) incidental to the article, provided that the value of those incidental services does not exceed that of the article itself.

United States means the 50 States, the District of Columbia, and outlying areas.

U.S.-made end product means an article that is mined, produced, or manufactured in the United States or that is substantially transformed in the United States into a new and different article of commerce with a name, character, or use distinct from that of the article or articles from which it was transformed.

WTO GPA country end product means an article that—

(1) Is wholly the growth, product, or manufacture of a WTO GPA country; or

(2) In the case of an article that consists in whole or in part of materials from another country, has been substantially transformed in a WTO GPA country into a new and different article of commerce with a name, character, or use distinct from that of the article or articles from which it was transformed. The term refers to a product offered for purchase under a supply contract, but for purposes of calculating the value of the end product includes services, (except transportation services) incidental to the article, provided that the value of those incidental services does not exceed that of the article itself.

(b) *Delivery of end products.* The Contracting Officer has determined that the WTO GPA and FTAs apply to this acquisition. Unless otherwise specified, these trade agreements apply to all items in the Schedule. The Contractor shall deliver under this contract only U.S.-made or designated country end products except to the extent that, in its offer, it specified delivery of other end products in the provision entitled "Trade Agreements Certificate."

(End of clause)

[FAC 97-15, 64 FR 72414, 12/27/99, effective 2/25/2000; FAC 97-17, 65 FR 24316, 4/25/2000, effective 4/25/2000; FAC 2001-02, 66 FR 65347, 12/18/2001, effective 12/18/2001; FAC 2001-04, 67 FR 6112, 2/8/2002, effective 2/20/2002; FAC 2001-10, 67 FR 70519, 11/22/2002, effective 11/22/2002; FAC 2001-14, 68 FR 28079, 5/22/2003, effective 6/23/2003; FAC 2001-16, 68 FR 56684, 10/1/2002, effective 10/31/2003; FAC 2001-24, 69 FR 1051, 1/7/2004, effective 1/12/2004; FAC 2001-24, 69 FR 34239, 6/18/2004, effective 6/18/2004; FAC 2001-25, 69 FR 59700, 10/5/2004, effective 10/5/2004; FAC 2001-27, interim rule, 69 FR 77870, 12/28/2004, effective 1/12/005; FAC 2005-07, 71 FR 219, 1/3/2006, effective 1/3/2006; FAC 2005-09, Interim rule, 71 FR 20306, 4/19/2006, effective 4/19/2006; FAC 2005-10, 71 FR 36935, 6/28/2006, effective 6/28/2006; FAC 2005-14, 71 FR 67776, 71 FR 67778, 11/22/2006, effective 11/22/2006; FAC 2005-19, 72 FR 46357, 46360, 46361, 8/17/2007, effective 8/17/2007; FAC 2005-21, 72 FR 63089, 11/7/2007, effective 11/7/2007; FAC 2005-24, 73 FR 10964, 2/28/2008, effective 2/28/2008; FAC 2005-31, 74 FR 11828, 3/19/2009, effective 3/19/2009; FAC 2005-33, Interim rule, 74 FR 28426; 6/15/2009, effective 6/15/2009; FAC 2005-36, 74 FR 40461, 8/11/2009, effective 8/11/2009; FAC 2005-39, 75 FR 13421, 3/19/2010, effective 3/19/2010; FAC 2005-42, 75 FR 34282, 6/16/2010, effective 6/16/2010; FAC 2005-54, FR 68039, 11/2/2011, effective 11/2/2011; FAC 2005-56, 77 FR 12935, 3/2/2012, effective 3/2/2012; FAC 2005-57, 77 FR 13952, 3/7/2012, effective 3/15/2012; Correction, 77 FR 14303, 3/9/2012, effective 3/9/2012; Correction, 77 FR 17353, 3/26/2012, effective 3/26/2012; FAC 2005-59, 77 FR 27548, 5/10/2012, effective 5/15/2012; FAC 2005-61, 77 FR 56739, 9/13/2012, effective 9/13/2012; FAC 2005-62, 77 FR 69723, 11/20/2012, effective 11/20/2012; FAC 2005-65, 78 FR 6188, 1/29/2013, effective 1/29/2013; FAC 2005-67, 78 FR 37695, 6/21/2013, effective 6/21/2013; FAC 2005-69, 78 FR 46792, 8/1/2013, effective 9/3/2013; FAC 2005-71, 78 FR 70480, 11/25/2013, effective 11/25/2013; FAC 2005-86, 80 FR 81892, 12/31/2015, effective 2/1/2016; FAC 2005-91, 81 FR 67774, 9/30/2016, effective 10/31/2016; FAC 2005-100, 83 FR 42571, 8/22/2018, effective 8/22/2018; FAC 2019-06, 84 FR 47866, 9/10/2019, effective 10/10/2019]

52.225-6 Trade Agreements Certificate.

As prescribed in 25.1101(c)(2), insert the following provision:

TRADE AGREEMENTS CERTIFICATE (MAY 2014)

(a) The offeror certifies that each end product, except those listed in paragraph (b) of this provision, is a U.S.-made, designated country end product, as defined in the clause of this solicitation entitled "Trade Agreements."

(b) The offeror shall list as other end products those supplies that are not U.S.-made, designated country end products, Caribbean Basin country, or FTA country end products.

Other End Products

Line Item No.: ———

Country of Origin: ———

[*List as necessary*]

(c) The Government will evaluate offers in accordance with the policies and procedures of Part 25 of the Federal Acquisition Regulation. For line items covered by the WTO GPA, the Government will evaluate offers of U.S.-made or designated country end products without regard to the restrictions of the Buy American statute. The Government will consider for award only offers of U.S.-made or designated country end products unless the Contracting Officer determines that there are no offers for such products or that the offers for those products are insufficient to fulfill the requirements of this solicitation.

(End of provision)

[FAC 97-15, 64 FR 72414, 12/27/99, effective 2/25/2000; FAC 2001-07, 67 FR 21534, 4/30/2002, effective 5/15/2002; FAC 2001-19, 69 FR 1051, 1/7/2004, effective 1/1/2004; FAC 2001-25, 69 FR 59700, 10/5/2004, effective 10/5/2004; FAC 2001-27, interim rule, 69 FR 77870, 12/28/2004, effective 1/1/2005; FAC 2005-07, 71 FR 219, 1/3/2006, effective 1/3/2006; FAC 2005-73, 79 FR 24192, 4/29/2014, effective 5/29/2014]

52.225-7 Waiver of Buy American Statute for Civil Aircraft and Related Articles.

As prescribed in 25.1101(d), insert the following provision:

WAIVER OF BUY AMERICAN STATUTE FOR CIVIL AIRCRAFT AND RELATED ARTICLES (FEB 2016)

(a) *Definition. Civil aircraft and related articles*, as used in this provision, means—

(1) All aircraft other than aircraft to be purchased for use by the Department of Defense or the U.S. Coast Guard;

(2) The engines (and parts and components for incorporation into the engines) of these aircraft;

(3) Any other parts, components, and subassemblies for incorporation into the aircraft; and

(4) Any ground flight simulators, and parts and components of these simulators, for use with respect to the aircraft, whether to be used as original or replacement equipment in the manufacture, repair, maintenance, rebuilding, modification, or conversion of the aircraft, and without regard to whether the aircraft or articles receive duty-free treatment under section 601(a)(2) of the Trade Agreements Act.

(b) The U.S. Trade Representative has waived the Buy American statute for acquisitions of civil aircraft and related articles from countries that are parties to the Agreement on Trade in Civil Aircraft. Those countries are Albania, Austria, Belgium, Bulgaria, Canada, Croatia, Cyprus, Czech Republic, Denmark, Egypt, Estonia, Finland, France, Georgia, Germany, Greece, Hungary, Ireland, Italy, Japan, Latvia, Lithuania, Luxembourg, Macao China, Malta, Montenegro, the Netherlands, Norway, Poland, Portugal, Romania, Slovakia, Slovenia, Spain, Sweden, Switzerland, Taiwan (Chinese Taipei), and the United Kingdom.

(c) For the purpose of this waiver, an article is a product of a country only if—

(1) It is wholly the growth, product, or manufacture of that country; or

(2) In the case of an article that consists in whole or in part of materials from another country, it has been substantially transformed into a new and different article of commerce with a name, character, or use distinct from that of the article or articles from which it was transformed.

(d) The waiver is subject to modification or withdrawal by the U.S. Trade Representative.

(End of provision)

[FAC 97-15, 64 FR 72414, 12/27/99, effective 2/25/2000; FAC 2005-56, 77 FR 12935, 3/2/2012, effective 3/2/2012; Correction, 77 FR 14303, 3/9/2012, effective 3/9/2012; Correction, 77 FR 17353, 3/26/2012, effective 3/26/2012; FAC 2005-71, 78 FR 70480, 11/25/2013, effective 11/25/2013; FAC 2005-73, 79 FR 24192, 4/29/2014, effective 5/29/2014; FAC 2005-86, 80 FR 81892, 12/31/2015, effective 2/1/2016]

52.225-8 Duty-Free Entry.

As prescribed in 25.1101(e), insert the following clause:

DUTY-FREE ENTRY (OCT 2010)

(a) *Definition. Customs territory of the United States* means the States, the District of Columbia, and Puerto Rico.

(b) Except as otherwise approved by the Contracting Officer, the Contractor shall not include in the contract price any amount for duties on supplies specifically identified in the Schedule to be accorded duty-free entry.

(c) Except as provided in paragraph (d) of this clause or elsewhere in this contract, the following procedures apply to supplies not identified in the Schedule to be accorded duty-free entry:

(1) The Contractor shall notify the Contracting Officer in writing of any purchase of foreign supplies (including, without limitation, raw materials, components, and intermediate assemblies) in excess of $15,000 that are to be imported into the customs territory of the United States for delivery to the Government under this contract, either as end products or for incorporation into end products. The Contractor shall furnish the notice to the Contracting Officer at least 20 calendar days before the importation. The notice shall identify the—

(i) Foreign supplies;

(ii) Estimated amount of duty; and

(iii) Country of origin.

(2) The Contracting Officer will determine whether any of these supplies should be accorded duty-free entry and will notify the Contractor within 10 calendar days after receipt of the Contractor's notification.

(3) Except as otherwise approved by the Contracting Officer, the contract price shall be reduced by (or the allowable cost shall not include) the amount of duty that would be payable if the supplies were not entered duty-free.

(d) The Contractor is not required to provide the notification under paragraph (c) of this clause for purchases of foreign supplies if—

(1) The supplies are identical in nature to items purchased by the Contractor or any subcontractor in connection with its commercial business; and

(2) Segregation of these supplies to ensure use only on Government contracts containing duty-free entry provisions is not economical or feasible.

(e) The Contractor shall claim duty-free entry only for supplies to be delivered to the Government under this contract, either as end products or incorporated into end products, and shall pay duty on supplies, or any portion of them, other than scrap, salvage, or competitive sale authorized by the Contracting Officer, diverted to nongovernmental use.

(f) The Government will execute any required duty-free entry certificates for supplies to be accorded duty-free entry and will assist the Contractor in obtaining duty-free entry for these supplies.

(g) Shipping documents for supplies to be accorded duty-free entry shall consign the shipments to the contracting agency in care of the Contractor and shall include the—

(1) Delivery address of the Contractor (or contracting agency, if appropriate);

(2) Government prime contract number;

(3) Identification of carrier;

(4) Notation "UNITED STATES GOVERNMENT, ____ [*agency*], ____ Duty-free entry to be claimed pursuant to Item No(s) ____ [*from Tariff Schedules*] ____, Harmonized Tariff Schedules of the United States. Upon arrival of shipment at port of entry, District Director of Customs, please release shipment under 19 CFR part 142 and notify [*cognizant contract administration office*] for execution of Customs Forms 7501 and 7501-A and any required duty-free entry certificates.";

(5) Gross weight in pounds (if freight is based on space tonnage, state cubic feet in addition to gross shipping weight); and

(6) Estimated value in United States dollars.

(h) The Contractor shall instruct the foreign supplier to—

(1) Consign the shipment as specified in paragraph (g) of this clause;

(2) Mark all packages with the words "UNITED STATES GOVERNMENT" and the title of the contracting agency; and

(3) Include with the shipment at least two copies of the bill of lading (or other shipping document) for use by the District Director of Customs at the port of entry.

(i) The Contractor shall provide written notice to the cognizant contract administration office immediately after notification by the Contracting Officer that duty-free entry will be accorded foreign supplies or, for duty-free supplies identified in the Schedule, upon award by the Contractor to the overseas supplier. The notice shall identify the—

(1) Foreign supplies;

(2) Country of origin;

(3) Contract number; and

(4) Scheduled delivery date(s).

(j) The Contractor shall include the substance of this clause in any subcontract if—

(1) Supplies identified in the Schedule to be accorded duty-free entry will be imported into the customs territory of the United States; or

(2) Other foreign supplies in excess of $15,000 may be imported into the customs territory of the United States.

(End of clause)

[FAC 97-15, 64 FR 72414, 12/27/99, effective 2/25/2000; FAC 2005-45, 75 FR 53129, 8/30/2010, effective 10/1/2010]

52.225-9 Buy American—Construction Materials.

As prescribed in 25.1102(a), insert the following clause:

BUY AMERICAN—CONSTRUCTION MATERIALS (MAY 2014)

(a) *Definitions.* As used in this clause—

Commercially available off-the-shelf (COTS) item— (1) Means any item of supply (including construction material) that is—

(i) A commercial item (as defined in paragraph (1) of the definition at FAR 2.101);

(ii) Sold in substantial quantities in the commercial marketplace; and

(iii) Offered to the Government, under a contract or subcontract at any tier, without modification, in the same form in which it is sold in the commercial marketplace; and

(2) Does not include bulk cargo, as defined in 46 U.S.C. 40102(4), such as agricultural products and petroleum products.

Component means an article, material, or supply incorporated directly into a construction material.

Construction material means an article, material, or supply brought to the construction site by the Contractor or a subcontractor for incorporation into the building or work. The term also includes an item brought to the site preassembled from articles, materials, or supplies. However, emergency life safety systems, such as emergency lighting, fire alarm, and audio evacuation systems, that are discrete systems incorporated into a public building or work and that are produced as complete systems, are evaluated as a single and distinct construction material regardless of when or how the individual parts or components of those systems are delivered to the construction site. Materials purchased directly by the Government are supplies, not construction material.

Cost of components means—

(1) For components purchased by the Contractor, the acquisition cost, including transportation costs to the place of incorporation into the construction material (whether or not such costs are paid to a domestic firm), and any applicable duty (whether or not a duty-free entry certificate is issued); or

(2) For components manufactured by the Contractor, all costs associated with the manufacture of the component, including transportation costs as described in paragraph (1) of this definition, plus allocable overhead costs, but excluding profit. Cost of components does not include any costs associated with the manufacture of the construction material.

Domestic construction material means—

(1) An unmanufactured construction material mined or produced in the United States;

(2) A construction material manufactured in the United States, if—

(i) The cost of its components mined, produced, or manufactured in the United States exceeds 50 percent of the cost of all its components. Components of foreign origin of the same class or kind for which nonavailability determinations have been made are treated as domestic; or

(ii) The construction material is a COTS item.

Foreign construction material means a construction material other than a domestic construction material.

United States means the 50 States, the District of Columbia, and outlying areas.

(b) *Domestic preference*. (1) This clause implements 41 U.S.C. chapter 83, Buy American, by providing a preference for domestic construction material. In accordance with 41 U.S.C. 1907, the component test of the Buy American statute is waived for construction material that is a COTS item. (See FAR 12.505(a)(2)). The Contractor shall use only domestic construction material in performing this contract, except as provided in paragraphs (b)(2) and (b)(3) of this clause.

(2) This requirement does not apply to information technology that is a commercial item or to the construction materials or components listed by the Government as follows:

(3) The Contracting Officer may add other foreign construction material to the list in paragraph (b)(2) of this clause if the Government determines that—

(i) The cost of domestic construction material would be unreasonable. The cost of a particular domestic construction material subject to the requirements of the Buy American statute is unreasonable when the cost of such material exceeds the cost of foreign material by more than 6 percent;

(ii) The application of the restriction of the Buy American statute to a particular construction material would be impracticable or inconsistent with the public interest; or

(iii) The construction material is not mined, produced, or manufactured in the United States in sufficient and reasonably available commercial quantities of a satisfactory quality.

(c) *Request for determination of inapplicability of the Buy American statute.*

(1)(i) Any Contractor request to use foreign construction material in accordance with paragraph (b)(3) of this clause shall include adequate information for Government evaluation of the request, including—

(A) A description of the foreign and domestic construction materials;

(B) Unit of measure;

(C) Quantity;

(D) Price;

(E) Time of delivery or availability;

(F) Location of the construction project;

(G) Name and address of the proposed supplier; and

(H) A detailed justification of the reason for use of foreign construction materials cited in accordance with paragraph (b)(3) of this clause.

(ii) A request based on unreasonable cost shall include a reasonable survey of the market and a completed price comparison table in the format in paragraph (d) of this clause.

(iii) The price of construction material shall include all delivery costs to the construction site and any applicable duty (whether or not a duty-free certificate may be issued).

(iv) Any Contractor request for a determination submitted after contract award shall explain why the Contractor could not reasonably foresee the need for such determination and could not have requested the determination before contract award. If the Contractor does not submit a satisfactory explanation, the Contracting Officer need not make a determination.

(2) If the Government determines after contract award that an exception to the Buy American statute applies and the Contracting Officer and the Contractor negotiate adequate consideration, the Contracting Officer will modify the contract to allow use of the foreign construction material. However, when the basis for the exception is the unreasonable price of a domestic construction material, adequate consideration is not less than the differential established in paragraph (b)(3)(i) of this clause.

(3) Unless the Government determines that an exception to the Buy American statute applies, use of foreign construction material is noncompliant with the Buy American statute.

(d) *Data.* To permit evaluation of requests under paragraph (c) of this clause based on unreasonable cost, the Contractor shall include the following information and any applicable supporting data based on the survey of suppliers:

Foreign and Domestic Construction Materials Price Comparison

Construction material description	Unit of measure	Quantity	Price (dollars)[1]
Item 1:			
Foreign construction material			
Domestic construction material			
Item 2:			
Foreign construction material			
Domestic construction material			

[1]Include all delivery costs to the construction site and any applicable duty (whether or not a duty-free entry certificate is issued).

List name, address, telephone number, and contact for suppliers surveyed. Attach copy of response; if oral, attach summary.

Include other applicable supporting information.

(End of clause)

[FAC 97-15, 64 FR 72414, 12/27/99, effective 2/25/2000, corrected 65 FR 4633, 1/31/2000; FAC 2001-02, 66 FR 65347, 12/18/2001, effective 2/19/2002; FAC 2001-07, 67 FR 21534, 4/20/2002, effective 5/15/2002; FAC 2001-14, 68 FR 28079, 5/22/2003, effective 6/23/2003; FAC 2001-27, interim rule, 69 FR 77870, 12/28/2004, effective 1/1/2005; FAC 2005-07, 71 FR 219, 1/3/2006, effective 1/3/2006; FAC 2005-30, 74 FR 2713, 1/15/2009, effective 2/17/2009; FAC 2005-46, 75 FR 60266, 9/29/2010, effective 9/29/2010; FAC 2005-52, 76 FR 31415, 5/31/2011, effective 5/31/2011; FAC 2005-73, 79 FR 24192, 4/29/2014, effective 5/29/2014]

52.225-10 Notice of Buy American Requirement—Construction Materials.

As prescribed in 25.1102(b)(1), insert the following provision:

NOTICE OF BUY AMERICAN REQUIREMENT—CONSTRUCTION MATERIALS (MAY 2014)

(a) *Definitions. Commercially available off-the-shelf (COTS) item, construction material, domestic construction material*, and *foreign construction material*, as used in this provision, are defined in the clause of this solicitation entitled *Buy American—Construction Materials* (Federal Acquisition Regulation (FAR) clause 52.225-9).

(b) *Requests for determinations of inapplicability.* An offeror requesting a determination regarding the inapplicability of the Buy American statute should submit the request to the Contracting Officer in time to allow a determination before submission of offers. The offeror shall include the information and applicable supporting data required by paragraphs (c) and (d) of the clause at FAR 52.225-9 in the request. If an offeror has not requested a determination regarding the inapplicability of the Buy American statute before submitting its offer, or has not received a response to a previous request, the offeror shall include the information and supporting data in the offer.

(c) *Evaluation of offers.*

(1) The Government will evaluate an offer requesting exception to the requirements of the Buy American statute, based on claimed unreasonable cost of domestic construction material, by adding to the offered price the appropriate percentage of the cost of such

foreign construction material, as specified in paragraph (b)(3)(i) of the clause at FAR 52.225-9.

(2) If evaluation results in a tie between an offeror that requested the substitution of foreign construction material based on unreasonable cost and an offeror that did not request an exception, the Contracting Officer will award to the offeror that did not request an exception based on unreasonable cost.

(d) *Alternate offers.*

(1) When an offer includes foreign construction material not listed by the Government in this solicitation in paragraph (b)(2) of the clause at FAR 52.225-9, the offeror also may submit an alternate offer based on use of equivalent domestic construction material.

(2) If an alternate offer is submitted, the offeror shall submit a separate Standard Form 1442 for the alternate offer, and a separate price comparison table prepared in accordance with paragraphs (c) and (d) of the clause at FAR 52.225-9 for the offer that is based on the use of any foreign construction material for which the Government has not yet determined an exception applies.

(3) If the Government determines that a particular exception requested in accordance with paragraph (c) of the clause at FAR 52.225-9 does not apply, the Government will evaluate only those offers based on use of the equivalent domestic construction material, and the offeror shall be required to furnish such domestic construction material. An offer based on use of the foreign construction material for which an exception was requested—

(i) Will be rejected as nonresponsive if this acquisition is conducted by sealed bidding; or

(ii) May be accepted if revised during negotiations.

(End of provision)

Alternate I (MAY 2014). As prescribed in 25.1102(b)(2), substitute the following paragraph (b) for paragraph (b) of the basic provision:

(b) *Requests for determinations of inapplicability.* An offeror requesting a determination regarding the inapplicability of the Buy American statute shall submit the request with its offer, including the information and applicable supporting data required by paragraphs (c) and (d) of the clause at FAR 52.225-9.

[FAC 97-15, 64 FR 72414, 12/27/99, effective 2/25/2000; FAC 2001-07, 67 FR 21534, 4/30/2002, effective 5/15/2002; FAC 2005-30, 74 FR 2713, 1/15/2009, effective 2/17/2009; FAC 2005-73, 79 FR 24192, 4/29/2014, effective 5/29/2014]

52.225-11 Buy American Act—Construction Materials under Trade Agreements.

As prescribed in 25.1102(c), insert the following clause:

BUY AMERICAN ACT —CONSTRUCTION MATERIALS UNDER TRADE AGREEMENTS (OCT 2019)

(a) *Definitions.* As used in this clause—

Caribbean Basin country construction material means a construction material that—

(1) Is wholly the growth, product, or manufacture of a Caribbean Basin country; or

(2) In the case of a construction material that consists in whole or in part of materials from another country, has been substantially transformed in a Caribbean Basin country into a new and different construction material distinct from the materials from which it was transformed.

Commercially available off-the-shelf (COTS) item— (1) Means any item of supply (including construction material) that is—

(i) A commercial item (as defined in paragraph (1) of the definition at FAR 2.101);

(ii) Sold in substantial quantities in the commercial marketplace; and

(iii) Offered to the Government, under a contract or subcontract at any tier, without modification, in the same form in which it is sold in the commercial marketplace; and

(2) Does not include bulk cargo, as defined in 46 U.S.C. 40102(4), such as agricultural products and petroleum products.

Component means an article, material, or supply incorporated directly into a construction material.

Construction material means an article, material, or supply brought to the construction site by the Contractor or subcontractor for incorporation into the building or work. The term also includes an item brought to the site preassembled from articles, materials, or supplies. However, emergency life safety systems, such as emergency lighting, fire alarm, and audio evacuation systems, that are discrete systems incorporated into a public building or work and that are produced as complete systems, are evaluated as a single and distinct construction material regardless of when or how the individual parts or components of those systems are delivered to the construction site. Materials purchased directly by the Government are supplies, not construction material.

Cost of components means—

(1) For components purchased by the Contractor, the acquisition cost, including transportation costs to the place of incorporation into the construction material (whether or not such costs are paid to a domestic firm), and any applicable duty (whether or not a duty-free entry certificate is issued); or

(2) For components manufactured by the Contractor, all costs associated with the manufacture of the component, including transportation costs as described in paragraph (1) of this definition, plus allocable overhead costs, but excluding profit. Cost of components does not include any costs associated with the manufacture of the construction material.

Designated country means any of the following countries:

(1) A World Trade Organization Government Procurement Agreement (WTO GPA) country (Armenia, Aruba, Australia, Austria, Belgium, Bulgaria, Canada, Croatia, Cyprus, Czech Republic, Denmark, Estonia, Finland, France, Germany, Greece, Hong Kong, Hungary, Iceland, Ireland, Israel, Italy, Japan, Korea (Republic of), Latvia, Liechtenstein, Lithuania, Luxembourg, Malta, Moldova, Montenegro, Netherlands, New Zealand, Norway, Poland, Portugal, Romania, Singapore, Slovak Republic, Slovenia, Spain, Sweden, Switzerland, Taiwan, Ukraine, or United Kingdom);

(2) A Free Trade Agreement (FTA) country (Australia, Bahrain, Canada, Chile, Colombia, Costa Rica, Dominican Republic, El Salvador, Guatemala, Honduras, Korea (Republic of), Mexico, Morocco, Nicaragua, Oman, Panama, Peru, or Singapore);

(3) A least developed country (Afghanistan, Angola, Bangladesh, Benin, Bhutan, Burkina Faso, Burundi, Cambodia, Central African Republic, Chad, Comoros, Democratic Republic of Congo, Djibouti, Equatorial Guinea, Eritrea, Ethiopia, Gambia, Guinea, Guinea-Bissau, Haiti, Kiribati, Laos, Lesotho, Liberia, Madagascar, Malawi, Mali, Mauritania, Mozambique, Nepal, Niger, Rwanda, Samoa, Sao Tome and Principe, Senegal, Sierra Leone, Solomon Islands, Somalia, South Sudan, Tanzania, Timor-Leste, Togo, Tuvalu, Uganda, Vanuatu, Yemen, or Zambia); or

(4) A Caribbean Basin country (Antigua and Barbuda, Aruba, Bahamas, Barbados, Belize, Bonaire, British Virgin Islands, Curacao, Dominica, Grenada, Guyana, Haiti, Jamaica, Montserrat, Saba, St. Kitts and Nevis, St. Lucia, St. Vincent and the Grenadines, Sint Eustatius, Sint Maarten, or Trinidad and Tobago).

Designated country construction material means a construction material that is a WTO GPA country construction material, an FTA country construction material, a least developed country construction material, or a Caribbean Basin country construction material.

Domestic construction material means—

(1) An unmanufactured construction material mined or produced in the United States;

(2) A construction material manufactured in the United States, if—

(i) The cost of its components mined, produced, or manufactured in the United States exceeds 50 percent of the cost of all its components. Components of foreign origin of the same class or kind for which nonavailability determinations have been made are treated as domestic; or

(ii) The construction material is a COTS item.

Foreign construction material means a construction material other than a domestic construction material.

Free Trade Agreement country construction material means a construction material that—

(1) Is wholly the growth, product, or manufacture of a Free Trade Agreement (FTA) country; or

(2) In the case of a construction material that consists in whole or in part of materials from another country, has been substantially transformed in a FTA country into a new and different construction material distinct from the materials from which it was transformed.

Least developed country construction material means a construction material that—

(1) Is wholly the growth, product, or manufacture of a least developed country; or

(2) In the case of a construction material that consists in whole or in part of materials from another country, has been substantially transformed in a least developed country into a new and different construction material distinct from the materials from which it transformed.

United States means the 50 States, the District of Columbia, and outlying areas.

WTO GPA country construction material means a construction material that—

(1) Is wholly the growth, product, or manufacture of a WTO GPA country; or

(2) In the case of a construction material that consists in whole or in part of a materials from another country, has been substantially transformed in a WTO GPA country into a new and different construction material distinct from the materials from which it was transformed.

(b) *Construction materials.* (1) This clause implements 41 U.S.C. chapter 83, Buy American, by providing a preference for domestic construction material. In accordance with 41 U.S.C. 1907, the component test of the Buy American statute is waived for construction material that is a COTS item. (See FAR 12.505(a)(2)). In addition, the Contracting Officer has determined that the WTO GPA and Free Trade Agreements (FTAs) apply to this acquisition. Therefore, the Buy American restrictions are waived for designated country construction materials.

(2) The Contractor shall use only domestic, or designated country, or FTA country construction material in performing this contract, except as provided in paragraphs (b)(3) and (b)(4) of this clause.

(3) The requirement in paragraph (b)(2) of this clause does not apply to information technology that is a commercial item or to the construction materials or components listed by the Government as follows:

[*Contracting Officer to list applicable excepted materials or indicate "none"*]

(4) The Contracting Officer may add other foreign construction material to the list in paragraph (b)(3) of this clause if the Government determines that—

(i) The cost of domestic construction material would be unreasonable. The cost of a particular domestic construction material subject to the restrictions of the Buy American statute is unreasonable when the cost of such material exceeds the cost of foreign material by more than 6 percent;

(ii) The application of the restriction of the Buy American statute to a particular construction material would be impracticable or inconsistent with the public interest; or

(iii) The construction material is not mined, produced, or manufactured in the United States in sufficient and reasonably available commercial quantities of a satisfactory quality.

(c) *Request for determination of inapplicability of the Buy American statute.* (1)(i) Any Contractor request to use foreign construction material in accordance with paragraph (b)(4) of this clause shall include adequate information for Government evaluation of the request, including—

(A) A description of the foreign and domestic construction materials;

(B) Unit of measure;

(C) Quantity;

(D) Price;

(E) Time of delivery or availability;

(F) Location of the construction project;

(G) Name and address of the proposed supplier; and

(H) A detailed justification of the reason for use of foreign construction materials cited in accordance with paragraph (b) (3) of this clause.

(ii) A request based on unreasonable cost shall include a reasonable survey of the market and a completed price comparison table in the format in paragraph (d) of this clause.

(iii) The price of construction material shall include all delivery costs to the construction site and any applicable duty (whether or not a duty-free certificate may be issued).

(iv) Any Contractor request for a determination submitted after contract award shall explain why the Contractor could not reasonably foresee the need for such determination and could not have requested the determination before contract award. If the Contractor does not submit a satisfactory explanation, the Contracting Officer need not make a determination.

(2) If the Government determines after contract award that an exception to the Buy American statute applies and the Contracting Officer and the Contractor negotiate adequate consideration, the Contracting Officer will modify the contract to allow use of the foreign construction material. However, when the basis for the exception is the unreasonable price of a domestic construction material, adequate consideration is not less than the differential established in paragraph (b) (4) (i) of this clause.

(3) Unless the Government determines that an exception to the Buy American statute applies, use of foreign construction material is noncompliant with the Buy American statute.

(d) *Data*. To permit evaluation of requests under paragraph (c) of this clause based on unreasonable cost, the Contractor shall include the following information and any applicable supporting data based on the survey of suppliers:

Foreign and Domestic Construction Materials Price Comparison

Construction material description	Unit of measure	Quantity	Price (dollars)[1]
Item 1:			
Foreign construction material			
Domestic construction material			
Item 2:			
Foreign construction material			
Domestic construction material			

[1]Include all delivery costs to the construction site and any applicable duty (whether or not a duty-free entry certificate is issued).

List name, address, telephone number, and contact for suppliers surveyed. Attach copy of response; if oral, attach summary.

Include other applicable supporting information.

(End of clause)

Alternate I (MAY 2014). As prescribed in 25.1102(c)(3), add the following definition of *Bahrainian, Mexican, or Omani construction material* and *Mexican construction material* to paragraph (a) of the basic clause, and substitute the following paragraphs (b)(1) and (b)(2) for paragraphs (b)(1) and (b)(2) of the basic clause:

Bahrainian, Mexican, or Omani construction material means a construction material that

(1) Is wholly the growth, product, or manufacture of Bahrain, Mexico, or Oman; or

(2) In the case of a construction material that consists in whole or in part of materials from another country, has been substantially transformed in Bahrain, Mexico, or Oman into a new and different construction material distinct from the materials from which it was transformed.

(b) *Construction materials.* (1) This clause implements 41 U.S.C. chapter 83, Buy American, by providing a preference for domestic construction material. In accordance with 41 U.S.C. 1907, the component test of the Buy American statute is waived for construction material that is a COTS item. (See FAR 12.505(a)(2)). In addition, the Contracting Officer has determined that the WTO GPA and all the Free Trade Agreements except the Bahrain FTA, NAFTA, and the Oman FTA apply to the this acquisition. Therefore, the Buy American statute restrictions are waived for designated country construction materials other than Bahrainian, Mexican, or Omani construction materials.

(2) The Contractor shall use only domestic or designated country construction material other than Bahrainian, Mexican, or Omani construction material in performing this contract, except as provided in paragraphs (b)(3) and (b)(4) of this clause.

[FAC 97-15, 64 FR 72414, 12/27/99, effective 2/25/2000, corrected 65 FR 4633, 1/31/2000; FAC 97-18, 65 FR 36014, 662000, effective 662000; FAC 2001-02, 66 FR 65347, 12/18/2001, effective 2/19/2002; FAC 2001-07, 67 FR 21534, 4/30/2002, effective 5/15/2002; FAC 2001-08, 67 FR 43520, 6/27/2002, effective 7/29/2002; FAC 2001-14, 68 FR 28079, 5/22/2003, effective 6/23/2003; FAC 2001-19, 69 FR 1051, 1/7/2004, effective 1/1/2004; FAC 2001-24, 69 FR 34239, 6/18/2004, effective 6/18/2004; FAC 2001-25, 69 FR 59700, 10/5/2004, effective 10/5/2004; FAC 2001-27, interim rule, 69 FR 77870, 12/28/2004, effective 1/12/005; FAC 2005-07, 71 FR 219, 1/3/2006, effective 1/3/2006; FAC 2005-09, Interim rule, 71 FR 20306, 4/19/2006, effective 4/19/2006; FAC 2005-10, 71 FR 36935, 6/28/2006, effective 6/28/2006; FAC 2005-10, 71 FR 36941, 6/28/2006, effective 6/28/2006; FAC 2005-14, 71 FR 67776, 71 FR 67778, 11/22/2006, effective 11/22/2006; FAC 2005-19, 72 FR 46357, 46360, 46361, 8/17/2007, effective 8/17/2007; FAC 2005-24, 73 FR 10964, 2/28/2008, effective 2/28/2008; FAC 2005-30, 74 FR 2713, 1/15/2009, effective 2/17/2009; FAC 2005-31, 74 FR 11828, 11832, 3/19/2009, effective 3/19/2009; FAC 2005-33, Interim rule, 74 FR 28426, 6/15/2009, effective 6/15/2009; FAC 2005-36, 74 FR 40461, 8/11/2009, effective 8/11/2009; FAC 2005-39, 75 FR 13421, 3/19/2010, effective 3/19/2010; FAC 2005-42, 75 FR 34282, 6/16/2010, effective 6/16/2010; FAC 2005-46, 75 FR 60266, 9/29/2010, effective 9/29/2010; FAC 2005-52, 76 FR 31415, 5/31/2011, effective 5/31/2011; FAC 2005-54, 76 FR 68039, 11/2/2011, effective 11/2/2011; FAC 2005-56, 77 FR 12935, 3/2/2012, effective 3/2/2012; FAC 2005-57, 77 FR 13952, 3/7/2012, effective 3/15/2012; Correction,77 FR 14303, 3/9/2012, effective 3/9/2012; Correction, 77 FR 17353, 3/26/2012, effective 3/26/2012; FAC 2005-59, 77 FR 27548, 5/10/2012, effective 5/15/2012; FAC 2005-61, 77 FR 56739, 9/13/2012, effective 9/13/2012; FAC 2005-62, 77 FR 69723, 11/20/2012, effective 11/20/2012; FAC 2005-65, 78 FR 6188, 1/29/2013, effective 1/29/2013; FAC 2005-67, 78 FR 37695, 6/21/2013, effective 6/21/2013; FAC 2005-69, 78 FR 46792, 8/1/2013, effective 9/3/2013; FAC 2005-71, 78 FR 70480, 11/25/2013, effective 11/25/2013; FAC 2005-73, 79 FR 24192, 4/29/2014, effective 5/29/2014; FAC 2005-86, 80 FR 81892, 12/31/2015, effective 2/1/2016; FAC 2005-91, 81 FR 67774, 9/30/2016, effective 10/31/2016; FAC 2019-06, 84 FR 47866, 9/10/2019, effective 10/10/2019]

52.225-12 Notice of Buy American Requirement—Construction Materials Under Trade Agreements.

As prescribed in 25.1102(d)(1), insert the following provision:

NOTICE OF BUY AMERICAN REQUIREMENT—CONSTRUCTION MATERIALS UNDER THE TRADE AGREEMENTS (MAY 2014)

(a) *Definitions. Commercially available off-the-shelf (COTS) item, construction material, designated country construction material, domestic construction material*, and *foreign construction material*, as used in this provision, are defined in the clause of this solicitation entitled *Buy American—Construction Materials Under Trade Agreements* (Federal Acquisition Regulation (FAR) clause 52.225-11).

(b) *Requests for determination of inapplicability.* An offeror requesting a determination regarding the inapplicability of the Buy American statute should submit the request to the Contracting Officer in time to allow a determination before submission of offers. The offeror shall include the information and applicable supporting data required by paragraphs (c) and (d) of FAR clause 52.225-11 in the request. If an offeror has not requested a determination regarding the inapplicability of the Buy American statute before submitting its offer, or has not received a response to a previous request, the offeror shall include the information and supporting data in the offer.

(c) *Evaluation of offers.*

(1) The Government will evaluate an offer requesting exception to the requirements of the Buy American statute, based on claimed unreasonable cost of domestic construction materials, by adding to the offered price the appropriate percentage of the cost of such foreign construction material, as specified in paragraph (b)(4)(i) of FAR clause 52.225-11.

(2) If evaluation results in a tie between an offeror that requested the substitution of foreign construction material based on unreasonable cost and an offeror that did not request an exception, the Contracting Officer will award to the offeror that did not request an exception based on unreasonable cost.

(d) *Alternate offers.* (1) When an offer includes foreign construction material, other than designated country construction material, that is not listed by the Government in this solicitation in paragraph (b)(3) of FAR clause 52.225-11, the offeror also may submit an alternate offer based on use of equivalent domestic or designated country construction material.

(2) If an alternate offer is submitted, the offeror shall submit a separate Standard Form 1442 for the alternate offer, and a separate price comparison table prepared in accordance with paragraphs (c) and (d) of FAR clause 52.225-11 for the offer that is based on the use of any foreign construction material for which the Government has not yet determined an exception applies.

(3) If the Government determines that a particular exception requested in accordance with paragraph (c) of FAR clause 52.225-11 based on use of the equivalent domestic or designated country construction material. An offer based on use of the foreign construction material for which an exception was requested—

(i) Will be rejected as nonresponsive if this acquisition is conducted by sealed bidding; or

(ii) May be accepted if revised during negotiations.

(End of provision)

Alternate I (MAY 2014). As prescribed in 25.1102(d)(2), substitute the following paragraph (b) for paragraph (b) of the basic provision:

(b) Requests for determination of inapplicability. An offeror requesting a determination regarding the inapplicability of the Buy American statute shall submit the request with its offer, including the information and applicable supporting data required by paragraphs (c) and (d) of FAR clause 52.225-11.

Alternate II (JUN 2009). As prescribed in 25.1102(d)(3), add the definition of *Bahrainian, Mexican, or Omani construction material* to paragraph (a) and substitute the following paragraph (d) for paragraph (d) of the basic provision:

(d) *Alternate offers.* (1) When an offer includes foreign construction material, except foreign construction material from a designated country other than Bahrain, Mexico, or Oman that is not listed by the Government in this solicitation in paragraph (b)(3) of FAR clause 52.225-11, the offeror also may submit an alternate offer based on use of equivalent domestic or designated country construction material other than Bahrainian, Mexican, or Omani construction material.

(2) If an alternate offer is submitted, the offeror shall submit a separate Standard Form 1442 for the alternate offer, and a separate price comparison table prepared in accordance with paragraphs (c) and (d) of FAR clause 52.225-11 for the offer that is based on the use of any foreign construction material for which the Government has not yet determined an exception applies.

(3) If the Government determines that a particular exception requested in accordance with paragraph (c) of FAR clause 52.225-11 does not apply, the Government will evaluate only those offers based on use of the equivalent domestic or designated country construction material other than Bahrainian, Mexican, or Omani construction material. An offer based on use of the foreign construction material for which an exception was requested—

(i) Will be rejected as nonresponsive if this acquisition is conducted by sealed bidding; or

(ii) May be accepted if revised during negotiations.

[FAC 97-15, 64 FR 72414, 12/27/99, effective 2/25/2000; FAC 97-18, 65 FR 36014, 6/6/2000, effective 6/6/2000; FAC 2001-07, 67 FR 21534, 4/30/2002, effective 5/15/2002; FAC 2001-19, Interim rule, 69 FR 1051, 1/7/2004, effective 1/1/2004; FAC 2001-25, Final rule, 69 FR 59700, 10/5/2004, effective 10/5/2004; FAC 2001-27, interim rule, 69 FR 77870, 12/28/2004, effective 1/1/2005; FAC 2005-07, 71 FR 219, 1/3/2006, effective 1/3/2006; FAC 2005-09, Interim rule, 71 FR 20306, 4/19/2006, effective 4/19/2006; FAC 2005-10, 71 FR 36935, 6/28/2006, effective 6/28/2006; FAC 2005-14, 71 FR 67776, 71 FR 67778, 11/22/2006, effective 11/22/2006; FAC 2005-19, 72 FR 46357, 46360, 46361, 8/17/2007, effective 8/17/2007; FAC 2005-24, 73 FR 10964, 2/28/2008, effective 2/28/2008; FAC 2005-30, 74 FR 2713, 1/15/2009, effective 2/17/2009; FAC 2005-33, Interim rule, 74 FR 28426, 6/15/2009, effective 6/15/2009; FAC 2005-39, 75 FR 13421, 3/19/2010, effective 3/19/2010; FAC 2005-73, 79 FR 24192, 4/29/2014, effective 5/29/2014]

52.225-13 Restrictions on Certain Foreign Purchases.

As prescribed in 25.1103(a), insert the following clause:

RESTRICTIONS ON CERTAIN FOREIGN PURCHASES (JUN 2008)

(a) Except as authorized by the Office of Foreign Assets Control (OFAC) in the Department of the Treasury, the Contractor shall not acquire, for use in the performance of this contract, any supplies or services if any proclamation, Executive order, or statute administered by OFAC, or if OFAC's implementing regulations at 31 CFR chapter V, would prohibit such a transaction by a person subject to the jurisdiction of the United States.

(b) Except as authorized by OFAC, most transactions involving Cuba, Iran, and Sudan are prohibited, as are most imports from Burma or North Korea, into the United States or its outlying areas. Lists of entities and individuals subject to economic sanctions are included in OFAC's List of Specially Designated Nationals and Blocked Persons at ***http://www.treas.gov/offices/enforcement/ofac/sdn***. More information about these restrictions, as well as updates, is available in the OFAC's regulations at 31 CFR chapter V and/or on OFAC's Web site at ***http://www.treas.gov/offices/enforcement/ofac***.

(c) The Contractor shall insert this clause, including this paragraph (c), in all subcontracts.

(End of clause)

[FAC 97-15, 64 FR 72414, 12/27/99, effective 2/25/2000; FAC 97-18, 65 FR 36014, 6/6/2000, effective 7/6/2000; FAC 2001-14,

68 FR 28079, 5/22/2003, effective 6/23/2003; FAC 2001-16, 68 FR 56685, 10/1/2003, effective 10/31/2003; FAC 2001-18, 68 FR 69258, 12/11/2003, effective 12/11/2003; FAC 2005-01, 70 FR 11763, 3/9/2005, effective 3/9/2005; FAC 2005-03, 70 FR 18959, 4/11/2005, effective 4/11/2005; FAC 2005-07, 71 FR 221, 1/3/2006, effective 1/3/2006; FAC 2005-26, 73 FR 33636, 6/12/2008, effective 6/12/2008; FAC 2005-36, 74 FR 40463, 8/11/2009, effective 8/11/2009]]

52.225-14 Inconsistency between English Version and Translation of Contract.

As prescribed in 25.1103(b), insert the following clause:

INCONSISTENCY BETWEEN ENGLISH VERSION AND TRANSLATION OF CONTRACT (FEB 2000)

In the event of inconsistency between any terms of this contract and any translation into another language, the English language meaning shall control.

(End of clause)

[FAC 97-15, 64 FR 72414, 12/27/99, effective 2/25/2000]

52.225-15 [Removed and Reserved]

[FAC 97-15, 64 FR 72414, 12/27/99, effective 2/25/2000; FAC 2005-09, Interim rule, 71 FR 20305, 4/19/2006, effective 4/19/2006; FAC 2005-14, 71 FR 67775, 11/22/2006, effective 11/22/2006]

52.225-16 [Removed and Reserved]

[FAC 97-15, 64 FR 72414, 12/27/99, effective 2/25/2000; FAC 2005-09, Interim rule, 71 FR 20305, 4/19/2006, effective 4/19/2006; FAC 2005-14, 71 FR 67775, 11/22/2006, effective 11/22/2006]

52.225-17 Evaluation of Foreign Currency Offers.

As prescribed in 25.1103(c), insert the following provision:

EVALUATION OF FOREIGN CURRENCY OFFERS (FEB 2000)

If the Government receives offers in more than one currency, the Government will evaluate offers by converting the foreign currency to United States currency using ____ [*Contracting Officer to insert source of rate*] in effect as follows:

(a) For acquisitions conducted using sealed bidding procedures, on the date of bid opening.

(b) For acquisitions conducted using negotiation procedures—

(1) On the date specified for receipt of offers, if award is based on initial offers; otherwise

(2) On the date specified for receipt of proposal revisions.

(End of provision)

[FAC 97-15, 64 FR 72414, 12/27/99, effective 2/25/2000; FAC 2005-21, 72 FR 63089, 11/7/2007, effective 11/7/2007; FAC 2005-21, 72 FR 63089, 11/7/2007, effective 11/7/2007]

52.225-18 Place of Manufacture.

As prescribed in 25.1101(f), insert the following solicitation provision:

PLACE OF MANUFACTURE (AUG 2018)

(a) *Definitions.* As used in this provision—

Manufactured end product means any end product in product and service codes (PSCs) 1000-9999, except—

(1) PSC 5510, Lumber and Related Basic Wood Materials;

(2) Product or Service Group (PSG) 87, Agricultural Supplies;

(3) PSG 88, Live Animals;

(4) PSG 89, Subsistence;

(5) PSC 9410, Crude Grades of Plant Materials;

(6) PSC 9430, Miscellaneous Crude Animal Products, Inedible;

(7) PSC 9440, Miscellaneous Crude Agricultural and Forestry Products;

(8) PSC 9610, Ores;

(9) PSC 9620, Minerals, Natural and Synthetic; and

(10) PSC 9630, Additive Metal Materials.

Place of manufacture means the place where an end product is assembled out of components, or otherwise made or processed from raw materials into the finished product that is to be provided to the Government. If a product is disassembled and reassembled, the place of reassembly is not the place of manufacture.

(b) For statistical purposes only, the offeror shall indicate whether the place of manufacture of the end products it expects to provide in response to this solicitation is predominantly—

(1) [] In the United States (Check this box if the total anticipated price of offered end products manufactured in the United States exceeds the total anticipated price of offered end products manufactured outside the United States); or

(2) []Outside the United States.

(End of provision)

[FAC 2205-13, 71 FR 57375, 9/28/2006, effective 9/28/2006; FAC 2005-19, 72 FR 46326, 8/17/2007, effective 8/17/2007; FAC 2005-80, 80 FR 4994, 1/29/2015, effective 3/2/2015; Correction, 80 FR 6909, 2/9/2015, effective 3/2/2015; FAC 2005-100, 83 FR 42571, 8/22/2018, effective 8/22/2018]

52.225-19 Contractor Personnel in a Designated Operational Area or Supporting a Diplomatic or Consular Mission Outside the United States.

As prescribed in 25.301-4, insert the following clause:

CONTRACTOR PERSONNEL IN A DESIGNATED OPERATIONAL AREA OR SUPPORTING A DIPLOMATIC OR CONSULAR MISSION OUTSIDE THE UNITED STATES (MAR 2008)

(a) *Definitions.* As used in this clause—

Chief of mission means the principal officer in charge of a diplomatic mission of the United States or of a United States office abroad which is designated by the Secretary of State as diplomatic in nature, including any individual assigned under section 502(c) of the Foreign Service Act of 1980 (Pub. L. 96-465) to be temporarily in charge of such a mission or office.

Combatant commander means the commander of a unified or specified combatant command established in accordance with 10 U.S.C. 161.

Designated operational area means a geographic area designated by the combatant commander or subordinate joint force commander for the conduct or support of specified military operations.

Supporting a diplomatic or consular mission means performing outside the United States under a contract administered by Federal agency personnel who are subject to the direction of a chief of mission.

(b) *General.* (1) This clause applies when Contractor personnel are required to perform outside the United States—

(i) In a designated operational area during—

(A) Contingency operations;

(B) Humanitarian or peacekeeping operations; or

(C) Other military operations; or military exercises, when designated by the Combatant Commander; or

(ii) When supporting a diplomatic or consular mission—

(A) That has been designated by the Department of State as a danger pay post (see *http://aoprals.state.gov/Web920/danger_pay_all.asp*); or

(B) That the Contracting Officer has indicated is subject to this clause.

(2) Contract performance may require work in dangerous or austere conditions. Except as otherwise provided in the contract, the Contractor accepts the risks associated with required contract performance in such operations.

(3) Contractor personnel are civilians.

(i) Except as provided in paragraph (b)(3)(ii) of this clause, and in accordance with paragraph (i)(3) of this clause, Contractor personnel are only authorized to use deadly force in self-defense.

(ii) Contractor personnel performing security functions are also authorized to use deadly force when use of such force reasonably appears necessary to execute their security mission to protect assets/persons, consistent with the terms and conditions contained in the contract or with their job description and terms of employment.

(4) Service performed by Contractor personnel subject to this clause is not active duty or service under 38 U.S.C. 106 note.

(c) *Support*. Unless specified elsewhere in the contract, the Contractor is responsible for all logistical and security support required for Contractor personnel engaged in this contract.

(d) *Compliance with laws and regulations*. The Contractor shall comply with, and shall ensure that its personnel in the designated operational area or supporting the diplomatic or consular mission are familiar with and comply with, all applicable—

(1) United States, host country, and third country national laws;

(2) Treaties and international agreements;

(3) United States regulations, directives, instructions, policies, and procedures; and

(4) Force protection, security, health, or safety orders, directives, and instructions issued by the Chief of Mission or the Combatant Commander; however, only the Contracting Officer is authorized to modify the terms and conditions of the contract.

(e) *Preliminary personnel requirements*. (1) Specific requirements for paragraphs (e)(2)(i) through (e)(2)(vi) of this clause will be set forth in the statement of work, or elsewhere in the contract.

(2) Before Contractor personnel depart from the United States or a third country, and before Contractor personnel residing in the host country begin contract performance in the designated operational area or supporting the diplomatic or consular mission, the Contractor shall ensure the following:

(i) All required security and background checks are complete and acceptable.

(ii) All personnel are medically and physically fit and have received all required vaccinations.

(iii) All personnel have all necessary passports, visas, entry permits, and other documents required for Contractor personnel to enter and exit the foreign country, including those required for in-transit countries.

(iv) All personnel have received—

(A) A country clearance or special area clearance, if required by the chief of mission; and

(B) Theater clearance, if required by the Combatant Commander.

(v) All personnel have received personal security training. The training must at a minimum—

(A) Cover safety and security issues facing employees overseas;

(B) Identify safety and security contingency planning activities; and

(C) Identify ways to utilize safety and security personnel and other resources appropriately.

(vi) All personnel have received isolated personnel training, if specified in the contract. Isolated personnel are military or civilian personnel separated from their unit or organization in an environment requiring them to survive, evade, or escape while awaiting rescue or recovery.

(vii) All personnel who are U.S. citizens are registered with the U.S. Embassy or Consulate with jurisdiction over the area of operations on-line at *http://www.travel.state.gov*.

(3) The Contractor shall notify all personnel who are not a host country national or ordinarily resident in the host country that—

(i) If this contract is with the Department of Defense, or the contract relates to supporting the mission of the Department of Defense outside the United States, such employees, and dependents residing with such employees, who engage in conduct outside the United States that would constitute an offense punishable by imprisonment for more than one year if the conduct had been engaged in within the special maritime and territorial jurisdiction of the United States, may potentially be subject to the criminal jurisdiction of the United States (see the

Military Extraterritorial Jurisdiction Act of 2000 (18 U.S.C. 3261 *et seq.*);

(ii) Pursuant to the War Crimes Act, 18 U.S.C. 2441, Federal criminal jurisdiction also extends to conduct that is determined to constitute a war crime when committed by a civilian national of the United States; and

(iii) Other laws may provide for prosecution of U.S. nationals who commit offenses on the premises of United States diplomatic, consular, military or other United States Government missions outside the United States (18 U.S.C. 7(9)).

(f) *Processing and departure points.* The Contractor shall require its personnel who are arriving from outside the area of performance to perform in the designated operational area or supporting the diplomatic or consular mission to—

(1) Process through the departure center designated in the contract or complete another process as directed by the Contracting Officer;

(2) Use a specific point of departure and transportation mode as directed by the Contracting Officer; and

(3) Process through a reception center as designated by the Contracting Officer upon arrival at the place of performance.

(g) *Personnel data.* (1) Unless personnel data requirements are otherwise specified in the contract, the Contractor shall establish and maintain with the designated Government official a current list of all Contractor personnel in the areas of performance. The Contracting Officer will inform the Contractor of the Government official designated to receive this data and the appropriate system to use for this effort.

(2) The Contractor shall ensure that all employees on this list have a current record of emergency data, for notification of next of kin, on file with both the Contractor and the designated Government official.

(h) *Contractor personnel.* The Contracting Officer may direct the Contractor, at its own expense, to remove and replace any Contractor personnel who fail to comply with or violate applicable requirements of this contract. Such action may be taken at the Government's discretion without prejudice to its rights under any other provision of this contract, including termination for default or cause.

(i) *Weapons.* (1) If the Contracting Officer, subject to the approval of the Combatant Commander or the Chief of Mission, authorizes the carrying of weapons—

(i) The Contracting Officer may authorize an approved Contractor to issue Contractor-owned weapons and ammunition to specified employees; or

(ii) The ____________ [*Contracting Officer to specify individual, e.g., Contracting Officer Representative, Regional Security Officer, etc,*] may issue Government-furnished weapons and ammunition to the Contractor for issuance to specified Contractor employees.

(2) The Contractor shall provide to the Contracting Officer a specific list of personnel for whom authorization to carry a weapon is requested.

(3) The Contractor shall ensure that its personnel who are authorized to carry weapons—

(i) Are adequately trained to carry and use them—

(A) Safely;

(B) With full understanding of, and adherence to, the rules of the use of force issued by the Combatant Commander or the Chief of Mission; and

(C) In compliance with applicable agency policies, agreements, rules, regulations, and other applicable law;

(ii) Are not barred from possession of a firearm by 18 U.S.C. 922; and

(iii) Adhere to all guidance and orders issued by the Combatant Commander or the Chief of Mission regarding possession, use, safety, and accountability of weapons and ammunition.

(4) Upon revocation by the Contracting Officer of the Contractor's authorization to possess weapons, the Contractor shall ensure that all Government-furnished weapons and unexpended ammunition are returned as directed by the Contracting Officer.

(5) Whether or not weapons are Government-furnished, all liability for the use of any weapon by Contractor personnel rests solely with the Contractor and the Contractor employee using such weapon.

(j) *Vehicle or equipment licenses.* Contractor personnel shall possess the required licenses to operate all vehicles or equipment necessary to perform the contract in the area of performance.

(k) *Military clothing and protective equipment.* (1) Contractor personnel are prohibited from wearing military clothing unless specifically authorized by the Combatant Commander. If authorized to wear military clothing, Contractor personnel must wear distinctive patches, armbands, nametags, or headgear, in order to be distinguishable from military personnel, consistent with force protection measures.

(2) Contractor personnel may wear specific items required for safety and security, such as ballistic, nuclear, biological, or chemical protective equipment.

(l) *Evacuation.* (1) If the Chief of Mission or Combatant Commander orders a mandatory evacuation of some or all personnel, the Government will provide to United States and third country national Contractor personnel the level of assistance provided to private United States citizens.

(2) In the event of a non-mandatory evacuation order, the Contractor shall maintain personnel on location sufficient to meet contractual obligations unless instructed to evacuate by the Contracting Officer.

(m) *Personnel recovery.* (1) In the case of isolated, missing, detained, captured or abducted Contractor personnel, the Government will assist in personnel recovery actions.

(2) Personnel recovery may occur through military action, action by non-governmental organizations, other Government-approved action, diplomatic initiatives, or through any combination of these options.

(3) The Department of Defense has primary responsibility for recovering DoD contract service employees and, when requested, will provide personnel recovery support to other agencies in accordance with DoD Directive 2310.2, Personnel Recovery.

(n) *Notification and return of personal effects.* (1) The Contractor shall be responsible for notification of the employee-designated next of kin, and notification as soon as possible to the U.S. Consul responsible for the area in which the event occurred, if the employee—

(i) Dies;

(ii) Requires evacuation due to an injury; or

(iii) Is isolated, missing, detained, captured, or abducted.

(2) The Contractor shall also be responsible for the return of all personal effects of deceased or missing Contractor personnel, if appropriate, to next of kin.

(o) *Mortuary affairs.* Mortuary affairs for Contractor personnel who die in the area of performance will be handled as follows:

(1) If this contract was awarded by DoD, the remains of Contractor personnel will be handled in accordance with DoD Directive 1300.22, Mortuary Affairs Policy.

(2) (i) If this contract was awarded by an agency other than DoD, the Contractor is responsible for the return of the remains of Contractor personnel from the point of identification of the remains to the location specified by the employee or next of kin, as applicable, except as provided in paragraph (o) (2) (ii) of this clause.

(ii) In accordance with 10 U.S.C. 1486, the Department of Defense may provide, on a reimbursable basis, mortuary support for the disposition of remains and personal effects of all U.S. citizens upon the request of the Department of State.

(p) *Changes.* In addition to the changes otherwise authorized by the Changes clause of this contract, the Contracting Officer may, at any time, by written order identified as a change order, make changes in place of performance or Government-furnished facilities, equipment, material, services, or site. Any change order issued in accordance with this paragraph shall be subject to the provisions of the Changes clause of this contract.

(q) *Subcontracts.* The Contractor shall incorporate the substance of this clause, including this paragraph (q), in all subcontracts that require subcontractor personnel to perform outside the United States—

(1) In a designated operational area during—

(i) Contingency operations;

(ii) Humanitarian or peacekeeping operations; or

(iii) Other military operations; or military exercises, when designated by the Combatant Commander; or

(2) When supporting a diplomatic or consular mission—

(i) That has been designated by the Department of State as a danger pay post (see *http://aoprals.state.gov/Web920/danger _pay _all.asp*); or

(ii) That the Contracting Officer has indicated is subject to this clause.

(End of clause)

[FAC 2005-24, 73 FR 19043, 2/28/2008, effective 3/31/2008]

52.225-20 Prohibition on Conducting Restricted Business Operations in Sudan—Certification.

As prescribed at 25.1103(d), insert the following provision:

PROHIBITION ON CONDUCTING RESTRICTED BUSINESS OPERATIONS IN SUDAN—CERTIFICATION (AUG 2009)

(a) *Definitions*. As used in this provision—

Business operations means engaging in commerce in any form, including by acquiring, developing, maintaining, owning, selling, possessing, leasing, or operating equipment, facilities, personnel, products, services, personal property, real property, or any other apparatus of business or commerce.

Marginalized populations of Sudan means—

(1) Adversely affected groups in regions authorized to receive assistance under section 8(c) of the Darfur Peace and Accountability Act (Pub. L. 109-344) (50 U.S.C. 1701 note); and

(2) Marginalized areas in Northern Sudan described in section 4(9) of such Act.

Restricted business operations means business operations in Sudan that include power production activities, mineral extraction activities, oil-related activities, or the production of military equipment, as those terms are defined in the Sudan Accountability and Divestment Act of 2007 (Pub. L. 110-174). Restricted business operations do not include business operations that the person (as that term is defined in Section 2 of the Sudan Accountability and Divestment Act of 2007) conducting the business can demonstrate—

(1) Are conducted under contract directly and exclusively with the regional government of southern Sudan;

(2) Are conducted pursuant to specific authorization from the Office of Foreign Assets Control in the Department of the Treasury, or are expressly exempted under Federal law from the requirement to be conducted under such authorization;

(3) Consist of providing goods or services to marginalized populations of Sudan;

(4) Consist of providing goods or services to an internationally recognized peacekeeping force or humanitarian organization;

(5) Consist of providing goods or services that are used only to promote health or education; or

(6) Have been voluntarily suspended.

(b) *Certification*. By submission of its offer, the offeror certifies that the offeror does not conduct any restricted business operations in Sudan.

(End of provision)

[FAC 2005-26, 73 FR 33636, 6/12/2008, effective 6/12/2008; FAC 2005-36, 74 FR 40463, 8/11/2009, effective 8/11/2009]

52.225-21 Required Use of American Iron, Steel, and

Manufactured Goods—Buy American Statute—Construction Materials.

As prescribed in 25.1102(e), insert the following clause:

REQUIRED OF AMERICAN IRON, STEEL, AND MANUFACTURED GOODS—BUY AMERICAN STATUTE—CONSTRUCTION MATERIALS (MAY 2014)

(a) *Definitions.* As used in this clause—

Component means an article, material, or supply incorporated directly into a construction material.

Construction material means an article, material, or supply brought to the construction site by the Contractor or a subcontractor for incorporation into the building or work. The term also includes an item brought to the site preassembled from articles, materials, or supplies. However, emergency life safety systems, such as emergency lighting, fire alarm, and audio evacuation systems, that are discrete systems incorporated into a public building or work and that are produced as complete systems, are evaluated as a single and distinct construction material regardless of when or how the individual parts or components of those systems are delivered to the construction site.

Domestic construction material means the following—

(1) An unmanufactured construction material mined or produced in the United States. (The Buy American statute applies.)

(2) A manufactured construction material that is manufactured in the United States and, if the construction material consists wholly or predominantly of iron or steel, the iron or steel was produced in the United States. (Section 1605 of the Recovery Act applies.)

Foreign construction material means a construction material other than a domestic construction material.

Manufactured construction material means any construction material that is not unmanufactured construction material.

Steel means an alloy that includes at least 50 percent iron, between .02 and 2 percent carbon, and may include other elements.

United States means the 50 States, the District of Columbia, and outlying areas.

Unmanufactured construction material means raw material brought to the construction site for incorporation into the building or work that has not been—

(1) Processed into a specific form and shape; or

(2) Combined with other raw material to create a material that has different properties than the properties of the individual raw materials.

(b) *Domestic preference.* (1) This clause implements—

(i) Section 1605 of the American Recovery and Reinvestment Act of 2009 (Recovery Act) (Pub. L. 111-5), by requiring, unless an exception applies, that all manufactured construction material in the project is manufactured in the United States and, if the construction material consists wholly or predominantly of iron or steel, the iron or steel was produced in the United States (produced in the United States means that all manufacturing processes of the iron or steel must take place in the United States, except metallurgical processes involving refinement of steel additives); and

(ii) 41 U.S.C. chapter 83, Buy American, by providing a preference for unmanufactured construction material mined or produced in the United States over unmanufactured construction material mined or produced in a foreign country.

(2) The Contractor shall use only domestic construction material in performing this contract, except as provided in paragraph (b)(3) and (b)(4) of this clause.

(3) This requirement does not apply to the construction material or components listed by the Government as follows:

[Contracting Officer to list applicable excepted materials or indicate "none"]

(4) The Contracting Officer may add other foreign construction material to the list in

paragraph (b)(3) of this clause if the Government determines that—

(i) The cost of domestic construction material would be unreasonable;

(A) The cost of domestic manufactured construction material, when compared to the cost of comparable foreign manufactured construction material, is unreasonable when the cumulative cost of such material will increase the cost of the contract by more than 25 percent;

(B) The cost of domestic unmanufactured construction material is unreasonable when the cost of such material exceeds the cost of comparable foreign unmanufactured construction material by more than 6 percent;

(ii) The construction material is not mined, produced, or manufactured in the United States in sufficient and reasonably available quantities and of a satisfactory quality;

(iii) The application of the restriction of section 1605 of the Recovery Act to a particular manufactured construction material would be inconsistent with the public interest or the application of the Buy American statute to a particular unmanufactured construction material would be impracticable or inconsistent with the public interest.

(c) *Request for determination of inapplicability of Section 1605 of the Recovery Act or the Buy American statute.* (1)(i) Any Contractor request to use foreign construction material in accordance with paragraph (b)(4) of this clause shall include adequate information for Government evaluation of the request, including—

(A) A description of the foreign and domestic construction materials;

(B) Unit of measure;

(C) Quantity;

(D) Cost;

(E) Time of delivery or availability;

(F) Location of the construction project;

(G) Name and address of the proposed supplier; and

(H) A detailed justification of the reason for use of foreign construction materials cited in accordance with paragraph (b)(4) of this clause.

(ii) A request based on unreasonable cost shall include a reasonable survey of the market and a completed cost comparison table in the format in paragraph (d) of this clause.

(iii) The cost of construction material shall include all delivery costs to the construction site and any applicable duty.

(iv) Any Contractor request for a determination submitted after contract award shall explain why the Contractor could not reasonably foresee the need for such determination and could not have requested the determination before contract award. If the Contractor does not submit a satisfactory explanation, the Contracting Officer need not make a determination.

(2) If the Government determines after contract award that an exception to section 1605 of the Recovery Act or the Buy American statute applies and the Contracting Officer and the Contractor negotiate adequate consideration, the Contracting Officer will modify the contract to allow use of the foreign construction material. However, when the basis for the exception is the unreasonable cost of a domestic construction material, adequate consideration is not less than the differential established in paragraph (b)(4)(i) of this clause.

(3) Unless the Government determines that an exception to section 1605 of the Recovery Act or the Buy American statute applies, use of foreign construction material is noncompliant with section 1605 of the American Recovery and Reinvestment Act or the Buy American statute.

(d) *Data.* To permit evaluation of requests under paragraph (c) of this clause based on unreasonable cost, the Contractor shall include the following information and any applicable supporting data based on the survey of suppliers:

FOREIGN AND DOMESTIC CONSTRUCTION MATERIALS COST COMPARISON

Construction material description	Unit of measure	Quantity	Cost (dollars)*
Item 1:			
Foreign construction material	____	____	____
Domestic construction material	____	____	____
Item 2			
Foreign construction material	____	____	____
Domestic construction material	____	____	____

[List name, address, telephone number, and contact for suppliers surveyed. Attach copy of response; if oral, attach summary.] [Include other applicable supporting information.]

** Include all delivery costs to the construction site.]*

(End of clause)

[FAC 2005-32, 74 FR 14623, 3/31/2009, effective 3/31/2009; FAC 2005-45, 75 FR 53153, 8/30/2010, effective 10/1/2010; FAC 2005-73, 79 FR 24192, 4/29/2014, effective 5/29/2014]

52.225-22 Notice of Required Use of American Iron, Steel, and Manufactured Goods—Buy American Statute—Construction Materials.

As prescribed in 25.1102(e), insert the following provision:

NOTICE OF REQUIRED USE OF AMERICAN IRON, STEEL, AND MANUFACTURED GOODS—BUY AMERICAN STATUTE—CONSTRUCTION MATERIALS (MAY 2014)

(a) *Definitions. Construction material, domestic construction material, foreign construction material, manufactured construction material, steel,* and *unmanufactured construction material,* as used in this provision, are defined in the clause of this solicitation entitled "Required Use of Iron, Steel, and Manufactured Goods—Buy American statute—Construction Materials" (Federal Acquisition Regulation (FAR) clause 52.225-21).

(b) *Requests for determinations of inapplicability.* An offeror requesting a determination regarding the inapplicability of section 1605 of the American Recovery and Reinvestment Act of 2009 (Pub. L. 111-5) (Recovery Act) or the Buy American statute should submit the request to the Contracting Officer in time to allow a determination before submission of offers. The offeror shall include the information and applicable supporting data required by paragraphs (c) and (d) of the clause at FAR 52.225-21 in the request. If an offeror has not requested a determination regarding the inapplicability of section 1605 of the Recovery Act or the Buy American statute before submitting its offer, or has not received a response to a previous request, the offeror shall include the information and supporting data in the offer.

(c) *Evaluation of offers.* (1) If the Government determines that an exception based on unreasonable cost of domestic construction material applies, in accordance with FAR 25.604, the Government will evaluate an offer requesting exception to the requirements of section 1605 of the Recovery Act or the Buy American statute by adding to the offered price of the contract—

(i) 25 percent of the offered price of the contract, if foreign manufactured construction material is incorporated in the offer based on an exception for unreasonable cost of comparable manufactured domestic construction material; and

(ii) 6 percent of the cost of foreign unmanufactured construction material included in the offer based on an exception for the unreasonable cost of comparable domestic unmanufactured construction material.

(2) If the solicitation specifies award on the basis of factors in addition to cost or price, the Contracting Officer will apply the evaluation factors as specified in paragraph (c) (1) of this provision and use the evaluated price in determining the offer that represents the best value to the Government.

(3) Unless paragraph (c) (2) of this provision applies, if two or more offers are equal in price, the Contracting Officer will give preference to an offer that does not include foreign construction material excepted at the request of the offeror on the basis of unreasonable cost of comparable domestic construction material.

(d) *Alternate offers.* (1) When an offer includes foreign construction material not listed by the Government in this solicitation in paragraph (b) (3) of the clause at FAR 52.225-21, the offeror also may submit an alternate offer based on use of equivalent domestic construction material.

(2) If an alternate offer is submitted, the offeror shall submit a separate Standard Form 1442 for the alternate offer and a separate cost comparison table prepared in accordance with paragraphs (c) and (d) of the clause at FAR 52.225-21 for the offer that is based on the use of any foreign construction material for which the Government has not yet determined an exception applies.

(3) If the Government determines that a particular exception requested in accordance with paragraph (c) of the clause at FAR 52.225-21 does not apply, the Government will evaluate only those offers based on use of the equivalent domestic construction material, and the offeror shall be required to furnish such domestic construction material. An offer based on use of the foreign construction material for which an exception was requested—

(i) Will be rejected as nonresponsive if this acquisition is conducted by sealed bidding; or

(ii) May be accepted if revised during negotiations.

(End of provision)

Alternate I (MAY 2014). As prescribed in 25.1102(e), substitute the following paragraph (b) for paragraph (b) of the basic provision:

(b) *Requests for determinations of inapplicability.* An offeror requesting a determination regarding the inapplicability of section 1605 of the American Recovery and Reinvestment Act of 2009 (Pub. L. 111-5) (Recovery Act) or the Buy American statute shall submit the request with its offer, including the information and applicable supporting data required by paragraphs (c) and (d) of the clause at FAR 52.225-21.

[FAC 2005-32, 74 FR 14623, 3/31/2009, effective 3/31/2009; FAC 2005-45, 75 FR 53153, 8/30/2010, effective 10/1/2010; FAC 2005-73, 79 FR 24192, 4/29/2014, effective 5/29/2014]

52.225-23 Required Use of American Iron, Steel, and Manufactured Goods—Buy American Statute—Construction Materials Under Trade Agreements.

As prescribed in 25.1102(e), insert the following clause:

REQUIRED USE OF AMERICAN IRON, STEEL, AND MANUFACTURED GOODS—BUY AMERICAN STATUTE—CONSTRUCTION MATERIALS UNDER TRADE AGREEMENTS (OCT 2019)

(a) *Definitions.* As used in this clause—

Component means an article, material, or supply incorporated directly into a construction material.

Construction material means an article, material, or supply brought to the construction site by the Contractor or subcontractor for incorporation into the building or work. The term also includes an item brought to the site preassembled from articles, materials, or supplies. However, emergency life safety systems, such as emergency lighting, fire alarm, and audio evacuation systems, that are discrete systems incorporated into a public building or work and that are produced as complete systems, are evaluated as a single and distinct construction material regardless of when or how the individual parts or components of those systems are delivered to the construction site.

Designated country means any of the following countries:

(1) A World Trade Organization Government Procurement Agreement (WTO GPA) country (Armenia, Aruba, Australia, Austria, Belgium, Bulgaria, Canada, Croatia, Cyprus, Czech Republic, Denmark, Estonia, Finland, France, Germany, Greece, Hong Kong, Hungary, Iceland, Ireland, Israel, Italy, Japan, Korea (Republic of), Latvia, Liechtenstein, Lithuania, Luxembourg, Malta, Moldova, Montenegro, Netherlands, New Zealand, Norway, Poland, Portugal, Romania, Singapore, Slovak Republic, Slovenia, Spain, Sweden, Switzerland, Taiwan, Ukraine, or United Kingdom);

(2) A Free Trade Agreement (FTA) country (Australia, Bahrain, Canada, Chile, Colombia, Costa Rica, Dominican Republic, El Salvador, Guatemala, Honduras, Korea (Republic of), Mexico, Morocco, Nicaragua, Oman, Panama, Peru, or Singapore);

(3) A least developed country (Afghanistan, Angola, Bangladesh, Benin, Bhutan, Burkina Faso, Burundi, Cambodia, Central African Republic, Chad, Comoros, Democratic Republic of Congo, Djibouti, Equatorial Guinea, Eritrea, Ethiopia, Gambia, Guinea, Guinea-Bissau, Haiti, Kiribati, Laos, Lesotho, Liberia, Madagascar, Malawi, Mali, Mauritania, Mozambique, Nepal, Niger, Rwanda, Samoa, Sao Tome and Principe, Senegal, Sierra Leone, Solomon Islands, Somalia, South Sudan, Tanzania, Timor-Leste, Togo, Tuvalu, Uganda, Vanuatu, Yemen, or Zambia); or

(4) A Caribbean Basin country (Antigua and Barbuda, Aruba, Bahamas, Barbados, Belize, Bonaire, British Virgin Islands, Curacao, Dominica, Grenada, Guyana, Haiti, Jamaica, Montserrat, Saba, St. Kitts and Nevis, St. Lucia, St. Vincent and the Grenadines, Sint Eustatius, Sint Maarten, or Trinidad and Tobago).

Designated country construction material means a construction material that is a WTO GPA country construction material, an FTA country construction material, a least developed country construction material, or a Caribbean Basin country construction material.

Domestic construction material means the following:

(1) An unmanufactured construction material mined or produced in the United States. (The Buy American statute applies.)

(2) A manufactured construction material that is manufactured in the United States and, if the construction material consists wholly or predominantly of iron or steel, the iron or steel was produced in the United States. (Section 1605 of the Recovery Act applies.)

Foreign construction material means a construction material other than a domestic construction material.

Free trade agreement (FTA) country construction material means a construction material that—

(1) Is wholly the growth, product, or manufacture of an FTA country; or

(2) In the case of a construction material that consists in whole or in part of materials from another country, has been substantially transformed in an FTA country into a new and different construction material distinct from the materials from which it was transformed.

Least developed country construction material means a construction material that—

(1) Is wholly the growth, product, or manufacture of a least developed country; or

(2) In the case of a construction material that consists in whole or in part of materials from another country, has been substantially transformed in a least developed country into a new and different construction material distinct from the materials from which it was transformed.

Manufactured construction material means any construction material that is not unmanufactured construction material.

Nondesignated country means a country other than the United States or a designated country.

Recovery Act designated country means any of the following countries:

(1) A World Trade Organization Government Procurement Agreement (WTO GPA)

country (Armenia, Aruba, Australia, Austria, Belgium, Bulgaria, Canada, Croatia, Cyprus, Czech Republic, Denmark, Estonia, Finland, France, Germany, Greece, Hong Kong, Hungary, Iceland, Ireland, Italy, Japan, Korea (Republic of), Latvia, Liechtenstein, Lithuania, Luxembourg, Malta, Moldova, Montenegro, Netherlands, New Zealand, Norway, Poland, Portugal, Romania, Singapore, Slovak Republic, Slovenia, Spain, Sweden, Switzerland, Taiwan, Ukraine, or United Kingdom);

(2) A Free Trade Agreement country (FTA) (Australia, Bahrain, Canada, Chile, Colombia, Costa Rica, Dominican Republic, El Salvador, Guatemala, Honduras, Korea (Republic of), Mexico, Morocco, Nicaragua, Oman, Panama, Peru, or Singapore); or

(3) A least developed country (Afghanistan, Angola, Bangladesh, Benin, Bhutan, Burkina Faso, Burundi, Cambodia, Central African Republic, Chad, Comoros, Democratic Republic of Congo, Djibouti, Equatorial Guinea, Eritrea, Ethiopia, Gambia, Guinea, Guinea-Bissau, Haiti, Kiribati, Laos, Lesotho, Liberia, Madagascar, Malawi, Mali, Mauritania, Mozambique, Nepal, Niger, Rwanda, Samoa, Sao Tome and Principe, Senegal, Sierra Leone, Solomon Islands, Somalia, South Sudan, Tanzania, Timor-Leste, Togo, Tuvalu, Uganda, Vanuatu, Yemen, or Zambia).

Recovery Act designated country construction material means a construction material that is a WTO GPA country construction material, an FTA country construction material, or a least developed country construction material.

Steel means an alloy that includes at least 50 percent iron, between .02 and 2 percent carbon, and may include other elements.

United States means the 50 States, the District of Columbia, and outlying areas.

Unmanufactured construction material means raw material brought to the construction site for incorporation into the building or work that has not been—

(1) Processed into a specific form and shape; or

(2) Combined with other raw material to create a material that has different properties than the properties of the individual raw materials.

WTO GPA country construction material means a construction material that—

(1) Is wholly the growth, product, or manufacture of a WTO GPA country; or

(2) In the case of a construction material that consists in whole or in part of materials from another country, has been substantially transformed in a WTO GPA country into a new and different construction material distinct from the materials from which it was transformed.

(b) *Construction materials.* (1) The restrictions of section 1605 of the American Recovery and Reinvestment Act of 2009 (Pub. L. 111-5) (Recovery Act) do not apply to Recovery Act designated country manufactured construction material. The restrictions of the Buy American statute do not apply to designated country unmanufactured construction material. Consistent with U.S. obligations under international agreements, this clause implements—

(i) Section 1605 of the Recovery Act by requiring, unless an exception applies, that all manufactured construction material in the project is manufactured in the United States and, if the construction material consists wholly or predominantly of iron or steel, the iron or steel was produced in the United States (produced in the United States means that all manufacturing processes of the iron or steel must take place in the United States, except metallurgical processes involving refinement of steel additives); and

(ii) The Buy American statute by providing a preference for unmanufactured construction material mined or produced in the United States over unmanufactured construction material mined or produced in a nondesignated country.

(2) The Contractor shall use only domestic construction material, Recovery Act designated country manufactured construction material, or designated country unmanufactured construction material in performing

this contract, except as provided in paragraphs (b)(3) and (b)(4) of this clause.

(3) The requirement in paragraph (b)(2) of this clause does not apply to the construction materials or components listed by the Government as follows:

[*Contracting Officer to list applicable excepted materials or indicate "none"*.]

(4) The Contracting Officer may add other construction material to the list in paragraph (b)(3) of this clause if the Government determines that—

(i) The cost of domestic construction material would be unreasonable;

(A) The cost of domestic manufactured construction material is unreasonable when the cumulative cost of such material, when compared to the cost of comparable foreign manufactured construction material, other than Recovery Act designated country construction material, will increase the overall cost of the contract by more than 25 percent;

(B) The cost of domestic unmanufactured construction material is unreasonable when the cost of such material exceeds the cost of comparable foreign unmanufactured construction material, other than designated country construction material, by more than 6 percent;

(ii) The construction material is not mined, produced, or manufactured in the United States in sufficient and reasonably available commercial quantities of a satisfactory quality; or

(iii) The application of the restriction of section 1605 of the Recovery Act to a particular manufactured construction material would be inconsistent with the public interest or the application of the Buy American statute to a particular unmanufactured construction material would be impracticable or inconsistent with the public interest.

(c) *Request for determination of inapplicability of section 1605 of the Recovery Act or the Buy American statute.*

(1)(i) Any Contractor request to use foreign construction material in accordance with paragraph (b)(4) of this clause shall include adequate information for Government evaluation of the request, including—

(A) A description of the foreign and domestic construction materials;

(B) Unit of measure;

(C) Quantity;

(D) Cost;

(E) Time of delivery or availability;

(F) Location of the construction project;

(G) Name and address of the proposed supplier; and

(H) A detailed justification of the reason for use of foreign construction materials cited in accordance with paragraph (b)(4) of this clause.

(ii) A request based on unreasonable cost shall include a reasonable survey of the market and a completed cost comparison table in the format in paragraph (d) of this clause.

(iii) The cost of construction material shall include all delivery costs to the construction site and any applicable duty.

(iv) Any Contractor request for a determination submitted after contract award shall explain why the Contractor could not reasonably foresee the need for such determination and could not have requested the determination before contract award. If the Contractor does not submit a satisfactory explanation, the Contracting Officer need not make a determination.

(2) If the Government determines after contract award that an exception to section 1605 of the Recovery Act or the Buy American statute applies and the Contracting Officer and the Contractor negotiate adequate consideration, the Contracting Officer will modify the contract to allow use of the foreign construction material. However, when the basis for the exception is the unreasonable cost of a domestic construction material, adequate consideration is not less than the differential established in paragraph (b)(4)(i) of this clause.

(3) Unless the Government determines that an exception to section 1605 of the Recovery Act or the Buy American statute applies, use of foreign construction material

other than manufactured construction material from a Recovery Act designated country or unmanufactured construction material from a designated country is noncompliant with the applicable statute.

(d) *Data*. To permit evaluation of requests under paragraph (c) of this clause based on unreasonable cost, the Contractor shall include the following information and any applicable supporting data based on the survey of suppliers:

FOREIGN (NONDESIGNATED COUNTRY) AND DOMESTIC CONSTRUCTION MATERIALS COST COMPARISON

Construction material description	Unit of measure	Quantity	Cost (dollars)*
Item 1:			
Foreign construction material	_____	_____	_____
Domestic construction material	_____	_____	_____
Item 2:			
Foreign construction material	_____	_____	_____
Domestic construction material	_____	_____	_____

[List name, address, telephone number, and contact for suppliers surveyed. Attach copy of response; if oral, attach summary.] [Include other applicable supporting information.]
[Include all delivery costs to the construction site.]*

(End of clause)

Alternate I (MAY 2014). As prescribed in 25.1102(e), add the following definition of *Bahrainian, Mexican, or Omani construction material* to paragraph (a) of the basic clause, and substitute the following paragraphs (b)(1) and (b)(2) for paragraphs (b)(1) and (b)(2) of the basic clause:

Bahrainian, Mexican, or Omani construction material means a construction material that—

(1) Is wholly the growth, product, or manufacture of Bahrain, Mexico, or Oman; or

(2) In the case of a construction material that consists in whole or in part of materials from another country, has been substantially transformed in Bahrain, Mexico, or Oman into a new and different construction material distinct from the materials from which it was transformed.

(b) *Construction materials.* (1) The restrictions of section 1605 of the American Recovery and Reinvestment Act of 2009 (Pub. L. 111-5) (Recovery Act) do not apply to Recovery Act designated country manufactured construction material. The restrictions of the Buy American statute do not apply to designated country unmanufactured construction material. Consistent with U.S. obligations under international agreements, this clause implements—

(i) Section 1605 of the Recovery Act, by requiring, unless an exception applies, that all manufactured construction material in the project is manufactured in the United States and, if the construction material consists wholly or predominantly of iron or steel, the iron or steel was produced in the United States (produced in the United States means that all manufacturing processes of the iron or steel must take place in the United States, except metallurgical processes involving refinement of steel additives); and

(ii) The Buy American statute by providing a preference for unmanufactured construction material mined or produced in the United States over unmanufactured construction material mined or produced in a nondesignated country.

(2) The Contractor shall use only domestic construction material, Recovery Act designated country manufactured construction material, or designated country unmanufactured construction material, other than Bahrainian, Mexican, or Omani construction

material, in performing this contract, except as provided in paragraphs (b)(3) and (b)(4) of this clause.

[FAC 2005-32, 74 FR 14623, 3/31/2009, effective 3/31/2009; FAC 2005-36, 74 FR 40461, 8/11/2009, effective 8/11/2009; FAC 2005-42, 75 FR 34282, 6/16/2010, effective 6/16/2010; FAC 2005-45, 75 FR 53153, 8/30/2010, effective 10/1/2010; FAC 2005-54, 76 FR 68039, 11/2/2011, effective 11/2/2011; FAC 2005-56, 77 FR 12935, 3/2/2012, effective 3/2/2012; FAC 2005-57, 77 FR 13952, 3/7/2012, effective 3/15/2012; Correction, 77 FR 14303, 3/9/2012, effective 3/9/2012; Correction, 77 FR 17353, 3/26/2012, effective 3/26/2012; FAC 2005-59, 77 FR 27548, 5/10/2012, effective 5/15/2012; FAC 2005-61, 77 FR 56739, 9/13/2012, effective 9/13/2012; FAC 2005-62, 77 FR 69723, 11/20/2012, effective 11/20/2012; FAC 2005-65, 78 FR 6188, 1/29/2013, effective 1/29/2013; FAC 2005-67, 78 FR 37695, 6/21/2013, effective 6/21/2013; FAC 2005-69, 78 FR 46792, 8/1/2013, effective 9/3/2013; FAC 2005-71, 78 FR 70480, 11/25/2013, effective 11/25/2013; FAC 2005-73, 79 FR 24192, 4/29/2014, effective 5/29/2014; FAC 2005-86, 80 FR 81892, 12/31/2015, effective 2/1/2016; FAC 2005-91, 81 FR 67774, 9/30/2016, effective 10/31/2016; FAC 2019-06, 84 FR 47866, 9/10/2019, effective 10/10/2019]

52.225-24 Notice of Required Use of American Iron, Steel, and Manufactured Goods—Buy American Statute—Construction Materials under Trade Agreements.

As prescribed in 25.1102(e), insert the following provision:

NOTICE OF REQUIRED USE OF AMERICAN IRON, STEEL, AND MANUFACTURED GOODS—BUY AMERICAN STATUTE—CONSTRUCTION MATERIALS UNDER TRADE AGREEMENTS (MAY 2014)

(a) *Definitions. Construction material, domestic construction material, foreign construction material, manufactured construction material, Recovery Act designated country construction material, steel,* and *unmanufactured construction material,* as used in this provision, are defined in the clause of this solicitation entitled "Required Use of Iron, Steel, and Manufactured Goods—Buy American statute—Construction Materials Under Trade Agreements" (Federal Acquisition Regulation (FAR) clause 52.225-23).

(b) *Requests for determination of inapplicability.* An offeror requesting a determination regarding the inapplicability of section 1605 of the American Recovery and Reinvestment Act of 2009 (Pub. L. 111-5) (Recovery Act) or the Buy American statute should submit the request to the Contracting Officer in time to allow a determination before submission of offers. The offeror shall include the information and applicable supporting data required by paragraphs (c) and (d) of FAR clause 52.225-23 in the request. If an offeror has not requested a determination regarding the inapplicability of section 1605 of the Recovery Act or the Buy American statute before submitting its offer, or has not received a response to a previous request, the offeror shall include the information and supporting data in the offer.

(c) *Evaluation of offers.* (1) If the Government determines that an exception based on unreasonable cost of domestic construction material applies in accordance with FAR 25.604, the Government will evaluate an offer requesting exception to the requirements of section 1605 of the Recovery Act or the Buy American statute by adding to the offered price of the contract—

(i) 25 percent of the offered price of the contract, if foreign manufactured construction material is included in the offer based on an exception for the unreasonable cost of comparable manufactured domestic construction material; and

(ii) 6 percent of the cost of foreign unmanufactured construction material included in the offer based on an exception for the unreasonable cost of comparable domestic unmanufactured construction material.

(2) If the solicitation specifies award on the basis of factors in addition to cost or price, the Contracting Officer will apply the evaluation factors as specified in paragraph (c)(1) of this provision and use the evaluated cost or price in determining the offer that

represents the best value to the Government.

(3) Unless paragraph (c)(2) of this provision applies, if two or more offers are equal in price, the Contracting Officer will give preference to an offer that does not include foreign construction material excepted at the request of the offeror on the basis of unreasonable cost.

(d) *Alternate offers.* (1) When an offer includes foreign construction material, other than Recovery Act designated country construction material, that is not listed by the Government in this solicitation in paragraph (b)(3) of FAR clause 52.225-23, the offeror also may submit an alternate offer based on use of equivalent domestic or Recovery Act designated country construction material.

(2) If an alternate offer is submitted, the offeror shall submit a separate Standard Form 1442 for the alternate offer and a separate cost comparison table prepared in accordance with paragraphs (c) and (d) of FAR clause 52.225-23 for the offer that is based on the use of any foreign construction material for which the Government has not yet determined an exception applies.

(3) If the Government determines that a particular exception requested in accordance with paragraph (c) of FAR clause 52.225-23 does not apply, the Government will evaluate only those offers based on use of the equivalent domestic or Recovery Act designated country construction material, and the offeror shall be required to furnish such domestic or Recovery Act designated country construction material. An offer based on use of the foreign construction material for which an exception was requested—

(i) Will be rejected as nonresponsive if this acquisition is conducted by sealed bidding; or

(ii) May be accepted if revised during negotiations.

(End of provision)

Alternate I (MAY 2014). As prescribed in 25.1102(e), substitute the following paragraph (b) for paragraph (b) of the basic provision:

(b) *Requests for determination of inapplicability.* An offeror requesting a determination regarding the inapplicability of section 1605 of the American Recovery and Reinvestment Act of 2009 (Pub. L. 111-5) (Recovery Act) or the Buy American statute shall submit the request with its offer, including the information and applicable supporting data required by paragraphs (c) and (d) of FAR clause 52.225-23.

Alternate II (MAR 2009). As prescribed in 25.1102(e), add the definition of "Bahrainian, Mexican, or Omani construction material" to paragraph (a) and substitute the following paragraph (d) for paragraph (d) of the basic provision:

(d) *Alternate offers.* (1) When an offer includes foreign construction material, except foreign construction material from a Recovery Act designated country other than Bahrain, Mexico, or Oman that is not listed by the Government in this solicitation in paragraph (b)(3) of FAR clause 52.225-23, the offeror also may submit an alternate offer based on use of equivalent domestic or Recovery Act designated country construction material other than Bahrainian, Mexican, or Omani construction material.

(2) If an alternate offer is submitted, the offeror shall submit a separate Standard Form 1442 for the alternate offer and a separate cost comparison table prepared in accordance with paragraphs (c) and (d) of FAR clause 52.225-23 for the offer that is based on the use of any foreign construction material for which the Government has not yet determined an exception applies.

(3) If the Government determines that a particular exception requested in accordance with paragraph (c) of FAR clause 52.225-23 does not apply, the Government will evaluate only those offers based on use of the equivalent domestic or Recovery Act designated country construction material other than Bahrainian, Mexican, or Omani construction material. An offer based on use of the foreign construction material for which an exception was requested—

(i) Will be rejected as nonresponsive if this acquisition is conducted by sealed bidding; or

(ii) May be accepted if revised during negotiations.

[FAC 2005-32, 74 FR 14623, 3/31/2009, effective 3/31/2009; FAC 2005-45, 75 FR 53153, 8/30/2010, effective 10/1/2010; FAC 2005-73, 79 FR 24192, 4/29/2014, effective 5/29/2014]

52.225-25 Prohibition on Contracting with Entities Engaging in Certain Activities or Transactions Relating to Iran—Representation and Certifications.

As prescribed at 25.1103(e), insert the following provision:

PROHIBITION ON CONTRACTING WITH ENTITIES ENGAGING IN CERTAIN ACTIVITIES OR TRANSACTIONS RELATING TO IRAN—REPRESENTATION AND CERTIFICATIONS (AUG 2018)

(a) *Definition. Person*—

(1) Means—

(i) A natural person;

(ii) A corporation, business association, partnership, society, trust, financial institution, insurer, underwriter, guarantor, and any other business organization, any other nongovernmental entity, organization, or group, and any governmental entity operating as a business enterprise; and

(iii) Any successor to any entity described in paragraph (1)(ii) of this definition; and

(2) Does not include a government or governmental entity that is not operating as a business enterprise.

(b) *Sensitive technology*—

(1) Means hardware, software, telecommunications equipment, or any other technology that is to be used specifically—

(i) To restrict the free flow of unbiased information in Iran; or

(ii) To disrupt, monitor, or otherwise restrict speech of the people of Iran; and

(2) Does not include information or informational materials the export of which the President does not have the authority to regulate or prohibit pursuant to section 203(b)(3) of the International Emergency Economic Powers Act (50 U.S.C. 1702(b)(3)).

(b) The offeror shall email questions concerning sensitive technology to the Department of State at *CISADA106@state.gov.*

(c) Except as provided in paragraph (d) of this provision or if a waiver has been granted in accordance with 25.703-4, by submission of its offer, the offeror—

(1) Represents, to the best of its knowledge and belief, that the offeror does not export any sensitive technology to the government of Iran or any entities or individuals owned or controlled by, or acting on behalf or at the direction of, the government of Iran;

(2) Certifies that the offeror, or any person owned or controlled by the offeror, does not engage in any activities for which sanctions may be imposed under section 5 of the Iran Sanctions Act. These sanctioned activities are in the areas of development of the petroleum resources of Iran, production of refined petroleum products in Iran, sale and provision of refined petroleum products to Iran, and contributing to Iran's ability to acquire or develop certain weapons or technologies; and

(3) Certifies that the offeror, and any person owned or controlled by the offeror, does not knowingly engage in any transaction that exceeds $3,500 with Iran's Revolutionary Guard Corps or any of its officials, agents, or affiliates, the property and interests in property of which are blocked pursuant to the International Emergency Economic Powers Act (50 U.S.C. 1701 *et seq.*) (see OFAC's Specially Designated Nationals and Blocked Persons List at *https://www.treasury.gov/resource-center/sanctions/SDN-List/Pages/default.aspx*).

(d) Exception for trade agreements. The representation requirement of paragraph (c)(1) and the certification requirements of paragraphs (c)(2) and (c)(3) of this provision do not apply if—

(1) This solicitation includes a trade agreements notice or certification (*e.g.*, 52.225–4, 52.225–6, 52.225–12, 52.225–24, or comparable agency provision); and

(2) The offeror has certified that all the offered products to be supplied are designated country end products or designated country construction material.

(End of provision)

[FAC 2005-46, 75 FR 60254, 9/29/2010, effective 9/29/2010; FAC 2005-54, 76 FR 68027, 68028, 11/2/2011, effective 11/2/2011; FAC 2005-58, 77 FR 23368, 4/18/2012, effective 5/18/2012; FAC 2005-63, 77 FR 73516, 12/10/2012, effective 12/10/2012; FAC 2005-69, 78 FR 46782, 8/1/2013, effective 8/1/2013; FAC 2005-83, 80 FR 38293, 7/2/2015, effective 10/1/2015; FAC 2005-100, 83 FR 42571, 8/22/2018, effective 8/22/2018]

52.225-26 Contractors Performing Private Security Functions Outside the United States.

As prescribed in 25.302-6, insert the following clause:

CONTRACTORS PERFORMING PRIVATE SECURITY FUNCTIONS OUTSIDE THE UNITED STATES (OCT 2016)

(a) *Definitions.* As used in this clause—

Area of combat operations means an area of operations designated as such by the Secretary of Defense when enhanced coordination of contractors performing private security functions working for Government agencies is required.

Full cooperation —

(1) Means disclosure to the Government of the information sufficient to identify the nature and extent of the incident and the individuals responsible for the conduct. It includes providing timely and complete responses to Government auditors' and investigators' requests for documents and access to employees with information;

(2) Does not foreclose any Contractor rights arising in law, the FAR, or the terms of the contract. It does not require—

(i) The Contractor to waive its attorney-client privilege or the protections afforded by the attorney work product doctrine; or

(ii) Any officer, director, owner, or employee of the Contractor, including a sole proprietor, to waive his or her attorney-client privilege or Fifth Amendment rights; and

(3) Does not restrict the Contractor from—

(i) Conducting an internal investigation; or

(ii) Defending a proceeding or dispute arising under the contract or related to a potential or disclosed violation.

Other significant military operations means activities, other than combat operations, as part of a contingency operation outside the United States that is carried out by United States Armed Forces in an uncontrolled or unpredictable high-threat environment where personnel performing security functions may be called upon to use deadly force.

(b) *Applicability.* If this contract is performed both in a designated area and in an area that is not designated, the clause only applies to performance in the following designated areas—

(1) Combat operations, as designated by the Secretary of Defense; or

(2) Other significant military operations, as designated by the Secretary of Defense, and only upon agreement of the Secretary of Defense and the Secretary of State.

(c) *Requirements.* The Contractor is required to—

(1) Ensure that all employees of the Contractor who are responsible for performing private security functions under this contract comply with 32 CFR part 159, and with any orders, directives, and instructions to Contractors performing private security functions that are identified in the contract for—

(i) Registering, processing, accounting for, managing, overseeing, and keeping appropriate records of personnel performing private security functions;

(ii) Authorizing and accounting for weapons to be carried by or available to be used by personnel performing private security functions;

(iii) Registering and identifying armored vehicles, helicopters, and other military vehicles operated by Contractors performing private security functions; and

(iv) Reporting incidents in which—

(A) A weapon is discharged by personnel performing private security functions;

(B) Personnel performing private security functions are attacked, killed, or injured;

(C) Persons are killed or injured or property is destroyed as a result of conduct by Contractor personnel;

(D) A weapon is discharged against personnel performing private security functions or personnel performing such functions believe a weapon was so discharged; or

(E) Active, non-lethal countermeasures (other than the discharge of a weapon) are employed by personnel performing private security functions in response to a perceived immediate threat;

(2) Ensure that the Contractor and all employees of the Contractor who are responsible for performing private security functions under this contract are briefed on and understand their obligation to comply with—

(i) Qualification, training, screening (including, if applicable, thorough background checks), and security requirements established by 32 CFR part 159, Private Security Contractors Operating in Contingency Operations;

(ii) Applicable laws and regulations of the United States and the host country and applicable treaties and international agreements regarding performance of private security functions;

(iii) Orders, directives, and instructions issued by the applicable commander of a combatant command or relevant Chief of Mission relating to weapons, equipment, force protection, security, health, safety, or relations and interaction with locals; and

(iv) Rules on the use of force issued by the applicable commander of a combatant command or relevant Chief of Mission for personnel performing private security functions; and

(3) Provide full cooperation with any Government-authorized investigation of incidents reported pursuant to paragraph (c)(1)(iv) of this clause and incidents of alleged misconduct by personnel performing private security functions under this contract by providing—

(i) Access to employees performing private security functions; and

(ii) Relevant information in the possession of the Contractor regarding the incident concerned.

(d) *Remedies.* In addition to other remedies available to the Government—

(1) The Contracting Officer may direct the Contractor, at its own expense, to remove and replace any Contractor or subcontractor personnel performing private security functions who fail to comply with or violate applicable requirements of this clause or 32 CFR part 159. Such action may be taken at the Government's discretion without prejudice to its rights under any other provision of this contract

(2) The Contractor's failure to comply with the requirements of this clause will be included in appropriate databases of past performance and considered in any responsibility determination or evaluation of past performance; and

(3) If this is an award-fee contract, the Contractor's failure to comply with the requirements of this clause shall be considered in the evaluation of the Contractor's performance during the relevant evaluation period, and the Contracting Officer may treat such failure to comply as a basis for reducing or denying award fees for such period or for recovering all or part of award fees previously paid for such period.

(e) *Rule of construction.* The duty of the Contractor to comply with the requirements of this clause shall not be reduced or diminished by the failure of a higher- or lower-tier Contractor or subcontractor to comply with the clause requirements or by a failure of the contracting activity to provide required oversight.

(f) *Subcontracts.* The Contractor shall include the substance of this clause, including this paragraph (f), in all subcontracts that will be performed outside the United States in areas of—

(1) Combat operations, as designated by the Secretary of Defense; or

(2) Other significant military operations, upon agreement of the Secretaries of Defense and State that the clause applies in that area.

(End of clause)

[FAC 2005-67, 78 FR 37670, 6/21/2013, effective 7/22/2013; FAC 2005-91, 81 FR 67776, 9/30/2016, effective 10/31/2016]

52.226-1 Utilization of Indian Organizations and Indian-Owned Economic Enterprises.

As prescribed in 26.104, insert the following clause:

UTILIZATION OF INDIAN ORGANIZATIONS AND INDIAN-OWNED ECONOMIC ENTERPRISES (JUN 2000)

(a) *Definitions*. As used in this clause:

Indian means any person who is a member of any Indian tribe, band, group, pueblo or community that is recognized by the Federal Government as eligible for services from the Bureau of Indian Affairs (BIA) in accordance with 25 U.S.C. 1452(c) and any *Native* as defined in the Alaska Native Claims Settlement Act (43 U.S.C. 1601).

Indian organization means the governing body of any Indian tribe or entity established or recognized by the governing body of an Indian tribe for the purposes of 25 U.S.C., chapter 17.

Indian-owned economic enterprise means any Indian-owned (as determined by the Secretary of the Interior) commercial, industrial, or business activity established or organized for the purpose of profit, provided that Indian ownership constitutes not less than 51 percent of the enterprise.

Indian tribe means any Indian tribe, band, group, pueblo or community, including native villages and native groups (including corporations organized by Kenai, Juneau, Sitka, and Kodiak) as defined in the Alaska Native Claims Settlement Act, that is recognized by the Federal Government as eligible for services from BIA in accordance with 25 U.S.C. 1542(c).

Interested party means a prime contractor or an actual or prospective offeror whose direct economic interest would be affected by the award of a subcontract or by the failure to award a subcontract.

(b) The Contractor shall use its best efforts to give Indian organizations and Indian-owned economic enterprises (25 U.S.C. 1544) the maximum practicable opportunity to participate in the subcontracts it awards to the fullest extent consistent with efficient performance of its contract.

(1) The Contracting Officer and the Contractor, acting in good faith, may rely on the representation of an Indian organization or Indian-owned economic enterprise as to its eligibility, unless an interested party challenges its status or the Contracting Officer has independent reason to question that status. In the event of a challenge to the representation of a subcontractor, the Contracting Officer will refer the matter to the U.S. Department of the Interior, Bureau of Indian Affairs (BIA), Attn: Chief, Division of Contracting and Grants Administration, 1849 C Street, NW., MS 2626-MIB, Washington, DC 20240-4000.

The BIA will determine the eligibility and notify the Contracting Officer. No incentive payment will be made within 50 working days of subcontract award or while a challenge is pending. If a subcontractor is determined to be an ineligible participant, no incentive payment will be made under the Indian Incentive Program.

(2) The Contractor may request an adjustment under the Indian Incentive Program to the following:

(i) The estimated cost of a cost-type contract.

(ii) The target cost of a cost-plus-incentive-fee prime contract.

(iii) The target cost and ceiling price of a fixed-price incentive prime contract.

(iv) The price of a firm-fixed-price prime contract.

(3) The amount of the adjustment to the prime contract is 5 percent of the estimated cost, target cost, or firm-fixed-price included in the subcontract initially awarded to the Indian organization or Indian-owned economic enterprise.

(4) The Contractor has the burden of proving the amount claimed and must assert its request for an adjustment prior to completion of contract performance.

(c) The Contracting Officer, subject to the terms and conditions of the contract and the availability of funds, will authorize an incentive payment of 5 percent of the amount paid to the subcontractor. The Contracting Officer will seek funding in accordance with agency procedures.

(End of clause)

[Interim Rule, FAC 90-7, 56 FR 41737, 8/22/91, effective 8/22/91; FAC 90-40, 61 FR 39186, 7/26/96, effective 9/24/96; FAC 97-10, 63 FR 70264, 12/18/98, effective 1/4/99; FAC 97-11, 64 FR 10530, 3/4/99, effective 5/3/99; FAC 97-15, 64 FR 72414, 12/27/99, effective 2/25/2000; FAC 97-17, 65 FR 24316, 4/25/2000, effective 6/26/2000].

52.226-2 Historically Black College or University and Minority Institution Representation.

As prescribed in 26.304, insert the following provision:

HISTORICALLY BLACK COLLEGE OR UNIVERSITY AND MINORITY INSTITUTION REPRESENTATION (OCT 2014)

(a) *Definitions.* As used in this provision—

Historically black college or university means an institution determined by the Secretary of Education to meet the requirements of 34 CFR 608.2.

Minority institution means an institution of higher education meeting the requirements of Section 365(3) of the Higher Education Act of 1965 (20 U.S.C. 1067k, including a Hispanic-serving institution of higher education, as defined in Section 502(a) of the Act (20 U.S.C. 1101a)).

(b) *Representation*. The offeror represents that it—

[ ] is [ ] is not a historically black college or university;

[ ] is [ ] is not a minority institution.

(End of provision)

[FAC 97-22, 66 FR 2116, 1/10/2001, effective 3/12/2001; Delay of effective date, 66 FR 14259, 3/9/2001, effective 5/11/2001; FAC 2005-27, 73 FR 53992, 9/17/2008, effective 10/17/2008; FAC 2005-77, 79 FR 61746, 10/14/2014, effective 10/14/2014]

52.226-3 Disaster or Emergency Area Representation.

As prescribed in 26.206(a), insert the following provision:

DISASTER OR EMERGENCY AREA REPRESENTATION (NOV 2007)

(a) *Set-aside area.* The area covered in this contract is: ____ [*Contracting Officer to fill in with definite geographic boundaries.*]

(b) *Representations.* The offeror represents that it _____does ______ does not reside or primarily do business in the set-aside area.

(c) An offeror is considered to be residing or primarily doing business in the set-aside area if, during the last twelve months—

(1) The offeror had its main operating office in the area; and

(2) That office generated at least half of the offeror's gross revenues and employed at least half of the offeror's permanent employees.

(d) If the offeror does not meet the criteria in paragraph (c) of this provision, factors to be considered in determining whether an offeror resides or primarily does business in the set-aside area include—

(1) Physical location(s) of the offeror's permanent office(s) and date any office in the set-aside area(s) was established;

(2) Current state licenses;

(3) Record of past work in the set-aside area(s) (*e.g.*, how much and for how long);

(4) Contractual history the offeror has had with subcontractors and/or suppliers in the set-aside area;

(5) Percentage of the offeror's gross revenues attributable to work performed in the set-aside area;

(6) Number of permanent employees the offeror employs in the set-aside area;

(7) Membership in local and state organizations in the set-aside area; and

(8) Other evidence that establishes the offeror resides or primarily does business in the set-aside area. For example, sole proprietorships may submit utility bills and bank statements.

(e) If the offeror represents it resides or primarily does business in the set-aside area, the offeror shall furnish documentation to support its representation if requested by the Contracting Officer. The solicitation may require the offeror to submit with its offer documentation to support the representation.

(End of provision)

[FAC 2005-12, 71 FR 44546, 8/4/2006, effective 8/4/2006; FAC 2005-21, 72 FR 63084, 11/7/2007, effective 11/7/2007; FAC 2005-27, 73 FR 53995, 9/17/2008, effective 10/17/2008; FAC 2005-37, 74 FR 52847, 10/14/2009, effective 10/14/2009; FAC 2005-43, 75 FR 38683, 7/2/2010, effective 8/2/2010]

52.226-4 Notice of Disaster or Emergency Area Set-Aside.

As prescribed in 26.206(b), insert the following clause:

NOTICE OF DISASTER OR EMERGENCY AREA SET-ASIDE (NOV 2007)

(a) *Set-aside area.* Offers are solicited only from businesses residing or primarily doing business in ____ [*Contracting Officer to fill in with definite geographic boundaries.*] Offers received from other businesses shall not be considered.

(b) This set-aside is in addition to any small business set-aside contained in this contract.

(End of clause)

[FAC 2005-12, 71 FR 44546, 8/4/2006, effective 8/4/2006; FAC 2005-21, 72 FR 63084, 11/7/2007, effective 11/7/2007; FAC 2005-27, 73 FR 53995, 9/17/2008, effective 10/17/2008; FAC 2005-37, 74 FR 52847, 10/14/2009, effective 10/14/2009; FAC 2005-43, 75 FR 38683, 7/2/2010, effective 8/2/2010]

52.226-5 Restrictions on Subcontracting Outside Disaster or Emergency Area.

As prescribed in 26.206(c), insert the following clause:

RESTRICTIONS ON SUBCONTRACTING OUTSIDE DISASTER OR EMERGENCY AREA (NOV 2007)

(a) *Definitions.* The definitions of the following terms used in this clause are found in the Small Business Administration regulations at 13 CFR 125.6(e): *cost of the contract, cost of contract performance incurred for personnel, cost of manufacturing, cost of materials, personnel,* and *subcontracting.*

(b) The Contractor agrees that in performance of the contract in the case of a contract for—

(1) *Services (except construction).* At least 50 percent of the cost of contract performance incurred for personnel shall be expended for employees of the Contractor or employees of other businesses residing or primarily doing business in the clause at FAR 52.226-4, Notice of Disaster or Emergency Area Set-Aside;

(2) *Supplies (other than procurement from a nonmanufacturer of such supplies).* The Contractor or employees of other businesses residing or primarily doing business in the set-aside area shall perform work for at least 50 percent of the cost of manufacturing the supplies, not including the cost of materials;

(3) *General construction.* The Contractor will perform at least 15 percent of the cost of the contract, not including the cost of materials, with its own employees or employees of other businesses residing or primarily doing business in the set-aside area; or

(4) *Construction by special trade Contractors.* The Contractor will perform at least 25 percent of the cost of the contract, not including the cost of materials, with its own employees or employees of other businesses residing or primarily doing business in the set-aside area.

(End of clause)

[FAC 2005-12, 71 FR 44546, 8/4/2006, effective 8/4/2006; FAC 2005-21, 72 FR 63084, 11/7/2007, effective 11/7/2007; FAC 2005-27, 73 FR 53995, 9/17/2008, effective 10/17/2008; FAC 2005-37, 74 FR 52847, 10/14/2009, effective 10/14/2009; FAC 2005-43, 75 FR 38683, 7/2/2010, effective 8/2/2010]

52.226-6 Promoting Excess Food Donation to Nonprofit Organizations.

As prescribed in 26.404, insert the following clause:

PROMOTING EXCESS FOOD DONATION TO NONPROFIT ORGANIZATIONS (MAY 2014)

(a) *Definitions*. As used in this clause—

Apparently wholesome food means food that meets all quality and labeling standards imposed by Federal, State, and local laws and regulations even though the food may not be readily marketable due to appearance, age, freshness, grade, size, surplus, or other conditions.

Excess food means food that—

(1) Is not required to meet the needs of the executive agencies; and

(2) Would otherwise be discarded.

Food-insecure means inconsistent access to sufficient, safe, and nutritious food.

Nonprofit organization means any organization that is—

(1) Described in section 501(c) of the Internal Revenue Code of 1986; and

(2) Exempt from tax under section 501(a) of that Code.

(b) In accordance with the Federal Food Donation Act of 2008 (42 U.S.C. 1792), the Contractor is encouraged, to the maximum extent practicable and safe, to donate excess, apparently wholesome food to nonprofit organizations that provide assistance to food-insecure people in the United States.

(c) *Costs*. (1) The Contractor, including any subcontractors, shall assume the responsibility for all the costs and the logistical support to collect, transport, maintain the safety of, or distribute the excess, apparently wholesome food to the nonprofit organization(s) that provides assistance to food-insecure people.

(2) The Contractor will not be reimbursed for any costs incurred or associated with the donation of excess foods. Any costs incurred for excess food donations are unallowable.

(d) *Liability*. The Government and the Contractor, including any subcontractors, shall be exempt from civil and criminal liability to the extent provided under the Bill Emerson Good Samaritan Food Donation Act (42 U.S.C. 1791). Nothing in this clause shall be construed to supersede State or local health regulations (subsection (f) of 42 U.S.C. 1791).

(e) *Flowdown*. The Contractor shall insert this clause in all contracts, task orders, delivery orders, purchase orders, and other similar instruments greater than $25,000 with its subcontractors or suppliers, at any tier, who will perform, under this contract, the provision, service, or sale of food in the United States.

(End of clause)

[FAC 2005-31, 74 FR 11829, 3/19/2009, effective 3/19/2009; FAC 2005-38, 74 FR 65607, 12/10/2009, effective 12/10/2009; FAC 2005-73, 79 FR 24192, 4/29/2014, effective 5/29/2014]

52.227-1 Authorization and Consent.

As prescribed at 27.201-2(a)(1), insert the following clause:

AUTHORIZATION AND CONSENT (DEC 2007)

(a) The Government authorizes and consents to all use and manufacture, in performing this contract or any subcontract at any tier, of any invention described in and covered by a United States patent—

(1) Embodied in the structure or composition of any article the delivery of which is accepted by the Government under this contract; or

(2) Used in machinery, tools, or methods whose use necessarily results from compliance by the Contractor or a subcontractor

with (i) specifications or written provisions forming a part of this contract or (ii) specific written instructions given by the Contracting Officer directing the manner of performance. The entire liability to the Government for infringement of a United States patent shall be determined solely by the provisions of the indemnity clause, if any, included in this contract or any subcontract hereunder (including any lower-tier subcontract), and the Government assumes liability for all other infringement to the extent of the authorization and consent hereinabove granted.

(b) The Contractor shall include the substance of this clause, including this paragraph (b), in all subcontracts that are expected to exceed the simplified acquisition threshold. However, omission of this clause from any subcontract, including those at or below the simplified acquisition threshold, does not affect this authorization and consent.

(End of clause)

Alternate I (APR 1984). As prescribed in 27-201-2 (a)(2), substitute the following paragraph (a) for paragraph (a) of the basic clause:

(a) The Government authorizes and consents to all use and manufacture of any invention described in and covered by a United States patent in the performance of this contract or any subcontract at any tier.

Alternate II (APR 1984). As prescribed in 27-201-2 (a)(3), substitute the following paragraph (a) for paragraph (a) of the basic clause:

(a) The Government authorizes and consents to all use and manufacture in the performance of any order at any tier or subcontract at any tier placed under this contract for communication services and facilities for which rates, charges, and tariffs are *not* established by a government regulatory body, of any invention described in and covered by a United States patent—

(1) Embodied in the structure or composition of any article the delivery of which is accepted by the Government under this contract; or

(2) Used in machinery, tools, or methods whose use necessarily results from compliance by the Contractor or a subcontractor with specifications or written provisions forming a part of this contract or with specific written instructions given by the Contracting Officer directing the manner of performance.

[FAC 84-1, 49 FR 12986, 3/30/84, effective 4/1/84; FAC 90-29, 60 FR 34732, 7/3/95, effective 7/3/95; FAC 90-32, 60 FR 48206, 9/18/95, effective 10/1/95; FAC 2005-21, 72 FR 63045, 11/7/2007, effective 12/7/2007]

52.227-2 Notice and Assistance Regarding Patent and Copyright Infringement.

As prescribed at 27.201-2, insert the following clause:

NOTICE AND ASSISTANCE REGARDING PATENT AND COPYRIGHT INFRINGEMENT (DEC 2007)

(a) The Contractor shall report to the Contracting Officer, promptly and in reasonable written detail, each notice or claim of patent or copyright infringement based on the performance of this contract of which the Contractor has knowledge.

(b) In the event of any claim or suit against the Government on account of any alleged patent or copyright infringement arising out of the performance of this contract or out of the use of any supplies furnished or work or services performed under this contract, the Contractor shall furnish to the Government, when requested by the Contracting Officer, all evidence and information in the Contractor's possession pertaining to such claim or suit. Such evidence and information shall be furnished at the expense of the Government except where the Contractor has agreed to indemnify the Government.

(c) The Contractor shall include the substance of this clause, including this paragraph (c), in all subcontracts that are expected to exceed the simplified acquisition threshold.

(End of clause)

[FAC 84-1, 49 FR 12987, 3/30/84, effective 4/1/84; FAC 90-32, 60 FR 48206, 9/18/95,

effective 10/1/95; FAC 90-40, 61 FR 39186, 7/26/96, effective 8/26/96; FAC 2005-21, 72 FR 63045, 11/7/2007, effective 12/7/2007]

52.227-3 Patent Indemnity.

Insert the following clause as prescribed at 27.201-2(c)(1), insert the following clause:

PATENT INDEMNITY (APR 1984)

(a) The Contractor shall indemnify the Government and its officers, agents, and employees against liability, including costs, for infringement of any United States patent (except a patent issued upon an application that is now or may hereafter be withheld from issue pursuant to a Secrecy Order under 35 U.S.C. 181) arising out of the manufacture or delivery of supplies, the performance of services, or the construction, alteration, modification, or repair of real property (hereinafter referred to as "construction work") under this contract, or out of the use or disposal by or for the account of the Government of such supplies or construction work.

(b) This indemnity shall not apply unless the Contractor shall have been informed as soon as practicable by the Government of the suit or action alleging such infringement and shall have been given such opportunity as is afforded by applicable laws, rules, or regulations to participate in its defense. Further, this indemnity shall not apply to

(1) An infringement resulting from compliance with specific written instructions of the Contracting Officer directing a change in the supplies to be delivered or in the materials or equipment to be used, or directing a manner of performance of the contract not normally used by the Contractor;

(2) An infringement resulting from addition to or change in supplies or components furnished or construction work performed that was made subsequent to delivery or performance; or

(3) A claimed infringement that is unreasonably settled without the consent of the Contractor, unless required by final decree of a court of competent jurisdiction.

(End of clause)

Alternate I (APR 1984). As prescribed in 27.201-2(c)(2), add the following paragraph (c) to the basic clause:

(c) This patent indemnification shall not apply to the following items: ____

[*Contracting Officer list and/or identify the items to be excluded from this indemnity*]

Alternate II (APR 1984). As prescribed in 27.201-2(c)(2), add the following paragraph (c) to the basic clause:

(c) This patent indemnification shall cover the following items: ____

[*List and/or identify the items to be included under this indemnity*]

Alternate III (JUL 1995). As prescribed in 27.201-2(c)(3), add the following paragraph to the basic clause:

( ) As to subcontracts at any tier for communication service, this clause shall apply only to individual communication service authorizations over the simplified acquisition threshold issued under this contract and covering those communications services and facilities;

(1) That are or have been sold or offered for sale by the Contractor to the public;

(2) That can be provided over commercially available equipment; or

(3) That involve relatively minor modifications.

[FAC 84-1, 49 FR 12987, 3/30/84, effective 4/1/84; FAC 90-4, 56 FR 15156, 4/15/91, effective 5/15/91; FAC 90-29, 60 FR 34732, 7/3/95, effective 7/3/95; FAC 90-32, 60 FR 48206, 9/18/95, effective 10/1/95; FAC 2005-21, 72 FR 63045, 11/7/2007, effective 12/7/2007]

52.227-4 Patent Indemnity—Construction Contracts.

As prescribed in 27.201-2(d)(1), insert the following clause:

PATENT INDEMNITY—CONSTRUCTION CONTRACTS (DEC 2007)

Except as otherwise provided, the Contractor shall indemnify the Government and its officers, agents, and employees against liability, including costs and expenses, for infringement of any United States patent (except a patent issued upon an application that is now or may hereafter be withheld from issue pursuant to a Secrecy Order under 35 U.S.C. 181) arising out of performing this contract or out of the use or disposal by or for the account of the Government of supplies furnished or work performed under this contract.

(End of clause)

Alternate I (DEC 2007). As prescribed in 27.201-2(d)(2), designate the first paragraph of the basic clause as paragraph (a) and add the following paragraph (b) to the basic clause:

(b) This patent indemnification shall not apply to the following items: ____

[*Contracting Officer list the items to be excluded.*]

[FAC 84-1, 49 FR 12987, 3/30/84, effective 4/1/84; FAC 90-32, 60 FR 48206, 9/18/95, effective 10/1/95; FAC 2005-21, 72 FR 63045, 11/7/2007, effective 12/7/2007]

52.227-5 Waiver of Indemnity.

As prescribed in 27.201-2(e), insert the following clause:

WAIVER OF INDEMNITY (APR 1984)

Any provision or clause of this contract to the contrary notwithstanding, the Government hereby authorizes and consents to the use and manufacture, solely in performing this contract, of any invention covered by the United States patents identified below and waives indemnification by the Contractor with respect to such patents: ____

[*Contracting Officer identify the patents by number or by other means if more appropriate.*]

(End of clause)

[FAC 84-1, 49 FR 12987, 3/30/84, effective 4/1/84; FAC 90-32, 60 FR 48206, 9/18/95, effective 10/1/95; FAC 2005-21, 72 FR 63045, 11/7/2007, effective 12/7/2007]

52.227-6 Royalty Information.

As prescribed in 27.202-5(a)(1), insert the following provision:

ROYALTY INFORMATION (APR 1984)

(a) *Cost or charges for royalties.* When the response to this solicitation contains costs or charges for royalties totaling more than $250, the following information shall be included in the response relating to each separate item of royalty or license fee:

(1) Name and address of licensor.

(2) Date of license agreement.

(3) Patent numbers, patent application serial numbers, or other basis on which the royalty is payable.

(4) Brief description, including any part or model numbers of each contract item or component on which the royalty is payable.

(5) Percentage or dollar rate of royalty per unit.

(6) Unit price of contract item.

(7) Number of units.

(8) Total dollar amount of royalties.

(b) *Copies of current licenses.* In addition, if specifically requested by the Contracting Officer before execution of the contract, the offeror shall furnish a copy of the current license agreement and an identification of applicable claims of specific patents.

(End of provision)

Alternate I (APR 1984). As prescribed in 27.202-5(a)(2), substitute the following for the introductory portion of paragraph (a) of the basic provision:

When the response to this solicitation covers charges for special construction or special assembly that contain costs or charges for royalties totaling more than $250, the following information shall be included in the response relating to each separate item of royalty or license fee:

[FAC 84-1, 49 FR 12987, 3/30/84, effective 4/1/84; FAC 90-32, 60 FR 48206, 9/18/95, effective 10/1/95; FAC 2005-21, 72 FR 63045, 11/7/2007, effective 12/7/2007]

52.227-7 Patents—Notice of Government Licensee.

As prescribed at 27.202-5(b), insert the following provision:

PATENTS—NOTICE OF GOVERNMENT LICENSEE (APR 1984)

The Government is obligated to pay a royalty applicable to the proposed acquisition because of a license agreement between the Government and the patent owner. The patent number is ___ [*Contracting Officer fill in*], and the royalty rate is ___ [*Contracting Officer fill in*]. If the offeror is the owner of, or a licensee under, the patent, indicate below:

[] Owner

[] Licensee

If an offeror does not indicate that it is the owner or a licensee of the patent, its offer will be evaluated by adding thereto an amount equal to the royalty.

(End of provision)

[FAC 84-1, 49 FR 12988, 3/30/84, effective 4/1/84; FAC 90-32, 60 FR 48206, 9/18/95, effective 10/1/95; FAC 2005-21, 72 FR 63045, 11/7/2007, effective 12/7/2007]

52.227-8 [Reserved]

52.227-9 Refund of Royalties.

As prescribed at 27.202-5(c), insert the following clause:

REFUND OF ROYALTIES (APR 1984)

(a) The contract price includes certain amounts for royalties payable by the Contractor or subcontractors or both, which amounts have been reported to the Contracting Officer.

(b) The term *royalties* as used in this clause refers to any costs or charges in the nature of royalties, license fees, patent or license amortization costs, or the like, for the use of or for rights in patents and patent applications in connection with performing this contract or any subcontract hereunder.

(c) The Contractor shall furnish to the Contracting Officer, before final payment under this contract, a statement of royalties paid or required to be paid in connection with performing this contract and subcontracts hereunder together with the reasons.

(d) The Contractor will be compensated for royalties reported under paragraph (c) of this clause, only to the extent that such royalties were included in the contract price and are determined by the Contracting Officer to be properly chargeable to the Government and allocable to the contract. To the extent that any royalties that are included in the contract price are not in fact paid by the Contractor or are determined by the Contracting Officer not to be properly chargeable to the Government and allocable to the contract, the contract price shall be reduced. Repayment or credit to the Government shall be made as the Contracting Officer directs.

(e) If, at any time within 3 years after final payment under this contract, the Contractor for any reason is relieved in whole or in part from the payment of the royalties included in the final contract price as adjusted pursuant to paragraph (d) of this clause, the Contractor shall promptly notify the Contracting Officer of that fact and shall reimburse the Government in a corresponding amount.

(f) The substance of this clause, including this paragraph (f), shall be included in any subcontract in which the amount of royalties reported during negotiation of the subcontract exceeds $250.

(End of clause)

[FAC 84-1, 49 FR 12988, 3/30/84, effective 4/1/84; FAC 90-32, 60 FR 48206, 9/18/95, effective 10/1/95; FAC 2005-21, 72 FR 63045, 11/7/2007, effective 12/7/2007]

52.227-10 Filing of Patent Applications—Classified Subject Matter.

As prescribed at 27.203-2, insert the following clause:

FILING OF PATENT APPLICATIONS—CLASSIFIED SUBJECT MATTER (DEC 2007)

(a) Before filing or causing to be filed a patent application in the United States disclosing any subject matter of this contract classified "Secret" or higher, the Contractor shall, citing the 30-day provision below, transmit the proposed application to the Contracting Officer. The government shall determine whether, for reasons of national security, the application should be placed under an order of secrecy, sealed in accordance with the provision of 35 U.S.C. 181-188, or the issuance of a patent otherwise delayed under pertinent United States statutes or regulations. The Contractor shall observe any instructions of the Contracting Officer regarding the manner of delivery of the patent application to the United States Patent Office, but the Contractor shall not be denied the right to file the application. If the Contracting Officer shall not have given any such instructions within 30 days from the date of mailing or other transmittal of the proposed application, the Contractor may file the application.

(b) Before filing a patent application in the United States disclosing any subject matter of this contract classified "Confidential," the Contractor shall furnish to the Contracting Officer a copy of the application for Government determination whether, for reasons of national security, the application should be placed under an order of secrecy or the issuance of a patent should be otherwise delayed under pertinent United States statutes or regulations.

(c) Where the subject matter of this contract is classified for reasons of security, the Contractor shall not file, or cause to be filed, in any country other than in the United States as provided in paragraphs (a) and (b) of this clause, an application or registration for a patent containing any of the subject matter of this contract without first obtaining written approval of the Contracting Officer.

(d) When filing any patent application coming within the scope of this clause, the Contractor shall observe all applicable security regulations covering the transmission of classified subject matter and shall promptly furnish to the Contracting Officer the serial number, filing date, and name of the country of any such application. When transmitting the application to the United States Patent Office, the Contractor shall by separate letter identify by agency and number the contract or contracts that require security classification markings to be placed on the application.

(e) The Contractor shall include the substance of this clause, including this paragraph (e), in all subcontracts that cover or are likely to cover classified subject matter.

(End of clause)

[FAC 84-1, 49 FR 12988, 3/30/84, effective 4/1/84; FAC 90-32, 60 FR 48206, 9/18/95, effective 10/1/95; FAC 2005-21, 72 FR 63045, 11/7/2007, effective 12/7/2007]

52.227-11 Patent Rights—Ownership by the Contractor.

As prescribed in 27.303((b)(1), insert the following clause:

PATENT RIGHTS—OWNERSHIP BY THE CONTRACTOR (MAY 2014)

(a) As used in this clause—

Invention means any invention or discovery that is or may be patentable or otherwise protectable under title 35 of the U.S. Code, or any variety of plant that is or may be protectable under the Plant Variety Protection Act (7 U.S.C. 2321, *et seq.*)

Made means—

(1) When used in relation to any invention other than a plant variety, the conception or first actual reduction to practice of the invention; or

(2) When used in relation to a plant variety, that the Contractor has at least tentatively determined that the variety has been reproduced with recognized characteristics.

Nonprofit organization means a university or other institution of higher education or an organization of the type described in section 501(c)(3) of the Internal Revenue Code of 1954 (26 U.S.C. 501(c)) and exempt from taxation under section 501(a) of the Internal Revenue Code (26 U.S.C. 501(a)), or any nonprofit scientific or educational organization qualified under a State nonprofit organization statute.

Practical application means to manufacture, in the case of a composition of product; to practice, in the case of a process or method; or to operate, in the case of a machine or system; and, in each case, under such conditions as to establish that the invention is being utilized and that its benefits are, to the extent permitted by law or Government regulations, available to the public on reasonable terms.

Subject invention means any invention of the Contractor made in the performance of work under this contract.

(b) *Contractor's rights.* (1) *Ownership.* The Contractor may retain ownership of each subject invention throughout the world in accordance with the provisions of this clause.

(2) *License.* (i) The Contractor shall retain a nonexclusive royalty-free license throughout the world in each subject invention to which the Government obtains title, unless the Contractor fails to disclose the invention within the times specified in paragraph (c) of this clause. The Contractor's license extends to any domestic subsidiaries and affiliates within the corporate structure of which the Contractor is a part, and includes the right to grant sublicenses to the extent the Contractor was legally obligated to do so at contract award. The license is transferable only with the written approval of the agency, except when transferred to the successor of that part of the Contractor's business to which the invention pertains.

(ii) The Contractor's license may be revoked or modified by the agency to the extent necessary to achieve expeditious practical application of the subject invention in a particular country in accordance with the procedures in FAR 27.302(i)(2) and 27.304-1(f).

(c) *Contractor's obligations.* (1) The Contractor shall disclose in writing each subject invention to the Contracting Officer within 2 months after the inventor discloses it in writing to Contractor personnel responsible for patent matters. The disclosure shall identify the inventor(s) and this contract under which the subject invention was made. It shall be sufficiently complete in technical detail to convey a clear understanding of the subject invention. The disclosure shall also identify any publication, on sale (*i.e.*, sale or offer for sale), or public use of the subject invention, or whether a manuscript describing the subject invention has been submitted for publication and, if so, whether it has been accepted for publication. In addition, after disclosure to the agency, the Contractor shall promptly notify the Contracting Officer of the acceptance of any manuscript describing the subject invention for publication and any on sale or public use.

(2) The Contractor shall elect in writing whether or not to retain ownership of any subject invention by notifying the Contracting Officer within 2 years of disclosure to the agency. However, in any case where publication, on sale, or public use has initiated the 1-year statutory period during which valid patent protection can be obtained in the United States, the period for election of title may be shortened by the agency to a date that is no more than 60 days prior to the end of the statutory period.

(3) The Contractor shall file either a provisional or a nonprovisional patent application or a Plant Variety Protection Application on an elected subject invention within 1 year after election. However, in any case where a publication, on sale, or public use has initiated the 1-year statutory period during which valid patent protection can be obtained in the United States, the Contractor shall file the application prior to the end of that statutory period. If the Contractor files a provisional application, it shall file a nonprovisional application within 10 months of the filing of the provisional application. The Contractor shall file patent applications in additional countries or international patent offices within either 10 months of the first filed patent application (whether provisional or nonprovisional) or 6 months from the date permission is granted by the Commissioner of Patents to file foreign patent applications where such filing has been prohibited by a Secrecy Order.

(4) The Contractor may request extensions of time for disclosure, election, or filing under paragraphs (c)(1), (c)(2), and (c)(3) of this clause.

(d) *Government's rights*—(1) *Ownership.* The Contractor shall assign to the agency, on written request, title to any subject invention—

(i) If the Contractor fails to disclose or elect ownership to the subject invention within the times specified in paragraph (c) of this clause, or elects not to retain ownership; provided, that the agency may request title only within 60 days after learning of the

Contractor's failure to disclose or elect within the specified times.

(ii) In those countries in which the Contractor fails to file patent applications within the times specified in paragraph (c) of this clause; provided, however, that if the Contractor has filed a patent application in a country after the times specified in paragraph (c) of this clause, but prior to its receipt of the written request of the agency, the Contractor shall continue to retain ownership in that country.

(iii) In any country in which the Contractor decides not to continue the prosecution of any application for, to pay the maintenance fees on, or defend in reexamination or opposition proceeding on, a patent on a subject invention.

(2) *License.* If the Contractor retains ownership of any subject invention, the Government shall have a nonexclusive, nontransferable, irrevocable, paid-up license to practice, or have practiced for or on its behalf, the subject invention throughout the world.

(e) *Contractor action to protect the Government's interest.* (1) The Contractor shall execute or have executed and promptly deliver to the agency all instruments necessary to—

(i) Establish or confirm the rights the Government has throughout the world in those subject inventions in which the Contractor elects to retain ownership; and

(ii) Assign title to the agency when requested under paragraph (d) of this clause and to enable the Government to obtain patent protection and plant variety protection for that subject invention in any country.

(2) The Contractor shall require, by written agreement, its employees, other than clerical and nontechnical employees, to disclose promptly in writing to personnel identified as responsible for the administration of patent matters and in the Contractor's format, each subject invention in order that the Contractor can comply with the disclosure provisions of paragraph (c) of this clause, and to execute all papers necessary to file patent applications on subject inventions and to establish the Government's rights in the subject inventions. The disclosure format should require, as a minimum, the information required by paragraph (c)(1) of this clause. The Contractor shall instruct such employees, through employee agreements or other suitable educational programs, as to the importance of reporting inventions in sufficient time to permit the filing of patent applications prior to U.S. or foreign statutory bars.

(3) The Contractor shall notify the Contracting Officer of any decisions not to file a nonprovisional patent application, continue the prosecution of a patent application, pay maintenance fees, or defend in a reexamination or opposition proceeding on a patent, in any country, not less than 30 days before the expiration of the response or filing period required by the relevant patent office.

(4) The Contractor shall include, within the specification of any United States nonprovisional patent or plant variety protection application and any patent or plant variety protection certificate issuing thereon covering a subject invention, the following statement, "This invention was made with Government support under (identify the contract) awarded by (identify the agency). The Government has certain rights in the invention."

(f) *Reporting on utilization of subject inventions.* The Contractor shall submit, on request, periodic reports no more frequently than annually on the utilization of a subject invention or on efforts at obtaining utilization of the subject invention that are being made by the Contractor or its licensees or assignees. The reports shall include information regarding the status of development, date of first commercial sale or use, gross royalties received by the Contractor, and other data and information as the agency may reasonably specify. The Contractor also shall provide additional reports as may be requested by the agency in connection with any march-in proceeding undertaken by the agency in accordance with paragraph (h) of this clause. The Contractor also shall mark any utilization report as confidential/proprietary to help prevent inadvertent release outside the Government. As required by 35 U.S.C. 202(c)(5), the agency will not disclose that information to persons outside the Government without the Contractor's permission.

(g) *Preference for United States industry.* Notwithstanding any other provision of this clause, neither the Contractor nor any assignee shall grant to any person the exclusive right to use or sell any subject invention in the United States unless the person agrees that any products embodying the subject invention or produced through the use of the subject invention will be manufactured substantially in the United States. However, in individual cases, the requirement for an agreement may be waived by the agency upon a showing by the Contractor or its assignee that reasonable but unsuccessful efforts have been made to grant licenses on similar terms to potential licensees that would be likely to manufacture substantially in the United States, or that under the circumstances domestic manufacture is not commercially feasible.

(h) *March-in rights.* The Contractor acknowledges that, with respect to any subject invention in which it has retained ownership, the agency has the right to require licensing pursuant to 35 U.S.C. 203 and 210(c), and in accordance with the procedures in 37 CFR 401.6 and any supplemental regulations of the agency in effect on the date of contract award.

(i) *Special provisions for contracts with nonprofit organizations.* If the Contractor is a nonprofit organization, it shall—

(1) Not assign rights to a subject invention in the United States without the written approval of the agency, except where an assignment is made to an organization that has as one of its primary functions the management of inventions, *provided,* that the assignee shall be subject to the same provisions as the Contractor;

(2) Share royalties collected on a subject invention with the inventor, including Federal employee co-inventors (but through their agency if the agency deems it appropriate) when the subject invention is assigned in accordance with 35 U.S.C. 202(e) and 37 CFR 401.10;

(3) Use the balance of any royalties or income earned by the Contractor with respect to subject inventions, after payment of expenses (including payments to inventors) incidental to the administration of subject inventions for the support of scientific research or education; and

(4) Make efforts that are reasonable under the circumstances to attract licensees of subject inventions that are small business concerns, and give a preference to a small business concern when licensing a subject invention if the Contractor determines that the small business concern has a plan or proposal for marketing the invention which, if executed, is equally as likely to bring the invention to practical application as any plans or proposals from applicants that are not small business concerns; *provided,* that the Contractor is also satisfied that the small business concern has the capability and resources to carry out its plan or proposal. The decision whether to give a preference in any specific case will be at the discretion of the Contractor.

(5) Allow the Secretary of Commerce to review the Contractor's licensing program and decisions regarding small business applicants, and negotiate changes to its licensing policies, procedures, or practices with the Secretary of Commerce when the Secretary's review discloses that the Contractor could take reasonable steps to more effectively implement the requirements of paragraph (i)(4) of this clause.

(j) *Communications.* [*Complete according to agency instructions.*]

(k) *Subcontracts.* (1) The Contractor shall include the substance of this clause, including this paragraph (k), in all subcontracts for experimental, developmental, or research work to be performed by a small business concern or nonprofit organization.

(2) The Contractor shall include in all other subcontracts for experimental, developmental, or research work the substance of the patent rights clause required by FAR Subpart 27.3.

(3) At all tiers, the patent rights clause must be modified to identify the parties as follows: references to the Government are not changed, and the subcontractor has all rights and obligations of the Contractor in

the clause. The Contractor shall not, as part of the consideration for awarding the subcontract, obtain rights in the subcontractor's subject inventions.

(4) In subcontracts, at any tier, the agency, the subcontractor, and the Contractor agree that the mutual obligations of the parties created by this clause constitute a contract between the subcontractor and the agency with respect to the matters covered by the clause; provided, however, that nothing in this paragraph is intended to confer any jurisdiction under the Contract Disputes statute in connection with proceedings under paragraph (h) of this clause.

(End of clause)

Alternate I (JUN 1989). As prescribed in 27.303(b)(3), add the following sentence at the end of paragraph (d)(2) of the basic clause:

The license shall include the right of the Government to sublicense foreign governments, their nationals and international organizations pursuant to the following treaties or international agreements: ______*

[* *Contracting Officer complete with the names of applicable existing treaties or international agreements. The above language is not intended to apply to treaties or agreements that are in effect on the date of the award but are not listed.*]

Alternate II (DEC 2007). As prescribed in 27.303(b)(4), add the following sentence at the end of paragraph (d)(2) of the basic clause:

The agency reserves the right to unilaterally amend this contract to identify specific treaties or international agreements entered into by the Government before or after the effective date of the contract and effectuate those license or other rights that are necessary for the Government to meet its obligations to foreign governments, their nationals, and international organizations under the treaties or international agreements with respect to subject inventions made after the date of the amendment.

Alternate III (JUN 1989). As prescribed in 27.303(b)(5), substitute the following paragraph (i)(3) in place of paragraph (i)(3) of the basic clause:

(3) After payment of patenting costs, licensing costs, payments to inventors, and other expenses incidental to the administration of subject inventions, the balance of any royalties or income earned and retained by the Contractor during any fiscal year on subject inventions under this or any successor contract containing the same requirement, up to any amount equal to 5 percent of the budget of the facility for that fiscal year, shall be used by the Contractor for the scientific research, development, and education consistent with the research and development mission and objectives of the facility, including activities that increase the licensing potential of other inventions of the facility. If the balance exceeds 5 percent, 75 percent of the excess above 5 percent shall be paid by the Contractor to the Treasury of the United States and the remaining 25 percent shall be used by the Contractor only for the same purposes as described above. To the extent it provides the most effective technology transfer, the licensing of subject inventions shall be administered by Contractor employees on location at the facility.

Alternate IV (JUN 1989). As prescribed in 27.303(b)(6), include the following paragraph (e)(5) in paragraph (e) of the basic clause:

(5) The Contractor shall establish and maintain active and effective procedures to ensure that subject inventions are promptly identified and timely disclosed, and shall submit a description of the procedures to the Contracting Officer so that the Contracting Officer may evaluate and determine their effectiveness.

Alternate V (DEC 2007). As prescribed in 27.303(b)(7), include the following paragraph (d)(3) in paragraph (d) of the basic clause:

(d)(3) *CRADA licensing.* If the Contractor performs services at a Government owned and operated laboratory or at a Government owned and Contractor operated laboratory directed by the Government to fulfill the Government's obligations under a Cooperative Research and Development Agreement

(CRADA) authorized by 15 U.S.C. 3710a, the Government may require the Contractor to negotiate an agreement with the CRADA collaborating party or parties regarding the allocation of rights to any subject invention the Contractor makes, solely or jointly, under the CRADA. The agreement shall be negotiated prior to the Contractor undertaking the CRADA work or, with the permission of the Government, upon the identification of a subject invention. In the absence of such an agreement, the Contractor agrees to grant the collaborating party or parties an option for a license in its inventions of the same scope and terms set forth in the CRADA for inventions made by the Government.

[Interim rule, FAC 84-48, 54 FR 25069, 6/12/89, effective 6/12/89; FAC 84-58, 55 FR 25525, 6/21/90, effective 7/23/90; Final rule, 62 FR 40236, 7/25/97, effective 6/30/97; FAC 2005-21, 72 FR 63045, 11/7/2007, effective 12/7/2007; FAC 2005-73, 79 FR 24192, 4/29/2014, effective 5/29/2014]

52.227-12 [Removed and Reserved]

[FAC 84-1, 49 FR 12991, 3/30/84, effective 4/1/84; Interim rule, FAC 84-48, 54 FR 25072, 6/12/89, effective 6/12/89; FAC 84-58, 55 FR 25525, 6/21/90, effective 7/23/90; Final rule, 55 FR 38518, 9/18/90; FAC 90-45, Final rule, 62 FR 224, 1/2/97, effective 1/1/97; FAC 2005-21, 72 FR 63045, 11/7/2007, effective 12/7/2007]

52.227-13 Patent Rights—Ownership by the Government.

As prescribed at 27.303(e), insert the following clause:

PATENT RIGHTS—OWNERSHIP BY THE GOVERNMENT (DEC 2007)

(a) *Definitions.* As used in this clause—

Invention means any invention or discovery that is or may be patentable or otherwise protectable under title 35 of the U.S. Code or any variety of plant that is or may be protectable under the Plant Variety Protection Act (7 U.S.C. 2321, *et seq.*)

Made means—

(1) When used in relation to any invention other than a plant variety, means the conception or first actual reduction to practice of the invention; or

(2) When used in relation to a plant variety, means that the Contractor has at least tentatively determined that the variety has been reproduced with recognized characteristics.

Practical application, means to manufacture, in the case of a composition or product; to practice, in the case of a process or method; or to operate, in the case of a machine or system; and, in each case, under such conditions as to establish that the invention is being utilized and that its benefits are, to the extent permitted by law or Government regulations, available to the public on reasonable terms.

Subject invention, means any invention of the Contractor made in the performance of work under this contract.

(b) *Ownership.* (1) *Assignment to the Government.* The Contractor shall assign to the Government title throughout the world to each subject invention, except to the extent that rights are retained under paragraphs (b)(2) and (d) of this clause.

(2) *Greater rights determinations.* (i) The Contractor, or an employee-inventor after consultation with the Contractor, may request greater rights than the nonexclusive license provided in paragraph (d) of this clause. The request for a greater rights must be submitted to the Contracting Officer at the time of the first disclosure of the subject invention pursuant to paragraph (e)(2) of this clause, or not later than 8 months thereafter, unless a longer period is authorized in writing by the Contracting Officer for good cause shown in writing by the Contractor. Each determination of greater rights under this contract normally shall be subject to paragraph (c) of this clause, and to the reservations and conditions deemed to be appropriate by the agency.

(ii) Upon request, the Contractor shall provide the filing date, serial number and title, a copy of the patent application (including an English-language version if filed in a language other than English), and patent number and issue date for any subject invention in any country for which the Contractor has retained title.

(iii) Upon request, the Contractor shall furnish the agency an irrevocable power to inspect and make copies of the patent application file.

(c) *Minimum rights acquired by the Government.* (1) Regarding each subject invention to which the Contractor retains ownership, the Contractor agrees as follows:

(i) The Government will have a nonexclusive, nontransferable, irrevocable, paid-up license to practice, or have practiced for or on its behalf, the subject invention throughout the world.

(ii) The agency has the right to require licensing pursuant to 35 U.S.C. 203 and 210(c) and in accordance with the procedures set forth in 37 CFR 401.6 and any supplemental regulations of the agency in effect on the date of the contract award.

(iii) Upon request, the Contractor shall submit periodic reports no more frequently than annually on the utilization, or efforts to obtain utilization, of a subject invention by the Contractor or its licensees or assignees. The reports shall include information regarding the status of development, date of first commercial sale or use, gross royalties received by the Contractor, and any other data and information as the agency may reasonably specify. The Contractor also shall provide additional reports as may be requested by the agency in connection with any march-in proceedings undertaken by the agency in accordance with paragraph (c)(1)(ii) of this clause. To the extent data or information supplied under this section is considered by the Contractor, or its licensees, or assignees to be privileged and confidential and is so marked, the agency, to the extent permitted by law, will not disclose such information to persons outside the Government.

(iv) When licensing a subject invention, the Contractor shall—

(A) Ensure that no royalties are charged on acquisitions involving Government funds, including funds derived through a Military Assistance Program of the Government or otherwise derived through the Government;

(B) Refund any amounts received as royalty charges on a subject invention in acquisitions for, or on behalf of, the Government;

(C) Provide for this refund in any instrument transferring rights in the subject invention to any party.

(v) When transferring rights in a subject invention, the Contractor shall provide for the Government's rights set forth in paragraphs (c)(1)(i) through (c)(1)(iv) of this clause.

(2) Nothing contained in paragraph (c) of this clause shall be deemed to grant to the Government rights in any invention other than a subject invention.

(d) *Minimum rights to the Contractor.* (1) The Contractor is hereby granted a revocable, nonexclusive, paid-up license in each patent application filed in any country on a subject invention and any resulting patent in which the Government obtains title, unless the Contractor fails to disclose the subject invention within the times specified in paragraph (e)(2) of this clause. The Contractor's license extends to any of its domestic subsidiaries and affiliates within the corporate structure of which the Contractor is a part, and includes the right to grant sublicenses to the extent the Contractor was legally obligated to do so at contract award. The license is transferable only with the written approval of the agency except when transferred to the successor of that part of the Contractor's business to which the subject invention pertains.

(2) The Contractor's license may be revoked or modified by the agency to the extent necessary to achieve expeditious practical application of the subject invention in a particular country in accordance with the procedures in FAR 27.302(i)(2) and 27.304-1(f).

(3) When the Government elects not to apply for a patent in any foreign country, the Contractor retains rights in that foreign country to apply for a patent, subject to the Government's rights in paragraph (c)(1) of this clause.

(e) *Invention identification, disclosures, and reports.* (1) The Contractor shall establish and maintain active and effective procedures to educate its employees in order to assure that subject inventions are promptly identified and disclosed to Contractor personnel responsible for patent matters. The procedures shall include the maintenance of laboratory notebooks or equivalent records and other records as are reasonably necessary to document the conception and/or the first actual reduction to practice of subject inventions, and records that show the procedures for identifying and disclosing subject inventions are followed. Upon request, the Contractor shall furnish the Contracting Officer a description of these procedures for evaluation and for a determination as to their effectiveness.

(2) The Contractor shall disclose in writing each subject invention to the Contracting Officer within 2 months after the inventor discloses it in writing to Contractor personnel responsible for patent matters or, if earlier, within 6 months after the Contractor becomes aware that a subject invention has been made, but in any event before any on sale (*i.e.*, sale or offer for sale), public use, or publication of the subject invention known to the Contractor. The disclosure shall identify the contract under which the subject invention was made and the inventor(s). It shall be sufficiently complete in technical detail to convey a clear understanding of the subject invention. The disclosure shall also identify any publication, on sale, or public use of the subject invention and whether a manuscript describing the subject invention has been submitted for publication and, if so, whether it has been accepted for publication. In addition, after disclosure to the agency, the Contractor shall promptly notify the Contracting Officer of the acceptance of any manuscript describing the subject invention for publication and any on sale or public use.

(3) The Contractor shall furnish the Contracting Officer the following:

(i) Interim reports every 12 months (or a longer period as may be specified by the Contracting Officer) from the date of the contract, listing subject inventions during that period, and stating that all subject inventions have been disclosed (or that there are none) and that the procedures required by paragraph (e)(1) of this clause have been followed.

(ii) A final report, within 3 months after completion of the contracted work, listing all subject inventions or stating that there were none, and listing all subcontracts at any tier containing a patent rights clause or stating that there were none.

(4) The Contractor shall require, by written agreement, its employees, other than clerical and nontechnical employees, to disclose promptly in writing to personnel identified as responsible for the administration of patent matters and in the Contractor's format each subject invention in order that the Contractor can comply with the disclosure provisions of paragraph (c) of this clause, and to execute all papers necessary to file patent applications on subject inventions and to establish the Government's rights in the subject inventions. This disclosure format should require, as a minimum, the information required by paragraph (e)(2) of this clause. The Contractor shall instruct such employees, through employee agreements or other suitable educational programs, as to the importance of reporting inventions in sufficient time to permit the filing of patent applications prior to U.S. or foreign statutory bars.

(5) Subject to FAR 27.302(i), the Contractor agrees that the Government may duplicate and disclose subject invention disclosures and all other reports and papers furnished or required to be furnished pursuant to this clause.

(f) *Examination of records relating to inventions.* (1) The Contracting Officer or any authorized representative shall, until 3 years after final payment under this contract, have the right to examine any books (including laboratory notebooks), records, and documents of the Contractor relating to the conception or first actual reduction to practice of inventions in the same field of technology as the work under this contract to determine whether—

(i) Any inventions are subject inventions;

(ii) The Contractor has established and maintains the procedures required by paragraphs (e)(1) and (e)(4) of this clause; and

(iii) The Contractor and its inventors have complied with the procedures.

(2) The Contractor shall disclose to the Contracting Officer, for the determination of ownership rights, any unreported invention that the Contracting Officer believes may be a subject invention.

(3) Any examination of records under paragraph (f) of this clause will be subject to appropriate conditions to protect the confidentiality of the information involved.

(g) *Withholding of payment. (This paragraph does not apply to subcontracts.)* (1) Any time before final payment under this contract, the Contracting Officer may, in the Government's interest, withhold payment until a reserve not exceeding $50,000 or 5 percent of the amount of this contract, whichever is less, shall have been set aside if, in the Contracting Officer's opinion, the Contractor fails to—

(i) Establish, maintain, and follow effective procedures for identifying and disclosing subject inventions pursuant to paragraph (e)(1) of this clause;

(ii) Disclose any subject invention pursuant to paragraph (e)(2) of this clause;

(iii) Deliver acceptable interim reports pursuant to paragraph (e)(3)(i) of this clause; or

(iv) Provide the information regarding subcontracts pursuant to paragraph (i)(4) of this clause.

(2) The Contracting Officer will withhold the reserve or balance until the Contracting Officer has determined that the Contractor has rectified whatever deficiencies exist and has delivered all reports, disclosures, and other information required by this clause.

(3) The Contracting Officer will not make final payment under this contract before the Contractor delivers to the Contracting Officer, as required by this clause, all disclosures of subject inventions, an acceptable final report, and all due confirmatory instruments.

(4) The Contracting Officer may decrease or increase the sums withheld up to the maximum authorized. The Contracting Officer will not withhold any amount under this paragraph while the amount specified by this paragraph is being withheld under other provisions of the contract. The withholding of any amount or the subsequent payment shall not be construed as a waiver of any Government rights.

(h) *Preference for United States industry.* Unless provided otherwise, neither the Contractor nor any assignee shall grant to any person the exclusive right to use or sell any subject invention in the United States unless the person agrees that any products embodying the subject invention or produced through the use of the subject invention will be manufactured substantially in the United States. However, in individual cases, the requirement may be waived by the agency upon a showing by the Contractor or assignee that reasonable but unsuccessful efforts have been made to grant licenses on similar terms to potential licensees that would be likely to manufacture substantially in the United States or that, under the circumstances, domestic manufacture is not commercially feasible.

(i) *Subcontracts.* (1) The Contractor shall include the substance of the patent rights clause required by FAR Subpart 27.3 in all subcontracts for experimental, developmental, or research work. The prescribed patent rights clause must be modified to identify the parties as follows: references to the Government are not changed, and the subcontractor has all rights and obligations of the Contractor in the clause. The Contractor shall not, as part of the consideration for awarding the subcontract, obtain rights in the subcontractor's subject inventions.

(2) In the event of a refusal by a prospective subcontractor to accept the clause, the Contractor—

(i) Shall promptly submit a written notice to the Contracting Officer setting forth the subcontractor's reasons for such refusal and other pertinent information that may expedite disposition of the matter; and

(ii) Shall not proceed with such subcontract without the written authorization of the Contracting Officer.

(3) In subcontracts at any tier, the agency, the subcontractor, and the Contractor agree that the mutual obligations of the parties created by the patent rights clause constitute a contract between the subcontractor and the agency with respect to those matters covered by this clause.

(4) The Contractor shall promptly notify the Contracting Officer in writing upon the award of any subcontract at any tier containing a patent rights clause by identifying the subcontractor, the applicable patent rights clause, the work to be performed under the subcontract, and the dates of award and estimated completion. Upon request of the Contracting Officer, the Contractor shall furnish a copy of such subcontract, and, no more frequently than annually, a listing of the subcontracts that have been awarded.

(End of clause)

Alternate I (JUN 1989). As prescribed in 27.303(e) (4), add the following sentence at the end of paragraph (c)(1)(i) of the basic clause:

The license will include the right of the Government to sublicense foreign governments, their nationals, and international organizations pursuant to the following treaties or international agreements: ______*

[**Contracting Officer complete with the names of applicable existing treaties or international agreements. The above language is not intended to apply to treaties or agreements that are in effect on the date of the award but are not listed.*]

Alternate II (DEC 2007). As prescribed in 27.303(e) (5), add the following sentence at the end of paragraph (c)(1)(i) of the basic clause:

The agency reserves the right to unilaterally amend this contract to identify specific treaties or international agreements entered into by the Government before or after the effective date of this contract, and effectuate those license or other rights that are necessary for the Government to meet its obligations to foreign governments, their nationals, and international organizations under treaties or international agreements with respect to subject inventions made after the date of the amendment.

[FAC 84-1, 49 FR 12994, 3/30/84, effective 4/1/84; Interim rule, FAC 84-48, 54 FR 25072, 6/12/89, effective 6/12/89; FAC 84-58, 55 FR 25525, 6/21/90, effective 7/23/90; FAC 90-45, Final rule, 62 FR 224, 1/2/97, effective 1/1/97; FAC 2005-21, 72 FR 63045, 11/7/2007, effective 12/7/2007]

52.227-14 Rights in Data—General.

As prescribed in 27.409(b)(1), insert the following clause with any appropriate alternates:

RIGHTS IN DATA—GENERAL (MAY 2014)

(a) *Definitions.* As used in this clause—

Computer database or *database* means a collection of recorded information in a form capable of, and for the purpose of, being stored in, processed, and operated on by a computer. The term does not include computer software.

Computer software—(1) Means (i) Computer programs that comprise a series of instructions, rules, routines, or statements, regardless of the media in which recorded, that allow or cause a computer to perform a specific operation or series of operations; and

(ii) Recorded information comprising source code listings, design details, algorithms, processes, flow charts, formulas, and related material that would enable the computer program to be produced, created, or compiled.

(2) Does not include computer databases or computer software documentation.

Computer software documentation means owner's manuals, user's manuals, installation instructions, operating instructions, and other similar items, regardless of storage medium, that explain the capabilities of the computer software or provide instructions for using the software.

Data means recorded information, regardless of form or the media on which it may be recorded. The term includes technical data and computer software. The term does not include information incidental to contract administration, such as financial, administrative, cost or pricing, or management information.

Form, fit, and function data means data relating to items, components, or processes that are sufficient to enable physical and functional interchangeability, and data identifying source, size, configuration, mating and attachment characteristics, functional characteristics, and performance requirements. For computer software it means data identifying source, functional characteristics, and performance requirements but specifically excludes the source code, algorithms, processes, formulas, and flow charts of the software.

Limited rights means the rights of the Government in limited rights data as set forth in the Limited Rights Notice of paragraph (g)(3) if included in this clause.

Limited rights data means data, other than computer software, that embody trade secrets or are commercial or financial and confidential or privileged, to the extent that such data pertain to items, components, or processes developed at private expense, including minor modifications.

Restricted computer software means computer software developed at private expense and that is a trade secret, is commercial or financial and confidential or privileged, or is copyrighted computer software, including minor modifications of the computer software.

Restricted rights, as used in this clause, means the rights of the Government in restricted computer software, as set forth in a Restricted Rights Notice of paragraph (g) if included in this clause, or as otherwise may be provided in a collateral agreement incorporated in and made part of this contract, including minor modifications of such computer software.

Technical data, means recorded information (regardless of the form or method of the recording) of a scientific or technical nature (including computer databases and computer software documentation). This term does not include computer software or financial, administrative, cost or pricing, or management data or other information incidental to contract administration. The term includes recorded information of a scientific or technical nature that is included in computer databases. (See 41 U.S.C. 116.)

Unlimited rights means the rights of the Government to use, disclose, reproduce, prepare derivative works, distribute copies to the public, and perform publicly and display publicly, in any manner and for any purpose, and to have or permit others to do so.

(b) *Allocation of rights.* (1) Except as provided in paragraph (c) of this clause, the Government shall have unlimited rights in—

(i) Data first produced in the performance of this contract;

(ii) Form, fit, and function data delivered under this contract;

(iii) Data delivered under this contract (except for restricted computer software) that constitute manuals or instructional and training material for installation, operation, or routine maintenance and repair of items, components, or processes delivered or furnished for use under this contract; and

(iv) All other data delivered under this contract unless provided otherwise for limited rights data or restricted computer software in accordance with paragraph (g) of this clause.

(2) The Contractor shall have the right to—

(i) Assert copyright in data first produced in the performance of this contract to the extent provided in paragraph (c)(1) of this clause;

(ii) Use, release to others, reproduce, distribute, or publish any data first produced or specifically used by the Contractor in the performance of this contract, unless provided otherwise in paragraph (d) of this clause;

(iii) Substantiate the use of, add, or correct limited rights, restricted rights, or copyright notices and to take other appropriate action, in accordance with paragraphs (e) and (f) of this clause; and

(iv) Protect from unauthorized disclosure and use those data that are limited rights data or restricted computer software to the extent provided in paragraph (g) of this clause.

(c) *Copyright*—(1) *Data first produced in the performance of this contract.* (i) Unless provided otherwise in paragraph (d) of this clause, the Contractor may, without prior approval of the Contracting Officer, assert copyright in scientific and technical articles based on or containing data first produced in the performance of this contract and published in academic, technical or professional journals, symposia proceedings, or similar works. The prior, express written permission of the Contracting Officer is required to assert copyright in all other data first produced in the performance of this contract.

(ii) When authorized to assert copyright to the data, the Contractor shall affix the applicable copyright notices of 17 U.S.C. 401 or 402, and an acknowledgment of Government sponsorship (including contract number).

(iii) For data other than computer software, the Contractor grants to the Government, and others acting on its behalf, a paid-up, nonexclusive, irrevocable, worldwide license in such copyrighted data to reproduce, prepare derivative works, distribute copies to the public, and perform publicly and display publicly by or on behalf of the Government. For computer software, the Contractor grants to the Government, and others acting on its behalf, a paid-up, nonexclusive, irrevocable, worldwide license in such copyrighted computer software to reproduce, prepare derivative works, and perform publicly and display publicly (but not to distribute copies to the public) by or on behalf of the Government.

(2) *Data not first produced in the performance of this contract.* The Contractor shall not, without the prior written permission of the Contracting Officer, incorporate in data delivered under this contract any data not first produced in the performance of this contract unless the Contractor—

(i) Identifies the data; and

(ii) Grants to the Government, or acquires on its behalf, a license of the same scope as set forth in paragraph (c)(1) of this clause or, if such data are restricted computer software, the Government shall acquire a copyright license as set forth in paragraph (g)(4) of this clause (if included in this contract) or as otherwise provided in a collateral agreement incorporated in or made part of this contract.

(3) *Removal of copyright notices.* The Government will not remove any authorized copyright notices placed on data pursuant to this paragraph (c), and will include such notices on all reproductions of the data.

(d) *Release, publication, and use of data.* The Contractor shall have the right to use, release to others, reproduce, distribute, or publish any data first produced or specifically used by the Contractor in the performance of this contract, except—

(1) As prohibited by Federal law or regulation (*e.g.*, export control or national security laws or regulations);

(2) As expressly set forth in this contract; or

(3) If the Contractor receives or is given access to data necessary for the performance of this contract that contain restrictive markings, the Contractor shall treat the data in accordance with such markings unless specifically authorized otherwise in writing by the Contracting Officer.

(e) *Unauthorized marking of data.* (1) Notwithstanding any other provisions of this contract concerning inspection or acceptance, if any data delivered under this contract are marked with the notices specified in paragraph (g)(3) or (g) (4) if included in this clause, and use of the notices is not authorized by this clause, or if the data bears any other restrictive or limiting markings not authorized by this contract, the Contracting Officer may at any time either return the data to the Contractor, or cancel or ignore the markings. However, pursuant to 41 U.S.C. 4703, the following procedures shall apply prior to canceling or ignoring the markings.

(i) The Contracting Officer will make written inquiry to the Contractor affording the Contractor 60 days from receipt of the inquiry to provide written justification to substantiate the propriety of the markings;

(ii) If the Contractor fails to respond or fails to provide written justification to substantiate the propriety of the markings within the 60-day period (or a longer time approved in writing by the Contracting Officer for good cause shown), the Government shall have the right to cancel or ignore the markings at any time after said period and the data will no longer be made subject to any disclosure prohibitions.

(iii) If the Contractor provides written justification to substantiate the propriety of the markings within the period set in paragraph (e)(1)(i) of this clause, the Contracting Officer will consider such written justification and determine whether or not the markings are to be cancelled or ignored. If the Contracting Officer determines that the markings are authorized, the Contractor will be so notified in writing. If the Contracting Officer determines, with concurrence of the head of the contracting activity, that the markings are not authorized, the Contracting Officer will furnish the Contractor a written determination, which determination will become the final agency decision regarding the appropriateness of the markings unless the Contractor files suit in a court of competent jurisdiction within 90 days of receipt of the Contracting Officer's decision. The Government will continue to abide by the markings under this paragraph (e)(1)(iii) until final resolution of the matter either by the Contracting Officer's determination becoming final (in which instance the Government will thereafter have the right to cancel or ignore the markings at any time and the data will no longer be made subject to any disclosure prohibitions), or by final disposition of the matter by court decision if suit is filed.

(2) The time limits in the procedures set forth in paragraph (e)(1) of this clause may be modified in accordance with agency regulations implementing the Freedom of Information Act (5 U.S.C. 552) if necessary to respond to a request thereunder.

(3) Except to the extent the Government's action occurs as the result of final disposition of the matter by a court of competent jurisdiction, the Contractor is not precluded by paragraph (e) of the clause from bringing a claim, in accordance with the Disputes clause of this contract, that may arise as the result of the Government removing or ignoring authorized markings on data delivered under this contract.

(f) *Omitted or incorrect markings.* (1) Data delivered to the Government without any restrictive markings shall be deemed to have been furnished with unlimited rights. The Government is not liable for the disclosure, use, or reproduction of such data.

(2) If the unmarked data has not been disclosed without restriction outside the Government, the Contractor may request, within 6 months (or a longer time approved by the Contracting Officer in writing for good cause shown) after delivery of the data, permission to have authorized notices placed on the data at the Contractor's expense. The Contracting Officer may agree to do so if the Contractor—

(i) Identifies the data to which the omitted notice is to be applied;

(ii) Demonstrates that the omission of the notice was inadvertent;

(iii) Establishes that the proposed notice is authorized; and

(iv) Acknowledges that the Government has no liability for the disclosure, use, or reproduction of any data made prior to the addition of the notice or resulting from the omission of the notice.

(3) If data has been marked with an incorrect notice, the Contracting Officer may—

(i) Permit correction of the notice at the Contractor's expense if the Contractor identifies the data and demonstrates that the correct notice is authorized; or

(ii) Correct any incorrect notices.

(g) *Protection of limited rights data and restricted computer software.* (1) The Contractor may withhold from delivery qualifying limited rights data or restricted computer software that are not data identified in paragraphs (b)(1)(i), (ii), and (iii) of this clause. As a condition to this withholding, the Contractor shall—

(i) Identify the data being withheld; and

(ii) Furnish form, fit, and function data instead.

(2) Limited rights data that are formatted as a computer database for delivery to the Government shall be treated as limited rights data and not restricted computer software.

(3) [Reserved]

(h) *Subcontracting*. The Contractor shall obtain from its subcontractors all data and rights therein necessary to fulfill the Contractor's obligations to the Government under this contract. If a subcontractor refuses to accept terms affording the Government those rights, the Contractor shall promptly notify the Contracting Officer of the refusal and shall not proceed with the subcontract award without authorization in writing from the Contracting Officer.

(i) *Relationship to patents or other rights.* Nothing contained in this clause shall imply a license to the Government under any patent or be construed as affecting the scope of any license or other right otherwise granted to the Government.

(End of clause)

Alternate I (DEC 2007). As prescribed in 27.409(b)(2), substitute the following definition for *limited rights data* in paragraph (a) of the basic clause:

Limited rights data means data, other than computer software, developed at private expense that embody trade secrets or are commercial or financial and confidential or privileged.

Alternate II (DEC 2007). As prescribed in 27.409(b)(3), insert the following paragraph (g)(3) in the basic clause:

(g)(3) Notwithstanding paragraph (g)(1) of this clause, the contract may identify and specify the delivery of limited rights data, or the Contracting Officer may require by written request the delivery of limited rights data that has been withheld or would otherwise be entitled to be withheld. If delivery of that data is required, the Contractor shall affix the following "Limited Rights Notice" to the data and the Government will treat the data, subject to the provisions of paragraphs (e) and (f) of this clause, in accordance with the notice:

LIMITED RIGHTS NOTICE (DEC 2007)

(a) These data are submitted with limited rights under Government Contract No. ____________ (and subcontract ____________, if appropriate). These data may be reproduced and used by the Government with the express limitation that they will not, without written permission of the Contractor, be used for purposes of manufacture nor disclosed outside the Government; except that the Government may disclose these data outside the Government for the following purposes, if any; provided that the Government makes such disclosure subject to prohibition against further use and disclosure: [*Agencies may list additional purposes as set forth in 27.404-2(c)(1) or if none, so state.*]

(b) This notice shall be marked on any reproduction of these data, in whole or in part.

(End of notice)

Alternate III (DEC 2007). As prescribed in 27.409(b)(4), insert the following paragraph (g)(4) in the basic clause:

(g)(4)(i) Notwithstanding paragraph (g)(1) of this clause, the contract may identify and specify the delivery of restricted computer software, or the Contracting Officer may require by written request the delivery of restricted computer software that has been withheld or would otherwise be entitled to be withheld. If delivery of that computer software is required, the Contractor shall affix the following "Restricted Rights Notice" to the computer software and the Government will treat the computer software, subject to paragraphs (e) and (f) of this clause, in accordance with the notice:

RESTRICTED RIGHTS NOTICE (DEC 2007)

(a) This computer software is submitted with restricted rights under Government Contract No. ____________ (and subcontract ____________, if appropriate).

It may not be used, reproduced, or disclosed by the Government except as provided in paragraph (b) of this notice or as otherwise expressly stated in the contract.

(b) This computer software may be—

(1) Used or copied for use with the computer(s) for which it was acquired, including use at any Government installation to which the computer(s) may be transferred;

(2) Used or copied for use with a backup computer if any computer for which it was acquired is inoperative;

(3) Reproduced for safekeeping (archives) or backup purposes;

(4) Modified, adapted, or combined with other computer software, *provided* that the modified, adapted, or combined portions of the derivative software incorporating any of the delivered, restricted computer software shall be subject to the same restricted rights;

(5) Disclosed to and reproduced for use by support service Contractors or their subcontractors in accordance with paragraphs (b)(1) through (4) of this notice; and

(6) Used or copied for use with a replacement computer.

(c) Notwithstanding the foregoing, if this computer software is copyrighted computer software, it is licensed to the Government with the minimum rights set forth in paragraph (b) of this notice.

(d) Any other rights or limitations regarding the use, duplication, or disclosure of this computer software are to be expressly stated in, or incorporated in, the contract.

(e) This notice shall be marked on any reproduction of this computer software, in whole or in part.

(End of notice)

(ii) Where it is impractical to include the Restricted Rights Notice on restricted computer software, the following short-form notice may be used instead:

RESTRICTED RIGHTS NOTICE SHORT FORM (JUN 1987)

Use, reproduction, or disclosure is subject to restrictions set forth in Contract No. ________ (and subcontract, if appropriate) with ________ (name of Contractor and subcontractor).

(End of notice)

(iii) If restricted computer software is delivered with the copyright notice of 17 U.S.C. 401, it will be presumed to be licensed to the Government without disclosure prohibitions, with the minimum rights set forth in paragraph (b) of this clause.

Alternate IV (DEC 2007). As prescribed in 27.409(b)(5), substitute the following paragraph (c)(1) for paragraph (c)(1) of the basic clause:

(c) *Copyright*—(1) *Data first produced in the performance of the contract.* Except as otherwise specifically provided in this contract, the Contractor may assert copyright in any data first produced in the performance of this contract. When asserting copyright, the Contractor shall affix the applicable copyright notice of 17 U.S.C. 401 or 402, and an acknowledgment of Government sponsorship (including contract number), to the data when such data are delivered to the Government, as well as when the data are published or deposited for registration as a published work in the U.S. Copyright Office. For data other than computer software, the Contractor grants to the Government, and others acting on its behalf, a paid-up, nonexclusive, irrevocable, worldwide license for all such data to reproduce, prepare derivative works, distribute copies to the public, and perform publicly and display publicly, by or on behalf of the Government. For computer software, the Contractor grants to the Government and others acting on its behalf, a paid-up, nonexclusive, irrevocable, worldwide license for all such computer software to reproduce, prepare derivative works, and perform publicly and display publicly (but not to distribute copies to the public), by or on behalf of the Government.

Alternate V (DEC 2007). As prescribed in 27.409(b)(6), add the following paragraph (j) to the basic clause:

(j) The Contractor agrees, except as may be otherwise specified in this contract for specific data deliverables listed as not subject to this paragraph, that the Contracting Officer may, up to three years after acceptance of all deliverables under this contract, inspect at the Contractor's facility any data withheld pursuant to paragraph (g)(1) of this clause, for purposes of verifying the Contractor's assertion of limited rights or restricted rights status of the data or for evaluating work performance. When the Contractor whose data are to be inspected demonstrates to the Contracting Officer that there would be a possible conflict of interest if a particular representative made the inspection, the Contracting Officer shall designate an alternate inspector.

[FAC 84-27, 52 FR 18150, 5/13/87, effective 6/1/87; FAC 2005-21, 72 FR 63045, 11/7/2007, effective 12/7/2007; FAC 2005-73, 79 FR 24192, 4/29/2014, effective 5/29/2014]

52.227-15 Representation of Limited Rights Data and Restricted Computer Software.

As prescribed in 27.409(c), insert the following provision:

REPRESENTATION OF LIMITED RIGHTS DATA AND RESTRICTED COMPUTER SOFTWARE (DEC 2007)

(a) This solicitation sets forth the Government's known delivery requirements for data (as defined in the clause at 52.227-14, Rights in Data—General). Any resulting contract may also provide the Government the option to order additional data under the Additional Data Requirements clause at 52.227-16, if included in the contract. Any data delivered under the resulting contract will be subject to the Rights in Data—General clause at 52.227-14 included in this contract. Under the latter clause, a Contractor may withhold from delivery data that qualify as limited rights data or restricted computer software, and deliver form, fit, and function data instead. The latter clause also may be used with its Alternates II and/or III to obtain delivery of limited rights data or restricted computer software, marked with limited rights or restricted rights notices, as appropriate. In addition, use of Alternate V with this latter clause provides the Government the right to inspect such data at the Contractor's facility.

(b) By completing the remainder of this paragraph, the offeror represents that it has reviewed the requirements for the delivery of technical data or computer software and states [*offeror check appropriate block*]—

() None of the data proposed for fulfilling the data delivery requirements qualifies as limited rights data or restricted computer software; or

() Data proposed for fulfilling the data delivery requirements qualify as limited rights data or restricted computer software and are identified as follows:

____

____

____

(c) Any identification of limited rights data or restricted computer software in the offeror's response is not determinative of the status of the data should a contract be awarded to the offeror.

(End of provision)

[FAC 97-11, 64 FR 10530, 3/4/99, effective 5/3/99; FAC 2005-21, 72 FR 63045, 11/7/2007, effective 12/7/2007]

52.227-16 Additional Data Requirements.

As prescribed in 27.409(d), insert the following clause:

ADDITIONAL DATA REQUIREMENTS (JUN 1987)

(a) In addition to the data (as defined in the clause at 52.227-14, Rights in Data—General clause or other equivalent included in this contract) specified elsewhere in this contract to be delivered, the Contracting Officer may, at any time during contract performance or within a period of 3 years after acceptance of all items to be delivered under this contract, order any data first produced or specifically used in the performance of this contract.

(b) The Rights in Data—General clause or other equivalent included in this contract is applicable to all data ordered under this Additional Data Requirements clause. Nothing contained in this clause shall require the Contractor to deliver any data the withholding of which is authorized by the Rights in Data—General or other equivalent clause of this contract, or data which are specifically identified in this contract as not subject to this clause.

(c) When data are to be delivered under this clause, the Contractor will be compensated for converting the data into the prescribed form, for reproduction, and for delivery.

(d) The Contracting Officer may release the Contractor from the requirements of this clause for specifically identified data items at any time during the 3-year period set forth in paragraph (a) of this clause.

(End of clause)

[FAC 84-27, 52 FR 18153, 5/13/87, effective 6/1/87; Final rule, 62 FR 40236, 7/25/97, effective 6/30/97; FAC 2005-21, 72 FR 63045, 11/7/2007, effective 12/7/2007]

52.227-17 Rights in Data—Special Works.

As prescribed in 27.409(e), insert the following clause:

RIGHTS IN DATA—SPECIAL WORKS (DEC 2007)

(a) *Definitions.* As used in this clause—

Data means recorded information, regardless of form or the media on which it may be recorded. The term includes technical data and computer software. The term does not include information incidental to contract administration, such as financial, administrative, cost or pricing, or management information.

Unlimited rights means the rights of the Government to use, disclose, reproduce, prepare derivative works, distribute copies to the public, and perform publicly and display publicly, in any manner and for any purpose, and to have or permit others to do so.

(b) *Allocation of Rights.* (1) The Government shall have—

(i) Unlimited rights in all data delivered under this contract, and in all data first produced in the performance of this contract, except as provided in paragraph (c) of this clause.

(ii) The right to limit assertion of copyright in data first produced in the performance of this contract, and to obtain assignment of copyright in that data, in accordance with paragraph (c)(1) of this clause.

(iii) The right to limit the release and use of certain data in accordance with paragraph (d) of this clause.

(2) The Contractor shall have, to the extent permission is granted in accordance with paragraph (c)(1) of this clause, the right to assert claim to copyright subsisting in data first produced in the performance of this contract.

(c) *Copyright*—(1) *Data first produced in the performance of this contract.* (i) The Contractor shall not assert or authorize others to assert any claim to copyright subsisting in any data first produced in the performance of this contract without prior written permission of the Contracting Officer. When copyright is asserted, the Contractor shall affix the appropriate copyright notice of 17 U.S.C. 401 or 402 and acknowledgment of Government sponsorship (including contract number) to the data when delivered to the Government, as well as when the data are published or deposited for registration as a published work in the U.S. Copyright Office. The Contractor grants to the Government, and others acting on its behalf, a paid-up, nonexclusive, irrevocable, worldwide license for all delivered data to reproduce, prepare derivative works, distribute copies to the public, and perform publicly and display publicly, by or on behalf of the Government.

(ii) If the Government desires to obtain copyright in data first produced in the performance of this contract and permission has not been granted as set forth in paragraph (c)(1)(i) of this clause, the Contracting Officer shall direct the Contractor to assign (with or without registration), or obtain the assignment of, the copyright to the Government or its designated assignee.

(2) *Data not first produced in the performance of this contract.* The Contractor shall not, without prior written permission of the Contracting Officer, incorporate in data delivered under this contract any data not first

produced in the performance of this contract and that contain the copyright notice of 17 U.S.C. 401 or 402, unless the Contractor identifies such data and grants to the Government, or acquires on its behalf, a license of the same scope as set forth in paragraph (c) (1) of this clause.

(d) *Release and use restrictions.* Except as otherwise specifically provided for in this contract, the Contractor shall not use, release, reproduce, distribute, or publish any data first produced in the performance of this contract, nor authorize others to do so, without written permission of the Contracting Officer.

(e) *Indemnity.* The Contractor shall indemnify the Government and its officers, agents, and employees acting for the Government against any liability, including costs and expenses, incurred as the result of the violation of trade secrets, copyrights, or right of privacy or publicity, arising out of the creation, delivery, publication, or use of any data furnished under this contract; or any libelous or other unlawful matter contained in such data. The provisions of this paragraph do not apply unless the Government provides notice to the Contractor as soon as practicable of any claim or suit, affords the Contractor an opportunity under applicable laws, rules, or regulations to participate in the defense of the claim or suit, and obtains the Contractor's consent to the settlement of any claim or suit other than as required by final decree of a court of competent jurisdiction; and these provisions do not apply to material furnished to the Contractor by the Government and incorporated in data to which this clause applies.

(End of clause)

[FAC 84-27, 52 FR 18153, 5/13/87, effective 6/1/87; FAC 84-51, 54 FR 34758, 8/21/89, effective 9/20/89; FAC 84-58, 55 FR 25532, 6/21/90, effective 7/23/90; FAC 2005-21, 72 FR 63045, 11/7/2007, effective 12/7/2007]

52.227-18 Rights in Data—Existing Works.

As prescribed in 27.409(f), insert the following clause:

RIGHTS IN DATA—EXISTING WORKS (DEC 2007)

(a) Except as otherwise provided in this contract, the Contractor grants to the Government, and others acting on its behalf, a paid-up nonexclusive, irrevocable, worldwide license to reproduce, prepare derivative works, and perform publicly and display publicly, by or on behalf of the Government, for all the material or subject matter called for under this contract, or for which this clause is specifically made applicable.

(b) The Contractor shall indemnify the Government and its officers, agents, and employees acting for the Government against any liability, including costs and expenses, incurred as the result of (1) the violation of trade secrets, copyrights, or right of privacy or publicity, arising out of the creation, delivery, publication or use of any data furnished under this contract; or (2) any libelous or other unlawful matter contained in such data. The provisions of this paragraph do not apply unless the Government provides notice to the Contractor as soon as practicable of any claim or suit, affords the Contractor an opportunity under applicable laws, rules, or regulations to participate in the defense of the claim or suit, and obtains the Contractor's consent to the settlement of any claim or suit other than as required by final decree of a court of competent jurisdiction; and do not apply to material furnished to the Contractor by the Government and incorporated in data to which this clause applies.

(End of clause)

[FAC 84-27, 52 FR 18154, 5/13/87, effective 6/1/87; FAC 2005-21, 72 FR 63045, 11/7/2007, effective 12/7/2007]

52.227-19 Commercial Computer Software License.

As prescribed in 27.409(g), insert the following clause:

COMMERCIAL COMPUTER SOFTWARE LICENSE (DEC 2007)

(a) Notwithstanding any contrary provisions contained in the Contractor's standard commercial license or lease agreement, the Contractor agrees that the Government will have the rights that are set forth in paragraph (b) of this clause to use, duplicate or disclose any commercial computer software delivered under this contract. The terms and provisions of this contract shall comply with Federal laws and the Federal Acquisition Regulation.

(b) (1) The commercial computer software delivered under this contract may not be used, reproduced, or disclosed by the Government except as provided in paragraph (b) (2) of this clause or as expressly stated otherwise in this contract.

(2) The commercial computer software may be—

(i) Used or copied for use with the computer(s) for which it was acquired, including use at any Government installation to which the computer(s) may be transferred;

(ii) Used or copied for use with a backup computer if any computer for which it was acquired is inoperative;

(iii) Reproduced for safekeeping (archives) or backup purposes;

(iv) Modified, adapted, or combined with other computer software, provided that the modified, adapted, or combined portions of the derivative software incorporating any of the delivered, commercial computer software shall be subject to same restrictions set forth in this contract;

(v) Disclosed to and reproduced for use by support service Contractors or their subcontractors, subject to the same restrictions set forth in this contract; and

(vi) Used or copied for use with a replacement computer.

(3) If the commercial computer software is otherwise available without disclosure restrictions, the Contractor licenses it to the Government without disclosure restrictions.

(c) The Contractor shall affix a notice substantially as follows to any commercial computer software delivered under this contract:

Notice—Notwithstanding any other lease or license agreement that may pertain to, or accompany the delivery of, this computer software, the rights of the Government regarding its use, reproduction and disclosure are as set forth in Government Contract No. _______________.

(End of clause)

[FAC 84-27, 52 FR 18154, 5/13/87, effective 6/1/87; FAC 2005-21, 72 FR 63045, 11/7/2007, effective 12/7/2007]

52.227-20 Rights in Data—SBIR Program.

As prescribed in 27.409(h), insert the following clause:

RIGHTS IN DATA—SBIR PROGRAM (MAY 2014)

(a) *Definitions.* As used in this clause—

Computer database or *database* means a collection of recorded information in a form capable of, and for the purpose of, being stored in, processed, and operated on by a computer. The term does not include computer software.

Computer software—(1) Means (i) Computer programs that comprise a series of instructions, rules, routines, or statements, regardless of the media in which recorded, that allow or cause a computer to perform a specific operation or series of operations; and

(ii) Recorded information comprising source code listings, design details, algorithms, processes, flow charts, formulas, and related material that would enable the computer program to be produced, created, or compiled.

(2) Does not include computer databases or computer software documentation.

Computer software documentation means owner's manuals, user's manuals, installation instructions, operating instructions, and other similar items, regardless of storage medium, that explain the capabilities of the computer software or provide instructions for using the software.

Data means recorded information, regardless of form or the media on which it may be recorded. The term includes technical data and computer software. The term does not include information incidental to contract administration, such as financial, administrative, cost or pricing or management information.

Form, fit, and function data means data relating to items, components, or processes that are sufficient to enable physical and functional interchangeability, and data identifying source, size, configuration, mating and attachment characteristics, functional characteristics, and performance requirements. For computer software it means data identifying source, functional characteristics, and performance requirements but specifically excludes the source code, algorithms, processes, formulas, and flow charts of the software.

Limited rights data means data (other than computer software) developed at private expense that embody trade secrets or are commercial or financial and confidential or privileged.

Restricted computer software means computer software developed at private expense and that is a trade secret, is commercial or financial and confidential or privileged, or is copyrighted computer software, including minor modifications of the computer software.

SBIR data means data first produced by a Contractor that is a small business concern in performance of a small business innovation research contract issued under the authority of 15 U.S.C. 638, which data are not generally known, and which data without obligation as to its confidentiality have not been made available to others by the Contractor or are not already available to the Government.

SBIR rights means the rights in SBIR data set forth in the SBIR Rights Notice of paragraph (d) of this clause.

Technical data means recorded information (regardless of the form or method of the recording) of a scientific or technical nature (including computer databases and computer software documentation). This term does not include computer software or financial, administrative, cost or pricing, or management data or other information incidental to contract administration. The term includes recorded information of a scientific or technical nature that is included in computer databases. (See 41 U.S.C. 116.)

Unlimited rights means the right of the Government to use, disclose, reproduce, prepare derivative works, distribute copies to the public, and perform publicly and display publicly, in any manner and for any purpose whatsoever, and to have or permit others to do so.

(b) *Allocation of rights.* (1) Except as provided in paragraph (c) of this clause regarding copyright, the Government shall have unlimited rights in—

(i) Data specifically identified in this contract as data to be delivered without restriction;

(ii) Form, fit, and function data delivered under this contract;

(iii) Data delivered under this contract (except for restricted computer software) that constitute manuals or instructional and training material for installation, operation, or routine maintenance and repair of items, components, or processes delivered or furnished for use under this contract; and

(iv) All other data delivered under this contract unless provided otherwise for SBIR data in accordance with paragraph (d) of this clause or for limited rights data or restricted computer software in accordance with paragraph (f) of this clause.

(2) The Contractor shall have the right to—

(i) Assert copyright in data first produced in the performance of this contract to the extent provided in paragraph (c)(1) of this clause;

(ii) Protect SBIR rights in SBIR data delivered under this contract in the manner and to the extent provided in paragraph (d) of this clause;

(iii) Substantiate use of, add, or correct SBIR rights or copyright notices and to take other appropriate action, in accordance with paragraph (e) of this clause; and

(iv) Withhold from delivery those data which are limited rights data or restricted computer software to the extent provided in paragraph (f) of this clause.

(c) *Copyright*—(1) *Data first produced in the performance of this contract.* (i) Except as otherwise specifically provided in this contract, the Contractor may assert copyright subsisting in any data first produced in the performance of this contract.

(ii) When asserting copyright, the Contractor shall affix the applicable copyright notice of 17 U.S.C. 401 or 402 and an acknowledgment of Government sponsorship (including contract number).

(iii) For data other than computer software, the Contractor grants to the Government, and others acting on its behalf, a paid-up nonexclusive, irrevocable, worldwide license to reproduce, prepare derivative works, distribute copies to the public, and perform publicly and display publicly, by or on behalf of the Government. For computer software, the Contractor grants to the Government, and others acting on its behalf, a paid-up, nonexclusive, irrevocable, worldwide license in such copyrighted computer software to reproduce, prepare derivative works, and perform publicly and display publicly, by or on behalf of the Government.

(2) *Data not first produced in the performance of this contract.* The Contractor shall not, without prior written permission of the Contracting Officer, incorporate in data delivered under this contract any data that are not first produced in the performance of this contract unless the Contractor (i) identifies such data and (ii) grants to the Government, or acquires on its behalf, a license of the same scope as set forth in paragraph (c)(1) of this clause.

(3) *Removal of copyright notices.* The Government will not remove any copyright notices placed on data pursuant to this paragraph (c), and will include such notices on all reproductions of the data.

(d) *Rights to SBIR data.* (1) The Contractor is authorized to affix the following "SBIR Rights Notice" to SBIR data delivered under this contract and the Government will treat the data, subject to the provisions of paragraphs (e) and (f) of this clause, in accordance with the notice:

SBIR RIGHTS NOTICE (DEC 2007)

These SBIR data are furnished with SBIR rights under Contract No.________ (and subcontract ________, if appropriate). For a period of 4 years, unless extended in accordance with FAR 27.409(h), after acceptance of all items to be delivered under this contract, the Government will use these data for Government purposes only, and they shall not be disclosed outside the Government (including disclosure for procurement purposes) during such period without permission of the Contractor, except that, subject to the foregoing use and disclosure prohibitions, these data may be disclosed for use by support Contractors. After the protection period, the Government has a paid-up license to use, and to authorize others to use on its behalf, these data for Government purposes, but is relieved of all disclosure prohibitions and assumes no liability for unauthorized use of these data by third parties. This notice shall be affixed to any reproductions of these data, in whole or in part.

(End of notice)

(2) The Government's sole obligation with respect to any SBIR data shall be as set forth in this paragraph (d).

(e) *Omitted or incorrect markings.* (1) Data delivered to the Government without any notice authorized by paragraph (d) of this clause shall be deemed to have been furnished with unlimited rights. The Government assumes no liability for the disclosure, use, or reproduction of such data.

(2) If the unmarked data has not been disclosed without restriction outside the Government, the Contractor may request, within 6 months (or a longer time approved by the Contracting Officer in writing for good cause shown) after delivery of the data, permission to have authorized notices placed on the data at the Contractor's expense, and the Contracting Officer may agree to do so if the Contractor—

(i) Identifies the data to which the omitted notice is to be applied;

(ii) Demonstrates that the omission of the notice was inadvertent;

(iii) Establishes that the use of the proposed notice is authorized; and

(iv) Acknowledges that the Government has no liability with respect to the disclosure or use of any such data made prior to the addition of the notice or resulting from the omission of the notice.

(3) If the data has been marked with an incorrect notice, the Contracting Officer may—

(i) Permit correction of the notice at the Contractor's expense, if the Contractor identifies the data and demonstrates that the correct notice is authorized, or

(ii) Correct any incorrect notices.

(f) *Protection of limited rights data and restricted computer software.* The Contractor may withhold from delivery qualifying limited rights data and restricted computer software that are not identified in paragraphs (b)(1)(i), (ii), and (iii) of this clause. As a condition to this withholding, the Contractor shall identify the data being withheld, and furnish form, fit, and function data instead.

(g) *Subcontracting.* The Contractor shall obtain from its subcontractors all data and rights therein necessary to fulfill the Contractor's obligations to the Government under this contract. If a subcontractor refuses to accept terms affording the Government those rights, the Contractor shall promptly notify the Contracting Officer of the refusal and not proceed with the subcontract award without further authorization in writing from the Contracting Officer.

(h) *Relationship to patents.* Nothing contained in this clause shall imply a license to the Government under any patent or be construed as affecting the scope of any license or other right otherwise granted to the Government.

(End of clause)

[FAC 84-27, 52 FR 18154, 5/13/87, effective 6/1/87; FAC 84-58, 55 FR 25532, 6/21/90, effective 7/23/90; Interim rule, FAC 90-20, 59 FR 11368, 3/10/94, effective 3/10/94, finalized without change, FAC 90-39, 61 FR 31612, 6/20/96, effective 6/20/96; FAC 2005-21, 72 FR 63045, 11/7/2007, effective 12/7/2007; FAC 2005-73, 79 FR 24192, 4/29/2014, effective 5/29/2014]

52.227-21 Technical Data Declaration, Revision, and Withholding of Payment—Major Systems.

As prescribed in 27.409(j), insert the following clause:

TECHNICAL DATA DECLARATION, REVISION, AND WITHHOLDING OF PAYMENT—MAJOR SYSTEMS (MAY 2014)

(a) *Scope of declaration.* The Contractor shall provide, in accordance with 41 U.S.C. 2302(e)(7), the following declaration with respect to all technical data that relate to a major system and that are delivered or required to be delivered under this contract or that are delivered within 3 years after acceptance of all items (other than technical data) delivered under this contract unless a different period is set forth in the contract. The Contracting Officer may release the Contractor from all or part of the requirements of this clause for specifically identified technical data items at any time during the period covered by this clause.

(b) *Technical data declaration.* (1) All technical data that are subject to this clause shall be accompanied by the following declaration upon delivery:

TECHNICAL DATA DECLARATION (JAN 1997)

The Contractor, ____________, hereby declares that, to the best of its knowledge and belief, the technical data delivered herewith under Government contract No. ____________ (and subcontract ____________, if appropriate) are complete, accurate, and comply with the requirements of the contract concerning such technical data.

(End of declaration)

(2) The Government may, at any time during the period covered by this clause, direct correction of any deficiencies that are not in compliance with contract requirements. The corrections shall be made at the expense of the Contractor. Unauthorized markings on data shall not be considered a deficiency for

the purpose of this clause, but will be treated in accordance with paragraph (e) of the Rights in Data—General clause included in this contract.

(c) *Technical data revision.* The Contractor also shall, at the request of the Contracting Officer, revise technical data that are subject to this clause to reflect engineering design changes made during the performance of this contract and affecting the form, fit, and function of any item (other than technical data) delivered under this contract. The Contractor may submit a request for an equitable adjustment to the terms and conditions of this contract for any revisions to technical data made pursuant to this paragraph.

(d) *Withholding of payment.* (1) At any time before final payment under this contract the Contracting Officer may withhold payment as a reserve up to an amount not exceeding $100,000 or 5 percent of the amount of this contract, whichever is less, if the Contractor fails to—

(i) Make timely delivery of the technical data;

(ii) Provide the declaration required by paragraph (b)(1) of this clause;

(iii) Make the corrections required by paragraph (b)(2) of this clause; or

(iv) Make revisions requested under paragraph (c) of this clause.

(2) The Contracting Officer may withhold the reserve until the Contractor has complied with the direction or requests of the Contracting Officer or determines that the deficiencies relating to delivered data, arose out of causes beyond the control of the Contractor and without the fault or negligence of the Contractor.

(3) The withholding of any reserve under this clause, or the subsequent payment of the reserve, shall not be construed as a waiver of any Government rights.

(End of clause)

[FAC 84-27, 52 FR 18155, 5/13/87, effective 6/1/87; FAC 90-45, Final rule, 62 FR 224, 1/2/97, effective 1/1/97; FAC 2005-21, 72 FR 63045, 11/7/2007, effective 12/7/2007; FAC 2005-73, 79 FR 24192, 4/29/2014, effective 5/29/2014]

52.227-22 Major System—Minimum Rights.

As prescribed in 27.409(k), insert the following clause:

MAJOR SYSTEM—MINIMUM RIGHTS (JUN 1987)

Notwithstanding any other provision of this contract, the Government shall have unlimited rights in any technical data, other than computer software, developed in the performance of this contract and relating to a major system or supplies for a major system procured or to be procured by the Government, to the extent that delivery of such technical data is required as an element of performance under this contract. The rights of the Government under this clause are in addition to and not in lieu of its rights under the other provisions of this contract.

(End of clause)

[FAC 84-27, 52 FR 18156, 5/13/87, effective 6/1/87; FAC 2005-21, 72 FR 63045, 11/7/2007, effective 12/7/2007]

52.227-23 Rights to Proposal Data (Technical).

As prescribed in 27.409(l), insert the following clause:

RIGHTS TO PROPOSAL DATA (TECHNICAL) (JUN 1987)

Except for data contained on pages __, it is agreed that as a condition of award of this contract, and notwithstanding the conditions of any notice appearing thereon, the Government shall have unlimited rights (as defined in the "Rights in Data—General" clause contained in this contract) in and to the technical data contained in the proposal dated __, upon which this contract is based.

(End of clause)

[FAC 84-27, 52 FR 18156, 5/13/87, effective 6/1/87; FAC 2005-21, 72 FR 63045, 11/7/2007, effective 12/7/2007]

52.228-1 Bid Guarantee.

As prescribed in 28.101-2, insert a provision or clause substantially as follows:

BID GUARANTEE (SEP 1996)

(a) Failure to furnish a bid guarantee in the proper form and amount, by the time set for opening of bids, may be cause for rejection of the bid.

(b) The bidder shall furnish a bid guarantee in the form of a firm commitment, e.g., bid bond supported by good and sufficient surety or sureties acceptable to the Government, postal money order, certified check, cashier's check, irrevocable letter of credit, or, under Treasury Department regulations, certain bonds or notes of the United States. The Contracting Officer will return bid guarantees, other than bid bonds, (1) to unsuccessful bidders as soon as practicable after the opening of bids, and (2) to the successful bidder upon execution of contractual documents and bonds (including any necessary coinsurance or reinsurance agreements), as required by the bid as accepted.

(c) The amount of the bid guarantee shall be __ percent of the bid price or $__, whichever is less.

(d) If the successful bidder, upon acceptance of its bid by the Government within the period specified for acceptance, fails to execute all contractual documents or furnish executed bond(s) within 10 days after receipt of the forms by the bidder, the Contracting Officer may terminate the contract for default.

(e) In the event the contract is terminated for default, the bidder is liable for any cost of acquiring the work that exceeds the amount of its bid, and the bid guarantee is available to offset the difference.

(End of provision)

[FAC 90-40, 61 FR 39186, 7/26/96, effective 9/24/96]

52.228-2 Additional Bond Security.

As prescribed in 28.106-4(a), insert the following clause:

ADDITIONAL BOND SECURITY (OCT 1997)

The Contractor shall promptly furnish additional security required to protect the Government and persons supplying labor or materials under this contract if—

(a) Any surety upon any bond, or issuing financial institution for other security, furnished with this contract becomes unacceptable to the Government;

(b) Any surety fails to furnish reports on its financial condition as required by the Government;

(c) The contract price is increased so that the penal sum of any bond becomes inadequate in the opinion of the Contracting Officer; or,

(d) An irrevocable letter of credit (ILC) used as security will expire before the end of the period of required security. If the Contractor does not furnish an acceptable extension or replacement ILC, or other acceptable substitute, at least 30 days before an ILC's scheduled expiration, the Contracting officer has the right to immediately draw on the ILC.

(End of clause)

[FAC 90-32, 60 FR 48206, 9/18/95, effective 10/1/95; FAC 90-39, 61 FR 31612, 6/20/96, effective 6/20/96; FAC 97-1, 62 FR 44802, 8/22/97, effective 10/21/97]

52.228-3 Workers' Compensation Insurance (Defense Base Act).

As prescribed in 28.309(a), insert the following clause:

WORKERS' COMPENSATION INSURANCE (DEFENSE BASE ACT) (JUL 2014)

(a) The Contractor shall—

(1) Before commencing performance under this contract, establish provisions to provide for the payment of disability compensation and medical benefits to covered employees and death benefits to their eligible survivors, by purchasing workers' compensation insurance or qualifying as a self-insurer under the Longshore and Harbor Workers' Compensation Act (33 U.S.C. 932) as extended by the Defense Base Act (42 U.S.C. 1651, *et seq.*), and continue to maintain provisions to provide such Defense Base Act benefits until contract performance is completed;

(2) Within ten days of an employee's injury or death or from the date the Contractor has knowledge of the injury or death, submit

Form LS-202 (Employee's First Report of Injury or Occupational Illness) to the Department of Labor in accordance with the Longshore and Harbor Workers' Compensation Act (33 U.S.C. 930(a), 20 CFR 702.201 to 702.203);

(3) Pay all compensation due for disability or death within the time frames required by the Longshore and Harbor Workers' Compensation Act (33 U.S.C. 914, 20 CFR 702.231 and 703.232);

(4) Provide for medical care as required by the Longshore and Harbor Workers' Compensation Act (33 U.S.C. 907, 20 CFR 702.402 and 702.419);

(5) If controverting the right to compensation, submit Form LS-207 (Notice of Controversion of Right to Compensation) to the Department of Labor in accordance with the Longshore and Harbor Workers' Compensation Act (33 U.S.C. 914(d), 20 CFR 702.251);

(6) Immediately upon making the first payment of compensation in any case, submit Form LS-206 (Payment Of Compensation Without Award) to the Department of Labor in accordance with the Longshore and Harbor Workers' Compensation Act (33 U.S.C. 914(c), 20 CFR 702.234);

(7) When payments are suspended or when making the final payment, submit Form LS-208 (Notice of Final Payment or Suspension of Compensation Payments) to the Department of Labor in accordance with the Longshore and Harbor Workers' Compensation Act (33 U.S.C. 914(c) and (g), 20 CFR 702.234 and 702.235); and

(8) Adhere to all other provisions of the Longshore and Harbor Workers' Compensation Act as extended by the Defense Base Act, and Department of Labor regulations at 20 CFR Parts 701 to 704.

(b) For additional information on the Longshore and Harbor Workers' Compensation Act requirements see *http://www.dol.gov/owcp/dlhwc/lsdba.htm*.

(c) The Contractor shall insert the substance of this clause, including this paragraph (c), in all subcontracts to which the Defense Base Act applies.

(End of clause)

[FAC 90-32, 60 FR 48206, 9/18/95, effective 10/1/95; FAC 2001-14, 68 FR 28079, 5/22/2003, effective 6/23/2003; FAC 2005-74, 79 FR 31201, 5/30/2014, effective 7/1/2014]

52.228-4 Workers' Compensation and War-Hazard Insurance Overseas.

As prescribed in 28.309(b), insert the following clause:

WORKERS' COMPENSATION AND WAR-HAZARD INSURANCE OVERSEAS (APR 1984)

(a) This paragraph applies if the Contractor employs any person who, but for a waiver granted by the Secretary of Labor, would be subject to workers' compensation insurance under the Defense Base Act (42 U.S.C. 1651 et seq.). On behalf of employees for whom the applicability of the Defense Base Act has been waived, the Contractor shall (1) provide, before commencing performance under this contract, at least that workers' compensation insurance or the equivalent as the laws of the country of which these employees are nationals may require and (2) continue to maintain it until performance is completed. The Contractor shall insert, in all subcontracts under this contract to which the Defense Base Act would apply but for the waiver, a clause similar to this paragraph (a) (including this sentence) imposing upon those subcontractors this requirement to provide such workers' compensation insurance coverage.

(b) This paragraph applies if the Contractor or any subcontractor under this contract employs any person who, but for a waiver granted by the Secretary of Labor, would be subject to the War Hazards Compensation Act (42 U.S.C. 1701, et seq.). On behalf of employees for whom the applicability of the Defense Base Act (and hence that of the War Hazards Compensation Act) has been waived, the Contractor shall, subject to reimbursement as provided elsewhere in this contract, afford the same protection as that provided in the War Hazards Compensation Act, except that the level of benefits shall conform to any law or international agreement controlling the benefits to which the employees may be entitled. In all other respects, the standards of the War Hazards Compensation Act shall apply; e.g., the definition of war-hazard risks (injury, death, capture, or detention as the result of a war hazard as defined in the Act), proof of loss, and exclusion of benefits otherwise covered by workers' compensation insurance or the equivalent. Unless the Contractor elects to assume directly the liability to subcontractor employees created by this clause, the Contractor shall insert, in all subcontracts under this contract to which the War Hazards Compensation Act would apply but for the waiver, a clause similar to this paragraph (b) (including this sentence) imposing upon those subcontractors this requirement to provide war-hazard benefits.

(End of clause)

[FAC 90-32, 60 FR 48206, 9/18/95, effective 10/1/95; FAC 2001-14, 68 FR 28079, 5/22/2003, effective 6/23/2003]

52.228-5 Insurance—Work on a Government Installation.

As prescribed in 28.310, insert the following clause:

INSURANCE—WORK ON A GOVERNMENT INSTALLATION (JAN 1997)

(a) The Contractor shall, at its own expense, provide and maintain during the entire performance period of this contract, at least the kinds and minimum amounts of insurance required in the schedule or elsewhere in the contract.

(b) Before commencing work under this contract, the Contractor shall notify the Contracting Officer in writing that the required insurance has been obtained. The policies evidencing required insurance shall contain an endorsement to the effect that any cancellation or any material change adversely affecting the Government's interest shall not be effective (1) for such period as the laws of the State in which this contract is to be performed prescribe or (2) until 30 days after the insurer or the Contractor gives written notice to the Contracting Officer, whichever period is longer.

(c) The Contractor shall insert the substance of this clause, including this paragraph (c), in subcontracts under this contract that require work on a Government installation and shall require subcontractors to provide and maintain the insurance required in the Schedule or elsewhere in the contract. The Contractor shall maintain a copy of all subcontractors' proofs of required insurance, and shall make copies available to the Contracting Officer upon request.

(End of clause)

[FAC 84-51, 54 FR 34758, 8/21/89, effective 9/20/89; FAC 90-45, Final rule, 62 FR 224, 1/2/97, effective 1/1/97]

52.228-6 [Reserved]

[Reserved, FAC 90-37, 61 FR 2626, 1/26/96, effective 3/26/96]

52.228-7 Insurance—Liability to Third Persons.

As prescribed in 28.311-1, insert the following clause:

INSURANCE—LIABILITY TO THIRD PERSONS (MAR 1996)

(a) (1) Except as provided in subparagraph (a)(2) of this clause, the Contractor shall provide and maintain workers' compensation, employer's liability, comprehensive general liability (bodily injury), comprehensive automobile liability (bodily injury and property damage) insurance, and such other insurance as the Contracting Officer may require under this contract.

(2) The Contractor may, with the approval of the Contracting Officer, maintain a self-insurance program; provided that, with respect to workers' compensation, the Contractor is qualified pursuant to statutory authority.

(3) All insurance required by this paragraph shall be in a form and amount and for those periods as the Contracting Officer may require or approve and with insurers approved by the Contracting Officer.

(b) The Contractor agrees to submit for the Contracting Officer's approval, to the extent and in the manner required by the Contracting Officer, any other insurance that is maintained by the Contractor in connection with the performance of this contract and for which the Contractor seeks reimbursement.

(c) The Contractor shall be reimbursed—

(1) For that portion (i) of the reasonable cost of insurance allocable to this contract and (ii) required or approved under this clause; and

(2) For certain liabilities (and expenses incidental to such liabilities) to third persons not compensated by insurance or otherwise without regard to and as an exception to the limitation of cost or the limitation of funds clause of this contract. These liabilities must arise out of the performance of this contract, whether or not caused by the negligence of the Contractor or of the Contractor's agents, servants, or employees, and must be represented by final judgments or settlements approved in writing by the Government. These liabilities are for—

(i) Loss of or damage to property (other than property owned, occupied, or used by the Contractor, rented to the Contractor, or in the care, custody, or control of the Contractor); or

(ii) Death or bodily injury.

(d) The Government's liability under paragraph (c) of this clause is subject to the availability of appropriated funds at the time a contingency occurs. Nothing in this contract shall be construed as implying that the Congress will, at a later date, appropriate funds sufficient to meet deficiencies.

(e) The Contractor shall not be reimbursed for liabilities (and expenses incidental to such liabilities)—

(1) For which the Contractor is otherwise responsible under the express terms of any clause specified in the Schedule or elsewhere in the contract;

(2) For which the Contractor has failed to insure or to maintain insurance as required by the Contracting Officer; or

(3) That result from willful misconduct or lack of good faith on the part of any of the Contractor's directors, officers, managers, superintendents, or other representatives who have supervision or direction of—

(i) All or substantially all of the Contractor's business;

(ii) All or substantially all of the Contractor's operations at any one plant or separate location in which this contract is being performed; or

(iii) A separate and complete major industrial operation in connection with the performance of this contract.

(f) The provisions of paragraph (e) of this clause shall not restrict the right of the Contractor to be reimbursed for the cost of insurance maintained by the Contractor in connection with the performance of this contract, other than insurance required in accordance with this clause; provided, that such cost is allowable under the Allowable Cost and Payment clause of this contract.

(g) If any suit or action is filed or any claim is made against the Contractor, the cost and expense of which may be reimbursable to the Contractor under this contract, and the risk of which is then uninsured or is insured for less than the amount claimed, the Contractor shall—

(1) Immediately notify the Contracting Officer and promptly furnish copies of all pertinent papers received;

(2) Authorize Government representatives to collaborate with counsel for the insurance carrier in settling or defending the claim when the amount of the liability claimed exceeds the amount of coverage; and

(3) Authorize Government representatives to settle or defend the claim and to represent the Contractor in or to take charge of any litigation, if required by the Government, when the liability is not insured or covered by bond. The Contractor may, at its own expense, be associated with the Government representatives in any such claim or litigation.

(End of clause)

[FAC 90-3, 55 FR 52799, 12/21/90, effective 1/22/91; FAC 90-32, 60 FR 48206, 9/18/95, effective 10/1/95; FAC 90-37, 61 FR 2626, 1/26/96, effective 3/26/96]

52.228-8 Liability and Insurance—Leased Motor Vehicles.

As prescribed in 28.312, insert the following clause:

LIABILITY AND INSURANCE—LEASED MOTOR VEHICLES (MAY 1999)

(a) The Government shall be responsible for loss of or damage to—

(1) Leased vehicles, except for (i) normal wear and tear and (ii) loss or damage caused by the negligence of the Contractor, its agents, or employees; and

(2) Property of third persons, or the injury or death of third persons, if the Government is liable for such loss, damage, injury, or death under the Federal Tort Claims Act (28 U.S.C. 2671-2680)

(b) The Contractor shall be liable for, and shall indemnify and hold harmless the Government against, all actions or claims for loss of or damage to property or the injury or death of persons, resulting from the fault, negligence, or wrongful act or omission of the Contractor, its agents, or employees.

(c) The Contractor shall provide and maintain insurance covering its liabilities under paragraph (b) of this clause, in amounts of at least $200,000 per person and $500,000 per occurrence for death or bodily injury and $20,000 per occurrence for property damage or loss.

(d) Before commencing work under this contract, the Contractor shall notify the Contracting Officer in writing that the required insurance has been obtained. The policies evidencing required insurance shall contain an endorsement to the effect that any cancellation or any material change adversely affecting the interests of the Government shall not be effective (1) for such period as the laws of the State in which this contract is to be performed prescribe or (2) until 30 days after written notice to the Contracting Officer, whichever period is longer. The policies shall exclude any claim by the insurer for subrogation against the Government by reason of any payment under the policies.

(e) The contract price shall not include any costs for insurance or contingency to cover losses, damage, injury, or death for which the Government is responsible under paragraph (a) of this clause.

(End of clause)

[Final rule, 55 FR 38518, 9/18/90; Final rule, FAC 90-20, 59 FR 11368, 3/10/94, effective 3/10/94; FAC 90-32, 60 FR 48206, 9/18/95, effective 10/1/95; FAC 90-45, Final rule, 62 FR 224, 1/2/97, effective 1/1/97; FAC 97-11, 64 FR 10530, 3/4/99, effective 5/3/99]

52.228-9 Cargo Insurance.

As prescribed in 28.313(a), insert the following clause:

CARGO INSURANCE (MAY 1999)

(a) The Contractor, at the Contractor's expense, shall provide and maintain, during the continuance of this contract, cargo insurance of $ __ per vehicle to cover the value of property on each vehicle and of $ __ to cover the total value of the property in the shipment.

(b) All insurance shall be written on companies acceptable to __ [*insert name of contracting agency*], and policies shall include such terms and conditions as required by __ [*insert name of contracting agency*]. The Contractor shall provide evidence of acceptable cargo insurance to __ [*insert name of contracting agency*] before commencing operations under this contract.

(c) Each cargo insurance policy shall include the following statement:

"It is a condition of this policy that the Company shall furnish—

(1) Written notice to __ [*insert name and address of contracting agency*], 30 days in advance of the effective date of any reduction in, or cancellation of, this policy; and

(2) Evidence of any renewal policy to the address specified in paragraph (1) of this statement, not less than 15 days prior to the expiration of any current policy on file with __ [*insert name of contracting agency*]."

(End of clause)

[FAC 97-11, 64 FR 10530, 3/4/99, effective 5/3/99]

52.228-10 Vehicular and General Public Liability Insurance.

As prescribed in 28.313(b), insert a clause substantially the same as the following in solicitations and contracts for transportation or for transportation-related services when the contracting officer determines that vehicular liability or general public liability insurance required by law is not sufficient:

VEHICULAR AND GENERAL PUBLIC LIABILITY INSURANCE (APR 1984)

(a) The Contractor, at the Contractor's expense, agrees to maintain, during the continuance of this contract, vehicular liability and general public liability insurance with limits of liability for—

(1) Bodily injury of not less than $__ for each person and $____ for each occurrence; and

(2) Property damage of not less than $____ for each accident and $____ in the aggregate.

(b) The Contractor also agrees to maintain workers' compensation and other legally required insurance with respect to the Contractor's own employees and agents.

(End of clause)

[FAC 90-32, 60 FR 48206, 9/18/95, effective 10/1/95]

52.228-11 Pledges of Assets.

As prescribed in 28.203-6, insert the following clause:

PLEDGES OF ASSETS (AUG 2018)

(a) Offerors shall obtain from each person acting as an individual surety on a bid guarantee, a performance bond, or a payment bond—

(1) Pledge of assets; and

(2) Standard Form 28, Affidavit of Individual Surety.

(b) Pledges of assets from each person acting as an individual surety shall be in the form of—

(1) Evidence of an escrow account containing cash, certificates of deposit, commercial or Government securities, or other assets described in FAR 28.203-2 (except see 28.203-2(b)(2) with respect to Government securities held in book entry form); and/or

(2) A recorded lien on real estate. The offeror will be required to provide—

(i) A mortgagee title insurance policy, in an insurance amount equal to the amount of the lien, or other evidence of title that is consistent with the requirements of Section 2 of the United States Department of Justice Title Standards at *https://www.justice.gov/enrd/page/file/922431/download*. This title evidence must show fee simple title vested in the surety along with any concurrent owners; whether any real estate taxes are due and payable; and any recorded encumbrances against the property, including the lien filed in favor of the Government as required by FAR 28.203-3(d);

(ii) Evidence of the amount due under any encumbrance shown in the evidence of title;

(iii) A copy of the current real estate tax assessment of the property or a current appraisal dated no earlier than 6 months prior to the date of the bond, prepared by a professional appraiser who certifies that the appraisal has been conducted in accordance with the generally accepted appraisal standards as reflected in the Uniform Standards of Professional Appraisal Practice, as promulgated by the Appraisal Foundation.

(End of clause)

[FAC 84-53, 54 FR 48995, 11/28/89, effective 2/26/90; FAC 90-9, 56 FR 67137, 12/27/91, effective 2/25/92; FAC 2005-36, 74 FR 40466, 8/11/2009, effective 9/10/2009; FAC 2005-55, 77 FR 204, 1/3/2012, effective 1/3/2012; FAC 2005-100, 83 FR 42571, 8/22/2018, effective 8/22/2018]

52.228-12 Prospective Subcontractor Requests for Bonds.

As prescribed in 28.106-4(b), use the following clause:

PROSPECTIVE SUBCONTRACTOR REQUESTS FOR BONDS (MAY 2014)

In accordance with section 806(a)(3) of Pub. L. 102-190, as amended by sections 2091 and 8105 of Pub. L. 103-355 (10 U.S.C. 2302 note), upon the request of a prospective subcontractor or supplier offering to furnish labor or material for the performance of this contract for which a payment bond has been furnished to the Government pursuant to 40 U.S.C. chapter 31, subchapter III, Bonds, the Contractor shall promptly provide a copy of such payment bond to the requester.

(End of clause)

[FAC 90-32, 60 FR 48206, 9/18/95, effective 10/1/95; FAC 2005-73, 79 FR 24192, 4/29/2014, effective 5/29/2014]

52.228-13 Alternative Payment Protections.

As prescribed in 28.102-3(b), insert the following clause:

ALTERNATIVE PAYMENT PROTECTIONS (JUL 2000)

(a) The Contractor shall submit one of the following payment protections:

____

____

____

(b) The amount of the payment protection shall be 100 percent of the contract price.

(c) The submission of the payment protection is required within ___ days of contract award.

(d) The payment protection shall provide protection for the full contract performance period plus a one-year period.

(e) Except for escrow agreements and payment bonds, which provide their own protection procedures, the Contracting Officer is authorized to access funds under the payment protection when it has been alleged in writing by a supplier of labor or material that a nonpayment has occurred, and to withhold such funds pending resolution by administrative or judicial proceedings or mutual agreement of the parties.

(f) When a tripartite escrow agreement is used, the Contractor shall utilize only suppliers of labor and material that signed the escrow agreement.

(End of clause)

[FAC 90-39, 61 FR 31612, 6/20/96, effective 6/20/96; FAC 97-1, 62 FR 44802, 8/22/97, effective 10/21/97; FAC 97-19, 65 FR 46052, 7/26/2000, effective 7/26/2000]

52.228-14 Irrevocable Letter of Credit.

As prescribed in 28.204-4, insert the following clause:

IRREVOCABLE LETTER OF CREDIT (NOV 2014)

(a) *Irrevocable letter of credit* (ILC), as used in this clause, means a written commitment by a federally insured financial institution to pay all or part of a stated amount of money, until the expiration date of the letter, upon presentation by the Government (the beneficiary) of a written demand therefor. Neither the financial institution nor the offeror/Contractor can revoke or condition the letter of credit.

(b) If the offeror intends to use an ILC in lieu of a bid bond, or to secure other types of bonds such as performance and payment bonds, the letter of credit and letter of confirmation formats in paragraphs (e) and (f) of this clause shall be used.

(c) The letter of credit shall be irrevocable, shall require presentation of no document other than a written demand and the ILC (including confirming letter, if any), shall be issued/confirmed by an acceptable federally insured financial institution as provided in paragraph (d) of this clause, and—

(1) If used as a bid guarantee, the ILC shall expire no earlier than 60 days after the close of the bid acceptance period;

(2) If used as an alternative to corporate or individual sureties as security for a performance or payment bond, the offeror/Contractor may submit an ILC with an initial expiration date estimated to cover the entire period for which financial security is required or may submit an ILC with an initial expiration date that is a minimum period of one year from the date of issuance. The ILC shall provide that, unless the issuer provides the beneficiary written notice of non-renewal at least 60 days in advance of the current expiration date, the ILC is automatically extended without amendment for one year from the expiration date, or any future expiration date, until the period of required cov-

erage is completed and the Contracting Officer provides the financial institution with a written statement waiving the right to payment. The period of required coverage shall be:

(i) For contracts subject to 40 U.S.C. chapter 31, subchapter III, Bonds, the later of—

(A) One year following the expected date of final payment;

(B) For performance bonds only, until completion of any warranty period; or

(C) For payment bonds only, until resolution of all claims filed against the payment bond during the one-year period following final payment.

(ii) For contracts not subject to 40 U.S.C. chapter 31, subchapter III, Bonds, the later of—

(A) 90 days following final payment; or

(B) For performance bonds only, until completion of any warranty period.

(d)(1) Only federally insured financial institutions rated investment grade by a commercial rating service shall issue or confirm the ILC.

(2) Unless the financial institution issuing the ILC had letter of credit business of at least $25 million in the past year, ILCs over $5 million must be confirmed by another acceptable financial institution that had letter of credit business of at least $25 million in the past year.

(3) The Offeror/Contractor shall provide the Contracting Officer a credit rating that indicates the financial institutions have the required credit rating as of the date of issuance of the ILC.

(4) The current rating for a financial institution is available through any of the following rating services registered with the U.S. Securities and Exchange Commission (SEC) as a Nationally Recognized Statistical Rating Organization (NRSRO). NRSRO's can be located at the Web site *http://www.sec.gov/answers/nrsro.htm* maintained by the SEC.

(e) The following format shall be used by the issuing financial institution to create an ILC:

____

[*Issuing Financial Institution's Letterhead or Name and Address*]

Issue Date ____

Irrevocable Letter of Credit No. __

Account party's name _____

Account party's address _____

For Solicitation No. _____ (*For reference only*)

TO: [*U.S. Government agency*]

[*U.S. Government agency's address*]

1. We hereby establish this irrevocable and transferable Letter of Credit in your favor for one or more drawings up to United States $___. This Letter of Credit is payable at [*issuing financial institution's and, if any, confirming financial institution's*] office at [*issuing financial institution's address and, if any, confirming financial institution's address*] and expires with our close of business on ___, or any automatically extended expiration date.

2. We hereby undertake to honor your or the transferee's sight draft(s) drawn on the issuing or, if any, the confirming financial institution, for all or any part of this credit if presented with this Letter of Credit and confirmation, if any, at the office specified in paragraph 1 of this Letter of Credit on or before the expiration date or any automatically extended expiration date.

3. [*This paragraph is omitted if used as a bid guarantee, and subsequent paragraphs are renumbered.*] It is a condition of this Letter of Credit that it is deemed to be automatically extended without amendment for one year from the expiration date hereof, or any future expiration date, unless at least 60 days prior to any expiration date, we notify you or the transferee by registered mail, or other receipted means of delivery, that we elect not to consider this Letter of Credit renewed for any such additional period. At the time we notify you, we also agree to notify the account party (and confirming financial institution, if any) by the same means of delivery.

4. This Letter of Credit is transferable. Transfers and assignments of proceeds are

to be effected without charge to either the beneficiary or the transferee/assignee of proceeds. Such transfer or assignment shall be only at the written direction of the Government (the beneficiary) in a form satisfactory to the issuing financial institution and the confirming financial institution, if any.

5. This Letter of Credit is subject to the Uniform Customs and Practice (UCP) for Documentary Credits, International Chamber of Commerce Publication No.___[*Insert version in effect at the time of ILC issuance, e.g., "Publication 600, 2006 edition"*] and to the extent not inconsistent therewith, to the laws of ___ [*State of confirming financial institution, if any, otherwise State of issuing financial institution*].

6. If this credit expires during an interruption of business of this financial institution as described in Article 17 of the UCP, the financial institution specifically agrees to effect payment if this credit is drawn against within 30 days after the resumption of our business.

Sincerely,

[*Issuing financial institution*]

(f) The following format shall be used by the financial institution to confirm an ILC:

[*Confirming Financial Institution's Letterhead or Name and Address*]

(*Date*)___

Our Letter of Credit Advice Number___,

Beneficiary:___, [*U.S. Government agency*]

Issuing Financial Institution: ___

Issuing Financial Institution's LC No.: ___

Gentlemen:

1. We hereby confirm the above indicated Letter of Credit, the original of which is attached, issued by ___ [*name of issuing financial institution*] for drawings of up to United States dollars ___/U.S. $___and expiring with our close of business on ___ [*the expiration date*], or any automatically extended expiration date.

2. Draft(s) drawn under the Letter of Credit and this Confirmation are payable at our office located at ___.

3. We hereby undertake to honor sight draft(s) drawn under and presented with the Letter of Credit and this Confirmation at our offices as specified herein.

4. [*This paragraph is omitted if used as a bid guarantee, and subsequent paragraphs are renumbered.*] It is a condition of this confirmation that it be deemed automatically extended without amendment for one year from the expiration date hereof, or any automatically extended expiration date, unless:

(a) At least 60 days prior to any such expiration date, we shall notify the Contracting Officer, or the transferee and the issuing financial institution, by registered mail or other receipted means of delivery, that we elect not to consider this confirmation extended for any such additional period; or

(b) The issuing financial institution shall have exercised its right to notify you or the transferee, the account party, and ourselves, of its election not to extend the expiration date of the Letter of Credit.

5. This confirmation is subject to the Uniform Customs and Practice (UCP) for Documentary Credits, 1993 Revision, International Chamber of Commerce Publication No. ___, [Insert version in effect at the time of ILC issuance, e.g., "Publication 600, 2006 edition") and to the extent not inconsistent therewith, to the laws of ___ [*State of confirming financial institution, if any, otherwise State of issuing financial institution*].

6. If this confirmation expires during an interruption of business of this financial institution as described in Article 17 of the UCP, we specifically agree to effect payment if this credit is drawn against within 30 days after the resumption of our business.

Sincerely,

___

[*Confirming financial institution*]

(g) The following format shall be used by the Contracting Officer for a sight draft to draw on the Letter of Credit:

SIGHT DRAFT

[*City, State*]

(*Date*)_____

[*Name and address of financial institution*]

Pay to the order of ___ [*Beneficiary Agency*] the sum of United States $___

This draft is drawn under Irrevocable Letter of Credit No. ___

[*Beneficiary Agency*]

By: ___

(End of clause)

[FAC 90-39, 61 FR 31612, 6/20/96, effective 6/20/96; FAC 90-43, 61 FR 67408, 12/20/96, effective 12/20/96; FAC 97-1, 62 FR 44802, 8/22/97, effective 10/21/97; FAC 97-15, 64 FR 72414, 12/27/99, effective 12/27/99; FAC 2005-73, 79 FR 24192, 4/29/2014, effective 5/29/2014; FAC 2005-77, 79 FR 61743, 10/14/2014, effective 11/13/2014]

52.228-15 Performance and Payment Bonds—Construction.

As prescribed in 28.102-3(a), insert a clause substantially as follows:

PERFORMANCE AND PAYMENT BONDS—CONSTRUCTION (OCT 2010)

(a) *Definitions*. As used in this clause—

Original contract price means the award price of the contract; or, for requirements contracts, the price payable for the estimated total quantity; or, for indefinite-quantity contracts, the price payable for the specified minimum quantity. Original contract price does not include the price of any options, except those options exercised at the time of contract award.

(b) *Amount of required bonds*. Unless the resulting contract price is $150,000 or less, the successful offeror shall furnish performance and payment bonds to the Contracting Officer as follows:

(1) *Performance bonds* (Standard Form 25). The penal amount of performance bonds at the time of contract award shall be 100 percent of the original contract price.

(2) *Payment bonds* (Standard Form 25-A). The penal amount of payment bonds at the time of contract award shall be 100 percent of the original contract price.

(3) *Additional bond protection*. (i) The Government may require additional performance and payment bond protection if the contract price is increased. The increase in protection generally will equal 100 percent of the increase in contract price.

(ii) The Government may secure the additional protection by directing the Contractor to increase the penal amount of the existing bond or to obtain an additional bond.

(c) *Furnishing executed bonds*. The Contractor shall furnish all executed bonds, including any necessary reinsurance agreements, to the Contracting Officer, within the time period specified in the Bid Guarantee provision of the solicitation, or otherwise specified by the Contracting Officer, but in any event, before starting work.

(d) *Surety or other security for bonds*. The bonds shall be in the form of firm commitment, supported by corporate sureties whose names appear on the list contained in Treasury Department Circular 570, individual sureties, or by other acceptable security such as postal money order, certified check, cashier's check, irrevocable letter of credit, or, in accordance with Treasury Department regulations, certain bonds or notes of the United States. Treasury Circular 570 is published in the *Federal Register* or may be obtained from the U.S. Department of the Treasury, Financial Management Service, Surety Bond Branch, 3700 East West Highway, Room 6F01, Hyattsville, MD 20782. Or via the internet at ***http://www.fms.treas.gov/c570/***.

(e) Notice of subcontractor waiver of protection (40 U.S.C. 3133(c)). Any waiver of the right to sue on the payment bond is void unless it is in writing, signed by the person whose right is waived, and executed after such person has first furnished labor or material for use in the performance of the contract.

(End of clause)

[FAC 97-19, 65 FR 46052, 7/26/2000, effective 7/26/2000; FAC 2005-06, 70 FR 57453, 9/30/2005, effective 9/30/2005; FAC 2005-14, 71 FR 67779, 11/22/2006, effective 11/22/2006; FAC 2005-45, 75 FR 53129, 8/30/2010, effective 10/1/2010]

52.228-16 Performance and Payment Bonds—Other Than Construction.

As prescribed in 28.103-4, insert a clause substantially as follows:

PERFORMANCE AND PAYMENT—BONDS OTHER THAN CONSTRUCTION (NOV 2006)

(a) *Definitions.* As used in this clause—

Original contract price means the award price of the contract or, for requirements contracts, the price payable for the estimated quantity; or, for indefinite-quantity contracts, the price payable for the specified minimum quantity. Original contract price does not include the price of any options, except those options exercised at the time of contract award.

(b) The Contractor shall furnish a performance bond (Standard Form 1418) for the protection of the Government in an amount equal to ___ percent of the original contract price and a payment bond (Standard Form 1416) in an amount equal to ___ percent of the original contract price.

(c) The Contractor shall furnish all executed bonds, including any necessary reinsurance agreements, to the Contracting Officer, within ___ days, but in any event, before starting work.

(d) The Government may require additional performance and payment bond protection if the contract price is increased. The Government may secure the additional protection by directing the Contractor to increase the penal amount of the existing bonds or to obtain additional bonds.

(e) The bonds shall be in the form of firm commitment, supported by corporate sureties whose names appear on the list contained in Treasury Department Circular 570, individual sureties, or by other acceptable security such as postal money order, certified check, cashier's check, irrevocable letter of credit, or, in accordance with Treasury Department regulations, certain bonds or notes of the United States. Treasury Circular 570 is published in the **Federal Register**, or may be obtained from the U.S. Department of the Treasury, Financial Management Service, Surety Bond Branch, 3700 East West Highway, Room 6F01, Hyattsville, MD 20782. Or via the internet at *http://www.fms.treas.gov/c570/*.

(End of clause)

Alternate I (JUL 2000). As prescribed in 28.103-4, substitute the following paragraphs (b) and (d) for paragraphs (b) and (d) of the basic clause:

(b) The Contractor shall furnish a performance bond (Standard Form 1418) for the protection to the Government in an amount equal to ___ percent of the original contract price.

(d) The Government may require additional performance bond protection if the contract price is increased. The Government may secure the additional protection by directing the Contractor to increase the penal amount of the existing bond or to obtain an additional bond.

[FAC 90-40, 61 FR 39186, 7/26/96, effective 9/24/96; FAC 97-19, 65 FR 46052, 7/26/2000, effective 7/26/2000; FAC 2005-14, 71 FR 67779, 11/22/2006, effective 11/22/2006]

52.229-1 State and Local Taxes.

As prescribed in 29.401-1, insert the following clause:

STATE AND LOCAL TAXES (APR 1984)

Notwithstanding the terms of the Federal, State, and Local Taxes clause, the contract price excludes all State and local taxes levied on or measured by the contract or sales price of the services or completed supplies furnished under this contract. The Contractor shall state separately on its invoices taxes excluded from the contract price, and the Government agrees either to pay the amount of the taxes to the Contractor or provide evidence necessary to sustain an exemption.

(End of clause)

[FAC 90-32, 60 FR 48206, 9/18/95, effective 10/1/95; FAC 2001-14, 68 FR 28079, 5/22/2003, effective 6/23/2003]

52.229-2 North Carolina State and Local Sales and Use Tax.

As prescribed in 29.401-2, insert the following clause in solicitations and contracts for construction to be performed in North Carolina:

NORTH CAROLINA STATE AND LOCAL SALES AND USE TAX (APR 1984)

(a) *Materials* as used in this clause, means building materials, supplies, fixtures, and equipment that become a part of or are annexed to any building or structure erected, altered, or repaired under this contract.

(b) If this is a fixed-price contract, the contract price includes North Carolina State and local sales and use taxes to be paid on materials, notwithstanding any other provision of this contract. If this is a cost-reimbursement contract, any North Carolina State and local sales and use taxes paid by the Contractor on materials shall constitute an allowable cost under this contract.

(c) At the time specified in paragraph (d) below, the Contractor shall furnish the Contracting Officer certified statements setting forth the cost of the materials purchased from each vendor and the amount of North Carolina State and local sales and use taxes paid. In the event the Contractor makes several purchases from the same vendor, the certified statement shall indicate the invoice numbers, the inclusive dates of the invoices, the total amount of the invoices, and the North Carolina State and local sales and use taxes paid. The statement shall also include the cost of any tangible personal property withdrawn from the Contractor's warehouse stock and the amount of North Carolina State and local sales or use tax paid on this property by the Contractor. Any local sales or use taxes included in the Contractor's statements must be shown separately from the State sales or use taxes. The Contractor shall furnish any additional information the Commissioner of Revenue of the State of North Carolina may require to substantiate a refund claim for sales or use taxes. The Contractor shall also obtain and furnish to the Contracting Officer similar certified statements by its subcontractors.

(d) If this contract is completed before the next October 1, the certified statements to be furnished pursuant to paragraph (c) above shall be submitted within 60 days after completion. If this contract is not completed before the next October 1, the certified statements shall be submitted on or before November 30 of each year and shall cover taxes paid during the 12-month period that ended the preceding September 30.

(e) The certified statements to be furnished pursuant to paragraph (c) above shall be in the following form:

I hereby certify that during the period ____ to ____ [*insert dates*], ____ [*insert name of Contractor or subcontractor*] paid North Carolina State and local sales and use taxes aggregating $___ (State) and $___ (local), with respect to building materials, supplies, fixtures, and equipment that have become a part of or annexed to a building or structure erected, altered, or repaired by ____ [*insert name of Contractor or subcontractor*] for the United States of America, and that the vendors from whom the property was purchased, the dates and numbers of the invoices covering the purchases, the total amount of the invoices of each vendor, the North Carolina State and local sales and use taxes paid on the property (shown separately), and the cost of property withdrawn from warehouse stock and North Carolina State and local sales or use taxes paid on this property are as set forth in the attachments.

(End of clause)

Alternate I (APR 1984). If the requirement is for vessel repair to be performed in North Carolina, substitute the following paragraph (a) for paragraph (a) of the basic clause:

(a) *Materials* as used in this clause, means materials, supplies, fixtures, and equipment that become a part of or are annexed to any vessel altered or repaired under this contract.

[FAC 84-5, 50 FR 1747, 1/11/85, effective 4/1/85; FAC 90-32, 60 FR 48206, 9/18/95, effective 10/1/95]

52.229-3 Federal, State, and Local Taxes.

As prescribed in 29.401-3, insert the following clause:

FEDERAL, STATE, AND LOCAL TAXES (FEB 2013)

(a) As used in this clause—

After-imposed Federal tax means any new or increased Federal excise tax or duty, or tax that was exempted or excluded on the contract date but whose exemption was later revoked or reduced during the contract period, on the transactions or property covered by this contract that the Contractor is required to pay or bear as the result of legislative, judicial, or administrative action taking effect after the contract date. It does not include social security tax or other employment taxes.

After-relieved Federal tax means any amount of Federal excise tax or duty, except social security or other employment taxes, that would otherwise have been payable on the transactions or property covered by this contract, but which the Contractor is not required to pay or bear, or for which the Contractor obtains a refund or drawback, as the result of legislative, judicial, or administrative action taking effect after the contract date.

All applicable Federal, State, and local taxes and duties means all taxes and duties, in effect on the contract date, that the taxing authority is imposing and collecting on the transactions or property covered by this contract.

Contract date means the date set for bid opening or, if this is a negotiated contract or a modification, the effective date of this contract or modification.

Local taxes includes taxes imposed by a possession or territory of the United States, Puerto Rico, or the Northern Mariana Islands, if the contract is performed wholly or partly in any of those areas.

(b)(1) The contract price includes all applicable Federal, State, and local taxes and duties, except as provided in subparagraph (b)(2)(i) of this clause.

(2) Taxes imposed under 26 U.S.C. 5000C may not be—

(i) Included in the contract price; nor

(ii) Reimbursed.

(c) The contract price shall be increased by the amount of any after-imposed Federal tax, provided the Contractor warrants in writing that no amount for such newly imposed Federal excise tax or duty or rate increase was included in the contract price, as a contingency reserve or otherwise.

(d) The contract price shall be decreased by the amount of any after-relieved Federal tax.

(e) The contract price shall be decreased by the amount of any Federal excise tax or duty, except social security or other employment taxes, that the Contractor is required to pay or bear, or does not obtain a refund of, through the Contractor's fault, negligence, or failure to follow instructions of the Contracting Officer.

(f) No adjustment shall be made in the contract price under this clause unless the amount of the adjustment exceeds $250.

(g) The Contractor shall promptly notify the Contracting Officer of all matters relating to any Federal excise tax or duty that reasonably may be expected to result in either an increase or decrease in the contract price and shall take appropriate action as the Contracting Officer directs.

(h) The Government shall, without liability, furnish evidence appropriate to establish exemption from any Federal, State, or local tax when the Contractor requests such evidence and a reasonable basis exists to sustain the exemption.

(End of clause)

[FAC 84-5, 50 FR 1747, 1/11/85, effective 4/1/85; FAC 90-3, 55 FR 52799, 12/21/90, effective 1/22/91; FAC 2001-13, 68 FR 13204, 3/18/2003, effective 4/17/2003; FAC 2005-65, 78 FR 6189, 1/29/2013, effective 2/28/2013]

52.229-4 Federal, State, and Local Taxes (State and Local Adjustments).

As prescribed in 29.401-3, insert the following clause:

FEDERAL, STATE, AND LOCAL TAXES (STATE AND LOCAL ADJUSTMENTS) (FEB 2013)

(a) As used in this clause—

After-imposed tax means any new or increased Federal, State, or local tax or duty, or tax that was excluded on the contract date but whose exclusion was later revoked or amount of exemption reduced during the contract period, other than an excepted tax, on the transactions or property covered by this contract that the Contractor is required to pay or bear as the result of legislative, judicial, or administrative action taking effect after the contract date.

After-relieved tax means any amount of Federal, State, or local tax or duty, other than an excepted tax, that would otherwise have been payable on the transactions or property covered by this contract, but which the Contractor is not required to pay or bear, or for which the Contractor obtains a refund or drawback, as the result of legislative, judicial, or administrative action taking effect after the contract date.

All applicable Federal, State, and local taxes and duties means all taxes and duties, in effect on the contract date, that the taxing authority is imposing and collecting on the transactions or property covered by this contract.

Contract date means the effective date of this contract and, for any modification to this contract, the effective date of the modification.

Excepted tax means social security or other employment taxes, net income and franchise taxes, excess profits taxes, capital stock taxes, transportation taxes, unemployment compensation taxes, and property taxes. *Excepted tax* does not include gross income taxes levied on or measured by sales or receipts from sales, property taxes assessed on completed supplies covered by this contract, or any tax assessed on the Contractor's possession of, interest in, or use of property, title to which is in the Government.

Local taxes includes taxes imposed by a possession or territory of the United States, Puerto Rico, or the Northern Mariana Islands, if the contract is performed wholly or partly in any of those areas.

(b) (1) Unless otherwise provided in this contract, the contract price includes all applicable Federal, State, and local taxes and duties, except as provided in subparagraph (b) (2) (i) of this clause.

(2) Taxes imposed under 26 U.S.C. 5000C may not be—

(i) Included in the contract price; nor

(ii) Reimbursed.

(c) The contract price shall be increased by the amount of any after-imposed tax, or of any tax or duty specifically excluded from the contract price by a term or condition of this contract that the Contractor is required to pay or bear, including any interest or penalty, if the Contractor states in writing that the contract price does not include any contingency for such tax and if liability for such tax, interest, or penalty was not incurred through the Contractor's fault, negligence, or failure to follow instructions of the Contracting Officer.

(d) The contract price shall be decreased by the amount of any after-relieved tax. The Government shall be entitled to interest received by the Contractor incident to a refund of taxes to the extent that such interest was earned after the Contractor was paid by the Government for such taxes. The Government shall be entitled to repayment of any penalty refunded to the Contractor to the extent that the penalty was paid by the Government.

(e) The contract price shall be decreased by the amount of any Federal, State, or local tax, other than an excepted tax, that was included in the contract price and that the Contractor is required to pay or bear, or does not obtain a refund of, through the Contractor's fault, negligence, or failure to follow instructions of the Contracting Officer.

(f) No adjustment shall be made in the contract price under this clause unless the amount of the adjustment exceeds $250.

(g) The Contractor shall promptly notify the Contracting Officer of all matters relating to Federal, State, and local taxes and duties that reasonably may be expected to result in either an increase or decrease in the contract price and shall take appropriate action as the Contracting Officer directs. The contract price shall be equitably adjusted to cover the costs of action taken by the Contractor at the direction of the Contracting Officer, including any interest, penalty, and reasonable attorneys' fees.

(h) The Government shall furnish evidence appropriate to establish exemption from any Federal, State, or local tax when (1) the Contractor requests such exemption and states in writing that it applies to a tax excluded from the contract price and (2) a reasonable basis exists to sustain the exemption.

(End of clause)

[FAC 90-3, 55 FR 52799, 12/21/90, effective 1/22/91; FAC 2001-13, 68 FR 13204, 3/18/2003, effective 4/17/2003; FAC 2005-65, 78 FR 6189, 1/29/2013, effective 2/28/2013]

52.229-5 [Removed and Reserved]

[FAC 90-32, 60 FR 48206, 9/18/95, effective 10/1/95; FAC 2001-13, 68 FR 13204, 3/18/2003, effective 4/17/2003]

52.229-6 Taxes—Foreign Fixed-Price Contracts.

As prescribed in 29.402-1(a), insert the following clause:

TAXES—FOREIGN FIXED-PRICE CONTRACTS (FEB 2013)

(a) To the extent that this contract provides for furnishing supplies or performing services outside the United States and its outlying areas, this clause applies in lieu of any Federal, State, and local taxes clause of the contract.

(b) *Definitions*. As used in this clause—

Contract date means the date set for bid opening or, if this is a negotiated contract or a modification, the effective date of this contract or modification.

Country concerned means any country, other than the United States and its outlying areas, in which expenditures under this contract are made.

Tax and *taxes* include fees and charges for doing business that are levied by the government of the country concerned or by its political subdivisions.

All applicable taxes and duties means all taxes and duties, in effect on the contract date, that the taxing authority is imposing and collecting on the transactions or property covered by this contract, pursuant to written ruling or regulation in effect on the contract date.

After-imposed tax means any new or increased tax or duty, or tax that was exempted or excluded on the contract date but whose exemption was later revoked or reduced during the contract period, other than excepted tax, on the transactions or property covered by this contract that the Contractor is required to pay or bear as the result of legislative, judicial, or administrative action taking effect after the contract date.

After-relieved tax means any amount of tax or duty, other than an excepted tax, that would otherwise have been payable on the transactions or property covered by this contract, but which the Contractor is not required to pay or bear, or for which the Contractor obtains a refund, as the result of legislative, judicial, or administrative action taking effect after the contract date.

Excepted tax means social security or other employment taxes, net income and franchise taxes, excess profits taxes, capital stock taxes, transportation taxes, unemployment compensation taxes, and property taxes. *Excepted tax* does not include gross income taxes levied on or measured by sales or receipts from sales, property taxes assessed on completed supplies covered by this contract, or any tax assessed on the Contractor's possession of, interest in, or use of property, title to which is in the U.S. Government.

(c) (1) Unless otherwise provided in this contract, the contract price includes all applicable taxes and duties, except taxes and duties that the Government of the United States and the government of the country concerned have agreed shall not be applicable to expenditures in such country by or on behalf of the United States, except as provided in subparagraph (c)(2) of this clause.

(2) Taxes imposed under 26 U.S.C. 5000C may not be—

(i) Included in the contract price; nor

(ii) Reimbursed.

(d)(1) Except as provided in subparagraph (d)(2) of this clause, the contract price shall be increased by the amount of any after-imposed tax or of any tax or duty specifically excluded from the contract price by a provision of this contract that the Contractor is required to pay or bear, including any interest or penalty, if the Contractor states in writing that the contract price does not include any contingency for such tax and if liability for such tax, interest, or penalty was not incurred through the Contractor's fault, negligence, or failure to follow instructions of the Contracting Officer or to comply with the provisions of paragraph (i) of this clause.

(2) The contract price may not be increased to offset taxes imposed under 26 U.S.C. 5000C.

(e) The contract price shall be decreased by the amount of any after-relieved tax, including any interest or penalty. The Government of the United States shall be entitled to interest received by the Contractor incident to a refund of taxes to the extent that such interest was earned after the Contractor was paid by the Government of the United States for such taxes. The Government of the United States shall be entitled to repayment of any penalty refunded to the Contractor to the extent that the penalty was paid by the Government.

(f) The contract price shall be decreased by the amount of any tax or duty, other than an excepted tax, that was included in the contract and that the Contractor is required to pay or bear, or does not obtain a refund of, through the Contractor's fault, negligence, or failure to follow instructions of the Contracting Officer or to comply with the provisions of paragraph (i) of this clause.

(g) No adjustment shall be made in the contract price under this clause unless the amount of the adjustment exceeds $250.

(h) If the Contractor obtains a reduction in tax liability under the United States Internal Revenue Code (Title 26, U.S. Code) because of the payment of any tax or duty that either was included in the contract price or was the basis of an increase in the contract price, the amount of the reduction shall be paid or credited to the Government of the United States as the Contracting Officer directs.

(i) The Contractor shall take all reasonable action to obtain exemption from or refund of any taxes or duties, including interest or penalty, from which the United States Government, the Contractor, any subcontractor, or the transactions or property covered by this contract are exempt under the laws of the country concerned or its political subdivisions or which the governments of the United States and of the country concerned have agreed shall not be applicable to expenditures in such country by or on behalf of the United States.

(j) The Contractor shall promptly notify the Contracting Officer of all matters relating to taxes or duties that reasonably may be expected to result in either an increase or decrease in the contract price and shall take appropriate action as the Contracting Officer directs. The contract price shall be equitably adjusted to cover the costs of action taken by the Contractor at the direction of the Contracting Officer, including any interest, penalty, and reasonable attorneys' fees.

(End of clause)

[FAC 90-3, 55 FR 52799, 12/21/90, effective 1/22/91; FAC 2001-14, 68 FR 28079, 5/22/2003, effective 6/23/2003; FAC 2005-65, 78 FR 6189, 1/29/2013, effective 2/28/2013]

52.229-7 Taxes—Fixed-Price Contracts with Foreign Governments.

As prescribed in 29.402-1(b), insert the following clause:

TAXES—FIXED-PRICE CONTRACTS WITH FOREIGN GOVERNMENTS (FEB 2013)

(a) *Contract date* as used in this clause, means the date set for bid opening or, if this is a negotiated contract or a modification, the effective date of this contract or modification.

(b) (1) The contract price, including the prices in any subcontracts under this contract, does not include any tax or duty that the Government of the United States and the Government of ____ [*insert name of the foreign government*] have agreed shall not apply to expenditures made by the United States in ____ [*insert name of country*], or any tax or duty not applicable to this contract or any subcontracts under this contract, pursuant to the laws of ____ [*insert name of country*]. If any such tax or duty has been included in the contract price, through error or otherwise, the contract price shall be correspondingly reduced.

(2) Taxes imposed under 26 U.S.C. 5000C may not be included in the contract price.

(c) If, after the contract date, the Government of the United States and the Government of ____ [*insert name of the foreign government*] agree that any tax or duty included in the contract price shall not apply to expenditures by the United States in ____ [*insert name of country*], the contract price shall be reduced accordingly.

(d) No adjustment shall be made in the contract price under this clause unless the amount of the adjustment exceeds $250.

(End of clause)

[FAC 90-3, 55 FR 52799, 12/21/90, effective 1/22/91; FAC 2005-65, 78 FR 6189, 1/29/2013, effective 2/28/2013; FAC 2005-66, 78 FR 13768, 2/28/2013, effective 2/28/2013]

52.229-8 Taxes—Foreign Cost-Reimbursement Contracts.

As prescribed in 29.402-2(a), insert the following clause:

TAXES—FOREIGN COST-REIMBURSEMENT CONTRACTS (MAR 1990)

(a) Any tax or duty from which the United States Government is exempt by agreement with the Government of ____ [*insert name of the foreign government*], or from which the Contractor or any subcontractor under this contract is exempt under the laws of ____ [*insert name of country*], shall not constitute an allowable cost under this contract.

(b) If the Contractor or subcontractor under this contract obtains a foreign tax credit that reduces its Federal income tax liability under the United States Internal Revenue Code (Title 26, U.S. Code) because of the payment of any tax or duty that was reimbursed under this contract, the amount of the reduction shall be paid or credited at the time of such offset to the Government of the United States as the Contracting Officer directs.

(End of clause)

[FAC 84-56, 55 FR 3889, 2/5/90, effective 3/7/90]

52.229-9 Taxes—Cost-Reimbursement Contracts with Foreign Governments.

As prescribed in 29.402-2(b), insert the following clause:

TAXES—COST-REIMBURSEMENT CONTRACTS WITH FOREIGN GOVERNMENTS (MAR 1990)

(a) Any tax or duty from which the United States Government is exempt by agreement with the Government of ____ [*insert name of the foreign government*], or from which any subcontractor under this contract is exempt under the laws of ____ [*insert name of country*], shall not constitute an allowable cost under this contract.

(b) If any subcontractor obtains a foreign tax credit that reduces its Federal income tax liability under the United States Internal Revenue Code (Title 26, U.S.C.) because of the payment of any tax or duty that was reimbursed under this contract, the amount of the reduction shall be paid (not credited to the contract) to the Treasurer of the

United States at the time the Federal income tax return is filed.

(End of clause)

[FAC 84-56, 55 FR 3889, 2/5/90, effective 3/7/90]

52.229-10 State of New Mexico Gross Receipts and Compensating Tax.

As prescribed in 29.401-4(b), insert the following clause:

STATE OF NEW MEXICO GROSS RECEIPTS AND COMPENSATING TAX (APR 2003)

(a) Within thirty (30) days after award of this contract, the Contractor shall advise the State of New Mexico of this contract by registering with the State of New Mexico, Taxation and Revenue Department, Revenue Division, pursuant to the Tax Administration Act of the State of New Mexico and shall identify the contract number.

(b) The Contractor shall pay the New Mexico gross receipts taxes, pursuant to the Gross Receipts and Compensating Tax Act of New Mexico, assessed against the contract fee and costs paid for performance of this contract, or of any part or portion thereof, within the State of New Mexico. The allowability of any gross receipts taxes or local option taxes lawfully paid to the State of New Mexico by the Contractor or its subcontractors will be determined in accordance with the Allowable Cost and Payment clause of this contract except as provided in paragraph (d) of this clause.

(c) The Contractor shall submit applications for Nontaxable Transaction Certificates, Form CSR-3C, to the State of New Mexico Taxation and Revenue Department, Revenue Division, P.O. Box 630, Santa Fe, New Mexico 87509. When the Type 15 Nontaxable Transaction Certificate is issued by the Revenue Division, the Contractor shall use these certificates strictly in accordance with this contract, and the agreement between the (* _) and the New Mexico Taxation and Revenue Department.

(d) The Contractor shall provide Type 15 Nontaxable Transaction Certificates to each vendor in New Mexico selling tangible personal property to the Contractor for use in the performance of this contract. Failure to provide a Type 15 Nontaxable Transaction Certificate to vendors will result in the vendor's liability for the gross receipt taxes and those taxes, which are then passed on to the Contractor, shall not be reimbursable as an allowable cost by the Government.

(e) The Contractor shall pay the New Mexico compensating user tax for any tangible personal property which is purchased pursuant to a Nontaxable Transaction Certificate if such property is not used for Federal purposes.

(f) Out-of-state purchase of tangible personal property by the Contractor which would be otherwise subject to compensation tax shall be governed by the principles of this clause. Accordingly, compensating tax shall be due from the Contractor only if such property is not used for Federal purposes.

(g) The (*_) may receive information regarding the Contractor from the Revenue Division of the New Mexico Taxation and Revenue Department and, at the discretion of the (*_), may participate in any matters or proceedings pertaining to this clause or the above-mentioned agreement. This shall not preclude the Contractor from having its own representative nor does it obligate the (*_) to represent its Contractor.

(h) The Contractor agrees to insert the substance of this clause, including this paragraph (h), in each subcontract which meets the criteria in 29.401-4(b)(1) through (3) of the Federal Acquisition Regulation, 48 CFR Part 29.

(i) Paragraphs (a) through (h) of this clause shall be null and void should the Agreement referred to in paragraph (c) of this clause be terminated; provided, however, that such termination shall not nullify obligations already incurred prior to the date of termination.

* (Insert appropriate agency name in blanks.)

(End of clause)

[FAC 84-39, 53 FR 34229, 9/2/88, effective 10/3/88; corrected 53 FR 36028, 9/16/88; FAC 2001-13, 68 FR 13204, 3/18/2003, effective 4/17/2003]

52.230-1 Cost Accounting Standards Notices and Certification.

As prescribed in 30.201-3, insert the following provision:

COST ACCOUNTING STANDARDS NOTICES AND CERTIFICATION (OCT 2015)

Note: This notice does not apply to small businesses or foreign governments. This notice is in three parts, identified by Roman numerals I through III.

Offerors shall examine each part and provide the requested information in order to determine Cost Accounting Standards (CAS) requirements applicable to any resultant contract.

If the offeror is an educational institution, Part II does not apply unless the contemplated contract will be subject to full or modified CAS coverage pursuant to 48 CFR 9903.201-2(c)(5) or 9903.201-2(c)(6), respectively.

I. DISCLOSURE STATEMENT—COST ACCOUNTING PRACTICES AND CERTIFICATION

(a) Any contract in excess of $750,000 resulting from this solicitation will be subject to the requirements of the Cost Accounting Standards Board (48 CFR Chapter 99), except for those contracts which are exempt as specified in 48 CFR 9903.201-1.

(b) Any offeror submitting a proposal which, if accepted, will result in a contract subject to the requirements of 48 CFR Chapter 99 must, as a condition of contracting, submit a Disclosure Statement as required by 48 CFR 9903.202. When required, the Disclosure Statement must be submitted as a part of the offeror's proposal under this solicitation unless the offeror has already submitted a Disclosure Statement disclosing the practices used in connection with the pricing of this proposal. If an applicable Disclosure Statement has already been submitted, the offeror may satisfy the requirement for submission by providing the information requested in paragraph (c) of Part I of this provision.

CAUTION: In the absence of specific regulations or agreement, a practice disclosed in a Disclosure Statement shall not, by virtue of such disclosure, be deemed to be a proper, approved, or agreed-to practice for pricing proposals or accumulating and reporting contract performance cost data.

(c) Check the appropriate box below:

[] (1) *Certificate of Concurrent Submission of Disclosure Statement.*

The offeror hereby certifies that, as a part of the offer, copies of the Disclosure Statement have been submitted as follows: (i) original and one copy to the cognizant Administrative Contracting Officer (ACO) or cognizant Federal agency official authorized to act in that capacity (Federal official), as applicable, and (ii) one copy to the cognizant Federal auditor.

(Disclosure must be on Form No. CASB DS-1 or CASB DS-2, as applicable. Forms may be obtained from the cognizant ACO or Federal official and/or from the loose-leaf version of the Federal Acquisition Regulation.)

Date of Disclosure Statement:

Name and Address of Cognizant ACO or Federal Official Where Filed:

The offeror further certifies that the practices used in estimating costs in pricing this proposal are consistent with the cost accounting practices disclosed in the Disclosure Statement.

[](2) *Certificate of Previously Submitted Disclosure Statement.*

The offeror hereby certifies that the required Disclosure Statement was filed as follows:

Date of Disclosure Statement:

Name and Address of Cognizant ACO or Federal Official Where Filed:

The offeror further certifies that the practices used in estimating costs in pricing this proposal are consistent with the cost accounting practices disclosed in the applicable Disclosure Statement.

[] (3) *Certificate of Monetary Exemption.*

The offeror hereby certifies that the offeror, together with all divisions, subsidiaries, and affiliates under common control, did not receive net awards of negotiated prime contracts and subcontracts subject to CAS totaling $50 million or more in the cost accounting period immediately preceding the period in which this proposal was submitted. The offeror further certifies that if such status changes before an award resulting from this proposal, the offeror will advise the Contracting Officer immediately.

[] (4) *Certificate of Interim Exemption.*

The offeror hereby certifies that (i) the offeror first exceeded the monetary exemption for disclosure, as defined in (3) of this subsection, in the cost accounting period immediately preceding the period in which this offer was submitted and (ii) in accordance with 48 CFR 9903.202-1, the offeror is not yet required to submit a Disclosure Statement. The offeror further certifies that if an award resulting from this proposal has not been made within 90 days after the end of that period, the offeror will immediately submit a revised certificate to the Contracting Officer, in the form specified under subparagraphs (c)(1) or (c)(2) of Part I of this provision, as appropriate, to verify submission of a completed Disclosure Statement.

CAUTION: Offerors currently required to disclose because they were awarded a CAS-covered prime contract or subcontract of $50 million or more in the current cost accounting period may not claim this exemption (4). Further, the exemption applies only in connection with proposals submitted before expiration of the 90-day period following the cost accounting period in which the monetary exemption was exceeded.

II. COST ACCOUNTING STANDARDS—ELIGIBILITY FOR MODIFIED CONTRACT COVERAGE

If the offeror is eligible to use the modified provisions of 48 CFR 9903.201-2(b) and elects to do so, the offeror shall indicate by checking the box below. Checking the box below shall mean that the resultant contract is subject to the Disclosure and Consistency of Cost Accounting Practices clause in lieu of the Cost Accounting Standards clause.

[] The offeror hereby claims an exemption from the Cost Accounting Standards clause under the provisions of 48 CFR 9903.201-2(b) and certifies that the offeror is eligible for use of the Disclosure and Consistency of Cost Accounting Practices clause because during the cost accounting period immediately preceding the period in which this proposal was submitted, the offeror received less than $50 million in awards of CAS-covered prime contracts and subcontracts. The offeror further certifies that if such status changes before an award resulting from this proposal, the offeror will advise the Contracting Officer immediately.

CAUTION: An offeror may not claim the above eligibility for modified contract coverage if this proposal is expected to result in the award of a CAS-covered contract of $50 million or more or if, during its current cost accounting period, the offeror has been awarded a single CAS-covered prime contract or subcontract of $50 million or more.

III. ADDITIONAL COST ACCOUNTING STANDARDS APPLICABLE TO EXISTING CONTRACTS

The offeror shall indicate below whether award of the contemplated contract would, in accordance with subparagraph (a)(3) of the Cost Accounting Standards clause, require a change in established cost accounting practices affecting existing contracts and subcontracts.

[] YES [] NO

(End of provision)

Alternate I (APR 1996).

As prescribed in 30.201-3(b), add the following subparagraph (c)(5) to Part I of the basic provision:

[] (5) *Certificate of Disclosure Statement Due Date by Educational Institution.*

If the offeror is an educational institution that, under the transition provisions of 48 CFR 9903.202-1(f), is or will be required to submit a Disclosure Statement after receipt of this award, the offeror hereby certifies that (check one and complete):

[] (i) A Disclosure Statement Filing Due Date of _____ has been established with the cognizant Federal agency.

[] (ii) The Disclosure Statement will be submitted within the 6-month period ending _____ months after receipt of this award.

Name and Address of Cognizant ACO or Federal Official Where Disclosure Statement is to be Filed:

____

[FAC 84-30, 9/30/87, effective 9/30/87; FAC 90-12, 57 FR 39591, 8/31/92, effective 8/31/92; Corrected, 57 FR 43409, 9/21/92; Corrected, 57 FR 43495, 9/21/92; FAC 90-23, 59 FR 67010, 12/28/94, effective 2/27/95, "Note" statement, (c)(1) and (c)(3), and (c)(4) "Caution" statement effective 11/4/93; FAC 90-38, 61 FR 18914, 4/29/96, effective 4/29/96; FAC 97-4, 63 FR 9048, 2/23/98, effective 4/24/98; FAC 97-18, 65 FR 36014, 6/6/2000, effective 6/6/2000, finalized without change, FAC 97-22, 66 FR 2135, 1/10/2001; FAC 2005-27, 73 FR 54011, 9/17/2008, effective 10/17/2008; FAC 2005-36, 74 FR 40467, 8/11/2009, effective 8/11/2009; FAC 2005-59, 77 FR 27550, 5/10/2012, effective 5/10/2012; FAC 2005-83, 80 FR 38293, 7/2/2015, effective 10/1/2015]

52.230-2 Cost Accounting Standards.

As prescribed in 30.201-4(a), insert the following clause:

COST ACCOUNTING STANDARDS (OCT 2015)

(a) Unless the contract is exempt under 48 CFR 9903.201-1 and 9903.201-2, the provisions of 48 CFR Part 9903 are incorporated herein by reference and the Contractor, in connection with this contract, shall—

(1) (*CAS-covered Contracts Only*) By submission of a Disclosure Statement, disclose in writing the Contractor's cost accounting practices as required by 48 CFR 9903.202-1 through 9903.202-5, including methods of distinguishing direct costs from indirect costs and the basis used for allocating indirect costs. The practices disclosed for this contract shall be the same as the practices currently disclosed and applied on all other contracts and subcontracts being performed by the Contractor and which contain a Cost Accounting Standards (CAS) clause. If the Contractor has notified the Contracting Officer that the Disclosure Statement contains trade secrets and commercial or financial information which is privileged and confidential, the Disclosure Statement shall be protected and shall not be released outside of the Government.

(2) Follow consistently the Contractor's cost accounting practices in accumulating and reporting contract performance cost data concerning this contract. If any change in cost accounting practices is made for the purposes of any contract or subcontract subject to CAS requirements, the change must be applied prospectively to this contract and the Disclosure Statement must be amended accordingly. If the contract price or cost allowance of this contract is affected by such changes, adjustment shall be made in accordance with subparagraph (a)(4) or (a)(5) of this clause, as appropriate.

(3) Comply with all CAS, including any modifications and interpretations indicated thereto contained in 48 CFR Part 9904, in effect on the date of award of this contract or, if the Contractor has submitted certified cost or pricing data, on the date of final agreement on price as shown on the Contractor's signed certificate of current cost or pricing data. The Contractor shall also comply with any CAS (or modifications to CAS) which hereafter become applicable to a contract or subcontract of the Contractor. Such compliance shall be required prospectively from the date of applicability to such contract or subcontract.

(4) (i) Agree to an equitable adjustment as provided in the Changes clause of this contract if the contract cost is affected by a

change which, pursuant to subparagraph (a)(3) of this clause, the Contractor is required to make to the Contractor's established cost accounting practices.

(ii) Negotiate with the Contracting Officer to determine the terms and conditions under which a change may be made to a cost accounting practice, other than a change made under other provisions of subparagraph (a)(4) of this clause; provided that no agreement may be made under this provision that will increase costs paid by the United States.

(iii) When the parties agree to a change to a cost accounting practice, other than a change under subdivision (a)(4)(i) of this clause, negotiate an equitable adjustment as provided in the Changes clause of this contract.

(5) Agree to an adjustment of the contract price or cost allowance, as appropriate, if the Contractor or a subcontractor fails to comply with an applicable Cost Accounting Standard, or to follow any cost accounting practice consistently and such failure results in any increased costs paid by the United States. Such adjustment shall provide for recovery of the increased costs to the United States, together with interest thereon computed at the annual rate established under section 6621(a)(2) of the Internal Revenue Code of 1986 (26 U.S.C. 6621(a)(2)) for such period, from the time the payment by the United States was made to the time the adjustment is effected. In no case shall the Government recover costs greater than the increased cost to the Government, in the aggregate, on the relevant contracts subject to the price adjustment, unless the Contractor made a change in its cost accounting practices of which it was aware or should have been aware at the time of price negotiations and which it failed to disclose to the Government.

(b) If the parties fail to agree whether the Contractor or a subcontractor has complied with an applicable CAS in 48 CFR, Part 9904 or a CAS rule or regulation in 48 CFR, Part 9903 and as to any cost adjustment demanded by the United States, such failure to agree will constitute a dispute under 41 U.S.C. chapter 71, Contract Disputes.

(c) The Contractor shall permit any authorized representatives of the Government to examine and make copies of any documents, papers, or records relating to compliance with the requirements of this clause.

(d) The Contractor shall include in all negotiated subcontracts which the Contractor enters into, the substance of this clause, except paragraph (b), and shall require such inclusion in all other subcontracts, of any tier, including the obligation to comply with all CAS in effect on the subcontractor's award date or if the subcontractor has submitted certified cost or pricing data, on the date of final agreement on price as shown on the subcontractor's signed Certificate of Current Cost or Pricing Data. If the subcontract is awarded to a business unit which pursuant to 48 CFR 9903.201-2 is subject to other types of CAS coverage, the substance of the applicable clause set forth in subsection 30.201-4 of the Federal Acquisition Regulation shall be inserted. This requirement shall apply only to negotiated subcontracts in excess of $750,000, except that the requirement shall not apply to negotiated subcontracts otherwise exempt from the requirement to include a CAS clause as specified in 48 CFR 9903.201-1.

(End of clause)

[FAC 90-12, 57 FR 39592, 8/31/92, effective 8/31/92; Corrected, 57 FR 45878, 10/5/92; FAC 90-38, 61 FR 18914, 4/29/96, effective 4/29/96; FAC 97-4, 63 FR 9048, 2/23/98, effective 4/24/98; FAC 2005-27, 73 FR 54011, 9/17/2008, effective 10/17/2008; FAC 2005-36, 74 FR 40467, 8/11/2009, effective 8/11/2009; FAC 2005-45, 75 FR 53135, 8/30/2010, effective 10/1/2010; FAC 2005-59, 77 FR 27550, 5/10/2012, effective 5/10/2012; FAC 2005-73, 79 FR 24192, 4/29/2014, effective 5/29/2014; FAC 2005-83, 80 FR 38293, 7/2/2015, effective 10/1/2015]

52.230-3 Disclosure and Consistency of Cost Accounting Practices.

As prescribed in 30.201-4(b)(1), insert the following clause:

DISCLOSURE AND CONSISTENCY OF COST ACCOUNTING PRACTICES (OCT 2015)

(a) The Contractor, in connection with this contract, shall—

(1) Comply with the requirements of 48 CFR 9904.401, Consistency in Estimating, Accumulating, and Reporting Costs; 48 CFR 9904.402, Consistency in Allocating Costs Incurred for the Same Purpose; 48 CFR 9904.405, Accounting for Unallowable Costs; and 48 CFR 9904.406, Cost Accounting Standard-Cost Accounting Period, in effect on the date of award of this contract as indicated in 48 CFR Part 9904.

(2) (*CAS-covered Contracts Only*) If it is a business unit of a company required to submit a Disclosure Statement, disclose in writing its cost accounting practices as required by 48 CFR 9903.202-1 through 9903.202-5. If the Contractor has notified the Contracting Officer that the Disclosure Statement contains trade secrets and commercial or financial information which is privileged and confidential, the Disclosure Statement shall be protected and shall not be released outside of the Government.

(3) (i) Follow consistently the Contractor's cost accounting practices. A change to such practices may be proposed, however, by either the Government or the Contractor, and the Contractor agrees to negotiate with the Contracting Officer the terms and conditions under which a change may be made. After the terms and conditions under which the change is to be made have been agreed to, the change must be applied prospectively to this contract, and the Disclosure Statement, if affected, must be amended accordingly.

(ii) The Contractor shall, when the parties agree to a change to a cost accounting practice and the Contracting Officer has made the finding required in 48 CFR 9903.201-6(c), that the change is desirable and not detrimental to the interests of the Government, negotiate an equitable adjustment as provided in the Changes clause of this contract. In the absence of the required finding, no agreement may be made under this contract clause that will increase costs paid by the United States.

(4) Agree to an adjustment of the contract price or cost allowance, as appropriate, if the Contractor or a subcontractor fails to comply with the applicable CAS or to follow any cost accounting practice, and such failure results in any increased costs paid by the United States. Such adjustment shall provide for recovery of the increased costs to the United States together with interest thereon computed at the annual rate of interest established under section 6621(a)(2) of the Internal Revenue Code of 1986 (26 U.S.C. 6621 (a)(2)), from the time the payment by the United States was made to the time the adjustment is effected.

(b) If the parties fail to agree whether the Contractor has complied with an applicable CAS, rule, or regulation as specified in 48 CFR, Parts 9903 and 9904 and as to any cost adjustment demanded by the United States, such failure to agree will constitute a dispute under 41 U.S.C. chapter 71, Contract Disputes.

(c) The Contractor shall permit any authorized representatives of the Government to examine and make copies of any documents, papers, and records relating to compliance with the requirements of this clause.

(d) The Contractor shall include in all negotiated subcontracts, which the Contractor enters into, the substance of this clause, except paragraph (b), and shall require such inclusion in all other subcontracts of any tier, except that—

(1) If the subcontract is awarded to a business unit which pursuant to 48 CFR 9903.201-2 is subject to other types of CAS coverage, the substance of the applicable clause set forth in subsection 30.201-4 of the Federal Acquisition Regulation shall be inserted.

(2) This requirement shall apply only to negotiated subcontracts in excess of $750,000.

(3) The requirement shall not apply to negotiated subcontracts otherwise exempt from the requirement to include a CAS clause as specified in 48 CFR 9903.201-1.

(End of clause)

[FAC 90-12, 57 FR 39592, 8/31/92, effective 8/31/92; Corrected, 57 FR 43495, 9/21/92; FAC 90-23, 59 FR 67010, 12/28/94, effective 11/4/93; FAC 90-38, 61 FR 18914, 4/29/96, effective 4/29/96; FAC 97-4, 63 FR 9048, 2/23/98, effective 4/24/98; FAC 2005-27, 73 FR 54011, 9/17/2008, effective 10/17/2008; FAC 2005-36, 74 FR 40467, 8/11/2009, effective 8/11/2009; FAC 2005-59, 77 FR 27550, 5/10/2012, effective 5/10/2012; FAC 2005-73, 79 FR 24192, 4/29/2014, effective 5/29/2014; FAC 2005-83, 80 FR 38293, 7/2/2015, effective 10/1/2015]

52.230-4 Disclosure and Consistency of Cost Accounting Practices—Foreign Concerns.

As prescribed in 30.201-4(c), insert the following clause:

DISCLOSURE AND CONSISTENCY OF COST ACCOUNTING PRACTICES-FOREIGN CONCERNS (OCT 2015)

(a) The Contractor, in connection with this contract, shall—

(1) Comply with the requirements of 48 CFR 9904.401, Consistency in Estimating, Accumulating, and Reporting Costs; and 48 CFR 9904.402, Consistency in Allocating Costs Incurred for the Same Purpose, in effect on the date of award of this contract, as indicated in 48 CFR 9904.

(2) (*Cost Accounting Standard (CAS)-covered Contracts Only*). If it is a business unit of a company required to submit a Disclosure Statement, disclose in writing its cost accounting practices as required by 48 CFR 9903.202-1 through 48 CFR 9903.202-5. If the Contractor has notified the Contracting Officer that the Disclosure Statement contains trade secrets and commercial or financial information which is privileged and confidential, the Disclosure Statement shall be protected and shall not be released outside of the U.S. Government.

(3) (i) Follow consistently the Contractor's cost accounting practices. A change to such practices may be proposed, however, by either the U.S. Government or the Contractor, and the Contractor agrees to negotiate with the Contracting Officer the terms and conditions under which a change may be made. After the terms and conditions under which the change is to be made have been agreed to, the change must be applied prospectively to this contract, and the Disclosure Statement, if affected, must be amended accordingly.

(ii) The Contractor shall, when the parties agree to a change to a cost accounting practice and the Contracting Officer has made the finding required in 48 CFR 9903.201-6(c) that the change is desirable and not detrimental to the interests of the U.S. Government, negotiate an equitable adjustment as provided in the Changes clause of this contract. In the absence of the required finding, no agreement may be made under this contract clause that will increase costs paid by the U.S. Government.

(4) Agree to an adjustment of the contract price or cost allowance, as appropriate, if the Contractor or a subcontractor fails to comply with the applicable CAS or to follow any cost accounting practice, and such failure results in any increased costs paid by the U.S. Government. Such adjustment shall provide for recovery of the increased costs to the U.S. Government, together with interest thereon computed at the annual rate established under section 6621(a)(2) of the Internal Revenue Code of 1986 (26 U.S.C. 6621(a)(2)) for such period, from the time the payment by the U.S. Government was made to the time the adjustment is effected.

(b) If the parties fail to agree whether the Contractor has complied with an applicable CAS rule, or regulation as specified in 48 CFR 9903 and 48 CFR 9904 and as to any cost adjustment demanded by the U.S. Government, such failure to agree will constitute a dispute under 41 U.S.C. chapter 71, Contract Disputes.

(c) The Contractor shall permit any authorized representatives of the U.S. Government to examine and make copies of any documents, papers, and records relating to compliance with the requirements of this clause.

(d) The Contractor shall include in all negotiated subcontracts, which the Contractor enters into, the substance of this clause, except paragraph (b), and shall require such inclusion in all other subcontracts of any tier, except that—

(1) If the subcontract is awarded to a business unit which pursuant to 48 CFR 9903.201-2 is subject to other types of CAS coverage, the substance of the applicable clause prescribed in FAR 30.201-4 shall be inserted.

(2) This requirement shall apply only to negotiated subcontracts in excess of $750,000.

(3) The requirement shall not apply to negotiated subcontracts otherwise exempt from the requirement to include a CAS clause as specified in 48 CFR 9903.201-1.

(End of clause)

[FAC 90-12, 57 FR 39593, 8/31/92, effective 8/31/92; FAC 2005-27, 73 FR 54011, 54013, 9/17/2008, effective 10/17/2008; FAC 2005-36, 74 FR 40467, 8/11/2009, effective 8/11/2009; FAC 2005-42, 75 FR 34283, 6/16/2010, effective 6/16/2010; FAC 2005-50, 76 FR 14570, 3/16/2011, effective 3/16/2011; FAC 2005-59, 77 FR 27550, 5/10/2012, effective 5/10/2012; FAC 2005-73, 79 FR 24192, 4/29/2014, effective 5/29/2014; FAC 2005-83, 80 FR 38293, 7/2/2015, effective 10/1/2015]

52.230-5 Cost Accounting Standards—Educational Institution.

As prescribed in 30.201-4(e), insert the following clause:

COST ACCOUNTING STANDARDS—EDUCATIONAL INSTITUTION (AUG 2016)

(a) Unless the contract is exempt under 48 CFR 9903.201-1 and 9903.201-2, the provisions of 48 CFR Part 9903 are incorporated herein by reference and the Contractor, in connection with this contract, shall—

(1) (*CAS-covered Contracts only*). If a business unit of an educational institution (defined as an institution of higher education in the OMB Uniform Guidance at 2 CFR part 200, subpart A and 20 U.S.C. 1001) is required to submit a Disclosure Statement, disclose in writing the Contractor's cost accounting practices as required by 48 CFR 9003.202-1 through 9903.202-5, including methods of distinguishing direct costs from indirect costs and the basis used for accumulating and allocating indirect costs. The practices disclosed for this contract shall be the same as the practices currently disclosed and applied on all other contracts and subcontracts being performed by the Contractor and which contain a Cost Accounting Standards (CAS) clause. If the Contractor has notified the Contracting Officer that the Disclosure Statement contains trade secrets, and commercial or financial information which is privileged and confidential, the Disclosure Statement shall be protected and shall not be released outside of the Government.

(2) Follow consistently the Contractor's cost accounting practices in accumulating and reporting contract performance cost data concerning this contract. If any change in cost accounting practices is made for the purposes of any contract or subcontract subject to CAS requirements, the change must be applied prospectively to this contract and the Disclosure Statement, if required, must be amended accordingly. If an accounting principle change mandated under OMB Uniform Guidance at 2 CFR part 200, subpart E and appendix III, requires that a change in the Contractor's cost accounting practices be made after the date of this contract award, the change must be applied prospectively to this contract and the Disclosure Statement, if required, must be amended accordingly. If the contract price or cost allowance of this contract is affected by such changes, adjustment shall be made in accordance with paragraph (a)(4) or (a)(5) of this clause, as appropriate.

(3) Comply with all CAS, including any modifications and interpretations indicated thereto contained in 48 CFR Part 9905 in effect on the date of award of this contract or, if the Contractor has submitted certified cost or pricing data, on the date of final agreement on price as shown on the Contractor's signed certificate of current cost or pricing data. The Contractor shall also comply with any CAS (or modifications to CAS) which hereafter become applicable to a contract or subcontract of the Contractor. Such

compliance shall be required prospectively from the date of applicability to such contract or subcontract.

(4) (i) Agree to an equitable adjustment as provided in the Changes clause of this contract if the contract cost is affected by a change which, pursuant to subparagraph (a)(3) of this clause, the Contractor is required to make to the Contractor's established cost accounting practices.

(ii) Negotiate with the Contracting Officer to determine the terms and conditions under which a change may be made to a cost accounting practice, other than a change made under other provisions of subparagraph (a)(4) of this clause; provided that no agreement may be made under this provision that will increase costs paid by the United States.

(iii) When the parties agree to a change to a cost accounting practice, other than a change under subdivision (a)(4)(i) or (a)(4)(iv) of this clause, negotiate an equitable adjustment as provided in the Changes clause of this contract.

(iv) Agree to an equitable adjustment as provided in the Changes clause of this contract, if the contract cost is materially affected by an accounting principle amendment required under the OMB Uniform Guidance at 2 CFR part 200, subpart E and appendix III, which, on becoming effective after the date of contract award, requires the Contractor to make a change to the Contractor's established cost accounting practices.

(5) Agree to an adjustment of the contract price or cost allowance, as appropriate, if the Contractor or a subcontractor fails to comply with an applicable Cost Accounting Standard, or to follow any cost accounting practice consistently and such failure results in any increased costs paid by the United States. Such adjustment shall provide for recovery of the increased costs to the United States, together with interest thereon computed at the annual rate established under section 6621 of the Internal Revenue Code of 1986 (26 U.S.C. 6621) for such period, from the time the payment by the United States was made to the time the adjustment is effected. In no case shall the Government recover costs greater than the increased cost to the Government, in the aggregate, on the relevant contracts subject to the price adjustment, unless the Contractor made a change in its cost accounting practices of which it was aware or should have been aware at the time of price negotiations and which it failed to disclose to the Government.

(b) If the parties fail to agree whether the Contractor or a subcontractor has complied with an applicable CAS or a CAS rule or regulation in 48 CFR Part 9903, and as to any cost adjustment demanded by the United States, such failure to agree will constitute a dispute under 41 U.S.C. chapter 71, Contract Disputes.

(c) The Contractor shall permit any authorized representatives of the Government to examine and make copies of any documents, papers, or records relating to compliance with the requirements of this clause.

(d) The Contractor shall include in all negotiated subcontracts which the Contractor enters into, the substance of this clause, except paragraph (b), and shall require such inclusion in all other subcontracts, of any tier, including the obligation to comply with all applicable CAS in effect on the subcontractor's award date or, if the subcontractor has submitted certified cost or pricing data, on the date of final agreement on price as shown on the subcontractor's signed Certificate of Current Cost or Pricing Data, except that—

(1) If the subcontract is awarded to a business unit which pursuant to 48 CFR 9903.201-2 is subject to other types of CAS coverage, the substance of the applicable clause set forth in 48 CFR 9903.201-4 shall be inserted;

(2) This requirement shall apply only to negotiated subcontracts in excess of $750,000; and

(3) The requirement shall not apply to negotiated subcontracts otherwise exempt from the requirement to include a CAS clause as specified in 48 CFR 9903.201-1.

(End of clause)

[FAC 90-38, 61 FR 18914, 4/29/96, effective 4/29/96; FAC 97-4, 63 FR 9048, 2/23/98,

effective 4/24/98; FAC 2005-27, 73 FR 53994, 9/17/2008, effective 10/17/2008; FAC 2005-36, 74 FR 40467, 8/11/2009, effective 8/11/2009; FAC 2005-45, 75 FR 53135, 8/30/2010, effective 10/1/2010; FAC 2005-59, 77 FR 27550, 5/10/2012, effective 5/10/2012; FAC 2005-73, 79 FR 24192, 4/29/2014, effective 5/29/2014; FAC 2005-83, 80 FR 38293, 7/2/2015, effective 10/1/2015; FAC 2005-89, 81 FR 45852, 7/14/2016, effective 8/15/2016]

52.230-6 Administration of Cost Accounting Standards.

As prescribed in 30.201-4(d)(1), insert the following clause:

ADMINISTRATION OF COST ACCOUNTING STANDARDS (JUL 2010)

For the purpose of administering the Cost Accounting Standards (CAS) requirements under this contract, the Contractor shall take the steps outlined in paragraphs (b) through (i) and (k) through (n) of this clause:

(a) *Definitions.* As used in this clause—

Affected CAS-covered contract or subcontract means a contract or subcontract subject to CAS rules and regulations for which a Contractor or subcontractor—

(1) Used one cost accounting practice to estimate costs and a changed cost accounting practice to accumulate and report costs under the contract or subcontract; or

(2) Used a noncompliant practice for purposes of estimating or accumulating and reporting costs under the contract or subcontract.

Cognizant Federal agency official (CFAO) means the Contracting Officer assigned by the cognizant Federal agency to administer the CAS.

Desirable change means a compliant change to a Contractor's established or disclosed cost accounting practices that the CFAO finds is desirable and not detrimental to the Government and is, therefore, not subject to the no increased cost prohibition provisions of CAS-covered contracts and subcontracts affected by the change.

Fixed-price contracts and subcontracts means—

(1) Fixed-price contracts and subcontracts described at FAR 16.202, 16.203, (except when price adjustments are based on actual costs of labor or material, described at 16.203-1(a)(2)), and 16.207;

(2) Fixed-price incentive contracts and subcontracts where the price is not adjusted based on actual costs incurred (FAR Subpart 16.4);

(3) Orders issued under indefinite-delivery contracts and subcontracts where final payment is not based on actual costs incurred (FAR Subpart 16.5); and

(4) The fixed-hourly rate portion of time-and-materials and labor-hours contracts and subcontracts (FAR Subpart 16.6).

Flexibly-priced contracts and subcontracts means—

(1) Fixed-price contracts and subcontracts described FAR 16.203-1(a)(2) at FAR 16.204, FAR 16.205, and FAR 16.206;

(2) Cost-reimbursement contracts and subcontracts (FAR Subpart 16.3);

(3) Incentive contracts and subcontracts where the price may be adjusted based on actual costs incurred (FAR Subpart 16.4);

(4) Orders issued under indefinite-delivery contracts and subcontracts where final payment is based on actual costs incurred (FAR Subpart 16.5); and

(5) The materials portion of time-and-materials contracts and subcontracts (FAR Subpart 16.6).

Noncompliance means a failure in estimating, accumulating, or reporting costs to—

(1) Comply with applicable CAS; or

(2) Consistently follow disclosed or established cost accounting practices.

Required change means—

(1) A change in cost accounting practice that a Contractor is required to make in order to comply with a CAS, or a modification or interpretation thereof, that subsequently becomes applicable to existing CAS-covered contracts or subcontracts due to the receipt of another CAS-covered contract or subcontract; or

(2) A prospective change to a disclosed or established cost accounting practice when the CFAO determines that the former practice was in compliance with applicable CAS and the change is necessary for the Contractor to remain in compliance.

Unilateral change means a change in cost accounting practice from one compliant practice to another compliant practice that a Contractor with a CAS-covered contract(s) or subcontract(s) elects to make that has not been deemed a desirable change by the CFAO and for which the Government will pay no aggregate increased costs.

(b) Submit to the CFAO a description of any cost accounting practice change as outlined in paragraphs (b)(1) through (3) of this clause (including revisions to the Disclosure Statement, if applicable), and any written statement that the cost impact of the change is immaterial. If a change in cost accounting practice is implemented without submitting the notice required by this paragraph, the CFAO may determine the change to be a failure to follow paragraph (a)(2) of the clause at FAR 52.230-2, Cost Accounting Standards; paragraph (a)(4) of the clause at FAR 52.230-3, Disclosure and Consistency of Cost Accounting Practices; paragraph (a)(4) of the clause at FAR 52.230-4, Disclosure and Consistency of Cost Accounting Practices—Foreign Concerns; or paragraph (a)(2) of the clause at FAR 52.230-5, Cost Accounting Standards—Educational Institution.

(1) When a description has been submitted for a change in cost accounting practice that is dependent on a contact award and that contract is subsequently awarded, notify the CFAO within 15 days after such award.

(2) For any change in cost accounting practice not covered by (b)(1) of this clause that is required in accordance with paragraphs (a)(3) and (a)(4)(i) of the clause at FAR 52.230-2; or paragraphs (a)(3), (a)(4)(i), or (a)(4)(iv) of the clause at FAR 52.230-5; submit a description of the change to the CFAO not less than 60 days (or such other date as may be mutually agreed to by the CFAO and the Contractor) before implementation of the change.

(3) For any change in cost accounting practices proposed in accordance with paragraph (a)(4)(ii) or (iii) of the clauses at FAR 52.230-2 and FAR 52.230-5; or with paragraph (a)(3) of the clauses at FAR 52.230-3 and FAR 52.230-4, submit a description of the change not less than 60 days (or such other date as may be mutually agreed to by the CFAO and the Contractor) before implementation of the change. If the change includes a proposed retroactive date submit supporting rationale.

(4) Submit a description of the change necessary to correct a failure to comply with an applicable CAS or to follow a disclosed practice (as contemplated by paragraph (a)(5) of the clause at FAR 52.230-2 and FAR 52.230-5; or by paragraph (a)(4) of the clauses at FAR 52.230-3 and FAR 52.230-4)—

(i) Within 60 days (or such other date as may be mutually agreed to by the CFAO and the Contractor) after the date of agreement with the CFAO that there is a noncompliance; or

(ii) In the event of Contractor disagreement, within 60 days after the CFAO notifies the Contractor of the determination of noncompliance.

(c) When requested by the CFAO, submit on or before a date specified by the CFAO—

(1) A general dollar magnitude (GDM) proposal in accordance with paragraph (d) or (g) of this clause. The Contractor may submit a detailed cost-impact (DCI) proposal in lieu of the requested GDM proposal provided the DCI proposal is in accordance with paragraph (e) or (h) of this clause;

(2) A detailed cost-impact (DCI) proposal in accordance with paragraph (e) or (h) of this clause;

(3) For any request for a desirable change that is based on the criteria in FAR 30.603-2(b)(3)(ii), the data necessary to demonstrate the required cost savings; and

(4) For any request for a desirable change that is based on criteria other than that in FAR 30.603-2(b)(3)(ii), a GDM proposal and any other data necessary for the CFAO to determine if the change is a desirable change.

(d) For any change in cost accounting practice subject to paragraph (b)(1), (b)(2), or (b)(3) of this clause, the GDM proposal shall—

(1) Calculate the cost impact in accordance with paragraph (f) of this clause;

(2) Use one or more of the following methods to determine the increase or decrease in cost accumulations:

(i) A representative sample of affected CAS-covered contracts and subcontracts.

(ii) The change in indirect rates multiplied by the total estimated base computed for each of the following groups:

(A) Fixed-price contracts and subcontracts.

(B) Flexibly-priced contracts and subcontracts.

(iii) Any other method that provides a reasonable approximation of the total increase or decrease in cost accumulations for all affected fixed-price and flexibly-priced contracts and subcontracts;

(3) Use a format acceptable to the CFAO but, as a minimum, include the following data:

(i) The estimated increase or decrease in cost accumulations by Executive agency, including any impact the change may have on contract and subcontract incentives, fees, and profits, for each of the following groups:

(A) Fixed-price contracts and subcontracts.

(B) Flexibly-priced contracts and subcontracts.

(ii) For unilateral changes, the increased or decreased costs to the Government for each of the following groups:

(A) Fixed-price contracts and subcontracts.

(B) Flexibly-priced contracts and subcontracts; and

(4) When requested by the CFAO, identify all affected CAS-covered contracts and subcontracts.

(e) For any change in cost accounting practice subject to paragraph (b)(1), (b)(2), or (b)(3) of this clause, the DCI proposal shall—

(1) Show the calculation of the cost impact in accordance with paragraph (f) of this clause;

(2) Show the estimated increase or decrease in cost accumulations for each affected CAS-covered contract and subcontract unless the CFAO and Contractor agree to include—

(i) Only those affected CAS-covered contracts and subcontracts having an estimate to complete exceeding a specified amount; and

(ii) An estimate of the total increase or decrease in cost accumulations for all affected CAS-covered contracts and subcontracts, using the results in paragraph (e)(2)(i) of this clause;

(3) Use a format acceptable to the CFAO but, as a minimum, include the information in paragraph (d)(3) of this clause; and

(4) When requested by the CFAO, identify all affected CAS-covered contracts and subcontracts.

(f) For GDM and DCI proposals that are subject to the requirements of paragraph (d) or (e) of this clause, calculate the cost impact as follows:

(1) The cost impact calculation shall include all affected CAS-covered contracts and subcontracts regardless of their status (*i.e.*, open or closed) or the fiscal year in which the costs were incurred (*i.e.*, whether or not the final indirect rates have been established).

(2) For unilateral changes—

(i) Determine the increased or decreased cost to the Government for flexibly-priced contracts and subcontracts as follows:

(A) When the estimated cost to complete using the changed practice exceeds the estimated cost to complete using the current practice, the difference is increased cost to the Government.

(B) When the estimated cost to complete using the changed practice is less than the estimated cost to complete using the current practice, the difference is decreased cost to the Government;

(ii) Determine the increased or decreased cost to the Government for fixed-priced contracts and subcontracts as follows:

(A) When the estimated cost to complete using the changed practice is less than the estimated cost to complete using the current practice, the difference is increased cost to the Government.

(B) When the estimated cost to complete using the changed practice exceeds the estimated cost to complete using the current practice, the difference is decreased cost to the Government;

(iii) Calculate the total increase or decrease in contract and subcontract incentives, fees, and profits associated with the increased or decreased costs to the Government in accordance with 48 CFR 9903.306(c). The associated increase or decrease is based on the difference between the negotiated incentives, fees, and profits and the amounts that would have been negotiated had the cost impact been known at the time the contracts and subcontracts were negotiated; and

(iv) Calculate the increased cost to the Government in the aggregate.

(3) For equitable adjustments for required or desirable changes—

(i) Estimated increased cost accumulations are the basis for increasing contract prices, target prices and cost ceilings; and

(ii) Estimated decreased cost accumulations are the basis for decreasing contract prices, target prices and cost ceilings.

(g) For any noncompliant cost accounting practice subject to paragraph (b)(4) of this clause, prepare the GDM proposal as follows:

(1) Calculate the cost impact in accordance with paragraph (i) of this clause.

(2) Use one or more of the following methods to determine the increase or decrease in contract and subcontract prices or cost accumulations, as applicable:

(i) A representative sample of affected CAS-covered contracts and subcontracts.

(ii) When the noncompliance involves cost accumulation the change in indirect rates multiplied by the applicable base for only flexibly-priced contracts and subcontracts.

(iii) Any other method that provides a reasonable approximation of the total increase or decrease.

(3) Use a format acceptable to the CFAO but, as a minimum, include the following data:

(i) The total increase or decrease in contract and subcontract price and cost accumulations, as applicable, by Executive agency, including any impact the noncompliance may have on contract and subcontract incentives, fees, and profits, for each of the following groups:

(A) Fixed-price contracts and subcontracts.

(B) Flexibly-priced contracts and subcontracts.

(ii) The increased or decreased cost to the Government for each of the following groups:

(A) Fixed-price contracts and subcontracts.

(B) Flexibly-priced contracts and subcontracts.

(iii) The total overpayments and underpayments made by the Government during the period of noncompliance.

(4) When requested by the CFAO, identify all CAS-covered contracts and subcontracts.

(h) For any noncompliant practice subject to paragraph (b)(4) of this clause, prepare the DCI proposal as follows:

(1) Calculate the cost impact in accordance with paragraph (i) of this clause.

(2) Show the increase or decrease in price and cost accumulations for each affected CAS-covered contract and subcontract unless the CFAO and Contractor agree to—

(i) Include only those affected CAS-covered contracts and subcontracts having—

(A) Contract and subcontract values exceeding a specified amount when the noncompliance involves estimating costs; and

(B) Incurred costs exceeding a specified amount when the noncompliance involves accumulating costs; and

(ii) Estimate the total increase or decrease in price and cost accumulations for all affected CAS-covered contracts and subcontracts using the results in paragraph (h) (2) (i) of this clause.

(3) Use a format acceptable to the CFAO that, as a minimum, include the information in paragraph (g) (3) of this clause.

(4) When requested by the CFAO, identify all CAS-covered contracts and subcontracts.

(i) For GDM and DCI proposals that are subject to the requirements of paragraph (g) or (h) of this clause, calculate the cost impact as follows:

(1) The cost impact calculation shall include all affected CAS-covered contracts and subcontracts regardless of their status (*i.e.*, open or closed) or the fiscal year in which the costs are incurred (*i.e.*, whether or not the final indirect rates have been established).

(2) For noncompliances that involve estimating costs, determine the increased or decreased cost to the Government for fixed-price contracts and subcontracts as follows:

(i) When the negotiated contract or subcontract price exceeds what the negotiated price would have been had the Contractor used a compliant practice, the difference is increased cost to the Government.

(ii) When the negotiated contract or subcontract price is less than what the negotiated price would have been had the Contractor used a compliant practice, the difference is decreased cost to the Government.

(3) For noncompliances that involve accumulating costs, determine the increased or decreased cost to the Government for flexibly-priced contracts and subcontracts as follows:

(i) When the costs that were accumulated under the noncompliant practice exceed the costs that would have been accumulated using a compliant practice (from the time the noncompliant practice was first implemented until the date the noncompliant practice was replaced with a compliant practice), the difference is increased cost to the Government.

(ii) When the costs that were accumulated under the noncompliant practice are less than the costs that would have been accumulated using a compliant practice (from the time the noncompliant practice was first implemented until the date the noncompliant practice was replaced with a compliant practice), the difference is decreased cost to the Government.

(4) Calculate the total increase or decrease in contract and subcontract incentives, fees, and profits associated with the increased or decreased cost to the Government in accordance with 48 CFR 9903.306(c). The associated increase or decrease is based on the difference between the negotiated incentives, fees, and profits and the amounts that would have been negotiated had the Contractor used a compliant practice.

(5) Calculate the increased cost to the Government in the aggregate.

(j) If the Contractor does not submit the information required by paragraph (b) or (c) of this clause within the specified time, or any extension granted by the CFAO, the CFAO may take one or both of the following actions:

(1) Withhold an amount not to exceed 10 percent of each subsequent amount payment to the Contractor's affected CAS-covered contracts, (up to the estimated general dollar magnitude of the cost impact), until such time as the Contractor provides the required information to the CFAO.

(2) Issue a final decision in accordance with FAR 33.211 and unilaterally adjust the contract(s) by the estimated amount of the cost impact.

(k) Agree to—

(1) Contract modifications to reflect adjustments required in accordance with paragraph (a) (4) (ii) or (a) (5) of the clauses at FAR 52.230-2 and 52.230-5; or with para-

graph (a)(3)(i) or (a)(4) of the clauses at FAR 52.230-3 and FAR 52.230-4; and

(2) Repay the Government for any aggregate increased cost paid to the Contractor.

(l) For all subcontracts subject to the clauses at FAR 52.230-2, 52.230-3, 52.230-4, or 52.230-5—

(1) So state in the body of the subcontract, in the letter of award, or in both (do not use self-deleting clauses);

(2) Include the substance of this clause in all negotiated subcontracts; and

(3) Within 30 days after award of the subcontract, submit the following information to the Contractor's CFAO:

(i) Subcontractor's name and subcontract number.

(ii) Dollar amount and date of award.

(iii) Name of Contractor making the award.

(m) Notify the CFAO in writing of any adjustments required to subcontracts under this contract and agree to an adjustment to this contract price or estimated cost and fee. The Contractor shall—

(1) Provide this notice within 30 days after the Contractor receives the proposed subcontract adjustments; and

(2) Include a proposal for adjusting the higher-tier subcontract or the contract appropriately.

(n) For subcontracts containing the clause or substance of the clause at FAR 52.230-2, FAR 52.230-3, FAR 52.230-4, or FAR 52.230-5, require the subcontractor to comply with all Standards in effect on the date of award or of final agreement on price, as shown on the subcontractor's signed Certificate of Current Cost or Pricing Data, whichever is earlier.

(End of clause)

[FAC 90-12, 57 FR 39593, 8/31/92, effective 8/31/92; Corrected, 57 FR 43495, 9/21/92; FAC 90-23, 59 FR 67010, 12/28/94, effective 2/27/95; Redesignated from 52.230-5, FAC 90-38, 61 FR 18914, 4/29/96, effective 4/29/96; FAC 97-14, 64 FR 51828, 9/24/99, effective 11/23/99; FAC 2005-01, 70 FR 11743, 3/9/2005, effective 4/8/2005; FAC 2005-24, 73 FR 19065, 2/28/2008, effective 3/31/2008; FAC 2005-42, 75 FR 34283, 6/16/2010, effective 6/16/2010; FAC 2005-50, 76 FR 14570, 3/16/2011, effective 3/16/2011]

52.230-7 Proposal Disclosure—Cost Accounting Practice Changes.

As prescribed in 30.201-3(c), insert the following provision:

PROPOSAL DISCLOSURE—COST ACCOUNTING PRACTICE CHANGES (APR 2005)

The offeror shall check "yes" below if the contract award will result in a required or unilateral change in cost accounting practice, including unilateral changes requested to be desirable changes.

☐ Yes ☐ No

If the offeror checked "Yes" above, the offeror shall—

(1) Prepare the price proposal in response to the solicitation using the changed practice for the period of performance for which the practice will be used; and

(2) Submit a description of the changed cost accounting practice to the Contracting Officer and the Cognizant Federal Agency Official as pricing support for the proposal.

(End of provision)

[FAC 2005-01, 70 FR 11743, 3/9/2005, effective 4/8/2005]

52.231 [Reserved]

52.232-1 Payments.

As prescribed in 32.111(a)(1), insert the following clause, appropriately modified with respect to payment due date in accordance with agency regulations, in solicitations and contracts when a fixed-price supply contract, a fixed-price service contract, or a contract for nonregulated communication services is contemplated.

PAYMENTS (APR 1984)

The Government shall pay the Contractor, upon the submission of proper invoices or vouchers, the prices stipulated in this contract for supplies delivered and accepted or services rendered and accepted, less any deductions provided in this contract. Unless otherwise specified in this contract, payment shall be made on partial deliveries accepted by the Government if—

(a) The amount due on the deliveries warrants it; or

(b) The Contractor requests it and the amount due on the deliveries is at least $1,000 or 50 percent of the total contract price.

(End of clause)

[FAC 90-7, 56 FR 41744, 8/22/91, effective 9/23/91; FAC 90-32, 60 FR 48206, 9/18/95, effective 10/1/95]

52.232-2 Payments under Fixed-Price Research and Development Contracts.

As prescribed in 32.111(a)(2), insert the following clause, as appropriately modified with respect to payment due dates in accordance with agency regulations, in solicitations and contracts when a fixed-price research and development contract is contemplated:

PAYMENTS UNDER FIXED-PRICE RESEARCH AND DEVELOPMENT CONTRACTS (APR 1984)

The Government shall pay the Contractor, upon submission of proper invoices or vouchers, the prices stipulated in this contract for work delivered or rendered and accepted, less any deductions provided in this contract. Unless otherwise specified, payment shall be made upon acceptance of any portion of the work delivered or rendered for which a price is separately stated in the contract.

(End of clause)

[FAC 90-32, 60 FR 48206, 9/18/95, effective 10/1/95]

52.232-3 Payments under Personal Services Contracts.

As prescribed in 32.111(a)(3), insert the following clause, appropriately modified with respect to payment due dates in accordance with agency regulations, in solicitations and contracts for personal services:

PAYMENTS UNDER PERSONAL SERVICES CONTRACTS (APR 1984)

The Government shall pay the Contractor for the services performed by the Contractor, as set forth in the Schedule of this contract, at the rates prescribed, upon the submission by the Contractor of proper invoices or time statements to the office or officer designated and at the time provided for in this contract. The Government shall also pay the Contractor (a) a per diem rate in lieu of subsistence for each day the Contractor is in a travel status away from home or regular place of employment in accordance with Federal Travel Regulations (41 CFR 101-7) as authorized in appropriate Travel Orders; and (b) any other transportation expenses if provided for in the Schedule.

(End of clause)

[FAC 90-32, 60 FR 48206, 9/18/95, effective 10/1/95]

52.232-4 Payments under Transportation Contracts and Transportation-Related Services Contracts.

As prescribed in 32.111(a)(4), insert the following clause, appropriately modified with respect to payment due dates in accordance with agency regulations, in solicitations and contracts for transportation or transportation-related services:

PAYMENTS UNDER TRANSPORTATION CONTRACTS AND TRANSPORTATION-RELATED SERVICES CONTRACTS (APR 1984)

The Government shall pay the Contractor upon the submission of properly certified invoices or vouchers, the amount due for services rendered and accepted, less deductions, if any, as herein provided.

(End of clause)

[FAC 90-32, 60 FR 48206, 9/18/95, effective 10/1/95]

52.232-5 Payments under Fixed-Price Construction Contracts.

As prescribed in 32.111(a)(5), insert the following clause:

PAYMENTS UNDER FIXED-PRICE CONSTRUCTION CONTRACTS (MAY 2014)

(a) *Payment of price*. The Government shall pay the Contractor the contract price as provided in this contract.

(b) *Progress payments*. The Government shall make progress payments monthly as the work proceeds, or at more frequent intervals as determined by the Contracting Officer, on estimates of work accomplished which meets the standards of quality established under the contract, as approved by the Contracting Officer.

(1) The Contractor's request for progress payments shall include the following substantiation:

(i) An itemization of the amounts requested, related to the various elements of work required by the contract covered by the payment requested.

(ii) A listing of the amount included for work performed by each subcontractor under the contract.

(iii) A listing of the total amount of each subcontract under the contract.

(iv) A listing of the amounts previously paid to each such subcontractor under the contract.

(v) Additional supporting data in a form and detail required by the Contracting Officer.

(2) In the preparation of estimates, the Contracting Officer may authorize material delivered on the site and preparatory work done to be taken into consideration. Material delivered to the Contractor at locations other than the site also may be taken into consideration if—

(i) Consideration is specifically authorized by this contract; and

(ii) The Contractor furnishes satisfactory evidence that it has acquired title to such material and that the material will be used to perform this contract.

(c) *Contractor certification*. Along with each request for progress payments, the Contractor shall furnish the following certification, or payment shall not be made: (However, if the Contractor elects to delete paragraph (c)(4) from the certification, the certification is still acceptable.)

I hereby certify, to the best of my knowledge and belief, that—

(1) The amounts requested are only for performance in accordance with the specifications, terms, and conditions of the contract;

(2) All payments due to subcontractors and suppliers from previous payments received under the contract have been made, and timely payments will be made from the proceeds of the payment covered by this certification, in accordance with subcontract agreements and the requirements of chapter 39 of Title 31, United States Code;

(3) This request for progress payments does not include any amounts which the prime contractor intends to withhold or retain from a subcontractor or supplier in accordance with the terms and conditions of the subcontract; and

(4) This certification is not to be construed as final acceptance of a subcontractor's performance.

____

(Name)

____

(Title)

____

(Date)

(d) *Refund of unearned amounts*. If the Contractor, after making a certified request for progress payments, discovers that a portion or all of such request constitutes a payment for performance by the Contractor that fails to conform to the specifications, terms, and conditions of this contract (hereinafter referred to as the "unearned amount"), the Contractor shall—

(1) Notify the Contracting Officer of such performance deficiency; and

(2) Be obligated to pay the Government an amount (computed by the Contracting Officer in the manner provided in paragraph (j) of this clause) equal to interest on the unearned amount from the 8th day after the

date of receipt of the unearned amount until—

(i) The date the Contractor notifies the Contracting Officer that the performance deficiency has been corrected; or

(ii) The date the Contractor reduces the amount of any subsequent certified request for progress payments by an amount equal to the unearned amount.

(e) *Retainage.* If the Contracting Officer finds that satisfactory progress was achieved during any period for which a progress payment is to be made, the Contracting Officer shall authorize payment to be made in full. However, if satisfactory progress has not been made, the Contracting Officer may retain a maximum of 10 percent of the amount of the payment until satisfactory progress is achieved. When the work is substantially complete, the Contracting Officer may retain from previously withheld funds and future progress payments that amount the Contracting Officer considers adequate for protection of the Government and shall release to the Contractor all the remaining withheld funds. Also, on completion and acceptance of each separate building, public work, or other division of the contract, for which the price is stated separately in the contract, payment shall be made for the completed work without retention of a percentage.

(f) *Title, liability, and reservation of rights.* All material and work covered by progress payments made shall, at the time of payment, become the sole property of the Government, but this shall not be construed as—

(1) Relieving the Contractor from the sole responsibility for all material and work upon which payments have been made or the restoration of any damaged work; or

(2) Waiving the right of the Government to require the fulfillment of all of the terms of the contract.

(g) *Reimbursement for bond premiums.* In making these progress payments, the Government shall, upon request, reimburse the Contractor for the amount of premiums paid for performance and payment bonds (including coinsurance and reinsurance agreements, when applicable) after the Contractor has furnished evidence of full payment to the surety. The retainage provisions in paragraph (e) of this clause shall not apply to that portion of progress payments attributable to bond premiums.

(h) *Final payment.* The Government shall pay the amount due the Contractor under this contract after—

(1) Completion and acceptance of all work;

(2) Presentation of a properly executed voucher; and

(3) Presentation of release of all claims against the Government arising by virtue of this contract, other than claims, in stated amounts, that the Contractor has specifically excepted from the operation of the release. A release may also be required of the assignee if the Contractor's claim to amounts payable under this contract has been assigned under the Assignment of Claims Act of 1940 (31 U.S.C. 3727 and 41 U.S.C. 6305).

(i) *Limitation because of undefinitized work.* Notwithstanding any provision of this contract, progress payments shall not exceed 80 percent on work accomplished on undefinitized contract actions. A "contract action" is any action resulting in a contract, as defined in FAR Subpart 2.1, including contract modifications for additional supplies or services, but not including contract modifications that are within the scope and under the terms of the contract, such as contract modifications issued pursuant to the Changes clause, or funding and other administrative changes.

(j) *Interest computation on unearned amounts.* In accordance with 31 U.S.C. 3903(c)(1), the amount payable under subparagraph (d)(2) of this clause shall be—

(1) Computed at the rate of average bond equivalent rates of 91-day Treasury bills auctioned at the most recent auction of such bills prior to the date the Contractor receives the unearned amount; and

(2) Deducted from the next available payment to the Contractor.

(End of clause)

[FAC 84-8, 50 FR 26904, 6/28/85, effective 7/1/85; FAC 84-12, 51 FR 2666, 1/17/86, effective 1/20/86; FAC 84-16, 51 FR 19717, 5/30/86, effective 5/30/86; FAC 84-29, 52 FR 30078, 8/12/87, effective 8/24/87; FAC 84-45, 54 FR 13337, 3/31/89, effective 4/1/89; FAC 90-46, 62 FR 12689, 3/17/97, effective 5/16/97; FAC 2001-09, 67 FR 56115, 8/30/2002, effective 8/30/2002; FAC 2005-73, 79 FR 24192, 4/29/2014, effective 5/29/2014]

52.232-6 Payment under Communication Service Contracts with Common Carriers.

As prescribed in 32.111(a)(6), insert the following clause, appropriately modified with respect to payment due dates in accordance with agency regulations, in solicitations and contracts for regulated communication services by common carriers:

PAYMENT UNDER COMMUNICATION SERVICE CONTRACTS WITH COMMON CARRIERS (APR 1984)

The Government shall pay the Contractor, in arrears, upon submission of invoices for services and facilities furnished in accordance with the terms of CSAs issued under this contract, the rates and charges for the services and facilities as set forth in the clause entitled "Rates, Charges and Services."

(End of clause)

[FAC 90-32, 60 FR 48206, 9/18/95, effective 10/1/95]

52.232-7 Payments under Time-and-Materials and Labor-Hour Contracts.

As prescribed in 32.111(a)(7), insert the following clause:

PAYMENTS UNDER TIME-AND-MATERIALS AND LABOR-HOUR CONTRACTS (AUG 2012)

The Government will pay the Contractor as follows upon the submission of vouchers approved by the Contracting Officer or the authorized representative:

(a) *Hourly rate.* (1) *Hourly rate* means the rate(s) prescribed in the contract for payment for labor that meets the labor category qualifications of a labor category specified in the contract that are—

(i) Performed by the Contractor;

(ii) Performed by the subcontractors; or

(iii) Transferred between divisions, subsidiaries, or affiliates of the Contractor under a common control.

(2) The amounts shall be computed by multiplying the appropriate hourly rates prescribed in the Schedule by the number of direct labor hours performed.

(3) The hourly rates shall be paid for all labor performed on the contract that meets the labor qualifications specified in the contract. Labor hours incurred to perform tasks for which labor qualifications were specified in the contract will not be paid to the extent the work is performed by employees that do not meet the qualifications specified in the contract, unless specifically authorized by the Contracting Officer.

(4) The hourly rates shall include wages, indirect costs, general and administrative expense, and profit. Fractional parts of an hour shall be payable on a prorated basis.

(5) Vouchers may be submitted not more than once every two weeks, to the Contracting Officer or authorized representative. A small business concern may receive more frequent payments than every two weeks. The Contractor shall substantiate vouchers (including any subcontractor hours reimbursed at the hourly rate in the schedule) by evidence of actual payment and by—

(i) Individual daily job timekeeping records;

(ii) Records that verify the employees meet the qualifications for the labor categories specified in the contract; or

(iii) Other substantiation approved by the Contracting Officer.

(6) Promptly after receipt of each substantiated voucher, the Government shall, except as otherwise provided in this contract, and subject to the terms of paragraph (e) of this clause, pay the voucher as approved by the Contracting Officer or authorized representative.

(7) Unless otherwise prescribed in the Schedule, the Contracting Officer may unilaterally issue a contract modification requiring the Contractor to withhold amounts from its billings until a reserve is set aside in an amount that the Contracting Officer considers necessary to protect the Government's interests. The Contracting Officer may require a withhold of 5 percent of the amounts due under paragraph (a) of this clause, but the total amount withheld for the contract shall not exceed $50,000. The amounts withheld shall be retained until the Contractor executes and delivers the release required by paragraph (g) of this clause.

(8) Unless the Schedule prescribes otherwise, the hourly rates in the Schedule shall not be varied by virtue of the Contractor having performed work on an overtime basis. If no overtime rates are provided in the Schedule and overtime work is approved in advance by the Contracting Officer, overtime rates shall be negotiated. Failure to agree upon these overtime rates shall be treated as a dispute under the Disputes clause of this contract. If the Schedule provides rates for overtime, the premium portion of those rates will be reimbursable only to the extent the overtime is approved by the Contracting Officer.

(b) *Materials.* (1) For the purposes of this clause—

(i) *Direct materials* means those materials that enter directly into the end product, or that are used or consumed directly in connection with the furnishing of the end product or service.

(ii) *Materials* means—

(A) Direct materials, including supplies transferred between divisions, subsidiaries, or affiliates of the Contractor under a common control;

(B) Subcontracts for supplies and incidental services for which there is not a labor category specified in the contract;

(C) Other direct costs (e.g., incidental services for which there is not a labor category specified in the contract, travel, computer usage charges, etc.); and

(D) Applicable indirect costs.

(2) If the Contractor furnishes its own materials that meet the definition of a commercial item at 2.101, the price to be paid for such materials shall not exceed the Contractor's established catalog or market price, adjusted to reflect the—

(i) Quantities being acquired; and

(ii) Actual cost of any modifications necessary because of contract requirements.

(3) Except as provided for in paragraph (b)(2) of this clause, the Government will reimburse the Contractor for allowable cost of materials provided the Contractor—

(i) Has made payments for materials in accordance with the terms and conditions of the agreement or invoice; or

(ii) Ordinarily makes these payments within 30 days of the submission of the Contractor's payment request to the Government and such payment is in accordance with the terms and conditions of the agreement or invoice.

(4) Payment for materials is subject to the Allowable Cost and Payment clause of this contract. The Contracting Officer will determine allowable costs of materials in accordance with Subpart 31.2 of the Federal Acquisition Regulation (FAR) in effect on the date of this contract.

(5) The Contractor may include allocable indirect costs and other direct costs to the extent they are—

(i) Comprised only of costs that are clearly excluded from the hourly rate;

(ii) Allocated in accordance with the Contractor's written or established accounting practices; and

(iii) Indirect costs are not applied to subcontracts that are paid at the hourly rates.

(6) To the extent able, the Contractor shall—

(i) Obtain materials at the most advantageous prices available with due regard to securing prompt delivery of satisfactory materials; and

(ii) Take all cash and trade discounts, rebates, allowances, credits, salvage, commissions, and other benefits. When unable to take advantage of the benefits, the Contractor shall promptly notify the Contracting Officer and give the reasons. The Contractor shall give credit to the Government for cash and trade discounts, rebates, scrap, commissions, and other amounts that have accrued to the benefit of the Contractor, or would have accrued except for the fault or neglect of the Contractor. The Contractor shall not deduct from gross costs the benefits lost without fault or neglect on the part of the Contractor, or lost through fault of the Government.

(7) Except as provided for in 31.205-26(e) and (f), the Government will not pay profit or fee to the prime Contractor on materials.

(c) If the Contractor enters into any subcontract that requires consent under the clause at 52.244-2, Subcontracts, without obtaining such consent, the Government is not required to reimburse the Contractor for any costs incurred under the subcontract prior to the date the Contractor obtains the required consent. Any reimbursement of subcontract costs incurred prior to the date the consent was obtained shall be at the sole discretion of the Government.

(d) *Total cost.* It is estimated that the total cost to the Government for the performance of this contract shall not exceed the ceiling price set forth in the Schedule, and the Contractor agrees to use its best efforts to perform the work specified in the Schedule and all obligations under this contract within such ceiling price. If at any time the Contractor has reason to believe that the hourly rate payments and material costs that will accrue in performing this contract in the next succeeding 30 days, if added to all other payments and costs previously accrued, will exceed 85 percent of the ceiling price in the Schedule, the Contractor shall notify the Contracting Officer giving a revised estimate of the total price to the Government for performing this contract with supporting reasons and documentation. If at any time during performing this contract, the Contractor has reason to believe that the total price to the Government for performing this contract will be substantially greater or less than the then stated ceiling price, the Contractor shall so notify the Contracting Officer, giving a revised estimate of the total price for performing this contract, with supporting reasons and documentation. If at any time during performing this contract, the Government has reason to believe that the work to be required in performing this contract will be substantially greater or less than the stated ceiling price, the Contracting Officer will so advise the Contractor, giving the then revised estimate of the total amount of effort to be required under the contract.

(e) *Ceiling price.* The Government will not be obligated to pay the Contractor any amount in excess of the ceiling price in the Schedule, and the Contractor shall not be obligated to continue performance if to do so would exceed the ceiling price set forth in the Schedule, unless and until the Contracting Officer notifies the Contractor in writing that the ceiling price has been increased and specifies in the notice a revised ceiling that shall constitute the ceiling price for performance under this contract. When and to the extent that the ceiling price set forth in the Schedule has been increased, any hours expended and material costs incurred by the Contractor in excess of the ceiling price before the increase shall be allowable to the same extent as if the hours expended and material costs had been incurred after the increase in the ceiling price.

(f) *Audit.* At any time before final payment under this contract, the Contracting Officer may request audit of the vouchers and supporting documentation. Each payment previously made shall be subject to reduction to the extent of amounts, on preceding vouchers, that are found by the Contracting Officer or authorized representative not to have been properly payable and shall also be subject to reduction for overpayments or to increase for underpayments. Upon receipt and approval of the voucher designated by the Contractor as the "completion voucher" and supporting documentation, and upon compliance by the Contractor with all terms of this contract (including, without limitation, terms relating to patents and the terms of paragraph (g) of this clause), the Government shall promptly pay any balance due the Contractor. The completion voucher, and supporting documentation, shall be submitted by the Contractor as promptly as practicable following completion of the work under this contract, but in no event later than 120 days (or such longer period as the Contracting Officer may approve in writing) from the date of completion.

(g) *Assignment and Release of Claims.* The Contractor, and each assignee under an assignment entered into under this contract and in effect at the time of final payment under this contract, shall execute and deliver, at the time of and as a condition precedent to final payment under this contract, a release discharging the Government, its officers, agents, and employees of and from all liabilities, obligations, and claims arising out of or under this contract, subject only to the following exceptions:

(1) Specified claims in stated amounts, or in estimated amounts if the amounts are not susceptible of exact statement by the Contractor.

(2) Claims, together with reasonable incidental expenses, based upon the liabilities of the Contractor to third parties arising out of performing this contract, that are not known to the Contractor on the date of the execution of the release, and of which the Contractor gives notice in writing to the Contracting Officer not more than 6 years after the date of the release or the date of any notice to the Contractor that the Government is prepared to make final payment, whichever is earlier.

(3) Claims for reimbursement of costs (other than expenses of the Contractor by reason of its indemnification of the Government against patent liability), including reasonable incidental expenses, incurred by the Contractor under the terms of this contract relating to patents.

(h) *Interim payments on contracts for other than services.* (1) Interim payments made prior to the final payment under the contract are contract financing payments. Contract financing payments are not subject to the interest penalty provisions of the Prompt Payment Act.

(2) The designated payment office will make interim payments for contract financing on the ________ [*Contracting Officer insert day as prescribed by agency head; if not prescribed, insert "30th"*] day after the designated billing office receives a proper payment request. In the event that the Government requires an audit or other review of a specific payment request to ensure compliance with the terms and conditions of the contract, the designated payment office is not compelled to make payment by the specified due date.

(i) *Interim payments on contracts for services.* For interim payments made prior to the final payment under this contract, the Government will make payment in accordance with the Prompt Payment Act (31 U.S.C. 3903) and prompt payment regulations at 5 CFR part 1315.

(End of clause)

[FAC 84-12, 51 FR 2667, 1/17/86, effective 1/20/86; FAC 90-32, 60 FR 48206, 9/18/95, effective 10/1/95; FAC 90-43, Final rule, 61 FR 67408, 12/20/96, effective 2/18/97; FAC 97-16, 65 FR 16274, 3/27/2000, effective 3/27/2000; FAC 2001-02, 66 FR 65347, 12/18/2001, effective 2/19/2002; FAC 2001-10, 67 FR 70520, 11/22/2002, effective 12/23/2002; FAC 2005-05, 70 FR 43580, 7/27/2005, effective 8/26/2005; FAC 2005-15, 71 FR 74656, 12/12/2006, effective 2/12/2007; Final rule, 72 FR 6881, 2/13/2007, effective 2/12/2007; FAC 2005-60, 77 FR 44059, 7/26/2012, effective 8/27/2012]

52.232-8 Discounts for Prompt Payment.

As prescribed in 32.111(b)(1), insert the following clause:

DISCOUNTS FOR PROMPT PAYMENT (FEB 2002)

(a) Discounts for prompt payment will not be considered in the evaluation of offers. However, any offered discount will form a part of the award, and will be taken if payment is made within the discount period indicated in the offer by the offeror. As an alternative to offering a discount for prompt payment in conjunction with the offer, offerors awarded contracts may include discounts for prompt payment on individual invoices.

(b) In connection with any discount offered for prompt payment, time shall be computed from the date of the invoice. If the Contractor has not placed a date on the invoice, the due date shall be calculated from the date the designated billing office receives a proper invoice, provided the agency annotates such invoice with the date of receipt at the time of receipt. For the purpose of computing the discount earned, payment shall be considered to have been made on the date that appears on the payment check or, for an electronic funds transfer, the specified payment date. When the discount date falls on a Saturday, Sunday, or legal holiday when Federal Government offices are closed and Government business is not expected to be conducted, payment may be made on the following business day.

(End of clause)

[FAC 84-8, 50 FR 26904, 6/28/85, effective 7/1/85; FAC 84-45, 54 FR 13337, 3/31/89, effective 4/1/89; FAC 90-46, 62 FR 12690, 3/17/97, effective 5/16/97; FAC 2001-02, 66 FR 65347, 12/18/2001, effective 2/19/2001; FAC 2005-05, 70 FR 43580, 7/27/2005, effective 8/26/2005]

52.232-9 Limitation on Withholding of Payments.

As prescribed in 32.111(b)(2), insert a clause substantially as follows, appropriately modified with respect to payment due dates in accordance with agency regulations, in solicitations and contracts when a supply contract, service contract, time-and-materials contract, labor-hour contract, or research and development contract is contemplated that includes two or more terms authorizing the temporary withholding of amounts otherwise payable to the contractor for supplies delivered or services performed:

LIMITATION ON WITHHOLDING OF PAYMENTS (APR 1984)

If more than one clause or Schedule term of this contract authorizes the temporary withholding of amounts otherwise payable to the Contractor for supplies delivered or services performed, the total of the amounts withheld at any one time shall not exceed the greatest amount that may be withheld under any one clause or Schedule term at that time; *provided*, that this limitation shall not apply to—

(a) Withholdings pursuant to any clause relating to wages or hours of employees;

(b) Withholdings not specifically provided for by this contract;

(c) The recovery of overpayments; and

(d) Any other withholding for which the Contracting Officer determines that this limitation is inappropriate.

(End of clause)

[FAC 90-32, 60 FR 48206, 9/18/95, effective 10/1/95; FAC 2005-05, 70 FR 43580, 7/27/2005, effective 8/26/2005]

52.232-10 Payments under Fixed-Price Architect-Engineer Contracts.

As prescribed in 32.111(c)(1), insert the following clause:

PAYMENTS UNDER FIXED-PRICE ARCHITECT-ENGINEER CONTRACTS (APR 2010)

(a) Estimates shall be made monthly of the amount and value of the work and services performed by the Contractor under this contract which meet the standards of quality established under this contract. The estimates, along with any supporting data required by the Contracting Officer, shall be prepared by the Contractor and submitted along with its voucher.

(b) After receipt of each substantiated voucher, the Government shall pay the voucher as approved by the Contracting Officer or authorized representative. The Contracting Officer shall require a withholding from amounts due under paragraph (a) of this clause of up to 10 percent only if the Contracting Officer determines that such a withholding is necessary to protect the Government's interest and ensure satisfactory completion of the contract. The amount withheld shall be determined based upon the Contractor's performance record under this contract. Whenever the Contracting Officer determines that the work is substantially complete and that the amount retained is in excess of the amount adequate for the protection of the Government, the Contracting

Officer shall release the excess amount to the Contractor.

(c) Upon satisfactory completion by the Contractor and final acceptance by the Contracting Officer of all the work done by the Contractor under the "Statement of Architect-Engineer Services", the Contractor will be paid the unpaid balance of any money due for work under the statement, including all withheld amounts.

(d) Before final payment under the contract, or before settlement upon termination of the contract, and as a condition precedent thereto, the Contractor shall execute and deliver to the Contracting Officer a release of all claims against the Government arising under or by virtue of this contract, other than any claims that are specifically excepted by the Contractor from the operation of the release in amounts stated in the release.

(e) Notwithstanding any other provision in this contract, and specifically paragraph (b) of this clause, progress payments shall not exceed 80 percent on work accomplished on undefinitized contract actions. A *contract action* is any action resulting in a contract, as defined in FAR Subpart 2.1, including contract modifications for additional supplies or services, but not including contract modifications that are within the scope and under the terms of the contract, such as contract modifications issued pursuant to the Changes clause, or funding and other administrative changes.

(End of clause)

[FAC 84-8, 50 FR 26904, 6/28/85, effective 7/1/85; FAC 84-29, 52 FR 30078, 8/12/87, effective 8/24/87; Final rule, 55 FR 38518, 9/18/90; FAC 2005-05, 70 FR 43580, 7/27/2005, effective 8/26/2005; FAC 2005-39, 75 FR 13422, 3/19/2010, effective 4/19/2010]

52.232-11 Extras.

As prescribed in 32.111(c)(2), insert the following clause, appropriately modified with respect to payment due dates in accordance with agency regulations, in solicitations and contracts when a fixed-price supply contract, fixed-price service contract, or transportation contract is contemplated:

EXTRAS (APR 1984)

Except as otherwise provided in this contract, no payment for extras shall be made unless such extras and the price therefor have been authorized in writing by the Contracting Officer.

(End of clause)

[FAC 90-32, 60 FR 48206, 9/18/95, effective 10/1/95; FAC 2005-05, 70 FR 43580, 7/27/2005, effective 8/26/2005]

52.232-12 Advance Payments.

As prescribed in 32.412(a), insert the following clause:

ADVANCE PAYMENTS (MAR 2001)

(a) *Requirements for payment.* Advance payments will be made under this contract (1) upon submission of properly certified invoices or vouchers by the Contractor, and approval by the administering office, ____ [*Insert the name of the office designated under agency procedures*], or (2) under a letter of credit. The amount of the invoice or voucher submitted plus all advance payments previously approved shall not exceed $____ If a letter of credit is used, the Contractor shall withdraw cash only when needed for disbursements acceptable under this contract and report cash disbursements and balances as required by the administering office. The Contractor shall apply terms similar to this clause to any advance payments to subcontractors.

(b) *Special bank account.* Until (1) the Contractor has liquidated all advance payments made under the contract and related interest charges and (2) the administering office has approved in writing the release of any funds due and payable to the Contractor, all advance payments and other payments under this contract shall be made by check payable to the Contractor marked for deposit only in the Contractor's special account with the ____ [*insert the name of the financial institution*]. None of the funds in the special account shall be mingled with other funds of the Contractor. Withdrawals from the special account may be made only by check of the Contractor countersigned by the Contracting Officer or a Government countersigning agent designated in writing by the Contracting Officer.

(c) *Use of funds.* The Contractor may withdraw funds from the special account only to pay for properly allocable, allowable, and reasonable costs for direct materials, direct labor, and indirect costs. Other withdrawals require approval in writing by the administering office. Determinations of whether costs are properly allocable, allowable, and reasonable shall be in accordance with generally accepted accounting principles, subject to any applicable subparts of Part 31 of the Federal Acquisition Regulation.

(d) *Repayment to the Government.* At any time, the Contractor may repay all or any part of the funds advanced by the Government. Whenever requested in writing to do so by the administering office, the Contractor shall repay to the Government any part of unliquidated advance payments considered by the administering office to exceed the Contractor's current requirements or the amount specified in paragraph (a) above. If the Contractor fails to repay the amount requested by the administering office, all or any part of the unliquidated advance payments may be withdrawn from the special account by check signed by only the countersigning agent and applied to reduction of the unliquidated advance payments under this contract.

(e) *Maximum payment.* When the sum of all unliquidated advance payments, unpaid interest charges, and other payments exceed $_ percent of the contract price, the Government shall withhold further payments to the Contractor. On completion or termination of the contract, the Government shall deduct from the amount due to the Contractor all unliquidated advance payments and all interest charges payable. If previous payments to the Contractor exceed the amount due, the excess amount shall be paid to the Government on demand. For purposes of this paragraph, the contract price shall be considered to be the stated contract price of $_____, less any subsequent price reductions under the contract, plus (1) any price increases resulting from any terms of this contract for price redetermination or escalation, and (2) any other price increases that do not, in the aggregate, exceed $_____ [*Insert an amount not higher than 10 percent of the stated contract amount inserted in this paragraph*]. Any payments withheld under this paragraph shall be applied to reduce the unliquidated advance payments. If full liquidation has been made, payments under the contract shall resume.

(f) *Interest.* (1) The Contractor shall pay interest to the Government on the daily unliquidated advance payments at the daily rate specified in subparagraph (f)(3) below. Interest shall be computed at the end of each calendar month for the actual number of days involved. For the purpose of computing the interest charge—

(i) Advance payments shall be considered as increasing the unliquidated balance as of the date of the advance payment check;

(ii) Repayments by Contractor check shall be considered as decreasing the unliquidated balance as of the date on which the check is received by the Government authority designated by the Contracting Officer; and

(iii) Liquidations by deductions from Government payments to the Contractor shall be considered as decreasing the unliquidated balance as of the date of the check for the reduced payment.

(2) Interest charges resulting from the monthly computation shall be deducted from payments, other than advance payments, due the Contractor. If the accrued interest exceeds the payment due, any excess interest shall be carried forward and deducted from subsequent payments. Interest carried forward shall not be compounded. Interest on advance payments shall cease to accrue upon satisfactory completion or termination of the contract for the convenience of the Government. The Contractor shall charge interest on advance payments to subcontractors in the manner described above and credit the interest to the Government. Interest need not be charged on advance payments to nonprofit educational or research subcontractors for experimental, developmental, or research work.

(3) If interest is required under the contract, the Contracting Officer shall determine a daily interest rate based on the higher of (i) the published prime rate of the financial institution (depository) in which the special account is established or (ii) the rate established by the Secretary of the Treasury under Pub. L. 92-41 (50 U.S.C. App. 1215(b)(2)). The Contracting Officer shall revise the daily interest rate during the contract period in keeping with any changes in the cited interest rates.

(4) If the full amount of interest charged under this paragraph has not been paid by deduction or otherwise upon completion or termination of this contract, the Contractor shall pay the remaining interest to the Government on demand.

(g) *Financial institution agreement.* Before an advance payment is made under this contract, the Contractor shall transmit to the administering office, in the form prescribed by the administering office, an agreement in triplicate from the financial institution in which the special account is established, clearly setting forth the special character of the account and the responsibilities of the financial institution under the account. The Contractor shall select a financial institution that is a member bank of the Federal Reserve System, is an "insured" bank within the meaning of the Federal Deposit Insurance Corporation Act (12 U.S.C. 1811), or a credit union insured by the National Credit Union Administration.

(h) *Lien on special bank account.* The Government shall have a lien upon any balance in the special account paramount to all other liens. The Government lien shall secure the repayment of any advance payments made under this contract and any related interest charges.

(i) *Lien on property under contract.* (1) All advance payments under this contract, together with interest charges, shall be secured, when made, by a lien in favor of the Government, paramount to all other liens, on the supplies or other things covered by this contract and on material and other property acquired for or allocated to the performance of this contract, except to the extent that the Government by virtue of any other terms of this contract, or otherwise, shall have valid title to the supplies, materials, or other property as against other creditors of the Contractor.

(2) The Contractor shall identify, by marking or segregation, all property that is subject to a lien in favor of the Government by virtue of any terms of this contract in such a way as to indicate that it is subject to a lien and that it has been acquired for or allocated to performing this contract. If, for any reason, the supplies, materials, or other property are not identified by marking or segregation, the Government shall be considered to have a lien to the extent of the Government's interest under this contract on any mass of property with which the supplies, materials, or other property are commingled. The Contractor shall maintain adequate accounting control over the property on its books and records.

(3) If, at any time during the progress of the work on the contract, it becomes necessary to deliver to a third person any items or materials on which the Government has a lien, the Contractor shall notify the third person of the lien and shall obtain from the third person a receipt in duplicate acknowledging the existence of the lien. The Contractor shall provide a copy of each receipt to the Contracting Officer.

(4) If, under the termination clause, the Contracting Officer authorizes the Contractor to sell or retain termination inventory, the approval shall constitute a release of the Government's lien to the extent that—

(i) The termination inventory is sold or retained; and

(ii) The sale proceeds or retention credits are applied to reduce any outstanding advance payments.

(j) *Insurance.* (1) The Contractor shall maintain with responsible insurance carriers—

(i) Insurance on plant and equipment against fire and other hazards, to the extent that similar properties are usually insured by others operating plants and properties of similar character in the same general locality;

(ii) Adequate insurance against liability on account of damage to persons or property; and

(iii) Adequate insurance under all applicable workers' compensation laws.

(2) Until work under this contract has been completed and all advance payments made under the contract have been liquidated, the Contractor shall—

(i) Maintain this insurance;

(ii) Maintain adequate insurance on any materials, parts, assemblies, subassemblies, supplies, equipment, and other property acquired for or allocable to this contract and subject to the Government lien under paragraph (i) of this clause; and

(iii) Furnish any evidence with respect to its insurance that the administering office may require.

(k) *Default.* (1) If any of the following events occurs, the Government may, by written notice to the Contractor, withhold further withdrawals from the special account and further payments on this contract:

(i) Termination of this contract for a fault of the Contractor.

(ii) A finding by the administering office that the Contractor has failed to—

(A) Observe any of the conditions of the advance payment terms;

(B) Comply with any material term of this contract;

(C) Make progress or maintain a financial condition adequate for performance of this contract;

(D) Limit inventory allocated to this contract to reasonable requirements; or

(E) Avoid delinquency in payment of taxes or of the costs of performing this contract in the ordinary course of business.

(iii) The appointment of a trustee, receiver, or liquidator for all or a substantial part of the Contractor's property, or the institution of proceedings by or against the Contractor for bankruptcy, reorganization, arrangement, or liquidation.

(iv) The service of any writ of attachment, levy of execution, or commencement of garnishment proceedings concerning the special bank account.

(v) The commission of an act of bankruptcy.

(2) If any of the events described in subparagraph (1) above continue for 30 days after the written notice to the Contractor, the Government may take any of the following additional actions:

(i) Withdraw by checks payable to the Treasurer of the United States, signed only by the countersigning agency, all or any part of the balance in the special account and apply the amounts to reduce outstanding advance payments and any other claims of the Government against the Contractor.

(ii) Charge interest, in the manner prescribed in paragraph (f) above, on outstanding advance payments during the period of any event described in subparagraph (k) (1) of this clause.

(iii) Demand immediate repayment by the Contractor of the unliquidated balance of advance payments.

(iv) Take possession of and, with or without advertisement, sell at public or private sale all or any part of the property on which the Government has a lien under this contract and, after deducting any expenses incident to the sale, apply the net proceeds of the sale to reduce the unliquidated balance of advance payments or other Government claims against the Contractor.

(3) The Government may take any of the actions described in subparagraphs (k) (1) and (2) of this clause it considers appropriate at its discretion and without limiting any other rights of the Government.

(l) *Prohibition against assignment.* Notwithstanding any other terms of this contract, the Contractor shall not assign this contract, any interest therein, or any claim under the contract to any party.

(m) *Information and access to records.* The Contractor shall furnish to the administering office (1) monthly or at other intervals as required, signed or certified balance sheets and profit and loss statements together with a report on the operation of the special bank account in the form prescribed by the administering office; and (2) if requested, other information concerning the operation of the Contractor's business. The Contractor shall provide the authorized Government representatives proper facilities for inspection of the Contractor's books, records, and accounts.

(n) *Other security*. The terms of this contract are considered to provide adequate security to the Government for advance payments; however, if the administering office considers the security inadequate, the Contractor shall furnish additional security satisfactory to the administering office, to the extent that the security is available.

(o) *Representations*. The Contractor represents the following:

(1) The balance sheet, the profit and loss statement, and any other supporting financial statements furnished to the administering office fairly reflect the financial condition of the Contractor at the date shown or the period covered, and there has been no subsequent materially adverse change in the financial condition of the Contractor.

(2) No litigation or proceedings are presently pending or threatened against the Contractor, except as shown in the financial statements.

(3) The Contractor has disclosed all contingent liabilities, except for liability resulting from the renegotiation of defense production contracts, in the financial statements furnished to the administering office.

(4) None of the terms in this clause conflict with the authority under which the Contractor is doing business or with the provision of any existing indenture or agreement of the Contractor.

(5) The Contractor has the power to enter into this contract and accept advance payments, and has taken all necessary action to authorize the acceptance under the terms of this contract.

(6) The assets of the Contractor are not subject to any lien or encumbrance of any character except for current taxes not delinquent, and except as shown in the financial statements furnished by the Contractor. There is no current assignment of claims under any contract affected by these advance payment provisions.

(7) All information furnished by the Contractor to the administering office in connection with each request for advance payments is true and correct.

(8) These representations shall be continuing and shall be considered to have been repeated by the submission of each invoice for advance payments.

(p) *Covenants*. To the extent the Government considers it necessary while any advance payments made under this contract remain outstanding, the Contractor, without the prior written consent of the administering office, shall not—

(1) Mortgage, pledge, or otherwise encumber or allow to be encumbered, any of the assets of the Contractor now owned or subsequently acquired, or permit any preexisting mortgages, liens, or other encumbrances to remain on or attach to any assets of the Contractor which are allocated to performing this contract and with respect to which the Government has a lien under this contract;

(2) Sell, assign, transfer, or otherwise dispose of accounts receivable, notes, or claims for money due or to become due;

(3) Declare or pay any dividends, except dividends payable in stock of the corporation, or make any other distribution on account of any shares of its capital stock, or purchase, redeem, or otherwise acquire for value any of its stock, except as required by sinking fund or redemption arrangements reported to the administering office incident to the establishment of these advance payment provisions;

(4) Sell, convey, or lease all or a substantial part of its assets;

(5) Acquire for value the stock or other securities of any corporation, municipality, or governmental authority, except direct obligations of the United States;

(6) Make any advance or loan or incur any liability as guarantor, surety, or accommodation endorser for any party;

(7) Permit a writ of attachment or any similar process to be issued against its property without getting a release or bonding the property within 30 days after the entry of the writ of attachment or other process;

(8) Pay any remuneration in any form to its directors, officers, or key employees higher than rates provided in existing agreements of which notice has been given to the administering office; accrue excess remuneration without first obtaining an agreement subordinating it to all claims of the Government; or employ any person at a rate of compensation over $____ a year;

(9) Change substantially the management, ownership, or control of the corporation;

(10) Merge or consolidate with any other firm or corporation, change the type of business, or engage in any transaction outside the ordinary course of the Contractor's business as presently conducted;

(11) Deposit any of its funds except in a bank or trust company insured by the Federal Deposit Insurance Corporation or a credit union insured by the National Credit Union Administration;

(12) Create or incur indebtedness for advances, other than advances to be made under the terms of this contract, or for borrowings;

(13) Make or covenant for capital expenditures exceeding $____ in total;

(14) Permit its net current assets, computed in accordance with generally accepted accounting principles, to become less than $____; or

(15) Make any payments on account of the obligations listed below, except in the manner and to the extent provided in this contract:

[*List the pertinent obligations*]

(End of clause)

Alternate I (APR 1984). If the agency desires to waive the countersignature requirement because of the Contractor's financial strength, good performance record, and favorable experience concerning cost disallowances, add the following sentence, if appropriate, to paragraph (b) of the basic clause:

However, for this contract, countersignature on behalf of the Government will not be required unless it is determined necessary by the administering office.

Alternate II (MAR 2001). If used in a cost-reimbursement contract, substitute the following paragraphs (c) and (e), and subparagraphs (f)(1) and (f)(2) for paragraphs (c) and (e) and subparagraphs (f)(1) and (2) of the basic clause:

(c) *Use of funds*. The Contractor shall withdraw funds from the special account only to pay for allowable costs as prescribed by the ____ clause of this contract. Payment for any other types of expenses shall be approved in writing by the administering office.

(e) *Maximum payment*. When the sum of all unliquidated advance payments, unpaid interest charges, and other payments equal the total estimated cost of $____ (not including fixed-fee, if any) for the work under this contract, the Government shall withhold further payments to the Contractor. Upon completion or termination of the contract, the Government shall deduct from the amount due to the Contractor all unliquidated advance payments and interest charges payable. The Contractor shall pay any deficiency to the Government upon demand. For purposes of this paragraph, the estimated cost shall be considered to be the stated estimated cost, less any subsequent reductions of the estimated cost, plus any increases in the estimated costs that do not, in the aggregate, exceed $____ [*Insert an amount not higher than 10 percent of the stated estimated cost inserted in this paragraph*]

The estimated cost shall include, without limitation, any reimbursable cost (as estimated by the Contracting Officer) incident to a termination for the convenience of the Government. Any payments withheld under this paragraph shall be applied to reduce the unliquidated advance payments. If full liquidation has been made, payments under the contract shall resume.

(f) *Interest*.

(1) The Contractor shall pay interest to the Government on the daily unliquidated advance payments at the daily rate specified in subparagraph (f)(3) below. Interest shall be computed at the end of each calendar month for the actual number of days involved. For the purpose of computing the interest charge, the following shall be observed:

(i) Advance payments shall be considered as increasing the unliquidated balance as of the date of the advance payment check.

(ii) Repayments by Contractor check shall be considered as decreasing the unliquidated balance as of the date on which the check is received by the Government authority designated by the Contracting Officer.

(iii) Liquidations by deductions from payments to the Contractor shall be considered as decreasing the unliquidated balance as of the dates on which the Contractor presents to the Contracting Officer full and accurate data for the preparation of each voucher. Credits resulting from these deductions shall be made upon the approval of the reimbursement vouchers by the Disbursing Officer, based upon the Contracting Officer's certification of the applicable dates.

(2) Interest charges resulting from the monthly computation shall be deducted from any payments on account of the fixed-fee due to the Contractor. If the accrued interest exceeds the payment due, any excess interest shall be carried forward and deducted from subsequent payments of the contract price or fixed-fee. Interest carried forward shall not be compounded. Interest on advance payments shall cease to accrue upon (i) satisfactory completion or (ii) termination of the contract for the convenience of the Government. The Contractor shall charge interest on advance payments to subcontractors in the manner described above and credit the interest to the Government. Interest need not be charged on advance payments to nonprofit educational or research subcontractors for experimental, developmental, or research work.

Alternate III (APR 1984). If the agency considers a more rapid liquidation appropriate, add the following sentence as the first sentence of paragraph (e) of the basic clause with the appropriate percentage specified:

To liquidate the principal amount of any advance payment made to the Contractor, there shall be deductions of _____ percent from all payments made by the Government under the contracts involved.

Alternate IV (APR 1984). If the agency provides advance payments under the contract at no interest to the prime contractor, add the following sentences as the beginning sentences of paragraph (f) of the clause:

No interest shall be charged to the prime Contractor for advance payments except for interest charged during a period of default. The terms of this paragraph concerning interest charges for advance payments shall not apply to the prime Contractor.

Alternate V (MAR 2001). If the requirement for a special bank account is eliminated in accordance with 32.409-3(e) or (g), insert the clause set forth below instead of the basic clause.

If this Alternate is used in combination with *Alternate II,* disregard the instructions concerning paragraph (c), Use of funds, in *Alternate II;* substitute paragraph (e), Maximum payment, in *Alternate II* for paragraph (d) below; and substitute paragraph (f), Interest, in *Alternate II* for paragraph (e) below and change the reference to paragraph (f)(3) in the first sentence of paragraph (f) of *Alternate II* to (e)(3).

If this Alternate is used in combination with *Alternate III,* insert the additional sentence set forth in *Alternate III* as the first sentence of paragraph (d) of this Alternate.

If this Alternate is used in combination with *Alternate IV,* insert the additional sentences set forth in *Alternate IV* as the beginning sentences of paragraph (e) of this Alternate.

ADVANCE PAYMENTS WITHOUT SPECIAL ACCOUNT (MAR 2001)

(a) *Requirements for payment.* Advance payments will be made under this contract (1) upon submission of properly certified invoices or vouchers by the contractor, and approval by the administering office, ___ [*insert the name of the office designated under agency procedures*], or (2) under a letter of credit. The amount of the invoice or voucher submitted plus all advance payments previously approved shall not exceed $___. If a letter of credit is used, the Contractor shall withdraw cash only when needed for disbursements acceptable under this contract and report cash disbursements and balances as required by the administering office. The Contractor shall apply terms similar to this clause to any advance payments to subcontractors.

(b) *Use of funds.* The Contractor may use advance payment funds only to pay for properly allocable, allowable, and reasonable costs for direct materials, direct labor, and indirect costs. Determinations of whether costs are properly allocable, allowable, and reasonable shall be in accordance with generally accepted accounting principles, subject to any applicable subparts of Part 31 of the Federal Acquisition Regulation.

(c) *Repayment to the Government.* At any time, the Contractor may repay all or any part of the funds advanced by the Government. Whenever requested in writing to do so by the administering office, the Contractor shall repay to the Government any part of unliquidated advance payments considered by the administering office to exceed the Contractor's current requirements or the amount specified in paragraph (a) of this clause.

(d) *Maximum payment.* When the sum of all unliquidated advance payments, unpaid interest charges, and other payments exceed ___ percent of the contract price, the Government shall withhold further payments to the Contractor. On completion or termination of the contract, the Government shall deduct from the amount due to the Contractor all unliquidated advance payments and all interest charges payable. If previous payments to the Contractor exceed the amount due, the excess amount shall be paid to the Government on demand. For purposes of this paragraph, the contract price shall be considered to be the stated contract price of $___, less any subsequent price reductions under the contract, plus (1) any price increases resulting from any terms of this contract for price redetermination or escalation, and (2) any other price increases that do not, in the aggregate, exceed $___ [*insert an amount not higher than 10 percent of the stated contract amount inserted in this paragraph*]. Any payments withheld under this paragraph shall be applied to reduce the unliquidated advance payments. If full liquidation has been made, payments under the contract shall resume.

(e) *Interest.* (1) The Contractor shall pay interest to the Government on the daily unliquidated advance payments at the daily rate in subparagraph (e)(3) of this clause. Interest shall be computed at the end of each calendar month for the actual number of days involved. For the purpose of computing the interest charge—

(i) Advance payments shall be considered as increasing the unliquidated balance as of the date of the advance payment check;

(ii) Repayments by Contractor check shall be considered as decreasing the unliquidated balance as of the date on which the check is received by the Government authority designated by the Contracting Officer; and

(iii) Liquidations by deductions from Government payments to the Contractor shall be considered as decreasing the unliquidated balance as of the date of the check for the reduced payment.

(2) Interest charges resulting from the monthly computation shall be deducted from payments, other than advance payments, due the Contractor. If the accrued interest exceeds the payment due, any excess interest shall be carried forward and deducted from subsequent payments. Interest carried forward shall not be compounded. Interest on advance payments shall cease to accrue upon satisfactory completion or termination of the contract for the convenience of the Government. The Contractor shall charge interest on advance payments to subcontractors in the manner described above and credit the interest to the Government. Interest need not be charged on advance payments to nonprofit educational or research

subcontractors, for experimental, developmental, or research work.

(3) If interest is required under the contract, the Contracting Officer shall determine a daily interest rate based on the rate established by the Secretary of the Treasury under Pub. L. 92-41 (50 U.S.C. App., 1215(b)(2)). The Contracting Officer shall revise the daily interest rate during the contract period in keeping with any changes in the cited interest rate.

(4) If the full amount of interest charged under this paragraph has not been paid by deduction or otherwise upon completion or termination of this contract, the Contractor shall pay the remaining interest to the Government on demand.

(f) *Lien on property under contract.* (1) All advance payments under this contract, together with interest charges, shall be secured, when made, by a lien in favor of the Government, paramount to all other liens, on the supplies or other things covered by this contract and on all material and other property acquired for or allocated to the performance of this contract, except to the extent that the Government by virtue of any other terms of this contract, or otherwise, shall have valid title to the supplies, materials, or other property as against other creditors of the Contractor.

(2) The Contractor shall identify, by marking or segregation, all property that is subject to a lien in favor of the Government by virtue of any terms of this contract in such a way as to indicate that it is subject to a lien and that it has been acquired for or allocated to performing this contract. If, for any reason, the supplies, materials, or other property are not identified by marking or segregation, the Government shall be considered to have a lien to the extent of the Government's interest under this contract on any mass of property with which the supplies, materials, or other property are commingled. The Contractor shall maintain adequate accounting control over the property on its books and records.

(3) If, at any time during the progress of the work on the contract, it becomes necessary to deliver to a third person any items or materials on which the Government has a lien, the Contractor shall notify the third person of the lien and shall obtain from the third person a receipt in duplicate acknowledging the existence of the lien. The Contractor shall provide a copy of each receipt to the Contracting Officer.

(4) If, under the termination clause, the Contracting Officer authorizes the contractor to sell or retain termination inventory, the approval shall constitute a release of the Government's lien to the extent that—

(i) The termination inventory is sold or retained; and

(ii) The sale proceeds or retention credits are applied to reduce any outstanding advance payments.

(g) *Insurance.* (1) The Contractor shall maintain with responsible insurance carriers—

(i) Insurance on plant and equipment against fire and other hazards, to the extent that similar properties are usually insured by others operating plants and properties of similar character in the same general locality;

(ii) Adequate insurance against liability on account of damage to persons or property; and

(iii) Adequate insurance under all applicable workers' compensation laws.

(2) Until work under this contract has been completed and all advance payments made under the contract have been liquidated, the Contractor shall—

(i) Maintain this insurance;

(ii) Maintain adequate insurance on any materials, parts, assemblies, subassemblies, supplies, equipment, and other property acquired for or allocable to this contract and subject to the Government lien under paragraph (f) of this clause; and

(iii) Furnish any evidence with respect to its insurance that the administering office may require.

(h) *Default.* (1) If any of the following events occur, the Government may, by written notice to the Contractor, withhold further payments on this contract:

(i) Termination of this contract for a fault of the Contractor.

(ii) A finding by the administering office that the Contractor has failed to—

(A) Observe any of the conditions of the advance payment terms;

(B) Comply with any material term of this contract;

(C) Make progress or maintain a financial condition adequate for performance of this contract;

(D) Limit inventory allocated to this contract to reasonable requirements; or

(E) Avoid delinquency in payment of taxes or of the costs of performing this contract in the ordinary course of business.

(iii) The appointment of a trustee, receiver, or liquidator for all or a substantial part of the Contractor's property, or the institution of proceedings by or against the Contractor for bankruptcy, reorganization, arrangement, or liquidation.

(iv) The commission of an act of bankruptcy.

(2) If any of the events described in subparagraph (h)(1) of this clause continue for 30 days after the written notice to the Contractor, the Government may take any of the following additional actions:

(i) Charge interest, in the manner prescribed in paragraph (e) of this clause, on outstanding advance payments during the period of any event described in subparagraph (h)(1) of this clause.

(ii) Demand immediate repayment by the Contractor of the unliquidated balance of advance payments.

(iii) Take possession of and, with or without advertisement, sell at public or private sale all or any part of the property on which the Government has a lien under this contract and, after deducting any expenses incident to the sale, apply the net proceeds of the sale to reduce the unliquidated balance of advance payments or other Government claims against the Contractor.

(3) The Government may take any of the actions described in subparagraphs (h)(1) and (h)(2) of this clause it considers appropriate at its discretion and without limiting any other rights of the Government.

(i) *Prohibition against assignment.* Notwithstanding any other terms of this contract, the Contractor shall not assign this contract, any interest therein, or any claim under the contract to any party.

(j) *Information and access to records.* The Contractor shall furnish to the administering office (1) monthly or at other intervals as required, signed or certified balance sheets and profit and loss statements, and, (2) if requested, other information concerning the operation of the contractor's business. The Contractor shall provide the authorized Government representatives proper facilities for inspection of the Contractor's books, records, and accounts.

(k) *Other security.* The terms of this contract are considered to provide adequate security to the Government for advance payments; however, if the administering office considers the security inadequate, the Contractor shall furnish additional security satisfactory to the administering office, to the extent that the security is available.

(l) *Representations.* The Contractor represents the following:

(1) The balance sheet, the profit and loss statement, and any other supporting financial statements furnished to the administering office fairly reflect the financial condition of the Contractor at the date shown or the period covered, and there has been no subsequent materially adverse change in the financial condition of the Contractor.

(2) No litigation or proceedings are presently pending or threatened against the Contractor, except as shown in the financial statements.

(3) The Contractor has disclosed all contingent liabilities, except for liability resulting from the renegotiation of defense production contracts, in the financial statements furnished to the administering office.

(4) None of the terms in this clause conflict with the authority under which the Con-

tractor is doing business or with the provision of any existing indenture or agreement of the Contractor.

(5) The Contractor has the power to enter into this contract and accept advance payments, and has taken all necessary action to authorize the acceptance under the terms of this contract.

(6) The assets of the Contractor are not subject to any lien or encumbrance of any character except for current taxes not delinquent, and except as shown in the financial statements furnished by the Contractor. There is no current assignment of claims under any contract affected by these advance payment provisions.

(7) All information furnished by the Contractor to the administering office in connection with each request for advance payments is true and correct.

(8) These representations shall be continuing and shall be considered to have been repeated by the submission of each invoice for advance payments.

(m) *Covenants.* To the extent the Government considers it necessary while any advance payments made under this contract remain outstanding, the Contractor, without the prior written consent of the administering office, shall not—

(1) Mortgage, pledge, or otherwise encumber or allow to be encumbered, any of the assets of the Contractor now owned or subsequently acquired, or permit any preexisting mortgages, liens, or other encumbrances to remain on or attach to any assets of the Contractor which are allocated to performing this contract and with respect to which the Government has a lien under this contract;

(2) Sell, assign, transfer, or otherwise dispose of accounts receivable, notes, or claims for money due or to become due;

(3) Declare or pay any dividends, except dividends payable in stock of the corporation, or make any other distribution on account of any shares of its capital stock, or purchase, redeem, or otherwise acquire for value any of its stock, except as required by sinking fund or redemption arrangements reported to the administering office incident to the establishment of these advance payment provisions;

(4) Sell, convey, or lease all or a substantial part of its assets;

(5) Acquire for value the stock or other securities of any corporation, municipality, or Governmental authority, except direct obligations of the United States;

(6) Make any advance or loan or incur any liability as guarantor, surety, or accommodation endorser for any party;

(7) Permit a writ of attachment or any similar process to be issued against its property without getting a release or bonding the property within 30 days after the entry of the writ of attachment or other process;

(8) Pay any remuneration in any form to its directors, officers, or key employees higher than rates provided in existing agreements of which notice has been given to the administering office; accrue excess remuneration without first obtaining an agreement subordinating it to all claims of the Government, or employ any person at a rate of compensation over $____ a year.

(9) Change substantially the management, ownership, or control of the corporation;

(10) Merge or consolidate with any other firm or corporation, change the type of business, or engage in any transaction outside the ordinary course of the Contractor's business as presently conducted;

(11) Deposit any of its funds except in a bank or trust company insured by the Federal Deposit Insurance Corporation or a credit union insured by the National Credit Union Administration;

(12) Create or incur indebtedness for advances, other than advances to be made under the terms of this contract, or for borrowings;

(13) Make or covenant for capital expenditures exceeding $____ in total;

(14) Permit its net current assets, computed in accordance with generally accepted accounting principles, to become less than $____; or

(15) Make any payments on account of the obligations listed below, except in the manner and to the extent provided in this contract:

[*List the pertinent obligations*]

[FAC 84-58, 55 FR 25532, 6/21/90, effective 7/23/90; FAC 90-32, 60 FR 48206, 9/18/95, effective 10/1/95; FAC 97-11, 64 FR 10530, 3/4/99, effective 5/3/99; FAC 97-22, 66 FR 2116, 1/10/2001, effective 3/12/2001; Delay of effective date, 66 FR 14259, 3/9/2001, effective 5/11/2001]

52.232-13 Notice of Progress Payments.

As prescribed in 32.502-3(a), insert the following provision in invitations for bids and requests for proposals that include a Progress Payments clause:

NOTICE OF PROGRESS PAYMENTS (APR 1984)

The need for customary progress payments conforming to the regulations in Subpart 32.5 of the Federal Acquisition Regulation (FAR) will not be considered as a handicap or adverse factor in the award of the contract. The Progress Payments clause included in this solicitation will be included in any resulting contract, modified or altered if necessary in accordance with subsection 52.232-16 and its Alternate I of the FAR. Even though the clause is included in the contract, the clause shall be inoperative during any time the contractor's accounting system and controls are determined by the Government to be inadequate for segregation and accumulation of contract costs.

(End of provision)

[FAC 90-32, 60 FR 48206, 9/18/95, effective 10/1/95]

52.232-14 Notice of Availability of Progress Payments Exclusively for Small Business Concerns.

As prescribed in 32.502-3(b)(2), insert the following provision in invitations for bids if it is anticipated that (a) both small business concerns and others may submit bids in response to the same invitation and (b) only the small business bidders would need progress payments:

NOTICE OF AVAILABILITY OF PROGRESS PAYMENTS EXCLUSIVELY FOR SMALL BUSINESS CONCERNS (APR 1984)

The Progress Payments clause will be available only to small business concerns. Any bid conditioned upon inclusion of a progress payment clause in the resulting contract will be rejected as nonresponsive if the bidder is not a small business concern.

(End of provision)

[FAC 90-32, 60 FR 48206, 9/18/95, effective 10/1/95]

52.232-15 Progress Payments Not Included.

As prescribed in 32.502-3(c), insert the following provision in invitations for bids if the solicitation will not contain one of the provisions prescribed in 32.502-3(a) and (b):

PROGRESS PAYMENTS NOT INCLUDED (APR 1984)

A progress payments clause is not included in this solicitation, and will not be added to the resulting contract at the time of award. Bids conditioned upon inclusion of a progress payment clause in the resulting contract will be rejected as nonresponsive.

(End of provision)

[FAC 90-32, 60 FR 48206, 9/18/95, effective 10/1/95]

52.232-16 Progress Payments.

As prescribed in 32.502-4(a), insert the following clause:

PROGRESS PAYMENTS (APR 2012)

The Government will make progress payments to the Contractor when requested as work progresses, but not more frequently than monthly, in amounts of $2,500 or more approved by the Contracting Officer, under the following conditions:

(a) *Computation of amounts.* (1) Unless the Contractor requests a smaller amount, the Government will compute each progress payment as 80 percent of the Contractor's total costs incurred under this contract whether or not actually paid, plus financing payments to subcontractors (see paragraph (j) of this clause), less the sum of all previous progress payments made by the Government under this contract. The Contracting Officer will consider cost of money that would be allowable under FAR 31.205-10 as an incurred cost for progress payment purposes.

(2) The amount of financing and other payments for supplies and services purchased directly for the contract are limited to the amounts that have been paid by cash, check, or other forms of payment, or that are determined due and will be paid to subcontractors—

(i) In accordance with the terms and conditions of a subcontract or invoice; and

(ii) Ordinarily within 30 days of the submission of the Contractor's payment request to the Government.

(3) The Government will exclude accrued costs of Contractor contributions under employee pension plans until actually paid unless—

(i) The Contractor's practice is to make contributions to the retirement fund quarterly or more frequently; and

(ii) The contribution does not remain unpaid 30 days after the end of the applicable quarter or shorter payment period (any contribution remaining unpaid shall be excluded from the Contractor's total costs for progress payments until paid).

(4) The Contractor shall not include the following in total costs for progress payment purposes in paragraph (a)(1) of this clause:

(i) Costs that are not reasonable, allocable to this contract, and consistent with sound and generally accepted accounting principles and practices.

(ii) Costs incurred by subcontractors or suppliers.

(iii) Costs ordinarily capitalized and subject to depreciation or amortization except for the properly depreciated or amortized portion of such costs.

(iv) Payments made or amounts payable to subcontractors or suppliers, except for—

(A) Completed work, including partial deliveries, to which the Contractor has acquired title; and

(B) Work under cost-reimbursement or time-and-material subcontracts to which the Contractor has acquired title.

(5) The amount of unliquidated progress payments may exceed neither (i) the progress payments made against incomplete work (including allowable unliquidated progress payments to subcontractors) nor (ii) the value, for progress payment purposes, of the incomplete work. Incomplete work shall be considered to be the supplies and services required by this contract, for which delivery and invoicing by the Contractor and acceptance by the Government are incomplete.

(6) The total amount of progress payments shall not exceed 80 percent of the total contract price.

(7) If a progress payment or the unliquidated progress payments exceed the amounts permitted by subparagraphs (a)(4) or (a)(5) above, the Contractor shall repay the amount of such excess to the Government on demand.

(8) Notwithstanding any other terms of the contract, the Contractor agrees not to request progress payments in dollar amounts of less than $2,500. The Contracting Officer may make exceptions.

(9) The costs applicable to items delivered, invoiced, and accepted shall not include costs in excess of the contract price of the items.

(b) *Liquidation*. Except as provided in the Termination for Convenience of the Government clause, all progress payments shall be liquidated by deducting from any payment under this contract, other than advance or progress payments, the unliquidated progress payments, or 80 percent of the amount invoiced, whichever is less. The Contractor shall repay to the Government any amounts required by a retroactive price reduction, after computing liquidations and payments on past invoices at the reduced prices and adjusting the unliquidated progress payments accordingly. The Government reserves the right to unilaterally change from the ordinary liquidation rate to an alternate rate when deemed appropriate for proper contract financing.

(c) *Reduction or suspension*. The Contracting Officer may reduce or suspend progress payments, increase the rate of liquidation, or take a combination of these actions, after finding on substantial evidence any of the following conditions:

(1) The Contractor failed to comply with any material requirement of this contract (which includes paragraphs (f) and (g) in this of this clause).

(2) Performance of this contract is endangered by the Contractor's (i) failure to make progress or (ii) unsatisfactory financial condition.

(3) Inventory allocated to this contract substantially exceeds reasonable requirements.

(4) The Contractor is delinquent in payment of the costs of performing this contract in the ordinary course of business.

(5) The fair value of the undelivered work is less than the amount of unliquidated progress payments for that work.

(6) The Contractor is realizing less profit than that reflected in the establishment of any alternate liquidation rate in paragraph (b) above, and that rate is less than the progress payment rate stated in subparagraph (a)(1) of this clause.

(d) *Title*. (1) Title to the property described in this paragraph (d) shall vest in the Government. Vestiture shall be immediately upon the date of this contract, for property acquired or produced before that date. Otherwise, vestiture shall occur when the property is or should have been allocable or properly chargeable to this contract.

(2) *Property,* as used in this clause, includes all of the below-described items acquired or produced by the Contractor that are or should be allocable or properly chargeable to this contract under sound and generally accepted accounting principles and practices.

(i) Parts, materials, inventories, and work in process;

(ii) Special tooling and special test equipment to which the Government is to acquire title;

(iii) Nondurable (i.e., noncapital) tools, jigs, dies, fixtures, molds, patterns, taps, gauges, test equipment, and other similar manufacturing aids, title to which would not be obtained as special tooling under subparagraph (ii) above; and

(iv) Drawings and technical data, to the extent the Contractor or subcontractors are required to deliver them to the Government by other clauses of this contract.

(3) Although title to property is in the Government under this clause, other applicable clauses of this contract, e.g., the termination clauses, shall determine the handling and disposition of the property.

(4) The Contractor may sell any scrap resulting from production under this contract without requesting the Contracting Officer's approval, but the proceeds shall be credited against the costs of performance.

(5) To acquire for its own use or dispose of property to which title is vested in the Government under this clause, the Contractor must obtain the Contracting Officer's advance approval of the action and the terms. The Contractor shall (i) exclude the allocable costs of the property from the costs of contract performance, and (ii) repay to the Government any amount of unliquidated progress payments allocable to the property. Repayment may be by cash or credit memorandum.

(6) When the Contractor completes all of the obligations under this contract, including liquidation of all progress payments, title shall vest in the Contractor for all property (or the proceeds thereof) not—

(i) Delivered to, and accepted by, the Government under this contract; or

(ii) Incorporated in supplies delivered to, and accepted by, the Government under this contract and to which title is vested in the Government under this clause.

(7) The terms of this contract concerning liability for Government-furnished property shall not apply to property to which the Government acquired title solely under this clause.

(e) *Risk of loss*. Before delivery to and acceptance by the Government, the Contractor shall bear the risk of loss for property, the title to which vests in the Government under this clause, except to the extent the Government expressly assumes the risk. The Contractor shall repay the Government an amount equal to the unliquidated progress payments that are based on costs allocable to property that is lost (see 45.101).

(f) *Control of costs and property.* The Contractor shall maintain an accounting system and controls adequate for the proper administration of this clause.

(g) *Reports, forms, and access to records.* (1) The Contractor shall promptly furnish reports, certificates, financial statements, and other pertinent information (including estimates to complete) reasonably requested by the Contracting Officer for the administration of this clause. Also, the Contractor shall give the Government reasonable opportunity to examine and verify the Contractor's books, records, and accounts.

(2) The Contractor shall furnish estimates to complete that have been developed or updated within six months of the date of the progress payment request. The estimates to complete shall represent the Contractor's best estimate of total costs to complete all remaining contract work required under the contract. The estimates shall include sufficient detail to permit Government verification.

(3) Each Contractor request for progress payment shall:

(i) Be submitted on Standard Form 1443, Contractor's Request for Progress Payment, or the electronic equivalent as required by agency regulations, in accordance with the form instructions and the contract terms; and

(ii) Include any additional supporting documentation requested by the Contracting Officer.

(h) *Special terms regarding default.* If this contract is terminated under the Default clause, (i) the Contractor shall, on demand, repay to the Government the amount of unliquidated progress payments and (ii) title shall vest in the Contractor, on full liquidation of progress payments, for all property for which the Government elects not to require delivery under the Default clause. The Government shall be liable for no payment except as provided by the Default clause.

(i) *Reservations of rights.* (1) No payment or vesting of title under this clause shall (i) excuse the Contractor from performance of obligations under this contract or (ii) constitute a waiver of any of the rights or remedies of the parties under the contract.

(2) The Government's rights and remedies under this clause (i) shall not be exclusive but rather shall be in addition to any other rights and remedies provided by law or this contract and (ii) shall not be affected by delayed, partial, or omitted exercise of any right, remedy, power, or privilege, nor shall such exercise or any single exercise preclude or impair any further exercise under this clause or the exercise of any other right, power, or privilege of the Government.

(j) *Financing payments to subcontractors.* The financing payments to subcontractors mentioned in paragraphs (a)(1) and (a)(2) of this clause shall be all financing payments to subcontractors or divisions, if the following conditions are met:

(1) The amounts included are limited to—

(i) The unliquidated remainder of financing payments made; plus

(ii) Any unpaid subcontractor requests for financing payments.

(2) The subcontract or interdivisional order is expected to involve a minimum of approximately 6 months between the beginning of work and the first delivery; or, if the subcontractor is a small business concern, 4 months.

(3) If the financing payments are in the form of progress payments, the terms of the subcontract or interdivisional order concerning progress payments—

(i) Are substantially similar to the terms of this clause for any subcontractor that is a large business concern, or this clause with its Alternate I for any subcontractor that is a small business concern;

(ii) Are at least as favorable to the Government as the terms of this clause;

(iii) Are not more favorable to the subcontractor or division than the terms of this clause are to the Contractor;

(iv) Are in conformance with the requirements of FAR 32.504(e); and

(v) Subordinate all subcontractor rights concerning property to which the Government has title under the subcontract to the Government's right to require delivery of the property to the Government if—

(A) The Contractor defaults; or

(B) The subcontractor becomes bankrupt or insolvent.

(4) If the financing payments are in the form of performance-based payments, the terms of the subcontract or interdivisional order concerning payments—

(i) Are substantially similar to the Performance-Based Payments clause at FAR 52.232-32 and meet the criteria for, and definition of, performance-based payments in FAR Part 32;

(ii) Are in conformance with the requirements of FAR 32.504(f); and

(iii) Subordinate all subcontractor rights concerning property to which the Government has title under the subcontract to the Government's right to require delivery of the property to the Government if—

(A) The Contractor defaults; or

(B) The subcontractor becomes bankrupt or insolvent.

(5) If the financing payments are in the form of commercial item financing payments, the terms of the subcontract or interdivisional order concerning payments—

(i) Are constructed in accordance with FAR 32.206(c) and included in a subcontract for a commercial item purchase that meets the definition and standards for acquisition of commercial items in FAR Parts 2 and 12;

(ii) Are in conformance with the requirements of FAR 32.504(g); and

(iii) Subordinate all subcontractor rights concerning property to which the Government has title under the subcontract to the Government's right to require delivery of the property to the Government if—

(A) The Contractor defaults; or

(B) The subcontractor becomes bankrupt or insolvent.

(6) If financing is in the form of progress payments, the progress payment rate in the subcontract is the customary rate used by the contracting agency, depending on whether the subcontractor is or is not a small business concern.

(7) Concerning any proceeds received by the Government for property to which title has vested in the Government under the subcontract terms, the parties agree that the proceeds shall be applied to reducing any unliquidated financing payments by the Government to the Contractor under this contract.

(8) If no unliquidated financing payments to the Contractor remain, but there are unliquidated financing payments that the Contractor has made to any subcontractor, the Contractor shall be subrogated to all the rights the Government obtained through the terms required by this clause to be in any subcontract, as if all such rights had been assigned and transferred to the Contractor.

(9) To facilitate small business participation in subcontracting under this contract, the Contractor shall provide financing payments to small business concerns, in conformity with the standards for customary contract financing payments stated in FAR 32.113. The Contractor shall not consider the need for such financing payments as a handicap or adverse factor in the award of subcontracts.

(k) *Limitations on Undefinitized Contract Actions.* Notwithstanding any other progress payment provisions in this contract, progress payments may not exceed 80 percent of costs incurred on work accomplished under undefinitized contract actions. A "contract action" is any action resulting in a contract, as defined in Subpart 2.1, including contract modifications for additional supplies or services, but not including contract modifications that are within the scope and under the terms of the contract, such as contract modifications issued pursuant to the Changes clause, or funding and other administrative changes. This limitation shall apply to the costs incurred, as computed in accordance with paragraph (a) of this clause, and shall remain in effect until the contract action is definitized. Costs incurred which are subject to this limitation shall be segregated on Contractor progress payment requests and invoices from those costs eligible for higher progress payment rates. For purposes of progress payment liquidation, as described in paragraph (b) of this clause, progress payments for undefinitized contract actions shall be liquidated at 80 percent of the amount invoiced for work performed under the undefinitized contract action as long as the contract action remains undefinitized. The amount of unliquidated progress payments for undefinitized contract actions shall not exceed 80 percent of the maximum liability of the Government under the undefinitized contract action or such lower limit specified elsewhere in the contract. Separate limits may be specified for separate actions.

(l) *Due date.* The designated payment office will make progress payments on the _____ [*Contracting Officer insert date as prescribed by agency head; if not prescribed, insert "30th"*] day after the designated billing office receives a proper progress payment request. In the event that the Government requires an audit or other review of a specific progress payment request to ensure compliance with the terms and conditions of the contract, the designated payment office is not compelled to make payment by the specified due date. Progress payments are considered contract financing and are not subject to the interest penalty provisions of the Prompt Payment Act.

(m) *Progress payments under indefinite—delivery contracts.* The Contractor shall account for and submit progress payment requests under individual orders as if the order constituted a separate contract, unless otherwise specified in this contract.

(End of clause)

Alternate I (MAR 2000). If the contract is with a small business concern, change each mention of the progress payment and liquidation rates excepting paragraph (k) to the customary rate of 85 percent for small business concerns (see FAR 32.501-1).

Alternate II (APR 2003). If the contract is a letter contract, add paragraphs (n) and (o). The amount specified in paragraph (o) shall not exceed 80 percent of the maximum liability of the Government under the letter contract. The contracting officer may specify separate limits for separate parts of the work.

(n) The Contracting Officer will liquidate progress payments made under this letter contract, unless previously liquidated under paragraph (b) of this clause, using the following procedures:

(1) If this letter contract is superseded by a definitive contract, unliquidated progress payments made under this letter contract shall be liquidated by deducting the amount from the first progress or other payments made under the definitive contract.

(2) If this letter contract is not superseded by a definitive contract calling for the furnishing of all or part of the articles or services covered under the letter contract, unliquidated progress payments made under the letter contract shall be liquidated by deduction from the amount payable under the Termination clause.

(3) If this letter contract is partly terminated and partly superseded by a contract, the Government will allocate the unliquidated progress payments to the terminated and unterminated portions as the Government deems equitable, and will liquidate each portion under the relevant procedure in paragraphs (n)(1) and (n)(2) of this clause.

(4) If the method of liquidating progress payments provided in this clause does not result in full liquidation, the Contractor shall immediately pay the unliquidated balance to the Government on demand.

(o) The amount of unliquidated progress payments shall not exceed _____ [*Contracting Officer specify dollar amount*].

Alternate III (APR 2003). As prescribed in 32.502-4(d), add the following paragraph (n) to the basic clause. If Alternate II is also being used, redesignate the following paragraph as paragraph (p):

(m) The provisions of this clause will not be applicable to individual orders at or below the simplified acquisition threshold.

[FAC 84-29, 52 FR 30079, 8/12/87, effective 8/24/87; Final rule, 55 FR 38516, 9/18/90; FAC 90-5, 56 FR 29138, 6/25/91, effective 7/25/91; FAC 97-16, 65 FR 16274, 3/27/2000, effective 3/27/2000; FAC 2001-02, 66 FR 65347, 12/18/2001, effective 2/19/2002; FAC 2001-09, 67 FR 56115, 8/30/2002, effective 9/30/2002; FAC 2001-10, 67 FR 70520, 11/22/2002, effective 12/23/2002; FAC 2001-13, 68 FR 13205, 3/18/2003, effective 4/17/2003; FAC 2005-19, 72 FR 46363, 8/17/2007, effective 8/17/2007; FAC 2005-33, 74 FR 28430, 6/15/2009, effective 7/15/2009; FAC 2005-43, 75 FR 38675, 7/2/2010, effective 8/2/2010; FAC 2005-56, 77 FR 12937, 3/2/2012, effective 4/2/2012]

52.232-17 Interest.

As prescribed in 32.611(a) and (b), insert the following clause:

INTEREST (MAY 2014)

(a) Except as otherwise provided in this contract under a Price Reduction for Defective Certified Cost or Pricing Data clause or a Cost Accounting Standards clause, all amounts that become payable by the Contractor to the Government under this contract shall bear simple interest from the date due until paid unless paid within 30 days of becoming due. The interest rate shall be the interest rate established by the Secretary of the Treasury as provided in 41 U.S.C. 7109, which is applicable to the period in which the amount becomes due, as provided in paragraph (e) of this clause, and then at the rate applicable for each six-month period as fixed by the Secretary until the amount is paid.

(b) The Government may issue a demand for payment to the Contractor upon finding a debt is due under the contract.

(c) *Final Decisions.* The Contracting Officer will issue a final decision as required by 33.211 if—

(1) The Contracting Officer and the Contractor are unable to reach agreement on the existence or amount of a debt in a timely manner;

(2) The Contractor fails to liquidate a debt previously demanded by the Contracting Officer within the timeline specified in the demand for payment unless the amounts were not repaid because the Contractor has requested an installment payment agreement; or

(3) The Contractor requests a deferment of collection on a debt previously demanded by the Contracting Officer (see 32.607-2).

(d) If a demand for payment was previously issued for the debt, the demand for payment included in the final decision shall identify the same due date as the original demand for payment.

(e) Amounts shall be due at the earliest of the following dates:

(1) The date fixed under this contract.

(2) The date of the first written demand for payment, including any demand for payment resulting from a default termination.

(f) The interest charge shall be computed for the actual number of calendar days involved beginning on the due date and ending on—

(1) The date on which the designated office receives payment from the Contractor;

(2) The date of issuance of a Government check to the Contractor from which an amount otherwise payable has been withheld as a credit against the contract debt; or

(3) The date on which an amount withheld and applied to the contract debt would otherwise have become payable to the Contractor.

(g) The interest charge made under this clause may be reduced under the procedures prescribed in 32.608-2 of the Federal Acquisition Regulation in effect on the date of this contract.

(End of clause)

[FAC 90-3, 55 FR 52799, 12/21/90, effective 1/22/91; FAC 90-38, 61 FR 18914, 4/29/96, effective 6/28/96; FAC 2005-27, 73 FR 53997, 9/17/2008, effective 10/17/2008; FAC 2005-45, 75 FR 53135, 8/30/2010, effective 10/1/2010; FAC 2005-73, 79 FR 24192, 4/29/2014, effective 5/29/2014]

52.232-18 Availability of Funds.

As prescribed in 32.706-1(a), insert the following clause:

AVAILABILITY OF FUNDS (APR 1984)

Funds are not presently available for this contract. The Government's obligation under this contract is contingent upon the availability of appropriated funds from which payment for contract purposes can be made. No legal liability on the part of the Government for any payment may arise until funds are made available to the Contracting Officer for this contract and until the Contractor receives notice of such availability, to be confirmed in writing by the Contracting Officer.

(End of clause)

[FAC 90-32, 60 FR 48206, 9/18/95, effective 10/1/95; FAC 2001-06, 67 FR 13048, 3/20/2002, effective 4/4/2002; FAC 2005-67, 78 FR 37686, 6/21/2013, effective 6/21/2013; FAC 2005-72, 78 FR 80382, 12/31/2013, effective 12/31/2013]

52.232-19 Availability of Funds for the Next Fiscal Year.

As prescribed in 32.706-1(b), insert the following clause:

AVAILABILITY OF FUNDS FOR THE NEXT FISCAL YEAR (APR 1984)

Funds are not presently available for performance under this contract beyond ____. The Government's obligation for performance of this contract beyond that date is contingent upon the availability of appropriated funds from which payment for contract purposes can be made. No legal liability on the part of the Government for any payment may arise for performance under this contract beyond ____, until funds are made available to the Contracting Officer for performance and until the Contractor receives notice of availability, to be confirmed in writing by the Contracting Officer.

(End of clause)

[FAC 90-32, 60 FR 48206, 9/18/95, effective 10/1/95; FAC 2005-67, 78 FR 37686, 6/21/2013, effective 6/21/2013; FAC 2005-72, 78 FR 80382, 12/31/2013, effective 12/31/2013]

52.232-20 Limitation of Cost.

As prescribed in 32.706–2(a), insert the following clause. The 60-day period may be varied from 30 to 90 days and the 75 percent from 75 to 85 percent. "Task Order" or other appropriate designation may be substituted for "Schedule" wherever that word appears in the clause:

LIMITATION OF COST (APR 1984)

(a) The parties estimate that performance of this contract, exclusive of any fee, will not cost the Government more than (1) the estimated cost specified in the Schedule or, (2) if this is a cost-sharing contract, the Government's share of the estimated cost specified in the Schedule. The Contractor agrees to use its best efforts to perform the work specified in the Schedule and all obligations under this contract within the estimated cost, which, if this is a cost-sharing contract, includes both the Government's and the Contractor's share of the cost.

(b) The Contractor shall notify the Contracting Officer in writing whenever it has reason to believe that—

(1) The costs the contractor expects to incur under this contract in the next 60 days, when added to all costs previously incurred, will exceed 75 percent of the estimated cost specified in the Schedule; or

(2) The total cost for the performance of this contract, exclusive of any fee, will be either greater or substantially less than had been previously estimated.

(c) As part of the notification, the Contractor shall provide the Contracting Officer a revised estimate of the total cost of performing this contract.

(d) Except as required by other provisions of this contract, specifically citing and stated to be an exception to this clause—

(1) The Government is not obligated to reimburse the Contractor for costs incurred in excess of (i) the estimated cost specified in the Schedule or, (ii) if this is a cost-sharing contract, the estimated cost to the Government specified in the Schedule; and

(2) The Contractor is not obligated to continue performance under this contract (including actions under the Termination clause of this contract) or otherwise incur costs in excess of the estimated cost specified in the Schedule, until the Contracting Officer (i) notifies the Contractor in writing that the estimated cost has been increased and (ii) provides a revised estimated total cost of performing this contract. If this is a cost-sharing contract, the increase shall be allocated in accordance with the formula specified in the Schedule.

(e) No notice, communication, or representation in any form other than that specified in subparagraph (d)(2) above, or from any person other than the Contracting Officer, shall affect this contract's estimated cost to the Government. In the absence of the specified notice, the Government is not obligated to reimburse the Contractor for any costs in excess of the estimated cost or, if this is a cost-sharing contract, for any costs in excess of the estimated cost to the Government specified in the Schedule, whether those excess costs were incurred during the course of the contract or as a result of termination.

(f) If the estimated cost specified in the Schedule is increased, any costs the Contractor incurs before the increase that are in excess of the previously estimated cost shall be allowable to the same extent as if incurred afterward, unless the Contracting Officer issues a termination or other notice directing that the increase is solely to cover termination or other specified expenses.

(g) Change orders shall not be considered an authorization to exceed the estimated cost to the Government specified in the Schedule, unless they contain a statement increasing the estimated cost.

(h) If this contract is terminated or the estimated cost is not increased, the Government and the Contractor shall negotiate an equitable distribution of all property produced or purchased under the contract, based upon the share of costs incurred by each.

(End of clause)

[FAC 90-32, 60 FR 48206, 9/18/95, effective 10/1/95; FAC 2005-17, 72 FR 27364, 5/15/2007, effective 6/14/2007; FAC 2005-67, 78 FR 37686, 6/21/2013, effective 6/21/2013; FAC 2005-72, 78 FR 80382, 12/31/2013, effective 12/31/2013]

52.232-21 [Removed and Reserved]

[FAC 90-32, 60 FR 48206, 9/18/95, effective 10/1/95; FAC 2005-17, 72 FR 27364, 5/15/2007, effective 6/14/2007]

52.232-22 Limitation of Funds.

As prescribed in 32.706–2(b), insert the following clause. The 60-day period may be varied from 30 to 90 days and the 75 percent from 75 to 85 percent. "Task Order" or other appropriate designation may be substituted for "Schedule" wherever that word appears in the clause:

LIMITATION OF FUNDS (APR 1984)

(a) The parties estimate that performance of this contract will not cost the Government more than (1) the estimated cost specified in the Schedule or, (2) if this is a cost-sharing contract, the Government's share of the estimated cost specified in the Schedule. The Contractor agrees to use its best efforts to perform the work specified in the Schedule and all obligations under this contract within the estimated cost, which, if this is a cost-sharing contract, includes both the Government's and the Contractor's share of the cost.

(b) The Schedule specifies the amount presently available for payment by the Government and allotted to this contract, the items covered, the Government's share of the cost if this is a cost-sharing contract, and the period of performance it is estimated the allotted amount will cover. The parties contemplate that the Government will allot additional funds incrementally to the contract up to the full estimated cost to the Government specified in the Schedule, exclusive of any fee. The Contractor agrees to perform, or have performed, work on the contract up to the point at which the total amount paid and payable by the Government under the contract approximates but does not exceed the total amount actually allotted by the Government to the contract.

(c) The Contractor shall notify the Contracting Officer in writing whenever it has reason to believe that the costs it expects to incur under this contract in the next 60 days, when added to all costs previously incurred, will exceed 75 percent of (1) the total amount so far allotted to the contract by the Government or, (2) if this is a cost-sharing contract, the amount then allotted to the contract by the Government plus the Contractor's corresponding share. The notice shall state the estimated amount of additional funds required to continue performance for the period specified in the Schedule.

(d) Sixty days before the end of the period specified in the Schedule, the Contractor shall notify the Contracting Officer in writing of the estimated amount of additional funds, if any, required to continue timely performance under the contract or for any further period specified in the Schedule or otherwise agreed upon, and when the funds will be required.

(e) If, after notification, additional funds are not allotted by the end of the period specified in the Schedule or another agreed-upon date, upon the Contractor's written request the Contracting Officer will terminate this contract on that date in accordance with the provisions of the Termination clause of this contract. If the Contractor estimates that the funds available will allow it to continue to discharge its obligations beyond that date, it may specify a later date in its request, and the Contracting Officer may terminate this contract on that later date.

(f) Except as required by other provisions of this contract, specifically citing and stated to be an exception to this clause—

(1) The Government is not obligated to reimburse the Contractor for costs incurred in excess of the total amount allotted by the Government to this contract; and

(2) The Contractor is not obligated to continue performance under this contract (including actions under the Termination clause of this contract) or otherwise incur costs in excess of (i) the amount then allotted to the contract by the Government or, (ii) if this is a cost-sharing contract, the amount then allotted by the Government to the contract plus the Contractor's corresponding share, until the Contracting Officer notifies the Contractor in writing that the amount allotted by the Government has been increased and specifies an increased amount, which shall then constitute the total amount allotted by the Government to this contract.

(g) The estimated cost shall be increased to the extent that (1) the amount allotted by the Government or, (2) if this is a cost-sharing contract, the amount then allotted by the Government to the contract plus the Contractor's corresponding share, exceeds the estimated cost specified in the Schedule. If this is a cost-sharing contract, the increase shall be allocated in accordance with the formula specified in the Schedule.

(h) No notice, communication, or representation in any form other than that specified in subparagraph (f)(2) above, or from any person other than the Contracting Officer, shall affect the amount allotted by the Government to this contract. In the absence of the specified notice, the Government is not obligated to reimburse the Contractor for any costs in excess of the total amount allotted by the Government to this contract, whether incurred during the course of the contract or as a result of termination.

(i) When and to the extent that the amount allotted by the Government to the contract is increased, any costs the Contractor incurs before the increase that are in excess of (1) the amount previously allotted by the Government or, (2) if this is a cost-sharing contract, the amount previously allotted by the Government to the contract plus the Contractor's corresponding share, shall be allowable to the same extent as if incurred afterward, unless the Contracting Officer issues a termination or other notice and directs that the increase is solely to cover termination or other specified expenses.

(j) Change orders shall not be considered an authorization to exceed the amount allotted by the Government specified in the Schedule, unless they contain a statement increasing the amount allotted.

(k) Nothing in this clause shall affect the right of the Government to terminate this contract. If this contract is terminated, the Government and the Contractor shall negotiate an equitable distribution of all property produced or purchased under the contract, based upon the share of costs incurred by each.

(l) If the Government does not allot sufficient funds to allow completion of the work, the Contractor is entitled to a percentage of the fee specified in the Schedule equalling the percentage of completion of the work contemplated by this contract.

(End of clause)

[FAC 90-32, 60 FR 48206, 9/18/95, effective 10/1/95; FAC 2005-17, 72 FR 27364, 5/15/2007, effective 6/14/2007; FAC 2005-67, 78 FR 37686, 6/21/2013, effective 6/21/2013; FAC 2005-72, 78 FR 80382, 12/31/2013, effective 12/31/2013]

52.232-23 Assignment of Claims.

As prescribed in 32.806(a)(1), insert the following clause:

ASSIGNMENT OF CLAIMS (MAY 2014)

(a) The Contractor, under the Assignment of Claims Act, as amended, 31 U.S.C. 3727, 41 U.S.C. 6305 (hereafter referred to as "the Act"), may assign its rights to be paid amounts due or to become due as a result of the performance of this contract to a bank, trust company, or other financing institution, including any Federal lending agency. The assignee under such an assignment may thereafter further assign or reassign its right under the original assignment to any type of financing institution described in the preceding sentence.

(b) Any assignment or reassignment authorized under the Act and this clause shall cover all unpaid amounts payable under this contract, and shall not be made to more than one party, except that an assignment or reassignment may be made to one party as agent or trustee for two or more parties participating in the financing of this contract.

(c) The Contractor shall not furnish or disclose to any assignee under this contract any classified document (including this contract) or information related to work under this contract until the Contracting Officer authorizes such action in writing.

(End of clause)

Alternate I (APR 1984). If a no-setoff commitment is to be included in the contract (see 32.801 and 32.803(d)), add the following sentence at the end of paragraph (a) of the basic clause:

Unless otherwise stated in this contract, payments to an assignee of any amounts due or to become due under this contract shall not, to the extent specified in the Act, be subject to reduction or setoff.

[FAC 84-12, 51 FR 2667, 1/17/86, effective 1/20/86; FAC 90-32, 60 FR 48206, 9/18/95, effective 10/1/95; FAC 2005-73, 79 FR 24192, 4/29/2014, effective 5/29/2014]

52.232-24 Prohibition of Assignment of Claims.

As prescribed in 32.806(b), insert the following clause:

PROHIBITION OF ASSIGNMENT OF CLAIMS (MAY 2014)

The assignment of claims under the Assignment of Claims Act of 1940 (31 U.S.C. 3727, 41 U.S.C. 6305) is prohibited for this contract.

(End of clause)

[FAC 84-12, 51 FR 2667, 1/17/86, effective 1/20/86; FAC 2005-73, 79 FR 24192, 4/29/2014, effective 5/29/2014]

52.232-25 Prompt Payment.

As prescribed in 32.908(c), insert the following clause:

PROMPT PAYMENT (JAN 2017)

Notwithstanding any other payment clause in this contract, the Government will make invoice payments under the terms and conditions specified in this clause. The Government considers payment as being made on the day a check is dated or the date of an electronic funds transfer (EFT). Definitions of pertinent terms are set forth in sections 2.101, 32.001, and 32.902 of the Federal Acquisition Regulation. All days referred to in this clause are calendar days, unless otherwise specified. (However, see paragraph (a)(4) of this clause concerning payments due on Saturdays, Sundays, and legal holidays.)

(a) *Invoice payments—(1) Due date.* (i) Except as indicated in paragraphs (a)(2) and (c) of this clause, the due date for making invoice payments by the designated payment office is the later of the following two events:

(A) The 30th day after the designated billing office receives a proper invoice from the Contractor (except as provided in paragraph (a)(1)(ii) of this clause).

(B) The 30th day after Government acceptance of supplies delivered or services performed. For a final invoice, when the payment amount is subject to contract settlement actions, acceptance is deemed to occur on the effective date of the contract settlement.

(ii) If the designated billing office fails to annotate the invoice with the actual date of receipt at the time of receipt, the invoice payment due date is the 30th day after the date of the Contractor's invoice, provided the designated billing office receives a proper invoice and there is no disagreement over quantity, quality, or Contractor compliance with contract requirements.

(2) *Certain food products and other payments.* (i) Due dates on Contractor invoices for meat, meat food products, or fish; perishable agricultural commodities; and dairy products, edible fats or oils, and food products prepared from edible fats or oils are—

(A) *For meat or meat food products,* as defined in section 2(a)(3) of the Packers and Stockyard Act of 1921 (7 U.S.C. 182(3)), and as further defined in Pub. L. 98-181, including any edible fresh or frozen poultry meat, any perishable poultry meat food product, fresh eggs, and any perishable egg product, as close as possible to, but not later than, the 7th day after product delivery.

(B) *For fresh or frozen fish,* as defined in section 204(3) of the Fish and Seafood Promotion Act of 1986 (16 U.S.C. 4003(3)), as close as possible to, but not later than, the 7th day after product delivery.

(C) *For perishable agricultural commodities,* as defined in section 1(4) of the Perishable Agricultural Commodities Act of 1930 (7 U.S.C. 499a(4)), as close as possible to, but not later than, the 10th day after product delivery, unless another date is specified in the contract.

(D) *For dairy products,* as defined in section 111(e) of the Dairy Production Stabilization Act of 1983 (7 U.S.C. 4502(e)), edible fats or oils, and food products prepared from edible fats or oils, as close as possible to, but not later than, the 10th day after the date on which a proper invoice has been received. Liquid milk, cheese, certain processed cheese products, butter, yogurt, ice cream, mayonnaise, salad dressings, and other similar products, fall within this classification. Nothing in the Act limits this classification to refrigerated products. When questions arise regarding the proper classification of a specific product, prevailing industry practices will be followed in specifying a contract payment due date. The burden of proof that a classification of a specific product is, in fact, prevailing industry practice is upon the Contractor making the representation.

(ii) If the contract does not require submission of an invoice for payment (e.g., periodic lease payments), the due date will be as specified in the contract.

(3) *Contractor's invoice.* The Contractor shall prepare and submit invoices to the designated billing office specified in the contract. A proper invoice must include the items listed in paragraphs (a)(3)(i) through (a)(3)(x) of this clause. If the invoice does not comply with these requirements, the designated billing office will return it within 7 days after receipt (3 days for meat, meat food products, or fish; 5 days for perishable agricultural commodities, dairy products, edible fats or oils, and food products prepared from edible fats or oils), with the reasons why it is not a proper invoice. The Government will take into account untimely notifica-

tion when computing any interest penalty owed the Contractor.

(i) Name and address of the Contractor.

(ii) Invoice date and invoice number. (The Contractor should date invoices as close as possible to the date of the mailing or transmission.)

(iii) Contract number or other authorization for supplies delivered or services performed (including order number and line item number).

(iv) Description, quantity, unit of measure, unit price, and extended price of supplies delivered or services performed.

(v) Shipping and payment terms (e.g., shipment number and date of shipment, discount for prompt payment terms). Bill of lading number and weight of shipment will be shown for shipments on Government bills of lading.

(vi) Name and address of Contractor official to whom payment is to be sent (must be the same as that in the contract or in a proper notice of assignment).

(vii) Name (where practicable), title, phone number, and mailing address of person to notify in the event of a defective invoice.

(viii) Taxpayer Identification Number (TIN). The Contractor shall include its TIN on the invoice only if required elsewhere in this contract.

(ix) Electronic funds transfer (EFT) banking information.

(A) The Contractor shall include EFT banking information on the invoice only if required elsewhere in this contract.

(B) If EFT banking information is not required to be on the invoice, in order for the invoice to be a proper invoice, the Contractor shall have submitted correct EFT banking information in accordance with the applicable solicitation provision (e.g., 52.232-38, Submission of Electronic Funds Transfer Information with Offer), contract clause (e.g., 52.232-33, Payment by Electronic Funds Transfer—System for Award Management, or 52.232-34, Payment by Electronic Funds Transfer—Other Than System for Award Management), or applicable agency procedures.

(C) EFT banking information is not required if the Government waived the requirement to pay by EFT.

(x) Any other information or documentation required by the contract (e.g., evidence of shipment).

(4) *Interest penalty*. The designated payment office will pay an interest penalty automatically, without request from the Contractor, if payment is not made by the due date and the conditions listed in paragraphs (a)(4)(i) through (a)(4)(iii) of this clause are met, if applicable. However, when the due date falls on a Saturday, Sunday, or legal holiday, the designated payment office may make payment on the following working day without incurring a late payment interest penalty.

(i) The designated billing office received a proper invoice.

(ii) The Government processed a receiving report or other Government documentation authorizing payment, and there was no disagreement over quantity, quality, or Contractor compliance with any contract term or condition.

(iii) In the case of a final invoice for any balance of funds due the Contractor for supplies delivered or services performed, the amount was not subject to further contract settlement actions between the Government and the Contractor.

(5) ***Computing penalty amount***. The Government will compute the interest penalty in accordance with the Office of Management and Budget prompt payment regulations at 5 CFR part 1315.

(i) For the sole purpose of computing an interest penalty that might be due the Contractor, Government acceptance is deemed to occur constructively on the 7th day (unless otherwise specified in this contract) after the Contractor delivers the supplies or performs the services in accordance with the terms and conditions of the contract, unless there is a disagreement over quantity, quality, or Contractor compliance with a contract provision. If actual acceptance occurs within the constructive acceptance period, the Government will base the determination of an interest penalty on the actual date of acceptance. The constructive acceptance requirement does not, however, compel Government officials to accept supplies or services, perform contract administration functions, or make payment prior to fulfilling their responsibilities.

(ii) The prompt payment regulations at 5 CFR 1315.10(c) do not require the Government to pay interest penalties if payment delays are due to disagreement between the Government and the Contractor over the payment amount or other issues involving contract compliance, or on amounts temporarily withheld or retained in accordance with the terms of the contract. The Government and the Contractor shall resolve claims involving disputes and any interest that may be payable in accordance with the clause at FAR 52.233-1, Disputes.

(6) *Discounts for prompt payment.* The designated payment office will pay an interest penalty automatically, without request from the Contractor, if the Government takes a discount for prompt payment improperly. The Government will calculate the interest penalty in accordance with the prompt payment regulations at 5 CFR part 1315.

(7) *Additional interest penalty.* (i) The designated payment office will pay a penalty amount, calculated in accordance with the prompt payment regulations at 5 CFR part 1315 in addition to the interest penalty amount only if—

(A) The Government owes an interest penalty of $1 or more;

(B) The designated payment office does not pay the interest penalty within 10 days after the date the invoice amount is paid; and

(C) The Contractor makes a written demand to the designated payment office for additional penalty payment, in accordance with paragraph (a)(7)(ii) of this clause, postmarked not later than 40 days after the invoice amount is paid.

(ii)(A) The Contractor shall support written demands for additional penalty payments with the following data. The Government will not request any additional data. The Contractor shall—

(1) Specifically assert that late payment interest is due under a specific invoice, and request payment of all overdue late payment interest penalty and such additional penalty as may be required;

(2) Attach a copy of the invoice on which the unpaid late payment interest is due; and

(3) State that payment of the principal has been received, including the date of receipt.

(B) If there is no postmark or the postmark is illegible—

(1) The designated payment office that receives the demand will annotate it with the date of receipt, provided the demand is received on or before the 40th day after payment was made; or

(2) If the designated payment office fails to make the required annotation, the Government will determine the demand's validity based on the date the Contractor has placed on the demand, provided such date is no later than the 40th day after payment was made.

(iii) The additional penalty does not apply to payments regulated by other Government regulations (e.g., payments under utility contracts subject to tariffs and regulation).

(b) *Contract financing payment.* If this contract provides for contract financing, the Government will make contract financing payments in accordance with the applicable contract financing clause.

(c) *Fast payment procedure due dates.* If this contract contains the clause at 52.213-1, Fast Payment Procedure, payments will be made within 15 days after the date of receipt of the invoice.

(d) *Overpayments.* If the Contractor becomes aware of a duplicate contract financing or invoice payment or that the Government has otherwise overpaid on a contract financing or invoice payment, the Contractor shall—

(1) Remit the overpayment amount to the payment office cited in the contract along with a description of the overpayment including the—

(i) Circumstances of the overpayment (e.g., duplicate payment, erroneous payment, liquidation errors, date(s) of overpayment);

(ii) Affected contract number and delivery order number if applicable;

(iii) Affected line item or subline item, if applicable; and

(iv) Contractor point of contact.

(2) Provide a copy of the remittance and supporting documentation to the Contracting Officer.

(End of clause)

Alternate I (FEB 2002). As prescribed in 32.908(c)(3), add the following paragraph (e) to the basic clause:

(e) *Invoices for interim payments.* For interim payments under this cost-reimbursement contract for services—

(1) Paragraphs (a)(2), (a)(3), (a)(4)(ii), (a)(4)(iii), and (a)(5)(i) do not apply;

(2) For purposes of computing late payment interest penalties that may apply, the due date for payment is the 30th day after the designated billing office receives a proper invoice; and

(3) The contractor shall submit invoices for interim payments in accordance with paragraph (a) of FAR 52.216-7, Allowable Cost and Payment. If the invoice does not comply with contract requirements, it will be returned within 7 days after the date the designated billing office received the invoice.

[FAC 84-33, 53 FR 3693, 2/8/88, effective 2/22/88; FAC 84-45, 54 FR 13338, 3/31/89, effective 4/1/89; FAC 84-49, 54 FR 29283, 7/11/89, effective 8/10/89; FAC 90-13, 57 FR 44268, 9/24/92, effective 9/24/92; Interim rule, FAC 90-20, 59 FR 11368, 3/10/94, effective 3/10/94, finalized without change, FAC 90-39, 61 FR 31612, 6/20/96, effective 6/20/96; FAC 90-46, 62 FR 12690, 3/17/97, effective 5/16/97; Final rule, 62 FR 40236, 7/25/97, effective 6/30/97; FAC 97-22, 66 FR 2117, 1/10/2001, effective 3/12/2001, effective date changed to 5/11/2001, 66 FR 14259, 3/9/2001; FAC 2001-01, 66 FR 53485, 10/22/2001, effective 10/22/2001; FAC 2001-02, 66 FR 65347, 12/18/2001, effective 2/19/2002; FAC 2001-14, 68 FR 28092, 5/22/2003, effective 5/22/2003; FAC 2001-16, 68 FR 56682, 10/1/2003, effective 10/31/2003; FAC 2005-27, 73 FR 53997, 9/17/2008, effective 10/17/2008; FAC 2005-67, 78 FR 37676, 6/21/2013, effective 7/22/2013; FAC 2005-95, 82 FR 4709, 1/13/2017, effective 1/13/2017]

52.232-26 Prompt Payment for Fixed-Price Architect-Engineer Contracts.

As prescribed in 32.908(a), insert the following clause:

PROMPT PAYMENT FOR FIXED-PRICE ARCHITECT-ENGINEER CONTRACTS (JAN 2017)

Notwithstanding any other payment terms in this contract, the Government will make invoice payments under the terms and conditions specified in this clause. The Government considers payment as being made on the day a check is dated or the date of an electronic funds transfer. Definitions of pertinent terms are set forth in sections 2.101, 32.001, and 32.902 of the Federal Acquisition Regulation. All days referred to in this clause are calendar days, unless otherwise specified. (However, see paragraph (a)(3) of this clause concerning payments due on Saturdays, Sundays, and legal holidays.)

(a) *Invoice payments—(1) Due date.* The due date for making invoice payments is—

(i) For work or services completed by the Contractor, the later of the following two events:

(A) The 30th day after the designated billing office receives a proper invoice from the Contractor (except as provided in paragraph (a)(1)(iii) of this clause).

(B) The 30th day after Government acceptance of the work or services completed by the Contractor. For a final invoice, when the payment amount is subject to contract settlement actions (e.g., release of claims), acceptance is deemed to occur on the effective date of the settlement.

(ii) The due date for progress payments is the 30th day after Government approval of Contractor estimates of work or services accomplished.

(iii) If the designated billing office fails to annotate the invoice or payment request with the actual date of receipt at the time of receipt, the payment due date is the 30th day after the date of the Contractor's invoice or payment request, provided the designated billing office receives a proper invoice or payment request and there is no disagreement over quantity, quality, or Contractor compliance with contract requirements.

(2) *Contractor's invoice.* The Contractor shall prepare and submit invoices to the designated billing office specified in the contract. A proper invoice must include the items listed in paragraphs (a)(2)(i) through (a)(2)(x) of this clause. If the invoice does not comply with these requirements, the designated billing office will return it within 7 days after receipt, with the reasons why it is not a proper invoice. When computing any interest penalty owed the Contractor, the Government will take into account if the Government notifies the Contractor of an improper invoice in an untimely manner.

(i) Name and address of the Contractor.

(ii) Invoice date and invoice number. (The Contractor should date invoices as close as possible to the date of mailing or transmission.)

(iii) Contract number or other authorization for work or services performed (including order number and line item number).

(iv) Description of work or services performed.

(v) Delivery and payment terms (e.g., discount for prompt payment terms).

(vi) Name and address of Contractor official to whom payment is to be sent (must be the same as that in the contract or in a proper notice of assignment).

(vii) Name (where practicable), title, phone number, and mailing address of person to be notified in the event of a defective invoice.

(viii) Taxpayer Identification Number (TIN). The Contractor shall include its TIN on the invoice only if required elsewhere in this contract.

(ix) Electronic funds transfer (EFT) banking information.

(A) The Contractor shall include EFT banking information on the invoice only if required elsewhere in this contract.

(B) If EFT banking information is not required to be on the invoice, in order for the invoice to be a proper invoice, the Contractor shall have submitted correct EFT banking information in accordance with the applicable solicitation provision (e.g., 52.232-38, Submission of Electronic Funds Transfer Information with Offer), contract clause (e.g., 52.232-33, Payment by Electronic Funds Transfer—System for Award Management, or 52.232-34, Payment by Electronic Funds Transfer—Other Than System for Award Management), or applicable agency procedures.

(C) EFT banking information is not required if the Government waived the requirement to pay by EFT.

(x) Any other information or documentation required by the contract.

(3) *Interest penalty.* The designated payment office will pay an interest penalty automatically, without request from the Contractor, if payment is not made by the due date and the conditions listed in paragraphs (a)(3)(i) through (a)(3)(iii) of this clause are met, if applicable. However, when the due date falls on a Saturday, Sunday, or legal holiday, the designated payment office may make payment on the following working day without incurring a late payment interest penalty.

(i) The designated billing office received a proper invoice.

(ii) The Government processed a receiving report or other Government documentation authorizing payment and there was no disagreement over quantity, quality, Contractor compliance with any contract term or condition, or requested progress payment amount.

(iii) In the case of a final invoice for any balance of funds due the Contractor for work or services performed, the amount was not subject to further contract settlement actions between the Government and the Contractor.

(4) *Computing penalty amount.* The Government will compute the interest penalty in accordance with the Office of Management and Budget prompt payment regulations at 5 CFR part 1315.

(i) For the sole purpose of computing an interest penalty that might be due the Contractor, Government acceptance or approval is deemed to occur constructively as shown in paragraphs (a)(4)(i)(A) and (B) of this clause. If actual acceptance or approval occurs within the constructive acceptance or approval period, the Government will base the determination of an interest penalty on the actual date of acceptance or approval. Constructive acceptance or constructive approval requirements do not apply if there is a disagreement over quantity, quality, Contractor compliance with a contract provision, or requested progress payment amounts. These requirements also do not compel Government officials to accept work or services, approve Contractor estimates, perform contract administration functions, or make payment prior to fulfilling their responsibilities.

(A) For work or services completed by the Contractor, Government acceptance is deemed to occur constructively on the 7th day after the Contractor completes the work or services in accordance with the terms and conditions of the contract.

(B) For progress payments, Government approval is deemed to occur on the 7th day after the designated billing office receives the Contractor estimates.

(ii) The prompt payment regulations at 5 CFR 1315.10(c) do not require the Government to pay interest penalties if payment delays are due to disagreement between the Government and the Contractor over the payment amount or other issues involving contract compliance, or on amounts temporarily withheld or retained in accordance with the terms of the contract. The Government and the Contractor shall resolve claims involving disputes, and any interest that may be payable in accordance with the clause at FAR 52.233-1, Disputes.

(5) *Discounts for prompt payment.* The designated payment office will pay an interest penalty automatically, without request from the Contractor, if the Government takes a discount for prompt payment improperly. The Government will calculate the interest penalty in accordance with 5 CFR part 1315.

(6) *Additional interest penalty.* (i) The designated payment office will pay a penalty amount, calculated in accordance with the prompt payment regulations at 5 CFR part 1315, in addition to the interest penalty amount only if—

(A) The Government owes an interest penalty of $1 or more;

(B) The designated payment office does not pay the interest penalty within 10 days after the date the invoice amount is paid; and

(C) The contractor makes a written demand to the designated payment office for additional penalty payment, in accordance with paragraph (a)(6)(ii) of this clause, postmarked not later than 40 days after the date the invoice amount is paid.

(ii)(A) The Contractor shall support written demands for additional penalty payments with the following data. The Government will not request any additional data. The Contractor shall—

(1) Specifically assert that late payment interest is due under a specific invoice, and request payment of all overdue late payment interest penalty and such additional penalty as may be required;

(2) Attach a copy of the invoice on which the unpaid late payment interest is due; and

(3) State that payment of the principal has been received, including the date of receipt.

(B) If there is no postmark or the postmark is illegible—

(1) The designated payment office that receives the demand will annotate it with the date of receipt, provided the demand is received on or before the 40th day after payment was made; or

(2) If the designated payment office fails to make the required annotation, the Government will determine the demand's validity based on the date the Contractor has

placed on the demand, provided such date is no later than the 40th day after payment was made.

(iii) The additional penalty does not apply to payments regulated by other Government regulations (e.g., payments under utility contracts subject to tariffs and regulation).

(b) *Contract financing payments.* If this contract provides for contract financing, the Government will make contract financing payments in accordance with the applicable contract financing clause.

(c) *Overpayments.* If the Contractor becomes aware of a duplicate contract financing or invoice payment or that the Government has otherwise overpaid on a contract financing or invoice payment, the Contractor shall—

(1) Remit the overpayment amount to the payment office cited in the contract along with a description of the overpayment including the—

(i) Circumstances of the overpayment (e.g., duplicate payment, erroneous payment, liquidation errors, date(s) of overpayment);

(ii) Affected contract number and delivery order number if applicable;

(iii) Affected line item or subline item, if applicable; and

(iv) Contractor point of contact.

(2) Provide a copy of the remittance and supporting documentation to the Contracting Officer.

(End of clause)

[FAC 2001-02, 66 FR 65347, 12/18/2001, effective 2/19/2002; FAC 2001-16, 68 FR 56682, 10/1/2003, effective 10/31/2003; FAC 2005-27, 73 FR 53997, 9/17/2008, effective 10/17/2008; FAC 2005-67, 78 FR 37676, 6/21/2013, effective 7/22/2013; FAC 2005-95, 82 FR 4709, 1/13/2017, effective 1/13/2017]

52.232-27 Prompt Payment for Construction Contracts.

As prescribed in 32.908(b), insert the following clause:

PROMPT PAYMENT FOR CONSTRUCTION CONTRACTS (JAN 2017)

Notwithstanding any other payment terms in this contract, the Government will make invoice payments under the terms and conditions specified in this clause. The Government considers payment as being made on the day a check is dated or the date of an electronic funds transfer. Definitions of pertinent terms are set forth in sections 2.101, 32.001, and 32.902 of the Federal Acquisition Regulation. All days referred to in this clause are calendar days, unless otherwise specified. (However, see paragraph (a)(3) concerning payments due on Saturdays, Sundays, and legal holidays.)

(a) *Invoice payments—(1) Types of invoice payments.* For purposes of this clause, there are several types of invoice payments that may occur under this contract, as follows:

(i) Progress payments, if provided for elsewhere in this contract, based on Contracting Officer approval of the estimated amount and value of work or services performed, including payments for reaching milestones in any project.

(A) The due date for making such payments is 14 days after the designated billing office receives a proper payment request. If the designated billing office fails to annotate the payment request with the actual date of receipt at the time of receipt, the payment due date is the 14th day after the date of the Contractor's payment request, provided the designated billing office receives a proper payment request and there is no disagreement over quantity, quality, or Contractor compliance with contract requirements.

(B) The due date for payment of any amounts retained by the Contracting Officer in accordance with the clause at 52.232-5, Payments Under Fixed-Price Construction Contracts, is as specified in the contract or, if not specified, 30 days after approval by the Contracting Officer for release to the Contractor.

(ii) Final payments based on completion and acceptance of all work and presentation of release of all claims against the Government arising by virtue of the contract, and payments for partial deliveries that have been accepted by the Government (e.g., each separate building, public work, or other division of the contract for which the price is stated separately in the contract).

(A) The due date for making such payments is the later of the following two events:

(1) The 30th day after the designated billing office receives a proper invoice from the Contractor.

(2) The 30th day after Government acceptance of the work or services completed by the Contractor. For a final invoice when the payment amount is subject to contract settlement actions (e.g., release of claims), acceptance is deemed to occur on the effective date of the contract settlement.

(B) If the designated billing office fails to annotate the invoice with the date of actual receipt at the time of receipt, the invoice payment due date is the 30th day after the date of the Contractor's invoice, provided the designated billing office receives a proper invoice and there is no disagreement over quantity, quality, or Contractor compliance with contract requirements.

(2) *Contractor's invoice.* The Contractor shall prepare and submit invoices to the designated billing office specified in the contract. A proper invoice must include the items listed in paragraphs (a)(2)(i) through (a)(2)(xi) of this clause. If the invoice does not comply with these requirements, the designated billing office must return it within 7 days after receipt, with the reasons why it is not a proper invoice. When computing any interest penalty owed the Contractor, the Government will take into account if the Government notifies the Contractor of an improper invoice in an untimely manner.

(i) Name and address of the Contractor.

(ii) Invoice date and invoice number. (The Contractor should date invoices as close as possible to the date of mailing or transmission.)

(iii) Contract number or other authorization for work or services performed (including order number and line item number).

(iv) Description of work or services performed.

(v) Delivery and payment terms (e.g., discount for prompt payment terms).

(vi) Name and address of Contractor official to whom payment is to be sent (must be the same as that in the contract or in a proper notice of assignment).

(vii) Name (where practicable), title, phone number, and mailing address of person to notify in the event of a defective invoice.

(viii) For payments described in paragraph (a)(1)(i) of this clause, substantiation of the amounts requested and certification in accordance with the requirements of the clause at 52.232-5, Payments Under Fixed-Price Construction Contracts.

(ix) Taxpayer Identification Number (TIN). The Contractor shall include its TIN on the invoice only if required elsewhere in this contract.

(x) Electronic funds transfer (EFT) banking information.

(A) The Contractor shall include EFT banking information on the invoice only if required elsewhere in this contract.

(B) If EFT banking information is not required to be on the invoice, in order for the invoice to be a proper invoice, the Contractor shall have submitted correct EFT banking information in accordance with the applicable solicitation provision (e.g., 52.232-38, Submission of Electronic Funds Transfer Information with Offer), contract clause (e.g., 52.232-33, Payment by Electronic Funds Transfer—System for Award Management, or 52.232-34, Payment by Electronic Funds Transfer—Other Than System for Award Management), or applicable agency procedures.

(C) EFT banking information is not required if the Government waived the requirement to pay by EFT.

(xi) Any other information or documentation required by the contract.

(3) *Interest penalty.* The designated payment office will pay an interest penalty automatically, without request from the Contractor, if payment is not made by the due date and the conditions listed in

paragraphs (a)(3)(i) through (a)(3)(iii) of this clause are met, if applicable. However, when the due date falls on a Saturday, Sunday, or legal holiday, the designated payment office may make payment on the following working day without incurring a late payment interest penalty.

(i) The designated billing office received a proper invoice.

(ii) The Government processed a receiving report or other Government documentation authorizing payment and there was no disagreement over quantity, quality, Contractor compliance with any contract term or condition, or requested progress payment amount.

(iii) In the case of a final invoice for any balance of funds due the Contractor for work or services performed, the amount was not subject to further contract settlement actions between the Government and the Contractor.

(4) *Computing penalty amount*. The Government will compute the interest penalty in accordance with the Office of Management and Budget prompt payment regulations at 5 CFR part 1315.

(i) For the sole purpose of computing an interest penalty that might be due the Contractor for payments described in paragraph (a)(1)(ii) of this clause, Government acceptance or approval is deemed to occur constructively on the 7th day after the Contractor has completed the work or services in accordance with the terms and conditions of the contract. If actual acceptance or approval occurs within the constructive acceptance or approval period, the Government will base the determination of an interest penalty on the actual date of acceptance or approval. Constructive acceptance or constructive approval requirements do not apply if there is a disagreement over quantity, quality, or Contractor compliance with a contract provision. These requirements also do not compel Government officials to accept work or services, approve Contractor estimates, perform contract administration functions, or make payment prior to fulfilling their responsibilities.

(ii) The prompt payment regulations at 5 CFR 1315.10(c) do not require the Government to pay interest penalties if payment delays are due to disagreement between the Government and the Contractor over the payment amount or other issues involving contract compliance, or on amounts temporarily withheld or retained in accordance with the terms of the contract. The Government and the Contractor shall resolve claims involving disputes, and any interest that may be payable in accordance with the clause at FAR 52.233-1, Disputes.

(5) *Discounts for prompt payment*. The designated payment office will pay an interest penalty automatically, without request from the Contractor, if the Government takes a discount for prompt payment improperly. The Government will calculate the interest penalty in accordance with the prompt payment regulations at 5 CFR part 1315.

(6) *Additional interest penalty*. (i) The designated payment office will pay a penalty amount, calculated in accordance with the prompt payment regulations at 5 CFR part 1315 in addition to the interest penalty amount only if—

(A) The Government owes an interest penalty of $1 or more;

(B) The designated payment office does not pay the interest penalty within 10 days after the date the invoice amount is paid; and

(C) The Contractor makes a written demand to the designated payment office for additional penalty payment, in accordance with paragraph (a)(6)(ii) of this clause, postmarked not later than 40 days after the date the invoice amount is paid.

(ii)(A) The Contractor shall support written demands for additional penalty payments with the following data. The Government will not request any additional data. The Contractor shall—

(1) Specifically assert that late payment interest is due under a specific invoice, and request payment of all overdue late payment interest penalty and such additional penalty as may be required;

(2) Attach a copy of the invoice on which the unpaid late payment interest was due; and

(3) State that payment of the principal has been received, including the date of receipt.

(B) If there is no postmark or the postmark is illegible—

(1) The designated payment office that receives the demand will annotate it with the date of receipt provided the demand is received on or before the 40th day after payment was made; or

(2) If the designated payment office fails to make the required annotation, the Government will determine the demand's validity based on the date the Contractor has placed on the demand, provided such date is no later than the 40th day after payment was made.

(b) *Contract financing payments.* If this contract provides for contract financing, the Government will make contract financing payments in accordance with the applicable contract financing clause.

(c) *Subcontract clause requirements.* The Contractor shall include in each subcontract for property or services (including a material supplier) for the purpose of performing this contract the following:

(1) *Prompt payment for subcontractors.* A payment clause that obligates the Contractor to pay the subcontractor for satisfactory performance under its subcontract not later than 7 days from receipt of payment out of such amounts as are paid to the Contractor under this contract.

(2) *Interest for subcontractors.* An interest penalty clause that obligates the Contractor to pay to the subcontractor an interest penalty for each payment not made in accordance with the payment clause—

(i) For the period beginning on the day after the required payment date and ending on the date on which payment of the amount due is made; and

(ii) Computed at the rate of interest established by the Secretary of the Treasury, and published in the Federal Register, for interest payments under 41 U.S.C. 7109 in effect at the time the Contractor accrues the obligation to pay an interest penalty.

(3) *Subcontractor clause flowdown.* A clause requiring each subcontractor to

(i) Include a payment clause and an interest penalty clause conforming to the standards set forth in paragraphs (c)(1) and (c)(2) of this clause in each of its subcontracts; and

(ii) Require each of its subcontractors to include such clauses in their subcontracts with each lower-tier subcontractor or supplier.

(d) *Subcontract clause interpretation.* The clauses required by paragraph (c) of this clause shall not be construed to impair the right of the Contractor or a subcontractor at any tier to negotiate, and to include in their subcontract, provisions that—

(1) *Retainage permitted.* Permit the Contractor or a subcontractor to retain (without cause) a specified percentage of each progress payment otherwise due to a subcontractor for satisfactory performance under the subcontract without incurring any obligation to pay a late payment interest penalty, in accordance with terms and conditions agreed to by the parties to the subcontract, giving such recognition as the parties deem appropriate to the ability of a subcontractor to furnish a performance bond and a payment bond;

(2) *Withholding permitted.* Permit the Contractor or subcontractor to make a determination that part or all of the subcontractor's request for payment may be withheld in accordance with the subcontract agreement; and

(3) *Withholding requirements.* Permit such withholding without incurring any obligation to pay a late payment penalty if—

(i) A notice conforming to the standards of paragraph (g) of this clause previously has been furnished to the subcontractor; and

(ii) The Contractor furnishes to the Contracting Officer a copy of any notice issued by a Contractor pursuant to paragraph (d)(3)(i) of this clause.

(e) *Subcontractor withholding procedures.* If a Contractor, after making a request for payment to the Government but before making a payment to a subcontractor for the subcontractor's performance covered by the payment request, discovers that all or a portion of the payment otherwise due such subcontractor is subject to withholding from the subcontractor in accordance with the subcontract agreement, then the Contractor shall—

(1) *Subcontractor notice.* Furnish to the subcontractor a notice conforming to the standards of paragraph (g) of this clause as soon as practicable upon ascertaining the cause giving rise to a withholding, but prior to the due date for subcontractor payment;

(2) *Contracting Officer notice.* Furnish to the Contracting Officer, as soon as practicable, a copy of the notice furnished to the subcontractor pursuant to paragraph (e)(1) of this clause;

(3) *Subcontractor progress payment reduction.* Reduce the subcontractor's progress payment by an amount not to exceed the amount specified in the notice of withholding furnished under paragraph (e)(1) of this clause;

(4) *Subsequent subcontractor payment.* Pay the subcontractor as soon as practicable after the correction of the identified subcontract performance deficiency, and—

(i) Make such payment within—

(A) Seven days after correction of the identified subcontract performance deficiency (unless the funds therefor must be recovered from the Government because of a reduction under paragraph (e)(5)(i)) of this clause; or

(B) Seven days after the Contractor recovers such funds from the Government; or

(ii) Incur an obligation to pay a late payment interest penalty computed at the rate of interest established by the Secretary of the Treasury, and published in the Federal Register, for interest payments under 41 U.S.C. 7109 in effect at the time the Contractor accrues the obligation to pay an interest penalty;

(5) *Notice to Contracting Officer.* Notify the Contracting Officer upon—

(i) Reduction of the amount of any subsequent certified application for payment; or

(ii) Payment to the subcontractor of any withheld amounts of a progress payment, specifying—

(A) The amounts withheld under paragraph (e)(1) of this clause; and

(B) The dates that such withholding began and ended; and

(6) *Interest to Government.* Be obligated to pay to the Government an amount equal to interest on the withheld payments (computed in the manner provided in 31 U.S.C. 3903(c)(1)), from the 8th day after receipt of the withheld amounts from the Government until—

(i) The day the identified subcontractor performance deficiency is corrected; or

(ii) The date that any subsequent payment is reduced under paragraph (e)(5)(i) of this clause.

(f) *Third-party deficiency reports—(1) Withholding from subcontractor.* If a Contractor, after making payment to a first-tier subcontractor, receives from a supplier or subcontractor of the first-tier subcontractor (hereafter referred to as a "second-tier subcontractor") a written notice in accordance with 40 U.S.C. 3133, asserting a deficiency in such first-tier subcontractor's performance under the contract for which the Contractor may be ultimately liable, and the Contractor determines that all or a portion of future payments otherwise due such first-tier subcontractor is subject to withholding in accordance with the subcontract agreement, the Contractor may, without incurring an obligation to pay an interest penalty under paragraph (e)(6) of this clause—

(i) Furnish to the first-tier subcontractor a notice conforming to the standards of paragraph (g) of this clause as soon as practicable upon making such determination; and

(ii) Withhold from the first-tier subcontractor's next available progress payment or payments an amount not to exceed the amount specified in the notice of withholding furnished under paragraph (f)(1)(i) of this clause.

(2) *Subsequent payment or interest charge.* As soon as practicable, but not later than 7 days after receipt of satisfactory written notification that the identified subcontract performance deficiency has been corrected, the Contractor shall—

(i) Pay the amount withheld under paragraph (f)(1)(ii) of this clause to such first-tier subcontractor; or

(ii) Incur an obligation to pay a late payment interest penalty to such first-tier subcontractor computed at the rate of interest established by the Secretary of the Treasury, and published in the Federal Register, for interest payments under 41 U.S.C. 7109 in effect at the time the Contractor accrues the obligation to pay an interest penalty.

(g) *Written notice of subcontractor withholding.* The Contractor shall issue a written notice of any withholding to a subcontractor (with a copy furnished to the Contracting Officer), specifying—

(1) The amount to be withheld;

(2) The specific causes for the withholding under the terms of the subcontract; and

(3) The remedial actions to be taken by the subcontractor in order to receive payment of the amounts withheld.

(h) *Subcontractor payment entitlement.* The Contractor may not request payment from the Government of any amount withheld or retained in accordance with paragraph (d) of this clause until such time as the Contractor has determined and certified to the Contracting Officer that the subcontractor is entitled to the payment of such amount.

(i) *Prime-subcontractor disputes.* A dispute between the Contractor and subcontractor relating to the amount or entitlement of a subcontractor to a payment or a late payment interest penalty under a clause included in the subcontract pursuant to paragraph (c) of this clause does not constitute a dispute to which the United States is a party. The Government may not be interpleaded in any judicial or administrative proceeding involving such a dispute.

(j) *Preservation of prime-subcontractor rights.* Except as provided in paragraph (i) of this clause, this clause shall not limit or impair any contractual, administrative, or judicial remedies otherwise available to the Contractor or a subcontractor in the event of a dispute involving late payment or nonpayment by the Contractor or deficient subcontract performance or nonperformance by a subcontractor.

(k) *Non-recourse for prime contractor interest penalty.* The Contractor's obligation to pay an interest penalty to a subcontractor pursuant to the clauses included in a subcontract under paragraph (c) of this clause shall not be construed to be an obligation of the Government for such interest penalty. A cost-reimbursement claim may not include any amount for reimbursement of such interest penalty.

(l) *Overpayments.* If the Contractor becomes aware of a duplicate contract financing or invoice payment or that the Government has otherwise overpaid on a contract financing or invoice payment, the Contractor shall—

(1) Remit the overpayment amount to the payment office cited in the contract along with a description of the overpayment including the—

(i) Circumstances of the overpayment (e.g., duplicate payment, erroneous payment, liquidation errors, date(s) of overpayment);

(ii) Affected contract number and delivery order number if applicable;

(iii) Affected line item or subline item, if applicable; and

(iv) Contractor point of contact.

(2) Provide a copy of the remittance and supporting documentation to the Contracting Officer.

(End of clause)

[FAC 2001-02, 66 FR 65347, 12/18/2001, effective 2/19/2002; FAC 2001-16, 68 FR 56682, 10/1/2003, effective 10/31/2003; FAC 2005-06, 70 FR 57453, 9/30/2005, effective 9/30/2005; FAC 2005-27, 9/17/2008, effective 10/17/2008; FAC 2005-67, 78 FR

37676, 6/21/2013, effective 7/22/2013; FAC 2005-73, 79 FR 24192, 4/29/2014, effective 5/29/2014; FAC 2005-95, 82 FR 4709, 1/13/2017, effective 1/13/2017]

52.232-28 Invitation to Propose Performance-Based Payments.

As prescribed in 32.1005(b)(1), insert the following provision:

INVITATION TO PROPOSE PERFORMANCE-BASED PAYMENTS (MAR 2000)

(a) The Government invites the offeror to propose terms under which the Government will make performance-based contract financing payments during contract performance. The Government will consider performance-based payment financing terms proposed by the offeror in the evaluation of the offeror's proposal. The Contracting Officer will incorporate the financing terms of the successful offeror and the FAR clause, Performance-Based Payments, at FAR 52.232-32, in any resulting contract.

(b) In the event of any conflict between the terms proposed by the offeror and the terms in the clause at FAR 52.232-32, Performance-Based Payments, the terms of the clause at FAR 52.232-32 shall govern.

(c) The Contracting Officer will not accept the offeror's proposed performance-based payment financing if the financing does not conform to the following limitations:

(1) The Government will make delivery payments only for supplies delivered and accepted, or services rendered and accepted in accordance with the payment terms of this contract.

(2) The terms and conditions of the performance-based payments must—

(i) Comply with FAR 32.1004;

(ii) Be reasonable and consistent with all other technical and cost information included in the offeror's proposal; and

(iii) Their total shall not exceed 90 percent of the contract price if on a whole contract basis, or 90 percent of the delivery item price if on a delivery item basis.

(3) The terms and conditions of the performance-based financing must be in the best interests of the Government.

(d) The offeror's proposal of performance-based payment financing shall include the following:

(1) The proposed contractual language describing the performance-based payments (see FAR 32.1004 for appropriate criteria for establishing performance bases and performance-based finance payment amounts).

(2) A listing of—

(i) The projected performance-based payment dates and the projected payment amounts; and

(ii) The projected delivery date and the projected payment amount.

(3) Information addressing the Contractor's investment in the contract.

(e) Evaluation of the offeror's proposed prices and financing terms will include whether the offeror's proposed performance-based payment events and payment amounts are reasonable and consistent with all other terms and conditions of the offeror's proposal.

(End of provision)

Alternate I (MAR 2000). As prescribed in FAR 32.1005(b)(2), add the following paragraph (f) to the basic provision:

(f) The Government will adjust each proposed price to reflect the cost of providing the proposed performance-based payments to determine the total cost to the Government of that particular combination of price and performance-based financing. The Government will make the adjustment using the procedure described in FAR 32.205(c).

[FAC 97-16, 65 FR 16274, 3/27/2000, effective 3/27/2000]

52.232-29 Terms for Financing of Purchases of Commercial Items.

As prescribed in 32.206(b)(2), insert the following clause:

TERMS FOR FINANCING OF PURCHASES OF COMMERCIAL ITEMS (FEB 2002)

(a) *Contractor entitlement to financing payments.* The Contractor may request, and the Government shall pay, a contract financing payment as specified elsewhere in this contract when: the payment requested is properly due in accordance with this contract; the supplies deliverable or services due under the contract will be delivered or performed in accordance with the contract; and there has been no impairment or diminution of the Government's security under this contract.

(b) *Special terms regarding termination for cause.* If this contract is terminated for cause, the Contractor shall, on demand, repay to the Government the amount of unliquidated contract financing payments. The Government shall be liable for no payment except as provided by the Termination for Cause paragraph of the clause at 52.212-4, Contract Terms and Conditions—Commercial Items.

(c) *Security for Government financing.* In the event the Contractor fails to provide adequate security, as required in this contract, no financing payment shall be made under this contract. Upon receipt of adequate security, financing payments shall be made, including all previous payments to which the Contractor is entitled, in accordance with the terms of the provisions for contract financing. If at any time the Contracting Officer determines that the security provided by the Contractor is insufficient, the Contractor shall promptly provide such additional security as the Contracting Officer determines necessary. In the event the Contractor fails to provide such additional security, the Contracting Officer may collect or liquidate such security that has been provided and suspend further payments to the Contractor; and the Contractor shall repay to the Government the amount of unliquidated financing payments as the Contracting Officer at his sole discretion deems repayable.

(d) *Reservation of rights.* (1) No payment or other action by the Government under this clause shall (i) excuse the Contractor from performance of obligations under this contract, or (ii) constitute a waiver of any of the rights or remedies of the parties under the contract.

(2) The Government's rights and remedies under this clause (i) shall not be exclusive, but rather shall be in addition to any other rights and remedies provided by law or this contract; and (ii) shall not be affected by delayed, partial, or omitted exercise of any right, remedy, power, or privilege, nor shall such exercise or any single exercise preclude or impair any further exercise under this clause or the exercise of any other right, power, or privilege of the Government.

(e) *Content of Contractor's request for financing payment.* The Contractor's request for financing payment shall contain the following:

(1) The name and address of the Contractor;

(2) The date of the request for financing payment;

(3) The contract number and/or other identifier of the contract or order under which the request is made; and

(4) An appropriately itemized and totaled statement of the financing payments requested and such other information as is necessary for computation of the payment, prepared in accordance with the direction of the Contracting Officer.

(f) *Limitation on frequency of financing payments.* Contractor financing payments shall be provided no more frequently than monthly.

(g) *Dates for payment.* A payment under this clause is a contract financing payment and not subject to the interest penalty provisions of the Prompt Payment Act. The designated payment office will pay approved payment requests within 30 days of submittal of a proper request for payment.

(h) *Conflict between terms of offeror and clause.* In the event of any conflict between the terms proposed by the offeror in response to an invitation to propose financing terms (52.232-31) and the terms in this clause, the terms of this clause shall govern.

(End of clause)

[FAC 90-33, 60 FR 49706, 9/26/95, effective 10/1/95; FAC 2001-02, 66 FR 65347, 12/18/2001, effective 2/19/2002]

52.232-30 Installment Payments for Commercial Items.

As prescribed in 32.206(g), insert the following clause:

INSTALLMENT PAYMENTS FOR COMMERCIAL ITEMS (JAN 2017)

(a) *Contractor entitlement to financing payments*. The Contractor may request, and the Government shall pay, a contract financing installment payment as specified in this contract when: the payment requested is properly due in accordance with this contract; the supplies deliverable or services due under the contract will be delivered or performed in accordance with the contract; and there has been no impairment or diminution of the Government's security under this contract.

(b) *Computation of amounts*. Installment payment financing shall be paid to the Contractor when requested for each separately priced unit of supply (but not for services) of each line item in amounts approved by the Contracting Officer pursuant to this clause.

(1) *Number of installment payments for each line item*. Each separately priced unit of each line item is authorized a fixed number of monthly installment payments. The number of installment payments authorized for each unit of a line item is equal to the number of months from the date of contract award to the date one month before the first delivery of the first separately priced unit of the line item. For example, if the first scheduled delivery of any separately priced unit of a line item is 9 months after award of the contract, all separately priced units of that line item are authorized 8 installment payments.

(2) *Amount of each installment payment*. The amount of each installment payment for each separately priced unit of each line item is equal to 70 percent of the unit price divided by the number of installment payments authorized for that unit.

(3) *Date of each installment payment*. Installment payments for any particular separately priced unit of a line item begin the number of months prior to the delivery of that unit that are equal to the number of installment payments authorized for that unit. For example, if 8 installment payments are authorized for each separately priced unit of a line item, the first installment payment for any particular unit of that line item would be 8 months before the scheduled delivery date for that unit. The last installment payment would be 1 month before scheduled delivery of a unit.

(4) *Limitation on payment*. Prior to the delivery payment for a separately priced unit of a line item, the sum of all installment payments for that unit shall not exceed 70 percent of the price of that unit.

(c) *Contractor request for installment payment*. The Contractor may submit requests for payment of installment payments not more frequently than monthly, in a form and manner acceptable to the Contracting Officer. Unless otherwise authorized by the Contracting Officer, all installment payments in any month for which payment is being requested shall be included in a single request, appropriately itemized and totaled.

(d) *Dates for payment*. An installment payment under this clause is a contract financing payment under the Prompt Payment clause of this contract, and except as provided in paragraph (e) of this clause, approved requests shall be paid within 30 days of submittal of a proper request for payment.

(e) *Liquidation of installment payments*. Installment payments shall be liquidated by deducting from the delivery payment of each item the total unliquidated amount of installment payments made for that separately priced unit of that line item. The liquidation amounts for each unit of each line item shall be clearly delineated in each request for delivery payment submitted by the Contractor.

(f) *Security for installment payment financing*. In the event the Contractor fails to provide adequate security as required in this contract, no financing payment shall be made under this contract. Upon receipt of adequate security, financing payments shall be made, including all previous payments to which the Contractor is entitled, in accordance with the terms of the contract. If at any time the Contracting Officer determines that the security provided by the Contractor is insufficient, the Contractor shall promptly provide such additional security as the Contracting Officer determines necessary. In the event the Contractor fails to provide such additional security, the Contracting Officer may collect or liquidate such security that has been provided, and suspend further payments to the Contractor; the Contractor shall repay to the Government the amount of unliquidated financing payments as the Contracting Officer at his sole discretion deems repayable.

(g) *Special terms regarding termination for cause.* If this contract is terminated for cause, the Contractor shall, on demand, repay to the Government the amount of unliquidated installment payments. The Government shall be liable for no payment except as provided by the Termination for Cause paragraph of the clause at 52.212-4, Contract Terms and Conditions—Commercial Items.

(h) *Reservation of rights.* (1) No payment, vesting of title under this clause, or other action taken by the Government under this clause shall (i) excuse the Contractor from performance of obligations under this contract, or (ii) constitute a waiver of any of the rights or remedies of the parties under the contract.

(2) The Government's rights and remedies under this clause (i) shall not be exclusive, but rather shall be in addition to any other rights and remedies provided by law or this contract, and (ii) shall not be affected by delayed, partial, or omitted exercise of any right, remedy, power, or privilege, nor shall such exercise or any single exercise preclude or impair any further exercise under this clause or the exercise of any other right, power, or privilege of the Government.

(i) *Content of Contractor's request for installment payment.* The Contractor's request for installment payment shall contain the following:

(1) The name and address of the Contractor;

(2) The date of the request for installment payment;

(3) The contract number and/or other identifier of the contract or order under which the request is made; and

(4) An itemized and totaled statement of the items, installment payment amount, and month for which payment is being requested, for each separately priced unit of each line item.

(End of clause)

[FAC 90-33, 60 FR 49706, 9/26/95, effective 10/1/95; FAC 2005-95, 82 FR 4709, 1/13/2017, effective 1/13/2017]

52.232-31 Invitation to Propose Financing Terms.

As prescribed in 32.205(b) and 32.206, insert the following provision:

INVITATION TO PROPOSE FINANCING TERMS (MAY 2014)

(a) The offeror is invited to propose terms under which the Government shall make contract financing payments during contract performance. The financing terms proposed by the offeror shall be a factor in the evaluation of the offeror's proposal. The financing terms of the successful offeror and the clause, Terms for Financing of Purchases of Commercial Items, at 52.232-29, shall be incorporated in any resulting contract.

(b) The offeror agrees that in the event of any conflict between the terms proposed by the offeror and the terms in the clause at 52.232-29, Terms for Financing of Purchases of Commercial Items, the terms of the clause at 52.232-29 shall govern.

(c) Because of statutory limitations (10 U.S.C. 2307(f) and 41 U.S.C. 4505), the offeror's proposed financing shall not be acceptable if it does not conform to the following limitations:

(1) Delivery payments shall be made only for supplies delivered and accepted, or services rendered and accepted in accordance with the payment terms of this contract;

(2) Contract financing payments shall not exceed 15 percent of the contract price in advance of any performance of work under the contract;

(3) The terms and conditions of the contract financing must be appropriate or customary in the commercial marketplace; and

(4) The terms and conditions of the contract financing must be in the best interests of the United States.

(d) The offeror's proposal of financing terms shall include the following:

(1) The proposed contractual language describing the contract financing (see FAR 32.202-2 for appropriate definitions of types of payments); and

(2) A listing of the earliest date and greatest amount at which each contract financing payment may be payable and the amount of each delivery payment. Any resulting contract shall provide that no contract financing payment shall be made at any earlier date or in a greater amount than shown in the offeror's listing.

(e) The offeror's proposed prices and financing terms shall be evaluated to determine the cost to the United States of the proposal using the interest rate and delivery schedule specified elsewhere in this solicitation.

(End of provision)

[FAC 90-33, 60 FR 49706, 9/26/95, effective 10/1/95; FAC 2005-73, 79 FR 24192, 4/29/2014, effective 5/29/2014]

52.232-32 Performance-Based Payments.

As prescribed in 32.1005, insert the following clause:

PERFORMANCE-BASED PAYMENTS (APR 2012)

(a) *Amount of payments and limitations on payments.* Subject to such other limitations and conditions as are specified in this contract and this clause, the amount of payments and limitations on payments shall be specified in the contract's description of the basis for payment.

(b) *Contractor request for performance-based payment.* The Contractor may submit requests for payment of performance-based payments not more frequently than monthly, in a form and manner acceptable to the Contracting Officer. Unless otherwise authorized by the Contracting Officer, all performance-based payments in any period for which payment is being requested shall be included in a single request, appropriately itemized and totaled. The Contractor's request shall contain the information and certification detailed in paragraphs (l) and (m) of this clause.

(c) *Approval and payment of requests.* (1) The Contractor shall not be entitled to payment of a request for performance-based payment prior to successful accomplishment of the event or performance criterion for which payment is requested. The Contracting Officer shall determine whether the event or performance criterion for which payment is requested has been successfully accomplished in accordance with the terms of the contract. The Contracting Officer may, at any time, require the Contractor to substantiate the successful performance of any event or performance criterion which has been or is represented as being payable.

(2) A payment under this performance-based payment clause is a contract financing payment under the Prompt Payment clause of this contract and not subject to the interest penalty provisions of the Prompt Payment Act. The designated payment office will pay approved requests on the ______ [*Contracting Officer insert day as prescribed by agency head; if not prescribed, insert "30th"*] day after receipt of the request for performance-based payment by the designated payment office. However, the designated payment office is not required to provide payment if the Contracting Officer requires substantiation as provided in paragraph (c)(1) of this clause, or inquires into the status of an event or performance criterion, or into any of the conditions listed in paragraph (e) of this clause, or into the Contractor certification. The payment period will not begin until the Contracting Officer approves the request.

(3) The approval by the Contracting Officer of a request for performance-based payment does not constitute an acceptance by the Government and does not excuse the Contractor from performance of obligations under this contract.

(d) *Liquidation of performance-based payments.* (1) Performance-based finance amounts paid prior to payment for delivery of an item shall be liquidated by deducting a percentage or a designated dollar amount from the delivery payment. If the performance-based finance payments are on a delivery item basis, the liquidation amount for each such line item shall be the percent of that delivery item price that was previously paid under performance-based finance payments or the designated dollar amount. If the performance-based finance payments are on a whole contract basis, liquidation shall be by either predesignated liquidation amounts or a liquidation percentage.

(2) If at any time the amount of payments under this contract exceeds any limitation in this contract, the Contractor shall repay to the Government the excess. Unless otherwise determined by the Contracting Officer, such excess shall be credited as a reduction in the unliquidated performance-based payment balance(s), after adjustment of invoice payments and balances for any retroactive price adjustments.

(e) *Reduction or suspension of performance-based payments.* The Contracting Officer may reduce or suspend performance-based payments, liquidate performance-based payments by deduction from any payment under the contract, or take a combination of these actions after finding upon substantial evidence any of the following conditions:

(1) The Contractor failed to comply with any material requirement of this contract (which includes paragraphs (h) and (i) of this clause).

(2) Performance of this contract is endangered by the Contractor's (i) failure to make progress, or (ii) unsatisfactory financial condition.

(3) The Contractor is delinquent in payment of any subcontractor or supplier under this contract in the ordinary course of business.

(f) *Title.* Title to the property described in this paragraph (f) shall vest in the Government. Vestiture shall be immediately upon the date of the first performance-based payment under this contract, for property acquired or produced before that date. Otherwise, vestiture shall occur when the property is or should have been allocable or properly chargeable to this contract.

(2) *Property,* as used in this clause, includes all of the following described items acquired or produced by the Contractor that are or should be allocable or properly chargeable to this contract under sound and generally accepted accounting principles and practices:

(i) Parts, materials, inventories, and work in process;

(ii) Special tooling and special test equipment to which the Government is to acquire title;

(iii) Nondurable (i.e., noncapital) tools, jigs, dies, fixtures, molds, patterns, taps, gauges, test equipment and other similar manufacturing aids, title to which would not be obtained as special tooling under subparagraph (f)(2)(ii) of this clause; and

(iv) Drawings and technical data, to the extent the Contractor or subcontractors are required to deliver them to the Government by other clauses of this contract.

(3) Although title to property is in the Government under this clause, other applicable clauses of this contract (e.g., the termination clauses) shall determine the handling and disposition of the property.

(4) The Contractor may sell any scrap resulting from production under this contract, without requesting the Contracting Officer's approval, provided that any significant reduction in the value of the property to which the Government has title under this clause is reported in writing to the Contracting Officer.

(5) In order to acquire for its own use or dispose of property to which title is vested in the Government under this clause, the Contractor shall obtain the Contracting Officer's

advance approval of the action and the terms. If approved, the basis for payment (the events or performance criteria) to which the property is related shall be deemed to be not in compliance with the terms of the contract and not payable (if the property is part of or needed for performance), and the Contractor shall refund the related performance-based payments in accordance with paragraph (d) of this clause.

(6) When the Contractor completes all of the obligations under this contract, including liquidation of all performance-based payments, title shall vest in the Contractor for all property (or the proceeds thereof) not—

(i) Delivered to, and accepted by, the Government under this contract; or

(ii) Incorporated in supplies delivered to, and accepted by, the Government under this contract and to which title is vested in the Government under this clause.

(7) The terms of this contract concerning liability for Government-furnished property shall not apply to property to which the Government acquired title solely under this clause.

(g) *Risk of loss.* Before delivery to and acceptance by the Government, the Contractor shall bear the risk of loss for property, the title to which vests in the Government under this clause, except to the extent the Government expressly assumes the risk. If any property is lost (see 45.101), the basis of payment (the events or performance criteria) to which the property is related shall be deemed to be not in compliance with the terms of the contract and not payable (if the property is part of or needed for performance), and the Contractor shall refund the related performance-based payments in accordance with paragraph (d) of this clause.

(h) *Records and controls.* The Contractor shall maintain records and controls adequate for administration of this clause. The Contractor shall have no entitlement to performance-based payments during any time the Contractor's records or controls are determined by the Contracting Officer to be inadequate for administration of this clause.

(i) *Reports and Government access.* The Contractor shall promptly furnish reports, certificates, financial statements, and other pertinent information requested by the Contracting Officer for the administration of this clause and to determine that an event or other criterion prompting a financing payment has been successfully accomplished. The Contractor shall give the Government reasonable opportunity to examine and verify the Contractor's records and to examine and verify the Contractor's performance of this contract for administration of this clause.

(j) *Special terms regarding default.* If this contract is terminated under the Default clause, (1) the Contractor shall, on demand, repay to the Government the amount of unliquidated performance-based payments, and (2) title shall vest in the Contractor, on full liquidation of all performance-based payments, for all property for which the Government elects not to require delivery under the Default clause of this contract. The Government shall be liable for no payment except as provided by the Default clause.

(k) *Reservation of rights.* (1) No payment or vesting of title under this clause shall (i) excuse the Contractor from performance of obligations under this contract, or (ii) constitute a waiver of any of the rights or remedies of the parties under the contract.

(2) The Government's rights and remedies under this clause (i) shall not be exclusive, but rather shall be in addition to any other rights and remedies provided by law or this contract, and (ii) shall not be affected by delayed, partial, or omitted exercise of any right, remedy, power, or privilege, nor shall such exercise or any single exercise preclude or impair any further exercise under this clause or the exercise of any other right, power, or privilege of the Government.

(l) *Content of Contractor's request for performance-based payment.* The Contractor's request for performance-based payment shall contain the following:

(1) The name and address of the Contractor;

(2) The date of the request for performance-based payment;

(3) The contract number and/or other identifier of the contract or order under which the request is made;

(4) Such information and documentation as is required by the contract's description of the basis for payment; and

(5) A certification by a Contractor official authorized to bind the Contractor, as specified in paragraph (m) of this clause.

(m) *Content of Contractor's certification.* As required in paragraph (l)(5) of this clause, the Contractor shall make the following certification in each request for performance-based payment:

I certify to the best of my knowledge and belief that—

(1) This request for performance-based payment is true and correct; this request (and attachments) has been prepared from the books and records of the Contractor, in accordance with the contract and the instructions of the Contracting Officer;

(2) (Except as reported in writing on), all payments to subcontractors and suppliers under this contract have been paid, or will be paid, currently, when due in the ordinary course of business;

(3) There are no encumbrances (except as reported in writing on) against the property acquired or produced for, and allocated or properly chargeable to, the contract which would affect or impair the government's title;

(4) There has been no materially adverse change in the financial condition of the Contractor since the submission by the Contractor to the Government of the most recent written information dated ___; and

(5) After the making of this requested performance-based payment, the amount of all payments for each deliverable item for which performance-based payments have been requested will not exceed any limitation in the contract, and the amount of all payments under the contract will not exceed any limitation in the contract.

(End of clause)

[FAC 90-33, 60 FR 49706, 9/26/95, effective 10/1/95; FAC 90-46, 62 FR 12690, 3/17/97, effective 5/16/97; FAC 2001-02, 66 FR 65347, 12/18/2001, effective 2/19/2002; FAC 2005-23, 72 FR 73219, 12/26/2007, effective 1/25/2008; FAC 2005-43, 75 FR 38675, 7/2/2010, effective 8/2/2010; FAC 2005-56, 77 FR 12937, 3/2/2012, effective 4/2/2012]

52.232-33 Payment by Electronic Funds Transfer—System for Award Management.

As prescribed in 32.1110(a)(1), insert the following clause:

PAYMENT BY ELECTRONIC FUNDS TRANSFER—SYSTEM FOR AWARD MANAGEMENT (OCT 2018)

(a) *Method of payment.* (1) All payments by the Government under this contract shall be made by electronic funds transfer (EFT), except as provided in paragraph (a)(2) of this clause. As used in this clause, the term *EFT* refers to the funds transfer and may also include the payment information transfer.

(2) In the event the Government is unable to release one or more payments by EFT, the Contractor agrees to either—

(i) Accept payment by check or some other mutually agreeable method of payment; or

(ii) Request the Government to extend the payment due date until such time as the Government can make payment by EFT (but see paragraph (d) of this clause).

(b) *Contractor's EFT information.* The Government shall make payment to the Contractor using the EFT information contained in the System for Award Management (SAM). In the event that the EFT information changes, the Contractor shall be responsible for providing the updated information to SAM.

(c) *Mechanisms for EFT payment.* The Government may make payment by EFT through either the Automated Clearing House (ACH) network, subject to the rules of the National Automated Clearing House

Association, or the Fedwire Transfer System. The rules governing Federal payments through the ACH are contained in 31 CFR part 210.

(d) *Suspension of payment.* If the Contractor's EFT information in SAM is incorrect, then the Government need not make payment to the Contractor under this contract until correct EFT information is entered into SAM; and any invoice or contract financing request shall be deemed not to be a proper invoice for the purpose of prompt payment under this contract. The prompt payment terms of the contract regarding notice of an improper invoice and delays in accrual of interest penalties apply.

(e) *Liability for uncompleted or erroneous transfers.* (1) If an uncompleted or erroneous transfer occurs because the Government used the Contractor's EFT information incorrectly, the Government remains responsible for—

(i) Making a correct payment;

(ii) Paying any prompt payment penalty due; and

(iii) Recovering any erroneously directed funds.

(2) If an uncompleted or erroneous transfer occurs because the Contractor's EFT information was incorrect, or was revised within 30 days of Government release of the EFT payment transaction instruction to the Federal Reserve System, and—

(i) If the funds are no longer under the control of the payment office, the Government is deemed to have made payment and the Contractor is responsible for recovery of any erroneously directed funds; or

(ii) If the funds remain under the control of the payment office, the Government shall not make payment, and the provisions of paragraph (d) of this clause shall apply.

(f) *EFT and prompt payment.* A payment shall be deemed to have been made in a timely manner in accordance with the prompt payment terms of this contract if, in the EFT payment transaction instruction released to the Federal Reserve System, the date specified for settlement of the payment is on or before the prompt payment due date, provided the specified payment date is a valid date under the rules of the Federal Reserve System.

(g) *EFT and assignment of claims.* If the Contractor assigns the proceeds of this contract as provided for in the assignment of claims terms of this contract, the Contractor shall require as a condition of any such assignment, that the assignee shall register separately in SAM and shall be paid by EFT in accordance with the terms of this clause. Notwithstanding any other requirement of this contract, payment to an ultimate recipient other than the Contractor, or a financial institution properly recognized under an assignment of claims pursuant to subpart 32.8, is not permitted. In all respects, the requirements of this clause shall apply to the assignee as if it were the Contractor. EFT information that shows the ultimate recipient of the transfer to be other than the Contractor, in the absence of a proper assignment of claims acceptable to the Government, is incorrect EFT information within the meaning of paragraph (d) of this clause.

(h) *Liability for change of EFT information by financial agent.* The Government is not liable for errors resulting from changes to EFT information made by the Contractor's financial agent.

(i) *Payment information.* The payment or disbursing office shall forward to the Contractor available payment information that is suitable for transmission as of the date of release of the EFT instruction to the Federal Reserve System. The Government may request the Contractor to designate a desired format and method(s) for delivery of payment information from a list of formats and methods the payment office is capable of executing. However, the Government does not guarantee that any particular format or method of delivery is available at any particular payment office and retains the latitude to use the format and delivery method most convenient to the Government. If the Government makes payment by check in accordance with paragraph (a) of this clause, the Government shall mail the payment information to the remittance address contained in SAM.

(End of clause)

[FAC 97-11, 64 FR 10530, 3/4/99, effective 5/3/99; FAC 2001-16, Final rule, 68 FR 56669, 10/1/2003, effective 10/1/2003; FAC 2005-67, 78 FR 37676, 6/21/2013, effective 7/22/2013; FAC 2005-101, 83 FR 48691, 9/26/2018, effective 10/26/2018]

52.232-34 Payment by Electronic Funds Transfer—Other than System for Award Management.

As prescribed in 32.1110(a)(2), insert the following clause:

PAYMENT BY ELECTRONIC FUNDS TRANSFER—OTHER THAN SYSTEM FOR AWARD MANAGEMENT (JUL 2013)

(a) *Method of payment.* (1) All payments by the Government under this contract shall be made by electronic funds transfer (EFT) except as provided in paragraph (a)(2) of this clause. As used in this clause, the term *EFT* refers to the funds transfer and may also include the payment information transfer.

(2) In the event the Government is unable to release one or more payments by EFT, the Contractor agrees to either—

(i) Accept payment by check or some other mutually agreeable method of payment; or

(ii) Request the Government to extend payment due dates until such time as the Government makes payment by EFT (but see paragraph (d) of this clause).

(b) *Mandatory submission of Contractor's EFT information.* (1) The Contractor is required to provide the Government with the information required to make payment by EFT (see paragraph (j) of this clause). The Contractor shall provide this information directly to the office designated in this contract to receive that information (hereafter: *designated office*) by _____ [*the Contracting Officer shall insert date, days after award, days before first request, the date specified for receipt of offers if the provision at 52.232-38 is utilized, or "concurrent with first request" as prescribed by the head of the agency; if not prescribed, insert "no later than 15 days prior to submission of the first request for payment"*]. If not otherwise specified in this contract, the payment office is the designated office for receipt of the Contractor's EFT information. If more than one designated office is named for the contract, the Contractor shall provide a separate notice to each office. In the event that the EFT information changes, the Contractor shall be responsible for providing the updated information to the designated office(s).

(2) If the Contractor provides EFT information applicable to multiple contracts, the Contractor shall specifically state the applicability of this EFT information in terms acceptable to the designated office. However, EFT information supplied to a designated office shall be applicable only to contracts that identify that designated office as the office to receive EFT information for that contract.

(c) *Mechanisms for EFT payment.* The Government may make payment by EFT through either the Automated Clearing House (ACH) network, subject to the rules of the National Automated Clearing House Association, or the Fedwire Transfer System. The rules governing Federal payments through the ACH are contained in 31 CFR part 210.

(d) *Suspension of payment.* (1) The Government is not required to make any payment under this contract until after receipt, by the designated office, of the correct EFT payment information from the Contractor. Until receipt of the correct EFT information, any invoice or contract financing request shall be deemed not to be a proper invoice for the purpose of prompt payment under this contract. The prompt payment terms of the contract regarding notice of an improper invoice and delays in accrual of interest penalties apply.

(2) If the EFT information changes after submission of correct EFT information, the Government shall begin using the changed EFT information no later than 30 days after its receipt by the designated office to the extent payment is made by EFT. However, the Contractor may request that no further payments be made until the updated EFT information is implemented by the payment office. If such suspension would result in a late payment under the prompt payment terms of this contract, the Contractor's re-

quest for suspension shall extend the due date for payment by the number of days of the suspension.

(e) *Liability for uncompleted or erroneous transfers.* (1) If an uncompleted or erroneous transfer occurs because the Government used the Contractor's EFT information incorrectly, the Government remains responsible for—

(i) Making a correct payment;

(ii) Paying any prompt payment penalty due; and

(iii) Recovering any erroneously directed funds.

(2) If an uncompleted or erroneous transfer occurs because the Contractor's EFT information was incorrect, or was revised within 30 days of Government release of the EFT payment transaction instruction to the Federal Reserve System, and—

(i) If the funds are no longer under the control of the payment office, the Government is deemed to have made payment and the Contractor is responsible for recovery of any erroneously directed funds; or

(ii) If the funds remain under the control of the payment office, the Government shall not make payment and the provisions of paragraph (d) shall apply.

(f) *EFT and prompt payment.* A payment shall be deemed to have been made in a timely manner in accordance with the prompt payment terms of this contract if, in the EFT payment transaction instruction released to the Federal Reserve System, the date specified for settlement of the payment is on or before the prompt payment due date, provided the specified payment date is a valid date under the rules of the Federal Reserve System.

(g) *EFT and assignment of claims.* If the Contractor assigns the proceeds of this contract as provided for in the assignment of claims terms of this contract, the Contractor shall require as a condition of any such assignment, that the assignee shall provide the EFT information required by paragraph (j) of this clause to the designated office, and shall be paid by EFT in accordance with the terms of this clause. In all respects, the requirements of this clause shall apply to the assignee as if it were the Contractor. EFT information that shows the ultimate recipient of the transfer to be other than the Contractor, in the absence of a proper assignment of claims acceptable to the Government, is incorrect EFT information within the meaning of paragraph (d) of this clause.

(h) *Liability for change of EFT information by financial agent.* The Government is not liable for errors resulting from changes to EFT information provided by the Contractor's financial agent.

(i) *Payment information.* The payment or disbursing office shall forward to the Contractor available payment information that is suitable for transmission as of the date of release of the EFT instruction to the Federal Reserve System. The Government may request the Contractor to designate a desired format and method(s) for delivery of payment information from a list of formats and methods the payment office is capable of executing. However, the Government does not guarantee that any particular format or method of delivery is available at any particular payment office and retains the latitude to use the format and delivery method most convenient to the Government. If the Government makes payment by check in accordance with paragraph (a) of this clause, the Government shall mail the payment information to the remittance address in the contract.

(j) *EFT information.* The Contractor shall provide the following information to the designated office. The Contractor may supply this data for this or multiple contracts (see paragraph (b) of this clause). The Contractor shall designate a single financial agent per contract capable of receiving and processing the EFT information using the EFT methods described in paragraph (c) of this clause.

(1) The contract number (or other procurement identification number).

(2) The Contractor's name and remittance address, as stated in the contract(s).

(3) The signature (manual or electronic, as appropriate), title, and telephone number

of the Contractor official authorized to provide this information.

(4) The name, address, and 9-digit Routing Transit Number of the Contractor's financial agent.

(5) The Contractor's account number and the type of account (checking, saving, or lockbox).

(6) If applicable, the Fedwire Transfer System telegraphic abbreviation of the Contractor's financial agent.

(7) If applicable, the Contractor shall also provide the name, address, telegraphic abbreviation, and 9-digit Routing Transit Number of the correspondent financial institution receiving the wire transfer payment if the Contractor's financial agent is not directly on-line to the Fedwire Transfer System; and, therefore, not the receiver of the wire transfer payment.

(End of clause)

[FAC 97-11, 64 FR 10530, 3/4/99, effective 5/3/99; FAC 2005-67, 78 FR 37676, 6/21/2013, effective 7/22/2013]

52.232-35 Designation of Office for Government Receipt of Electronic Funds Transfer Information.

As prescribed in 32.1110(c), insert the following clause:

DESIGNATION OF OFFICE FOR GOVERNMENT RECEIPT OF ELECTRONIC FUNDS TRANSFER INFORMATION (JUL 2013)

(a) As provided in paragraph (b) of the clause at 52.232-34, Payment by Electronic Funds Transfer—Other than System for Award Management, the Government has designated the office cited in paragraph (c) of this clause as the office to receive the Contractor's electronic funds transfer (EFT) information, in lieu of the payment office of this contract.

(b) The Contractor shall send all EFT information, and any changes to EFT information to the office designated in paragraph (c) of this clause. The Contractor shall not send EFT information to the payment office, or any other office than that designated in paragraph (c). The Government need not use any EFT information sent to any office other than that designated in paragraph (c).

(c) Designated Office:

Name:

____

____

Mailing Address:

____

____

____

Telephone Number:

____

Person to Contact:

____

Electronic Address:

____

(End of clause)

[FAC 97-11, 64 FR 10530, 3/4/99, effective 5/3/99; FAC 2005-67, 78 FR 37676, 6/21/2013, effective 7/22/2013]

52.232-36 Payment by Third Party.

As prescribed in 32.1110(d), insert the following clause:

PAYMENT BY THIRD PARTY (MAY 2014)

(a) *General.* (1) Except as provided in paragraph (a)(2) of this clause, the Contractor agrees to accept payments due under this contract, through payment by a third party in lieu of payment directly from the Government, in accordance with the terms of this clause. The third party and, if applicable, the particular Governmentwide commercial purchase card to be used are identified elsewhere in this contract.

(2) The Governmentwide commercial purchase card is not authorized as a method of payment during any period the System for Award Management (SAM) indicates that the Contractor has delinquent debt that is subject to collection under the Treasury Offset Program (TOP). Information on TOP is available at *http://fms.treas.gov/debt/index.html.* If the SAM subsequently indicates that the Contractor no longer has delinquent

debt, the Contractor may request the Contracting Officer to authorize payment by Governmentwide commercial purchase card.

(b) *Contractor payment request.* (1) Except as provided in paragraph (b)(2) of this clause, the Contractor shall make payment requests through a charge to the Government account with the third party, at the time and for the amount due in accordance with those clauses of this contract that authorize the Contractor to submit invoices, contract financing requests, other payment requests, or as provided in other clauses providing for payment to the Contractor.

(2) When the Contracting Officer has notified the Contractor that the Governmentwide commercial purchase card is no longer an authorized method of payment, the Contractor shall make such payment requests in accordance with instructions provided by the Contracting Officer during the period when the purchase card is not authorized.

(c) *Payment.* The Contractor and the third party shall agree that payments due under this contract shall be made upon submittal of payment requests to the third party in accordance with the terms and conditions of an agreement between the Contractor, the Contractor's financial agent (if any), and the third party and its agents (if any). No payment shall be due the Contractor until such agreement is made. Payments made or due by the third party under this clause are not payments made by the Government and are not subject to the Prompt Payment Act or any implementation thereof in this contract.

(d) *Documentation.* Documentation of each charge against the Government's account shall be provided to the Contracting Officer upon request.

(e) *Assignment of claims.* Notwithstanding any other provision of this contract, if any payment is made under this clause, then no payment under this contract shall be assigned under the provisions of the assignment of claims terms of this contract or the Assignment of Claims Act of 1940, as amended, (31 U.S.C. 3727, 41 U.S.C. 6505).

(f) *Other payment terms.* The other payment terms of this contract shall govern the content and submission of payment requests. If any clause requires information or documents in or with the payment request, that is not provided in the third party agreement referenced in paragraph (c) of this clause, the Contractor shall obtain instructions from the Contracting Officer before submitting such a payment request.

(End of clause)

[FAC 97-11, 64 FR 10530, 3/4/99, effective 5/3/99; FAC 2005-38, 74 FR 65600, 12/10/2009, effective 2/1/2010; FAC 2005-67, 78 FR 37676, 6/21/2013, effective 7/22/2013; FAC 2005-73, 79 FR 24192, 4/29/2014, effective 5/29/2014]

52.232-37 Multiple Payment Arrangements.

As prescribed in 32.1110(e), insert the following clause:

MULTIPLE PAYMENT ARRANGEMENTS (MAY 1999)

This contract or agreement provides for payments to the Contractor through several alternative methods. The applicability of specific methods of payment and the designation of the payment office(s) are either stated—

(a) Elsewhere in this contract or agreement; or

(b) In individual orders placed under this contract or agreement.

(End of clause)

[FAC 97-11, 64 FR 10530, 3/4/99, effective 5/3/99]

52.232-38 Submission of Electronic Funds Transfer Information with Offer.

As prescribed in 32.1110(g), insert the following provision:

SUBMISSION OF ELECTRONIC FUNDS TRANSFER INFORMATION WITH OFFER (JUL 2013)

The offeror shall provide, with its offer, the following information that is required to make payment by electronic funds transfer (EFT) under any contract that results from this solicitation. This submission satisfies the requirement to provide EFT information under paragraphs (b)(1) and (j) of the clause at 52.232-34, Payment by Electronic Funds Transfer—Other than System for Award Management.

(1) The solicitation number (or other procurement identification number).

(2) The offeror's name and remittance address, as stated in the offer.

(3) The signature (manual or electronic, as appropriate), title, and telephone number of the offeror's official authorized to provide this information.

(4) The name, address, and 9-digit Routing Transit Number of the offeror's financial agent.

(5) The offeror's account number and the type of account (checking, savings, or lockbox).

(6) If applicable, the Fedwire Transfer System telegraphic abbreviation of the offeror's financial agent.

(7) If applicable, the offeror shall also provide the name, address, telegraphic abbreviation, and 9-digit Routing Transit Number of the correspondent financial institution receiving the wire transfer payment if the offeror's financial agent is not directly on-line to the Fedwire and, therefore, not the receiver of the wire transfer payment.

[FAC 97-11, 64 FR 10530, 3/4/99, effective 5/3/99; FAC 2005-67, 78 FR 37676, 6/21/2013, effective 7/22/2013]

52.232-39 Unenforceability of Unauthorized Obligations.

As prescribed in 32.706–3, insert the following clause:

UNENFORCEABILITY OF UNAUTHORIZED OBLIGATIONS (JUN 2013)

(a) Except as stated in paragraph (b) of this clause, when any supply or service acquired under this contract is subject to any End User License Agreement (EULA), Terms of Service (TOS), or similar legal instrument or agreement, that includes any clause requiring the Government to indemnify the Contractor or any person or entity for damages, costs, fees, or any other loss or liability that would create an Anti-Deficiency Act violation (31 U.S.C. 1341), the following shall govern:

(1) Any such clause is unenforceable against the Government.

(2) Neither the Government nor any Government authorized end user shall be deemed to have agreed to such clause by virtue of it appearing in the EULA, TOS, or similar legal instrument or agreement. If the EULA, TOS, or similar legal instrument or agreement is invoked through an "I agree" click box or other comparable mechanism (e.g., "click-wrap" or "browse-wrap" agreements), execution does not bind the Government or any Government authorized end user to such clause.

(3) Any such clause is deemed to be stricken from the EULA, TOS, or similar legal instrument or agreement.

(b) Paragraph (a) of this clause does not apply to indemnification by the Government that is expressly authorized by statute and specifically authorized under applicable agency regulations and procedures.

(End of clause)

[FAC 2005-67, 78 FR 37686, 6/21/2013, effective 6/21/2013; FAC 2005-72, 78 FR 80382, 12/31/2013, effective 12/31/2013]

52.232-40 Providing Accelerated Payments to Small Business Subcontractors.

As prescribed in 32.009-2, insert the following clause:

PROVIDING ACCELERATED PAYMENTS TO SMALL BUSINESS SUBCONTRACTORS (DEC 2013)

(a) Upon receipt of accelerated payments from the Government, the Contractor shall make accelerated payments to its small business subcontractors under this contract, to the maximum extent practicable and prior to when such payment is otherwise required under the applicable contract or subcontract, after receipt of a proper invoice and all other required documentation from the small business subcontractor.

(b) The acceleration of payments under this clause does not provide any new rights under the Prompt Payment Act.

(c) Include the substance of this clause, including this paragraph (c), in all subcontracts with small business concerns, including subcontracts with small business concerns for the acquisition of commercial items.

(End of clause)

[FAC 2005-71, 78 FR 70477, 11/25/2013, effective 12/26/2013]

52.233-1 Disputes.

As prescribed in 33.215, insert the following clause:

DISPUTES (MAY 2014)

(a) This contract is subject to 41 U.S.C. chapter 71, Contract Disputes.

(b) Except as provided in 41 U.S.C. chapter 71, all disputes arising under or relating to this contract shall be resolved under this clause.

(c) *Claim*, as used in this clause, means a written demand or written assertion by one of the contracting parties seeking, as a matter of right, the payment of money in a sum certain, the adjustment or interpretation of contract terms, or other relief arising under or relating to this contract. However, a written demand or written assertion by the Contractor seeking the payment of money exceeding $100,000 is not a claim under 41 U.S.C. chapter 71 until certified. A voucher, invoice, or other routine request for payment that is not in dispute when submitted is not a claim under 41 U.S.C. chapter 71. The submission may be converted to a claim under 41 U.S.C. chapter 71, by complying with the submission and certification requirements of this clause, if it is disputed either as to liability or amount or is not acted upon in a reasonable time.

(d) (1) A claim by the Contractor shall be made in writing and, unless otherwise stated in this contract, submitted within 6 years after accrual of the claim to the Contracting Officer for a written decision. A claim by the Government against the Contractor shall be subject to a written decision by the Contracting Officer.

(d) (2) (i) Contractors shall provide the certification specified in subparagraph (d) (2) (iii) of this clause when submitting any claim exceeding $100,000.

(ii) The certification requirement does not apply to issues in controversy that have not been submitted as all or part of a claim.

(iii) The certification shall state as follows: "I certify that the claim is made in good faith; that the supporting data are accurate and complete to the best of my knowledge and belief; that the amount requested accurately reflects the contract adjustment for which the Contractor believes the Government is liable; and that I am authorized to certify the claim on behalf of the Contractor."

(3) The certification may be executed by any person authorized to bind the Contractor with respect to the claim.

(e) For Contractor claims of $100,000 or less, the Contracting Officer must, if requested in writing by the Contractor, render a decision within 60 days of the request. For Contractor-certified claims over $100,000, the Contracting Officer must, within 60 days, decide the claim or notify the Contractor of the date by which the decision will be made.

(f) The Contracting Officer's decision shall be final unless the Contractor appeals or files a suit as provided in 41 U.S.C. chapter 71.

(g) If the claim by the Contractor is submitted to the Contracting Officer or a claim by the Government is presented to the Contractor, the parties, by mutual consent, may agree to use alternative dispute resolution (ADR). If the Contractor refuses an offer for ADR, the Contractor shall inform the Contracting Officer, in writing, of the Contractor's specific reasons for rejecting the offer.

(h) The government shall pay interest on the amount found due and unpaid from (1) the date that the Contracting Officer receives the claim (certified, if required); or (2) the date that payment otherwise would be due, if that date is later, until the date of payment. With regard to claims having defective certifications, as defined in (FAR) 48

CFR 33.201, interest shall be paid from the date that the Contracting Officer initially receives the claim. Simple interest on claim shall be paid at the rate, fixed by the Secretary of the Treasury as provided in the Act, which is applicable to the period during which the Contracting Officer receives the claim and then at the rate applicable for each 6-month period as fixed by the Treasury Secretary during the pendency of the claim.

(i) The Contractor shall proceed diligently with performance of this contract, pending final resolution of any request for relief, claim, appeal, or action arising under the contract, and comply with any decision of the Contracting Officer.

(End of clause)

Alternate I (DEC 1991). As prescribed in 33.215, substitute the following paragraph (i) for paragraph (i) of the basic clause:

(i) The Contractor shall proceed diligently with performance of this contract, pending final resolution of any request for relief, claim, appeal, or action arising under or relating to the contract, and comply with any decision of the Contracting Officer.

[FAC 84-23, 51 FR 36972, 10/16/86, effective 9/30/86; Interim rule, FAC 90-10, 56 FR 67417, 12/30/91, effective 12/30/91; FAC 90-20, 59 FR 11368, 3/10/94, effective 3/10/94, finalized without change, FAC 90-39, 61 FR 31612, 6/20/96, effective 6/20/96; FAC 90-32, 60 FR 48206, 9/18/95, effective 10/1/95; FAC 97-9, 63 FR 58587, 10/30/98, effective 12/29/98; FAC 2001-08, 67 FR 43513, 6/27/2002, effective 7/29/2002; FAC 2005-73, 79 FR 24192, 4/29/2014, effective 5/29/2014]

52.233-2 Service of Protest.

As prescribed in 33.106(a), insert the following provision:

SERVICE OF PROTEST (SEP 2006)

(a) *Protests*, as defined in section 33.101 of the Federal Acquisition Regulation, that are filed directly with an agency, and copies of any protests that are filed with the Government Accountability Office (GAO), shall be served on the Contracting Officer (addressed as follows) by obtaining written and dated acknowledgment of receipt from __________ [*Contracting Officer designate the official or location where a protest may be served on the Contracting Officer*].

(b) The copy of any protest shall be received in the office designated above within one day of filing a protest with the GAO.

(End of provision)

[FAC 90-41, 61 FR 41466, 8/8/96, effective 8/8/96, finalized without change, FAC 97-3, 62 FR 64912, 12/9/97, effective 2/9/98; FAC 2005-13, 71 FR 57380, 9/28/2006, effective 9/28/2006]

52.233-3 Protest after Award.

As prescribed in 33.106(b), insert the following clause:

PROTEST AFTER AWARD (AUG 1996)

(a) Upon receipt of a notice of protest (as defined in FAR 33.101) or a determination that a protest is likely (see FAR 33.102(d)), the Contracting Officer may, by written order to the Contractor, direct the Contractor to stop performance of the work called for by this contract. The order shall be specifically identified as a stop-work order issued under this clause. Upon receipt of the order, the Contractor shall immediately comply with its terms and take all reasonable steps to minimize the incurrence of costs allocable to the work covered by the order during the period of work stoppage. Upon receipt of the final decision in the protest, the Contracting Officer shall either—

(1) Cancel the stop-work order; or

(2) Terminate the work covered by the order as provided in the Default, or the Termination for Convenience of the Government, clause of this contract.

(b) If a stop-work order issued under this clause is canceled either before or after a final decision in the protest, the Contractor shall resume work. The Contracting Officer shall make an equitable adjustment in the delivery schedule or contract price, or both, and the contract shall be modified, in writing, accordingly, if—

(1) The stop-work order results in an increase in the time required for, or in the

Contractor's cost properly allocable to, the performance of any part of this contract; and

(2) The Contractor asserts its right to an adjustment within 30 days after the end of the period of work stoppage; provided, that if the Contracting Officer decides the facts justify the action, the Contracting Officer may receive and act upon a proposal submitted at any time before final payment under this contract.

(c) If a stop-work order is not canceled and the work covered by the order is terminated for the convenience of the Government, the Contracting Officer shall allow reasonable costs resulting from the stop-work order in arriving at the termination settlement.

(d) If a stop-work order is not canceled and the work covered by the order is terminated for default, the Contracting Officer shall allow, by equitable adjustment or otherwise, reasonable costs resulting from the stop-work order.

(e) The Government's rights to terminate this contract at any time are not affected by action taken under this clause.

(f) If, as the result of the Contractor's intentional or negligent misstatement, misrepresentation, or miscertification, a protest related to this contract is sustained, and the Government pays costs, as provided in FAR 33.102(b)(2) or 33.104(h)(1), the Government may require the Contractor to reimburse the Government the amount of such costs. In addition to any other remedy available, and pursuant to the requirements of Subpart 32.6, the Government may collect this debt by offsetting the amount against any payment due the Contractor under any contract between the Contractor and the Government.

(End of clause)

Alternate I (JUN 1985). As prescribed in 33.106(b), substitute in paragraph (a)(2) the words "the Termination clause of this contract" for the words "the Default, or the Termination for Convenience of the Government clause of this contract." In paragraph (b) substitute the words "an equitable adjustment in the delivery schedule, the estimated cost, the fee, or a combination thereof, and in any other terms of the contract that may be affected" for the words "an equitable adjustment in the delivery schedule or contract price, or both."

[FAC 84-9, 50 FR 25681, 6/20/85, effective 6/20/85; FAC 84-49, 54 FR 29284, 7/11/89, effective 8/10/89; FAC 90-32, 60 FR 48206, 9/18/95, effective 10/1/95; FAC 90-41, 61 FR 41466, 8/8/96, effective 8/8/96, finalized without change, FAC 97-3, 62 FR 64912, 12/9/97, effective 2/9/98]

52.233-4 Applicable Law for Breach of Contract Claim.

As prescribed in 33.215(b), insert the following clause:

APPLICABLE LAW FOR BREACH OF CONTRACT CLAIM (OCT 2004)

United States law will apply to resolve any claim of breach of this contract.

(End of clause)

[FAC 2001-25, 69 FR 59700, 10/5/2004, effective 10/5/2004]

52.234-1 Industrial Resources Developed Under Title III, Defense Production Act.

As prescribed at 34.104, insert the following clause:

INDUSTRIAL RESOURCES DEVELOPED UNDER TITLE III, DEFENSE PRODUCTION ACT (SEP 2016)

(a) *Definitions.*

Title III industrial resource means materials, services, processes, or manufacturing equipment (including the processes, technologies, and ancillary services for the use of such equipment) established or maintained under the authority of Title III, Defense Production Act (50 U.S.C. App. 2091-2093).

Title III project contractor means a contractor that has received assistance for the development or manufacture of an industrial resource under Title III of Defense Production Act (50 U.S.C. App. 2091–2093).

(b) The Contractor shall refer any request from a Title III project contractor for testing and qualification of a Title III industrial resource to the Contracting Officer.

(c) Upon the direction of the Contracting Officer, the Contractor shall test Title III industrial resources for qualification. The Contractor shall provide the test results to the Defense Production Act Office, Title III Program, located at Wright Patterson Air Force Base, Ohio 45433-7739.

(d) When the Contracting Officer modifies the contract to direct testing pursuant to this clause, the Government will provide the Title III industrial resource to be tested and will make an equitable adjustment in the contract for the costs of testing and qualification of the Title III industrial resource.

(e) The Contractor agrees to insert the substance of this clause, including paragraph (e), in every subcontract issued in performance of this contract.

(End of clause)

[FAC 90-23, 59 FR 67010, 12/28/94, effective 12/28/94, corrected 60 FR 5869, 1/31/95, finalized without change, FAC 90-39, 61 FR 31612, 6/20/96, effective 6/20/96; FAC 2005-91, 81 FR 67781, 9/30/2016, effective 9/30/2016]

52.234-2 Notice of Earned Value Management System—Preaward Integrated Baseline Review.

As prescribed in 34.203(a) use the following provision:

NOTICE OF EARNED VALUE MANAGEMENT SYSTEM-PREAWARD INTEGRATED BASELINE REVIEW (NOV 2016)

(a) The offeror shall provide documentation that the Cognizant Federal Agency has determined that the proposed earned value management system (EVMS) complies with the EVMS guidelines in Electronic Industries Alliance Standard 748(EIA-748) (current version at time of solicitation).

(b) If the offeror proposes to use a system that has not been determined to be in compliance with the requirements of paragraph (a) of this provision, the offeror shall submit a comprehensive plan for compliance with the EVMS guidelines.

(1) The plan shall—

(i) Describe the EVMS the offeror intends to use in performance of the contracts;

(ii) Distinguish between the offeror's existing management system and modifications proposed to meet the guidelines;

(iii) Describe the management system and its application in terms of the EVMS guidelines;

(iv) Describe the proposed procedure for administration of the guidelines, as applied to subcontractors; and

(v) Provide documentation describing the process and results of any third-party or self-evaluation of the system's compliance with the EVMS guidelines.

(2) The offeror shall provide information and assistance as required by the Contracting Officer to support review of the plan.

(3) The Government will review and approve the offeror's plan for an EVMS before contract award.

(4) The offeror's EVMS plan must provide milestones that indicate when the offeror anticipates that the EVM system will be compliant with the EIA-748 guidelines.

(c) Offerors shall identify the major subcontractors, or major subcontracted effort if major subcontractors have not been selected subject to the guidelines. The prime Contractor and the Government shall agree to subcontractors selected for application of the EVMS guidelines.

(d) The Government will conduct an Integrated Baseline Review (IBR), as designated by the agency, prior to contract award. The objective of the IBR is for the Government and the Contractor to jointly assess technical areas, such as the Contractor's planning, to ensure complete coverage of the contract requirements, logical scheduling of the work activities, adequate resources, methodologies for earned value (budgeted cost for work performed (BCWP)), and identification of inherent risks.

(End of provision)

[FAC 2005-11, 71 FR 38238, 7/5/2006, effective 7/5/2006; FAC 2005-92 81 FR 83103, 11/18/2016, effective 11/18/2016]

52.234-3 Notice of Earned Value Management System—Postaward Integrated Baseline Review.

As prescribed in 34.203(b) use the following provision:

NOTICE OF EARNED VALUE MANAGEMENT SYSTEM-POSTAWARD INTEGRATED BASELINE REVIEW (NOV 2016)

(a) The offeror shall provide documentation that the Cognizant Federal Agency has determined that the proposed earned value management system (EVMS) complies with the EVMS guidelines in Electronic Industries Alliance Standard 748 (EIA-748) (current version at time of solicitation).

(b) If the offeror proposes to use a system that has not been determined to be in compliance with the requirements of paragraph (a) of this provision, the offeror shall submit a comprehensive plan for compliance with the EVMS guidelines.

(1) The plan shall—

(i) Describe the EVMS the offeror intends to use in performance of the contracts;

(ii) Distinguish between the offeror's existing management system and modifications proposed to meet the guidelines;

(iii) Describe the management system and its application in terms of the EVMS guidelines;

(iv) Describe the proposed procedure for administration of the guidelines, as applied to subcontractors; and

(v) Provide documentation describing the process and results of any third-party or self-evaluation of the system's compliance with the EVMS guidelines.

(2) The offeror shall provide information and assistance as required by the Contracting Officer to support review of the plan.

(3) The Government will review and approve the offeror's plan for an EVMS before contract award.

(4) The offeror's EVMS plan must provide milestones that indicate when the offeror anticipates that the EVM system will be compliant with the EIA-748 guidelines.

(c) Offerors shall identify the major subcontractors, or major subcontracted effort if major subcontractors have not been selected, planned for application of the guidelines. The prime Contractor and the Government shall agree to subcontractors selected for application of the EVMS guidelines.

(End of provision)

[FAC 2005-11, 71 FR 38238, 7/5/2006, effective 7/5/2006; FAC 2005-92 81 FR 83103, 11/18/2016, effective 11/18/2016]

52.234-4 Earned Value Management System.

As prescribed in 34.203(c), insert the following clause:

EARNED VALUE MANAGEMENT SYSTEM (NOV 2016)

(a) The Contractor shall use an earned value management system (EVMS) that has been determined by the Cognizant Federal Agency (CFA) to be compliant with the guidelines in Electronic Industries Alliance Standard 748 (EIA-748) (current version at the time of award) to manage this contract. If the Contractor's current EVMS has not been determined compliant at the time of award, see paragraph (b) of this clause. The Contractor shall submit reports in accordance with the requirements of this contract.

(b) If, at the time of award, the Contractor's EVM System has not been determined by the CFA as complying with EVMS guidelines or the Contractor does not have an existing cost/schedule control system that is compliant with the guidelines in EIA-748 (current version at time of award), the Contractor shall—

(1) Apply the current system to the contract; and

(2) Take necessary actions to meet the milestones in the Contractor's EVMS plan approved by the Contracting Officer.

(c) The Government will conduct an Integrated Baseline Review (IBR). If a pre-award IBR has not been conducted, a post award IBR shall be conducted as early as practicable after contract award.

(d) The Contracting Officer may require an IBR at—

(1) Exercise of significant options; or

(2) Incorporation of major modifications.

(e) Unless a waiver is granted by the CFA, Contractor proposed EVMS changes require approval of the CFA prior to implementation. The CFA will advise the Contractor of the acceptability of such changes within 30 calendar days after receipt of the notice of proposed changes from the Contractor. If the advance approval requirements are waived by the CFA, the Contractor shall disclose EVMS changes to the CFA at least 14 calendar days prior to the effective date of implementation.

(f) The Contractor shall provide access to all pertinent records and data requested by the Contracting Officer or an authorized representative as necessary to permit Government surveillance to ensure that the EVMS conforms, and continues to conform, with the performance criteria referenced in paragraph (a) of this clause.

(g) The Contractor shall require the subcontractors specified below to comply with the requirements of this clause: [Insert list of applicable subcontractors.]

(End of clause)

[FAC 2005-11, 71 FR 38238, 7/5/2006, effective 7/5/2006; FAC 2005-73, 79 FR 24192, 4/29/2014, effective 5/29/2014; FAC 2005-92 81 FR 83103, 11/18/2016, effective 11/18/2016]

52.235 [Reserved]

52.236-1 Performance of Work by the Contractor.

As prescribed in 36.501(b), insert the following clause: [*Complete the clause by inserting the appropriate percentage consistent with the complexity and magnitude of the work and customary or necessary specialty subcontracting (see 36.501(a)).*]

PERFORMANCE OF WORK BY THE CONTRACTOR (APR 1984)

The Contractor shall perform on the site, and with its own organization, work equivalent to at least ____ [*insert the appropriate number in words followed by numerals in parentheses*] percent of the total amount of work to be performed under the contract. This percentage may be reduced by a supplemental agreement to this contract if, during performing the work, the Contractor requests a reduction and the Contracting Officer determines that the reduction would be to the advantage of the Government.

(End of clause)

[FAC 90-32, 60 FR 48206, 9/18/95, effective 10/1/95; FAC 2005-13, 71 FR 57363, 9/28/2006, effective 9/28/2006]

52.236-2 Differing Site Conditions.

As prescribed in 36.502, insert the following clause:

DIFFERING SITE CONDITIONS (APR 1984)

(a) The Contractor shall promptly, and before the conditions are disturbed, give a written notice to the Contracting Officer of (1) subsurface or latent physical conditions at the site which differ materially from those indicated in this contract, or (2) unknown physical conditions at the site, of an unusual nature, which differ materially from those ordinarily encountered and generally recognized as inhering in work of the character provided for in the contract.

(b) The Contracting Officer shall investigate the site conditions promptly after receiving the notice. If the conditions do materially so differ and cause an increase or decrease in the Contractor's cost of, or the time required for, performing any part of the work under this contract, whether or not changed as a result of the conditions, an equitable adjustment shall be made under this clause and the contract modified in writing accordingly.

(c) No request by the Contractor for an equitable adjustment to the contract under this clause shall be allowed, unless the Contractor has given the written notice required; *provided*, that the time prescribed in (a) above for giving written notice may be extended by the Contracting Officer.

(d) No request by the Contractor for an equitable adjustment to the contract for differing site conditions shall be allowed if made after final payment under this contract.

(End of clause)

[FAC 90-29, 60 FR 34732, 7/3/95, effective 7/3/95]

52.236-3 Site Investigation and Conditions Affecting the Work.

As prescribed in 36.503, insert the following clause:

SITE INVESTIGATION AND CONDITIONS AFFECTING THE WORK (APR 1984)

(a) The Contractor acknowledges that it has taken steps reasonably necessary to ascertain the nature and location of the work, and that it has investigated and satisfied itself as to the general and local conditions which can affect the work or its cost, including but not limited to (1) conditions bearing upon transportation, disposal, handling, and storage of materials; (2) the availability of labor, water, electric power, and roads; (3) uncertainties of weather, river stages, tides, or similar physical conditions at the site; (4) the conformation and conditions of the ground; and (5) the character of equipment and facilities needed preliminary to and during work performance. The Contractor also acknowledges that it has satisfied itself as to the character, quality, and quantity of surface and subsurface materials or obstacles to be encountered insofar as this information is reasonably ascertainable from an inspection of the site, including all exploratory work done by the Government, as well as from the drawings and specifications made a part of this contract. Any failure of the Contractor to take the actions described and acknowledged in this paragraph will not relieve the Contractor from responsibility for estimating properly the difficulty and cost of successfully performing the work, or for proceeding to successfully perform the work without additional expense to the Government.

(b) The Government assumes no responsibility for any conclusions or interpretations made by the Contractor based on the information made available by the Government. Nor does the Government assume responsibility for any understanding reached or representation made concerning conditions which can affect the work by any of its officers or agents before the execution of this contract, unless that understanding or representation is expressly stated in this contract.

(End of clause)

[FAC 90-29, 60 FR 34732, 7/3/95, effective 7/3/95]

52.236-4 Physical Data.

As prescribed in 36.504, insert the following clause in solicitations and contracts when a fixed-price construction contract is contemplated and physical data (e.g., test borings, hydrographic, weather conditions data) will be furnished or made available to offerors. All information to be furnished or made available to offerors before award that pertains to the performance of the work should be identified in the clause. When subparagraphs are not applicable they may be deleted.

PHYSICAL DATA (APR 1984)

Data and information furnished or referred to below is for the Contractor's information. The Government shall not be responsible for any interpretation of or conclusion drawn from the data or information by the Contractor.

(a) The indications of physical conditions on the drawings and in the specifications are the result of site investigations by ______ [*insert a description of investigational methods used, such as surveys, auger borings, core borings, test pits, probings, test tunnels*].

(b) Weather conditions ______ [*insert a summary of weather records and warnings*].

(c) Transportation facilities ______ [*insert a summary of transportation facilities providing access from the site, including information about their availability and limitations*].

(d) ______ [*insert other pertinent information*].

(End of clause)

[FAC 90-32, 60 FR 48206, 9/18/95, effective 10/1/95]

52.236-5 Material and Workmanship.

As prescribed in 36.505, insert the following clause:

MATERIAL AND WORKMANSHIP (APR 1984)

(a) All equipment, material, and articles incorporated into the work covered by this contract shall be new and of the most suitable grade for the purpose intended, unless otherwise specifically provided in this contract. References in the specifications to equipment, material, articles, or patented processes by trade name, make, or catalog number, shall be regarded as establishing a standard of quality and shall not be construed as limiting competition. The Contractor may, at its option, use any equipment, material, article, or process that, in the judgment of the Contracting Officer, is equal to that named in the specifications, unless otherwise specifically provided in this contract.

(b) The Contractor shall obtain the Contracting Officer's approval of the machinery and mechanical and other equipment to be incorporated into the work. When requesting approval, the Contractor shall furnish to the Contracting Officer the name of the manufacturer, the model number, and other information concerning the performance, capacity, nature, and rating of the machinery and mechanical and other equipment. When required by this contract or by the Contracting Officer, the Contractor shall also obtain the Contracting Officer's approval of the material or articles which the Contractor contemplates incorporating into the work. When requesting approval, the Contractor shall provide full information concerning the material or articles. When directed to do so, the Contractor shall submit samples for approval at the Contractor's expense, with all shipping charges prepaid. Machinery, equipment, material, and articles that do not have the required approval shall be installed or used at the risk of subsequent rejection.

(c) All work under this contract shall be performed in a skillful and workmanlike manner. The Contracting Officer may require, in writing, that the Contractor remove from the work any employee the Contracting Officer deems incompetent, careless, or otherwise objectionable.

(End of clause)

[FAC 84-53, 54 FR 48995, 11/28/89, effective 12/28/89; FAC 90-32, 60 FR 48206, 9/18/95, effective 10/1/95]

52.236-6 Superintendence by the Contractor.

As prescribed in 36.506, insert the following clause:

SUPERINTENDENCE BY THE CONTRACTOR (APR 1984)

At all times during performance of this contract and until the work is completed and accepted, the Contractor shall directly superintend the work or assign and have on the worksite a competent superintendent who is satisfactory to the Contracting Officer and has authority to act for the Contractor.

(End of clause)

[FAC 90-29, 60 FR 34732, 7/3/95, effective 7/3/95]

52.236-7 Permits and Responsibilities.

As prescribed in 36.507, insert the following clause:

PERMITS AND RESPONSIBILITIES (NOV 1991)

The Contractor shall, without additional expense to the Government, be responsible for obtaining any necessary licenses and permits, and for complying with any Federal, State, and municipal laws, codes, and regulations applicable to the performance of the work. The Contractor shall also be responsible for all damages to persons or property that occur as a result of the Contractor's fault or negligence. The Contractor shall also be responsible for all materials delivered and work performed until completion and acceptance of the entire work, except for any completed unit of work which may have been accepted under the contract.

(End of clause)

[FAC 84-53, 54 FR 48995, 11/28/89, effective 12/28/89; FAC 90-8, 56 FR 55376, 10/25/91, effective 11/25/91]

52.236-8 Other Contracts.

As prescribed in 36.508, insert the following clause:

OTHER CONTRACTS (APR 1984)

The Government may undertake or award other contracts for additional work at or near the site of the work under this contract. The Contractor shall fully cooperate with the other contractors and with Government employees and shall carefully adapt scheduling and performing the work under this contract to accommodate the additional work, heeding any direction that may be provided by the Contracting Officer. The Contractor shall not commit or permit any act that will interfere with the performance of work by any other contractor or by Government employees.

(End of clause)

[FAC 90-29, 60 FR 34732, 7/3/95, effective 7/3/95]

52.236-9 Protection of Existing Vegetation, Structures, Equipment, Utilities, and Improvements.

As prescribed in 36.509, insert the following clause:

PROTECTION OF EXISTING VEGETATION, STRUCTURES, EQUIPMENT, UTILITIES, AND IMPROVEMENTS (APR 1984)

(a) The Contractor shall preserve and protect all structures, equipment, and vegetation (such as trees, shrubs, and grass) on or adjacent to the work site, which are not to be removed and which do not unreasonably interfere with the work required under this contract. The Contractor shall only remove trees when specifically authorized to do so, and shall avoid damaging vegetation that will remain in place. If any limbs or branches of trees are broken during contract performance, or by the careless operation of equipment, or by workmen, the Contractor shall trim those limbs or branches with a clean cut and paint the cut with a tree-pruning compound as directed by the Contracting Officer.

(b) The Contractor shall protect from damage all existing improvements and utilities (1) at or near the work site, and (2) on adjacent property of a third party, the locations of which are made known to or should be known by the Contractor. The Contractor shall repair any damage to those facilities, including those that are the property of a third party, resulting from failure to comply with the requirements of this contract or failure to exercise reasonable care in performing the work. If the Contractor fails or refuses to repair the damage promptly, the Contracting Officer may have the necessary work performed and charge the cost to the Contractor.

(End of clause)

[FAC 90-29, 60 FR 34732, 7/3/95, effective 7/3/95]

52.236-10 Operations and Storage Areas.

As prescribed in 36.510, insert the following clause:

OPERATIONS AND STORAGE AREAS (APR 1984)

(a) The Contractor shall confine all operations (including storage of materials) on Government premises to areas authorized or approved by the Contracting Officer. The Contractor shall hold and save the Government, its officers and agents, free and harmless from liability of any nature occasioned by the Contractor's performance.

(b) Temporary buildings (e.g., storage sheds, shops, offices) and utilities may be erected by the Contractor only with the approval of the Contracting Officer and shall be built with labor and materials furnished by the Contractor without expense to the Government. The temporary buildings and utilities shall remain the property of the Contractor and shall be removed by the Contractor at its expense upon completion of the work. With the written consent of the Contracting Officer, the buildings and utilities may be abandoned and need not be removed.

(c) The Contractor shall, under regulations prescribed by the Contracting Officer, use only established roadways, or use temporary roadways constructed by the Contractor when and as authorized by the Contracting Officer. When materials are transported in prosecuting the work, vehicles shall not be loaded beyond the loading capacity recommended by the manufacturer of the vehicle or prescribed by any Federal, State, or local law or regulation. When it is necessary to cross curbs or sidewalks, the Contractor shall protect them from damage. The Contractor shall repair or pay for the repair of any damaged curbs, sidewalks, or roads.

(End of clause)

[FAC 90-29, 60 FR 34732, 7/3/95, effective 7/3/95]

52.236-11 Use and Possession Prior to Completion.

As prescribed in 36.511, insert the following clause:

USE AND POSSESSION PRIOR TO COMPLETION (APR 1984)

(a) The Government shall have the right to take possession of or use any completed or partially completed part of the work. Before taking possession of or using any work, the Contracting Officer shall furnish the Contractor a list of items of work remaining to be performed or corrected on those portions of the work that the Government intends to take possession of or use. However, failure of the Contracting Officer to list any item of work shall not relieve the Contractor of responsibility for complying with the terms of the contract. The Government's possession or use shall not be deemed an acceptance of any work under the contract.

(b) While the Government has such possession or use, the Contractor shall be relieved of the responsibility for the loss of or damage to the work resulting from the Government's possession or use, notwithstanding the terms of the clause in this contract entitled "Permits and Responsibilities." If prior possession or use by the Government delays the progress of the work or causes additional expense to the Contractor, an equitable adjustment shall be made in the contract price or the time of completion, and the contract shall be modified in writing accordingly.

(End of clause)

[FAC 90-29, 60 FR 34732, 7/3/95, effective 7/3/95]

52.236-12 Cleaning Up.

As prescribed in 36.512, insert the following clause:

CLEANING UP (APR 1984)

The Contractor shall at all times keep the work area, including storage areas, free from accumulations of waste materials. Before completing the work, the Contractor shall remove from the work and premises any rubbish, tools, scaffolding, equipment, and materials that are not the property of the Government. Upon completing the work, the Contractor shall leave the work area in a clean, neat, and orderly condition satisfactory to the Contracting Officer.

(End of clause)

[FAC 90-29, 60 FR 34732, 7/3/95, effective 7/3/95]

52.236-13 Accident Prevention.

As prescribed in 36.513, insert the following clause:

ACCIDENT PREVENTION (NOV 1991)

(a) The Contractor shall provide and maintain work environments and procedures which will (1) safeguard the public and Government personnel, property, materials, supplies, and equipment exposed to Contractor operations and activities; (2) avoid interruptions of Government operations and delays in project completion dates; and (3) control costs in the performance of this contract.

(b) For these purposes on contracts for construction or dismantling, demolition, or removal of improvements, the Contractor shall—

(1) Provide appropriate safety barricades, signs, and signal lights;

(2) Comply with the standards issued by the Secretary of Labor at 29 CFR part 1926 and 29 CFR part 1910; and

(3) Ensure that any additional measures the Contracting Officer determines to be reasonably necessary for the purposes are taken.

(c) If this contract is for construction or dismantling, demolition or removal of improvements with any Department of Defense agency or component, the Contractor shall comply with all pertinent provisions of the latest version of U.S. Army Corps of Engineers Safety and Health Requirements Manual, EM 385-1-1, in effect on the date of the solicitation.

(d) Whenever the Contracting Officer becomes aware of any noncompliance with these requirements or any condition which poses a serious or imminent danger to the health or safety of the public or Government personnel, the Contracting Officer shall notify the Contractor orally, with written confirmation, and request immediate initiation of corrective action. This notice, when delivered to the Contractor or the Contractor's representative at the work site, shall be deemed sufficient notice of the noncompliance and that corrective action is required. After receiving the notice, the Contractor shall immediately take corrective action. If the Contractor fails or refuses to promptly take corrective action, the Contracting Officer may issue an order stopping all or part of the work until satisfactory corrective action has been taken. The Contractor shall not be entitled to any equitable adjustment of the contract price or extension of the performance schedule on any stop work order issued under this clause.

(e) The Contractor shall insert this clause, including this paragraph (e), with appropriate changes in the designation of the parties, in subcontracts.

(End of clause)

Alternate I (NOV 1991). If the contract will involve (a) work of a long duration or hazardous nature, or (b) performance on a Government facility that on the advice of technical representatives involves hazardous materials or operations that might endanger the safety of the public and/or Government personnel or property, add the following paragraph (f) to the basic clause:

(f) Before commencing the work, the Contractor shall—

(1) Submit a written proposed plan for implementing this clause. The plan shall include an analysis of the significant hazards to life, limb, and property inherent in contract work performance and a plan for controlling these hazards; and

(2) Meet with representatives of the Contracting Officer to discuss and develop a mutual understanding relative to administration of the overall safety program.

[FAC 90-8, 56 FR 55376, 10/25/91, effective 11/25/91]

52.236-14 Availability and Use of Utility Services.

As prescribed in 36.514, insert the following clause in solicitations and contracts when a fixed-price construction contract or a fixed-price dismantling, demolition, or removal of improvements contract is contemplated, the contract is to be performed on Government sites when the contracting officer decides (a) that the existing utility system is adequate for the needs of both the Government and the contractor, and (b) furnishing it is in the Government's interest. When this clause is used, the contracting officer shall list the available utilities in the contract.

AVAILABILITY AND USE OF UTILITY SERVICES (APR 1984)

(a) The Government shall make all reasonably required amounts of utilities available to the Contractor from existing outlets and supplies, as specified in the contract. Unless otherwise provided in the contract, the amount of each utility service consumed shall be charged to or paid for by the Contractor at prevailing rates charged to the Government or, where the utility is produced by the Government, at reasonable rates determined by the Contracting Officer. The Contractor shall carefully conserve any utilities furnished without charge.

(b) The Contractor, at its expense and in a workmanlike manner satisfactory to the Contracting Officer, shall install and maintain all necessary temporary connections and distribution lines, and all meters required to measure the amount of each utility used for the purpose of determining charges. Before final acceptance of the work by the Government, the Contractor shall remove all the temporary connections, distribution lines, meters, and associated paraphernalia.

(End of clause)

[FAC 90-32, 60 FR 48206, 9/18/95, effective 10/1/95]

52.236-15 Schedules for Construction Contracts.

As prescribed in 36.515, insert the following clause:

SCHEDULES FOR CONSTRUCTION CONTRACTS (APR 1984)

(a) The Contractor shall, within five days after the work commences on the contract or another period of time determined by the Contracting Officer, prepare and submit to the Contracting Officer for approval three copies of a practicable schedule showing the order in which the Contractor proposes to perform the work, and the dates on which the Contractor contemplates starting and completing the several salient features of the work (including acquiring materials, plant, and equipment). The schedule shall be in the form of a progress chart of suitable scale to indicate appropriately the percentage of work scheduled for completion by any given date during the period. If the Contractor fails to submit a schedule within the time prescribed, the Contracting Officer may withhold approval of progress payments until the Contractor submits the required schedule.

(b) The Contractor shall enter the actual progress on the chart as directed by the Contracting Officer, and upon doing so shall immediately deliver three copies of the annotated schedule to the Contracting Officer. If, in the opinion of the Contracting Officer, the Contractor falls behind the approved schedule, the Contractor shall take steps necessary to improve its progress, including those that may be required by the Contracting Officer, without additional cost to the Government. In this circumstance, the Contracting Officer may require the Contractor to increase the number of shifts, overtime operations, days of work, and/or the amount of construction plant, and to submit for approval any supplementary schedule or schedules in chart form as the Contracting Officer deems necessary to demonstrate how the approved rate of progress will be regained.

(c) Failure of the Contractor to comply with the requirements of the Contracting Officer under this clause shall be grounds for a determination by the Contracting Officer that the Contractor is not prosecuting the work with sufficient diligence to ensure completion within the time specified in the contract. Upon making this determination, the Contracting Officer may terminate the Contractor's right to proceed with the work, or any separable part of it, in accordance with the default terms of this contract.

(End of clause)

[FAC 90-29, 60 FR 34732, 7/3/95, effective 7/3/95]

52.236-16 Quantity Surveys.

As prescribed in 36.516, the contracting officer may insert the following clause in solicitations and contracts when a fixed-price construction contract providing for unit pricing of items and for payment based on quantity surveys is contemplated:

QUANTITY SURVEYS (APR 1984)

(a) Quantity surveys shall be conducted, and the data derived from these surveys shall be used in computing the quantities of work performed and the actual construction completed and in place.

(b) The Government shall conduct the original and final surveys and make the computations based on them. The Contractor shall conduct the surveys for any periods for which progress payments are requested and shall make the computations based on these surveys. All surveys conducted by the Contractor shall be conducted under the direction of a representative of the Contracting Officer, unless the Contracting Officer waives this requirement in a specific instance.

(c) Promptly upon completing a survey, the Contractor shall furnish the originals of all field notes and all other records relating to the survey or to the layout of the work to the Contracting Officer, who shall use them as necessary to determine the amount of progress payments. The Contractor shall retain copies of all such material furnished to the Contracting Officer.

(End of clause)

Alternate I (APR 1984). If it is determined at a level above that of the contracting officer that it is impracticable for Government personnel to perform the original and final surveys, and the Government wishes the contractor to perform these surveys, substitute the following paragraph (b) for paragraph (b) of the basic clause:

(b) The Contractor shall conduct the original and final surveys and surveys for any periods for which progress payments are requested. All these surveys shall be conducted under the direction of a representative of the Contracting Officer, unless the Contracting Officer waives this requirement in a specific instance. The Government shall make such computations as are necessary to determine the quantities of work performed or finally in place. The Contractor shall make the computations based on the surveys for any periods for which progress payments are requested.

[FAC 90-32, 60 FR 48206, 9/18/95, effective 10/1/95]

52.236-17 Layout of Work.

As prescribed in 36.517, insert the following clause in solicitations and contracts when a fixed-price construction contract is contemplated and use of this clause is appropriate due to a need for accurate work layout and for siting verification during work performance:

LAYOUT OF WORK (APR 1984)

The Contractor shall lay out its work from Government-established base lines and bench marks indicated on the drawings, and shall be responsible for all measurements in connection with the layout. The Contractor shall furnish, at its own expense, all stakes, templates, platforms, equipment, tools, materials, and labor required to lay out any part of the work. The Contractor shall be responsible for executing the work to the lines and grades that may be established or indicated by the Contracting Officer. The Contractor shall also be responsible for maintaining and preserving all stakes and other marks established by the Contracting Officer until authorized to remove them. If such marks are destroyed by the Contractor or through its negligence before their removal is authorized, the Contracting Officer may replace them and deduct the expense of the replacement from any amounts due or to become due to the Contractor.

(End of clause)

[FAC 90-32, 60 FR 48206, 9/18/95, effective 10/1/95]

52.236-18 Work Oversight in Cost-Reimbursement Construction Contracts.

As prescribed in 36.518, insert the following clause in solicitations and contracts when cost-reimbursement construction contracts are contemplated:

WORK OVERSIGHT IN COST-REIMBURSEMENT CONSTRUCTION CONTRACTS (APR 1984)

The extent and character of the work to be done by the Contractor shall be subject to the general supervision, direction, control, and approval of the Contracting Officer.

(End of clause)

[FAC 90-32, 60 FR 48206, 9/18/95, effective 10/1/95]

52.236-19 Organization and Direction of the Work.

As prescribed in 36.519, insert the following clause in solicitations and contracts when a cost-reimbursement construction contract is contemplated:

ORGANIZATION AND DIRECTION OF THE WORK (APR 1984)

(a) When this contract is executed, the Contractor shall submit to the Contracting Officer a chart showing the general executive and administrative organization, the personnel to be employed in connection with the work under this contract, and their respective duties. The Contractor shall keep the data furnished current by supplementing it as additional information becomes available.

(b) Work performance under this contract shall be under the full-time resident direction of: (1) the Contractor, if the Contractor is an individual; (2) one or more principal partners, if the Contractor is a partnership; or (3) one or more senior officers, if Contractor is a corporation, association, or similar legal entity. However, if the Contracting Officer approves, the Contractor may be represented in the direction of the work by a specific person or persons holding positions other than those identified in this paragraph.

(End of clause)

[FAC 90-32, 60 FR 48206, 9/18/95, effective 10/1/95]

52.236-20 [Reserved]

[Reserved, FAC 84-53, 54 FR 48995, 11/28/89, effective 2/26/90]

52.236-21 Specifications and Drawings for Construction.

As prescribed in 36.521, insert the following clause:

SPECIFICATIONS AND DRAWINGS FOR CONSTRUCTION (FEB 1997)

(a) The Contractor shall keep on the work site a copy of the drawings and specifications and shall at all times give the Contracting Officer access thereto. Anything mentioned in the specifications and not shown on the drawings, or shown on the drawings and not mentioned in the specifications, shall be of like effect as if shown or mentioned in both. In case of difference between drawings and specifications, the specifications shall govern. In case of discrepancy in the figures, in the drawings, or in the specifications, the matter shall be promptly submitted to the Contracting Officer, who shall promptly make a determination in writing. Any adjustment by the Contractor without such a determination shall be at its own risk and expense. The Contracting Officer shall furnish from time to time such detailed drawings and other information as considered necessary, unless otherwise provided.

(b) Wherever in the specifications or upon the drawings the words *directed*, *required*, *ordered*, *designated,prescribed*, or words of like import are used, it shall be understood that the *direction*, *requirement*, *order*, *designation*, or *prescription*, of the Contracting Officer is intended and similarly the words *approved*, *acceptable*, *satisfactory*, or words of like import shall mean *approved by*, or *acceptable to*, or *satisfactory to* the Contracting Officer, unless otherwise expressly stated.

(c) Where *as shown*, *as indicated*, *as detailed*, or words of similar import are used, it shall be understood that the reference is made to the drawings accompanying this contract unless stated otherwise. The word *provided* as used herein shall be understood to mean *provide complete in place*, that is *furnished and installed*.

(d) Shop drawings means drawings, submitted to the Government by the Contractor, subcontractor, or any lower tier subcontractor pursuant to a construction contract, showing in detail (1) the proposed fabrication and assembly of structural elements and (2) the installation (i.e., form, fit, and attachment details) of materials of equipment. It includes drawings, diagrams, layouts, schematics, descriptive literature, illustrations, schedules, performance and test data, and similar materials furnished by the contractor to explain in detail specific portions of the work required by the contract. The Government may duplicate, use, and disclose in any manner and for any purpose shop drawings delivered under this contract.

(e) If this contract requires shop drawings, the Contractor shall coordinate all such drawings, and review them for accuracy, completeness, and compliance with contract requirements and shall indicate its approval thereon as evidence of such coordination and review. Shop drawings submitted to the Contracting Officer without evidence of the Contractor's approval may be returned for resubmission. The Contracting Officer will indicate an approval or disapproval of the shop drawings and if not approved as submitted shall indicate the Government's reasons therefor. Any work done before such approval shall be at the Contractor's risk. Approval by the Contracting Officer shall not relieve the Contractor from responsibility for any errors or omissions in such drawings, nor from responsibility for complying with the requirements of this contract, except with respect to variations described and approved in accordance with (f) below.

(f) If shop drawings show variations from the contract requirements, the Contractor shall describe such variations in writing, separate from the drawings, at the time of submission. If the Contracting Officer approves any such variation, the Contracting Officer shall issue an appropriate contract modification, except that, if the variation is minor or does not involve a change in price or in time of performance, a modification need not be issued.

(g) The Contractor shall submit to the Contracting Officer for approval four copies (unless otherwise indicated) of all shop drawings as called for under the various headings of these specifications. Three sets (unless otherwise indicated) of all shop drawings, will be retained by the Contracting Officer and one set will be returned to the Contractor.

(End of clause)

Alternate I (APR 1984). When record shop drawings are required and reproducible shop drawings are needed, add the following sentences to paragraph (g) of the basic clause:

Upon completing the work under this contract, the Contractor shall furnish a complete set of all shop drawings as finally approved. These drawings shall show all changes and revisions made up to the time the equipment is completed and accepted.

Alternate II (APR 1984). When record shop drawings are required and reproducible shop drawings are not needed, the following sentences shall be added to paragraph (g) of the basic clause:

Upon completing the work under this contract, the Contractor shall furnish ____ [*Contracting Officer complete by inserting desired amount*] sets of prints of all shop drawings as finally approved. These drawings shall show changes and revisions made up to the time the equipment is completed and accepted.

[Final rule, 55 FR 38518, 9/18/90; FAC 90-7, 56 FR 41744, 8/22/91, effective 9/23/91; FAC 90-29, 60 FR 34732, 7/3/95, effective 7/3/95; FAC 90-32, 60 FR 48206, 9/18/95, effective 10/1/95; FAC 90-43, Final rule, 61 FR 67408, 12/20/96, effective 2/18/97]

52.236-22 Design within Funding Limitations.

As prescribed in 36.609-1(c), insert the following clause:

DESIGN WITHIN FUNDING LIMITATIONS (APR 1984)

(a) The Contractor shall accomplish the design services required under this contract so as to permit the award of a contract, using standard Federal Acquisition Regulation procedures for the construction of the facilities designed at a price that does not exceed the estimated construction contract price as set forth in paragraph (c) below. When bids or proposals for the construction contract are received that exceed the estimated price, the contractor shall perform such redesign and other services as are necessary to permit contract award within the funding limitation. These additional services shall be performed at no increase in the price of this contract. However, the Contractor shall not be required to perform such additional services at no cost to the Government if the unfavorable bids or proposals are the result of conditions beyond its reasonable control.

(b) The Contractor will promptly advise the Contracting Officer if it finds that the project being designed will exceed or is likely to exceed the funding limitations and it is unable to design a usable facility within these limitations. Upon receipt of such information, the Contracting Officer will review the Contractor's revised estimate of construction cost. The Government may, if it determines that the estimated construction contract price set forth in this contract is so low that award of a construction contract not in excess of such estimate is improbable, authorize a change in scope or materials as required to reduce the estimated construction cost to an amount within the estimated construction contract price set forth in paragraph (c) below, or the Government may adjust such estimated construction contract price. When bids or proposals are not solicited or are unreasonably delayed, the Government shall prepare an estimate of constructing the design submitted and such estimate shall be used in lieu of bids or proposals to determine compliance with the funding limitation.

(c) The estimated construction contract price for the project described in this contract is $________.

(End of clause)

[FAC 84-8, 50 FR 26904, 6/28/85, effective 7/1/85; FAC 90-32, 60 FR 48206, 9/18/95, effective 10/1/95]

52.236-23 Responsibility of the Architect-Engineer Contractor.

As prescribed in 36.609-2(b), insert the following clause:

RESPONSIBILITY OF THE ARCHITECT-ENGINEER CONTRACTOR (APR 1984)

(a) The Contractor shall be responsible for the professional quality, technical accuracy, and the coordination of all designs, drawings, specifications, and other services furnished by the Contractor under this contract. The Contractor shall, without additional compensation, correct or revise any errors or deficiencies in its designs, drawings, specifications, and other services.

(b) Neither the Government's review, approval or acceptance of, nor payment for, the services required under this contract shall be construed to operate as a waiver of any rights under this contract or of any cause of action arising out of the performance of this contract, and the Contractor shall be and remain liable to the Government in accordance with applicable law for all damages to the Government caused by the Contractor's negligent performance of any of the services furnished under this contract.

(c) The rights and remedies of the Government provided for under this contract are in addition to any other rights and remedies provided by law.

(d) If the Contractor is comprised of more than one legal entity, each such entity shall be jointly and severally liable hereunder.

(End of clause)

[FAC 84-8, 50 FR 26904 6/28/85, effective 7/1/85; FAC 90-32, 60 FR 48206, 9/18/95, effective 10/1/95]

52.236-24 Work Oversight in Architect-Engineer Contracts.

As prescribed in 36.609-3, insert the following clause:

WORK OVERSIGHT IN ARCHITECT-ENGINEER CONTRACTS (APR 1984)

The extent and character of the work to be done by the Contractor shall be subject to the general oversight, supervision, direction, control, and approval of the Contracting Officer.

(End of clause)

[FAC 84-8, 50 FR 26904, 6/28/85, effective 7/1/85; FAC 90-32, 60 FR 48206, 9/18/95, effective 10/1/95]

52.236-25 Requirements for Registration of Designers.

As prescribed in 36.609-4, insert the following clause:

REQUIREMENTS FOR REGISTRATION OF DESIGNERS (JUN 2003)

Architects or engineers registered to practice in the particular professional field involved in a State, the District of Columbia, or an outlying area of the United States shall prepare or review and approve the design of architectural, structural, mechanical, electrical, civil, or other engineering features of the work.

(End of clause)

[FAC 90-32, 60 FR 48206, 9/18/95, effective 10/1/95; FAC 97-14, 64 FR 51828, 9/24/99, effective 11/23/99; FAC 2001-14, 68 FR 28079, 5/22/2003, effective 6/23/2003]

52.236-26 Preconstruction Conference.

As prescribed in 36.522, insert the following clause:

PREDONSTRUCTION CONFERENCE (FEB 1995)

If the Contracting Officer decides to conduct a preconstruction conference, the successful offeror will be notified and will be required to attend. The Contracting Officer's notification will include specific details regarding the date, time, and location of the conference, any need for attendance by subcontractors, and information regarding the items to be discussed.

(End of clause)

[FAC 90-23, 59 FR 67010, 12/28/94, effective 2/27/95]

52.236-27 Site Visit (Construction).

As prescribed in 36.523, insert a provision substantially the same as the following:

SITE VISIT (CONSTRUCTION) (FEB 1995)

(a) The clauses at 52.236-2, Differing Site Conditions, and 52.236-3, Site Investigations and Conditions Affecting the Work, will be included in any contract awarded as a result of this solicitation. Accordingly, offerors or quoters are urged and expected to inspect the site where the work will be performed.

(b) Site visits may be arranged during normal duty hours by contacting:

Name:________________________

Address:________________________

Telephone:________________________

(End of provision)

Alternate I (FEB 1995). If an organized site visit will be conducted, substitute a paragraph substantially the same as the following for paragraph (b) of the basic provision:

(b) An organized site visit has been scheduled for—

___ (Insert date and time)

(c) Participants will meet at—

___ (Insert location)

(End of provision)

[FAC 90-23, 59 FR 67010, 12/28/94, effective 2/27/95]

52.236-28 Preparation of Proposals—Construction.

As prescribed in 36.520, insert the following provision:

PREPARATION OF PROPOSALS—CONSTRUCTION (OCT 1997)

(a) Proposals must be (1) submitted on the forms furnished by the Government or on copies of those forms, and (2) manually signed. The person signing a proposal must initial each erasure or change appearing on any proposal form.

(b) The proposal form may require offerors to submit proposed prices for one or more items on various bases, including—

(1) Lump sum price;

(2) Alternate prices;

(3) Units of construction; or

(4) Any combination of paragraphs (b)(1) through (b)(3) of this provision.

(c) If the solicitation requires submission of a proposal on all items, failure to do so may result in the proposal being rejected without further consideration. If a proposal on all items is not required, offerors should insert the words "no proposal" in the space provided for any item on which no price is submitted.

(d) Alternate proposals will not be considered unless this solicitation authorizes their submission.

(End of provision)

[FAC 97-2, 62 FR 51224, 9/30/97, effective 10/10/97]

52.237-1 Site Visit.

As prescribed in 37.110(a), insert the following provision in solicitations for services to be performed on Government installations, unless the solicitation is for construction:

SITE VISIT (APR 1984)

Offerors or quoters are urged and expected to inspect the site where services are to be performed and to satisfy themselves regarding all general and local conditions that may affect the cost of contract performance, to the extent that the information is reasonably obtainable. In no event shall failure to inspect the site constitute grounds for a claim after contract award.

(End of provision)

[FAC 90-32, 60 FR 48206, 9/18/95, effective 10/1/95]

52.237-2 Protection of Government Buildings, Equipment, and Vegetation.

As prescribed in 37.110(b), insert the following clause in solicitations and contracts for services to be performed on Government installations, unless a construction contract is contemplated:

PROTECTION OF GOVERNMENT BUILDINGS, EQUIPMENT, AND VEGETATION (APR 1984)

The Contractor shall use reasonable care to avoid damaging existing buildings, equipment, and vegetation on the Government installation. If the Contractor's failure to use reasonable care causes damage to any of this property, the Contractor shall replace or repair the damage at no expense to the Government as the Contracting Officer directs. If the Contractor fails or refuses to make such repair or replacement, the Contractor shall be liable for the cost, which may be deducted from the contract price.

(End of clause)

[FAC 90-32, 60 FR 48206, 9/18/95, effective 10/1/95]

52.237-3 Continuity of Services.

As prescribed in 37.110(c), the following clause:

CONTINUITY OF SERVICES (JAN 1991)

(a) The Contractor recognizes that the services under this contract are vital to the Government and must be continued without interruption and that, upon contract expiration, a successor, either the Government or another contractor, may continue them. The Contractor agrees to (1) furnish phase-in training and (2) exercise its best efforts and cooperation to effect an orderly and efficient transition to a successor.

(b) The Contractor shall, upon the Contracting Officer's written notice, (1) furnish phase-in, phase-out services for up to 90 days after this contract expires and (2) negotiate in good faith a plan with a successor to determine the nature and extent of phase-in, phase-out services required. The plan shall specify a training program and a date for transferring responsibilities for each division of work described in the plan, and shall be subject to the Contracting Officer's approval. The Contractor shall provide sufficient experienced personnel during the phase-in, phase-out period to ensure that the services called for by this contract are maintained at the required level of proficiency.

(c) The Contractor shall allow as many personnel as practicable to remain on the job to help the successor maintain the continuity and consistency of the services required by this contract. The Contractor also shall disclose necessary personnel records and allow the successor to conduct on-site interviews with these employees. If selected employees are agreeable to the change, the Contractor shall release them at a mutually agreeable date and negotiate transfer of their earned fringe benefits to the successor.

(d) The Contractor shall be reimbursed for all reasonable phase-in, phase-out costs (i.e., costs incurred within the agreed period after contract expiration that result from phase-in, phase-out operations) and a fee (profit) not to exceed a pro rata portion of the fee (profit) under this contract.

(End of clause)

[FAC 90-3, 55 FR 52799, 12/21/90, effective 1/22/91; Final rule, 62 FR 40236, 7/25/97, effective 6/30/97]

52.237-4 Payment by Government to Contractor.

As prescribed in 37.304(a), insert the following clause in solicitations and contracts solely for dismantling, demolition, or removal of improvements whenever the contracting officer determines that the Government shall make payment to the contractor in addition to any title to property that the contractor may receive under the contract:

PAYMENT BY GOVERNMENT TO CONTRACTOR (APR 1984)

(a) In ____ [*insert "full" if Alternate I is used; otherwise insert "partial"*] consideration of the performance of the work called for in the Schedule, the Government will pay to the Contractor ____ [*fill in amount*].

(b) The Government shall make progress payments monthly as the work proceeds, or at more frequent intervals as determined by the Contracting Officer, on estimates approved by the Contracting Officer. Except as provided in paragraph (c) below, in making progress payments the Contracting Officer shall retain 10 percent of the estimated payment until final completion and acceptance of the contract work. However, if the Contracting Officer finds that satisfactory progress was achieved during any period for which a progress payment is to be made, the Contracting Officer may authorize such payment in full, without retaining a percentage. Also, on completion and acceptance of each unit or division for which the price is stated separately, the Contracting Officer may authorize full payment for that unit or division without retaining a percentage.

(c) When the work is substantially completed, the Contracting Officer shall retain an amount considered adequate for the protection of the Government and, at the Contracting Officer's discretion, may release all or a portion of any excess amount.

(d) In further consideration of performance, the Contractor shall receive title to all property to be dismantled or demolished that is not specifically designated as being retained by the Government. The title shall vest in the Contractor immediately upon the Government's issuing the notice of award, or if a performance bond is to be furnished after award, upon the Government's issuance of a notice to proceed with the work. The Government shall not be responsible for the condition of, or any loss or damage to, the property. If the Contractor does not wish to remove from the site any of the property acquired, the Contracting Officer may, upon written request, grant the Contractor permission to leave the property on the premises. As a condition to the granting of this permission, the Contractor agrees to waive any right, title, claim, or interest in and to the property.

(e) Upon completion and acceptance of all work and receipt of a properly executed voucher, the Government shall make final payment of the amount due the Contractor under this contract. If requested, the Contractor shall release all claims against the Government arising under this contract, other than any claims the Contractor specifically excepts, in stated amounts, from operation of this release.

(End of clause)

Alternate I (APR 1984). If the contracting officer determines that the Government shall retain all material resulting from the dismantling or demolition work, delete paragraph (d) from the basic clause and renumber the remaining paragraphs.

[FAC 90-32, 60 FR 48206, 9/18/95, effective 10/1/95]

52.237-5 Payment by Contractor to Government.

As prescribed in 37.304(b), insert the following clause in solicitations and contracts for dismantling, demolition, or removal of improvements whenever the contractor is to receive title to dismantled or demolished property and a net amount of compensation is due to the Government, except if the contracting officer determines that it would be advantageous to the Government for the contractor to pay in increments and the Government to transfer title to the contractor for increments of property only upon receipt of those payments:

PAYMENT BY CONTRACTOR TO GOVERNMENT (APR 1984)

(a) The Contractor shall receive title to all property to be dismantled, demolished, or removed under this contract and not specifically designated in the Schedule as being retained by the Government. The title shall vest in the Contractor immediately upon the Government's issuing the notice of award, or if a performance bond is to be furnished, upon the Government's issuing a notice to proceed with the work. The Government shall not be responsible for the condition of, or any loss or damage to, the property.

(b) The Contractor shall promptly remove from the site all property acquired by the Contractor. The Government shall not permit storage of property on the site beyond the completion date. If the Contractor does not wish to remove from the site any of the property acquired, the Contracting Officer may, upon written request, grant the Contractor permission to leave the property on the premises. As a condition of the granting of the permission, the Contractor agrees to waive any right, title, claim, or interest in and to the property.

(c) The Contractor shall perform the work called for under this contract and within ____ days of receipt of notice of award, unless otherwise provided in the Schedule and before proceeding with the work, shall pay ____ [*fill in amount*]. Checks shall be made payable to the office designated in the contract and shall be forwarded to the Contracting Officer.

(End of clause)

[FAC 90-32, 60 FR 48206, 9/18/95, effective 10/1/95]

52.237-6 Incremental Payment by Contractor to Government.

As prescribed in 37.304(c), insert the following clause in solicitations and contracts for dismantling, demolition, or removal of improvements (a) if the contractor is to receive title to dismantled or demolished property and a net amount of compensation is due the Government, and (b) if the contracting officer determines that it would be advantageous to the Government for the contractor to pay in increments, and for the Government to transfer title to the contractor for increments of property, only upon receipt of those payments:

INCREMENTAL PAYMENT BY CONTRACTOR TO GOVERNMENT (APR 1984)

(a) The Contractor shall perform the work called for under this contract and within ____ days of receipt of notice of award, unless otherwise provided in the Schedule, and before proceeding with the work, shall pay ____ [*fill in amount*]. Thereafter, the Contractor shall make payment to the Government in the amount and frequency specified in the Schedule. Checks shall be made payable to the office designated in the contract and shall be forwarded to the Contracting Officer.

(b) Upon the Government's receipt of each increment of payment, the Contractor shall receive title to such property as the Contracting Officer determines to be fair and reasonable for that increment of payment. Upon receipt of the Contractor's final payment, all title that has not passed to the Contractor shall vest in the Contractor, unless specifically designated in the Schedule as being retained by the Government. The Government shall not be responsible for the condition of, or any loss or damage to, the property.

(c) The Contractor shall promptly remove from the site all property acquired by the Contractor. The Government will not permit storage of property on the site beyond the completion date. If the Contractor does not wish to remove from the site any of the property acquired, the Contracting Officer may, upon written request, grant the Contractor permission to leave the property on the premises. As a condition of the granting of this permission, the Contractor agrees to waive any right, title, claim, or interest in and to the property.

(End of clause)

[FAC 90-32, 60 FR 48206, 9/18/95, effective 10/1/95]

52.237-7 Indemnification and Medical Liability Insurance.

As prescribed in 37.403, insert the following clause:

INDEMNIFICATION AND MEDICAL LIABILITY INSURANCE (JAN 1997)

(a) It is expressly agreed and understood that this is a nonpersonal services contract, as defined in Federal Acquisition Regulation (FAR) 37.101, under which the professional services rendered by the Contractor are rendered in its capacity as an independent contractor. The Government may evaluate the quality of professional and administrative services provided, but retains no control over professional aspects of the services rendered, including by example, the Contractor's professional medical judgment, diagnosis, or specific medical treatments. The Contractor shall be solely liable for and expressly agrees to indemnify the Government with respect to any liability producing acts or omissions by it or by its employees or agents. The Contractor shall maintain during the term of this contract liability insurance issued by a responsible insurance carrier of not less than the following amount(s) per specialty per occurrence:___.

(b) An apparently successful offeror, upon request by the Contracting Officer, shall furnish prior to contract award evidence of its insurability concerning the medical liability insurance required by paragraph (a) of this clause.

(c) Liability insurance may be on either an occurrences basis or on a claims-made basis. If the policy is on a claims-made basis, an extended reporting endorsement (tail) for a period of not less than 3 years after the end of the contract term must also be provided.

(d) Evidence of insurance documenting the required coverage for each health care provider who will perform under this contract shall be provided to the Contracting Officer prior to the commencement of services under this contract. If the insurance is on a claims-made basis and evidence of an extended reporting endorsement is not provided prior to the commencement of services, evidence of such endorsement shall be provided to the Contracting Officer prior to the expiration of this contract. Final payment under this contract shall be withheld until evidence of the extended reporting endorsement is provided to the Contracting Officer.

(e) The policies evidencing required insurance shall also contain an endorsement to the effect that any cancellation or material change adversely affecting the Government's interest shall not be effective until 30 days after the insurer or the Contractor gives written notice to the Contracting Officer. If during the performance period of the contract the Contractor changes insurance providers, the Contractor must provide evidence that the Government will be indemnified to the limits specified in paragraph (a) of this clause, for the entire period of the contract, either under the new policy, or a combination of old and new policies.

(f) The Contractor shall insert the substance of this clause, including this paragraph (f), in all subcontracts under this contract for health care services and shall require such subcontractors to provide evidence of and maintain insurance in accordance with paragraph (a) of this clause. At least 5 days before the commencement of work by any subcontractor, the Contractor shall furnish to the Contracting Officer evidence of such insurance.

(End of clause)

* Contracting Officer insert the dollar value(s) of standard coverage(s) prevailing within the local community as to the specific medical specialty, or specialties, concerned, or such higher amount as the Contracting Officer deems necessary to protect the Government's interests.

* (Insert appropriate agency name in blanks.)

[FAC 84-42, 54 FR 5058, 1/31/89, effective 3/2/89; FAC 84-51, 54 FR 34758, 8/21/89, effective 9/20/89; FAC 90-45, Final rule, 62 FR 224, 1/2/97, effective 1/1/97]

52.237-8 Restriction on Severance Payments to Foreign Nationals.

As prescribed in 37.113-2(a), use the following provision:

RESTRICTION ON SEVERANCE PAYMENTS TO FOREIGN NATIONALS (AUG 2003)

(a) The Federal Acquisition Regulation (FAR), at 31.205-6(g)(6), limits the cost allowability of severance payments to foreign nationals employed under a service contract performed outside the United States unless the agency grants a waiver pursuant to FAR 37.113-1 before contract award.

(b) In making the determination concerning the granting of a waiver, the agency will determine that—

(1) The application of the severance pay limitations to the contract would adversely affect the continuation of a program, project, or activity that provides significant support services for (i) members of the armed forces stationed or deployed outside the United States, or (ii) employees of an executive agency posted outside the United States;

(2) The Contractor has taken (or has established plans to take) appropriate actions within its control to minimize the amount and number of incidents of the payment of severance pay to employees under the contract who are foreign nationals; and

(3) The payment of severance pay is necessary in order to comply with a law that is generally applicable to a significant number of businesses in the country in which the foreign national receiving the payment performed services under the contract, or is necessary to comply with a collective bargaining agreement.

(End of provision)

[FAC 90-31, 60 FR 42648, 8/16/95, effective 10/1/95; FAC 2001-15, 68 FR 43863, 7/24/2003, effective 8/25/2003]

52.237-9 Waiver of Limitation on Severance Payments to Foreign Nationals.

As prescribed in 37.113-2(b), use the following clause:

WAIVER OF LIMITATION ON SEVERANCE PAYMENTS TO FOREIGN NATIONALS (MAY 2014)

(a) Pursuant to 10 U.S.C. 2324(e)(3)(A) or 41 U.S.C. 4304(b)(1), as applicable, the cost allowability limitations in FAR 31.205-6(g)(6) are waived.

(b) This clause may be incorporated into subcontracts issued under this contract, if approved by the Contracting Officer.

(End of clause)

[FAC 90-31, 60 FR 42648, 8/16/95, effective 10/1/95; FAC 2001-15, 68 FR 43863, 7/24/2003, effective 8/25/2003; FAC 2005-73, 79 FR 24192, 4/29/2014, effective 5/29/2014]

52.237-10 Identification of Uncompensated Overtime.

As prescribed in 37.115-3, insert the following provision:

IDENTIFICATION OF UNCOMPENSATED OVERTIME (MAR 2015)

(a) *Definitions.* As used in this provision—

Adjusted hourly rate (including uncompensated overtime) is the rate that results from multiplying the hourly rate for a 40-hour work week by 40, and then dividing by the proposed hours per week which includes uncompensated overtime hours over and above the standard 40-hour work week. For example, 45 hours proposed on a 40-hour work week basis at $20 per hour would be converted to an uncompensated overtime rate of $17.78 per hour ($20.00 × 40 divided by 45 = $17.78).

(b) (1) Whenever there is uncompensated overtime, the adjusted hourly rate (including uncompensated overtime), rather than the hourly rate, shall be applied to all proposed hours, whether regular or overtime hours.

(2) All proposed labor hours subject to the adjusted hourly rate (including uncompensated overtime) shall be identified as either regular or overtime hours, by labor categories, and described at the same level of detail. This is applicable to all proposals whether the labor hours are at the prime or subcontract level. This includes uncompensated overtime hours that are in indirect cost pools for personnel whose regular hours are normally charged direct.

(c) The offeror's accounting practices used to estimate uncompensated overtime must be consistent with its cost accounting practices used to accumulate and report uncompensated overtime hours.

(d) Proposals that include unrealistically low labor rates, or that do not otherwise demonstrate cost realism, will be considered in a risk assessment and will be evaluated for award in accordance with that assessment.

(e) The offeror shall include a copy of its policy addressing uncompensated overtime with its proposal.

(End of provision)

[FAC 97-1, 62 FR 44802, 8/22/97, effective 10/21/97; FAC 2005-80, 80 FR 4992, 1/29/2015, effective 3/2/2015; Correction, 80 FR 6909, 2/9/2015, effective 3/2/2015]

52.237-11 [Removed]

[FAC 2005-19, 72 FR 46361, 8/17/2007, effective 8/17/2007; FAC 2005-27, 73 FR 54014, 9/17/2008, effective 9/17/2008; FAC 2005-101, 83 FR 48700, 9/26/2018, effective 10/26/2018]

52.238 [Reserved]

52.239-1 Privacy or Security Safeguards.

As prescribed in 39.106, insert a clause substantially the same as the following:

PRIVACY OR SECURITY SAFEGUARDS (AUG 1996)

(a) The Contractor shall not publish or disclose in any manner, without the Contracting Officer's written consent, the details of any safeguards either designed or developed by the Contractor under this contract or otherwise provided by the Government.

(b) To the extent required to carry out a program of inspection to safeguard against threats and hazards to the security, integrity, and confidentiality of Government data, the Contractor shall afford the Government access to the Contractor's facilities, installations, technical capabilities, operations, documentation, records, and databases.

(c) If new or unanticipated threats or hazards are discovered by either the Government or the Contractor, or if existing safeguards have ceased to function, the discoverer shall immediately bring the situation to the attention of the other party.

(End of clause)

[FAC 90-41, 61 FR 41466, 8/8/96, effective 8/8/96, finalized without change, FAC 97-3, 62 FR 64912, 12/9/97, effective 2/9/98; FAC 90-45, Final rule, 62 FR 224, 1/2/97, effective 1/1/97; FAC 2005-78, 79 FR 70343, 11/25/2014, effective 12/26/2014]

52.240 [Reserved]

52.241-1 Electric Service Territory Compliance Representation.

As prescribed in 41.501(b), insert a provision substantially the same as the following:

ELECTRIC SERVICE TERRITORY COMPLIANCE REPRESENTATION (MAY 1999)

(a) Section 8093 of Public Law 100-202 generally requires purchases of electricity by any department, agency, or instrumentality of the United States to be consistent with State law governing the provision of electric utility service, including State utility commission rulings and electric utility franchises or service territories established pursuant to State statute, State regulation, or State-approved territorial agreements.

(b) By signing this offer, the offeror represents that this offer to sell electricity is consistent with Section 8093 of Public Law 100-202.

(c) Upon request of the Contracting Officer, the offeror shall submit supporting legal and factual rationale for this representation.

[FAC 97-11, 64 FR 10530, 3/4/99, effective 5/3/99]

52.241-2 Order of Precedence—Utilities.

As prescribed in 41.501(c)(1), insert a clause substantially the same as the following:

ORDER OF PRECEDENCE—UTILITIES (FEB 1995)

In the event of any inconsistency between the terms of this contract (including the specifications) and any rate schedule, rider, or exhibit incorporated in this contract by reference or otherwise, or any of the Contractor's rules and regulations, the terms of this contract shall control.

(End of clause)

[FAC 90-23, 59 FR 67010, 12/28/94, effective 2/27/95]

52.241-3 Scope and Duration of Contract.

As prescribed in 41.501(c)(2), insert a clause substantially the same as the following:

SCOPE AND DURATION OF CONTRACT (FEB 1995)

(a) For the period ___ [*insert period of service*] the Contractor agrees to furnish and the Government agrees to purchase ___ [*insert type of service*] utility service in accordance with the applicable tariff(s), rules, and regulations as approved by the applicable governing regulatory body and as set forth in the contract.

(b) It is expressly understood that neither the Contractor nor the Government is under any obligation to continue any service under the terms and conditions of this contract beyond the expiration date.

(c) The Contractor shall provide the Government with one complete set of rates, terms, and conditions of service which are in effect as of the date of this contract and any subsequently approved rates.

(d) The Contractor shall be paid at the applicable rate(s) under the tariff and the Government shall be liable for the minimum monthly charge, if any, specified in this contract commencing with the period in which service is initially furnished and continuing for the term of this contract. Any minimum monthly charge specified in this contract shall be equitably prorated for the periods in which commencement and termination of this contract become effective.

(End of clause)

[FAC 90-23, 59 FR 67010, 12/28/94, effective 2/27/95]

52.241-4 Change in Class of Service.

As prescribed in 41.501(c)(3), insert a clause substantially the same as the following:

CHANGE IN CLASS OF SERVICE (FEB 1995)

(a) In the event of a change in the class of service, such service shall be provided at the Contractor's lowest available rate schedule applicable to the class of service furnished.

(b) Where the Contractor does not have on file with the regulatory body approved rate schedules applicable to services provided, no clause in this contract shall preclude the parties from negotiating a rate schedule applicable to the class of service furnished.

(End of clause)

[FAC 90-23, 59 FR 67010, 12/28/94, effective 2/27/95]

52.241-5 Contractor's Facilities.

As prescribed in 41.501(c)(4), insert a clause substantially the same as the following:

CONTRACTOR'S FACILITIES (FEB 1995)

(a) The Contractor, at its expense, unless otherwise provided for in this contract, shall furnish, install, operate, and maintain all facilities required to furnish service hereunder, and measure such service at the point of delivery specified in the Service Specifications. Title to all such facilities shall remain with the Contractor and the Contractor shall be responsible for loss or damage to such facilities, except that the Government shall be responsible to the extent that loss or damage has been caused by the Government's negligent acts or omissions.

(b) Notwithstanding any terms expressed in this clause, the Contractor shall obtain approval from the Contracting Officer prior to any equipment installation, construction, or removal. The Government hereby grants to the Contractor, free of any rental or similar charge, but subject to the limitations specified in this contract, a revocable permit or license to enter the service location for any proper purpose under this contract. This permit or license includes use of the site or sites agreed upon by the parties hereto for the installation, operation, maintenance, and repair of the facilities of the Contractor required to be located upon Government premises. All applicable taxes and other charges in connection therewith, together with all liability of the Contractor in construction, operation, maintenance and repair of such facilities, shall be the obligation of the Contractor.

(c) Authorized representatives of the Contractor will be allowed access to the facilities on Government premises at reasonable times to perform the obligations of the Contractor regarding such facilities. It is expressly understood that the Government may limit or restrict the right of access herein granted in any manner considered necessary (e.g., national security, public safety).

(d) Unless otherwise specified in this contract, the Contractor shall, at its expense, remove such facilities and restore Government premises to their original condition as near as practicable within a reasonable time after the Government terminates this contract. In the event such termination of this contract is due to the fault of the Contractor, such facilities may be retained in place at the option of the Government for a reasonable time while the Government attempts to obtain service elsewhere comparable to that provided for hereunder.

(End of clause)

[FAC 90-23, 59 FR 67010, 12/28/94, effective 2/27/95]

52.241-6 Service Provisions.

As prescribed in 41.501(c)(5), insert a clause substantially the same as the following:

SERVICE PROVISIONS (FEB 1995)

(a) *Measurement of service*. (1) All service furnished by the Contractor shall be measured by suitable metering equipment of standard manufacture, to be furnished, installed, maintained, repaired, calibrated, and read by the Contractor at its expense. When more than a single meter is installed at a service location, the readings thereof may be billed conjunctively, if appropriate. In the event any meter fails to register (or registers incorrectly) the service furnished, the parties shall agree upon the length of time of meter malfunction and the quantity of service delivered during such period of time. An appropriate adjustment shall be made to the next invoice for the purpose of correcting such errors. However, any meter which registers not more than ___ percent slow or fast shall be deemed correct.

(2) The Contractor shall read all meters at periodic intervals of approximately 30 days or in accordance with the policy of the cognizant regulatory body or applicable bylaws. All billings based on meter readings of less than ___ days shall be prorated accordingly.

(b) *Meter test.* (1) The Contractor, at its expense, shall periodically inspect and test Contractor-installed meters at intervals not exceeding __ year(s). The Government has the right to have representation during the inspection and test.

(2) At the written request of the Contracting Officer, the Contractor shall make additional tests of any or all such meters in the presence of Government representatives. The cost of such additional tests shall be borne by the Government if the percentage of errors is found to be not more than ___ percent slow or fast.

(3) No meter shall be placed in service or allowed to remain in service which has an error in registration in excess of ___ percent under normal operating conditions.

(c) *Change in volume or character.* Reasonable notice shall be given by the Contracting Officer to the Contractor regarding any material changes anticipated in the volume or characteristics of the utility service required at each location.

(d) *Continuity of service and consumption.* The Contractor shall use reasonable diligence to provide a regular and uninterrupted supply of service at each service location, but shall not be liable for damages, breach of contract or otherwise, to the Government for failure, suspension, diminution, or other variations of service occasioned by or in consequence of any cause beyond the control of the Contractor, including but not limited to acts of God or of the public enemy, fires, floods, earthquakes, or other catastrophe, strikes, or failure or breakdown of transmission or other facilities. If any such failure, suspension, diminution, or other variation of service shall aggregate more than __ hour(s) during any billing period hereunder, an equitable adjustment shall be made in the monthly billing specified in this contract (including the minimum monthly charge).

(End of clause)

[FAC 90-23, 59 FR 67010, 12/28/94, effective 2/27/95; Corrected 60 FR 5869, 1/31/95]

52.241-7 Change in Rates or Terms and Conditions of Service for Regulated Services.

As prescribed in 41.501(d)(1), insert a clause substantially the same as the following:

CHANGE IN RATES OR TERMS AND CONDITIONS OF SERVICE FOR REGULATED SERVICES (FEB 1995)

(a) This clause applies to the extent services furnished under this contract are subject to regulation by a regulatory body. The Contractor agrees to give ____ written notice of (1) the filing of an application for change in rates or terms and conditions of service concurrently with the filing of the application and (2) any changes pending with the regulatory body as of the date of contract award. Such notice shall fully describe the proposed change. If, during the term of this contract, the regulatory body having jurisdiction approves any changes, the Contractor shall forward to the Contracting Officer a copy of such changes within 15 days after the effective date thereof. The Contractor agrees to continue furnishing service under this contract in accordance with the amended tariff, and the Government agrees to pay for such service at the higher or lower rates as of the date when such rates are made effective.

(b) The Contractor agrees that throughout the life of this contract the applicable published and unpublished rate schedule(s) shall not be in excess of the lowest cost published and unpublished rate schedule(s) available to any other customers of the same class under similar conditions of use and service.

(c) In the event that the regulatory body promulgates any regulation concerning matters other than rates which affects this contract, the Contractor shall immediately provide a copy to the Contracting Officer. The Government shall not be bound to accept any new regulation inconsistent with Federal laws or regulations.

(d) Any changes to rates or terms and conditions of service shall be made a part of this contract by the issuance of a contract modification unless otherwise specified in the contract. The effective date of the change shall be the effective date by the regulatory body. Any factors not governed by the regulatory body will have an effective date as agreed to by the parties.

(End of clause)

Note: Insert language prescribed in 41.501(d)(1)

[FAC 90-23, 59 FR 67010, 12/28/94, effective 2/27/95]

52.241-8 Change in Rates or Terms and Conditions of Service for Unregulated Services.

As prescribed in 41.501(d)(2), insert a clause substantially the same as the following:

CHANGE IN RATES OR TERMS AND CONDITIONS OF SERVICE FOR UNREGULATED SERVICES (FEB 1995)

(a) This clause applies to the extent that services furnished hereunder are not subject to regulation by a regulatory body.

(b) After ___ [*insert date*], either party may request a change in rates or terms and conditions of service, unless otherwise provided in this contract. Both parties agree to enter in negotiations concerning such changes upon receipt of a written request detailing the proposed changes and specifying the reasons for the proposed changes.

(c) The effective date of any change shall be as agreed to by the parties. The Contractor agrees that throughout the life of this contract the rates so negotiated will not be in excess of published and unpublished rates charged to any other customer of the same class under similar terms and conditions of use and service.

(d) The failure of the parties to agree upon any change after a reasonable period of time shall be a dispute under the Disputes clause of this contract.

(e) Any changes to rates, terms, or conditions as a result of such negotiations shall be made a part of this contract by the issuance of a contract modification.

(End of clause)

[FAC 90-23, 59 FR 67010, 12/28/94, effective 2/27/95]

52.241-9 Connection Charge.

As prescribed in 41.501(d)(3), insert a clause substantially the same as the following:

CONNECTION CHARGE (FEB 1995)

(a) *Charge.* In consideration of the Contractor furnishing and installing at its expense the new connection facilities described herein, the Government shall pay the Contractor a connection charge. The payment shall be in the form of progress payments, advance payments or as a lump sum, as agreed to by the parties and as permitted by applicable law. The total amount payable shall be either the estimated cost of $___ less the agreed to salvage value of $___, or the actual cost less the salvage value, whichever is less. As a condition precedent to final payment, the Contractor shall execute a release of any claims against the Government arising under or by the virtue of such installation.

(b) *Ownership, operation, maintenance and repair of new facilities to be provided.* The facilities to be supplied by the Contractor under this clause, notwithstanding the payment by the Government of a connection charge, shall be and remain the property of the Contractor and shall, at all times during the life of this contract or any renewals thereof, be operated, maintained, and repaired by the Contractor at its expense. All taxes and other charges in connection therewith, together with all liability arising out of the construction, operations, maintenance, or repair of such facilities, shall be the obligation of the Contractor.

(c) *Credits.* (1) The Contractor agrees to allow the Government, on each monthly bill for service furnished under this contract to the service location, a credit of ___ percent of the amount of each such bill as rendered until the accumulation of credits shall equal the amount of such connection charge, provided that the Contractor may at any time allow a credit up to 100 percent of the amount of each such bill.

(2) In the event the Contractor, before any termination of this contract but after completion of the facilities provided for in this clause, serves any customer other than the Government (regardless of whether the Government is being served simultaneously, intermittently, or not at all) by means of these facilities, the Contractor shall promptly notify the Government in writing. Unless otherwise agreed by the parties in writing at that time, the Contractor shall promptly accelerate the credits provided for under subparagraph (c)(1) of this clause, up to 100 percent of each monthly bill until there is refunded the amount that reflects the Government's connection costs for that portion of the facilities used in serving others.

(3) In the event the Contractor terminates this contract, or defaults in performance, prior to full credit of any connection charge paid by the Government, the Contractor shall pay to the Government an amount equal to the uncredited balance of the connection charge as of the date of the termination or default.

(d) *Termination before completion of facilities.* The Government reserves the right to terminate this contract at any time before completion of the facilities with respect to which the Government is to pay a connection charge. In the event the Government exercises this right, the Contractor shall be paid the cost of any work accomplished, including direct and indirect costs reasonably allocable to the completed work prior to the time of termination by the Government, plus the cost of removal, less the salvage value.

(e) *Termination after completion of facilities.* In the event the Government terminates this contract after completion of the facilities with respect to which the Government has paid a connection charge, but before the crediting in full by the Contractor of any connection charge in accordance with the terms of this contract, the Contractor shall have the following options:

(1) To retain in place for ___ months after the notice of termination by the Government such facilities on condition that—

(i) If, during such ___ month period, the Contractor serves any other customer by means of such facilities, the Contractor, shall, in lieu of allowing credits, pay the Government during such period installments in like amount, manner, and extent as the credit provided for under paragraph (c) of this clause before such termination; and

(ii) Immediately after such ___ month period the Contractor shall promptly pay in full to the Government the uncredited balance of the connection charge.

(2) To remove such facilities at the Contractor's own expense within ___ months after the effective date of the termination by the Government. If the Contractor elects to remove such facilities, the Government shall then have the option of purchasing such facilities at the agreed salvage value set forth herein; and provided further, that the Contractor shall, at the direction of the Government, leave in place such facilities located on Government property which the Government elects to purchase at the agreed salvage value.

(End of clause)

Alternate I (FEB 1995). If the Contracting Officer determines that a nonrefundable charge is to be paid and no credits are due the Government, delete paragraphs (c) and (e), renumber paragraph (d) as (c) and add the following as paragraph (d):

(d) *Termination after completion of facilities.* In the event the Government terminates this contract after completion of the facilities with respect to which the Government is to pay a connection charge, the Contractor shall have the following options:

(1) To retain in place for ___ months after the notice of termination by the Government. If the Contractor and the Government have not agreed on terms for retention in place beyond ___ months, then the Contractor must remove the facilities pursuant to the terms of subparagraph (d)(2) of this clause.

(2) To remove such facilities at the Contractor's own expense within ___ months after the effective date of the termination by the Government. If the Contractor elects to remove such facilities, the Government shall then have the option of purchasing such facilities at the agreed salvage value set forth herein; and provided further, that the Contractor shall, at the direction of the Government, leave in place such facilities located on Government property which the Government elects to purchase at the agreed salvage value.

[FAC 90-23, 59 FR 67010, 12/28/94, effective 2/27/95]

52.241-10 Termination Liability.

As prescribed in 41.501(d)(4), insert a clause substantially the same as the following:

TERMINATION LIABILITY (FEB 1995)

(a) If the Government discontinues utility service under this contract before completion of the facilities cost recovery period specified in paragraph (b) of this clause, in consideration of the Contractor furnishing and installing at its expense, the new facility described herein, the Government shall pay termination charges, calculated as set forth in this clause.

(b) *Facility cost recovery period.* The period of time, not exceeding the term of this contract, during which the net cost of the new facility, shall be recovered by the Contractor is—

___ months. [*Insert negotiated duration.*]

(c) *Net facility cost.* The cost of the new facility, less the agreed upon salvage value of such facility, is—

$___. [*Insert appropriate dollar amount.*]

(d) *Monthly facility cost recovery rate.* The monthly facility cost recovery rate which the Government shall pay the Contractor whether or not service is received is—

$___. [*Divide the net facility cost in paragraph (c) of this clause by the facility's cost recovery period in paragraph (b) of this clause and insert the resultant figure.*]

(e) *Termination charges.* Termination charges = $ [*Multiply the remaining months of the facility's cost recovery period specified in paragraph (b) of this clause by the monthly facility cost recovery rate in paragraph (d) of this clause and insert the resultant figure.*]

(f) If the Contractor has recovered its capital costs at the time of termination there will be no termination liability charge.

(End of clause)

[FAC 90-23, 59 FR 67010, 12/28/94, effective 2/27/95]

52.241-11 Multiple Service Locations.

As prescribed in 41.501(d)(5), insert a clause substantially the same as the following:

MULTIPLE SERVICE LOCATIONS (FEB 1995)

(a) At any time by written order, the Contracting Officer may designate any location within the service area of the Contractor at which utility service shall commence or be discontinued. Any changes to the service specifications shall be made a part of the contract by the issuance of a contract modification to include the name and location of the service, specifying any different rate, the point of delivery, different service specifications, and any other terms and conditions.

(b) The applicable monthly charge specified in this contract shall be equitably prorated from the period in which commencement or discontinuance of service at any service location designated under the Service Specifications shall become effective.

(End of clause)

[FAC 90-23, 59 FR 67010, 12/28/94, effective 2/27/95]

52.241-12 Nonrefundable, Nonrecurring Service Charge.

As prescribed in 41.501(d)(6), insert a clause substantially the same as the following:

NONREFUNDABLE, NONRECURRING SERVICE CHARGE (FEB 1995)

As provided herein, the Government will pay a nonrefundable, nonrecurring charge when the rules and regulations of a Contractor require that a customer pay (1) a charge for the initiation of service, (2) a contribution in aid of construction, or (3) a nonrefundable membership fee. This charge may be in addition to or in lieu of a connection charge. Therefore, there is hereby added to the Contractor's schedule a nonrefundable, nonrecurring charge for ___ in the amount of $___ dollars payable [*specify dates or schedules*].

(End of clause)

[FAC 90-23, 59 FR 67010, 12/28/94, effective 2/27/95]

52.241-13 Capital Credits.

As prescribed in 41.501(d)(7), insert a clause substantially the same as the following:

CAPITAL CREDITS (FEB 1995)

(a) The Government is a member of the ___ [*insert cooperative name*], and as any other member, is entitled to capital credits consistent with the bylaws of the cooperative, which states the obligation of the Contractor to pay capital credits and which specifies the method and time of payment.

(b) The Contractor shall furnish to the Contracting Officer, or the designated representative of the Contracting Officer, in writing, on an ___ basis [*insert period of time*] a list of accrued credits by contract number, year, and delivery point.

(c) Payment of capital credits will be made by check, payable to the ___[*insert agency name*], and forwarded to the Contracting Officer at ___ [*insert agency address*], unless otherwise directed in writing by the Contracting Officer. Checks shall cite the current or last contract number and indicate whether the check is partial or final payment for all capital credits accrued.

(End of clause)

[FAC 90-23, 59 FR 67010, 12/28/94, effective 2/27/95]

52.242-1 Notice of Intent to Disallow Costs.

As prescribed in 42.802, insert the following clause in solicitations and contracts when a cost-reimbursement contract, a fixed-price incentive contract, or a contract providing for price redetermination is contemplated:

NOTICE OF INTENT TO DISALLOW COSTS (APR 1984)

(a) Notwithstanding any other clause of this contract—

(1) The Contracting Officer may at any time issue to the Contractor a written notice of intent to disallow specified costs incurred or planned for incurrence under this contract that have been determined not to be allowable under the contract terms; and

(2) The Contractor may, after receiving a notice under subparagraph (1) above, submit a written response to the Contracting Officer, with justification for allowance of the costs. If the Contractor does respond within 60 days, the Contracting Officer shall, within 60 days of receiving the response, either make a written withdrawal of the notice or issue a written decision.

(b) Failure to issue a notice under this Notice of Intent to Disallow Costs clause shall not affect the Government's rights to take exception to incurred costs.

(End of clause)

[FAC 90-32, 60 FR 48206, 9/18/95, effective 10/1/95]

52.242-2 Production Progress Reports.

As prescribed in 42.1107(a), insert the following clause:

PRODUCTION PROGRESS REPORTS (APR 1991)

(a) The Contractor shall prepare and submit to the Contracting Officer the production progress reports specified in the contract Schedule.

(b) During any delay in furnishing a production progress report required under this contract, the Contracting Officer may withhold from payment an amount not exceeding $25,000 or 5 percent of the amount of this contract, whichever is less.

(End of clause)

[FAC 90-4, 56 FR 15156, 4/15/91, effective 5/15/91]

52.242-3 Penalties for Unallowable Costs.

As prescribed in 42.709-6, use the following clause:

PENALTIES FOR UNALLOWABLE COSTS (MAY 2014)

(a) *Definition. Proposal,* as used in this clause, means either—

(1) A final indirect cost rate proposal submitted by the Contractor after the expiration of its fiscal year which—

(i) Relates to any payment made on the basis of billing rates; or

(ii) Will be used in negotiating the final contract price; or

(2) The final statement of costs incurred and estimated to be incurred under the Incentive Price Revision clause (if applicable), which is used to establish the final contract price.

(b) Contractors which include unallowable indirect costs in a proposal may be subject to penalties. The penalties are prescribed in 10 U.S.C. 2324 or 41 U.S.C. chapter 43, as applicable, which is implemented in Section 42.709 of the Federal Acquisition Regulation (FAR).

(c) The Contractor shall not include in any proposal any cost that is unallowable, as defined in Subpart 2.1 of the FAR, or an executive agency supplement to the FAR.

(d) If the Contracting Officer determines that a cost submitted by the Contractor in its proposal is expressly unallowable under a cost principle in the FAR, or an executive agency supplement to the FAR, that defines the allowability of specific selected costs, the Contractor shall be assessed a penalty equal to—

(1) The amount of the disallowed cost allocated to this contract; plus

(2) Simple interest, to be computed—

(i) On the amount the Contractor was paid (whether as a progress or billing payment) in excess of the amount to which the Contractor was entitled; and

(ii) Using the applicable rate effective for each six-month interval prescribed by the Secretary of the Treasury pursuant to Pub. L. 92-41 (85 Stat. 97).

(e) If the Contracting Officer determines that a cost submitted by the Contractor in its proposal includes a cost previously determined to be unallowable for that Contractor, then the Contractor will be assessed a penalty in an amount equal to two times the amount of the disallowed cost allocated to this contract.

(f) Determinations under paragraphs (d) and (e) of this clause are final decisions within the meaning of 41 U.S.C. chapter 71, Contract Disputes.

(g) Pursuant to the criteria in FAR 42.709-5, the Contracting Officer may waive the penalties in paragraph (d) or (e) of this clause.

(h) Payment by the Contractor of any penalty assessed under this clause does not constitute repayment to the Government of any unallowable cost which has been paid by the Government to the Contractor.

(End of clause)

[FAC 90-31, 60 FR 42648, 8/16/95, effective 10/1/95; FAC 97-22, 66 FR 2116, 1/10/2001, effective 3/12/2001; Delay of effective date, 66 FR 14259, 3/9/2001, effective 5/11/2001; FAC 2005-73, 79 FR 24192, 4/29/2014, effective 5/29/2014]

52.242-4 Certification of Final Indirect Costs.

As prescribed in 42.703-2(f), insert the following clause:

CERTIFICATION OF FINAL INDIRECT COSTS (JAN 1997)

(a) The Contractor shall—

(1) Certify any proposal to establish or modify final indirect cost rates;

(2) Use the format in paragraph (c) of this clause to certify; and

(3) Have the certificate signed by an individual of the Contractor's organization at a level no lower than a vice president or chief financial officer of the business segment of the Contractor that submits the proposal.

(b) Failure by the Contractor to submit a signed certificate, as described in this clause, may result in final indirect costs at rates unilaterally established by the Contracting Officer.

(c) The certificate of final indirect costs shall read as follows:

CERTIFICATE OF FINAL INDIRECT COSTS

This is to certify that I have reviewed this proposal to establish final indirect cost rates and to the best of my knowledge and belief:

1. All costs included in this proposal (identify proposal and date) to establish final indirect cost rates for (identify period covered by rate) are allowable in accordance with the cost principles of the Federal Acquisition Regulation (FAR) and its supplements applicable to the contracts to which the final indirect cost rates will apply; and

2. This proposal does not include any costs which are expressly unallowable under applicable cost principles of the FAR or its supplements.

Firm: ______________________

Signature: ______________________

Name of Certifying Official: ____________

Title: ______________________

Date of Execution: ______________

(End of clause)

[FAC 90-31, 60 FR 42648, 8/16/95, effective 10/1/95; FAC 90-45, Final rule, 62 FR 224, 1/2/97, effective 1/1/97]

52.242-5 Payments to Small Business Subcontractors.

As prescribed in 42.1504, insert the following clause:

PAYMENTS TO SMALL BUSINESS SUBCONTRACTORS (JAN 2017)

(a) *Definitions*. As used in this clause—

Reduced payment means a payment that is for less than the amount agreed upon in a subcontract in accordance with its terms and conditions, for supplies and services for which the Government has paid the prime contractor.

Untimely payment means a payment that is more than 90 days past due under the terms and conditions of a subcontract, for supplies and services for which the Government has paid the prime contractor.

(b) *Notice*. The Contractor shall notify the Contracting Officer, in writing, not later than 14 days after—

(1) A small business subcontractor was entitled to payment under the terms and conditions of the subcontract; and

(2) The Contractor—

(i) Made a reduced or untimely payment to the small business subcontractor; or

(ii) Failed to make a payment, which is now untimely.

(c) *Content of notice*. The Contractor shall include the reason(s) for making the reduced or untimely payment in any notice required under paragraph (b) of this clause.

(End of clause)

[Final rule, 81 FR 93481, 12/20/2016, effective 1/19/2017]

52.242-6 [Reserved]

52.242-7 [Reserved]

52.242-8 [Reserved]

52.242-9 [Reserved]

52.242-10 [Removed and Reserved]

[FAC 2005-07, 71 FR 200, 1/3/2006, effective 2/2/2006]

52.242-11 [Removed and Reserved]

[FAC 2005-07, 71 FR 200, 1/3/2006, effective 2/2/2006]

52.242-12 [Removed and Reserved]

[FAC 84-53, 54 FR 48995, 11/28/89, effective 12/28/89; FAC 90-29, 60 FR 34732, 7/3/95, effective 7/3/95; FAC 2001-14, 68 FR 28079, 5/22/2003, effective 6/23/2003; FAC 2005-07, 71 FR 200, 1/3/2006, effective 2/2/2006]

52.242-13 Bankruptcy.

As prescribed in 42.903, insert the following clause:

BANKRUPTCY (JUL 1995)

In the event the Contractor enters into proceedings relating to bankruptcy, whether voluntary or involuntary, the Contractor agrees to furnish, by certified mail or electronic commerce method authorized by the contract, written notification of the bankruptcy to the Contracting Officer responsible for administering the contract. This notification shall be furnished within five days of the initiation of the proceedings relating to bankruptcy filing. This notification shall include the date on which the bankruptcy petition was filed, the identity of the court in which the bankruptcy petition was filed, and a listing of Government contract numbers and contracting offices for all Government contracts against which final payment has not been made. This obligation remains in effect until final payment under this contract.

(End of clause)

[FAC 90-4, 56 FR 15156, 4/15/91, effective 5/15/91; FAC 90-29, 60 FR 34732, 7/3/95, effective 7/3/95]

52.242-14 Suspension of Work.

As prescribed in 42.1305(a), insert the following clause in solicitations and contracts when a fixed-price construction or architect-engineer contract is contemplated:

SUSPENSION OF WORK (APR 1984)

(a) The Contracting Officer may order the Contractor, in writing, to suspend, delay, or interrupt all or any part of the work of this contract for the period of time that the Contracting Officer determines appropriate for the convenience of the Government.

(b) If the performance of all or any part of the work is, for an unreasonable period of time, suspended, delayed, or interrupted (1) by an act of the Contracting Officer in the administration of this contract, or (2) by the Contracting Officer's failure to act within the time specified in this contract (or within a reasonable time if not specified), an adjustment shall be made for any increase in the cost of performance of this contract (excluding profit) necessarily caused by the unreasonable suspension, delay, or interruption, and the contract modified in writing accordingly. However, no adjustment shall be made under this clause for any suspension, delay, or interruption to the extent that performance would have been so suspended, delayed, or interrupted by any other cause, including the fault or negligence of the Contractor, or for which an equitable adjustment is provided for or excluded under any other term or condition of this contract.

(c) A claim under this clause shall not be allowed (1) for any costs incurred more than 20 days before the Contractor shall have notified the Contracting Officer in writing of the act or failure to act involved (but this requirement shall not apply as to a claim resulting from a suspension order), and (2) unless the claim, in an amount stated, is asserted in writing as soon as practicable after the termination of the suspension, delay, or interruption, but not later than the date of final payment under the contract.

(End of clause)

[Redesignated from 52.212-12, FAC 90-32, 60 FR 48206, 9/18/95, effective 10/1/95]

52.242-15 Stop-Work Order.

As prescribed in 42.1305(b), insert the following clause. The "90-day" period stated in the clause may be reduced to less than 90 days.

STOP-WORK ORDER (AUG 1989)

(a) The Contracting Officer may, at any time, by written order to the Contractor, require the Contractor to stop all, or any part, of the work called for by this contract for a period of 90 days after the order is delivered to the Contractor, and for any further period to which the parties may agree. The order shall be specifically identified as a stop-work order issued under this clause. Upon receipt of the order, the Contractor shall immediately comply with its terms and take all reasonable steps to minimize the incurrence of costs allocable to the work covered by the order during the period of work stoppage. Within a period of 90 days after a stop-work order is delivered to the Contractor, or within any extension of that period to which the parties shall have agreed, the Contracting Officer shall either—

(1) Cancel the stop-work order; or

(2) Terminate the work covered by the order as provided in the Default, or the Termination for Convenience of the Government, clause of this contract.

(b) If a stop-work order issued under this clause is canceled or the period of the order or any extension thereof expires, the Contractor shall resume work. The Contracting Officer shall make an equitable adjustment in the delivery schedule or contract price, or both, and the contract shall be modified, in writing, accordingly, if—

(1) The stop-work order results in an increase in the time required for, or in the Contractor's cost properly allocable to, the performance of any part of this contract; and

(2) The Contractor asserts its right to the adjustment within 30 days after the end of the period of work stoppage; *provided*, that, if the Contracting Officer decides the facts justify the action, the Contracting Officer may receive and act upon a proposal submitted at any time before final payment under this contract.

(c) If a stop-work order is not canceled and the work covered by the order is terminated for the convenience of the Government, the Contracting Officer shall allow reasonable costs resulting from the stop-work order in arriving at the termination settlement.

(d) If a stop-work order is not canceled and the work covered by the order is terminated for default, the Contracting Officer shall allow, by equitable adjustment or otherwise, reasonable costs resulting from the stop-work order.

(End of clause)

Alternate I (APR 1984). If this clause is inserted in a cost-reimbursement contract, substitute in paragraph (a)(2) the words "the Termination clause of this contract" for the words "the Default, or the Termination for Convenience of the Government clause of this contract." In paragraph (b) substitute the words "an equitable adjustment in the delivery schedule, the estimated cost, the fee, or a combination thereof, and in any other terms of the contract that may be affected" for the words "an equitable adjustment in the delivery schedule or contract price, or both."

[FAC 84-6, 50 FR 2272, 1/15/85, effective 1/15/85; FAC 84-49, 54 FR 29283, 7/11/89, effective 8/10/89; Redesignated from 52.212-13, FAC 90-32, 60 FR 48206, 9/18/95, effective 10/1/95]

52.242-16 [Removed and Reserved]

[FAC 84-49, 54 FR 29283, 7/11/89, effective 8/10/89; Redesignated from 52.212-14, FAC 90-32, 60 FR 48206, 9/18/95, effective 10/1/95; FAC 2005-17, 72 FR 27364, 5/15/2007, effective 6/14/2007]

52.242-17 Government Delay of Work.

As prescribed in 42.1305(c), insert the following clause in solicitations and contracts when a fixed-price contract is contemplated for supplies other than commercial or modified-commercial items. The clause use is optional when a fixed-price contract is contemplated for services, or for supplies that are commercial or modified-commercial items.

GOVERNMENT DELAY OF WORK (APR 1984)

(a) If the performance of all or any part of the work of this contract is delayed or interrupted (1) by an act of the Contracting Officer in the administration of this contract that is not expressly or impliedly authorized by this contract, or (2) by a failure of the Contracting Officer to act within the time specified in this contract, or within a reasonable time if not specified, an adjustment (excluding profit) shall be made for any increase in the cost of performance of this contract caused by the delay or interruption and the contract shall be modified in writing accordingly. Adjustment shall also be made in the delivery or performance dates and any other contractual term or condition affected by the delay or interruption. However, no adjustment shall be made under this clause for any delay or interruption to the extent that performance would have been delayed or interrupted by any other cause, including the fault or negligence of the Contractor, or for which an adjustment is provided or excluded under any other term or condition of this contract.

(b) A claim under this clause shall not be allowed (1) for any costs incurred more than 20 days before the Contractor shall have notified the Contracting Officer in writing of the act or failure to act involved, and (2) unless the claim, in an amount stated, is asserted in writing as soon as practicable after the termination of the delay or interruption, but not later than the day of final payment under the contract.

(End of clause)

[Redesignated from 52.212-15, FAC 90-32, 60 FR 48206, 9/18/95, effective 10/1/95; FAC 2005-17, 72 FR 27364, 5/15/2007, effective 6/14/2007]

52.243-1 Changes—Fixed-Price.

As prescribed in 43.205(a)(1), insert the following clause. The 30-day period may be varied according to agency procedures.

CHANGES—FIXED-PRICE (AUG 1987)

(a) The Contracting Officer may at any time, by written order, and without notice to the sureties, if any, make changes within the general scope of this contract in any one or more of the following:

(1) Drawings, designs, or specifications when the supplies to be furnished are to be specially manufactured for the Government in accordance with the drawings, designs, or specifications.

(2) Method of shipment or packing.

(3) Place of delivery.

(b) If any such change causes an increase or decrease in the cost of, or the time required for, performance of any part of the work under this contract, whether or not changed by the order, the Contracting Officer shall make an equitable adjustment in the contract price, the delivery schedule, or both, and shall modify the contract.

(c) The Contractor must assert its right to an adjustment under this clause within 30 days from the date of receipt of the written order. However, if the Contracting Officer decides that the facts justify it, the Contracting Officer may receive and act upon a proposal submitted before final payment of the contract.

(d) If the Contractor's proposal includes the cost of property made obsolete or excess by the change, the Contracting Officer shall have the right to prescribe the manner of the disposition of the property.

(e) Failure to agree to any adjustment shall be a dispute under the Disputes clause. However, nothing in this clause shall excuse the Contractor from proceeding with the contract as changed.

(End of clause)

Alternate I (APR 1984). If the requirement is for services, other than architect-engineer or other professional services, and no supplies are to be furnished, substitute the following paragraph (a) for paragraph (a) of the basic clause:

(a) The Contracting Officer may at any time, by written order, and without notice to the sureties, if any, make changes within the general scope of this contract in any one or more of the following:

(1) Description of services to be performed.

(2) Time of performance (i.e., hours of the day, days of the week, etc.).

(3) Place of performance of the services.

Alternate II (APR 1984). If the requirement is for services (other than architect-engineer services, transportation, or research and development) and supplies are to be furnished, substitute the following paragraph (a) for paragraph (a) of the basic clause:

(a) The Contracting Officer may at any time, by written order, and without notice to the sureties, if any, make changes within the general scope of this contract in any one or more of the following:

(1) Description of services to be performed.

(2) Time of performance (i.e., hours of the day, days of the week, etc.).

(3) Place of performance of the services.

(4) Drawings, designs, or specifications when the supplies to be furnished are to be specially manufactured for the Government in accordance with the drawings, designs, or specifications.

(5) Method of shipment or packing of supplies.

(6) Place of delivery.

Alternate III (APR 1984). If the requirement is for architect-engineer or other professional services, substitute the following paragraph (a) for paragraph (a) of the basic clause and add the following paragraph (f):

(a) The Contracting Officer may at any time, by written order, and without notice to the sureties, if any, make changes within the general scope of this contract in the services to be performed.

(f) No services for which an additional cost or fee will be charged by the Contractor shall be furnished without the prior written authorization of the Contracting Officer.

Alternate IV (APR 1984). If the requirement is for transportation services, substitute the following paragraph (a) for paragraph (a) of the basic clause:

(a) The Contracting Officer may at any time, by written order, and without notice to the sureties, if any, make changes within the general scope of this contract in any one or more of the following:

(1) Specifications.

(2) Work or services.

(3) Place of origin.

(4) Place of delivery.

(5) Tonnage to be shipped.

(6) Amount of Government-furnished property.

Alternate V (APR 1984). If the requirement is for research and development and it is desired to include the clause, substitute the following subparagraphs (a)(1) and (a)(3) and paragraph (b) for subparagraphs (a)(1) and (a)(3) and paragraph (b) of the basic clause:

(1) Drawings, designs, or specifications.

(3) Place of inspection, delivery, or acceptance.

(b) If any such change causes an increase or decrease in the cost of, or time required for, performing this contract, whether or not changed by the order, the Contracting Officer shall make an equitable adjustment in (1) the contract price, the time of performance, or both; and (2) other affected terms of the contract, and shall modify the contract accordingly.

[FAC 84-29, 52 FR 30079, 8/12/87, effective 8/24/87; FAC 84-53, 54 FR 48995, 11/28/89, effective 12/28/89; FAC 90-32, 60 FR 48206, 9/18/95, effective 10/1/95; FAC 2005-100, 83 FR 42571, 8/22/2018, effective 8/22/2018]

52.243-2 Changes—Cost-Reimbursement.

As prescribed in 43.205(b)(1), insert the following clause. The 30-day period may be varied according to agency procedures.

CHANGES—COST-REIMBURSEMENT (AUG 1987)

(a) The Contracting Officer may at any time, by written order, and without notice to the sureties, if any, make changes within the general scope of this contract in any one or more of the following:

(1) Drawings, designs, or specifications when the supplies to be furnished are to be specially manufactured for the Government in accordance with the drawings, designs, or specifications.

(2) Method of shipment or packing.

(3) Place of delivery.

(b) If any such change causes an increase or decrease in the estimated cost of, or the time required for, performance of any part of the work under this contract, whether or not changed by the order, or otherwise affects any other terms and conditions of this contract, the Contracting Officer shall make an equitable adjustment in the (1) estimated cost, delivery or completion schedule, or both; (2) amount of any fixed fee; and (3) other affected terms and shall modify the contract accordingly.

(c) The Contractor must assert its right to an adjustment under this clause within 30 days from the date of receipt of the written order. However, if the Contracting Officer decides that the facts justify it, the Contracting Officer may receive and act upon a proposal submitted before final payment of the contract.

(d) Failure to agree to any adjustment shall be a dispute under the Disputes clause. However, nothing in this clause shall excuse the Contractor from proceeding with the contract as changed.

(e) Notwithstanding the terms and conditions of paragraphs (a) and (b) above, the estimated cost of this contract and, if this contract is incrementally funded, the funds allotted for the performance of this contract, shall not be increased or considered to be increased except by specific written modification of the contract indicating the new contract estimated cost and, if this contract is incrementally funded, the new amount allotted to the contract. Until this modification is made, the Contractor shall not be obligated to continue performance or incur costs beyond the point established in the Limitation of Cost or Limitation of Funds clause of this contract.

(End of clause)

Alternate I (APR 1984). If the requirement is for services and no supplies are to be furnished, substitute the following paragraph (a) for paragraph (a) of the basic clause:

(a) The Contracting Officer may at any time, by written order, and without notice to the sureties, if any, make changes within the general scope of this contract in any one or more of the following:

(1) Description of services to be performed.

(2) Time of performance (i.e., hours of the day, days of the week, etc.).

(3) Place of performance of the services.

Alternate II (APR 1984). If the requirement is for services and supplies are to be furnished, substitute the following paragraph (a) for paragraph (a) of the basic clause:

(a) The Contracting Officer may at any time, by written order, and without notice to the sureties, if any, make changes within the general scope of this contract in any one or more of the following:

(1) Description of services to be performed.

(2) Time of performance (i.e., hours of the day, days of the week, etc.).

(3) Place of performance of the services.

(4) Drawings, designs, or specifications when the supplies to be furnished are to be specially manufactured for the Government in accordance with the drawings, designs, or specifications.

(5) Method of shipment or packing of supplies.

(6) Place of delivery.

Alternate III (APR 1984). If the requirement is for construction, substitute the following paragraph (a) for paragraph (a) of the basic clause:

(a) The Contracting Officer may at any time, by written order, and without notice to the sureties, if any, make changes within the general scope of this contract in the plans and specifications or instructions incorporated in the contract.

[Removed and reserved]

Alternate V (APR 1984). If the requirement is for research and development, and it is desired to include the clause, substitute the following subparagraphs (a)(1) and (a)(3) for subparagraphs (a)(1) and (a)(3) of the basic clause:

(1) Drawings, designs, or specifications.

(3) Place of inspection, delivery, or acceptance.

[FAC 84-29, 52 FR 30079, 8/12/87, effective 8/24/87; FAC 90-32, 60 FR 48206, 9/18/95, effective 10/1/95; FAC 2005-17, 72 FR 27364, 5/15/2007, effective 6/14/2007]

52.243-3 Changes—Time-and-Materials or Labor-Hours.

As prescribed in 43.205(c), insert the following clause:

CHANGES—TIME-AND-MATERIALS OR LABOR-HOURS (SEP 2000)

(a) The Contracting Officer may at any time, by written order, and without notice to the sureties, if any, make changes within the general scope of this contract in any one or more of the following:

(1) Description of services to be performed.

(2) Time of performance (i.e., hours of the day, days of the week, etc.).

(3) Place of performance of the services.

(4) Drawings, designs, or specifications when the supplies to be furnished are to be specially manufactured for the Government in accordance with the drawings, designs, or specifications.

(5) Method of shipment or packing of supplies.

(6) Place of delivery.

(7) Amount of Government-furnished property.

(b) If any change causes an increase or decrease in any hourly rate, the ceiling price, or the time required for performance of any part of the work under this contract, whether or not changed by the order, or otherwise affects any other terms and conditions of this contract, the Contracting Officer will make an equitable adjustment in any one or more of the following and will modify the contract accordingly:

(1) Ceiling price.

(2) Hourly rates.

(3) Delivery schedule.

(4) Other affected terms.

(c) The Contractor shall assert its right to an adjustment under this clause within 30 days from the date of receipt of the written order. However, if the Contracting Officer decides that the facts justify it, the Contracting Officer may receive and act upon a proposal submitted before final payment of the contract.

(d) Failure to agree to any adjustment will be a dispute under the Disputes clause. However, nothing in this clause excuses the

Contractor from proceeding with the contract as changed.

[FAC 97-19, 65 FR 46052, 7/26/2000, effective 9/25/2000]

52.243-4 Changes.

As prescribed in 43.205(d), insert the following clause. The 30-day period may be varied according to agency procedures.

CHANGES (JUN 2007)

(a) The Contracting Officer may, at any time, without notice to the sureties, if any, by written order designated or indicated to be a change order, make changes in the work within the general scope of the contract, including changes—

(1) In the specifications (including drawings and designs);

(2) In the method or manner of performance of the work;

(3) In the Government-furnished property or services; or

(4) Directing acceleration in the performance of the work.

(b) Any other written or oral order (which, as used in this paragraph (b), includes direction, instruction, interpretation, or determination) from the Contracting Officer that causes a change shall be treated as a change order under this clause; *provided*, that the Contractor gives the Contracting Officer written notice stating (1) the date, circumstances, and source of the order and (2) that the Contractor regards the order as a change order.

(c) Except as provided in this clause, no order, statement, or conduct of the Contracting Officer shall be treated as a change under this clause or entitle the Contractor to an equitable adjustment.

(d) If any change under this clause causes an increase or decrease in the Contractor's cost of, or the time required for, the performance of any part of the work under this contract, whether or not changed by any such order, the Contracting Officer shall make an equitable adjustment and modify the contract in writing. However, except for an adjustment based on defective specifications, no adjustment for any change under paragraph (b) of this clause shall be made for any costs incurred more than 20 days before the Contractor gives written notice as required. In the case of defective specifications for which the Government is responsible, the equitable adjustment shall include any increased cost reasonably incurred by the Contractor in attempting to comply with the defective specifications.

(e) The Contractor must assert its right to an adjustment under this clause within 30 days after (1) receipt of a written change order under paragraph (a) of this clause or (2) the furnishing of a written notice under paragraph (b) of this clause, by submitting to the Contracting Officer a written statement describing the general nature and amount of proposal, unless this period is extended by the Government. The statement of proposal for adjustment may be included in the notice under paragraph (b) above.

(f) No proposal by the Contractor for an equitable adjustment shall be allowed if asserted after final payment under this contract.

(End of clause)

[FAC 84-29, 52 FR 30079, 8/12/87, effective 8/24/87; FAC 2005-17, 72 FR 27364, 5/15/2007, effective 6/14/2007]

52.243-5 Changes and Changed Conditions.

As prescribed in 43.205(e), insert the following clause:

CHANGES AND CHANGED CONDITIONS (APR 1984)

(a) The Contracting Officer may, in writing, order changes in the drawings and specifications within the general scope of the contract.

(b) The Contractor shall promptly notify the Contracting Officer, in writing, of subsurface or latent physical conditions differing materially from those indicated in this contract or unknown unusual physical conditions at the site before proceeding with the work.

(c) If changes under paragraph (a) or conditions under paragraph (b) increase or decrease the cost of, or time required for performing the work, the Contracting Officer shall make an equitable adjustment (see paragraph (d)) upon submittal of a "proposal for adjustment" (hereafter referred to as proposal) by the Contractor before final payment under the contract.

(d) The Contracting Officer shall not make an equitable adjustment under paragraph (b) unless—

(1) The Contractor has submitted and the Contracting Officer has received the required written notice; or

(2) The Contracting Officer waives the requirement for the written notice.

(e) Failure to agree to any adjustment shall be a dispute under the Disputes clause.

(End of clause)

[FAC 90-29, 60 FR 34732, 7/3/95, effective 7/3/95]

52.243-6 Change Order Accounting.

As prescribed in 43.205(f), the contracting officer may insert a clause, substantially the same as follows:

CHANGE ORDER ACCOUNTING (APR 1984)

The Contracting Officer may require change order accounting whenever the estimated cost of a change or series of related changes exceeds $100,000. The Contractor, for each change or series of related changes, shall maintain separate accounts, by job order or other suitable accounting procedure, of all incurred segregable, direct costs (less allocable credits) of work, both changed and not changed, allocable to the change. The Contractor shall maintain such accounts until the parties agree to an equitable adjustment for the changes ordered by the Contracting Officer or the matter is conclusively disposed of in accordance with the Disputes clause.

(End of clause)

[FAC 90-4, 56 FR 15156, 4/15/91, effective 5/15/91; FAC 90-32, 60 FR 48206, 9/18/95, effective 10/1/95]

52.243-7 Notification of Changes.

As prescribed in 43.107, insert the following clause:

NOTIFICATION OF CHANGES (JAN 2017)

(a) *Definitions. Contracting Officer* as used in this clause, does not include any representative of the Contracting Officer. *Specifically Authorized Representative (SAR)* as used in this clause, means any person the Contracting Officer has so designated by written notice (a copy of which shall be provided to the Contractor) which shall refer to this subparagraph and shall be issued to the designated representative before the SAR exercises such authority.

(b) *Notice*. The primary purpose of this clause is to obtain prompt reporting of Government conduct that the Contractor considers to constitute a change to this contract. Except for changes identified as such in writing and signed by the Contracting Officer, the Contractor shall notify the Administrative Contracting Officer in writing promptly, within ____ (to be negotiated) calendar days from the date that the Contractor identifies any Government conduct (including actions, inactions, and written or oral communications) that the Contractor regards as a change to the contract terms and conditions. On the basis of the most accurate information available to the Contractor, the notice shall state—

(1) The date, nature, and circumstances of the conduct regarded as a change;

(2) The name, function, and activity of each Government individual and Contractor official or employee involved in or knowledgeable about such conduct;

(3) The identification of any documents and the substance of any oral communication involved in such conduct;

(4) In the instance of alleged acceleration of scheduled performance or delivery, the basis upon which it arose;

(5) The particular elements of contract performance for which the Contractor may seek an equitable adjustment under this clause, including—

(i) What line items have been or may be affected by the alleged change;

(ii) What labor or materials or both have been or may be added, deleted, or wasted by the alleged change;

(iii) To the extent practicable, what delay and disruption in the manner and sequence of performance and effect on continued performance have been or may be caused by the alleged change;

(iv) What adjustments to contract price, delivery schedule, and other provisions affected by the alleged change are estimated; and

(6) The Contractor's estimate of the time by which the Government must respond to the Contractor's notice to minimize cost, delay or disruption of performance.

(c) *Continued performance.* Following submission of the notice required by paragraph (b) of this clause, the Contractor shall diligently continue performance of this contract to the maximum extent possible in accordance with its terms and conditions as construed by the Contractor, unless the notice reports a direction of the Contracting Officer or a communication from a SAR of the Contracting Officer, in either of which events the Contractor shall continue performance; provided, however, that if the Contractor regards the direction or communication as a change as described in paragraph (b) of this clause, notice shall be given in the manner provided. All directions, communications, interpretations, orders and similar actions of the SAR shall be reduced to writing promptly and copies furnished to the Contractor and to the Contracting Officer. The Contracting Officer shall promptly countermand any action which exceeds the authority of the SAR.

(d) *Government response.* The Contracting Officer shall promptly, within ____ (to be negotiated) calendar days after receipt of notice, respond to the notice in writing. In responding, the Contracting Officer shall either—

(1) Confirm that the conduct of which the Contractor gave notice constitutes a change and when necessary direct the mode of further performance;

(2) Countermand any communication regarded as a change;

(3) Deny that the conduct of which the Contractor gave notice constitutes a change and when necessary direct the mode of further performance; or

(4) In the event the Contractor's notice information is inadequate to make a decision under paragraphs (d)(1), (2), or (3) of this clause, advise the Contractor what additional information is required, and establish the date by which it should be furnished and the date thereafter by which the Government will respond.

(e) *Equitable adjustments.* (1) If the Contracting Officer confirms that Government conduct effected a change as alleged by the Contractor, and the conduct causes an increase or decrease in the Contractor's cost of, or the time required for, performance of any part of the work under this contract, whether changed or not changed by such conduct, an equitable adjustment shall be made—

(i) In the contract price or delivery schedule or both; and

(ii) In such other provisions of the contract as may be affected.

(2) The contract shall be modified in writing accordingly. In the case of drawings, designs or specifications which are defective and for which the Government is responsible, the equitable adjustment shall include the cost and time extension for delay reasonably incurred by the Contractor in attempting to comply with the defective drawings, designs or specifications before the Contractor identified, or reasonably should have identified, such defect. When the cost of property made obsolete or excess as a result of a change confirmed by the Contracting Officer under this clause is included in the equitable adjustment, the Contracting Officer shall have the right to prescribe the manner of disposition of the property. The equitable adjustment shall not include increased costs or time extensions for delay resulting from the Contractor's failure to

provide notice or to continue performance as provided, respectively, in paragraphs (b) and (c) above.

NOTE: The phrases *contract price* and *cost* wherever they appear in the clause, may be appropriately modified to apply to cost-reimbursement or incentive contracts, or to combinations thereof.

(End of clause)

[FAC 84-58, 55 FR 25534, 6/21/90, effective 7/23/90; Final rule, 55 FR 38518, 9/18/90; FAC 90-32, 60 FR 48206, 9/18/95, effective 10/1/95; FAC 2005-13, 71 FR 57363, 9/28/2006, effective 9/28/2006; FAC 2005-95, 82 FR 4709, 1/13/2017, effective 1/13/2017]

52.244-1 [Reserved]

[Removed and reserved, FAC 97-5, 63 FR 34058, 6/22/98, effective 8/21/98]

52.244-2 Subcontracts.

As prescribed in 44.204(a)(1), insert the following clause:

SUBCONTRACTS (OCT 2010)

(a) *Definitions.* As used in this clause—

Approved purchasing system means a Contractor's purchasing system that has been reviewed and approved in accordance with Part 44 of the Federal Acquisition Regulation (FAR).

Consent to subcontract means the Contracting Officer's written consent for the Contractor to enter into a particular subcontract.

Subcontract means any contract, as defined in FAR Subpart 2.1, entered into by a subcontractor to furnish supplies or services for performance of the prime contract or a subcontract. It includes, but is not limited to, purchase orders, and changes and modifications to purchase orders.

(b) When this clause is included in a fixed-price type contract, consent to subcontract is required only on unpriced contract actions (including unpriced modifications or unpriced delivery orders), and only if required in accordance with paragraph (c) or (d) of this clause.

(c) If the Contractor does not have an approved purchasing system, consent to subcontract is required for any subcontract that—

(1) Is of the cost-reimbursement, time-and-materials, or labor-hour type; or

(2) Is fixed-price and exceeds—

(i) For a contract awarded by the Department of Defense, the Coast Guard, or the National Aeronautics and Space Administration, the greater of the simplified acquisition threshold or 5 percent of the total estimated cost of the contract; or

(ii) For a contract awarded by a civilian agency other than the Coast Guard and the National Aeronautics and Space Administration, either the simplified acquisition threshold or 5 percent of the total estimated cost of the contract.

(d) If the Contractor has an approved purchasing system, the Contractor nevertheless shall obtain the Contracting Officer's written consent before placing the following subcontracts:

____

____

____

(e)(1) The Contractor shall notify the Contracting Officer reasonably in advance of placing any subcontract or modification thereof for which consent is required under paragraph (b), (c), or (d) of this clause, including the following information:

(i) A description of the supplies or services to be subcontracted.

(ii) Identification of the type of subcontract to be used.

(iii) Identification of the proposed subcontractor.

(iv) The proposed subcontract price.

(v) The subcontractor's current, complete, and accurate certified cost or pricing data and Certificate of Current Cost or Pricing Data, if required by other contract provisions.

(vi) The subcontractor's Disclosure Statement or Certificate relating to Cost Accounting Standards when such data are required by other provisions of this contract.

(vii) A negotiation memorandum reflecting—

(A) The principal elements of the subcontract price negotiations;

(B) The most significant considerations controlling establishment of initial or revised prices;

(C) The reason certified cost or pricing data were or were not required;

(D) The extent, if any, to which the Contractor did not rely on the subcontractor's certified cost or pricing data in determining the price objective and in negotiating the final price;

(E) The extent to which it was recognized in the negotiation that the subcontractor's certified cost or pricing data were not accurate, complete, or current; the action taken by the Contractor and the subcontractor; and the effect of any such defective data on the total price negotiated;

(F) The reasons for any significant difference between the Contractor's price objective and the price negotiated; and

(G) A complete explanation of the incentive fee or profit plan when incentives are used. The explanation shall identify each critical performance element, management decisions used to quantify each incentive element, reasons for the incentives, and a summary of all trade-off possibilities considered.

(2) The Contractor is not required to notify the Contracting Officer in advance of entering into any subcontract for which consent is not required under paragraph (b), (c), or (d) of this clause.

(f) Unless the consent or approval specifically provides otherwise, neither consent by the Contracting Officer to any subcontract nor approval of the Contractor's purchasing system shall constitute a determination—

(1) Of the acceptability of any subcontract terms or conditions;

(2) Of the allowability of any cost under this contract; or

(3) To relieve the Contractor of any responsibility for performing this contract.

(g) No subcontract or modification thereof placed under this contract shall provide for payment on a cost-plus-a-percentage-of-cost basis, and any fee payable under cost-reimbursement type subcontracts shall not exceed the fee limitations in FAR 15.404-4(c)(4)(i).

(h) The Contractor shall give the Contracting Officer immediate written notice of any action or suit filed and prompt notice of any claim made against the Contractor by any subcontractor or vendor that, in the opinion of the Contractor, may result in litigation related in any way to this contract, with respect to which the Contractor may be entitled to reimbursement from the Government.

(i) The Government reserves the right to review the Contractor's purchasing system as set forth in FAR Subpart 44.3.

(j) Paragraphs (c) and (e) of this clause do not apply to the following subcontracts, which were evaluated during negotiations:

____

____

____

(End of clause)

Alternate I (JUN 2007). As prescribed in 44.204(a)(2), substitute the following paragraph (e)(2) for paragraph (e)(2) of the basic clause:

(e)(2) If the Contractor has an approved purchasing system and consent is not required under paragraph (c), or (d) of this clause, the Contractor nevertheless shall notify the Contracting Officer reasonably in advance of entering into any (i) cost-plus-fixed-fee subcontract, or (ii) fixed-price subcontract that exceeds either the simplified acquisition threshold or 5 percent of the total estimated cost of this contract. The notification shall include the information required by paragraphs (e)(1)(i) through (e)(1)(iv) of this clause.

[FAC 97-5, 63 FR 34058, 6/22/98, effective 8/21/98; FAC 2005-01, 70 FR 11761, 3/9/2005, effective 3/9/2005; FAC 2005-07,

71 FR 225, 1/3/2006, effective 1/3/2006; FAC 2005-17, 72 FR 27364, 5/15/2007, effective 6/14/2007; FAC 2005-45, 75 FR 53135, 8/30/2010, effective 10/1/2010]

52.244-3 [Reserved]

[Removed and reserved, FAC 97-5, 63 FR 34058, 6/22/98, effective 8/21/98]

52.244-4 Subcontractors and Outside Associates and Consultants (Architect-Engineer Services).

As prescribed in 44.204(b), insert the following clause:

SUBCONTRACTORS AND OUTSIDE ASSOCIATES AND CONSULTANTS (ARCHITECT-ENGINEER SERVICES) (AUG 1998)

Any subcontractors and outside associates or consultants required by the Contractor in connection with the services covered by the contract will be limited to individuals or firms that were specifically identified and agreed to during negotiations. The Contractor shall obtain the Contracting Officer's written consent before making any substitution for these subcontractors, associates, or consultants.

(End of clause)

[FAC 90-32, 60 FR 48206, 9/18/95, effective 10/1/95; FAC 97-5, 63 FR 34058, 6/22/98, effective 8/21/98]

52.244-5 Competition in Subcontracting.

As prescribed in 44.204(c), insert the following clause:

COMPETITION IN SUBCONTRACTING (DEC 1996)

(a) The Contractor shall select subcontractors (including suppliers) on a competitive basis to the maximum practical extent consistent with the objectives and requirements of the contract.

(b) If the Contractor is an approved mentor under the Department of Defense Pilot Mentor-Protege Program (Pub. L. 101-510, section 831 as amended), the Contractor may award subcontracts under this contract on a noncompetitive basis to its proteges.

(End of clause)

[FAC 90-29, 60 FR 34732, 7/3/95, effective 7/3/95; FAC 90-37, 61 FR 2626, 1/26/96, effective 1/26/96; FAC 90-43, Interim rule, 61 FR 67408, 12/20/96, effective 2/18/97; FAC 97-5, 63 FR 34058, 6/22/98, effective 8/21/98]

52.244-6 Subcontracts for Commercial Items.

As prescribed in 44.403, insert the following clause:

SUBCONTRACTS FOR COMMERCIAL ITEMS (AUG 2019)

(a) *Definitions.* As used in this clause—

Commercial item and *commercially available off-the-shelf item* have the meanings contained in Federal Acquisition Regulation 2.101, Definitions.

Subcontract includes a transfer of commercial items between divisions, subsidiaries, or affiliates of the Contractor or subcontractor at any tier.

(b) To the maximum extent practicable, the Contractor shall incorporate, and require its subcontractors at all tiers to incorporate, commercial items or nondevelopmental items as components of items to be supplied under this contract.

(c) (1) The Contractor shall insert the following clauses in subcontracts for commercial items:

(i) 52.203-13, Contractor Code of Business Ethics and Conduct (Oct 2015) (41 U.S.C. 3509), if the subcontract exceeds $5.5 million and has a performance period of more than 120 days. In altering this clause to identify the appropriate parties, all disclosures of violation of the civil False Claims Act or of Federal criminal law shall be directed to the agency Office of the Inspector General, with a copy to the Contracting Officer.

(ii) 52.203-15, Whistleblower Protections Under the American Recovery and Reinvestment Act of 2009 (JUN 2010) (Section 1553 of Pub. L. 111-5), if the subcontract is funded under the Recovery Act.

(iii) 52.203-19, Prohibition on Requiring Certain Internal Confidentiality Agreements or Statements (JAN 2017).

(iv) 52.204-21, Basic Safeguarding of Covered Contractor Information Systems (JUN 2016), other than subcontracts for commercially available off-the-shelf items, if flow down is required in accordance with paragraph (c) of FAR clause 52.204-21.

(v) 52.204-23, Prohibition on Contracting for Hardware, Software, and Services Developed or Provided by Kaspersky Lab and Other Covered Entities (JUL 2018) (Section 1634 of Pub. L. 115-91).

(vi) 52.204-25, Prohibition on Contracting for Certain Telecommunications and Video Surveillance Services or Equipment. (AUG 2019) (Section 889(a)(1)(A) of Pub. L. 115-232).

(vii) 52.219-8, Utilization of Small Business Concerns (OCT 2018) (15 U.S.C. 637(d)(2) and (3)), if the subcontract offers further subcontracting opportunities. If the subcontract (except subcontracts to small business concerns) exceeds $700,000 ($1.5 million for construction of any public facility), the subcontractor must include 52.219-8 in lower tier subcontracts that offer subcontracting opportunities.

(viii) 52.222-21, Prohibition of Segregated Facilities (APR 2015).

(ix) 52.222-26, Equal Opportunity (SEP 2016) (E.O. 11246).

(x) 52.222-35, Equal Opportunity for Veterans (OCT 2015) (38 U.S.C. 4212(a));

(xi) 52.222-36, Equal Opportunity for Workers with Disabilities (JUL 2014) (29 U.S.C. 793).

(xii) 52.222-37, Employment Reports on Veterans (FEB 2016) (38 U.S.C. 4212).

(xiii) 52.222-40, Notification of Employee Rights Under the National Labor Relations Act (DEC 2010) (E.O. 13496), if flow down is required in accordance with paragraph (f) of FAR clause 52.222-40.

(xiv)(A) 52.222-50, Combating Trafficking in Persons (JAN 2019) (22 U.S.C. chapter 78 and E.O. 13627).

(B) Alternate I (MAR 2015) of 52.222-50 (22 U.S.C. chapter 78 and E.O. 13627).

(xv) 52.222–55, Minimum Wages under Executive Order 13658 (DEC 2015), if flowdown is required in accordance with paragraph (k) of FAR clause 52.222-55.

(xvi) 52.222-62, Paid Sick Leave Under Executive Order 13706 (JAN 2017) (E.O. 13706), if flow down is required in accordance with paragraph (m) of FAR clause 52.222-62.

(xvii)(A) 52.224-3, Privacy Training (JAN 2017) (5 U.S.C. 552a) if flow down is required in accordance with 52.224-3(f).

(B) Alternate I (JAN 2017) of 52.224-3, if flow down is required in accordance with 52.224-3(f) and the agency specifies that only its agency-provided training is acceptable).

(xviii) 52.225-26, Contractors Performing Private Security Functions Outside the United States (OCT 2016) (Section 862, as amended, of the National Defense Authorization Act for Fiscal Year 2008; 10 U.S.C. 2302 Note).

(xvix) 52.232-40, Providing Accelerated Payments to Small Business Subcontractors (DEC 2013), if flow down is required in accordance with paragraph (c) of FAR clause 52.232-40.

(xx) 52.247-64, Preference for Privately Owned U.S.-Flag Commercial Vessels (FEB 2006) (46 U.S.C. App. 1241 and 10 U.S.C. 2631), if flow down is required in accordance with paragraph (d) of FAR clause 52.247-64.

(2) While not required, the Contractor may flow down to subcontracts for commercial items a minimal number of additional clauses necessary to satisfy its contractual obligations.

(d) The Contractor shall include the terms of this clause, including this paragraph (d), in subcontracts awarded under this contract.

(End of clause)

[FAC 90-32, 60 FR 48206, 9/18/95, effective 10/1/95; FAC 97-4, 63 FR 9048, 2/23/98, effective 4/24/98; FAC 97-9, 63 FR 58587, 10/30/98, effective 10/30/98; FAC 97-22, 66 FR 2117, 1/10/2001, effective 3/12/2001; Delay of effective date, 66 FR 14259, 3/9/2001, effective 5/11/2001; FAC 2001-01, 66 FR 53478, 10/22/2001, effective

12/21/2001; Corrected 67 FR 3441, 1/24/2002; FAC 2001-07, 67 FR 21538, 4/30/2002, effective 5/15/2002; FAC 2001-13, 68 FR 13202, 3/18/2003, effective 4/17/2003; FAC 2001-14, 68 FR 28098, 5/22/2003, effective 5/22/2003; FAC 2001-23, 69 FR 25273, 5/5/2004, effective 5/5/2004; FAC 2001-24, 69 FR 34228, 6/18/2004, effective 7/19/2004; FAC 2001-26, 69 FR 76351, 12/20/2004, effective 12/20/2004; FAC 2005-02, 70 FR 14950, 3/23/2005, effective 3/23/2005; FAC 2005-04, 70 FR 33655, 6/8/2005, effective 6/8/2005; FAC 2005-07, 71 FR 200, 1/3/2006, effective 2/2/2006; FAC 2005-13, 71 FR 57363, 9/28/2006, effective 9/28/2006; FAC 2005-16, 72 FR 13586, 3/22/2007, effective 3/22/2007; FAC 2005-23, 72 FR 73218, 12/26/2007, effective 12/26/2007; FAC 2005-28, 73 FR 67064, 11/12/2008, effective 12/12/2008; FAC 2005-30, 74 FR 2741, 1/15/2009, effective 2/17/2009; FAC 2005-32, 74 FR 14633, 3/31/2009, effective 3/31/2009; FAC 2005-36, 74 FR 40468, 8/11/2009, effective 8/11/2009; FAC 2005-37, 74 FR 52860, 10/14/2009, effective 10/14/2009; FAC 2005-38, 74 FR 65599, 12/10/2009, effective 12/10/2009; FAC 2005-40, 75 FR 14059, 3/23/2010, effective 4/22/2010; FAC 2005-42, 75 FR 34258, 34277, 6/16/2010, effective 6/16/2010; FAC 2005-45, 75 FR 53129, 8/30/2010, effective 10/1/2010; FAC 2005-46, 75 FR 60249, 9/29/2010, effective 9/29/2010; FAC 2005-47, 75 FR 77723, 77737, 12/13/2010, effective 12/13/2010; FAC 2005-50, 76 FR 14562, 3/16/2011, effective 4/15/2011; FAC 2005-53, 76 FR 39233, 7/5/2011, effective 8/4/2011; FAC 2005-54, 76 FR 68015, 68026, 11/2/2011, effective 11/2/2011; FAC 2005-67, 78 FR 37670, 78 FR 37676, 6/21/2013, effective 7/22/2013; FAC 2005-71, 78 FR 70477, 11/26/2013, effective 12/26/2013; FAC 2005-73, 79 FR 24192, 4/29/2014, effective 5/29/2014; FAC 2005-76, 79 FR 4575, 7/25/2014, effective 7/25/2014; FAC 2005-77, 79 FR 61746, 10/14/2014, effective 10/14/2014; FAC 2005-80, 80 FR 4967, 1/29/2015, effective 3/2/2015; Correction, 80 FR 6908, 2/9/2015, effective 3/2/2015; FAC 2005-81, 80 FR 19504, 4/10/2015, effective 4/10/2015; FAC 2005-82, 80 FR 26423, 5/7/2015, effective 5/7/2015; FAC 2005-83, 80 FR 38293, 7/2/2015, effective 10/1/2015; FAC 2005-85, 80 FR 75907, 80 FR 75915, 12/4/2015, effective 12/4/2015; FAC 2005-85, 80 FR 75908, 12/4/2015, effective 2/26/2016; FAC 2005-88, 81 FR 30439, 5/16/2016, effective 6/15/2016; FAC 2005-89, 81 FR 45833, 7/14/2016, effective 11/1/2016; FAC 2005-90, 81 FR 58562, 8/25/2016, effective 10/25/2016; FAC 2005-91, 81 FR 67731, 9/30/2016, effective 9/30/2016; FAC 2005-91, 81 FR 67732, 9/30/2016, effective 9/30/2016; FAC 2005-91, 81 FR 67776, 9/30/2016, effective 10/31/2016; FAC 2005-93, 81 FR 91636, 12/16/2016, effective 12/16/2016; FAC 2005-93, 81 FR 91627, 12/16/2016, effective 1/1/2017; FAC 2005-94, 81 FR 93476, 12/20/2016, effective 1/19/2017; FAC 2005-95, 82 FR 4717, 1/13/2017, effective 1/19/2017; FAC 2005-96, 82 FR 51773, 11/8/2017, effective 11/6/2017; FAC 2005-99, 83 FR 28141, 6/15/2018, effective 7/16/2018; FAC 2005-100, 83 FR 42569, 8/22/2018, effective 8/22/2018; FAC 2005-100, 83 FR 42570, 8/22/2018, effective 8/22/2018; FAC 2005-100, 83 FR 42571, 8/22/2018, effective 8/22/2018; FAC 2005-101, 83 FR 48691, 9/26/2018, effective 10/26/2018; FAC 2019-01, 83 FR 65466, 12/20/2018, effective 1/22/2019; FAC 2019-05, 84 FR 40216, 8/13/2019, effective 8/13/2019; FAC 2019-06, 84 FR 47861, 9/10/2019, effective 9/10/2019]

52.245-1 Government Property.

As prescribed in 45.107(a), insert the following clause:

GOVERNMENT PROPERTY (JAN 2017)

(a) *Definitions*. As used in this clause—

Cannibalize means to remove parts from Government property for use or for installation on other Government property.

Contractor-acquired property means property acquired, fabricated, or otherwise provided by the Contractor for performing a contract, and to which the Government has title.

Contractor inventory means—

(1) Any property acquired by and in the possession of a Contractor or subcontractor

under a contract for which title is vested in the Government and which exceeds the amounts needed to complete full performance under the entire contract;

(2) Any property that the Government is obligated or has the option to take over under any type of contract, e.g., as a result either of any changes in the specifications or plans thereunder or of the termination of the contract (or subcontract thereunder), before completion of the work, for the convenience or at the option of the Government; and

(3) Government-furnished property that exceeds the amounts needed to complete full performance under the entire contract.

Contractor's managerial personnel means the Contractor's directors, officers, managers, superintendents, or equivalent representatives who have supervision or direction of—

(1) All or substantially all of the Contractor's business;

(2) All or substantially all of the Contractor's operation at any one plant or separate location; or

(3) A separate and complete major industrial operation.

Demilitarization means rendering a product unusable for, and not restorable to, the purpose for which it was designed or is customarily used.

Discrepancies incident to shipment means any differences (e.g., count or condition) between the items documented to have been shipped and items actually received.

Equipment means a tangible item that is functionally complete for its intended purpose, durable, nonexpendable, and needed for the performance of a contract. Equipment is not intended for sale, and does not ordinarily lose its identity or become a component part of another article when put into use. Equipment does not include material, real property, special test equipment or special tooling.

Government-furnished property means property in the possession of, or directly acquired by, the Government and subsequently furnished to the Contractor for performance of a contract. Government-furnished property includes, but is not limited to, spares and property furnished for repair, maintenance, overhaul, or modification. Government-furnished property also includes contractor-acquired property if the contractor-acquired property is a deliverable under a cost contract when accepted by the Government for continued use under the contract.

Government property means all property owned or leased by the Government. Government property includes both Government-furnished and Contractor-acquired property. Government property includes material, equipment, special tooling, special test equipment, and real property. Government property does not include intellectual property and software.

Loss of Government property means unintended, unforeseen or accidental loss, damage or destruction to Government property that reduces the Government's expected economic benefits of the property. Loss of Government property does not include purposeful destructive testing, obsolescence, normal wear and tear or manufacturing defects. Loss of Government property includes, but is not limited to—

(1) Items that cannot be found after a reasonable search;

(2) Theft;

(3) Damage resulting in unexpected harm to property requiring repair to restore the item to usable condition; or

(4) Destruction resulting from incidents that render the item useless for its intended purpose or beyond economical repair.

Material means property that may be consumed or expended during the performance of a contract, component parts of a higher assembly, or items that lose their individual identity through incorporation into an end item. Material does not include equipment, special tooling, special test equipment or real property.

Nonseverable means property that cannot be removed after construction or installation without substantial loss of value or damage to the installed property or to the premises where installed.

Precious metals means silver, gold, platinum, palladium, iridium, osmium, rhodium, and ruthenium.

Production scrap means unusable material resulting from production, engineering, operations and maintenance, repair, and research and development contract activities. Production scrap may have value when remelted or reprocessed, *e.g.,* textile and metal clippings, borings, and faulty castings and forgings.

Property means all tangible property, both real and personal.

Property Administrator means an authorized representative of the Contracting Officer appointed in accordance with agency procedures, responsible for administering the contract requirements and obligations relating to Government property in the possession of a Contractor.

Property records means the records created and maintained by the contractor in support of its stewardship responsibilities for the management of Government property.

Provide means to furnish, as in Government-furnished property, or to acquire, as in contractor-acquired property.

Real property. See Federal Management Regulation 102-71.20 (41 CFR 102-71.20).

Sensitive property means property potentially dangerous to the public safety or security if stolen, lost, or misplaced, or that shall be subject to exceptional physical security, protection, control, and accountability. Examples include weapons, ammunition, explosives, controlled substances, radioactive materials, hazardous materials or wastes, or precious metals.

Unit acquisition cost means—

(1) For Government-furnished property, the dollar value assigned by the Government and identified in the contract; and

(2) For contractor-acquired property, the cost derived from the Contractor's records that reflect consistently applied generally accepted accounting principles.

(b) *Property management.* (1) The Contractor shall have a system of internal controls to manage (control, use, preserve, protect, repair, and maintain) Government property in its possession. The system shall be adequate to satisfy the requirements of this clause. In doing so, the Contractor shall initiate and maintain the processes, systems, procedures, records, and methodologies necessary for effective and efficient control of Government property. The Contractor shall disclose any significant changes to its property management system to the Property Administrator prior to implementation of the changes. The Contractor may employ customary commercial practices, voluntary consensus standards, or industry-leading practices and standards that provide effective and efficient Government property management that are necessary and appropriate for the performance of this contract (except where inconsistent with law or regulation).

(2) The Contractor's responsibility extends from the initial acquisition and receipt of property, through stewardship, custody, and use until formally relieved of responsibility by authorized means, including delivery, consumption, expending, sale (as surplus property), or other disposition, or via a completed investigation, evaluation, and final determination for lost property. This requirement applies to all Government property under the Contractor's accountability, stewardship, possession or control, including its vendors or subcontractors (see paragraph (f)(1)(v) of this clause).

(3) The Contractor shall include the requirements of this clause in all subcontracts under which Government property is acquired or furnished for subcontract performance.

(4) The Contractor shall establish and maintain procedures necessary to assess its property management system effectiveness and shall perform periodic internal reviews, surveillances, self assessments, or audits. Significant findings or results of such reviews and audits pertaining to Government property shall be made available to the Property Administrator.

(c) *Use of Government property.* (1) The Contractor shall use Government property, either furnished or acquired under this contract, only for performing this contract, unless otherwise provided for in this contract or approved by the Contracting Officer.

(2) Modifications or alterations of Government property are prohibited, unless they are—

(i) Reasonable and necessary due to the scope of work under this contract or its terms and conditions;

(ii) Required for normal maintenance; or

(iii) Otherwise authorized by the Contracting Officer.

(3) The Contractor shall not cannibalize Government property unless otherwise provided for in this contract or approved by the Contracting Officer.

(d) *Government-furnished property.* (1) The Government shall deliver to the Contractor the Government-furnished property described in this contract. The Government shall furnish related data and information needed for the intended use of the property. The warranties of suitability of use and timely delivery of Government-furnished property do not apply to property acquired or fabricated by the Contractor as contractor-acquired property and subsequently transferred to another contract with this Contractor.

(2) The delivery and/or performance dates specified in this contract are based upon the expectation that the Government-furnished property will be suitable for contract performance and will be delivered to the Contractor by the dates stated in the contract.

(i) If the property is not delivered to the Contractor by the dates stated in the contract, the Contracting Officer shall, upon the Contractor's timely written request, consider an equitable adjustment to the contract.

(ii) In the event property is received by the Contractor, or for Government-furnished property after receipt and installation, in a condition not suitable for its intended use, the Contracting Officer shall, upon the Contractor's timely written request, advise the Contractor on a course of action to remedy the problem. Such action may include repairing, replacing, modifying, returning, or otherwise disposing of the property at the Government's expense. Upon completion of the required action(s), the Contracting Officer shall consider an equitable adjustment to the contract (see also paragraph (f)(1)(ii)(A) of this clause).

(iii) The Government may, at its option, furnish property in an "as-is" condition. The Contractor will be given the opportunity to inspect such property prior to the property being provided. In such cases, the Government makes no warranty with respect to the serviceability and/or suitability of the property for contract performance. Any repairs, replacement, and/or refurbishment shall be at the Contractor's expense.

(3)(i) The Contracting Officer may by written notice, at any time—

(A) Increase or decrease the amount of Government-furnished property under this contract;

(B) Substitute other Government-furnished property for the property previously furnished, to be furnished, or to be acquired by the Contractor for the Government under this contract; or

(C) Withdraw authority to use property.

(ii) Upon completion of any action(s) under paragraph (d)(3)(i) of this clause, and the Contractor's timely written request, the Contracting Officer shall consider an equitable adjustment to the contract.

(e) *Title to Government property.* (1) All Government-furnished property and all property acquired by the Contractor, title to which vests in the Government under this paragraph (collectively referred to as "Government property"), is subject to the provisions of this clause. The Government shall retain title to all Government-furnished property. Title to Government property shall not be affected by its incorporation into or attachment to any property not owned by the Government, nor shall Government property become a fixture or lose its identity as personal property by being attached to any real property.

(2) Title vests in the Government for all property acquired or fabricated by the Con-

tractor in accordance with the financing provisions or other specific requirements for passage of title in the contract. Under fixed price type contracts, in the absence of financing provisions or other specific requirements for passage of title in the contract, the Contractor retains title to all property acquired by the Contractor for use on the contract, except for property identified as a deliverable end item. If a deliverable item is to be retained by the Contractor for use after inspection and acceptance by the Government, it shall be made accountable to the contract through a contract modification listing the item as Government-furnished property.

(3) *Title under Cost-Reimbursement or Time-and-Material Contracts or Cost-Reimbursable line items under Fixed-Price contracts.* (i) Title to all property purchased by the Contractor for which the Contractor is entitled to be reimbursed as a direct item of cost under this contract shall pass to and vest in the Government upon the vendor's delivery of such property.

(ii) Title to all other property, the cost of which is reimbursable to the Contractor, shall pass to and vest in the Government upon—

(A) Issuance of the property for use in contract performance;

(B) Commencement of processing of the property for use in contract performance; or

(C) Reimbursement of the cost of the property by the Government, whichever occurs first.

(f) *Contractor plans and systems.* (1) Contractors shall establish and implement property management plans, systems, and procedures at the contract, program, site or entity level to enable the following outcomes:

(i) *Acquisition of Property.* The Contractor shall document that all property was acquired consistent with its engineering, production planning, and property control operations.

(ii) *Receipt of Government Property.* The Contractor shall receive Government property and document the receipt, record the information necessary to meet the record requirements of paragraph (f)(1)(iii)(A)(1) through (5) of this clause, identify as Government owned in a manner appropriate to the type of property (e.g., stamp, tag, mark, or other identification), and manage any discrepancies incident to shipment.

(A) *Government-furnished property.* The Contractor shall furnish a written statement to the Property Administrator containing all relevant facts, such as cause or condition and a recommended course(s) of action, if overages, shortages, or damages and/or other discrepancies are discovered upon receipt of Government-furnished property.

(B) *Contractor-acquired property.* The Contractor shall take all actions necessary to adjust for overages, shortages, damage and/or other discrepancies discovered upon receipt, in shipment of Contractor-acquired property from a vendor or supplier, so as to ensure the proper allocability and allowability of associated costs.

(iii) *Records of Government property.* The Contractor shall create and maintain records of all Government property accountable to the contract, including Government-furnished and Contractor-acquired property.

(A) Property records shall enable a complete, current, auditable record of all transactions and shall, unless otherwise approved by the Property Administrator, contain the following:

(1) The name, part number and description, National Stock Number (if needed for additional item identification tracking and/or disposition), and other data elements as necessary and required in accordance with the terms and conditions of the contract.

(2) Quantity received (or fabricated), issued, and balance-on-hand.

(3) Unit acquisition cost.

(4) Unique-item identifier or equivalent (if available and necessary for individual item tracking).

(5) Unit of measure.

(6) Accountable contract number or equivalent code designation.

(7) Location.

(8) Disposition.

(9) Posting reference and date of transaction.

(10) Date placed in service (if required in accordance with the terms and conditions of the contract).

(B) *Use of a Receipt and Issue System for Government Material.* When approved by the Property Administrator, the Contractor may maintain, in lieu of formal property records, a file of appropriately cross-referenced documents evidencing receipt, issue, and use of material that is issued for immediate consumption.

(iv) *Physical inventory.* The Contractor shall periodically perform, record, and disclose physical inventory results. A final physical inventory shall be performed upon contract completion or termination. The Property Administrator may waive this final inventory requirement, depending on the circumstances (e.g., overall reliability of the Contractor's system or the property is to be transferred to a follow-on contract).

(v) *Subcontractor control.*

(A) The Contractor shall award subcontracts that clearly identify items to be provided and the extent of any restrictions or limitations on their use. The Contractor shall ensure appropriate flow down of contract terms and conditions (*e.g.,* extent of liability for loss of Government property.

(B) The Contractor shall assure its subcontracts are properly administered and reviews are periodically performed to determine the adequacy of the subcontractor's property management system.

(vi) *Reports.* The Contractor shall have a process to create and provide reports of discrepancies, loss of Government property, physical inventory results, audits and self-assessments, corrective actions, and other property-related reports as directed by the Contracting Officer.

(vii) *Relief of stewardship responsibility and liability.* The Contractor shall have a process to enable the prompt recognition, investigation, disclosure and reporting of loss of Government property, including losses that occur at subcontractor or alternate site locations.

(A) This process shall include the corrective actions necessary to prevent recurrence.

(B) Unless otherwise directed by the Property Administrator, the Contractor shall investigate and report to the Government all incidents of property loss as soon as the facts become known. Such reports shall, at a minimum, contain the following information:

(1) Date of incident (if known).

(2) The data elements required under paragraph (f) (1) (iii) (A) of this clause.

(3) Quantity.

(4) Accountable contract number.

(5) A statement indicating current or future need.

(6) Unit acquisition cost, or if applicable, estimated sales proceeds, estimated repair or replacement costs.

(7) All known interests in commingled material of which includes Government material.

(8) Cause and corrective action taken or to be taken to prevent recurrence.

(9) A statement that the Government will receive compensation covering the loss of Government property, in the event the Contractor was or will be reimbursed or compensated.

(10) Copies of all supporting documentation.

(11) Last known location.

(12) A statement that the property did or did not contain sensitive, export controlled, hazardous, or toxic material, and that the appropriate agencies and authorities were notified.

(C) Unless the contract provides otherwise, the Contractor shall be relieved of stewardship responsibility and liability for property when—

(*1*) Such property is consumed or expended, reasonably and properly, or otherwise accounted for, in the performance of the contract, including reasonable inventory adjustments of material as determined by the Property Administrator;

(*2*) Property Administrator grants relief of responsibility and liability for loss of Government property;

(*3*) Property is delivered or shipped from the Contractor's plant, under Government instructions, except when shipment is to a subcontractor or other location of the Contractor; or

(*4*) Property is disposed of in accordance with paragraphs (j) and (k) of this clause.

(viii) *Utilizing Government property.* (A) The Contractor shall utilize, consume, move, and store Government Property only as authorized under this contract. The Contractor shall promptly disclose and report Government property in its possession that is excess to contract performance.

(B) Unless otherwise authorized in this contract or by the Property Administrator the Contractor shall not commingle Government material with material not owned by the Government.

(ix) *Maintenance.* The Contractor shall properly maintain Government property. The Contractor's maintenance program shall enable the identification, disclosure, and performance of normal and routine preventative maintenance and repair. The Contractor shall disclose and report to the Property Administrator the need for replacement and/or capital rehabilitation.

(x) *Property closeout.* The Contractor shall promptly perform and report to the Property Administrator contract property closeout, to include reporting, investigating and securing closure of all loss of Government property cases; physically inventorying all property upon termination or completion of this contract; and disposing of items at the time they are determined to be excess to contractual needs.

(2) The Contractor shall establish and maintain Government accounting source data, as may be required by this contract, particularly in the areas of recognition of acquisitions, loss of Government property, and disposition of material and equipment.

(g) *Systems analysis.* (1) The Government shall have access to the Contractor's premises and all Government property, at reasonable times, for the purposes of reviewing, inspecting and evaluating the Contractor's property management plan(s), systems, procedures, records, and supporting documentation that pertains to Government property. This access includes all site locations and, with the Contractor's consent, all subcontractor premises.

(2) Records of Government property shall be readily available to authorized Government personnel and shall be appropriately safeguarded.

(3) Should it be determined by the Government that the Contractor's (or subcontractor's) property management practices are inadequate or not acceptable for the effective management and control of Government property under this contract, or present an undue risk to the Government, the Contractor shall prepare a corrective action plan when requested by the Property Administrator and take all necessary corrective actions as specified by the schedule within the corrective action plan.

(h) *Contractor Liability for Government Property.*

(1) Unless otherwise provided for in the contract, the Contractor shall not be liable for loss of Government property furnished or acquired under this contract, except when any one of the following applies—

(i) The risk is covered by insurance or the Contractor is otherwise reimbursed (to the extent of such insurance or reimbursement). The allowability of insurance costs shall be determined in accordance with 31.205-19.

(ii) Loss of Government property that is the result of willful misconduct or lack of good faith on the part of the Contractor's managerial personnel.

(iii) The Contracting Officer has, in writing, revoked the Government's assumption of risk for loss of Government property due to a determination under paragraph (g) of this clause that the Contractor's property management practices are inadequate, and/or present an undue risk to the Government, and the Contractor failed to take timely corrective action. If the Contractor can establish by clear and convincing evidence that the loss of Government property occurred while the Contractor had adequate property management practices or the loss did not result from the Contractor's failure to maintain adequate property management practices, the Contractor shall not be held liable.

(2) The Contractor shall take all reasonable actions necessary to protect the property from further loss. The Contractor shall separate the damaged and undamaged property, place all the affected property in the best possible order, and take such other action as the Property Administrator directs.

(3) The Contractor shall do nothing to prejudice the Government's rights to recover against third parties for any loss of Government property.

(4) The Contractor shall reimburse the Government for loss of Government property, to the extent that the Contractor is financially liable for such loss, as directed by the Contracting Officer.

(5) Upon the request of the Contracting Officer, the Contractor shall, at the Government's expense, furnish to the Government all reasonable assistance and cooperation, including the prosecution of suit and the execution of instruments of assignment in favor of the Government in obtaining recovery.

(i) *Equitable adjustment.* Equitable adjustments under this clause shall be made in accordance with the procedures of the Changes clause. However, the Government shall not be liable for breach of contract for the following:

(1) Any delay in delivery of Government-furnished property.

(2) Delivery of Government-furnished property in a condition not suitable for its intended use.

(3) An increase, decrease, or substitution of Government-furnished property.

(4) Failure to repair or replace Government property for which the Government is responsible.

(j) *Contractor inventory disposal.* Except as otherwise provided for in this contract, the Contractor shall not dispose of Contractor inventory until authorized to do so by the Plant Clearance Office or authorizing official.

(1) *Predisposal requirements.* (i) If the Contractor determines that the property has the potential to fulfill requirements under other contracts, the Contractor, in consultation with the Property Administrator, shall request that the Contracting Officer transfer the property to the contract in question, or provide authorization for use, as appropriate. In lieu of transferring the property, the Contracting Officer may authorize the Contractor to credit the costs of Contractor-acquired property (material only) to the losing contract, and debit the gaining contract with the corresponding cost, when such material is needed for use on another contract. Property no longer needed shall be considered contractor inventory.

(ii) For any remaining Contractor-acquired property, the Contractor may purchase the property at the unit acquisition cost if desired or make reasonable efforts to return unused property to the appropriate supplier at fair market value (less, if applicable, a reasonable restocking fee that is consistent with the supplier's customary practices.)

(2) *Inventory disposal schedules.* (i) Absent separate contract terms and conditions for property disposition, and provided the property was not reutilized, transferred, or otherwise disposed of, the Contractor, as directed by the Plant Clearance Officer or authorizing official, shall use Standard Form 1428, Inventory Disposal Schedule or electronic equivalent, to identify and report—

(A) Government-furnished property that is no longer required for performance of this contract;

(B) Contractor-acquired property, to which the Government has obtained title under paragraph (e) of this clause, which is no longer required for performance of that contract; and

(C) Termination inventory.

(ii) The Contractor may annotate inventory disposal schedules to identify property the Contractor wishes to purchase from the Government, in the event that the property is offered for sale.

(iii) Separate inventory disposal schedules are required for aircraft in any condition, flight safety critical aircraft parts, and other items as directed by the Plant Clearance Officer.

(iv) The Contractor shall provide the information required by FAR 52.245-1(f)(1)(iii) along with the following:

(A) Any additional information that may facilitate understanding of the property's intended use.

(B) For work-in-progress, the estimated percentage of completion.

(C) For precious metals in raw or bulk form, the type of metal and estimated weight.

(D) For hazardous material or property contaminated with hazardous material, the type of hazardous material.

(E) For metals in mill product form, the form, shape, treatment, hardness, temper, specification (commercial or Government) and dimensions (thickness, width and length).

(v) Property with the same description, condition code, and reporting location may be grouped in a single line item.

(vi) Scrap should be reported by *lot* along with metal content, estimated weight and estimated value.

(3) *Submission requirements.* (i) The Contractor shall submit inventory disposal schedules to the Plant Clearance Officer no later than—

(A) 30 days following the Contractor's determination that a property item is no longer required for performance of this contract;

(B) 60 days, or such longer period as may be approved by the Plant Clearance Officer, following completion of contract deliveries or performance; or

(C) 120 days, or such longer period as may be approved by the Termination Contracting Officer, following contract termination in whole or in part.

(ii) Unless the Plant Clearance Officer determines otherwise, the Contractor need not identify or report production scrap on inventory disposal schedules, and may process and dispose of production scrap in accordance with its own internal scrap procedures. The processing and disposal of other types of Government-owned scrap will be conducted in accordance with the terms and conditions of the contract or Plant Clearance Officer direction, as appropriate.

(4) *Corrections.* The Plant Clearance Officer may—

(i) Reject a schedule for cause (*e.g.*, contains errors, determined to be inaccurate); and

(ii) Require the Contractor to correct an inventory disposal schedule.

(5) *Postsubmission adjustments.* The Contractor shall notify the Plant Clearance Officer at least 10 working days in advance of its intent to remove an item from an approved inventory disposal schedule. Upon approval of the Plant Clearance Officer, or upon expiration of the notice period, the Contractor may make the necessary adjustments to the inventory schedule.

(6) *Storage.* (i) The Contractor shall store the property identified on an inventory disposal schedule pending receipt of disposal instructions. The Government's failure to furnish disposal instructions within 120 days following acceptance of an inventory disposal schedule may entitle the Contractor to an equitable adjustment for costs incurred to store such property on or after the 21stday.

(ii) The Contractor shall obtain the Plant Clearance Officer's approval to remove property from the premises where the property is currently located prior to receipt of final disposition instructions. If approval is granted, any costs incurred by the Contractor to transport or store the property shall not increase the price or fee of any Government contract. The storage area shall be appropriate for assuring the property's physical safety and suitability for use. Approval does not relieve the Contractor of any liability for such property under this contract.

(7) *Disposition instructions.*

(i) The Contractor shall prepare for shipment, deliver f.o.b. origin, or dispose of Contractor inventory as directed by the Plant Clearance Officer. Unless otherwise directed by the Contracting Officer or by the Plant Clearance Officer, the Contractor shall remove and destroy any markings identifying the property as U.S. Government-owned property prior to its disposal.

(ii) The Contracting Officer may require the Contractor to demilitarize the property prior to shipment or disposal. In such cases, the Contractor may be entitled to an equitable adjustment under paragraph (i) of this clause.

(8) *Disposal proceeds.* As directed by the Contracting Officer, the Contractor shall credit the net proceeds from the disposal of Contractor inventory to the contract, or to the Treasury of the United States as miscellaneous receipts.

(9) *Subcontractor inventory disposal schedules.* The Contractor shall require its Subcontractors to submit inventory disposal schedules to the Contractor in accordance with the requirements of paragraph (j)(3) of this clause.

(k) *Abandonment of Government property.* (1) The Government shall not abandon sensitive property or termination inventory without the Contractor's written consent.

(2) The Government, upon notice to the Contractor, may abandon any nonsensitive property in place, at which time all obligations of the Government regarding such property shall cease.

(3) Absent contract terms and conditions to the contrary, the Government may abandon parts removed and replaced from property as a result of normal maintenance actions, or removed from property as a result of the repair, maintenance, overhaul, or modification process.

(4) The Government has no obligation to restore or rehabilitate the Contractor's premises under any circumstances; however, if Government—furnished property is withdrawn or is unsuitable for the intended use, or if other Government property is substituted, then the equitable adjustment under paragraph (i) of this clause may properly include restoration or rehabilitation costs.

(l) *Communication.* All communications under this clause shall be in writing.

(m) *Contracts outside the United States.* If this contract is to be performed outside of the United States and its outlying areas, the words "Government" and "Government-furnished" (wherever they appear in this clause) shall be construed as "United States Government" and "United States Government-furnished," respectively.

(End of clause)

Alternate I (APR 2012). As prescribed in 45.107(a)(2), substitute the following for paragraph (h)(1) of the basic clause:

(h)(1) The Contractor assumes the risk of, and shall be responsible for, any loss of Government property upon its delivery to the Contractor as Government-furnished property. However, the Contractor is not responsible for reasonable wear and tear to Government property or for Government property properly consumed in performing this contract.

Alternate II (APR 2012). As prescribed in 45.107(a)(3), substitute the following for paragraph (e)(3) of the basic clause:

(e)(3) Title to property (and other tangible personal property) purchased with funds available for research and having a unit acquisition cost of less than $5,000 shall vest in the Contractor upon acquisition or as soon thereafter as feasible; provided that the Contractor obtained the Contracting Officer's approval before each acquisition. Title to property purchased with funds available for research and having a unit acquisition cost of $5,000 or more shall vest as set forth in this contract. If title to property vests in the Contractor under this paragraph, the Contractor agrees that no costs shall be allowed for any depreciation, amortization, or use under any existing or future Government contract or subcontract thereunder. The Contractor shall furnish the Contracting Officer a list of all property to which title is vested in the Contractor under this paragraph within 10 days following the end of the calendar quarter during which it was received. Vesting title under this paragraph is subject to civil rights legislation, 42 U.S.C. 2000d. Before title is vested and by signing this contract, the Contractor accepts and agrees that—

"No person in the United States or its outlying areas shall, on the ground of race, color, or national origin, be excluded from participation in, be denied the benefits of, or be otherwise subjected to discrimination under this contemplated financial assistance (title to property)."

[FAC 90-32, 60 FR 48206, 9/18/95, effective 10/1/95; FAC 2005-17, 72 FR 27364, 5/15/2007, effective 6/14/2007; FAC 2005-19, 72 FR 46363, 8/17/2007, effective 8/17/2007; FAC 2005-43, 75 FR 38675, 7/2/2010, effective 8/2/2010; FAC 2005-56, 77 FR 12937, 3/2/2012, effective 4/2/2012; FAC 2005-95, 82 FR 4709, 1/13/2017, effective 1/13/2017]

52.245-2 Government Property Installation Operation Services.

As prescribed in 45.107(b), insert the following clause:

GOVERNMENT PROPERTY INSTALLATION OPERATION SERVICES (APR 2012)

(a) This Government Property listed in paragraph (e) of this clause is furnished to the Contractor in an "as-is, where is" condition. The Government makes no warranty regarding the suitability for use of the Government property specified in this contract. The Contractor shall be afforded the opportunity to inspect the Government property as specified in the solicitation.

(b) The Government bears no responsibility for repair or replacement of any lost Government property. If any or all of the Government property is lost or becomes no longer usable, the Contractor shall be responsible for replacement of the property at Contractor expense. The Contractor shall have title to all replacement property and shall continue to be responsible for contract performance.

(c) Unless the Contracting Officer determines otherwise, the Government abandons all rights and title to unserviceable and scrap property resulting from contract performance. Upon notification to the Contracting Officer, the Contractor shall remove such property from the Government premises and dispose of it at Contractor expense.

(d) Except as provided in this clause, Government property furnished under this contract shall be governed by the Government Property clause of this contract.

(e) Government property provided under this clause:

____

____

____

(End of clause)

[FAC 84-8, 50 FR 26904, 6/28/85, effective 7/1/85; FAC 84-53, 54 FR 48995, 11/28/89, effective 12/28/89; FAC 90-32, 60 FR 48206, 9/18/95, effective 10/1/95; FAC 2001-14, 68 FR 28079, 5/22/2003, effective 6/23/2003; FAC 2001-22, 69 FR 17741, 4/5/2004, effective 5/5/2004; FAC 2005-17, 72 FR 27364, 5/15/2007, effective 6/14/2007; FAC 2005-43, 75 FR 38675, 7/2/2010, effective 8/2/2010; FAC 2005-56, 77 FR 12937, 3/2/2012, effective 4/2/2012]

52.245-3 [Removed and Reserved]

[FAC 90-32, 60 FR 48206, 9/18/95, effective 10/1/95; FAC 2005-17, 72 FR 27364, 5/15/2007, effective 6/14/2007]

52.245-4 [Removed and Reserved]

[FAC 84-32, 53 FR 663, 1/11/88, effective 1/29/88; FAC 90-32, 60 FR 48206, 9/18/95, effective 10/1/95; FAC 2001-14, 68 FR 28079, 5/22/2003, effective 6/23/2003; FAC 2005-17, 72 FR 27364, 5/15/2007, effective 6/14/2007]

52.245-5 [Removed and Reserved]

[FAC 84-8, 50 FR 26904, 6/28/85, effective 7/1/85; FAC 84-12, 51 FR 2667, 1/17/86, effective 1/20/86; FAC 84-56, 55 FR 3889, 2/5/90, effective 3/7/90; FAC 2001-14, 68 FR 28079, 5/22/2003, effective 6/23/2003; FAC 2001-22, 69 FR 17741, 4/5/2004, effective 5/5/2004; FAC 2005-17, 72 FR 27364, 5/15/2007, effective 6/14/2007]

52.245-6 [Removed and Reserved]

[FAC 90-32, 60 FR 48206, 9/18/95, effective 10/1/95; FAC 2005-17, 72 FR 27364, 5/15/2007, effective 6/14/2007]

52.245-7 [Removed and Reserved]

[FAC 90-32, 60 FR 48206, 9/18/95, effective 10/1/95; FAC 90-37, 61 FR 2626, 1/26/96, effective 3/26/96; FAC 2005-17, 72 FR 27364, 5/15/2007, effective 6/14/2007]

52.245-8 [Removed and Reserved]

[FAC 90-32, 60 FR 48206, 9/18/95, effective 10/1/95; FAC 90-45, Final rule, 62 FR 224, 1/2/97, effective 1/1/97; FAC 2005-17, 72 FR 27364, 5/15/2007, effective 6/14/2007]

52.245-9 Use and Charges.

As prescribed in 45.107(c), insert the following clause:

USE AND CHARGES (APR 2012)

(a) *Definitions.* Definitions applicable to this contract are provided in the clause at 52.245-1, Government Property. Additional definitions as used in this clause include:

Rental period means the calendar period during which Government property is made available for nongovernmental purposes.

Rental time means the number of hours, to the nearest whole hour, rented property is actually used for nongovernmental purposes. It includes time to set up the property for such purposes, perform required maintenance, and restore the property to its condition prior to rental (less normal wear and tear).

(b) *Use of Government property.* The Contractor may use the Government property without charge in the performance of—

(1) Contracts with the Government that specifically authorize such use without charge;

(2) Subcontracts of any tier under Government prime contracts if the Contracting Officer having cognizance of the prime contract—

(i) Approves a subcontract specifically authorizing such use; or

(ii) Otherwise authorizes such use in writing; and

(3) Other work, if the Contracting Officer specifically authorizes in writing use without charge for such work.

(c) *Rental.* If granted written permission by the Contracting Officer, or if it is specifically provided for in the Schedule, the Contractor may use the Government property (except material) for a rental fee for work other than that provided in paragraph (b) of this clause. Authorizing such use of the Government property does not waive any rights of the Government to terminate the Contractor's right to use the Government property. The rental fee shall be determined in accordance with the following paragraphs.

(d) *General.* (1) Rental requests shall be submitted to the Administrative Contracting Officer (ACO), identify the property for which rental is requested, propose a rental period, and compute an estimated rental charge by using the Contractor's best estimate of rental time in the formulae described in paragraph (e) of this clause.

(2) The Contractor shall not use Government property for nongovernmental purposes, including Independent Research and Development, until a rental charge for real property, or estimated rental charge for other property, is agreed upon. Rented property shall be used only on a non-interference basis.

(e) *Rental charge.—(1) Real property and associated fixtures.* (i) The Contractor shall obtain, at its expense, a property appraisal from an independent licensed, accredited, or certified appraiser that computes a monthly, daily, or hourly rental rate for comparable commercial property. The appraisal may be used to compute rentals under this clause throughout its effective period or, if an effective period is not stated in the appraisal, for one year following the date the appraisal was performed. The Contractor shall submit the appraisal to the ACO at least 30 days prior to the date the property is needed for nongovernmental use. Except as provided in paragraph (e)(1)(iii) of this clause, the ACO shall use the appraisal rental rate to determine a reasonable rental charge.

(ii) Rental charges shall be determined by multiplying the rental time by the appraisal rental rate expressed as a rate per hour. Monthly or daily appraisal rental rates shall be divided by 720 or 24, respectively, to determine an hourly rental rate.

(iii) When the ACO believes the appraisal rental rate is unreasonable, the ACO shall promptly notify the Contractor. The parties may agree on an alternative means for computing a reasonable rental charge.

(iv) The Contractor shall obtain, at its expense, additional property appraisals in the same manner as provided in paragraph (e)(1)(i) if the effective period has expired and the Contractor desires the continued use of property for nongovernmental use. The Contractor may obtain additional appraisals within the effective period of the current appraisal if the market prices decrease substantially.

(2) *Other Government property.* The Contractor may elect to compute the rental charge using the appraisal method described in paragraph (e)(1) of this clause subject to the constraints therein or the following formula in which rental time shall be expressed in increments of not less than one hour with portions of hours rounded to the next higher hour: The hourly rental charge is calculated by multiplying 2 percent of the acquisition cost by the hours of rental time, and dividing by 720.

(3) *Alternative methodology.* The Contractor may request consideration of an alternative basis for computing the rental charge if it considers the monthly rental rate or a time-based rental unreasonable or impractical.

(f) *Rental payments.* (1) Rent is due 60 days following completion of the rental period or as otherwise specified in the contract. The Contractor shall compute the rental due, and furnish records or other supporting data in sufficient detail to permit the ACO to verify the rental time and computation. Payment shall be made by check payable to the Treasurer of the United States and sent to the contract administration office identified in this contract, unless otherwise specified by the Contracting Officer.

(2) Interest will be charged if payment is not made by the date specified in paragraph (f)(1) of this clause. Interest will accrue at the "Renegotiation Board Interest Rate" (published in the Federal Register semiannually on or about January 1 and July 1) for the period in which the rent is due.

(3) The Government's acceptance of any rental payment under this clause, in whole or in part, shall not be construed as a waiver or relinquishment of any rights it may have against the Contractor stemming from the Contractor's unauthorized use of Government property or any other failure to perform this contract according to its terms.

(g) *Use revocation.* At any time during the rental period, the Government may revoke nongovernmental use authorization and require the Contractor, at the Contractor's expense, to return the property to the Government, restore the property to its pre-rental condition (less normal wear and tear), or both.

(h) *Unauthorized use.* The unauthorized use of Government property can subject a person to fines, imprisonment, or both, under 18 U.S.C. 641.

(End of clause)

[FAC 90-32, 60 FR 48206, 9/18/95, effective 10/1/95; FAC 2005-05, 70 FR 43583, 7/27/2005, effective 8/26/2005; FAC 2005-17, 72 FR 27364, 5/15/2007, effective 6/14/2007; FAC 2005-43, 75 FR 38675, 7/2/2010, effective 8/2/2010; FAC 2005-56, 77 FR 12937, 3/2/2012, effective 4/2/2012]

52.245-10 [Removed]

[FAC 90-32, 60 FR 48206, 9/18/95, effective 10/1/95; FAC 90-37, 61 FR 2626, 1/26/96, effective 3/26/96; FAC 2005-05, 70 FR 43583, 7/27/2005, effective 8/26/2005; FAC 2005-17, 72 FR 27364, 5/15/2007, effective 6/14/2007]

52.245-11 [Removed]

[FAC 84-8, 50 FR 26904, 6/28/85, effective 7/1/85; FAC 90-32, 60 FR 48206, 9/18/95, effective 10/1/95; FAC 2001-14, 68 FR 28079, 5/22/2003, effective 6/23/2003; FAC

2005-05, 70 FR 43583, 7/27/2005, effective 8/26/2005; FAC 2005-17, 72 FR 27364, 5/15/2007, effective 6/14/2007]

52.245-12 [Removed]

[FAC 90-32, 60 FR 48206, 9/18/95, effective 10/1/95; FAC 2005-17, 72 FR 27364, 5/15/2007, effective 6/14/2007]

52.245-13 [Removed]

[FAC 90-32, 60 FR 48206, 9/18/95, effective 10/1/95; FAC 2005-17, 72 FR 27364, 5/15/2007, effective 6/14/2007]

52.245-14 [Removed]

[FAC 90-32, 60 FR 48206, 9/18/95, effective 10/1/95; FAC 2005-17, 72 FR 27364, 5/15/2007, effective 6/14/2007]

52.245-15 [Removed]

[FAC 84-8, 50 FR 26905, 6/28/95, effective 7/1/85; FAC 2001-14, 68 FR 28079, 5/22/2003, effective 6/23/2003; FAC 2005-17, 72 FR 27364, 5/15/2007, effective 6/14/2007]

52.245-16 [Removed]

[FAC 84-5, 50 FR 1748, 1/11/85, effective 4/1/85; FAC 84-13, 50 FR 52434, 12/23/85, effective 2/3/86; FAC 2005-17, 72 FR 27364, 5/15/2007, effective 6/14/2007]

52.245-17 [Removed]

[FAC 84-53, 54 FR 48995, 11/28/89, effective 12/28/89; FAC 2001-22, 69 FR 17741, 4/5/2004, effective 5/5/2004; FAC 2005-17, 72 FR 27364, 5/15/2007, effective 6/14/2007]

52.245-18 [Removed]

[FAC 84-38, 53 FR 27468, 7/20/88, effective 8/19/88; corrected 53 FR 36028, 9/16/88; FAC 84-53, 54 FR 48997, 11/28/89, effective 12/28/89; FAC 90-16, 57 FR 60588, 12/21/92, effective 2/19/93; FAC 2005-17, 72 FR 27364, 5/15/2007, effective 6/14/2007]

52.245-19 [Removed]

[FAC 90-32, 60 FR 48206, 9/18/95, effective 10/1/95; FAC 2005-17, 72 FR 27364, 5/15/2007, effective 6/14/2007]

52.246-1 Contractor Inspection Requirements.

As prescribed in 46.301, insert the following clause:

CONTRACTOR INSPECTION REQUIREMENTS (APR 1984)

The Contractor is responsible for performing or having performed all inspections and tests necessary to substantiate that the supplies or services furnished under this contract conform to contract requirements, including any applicable technical requirements for specified manufacturers' parts. This clause takes precedence over any Government inspection and testing required in the contract's specifications, except for specialized inspections or tests specified to be performed solely by the Government.

(End of clause)

[FAC 90-29, 60 FR 34732, 7/3/95, effective 7/3/95]

52.246-2 Inspection of Supplies—Fixed-Price.

As prescribed in 46.302, insert the following clause:

INSPECTION OF SUPPLIES—FIXED-PRICE (AUG 1996)

(a) *Definition. Supplies,* as used in this clause, includes but is not limited to raw materials, components, intermediate assemblies, end products, and lots of supplies.

(b) The Contractor shall provide and maintain an inspection system acceptable to the Government covering supplies under this contract and shall tender to the Government for acceptance only supplies that have been inspected in accordance with the inspection system and have been found by the Contractor to be in conformity with contract requirements. As part of the system, the Contractor shall prepare records evidencing all inspections made under the system and the outcome. These records shall be kept complete and made available to the Government during contract performance and for as long afterwards as the contract requires. The Government may perform reviews and evaluations as reasonably necessary to ascertain compliance with this paragraph.

These reviews and evaluations shall be conducted in a manner that will not unduly delay the contract work. The right of review, whether exercised or not, does not relieve the Contractor of the obligations under the contract.

(c) The Government has the right to inspect and test all supplies called for by the contract, to the extent practicable, at all places and times, including the period of manufacture, and in any event before acceptance. The Government shall perform inspections and tests in a manner that will not unduly delay the work. The Government assumes no contractual obligation to perform any inspection and test for the benefit of the Contractor unless specifically set forth elsewhere in this contract.

(d) If the Government performs inspection or test on the premises of the Contractor or a subcontractor, the Contractor shall furnish, and shall require subcontractors to furnish, at no increase in contract price, all reasonable facilities and assistance for the safe and convenient performance of these duties. Except as otherwise provided in the contract, the Government shall bear the expense of Government inspections or tests made at other than the Contractor's or subcontractor's premises; *provided*, that in case of rejection, the Government shall not be liable for any reduction in the value of inspection or test samples.

(e) (1) When supplies are not ready at the time specified by the Contractor for inspection or test, the Contracting Officer may charge to the Contractor the additional cost of inspection or test.

(2) The Contracting Officer may also charge the Contractor for any additional cost of inspection or test when prior rejection makes reinspection or retest necessary.

(f) The Government has the right either to reject or to require correction of nonconforming supplies. Supplies are nonconforming when they are defective in material or workmanship or are otherwise not in conformity with contract requirements. The Government may reject nonconforming supplies with or without disposition instructions.

(g) The Contractor shall remove supplies rejected or required to be corrected. However, the Contracting Officer may require or permit correction in place, promptly after notice, by and at the expense of the Contractor. The Contractor shall not tender for acceptance corrected or rejected supplies without disclosing the former rejection or requirement for correction, and, when required, shall disclose the corrective action taken.

(h) If the Contractor fails to promptly remove, replace, or correct rejected supplies that are required to be removed or to be replaced or corrected, the Government may either (1) by contract or otherwise, remove, replace, or correct the supplies and charge the cost to the Contractor or (2) terminate the contract for default. Unless the Contractor corrects or replaces the supplies within the delivery schedule, the Contracting Officer may require their delivery and make an equitable price reduction. Failure to agree to a price reduction shall be a dispute.

(i) (1) If this contract provides for the performance of Government quality assurance at source, and if requested by the Government, the Contractor shall furnish advance notification of the time (i) when Contractor inspection or tests will be performed in accordance with the terms and conditions of the contract and (ii) when the supplies will be ready for Government inspection.

(2) The Government's request shall specify the period and method of the advance notification and the Government representative to whom it shall be furnished. Requests shall not require more than 2 workdays of advance notification if the Government representative is in residence in the Contractor's plant, nor more than 7 workdays in other instances.

(j) The Government shall accept or reject supplies as promptly as practicable after delivery, unless otherwise provided in the contract. Government failure to inspect and accept or reject the supplies shall not relieve the Contractor from responsibility, nor impose liability on the Government, for nonconforming supplies.

(k) Inspections and tests by the Government do not relieve the Contractor of responsibility for defects or other failures to meet contract requirements discovered before acceptance. Acceptance shall be conclusive, except for latent defects, fraud, gross mistakes amounting to fraud, or as otherwise provided in the contract.

(l) If acceptance is not conclusive for any of the reasons in paragraph (k) hereof, the Government, in addition to any other rights and remedies provided by law, or under other provisions of this contract, shall have the right to require the Contractor (1) at no increase in contract price, to correct or replace the defective or nonconforming supplies at the original point of delivery or at the Contractor's plant at the Contracting Officer's election, and in accordance with a reasonable delivery schedule as may be agreed upon between the Contractor and the Contracting Officer; *provided*, that the Contracting Officer may require a reduction in contract price if the Contractor fails to meet such delivery schedule, or (2) within a reasonable time after receipt by the Contractor of notice of defects or nonconformance, to repay such portion of the contract as is equitable under the circumstances if the Contracting Officer elects not to require correction or replacement. When supplies are returned to the Contractor, the Contractor shall bear the transportation cost from the original point of delivery to the Contractor's plant and return to the original point when that point is not the Contractor's plant. If the Contractor fails to perform or act as required in (1) or (2) above and does not cure such failure within a period of 10 days (or such longer period as the Contracting Officer may authorize in writing) after receipt of notice from the Contracting Officer specifying such failure, the Government shall have the right by contract or otherwise to replace or correct such supplies and charge to the Contractor the cost occasioned the Government thereby.

(End of clause)

Alternate I (JUL 1985). If a fixed-price incentive contract is contemplated, substitute paragraphs (g), (h), and (l) below for paragraphs (g), (h), and (l) of the basic clause.

(g) The Contractor shall remove supplies rejected or required to be corrected. However, the Contracting Officer may require or permit correction in place, promptly after notice. The Contractor shall not tender for acceptance corrected or rejected supplies without disclosing the former rejection or requirement for correction, and when required shall disclose the corrective action taken. Cost of removal, replacement, or correction shall be considered a cost incurred, or to be incurred, in the total final negotiated cost fixed under the incentive price revision clause. However, replacements or corrections by the Contractor after the establishment of the total final price shall be at no increase in the total final price.

(h) If the Contractor fails to promptly remove, replace, or correct rejected supplies that are required to be removed or to be replaced or corrected, the Government may either (1) by contract or otherwise, remove, replace, or correct the supplies and equitably reduce the target price or, if established, the total final price or (2) may terminate the contract for default. Unless the Contractor corrects or replaces the nonconforming supplies within the delivery schedule, the Contracting Officer may require their delivery and equitably reduce any target price or, if it is established, the total final contract price. Failure to agree upon an equitable price reduction shall be a dispute.

(l) If acceptance is not conclusive for any of the reasons in paragraph (k) hereof, the Government, in addition to any other rights and remedies provided by law, or under other provisions of this contract, shall have the right to require the Contractor (1) at no increase in any target price or, if it is established, the total final price of this contract, to correct or replace the defective or nonconforming supplies at the original point of delivery or at the Contractor's plant at the Contracting Officer's election, and in accordance with a reasonable delivery schedule as may be agreed upon between the Contractor and the Contracting Officer; *provided*, that the Contracting Officer may require a reduction in any target price, or, if it is established, the total final price of this contract, if the Contractor fails to meet such delivery schedule; or (2) within a reasonable time after receipt by the Contractor of notice of defects or nonconformance, to repay such portion of the total final price as is equitable under the circumstances if the Contracting Officer elects not to require correction or replacement. When supplies are returned to the Contractor, the Contractor shall bear the transportation costs from the original point of delivery to the Contractor's plant and return to the original point when that point is not the Contractor's plant. If the Contractor fails to perform or act as required in (1) or (2) above and does not cure such failure within a period of 10 days (or such longer period as the Contracting Officer may authorize in writing) after receipt of notice from the Contracting Officer specifying such failure, the Government shall have the right by contract or otherwise to replace or correct such supplies and equitably reduce any target price or, if it is established, the total final price of this contract.

Alternate II (JUL 1985). If a fixed-ceiling-price contract with retroactive price redetermination is contemplated, substitute paragraphs (g), (h), and (l) below for paragraphs (g), (h), and (l) of the basic clause:

(g) The Contractor shall remove supplies rejected or required to be corrected. However, the Contracting Officer may require or permit correction in place, promptly after notice. The Contractor shall not tender for acceptance corrected or rejected supplies without disclosing the former rejection or requirement for correction, and when required shall disclose the corrective action taken. Cost of removal, replacement, or correction shall be considered a cost incurred, or to be incurred, when redetermining the prices under the price redetermination clause. However, replacements or corrections by the Contractor after the establishment of the redetermined prices shall be at no increase in the redetermined price.

(h) If the Contractor fails to promptly remove, replace, or correct rejected supplies that are required to be removed or to be replaced or corrected, the Government may either (1) by contract or otherwise, remove, replace, or correct the supplies and equitably reduce the initial contract prices or, if established, the redetermined contract prices or (2) terminate the contract for default. Unless the Contractor corrects or replaces the nonconforming supplies within the delivery schedule, the Contracting Officer may require their delivery and equitably reduce the initial contract price or, if it is established, the redetermined contract prices. Failure to agree upon an equitable price reduction shall be a dispute.

(l) If acceptance is not conclusive for any of the reasons in paragraph (k) hereof, the Government, in addition to any other rights and remedies provided by law, or under other provisions of this contract, shall have the right to require the Contractor (1) at no increase in the initial contract prices, or, if it is established, the redetermined prices of this contract, to correct or replace the defective or nonconforming supplies at the original point of delivery or at the Contractor's plant at the Contracting Officer's election, and in accordance with a reasonable delivery schedule as may be agreed upon between the Contractor and the Contracting Officer; *provided*, that the Contracting Officer may require a reduction in the initial contract prices, or, if it is established, the redetermined prices of this contract, if the Contractor fails to meet such delivery schedule; or (2) within a reasonable time after receipt by the Contractor of notice of defects or nonconformance, to repay such portion of the initial contract prices, or, if it is established, the redetermined prices of this contract, as is equitable under the circumstances if the Contracting Officer elects not to require correction or replacement. When supplies are returned to the Contractor, the Contractor shall bear the transportation costs from the original point of delivery to the Contractor's plant and return to the original point when that point is not the Contractor's plant. If the Contractor fails to perform or act as required in (1) or (2) above and does not cure such failure within a period of 10 days (or such longer period as the Contracting Officer may authorize in writing) after receipt of notice from the Contracting Officer specifying such failure, the Government shall have the right by contract or otherwise to replace or correct such supplies and equitably reduce the initial contract prices, or, if it is established, the redetermined prices of this contract.

[FAC 84-8, 50 FR 26905, 6/28/85, effective 7/1/85; FAC 90-7, 56 FR 41744, 8/22/91, effective 9/23/91; FAC 90-39, 61 FR 31612, 6/20/96, effective 8/19/96]

52.246-3 Inspection of Supplies—Cost-Reimbursement.

As prescribed in 46.303, insert the following clause in solicitations and contracts for supplies, or services that involve the furnishing of supplies, when a cost-reimbursement contract is contemplated:

INSPECTION OF SUPPLIES—COST-REIMBURSEMENT (MAY 2001)

(a) *Definitions*. As used in this clause—

Contractor's managerial personnel means any of the Contractor's directors, officers, managers, superintendents, or equivalent representatives who have supervision or direction of—

(1) All or substantially all of the Contractor's business;

(2) All or substantially all of the Contractor's operation at a plant or separate location where the contract is being performed; or

(3) A separate and complete major industrial operation connected with performing this contract.

Supplies includes but is not limited to raw materials, components, intermediate assemblies, end products, lots of supplies, and, when the contract does not include the Warranty of Data clause, data.

(b) The Contractor shall provide and maintain an inspection system acceptable to the Government covering the supplies, fabricating methods, and special tooling under this contract. Complete records of all inspection work performed by the Contractor shall be maintained and made available to the Government during contract performance and for as long afterwards as the contract requires.

(c) The Government has the right to inspect and test the contract supplies, to the extent practicable at all places and times, including the period of manufacture, and in any event before acceptance. The Government may also inspect the plant or plants of the Contractor or any subcontractor engaged in the contract performance. The Government shall perform inspections and tests in a manner that will not unduly delay the work.

(d) If the Government performs inspection or test on the premises of the Contractor or a subcontractor, the Contractor shall furnish and shall require subcontractors to furnish all reasonable facilities and assistance for the safe and convenient performance of these duties.

(e) Unless otherwise specified in the contract, the Government shall accept supplies as promptly as practicable after delivery, and supplies shall be deemed accepted 60 days after delivery, unless accepted earlier.

(f) At any time during contract performance, but no later than 6 months (or such other time as may be specified in the contract) after acceptance of the supplies to be delivered under the contract, the Government may require the Contractor to replace or correct any supplies that are nonconforming at time of delivery. Supplies are nonconforming when they are defective in material or workmanship or are otherwise not in conformity with contract requirements. Except as otherwise provided in paragraph (h) below, the cost of replacement or correction shall be included in allowable cost, determined as provided in the Allowable Cost and Payment clause, but no additional fee shall be paid. The Contractor shall not tender for acceptance supplies required to be replaced or corrected without disclosing the former requirement for replacement or correction, and, when required, shall disclose the corrective action taken.

(g) (1) If the Contractor fails to proceed with reasonable promptness to perform required replacement or correction, the Government may—

(i) By contract or otherwise, perform the replacement or correction and charge to the Contractor any increased cost or make an equitable reduction in any fixed fee paid or payable under the contract;

(ii) Require delivery of undelivered supplies at an equitable reduction in any fixed fee paid or payable under the contract; or

(iii) Terminate the contract for default.

(2) Failure to agree on the amount of increased cost to be charged to the Contractor or to the reduction in the fixed fee shall be a dispute.

(h) Notwithstanding paragraphs (f) and (g) above, the Government may at any time require the Contractor to correct or replace, without cost to the Government, nonconforming supplies, if the nonconformances are due to (1) fraud, lack of good faith, or willful misconduct on the part of the Contractor's managerial personnel or (2) the conduct of one or more of the Contractor's employees selected or retained by the Contractor after any of the Contractor's managerial personnel has reasonable grounds to believe that the employee is habitually careless or unqualified.

(i) This clause applies in the same manner to corrected or replacement supplies as to supplies originally delivered.

(j) The Contractor shall have no obligation or liability under this contract to replace supplies that were nonconforming at the time of delivery, except as provided in this clause or as may be otherwise provided in the contract.

(k) Except as otherwise specified in the contract, the Contractor's obligation to correct or replace Government-furnished property shall be governed by the clause pertaining to Government property.

(End of clause)

[FAC 90-32, 60 FR 48206, 9/18/95, effective 10/1/95; FAC 97-22, 66 FR 2116, 1/10/2001, effective 3/12/2001; Delay of effective date, 66 FR 14259, 3/9/2001, effective 5/11/2001]

52.246-4 Inspection of Services—Fixed-Price.

As prescribed in 46.304, insert the following clause:

INSPECTION OF SERVICES—FIXED-PRICE (AUG 1996)

(a) *Definition. Services* as used in this clause, includes services performed, workmanship, and material furnished or utilized in the performance of services.

(b) The Contractor shall provide and maintain an inspection system acceptable to the Government covering the services under this contract. Complete records of all inspection work performed by the Contractor shall be maintained and made available to the Government during contract performance and for as long afterwards as the contract requires.

(c) The Government has the right to inspect and test all services called for by the contract, to the extent practicable at all times and places during the term of the contract. The Government shall perform inspections and tests in a manner that will not unduly delay the work.

(d) If the Government performs inspections or tests on the premises of the Contractor or a subcontractor, the Contractor shall furnish, and shall require subcontractors to furnish, at no increase in contract price, all reasonable facilities and assistance for the safe and convenient performance of these duties.

(e) If any of the services do not conform with contract requirements, the Government may require the Contractor to perform the services again in conformity with contract requirements, at no increase in contract amount. When the defects in services cannot be corrected by reperformance, the Government may (1) require the Contractor to take necessary action to ensure that future performance conforms to contract requirements and (2) reduce the contract price to reflect the reduced value of the services performed.

(f) If the Contractor fails to promptly perform the services again or to take the necessary action to ensure future performance in conformity with contract requirements, the Government may (1) by contract or otherwise, perform the services and charge to the Contractor any cost incurred by the Government that is directly related to the performance of such service or (2) terminate the contract for default.

(End of clause)

[FAC 90-9, 56 FR 67136, 12/27/91, effective 2/25/92; FAC 90-39, 61 FR 31612, 6/20/96, effective 8/19/96]

52.246-5 Inspection of Services—Cost-Reimbursement.

As prescribed in 46.305, insert the following clause in solicitations and contracts for services, or supplies that involve the furnishing of services, when a cost-reimbursement contract is contemplated:

INSPECTION OF SERVICES—COST-REIMBURSEMENT (APR 1984)

(a) *Definition. Services,* as used in this clause, includes services performed, workmanship, and material furnished or used in performing services.

(b) The Contractor shall provide and maintain an inspection system acceptable to the Government covering the services under this contract. Complete records of all inspection work performed by the Contractor shall be maintained and made available to the Government during contract performance and for as long afterwards as the contract requires.

(c) The Government has the right to inspect and test all services called for by the contract, to the extent practicable at all places and times during the term of the contract. The Government shall perform inspections and tests in a manner that will not unduly delay the work.

(d) If any of the services performed do not conform with contract requirements, the Government may require the Contractor to perform the services again in conformity with contract requirements, for no additional fee. When the defects in services cannot be corrected by reperformance, the Government may (1) require the Contractor to take necessary action to ensure that future performance conforms to contract requirements and (2) reduce any fee payable under the contract to reflect the reduced value of the services performed.

(e) If the Contractor fails to promptly perform the services again or take the action necessary to ensure future performance in conformity with contract requirements, the Government may (1) by contract or otherwise, perform the services and reduce any fee payable by an amount that is equitable under the circumstances or (2) terminate the contract for default.

(End of clause)

[FAC 90-32, 60 FR 48206, 9/18/95, effective 10/1/95]

52.246-6 Inspection—Time-and-Material and Labor-Hour.

As prescribed in 46.306, insert the following clause:

INSPECTION—TIME-AND-MATERIAL AND LABOR-HOUR (MAY 2001)

(a) *Definitions*. As used in this clause—

Contractor's managerial personnel means any of the Contractor's directors, officers, managers, superintendents, or equivalent representatives who have supervision or direction of—

(1) All or substantially all of the Contractor's business;

(2) All or substantially all of the Contractor's operation at any one plant or separate location where the contract is being performed; or

(3) A separate and complete major industrial operation connected with the performance of this contract.

Materials includes data when the contract does not include the Warranty of Data clause.

(b) The Contractor shall provide and maintain an inspection system acceptable to the Government covering the material, fabricating methods, work, and services under this contract. Complete records of all inspection work performed by the Contractor shall be maintained and made available to the Government during contract performance and for as long afterwards as the contract requires.

(c) The Government has the right to inspect and test all materials furnished and services performed under this contract, to the extent practicable at all places and times, including the period of performance, and in any event before acceptance. The Government may also inspect the plant or plants of the Contractor or any subcontractor engaged in contract performance. The Government shall perform inspections and tests in a manner that will not unduly delay the work.

(d) If the Government performs inspection or test on the premises of the Contractor or a subcontractor, the Contractor shall furnish and shall require subcontractors to furnish all reasonable facilities and assistance for the safe and convenient performance of these duties.

(e) Unless otherwise specified in the contract, the Government shall accept or reject services and materials at the place of delivery as promptly as practicable after delivery, and they shall be presumed accepted 60 days after the date of delivery, unless accepted earlier.

(f) At any time during contract performance, but not later than 6 months (or such other time as may be specified in the contract) after acceptance of the services or materials last delivered under this contract, the Government may require the Contractor to replace or correct services or materials that at time of delivery failed to meet contract requirements. Except as otherwise specified in paragraph (h) below, the cost of replacement or correction shall be determined under the Payments Under Time-and-Materials and Labor-Hour Contracts clause, but the "hourly rate" for labor hours incurred in the replacement or correction shall be reduced to exclude that portion of the rate attributable to profit. The Contractor shall not tender for acceptance materials and services required to be replaced or corrected without disclosing the former requirement for replacement or correction, and, when required, shall disclose the corrective action taken.

(g) (1) If the Contractor fails to proceed with reasonable promptness to perform required replacement or correction, and if the replacement or correction can be performed within the ceiling price (or the ceiling price as increased by the Government), the Government may—

(i) By contract or otherwise, perform the replacement or correction, charge to the Contractor any increased cost, or deduct such increased cost from any amounts paid or due under this contract; or

(ii) Terminate this contract for default.

(2) Failure to agree to the amount of increased cost to be charged to the Contractor shall be a dispute.

(h) Notwithstanding paragraphs (f) and (g) above, the Government may at any time require the Contractor to remedy by correction or replacement, without cost to the Government, any failure by the Contractor to comply with the requirements of this contract, if the failure is due to (1) fraud, lack of good faith, or willful misconduct on the part of the Contractor's managerial personnel or (2) the conduct of one or more of the Contractor's employees selected or retained by the Contractor after any of the Contractor's managerial personnel has reasonable grounds to believe that the employee is habitually careless or unqualified.

(i) This clause applies in the same manner and to the same extent to corrected or replacement materials or services as to materials and services originally delivered under this contract.

(j) The Contractor has no obligation or liability under this contract to correct or replace materials and services that at time of delivery do not meet contract requirements, except as provided in this clause or as may be otherwise specified in the contract.

(k) Unless otherwise specified in the contract, the Contractor's obligation to correct or replace Government-furnished property shall be governed by the clause pertaining to Government property.

(End of clause)

Alternate I (APR 1984). If Government inspection and acceptance are to be performed at the contractor's plant, paragraph (e) below may be substituted for paragraph (e) of the basic clause:

(e) The Government shall inspect for acceptance all items (other than aircraft to be flown away, if any) to be furnished under this contract at the Contractor's plant or plants specified in the contract, or at any other plant or plants approved for such purpose in writing by the Contracting Officer. The Contractor shall inform the contract administration office or Contracting Officer when the work is ready for inspection. The Government reserves the right to charge to the Contractor any additional cost of Government inspection and test when items are not ready at the time for which inspection and test is requested by the Contractor.

[FAC 84-12, 51 FR 2667, 1/17/86, effective 1/20/86; FAC 90-32, 60 FR 48206, 9/18/95, effective 10/1/95; FAC 97-22, 66 FR 2116, 1/10/2001, effective 3/12/2001; Delay of effective date, 66 FR 14259, 3/9/2001, effective 5/11/2001]

52.246-7 Inspection of Research and Development—Fixed-Price.

As prescribed in 46.307(a), insert the following clause:

INSPECTION OF RESEARCH AND DEVELOPMENT—FIXED-PRICE (AUG 1996)

(a) The Contractor shall provide and maintain an inspection system acceptable to the Government covering the work under this contract. Complete records of all inspection work performed by the Contractor shall be maintained and made available to the Government during contract performance and for as long afterwards as the contract requires.

(b) The Government has the right to inspect and test all work called for by the contract, to the extent practicable at all places and times, including the period of performance, and in any event before acceptance. The Government may also inspect the premises of the Contractor or any subcontractor engaged in contract performance. The Government shall perform inspections and tests in a manner that will not unduly delay the work.

(c) If the Government performs any inspection or test on the premises of the Contractor or a subcontractor, the Contractor shall furnish and shall require subcontractors to furnish, at no increase in contract price, all reasonable facilities and assistance for the safe and convenient performance of these duties. Except as otherwise provided in the contract, the Government shall bear the expense of Government inspections or tests made at other than the Contractor's or subcontractor's premises.

(d) The Government shall accept or reject the work as promptly as practicable after delivery, unless otherwise specified in the contract. Government failure to inspect and accept or reject the work shall not relieve the Contractor from responsibility, nor impose liability on the Government, for nonconforming work. Work is nonconforming when it is defective in material or workmanship or is otherwise not in conformity with contract requirements.

(e) The Government has the right to reject nonconforming work. If the Contractor fails or is unable to correct or to replace nonconforming work within the delivery schedule (or such later time as the Contracting Officer may authorize), the Contracting Officer may accept the work and make an equitable price reduction. Failure to agree on a price reduction shall be a dispute.

(f) Inspection and test by the Government does not relieve the Contractor from responsibility for defects or other failures to meet the contract requirements that may be discovered before acceptance. Acceptance shall be conclusive, except for latent defects, fraud, gross mistakes amounting to fraud, or as otherwise specified in the contract. If acceptance is not conclusive for any of these causes, the Government, in addition to any other rights and remedies provided by law, or under other provisions of this contract, shall have the right to require the Contractor (1) at no increase in contract price, to correct or replace the defective or nonconforming supplies (work) at the original point of delivery or at the Contractor's plant at the Contracting Officer's election, and in accordance with a reasonable delivery schedule as may be agreed upon between the Contractor and the Contracting Officer; *provided*, the Contracting Officer may require a reduction in contract price if the Contractor fails to meet such delivery schedule; or (2) within a reasonable time after the Contractor's receipt of notice of defects or nonconformance, to repayment of such portion of the contract price as is equitable under the circumstances if the Government elects not to require correction or replacement. When supplies (work) are (is) returned to the Contractor, the Contractor shall bear transportation costs from the original point of delivery to the Contractor's plant and return to the original point of delivery when that point is not the Contractor's plant.

(End of clause)

[FAC 90-29, 60 FR 34732, 7/3/95, effective 7/3/95; FAC 90-39, 61 FR 31612, 6/20/96, effective 8/19/96]

52.246-8 Inspection of Research and Development—Cost-Reimbursement.

As prescribed in 46.308, insert the following clause in solicitations and contracts for research and development when (a) the primary objective is the delivery of end items other than designs, drawings, or reports, and (b) a cost-reimbursement contract is contemplated; unless use of the clause is impractical and the clause prescribed in 46.309 is considered to be more appropriate:

INSPECTION OF RESEARCH AND DEVELOPMENT—COST-REIMBURSEMENT (MAY 2001)

(a) *Definitions*. As used in this clause—

Contractor's managerial personnel means the Contractor's directors, officers, managers, superintendents, or equivalent representatives who have supervision or direction of—

(1) All or substantially all of the Contractor's business;

(2) All or substantially all of the Contractor's operation at any one plant or separate location where the contract is being performed; or

(3) A separate and complete major industrial operation connected with performing this contract.

Work includes data when the contract does not include the Warranty of Data clause.

(b) The Contractor shall provide and maintain an inspection system acceptable to the Government covering the work under this contract. Complete records of all inspection work performed by the Contractor shall be maintained and made available to the Government during contract performance and for as long afterwards as the contract requires.

(c) The Government has the right to inspect and test all work called for by the contract, to the extent practicable at all places and times, including the period of performance, and in any event before acceptance. The Government may also inspect the plant or plants of the Contractor or its subcontractors engaged in the contract performance. The Government shall perform inspections and tests in a manner that will not unduly delay the work.

(d) If the Government performs any inspection or test on the premises of the Contractor or a subcontractor, the Contractor shall furnish and shall require subcontractors to furnish all reasonable facilities and assistance for the safe and convenient performance of these duties.

(e) Unless otherwise provided in the contract, the Government shall accept work as promptly as practicable after delivery, and work shall be deemed accepted 90 days after delivery, unless accepted earlier.

(f) At any time during contract performance, but no later than 6 months (or such other time as may be specified in the contract) after acceptance of all of the end items (other than designs, drawings, or reports) to be delivered under the contract, the Government may require the Contractor to replace or correct work not meeting contract requirements. Time devoted to the replacement or correction of such work shall not be included in the computation of the above time period. Except as otherwise provided in paragraph (h) below, the cost of replacement or correction shall be determined as specified in the Allowable Cost and Payment clause, but no additional fee shall be paid.

The Contractor shall not tender for acceptance work required to be replaced or corrected without disclosing the former requirement for replacement or correction, and, when required, shall disclose the corrective action taken.

(g) (1) If the Contractor fails to proceed with reasonable promptness to perform required replacement or correction, the Government may—

(i) By contract or otherwise, perform the replacement or correction, charge to the Contractor any increased cost, or make an equitable reduction in any fixed fee paid or payable under the contract;

(ii) Require delivery of any undelivered articles and shall have the right to make an equitable reduction in any fixed fee paid or payable under the contract; or

(iii) Terminate the contract for default.

(2) Failure to agree on the amount of increased cost to be charged the Contractor or to the reduction in fixed fee shall be a dispute.

(h) Notwithstanding paragraphs (f) and (g) above, the Government may at any time require the Contractor to remedy by correction or replacement, without cost to the Government, any failure by the Contractor to comply with the requirements of this contract, if the failure is due to (1) fraud, lack of good faith, or willful misconduct on the part of the Contractor's managerial personnel or (2) the conduct of one or more of the Contractor's employees selected or retained by the Contractor after any of the Contractor's managerial personnel has reasonable grounds to believe that the employee is habitually careless or unqualified.

(i) This clause shall apply in the same manner to a corrected or replacement end item or components as to work originally delivered.

(j) The Contractor has no obligation or liability under the contract to correct or replace articles not meeting contract requirements at time of delivery, except as provided in this clause or as may otherwise be specified in the contract.

(k) Unless otherwise provided in the contract, the Contractor's obligations to correct or replace Government-furnished property shall be governed by the clause pertaining to Government property.

(End of clause)

Alternate I (APR 1984). If it is contemplated that the contract will be on a no-fee basis, substitute paragraphs (f) and (g) below for paragraphs (f) and (g) of the basic clause.

(f) At any time during contract performance, but not later than 6 months (or such other time as may be specified in the contract) after acceptance of all of the end items (other than designs, drawings, or reports) to be delivered under the contract, the Government may require the Contractor to correct or replace work not meeting contract requirements. Time devoted to the correction or replacement of such work shall not be included in the computation of the above time period. Except as otherwise provided in paragraph (g) below, the allowability of the cost of any such replacement or correction shall be determined as specified in the Allowable Cost and Payment clause. The Contractor shall not tender for acceptance corrected work without disclosing the former requirement for correction, and, when required, shall disclose the corrective action taken.

(g) If the Contractor fails to proceed with reasonable promptness to perform required replacement or correction, the Government may (1) by contract or otherwise, perform the replacement or correction and charge to the Contractor any increased cost, (2) require delivery of any undelivered articles, or (3) terminate the contract for default. Failure to agree on the amount of increased cost to be charged to the Contractor shall be a dispute.

[FAC 90-32, 60 FR 48206, 9/18/95, effective 10/1/95; FAC 97-22, 66 FR 2116, 1/10/2001, effective 3/12/2001; Delay of effective date, 66 FR 14259, 3/9/2001, effective 5/11/2001]

52.246-9 Inspection of Research and Development (Short Form).

As prescribed in 46.309, insert the following clause:

INSPECTION OF RESEARCH AND DEVELOPMENT (SHORT FORM) (APR 1984)

The Government has the right to inspect and evaluate the work performed or being performed under the contract, and the premises where the work is being performed, at all reasonable times and in a manner that will not unduly delay the work. If the Government performs inspection or evaluation on the premises of the Contractor or a subcontractor, the Contractor shall furnish and shall require subcontractors to furnish all reasonable facilities and assistance for the safe and convenient performance of these duties.

(End of clause)

[FAC 84-18, 51 FR 27120, 7/29/86, effective 7/30/86; FAC 90-32, 60 FR 48206, 9/18/95, effective 10/1/95]

52.246-10 [Removed and Reserved]

[FAC 90-32, 60 FR 48206, 9/18/95, effective 10/1/95; FAC 2005-17, 72 FR 27364, 5/15/2007, effective 6/14/2007]

52.246-11 Higher-Level Contract Quality Requirement.

As prescribed in 46.311, insert the following clause:

HIGHER-LEVEL CONTRACT QUALITY REQUIREMENT (DEC 2014)

(a) The Contractor shall comply with the higher-level quality standard(s) listed below. [*Contracting Officer insert the title, number, date, and tailoring (if any) of the higher-level quality standards.*]

(b) The Contractor shall include applicable requirements of the higher-level quality standard(s) listed in paragraph (a) of this clause and the requirement to flow down such standards, as applicable, to lower-tier subcontracts, in—

(1) Any subcontract for critical and complex items (see 46.203(b) and (c)); or

(2) When the technical requirements of a subcontract require—

(i) Control of such things as design, work operations, in-process control, testing, and inspection; or

(ii) Attention to such factors as organization, planning, work instructions, documentation control, and advanced metrology.

(End of clause)

[FAC 97-10, 63 FR 70264, 12/18/98, effective 2/16/99; FAC 2005-78, 79 FR 70344, 11/25/2014, effective 12/26/2014]

52.246-12 Inspection of Construction.

As prescribed in 46.312, insert the following clause:

INSPECTION OF CONSTRUCTION (AUG 1996)

(a) *Definition. Work* includes, but is not limited to, materials, workmanship, and manufacture and fabrication of components.

(b) The Contractor shall maintain an adequate inspection system and perform such inspections as will ensure that the work performed under the contract conforms to contract requirements. The Contractor shall maintain complete inspection records and make them available to the Government. All work shall be conducted under the general direction of the Contracting Officer and is subject to Government inspection and test at all places and at all reasonable times before acceptance to ensure strict compliance with the terms of the contract.

(c) Government inspections and tests are for the sole benefit of the Government and do not—

(1) Relieve the Contractor of responsibility for providing adequate quality control measures;

(2) Relieve the Contractor of responsibility for damage to or loss of the material before acceptance;

(3) Constitute or imply acceptance; or

(4) Affect the continuing rights of the Government after acceptance of the completed work under paragraph (i) below.

(d) The presence or absence of a Government inspector does not relieve the Contractor from any contract requirement, nor is the inspector authorized to change any term or condition of the specification without the Contracting Officer's written authorization.

(e) The Contractor shall promptly furnish, at no increase in contract price, all facilities, labor, and material reasonably needed for performing such safe and convenient inspections and tests as may be required by the Contracting Officer. The Government may charge to the Contractor any additional cost of inspection or test when work is not ready at the time specified by the Contractor for inspection or test, or when prior rejection makes reinspection or retest necessary. The Government shall perform all inspections and tests in a manner that will not unnecessarily delay the work. Special, full size, and performance tests shall be performed as described in the contract.

(f) The Contractor shall, without charge, replace or correct work found by the Government not to conform to contract requirements, unless in the public interest the Government consents to accept the work with an appropriate adjustment in contract price. The Contractor shall promptly segregate and remove rejected material from the premises.

(g) If the Contractor does not promptly replace or correct rejected work, the Government may (1) by contract or otherwise, replace or correct the work and charge the cost to the Contractor or (2) terminate for default the Contractor's right to proceed.

(h) If, before acceptance of the entire work, the Government decides to examine already completed work by removing it or tearing it out, the Contractor, on request, shall promptly furnish all necessary facilities, labor, and material. If the work is found to be defective or nonconforming in any material respect due to the fault of the Contractor or its subcontractors, the Contractor shall defray the expenses of the examination and of satisfactory reconstruction. However, if the work is found to meet contract requirements, the Contracting Officer shall make an equitable adjustment for the additional services involved in the examination and reconstruction, including, if completion of the work was thereby delayed, an extension of time.

(i) Unless otherwise specified in the contract, the Government shall accept, as promptly as practicable after completion and inspection, all work required by the contract or that portion of the work the Contracting Officer determines can be accepted separately. Acceptance shall be final and conclusive except for latent defects, fraud, gross mistakes amounting to fraud, or the Government's rights under any warranty or guarantee.

(End of clause)

[FAC 84-18, 51 FR 27120, 7/29/86, effective 7/30/86; FAC 90-29, 60 FR 34732, 7/3/95, effective 7/3/95; FAC 90-39, 61 FR 31612, 6/20/96, effective 8/19/96]

52.246-13 Inspection—Dismantling, Demolition, or Removal of Improvements.

As prescribed in 46.313, insert the following clause in solicitations and contracts for dismantling, demolition, or removal of improvements:

INSPECTION—DISMANTLING, DEMOLITION, OR REMOVAL OF IMPROVEMENTS (AUG 1996)

(a) Unless otherwise designated by the specifications, all workmanship performed under the contract is subject to Government inspection at all times and places where dismantling or demolition work is being performed. The Contractor shall furnish promptly, and at no increase in contract price all reasonable facilities, labor, and materials necessary for safe and convenient inspection by the Government. The Government shall perform inspections in a manner that will not unduly delay the work.

(b) The Contractor is responsible for damage to property caused by defective workmanship. The Contractor shall promptly segregate and remove from the premises any unsatisfactory facilities, materials, and equipment used in contract performance, and promptly replace them with satisfactory items. If the Contractor fails to proceed at once in a workmanlike manner with performance of the work or with the correction of defective workmanship, the Government may (1) by contract or otherwise, replace the facilities, materials, and equipment or correct the workmanship and charge the cost to the Contractor and (2) terminate for default the Contractor's right to proceed. The Contractor and any surety shall be liable, to the extent specified in the contract for any damage or cost of repair or replacement.

(End of clause)

[FAC 90-32, 60 FR 48206, 9/18/95, effective 10/1/95; FAC 90-39, 61 FR 31612, 6/20/96, effective 8/19/96]

52.246-14 Inspection of Transportation.

As prescribed in 46.314, insert the following clause in solicitations and contracts for freight transportation services (including local drayage) by rail, motor (including bus), domestic freight forwarder, and domestic water carriers (including inland, coastwise, and intercoastal). The contracting officer shall not use the clause for the acquisition of transportation services by domestic or international air carriers or by international ocean carriers, or to freight services provided under bills of lading or to those negotiated for reduced rates under 49 U.S.C. 10721 or 13712. (See Part 47, Transportation.)

INSPECTION OF TRANSPORTATION (APR 1984)

The Government has the right to inspect and test the Contractor's services, facilities, and equipment at all reasonable times. The Contractor shall furnish Government representatives with the free access and reasonable facilities and assistance required to accomplish their inspections and tests.

(End of clause)

[FAC 90-32, 60 FR 48206, 9/18/95, effective 10/1/95; FAC 2005-07, 71 FR 200, 1/3/2006, effective 2/2/2006]

52.246-15 Certificate of Conformance.

As prescribed in 46.315, insert the following clause in solicitations and contracts for supplies or services when the conditions in 46.504 apply:

CERTIFICATE OF CONFORMANCE (APR 1984)

(a) When authorized in writing by the cognizant Contract Administration Office (CAO), the Contractor shall ship with a Certificate of Conformance any supplies for which the contract would otherwise require inspection at source. In no case shall the Government's right to inspect supplies under the inspection provisions of this contract be prejudiced. Shipments of such supplies will not be made under this contract until use of the Certificate of Conformance has been authorized in writing by the CAO, or inspection and acceptance have occurred.

(b) The Contractor's signed certificate shall be attached to or included on the top copy of the inspection or receiving report distributed to the payment office or attached to the CAO copy when contract administration (Block 10 of the DD Form 250) is performed by the Defense Contract Administration Services. In addition, a copy of the signed certificate shall also be attached to or entered on copies of the inspection or receiving report accompanying the shipment.

(c) The Government has the right to reject defective supplies or services within a reasonable time after delivery by written notification to the Contractor. The Contractor shall in such event promptly replace, correct, or repair the rejected supplies or services at the Contractor's expense.

(d) The certificate shall read as follows:

"I certify that on ____ [*insert date*], the ____ [*insert Contractor's name*] furnished the supplies or services called for by Contract No. ____ via ____*[Carrier]* on ____*[identify the bill of lading or shipping document]* in accordance with all applicable requirements. I further certify that the supplies or services are of the quality specified and conform in all respects with the contract requirements, including specifications, drawings, preservation, packaging, packing, marking requirements, and physical item identification (part number), and are in the quantity shown on this or on the attached acceptance document."

Date of Execution:

Signature:

Title:

(End of clause)

[FAC 90-32, 60 FR 48206, 9/18/95, effective 10/1/95]

52.246-16 Responsibility for Supplies.

As prescribed in 46.316, insert the following clause:

RESPONSIBILITY FOR SUPPLIES (APR 1984)

(a) Title to supplies furnished under this contract shall pass to the Government upon formal acceptance, regardless of when or where the Government takes physical possession, unless the contract specifically provides for earlier passage of title.

(b) Unless the contract specifically provides otherwise, risk of loss of or damage to supplies shall remain with the Contractor until, and shall pass to the Government upon—

(1) Delivery of the supplies to a carrier, if transportation is f.o.b. origin; or

(2) Acceptance by the Government or delivery of the supplies to the Government at the destination specified in the contract, whichever is later, if transportation is f.o.b. destination.

(c) Paragraph (b) above shall not apply to supplies that so fail to conform to contract requirements as to give a right of rejection. The risk of loss of or damage to such nonconforming supplies remains with the Contractor until cure or acceptance. After cure or acceptance, paragraph (b) above shall apply.

(d) Under paragraph (b) above, the Contractor shall not be liable for loss of or damage to supplies caused by the negligence of officers, agents, or employees of the Government acting within the scope of their employment.

(End of clause)

[FAC 90-29, 60 FR 34732, 7/3/95, effective 7/3/95]

52.246-17 Warranty of Supplies of a Noncomplex Nature.

As prescribed in 46.710(a)(1), insert a clause substantially as follows:

WARRANTY OF SUPPLIES OF A NONCOMPLEX NATURE (JUN 2003)

(a) *Definitions*. As used in this clause—

Acceptance means the act of an authorized representative of the Government by which the Government assumes for itself, or as an agent of another, ownership of existing supplies, or approves specific services as partial or complete performance of the contract.

Supplies means the end items furnished by the Contractor and related services required under this contract. The word does not include *data*.

(b) *Contractor's obligations*. (1) Notwithstanding inspection and acceptance by the Government of supplies furnished under this contract, or any condition of this contract concerning the conclusiveness thereof, the Contractor warrants that for ____ [*Contracting Officer shall state specific period of time after delivery, or the specified event whose occurrence will terminate the warranty period; e.g., the number of miles or hours of use, or combinations of any applicable events or periods of time*]—

(i) All supplies furnished under this contract will be free from defects in material or workmanship and will conform with all requirements of this contract; and

(ii) The preservation, packaging, packing, and marking, and the preparation for, and method of, shipment of such supplies will conform with the requirements of this contract.

(2) When return, correction, or replacement is required, transportation charges and responsibility for the supplies while in transit shall be borne by the Contractor. However, the Contractor's liability for the transportation charges shall not exceed an amount equal to the cost of transportation by the usual commercial method of shipment between the place of delivery specified in this contract and the Contractor's plant, and return.

(3) Any supplies or parts thereof, corrected or furnished in replacement under this clause, shall also be subject to the terms of this clause to the same extent as supplies initially delivered. The warranty, with respect to supplies or parts thereof, shall be equal in duration to that in paragraph (b)(1) of this clause and shall run from the date of delivery of the corrected or replaced supplies.

(4) All implied warranties of merchantability and "fitness for a particular purpose" are excluded from any obligation contained in this contract.

(c) *Remedies available to the Government.* (1) The Contracting Officer shall give written notice to the Contractor of any breach of warranties in paragraph (b)(1) of this clause within ___ [*Contracting Officer shall insert specific period of time; e.g., "45 days of the last delivery under this contract," or "45 days after discovery of the defect"*].

(2) Within a reasonable time after the notice, the Contracting Officer may either—

(i) Require, by written notice, the prompt correction or replacement of any supplies or parts thereof (including preservation, packaging, packing, and marking) that do not conform with the requirements of this contract within the meaning of paragraph (b)(1) of this clause; or

(ii) Retain such supplies and reduce the contract price by an amount equitable under the circumstances.

(3) (i) If the contract provides for inspection of supplies by sampling procedures, conformance of supplies or components subject to warranty action shall be determined by the applicable sampling procedures in the contract. The Contracting Officer—

(A) May, for sampling purposes, group any supplies delivered under this contract;

(B) Shall require the size of the sample to be that required by sampling procedures specified in the contract for the quantity of supplies on which warranty action is proposed;

(C) May project warranty sampling results over supplies in the same shipment or other supplies contained in other shipments even though all of such supplies are not present at the point of reinspection; *provided*, that the supplies remaining are reasonably representative of the quantity on which warranty action is proposed; and

(D) Need not use the same lot size as on original inspection or reconstitute the original inspection lots.

(ii) Within a reasonable time after notice of any breach of the warranties specified in paragraph (b)(1) of this clause, the Contracting Officer may exercise one or more of the following options:

(A) Require an equitable adjustment in the contract price for any group of supplies.

(B) Screen the supplies grouped for warranty action under this clause at the Contractor's expense and return all nonconforming supplies to the Contractor for correction or replacement.

(C) Require the Contractor to screen the supplies at locations designated by the Government within the contiguous United States and to correct or replace all nonconforming supplies.

(D) Return the supplies grouped for warranty action under this clause to the Contractor (irrespective of the f.o.b. point or the point of acceptance) for screening and correction or replacement.

(4) (i) The Contracting Officer may, by contract or otherwise, correct or replace the nonconforming supplies with similar supplies from another source and charge to the Contractor the cost occasioned to the Government thereby if the Contractor—

(A) Fails to make redelivery of the corrected or replaced supplies within the time established for their return; or

(B) Fails either to accept return of the nonconforming supplies or fails to make progress after their return to correct or replace them so as to endanger performance of the delivery schedule, and in either of these circumstances does not cure such failure within a period of 10 days (or such longer period as the Contracting Officer may authorize in writing) after receipt of notice from the Contracting Officer specifying such failure.

(ii) Instead of correction or replacement by the Government, the Contracting Officer may require an equitable adjustment of the contract price. In addition, if the Contractor fails to furnish timely disposition instructions, the Contracting Officer may dispose of the nonconforming supplies for the Contractor's account in a reasonable manner. The Government is entitled to reimbursement from the Contractor, or from the proceeds of such disposal, for the reasonable expenses of the care and disposition of the nonconforming supplies, as well as for excess costs incurred or to be incurred.

(5) The rights and remedies of the Government provided in this clause are in addition to and do not limit any rights afforded to the Government by any other clause of this contract.

(End of clause)

Alternate I [Reserved].

Alternate II (APR 1984). If it is desirable to specify that necessary transportation incident to correction or replacement will be at the Government's expense (as might be the case if, for example, the cost of a warranty would otherwise be prohibitive), substitute a paragraph substantially the same as the following paragraph (b)(2) for paragraph (b)(2) of the basic clause:

(2) If correction or replacement is required and transportation of supplies in connection with correction or replacement is necessary, transportation charges and responsibility for the supplies while in transit shall be borne by the Government.

Alternate III (APR 1984). If the supplies cannot be obtained from another source, substitute a paragraph substantially the same as the following paragraph (c)(4) for paragraph (c)(4) of the basic clause:

(4) If the Contractor does not agree as to responsibility to correct or replace the supplies delivered, the Contractor shall nevertheless proceed in accordance with the written request issued by the Contracting Officer under paragraph (c)(2) of this clause to correct or replace the defective or nonconforming supplies. In the event it is later determined that the supplies were not defective or nonconforming within the terms and conditions of this clause, the contract price will be equitably adjusted.

Alternate IV (APR 1984). If a fixed-price incentive contract is contemplated, add a paragraph substantially the same as the following paragraph (c)(6) to the basic clause:

(6) All costs incurred or estimated to be incurred by the Contractor in complying with this clause shall be considered when negotiating the total final price under the Incentive Price Revision clause of this contract. After establishment of the total final price, Contractor compliance with this clause shall be at no increase in the total final price. Any equitable adjustment made under paragraph (c)(2) of this clause shall be governed by the paragraph entitled "Equitable Adjustments Under Other Clauses" in the Incentive Price Revision clause of this contract.

Alternate V (APR 1984). If it is anticipated that recovery of the warranted item will involve considerable Government expense for disassembly and/or reassembly of larger items, add a paragraph substantially the same as the following paragraph (c)(6) to the basic clause. Redesignate the additional paragraph as "(c)(7)" if Alternate IV is also being used.

(6) The Contractor shall be liable for the reasonable costs of disassembly and/or reassembly of larger items when it is necessary to remove the supplies to be inspected and/or returned for correction or replacement.

[Final rule, 55 FR 38518, 9/18/90; FAC 90-32, 60 FR 48206, 9/18/95, effective 10/1/95; FAC 97-22, 66 FR 2116, 1/10/2001, effective 3/12/2001; Delay of effective date, 66 FR 14259, 3/9/2001, effective 5/11/2001; FAC 2001-14, 68 FR 28079, 5/22/2003, effective 6/23/2003]

52.246-18 Warranty of Supplies of a Complex Nature.

As prescribed in 46.710(b)(1), insert a clause substantially as follows:

WARRANTY OF SUPPLIES OF A COMPLEX NATURE (MAY 2001)

(a) *Definitions*. As used in this clause—

Acceptance means the act of an authorized representative of the Government by which the Government assumes for itself, or as an agent of another, ownership of existing and identified supplies, or approves specific services rendered, as partial or complete performance of the contract.

Supplies means the end items furnished by the Contractor and related services required under this contract. The word does not include *data.*

(b) *Contractor's obligations.*

(1) The Contractor warrants that for ____ [*Contracting Officer shall state the specific warranty period after delivery, or the specified event whose occurrence will terminate the warranty period; e.g., the number of miles or hours of use, or combinations of any applicable events or periods of time*] all supplies furnished under this contract will be free from defects in material and workmanship and will conform with all requirements of this contract; *provided, however,* that with respect to Government-furnished property, the Contractor's warranty shall extend only to its proper installation, unless the Contractor performs some modification or other work on the property, in which case the Contractor's warranty shall extend to the modification or other work.

(2) Any supplies or parts thereof corrected or furnished in replacement shall be subject to the conditions of this clause to the same extent as supplies initially delivered. This warranty shall be equal in duration to that set forth in paragraph (b)(1) of this clause and shall run from the date of delivery of the corrected or replaced supplies.

(3) The Contractor shall not be obligated to correct or replace supplies if the facilities, tooling, drawings, or other equipment or supplies necessary to accomplish the correction or replacement have been made unavailable to the Contractor by action of the Government. In the event that correction or replacement has been directed, the Contractor shall promptly notify the Contracting Officer, in writing, of the nonavailability.

(4) The Contractor shall also prepare and furnish to the Government data and reports applicable to any correction required (including revision and updating of all affected data called for under this contract) at no increase in the contract price.

(5) When supplies are returned to the Contractor, the Contractor shall bear the transportation costs from the place of delivery specified in the contract (irrespective of the f.o.b. point or the point of acceptance) to the Contractor's plant and return.

(6) All implied warranties of merchantability and "fitness for a particular purpose" are excluded from any obligation contained in this contract.

(c) Remedies available to the Government. (1) In the event of a breach of the Contractor's warranty in paragraph (b)(1) of this clause, the Government may, at no increase in contract price—

(i) Require the Contractor, at the place of delivery specified in the contract (irrespective of the f.o.b. point or the point of acceptance) or at the Contractor's plant, to repair or replace, at the Contractor's election, defective or nonconforming supplies; or

(ii) Require the Contractor to furnish at the Contractor's plant the materials or parts and installation instructions required to successfully accomplish the correction.

(2) If the Contracting Officer does not require correction or replacement of defective or nonconforming supplies or the Contractor is not obligated to correct or replace under paragraph (b)(3) of this clause, the Government shall be entitled to an equitable reduction in the contract price.

(3) The Contracting Officer shall notify the Contractor in writing of any breach of the warranty in paragraph (b) of this clause within ____ [*Contracting Officer shall insert specific period of time in which notice shall be given to the Contractor; e.g., "45 days after delivery of the nonconforming supplies."; "45 days of the last delivery under this contract."; or "45 days after discovery of the defect."*] The Contractor shall submit to the Contracting Officer a written recommendation within ____ [*Contracting Officer shall insert period of time*] as to the corrective action required to remedy the breach. After the notice of breach, but not later than ____ [*Contracting*

Officer shall insert period within which the warranty remedies should be exercised] after receipt of the Contractor's recommendation for corrective action, the Contracting Officer may, in writing, direct correction or replacement as in paragraph (c)(1) of this clause, and the Contractor shall, notwithstanding any disagreement regarding the existence of a breach of warranty, comply with this direction. If it is later determined that the Contractor did not breach the warranty in paragraph (b)(1) of this clause, the contract price will be equitably adjusted.

(4) If supplies are corrected or replaced, the period for notification of a breach of the Contractor's warranty in paragraph (c)(3) of this clause shall be ____ [*Contracting Officer shall insert period within which the Contractor must be notified of a breach as to corrected or replaced supplies*] from the furnishing or return by the Contractor to the Government of the corrected or replaced supplies or parts thereof, or, if correction or replacement is effected by the Contractor at a Government or other activity, for ____ [*Contracting Officer shall insert period within which the Contractor must be notified of a breach of warranty as to corrected or replaced supplies*] thereafter.

(5) The rights and remedies of the Government provided in this clause are in addition to and do not limit any rights afforded to the Government by any other clause of the contract.

(End of clause)

Alternate I [Reserved].

Alternate II (APR 1984). If it is desirable to specify that necessary transportation incident to correction or replacement will be at the Government's expense (as might be the case if, for example, the cost of a warranty would otherwise be prohibitive), substitute a paragraph substantially the same as the following paragraph (b)(5) for paragraph (b)(5) of the basic clause:

(5) If correction or replacement is required and transportation of supplies in connection with correction or replacement is necessary, transportation charges and responsibility for the supplies while in transit shall be borne by the Government.

Alternate III (APR 1984). If a fixed-price incentive contract is contemplated, add a paragraph substantially the same as the following paragraph (c)(6) to the basic clause:

(6) All costs incurred or estimated to be incurred by the Contractor in complying with this clause shall be considered when negotiating the total final price under the Incentive Price Revision clause of this contract. After establishment of the total final price, Contractor compliance with this clause shall be at no increase in the total final price. Any equitable adjustments made under paragraph (c)(2) of this clause shall be governed by the paragraph entitled "Equitable Adjustments Under Other Clauses" in the Incentive Price Revision clause of this contract.

Alternate IV (APR 1984). If it is anticipated that recovery of the warranted item will involve considerable Government expense for disassembly and/or reassembly of larger items, add a paragraph substantially the same as the following paragraph (c)(6) to the basic clause. Redesignate the additional paragraph as "(c)(7)" if Alternate III is also used:

(6) The Contractor shall be liable for the reasonable costs of disassembly and/or reassembly of larger items when it is necessary to remove the supplies to be inspected and/or returned for correction or replacement.

[FAC 90-32, 60 FR 48206, 9/18/95, effective 10/1/95; FAC 97-22, 66 FR 2116, 1/10/2001, effective 3/12/2001; Delay of effective date, 66 FR 14259, 3/9/2001, effective 5/11/2001]

52.246-19 Warranty of Systems and Equipment under Performance Specifications or Design Criteria.

As prescribed in 46.710(c)(1), the contracting officer may insert a clause substantially as follows:

WARRANTY OF SYSTEMS AND EQUIPMENT UNDER PERFORMANCE SPECIFICATIONS OR DESIGN CRITERIA (MAY 2001)

(a) *Definitions*. As used in this clause—

Acceptance means the act of an authorized representative of the Government by which the Government assumes for itself, or as an agent of another, ownership of existing and identified supplies, or approves specific services rendered, as partial or complete performance of the contract.

Defect means any condition or characteristic in any supplies or services furnished by the Contractor under the contract that is not in compliance with the requirements of the contract.

Supplies means the end items furnished by the Contractor and related services required under this contract. Except when this contract includes the clause entitled Warranty of Data, supplies also mean *data*.

(b) *Contractor's obligations.*

(1) The Contractor's warranties under this clause shall apply only to those defects discovered by either the Government or the Contractor ____ [*Contracting Officer shall state the warranty period; e.g., "at the time of delivery;" "within 45 days after delivery," or the specified event whose occurrence will terminate the warranty period; e.g., the number of miles or hours of use, or combination of any applicable events or periods of time.*]

(2) If the Contractor becomes aware at any time before acceptance by the Government (whether before or after tender to the Government) that a defect exists in any supplies or services, the Contractor shall (i) promptly correct the defect or (ii) promptly notify the Contracting Officer, in writing, of the defect, using the same procedures prescribed in paragraph (b)(3) of this clause.

(3) If the Contracting Officer determines that a defect exists in any of the supplies or services accepted by the Government under this contract, the Contracting Officer shall promptly notify the Contractor of the defect, in writing, within ____ [*Contracting Officer shall insert the specific period of time in which notice shall be given to the Contractor; e.g., "30 days after delivery of the nonconforming supplies;" "90 days of the last delivery under this contract;" or "90 days after discovery of the defect."*] Upon timely notification of the existence of a defect, or if the Contractor independently discovers a defect in accepted supplies or services, the Contractor shall submit to the Contracting Officer, in writing, within ____ [*Contracting Officer shall insert period of time*] a recommendation for corrective actions, together with supporting information in sufficient detail for the Contracting Officer to determine what corrective action, if any, shall be undertaken.

(4) The Contractor shall promptly comply with any timely written direction from the Contracting Officer to correct or partially correct a defect, at no increase in the contract price.

(5) The Contractor shall also prepare and furnish to the Contracting Officer data and reports applicable to any correction required under this clause (including revision and updating of all other affected data called for under this contract) at no increase in the contract price.

(6) In the event of timely notice of a decision not to correct or only to partially correct, the Contractor shall submit a technical and cost proposal within ____ [*Contracting Officer shall insert period of time*] to amend the contract to permit acceptance of the affected supplies or services in accordance with the revised requirement, and an equitable reduction in the contract price shall promptly be negotiated by the parties and be reflected in a supplemental agreement to this contract.

(7) Any supplies or parts thereof corrected or furnished in replacement and any services reperformed shall also be subject to the conditions of this clause to the same extent as supplies or services initially accepted. The warranty, with respect to these supplies, parts, or services, shall be equal in duration to that set forth in paragraph (b)(1) of this clause, and shall run from the date of delivery of the corrected or replaced supplies.

(8) The Contractor shall not be responsible under this clause for the correction of defects in Government-furnished property, except for defects in installation, unless the Contractor performs, or is obligated to perform, any modifications or other work on such property. In that event, the Contractor shall be responsible for correction of defects that result from the modifications or other work.

(9) If the Government returns supplies to the Contractor for correction or replacement under this clause, the Contractor shall be liable for transportation charges up to an amount equal to the cost of transportation by the usual commercial method of shipment from the place of delivery specified in this contract (irrespective of the f.o.b. point or the point of acceptance) to the Contractor's plant and return to the place of delivery specified in this contract. The Contractor shall also bear the responsibility for the supplies while in transit.

(10) All implied warranties of merchantability and "fitness for a particular purpose" are excluded from any obligation under this contract.

(c) *Remedies available to the Government.* (1) The rights and remedies of the Government provided in this clause—

(i) Shall not be affected in any way by any terms or conditions of this contract concerning the conclusiveness of inspection and acceptance; and

(ii) Are in addition to, and do not limit, any rights afforded to the Government by any other clause of this contract.

(2) Within _____ [*Contracting Officer shall insert period of time*] after receipt of the Contractor's recommendations for corrective action and adequate supporting information, the Contracting Officer, using sole discretion, shall give the Contractor written notice not to correct any defect, or to correct or partially correct any defect within a reasonable time at _____ [*Contracting Officer shall insert locations where corrections may be performed*].

(3) In no event shall the Government be responsible for any extension or delays in the scheduled deliveries or periods of performance under this contract as a result of the Contractor's obligations to correct defects, nor shall there be any adjustment of the delivery schedule or period of performance as a result of the correction of defects unless provided by a supplemental agreement with adequate consideration.

(4) This clause shall not be construed as obligating the Government to increase the contract price.

(5) (i) The Contracting Officer shall give the Contractor a written notice specifying any failure or refusal of the Contractor to—

(A) Present a detailed recommendation for corrective action as required by paragraph (b)(3) of this clause;

(B) Correct defects as directed under paragraph (b)(4) of this clause; or

(C) Prepare and furnish data and reports as required by paragraph (b)(5) of this clause.

(ii) The notice shall specify a period of time following receipt of the notice by the Contractor in which the Contractor must remedy the failure or refusal specified in the notice.

(6) If the Contractor does not comply with the Contracting Officer's written notice in paragraph (c)(5)(i) of this clause, the Contracting Officer may by contract or otherwise—

(i) Obtain detailed recommendations for corrective action and either—

(A) Correct the supplies or services; or

(B) Replace the supplies or services, and if the Contractor fails to furnish timely disposition instructions, the Contracting Officer may dispose of the nonconforming supplies for the Contractor's account in a reasonable manner, in which case the Government is entitled to reimbursement from the Contractor, or from the proceeds, for the reasonable expenses of care and disposition, as well as for excess costs incurred or to be incurred;

(ii) Obtain applicable data and reports; and

(iii) Charge the Contractor for the costs incurred by the Government.

(End of clause)

Alternate I (APR 1984). If it is desirable to specify that necessary transportation incident to correction or replacement will be at the Government's expense (as might be the case if, for example, the cost of a warranty would otherwise be prohibitive), substitute a paragraph substantially the same as the following paragraph (b)(9) for paragraph (b)(9) of the basic clause:

(9) If correction or replacement is required, and transportation of supplies in connection with correction or replacement is necessary, transportation charges and responsibility for the supplies while in transit shall be borne by the Government.

Alternate II (APR 1984). If a fixed-price incentive contract is contemplated, add a paragraph substantially the same as the following paragraph (c)(7) to the basic clause:

(7) All costs incurred or estimated to be incurred by the Contractor in complying with this clause shall be considered when negotiating the total final price under the Incentive Price Revision clause of this contract. After establishment of the total final price, Contractor compliance with this clause shall be at no increase in the total final price. Any equitable adjustments made under paragraph (b)(6) of this clause shall be governed by the paragraph entitled "Equitable Adjustments Under Other Clauses" in the Incentive Price Revision clause of this contract.

Alternate III (APR 1984). If it is anticipated that recovery of the warranted item will involve considerable Government expense for disassembly and/or reassembly of larger items, add a paragraph substantially the same as the following paragraph (c)(7) to the basic clause. Redesignate the additional paragraph as "(c)(8)" if Alternate II is also being used:

(7) The Contractor shall be liable for the reasonable costs of disassembly and/or reassembly of larger items when it is necessary to remove the supplies to be inspected and/or returned for correction or replacement.

[FAC 84-53, 54 FR 48997, 11/28/89, effective 12/28/89; FAC 90-32, 60 FR 48206, 9/18/95, effective 10/1/95; FAC 97-22, 66 FR 2116, 1/10/2001, effective 3/12/2001; Delay of effective date, 66 FR 14259, 3/9/2001, effective 5/11/2001]

52.246-20 Warranty of Services.

As prescribed in 46.710(d), insert a clause substantially as follows:

WARRANTY OF SERVICES (MAY 2001)

(a) *Definition. Acceptance,* as used in this clause, means the act of an authorized representative of the Government by which the Government assumes for itself, or as an agent of another, ownership of existing and identified supplies, or approves specific services, as partial or complete performance of the contract.

(b) Notwithstanding inspection and acceptance by the Government or any provision concerning the conclusiveness thereof, the Contractor warrants that all services performed under this contract will, at the time of acceptance, be free from defects in workmanship and conform to the requirements of this contract. The Contracting Officer shall give written notice of any defect or nonconformance to the Contractor ____ [*Contracting Officer shall insert the specific period of time in which notice shall be given to the Contractor; e.g., "within 30 days from the date of acceptance by the Government,"; within 1000 hours of use by the Government,"; or other specified event whose occurrence will terminate the period of notice, or combination of any applicable events or period of time*]. This notice shall state either (1) that the Contractor shall correct or reperform any defective or nonconforming services, or (2) that the Government does not require correction or reperformance.

(c) If the Contractor is required to correct or reperform, it shall be at no cost to the Government, and any services corrected or reperformed by the Contractor shall be subject to this clause to the same extent as work initially performed. If the Contractor fails or refuses to correct or reperform, the Contracting Officer may, by contract or otherwise, correct or replace with similar services and charge to the Contractor the cost occasioned to the Government thereby, or make an equitable adjustment in the contract price.

(d) If the Government does not require correction or reperformance, the Contracting Officer shall make an equitable adjustment in the contract price.

(End of clause)

[FAC 90-32, 60 FR 48206, 9/18/95, effective 10/1/95; FAC 97-22, 66 FR 2116, 1/10/2001, effective 3/12/2001; Delay of effective date, 66 FR 14259, 3/9/2001, effective 5/11/2001]

52.246-21 Warranty of Construction.

As prescribed in 46.710(e)(1), the contracting officer may insert a clause substantially as follows in solicitations and contracts when a fixed-price construction contract (see 46.705(c)) is contemplated, and the use of a warranty clause has been approved under agency procedures:

WARRANTY OF CONSTRUCTION (MAR 1994)

(a) In addition to any other warranties in this contract, the Contractor warrants, except as provided in paragraph (i) of this clause, that work performed under this contract conforms to the contract requirements and is free of any defect in equipment, material, or design furnished, or workmanship performed by the Contractor or any subcontractor or supplier at any tier.

(b) This warranty shall continue for a period of 1 year from the date of final acceptance of the work. If the Government takes possession of any part of the work before final acceptance, this warranty shall continue for a period of 1 year from the date the Government takes possession.

(c) The Contractor shall remedy at the Contractor's expense any failure to conform, or any defect. In addition, the Contractor shall remedy at the Contractor's expense any damage to Government-owned or controlled real or personal property, when that damage is the result of—

(1) The Contractor's failure to conform to contract requirements; or

(2) Any defect of equipment, material, workmanship, or design furnished.

(d) The Contractor shall restore any work damaged in fulfilling the terms and conditions of this clause. The Contractor's warranty with respect to work repaired or replaced will run for 1 year from the date of repair or replacement.

(e) The Contracting Officer shall notify the Contractor, in writing, within a reasonable time after the discovery of any failure, defect, or damage.

(f) If the Contractor fails to remedy any failure, defect, or damage within a reasonable time after receipt of notice, the Government shall have the right to replace, repair, or otherwise remedy the failure, defect, or damage at the Contractor's expense.

(g) With respect to all warranties, express or implied, from subcontractors, manufacturers, or suppliers for work performed and materials furnished under this contract, the Contractor shall—

(1) Obtain all warranties that would be given in normal commercial practice;

(2) Require all warranties to be executed, in writing, for the benefit of the Government, if directed by the Contracting Officer; and

(3) Enforce all warranties for the benefit of the Government, if directed by the Contracting Officer.

(h) In the event the Contractor's warranty under paragraph (b) of this clause has expired, the Government may bring suit at its expense to enforce a subcontractor's, manufacturer's, or supplier's warranty.

(i) Unless a defect is caused by the negligence of the Contractor or subcontractor or supplier at any tier, the Contractor shall not be liable for the repair of any defects of material or design furnished by the Government nor for the repair of any damage that results from any defect in Government-furnished material or design.

(j) This warranty shall not limit the Government's rights under the Inspection and Acceptance clause of this contract with respect to latent defects, gross mistakes, or fraud.

(End of clause)

Alternate I (APR 1984). If the Government specifies in the contract the use of any equipment by "brand name and model", the contracting officer may add a paragraph substantially the same as the following paragraph (k) to the basic clause:

(k) Defects in design or manufacture of equipment specified by the Government on a "brand name and model" basis, shall not be included in this warranty. In this event, the Contractor shall require any subcontractors, manufacturers, or suppliers thereof to execute their warranties, in writing, directly to the Government.

[Final rule, FAC 90-20, 59 FR 11368, 3/10/94, effective 3/10/94; FAC 2019-04, 84 FR 38838, 8/7/2019, effective 8/7/2019]

52.246-22 [Reserved]

52.246-23 Limitation of Liability.

As prescribed in 46.805, insert the following clause:

LIMITATION OF LIABILITY (FEB 1997)

(a) Except as provided in paragraphs (b) and (c) below, and except for remedies expressly provided elsewhere in this contract, the Contractor shall not be liable for loss of or damage to property of the Government (excluding the supplies delivered under this contract) that (1) occurs after Government acceptance of the supplies delivered under this contract and (2) results from any defects or deficiencies in the supplies.

(b) The limitation of liability under paragraph (a) above shall not apply when a defect or deficiency in, or the Government's acceptance of, the supplies results from willful misconduct or lack of good faith on the part of any of the Contractor's managerial personnel. The term *Contractor's managerial personnel*, as used in this clause, means the Contractor's directors, officers, and any of the Contractor's managers, superintendents, or equivalent representatives who have supervision or direction of—

(1) All or substantially all of the Contractor's business;

(2) All or substantially all of the Contractor's operations at any one plant, laboratory, or separate location at which the contract is being performed; or

(3) A separate and complete major industrial operation connected with the performance of this contract.

(c) If the Contractor carries insurance, or has established a reserve for self-insurance, covering liability for loss or damage suffered by the Government through purchase or use of the supplies required to be delivered under this contract, the Contractor shall be liable to the Government, to the extent of such insurance or reserve, for loss of or damage to property of the Government occurring after Government acceptance of, and resulting from any defects or deficiencies in, the supplies delivered under this contract.

(End of clause)

[FAC 90-29, 60 FR 34732, 7/3/95, effective 7/3/95; FAC 90-43, Final rule, 61 FR 67408, 12/20/96, effective 2/18/97]

52.246-24 Limitation of Liability—High-Value Items.

As prescribed in 46.805, insert the following clause:

LIMITATION OF LIABILITY—HIGH-VALUE ITEMS (FEB 1997)

(a) Except as provided in paragraphs (b) through (e) below, and notwithstanding any other provision of this contract, the Contractor shall not be liable for loss of or damage to property of the Government (including the supplies delivered under this contract) that (1) occurs after Government acceptance of the supplies delivered under this contract and (2) results from any defects or deficiencies in the supplies.

(b) The limitation of liability under paragraph (a) above shall not apply when a defect or deficiency in, or the Government's acceptance of, the supplies results from willful misconduct or lack of good faith on the part of any of the Contractor's managerial personnel. The term *Contractor's managerial personnel* as used in this clause, means the Contractor's directors, officers, and any of the Contractor's managers, superintendents, or equivalent representatives who have supervision or direction of—

(1) All or substantially all of the Contractor's business;

(2) All or substantially all of the Contractor's operations at any one plant, laboratory,

or separate location at which the contract is being performed; or

(3) A separate and complete major industrial operation connected with the performance of this contract.

(c) If the Contractor carries insurance, or has established a reserve for self-insurance, covering liability for loss or damage suffered by the Government through purchase or use of the supplies required to be delivered under this contract, the Contractor shall be liable to the Government, to the extent of such insurance or reserve, for loss of or damage to property of the Government occurring after Government acceptance of, and resulting from any defects or deficiencies in, the supplies delivered under this contract.

(d) (1) This clause does not diminish the Contractor's obligations, to the extent that they arise otherwise under this contract, relating to correction, repair, replacement, or other relief for any defect or deficiency in supplies delivered under this contract.

(2) Unless this is a cost-reimbursement contract, if loss or damage occurs and correction, repair, or replacement is not feasible or desired by the Government, the Contractor shall, as determined by the Contracting Officer—

(i) Pay the Government the amount it would have cost the Contractor to make correction, repair, or replacement before the loss or damage occurred; or

(ii) Provide other equitable relief.

(e) This clause shall not limit or otherwise affect the Government's rights under clauses, if included in this contract, that cover—

(1) Warranty of technical data;

(2) Ground and flight risks or aircraft flight risks; or

(3) Government property.

(End of clause)

Alternate I (APR 1984). If the contract is for both high-value items and other end items, the contracting officer shall identify the high-value items by line item and insert the following preamble before paragraph (a):

(This clause shall apply only to those items identified in this contract as being subject to this clause.)

[FAC 90-29, 60 FR 34732, 7/3/95, effective 7/3/95; FAC 90-32, 60 FR 48206, 9/18/95, effective 10/1/95; FAC 90-43, Final rule, 61 FR 67408, 12/20/96, effective 2/18/97]

52.246-25 Limitation of Liability—Services.

As prescribed in 46.805, insert the following clause:

LIMITATION OF LIABILITY—SERVICES (FEB 1997)

(a) Except as provided in paragraphs (b) and (c) below, and except to the extent that the Contractor is expressly responsible under this contract for deficiencies in the services required to be performed under it (including any materials furnished in conjunction with those services), the Contractor shall not be liable for loss of or damage to property of the Government that (1) occurs after Government acceptance of services performed under this contract and (2) results from any defects or deficiencies in the services performed or materials furnished.

(b) The limitation of liability under paragraph (a) above shall not apply when a defect or deficiency in, or the Government's acceptance of, services performed or materials furnished results from willful misconduct or lack of good faith on the part of any of the Contractor's managerial personnel. The term *Contractor's managerial personnel* as used in this clause, means the Contractor's directors, officers, and any of the Contractor's managers, superintendents, or equivalent representatives who have supervision or direction of—

(1) All or substantially all of the Contractor's business;

(2) All or substantially all of the Contractor's operations at any one plant, laboratory, or separate location at which the contract is being performed; or

(3) A separate and complete major industrial operation connected with the performance of this contract.

(c) If the Contractor carries insurance, or has established a reserve for self-insurance, covering liability for loss or damage suffered by the Government through the Contractor's performance of services or furnishing of materials under this contract, the Contractor shall be liable to the Government, to the extent of such insurance or reserve, for loss of or damage to property of the Government occurring after Government acceptance of, and resulting from any defects and deficiencies in, services performed or materials furnished under this contract.

(End of clause)

[FAC 90-29, 60 FR 34732, 7/3/95, effective 7/3/95; FAC 90-43, Final rule, 61 FR 67408, 12/20/96, effective 2/18/97]

52.246-26 Reporting Nonconforming Items.

As prescribed in 46.317, insert the following clause:

REPORTING NONCONFORMING ITEMS (DEC 2019)

(a) *Definitions.* As used in this clause—

Common item means an item that has multiple applications versus a single or peculiar application.

Counterfeit item means an unlawful or unauthorized reproduction, substitution, or alteration that has been knowingly mismarked, misidentified, or otherwise misrepresented to be an authentic, unmodified item from the original manufacturer, or a source with the express written authority of the original manufacturer or current design activity, including an authorized aftermarket manufacturer. Unlawful or unauthorized substitution includes used items represented as new, or the false identification of grade, serial number, lot number, date code, or performance characteristics.

Critical item means an item, the failure of which is likely to result in hazardous or unsafe conditions for individuals using, maintaining, or depending upon the item; or is likely to prevent performance of a vital agency mission.

Critical nonconformance means a nonconformance that is likely to result in hazardous or unsafe conditions for individuals using, maintaining, or depending upon the supplies or services; or is likely to prevent performance of a vital agency mission.

Design activity means an organization, Government or contractor, that has responsibility for the design and configuration of an item, including the preparation or maintenance of design documents. Design activity could be the original organization, or an organization to which design responsibility has been transferred.

Major nonconformance means a nonconformance, other than critical, that is likely to result in failure of the supplies or services, or to materially reduce the usability of the supplies or services for their intended purpose.

Suspect counterfeit item means an item for which credible evidence (including but not limited to, visual inspection or testing) provides reasonable doubt that the item is authentic.

(b) The Contractor shall—

(1) Screen Government-Industry Data Exchange Program (GIDEP) reports, available at *www.gidep.org*, as a part of the Contractor's inspection system or program for the control of quality, to avoid the use and delivery of counterfeit or suspect counterfeit items or delivery of items that contain a major or critical nonconformance. This requirement does not apply if the Contractor is a foreign corporation or partnership that does not have an office, place of business, or fiscal paying agent in the United States;

(2) Provide written notification to the Contracting Officer within 60 days of becoming aware or having reason to suspect, such as through inspection, testing, record review, or notification from another source (*e.g.*, seller, customer, third party) that any end item, component, subassembly, part, or material contained in supplies purchased by the Contractor for delivery to, or for, the Government is counterfeit or suspect counterfeit;

(3) Retain counterfeit or suspect counterfeit items in its possession at the time of discovery until disposition instructions have

been provided by the Contracting Officer; and

(4) Except as provided in paragraph (c) of this clause, submit a report to GIDEP at *www.gidep.org* within 60 days of becoming aware or having reason to suspect, such as through inspection, testing, record review, or notification from another source (*e.g.*, seller, customer, third party) that an item purchased by the Contractor for delivery to, or for, the Government is—

(i) A counterfeit or suspect counterfeit item; or

(ii) A common item that has a major or critical nonconformance.

(c) The Contractor shall not submit a report as required by paragraph (b)(4) of this clause, if—

(1) The Contractor is a foreign corporation or partnership that does not have an office, place of business, or fiscal paying agent in the United States;

(2) The Contractor is aware that the counterfeit, suspect counterfeit, or nonconforming item is the subject of an on-going criminal investigation, unless the report is approved by the cognizant law-enforcement agency; or

(3) For nonconforming items other than counterfeit or suspect counterfeit items, it can be confirmed that the organization where the defect was generated (*e.g.*, original component manufacturer, original equipment manufacturer, aftermarket manufacturer, or distributor that alters item properties or configuration) has not released the item to more than one customer.

(d) Reports submitted in accordance with paragraph (b)(4) of this clause shall not include—

(1) Trade secrets or confidential commercial or financial information protected under the Trade Secrets Act (18 U.S.C. 1905); or

(2) Any other information prohibited from disclosure by statute or regulation.

(e) Additional guidance on the use of GIDEP is provided at *http://www.gidep.org/about/opmanual/opmanual.htm*.

(f) If this is a contract with the Department of Defense, as provided in paragraph (c)(5) of section 818 of the National Defense Authorization Act for Fiscal Year 2012 (Pub. L. 112-81), the Contractor or subcontractor that provides a written report or notification under this clause that the end item, component, part, or material contained electronic parts (*i.e.*, an integrated circuit, a discrete electronic component (including, but not limited to, a transistor, capacitor, resistor, or diode), or a circuit assembly)) that are counterfeit electronic parts or suspect counterfeit electronic parts shall not be subject to civil liability on the basis of such reporting, provided that the Contractor or any subcontractor made a reasonable effort to determine that the report was factual.

(g) *Subcontracts*.

(1) Except as provided in paragraph (g)(2) of this clause, the Contractor shall insert this clause, including this paragraph (g), in subcontracts that are for—

(i) Items subject to higher-level quality standards in accordance with the clause at FAR 52.246-11, Higher-Level Contract Quality Requirement;

(ii) Items that the Contractor determines to be critical items for which use of the clause is appropriate;

(iii) Electronic parts or end items, components, parts, or materials containing electronic parts, whether or not covered in paragraph (g)(1)(i) or (ii) of this clause, if the subcontract exceeds the simplified acquisition threshold and this contract is by, or for, the Department of Defense (as required by paragraph (c)(4) of section 818 of the National Defense Authorization Act for Fiscal Year 2012 (Pub. L. 112-81)); or

(iv) For the acquisition of services, if the subcontractor will furnish, as part of the service, any items that meet the criteria specified in paragraphs (g)(1)(i) through (g)(1)(iii) of this clause.

(2) The Contractor shall not insert the clause in subcontracts for—

(i) Commercial items; or

(ii) Medical devices that are subject to the Food and Drug Administration reporting requirements at 21 CFR 803.

(3) The Contractor shall not alter the clause other than to identify the appropriate parties.

(End of clause)

[FAC 90-29, 60 FR 34732, 7/3/95, effective 7/3/95; FAC 90-43, Final rule, 61 FR 67408, 12/20/96, effective 2/18/97; FAC 2020-02, 84 FR 64680, 11/22/2019, effective 12/23/2019]

52.247-1 Commercial Bill of Lading Notations.

(a) As prescribed in 47.104-4, insert the following clause:

COMMERCIAL BILL OF LADING NOTATIONS (FEB 2006)

When the Contracting Officer authorizes supplies to be shipped on a commercial bill of lading and the Contractor will be reimbursed these transportation costs as direct allowable costs, the Contractor shall ensure before shipment is made that the commercial shipping documents are annotated with either of the following notations, as appropriate:

(a) If the Government is shown as the consignor or the consignee, the annotation shall be:

"Transportation is for the ____ [*name the specific agency*] and the actual total transportation charges paid to the carrier(s) by the consignor or consignee are assignable to, and shall be reimbursed by, the Government."

(b) If the Government is not shown as the consignor or the consignee, the annotation shall be:

"Transportation is for the ____ [*name the specific agency*] and the actual total transportation charges paid to the carrier(s) by the consignor or consignee shall be reimbursed by the Government, pursuant to cost-reimbursement contract No. ____ This may be confirmed by contacting ____ [*name and address of the contract administration office listed in the contract*]."

(End of clause)

[FAC 84-53, 54 FR 48997, 11/28/89, effective 12/28/89; Final rule, 55 FR 38518, 9/18/90; FAC 90-29, 60 FR 34732, 7/3/95, effective 7/3/95; FAC 2005-07, 71 FR 200, 1/3/2006, effective 2/2/2006]

52.247-2 Permits, Authorities, or Franchises.

As prescribed in 47.207-1(a), insert the following clause:

PERMITS, AUTHORITIES, OR FRANCHISES (JAN 1997)

(a) The offeror does [], does not [], hold authorization from the Federal Highway Administration (FHWA) or other cognizant regulatory body. If authorization is held, it is as follows:

____

(Name of regulatory body)

____

(Authorization No.)

(b) The offeror shall furnish to the Government, if requested, copies of the authorization before moving the material under any contract awarded. In addition, the offeror shall, at the offeror's expense, obtain and maintain any permits, franchises, licenses, and other authorities issued by State and local governments.

(End of clause)

[FAC 90-32, 60 FR 48206, 9/18/95, effective 10/1/95; FAC 90-45, Final rule, 62 FR 224, 1/2/97, effective 1/1/97]

52.247-3 Capability to Perform a Contract for the Relocation of a Federal Office.

As prescribed in 47.207-1(b), insert the following clause in solicitations and contracts for transportation or for transportation-related services when a Federal office is relocated, to ensure that offerors are capable to perform interstate or intrastate moving contracts involving the relocation of Federal offices:

CAPABILITY TO PERFORM A CONTRACT FOR THE RELOCATION OF A FEDERAL OFFICE (FEB 2006)

(a) If the move specified in this contract is to be performed by the Contractor as a carrier within the borders of more than one State, including the District of Columbia, (i.e., an interstate move), the Contractor shall have obtained and hold appropriate and current operating authority from the Federal Motor Carrier Safety Administration.

(b) (1) If the move specified in this contract is to be performed by the Contractor as a carrier wholly within the borders of one State or the District of Columbia (i.e., an intrastate move), the Contractor shall, when required by the State, or the District of Columbia, in which the move is to take place, have obtained and hold appropriate and current operating authority from that jurisdiction in the form of a certificate, permit, or equivalent license to operate.

(2) If no authority to operate is required by the State or the District of Columbia, the Contractor as carrier shall maintain facilities, equipment, and a business address within the jurisdiction in which the move is to take place. However, if the move is to originate and/or terminate within an area of one State, or the District of Columbia, that comprises a part of a recognized Commercial Zone (see Subpart B of 49 CFR part 372) the boundaries of which encompass portions of more than one State or the District of Columbia, it shall be sufficient if the Contractor as carrier maintains facilities, equipment, and a business address within the Commercial Zone and holds appropriate operating authority, if required, from the jurisdiction within which the Contractor maintains the facilities, equipment, and business address.

(c) If the move specified in this contract will not be performed by the Contractor as carrier, it must be performed for the Contractor by a carrier operating under a subcontract with the Contractor. In this case, the Contractor shall not be subject to the requirements of paragraphs (a) and (b) above, but shall be responsible for requiring and ensuring that the subcontractor carrier complies with those requirements in every respect.

(d) The Contractor shall be in compliance with the applicable requirements of this clause at least 14 days before the date on which performance of the contract shall commence under the terms specified; *except* that, if the period from the date of award of the contract to the date that performance shall commence is less than 28 days, the Contractor shall comply with the applicable requirements of this clause midway between the time of award and the time of commencement of performance.

(End of clause)

Alternate I (APR 1984). If a Federal office move is intrastate and the contracting officer determines that it is in the Government's interest not to apply the requirements for holding or obtaining State authority to operate within the State, and to maintain a facility within the State or Commercial zone, delete paragraph (b) of the basic clause and redesignate the remaining paragraphs "(b) and (c)." In the 6th line of the new paragraph (b), delete the words "paragraphs (a) and (b) above" and replace them with "paragraph (a) above."

[FAC 90-32, 60 FR 48206, 9/18/95, effective 10/1/95; FAC 2005-07, 71 FR 200, 1/3/2006, effective 2/2/2006]

52.247-4 Inspection of Shipping and Receiving Facilities.

As prescribed in 47.207-1(c), insert the following provision in solicitations for transportation or for transportation-related services when it is desired for offerors to inspect the shipping, receiving, or other sites to ensure realistic bids:

INSPECTION OF SHIPPING AND RECEIVING FACILITIES (APR 1984)

(a) Offerors are urged to inspect the shipping and receiving facilities where services are to be performed and to satisfy themselves regarding all general and local conditions that may affect the cost of contract performance.

(b) Site visits have been scheduled as follows:

(locations)

(dates)

(times)

(c) For further information offerors may contact:

(name)

(telephone)

(End of provision)

[FAC 90-32, 60 FR 48206, 9/18/95, effective 10/1/95]

52.247-5 Familiarization with Conditions.

As prescribed in 47.207-1(d), insert the following clause in solicitations and contracts for transportation or for transportation-related services to ensure that offerors become familiar with conditions under which and where the services will be performed:

FAMILIARIZATION WITH CONDITIONS (APR 1984)

The offeror shall become familiar with all available information regarding difficulties that may be encountered and the conditions, including safety precautions, under which the work must be accomplished under the contract. The offeror shall not be relieved from assuming all responsibility for properly estimating the difficulties and the cost of performing the services required in this contract because the offeror failed to investigate the conditions or to become acquainted with all information concerning the services to be performed.

(End of clause)

[FAC 90-32, 60 FR 48206, 9/18/95, effective 10/1/95]

52.247-6 Financial Statement.

As prescribed in 47.207-1(e), insert the following provision in solicitations for transportation or for transportation-related services to ensure that offerors are prepared to furnish financial statements:

FINANCIAL STATEMENT (APR 1984)

The offeror shall, upon request, promptly furnish the Government with a current certified statement of the offeror's financial condition and such data as the Government may request with respect to the offeror's operations. The Government will use this information to determine the offeror's financial responsibility and ability to perform under the contract. Failure of an offeror to comply with a request for information will subject the offer to possible rejection on responsibility grounds.

(End of provision)

[FAC 90-32, 60 FR 48206, 9/18/95, effective 10/1/95]

52.247-7 Freight Excluded.

As prescribed in 47.207-3(d)(2), insert a clause substantially as follows in solicitations and contracts for transportation or for transportation-related services when any commodities or types of shipments have been identified for exclusion:

FREIGHT EXCLUDED (APR 1984)

Excluded from the scope of this contract are shipments that can be more advantageously or economically moved via parcel post or small package carrier; shipments of unusual value, explosives and other dangerous articles, household goods, commodities in bulk, commodities injurious or contaminating to other freight; and shipments that the Government may elect to move in Government vehicles.

(End of clause)

[FAC 90-32, 60 FR 48206, 9/18/95, effective 10/1/95]

52.247-8 Estimated Weights or Quantities Not Guaranteed.

As prescribed in 47.207-3(e)(2), insert the following clause in solicitations and contracts for transportation or for transportation-related services when weights or quantities are estimates:

ESTIMATED WEIGHTS OR QUANTITIES NOT GUARANTEED (APR 1984)

The estimated weights or quantities are not a guarantee of actual weights or quantities, as the Government does not guarantee any particular volume of traffic described in this contract. However, to the extent services are required as described in this contract and in accordance with the terms of this contract, orders for these services will be placed with the Contractor.

(End of clause)

[FAC 90-32, 60 FR 48206, 9/18/95, effective 10/1/95]

52.247-9 Agreed Weight—General Freight.

As prescribed in 47.207-4(a)(1), insert the following clause in solicitations and contracts for transportation or for transportation-related services when the shipping activity determines the weight of shipments of freight other than household goods or office furniture:

AGREED WEIGHT—GENERAL FREIGHT (APR 1984)

The shipping activity shall determine the weight of each shipment. The weight shall be shown on the covering shipping document and shall be accepted by the Contractor as the agreed weight.

(End of clause)

[FAC 90-32, 60 FR 48206, 9/18/95, effective 10/1/95]

52.247-10 Net Weight—General Freight.

As prescribed in 47.207-4(a)(2), insert the following clause in solicitations and contracts for transportation or for transportation-related services when the weight of shipments of freight other than household goods or office furniture is not known at the time of shipment and the contractor is responsible for determining the net weight of the shipments:

NET WEIGHT—GENERAL FREIGHT (APR 1984)

(a) The net weight of the shipment shall be determined by deducting the tare weight of the vehicle (determined by having the empty vehicle with a full tank of fuel weighed by a certified weighmaster on a certified scale) from the gross weight of the vehicle (determined by having the loaded vehicle with a full tank of fuel weighed by a certified weighmaster on a certified scale).

(b) The Contractor shall attach the original copies of the empty and loaded weight certificates to the invoice for services.

(End of clause)

[FAC 90-32, 60 FR 48206, 9/18/95, effective 10/1/95]

52.247-11 Net Weight—Household Goods or Office Furniture.

As prescribed in 47.207-4(b), insert the following clause in contracts for transportation or for transportation-related services when movements of Government employees' household goods or relocations of Government offices are involved:

NET WEIGHT—HOUSEHOLD GOODS OR OFFICE FURNITURE (APR 1984)

(a) *Net weight—full loads.* The net weight of the shipment shall be determined by deducting the tare weight of the vehicle (determined by having a certified weighmaster weigh on a certified scale the empty vehicle with all blankets, pads, chains, dollies, hand trucks, and all other necessary equipment inside the vehicle) from the gross weight of the vehicle (determined by having a certified weighmaster weigh on a certified scale the fully loaded vehicle before arrival at destination).

(b) *Net weight—part loads.* The net weight of the first part load shall be determined in the same manner as specified for a full load. The net weight of the second part load shall be determined by using as the tare weight of the vehicle the gross weight of the vehicle containing the first part load and deducting this weight from the new gross weight (determined by having the loaded vehicle weighed again, in the same manner as specified for the full load). The same procedure shall apply for each succeeding part load.

(c) *Weight certificates.* The contractor shall attach the original copy of each weight certificate to the invoice for services.

(End of clause)

[FAC 90-32, 60 FR 48206, 9/18/95, effective 10/1/95]

52.247-12 Supervision, Labor, or Materials.

As prescribed in 47.207-5(b), insert a clause substantially as follows in solicitations and contracts for transportation or for transportation-related services when the contractor is required to furnish supervision, labor, or materials:

SUPERVISION, LABOR, OR MATERIALS (APR 1984)

The Contractor shall furnish adequate supervision, labor, materials, supplies, and equipment necessary to perform all the services contemplated under this contract in an orderly, timely, and efficient manner.

(End of clause)

[FAC 90-32, 60 FR 48206, 9/18/95, effective 10/1/95]

52.247-13 Accessorial Services—Moving Contracts.

As prescribed in 47.207-5(c), insert a clause substantially as follows in solicitations and contracts for the transportation of household goods or office furniture:

ACCESSORIAL SERVICES—MOVING CONTRACTS (APR 1984)

(a) *Packing and/or crating and padding.* The Contractor shall—

(1) Perform all of the packing and/or crating and padding necessary for the protection of the goods to be transported;

(2) Furnish packing containers, including, but not limited to, barrels, boxes, wardrobes, and cartons; all crating materials; and all padding materials and equipment;

(3) Furnish or cause to be furnished, when necessary, padding or other protective material for the interior of the buildings, including elevators, from and to which the property will be moved under this contract; and

(4) Ensure that all containers and materials are clean and of quality sufficient for protection of the goods.

(b) *Disassembling and reassembling of property and servicing appliances.* The disassembling of property; e.g., beds and sectional bookcases, and the preparing of appliances; e.g., washers, driers, and record players, for shipment shall be performed by the Contractor. The Contractor shall reassemble the property and service the appliances upon delivery at the new location.

(c) *Unpacking and/or uncrating and placement of property.* The Contractor shall unpack and/or uncrate all property that was packed and/or crated for movement under this contract. The Contractor shall also place the property in the new location as instructed by the owner of the property or authorized representative, and shall remove all packing and similar or related material from the premises as requested by the owner.

(End of clause)

[FAC 90-32, 60 FR 48206, 9/18/95, effective 10/1/95]

52.247-14 Contractor Responsibility for Receipt of Shipment.

As prescribed in 47.207-5(d), insert the following clause in solicitations and contracts for transportation or for transportation-related services:

CONTRACTOR RESPONSIBILITY FOR RECEIPT OF SHIPMENT (APR 1984)

The Contractor shall diligently count and examine all goods tendered for shipment, receipt for them, and make appropriate written exception for any goods not in apparent good order.

(End of clause)

[FAC 90-32, 60 FR 48206, 9/18/95, effective 10/1/95]

52.247-15 Contractor Responsibility for Loading and Unloading.

As prescribed in 47.207-5(e), insert the following clause in solicitations and contracts for transportation or for transportation-related services when the contractor is responsible for loading and unloading shipments:

CONTRACTOR RESPONSIBILITY FOR LOADING AND UNLOADING (APR 1984)

(a) (1) Unless otherwise specified in this contract to cover store-door or inside delivery, the Contractor shall load and unload shipments at no additional expense to the Government.

(2) The Government or its agent will place or receive freight at the tailgate of the Contractor's vehicle. Tailgate delivery, for purposes of this contract, is defined as that which enables a forklift truck or similar equipment, with operator only, to place or remove cargo from the tailgate of the Contractor's vehicle.

(b) If loading is the responsibility of the Contractor, the Contractor shall perform all shoring, blocking, and bracing. The Contractor shall provide dunnage at the Contractor's expense.

(End of clause)

[FAC 90-32, 60 FR 48206, 9/18/95, effective 10/1/95]

52.247-16 Contractor Responsibility for Returning Undelivered Freight.

As prescribed in 47.207-5(f), insert the following clause in solicitations and contracts for transportation or for transportation-related services when the contractor is responsible for returning undelivered freight:

CONTRACTOR RESPONSIBILITY FOR RETURNING UNDELIVERED FREIGHT (APR 1984)

(a) When, through no fault of the Contractor, a shipment cannot be delivered, the Contractor shall contact the shipper for disposition instructions. If the shipment is ordered returned to the origin point, the charges assessed for the return trip shall be the same as the charges assessed for the outbound trip. The shipper shall maintain a record of the goods that, through no fault of the Contractor, could not be delivered and are returned to the shipper. If, at a future date, the returned goods are determined to be related to a claim against the Contractor, the claim will be adjusted accordingly.

(b) When, through the fault of the Contractor, a shipment cannot be delivered, the Contractor shall return the shipment to the origin point at no charge to the Government. Any charges incurred for redelivery, which are in excess of the charges that would have been incurred under this contract, shall be for the Contractor's account in accordance with the Default clause of the contract.

(End of clause)

[FAC 90-32, 60 FR 48206, 9/18/95, effective 10/1/95]

52.247-17 Charges.

As prescribed in 47.207-6(a)(2), insert the following clause in solicitations and contracts for transportation or for transportation-related services:

CHARGES (APR 1984)

In no event shall charges under this contract be in excess of charges based on the Contractor's lowest rate available to the general public, or be in excess of charges based on rates otherwise tendered to the Government by the Contractor for the same type of service.

(End of clause)

[FAC 90-32, 60 FR 48206, 9/18/95, effective 10/1/95]

52.247-18 Multiple Shipments.

As prescribed in 47.207-6(c)(5)(i), insert the following clause in solicitations and contracts for transportation or for transportation-related services when multiple shipments are tendered at one time to the contractor for transportation from one origin to two or more consignees at the same destination:

MULTIPLE SHIPMENTS (APR 1984)

When multiple shipments are tendered at one time to the Contractor for movement from one origin to multiple consignees at the same destination, the rate charged for each shipment shall be the rate applicable to the aggregate weight.

(End of clause)

[FAC 90-32, 60 FR 48206, 9/18/95, effective 10/1/95]

52.247-19 Stopping in Transit for Partial Unloading.

As prescribed in 47.207-6(c)(5)(ii), insert the following clause in solicitations and contracts for transportation or for transportation-related services when multiple shipments are tendered at one time to the contractor for transportation from one origin to two or more consignees along the route between origin and last destination:

STOPPING IN TRANSIT FOR PARTIAL UNLOADING (APR 1984)

When multiple shipments are tendered at one time to the Contractor for movement from one origin to two or more consignees along the route between the origin and the last destination, the rate charged shall be the rate applicable to the aggregate weight, plus a charge of $____ for each shipment unloaded at an intermediate point en route to the last destination.

(End of clause)

[FAC 90-32, 60 FR 48206, 9/18/95, effective 10/1/95]

52.247-20 Estimated Quantities or Weights for Evaluation of Offers.

As prescribed in 47.207-6(c)(6), insert the following provision in solicitations for transportation or for transportation-related services when quantities or weights of shipments between each origin and destination are not known, stating estimated quantity or weight for each origin/destination pair:

ESTIMATED QUANTITIES OR WEIGHTS FOR EVALUATION OF OFFERS (APR 1984)

For the purpose of evaluating offers, and for no other purpose, the following estimated quantities or weights will be considered as the quantities or weights to be shipped between each origin and destination listed:

Origin	Destination	Estimated quantity or weight

(End of provision)

[FAC 90-32, 60 FR 48206, 9/18/95, effective 10/1/95]

52.247-21 Contractor Liability for Personal Injury and/or Property Damage.

As prescribed in 47.207-7(c), insert the following clause in solicitations and contracts for transportation or for transportation-related services:

CONTRACTOR LIABILITY FOR PERSONAL INJURY AND/OR PROPERTY DAMAGE (APR 1984)

(a) The Contractor assumes responsibility for all damage or injury to persons or property occasioned through the use, maintenance, and operation of the Contractor's vehicles or other equipment by, or the action of, the Contractor or the Contractor's employees and agents.

(b) The Contractor, at the Contractor's expense, shall maintain adequate public liability and property damage insurance during the continuance of this contract, insuring the Contractor against all claims for injury or damage.

(c) The Contractor shall maintain Workers' Compensation and other legally required insurance with respect to the Contractor's own employees and agents.

(d) The Government shall in no event be liable or responsible for damage or injury to any person or property occasioned through the use, maintenance, or operation of any vehicle or other equipment by, or the action of, the Contractor or the Contractor's employees and agents in performing under this contract, and the Government shall be indemnified and saved harmless against claims for damage or injury in such cases.

(End of clause)

[FAC 90-32, 60 FR 48206, 9/18/95, effective 10/1/95]

52.247-22 Contractor Liability for Loss of and/or Damage to Freight other than Household Goods.

As prescribed in 47.207-7(d), insert the following clause in solicitations and contracts for the transportation of freight other than household goods:

CONTRACTOR LIABILITY FOR LOSS OF AND/OR DAMAGE TO FREIGHT OTHER THAN HOUSEHOLD GOODS (APR 1984)

Except when loss and/or damage arises out of causes beyond the control and without the fault or negligence of the Contractor, the Contractor shall assume full liability for any and all goods lost and/or damaged in the movement covered by this contract.

(End of clause)

[FAC 90-32, 60 FR 48206, 9/18/95, effective 10/1/95]

52.247-23 Contractor Liability for Loss of and/or Damage to Household Goods.

As prescribed in 47.207-7(e), insert the following clause:

CONTRACTOR LIABILITY FOR LOSS OF AND/OR DAMAGE TO HOUSEHOLD GOODS (JAN 1991)

(a) Except when loss and/or damage arise out of causes beyond the control and without the fault or negligence of the Contractor, the Contractor shall be liable to the owner for the loss of and/or damage to any article while being—

(1) Packed, picked up, loaded, transported, delivered, unloaded, or unpacked;

(2) Stored in transit; or

(3) Serviced (appliances, etc.) by a third person hired by the Contractor to perform the servicing.

(b) The Contractor shall be liable for loss and/or damage discovered by the owner if written notice of such loss and/or damage is dispatched to the Contractor not later than 75 days following the date of delivery.

(c) The Contractor shall indemnify the owner of the goods at a rate of ____ cents per pound per article.

(End of clause)

[FAC 90-3, 55 FR 52800, 12/21/90, effective 1/22/91]

52.247-24 Advance Notification by the Government.

As prescribed in 47.207-8(a)(1), insert the following clause in solicitations and contracts for transportation or for transportation-related services when the Government is responsible for notifying the contractor of specific service times or unusual shipments:

ADVANCE NOTIFICATION BY THE GOVERNMENT (APR 1984)

The Government will notify the Contractor ____ hours in advance of the number of pieces and weight of all normal shipments and the time the shipment will be available for pickup. On other-than-normal shipments, the Government will furnish additional information; e.g., dimension of oversized pieces, as necessary to determine the amount of equipment and/or manpower needed to perform the required services.

(End of clause)

[FAC 90-32, 60 FR 48206, 9/18/95, effective 10/1/95]

52.247-25 Government-Furnished Equipment with or without Operators.

As prescribed in 47.207-8(a)(2)(i), insert the following clause in solicitations and contracts for transportation or for transportation-related services when the Government furnishes equipment with or without operators:

GOVERNMENT-FURNISHED EQUIPMENT WITH OR WITHOUT OPERATORS (APR 1984)

The Government will provide ____ [*insert equipment; e.g., forklifts*] with or without operators at ____ [*strike out "with" or "without," as applicable, and insert origin, destination, or both*] to assist in ____ [*insert loading, unloading, or both*], when required.

(End of clause)

[FAC 90-32, 60 FR 48206, 9/18/95, effective 10/1/95]

52.247-26 Government Direction and Marking.

As prescribed in 47.207-8(a)(3), insert the following clause in solicitations and contracts for transportation or for transportation-related services when office relocations are involved:

GOVERNMENT DIRECTION AND MARKING (APR 1984)

The agency being relocated shall tag or mark property, showing floor, room number, and location where property is to be placed in the new building. The agency shall provide sufficient personnel to direct the Contractor's personnel in the placement of the property at destination.

(End of clause)

[FAC 90-32, 60 FR 48206, 9/18/95, effective 10/1/95]

52.247-27 Contract Not Affected by Oral Agreement.

As prescribed in 47.207-8(b), insert the following clause in solicitations and contracts for transportation or for transportation-related services:

CONTRACT NOT AFFECTED BY ORAL AGREEMENT (APR 1984)

No oral statement of any person shall modify or otherwise affect the terms, conditions, or specifications stated in this contract. All modifications to the contract must be made in writing by the Contracting Officer or an authorized representative.

(End of clause)

[FAC 90-32, 60 FR 48206, 9/18/95, effective 10/1/95]

52.247-28 Contractor's Invoices.

As prescribed in 47.207-9(c), insert the following clause in solicitations and contracts for drayage or other term contracts for transportation or for transportation-related services:

CONTRACTOR'S INVOICES (APR 1984)

The Contractor shall submit itemized invoices as instructed by the agency ordering services under this contract. The Contractor shall annotate each invoice with the contract number and other ordering office document identification.

(End of clause)

[FAC 90-32, 60 FR 48206, 9/18/95, effective 10/1/95]

52.247-29 F.o.b. Origin.

As prescribed in 47.303-1(c), insert the following clause:

F.O.B. ORIGIN (FEB 2006)

(a) The term *f.o.b. origin* as used in this clause, means free of expense to the Government delivered—

(1) On board the indicated type of conveyance of the carrier (or of the Government, if specified) at a designated point in the city, county, and State from which the shipment will be made and from which line-haul transportation service (as distinguished from switching, local drayage, or other terminal service) will begin;

(2) To, and placed on, the carrier's wharf (at shipside, within reach of the ship's loading tackle, when the shipping point is within a port area having water transportation service) or the carrier's freight station;

(3) To a U.S. Postal Service facility; or

(4) If stated in the solicitation, to any Government designated point located within the same city or commercial zone as the f.o.b. origin point specified in the contract (the Federal Motor Carrier Safety Administration prescribes commercial zones at Subpart B of 49 CFR part 372).

(b) The Contractor shall—

(1) (i) Pack and mark the shipment to comply with contract specifications; or

(ii) In the absence of specifications, prepare the shipment in conformance with carrier requirements to protect the goods and to ensure assessment of the lowest applicable transportation charge;

(2) (i) Order specified carrier equipment when requested by the Government; or

(ii) If not specified, order appropriate carrier equipment not in excess of capacity to accommodate shipment;

(3) Deliver the shipment in good order and condition to the carrier, and load, stow, trim, block, and/or brace carload or truckload shipment (when loaded by the Contractor) on or in the carrier's conveyance as required by carrier rules and regulations;

(4) Be responsible for any loss of and/or damage to the goods—

(i) Occurring before delivery to the carrier;

(ii) Resulting from improper packing and marking; or

(iii) Resulting from improper loading, stowing, trimming, blocking, and/or bracing of the shipment, if loaded by the Contractor on or in the carrier's conveyance;

(5) Complete the Government bill of lading supplied by the ordering agency or, when a Government bill of lading is not supplied, prepare a commercial bill of lading or other transportation receipt. The bill of lading shall show—

(i) A description of the shipment in terms of the governing freight classification or tariff (or Government rate tender) under which lowest freight rates are applicable;

(ii) The seals affixed to the conveyance with their serial numbers or other identification;

(iii) Lengths and capacities of cars or trucks ordered and furnished;

(iv) Other pertinent information required to effect prompt delivery to the consignee, including name, delivery address, postal address and ZIP code of consignee, routing, etc.;

(v) Special instructions or annotations requested by the ordering agency for commercial bills of lading; e.g., "This shipment is the property of, and the freight charges paid to the carrier(s) will be reimbursed by, the Government"; and

(vi) The signature of the carrier's agent and the date the shipment is received by the carrier; and

(6) Distribute the copies of the bill of lading, or other transportation receipts, as directed by the ordering agency.

(c) These Contractor responsibilities are specified for performance at the plant or plants at which the supplies are to be finally inspected and accepted, unless the facilities for shipment by carrier's equipment are not available at the Contractor's plant, in which case the responsibilities shall be performed f.o.b. the point or points in the same or nearest city where the specified carrier's facilities are available; subject, however, to the following qualifications:

(1) If the Contractor's shipping plant is located in the State of Alaska or Hawaii, the Contractor shall deliver the supplies listed for shipment outside Alaska or Hawaii to the port of loading in Alaska or Hawaii, respectively, as specified in the contract, at Contractor's expense, and to that extent the contract shall be "f.o.b. destination."

(2) Notwithstanding subparagraph (c)(1) of this clause, if the Contractor's shipping plant is located in the State of Hawaii, and the contract requires delivery to be made by container service, the Contractor shall deliver the supplies, at the Contractor's expense, to the container yard in the same or nearest city where seavan container service is available.

(End of clause)

[FAC 84-37, 53 FR 17860, 5/18/88, effective 6/17/88; FAC 2005-07, 71 FR 200, 1/3/2006, effective 2/2/2006]

52.247-30 F.o.b. Origin, Contractor's Facility.

As prescribed in 47.303-2(c), insert the following clause in solicitations and contracts when the delivery term is f.o.b. origin, contractor's facility:

F.O.B. ORIGIN, CONTRACTOR'S FACILITY (FEB 2006)

(a) The term *f.o.b. origin, contractor's facility* as used in this clause, means free of expense to the Government delivered on board the indicated type of conveyance of the carrier (or of the Government, if specified) at the designated facility, on the named street or highway, in the city, county, and State from which the shipment will be made.

(b) The Contractor shall—

(1) (i) Pack and mark the shipment to comply with contract specifications; or

(ii) In the absence of specifications, prepare the shipment in conformance with carrier requirements to protect the goods and to ensure assessment of the lowest applicable transportation charge;

(2) (i) Order specified carrier equipment when requested by the Government; or

(ii) If not specified, order appropriate carrier equipment not in excess of capacity to accommodate shipment;

(3) Deliver the shipment in good order and condition to the carrier, and load, stow, trim, block, and/or brace carload or truckload shipment (when loaded by the Contractor) on or in the carrier's conveyance as required by carrier rules and regulations;

(4) Be responsible for any loss of and/or damage to the goods—

(i) Occurring before delivery to the carrier;

(ii) Resulting from improper packing and marking; or

(iii) Resulting from improper loading, stowing, trimming, blocking, and/or bracing of the shipment, if loaded by the Contractor on or in the carrier's conveyance;

(5) Complete the Government bill of lading supplied by the ordering agency or, when a Government bill of lading is not supplied, prepare a commercial bill of lading or other transportation receipt. The bill of lading shall show—

(i) A description of the shipment in terms of the governing freight classification or tariff (or Government rate tender) under which lowest freight rates are applicable;

(ii) The seals affixed to the conveyance with their serial numbers or other identification;

(iii) Lengths and capacities of cars or trucks ordered and furnished;

(iv) Other pertinent information required to effect prompt delivery to the consignee, including name, delivery address, postal address and ZIP code of consignee, routing, etc.;

(v) Special instructions or annotations requested by the ordering agency for bills of lading; e.g., "This shipment is the property of, and the freight charges paid to the carrier(s) will be reimbursed by, the Government"; and

(vi) The signature of the carrier's agent and the date the shipment is received by the carrier; and

(6) Distribute the copies of the bill of lading, or other transportation receipts, as directed by the ordering agency.

(End of clause)

[FAC 90-32, 60 FR 48206, 9/18/95, effective 10/1/95; FAC 2005-07, 71 FR 200, 1/3/2006, effective 2/2/2006]

52.247-31 F.o.b. Origin, Freight Allowed.

As prescribed in 47.303-3(c), insert the following clause:

F.O.B. ORIGIN, FREIGHT ALLOWED (FEB 2006)

(a) The term *f.o.b. origin, freight allowed* as used in this clause, means—

(1) Free of expense to the Government delivered—

(i) On board the indicated type of conveyance of the carrier (or of the Government, if specified) at a designated point in the city, county, and State from which the shipments will be made and from which line-haul transportation service (as distinguished from switching, local drayage, or other terminal service) will begin;

(ii) To, and placed on, the carrier's wharf (at shipside within reach of the ship's loading tackle when the shipping point is within a port area having water transportation service) or the carrier's freight station;

(iii) To a U.S. Postal Service facility; or

(iv) If stated in the solicitation, to any Government-designated point located within the same city or commercial zone as the f.o.b. origin point specified in the contract the Federal Motor Carrier Safety Administration prescribes commercial zones at Subpart B of 49 CFR part 372; and

(2) An allowance for freight, based on applicable published tariff rates (or Government rate tenders) between the points specified in the contract, is deducted from the contract price.

(b) The Contractor shall—

(1) (i) Pack and mark the shipment to comply with contract specifications; or

(ii) In the absence of specifications, prepare the shipment in conformance with carrier requirements to protect the goods and to ensure assessment of the lowest applicable transportation charge;

(2) (i) Order specified carrier equipment when requested by the Government; or

(ii) If not specified, order appropriate carrier equipment not in excess of capacity to accommodate shipment;

(3) Deliver the shipment in good order and condition to the carrier, and load, stow, trim, block, and/or brace carload or truckload shipment (when loaded by the Contractor) on or in the carrier's conveyance as required by carrier rules and regulations;

(4) Be responsible for any loss of and/or damage to the goods—

(i) Occurring before delivery to the carrier;

(ii) Resulting from improper packing and marking; or

(iii) Resulting from improper loading, stowing, trimming, blocking, and/or bracing of the shipment, if loaded by the Contractor on or in the carrier's conveyance;

(5) Complete the Government bill of lading supplied by the ordering agency, or when a Government bill of lading is not supplied, prepare a commercial bill of lading or other transportation receipt. The bill of lading shall show—

(i) A description of the shipment in terms of the governing freight classification or tariff (or Government rate tender) under which lowest freight rates are applicable;

(ii) The seals affixed to the conveyance with their serial numbers or other identification;

(iii) Lengths and capacities of cars or trucks ordered and furnished;

(iv) Other pertinent information required to effect prompt delivery to the consignee, including name, delivery address, postal address and ZIP code of consignee, routing, etc.;

(v) Special instructions or annotations requested by the ordering agency for commercial bills of lading; e.g., "This shipment is the property of, and the freight charges paid to the carrier(s) will be reimbursed by, the Government"; and

(vi) The signature of the carrier's agent and the date the shipment is received by the carrier; and

(6) Distribute the copies of the bill of lading, or other transportation receipts, as directed by the ordering agency.

(c) These Contractor responsibilities are specified for performance at the plant or plants at which the supplies are to be finally inspected and accepted, unless the facilities for shipment by carrier's equipment are not available at the Contractor's plant, in which case the responsibilities shall be performed f.o.b. the point or points in the same or nearest city where the specified carrier's facilities are available; subject, however, to the following qualifications:

(1) If the Contractor's shipping plant is located in the State of Alaska or Hawaii, the Contractor shall deliver the supplies listed for shipment outside Alaska or Hawaii to the port of loading in Alaska or Hawaii, respectively, as specified in the contract, at Contractor's expense, and to that extent the contract shall be "f.o.b. destination."

(2) Notwithstanding subparagraph (c)(1) of this clause, if the Contractor's shipping plant is located in the State of Hawaii, and the contract requires delivery to be made by container service, the Contractor shall deliver the supplies, at Contractor's expense, to the container yard in the same or nearest city where seavan container service is available.

(End of clause)

[FAC 84-37, 53 FR 17860, 5/18/88, effective 6/17/88; FAC 2005-07, 71 FR 200, 1/3/2006, effective 2/2/2006]

52.247-32 F.o.b. Origin, Freight Prepaid.

As prescribed in 47.303-4(c), insert the following clause:

F.O.B. ORIGIN, FREIGHT PREPAID (FEB 2006)

(a) The term *f.o.b. origin, freight prepaid* as used in this clause, means—

(1) Free of expense to the Government delivered—

(i) On board the indicated type of conveyance of the carrier (or of the Government if specified) at a designated point in the city, county, and State from which the shipments will be made and from which line-haul transportation service (as distinguished from switching, local drayage, or other terminal service) will begin;

(ii) To, and placed on, the carrier's wharf (at shipside, within reach of the ship's loading tackle, when the shipping point is within a port area having water transportation service) or the carrier's freight station;

(iii) To a U.S. Postal Service facility; or

(iv) If stated in the solicitation, to any Government designated point located within the same city or commercial zone as the f.o.b. origin point specified in the contract (the Federal Motor Carrier Safety Administration prescribes at Subpart B of 49 CFR part 372); and

(2) The cost of transportation, ultimately the Government's obligation, is prepaid by the contractor to the point specified in the contract.

(b) The Contractor shall—

(1) (i) Pack and mark the shipment to comply with contract specifications; or

(ii) In the absence of specifications, prepare the shipment in conformance with carrier requirements to protect the goods and to ensure assessment of the lowest applicable transportation charge;

(2) (i) Order specified carrier equipment when requested by the Government; or

(ii) If not specified, order appropriate carrier equipment not in excess of capacity to accommodate shipment;

(3) Deliver the shipment in good order and condition to the carrier, and load, stow, trim, block, and/or brace carload or truckload shipment (when loaded by the Contractor) on or in the carrier's conveyance as required by carrier rules and regulations;

(4) Be responsible for any loss of and/or damage to the goods—

(i) Occurring before delivery to the carrier;

(ii) Resulting from improper packing or marking; or

(iii) Resulting from improper loading, stowing, trimming, blocking, and/or bracing of the shipment, if loaded by the Contractor on or in the carrier's conveyance;

(5) Prepare a commercial bill of lading or other transportation receipt. The bill of lading shall show—

(i) A description of the shipment in terms of the governing freight classification or tariff (or Government rate tender) under which lowest freight rates are applicable;

(ii) The seals affixed to the conveyance with their serial numbers or other identification;

(iii) Lengths and capacities of cars or trucks ordered and furnished;

(iv) Other pertinent information required to effect prompt delivery to the consignee, including name, delivery address, postal address and ZIP code of consignee, routing, etc.;

(v) Special instructions or annotations requested by the ordering agency for bills of lading; e.g., "This shipment is the property of, and the freight charges paid to the carrier (s) will be reimbursed by the Government"; and

(vi) The signature of the carrier's agent and the date the shipment is received by the carrier;

(6) Distribute the copies of the bill of lading, or other transportation receipts, as directed by the ordering agency; and

(7) Prepay all freight charges to the extent specified in the contract.

(c) These Contractor responsibilities are specified for performance at the plant or plants at which these supplies are to be finally inspected and accepted, unless the facilities for shipment by carrier's equipment are not available at the Contractor's plant, in which case the responsibilities shall be performed f.o.b. the point or points in the same or nearest city where the specified carrier's facilities are available; subject, however, to the following qualifications:

(1) If the Contractor's shipping plant is located in the State of Alaska or Hawaii, the Contractor shall deliver the supplies listed for shipment outside Alaska or Hawaii to the port of loading in Alaska or Hawaii, respectively, as specified in the contract, at Contractor's expense, and to that extent the contract shall be "f.o.b. destination."

(2) Notwithstanding subparagraph (c)(1) of this clause, if the Contractor's shipping plant is located in the State of Hawaii, and the contract requires delivery to be made by container service, the Contractor shall deliver the supplies, at the Contractor's expense, to the container yard in the same or nearest city where seavan container service is available.

(End of clause)

[FAC 84-37, 53 FR 17861, 5/18/88, effective 6/17/88; FAC 2005-07, 71 FR 200, 1/3/2006, effective 2/2/2006]

52.247-33 F.o.b. Origin, with Differentials.

As prescribed in 47.303-5(c), insert the following clause:

F.O.B. ORIGIN, WITH DIFFERENTIALS (FEB 2006)

(a) The term *f.o.b. origin, with differentials* as used in this clause, means—

(1) Free of expense to the Government delivered—

(i) On board the indicated type of conveyance of the carrier (or of the Government, if specified) at a designated point in the city, county, and State from which the shipments will be made and from which line-haul transportation service (as distinguished from switching, local drayage, or other terminal service) will begin;

(ii) To, and placed on, the carrier's wharf (at shipside, within reach of the ship's loading tackle, when the shipping point is within a port area having water transportation service) or the carrier's freight station;

(iii) To a U.S. Postal Service facility; or

(iv) If stated in the solicitation, to any Government-designated point located within the same city or commercial zone as the f.o.b. origin point specified in the contract (the Federal Motor Carrier Safety Administration prescribes commercial zones at Subpart B of 49 CFR part 372); and

(2) Differentials for mode of transportation, type of vehicle, or place of delivery as indicated in Contractor's offer may be added to the contract price.

(b) The Contractor shall—

(1) (i) Pack and mark the shipment to comply with contract specification; or

(ii) In the absence of specifications, prepare the shipment in conformance with carrier requirements to protect the goods and to ensure assessment of the lowest applicable transportation charge;

(2) (i) Order specified carrier equipment when requested by the Government; or

(ii) If not specified, order appropriate carrier equipment not in excess of capacity to accommodate shipment;

(3) Deliver the shipment in good order and condition to the carrier, and load, stow, trim, block, and/or brace carload or truckload shipment (when loaded by the Contractor) on or in the carrier's conveyance as required by carrier rules and regulations;

(4) Be responsible for any loss of and/or damage to the goods—

(i) Occurring before delivery to the carrier;

(ii) Resulting from improper packing and marking; or

(iii) Resulting from improper loading, stowing, trimming, blocking, and/or bracing of the shipment, if loaded by the Contractor on or in the carrier's conveyance;

(5) Complete the Government bill of lading supplied by the ordering agency or, when a Government bill of lading is not supplied, prepare a commercial bill of lading or other transportation receipt. The bill of lading shall show—

(i) A description of the shipment in terms of the governing freight classification or tariff (or Government rate tender) under which lowest freight rates are applicable;

(ii) The seals affixed to the conveyance with their serial numbers or other identification;

(iii) Lengths and capacities of cars or trucks ordered and furnished;

(iv) Other pertinent information required to effect prompt delivery to the consignee, including name, delivery address, postal address and ZIP code of consignee, routing, etc.;

(v) Special instructions or annotations requested by the ordering agency for commercial bills of lading; e.g., "This shipment is the property of, and the freight charges paid to the carrier will be reimbursed by, the Government"; and

(vi) The signature of the carrier's agent and the date the shipment is received by carrier; and

(6) Distribute the copies of the bill of lading, or other transportation receipts, as directed by the ordering agency.

(c) (1) It may be advantageous to the offeror to submit f.o.b. origin prices that include only the lowest cost to the Contractor for loading of shipment at the Contractor's plant or most favorable shipping point. The cost beyond that plant or point of bringing the supplies to the place of delivery and the cost of loading, blocking, and bracing on the type vehicle specified by the Government at the time of shipment may exceed the offeror's lowest cost when the offeror ships for the offeror's account. Accordingly, the offeror may indicate differentials that may be added to the offered price. These differentials shall be expressed as a rate in cents for each 100 pounds (CWT) of the supplies for one or more of the options under this clause that the Government may specify at the time of shipment.

(2) These differential(s) will be considered in the evaluation of offers to determine the lowest overall cost to the Government. If, at the time of shipment, the Government specifies a mode of transportation, type of vehicle, or place of delivery for which the offeror has set forth a differential, the Contractor shall include the total of such differential costs (the applicable differential multiplied by the actual weight) as a separate reimbursable item on the Contractor's invoice for the supplies.

(3) The Government shall have the option of performing or arranging at its own expense any transportation from Contractor's shipping plant or point to carrier's facility at the time of shipment and, whenever this option is exercised, the Government shall make no reimbursement based on a quoted differential.

(4) Offeror's differentials in cents for each 100 pounds for optional mode of transportation, types of vehicle, transportation within a mode, or place of delivery, specified by the Government at the time of shipment and not included in the f.o.b. origin price indicated in the Schedule by the offeror, are as follows:

_____ (*carload, truckload, less-load,*

_____*wharf, flatcar, driveaway, etc.*)

(End of clause)

[FAC 84-37, 53 FR 17861, 5/18/88, effective 6/17/88; FAC 2005-07, 71 FR 200, 1/3/2006, effective 2/2/2006]

52.247-34 F.o.b. Destination.

As prescribed in 47.303-6(c), insert the following clause:

F.O.B. DESTINATION (NOV 1991)

(a) The term *f.o.b. destination* as used in this clause, means—

(1) Free of expense to the Government, on board the carrier's conveyance, at a specified delivery point where the consignee's facility (plant, warehouse, store, lot, or other location to which shipment can be made) is located; and

(2) Supplies shall be delivered to the destination consignee's wharf (if destination is a port city and supplies are for export), warehouse unloading platform, or receiving dock, at the expense of the Contractor. The Government shall not be liable for any delivery, storage, demurrage, accessorial, or other charges involved before the actual delivery (or "constructive placement" as defined in carrier tariffs) of the supplies to the destination, unless such charges are caused by an act or order of the Government acting in its contractual capacity. If rail carrier is used, supplies shall be delivered to the specified unloading platform of the consignee. If motor carrier (including "piggyback") is used, supplies shall be delivered to truck tailgate at the unloading platform of the consignee, except when the supplies delivered meet the requirements of Item 568 of the National Motor Freight Classification for "heavy or bulky freight." When supplies meeting the requirements of the referenced Item 568 are delivered, unloading (including movement to the tailgate) shall be performed by the consignee, with assistance from the truck driver, if requested. If the contractor uses rail carrier or freight forwarder for less than carload shipments, the contractor shall ensure that the carrier will furnish tailgate delivery, when required, if transfer to truck is required to complete delivery to consignee.

(b) The Contractor shall—

(1) (i) Pack and mark the shipment to comply with contract specifications; or

(ii) In the absence of specifications, prepare the shipment in conformance with carrier requirements;

(2) Prepare and distribute commercial bills of lading;

(3) Deliver the shipment in good order and condition to the point of delivery specified in the contract;

(4) Be responsible for any loss of and/or damage to the goods occurring before receipt of the shipment by the consignee at the delivery point specified in the contract;

(5) Furnish a delivery schedule and designate the mode of delivering carrier; and

(6) Pay and bear all charges to the specified point of delivery.

(End of clause)

[FAC 90-3, 55 FR 52800, 12/21/90, effective 1/22/91]

52.247-35 F.o.b. Destination, within Consignee's Premises.

As prescribed in 47.303-7(c), insert the following clause in solicitations and contracts when the delivery term is f.o.b. destination, within consignee's premises:

F.O.B. DESTINATION, WITHIN CONSIGNEE'S PREMISES (APR 1984)

(a) The term *f.o.b. destination, within consignee's premises* as used in this clause, means free of expense to the Government delivered and laid down within the doors of the consignee's premises, including delivery to specific rooms within a building if so specified.

(b) The Contractor shall—

(1) (i) Pack and mark the shipment to comply with contract specifications; or

(ii) In the absence of specifications, prepare the shipment in conformance with carrier requirements;

(2) Prepare and distribute commercial bills of lading;

(3) Deliver the shipment in good order and condition to the point of delivery specified in the contract;

(4) Be responsible for any loss of and/or damage to the goods occurring before receipt of the shipment by the consignee at the delivery point specified in the contract;

(5) Furnish a delivery schedule and designate the mode of delivering carrier; and

(6) Pay and bear all charges to the specified point of delivery.

(End of clause)

[FAC 90-32, 60 FR 48206, 9/18/95, effective 10/1/95]

52.247-36 F.a.s. Vessel, Port of Shipment.

As prescribed in 47.303-8(c), insert the following clause in solicitations and contracts when the delivery term is f.a.s. vessel, port of shipment:

F.A.S. VESSEL, PORT OF SHIPMENT (APR 1984)

(a) The term *f.a.s. vessel, port of shipment* as used in this clause, means free of expense to the Government delivered alongside the ocean vessel and within reach of its loading tackle at the specified port of shipment.

(b) The Contractor shall—

(1) (i) Pack and mark the shipment to comply with contract specifications; or

(ii) In the absence of specifications, prepare the shipment for ocean transportation in conformance with carrier requirements to protect the goods and to ensure assessment of the lowest applicable transportation charge;

(2) (i) Deliver the shipment in good order and condition alongside the ocean vessel and within reach of its loading tackle, at the point of delivery and on the date or within the period specified in the contract; and

(ii) Pay and bear all applicable charges, including transportation costs, wharfage, handling, and heavy lift charges, if necessary, up to this point;

(3) Provide a clean dock or ship's receipt;

(4) Be responsible for any loss of and/or damage to the goods occurring before delivery of the shipment to the point specified in the contract; and

(5) At the Government's request and expense, assist obtaining the documents required for (i) exportation or (ii) importation at destination.

(End of clause)

[FAC 90-32, 60 FR 48206, 9/18/95, effective 10/1/95]

52.247-37 F.o.b. Vessel, Port of Shipment.

As prescribed in 47.303-9(c), insert the following clause in solicitations and contracts when the delivery term is f.o.b. vessel, port of shipment:

F.O.B. VESSEL, PORT OF SHIPMENT (APR 1984)

(a) The term *f.o.b. vessel, port of shipment,* as used in this clause, means free of expense to the Government loaded, stowed, and trimmed on board the ocean vessel at the specified port of shipment.

(b) The Contractor shall—

(1) (i) Pack and mark the shipment to comply with contract specifications; or

(ii) In the absence of specifications, prepare the shipment for ocean transportation in conformance with carrier requirements to protect the goods and to ensure assessment of the lowest applicable transportation charge;

(2) (i) Deliver the shipment on board the ocean vessel in good order and condition on the date or within the period fixed; and

(ii) Pay and bear all charges incurred in placing the shipment actually on board;

(3) Provide a clean ship's receipt or on-board ocean bill of lading;

(4) Be responsible for any loss of and/or damage to the goods occurring before delivery of the shipment on board the ocean vessel; and

(5) At the Government's request and expense, assist in obtaining the documents required for (i) exportation or (ii) importation at destination.

(End of clause)

[FAC 90-32, 60 FR 48206, 9/18/95, effective 10/1/95]

52.247-38 F.o.b. Inland Carrier, Point of Exportation.

As prescribed in 47.303-10(c), insert the following clause in solicitations and contracts when the delivery term is f.o.b. inland carrier, point of exportation:

F.O.B. INLAND CARRIER, POINT OF EXPORTATION (FEB 2006)

(a) The term *f.o.b. inland carrier, point of exportation* as used in this clause, means free of expense to the Government, on board the conveyance of the inland carrier, delivered to the specified point of exportation.

(b) The Contractor shall—

(1) (i) Pack and mark the shipment to comply with contract specifications; or

(ii) In the absence of specifications, prepare the shipment for ocean transportation in conformance with carrier requirements to protect the goods and to ensure assessment of the lowest applicable transportation charge;

(2) Prepare and distribute commercial bills of lading or other transportation receipt;

(3) (i) Deliver the shipment in good order and condition in or on the conveyance of the carrier on the date or within the period specified; and

(ii) Pay and bear all applicable charges, including transportation costs, to the point of delivery specified in the contract;

(4) Be responsible for any loss of and/or damage to the goods occurring before delivery of the shipment to the point of delivery in the contract; and

(5) At the Government's request and expense, assist in obtaining the documents required for (i) exportation or (ii) importation at destination.

(End of clause)

[FAC 90-32, 60 FR 48206, 9/18/95, effective 10/1/95; FAC 2005-07, 71 FR 200, 1/3/2006, effective 2/2/2006]

52.247-39 F.o.b. Inland Point, Country of Importation.

As prescribed in 47.303-11(c), insert the following clause in solicitations and contracts when the delivery term is f.o.b. inland point, country of importation:

F.O.B. INLAND POINT, COUNTRY OF IMPORTATION (APR 1984)

(a) The term *f.o.b. inland point, country of importation* as used in this clause, means free of expense to the Government, on board the indicated type of conveyance of the carrier, delivered to the specified inland point where the consignee's facility is located.

(b) The Contractor shall—

(1) (i) Pack and mark the shipment to comply with contract specifications; or

(ii) In the absence of specifications, prepare the shipment for ocean transportation in conformance with carrier requirements to protect the goods;

(2) (i) Deliver, in or on the inland carrier's conveyance, the shipment in good order and condition to the specified inland point where the consignee's facility is located; and

(ii) Pay and bear all applicable charges incurred up to the point of delivery, including transportation costs; export, import, or other fees or taxes; costs of landing; wharfage costs; customs duties and costs of certificates of origin; consular invoices; and other documents that may be required for importation; and

(3) Be responsible for any loss of and/or damage to the goods until their arrival on or in the carrier's conveyance at the specified inland point.

(End of clause)

[FAC 90-32, 60 FR 48206, 9/18/95, effective 10/1/95]

52.247-40 Ex Dock, Pier, or Warehouse, Port of Importation.

As prescribed in 47.303-12(c), insert the following clause in solicitations and contracts when the delivery term is ex dock, pier, or warehouse, port of importation:

EX DOCK, PIER, OR WAREHOUSE, PORT OF IMPORTATION (APR 1984)

(a) The term *ex dock, pier, or warehouse, port of importation* as used in this clause, means free of expense to the Government delivered on the designated dock or pier or in the warehouse at the specified port of importation.

(b) The Contractor shall—

(1) (i) Pack and mark the shipment to comply with contract specifications; or

(ii) In the absence of specifications, prepare the shipment for ocean transportation in conformance with carrier requirements to protect the goods;

(2) (i) Deliver shipment in good order and condition; and

(ii) Pay and bear all charges up to the point of delivery specified in the contract, including transportation costs; export, import, or other fees or taxes; costs of wharfage and landing, if any; customs duties; and costs of certificates of origin, consular invoices, or other documents that may be required for exportation or importation; and

(3) Be responsible for any loss of and/or damage to the goods occurring before delivery of the shipment to the point of delivery specified in the contract.

(End of clause)

[FAC 90-32, 60 FR 48206, 9/18/95, effective 10/1/95]

52.247-41 C.&f. Destination.

As prescribed in 47.303-13(c), insert the following clause in solicitations and contracts when the delivery term is c.&f. destination:

C.&F. DESTINATION (APR 1984)

(a) The term *c.&f. destination* as used in this clause, means free of expense to the Government delivered on board the ocean vessel to the specified point of destination, with the cost of transportation paid by the Contractor.

(b) The Contractor shall—

(1) (i) Pack and mark the shipment to comply with contract specifications; or

(ii) In the absence of specifications, prepare the shipment for ocean transportation in conformance with carrier requirements;

(2) (i) Deliver the shipment in good order and condition; and

(ii) Pay and bear all applicable charges to the point of destination specified in the contract, including transportation costs and export taxes or other fees or charges levied because of exportation;

(3) Obtain and dispatch promptly to the Government clean on-board ocean bills of lading to the specified point of destination;

(4) Be responsible for any loss of and/or damage to the goods occurring before delivery; and

(5) At the Government's request and expense, provide certificates of origin, consular invoices, or any other documents issued in the country of origin or of shipment, or both, that may be required for importation into the country of destination.

(End of clause)

[FAC 90-32, 60 FR 48206, 9/18/95, effective 10/1/95]

52.247-42 C.i.f. Destination.

As prescribed in 47.303-14(c), insert the following clause in solicitations and contracts when the delivery term is c.i.f. destination:

C.I.F. DESTINATION (APR 1984)

(a) The term *c.i.f. destination* as used in this clause, means free of expense to the Government delivered on board the ocean vessel to the specified point of destination, with the cost of transportation and marine insurance paid by the Contractor.

(b) The Contractor shall—

(1) (i) Pack and mark the shipment to comply with contract specifications; or

(ii) In the absence of specifications, prepare the shipment for ocean transportation in conformance with carrier requirements;

(2) (i) Deliver the shipment in good order and condition; and

(ii) Pay and bear all applicable charges to the point of destination specified in the contract, including transportation costs and export taxes or other fees or charges levied because of exportation;

(3) Obtain and dispatch promptly to the Government clean on-board ocean bills of lading to the specified point of destination;

(4) Be responsible for any loss of and/or damage to the goods occurring before delivery;

(5) At the Government's request and expense, provide certificates of origin, consular invoices, or any other documents issued in the country of origin or of shipment, or both, that may be required for importation into the country of destination; and

(6) Obtain and dispatch to the Government an insurance policy or certificate providing the amount and extent of marine insurance coverage specified in the contract

or agreed upon by the Government Contracting Officer.

(End of clause)

[FAC 90-32, 60 FR 48206, 9/18/95, effective 10/1/95]

52.247-43 F.o.b. Designated Air Carrier's Terminal, Point of Exportation.

As prescribed in 47.303-15(c), insert the following clause in solicitations and contracts when the delivery term is f.o.b. designated air carrier's terminal, point of exportation:

F.O.B. DESIGNATED AIR CARRIER'S TERMINAL, POINT OF EXPORTATION (FEB 2006)

(a) The term *f.o.b. designated air carrier's terminal, point of exportation* as used in this clause, means free of expense to the Government loaded aboard the aircraft, or delivered to the custody of the air carrier (if only the air carrier performs the loading), at the air carrier's terminal specified in the contract.

(b) The Contractor shall—

(1) (i) Pack and mark the shipment to comply with contract specifications; or

(ii) In the absence of specifications, prepare the shipment for air transportation in conformance with carrier requirements to protect the goods and to ensure assessment of the lowest applicable transportation charge;

(2) (i) Deliver the shipment in good order and condition into the conveyance of the carrier, or to the custody of the carrier (if only the carrier performs the loading), at the point of delivery and on the date or within the period specified in the contract; and

(ii) Pay and bear all applicable charges up to this point;

(3) Provide a clean bill of lading and/or air waybill;

(4) Be responsible for any loss of and/or damage to the goods occurring before delivery of the goods to the point specified in the contract; and

(5) At the Government's request and expense, assist in obtaining the documents required for the purpose of exportation.

(End of clause)

[FAC 90-32, 60 FR 48206, 9/18/95, effective 10/1/95; FAC 2005-07, 71 FR 200, 1/3/2006, effective 2/2/2006]

52.247-44 F.o.b. Designated Air Carrier's Terminal, Point of Importation.

As prescribed in 47.303-16(c), insert the following clause in solicitations and contracts when the delivery term is f.o.b. designated air carrier's terminal, point of importation:

F.O.B. DESIGNATED AIR CARRIER'S TERMINAL, POINT OF IMPORTATION (APR 1984)

(a) The term *f.o.b. designated air carrier's terminal, point of importation* as used in this clause, means free of expense to the Government delivered to the air carrier's terminal at the point of importation specified in the contract.

(b) The Contractor shall—

(1) (i) Pack and mark the shipment to comply with contract specifications; or

(ii) In the absence of specifications, prepare the shipment for air transportation in conformance with carrier requirements to protect the goods;

(2) Prepare and distribute bills of lading or air waybills;

(3) (i) Deliver the shipment in good order and condition to the point of delivery specified in the contract; and

(ii) Pay and bear all charges incurred up to the point of delivery specified in the contract, including transportation costs; export, import, or other fees or taxes; cost of landing, if any; customs duties; and costs of certificates of origin, consular invoices, or other documents that may be required for exportation or importation; and

(4) Be responsible for any loss of and/or damage to the goods until delivery of the goods to the Government at the designated air carrier's terminal.

(End of clause)

[FAC 90-32, 60 FR 48206, 9/18/95, effective 10/1/95]

52.247-45 F.o.b. Origin and/or F.o.b. Destination Evaluation.

As prescribed in 47.305-2(b), insert the following provision in solicitations when offers are solicited on the basis of both f.o.b. origin and f.o.b. destination:

F.O.B. ORIGIN AND/OR F.O.B. DESTINATION EVALUATION (APR 1984)

Offers are invited on the basis of both f.o.b. origin and f.o.b. destination, and the Government will award on the basis the Contracting Officer determines to be most advantageous to the Government. An offer on the basis of f.o.b. origin only or f.o.b. destination only is acceptable, but will be evaluated only on the basis submitted.

(End of provision)

[FAC 90-32, 60 FR 48206, 9/18/95, effective 10/1/95]

52.247-46 Shipping Point(s) Used in Evaluation of F.o.b. Origin Offers.

As prescribed in 47.305-3(b)(4)(ii), insert the following provision in f.o.b. origin solicitations when price evaluation for shipments from various shipping points is contemplated:

SHIPPING POINT(S) USED IN EVALUATION OF F.O.B. ORIGIN OFFERS (APR 1984)

(a) If more than one shipping point or plant is designated by the offeror and the offeror fails to indicate the quantity per shipping point or plant before bid opening, the Government will evaluate the offer on the basis of delivery of the entire quantity from the point or plant where cost of transportation is most favorable to the Government.

(b) If the offeror, before bid opening (or the closing date specified for receipt of offers) fails to indicate any shipping point or plant, the Government will evaluate the offer on the basis of delivery from the plant at which the contract will be performed, as indicated in the offer. If no plant is indicated in the offer, the offer will be evaluated on the basis of delivery from the Contractor's business address indicated in the offer.

(c) If the offeror uses a shipping point other than that which has been used by the Government as a basis for the evaluation of offers, any increase of transportation costs shall be borne by the Contractor and any savings shall revert to the Government.

(End of provision)

[FAC 90-32, 60 FR 48206, 9/18/95, effective 10/1/95]

52.247-47 Evaluation—F.o.b. Origin.

As prescribed in 47.305-3(f)(2), insert the following provision. When it is appropriate to use methods other than land transportation in evaluating offers; e.g., air, pipeline, barge, or ocean tanker, modify the provision accordingly.

EVALUATION—F.O.B. ORIGIN (JUN 2003)

(a) The Government normally uses land methods of transportation by regulated common carrier for shipment within the contiguous United States.

(b) To evaluate offers, the Government will consider only these methods to establish the cost of transportation between offeror's shipping point and destination (tentative or firm, whichever is applicable) in the contiguous United States.

(c) This transportation cost will be added to the offer price to determine the Government's overall cost.

(d) When tentative destinations are indicated, the Government will use them only for evaluation purposes. The Government has the right to use any other means of transportation or any other destination at the time of shipment.

(End of provision)

[FAC 84-21, 51 FR 34127, 9/3/86, effective 8/29/86; FAC 90-32, 60 FR 48206, 9/18/95, effective 10/1/95; FAC 2001-14, 68 FR 28079, 5/22/2003, effective 6/23/2003]

52.247-48 F.o.b. Destination—Evidence of Shipment.

As prescribed in 47.305-4(c), insert the following clause:

F.O.B. DESTINATION—EVIDENCE OF SHIPMENT (FEB 1999)

(a) If this contract is awarded on a free on board (f.o.b.) destination basis, the Contractor—

(1) Shall not submit an invoice for payment until the supplies covered by the invoice have been shipped to the destination; and

(2) Shall retain, and make available to the Government for review as necessary, the following evidence of shipment documentation for a period of 3 years after final payment under the contract:

(i) If transportation is accomplished by common carrier, a signed copy of the commercial bill of lading for the supplies covered by the Contractor's invoice, indicating the carrier's intent to ship the supplies to the destination specified in the contract.

(ii) If transportation is accomplished by parcel post, a copy of the certificate of mailing.

(iii) If transportation is accomplished by other than common carrier or parcel post, a copy of the delivery document showing receipt at the destination specified in the contract.

(b) The Contractor is not required to submit evidence of shipment documentation with its invoice.

(End of clause)

[FAC 97-10, 63 FR 70264, 12/18/98, effective 2/16/99]

52.247-49 Destination Unknown.

As prescribed in 47.305-5(b)(2), insert the following provision in solicitations when destinations are tentative and only for the purpose of evaluating offers:

DESTINATION UNKNOWN (APR 1984)

For the purpose of evaluating offers and for no other purpose, the final destination(s) for the supplies will be considered to be as follows: ________.

(End of provision)

[FAC 90-32, 60 FR 48206, 9/18/95, effective 10/1/95]

52.247-50 No Evaluation of Transportation Costs.

As prescribed in 47.305-5(c)(1), insert the following provision in solicitations when exact destinations are not known and it is impractical to establish tentative or general delivery places for the purpose of evaluating transportation costs:

NO EVALUATION OF TRANSPORTATION COSTS (APR 1984)

Costs of transporting supplies to be delivered under this contract will not be an evaluation factor for award.

(End of provision)

[FAC 90-32, 60 FR 48206, 9/18/95, effective 10/1/95]

52.247-51 Evaluation of Export Offers.

As prescribed in 47.305-6(e), insert the following provision:

EVALUATION OF EXPORT OFFERS (JAN 2001)

(a) *Port handling and ocean charges—other than DOD water terminals.* Port handling and ocean charges in tariffs on file with the Bureau of Domestic Regulation, Federal Maritime Commission, or other appropriate regulatory authorities as of the date of bid opening (or the closing date specified for receipt of offers) and which will be effective for the date of the expected initial shipment will be used in the evaluation of offers.

(b) *F.o.b. origin, transportation under Government bill of lading.* (1) Offers shall be evaluated and awards made on the basis of the lowest laid down cost to the Government at the overseas port of discharge, via methods and ports compatible with required delivery dates and conditions affecting transportation known at the time of evaluation. Included in this evaluation, in addition to the f.o.b. origin price of the item, shall be the inland transportation costs from the point of origin in the United States to the port of loading, port handling charges at the port of loading, and ocean shipping costs from the United States port of loading (see paragraph (d) below) to the overseas port of discharge. The Government may designate the mode of routing of shipment and may load from other than those ports specified for evaluation purposes.

(2) Offers shall be evaluated on the basis of shipment through one of the ports set forth in paragraph (d) below to the overseas port of discharge. Evaluation shall be made on the basis of shipment through the port that will result in the lowest cost to the Government.

(3) Ports of loading shall be considered as destinations within the meaning of the term "f.o.b. destination" as that term is used in the F.o.b. Origin clause of this contract.

(c) *F.o.b. port of loading with inspection and acceptance at origin*. (1) Offers shall be evaluated on the basis of the lowest laid down cost to the Government at the overseas port of discharge via methods compatible with required delivery dates and conditions affecting transportation known at the time of evaluation. Included in this evaluation, in addition to the price to the United States port of loading (see paragraph (2) below), shall be the port handling charges at the port of loading and the ocean shipping cost from the port of loading (see paragraph (d) below) to the overseas port of discharge.

(2) Unless offers are applicable only to f.o.b. origin delivery under Government bills of lading (see paragraph (b) above), offerors shall designate below at least one of the ports of loading listed in paragraph (d) below as their place of delivery. Failure to designate at least one of the ports as the point to which delivery will be made by the Contractor may render the offer nonresponsive.

PLACE OF DELIVERY:

[Offerors insert at least one of the ports listed in paragraph (d) below.]

(d) *Ports of loading for evaluation of offers.* Terminals to be used by the Government in evaluating offers are as follows: [For the information of the offerors, ocean and port handling charges are set forth if the terminal named is a DOD water terminal.]

Ports/Terminals of Loading

____

____

____

Combined Ocean and Port Handling Charges to [Indicate Country]

____

____

____

Unit of Measure: i.e., metric ton, measurement ton, cubic foot, etc.

____

____

____

(e) *Ports of loading nominated by offeror.* The ports of loading named in paragraph (d) above are considered by the Government to be appropriate for this solicitation due to their compatibility with methods and facilities required to handle the cargo and types of vessels and to meet the required overseas delivery dates. Notwithstanding the foregoing, offerors may nominate additional ports of loading that the offeror considers to be more favorable to the Government. The Government may disregard such nominated ports if, after considering the quantity and nature of the supplies concerned, the requisite cargo handling capability, the available sailings on U.S.-flag vessels, and other pertinent transportation factors, it determines that use of the nominated ports is not compatible with the required overseas delivery date. United States Great Lakes ports of loading may be considered in the evaluation of offers only for those items scheduled in this provision for delivery during the ice-free or navigable period as proclaimed by the authorities of the St. Lawrence Seaway (normal period is between April 15 and November 30 annually). All ports named, including those nominated by offerors and determined to be eligible as provided in this provision, shall be considered in evaluating all offers received in order to establish the lowest laid down cost to the Government at the overseas port of discharge. All determinations shall be based on availability of ocean services by U.S.-flag vessels only. Additional U.S. port(s) of loading nominated by offeror, if any: ____

(f) *Price basis*: Offeror shall indicate whether prices are based on—

() Paragraph (b), f.o.b. origin, transportation by GBL to port listed in paragraph (d);

( ) Paragraph (c), f.o.b. destination (i.e., a port listed in paragraph (d));

( ) Paragraph (e), f.o.b. origin, transportation by GBL to port nominated in paragraph (e); and/or

() Paragraph (e), f.o.b. destination (i.e., a port nominated in paragraph (e)).

(End of provision)

Alternate I (FEB 2006). When the CONUS ports of export are DOD water terminals, delete paragraph (a) from the basic provision and substitute for it the following paragraph (a):

(a) *Port handling and ocean charges—DOD water terminals*. The port handling and ocean charges are set forth in paragraph (d) of this provision for the information of offerors and are current as of the time of issuance of the solicitation. For evaluation of offers, the Government will use the port handling and ocean charges made available by the Directorate of International Traffic, Military Surface Deployment and Distribution Command (SDDC) rate information letters, on file as of the date of bid opening (or the closing date specified for receipt of offers) and which will be effective for the date of the expected initial shipment.

Alternate II (APR 1984). When offers are solicited on an f.o.b. origin only basis, delete paragraphs (c) and (f) from the basic provision, but do not redesignate the ensuing paragraphs. Add the following basic paragraph (g) to the provision:

(g) Paragraphs (c) and (f) have been deleted but ensuing paragraphs have not been redesignated.

Alternate III (APR 1984). When offers are solicited on an f.o.b. destination only basis, delete paragraph (b) from the basic provision but do not redesignate the ensuing paragraphs. Delete subparagraph (c)(2) and paragraph (f) from the provision and substitute the following subparagraph (c)(2) and paragraph (f). Add paragraph (g) below.

(c)(2) Offerors shall designate below at least one of the ports of loading listed in paragraph (d) below as their place of delivery. Failure to designate at least one of the ports as the point to which delivery will be made by the Contractor may render the offer nonresponsive.

PLACE OF DELIVERY:

[*Offerors insert at least one of the ports listed in paragraph (d) below.*]

(f) *Price basis*. Offerors shall indicate whether prices are based on—

() Paragraph (c), f.o.b. destination (i.e., a port listed in paragraph (d)); or

() Paragraph (e), f.o.b. destination (i.e., a port nominated in paragraph (e)).

(g) Paragraph (b) has been deleted, but ensuing paragraphs have not been redesignated.

[FAC 90-23, 59 FR 67010, 12/28/94, effective 2/27/95; FAC 90-32, 60 FR 48206, 9/18/95, effective 10/1/95; FAC 97-22, 66 FR 2117, 1/10/2001, effective 1/10/2001; FAC 2005-07, 71 FR 200, 1/3/2006, effective 2/2/2006]

52.247-52 Clearance and Documentation Requirements—Shipments to DOD Air or Water Terminal Transshipment Points.

As prescribed in 47.305-6(f)(2), insert the following clause in solicitations and contracts when shipments will be consigned to DOD air or water terminal transshipment points:

CLEARANCE AND DOCUMENTATION REQUIREMENTS—SHIPMENTS TO DOD AIR OR WATER TERMINAL TRANSSHIPMENT POINTS (FEB 2006)

All shipments to water or air ports for transshipment to overseas destinations are subject to the following requirements unless clearance and documentation requirements have been expressly delegated to the Contractor:

(a) At least 10 days before shipping cargo to a water port, the Contractor shall obtain an Export Release from the Government transportation office for—

(1) Each shipment weighing 10,000 pounds or more; and

(2) Each shipment weighing less than 10,000 pounds; if the cargo either—

(i) Is classified TOP SECRET, SECRET, OR CONFIDENTIAL;

(ii) Will require exclusive use of a motor vehicle;

(iii) Will occupy full visible capacity of a railway car or motor vehicle;

(iv) Is less than a carload or truckload, but will be tendered as a carload or truckload; or

(v) Is to be shipped to an ammunition outloading port for water shipment; or

(3) Each shipment weighing less than 10,000 pounds if the cargo consists of—

(i) Narcotics;

(ii) Perishable biological material;

(iii) Vehicles to be offered for driveaway service;

(iv) Explosives, ammunition, poisons or other dangerous articles classified as class 1, division 1.1, 1.2, 1.3, 1.4; class 2, division 2.3; and class 6, division 6.1; or

(v) Radioactive material, as defined in 49 CFR 173.403, class 7.

(b) The Contractor is cautioned not to order railway cars or motor vehicles for loading until an Export Release has been received.

(c) If the Contracting Officer directs delivery within a shorter period than 10 days, the Contractor shall advise the transportation office of the date on which the cargo will be ready for shipment.

(d) At least 5 days before shipping cargo to either a water port or an airport (regardless of the weight, security classification, or the commodity description), the Contractor shall provide the Government transportation office the information shown in paragraph (e) below to permit preparation of a Transportation Control and Movement Document (TCMD).

(e) When applying for the Export Release in paragraph (a) above or when providing information for preparation of the TCMD in accordance with paragraph (d) above, the Contractor shall furnish the—

(1) Proposed date or dates of shipment;

(2) Number and type of containers;

(3) Gross weight and cube of the shipment;

(4) Number of cars or trucks that will be involved;

(5) Transportation Control Number(s) (TCN) as required for marking under MIL-STD-129 or Federal Standard 123; and

(6) Proper shipping name as specified in 46 CFR 146.05 for all items classified as dangerous substances as required for marking under MIL-STD-129.

(f) All movement documents (Government or commercial bills of lading or other delivery documents) shall be annotated by the Contractor with the—

(1) Transportation Control Number, Consignor Code of activity directing the shipment; *i.e.*, cognizant contract administration office, purchasing office when contract administration has been retained, or a Contractor specifically delegated transportation responsibilities under DoD 4500.9-R, Defense Transportation Regulation, responsibilities in the contract, whichever is appropriate, Consignee Code, and Transportation Priority for each shipment unit;

(2) Export Release Number and valid shipping period, if stated (if expired, the Contractor shall request a renewal); and

(3) Cubic foot measurement of each shipment unit.

(g) All annotations on the movement documents shall be made in the "Description of Articles" space except, on Government bills of lading the Export Release number and shipping period shall be entered in the space entitled "Route Order/Release No."

(h) The Contractor shall—

(1) Mail a copy of the bill of lading or other movement document to the transshipment point; and

(2) Give a copy of the bill of lading or other movement document to the carrier for

presentation to the transshipment point with delivery of the shipment.

(End of clause)

[FAC 90-32, 60 FR 48206, 9/18/95, effective 10/1/95; FAC 2005-07, 71 FR 200, 1/3/2006, effective 2/2/2006]

52.247-53 Freight Classification Description.

As prescribed in 47.305-9(b)(1), insert the following provision in solicitations when the supplies being acquired are new to the supply system, nonstandard, or modifications of previously shipped items, and different freight classifications may apply:

FREIGHT CLASSIFICATION DESCRIPTION (APR 1984)

Offerors are requested to indicate below the full Uniform Freight Classification (rail) description, or the National Motor Freight Classification description applicable to the supplies, the same as offeror uses for commercial shipment. This description should include the packing of the commodity (box, crate, bundle, loose, setup, knocked down, compressed, unwrapped, etc.), the container material (fiberboard, wooden, etc.), unusual shipping dimensions, and other conditions affecting traffic descriptions. The Government will use these descriptions as well as other information available to determine the classification description most appropriate and advantageous to the Government. Offeror understands that shipments on any f.o.b. origin contract awarded, as a result of this solicitation, will be made in conformity with the shipping classification description specified by the Government, which may be different from the classification description furnished below.

FOR FREIGHT CLASSIFICATION PURPOSES, OFFEROR DESCRIBES THIS COMMODITY AS ____

(End of provision)

[FAC 90-32, 60 FR 48206, 9/18/95, effective 10/1/95]

52.247-54 [Reserved]

[Removed and reserved, FAC 90-45, Final rule, 62 FR 224, 1/2/97, effective 1/1/97]

52.247-55 F.o.b. Point for Delivery of Government-Furnished Property.

As prescribed in 47.305-12(a)(2), insert the following clause:

F.O.B. POINT FOR DELIVERY OF GOVERNMENT-FURNISHED PROPERTY (JUN 2003)

(a) Unless otherwise specified in this solicitation, the Government will deliver any Government-furnished property for use within the contiguous United States or Canada to a point specified by the Contractor in the offer. If the Government makes delivery by railroad, the f.o.b. point will be private siding, Contractor's plant. If the Contractor's plant is not served by rail, the f.o.b. point will be railroad cars in the same or nearest city having rail service. The Government may choose the mode of transportation and the carriers and will bear the cost of all line-haul transportation to the specified destination.

(b) If the destination of the Government-furnished property is a Contractor's plant located outside the contiguous United States or Canada, the f.o.b. point for Government delivery of Government-furnished property will be a Contractor-specified location in the contiguous United States. If the Contractor fails to name a point, the Government will select as the f.o.b. point the port city in the contiguous United States nearest to the Government-furnished property that has regular commercial water transportation services to the offshore port nearest the Contractor's plant.

(c) Unless otherwise directed by the Contracting Officer or provided in the contract, the Contractor shall return all Government-furnished equipment, supplies, and property, including all property not returned in the form of acceptable end items, to the point at which the Government property was originally furnished to the Contractor under the contract. Notwithstanding the fact that the Government may have furnished the property at the Contractor's plant, the Contracting Officer may direct the Contractor to deliver the Government property being returned to, and load, block and brace it in, railway cars in the city in which the Contractor's plant is located, or, if the Contractor's city is not served by rail service, in the nearest city having rail service. Unless otherwise specified in the contract, all property shall be packed in containers conforming with the rules of common carrier published tariffs so as to be free of penalty charges by the carrier designated for shipment by the Government.

(End of clause)

[FAC 90-32, 60 FR 48206, 9/18/95, effective 10/1/95; FAC 2001-14, 68 FR 28079, 5/22/2003, effective 6/23/2003]

52.247-56 Transit Arrangements.

As prescribed in 47.305-13(a)(3)(ii), insert the following provision in solicitations when benefits may accrue to the Government because transit arrangements may apply:

TRANSIT ARRANGEMENTS (APR 1984)

The lowest appropriate common carrier transportation costs, including offeror's through transit rates and charges when applicable, from offeror's shipping points, via the transit point, to the ultimate destination will be used in evaluating offers.

Transit point(s) Destination(s)

____

____

____

(End of provision)

[FAC 90-32, 60 FR 48206, 9/18/95, effective 10/1/95]

52.247-57 Transportation Transit Privilege Credits.

As prescribed in 47.305-13(b)(4), insert the following clause in solicitations and contracts when supplies are of such a nature, or when it is the custom of the trade, that offerors may have potential transit credits available and the Government may reduce transportation costs through the use of transit credits:

TRANSPORTATION TRANSIT PRIVILEGE CREDITS (APR 1984)

(a) If the offeror has established with regulated common carriers transit privileges that can be applied to the supplies when shipped from the original source, the offeror is invited to propose to use these credits for shipping the supplies to the designated Government destinations. The offeror will ship these supplies under commercial bills of lading, paying all remaining transportation charges connected with the shipment, subject to reimbursement by the Government in an amount equal to the remaining charges but not exceeding the amount quoted by the offeror.

(b) After loading on the carrier's equipment and acceptance by the carrier, these shipments under paid commercial bills of lading will move for the account of and at the risk of the Government (unless, pursuant to the Changes clause, the office administering the contract directs use of Government bills of lading).

(c) The amount quoted below by the offeror represents the transportation costs in cents per 100 pounds (freight rate) for full carload/truckload shipments of the supplies from offeror's original source, via offeror's transit plant or point, to the Government destination(s) including the carrier's transit privilege charge, less the applicable transit credit (*i.e.*, the amount (rate) initially paid to the carrier for shipment from original source to offeror's transit plant or point).

(d) The rate per CWT quoted will be used by the Government to evaluate the offered f.o.b. origin price unless a lower rate is applicable on the date of bid opening (or closing date specified for receipt of offers). To have the offer evaluated on this basis, the offeror must insert below the remaining transportation charges that the offeror agrees to pay, including any transit charges, subject to reimbursement by the Government, as explained in this clause, to destinations, listed in the Schedule as follows:

RATE PER CWT IN CENTS: ____

TO DESTINATION: ____

(End of clause)

[FAC 90-32, 60 FR 48206, 9/18/95, effective 10/1/95]

52.247-58 Loading, Blocking, and Bracing of Freight Car Shipments.

As prescribed in 47.305-15(a)(2), insert the following clause in solicitations and contracts when supplies may be shipped in carload lots by rail:

LOADING, BLOCKING, AND BRACING OF FREIGHT CAR SHIPMENTS (APR 1984)

(a) Upon receipt of shipping instructions, as provided in this contract, the supplies to be included in any carload shipment by rail shall be loaded, blocked, and braced by the Contractor in accordance with the standards published by the Association of American Railroads and effective at the time of shipment.

(b) Shipments, for which the Association of American Railroads has published no such standards, shall be loaded, blocked, and braced in accordance with standards established by the shipper as evidenced by written acceptance of an authorized representative of the carrier.

(c) The Contractor shall be liable for payment of any damage to any supplies caused by the failure to load, block, and brace in accordance with acceptable standards set forth herein.

(d) A copy of the appropriate pamphlet of the Association of American Railroads may be obtained from that Association.

(End of clause)

[FAC 90-32, 60 FR 48206, 9/18/95, effective 10/1/95]

52.247-59 F.o.b. Origin—Carload and Truckload Shipments.

As prescribed in 47.305-16(a), insert the following clause in solicitations and contracts when it is contemplated that they may result in f.o.b. origin contracts with shipments in carloads or truckloads. This will facilitate realistic freight cost evaluations of offers and ensure that contractors produce economical shipments of agreed size.

F.O.B. ORIGIN—CARLOAD AND TRUCKLOAD SHIPMENTS (APR 1984)

(a) The Contractor agrees that shipment shall be made in carload or truckload lots when the quantity to be delivered to any one destination in any delivery period pursuant to the contract schedule of deliveries is sufficient to constitute a carload or truckload shipment, except as may otherwise be permitted or directed, in writing, by the Contracting Officer.

(b) For evaluation purposes, the agreed weight of a carload or truckload shall be the highest applicable minimum weight that will result in the lowest freight rate (or per car charge) on file or published in common carrier tariffs or tenders as of the date of bid opening (or the closing date specified for receipt of proposals).

(c) For purposes of actual delivery, the agreed weight of a carload or truckload will be the highest applicable minimum weight that will result in the lowest possible freight rate (or per car charge) on file or published as of date of shipment.

(d) If the total weight of any scheduled quantity to a destination is less than the highest carload/truckload minimum weight used for evaluation of offers, the Contractor agrees to ship such scheduled quantity in one shipment.

(e) The Contractor shall be liable to the Government for any increased costs to the Government resulting from failure to comply with the above requirements.

(End of clause)

[FAC 90-32, 60 FR 48206, 9/18/95, effective 10/1/95]

52.247-60 Guaranteed Shipping Characteristics.

As prescribed in 47.305-16(b)(1), insert the following clause:

GUARANTEED SHIPPING CHARACTERISTICS (JAN 2017)

(a) The offeror is requested to complete subparagraph (a)(1) of this clause, for each part or component which is packed or packaged separately. This information will be used to determine transportation costs for evaluation purposes. If the offeror does not furnish sufficient data in subparagraph (a)(1) of this clause, to permit determination by the Government of the item shipping costs, evaluation will be based on the shipping characteristics submitted by the offeror whose offer produces the highest transportation costs or in the absence thereof, by the Contracting Officer's best estimate of the actual transportation costs. If the item shipping costs, based on the actual shipping characteristics, exceed the item shipping costs used for evaluation purposes, the Contractor agrees that the contract price shall be reduced by an amount equal to the difference between the transportation costs actually incurred, and the costs which would have been incurred if the evaluated shipping characteristics had been accurate.

(1) To be completed by the offeror:

(i) *Type of container*: Wood Box __, Fiber Box __, Barrel __, Reel __, Drum __, Other (Specify) __;

(ii) *Shipping configuration*: Knocked-down __, Set-up __, Nested __, Other (specify) __;

(iii) *Size of container*: __" (Length), × __" (Width), × __" (Height) = __ Cubic Ft;

(iv) Number of items per container __ Each;

(v) Gross weight of container and contents __ LBS;

(vi) Palletized/skidded __ Yes __ No;

(vii) Number of containers per pallet/skid __;

(viii) Weight of empty pallet bottom/skid and sides__ LBS;

(ix) Size of pallet/skid and contents __ LBS Cube __;

(x) Number of containers or pallets/skid per railcar __*

Size of railcar __

Type of railcar __

(xi) Number of containers or pallets/skids per trailer __* Number of complete units (line item) to be shipped in carrier's equipment.

Size of trailer __ FT

Type of trailer __

(2) To be completed by the Government after evaluation but before contract award:

(i) Rate used in evaluation __;

(ii) Tender/Tariff__;

(iii) Item __.

* Number of complete units (line item) to be shipped in carrier's equipment.

(b) The guaranteed shipping characteristics requested in subparagraph (a)(1) of this clause do not establish actual transportation requirements, which are specified elsewhere in this solicitation. The guaranteed shipping characteristics will be used only for the purpose of evaluating offers and establishing any liability of the successful offeror for increased transportation costs resulting from actual shipping characteristics which differ from those used for evaluation in accordance with paragraph (a) of this clause.

(End of clause)

[FAC 84-53, 54 FR 48997, 11/28/89, effective 12/28/89; Corrected, 54 FR 30, 1/2/90; FAC 2005-95, 82 FR 4709, 1/13/2017, effective 1/13/2017]

52.247-61 F.o.b. Origin—Minimum Size of Shipments.

As prescribed in 47.305-16(c), insert the following clause in solicitations and contracts when volume rates may apply:

F.O.B. ORIGIN—MINIMUM SIZE OF SHIPMENTS (APR 1984)

The Contractor agrees that shipment will be made in carload and truckload lots when the quantity to be delivered to any one destination in any delivery period pursuant to the contract schedule of deliveries is sufficient to constitute a carload or truckload shipment, except as may otherwise be permitted or directed in writing by the Contracting Officer. The agreed weight of a carload or truckload will be the highest applicable minimum weight which will result in the lowest freight rate (or per car charge) on file or published in common carrier tariffs or tenders as of date of shipment. In the event the total weight of any scheduled quantity to a destination is less than the highest carload/truckload minimum weight, the Contractor agrees to ship such scheduled quantity in one shipment. The Contractor shall be liable to the Government for any increased costs to the Government resulting from failure to comply with the above requirements. This liability shall not attach if supplies are outsized or of such nature that they cannot be loaded at the highest minimum weight bracket.

(End of clause)

[FAC 90-32, 60 FR 48206, 9/18/95, effective 10/1/95]

52.247-62 Specific Quantities Unknown.

As prescribed in 47.305-16(d)(2), insert the following clause in solicitations and contracts when total requirements and destinations to which shipments will be made are known, but the specific quantity to be shipped to each destination cannot be predetermined. This clause protects the interests of both the Government and the contractor during the course of the performance of the contract.

SPECIFIC QUANTITIES UNKNOWN (APR 1984)

(a) For the purpose of evaluating *f.o.b. destination* offers, the Government estimates that the quantity specified will be shipped to the destinations indicated:

Estimated quantity	Destination(s)

(b) If the quantity shipped to each destination varies from the quantity estimated, and if the variation results in a change in the transportation costs, appropriate adjustment shall be made.

(End of clause)

[FAC 90-32, 60 FR 48206, 9/18/95, effective 10/1/95]

52.247-63 Preference for U.S.-Flag Air Carriers.

As prescribed in 47.405, insert the following clause:

PREFERENCE FOR U.S.-FLAG AIR CARRIERS (JUN 2003)

(a) *Definitions*. As used in this clause—

International air transportation means transportation by air between a place in the United States and a place outside the United States or between two places both of which are outside the United States.

United States means the 50 States, the District of Columbia, and outlying areas.

U.S.-flag air carrier means an air carrier holding a certificate under 49 U.S.C. Chapter 411.

(b) Section 5 of the International Air Transportation Fair Competitive Practices Act of 1974 (49 U.S.C. 40118) (Fly America Act) requires that all Federal agencies and Government contractors and subcontractors use U.S.-flag air carriers for U.S. Government-financed international air transportation of personnel (and their personal effects) or property, to the extent that service by those carriers is available. It requires the Comptroller General of the United States, in the absence of satisfactory proof of the necessity for foreign-flag air transportation, to disallow expenditures from funds, appropriated or otherwise established for the account of the United States, for international air transportation secured aboard a foreign-flag air carrier if a U.S.-flag air carrier is available to provide such services.

(c) If available, the Contractor, in performing work under this contract, shall use U.S.-flag carriers for international air transportation of personnel (and their personal effects) or property.

(d) In the event that the Contractor selects a carrier other than a U.S.-flag air carrier for international air transportation, the Contractor shall include a statement on vouchers involving such transportation essentially as follows:

STATEMENT OF UNAVAILABILITY OF U.S.-FLAG AIR CARRIERS

International air transportation of persons (and their personal effects) or property by U.S.-flag air carrier was not available or it was necessary to use foreign-flag air carrier service for the following reasons (see47.403): [*state reasons*]: ______

(e) The Contractor shall include the substance of this clause, including this paragraph (e), in each subcontract or purchase under this contract that may involve international air transportation.

(End of clause)

[FAC 84-38, 53 FR 27468, 7/20/88, effective 8/19/88; FAC 90-32, 60 FR 48206, 9/18/95, effective 10/1/95; FAC 90-45, Final rule, 62 FR 224, 1/2/97, effective 1/1/97; FAC 2001-14, 68 FR 28079, 5/22/2003, effective 6/23/2003]

52.247-64 Preference for Privately Owned U.S.-Flag Commercial Vessels.

As prescribed in 47.507(a), insert the following clause:

PREFERENCE FOR PRIVATELY OWNED U.S.-FLAG COMMERCIAL VESSELS (FEB 2006)

(a) Except as provided in paragraph (e) of this clause, the Cargo Preference Act of 1954 (46 U.S.C. Appx 1241(b)) requires that Federal departments and agencies shall transport in privately owned U.S.-flag commercial vessels at least 50 percent of the gross tonnage of equipment, materials, or commodities that may be transported in ocean vessels (computed separately for dry bulk carriers, dry cargo liners, and tankers). Such transportation shall be accomplished when any equipment, materials, or commodities, located within or outside the United States, that may be transported by ocean vessel are—

(1) Acquired for a U.S. Government agency account;

(2) Furnished to, or for the account of, any foreign nation without provision for reimbursement;

(3) Furnished for the account of a foreign nation in connection with which the United States advances funds or credits, or guarantees the convertibility of foreign currencies; or

(4) Acquired with advance of funds, loans, or guaranties made by or on behalf of the United States.

(b) The Contractor shall use privately owned U.S.-flag commercial vessels to ship at least 50 percent of the gross tonnage involved under this contract (computed separately for dry bulk carriers, dry cargo liners, and tankers) whenever shipping any equipment, materials, or commodities under the conditions set forth in paragraph (a) above, to the extent that such vessels are available at rates that are fair and reasonable for privately owned U.S.-flag commercial vessels.

(c) (1) The Contractor shall submit one legible copy of a rated on-board ocean bill of lading for each shipment to both—

(i) The Contracting Officer, and

(ii) The Office of Cargo Preference, Maritime Administration (MAR-590), 400 Seventh Street, SW, Washington, DC 20590.

Subcontractor bills of lading shall be submitted through the Prime Contractor.

(2) The Contractor shall furnish these bill of lading copies (i) within 20 working days of the date of loading for shipments originating in the United States, or (ii) within 30 working days for shipments originating outside the United States. Each bill of lading copy shall contain the following information:

(A) Sponsoring U.S. Government agency.

(B) Name of vessel.

(C) Vessel flag of registry.

(D) Date of loading.

(E) Port of loading.

(F) Port of final discharge.

(G) Description of commodity.

(H) Gross weight in pounds and cubic feet if available.

(I) Total ocean freight revenue in U.S. dollars.

(d) The Contractor shall insert the substance of this clause, including this paragraph (d), in all subcontracts or purchase orders under this contract except those described in paragraph (e)(4).

(e) The requirement in paragraph (a) does not apply to—

(1) Cargoes carried in vessels as required or authorized by law or treaty;

(2) Ocean transportation between foreign countries of supplies purchased with foreign

currencies made available, or derived from funds that are made available, under the Foreign Assistance Act of 1961 (22 U.S.C. 2353);

(3) Shipments of classified supplies when the classification prohibits the use of non-Government vessels; and

(4) Subcontracts or purchase orders for the acquisition of commercial items unless—

(i) This contract is—

(A) A contract or agreement for ocean transportation services; or

(B) A construction contract; or

(ii) The supplies being transported are—

(A) Items the Contractor is reselling or distributing to the Government without adding value. (Generally, the Contractor does not add value to the items when it subcontracts items for f.o.b. destination shipment); or

(B) Shipped in direct support of U.S. military—

(1) Contingency operations;

(2) Exercises; or

(3) Forces deployed in connection with United Nations or

North Atlantic Treaty Organization humanitarian or peacekeeping operations.

(f) Guidance regarding fair and reasonable rates for privately owned U.S.-flag commercial vessels may be obtained from the Office of Costs and Rates, Maritime Administration, 400 Seventh Street, SW, Washington, DC 20590, Phone: 202-366-4610.

(End of clause)

Alternate I (APR 2003). As prescribed in 47.507(a)(2), substitute the following paragraphs (a) and (b) for paragraphs (a) and (b) of the basic clause:

(a) Except as provided in paragraphs (b) and (e) of this clause, the Contractor shall use privately owned U.S.-flag commercial vessels, and no others, in the ocean transportation of any supplies to be furnished under this contract.

(b) If such vessels are not available for timely shipment at rates that are fair and reasonable for privately owned U.S.-flag commercial vessels, the Contractor shall notify the Contracting Officer and request (1) authorization to ship in foreign-flag vessels or (2) designation of available U.S.-flag vessels. If the Contractor is authorized in writing by the Contracting Officer to ship the supplies in foreign-flag vessels, the contract price shall be equitably adjusted to reflect the difference in costs of shipping the supplies in privately owned U.S.-flag commercial vessels and in foreign-flag vessels.

Alternate II (FEB 2006). As prescribed in 47.507(a)(3), substitute the following paragraph (e) for paragraph (e) of the basic clause:

(e) The requirement in paragraph (a) does not apply to—

(1) Cargoes carried in vessels as required or authorized by law or treaty;

(2) Ocean transportation between foreign countries of supplies purchased with foreign currencies made available, or derived from funds that are made available, under the Foreign Assistance Act of 1961 (22 U.S.C. 2353); and

(3) Shipments of classified supplies when the classification prohibits the use of non-Government vessels.

(4) Subcontracts or purchase orders under this contract for the acquisition of commercial items unless the supplies being transported are—

(i) Items the Contractor is reselling or distributing to the Government without adding value. (Generally, the Contractor does not add value to the items when it subcontracts items for f.o.b. destination shipment); or

(ii) Shipments in direct support of U.S. military—

(A) Contingency operations;

(B) Exercises; or

(C) Forces deployed in connection with United Nations or North Atlantic Treaty Organization humanitarian or peacekeeping operations. (Note: This contract requires shipment of commercial items in direct support of U.S. military contingency operations, exercises, or forces deployed in connection with United Nations or North Atlantic Treaty Organization humanitarian or peacekeeping operations.)

[FAC 90-29, 60 FR 34732, 7/3/95, effective 7/3/95; FAC 90-32, 60 FR 48206, 9/18/95, effective 10/1/95; FAC 90-40, 61 FR 39186, 7/26/96, effective 8/26/96; Final rule, 62 FR 40236, 7/25/97, effective 6/30/97, corrected 62 FR 51379, 10/1/97, effective 10/1/97; FAC 97-17, 65 FR 24316, 4/25/2000, effective 6/26/2000; FAC 2001-13, 68 FR 13202, 3/18/2003, effective 4/17/2003; FAC 2001-14, 68 FR 28098, 5/22/2003, effective 5/22/2003; FAC 2005-07, 71 FR 200, 1/3/2006, effective 2/2/2006]

52.247-65 F.o.b. Origin, Prepaid Freight—Small Package Shipments.

As prescribed in 47.303-17(f), insert the following clause:

F.O.B. ORIGIN, PREPAID FREIGHT—SMALL PACKAGE SHIPMENTS (JAN 1991)

(a) When authorized by the Contracting Officer, f.o.b. origin freight shipments which do not have a security classification shall move on prepaid commercial bills of lading or other shipping documents to domestic destinations, including air and water terminals. Weight of individual shipments shall be governed by carrier restrictions but shall not exceed 150 pounds by any form of commercial air or 1,000 pounds by other commercial carriers. The Government will reimburse the Contractor for reasonable freight charges.

(b) The Contractor shall annotate the commercial bill of lading as required by the clause of this contract entitled "Commercial Bill of Lading Notations."

(c) The Contractor shall consolidate prepaid shipments in accordance with procedures established by the cognizant transportation office. The Contractor is authorized to combine Government prepaid shipments with the Contractor's commercial shipments for delivery to one or more consignees and the Government will reimburse its pro rata share of the total freight costs. The Contractor shall provide a copy of the commercial bill of lading promptly to each consignee. Quantities shall not be divided into mailable lots for the purpose of avoiding movement by other modes of transportation.

(d) Transportation charges will be billed as a separate item on the invoice for each shipment made. A copy of the pertinent bill of lading, shipment receipt, or freight bill shall accompany the invoice unless otherwise specified in the contract.

(e) Loss and damage claims will be processed by the Government.

(End of clause)

[FAC 90-3, 55 FR 52800, 12/21/90, effective 1/22/91]

52.247-66 Returnable Cylinders.

As prescribed in 47.305-17, insert the following clause:

RETURNABLE CYLINDERS (MAY 1994)

(a) Cylinder, referred to in this clause, is a pressure vessel designed for pressures higher than 40 psia and having a circular cross section excluding a portable tank, multi—tank car tank, cargo tank or tank car.

(b) Returnable cylinders shall remain the Contractor's property but shall be loaned without charge to the Government for a period of __ days [*Contracting Officer shall insert number of days*] (hereafter referred to as loan period) following the day of delivery to the f.o.b. point specified in the contract. Any cylinder not returned within the loan period shall be charged a daily rental beginning with the first day after the loan period expires, to and including the day the cylinders are delivered to the Contractor (if the original delivery was f.o.b. origin) or are delivered or made available for delivery to the Contractor's designated carrier (if the original delivery was f.o.b. destination). The Government shall pay the Contractor a rental of $__ [*Contracting Officer shall insert dollar amount for rental, after evaluation of offers*] per cylinder, per day, computed separately for cylinders by type, size, and capacity and for each point of delivery named in the contract. No rental shall accrue to the Contractor in excess of replacement value per cylinder specified in paragraph (c) of this clause.

(c) For each cylinder lost or damaged beyond repair while in the Government's possession, the Government shall pay to the Contractor the replacement value, less the allocable rental paid for that cylinder as follows: ______ [*Contracting Officer shall insert the cylinder types, sizes, capacities, and associated replacement values.*] These cylinders shall become Government property.

(d) If any lost cylinder is located within ______ [*Contracting Officer shall insert number of days*] calendar days after payment by the Government, it may be returned to the Contractor by the Government, and the Contractor shall pay to the Government an amount equal to the replacement value, less rental computed in accordance with paragraph (b) of this clause, beginning at the expiration of the loan period specified in paragraph (b) of this clause, and continuing to the date on which the cylinder was delivered to the Contractor.

(End of clause)

[FAC 90-20, 59 FR 11368, 3/10/94, effective 5/9/94]

52.247-67 Submission of Transportation Documents for Audit.

As prescribed in 47.103-2, insert the following clause:

SUBMISSION OF TRANSPORTATION DOCUMENTS FOR AUDIT (FEB 2006)

(a) The Contractor shall submit to the address identified below, for prepayment audit, transportation documents on which the United States will assume freight charges that were paid—

(1) By the Contractor under a cost-reimbursement contract; and

(2) By a first-tier subcontractor under a cost-reimbursement subcontract thereunder.

(b) Cost-reimbursement Contractors shall only submit for audit those bills of lading with freight shipment charges exceeding $100. Bills under $100 shall be retained on-site by the Contractor and made available for on-site audits. This exception only applies to freight shipment bills and is not intended to apply to bills and invoices for any other transportation services.

(c) Contractors shall submit the above referenced transportation documents to—

____

____

____

[To be filled in by Contracting Officer]

(End of clause)

[FAC 90-23, 59 FR 67010, 12/28/94, effective 2/27/95; Final rule, 62 FR 40236, 7/25/97, effective 6/30/97; FAC 2005-07, 71 FR 200, 1/3/2006, effective 2/2/2006]

52.247-68 Report of Shipment (REPSHIP).

As prescribed in 47.208-2, insert the following clause:

REPORT OF SHIPMENT (REPSHIP) (FEB 2006)

As prescribed in 47.208-2, insert the following clause:

(a) *Definition. Domestic destination*, as used in this clause, means—

(1) A destination within the contiguous United States; or

(2) If shipment originates in Alaska or Hawaii, a destination in Alaska or Hawaii, respectively.

(b) Unless otherwise directed by the Contracting Officer, the Contractor shall—

(1) Send a prepaid notice of shipment to the consignee transportation officer—

(i) For all shipments of—

(A) Classified material, protected sensitive, and protected controlled material;

(B) Explosives and poisons, class 1, division 1.1, 1.2 and 1.3; class 2, division 2.3 and class 6, division 6.1;

(C) Radioactive materials requiring the use of a III bar label; or

(ii) When a truckload/carload shipment of supplies weighing 20,000 pounds or more, or a shipment of less weight that occupies the full visible capacity of a railway car or motor vehicle, is given to any carrier (common, contract, or private) for transportation to a domestic destination (other than a port for export);

(2) *Transmits the notice by rapid* means to be received by the consignee transportation officer at least 24 hours before the arrival of the shipment; and

(3) Send, to the receiving transportation officer, the bill of lading or letter or other document containing the following information and prominently identified as a "Report of Shipment" or "REPSHIP FOR T.O."

REPSHIP FOR T.O. 81 JUN 01

TRANSPORTATION OFFICER

DEFENSE DEPOT, MEMPHIS, TN.

SHIPPED YOUR DEPOT 1981 JUN 1 540 CTNS MENS COTTON TROUSERS, 30,240 LB, 1782 CUBE, VIA XX-YY*

IN CAR NO. XX 123456**-BL***-C98000031****CONTRACT DLA———— ETA*****-JUNE 5 JONES & CO., JERSEY CITY, N.J.

*Name of rail carrier, trucker, or other carrier.

**Vehicle identification.

***Bill of lading.

****If not shipped by BL, identify lading document and state whether paid by contractor.

*****Estimated time of arrival.

(End of clause)

[FAC 2005-07, 71 FR 200, 1/3/2006, effective 2/2/2006]

52.248-1 Value Engineering.

As prescribed in 48.201, insert the following clause:

VALUE ENGINEERING (OCT 2010)

(a) *General*. The Contractor is encouraged to develop, prepare, and submit value engineering change proposals (VECP's) voluntarily. The Contractor shall share in any net acquisition savings realized from accepted VECP's, in accordance with the incentive sharing rates in paragraph (f) below.

(b) *Definitions*.

Acquisition savings as used in this clause, means savings resulting from the application of a VECP to contracts awarded by the same contracting office or its successor for essentially the same unit. Acquisition savings include—

(1) Instant contract savings, which are the net cost reductions on this, the instant contract, and which are equal to the instant unit cost reduction multiplied by the number of instant contract units affected by the VECP, less the Contractor's allowable development and implementation costs;

(2) Concurrent contract savings, which are net reductions in the prices of other contracts that are definitized and ongoing at the time the VECP is accepted; and

(3) Future contract savings, which are the product of the future unit cost reduction multiplied by the number of future contract units in the sharing base. On an instant contract, future contract savings include savings on increases in quantities after VECP acceptance that are due to contract modifications, exercise of options, additional orders, and funding of subsequent year requirements on a multiyear contract.

Collateral costs, as used in this clause, means agency cost of operation, maintenance, logistic support, or Government-furnished property.

Collateral savings, as used in this clause, means those measurable net reductions resulting from a VECP in the agency's overall projected collateral costs, exclusive of acquisition savings, whether or not the acquisition cost changes.

Contracting office includes any contracting office that the acquisition is transferred to, such as another branch of the agency or another agency's office that is performing a joint acquisition action.

Contractor's development and implementation costs, as used in this clause, means those costs the Contractor incurs on a VECP specifically in developing, testing, preparing, and submitting the VECP, as well as those costs the Contractor incurs to make the contractual changes required by Government acceptance of a VECP.

Future unit cost reduction as used in this clause, means the instant unit cost reduction adjusted as the Contracting Officer considers necessary for projected learning or changes in quantity during the sharing period. It is calculated at the time the VECP is accepted and applies either—

(1) Throughout the sharing period, unless the Contracting Officer decides that recalculation is necessary because conditions are significantly different from those previously anticipated; or

(2) To the calculation of a lump-sum payment, which cannot later be revised.

Government costs, as used in this clause, means those agency costs that result directly from developing and implementing the VECP, such as any net increases in the cost of testing, operations, maintenance, and logistics support. The term does not include the normal administrative costs of processing the VECP or any increase in this contract's cost or price resulting from negative instant contract savings.

Instant contract, as used in this clause, means this contract, under which the VECP is submitted. It does not include increases in quantities after acceptance of the VECP that are due to contract modifications, exercise of options, or additional orders. If this is a multiyear contract, the term does not include quantities funded after VECP acceptance. If this contract is a fixed-price contract with prospective price redetermination, the term refers to the period for which firm prices have been established.

Instant unit cost reduction means the amount of the decrease in unit cost of performance (without deducting any Contractor's development or implementation costs) resulting from using the VECP on this, the instant contract. If this is a service contract, the instant unit cost reduction is normally equal to the number of hours per line-item task saved by using the VECP on this contract, multiplied by the appropriate contract labor rate.

Negative instant contract savings means the increase in the cost or price of this contract when the acceptance of a VECP results in an excess of the Contractor's allowable development and implementation costs over the product of the instant unit cost reduction multiplied by the number of instant contract units affected.

Net acquisition savings means total acquisition savings, including instant, concurrent, and future contract savings, less Government costs.

Sharing base, as used in this clause, means the number of affected end items on contracts of the contracting office accepting the VECP.

Sharing period, as used in this clause, means the period beginning with acceptance of the first unit incorporating the VECP and ending at a calendar date or event determined by the contracting officer for each VECP.

Unit, as used in this clause, means the item or task to which the Contracting Officer and the Contractor agree the VECP applies.

Value engineering change proposal (VECP) means a proposal that—

(1) Requires a change to this, the instant contract, to implement; and

(2) Results in reducing the overall projected cost to the agency without impairing essential functions or characteristics; *provided,* that it does not involve a change—

(i) In deliverable end item quantities only;

(ii) In research and development (R&D) end items or R&D test quantities that is due solely to results of previous testing under this contract; or

(iii) To the contract type only.

(c) *VECP preparation.* As a minimum, the Contractor shall include in each VECP the information described in subparagraphs (c)(1) through (8) below. If the proposed change is affected by contractually required configuration management or similar procedures, the instructions in those procedures relating to format, identification, and priority assignment shall govern VECP preparation. The VECP shall include the following:

(1) A description of the difference between the existing contract requirement and the proposed requirement, the comparative

advantages and disadvantages of each, a justification when an item's function or characteristics are being altered, the effect of the change on the end item's performance, and any pertinent objective test data.

(2) A list and analysis of the contract requirements that must be changed if the VECP is accepted, including any suggested specification revisions.

(3) Identification of the unit to which the VECP applies.

(4) A separate, detailed cost estimate for (i) the affected portions of the existing contract requirement and (ii) the VECP. The cost reduction associated with the VECP shall take into account the Contractor's allowable development and implementation costs, including any amount attributable to subcontracts under the Subcontracts paragraph of this clause, below.

(5) A description and estimate of costs the Government may incur in implementing the VECP, such as test and evaluation and operating and support costs.

(6) A prediction of any effects the proposed change would have on collateral costs to the agency.

(7) A statement of the time by which a contract modification accepting the VECP must be issued in order to achieve the maximum cost reduction, noting any effect on the contract completion time or delivery schedule.

(8) Identification of any previous submissions of the VECP, including the dates submitted, the agencies and contract numbers involved, and previous Government actions, if known.

(d) *Submission*. The Contractor shall submit VECP's to the Contracting Officer, unless this contract states otherwise. If this contract is administered by other than the contracting office, the Contractor shall submit a copy of the VECP simultaneously to the Contracting Officer and to the Administrative Contracting Officer.

(e) *Government action*. (1) The Contracting Officer will notify the Contractor of the status of the VECP within 45 calendar days after the contracting office receives it. If additional time is required, the Contracting Officer will notify the Contractor within the 45-day period and provide the reason for the delay and the expected date of the decision. The Government will process VECP's expeditiously; however, it shall not be liable for any delay in acting upon a VECP.

(2) If the VECP is not accepted, the Contracting Officer will notify the Contractor in writing, explaining the reasons for rejection. The Contractor may withdraw any VECP, in whole or in part, at any time before it is accepted by the Government. The Contracting Officer may require that the Contractor provide written notification before undertaking significant expenditures for VECP effort.

(3) Any VECP may be accepted, in whole or in part, by the Contracting Officer's award of a modification to this contract citing this clause and made either before or within a reasonable time after contract performance is completed. Until such a contract modification applies a VECP to this contract, the Contractor shall perform in accordance with the existing contract. The decision to accept or reject all or part of any VECP is a unilateral decision made solely at the discretion of the Contracting Officer.

(f) *Sharing rates*. If a VECP is accepted, the Contractor shall share in net acquisition savings according to the percentages shown in the table below. The percentage paid the Contractor depends upon—

(1) This contract's type (fixed-price, incentive, or cost-reimbursement);

(2) The sharing arrangement specified in paragraph (a) above (incentive, program requirement, or a combination as delineated in the Schedule); and

(3) The source of the savings (the instant contract, or concurrent and future contracts), as follows:

Contractor's Share of Net Acquisition Savings
[Figures in percent]

Contract type	Sharing arrangement: Incentive (voluntary) — Instant contract rate	Incentive (voluntary) — Concurrent and future contract rate	Program requirement (mandatory) — Instant contract rate	Program requirement (mandatory) — Concurrent and future contract rate
Fixed-price (includes fixed-price-award-fee; excludes other fixed-price incentive contracts)	* 50	* 50	25	25
Incentive (fixed-price or cost) (other than award fee)	(**)	* 50	(**)	25
Cost-reimbursement (includes cost-plus-award fee; excludes other cost-type incentive contracts)	*** 25	*** 25	15	15

* The contracting officer may increase the contractor's sharing rate to as high as 75 percent for each VECP.
** Same sharing arrangement as the contract's profit or fee adjustment formula.
*** The contracting officer may increase the contractor's sharing rate to as high as 50 percent for each VECP.

(g) *Calculating net acquisition savings.* (1) Acquisition savings are realized when (i) the cost or price is reduced on the instant contract, (ii) reductions are negotiated in concurrent contracts, (iii) future contracts are awarded, or (iv) agreement is reached on a lump-sum payment for future contract savings (see subparagraph (i)(4) below). Net acquisition savings are first realized, and the Contractor shall be paid a share, when Government costs and any negative instant contract savings have been fully offset against acquisition savings.

(2) Except in incentive contracts, Government costs and any price or cost increases resulting from negative instant contract savings shall be offset against acquisition savings each time such savings are realized until they are fully offset. Then, the Contractor's share is calculated by multiplying net acquisition savings by the appropriate Contractor's percentage sharing rate (see paragraph (f) above). Additional Contractor shares of net acquisition savings shall be paid to the Contractor at the time realized.

(3) If this is an incentive contract, recovery of Government costs on the instant contract shall be deferred and offset against concurrent and future contract savings. The Contractor shall share through the contract incentive structure in savings on the instant contract items affected. Any negative instant contract savings shall be added to the target cost or to the target price and ceiling price, and the amount shall be offset against concurrent and future contract savings.

(4) If the Government does not receive and accept all items on which it paid the Contractor's share, the Contractor shall reimburse the Government for the proportionate share of these payments.

(h) *Contract adjustment.* The modification accepting the VECP (or a subsequent modification issued as soon as possible after any negotiations are completed) shall—

(1) Reduce the contract price or estimated cost by the amount of instant contract savings, unless this is an incentive contract;

(2) When the amount of instant contract savings is negative, increase the contract price, target price and ceiling price, target cost, or estimated cost by that amount;

(3) Specify the Contractor's dollar share per unit on future contracts, or provide the lump-sum payment;

(4) Specify the amount of any Government costs or negative instant contract savings to be offset in determining net acquisition savings realized from concurrent or future contract savings; and

(5) Provide the Contractor's share of any net acquisition savings under the instant contract in accordance with the following:

(i) Fixed-price contracts—add to contract price.

(ii) Cost-reimbursement contracts—add to contract fee.

(i) *Concurrent and future contract savings.* (1) Payments of the Contractor's share of concurrent and future contract savings shall be made by a modification to the instant contract in accordance with subparagraph (h)(5) above. For incentive contracts, shares shall be added as a separate firm-fixed-price line item on the instant contract. The Contractor shall maintain records adequate to identify the first delivered unit for 3 years after final payment under this contract.

(2) The Contracting Officer shall calculate the Contractor's share of concurrent contract savings by—

(i) Subtracting from the reduction in price negotiated on the concurrent contract any Government costs or negative instant contract savings not yet offset; and by

(ii) Multiplying the result by the Contractor's sharing rate.

(3) The Contracting Officer shall calculate the Contractor's share of future contract savings by—

(i) Multiplying the future unit cost reduction by the number of future contract units scheduled for delivery during the sharing period;

(ii) Subtracting any Government costs or negative instant contract savings not yet offset; and

(iii) Multiplying the result by the Contractor's sharing rate.

(4) When the Government wishes and the Contractor agrees, the Contractor's share of future contract savings may be paid in a single lump sum rather than in a series of payments over time as future contracts are awarded. Under this alternate procedure, the future contract savings may be calculated when the VECP is accepted, on the basis of the Contracting Officer's forecast of the number of units that will be delivered during the sharing period. The Contractor's share shall be included in a modification to this contract (see subparagraph (h)(3) above) and shall not be subject to subsequent adjustment.

(5) *Alternate no-cost settlement method.* When, in accordance with subsection 48.104-4 of the Federal Acquisition Regulation, the Government and the Contractor mutually agree to use the no-cost settlement method, the following applies:

(i) The Contractor will keep all the savings on the instant contract and on its concurrent contracts only.

(ii) The Government will keep all the savings resulting from concurrent contracts placed on other sources, savings from all future contracts, and all collateral savings.

(j) *Collateral savings.* If a VECP is accepted, the Contracting Officer will increase the instant contract amount, as specified in paragraph (h)(5) of this clause, by a rate from 20 to 100 percent, as determined by the Contracting Officer, of any projected collateral savings determined to be realized in a typical year of use after subtracting any Government costs not previously offset. However, the Contractor's share of collateral savings will not exceed the contract's firm-fixed-price, target price, target cost, or estimated cost, at the time the VECP is accepted, or $100,000, whichever is greater. The Contracting Officer will be the sole determiner of the amount of collateral savings.

(k) *Relationship to other incentives.* Only those benefits of an accepted VECP not rewardable under performance, design-to-cost (production unit cost, operating and support costs, reliability and maintainability), or similar incentives shall be rewarded under this clause. However, the targets of such incentives affected by the VECP shall not be adjusted because of VECP acceptance. If this contract specifies targets but provides no incentive to surpass them, the value engineering sharing shall apply only to the amount of achievement better than target.

(l) *Subcontracts.* The Contractor shall include an appropriate value engineering clause in any subcontract of $150,000 or more and may include one in subcontracts of lesser value. In calculating any adjustment in this contract's price for instant contract savings (or negative instant contract savings), the Contractor's allowable development and implementation costs shall include any subcontractor's allowable development and implementation costs, and any value engineering incentive payments to a subcontractor, clearly resulting from a VECP accepted by the Government under this contract. The Contractor may choose any arrangement for subcontractor value engineering incentive payments; *provided,* that the payments shall not reduce the Government's share of concurrent or future contract savings or collateral savings.

(m) *Data.* The Contractor may restrict the Government's right to use any part of a VECP or the supporting data by marking the following legend on the affected parts:

"These data, furnished under the Value Engineering clause of contract ____, shall not be disclosed outside the Government or duplicated, used, or disclosed, in whole or in part, for any purpose other than to evaluate a value engineering change proposal submitted under the clause. This restriction does not limit the Government's right to use information contained in these data if it has been obtained or is otherwise available from the Contractor or from another source without limitations."

If a VECP is accepted, the Contractor hereby grants the Government unlimited rights in the VECP and supporting data, except that, with respect to data qualifying and submitted as limited rights technical data, the Government shall have the rights specified in the contract modification implementing the VECP and shall appropriately mark the data. (The terms "unlimited rights" and "limited rights" are defined in Part 27 of the Federal Acquisition Regulation.)

(End of clause)

Alternate I (APR 1984). If the contracting officer selects a mandatory value engineering program requirement, substitute the following paragraph (a) for paragraph (a) of the basic clause:

(a) *General.* The Contractor shall (1) engage in a value engineering program, and submit value engineering progress reports, as specified in the Schedule and (2) submit to the Contracting Officer any resulting value engineering change proposals (VECP's). In addition to being paid as the Schedule specifies for this mandatory program, the Contractor shall share in any net acquisition savings realized from accepted VECP's, in accordance with the program requirement sharing rates in paragraph (f) below.

Alternate II (JAN 2017). If the contracting officer selects both a value engineering incentive and mandatory value engineering program requirement, substitute the following paragraph (a) for paragraph (a) of the basic clause:

(a) *General.* For those line items designated in the Schedule as subject to the value engineering program requirement, the Contractor shall (1) engage in a value engineering program, and submit value engineering progress reports, as specified in the Schedule and (2) submit to the Contracting Officer any resulting VECP's. In addition to being paid as the Schedule specifies for this mandatory program, the Contractor shall share in any net acquisition savings realized from VECP's accepted under the program, in accordance with the program requirement sharing rates in paragraph (f) below. For remaining areas of the contract, the Contractor is encouraged to develop, prepare, and submit VECP's voluntarily; for VECP's accepted under these remaining areas, the incentive sharing rates apply. The decision on which rate applies is a unilateral decision made solely at the discretion of the Government.

Alternate III (APR 1984). When the head of the contracting activity determines that the cost of calculating and tracking collateral savings will exceed the benefits to be derived in a contract calling for a value engineering incentive, delete paragraph (j) from the basic clause and redesignate the remaining paragraphs accordingly.

[FAC 84-42, 54 FR 5059, 1/31/89, effective 3/2/89; FAC 90-32, 60 FR 48206, 9/18/95, effective 10/1/95; FAC 97-14, 64 FR 51828, 9/24/99, effective 11/23/99; FAC 97-15, 64 FR 72414, 12/27/99, effective 2/25/2000; FAC 2005-45, 75 FR 53129, 8/30/2010, effective 10/1/2010; FAC 2005-95, 82 FR 4709, 1/13/2017, effective 1/13/2017]

52.248-2 Value Engineering—Architect-Engineer.

As prescribed in 48.201(f), insert the following clause:

VALUE ENGINEERING—ARCHITECT-ENGINEER (MAR 1990)

(a) *General*. The Contractor shall (1) perform value engineering (VE) services and submit progress reports as specified in the Schedule; and (2) submit to the Contracting Officer any resulting value engineering proposals (VEP's). Value engineering activities shall be performed concurrently with, and without delay to, the schedule set forth in the contract. The services shall include VE evaluation and review and study of design documents immediately following completion of the 35 percent design state or at such stages as the Contracting Officer may direct. Each separately priced line item for VE services shall define specifically the scope of work to be accomplished and may include VE studies of items other than design documents. The Contractor shall be paid as the contract specifies for this effort, but shall not share in savings which may result from acceptance and use of VEP's by the Government.

(b) *Definitions. Life cycle cost*, as used in this clause, is the sum of all costs over the useful life of a building, system or product. It includes the cost of design, construction, acquisition, operation, maintenance, and salvage (resale) value, if any.

Value engineering, as used in this clause, means an organized effort to analyze the functions of systems, equipment, facilities, services, and supplies for the purpose of achieving the essential functions at the lowest life cycle cost consistent with required performance, reliability, quality, and safety.

Value engineering proposal, as used in this clause, means, in connection with an A-E contract, a change proposal developed by employees of the Federal Government or contractor value engineering personnel under contract to an agency to provide value engineering services for the contract or program.

(c) *Submissions*. After award of an architect-engineering contract the contractor shall—

(1) Provide the Government with a fee breakdown schedule for the VE services (such as criteria review, task team review, and bid package review) included in the contract schedule;

(2) Submit, for approval by the Contracting Officer, a list of team members and their respective resumes representing the engineering disciplines required to complete the study effort, and evidence of the team leader's qualifications and engineering discipline. Subsequent changes or substitutions to the approved VE team shall be submitted in writing to the Contracting Officer for approval; and

(3) The team leader shall be responsible for pre—study work assembly and shall edit, reproduce, and sign the final report and each VEP. All VEP's, even if submitted earlier as an individual submission, shall be contained in the final report.

(d) *VEP preparation*. As a minimum, the contractor shall include the following information in each VEP:

(1) A description of the difference between the existing and the proposed design, the comparative advantages and disadvantages of each, a justification when an item's function is being altered, the effect of the change on system or facility performance, and any pertinent objective test data.

(2) A list and analysis of design criteria or specifications that must be changed if the VEP is accepted.

(3) A separate detailed estimate of the impact on project cost of each VEP, if accepted and implemented by the Government.

(4) A description and estimate of costs the Government may incur in implementing the VEP, such as design change cost and test and evaluation cost.

(5) A prediction of any effects the proposed change may have on life cycle cost.

(6) The effect the VEP will have on design or construction schedules.

(e) *VEP acceptance*. Approved VEP's shall be implemented by bilateral modification to this contract.

(End of clause.)

[FAC 84-56, 55 FR 3889, 2/5/90, effective 3/7/90]

52.248-3 Value Engineering—Construction.

As prescribed in 48.202, insert the following clause:

VALUE ENGINEERING-CONSTRUCTION (OCT 2015)

(a) *General*. The Contractor is encouraged to develop, prepare, and submit value engineering change proposals (VECP's) voluntarily. The Contractor shall share in any instant contract savings realized from accepted VECP's, in accordance with paragraph (f) below.

(b) *Definitions*. *Collateral costs,* as used in this clause, means agency costs of operation, maintenance, logistic support, or Government-furnished property.

Collateral savings, as used in this clause, means those measurable net reductions resulting from a VECP in the agency's overall projected collateral costs, exclusive of acquisition savings, whether or not the acquisition cost changes.

Contractor's development and implementation costs, as used in this clause, means those costs the Contractor incurs on a VECP specifically in developing, testing, preparing, and submitting the VECP, as well as those costs the Contractor incurs to make the contractual changes required by Government acceptance of a VECP.

Government costs, as used in this clause, means those agency costs that result directly from developing and implementing the VECP, such as any net increases in the cost of testing, operations, maintenance, and logistic support. The term does not include the normal administrative costs of processing the VECP.

Instant contract savings, as used in this clause, means the estimated reduction in Contractor cost of performance resulting from acceptance of the VECP, minus allowable Contractor's development and implementation costs, including subcontractors' development and implementation costs (see paragraph (h) below).

Value engineering change proposal (VECP) means a proposal that—

(1) Requires a change to this, the instant contract, to implement; and

(2) Results in reducing the contract price or estimated cost without impairing essential functions or characteristics; *provided*, that it does not involve a change—

(i) In deliverable end item quantities only; or

(ii) To the contract type only.

(c) *VECP preparation*. As a minimum, the Contractor shall include in each VECP the information described in subparagraphs (c)(1) through (7) below. If the proposed change is affected by contractually required configuration management or similar procedures, the instructions in those procedures relating to format, identification, and priority assignment shall govern VECP preparation. The VECP shall include the following:

(1) A description of the difference between the existing contract requirement and that proposed, the comparative advantages and disadvantages of each, a justification when an item's function or characteristics are being altered, and the effect of the change on the end item's performance.

(2) A list and analysis of the contract requirements that must be changed if the VECP is accepted, including any suggested specification revisions.

(3) A separate, detailed cost estimate for (i) the affected portions of the existing contract requirement and (ii) the VECP. The cost reduction associated with the VECP shall take into account the Contractor's allowable development and implementation costs, including any amount attributable to subcontracts under paragraph (h) below.

(4) A description and estimate of costs the Government may incur in implementing the VECP, such as test and evaluation and operating and support costs.

(5) A prediction of any effects the proposed change would have on collateral costs to the agency.

(6) A statement of the time by which a contract modification accepting the VECP must be issued in order to achieve the maximum cost reduction, noting any effect on the contract completion time or delivery schedule.

(7) Identification of any previous submissions of the VECP, including the dates submitted, the agencies and contract numbers involved, and previous Government actions, if known.

(d) *Submission*. The Contractor shall submit VECP's to the Resident Engineer at the worksite, with a copy to the Contracting Officer.

(e) *Government action*. (1) The Contracting Officer will notify the Contractor of the status of the VECP within 45 calendar days after the contracting office receives it. If additional time is required, the Contracting Officer will notify the Contractor within the 45-day period and provide the reason for the delay and the expected date of the decision. The Government will process VECP's expeditiously; however, it will not be liable for any delay in acting upon a VECP.

(2) If the VECP is not accepted, the Contracting Officer will notify the Contractor in writing, explaining the reasons for rejection. The Contractor may withdraw any VECP, in whole or in part, at any time before it is accepted by the Government. The Contracting Officer may require that the Contractor provide written notification before undertaking significant expenditures for VECP effort.

(3) Any VECP may be accepted, in whole or in part, by the Contracting Officer's award of a modification to this contract citing this clause. The Contracting Officer may accept the VECP, even though an agreement on price reduction has not been reached, by issuing the Contractor a notice to proceed with the change. Until a notice to proceed is issued or a contract modification applies a VECP to this contract, the Contractor shall perform in accordance with the existing contract. The decision to accept or reject all or part of any VECP is a unilateral decision made solely at the discretion of the Contracting Officer.

(f) *Sharing*—

(1) *Rates*. The Government's share of savings is determined by subtracting Government costs from instant contract savings and multiplying the result by—

(i) 45 percent for fixed-price contracts; or

(ii) 75 percent for cost-reimbursement contracts.

(2) *Payment*. Payment of any share due the Contractor for use of a VECP on this contract shall be authorized by a modification to this contract to—

(i) Accept the VECP;

(ii) Reduce the contract price or estimated cost by the amount of instant contract savings; and

(iii) Provide the Contractor's share of savings by adding the amount calculated to the contract price or fee.

(g) *Collateral savings*. If a VECP is accepted, the Contracting Officer will increase the instant contract amount by 20 percent of any projected collateral savings determined to be realized in a typical year of use after subtracting any Government costs not previously offset. However, the Contractor's share of collateral savings will not exceed the contract's firm-fixed-price or estimated cost, at the time the VECP is accepted, or $100,000, whichever is greater. The Contracting Officer is the sole determiner of the amount of collateral savings.

(h) *Subcontracts*. The Contractor shall include an appropriate value engineering clause in any subcontract of $70,000 or more and may include one in subcontracts of lesser value. In computing any adjustment in this contract's price under paragraph (f) above, the Contractor's allowable development and implementation costs shall include any subcontractor's allowable development and implementation costs clearly resulting from a VECP accepted by the Government under this contract, but shall exclude any value engineering incentive payments to a subcontractor. The Contractor may choose any arrangement for subcontractor value engineering incentive payments; *provided*, that these payments shall not reduce the Government's share of the savings resulting from the VECP.

(i) *Data*. The Contractor may restrict the Government's right to use any part of a VECP or the supporting data by marking the following legend on the affected parts:

"These data, furnished under the Value Engineering—Construction clause of contract ____, shall not be disclosed outside the Government or duplicated, used, or disclosed, in whole or in part, for any purpose other than to evaluate a value engineering change proposal submitted under the clause. This restriction does not limit the Government's right to use information contained in these data if it has been obtained or is otherwise available from the Contractor or from another source without limitations."

If a VECP is accepted, the Contractor hereby grants the Government unlimited rights in the VECP and supporting data, except that, with respect to data qualifying and submitted as limited rights technical data, the Government shall have the rights specified in the contract modification implementing the VECP and shall appropriately mark the data. (The terms "unlimited rights" and "limited rights" are defined in Part 27 of the Federal Acquisition Regulation.)

(End of clause)

Alternate I (APR 1984). When the head of the contracting activity determines that the cost of calculating and tracking collateral savings will exceed the benefits to be derived in a construction contract, delete paragraph (g) from the basic clause and redesignate the remaining paragraphs accordingly.

[FAC 84-42, 54 FR 5059, 1/31/89, effective 3/2/89; FAC 97-15, 64 FR 72414, 12/27/99, effective 2/25/2000; FAC 2005-13, 71 FR 57363, 9/28/2006, effective 9/28/2006; FAC 2005-45, 75 FR 53129, 8/30/2010, effective 10/1/2010; FAC 2005-83, 80 FR 38293, 7/2/2015, effective 10/1/2015]

52.249-1 Termination for Convenience of the Government (Fixed-Price) (Short Form).

As prescribed in 49.502(a)(1), insert the following clause:

TERMINATION FOR CONVENIENCE OF THE GOVERNMENT (FIXED-PRICE) (SHORT FORM) (APR 1984)

The Contracting Officer, by written notice, may terminate this contract, in whole or in part, when it is in the Government's interest. If this contract is terminated, the rights, duties, and obligations of the parties, including compensation to the Contractor, shall be in accordance with Part 49 of the Federal Acquisition Regulation in effect on the date of this contract.

(End of clause)

Alternate I (APR 1984). If the contract is for dismantling, demolition, or removal of improvements, designate the basic clause as paragraph (a) and add the following paragraph (b):

(b) Upon receipt of the termination notice, if title to property is vested in the Contractor under this contract, it shall revest in the Government regardless of any other clause of the contract, except for property that the Contractor (a) disposed of by bona fide sale or (b) removed from the site.

[FAC 90-32, 60 FR 48206, 9/18/95, effective 10/1/95; FAC 2005-13, 71 FR 57363, 9/28/2006, effective 9/28/2006]

52.249-2 Termination for Convenience of the Government (Fixed-Price).

As prescribed in 49.502(b)(1)(i), insert the following clause:

TERMINATION FOR CONVENIENCE OF THE GOVERNMENT (FIXED-PRICE) (APR 2012)

(a) The Government may terminate performance of work under this contract in whole or, from time to time, in part if the Contracting Officer determines that a termination is in the Government's interest. The Contracting Officer shall terminate by delivering to the Contractor a Notice of Termination specifying the extent of termination and the effective date.

(b) After receipt of a Notice of Termination, and except as directed by the Contracting Officer, the Contractor shall immediately proceed with the following obligations, regardless of any delay in determining or adjusting any amounts due under this clause:

(1) Stop work as specified in the notice.

(2) Place no further subcontracts or orders (referred to as subcontracts in this clause) for materials, services, or facilities, except as necessary to complete the continued portion of the contract.

(3) Terminate all subcontracts to the extent they relate to the work terminated.

(4) Assign to the Government, as directed by the Contracting Officer, all right, title, and interest of the Contractor under the subcontracts terminated, in which case the Government shall have the right to settle or to pay any termination settlement proposal arising out of those terminations.

(5) With approval or ratification to the extent required by the Contracting Officer, settle all outstanding liabilities and termination settlement proposals arising from the termination of subcontracts; the approval or ratification will be final for purposes of this clause.

(6) As directed by the Contracting Officer, transfer title and deliver to the Government—

(i) The fabricated or unfabricated parts, work in process, completed work, supplies, and other material produced or acquired for the work terminated; and

(ii) The completed or partially completed plans, drawings, information, and other property that, if the contract had been completed, would be required to be furnished to the Government.

(7) Complete performance of the work not terminated.

(8) Take any action that may be necessary, or that the Contracting Officer may direct, for the protection and preservation of the property related to this contract that is in the possession of the Contractor and in which the Government has or may acquire an interest.

(9) Use its best efforts to sell, as directed or authorized by the Contracting Officer, any property of the types referred to in subparagraph (b)(6) of this clause; *provided*, however, that the Contractor (i) is not required to extend credit to any purchaser and (ii) may acquire the property under the conditions prescribed by, and at prices approved by, the Contracting Officer. The proceeds of any transfer or disposition will be applied to reduce any payments to be made by the Government under this contract, credited to the price or cost of the work, or paid in any other manner directed by the Contracting Officer.

(c) The Contractor shall submit complete termination inventory schedules no later than 120 days from the effective date of termination, unless extended in writing by the Contracting Officer upon written request of the Contractor within this 120-day period.

(d) After expiration of the plant clearance period as defined in Subpart 49.001 of the Federal Acquisition Regulation, the Contractor may submit to the Contracting Officer a list, certified as to quantity and quality, of termination inventory not previously disposed of, excluding items authorized for disposition by the Contracting Officer. The Contractor may request the Government to remove those items or enter into an agreement for their storage. Within 15 days, the Government will accept title to those items and remove them or enter into a storage agreement. The Contracting Officer may verify the list upon removal of the items, or if stored, within 45 days from submission of the list, and shall correct the list, as necessary, before final settlement.

(e) After termination, the Contractor shall submit a final termination settlement proposal to the Contracting Officer in the form and with the certification prescribed by the Contracting Officer. The Contractor shall submit the proposal promptly, but no later than 1 year from the effective date of termination, unless extended in writing by the Contracting Officer upon written request of the Contractor within this 1-year period. However, if the Contracting Officer determines that the facts justify it, a termination settlement proposal may be received and acted on after 1 year or any extension. If the Contractor fails to submit the proposal within the time allowed, the Contracting Officer may determine, on the basis of information available, the amount, if any, due the Contractor because of the termination and shall pay the amount determined.

(f) Subject to paragraph (e) of this clause, the Contractor and the Contracting Officer may agree upon the whole or any part of the amount to be paid or remaining to be paid because of the termination. The amount may include a reasonable allowance for profit on work done. However, the agreed amount, whether under this paragraph (f) or paragraph (g) of this clause, exclusive of costs shown in subparagraph (g)(3) of this clause, may not exceed the total contract price as reduced by (1) the amount of payments previously made and (2) the contract price of work not terminated. The contract shall be modified, and the Contractor paid the agreed amount. Paragraph (g) of this clause shall not limit, restrict, or affect the amount that may be agreed upon to be paid under this paragraph.

(g) If the Contractor and the Contracting Officer fail to agree on the whole amount to be paid because of the termination of work, the Contracting Officer shall pay the Contractor the amounts determined by the Contracting Officer as follows, but without duplication of any amounts agreed on under paragraph (f) of this clause:

(1) The contract price for completed supplies or services accepted by the Government (or sold or acquired under subparagraph (b)(9) of this clause) not previously paid for, adjusted for any saving of freight and other charges.

(2) The total of—

(i) The costs incurred in the performance of the work terminated, including initial costs and preparatory expense allocable thereto, but excluding any costs attributable to supplies or services paid or to be paid under subparagraph (g)(1) of this clause;

(ii) The cost of settling and paying termination settlement proposals under terminated subcontracts that are properly chargeable to the terminated portion of the contract if not included in subdivision (g)(2)(i) of this clause; and

(iii) A sum, as profit on subdivision (g)(2)(i) of this clause, determined by the Contracting Officer under 49.202 of the Federal Acquisition Regulation, in effect on the date of this contract, to be fair and reasonable; however, if it appears that the Contractor would have sustained a loss on the entire contract had it been completed, the Contracting Officer shall allow no profit under this subdivision (g)(2)(iii) and shall reduce the settlement to reflect the indicated rate of loss.

(3) The reasonable costs of settlement of the work terminated, including—

(i) Accounting, legal, clerical, and other expenses reasonably necessary for the preparation of termination settlement proposals and supporting data;

(ii) The termination and settlement of subcontracts (excluding the amounts of such settlements); and

(iii) Storage, transportation, and other costs incurred, reasonably necessary for the preservation, protection, or disposition of the termination inventory.

(h) Except for normal spoilage, and except to the extent that the Government expressly assumed the risk of loss, the Contracting Officer shall exclude from the amounts payable to the Contractor under paragraph (g) of this clause, the fair value as determined by the Contracting Officer, for the loss of the Government property.

(i) The cost principles and procedures of part 31 of the Federal Acquisition Regulation, in effect on the date of this contract, shall govern all costs claimed, agreed to, or determined under this clause.

(j) The Contractor shall have the right of appeal, under the Disputes clause, from any determination made by the Contracting Officer under paragraph (e), (g), or (l) of this clause, except that if the Contractor failed to submit the termination settlement proposal or request for equitable adjustment within the time provided in paragraph (e) or (l), respectively, and failed to request a time extension, there is no right of appeal.

(k) In arriving at the amount due the Contractor under this clause, there shall be deducted—

(1) All unliquidated advance or other payments to the Contractor under the terminated portion of this contract;

(2) Any claim which the Government has against the Contractor under this contract; and

(3) The agreed price for, or the proceeds of sale of, materials, supplies, or other things acquired by the Contractor or sold under the provisions of this clause and not recovered by or credited to the Government.

(l) If the termination is partial, the Contractor may file a proposal with the Contracting Officer for an equitable adjustment of the price(s) of the continued portion of the contract. The Contracting Officer shall make any equitable adjustment agreed upon. Any proposal by the Contractor for an equitable adjustment under this clause shall be requested within 90 days from the effective date of termination unless extended in writing by the Contracting Officer.

(m)(1) The Government may, under the terms and conditions it prescribes, make partial payments and payments against costs incurred by the Contractor for the terminated portion of the contract, if the Contracting Officer believes the total of these payments will not exceed the amount to which the Contractor will be entitled.

(2) If the total payments exceed the amount finally determined to be due, the Contractor shall repay the excess to the Government upon demand, together with interest computed at the rate established by the Secretary of the Treasury under 50 U.S.C. App. 1215(b)(2). Interest shall be computed for the period from the date the excess payment is received by the Contractor to the date the excess is repaid. Interest shall not be charged on any excess payment due to a reduction in the Contractor's termination settlement proposal because of retention or other disposition of termination inventory until 10 days after the date of the retention or disposition, or a later date determined by the Contracting Officer because of the circumstances.

(n) Unless otherwise provided in this contract or by statute, the Contractor shall maintain all records and documents relating to the terminated portion of this contract for 3 years after final settlement. This includes all books and other evidence bearing on the Contractor's costs and expenses under this contract. The Contractor shall make these records and documents available to the Government, at the Contractor's office, at all reasonable times, without any direct charge. If approved by the Contracting Officer, photographs, microphotographs, or other authentic reproductions may be maintained instead of original records and documents.

(End of clause)

Alternate I (SEP 1996). If the contract is for construction, substitute the following paragraph (g) for paragraph (g) of the basic clause:

(g) If the Contractor and Contracting Officer fail to agree on the whole amount to be paid the Contractor because of the termination of work, the Contracting Officer shall pay the Contractor the amounts determined as follows, but without duplication of any amounts agreed upon under paragraph (f) of this clause:

(1) For contract work performed before the effective date of termination, the total (without duplication of any items) of—

(i) The cost of this work;

(ii) The cost of settling and paying termination settlement proposals under terminated subcontracts that are properly chargeable to the terminated portion of the contract if not included in subdivision (g)(1)(i) of this clause; and

(iii) A sum, as profit on subdivision (g)(1)(i) of this clause, determined by the Contracting Officer under 49.202 of the Federal Acquisition Regulation, in effect on the date of this contract, to be fair and reasonable; however, if it appears that the Contractor would have sustained a loss on the entire contract had it been completed, the Contracting Officer shall allow no profit under this subdivision (g)(1)(iii) and shall reduce the settlement to reflect the indicated rate of loss.

(2) The reasonable costs of settlement of the work terminated, including—

(i) Accounting, legal, clerical, and other expenses reasonably necessary for the preparation of termination settlement proposals and supporting data;

(ii) The termination and settlement of subcontracts (excluding the amounts of such settlements); and

(iii) Storage, transportation, and other costs incurred, reasonably necessary for the preservation, protection, or disposition of the termination inventory.

Alternate II (SEP 1996). If the contract is with an agency of the U.S. Government or with State, local, or foreign governments or their agencies, and if the Contracting Officer determines that the requirement to pay interest on excess partial payments is inappropriate, delete subparagraph (m)(2) of the basic clause.

Alternate III (SEP 1996). If the contract is for construction and with an agency of the U.S. Government or with State, local, or foreign governments or their agencies, substitute the following paragraph (g) for paragraph (g) of the basic clause. Subparagraph (m)(2) may be deleted from the basic clause if the Contracting Officer determines that the requirement to pay interest on excess partial payments is inappropriate.

(g) If the Contractor and Contracting Officer fail to agree on the whole amount to be paid the Contractor because of the termination of work, the Contracting Officer shall pay the Contractor the amounts determined as follows, but without duplication of any amounts agreed upon under paragraph (f) of this clause:

(1) For contract work performed before the effective date of termination, the total (without duplication of any items) of—

(i) The cost of this work;

(ii) The cost of settling and paying termination settlement proposals under terminated subcontracts that are properly chargeable to the terminated portion of the contract if not included in subdivision (g)(1)(i) of this clause; and

(iii) A sum, as profit on subdivision (g)(1)(i) of this clause, determined by the Contracting Officer under 49.202 of the Federal Acquisition Regulation, in effect on the date of this contract, to be fair and reasonable; however, if it appears that the Contractor would have sustained a loss on the entire contract had it been completed, the Contracting Officer shall allow no profit under this subdivision (iii) and shall reduce the settlement to reflect the indicated rate of loss.

(2) The reasonable costs of settlement of the work terminated, including—

(i) Accounting, legal, clerical, and other expenses reasonably necessary for the preparation of termination settlement proposals and supporting data;

(ii) The termination and settlement of subcontracts (excluding the amounts of such settlements); and

(iii) Storage, transportation, and other costs incurred, reasonably necessary for the preservation, protection, or disposition of the termination inventory.

[Final rule, 55 FR 38518, 9/18/90; FAC 90-32, 60 FR 48206, 9/18/95, effective 10/1/95; FAC 90-39, 61 FR 31612, 6/20/96, effective 8/19/96; FAC 90-40, 61 FR 39186, 7/29/96, effective 9/24/96; FAC 2001-22, 69 FR 17741, 4/5/2004, effective 5/5/2004; FAC 2005-56, 77 FR 12937, 3/2/2012, effective 4/2/2012; CFR Correction, 78 FR 26518, 5/7/2013, effective 5/7/2013]

52.249-3 Termination for Convenience of the Government (Dismantling, Demolition, or Removal of Improvements).

As prescribed in 49.502(b)(2), insert the following clause:

TERMINATION FOR CONVENIENCE OF THE GOVERNMENT (DISMANTLING, DEMOLITION, OR REMOVAL OF IMPROVEMENTS) (APR 2012)

(a) The Government may terminate performance of work under this contract, in whole or, from time to time, in part if the Contracting Officer determines that a termination is in the Government's interest. The Contracting Officer shall terminate by delivering to the Contractor a Notice of Termination specifying the extent of termination and the effective date. Upon receipt of the notice, if title to property is vested in the Contractor under this contract, it shall revest in the Government regardless of any other clause of this contract, except for property that the Contractor disposed of by bona fide sale or removed from the site.

(b) After receipt of a Notice of Termination, and except as directed by the Contracting Officer, the Contractor shall immediately proceed with the following obligations, regardless of delay in determining or adjusting any amounts due under this clause:

(1) Stop work as specified in the notice.

(2) Place no further subcontracts or orders (referred to as subcontracts in this clause) for materials, services, or facilities, except as necessary to complete the continued portion of the contract.

(3) Terminate all subcontracts to the extent they relate to the work terminated.

(4) Assign to the Government, as directed by the Contracting Officer, all right, title, and interest of the Contractor under the subcontracts terminated, in which case the Government shall have the right to settle or to pay any termination settlement proposal arising out of those terminations.

(5) With approval or ratification to the extent required by the Contracting Officer, settle all outstanding liabilities and termination settlement proposals arising from the termination of subcontracts; the approval or ratification will be final for purposes of this clause.

(6) As directed by the Contracting Officer, transfer title and deliver to the Government—

(i) The fabricated or unfabricated parts, work in process, completed work, supplies, and other material produced or acquired for the work terminated; and

(ii) The completed or partially completed plans, drawings, information, and other property that, if the contract has been completed, would be required to be furnished to the Government.

(7) Complete performance of the work not terminated.

(8) Take any action that may be necessary, or that the Contracting Officer may direct, for the protection and preservation of the property related to this contract that is in the possession of the Contractor and in which the Government has or may acquire an interest.

(9) Use its best efforts to sell, as directed or authorized by the Contracting Officer, any property of the types referred to in subparagraph (b)(6) of this clause; provided, however, that the Contractor (i) is not required to extend credit to any purchaser and (ii) may acquire the property under the conditions prescribed by, and at prices approved by, the Contracting Officer. The proceeds of any transfer or disposition will be applied to reduce any payments to be made by the Government under this contract, credited to the price or cost of the work, or paid in any other manner directed by the Contracting Officer.

(c) The Contractor shall submit complete termination inventory schedules no later than 120 days from the effective date of termination, unless extended in writing by the Contracting Officer upon written request of the Contractor within this 120-day period.

(d) After expiration of the plant clearance period as defined in Subpart 49.001 of the Federal Acquisition Regulation, the Contractor may submit to the Contracting Officer a list, certified as to quantity and quality, of termination inventory not previously disposed of, excluding items authorized for disposition by the Contracting Officer. The Contractor may request the Government to remove those items or enter into an agreement for their storage. Within 15 days, the Government will accept title to those items and remove them or enter into a storage agreement. The Contracting Officer may verify the list upon removal of the items, or if stored, within 45 days from submission of the list, and shall correct the list, as necessary, before final settlement.

(e) After termination, the Contractor shall submit a final termination settlement proposal to the Contracting Officer in the form and with the certification prescribed by the Contracting Officer. The Contractor shall submit the proposal promptly, but no later than 1 year from the effective date of termination, unless extended in writing by the Contracting Officer upon written request of the Contractor within this 1-year period. However, if the Contracting Officer determines that the facts justify it, a termination settlement proposal may be received and acted on after 1 year or any extension. If the Contractor fails to submit the proposal within the time allowed, the Contracting Officer may determine, on the basis of information available, the amount, if any, due the Contractor because of the termination and shall pay the amount determined.

(f) Subject to paragraph (e) of this clause, the Contractor and the Contracting Officer may agree upon the whole or any part of the amount to be paid because of the termination. The amount may include a reasonable allowance for profit on work done. However, the agreed amount, whether under this paragraph (f) or paragraph (g) of this clause, exclusive of settlement costs, may not exceed the total contract price as reduced by (1) the amount of payments previously made and (2) the contract price of work not terminated. The contract shall be amended and the Contractor paid the agreed amount. Paragraph (g) of this clause shall not limit, restrict, or affect the amount that may be agreed upon to be paid under this paragraph.

(g) If the Contractor and the Contracting Officer fail to agree on the whole amount to be paid because of the termination of work, the Contracting Officer shall pay the Contractor the amounts determined by the Contracting Officer as follows, but without duplication of any amounts agreed on under paragraph (f) of this clause:

(1) For contract work performed before the effective date of termination, the total (without duplication of any items) of—

(i) The cost of this work;

(ii) The cost of settling and paying termination settlement proposals under terminated subcontracts that are properly chargeable to the terminated portion of the contract, if not included in subdivision (g)(1)(i) of this clause; and

(iii) A sum, as profit on subdivision (g)(1)(i) of this clause, determined by the Contracting Officer under section 49.202 of the Federal Acquisition Regulation, in effect on the date of this contract, to be fair and reasonable; however, if it appears that the Contractor would have sustained a loss on the entire contract had it been completed, the Contracting Officer shall allow no profit under this subdivision (iii) and shall reduce the amount of the settlement to reflect the indicated rate of loss.

(2) The reasonable costs of settlement of the work terminated, including—

(i) Accounting, legal, clerical, and other expenses reasonably necessary for the preparation of termination settlement proposals and supporting data;

(ii) The termination and settlement of subcontracts (excluding the amounts of such settlements); and

(iii) Preservation and protection of property under subparagraph (b)(8) of this clause.

(h) Except for normal spoilage, and except to the extent that the Government expressly assumed the risk of loss, the Contracting Officer shall exclude from the amounts payable to the Contractor under paragraph (g) of this clause, the fair value, as determined by the Contracting Officer, for the loss of the Government property.

(i) The cost principles and procedures of Part 31 of the Federal Acquisition Regulation, in effect on the date of this contract, shall govern all costs claimed, agreed to, or determined under this clause.

(j) The Contractor shall have the right of appeal, under the Disputes clause, from any determination made by the Contracting Officer under paragraph (e), (g), or (l) of this clause, except that if the Contractor failed to submit the termination settlement proposal within the time provided in paragraph (e) or (l) and failed to request a time extension, there is no right of appeal. If the Contracting Officer has made a determination of the amount due under paragraph (e), (g), or (l) of this clause, the Government shall pay the Contractor—

(1) The amount determined by the Contracting Officer, if there is no right of appeal or if no timely appeal has been taken; or

(2) The amount finally determined on an appeal.

(k) In arriving at the amount due the Contractor under this clause, there shall be deducted—

(1) All unliquidated advance or other payments to the Contractor under the terminated portion of this contract;

(2) Any claim which the Government has against the Contractor under this contract; and

(3) The agreed price for, or the proceeds of sale of, materials, supplies, or other things acquired by the Contractor or sold under the provisions of this clause and not recovered by or credited to the Government.

(l) If the termination is partial, the Contractor may file a proposal with the Contracting Officer for an equitable adjustment of the price(s) of the continued portion of the contract. The Contracting Officer shall make any equitable adjustment agreed upon. Any proposal by the Contractor for an equitable adjustment under this clause shall be requested within 90 days from the effective date of termination unless extended in writing by the Contracting Officer.

(m)(1) The Government may, under the terms and conditions it prescribes, make partial payments and payments against cost incurred by the Contractor for the terminated portion of the contract, if the Contracting Officer believes the total of these payments will not exceed the amount to which the Contractor will be entitled.

(2) If the total payments exceed the amount finally determined to be due, the Contractor shall repay the excess to the Government upon demand, together with interest computed at the rate established by the Secretary of the Treasury under 50 U.S.C. App. 1215(b)(2). Interest shall be computed for the period from the date the excess payment is received by the Contractor to the date the excess is repaid. Interest shall not be charged on any excess payment due to a reduction in the Contractor's termination settlement proposal because of retention or other disposition of termination inventory until 10 days after the date of the retention or disposition, or a later date determined by the Contracting Officer because of the circumstances.

(n) Unless otherwise provided in this contract or by statute, the Contractor shall maintain all records and documents relating to the terminated portion of this contract for 3 years after final settlement. This includes all books and other evidence bearing on the Contractor's costs and expenses under this contract. The Contractor shall make these records and documents available to the Government, at the Contractor's office, at all reasonable times, without any direct charge. If approved by the Contracting Officer, photographs, microphotographs, or other authentic reproductions may be maintained instead of original records and documents.

(End of clause)

Alternate I (SEP 1996). If the contract is with an agency of the U.S. Government or with State, local, or foreign governments or their agencies, and if the contracting officer determines that the requirement to pay interest on excess partial payments is inappropriate, delete subparagraph (m)(2) from the basic clause.

[FAC 90-32, 60 FR 48206, 9/18/95, effective 10/1/95; FAC 90-40, 61 FR 39186, 7/26/96, effective 9/24/96; FAC 2001-22, 69 FR 17741, 4/5/2004, effective 5/5/2004; FAC 2005-56, 77 FR 12937, 3/2/2012, effective 4/2/2012]

52.249-4 Termination for Convenience of the Government (Services) (Short Form).

As prescribed in 49.502(c), insert the following clause in solicitations and contracts for services, regardless of value, when a fixed-price contract is contemplated and the Contracting Officer determines that because of the kind of services required, the successful offeror will not incur substantial charges in preparation for and in carrying out the contract, and would, if terminated for the convenience of the Government, limit termination settlement charges to services rendered before the date of termination:

TERMINATION FOR CONVENIENCE OF THE GOVERNMENT (SERVICES) (SHORT FORM) (APR 1984)

The Contracting Officer, by written notice, may terminate this contract, in whole or in part, when it is in the Government's interest. If this contract is terminated, the Government shall be liable only for payment under the payment provisions of this contract for services rendered before the effective date of termination.

(End of clause)

[FAC 90-32, 60 FR 48206, 9/18/95, effective 10/1/95]

52.249-5 Termination for Convenience of the Government (Educational and Other Nonprofit Institutions).

As prescribed in 49.502(d), insert the following clause:

TERMINATION FOR CONVENIENCE OF THE GOVERNMENT (EDUCATIONAL AND OTHER NONPROFIT INSTITUTIONS) (AUG 2016)

(a) The Government may terminate performance of work under this contract in whole or, from time to time, in part if the Contracting Officer determines that a termination is in the Government's interest. The Contracting Officer shall terminate by delivering to the Contractor a Notice of Termination specifying the extent of termination and the effective date.

(b) After receipt of a Notice of Termination and except as directed by the Contracting Officer, the Contractor shall immediately proceed with the following obligations:

(1) Stop work as specified in the notice.

(2) Place no further subcontracts or orders (referred to as subcontracts in this clause), except as necessary to complete the continued portion of the contract.

(3) Terminate all applicable subcontracts and cancel or divert applicable commitments covering personal services that extend beyond the effective date of termination.

(4) Assign to the Government, as directed by the Contracting Officer, all right, title, and interest of the Contractor under the subcontracts terminated, in which case the Government shall have the right to settle or pay any termination settlement proposal arising out of those terminations.

(5) With approval or ratification to the extent required by the Contracting Officer, settle all outstanding liabilities and termination settlement proposals arising from the termination of subcontracts; approval or ratification will be final for purposes of this clause.

(6) Transfer title (if not already transferred) and, as directed by the Contracting Officer, deliver to the Government any information and items that, if the contract had been completed, would have been required to be furnished, including—

(i) Materials or equipment produced, in process, or acquired for the work terminated; and

(ii) Completed or partially completed plans, drawings, and information.

(7) Complete performance of the work not terminated.

(8) Take any action that may be necessary, or that the Contracting Officer may direct, for the protection and preservation of the property related to this contract that is in the possession of the Contractor and in which the Government has or may acquire an interest.

(9) Use its best efforts to sell, as directed or authorized by the Contracting Officer, termination inventory other than that retained by the Government under subparagraph (b)(6) of this clause; *provided, however*, that the Contractor (i) is not required to extend credit to any purchaser and (ii) may acquire the property under the conditions prescribed by, and at prices approved by, the Contracting Officer. The proceeds of any transfer or disposition will be applied to reduce any payments to be made by the Government under this contract, credited to the price or cost of the work, or paid in any

other manner directed by the Contracting Officer.

(c) The Contractor shall submit complete termination inventory schedules no later than 120 days from the effective date of termination, unless extended in writing by the Contracting Officer upon written request of the Contractor within this 120-day period.

(d) After termination, the Contractor shall submit a final termination settlement proposal to the Contracting Officer in the form and with the certification prescribed by the Contracting Officer. The Contractor shall submit the proposal promptly but no later than 1 year from the effective date of termination unless extended in writing by the Contracting Officer upon written request of the Contractor within this 1-year period. If the Contractor fails to submit the termination settlement proposal within the time allowed, the Contracting Officer may determine, on the basis of information available, the amount, if any, due the Contractor because of the termination and shall pay the amount determined.

(e) Subject to paragraph (d) of this clause, the Contractor and the Contracting Officer may agree upon the whole or any part of the amount to be paid because of the termination. This amount may include reasonable cancellation charges incurred by the Contractor and any reasonable loss on outstanding commitments for personal services that the Contractor is unable to cancel; *provided*, that the Contractor exercised reasonable diligence in diverting such commitments to other operations. The contract shall be amended and the Contractor paid the agreed amount.

(f) The cost principles and procedures in subpart 31.3 of the Federal Acquisition Regulation (FAR), Contracts with Educational Institutions (defined as institutions of higher education in the OMB Uniform Guidance in 2 CFR part 200, subpart A, and 20 U.S.C. 1001), as in effect on the date of the contract, shall govern all costs claimed, agreed to, or determined under this clause; however, if the Contractor is not an educational institution and is a nonprofit organization (as defined in the OMB Uniform Guidance at 2 CFR part 200), the cost principles and procedures in subpart 31.7 of the FAR, Contracts with Nonprofit Organizations, shall apply; unless the Contractor is a nonprofit institution listed in the OMB Uniform Guidance at 2 CFR part 200, appendix VIII, as exempted from the cost principles in subpart E, in which case the cost principles at FAR 31.2 for commercial organizations shall apply to such contractor.

(g) The Government may, under the terms and conditions it prescribes, make partial payments against costs incurred by the Contractor for the terminated portion of this contract, if the Contracting Officer believes the total of these payments will not exceed the amount to which the Contractor will be entitled.

(h) The Contractor has the right of appeal as provided under the Disputes clause, except that if the Contractor failed to submit the termination settlement proposal within the time provided in paragraph (d) of this clause and failed to request a time extension, there is no right of appeal.

(End of clause)

[FAC 90-32, 60 FR 48206, 9/18/95, effective 10/1/95; FAC 90-40, 61 FR 39186, 7/26/96, effective 9/24/96; FAC 2005-89, 81 FR 45852, 7/14/2016, effective 8/15/2016]

52.249-6 Termination (Cost-Reimbursement).

As prescribed in 49.503(a)(1), insert the following clause:

TERMINATION (COST-REIMBURSEMENT) (MAY 2004)

(a) The Government may terminate performance of work under this contract in whole or, from time to time, in part, if—

(1) The Contracting Officer determines that a termination is in the Government's interest; or

(2) The Contractor defaults in performing this contract and fails to cure the default within 10 days (unless extended by the Contracting Officer) after receiving a notice specifying the default. "Default" includes failure to make progress in the work so as to endanger performance.

(b) The Contracting Officer shall terminate by delivering to the Contractor a Notice of Termination specifying whether termination is for default of the Contractor or for convenience of the Government, the extent of termination, and the effective date. If, after termination for default, it is determined that the Contractor was not in default or that the Contractor's failure to perform or to make progress in performance is due to causes beyond the control and without the fault or negligence of the Contractor as set forth in the Excusable Delays clause, the rights and obligations of the parties will be the same as if the termination was for the convenience of the Government.

(c) After receipt of a Notice of Termination, and except as directed by the Contracting Officer, the Contractor shall immediately proceed with the following obligations, regardless of any delay in determining or adjusting any amounts due under this clause:

(1) Stop work as specified in the notice.

(2) Place no further subcontracts or orders (referred to as subcontracts in this clause), except as necessary to complete the continued portion of the contract.

(3) Terminate all subcontracts to the extent they relate to the work terminated.

(4) Assign to the Government, as directed by the Contracting Officer, all right, title, and interest of the Contractor under the subcontracts terminated, in which case the Government shall have the right to settle or to pay any termination settlement proposal arising out of those terminations.

(5) With approval or ratification to the extent required by the Contracting Officer, settle all outstanding liabilities and termination settlement proposals arising from the termination of subcontracts, the cost of which would be reimbursable in whole or in part, under this contract; approval or ratification will be final for purposes of this clause.

(6) Transfer title (if not already transferred) and, as directed by the Contracting Officer, deliver to the Government—

(i) The fabricated or unfabricated parts, work in process, completed work, supplies, and other material produced or acquired for the work terminated;

(ii) The completed or partially completed plans, drawings, information, and other property that, if the contract had been completed, would be required to be furnished to the Government; and

(iii) The jigs, dies, fixtures, and other special tools and tooling acquired or manufactured for this contract, the cost of which the Contractor has been or will be reimbursed under this contract.

(7) Complete performance of the work not terminated.

(8) Take any action that may be necessary, or that the Contracting Officer may direct, for the protection and preservation of the property related to this contract that is in the possession of the Contractor and in which the Government has or may acquire an interest.

(9) Use its best efforts to sell, as directed or authorized by the Contracting Officer, any property of the types referred to in subparagraph (c)(6) of this clause; *provided, however*, that the Contractor (i) is not required to extend credit to any purchaser and (ii) may acquire the property under the conditions prescribed by, and at prices approved by, the Contracting Officer. The proceeds of any transfer or disposition will be applied to reduce any payments to be made by the Government under this contract, credited to the price or cost of the work, or paid in any other manner directed by the Contracting Officer.

(d) The Contractor shall submit complete termination inventory schedules no later than 120 days from the effective date of termination, unless extended in writing by the Contracting Officer upon written request of the Contractor within this 120-day period.

(e) After expiration of the plant clearance period as defined in Subpart 49.001 of the Federal Acquisition Regulation, the Contractor may submit to the Contracting Officer a list, certified as to quantity and quality, of termination inventory not previously disposed of, excluding items authorized for disposition by the Contracting Officer. The

Contractor may request the Government to remove those items or enter into an agreement for their storage. Within 15 days, the Government will accept the items and remove them or enter into a storage agreement. The Contracting Officer may verify the list upon removal of the items, or if stored, within 45 days from submission of the list, and shall correct the list, as necessary, before final settlement.

(f) After termination, the Contractor shall submit a final termination settlement proposal to the Contracting Officer in the form and with the certification prescribed by the Contracting Officer. The Contractor shall submit the proposal promptly, but no later than 1 year from the effective date of termination, unless extended in writing by the Contracting Officer upon written request of the Contractor within this 1-year period. However, if the Contracting Officer determines that the facts justify it, a termination settlement proposal may be received and acted on after 1 year or any extension. If the Contractor fails to submit the proposal within the time allowed, the Contracting Officer may determine, on the basis of information available, the amount, if any, due the Contractor because of the termination and shall pay the amount determined.

(g) Subject to paragraph (f) of this clause, the Contractor and the Contracting Officer may agree on the whole or any part of the amount to be paid (including an allowance for fee) because of the termination. The contract shall be amended, and the Contractor paid the agreed amount.

(h) If the Contractor and the Contracting Officer fail to agree in whole or in part on the amount of costs and/or fee to be paid because of the termination of work, the Contracting Officer shall determine, on the basis of information available, the amount, if any, due the Contractor, and shall pay that amount, which shall include the following:

(1) All costs reimbursable under this contract, not previously paid, for the performance of this contract before the effective date of the termination, and those costs that may continue for a reasonable time with the approval of or as directed by the Contracting Officer; however, the Contractor shall discontinue these costs as rapidly as practicable.

(2) The cost of settling and paying termination settlement proposals under terminated subcontracts that are properly chargeable to the terminated portion of the contract if not included in subparagraph (h) (1) of this clause.

(3) The reasonable costs of settlement of the work terminated, including—

(i) Accounting, legal, clerical, and other expenses reasonably necessary for the preparation of termination settlement proposals and supporting data;

(ii) The termination and settlement of subcontracts (excluding the amounts of such settlements); and

(iii) Storage, transportation, and other costs incurred, reasonably necessary for the preservation, protection, or disposition of the termination inventory. If the termination is for default, no amounts for the preparation of the Contractor's termination settlement proposal may be included.

(4) A portion of the fee payable under the contract, determined as follows:

(i) If the contract is terminated for the convenience of the Government, the settlement shall include a percentage of the fee equal to the percentage of completion of work contemplated under the contract, but excluding subcontract effort included in subcontractors' termination proposals, less previous payments for fee.

(ii) If the contract is terminated for default, the total fee payable shall be such proportionate part of the fee as the total number of articles (or amount of services) delivered to and accepted by the Government is to the total number of articles (or amount of services) of a like kind required by the contract.

(5) If the settlement includes only fee, it will be determined under subparagraph (h) (4) of this clause.

(i) The cost principles and procedures in Part 31 of the Federal Acquisition Regulation, in effect on the date of this contract, shall govern all costs claimed, agreed to, or determined under this clause.

(j) The Contractor shall have the right of appeal, under the Disputes clause, from any determination made by the Contracting Officer under paragraph (f), or (h), or (l) of this clause, except that if the Contractor failed to submit the termination settlement proposal within the time provided in paragraph (f) and failed to request a time extension, there is no right of appeal. If the Contracting Officer has made a determination of the amount due under paragraph (f), (h) or (l) of this clause, the Government shall pay the Contractor—

(1) The amount determined by the Contracting Officer if there is no right of appeal or if no timely appeal has been taken; or

(2) The amount finally determined on an appeal.

(k) In arriving at the amount due the Contractor under this clause, there shall be deducted—

(1) All unliquidated advance or other payments to the Contractor, under the terminated portion of this contract;

(2) Any claim which the Government has against the Contractor under this contract; and

(3) The agreed price for, or the proceeds of sale of materials, supplies, or other things acquired by the Contractor or sold under this clause and not recovered by or credited to the Government.

(l) The Contractor and Contracting Officer must agree to any equitable adjustment in fee for the continued portion of the contract when there is a partial termination. The Contracting Officer shall amend the contract to reflect the agreement.

(m) (1) The Government may, under the terms and conditions it prescribes, make partial payments and payments against costs incurred by the Contractor for the terminated portion of the contract, if the Contracting Officer believes the total of these payments will not exceed the amount to which the Contractor will be entitled.

(2) If the total payments exceed the amount finally determined to be due, the Contractor shall repay the excess to the Government upon demand, together with interest computed at the rate established by the Secretary of the Treasury under 50 U.S.C. App. 1215(b)(2). Interest shall be computed for the period from the date the excess payment is received by the Contractor to the date the excess is repaid. Interest shall not be charged on any excess payment due to a reduction in the Contractor's termination settlement proposal because of retention or other disposition of termination inventory until 10 days after the date of the retention or disposition, or a later date determined by the Contracting Officer because of the circumstances.

(n) The provisions of this clause relating to fee are inapplicable if this contract does not include a fee.

(End of clause)

Alternate I (SEP 1996). If the contract is for construction, substitute the following subparagraph (h)(4) for subparagraph (h)(4) of the basic clause:

(4) A portion of the fee payable under the contract determined as follows:

(i) If the contract is terminated for the convenience of the Government, the settlement shall include a percentage of the fee equal to the percentage of completion of work contemplated under the contract, but excluding subcontract effort included in subcontractors' termination settlement proposals, less previous payments for fee.

(ii) If the contract is terminated for default, the total fee payable shall be such proportionate part of the fee as the actual work in place is to the total work in place required by the contract.

Alternate II (SEP 1996). If the contract is with an agency of the U.S. Government or with State, local, or foreign governments or their agencies, and if the contracting officer determines that the requirement to pay interest on excess partial payments is inappropriate, delete subparagraph (m)(2) from the basic clause.

Alternate III (SEP 1996). If the contract is for construction with an agency of the U.S. Government or with State, local, or foreign governments or their agencies, the following subparagraph (h)(4) shall be substituted for subparagraph (h)(4) of the basic clause. Subparagraph (m)(2) may be deleted from the basic clause if the contracting officer determines that the requirement to pay interest on excess partial payments is inappropriate.

(4) A portion of the fee payable under the contract determined as follows:

(i) If the contract is terminated for the convenience of the Government, the settlement shall include a percentage of the fee equal to the percentage of completion of work contemplated under the contract, but excluding subcontract effort included in subcontractors' termination settlement proposals, less previous payments for fee.

(ii) If the contract is terminated for default, the total fee payable shall be such proportionate part of the fee as the actual work in place is to the total work in place required by the contract.

Alternate IV (SEP 1996). If the contract is a time-and-material or labor-hour contract, substitute the following paragraphs (h) and (l) for paragraphs (h) and (l) of the basic clause:

(h) If the Contractor and the Contracting Officer fail to agree in whole or in part on the amount to be paid because of the termination of work, the Contracting Officer shall determine, on the basis of information available, the amount, if any, due the Contractor and shall pay the amount determined as follows:

(1) If the termination is for the convenience of the Government, include—

(i) An amount for direct labor hours (as defined in the Schedule of the contract) determined by multiplying the number of direct labor hours expended before the effective date of termination by the hourly rate(s) in the Schedule, less any hourly rate payments already made to the Contractor;

(ii) An amount (computed under the provisions for payment of materials) for material expenses incurred before the effective date of termination, not previously paid to the Contractor;

(iii) An amount for labor and material expenses computed as if the expenses were incurred before the effective date of termination, if they are reasonably incurred after the effective date, with the approval of or as directed by the Contracting Officer; however, the Contractor shall discontinue these expenses as rapidly as practicable;

(iv) If not included in subdivision (h)(1)(i), (ii), or (iii) of this clause, the cost of settling and paying termination settlement proposals under terminated subcontracts that are properly chargeable to the terminated portion of the contract; and

(v) The reasonable costs of settlement of the work terminated, including—

(A) Accounting, legal, clerical, and other expenses reasonably necessary for the preparation of termination settlement proposals and supporting data;

(B) The termination and settlement of subcontracts (excluding the amounts of such settlements); and

(C) Storage, transportation, and other costs incurred, reasonably necessary for the protection or disposition of the termination inventory.

(2) If the termination is for default of the Contractor, include the amounts computed under subparagraph (h)(1) of this clause but omit—

(i) Any amount for preparation of the Contractor's termination settlement proposal; and

(ii) The portion of the hourly rate allocable to profit for any direct labor hours expended in furnishing materials and services not delivered to and accepted by the Government.

(l) If the termination is partial, the Contractor may file with the Contracting Officer a proposal for an equitable adjustment of the price(s) for the continued portion of the contract. The Contracting Officer shall make any equitable adjustment agreed upon. Any proposal by the Contractor for an equitable adjustment under this clause shall be requested within 90 days from the effective date of termination, unless extended in writing by the Contracting Officer.

Alternate V (SEP 1996). If the contract is a time-and-material or labor-hour contract with an agency of the U.S. Government or with State, local or foreign governments or their agencies, substitute the following paragraphs (h) and (l) for paragraphs (h) and (l) of the basic clause. Subparagraph (m)(2) may be deleted from the basic clause if the contracting officer determines that the requirement to pay interest on excess partial payments is inappropriate.

(h) If the Contractor and the Contracting Officer fail to agree in whole or in part on the amount to be paid because of the termination of work, the Contracting Officer shall determine, on the basis of information available, the amount, if any, due the Contractor and shall pay the amount determined as follows:

(1) If the termination is for the convenience of the Government, include—

(i) An amount for direct labor hours (as defined in the Schedule of the contract) determined by multiplying the number of direct labor hours expended before the effective date of termination by the hourly rate(s) in the Schedule, less any hourly rate payments already made to the Contractor;

(ii) An amount (computed under the provisions for payment of materials) for material expenses incurred before the effective date of termination, not previously paid to the Contractor;

(iii) An amount for labor and material expenses computed as if the expenses were incurred before the effective date of termination, if they are reasonably incurred after the effective date, with the approval of or as directed by the Contracting Officer; however, the Contractor shall discontinue these expenses as rapidly as practicable;

(iv) If not included in subdivision (h)(1)(i), (ii), or (iii) of this clause, the cost of settling and paying termination settlement proposals under terminated subcontracts that are properly chargeable to the terminated portion of the contract; and

(v) The reasonable costs of settlement of the work terminated, including—

(A) Accounting, legal, clerical, and other expenses reasonably necessary for the preparation of termination settlement proposals and supporting data;

(B) The termination and settlement of subcontracts (excluding the amounts of such settlements); and

(C) Storage, transportation, and other costs incurred, reasonably necessary for the protection or disposition of the termination inventory.

(2) If the termination is for default of the Contractor, include the amounts computed under subparagraph (h)(1) of this clause but omit—

(i) Any amount for preparation of the Contractor's termination settlement proposal; and

(ii) The portion of the hourly rate allocable to profit for any direct labor hours expended in furnishing materials and services not delivered to and accepted by the Government.

(l) If the termination is partial, the Contractor may file with the Contracting Officer a proposal for an equitable adjustment of the price(s) for the continued portion of the contract. The Contracting Officer shall make any equitable adjustment agreed upon. Any proposal by the Contractor for an equitable adjustment under this clause shall be requested within 90 days from the effective date of termination, unless extended in writing by the Contracting Officer.

[FAC 84-16, 51 FR 19717, 5/30/86, effective 5/30/86; FAC 90-32, 60 FR 48206, 9/18/95, effective 10/1/95; FAC 90-40, 61 FR 39186, 7/26/96, effective 9/24/96; FAC 2001-22, 69 FR 17741, 4/5/2004, effective 5/5/2004]

52.249-7 Termination (Fixed-Price Architect-Engineer).

As prescribed in 49.503(b), insert the following clause in solicitations and contracts for architect-engineer services when a fixed-price contract is contemplated:

TERMINATION (FIXED-PRICE ARCHITECT-ENGINEER) (APR 1984)

(a) The Government may terminate this contract in whole or, from time to time, in part, for the Government's convenience or because of the failure of the Contractor to fulfill the contract obligations. The Contracting Officer shall terminate by delivering to the Contractor a Notice of Termination specifying the nature, extent, and effective date of the termination. Upon receipt of the notice, the Contractor shall—

(1) Immediately discontinue all services affected (unless the notice directs otherwise); and

(2) Deliver to the Contracting Officer all data, drawings, specifications, reports, estimates, summaries, and other information and materials accumulated in performing this contract, whether completed or in process.

(b) If the termination is for the convenience of the Government, the Contracting Officer shall make an equitable adjustment in the contract price but shall allow no anticipated profit on unperformed services.

(c) If the termination is for failure of the Contractor to fulfill the contract obligations, the Government may complete the work by contract or otherwise and the Contractor shall be liable for any additional cost incurred by the Government.

(d) If, after termination for failure to fulfill contract obligations, it is determined that the Contractor had not failed, the rights and obligations of the parties shall be the same as if the termination had been issued for the convenience of the Government.

(e) The rights and remedies of the Government provided in this clause are in addition to any other rights and remedies provided by law or under this contract.

(End of clause)

[FAC 90-32, 60 FR 48206, 9/18/95, effective 10/1/95]

52.249-8 Default (Fixed-Price Supply and Service).

As prescribed in 49.504(a)(1), insert the following clause:

DEFAULT (FIXED-PRICE SUPPLY AND SERVICE) (APR 1984)

(a)(1) The Government may, subject to paragraphs (c) and (d) of this clause, by written notice of default to the Contractor, terminate this contract in whole or in part if the Contractor fails to—

(i) Deliver the supplies or to perform the services within the time specified in this contract or any extension;

(ii) Make progress, so as to endanger performance of this contract (but see subparagraph (a)(2) of this clause); or

(iii) Perform any of the other provisions of this contract (but see subparagraph (a)(2) of this clause).

(2) The Government's right to terminate this contract under subdivisions (a)(1)(ii) and (1)(iii) above, may be exercised if the Contractor does not cure such failure within 10 days (or more if authorized in writing by the Contracting Officer) after receipt of the notice from the Contracting Officer specifying the failure.

(b) If the Government terminates this contract in whole or in part, it may acquire, under the terms and in the manner the Contracting Officer considers appropriate, supplies or services similar to those terminated, and the Contractor will be liable to the Government for any excess costs for those supplies or services. However, the Contractor shall continue the work not terminated.

(c) Except for defaults of subcontractors at any tier, the Contractor shall not be liable for any excess costs if the failure to perform the contract arises from causes beyond the control and without the fault or negligence of the Contractor. Examples of such causes include (1) acts of God or of the public enemy, (2) acts of the Government in either its sovereign or contractual capacity, (3) fires, (4) floods, (5) epidemics, (6) quarantine restrictions, (7) strikes, (8) freight embargoes, and (9) unusually severe weather. In each instance the failure to perform must be beyond the control and without the fault or negligence of the Contractor.

(d) If the failure to perform is caused by the default of a subcontractor at any tier, and if the cause of the default is beyond the control of both the Contractor and subcontractor, and without the fault or negligence of either, the Contractor shall not be liable for any excess costs for failure to perform, unless the subcontracted supplies or services were obtainable from other sources in sufficient time for the Contractor to meet the required delivery schedule.

(e) If this contract is terminated for default, the Government may require the Contractor to transfer title and deliver to the Government, as directed by the Contracting Officer, any (1) completed supplies, and (2) partially completed supplies and materials, parts, tools, dies, jigs, fixtures, plans, drawings, information, and contract rights (collectively referred to as "manufacturing materials" in this clause) that the Contractor has specifically produced or acquired for the terminated portion of this contract. Upon direction of the Contracting Officer, the Contractor shall also protect and preserve property in its possession in which the Government has an interest.

(f) The Government shall pay contract price for completed supplies delivered and accepted. The Contractor and Contracting Officer shall agree on the amount of payment for manufacturing materials delivered and accepted and for the protection and preservation of the property. Failure to agree will be a dispute under the Disputes clause. The Government may withhold from these amounts any sum the Contracting Officer determines to be necessary to protect the Government against loss because of outstanding liens or claims of former lien holders.

(g) If, after termination, it is determined that the Contractor was not in default, or that the default was excusable, the rights and obligations of the parties shall be the same as if the termination had been issued for the convenience of the Government.

(h) The rights and remedies of the Government in this clause are in addition to any other rights and remedies provided by law or under this contract.

(End of clause)

Alternate I (APR 1984). If the contract is for transportation or transportation-related services, delete paragraph (f) of the basic clause, redesignate the remaining paragraphs accordingly, and substitute the following paragraphs (a) and (e) for paragraphs (a) and (e) of the basic clause:

(a) (1) The Government may, subject to paragraphs (c) and (d) of this clause, by written notice of default to the Contractor, terminate this contract in whole or in part if the Contractor fails to—

(i) Pick up the commodities or to perform the services, including delivery services, within the time specified in this contract or any extension;

(ii) Make progress, so as to endanger performance of this contract (but see subparagraph (a) (2) of this clause); or

(iii) Perform any of the other provisions of this contract (but see subparagraph (a) (2) of this clause).

(2) The Government's right to terminate this contract under subdivisions (a) (1) (ii) and (iii) of this clause, may be exercised if the Contractor does not cure such failure within 10 days (or more if authorized in writing by the Contracting Officer) after receipt of the notice from the Contracting Officer specifying the failure.

(e) If this contract is terminated while the Contractor has possession of Government goods, the Contractor shall, upon direction of the Contracting Officer, protect and preserve the goods until surrendered to the Government or its agent. The Contractor and Contracting Officer shall agree on payment for the preservation and protection of goods. Failure to agree on an amount will be a dispute under the Disputes clause.

[FAC 90-29, 60 FR 34732, 7/3/95, effective 7/3/95; FAC 90-32, 60 FR 48206, 9/18/95, effective 10/1/95]

52.249-9 Default (Fixed-Price Research and Development).

As prescribed in 49.504(b), insert the following clause:

DEFAULT (FIXED-PRICE RESEARCH AND DEVELOPMENT) (APR 1984)

(a)(1) The Government may, subject to paragraphs (c) and (d) of this clause, by written Notice of Default to the Contractor, terminate this contract in whole or in part if the Contractor fails to—

(i) Perform the work under the contract within the time specified in this contract or any extension;

(ii) Prosecute the work so as to endanger performance of this contract (but see subparagraph (a)(2) of this clause); or

(iii) Perform any of the other provisions of this contract (but see subparagraph (a)(2) below).

(2) The Government's right to terminate this contract under subdivisions (a)(1)(ii) and (iii) of this paragraph may be exercised if the Contractor does not cure such failure within 10 days (or more, if authorized in writing by the Contracting Officer) after receipt of the notice from the Contracting Officer specifying the failure.

(b) If the Government terminates this contract in whole or in part, it may acquire, under the terms and in the manner the Contracting Officer considers appropriate, work similar to the work terminated, and the Contractor will be liable to the Government for any excess costs for the similar work. However, the Contractor shall continue the work not terminated.

(c) Except for defaults of subcontractors at any tier, the Contractor shall not be liable for any excess costs if the failure to perform the contract arises from causes beyond the control and without the fault or negligence of the Contractor. Examples of such causes include (1) acts of God or of the public enemy, (2) acts of the Government in either its sovereign or contractual capacity, (3) fires, (4) floods, (5) epidemics, (6) quarantine restrictions, (7) strikes, (8) freight embargoes, and (9) unusually severe weather. In each instance the failure to perform must be beyond the control and without the fault or negligence of the Contractor.

(d) If the failure to perform is caused by the default of a subcontractor at any tier, and if the cause of the default is beyond the control of both the Contractor and subcontractor, and without the fault or negligence of either, the Contractor shall not be liable for any excess costs for failure to perform, unless the subcontracted supplies or services were obtainable from other sources in sufficient time for the Contractor to meet the required delivery schedule or other performance requirements.

(e) If this contract is terminated for default, the Government may require the Contractor to transfer title and deliver to the Government, as directed by the Contracting Officer, any (1) completed or partially completed work not previously delivered to, and accepted by, the Government and (2) other property, including contract rights, specifically produced or acquired for the terminated portion of this contract. Upon direction of the Contracting Officer, the Contractor shall also protect and preserve property in its possession in which the Government has an interest.

(f) The Government shall pay the contract price, if separately stated, for completed work it has accepted and the amount agreed upon by the Contractor and the Contracting Officer for (1) completed work for which no separate price is stated, (2) partially completed work, (3) other property described above that it accepts, and (4) the protection and preservation of the property. Failure to agree will be a dispute under the Disputes clause. The Government may withhold from these amounts any sum the Contracting Officer determines to be necessary to protect the Government against loss from outstanding liens or claims of former lien holders.

(g) If, after termination, it is determined that the Contractor was not in default, or that the default was excusable, the rights and obligations of the parties shall be the same as if the termination had been issued for the convenience of the Government.

(h) The rights and remedies of the Government in this clause are in addition to any other rights and remedies provided by law or under this contract.

(End of clause)

[FAC 90-29, 60 FR 34732, 7/3/95, effective 7/3/95]

52.249-10 Default (Fixed-Price Construction).

As prescribed in 49.504(c)(1), insert the following clause:

DEFAULT (FIXED-PRICE CONSTRUCTION) (APR 1984)

(a) If the Contractor refuses or fails to prosecute the work or any separable part, with the diligence that will insure its completion within the time specified in this contract including any extension, or fails to complete the work within this time, the Government may, by written notice to the Contractor, terminate the right to proceed with the work (or the separable part of the work) that has been delayed. In this event, the Government may take over the work and complete it by contract or otherwise, and may take possession of and use any materials, appliances, and plant on the work site necessary for completing the work. The Contractor and its sureties shall be liable for any damage to the Government resulting from the Contractor's refusal or failure to complete the work within the specified time, whether or not the Contractor's right to proceed with the work is terminated. This liability includes any increased costs incurred by the Government in completing the work.

(b) The Contractor's right to proceed shall not be terminated nor the Contractor charged with damages under this clause, if—

(1) The delay in completing the work arises from unforeseeable causes beyond the control and without the fault or negligence of the Contractor. Examples of such causes include—

(i) Acts of God or of the public enemy,

(ii) Acts of the Government in either its sovereign or contractual capacity,

(iii) Acts of another Contractor in the performance of a contract with the Government,

(iv) Fires,

(v) Floods,

(vi) Epidemics,

(vii) Quarantine restrictions,

(viii) Strikes,

(ix) Freight embargoes,

(x) Unusually severe weather, or

(xi) Delays of subcontractors or suppliers at any tier arising from unforeseeable causes beyond the control and without the fault or negligence of both the Contractor and the subcontractors or suppliers; and

(2) The Contractor, within 10 days from the beginning of any delay (unless extended by the Contracting Officer), notifies the Contracting Officer in writing of the causes of delay. The Contracting Officer shall ascertain the facts and the extent of delay. If, in the judgment of the Contracting Officer, the findings of fact warrant such action, the time for completing the work shall be extended. The findings of the Contracting Officer shall be final and conclusive on the parties, but subject to appeal under the Disputes clause.

(c) If, after termination of the Contractor's right to proceed, it is determined that the Contractor was not in default, or that the delay was excusable, the rights and obligations of the parties will be the same as if the termination had been issued for the convenience of the Government.

(d) The rights and remedies of the Government in this clause are in addition to any other rights and remedies provided by law or under this contract.

(End of clause)

Alternate I (APR 1984). If the contract is for dismantling, demolition, or removal of improvements, substitute the following paragraph (a) for paragraph (a) of the basic clause:

(a) (1) If the Contractor refuses or fails to prosecute the work, or any separable part, with the diligence that will insure its completion within the time specified in this contract, including any extension, or fails to complete the work within this time, the Government may, by written notice to the Contractor, terminate the right to proceed with the work or the part of the work that has been delayed. In this event, the Government may take over the work and complete it by contract or otherwise, and may take possession of and use any materials, appliances, and plant on the work site necessary for completing the work.

(2) If title to property is vested in the Contractor under this contract, it shall revest in the Government regardless of any other clause of this contract, except for property that the Contractor has disposed of by bona fide sale or removed from the site.

(3) The Contractor and its sureties shall be liable for any damage to the Government resulting from the Contractor's refusal or failure to complete the work within the specified time, whether or not the Contractor's right to proceed with the work is terminated. This liability includes any increased costs incurred by the Government in completing the work.

Alternate II (APR 1984). If the contract is to be awarded during a period of national emergency, subparagraph (b)(1) below may be substituted for subparagraph (b)(1) of the basic clause:

(1) The delay in completing the work arises from causes other than normal weather beyond the control and without the fault or negligence of the Contractor. Examples of such causes include—

(i) Acts of God or of the public enemy,

(ii) Acts of the Government in either its sovereign or contractual capacity,

(iii) Acts of another Contractor in the performance of a contract with the Government,

(iv) Fires,

(v) Floods,

(vi) Epidemics,

(vii) Quarantine restrictions,

(viii) Strikes,

(ix) Freight embargoes,

(x) Unusually severe weather, or

(xi) Delays of subcontractors or suppliers at any tier arising from causes other than normal weather beyond the control and without the fault or negligence of both the Contractor and the subcontractors or suppliers; and

Alternate III (APR 1984). If the contract is for dismantling, demolition, or removal of improvements and is to be awarded during a period of national emergency, substitute the following paragraph (a) for paragraph (a) of the basic clause. The following subparagraph (b)(1) may be substituted for subparagraph (b)(1) of the basic clause:

(a)(1) If the Contractor refuses or fails to prosecute the work, or any separable part, with the diligence that will insure its completion within the time specified in this contract, including any extension, or fails to complete the work within this time, the Government may, by written notice to the Contractor, terminate the right to proceed with the work or the part of the work that has been delayed. In this event, the Government may take over the work and complete it by contract or otherwise, and may take possession of and use any materials, appliances, and plant on the work site necessary for completing the work.

(2) If title to property is vested in the Contractor under this contract, it shall revest in the Government regardless of any other clause of this contract, except for property that the Contractor has disposed of by bona fide sale or removed from the site.

(3) The Contractor and its sureties shall be liable for any damage to the Government resulting from the Contractor's refusal or failure to complete the work within the specified time, whether or not the Contractor's right to proceed with the work is terminated. This liability includes any increased costs incurred by the Government in completing the work.

(b) The Contractor's right to proceed shall not be terminated nor the Contractor charged with damages under this clause, if—

(1) The delay in completing the work arises from causes other than normal weather beyond the control and without the fault or negligence of the Contractor. Examples of such causes include—

(i) Acts of God or of the public enemy,

(ii) Acts of the Government in either its sovereign or contractual capacity,

(iii) Acts of another Contractor in the performance of a contract with the Government,

(iv) Fires,

(v) Floods,

(vi) Epidemics,

(vii) Quarantine restrictions,

(viii) Strikes,

(ix) Freight embargoes,

(x) Unusually severe weather, or

(xi) Delays of subcontractors or suppliers at any tier arising from causes other than normal weather beyond the control and without the fault or negligence of both the Contractor and the subcontractors or suppliers; and

[FAC 90-29, 60 FR 34732, 7/3/95, effective 7/3/95; FAC 90-32, 60 FR 48206, 9/18/95, effective 10/1/95]

52.249-11 [Removed and Reserved]

[FAC 90-32, 60 FR 48206, 9/18/95, effective 10/1/95; FAC 90-40, 61 FR 39186, 7/26/96, effective 9/24/96; FAC 2001-22, 69 FR 17741, 4/5/2004, effective 5/5/2004; FAC 2005-17, 72 FR 27364, 5/15/2007, effective 6/14/2007]

52.249-12 Termination (Personal Services).

As prescribed in 49.505(a), insert the following clause in solicitations and contracts for personal services (see Part 37):

TERMINATION (PERSONAL SERVICES) (APR 1984)

The Government may terminate this contract at any time upon at least 15 days' written notice by the Contracting Officer to the Contractor. The Contractor, with the written consent of the Contracting Officer, may terminate this contract upon at least 15 days' written notice to the Contracting Officer.

(End of clause)

[FAC 90-32, 60 FR 48206, 9/18/95, effective 10/1/95; FAC 2005-17, 72 FR 27364, 5/15/2007, effective 6/14/2007]

52.249-13 [Removed and Reserved]

[FAC 90-32, 60 FR 48206, 9/18/95, effective 10/1/95; FAC 2005-17, 72 FR 27364, 5/15/2007, effective 6/14/2007]

52.249-14 Excusable Delays.

As prescribed in 49.505(b), insert the following clause in solicitations and contracts for supplies, services, construction, and research and development on a fee basis whenever a cost-reimbursement contract is contemplated. Also insert the clause in time-and-material contracts, and labor-hour contracts. When used in construction contracts, substitute the words "completion time" for "delivery schedule" in the last sentence of the clause. When used in facilities contracts, substitute the words "termination of work" for "termination" in the last sentence of the clause.

EXCUSABLE DELAYS (APR 1984)

(a) Except for defaults of subcontractors at any tier, the Contractor shall not be in default because of any failure to perform this contract under its terms if the failure arises from causes beyond the control and without the fault or negligence of the Contractor. Examples of these causes are (1) acts of God or of the public enemy, (2) acts of the Government in either its sovereign or contractual capacity, (3) fires, (4) floods, (5) epidemics, (6) quarantine restrictions, (7) strikes, (8) freight embargoes, and (9) unusually severe weather. In each instance, the failure to perform must be beyond the control and without the fault or negligence of the Contractor. "Default" includes failure to make progress in the work so as to endanger performance.

(b) If the failure to perform is caused by the failure of a subcontractor at any tier to perform or make progress, and if the cause of the failure was beyond the control of both the Contractor and subcontractor, and without the fault or negligence of either, the Contractor shall not be deemed to be in default, unless—

(1) The subcontracted supplies or services were obtainable from other sources;

(2) The Contracting Officer ordered the Contractor in writing to purchase these supplies or services from the other source; and

(3) The Contractor failed to comply reasonably with this order.

(c) Upon request of the Contractor, the Contracting Officer shall ascertain the facts and extent of the failure. If the Contracting Officer determines that any failure to perform results from one or more of the causes above, the delivery schedule shall be revised, subject to the rights of the Government under the termination clause of this contract.

(End of clause)

[FAC 90-32, 60 FR 48206, 9/18/95, effective 10/1/95; FAC 2005-17, 72 FR 27364, 5/15/2007, effective 6/14/2007]

52.250-1 Indemnification under Public Law 85-804.

As prescribed in 50.104-4, insert the following clause:

INDEMNIFICATION UNDER PUBLIC LAW 85-804 (APR 1984)

(a) *Contractor's principal officials,* as used in this clause, means directors, officers, managers, superintendents, or other representatives supervising or directing—

(1) All or substantially all of the Contractor's business;

(2) All or substantially all of the Contractor's operations at any one plant or separate location in which this contract is being performed; or

(3) A separate and complete major industrial operation in connection with the performance of this contract.

(b) Under Public Law 85-804 (50 U.S.C 1431-1435) and Executive Order 10789, as amended, and regardless of any other provisions of this contract, the Government shall, subject to the limitations contained in the other paragraphs of this clause, indemnify the Contractor against—

(1) Claims (including reasonable expenses of litigation or settlement) by third persons (including employees of the Contractor) for death; personal injury; or loss of, damage to, or loss of use of property;

(2) Loss of, damage to, or loss of use of Contractor property, excluding loss of profit; and

(3) Loss of, damage to, or loss of use of Government property, excluding loss of profit.

(c) This indemnification applies only to the extent that the claim, loss, or damage (1) arises out of or results from a risk defined in this contract as unusually hazardous or nuclear and (2) is not compensated for by insurance or otherwise. Any such claim, loss, or damage, to the extent that it is within the deductible amounts of the Contractor's insurance, is not covered under this clause. If insurance coverage or other financial protection in effect on the date the approving official authorizes use of this clause is reduced, the Government's liability under this clause shall not increase as a result.

(d) When the claim, loss, or damage is caused by willful misconduct or lack of good faith on the part of any of the Contractor's principal officials, the Contractor shall not be indemnified for—

(1) Government claims against the Contractor (other than those arising through subrogation); or

(2) Loss or damage affecting the Contractor's property.

(e) With the Contracting Officer's prior written approval, the Contractor may, in any subcontract under this contract, indemnify the subcontractor against any risk defined in this contract as unusually hazardous or nuclear. This indemnification shall provide, between the Contractor and the subcontractor, the same rights and duties, and the same provisions for notice, furnishing of evidence or proof, and Government settlement or defense of claims as this clause provides. The Contracting Officer may also approve indemnification of subcontractors at any lower tier, under the same terms and conditions. The Government shall indemnify the Contractor against liability to subcontractors incurred under subcontract provisions approved by the Contracting Officer.

(f) The rights and obligations of the parties under this clause shall survive this contract's termination, expiration, or completion. The Government shall make no payment under this clause unless the agency head determines that the amount is just and reasonable. The Government may pay the Contractor or subcontractors, or may directly pay parties to whom the Contractor or subcontractors may be liable.

(g) The Contractor shall—

(1) Promptly notify the Contracting Officer of any claim or action against, or any loss by, the Contractor or any subcontractors that may reasonably be expected to involve indemnification under this clause;

(2) Immediately furnish to the Government copies of all pertinent papers the Contractor receives;

(3) Furnish evidence or proof of any claim, loss, or damage covered by this clause in the manner and form the Government requires; and

(4) Comply with the Government's directions and execute any authorizations required in connection with settlement or defense of claims or actions.

(h) The Government may direct, control, or assist in settling or defending any claim or action that may involve indemnification under this clause.

(End of clause)

Alternate I (APR 1984). In cost-reimbursement contracts, add the following paragraph (i) to the basic clause

(i) The cost of insurance (including self-insurance programs) covering a risk defined in this contract as unusually hazardous or nuclear shall not be reimbursed except to the extent that the Contracting Officer has required or approved this insurance. The Government's obligations under this clause are—

(1) Excepted from the release required under this contract's clause relating to allowable cost; and

(2) Not affected by this contract's Limitation of Cost or Limitation of Funds clause.

[FAC 90-32, 60 FR 48206, 9/18/95, effective 10/1/95; FAC 2005-17, 72 FR 27364, 5/15/2007, effective 6/14/2007; FAC 2005-21, 72 FR 63027, 11/7/2007, effective 11/7/2007; FAC 2005-30, 74 FR 2733, 1/15/2009, effective 2/17/2009]

52.250-2 SAFETY Act Coverage Not Applicable.

As prescribed in 50.206(a), insert the following provision:

SAFETY ACT COVERAGE NOT APPLICABLE (FEB 2009)

The Government has determined that for purposes of this solicitation the product(s) or service(s) being acquired by this action are neither presumptively nor actually entitled to a pre-determination that the products or services are qualified anti-terrorism technologies as that term is defined by the Support Anti-terrorism by Fostering Effective Technologies Act of 2002 (SAFETY Act), 6 U.S.C. 441-444. This determination does not prevent sellers of technologies from applying for SAFETY Act protections in other contexts. Proposals in which either acceptance or pricing is made contingent upon SAFETY Act designation as a qualified anti-terrorism technology or SAFETY Act certification as an approved product for homeland security of the proposed product or service will not be considered for award. See Federal Acquisition Regulation Subpart 50.2.

(End of provision)

[FAC 2005-21, 72 FR 63027, 11/7/2007, effective 11/7/2007; FAC 2005-30, 74 FR 2733, 1/15/2009, effective 2/17/2009]

52.250-3 SAFETY Act Block Designation/Certification.

As prescribed in 50.206(b)(1), insert the following provision:

SAFETY ACT BLOCK DESIGNATION/ CERTIFICATION (FEB 2009)

(a) *Definitions.* As used in this provision—

Act of terrorism means any act determined to have met the following requirements or such other requirements as defined and specified by the Secretary of Homeland Security:

(1) Is unlawful.

(2) Causes harm, including financial harm, to a person, property, or entity, in the United States, or in the case of a domestic United States air carrier or a United States-flag vessel (or a vessel based principally in the United States on which United States income tax is paid and whose insurance coverage is subject to regulation in the United States), in or outside the United States.

(3) Uses or attempts to use instrumentalities, weapons or other methods designed or intended to cause mass destruction, injury or other loss to citizens or institutions of the United States.

Block certification means SAFETY Act certification of a technology class that the Department of Homeland Security (DHS) has determined to be an approved class of approved products for homeland security.

Block designation means SAFETY Act designation of a technology class that the DHS has determined to be a Qualified Anti-Terrorism Technology (QATT).

Qualified Anti-Terrorism Technology (QATT) means any technology designed, developed, modified, procured, or sold for the purpose of preventing, detecting, identifying, or deterring acts of terrorism or limiting the harm such acts might otherwise cause, for which a SAFETY Act designation has been issued. For purposes of defining a QATT, technology means any product, equipment, service (including support services), device, or technology (including information technology) or any combination of the foregoing. Design services, consulting services, engineering services, software development services, software integration services, threat assessments, vulnerability studies, and other analyses relevant to homeland security may be deemed a technology.

SAFETY Act certification means a determination by DHS pursuant to 6 U.S.C. 442(d), as further delineated in 6 CFR 25.9, that a QATT for which a SAFETY Act designation has been issued is an approved product for homeland security, i.e., it will perform as intended, conforms to the seller's specifications, and is safe for use as intended.

SAFETY Act designation means a determination by DHS pursuant to 6 U.S.C. 441(b) and 6 U.S.C. 443(a), as further delineated in 6 CFR 25.4, that a particular Anti-Terrorism Technology constitutes a QATT under the SAFETY Act.

(b) The Support Anti-terrorism by Fostering Effective Technologies Act of 2002 (SAFETY Act), 6 U.S.C. 441-444, creates certain liability limitations for claims arising out of, relating to, or resulting from an act of terrorism where QATTs have been deployed. It also confers other important benefits. SAFETY Act designation and SAFETY Act certification are designed to support effective technologies aimed at preventing, detecting, identifying, or deterring acts of terrorism, or limiting the harm that such acts might otherwise cause, and which also meet other prescribed criteria. For some classes of technologies, DHS may issue a block designation/certification in order to lessen the burdens for filing for SAFETY Act designation or SAFETY Act certifications by not requiring applicants to provide certain information otherwise required and in order to offer expedited review of any application submitted pursuant to a block designation/certification. Block designations/certifications will be issued only for technologies that rely on established performance standards or defined technical characteristics.

(c)(1) DHS has issued a block designation or block certification for the technology to be acquired under this solicitation.

(2) This block designation or block certification is attached to this solicitation and contains essential information, including—

(i) A detailed description of and specification for the technology covered by the block designation or block certification;

(ii) A listing of those portions of the SAFETY Act application kit that must be completed and submitted by applicants;

(iii) The date of its expiration; and

(iv) Any other terms and conditions.

(3) Offerors should read this block designation or block certification carefully to make sure they comply with its terms if they

plan to take advantage of SAFETY Act coverage for their technology(ies).

(d) All determinations by DHS are based on factors set forth in the SAFETY Act and its implementing regulations. A determination by DHS to issue a SAFETY Act designation, or not to issue a SAFETY Act designation for a particular technology as a QATT is not a determination that the technology meets, or fails to meet, the requirements of any solicitation issued by any Federal, State, local or tribal governments. Determinations by DHS with respect to whether to issue a SAFETY Act designation for technologies submitted for DHS review are based on the factors identified in 6 CFR 25.4(b).

(e) Neither SAFETY Act designation nor certification is in any way a requirement of this action. Whether to seek the benefits of the SAFETY Act for a proposed product or service is entirely up to the offeror. Additional information about the SAFETY Act and this block designation/certification may be found at the SAFETY Act website at *http://www.SAFETYAct.gov* or requests may be mailed to: Directorate of Science and Technology, SAFETY Act/Room 4320, Department of Homeland Security, Washington, DC 20528.

(f) Proposals in which pricing or any other terms or conditions are offered contingent upon SAFETY Act designation or SAFETY Act certification of the proposed product(s) or service(s) will not be considered for award.

(End of provision)

Alternate I (FEB 2009). As prescribed in 50.206(b)(2), substitute the following paragraph (f):

(f)(1) Offerors are authorized to submit proposals made contingent upon SAFETY Act designation (or SAFETY Act certification, if a block certification exists) before award. When an offer is made contingent upon SAFETY Act designation or certification, the offeror also may submit an alternate offer without the contingency.

(2) If an offer is submitted contingent upon receipt of SAFETY Act designation (or SAFETY Act certification, if a block certification exists) prior to contract award, then the Government may not award a contract based on such offer unless the offeror demonstrates prior to award that DHS has issued a SAFETY Act designation (or SAFETY Act certification, if a block certification exists) for the offeror's technology.

(3) The Government reserves the right to award the contract based on a noncontingent offer, prior to DHS resolution of the offeror's application for SAFETY Act designation (or SAFETY Act certification, if a block certification exists).

Alternate II (FEB 2009). As prescribed in 50.206(b)(3), substitute the following paragraph (f):

(f)(1) Offerors are authorized to submit offers presuming that SAFETY Act designation (or SAFETY Act certification, if a block certification exists) will be obtained before or after award.

(2) An offeror is eligible for award only if the offeror—

(i) Files a SAFETY Act designation (or SAFETY Act certification) application, limited to the scope of the applicable block designation (or block certification), within 15 days after submission of the proposal;

(ii) Pursues its SAFETY Act designation (or SAFETY Act certification) application in good faith; and

(iii) Agrees to obtain the amount of insurance DHS requires for issuing the offeror's SAFETY Act designation (or SAFETY Act certification).

(3) If DHS has not issued a SAFETY Act designation (or SAFETY Act certification) to the successful offeror before contract award, the contracting officer will include the clause at 52.250-5 in the resulting contract.

[FAC 2005-21, 72 FR 63027, 11/7/2007, effective 11/7/2007; FAC 2005-30, 74 FR 2733, 1/15/2009, effective 2/17/2009]

52.250-4 SAFETY Act Prequalification Designation Notice.

As prescribed in 50.206(c)(1), insert the following provision:

SAFETY ACT PRE-QUALIFICATION DESIGNATION NOTICE (FEB 2009)

(a) *Definitions.* As used in this provision—

Act of terrorism means any act determined to have met the following requirements or such other requirements as defined and specified by the Secretary of Homeland Security:

(1) Is unlawful.

(2) Causes harm, including financial harm, to a person, property, or entity, in the United States, or in the case of a domestic United States air carrier or a United States-flag vessel (or a vessel based principally in the United States on which United States income tax is paid and whose insurance coverage is subject to regulation in the United States), in or outside the United States.

(3) Uses or attempts to use instrumentalities, weapons or other methods designed or intended to cause mass destruction, injury or other loss to citizens or institutions of the United States.

Block certification means SAFETY Act certification of a technology class that the Department of Homeland Security (DHS) has determined to be an approved class of approved products for homeland security.

Block designation means SAFETY Act designation of a technology class that the DHS has determined to be a Qualified Anti-Terrorism Technology (QATT).

Pre-qualification designation notice means a notice in a procurement solicitation or other publication by the Government stating that the technology to be procured either affirmatively or presumptively satisfies the technical criteria necessary to be deemed a qualified anti-terrorism technology. A pre-qualification designation notice authorizes offeror(s) to submit streamlined SAFETY Act applications for SAFETY Act designation and receive expedited processing of those applications.

Qualified Anti-Terrorism Technology (QATT) means any technology designed, developed, modified, procured, or sold for the purpose of preventing, detecting, identifying, or deterring acts of terrorism or limiting the harm such acts might otherwise cause, for which a SAFETY Act designation has been issued. For purposes of defining a QATT, technology means any product, equipment, service (including support services), device, or technology (including information technology) or any combination of the foregoing. Design services, consulting services, engineering services, software development services, software integration services, threat assessments, vulnerability studies, and other analyses relevant to homeland security may be deemed a technology.

SAFETY Act certification means a determination by DHS pursuant to 6 U.S.C. 442(d), as further delineated in 6 CFR 25.9, that a QATT for which a SAFETY Act designation has been issued is an approved product for homeland security, i.e., it will perform as intended, conforms to the seller's specifications, and is safe for use as intended.

SAFETY Act designation means a determination by DHS pursuant to 6 U.S.C. 441(b) and 6 U.S.C. 443(a), as further delineated in 6 CFR 25.4, that a particular Anti-Terrorism Technology constitutes a QATT under the SAFETY Act.

(b) The Support Anti-terrorism by Fostering Effective Technologies Act of 2002 (SAFETY Act), 6 U.S.C. 441-444, creates certain liability limitations for claims arising out of, relating to, or resulting from an act of terrorism where QATTs have been deployed. It also confers other important benefits. SAFETY Act designation and SAFETY Act certification are designed to support effective technologies aimed at preventing, detecting, identifying, or deterring acts of terrorism, or limiting the harm that such acts might otherwise cause, and which also meet other prescribed criteria.

(c) (1) DHS has issued a SAFETY Act pre-qualification designation notice for the technology to be acquired under this solicitation.

(2) This notice is attached to this solicitation and contains essential information, including—

(i) A detailed description of and specification for the technology covered by the notice;

(ii) A statement that the technology described and specified in the notice satisfies the technical criteria to be deemed a QATT and the offeror's proposed technology either may presumptively or will qualify for the issuance of a designation provided the offeror complies with terms and conditions in the notice and its application is approved;

(iii) The period of time within which DHS will take action upon submission of a SAFETY Act application submitted pursuant to the notice;

(iv) A listing of those portions of the application that must be completed and submitted by selected awardees and the time periods for such submissions;

(v) The date of expiration of the notice; and

(vi) Any other terms and conditions concerning the notice.

(3) Offerors should read this notice carefully to make sure they comply with the terms of the notice if they plan on taking advantage of SAFETY Act coverage for their technologies.

(d) All determinations by DHS are based on factors set forth in the SAFETY Act and its implementing regulations. A determination by DHS to issue a SAFETY Act designation, or not to issue a SAFETY Act designation for a particular Technology as a QATT is not a determination that the Technology meets, or fails to meet, the requirements of any solicitation issued by any Federal, State, local or tribal governments. Determinations by DHS with respect to whether to issue a SAFETY Act designation for Technologies submitted for DHS review are based on the factors identified in 6 CFR 25.4(b).

(e) Neither SAFETY Act designation nor certification is in any way a requirement of this action. Whether to seek the benefits of the SAFETY Act for a proposed product or service is entirely up to the offeror. Additional information about the SAFETY Act may be found at the SAFETY Act website at *http://www.SAFETYAct.gov*.

(f) Proposals in which pricing or any other terms or conditions are offered contingent upon SAFETY Act designation or certification of the proposed product(s) or service(s) will not be considered for award.

(End of provision)

Alternate I (FEB 2009). As prescribed in 50.206(c)(2), substitute the following paragraph (f):

(f)(1) Offerors are authorized to submit proposals made contingent upon SAFETY Act designation before award. When an offer is made contingent upon SAFETY Act designation, the offeror also may submit an alternate offer without the contingency.

(2) If an offer is submitted contingent upon receipt of SAFETY Act designation prior to contract award, then the Government may not award a contract based on such offer unless the offeror demonstrates prior to award that DHS has issued a SAFETY Act designation for the offeror's technology.

(3) The Government reserves the right to award the contract based on a noncontingent offer, prior to DHS resolution of the offeror's application for SAFETY Act designation.

Alternate II (FEB 2009). As prescribed in 50.206(c)(3), substitute the following paragraph (f):

(f)(1) Offerors are authorized to submit proposals presuming SAFETY Act designation before or after award.

(2) An offeror is eligible for award only if the offeror—

(i) Files a SAFETY Act designation application, limited to the scope of the applicable prequalification designation notice, within 15 days after submission of the proposal;

(ii) Pursues its SAFETY Act designation application in good faith; and

(iii) Agrees to obtain the amount of insurance DHS requires for issuing the offeror's SAFETY Act designation.

(3) If DHS has not issued a SAFETY Act designation to the successful offeror before contract award, the contracting officer will include the clause at 52.250-5 in the resulting contract.

[FAC 2005-21, 72 FR 63027, 11/7/2007, effective 11/7/2007; FAC 2005-30, 74 FR 2733, 1/15/2009, effective 2/17/2009]

52.250-5 SAFETY Act—Equitable Adjustment.

As prescribed in 50.206(d), insert the following clause:

SAFETY ACT—EQUITABLE ADJUSTMENT (FEB 2009)

(a) *Definitions.* As used in this clause—

Act of terrorism means any act determined to have met the following requirements or such other requirements as defined and specified by the Secretary of Homeland Security:

(1) Is unlawful.

(2) Causes harm, including financial harm, to a person, property, or entity, in the United States, or in the case of a domestic United States air carrier or a United States-flag vessel (or a vessel based principally in the United States on which United States income tax is paid and whose insurance coverage is subject to regulation in the United States), in or outside the United States.

(3) Uses or attempts to use instrumentalities, weapons or other methods designed or intended to cause mass destruction, injury or other loss to citizens or institutions of the United States.

Block certification means SAFETY Act certification of a technology class that the Department of Homeland Security (DHS) has determined to be an approved class of approved products for homeland security.

Block designation means SAFETY Act designation of a technology class that the DHS has determined to be a Qualified Anti-Terrorism Technology (QATT).

Qualified Anti-Terrorism Technology (QATT) means any technology designed, developed, modified, procured, or sold for the purpose of preventing, detecting, identifying, or deterring acts of terrorism or limiting the harm such acts might otherwise cause, for which a SAFETY Act designation has been issued. For purposes of defining a QATT, technology means any product, equipment, service (including support services), device, or technology (including information technology) or any combination of the foregoing. Design services, consulting services, engineering services, software development services, software integration services, threat assessments, vulnerability studies, and other analyses relevant to homeland security may be deemed a technology.

SAFETY Act certification means a determination by DHS pursuant to 6 U.S.C. 442(d), as further delineated in 6 CFR 25.9, that a QATT for which a SAFETY Act designation has been issued is an approved product for homeland security, i.e., it will perform as intended, conforms to the seller's specifications, and is safe for use as intended.

SAFETY Act designation means a determination by DHS pursuant to 6 U.S.C. 441(b) and 6 U.S.C. 443(a), as further delineated in 6 CFR 25.4, that a particular Anti-Terrorism Technology constitutes a QATT under the SAFETY Act.

(b) Prices for the items covered by the pre-qualification designation notice, block designation, or block certification in the contract were established presuming DHS will issue a SAFETY Act designation (or SAFETY Act certification) for those items.

(c) In order to qualify for an equitable adjustment in accordance with paragraph (d) of this clause the Contractor shall in good faith pursue obtaining—

(1) SAFETY Act designation (or SAFETY Act certification); and

(2) The amount of insurance DHS requires for issuing any SAFETY Act designation (or SAFETY Act certification).

(d)(1) If DHS denies the Contractor's SAFETY Act designation (or certification) application, the Contractor may submit a request for an equitable adjustment within 30 days of DHS's notification of denial.

(2) The Contracting Officer shall either—

(i) Make an equitable adjustment to the contract price based on evidence of the resulting increase or decrease in the Contractor's costs and/or an equitable adjustment to other terms and conditions based on lack of

SAFETY Act designation (or certification); or

(ii) At the sole option of the Government, terminate this contract for the convenience of the Government in place of an equitable adjustment.

(3) A failure of the parties to agree on the equitable adjustment will be considered to be a dispute in accordance with the "Disputes" clause of this contract.

(4) Unless first terminated, the Contractor shall continue contract performance during establishment of any equitable adjustment.

(End of clause)

[FAC 2005-21, 72 FR 63027, 11/7/2007, effective 11/7/2007; FAC 2005-30, 74 FR 2733, 1/15/2009, effective 2/17/2009]

52.251-1 Government Supply Sources.

As prescribed in 51.107, insert the following clause in solicitations and contracts when the contracting officer may authorize the contractor to acquire supplies or services from a Government supply source:

GOVERNMENT SUPPLY SOURCES (APR 2012)

The Contracting Officer may issue the Contractor an authorization to use Government supply sources in the performance of this contract. Title to all property acquired by the Contractor under such an authorization shall vest in the Government unless otherwise specified in the contract. The provisions of the clause at FAR 52.245-1, Government Property, apply to all property acquired under such authorization.

(End of clause)

[FAC 90-32, 60 FR 48206, 9/18/95, effective 10/1/95; FAC 2005-17, 72 FR 27364, 5/15/2007, effective 6/14/2007; FAC 2005-43, 75 FR 38675, 7/2/2010, effective 8/2/2010; FAC 2005-56, 77 FR 12937, 3/2/2012, effective 4/2/2012]

52.251-2 Interagency Fleet Management System Vehicles and Related Services.

As prescribed in 51.205, insert the following clause:

INTERAGENCY FLEET MANAGEMENT SYSTEM VEHICLES AND RELATED SERVICES (JAN 1991)

The Contracting Officer may issue the Contractor an authorization to obtain interagency fleet management system (IFMS) vehicles and related services for use in the performance of this contract. The use, service, and maintenance of interagency fleet management system vehicles and the use of related services by the Contractor shall be in accordance with 41 CFR 101-39 and 41 CFR 101-38.301-1.

(End of clause)

[FAC 84-49, 54 FR 29284, 7/11/89, effective 8/10/89; FAC 90-3, 55 FR 52782, 12/21/90, effective 1/22/91]

52.252-1 Solicitation Provisions Incorporated by Reference.

As prescribed in 52.107(a), insert the following provision:

SOLICITATION PROVISIONS INCORPORATED BY REFERENCE (FEB 1998)

This solicitation incorporates one or more solicitation provisions by reference, with the same force and effect as if they were given in full text. Upon request, the Contracting Officer will make their full text available. The offeror is cautioned that the listed provisions may include blocks that must be completed by the offeror and submitted with its quotation or offer. In lieu of submitting the full text of those provisions, the offeror may identify the provision by paragraph identifier and provide the appropriate information with its quotation or offer. Also, the full text of a solicitation provision may be accessed electronically at this/these address(es):

____

____

[*Insert one or more Internet addresses*]

(End of provision)

[FAC 97-3, 62 FR 64912, 12/9/97, effective 2/9/98]

52.252-2 Clauses Incorporated by Reference.

As prescribed in 52.107(b), insert the following clause:

CLAUSES INCORPORATED BY REFERENCE (FEB 1998)

This contract incorporates one or more clauses by reference, with the same force and effect as if they were given in full text. Upon request, the Contracting Officer will make their full text available. Also, the full text of a clause may be accessed electronically at this/these address(es):

____

____

[*Insert one or more Internet addresses*]

(End of clause)

[FAC 97-3, 62 FR 64912, 12/9/97, effective 2/9/98]

52.252-3 Alterations in Solicitation.

As prescribed in 52.107(c), insert the following provision in solicitations in order to revise or supplement, as necessary, other parts of the solicitation that apply to the solicitation phase only, except for any provision authorized for use with a deviation. Include clear identification of what is being altered.

ALTERATIONS IN SOLICITATION (APR 1984)

Portions of this solicitation are altered as follows:

____

____

(End of provision)

[FAC 90-32, 60 FR 48206, 9/18/95, effective 10/1/95]

52.252-4 Alterations in Contract.

As prescribed in 52.107(d), insert the following clause in solicitations and contracts in order to revise or supplement, as necessary, other parts of the contract, or parts of the solicitation that apply after contract award, except for any clause authorized for use with a deviation. Include clear identification of what is being altered.

ALTERATIONS IN CONTRACT (APR 1984)

Portions of this contract are altered as follows:

____

____

(End of clause)

[FAC 90-32, 60 FR 48206, 9/18/95, effective 10/1/95]

52.252-5 Authorized Deviations in Provisions.

As prescribed in 52.107(e), insert the following provision in solicitations that include any FAR or supplemental provision with an authorized deviation. Whenever any FAR or supplemental provision is used with an authorized deviation, the contracting officer shall identify it by the same number, title, and date assigned to the provision when it is used without deviation, include regulation name for any supplemental provision, except that the contracting officer shall insert "(DEVIATION)" after the date of the provision.

AUTHORIZED DEVIATIONS IN PROVISIONS (APR 1984)

(a) The use in this solicitation of any Federal Acquisition Regulation (48 CFR Chapter 1) provision with an authorized deviation is indicated by the addition of "(DEVIATION)" after the date of the provision.

(b) The use in this solicitation of any ___ [*insert regulation name*] (48 CFR Chapter ___) provision with an authorized deviation is indicated by the addition of "(DEVIATION)" after the name of the regulation.

(End of provision)

[FAC 90-32, 60 FR 48206, 9/18/95, effective 10/1/95]

52.252-6 Authorized Deviations in Clauses.

As prescribed in 52.107(f), insert the following clause in solicitations and contracts that include any FAR or supplemental clause with an authorized deviation. Whenever any FAR or supplemental clause is used with an authorized deviation, the contracting officer shall identify it by the same number, title, and date assigned to the clause when it is used without deviation, include regulation name for any supplemental clause, except that the contracting officer shall insert "(DEVIATION)" after the date of the clause.

AUTHORIZED DEVIATIONS IN CLAUSES (APR 1984)

(a) The use in this solicitation or contract of any Federal Acquisition Regulation (48 CFR Chapter 1) clause with an authorized deviation is indicated by the addition of "(DEVIATION)" after the date of the clause.

(b) The use in this solicitation or contract of any ____ [*insert regulation name*] (48 CFR ____) clause with an authorized deviation is indicated by the addition of "(DEVIATION)" after the name of the regulation.

(End of clause)

[FAC 90-32, 60 FR 48206, 9/18/95, effective 10/1/95]

52.253-1 Computer Generated Forms.

As prescribed in FAR 53.111, insert the following clause:

COMPUTER GENERATED FORMS (JAN 1991)

(a) Any data required to be submitted on a Standard or Optional Form prescribed by the Federal Acquisition Regulation (FAR) may be submitted on a computer generated version of the form, provided there is no change to the name, content, or sequence of the data elements on the form, and *provided* the form carries the Standard or Optional Form number and edition date.

(b) Unless prohibited by agency regulations, any data required to be submitted on an agency unique form prescribed by an agency supplement to the FAR may be submitted on a computer generated version of the form provided there is no change to the name, content, or sequence of the data elements on the form and provided the form carries the agency form number and edition date.

(c) If the Contractor submits a computer generated version of a form that is different than the required form, then the rights and obligations of the parties will be determined based on the content of the required form.

(End of clause)

[FAC 90-3, 55 FR 52800, 12/21/90, effective 1/22/91]

SUBPART 52.3—PROVISION AND CLAUSE MATRIX

52.300 Scope of subpart.

The matrix in this subpart contains a column for each principal type and/or purpose of contract (see 52.101(e)).

[FAC 84-56, 55 FR 3890, 2/5/90, effective 3/7/90]

[FAR MATRIX]

52.301 Solicitation provisions and contract clauses (Matrix).

[Current through FAC 2020-03, 84 FR 68314, 12/13/2019]

Federal Acquisition Regulation Matrix Table

Provision or Clause	Prescribed in	P or C	IBR	UCF	FP SUP	CR SUP	FP R&D	CR R&D	FP SVC	CR SVC	FP CON	CR CON	T&M LH	LMV	COM SVC	DDR	A&E	FAC	IND DEL	TRN	SAP	UTL SVC	CI
52.202-1 Definitions.	2.201	C	Yes	I	R	R	A	R	R	R		R	R	R	R		R	R	R	R		R	
52.203-2 Certificate of Independent Price Determination.	3.103-1	P	No	K	A		A		A		A			A	A	A	A	A	A	A		A	
52.203-3 Gratuities.	3.202	C	Yes	I	A	A	A	A	A	A	A	A	A	A	A	A	A	A	A	A		A	
52.203-5 Covenant Against Contingent Fees.	3.404	C	Yes	I	R	R	R	R	R	R	R	R	R	R	R	R	R	R	R	R		R	
52.203-6 Restrictions on Subcontractor Sales to the Government.	3.503-2	C	Yes	I	R	R			R	R									R			R	
52.203-6_Alternate I	3.503-2	C	Yes	I	R	R			R	R									R			R	
52.203-7 Anti-Kickback Procedures.	3.502-3	C	Yes	I	R	R	R	R	R	R	R	R	R	R	R	R	R	R	R	R		R	
52.203-8 Cancellation, Rescission, and Recovery of Funds for Illegal or Improper Activity.	3.104-9(a)	C	Yes	I	A	A	A	A	A	A	A	A	A	A	A	A	A	A	A	A		A	
52.203-10 Price or Fee Adjustment for Illegal or Improper Activity.	3.104-9(b)	C	Yes	I	A	A	A	A	A	A	A	A	A	A	A	A	A	A	A	A		A	
52.203-11 Certification and Disclosure Regarding Payments to Influence Certain Federal Transactions.	3.808(a)	P	Yes	K	A	A	A	A	A	A	A	A	A	A	A	A	A	A	A	A		A	
52.203-12 Limitation on Payments to Influence Certain Federal Transactions.	3.808(b)	C	Yes	I	A	A	A	A	A	A	A	A	A	A	A	A	A	A	A	A		A	
52.203-13 Contractor Code of Business Ethics and Conduct.	3.1004(a)	C	Yes	I	A	A	A	A	A	A	A	A	A	A	A	A	A	A	A	A		A	
52.203-14 Display of Hotline Poster(s).	3.1004	C	Yes	I	A	A	A	A	A	A	A	A	A	A	A	A	A	A	A	A		A	
52.203-15 Whistleblower Protections Under the American Recovery and Reinvestment Act of 2009.	3.907-7	C	Yes	I	A	A	A	A	A	A	A	A	A	A	A	A	A	A	A	A	A	A	A
52.203-16 Preventing Personal Conflicts of Interest.	3.1106	C	Yes	I	A	A	A	A	A	A	A	A	A	A	A	A	A	A	A	A		A	A
52.203-17 Contractor Employee Whistleblower Rights and Requirement To Inform Employees of Whistleblower Rights.	3.908-9	C	Yes	I	R	R	R	R	R	R	R	R	R	R	R	R	R	R	R	R		R	
52.203-18 Prohibition on Contracting with	3.909-3(a)	P	Yes	K	A	A	A	A	A	A	A	A	A	A	A	A	A	A	A	A	A	A	A

Provision or Clause	Prescribed in	P or C	IBR	UCF	FP SUP	CR SUP	FP R&D	CR R&D	FP SVC	CR SVC	FP CON	CR CON	T&M LH	LMV	COM SVC	DDR	A&E	FAC	IND DEL	TRN	SAP	UTL SVC	CI
Entities that Require Certain Internal Confidentiality Agreements or Statements-Representation.																							
52.203-19 Prohibition on Requiring Certain Internal Confidentiality Agreements or Statements.	3.909-3(b)	C	Yes	I	A	A	A	A	A	A	A	A	A	A	A	A	A	A	A	A	A	A	A
52.204-1 Approval of Contract.	4.103	C	No	I	A	A	A	A	A	A	A	A	A	A	A	A	A	A	A	A	A	A	
52.204-2 Security Requirements.	4.404(a)	C	Yes	I	A	A	A	A	A	A	A	A	A	A	A	A	A	A	A	A	A	A	
52.204-2_Alternate I	4.404(a)	C	Yes	I	A	A	A	A	A	A	A	A	A	A	A	A	A	A	A	A	A	A	
52.204-2_Alternate II	4.404(a)	C	Yes	I	A	A	A	A	A	A	A	A	A	A	A	A	A	A	A	A	A	A	
52.204-3 Taxpayer Identification.	4.905	P	No	K	A	A	A	A	A	A	A	A	A	A	A	A	A	A	A	A	A	A	
52.204-4 Printed or Copied Double-Sided on Postconsumer Fiber Content Paper.	4.303	C	Yes	I	A	A	A	A	A	A	A	A	A	A	A	A	A	A	A	A		A	A
52.204-5 Women-Owned Business (Other Than Small Business).	4.607(a)	P	Yes	K	A	A	A	A	A	A	A	A	A	A	A	A	A	A	A	A		A	
52.204-6 Unique Entity Identifier.	4.607(b)	P	Yes	L	A	A	A	A	A	A	A	A	A	A	A	A	A	A	A	A	A	A	A
52.204-7 System for Award Management.	4.1105(a)(1)	P	Yes	L	A	A	A	A	A	A	A	A	A	A	A	A	A	A	A	A	A	A	A
52.204-7_Alternate I	4.1105(a)(2)	P	Yes	L	A	A	A	A	A	A	A	A	A	A	A	A	A	A	A	A	A	A	A
52.204-8 Annual Representations and Certifications.	4.1202(a)	P	No	K	A	A	A	A	A	A	A	A	A	A	A	A	A	A	A	A	A	A	
52.204-9 Personal Identity Verification of Contractor Personnel.	4.1303	C	Yes	I	A	A	A	A	A	A	A	A	A		A	A	A	A	A	A	A	A	A
52.204-10 Reporting Executive Compensation and First-Tier Subcontract Awards.	4.1403(a)	C	Yes	I	A	A	A	A	A	A	A	A	A	A	A	A	A	A	A	A	A	A	A
52.204-12 Unique Entity Identifier Maintenance.	4.607(c)	C	Yes	I	A	A	A	A	A	A	A	A	A	A	A	A	A	A	A	A	A	A	A
52.204-13 System for Award Management Maintenance.	4.1105(b)	C	Yes	I	A	A	A	A	A	A	A	A	A	A	A	A	A	A	A	A	A	A	A
52.204-14 Service Contract Reporting Requirements.	4.1705(a)	C	Yes						A	A	A	A	A		A	A	A	A		A			A
52.204-15 Service Contract Reporting Requirements for Indefinite-Delivery Contracts.	4.1705(b)	C	Yes						A	A	A	A	A		A	A	A	A	A	A			A

Provision or Clause	Prescribed in	P or C	IBR	UCF	FP SUP	CR SUP	FP R&D	CR R&D	FP SVC	CR SVC	FP CON	CR CON	T&M LH	LMV	COM SVC	DDR	A&E	FAC	IND DEL	TRN	SAP	UTL SVC	CI
52.204-16 Commercial and Government Entity Code Reporting.	4.1804(a)	P	Yes	L	A	A	A	A	A	A	A	A	A	A	A	A	A	A	A	A	A	A	A
52.204-17 Ownership or Control of Offeror.	4.1804(b)	P	Yes	K	A	A	A	A	A	A	A	A	A	A	A	A	A	A	A	A	A	A	A
52.204-18 Commercial and Government Entity Code Maintenance.	4.1804(c)	C	Yes	I	A	A	A	A	A	A	A	A	A	A	A	A	A	A	A	A	A	A	A
52.204-19 Incorporation by Reference of Representations and Certifications.	4.1202(b)	C	Yes	I	R	R	R	R	R	R	R	R	R	R	R	R	R	R	R	R	R	R	R
52.204-20 Predecessor of Offeror.	4.1804	P	No	K	A	A	A	A	A	A	A	A	A	A	A	A	A	A	A	A	A	A	A
52.204-21 Basic Safeguarding of Covered Contractor Information Systems.	4.1903	C	No	I	A	A	A	A	A	A	A	A	A	A	A	A	A	A	A	A	A	A	A
52.204-22 Alternative Line Item Proposal.	4.1008	P	Yes	L	A	A	A	A	A	A	A	A	A	A	A	A	A	A	A	A	A	A	A
52.204-23 Prohibition on Contracting for Hardware, Software, and Services Developed or Provided by Kaspersky Lab and Other Covered Entities.	4.2004	C	Yes	I	A	A	A	A	A	A	A	A	A	A	A	A	A	A	A	A	A	A	A
52.204-24 Representation Regarding Certain Telecommunications and Video Surveillance Services or Equipment.	4.2105(a)	P	No	K	R	R	R	R	R	R	R	R	R	R	R	R	R	R	R	R	R	R	R
52.204-25 Prohibition on Contracting for Certain Telecommunications and Video Surveillance Services or Equipment.	4.2105(b)	C	Yes	I	R	R	R	R	R	R	R	R	R	R	R	R	R	R	R	R	R	R	R
52.204-26 Covered Telecommunications Equipment or Services-Representation.	4.2105(c)	P	No	K	R	R	R	R	R	R	R	R	R	R	R	R	R	R	R	R	R	R	R
52.207-1 Notice of Standard Competition.	7.305(a)	P	Yes	L	A		A		A		A			A	A	A				A			
52.207-2 Notice of Streamlined Competition.	7.305(b)	P	Yes	L	A	A	A	A	A	A	A	A	A	A	A	A	A		A	A		A	
52.207-3 Right of First Refusal of Employment.	7.305(c)	C	Yes	I	A	A	A	A	A	A	A	A	A	A	A	A	A		A	A		A	
52.207-4 Economic Purchase Quantity-Supplies.	7.203	P	No	K	A	A													A		A		
52.207-5 Option to Purchase Equipment.	7.404	C	Yes	I	A	A	A	A	A	A	A	A	A	A	A	A	A	A	A	A	A	A	
52.207-6 Solicitation of Offers from Small Business Concerns and Small Business Teaming Arrangements or Joint Ventures (Multiple-Award Contracts).	7.107-6	P	Yes	L	A	A	A	A	A	A	A	A	A	A	A	A	A	A	A	A	A	A	A
52.208-4 Vehicle Lease Payments.	8.1104(a)	C	Yes	I										A							A		

Provision or Clause	Prescribed in	P or C	IBR	UCF	FP SUP	CR SUP	FP R&D	CR R&D	FP SVC	CR SVC	FP CON	CR CON	T&M LH	LMV	COM SVC	DDR	A&E	FAC	IND DEL	TRN	SAP	UTL SVC	CI
52.208-5 Condition of Leased Vehicles.	8.1104(b)	C	Yes	I										A							A		
52.208-6 Marking of Leased Vehicles.	8.1104(c)	C	Yes	I										A							A		
52.208-7 Tagging of Leased Vehicles.	8.1104(d)	C	Yes	I										A							A		
52.208-8 Required Sources for Helium and Helium Usage Data.	8.505	C	No	I	A	A	A	A	A	A	A	A	A	A	A	A	A	A	A	A	A	A	
52.208-9 Contractor Use of Mandatory Sources of Supply or Services.	8.005	C	Yes	I	A	A													A		A		
52.209-1 Qualification Requirements.	9.209-6	C	No	I	A	A			A	A				A					A		A		
52.209-2 Prohibition on Contracting with Inverted Domestic Corporations-Representation.	9.108-5(a)	P	Yes	K	A	A	A	A	A	A	A	A	A	A	A	A	A	A	A	A	A	A	A
52.209-3 First Article Approval-Contractor Testing.	9.308-1(a)	C	Yes	I	A	O								A					A		A		
52.209-3_Alternate I	9.308-1(a)(2)	C	Yes	I	A	O								A					A		A		
52.209-3_Alternate II	9.308-1(a)(3)	C	Yes	I	A	O								A					A		A		
52.209-4 First Article Approval-Government Testing.	9.308-2(a) and (b)	C	Yes	I	A	O								A					A		A		
52.209-4_Alternate I	9.308-2(a)(2)	C	Yes	I	A	O								A					A		A		
52.209-4_Alternate II	9.308-2(a)(3)	C	Yes	I	A	O								A					A		A		
52.209-5 Certification Regarding Responsibility Matters.	9.104-7(a)	P	No	K	A	A	A	A	A	A	A	A	A	A	A	A	A	A	A	A		A	
52.209-6 Protecting the Government's Interest When Subcontracting with Contractors Debarred, Suspended, or Proposed for Debarment.	9.409	C	Yes	I	A	A	A	A	A	A	A	A	A	A	A	A	A	A	A	A		A	
52.209-7 Information Regarding Responsibility Matters.	9.104-7	P	No	K	A	A	A	A	A	A	A	A	A	A	A	A	A	A	A	A	A	A	A
52.209-9 Updates of Publicly Available Information Regarding Responsibility Matters.	9.104-7	C	Yes	I	A	A	A	A	A	A	A	A	A	A	A	A	A	A	A	A	A	A	A
52.209-10 Prohibition on Contracting with Inverted Domestic Corporations.	9.108-5(b)	C	Yes	I	A	A	A	A	A	A	A	A	A	A	A	A	A	A	A	A	A	A	A
52.209-11 Representation by Corporations Regarding Delinquent Tax Liability or a Felony Conviction under any Federal Law.	9.104-7	P	No	K	A	A	A	A	A	A	A	A	A	A	A	A	A	A	A	A	A	A	A

Provision or Clause	Prescribed in	P or C	IBR	UCF	FP SUP	CR SUP	FP R&D	CR R&D	FP SVC	CR SVC	FP CON	CR CON	T&M LH	LMV	COM SVC	DDR	A&E	FAC	IND DEL	TRN	SAP	UTL SVC	CI
52.209-12 Certification Regarding Tax Matters.	9.104-7	P	No	K	A	A	A	A	A	A	A	A	A	A	A	A	A	A	A	A	A	A	A
52.209-13 Violation of Arms Control Treaties or Agreements-Certification.	9.109-5	P	No	K	A	A	A	A	A	A	A	A	A	A	A	A	A	A	A	A		A	
52.210-1 Market Research.	10.003	C	Yes	I	A	A	A	A	A	A	A	A	A		A	A	A	A	A	A		A	
52.211-1 Availability of Specifications Listed in the GSA Index of Federal Specifications, Standards and Commercial Item Descriptions, FPMR Part101-29.	11.204(a)	P	No	L	A	A	A	A	A	A	A			A	A			A	A		A		
52.211-2 Availability of Specifications, Standards, and Data Item Descriptions Listed in the Acquisition Streamlining and Standardization Information System (ASSIST).	11.204(b)	P	No	L	A	A	A	A	A	A	A			A	A			A	A		A		
52.211-3 Availability of Specifications Not Listed in the GSA Index of Federal Specifications, Standards and Commercial Item Descriptions.	11.204(c)	P	No	L	A	A	A	A	A	A	A			A	A			A	A		A		
52.211-4 Availability for Examination of Specifications Not Listed in the GSA Index of Federal Specifications, Standards and Commercial Item Descriptions.	11.204(d)	P	No	L	A	A	A	A	A	A	A			A	A			A	A	A	A		
52.211-5 Material Requirements.	11.304	C	Yes	I	R	R															A		
52.211-6 Brand Name or Equal.	11.107(a)	P	Yes	L	A	A							A						A		A		
52.211-7 Alternatives to Government-Unique Standards.	11.107(b)	P	Yes	L	A	A	A	A	A	A	A	A	A	A	A	A	A	A	A	A	A	A	
52.211-8 Time of Delivery.	11.404(a)(2)	C	No	F	O	O	O	O	O	O	O	O	O	O	O	O	O	O	O	O	O	O	
52.211-8_Alternate I	11.404(a)(2)	C	No	F	O	O	O	O	O	O	O	O	O	O	O	O	O	O	O	O	O	O	
52.211-8_Alternate II	11.404(a)(2)	C	No	F	O	O	O	O	O	O	O	O	O	O	O	O	O	O	O	O	O	O	
52.211-8_Alternate III	11.404(a)(2)	C	No	F	O	O	O	O	O	O	O	O	O	O	O	O	O	O	O	O	O	O	
52.211-9 Desired and Required Time of Delivery.	11.404(a)(3)	C	No	F	O	O	O	O	O	O	O	O	O	O	O	O	O	O	O	O	O	O	
52.211-9_Alternate I	11.404(a)(3)	C	No	F	O	O	O	O	O	O	O	O	O	O	O	O	O	O	O	O	O	O	
52.211-9_Alternate II	11.404(a)(3)	C	No	F	O	O	O	O	O	O	O	O	O	O	O	O	O	O	O	O	O	O	
52.211-9_Alternate III	11.404(a)(3)	C	No	F	O	O	O	O	O	O	O	O	O	O	O	O	O	O	O	O	O	O	

Provision or Clause	Prescribed in	P or C	IBR	UCF	FP SUP	CR SUP	FP R&D	CR R&D	FP SVC	CR SVC	FP CON	CR CON	T&M LH	LMV	COM SVC	DDR	A&E	FAC	IND DEL	TRN	SAP	UTL SVC	CI
52.211-10 Commencement, Prosecution, and Completion of Work.	11.404(b)	C	Yes								R												
52.211-10_Alternate I	11.404(b)	C	Yes								R												
52.211-11 Liquidated Damages-Supplies, Services, or Research and Development.	11.503(a)	C	Yes	I	O		O		O					O							O	O	
52.211-12 Liquidated Damages-Construction.	11.503(b)	C	Yes								O	O									O		
52.211-13 Time Extensions.	11.503(c)	C	Yes								A	A									A		
52.211-14 Notice of Priority Rating for National Defense, Emergency Preparedness, and Energy Program Use.	11.604(a)	P	Yes	L	A	A	A	A	A	A	A	A	A	A	A	A	A	A	A	A	A	A	
52.211-15 Defense Priority and Allocation Requirements.	11.604(b)	C	Yes	I	A	A	A	A	A	A	A	A	A	A	A	A	A	A	A	A	A	A	
52.211-16 Variation in Quantity.	11.703(a)	C	Yes	F	A				A					A					A		A		
52.211-17 Delivery of Excess Quantities.	11.703(b)	C	Yes	F	O									O					O		O		
52.211-18 Variation in Estimated Quantity.	11.703(c)	C	Yes								A										A		
52.212-1 Instructions to Offerors-Commercial Items.	12.301(b)(1)	P	Yes	NA	A		A		A		A			A	A	A	A	A	A	A	A	A	R
52.212-2 Evaluation-Commercial Items.	12.301(c)	P	No	NA	O		O		O		O			O	O	O	O	O	O	O	O	O	O
52.212-3 Offeror Representations and Certifications-Commercial Items.	12.301(b)(2)	P	No	NA	A		A		A		A			A	A	A	A	A	A	A	A	A	R
52.212-3_Alternate I	12.301(b)(2)	P	No	NA	A		A		A		A			A	A	A	A	A	A	A	A	A	R
52.212-4 Contract Terms and Conditions-Commercial Items.	12.301(b)(3)	C	Yes	NA	A		A		A		A			A	A	A	A	A	A	A	A	A	R
52.212-4_Alternate I	32.608-2	C	Yes	NA	A		A		A		A			A	A	A	A	A	A	A	A	A	R
52.212-5 Contract Terms and Conditions Required to Implement Statutes or Executive Orders-Commercial Items.	12.301(b)(4)	C	Yes		A	A	A	A	A	A	A	A	A	A	A	A	A	A	A	A	A	A	R
52.212-5_Alternate I	12.301(b)(4)(i)	C	Yes		A	A	A	A	A	A	A	A	A	A	A	A	A	A	A	A	A	A	R
52.212-5_Alternate II	12.301(b)(4)(ii)	C	Yes		A	A	A	A	A	A	A	A	A	A	A	A	A	A	A	A	A	A	A
52.213-1 Fast Payment Procedure.	13.404	C	Yes	G	A									A					A		A		
52.213-2 Invoices.	13.302-5(b)	C	Yes																		A		

Provision or Clause	Prescribed in	P or C	IBR	UCF	FP SUP	CR SUP	FP R&D	CR R&D	FP SVC	CR SVC	FP CON	CR CON	T&M LH	LMV	COM SVC	DDR	A&E	FAC	IND DEL	TRN	SAP	UTL SVC	CI
52.213-3 Notice to Supplier.	13.302-5(c)	C	Yes																		A		
52.213-4 Terms and Conditions-Simplified Acquisitions (Other Than Commercial Items).	13.302-5(d)	C	Yes	I	A	A	A	A	A	A	A	A	A	A	A	A	A	A	A	A	A	A	
52.214-3 Amendments to Invitations for Bids.	14.201-6(b)(1)	P	Yes	L	A				A		A			A	A	A			A	A		A	
52.214-4 False Statements in Bids.	14.201-6(b)(2)	P	Yes	L	A				A		A			A	A	A			A	A		A	
52.214-5 Submission of Bids.	14.201-6(c)(1)	P	Yes	L	A				A		A			A	A	A			A	A		A	
52.214-6 Explanation to Prospective Bidders.	14.201-6(c)(2)	P	Yes	L	A				A		A			A	A	A			A	A		A	
52.214-7 Late Submissions, Modifications, and Withdrawals of Bids.	14.201-6(c)(3)	P	Yes	L	A				A		A			A	A	A			A	A		A	
52.214-10 Contract Award-Sealed Bidding.	14.201-6(e)	P	Yes	L	A				A					A	A	A			A	A		A	
52.214-12 Preparation of Bids.	14.201-6(f)	P	Yes	L	A				A					A	A	A			A	A		A	
52.214-14 Place of Performance-Sealed Bidding.	14.201-6(h)	P	No	K	A				A					A	A	A			A	A		A	
52.214-15 Period for Acceptance of Bids.	14.201-6(i)	P	Yes	L	A				A					A	A	A			A	A		A	
52.214-16 Minimum Bid Acceptance Period.	14.201-6(j)	P	No	K	A				A					A	A	A			A	A		A	
52.214-18 Preparation of Bids-Construction.	14.201-6(l)	P	Yes								A												
52.214-19 Contract Award-Sealed Bidding-Construction.	14.201-6(m)	P	Yes								A					A							
52.214-20 Bid Samples.	14.201-6(o)(1)	P	Yes	L	A				A					A					A				
52.214-20_Alternate I	14.201-6(o)(2)(i)	P	Yes	L	A				A					A					A				
52.214-20_Alternate II	14.201-6(o)(2)(ii)	P	Yes	L	A				A					A					A				
52.214-21 Descriptive Literature.	14.201-6(p)	P	Yes	L	A				A					A					A				
52.214-21_Alternate I	14.201-6(p)(2)	P	Yes	L	A				A					A					A				
52.214-22 Evaluation of Bids for Multiple Awards.	14.201-6(q)	P	Yes	M	A				A		A			A	A	A			A	A			
52.214-23 Late Submissions, Modifications,	14.201-6(r)	P	Yes	L	A		A		A		A			A	A	A			A				

Provision or Clause	Prescribed in	P or C	IBR	UCF	FP SUP	CR SUP	FP R&D	CR R&D	FP SVC	CR SVC	FP CON	CR CON	T&M LH	LMV	COM SVC	DDR	A&E	FAC	IND DEL	TRN	SAP	UTL SVC	CI
Revisions, and Withdrawals of Technical Proposals under Two-Step Sealed Bidding.																							
52.214-24 Multiple Technical Proposals.	14.201-6(s)	P	Yes	M	A		A		A		A			A					A				
52.214-25 Step Two of Two-Step Sealed Bidding.	14.201-6(t)	P	Yes	L	A				A		A			A	A	A							
52.214-26 Audit and Records-Sealed Bidding.	14.201-7(a)(1)	C	Yes	I	A				A		A			A	A	A			A	A			
52.214-26_Alternate I	14.201-7(a)(2)	C	Yes	I	A				A		A			A	A	A			A	A			
52.214-27 Price Reduction for Defective Certified Cost or Pricing Data-Modifications-Sealed Bidding.	14.201-7(b)	C	Yes	I	A				A		A			A	A	A			A	A			
52.214-28 Subcontractor Certified Cost or Pricing Data-Modifications-Sealed Bidding.	14.201-7(c)	C	Yes	I	A				A		A			A	A	A			A	A			
52.214-29 Order of Precedence-Sealed Bidding.	14.201-7(d)	C	Yes	I	A				A		A			A	A	A			A	A			
52.214-31 Facsimile Bids.	14.201-6(v)	P	Yes	L	A				A					A	A	A			A	A		A	
52.214-34 Submission of Offers in the English Language.	14.201-6(w)	P	Yes	L	A	A	A	A	A	A	A	A	A	A	A	A	A	A	A	A	A	A	
52.214-35 Submission of Offers in U.S. Currency.	14.201-6(x)	P	Yes	L	A	A	A	A	A	A	A	A	A	A	A	A	A	A	A	A	A	A	
52.215-1 Instructions to Offerors-Competitive Acquisition.	15.209(a)	P	Yes	L	A	A	A	A	A	A	A	A	A	A	A		A	A	A	A		A	
52.215-1_Alternate I	15.209(a)(1)	P	Yes	L	A	A	A	A	A	A	A	A	A	A	A		A	A	A	A		A	
52.215-1_Alternate II	15.209(a)(2)	P	Yes	L	A	A	A	A	A	A	A	A	A	A	A		A	A	A	A		A	
52.215-2 Audit and Records-Negotiation.	15.209(b)	C	Yes	I	A	A	A	A	A	A	A	A	A	A	A	A	A			A		A	
52.215-2_Alternate I	15.209(b)(2)	C	Yes	I	A	A	A	A	A	A	A	A	A	A	A	A	A			A		A	
52.215-2_Alternate II	15.209(b)(3)	C	Yes	I	A	A	A	A	A	A	A	A	A	A	A	A	A			A		A	
52.215-2_Alternate III	15.209(b)(4)	C	Yes	I	A	A	A	A	A	A	A	A	A	A	A	A	A			A		A	
52.215-3 Request for Information or Solicitation for Planning Purposes.	15.209(c)	P	Yes	L	A	A	A	A	A	A	A	A	A	A	A	A	A	A	A	A		A	
52.215-5 Facsimile Proposals.	15.209(e)	P	Yes	L	A	A	A	A	A	A	A	A	A	A	A	A	A	A	A	A		A	
52.215-6 Place of Performance.	15.209(f)	P	No	K	A	A	A	A	A	A	A	A	A	A	A		A	A	A	A			
52.215-8 Order of Precedence-Uniform	15.209(h)	C	Yes	I	A	A	A	A	A	A	A	A	A	A	A		A	A	A	A		A	

Provision or Clause	Prescribed in	P or C	IBR	UCF	FP SUP	CR SUP	FP R&D	CR R&D	FP SVC	CR SVC	FP CON	CR CON	T&M LH	LMV	COM SVC	DDR	A&E	FAC	IND DEL	TRN	SAP	UTL SVC	CI
Contract Format.																							
52.215-9 Changes or Additions to Make-or-Buy Program.	15.408(a)	C	Yes	I	A	A	A	A	A	A			A	A	A	A	A	A	A	A		A	
52.215-9_Alternate I	15.408(a)(1)	C	Yes	I	A	A	A	A	A	A			A	A	A	A	A	A	A	A		A	
52.215-9_Alternate II	15.408(a)(2)	C	Yes	I	A	A	A	A	A	A			A	A	A	A	A	A	A	A		A	
52.215-10 Price Reduction for Defective Certified Cost or Pricing Data.	15.408(b)	C	Yes	I	A	A	A	A	A	A	A	A	A	A	A	A	A	A	A	A		A	
52.215-11 Price Reduction for Defective Certified Cost or Pricing Data-Modifications.	15.408(c)	C	Yes	I	A	A	A	A	A	A	A	A	A	A	A	A	A	A	A	A		A	
52.215-12 Subcontractor Certified Cost or Pricing Data.	15.408(d)	C	Yes	I	A	A	A	A	A	A	A	A	A	A	A	A	A	A	A	A		A	
52.215-13 Subcontractor Certified Cost or Pricing Data-Modifications.	15.408(e)	C	Yes	I	A	A	A	A	A	A	A	A	A	A	A	A	A	A	A	A		A	
52.215-14 Integrity of Unit Prices.	15.408(f)(1)	C	Yes	I	A	A	A	A	A	A			A	A	A	A		A	A	A			
52.215-14_Alternate I	15.408(f)(2)	C	Yes	I	A	A	A	A	A	A			A	A	A	A		A	A	A			
52.215-15 Pension Adjustments and Asset Reversions.	15.408(g)	C	Yes	I	A	A	A	A	A	A	A	A	A	A	A		A	A	A	A		A	
52.215-16 Facilities Capital Cost of Money.	15.408(h)	P	Yes	L	A	A	A	A	A	A	A	A	A	A	A		A	A	A	A		A	
52.215-17 Waiver of Facilities Capital Cost of Money.	15.408(i)	C	Yes	I	A	A	A	A	A	A	A	A	A	A	A		A	A	A	A		A	
52.215-18 Reversion or Adjustment of Plans for Postretirement Benefits (PRB) Other Than Pensions.	15.408(j)	C	Yes	I	A	A	A	A	A	A	A	A	A	A	A	A	A	A	A	A		A	
52.215-19 Notification of Ownership Changes.	15.408(k)	C	Yes	I	A	A	A	A	A	A	A	A	A	A	A	A	A	A	A	A		A	
52.215-20 Requirements for Certified Cost or Pricing Data and Data Other Than Certified Cost or Pricing Data.	15.408(l)	P	Yes	L	O	O	O	O	O	O	O	O	O	O	O	O	O	O	O	O	O	O	
52.215-20_Alternate I	15.408(l)	P	Yes	L	O	O	O	O	O	O	O	O	O	O	O	O	O	O	O	O	O	O	
52.215-20_Alternate II	15.408(l)	P	Yes	L	O	O	O	O	O	O	O	O	O	O	O	O	O	O	O	O	O	O	
52.215-20_Alternate III	15.408(l)	P	Yes	L	O	O	O	O	O	O	O	O	O	O	O	O	O	O	O	O	O	O	
52.215-20_Alternate IV	15.408(l)	P	Yes	L	O	O	O	O	O	O	O	O	O	O	O	O	O	O	O	O	O	O	
52.215-21 Requirements for Certified Cost or Pricing Data and Data Other Than Certified	15.408(m)	C	Yes	I	O	O	O	O	O	O	O	O	O	O	O	O	O	O	O	O	O	O	

Provision or Clause	Prescribed in	P or C	IBR	UCF	FP SUP	CR SUP	FP R&D	CR R&D	FP SVC	CR SVC	FP CON	CR CON	T&M LH	LMV	COM SVC	DDR	A&E	FAC	IND DEL	TRN	SAP	UTL SVC	CI
Cost or Pricing Data-Modifications.																							
52.215-21_Alternate I	15.408(m)	C	Yes	I	O	O	O	O	O	O	O	O	O	O	O	O	O	O	O	O	O	O	
52.215-21_Alternate II	15.408(m)	C	Yes	I	O	O	O	O	O	O	O	O	O	O	O	O	O	O	O	O	O	O	
52.215-21_Alternate III	15.408(m)	C	Yes	I	O	O	O	O	O	O	O	O	O	O	O	O	O	O	O	O	O	O	
52.215-21_Alternate IV	15.408(m)	C	Yes	I	O	O	O	O	O	O	O	O	O	O	O	O	O	O	O	O	O	O	
52.215-22 Limitations on Pass-Through Charges-Identification of Subcontract Effort.	15.408(n)(1)	P	Yes	L	A	R	A	R	A	R	A	R	A	A		A	A	A	A	A		A	
52.215-23 Limitations on Pass-Through Charges.	15.408(n)(2)	C	Yes	I	A	R	A	R	A	R	A	R	A	A		A	A	A	A	A		A	
52.215-23_Alternate I	15.408(n)(2)(iii)	C	Yes	I	A	R	A	R	A	R	A	R	A	A		A	A	A	A	A		A	
52.216-1 Type of Contract.	16.105	P	No	L	A	A	A	A	A	A	A	A	A	A	A	A	A	A	A	A	A	A	
52.216-2 Economic Price Adjustment-Standard Supplies.	16.203-4(a)	C	No	I	O									O					O				
52.216-3 Economic Price Adjustment-Semistandard Supplies.	16.203-4(b)	C	No	I	O									O					O				
52.216-4 Economic Price Adjustment-Labor and Material.	16.203-4(c)	C	Yes	I	O				O		O		O	O	O	O	O	O	O				
52.216-5 Price Redetermination-Prospective.	16.205-4	C	Yes	I			A		A		A		A	A	A	A	A	A	A				
52.216-6 Price Redetermination-Retroactive.	16.206-4	C	Yes	I			A		A		A		A	A		A		A	A				
52.216-7 Allowable Cost and Payment.	16.307(a)	C	Yes	I		A		A		A		A	A	A	A	A	A		A	A			
52.216-7_Alternate I	16.307(a)(2)	C	Yes	I		A		A		A		A	A	A	A	A	A		A	A			
52.216-7_Alternate II	16.307(a)(3)	C	Yes	I		A		A		A		A	A	A	A	A	A		A	A			
52.216-7_Alternate III	16.307(a)(4)	C	Yes	I		A		A		A		A	A	A	A	A	A		A	A			
52.216-7_Alternate IV	16.307(a)(5)	C	Yes	I		A		A		A		A	A	A	A	A	A		A	A			
52.216-8 Fixed Fee.	16.307(b)	C	Yes	I		A		A		A			A	A	A	A	A	A	A	A			
52.216-9 Fixed Fee-Construction.	16.307(c)	C	Yes									A											
52.216-10 Incentive Fee.	16.307(d)	C	Yes	I		A		A		A			A		A	A			A	A			
52.216-11 Cost Contract-No Fee.	16.307(e)	C	Yes	I		A		A		A		A	A	A	A	A		A	A	A			
52.216-11_Alternate I	16.307(e)	C	Yes	I		A		A		A		A	A	A	A	A		A	A	A			
52.216-12 Cost-Sharing Contract-No Fee.	16.307(f)	C	Yes	I		A		A		A		A			A	A	A	A	A	A			
52.216-12_Alternate I	16.307(f)	C	Yes	I		A		A		A		A			A	A	A	A	A	A			

Provision or Clause	Prescribed in	P or C	IBR	UCF	FP SUP	CR SUP	FP R&D	CR R&D	FP SVC	CR SVC	FP CON	CR CON	T&M LH	LMV	COM SVC	DDR	A&E	FAC	IND DEL	TRN	SAP	UTL SVC	CI
52.216-15 Predetermined Indirect Cost Rates.	16.307(g)	C	Yes	I				A															
52.216-16 Incentive Price Revision-Firm Target.	16.406(a)	C	Yes	I	A		A		A		A		A	A	A	A	A		A				
52.216-16_Alternate I	16.406(a)	C	Yes	I	A		A		A		A		A	A	A	A	A		A				
52.216-17 Incentive Price Revision-Successive Targets.	16.406(b)	C	Yes	I	A		A		A		A		A	A	A	A	A		A				
52.216-17_Alternate I	16.406(b)	C	Yes	I	A		A		A		A		A	A	A	A	A		A				
52.216-18 Ordering.	16.506(a)	C	No	I															A				
52.216-19 Order Limitations.	16.506(b)	C	No	I															A				
52.216-20 Definite Quantity.	16.506(c)	C	Yes	I															A				
52.216-21 Requirements.	16.506(d)	C	No	I															A				
52.216-21_Alternate I	16.506(d)	C	No	I															A				
52.216-21_Alternate II	16.506(d)	C	No	I															A				
52.216-21_Alternate III	16.506(d)	C	No	I															A				
52.216-21_Alternate IV	16.506(d)	C	No	I															A				
52.216-22 Indefinite Quantity.	16.506(e)	C	No	I															A				
52.216-23 Execution and Commencement of Work.	16.603-4(b)(1)	C	No	I	A	A	A	A	A	A	A	A	A	A	A	A	A	A	A	A	A	A	A
52.216-24 Limitation of Government Liability.	16.603-4(b)(2)	C	No	I	R	R	R	R	R	R	R	R	R	R	R	R	R	R	R	R	R	R	R
52.216-25 Contract Definitization.	16.603-4(b)(3)	C	No	I	R	R	R	R	R	R	R	R	R	R	R	R	R	R	R	R	R	R	R
52.216-25_Alternate I	16.603-4(b)(3)	C	No	I	R	R	R	R	R	R	R	R	R	R	R	R	R	R	R	R	R	R	R
52.216-26 Payments of Allowable Costs Before Definitization.	16.603-4(c)	C	Yes	I		A		A		A		A			A	A	A	A	A				
52.216-27 Single or Multiple Awards.	16.506(f)	P	Yes	L															A				
52.216-28 Multiple Awards for Advisory and Assistance Services.	16.506(g)	P	Yes	L															A				
52.216-29 Time-and-Materials/Labor-Hour Proposal Requirements-Non-Commercial Item Acquisition With Adequate Price Competition.	16.601(f)(1)	P	Yes	L									A										

Provision or Clause	Prescribed in	P or C	IBR	UCF	FP SUP	CR SUP	FP R&D	CR R&D	FP SVC	CR SVC	FP CON	CR CON	T&M LH	LMV	COM SVC	DDR	A&E	FAC	IND DEL	TRN	SAP	UTL SVC	CI
52.216-30 Time-and-Materials/Labor-Hour Proposal Requirements-Non-Commercial Item Acquisition Without Adequate Price Competition.	16.601(f)(2)	P	No	L									A										
52.216-31 Time-and-Materials/Labor-Hour Proposal Requirements-Commercial Item Acquisition.	16.601(f)(3)	P	Yes	I									A										
52.216-32 Task-Order and Delivery-Order Ombudsman.	16.506(j)	C	Yes	G															A				
52.216-32_Alternate I	16.506(j)	C	Yes	G															A				
52.217-2 Cancellation Under Multi-year Contracts.	17.109(a)	C	Yes	I	A				A					A					A				
52.217-3 Evaluation Exclusive of Options.	17.208(a)	P	Yes	M	A	A			A	A			A	A					A	A			O
52.217-4 Evaluation of Options Exercised at Time of Contract Award.	17.208(b)	P	Yes	M	A	A			A	A			A	A					A	A			O
52.217-5 Evaluation of Options.	17.208(c)	P	Yes	M	A	A			A	A			A	A					A	A			O
52.217-6 Option for Increased Quantity.	17.208(d)	C	Yes	I	A				A					A					A	A			O
52.217-7 Option for Increased Quantity-Separately Priced Line Item.	17.208(e)	C	Yes	I	A	A							A	A					A				O
52.217-8 Option to Extend Services.	17.208(f)	C	Yes	I					A	A			A						A	A			O
52.217-9 Option to Extend the Term of the Contract.	17.208(g)	C	No	I					A	A			A						A	A			O
52.219-1 Small Business Program Representations.	19.309(a)(1)	P	No	K	A	A	A	A	A	A	A	A	A	A	A	A	A	A	A	A	A	A	
52.219-1_Alternate I	19.309(a)(2)	P	No	K	A	A	A	A	A	A	A	A	A	A	A	A	A	A	A	A	A	A	
52.219-2 Equal Low Bids.	19.309(b)	P	No	K	A				A		A			A	A	A			A	A		A	
52.219-3 Notice of HUBZone Set-Aside or Sole Source Award.	19.1309(a)	C	Yes	I	A	A	A	A	A	A	A	A	A	A	A	A	A	A	A	A	A	A	A
52.219-3_Alternate I	19.1309(a)(1)	C	Yes	I	A	A	A	A	A	A	A	A	A	A	A	A	A	A	A	A	A	A	A
52.219-4 Notice of Price Evaluation Preference for HUBZone Small Business Concerns.	19.1309(b)	C	Yes	I	A	A	A	A	A	A	A	A	A	A	A	A		A	A	A	A	A	A
52.219-4_Alternate I	19.1309(b)(1)	C	Yes	I	A	A	A	A	A	A	A	A	A	A	A	A		A	A	A	A	A	A

Provision or Clause	Prescribed in	P or C	IBR	UCF	FP SUP	CR SUP	FP R&D	CR R&D	FP SVC	CR SVC	FP CON	CR CON	T&M LH	LMV	COM SVC	DDR	A&E	FAC	IND DEL	TRN	SAP	UTL SVC	CI
52.219-6 Notice of Total Small Business Set-Aside.	19.508(c)	C	Yes	I	A	A	A	A	A	A	A	A	A	A	A	A	A	A	A	A	A	A	
52.219-6_Alternate I	19.508(c)	C	Yes	I	A	A	A	A	A	A	A	A	A	A	A	A	A	A	A	A	A	A	
52.219-6_Alternate II	19.508(c)	C	Yes	I	A	A	A	A	A	A	A	A	A	A	A	A	A	A	A	A	A	A	
52.219-7 Notice of Partial Small Business Set-Aside.	19.508(d)	C	Yes	I	A	A	A	A	A	A	A	A	A	A	A	A	A	A	A	A		A	
52.219-7_Alternate I	19.508(d)	C	Yes	I	A	A	A	A	A	A	A	A	A	A	A	A	A	A	A	A		A	
52.219-7_Alternate II	19.508(d)	C	Yes	I	A	A	A	A	A	A	A	A	A	A	A	A	A	A	A	A		A	
52.219-8 Utilization of Small Business Concerns.	19.708(a)	C	Yes	I	A	A	A	A	A	A	A	A	A	A	A	A	A	A	A	A		A	
52.219-9 Small Business Subcontracting Plan.	19.708(b)	C	Yes	I	A	A	A	A	A	A	A	A	A	A	A	A	A	A	A	A		A	A
52.219-9_Alternate I	19.708(b)(1)(i)	C	Yes	I	A	A	A	A	A	A	A	A	A	A	A	A	A	A	A	A		A	A
52.219-9_Alternate II	19.708(b)(1)(ii)	C	Yes	I	A	A	A	A	A	A	A	A	A	A	A	A	A	A	A	A		A	A
52.219-9_Alternate III	19.708(b)(1)(iii)	C	Yes	I	A	A	A	A	A	A	A	A	A	A	A	A	A	A	A	A		A	A
52.219-9_Alternate IV	19.708(b)(1)(iv)	C	Yes	I	A	A	A	A	A	A	A	A	A	A	A	A	A	A	A	A		A	A
52.219-10 Incentive Subcontracting Program.	19.708(c)(1)	C	Yes	I	O	O	O	O	O	O	O	O	O	O	O		O	O	O	O		O	
52.219-13 Notice of Set-Aside of Orders.	19.508(f)	C	No	I															A				
52.219-14 Limitations on Subcontracting.	19.508(e)	C	Yes	I	A	A	A	A	A	A	A	A	A	A	A	A	A	A	A	A		A	
52.219-16 Liquidated Damages-Subcontracting Plan.	19.708(b)(2)	C	Yes	I	A	A	A	A	A	A	A	A	A	A	A	A	A	A	A	A		A	
52.219-27 Notice of Service-Disabled Veteran-Owned Small Business Set-Aside.	19.1407	C	Yes	I	A	A	A	A	A	A	A	A	A	A	A	A	A	A	A	A	A	A	A
52.219-28 Post-Award Small Business Program Rerepresentation.	19.309(c)	C	Yes	I	A	A	A	A	A	A	A	A	A	A	A	A	A	A	A	A	A	A	A
52.219-29 Notice of Set-Aside for, or Sole Source Award to, Economically Disadvantaged Women-Owned Small Business Concerns.	19.1507	C	Yes	I	A	A	A	A	A	A	A	A	A	A	A	A	A	A	A	A	A	A	A
52.219-30 Notice of Set-Aside for, or Sole	19.1507	C	Yes	I	A	A	A	A	A	A	A	A	A	A	A	A	A	A	A	A	A	A	A

Provision or Clause	Prescribed in	P or C	IBR	UCF	FP SUP	CR SUP	FP R&D	CR R&D	FP SVC	CR SVC	FP CON	CR CON	T&M LH	LMV	COM SVC	DDR	A&E	FAC	IND DEL	TRN	SAP	UTL SVC	CI
Source Award to, Women-Owned Small Business Concerns Eligible Under the Women-Owned Small Business Program.																							
52.222-1 Notice to the Government of Labor Disputes.	22.103-5(a)	C	Yes	I	A	A	A	A	A	A	A	A	A	A	A	A	A	A	A	A	A	A	
52.222-2 Payment for Overtime Premiums.	22.103-5(b)	C	Yes	I		A		A		A		A			A	A	A		A	A			
52.222-3 Convict Labor.	22.202	C	Yes	I	A	A	A	A	A	A	A	A	A	A	A	A	A	A	A	A	A	A	
52.222-4 Contract Work Hours and Safety Standards -Overtime Compensation.	22.305	C	Yes	I	A	A	A	A	A	A	A	A	A	A	A	A		A	A	A		A	
52.222-5 Construction Wage Rate Requirements-Secondary Site of the Work.	22.407(h)	P	No	L							A	A									A		
52.222-6 Construction Wage Rate Requirements.	22.407(a)	C	Yes	I							A	A									A		
52.222-7 Withholding of Funds.	22.407(a)	C	Yes	I							A	A											
52.222-8 Payrolls and Basic Records.	22.407(a)	C	Yes	I							A	A											
52.222-9 Apprentices and Trainees.	22.407(a)	C	Yes	I							A	A											
52.222-10 Compliance with Copeland Act Requirements.	22.407(a)	C	Yes	I							A	A											
52.222-11 Subcontracts (Labor Standards).	22.407(a)	C	Yes	I							A	A											
52.222-12 Contract Termination-Debarment.	22.407(a)	C	Yes	I							A	A									A		
52.222-13 Compliance with Construction Wage Rate Requirements and Related Regulations.	22.407(a)	C	Yes	I							A	A									A		
52.222-14 Disputes Concerning Labor Standards.	22.407(a)	C	Yes	I							A	A									A		
52.222-15 Certification of Eligibility.	22.407(a)	C	Yes	I							A	A									A		
52.222-16 Approval of Wage Rates.	22.407(b)	C	Yes	I								A											
52.222-17 Nondisplacement of Qualified Workers.	22.1207	C	Yes	I					R	R			R					A	A				A
52.222-18 Certification Regarding Knowledge of Child Labor for Listed End Products.	22.1505(a)	P	No	K	A	A													A		A		A
52.222-19 Child Labor-Cooperation with Authorities and Remedies.	22.1505(b)	C	Yes	I	A	A													A		A		A
52.222-20 Contracts for Materials, Supplies,	22.610	C	Yes	I	A	A	A	A	A	A	A	A	A	A	A	A	A	A	A	A	A		

Provision or Clause	Prescribed in	P or C	IBR	UCF	FP SUP	CR SUP	FP R&D	CR R&D	FP SVC	CR SVC	FP CON	CR CON	T&M LH	LMV	COM SVC	DDR	A&E	FAC	IND DEL	TRN	SAP	UTL SVC	CI
Articles, and Equipment Exceeding $15,000.																							
52.222-21 Prohibition of Segregated Facilities.	22.810(a)(1)	C	Yes	I	A	A	A	A	A	A	A	A	A	A	A	A	A	A	A	A	A	A	
52.222-22 Previous Contracts and Compliance Reports.	22.810(a)(2)	P	No	K	A	A	A	A	A	A	A	A	A	A	A	A	A	A	A	A	A	A	
52.222-23 Notice of Requirement for Affirmative Action to Ensure Equal Employment Opportunity for Construction.	22.810(b)	P	Yes								A	A									A		
52.222-24 Preaward On-Site Equal Opportunity Compliance Evaluation.	22.810(c)	P	Yes	L	A	A	A	A	A	A			A	A	A	A	A	A	A	A		A	
52.222-25 Affirmative Action Compliance.	22.810(d)	P	No	K	A	A	A	A	A	A			A	A	A	A	A	A	A	A	A	A	
52.222-26 Equal Opportunity.	22.810(e)	C	Yes	I	A	A	A	A	A	A	A	A	A	A	A	A	A	A	A	A	A	A	
52.222-26_Alternate I	22.810(e)	C	Yes	I	A	A	A	A	A	A	A	A	A	A	A	A	A	A	A	A	A	A	
52.222-27 Affirmative Action Compliance Requirements for Construction.	22.810(f)	C	Yes								A	A									A		
52.222-29 Notification of Visa Denial.	22.810(g)	C	Yes	I	A	A	A	A	A	A	A	A	A	A	A	A	A	A	A	A	A	A	
52.222-30 Construction Wage Rate Requirements-Price Adjustment (None or Separately Specified Method).	22.407(e)	C									A	A											
52.222-31 Construction Wage Rate Requirements-Price Adjustment (Percentage Method).	22.407(f)	C									A	A											
52.222-32 Construction Wage Rate Requirements-Price Adjustment (Actual Method).	22.407(g)	C									A	A											
52.222-33 Notice of Requirement for Project Labor Agreement.	22.505(a)(1)	P	Yes								A	A											
52.222-33_Alternate I	22.505(a)(1)	P	Yes								A	A											
52.222-33_Alternate II	22.505(a)(2)	P	Yes								A	A											
52.222-34 Project Labor Agreement.	22.505(b)(1)	C	Yes								A	A											
52.222-34_Alternate I	22.505(b)(2)	C	Yes								A	A											
52.222-35 Equal Opportunity for Veterans.	22.1310(a)(1)	C	No	I	A	A	A	A	A	A	A	A	A	A	A	A	A	A	A	A	A	A	
52.222-35_Alternate I	22.1310(a)	C	No	I	A	A	A	A	A	A	A	A	A	A	A	A	A	A	A	A	A	A	

Provision or Clause	Prescribed in	P or C	IBR	UCF	FP SUP	CR SUP	FP R&D	CR R&D	FP SVC	CR SVC	FP CON	CR CON	T&M LH	LMV	COM SVC	DDR	A&E	FAC	IND DEL	TRN	SAP	UTL SVC	CI
	(2)																						
52.222-36 Equal Opportunity for Workers with Disabilities.	22.1408(a)	C	No	I	A	A	A	A	A	A	A	A	A	A	A	A	A	A	A	A	A	A	
52.222-36_Alternate I	22.1408(b)	C	No	I	A	A	A	A	A	A	A	A	A	A	A	A	A	A	A	A	A	A	
52.222-37 Employment Reports on Veterans.	22.1310(b)	C	Yes	I	A	A	A	A	A	A	A	A	A	A	A	A	A	A	A	A	A	A	
52.222-38 Compliance with Veterans' Employment Reporting Requirements.	22.1310(c)	P	Yes	K	A	A	A	A	A	A	a	A	A	A	A	A	A	A	A	A	A	A	
52.222-40 Notification of Employee Rights Under the National Labor Relations Act.	22.1605	C	Yes	I	A	A	A	A	A	A	A	A	A	A	A	A	A	A	A	A		A	A
52.222-41 Service Contract Labor Standards.	22.1006(a)	C	Yes	I					A	A			A		A	A	A			A	A		
52.222-42 Statement of Equivalent Rates for Federal Hires.	22.1006(b)	C	No	I					A	A			A		A	A	A			A	A		
52.222-43 Fair Labor Standards Act and Service Contract Labor Standards-Price Adjustment (Multiple Year and Option Contracts).	22.1006(c)(1)	C	Yes	I					A				A		A	A	A			A	A		
52.222-44 Fair Labor Standards Act and Service Contract Labor Standards-Price Adjustment.	22.1006(c)(2)	C	Yes	I					A				A		A	A	A			A	A		
52.222-46 Evaluation of Compensation for Professional Employees.	22.1103	P	Yes	L					A	A													
52.222-48 Exemption from Application of the Service Contract Labor Standards to Contracts for Maintenance, Calibration, or Repair of Certain Equipment-Certification.	22.1006(e)(1)	P	Yes	K					A	A			A								A		
52.222-49 Service Contract Labor Standards-Place of Performance Unknown.	22.1006(f)	C	Yes	I					A	A			A		A	A				A	A		
52.222-50 Combating Trafficking in Persons.	22.1705(a)(1)	C	Yes	I	R	R	R	R	R	R	R	R	R	R	R	R	R	R	R	R	R	R	
52.222-51 Exemption from Application of the Service Contract Labor Standards to Contracts for Maintenance, Calibration, or Repair of Certain Equipment-Requirements.	22.1006(e)(2)	C	Yes	I					A	A			A								A		
52.222-52 Exemption from Application of the Service Contract Labor Standards to Contracts for Certain Services-Certification.	22.1006(e)(3)	P	Yes	K					A	A			A								A		

Provision or Clause	Prescribed in	P or C	IBR	UCF	FP SUP	CR SUP	FP R&D	CR R&D	FP SVC	CR SVC	FP CON	CR CON	T&M LH	LMV	COM SVC	DDR	A&E	FAC	IND DEL	TRN	SAP	UTL SVC	CI
52.222-53 Exemption from Application of the Service Contract Labor Standards to Contracts for Certain Services-Requirements.	22.1006(e)(4)	C	Yes	I					A	A			A								A		
52.222-54 Employment Eligibility Verification.	22.1803	C	Yes	I	A	A	A	A	A	A	A	A	A		A	A	A	A	A	A		A	
52.222-55 Minimum Wages Under Executive Order 13658.	22.1906	C	Yes	I					A	A	A	A	A		A	A				A	A		A
52.222-56 Certification Regarding Trafficking in Persons Compliance Plan.	22.1705(b)	P	Yes	L	A	A	A	A	A	A	A	A	A	A	A	A	A	A	A	A		A	A
52.222-62 Paid Sick Leave Under Executive Order 13706.	22.2110	C	Yes	I	A	A	A	A	A	A	A	A	A	A	A	A	A	A	A	A	A	A	
52.223-1 Biobased Product Certification.	23.406(a)	P	Yes	K	A	A	A	A	A	A	A	A	A	A	A	A		A	A	A	A	A	A
52.223-2 Affirmative Procurement of Biobased Products Under Service and Construction Contracts.	23.406(b)	C	Yes	I					A	A	A	A	A		A	A		A	A	A	A		A
52.223-3 Hazardous Material Identification and Material Safety Data.	23.303	C	Yes	I	A	A	A	A	A	A	A	A	A	A	A	A	A	A	A	A	A	A	
52.223-3_Alternate I	23.303	C	Yes	I	A	A	A	A	A	A	A	A	A	A	A	A	A	A	A	A	A	A	
52.223-4 Recovered Material Certification.	23.406(c)	P	Yes	K	A	A	A	A	A	A	A	A	A	A	A	A		A	A	A	A	A	A
52.223-5 Pollution Prevention and Right-to-Know Information.	23.1005	C	Yes	I	A	A	A	A	A	A	A	A	A	A	A	A	A	A	A	A	A	A	
52.223-5_Alternate I	23.1005(b)	C	Yes	I	A	A	A	A	A	A	A	A	A	A	A	A	A	A	A	A	A	A	
52.223-5_Alternate II	23.1005(c)	C	Yes	I	A	A	A	A	A	A	A	A	A	A	A	A	A	A	A	A	A	A	
52.223-6 Drug-Free Workplace.	23.505	C	Yes	I	A	A	A	A	A	A	A	A	A	A	A	A	A	A	A	A	A	A	
52.223-7 Notice of Radioactive Materials.	23.602	C	No	I	A	A	A	A	A	A	A	A	A			A		A	A		A		
52.223-9 Estimate of Percentage of Recovered Material Content for EPA-Designated Items.	23.406(d)	C	No	I	A	A	A	A	A	A	A	A	A	A	A	A	A	A	A	A		A	A
52.223-9_Alternate I	23.406(d)	C	No	I	A	A	A	A	A	A	A	A	A	A	A	A	A	A	A	A		A	A
52.223-10 Waste Reduction Program.	23.705(a)	C	Yes	I					A	A					A			A					
52.223-11 Ozone-Depleting Substances and High Global Warming Potential Hydrofluorocarbons.	23.804(a)(1)	C	Yes	I	A	A	A	A	A	A	A	A	A	A	A	A	A	A	A	A	A	A	A
52.223-12 Maintenance, Service, Repair, or Disposal of Refrigeration Equipment and Air	23.804(a)(2)	C	Yes	I	A	A	A	A	A	A	A	A	A	A	A	A	A	A	A	A	A	A	A

Provision or Clause	Prescribed in	P or C	IBR	UCF	FP SUP	CR SUP	FP R&D	CR R&D	FP SVC	CR SVC	FP CON	CR CON	T&M LH	LMV	COM SVC	DDR	A&E	FAC	IND DEL	TRN	SAP	UTL SVC	CI
Conditioners.																							
52.223-13 Acquisition of EPEAT®–Registered Imaging Equipment.	23.705(b)(1)	C	Yes	I	A	A	A	A	A	A			A	A	A				A		A		A
52.223-13_Alternate I	23.705(c)(2)	C	Yes	I	A	A	A	A	A	A			A	A	A				A		A		A
52.223-14 Acquisition of EPEAT®-Registered Televisions.	23.705(d)(1)	C	Yes	I	A	A	A	A	A	A			A	A	A				A		A		A
52.223-14_Alternate I	23.705(d)(2)	C	Yes	I	A	A	A	A	A	A			A	A	A				A		A		A
52.223-15 Energy Efficiency in Energy-Consuming Products.	23.206	C	Yes	I	A	A	A	A	A	A	A	A	A		A	A		A	A	A	A	A	A
52.223-16 Acquisition of EPEAT®-Registered Personal Computer Products.	23.705(b)(1)	C	Yes	I	A	A	A	A	A	A			A	A	A				A		A		A
52.223-16_Alternate I	23.705(b)(2)	C	Yes	I	A	A	A	A	A	A			A	A	A				A		A		A
52.223-17 Affirmative Procurement of EPA-designated Items in Service and Construction Contracts.	23.406(e)	C	Yes	I					A	A	A	A	A		A	A	A	A	A	A	A		
52.223-18 Encouraging Contractor Policies to Ban Text Messaging While Driving.	23.1105	C	Yes	I	R	R	R	R	R	R	R	R	R	R	R	R	R	R	R	R	R	R	R
52.223-19 Compliance with Environmental Management Systems.	23.903	C	Yes	I			A	A	A	A	A	A	A	A	A	A		A	A	A	A	A	
52.223-20 Aerosols.	23.804(a)(3)	C	Yes	I	A	A	A	A	A	A	A	A	A	A	A	A	A	A	A	A	A	A	A
52.223-21 Foams.	23.804(a)(4)	C	Yes	I	A	A	A	A	A	A	A	A	A	A	A	A	A	A	A	A	A	A	A
52.223-22 Public Disclosure of Greenhouse Gas Emissions and Reduction Goals-Representation.	23.804(b)	P		K	A	A	A	A	A	A	A	A	A	A	A	A	A	A	A	A	A	A	A
52.224-1 Privacy Act Notification.	24.104	C	Yes	I	A	A	A	A	A	A	A	A	A	A	A	A	A	A	A	A	A		
52.224-2 Privacy Act.	24.104	C	Yes	I	A	A	A	A	A	A	A	A	A	A	A	A	A	A	A	A	A		
52.224-3 Privacy Training.	24.302	C	Yes	I	A	A	A	A	A	A	A	A	A	A	A	A	A	A	A	A	A	A	A
52.224-3_Alternate I	24.302(b)	C	Yes	I	A	A	A	A	A	A	A	A	A	A	A	A	A	A	A	A	A	A	A
52.225-1 Buy American-Supplies	25.1101(a)(1)	C	Yes	I	A	A	A	A	A	A			A	A	A				A		A		A
52.225-2 Buy American Certificate.	25.1101(a)(2)	P	No	K	A	A	A	A	A	A			A	A	A				A		A		
52.225-3 Buy American-Free Trade Agreements-Israeli Trade Act.	25.1101(b)(1)	C	Yes	I	A	A							A	A					A		A		A

Provision or Clause	Prescribed in	P or C	IBR	UCF	FP SUP	CR SUP	FP R&D	CR R&D	FP SVC	CR SVC	FP CON	CR CON	T&M LH	LMV	COM SVC	DDR	A&E	FAC	IND DEL	TRN	SAP	UTL SVC	CI
52.225-3_Alternate I	25.1101(b)(1)(ii)	C	Yes	I	A	A							A	A					A		A		A
52.225-3_Alternate II	25.1101(b)(1)(iii)	C	Yes	I	A	A							A	A					A		A		A
52.225-3_Alternate III	25.1101(b)(1)(iv)	C	Yes	I	A	A							A	A					A		A		A
52.225-4 Buy American-Free Trade Agreements-Israeli Trade Act Certificate.	25.1101(b)(2)	P	No	K	A	A							A	A					A		A		
52.225-4_Alternate I	25.1101(b)(2)(ii)	P	No	K	A	A							A	A					A		A		
52.225-4_Alternate II	25.1101(b)(2)(iii)	P	No	K	A	A							A	A					A		A		
52.225-4_Alternate III	25.1101(b)(2)(iv)	P	No	K	A	A							A	A					A		A		
52.225-5 Trade Agreements.	25.1101(c)(1)	C	Yes	I	A	A													A		A		A
52.225-6 Trade Agreements Certificate.	25.1101(c)(2)	P	No	K	A	A													A		A		
52.225-7 Waiver of Buy American Statute for Civil Aircraft and Related Articles.	25.1101(d)	P	Yes	L	A	A	A	A											A		A		A
52.225-8 Duty-Free Entry.	25.1101(e)	C	Yes	I	A	A	A	A					A	A	A				A		A		A
52.225-9 Buy American-Construction Materials.	25.1102(a)	C	No								A	A											
52.225-10 Notice of Buy American Requirement-Construction Materials.	25.1102(b)(1)	P	No								A	A											
52.225-10_Alternate I	25.1102(b)(2)	P	No								A	A											
52.225-11 Buy American-Construction Materials under Trade Agreements.	25.1102(c)	C	No								A	A											
52.225-11_Alternate I	25.1102(c)(3)	C	No								A	A											
52.225-12 Notice of Buy American Requirement-Construction Materials Under Trade Agreements.	25.1102(d)(1)	P	No								A	A											
52.225-12_Alternate I	25.1102(d)(2)	P	No								A	A											
52.225-12_Alternate II	25.1102(d)(3)	P	No								A	A											

Provision or Clause	Prescribed in	P or C	IBR	UCF	FP SUP	CR SUP	FP R&D	CR R&D	FP SVC	CR SVC	FP CON	CR CON	T&M LH	LMV	COM SVC	DDR	A&E	FAC	IND DEL	TRN	SAP	UTL SVC	CI
52.225-13 Restrictions on Certain Foreign Purchases.	25.1103(a)	C	Yes	I	R	R	R	R	R	R	R	R	R	R	R	R	R	R	R	R	R	R	R
52.225-14 Inconsistency between English Version and Translation of Contract.	25.1103	C	Yes	I	A	A	A	A	A	A	A	A	A	A	A	A	A	A	A	A	A	A	A
52.225-17 Evaluation of Foreign Currency Offers.	25.1103(c)	P	Yes	M	A	A	A	A	A	A	A	A	A	A	A	A	A	A	A	A	A	A	A
52.225-18 Place of Manufacture.	25.1101(f)	P	No	K	R	R							A						A		A		A
52.225-19 Contractor Personnel in a Designated Operational Area or Supporting a Diplomatic or Consular Mission Outside the United States.	25.301-4	C	Yes	I	A	A	A	A	A	A	A	A	A	A	A	A	A	A	A	A	A	A	A
52.225-20 Prohibition on Conducting Restricted Business Operations in Sudan-Certification.	25.1103	P	No	K	A	A	A	A	A	A	A	A	A	A	A	A	A	A	A	A	A	A	A
52.225-21 Required Use of American Iron, Steel, and Manufactured Goods-Buy American Statute-Construction Materials.	25.1102(e)	C	No								A	A											
52.225-22 Notice of Required Use of American Iron, Steel, and Manufactured Goods-Buy American Statute-Construction Materials.	25.1102(e)	P	No								A	A											
52.225-22_Alternate I	25.1102(e)	P	No								A	A											
52.225-23 Required Use of American Iron, Steel, and Manufactured Goods-Buy American Statute-Construction Materials under Trade Agreements.	25.1102(e)	C	No								A	A											
52.225-23_Alternate I	25.1102(e)	C	No								A	A											
52.225-24 Notice of Required Use of American Iron, Steel, and Manufactured Goods-Buy American Statute-Construction Materials Under Trade Agreements.	25.1102(e)	P	No								A	A											
52.225-24_Alternate I	25.1102(e)	P	No								A	A											
52.225-24_Alternate II	25.1102(e)	P	No								A	A											
52.225-25 Prohibition on Contracting with Entities Engaging in Certain Activities or Transactions Relating to Iran-Representation	25.1103	P	Yes	K	R	R	R	R	R	R	R	R	R	R	R	R	R	R	R	R	R	R	R

Provision or Clause	Prescribed in	P or C	IBR	UCF	FP SUP	CR SUP	FP R&D	CR R&D	FP SVC	CR SVC	FP CON	CR CON	T&M LH	LMV	COM SVC	DDR	A&E	FAC	IND DEL	TRN	SAP	UTL SVC	CI
and Certifications.																							
52.225-26 Contractors Performing Private Security Functions Outside the United States.	25.302-6	C	Yes	I	A	A	A	A	A	A	A	A	O	A	A	A	A	A	A	A	A	A	A
52.226-1 Utilization of Indian Organizations and Indian-Owned Economic Enterprises.	26.104	C	Yes	I	A	A	A	A	A	A	A	A	A	A	A	A	A	A	A	A		A	
52.226-2 Historically Black College or University and Minority Institution Representation.	26.404	P	No	K	A	A	A	A	A	A			A		A				A		A		
52.226-3 Disaster or Emergency Area Representation.	26.206(a)	P	No	K	A	A			A	A	A	A	A	A	A	A	A	A	A	A		A	A
52.226-4 Notice of Disaster or Emergency Area Set-Aside.	26.206(b)	C	Yes	I	A	A			A	A	A	A	A	A	A	A	A	A	A	A		A	A
52.226-5 Restrictions on Subcontracting Outside Disaster or Emergency Area.	26.206(c)	C	Yes	I	A	A			A	A	A	A	A	A	A	A	A	A	A	A		A	A
52.226-6 Promoting Excess Food Donation to Nonprofit Organizations.	26.404	C	Yes	I	A	A			A	A									A		A		A
52.227-1 Authorization and Consent.	27.201-2(a)(1)	C	Yes	I	A	A			A		A	A			A	A	A	A	A		O		
52.227-1_Alternate I	27.201-2(a)(2)	C	Yes	I	A	A			A		A	A			A	A	A	A	A		O		
52.227-1_Alternate II	27.201-2(a)(3)	C	Yes	I	A	A			A		A	A			A	A	A	A	A		O		
52.227-2 Notice and Assistance Regarding Patent and Copyright Infringement.	27.201-2(b)	C	Yes	I	A	A																	
52.227-3 Patent Indemnity.	27.201-2(c)(1)	C	Yes	I	A	A			A	A									A				
52.227-3_Alternate I	27.201-2(c)(2)	C	Yes	I	A	A			A	A									A				
52.227-3_Alternate II	27.201-2(c)(2)	C	Yes	I	A	A			A	A									A				
52.227-3_Alternate III	27.201-2(c)(3)	C	Yes	I	A	A			A	A									A				
52.227-4 Patent Indemnity-Construction Contracts.	27.201-2(d)(1)	C	Yes								A	A				A							
52.227-4_Alternate I	27.201-2(d)	C	Yes								A	A				A							

Provision or Clause	Prescribed in	P or C	IBR	UCF	FP SUP	CR SUP	FP R&D	CR R&D	FP SVC	CR SVC	FP CON	CR CON	T&M LH	LMV	COM SVC	DDR	A&E	FAC	IND DEL	TRN	SAP	UTL SVC	CI
	(2)																						
52.227-5 Waiver of Indemnity.	27.201-2(e)	C	Yes	I	A	A	A	A	A	A	A	A				A		A	A				
52.227-6 Royalty Information.	27.202-5(a)(1)	P	No	K	A	A	A	A	A	A	A	A				A		A	A				
52.227-6_Alternate I	27.202-5(a)(2)	P	No	K	A	A	A	A	A	A	A	A				A		A	A				
52.227-7 Patents-Notice of Government Licensee.	27.202-5	P	No	K	A	A	A	A	A	A	A	A			A	A		A	A				
52.227-9 Refund of Royalties.	27.202-5(c)	C	Yes	I	A		A		A		A				A	A		A	A				
52.227-10 Filing of Patent Applications-Classified Subject Matter.	27.203-2	C	Yes	I	A	A	A	A	A	A	A	A			A	A		A	A				
52.227-11 Patent Rights-Ownership by the Contractor.	27.303(b)(1)	C	Yes	I			A	A			A	A					A						
52.227-11_Alternate I	27.303(b)(3)	C	Yes	I			A	A			A	A					A						
52.227-11_Alternate II	27.303(b)(4)	C	Yes	I			A	A			A	A					A						
52.227-11_Alternate III	27.303(b)(5)	C	Yes	I			A	A			A	A					A						
52.227-11_Alternate IV	27.303(b)(6)	C	Yes	I			A	A			A	A					A						
52.227-11_Alternate V	27.303(b)(7)	C	Yes	I			A	A			A	A					A						
52.227-13 Patent Rights-Ownership by the Government.	27.303	C	Yes	I			A	A			A	A					A						
52.227-13_Alternate I	27.303(e)	C	Yes	I			A	A			A	A					A						
52.227-13_Alternate II	27.303(e)(5)	C	Yes	I			A	A			A	A					A						
52.227-14 Rights in Data-General.	27.409(b)(1)	C	Yes	I	A	A	A	A	A	A			A	A	A	A		A	A	A	A		
52.227-14_Alternate I	27.409(b)(2)	C	Yes	I	A	A	A	A	A	A			A	A	A	A		A	A	A	A		
52.227-14_Alternate II	27.409(b)(3)	C	Yes	I	A	A	A	A	A	A			A	A	A	A		A	A	A	A		
52.227-14_Alternate III	27.409(b)(4)	C	Yes	I	A	A	A	A	A	A			A	A	A	A		A	A	A	A		
52.227-14_Alternate IV	27.409(b)(5)	C	Yes	I	A	A	A	A	A	A			A	A	A	A		A	A	A	A		
52.227-14_Alternate V	27.409(b)(6)	C	Yes	I	A	A	A	A	A	A			A	A	A	A		A	A	A	A		
52.227-15 Representation of Limited Rights Data and Restricted Computer Software.	27.409(c)	P	No	K	A	A	A	A	A	A	A	A	A	A	A	A	A	A	A	A	A	A	
52.227-16 Additional Data Requirements.	27.409(d)	C	Yes	I			A	A													A		
52.227-17 Rights in Data-Special Works.	27.409(e)	C	Yes	I	A	A	A	A	A	A	O	O	A		A		O				A		

Provision or Clause	Prescribed in	P or C	IBR	UCF	FP SUP	CR SUP	FP R&D	CR R&D	FP SVC	CR SVC	FP CON	CR CON	T&M LH	LMV	COM SVC	DDR	A&E	FAC	IND DEL	TRN	SAP	UTL SVC	CI
52.227-18 Rights in Data-Existing Works.	27.409(f)	C	Yes	I	A	A	A	A	A	A			A		A		A		A		A		
52.227-19 Commercial Computer Software License.	27.409(g)	C	Yes	I	A				A						A						A		
52.227-20 Rights in Data-SBIR Program.	27.409(h)	C	Yes	I			A	A															
52.227-21 Technical Data Declaration, Revision, and Withholding of Payment-Major Systems.	27.409(j)	C	Yes	I	A	A	A	A	A	A	A	A	A	A	A	A	A	A	A	A	A		
52.227-22 Major System-Minimum Rights.	27.409(k)	C	Yes	I	A	A	A	A	A	A	A	A	A	A	A	A	A	A	A	A	A		
52.227-23 Rights to Proposal Data (Technical).	27.409(l)	C	Yes	I	A	A	A	A	A	A	A	A	A	A	A	A	A	A	A	A	A		
52.228-1 Bid Guarantee.	28.101-2	P	Yes	L	A	A	A	A	A	A	A	A	A	A	A	A	A	A	A	A	A	A	
52.228-2 Additional Bond Security.	28.106-4(a)	C	Yes	I	A	A	A	A	A	A	A	A	A	A	A	A	A	A	A	A	A	A	
52.228-3 Workers' Compensation Insurance (Defense Base Act).	28.309(a)	C	Yes	I					A	A	A	A	A				A						
52.228-4 Workers' Compensation and War-Hazard Insurance Overseas.	28.309(b)	C	Yes	I					A	A	A	A	A				A						
52.228-5 Insurance-Work on a Government Installation.	28.310	C	Yes	I	A		A		A		A	A		A	A	A	A		A				
52.228-7 Insurance-Liability to Third Persons.	28.311-1	C	Yes	I		A		A		A					A			A	A				
52.228-8 Liability and Insurance-Leased Motor Vehicles.	28.312	C	Yes	I										R							A		
52.228-9 Cargo Insurance.	28.313(a)	C	Yes	I																A	A		
52.228-10 Vehicular and General Public Liability Insurance.	28.313(b)	C	Yes	I																A			
52.228-11 Pledges of Assets.	28.203-6	C	Yes	I	A	A	A	A	A	A	A	A	A	A	A	A	A	A	A	A	A	A	
52.228-12 Prospective Subcontractor Requests for Bonds.	28.106-4(b)	C	Yes	I							A	A	A			A							
52.228-13 Alternative Payment Protections.	28.102-3(b)	C	Yes	I							A	A	A			A							
52.228-14 Irrevocable Letter of Credit.	28.204-4	C	Yes	I	A	A	A	A	A	A	A	A	A	A	A	A	A	A	A	A	A	A	
52.228-15 Performance and Payment Bonds-Construction.	28.102-3(a)	C	Yes	I							A	A				A							
52.228-16 Performance and Payment Bonds-Other Than Construction.	28.103-4	C	No	I	A	A	A	A	A	A			A	A	A		A	A	A	A		A	
52.228-16_Alternate I	28.103-4	C	No	I	A	A	A	A	A	A			A	A	A		A	A	A	A		A	

Provision or Clause	Prescribed in	P or C	IBR	UCF	FP SUP	CR SUP	FP R&D	CR R&D	FP SVC	CR SVC	FP CON	CR CON	T&M LH	LMV	COM SVC	DDR	A&E	FAC	IND DEL	TRN	SAP	UTL SVC	CI
52.229-1 State and Local Taxes.	29.401-1	C	Yes	I																A			
52.229-2 North Carolina State and Local Sales and Use Tax.	29.401-2	C	Yes	I							A	A											
52.229-2_Alternate I	29.401-2	C	Yes	I							A	A											
52.229-3 Federal, State, and Local Taxes.	29.401-3	C	Yes	I	A		A		A		A		A	A	A	A	A	A	A	A			
52.229-4 Federal, State, and Local Taxes (State and Local Adjustments).	29.401-3	C	Yes	I	A		A		A		A		A	A	A	A	A	A	A	A			
52.229-6 Taxes-Foreign Fixed-Price Contracts.	29.402-1(a)	C	Yes	I	A		A		A		A		A	A	A	A	A	A	A	A			
52.229-7 Taxes-Fixed-Price Contracts with Foreign Governments.	29.402-1(b)	C	Yes	I	A		A		A		A		A	A	A	A	A	A	A	A	A		
52.229-8 Taxes-Foreign Cost-Reimbursement Contracts.	29.402-2(a)	C	Yes	I		A		A		A		A		A	A	A	A	A	A	A			
52.229-9 Taxes-Cost-Reimbursement Contracts with Foreign Governments.	29.402-2(b)	C	Yes	I		A		A		A		A		A	A	A	A	A	A	A			
52.229-10 State of New Mexico Gross Receipts and Compensating Tax.	29.401-4(b)	C	Yes	I		A		A		A		A	A	A	A	A	A	A	A	A			
52.230-1 Cost Accounting Standards Notices and Certification.	30.201-3	P	No	K	A	A	A	A	A	A	A	A	A	A	A	A	A	A	A	A		A	
52.230-1_Alternate I	30.201-3(b)	P	No	K	A	A	A	A	A	A	A	A	A	A	A	A	A	A	A	A		A	
52.230-2 Cost Accounting Standards.	30.201-4(a)	C	Yes	I	A	A	A	A	A	A	A	A	A	A	A	A	A	A	A	A		A	
52.230-3 Disclosure and Consistency of Cost Accounting Practices.	30.201-4(b)(1)	C	Yes	I	A	A	A	A	A	A	A	A	A	A	A	A	A	A	A	A		A	
52.230-4 Disclosure and Consistency of Cost Accounting Practices-Foreign Concerns.	30.201-4(c)	C	Yes	I	A	A	A	A	A	A	A	A	A	A	A	A	A	A	A	A		A	
52.230-5 Cost Accounting Standards-Educational Institution.	30.201-4(e)	C	Yes	I	A	A	A	A	A	A	A	A	A	A	A	A	A	A	A	A		A	
52.230-6 Administration of Cost Accounting Standards.	30.201-4(d)(1)	C	Yes	I	A	A	A	A	A	A	A	A	A	A	A	A	A	A	A	A		A	
52.230-7 Proposal Disclosure-Cost Accounting Practice Changes.	30.201-3(c)	P	No	K	A	A	A	A	A	A	A	A	A	A	A	A	A	A	A	A		A	
52.232-1 Payments.	32.111(a)(1)	C	Yes	I	R				R						A						A	A	
52.232-2 Payments under Fixed-Price Research and Development Contracts.	32.111(a)(2)	C	Yes	I			R																

Provision or Clause	Prescribed in	P or C	IBR	UCF	FP SUP	CR SUP	FP R&D	CR R&D	FP SVC	CR SVC	FP CON	CR CON	T&M LH	LMV	COM SVC	DDR	A&E	FAC	IND DEL	TRN	SAP	UTL SVC	CI
52.232-3 Payments under Personal Services Contracts.	32.111(a)(3)	C	Yes	I					A	A													
52.232-4 Payments under Transportation Contracts and Transportation-Related Services Contracts.	32.111(a)(4)	C	Yes	I																R	A		
52.232-5 Payments under Fixed-Price Construction Contracts.	32.111(a)(5)	C	Yes								R												
52.232-6 Payment under Communication Service Contracts with Common Carriers.	32.111(a)(6)	C	Yes	I											A						A		
52.232-7 Payments under Time-and-Materials and Labor-Hour Contracts.	32.111(a)(7)	C	Yes	I									A										
52.232-8 Discounts for Prompt Payment.	32.111(b)(1)	C	Yes	I	A				A				A	A							A		
52.232-9 Limitation on Withholding of Payments.	32.111(b)(2)	C	Yes	I	A	A	A	A	A	A			A	A									
52.232-10 Payments under Fixed-Price Architect-Engineer Contracts.	32.111(c)(1)	C	Yes														A						
52.232-11 Extras.	32.111(c)(2)	C	Yes	I	A				A					A						A	A	A	
52.232-12 Advance Payments.	32.412(a)	C	No	I	A	A	A	A	A	A	A	A	A	A	A	A	A	A	A	A	A	A	
52.232-12_Alternate I	32.412(a)	C	No	I	A	A	A	A	A	A	A	A	A	A	A	A	A	A	A	A	A	A	
52.232-12_Alternate II	32.412(a)	C	No	I	A	A	A	A	A	A	A	A	A	A	A	A	A	A	A	A	A	A	
52.232-12_Alternate III	32.412(a)	C	No	I	A	A	A	A	A	A	A	A	A	A	A	A	A	A	A	A	A	A	
52.232-12_Alternate IV	32.412(a)	C	No	I	A	A	A	A	A	A	A	A	A	A	A	A	A	A	A	A	A	A	
52.232-12_Alternate V	32.412(a)	C	No	I	A	A	A	A	A	A	A	A	A	A	A	A	A	A	A	A	A	A	
52.232-13 Notice of Progress Payments.	32.502-3(a)	P	Yes	L	A		A		A					A	A		A	A	A	A			
52.232-14 Notice of Availability of Progress Payments Exclusively for Small Business Concerns.	32.502-3(b)(2)	P	Yes	L	A		A		A		A			A	A			A	A	A			
52.232-15 Progress Payments Not Included.	32.502-3(c)	P	Yes	M	A		A		A					A	A			A	A	A			
52.232-16 Progress Payments.	32.502-4(a)	C	Yes	I	A		A		A		A	A		A	A		A	A	A	A			
52.232-16_Alternate I	32.502-4(a)	C	Yes	I	A		A		A		A	A		A	A		A	A	A	A			
52.232-16_Alternate II	32.502-4(a)	C	Yes	I	A		A		A		A	A		A	A		A	A	A	A			
52.232-16_Alternate III	32.502-4(d)	C	Yes	I	A		A		A		A	A		A	A		A	A	A	A			
52.232-17 Interest.	32.611(a)	C	Yes	I	A	A	A	A	A	A	A	A	A	A	A	A	A	A	A	A		A	

Provision or Clause	Prescribed in	P or C	IBR	UCF	FP SUP	CR SUP	FP R&D	CR R&D	FP SVC	CR SVC	FP CON	CR CON	T&M LH	LMV	COM SVC	DDR	A&E	FAC	IND DEL	TRN	SAP	UTL SVC	CI
52.232-18 Availability of Funds.	32.706-1(a)	C	Yes	I	A	A	A	A	A	A	A	A	A	A	A	A	A	A	A	A	A	A	
52.232-19 Availability of Funds for the Next Fiscal Year.	32.706-1(b)	C	No	I					A	A									A			A	
52.232-20 Limitation of Cost.	32.706-2(a)	C	Yes	I		A		A		A				A	A	A		A	A	A		A	
52.232-22 Limitation of Funds.	32.706-2(b)	C	Yes	I		A		A		A				A	A	A		A	A	A			
52.232-23 Assignment of Claims.	32.806(a)(1)	C	Yes	I	A	A	A	A	A	A	A	A	A	A	A	A	A	A	A	A	A	A	
52.232-23_Alternate I	32.806(a)(1)	C	Yes	I	A	A	A	A	A	A	A	A	A	A	A	A	A	A	A	A	A	A	
52.232-24 Prohibition of Assignment of Claims.	32.806(b)	C	Yes	I	A	A	A	A	A	A	A	A	A	A	A	A	A	A	A	A	A	A	
52.232-25 Prompt Payment.	32.908(c)	C	Yes	I	A	A	A	A	A	A			A	A	A	A	A	A	A	A	A	A	
52.232-25_Alternate I	32.908(c)(3)	C	Yes	I	A	A	A	A	A	A			A	A	A	A	A	A	A	A	A	A	
52.232-26 Prompt Payment for Fixed-Price Architect-Engineer Contracts.	32.908(a)	C	Yes	I													A						
52.232-27 Prompt Payment for Construction Contracts.	32.908(b)	C	Yes	I							R	R											
52.232-28 Invitation to Propose Performance-Based Payments.	32.1005(b)(1)	P	No	L	A		A		A		A					A	A	A	A	A		A	
52.232-28_Alternate I	32.1005(b)(1)	P	No	L	A		A		A		A					A	A	A	A	A		A	
52.232-29 Terms for Financing of Purchases of Commercial Items.	32.206(b)(2)	C	No	I	A				A														A
52.232-30 Installment Payments for Commercial Items.	32.206(g)	C	Yes	I	A				A														A
52.232-31 Invitation to Propose Financing Terms.	32.205(b)	P	No	L	A				A														
52.232-32 Performance-Based Payments.	32.1005	C	No	I	A				A														
52.232-33 Payment by Electronic Funds Transfer-System for Award Management.	32.1110(a)(1)	C	Yes	I	A	A	A	A	A	A	A	A	A	A	A	A	A	A	A	A	A	A	A
52.232-34 Payment by Electronic Funds Transfer-Other than System for Award Management.	32.1110(a)(2)	C	Yes	I	A	A	A	A	A	A	A	A	A	A	A	A	A	A	A	A	A	A	A
52.232-35 Designation of Office for Government Receipt of Electronic Funds Transfer Information.	32.1110(c)	C	Yes	I	A	A	A	A	A	A	A	A	A	A	A	A	A	A	A	A	A	A	A

Provision or Clause	Prescribed in	P or C	IBR	UCF	FP SUP	CR SUP	FP R&D	CR R&D	FP SVC	CR SVC	FP CON	CR CON	T&M LH	LMV	COM SVC	DDR	A&E	FAC	IND DEL	TRN	SAP	UTL SVC	CI
52.232-36 Payment by Third Party.	32.1110(d)	C	Yes	I	A	A	A	A	A	A	A	A	A	A	A	A	A	A	A	A	A	A	A
52.232-37 Multiple Payment Arrangements.	32.1110(e)	C	Yes	I	A	A	A	A	A	A	A	A	A	A	A	A	A	A	A	A	A	A	A
52.232-38 Submission of Electronic Funds Transfer Information with Offer.	32.1110(g)	P	Yes	L	A	A	A	A	A	A	A	A	A	A	A	A	A	A	A	A	A	A	A
52.232-39 Unenforceability of Unauthorized Obligations.	32.706-3	C	Yes	I	R	R	R	R	R	R	R	R	R	R	R	R	R	R	R	R	R	R	
52.232-40 Providing Accelerated Payments to Small Business Subcontractors.	32.009-2	C	Yes	I	A	A	A	A	A	A	A	A	A	A	A	A	A	A	A	A	A	A	A
52.233-1 Disputes.	33.215	C	Yes	I	A	A	A	A	A	A	A	A	A	A	A	A	A	A	A	A	A	A	
52.233-1_Alternate I	33.215	C	Yes	I	A	A	A	A	A	A	A	A	A	A	A	A	A	A	A	A	A	A	
52.233-2 Service of Protest.	33.106	P	No	L	R	R	R	R	R	R	R	R	R	R	R	R	R	R	R	R		R	
52.233-3 Protest after Award.	33.106(b)	C	Yes	I	R		R		R		R		R	R	A	R	A	A	R	A	R	R	
52.233-3_Alternate I	33.106(b)	C	Yes	I	R		R		R		R		R	R	A	R	A	A	R	A	R	R	
52.233-4 Applicable Law for Breach of Contract Claim.	33.215(b)	C	Yes	I	R	R	R	R	R	R	R	R	R	R	R	R	R	R	R	R	R	R	R
52.234-1 Industrial Resources Developed Under Title III, Defense Production Act.	34.104	C	No	I	A	A	A	A															
52.234-2 Notice of Earned Value Management System-Preaward Integrated Baseline Review.	34.203(a)	P	No	K	A	A	A	A	A	A	A	A	A	A	A	A	A	A	A	A	A	A	A
52.234-3 Notice of Earned Value Management System-Post Award Postaward Integrated Baseline Review.	34.203(b)	P	No	K	A	A	A	A	A	A	A	A	A	A	A	A	A	A	A	A	A	A	A
52.234-4 Earned Value Management System.	34.203(c)	C	Yes	H	A	A	A	A	A	A	A	A	A	A	A	A	A	A	A	A	A	A	A
52.236-1 Performance of Work by the Contractor.	36.501(b)	C	Yes								A												
52.236-2 Differing Site Conditions.	36.502	C	Yes								A					A					O		
52.236-3 Site Investigation and Conditions Affecting the Work.	36.503	C	Yes								A					A					O		
52.236-4 Physical Data.	36.504	C	No								A										A		
52.236-5 Material and Workmanship.	36.505	C	Yes								R	R									A		
52.236-6 Superintendence by the Contractor.	36.506	C	Yes								A					A					O		
52.236-7 Permits and Responsibilities.	36.507	C	Yes								R	R				A					A		

Provision or Clause	Prescribed in	P or C	IBR	UCF	FP SUP	CR SUP	FP R&D	CR R&D	FP SVC	CR SVC	FP CON	CR CON	T&M LH	LMV	COM SVC	DDR	A&E	FAC	IND DEL	TRN	SAP	UTL SVC	CI
52.236-8 Other Contracts.	36.508	C	Yes								A					A					O		
52.236-9 Protection of Existing Vegetation, Structures, Equipment, Utilities, and Improvements.	36.509	C	Yes								A					A					O		
52.236-10 Operations and Storage Areas.	36.510	C	Yes								A					A					O		
52.236-11 Use and Possession Prior to Completion.	36.511	C	Yes								A										O		
52.236-12 Cleaning Up.	36.512	C	Yes								A					A					O		
52.236-13 Accident Prevention.	36.513	C	Yes								A					A					O		
52.236-13_Alternate I	36.513	C	Yes								A					A					O		
52.236-14 Availability and Use of Utility Services.	36.514	C	Yes								A					A					A		
52.236-15 Schedules for Construction Contracts.	36.515	C	Yes								O												
52.236-16 Quantity Surveys.	36.516	C	Yes								O										O		
52.236-16_Alternate I	36.516	C	Yes								O										O		
52.236-17 Layout of Work.	36.517	C	Yes								A										A		
52.236-18 Work Oversight in Cost-Reimbursement Construction Contracts.	36.518	C	Yes									R											
52.236-19 Organization and Direction of the Work.	36.519	C	Yes									R											
52.236-21 Specifications and Drawings for Construction.	36.521	C	Yes								A					A					O		
52.236-21_Alternate I	36.521	C	Yes								A					A					O		
52.236-21_Alternate II	36.521	C	Yes								A					A					O		
52.236-22 Design Within Funding Limitations.	36.609-1(c)	C	Yes														A				O		
52.236-23 Responsibility of the Architect-Engineer Contractor.	36.609-2(b)	C	Yes														A						
52.236-24 Work Oversight in Architect-Engineer Contracts.	36.609-3	C	Yes														A						
52.236-25 Requirements for Registration of Designers.	36.609-4	C	Yes														A						
52.236-26 Preconstruction Conference.	36.522	C	Yes	I							A					A							

Provision or Clause	Prescribed in	P or C	IBR	UCF	FP SUP	CR SUP	FP R&D	CR R&D	FP SVC	CR SVC	FP CON	CR CON	T&M LH	LMV	COM SVC	DDR	A&E	FAC	IND DEL	TRN	SAP	UTL SVC	CI
52.236-27 Site Visit (Construction).	36.523	P	Yes	L							A					A							
52.236-27_Alternate I	36.523	P	Yes	L							A					A							
52.236-28 Preparation of Proposals-Construction.	36.520	P	Yes	K							R	R											
52.237-1 Site Visit.	37.110(a)	P	Yes	L			A	A	A	A			A	A	A	A	A	A	A	A	A	A	
52.237-2 Protection of Government Buildings, Equipment, and Vegetation.	37.110(b)	C	Yes	I			A	A	A	A			A	A	A	A	A	A	A	A	A	A	
52.237-3 Continuity of Services.	37.110(c)	C	Yes	I					O	O											O		
52.237-4 Payment by Government to Contractor.	37.304(a)	C	Yes	I												A					A		
52.237-4_Alternate I	37.304(a)	C	Yes	I												A					A		
52.237-5 Payment by Contractor to Government.	37.304(b)	C	Yes	I												A					A		
52.237-6 Incremental Payment by Contractor to Government.	37.304(c)	C	Yes	I												A					A		
52.237-7 Indemnification and Medical Liability Insurance.	37.403	C	Yes	I					A	A			A						A		O		
52.237-8 Restriction on Severance Payments to Foreign Nationals.	37.113-2(a)	P	Yes	K		A		A		A		A	A	A	A	A	A		A	A			
52.237-9 Waiver of Limitation on Severance Payments to Foreign Nationals.	37.113-2(b)	C	Yes	I		A		A		A		A	A	A	A	A	A		A	A			
52.237-10 Identification of Uncompensated Overtime.	37.115-3	P	Yes	L					A	A			A										
52.239-1 Privacy or Security Safeguards.	39.106	C	Yes	I	A	A	A	A	A	A			A					A	A		A		A
52.241-1 Electric Service Territory Compliance Representation.	41.501(b)	P	No	K																	A	A	
52.241-2 Order of Precedence-Utilities.	41.501(c)(1)	C	Yes	I																	O	R	
52.241-3 Scope and Duration of Contract.	41.501(c)(2)	C	No	I																	O	R	
52.241-4 Change in Class of Service.	41.501(c)(3)	C	Yes	I																	O	R	
52.241-5 Contractor's Facilities.	41.501(c)(4)	C	Yes	I																	O	R	
52.241-6 Service Provisions.	41.501(c)(5)	C	No	I																	O	R	
52.241-7 Change in Rates or Terms and Conditions of Service for Regulated Services.	41.501(d)(1)	C	No	I																	O	A	

Provision or Clause	Prescribed in	P or C	IBR	UCF	FP SUP	CR SUP	FP R&D	CR R&D	FP SVC	CR SVC	FP CON	CR CON	T&M LH	LMV	COM SVC	DDR	A&E	FAC	IND DEL	TRN	SAP	UTL SVC	CI
52.241-8 Change in Rates or Terms and Conditions of Service for Unregulated Services.	41.501(d)(2)	C	No	I																	O	A	
52.241-9 Connection Charge.	41.501(d)(3)	C	No	I																	O	A	
52.241-9_Alternate I	41.501(d)(3)	C	No	I																	O	A	
52.241-10 Termination Liability.	41.501(d)(4)	C	No	I																	O	A	
52.241-11 Multiple Service Locations.	41.501(d)(5)	C	Yes	I																	O	A	
52.241-12 Nonrefundable, Nonrecurring Service Charge.	41.501(d)(6)	C	No	I																	O	A	
52.241-13 Capital Credits.	41.501(d)(7)	C	No	I																	O	A	
52.242-1 Notice of Intent to Disallow Costs.	42.802	C	Yes	I	A	R	A	R	A	R	A	R	A	A	A	A	A	R	A	A		A	
52.242-2 Production Progress Reports.	42.1107	C	Yes	I	A	A	A	A	A	A			A	A			A		A				
52.242-3 Penalties for Unallowable Costs.	42.709-7	C	Yes	I		A		A		A		A	A	A	A	A	A		A	A			
52.242-4 Certification of Final Indirect Costs.	42.703-2(f)	C	Yes	I		A		A		A		A	A	A	A	A	A		A	A			
52.242-5 Payments to Small Business Subcontractors.	42.1504	C	Yes	I	A	A	A	A	A	A	A	A	A	A	A	A	A	A	A	A		A	A
52.242-13 Bankruptcy.	42.903	C	Yes	I	A	A	A	A	A	A	A	A	A	A	A	A	A	A	A	A	O	R	
52.242-14 Suspension of Work.	42.1305(a)	C	Yes								A						A				A		
52.242-15 Stop-Work Order.	42.1305(b)	C	Yes	F	O	O	O	O	O	O				O							O		
52.242-15_Alternate I	42.1305(b)	C	Yes	F	O	O	O	O	O	O				O							O		
52.242-17 Government Delay of Work.	42.1305(c)	C	Yes	F	A				O					A							A		
52.243-1 Changes-Fixed-Price.	43.205(a)(1)	C	Yes	I	R									R					A		A		
52.243-1_Alternate I	43.205(a)(1)	C	Yes	I	R									R					A		A		
52.243-1_Alternate II	43.205(a)(1)	C	Yes	I	R									R					A		A		
52.243-1_Alternate III	43.205(a)(1)	C	Yes	I	R									R					A		A		
52.243-1_Alternate IV	43.205(a)(1)	C	Yes	I	R									R					A		A		
52.243-1_Alternate V	43.205(a)(1)	C	Yes	I	R									R					A		A		
52.243-2 Changes-Cost-Reimbursement.	43.205(b)(1)	C	Yes	I		R																	
52.243-2_Alternate I	43.205(b)(1)	C	Yes	I		R																	
52.243-2_Alternate II	43.205(b)(1)	C	Yes	I		R																	
52.243-2_Alternate III	43.205(b)(1)	C	Yes	I		R																	
52.243-2_Alternate IV	43.205(b)(1)	C	Yes	I		R																	

Provision or Clause	Prescribed in	P or C	IBR	UCF	FP SUP	CR SUP	FP R&D	CR R&D	FP SVC	CR SVC	FP CON	CR CON	T&M LH	LMV	COM SVC	DDR	A&E	FAC	IND DEL	TRN	SAP	UTL SVC	CI
52.243-2_Alternate V	43.205(b)(1)	C	Yes	I		R																	
52.243-3 Changes-Time-and-Materials or Labor-Hours.	43.205(c)	C	Yes	I									R										
52.243-4 Changes.	43.205(d)	C	Yes	I							A					R							
52.243-5 Changes and Changed Conditions.	43.205(e)	C	Yes	I							A										A		
52.243-6 Change Order Accounting.	43.205(f)	C	Yes	I	O	O	O	O						O									
52.243-7 Notification of Changes.	43.107	C	Yes	I	A	A	A	A	A	A	A	A	A	A	A	A	A	A	A	A	A	O	
52.244-2 Subcontracts.	44.204(a)(1)	C	Yes	I	A	A	A	A	A	A	A	A	A	A	A	A	A	A	A	A		A	
52.244-2_Alternate I	44.204(a)(2)	C	Yes	I	A	A	A	A	A	A	A	A	A	A	A	A	A	A	A	A		A	
52.244-4 Subcontractors and Outside Associates and Consultants (Architect-Engineer Services).	44.204(b)	C	Yes	I													A						
52.244-5 Competition in Subcontracting.	44.204(c)	C	Yes	I	A	A	A	A	A	A		A		A		A	A	A		A		A	
52.244-6 Subcontracts for Commercial Items.	44.403	C	Yes	I	R	R	R	R	R	R	R	R	R	R	R	R	R	R	R	R	R	R	
52.245-1 Government Property.	45.107(a)	C	Yes	I	A	A	A	A	A	A	A	A	A	A	A	A	A	A	A	A	A	A	
52.245-1_Alternate I	45.107(a)(2)	C	Yes	I	A	A	A	A	A	A	A	A	A	A	A	A	A	A	A	A	A	A	
52.245-1_Alternate II	45.107(a)(3)	C	Yes	I	A	A	A	A	A	A	A	A	A	A	A	A	A	A	A	A	A	A	
52.245-2 Government Property Installation Operation Services.	45.107(b)	C	No	I	A	A	A	A	A	A	A	A	A	A	A	A	A	A	A	A	A	A	
52.245-9 Use and Charges.	45.107(c)	C	Yes	I	A	A	A	A	A	A	A	A	A	A	A	A	A	A	A	A	A	A	
52.246-1 Contractor Inspection Requirements.	46.301	C	Yes																		A		
52.246-2 Inspection of Supplies-Fixed-Price.	46.302	C	Yes	E	A		A		A					A					A		O		
52.246-2_Alternate I	46.302	C	Yes	E	A		A		A					A					A		O		
52.246-2_Alternate II	46.302	C	Yes	E	A		A		A					A					A		O		
52.246-3 Inspection of Supplies-Cost-Reimbursement.	46.303	C	Yes	E		A		A		A													
52.246-4 Inspection of Services-Fixed-Price.	46.304	C	Yes	E	A		A		A					A					A		O		
52.246-5 Inspection of Services-Cost-Reimbursement.	46.305	C	Yes	E		A		A		A													
52.246-6 Inspection-Time-and-Material and Labor-Hour.	46.306	C	Yes	E									R										

Provision or Clause	Prescribed in	P or C	IBR	UCF	FP SUP	CR SUP	FP R&D	CR R&D	FP SVC	CR SVC	FP CON	CR CON	T&M LH	LMV	COM SVC	DDR	A&E	FAC	IND DEL	TRN	SAP	UTL SVC	CI
52.246-6_Alternate I	46.306	C	Yes	E									R										
52.246-7 Inspection of Research and Development-Fixed-Price.	46.307(a)	C	Yes	E			A														O		
52.246-8 Inspection of Research and Development-Cost-Reimbursement.	46.308	C	Yes	E				A															
52.246-8_Alternate I	46.308	C	Yes	E				A															
52.246-9 Inspection of Research and Development (Short Form).	46.309	C	Yes	E			A	A													O		
52.246-11 Higher-Level Contract Quality Requirement.	46.311	C	Yes	E	A	A	A	A	A	A	A	A	A	A	A	A	A	A	A	A	A		
52.246-12 Inspection of Construction.	46.312	C	Yes								A	A									O		
52.246-13 Inspection-Dismantling, Demolition, or Removal of Improvements.	46.313	C	Yes													R					A		
52.246-14 Inspection of Transportation.	46.314	C	Yes	E																A	A		
52.246-15 Certificate of Conformance.	46.315	C	Yes	E	A	A	A	A	A	A				A					A		A		
52.246-16 Responsibility for Supplies.	46.316	C	Yes	E	A		A		A					A							O		
52.246-17 Warranty of Supplies of a Noncomplex Nature.	46.710(a)(1)	C	Yes	I	O									O					O				
52.246-17_Alternate I	46.710(a)(1)	C	Yes	I	O									O					O				
52.246-17_Alternate II	46.710(a)(1)	C	Yes	I	O									O					O				
52.246-17_Alternate III	46.710(a)(1)	C	Yes	I	O									O					O				
52.246-17_Alternate IV	46.710(a)(1)	C	Yes	I	O									O					O				
52.246-17_Alternate V	46.710(a)(1)	C	Yes	I	O									O					O				
52.246-18 Warranty of Supplies of a Complex Nature.	46.710(b)(1)	C	Yes	I	O		O							O					O				
52.246-18_Alternate I	46.710(b)(1)	C	Yes	I	O		O							O					O				
52.246-18_Alternate II	46.710(b)(1)	C	Yes	I	O		O							O					O				
52.246-18_Alternate III	46.710(b)(1)	C	Yes	I	O		O							O					O				
52.246-18_Alternate IV	46.710(b)(1)	C	Yes	I	O		O							O					O				
52.246-19 Warranty of Systems and Equipment under Performance Specifications or Design Criteria.	46.710(c)(1)	C	Yes	I	O		O		O					O									
52.246-19_Alternate I	46.710(c)(1)	C	Yes	I	O		O		O					O									

Provision or Clause	Prescribed in	P or C	IBR	UCF	FP SUP	CR SUP	FP R&D	CR R&D	FP SVC	CR SVC	FP CON	CR CON	T&M LH	LMV	COM SVC	DDR	A&E	FAC	IND DEL	TRN	SAP	UTL SVC	CI
52.246-19_Alternate II	46.710(c)(1)	C	Yes	I	O		O		O					O									
52.246-19_Alternate III	46.710(c)(1)	C	Yes	I	O		O		O					O									
52.246-20 Warranty of Services.	46.710(d)	C	Yes	I					O						O				O	O			
52.246-21 Warranty of Construction.	46.710(e)(1)	C	Yes								O										O		
52.246-21_Alternate I	46.710(e)(1)	C	Yes								O										O		
52.246-23 Limitation of Liability.	46.805	C	Yes	I	A	A	A	A						A					A		O		
52.246-24 Limitation of Liability-High-Value Items.	46.805	C	Yes	I	A	A	A	A						A					A				
52.246-24_Alternate I	46.805	C	Yes	I	A	A	A	A						A					A				
52.246-25 Limitation of Liability-Services.	46.805	C	Yes	I			A	A	A	A			A					A	A	A	O	A	
52.246-26 Reporting Nonconforming Items.	46.317	C	Yes	I	A	A	A	A	A	A	A	A	A	A	A	A	A	A	A	A			
52.247-1 Commercial Bill of Lading Notations.	47.104-4	C	Yes	I	A	A	A	A	A	A	A	A	A	A	A	A	A	A	A	A	O	A	
52.247-2 Permits, Authorities, or Franchises.	47.207-1(a)	C	No	I																A	A		
52.247-3 Capability to Perform a Contract for the Relocation of a Federal Office.	47.207-1(b)	C	Yes	I																A	A		
52.247-3_Alternate I	47.207-1(b)	C	Yes	I																A	A		
52.247-4 Inspection of Shipping and Receiving Facilities.	47.207-1(c)	P	Yes	L																A			
52.247-5 Familiarization with Conditions.	47.207-1(d)	C	Yes	I																A	A		
52.247-6 Financial Statement.	47.207-1(e)	P	Yes	L																A	A		
52.247-7 Freight Excluded.	47.207-3(d)(2)	C	Yes	I																A	A		
52.247-8 Estimated Weights or Quantities Not Guaranteed.	47.207-3(e)(2)	C	Yes	I																A	A		
52.247-9 Agreed Weight-General Freight.	47.207-4(a)(1)	C	Yes	I																A	A		
52.247-10 Net Weight-General Freight.	47.207-4(a)(2)	C	Yes	I																A	A		
52.247-11 Net Weight-Household Goods or Office Furniture.	47.207-4(b)	C	Yes	I																A	A		
52.247-12 Supervision, Labor, or Materials.	47.207-5(b)	C	Yes	I																A	A		
52.247-13 Accessorial Services-Moving	47.207-5(c)	C	Yes	I																A	A		

Provision or Clause	Prescribed in	P or C	IBR	UCF	FP SUP	CR SUP	FP R&D	CR R&D	FP SVC	CR SVC	FP CON	CR CON	T&M LH	LMV	COM SVC	DDR	A&E	FAC	IND DEL	TRN	SAP	UTL SVC	CI
Contracts.																							
52.247-14 Contractor Responsibility for Receipt of Shipment.	47.207-5(d)	C	Yes	I																A	A		
52.247-15 Contractor Responsibility for Loading and Unloading.	47.207-5(e)	C	Yes	I																A	A		
52.247-16 Contractor Responsibility for Returning Undelivered Freight.	47.207-5(f)	C	Yes	I																A	A		
52.247-17 Charges.	47.207-6(a)(2)	C	Yes	I																A	A		
52.247-18 Multiple Shipments.	47.207-6(c)(5)	C	Yes	I																A	A		
52.247-19 Stopping in Transit for Partial Unloading.	47.207-6(c)(5)	C	No	I																A	A		
52.247-20 Estimated Quantities or Weights for Evaluation of Offers.	47.207-6(c)(6)	P	Yes	M																A	A		
52.247-21 Contractor Liability for Personal Injury and/or Property Damage.	47.207-7(c)	C	Yes	I																A	A		
52.247-22 Contractor Liability for Loss of and/or Damage to Freight other than Household Goods.	47.207-7(d)	C	Yes	I																A	A		
52.247-23 Contractor Liability for Loss of and/or Damage to Household Goods.	47.207-7(e)	C	Yes	I																A	A		
52.247-24 Advance Notification by the Government.	47.207-8(a)(1)	C	Yes	I																A	A		
52.247-25 Government-Furnished Equipment With or Without Operators.	47.207-8(a)(2)	C	Yes	I																A	A		
52.247-26 Government Direction and Marking.	47.207-8(a)(3)	C	Yes	I																A	A		
52.247-27 Contract Not Affected by Oral Agreement.	47.207-8(b)	C	Yes	I																A	A		
52.247-28 Contractor's Invoices.	47.207-9(c)	C	Yes	I																A	A		
52.247-29 F.o.b. Origin.	47.303-1(c)	C	Yes	F	A									A					A		A		
52.247-30 F.o.b. Origin, Contractor's Facility.	47.303-2(c)	C	Yes	F	A									A					A		A		
52.247-31 F.o.b. Origin, Freight Allowed.	47.303-3(c)	C	Yes	F	A									A					A		A		

Provision or Clause	Prescribed in	P or C	IBR	UCF	FP SUP	CR SUP	FP R&D	CR R&D	FP SVC	CR SVC	FP CON	CR CON	T&M LH	LMV	COM SVC	DDR	A&E	FAC	IND DEL	TRN	SAP	UTL SVC	CI
52.247-32 F.o.b. Origin, Freight Prepaid.	47.303-4(c)	C	Yes	F	A									A					A		A		
52.247-33 F.o.b. Origin, with Differentials.	47.303-5(c)	C	No	F	A						A			A					A		A		
52.247-34 F.o.b. Destination.	47.303-6(c)	C	Yes	F	A									A					A		A		
52.247-35 F.o.b. Destination, Within Consignee's Premises.	47.303-7(c)	C	Yes	F	A									A					A		A		
52.247-36 F.a.s. Vessel, Port of Shipment.	47.303-8(c)	C	Yes	F	A									A					A		A		
52.247-37 F.o.b. Vessel, Port of Shipment.	47.303-9(c)	C	Yes	F	A									A					A		A		
52.247-38 F.o.b. Inland Carrier, Point of Exportation.	47.303-10(c)	C	Yes	F	A									A					A		A		
52.247-39 F.o.b. Inland Point, Country of Importation.	47.303-11(c)	C	Yes	F	A									A					A		A		
52.247-40 Ex Dock, Pier, or Warehouse, Port of Importation.	47.303-12(c)	C	Yes	F	A									A					A		A		
52.247-41 C.& f. Destination.	47.303-13(c)	C	Yes	F	A									A					A		A		
52.247-42 C.i.f. Destination.	47.303-14(c)	C	Yes	F	A									A					A		A		
52.247-43 F.o.b. Designated Air Carrier's Terminal, Point of Exportation.	47.303-15(c)	C	Yes	F	A									A					A		A		
52.247-44 F.o.b. Designated Air Carrier's Terminal, Point of Importation.	47.303-16(c)	C	Yes	F	A									A					A		A		
52.247-45 F.o.b. Origin and/or F.o.b. Destination Evaluation.	47.305-2(b)	P	Yes	L	A									A					A		A		
52.247-46 Shipping Point(s) Used in Evaluation of F.o.b. Origin Offers.	47.305-3(b)(4)	P	Yes	L	A									A					A		A		
52.247-47 Evaluation-F.o.b. Origin.	47.305-3(f)(2)	P	Yes	M	A									A					A		A		
52.247-48 F.o.b. Destination-Evidence of Shipment.	47.305-4(c)	C	Yes	F	A									A					A		A		
52.247-49 Destination Unknown.	47.305-5(b)(2)	P	Yes	M	A									A					A		A		
52.247-50 No Evaluation of Transportation Costs.	47.305-5(c)(1)	P	Yes	M	A									A					A		A		
52.247-51 Evaluation of Export Offers.	47.305-6(e)	P	No	M	A									A					A		A		
52.247-51_Alternate I	47.305-6(e)	P	No	M	A									A					A		A		
52.247-51_Alternate II	47.305-6(e)	P	No	M	A									A					A		A		

Provision or Clause	Prescribed in	P or C	IBR	UCF	FP SUP	CR SUP	FP R&D	CR R&D	FP SVC	CR SVC	FP CON	CR CON	T&M LH	LMV	COM SVC	DDR	A&E	FAC	IND DEL	TRN	SAP	UTL SVC	CI
52.247-51_Alternate III	47.305-6(e)	P	No	M	A									A					A		A		
52.247-52 Clearance and Documentation Requirements-Shipments to DoD Air or Water Terminal Transshipment Points.	47.305-6(f)(2)	C	Yes	F	A						A			A					A		A		
52.247-53 Freight Classification Description.	47.305-9(b)(1)	P	No	K	A									A					A		A		
52.247-55 F.o.b. Point for Delivery of Government-Furnished Property.	47.305-12(a)(2)	C	Yes	F	A									A					A		A		
52.247-56 Transit Arrangements.	47.305-13(a)(3)	P	No	M	A									A					A				
52.247-57 Transportation Transit Privilege Credits.	47.305-13(b)(4)	C	No	F	A									A					A		A		
52.247-58 Loading, Blocking, and Bracing of Freight Car Shipments.	47.305-15(a)(2)	C	Yes	F	A									A					A		A		
52.247-59 F.o.b. Origin-Carload and Truckload Shipments.	47.305-16(a)	C	Yes	F	A									A					A		A		
52.247-60 Guaranteed Shipping Characteristics.	47.305-16(b)(1)	C	No	F	A									A					A				
52.247-61 F.o.b. Origin-Minimum Size of Shipments.	47.305-16(c)	C	Yes	F	A									A					A		A		
52.247-62 Specific Quantities Unknown.	47.305-16(d)(2)	C	No	F	A									A					A		A		
52.247-63 Preference for U.S.-Flag Air Carriers.	47.405	C	Yes	I	A	A	A	A	A	A	A	A	A	A	A	A	A	A	A	A		A	
52.247-64 Preference for Privately Owned U.S.-Flag Commercial Vessels.	47.507(a)	C	Yes	I	A	A	A	A	A	A	A	A	A	A	A	A		A	A	A		A	
52.247-64_Alternate I	47.507(a)(2)	C	Yes	I	A	A	A	A	A	A	A	A	A	A	A	A		A	A	A		A	
52.247-64_Alternate II	47.507(a)(3)	C	Yes	I	A	A	A	A	A	A	A	A	A	A	A	A		A	A	A		A	
52.247-65 F.o.b. Origin, Prepaid Freight-Small Package Shipments.	47.305-17(f)	C	Yes	F	A									A					A		A		
52.247-66 Returnable Cylinders.	47.305-17	C	No	I	A				A		A				A				A				
52.247-67 Submission of Transportation Documents for Audit.	47.103-2	C	No	I		A		A	A	A		A	A			A			A	A	A		
52.247-68 Report of Shipment (REPSHIP).	47.208-2	C	Yes	I	A	A	A	A	A	A			A	A	A		A	A	A		A		

Provision or Clause	Prescribed in	P or C	IBR	UCF	FP SUP	CR SUP	FP R&D	CR R&D	FP SVC	CR SVC	FP CON	CR CON	T&M LH	LMV	COM SVC	DDR	A&E	FAC	IND DEL	TRN	SAP	UTL SVC	CI
52.248-1 Value Engineering.	48.201	C	Yes	I	A	A	A	A	A	A			A	A	A	A		A	A	A		A	
52.248-1_Alternate I	48.201	C	Yes	I	A	A	A	A	A	A			A	A	A	A		A	A	A		A	
52.248-1_Alternate II	48.201	C	Yes	I	A	A	A	A	A	A			A	A	A	A		A	A	A		A	
52.248-1_Alternate III	48.201	C	Yes	I	A	A	A	A	A	A			A	A	A	A		A	A	A		A	
52.248-2 Value Engineering-Architect-Engineer.	48.201(f)	C	Yes														A						
52.248-3 Value Engineering-Construction.	48.202	C	Yes								A	A											
52.248-3_Alternate I	48.202	C	Yes								A	A											
52.249-1 Termination for Convenience of the Government (Fixed-Price) (Short Form).	49.502(a)(1)	C	Yes	I	A		A		A				A	A		A			A	A	A	A	
52.249-1_Alternate I	49.502(a)(1)	C	Yes	I	A		A		A				A	A		A			A	A	A	A	
52.249-2 Termination for Convenience of the Government (Fixed-Price).	49.502(b)(1)	C	Yes	I	A		A		A				A	A					A	A		A	
52.249-2_Alternate I	49.502(b)(1)(i)	C	Yes	I	A		A		A				A	A					A	A		A	
52.249-2_Alternate II	49.502(b)(1)(i)	C	Yes	I	A		A		A				A	A					A	A		A	
52.249-2_Alternate III	49.502(b)(1)(i)	C	Yes	I	A		A		A				A	A					A	A		A	
52.249-3 Termination for Convenience of the Government (Dismantling, Demolition, or Removal of Improvements).	49.502(b)(2)	C	Yes	I												A							
52.249-3_Alternate I	49.502(b)(2)	C	Yes	I												A							
52.249-4 Termination for Convenience of the Government (Services) (Short Form).	49.502(c)	C	Yes	I					A												A	A	
52.249-5 Termination for Convenience of the Government (Educational and Other Nonprofit Institutions).	49.502(d)	C	Yes	I			A	A													A		
52.249-6 Termination (Cost-Reimbursement).	49.503(a)(1)	C	Yes	I		A		A		A				A	A	A		A	A	A		A	
52.249-6_Alternate I	49.503(a)(1)	C	Yes	I		A		A		A				A	A	A		A	A	A		A	
52.249-6_Alternate II	49.503(a)(1)	C	Yes	I		A		A		A				A	A	A		A	A	A		A	
52.249-6_Alternate III	49.503(a)(1)	C	Yes	I		A		A		A				A	A	A		A	A	A		A	
52.249-6_Alternate IV	49.503(a)(1)	C	Yes	I		A		A		A				A	A	A		A	A	A		A	

Provision or Clause	Prescribed in	P or C	IBR	UCF	FP SUP	CR SUP	FP R&D	CR R&D	FP SVC	CR SVC	FP CON	CR CON	T&M LH	LMV	COM SVC	DDR	A&E	FAC	IND DEL	TRN	SAP	UTL SVC	CI
52.252-2 Clauses Incorporated by Reference.	52.107(b)	C	No	I	A	A	A	A	A	A	A	A	A	A	A	A	A	A	A	A	A	A	
52.252-3 Alterations in Solicitation.	52.107(c)	P	No	L	A	A	A	A	A	A	A	A	A	A	A	A	A	A	A	A	A	A	
52.252-4 Alterations in Contract.	52.107(d)	C	No	I	A	A	A	A	A	A	A	A	A	A	A	A	A	A	A	A	A	A	
52.252-5 Authorized Deviations in Provisions.	52.107(e)	P	No	L	A	A	A	A	A	A	A	A	A	A	A	A	A	A	A	A	A	A	
52.252-6 Authorized Deviations in Clauses.	52.107(f)	C	No	I	A	A	A	A	A	A	A	A	A	A	A	A	A	A	A	A	A	A	
52.253-1 Computer Generated Forms.	53.111	C	Yes	I	A	A	A	A	A	A	A	A	A	A	A	A	A	A	A	A	A	A	

Federal Acquisition Regulation
Part 53
Forms

Table of Contents

Part 53—Forms 2035

PART 53—FORMS

Table of Contents

Scope of part 53.000
Definitions 53.001

Subpart 53.1—General

Scope of subpart 53.100
Requirements for use of forms 53.101
Current editions 53.102
Exceptions 53.103
Overprinting 53.104
Computer generation 53.105
Special construction and printing 53.106
Obtaining forms 53.107
Recommendations concerning forms 53.108
Forms prescribed by other regulations 53.109
Continuation sheets 53.110
Contract clause 53.111

Subpart 53.2—Prescription of Forms

Scope of subpart 53.200
Federal acquisition system 53.201
Contracting authority and responsibilities (SF 1402) 53.201-1
[Reserved] 53.202
[Reserved] 53.203
Administrative matters 53.204
Safeguarding classified information within industry (DD Form-254, DD Form-441) 53.204-1
[Reserved] 53.204-2
Publicizing contract actions 53.205
Paid advertisements 53.205-1
[Reserved] 53.206
[Reserved] 53.207
[Reserved] 53.208
Contractor qualifications 53.209
Responsible prospective contractors 53.209-1
Acquisition of commercial items 53.212
Simplified acquisition procedures (SF's 18, 30, 44, 1165, 1449 and OF's 336, 347, 348) 53.213
Sealed bidding 53.214
Contracting by negotiation 53.215
Solicitation and receipt of proposals 53.215-1
Types of contracts 53.216
Delivery orders and orders under basic ordering agreements (OF 347) . 53.216-1
[Reserved] 53.217
[Reserved] 53.218
Small business programs 53.219
[Reserved] 53.220
[Reserved] 53.221
Application of labor laws to Government acquisitions (SF's 307, 1413, 1445, 1446, WH-347) 53.222
Bonds and insurance 53.228
Taxes (SF's 1094, 1094-A) 53.229
[Reserved] 53.230
Contract financing (SF 1443) 53.232
Research and Development Contracting (SF 298) 53.235

Construction and architect-engineer contracts . . . 53.236
Construction . . . 53.236-1
Architect-engineer services (SF's 252 and 330) . . . 53.236-2
[Reserved] . . . 53.237
[Reserved] . . . 53.238
[Reserved] . . . 53.239
[Reserved] . . . 53.240
[Reserved] . . . 53.241
Contract administration . . . 53.242
Novation and change-of-name agreements (SF 30) . . . 53.242-1
Contract modifications (SF 30) . . . 53.243
[Reserved] . . . 53.244
Government property . . . 53.245
[Reserved] . . . 53.246
Transportation (U.S. Commercial Bill of Lading) . . . 53.247
[Reserved] . . . 53.248
Termination of contracts . . . 53.249
[Reserved] . . . 53.250
Contractor use of Government supply sources (OF 347) . . . 53.251

Subpart 53.3—Forms Used in Acquisitions

Listing of Standard, Optional, and Agency forms . . . 53.300
Standard forms . . . 53.301
Architect-Engineer Qualification 53.301-330
Optional forms . . . 53.302
Agency forms . . . 53.303
Standard Form 18, Request for Quotations . . . 53.301-18
Standard Form 24, Bid Bond . . . 53.301-24
Standard Form 25, Performance Bond . . . 53.301-25
Standard Form 25-A, Payment Bond . . . 53.301-25-A
Standard Form 25-B, Continuation Sheet (For Standard Forms 24, 25, and 25-A) . . . 53.301-25-B
Standard Form 26, Award/Contract . . . 53.301-26
Standard Form 28, Affidavit of Individual Surety . . . 53.301-28
Standard Form 30, Amendment of Solicitation/Modification of Contract . 53.301-30
Standard Form 33, Solicitation, Offer and Award . . . 53.301-33
Standard Form 34, Annual Bid Bond . . . 53.301-34
Standard Form 35, Annual Performance Bond . . . 53.301-35
Standard Form 44, Purchase Order—Invoice— Voucher . . . 53.301-44
[Removed] . . . 53.301-98
[Removed] . . . 53.301-98a
[Removed] . . . 53.301-99
Standard Form 120, Report of Excess Personal Property . . . 53.301-120
Standard Form 120-A, Continuation Sheet (Report of Excess Personal Property) . . . 53.301-120-A
Standard Form 126, Report of Personal Property for Sale . . . 53.301-126
Standard Form 126-A, Report of Personal Property for Sale (Continuation Sheet) . . . 53.301-126-A
[Removed] . . . 53.301-129
Standard Form 252, Architect-Engineer Contract . . . 53.301-252
[Removed] . . . 53.301-254
[Removed] . . . 53.301-255
Standard Form 273, Reinsurance Agreement for a Bond Statute Performance Bond . . . 53.301-273
Standard Form 274, Reinsurance Agreement for a Bond Statute Payment Bond . . . 53.301-274

Standard Form 275, Reinsurance Agreement in Favor of the United States 53.301-275
[Removed] 53.301-279
[Removed] 53.301-281
Subcontracting Report for Individual Contracts 53.301-294
[Removed] 53.301-295
Standard Form 298, Report Documentation Page 53.301-298
Standard Form 308, Request for Wage Determination and Response to Request 53.301-308
Standard Form 1034, Public Voucher for Purchases and Services Other Than Personal 53.301-1034
Standard Form 1034-A, Public Voucher for Purchases and Services Other Than Personal—Memorandum Copy 53.301-1034-A
Standard Form 1035, Public Voucher for Purchases and Services Other Than Personal, Continuation Sheet 53.301-1035
Standard Form 1035-A, Public Voucher for Purchases and Services Other Than Personal—Memorandum, Continuation Sheet 53.301-1035-A
[Removed] 53.301-1093
Standard Form 1094, U.S. Tax Exemption Form 53.301-1094
Standard Form 1094-A, Tax Exemption Forms Accountability Record 53.301-1094-A
Standard Form 1165, Receipt for Cash—Subvoucher 53.301-1165
Standard Form 1402, Certificate of Appointment 53.301-1402
Standard Form 1403, Preaward Survey of Prospective Contractor (General) 53.301-1403
Standard Form 1404, Preaward Survey of Prospective Contractor—Technical 53.301-1404
Standard Form 1405, Preaward Survey of Prospective Contractor—Production 53.301-1405
Standard Form 1406, Preaward Survey of Prospective Contractor—Quality Assurance 53.301-1406
Standard Form 1407, Preaward Survey of Prospective Contractor—Financial Capability 53.301-1407
Standard Form 1408, Preaward Survey of Prospective Contractor—Accounting System 53.301-1408
Standard Form 1409, Abstract of Offers 53.301-1409
Standard Form 1410, Abstract of Offers—Continuation 53.301-1410
Standard Form 1413, Statement and Acknowledgment 53.301-1413
Standard Form 1414, Consent of Surety 53.301-1414
Standard Form 1415, Consent of Surety and Increase of Penalty 53.301-1415
Standard Form 1416, Payment Bond for Other than Construction Contracts 53.301-1416
[Removed] 53.301-1417
Standard Form 1418, Performance Bond for Other Than Construction Contracts 53.301-1418
[Removed] 53.301-1420
[Removed] 53.301-1421
Standard Form 1423, Inventory Verification Survey 53.301-1423
Standard Form 1424, Inventory Disposal Report 53.301-1424
[Removed] 53.301-1426
Standard Form 1427, Inventory Schedule A—Continuation Sheet (Metals in Mill Product Form) 53.301-1427
Inventory Disposal Schedule 53.301-1428
Inventory Disposal Schedule—Continuation Sheet 53.301-1429
[Removed] 53.301-1430
[Removed] 53.301-1431
[Removed] 53.301-1432

[Removed] 53.301-1433
Standard Form 1434, Termination Inventory Schedule E (Short Form for Use with SF 1438 Only) 53.301-1434
Standard Form 1435, Settlement Proposal (Inventory Basis) 53.301-1435
Settlement Proposal (Total Cost Basis) 53.301-1436
Standard Form 1437, Settlement Proposal for Cost-Reimbursement Type Contracts 53.301-1437
Settlement Proposal (Short Form) 53.301-1438
Standard Form 1439, Schedule of Accounting Information 53.301-1439
Standard Form 1440, Application for Partial Payment 53.301-1440
Standard Form 1442, Solicitation, Offer, and Award (Construction, Alteration, or Repair) 53.301-1442
Standard Form 1443, Contractor's Request for Progress Payment 53.301-1443
Standard Form 1444, Request for Authorization of Additional Classification and Rate 53.301-1444
Standard Form 1445, Labor Standards Interview 53.301-1445
Standard Form 1446, Labor Standards Investigation Summary Sheet 53.301-1446
Solicitation/Contract 53.301-1447
Standard Form 1449, Solicitation/Contract/Order for Commercial Items 53.301-1449
Optional Form 17, Offer Label 53.302-17
Optional Form 90, Release of Lien on Real Property 53.302-90
Optional Form 91, Release of Personal Property from Escrow 53.302-91
Optional Form 307, Contract Award 53.302-307
Optional Form 308, Solicitation and Offer—Negotiated Acquisition 53.302-308
Optional Form 309, Amendment of Solicitation 53.302-309
[Removed] 53.302-312
Optional Form 336, Continuation Sheet 53.302-336
Optional Form 347, Order for Supplies or Services 53.302-347
Optional Form 348, Order for Supplies or Services Schedule—Continuation 53.302-348
Optional Form 1419, Abstract of Offers—Construction 53.302-1419
Optional Form 1419A, Abstract of Offers—Construction, Continuation Sheet 53.302-1419A
Department of Defense DD Form 254, Contract Security Classification Specification 53.303-DD-254
Department of Defense DD Form 441, Security Agreement 53.303-DD-441
Department of Labor Form WH-347, Payroll (For Contractor's Optional Use) 53.303-WH-347

PART 53—FORMS

53.000 Scope of part.

This part—

(a) Prescribes standard forms (SF's) and references optional forms (OF's) and agency-prescribed forms for use in acquisition; and

(b) Contains requirements and information generally applicable to the forms.

[FAC 2005-100, 83 FR 42571, 8/22/2018, effective 8/22/2018]

53.001 Definitions.

Exception, as used in this part, means an approved departure from the established design, content, printing specifications, or conditions for use of any standard form.

SUBPART 53.1—GENERAL

53.100 Scope of subpart.

This subpart contains requirements and information generally applicable to the forms prescribed in this regulation.

53.101 Requirements for use of forms.

The requirements for use of the forms prescribed or referenced in this part are contained in Parts 1 through 52, where the subject matter applicable to each form is addressed. The specific location of each requirement is identified in Subpart 53.2.

[FAC 97-5, 63 FR 34058, 6/22/98, effective 6/22/98]

53.102 Current editions.

The form prescriptions in subpart 53.2 and the FAR forms located at *https://www.gsa.gov/forms* contain current edition dates. Contracting officers shall use the current editions unless otherwise authorized under this regulation.

[FAC 2005-100, 83 FR 42571, 8/22/2018, effective 8/22/2018]

53.103 Exceptions.

Agencies shall not—

(a) Alter a standard form prescribed by this regulation, or

(b) Use for the same purpose any form other than the standard form prescribed by this regulation without receiving in advance an exception to the form.

[FAC 84-40, 53 FR 43395, 10/26/88, effective 11/25/88; Final rule, 62 FR 40236, 7/25/97, effective 6/30/97]

53.104 Overprinting.

Standard and optional forms (obtained as required by 53.107) may be overprinted with names, addresses, and other uniform entries that are consistent with the purpose of the form and that do not alter the form in any way. Exception approval for overprinting is not needed.

53.105 Computer generation.

(a) The forms prescribed by this part may be computer generated—without exception approval (see 53.103), provided—

(1) There is no change to the name, content, or sequence of the data elements, and the form carries the Standard or Optional Form number and edition date (see 53.111); or

(2) The form is in an electronic format covered by the American National Standards Institute (ANSI) X12 Standards published by the Accredited Standards Committee X12 on Electronic Data Interchange or a format that can be translated into one of those standards.

(b) The standards listed in paragraph (a)(2) of this section may also be used for submission of data set forth in other parts for which specific forms have not been prescribed.

[FAC 90-29, 60 FR 34732, 7/3/95, effective 7/3/95; FAC 2005-60, 77 FR 44064, 7/26/2012, effective 8/27/2012]

53.106 Special construction and printing.

Contracting offices may request exceptions (see 53.103) to standard forms for special construction and printing. Examples of common exceptions are as follows:

	Standard Forms	Special Construction and Printing
(a)	SF 18— . .	(1) With vertical lines omitted (for listing of supplies and services, unit, etc.); (2) As reproducible masters; and/or (3) In carbon interleaved pads or sets.
(b)	SF's 26, 30, 33, 1447—	As die-cut stencils or reproducible masters.
(c)	SF 44— . .	(1) With serial numbers and contracting office name and address; and/or (2) On special weight of paper and with the type of construction, number of sets per book, and number of parts per set as specified by the contracting officer. (Executive agencies may supplement the administrative instructions on the inside front cover of the book.)
(d)	SF 1442—.	(1) As die-cut stencils or reproducible masters; and/or (2) With additional wording as required by the executive agency. (However, the sequence and wording of the items appearing on the prescribed form should not be altered.)

[FAC 84-18, 51 FR 27121, 7/29/86, effective 7/30/86; FAC 84-53, 54 FR 48998, 11/28/89, effective 12/28/89]

53.107 Obtaining forms.

Executive agencies shall obtain standard and optional forms from the General Services Administration (GSA) Forms Library at *https://www.gsa.gov/forms*. Agency forms are available from the prescribing agency.

[FAC 2019-02, 84 FR 19839, 5/6/2019, effective 5/6/2019]

53.108 Recommendations concerning forms.

Users of this regulation may recommend new forms or the revision, elimination, or consolidation of the forms prescribed or referenced in this regulation. Recommendations from within an executive agency shall be submitted to the cognizant council in accordance with agency procedures. Recommendations from other than executive agencies should be submitted directly to the FAR Secretariat.

53.109 Forms prescribed by other regulations.

Certain forms referred to in Subpart 53.2 are prescribed in other regulations and are specified by the FAR for use in acquisition. For each of these forms, the prescribing agency is identified by means of a parenthetical notation after the form number. For example, SF 1165, which is prescribed by the Government Accountability Office (GAO), is identified as SF 1165 (GAO).

[FAC 2005-13, 71 FR 57380, 9/28/2006, effective 9/28/2006]

53.110 Continuation sheets.

Except as may be otherwise indicated in the FAR, all standard forms prescribed by the FAR may be continued on (a) plain paper of similar specification, or (b) specially constructed continuation sheets (*e.g.*, OF 336). Continuation sheets shall be annotated in the upper right-hand corner with the reference number of the document being continued and the serial page number.

[FAC 84-18, 51 FR 27121, 7/29/86, effective 7/30/86]

53.111 Contract clause.

Contracting officers shall insert the clause at 52.253-1, Computer Generated Forms, in solicitations and contracts that require the contractor to submit data on Standard or Optional Forms prescribed by this regulation; and, unless prohibited by agency regulations, forms prescribed by agency supplements.

[FAC 90-3, 55 FR 52800, 12/21/90, effective 1/22/91]

SUBPART 53.2—PRESCRIPTION OF FORMS

53.200 Scope of subpart.

This subpart prescribes standard forms and references optional forms and agency-prescribed forms for use in acquisition. Consistent with the approach used in Subpart 52.2, this subpart is arranged by subject matter, in the same order as, and keyed to, the parts of the FAR in which the form usage requirements are addressed. For example, forms addressed in FAR Part 14, Sealed Bidding, are treated in this subpart in section 53.214, Sealed Bidding; forms addressed in FAR Part 43, Contract Modifications, are treated in this subpart in section 53.243, Contract modifications. The following example illustrates how the subjects are keyed to the parts in which they are addressed:

53.243 Contract Modification (SF 30).

SECTION (KEYED TO FAR PART CONTAINING SUBJECT MATTER: USAGE REQUIREMENTS FOR SF 30 ARE ADDRESSED IN PART 43. CONTRACT MODIFICATIONS)

PART AND SUBPART (INVARIABLE)

[FAC 84-5, 50 FR 1748, 1/11/85, effective 4/1/85]

53.201 Federal acquisition system. (No Text)

53.201-1 Contracting authority and responsibilities (SF 1402).

SF 1402 (10/83), Certificate of Appointment. SF 1402 is prescribed for use in appointing contracting officers, as specified in 1.603-3.

53.202 [Reserved]

53.203 [Reserved]

[Removed and reserved, FAC 90-45, Final rule, 62 FR 224, 1/2/97, effective 1/1/97]

53.204 Administrative matters. (No Text)

53.204-1 Safeguarding classified information within industry (DD Form 254, DD Form 441).

The following forms, which are prescribed by the Department of Defense, shall be used by agencies covered by the Defense Industrial Security Program if contractor access to classified information is required, as specified in Subpart 4.4 and the clause at 52.204-2:

(a) *DD Form 254 (Department of Defense (DOD)), Contract Security Classification Specification.* (See 4.403(c)(1).)

(b) *DD Form 441 (DOD), Security Agreement.* (See paragraph (b) of the clause at 52.204-2.)

53.204-2 [Reserved]

[FAC 2001-02, 66 FR 65347, 12/18/2001, effective 2/19/2002; FAC 2001-18, 68 FR 69248, 12/11/2003, effective 12/11/2003]

53.205 Publicizing contract actions. (No Text)

53.205-1 Paid advertisements.

SF 1449, prescribed in 53.212, shall be used to place orders for paid advertisements, as specified in 5.503.

[FAC 90-40, 61 FR 39186, 7/26/96, effective 8/26/96]

53.206 [Reserved]

53.207 [Reserved]

53.208 [Reserved]

53.209 Contractor qualifications. (No Text)

53.209-1 Responsible prospective contractors.

The following forms are prescribed for use in conducting preaward surveys of prospective contractors, as specified in 9.106-1, 9.106-2, and 9.106-4. These forms are authorized for local reproduction and can be found at the GSA Forms Library at *https://www.gsa.gov/forms.*

(a) SF 1403 (Rev. 01/2014), Preaward Survey of Prospective Contractor (General).

(b) SF 1404 (Rev. 01/2014), Preaward Survey of Prospective Contractor—Technical.

(c) SF 1405 (Rev. 01/2014), Preaward Survey of Prospective Contractor—Production.

(d) SF 1406 (Rev. 01/2014), Preaward Survey of Prospective Contractor—Quality Assurance.

(e) SF 1407 (Rev. 01/2014), Preaward Survey of Prospective Contractor—Financial Capability.

(f) SF 1408 (Rev. 01/2014), Preaward Survey of Prospective Contractor—Accounting System.

[FAC 84-58, 55 FR 25534, 6/21/90, effective 7/23/90; FAC 97-3, 62 FR 64912, 12/9/97, effective 2/9/98; FAC 2005-100, 83 FR 42571, 8/22/2018, effective 8/22/2018]

53.212 Acquisition of commercial items.

SF 1449 (Rev. 2/2012), Solicitation/Contract/Order for Commercial Items. SF 1449 is prescribed for use in solicitations and contracts for commercial items. Agencies may prescribe additional detailed instructions for use of the form.

[FAC 90-32, 60 FR 48206, 9/18/95, effective 10/1/95; FAC 2001-06, 67 FR 13048, 3/20/2002, effective 4/4/2002; FAC 2005-02, 70 FR 14950, 3/23/2005, effective 3/23/2005; FAC 2005-48, 75 FR 82567, 12/30/2010, effective 1/31/2011; FAC 2005-56, 77 FR 12913, 3/2/2012, effective 4/2/2012]

53.213 Simplified acquisition procedures (SF's 18, 30, 44, 1165, 1449, and OF's 336, 347, and 348).

The following forms are prescribed as stated in this section for use in simplified acquisition procedures, orders under existing contracts or agreements, and orders from required sources of supplies and services:

(a) *SF 18 (Rev. 6/95), Request for Quotations, or SF 1449, (Rev. 2/2012), Solicitation/Contract/Order for Commercial Items.* SF 18 is prescribed for use in obtaining price, cost, delivery, and related information from suppliers as specified in 13.307(b). SF 1449, as prescribed in 53.212, or other agency forms/automated formats, may also be used to obtain price, cost, delivery, and related information from suppliers as specified in 13.307(b).

(b) *SF 30 (Rev. 11/2016), Amendment of Solicitation/Modification of Contract.* SF 30, prescribed in 53.243, may be used for modifying purchase orders, as specified in 13.307(c)(3).

(c) *SF 44 (Rev. 10/83), Purchase Order Invoice Voucher.* SF 44 is prescribed for use in simplified acquisition procedures, as specified in 13.306.

(d) *SF 1165 (6/83 Ed.), Receipt for Cash-Subvoucher.* SF 1165 (GAO) may be used for imprest fund purchases, as specified in 13.307(e).

(e) *OF 336 (4/86 Ed.), Continuation Sheet.* OF 336, prescribed in 53.214(h), may be used as a continuation sheet in solicitations, as specified in 13.307(c)(1).

(f) *SF 1449, (Rev. 2/2012) Solicitation/Contract/Order for Commercial Items prescribed in 53.212, OF 347, (Rev. 10/2010), Order for Supplies or Services, and OF 348 (Rev. 4/06), Order for Supplies or Services—Schedule Continuation.* SF 1449, OF's 347 and 348 (or approved agency forms/automated formats) may be used as follows:

(1) To accomplish acquisitions under simplified acquisition procedures, as specified in 13.307.

(2) To establish blanket purchase agreements (BPA's), as specified in 13.303-2, and to make purchases under BPA's, as specified in 13.303-5.

(3) To issue orders under basic ordering agreements, as specified in 16.703(d)(2)(i).

(4) As otherwise specified in this chapter (*e.g.*, see 5.503(a)(2), 8.406-1, 36.701(b), and 51.102(e)(3)(ii)).

[FAC 90-40, 61 FR 39186, 7/26/96, effective 8/26/96; FAC 97-2, 62 FR 51224, 9/30/97, effective 10/10/97; FAC 97-3, 62 FR 64912, 12/9/97, effective 2/9/98; FAC 2001-06, 67 FR 13048, 3/20/2002, effective 4/4/2002; FAC 2001-24, 69 FR 34231, 6/18/2004, effective 7/19/2004; FAC 2001-25, 69 FR 59699, 10/5/2004, effective 11/4/2004; FAC 2005-02, 70 FR 14950,

3/23/2005, effective 3/23/2005; FAC 2005-21, 72 FR 63089, 11/7/2007, effective 11/7/2007; FAC 2005-48, 75 FR 82567, 12/30/2010, effective 1/31/2011; FAC 2005-56, 77 FR 12913, 3/2/2012, effective 4/2/2012; FAC 2005-92, 81 FR 83097, 11/18/2016, effective 12/19/2016]

53.214 Sealed bidding.

The following forms are prescribed for use in contracting by sealed bidding (except for construction and architect-engineer services):

(a) *SF 26 (Rev. 3/2013), Award/Contract.* SF 26 is prescribed for use in awarding sealed bid contracts for supplies or services in which bids were obtained on SF 33, Solicitation, Offer and Award, as specified in 14.408-1(d)(1). Block 18 may only be used for sealed-bid procurements.

(b) *SF 30, Amendment of Solicitation/ Modification of Contract.* SF 30, prescribed in 53.243, shall be used in amending invitations for bids, as specified in 14.208(a).

(c) *SF 33 (Rev. 9/97), Solicitation, Offer and Award.* SF 33 is prescribed for use in soliciting bids for supplies or services and for awarding the contracts that result from the bids, as specified in 14.201-2(a)(1), unless award is accomplished by SF 26.

(d) *SF 1447 (Rev. 8/2016), Solicitation/ Contract.* SF 1447 is prescribed for use in soliciting supplies or services and for awarding contracts that result from the bids. It shall be used when the simplified contract format is used (see 14.201-9) and may be used in place of the SF 26 or SF 33 with other solicitations and awards. Agencies may prescribe additional detailed instructions for use of the form.

(e) [Removed and Reserved]

(f) *SF 1409 (Rev. 9/88), Abstract of Offers, and SF 1410 (9/88), Abstract of Offers—Continuation.*SF 1409 and SF 1410 are prescribed for use in recording bids, as specified in 14.403(a).

(g) *OF 17 (Rev. 12/93), Offer Label.* OF 17 may be furnished with each invitation for bids to facilitate identification and handling of bids, as specified in 14.202-3(b).

(h) *OF 336 (Rev. 3/86), Continuation Sheet.* OF 336 may be used as a continuation sheet in solicitations, as specified in 14.201-2(b).

[FAC 84-5, 50 FR 1748, 1/11/85, effective 4/1/85; FAC 84-18, 51 FR 27121, 7/29/86, effective 7/30/86; FAC 84-26, 52 FR 19805, 5/27/87, effective 7/30/87; FAC 84-49, 54 FR 29284, 7/11/89, effective 8/10/89; FAC 84-53, 54 FR 48998, 11/28/89, effective 12/28/89; Final rule, FAC 90-20, 59 FR 11368, 3/10/94, effective 3/10/94; FAC 90-23, 59 FR 67010, 12/28/94, effective 2/27/95; FAC 90-29, 60 FR 34732, 7/3/95, effective 7/3/95; FAC 90-45, Final rule, 62 FR 224, 1/2/97, effective 1/1/97; FAC 97-2, 62 FR 51224, 9/30/97, effective 10/10/97; FAC 97-3, 62 FR 64912, 12/9/97, effective 12/9/97; FAC 97-12, 64 FR 32740, 6/17/99, effective 6/17/99; FAC 2001-15, 68 FR 43854, 7/24/2003, effective 8/25/2003; FAC 2005-02, 70 FR 14950, 3/23/2005, effective 3/23/2005; FAC 2005-25, 73 FR 21783, 4/22/2008, effective 4/22/2008; FAC 2005-39, 75 FR 13415, 3/19/2010, effective 4/19/2010; FAC 2005-48, 75 FR 82567, 12/30/2010, effective 1/31/2011; FAC 2005-51, 76 FR 18322, 4/1/2011, effective 5/2/2011; FAC 2005-56, 77 FR 12913, 3/2/2012, effective 4/2/2012; FAC 2005-73, 79 FR 24192, 4/29/2014, effective 5/29/2014; FAC 2005-91, 81 FR 67736, 9/30/2016, effective 10/31/2016]

53.215 Contracting by negotiation. (No Text)

53.215-1 Solicitation and receipt of proposals.

The following forms are prescribed, as stated in the following paragraphs, for use in contracting by negotiation (except for construction, architect-engineer services, or acquisitions made using simplified acquisition procedures):

(a) *SF 26 (Rev. 3/2013), Award/Contract.* SF 26, prescribed in 53.214(a), may be used in entering into negotiated contracts in which the signature of both parties on a single document is appropriate, as specified in 15.509. Block 18 may not be used for negotiated procurements.

(b) *SF 30 (11/2016), Amendment of Solicitation/Modification of Contract.* SF 30, prescribed in 53.243, may be used for amending requests for proposals and for amending requests for information, as specified in 15.210(b).

(c) *SF 33 (Rev. 9/97), Solicitation, Offer and Award.* SF 33, prescribed in 53.214(c), may be used in connection with the solicitation and award of negotiated contracts. Award of such contracts may be made by either OF 307, SF 33, or SF 26, as specified in 53.214(c) and 15.509.

(d) *OF 17 (Rev. 12/93), Offer Label.* OF 17 may be furnished with each request for proposals to facilitate identification and handling of proposals, as specified in 15.210(c).

(e) *OF 307 (Rev. 8/2016), Contract Award.* OF 307 may be used to award negotiated contracts as specified in 15.509.

(f) *OF 308 (Rev. 9/97), Solicitation and Offer-Negotiated Acquisition.* OF 308 may be used to support solicitation of negotiated contracts as specified in 15.210(a). Award of such contracts may be made by OF 307, as specified in 15.509.

(g) *OF 309 (Rev. 9/97), Amendment of Solicitation.* OF 309 may be used to amend solicitations of negotiated contracts, as specified in 15.210(b).

[FAC 97-2, 62 FR 51224, 9/30/97, effective 10/10/97; FAC 97-3, 62 FR 64912, 12/9/97, effective 12/9/97; FAC 97-12, 64 FR 32740, 6/17/99, effective 6/17/99; FAC 97-22, 66 FR 2117, 1/10/2001, effective 1/10/2001; FAC 2005-25, 73 FR 21783, 4/22/2008, effective 4/22/2008; FAC 2005-39, 75 FR 13415, 3/19/2010, effective 4/19/2010; FAC 2005-51, 76 FR 18322, 4/1/2011, effective 5/2/2011; FAC 2005-73, 79 FR 24192, 4/29/2014, effective 5/29/2014; FAC 2005-91, 81 FR 67736, 9/30/2016, effective 10/31/2016; FAC 2005-92, 81 FR 83097, 11/18/2016, effective 12/19/2016]

53.216 Types of contracts. (No Text)

53.216-1 Delivery orders and orders under basic ordering agreements (OF 347).

OF 347, Order for Supplies or Services. OF 347, prescribed in 53.213(f) (or an approved agency form), may be used to place orders under indefinite delivery contracts and basic ordering agreements, as specified in 16.703(d)(2)(i). [FAC 90-40, 61 FR 39186, 7/26/96, effective 8/26/96]

53.217 [Reserved]

53.218 [Reserved]

53.219 Small business programs.

The following standard form is prescribed for use in reporting small business (including Alaska Native Corporations and Indian tribes), veteran-owned small business, service-disabled veteran-owned small business, HUBZone small business, small disadvantaged business (including Alaska Native Corporations and Indian tribes) and women-owned small business subcontracting data, as specified in part 19: SF 294, (Rev. 8/2016) Subcontracting Report for Individual Contracts. SF 294 is authorized for local reproduction.

[FAC 90-32, 60 FR 48206, 9/18/95, effective 10/1/95; FAC 90-43, Interim rule, 61 FR 67408, 12/20/96, effective 12/20/96, finalized without change, FAC 97-4, 63 FR 9048, 2/23/98, effective 4/24/98; FAC 97-5, 63 FR 34058, 6/22/98, effective 8/21/98; FAC 97-7, 63 FR 36120, 7/1/98, effective 1/1/99, finalized without change, FAC 97-13, 7/2/99; FAC 97-10, 63 FR 70264, 12/18/98, effective 1/4/99; FAC 97-19, 65 FR 46052, 7/26/2000, effective 10/1/2000, finalized without change by FAC 2001-02, 66 FR 65347, 12/18/2001, effective 12/18/2001; FAC 97-20, 65 FR 60542, 10/11/2000, effective 10/11/2000; FAC 2001-01, 66 FR 53478, 10/22/2001, effective 10/22/2001; FAC 2005-13, 71 FR 57363, 9/28/2006, effective 9/28/2006; FAC 2005-19, 72 FR 46345, 8/17/2007, effective 9/17/2007; FAC 2005-25, 73 FR 21779, 4/22/2008, effective 4/22/2008; FAC 2005-42, 75 FR 34260, 6/16/2010, effective 7/16/2010; FAC 2005-77, 79 FR 61746, 10/14/2014, effective 10/14/2014; FAC 2005-78, 79 FR 70348, 11/25/2014, effective 11/25/2014; FAC 2005-83, 80 FR 38293, 7/2/2015, effective 10/1/2015; FAC 2005-91, 81 FR 67736, 9/30/2016, effective 10/31/2016]

53.220 [Reserved]

53.221 [Reserved]

53.222 Application of labor laws to Government acquisitions (SF's 307, 1413, 1445, 1446, WH-347).

The following forms are prescribed as stated below, for use in connection with the application of labor laws:

(a) [Reserved]

(b) [Removed and Reserved]

(c) *SF 1445 (DOL) (Rev. 2/2013), Request for Wage Determination and Response to Request.* (See 22.404-3 (a) and (b).)

(d) [Removed and Reserved]

(e) *SF 1413 (Rev. 4/2013), Statement and Acknowledgment.* SF 1413 is prescribed for use in obtaining contractor acknowledgment of inclusion of required clauses in subcontracts, as specified in 22.406-5.

(f) *Form SF 1444 (Rev. 4/2013), Request for Authorization of Additional Classification and Rate.* (See 22.406-3(a) and 22.1019.)

(g) *SF 1445 (Rev. 12/96), Labor Standards Interview.*

(h) *SF 1446 (Rev. 4/2013), Labor Standards Investigation Summary Sheet.* (See 22.406-8(d).)

(i) *Form WH-347 (DOL), Payroll (For Contractor's Optional Use).* (See 22.406-6(a).)

[FAC 84-1, 49 FR 12997, 3/30/84, effective 4/1/84; FAC 84-34, 53 FR 4948, 2/18/88, effective 2/29/88; FAC 84-38, 53 FR 27468, 7/20/88, effective 8/18/88; FAC 84-53, 54 FR 48998, 11/28/89, effective 12/28/89; Final rule, 55 FR 38518, 9/18/90; Final rule, FAC 90-20, 59 FR 11368, 3/10/94, effective 3/10/94; FAC 90-45, Final rule, 62 FR 224, 1/2/97, effective 1/1/97; FAC 2005-04, 70 FR 33662, 6/8/2005, effective 7/8/2005; FAC 2005-10, 71 FR 36930, 6/28/2006, effective 6/28/2006; FAC 2005-16, 72 FR 13585, 3/22/2007, effective 3/22/2007; FAC 2005-73, 79 FR 24192, 4/29/2014, effective 5/29/2014; FAC 2005-78, 79 FR 70342, 11/25/2014, effective 12/26/2014]

53.228 Bonds and insurance.

The following standard forms are prescribed for use for bond and insurance requirements, as specified in part 28. These forms can be found at the GSA Forms Library at *https://www.gsa.gov/forms.* All the following forms are authorized for local reproduction, except for SF 25B.

(a) SF 24 (Rev. 8/2016) Bid Bond. (See 28.106-1.)

(b) SF 25 (Rev. 8/2016) Performance Bond. (See 28.106-1(b).)

(c) SF 25A (Rev. 8/2016) Payment Bond. (See 28.106-1(c).)

(d) SF 25B (For Standard Forms 24, 25, and 25A) (Rev. 10/1983) Continuation Sheet for Standard Forms 24, 25 and 25A. (See 28.106-1(c).)

(e) SF 28 (Rev. 6/2003) Affidavit of Individual Surety. (See 28.106-1(e) and 28.203(b).)

(f) SF 34 (Rev 8/2016) Annual Bid Bond. (See 28.106–1(f).)

(g) SF 35 (Rev. 8/2016) Annual Performance Bond. (See 28.106-1.)

(h) SF 273 (Rev. 4/2013) Reinsurance Agreement for a Bonds statute Performance Bond. (See 28.106-1(h) and 28.202-1(a)(4).)

(i) SF 274 (Rev. 4/2013) Reinsurance Agreement for a Bonds statute Payment Bond. (See 28.106-1(i) and 28.202–1(a)(4).)

(j) SF 275 (Rev. 10/1998) Reinsurance Agreement in Favor of the United States. (See 28.106-1(j) and 28.202–1(a)(4).)

(k) SF 1414 (Rev. 05/1997), Consent of Surety.

(l) SF 1415 (Rev. 7/1993), Consent of Surety and Increase of Penalty. (See 28.108-1(l).)

(m) SF 1416 (Rev. 10/1998) Payment Bond for Other than Construction Contracts. (See 28.106-1(m).)

(n) SF 1418 (Rev. 2/1999) Performance Bond For Other Than Construction Contracts. (See 28.106-1(n).)

(o) OF 90 (Rev. 1/1990), Release of Lien on Real Property. (See 28.106-1(o) and 28.203-5(a).)

(p) OF 91 (Rev. 1/1990), Release of Personal Property from Escrow. (See 28.106-1(p) and 28.203-5(a).)

[FAC 84-7, 50 FR 23607, 6/4/85, effective 4/30/85; FAC 84-40, 53 FR 43395, 10/26/88, effective 11/25/88; FAC 84-53, 54 FR 48998, 11/28/89, effective 2/26/90; FAC 84-58, 55 FR 25534, 6/21/90, effective 7/23/90; FAC 90-3, 55 FR 52801, 12/21/90, effective 1/22/91; FAC 90-23, 59 FR 67010, 12/28/94, effective 2/27/95; FAC 90-40, 61 FR 39186, 7/26/96, effective 9/24/96; FAC 97-9, 63 FR 58587, 10/30/98, effective 10/30/98; FAC 97-10, 63 FR 70264, 12/18/98, effective 1/4/99; FAC 97-11, 64 FR 10530, 3/4/99, effective 3/4/99; FAC 2001-14, 68 FR 28079, 5/22/2003, effective 6/23/2003; FAC 2005-73, 79 FR 24192, 4/29/2014, effective 5/29/2014; FAC 2005-89, 81 FR 45855, 7/14/2016, effective 8/15/2016; FAC 2005-100, 83 FR 42571, 8/22/2018, effective 8/22/2018]

53.229 Taxes (SF's 1094, 1094-A).

SF 1094 (Rev. 12/96, U.S. Tax Exemption Form, and SF 1094-A (Rev. 12/96), Tax Exemption Forms Accountability Record. SF's 1094 and 1094-Aare prescribed for use in establishing exemption from State or local taxes, as specified in 29.302(b).

[FAC 90-45, Final rule, 62 FR 224, 1/2/97, effective 1/1/97]

53.230 [Reserved]

53.232 Contract financing (SF 1443).

SF 1443 (JUL 2009), Contractor's Request for Progress Payment. SF 1443 is prescribed for use in obtaining contractors' requests for progress payments.

[FAC 2005-33, 74 FR 28430, 6/15/2009, effective 7/15/2009]

53.235 Research and Development Contracting (SF 298).

SF 298 (2/89), Report Documentation Page. SF 298 is prescribed for use in submitting scientific and technical reports to contracting officers and to technical information libraries, as specified in 35.010.

[FAC 84-56, 55 FR 3890, 2/5/90, effective 3/7/90]

53.236 Construction and architect-engineer contracts. (No Text)

53.236-1 Construction.

The following forms are prescribed, as stated below, for use in contracting for construction, alteration, or repair, or dismantling, demolition, or removal of improvements.

(a) [Removed and reserved]

(b) [Reserved]

(c) [Reserved]

(d) *SF 1442 (4/85), Solicitation, Offer and Award (Construction, Alteration, or Repair).* SF 1442 is prescribed for use in soliciting offers and awarding contracts expected to exceed the simplified acquisition threshold for (1) construction, alteration, or repair, or (2) dismantling, demolition, or removal of improvements (and may be used for contracts within the simplified acquisition threshold), as specified in 36.701(a).

(e) *OF 347, (10/83) Order for Supplies or Services.* OF 347*(Rev. 2/2012)*, prescribed in 53.213(f), (or an approved agency form) may be used for contracts under the simplified acquisition threshold for (1) construction, alteration, or repair, or (2) dismantling, demolition, or removal of improvements, as specified in 36.701(b).

(f) *OF 1419 (11/88), Abstract of Offers-Construction, and OF 1419A (11/88), Abstract of Offers—Construction, Continuation Sheet.* OF's 1419 and 1419A are prescribed for use in recording bids (and may be used for recording proposal evaluation information), as specified in 36.701(c).

[FAC 84-5, 50 FR 1748, 1/11/85, effective 4/1/85; FAC 84-34, 53 FR 4948, 2/18/88, effective 2/29/88; FAC 84-49, 54 FR 29284, 7/11/89, effective 8/10/89; FAC 90-3, 55 FR 52801, 12/21/90, effective 1/22/91; FAC 90-29, 60 FR 34732, 7/3/95, effective 7/3/95; FAC 90-40, 61 FR 39186, 7/26/96, effective 8/26/96; FAC 2001-25, 69 FR 59699, 10/5/2004, effective 11/4/2004; FAC 2005-02, 70 FR 14950, 3/23/2005, effective 3/23/2005; FAC 2005-34, 74 FR 31557, 7/1/2009, effective 7/1/2009; FAC 2005-48, 75 FR 82567, 12/30/2010, effective

1/31/2011; FAC 2005-56, 77 FR 12913, 3/2/2012, effective 4/2/2012]

53.236-2 Architect-engineer services (SF's 252 and 330).

The following forms are prescribed for use in contracting for architect-engineer and related services:

(a) *SF 252 (Rev. 10/83), Architect-Engineer Contract.* SF 252 is prescribed for use in awarding fixed-price contracts for architect-engineer services, as specified in 36.702(a). Pending issuance of a new edition of the form, Block 8, Negotiation Authority, is deleted.

(b) *SF 330 (Rev. 8/2016), Architect-Engineer Qualifications.* SF 330 is prescribed for use in obtaining information from architect-engineer firms regarding their professional qualifications, as specified in 36.702(b)(1) and (b)(2).

[FAC 84-5, 50 FR 1748, 1/11/85, effective 4/1/85; FAC 84-23, 51 FR 36972, 10/16/86, effective 9/30/86; FAC 90-16, 57 FR 60591, 12/21/92, effective 2/19/93; FAC 2001-18, Final rule, 68 FR 69227, 12/11/2003, effective 1/12/2004, delay of effective date, 6/8/2004; FAC 2001-19, Final rule, 69 FR 1050, 1/7/2004, effective 1/7/2004; FAC 2005-34, 74 FR 31557, 7/1/2009, effective 7/1/2009; FAC 2005-73, 79 FR 24192, 4/29/2014, effective 5/29/2014; FAC 2005-91, 81 FR 67736, 9/30/2016, effective 10/31/2016]

53.237 [Reserved]

53.238 [Reserved]

53.239 [Reserved]

53.240 [Reserved]

53.241 [Reserved]

53.242 Contract administration. (No Text)

53.242-1 Novation and change-of-name agreements (SF 30).

SF 30, Amendment of Solicitation/Modification of Contract. SF 30, prescribed in 53.243, shall be used in connection with novation and change of name agreements, as specified in 42.1203(h). [FAC 97-3, 62 FR 64912, 12/9/97, effective 2/9/98]

53.243 Contract modifications (SF 30).

SF 30 (Rev. 11/2016), Amendment of Solicitation/Modification of Contract. SF 30 is prescribed for use in amending invitation for bids, as specified in 14.208; modifying purchase and delivery orders, as specified in 13.302-3; and modifying contracts, as specified in 42.1203(h), 43.301, 49.602-5, and elsewhere in this regulation. The form may also be used to amend solicitations for negotiated contracts, as specified in 15.210(b). Pending the publication of a new edition of the form, Instruction (b), Item 3 (effective date), is revised in paragraphs (3) and (5) as follows:

(b) Item 3 (effective date).

* * *

(3) For a modification issued as a confirming notice of termination for the convenience of the Government, the effective date of the confirming notice shall be the same as the effective date of the initial notice.

* * *

(5) For a modification confirming the termination contracting officer's previous letter determination of the amount due in settlement of a contract termination for convenience, the effective date shall be the same as the effective date of the previous letter determination.

[FAC 97-2, 62 FR 51224, 9/30/97, effective 10/10/97; FAC 97-3, 62 FR 64912, 12/9/97, effective 2/9/98; FAC 2005-92, 81 FR 83097, 11/18/2016, effective 12/19/2016]

53.244 [Reserved]

53.245 Government Property.

The following forms are prescribed, as specified in this section, for use in reporting, reutilization, and disposal of Government property and in accounting for this property:

(a) *SF 120 (GSA), Report of Excess Personal Property, and SF 120-A(GSA), Continuation Sheet (Report of Excess Personal Property).* See 45.602-3 and 41 CFR 102-36.215.)

(b) *SF 126 (GSA), Report of Personal Property for Sale, and SF 126-A(GSA), Report of Personal Property for Sale (Continuation Sheet).* See FPMR 101-45.303 (41 CFR 101-45.303.))

(c) *SF 1423 (Rev. 5/04), Inventory Verification Survey.* See 45.602-1(b)(1).)

(d) *SF 1424 (Rev. 5/04), Inventory Disposal Report* (See 45.605). SF 1424 is authorized for local reproduction.

(e) *SF 1428 (Rev. 6/2007), Inventory Disposal Schedule, and SF 1429(Rev. 5/04), Inventory Disposal Schedule—Continuation Sheet.* (See 45.602-1, 49.303-2, 52.245-1, and 53.249(b).) SF's 1428 and 1429 are authorized for local reproduction.

(f) *SF 1426 (Rev. 12/96), Inventory Schedule A (Metals in Mill Product Form), and SF 1427(Rev. 7/89), Inventory Schedule A-Continuation Sheet (Metals in Mill Product Form).* (See 45.606 and 49.602-2(e).) Standard Form 1426 and Standard Form 1427 are authorized for local reproduction and copies are furnished for this purpose in Part 53 of the loose-leaf edition of the FAR.

(g) *SF 1428 (Rev. 12/96), Inventory Schedule B, and SF 1429(Rev. 7/89), Inventory Schedule B-Continuation Sheet.* (See 45.606 and 49.602-2(b).) Standard Form 1428 and Standard Form 1429 are authorized for local reproduction and copies are furnished for this purpose in Part 53 of the loose-leaf edition of the FAR.

(h) *SF 1430 (Rev. 12/96), Inventory Schedule C (Work-in-Process) and SF 1431(Rev. 7/89), Inventory Schedule C-Continuation Sheet (Work-in-Process).* (See 45.606 and 49.602-2(c).) Standard Form 1430 and Standard Form 1431 are authorized for local reproduction and copies are furnished for this purpose in Part 53 of the loose-leaf edition of the FAR.

(i) *SF 1432 (Rev. 12/96), Inventory Schedule D (Special Tooling and Special Test Equipment), and SF 1433(Rev. 7/89), Inventory Schedule D-Continuation Sheet (Special Tooling and Special Test Equipment).* (See 45.606 and 49.602-2(d).) Standard Form 1432 and Standard Form 1433 are authorized for local reproduction and copies are furnished for this purpose in Part 53 of the loose-leaf edition of the FAR.

(j) *SF 1434 (Rev. 12/96), Termination Inventory Schedule E (Short Form for Use with SF 38 Only).* (See 45.606 and 49.602-2(e).) Standard Form 1434 is authorized for local reproduction and a copy is furnished for this purpose in Part 53 of the loose-leaf edition of the FAR.

[FAC 84-56, 55 FR 3890, 2/5/90, effective 3/7/90; FAC 90-41, 61 FR 41466, 8/8/96, effective 8/8/96, finalized without change, FAC 97-3, 62 FR 64912, 12/9/97, effective 2/9/98; FAC 90-45, Final rule, 62 FR 224, 1/2/97, effective 1/1/97; FAC 2001-22, Final rule, 69 FR 17741, 4/5/2004, effective 5/5/2004; FAC 2005-17, 72 FR 27364, 5/15/2007, effective 6/14/2007]

53.246 [Reserved]

53.247 Transportation (U.S. Commercial Bill of Lading).

The commercial bill of lading is the preferred document for the transportation of property, as specified in 47.101.

[FAC 2005-07, 71 FR 200, 1/3/2006, effective 2/2/2006]

53.248 [Reserved]

53.249 Termination of contracts.

(a) The following forms are prescribed for use in connection with the termination of contracts, as specified in subpart 49.6. These forms are available at the GSA Forms Library at *https://www.gsa.gov/forms.* These forms are authorized for local reproduction except for SF 1034.

(1) SF 1034 (GAO), Public Voucher for Purchases and Services Other Than Personal. (See 49.302(a).)

(2) SF 1435 (Rev. 03/2016), Settlement Proposal (Inventory Basis). (See 49.602-1(a).)

(3) SF 1436 (Rev. 5/2004), Settlement Proposal (Total Cost Basis). (See 49.602-1(b).)

(4) SF 1437 (Rev. 9/1997), Settlement Proposal for Cost-Reimbursement Type Contracts. (See 49.602-1(c) and 49.302.)

(5) SF 1438 (Rev. 5/2004), Settlement Proposal (Short Form). (See 49.602-1(d).)

(6) SF 1439 (Rev. 7/1989), Schedule of Accounting Information. (See 49.602-3.)

(7) SF 1440 (Rev. 01/1995), Application for Partial Payment. (See 49.602-4.)

(b) SF 1428 (Rev. 6/2007), Inventory Disposal Schedule, and Standard Form 1429 (Rev. 1/2016), Inventory Disposal Schedule—Continuation Sheet, shall be used to support termination settlement proposals listed in paragraph (a) of this section, as specified in 49.602-2. These forms are available at the GSA Forms Library at *https://www.gsa.gov/forms.*

[FAC 84-29, 52 FR 30079, 8/12/87, effective 8/24/87; FAC 84-56, 55 FR 3890, 2/5/90, effective 3/7/90; FAC 97-2, 62 FR 51224, 9/30/97, effective 10/10/97; FAC 97-3, 62 FR 64912, 12/9/97, effective 12/9/97; FAC 2001-22, 69 FR 17741, 4/5/2004, effective 5/5/2004; FAC 2005-17, 72 FR 27364, 5/15/2007, effective 6/14/2007; FAC 2005-100, 83 FR 42571, 8/22/2018, effective 8/22/2018]

53.250 [Reserved]

53.251 Contractor use of Government supply sources (OF 347).

OF 347, Order for Supplies or Services. OF 347, prescribed in 53.213(f), may be used by contractors when requisitioning from the VA, as specified in 51.102(e)(3)(ii).

[FAC 90-40, 61 FR 39186, 7/26/96, effective 8/26/96]

SUBPART 53.3—FORMS USED IN ACQUISITIONS

53.300 Listing of Standard, Optional, and Agency forms.

This subpart identifies, in numerical sequence, Standard Forms (SF), Optional Forms (OF) and agency forms that are specified by the FAR for use in acquisitions.

(a) You can access the forms in Table 53-1 at the GSA Forms Library at *https://www.gsa.gov/forms.*

Table 53-1–Forms in the GSA Forms Library

Form Number	Form Title
SF 18	Request for Quotation
SF 24	Bid Bond
SF 25	Performance Bond
SF 25A	Payment Bond
SF 25B	Continuation Sheet for 24, 25, and 25A
SF 26	Award/Contract

SF 28	Affidavit of Individual Surety
SF 30	Amendment of Solicitation/Modification of Contract
SF 33	Solicitation, Offer and Award
SF 34	Annual Bid Bond
SF 35	Annual Performance Bond
SF 44	U.S. Government Purchase Order—Invoice—Voucher
SF 120	Report of Excess Personal Property
SF 120A	Continuation Sheet (Report of Excess Personal Property)
SF 126	Report of Personal Property for Sale
SF 126A	Report of Personal Property for Sale (Continuation Sheet)
SF 252	Architect-Engineer Contract
SF 273	Reinsurance Agreement for a Bonds Statute Performance Bid
SF 274	Reinsurance Agreement for a Bonds Statute Payment Bond
SF 275	Reinsurance Agreement in Favor of the United States
SF 294	Subcontracting Report for Individual Contracts
SF 298	Report Documentation Page
SF 308	Request For Wage Determination and Response to Request

SF 330	Architect-Engineer Qualifications
SF 1034	Public Voucher for Purchases and Services Other Than Personal
SF 1035	Public Voucher for Purchases and Services Other Than Personal (Continuation Sheet)
SF 1094	United States Tax Exemption Form
SF 1094A	Tax Exemption Accountability Record
SF 1165	Receipt for Cash-Subvoucher
SF 1402	Certificate of Appointment
SF 1403	Preaward Survey of Prospective Contractor (General)
SF 1404	Preaward Survey of Prospective Contractor (Technical)
SF 1405	Preaward Survey of Prospective Contractor (Production)
SF 1406	Preaward Survey of Prospective Contractor (Quality Assurance)
SF 1407	Preaward Survey of Prospective Contractor Financial Capability
SF 1408	Preaward Survey of Prospective Contractor Accounting System
SF 1409	Abstract of Offers
SF 1410	Abstract of Offers -Continuation
SF 1413	Statement and Acknowledgment

SF 1414	Consent of Surety
SF 1415	Consent of Surety and Increase of Penalty
SF 1416	Payment Bond For Other Than Construction Contracts
SF 1418	Performance Bond for Other Than Construction Contracts
SF 1423	Inventory Verification Survey
SF 1424	Inventory Disposal Report
SF 1428	Inventory Disposal Schedule
SF 1429	Inventory Disposal Schedule-Continuation Sheet
SF 1435	Settlement Proposal (Inventory Basis)
SF 1436	Settlement Proposal (Total Cost Basis)
SF 1437	Settlement Proposal for Cost-Reimbursement Type Contracts
SF 1438	Settlement Proposal (Short Form)
SF 1439	Schedule of Accounting Information
SF 1440	Application For Partial Payment
SF 1442	Solicitation, Offer, and Award (Construction, Alteration, or Repair)
SF 1443	Contractor's Request For Progress Payment
SF 1444	Request For Authorization of Additional Classification and Rate

SF 1445	Labor Standards Interview
SF 1446	Labor Standards Investigation Summary Sheet
SF 1447	Solicitation/Contract
SF 1449	Solicitation/Contract/Order for Commercial Items
OF 17	Offer Label
OF 90	Release of Lien on Real Property
OF 91	Release of Personal Property From Escrow
OF 307	Contract Award
OF 308	Solicitation and Offer-Negotiated Acquisition
OF 309	Amendment of Solicitation (Negotiated Procurements)
OF 336	Continuation Sheet
OF 347	Order for Supplies or Services
OF 348	Order For Supplies or Services - Schedule - Continuation
OF 1419	Abstract of Offers - Construction
OF 1419A	Abstract of Offers-Construction Continuation Sheet

(b) You can access the forms in Table 53-2 at the websites listed in the table.

Table 53-2–Other Forms

Form DD 254	Department of Defense Contract Security Classification Specification	http://www.dtic.mil/whs/directives/forms/eforms/dd0254.pdf
Form DD 441	Department of Defense Security Agreement	http://www.dtic.mil/whs/directives/forms/eforms/dd0441 2017.pdf
Form WH-347	Payroll-U.S. Department of Labor	https://www.dol.gov/whd/forms/wh347.pdf

[FAC 2005-100, 83 FR 42571, 8/22/2018, effective 8/22/2018]

53.301 Standard forms.

This section illustrates the standard forms that are specified by the FAR for use in acquisitions. The forms are illustrated in numerical order. The subsection numbers correspond with the standard form numbers (*e.g.*, Standard Form 18 appears as 53.301-18).

53.301-18 Standard Form 18 (REV 6/95), Request for Quotations

[FAC 90-29, 60 FR 34732, 7/3/95, effective 7/3/95]

REQUEST FOR QUOTATION (THIS IS NOT AN ORDER)

THIS RFQ ☐ IS ☐ IS NOT A SMALL BUSINESS SET-ASIDE

PAGE OF PAGES

1. REQUEST NO.
2. DATE ISSUED
3. REQUISITION/PURCHASE REQUEST NO.
4. CERT. FOR NAT. DEF. UNDER BDSA REG. 2 AND/OR DMS REG. 1 ▶ RATING

5a. ISSUED BY

6. DELIVER BY *(Date)*

5b. FOR INFORMATION CALL *(NO COLLECT CALLS)*

NAME — TELEPHONE NUMBER: AREA CODE, NUMBER

7. DELIVERY ☐ FOB DESTINATION ☐ OTHER *(See Schedule)*

9. DESTINATION
a. NAME OF CONSIGNEE
b. STREET ADDRESS
c. CITY
d. STATE
e. ZIP CODE

8. TO:
a. NAME
b. COMPANY
c. STREET ADDRESS
d. CITY
e. STATE
f. ZIP CODE

10. PLEASE FURNISH QUOTATIONS TO THE ISSUING OFFICE IN BLOCK 5a ON OR BEFORE CLOSE OF BUSINESS *(Date)*

IMPORTANT: This is a request for information, and quotations furnished are not officers. If you are unable to quote, please so indicate on this form and return it to the address in Block 5a. This request does not commit the Government to pay any costs incurred in the preparation of the submission of this quotation or to contract for supplies or service. Supplies are of domestic origin unless otherwise indicated by quoter. Any representations and/or certifications attached to this Request for Quotation must be completed by the quoter.

11. SCHEDULE *(Include applicable Federal, State and local taxes)*

ITEM NO. (a)	SUPPLIES/SERVICES (b)	QUANTITY (c)	UNIT (d)	UNIT PRICE (e)	AMOUNT (f)

12. DISCOUNT FOR PROMPT PAYMENT ▶	a. 10 CALENDAR DAYS (%)	b. 20 CALENDAR DAYS (%)	c. 30 CALENDAR DAYS (%)	d. CALENDAR DAYS NUMBER	PERCENTAGE

NOTE: Additional provisions and representations ☐ are ☐ are not attached.

13. NAME AND ADDRESS OF QUOTER
a. NAME OF QUOTER
b. STREET ADDRESS
c. COUNTY
d. CITY
e. STATE
f. ZIP CODE

14. SIGNATURE OF PERSON AUTHORIZED TO SIGN QUOTATION

15. DATE OF QUOTATION

16. SIGNER
a. NAME *(Type or print)*
b. TELEPHONE: AREA CODE, NUMBER
c. TITLE *(Type or print)*

AUTHORIZED FOR LOCAL REPRODUCTION
Previous edition not usable

STANDARD FORM 18 (REV. 6-95)
Prescribed by GSA-FAR (48 CFR) 53.215-1(a)

53.301-24 Bid Bond

[FAC 84-58, 55 FR 25535, 6/21/90, effective 7/23/90; FAC 97-10, 63 FR 70264, 12/18/98, effective 1/4/99; FAC 2005-89, 81 FR 45855, 7/14/2016, effective 8/15/2016]

BID BOND (See instructions on reverse)	DATE BOND EXECUTED *(Must not be later than bid opening date)*	**OMB Control Number: 9000-0045** **Expiration Date: DATE**

Paperwork Reduction Act Statement - This information collection meets the requirements of 44 USC § 3507, as amended by section 2 of the Paperwork Reduction Act of 1995. You do not need to answer these questions unless we display a valid Office of Management and Budget (OMB) control number. The OMB control number for this collection is 9000-0045. We estimate that it will take 25 minutes to read the instructions, gather the facts, and answer the questions. Send only comments relating to our time estimate, including suggestions for reducing this burden, or any other aspects of this collection of information to: General Services Administration, Regulatory Secretariat Division (M1V1CB), 1800 F Street, NW, Washington, DC 20405.

PRINCIPAL *(Legal name and business address)*	TYPE OF ORGANIZATION *("X" one)* ☐ INDIVIDUAL ☐ PARTNERSHIP ☐ JOINT VENTURE ☐ CORPORATION ☐ OTHER *(Specify)*
	STATE OF INCORPORATION

SURETY(IES) *(Name and business address)*

PENAL SUM OF BOND					BID IDENTIFICATION	
PERCENT OF BID PRICE	AMOUNT NOT TO EXCEED				BID DATE	INVITATION NUMBER
	MILLION(S)	THOUSAND(S)	HUNDRED(S)	CENTS	FOR *(Construction, Supplies or Services)*	

OBLIGATION:

We, the Principal and Surety(ies) are firmly bound to the United States of America (hereinafter called the Government) in the above penal sum. For payment of the penal sum, we bind ourselves, our heirs, executors, administrators, and successors, jointly and severally. However, where the Sureties are corporations acting as co-sureties, we, the Sureties, bind ourselves in such sum "jointly and severally" as well as "severally" only for the purpose of allowing a joint action or actions against any or all of us. For all other purposes, each Surety binds itself, jointly and severally with the Principal, for the payment of the sum shown opposite the name of the Surety. If no limit of liability is indicated, the limit of liability is the full amount of the penal sum.

CONDITIONS:

The Principal has submitted the bid identified above.

THEREFORE:

The above obligation is void if the Principal - (a) upon acceptance by the Government of the bid identified above, within the period specified therein for acceptance (sixty (60) days if no period is specified), executes the further contractual documents and gives the bond(s) required by the terms of the bid as accepted within the time specified (ten (10) days if no period is specified) after receipt of the forms by the principal; or (b) in the event of failure to execute such further contractual documents and give such bonds, pays the Government for any cost of procuring the work which exceeds the amount of the bid.

Each Surety executing this instrument agrees that its obligation is not impaired by any extension(s) of the time for acceptance of the bid that the Principal may grant to the Government. Notice to the surety(ies) of extension(s) is waived. However, waiver of the notice applies only to extensions aggregating not more than sixty (60) calendar days in addition to the period originally allowed for acceptance of the bid.

WITNESS:

The Principal and Surety(ies) executed this bid bond and affixed their seals on the above date.

PRINCIPAL

SIGNATURE(S)	1. (Seal)	2. (Seal)	3. (Seal)	Corporate Seal
NAME(S) & TITLE(S) *(Typed)*	1.	2.	3.	

INDIVIDUAL SURETY(IES)

SIGNATURE(S)	1. (Seal)	2. (Seal)
NAME(S) *(Typed)*	1.	2.

CORPORATE SURETY(IES)

SURETY A	NAME & ADDRESS		STATE OF INCORPORATION	LIABILITY LIMIT ($)	Corporate Seal
	SIGNATURE(S)	1.	2.		
	NAME(S) & TITLE(S) *(Typed)*	1.	2.		

AUTHORIZED FOR LOCAL REPRODUCTION
Previous edition is NOT usable

STANDARD FORM 24 (REV. DATE)
Prescribed by GSA - FAR (48 CFR) 53.228(a)

			STATE OF INCORPORATION	LIABILITY LIMIT ($)	
SURETY B	NAME & ADDRESS				Corporate Seal
	SIGNATURE(S)	1.	2.		
	NAME(S) & TITLE(S) *(Typed)*	1.	2.		
SURETY C	NAME & ADDRESS		STATE OF INCORPORATION	LIABILITY LIMIT ($)	Corporate Seal
	SIGNATURE(S)	1.	2.		
	NAME(S) & TITLE(S) *(Typed)*	1.	2.		
SURETY D	NAME & ADDRESS		STATE OF INCORPORATION	LIABILITY LIMIT ($)	Corporate Seal
	SIGNATURE(S)	1.	2.		
	NAME(S) & TITLE(S) *(Typed)*	1.	2.		
SURETY E	NAME & ADDRESS		STATE OF INCORPORATION	LIABILITY LIMIT ($)	Corporate Seal
	SIGNATURE(S)	1.	2.		
	NAME(S) & TITLE(S) *(Typed)*	1.	2.		
SURETY F	NAME & ADDRESS		STATE OF INCORPORATION	LIABILITY LIMIT ($)	Corporate Seal
	SIGNATURE(S)	1.	2.		
	NAME(S) & TITLE(S) *(Typed)*	1.	2.		
SURETY G	NAME & ADDRESS		STATE OF INCORPORATION	LIABILITY LIMIT ($)	Corporate Seal
	SIGNATURE(S)	1.	2.		
	NAME(S) & TITLE(S) *(Typed)*	1.	2.		

INSTRUCTIONS

1. This form is authorized for use when a bid guaranty is required. Any deviation from this form will require the written approval of the Administrator of General Services.

2. Insert the full legal name and business address of the Principal in the space designated "Principal" on the face of the form. An authorized person shall sign the bond. Any person signing in a representative capacity (e.g., an attorney-in-fact) must furnish evidence of authority if that representative is not a member of the firm, partnership, or joint venture, or an officer of the corporation involved.

3. The bond may express penal sum as a percentage of the bid price. In these cases, the bond may state a maximum dollar limitation (e.g., 20% of the bid price but the amount not to exceed __________ dollars).

4. (a) Corporations executing the bond as sureties must appear on the Department of the Treasury's list of approved sureties and must act within the limitations listed therein. The value put into the LIABILITY LIMIT block is the penal sum (i.e., the face value) of the bond, unless a co-surety arrangement is proposed.

(b) When multiple corporate sureties are involved, their names and addresses shall appear in the spaces (Surety A, Surety B, etc.) headed "CORPORATE SURETY(IES)." In the space designated "SURETY(IES)" on the face of the form, insert only the letter identifier corresponding to each of the sureties. Moreover, when co-surety arrangements exist, the parties may allocate their respective limitations of liability under the bond, provided that the sum total of their liability equals 100% of the bond penal sum.

(c) When individual sureties are involved, a completed Affidavit of Individual Surety (Standard Form 28) for each individual surety, shall accompany the bond. The Government may require the surety to furnish additional substantiating information concerning its financial capability.

5. Corporations executing the bond shall affix their corporate seals. Individuals shall execute the bond opposite the word "Corporate Seal"; and shall affix an adhesive seal if executed in Maine, New Hampshire, or any other jurisdiction requiring adhesive seals.

6. Type the name and title of each person signing this bond in the space provided.

7. In its application to negotiated contracts, the terms "bid" and "bidder" shall include "proposal" and "offeror."

STANDARD FORM 24 (REV. DATE) **BACK**

53.301-25 Performance Bond

[Final rule, 62 FR 40236, 7/25/97, effective 6/30/97; FAC 97-10, 63 FR 70264, 12/18/98, effective 1/4/99; FAC 2005-73, 79 FR 24192, 4/29/2014, effective 5/29/2014; FAC 2005-89, 81 FR 45855, 7/14/2016, effective 8/15/2016]

PERFORMANCE BOND *(See instructions on reverse)*	DATE BOND EXECUTED *(Must be same or later than date of contract)*	**OMB Control Number: 9000-0045** **Expiration Date: DATE**

Paperwork Reduction Act Statement - This information collection meets the requirements of 44 USC § 3507, as amended by section 2 of the Paperwork Reduction Act of 1995. You do not need to answer these questions unless we display a valid Office of Management and Budget (OMB) control number. The OMB control number for this collection is 9000-0045. We estimate that it will take 60 minutes to read the instructions, gather the facts, and answer the questions. Send only comments relating to our time estimate, including suggestions for reducing this burden, or any other aspects of this collection of information to: General Services Administration, Regulatory Secretariat Division (M1V1CB), 1800 F Street, NW, Washington, DC 20405.

PRINCIPAL *(Legal name and business address)*	TYPE OF ORGANIZATION *("X" one)* ☐ INDIVIDUAL ☐ PARTNERSHIP ☐ JOINT VENTURE ☐ CORPORATION ☐ OTHER *(Specify)*
	STATE OF INCORPORATION
SURETY(IES) *(Name(s) and business address(es))*	PENAL SUM OF BOND: MILLION(S) / THOUSAND(S) / HUNDRED(S) / CENTS
	CONTRACT DATE / CONTRACT NUMBER

OBLIGATION:

We, the Principal and Surety(ies), are firmly bound to the United States of America (hereinafter called the Government) in the above penal sum. For payment of the penal sum, we bind ourselves, our heirs, executors, administrators, and successors, jointly and severally. However, where the Sureties are corporations acting as co-sureties, we, the Sureties, bind ourselves in such sum "jointly and severally" as well as "severally" only for the purpose of allowing a joint action or actions against any or all of us. For all other purposes, each Surety binds itself, jointly and severally with the Principal, for the payment of the sum shown opposite the name of the Surety. If no limit of liability is indicated, the limit of liability is the full amount of the penal sum.

CONDITIONS:

The Principal has entered into the contract identified above.

THEREFORE:

The above obligation is void if the Principal-

(a)(1) Performs and fulfills all the understanding, covenants, terms, conditions, and agreements of the contract during the original term of the contract and any extensions thereof that are granted by the Government, with or without notice of the Surety(ies) and during the life of any guaranty required under the contract, and

(2) Performs and fulfills all the undertakings, covenants, terms, conditions, and agreements of any and all duly authorized modifications of the contract that hereafter are made. Notice of those modifications to the Surety(ies) are waived.

(b) Pays to the Government the full amount of the taxes imposed by the Government, if the said contract is subject to 41 USC Chapter 31, Subchapter III, Bonds, which are collected, deducted, or withheld from wages paid by the Principal in carrying out the construction contract with respect to which this bond is furnished.

WITNESS:

The Principal and Surety(ies) executed this performance bond and affixed their seals on the above date.

PRINCIPAL

SIGNATURE(S)	1. (Seal)	2. (Seal)	3. (Seal)	Corporate Seal
NAME(S) & TITLE(S) *(Typed)*	1.	2.	3.	

INDIVIDUAL SURETY(IES)

SIGNATURE(S)	1. (Seal)	2. (Seal)
NAME(S) *(Typed)*	1.	2.

CORPORATE SURETY(IES)

SURETY A	NAME & ADDRESS		STATE OF INCORPORATION	LIABILITY LIMIT ($)	Corporate Seal
	SIGNATURE(S)	1.	2.		
	NAME(S) & TITLE(S) *(Typed)*	1.	2.		

AUTHORIZED FOR LOCAL REPRODUCTION
Previous edition is NOT usable

STANDARD FORM 25 (REV. DATE)
Prescribed by GSA-FAR (48 CFR) 53.228(b)

CORPORATE SURETY(IES) *(Continued)*					
SURETY B	NAME & ADDRESS		STATE OF INCORPORATION	LIABILITY LIMIT ($)	
	SIGNATURE(S)	1.	2.		Corporate Seal
	NAME(S) & TITLE(S) *(Typed)*	1.	2.		
SURETY C	NAME & ADDRESS		STATE OF INCORPORATION	LIABILITY LIMIT ($)	
	SIGNATURE(S)	1.	2.		Corporate Seal
	NAME(S) & TITLE(S) *(Typed)*	1.	2.		
SURETY D	NAME & ADDRESS		STATE OF INCORPORATION	LIABILITY LIMIT ($)	
	SIGNATURE(S)	1.	2.		Corporate Seal
	NAME(S) & TITLE(S) *(Typed)*	1.	2.		
SURETY E	NAME & ADDRESS		STATE OF INCORPORATION	LIABILITY LIMIT ($)	
	SIGNATURE(S)	1.	2.		Corporate Seal
	NAME(S) & TITLE(S) *(Typed)*	1.	2.		
SURETY F	NAME & ADDRESS		STATE OF INCORPORATION	LIABILITY LIMIT ($)	
	SIGNATURE(S)	1.	2.		Corporate Seal
	NAME(S) & TITLE(S) *(Typed)*	1.	2.		
SURETY G	NAME & ADDRESS		STATE OF INCORPORATION	LIABILITY LIMIT ($)	
	SIGNATURE(S)	1.	2.		Corporate Seal
	NAME(S) & TITLE(S) *(Typed)*	1.	2.		

BOND PREMIUM ▶	RATE PER THOUSAND ($)	TOTAL ($)

INSTRUCTIONS

1. This form is authorized for use in connection with Government contracts. Any deviation from this form will require the written approval of the Administrator of General Services.

2. Insert the full legal name and business address of the Principal in the space designated "Principal" on the face of the form. An authorized person shall sign the bond. Any person signing in a representative capacity (e.g., an attorney-in-fact) must furnish evidence of authority if that representative is not a member of the firm, partnership, or joint venture, or an officer of the corporation involved.

3. (a) Corporations executing the bond as sureties must appear on the Department of the Treasury's list of approved sureties and must act within the limitations listed therein. The value put into the LIABILITY LIMIT block is the penal sum (i.e., the face value) of bonds, unless a co-surety arrangement is proposed.

(b) When multiple corporate sureties are involved, their names and addresses shall appear in the spaces (Surety A, Surety B, etc.) headed "CORPORATE SURETY(IES)." In the space designated "SURETY(IES)" on the face of the form, insert only the letter identifier corresponding to each of the sureties. Moreover, when co-surety arrangements exist, the parties may allocate their respective limitations of liability under the bonds, provided that the sum total of their liability equals 100% of the bond penal sum.

(c) When individual sureties are involved, a completed Affidavit of Individual Surety (Standard Form 28) for each individual surety shall accompany the bond. The government may require the surety to furnish additional substantiating information concerning its financial capability.

4. Corporations executing the bond shall affix their corporate seals. Individuals shall execute the bond opposite the words "Corporate Seal", and shall affix an adhesive seal if executed in Maine, New Hampshire, or any other jurisdiction requiring adhesive seals.

5. Type the name and title of each person signing this bond in the space provided.

STANDARD FORM 25 (REV. DATE) **BACK**

53.301-25-A Payment Bond

[FAC 84-58, 55 FR 25535, 6/21/90, effective 7/23/90; FAC 97-10, 63 FR 70264, 12/18/98, effective 1/4/99; FAC 2005-73, 79 FR 24192, 4/29/2014, effective 5/29/2014; FAC 2005-89, 81 FR 45855, 7/14/2016, effective 8/15/2016]

PAYMENT BOND *(See instructions on reverse)*	DATE BOND EXECUTED *(Must be same or later than date of contract)*	**OMB Control Number: 9000-0045** **Expiration Date: DATE**

Paperwork Reduction Act Statement - This information collection meets the requirements of 44 USC § 3507, as amended by section 2 of the Paperwork Reduction Act of 1995. You do not need to answer these questions unless we display a valid Office of Management and Budget (OMB) control number. The OMB control number for this collection is 9000-0045. We estimate that it will take 60 minutes to read the instructions, gather the facts, and answer the questions. Send only comments relating to our time estimate, including suggestions for reducing this burden, or any other aspects of this collection of information to: General Services Administration, Regulatory Secretariat Division (M1V1CB), 1800 F Street, NW, Washington, DC 20405.

PRINCIPAL *(Legal name and business address)*	TYPE OF ORGANIZATION *("X" one)* ☐ INDIVIDUAL ☐ PARTNERSHIP ☐ JOINT VENTURE ☐ CORPORATION ☐ OTHER *(Specify)*			
	STATE OF INCORPORATION			
SURETY(IES) *(Name(s) and business address(es))*	PENAL SUM OF BOND			
	MILLION(S)	THOUSAND(S)	HUNDRED(S)	CENTS
	CONTRACT DATE	CONTRACT NUMBER		

OBLIGATION:

We, the Principal and Surety(ies), are firmly bound to the United States of America (hereinafter called the Government) in the above penal sum. For payment of the penal sum, we bind ourselves, our heirs, executors, administrators, and successors, jointly and severally. However, where the Sureties are corporations acting as co-sureties, we, the Sureties, bind ourselves in such sum "jointly and severally" as well as "severally" only for the purpose of allowing a joint action or actions against any or all of us. For all other purposes, each Surety binds itself, jointly and severally with the Principal, for the payment of the sum shown opposite the name of the Surety. If no limit is indicated, the limit of liability is the full amount of the penal sum.

CONDITIONS:

The above obligation is void if the Principal promptly makes payment to all persons having a direct relationship with the Principal or a subcontractor of the Principal for furnishing labor, material or both in the prosecution of the work provided for in the contract identified above, and any authorized modifications of the contract that subsequently are made. Notice of those modifications to the Surety(ies) are waived.

WITNESS:

The Principal and Surety(ies) executed this payment bond and affixed their seals on the above date.

PRINCIPAL

SIGNATURE(S)	1. (Seal)	2. (Seal)	3. (Seal)	Corporate Seal
NAME(S) & TITLE(S) *(Typed)*	1.	2.	3.	

INDIVIDUAL SURETY(IES)

SIGNATURE(S)	1. (Seal)	2. (Seal)
NAME(S) *(Typed)*	1.	2.

CORPORATE SURETY(IES)

SURETY A	NAME & ADDRESS		STATE OF INCORPORATION	LIABILITY LIMIT $	Corporate Seal
	SIGNATURE(S)	1.	2.		
	NAME(S) & TITLE(S) *(Typed)*	1.	2.		

AUTHORIZED FOR LOCAL REPRODUCTION
Previous edition is NOT usable

STANDARD FORM 25A (REV. DATE)
Prescribed by GSA-FAR (48 CFR) 53.228(c)

CORPORATE SURETY(IES) *(Continued)*					
SURETY B	NAME & ADDRESS		STATE OF INCORPORATION	LIABILITY LIMIT $	Corporate Seal
	SIGNATURE(S)	1.	2.		
	NAME(S) & TITLE(S) *(Typed)*	1.	2.		
SURETY C	NAME & ADDRESS		STATE OF INCORPORATION	LIABILITY LIMIT $	Corporate Seal
	SIGNATURE(S)	1.	2.		
	NAME(S) & TITLE(S) *(Typed)*	1.	2.		
SURETY D	NAME & ADDRESS		STATE OF INCORPORATION	LIABILITY LIMIT $	Corporate Seal
	SIGNATURE(S)	1.	2.		
	NAME(S) & TITLE(S) *(Typed)*	1.	2.		
SURETY E	NAME & ADDRESS		STATE OF INCORPORATION	LIABILITY LIMIT $	Corporate Seal
	SIGNATURE(S)	1.	2.		
	NAME(S) & TITLE(S) *(Typed)*	1.	2.		
SURETY F	NAME & ADDRESS		STATE OF INCORPORATION	LIABILITY LIMIT $	Corporate Seal
	SIGNATURE(S)	1.	2.		
	NAME(S) & TITLE(S) *(Typed)*	1.	2.		
SURETY G	NAME & ADDRESS		STATE OF INCORPORATION	LIABILITY LIMIT $	Corporate Seal
	SIGNATURE(S)	1.	2.		
	NAME(S) & TITLE(S) *(Typed)*	1.	2.		

INSTRUCTIONS

1. This form, for the protection of persons supplying labor and material, is used when a payment bond is required under 40 USC Chapter 31, Subchapter III, Bonds. Any deviation from this form will require the written approval of the Administrator of General Services.

2. Insert the full legal name and business address of the Principal in the space designated "Principal" on the face of the form. An authorized person shall sign the bond. Any person signing in a representative capacity (e.g., an attorney-in-fact) must furnish evidence of authority if that representative is not a member of the firm, partnership, or joint venture, or an officer of the corporation involved.

3. (a) Corporations executing the bond as sureties must appear on the Department of the Treasury's list of approved sureties and must act within the limitations listed therein. The value put into the LIABILITY LIMIT block is the penal sum (i.e., the face value) of the bond, unless a co-surety arrangement is proposed.

(b) When multiple corporate sureties are involved, their names and addresses shall appear in the spaces (Surety A, Surety B, etc.) headed "CORPORATE SURETY(IES)." In the space designated "SURETY(IES)" on the face of the form, insert only the letter identifier corresponding to each of the sureties. Moreover, when co-surety arrangements exist, the parties may allocate their respective limitations of liability under the bonds, provided that the sum total of their liability equals 100% of the bond penal sum.

(c) When individual sureties are involved, a completed Affidavit of Individual Surety (Standard Form 28) for each individual surety shall accompany the bond. The Government may require the surety to furnish additional substantiating information concerning its financial capability.

4. Corporations executing the bond shall affix their corporate seals. Individuals shall execute the bond opposite the words "Corporate Seal", and shall affix an adhesive seal if executed in Maine, New Hampshire, or any other jurisdiction requiring adhesive seals.

5. Type the name and title of each person signing this bond in the space provided.

STANDARD FORM 25A (REV. DATE) **BACK**

53.301-25-B Standard Form 25-B, Continuation Sheet (For Standard Forms 24, 25, and 25-A)

CONTINUATION SHEET
(For Standard Forms 24, 25 and 25-A)

NAME OF PRINCIPAL *(Legal name and business address)*	TYPE OF BOND ☐ BID ☐ PERFORMANCE ☐ PAYMENT
	FURNISHED IN CONNECTION WITH - ☐ BID ☐ CONTRACT DATED -

CORPORATE SURETY(IES)

SURETY H	Name & Address		STATE OF INC.	LIABILITY LIMIT $	
	Signature(s)	1.	2.		*Corporate Seal*
	Name(s) & Title(s) *(Typed)*	1.	2.		
SURETY I	Name & Address		STATE OF INC.	LIABILITY LIMIT $	
	Signature(s)	1.	2.		*Corporate Seal*
	Name(s) & Title(s) *(Typed)*	1.	2.		
SURETY J	Name & Address		STATE OF INC.	LIABILITY LIMIT $	
	Signature(s)	1.	2.		*Corporate Seal*
	Name(s) & Title(s) *(Typed)*	1.	2.		
SURETY K	Name & Address		STATE OF INC.	LIABILITY LIMIT $	
	Signature(s)	1.	2.		*Corporate Seal*
	Name(s) & Title(s) *(Typed)*	1.	2.		
SURETY L	Name & Address		STATE OF INC.	LIABILITY LIMIT $	
	Signature(s)	1.	2.		*Corporate Seal*
	Name(s) & Title(s) *(Typed)*	1.	2.		
SURETY M	Name & Address		STATE OF INC.	LIABILITY LIMIT $	
	Signature(s)	1.	2.		*Corporate Seal*
	Name(s) & Title(s) *(Typed)*	1.	2.		
SURETY N	Name & Address		STATE OF INC.	LIABILITY LIMIT $	
	Signature(s)	1.	2.		*Corporate Seal*
	Name(s) & Title(s) *(Typed)*	1.	2.		
SURETY O	Name & Address		STATE OF INC.	LIABILITY LIMIT $	
	Signature(s)	1.	2.		*Corporate Seal*
	Name(s) & Title(s) *(Typed)*	1.	2.		

NSN 7540-01-152-8062
PREVIOUS EDITION USABLE

25-302

STANDARD FORM 25-B (REV. 10-83)
Prescribed by GSA
FAR (48 CFR 53.228(d))

CORPORATE SURETY(IES) *(Continued)*

SURETY P	Name & Address		STATE OF INC.	LIABILITY LIMIT $		*Corporate Seal*
	Signature(s)	1.	2.			
	Name(s) & Title(s) *(Typed)*	1.	2.			
SURETY Q	Name & Address		STATE OF INC.	LIABILITY LIMIT $		*Corporate Seal*
	Signature(s)	1.	2.			
	Name(s) & Title(s) *(Typed)*	1.	2.			
SURETY R	Name & Address		STATE OF INC.	LIABILITY LIMIT $		*Corporate Seal*
	Signature(s)	1.	2.			
	Name(s) & Title(s) *(Typed)*	1.	2.			
SURETY S	Name & Address		STATE OF INC.	LIABILITY LIMIT $		*Corporate Seal*
	Signature(s)	1.	2.			
	Name(s) & Title(s) *(Typed)*	1.	2.			
SURETY T	Name & Address		STATE OF INC.	LIABILITY LIMIT $		*Corporate Seal*
	Signature(s)	1.	2.			
	Name(s) & Title(s) *(Typed)*	1.	2.			
SURETY U	Name & Address		STATE OF INC.	LIABILITY LIMIT $		*Corporate Seal*
	Signature(s)	1.	2.			
	Name(s) & Title(s) *(Typed)*	1.	2.			
SURETY V	Name & Address		STATE OF INC.	LIABILITY LIMIT $		*Corporate Seal*
	Signature(s)	1.	2.			
	Name(s) & Title(s) *(Typed)*	1.	2.			
SURETY W	Name & Address		STATE OF INC.	LIABILITY LIMIT $		*Corporate Seal*
	Signature(s)	1.	2.			
	Name(s) & Title(s) *(Typed)*	1.	2.			
SURETY X	Name & Address		STATE OF INC.	LIABILITY LIMIT $		*Corporate Seal*
	Signature(s)	1.	2.			
	Name(s) & Title(s) *(Typed)*	1.	2.			
SURETY Y	Name & Address		STATE OF INC.	LIABILITY LIMIT $		*Corporate Seal*
	Signature(s)	1.	2.			
	Name(s) & Title(s) *(Typed)*	1.	2.			

STANDARD FORM 25-B PAGE 2 (REV. 10-83)

53.301-26 Standard Form 26, Award/Contract

[FAC 2005-25, 73 FR 21783, 4/22/2008, effective 4/22/2008; FAC 2005-51, 76 FR 18322, 4/1/2011, effective 5/2/2011; FAC 2005-73, 79 FR 24192, 4/29/2014, effective 5/29/2014]

AWARD/CONTRACT

1. THIS CONTRACT IS A RATED ORDER UNDER DPAS (15 CFR 700) ▶ | RATING | PAGE OF PAGES

2. CONTRACT (*Proc. Inst. Ident.*) NO. | 3. EFFECTIVE DATE | 4. REQUISITION/PURCHASE REQUEST/PROJECT NO.

5. ISSUED BY CODE | 6. ADMINISTERED BY (*If other than Item 5*) CODE

7. NAME AND ADDRESS OF CONTRACTOR (*No., street, county, State and ZIP Code*)

CODE | FACILITY CODE

8. DELIVERY

☐ FOB ORIGIN ☐ OTHER (*See below*)

9. DISCOUNT FOR PROMPT PAYMENT

10. SUBMIT INVOICES (*4 copies unless otherwise specified*) TO THE ADDRESS SHOWN IN ▶ | ITEM

11. SHIP TO/MARK FOR CODE | 12. PAYMENT WILL BE MADE BY CODE

13. AUTHORITY FOR USING OTHER THAN FULL AND OPEN COMPETITION:

☐ 10 U.S.C. 2304(c)( ) ☐ 41 U.S.C. 3304(a)( )

14. ACCOUNTING AND APPROPRIATION DATA

15A. ITEM NO.	15B. SUPPLIES/SERVICES	15C. QUANTITY	15D.UNIT	15E. UNIT PRICE	15F. AMOUNT

15G. TOTAL AMOUNT OF CONTRACT ▶ $

16. TABLE OF CONTENTS

(X)	SEC.	DESCRIPTION	PAGE(S)	(X)	SEC.	DESCRIPTION	PAGE(S)
		PART I - THE SCHEDULE				PART II - CONTRACT CLAUSES	
	A	SOLICITATION/CONTRACT FORM			I	CONTRACT CLAUSES	
	B	SUPPLIES OR SERVICES AND PRICES/COSTS				PART III - LIST OF DOCUMENTS, EXHIBITS AND OTHER ATTACH.	
	C	DESCRIPTION/SPECS./WORK STATEMENT			J	LIST OF ATTACHMENTS	
	D	PACKAGING AND MARKING				PART IV - REPRESENTATIONS AND INSTRUCTIONS	
	E	INSPECTION AND ACCEPTANCE			K	REPRESENTATIONS, CERTIFICATIONS AND OTHER STATEMENTS OF OFFERORS	
	F	DELIVERIES OR PERFORMANCE					
	G	CONTRACT ADMINISTRATION DATA			L	INSTRS., CONDS., AND NOTICES TO OFFERORS	
	H	SPECIAL CONTRACT REQUIREMENTS			M	EVALUATION FACTORS FOR AWARD	

CONTRACTING OFFICER WILL COMPLETE ITEM 17 (SEALED-BID OR NEGOTIATED PROCUREMENT) OR 18 (SEALED-BID PROCUREMENT) AS APPLICABLE

17. ☐ CONTRACTOR'S NEGOTIATED AGREEMENT (*Contractor is required to sign this document and return ____________ copies to issuing office.*) Contractor agrees to furnish and deliver all items or perform all the services set forth or otherwise identified above and on any continuation sheets for the consideration stated herein. The rights and obligations of the parties to this contract shall be subject to and governed by the following documents: (a) this award/contract, (b) the solicitation, if any, and (c) such provisions, representations, certifications, and specifications, as are attached or incorporated by reference herein. (*Attachments are listed herein.*)

18. ☐ SEALED-BID AWARD (*Contractor is not required to sign this document.*) Your bid on Solicitation Number ____________ including the additions or changes made by you which additions or changes are set forth in full above, is hereby accepted as to the terms listed above and on any continuation sheets. This award consummates the contract which consists of the following documents: (a) the Government's solicitation and your bid, and (b) this award/contract. No further contractual document is necessary. (Block 18 should be checked only when awarding a sealed-bid contract.)

19A. NAME AND TITLE OF SIGNER (*Type or Print*) | 20A. NAME OF CONTRACTING OFFICER

19B. NAME OF CONTRACTOR | 19C. DATE SIGNED | 20B. UNITED STATES OF AMERICA | 20C. DATE SIGNED

BY ____________________ (*Signature of person authorized to sign*)

BY ____________________ (*Signature of Contracting Officer*)

AUTHORIZED FOR LOCAL REPRODUCTION
Previous edition is NOT usable

STANDARD FORM 26 (REV. 3/2013)
Prescribed by GSA - FAR (48 CFR) 53.214(a)

53.301-28 Standard Form 28, Affidavit of Individual Surety

[Final rule, 62 FR 40236, 7/25/97, effective 6/30/97; FAC 97-10, 63 FR 70264, 12/18/98, effective 1/4/99; FAC 2001-14, 68 FR 28079, 5/22/2003, effective 6/23/2003]

AFFIDAVIT OF INDIVIDUAL SURETY
(See instructions on reverse)

OMB No.: **9000-0001**

Public reporting burden for this collection of information is estimated to average 3 hours per response, including the time for reviewing instructions, searching existing data sources, gathering and maintaining the data needed, and completing and reviewing the collection of information. Send comments regarding this burden estimate or any other aspect of this collection of information, including suggestions for reducing this burden, to the Regulatory Secretariat (MVA), Office of Acquisition Policy, GSA, Washington, DC 20405.

STATE OF

SS.

COUNTY OF

I, the undersigned, being duly sworn, depose and say that I am: (1) the surety to the attached bond(s); (2) a citizen of the United States; and of full age and legally competent. I also depose and say that, concerning any stocks or bonds included in the assets listed below, that there are no restrictions on the resale of these securities pursuant to the registration provisions of Section 5 of the Securities Act of 1933. I recognize that statements contained herein concern a matter within the jurisdiction of an agency of the United States and the making of a false, fictitious or fraudulent statement may render the maker subject to prosecution under Title 18, United States Code Sections 1001 and 494. This affidavit is made to induce the United States of America to accept me as surety on the attached bond.

1. NAME *(First, Middle, Last) (Type or Print)*	2. HOME ADDRESS *(Number, Street, City, State, ZIP Code)*
3. TYPE AND DURATION OF OCCUPATION	4. NAME AND ADDRESS OF EMPLOYER *(If Self-employed, so State)*
5. NAME AND ADDRESS OF INDIVIDUAL SURETY BROKER USED *(If any)* *(Number, Street, City, State, ZIP Code)*	6. TELEPHONE NUMBER HOME - BUSINESS -

7. THE FOLLOWING IS A TRUE REPRESENTATION OF THE ASSETS I HAVE PLEDGED TO THE UNITED STATES IN SUPPORT OF THE ATTACHED BOND:

(a) Real estate *(Include a legal description, street address and other identifying description; the market value; attach supporting certified documents including recorded lien; evidence of title and the current tax assessment of the property. For market value approach, also provide a current appraisal.)*

(b) Assets other than real estate *(describe the assets, the details of the escrow account, and attach certified evidence thereof).*

8. IDENTIFY ALL MORTGAGES, LIENS, JUDGEMENTS, OR ANY OTHER ENCUMBRANCES INVOLVING SUBJECT ASSETS INCLUDING REAL ESTATE TAXES DUE AND PAYABLE.

9. IDENTIFY ALL BONDS, INCLUDING BID GUARANTEES, FOR WHICH THE SUBJECT ASSETS HAVE BEEN PLEDGED WITHIN 3 YEARS PRIOR TO THE DATE OF EXECUTION OF THIS AFFIDAVIT.

DOCUMENTATION OF THE PLEDGED ASSET MUST BE ATTACHED.

10. SIGNATURE	11. BOND AND CONTRACT TO WHICH THIS AFFIDAVIT RELATES *(Where appropriate)*

12. SUBSCRIBED AND SWORN TO BEFORE ME AS FOLLOWS:

a. DATE OATH ADMINISTERED MONTH DAY YEAR	b. CITY AND STATE *(Or other jurisdiction)*		Official Seal
c. NAME AND TITLE OF OFFICIAL ADMINISTERING OATH *(Type or print)*	d. SIGNATURE	e. MY COMMISSION EXPIRES	

AUTHORIZED FOR LOCAL REPRODUCTION
Previous edition is not usable

STANDARD FORM 28 (REV. 6/2003)
Prescribed by GSA-FAR (48 CFR) 53.228(e)

INSTRUCTIONS

1. Individual sureties on bonds executed in connection with Government contracts must complete and submit this form with the bond. (See 48 CFR 28.203, 53.228(e).) The surety must have the completed form notarized.

2. No corporation, partnership, or other unincorporated association or firm, as such, is acceptable as an individual surety. Likewise, members of a partnership are not acceptable as sureties on bonds that a partnership or an association, or any co-partner or member thereof, is the principal obligor. However, stockholders of corporate principals are acceptable provided (a) their qualifications are independent of their stockholdings or financial interest therein, and (b) that the fact is expressed in the affidavit of justification. An individual surety will not include any financial interest in assets connected with the principal on the bond that this affidavit supports.

3. United States citizenship is a requirement for individual sureties for contracts and bonds when the contract is awarded in the United States. However, when the Contracting Officer is located in an outlying area or a foreign country, the individual surety is only required to be a permanent resident of the area or country in which the contracting officer is located.

4. All signatures of the affidavit submitted must be originals. Affidavits bearing reproduced signatures are not acceptable. An authorized person must sign the bond. Any person signing in a representative capacity (e.g., an attorney-in-fact) must furnish evidence of authority if that representative is not a member of a firm, partnership, or joint venture, or an officer of the corporation involved.

STANDARD FORM 28 (REV. 6/2003) **BACK**

53.301-30 Standard Form 30, Amendment of Solicitation/ Modification of Contract

AMENDMENT OF SOLICITATION/MODIFICATION OF CONTRACT

1. CONTRACT ID CODE	PAGE OF PAGES

2. AMENDMENT/MODIFICATION NUMBER	3. EFFECTIVE DATE	4. REQUISITION/PURCHASE REQUISITION NUMBER	5. PROJECT NUMBER *(If applicable)*

6. ISSUED BY	CODE	7. ADMINISTERED BY *(If other than Item 6)*	CODE

8. NAME AND ADDRESS OF CONTRACTOR *(Number, street, county, State and ZIP Code)*	(X)	9A. AMENDMENT OF SOLICITATION NUMBER
	☐	9B. DATED *(SEE ITEM 11)*
		10A. MODIFICATION OF CONTRACT/ORDER NUMBER
	☐	10B. DATED *(SEE ITEM 13)*
CODE / FACILITY CODE		

11. THIS ITEM ONLY APPLIES TO AMENDMENTS OF SOLICITATIONS

☐ The above numbered solicitation is amended as set forth in Item 14. The hour and date specified for receipt of Offers ☐ is extended. ☐ is not extended.

Offers must acknowledge receipt of this amendment prior to the hour and date specified in the solicitation or as amended, by one of the following methods:
(a) By completing items 8 and 15, and returning ________ copies of the amendment; (b) By acknowledging receipt of this amendment on each copy of the offer submitted; or (c) By separate letter or electronic communication which includes a reference to the solicitation and amendment numbers. FAILURE OF YOUR ACKNOWLEDGMENT TO BE RECEIVED AT THE PLACE DESIGNATED FOR THE RECEIPT OF OFFERS PRIOR TO THE HOUR AND DATE SPECIFIED MAY RESULT IN REJECTION OF YOUR OFFER. If by virtue of this amendment you desire to change an offer already submitted, such change may be made by letter or electronic communication, provided each letter or electronic communication makes reference to the solicitation and this amendment, and is received prior to the opening hour and date specified.

12. ACCOUNTING AND APPROPRIATION DATA *(If required)*

13. THIS ITEM APPLIES ONLY TO MODIFICATIONS OF CONTRACTS/ORDERS. IT MODIFIES THE CONTRACT/ORDER NUMBER AS DESCRIBED IN ITEM 14.

CHECK ONE	
☐	A. THIS CHANGE ORDER IS ISSUED PURSUANT TO: *(Specify authority)* THE CHANGES SET FORTH IN ITEM 14 ARE MADE IN THE CONTRACT ORDER NUMBER IN ITEM 10A.
☐	B. THE ABOVE NUMBERED CONTRACT/ORDER IS MODIFIED TO REFLECT THE ADMINISTRATIVE CHANGES *(such as changes in paying office, appropriation data, etc.)* SET FORTH IN ITEM 14, PURSUANT TO THE AUTHORITY OF FAR 43.103(b).
☐	C. THIS SUPPLEMENTAL AGREEMENT IS ENTERED INTO PURSUANT TO AUTHORITY OF:
☐	D. OTHER *(Specify type of modification and authority)*

E. IMPORTANT: Contractor ☐ is not ☐ is required to sign this document and return ________ copies to the issuing office.

14. DESCRIPTION OF AMENDMENT/MODIFICATION *(Organized by UCF section headings, including solicitation/contract subject matter where feasible.)*

Except as provided herein, all terms and conditions of the document referenced in Item 9A or 10A, as heretofore changed, remains unchanged and in full force and effect.

15A. NAME AND TITLE OF SIGNER *(Type or print)*		16A. NAME AND TITLE OF CONTRACTING OFFICER *(Type or print)*	
15B. CONTRACTOR/OFFEROR	15C. DATE SIGNED	16B. UNITED STATES OF AMERICA	16C. DATE SIGNED
(Signature of person authorized to sign)		*(Signature of Contracting Officer)*	

Previous edition unusable

STANDARD FORM 30 (REV. 11/2016)
Prescribed by GSA FAR (48 CFR) 53.243

INSTRUCTIONS *(Back Page)*:

Instructions for items other than those that are self-explanatory, are as follows:

(a) Item 1 (Contract ID Code). Insert the contract type identification code that appears in the title block of the contract being modified.

(b) Item 3 (Effective date).

(1) For a solicitation amendment, change order, or administrative change, the effective date shall be the issue date of the amendment, change order, or administrative change.

(2) For a supplemental agreement, the effective date shall be the date agreed to by the contracting parties.

(3) For a modification issued as an initial or confirming notice of termination for the convenience of the Government, the effective date and the modification number of the confirming notice shall be the same as the effective date and modification number of the initial notice.

(4) For a modification converting a termination for default to a termination for the convenience of the Government, the effective date shall be the same as the effective date of the termination for default.

(5) For a modification confirming the contracting officer's determination of the amount due in settlement of a contract termination, the effective date shall be the same as the effective date of the initial decision.

(c) Item 6 (Issued By). Insert the name and address of the issuing office. If applicable, insert the appropriate issuing office code in the code block.

(d) Item 8 (Name and Address of Contractor). For modifications to a contract or order, enter the contractor's name, address, and code as shown in the original contract or order, unless changed by this or a previous modification.

(e) Items 9, (Amendment of Solicitation Number - Dated), and 10, (Modification of Contract/Order Number - Dated). Check the appropriate box and in the corresponding blanks insert the number and date of the original solicitation, contract, or order.

(f) Item 12 (Accounting and Appropriation Data). When appropriate, indicate the impact of the modification on each affected accounting classification by inserting one of the following entries:

(1) Accounting classification ....
Net increase $ ....

(2) Accounting classification ....
Net decrease $ ....

NOTE: If there are changes to multiple accounting classifications that cannot be placed in block 12, insert an asterisk and the words "See continuation sheet".

(g) Item 13. Check the appropriate box to indicate the type of modification. Insert in the corresponding blank the authority under which the modification is issued. Check whether or not contractor must sign this document. (See FAR 43.103.)

(h) Item 14 (Description of Amendment/Modification).

(1) Organize amendments or modifications under the appropriate Uniform Contract Format (UCF) section headings from the applicable solicitation or contract. The UCF table of contents, however, shall not be set forth in this document.

(2) Indicate the impact of the modification on the overall total contract price by inserting one of the following entries:

(i) Total contract price increased by $ ....

(ii) Total contract price decreased by $..................

(iii) Total contract price unchanged.

(3) State reason for modification.

(4) When removing, reinstating, or adding funds, identify the contract items and accounting classifications.

(5) When the SF 30 is used to reflect a determination by the contracting officer of the amount due in settlement of a contract terminated for the convenience of the Government, the entry in Item 14 of the modification may be limited to --

(i) A reference to the letter determination; and

(ii) A statement of the net amount determined to be due in settlement of the contract.

(6) Include subject matter or short title of solicitation/contract where feasible.

(i) Item 16B. The contracting officer's signature is not required on solicitation amendments. The contracting officer's signature is normally affixed last on supplemental agreements.

STANDARD FORM 30 (REV. 11/2016) **BACK**

[FAC 2005-92, 81 FR 83097, 11/18/2016, effective 12/19/2016]

53.301-33 Standard Form 33, Solicitation, Offer, and Award

[FAC 97-3, 62 FR 64912, 12/9/97, effective 2/9/98]

OMB Approved No. 9000-0008

SOLICITATION, OFFER AND AWARD	1. THIS CONTRACT IS A RATED ORDER UNDER DPAS (15 CFR 700) ▶	RATING	PAGE OF PAGES

2. CONTRACT NUMBER	3. SOLICITATION NUMBER	4. TYPE OF SOLICITATION ☐ SEALED BID (IFB) ☐ NEGOTIATED (RFP)	5. DATE ISSUED	6. REQUISITION/PURCHASE NUMBER

7. ISSUED BY CODE	8. ADDRESS OFFER TO *(If other than Item 7)*

NOTE: In sealed bid solicitations offer and offeror" mean "bid" and "bidder".

SOLICITATION

9. Sealed offers in original and ______ copies for furnishing the supplies or services in the Schedule will be received at the place specified in Item 8, or if handcarried, in the depository located in ______ until ______ local time ______
(Hour) *(Date)*

CAUTION - LATE Submissions, Modifications, and Withdrawals: See Section L, Provision No. 52.214-7 or 52.215-1. All offers are subject to all terms and conditions contained in this solicitation.

10. FOR INFORMATION CALL: ▶	A. NAME	B. TELEPHONE *(NO COLLECT CALLS)* AREA CODE / NUMBER / EXT.	C. E-MAIL ADDRESS

11. TABLE OF CONTENTS

(X)	SEC.	DESCRIPTION	PAGE(S)	(X)	SEC.	DESCRIPTION	PAGE(S)
		PART I - THE SCHEDULE				PART II - CONTRACT CLAUSES	
	A	SOLICITATION/CONTRACT FORM			I	CONTRACT CLAUSES	
	B	SUPPLIES OR SERVICES AND PRICES/COSTS				PART III - LIST OF DOCUMENTS, EXHIBITS AND OTHER ATTACH.	
	C	DESCRIPTION/SPECS./WORK STATEMENT			J	LIST OF ATTACHMENTS	
	D	PACKAGING AND MARKING				PART IV - REPRESENTATIONS AND INSTRUCTIONS	
	E	INSPECTION AND ACCEPTANCE			K	REPRESENTATIONS, CERTIFICATIONS AND OTHER	
	F	DELIVERIES OR PERFORMANCE				STATEMENTS OF OFFERORS	
	G	CONTRACT ADMINISTRATION DATA			L	INSTRS., CONDS., AND NOTICES TO OFFERORS	
	H	SPECIAL CONTRACT REQUIREMENTS			M	EVALUATION FACTORS FOR AWARD	

OFFER *(Must be fully completed by offeror)*

NOTE: Item 12 does not apply it the solicitation includes the provisions at 52.214-16, Minimum Bid Acceptance Period.

12. In compliance with the above, the undersigned agrees, if this offer is accepted within ______ calendar days *(60 calendar days unless a different period is inserted by the offeror)* from the date for receipt of offers specified above, to furnish any or all items upon which prices are offered at the price set opposite each item, delivered at the designated point(s), within the time specified in the schedule.

13. DISCOUNT FOR PROMPT PAYMENT *(See Section I, Clause No. 52-232-8)* ▶	10 CALENDAR DAYS (%)	20 CALENDAR DAYS (%)	30 CALENDAR DAYS (%)	CALENDAR DAYS (%)

14. ACKNOWLEDGMENT OF AMENDMENTS *(The offeror acknowledges receipt of amendments to the SOLICITATION for offerors and related documents numbered and dated:*	AMENDMENT NO.	DATE	AMENDMENT NO.	DATE

15A. NAME AND ADDRESS OF OFFEROR CODE / FACILITY	16. NAME AND TITLE OF PERSON AUTHORIZED TO SIGN OFFER *(Type or print)*
15B. TELEPHONE NUMBER AREA CODE / NUMBER / EXT. ☐ 15C. CHECK IF REMITTANCE ADDRESS IS DIFFERENT FROM ABOVE - ENTER SUCH ADDRESS IN SCHEDULE.	17. SIGNATURE / 18. OFFER DATE

AWARD *(To be completed by Government)*

19. ACCEPTED AS TO ITEMS NUMBERED	20. AMOUNT	21. ACCOUNTING AND APPROPRIATION

22. AUTHORITY FOR USING OTHER THAN FULL AND OPEN COMPETITION:
☐ 10 U.S.C. 2304(c)( ) ☐ 41 U.S.C. 253(c)( )

24. ADMINISTERED BY *(If other than Item 7)* CODE	23. SUBMIT INVOICES TO ADDRESS SHOWN IN *(4 copies unless otherwise specified)* ▶ ITEM
	25. PAYMENT WILL BE MADE BY CODE

26. NAME OF CONTRACTING OFFICER *(Type or print)*	27. UNITED STATES OF AMERICA *(Signature of Contracting Officer)*	28. AWARD DATE

IMPORTANT - Award will be made on this Form, or on Standard Form 26, or by other authorized official written notice.

AUTHORIZED FOR LOCAL REPRODUCTION
Previous edition is unusable

33-134

STANDARD FORM 33 (Rev. 9-97)
Prescribed by GSA - FAR CFR) 53.214(c)

53.301-34 Standard Form 34, Annual Bid Bond

[FAC 84-58, 55 FR 25543, 6/21/90, effective 7/23/90; FAC 2005-89, 81 FR 45855, 7/14/2016, effective 8/15/2016]

ANNUAL BID BOND
(See instructions on reverse)

DATE BOND EXECUTED

OMB Control Number: 9000-0045
Expiration Date: DATE

Paperwork Reduction Act Statement - This information collection meets the requirements of 44 USC § 3507, as amended by section 2 of the Paperwork Reduction Act of 1995. You do not need to answer these questions unless we display a valid Office of Management and Budget (OMB) control number. The OMB control number for this collection is 9000-0045. We estimate that it will take 60 minutes to read the instructions, gather the facts, and answer the questions. Send only comments relating to our time estimate, including suggestions for reducing this burden, or any other aspects of this collection of information to: General Services Administration, Regulatory Secretariat Division (M1V1CB), 1800 F Street, NW, Washington, DC 20405.

PRINCIPAL *(Legal name and business address)*

TYPE OF ORGANIZATION *("X" one)*
☐ INDIVIDUAL ☐ PARTNERSHIP ☐ JOINT VENTURE
☐ CORPORATION ☐ OTHER *(Specify)*

STATE OF INCORPORATION

SURETY(IES) *(Name, business address, and state of incorporation)*

PENAL SUM OF BOND

MILLION(S)	THOUSAND(S)	HUNDRED(S)	CENTS

BIDS TO BE SUBMITTED DURING FISCAL YEAR ENDING

September 30, 20 ____

AGENCY TO WHICH BIDS ARE TO BE SUBMITTED

OBLIGATION:

We, the Principal and Surety(ies), are firmly bound to the United States of America (hereinafter called the Government) in the penal sum or sums that is sufficient to indemnify the Government in case of the default of the Principal as provided herein. For payment of the penal sum or sums, we bind ourselves, our heirs, executors, administrators, and successors, jointly and severally.

CONDITIONS:

The Principal contemplates submitting bids from time to time during the fiscal year shown above to the department or agency named above for furnishing supplies or services to the Government. The Principal desires that all of those bids submitted for opening during the fiscal year be covered by a single bond instead of by a separate bid bond for each bid.

THEREFORE:

The above obligation is void and of no effect if the Principal - (a) upon acceptance by the Government of any such bid within the period specified therein for acceptance (sixty (60) days if no period is specified), executes the further contractual documents and gives the bond(s) required by the terms of the bid as accepted within the time specified (ten (10) days if no period is specified) after receipt of forms by the Principal; or (b) in the event of failure to execute the further contractual documents and give the bond(s), pays the Government for any cost of acquiring the work which exceeds the amount of the bid.

WITNESS:

The Principal and Surety(ies) executed this bid bond and affixed their seals on the above date.

SIGNATURES	NAMES AND TITLES *(Typed)*	
	PRINCIPAL	
1. (Seal)	1.	Corporate Seal
2. (Seal)	2.	
3. (Seal)	3.	
	INDIVIDUAL SURETIES	
1. (Seal)	1.	
2. (Seal)	2.	
	CORPORATE SURETY	
1.	1.	Corporate Seal
2.	2.	

AUTHORIZED FOR LOCAL REPRODUCTION
Previous edition is NOT usable

STANDARD FORM 34 (REV. DATE)
Prescribed by GSA - FAR (48 CFR) 53.228(f)

INSTRUCTIONS

1. This form is authorized for use in the acquisition of supplies and services, excluding construction, in lieu of Standard Form 24 (Bid Bond). Any deviation from this form will require the written approval of the Administrator of General Services.

2. Insert the full legal name and business address of the Principal in the space designated "Principal" on the face of the form. An authorized person shall sign the bond. Any person signing in a representative capacity (e.g., an attorney-in-fact) must furnish evidence of authority if that representative is not a member of the firm, partnership, or joint venture, or an officer of the corporation involved.

3. (a) Corporations executing the bond as sureties must appear on the Department of the Treasury's list of approved sureties and must act within the limitations listed therein.

(b) When individual sureties are involved, a completed Affidavit of Individual Surety (Standard Form 28) for each individual surety shall accompany the bond. The Government may require the surety to furnish additional substantiating information concerning its financial capability.

4. Corporations executing the bond shall affix their corporate seals. Individuals shall execute the bond opposite the word "Corporate Seal", and shall affix an adhesive seal if executed in Maine, New Hampshire, or any other jurisdiction requiring adhesive seals.

5. Type the name and title of each person signing this bond in the space provided.

6. In its application to negotiated contracts, the terms "bid" and "bidder" shall include "proposal" and "offeror."

STANDARD FORM 34 (REV. DATE) **BACK**

53.301-35 Annual Performance Bond

[FAC 84-58, 55 FR 25546, 6/21/90, effective 7/23/90; FAC 2005-89, 81 FR 45855, 7/14/2016, effective 8/15/2016]

ANNUAL PERFORMANCE BOND
(See instructions on reverse)

DATE BOND EXECUTED

OMB Control Number: 9000-0045
Expiration Date: DATE

Paperwork Reduction Act Statement - This information collection meets the requirements of 44 USC § 3507, as amended by section 2 of the Paperwork Reduction Act of 1995. You do not need to answer these questions unless we display a valid Office of Management and Budget (OMB) control number. The OMB control number for this collection is 9000-0045. We estimate that it will take 25 minutes to read the instructions, gather the facts, and answer the questions. Send only comments relating to our time estimate, including suggestions for reducing this burden, or any other aspects of this collection of information to: General Services Administration, Regulatory Secretariat Division (M1V1CB), 1800 F Street, NW, Washington, DC 20405.

PRINCIPAL *(Legal name and business address)*

TYPE OF ORGANIZATION *("X" one)*

☐ INDIVIDUAL ☐ PARTNERSHIP ☐ JOINT VENTURE

☐ CORPORATION ☐ OTHER *(Specify)*

STATE OF INCORPORATION

SURETY(IES) *(Name(s) and business address(es))*

PENAL SUM OF BOND			
MILLION(S)	THOUSAND(S)	HUNDRED(S)	CENTS

FISCAL YEAR ENDING

September 30, 20___

AGENCY REPRESENTING THE GOVERNMENT

OBLIGATION:

We, the Principal and Surety(ies), are firmly bound to the United States of America (hereinafter called the Government) in the above penal sum. For payment of the penal sum, we bind ourselves, our heirs, executors, administrators, and successors, jointly and severally.

CONDITIONS:

The Principal contemplates entering into contracts, from time to time during the fiscal year shown above, with the Government department or agency shown above, for furnishing supplies or services to the Government. The Principal desires that all of those contracts be covered by one bond instead of by a separate performance bond for each contract.

THEREFORE:

The above obligation is void if the Principal - (a) performs and fulfills all the undertakings, covenants, terms, conditions, and agreements of any and all of those contracts entered into during the original term and any extensions granted by the Government with or without notice to the surety(ies) and during the life of any guaranty required under the contracts; and (b) performs and fulfills all the undertakings, covenants, terms, conditions, and agreements of any and all duly authorized modifications of those contracts, that subsequently are made. Notice of those modifications to the surety(ies) is waived.

WITNESS:

The Principal and Surety(ies) executed this performance bond and affixed their seals on the above date.

SIGNATURES	NAMES AND TITLES *(Typed)*	
PRINCIPAL		
1. (Seal)	1.	Corporate Seal
2. (Seal)	2.	
3. (Seal)	3.	
INDIVIDUAL SURETIES		
1. (Seal)	1.	
2. (Seal)	2.	
CORPORATE SURETY		
1.	1.	Corporate Seal
2.	2.	

AUTHORIZED FOR LOCAL REPRODUCTION
Previous edition is NOT usable

STANDARD FORM 35 (REV. DATE)
Prescribed by GSA - FAR (48 CFR) 53.228(g)

INSTRUCTIONS

1. This form is authorized for use in the acquisition of supplies and services, excluding construction, in lieu of Standard Form 25 (Performance Bond). Any deviation from this form will require the written approval of the Administrator of General Services.

2. Insert the full legal name and business address of the Principal in the space designated "Principal" on the face of the form. An authorized person shall sign the bond. Any person signing in a representative capacity (e.g., an attorney-in-fact) must furnish evidence of authority if that representative is not a member of the firm, partnership, or joint venture, or an officer of the corporation involved.

3. (a) Corporations executing the bond as sureties must appear on the Department of the Treasury's list of approved sureties and must act within the limitations listed therein.

(b) When individual sureties are involved, a completed Affidavit of Individual Surety (Standard Form 28) for each individual surety shall accompany the bond. The Government may require the surety to furnish additional substantiating information concerning its financial capability.

4. Corporations executing the bond shall affix their corporate seals. Individuals shall execute the bond opposite the word "Corporate Seal"; and shall affix an adhesive seal if executed in Maine, New Hampshire, or any other jurisdiction requiring adhesive seals.

5. Type the name and title of each person signing this bond in the space provided.

6. In its application to negotiated contracts, the terms "bid" and "bidder" shall include "proposal" and "offeror".

STANDARD FORM 35 (REV. DATE) **BACK**

53.301-44 Standard Form 44, Purchase Order—Invoice Voucher

U.S. GOVERNMENT

PURCHASE ORDER - INVOICE - VOUCHER

Anyone who finds this booklet, please notify:

OFFICE:

TELEPHONE NUMBER:

NSN 7540-01-152-8068
PREVIOUS EDITION USABLE
44-108

STANDARD FORM 44 (Rev. 10-83)
PRESCRIBED BY GSA,
FAR (48 CFR) 53.213(c)

INSTRUCTIONS

(This form is for official Government use only)

1. Filling in the Form

(a) All copies of the form must be legible. To insure legibility, indelible pencil or ball-point pen should be used. SELLER'S NAME AND ADDRESS MUST BE PRINTED.

(b) Items ordered will be individually listed. General descriptions such as "hardware" are not acceptable. Show discount terms.

(c) Enter project reference or other identifying description in space captioned "PURPOSE." Also, enter proper accounting information, if known.

2. Distributing Copies

Copy No. 1 - Give to seller for use as the invoice or as an attachment to his commercial invoice.

Copy No. 2 - Give to seller for use as a record of the order.

Copy No. 3 -

(1) On over-the-counter transactions where delivery has been made, complete receiving report section and forward this copy to the proper administrative office.

(2) On other than completed over-the-counter transactions, forward this copy to location specified for delivery. (Upon delivery, receiving report section is to be completed and this copy then forwarded to the proper administrative office.)

Copy No. 4 - Retain in the book, unless otherwise instructed.

3. When Paying Cash at Time of Purchase

(a) Enter the amount of cash paid and obtain seller's signature in the space provided in the Seller section of Copy No. 1. If seller prefers to provide a commercial cash receipt, attach it to Copy No. 1 and check the "paid in cash" block at the bottom of the form.

(b) Distribution of copies when payment is by cash is the same as described above, except that Copy No. 1 is retained by Government representative when cash payment is made. Copy No. 1 is used thereafter in accordance with agency instructions pertaining to handling receipts for cash payment.

U.S. GOVERNMENT

PURCHASE ORDER - INVOICE - VOUCHER

DATE OF ORDER	ORDER NO.

PAYEE — PRINT NAME AND ADDRESS OF SELLER (Number, Street, City, and State)*

FURNISH SUPPLIES OR SERVICES TO (Name and address)*

SUPPLIES OR SERVICES	QUANTITY	UNIT PRICE	AMOUNT

PAYOR — AGENCY NAME AND BILLING ADDRESS*

TOTAL

DISCOUNT TERMS

.... % .... DAYS

DATE INVOICE RECEIVED

ORDERED BY (Signature and title)

PURPOSE AND ACCOUNTING DATA

PURCHASER - *To sign below for over-the-counter delivery of items*

RECEIVED BY

TITLE | DATE

SELLER - *Please read instructions on Copy 2*

☐ PAYMENT RECEIVED **$** .... ☐ PAYMENT REQUESTED **$** ....

NO FURTHER INVOICE NEED BE SUBMITTED

SELLER | DATE

BY ....

(Signature)

I certify that this account is correct and proper for payment in the amount of

$ ....

(Authorized certifying officer)

DIFFERENCES

ACCOUNT VERIFIED: CORRECT FOR

BY ....

PAID BY ☐ **CASH** **OR** *(Check No.)* | **DATE PAID** | **VOUCHER NO.**

***PLEASE INCLUDE ZIP CODE**

1. SELLER'S INVOICE *(See Instructions on Copy 2)*

STANDARD FORM 44a (Rev. 10-83) PRESCRIBED BY GSA, FAR (48 CFR) 53.213(c)

U.S. GOVERNMENT

PURCHASE ORDER - INVOICE - VOUCHER

DATE OF ORDER	ORDER NO.

PRINT NAME AND ADDRESS OF SELLER (Number, Street, City, and State)*

P A Y E E

FURNISH SUPPLIES OR SERVICES TO (Name and address)*

SUPPLIES OR SERVICES	QUANTITY	UNIT PRICE	AMOUNT

AGENCY NAME AND BILLING ADDRESS*

P A Y O R

TOTAL

DISCOUNT TERMS

.... % .... DAYS

DATE INVOICE RECEIVED

ORDERED BY (Signature and title)

PURPOSE AND ACCOUNTING DATA

PURCHASER - *To sign below for over-the-counter delivery of items*

RECEIVED BY

TITLE | DATE

SELLER - *Please read instructions on Copy 2*

☐ PAYMENT RECEIVED $ .... ☐ PAYMENT REQUESTED $ ....

NO FURTHER INVOICE NEED BE SUBMITTED

SELLER | DATE

BY ....

(*Signature*)

INSTRUCTIONS TO SELLER

After satisfactory identification of the Government representative presenting this purchase order, verify the itemization, including quantity, unit price, amount, total and discount sections.

This form is so designed that Copy 1 may be used as a cash payment receipt or as your invoice by completing, as appropriate, either the Payment Received or Payment Request blocks and signing the Seller Section.

If you would rather submit your own invoice, DO NOT SIGN COPY 1, but attach it unsigned to your invoice to expedite verification and processing for payment.

2. SELLER'S COPY OF ORDER

STANDARD FORM 44b (Rev. 10-83)
PRESCRIBED BY GSA,
FAR (48 CFR) 53.213(c)

U.S. GOVERNMENT

PURCHASE ORDER - INVOICE - VOUCHER

DATE OF ORDER	ORDER NO.

PRINT NAME AND ADDRESS OF SELLER (Number, Street, City, and State)*

P A Y E E

FURNISH SUPPLIES OR SERVICES TO (Name and address)*

SUPPLIES OR SERVICES	QUANTITY	UNIT PRICE	AMOUNT

AGENCY NAME AND BILLING ADDRESS*

P A Y O R

TOTAL

DISCOUNT TERMS

.... % .... DAYS

DATE INVOICE RECEIVED

ORDERED BY (Signature and title)

PURPOSE AND ACCOUNTING DATA

PURCHASER - *To sign below for over-the-counter delivery of items*

RECEIVED BY

TITLE | DATE

SELLER - *Please read instructions on Copy 2*

☐ PAYMENT RECEIVED $ .... ☐ PAYMENT REQUESTED $ ....

NO FURTHER INVOICE NEED BE SUBMITTED

SELLER | DATE

BY ....

(*Signature*)

REMARKS

DIFFERENCES

ACCOUNT VERIFIED: CORRECT FOR

BY ....

3. RECEIVING REPORT - ACCOUNTING COPY

STANDARD FORM 44c (Rev. 10-83)
PRESCRIBED BY GSA
FAR (48 CFR) 53.213(c)

U.S. GOVERNMENT

PURCHASE ORDER - INVOICE - VOUCHER

DATE OF ORDER | ORDER NO.

PRINT NAME AND ADDRESS OF SELLER (Number, Street, City, and State)*

PAYEE

FURNISH SUPPLIES OR SERVICES TO (Name and address)*

SUPPLIES OR SERVICES	QUANTITY	UNIT PRICE	AMOUNT

AGENCY NAME AND BILLING ADDRESS*

PAYOR

TOTAL

DISCOUNT TERMS

.... % .... DAYS

DATE INVOICE RECEIVED

ORDERED BY (Signature and title)

PURPOSE AND ACCOUNTING DATA

PURCHASER - *To sign below for over-the-counter delivery of items*

RECEIVED BY

TITLE | DATE

SELLER - *Please read instructions on Copy 2*

☐ PAYMENT RECEIVED $ .... ☐ PAYMENT REQUESTED $ ....

NO FURTHER INVOICE NEED BE SUBMITTED

SELLER | DATE

BY ....

(Signature)

REMARKS

4. MEMORANDUM COPY *(Optional Use)*

STANDARD FORM 44d (Rev. 10-83)
PRESCRIBED BY GSA,
FAR (48 CFR) 53.213(c)

RECORD OF PURCHASES

ORDER NO.	NAME OF CONTRACTOR	DATE OF PURCHASE	AMOUNT

53.301-98 [Removed]

[FAC 2005-10, 71 FR 36930, 6/28/2006, effective 6/28/2006]

53.301-98a [Removed]

[FAC 2005-10, 71 FR 36930, 6/28/2006, effective 6/28/2006]

53.301-99 [Removed]

[FAC 2005-10, 71 FR 36930, 6/28/2006, effective 6/28/2006]

53.301-120 Standard Form 120, Report of Excess Personal Property

PAGE 1 OF

STANDARD FORM 120 REV.
APRIL 1957
GEN. SERV. ADMIN.
FPMR (41 CFR) 101 - 43.311

REPORT OF EXCESS PERSONAL PROPERTY

1. REPORT NO.

2. DATE MAILED

3. TOTAL COST $

4. TYPE OF REPORT (Check one only of "a", "b", "c", or "d") — a. ORIGINAL / b. CORRECTED / c. PARTIAL W/D / d. TOTAL W/D (Also check "e" and/or "f" if appropriate) — e. OVERSEAS / f. CONTRACTORS INV

5. TO (Name and Address of Agency to which report is made) THRU

6. APPROP. OR FUND TO BE REIMBURSED (If any)

7. FROM (Name and Address of Reporting Agency)

8. REPORT APPROVED BY (Name and Title)

9. FOR FURTHER INFORMATION CONTACT (Title, Address and Telephone No.)

10. AGENCY APPROVAL (If applicable)

11. SEND PURCHASE ORDERS OR DISPOSAL INSTRUCTIONS TO (Title, Address and Telephone No.)

12. GSA CONTROL NO.

13. FSC GROUP NO.

14. LOCATION OF PROPERTY (If location is to be abandoned give date)

15. REIM/REQD — YES / NO

16. AGENCY CONTROL NO.

17. SURPLUS RELEASE DATE

18. EXCESS PROPERTY LIST

ITEM NO. (a)	DESCRIPTION (b)	COND. (c)	UNIT (d)	NUMBER OF UNITS (e)	ACQUISITION COST PER UNIT (f)	ACQUISITION COST TOTAL (g)	FAIR VALUE % (h)

STANDARD FORM 120 REV. APRIL 1957 EDITION

(Use Standard Form 120A for Continuation Sheets)
NSN 7540-00-634-4074

120-105

PREVIOUS EDITION USABLE

53.301-120-A Standard Form 120-A, Continuation Sheet (Report of Excess Personal Property)

STANDARD FORM 120-A
APRIL 1957
GEN. SERV. ADMIN.
FPMR (41 CFR) 101-43.311

CONTINUATION SHEET
(Report of Excess Personal Property)

PAGE ______

FROM *(Name and Address of Reporting Agency)*

REPORT NO.

AGENCY CONTROL NO.

EXCESS PROPERTY LIST *(Continued)*

ITEM NO. (a)	DESCRIPTION (b)	COND. (c)	UNIT (d)	NUMBER OF UNITS (e)	ACQUISITION COST		FAIR VALUE % (h)
					PER UNIT (f)	TOTAL (g)	

STANDARD FORM 120A
APRIL 1957 EDITION

120-204

53.301-126 Standard Form 126, Report of Personal Property for Sale

REPORT OF PERSONAL PROPERTY FOR SALE — PAGE 1 OF

1. FROM (NAME, ADDRESS AND ZIP CODE OF OWNING AGENCY)
2. REPORT NO.
3. DATE
4. FSC GROUP
5. TOTAL ACQUISITION COST
6. PUBLIC MAY INSPECT PROPERTY BY CONTACTING (NAME, ADDRESS, ZIP CODE AND TELEPHONE NO.)
7. PROPERTY LOCATED AT

8. TO
General Services Administration

9. LOADING BY GOV'T
a. ACTIVITY WILL LOAD FOR PURCHASER ☐ (1) YES ☐ (2) NO
b. EXTENT (IF CHECKED "YES")

10. PROPERTY IS EXCHANGE/SALE ☐ a. YES ☐ b. NO
11. PROPERTY IS REIMBURSABLE ☐ a. YES ☐ b. NO

12. SEND EXECUTED SALES DOCUMENTS TO (NAME, ADDRESS AND ZIP CODE)
13. DEPOSIT PROCEEDS TO (APPROPRIATE FUND SYMBOL AND TITLE)
14. STATION DEPOSIT SYMBOL OR STATION ACCOUNT NUMBER

15. UTILIZATION AND DONATION SCREENING REQUIREMENTS COMPLETED. PROPERTY IS AVAILABLE FOR SALE ➤ BY (SIGNATURE AND TITLE)

16. **PROPERTY LIST** *(USE CONTINUATION SHEET, IF NECESSARY)*

ITEM NO. (a)	ITEM NO. ASSIGNED BY GSA (b)	COMMERCIAL DESCRIPTION AND CONDITION (c)	UNIT (d)	NUMBER OF UNITS (e)	ACQUISITION COST PER UNIT (f)	ACQUISITION COST TOTAL (g)

17. RECEIPT OF PROPERTY AT GSA SALES SITE OR CENTER ACKNOWLEDGED
SIGNATURE AND TITLE | DATE

18. RECEIPT OF REPORT IS HEREBY ACKNOWLEDGED
SIGNATURE AND TITLE | DATE

FOR GSA INTERNAL USE ONLY

19. SALE NO.
20. TYPE OF SALE
21. INSPECTION DATES
22. BID OPENING DATE AND TIME

126-103

STANDARD FORM 126 (REV. 7-78)
Prescribed by GSA, FPMR (41 CFR) 101-45.303

53.301-126-A Standard Form 126-A, Report of Personal Property for Sale (Continuation Sheet)

Standard Form 126-A
February 1965
Prescribed by General Services Administration
FPMR (41 CFR) 101-45.303

REPORT OF PERSONAL PROPERTY FOR SALE
(CONTINUATION SHEET)

PAGE OF PAGES

FROM (Name and address of owning agency. Please include ZIP Code) | FSC GROUP | REPORT NO.

PROPERTY LIST

ITEM NO. (a)	ITEM NO. ASSIGNED BY GSA (b)	COMMERCIAL DESCRIPTION AND CONDITION (c)	UNIT (d)	NUMBER OF UNITS (e)	ACQUISITION COST PER UNIT (f)	ACQUISITION COST TOTAL (g)

126-201

53.301-129 [Removed]

[FAC 90-45, Final rule, 62 FR 224, 1/2/97, effective 1/1/97; FAC 2001-15, 68 FR 43854, 7/24/2003, effective 8/25/2003]

53.301-252 Standard Form 252, Architect-Engineer Contract

ARCHITECT-ENGINEER CONTRACT	1. CONTRACT NO. 2. DATE OF CONTRACT
3A. NAME OF ARCHITECT-ENGINEER	3B. TELEPHONE NO. *(include Area Code)*
3C. ADDRESS OF ARCHITECT-ENGINEER *(Include ZIP Code)*	
4. DEPARTMENT OR AGENCY AND ADDRESS *(Include ZIP Code)*	
5. PROJECT TITLE AND LOCATION	
6. CONTRACT FOR *(General description of services to be provided)*	
7. CONTRACT AMOUNT *(Express in words and figures)*	
8. NEGOTIATION AUTHORITY	
9. ADMINISTRATIVE, APPROPRIATION, AND ACCOUNTING DATA	

NSN 7540-01-152-8072
PREVIOUS EDITION NOT USABLE

252-102

STANDARD FORM 252 (REV. 10-83)
Prescribed by GSA
FAR (48 CFR) 53.236-2(a)

10. The United States of America (called the Government) represented by the Contracting Officer executing this contract, and the Architect-Engineer agree to perform this contract in strict accordance with the clauses and the documents identified as follows, all of which are made a part of this contract:

If the parties to this contract are comprised of more than one legal entity, each entity shall be jointly and severally liable under this contract.
The parties hereto have executed this contract as of the date recorded in Item 2.

	SIGNATURES	NAMES AND TITLES *(Typed)*
11. ARCHITECT-ENGINEER OR OTHER PROFESSIONAL SERVICES CONTRACTOR		
A		
B		
C		
D		
12. THE UNITED STATES OF AMERICA		
		Contracting Officer

STANDARD FORM 252 PAGE 2 (REV. 10-83)

53.301-254 [Removed]

[Final rule, FAC 90-20, 59 FR 11368, 3/10/94, effective 3/10/94; [Removed] FAC 2001-24, 69 FR 34244, 6/18/2004, effective 6/18/2004]

53.301-255 [Removed]

[Final rule, FAC 90-20, 59 FR 11368, 3/10/94, effective 3/10/94; [Removed] FAC 2001-24, 69 FR 34244, 6/18/2004, effective 6/18/2004]

53.301-273 Standard Form 273, Reinsurance Agreement for a Bond Statute Performance Bond

[FAC 2005-73, 79 FR 24192, 4/29/2014, effective 5/29/2014]

REINSURANCE AGREEMENT FOR A BONDS STATUTE PERFORMANCE BOND
(See instructions on reverse)

OMB Number: 9000-0045
Expiration Date: 6/30/2016

PAPERWORK REDUCTION ACT STATEMENT: Public reporting burden for this collection of information is estimated to average 60 minutes per response, including the time for reviewing instructions, searching existing data sources, gathering and maintaining the data needed, and completing and reviewing the collection of information. Send comments regarding this burden estimate or any other aspects of this collection of information, including suggestions for reducing this burden, to U.S. General Services Administration, Regulatory Secretariat (MVCB)/IC 9000-0045, Office of Governmentwide Acquisition Policy,1800 F Street, NW, Washington, DC 20405.

1. DIRECT WRITING COMPANY*	1A. DATE DIRECT WRITING COMPANY EXECUTES THIS AGREEMENT
	1B. STATE OF INCORPORATION
2. REINSURING COMPANY*	2A. AMOUNT OF THIS REINSURANCE ($)
	2B. DATE REINSURING COMPANY EXECUTES THIS AGREEMENT
	2C. STATE OF INCORPORATION

3. DESCRIPTION OF CONTRACT		4. DESCRIPTION OF BOND	
3A. AMOUNT OF CONTRACT		4A. PENAL SUM OF BOND	
3B. CONTRACT DATE	3C. CONTRACT NO.	4B. DATE OF BOND	4C. BOND NO.
3D. DESCRIPTION OF CONTRACT		4D. PRINCIPAL*	
3E. CONTRACTING AGENCY		4E. STATE OF INCORPORATION (*If Corporate Principal*)	

AGREEMENT:

(a) The Direct Writing Company named above is bound as surety to the United States of America on the performance bond described above, wherein the above described is the principal, for the protection of the United States on the contract described above. The contract is for the construction, alteration, or repair of a public building or public work of the United States, and the performance bond was furnished to the United States under 40 U.S.C. chapter 31, subchapter III, Bonds, known as the Bonds Statute. The Direct Writing Company has applied to the Reinsuring Company named above to be reinsured and countersecured in the amount shown opposite the name of the Reinsuring Company (referred to as the "Amount of this Reinsurance"), or for whatever amount less than the "Amount of this Reinsurance" the Direct Writing Company is liable to pay under or by virtue of the performance bond.

(b) For a sum mutually agreed upon, paid by the Direct Writing Company to the Reinsuring Company which acknowledges its receipt, the parties to this Agreement covenant and agree to the terms and conditions of the agreement.

TERMS AND CONDITIONS:

(a) The purpose and intent of this agreement is to guarantee and indemnify the United States against loss under the performance and to the extent of the "Amount of this Reinsurance," or any sum less than the "Amount of this Reinsurance" that is owing and unpaid by the Direct Writing Company to the United States under the performance bond.

(b) If the Direct Writing Company fails to pay any default under the performance bond equal to or in excess of the "Amount of this Reinsurance," the Reinsuring Company covenants and agrees to pay to the United States, the obligee on the performance bond, the "Amount of this Reinsurance." If the Direct Writing Company fails to pay to the United States any default for a sum less than the "Amount of this Reinsurance" the Reinsuring Company covenants and agrees to pay to the United States the full amount of the default, or so much thereof that is not paid to the United States by the Direct Writing Company.

(c) If there is a default on the performance bond for the "Amount of this Reinsurance," or more, the Reinsuring Company and the Direct Writing Company hereby covenant and agree that the United States may bring suit against the Reinsuring Company for the "Amount of this Reinsurance" or, in case the amount of the default is for less than the "Amount of this Reinsurance," for the full amount of the default.

WITNESS:

The Direct Writing Company and the Reinsuring Company, respectively, have caused this Agreement to be signed and impressed with their respective corporate seals by officers possessing power to sign this instrument, and to be duly attested by officers empowered thereto, on the day and date above written opposite their respective names.

**Items 1, 2, 4D - Furnish legal name, business address and ZIP Code.* (Over)

AUTHORIZED FOR LOCAL REPRODUCTION
Previous edition is usable

STANDARD FORM 273 (REV. 4-2013)
Prescribed by GSA - FAR (48 CFR) 53.228(h)

5. DIRECT WRITING COMPANY		
5A(1) SIGNATURE	(2) ATTEST: SIGNATURE	Corporate Seal
5B(1) NAME AND TITLE *(Typed)*	(2) NAME AND TITLE *(Typed)*	

6. REINSURING COMPANY		
6A (1) SIGNATURE	(2) ATTEST: SIGNATURE	Corporate Seal
6B(1) NAME AND TITLE *(Typed)*	(2) NAME AND TITLE *(Typed)*	

INSTRUCTIONS

This form is to be used in cases where it is desired to cover the excess of a Direct Writing Company's underwriting limitation by reinsurance instead of co-insurance on Bonds Statute performance bonds running to the United States. See FAR (48 CFR) 28.202-1 and 53.228(h).

Execute and file this form as follows:

Original and copies (as specified by the bond-approving officer), signed and sealed, shall accompany the bond or be filed within the time period shown in the bid or proposal.

One copy, signed and sealed, shall accompany the Direct Writing Company's quarterly Schedule of Excess Risks filed with the Department of the Treasury.

Other copies may be prepared for the use of the Direct Writing Company and Reinsuring Company. Each Reinsuring Company should use a separate form.

STANDARD FORM 273 (REV. 4/2013) BACK

53.301-274 Standard Form 274, Reinsurance Agreement for a Bond Statute Payment Bond

[FAC 2005-73, 79 FR 24192, 4/29/2014, effective 5/29/2014]

REINSURANCE AGREEMENT FOR A BONDS STATUTE PAYMENT BOND
(See instruction on reverse)

OMB Control Number: 9000-0045
Expiration Date: 6/30/2016

PAPERWORK REDUCTION ACT STATEMENT: Public reporting burden for this collection of information is estimated to average 60 minutes per response, including the time for reviewing instructions, searching existing data sources, gathering and maintaining the data needed, and completing and reviewing the collection of information. Send comments regarding this burden estimate or any other aspects of this collection of information, including suggestions for reducing this burden, to U.S. General Services Administration, Regulatory Secretariat (MVCB)/IC 9000-0045, Office of Governmentwide Acquisition Policy,1800 F Street, NW, Washington, DC 20405.

1. DIRECT WRITING COMPANY*	1A. DATE DIRECT WRITING COMPANY EXECUTES THIS AGREEMENT
	1B. STATE OF INCORPORATION
2. REINSURING COMPANY*	2A. AMOUNT OF THIS REINSURANCE $
	2B. DATE REINSURING COMPANY EXECUTES THIS AGREEMENT
	2C. STATE OF INCORPORATION

3. DESCRIPTION OF CONTRACT		4. DESCRIPTION OF BOND	
3A. AMOUNT OF CONTRACT		4A. PENAL SUM OF BOND	
3B. CONTRACT DATE	3C. CONTRACT NO.	4B. DATE OF BOND	4C. BOND NO.
3D. DESCRIPTION OF CONTRACT		4D. PRINCIPAL*	
3E. CONTRACTING AGENCY		4E. STATE OF INCORPORATION *(If Corporate Principal)*	

AGREEMENT:

(a) The Direct Writing Company named above is bound as a surety on the payment bond described above, wherein the above described is the principal, for the protection of all persons supplying labor and material on the contract described above, which is for the construction, alteration, or repair of a public building or public work of the United States. The payment bond is for the use of persons supplying labor or material, and is furnished to the United States under 40 U.S.C. chapter 31, subchapter III, Bonds, known as the Bonds Statute. The Direct Writing Company has applied to the Reinsuring Company named above to be reinsured and countersecured in the amount above opposite the name of the Reinsuring Company (referred to as "Amount of this Reinsurance"), or for whatever amount less than the "Amount of this Reinsurance" the Direct Writing Company is liable to pay under or by virtue of the payments bond.

(b) For a sum mutually agreed upon, paid by the Direct Writing Company to the Reinsuring Company which acknowledges its receipt, the parties to this Agreement covenant and agree to the terms and conditions of this agreement.

TERMS AND CONDITIONS:

The purpose and intent of this agreement is (a) to guarantee and indemnify the persons who have furnished or supplied labor or material in the prosecution of the work provided for in the contract referred to above (hereinafter referred to as "laborers and materialmen," the term "materialmen" including persons having a direct contractual relation with a subcontractor but no contractual relationship expressed or implied with the contractor who has furnished the said payment bond) against loss under the payment bond to the extent of the "Amount of this Reinsurance," or for any sum less than the "Amount of this Reinsurance," that is owing and unpaid by the Direct Writing Company to the "laborers and materialmen" on the payment bond; and (b) to make the "laborers and materialmen" obligees under this Reinsurance Agreement to the same extent as if their respective names were written herein.

THEREFORE:

1. The Reinsuring Company covenants and agrees -

(a) To pay the "Amount of this Reinsurance" to the "laborers and materialmen" in the event of the Direct Writing Company's failure to pay to the "laborers and materialmen" any default under the payment bond equal to or in excess of the "Amount of this Reinsurance;" and

(b) To pay (1) the full amount to the "laborers and materialmen," or (2) the amount not paid to them by the Direct Writing Company, in case the Direct Writing Company fails to pay the "laborers and materialmen" any default under the payment bond less than the "Amount of this Reinsurance."

*Items 1, 2 ,4D - furnished legal name, business address and ZIP Code. *(Over)*

AUTHORIZED FOR LOCAL REPRODUCTION
Previous edition is usable

STANDARD FORM 274 (REV. 4-2013)
Prescribed by GSA - FAR (48 CFR) 53.228(l)

2. The Reinsuring Company and the Direct Writing Company covenant and agree that, in the case of default on the payment bond for the "Amount of this Reinsurance," or more, the persons given a "right of action" or a "right to sue" on the payment bond by 40 U.S.C. 3133 may bring suit against the Reinsuring Company in the United States District Court for the district in which the contract described above is to be performed and executed for the "Amount of this Reinsurance" or, if the amount of the default is for less than the "Amount of this Reinsurance," for whatever the full amount of the default may be. The Reinsuring Company further covenants and agrees to comply with all requirements necessary to give such court jurisdiction, and to consent to determination of matters arising under this Reinsurance Agreement in accordance with the law and practice of the court. It is expressly understood by the parties that the rights, powers, and privileges given in this paragraph to persons are in addition to or supplemental to or in accordance with other rights, powers, and privileges which they might have under the statutes of the United States, any States, or the other laws of either, and should not be construed as limitations.

3. The Reinsuring Company and the Direct Writing Company further covenant and agree that the Reinsuring Company designates the process agent, appointed by the Direct Writing Company in the district in which the contract is to be performed and executed, as an agent to accept service of process in any suit instituted on this Reinsurance Agreement, and that the process agent shall send, by registered mail, to the Reinsuring Company at its principal place of business shown above, a copy of the process.

4. The Reinsuring Company and the Direct Writing Company further covenant and agree that this Reinsurance Agreement is an integral part of the payment bond.

WITNESS:

The Direct Writing Company and the Reinsuring Company, respectively, have caused this Agreement to be signed and impressed with their respective corporate seals by officers possessing the power to sign this instrument, and to be duly attested to by officers empowered thereto, on the day and date in item 1A written opposite their respective names.

5. DIRECT WRITING COMPANY		
5A. (1) SIGNATURE	(2) ATTEST SIGNATURE	*Corporate*
5B. (1) NAME AND TITLE *(Typed)*	(2) NAME AND TITLE *(Typed)*	*Seal*

6. REINSURING COMPANY		
6A. (1) SIGNATURE	(2) ATTEST SIGNATURE	*Corporate*
6B. (1) NAME AND TITLE *(Typed)*	(2) NAME AND TITLE *(Typed)*	*Seal*

INSTRUCTIONS

This form is to be used in cases where it is desired to cover the excess of a Direct Writing Company's underwriting limitation by reinsurance instead of co-insurance on Bonds Statute payment bonds running to the United States. See FAR (48 CFR) 28.202-1 and 53.228(i).

Execute and file this form as follows:

Original and copies (as specified by the bond-approving officer), signed and sealed, shall accompany the bond or be filed within the time period shown in bid or proposal.

One copy, signed and sealed, shall accompany the Direct Writing Company's quarterly Schedule of Excess Risks filled with the Department of Treasury.

Other copies may be prepared for the use of the Direct Writing Company and Reinsuring Company. Each Reinsuring Company should use a separate form.

STANDARD FORM 274 (REV. 4-2013) BACK

53.301-275 Standard Form 275, Reinsurance Agreement in Favor of the United States

[FAC 97-10, 63 FR 70264, 12/18/98, effective 1/4/99]

REINSURANCE AGREEMENT IN FAVOR OF THE UNITED STATES *(See instructions on reverse)*	OMB No.: 9000-0045

Public reporting burden for this collection of information is estimated to average 25 minutes per response, including the time for reviewing instructions, searching existing data sources, gathering and maintaining the data needed, and completing and reviewing the collection of information. Send comments regarding this burden estimate or any other aspect of this collection of information, including suggestions for reducing this burden, to the FAR Secretariat (MVR), Federal Acquisition Policy Division, GSA, Washington, DC 20405.

1. DIRECT WRITING COMPANY*	1A. DATE DIRECT WRITING COMPANY EXECUTES THIS AGREEMENT
	1B. STATE OF INCORPORATION
2. REINSURING COMPANY*	2A. AMOUNT OF THIS REINSURANCE ($)
	2B. DATE REINSURING COMPANY EXECUTES THIS AGREEMENT
	2C. STATE OF INCORPORATION

3. DESCRIPTION OF BOND		
3A. DESCRIPTION OF BOND *(Type, purpose etc.) (If associated with contract number, date, amount, etc., include name of Government agency involved.)*	3B. PENAL SUM OF BOND $	
	3C. DATE OF BOND	3D. BOND NO.
	3E. PRINCIPAL*	
	3F. STATE OF INCORPORATION *(If Corporate Principal)*	

AGREEMENT:

(a) The Direct Writing Company named above is bound as surety to the United States of America, on the bond described above, wherein the above-named is the principal. The bond is given for the protection of the United States and the Direct Writing Company has applied to the above Reinsuring Company to be reinsured and counter-secured in the amount shown opposite the name of the Reinsuring Company (referred to as the "Amount of this Reinsurance"), or for whatever amount less than the "Amount of this Reinsurance" the Direct Writing Company is liable to pay under or by virtue of the bond.

(b) For a sum mutually agreed upon, paid by the Direct Writing Company to the Reinsuring Company which acknowledges its receipt, the parties to this Agreement covenant and agree to the terms and conditions of this agreement.

TERMS AND CONDITIONS:

The purpose and intent of this agreement is to guarantee and indemnify the United States against loss under the bond to the extent of the "Amount of this Reinsurance," or for any less sum than the "Amount of this Reinsurance," that is owing and unpaid by the Direct Writing Company to the United States.

THEREFORE:

1. If the Direct Writing Company fails to pay any default under the bond equal to or in excess of the "Amount of this Reinsurance," the Reinsuring Company covenants and agrees to pay to the United States, the obligee on the bond, the "Amount of this Reinsurance." If the Direct Writing Company fails to pay to the United States any default for a sum less than the "Amount of this Reinsurance," the Reinsuring Company covenants and agrees to pay to the United States the full amount of the default, or so much thereof that is not paid to the United States by the Direct Writing Company.

2. The Reinsuring Company further covenants and agrees that in case of default on the bond for the "Amount of this Reinsurance," or more, the United States may sue the Reinsuring Company for the "Amount of this Reinsurance" or for the full amount of the default when the default is less than the "Amount of this Reinsurance."

WITNESS

The Direct Writing Company and the Reinsuring Company, respectively, have caused this Agreement to be signed and impressed with their respective corporate seals by officers possessing power to sign this instrument, and to be duly attested to by officers empowered thereto, on the day and date above -- written opposite their respective names.

(Over)

**Items 1, 2, 3E - Furnish legal name, business address and ZIP Code.*

AUTHORIZED FOR LOCAL REPRODUCTION
Previous edition usable

STANDARD FORM 275 (REV. 10-98)
Prescribed by GSA-FAR (48 CFR) 53.228(j)

4. DIRECT WRITING COMPANY		
4A.(1). SIGNATURE	(2). ATTEST: SIGNATURE	Corporate Seal
4B.(1) NAME AND TITLE *(Typed)*	4B.(2). NAME AND TITLE *(Typed)*	

5. REINSURING COMPANY		
5A.(1). SIGNATURE	(2). ATTEST: SIGNATURE	Corporate Seal
5B.(1). NAME AND TITLE *(Typed)*	5B.(2). NAME AND TITLE *(Typed)*	

INSTRUCTIONS

This form is to be used in cases where it is desired to cover the excess of a Direct Writing Company's underwriting limitation by reinsurance instead of co-insurance on bonds running to the United States except Miller Act Performance and Payment Bonds. See FAR (48 CFR) 28.202-1 and 53.228(j) and 31 CFR 223.11(b)(1). If this form is used to reinsure a bid bond, the "Penal Sum of Bond" and "Amount of this Reinsurance" may be expressed as percentage of the bid provided the actual amounts will not exceed the companies' respective underwriting limitations.

Execute and file this form as follows:

Original and copies (as specified by the bond-approving officer), signed and sealed, shall accompany the bond or be filed within the time period shown in the bid or proposal.

One carbon copy, signed and sealed, shall accompany the Direct Writing Company's quarterly Schedule of Excess Risks filed with the Department of Treasury.

Other copies may be prepared for the use of the Direct Writing Company and Reinsuring Company. Each Reinsuring Company should use a separate form.

STANDARD FORM 275 (REV. 10-98) **BACK**

53.301-279 [Removed]

[FAC 2001-02, 66 FR 65347, 12/18/2001, effective 2/19/2002; FAC 2001-18, 68 FR 69248, 12/11/2003, effective 12/11/2003]

53.301.281 [Removed]

[Removed, FAC 2001-18, 68 FR 69248, 12/11/2003, effective 12/11/2003]

53.301-294 Subcontracting Report for Individual Contracts

SUBCONTRACTING REPORT FOR INDIVIDUAL CONTRACTS
(See instructions on reverse)

OMB Control Number: 9000-0006
Expiration Date: 2/28/2019

Paperwork Reduction Act Statement - This information collection meets the requirements of 44 USC § 3507, as amended by section 2 of the Paperwork Reduction Act of 1995. You do not need to answer these questions unless we display a valid Office of Management and Budget (OMB) control number. The OMB control number for this collection is 9000-0006. We estimate that it will take 13.5 hours to read the instructions, gather the facts, and answer the questions. Send only comments relating to our time estimate, including suggestions for reducing this burden, or any other aspects of this collection of information to: General Services Administration, Regulatory Secretariat Division (M1V1CB), 1800 F Street, NW, Washington, DC 20405.

1. CORPORATION, COMPANY, OR SUBDIVISION COVERED
a. COMPANY NAME
b. STREET ADDRESS
c. CITY | d. STATE | e. ZIP CODE

2. CONTRACTOR IDENTIFICATION NUMBER

3. DATE SUBMITTED

4. REPORTING PERIOD FROM INCEPTION OF CONTRACT THRU:
☐ MAR 31 ☐ SEPT 30 YEAR

5. TYPE OF REPORT
☐ REGULAR ☐ FINAL ☐ REVISED

6. ADMINISTERING ACTIVITY *(Please check applicable box)*

☐ ARMY ☐ GSA ☐ NASA
☐ NAVY ☐ DOE ☐ OTHER FEDERAL AGENCY *(Specify)*
☐ AIR FORCE ☐ DEFENSE CONTRACT MANAGEMENT AGENCY

7. REPORT SUBMITTED AS *(Check one and provide appropriate number)*
☐ PRIME CONTRACTOR — PRIME CONTRACT NUMBER
☐ SUBCONTRACTOR — SUBCONTRACT NUMBER

8. AGENCY OR CONTRACTOR AWARDING CONTRACT
a. AGENCY'S OR CONTRACTOR'S NAME
b. STREET ADDRESS
c. CITY | d. STATE | e. ZIP CODE

9. DOLLARS AND PERCENTAGES IN THE FOLLOWING BLOCKS:
☐ DO INCLUDE INDIRECT COSTS ☐ DO NOT INCLUDE INDIRECT COSTS

SUBCONTRACT AWARDS

TYPE	CURRENT GOAL		ACTUAL CUMULATIVE	
	WHOLE DOLLARS	PERCENT	WHOLE DOLLARS	PERCENT
10a. SMALL BUSINESS CONCERNS *(Dollar Amount and Percent of 10c.)* (SEE SPECIFIC INSTRUCTIONS)				
10b. LARGE BUSINESS CONCERNS *(Dollar Amount and Percent of 10c.)* (SEE SPECIFIC INSTRUCTIONS)				
10c. TOTAL *(Sum of 10a and 10b.)*		100.0%		100.0%
11. SMALL DISADVANTAGED BUSINESS (SDB) CONCERNS *(Dollar Amount and Percent of 10c.)* (SEE SPECIFIC INSTRUCTIONS)				
12. WOMEN-OWNED SMALL BUSINESS (WOSB) CONCERNS *(Dollar Amount and Percent of 10c.)* (SEE SPECIFIC INSTRUCTIONS)				
13. HISTORICALLY BLACK COLLEGES AND UNIVERSITIES (HBCU) AND MINORITY INSTITUTIONS (MI) *(If applicable) (Dollar Amount and Percent of 10c.)* (SEE SPECIFIC INSTRUCTIONS)				
14. HUBZone SMALL BUSINESS (HUBZone SB) CONCERNS *(Dollar Amount and Percent of 10c.)* (SEE SPECIFIC INSTRUCTIONS)				
15. VETERAN-OWNED SMALL BUSINESS CONCERNS *(Dollar Amount and Percent of 10c.)* (SEE SPECIFIC INSTRUCTIONS)				
16. SERVICE-DISABLED VETERAN-OWNED SMALL BUSINESS CONCERNS *(Dollar Amount and Percent of 10c)* (SEE SPECIFIC INSTRUCTIONS)				
17. ALASKA NATIVE CORPORATIONS (ANCs) AND INDIAN TRIBES THAT HAVE NOT BEEN CERTIFIED BY THE SMALL BUSINESS ADMINISTRATION AS SMALL DISADVANTAGED BUSINESSES *(Dollar Amount)* (SEE SPECIFIC INSTRUCTIONS)				
18. ALASKA NATIVE CORPORATIONS (ANCs) AND INDIAN TRIBES THAT ARE NOT SMALL BUSINESSES *(Dollar Amount)* (SEE SPECIFIC INSTRUCTIONS)				

Previous Edition is NOT Usable

STANDARD FORM 294 (REV. 8/2016)
Prescribed by GSA-FAR (48 CFR 53.219)

19. REMARKS		
20a. NAME OF INDIVIDUAL ADMINISTERING SUBCONTRACTING PLAN	**20b. TELEPHONE NUMBER**	
	AREA CODE	NUMBER

STANDARD FORM 294 (REV. 8/2016) **PAGE 2**

GENERAL INSTRUCTIONS

1. This report is not required for small businesses.

2. This report is not required for commercial items for which a commercial plan has been approved, nor from large businesses in the Department of Defense (DOD) Test Program for Negotiation of Comprehensive Subcontracting plans. The Summary Subcontract Report (SSR) is required for contractors operating under one of these two conditions and should be submitted to the Government in accordance with the instructions on that form.

3. This form collects subcontract award data from prime contractors/ subcontractors that : (a) hold one or more contracts over $700,000 (over $1,500,000 for construction of a public facility); and (b) are required to report subcontracts awarded to Small Business (SB), Small Disadvantaged Business (SDB), Women-Owned Small Business (WOSB), HUBZone Small Business (HUBZone SB), Veteran-Owned Small Business (VOSB) and Service-Disabled Veteran-Owned Small Business concerns under a subcontracting plan. For the Department of Defense (DOD), the National Aeronautics and Space Administration (NASA), and the Coast Guard, this form also collects subcontract award data for Historically Black Colleges and Universities (HBCUs) and Minority Institutions (MIs).

4. This report is required for each contract containing a subcontracting plan and must be submitted to the administrative contracting officer (ACO) or contracting officer if no ACO is assigned, semi-annually, during contract performance for the periods ended March 31st and September 30th. A separate report is required for each contract at contract completion. Reports are due 30 days after the close of each reporting period unless otherwise directed by the contracting officer. Reports are required when due, regardless of whether there has been any subcontracting activity since the inception of the contract or since the previous report.

5. Only subcontracts involving performance in the United States or its outlying areas should be included in this report with the exception of subcontracts under a contract awarded by the State Department or any other agency that has statutory or regulatory authority to require subcontracting plans for subcontracts performed outside the United States and its outlying areas.

6. Purchases from a corporation, company, or subdivision that is an affiliate of the prime/subcontractor are not included in this report.

7. Subcontract award data reported on this form by prime contractors/ subcontractors shall be limited to awards made to their immediate subcontractors. Credit cannot be taken for awards made to lower tier subcontractors unless you have been designated to receive an SB and SDB credit from an Alaska Native Corporation (ANC) or Indian tribe.

8. FAR 19.703 sets forth the eligibility requirements for participating in the subcontracting program.

9. Actual achievements must be reported on the same basis as the goals set forth in the contract. For example, if goals in the plan do not include indirect and overhead items, the achievements shown on this report should not include them either.

SPECIFIC INSTRUCTIONS

BLOCK 2: For the Contractor Identification Number, enter the unique entity identifier that identifies the specific contractor establishment. If there is no unique entity identifier that identifies the exact name and address entered in Block 1, contact the entity designated at SAM for establishment of the unique entity identifier.

BLOCK 4: Check only one. Note that all subcontract award data reported on this form represents activity since the inception of the contract through the date indicated on this block.

BLOCK 5: Check whether this report is a "Regular," "Final," and/or "Revised" report. A "Final" report should be checked only if the contractor has completed the contract or subcontract reported in Block 7. A "Revised" report is a change to a report previously submitted for the same period.

BLOCK 6: Identify the department or agency administering the majority of subcontracting plans.

BLOCK 7: Indicate whether the reporting contractor is submitting this report as a prime contractor or subcontractor and the prime contract or subcontract number.

BLOCK 8: Enter the name and address of the Federal department or agency awarding the contract or the prime contractor awarding the subcontract.

BLOCK 9: Check the appropriate block to indicate whether indirect costs are included in the dollar amounts in blocks 10a through 16. To ensure comparability between the goal and actual columns, the contractor may include indirect costs in the actual column only if the subcontracting plan included indirect costs in the goal.

BLOCKS 10a through 18: Under "Current Goal," enter the dollar and percent goals in each category (SB, SDB, WOSB, VOSB, service-disabled VOSB, and HUBZone SB) from the subcontracting plan approved for this contract. (If the original goals agreed upon at contract award have been revised as a result of contract modifications, enter the original goals in Block 19. The amounts entered in Blocks 10a through 16 should reflect the revised goals.) There are no goals for Blocks 17 and 18. Under "Actual Cumulative," enter actual subcontract achievements (dollars and percent) from the inception of the contract through the date of the report shown in Block 4. In cases where indirect costs are included, the amounts should include both direct awards and an appropriate prorated portion of indirect awards. However, the dollar amounts reported under "Actual Cumulative" must be for the same period of time as the dollar amounts shown under "Current Goal." For a contract with options, the current goal should represent the aggregate goal since the inception of the contract. For example, if the contractor is submitting the report during Option 2 of a multiple year contract, the current goal would be the cumulative goal for the base period plus the goal for Option 1 and the goal for Option 2.

BLOCK 10a: Report all subcontracts awarded to SBs including subcontracts to SDBs, WOSB, VOSB, service-disabled VOSB, and HUBZone SBs. For DOD, NASA, and Coast Guard contracts, include subcontracting awards to HBCUs and MIs. Include subcontracts awarded to ANCs and Indian tribes that are not small businesses and that are not certified by the SBA as SDBs where you have been designated to receive their SB and SDB credit. Where your company and other companies have been designated by an ANC or Indian tribe to receive SB and SDB credit for a subcontract awarded to the ANC or Indian tribe, report only the portion of the total amount of the subcontract that has been designated to your company.

BLOCK 10b: Report all subcontracts awarded to large businesses (LBs) and any other-than-small businesses. Do not include subcontracts awarded to ANCs and Indian tribes that have been reported in 10a above.

BLOCK 10c: Report on this line the total of all subcontracts awarded under this contract (the sum of lines 10a and 10b).

BLOCKS 11 - 16: Each of these items is a subcategory of Block 10a. Note that in some cases the same dollars may be reported in more than one block (e.g., SDBs owned by women or veterans).

BLOCK 11: Report all subcontracts awarded to SDBs (including WOSB, VOSB, service-disabled VOSBs, and HUBZone SB SDBs). Include subcontracts awarded to ANCs and Indian tribes that have not been certified by SBA as SDBs where you have been designated to receive their SDB credit. Where your company and other companies have been designated by an ANC or Indian tribe to receive their SDB credit for a subcontract awarded to the ANC or Indian tribe, report only the portion of the total amount of the subcontract that has been designated to your company. For DoD, NASA, and Coast Guard contracts, include subcontracting awards to HBCUs and MIs.

BLOCK 12: Report all subcontracts awarded to WOSBs (including SDBs, VOSBs (including service-disabled VOSBs), and HUBZone SBs that are also WOSBs).

BLOCK 13: (For contracts with DoD, NASA, and Coast Guard): Report all subcontracts with HBCUs/MIs. Complete the column under "Current Goal" only when the subcontracting plan establishes a goal.

BLOCK 14: Report all subcontracts awarded to HUBZone SBs (including WOSBs, VOSBs (including service-disabled VOSBs), and SDBs that are also HUBZone SBs).

BLOCK 15: Report all subcontracts awarded to VOSBs including service-disabled VOSBs (and including SDBs, WOSBs, and HUBZone SBs that are also VOSBs).

BLOCK 16: Report all subcontracts awarded to service-disabled VOSBs (including SDBs, WOSBs, and HUBZone SBs that are also service-disabled VOSBs).

BLOCK 17: Report all subcontracts awarded to ANCs and Indian tribes that are reported in Block 11, but have not been certified by SBA as SDBs.

STANDARD FORM 294 (REV. 8/2016) **PAGE 3**

BLOCK 18: Report all subcontracts awarded to ANCs and Indian tribes that are reported in Block 10a, but are not small businesses.

BLOCK 19: Enter a short narrative explanation if (a) SB, SDB, WOSB, VOSB, service-disabled VOSB, or HUBZone SB accomplishments fall below that which would be expected using a straight-line projection of goals through the period of contract performance; or (b) if this is a final report, any one of the six goals were not met.

DEFINITIONS

1. Direct Subcontract Awards are those that are identified with the performance of one or more specific Government contract(s).

2. Indirect costs are those which, because of incurrence for common or joint purposes, are not identified with specific Government contracts; these awards are related to Government contract performance but remain for allocation after direct awards have been determined and identified to specific Government contracts.

DISTRIBUTION OF THIS REPORT

For the Awarding Agency or Contractor:

The original copy of this report should be provided to the contracting officer at the agency or contractor identified in Block 8. For contracts with DOD, a copy should also be provided to the Defense Contract Management Agency (DCMA) at the cognizant Defense Contract Management Area Operations (DCMAO) office.

For the Small Business Administration (SBA):

A copy of this report must be provided to the cognizant Commercial Market Representative (CMR) at the time of a compliance review. It is NOT necessary to mail the SF 294 to SBA unless specifically requested by the CMR.

STANDARD FORM 294 (REV. 8/2016) **PAGE 4**

[FAC 90-43, Interim rule, 61 FR 67408, 12/20/96, effective 12/20/96, finalized without change, FAC 97-4, 63 FR 9048, 2/23/98, effective 4/24/98; FAC 97-5, 63 FR 34058, 6/22/98, effective 8/21/98; FAC 97-10, 63 FR 70264, 12/18/98, effective 1/4/99; FAC 97-20, 65 FR 60542, 10/11/2000, effective 10/11/2000; FAC 2001-01, 66 FR 53478, 10/22/2001, effective 10/22/2001; FAC 2005-13, 71 FR 57363, 9/28/2006, 9/28/2006; FAC 2005-19, 72 FR 46345, 8/17/2007, effective 9/17/2007; Removed, FAC 2005-25, 73 FR 21779, 4/22/2008, effective 4/22/2008; FAC 2005-42, 75 FR 34260, 6/16/2010, effective 7/16/2010; FAC 2005-77, 79 FR 61746, 10/14/2014, effective 10/14/2014; FAC 2005-83, 80 FR 38293, 7/2/2015, effective 10/1/2015; FAC 2005-91, 81 FR 67736, 9/30/2016, effective 10/31/2016]

53.301-295 [Removed]

[FAC 90-43, Interim rule, 61 FR 67408, 12/20/96, effective 12/20/96, finalized without change, FAC 97-4, 63 FR 9048, 2/23/98, effective 4/24/98; FAC 97-5, 63 FR 34058, 6/22/98, effective 8/21/98; FAC 97-10, 63 FR 70264, 12/18/98, effective 1/4/99; FAC 97-20, 65 FR 60542, 10/11/2000, effective 10/11/2000; FAC 2001-01, 66 FR 53478, 10/22/2001, effective 10/22/2001; FAC 2005-13, 71 FR 57363, 9/28/2006, effective 9/28/2006; FAC 2005-19, 72 FR 46345, 8/17/2007, effective 9/17/2007; Removed, FAC 2005-25, 73 FR 21779, 4/22/2008, effective 4/22/2008; FAC 2005-42, 75 FR 34260, 6/16/2010, effective 7/16/2010]

53.301-298 Standard Form 298, Report Documentation Page

[FAC 84-56, 55 FR 3890, 2/5/90, effective 3/7/90]

REPORT DOCUMENTATION PAGE

Form Approved
OMB No. 0704-0188

The public reporting burden for this collection of information is estimated to average 1 hour per response, including the time for reviewing instructions, searching existing data sources, gathering and maintaining the data needed, and completing and reviewing the collection of information. Send comments regarding this burden estimate or any other aspect of this collection of information, including suggestions for reducing the burden, to Department of Defense, Washington Headquarters Services, Directorate for Information Operations and Reports (0704-0188), 1215 Jefferson Davis Highway, Suite 1204, Arlington, VA 22202-4302. Respondents should be aware that notwithstanding any other provision of law, no person shall be subject to any penalty for failing to comply with a collection of information if it does not display a currently valid OMB control number.

PLEASE DO NOT RETURN YOUR FORM TO THE ABOVE ADDRESS.

1. REPORT DATE *(DD-MM-YYYY)*
2. REPORT TYPE
3. DATES COVERED *(From - To)*
4. TITLE AND SUBTITLE
5a. CONTRACT NUMBER
5b. GRANT NUMBER
5c. PROGRAM ELEMENT NUMBER
6. AUTHOR(S)
5d. PROJECT NUMBER
5e. TASK NUMBER
5f. WORK UNIT NUMBER
7. PERFORMING ORGANIZATION NAME(S) AND ADDRESS(ES)
8. PERFORMING ORGANIZATION REPORT NUMBER
9. SPONSORING/MONITORING AGENCY NAME(S) AND ADDRESS(ES)
10. SPONSOR/MONITOR'S ACRONYM(S)
11. SPONSOR/MONITOR'S REPORT NUMBER(S)
12. DISTRIBUTION/AVAILABILITY STATEMENT
13. SUPPLEMENTARY NOTES
14. ABSTRACT
15. SUBJECT TERMS

16. SECURITY CLASSIFICATION OF:			17. LIMITATION OF ABSTRACT	18. NUMBER OF PAGES	19a. NAME OF RESPONSIBLE PERSON
a. REPORT	b. ABSTRACT	c. THIS PAGE			19b. TELEPHONE NUMBER *(Include area code)*

Standard Form 298 (Rev. 8/98)
Prescribed by ANSI Std. Z39.18

INSTRUCTIONS FOR COMPLETING SF 298

1. REPORT DATE. Full publication date, including day, month, if available. Must cite at least the year and be Year 2000 compliant, e.g. 30-06-1998; xx-06-1998; xx-xx-1998.

2. REPORT TYPE. State the type of report, such as final, technical, interim, memorandum, master's thesis, progress, quarterly, research, special, group study, etc.

3. DATES COVERED. Indicate the time during which the work was performed and the report was written, e.g., Jun 1997 - Jun 1998; 1-10 Jun 1996; May - Nov 1998; Nov 1998.

4. TITLE. Enter title and subtitle with volume number and part number, if applicable. On classified documents, enter the title classification in parentheses.

5a. CONTRACT NUMBER. Enter all contract numbers as they appear in the report, e.g. F33615-86-C-5169.

5b. GRANT NUMBER. Enter all grant numbers as they appear in the report, e.g. AFOSR-82-1234.

5c. PROGRAM ELEMENT NUMBER. Enter all program element numbers as they appear in the report, e.g. 61101A.

5d. PROJECT NUMBER. Enter all project numbers as they appear in the report, e.g. 1F665702D1257; ILIR.

5e. TASK NUMBER. Enter all task numbers as they appear in the report, e.g. 05; RF0330201; T4112.

5f. WORK UNIT NUMBER. Enter all work unit numbers as they appear in the report, e.g. 001; AFAPL30480105.

6. AUTHOR(S). Enter name(s) of person(s) responsible for writing the report, performing the research, or credited with the content of the report. The form of entry is the last name, first name, middle initial, and additional qualifiers separated by commas, e.g. Smith, Richard, J, Jr.

7. PERFORMING ORGANIZATION NAME(S) AND ADDRESS(ES). Self-explanatory.

8. PERFORMING ORGANIZATION REPORT NUMBER. Enter all unique alphanumeric report numbers assigned by the performing organization, e.g. BRL-1234; AFWL-TR-85-4017-Vol-21-PT-2.

9. SPONSORING/MONITORING AGENCY NAME(S) AND ADDRESS(ES). Enter the name and address of the organization(s) financially responsible for and monitoring the work.

10. SPONSOR/MONITOR'S ACRONYM(S). Enter, if available, e.g. BRL, ARDEC, NADC.

11. SPONSOR/MONITOR'S REPORT NUMBER(S). Enter report number as assigned by the sponsoring/ monitoring agency, if available, e.g. BRL-TR-829; -215.

12. DISTRIBUTION/AVAILABILITY STATEMENT. Use agency-mandated availability statements to indicate the public availability or distribution limitations of the report. If additional limitations/ restrictions or special markings are indicated, follow agency authorization procedures, e.g. RD/FRD, PROPIN, ITAR, etc. Include copyright information.

13. SUPPLEMENTARY NOTES. Enter information not included elsewhere such as: prepared in cooperation with; translation of; report supersedes; old edition number, etc.

14. ABSTRACT. A brief (approximately 200 words) factual summary of the most significant information.

15. SUBJECT TERMS. Key words or phrases identifying major concepts in the report.

16. SECURITY CLASSIFICATION. Enter security classification in accordance with security classification regulations, e.g. U, C, S, etc. If this form contains classified information, stamp classification level on the top and bottom of this page.

17. LIMITATION OF ABSTRACT. This block must be completed to assign a distribution limitation to the abstract. Enter UU (Unclassified Unlimited) or SAR (Same as Report). An entry in this block is necessary if the abstract is to be limited.

Standard Form 298 Back (Rev. 8/98)

53.301-308 Standard Form 308, Request for Determination and Response to Request

[FAC 2005-73, 79 FR 24192, 4/29/2014, effective 5/29/2014]

Request For Wage Determination And Response To Request
(Construction Wage Rate Requirements Statute and Related Statutes)

U.S. Department of Labor
Wage and Hour Division

FOR DEPARTMENT OF LABOR USE

Response To Request

☐ Use area determination issued for this area

☐ The attached decision noted below is applicable to this project

Decision Number

Date of Decision

Expires

Supersedes Decision Number

Approved

Mail Your Request To:
U.S. Department of Labor
Wage and Hour Division
Branch of Construction Contract Wage Determinations
Washington, D.C. 20210

Requesting Officer (Typed name *and signature*)

Department, Agency, or Bureau		Phone Number
Date of Request	Estimated Advertising Date	Estimated Bid Opening Date
Prior Decision Number (if any)	Estimated $ Value of Contract ☐ Under 1/2 Mil ☐ 1 to 5 Mil ☐ 1/2 to 1 Mil ☐ Over 5 Mil	Type of Work ☐ Bldg. ☐ Highway ☐ Resid. ☐ Heavy

Address to which wage determination should be mailed. (Print or type)

Location of Project (*City, County, State, Zip Code*)

Description of Work (*Be specific*) (*Print or type*)

CHECK OR LIST CRAFTS NEEDED
(Attach continuation sheet if needed)

- Asbestos workers
- Boilermakers
- Bricklayers
- Carpenters
- Cement masons
- Electricians
- Glaziers
- Ironworkers
- Laborers (Specify classes)
- Lathers
- Marble & tile setters, terrazzo workers
- Painters
- Piledrivermen
- Plasterers
- Plumbers
- Roofers
- Sheet metal workers
- Soft floor layers
- Steamfitters
- Welders-rate for craft
- Truck drivers
- Power equipment operators (*Specify types*)

Other Crafts

Standard Form 308 (Rev. 2/2013)
U.S. Department of Labor -29 CFR Part 1

53.301-330 Architect-Engineer Qualifications

ARCHITECT-ENGINEER QUALIFICATIONS

OMB Control Number: 9000-0157
Expiration Date: 11/30/2017

Paperwork Reduction Act Statement - This information collection meets the requirements of 44 USC § 3507, as amended by section 2 of the Paperwork Reduction Act of 1995. You do not need to answer these questions unless we display a valid Office of Management and Budget (OMB) control number. The OMB control number for this collection is 9000-0157. We estimate that it will take 29 hours (25 hours for part 1 and 4 hours for Part 2) to read the instructions, gather the facts, and answer the questions. Send only comments relating to our time estimate, including suggestions for reducing this burden, or any other aspects of this collection of information to: General Services Administration, Regulatory Secretariat Division (M1V1CB), 1800 F Street, NW, Washington, DC 20405.

PURPOSE

Federal agencies use this form to obtain information from architect-engineer (A-E) firms about their professional qualifications. Federal agencies select firms for A-E contracts on the basis of professional qualifications as required by 40 U.S.C. chapter 11, Selection of Architects Engineers, and Part 36 of the Federal Acquisition Regulation (FAR).

The Selection of Architects and Engineers statute requires the public announcement of requirements for A-E services (with some exceptions provided by other statutes), and the selection of at least three of the most highly qualified firms based on demonstrated competence and professional qualifications according to specific criteria published in the announcement. The Act then requires the negotiation of a contract at a fair and reasonable price starting first with the most highly qualified firm.

The information used to evaluate firms is from this form and other sources, including performance evaluations, any additional data requested by the agency, and interviews with the most highly qualified firms and their references.

GENERAL INSTRUCTIONS

Part I presents the qualifications for a specific contract.

Part II presents the general qualifications of a firm or a specific branch office of a firm. Part II has two uses:

1. An A-E firm may submit Part II to the appropriate central, regional or local office of each Federal agency to be kept on file. A public announcement is not required for certain contracts, and agencies may use Part II as a basis for selecting at least three of the most highly qualified firms for discussions prior to requesting submission of Part I. Firms are encouraged to update Part II on file with agency offices, as appropriate, according to FAR Part 36. If a firm has branch offices, submit a separate Part II for each branch office seeking work.

2. Prepare a separate Part II for each firm that will be part of the team proposed for a specific contract and submitted with Part I. If a firm has branch offices, submit a separate Part II for each branch office that has a key role on the team.

INDIVIDUAL AGENCY INSTRUCTIONS

Individual agencies may supplement these instructions. For example, they may limit the number of projects or number of pages submitted in Part I in response to a public announcement for a particular project. Carefully comply with any agency instructions when preparing and submitting this form. Be as concise as possible and provide only the information requested by the agency.

DEFINITIONS

Architect-Engineer Services: Defined in FAR 2.101.

Branch Office: A geographically distinct place of business or subsidiary office of a firm that has a key role on the team.

Discipline: Primary technical capabilities of key personnel, as evidenced by academic degree, professional registration, certification, and/or extensive experience.

Firm: Defined in FAR 36.102.

Key Personnel: Individuals who will have major contract responsibilities and/or provide unusual or unique expertise.

SPECIFIC INSTRUCTIONS

Part I - Contract-Specific Qualifications

Section A. Contract Information.

1. Title and Location. Enter the title and location of the contract for which this form is being submitted, exactly as shown in the public announcement or agency request.

2. Public Notice Date. Enter the posted date of the agency's notice on the Federal Business Opportunity website (FedBizOpps), other form of public announcement or agency request for this contract.

3. Solicitation or Project Number. Enter the agency's solicitation number and/or project number, if applicable, exactly as shown in the public announcement or agency request for this contract.

Section B. Architect-Engineer Point of Contact.

4-8. Name, Title, Name of Firm, Telephone Number, Fax (Facsimile) Number and E-mail (Electronic Mail) Address. Provide information for a representative of the prime contractor or joint venture that the agency can contact for additional information.

AUTHORIZED FOR LOCAL REPRODUCTION

STANDARD FORM 330 (REV. 8/2016) PAGE 1 OF INSTRUCTIONS
Prescribed by GSA - FAR (48 CFR) 53.236-2(b)

Section C. Proposed Team.

9-11. Firm Name, Address, and Role in This Contract. Provide the contractual relationship, name, full mailing address, and a brief description of the role of each firm that will be involved in performance of this contract. List the prime contractor or joint venture partners first. If a firm has branch offices, indicate each individual branch office that will have a key role on the team. The named subcontractors and outside associates or consultants must be used, and any change must be approved by the contracting officer. (See FAR Part 52 Clause "Subcontractors and Outside Associates and Consultants (Architect-Engineer Services)"). Attach an additional sheet in the same format as Section C if needed.

Section D. Organizational Chart of Proposed Team.

As an attachment after Section C, present an organizational chart of the proposed team showing the names and roles of all key personnel listed in Section E and the firm they are associated with as listed in Section C.

Section E. Resumes of Key Personnel Proposed for this Contract.

Complete this section for each key person who will participate in this contract. Group by firm, with personnel of the prime contractor or joint venture partner firms first. The following blocks must be completed for each resume:

12. Name. Self-explanatory.

13. Role in this contract. Self-explanatory.

14. Years Experience. Total years of relevant experience (block 14a), and years of relevant experience with current firm, but not necessarily the same branch office (block 14b).

15. Firm Name and Location. Name, city and state of the firm where the person currently works, which must correspond with one of the firms (or branch office of a firm, if appropriate) listed in Section C.

16. Education. Provide information on the highest relevant academic degree(s) received. Indicate the area(s) of specialization for each degree.

17. Current Professional Registration. Provide information on current relevant professional registration(s) in a State or possession of the United States, Puerto Rico, or the District of Columbia according to FAR Part 36.

18. Other Professional Qualifications. Provide information on any other professional qualifications relating to this contract, such as education, professional registration, publications, organizational memberships, certifications, training, awards, and foreign language capabilities.

19. Relevant Projects. Provide information on up to five projects in which the person had a significant role that demonstrates the person's capability relevant to her/his proposed role in this contract. These projects do not necessarily have to be any of the projects presented in Section F for the project team if the person was not involved in any of those projects or the person worked on other projects that were more relevant than the team projects in Section F. Use the check box provided to indicate if the project was performed with any office of the current firm. If any of the professional services or construction projects are not complete, leave Year Completed blank and indicate the status in Brief Description and Specific Role (block (3)).

Section F. Example Projects Which Best Illustrate Proposed Team's Qualifications for this Contract.

Select projects where multiple team members worked together, if possible, that demonstrate the team's capability to perform work similar to that required for this contract. Complete one Section F for each project. Present ten projects, unless otherwise specified by the agency. Complete the following blocks for each project:

20. Example Project Key Number. Start with "1" for the first project and number consecutively.

21. Title and Location. Title and location of project or contract. For an indefinite delivery contract, the location is the geographic scope of the contract.

22. Year Completed. Enter the year completed of the professional services (such as planning, engineering study, design, or surveying), and/or the year completed of construction, if applicable. If any of the professional services or the construction projects are not complete, leave Year Completed blank and indicate the status in Brief Description of Project and Relevance to this Contract (block 24).

23a. Project Owner. Project owner or user, such as a government agency or installation, an institution, a corporation or private individual.

23b. Point of Contact Name. Provide name of a person associated with the project owner or the organization which contracted for the professional services, who is very familiar with the project and the firm's (or firms') performance.

23c. Point of Contact Telephone Number. Self-explanatory.

24. Brief Description of Project and Relevance to this Contract. Indicate scope, size, cost, principal elements and special features of the project. Discuss the relevance of the example project to this contract. Enter any other information requested by the agency for each example project.

STANDARD FORM 330 (REV. 8/2016)
PAGE 2 OF INSTRUCTIONS

25. Firms from Section C Involved with this Project. Indicate which firms (or branch offices, if appropriate) on the project team were involved in the example project, and their roles. List in the same order as Section C.

Section G. Key Personnel Participation in Example Projects.

This matrix is intended to graphically depict which key personnel identified in Section E worked on the example projects listed in Section F. Complete the following blocks (see example below).

26. and 27. Names of Key Personnel and Role in this Contract. List the names of the key personnel and their proposed roles in this contract in the same order as they appear in Section E.

28. Example Projects Listed in Section F. In the column under each project key number (see block 29) and for each key person, place an "X" under the project key number for participation in the same or similar role.

29. Example Projects Key. List the key numbers and titles of the example projects in the same order as they appear in Section F.

Section H. Additional Information.

30. Use this section to provide additional information specifically requested by the agency or to address selection criteria that are not covered by the information provided in Sections A-G.

Section I. Authorized Representative.

31. and 32. Signature of Authorized Representative and Date. An authorized representative of a joint venture or the prime contractor must sign and date the completed form. Signing attests that the information provided is current and factual, and that all firms on the proposed team agree to work on the project. Joint ventures selected for negotiations must make available a statement of participation by a principal of each member of the joint venture.

33. Name and Title. Self-explanatory.

SAMPLE ENTRIES FOR SECTION G *(MATRIX)*

26. NAMES OF KEY PERSONNEL *(From Section E, Block 12)*	27. ROLE IN THIS CONTRACT *(From Section E, Block 13)*	28. EXAMPLE PROJECTS LISTED IN SECTION F *(Fill in "Example Projects Key" section below first, before completing table. Place "X" under project key number for participation in same or similar role.)*									
		1	2	3	4	5	6	7	8	9	10
Jane A. Smith	Chief Architect	X		X							
Joseph B. Williams	Chief Mechanical Engineer	X	X	X	X						
Tara C. Donovan	Chief Electricial Engineer	X	X		X						

29. EXAMPLE PROJECTS KEY

NUMBER	TITLE OF EXAMPLE PROJECT *(From Section F)*	NUMBER	TITLE OF EXAMPLE PROJECT *(From Section F)*
1	Federal Courthouse, Denver, CO	6	XYZ Corporation Headquarters, Boston, MA
2	Justin J. Wilson Federal Building, Baton Rouge, LA	7	Founder's Museum, Newport, RI

STANDARD FORM 330 (REV. 8/2016)
PAGE 3 OF INSTRUCTIONS

Part II - General Qualifications

See the "**General Instructions**" on page 1 for firms with branch offices. Prepare Part II for the specific branch office seeking work if the firm has branch offices.

1. Solicitation Number. If Part II is submitted for a specific contract, insert the agency's solicitation number and/or project number, if applicable, exactly as shown in the public announcement or agency request.

2a-2e. Firm (or Branch Office) Name and Address. Self-explanatory.

3. Year Established. Enter the year the firm (or branch office, if appropriate) was established under the current name.

4. Unique Entity Identifier. Insert the unique entity identifier issued by the entity designated at SAM. See FAR part 4.6.

5. Ownership.

a. Type. Enter the type of ownership or legal structure of the firm (sole proprietor, partnership, corporation, joint venture, etc.).

b. Small Business Status. Refer to the North American Industry Classification System (NAICS) code in the public announcement, and indicate if the firm is a small business according to the current size standard for that NAICS code (for example, Engineering Services (part of NAICS 541330), Architectural Services (NAICS 541310), Surveying and Mapping Services (NAICS 541370)). The small business categories and the internet website for the NAICS codes appear in FAR part 19. Contact the requesting agency for any questions. Contact your local U.S. Small Business Administration office for any questions regarding Business Status.

6a-6c. Point of Contact. Provide this information for a representative of the firm that the agency can contact for additional information. The representative must be empowered to speak on contractual and policy matters.

7. Name of Firm. Enter the name of the firm if Part II is prepared for a branch office.

8a-8c. Former Firm Names. Indicate any other previous names for the firm (or branch office) during the last six years. Insert the year that this corporate name change was effective and the associated unique entity identifier. This information is used to review past performance on Federal contracts.

9. Employees by Discipline. Use the relevant disciplines and associated function codes shown at the end of these instructions and list in the same numerical order. After the listed disciplines, write in any additional disciplines and leave the function code blank. List no more than 20 disciplines. Group remaining employees under "Other Employees" in column b. Each person can be counted only once according to his/her primary function. If Part II is prepared for a firm (including all branch offices), enter the number of employees by disciplines in column c(1). If Part II is prepared for a branch office, enter the number of employees by discipline in column c(2) and for the firm in column c(1).

10. Profile of Firm's Experience and Annual Average Revenue for Last 5 Years. Complete this block for the firm or branch office for which this Part II is prepared. Enter the experience categories which most accurately reflect the firm's technical capabilities and project experience. Use the relevant experience categories and associated profile codes shown at the end of these instructions, and list in the same numerical order. After the listed experience categories, write in any unlisted relevant project experience categories and leave the profile codes blank. For each type of experience, enter the appropriate revenue index number to reflect the professional services revenues received annually (averaged over the last 5 years) by the firm or branch office for performing that type of work. A particular project may be identified with one experience category or it may be broken into components, as best reflects the capabilities and types of work performed by the firm. However, do not double count the revenues received on a particular project.

11. Annual Average Professional Services Revenues of Firm for Last 3 Years. Complete this block for the firm or branch office for which this Part II is prepared. Enter the appropriate revenue index numbers to reflect the professional services revenues received annually (averaged over the last 3 years) by the firm or branch office. Indicate Federal work (performed directly for the Federal Government, either as the prime contractor or subcontractor), non-Federal work (all other domestic and foreign work, including Federally-assisted projects), and the total. If the firm has been in existence for less than 3 years, see the definition for "Annual Receipts" under FAR 19.101.

12. Authorized Representative. An authorized representative of the firm or branch office must sign and date the completed form. Signing attests that the information provided is current and factual. Provide the name and title of the authorized representative who signed the form.

STANDARD FORM 330 (REV. 8/2016)
PAGE 4 OF INSTRUCTIONS

List of Disciplines *(Function Codes)*

Code	Description	Code	Description
01	Acoustical Engineer	32	Hydraulic Engineer
02	Administrative	33	Hydrographic Surveyor
03	Aerial Photographer	34	Hydrologist
04	Aeronautical Engineer	35	Industrial Engineer
05	Archeologist	36	Industrial Hygienist
06	Architect	37	Interior Designer
07	Biologist	38	Land Surveyor
08	CADD Technician	39	Landscape Architect
09	Cartographer	40	Materials Engineer
10	Chemical Engineer	41	Materials Handling Engineer
11	Chemist	42	Mechanical Engineer
12	Civil Engineer	43	Mining Engineer
13	Communications Engineer	44	Oceanographer
14	Computer Programmer	45	Photo Interpreter
15	Construction Inspector	46	Photogrammetrist
16	Construction Manager	47	Planner: Urban/Regional
17	Corrosion Engineer	48	Project Manager
18	Cost Engineer/Estimator	49	Remote Sensing Specialist
19	Ecologist	50	Risk Assessor
20	Economist	51	Safety/Occupational Health Engineer
21	Electrical Engineer	52	Sanitary Engineer
22	Electronics Engineer	53	Scheduler
23	Environmental Engineer	54	Security Specialist
24	Environmental Scientist	55	Soils Engineer
25	Fire Protection Engineer	56	Specifications Writer
26	Forensic Engineer	57	Structural Engineer
27	Foundation/Geotechnical Engineer	58	Technician/Analyst
28	Geodetic Surveyor	59	Toxicologist
29	Geographic Information System Specialist	60	Transportation Engineer
30	Geologist	61	Value Engineer
31	Health Facility Planner	62	Water Resources Engineer

STANDARD FORM 330 (REV. 8/2016)
PAGE 5 OF INSTRUCTIONS

List of Experience Categories *(Profile Codes)*

Code	Description
A01	Acoustics, Noise Abatement
A02	Aerial Photography; Airborne Data and Imagery Collection and Analysis
A03	Agricultural Development; Grain Storage; Farm Mechanization
A04	Air Pollution Control
A05	Airports; Navaids; Airport Lighting; Aircraft Fueling
A06	Airports; Terminals and Hangars; Freight Handling
A07	Arctic Facilities
A08	Animal Facilities
A09	Anti-Terrorism/Force Protection
A10	Asbestos Abatement
A11	Auditoriums & Theaters
A12	Automation; Controls; Instrumentation
B01	Barracks; Dormitories
B02	Bridges
C01	Cartography
C02	Cemeteries *(Planning & Relocation)*
C03	Charting: Nautical and Aeronautical
C04	Chemical Processing & Storage
C05	Child Care/Development Facilities
C06	Churches; Chapels
C07	Coastal Engineering
C08	Codes; Standards; Ordinances
C09	Cold Storage; Refrigeration and Fast Freeze
C10	Commercial Building *(low rise)* ; Shopping Centers
C11	Community Facilities
C12	Communications Systems; TV; Microwave
C13	Computer Facilities; Computer Service
C14	Conservation and Resource Management
C15	Construction Management
C16	Construction Surveying
C17	Corrosion Control; Cathodic Protection; Electrolysis
C18	Cost Estimating; Cost Engineering and Analysis; Parametric Costing; Forecasting
C19	Cryogenic Facilities
D01	Dams *(Concrete; Arch)*
D02	Dams *(Earth; Rock)*; Dikes; Levees
D03	Desalinization *(Process & Facilities)*
D04	Design-Build - Preparation of Requests for Proposals
D05	Digital Elevation and Terrain Model Development
D06	Digital Orthophotography
D07	Dining Halls; Clubs; Restaurants
D08	Dredging Studies and Design
E01	Ecological & Archeological Investigations
E02	Educational Facilities; Classrooms
E03	Electrical Studies and Design
E04	Electronics
E05	Elevators; Escalators; People-Movers
E06	Embassies and Chanceries
E07	Energy Conservation; New Energy Sources
E08	Engineering Economics
E09	Environmental Impact Studies, Assessments or Statements
E10	Environmental and Natural Resource Mapping
E11	Environmental Planning
E12	Environmental Remediation
E13	Environmental Testing and Analysis
F01	Fallout Shelters; Blast-Resistant Design
F02	Field Houses; Gyms; Stadiums
F03	Fire Protection
F04	Fisheries; Fish ladders
F05	Forensic Engineering
F06	Forestry & Forest products
G01	Garages; Vehicle Maintenance Facilities; Parking Decks
G02	Gas Systems (Propane; Natural, Etc.)
G03	Geodetic Surveying: Ground and Air-borne
G04	Geographic Information System Services: Development, Analysis, and Data Collection
G05	Geospatial Data Conversion: Scanning, Digitizing, Compilation, Attributing, Scribing, Drafting
G06	Graphic Design
H01	Harbors; Jetties; Piers, Ship Terminal Facilities
H02	Hazardous Materials Handling and Storage
H03	Hazardous, Toxic, Radioactive Waste Remediation
H04	Heating; Ventilating; Air Conditioning
H05	Health Systems Planning
H06	Highrise; Air-Rights-Type Buildings
H07	Highways; Streets; Airfield Paving; Parking Lots
H08	Historical Preservation
H09	Hospital & Medical Facilities
H10	Hotels; Motels
H11	Housing *(Residential, Multi-Family; Apartments; Condominiums)*
H12	Hydraulics & Pneumatics
H13	Hydrographic Surveying

STANDARD FORM 330 (REV. 8/2016)
PAGE 6 OF INSTRUCTIONS

List of Experience Categories *(Profile Codes continued)*

Code	Description
I01	Industrial Buildings; Manufacturing Plants
I02	Industrial Processes; Quality Control
I03	Industrial Waste Treatment
I04	Intelligent Transportation Systems
I05	Interior Design; Space Planning
I06	Irrigation; Drainage
J01	Judicial and Courtroom Facilities
L01	Laboratories; Medical Research Facilities
L02	Land Surveying
L03	Landscape Architecture
L04	Libraries; Museums; Galleries
L05	Lighting (Interior; Display; Theater, Etc.)
L06	Lighting (Exteriors; Streets; Memorials; Athletic Fields, Etc.)
M01	Mapping Location/Addressing Systems
M02	Materials Handling Systems; Conveyors; Sorters
M03	Metallurgy
M04	Microclimatology; Tropical Engineering
M05	Military Design Standards
M06	Mining & Mineralogy
M07	Missile Facilities (Silos; Fuels; Transport)
M08	Modular Systems Design; Pre-Fabricated Structures or Components
N01	Naval Architecture; Off-Shore Platforms
N02	Navigation Structures; Locks
N03	Nuclear Facilities; Nuclear Shielding
O01	Office Buildings; Industrial Parks
O02	Oceanographic Engineering
O03	Ordnance; Munitions; Special Weapons
P01	Petroleum Exploration; Refining
P02	Petroleum and Fuel (Storage and Distribution)
P03	Photogrammetry
P04	Pipelines (Cross-Country - Liquid & Gas)
P05	Planning (Community, Regional, Areawide and State)
P06	Planning (Site, Installation, and Project)
P07	Plumbing & Piping Design
P08	Prisons & Correctional Facilities

Code	Description
P09	Product, Machine Equipment Design
P10	Pneumatic Structures, Air-Support Buildings
P11	Postal Facilities
P12	Power Generation, Transmission, Distribution
P13	Public Safety Facilities
R01	Radar; Sonar; Radio & Radar Telescopes
R02	Radio Frequency Systems & Shieldings
R03	Railroad; Rapid Transit
R04	Recreation Facilities (Parks, Marinas, Etc.)
R05	Refrigeration Plants/Systems
R06	Rehabilitation (Buildings; Structures; Facilities)
R07	Remote Sensing
R08	Research Facilities
R09	Resources Recovery; Recycling
R10	Risk Analysis
R11	Rivers; Canals; Waterways; Flood Control
R12	Roofing
S01	Safety Engineering; Accident Studies; OSHA Studies
S02	Security Systems; Intruder & Smoke Detection
S03	Seismic Designs & Studies
S04	Sewage Collection, Treatment and Disposal
S05	Soils & Geologic Studies; Foundations
S06	Solar Energy Utilization
S07	Solid Wastes; Incineration; Landfill
S08	Special Environments; Clean Rooms, Etc.
S09	Structural Design; Special Structures
S10	Surveying; Platting; Mapping; Flood Plain Studies
S11	Sustainable Design
S12	Swimming Pools
S13	Storm Water Handling & Facilities
T01	Telephone Systems *(Rural; Mobile; Intercom, Etc.)*
T02	Testing & Inspection Services
T03	Traffic & Transportation Engineering
T04	Topographic Surveying and Mapping
T05	Towers *(Self-Supporting & Guyed Systems)*
T06	Tunnels & Subways

STANDARD FORM 330 (REV. 8/2016)
PAGE 7 OF INSTRUCTIONS

List of Experience Categories *(Profile Codes continued)*

Code	Description
U01	Unexploded Ordnance Remediation
U02	Urban Renewals; Community Development
U03	Utilities (Gas and Steam)
V01	Value Analysis; Life-Cycle Costing
W01	Warehouses & Depots
W02	Water Resources; Hydrology; Ground Water
W03	Water Supply; Treatment and Distribution
W04	Wind Tunnels; Research/Testing Facilities Design
Z01	Zoning; Land Use Studies

ARCHITECT - ENGINEER QUALIFICATIONS

PART I - CONTRACT-SPECIFIC QUALIFICATIONS

A. CONTRACT INFORMATION

1. TITLE AND LOCATION *(City and State)*

2. PUBLIC NOTICE DATE	3. SOLICITATION OR PROJECT NUMBER

B. ARCHITECT-ENGINEER POINT OF CONTACT

4. NAME AND TITLE

5. NAME OF FIRM

6. TELEPHONE NUMBER	7. FAX NUMBER	8. E-MAIL ADDRESS

C. PROPOSED TEAM

(Complete this section for the prime contractor and all key subcontractors.)

	(Check) PRIME	(Check) J-V PARTNER	(Check) SUBCON-TRACTOR	9. FIRM NAME	10. ADDRESS	11. ROLE IN THIS CONTRACT
a.				☐ CHECK IF BRANCH OFFICE		
b.				☐ CHECK IF BRANCH OFFICE		
c.				☐ CHECK IF BRANCH OFFICE		
d.				☐ CHECK IF BRANCH OFFICE		
e.				☐ CHECK IF BRANCH OFFICE		
f.				☐ CHECK IF BRANCH OFFICE		

D. ORGANIZATIONAL CHART OF PROPOSED TEAM

☐ *(Attached)*

AUTHORIZED FOR LOCAL REPRODUCTION STANDARD FORM 330 (REV. 8/2016)

E. RESUMES OF KEY PERSONNEL PROPOSED FOR THIS CONTRACT

(Complete one Section E for each key person.)

12. NAME	13. ROLE IN THIS CONTRACT	14. YEARS EXPERIENCE	
		a. TOTAL	b. WITH CURRENT FIRM

15. FIRM NAME AND LOCATION *(City and State)*

16. EDUCATION *(Degree and Specialization)*	17. CURRENT PROFESSIONAL REGISTRATION *(State and Discipline)*

18. OTHER PROFESSIONAL QUALIFICATIONS *(Publications, Organizations, Training, Awards, etc.)*

19. RELEVANT PROJECTS

	(1) TITLE AND LOCATION *(City and State)*	(2) YEAR COMPLETED	
		PROFESSIONAL SERVICES	CONSTRUCTION *(If applicable)*
a.	(3) BRIEF DESCRIPTION *(Brief scope, size, cost, etc.)* AND SPECIFIC ROLE	☐ Check if project performed with current firm	
	(1) TITLE AND LOCATION *(City and State)*	(2) YEAR COMPLETED	
		PROFESSIONAL SERVICES	CONSTRUCTION *(If applicable)*
b.	(3) BRIEF DESCRIPTION *(Brief scope, size, cost, etc.)* AND SPECIFIC ROLE	☐ Check if project performed with current firm	
	(1) TITLE AND LOCATION *(City and State)*	(2) YEAR COMPLETED	
		PROFESSIONAL SERVICES	CONSTRUCTION *(If applicable)*
c.	(3) BRIEF DESCRIPTION *(Brief scope, size, cost, etc.)* AND SPECIFIC ROLE	☐ Check if project performed with current firm	
	(1) TITLE AND LOCATION *(City and State)*	(2) YEAR COMPLETED	
		PROFESSIONAL SERVICES	CONSTRUCTION *(If applicable)*
d.	(3) BRIEF DESCRIPTION *(Brief scope, size, cost, etc.)* AND SPECIFIC ROLE	☐ Check if project performed with current firm	
	(1) TITLE AND LOCATION *(City and State)*	(2) YEAR COMPLETED	
		PROFESSIONAL SERVICES	CONSTRUCTION *(If applicable)*
e.	(3) BRIEF DESCRIPTION *(Brief scope, size, cost, etc.)* AND SPECIFIC ROLE	☐ Check if project performed with current firm	

STANDARD FORM 330 (REV. 8/2016) **PAGE 2**

<table>
<tr><td colspan="3">F. EXAMPLE PROJECTS WHICH BEST ILLUSTRATE PROPOSED TEAM'S QUALIFICATIONS FOR THIS CONTRACT
(Present as many projects as requested by the agency, or 10 projects, if not specified. Complete one Section F for each project.)</td><td colspan="2">20. EXAMPLE PROJECT KEY NUMBER</td></tr>
<tr><td colspan="3" rowspan="2">21. TITLE AND LOCATION (City and State)</td><td colspan="2">22. YEAR COMPLETED</td></tr>
<tr><td>PROFESSIONAL SERVICES</td><td>CONSTRUCTION (If applicable)</td></tr>
<tr><td colspan="5">23. PROJECT OWNER'S INFORMATION</td></tr>
<tr><td>a. PROJECT OWNER</td><td colspan="2">b. POINT OF CONTACT NAME</td><td colspan="2">c. POINT OF CONTACT TELEPHONE NUMBER</td></tr>
<tr><td colspan="5">24. BRIEF DESCRIPTION OF PROJECT AND RELEVANCE TO THIS CONTRACT (Include scope, size, and cost)</td></tr>
</table>

25. FIRMS FROM SECTION C INVOLVED WITH THIS PROJECT

	(1) FIRM NAME	(2) FIRM LOCATION *(City and State)*	(3) ROLE
a.			
b.			
c.			
d.			
e.			
f.			

STANDARD FORM 330 (REV. 8/2016) PAGE 3

G. KEY PERSONNEL PARTICIPATION IN EXAMPLE PROJECTS

26. NAMES OF KEY PERSONNEL *(From Section E, Block 12)*	27. ROLE IN THIS CONTRACT *(From Section E, Block 13)*	28. EXAMPLE PROJECTS LISTED IN SECTION F *(Fill in "Example Projects Key" section below before completing table. Place "X" under project key number for participation in same or similar role.)*									
		1	2	3	4	5	6	7	8	9	10

29. EXAMPLE PROJECTS KEY

NUMBER	TITLE OF EXAMPLE PROJECT *(From Section F)*	NUMBER	TITLE OF EXAMPLE PROJECT *(From Section F)*
1		6	
2		7	
3		8	
4		9	
5		10	

STANDARD FORM 330 (REV. 8/2016) **PAGE 4**

H. ADDITIONAL INFORMATION

30. PROVIDE ANY ADDITIONAL INFORMATION REQUESTED BY THE AGENCY. ATTACH ADDITIONAL SHEETS AS NEEDED.

I. AUTHORIZED REPRESENTATIVE

The foregoing is a statement of facts.

31. SIGNATURE	32. DATE

33. NAME AND TITLE

STANDARD FORM 330 (REV. 8/2016) **PAGE 5**

ARCHITECT-ENGINEER QUALIFICATIONS

1. SOLICITATION NUMBER *(If any)*

PART II - GENERAL QUALIFICATIONS

(If a firm has branch offices, complete for each specific branch office seeking work.)

2a. FIRM *(or Branch Office)* NAME

3. YEAR ESTABLISHED

4. UNIQUE ENTITY IDENTIFIER

2b. STREET

5. OWNERSHIP

a. TYPE

2c. CITY

2d. STATE

2e. ZIP CODE

b. SMALL BUSINESS STATUS

6a. POINT OF CONTACT NAME AND TITLE

7. NAME OF FIRM *(If Block 2a is a Branch Office)*

6b. TELEPHONE NUMBER

6c. E-MAIL ADDRESS

8a. FORMER FIRM NAME(S) *(If any)*	8b. YEAR ESTABLISHED	8c. UNIQUE ENTITY IDENTIFIER

9. EMPLOYEES BY DISCIPLINE

a. Function Code	b. Discipline	c. Number of Employees (1) FIRM	c. Number of Employees (2) BRANCH
	Other Employees		
	Total		

10. PROFILE OF FIRM'S EXPERIENCE AND ANNUAL AVERAGE REVENUE FOR LAST 5 YEARS

a. Profile Code	b. Experience	c. Revenue Index Number *(see below)*

11. ANNUAL AVERAGE PROFESSIONAL SERVICES REVENUES OF FIRM FOR LAST 3 YEARS

(Insert revenue index number shown at right)

a. Federal Work	
b. Non-Federal Work	
c. Total Work	

PROFESSIONAL SERVICES REVENUE INDEX NUMBER

1. Less than $100,000
2. $100,000 to less than $250,000
3. $250,000 to less than $500,000
4. $500,000 to less than $1 million
5. $1 million to less than $2 million
6. $2 million to less than $5 million
7. $5 million to less than $10 million
8. $10 million to less than $25 million
9. $25 million to less than $50 million
10. $50 million or greater

12. AUTHORIZED REPRESENTATIVE

The foregoing is a statement of facts.

a. SIGNATURE

b. DATE

c. NAME AND TITLE

STANDARD FORM 330 (REV. 8/2016) PAGE 6

[FAC 2001-18, 68 FR 69227, 12/11/2003, effective 1/12/2004; FAC 2001-19, revised pages, 5/28/2004, effective 6/8/2004; FAC 2005-73, 79 FR 24192, 4/29/2014, effective 5/29/2014; FAC 2005-91, 81 FR 67736, 9/30/2016, effective 10/31/2016]

Section C. Proposed Team.

9-11. Firm Name, Address, and Role in This Contract. Provide the contractual relationship, name, full mailing address, and a brief description of the role of each firm that will be involved in performance of this contract. List the prime contractor or joint venture partners first. If a firm has branch offices, indicate each individual branch office that will have a key role on the team. The named subcontractors and outside associates or consultants must be used, and any change must be approved by the contracting officer. (See FAR Part 52 Clause "Subcontractors and Outside Associates and Consultants (Architect-Engineer Services)".) Attach an additional sheet in the same format as Section C if needed.

Section D. Organizational Chart of Proposed Team.

As an attachment after Section C, present an organizational chart of the proposed team showing the names and roles of all key personnel listed in Section E and the firm they are associated with as listed in Section C.

Section E. Resumes of Key Personnel Proposed for This Contract.

Complete this section for each key person who will participate in this contract. Group by firm, with personnel of the prime contractor or joint venture partner firms first. The following blocks must be completed for each resume:

12. Name. Self-explanatory.

13. Role in This Contract. Self-explanatory.

14. Years Experience. Total years of relevant experience (block 14a), and years of relevant experience with current firm, but not necessarily the same branch office (block 14b).

15. Firm Name and Location. Name, city and state of the firm where the person currently works, which must correspond with one of the firms (or branch office of a firm, if appropriate) listed in Section C.

16. Education. Provide information on the highest relevant academic degree(s) received. Indicate the area(s) of specialization for each degree.

17. Current Professional Registration. Provide information on current relevant professional registration(s) in a State or possession of the United States, Puerto Rico, or the District of Columbia according to FAR Part 36.

18. Other Professional Qualifications. Provide information on any other professional qualifications relating to this contract, such as education, professional registration, publications, organizational memberships, certifications, training, awards, and foreign language capabilities.

19. Relevant Projects. Provide information on up to five projects in which the person had a significant role that demonstrates the person's capability relevant to her/his proposed role in this contract. These projects do not necessarily have to be any of the projects presented in Section F for the project team if the person was not involved in any of those projects or the person worked on other projects that were more relevant than the team projects in Section F. Use the check box provided to indicate if the project was performed with any office of the current firm. If any of the professional services or construction projects are not complete, leave Year Completed blank and indicate the status in Brief Description and Specific Role (block (3)).

Section F. Example Projects Which Best Illustrate Proposed Team's Qualifications for This Contract.

Select projects where multiple team members worked together, if possible, that demonstrate the team's capability to perform work similar to that required for this contract. Complete one Section F for each project. Present ten projects, unless otherwise specified by the agency. Complete the following blocks for each project:

20. Example Project Key Number. Start with "1" for the first project and number consecutively.

21. Title and Location. Title and location of project or contract. For an indefinite delivery contract, the location is the geographic scope of the contract.

22. Year Completed. Enter the year completed of the professional services (such as planning, engineering study, design, or surveying), and/or the year completed of construction, if applicable. If any of the professional services or the construction projects are not complete, leave Year Completed blank and indicate the status in Brief Description of Project and Relevance to This Contract (block 24).

23a. Project Owner. Project owner or user, such as a government agency or installation, an institution, a corporation or private individual.

23b. Point of Contact Name. Provide name of a person associated with the project owner or the organization which contracted for the professional services, who is very familiar with the project and the firm's (or firms') performance.

23c. Point of Contact Telephone Number Self-explanatory.

24. Brief Description of Project and Relevance to This Contract. Indicate scope, size, cost, principal elements and special features of the project. Discuss the relevance of the example project to this contract. Enter any other information requested by the agency for each example project.

STANDARD FORM 330 (REV. 3/2013) **PAGE 2 OF INSTRUCTIONS**

25. Firms from Section C Involved with This Project. Indicate which firms (or branch offices, if appropriate) on the project team were involved in the example project, and their roles. List in the same order as Section C.

Section G. Key Personnel Participation in Example Projects.

This matrix is intended to graphically depict which key personnel identified in Section E worked on the example projects listed in Section F. Complete the following blocks (see example below).

26. and 27. Names of Key Personnel and Role in This Contract. List the names of the key personnel and their proposed roles in this contract in the same order as they appear in Section E.

28. Example Projects Listed in Section F. In the column under each project key number (see block 29) and for each key person, place an "X" under the project key number for participation in the same or similar role.

29. Example Projects Key. List the key numbers and titles of the example projects in the same order as they appear in Section F.

Section H. Additional Information.

30. Use this section to provide additional information specifically requested by the agency or to address selection criteria that are not covered by the information provided in Sections A-G.

Section I. Authorized Representative.

31. and 32. Signature of Authorized Representative and Date. An authorized representative of a joint venture or the prime contractor must sign and date the completed form. Signing attests that the information provided is current and factual, and that all firms on the proposed team agree to work on the project. Joint ventures selected for negotiations must make available a statement of participation by a principal of each member of the joint venture.

33. Name and Title. Self-explanatory.

SAMPLE ENTRIES FOR SECTION G (MATRIX)

26. NAMES OF KEY PERSONNEL (From Section E, Block 12)	27. ROLE IN THIS CONTRACT (From Section E, Block 13)	28. EXAMPLE PROJECTS LISTED IN SECTION F (Fill in "Example Projects Key" section below first, before completing table. Place "X" under project key number for participation in same or similar role.)									
		1	2	3	4	5	6	7	8	9	10
Jane A. Smith	Chief Architect	X		X							
Joseph B. Williams	Chief Mech. Engineer	X	X	X	X						
Tara C. Donovan	Chief Elec. Engineer	X	X		X						

29. EXAMPLE PROJECTS KEY

NO.	TITLE OF EXAMPLE PROJECT (FROM SECTION F)	NO.	TITLE OF EXAMPLE PROJECT (FROM SECTION F)
1	Federal Courthouse, Denver, CO	6	XYZ Corporation Headquarters, Boston, MA
2	Justin J. Wilson Federal Building, Baton Rouge, LA	7	Founder's Museum, Newport RI

Part II - General Qualifications

See the " **General Instructions** " on page 1 for firms with branch offices. Prepare Part II for the specific branch office seeking work if the firm has branch offices.

1. Solicitation Number. If Part II is submitted for a specific contract, insert the agency's solicitation number and/or project number, if applicable, exactly as shown in the public announcement or agency request.

2a-2e. Firm (or Branch Office) Name and Address. Self-explanatory.

3. Year Established. Enter the year the firm (or branch office, if appropriate) was established under the current name.

4. DUNS Number. Insert the Data Universal Numbering System number issued by Dun and Bradstreet Information Services. Firms must have a DUNS number. See FAR Part 4.6.

5. Ownership.

a. Type. Enter the type of ownership or legal structure of the firm (sole proprietor, partnership, corporation, joint venture, etc.).

b. Small Business Status. Refer to the North American Industry Classification System (NAICS) code in the public announcement, and indicate if the firm is a small business according to the current size standard for that NAICS code (for example, Engineering Services (part of NAICS 541330), Architectural Services (NAICS 541310), Surveying and Mapping Services (NAICS 541370)). The small business categories and the internet website for the NAICS codes appear in FAR Part 19. Contact the requesting agency for any questions. Contact your local U.S. Small Business Administration office for any questions regarding Business Status.

6a-6c. Point of Contact. Provide this information for a representative of the firm that the agency can contact for additional information. The representative must be empowered to speak on contractual and policy matters.

7. Name of Firm. Enter the name of the firm if Part II is prepared for a branch office.

8a-8c. Former Firm Names. Indicate any other previous names for the firm (or branch office) during the last six years. Insert the year that this corporate name change was effective and the associated DUNS Number. This information is used to review past performance on Federal contracts.

9. Employees by Discipline. Use the relevant disciplines and associated function codes shown at the end of these instructions and list in the same numerical order. After the listed disciplines, write in any additional disciplines and leave the function code blank. List no more than 20 disciplines. Group remaining employees under "Other Employees" in column b. Each person can be counted only once according to his/her primary function. If Part II is prepared for a firm (including all branch offices), enter the number of employees by disciplines in column c(1). If Part II is prepared for a branch office, enter the number of employees by discipline in column c(2) and for the firm in column c(1).

10. Profile of Firm's Experience and Annual Average Revenue for Last 5 Years. Complete this block for the firm or branch office for which this Part II is prepared. Enter the experience categories which most accurately reflect the firm's technical capabilities and project experience. Use the relevant experience categories and associated profile codes shown at the end of these instructions, and list in the same numerical order. After the listed experience categories, write in any unlisted relevant project experience categories and leave the profile codes blank. For each type of experience, enter the appropriate revenue index number to reflect the professional services revenues received annually (averaged over the last 5 years) by the firm or branch office for performing that type of work. A particular project may be identified with one experience category or it may be broken into components, as best reflects the capabilities and types of work performed by the firm. However, do not double count the revenues received on a particular project.

11. Annual Average Professional Services Revenues of Firm for Last 3 Years. Complete this block for the firm or branch office for which this Part II is prepared. Enter the appropriate revenue index numbers to reflect the professional services revenues received annually (averaged over the last 3 years) by the firm or branch office. Indicate Federal work (performed directly for the Federal Government, either as the prime contractor or subcontractor), non-Federal work (all other domestic and foreign work, including Federally-assisted projects), and the total. If the firm has been in existence for less than 3 years, see the definition for "Annual Receipts" under FAR 19.101.

12. Authorized Representative. An authorized representative of the firm or branch office must sign and date the completed form. Signing attests that the information provided is current and factual. Provide the name and title of the authorized representative who signed the form.

STANDARD FORM 330 (REV. 3/2013) PAGE 4 OF INSTRUCTIONS

List of Disciplines (Function Codes)

Code	Description	Code	Description
01	Acoustical Engineer	32	Hydraulic Engineer
02	Administrative	33	Hydrographic Surveyor
03	Aerial Photographer	34	Hydrologist
04	Aeronautical Engineer	35	Industrial Engineer
05	Archeologist	36	Industrial Hygienist
06	Architect	37	Interior Designer
07	Biologist	38	Land Surveyor
08	CADD Technician	39	Landscape Architect
09	Cartographer	40	Materials Engineer
10	Chemical Engineer	41	Materials Handling Engineer
11	Chemist	42	Mechanical Engineer
12	Civil Engineer	43	Mining Engineer
13	Communications Engineer	44	Oceanographer
14	Computer Programmer	45	Photo Interpreter
15	Construction Inspector	46	Photogrammetrist
16	Construction Manager	47	Planner: Urban/Regional
17	Corrosion Engineer	48	Project Manager
18	Cost Engineer/Estimator	49	Remote Sensing Specialist
19	Ecologist	50	Risk Assessor
20	Economist	51	Safety/Occupational Health Engineer
21	Electrical Engineer	52	Sanitary Engineer
22	Electronics Engineer	53	Scheduler
23	Environmental Engineer	54	Security Specialist
24	Environmental Scientist	55	Soils Engineer
25	Fire Protection Engineer	56	Specifications Writer
26	Forensic Engineer	57	Structural Engineer
27	Foundation/Geotechnical Engineer	58	Technician/Analyst
28	Geodetic Surveyor	59	Toxicologist
29	Geographic Information System Specialist	60	Transportation Engineer
30	Geologist	61	Value Engineer
31	Health Facility Planner	62	Water Resources Engineer

STANDARD FORM 330 (REV. 3/2013) PAGE 5 OF INSTRUCTIONS

List of Experience Categories (Profile Codes)

Code	Description
A01	Acoustics, Noise Abatement
A02	Aerial Photography; Airborne Data and Imagery Collection and Analysis
A03	Agricultural Development; Grain Storage; Farm Mechanization
A04	Air Pollution Control
A05	Airports; Navaids; Airport Lighting; Aircraft Fueling
A06	Airports; Terminals and Hangars; Freight Handling
A07	Arctic Facilities
A08	Animal Facilities
A09	Anti-Terrorism/Force Protection
A10	Asbestos Abatement
A11	Auditoriums & Theaters
A12	Automation; Controls; Instrumentation
B01	Barracks; Dormitories
B02	Bridges
C01	Cartography
C02	Cemeteries *(Planning & Relocation)*
C03	Charting: Nautical and Aeronautical
C04	Chemical Processing & Storage
C05	Child Care/Development Facilities
C06	Churches; Chapels
C07	Coastal Engineering
C08	Codes; Standards; Ordinances
C09	Cold Storage; Refrigeration and Fast Freeze
C10	Commercial Building *(low rise)* ; Shopping Centers
C11	Community Facilities
C12	Communications Systems; TV; Microwave
C13	Computer Facilities; Computer Service
C14	Conservation and Resource Management
C15	Construction Management
C16	Construction Surveying
C17	Corrosion Control; Cathodic Protection; Electrolysis
C18	Cost Estimating; Cost Engineering and Analysis; Parametric Costing; Forecasting
C19	Cryogenic Facilities
D01	Dams *(Concrete; Arch)*
D02	Dams *(Earth; Rock);* Dikes; Levees
D03	Desalinization *(Process & Facilities)*
D04	Design-Build - Preparation of Requests for Proposals
D05	Digital Elevation and Terrain Model Development
D06	Digital Orthophotography
D07	Dining Halls; Clubs; Restaurants
D08	Dredging Studies and Design
E01	Ecological & Archeological Investigations
E02	Educational Facilities; Classrooms
E03	Electrical Studies and Design
E04	Electronics
E05	Elevators; Escalators; People-Movers
E06	Embassies and Chanceries
E07	Energy Conservation; New Energy Sources
E08	Engineering Economics
E09	Environmental Impact Studies, Assessments or Statements
E10	Environmental and Natural Resource Mapping
E11	Environmental Planning
E12	Environmental Remediation
E13	Environmental Testing and Analysis
F01	Fallout Shelters; Blast-Resistant Design
F02	Field Houses; Gyms; Stadiums
F03	Fire Protection
F04	Fisheries; Fish ladders
F05	Forensic Engineering
F06	Forestry & Forest products
G01	Garages; Vehicle Maintenance Facilities; Parking Decks
G02	Gas Systems (Propane; Natural, Etc.)
G03	Geodetic Surveying: Ground and Air-borne
G04	Geographic Information System Services: Development, Analysis, and Data Collection
G05	Geospatial Data Conversion: Scanning, Digitizing, Compilation, Attributing, Scribing, Drafting
G06	Graphic Design
H01	Harbors; Jetties; Piers, Ship Terminal Facilities
H02	Hazardous Materials Handling and Storage
H03	Hazardous, Toxic, Radioactive Waste Remediation
H04	Heating; Ventilating; Air Conditioning
H05	Health Systems Planning
H06	Highrise; Air-Rights-Type Buildings
H07	Highways; Streets; Airfield Paving; Parking Lots
H08	Historical Preservation
H09	Hospital & Medical Facilities
H10	Hotels; Motels
H11	Housing *(Residential, Multi-Family; Apartments; Condominiums)*
H12	Hydraulics & Pneumatics
H13	Hydrographic Surveying

STANDARD FORM 330 (REV. 3/2013) **PAGE 6 OF INSTRUCTIONS**

List of Experience Categories (Profile Codes)

Code	Description
I01	Industrial Buildings; Manufacturing Plants
I02	Industrial Processes; Quality Control
I03	Industrial Waste Treatment
I04	Intelligent Transportation Systems
I05	Interior Design; Space Planning
I06	Irrigation; Drainage
J01	Judicial and Courtroom Facilities
L01	Laboratories; Medical Research Facilities
L02	Land Surveying
L03	Landscape Architecture
L04	Libraries; Museums; Galleries
L05	Lighting (Interior; Display; Theater, Etc.)
L06	Lighting (Exteriors; Streets; Memorials; Athletic Fields, Etc.)
M01	Mapping Location/Addressing Systems
M02	Materials Handling Systems; Conveyors; Sorters
M03	Metallurgy
M04	Microclimatology; Tropical Engineering
M05	Military Design Standards
M06	Mining & Mineralogy
M07	Missile Facilities (Silos; Fuels; Transport)
M08	Modular Systems Design; Pre-Fabricated Structures or Components
N01	Naval Architecture; Off-Shore Platforms
N02	Navigation Structures; Locks
N03	Nuclear Facilities; Nuclear Shielding
O01	Office Buildings; Industrial Parks
O02	Oceanographic Engineering
O03	Ordnance; Munitions; Special Weapons
P01	Petroleum Exploration; Refining
P02	Petroleum and Fuel (Storage and Distribution)
P03	Photogrammetry
P04	Pipelines (Cross-Country - Liquid & Gas)
P05	Planning (Community, Regional, Areawide and State)
P06	Planning (Site, Installation, and Project)
P07	Plumbing & Piping Design
P08	Prisons & Correctional Facilities

Code	Description
P09	Product, Machine Equipment Design
P10	Pneumatic Structures, Air-Support Buildings
P11	Postal Facilities
P12	Power Generation, Transmission, Distribution
P13	Public Safety Facilities
R01	Radar; Sonar; Radio & Radar Telescopes
R02	Radio Frequency Systems & Shieldings
R03	Railroad; Rapid Transit
R04	Recreation Facilities (Parks, Marinas, Etc.)
R05	Refrigeration Plants/Systems
R06	Rehabilitation (Buildings; Structures; Facilities)
R07	Remote Sensing
R08	Research Facilities
R09	Resources Recovery; Recycling
R10	Risk Analysis
R11	Rivers; Canals; Waterways; Flood Control
R12	Roofing
S01	Safety Engineering; Accident Studies; OSHA Studies
S02	Security Systems; Intruder & Smoke Detection
S03	Seismic Designs & Studies
S04	Sewage Collection, Treatment and Disposal
S05	Soils & Geologic Studies; Foundations
S06	Solar Energy Utilization
S07	Solid Wastes; Incineration; Landfill
S08	Special Environments; Clean Rooms, Etc.
S09	Structural Design; Special Structures
S10	Surveying; Platting; Mapping; Flood Plain Studies
S11	Sustainable Design
S12	Swimming Pools
S13	Storm Water Handling & Facilities
T01	Telephone Systems *(Rural; Mobile; Intercom, Etc.)*
T02	Testing & Inspection Services
T03	Traffic & Transportation Engineering
T04	Topographic Surveying and Mapping
T05	Towers *(Self-Supporting & Guyed Systems)*
T06	Tunnels & Subways

List of Experience Categories (Profile Codes)

Code	Description
U01	Unexploded Ordnance Remediation
U02	Urban Renewals; Community Development
U03	Utilities (Gas and Steam)
V01	Value Analysis; Life-Cycle Costing
W01	Warehouses & Depots
W02	Water Resources; Hydrology; Ground Water
W03	Water Supply; Treatment and Distribution
W04	Wind Tunnels; Research/Testing Facilities Design
Z01	Zoning; Land Use Studies

ARCHITECT - ENGINEER QUALIFICATIONS

PART I - CONTRACT-SPECIFIC QUALIFICATIONS

A. CONTRACT INFORMATION

1. TITLE AND LOCATION *(City and State)*

2. PUBLIC NOTICE DATE	3. SOLICITATION OR PROJECT NUMBER

B. ARCHITECT-ENGINEER POINT OF CONTACT

4. NAME AND TITLE

5. NAME OF FIRM

6. TELEPHONE NUMBER	7. FAX NUMBER	8. E-MAIL ADDRESS

C. PROPOSED TEAM

(Complete this section for the prime contractor and all key subcontractors.)

	(Check) PRIME	J-V PARTNER	SUBCON-TRACTOR	9. FIRM NAME	10. ADDRESS	11. ROLE IN THIS CONTRACT
a.				☐ CHECK IF BRANCH OFFICE		
b.				☐ CHECK IF BRANCH OFFICE		
c.				☐ CHECK IF BRANCH OFFICE		
d.				☐ CHECK IF BRANCH OFFICE		
e.				☐ CHECK IF BRANCH OFFICE		
f.				☐ CHECK IF BRANCH OFFICE		

D. ORGANIZATIONAL CHART OF PROPOSED TEAM ☐ *(Attached)*

AUTHORIZED FOR LOCAL REPRODUCTION

STANDARD FORM 330 (REV. 3/2013) **PAGE 1**

E. RESUMES OF KEY PERSONNEL PROPOSED FOR THIS CONTRACT

(Complete one Section E for each key person.)

12. NAME	13. ROLE IN THIS CONTRACT	14. YEARS EXPERIENCE	
		a. TOTAL	b. WITH CURRENT FIRM

15. FIRM NAME AND LOCATION *(City and State)*

16. EDUCATION *(DEGREE AND SPECIALIZATION)*	17. CURRENT PROFESSIONAL REGISTRATION *(STATE AND DISCIPLINE)*

18. OTHER PROFESSIONAL QUALIFICATIONS *(Publications, Organizations, Training, Awards, etc.)*

19. RELEVANT PROJECTS

		(2) YEAR COMPLETED	
a.	(1) TITLE AND LOCATION *(City and State)*	PROFESSIONAL SERVICES	CONSTRUCTION *(If applicable)*
	(3) BRIEF DESCRIPTION *(Brief scope, size, cost, etc.)* AND SPECIFIC ROLE	☐ Check if project performed with current firm	
b.	(1) TITLE AND LOCATION *(City and State)*	PROFESSIONAL SERVICES	CONSTRUCTION *(If applicable)*
	(3) BRIEF DESCRIPTION *(Brief scope, size, cost, etc.)* AND SPECIFIC ROLE	☐ Check if project performed with current firm	
c.	(1) TITLE AND LOCATION *(City and State)*	PROFESSIONAL SERVICES	CONSTRUCTION *(If applicable)*
	(3) BRIEF DESCRIPTION *(Brief scope, size, cost, etc.)* AND SPECIFIC ROLE	☐ Check if project performed with current firm	
d.	(1) TITLE AND LOCATION *(City and State)*	PROFESSIONAL SERVICES	CONSTRUCTION *(If applicable)*
	(3) BRIEF DESCRIPTION *(Brief scope, size, cost, etc.)* AND SPECIFIC ROLE	☐ Check if project performed with current firm	
e.	(1) TITLE AND LOCATION *(City and State)*	PROFESSIONAL SERVICES	CONSTRUCTION *(If applicable)*
	(3) BRIEF DESCRIPTION *(Brief scope, size, cost, etc.)* AND SPECIFIC ROLE	☐ Check if project performed with current firm	

STANDARD FORM 330 (REV. 3/2013) **PAGE 2**

F. EXAMPLE PROJECTS WHICH BEST ILLUSTRATE PROPOSED TEAM'S QUALIFICATIONS FOR THIS CONTRACT *(Present as many projects as requested by the agency, or 10 projects, if not specified. Complete one Section F for each project.)*		20. EXAMPLE PROJECT KEY NUMBER
21. TITLE AND LOCATION *(City and State)*	22. YEAR COMPLETED	
	PROFESSIONAL SERVICES	CONSTRUCTION *(If applicable)*

23. PROJECT OWNER'S INFORMATION

a. PROJECT OWNER	b. POINT OF CONTACT NAME	c. POINT OF CONTACT TELEPHONE NUMBER

24. BRIEF DESCRIPTION OF PROJECT AND RELEVANCE TO THIS CONTRACT *(Include scope, size, and cost)*

25. FIRMS FROM SECTION C INVOLVED WITH THIS PROJECT

a.	(1) FIRM NAME	(2) FIRM LOCATION *(City and State)*	(3) ROLE
b.	(1) FIRM NAME	(2) FIRM LOCATION *(City and State)*	(3) ROLE
c.	(1) FIRM NAME	(2) FIRM LOCATION *(City and State)*	(3) ROLE
d.	(1) FIRM NAME	(2) FIRM LOCATION *(City and State)*	(3) ROLE
e.	(1) FIRM NAME	(2) FIRM LOCATION *(City and State)*	(3) ROLE
f.	(1) FIRM NAME	(2) FIRM LOCATION *(City and State)*	(3) ROLE

STANDARD FORM 330 (REV. 3/2013) **PAGE 3**

G. KEY PERSONNEL PARTICIPATION IN EXAMPLE PROJECTS

26. NAMES OF KEY PERSONNEL (From Section E, Block 12)	27. ROLE IN THIS CONTRACT (From Section E, Block 13)	28. EXAMPLE PROJECTS LISTED IN SECTION F (Fill in "Example Projects Key" section below before completing table. Place "X" under project key number for participation in same or similar role.)									
		1	2	3	4	5	6	7	8	9	10

29. EXAMPLE PROJECTS KEY

NO.	TITLE OF EXAMPLE PROJECT (FROM SECTION F)	NO.	TITLE OF EXAMPLE PROJECT (FROM SECTION F)
1		6	
2		7	
3		8	
4		9	
5		10	

STANDARD FORM 330 (REV. 3/2013) **PAGE 4**

H. ADDITIONAL INFORMATION

30. PROVIDE ANY ADDITIONAL INFORMATION REQUESTED BY THE AGENCY. ATTACH ADDITIONAL SHEETS AS NEEDED.

I. AUTHORIZED REPRESENTATIVE

The foregoing is a statement of facts.

31. SIGNATURE	32. DATE
33. NAME AND TITLE	

STANDARD FORM 330 (REV. 3/2013) PAGE 5

ARCHITECT-ENGINEER QUALIFICATIONS

1. SOLICITATION NUMBER *(If any)*

PART II - GENERAL QUALIFICATIONS

(If a firm has branch offices, complete for each specific branch office seeking work.)

2a. FIRM (OR BRANCH OFFICE) NAME			3. YEAR ESTABLISHED	4. DUNS NUMBER
2b. STREET			5. OWNERSHIP a. TYPE	
2c. CITY	2d. STATE	2e. ZIP CODE	b. SMALL BUSINESS STATUS	
6a. POINT OF CONTACT NAME AND TITLE			7. NAME OF FIRM *(If block 2a is a branch office)*	
6b. TELEPHONE NUMBER	6c. E-MAIL ADDRESS			

8a. FORMER FIRM NAME(S) *(If any)*	8b. YR. ESTABLISHED	8c. DUNS NUMBER

9. EMPLOYEES BY DISCIPLINE				10. PROFILE OF FIRM'S EXPERIENCE AND ANNUAL AVERAGE REVENUE FOR LAST 5 YEARS		
a. Function Code	b. Discipline	c. No. of Employees (1) FIRM	(2) BRANCH	a. Profile Code	b. Experience	c. Revenue Index Number *(see below)*
	Other Employees					
	Total					

11. ANNUAL AVERAGE PROFESSIONAL SERVICES REVENUES OF FIRM FOR LAST 3 YEARS
(Insert revenue index number shown at right)

a. Federal Work	
b. Non-Federal Work	
c. Total Work	

PROFESSIONAL SERVICES REVENUE INDEX NUMBER

1. Less than $100,000
2. $100,00 to less than $250,000
3. $250,000 to less than $500,000
4. $500,000 to less than $1 million
5. $1 million to less than $2 million
6. $2 million to less than $5 million
7. $5 million to less than $10 million
8. $10 million to less than $25 million
9. $25 million to less than $50 million
10. $50 million or greater

12. AUTHORIZED REPRESENTATIVE
The foregoing is a statement of facts.

a. SIGNATURE	b. DATE
c. NAME AND TITLE	

AUTHORIZED FOR LOCAL REPRODUCTION

STANDARD FORM 330 (REV. 3/2013) **PAGE 6**

53.301-1034 Standard Form 1034, Public Voucher for Purchases and Services Other Than Personal

Standard Form 1034
Revised October 1987
Department of the Treasury
1 TFM 4-2000

PUBLIC VOUCHER FOR PURCHASES AND SERVICES OTHER THAN PERSONAL

VOUCHER NO.

U.S. DEPARTMENT, BUREAU, OR ESTABLISHMENT AND LOCATION

DATE VOUCHER PREPARED

SCHEDULE NO.

CONTRACT NUMBER AND DATE

PAID BY

REQUISITION NUMBER AND DATE

PAYEE'S NAME AND ADDRESS

DATE INVOICE RECEIVED

DISCOUNT TERMS

PAYEE'S ACCOUNT NUMBER

SHIPPED FROM | TO | WEIGHT | GOVERNMENT B/L NUMBER

NUMBER AND DATE OF ORDER	DATE OF DELIVERY OR SERVICE	ARTICLES OR SERVICES *(Enter description, item number of contract or Federal supply schedule, and other information deemed necessary)*	QUAN-TITY	UNIT PRICE COST	UNIT PRICE PER	AMOUNT (1)

(Use continuation sheet(s) if necessary)

(Payee must NOT use the space below)

TOTAL

PAYMENT:
- PROVISIONAL
- COMPLETE
- PARTIAL
- FINAL
- PROGRESS
- ADVANCE

APPROVED FOR = $

EXCHANGE RATE = $1.00

DIFFERENCES

BY 2

TITLE

Amount verified; correct for

(Signature or initials)

Pursuant to authority vested in me, I certify that this voucher is correct and proper for payment.

(Date) *(Authorized Certifying Officer)* 2 *(Title)*

ACCOUNTING CLASSIFICATION

PAID BY

CHECK NUMBER | ON ACCOUNT OF U.S. TREASURY | CHECK NUMBER | ON *(Name of bank)*

CASH $ | DATE | PAYEE 3

1 When stated in foreign currency, insert name of currency.
2 If the ability to certify and authority to approve are combined in one person, one signature only is necessary; otherwise the approving officer will sign in the space provided, over his official title.
3 When a voucher is receipted in the name of a company or corporation, the name of the person writing the company or corporate name, as well as the capacity in which he signs, must appear. For example: "John Doe Company, per John

PER

TITLE

Previous edition usable.

NSN 7540-00-900-2234

PRIVACY ACT STATEMENT

The information requested on this form is required under the provisions of 31 U.S.C. 82b and 82c, for the purpose of disbursing Federal money. The information requested is to identify the particular creditor and the amounts to be paid. Failure to furnish this information will hinder discharge of the payment obligation.

Standard Form 1034
Revised October 1987
Department of the Treasury
1 TFM 4-2000

PUBLIC VOUCHER FOR PURCHASES AND SERVICES OTHER THAN PERSONAL

VOUCHER NO.

U.S. DEPARTMENT, BUREAU, OR ESTABLISHMENT AND LOCATION

DATE VOUCHER PREPARED

SCHEDULE NO.

CONTRACT NUMBER AND DATE

PAID BY

REQUISITION NUMBER AND DATE

PAYEE'S NAME AND ADDRESS

DATE INVOICE RECEIVED

DISCOUNT TERMS

PAYEE'S ACCOUNT NUMBER

SHIPPED FROM | TO | WEIGHT | GOVERNMENT B/L NUMBER

NUMBER AND DATE OF ORDER	DATE OF DELIVERY OR SERVICE	ARTICLES OR SERVICES (*Enter description, item number of contract or Federal supply schedule, and other information deemed necessary*)	QUAN-TITY	UNIT PRICE		AMOUNT
				COST	PER	(1)

(Use continuation sheet(s) if necessary)

(Payee must NOT use the space below)

TOTAL

PAYMENT:
- PROVISIONAL
- COMPLETE
- PARTIAL
- FINAL
- PROGRESS
- ADVANCE

APPROVED FOR = $

EXCHANGE RATE = $1.00

DIFFERENCES

BY 2

TITLE

Amount verified; correct for
(Signature or initials)

MEMORANDUM

ACCOUNTING CLASSIFICATION

PAID BY

CHECK NUMBER	ON ACCOUNT OF U.S. TREASURY	CHECK NUMBER	ON *(Name of bank)*
CASH $	DATE	PAYEE 3	

PRIVACY ACT STATEMENT

The information requested on this form is required under the provisions of 31 U.S.C. 82b and 82c, for the purpose of disbursing Federal money. The information requested is to identify the particular creditor and the amounts to be paid. Failure to furnish this information will hinder discharge of the payment obligation.

53.301-1034-A Standard Form 1034-A, Public Voucher for Purchases and Services Other Than Personal—Memorandum Copy

FEDERAL ACQUISITION REGULATION (FAR)

Standard Form 1034 A
Revised January 1980
Department of the Treasury
I TFRM 4-2000

PUBLIC VOUCHER FOR PURCHASES AND SERVICES OTHER THAN PERSONAL

VOUCHER NO.

U.S. DEPARTMENT, BUREAU, OR ESTABLISHMENT AND LOCATION

DATE VOUCHER PREPARED

SCHEDULE NO.

CONTRACT NUMBER AND DATE

PAID BY

REQUISITION NUMBER AND DATE

PAYEE'S NAME AND ADDRESS

DATE INVOICE RECEIVED

DISCOUNT TERMS

PAYEE'S ACCOUNT NUMBER

SHIPPED FROM | TO | WEIGHT

GOVERNMENT B/L NUMBER

NUMBER AND DATE OF ORDER	DATE OF DELIVERY OR SERVICE	ARTICLES OR SERVICES (*Enter description, item number of contract of Federal supply schedule, and other information deemed necessary*)	QUAN-TITY	UNIT PRICE COST	UNIT PRICE PER	AMOUNT

(Use continuation sheet(s) if necessary) **(Payee must NOT use the space below)** TOTAL

PAYMENT:
- PROVISIONAL
- COMPLETE
- PARTIAL
- FINAL
- PROGRESS
- ADVANCE

DIFFERENCES

Amount verified; correct for

(*Signature of initials*)

MEMORANDUM

ACCOUNTING CLASSIFICATION

PAID BY | CHECK NUMBER | ON ACCOUNT OF U.S. TREASURY | CHECK NUMBER | ON (*Name of bank*)

CASH $ | DATE

1034-213

NSN: 7540-00-634-4207

PRIVACY ACT STATEMENT

The information requested on this form is required under the provisions of 31 U.S.C. 82b and 82c, for the purpose of disbursing Federal money. The information requested is to identify the particular creditor and the amounts to be paid. Failure to furnish this information will hinder discharge of the payment obligation.

53.301-1035 Standard Form 1035, Public Voucher for Purchases and Services Other Than Personal, Continuation Sheet

Standard Form 1035 September 1973 4 Treasury FRM 2000 1035-110	PUBLIC VOUCHER FOR PURCHASES AND SERVICES OTHER THAN PERSONAL *CONTINUATION SHEET*	VOUCHER NO. SCHEDULE NO. SHEET NO.
U.S. DEPARTMENT, BUREAU, OR ESTABLISHMENT		

NUMBER AND DATE OF ORDER	DATE OF DELIVERY OR SERVICE	ARTICLES OR SERVICES *(Enter description, item number of contract or Federal supply schedule, and other information deemed necessary)*	QUAN-TITY	UNIT PRICE		AMOUNT
				COST	PER	

53.301-1035-A Standard Form 1035-A, Public Voucher for Purchases and Services Other Than Personal—Memorandum, Continuation Sheet

FEDERAL ACQUISITION REGULATION (FAR)

Standard Form No. 1035-A September 1973 4 Treasury FRM 2000 1035-209-01	PUBLIC VOUCHER FOR PURCHASES AND SERVICES OTHER THAN PERSONAL MEMORANDUM *CONTINUATION SHEET*	VOUCHER NO. SCHEDULE NO. SHEET NO.

U.S. DEPARTMENT, BUREAU, OR ESTABLISHMENT

NUMBER AND DATE OF ORDER	DATE OF DELIVERY OR SERVICE	ARTICLES OR SERVICES *(Enter description, item number of contract or Federal supply schedule, and other information deemed necessary)*	QUAN-TITY	UNIT PRICE		AMOUNT
				COST	PER	

53.301-1093 [Removed]

[FAC 2005-73, 79 FR 24192, 4/29/2014, effective 5/29/2014; FAC 2005-78, 79 FR 70342, 11/25/2014, effective 12/26/2014]

53.301-1094 Standard Form 1094, U.S. Tax Exemption Form

[FAC 90-45, Final rule, 62 FR 224, 1/2/97, effective 1/1/97]

Book No.

UNITED STATES TAX EXEMPTION FORMS

NSN 7540-01-152-8080 PREVIOUS EDITION NOT USABLE

These Are Accountable Forms

In case this book of United States Tax Exemption Forms is lost. finder will please put band or string around cover and mail to:

GENERAL SERVICES ADMINISTRATION
FEDERAL SUPPLY SERVICE
GENERAL PRODUCTS COMMODITY CENTER
ATTN: 7FXM
819 TAYLOR STREET
FORT WORTH TX 76102

FAR 53.301-1094

INSTRUCTIONS

1. This form will be used to establish the Government's exemption or immunity from State or Local taxes whenever no other evidence is available.

2. This form shall NOT be used for:

(a) Purchases of quarters or subsistence made by employees in travel status.

(b) Expenses incident to use of a privately owned motor vehicle for which mileage allowance has been authorized, or

(c) Merchandise purchased which is subject only to Federal Tax.

3. If the spaces provided on the face of this form are inadequate, attach a separate statement containing the required information.

4. If both State and local taxes are involved, use a separate form for each tax. The form will be provided to the vendor when the prices exclude State or local tax.

5. The serial number of each form prepared will be shown on the payment voucher.

THE FRAUDULENT USE OF THIS FORM FOR THE PURPOSE OF OBTAINING EXCEPTION FROM OR ADJUSTMENT OF TAXES IS PROHIBITED.

STANDARD FORM 1094 (REV. 12-96) **PAGE 2**

U.S. TAX EXEMPTION FORM | Read the Instructions | DEPARTMENT, AGENCY, OR OFFICE | SERIAL NO.

ITEM PURCHASED FOR EXCLUSIVE USE OF THE U.S. GOVERNMENT (Describe) | QUANTITY | UNIT PRICE ($)

VENDOR FROM WHICH PUR-CHASED: NAME; ADDRESS (No., Street, City. State, and ZIP Code)

A tax exemption form has not previously been issued and the described item(s) has (have) been delivered and invoiced pursuant to:

P.O. OR CONTRACT NO.

AMOUNT OF TAX EXCLUDED ($): STATE; LOCAL

The information on this form is true and correct to the best of my knowledge and belief.

PURCHASER'S SIGNATURE, OFFICE TITLE AND ADDRESS ▶ | DATE

SIGNATURE AND TITLE OF VENDOR'S REPRESENTATIVE ▶ | DATE

DATES

FOR ADMINISTRATIVE OFFICE: D.O. SYMBOL NO.; VOUCHER NO.; DATE:

STANDARD FORM 1094 (REV. 12-96)
Prescribed by GSA-FAR (48 CFR) 53.229

53.301-1094-A Standard Form 1094-A, Tax Exemption Forms Accountability Record

[FAC 90-45, Final rule, 62 FR 224, 1/2/97, effective 1/1/97]

TAX EXEMPTION FORMS ACCOUNTABILITY RECORD	To be used for convenience of the issuing agency for maintaining a control record of tax exemption forms issued.				
TAX EXEMPTION FORMS IN THIS BOOK NUMBERED ▶	FROM	THROUGH	TAX EXEMPTION FORMS RETURNED UNUSED FOR REISSUE ▶	FROM	THROUGH
ISSUED TO			REISSUED TO		
NAME			NAME		
TITLE			TITLE		
OFFICE DESIGNATION			OFFICE DESIGNATION		
ISSUING OFFICER	SIGNATURE	DATE ISSUED	ISSUING OFFICER	SIGNATURE	DATE ISSUED
	TITLE AND OFFICE DESIGNATION			TITLE AND OFFICE DESIGNATION	

STAND FORM 1094A (REV. 12-96)
Prescribed by GSA-FAR (48 CFR) 53.229

FORM		Mark "X" in appropriate column to indicate type of tax ▶		TAX EXCLUDED (Amount $)	STATE	LOCAL	TRANSACTION REFERENCE
NO.	DATE	VENDOR NAME AND ADDRESS	ITEM PURCHASED				
							Voucher No.:
							Voucher Date:
							PO/Cont. No.:
							Voucher No.:
							Voucher Date:
							PO/Cont. No.:
							Voucher No.:
							Voucher Date:
							PO/Cont. No.:
							Voucher No.:
							Voucher Date:
							PO/Cont. No.:

STANDARD FORM 1094A (REV, 12-96) **PAGE 2**

Prescribed by GSA-FAR (48 CFR) 53.229

53.301-1165 Standard Form 1165, Receipt for Cash-Subvoucher

INTERIM RECEIPT FOR CASH

DATE ____________

Received of Imprest Fund Cashier
$ ____________ **for which I hold myself accountable to the United States.**

____
(Signature)

NOTE TO SIGNER
Be sure this receipt is marked "VOID" and returned to you when the transaction is completed or the funds returned to the Cashier.

Standard Form 1165
7 GAO 5100
1165-105

RECEIPT FOR CASH— SUBVOUCHER

(To be used when invoice is not available)

Subvoucher No. ____________

Date ____________

Received in cash from ____________

____________ **and** ______ 100 **($** ______ **) for the following:**

QUANTITY	ARTICLES OR SERVICES	AMOUNT

Vendor ____________

Address ____________ **By** ____________
(Signature of Vendor/Agent)

____________ **Title** ____________
(DO NOT SIGN IN DUPLICATE)

PURPOSE (Project, etc.)	APPROPRIATION AND ACCOUNTING CLASSIFICATION

53.301-1402 Standard Form 1402, Certificate of Appointment

Certificate of Appointment

Under authority vested in the undersigned and in conformance with
Subpart 1.6 of the Federal Acquisition Regulation

is appointed

Contracting Officer

for the

United States of America

Subject to the limitations contained in the Federal Acquisition Regulation and to the following:

Unless sooner terminated, this appointment is effective as long as the apointee is assigned to: ______________________ (Organization)

______________________ (Agency/Department)

______________________ (Signature and Title)

______________ (Date)

______________ (No.)

NSN7540-01-152-5812
1402-101

STANDARD FORM 1402 (10-83)
Prescribed by GSA
FAR (48 CFR) 53.201 -1

53.301-1403 Standard Form 1403, Preaward Survey of Prospective Contractor (General)

[FAC 84-58, 55 FR 25535, 6/21/90, effective 7/23/90]

PREAWARD SURVEY OF PROSPECTIVE CONTRACTOR (GENERAL) | 1. SERIAL NO. (For surveying activity use) | FORM APPROVED OMB NO. 9000-0011

Public reporting burden for this collection of information is estimated to average 24 hours per response, including the time for reviewing instructions, searching existing data sources, gathering and maintaining the data needed, and completing and reviewing the collection of information. Send comments regarding this burden estimate or any other aspect of this collection of information, including suggestions for reducing this burden, to the FAR Secretariat (VRS), Office of Federal Acquisition and Regulatory Policy, GSA, Washington, D.C. 20405; and to the Office of Management and Budget, Paperwork Reduction Project (9000-0011), Washington, D.C. 20503.

SECTION I - REQUEST (For Completion by Contracting Office)

2. NAME AND ADDRESS OF SURVEYING ACTIVITY

3. SOLICITATION NO.

4. TOTAL OFFERED PRICE
$

5. TYPE OF CONTRACT

6A. NAME AND ADDRESS OF SECONDARY SURVEY ACTIVITY (For surveying activity use)

7A. NAME AND ADDRESS PROSPECTIVE CONTRACTOR

6B. TELEPHONE NO. (include AUTOVON, WATS or FTS, it available)

7B. FIRM'S CONTACT

7C. TELEPHONE NO. (with area code)

8. WILL CONTRACTING OFFICE PARTICIPATE IN SURVEY?
☐ YES ☐ NO

13. NAME AND ADDRESS OF PARENT COMPANY (if applicable)

9. DATE OF THIS REQUEST

10. DATE REPORT REQUIRED

11. PROSPECTIVE CONTRACTOR REPRESENTS THAT IT ☐ IS, ☐ IS NOT A SMALL BUSINESS CONCERN.

12. WALSH-HEALEY CONTRACTS ACT (Check applicable box(es))
A. IS NOT APPLICABLE
B. IS APPLICABLE AND PROSPECTIVE CONTRACTOR REPRESENTS HIS CLASSIFICATION AS:
☐ MANUFACTURER ☐ REGULAR DEALER
☐ OTHER (Specify)

14A. PLANT AND LOCATION (If different from Item 7, above)

15A. NAME OF REQUESTING ACTIVITY CONTRACTING OFFICER

14B. POINT OF CONTACT

14C. TELEPHONE NO. (with area code)

15B. SIGNATURE

16A. NAME OF CONTACT POINT AT REQUESTING ACTIVITY (if different from Item 15A)

15C. TELEPHONE NO. (Include AUTOVON, WATS or FTS, if available)

17. RETURN PREAWARD SURVEY TO THIS ADDRESS:

ATTN:

16B. TELEPHONE NO. (Include AUTOVON, WATS or FTS, if available)

SECTION II - DATA (For Completion by Contracting Office)

18A. ITEM NO.	18B. NATIONAL STOCK NUMBER (NEW) AND NOMENCLATURE		18C. TOTAL QUANTITY	18D. UNIT PRICE	18E. DELIVERY SCHEDULE (a)	(b)	(c)	(d)	(e)
		SOLICITED							
		OFFERED		$					
		SOLICITED							
		OFFERED		$					
		SOLICITED							
		OFFERED		$					
		SOLICITED							
		OFFERED		$					
		SOLICITED							
		OFFERED		$					
		SOLICITED							
		OFFERED		$					
		SOLICITED							
		OFFERED		$					
		SOLICITED							
		OFFERED		$					

AUTHORIZED FOR LOCAL REPRODUCTION
Previous edition is usable.
EXPIRATION DATE: 9-30-91
1403-103
STANDARD FORM 1403 (Rev. 9-88)
Prescribed by GSA - FAR (48 CFR) 53.209 -1(a)

FEDERAL ACQUISITION REGULATION (FAR)

SECTION III - FACTORS TO BE INVESTIGATED

19. MAJOR FACTORS	CHK. (a)	SAT. (b)	UN-SAT. (c)	20. OTHER FACTORS (Provide specific requirements in Remarks)	CHK. (a)	SAT. (b)	UN-SAT. (c)
A. TECHNICAL CAPABILITY				A. GOVERNMENT PROPERTY CONTROL			
B. PRODUCTION CAPABILITY				B. TRANSPORTATION			
C. QUALITY ASSURANCE CAPABILITY				C. PACKAGING			
D. FINANCIAL CAPABILITY				D. SECURITY			
E. ACCOUNTING SYSTEM				E. SAFETY			
21. IS THIS A SHORT FORM PREAWARD REPORT? (For completion by surveying activity) ☐ YES ☐ NO				F. ENVIRONMENTAL/ENERGY CONSIDERATIONS			
				G. FLIGHT OPERATIONS/FLIGHT SAFETY			
22. IS A FINANCIAL ASSISTANCE PAYMENT PROVISION IN THE SOLICITATION? (For completion by contracting activity) ☐ YES ☐ NO				H. OTHER (Specify)			

23. REMARKS (For Contracting Activity Use)

SECTION IV - SURVEYING ACTIVITY RECOMMENDATIONS

24. RECOMMEND	25A. NAME AND TITLE OF SURVEY APPROVING OFFICIAL	25B. TELEPHONE NO.
☐ A. COMPLETE AWARD ☐ B. PARTIAL AWARD (Quantity ______) ☐ C. NO AWARD	25C. SIGNATURE	25D. DATE

STANDARD FORM 1403 (REV. 9-88) PAGE 2

53.301-1404 Standard Form 1404, Preaward Survey of Prospective Contractor—Technical

[FAC 84-58, 55 FR 25535, 6/21/90, effective 7/23/90]

PREAWARD SURVEY OF PROSPECTIVE CONTRACTOR TECHNICAL	SERIAL NO. (For surveying activity use)	FORM APPROVED OMB NUMBER 9000-0011
	PROSPECTIVE CONTRACTOR	

Public reporting burden for this collection of information is estimated to average 24 hours per response, including the time for reviewing instructions, searching existing data sources, gathering and maintaining the data needed, and completing and reviewing the collection of information. Send comments regarding this burden estimate or any other aspect of this collection of information, including suggestions for reducing this burden, to the FAR Secretariat (VRS), Office of Federal Acquisition and Regulatory Policy, GSA, Washington, DC 20405; and to the Office of Management and Budget, Paperwork Reduction Project (9000-0011), Washington, DC 20503.

1. RECOMMENDED
☐ a. COMPLETE AWARD ☐ b. PARTIAL AWARD (Quantity: ____________) ☐ c. NO AWARD

2. NARRATIVE (Include the following information concerning key personnel who will be involved with the prospective contract: (1) Names, qualification s/experience and length of affiliation with prospective contractor; (2) Evaluate technical capabilities with respect to the requirements of the proposed contract or item classification; (3) Description of any technical capabilities which the prospective contractor lacks. Comment on the prospective contractor's efforts to obtain the needed technical capabilities.)

IF CONTINUATION SHEETS ATTACHED - MARK HERE ☐

3. FIRM HAS AND/OR UNDERSTANDS (Give explanation for any items marked "NO" in 2. narrative)

a. SPECIFICATIONS	☐ YES	☐ NO	b. EXHIBITS	☐ YES	☐ NO
c. DRAWINGS	☐ YES	☐ NO	d. TECHNICAL DATA REQUIREMENTS	☐ YES	☐ NO

4. SURVEY MADE BY	a. SIGNATURE AND OFFICE (Include typed or printed name)	b. TELEPHONE NO. (include area code)	c. DATE SIGNED
5. SURVEY REVIEWING OFFICIAL	a. SIGNATURE AND OFFICE (Include typed or printed name)	b. TELEPHONE NO. (Include area code)	c. DATE REVIEWED

AUTHORIZED FOR LOCAL REPRODUCTION EXPIRATION DATE: 9-30-91 1404-103 **STANDARD FORM 1404** (REV. 9-88)
Previous edition is usable. Prescribed by GSA - FAR (48 CFR) 53.209-1 (b)

53.301-1405 Standard Form 1405, Preaward Survey of Prospective Contractor—Production

[FAC 84-58, 55 FR 25559, 6/21/90, effective 7/23/90]

PREAWARD SURVEY OF PROSPECTIVE CONTRACTOR PRODUCTION	SERIAL NO. (For surveying activity use)	FORM APPROVED OMB NO. 9000-0011
	PROSPECTIVE CONTRACTOR	

Public reporting burden for this collection of information is estimated to average 24 hours per response, including the time for reviewing instructions, searching existing data sources, gathering and maintaining the data needed, and completing and reviewing the collection of information. Send comments regarding this burden estimate or any other aspect of this collection of information, including suggestions for reducing this burden, to the FAR Secretariat (VRS), Office of Federal Acquisition and Regulatory Policy, GSA, Washington, DC 20405; and to the Off ice of Management and Budget, Paperwork Reduction Project (9000-0011), Washington, DC 20503.

SECTION I - RECOMMENDATION

1. RECOMMENDED

☐ a. COMPLETE AWARD ☐ b. PARTIAL AWARD (Quantity:____________) ☐ c. NO AWARD

2. NARRATIVE (Cite those sections of this report which substantiate the recommendations. List any other backup information in this space or on attached sheet if necessary. Identify any formal systems reviews and state results.)

IF CONTINUATION SHEETS ATTACHED - MARK HERE ☐

3. SURVEY MADE BY	a. SIGNATURE AND OFFICE (Include typed or printed name)	b. TELEPHONE NO. (Include area code)	c. DATE SIGNED
4. SURVEY REVIEWING OFFICIAL	a. SIGNATURE AND OFFICE (Include typed or printed name)	b. TELEPHONE NO. (Include area code)	c. DATE REVIEWED

AUTHORIZED FOR LOCAL REPRODUCTION EXPIRATION DATE: 9-30-91 1405-103 **STANDARD FORM 1405** (REV. 9-88)
Previous edition is usable. Prescribed by GSA - FAR (48 CFR) 53.209-1 (c)

SECTION II - PLANT FACILITIES

1. SIZE OF TRACT		4. DESCRIPTION AND TYPE OF BUILDING(S)
2. SQUARE FEET UNDER ROOF	3. NO. OF BUILDINGS	☐ OWNED ☐ LEASED (Give expiration date)

5. SPACE					6. MISCELLANEOUS PLANT OBSERVATIONS		
	TYPE	SQUARE FEET	ADEQUATE	INADEQUATE	(Explain any items marked "NO" on an attached sheet.)	YES	NO
MANUFACTURING	a. TOTAL MANUFACTURING SPACE				a. GOOD HOUSEKEEPING MAINTAINED		
					b. POWER AND FUEL SUPPLY ADEQUATE TO MEET PRODUCTION REQUIREMENTS		
	b. SPACE AVAILABLE FOR OFFERED ITEM				c. ALTERNATE POWER AND FUEL SOURCE AVAILABLE		
STORAGE	c. TOTAL STORAGE SPACE				d. ADEQUATE MATERIAL HANDLING EQUIPMENT AVAILABLE		
	d. FOR INSPECTION LOTS				e. TRANSPORTATION FACILITIES AVAILABLE FOR SHIPPING PRODUCT		
	e. FOR SHIPPING QUANTITIES						
	f. SPACE AVAILABLE FOR OFFERED ITEM				OTHER (Specify) f.		
					g.		
	g. AMOUNT OF STORAGE THAT CAN BE CONVERTED FOR MANUFACTURING, IF REQUIRED				h.		

SECTION III - PRODUCTION EQUIPMENT

	LIST MAJOR EQUIPMENT REQUIRED (Include GFP and annotate it as such)	QUANTITY REQUIRED FOR PROPOSED CONTRACT	TOTAL QTY. REQD.DURING LIFE OF PROPOSED CONTRACT	QUANTITY ON HAND	CONDITION (e)			QUANTITY SHORT* (Col. (c) minus (d))	SOURCE, IF NOT ON HAND	VERIFIED DELIVERY DATE
	MANUFACTURING	(b)	(c)	(d)	G	F	P	(f)	(g)	(h)
MANUFACTURING	1.									
SPECIAL TOOLING	2.									
SPECIAL TEST	3.									

* Coordinate shortage information for financial implications.

SECTION IV - MATERIALS, PURCHASED PARTS AND SUBCONTRACTS

1. PARTS/MATERIALS/SUBCONTRACTS WITH LONGEST LEAD TIME OR CRUCIAL ITEMS

DESCRIPTION (a)	SOURCE (b)	VERIFIED DELIVERY DATE TO MEET PROD. (c)

2. DESCRIBE THE MATERIAL CONTROL SYSTEM, INDICATING WHETHER IT IS CURRENTLY OPERATIONAL, AND EVALUATE ITS ABILITY TO MEET THE NEEDS OF THE PROPOSED ACQUISITION.

SECTION V - PERSONNEL

1. NUMBER AND SOURCE OF EMPLOYEES

TYPE OF EMPLOYEES	NO. ON BOARD	ADD. NO. REQUIRED	AVAIL. YES	AVAIL. NO	SOURCE
a. Skilled Production					
b. Unskilled Production					
c. Engineering					
d. Administrative					
e. TOT. (Lines a thru d)					

2. SHIFTS ON WHICH WORK IS TO BE PERFORMED

☐ FIRST ☐ SECOND ☐ THIRD

3. UNION AFFILIATION

AGREEMENT EXPIRATION DATE ▶

4. RELATIONSHIP WITH LABOR INDICATES PROBLEMS AFFECTING TIMELY PERFORMANCE OF PROPOSED CONTRACT (if "Yes," explain on attached sheet)

☐ YES ☐ NO

SECTION VI - DELIVERY PERFORMANCE RECORD

STANDARD FORM 1405 (REV. 9-88) PAGE 3

SECTION VII - RELATED PREVIOUS PRODUCTION (Government)

PAST YEAR PRODUCTION		GOVERNMENT CONTRACT NUMBER 1/ (c)	PERFORMANCE		QUANTITY (f)	DOLLAR VALUE ($000) (g)
ITEM NOMENCLATURE (a)	NATIONAL STOCK NO. (NSN) (b)		ON SCHED. (d)	DELIN-QUENT (e)		

1/ Identify identical items by an asterisk (*) after the Government contract number.

SECTION VIII - CURRENT PRODUCTION

(Government and civilian concurrent production schedule using same equipment and/or personnel as offered item.)

	ITEM(S) (Include Government Contract No., if applicable. Identify unsatisfactory performance with asterisk (*).)	MONTHLY SCHEDULE OF CONCURRENT DELIVERIES (Quantity)										
		1st	2nd	3rd	4th	5th	6th	7th	8th	9th	10th	BAL.
BEING PRODUCED	1.											
PENDING AWARD	2.											

SECTION IX - ORGANIZATION AND MANAGEMENT DATA

Provide the following information in SECTION I NARRATIVE:

1. Describe the relationship between management, production, and inspection. Attach an organizational chart, if available.

2. Describe the prospective contractor's production control system. State whether or not it is operational.

3. Evaluate the prospective contractor's production control system in terms of (a) historical effectiveness, (b) the proposed contract, and (c) total production during performance of the proposed contract.

4. Comment on or evaluate other areas unique to this survey (include all special requests by the contracting office and any other information pertinent to the proposed contract or item classification).

STANDARD FORM 1405 (REV. 9-88) **PAGE 4**

53.301-1406 Standard Form 1406, Preaward Survey of Prospective Contractor—Quality Assurance

[FAC 97-3, 62 FR 64912, 12/9/97, effective 2/9/98]

PREAWARD SURVEY OF PROSPECTIVE CONTRACTOR QUALITY ASSURANCE	SERIAL NO. (For surveying activity use)	OMB No.: 9000-0011 Expires: 10/31/2000
	PROSPECTIVE CONTRACTOR	

Public reporting burden for this collection of information is estimated to average 24 hours per response, including the time for reviewing instructions, searching existing data sources, gathering and maintaining the data needed, and completing and reviewing the collection of information. Send comments regarding this burden estimate or any other aspect of this collection of information, including suggestions for reducing this burden, to the FAR Secretariat (MVR), Federal Acquisition Policy Division, GSA, Washington, D.C. 20405.

SECTION I - RECOMMENDATION

1. RECOMMEND: ☐ AWARD ☐ NO AWARD *(Provide full substantiation for recommendation in 4. NARRATIVE)*

2 . IF PROSPECTIVE CONTRACTOR RECEIVES AWARD, A POST AWARD CONFERENCE IS RECOMMENDED. ☐ YES ☐ NO

3. AN ON-SITE SURVEY WAS PERFORMED. ☐ YES ☐ NO

4. NARRATIVE

IF CONTINUATION SHEETS - MARK HERE ☐

5. SURVEY MADE BY			6. SURVEY REVIEWING OFFICIAL		
A. SIGNATURE		B. DATE SIGNED	A. SIGNATURE		B. DATE REVIEWED
C. NAME			C. NAME		
D. OFFICE			D. OFFICE		
E. AREA CODE	F. TELEPHONE NUMBER	G. EXT.	E. AREA CODE	F. TELEPHONE NUMBER	G. EXT.

AUTHORIZED FOR LOCAL REPRODUCTION
Previous edition is not usable.

STANDARD FORM 1406 (REV. 11-97)
Prescribed by GSA
FAR (48 CFR) 53.209-1(d)

SECTION II - COMPANY AND SOLICITATION DATA

1. BRIEFLY DESCRIBE HOW QUALITY ASSURANCE RESPONSIBILITIES ARE ACCOMPLISHED.

2. QUALITY ASSURANCE OFFICIALS CONTACTED

A. NAME	B. TITLE	C. YEARS OF QUALITY ASSURANCE EXPERIENCE

3. APPLICABLE CONTRACT QUALITY REQUIREMENTS

A. NUMBER	B. TITLE	C. TAILORING *(If any)*

4. ☐ IDENTICAL OR ☐ SIMILAR ITEMS HAVE BEEN ☐ PRODUCED, ☐ SUPPLIED, OR ☐ SERVICED BY PROSPECTIVE CONTRACTOR

(If similar items, identify:

SECTION III - EVALUATION CHECKLIST

STATEMENTS		YES	NO
1. These items (where applicable to the contract) are understood by the prospective contractor.	A. Exhibits, technical data, drawings, specifications, and approval requirements.		
	B. Preservation, packaging, packing, and marking requirements.		
	C. Other *(Specify)*		
2. Records available indicate that the prospective contractor has a satisfactory quality performance record during the past twelve (12) months for similar items.			
3. Used, reconditioned, or remanufactured material and former Government surplus material will be furnished by the prospective contractor. *(If Yes, explain in Section I NARRATIVE)*			
4. Prospective contractor will require unusual assistance from the Government. *(If Yes, explain in Section I NARRATIVE)*			
5. Did prospective contractor fulfill commitments to correct deficiencies, as proposed on previous surveys, when awarded that contract? *(If No, explain in Section I NARRATIVE)*			
6. Quality verification personnel	NUMBER SKILLED / NUMBER SEMI-SKILLED		
7. Quality verification to production personnel ratio.	RATIO		
THE FOLLOWING ARE AVAILABLE AND ADEQUATE. *(If not applicable, show "NIA" in "Yes" column.)*			
8. Inspection and test equipment, gauges, and instruments for first article and production *(including solicitation specified equipment)*.			
9. Calibration/metrology program.			
10. Quality system procedures and controls.			
11. Control of specifications, drawings, changes and modifications, work/process instructions.			
12. System for determining inspection, test, and measurement requirements.			
13. Purchasing: Processes for selecting qualified suppliers and assuring the quality of purchased materials.			
14. Product identification, segregation, traceability, and maintenance.			
15. Government furnished property controls.			
16. Process controls.			
17. Nonconforming product: System for timely identification, disposition, correction of deficiencies, and corrective and preventative action.			
18. Preservation, storage, packaging, packing, marking, and delivery controls.			
19. Records *(such as: inspection, test, status, corrective actions, calibration, etc.)*			
20. Controls for investigation of customer complaints and correction of deficiencies.			
21. Design controls system.			
22. Computer software *(deliverable and/or non-deliverable)* quality assurance program.			
23. Management review and internal quality audits.			
24. Quality assurance training program.			
25. Installation and servicing quality assurance program.			
26. Statistical techniques.			

STANDARD FORM 1406 (REV. 11-97) PAGE 2

53.301-1407 Standard Form 1407, Preaward Survey of Prospective Contractor—Financial Capability

[FAC 84-58, 55 FR 25564, 6/21/90, effective 7/23/90]

PREAWARD SURVEY OF PROSPECTIVE CONTRACTOR FINANCIAL CAPABILITY	SERIAL NO. (For surveying activity use)	FORM APPROVED OMB NO. 9000-0011
	PROSPECTIVE CONTRACTOR	

Public reporting burden for this collection of information is estimated to average 24 hours per response, including the time for reviewing instructions, searching existing data sources, gathering and maintaining the data needed, and completing and reviewing the collection of information. Send comments regarding this burden estimate or any other aspect of this collection of information, including suggestions for reducing this burden, to the FAR Secretariat (VRS), Office of Federal Acquisition and Regulatory Policy, GSA, Washington, D.C. 20405; and to the Off ice of Management and Budget, Paperwork Reduction Project (9000-0011), Washington, D.C. 20503.

SECTION I - RECOMMENDATION

1. RECOMMENDED

☐ a. COMPLETE AWARD ☐ b. PARTIAL AWARD (Quantity:_____________) ☐ c. NO AWARD

2. TOTAL OFFERED PRICE

3. NARRATIVE (Cite those sections of the report which substantiate the recommendations. Give any other backup information in this space or on an attached sheet, if necessary.)

IF CONTINUATION SHEETS ATTACHED - MARK HERE ☐

	a. SIGNATURE AND OFFICE (Include typed or printed name)	b. TELEPHONE NO. (include area code)	c. DATE SIGNED
4. SURVEY MADE BY			
5. SURVEY REVIEWING OFFICIAL	a. SIGNATURE AND OFFICE (include typed or printed name)	b. TELEPHONE NO. (Include area code)	c. DATE REVIEWED

AUTHORIZED FOR LOCAL REPRODUCTION Previous edition is usable. EXPIRATION DATE: 9-30-91 1407-103 STANDARD FORM 1407 (REV. 9-88) Prescribed by GSA - FAR (48 CFR) 53.209-1 (e)

SECTION II - GENERAL

1. TYPE OF COMPANY	3. NAME AND ADDRESS OF:
☐ CORPORATION ☐ PARTNERSHIP	a. PARENT CO.
☐ SUBSIDIARY ☐ DIVISION	
☐ PROPRIETORSHIP ☐ OTHER (Specify)	b. SUBSIDIARIES
2. YEAR ESTABLISHED:	

SECTION III - BALANCE SHEET/PROFIT AND LOSS STATEMENT

PART A - LATEST BALANCE SHEET		PART B - LATEST PROFIT AND LOSS STATEMENT		
1. DATE	2. FILED WITH	1. CURRENT PERIOD a. FROM	b. TO	2. FILED WITH

3. FINANCIAL POSITION				
a. Cash	$	3. NET SALES	a. CURRENT PERIOD	$
b. Accounts Receivable			b. First prior fiscal year	
c. Inventory			c. Second prior fiscal year	
d. Other Current Assets		4. NET PROFITS BEFORE TAXES		
e. Total Current Assets			a. CURRENT PERIOD	$
f. Fixed Assets			b. First prior fiscal year	
g. Current Liabilities			c. Second prior fiscal year	
h. Long Term Liabilities		PART C - OTHER		
i. Total Liabilities		1. FISCAL YEAR ENDS (Date):		
j. Net Worth		2. BALANCE SHEETS AND PROFIT AND LOSS STATEMENTS HAVE BEEN CERTIFIED ▶	a. THROUGH (Date)	b. BY (Signature)
4. WORKING CAPITAL (Current Assets less Current Liabilities)				

5. RATIOS			3. OTHER PERTINENT DATA
a. CURRENT ASSETS TO CURRENT LIABILITIES	b. ACID TEST (Cash, investments held in lieu of cash and current receivables to current liabilities)	c. TOTAL LIABILITIES TO NET WORTH	

SECTION IV - PROSPECTIVE CONTRACTOR'S FINANCIAL ARRANGEMENTS

Mark "X" in appropriate column.	YES	NO
1. USE OF OWN RESOURCES		
2. USE OF BANK CREDITS		
3. OTHER (Specify)		

4. INDEPENDENT ANALYSIS OF FINANCIAL POSITION SUPPORTS THE STATEMENTS SHOWN IN ITEMS 1, 2, AND 3 ☐ YES ☐ NO (if "NO", explain)

SECTION V - GOVERNMENT FINANCIAL AID

1 TO BE REQUESTED IN CONNECTION WITH PERFORMANCE OF PROPOSED CONTRACT

Mark X" in appropriate column.	YES	NO
a. PROGRESS PAYMENT(S)		
b. GUARANTEED LOAN		
c. ADVANCE PAYMENTS		

2. EXPLAIN ANY "YES" ANSWERS TO ITEMS 1a, b, AND c

3. FINANCIAL AID CURRENTLY OBTAINED FROM THE GOVERNMENT

Complete items below only if Item a., is marked "YES."

a PROSPECTIVE CONTRACTOR RECEIVES GOVERNMENT FINANCING AT PRESENT	b. IS LIQUIDATION CURRENT?	c. AMOUNT OF UNLIQUIDATED PROGRESS PAYMENTS OUTSTANDING	DOLLAR AMOUNTS	(a) AUTHORIZED	(b) IN USE
			a. Guaranteed loans	$	$
☐ YES ☐ NO	☐ YES ☐ NO	$	b. Advance payments	$	$

4. LIST THE GOVERNMENT AGENCIES INVOLVED	5. SHOW THE APPLICABLE CONTRACT NOS.

STANDARD FORM 1407 (REV. 9-88) **PAGE 2**

SECTION VI - BUSINESS AND FINANCIAL REPUTATION

1. COMMENTS OF PROSPECTIVE CONTRACTOR'S BANK

2. COMMENTS OF TRADE CREDITORS

3. COMMENTS AND REPORTS OF COMMERCIAL FINANCIAL SERVICES AND CREDIT ORGANIZATIONS (Such as, Dun & Bradstreet, Standard and Poor, etc.)

4. MOST RECENT CREDIT RATING	a. DATE	b. BY

5. DOES PRICE APPEAR UNREALISTICALLY LOW? ☐ YES ☐ NO (If YES, explain in Section I NARRATIVE)

6. DESCRIBE ANY OUTSTANDING LIENS OR JUDGEMENTS

SECTION VII - SALES (000'S) FOR NEXT SIX QUARTERS

CATEGORY	1	2	3	4	5	6	TOTAL
1. CURRENT CONTRACT SALES (Backlog)	$	$	$	$	$	$	$
A. GOVERNMENT (Prime & Subcontractor)							
B. COMMERCIAL							
2. ANTICIPATED ADDITIONAL SALES							
A. GOVERNMENT (Prime and Subcontractor)							
B. COMMERCIAL							
3. TOTALS							

53.301-1408 Standard Form 1408, Preaward Survey of Prospective Contractor—Accounting System

[Final rule, 62 FR 40236, 7/25/97, effective 6/30/97]

PREAWARD SURVEY OF PROSPECTIVE CONTRACTOR ACCOUNTING SYSTEM	SERIAL NO. (For surveying activity use)	FORM APPROVED OMB NO. 9000-0011
	PROSPECTIVE CONTRACTOR	

Public reporting burden for this collection of information is estimated to average 24 hours per response, including the time for reviewing instructions, searching existing data sources, gathering and maintaining the data needed, and completing and reviewing the collection of information. Send comments regarding this burden estimate or any other aspect of this collection of information, including suggestions for reducing this burden, to the FAR Secretariat (VRS), Office of Federal Acquisition and Regulatory Policy, GSA, Washington, D.C. 20405; and to the Office of Management and Budget, Paperwork Reduction Project (9000-0011), Washington, D.C. 20503.

SECTION I - RECOMMENDATION

1. PROSPECTIVE CONTRACTOR'S ACCOUNTING SYSTEM IS ACCEPTABLE FOR AWARD OF PROSPECTIVE CONTRACT.

☐ YES ☐ NO (Explain in 2. NARRATIVE)

☐ YES, WITH A RECOMMENDATION THAT A FOLLOW ON ACCOUNTING SYSTEM REVIEW BE PERFORMED AFTER CONTRACT AWARD (Explain in 2. NARRATIVE)

2 NARRATIVE (Clarification of deficiencies, and other pertinent comments. If additional space is required, continue on plain sheets of paper.)

IF CONTINUATION SHEETS ATTACHED - MARK HERE ☐

	a. SIGNATURE AND OFFICE (Include typed or printed name)	b. TELEPHONE NO. (Include area code)	c. DATE SIGNED
3. SURVEY MADE BY			
4. SURVEY REVIEWING OFFICIAL	a. SIGNATURE AND OFFICE (Include typed or printed name)	b. TELEPHONE NO. (Include area code)	c. DATE REVIEWED

AUTHORIZED FOR LOCAL REPRODUCTION EXPIRATION DATE: 9-30-91 1408-103 **STANDARD FORM 1408** (REV. 9-88)
Previous edition is usable. Prescribed by GSA - FAR (48 CFR) 53.209-1 (f)

SECTION II - EVALUATION CHECKLIST

MARK "X" IN THE APPROPRIATE COLUMN (Explain any deficiencies in SECTION I NARRATIVE)	YES	NO	NOT APPLI-CABLE
1. EXCEPT AS STATED IN SECTION I NARRATIVE, IS THE ACCOUNTING SYSTEM IN ACCORD WITH GENERALLY ACCEPTED ACCOUNTING PRINCIPLES APPLICABLE IN THE CIRCUMSTANCES?			
2. ACCOUNTING SYSTEM PROVIDES FOR:			
a. Proper segregation of direct costs from indirect costs.			
b. Identification and accumulation of direct costs by contract.			
c. A logical and consistent method for the allocation of indirect costs to intermediate and final cost objectives. (A contract is a final cost objective.)			
d. Accumulation of costs under general ledger control.			
e. A timekeeping system that identifies employees' labor by intermediate or final cost objectives.			
f. A labor distribution system that charges direct and indirect labor to the appropriate cost objectives.			
g. Interim (at least monthly) determination of costs charged to a contract through routine posting of books of account.			
h. Exclusion from costs charged to government contracts of amounts which are not allowable in terms of FAR 31, Contract Cost Principles and Procedures, or other contract provisions.			
i. Identification of costs by contract line item and by units (as if each unit or line item were a separate contract) if required by the proposed contract.			
j. Segregation of preproduction costs from production costs.			
3. ACCOUNTING SYSTEM PROVIDES FINANCIAL INFORMATION:			
a. Required by contract clauses concerning limitation of cost (FAR 52.232-20 and 21) or limitation on payments (FAR 52.216-16).			
b. Required to support requests for progress payments.			
4. IS THE ACCOUNTING SYSTEM DESIGNED AND ARE THE RECORDS MAINTAINED IN SUCH A MANNER THAT ADEQUATE, RELIABLE DATA ARE DEVELOPED FOR USE IN PRICING FOLLOW-ON ACQUISITIONS?			
5. IS THE ACCOUNTING SYSTEM CURRENTLY IN FULL OPERATION? (If not, describe in Section I Narrative which portions are (1) in operation, (2) set up, but not yet in operation, (3) anticipated, or (4) nonexistent.)			

STANDARD FORM 1408 (REV. 9-88) PAGE 2

53.301-1409 Standard Form 1409, Abstract of Offers

[FAC 84-58, 55 FR 25566, 6/21/90, effective 7/23/90]

ABSTRACT OF OFFERS	SOLICITATION NO.	OPENING DATE	PAGE OF PAGES
ISSUING OFFICE		SUPPLIES OR SERVICES (General Description)	

NO.	NAME OF OFFEROR	ACCEPTANCE TIME * (Days)	BUSINESS SIZE L	BUSINESS SIZE S	ITEM NO. ▶ QUANTITY ▶ UNIT ▶				DELIVERY TIME**	F.O.B. POINT	REMARKS
						$	$	$			

* Indicate by an X a 60-day acceptance.
** Indicate by an X if offer conforms to delivery time specified in solicitation.

I CERTIFY THAT I HAVE OPENED, READ AND RECORDED ON THIS ABSTRACT (AND CONTINUATION SHEETS, IF ANY) ALL OFFERS RECEIVED IN RESPONSE TO THE SOLICITATION.

TYPED NAME AND TITLE

SIGNATURE

DATE

NSN 7540-01-142-9844 1409-102 **STANDARD FORM 1409** (Rev. 9-88)
Prescribed by GSA, FAR (48 CFR) 53.214(f)

53.301-1410 Standard Form 1410, Abstract of Offers—Continuation

[FAC 84-49, 54 FR 29286, 7/11/89, effective 8/10/89]

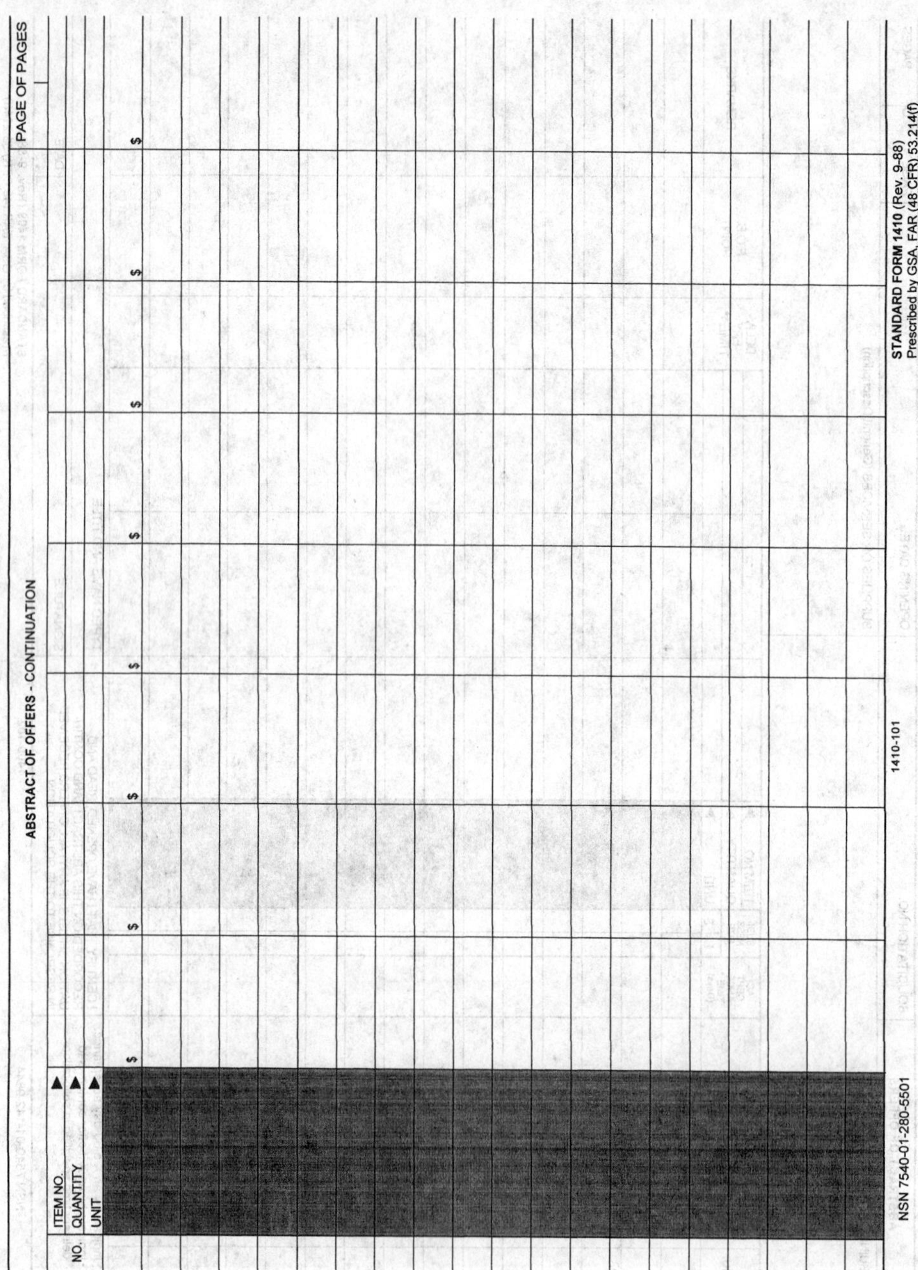
ABSTRACT OF OFFERS - CONTINUATION

PAGE OF PAGES

NO. | ITEM NO. | QUANTITY | UNIT

$ $ $ $ $ $ $ $

NSN 7540-01-280-5501

1410-101

STANDARD FORM 1410 (Rev. 9-88)
Prescribed by GSA, FAR (48 CFR) 53.214(f)

53.301-1413 Standard Form 1413, Statement and Acknowledgment

[FAC 84-53, 54 FR 48999, 11/28/89, effective 2/26/90; FAC 2005-04, 70 FR 33662, 6/8/2005, effective 7/8/2005;FAC 2005-73, 79 FR 24192, 4/29/2014, effective 5/29/2014]

STATEMENT AND ACKNOWLEDGMENT

OMB No.: 9000-0014
Expires: 6/30/2014

PAPERWORK REDUCTION ACT STATEMENT: Public reporting burden for this collection of information is estimated to average .05 hours per response, including the time for reviewing instructions, searching existing data sources, gathering and maintaining the data needed, and completing and reviewing the collection of information. Send comments regarding this burden estimate or any other aspects of this collection of information, including suggestions for reducing this burden, to U.S. General Services Administration, Regulatory Secretariat (MVCB)/IC 9000-0014, Office of Governmentwide Acquisition Policy,1800 F Street, NW, Washington, DC 20405.

PART I - STATEMENT OF PRIME CONTRACTOR

1. PRIME CONTRACT NO.	2. DATE SUBCONTRACT AWARDED	3. SUBCONTRACT NUMBER

4. PRIME CONTRACTOR			5. SUBCONTRACTOR		
a. NAME			a. NAME		
b. STREET ADDRESS			b. STREET ADDRESS		
c. CITY	d. STATE	e. ZIP CODE	c. CITY	d. STATE	e. ZIP CODE

6. The prime contract ☐ does, ☐ does not contain the clause entitled "Contract Work Hours and Safety Standards Act – Overtime Compensation."

7. The prime contractor states that under the contract shown in Item 1, a subcontract was awarded on the date shown in Item 2 to the subcontractor identified in item 5 by the following firm:

a. NAME OF AWARDING FIRM

b. DESCRIPTION OF WORK BY SUBCONTRACTOR

8. PROJECT	9. LOCATION

10a. NAME OF PERSON SIGNING	11. BY *(Signature)*	12. DATE SIGNED
10b. TITLE OF PERSON SIGNING		

PART II - ACKNOWLEDGMENT OF SUBCONTRACTOR

13. The subcontractor acknowledges that the following clauses of the contract shown in Item 1 are included in this subcontract:

- Contract Work Hours and Safety Standards Act - Overtime Compensation (If included in prime contract see Block 6)
- Payrolls and Basic Records
- Withholding of Funds
- Disputes Concerning Labor Standards
- Compliance with Construction Wage Rate Requirements and Related Regulations
- Construction Wage Rate Requirements
- Apprentices and Trainees
- Compliance with Copeland Act Requirements
- Subcontracts (Labor Standards)
- Contract Termination - Debarment
- Certification of Eligibility

14. NAME(S) OF ANY INTERMEDIATE SUBCONTRACTORS, IF ANY

A		C	
B		D	

15a. NAME OF PERSON SIGNING	16. BY *(Signature)*	17. DATE SIGNED
15b. TITLE OF PERSON SIGNING		

AUTHORIZED FOR LOCAL REPRODUCTION
PREVIOUS EDITION IS NOT USABLE

STANDARD FORM 1413 (REV. 4/2013)
Prescribed by GSA/FAR (48 CFR) 53.222(e)

53.301-1414 Standard Form 1414 (REV 10/93), Consent of Surety

[FAC 90-23, 59 FR 67010, 12/28/94, effective 2/27/95]

CONSENT OF SURETY	1. CONTRACT NUMBER	2. MODIFICATION NUMBER	3. DATED

The Surety (Co-Sureties) consents (consent) to the foregoing contract modification and agrees (agree) that its (their) bond or bonds shall apply and extend to the contract as modified or amended.

4. INDIVIDUAL PRINCIPAL	a. NAME OF PRINCIPAL			c. SIGNATURE	(Affix Seal)
	b. BUSINESS ADDRESS			d. TYPED NAME	
	STREET ADDRESS			e. TYPED TITLE	
	CITY	STATE	ZIP CODE	f. DATE THIS CONSENT EXECUTED	
5. CORPORATE PRINCIPAL	a. CORPORATE NAME			c. PERSON EXECUTING CONSENT *(Signature)*	(Affix Seal)
	b. BUSINESS ADDRESS			d. TYPED NAME	
	STREET ADDRESS			e. TYPED TITLE	
	CITY	STATE	ZIP CODE	f. DATE THIS CONSENT EXECUTED	

6. CORPORATE/INDIVIDUAL SURETY (CO-SURETIES)

The Principal or authorized representative shall execute this consent of surety with the modification to which it pertains. If the representative (e.g., attorney-in-fact) that signs the consent is not a member of the partnership, or joint venture, or an officer of the corporation involved, a Power-of-Attorney or a Certificate of Corporate Principal must accompany the consent.

A	a. CORPORATE/INDIVIDUAL SURETY'S NAME			c. PERSON EXECUTING CONSENT *(Signature)*	(Affix Seal)
	b. BUSINESS ADDRESS			d. TYPED NAME	
	STREET ADDRESS			e. TYPED TITLE	
	CITY	STATE	ZIP CODE	f. DATE THIS CONSENT EXECUTED	
B	a. CORPORATE/INDIVIDUAL SURETY'S NAME			c. PERSON EXECUTING CONSENT *(Signature)*	(Affix Seal)
	b. BUSINESS ADDRESS			d. TYPED NAME	
	STREET ADDRESS			e. TYPED TITLE	
	CITY	STATE	ZIP CODE	f. DATE THIS CONSENT EXECUTED	
C	a. CORPORATE/INDIVIDUAL SURETY'S NAME			c. PERSON EXECUTING CONSENT *(Signature)*	(Affix Seal)
	b. BUSINESS ADDRESS			d. TYPED NAME	
	STREET ADDRESS			e. TYPED TITLE	
	CITY	STATE	ZIP CODE	f. DATE THIS CONSENT EXECUTED	

(Add similar signature blocks on the back of this form if necessary for additional co-Sureties)

AUTHORIZED FOR LOCAL REPRODUCTION
Previous edition is usable

STANDARD FORM 1414 (REV 97)
Prescribed by GSA - FAR (48 CFR) 53.228(k)

CCH G90127 0430

53.301-1415 Standard Form 1415 (REV 7/93), Consent of Surety and Increase of Penalty

[FAC 90-23, 59 FR 67010, 12/28/94, effective 2/27/95]

CONSENT OF SURETY AND INCREASE OF PENALTY	1. CONTRACT NUMBER	2. MODIFICATION NUMBER	3. DATED

4. The surety (co-sureties) consents (consent) to the foregoing contract modification and agrees (agree) that its (their) bond or bonds shall apply and extend to the contract as modified or amended. The principal and surety (co-sureties) further agree that on or after the execution of this consent, the penalty of the performance bond or bonds is increased by ______________ dollars ($______________) and the penalty of the payment bond or bonds is increased by ______________ dollars ($______________). However, the increase of the liability of each co-surety resulting from this consent shall not exceed the sums shown below.

5. NAME OF SURETY(IES)	6. INCREASE IN LIABILITY LIMIT UNDER PERFORMANCE BOND	7. INCREASE IN LIABILITY LIMIT UNDER PAYMENT BOND
a.	$	$
b.		
c.		

8. INDIVIDUAL PRINCIPAL	a. BUSINESS ADDRESS	b. SIGNATURE * c. TYPED NAME AND TITLE d. DATE THIS CONSENT EXECUTED	*(Affix Seal)*
9. CORPORATE PRINCIPAL	a. CORPORATE NAME AND BUSINESS ADDRESS	b. PERSON EXECUTING CONSENT *(Signature)** BY c. TYPED NAME AND TITLE d. DATE THIS CONSENT EXECUTED	*(Affix Corporate Seal)*

*The Principal or authorized representative shall execute this Consent of Surety and Increase of Penalty with the modification to which it pertains. If the representative (e.g., attorney-in-fact) that signs the consent is not a member of the partnership, or joint venture, or an officer of the corporation involved, a Power-of-Attorney or a Certificate of Corporate Principal must accompany the consent.

10. CORPORATE/INDIVIDUAL SURETY (CO-SURETIES)

A	a. CORPORATE/INDIVIDUAL SURETY'S NAME AND ADDRESS	b. PERSON EXECUTING CONSENT *(Signature)* BY c. TYPED NAME AND TITLE d. DATE THIS CONSENT EXECUTED	*(Affix Seal)*
B	a. CORPORATE/INDIVIDUAL SURETY'S NAME AND ADDRESS	b. PERSON EXECUTING CONSENT *(Signature)* BY c. TYPED NAME AND TITLE d. DATE THIS CONSENT EXECUTED	*(Affix Seal)*
C	a. CORPORATE/INDIVIDUAL SURETY'S NAME AND ADDRESS	b. PERSON EXECUTING CONSENT *(Signature)* BY c. TYPED NAME AND TITLE d. DATE THIS CONSENT EXECUTED	*(Affix Seal)*

Add similar signature blocks on the back of this form if necessary for additional co-sureties.

Previous editions not usable

AUTHORIZED FOR LOCAL REPRODUCTION

STANDARD FORM 1415 (REV. 7-93)
Prescribed by GSA - FAR (48 CFR) 53.228(l)

53.301-1416 Standard Form 1416, Payment Bond for Other than Construction Contracts

[FAC 84-58, 55 FR 25568, 6/21/90, effective 7/23/90; FAC 97-10, 63 FR 70264, 12/18/98, effective 1/4/99]

PAYMENT BOND FOR OTHER THAN CONSTRUCTION CONTRACTS (See instructions on reverse)	DATE BOND EXECUTED (Must not be later than bid opening date)	OMB NO.:9000-0045

Public reporting burden for this collection of information is estimated to average 25 minutes per response, including the time for reviewing instructions, searching existing data sources, gathering and maintaining the data needed, and completing and reviewing the collection of information. Send comments regarding this burden estimate or any other aspect of this collection of information, including suggestions for reducing this burden, to the FAR Secretariat (MVR), Federal Acquisition Policy Division, GSA, Washington, DC 20405.

PRINCIPAL (Legal name and business address)	TYPE OF ORGANIZATION ("X" one) ☐ INDIVIDUAL ☐ PARTNERSHIP ☐ JOINT VENTURE ☐ CORPORATION
	STATE OF INCORPORATION
SURETY(IES) (Name(s) and business address(es)) (include ZIP code)	PENAL SUM OF BOND: MILLION(S) / THOUSAND(S) / HUNDRED(S) / CENTS
	CONTRACT DATE / CONTRACT NO.

We, the Principal and Surety(ies) are firmly bound to the United States of America (hereinafter called the Government) in the above penal sum. For payment of the penal sum, we bind ourselves, our heirs, executors, administrators, and successors, jointly and severally. However, where the Sureties are corporations acting as co-sureties, we, the Sureties, bind ourselves in such sum "jointly and severally" as well as "severally" only for the purpose of allowing a joint action or actions against any or all of us. For all other purposes, each Surety binds itself, jointly and severally with the Principal, for the payment of the sum shown opposite the name of the Surety. If no limit of liability is indicated, the limit of liability is the full amount of the penal sum.

CONDITIONS:

The Principal has entered into the contract identified above.

THEREFORE:

(a) The above obligation is void if the Principal promptly makes payment to all persons (claimants) having a contract relationship with the Principal or a subcontractor of the Principal for furnishing labor, material or both in the prosecution of the work provided for in the contract identified above and any duly authorized modifications thereof. Notice of those modifications to the Surety(ies) are waived.

(b) The above obligation shall remain in full force if the Principal does not promptly make payments to all persons (claimants) having a contract relationship with the principal or a subcontractor of the Principal for furnishing labor, material or both in the prosecution of the contract identified above. In these cases, persons not paid in full before the expiration of ninety (90) days after the date of which the last labor was performed or material furnishing, have a direct right of action against the principal and Surety(ies) on this bond for the sum or sums justly due. The claimant, however, may not bring a suit or any action -

(1) Unless claimant, other than one having a direct contract with the Principal, had given written notice to the Principal within ninety (90) days after the claimant did or performed the last of the work or labor, or furnished or supplied the last of the materials for which the claim is made. The notice is to state with substantial accuracy the amount claimed and the name of the party to whom the materials were furnished or supplied, or for whom the work or labor was done or performed. Such notice shall be served by mailing the same by registered or certified mail, postage prepaid, in an envelope addressed to the Principal at any place where an office is regularly maintained for the transaction of business, or served in any manner in which legal process is served in the state in which the contract is being performed, save that such service need not be made by a public officer.

(2) After the expiration one (1) year following the date on which claimant did or performed the last of the work or labor, or furnished or suppled the last of the materials for which the suit is brought.

(3) Other than in the United States District court for the district in which the the contract, or any part thereof, was performed and executed, and not elsewhere.

WITNESS:

The Principal and Surety(ies) executed this bid bond and affixed their seals on the above date.

AUTHORIZED FOR LOCAL REPRODUCTION
Previous edition is usable

STANDARD FORM 1416 (REV. 10-98)
Prescribed by GSA - FAR (48 CFR) 53.228(m)

PRINCIPAL				
SIGNATURE(S)	1. (Seal)	2. (Seal)	3. (Seal)	Corporate Seal
NAME(S) & TITLE(S) (Typed)	1.	2.	3.	

INDIVIDUAL SURETY(IES)		
SIGNATURE(S)	1. (Seal)	2. (Seal)
NAME(S) & TITLE(S) (Typed)	1.	2.

CORPORATE SURETY(IES)					
SURETY A	NAME & ADDRESS		STATE OF INC.	LIABILITY LIMIT $	Corporate Seal
	SIGNATURE(S)	1.	2.		
	NAME(S) & TITLE(S) (Typed)	1.	2.		
SURETY B	NAME & ADDRESS		STATE OF INC.	LIABILITY LIMIT $	Corporate Seal
	SIGNATURE(S)	1.	2.		
	NAME(S) & TITLE(S) (Typed)	1.	2.		

INSTRUCTIONS

1. This form is authorized for use when payment bonds are required under FAR (48 CFR) 28.103-3, i.e., payment bonds for other than construction contracts. Any deviation from this form will require the written approval of the Administrator of General Services.

2. Insert the full legal name and business address of the Principal in the space designated "Principal" on the face of the form. An authorized person shall sign the bond. Any person signing in a representative capacity (e.g., an attorney-in-fact) must furnish evidence of authority if that representative is not a member of the firm, partnership, or joint venture, or an officer of the corporation involved.

3. (a) Corporations executing the bond as sureties must appear on the Department of the Treasury's list of approved sureties and must act within the limitation listed therein. Where more than one corporate surety is involved, their names and addresses shall appear in the spaces (Surety A, Surety B, etc.) headed "CORPORATE SURETY(IES)." In the space designed "SURETY(IES)" on the face of the form, insert only the letter identification of the sureties.

(b) Where individual Sureties are involved, a completed Affidavit of Individual Surety (Standard Form 28), for each individual surety, shall accompany the bond. The Government may require the surety to furnish additional substantiating information concerning its financial capability.

4. Corporations executing the bond shall affix their corporate seals. Individuals shall execute the bond opposite the word "Corporate Seal"; and shall affix an adhesive seal if executed in Maine, New Hampshire, or any other jurisdiction requiring adhesive seals.

5. Type the name and title of each person signing this bond in the space provided.

STANDARD FORM 1416 (REV. 10-98) **BACK**

53.301-1417 [Removed]

[FAC 84-49, 54 FR 29288, 7/11/89, effective 8/10/89; FAC 2001-25, 69 FR 59699, 10/5/2004, effective 11/4/2004]

53.301-1418 Standard Form 1418, Performance Bond for Other Than Construction Contracts

[FAC 90-40, 61 FR 39186, 7/26/96, effective 9/24/96; FAC 97-11, 64 FR 10530, 3/4/99, effective 3/4/99]

PERFORMANCE BOND FOR OTHER THAN CONSTRUCTION CONTRACTS *(See instructions on reverse)*	DATE BOND EXECUTED *(Must be same or later than date of contract)*	OMB No.: 9000-0045

Public reporting burden for this collection of information is estimated to average 25 minutes per response, including the time for reviewing instructions, searching existing data sources, gathering and maintaining the data needed, and completing and reviewing the collection of information. Send comments regarding this burden estimate or any other aspect of this collection of information, including suggestions for reducing this burden, to the FAR Secretariat (MVR), Federal Acquisition Policy Division, GSA, Washington, DC 20405

PRINCIPAL *(Legal name and business address)*	TYPE OF ORGANIZATION *("X" one)* ☐ INDIVIDUAL ☐ PARTNERSHIP ☐ JOINT VENTURE ☐ CORPORATION			
	STATE OF INCORPORATION			
SURETY(IES) *(Name(s) and business address(es))*	PENAL SUM OF BOND			
	MILLION(S)	THOUSAND(S)	HUNDRED(S)	CENTS
	CONTRACT DATE	CONTRACT NO.		
	OPTION DATE	OPTION NO.		

OBLIGATION:

We, the Principal and Surety(ies), are firmly bound to the United States of America (hereinafter called the Government) in the above penal sum. For payment of the penal sum, we bind ourselves, our heirs, executors, administrators, and successors, jointly and severally. However, where the Sureties are corporations acting as co-sureties, we the Sureties, bind ourselves in such sum "jointly and severally" as well as "severally" only for the purpose of allowing a joint action or actions against any or all of us. For all other purposes, each Surety binds itself, jointly and severally with the Principal, for the payment of the sum shown opposite the name of the Surety. If no limit of liability is indicated, the limit of liability is the full amount of the penal sum.

CONDITIONS:

The Principal has entered into the contract identified above.

THEREFORE:

The above obligation is void if the Principal: (1) Performs and fulfills all the undertakings, covenants, terms, conditions, and agreements of the contract during either the base term or an optional term of the contract and any extensions thereof that are granted by the Government, with or without notice to the Surety(ies), and during the life of any guaranty required under the contract, and (2) performs and fulfills all the undertakings, covenants, terms, conditions, and agreements of any and all duly authorized modifications of the contract that hereafter are made. Notice of those modifications to the Surety(ies) is waived.

The guaranty for a base term covers the initial period of performance of the contract and any extensions thereof excluding any options. The guaranty for an option term covers the period of performance for the option being exercised and any extensions thereof.

The failure of a surety to renew a bond for any option term shall not result in a default of any bond previously furnished covering any base or option term.

WITNESS:

The Principal and Surety(ies) executed this performance bond and affixed their seals on the above date.

PRINCIPAL

SIGNATURE(S)	1. (Seal)	2. (Seal)	Corporate Seal
NAME(S) & TITLE(S) *(Typed)*	1.	2.	

INDIVIDUAL SURETY(IES)

SIGNATURE(S)	1. (Seal)	2. (Seal)
NAME(S) *(Typed)*	1.	2.

CORPORATE SURETY(IES)

SURETY A	NAME & ADDRESS		STATE OF INC.	LIABILITY LIMIT $	Corporate Seal
	SIGNATURE(S)	1.	2.		
	NAME(S) & TITLE(S) *(Typed)*	1.	2.		

AUTHORIZED FOR LOCAL REPRODUCTION
Previous edition not usable

STANDARD FORM 1418 (REV. 2-99)
Prescribed by GSA-FAR (48 CFR) 53.228(b)

SURETY B	NAME & ADDRESS		STATE OF INC.	LIABILITY LIMIT $	Corporate Seal
	SIGNATURE(S)	1.	2.		
	NAME(S) & TITLE(S) (Typed)	1.	2.		
SURETY C	NAME & ADDRESS		STATE OF INC.	LIABILITY LIMIT $	Corporate Seal
	SIGNATURE(S)	1.	2.		
	NAME(S) & TITLE(S) (Typed)	1.	2.		
SURETY D	NAME & ADDRESS		STATE OF INC.	LIABILITY LIMIT $	Corporate Seal
	SIGNATURE(S)	1.	2.		
	NAME(S) & TITLE(S) (Typed)	1.	2.		
SURETY E	NAME & ADDRESS		STATE OF INC.	LIABILITY LIMIT $	Corporate Seal
	SIGNATURE(S)	1.	2.		
	NAME(S) & TITLE(S) (Typed)	1.	2.		
SURETY F	NAME & ADDRESS		STATE OF INC.	LIABILITY LIMIT $	Corporate Seal
	SIGNATURE(S)	1.	2.		
	NAME(S) & TITLE(S) (Typed)	1.	2.		
SURETY G	NAME & ADDRESS		STATE OF INC.	LIABILITY LIMIT $	Corporate Seal
	SIGNATURE(S)	1.	2.		
	NAME(S) & TITLE(S) (Typed)	1.	2.		

BOND PREMIUM	RATE PER THOUSAND ($)	TOTAL ($)

INSTRUCTIONS

1. This form is authorized for use in connection with Government contracts. Any deviation from this form will require the written approval of the Administrator of General Services.

2. Insert the full legal name and business address of the Principal in the space designated "Principal" on the face of the form. An authorized person shall sign the bond. Any person signing in a representative capacity (e.g., an attorney-in-fact) must furnish evidence of authority if that representative is not a member of the firm, partnership, or joint venture, or an officer of the coporation involved.

3. (a) Corporations executing the bond as sureties must appear on the Department of the Treasury's list of approved sureties and must act within the limitation listed therein. Where more than one corporate surety is involved, their names and addresses shall appear in the spaces (Surety A, Surety B, etc.) headed "CORPORATE SURETY(IES)." In the space designated "SURETY(IES)" on the face of the form, insert only the letter identification of the sureties.

(b) Where individual sureties are involved, a completed Affidavit of Individual Surety (Standard Form 28) for each individual surety, shall accompany the bond. The Government may require the surety to furnish additional substantiating information concerning their financial capability.

4. Corporations executing the bond shall affix their corporate seals. Individuals shall execute the bond opposite the word "Corporate Seal", and shall affix an adhesive seal if executed in Maine, New Hampshire, or any other jurisdiction requiring adhesive seals.

5. Type the name and title of each person signing this bond in the space provided.

6. Unless otherwise specified, the bond shall be submitted to the contracting office that awarded the contract.

STANDARD FORM 1418 (REV. 2-99) BACK

53.301-1420 [Removed]

[FAC 2005-34, 74 FR 31557, 7/1/2009, effective 7/1/2009]

53.301-1421 [Removed]

[FAC 2005-34, 74 FR 31557, 7/1/2009, effective 7/1/2009]

53.301-1423 Standard Form 1423, Inventory Verification Survey

[FAC 90-45, Final rule, 62 FR 224, 1/2/97, effective 1/1/97; FAC 2001-22, Final rule 69 FR 17741, 4/5/2004, effective 5/5/2004]

INVENTORY VERIFICATION SURVEY
(See FAR 45.602-1(b)(1))

DATE

SECTION I - GENERAL

1. FROM: *(Include ZIP Code)*

2. TO: *(Include ZIP Code)*

3. CONTRACT NUMBER AND TYPE

4. CONTRACTOR/SUBCONTRACTOR

5A. SCHEDULES OF INVENTORY TO BE INSPECTED AND VERIFIED

REFERENCE NUMBER	PAGES		AMOUNT ($)
	START NO.	END NO.	

5B. PLANT CLEARANCE CASE NUMBER/DOCUMENT NUMBER

SECTION II - TECHNICAL VERIFICATION

	YES	NO
6. IS PROPERTY LISTED ON THE INVENTORY DISPOSAL SCHEDULES ON HAND AND IN THE QUANTITIES INDICATED?		*
7. IS THE PROPERTY CORRECTLY DESCRIBED ON THE INVENTORY DISPOSAL SCHEDULES?		*
8. IS THE PROPERTY SEGREGATED OR ADEQUATELY PROTECTED?		*
9. IS THE PROPERTY PROPERLY TAGGED?		*
10. ARE THE CONDITION CODES ACCURATE?		*
11. IS THE PROPERTY CLASSIFICATION CORRECTLY IDENTIFIED?		*

	YES	NO
12. ARE THE WEIGHTS OF THE ITEMS APPROXIMATELY CORRECT?		*
IF WEIGHTS ARE NOT SHOWN, GIVE ESTIMATE OF WEIGHT BY BASIC MATERIAL CONTENT: ________		
13. DO THE ITEMS APPEAR TO HAVE COMMERCIAL VALUE OTHER THAN SCRAP?	*	*
14. DID CONTRACTOR MAKE REASONABLE EFFORTS TO RETURN THE PROPERTY?		*
15. DO ANY ITEMS REQUIRE DEMILITARIZATION OR SPECIAL PROCESSING *(sensitive items)*?	*	
16. ARE COMMON ITEMS INCLUDED ON THE INVENTORY DISPOSAL SCHEDULE?	*	

SECTION III - TERMINATION INVENTORY

COMPLETION OF THIS SECTION ☐ IS ☐ IS NOT REQUIRED *(Requester, check one)*

	YES	NO
17. DID WORK STOP PROMPTLY UPON RECEIPT OF THE TERMINATION NOTICE?		*
DATE OF NOTICE: ________		
18a. DO THE QUANTITIES OF MATERIAL EXCEED THE AMOUNTS THAT WOULD HAVE BEEN REQUIRED TO COMPLETE THE TERMIINATED PORTION OF THE CONTRACT?	*	
b. CAN THE ITEMS OF TERMINATION INVENTORY BE USED ON THE CONTINUING PORTION OF THE CONTRACT?	*	
19. ARE ALL ITEMS AND QUANTITIES ALLOCABLE TO THE TERMINATION PORTION OF THIS CONTRACT OR ORDER?		*

	YES	NO
20. DOES THE INVENTORY INCLUDE REJECTS? IF YES, EXPLAIN SPECIFIC LINE ITEM ENTRIES. OBTAIN FROM CONTRACTOR ESTIMATED COST OF REWORKING REJECTS ON SPECIFIC LINE ITEM BASIS.	*	
21a. HAVE COMPLETED ARTICLES BEEN INSPECTED AS TO QUALITY AND CONFORMANCE TO SPECIFICATIONS?		*
b. DO THE COMPLETED ITEMS INSPECTED CONFORM TO CONTRACT SPECIFICATIONS?		*
c, DO OTHER THAN COMPLETED ITEMS CONFORM WITH TECHNICAL REQUIREMENTS OF THE CONTRACT OR ORDER?		*
22. FOR WORK-IN-PROCESS, IS THE PERCENTAGE OF COMPLETION ACCURATE?		*

23. REQUESTING OFFICE REMARKS *(Where the answer to any question is placed in a block containing an asterisk (*) detailed comments of the verifier shall be included on the reverse of this form and identified by section and item number.)*

24. SIGNATURE OF REQUESTER

INVENTORY VERIFICATION
The above information is based on a physical verification of inventory listed under Item 5.

25. NAME AND TITLE	26. SIGNATURE OF VERIFIER	27. DATE

AUTHORIZED FOR LOCAL REPRODUCTION
Previous edition not usable

STANDARD FORM 1423 (REV. 5/2004)
Prescribed by GSA-FAR (48 CFR) 53.245(c)

53.301-1424 Standard Form 1424, Inventory Disposal Report

[FAC 84-56, 55 FR 3893, 2/5/90, effective 3/7/90; FAC 2001-22, 69 FR 17741, 4/5/2004, effective 5/5/2004]

INVENTORY DISPOSAL REPORT
(See FAR 45.605)

PLANT CLEARANCE CASE NUMBER

TO: *(Include ZIP Code)*	FROM: *(Include ZIP Code)*

1. DATE PLANT CLEARANCE CASE OPENED	2. DATE PLANT CLEARANCE CASE CLOSED	3. NUMBER OF DAYS BETWEEN OPENING AND CLOSING

4. NAME AND ADDRESS OF CONTRACTOR/SUBCONTRACTOR *(Include ZIP Code)*	5. IF SUBCONTRACTOR, STATE NAME AND ADDRESS OF PRIME CONTRACTOR *(Include ZIP Code)*

6. LOCATION OF PROPERTY *(City and State)*	7. CONTRACT NUMBER	8. DOCKET NUMBER *(Termination only)*
	9. SUBCONTRACT NUMBER	10. CONTRACTOR REFERENCE NUMBER

DISPOSITION OF PROPERTY

ITEM DESCRIPTION	LINE ITEMS	ACQUISITION COST	PROCEEDS
11. **TOTAL INVENTORY AS SUBMITTED**			
12. ADJUSTMENTS (*Pricing errors, shortages, etc.)*			
13. ADJUSTED INVENTORY *(Line 11 + or - Line 12)*			
14. PURCHASE OR RETENTION AT COST			
15. RETURN TO SUPPLIERS *(Net Proceeds)*			
16. REDISTRIBUTIONS			
A. WITHIN OWNING AGENCY			
B. OTHER AGENCIES			
TOTAL			
17. DONATIONS			
18. SALES			
19. SALES - SCRAP PROCEEDS TO OVERHEAD			
20.			
21.			
22. **TOTAL PROCEEDS CREDIT** ***(Total Lines 14, 15, and 18)***			
23. ABANDONED			
24. DESTROYED/ABANDONED			
25. DESTROYED/SCRAPPED			
26. OTHER *(Explain in Item 28, Remarks)*			
27. **TOTAL DISPOSITIONS**			

28. REMARKS *(Identify contract number in which proceeds were applied, or disbursing office where proceeds were deposited)*

To the best of my knowledge, disposition of all property on this case has been effected in accordance with existing regulations, all property has been accounted for and all disposal credits properly applied.

CONTRACT ADMINISTRATION OFFICE *(Authorized signature and title)*	DATE

AUTHORIZED FOR LOCAL REPRODUCTION
Previous edition is not usable

STANDARD FORM 1424 (REV. 5/2004)
Prescribed by GSA - FAR (48 CFR) 53.245(d)

53.301-1427 Standard Form 1427, Inventory Schedule A—Continuation Sheet (Metals in Mill Product Form)

[FAC 84-56, 55 FR 3897, 2/5/90, effective 3/7/90]

INVENTORY SCHEDULE A - CONTINUATION SHEET (METALS IN MILL PRODUCT FORM)

TYPE ☐ TERMINATION ☐ NONTERMINATION | DATE | FORM APPROVED OMB NO. 9000-0015

Public reporting burden for this collection of information is estimated to average 1 hour per response, including the time for reviewing instructions, searching existing data sources, gathering and maintaining the data needed, and completing and reviewing the collection of information. Send comments regarding this burden estimate or any other aspect of this collection of information, including suggestions for reducing this burden, to the FAR Secretariat (VRS), Office of Federal Acquisition and Regulatory Policy, GSA, Washington, D.C. 20405; and to the Office of Management and Budget, Paperwork Reduction Project (9000-0015), Washington, D.C. 20503.

GOVERNMENT PRIME CONTRACT NO.	SUBCONTRACTOR P.O. NO.	REFERENCE NO.	PROPERTY CLASSIFICATION	PAGE NO.	NO. OF PAGES

FOR USE OF CONTRACTING AGENCY ONLY	ITEM NO.	DESCRIPTION			DIMENSIONS				CONDITION (Use code)	QUANTITY	UNIT OF MEASURE	COST		CONTRACTOR'S OFFER	FOR USE OF CONTRACTING AGENCY ONLY
		FORM, SHAPE, ROLLING TREATMENT	HEAT TREATMENT, TEMPER, HARDNESS, FINISH, ETC.	SPECIFICATIONS, AND ALLOY OR OTHER VARIABLE DESIGNATION IN THE SPECIFICATION	THICKNESS	WIDTH	LENGTH (b5)					UNIT	TOTAL		
							FEET	INCHES							
	(a)	(b)	(b1)	(b2)	(b3)	(b4)			(c)	(d)	(d1)	(e)	(f)	(g)	

AUTHORIZED FOR LOCAL REPRODUCTION
Previous edition is usable

EXPIRATION DATE: 4-30-92

1427-102

STANDARD FORM 1427 (REV. 7-89)
Prescribed by GSA - FAR (48 CFR) 53.245(f)

53.301-1428 Inventory Disposal Schedule

[FAC 90-45, Final rule, 62 FR 224, 1/2/97, effective 1/1/97; FAC 2001-22, 69 FR 17741, 4/5/2004, effective 5/5/2004; FAC 2005-17, 72 FR 27364, 5/15/2007, effective 6/14/2007]

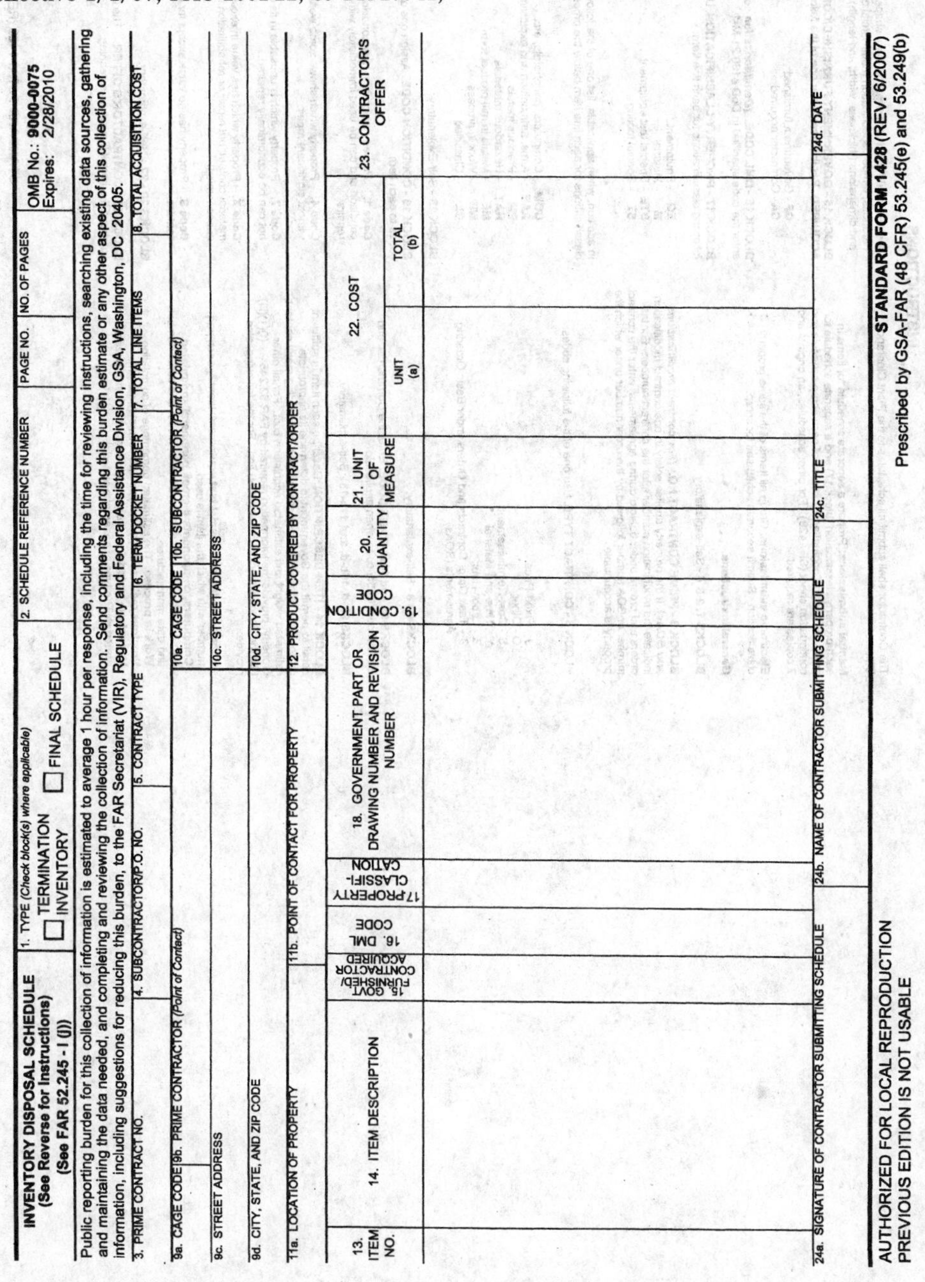

INVENTORY DISPOSAL SCHEDULE
(See Reverse for Instructions)
(See FAR 52.245 - I (j))

1. TYPE (*Check block(s) where applicable*)
☐ TERMINATION INVENTORY ☐ FINAL SCHEDULE

2. SCHEDULE REFERENCE NUMBER | PAGE NO. | NO. OF PAGES

OMB No.: **9000-0075**
Expires: 2/28/2010

Public reporting burden for this collection of information is estimated to average 1 hour per response, including the time for reviewing instructions, searching existing data sources, gathering and maintaining the data needed, and completing and reviewing the collection of information. Send comments regarding this burden estimate or any other aspect of this collection of information, including suggestions for reducing this burden, to the FAR Secretariat (VIR), Regulatory and Federal Assistance Division, GSA, Washington, DC 20405.

3. PRIME CONTRACT NO.	4. SUBCONTRACTOR/P.O. NO.	5. CONTRACT TYPE	6. TERM DOCKET NUMBER	7. TOTAL LINE ITEMS	8. TOTAL ACQUISITION COST

9a. CAGE CODE	9b. PRIME CONTRACTOR (*Point of Contact*)	10a. CAGE CODE	10b. SUBCONTRACTOR (*Point of Contact*)
9c. STREET ADDRESS		10c. STREET ADDRESS	
9d. CITY, STATE, AND ZIP CODE		10d. CITY, STATE, AND ZIP CODE	
11a. LOCATION OF PROPERTY	11b. POINT OF CONTACT FOR PROPERTY	12. PRODUCT COVERED BY CONTRACT/ORDER	

13. ITEM NO.	14. ITEM DESCRIPTION	15. GOVT FURNISHED/ CONTRACTOR ACQUIRED	16. DML CODE	17. PROPERTY CLASSIFI-CATION	18. GOVERNMENT PART OR DRAWING NUMBER AND REVISION NUMBER	19. CONDITION CODE	20. QUANTITY	21. UNIT OF MEASURE	22. COST UNIT (a)	22. COST TOTAL (b)	23. CONTRACTOR'S OFFER

24a. SIGNATURE OF CONTRACTOR SUBMITTING SCHEDULE	24b. NAME OF CONTRACTOR SUBMITTING SCHEDULE	24c. TITLE	24d. DATE

AUTHORIZED FOR LOCAL REPRODUCTION
PREVIOUS EDITION IS NOT USABLE

STANDARD FORM 1428 (REV. 6/2007)
Prescribed by GSA-FAR (48 CFR) 53.245(e) and 53.249(b)

INSTRUCTIONS

The Contractor shall submit all schedules to the Plant Clearance Officer.

Manual submissions. Prepare a separate schedule for items in each property classification (block 17) and a separate schedule for scrap. Submit an original and 2 copies of each scrap schedule and continuation sheet (SF 1429). For other schedules, an original and 7 copies are required.

Electronic submissions. Group all items of the same property classification. Submit separate schedules for scrap.

General instructions.

BLOCKS 1, 2 & 4 - Self-explanatory.

BLOCK 3 - PRIME CONTRACT NO. ***(For contract modifications and BOAs).*** If the property applies solely to one contract modification indicate the modification number after the contract number. For task orders and orders under basic ordering agreements, enter the contract number or BOA number followed by the order number under which the property is accountable.

BLOCK 5 - CONTRACT TYPE. Use one of the following codes:

J - Fixed-Price
O - Other
S - Cost-Reimbursement
Y - Time-and-Material
Z - Labor-Hour
9 - Task Order Contracts and Orders under Basic Ordering Agreements (BOAs)

BLOCKS 6 - 8 - Self-explanatory.

BLOCKS 9a and 10a - CAGE CODE. Enter the Commercial and Government Entity code when applicable.

BLOCKS 9b-d, 10b-d, and 11a-13 - Self-explanatory.

BLOCK 14 - ITEM DESCRIPTION. Describe each item in sufficient detail to permit the Government to determine its appropriate disposition. Scrap may be described as a lot including metal content, estimated weight and estimated acquisition cost. For all other property, provide the information required by FAR 52.245 - 1 (f)(1)(iii). List the national stock number (NSN) first. For the following, also provide:

Special tooling and special test equipment. Identify each part number with which the item is used.
Computers, components thereof, peripheral and related equipment. The manufacturer's name, model and serial number, and date manufactured.
Work in process. The estimated percentage of completion.
Precious metals. The metal type and estimated weight.
Hazardous material or property contaminated with hazardous material. The type of hazardous material.
Metals in mill product form. The form, shape, treatments, hardness, temper, specification (commercial or Government), and dimensions (thickness, width, and length).

BLOCK 15 - GOVERNMENT FURNISHED/CONTRACTOR ACQUIRED. Per line item, enter one of the following:

GF - Government furnished
CA - Contractor acquired

BLOCK 16 - DML CODE. ***(Demilitarization code).*** If applicable, enter the code specified in DoD 4160.21-M-1.

BLOCK 17 - PROPERTY CLASSIFICATION. Use one of the following classifications for each line item:

EQ - Equipment
M - Material
STE - Special test equipment
ST - Special tooling

In addition, when applicable, list one of the following sub classifications for each line item below the property classification:

COM - Computers, peripherals, etc.
AAE - Arms, ammunition and explosives
PM - Precious metals
HAZ - Hazardous materials
ME - Metals in mill product form
WIP - Work in process
CL - Classified

BLOCK 18 - Self-Explanatory.

BLOCK 19 - CONDITION CODE. Assign one of the following codes to each item:

Code 1. Property which is in new condition or unused condition and can be used immediately without modifications or repairs.

Code 4. Property which shows some wear, but can be used without significant repair.

Code 7. Property which is unusable in its current condition but can be economically repaired.

Code X. Property which has value in excess of its basic material content, but repair or rehabilitation is impractical and/or uneconomical.

Code S. Property has no value except for its basic material content.

BLOCKS 20 - 22 - Self-explanatory.

BLOCK 23 - CONTRACTOR'S OFFER. The Contractor's offer to purchase the item if it survives screening.

STANDARD FORM 1428 (REV. 6/2007) **BACK**

53.301-1429 Inventory Disposal Schedule—Continuation Sheet

[FAC 84-56, 55 3901, 2/5/90, effective 3/7/90; FAC 2001-22, 69 FR 17741, 4/5/2004, effective 5/5/2004]

INVENTORY DISPOSAL SCHEDULE - CONTINUATION SHEET	2. SCHEDULE REFERENCE NUMBER	PAGE NO.	NO. OF PAGES	OMB No.:9000-0075 Expires: 10/31/2006

Public reporting burden for this collection of information is estimated to average 1 hour per response, including the time for reviewing instructions, searching existing data sources, gathering and maintaining the data needed, and completing and reviewing the collection of information. Send comments regarding this burden estimate or any other aspect of this collection of information, including suggestions for reducing this burden, to the FAR Secretariat (MVA), Regulatory and Federal Assistance Publciations Division, GSA, Washington, DC 20405.

13. ITEM NO.	14. ITEM DESCRIPTION	15. GOVT. FURNISHED/ CONTRACTOR ACQUIRED	16. DML CODE	17. PROPERTY CLASSIFI-CATION	18. GOVERNMENT PART OR DRAWING NUMBER AND REVISION NUMBER	19. CONDITION CODE	20. QUAN-TITY	21. UNIT OF MEASURE	22. COST		23. CONTRACTOR'S OFFER
									UNIT (a)	TOTAL (b)	

AUTHORIZED FOR LOCAL REPRODUCTION
Previous edition not usable

STANDARD FORM 1429 (REV. 5/2004)
Prescribed by GSA-FAR (48 CFR) 53.245(e) and 53.249(b)

53.301-1435 Standard Form 1435, Settlement Proposal (Inventory Basis)

[FAC 97-3, 62 FR 64912, 12/9/97, effective 2/9/98]

SETTLEMENT PROPOSAL (INVENTORY BASIS)

OMB No.: 9000-0012
Expires: 05/31/98

Public reporting burden for this collection of information is estimated to average 2.5 hours per response, including the time for reviewing instructions, searching existing data sources, gathering and maintaining the data needed, and completing and reviewing the collection of information. Send comments regarding this burden estimate or any other aspect of this collection of information, including suggestions for reducing this burden, to the FAR Secretariat (MVR), Federal Acquisition Policy Division, GSA, Washington, D.C. 20405.

FOR USE BY A FIXED-PRICE PRIME CONTRACTOR OR FIXED- PRICE SUBCONTRACTOR

THIS PROPOSAL APPLIES TO (Check one) ☐ A PRIME CONTRACT WITH THE GOVERNMENT ☐ SUBCONTRACT OR PURCHASE ORDER	COMPANY
SUBCONTRACT OR PURCHASE ORDER NO(S).	STREET ADDRESS
CONTRACTOR WHO SENT NOTICE OF TERMINATION	CITY AND STATE *(Include ZIP Code)*
NAME	NAME OF GOVERNMENT AGENCY
ADDRESS *(include ZIP Code)*	GOVERNMENT PRIME CONTRACT NO. / CONTRACTOR'S REFERENCE NO.
If moneys payable under the contract have been assigned, give the following: NAME OF ASSIGNEE	EFFECTIVE DATE OF TERMINATION
ADDRESS *(include ZIP Code)*	PROPOSAL NO. / CHECK ONE ☐ INTERIM ☐ FINAL
SF 1439, SCHEDULE OF ACCOUNTING INFORMATION ☐ IS ☐ IS NOT ATTACHED *(If not, explain)*	

SECTION I - STATUS OF CONTRACT OR ORDER AT EFFECTIVE DATE OF TERMINATION

PRODUCTS COVERED BY TERMINATED CONTRACT OR PURCHASE ORDER (a)		FINISHED: PREVIOUSLY SHIPPED AND INVOICED (b)	FINISHED ON HAND: PAYMENT TO BE RECEIVED THROUGH INVOICING (c)	FINISHED ON HAND: INCLUDED IN THIS PROPOSAL (d)	UNFINISHED OR NOT COMMENCED: TO BE COMPLETED (Partial termination only) (e)	UNFINISHED OR NOT COMMENCED: NOT TO BE COMPLETED (f)	TOTAL COVERED BY CONTRACT OR ORDER (g)
	QUANTITY						
	$						
	QUANTITY						
	$						
	QUANTITY						
	$						

SECTION II - PROPOSED SETTLEMENT

NO.	ITEM (a)	(Use Columns (b) and (c) only where previous proposal has been filed) TOTAL PREVIOUSLY PROPOSED (b)	INCREASE OR DECREASE BY THIS PROPOSAL (c)	TOTAL PROPOSED TO DATE (d)	FOR USE OF CONTRACTING AGENCY ONLY (e)
1	METALS				
2	RAW MATERIALS *(other than metals)*				
3	PURCHASED PARTS				
4	FINISHED COMPONENTS				
5	MISCELLANEOUS INVENTORY				
6	WORK-IN-PROGRESS				
7	SPECIAL TOOLING AND SPECIAL TEST EQUIPMENT				
8	OTHER COSTS *(from Schedule B)*				
9	GENERAL AND ADMINISTRATIVE EXPENSES *(from Schedule C)*				
10	**TOTAL** *(Items 1 to 9 Inclusive)*				
11	PROFIT *(explain in Schedule D)*				
12	SETTLEMENT EXPENSES *(from Schedule E)*				
13	**TOTAL** *(Items 10 to 12 Inclusive)*				
14	SETTLEMENTS WITH SUBCONTRACTORS *(from Schedule F)*				
15	ACCEPTABLE FINISHED PRODUCT				
16	GROSS PROPOSED SETTLEMENT *(Items 13 through 15)*				
17	DISPOSAL AND OTHER CREDITS *(from Schedule G)*				
18	NET PROPOSED SETTLEMENT *(Item 16 less 17)*				
19	ADVANCE, PROGRESS & PARTIAL PAYMENTS *(from Schedule H)*				
20	**NET PAYMENT REQUESTED** *(Item 18 less 19)*				

(When the space provided for any information is insufficient, continue on a separate sheet.)

AUTHORIZED FOR LOCAL REPRODUCTION
Previous edition is unusable

STANDARD FORM 1435 (REV. 9-97)
Prescribed by GSA - FAR (48 CFR) 53.249(a)(2)

SCHEDULE A -ANALYSIS OF INVENTORY COST *(Items 4 and 6)*

Furnish the following information (unless not reasonably available) for inventories of finished components and work-in-progress included in this proposal:

	TOTAL DIRECT LABOR	TOTAL DIRECT MATERIALS	TOTAL INDIRECT EXPENSES	TOTAL
FINISHED COMPONENTS				
WORK-IN-PROGRESS				

NOTE: Individual items of small amounts may be grouped into a single entry in Schedules B, C, D, E, and G.

SCHEDULE B - OTHER COSTS *(Item 8)*

ITEM	EXPLANATION	AMOUNT	FOR USE OF CONTRACTING AGENCY ONLY

SCHEDULE C - GENERAL AND ADMINISTRATIVE EXPENSES *(Item 9)*

DETAIL OF EXPENSES	AMOUNT	FOR USE OF CONTRACTING AGENCY ONLY

SCHEDULE D - PROFIT *(Item 11)*

EXPLANATION	AMOUNT	FOR USE OF CONTRACTING AGENCY ONLY

(Where the space provided for any information is insufficient, continue on a separate sheet.)

STANDARD FORM 1435 (REV. 9-97) **PAGE 2**

SCHEDULE E - SETTLEMENT EXPENSES *(Item 12)*			
ITEM	EXPLANATION	AMOUNT	FOR USE OF CONTRACTING AGENCY ONLY

SCHEDULE F - SETTLEMENTS WITH IMMEDIATE SUBCONTRACTORS AND SUPPLIERS *(Item 14)*			
NAME AND ADDRESS OF SUBCONTRACTOR	BRIEF DESCRIPTION OF PRODUCT CANCELED	AMOUNT OF SETTLEMENT	FOR USE OF CONTRACTING AGENCY ONLY

SCHEDULE G - DISPOSAL AND OTHER CREDITS *(Item 17)*		
DESCRIPTION	AMOUNT	FOR USE OF CONTRACTING AGENCY ONLY

(If practicable, show separately amount of disposal credits applicable to acceptable finished product included in Item 15.)

(Where the space provided for any information is insufficient, continue on a separate sheet.)

STANDARD FORM 1435 (REV. 9-97) **PAGE 3**

SCHEDULE H -ADVANCE, PROGRESS AND PARTIAL PAYMENTS *(Item 19)*			
DATE	TYPE OF PAYMENT	AMOUNT	FOR USE OF CONTRACTING AGENCY ONLY

(Where the space provided for any information is insufficient, continue on a separate sheet.)

CERTIFICATE

This is to certify that the undersigned, individually, and as an authorized representative of the Contractor, has examined this termination settlement proposal and that, to the best knowledge and belief of the undersigned:

(a) AS TO THE CONTRACTOR'S OWN CHARGES. The proposed settlement (exclusive of charges set forth in Item 14) and supporting schedules and explanations have been prepared from the books of account and records of the Contractor in accordance with recognized commercial accounting practices; they include only those charges allocable to the termination portion of this contract; they have been prepared with knowledge that they will, or may, be used directly or indirectly as the basis of settlement of a termination settlement proposal or claim against an agency of the United States; and the charges as stated are fair and reasonable.

(b) AS TO THE SUBCONTRACTORS' CHARGES. (1) The Contractor has examined, or caused to be examined, to an extent it considered adequate in the circumstances, the termination settlement proposals of its immediate subcontractors (exclusive of proposals filed against these immediate subcontractors by their subcontractors) ; (2) The settlements on account of immediate subcontractors' own charges are fair and reasonable, the charges are allocable to the terminated portion of this contract, and the settlements were negotiated in good faith and are not more favorable to its immediate subcontractors than those that the Contractor would make if reimbursement by the Government were not involved; (3) The Contractor has received from all its immediate subcontractors appropriate certificates with respect to their termination settlement proposals, which certificates are substantially in the form of this certificate; and (4) The Contractor has no information leading it to doubt (i) the reasonableness of the settlements with more remote subcontractors or (ii) that the charges for them are allocable to this contract. Upon receipt by the Contractor of amounts covering settlements with its immediate subcontractors, the Contractor will pay or credit them promptly with the amounts so received, to the extent that it has not previously done so. The term "subcontractors," as used above, includes suppliers.

NOTE: The Contractor shall, under conditions stated in FAR 15.403, be required to submit a Certificate of Current Cost or Pricing Data (see FAR 15.406-2 and 15.408 Table 15-2).

NAME OF CONTRACTOR	BY *(Signature of authorized official)*	
	TITLE	DATE
NAME OF SUPERVISORY ACCOUNTING OFFICIAL	TITLE	

STANDARD FORM 1435 (REV. 9-97) **PAGE 4**

53.301-1436 Settlement Proposal (Total Cost Basis)

[FAC 97-3, 62 FR 64912, 12/9/97, effective 2/9/98; FAC 2001-22, 69 FR 17741, 4/5/2004, effective 5/5/2004]

SETTLEMENT PROPOSAL (TOTAL COST BASIS)

OMB No.: **9000-0012**
Expires: 06/30/2004

Public reporting burden for this collection of information is estimated to average 2.5 hours per response, including the time for reviewing instructions, searching existing data sources, gathering and maintaining the data needed, and completing and reviewing the collection of information. Send comments regarding this burden estimate or any other aspect of this collection of information, including suggestions for reducing this burden, to the FAR Secretariat (MVA), Regulatory and Federal Assistance Publications Division, GSA, Washington, DC 20405.

FOR USE BY A FIXED-PRICE PRIME CONTRACTOR OR FIXED-PRICE SUBCONTRACTOR

THIS PROPOSAL APPLIES TO *(Check one)* ☐ A PRIME CONTRACT WITH THE GOVERNMENT ☐ SUBCONTRACT OR PURCHASE ORDER	COMPANY
SUBCONTRACT OR PURCHASE ORDER NO(S).	STREET ADDRESS
CONTRACTOR WHO SENT NOTICE OF TERMINATION	CITY AND STATE *(Include ZIP Code)*
NAME	NAME OF GOVERNMENT AGENCY
ADDRESS *(Include ZIP Code)*	GOVERNMENT PRIME CONTRACT NO. / CONTRACTOR'S REFERENCE NO.
If moneys payable under the contract have been assigned, give the following: NAME OF ASSIGNEE	EFFECTIVE DATE OF TERMINATION
ADDRESS *(Include ZIP Code)*	PROPOSAL NO. / CHECK ONE ☐ INTERIM ☐ FINAL

SF 1439, SCHEDULE OF ACCOUNTING INFORMATION ☐ IS ☐ IS NOT ATTACHED *(If not, explain below)*

SECTION I - STATUS OF CONTRACT OR ORDER AT EFFECTIVE DATE OF TERMINATION

PRODUCTS COVERED BY TERMINATED CONTRACT OR PURCHASE ORDER (a)		FINISHED: PREVIOUSLY SHIPPED AND INVOICED (b)	FINISHED ON HAND: PAYMENT TO BE RECEIVED THROUGH INVOICING (c)	FINISHED ON HAND: PAYMENT NOT TO BE RECEIVED THROUGH INVOICING (d)	UNFINISHED OR NOT COMMENCED: SUBSEQUENTLY COMPLETED AND INVOICED* (e)	UNFINISHED OR NOT COMMENCED: NOT TO BE COMPLETED (f)	TOTAL COVERED BY CONTRACT OR ORDER (g)
	QUANTITY						
	$						
	QUANTITY						
	$						
	QUANTITY						
	$						

SECTION II - PROPOSED SETTLEMENT

(Use Columns (b) and (c) only where previous proposal has been filed)

NO.	ITEM (a)	TOTAL PREVIOUSLY PROPOSED (b)	INCREASE OR DECREASE BY THIS PROPOSAL (c)	TOTAL PROPOSED TO DATE (d)	FOR USE OF CONTRACTING AGENCY ONLY (e)
1	DIRECT MATERIAL				
2	DIRECT LABOR				
3	INDIRECT FACTORY EXPENSE *(from Schedule A)*				
4	SPECIAL TOOLING AND SPECIAL TEST EQUIPMENT *(SF 1428)*				
5	OTHER COSTS *(from Schedule B)*				
6	GENERAL AND ADMINISTRATIVE EXPENSES *(from Schedule C)*				
7	**TOTAL COSTS *(Items 1 thru 6)***				
8	PROFIT *(Explain in Schedule D)*				
9	**TOTAL *(Items 7 and 8)***				
10	DEDUCT FINISHED PRODUCT INVOICED OR TO BE INVOICED*				
11	**TOTAL *(Item 9 less Item 10)***				
12	SETTLEMENT EXPENSES *(from Schedule E)*				
13	**TOTAL *(Items 11 and 12)***				
14	SETTLEMENTS WITH SUBCONTRACTORS *(from Schedule F)*				
15	GROSS PROPOSED SETTLEMENT *(Items 13 thru 14)*				
16	DISPOSAL AND OTHER CREDITS *(from Schedule G)*				
17	NET PROPOSED SETTLEMENT *(Item 15 less 16)*				
18	ADVANCE, PROGRESS & PARTIAL PAYMENTS *(from Schedule H)*				
19	**NET PAYMENT REQUESTED *(Item 17 less 18)***				

*Column (e), Section I, should only be used in the event of a partial termination, in which the total cost reported in Section II should be accumulated to date of completion of the continued portion of the contract and the deduction for finished product (Item 10, Section II) should be the contract price of finished product in Column (b), (c), and (e), Section I.

NOTE: File inventory schedule (SF 1428) for allocable inventories on hand at date of termination (See 49.206).

(When the space provided for any information is insufficient, continue on a separate sheet.)

AUTHORIZED FOR LOCAL REPRODUCTION
Previous edition is unusable

STANDARD FORM 1436 (REV. 5/2004)
Prescribed by GSA - FAR (48 CFR) 53.249(a)(3)

SCHEDULE A - INDIRECT FACTORY EXPENSE *(Item 3)*

DETAIL OF EXPENSES	METHOD OF ALLOCATION	AMOUNT	FOR USE OF CONTRACTING AGENCY ONLY

NOTE: Individual items of small amounts may be grouped into a single entry in Schedules B, C, D, E, and G.

SCHEDULE B - OTHER COSTS *(Item 5)*

ITEM	EXPLANATION	AMOUNT	FOR USE OF CONTRACTING AGENCY ONLY

SCHEDULE C - GENERAL AND ADMINISTRATIVE EXPENSES *(Item 6)*

DETAIL OF EXPENSES	METHOD OF ALLOCATION	AMOUNT	FOR USE OF CONTRACTING AGENCY ONLY

SCHEDULE D - PROFIT *(Item 8)*

EXPLANATION	AMOUNT	FOR USE OF CONTRACTING AGENCY ONLY

(Where the space provided for any information is insufficient, continue on a separate sheet.)

STANDARD FORM 1436 (REV. 5/2004) PAGE 2

SCHEDULE E - SETTLEMENT EXPENSES *(Item 12)*

ITEM	EXPLANATION	AMOUNT	FOR USE OF CONTRACTING AGENCY ONLY

SCHEDULE F - SETTLEMENTS WITH IMMEDIATE SUBCONTRACTORS AND SUPPLIERS *(Item 14)*

NAME AND ADDRESS OF SUBCONTRACTOR	BRIEF DESCRIPTION OF PRODUCT CANCELED	AMOUNT OF SETTLEMENT	FOR USE OF CONTRACTING AGENCY ONLY

SCHEDULE G - DISPOSAL AND OTHER CREDITS *(Item 16)*

DESCRIPTION	AMOUNT	FOR USE OF CONTRACTING AGENCY ONLY

(If practicable, show separately amount of disposal credits applicable to acceptable finished product included on SF 1428.)

(Where the space provided for any information is insufficient, continue on a separate sheet.)

STANDARD FORM 1436 (REV. 5/2004) **PAGE 3**

SCHEDULE H - ADVANCE, PROGRESS AND PARTIAL PAYMENTS *(Item 19)*

DATE	TYPE OF PAYMENT	AMOUNT	FOR USE OF CONTRACTING AGENCY ONLY

(Where the space provided for any information is insufficient, continue on a separate sheet.)

CERTIFICATE

This is to certify that the undersigned, individually, and as an authorized representative of the Contractor, has examined this termination settlement proposal and that, to the best knowledge and belief of the undersigned:

(a) AS TO THE CONTRACTOR'S OWN CHARGES. The proposed settlement (exclusive of charges set forth in Item 14) and supporting schedules and explanations have been prepared from the books of account and records of the Contractor in accordance with recognized commercial accounting practices; they include only those charges allocable to the terminated portion of this contract; they have been prepared with knowledge that they will, or may, be used directly or indirectly as the basis of settlement of a termination settlement proposal or claim against an agency of the United States; and the charges as stated are fair and reasonable.

(b) AS TO THE SUBCONTRACTORS' CHARGES. (1) The Contractor has examined, or caused to be examined, to an extent it considered adequate in the circumstances, the termination settlement proposals of its immediate subcontractors (exclusive of proposals filed against these immediate subcontractors by their subcontractors); (2) The settlements on account of immediate subcontractors own charges are fair and reasonable, the charges are allocable to the terminated portion of this contract, and the settlements were negotiated in good faith and are not more favorable to its immediate subcontractors than those that the Contractor would make if reimbursement by the Government were not involved; (3) The Contractor has received from all its immediate subcontractors appropriate certificates with respect to their termination settlement proposals, which certificates are substantially in the form of this certificate; and (4) The Contractor has no information leading it to doubt (i) the reasonableness of the settlements with more remote subcontractors or (ii) that the charges for them are allocable to this contract. Upon receipt by the Contractor of amounts covering settlements with its immediate subcontractors, the Contractor will pay or credit them promptly with the amounts so received, to the extent that it has not previously done so. The term "subcontractors," as used above, includes suppliers.

NOTE: The Contractor shall, under conditions stated in FAR 15.403, be required to submit a Certificate of Current Cost or Pricing Data (see FAR 15.406-2 and 15.408 Table 15-2).

NAME OF CONTRACTOR	BY *(Signature of authorized official)*	
	TITLE	DATE
NAME OF SUPERVISORY ACCOUNTING OFFICIAL	TITLE	

53.301-1437 Standard Form 1437, Settlement Proposal for Cost-Reimbursement Type Contracts

[FAC 97-3, 62 FR 64912, 12/9/97, effective 2/9/98]

SETTLEMENT PROPOSAL FOR COST-REIMBURSEMENT TYPE CONTRACTS	OMB No.: 9000-0012 Expires: 05/31/98

Public reporting burden for this collection of information is estimated to average 2.5 hours per response, including the time for reviewing instructions, searching existing data sources, gathering and maintaining the data needed, and completing and reviewing the collection of information. Send comments regarding this burden estimate or any other aspect of this collection of information, including suggestions for reducing this burden, to the FAR Secretariat (MVR), Federal Acquisition Policy Division, GSA, Washington, D.C. 20405.

To be used by prime contractors submitting settlement proposals on cost-reimbursement type contracts under Part 49 of the Federal Acquisition Regulation. Also suitable for use in connection with terminated cost-reimbursement type subcontracts.

COMPANY	PROPOSAL NUMBER	CHECK ONE ☐ PARTIAL ☐ FINAL
STREET ADDRESS	GOVERNMENT PRIME CONTRACT NO.	REFERENCE NO.
CITY AND STATE *(Include ZIP Code)*	EFFECTIVE DATE OF TERMINATION	

ITEM (a)	TOTAL PREVIOUSLY SUBMITTED (b)	INCREASE OR DECREASE BY THIS PROPOSAL (c)	TOTAL SUBMITTED TO DATE (d)
1. DIRECT MATERIAL	$	$	$
2. DIRECT LABOR			
3. INDIRECT FACTORY EXPENSE			
4. SPECIAL TOOLING AND SPECIAL TEST EQUIPMENT			
5. OTHER COSTS			
6. GENERAL AND ADMINISTRATIVE EXPENSE			
7. TOTAL COSTS *(Items 1 thru 6)*	$	$	$
8. FEE			
9. SETTLEMENT EXPENSES			
10. SETTLEMENTS WITH SUBCONTRACTORS			
11. GROSS PROPOSED SETTLEMENT *(Items 7 thru 10)*			
12. DISPOSAL AND OTHER CREDITS			
13. NET PROPOSED SETTLEMENT *(Item 11 less 12)*	$	$	$
14. PRIOR PAYMENTS TO CONTRACTOR	$	$	$
15. NET PAYMENT REQUESTED *(Item 13 less 14)*	$	$	$

CERTIFICATE

This is to certify that the undersigned, individually, and as an authorized representative of the Contractor, has examined this termination settlement proposal and that, to the best knowledge and belief of the undersigned:

(a) AS TO THE CONTRACTOR'S OWN CHARGES. The proposed settlement (exclusive of charges set forth in Item 10) and supporting schedules and explanations have been prepared from the books of account and records of the Contractor in accordance with recognized commercial accounting practices; they include only those charges allocable to the terminated portion of this contract; they have been prepared with knowledge that they will, or may, be used directly or indirectly as the basis of settlement of a termination settlement proposal or claim against an agency of the United States; and the charges as stated are fair and reasonable.

(b) AS TO THE SUBCONTRACTORS' CHARGES. (1) The Contractor has examined, or caused to be examined, to an extent it considered adequate in the circumstances, the termination settlement proposals of its immediate subcontractors (exclusive of proposals filed against these immediate subcontractors by their subcontractors); (2) The settlements on account of immediate subcontractors' own charges are fair and reasonable, the charges are allocable to the terminated portion of this contract, and the settlements were negotiated in good faith and are not more favorable to its immediate subcontractors than those that the Contractor would make if reimbursement by the Government were not involved; (3) The Contractor has received from all its immediate subcontractors appropriate certificates with respect to their termination settlement proposals, which certificates are substantially in the form of this certificate; and (4) The Contractor has no information leading it to doubt (i) the reasonableness of the settlements with more remote subcontractors or (ii) that the charges for them are allocable to this contract. Upon receipt by the Contractor of amounts covering settlements with its immediate subcontractors, the Contractor will pay or credit them promptly with the amounts so received, to the extent that it has not previously done so. The term "subcontractors," as used above, includes suppliers.

NOTE: The Contractor shall, under conditions stated in FAR 15.403, be required to submit a Certificate of Current Cost or Pricing Data (see FAR 15.406-2 and 15.408 Table 15-2).

NAME OF CONTRACTOR	BY *(Signature of authorized official)*	
	TITLE	DATE
NAME OF SUPERVISORY ACCOUNTING OFFICIAL	TITLE	

AUTHORIZED FOR LOCAL REPRODUCTION
Previous edition is unusable

STANDARD FORM 1437 (REV. 9-97)
Prescribed by GSA - FAR (48 CFR) 53.249(a)(4)

53.301-1438 Settlement Proposal (Short Form)

[FAC 84-56, 55 FR 3925, 2/5/90, effective 3/7/90; FAC 2001-22, 60 FR 17741, 4/5/2004, effective 5/5/2004]

SETTLEMENT PROPOSAL (SHORT FORM)

OMB No.: 9000-0012
Expires: 06/30/2004

Public reporting burden for this collection of information is estimated to average 2.5 hours per response, including the time for reviewing instructions, searching existing data sources, gathering and maintaining the data needed, and completing and reviewing the collection of information. Send comments regarding this burden estimate or any other aspect of this collection of information, including suggestions for reducing this burden, to the FAR Secretariat (MVA), Regulatory and Federal Assistance Publications Division, GSA, Washington, DC 20405.

For Use by a Prime Contractor or Subcontractor in Settlement of a Fixed Price Terminated Contract When Total Charges Claimed Are Less Than $10,000.

THIS PROPOSAL APPLIES TO *(Check one)* ☐ A PRIME CONTRACT WITH THE GOVERNMENT ☐ SUBCONTRACT OR PURCHASE ORDER	COMPANY *(Prime or Subcontractor)*
SUBCONTRACT OR PURCHASE ORDER NO.(S)	STREET ADDRESS
CONTRACTOR WHO SENT NOTICE OF TERMINATION NAME	CITY AND STATE *(Include ZIP code)*
ADDRESS *(Include ZIP Code)*	NAME OF GOVERNMENT AGENCY / GOVERNMENT PRIME CONTRACT NO.
If moneys payable under the contract have been assigned, give the following: NAME OF ASSIGNEE	CONTRACTOR'S REFERENCE NO. / EFFECTIVE DATE OF TERMINATION
ADDRESS *(Include ZIP Code)*	

SECTION I - STATUS OF CONTRACT OR ORDER AT EFFECTIVE DATE OF TERMINATION

PRODUCTS COVERED BY TERMINATED CONTRACT OR PURCHASE ORDER (a)		PREVIOUSLY SHIPPED AND INVOICED (b)	FINISHED ON HAND: PAYMENT TO BE RECEIVED THROUGH INVOICING (c)	FINISHED ON HAND: INCLUDED IN THIS PROPOSAL (d)	UNFINISHED OR NOT COMMENCED: TO BE COMPLETED *(Partial termination only)* (e)	UNFINISHED OR NOT COMMENCED: NOT TO BE COMPLETED (f)	TOTAL COVERED BY CONTRACT OR ORDER (g)
	QUANTITY						
	$						
	QUANTITY						
	$						
	QUANTITY						
	$						

SECTION II - PROPOSED SETTLEMENT

NO.	ITEM *(Include only items allocable to the terminated portion of contract)*	AMOUNT OF CHARGE ($)
1	CHARGE FOR ACCEPTABLE FINISHED PRODUCT NOT COVERED BY INVOICING *(from SF 1428)*	
2	CHARGE FOR WORK-IN-PROGRESS, RAW MATERIAL, ETC. ON HAND *(from SF 1428)*	
3	OTHER CHARGES INCLUDING PROFIT AND SETTLEMENT EXPENSES	
4	CHARGES FOR SETTLEMENT(S) WITH SUBCONTRACTORS	
5	GROSS PROPOSED SETTLEMENT *(Sum of Items 1 thru 4)*	
6	DISPOSAL AND OTHER CREDITS *(from SF 1424, Item 27, Col. 3)*	
7	NET PROPOSED SETTLEMENT *(Item 5 less 6)*	
8	ADVANCE, PROGRESS, AND PARTIAL PAYMENTS	
9	NET PAYMENT REQUESTED *(Item 7 less 8)*	

List your inventory on SF 1428 and attach a copy thereto. Retain for the applicable period specified in the prime contract all papers and records relating to this proposal for future examination.

GIVE A BRIEF EXPLANATION OF HOW YOU ARRIVED AT THE AMOUNTS SHOWN IN ITEMS 3, 4, 6, AND 7

I CERTIFY that the above proposed settlement includes only charges allocable to the terminated portion of the contract or purchase order, that the total charges (Item 5) and the disposal credits (Item 6) are fair and reasonable, and that this proposal has been prepared with knowledge that it will, or may, be used directly or indirectly as a basis for reimbursement under a settlement proposal(s) against agencies of the United States.	NAME OF YOUR COMPANY BY *(Signature of authorized official)* TITLE	DATE

(Where the space provided for any information is insufficient, continue on a separate sheet.)

AUTHORIZED FOR LOCAL REPRODUCTION
Previous edition is not usable

STANDARD FORM 1438 (REV. 5/2004)
Prescribed by GSA-FAR (48 CFR) 53.249(a)(5)

INSTRUCTIONS

1. This settlement proposal should be submitted to the contracting officer, if you are a prime contractor, or to your customer, if you are a subcontractor. The term contract as used hereinafter includes a subcontract or a purchase order.

2. Proposals that would normally be included in a single settlement proposal, such as those based on a series of separate orders for the same item under one contract should be consolidated wherever possible, and must not be divided in such a way as to bring them below $10,000.

3. You should review any aspects of your contract relating to termination and consult your customer or contracting officer for further information. Government regulations pertaining to the basis for determining a fair and reasonable termination settlement are contained in Part 49 of the Federal Acquisition Regulation. Your proposal for fair compensation should be prepared on the basis of the costs shown by your accounting records. Where your costs are not so shown, you may use any reasonable basis for estimating your costs which will provide for fair compensation for the preparations made and work done for the terminated portion of the contract, including a reasonable profit on such preparation and work.

4. Generally your settlement proposal may include under Items 2, 3, and 4, the following:

a. COSTS - Costs incurred which are reasonably necessary and are properly allocable to the terminated portion of your contract under recognized commerical accounting practices, including direct and indirect manufacturing, selling and distribution, administrative, and other costs and expenses incurred.

b. SETTLEMENT WITH SUBCONTRACTORS - Reasonable settlements of proposals of subcontractors allocable to the terminated portion of the subcontract. Copies of such settlements will be attached hereto.

c. SETTLEMENT EXPENSES - Reasonable costs of protecting and preserving termination inventory in your possession and preparing your proposal.

d. PROFIT - A reasonable profit with respect to the preparations you have made and work you have actually done for the terminated portion of your contract. No profit should be included for work which has not been done, nor shall profit be included for settlement expenses, or for settlement with subcontractors.

5. If you use this form, your total charges being proposed (line 5), must be less than $10,000. The Government has the right to examine your books and records relative to this proposal, and if you are a subcontractor, your customer must be satisfied with your proposal.

STANDARD FORM 1438 (REV. 5/2004) **BACK**

[FR Doc. 04–7405 Filed 4–2–04; 8:45 am]

BILLING CODE 6820–EP–C

53.301-1439 Standard Form 1439, Schedule of Accounting Information

[FAC 84-56, 55 FR 3928, 2/5/90, effective 3/7/90]

SCHEDULE OF ACCOUNTING INFORMATION — FORM APPROVED OMB NO. 9000-0012

Public reporting burden for this collection of information is estimated to average 2.5 hours per response, including the time for reviewing instructions, searching existing data sources, gathering and maintaining the data needed, and completing and reviewing the collection of information. Send comments regarding this burden estimate or any other aspect of this collection of information, including suggestions for reducing this burden, to the FAR Secretariat (VRS), Office of Federal Acquisition and Regulatory Policy, GSA, Washington, D.C. 20405; and the Office of Management and Budget, Paperwork Reduction Project (9000-0012), Washington, D.C. 20503.

To be used by prime contractors submitting termination proposals under Part 49 of the Federal Acquisition Regulation. Also suitable for use by subcontractor in effecting subcontract settlements with prime contractor or immediate subcontractor.

THIS PROPOSAL APPLIES TO (Check one) ☐ A PRIME CONTRACT WITH THE GOVERNMENT ☐ SUBCONTRACT OR PURCHASE ORDER	COMPANY (Prime or Subcontractor)		
SUBCONTRACT OR PURCHASE ORDER NO.(S)	STREET ADDRESS		
CONTRACTOR WHO SENT NOTICE OF TERMINATION NAME AND ADDRESS (include ZIP Code)	CITY AND STATE (Include ZIP Code)		
	NAME OF GOVERNMENT AGENCY		
	GOVERNMENT PRIME CONTRACT NO. New Hampshire City-New ScCDE4	CONTRACTOR'S REFERENCE NO.	EFFECTIVE DATE OF TERMINATION

1. INDIVIDUAL IN YOUR ORGANIZATION FROM WHOM ADDITIONAL INFORMATION MAY BE REQUESTED ON QUESTIONS RELATING TO:

ACCOUNTING MATTERS		PROPERTY DISPOSAL	
NAME		NAME	
TITLE	TELEPHONE NO.	TITLE	TELEPHONE NO.
ADDRESS (Include ZIP Code)		ADDRESS (Include ZIP Code)	

2. ARE THE ACCOUNTS OF THE CONTRACTOR SUBJECT TO REGULAR PERIODIC EXAMINATION BY INDEPENDENT PUBLIC ACCOUNTANTS?
☐ YES ☐ NO (Name and address of accountants)

3. INDEPENDENT ACCOUNTANTS, IF ANY, WHO HAVE REVIEWED OR ASSISTED IN THE PREPARATION OF THE ATTACHED PROPOSAL

NAME	ADDRESS (Include ZIP Code)

4. GOVERNMENTAL AGENCY(IES) WHICH HAVE REVIEWED YOUR ACCOUNTS IN CONNECTION WITH PRIOR SETTLEMENT PROPOSALS DURING THE CURRENT AND PRECEDING FISCAL YEAR

NAME	ADDRESS (Include ZIP Code)

5. HAVE THERE BEEN ANY SIGNIFICANT DEVIATIONS FROM YOUR REGULAR ACCOUNTING PROCEDURES AND POLICIES IN ARRIVING AT THE COSTS SET FORTH IN THE ATTACHED PROPOSAL? (If "Yes," explain briefly)
☐ YES ☐ NO

6. WERE THE DETAILED COST RECORDS USED IN PREPARING THE PROPOSAL CONTROLLED BY AND IN AGREEMENT WITH YOUR GENERAL BOOKS OF ACCOUNT? ☐ YES ☐ NO

7. STATE METHOD OF ACCOUNTING FOR TRADE AND CASH DISCOUNTS EARNED, REBATES, ALLOWANCES, AND VOLUME PRICE ADJUSTMENTS. ARE SUCH ITEMS EXCLUDED FROM COSTS PROPOSED? ☐ YES ☐ NO

(Where the space provided for any information is insufficient, continue on a separate sheet.)

AUTHORIZED FOR LOCAL REPRODUCTION
Previous edition is usable
EXPIRATION DATE: 4-30-92
1439-102
STANDARD FORM 1439 (REV. 7-89)
Prescribed by GSA - FAR (48 CFR) 53.249(a)(6)

8. STATE METHOD OF RECORDING AND ABSORBING (1) GENERAL ENGINEERING AND GENERAL DEVELOPMENT EXPENSE AND (2) ENGINEERING AND DEVELOPMENT EXPENSE DIRECTLY APPLICABLE TO THE TERMINATED CONTRACT.

9. STATE TYPES AND SOURCE OF MISCELLANEOUS INCOME AND CREDITS AND MANNER OF RECORDING IN THE INCOME OR THE COST ACCOUNTS SUCH AS RENTAL OF YOUR FACILITIES TO OUTSIDE PARTIES, ETC.

10. METHOD OF ALLOCATING GENERAL AND ADMINISTRATIVE EXPENSE.

11. ARE COSTS AND INCOME FROM CHANGE ORDERS SEGREGATED FROM OTHER CONTRACT COSTS AND INCOME? (If "Yes," by what method?)

☐ YES ☐ NO

12. METHOD OF COMPUTING PROFIT SHOWN IN THE ATTACHED PROPOSAL AND REASON FOR SELECTING THE METHOD USED. FURNISH ESTIMATE OF AMOUNT OR RATE OF PROFIT IN DOLLARS OR PERCENT ANTICIPATED HAD THE CONTRACT BEEN COMPLETED.

13. ARE SETTLEMENT EXPENSES APPLICABLE TO PREVIOUSLY TERMINATED CONTRACTS EXCLUDED FROM THE ATTACHED PROPOSALS? (If "NO," explain)

☐ YES ☐ NO

14. DOES THIS PROPOSAL INCLUDE CHARGES FOR MAJOR INVENTORY ITEMS AND PROPOSALS OF SUBCONTRACTORS COMMON TO THIS TERMINATED CONTRACT AND OTHER WORK OF THE CONTRACTOR? (If "Yes," explain the method used in allocating amounts to the terminated portion of this contract.)

☐ YES ☐ NO

15. EXPLAIN BRIEFLY YOUR METHOD OF PRICING INVENTORIES, INDICATING WHETHER MATERIAL HANDLING COST HAS BEEN INCLUDED IN CHARGES FOR MATERIALS.

16. ARE ANY PARTS, MATERIALS, OR FINISHED PRODUCT, KNOWN TO BE DEFECTIVE, INCLUDED IN THE INVENTORIES? (If "Yes," explain.)

☐ YES ☐ NO

(Where the space provided for any information is insufficient, continue on a separate sheet.)

STANDARD FORM 1439 (REV. 7-89) **PAGE 2**

17. WERE INVENTORY QUANTITIES BASED ON A PHYSICAL COUNT AS OF THE DATE OF TERMINATION? (If "NO," explain exceptions.)

☐ YES ☐ NO

18. DESCRIBE BRIEFLY THE NATURE OF INDIRECT EXPENSE ITEMS INCLUDED IN INVENTORY COSTS (See Schedule A, SF 1435) AND EXPLAIN YOUR METHOD OF ALLOCATION USED IN PREPARING THIS PROPOSAL, INCLUDING IF PRACTICABLE, THE RATES USED AND THE PERIOD OF TIME UPON WHICH THEY ARE BASED.

19. STATE GENERAL POLICIES RELATING TO DEPRECIATION AND AMORTIZATION OF FIXED ASSETS, BASES, UNDERLYING POLICIES.

20. DO THE COSTS SET FORTH IN THE ATTACHED PROPOSAL INCLUDE PROVISIONS FOR ANY RESERVES OTHER THAN DEPRECIATION RESERVES? (If "Yes," list such reserves)

☐ YES ☐ NO

21. STATE POLICY OR PROCEDURE FOR RECORDING AND WRITING OFF STARTING LOAD.

22. STATE POLICIES FOR DISTINGUISHING BETWEEN CHARGES TO CAPITAL (FIXED) ASSET ACCOUNTS AND TO REPAIR AND MAINTENANCE ACCOUNTS.

23. ARE PERISHABLE TOOLS AND MANUFACTURING SUPPLIES CHARGED DIRECTLY TO CONTRACT COSTS OR INCLUDED IN INDIRECT EXPENSES?

(Where the space provided for any information is insufficient, continue on a separate sheet.)

STANDARD FORM 1439 (REV. 7-89) **PAGE 3**

24. HAVE ANY CHARGES FOR SEVERANCE, DISMISSAL, OR SEPARATION PAY BEEN INCLUDED IN THIS PROPOSAL? (If "Yes," furnish brief explanation and estimates of amounts included.)

☐ YES ☐ NO

25. STATE POLICIES RELATING TO RECORDING OF OVERTIME SHIFT PREMIUMS AND PRODUCTION BONUSES.

26. DOES CONTRACTOR HAVE A PENSION PLAN? (If "Yes," state method of funding and absorption of past and current pension service costs.)

☐ YES ☐ NO

27. IS THIS SETTLEMENT PROPOSAL BASED ON STANDARD COSTS?

☐ YES (If "Yes," has adjustment to actual cost or adjustment for any significant variations been made? ☐ YES ☐ NO (If "NO," explain.)

☐ NO

28. DOES THIS PROPOSAL INCLUDE ANY ELEMENT OF PROFIT TO THE CONTRACTOR OR RELATED ORGANIZATION, OTHER THAN (a) PROFIT SET FORTH SEPARATELY IN THE PROPOSAL OR (b) PROFIT INCLUDED IN THE CONTRACT PRICE AT WHICH ACCEPTABLE FINISHED PRODUCT, IF ANY, IS INCLUDED IN THE PROPOSAL? (If "Yes," explain briefly.)

☐ YES ☐ NO

29. WHAT IS LENGTH OF TIME (PRODUCTION CYCLE) REQUIRED TO PRODUCE ONE OF THE END ITEMS FROM THE TIME THE MATERIAL ENTERS THE PRODUCTION LINE TO THE COMPLETION AS THE FINISHED PRODUCT?

30. STATE POLICY AND PROCEDURE FOR VERIFICATION AND NEGOTIATION OF SETTLEMENTS WITH SUBCONTRACTORS AND VENDORS.

CERTIFICATE

THIS CERTIFIES THAT, TO THE BEST KNOWLEDGE AND BELIEF OF THE UNDERSIGNED, THE ABOVE STATEMENTS ARE TRUE AND CORRECT.

NAME OF CONTRACTOR	BY (Signature of supervisory accounting official)	
	TITLE	DATE

(Where the space provided for any information is insufficient, continue on a separate sheet.)

STANDARD FORM 1439 (REV. 7-89) **PAGE 4**

53.301-1440 Standard Form 1440, Application for Partial Payment

[FAC 84-56, 55 FR 3933, 2/5/90, effective 3/7/90]

APPLICATION FOR PARTIAL PAYMENT

OMB No.: **9000-0012**
Expires: 05/31/96

Public reporting burden for this collection of information is estimated to average 2.5 hours per response, including the time for reviewing instructions, searching existing data sources, gathering and maintaining the data needed, and completing and reviewing the collection of information. Send comments regarding this burden estimate or any other aspect of this collection of information, including suggestions for reducing this burden, to the FAR Secretariat (VRS), Office of Federal Acquisiton Policy, GSA, Washington, DC 20405; and to the Office of Management and Budget, Paperwork Reduction Project (9000-0012), Washington, DC 20503.

For use by Prime Contractor or Subcontractor under contracts terminated for the convenience of the Government

THIS APPLICATION APPLIES TO *(Check one)* ☐ A PRIME CONTRACT WITH THE GOVERNMENT ☐ SUBCONTRACT OR PURCHASE ORDER	APPLICANT
SUBCONTRACT OR PURCHASE ORDER NUMBER(S)	STREET ADDRESS
CONTRACTOR WHO SENT NOTICE OF TERMINATION	
NAME	CITY AND STATE *(Include ZIP Code)*
ADDRESS *(Include ZIP Code)*	NAME OF GOVERNMENT AGENCY
IF CONTRACTOR HAS GUARANTEED LOANS OR HAS ASSIGNED MONEYS DUE UNDER THE CONTRACT, GIVE THE FOLLOWING:	GOVERNMENT PRIME CONTRACT NUMBER
NAME AND ADDRESS OF FINANCING INSTITUTION *(Include ZIP Code)*	CONTRACTOR'S REFERENCE NUMBER

NAME AND ADDRESS OF GUARANTOR *(Include ZIP Code)*	EFFECTIVE DATE OF TERMINATION	DATE OF THIS APPLICATION
NAME AND ADDRESS OF ASSIGNEE *(Include ZIP Code)*	AMOUNT REQUESTED $	APPLICATION NUMBER UNDER THIS TERMINATION

SECTION I - STATUS OF CONTRACT OR ORDER AT EFFECTIVE DATE OF TERMINATION

PRODUCTS COVERED BY TERMINATED CONTRACT OR PURCHASE ORDER		FINISHED			UNFINISHED OR NOT COMMENCED		TOTAL COVERED BY CONTRACT OR ORDER
		PREVIOUSLY SHIPPED AND INVOICED	ON HAND: PAYMENT TO BE RECEIVED THROUGH INVOICING	ON HAND: INCLUDED IN THIS APPLICATION	TO BE COMPLETED	NOT TO BE COMPLETED	
(a)		(b)	(c)	(d)	(e)	(f)	(g)
	QUANTITY						
	$						
	QUANTITY						
	$						
	QUANTITY						
	$						

SECTION II - APPLICANT'S OWN TERMINATION CHARGES
(Exclusive of its Subcontractors' Charges)

SETTLEMENT PROPOSAL
☐ ATTACHED
☐ PREVIOUSLY SUBMITTED

NO.	ITEM	CHARGES AS LISTED IN SETTLEMENT PROPOSAL
1.	ACCEPTABLE FURNISHED PRODUCT *(at contract price)*	$
2.	WORK-IN-PROCESS	
3.	RAW MATERIALS, PURCHASED PARTS, AND SUPPLIES	
4.	GENERAL AND ADMINISTRATIVE EXPENSES	
5.	**TOTAL *(Sum of lines 1, 2, 3, and 4)***	$
6.	SPECIAL TOOLING AND SPECIAL TEST EQUIPMENT	
7.	OTHER COSTS	
8.	SETTLEMENT EXPENSES	
9.	**TOTAL *(Sum of lines 5, 6, 7, and 8)***	$
10.	SUBCONTRACTOR SETTLEMENTS APPROVED BY CONTRACTING OFFICER OR SETTLED UNDER A DELEGATION OF AUTHORITY AND PAID BY APPLICANT	$
11. AMOUNT RECEIVED		$
(a)	UNLIQUIDATED PARTIAL, PROGRESS, AND ADVANCE PAYMENTS RECEIVED	
(b)	DISPOSAL AND OTHER CREDITS	
(c)	**TOTAL *(Sum of lines a and b)***	
(d)	AMOUNT OF PARTIAL PAYMENT REQUESTED	
(e)	**TOTAL *(Sum of lines c and d)***	$

AUTHORIZED FOR LOCAL REPRODUCTION
Previous edition is usable

STANDARD FORM 1440 (REV. 1-95)
Prescribed by GSA-FAR (48 CFR) 53.249(a)(7)

53.301-1442 Standard Form 1442, Solicitation, Offer, and Award (Construction, Alteration, or Repair)

SOLICITATION, OFFER, AND AWARD *(Construction, Alteration, or Repair)*	1. SOLICITATION NO.	2. TYPE OF SOLICITATION ☐ SEALED BID (IFB) ☐ NEGOTIATED *(RFP)*	3. DATE ISSUED	PAGE OF PAGES

IMPORTANT - The "offer" section on the reverse must be fully completed by offeror.

4. CONTRACT NO.	5. REQUISITION/PURCHASE REQUEST NO.	6. PROJECT NO.

7. ISSUED BY	CODE	8. ADDRESS OFFER TO

9. FOR INFORMATION CALL:	A. NAME	B. TELEPHONE NO. *(Include area code) (NO COLLECT CALLS)*

SOLICITATION

NOTE: In sealed bid solicitations "offer" and "offeror" mean "bid" and "bidder".

10. THE GOVERNMENT REQUIRES PERFORMANCE OF THE WORK DESCRIBED IN THESE DOCUMENTS *(Title, identifying no., date):*

11. The Contractor shall begin performance within ________ calendar days and complete it within ________ calendar days after receiving ☐ award, ☐ notice to proceed. This performance period is ☐ mandatory, ☐ negotiable. *(See* ______________________.)

12A. THE CONTRACTOR MUST FURNISH ANY REQUIRED PERFORMANCE AND PAYMENT BONDS? *(If "YES," indicate within how many calendar days after award in Item 12B.)* ☐ YES ☐ NO	12B. CALENDAR DAYS

13. ADDITIONAL SOLICITATION REQUIREMENTS:

A. Sealed offers in original and ______ copies to perform the work required are due at the place specified in Item 8 by ________ *(hour)* local time ________________ *(date)*. If this is a sealed bid solicitation, offers must be publicly opened at that time. Sealed envelopes containing offers shall be marked to show the offeror's name and address, the solicitation number, and the date and time offers are due.

B. An offer guarantee ☐ is, ☐ is not required.

C. All offers are subject to the (1) work requirements, and (2) other provisions and clauses incorporated in the solicitation in full text or by reference.

D. Offers providing less than ______ calendar days for Government acceptance after the date offers are due will not be considered and will be rejected.

NSN 7540-01-155-3212 1442-101 **STANDARD FORM 1442** (REV. 4-85) Prescribed by GSA FAR (48 CFR) 53.236-1 (e)

OFFER *(Must be fully completed by offeror)*

14. NAME AND ADDRESS OF OFFEROR *(Include ZIP Code)*

15. TELEPHONE NO. *(Include area code)*

16. REMITTANCE ADDRESS *(Include only if different than Item 14)*

CODE FACILITY CODE

17. The offeror agrees to perform the work required at the prices specified below in strict accordance with the terms of this solicitation, if this offer is accepted by the Government in writing within ________ calendar days after the date offers are due. *(Insert any number equal to or greater than the minimum requirement stated in Item 13D. Failure to insert any number means the offeror accepts the minimum in Item 13D.*

AMOUNTS ▶

18. The offeror agrees to furnish any required performance and payment bonds.

19. ACKNOWLEDGMENT OF AMENDMENTS
(The offeror acknowledges receipt of amendments to the solicitation - give number and date of each)

AMENDMENT NO.									
DATE									

20A. NAME AND TITLE OF PERSON AUTHORIZED TO SIGN OFFER *(Type or print)*

20B. SIGNATURE

20C. OFFER DATE

AWARD *(To be completed by Government)*

21. ITEMS ACCEPTED:

22. AMOUNT

23. ACCOUNTING AND APPROPRIATION DATA

24. SUBMIT INVOICES TO ADDRESS SHOWN IN *(4 copies unless otherwise specified)* ▶ ITEM

25. OTHER THAN FULL AND OPEN COMPETITION PURSUANT TO
☐ 10 U.S.C. 2304(c)( ) ☐ 41 U.S.C. 253(c)( )

26. ADMINISTERED BY CODE

27. PAYMENT WILL BE MADE BY

CONTRACTING OFFICER WILL COMPLETE ITEM 28 OR 29 AS APPLICABLE

☐ 28. NEGOTIATED AGREEMENT *(Contractor is required to sign this document and return ________ copies to issuing office.)* Contractor agrees to furnish and deliver all items or perform all work, requisitions identified on this form and any continuation sheets for the consideration slated in this contract. The rights and obligations of the parties to this contract shall be governed by (a) this contract award, (b) the solicitation, and (c) the clauses, representations, certifications, and specifications or incorporated by reference in or attached to this contract.

☐ 29. AWARD *(Contractor is not required to sign this document.)* Your offer on this solicitation, is hereby accepted as to the items listed. This award consummates the contract, which consists of (a) the Government solicitation and your offer, and (b) this contract award. No further contractual document is necessary.

30A. NAME AND TITLE OF CONTRACTOR OR PERSON AUTHORIZED TO SIGN *(Type or print)*

31A. NAME OF CONTRACTING OFFICER *(Type or print)*

30B. SIGNATURE

30C. DATE

31B. UNITED STATES OF AMERICA

BY

31C. AWARD DATE

STANDARD FORM 1442 PAGE 2 (REV. 4-85)

53.301-1443 Standard Form 1443 Contractor's Request for Progress Payment

[FAC 2005-33, 74 FR 28430, 6/15/2009, effective 7/15/2009]

CONTRACTOR'S REQUEST FOR PROGRESS PAYMENT

Form Approved
OMB Number 9000-0010

IMPORTANT: This form is to be completed in accordance with instructions on the reverse.

SECTION I - IDENTIFICATION INFORMATION

1 TO NAME AND ADDRESS OF CONTRACTING OFFICE ADMINISTERING THE CONTRACT *(Include ZIP Code)*	2 FROM NAME AND ADDRESS OF CONTRACTOR *(Include ZIP Code)*		
PAYING OFFICE	3 SMALL BUSINESS ☐YES ☐NO	4 CONTRACT NUMBER A BASIC CONTRACT NUMBER	B TASK OR DELIVERY ORDER NUMBER
	5 CONTRACT PRICE $		

6. RATES		7. DATE OF INITIAL AWARD		8A PROGRESS PAYMENT REQUEST NUMBER	8B DATE OF THIS REQUEST
A PROGRESS PAYMENTS	B LIQUIDATION	A YEAR	B MONTH		
0 %	0 %				

SECTION II - STATEMENT OF COSTS UNDER THIS CONTRACT THROUGH ________ *(Date)*

9. RESERVED		
10. RESERVED		
11. COSTS ELIGIBLE FOR PROGRESS PAYMENTS UNDER THE PROGRESS PAYMENTS CLAUSE		
12a. TOTAL CONTRACT COST(S) INCURRED TO DATE		
b. ESTIMATED COST TO COMPLETE	c. TOTAL ESTIMATED COST OF PERFORMANCE	
13. ITEM 11 MULTIPLIED BY ITEM 6a		
14a. FINANCING PAYMENTS PAID TO SUBCONTRACTORS		
b. LIQUIDATED FINANCING PAYMENTS TO SUBCONTRACTORS		
c. UNLIQUIDATED FINANCING PAYMENTS PAID TO SUBCONTRACTORS *(Item 14a less 14b)*		
d. SUBCONTRACT FINANCING PAYMENTS APPROVED FOR CURRENT PAYMENT		
e. ELIGIBLE SUBCONTRACTOR FINANCING PAYMENTS *(Item 14c plus 14d)*		
15. TOTAL DOLLAR AMOUNT *(Item 13 plus 14e)*		
16. ITEM 5 MULTIPLIED BY ITEM 6b		
17. LESSER OF ITEM 15 OR ITEM 16		
18. TOTAL AMOUNT OF PREVIOUS PROGRESS PAYMENTS REQUESTED		
19 MAXIMUM BALANCE ELIGIBLE FOR PROGRESS PAYMENTS *(Item 17 less 18)*		

SECTION III - COMPUTATION OF LIMITS FOR OUTSTANDING PROGRESS PAYMENTS

Item		
20. COMPUTATION OF PROGRESS PAYMENT CLAUSE LIMITATION		
a. COSTS INCLUDED IN ITEM 11, APPLICABLE TO ITEMS DELIVERED, INVOICED, AND ACCEPTED TO THE DATE IN HEADING OF SECTION II		
b. COSTS ELIGIBLE FOR PROGRESS PAYMENTS, APPLICABLE TO UNDELIVERED ITEMS AND TO DELIVERED ITEMS NOT INVOICED AND ACCEPTED *(Item 11 less 20a)*		
c. ITEM 20b MULTIPLIED BY ITEM 6a		
d. ELIGIBLE SUBCONTRACTOR FINANCING PAYMENTS *(Same as Item 14e)*		
e. LIMITATION *(Item 20c plus 20d)*		
21. COMPUTATION OF PROGRESS PAYMENT CLAUSE LIMITATION		
a. CONTRACT PRICE OF ITEMS DELIVERED, ACCEPTED AND INVOICED AS OF THE DATE SHOWN IN THE HEADING OF SECTION II		
b. CONTRACT PRICE OF ITEMS NOT DELIVERED, ACCEPTED AND INVOICED *(Item 5 less 21a)*		
c. ITEM 21b MULTIPLIED BY ITEM 6b		
d. UNLIQUIDATED ADVANCE PAYMENTS PLUS ACCRUED INTEREST		
e. LIMITATION *(Item 21c less 21d)*		
22. MAXIMUM UNLIQUIDATED PROGRESS PAYMENTS *(Lesser of Item 20e or 21e)*		
23 TOTAL AMOUNT LIQUIDATED AND TO BE LIQUIDATED		
24. UNLIQUIDATED PROGRESS PAYMENTS *(Item 18 less 23)*		
25. MAXIMUM PERMISSIBLE PROGRESS PAYMENTS *(Item 22 less 24)*		
26. AMOUNT OF CURRENT INVOICE FOR PROGRESS PAYMENT *(Lesser of item 25 or 19)*		
27. AMOUNT APPROVED BY CONTRACTING OFFICER		

CERTIFICATION

DATE ________

I Certify that

(a) The above statement (with attachments) has been prepared from the books and records of the above-named contractor in accordance with the contract and the instructions hereon, and to the best of my knowledge and belief, that it is correct,
(b) All the costs of contract performance (except as herewith reported in writing) have been paid to the extent shown herein, or where not shown as paid have been paid or will be paid currently, by the contractor, when due, in the ordinary course of business,
(c) The work reflected above has been performed,
(d) The quantities and amounts involved are consistent with the requirements of the contract,
(e) There are no encumbrances (except as reported in writing herewith, or on previous progress payment request number ________________) against the property acquired or produced for, and allocated or property chargeable to the contract which would affect or impair the Government's title,
(f) There has been no materially adverse change in the financial condition of the contractor since the contractor's (insert 'as of date of financial information) ________________ submission of its last financial information dated (insert date of prior submission/certification) ________________ to the Government in connection with the contract,
(g) To the extent of any contract provision limiting progress payments pending first article approval, such provision has been complied with, and
(h) After the making of the requested progress payment the unliquidated progress payments will not exceed the maximum unliquidated progress payments permitted by the contract

NAME AND TITLE OF CONTRACTOR REPRESENTATIVE SIGNING THIS FORM	SIGNATURE
NAME AND TITLE OF CONTRACTING OFFICER	SIGNATURE

NSN 7540-01-140-5523

STANDARD FORM 1443 (REV. 6/2009)
Prescribed by GSA FAR (48 CFR 53 232)

INSTRUCTIONS

GENERAL - All dollar amounts must be shown in whole dollars, rounded using a consistent methodology (e.g., always round up, always round down, always round to the nearest dollar). All line item numbers not included in the instructions below are self-explanatory.

SECTION I - IDENTIFICATION INFORMATION. Complete items 1 through 8b in accordance with the following instructions.

Item 1. TO - Enter the name and address of the cognizant Contract Administration Office (the office administering the contract).
PAYING OFFICE - Enter the designation of the paying office, as indicated on the contract.

Item 2. FROM - CONTRACTOR'S NAME AND ADDRESS/ZIP CODE - Enter the name and mailing address of the contractor. If applicable, the division of the company performing the contract should be entered immediately following the contractor's name.

Item 3 Enter an "X" in the appropriate block to indicate whether or not the contractor is a small business concern.

Item 4. Enter the contract number, including the task or delivery order number if applicable. Progress payment requests under individual orders shall be submitted as if the order constituted a separate contract, unless otherwise specified in this contract (FAR 52.232-16(m)).

Item 5. Enter the total contract price in accordance with the following (See FAR 32.501-3):

(1) Under firm-fixed-price contracts, the contract price is the current amount fixed by the contract plus the not-to-exceed amount for any unpriced modifications.

(2) If the contract is redeterminable or subject to economic price adjustment, the contract price is the initial price until modified.

(3) Under a fixed-price incentive contract, the contract price is the target price plus the not-to-exceed amount for any unpriced modifications. However, if the contractor's properly incurred costs exceed the target price, the contracting officer may provisionally increase the price up to the ceiling or maximum price.

(4) Under a letter contract, the contract price is the maximum amount obligated by the contract as modified

(5) Under an unpriced order issued against a basic ordering agreement, the contract price is the maximum amount obligated by the order, as modified.

(6) Any portion of the contract specifically providing for reimbursement of costs only shall be excluded from the contract price.

Item 6A. PROGRESS PAYMENT RATES - Enter the 2-digit progress payment percentage rate shown in paragraph (a) (1) of the progress payment clause

Item 6B. LIQUIDATED RATE - Enter the current progress payment liquidation rate prescribed in the contract (FAR 52.232-16(b)) using three digits - Example. show 80% as 800 - show 72.3% as 723. Decimals between tenths must be rounded up to the next highest tenth (not necessarily the nearest tenth), since rounding down would produce a rate below the minimum rate calculated (FAR 32.503-10(b) (4)).

Item 7. DATE OF INITIAL AWARD - Enter the four digit calendar year Use two digits to indicate the month. Example: Show January 2005 as 2005/01.

Item 8A. PROGRESS PAYMENT REQUEST NUMBER - Enter the number assigned to this request. All requests under a single contract must be numbered consecutively, beginning with 1 Each subsequent request under the same contract must continue in sequence, using the same series of numbers without omission.

Item 8B. Enter the date of the request.

SECTION II - STATEMENT OF COSTS UNDER THIS CONTRACT.
Date. In the space provided in the heading enter the date through which costs have been accumulated from inception for inclusion in this request. This date is applicable to item entries in Sections II and III.

Cost Basis. In accordance with FAR 52.232-16 (a) (1), the basis for progress payments is the contractor's total costs incurred under this contract, whether or not actually paid, plus financing payments to subcontractors (computed in accordance with FAR 52.232-16(j)), less the sum of all previous progress payments made by the Government under this contract.

Item 11. Costs eligible for progress payments under the progress payments clause. Compute the eligible costs in accordance with the requirements at FAR 52.232-16(a)(1) through (4) First articles· Before first article approval, the acquisition of materials or components for, or the commencement of production of, the balance of the contract quantity is at the sole risk of the contractor. Before the first article approval, the costs thereof shall not be allowable for purposes of progress payments (See FAR 52.209-3(g) and FAR 52.209-4(h))

Item 12a. Enter the total contract costs incurred to date, if the actual amount is not known, enter the best possible estimate If an estimate is used, enter (E) after the amount

Item 12b Enter the estimated cost to complete the contract. The contractor shall furnish estimates to complete that have been developed or updated within six months of the date of the progress payment request. The estimates to complete shall represent the contractor's best estimate of total costs to complete all remaining contract work required under the contract. The estimates shall include sufficient detail to permit Government verification.

Items 14a through 14e. Include only financing payments (progress payments, performance-based payments, and commercial item financing) on subcontracts which are in accordance with the requirements of FAR 52.232-16(j) Do not include interim payments under a cost reimbursement contract

Item 14a. Enter only financing payments actually paid.

Item 14b. Enter total financing payments recouped from subcontractors.

Item 14d. Include the amount of unpaid subcontract progress payment billings which have been approved by the contractor for the current payment in the ordinary course of business.

SECTION III - ADVANCE PAYMENTS/ACCEPTED ITEMS. This Section must be completed only if the contractor has received advance payments against this contract, or if the items have been delivered, invoiced and accepted as of the date indicated in the heading of Section II above.
EXCEPTION· Item 27 must be completed for all progress payment requests where the line 12c amount exceeds the amount on Line 5

Item 20a. Of the costs reported in Item 11, compute and enter only costs which are properly allocable to items delivered, invoiced and accepted to the applicable date. In order of preference, these costs are to be computed on the basis of one of the following: (a) The actual unit cost of items delivered, giving proper consideration to the deferment of the starting load costs or (b) projected unit costs (based on experienced costs plus the estimated cost to complete the contract), where the contractor maintains cost data which will clearly establish the reliability of such estimates.

Item 23. Enter total progress payments liquidated (monies recouped from the contractor on prior billings) and those to be liquidated from billings submitted but not yet paid (monies to be recouped from the contractor on submitted but unpaid billings).

CERTIFICATION
Paragraph (f). If no financial information has been provided previously in connection with this contract, insert "N/A" in the submission date block and the financial information date block Otherwise, insert respectively, the "as of" date of the financial information submitted last and the date of the last submission.

STANDARD FORM 1443 (REV 6/2009) **BACK**

53.301-1444 Standard Form 1444, Request for Authorization of Additional Classification and Rate

[FAC 2005-73, 79 FR 24192, 4/29/2014, effective 5/29/2014]

AUTHORIZED FOR LOCAL REPRODUCTION

REQUEST FOR AUTHORIZATION OF ADDITIONAL CLASSIFICATION AND RATE

CHECK APPROPRIATE BOX
☐ SERVICE CONTRACT
☐ CONSTRUCTION CONTRACT

OMB Number: 9000-0089
Expiration Date: 7/31/2014

PAPERWORK REDUCTION ACT STATEMENT: Public reporting burden for this collection of information is estimated to average .5 hours per response, including the time for reviewing instructions, searching existing data sources, gathering and maintaining the data needed, and completing and reviewing the collection of information. Send comments regarding this burden estimate or any other aspects of this collection of information, including suggestions for reducing this burden, to U.S. General Services Administration, Regulatory Secretariat (MVCB)/IC 9000-0089, Office of Governmentwide Acquisition Policy, 1800 F Street, NW, Washington, DC 20405.

INSTRUCTIONS: THE CONTRACTOR SHALL COMPLETE ITEMS 3 THROUGH 16, KEEP A PENDING COPY, AND SUBMIT THE REQUEST, IN QUADRUPLICATE, TO THE CONTRACTING OFFICER.

1. TO: ADMINISTRATOR, WAGE AND HOUR DIVISION, U.S. DEPARTMENT OF LABOR, WASHINGTON, D.C. 20210	2. FROM: *(REPORTING OFFICE)*
3. CONTRACTOR	4. DATE OF REQUEST

5. CONTRACT NUMBER	6. DATE BID OPENED *(SEALED BIDDING)*	7. DATE OF AWARD	8. DATE CONTRACT WORK STARTED	9. DATE OPTION EXERCISED *(IF APPLICABLE) (SERVICE CONTRACT ONLY)*

10. SUBCONTRACTOR *(IF ANY)*

11. PROJECT AND DESCRIPTION OF WORK *(ATTACH ADDITIONAL SHEET IF NEEDED)*

12. LOCATION *(CITY, COUNTY AND STATE)*

13. IN ORDER TO COMPLETE THE WORK PROVIDED FOR UNDER THE ABOVE CONTRACT, IT IS NECESSARY TO ESTABLISH THE FOLLOWING RATE(S) FOR THE INDICATED CLASSIFICATION(S) NOT INCLUDED IN THE DEPARTMENT OF LABOR DETERMINATION

NUMBER: DATED:

a. LIST IN ORDER: PROPOSED CLASSIFICATION TITLE(S); JOB DESCRIPTION(S); DUTIES; AND RATIONALE FOR PROPOSED CLASSIFICATIONS *(Service contracts only)* *(Use reverse or attach additional sheets, if necessary)*	b. WAGE RATE(S)	c. FRINGE BENEFITS PAYMENTS

14. SIGNATURE AND TITLE OF SUBCONTRACTOR REPRESENTATIVE *(IF ANY)*	15. SIGNATURE AND TITLE OF PRIME CONTRACTOR REPRESENTATIVE	
16. SIGNATURE OF EMPLOYEE OR REPRESENTATIVE	TITLE	CHECK APPROPRIATE BOX-REFERENCING BLOCK 13. ☐ AGREE ☐ DISAGREE

TO BE COMPLETED BY CONTRACTING OFFICER *(CHECK AS APPROPRIATE - SEE FAR 22.1019 (SERVICE CONTRACT LABOR STANDARDS) OR FAR 22.406-3 (CONSTRUCTION WAGE RATE REQUIREMENTS))*

☐ THE INTERESTED PARTIES AGREE AND THE CONTRACTING OFFICER RECOMMENDS APPROVAL BY THE WAGE AND HOUR DIVISION. AVAILABLE INFORMATION AND RECOMMENDATIONS ARE ATTACHED.

☐ THE INTERESTED PARTIES CANNOT AGREE ON THE PROPOSED CLASSIFICATION AND WAGE RATE. A DETERMINATION OF THE QUESTION BY THE WAGE AND HOUR DIVISION IS THEREFORE REQUESTED. AVAILABLE INFORMATION AND RECOMMENDATIONS ARE ATTACHED.
(Send 3 copies to the Department of Labor)

SIGNATURE OF CONTRACTING OFFICER OR REPRESENTATIVE	TITLE AND COMMERCIAL TELEPHONE NUMBER	DATE SUBMITTED

PREVIOUS EDITION IS USABLE

STANDARD FORM 1444 (REV. 4/2013)
Prescribed by GSA-FAR (48 CFR) 53.222(f)

53.301-1445 Standard Form 1445, Labor Standards Interview

[FAC 90-45, Final rule, 62 FR 224, 1/2/97, effective 1/1/97]

LABOR STANDARDS INTERVIEW

CONTRACT NUMBER			EMPLOYEE INFORMATION			
			LAST NAME	FIRST NAME		MI
NAME OF PRIME CONTRACTOR			STREET ADDRESS			
NAME OF EMPLOYER			CITY		STATE	ZIP CODE
SUPERVISOR'S NAME						
LAST NAME	FIRST NAME	MI	WORK CLASSIFICATION		WAGE RATE	

ACTION	CHECK BELOW YES	NO
Do you work over 8 hours per day?		
Do you work over 40 hours per week?		
Are you paid at least time and a half for overtime hours?		
Are you receiving any cash payments for fringe benefits required by the posted wage determination decision?		

WHAT DEDUCTIONS OTHER THAN TAXES AND SOCIAL SECURITY ARE MADE FROM YOUR PAY?

	TOOLS YOU USE	
HOW MANY HOURS DID YOU WORK ON YOUR LAST WORK DAY BEFORE THIS INTERVIEW?		
DATE OF LAST WORK DAY BEFORE INTERVIEW *(YYMMDD)*		
DATE YOU BEGAN WORK ON THIS PROJECT *(YYMMDD)*		

THE ABOVE IS CORRECT TO THE BEST OF MY KNOWLEDGE

EMPLOYEE'S SIGNATURE			DATE *(YYMMDD)*
INTERVIEWER	SIGNATURE	TYPED OR PRINTED NAME	DATE *(YYMMDD)*

INTERVIEWER'S COMMENTS

WORK EMPLOYEE WAS DOING WHEN INTERVIEWED	ACTION *(If explanation is needed, use comments section)*	YES	NO
	IS EMPLOYEE PROPERLY CLASSIFIED AND PAID?		
	ARE WAGE RATES AND POSTERS DISPLAYED?		

FOR USE BY PAYROLL CHECKER

IS ABOVE INFORMATION IN AGREEMENT WITH PAYROLL DATA?

☐ YES ☐ NO

COMMENTS

CHECKER

LAST NAME	FIRST NAME	MI	JOB TITLE
SIGNATURE			DATE *(YYMMDD)*

AUTHORIZED FOR LOCAL REPRODUCTION
Previous edition not usable
LHA

STANDARD FORM 1445 (REV. 12-96)
Prescribed by GSA - FAR (48 CFR) 53.222(g)

53.301-1446 Standard Form 1446, Labor Standards Investigation Summary Sheet

[FAC 2005-73, 79 FR 24192, 4/29/2014, effective 5/29/2014]

LABOR STANDARDS INVESTIGATION SUMMARY SHEET

REPORTING OFFICE	CONTRACT NUMBER	CONTRACT AMOUNT	DATE OF CONTRACT

TYPE OF CONTRACT
☐ FIXED PRICE ☐ CPFF ☐ OTHER *(Specify)*

CONTRACTOR'S NAME AND ADDRESS *(Include ZIP Code)*	EMPLOYER'S NAME AND ADDRESS *(Include ZIP Code)* *(If other than prime contractor)*

PROJECT AND LOCATION

DESCRIPTION OF WORK

BASIS FOR INVESTIGATION

WAGE DETERMINATION NUMBER	WAGE DETERMINATION DATE

NATURE AND EXTENT OF VIOLATION

NO. EMPLOYEES INVOLVED	ARE VIOLATIONS CONSIDERED WILLFUL? ☐ Yes ☐ No	COPELAND ACT VIOLATIONS ☐ Yes ☐ No
CONSTRUCTION WAGE RATE REQUIREMENTS STATUTE UNDERPAYMENTS $	CWHSS* UNDERPAYMENTS $	CWHSS * LAW VIOLATIONS $

CORRECTIVE ACTIONS TAKEN

RESTITUTION MADE ☐ Yes ☐ No	AMOUNT OF RESTITUTION $	CONTRACTORS PAYMENT WITHHELD ☐ Yes ☐ No
WITHHELD FOR CONSTRUCTION WAGE RATE REQUIREMENTS STATUTE VIOLATIONS $	WITHHELD FOR CWHSS* UNDERPAYMENTS $	WITHHELD FOR CWHSS* VIOLATIONS $

REMARKS

PREPARED BY

DATE	TITLE	SIGNATURE

*Contract Work Hours and Safety Standards Statute

AUTHORIZED FOR LOCAL REPRODUCTION
Previous edition is usable

STANDARD FORM 1446 (REV. 4-2013)
Prescribed by GSA-FAR (48 CFR) 53.222(h)

53.301-1447 Solicitation/Contract

SOLICITATION/CONTRACT

BIDDER/OFFEROR TO COMPLETE BLOCKS 11, 13, 15, 21, 22, & 27

1. THIS CONTRACT IS A RATED ORDER UNDER DPAS (15 CFR 700) | RATING | PAGE OF

2. CONTRACT NUMBER | 3. AWARD/EFFECTIVE DATE | 4. SOLICITATION NUMBER | 5. SOLICITATION TYPE ☐ SEALED BIDS (IFB) ☐ NEGOTIATED (RFP) | 6. SOLICITATION ISSUE DATE

7. ISSUED BY CODE | NO COLLECT CALLS

8. THIS ACQUISITION IS ☐ UNRESTRICTED OR ☐ SET ASIDE: % FOR:
☐ SMALL BUSINESS ☐ WOMEN-OWNED SMALL BUSINESS (WOSB) ELIGIBLE UNDER THE WOSB PROGRAM
☐ HUBZONE SMALL BUSINESS ☐ EDWOSB
☐ SERVICE-DISABLED VETERAN-OWNED SMALL BUSINESS NAICS:
☐ 8(A) SIZE STANDARD:

9. *(Agency Use)*

10. ITEMS TO BE PURCHASED *(Brief Description)*
☐ SUPPLIES ☐ SERVICES

11. IF OFFER IS ACCEPTED BY THE GOVERNMENT WITHIN ______ CALENDAR DAYS (60 CALENDAR DAYS UNLESS OFFEROR INSERTS A DIFFERENT PERIOD) FROM THE DATE SET FORTH IN BLOCK 9 ABOVE, THE CONTRACTOR AGREES TO HOLD ITS OFFERED PRICES FIRM FOR THE ITEMS SOLICITED HEREIN AND TO ACCEPT ANY RESULTING CONTRACT SUBJECT TO THE TERMS AND CONDITIONS STATED HEREIN.

12. ADMINISTERED BY CODE

13. CONTRACTOR OFFEROR CODE | FACILITY CODE

TELEPHONE NUMBER | UNIQUE ENTITY IDENTIFIER

☐ CHECK IF REMITTANCE IS DIFFERENT AND PUT SUCH ADDRESS IN OFFER

14. PAYMENT WILL BE MADE BY CODE

SUBMIT INVOICES TO ADDRESS SHOWN IN BLOCK:

15. PROMPT PAYMENT DISCOUNT

16. AUTHORITY FOR USING OTHER THAN FULL AND OPEN COMPETITION ☐ 10 U.S.C. 2304 ( ) ☐ 41 U.S.C. 253 ( )

17. ITEM NUMBER	18. SCHEDULE OF SUPPLIES/SERVICES	19. QUANTITY	20. UNIT	21. UNIT PRICE	22. AMOUNT

23. ACCOUNTING AND APPROPRIATION DATA | 24. TOTAL AWARD AMOUNT *(For Government Use Only)*

25. ☐ CONTRACTOR IS REQUIRED TO SIGN THIS DOCUMENT AND RETURN ______ COPIES TO ISSUING OFFICE. CONTRACTOR AGREES TO FURNISH AND DELIVER ALL ITEMS SET FORTH OR OTHERWISE IDENTIFIED ABOVE AND ON ANY CONTINUATION SHEETS SUBJECT TO THE TERMS AND CONDITIONS SPECIFIED HEREIN.

26. ☐ AWARD OF CONTRACT: YOUR OFFER ON SOLICITATION NUMBER SHOWN IN BLOCK 4 INCLUDING ANY ADDITIONS OR CHANGES WHICH ARE SET FORTH HEREIN, IS ACCEPTED AS TO ITEMS:

27. SIGNATURE OF OFFEROR/CONTRACTOR | 28. UNITED STATES OF AMERICA *(Signature of Contracting Officer)*

NAME AND TITLE OF SIGNER *(Type or Print)* | DATE SIGNED | NAME OF CONTRACTING OFFICER | DATE SIGNED

AUTHORIZED FOR LOCAL REPRODUCTION
PREVIOUS EDITION NOT USABLE

STANDARD FORM 1447 (REV. 8/2016)
Prescribed by GSA - FAR (48 CFR) 53.214(d)

NO RESPONSE FOR REASONS CHECKED			
	CANNOT COMPLY WITH SPECIFICATIONS		CANNOT MEET DELIVERY REQUIREMENT
	UNABLE TO IDENTIFY THE ITEM(S)		DO NOT REGULARLY MANUFACTURE OR SELL THE TYPE OF ITEMS INVOLVED
	OTHER *(Specify)*		
	WE DO		WE DO NOT, DESIRE TO BE RETAINED ON THE MAILING LIST FOR FUTURE PROCUREMENT OF THE TYPE OF ITEMS INVOLVED

NAME AND ADDRESS OF FIRM *(Include Zip Code)*	SIGNATURE
	TYPE OR PRINT NAME AND TITLE OF SIGNER

FROM:

AFFIX STAMP HERE

TO:

SOLICITATION NUMBER ________

DATE AND LOCAL TIME ________

STANDARD FORM 1447 (REV. 8/2016) BACK

[FAC 84-53, 54 FR 49002, 11/28/89, effective 2/26/90; FAC 2005-02, 70 FR 14950, 3/23/2005, effective 3/23/2005; FAC 2005-25, 73 FR 21783, 4/22/2008, effective 4/22/2008; FAC 2005-48, 75 FR 82567, 12/30/2010, effective 1/31/2011; FAC 2005-51, 76 FR 18304, 4/1/2011, effective 4/1/2011; FAC 2005-52, 76 FR 31416, 5/31/2011, effective 5/31/2011; FAC 2005-56, 77 FR 12913, 3/2/2012, effective 4/2/2012; FAC 2005-91, 81 FR 67736, 9/30/2016, effective 10/31/2016]

53.301-1449 Standard Form 1449, (APR 2002), Solicitation/Contract/Order for Commercial Items

[FAC 2001-06, 67 FR 13048, 3/20/2002, effective 4/4/2002; FAC 2005-02, 70 FR 14950, 3/23/2005, effective 3/23/2005; FAC 2005-48, 75 FR 82567, 12/30/2010, effective 1/31/2011; FAC 2005-51, 76 FR 18304, 4/1/2011, effective 4/1/2011; FAC 2005-52, 76 FR 31416, 5/31/2011, effective 5/31/2011; FAC 2005-56, 77 FR 12913, 3/2/2012, effective 4/2/2012]

SOLICITATION/CONTRACT/ORDER FOR COMMERCIAL ITEMS
OFFEROR TO COMPLETE BLOCKS 12, 17, 23, 24, & 30

1. REQUISITION NUMBER | PAGE 1 OF

2. CONTRACT NO. | 3. AWARD/EFFECTIVE DATE | 4. ORDER NUMBER | 5. SOLICITATION NUMBER | 6. SOLICITATION ISSUE DATE

7. FOR SOLICITATION INFORMATION CALL: ▶ a. NAME | b. TELEPHONE NUMBER *(No collect calls)* | 8. OFFER DUE DATE/ LOCAL TIME

9. ISSUED BY CODE

10. THIS ACQUISITION IS ☐ UNRESTRICTED OR ☐ SET ASIDE: ____ % FOR:
☐ SMALL BUSINESS
☐ HUBZONE SMALL BUSINESS
☐ SERVICE-DISABLED VETERAN-OWNED SMALL BUSINESS
☐ WOMEN-OWNED SMALL BUSINESS (WOSB) ELIGIBLE UNDER THE WOMEN-OWNED SMALL BUSINESS PROGRAM
☐ EDWOSB
☐ 8 (A)
NAICS:
SIZE STANDARD:

11. DELIVERY FOR FOB DESTINATION UNLESS BLOCK IS MARKED
☐ SEE SCHEDULE

12. DISCOUNT TERMS

☐ 13a. THIS CONTRACT IS A RATED ORDER UNDER DPAS (15 CFR 700)

13b. RATING

14. METHOD OF SOLICITATION ☐ RFQ ☐ IFB ☐ RFP

15. DELIVER TO CODE

16. ADMINISTERED BY CODE

17a. CONTRACTOR/ OFFEROR CODE | FACILITY CODE

TELEPHONE NO.

18a. PAYMENT WILL BE MADE BY CODE

☐ 17b. CHECK IF REMITTANCE IS DIFFERENT AND PUT SUCH ADDRESS IN OFFER

18b. SUBMIT INVOICES TO ADDRESS SHOWN IN BLOCK 18a UNLESS BLOCK BELOW IS CHECKED ☐ SEE ADDENDUM

19. ITEM NO.	20. SCHEDULE OF SUPPLIES/SERVICES	21. QUANTITY	22. UNIT	23. UNIT PRICE	24. AMOUNT
	(Use Reverse and/or Attach Additional Sheets as Necessary)				

25. ACCOUNTING AND APPROPRIATION DATA

26. TOTAL AWARD AMOUNT *(For Govt. Use Only)*

☐ 27a. SOLICITATION INCORPORATES BY REFERENCE FAR 52.212-1, 52.212-4. FAR 52.212-3 AND 52.212-5 ARE ATTACHED. ADDENDA ☐ ARE ☐ ARE NOT ATTACHED

☐ 27b. CONTRACT/PURCHASE ORDER INCORPORATES BY REFERENCE FAR 52.212-4. FAR 52.212-5 IS ATTACHED. ADDENDA ☐ ARE ☐ ARE NOT ATTACHED

☐ 28. CONTRACTOR IS REQUIRED TO SIGN THIS DOCUMENT AND RETURN ______ COPIES TO ISSUING OFFICE. CONTRACTOR AGREES TO FURNISH AND DELIVER ALL ITEMS SET FORTH OR OTHERWISE IDENTIFIED ABOVE AND ON ANY ADDITIONAL SHEETS SUBJECT TO THE TERMS AND CONDITIONS SPECIFIED

☐ 29. AWARD OF CONTRACT: REF. ______________ OFFER DATED ______________. YOUR OFFER ON SOLICITATION (BLOCK 5), INCLUDING ANY ADDITIONS OR CHANGES WHICH ARE SET FORTH HEREIN, IS ACCEPTED AS TO ITEMS:

30a. SIGNATURE OF OFFEROR/CONTRACTOR

31a. UNITED STATES OF AMERICA *(SIGNATURE OF CONTRACTING OFFICER)*

30b. NAME AND TITLE OF SIGNER *(Type or print)* | 30c. DATE SIGNED | 31b. NAME OF CONTRACTING OFFICER *(Type or print)* | 31c. DATE SIGNED

AUTHORIZED FOR LOCAL REPRODUCTION
PREVIOUS EDITION IS NOT USABLE

STANDARD FORM 1449 (REV. 2/2012)
Prescribed by GSA - FAR (48 CFR) 53.212

19. ITEM NO.	20. SCHEDULE OF SUPPLIES/SERVICES	21. QUANTITY	22. UNIT	23. UNIT PRICE	24. AMOUNT

32a. QUANTITY IN COLUMN 21 HAS BEEN

☐ RECEIVED ☐ INSPECTED ☐ ACCEPTED, AND CONFORMS TO THE CONTRACT, EXCEPT AS NOTED: ________

32b. SIGNATURE OF AUTHORIZED GOVERNMENT REPRESENTATIVE	32c. DATE	32d. PRINTED NAME AND TITLE OF AUTHORIZED GOVERNMENT REPRESENTATIVE

32e. MAILING ADDRESS OF AUTHORIZED GOVERNMENT REPRESENTATIVE	32f. TELEPHONE NUMBER OF AUTHORIZED GOVERNMENT REPRESENTATIVE
	32g. E-MAIL OF AUTHORIZED GOVERNMENT REPRESENTATIVE

33. SHIP NUMBER	34. VOUCHER NUMBER	35. AMOUNT VERIFIED CORRECT FOR	36. PAYMENT	37. CHECK NUMBER
☐ PARTIAL ☐ FINAL			☐ COMPLETE ☐ PARTIAL ☐ FINAL	
38. S/R ACCOUNT NO.	39. S/R VOUCHER NUMBER	40. PAID BY		

41a. I CERTIFY THIS ACCOUNT IS CORRECT AND PROPER FOR PAYMENT		42a. RECEIVED BY *(Print)*	
41b. SIGNATURE AND TITLE OF CERTIFYING OFFICER	41c. DATE	42b. RECEIVED AT *(Location)*	
		42c. DATE REC'D *(YY/MM/DD)*	42d. TOTAL CONTAINERS

STANDARD FORM 1449 (REV. 2/2012) BACK

53.302 Optional forms.

This section illustrates the optional forms that are specified by the FAR for use in acquisitions. The numbering system is as indicated in 53.301.

53.302-17 Optional Form 17, Offer Label

[FAC 90-23, 59 FR 67010, 12/28/94, effective 2/27/95]

OF-17 (12/93)
Offer Label

FAR (48) CFR 53.214(g))
FAR (48) CFR 53.215-1(h))

NOTICE TO OFFEROR

1. THIS LABEL MAY ONLY BE USED ON ENVELOPES LARGER THAN 156mm (6 1/8 INCHES) IN HEIGHT AND 292 mm (11 1/2 INCHES) IN LENGTH.
2. Print or type your name and address in the UPPER left comer of the envelope containing your offer.
3. Complete the bottom portion of this form and paste it on the LOWER left corner of the envelope, unless the envelope is 156 mm by 292 mm (6 1/8 inches by 11 1/2 inches) or smaller.

OFFER

SOLICITATION NO.	
DATE FOR RECEIPT OF OFFERS	
TIME FOR RECEIPT OF OFFERS	
AM	PM
OFFICE DESIGNATED TO RECEIVE OFFERS	

53.302-90 Optional Form 90, Release of Lien on Real Property

[FAC 84-58, 55 FR 25569, 6/21/90, effective 7/23/90]

RELEASE OF LIEN ON REAL PROPERTY

Whereas ____________________, of ____________________, by a bond
(Name) (Place of Residence)
for the performance of U.S. Government Contract Number ____________________,
became a surety for the complete and successful performance of said contract, which bond includes a lien upon certain real property further described hereafter, and

Whereas said surety established the said lien upon the following property

and recorded this pledge on ____________________
(Name of Land Records)
in the ____________________ of ____________________,
(Locality) (State)
and

Whereas, I, ____________________, being a duly authorized representative of the United States Government as a warranted contracting officer, have determined that the lien is no longer required to ensure further performance of the said Government contract or satisfaction of claims arising therefrom, and

Whereas the surety remains liable to the United States Government for continued performance of the said Government contract and satisfaction of claims pertaining thereto.

Now, therefore, this agreement witnesseth that the Government hereby releases the aforementioned lien.

[Date] [Signature]

Seal

AUTHORIZED FOR LOCAL REPRODUCTION

OPTIONAL FORM 90 (REV. 1-90)
Prescribed by GSA
FAR (48 CFR) 53.228(n)

53.302-91 Optional Form 91, Release of Personal Property from Escrow

[Final rule, FAC 90-20, 59 FR 11368, 3/10/94, effective 3/10/94]

RELEASE OF PERSONAL PROPERTY FROM ESCROW

Whereas ______________________ (Name), of ______________________ (Place of Residence), by a bond for the performance of U.S. Government Contract Number ______________ became a surety for the complete and successful performance of said contract, and

Whereas said surety has placed certain personal property in escrow

in Account Number ______________________ on deposit

at ______________________ (Name of Financial Institution)

located at ______________________ (Address of Financial Institution), and

Whereas I, ______________________, being a duly authorized representative of the United States Government as a warranted contracting officer, have determined that retention in escrow of the following property is no longer required to ensure further performance of the said Government contract or satisfaction of claims arising therefrom:

and

Whereas the surety remains liable to the United States Government for the continued performance of the said Government contract and satisfaction of claims pertaining thereto.

Now, therefore, this agreement witnesseth that the Government hereby releases from escrow the property listed above, and directs the custodian of the aforementioned escrow account to deliver the listed property to the surety. If the listed property comprises the whole of the property placed in escrow in the aforementioned escrow account, the Government further directs the custodian to close the account and to return all property therein to the surety, along with any interest accruing which remains after the deduction of any fees lawfully owed to ______________________ (Name of Financial Institution)

[Date] [Signature]

Seal

AUTHORIZED FOR LOCAL REPRODUCTION

OPTIONAL FORM 91 (REV. 1 -90)
Prescribed by GSA
FAR (48 CFR) 53.228(o)

53.302-307 Optional Form 307, Contract Award

CONTRACT AWARD — PAGE OF PAGES

1. CONTRACT NUMBER
2. EFFECTIVE DATE
3. SOLICITATION NUMBER
4. REQUISITION/PROJECT NUMBER
5. ISSUED BY — CODE
6. ADMINISTERED BY *(If other than Item 5)* — CODE
7. NAME AND ADDRESS OF CONTRACTOR — CODE
8. PAYMENT WILL BE MADE BY

9A. UNIQUE ENTITY IDENTIFIER
9B. TAXPAYER'S IDENTIFICATION NUMBER
10. SUBMIT INVOICES *(4 copies unless otherwise specified)* TO
☐ ITEM 5 ☐ ITEM 6 ☐ ITEM 8 ☐ OTHER *(Specify)*

11. TABLE OF CONTENTS

(X)	SECTION	DESCRIPTION	PAGE(S)	(X)	SECTION	DESCRIPTION	PAGE(S)
		PART I - THE SCHEDULE				PART II - CONTRACT CLAUSES	
	A	SOLICITATION/CONTRACT TEAM			I	CONTRACT CLAUSES	
	B	SUPPLIES OR SERVICES AND PRICES/COSTS				PART III - LIST OF DOCUMENTS, EXHIBITS AND OTHER ATTACHMENTS	
	C	DESCRIPTION/SPECIFICATIONS/WORK STATEMENT			J	LIST OF ATTACHMENTS	
	D	PACKAGING AND MARKING				PART IV - REPRESENTATIONS AND INSTRUCTIONS	
	E	INSPECTION AND ACCEPTANCE			K	REPRESENTATIONS, CERTIFICATIONS AND OTHER STATEMENTS OF OFFERORS	
	F	DELIVERIES OR PERFORMANCE					
	G	CONTRACT ADMINISTRATION DATA			L	INSTRUCTIONS, CONDITIONS, AND NOTICES TO OFFERORS	
	H	SPECIAL CONTRACT REQUIREMENTS			M	EVALUATION FACTORS FOR AWARD	

12. BRIEF DESCRIPTION

13. TOTAL AMOUNT OF CONTRACT ▶

14. CONTRACTOR'S AGREEMENT. Contractor agrees to furnish and deliver the items or perform services to the extent stated in this document for the consideration stated. The rights and obligations of the parties to this contract shall be subject to and governed by this document and any documents attached or incorporated by reference.

☐ A. CONTRACTOR IS REQUIRED TO SIGN THIS DOCUMENT AND RETURN FOUR COPIES TO THE ISSUING OFFICE. *(Check if applicable)*

B. SIGNATURE OF PERSON AUTHORIZED TO SIGN

C. NAME OF SIGNER

D. TITLE OF SIGNER

E. DATE

15. AWARD. The Government hereby accepts your offer on the solicitation identified in item 3 above as reflected in this award document. The rights and obligations of the parties to this contract shall be subject to and governed by this document and any documents attached or incorporated by reference.

A. UNITED STATES OF AMERICA *(Signature of Contracting Officer)*

B. NAME OF CONTRACTING OFFICER

C. DATE

AUTHORIZED FOR LOCAL REPRODUCTION

OPTIONAL FORM 307 (REV. 8/2016)
Prescribed by GSA - FAR (48 CFR) 53.215-1(e)

[FAC 97-2, 62 FR 51224, 9/30/97, effective 10/10/97; FAC 2005-91, 81 FR 67736, 9/30/2016, effective 10/31/2016]

53.302-308 Optional Form 308, Solicitation and Offer—Negotiated Acquisition

[FAC 97-2, 62 FR 51224, 9/30/97, effective 10/10/97]

SOLICITATION AND OFFER - NEGOTIATED ACQUISITION | PAGE | OF | PAGES

I. SOLICITATION

1. SOLICITATION NUMBER	2. DATE ISSUED	3. OFFERS DUE BY	4. OFFERS VALID FOR 60 DAYS UNLESS A DIFFERENT PERIOD IS ENTERED HERE

5. ISSUED BY	6. ADDRESS OFFER TO (If other than Item 5)

7. FOR INFORMATION CALL (No collect calls)

A. NAME	B. TELEPHONE		C. E-MAIL ADDRESS
	AREA CODE	PHONE NUMBER	

8. BRIEF DESCRIPTION

9. TABLE OF CONTENTS

(X)	SEC.	DESCRIPTION	PAGE(S)	(X)	SEC.	DESCRIPTION	PAGE(S)
		PART I - THE SCHEDULE				PART II - CONTRACT CLAUSES	
	A	SOLICITATION/CONTRACT FORM			I	CONTRACT CLAUSES	
	B	SUPPLIES OR SERVICES AND PRICES/COSTS				PART III - LIST OF DOCUMENTS, EXHIBITS AND OTHER ATTACH.	
	C	DESCRIPTION/SPECS./WORK STATEMENT			J	LIST OF ATTACHMENTS	
	D	PACKAGING AND MARKING				PART IV - REPRESENTATIONS AND INSTRUCTIONS	
	E	INSPECTION AND ACCEPTANCE			K	REPRESENTATIONS, CERTIFICATIONS AND OTHER STATEMENTS OF OFFERORS	
	F	DELIVERIES OR PERFORMANCE					
	G	CONTRACT ADMINISTRATION DATA			L	INSTRS., CONDS., AND NOTICES TO OFFERORS	
	H	SPECIAL CONTRACT REQUIREMENTS			M	EVALUATION FACTORS FOR AWARD	

II. OFFER

The undersigned agrees to furnish and deliver the items or perform services to the extent stated in this document for the consideration stated. The rights and obligations of the parties to the resultant contract shall be subject to and governed by this document and any documents attached or incorporated by reference.

10A. PERSONS AUTHORIZED TO NEGOTIATE	10B. TITLE	10C. TELEPHONE	
		AREA CODE	NUMBER

11. NAME AND ADDRESS OF OFFEROR	12A. SIGNATURE OF PERSON AUTHORIZED TO SIGN		
	12B. NAME OF SIGNER		
	12C. TITLE OF SIGNER		
	12D. DATE	12E. TELEPHONE	
		AREA CODE	NUMBER

OPTIONAL FORM 308 (9-97)
Prescribed by GSA - FAR (48 CFR) 53.215-1(f)

53.302-309 Optional Form 309, Amendment of Solicitation

[FAC 97-2, 62 FR 51224, 9/30/97, effective 10/10/97]

AMENDMENT OF SOLICITATION
(Negotiated Procurements)

PAGE OF PAGES

NOTICE: Offerors must acknowledge receipt of this amendment in writing, by the date and time specified for proposal submissions or the date and time specified in Block 6, whichever is later. IF YOUR ACKNOWLEDGMENT IS NOT RECEIVED AT THE DESIGNATED LOCATION BY THE SPECIFIED DATE AND TIME, YOUR OFFER MAY BE REJECTED. If, by virtue of this amendment, you wish to change your offer, such change must make reference to the solicitation and this amendment and be received prior to the date and time specified in Block 6.

I. AMENDMENT

1. SOLICITATION NUMBER	2. SOLICITATION DATE	3. AMENDMENT NUMBER	4. AMENDMENT DATE

5. ISSUED BY

4. DUE DATE

THIS AMENDMENT DOES NOT CHANGE THE DATE BY WHICH OFFERS ARE DUE UNLESS A DATE AND TIME IS INSERTED BELOW.

A. DATE	B. TIME

7. FOR INFORMATION CALL (No collect calls)

A. NAME	B. TELEPHONE		C. E-MAIL ADDRESS
	AREA CODE	PHONE NUMBER	

8. DESCRIPTION OF AMENDMENT

Expect as provided herein, all terms and conditions of the solicitation remain unchanged and in full force and effect.

II. ACKNOWLEDGMENT OF AMENDMENT

In lieu of other written methods of acknowledgment, the offeror may complete Blocks 9 and 10 and return this amendment to the address in Block 5.

9. NAME AND ADDRESS OF OFFEROR	10A. OFFEROR (Signature of person authorized to sign)
	10B. NAME OF SIGNER
	10C. TITLE OF SIGNER
	10D. DATE

OPTIONAL FORM 309 (9-97)
Prescribed by GSA - FAR (48 CFR) 53.215-1(g)

53.302-312 [Removed]

[FAC 97-7, 63 FR 36120, 7/1/98, effective 1/1/99, finalized without change, 97-13, 7/2/99; FAC 97-19, 65 FR 46052, 7/26/2000, effective 10/1/2000, finalized without change by FAC 2001-02, 66 FR 65347, 12/18/2001, effective 12/18/2001; FAC 2005-77, 79 FR 61746, 10/14/2014, effective 10/14/2014]

53.302-336 Optional Form 336, Continuation Sheet

CONTINUATION SHEET	REFERENCE NO. OF DOCUMENT BEING CONTINUED	PAGE

NAME OF OFFEROR OR CONTRACTOR

ITEM NO.	SUPPLIES/SERVICES	QUANTITY	UNIT	UNIT PRICE	AMOUNT

NSN 7540-01-152-8067

50336-101

OPTIONAL FORM 336 (4-86)
Sponsored by GSA
FAR (48 CFR) 53.110

53.302-347 Optional Form 347, Order for Supplies or Services

[FAC 90-29, 60 FR 34732, 7/3/95, effective 7/3/95; FAC 2005-02, 70 FR 14950, 3/23/2005, effective 3/23/2005; FAC 2005-21, 72 FR 63089, 11/7/2007, effective 11/7/2007; FAC 2005-48, 75 FR 82567, 12/30/2010, effective 1/31/2011; FAC 2005-51, 76 FR 18304, 4/1/2011, effective 4/1/2011; FAC 2005-52, 76 FR 31416, 5/31/2011, effective 5/31/2011; FAC 2005-56, 77 FR 12913, 3/2/2012, effective 4/2/2012]

ORDER FOR SUPPLIES OR SERVICES — PAGE OF PAGES

IMPORTANT: Mark all packages and papers with contract and/or order numbers.

1. DATE OF ORDER
2. CONTRACT NO. *(If any)*
3. ORDER NO.
4. REQUISITION/REFERENCE NO.
5. ISSUING OFFICE *(Address correspondence to)*

6. SHIP TO:
a. NAME OF CONSIGNEE
b. STREET ADDRESS
c. CITY | d. STATE | e. ZIP CODE
f. SHIP VIA

7. TO:
a. NAME OF CONTRACTOR
b. COMPANY NAME
c. STREET ADDRESS
d. CITY | e. STATE | f. ZIP CODE

8. TYPE OF ORDER

☐ a. PURCHASE
REFERENCE YOUR ______________
Please furnish the following on the terms and conditions specified on both sides of this order and on the attached sheet, if any, including delivery as indicated.

☐ b. DELIVERY – Except for billing instructions on the reverse, this delivery order is subject to instructions contained on this side only of this form and is issued subject to the terms and conditions of the above-numbered contract.

9. ACCOUNTING AND APPROPRIATION DATA

10. REQUISITIONING OFFICE

11. BUSINESS CLASSIFICATION *(Check appropriate box(es))*
☐ a. SMALL ☐ b. OTHER THAN SMALL ☐ c. DISADVANTAGED ☐ d. WOMEN-OWNED ☐ e. HUBZone
☐ f. SERVICE-DISABLED VETERAN-OWNED ☐ g. WOMEN-OWNED SMALL BUSINESS (WOSB) ELIGIBLE UNDER THE WOSB PROGRAM ☐ h. EDWOSB

12. F.O.B. POINT

13. PLACE OF
a. INSPECTION | b. ACCEPTANCE

14. GOVERNMENT B/L NO.

15. DELIVER TO F.O.B. POINT ON OR BEFORE *(Date)*

16. DISCOUNT TERMS

17. SCHEDULE *(See reverse for Rejections)*

ITEM NO. (a)	SUPPLIES OR SERVICES (b)	QUANTITY ORDERED (c)	UNIT (d)	UNIT PRICE (e)	AMOUNT (f)	QUANTITY ACCEPTED (g)

SEE BILLING INSTRUCTIONS ON REVERSE

18. SHIPPING POINT
19. GROSS SHIPPING WEIGHT
20. INVOICE NO.

17(h) TOT. *(Cont. pages)*

21. MAIL INVOICE TO:
a. NAME
b. STREET ADDRESS *(or P.O. Box)*
c. CITY | d. STATE | e. ZIP CODE

$ 17(i) GRAND TOTAL

22. UNITED STATES OF AMERICA BY *(Signature)*

23. NAME *(Typed)*

TITLE: CONTRACTING/ORDERING OFFICER

AUTHORIZED FOR LOCAL REPRODUCTION
PREVIOUS EDITION NOT USABLE

OPTIONAL FORM 347 (REV. 2/2012)
Prescribed by GSA/FAR 48 CFR 53.213(f)

SUPPLEMENTAL INVOICING INFORMATION

If desired, this order (or a copy thereof) may be used by the Contractor as the Contractor's invoice, instead of a separate invoice, provided the following statement, (signed and dated) is on (or attached to) the order: "Payment is requested in the amount of $ ____________. No other invoice will be submitted." However, if the Contractor wishes to submit an invoice, the following information must be provided: contract number (if any), order number, item number(s), description of supplies or service, sizes, quantities, unit prices, and extended totals. Prepaid shipping costs will be indicated as a separate item on the invoice. Where shipping costs exceed $10 (except for parcel post), the billing must be supported by a bill of lading or receipt. When several orders are invoiced to an ordering activity during the same billing period, consolidated periodic billings are encouraged.

RECEIVING REPORT

Quantity in the "Quantity Accepted" column on the face of this order has been: ☐ inspected, ☐ accepted, ☐ received by me and conforms to contract. Items listed below have been rejected for the reasons indicated.

SHIPMENT NUMBER	PARTIAL		DATE RECEIVED	SIGNATURE OF AUTHORIZED U.S. GOV'T REP.	DATE
	FINAL				
TOTAL CONTAINERS		GROSS WEIGHT	RECEIVED AT	TITLE	

REPORT OF REJECTIONS

ITEM NO.	SUPPLIES OR SERVICES	UNIT	QUANTITY REJECTED	REASON FOR REJECTION

OPTIONAL FORM 347 (REV. 2/2012) BACK

53.302-348 Optional Form 348, Order for Supplies or Services Schedule—Continuation

[FAC 2005-21, 72 FR 63089, 11/7/2007, effective 11/7/2007]

ORDER FOR SUPPLIES OR SERVICES
SCHEDULE - CONTINUATION

PAGE NO.

IMPORTANT: Mark all packages and papers with contract and/or order numbers.

DATE OF ORDER	CONTRACT NO.	ORDER NO.

ITEM NO. (a)	SUPPLIES OR SERVICES (b)	QUANTITY ORDERED (c)	UNIT (d)	UNIT PRICE (e)	AMOUNT (f)	QUANTITY ACCEPTED (g)
	TOTAL CARRIED FORWARD TO 1ST PAGE (ITEM 17h))					

AUTHORIZED FOR LOCAL REPRODUCTION
PREVIOUS EDITION NOT USABLE

OPTIONAL FORM 348 REV. (4/2006)
Prescribed by GSA - FAR (48 CFR) 53.213(f)

53.302-1419 Optional Form 1419, Abstract of Offers—Construction

[FAC 84-49, 54 FR 29290, 7/11/89, effective 8/10/89]

ABSTRACT OF OFFERS - CONSTRUCTION	1. SOLICITATION NUMBER	2. DATE ISSUED	3. DATE OPENED	PAGE OF PAGES
4. ISSUING OFFICE	I CERTIFY that I have opened, read, and recorded on this abstract all offers received in response to this solicitation. ▶	NAME AND TITLE OF CERTIFYING OFFICIAL (TYPE)		
		SIGNATURE		DATE SIGNED

5. PROJECT TITLE	8. GOVERNMENT ESTIMATE (Check A, B or C and complete D, E, and F.)	9. OFFERS NO. 1	9. OFFERS NO. 2
	A. HIRED LABOR	A. OFFEROR	A. OFFEROR
	B. REASONABLE CONTRACT (Without Profit)	B. BID SECURITY (Type and amount)	B. BID SECURITY (Type and amount)
6. NUMBER OF AMENDMENTS ISSUED	C. REASONABLE CONTRACT (Including Profit)	C. AMENDMENTS ACKNOWLEDGED	C. AMENDMENTS ACKNOWLEDGED

7A. ITEM NO.	7B. DESCRIPTION OF OFFERED ITEM	7C. EST. QUANTITY	D. UNIT	E. UNIT PRICE	F. ESTIMATED AMOUNT	D. UNIT PRICE	E. ESTIMATED AMOUNT	D. UNIT PRICE	E. ESTIMATED AMOUNT

NSN 7540-01-150-0981 501419-101 NOTE: If more than two offers are received, continue on OF 1419A. **OPTIONAL FORM 1419** (11-88) Prescribed by GSA - FAR (48 CFR) 53.236-1

53.302-1419A Optional Form 1419A, Abstract of Offers—Construction, Continuation Sheet

[FAC 84-49, 54 FR 29292, 7/11/89, effective 8/10/89]

ABSTRACT OF OFFERS - CONSTRUCTION CONTINUATION SHEET

1. SOLICITATION NUMBER

PAGE OF ___ PAGES

INSTRUCTIONS - Attach this form to OF 1419, Abstract of Offers - Construction, when more than 2 offers are received on a construction project. Each Continuation Sheet will accomodate 14 contract items to conform to the number of items which can be entered on the OF 1419. Use additional OF 1419's for contract items in excess of 14 and attach additional Continuation Sheets (OF 1419A) as needed.

2. PROJECT TITLE

4. OFFERS (Continued)

Offer	A. OFFEROR	NO:	B. BID SECURITY (Type and amount)	C. AMENDMENTS ACKNOWLEDGED
1				
2				
3				
4				

3. CONTRACT ITEMS A. ITEM NO.	B. ESTIMATED QUANTITY	C. UNIT	D. UNIT PRICE	E. ESTIMATED AMOUNT	D. UNIT PRICE	E. ESTIMATED AMOUNT	D. UNIT PRICE	E. ESTIMATED AMOUNT	D. UNIT PRICE	E. ESTIMATED AMOUNT

NSN 7540-01-280-5502 501419-201 **OPTIONAL FORM 1419A** (11-88) Prescribed by GSA - FAR (48 CFR) 53.236-1

53.303 Agency forms.

This section illustrates agency forms that are specified by the FAR for use in acquisitions. The forms are arranged numerically by agency. The numbering system is as indicated in 53.301.

53.303-DD-254 Department of Defense DD Form 254, Contract Security Classification Specification

[FAC 90-7, 56 FR 41742, 8/22/91, effective 9/23/91]

DEPARTMENT OF DEFENSE
CONTRACT SECURITY CLASSIFICATION SPECIFICATION
(The requirements of the DoD Industrial Security Manual apply to all security aspects of this effort.)

1. CLEARANCE AND SAFEGUARDING
a. FACILITY CLEARANCE REQUIRED
b. LEVEL OF SAFEGUARDING REQUIRED

2. THIS SPECIFICATION IS FOR: *(X and complete as applicable)*

	a. PRIME CONTRACT NUMBER	
	b. SUBCONTRACT NUMBER	
	c. SOLICITATION OR OTHER NUMBER	DUE DATE *(YYYYMMDD)*

3. THIS SPECIFICATION IS: *(X and complete as applicable)*

	a. ORIGINAL *(Complete date in all cases)*		DATE *(YYYYMMDD)*
	b. REVISED *(Supersedes all previous specs)*	REVISION NO.	DATE *(YYYYMMDD)*
	c. FINAL *(Complete Item 5 in all cases)*		DATE *(YYYYMMDD)*

4. IS THIS A FOLLOW-ON CONTRACT? ☐ YES ☐ NO. If Yes, complete the following:
Classified material received or generated under ______ *(Preceding Contract Number)* is transferred to this follow-on contract.

5. IS THIS A FINAL DD FORM 254? ☐ YES ☐ NO. If Yes, complete the following:
In response to the contractor's request dated ______, retention of the classified material is authorized for the period of ______

6. CONTRACTOR *(Include Commercial and Government Entity (CAGE) Code)*

a. NAME, ADDRESS, AND ZIP CODE	b. CAGE CODE	c. COGNIZANT SECURITY OFFICE *(Name, Address, and Zip Code)*

7. SUBCONTRACTOR

a. NAME, ADDRESS, AND ZIP CODE	b. CAGE CODE	c. COGNIZANT SECURITY OFFICE *(Name, Address, and Zip Code)*

8. ACTUAL PERFORMANCE

a. LOCATION	b. CAGE CODE	c. COGNIZANT SECURITY OFFICE *(Name, Address, and Zip Code)*

9. GENERAL IDENTIFICATION OF THIS PROCUREMENT

10. CONTRACTOR WILL REQUIRE ACCESS TO:	YES	NO	11. IN PERFORMING THIS CONTRACT, THE CONTRACTOR WILL:	YES	NO
a. COMMUNICATIONS SECURITY (COMSEC) INFORMATION			a. HAVE ACCESS TO CLASSIFIED INFORMATION ONLY AT ANOTHER CONTRACTOR'S FACILITY OR A GOVERNMENT ACTIVITY		
b. RESTRICTED DATA			b. RECEIVE CLASSIFIED DOCUMENTS ONLY		
c. CRITICAL NUCLEAR WEAPON DESIGN INFORMATION			c. RECEIVE AND GENERATE CLASSIFIED MATERIAL		
d. FORMERLY RESTRICTED DATA			d. FABRICATE, MODIFY, OR STORE CLASSIFIED HARDWARE		
e. INTELLIGENCE INFORMATION			e. PERFORM SERVICES ONLY		
(1) Sensitive Compartmented Information (SCI)			f. HAVE ACCESS TO U. S. CLASSIFIED INFORMATION OUTSIDE THE U.S., PUERTO RICO, U. S. POSSESSIONS AND TRUST TERRITORIES		
(2) Non-SCI			g. BE AUTHORIZED TO USE THE SERVICES OF DEFENSE TECHNICAL INFORMATION CENTER (DTIC) OR OTHER SECONDARY DISTRIBUTION CENTER		
f. SPECIAL ACCESS INFORMATION			h. REQUIRE A COMSEC ACCOUNT		
g. NATO INFORMATION			i. HAVE TEMPEST REQUIREMENTS		
h. FOREIGN GOVERNMENT INFORMATION			j. HAVE OPERATIONS SECURITY (OPSEC) REQUIREMENTS		
i. LIMITED DISSEMINATION INFORMATION			k. BE AUTHORIZED TO USE THE DEFENSE COURIER SERVICE		
j. FOR OFFICIAL USE ONLY INFORMATION			l. OTHER *(Specify)*		
k. OTHER *(Specify)*					

DD FORM 254, DEC 1999 PREVIOUS EDITION IS OBSOLETE.

Reset

12. **PUBLIC RELEASE.** Any information *(classified or unclassified)* pertaining to this contract shall not be released for public dissemination except as provided by the Industrial Security Manual or unless it has been approved for public release by appropriate U.S. Government authority. Proposed public releases shall be submitted for approval prior to release ☐ Direct ☐ Through *(Specify)*

to the Directorate for Freedom of Information and Security Review, Office of the Assistant Secretary of Defense (Public Affairs)* for review.
* In the case of non-DoD User Agencies, requests for disclosure shall be submitted to that agency.

13. **SECURITY GUIDANCE.** The security classification guidance needed for this classified effort is identified below. If any difficulty is encountered in applying this guidance or if any other contributing factor indicates a need for changes in this guidance, the contractor is authorized and encouraged to provide recommended changes; to challenge the guidance or the classification assigned to any information or material furnished or generated under this contract; and to submit any questions for interpretation of this guidance to the official identified below. Pending final decision, the information involved shall be handled and protected at the highest level of classification assigned or recommended. *(Fill in as appropriate for the classified effort. Attach, or forward under separate correspondence, any documents/guides/extracts referenced herein. Add additional pages as needed to provide complete guidance.)*

14. **ADDITIONAL SECURITY REQUIREMENTS.** Requirements, in addition to ISM requirements, are established for this contract. ☐ Yes ☐ No
(If Yes, identify the pertinent contractual clauses in the contract document itself, or provide an appropriate statement which identifies the additional requirements. Provide a copy of the requirements to the cognizant security office. Use Item 13 if additional space is needed.)

15. **INSPECTIONS.** Elements of this contract are outside the inspection responsibility of the cognizant security office. ☐ Yes ☐ No
(If Yes, explain and identify specific areas or elements carved out and the activity responsible for inspections. Use Item 13 if additional space is needed.)

16. **CERTIFICATION AND SIGNATURE. Security requirements stated herein are complete and adequate for safeguarding the classified information to be released or generated under this classified effort. All questions shall be referred to the official named below.**

a. TYPED NAME OF CERTIFYING OFFICIAL	b. TITLE	c. TELEPHONE (Include Area Code)
d. ADDRESS *(Include Zip Code)*		
e. SIGNATURE		

17. **REQUIRED DISTRIBUTION**
- ☐ a. CONTRACTOR
- ☐ b. SUBCONTRACTOR
- ☐ c. COGNIZANT SECURITY OFFICE FOR PRIME AND SUBCONTRACTOR
- ☐ d. U.S. ACTIVITY RESPONSIBLE FOR OVERSEAS SECURITY ADMINISTRATION
- ☐ e. ADMINISTRATIVE CONTRACTING OFFICER
- ☐ f. OTHERS AS NECESSARY

DD FORM 254 (BACK), DEC 1999

53.303-DD-441 Department of Defense DD Form 441, Security Agreement

DEPARTMENT OF DEFENSE
SECURITY AGREEMENT

Form Approved
OMB No. 0704-0194
Expires Jun 30, 2004

The public reporting burden for this collection of information is estimated to average 14 minutes per response, including the time for reviewing instructions, searching existing data sources, gathering and maintaining the data needed, and completing and reviewing the collection of information. Send comments regarding this burden estimate or any other aspect of this collection of information, including suggestions for reducing the burden, to Department of Defense, Washington Headquarters Services, Directorate for Information Operations and Reports (0704-0194), 1215 Jefferson Davis Highway, Suite 1204, Arlington, VA 22202-4302. Respondents should be aware that notwithstanding any other provision of law, no person shall be subject to any penalty for failing to comply with a collection of information if it does not display a currently valid OMB control number.

PLEASE DO NOT RETURN YOUR FORM TO THE ABOVE ADDRESS. RETURN COMPLETED FORM TO YOUR RESPECTIVE COGNIZANT SECURITY OFFICE.

This DEPARTMENT OF DEFENSE SECURITY AGREEMENT *(hereinafter called the Agreement)*, entered into this ________ day of

________________, ________ by and between THE UNITED STATES OF AMERICA through the Defense Security Service acting for the Department of Defense and other governmental User Agencies *(hereinafter called the Government)*, and

____ *(hereinafter called the Contractor)*, which is:

(1) a corporation organized and existing under the laws of the state of ________________

(2) a partnership consisting of ________________

(3) an individual trading as ________________

with its principal office and place of business at *(Street, City, State and ZIP Code)*

____

WITNESSETH THAT:

WHEREAS, the Government has in the past purchased or may in the future purchase from the Contractor supplies or services, which are required and necessary to the national security of the United States; or may invite bids or request quotations on proposed contracts for the purchase of supplies or services, which are required and necessary to the national security of the United States; and

WHEREAS, it is essential that certain security measures be taken by the Contractor prior to and after being accorded access to classified information; and

WHEREAS, the parties desire to define and set forth the precautions and specific safeguards to be taken by the Contractor and the Government in order to preserve and maintain the security of the United States through the prevention of improper disclosure of classified information, sabotage, or any other acts detrimental to the security of the United States;

NOW, THEREFORE, in consideration of the foregoing and of the mutual promises herein contained, the parties hereto agree as follows.

Section I - SECURITY CONTROLS

(A) The Contractor agrees to provide and maintain a system of security controls within the organization in accordance with the requirements of the "National Industrial Security Program Operating Manual," DoD 5220.22-M (hereinafter called the Manual) attached hereto and made a part of this agreement, subject, however, (i) to any revisions of the Manual required by the demands of national security as determined by the Government, notice of which shall be furnished to the Contractor, and (ii) to mutual agreements entered into by the parties in order to adapt the Manual to the Contractor's business and necessary procedures thereunder. In order to place in effect such security controls, the Contractor further agrees to prepare Standard Practice Procedures for internal use, such procedures to be consistent with the Manual. In the event of any inconsistency between the Manual, as revised, and the Contractor's Standard Practice Procedures, the Manual shall control.

(B) The Government agrees that it shall indicate when necessary, by security classification (TOP SECRET, SECRET, or CONFIDENTIAL), the degree of importance to the national security of information pertaining to supplies, services, and other matters to be furnished by the Contractor to the Government or by the Government to the Contractor, and the Government shall give written notice of such security classification to the Contractor and of any subsequent changes thereof; provided, however, that matters requiring security classification will be assigned the least restricted security classification consistent with proper safeguarding of the matter concerned, since overclassification causes unnecessary operational delays and depreciates the importance of correctly classified matter. Further, the Government agrees that when Atomic Energy information is involved it will, when necessary, indicate by a marking additional to the classification marking that the information is "RESTRICTED DATA." The "Department of Defense Contract Security Classification Specification" (DD Form 254) is the basic document by which classification, regrading, and declassification specifications are documented and conveyed to the Contractor.

(C) The Government agrees, on written application, to grant personnel security clearances to eligible employees of the Contractor who require access to information classified TOP SECRET, SECRET, or CONFIDENTIAL.

(D) The Contractor agrees to determine that any subcontractor, subbidder, individual, or organization proposed for the furnishing of supplies or services which will involve access to classified information, has been granted an appropriate facility security clearance, which is still in effect prior to according access to such classified information.

Section II - SECURITY REVIEWS

Designated representatives of the Government responsible for reviews pertaining to industrial plant security shall have the right to review, at reasonable intervals, the procedures, methods, and facilities utilized by the Contractor in complying with the requirements of the terms and conditions of the Manual. Should the Government, through its authorized representative, determine that the Contractor's security methods, procedures, or facilities do not comply with such requirements, it shall submit a written report to the Contractor advising of the deficiencies.

DD FORM 441, JUL 2001 PREVIOUS EDITION IS OBSOLETE.

Section III - MODIFICATION

Modification of this Agreement may be made only by written agreement of the parties hereto. The Manual may be modified in accordance with Section I of this Agreement.

Section IV - TERMINATION

This Agreement shall remain in effect until terminated through the giving of 30 days' written notice to the other party of intention to terminate; provided, however, notwithstanding any such termination, the terms and conditions of this Agreement shall continue in effect so long as the Contractor possesses classified information.

Section V - PRIOR SECURITY AGREEMENTS

As of the date hereof, this Agreement replaces and succeeds any and all prior security or secrecy agreements, understandings, and representations, with respect to the subject matter included herein, entered into between the Contractor and the Government; provided, that the term "security or secrecy agreements, understandings, and representations" shall not include agreements, understandings, and representations contained in contracts for the furnishing of supplies or services to the Government which were previously entered into between the Contractor and the Government.

Section VI - SECURITY COSTS

This Agreement does not obligate Government funds, and the Government shall not be liable for any costs or claims of the Contractor arising out of this Agreement or instructions issued hereunder. It is recognized, however, that the parties may provide in other written contracts for security costs, which may be properly chargeable thereto.

IN WITNESS WHEREOF, the parties hereto have executed this Agreement as of the day and year written above:

THE UNITED STATES OF AMERICA

By ______________________________

(Signature of Authorized Government Representative)

____

(Typed Name of Authorized Government Representative)

____

(Typed Name of Authorized Government Agency)

WITNESS

____

(Typed Name of Contractor Entering Agreement)

____

By ______________________________

(Signature of Authorized Contractor Representative)

____

____

(Typed Name of Authorized Contractor Representative)

____

(Title of Authorized Contractor Representative)

NOTE: In case of a corporation, a witness is not required but the certificate must be completed. Type or print names under all signatures.

____

(Contractor Address)

____

(Contractor Address)

NOTE: Contractor, if a corporation, should cause the following certificate to be executed under its corporate seal, provided that the same officer shall not execute both the Agreement and the Certificate.

CERTIFICATE

I, ______________________________ , certify that I am the ______________________________

of the corporation named as Contractor herein; that ______________________________

who signed this Agreement on behalf of the Contractor, was then ______________________________

of said corporation; that said Agreement was duly signed for and in behalf of said corporation by authority of its governing body, and is within the scope of its corporate powers.

(Corporate Seal)

____

(Signature and Date)

DD FORM 441 (BACK), JUL 2001

53.303-WH-347 Department of Labor Form WH-347, Payroll (For Contractor's Optional Use)

[FAC 2005-42, 75 FR 34286, 6/16/2010, effective 6/16/2010; FAC 2005-48, 75 FR 82577, 12/30/2010, effective 12/30/2010]

U.S. Department of Labor
Wage and Hour Division

PAYROLL

(For Contractor's Optional Use; See Instructions at www.dol.gov/whd/forms/wh347instr.htm)

Persons are not required to respond to the collection of information unless it displays a currently valid OMB control number.

WHD
U.S. Wage and Hour Division
Rev. Dec. 2008

OMB No.: 1215-0149
Expires: 12/31/2011

NAME OF CONTRACTOR ☐ OR SUBCONTRACTOR ☐ | ADDRESS

PAYROLL NO. | FOR WEEK ENDING | PROJECT AND LOCATION | PROJECT OR CONTRACT NO.

(1) NAME AND INDIVIDUAL IDENTIFYING NUMBER (e.g., LAST FOUR DIGITS OF SOCIAL SECURITY NUMBER) OF WORKER	(2) NO. OF WITHHOLDING EXEMPTIONS	(3) WORK CLASSIFICATION	OT. OR ST.	(4) DAY AND DATE / HOURS WORKED EACH DAY							(5) TOTAL HOURS	(6) RATE OF PAY	(7) GROSS AMOUNT EARNED	(8) DEDUCTIONS: FICA	WITH-HOLDING TAX			OTHER	TOTAL DEDUCTIONS	(9) NET WAGES PAID FOR WEEK
			O																	
			S																	
			O																	
			S																	
			O																	
			S																	
			O																	
			S																	
			O																	
			S																	
			O																	
			S																	
			O																	
			S																	
			O																	
			S																	

While completion of Form WH-347 is optional, it is mandatory for covered contractors and subcontractors performing work on Federally financed or assisted construction contracts to respond to the information collection contained in 29 C.F.R. §§ 3.3, 5.5(a). The Copeland Act (40 U.S.C. § 3145) contractors and subcontractors performing work on Federally financed or assisted construction contracts to "furnish weekly a statement with respect to the wages paid each employee during the preceding week." U.S. Department of Labor (DOL) regulations at 29 C.F.R. § 5.5(a)(3)(ii) require contractors to submit weekly a copy of all payrolls to the Federal agency contracting for or financing the construction project, accompanied by a signed "Statement of Compliance" indicating that the payrolls are correct and complete and that each laborer or mechanic has been paid not less than the proper Davis-Bacon prevailing wage rate for the work performed. DOL and federal contracting agencies receiving this information review the information to determine that employees have received legally required wages and fringe benefits.

Public Burden Statement

We estimate that is will take an average of 55 minutes to complete this collection, including time for reviewing instructions, searching existing data sources, gathering and maintaining the data needed, and completing and reviewing the collection of information. If you have any comments regarding these estimates or any other aspect of this collection, including suggestions for reducing this burden, send them to the Administrator, Wage and Hour Division, U.S. Department of Labor, Room S3502, 200 Constitution Avenue, N.W. Washington, D.C. 20210

(over)

Date ______________

I, ______________________________ ______________________________
(Name of Signatory Party) (Title)

do hereby state:

(1) That I pay or supervise the payment of the persons employed by

____ on the
(Contractor or Subcontractor)

______________________________; that during the payroll period commencing on the
(Building or Work)

_____ day of __________, _____, and ending the _____ day of __________, _____,

all persons employed on said project have been paid the full weekly wages earned, that no rebates have been or will be made either directly or indirectly to or on behalf of said

____ from the full
(Contractor or Subcontractor)

weekly wages earned by any person and that no deductions have been made either directly or indirectly from the full wages earned by any person, other than permissible deductions as defined in Regulations, Part 3 (29 C.F.R. Subtitle A), issued by the Secretary of Labor under the Copeland Act, as amended (48 Stat. 948, 63 Start. 108, 72 Stat. 967; 76 Stat. 357; 40 U.S.C. § 3145), and described below:

(2) That any payrolls otherwise under this contract required to be submitted for the above period are correct and complete; that the wage rates for laborers or mechanics contained therein are not less than the applicable wage rates contained in any wage determination incorporated into the contract; that the classifications set forth therein for each laborer or mechanic conform with the work he performed.

(3) That any apprentices employed in the above period are duly registered in a bona fide apprenticeship program registered with a State apprenticeship agency recognized by the Bureau of Apprenticeship and Training, United States Department of Labor, or if no such recognized agency exists in a State, are registered with the Bureau of Apprenticeship and Training, United States Department of Labor.

(4) That:

(a) WHERE FRINGE BENEFITS ARE PAID TO APPROVED PLANS, FUNDS, OR PROGRAMS

☐ – in addition to the basic hourly wage rates paid to each laborer or mechanic listed in the above referenced payroll, payments of fringe benefits as listed in the contract have been or will be made to appropriate programs for the benefit of such employees, except as noted in section 4(c) below.

(b) WHERE FRINGE BENEFITS ARE PAID IN CASH

☐ – Each laborer or mechanic listed in the above referenced payroll has been paid, as indicated on the payroll, an amount not less than the sum of the applicable basic hourly wage rate plus the amount of the required fringe benefits as listed in the contract, except as noted in section 4(c) below.

(c) EXCEPTIONS

EXCEPTION (CRAFT)	EXPLANATION

REMARKS:	
NAME AND TITLE	SIGNATURE

THE WILLFUL FALSIFICATION OF ANY OF THE ABOVE STATEMENTS MAY SUBJECT THE CONTRACTOR OR SUBCONTRACTOR TO CIVIL OR CRIMINAL PROSECUTION. SEE SECTION 1001 OF TITLE 18 AND SECTION 231 OF TITLE 31 OF THE UNITED STATES CODE.

APPENDIX TO THE FAR

APPENDIX

[Not reproduced]

The FAR Appendix contains the cost accounting standards and the related rules and regulations of the Cost Accounting Standards Board.

Federal Acquisition Regulation Topical Index

Table of Contents

Topical Index 2223

Federal Acquisition Regulation

Topical Index
References are to section (§) numbers

A

AbilityOne program (formerly Javits-Wagner-O'Day (JWOD) Act)—see also Nonprofit organizations
. emergency acquisitions . . . 18.107
. purchase priorities . . . 8.603

Acceptable material, requirements
. contract clause . . . 11.304; 52.211-5
. definitions . . . 11.301
. policy . . . 11.302
. special requirements for printing and writing paper . . . 11.303

Acceptance of performance—see also First article testing and approval; Quality assurance; Warranties
. certificate of conformance . . . 46.504
. commercial items acquisition . . . 12.402
. general . . . 46.501
. material inspection and receiving reports . . . 46.601
. place of acceptance . . . 46.503
. responsibility for acceptance . . . 46.502
. risk of loss . . . 46.505
. transfer of title . . . 46.505

Acquisition planning—see also Agency needs, describing; Competition requirements
. acquisition-related dollar thresholds, adjustment for inflation . . . 1.109
. acquisitions involving consolidation, bundling, or substantial bundling . . . 7.107
. . bundling . . . 7.107-3
. . consolidation . . . 7.107-2
. . general . . . 7.107-1
. . notifications . . . 7.107-5
. . solicitation provision . . . 7.107-6
. . substantial bundling . . . 7.107-4
. contract clauses and solicitation provisions
. . commencement, prosecution, and completion of work . . . 11.404; 52.211-10
. . desired and required time of delivery . . . 11.404; 52.211-9
. . economic purchase quantity—supplies . . . 7.203; 52.207-4
. . notice of standard competition . . . 52.207-1
. . notice of streamlined competition . . . 52.207-2
. . option to purchase equipment . . . 7.404; 52.207-5
. . right of first refusal of employment . . . 52.207-3
. . time of delivery . . . 11.404; 52.211-8
. delivery or performance schedules
. . factors to consider . . . 11.402
. . general . . . 11.401
. . supplies or services . . . 11.403
. economic quantities of supplies
. . contracting officers' responsibilities . . . 7.204
. . policy . . . 7.202; 14.212
. . scope . . . 7.200

Acquisition planning—see also Agency needs, describing; Competition requirements—continued
. economic quantities of supplies—continued
. . solicitation provision prescription . . . 7.203
. equipment lease or purchase
. . acquisition considerations . . . 7.401
. . acquisition methods . . . 7.402
. . contract clause prescription . . . 7.404
. . General Services Administration assistance . . . 7.403
. . scope . . . 7.400
. general
. . agency-head responsibilities . . . 7.103
. . definitions . . . 7.101
. . policy . . . 7.102
. . procedures . . . 7.104
. government versus contractor performance
. . policy . . . 7.302
. . solicitation provisions and contract clause prescriptions . . . 7.305
. inherently governmental functions
. . applicability . . . 7.502
. . policy . . . 7.503
. . scope . . . 7.500
. long-range acquisition estimates . . . 5.404
. . announcements . . . 5.404-2
. . release procedures . . . 5.404-1
. market research
. . policy . . . 10.001
. . procedures . . . 10.002
. . scope . . . 10.000
. plans
. . acquisitions involving bundling of contract requirements . . . 7.107
. . contents . . . 7.105
. . major systems . . . 7.106
. . telecommuting . . . 7.108
. requirements documents
. . contract clause and solicitation provision prescriptions . . . 11.107
. . contract clauses and solicitation provisions . . . 11.204
. . customer satisfaction . . . 11.203
. . identification and availability of specifications . . . 11.201
. . items peculiar to one manufacturer . . . 11.105
. . maintenance of standardization documents . . . 11.202
. . market acceptance . . . 11.103
. . order of precedence . . . 11.101
. . service contracts, purchase descriptions for . . . 11.106
. . standardization program . . . 11.102
. . use of brand name or equal purchase descriptions . . . 11.104

Advance agreements
. cost principles and procedures . . . 31.109
Advance payments—see also Contract financing
. emergency acquisitions . . . 18.120
. non-commercial items
. . agreement for special account at a financial institution . . . 32.411
. . applicability . . . 32.403
. . application criteria . . . 32.408
. . approval recommendation . . . 32.409-1
. . authorization . . . 32.410
. . contract clause prescription . . . 32.412
. . contracting officer action . . . 32.409
. . determination . . . 32.410
. . disapproval recommendation . . . 32.409-2
. . exclusions . . . 32.404
. . findings . . . 32.410
. . general . . . 32.402
. . interest . . . 32.407
. . letters of credit . . . 32.406
. . PL 85-804 applicability . . . 32.405
. . scope . . . 32.400
. . security, supervision, covenants . . . 32.409-3
. . statutory authority . . . 32.401
Advertising costs . . . 31.205-1
Advisory and assistance services
. contract clause
. . multiple awards for advisory and assistance services . . . 16.506; 52.216-28
. contracting officer responsibilities . . . 37.205
. definition of covered personnel . . . 37.201
. exclusions . . . 37.202
. guidelines for determining availability of personnel . . . 37.204
. policy . . . 37.203
. scope . . . 37.200
Affirmative action programs—see also Equal employment opportunity; Labor laws
. construction contracts . . . 22.804-2
. nonconstruction contracts . . . 22.804-1
Age discrimination
. complaints . . . 22.902
. policy . . . 22.901
Agencies
. cognizant federal agency . . . 42.003
. competition advocates
. . duties and responsibilities . . . 6.502
. . requirement . . . 6.501
. protests to . . . 33.103
. quality assurance responsibilities . . . 46.103; 46.104
Agency acquisition regulations
. agency control and compliance procedures . . . 1.304
. interagency acquisitions
. . definition . . . 2.101
. . emergency acquisitions . . . 18.113
. . general . . . 17.501
. . procedures . . . 17.502-1
Agency acquisition regulations—continued
. interagency acquisitions—continued
. . scope . . . 17.500
. . transfer costs . . . 45.602-4
. . under Economy Act . . . 17.502-2
. . utilities services . . . 41.206
. interagency acquisitions by nondefense agencies on DoD's behalf
. . applicability . . . 17.702
. . definitions . . . 17.701,
. . policy . . . 17.703
. . scope . . . 17.700
. limitations . . . 1.302
. numbering of clauses and provisions . . . 52.101
. policy . . . 1.301
. publication and codification . . . 1.303
Agency and public participation
. definition . . . 1.501-1
. exceptions . . . 1.501-3
. opportunity for public comments . . . 1.501-2
. public meetings . . . 1.503
. solicitation of agency and public views . . . 1.501
. unsolicited proposed revisions . . . 1.502
Agency heads
. acquisition planning responsibilities . . . 7.103
. appointment of contracting officers . . . 1.603-3
. definition . . . 2.101
. general responsibilities . . . 1.601; 1.602-1; 1.603-1
. management of service contracts . . . 37.503
. ratification of unauthorized commitments . . . 1.602-3
. selection of contracting officers . . . 1.603-2
. termination of contracting officer appointment . . . 1.603-4
Agency needs, describing
. acceptable material
. . contract clause . . . 11.304; 52.211-5
. . definitions . . . 11.301
. . policy . . . 11.302
. . special requirements for printing and writing paper . . . 11.303
. commercial items acquisition . . . 12.202
. construction contracts . . . 11.702
. contract clauses and solicitation provisions . . . 11.204; 11.604; 11.703
. . alternatives to government-unique standards . . . 11.107; 52.211-7
. . availability for examination of specifications not listed in the GSA Index of Federal Specifications, Standards and Commercial Item Descriptions . . . 11.204; 52.211-4
. . availability of specifications listed in the GSA Index of Federal Specifications, Standards and Commercial Item Descriptions . . . 11.204; 52.211-1
. . availability of specifications not listed in the GSA Index of Federal Specifications, Standards and Commercial Item Descriptions . . . 11.204; 52.211-3

Agency needs, describing—continued
. contract clauses and solicitation provisions—continued
. . availability of specifications, standards, and data item descriptions listed in the Acquisition Streamlining and Standardization Information System (ASSIST) . . . 11.204; 52.211-2
. . brand name or equal . . . 11.107; 52.211-6
. . commencement, prosecution, and completion of work . . . 11.404; 52.211-10
. . defense priority and allocation requirements . . . 11.604; 52.211-15
. . delivery of excess quantities . . . 11.703; 52.211-17
. . desired and required time of delivery . . . 11.404; 52.211-9
. . liquidated damages—construction . . . 11.503; 52.211-12
. . liquidated damages—supplies, services, or research and development . . . 11.503; 52.211-11
. . material requirements . . . 11.304; 52.211-5
. . notice of priority rating for national defense use . . . 11.604; 52.211-14
. . time extensions . . . 11.503; 52.211-13
. . time of delivery . . . 11.404; 52.211-8
. . variation in estimated quantity . . . 11.703; 52.211-18
. . variation in quantity . . . 11.703; 52.211-16
. delivery or performance schedules
. . contract clause prescriptions . . . 11.404
. . factors to consider . . . 11.402
. . general . . . 11.401
. . supplies or services . . . 11.403
. general
. . definitions . . . 11.001
. . policy . . . 11.002
. . scope . . . 11.000
. liquidated damages clauses
. . contract clause prescriptions . . . 11.503
. . policy . . . 11.501
. . procedures . . . 11.502
. . scope . . . 11.500
. priorities and allocations
. . contract clause and solicitation provision prescriptions . . . 11.604
. . definitions . . . 11.601
. . general . . . 11.602
. . procedures . . . 11.603
. . scope . . . 11.600
. requirements documents
. . contract clause prescriptions . . . 11.204
. . customer satisfaction . . . 11.203
. . identification and availability of specifications . . . 11.201
. . items peculiar to one manufacturer . . . 11.105
. . maintenance of standardization documents . . . 11.202
. . market acceptance . . . 11.103
. . order of precedence . . . 11.101

Agency needs, describing—continued
. requirements documents—continued
. . service contracts, purchase descriptions for . . . 11.106
. . solicitation provision prescriptions . . . 11.107; 11.204
. . standardization program . . . 11.102
. . use of brand name or equal purchase descriptions . . . 11.104
. testing
. . preaward in-use evaluation . . . 11.801
. variation in quantity
. . construction contracts . . . 11.702
. . contract clause prescriptions . . . 11.703
. . supply contracts . . . 11.701

Agents, contract signatures . . . 4.102

Agreements—see also Blanket purchase agreements (BPAs)
. basic agreements . . . 16.702
. basic ordering agreements . . . 16.703
. scope . . . 16.701

Alternative dispute resolution (ADR) . . . 33.214

American Recovery and Reinvestment Act
. construction materials . . . 25.600—25-607
. . contract clauses . . . 52.225-21—52.225-24
. publicizing requirements . . . 5.701—5-705
. reporting requirements . . . 4.1500—4-1502
. . contract clause . . . 52.204-11
. whistleblower protections . . . 3.907
. . contract clause . . . 52.203-15

Anti-Kickback Act of 1986 . . . 3.502-2

Anti-Terrorism
. SAFETY Act of 2002
. . authorities . . . 50.202
. . definitions . . . 50.201
. . generally . . . 50.203
. . policy . . . 50.204
. . procedures . . . 50.205
. . procedures, authorization of offers contingent upon designation or certification before contract award . . . 50.205-3
. . procedures, considerations . . . 50.205-1
. . procedures, pre-qualification designation notice . . . 50.205-2
. . solicitation provision and contract award . . . 50.206

Antitrust violations—see also Prohibited practices
. definitions . . . 3.302
. general . . . 3.301
. reporting . . . 3.303

Apprentices and trainees
. construction contracts . . . 22.406-4

Architect-engineer services—see also Construction contracts
. contract clauses and solicitation provisions
. . design within funding limitations . . . 52.236-22; 36.609-1
. . preconstruction conference . . . 52.236-26

Architect-engineer services—see also Construction contracts—continued
. contract clauses and solicitation provisions—continued
. . preparation of proposals—construction . . . 36.520; 52.236-28
. . requirements for registration of designers . . . 52.236-25; 36.609-4
. . responsibility of the architect-engineer contractor . . . 52.236-23; 36.609-2
. . site visit (construction) . . . 52.236-27
. . work oversight . . . 52.236-24; 36.609-3
. . work oversight in architect-engineer contracts . . . 52.236-24; 36.609-3
. cost principles and procedures . . . 31.105; 31.201-7
. design responsibility
. . funding limitations . . . 36.609-1
. . liability for defects . . . 36.608
. . redesign . . . 36.609-2
. . requirements for registration of designers . . . 36.609-4
. forms
. . architect-engineer contract, SF 252 . . . 53.301-252
. . architect-engineer qualifications, SF 330 . . . 53.301-330
. . prescriptions . . . 36.702; 53.236-1
. . scope . . . 36.700
. general
. . applicability of regulations . . . 36.101
. . definitions . . . 36.102
. . methods of contracting . . . 36.103
. . policy . . . 36.104
. . scope . . . 36.000
. performance evaluation
. . government cost estimate . . . 36.605
. policy
. . applicable contracting procedures . . . 36.601-3
. . competition . . . 36.601-2
. . implementation . . . 36.601-4
. . public announcement . . . 36.601-1
. publicizing contracts . . . 5.205; 36.601-1
. registration of designers . . . 36.609-4
. selection of firms
. . collection of qualification data . . . 36.603
. . evaluation boards . . . 36.602-2
. . functions of evaluation board . . . 36.602-3
. . negotiations . . . 36.606
. . performance evaluation use . . . 36.604
. . qualifications of firms . . . 36.603
. . release of information . . . 36.607
. . selection authority . . . 36.602-4
. . selection criteria . . . 36.602-1
. . short selection process . . . 36.602-5
. work oversight . . . 36.609-3

Assignment of claims—see also Contract financing
. conditions . . . 32.802
. contract clauses and solicitation provisions
. . assignment of claims . . . 32.806; 52.232-23

Assignment of claims—see also Contract financing—continued
. contract clauses and solicitation provisions—continued
. . prohibition of assignment of claims . . . 32.806; 52.232-24
. definitions . . . 32.801
. electronic funds transfer . . . 32.1105
. emergency acquisitions . . . 18.123
. extent of assignee's protection . . . 32.804
. guaranteed loans . . . 32.304-5
. loan guarantees for defense production . . . 32.304-5
. policies . . . 32.803
. procedure . . . 32.805
. scope . . . 32.800

Audits
. assignment of contract audit services . . . 42.102
. contract audit responsibilities . . . 42.101
. contract audit services directory . . . 42.103
. contractor's system compliance . . . 45.105
. settlement proposals . . . 49.107; 49.303-3

Authority—see also Contract administration; Contracting officers
. advance payments . . . 32.410
. appointment of contracting officers . . . 1.603-3
. general . . . 1.601; 1.602-1; 1.603-1
. ratification of unauthorized commitments . . . 1.602-3
. responsibilities of contracting officers . . . 1.602-2
. selection of contracting officers . . . 1.603-2
. signature authority, determinations and findings . . . 1.707
. termination of contracting officer appointment . . . 1.603-4

Award of contract
. documentation of . . . 14.408-7
. economic price adjustment . . . 14.408-4
. equal low bids . . . 14.408-6
. forms
. . award/contract, SF 26 . . . 53.301-26
. general procedures . . . 14.408-1
. information to bidders
. . classified contracts . . . 14.409-2
. . notifications of award . . . 15.504
. . notifications to unsuccessful offerors . . . 15.503
. . postaward debriefing . . . 15.506
. . preaward debriefing . . . 15.505
. . unclassified contracts . . . 14.409-1
. liquidated damages . . . 19.705-7
. management and operating contracts . . . 17.605
. prompt payment discounts . . . 14.408-3
. protests against . . . 15.507; 14.408-8
. reasonableness of price . . . 14.408-2
. research and development contracts . . . 35.008
. responsible bidder, determination of . . . 14.408-2
. simplified acquisition procedures . . . 13.106-2
. subcontracting plans . . . 19.705-5; 19.705-6
. subcontracts
. . reporting requirements . . . 4.1400
. synopses . . . 5.301

B

Backpay . . . 31.205-6

Bad debts . . . 31.205-3

Bankruptcy
. general . . . 42.901
. procedures . . . 42.902
. scope . . . 42.900
. solicitation provision and contract clause . . . 42.903; 52.242-13

Basic agreements
. basic ordering agreements . . . 16.703
. description . . . 16.702

Benefits
. construction contracts . . . 22.406-2
. deferred compensation . . . 31.205-6
. postretirement . . . 15.408; 52.215-15; 52.215-18

Best value continuum . . . 15.101
. lowest price technically acceptable . . . 15.101-2
. tradeoff process . . . 15.101-1

Bid and proposal costs . . . 31.205-18

Bid evaluation—see also Sealed bidding
. architect-engineer services . . . 36.602
. award . . . 14.408-1
. Buy American statute, construction materials . . . 25.204
. disclosure, protection, and marking of bids . . . 3.700; 3.104-4
. negotiated procurement . . . 15.305
. . evaluating factors and significant subfactors . . . 15.304
. . information to support . . . 15.404-2
. . profit . . . 15.404-4
. . subcontract pricing considerations . . . 15.404-3
. . techniques . . . 15.305; 15.404-1
. options . . . 17.206
. research and development contracts . . . 35.008
. simplified acquisition procedures . . . 13.106-2

Bid guarantees
. bonds
. . authority of an attorney-in-fact . . . 28.101-3
. . contract clauses prescriptions . . . 28.101-2
. . emergency acquisitions . . . 18.118
. . noncompliance with requirements . . . 28.101-4
. . policy . . . 28.101-1
. waiver of for emergency acquisitions . . . 18.119

Bid opening
. classified bids . . . 14.402-2
. minor informalities or irregularities . . . 14.405
. mistakes in bids
. . apparent clerical mistakes . . . 14.407-2
. . general . . . 14.407-1
. . mistakes after award . . . 15.508; 14.407-4
. . other mistakes disclosed before award . . . 14.407-3
. postponement of openings . . . 14.402-3
. receipt and safeguarding of bids . . . 14.401
. recording of bids . . . 14.204; 14.403

Bid opening—continued
. rejection of bids
. . all or none qualifications . . . 14.404-5
. . cancellation after opening . . . 14.404-1
. . disclosure of descriptive literature . . . 14.404-4
. . notice to bidders . . . 14.404-3
. . rejection of individual bids . . . 14.404-2
. scope . . . 14.400
. unclassified bids . . . 14.402-1
. unreadable electronic bids . . . 14.406

Bid solicitation—see also Publicizing contract actions
. amendment of invitations . . . 14.208
. cancellation of invitations . . . 14.209; 14.404-1
. construction contracts . . . 36.211; 36.213-3
. economic purchase quantities (supplies) . . . 14.212
. encouraging small business concerns . . . 19.202-4
. general rules . . . 14.202
. . bid envelopes . . . 14.202-3
. . bid samples . . . 14.202-4
. . bidding time . . . 14.202-1
. . descriptive literature . . . 14.202-5
. . electronic bids . . . 14.202-8
. . facsimile bids . . . 14.202-7
. . final IFB review . . . 14.202-6
. government property, use of . . . 45.201
. methods . . . 14.203
. . dissemination of information . . . 14.203-2
. . master solicitation . . . 14.203-3
. . transmittal to prospective bidders . . . 14.203-1
. mission-oriented solicitation . . . 34.005-2
. multi-year contracts . . . 17.106-1
. negotiated procurement
. . advisory multi-step process . . . 15.202
. . amending the solicitation . . . 15.206
. . contract clause and solicitation provision prescriptions . . . 15.209
. . contract format . . . 15.204
. . exchanges with industry before receipt of proposals . . . 15.201
. . forms prescriptions . . . 15.210
. . handling proposals and information . . . 15.207
. . issuing solicitations . . . 15.205
. . requests for proposals . . . 15.203
. . requests for proposals (RFPs) . . . 15.203
. . scope . . . 15.200
. . submission, modification, revision, and withdrawal . . . 15.208
. . uniform contract format . . . 15.204-1
. option provisions . . . 17.203
. pre-bid conference . . . 14.207
. preparation of invitations . . . 14.201
. presolicitation notices . . . 14.205
. records of invitations and bids . . . 14.204; 14.403
. release of acquisition information . . . 14.211
. research and development contracts . . . 35.007
. simplified acquisition procedures . . . 13.106-1; 13.106-3
. transportation contracts . . . 47.202; 47.206

Bid solicitation—see also Publicizing contract actions—continued
. uniform contract format . . . 14.201-1; 15.204-1
. . contract clause prescriptions . . . 14.201-7
. . part I—the schedule . . . 14.201-2; 15.204-2
. . part II—contract clauses . . . 14.201-3; 15.204-3
. . part III—documents, exhibits, and other attachments . . . 14.201-4; 15.204-4
. . part IV—representations and instructions . . . 14.201-5; 15.204-5
. . price-related factors . . . 14.201-8
. . simplified format . . . 14.201-9
. . solicitation provision prescriptions . . . 14.201-6
Bid submission
. disclosure, protection, and marking of bids . . . 3.700; 3.104-4
. modification or withdrawal of bids . . . 14.303; 14.304
. procedure . . . 14.302
. responsiveness of bids . . . 14.301
Biobased products
. affirmative procurement . . . 23.406
. . contract clause . . . 52.223-2
. certification requirement . . . 23.406
. . contract clause . . . 52.223-1
Blanket purchase agreements (BPAs)
. completion of . . . 13.303-7
. contract clause prescriptions . . . 13.303-4; 13.303-8
. emergency acquisitions . . . 18.105
. establishment of . . . 13.303-2
. Federal Supply Schedules . . . 8.405-3
. general . . . 13.303-1
. optional clause . . . 13.303-8
. preparation of . . . 13.303-3
. purchases under . . . 13.303-5
. review procedures . . . 13.303-6
Bonds—see also Sureties
. administration
. . additional bond . . . 28.106-3
. . consent of surety . . . 28.106-5
. . contract clause prescription . . . 28.106-4
. . form prescriptions . . . 28.106-1
. . furnishing information . . . 28.106-6
. . payment to subcontractors or suppliers . . . 28.106-8
. . substitution of surety bonds . . . 28.106-2
. . withholding contract payments . . . 28.106-7
. advance payment bonds . . . 28.105-1
. annual performance bonds . . . 28.104
. bid guarantees
. . authority of an attorney-in-fact . . . 28.101-3
. . contract clause and solicitation provision prescription . . . 28.101-2
. . emergency acquisitions . . . 18.118
. . noncompliance with requirements . . . 28.101-4
. . policy . . . 28.101-1
. bonding costs . . . 31.205-4
. construction contracts
. . amount required . . . 28.102-2

Bonds—see also Sureties—continued
. construction contracts—continued
. . contract clauses . . . 28.102-3
. . general . . . 28.102-1
. contract clauses and solicitation provisions
. . additional bond security . . . 28.106-4; 52.228-2
. . alternative payment protections . . . 28.102-3; 52.228-13
. . bid guarantee . . . 28.101-2; 52.228-1
. . cargo insurance . . . 28.313; 52.228-9
. . insurance—liability to third persons . . . 52.228-7; 28.311-1
. . insurance—work on a government installation . . . 28.310; 52.228-5
. . irrevocable letter of credit . . . 28.204-4; 52.228-14
. . liability and insurance—leased motor vehicles . . . 28.312; 52.228-8
. . performance and payment bonds—construction . . . 28.102-3; 52.228-15
. . performance and payment bonds—other than construction . . . 28.103-4; 52.228-16
. . pledges of assets . . . 28.203-6; 52.228-11
. . prospective subcontractor requests for bonds . . . 28.106-4; 52.228-12
. . vehicular and general public liability insurance . . . 28.313; 52.228-10
. . workers' compensation and war-hazard insurance overseas . . . 28.309; 52.228-4
. . workers' compensation insurance . . . 28.309; 52.228-3
. definitions . . . 28.001
. dismantling, demolition, or removal of improvements . . . 37.302
. forms
. . annual bid bond, SF 34 . . . 53.301-34
. . annual performance bond, SF 35 . . . 53.301-35
. . bid bond, SF 24 . . . 53.301-24
. . payment bond for other than construction contracts, SF 1416 . . . 53.301-1416
. . payment bond, SF 25-A . . . 53.301-25A
. . performance bond for other than construction contracts, SF 1418 . . . 53.301-1418
. . performance bond, SF 25 . . . 53.301-25
. . prescriptions . . . 53.228
. . reinsurance agreement for Miller Act payment bond, SF 274 . . . 53.301-274
. . reinsurance agreement for Miller Act performance bond, SF 273 . . . 53.301-273
. . reinsurance agreement in favor of the United States, SF 275 . . . 53.301-275
. nonconstruction contracts
. . contract clauses . . . 28.103-4
. . general . . . 28.103-1
. . payment bonds . . . 28.103-3
. . performance bonds . . . 28.103-2
. patent infringement bonds . . . 28.105-2
. scope . . . 28.000; 28.100
Bonuses and incentive compensation . . . 31.205-6
Brand name acquisitions . . . 6.302-1

Business expenses . . . 31.205-28

Business Partner Network (BPN)
. definition . . . 2.101

Buy American
. applicability . . . 25.002
. construction materials
. . American Recovery and Reinvestment Act . . . 25.600—25-607
. . evaluations of offers of foreign construction material . . . 25.204
. . exceptions . . . 25.202
. . noncompliance . . . 25.206
. . policy . . . 25.201
. . postaward determinations . . . 25.205
. . preaward determinations . . . 25.203
. . scope . . . 25.200
. contract clauses and solicitation provisions
. . Buy American—construction materials . . . 25.1102; 52.225-9
. . Buy American Act—construction materials under trade agreements . . . 25.1102
. . Buy American—construction materials under trade agreements . . . 52.225-11
. . Buy American—Free Trade Agreements—Israeli Trade Act . . . 25.1101
. . Buy American—Free Trade Agreements—Israeli Trade Act certificate . . . 25.1101
. . Buy American—Free Trade Agreements—Israeli Trade Act . . . 52.225-3
. . Buy American—Free Trade Agreements—Israeli Trade Act certificate . . . 52.225-4
. . Buy American—supplies . . . 25.1101; 52.225-1
. . Buy American certificate . . . 25.1101; 52.225-2
. . duty-free entry . . . 25.1101; 52.225-8
. . evaluation of foreign currency offers . . . 25.1103; 52.225-17
. . inconsistency between English version and translation of contract . . . 25.1103; 52.225-14
. . notice of Buy American requirement—construction materials . . . 25.1102
. . notice of Buy American requirement—construction materials under trade agreements . . . 25.1102
. . notice of Buy American requirement—construction materials . . . 52.225-10
. . notice of Buy American requirement—construction materials under trade agreements . . . 52.225-12
. . notice of required use of American construction materials . . . 52.225-22
. . notice of required use of American construction materials under trade agreements . . . 52.225-24
. . required use of American iron, steel, and other manufactured goods . . . 52.225-21
. . required use of American iron, steel, and other manufactured goods under trade agreements . . . 52.225-23
. . restrictions on certain foreign purchases . . . 25.1103; 52.225-13
. . trade agreements . . . 25.1101; 52.225-5

Buy American—continued
. contract clauses and solicitation provisions—continued
. . trade agreements certificate . . . 25.1101; 52.225-6
. . waiver of Buy American statute for civil aircraft and related articles . . . 25.1101; 52.225-7
. definitions . . . 25.003
. evaluation example . . . 25.504-1
. scope . . . 25.001; 25.100; 25.200
. supplies
. . contract clause prescriptions . . . 25.1101
. . cost reasonableness determination . . . 25.105
. . exceptions . . . 25.103
. . general . . . 25.101
. . nonavailable articles . . . 25.104
. . policy . . . 25.102
. . scope . . . 25.100

Buying-in—see also Prohibited practices
. definition . . . 3.501-1
. general . . . 3.501-2

C

Cancellation of contracts—see also Termination of contracts
. multi-year contracts . . . 17.103; 17.106-1

Cancellation of solicitation
. after bid opening . . . 14.209; 14.404-1

Career development
. appointment of contracting officers . . . 1.603-3
. general . . . 1.601; 1.602-1; 1.603-1
. responsibilities of contracting officers . . . 1.602-2
. selection of contracting officers . . . 1.603-2
. termination of contracting officer appointment . . . 1.603-4

Caribbean Basin Trade Initiative
. definitions . . . 25.003
. evaluation example . . . 25.504-2
. general . . . 25.405

Certificate of current cost or pricing data . . . 15.406-2

Certificates of competency—see also Small business programs
. awarding the contract . . . 19.602-4
. eligibility determinations . . . 19.601
. general . . . 19.601
. issuing or denying . . . 19.602-2
. referral . . . 19.602-1
. resolving differences . . . 19.602-3
. service contracts . . . 37.108

Child labor
. definitions . . . 22.1501
. policy . . . 22.1502
. products requiring contractor certification as to forced or indentured child labor . . . 22.1503
. scope . . . 22.1500
. solicitation provision and contract clause . . . 22.1505

Civil penalties, improper business practices . . . 3.807; 3.104-8

Civilian Agency Acquisition Council (CAA Council) . . . 1.201-1

Classified information safeguards—see also Contract administration
. award of classified contracts . . . 14.409-2
. contract clause prescription . . . 4.404
. contracting officer responsibilities . . . 4.403
. Federal Prison Industries, Inc., as supplier . . . 8.608
. forms
. . security agreement, DD Form 441 . . . 53.303-DD
. . security classification specification, DD Form 254 . . . 53.303-DD
. general . . . 4.402
. opening of classified bids . . . 14.402-2

Coast Guard
. multi-year contracts . . . 17.106-3

Collective bargaining agreements
. disabilities, workers with . . . 22.1405
. veterans . . . 22.1307
. wage determinations based on . . . 22.1002-3; 22.1012-2

Commercial items
. applicability of certain laws
. . acquisition of COTS items . . . 12.505
. . applicability of subpart . . . 12.501
. . procedures . . . 12.502
. . scope . . . 12.500
. . to executive agency contracts . . . 12.503
. . to subcontracts . . . 12.504
. commercially available off-the-shelf items . . . 12.103
. contract clauses and solicitation provisions
. . contract format . . . 12.303
. . contract terms and conditions—commercial items . . . 12.302; 52.212-4
. . contract terms and conditions required to implement statutes or executive orders—commercial items . . . 52.212-5
. . evaluation—commercial items . . . 52.212-2
. . installment payments for commercial items . . . 52.232-30
. . instructions to offerors—commercial items . . . 52.212-1
. . invitation to propose financing terms . . . 52.232-31
. . invitation to propose performance-based payments . . . 52.232-28
. . offeror representations and certifications—commercial items . . . 52.212-3
. . performance-based payments . . . 52.232-32
. . prescriptions . . . 12.301
. . scope . . . 12.300
. . tailoring of provisions and clauses . . . 12.302
. . terms for financing of purchases of commercial items . . . 52.232-29
. contract financing
. . administration and payment of commercial financing payments . . . 32.207

Commercial items—continued
. contract financing—continued
. . authority . . . 32.201
. . contract clauses and solicitation provisions . . . 32.206
. . determining financing terms . . . 32.203
. . market research about financing terms, conducting . . . 32.202-3
. . policy . . . 12.210; 32.202-1
. . procedures for contracting officer-specified financing . . . 32.204
. . procedures for offeror-proposed financing . . . 32.205
. . scope . . . 32.200
. . security for government financing . . . 32.202-4
. . statutory authority . . . 32.201
. . types of payments for purchases . . . 32.202-2
. definitions . . . 12.00; 2.101
. emergency acquisitions . . . 18.202
. evaluation and solicitation
. . general . . . 12.601
. . streamlined evaluation of offers . . . 12.602
. . streamlined solicitation . . . 12.603
. forms prescription . . . 53.212; 13.307
. general
. . applicability . . . 12.102
. . definition of subcontract . . . 12.001
. . policy . . . 12.101
. . scope . . . 12.000
. pricing . . . 12.209
. special requirements
. . agency need . . . 12.202
. . computer software . . . 12.212
. . contract financing . . . 12.210
. . contract type . . . 12.207
. . cost accounting standards . . . 12.214
. . customary commercial practices . . . 12.213
. . general . . . 12.201
. . market research . . . 12.202
. . notification of overpayment . . . 12.215
. . offers . . . 12.205
. . past performance, use of . . . 12.206
. . price reasonableness, determination of . . . 12.209
. . quality assurance . . . 12.208
. . solicitation/contract form . . . 12.204
. . solicitation, evaluation, and award . . . 12.203
. . technical data . . . 12.211
. . terms and conditions . . . 12.213
. subcontracts
. . applicability . . . 44.401
. . definition . . . 12.001
. . policy requirements . . . 44.402
. . prescription . . . 44.403
. terms and conditions, unique requirements
. . acceptance . . . 12.402
. . general . . . 12.401
. . termination . . . 12.403
. . warranties . . . 12.404
. test program
. . general . . . 13.500

Commercial items—continued
. test program—continued
. . special documentation requirements . . . 13.501
. unenforceability of unauthorized obligations . . . 12.216
. . contract clause . . . 52.232-39
. warranties . . . 12.404; 46.709

Competition requirements
. architect-engineer services . . . 36.601-2
. competition advocates
. . duties and responsibilities . . . 6.502
. . requirement . . . 6.501
. contractor qualifications requirements . . . 9.206-3
. full and open competition
. . after exclusion of sources . . . 6.200
. . policy . . . 6.101
. . scope . . . 6.100
. . use of competitive procedures . . . 6.102
. full and open competition after exclusion of sources
. . establishing or maintaining alternative sources . . . 6.202
. . policy . . . 6.201
. . scope . . . 6.200
. . section 8(a) competition . . . 6.204
. . set-asides for HUBZone small business concerns . . . 6.205
. . set-asides for service-disabled veteran-owned small business concerns . . . 6.206
. . set-asides for small business concerns . . . 6.203
. general
. . applicability . . . 6.001
. . limitations . . . 6.002
. . scope . . . 6.000
. major system acquisition . . . 34.005-1
. negotiated procurement . . . 15.002
. other than full and open competition
. . availability of justification . . . 6.305
. . circumstances permitting . . . 6.302
. . content of justification . . . 6.303-2
. . engineering, developmental, or research capability . . . 6.302-3
. . expert services . . . 6.302-3
. . industrial mobilization . . . 6.302-3
. . international agreements . . . 6.302-4
. . justification, approval of . . . 6.304
. . justification, availability to public . . . 6.305
. . justification content . . . 6.303-2
. . justification requirements . . . 6.303-1
. . national security . . . 6.302-6
. . policy . . . 6.301
. . public interest . . . 6.302-7
. . requirements . . . 6.303-1
. . scope . . . 6.300
. . sole source . . . 6.302-1
. . statutory acquisition requirements . . . 6.302-5
. . unusual or compelling urgency . . . 6.302-2
. preference for local area contractor
. . set-asides for local firms during disasters or emergencies . . . 6.207

Competition requirements—continued
. sealed bidding and competitive proposals . . . 6.401
. Section 8(a) program
. . estimating fair market price . . . 19.807
. . general . . . 19.805-1
. . pricing . . . 19.806
. . procedures . . . 19.805-2
. service contracts . . . 37.105
. simplified acquisition procedures and . . . 13.104; 13.106-1

Compliance checking
. construction contracts . . . 22.406-7

Computer software—see also Rights in data and copyrights
. commercial items acquisition . . . 12.212

Concept exploration contracts . . . 34.005-3

Conferences—see also Postaward orientation
. pre-bid conference . . . 14.207
. preconstruction conference . . . 52.236-26

Conflicts of interest—see also Prohibited practices
. contracts with government employees
. . contracting officer responsibilities . . . 3.603
. . exceptions . . . 3.602
. . policy . . . 3.601
. organizational or consultant conflicts
. . applicability . . . 9.502
. . contract clause . . . 9.507-2
. . contracting officer responsibilities . . . 9.504
. . evaluation services . . . 9.505-3
. . examples . . . 9.508
. . preparation of specifications or work statements . . . 9.505-2
. . procedures . . . 9.506
. . proprietary information, obtaining access to . . . 9.505-4
. . solicitation provisions . . . 9.507-1
. . systems engineering and technical direction . . . 9.505-1
. . waiver . . . 9.503
. preventing personal conflicts of interest for contractor employees performing acquisition functions
. . contract clause . . . 52.203-16
. . contract clause prescription . . . 3.1106
. . definitions . . . 3.1101
. . mitigation . . . 3.1104
. . policy . . . 3.1102
. . procedures . . . 3.1103
. . scope of subpart . . . 3.1100
. . violations . . . 3.1105
. . waiver . . . 3.1104

Construction contracts
. adjustment of fee, general . . . 49.305-1
. affirmative action programs . . . 22.804-2
. American Recovery and Reinvestment Act—Buy American . . 25.600—25-607
. architect-engineer firms as construction contractors . . . 36.209

Construction contracts—continued
. brand name or equal purchase descriptions . . . 36.202
. contract clauses and solicitation provisions
. . accident prevention . . . 36.513; 52.236-13
. . affirmative procurement of EPA-designated items in service and construction contracts . . . 52.223-17
. . availability and use of utility services . . . 36.514; 52.236-14
. . certificate of conformance . . . 46.315; 52.246-15
. . changes . . . 43.205; 52.243-4
. . changes and changed conditions . . . 43.205; 52.243-5
. . cleaning up . . . 36.512; 52.236-12
. . delivery of excess quantities . . . 11.703; 52.211-17
. . design within funding limitations . . . 52.236-22; 36.609-1
. . differing site conditions . . . 36.502; 52.236-2
. . inspection of construction . . . 46.311; 52.246-12
. . inspection of transportation . . . 46.314; 52.246-14
. . layout of work . . . 36.517; 52.236-17
. . liquidated damages—construction . . . 11.503; 52.211-12
. . material and workmanship . . . 36.505; 52.236-5
. . operations and storage areas . . . 36.510; 52.236-10
. . organization and direction of work . . . 36.519; 52.236-19
. . other contracts . . . 36.508; 52.236-8
. . performance of work by contractor . . . 36.501; 52.236-1
. . permits and responsibilities . . . 36.507; 52.236-7
. . physical data . . . 36.504; 52.236-4
. . preconstruction conference . . . 36.522; 52.236-26
. . preparation of proposals . . . 36.520; 52.236-28
. . protection of existing vegetation, structures, equipment, utilities, and improvements . . . 36.509; 52.236-9
. . quantity surveys . . . 36.516; 52.236-16
. . responsibility for supplies . . . 46.316; 52.246-16
. . responsibility of the architect-engineer contractor . . . 52.236-23; 36.609-2
. . schedules for construction contracting . . . 36.515; 52.236-15
. . scope . . . 36.500
. . site investigation and conditions affecting work . . . 36.503; 52.236-3
. . site visit . . . 36.523; 52.236-27
. . specifications and drawings for construction . . . 36.521; 52.236-21
. . stop-work order . . . 42.1305; 52.242-15
. . superintendence by the contractor . . . 36.506; 52.236-6
. . suspension of work . . . 42.1305; 52.242-14
. . use and possession prior to completion . . . 36.511; 52.236-11
. . work oversight in cost-reimbursement construction contracts . . . 36.518; 52.236-18
. cost principles and procedures . . . 31.105
. data examination . . . 36.210

Construction contracts—continued
. disclosure of magnitude of project . . . 36.204
. economic price adjustment . . . 36.207
. evaluation of contractor performance . . . 36.201
. firm fixed-price contracts, concurrent performance . . . 36.208
. forms
. . prescription . . . 36.701; 53.236-1
. . request for authorization of additional classification and rate, SF 1444 . . . 53.301-1444
. general
. . applicability of regulations . . . 36.101
. . definitions . . . 36.102
. . methods of contracting . . . 36.103
. . policy . . . 36.104
. . scope . . . 36.000
. government estimate of cost . . . 36.203
. liquidated damages . . . 36.206
. lump sum pricing . . . 36.207
. negotiated procurement
. . cost-reimbursement contracts . . . 36.215
. . price negotiation . . . 36.214; 15.405
. . procedures for price negotiation . . . 36.214
. notice of contracting . . . 36.211
. ocean transportation . . . 47.505
. performance and payment bonds
. . amount required . . . 28.102-2
. . contract clauses . . . 28.102-3
. . general . . . 28.102-1
. performance evaluation . . . 36.201
. preconstruction orientation . . . 36.212
. price negotiation . . . 36.214; 15./405
. pricing fixed-price contracts . . . 36.207
. sealed bidding
. . general . . . 36.213-1
. . invitations for bids . . . 36.213-3
. . notice of award . . . 36.213-4
. . presolicitation notices . . . 36.213-2
. site inspection . . . 36.210
. solicitation distribution . . . 36.211
. specifications . . . 36.202
. statutory cost limitations . . . 36.205
. two-phase design-build selection procedures
. . phase one . . . 36.303-1
. . phase two . . . 36.303-2
. . procedures . . . 36.303
. . scope . . . 36.300
. . scope of work . . . 36.302
. . use . . . 36.301
. value engineering
. . contract clauses . . . 48.202
. . sharing acquisition savings . . . 48.104-2
. variation in estimated quantity . . . 52.211-18
. variation in quantity . . . 11.702; 11.703

Construction contracts, labor standards
. administration and enforcement . . . 22.406
. . additional classifications . . . 22.406-3
. . apprentices and trainees . . . 22.406-4
. . compliance checking . . . 22.406-7

Construction contracts, labor standards—continued
. administration and enforcement—continued
. . contract clause prescriptions and solicitation provisions . . . 22.407
. . cooperation with the Department of Labor . . . 22.406-12
. . disposition of disputes . . . 22.406-10
. . investigations . . . 22.406-8
. . payrolls and statements . . . 22.406-6
. . policy . . . 22.406-1
. . semiannual enforcement reports . . . 22.406-13
. . subcontracts . . . 22.406-5
. . termination of contracts . . . 22.406-11
. . wages, fringe benefits, and overtime . . . 22.406-2
. . withholding from or suspension of payments . . . 22.406-9
. applicability . . . 22.402
. construction wage rate requirements statute wage determinations . . . 22.404
. . appeals . . . 22.404-11
. . award without required wage determination . . . 22.404-9
. . corrections of clerical errors . . . 22.404-7
. . expiration . . . 22.404-5
. . general requirements . . . 22.404-2
. . modifications . . . 22.404-6
. . notification of improper wage determination before award . . . 22.404-8
. . options extending term of contract . . . 22.404-12
. . posting and notice . . . 22.404-10
. . procedures for requesting . . . 22.404-3
. . solicitations issued without wage determinations . . . 22.404-4
. . types of . . . 22.404-1
. definitions . . . 22.401
. Department of Labor cooperation . . . 22.406-12
. disputes . . . 22.406-10
. investigations . . . 22.406-8
. labor standards . . . 22.400
. payrolls and statements . . . 22.406-6
. project labor agreements
. . definitions . . . 22.502
. . general requirements . . . 22.504
. . notice of requirement for project labor agreement clause . . . 52.222-33
. . policy . . . 22.503
. . project labor agreement clause . . . 52.222-34
. . scope of subpart . . . 22.501
. . solicitation provision and contract clause prescription . . . 22.505
. scope . . . 22.400
. statutory and regulatory requirements
. . contract work hours and safety standards . . . 22.403-3
. . Copeland Act . . . 22.403-2
. . construction wage rate requirements statute . . . 22.403-1
. . Department of Labor regulations involving construction . . . 22.403-6

Construction contracts, labor standards—continued
. statutory and regulatory requirements—continued
. . Executive Order 13658 . . . 22.403-4
. . Executive Order 13706 . . . 22.403-5
. wage determination request and response, SF 308 . . . 53.301-308

Construction wage rate requirements (formerly Davis-Bacon Act)
. contract clauses and solicitation provisions . . . 22.407; 52.222-13; 52.222-30; 52.222-31; 52.222-32; 52.222-4; 52.222-5; 52.222-6
. requirements . . . 22.403-1
. wage determinations . . . 22.404
. . appeals . . . 22.404-11
. . award without required wage determination . . . 22.404-9
. . corrections of clerical errors . . . 22.404-7
. . expiration . . . 22.404-5
. . general requirements . . . 22.404-2
. . modifications . . . 22.404-6
. . notification of improper wage determination before award . . . 22.404-8
. . options extending term of contract . . . 22.404-12
. . posting and notice . . . 22.404-10
. . procedures for requesting . . . 22.404-3
. . solicitations issued without wage determinations . . . 22.404-4
. . types of . . . 22.404-1

Consultants
. conflicts of interest
. . applicability . . . 9.502
. . contract clause . . . 9.507-2
. . contracting officer responsibilities . . . 9.504
. . evaluation services . . . 9.505-3
. . examples . . . 9.508
. . preparation of specifications or work statements . . . 9.505-2
. . procedures . . . 9.506
. . proprietary information, obtaining access to . . . 9.505-4
. . solicitation provisions . . . 9.507-1
. . systems engineering and technical direction . . . 9.505-1
. . waiver . . . 9.503
. cost principles . . . 31.205-33
. professional and consultant services, defined . . . 31.205-33

Contingencies costs . . . 31.205-7

Contingent fees, restriction of—see also Prohibited practices
. applicability . . . 3.403
. contract clause prescription . . . 3.404
. definitions . . . 3.401
. record preservation . . . 3.406
. scope . . . 3.400
. statutory requirements . . . 3.402
. violation of covenant . . . 3.405

Contract administration—see also Cost accounting standards; Cost principles
. administration services
. . assignment of . . . 42.202
. . cognizant federal agency . . . 42.003
. . contract administration services directory . . . 42.203
. . interagency agreements . . . 42.002
. . responsibilities . . . 42.201
. . scope . . . 42.000
. annual representations and certifications
. . policy . . . 4.1201
. . scope . . . 4.1200
. . solicitation provision and contract clause . . . 4.1202; 52.204-8
. audit services
. . assignment of contract audit services . . . 42.102
. . contract audit responsibilities . . . 42.101
. . contract audit services directory . . . 42.103
. bankruptcy
. . general . . . 42.901
. . procedures . . . 42.902
. . scope . . . 42.900
. . solicitation provision and contract clause . . . 52.242-13; 42.903
. System for Award Management (SAM) database
. . definition of agreement . . . 4.1101
. . disaster response registry . . . 4.1104
. . policy . . . 4.1102
. . procedures . . . 4.1103
. . scope . . . 4.1100
. . solicitation provision and contract clause . . . 4.1105; 52.204-7
. . contract clause, maintenance . . . 52.204-13
. classified information safeguards
. . contract clause prescription . . . 4.404
. . contracting officer responsibilities . . . 4.403
. . general . . . 4.402
. cognizant federal agency . . . 42.003
. commercial contract financing payments . . . 32.207
. construction contracts . . . 22.406
. . additional classifications . . . 22.406-3
. . apprentices and trainees . . . 22.406-4
. . compliance checking . . . 22.406-7
. . contract clause and solicitation provision prescriptions . . . 22.407
. . cooperation with the Department of Labor . . . 22.406-12
. . disposition of disputes . . . 22.406-10
. . investigations . . . 22.406-8
. . payrolls and statements . . . 22.406-6
. . policy . . . 22.406-1
. . semiannual enforcement reports . . . 22.406-13
. . subcontracts . . . 22.406-5
. . termination of contract . . . 22.406-11
. . wages, fringe benefits, and overtime . . . 22.406-2
. . withholding from or suspension of payments . . . 22.406-9
. contract clauses and solicitation provisions
. . approval of contract . . . 52.204-1

Contract administration—see also Cost accounting standards; Cost principles—continued
. contract clauses and solicitation provisions—continued
. . bankruptcy . . . 52.242-13
. . certification of final indirect costs . . . 52.242-4
. . notice of intent to disallow costs . . . 52.242-1
. . payments to small business subcontractors . . . 52.242-5
. . penalties for unallowable costs . . . 52.242-3
. . printed or copied double-sided on recycled paper . . . 52.204-4; 4.303
. . production progress reports . . . 52.242-2
. . prohibition on contracting for hardware, software, and services developed or provided by Kaspersky Lab and other covered entities . . . 52.204-23
. . security requirements . . . 52.204-2
. . women-owned business other than small business . . . 52.204-5
. contract line items, policy . . . 4.1001
. contractor performance information
. . contract clause prescription, payments to small business subcontractors . . . 42.1504
. . general . . . 42.1501
. . policy . . . 42.1502
. . procedures . . . 42.1503
. . scope . . . 42.1500
. contractor records retention
. . acquisition and supply records . . . 4.705-3
. . applicability . . . 4.702
. . calculation of retention periods . . . 4.704
. . construction contracts pay administration records . . . 4.705-2
. . financial and cost accounting records . . . 4.705-1
. . pay administration records . . . 4.705-2
. . policy . . . 4.703
. . purpose . . . 4.701
. . scope . . . 4.700
. . specific retention periods . . . 4.705
. corporate administrative contracting officer
. . assignment and location . . . 42.602
. . general . . . 42.601
. . responsibilities . . . 42.603
. correspondence . . . 42.401
. data universal numbering system number . . . 52.204-6
. data universal numbering system number maintenance . . . 52.204-12
. disallowance of costs
. . after incurrence . . . 42.803
. . air transportation, U.S.-flag carriers . . . 47.403-3
. . contract clause prescription . . . 42.802
. . notice of intent to disallow . . . 42.801
. . scope . . . 42.800
. distribution of contracts
. . agency requirements . . . 4.202
. . procedures . . . 4.201
. . taxpayer identification number information . . . 4.203

Contract administration—see also Cost accounting standards; Cost principles—continued
. electronic commerce
. . policy . . . 4.502
. execution of contracts
. . contract clause prescription . . . 4.103
. . contracting officer's signature . . . 4.101
. . contractor's signature . . . 4.102
. final indirect cost rates . . . 42.705
. forms prescription . . . 53.204-1
. forward pricing rate agreements . . . 42.1701
. government contract files
. . closeout by the office administering the contract . . . 4.804-1
. . closeout if another office administers the contract . . . 4.804-2
. . closeout of paying office files . . . 4.804-3
. . closeout procedures . . . 4.804-5
. . contents . . . 4.803
. . documentation requirements . . . 13.501
. . general . . . 4.801
. . physically completed contracts . . . 4.804-4
. . scope . . . 4.800
. . storage, handling, and disposal . . . 4.805
. . types of files . . . 4.802
. government delay of work . . . 42.1304
. information reporting
. . contract information . . . 4.903
. . definition . . . 4.901
. . payment information . . . 4.904
. . scope . . . 4.900
. . solicitation provision . . . 4.905
. instructions for submission of cost/price proposals . . . 15.408
. interagency agreements . . . 42.002
. labor laws
. . federal and state requirements . . . 22.102-2
. . labor disputes . . . 22.101-2
. novation agreement
. . processing . . . 42.1204
. . responsibility for execution . . . 42.1202
. . scope . . . 42.1200
. novation and change-of-name agreements
. . applicability . . . 42.1204
. . definition . . . 2.101
. . form prescription . . . 53.110
. office functions
. . contract administration functions . . . 42.302
. . evaluation . . . 42.403
. . general . . . 42.301
. paper documents
. . contract clause prescription . . . 4.303
. . definition . . . 4.301
. . policy . . . 4.302
. . scope . . . 4.300
. performance-based payments . . . 32.1007
. personal identity verification of contractor personnel
. . contract clause prescription . . . 4.1303
. . obligation to verify . . . 4.1302
. . policy . . . 4.1301

Contract administration—see also Cost accounting standards; Cost principles—continued
. postaward orientation
. . conference arrangements . . . 42.503-1
. . conference procedure . . . 42.503-2
. . conference report . . . 42.503-3
. . contract selection . . . 42.502
. . general . . . 42.501
. . letters . . . 42.504
. . preconstruction orientation . . . 36.212
. . scope . . . 42.500
. . subcontractor conferences . . . 42.505
. processing . . . 42.1203
. . responsibility for execution . . . 42.1202
. . scope . . . 42.1200
. production surveillance and reporting
. . applicability . . . 42.1102
. . contract clause prescription . . . 42.1107
. . criticality designator . . . 42.1105
. . general . . . 42.1101
. . policy . . . 42.1103
. . reporting requirements . . . 42.1106
. . requirements . . . 42.1104
. progress payments . . . 32.503-5
. prohibition on contracting for hardware, software, and services developed or provided by Kaspersky Lab
. . contract clause prescription . . . 4.2004
. . definitions . . . 4.2001
. . notification . . . 4.2003
. . prohibition . . . 4.2002
. reporting
. . general requirements . . . 4.602
. . policy . . . 4.603
. . procedures . . . 4.605
. . definitions . . . 4.601
. . reporting data . . . 4.606
. . responsibilities . . . 4.604
. . scope . . . 4.600
. . solicitation provisions . . . 4.607
. scope . . . 4.000; 42.000
. Section 8(a) program . . . 19.812
. selection of contract type
. . factors in selecting type of contract . . . 16.104
. . general considerations . . . 16.101
. . negotiating contract type . . . 16.103
. . policies . . . 16.102
. . solicitation provision . . . 16.105; 52.216-1
. small business . . . 42.1601
. suspension of work, stop-work orders, and government delay of work
. . contract clause prescriptions . . . 42.1305
. . general . . . 42.1301
. . government delay of work . . . 42.1304
. . stop-work orders . . . 42.1303
. . suspension of work . . . 42.1302
. under service contract labor standards . . . 22.1003-4
. uniform contract format . . . 14.201-1; 15.204-1
. . contract clause prescriptions . . . 14.201-7
. . part I—the schedule . . . 14.201-2; 15.204-2
. . part II—contract clauses . . . 14.201-3; 15.204-3

Contract administration—see also Cost accounting standards; Cost principles—continued
. uniform contract format—continued
. . part III—documents, exhibits, and other attachments . . . 14.201-4; 15.204-4
. . part IV—representations and instructions . . . 14.201-5; 15.204-5
. . price-related factors . . . 14.201-8
. . simplified format . . . 14.201-9
. . solicitation provision prescriptions . . . 14.201-6
. utilities service contracts
. . monthly and annual review . . . 41.401
. . rate changes and regulatory intervention . . . 41.402
. visits to contractors' facilities . . . 42.402

Contract clauses and solicitation provisions
. accessorial services—moving contracts . . . 52.247-13
. . prescription . . . 47.207-5
. accident prevention . . . 52.236-13
. . prescription . . . 36.513
. acquisition of EPEAT-registered personal computer products . . . 52.223-16
. . prescription . . . 23.705
. acquisition of EPEAT®-registered imaging equipment . . . 52.223-13
. . prescription . . . 23.705
. acquisition of EPEAT®-registered televisions . . . 52.223-14
. . prescription . . . 23.705
. additional bond security . . . 52.228-2
. . prescription . . . 28.106-4
. administration of cost accounting standards . . . 52.230-6
. . prescription . . . 30.201-4
. advance notification by the government . . . 52.247-24
. . prescription . . . 47.207-8
. advance payments . . . 52.232-12
. . prescription . . . 32.412
. affirmative action compliance . . . 52.222-25
. . prescription . . . 22.810
. affirmative action compliance requirements for construction . . . 52.222-27
. . prescription . . . 22.810
. affirmative action for workers with disabilities . . . 52.222-36
. . prescription . . . 22.1408
. affirmative procurement of EPA-designated items in service and construction contracts . . . 52.223-17
. . prescription . . . 23.406
. agreed weight—general freight . . . 52.247-9
. . prescription . . . 47.207-4
. allowable cost and payment . . . 52.216-7
. . prescription . . . 16.307; 16.406
. allowable cost and payment—facilities . . . 52.216-13
. . prescription . . . 16.307
. allowable cost and payment—facilities use . . . 52.216-14
. . prescription . . . 16.307

Contract clauses and solicitation provisions—continued
. alterations in contract . . . 52.252-4
. . prescription . . . 52.107
. alterations in solicitation . . . 52.252-3
. . prescription . . . 52.107
. alternative payment protections . . . 52.228-13
. . prescription . . . 28.102-3
. alternatives to government-unique standards . . . 52.211-7
. . prescription . . . 11.107
. alternatives to government unique standards
. . prescription . . . 11.107
. amendments to invitations for bids . . . 52.214-3
. . prescription . . . 14.201-6
. American Recovery and Reinvestment Act reporting requirements . . . 52.204-11
. . prescription . . . 4.1502
. annual representations and certifications . . . 52.204-8
. . prescription . . . 4.1202
. anti-kickback procedures . . . 52.203-7
. . prescription . . . 3.502-3
. applicable law for breach of contract claim . . . 52.233-4
. . prescription . . . 33.215
. apprentices and trainees . . . 52.222-9
. . prescription . . . 22.407
. approval of contract . . . 52.204-1
. . prescription . . . 4.103
. approval of wage rates . . . 52.222-16
. . prescription . . . 22.407
. assignment of claims . . . 52.232-23
. . prescription . . . 32.806
. audit and records—sealed bidding . . . 52.214-26
. . prescription . . . 14.201-7
. audits and records—negotiation . . . 52.215-2
. . prescription . . . 15.209
. authorized deviations in clauses . . . 52.252-6
. . prescription . . . 52.107
. authorized deviations in provisions . . . 52.252-5
. . prescription . . . 52.107
. availability and use of utility services . . . 52.236-14
. . prescription . . . 36.514
. availability for examination of specifications not listed in the GSA Index of Federal Specifications, Standards and Commercial Item Descriptions . . . 52.211-4
. . prescription . . . 11.204
. availability of funds . . . 52.232-18
. . prescription . . . 32.706-1
. availability of funds for the next fiscal year . . . 52.232-19
. . prescription . . . 32.706-1
. availability of specifications listed in the GSA Index of Federal Specifications, Standards and Commercial Item Descriptions, FPMR Part 101-29 . . . 52.211-1
. . prescription . . . 11.204

Contract clauses and solicitation provisions—
continued
. availability of specifications not listed in the GSA Index of Federal Specifications, Standards and Commercial Item Descriptions . . . 52.211-3
. . prescription . . . 11.204
. availability of specifications, standards, and data item descriptions listed in the Acquisition Streamlining and Standardization Information System (ASSIST) . . . 52.211-2
. . prescription . . . 11.204
. bankruptcy . . . 52.242-13
. . prescription . . . 42.903
. bid guarantee . . . 52.228-1
. . prescription . . . 28.101-2
. bid samples . . . 52.214-20
. . prescription . . . 14.201-6
. brand name or equal . . . 52.211-6
. . prescription . . . 11.107
. Buy American—construction materials . . . 52.225-9
. . prescription . . . 25.1102
. Buy American—construction materials under trade agreements . . . 52.225-11
. . prescription . . . 25.1102
. Buy American—Free Trade Agreements—Israeli Trade Act . . . 52.225-3
. Buy American—Free Trade Agreements—Israeli Trade Act certificate . . . 52.225-4
. . prescription . . . 25.1101
. Buy American—Free Trade Agreements—Israeli Trade Act
. . prescription . . . 25.1101
. Buy American—supplies . . . 52.225-1
. . prescription . . . 25.1101; 13.302-5
. Buy American certificate . . . 52.225-2
. . prescription . . . 25.1101
. c. & f. destination . . . 52.247-41
. . prescription . . . 47.303-13
. cancellation, rescission, and recovery of funds for illegal or improper activity . . . 52.203-8
. . prescription . . . 3.104-9
. cancellation under multi-year contracts . . . 52.217-2
. . prescription . . . 17.109
. capability to perform contract for relocation of a federal office . . . 52.247-3
. . prescription . . . 47.207-1
. capital credits . . . 52.241-13
. . prescription . . . 41.501
. cargo insurance . . . 52.228-9
. . prescription . . . 28.313
. system for award management (SAM) database . . . 52.204-7
. System for Award Management (SAM) database
. . prescription . . . 4.1105
. system for award management (SAM) database, maintenance . . . 52.204-13
. certificate of conformance . . . 52.246-15
. . prescription . . . 46.315

Contract clauses and solicitation provisions—
continued
. certificate of independent price determination . . . 52.203-2
. . prescription . . . 3.103-1
. certification and disclosure regarding payments to influence certain federal transactions . . . 52.203-11
. certification of eligibility . . . 52.222-15
. . prescription . . . 22.407
. certification of final indirect costs . . . 52.242-4
. . prescription . . . 42.703-2
. certification regarding debarment, suspension, proposed debarment, and other responsibility matters . . . 52.209-5
. . prescription . . . 9.409
. certification regarding knowledge of child labor for listed end products . . . 52.222-18
. . prescription . . . 22.1505
. certification regarding tax matter . . . 52.209-12
. . prescription . . . 9.104-7
. certification regarding trafficking in persons compliance plan . . . 52.222-50
. . prescription . . . 22.1705
. change in class of service . . . 52.241-4
. . prescription . . . 41.501
. change in rates or terms and conditions of service for regulated services . . . 52.241-7
. change in rates or terms and conditions of service for unregulated services . . . 52.241-8
. . prescription . . . 41.501
. change in rates or terms and conditions of service for regulated services
. . prescription . . . 41.501
. change order accounting . . . 52.243-6
. . prescription . . . 43.205
. changes . . . 52.243-4
. . prescription . . . 43.205
. changes—cost-reimbursement . . . 52.243-2
. . prescription . . . 43.205
. changes—fixed-price . . . 52.243-1
. . prescription . . . 43.205
. changes—time-and-materials or labor-hours . . . 52.243-3
. . prescription . . . 43.205
. changes and changed conditions . . . 52.243-5
. . prescription . . . 43.205
. changes or additions to make-or-buy program . . . 52.215-9
. . prescription . . . 15.408
. charges . . . 52.247-17
. . prescription . . . 47.207-6
. child labor—cooperation with authorities and remedies . . . 52.222-19
. . prescription . . . 22.1505
. c.i.f. destination . . . 52.247-42
. . prescription . . . 47.303-14
. clauses incorporated by reference . . . 52.252-2
. . prescription . . . 52.107

Contract clauses and solicitation provisions— continued
. cleaning up . . . 52.236-12
. . prescription . . . 36.512
. clearance and documentation requirements—shipments to DoD air or water terminal transshipment points . . . 52.247-52
. . prescription . . . 47.305-6
. combating trafficking in persons . . . 52.222-50
. . prescription . . . 22.1705
. commencement, prosecution, and completion of work . . . 52.211-10
. . prescription . . . 11.404
. commercial bill of lading notations . . . 52.247-1
. . prescription . . . 47.104-4
. competition in subcontracting . . . 52.244-5
. . prescription . . . 44.204
. compliance with Copeland Act requirements . . . 52.222-10
. . prescription . . . 22.407
. compliance with construction wage rate requirements and related regulations . . . 52.222-13
. . prescription . . . 22.407
. compliance with environmental management systems . . . 52.223-19
. . prescription . . . 23.903
. compliance with veterans' employment reporting requirements . . . 52.222-38
. . prescription . . . 22.1310
. computer generated forms . . . 52.253-1
. . prescription . . . 53.111
. condition of leased vehicles . . . 52.208-5
. . prescription . . . 8.1104
. connection charge . . . 52.241-9
. construction wage rate requirements—secondary site of the work . . . 52.222-5
. continuity of services . . . 52.237-3
. . prescription . . . 37.110
. contract award—sealed bidding . . . 52.214-10
. . prescription . . . 14.201-6
. contract award—sealed bidding—construction . . . 52.214-19
. . prescription . . . 14.201-6
. contract clauses . . . 32.908
. contract definitization . . . 52.216-25
. . prescription . . . 16.603-4
. contract not affected by oral agreement . . . 52.247-27
. . prescription . . . 47.207-8
. contract termination—debarment . . . 52.222-12
. . prescription . . . 22.407
. contract terms and conditions—commercial items . . . 52.212-4
. . prescription . . . 32.206; 12.301
. contract terms and conditions required to implement statutes or executive orders—commercial items . . . 52.212-5
. . prescription . . . 12.301

Contract clauses and solicitation provisions— continued
. contract work hours and safety standards—overtime compensation . . . 52.222-4
. . prescription . . . 22.305
. contractor employee whistleblower rights and requirement to inform employees of rights . . . 52.203-17
. . prescription . . . 3.908-9
. contractor inspection requirements . . . 52.246-1
. . prescription . . . 46.301
. contractor liability for loss and/or damage to freight other than household goods . . . 52.247-22
. . prescription . . . 47.207-7
. contractor liability for loss and/or damage to household goods
. . prescription . . . 47.207-7
. contractor liability for loss of and/or damage to household goods . . . 52.247-23
. contractor liability for personal injury and/or property damage . . . 52.247-21
. . prescription . . . 47.207-7
. contractor personnel in designated operational area or supporting diplomatic or consular mission outside the United States . . . 52.225-19
. . prescription . . . 25.301-4
. contractor policy to ban text messaging while driving . . . 52.223-18
. . prescription . . . 23.1105
. contractor responsibility for loading and unloading . . . 52.247-15
. . prescription . . . 47.207-5
. contractor responsibility for receipt of shipment . . . 52.247-14
. . prescription . . . 47.207-5
. contractor responsibility for returning undelivered freight . . . 52.247-16
. . prescription . . . 47.207-5
. contractor use of mandatory sources of supply
. . prescription . . . 8.005
. contractor use of mandatory sources of supply or services . . . 52.208-9
. contractor's facilities . . . 52.241-5
. . prescription . . . 41.501
. contractor's invoices . . . 52.247-28
. . prescription . . . 47.207-9
. contractors performing private security functions outside the United States . . . 52.225-26
. . prescription . . . 25.302-6
. convict labor . . . 52.222-3
. . prescription . . . 22.202
. cost accounting standards . . . 52.230-2
. . prescription . . . 30.201-4
. cost accounting standards—educational institution . . . 52.230-5
. . prescription . . . 30.201-4
. cost accounting standards notices and certification . . . 52.230-1
. . prescription . . . 30.201-3

Contract clauses and solicitation provisions— continued
. cost contract—no fee . . . 52.216-11
. . prescription . . . 16.307
. cost-sharing contract—no fee . . . 52.216-12
. . prescription . . . 16.307
. covenant against contingent fees . . . 52.203-5
. . prescription . . . 3.404
. data universal numbering system number . . . 52.204-6
. data universal numbering system number maintenance . . . 52.204-12
. construction wage rate requirements . . . 52.222-6
. . prescription . . . 22.407
. construction wage rate requirements—price adjustment (actual method) . . . 52.222-32
. . prescription . . . 22.407
. construction wage rate requirements—price adjustment (none or separately specified method) . . . 52.222-30
. . prescription . . . 22.407
. construction wage rate requirements—price adjustment (percentage method) . . . 52.222-31
. . prescription . . . 22.407
. construction wage rate requirements—secondary site of the work . . . 52.222-5
. . prescription . . . 22.407
. default (fixed-price construction) . . . 52.249-10
. . prescription . . . 49.504
. default (fixed-price research and development) . . . 52.249-9
. . prescription . . . 49.504
. default (fixed-price supply and service) . . . 52.249-8
. . prescription . . . 49.504
. defense priority and allocation requirements . . . 52.211-15
. . prescription . . . 11.604
. definite quantity . . . 52.216-20
. . prescription . . . 16.506
. definitions
. . prescription . . . 2.201
. delivery of excess quantities . . . 52.211-17
. . prescription . . . 11.703
. descriptive literature . . . 52.214-21
. . prescription . . . 14.201-6
. design within funding limitations . . . 52.236-22
. . prescription . . . 36.609-1
. designation of office for government receipt of electronic funds transfer information . . . 52.232-35
. . prescription . . . 32.1110
. desired and required time of delivery . . . 52.211-9
. . prescription . . . 11.404
. destination unknown . . . 52.247-49
. . prescription . . . 47.305-5
. differing site conditions . . . 52.236-2
. . prescription . . . 36.502
. disaster or emergency area representation . . . 52.226-3
. . prescription . . . 26.206

Contract clauses and solicitation provisions— continued
. disclosure and consistency of cost accounting practices . . . 52.230-3
. disclosure and consistency of cost accounting practices; foreign concerns . . . 52.230-4
. disclosure and consistency of cost accounting practices
. . prescription . . . 30.201-4
. discounts for prompt payment . . . 52.232-8
. . prescription . . . 32.111
. disputes . . . 52.233-1
. . prescription . . . 33.215
. disputes concerning labor standards . . . 52.222-14
. . prescription . . . 22.407
. drug-free workplace . . . 52.223-6
. . prescription . . . 23.505
. duty-free entry . . . 52.225-8
. . prescription . . . 25.1101; 25.1103
. earned value management system . . . 52.234-4
. . prescription . . . 34.203
. economic price adjustment—labor and material . . . 52.216-4
. . prescription . . . 16.203-4
. economic price adjustment—semistandard supplies . . . 52.216-3
. . prescription . . . 16.203-4
. economic price adjustment—standard supplies . . . 52.216-2
. . prescription . . . 16.203-4
. economic purchase quantity—supplies . . . 52.207-4
. . prescription . . . 7.203
. electric service territory compliance representation . . . 52.241-1
. . prescription . . . 41.501
. employment eligibility verification . . . 52.222-54
. . prescription . . . 22.1803
. employment reports on veterans . . . 52.222-37
. . prescription . . . 22.1310
. equal low bids . . . 52.219-2
. . prescription . . . 19.307
. equal opportunity . . . 52.222-26
. . prescription . . . 22.810
. equal opportunity for veterans . . . 52.222-35
. . prescription . . . 22.1310; 22.1310
. establishing a minimum wage for contractors . . . 52.222-55
. . prescription . . . 22.1906
. estimated quantities or weights for evaluation of offers . . . 52.247-20
. . prescription . . . 47.207-6
. estimated weights or quantities not guaranteed . . . 52.247-8
. . prescription . . . 47.207-3
. evaluation—commercial items . . . 52.212-2
. . prescription . . . 12.301
. evaluation—f.o.b. origin . . . 52.247-47
. . prescription . . . 47.305-3
. evaluation exclusive of options . . . 52.217-3
. . prescription . . . 17.208

Contract clauses and solicitation provisions— continued
. evaluation of bids for multiple awards . . . 52.214-22
. . prescription . . . 14.201-6
. evaluation of compensation for professional employees . . . 52.222-46
. . prescription . . . 22.1103
. evaluation of export offers . . . 52.247-51
. evaluation of foreign currency offers . . . 52.225-17
. . prescription . . . 25.1103
. evaluation of options . . . 52.217-5
. . prescription . . . 17.208
. evaluation of options exercised at time of contract award . . . 52.217-4
. . prescription . . . 17.208
. ex dock, pier, or warehouse, port of importation . . . 52.247-40
. . prescription . . . 47.303-12
. excusable delays . . . 52.249-14
. . prescription . . . 49.505
. execution and commencement of work . . . 52.216-23
. . prescription . . . 16.603-4
. exemption from application of service contract labor standards—certification . . . 52.222-48; 52.222-52
. . prescription . . . 22.1006
. exemption from application of service contract labor standards—requirements . . . 52.222-51; 52.222-53
. . prescription . . . 22.1006
. exemption from application of service contract labor standards—certification
. . prescription . . . 22.1006
. explanation to prospective bidders . . . 52.214-6
. . prescription . . . 14.201-6
. extras . . . 52.232-11
. . prescription . . . 32.111
. facilities capital cost of money . . . 52.215-16
. . prescription . . . 15.408
. facsimile bids . . . 52.214-31
. . prescription . . . 14.201-6
. facsimile proposals . . . 52.215-5
. . prescription . . . 15.209
. Fair Labor Standards Act and service contract labor standards—price adjustment (multiple year and option contracts) . . . 52.222-43
. Fair Labor Standards Act and service contract labor standards—price adjustment
. . prescription . . . 22.1006; 52.222-44
. Fair Labor Standards Act and service contract labor standards—price adjustment (multiple year and option contracts)
. . prescription . . . 22.1006
. false statements in bids . . . 52.214-4
. . prescription . . . 14.201-6
. familiarization with conditions . . . 52.247-5
. . prescription . . . 47.207-1
. f.a.s. vessel, port of shipment . . . 52.247-36
. . prescription . . . 47.303-8
. fast payment procedure . . . 52.213-1
. . prescription . . . 13.404

Contract clauses and solicitation provisions— continued
. federal, state, and local taxes . . . 52.229-3
. . prescription . . . 29.401-3
. federal, state, and local taxes (state and local adjustments) . . . 52.229-4
. . prescription . . . 29.401-4
. financial statement . . . 52.247-6
. . prescription . . . 47.207-1
. first article approval—contractor testing . . . 52.209-3
. . prescription . . . 9.308-1
. first article approval—government testing . . . 52.209-4
. . prescription . . . 9.308-2
. fixed-fee . . . 52.216-8
. . prescription . . . 16.307
. fixed-fee—construction . . . 52.216-9
. . prescription . . . 16.307
. f.o.b. designated air carrier's terminal, point of exportation . . . 52.247-43
. . prescription . . . 47.303-15
. f.o.b. designated air carrier's terminal, point of importation . . . 52.247-44
. . prescription . . . 47.303-16
. f.o.b. destination . . . 52.247-34
. . prescription . . . 47.303-6
. f.o.b. destination—evidence of shipment . . . 52.247-48
. . prescription . . . 47.305-4
. f.o.b. destination, within consignee's premises . . . 52.247-35
. . prescription . . . 47.303-7
. f.o.b. inland carrier, point of exportation . . . 52.247-38
. . prescription . . . 47.303-10
. f.o.b. inland point, country of importation . . . 52.247-39
. . prescription . . . 47.303-11
. f.o.b. origin . . . 52.247-29
. . prescription . . . 47.303-1
. f.o.b. origin—carload and truckload shipments . . . 52.247-59
. . prescription . . . 47.305-16
. f.o.b. origin—minimum size of shipments . . . 52.247-61
. . prescription . . . 47.305-16
. f.o.b. origin and/or f.o.b. destination evaluation . . . 52.247-45
. . prescription . . . 47.305-2
. f.o.b. origin, contractor's facility . . . 52.247-30
. . prescription . . . 47.303-2
. f.o.b. origin, freight allowed . . . 52.247-31
. . prescription . . . 47.303-3
. f.o.b. origin, freight prepaid . . . 52.247-32
. . prescription . . . 47.303-4
. f.o.b. origin, prepaid freight—small package shipments . . . 52.247-65
. . prescription . . . 47.303-17
. f.o.b. origin, with differentials . . . 52.247-33
. . prescription . . . 47.303-5

Contract clauses and solicitation provisions— continued
. f.o.b. point for delivery of government-furnished property . . . 52.247-55
. . prescription . . . 47.305-12
. f.o.b. vessel, port of shipment . . . 52.247-37
. . prescription . . . 47.303-9
. freight classification description . . . 52.247-53
. . prescription . . . 47.305-9
. freight excluded . . . 52.247-7
. . prescription . . . 47.207-3
. government delay of work . . . 52.242-17
. . prescription . . . 42.1305
. government direction and marking . . . 52.247-26
. . prescription . . . 47.207-8
. government-furnished equipment
. . prescription . . . 47.207-8
. government-furnished equipment with or without operators . . . 52.247-25
. government property . . . 52.245-1
. . prescription . . . 45.107
. government property installation operation services . . . 52.245-2
. . prescription . . . 45.107
. government supply sources . . . 52.251-1
. . prescription . . . 51.107
. gratuities . . . 52.203-3
. . prescription . . . 3.202
. guaranteed shipping characteristics . . . 52.247-60
. . prescription . . . 47.305-16
. hazardous material identification and material safety data . . . 52.223-3
. . prescription . . . 23.303
. helium requirement forecast and required sources for helium
. . prescription . . . 8.505
. higher-level contract quality requirement . . . 52.246-11
. . prescription . . . 46.311
. historically black college or university and minority institution representation . . . 52.226-2
. . prescription . . . 26.304
. identification of uncompensated overtime . . . 52.237-10
. . prescription . . . 37.115-3
. incentive fee . . . 52.216-10
. . prescription . . . 16.307; 16.406
. incentive price revision—firm target . . . 52.216-16
. . prescription . . . 16.406
. incentive price revision—successive targets . . . 52.216-17
. . prescription . . . 16.406
. incentive subcontracting program . . . 52.219-10
. . prescription . . . 19.708
. inconsistency between English version and translation of contract . . . 52.225-14
. . prescription . . . 25.1103
. incorporation by reference of representations and certifications . . . 52.204-19
. . prescription . . . 4.1202

Contract clauses and solicitation provisions— continued
. incremental payment by contractor to government . . . 52.237-6
. . prescription . . . 37.304
. indefinite quantity . . . 52.216-22
. . prescription . . . 16.506
. indemnification and medical liability insurance . . . 52.237-7
. . prescription . . . 37.403
. industrial resources developed under Defense Production Act, Title III . . . 52.234-1
. . prescription . . . 34.101
. information regarding responsibility matters . . . 52.209-7
. . prescription . . . 9.104-7
. inspection—dismantling, demolition, or removal of improvements . . . 52.246-13
. . prescription . . . 46.313
. inspection—time-and-material and labor-hour . . . 52.246-6
. . prescription . . . 46.306
. inspection of construction . . . 52.246-12
. . prescription . . . 46.312
. inspection of research and development—cost-reimbursement . . . 52.246-8
. . prescription . . . 46.308
. inspection of research and development—fixed-price . . . 52.246-7
. . prescription . . . 46.307
. inspection of research and development (short form) . . . 52.246-9
. . prescription . . . 46.309
. inspection of services—cost-reimbursement . . . 52.246-5
. . prescription . . . 46.305
. inspection of services—fixed-price . . . 52.246-4
. . prescription . . . 46.304
. inspection of shipping and receiving facilities . . . 52.247-4
. . prescription . . . 47.207-1
. inspection of supplies—cost-reimbursement . . . 52.246-3
. . prescription . . . 46.303
. inspection of supplies—fixed-price . . . 52.246-2
. . prescription . . . 46.302
. inspection of transportation . . . 52.246-14
. . prescription . . . 46.314
. installment payments for commercial items . . . 52.232-30
. . prescription . . . 32.206
. instructions to offerors—commercial items . . . 52.212-1
. . prescription . . . 12.301
. instructions to offerors—competitive acquisition . . . 52.215-1
. . prescription . . . 15.209
. insurance—liability to third persons . . . 52.228-7
. . prescription . . . 28.311-1

Contract clauses and solicitation provisions— continued
. insurance—work on a government installation . . . 52.228-5
. . prescription . . . 28.310
. integrity of unit prices . . . 52.215-14
. . prescription . . . 15.408
. interagency fleet management system vehicles and related services . . . 52.251-2
. . prescription . . . 51.205
. interest . . . 52.232-17
. . prescription . . . 32.617
. inverted domestic corporation . . . 9.108-1
. invitation to propose financing terms . . . 52.232-31
. . prescription . . . 32.206
. invitation to propose performance-based payments . . . 52.232-28
. . prescription . . . 32.1005
. invoices . . . 52.213-2
. . prescription . . . 13.302-5
. irrevocable letter of credit . . . 52.228-14
. . prescription . . . 28.204-4
. labor standards for construction work—facilities contracts . . . 52.222-17
. . prescription . . . 22.407
. late submissions, modifications, and withdrawals of technical proposals under two-step sealed bidding . . . 52.214-23
. late submissions, modifications, and withdrawals of bids . . . 52.214-7
. . prescription . . . 14.201-6
. late submissions, modifications, and withdrawals of technical proposals under two-step sealed bidding
. . prescription . . . 14.201-6
. layout of work . . . 52.236-17
. . prescription . . . 36.517
. liability and insurance—leased motor vehicles . . . 52.228-8
. . prescription . . . 28.312
. limitation of cost . . . 52.232-20
. . prescription . . . 32.705-2
. limitation of funds . . . 52.232-22
. . prescription . . . 32.705-2
. limitation of government liability . . . 52.216-24
. . prescription . . . 16.603-4
. limitation of liability . . . 52.246-23
. . prescription . . . 46.805
. limitation of liability—high-value items . . . 52.246-24
. . prescription . . . 46.805
. limitation of liability—services . . . 52.246-25
. . prescription . . . 46.805
. limitation on payments to influence certain federal transactions . . . 52.203-12
. . prescription . . . 3.808
. limitation on withholding of payments . . . 52.232-9
. . prescription . . . 32.111
. limitations on pass-through charges . . . 52.215-23
. . prescription . . . 15.408

Contract clauses and solicitation provisions— continued
. limitations on pass-through charges; identification of subcontract effort . . . 52.215-22
. . prescription . . . 15.408
. limitations on subcontracting . . . 52.219-14
. . prescription . . . 19.508; 19.811-3
. liquidated damages—construction . . . 52.211-12
. . prescription . . . 11.503
. liquidated damages—subcontracting plan . . . 52.219-16
. . prescription . . . 19.708
. liquidated damages—supplies, services, or research and development . . . 52.211-11
. . prescription . . . 11.503
. loading, blocking, and bracing of freight car shipments . . . 52.247-58
. market research . . . 52.210-1
. . prescription . . . 10.003
. marking of leased vehicles . . . 52.208-6
. . prescription . . . 8.1104
. material and workmanship . . . 52.236-5
. . prescription . . . 36.505
. material requirements . . . 52.211-5
. . prescription . . . 11.304
. matrix
. . how to use . . . 52.101
. . scope . . . 52.300
. . solicitation provisions and contract clauses . . . 52.301
. minimum bid acceptance period . . . 52.214-16
. . prescription . . . 14.201-6
. multiple awards for advisory and assistance services . . . 52.216-28
. . prescription . . . 16.506
. multiple payment arrangements . . . 52.232-37
. . prescription . . . 32.1110
. multiple service locations . . . 52.241-11
. . prescription . . . 41.501
. multiple shipments . . . 52.247-18
. . prescription . . . 47.207-6
. multiple technical proposals . . . 52.214-24
. . prescription . . . 14.201-6
. net weight—general freight . . . 52.247-10
. . prescription . . . 47.207-4
. net weight—household goods or office furniture . . . 52.247-11
. . prescription . . . 47.207
. no evaluation of transportation costs . . . 52.247-50
. . prescription . . . 47.305-5
. nonrefundable, nonrecurring service charge . . . 52.241-12
. . prescription . . . 41.501
. North Carolina state and local sales and use tax . . . 52.229-2
. . prescription . . . 29.401-2
. notice of availability of progress payments exclusively for small business concerns . . . 52.232-14
. . prescription . . . 32.502-3

Contract clauses and solicitation provisions—continued
. notice of Buy American requirement—construction materials . . . 52.225-10
. notice of Buy American requirement—construction materials under trade agreements . . . 52.225-12
. . prescription . . . 25.1102
. notice of Buy American requirement—construction materials
. . prescription . . . 25.1102
. notice of cost comparison (negotiated) . . . 52.207-2
. . prescription . . . 7.305
. notice of cost comparison (sealed-bid) . . . 52.207-1
. . prescription . . . 7.305
. notice of disaster or emergency area set-aside . . . 52.226-4
. . prescription . . . 26.206
. notice of earned value management system—postaward IBR . . . 52.234-3
. . prescription . . . 34.203
. notice of earned value management system—preaward IBR . . . 52.234-2
. . prescription . . . 34.203
. notice of HUBZone set-aside or sole source award . . . 52.219-3
. . prescription . . . 19.1309
. notice of intent to disallow costs . . . 52.242-1
. . prescription . . . 42.802
. notice of partial small business set-aside . . . 52.219-7
. . prescription . . . 19.508
. notice of price evaluation preference for HUBZone small business concerns . . . 52.219-4
. notice of priority rating for national defense use . . . 52.211-14
. . prescription . . . 11.604
. notice of progress payments . . . 52.232-13
. . prescription . . . 32.502-3
. notice of radioactive materials . . . 52.223-7
. . prescription . . . 23.602
. notice of required use of American construction materials . . . 52.225-22
. notice of required use of American construction materials under trade agreements
. . prescription . . . 25.1102
. notice of required use of American construction materials
. . prescription . . . 25.1102
. notice of requirement for affirmative action to ensure equal employment opportunity for construction . . . 52.222-23
. . prescription . . . 22.810
. notice of requirement for project labor agreement . . . 52.222-33
. . prescription . . . 22.505
. notice of set-aside of orders . . . 52.219-13
. . prescription . . . 19.508
. notice of set-aside for, or sole source award to, EDWOSB concerns . . . 52.219-29
. . prescription . . . 19.1507

Contract clauses and solicitation provisions—continued
. notice of set-aside for, or sole source award to, WOSB concerns
. . prescription . . . 19.1507
. notice of set-aside for, or sole source award to, WOSB eligible concerns . . . 52.219-30
. notice of set-aside for WOSB eligible concerns
. . prescription . . . 19.1506
. notice of total small business set-aside . . . 52.219-6
. . prescription . . . 19.508
. notice to government of labor disputes . . . 52.222-1
. . prescription . . . 22.103-5
. notice to supplier . . . 52.213-3
. . prescription . . . 13.302-5
. notification of changes . . . 52.243-7
. . prescription . . . 43.107
. notification of competition limited to eligible 8(a) concerns . . . 52.219-18
. . prescription . . . 19.811-3
. notification of employee rights under National Labor Relations Act . . . 52.222-40
. . prescription . . . 22.1605
. notification of ownership changes . . . 52.215-19
. . prescription . . . 15.408
. notification of visa denial . . . 52.222-29
. . prescription . . . 22.810
. offeror representations and certifications—commercial items . . . 52.212-3
. . prescription . . . 12.301
. operations and storage areas . . . 52.236-10
. . prescription . . . 36.510
. option for increased quantity . . . 52.217-6
. . prescription . . . 17.208
. option for increased quantity—separately priced line item . . . 52.217-7
. . prescription . . . 17.208
. option to extend services . . . 52.217-8
. . prescription . . . 17.208
. option to extend term of contract . . . 52.217-9
. . prescription . . . 17.208
. option to purchase equipment . . . 52.207-5
. . prescription . . . 7.404
. order limitations . . . 52.216-19
. . prescription . . . 16.506
. order of precedence—sealed bidding . . . 52.214-29
. . prescription . . . 14.201-7
. order of precedence—uniform contract format . . . 52.215-8
. . prescription . . . 15.209
. order of precedence—utilities . . . 52.241-2
. . prescription . . . 41.501
. ordering . . . 52.216-18
. . prescription . . . 16.506
. organization and direction of work . . . 52.236-19
. . prescription . . . 36.519
. other contracts . . . 52.236-8
. . prescription . . . 36.508
. ozone-depleting substances . . . 52.223-11
. . prescription . . . 23.804

Contract clauses and solicitation provisions— continued
. paid sick leave under Executive Order 13706 . . . 52.222-62
. . prescription . . . 22.2110
. payment by contractor to government . . . 52.237-5
. . prescription . . . 37.304
. payment by electronic funds transfer—system for award management . . . 52.232-33
. . prescription . . . 32.1110
. payment by electronic funds transfer—other than system for award management
. . prescription . . . 32.1110
. payment by government to contractor . . . 52.237-4
. . prescription . . . 37.304
. payment by third party . . . 52.232-36
. . prescription . . . 32.1110
. payment for overtime premiums . . . 52.222-2
. . prescription . . . 22.103-5
. payment under communication service contracts with common carriers . . . 52.232-6
. . prescription . . . 32.111
. payments . . . 52.232-1
. . prescription . . . 8.1104; 32.111
. payments of allowable costs before definitization . . . 52.216-26
. . prescription . . . 16.603-4
. payments to small business subcontractors . . . 52.242-5
. . prescription . . . 52.242-5
. payments under fixed-price architect-engineer contracts . . . 52.232-10
. . prescription . . . 32.111
. payments under fixed-price construction contracts . . . 52.232-5
. . prescription . . . 32.111
. payments under fixed-price research and development contracts . . . 52.232-2
. . prescription . . . 32.111
. payments under personal services contracts . . . 52.232-3
. . prescription . . . 32.111
. payments under time-and-materials and labor-hour contracts . . . 52.232-7
. . prescription . . . 32.111
. payments under transportation contracts and transportation-related services contracts . . . 52.232-4
. . prescription . . . 32.111
. payrolls and basic records . . . 52.222-8
. . prescription . . . 22.407
. penalties for unallowable costs . . . 52.242-3
. . prescription . . . 42.709-6
. pension adjustments and asset reversions . . . 52.215-15
. pension adjustments and asset revisions
. . prescription . . . 15.408
. performance and payment bonds—construction . . . 52.228-15
. . prescription . . . 28.102-3

Contract clauses and solicitation provisions— continued
. performance and payment bonds—other than construction . . . 52.228-16
. performance-based payments . . . 52.232-32
. . prescription . . . 32.1005
. performance of work by contractor . . . 52.236-1
. . prescription . . . 36.501
. period for acceptance of bids . . . 52.214-15
. . prescription . . . 14.201-6
. permits and responsibilities . . . 52.236-7
. . prescription . . . 36.507
. permits, authorities, or franchises . . . 52.247-2
. . prescription . . . 47.207-1
. personal identity verification of contractor personnel . . . 52.204-9
. . prescription . . . 4.1303
. physical data . . . 52.236-4
. . prescription . . . 36.504
. place of manufacture . . . 52.225-18
. . prescription . . . 25.1101
. place of performance . . . 52.215-6
. . prescription . . . 15.209
. place of performance—sealed bidding . . . 52.214-14
. . prescription . . . 14.201-6
. pledges of assets . . . 52.228-11
. . prescription . . . 28.203-6
. pollution prevention and right-to-know information . . . 52.223-5
. . prescription . . . 23.1005
. preaward on-site equal opportunity compliance evaluation . . . 52.222-24
. . prescription . . . 22.810
. preconstruction conference . . . 52.236-26
. . prescription . . . 36.522
. predecessor of offeror . . . 52.204-20
. . prescription . . . 4.1804
. predetermined indirect cost rates . . . 52.216-15
. . prescription . . . 16.307
. preference for privately owned U.S.-flag commercial vessels . . . 52.247-64
. . prescription . . . 47.507
. preference for U.S.-flag air carriers . . . 52.247-63
. . prescription . . . 47.405
. preparation of bids . . . 52.214-12
. . prescription . . . 14.201-6
. preparation of bids—construction . . . 52.214-18
. . prescription . . . 14.201-6
. preparation of proposals—construction . . . 52.236-28
. . prescription . . . 36.520
. preventing personal conflicts of interest . . . 52.203-16
. . prescription . . . 3.1106
. previous contracts and compliance reports . . . 52.222-22
. . prescription . . . 22.810
. price or fee adjustment for illegal or improper activity . . . 52.203-10
. . prescription . . . 3.104-9
. price redetermination—prospective . . . 52.216-5
. . prescription . . . 16.205-4

Contract clauses and solicitation provisions—continued
. price redetermination—retroactive . . . 52.216-6
. . prescription . . . 16.206-4
. price reduction for defective certified cost or pricing data—modifications—sealed bidding . . . 52.214-27
. price reduction for defective certified cost or pricing data . . . 52.215-10
. price reduction for defective certified cost or pricing data—modifications . . . 52.215-11
. price reduction for defective cost or pricing data—modifications
. . prescription . . . 15.408
. price reduction for defective cost or pricing data
. . prescription . . . 15.408
. price reduction for defective cost or pricing data—modifications—sealed bidding
. . prescription . . . 14.201-7
. printed or copied double-sided on recycled paper . . . 52.204-4
. . prescription . . . 4.303
. Privacy Act . . . 52.224-2
. . prescription . . . 24.104
. Privacy Act notification . . . 52.224-1
. . prescription . . . 24.104
. privacy or security safeguards . . . 52.239-1
. . prescription . . . 39.106
. production progress reports . . . 52.242-2
. . prescription . . . 42.1107
. progress payments . . . 52.232-16
. . prescription . . . 32.502-4
. progress payments not included . . . 52.232-15
. . prescription . . . 32.502-3
. prohibition of assignment of claims . . . 52.232-24
. . prescription . . . 32.806
. prohibition of segregated facilities . . . 52.222-21
. . prescription . . . 22.810
. prohibition on conducting restricted business operations in Sudan . . . 52.225-20
. prohibition on conducting restricted business operations in sudan
. . prescription . . . 25.1103
. prohibition on contracting for hardware, software, and services developed or provided by Kaspersky Lab and other covered entities . . . 52.204-23
. . prescription . . . 4.2004
. prohibition on contracting with entities that require certain internal confidentiality agreements or statements-representation . . . 52.203-18
. . prescription . . . 3.909-3
. prohibition on contracting with inverted domestic corporations . . . 52.209-10; 52.209-2
. . prescription . . . 9.108-5; 9.108-5
. prohibition on contracting with entities engaging in certain activities or transactions relating to Iran, representation and certifications . . . 52.225-25
. prohibition on engaging in sanctioned activities relating to Iran, certification
. . prescription . . . 25.1103

Contract clauses and solicitation provisions—continued
. prohibition on requiring certain internal confidentiality agreements or statements . . . 52.203-19
. . prescription . . . 52.203-19
. project labor agreement . . . 52.222-34
. . prescription . . . 22.505
. promoting excess food donation . . . 52.226-6
. . prescription . . . 26.404
. prompt payment . . . 52.232-25
. . prescription . . . 32.908
. prompt payment for construction contracts . . . 52.232-27
. . prescription . . . 32.908
. prompt payment for fixed-price architect-engineer contracts . . . 52.232-26
. proposal disclosure—cost accounting practice changes . . . 52.230-7
. . prescription . . . 30.201-3
. prospective subcontractor requests for bonds . . . 52.228-12
. . prescription . . . 28.106-4
. protecting the government's interest when subcontracting with contractors debarred, suspended, or proposed for debarment . . . 52.209-6
. . prescription . . . 9.409
. protection of existing vegetation, structures, equipment, utilities, and improvements . . . 52.236-9
. . prescription . . . 36.509
. protection of government buildings, equipment, and vegetation . . . 52.237-2
. . prescription . . . 37.110
. protest after award . . . 52.233-3
. . prescription . . . 33.106
. providing accelerated payments to small business contractors . . . 52.232-40
. . prescription . . . 32.009-2
. public disclosure of greenhouse gas emissions and reduction goals-representation . . . 52.223-22
. . prescription . . . 23.804
. qualification requirements . . . 52.209-1
. . prescription . . . 9.206-2
. quantity surveys . . . 52.236-16
. . prescription . . . 36.516
. recovered material certification . . . 52.223-4
. . prescription . . . 23.406
. refrigeration equipment and air conditioners . . . 52.223-12
. . prescription . . . 23.804
. report of shipment (REPSHIP)
. . prescription . . . 47.208-2
. report of shipment (RESHIP) . . . 52.247-68
. . prescription . . . 47.208-2
. reporting executive compensation and first-tier subcontractor awards . . . 52.204-10
. . prescription . . . 4.1403

Contract clauses and solicitation provisions— continued
. representation by corporations regarding delinquent tax liability or a felony conviction under any federal law . . . 52.209-11
. . prescription . . . 9.104-7
. request for information or solicitation for planning purposes . . . 52.215-3
. . prescription . . . 15.209
. required sources for helium and helium usage data . . . 52.208-8
. required use of American iron, steel, and other manufactured goods . . . 52.225-21
. . prescription . . . 25.1102
. required use of American iron, steel, and other manufactured goods under trade agreements
. . prescription . . . 25.1102
. requirements . . . 52.216-21
. . prescription . . . 16.506
. requirements for certified cost or pricing data or information other than certified cost or pricing data . . . 52.215-20
. requirements for certified cost or pricing data or information other than certified cost or pricing data—modifications . . . 52.215-21
. requirements for cost or pricing data or information other than cost or pricing data—modifications
. . prescription . . . 15.408
. requirements for cost or pricing data or information other than cost or pricing data
. . prescription . . . 15.408
. requirements for registration of designers . . . 52.236-25
. . prescription . . . 36.609-4
. responsibility for supplies . . . 52.246-16
. . prescription . . . 8.1104; 46.316
. responsibility of the architect-engineer contractor . . . 52.236-23
. . prescription . . . 36.609-2
. restriction on severance payments to foreign nationals . . . 52.237-8
. . prescription . . . 37.113-2
. restrictions on certain foreign purchases . . . 52.225-13
. . prescription . . . 25.1103
. restrictions on subcontracting outside disaster or emergency area . . . 52.226-5
. . prescription . . . 26.206
. restrictions on subcontractor sales to the government . . . 52.203-6
. . prescription . . . 3.503-2
. returnable cylinders . . . 52.247-66
. . prescription . . . 47.305-17
. reversion or adjustment of plans for postretirement benefits (PRB) other than pensions . . . 52.215-18
. . prescription . . . 15.408
. right of first refusal of employment . . . 52.207-3
. . prescription . . . 7.305
. schedules for construction contracts . . . 52.236-15
. . prescription . . . 36.515

Contract clauses and solicitation provisions— continued
. scope and duration of contract . . . 52.241-3
. . prescription . . . 41.501
. scope of FAR Part 52 . . . 52.000
. section 8(a) award . . . 52.219-17
. . prescription . . . 19.811-3
. security requirements . . . 52.204-2
. . prescription . . . 4.404
. service contract labor standards—place of performance unknown . . . 52.222-49
. . prescription . . . 22.1006
. service contract labor standards . . . 52.222-41
. . prescription . . . 22.1006
. service contract contracts reporting requirements . . . 52.204-14
. service contract contracts reporting requirements, indefinite-delivery contracts . . . 52.204-15
. . prescription . . . 4.1705
. service contract contracts reporting requirements
. . prescription . . . 4.1705
. service of protest . . . 52.233-2
. . prescription . . . 33.106
. service provisions . . . 52.241-6
. . prescription . . . 41.501
. shipping point(s) used in evaluation of f.o.b. origin offers . . . 52.247-46
. . prescription . . . 47.305-3
. single or multiple awards . . . 52.216-27
. . prescription . . . 16.506
. site investigation and conditions affecting work . . . 52.236-3
. . prescription . . . 36.503
. site visit . . . 52.237-1
. . prescription . . . 37.110
. site visit (construction) . . . 52.236-27
. . prescription . . . 36.523
. small business concern representation for the small business competitiveness demonstration program . . . 52.219-28
. small business program representations . . . 52.219-1; 52.219-28
. . prescription . . . 19.307; 19.308
. small business subcontracting plan . . . 52.219-9
. . prescription . . . 19.708
. small disadvantaged business participation program—disadvantaged status and reporting
. . prescription . . . 19.1204
. small disadvantaged business participation program—incentive subcontracting
. . prescription . . . 19.1204
. small disadvantaged business participation program—targets
. . prescription . . . 19.1204
. small disadvantaged business participation program—disadvantaged status and reporting
. . prescription . . . 19.307
. solicitation definitions—sealed bidding
. . prescription . . . 14.201-6

Contract clauses and solicitation provisions— continued
. solicitation of offers from small business concerns and small business teaming arrangements or joint ventures (multiple-award contracts) . . . 52.207-6
. . prescription . . . 7.107-6
. solicitation provisions incorporated by reference . . . 52.252-1
. . prescription . . . 52.107
. special 8(a) contract conditions . . . 52.219-11
. . prescription . . . 19.811-3
. special 8(a) subcontract conditions . . . 52.219-12
. . prescription . . . 19.811-3
. specific quantities unknown . . . 52.247-62
. . prescription . . . 47.305-16
. specifications and drawings for construction . . . 52.236-21
. . prescription . . . 36.521
. state and local taxes . . . 52.229-1
. . prescription . . . 29.401-1
. State of New Mexico Gross Receipts and Compensating Tax . . . 52.229-10
. . prescription . . . 29.404-6
. statement of equivalent rates for federal hires . . . 52.222-42
. . prescription . . . 22.1006
. step two of two-step sealed bidding . . . 52.214-25
. . prescription . . . 14.201-6
. stopping in transit for partial unloading . . . 52.247-19
. . prescription . . . 47.207-6
. subcontractor certified cost or pricing data . . . 52.215-12
. subcontractor cost or pricing data
. . prescription . . . 15.408
. subcontractor certified cost or pricing data—modifications . . . 52.215-13
. subcontractor cost or pricing data—modifications
. . prescription . . . 15.408
. subcontractor certified cost or pricing data—modifications—sealed bidding . . . 52.214-28
. subcontractor cost or pricing data—modifications—sealed bidding
. . prescription . . . 14.201-7
. subcontractors and outside associates and consultants (architect-engineer services) . . . 52.244-4
. . prescription . . . 44.204
. subcontracts . . . 52.244-2
. . prescription . . . 44.204
. subcontracts for commercial items . . . 52.244-6
. . prescription . . . 44.403
. subcontracts (labor standards) . . . 52.222-11
. . prescription . . . 22.407
. submission of bids . . . 52.214-5
. . prescription . . . 14.201-6
. submission of electronic funds transfer information with offer . . . 52.232-38
. . prescription . . . 32.1110

Contract clauses and solicitation provisions— continued
. submission of offers in the English language . . . 52.214-34
. . prescription . . . 14.201-6
. submission of offers in U.S. currency . . . 52.214-35
. . prescription . . . 14.201-6
. submission of transportation documents for audit . . . 52.247-67
. . prescription . . . 47.104-4
. superintendence by the contractor . . . 52.236-6
. . prescription . . . 36.506
. supervision, labor, or materials . . . 52.247-12
. . prescription . . . 47.207-5
. suspension of work . . . 52.242-14
. . prescription . . . 42.1305
. suspension of work, stop-work order, and government delay of work
. . prescription . . . 42.1305
. tagging of leased vehicles . . . 52.208-7
. . prescription . . . 8.1104
. taxes—cost-reimbursement contracts with foreign governments . . . 52.229-9
. . prescription . . . 29.402-2
. taxes—fixed-price contracts with foreign governments . . . 52.229-7
. . prescription . . . 29.402-1
. taxes—foreign cost-reimbursement contracts . . . 52.229-8
. . prescription . . . 29.402-2
. taxes—foreign fixed-price contracts . . . 52.229-6
. . prescription . . . 29.402-1
. taxpayer identification . . . 52.204-3
. . prescription . . . 4.905
. telegraphic bids
. . prescription . . . 14.201-6
. termination (cost-reimbursement) . . . 52.249-6
. . prescription . . . 49.503
. termination (fixed-price architect-engineer) . . . 52.249-7
. . prescription . . . 49.503
. termination for convenience of the government (dismantling, demolition, or removal of improvements) . . . 52.249-3
. . prescription . . . 49.502
. termination for convenience of the government (educational and other nonprofit institutions) . . . 52.249-5
. . prescription . . . 49.502
. termination for convenience of the government (fixed-price) (short form) . . . 52.249-1
. termination for convenience of the government (fixed-price) . . . 52.249-2
. . prescription . . . 49.502
. termination for convenience of the government (fixed-price) (short form)
. . prescription . . . 49.502
. termination for convenience of the government (services) (short form) . . . 52.249-4
. . prescription . . . 49.502

Contract clauses and solicitation provisions—
continued
. termination liability . . . 52.241-10
. . prescription . . . 41.501
. termination (personal services) . . . 52.249-12
. . prescription . . . 49.505
. terms and conditions—simplified acquisitions (other than commercial items) . . . 52.213-4
. . prescription . . . 13.302-5
. terms for financing of purchases of commercial items . . . 52.232-29
. . prescription . . . 32.206
. text of provisions and clauses
. . definitions . . . 52.202-1
. . scope . . . 52.200
. time-and-materials/labor-hour proposal requirements—non-commercial item acquisition with adequate price competition . . . 52.216-29
. time-and-materials/labor-hour proposal requirements—non-commercial item acquisition without adequate price competition . . . 52.216-30
. time-and-materials/labor-hour proposal requirements—commercial item acquisition . . . 52.216-31
. . prescription . . . 16.601
. time-and-materials/labor-hour proposal requirements—non-commercial item acquisition without adequate price competition
. . prescription . . . 16.601
. time-and-materials/labor-hour proposal requirements—non-commercial item acquisition with adequate price competition
. . prescription . . . 16.601
. time extensions . . . 52.211-13
. . prescription . . . 11.503
. time of delivery . . . 52.211-8
. . prescription . . . 11.404
. toxic chemical release reporting
. . prescription . . . 23.302
. trade agreements . . . 52.225-5
. . prescription . . . 25.1101
. trade agreements certificate . . . 52.225-6
. . prescription . . . 25.1101
. transit arrangements . . . 52.247-56
. . prescription . . . 47.305-13
. transportation transit privilege credits . . . 52.247-57
. type of business organization
. . prescription . . . 15.209
. type of contract . . . 52.216-1
. . prescription . . . 16.105
. unenforceability of unauthorized obligations . . . 52.232-39
. . prescription . . . 32.706-3
. updates of publicly available information regarding responsibility matters . . . 52.209-9
. . prescription . . . 9.104-7
. use and possession prior to completion . . . 52.236-11
. . prescription . . . 36.511

Contract clauses and solicitation provisions—
continued
. utilization of Indian organizations and Indian-owned economic enterprises . . . 52.226-1
. . prescription . . . 26.104
. utilization of small business concerns . . . 52.219-8
. . prescription . . . 19.708
. value engineering . . . 52.248-1
. . prescription . . . 48.201
. value engineering—architect-engineer . . . 52.248-2
. . prescription . . . 48.201
. value engineering—construction . . . 52.248-3
. . prescription . . . 48.202
. variation in estimated quantity . . . 52.211-18
. . prescription . . . 11.703
. variation in quantity . . . 52.211-16
. . prescription . . . 8.1104; 11.703
. vehicle lease payments . . . 52.208-4
. . prescription . . . 8.1104
. vehicular and general public liability insurance . . . 52.228-10
. . prescription . . . 28.313
. violation of arms control treaties or agreements-certification . . . 52.209-13
. . prescription . . . 9.109-5
. waiver of Buy American statute for civil aircraft and related articles . . . 52.225-7
. . prescription . . . 25.1101
. waiver of facilities capital cost of money . . . 52.215-17
. . prescription . . . 15.408
. waiver of limitation on severance payments to foreign nationals . . . 52.237-9
. . prescription . . . 37.113-2
. contracts for materials, supplies, articles, and equipment exceeding $15,000 . . . 52.222-20
. . prescription . . . 8.1104; 22.610
. warranty of construction . . . 52.246-21
. . prescription . . . 46.710
. warranty of services . . . 52.246-20
. . prescription . . . 46.710
. warranty of supplies of complex nature . . . 52.246-18
. . prescription . . . 46.710
. warranty of supplies of noncomplex nature . . . 52.246-17
. . prescription . . . 46.710
. warranty of systems and equipment under performance specifications or design criteria . . . 52.246-19
. . prescription . . . 46.710
. waste reduction program . . . 52.223-10
. . prescription . . . 23.705
. whistleblower protections . . . 52.203-15
. . prescription . . . 3.907-7
. withholding of funds . . . 52.222-7
. . prescription . . . 22.407
. women-owned business other than small business . . . 52.204-5
. . prescription . . . 4.607

Contract clauses and solicitation provisions—continued
. work oversight in architect-engineer contracts . . . 52.236-24
. . prescription . . . 36.609-3
. work oversight in cost-reimbursement construction contracts . . . 52.236-18
. . prescription . . . 36.518
. workers' compensation and war-hazard insurance overseas . . . 52.228-4
. . prescription . . . 28.309
. workers' compensation insurance (Defense Base Act) . . . 52.228-3
. . prescription . . . 28.309

Contract clauses and solicitation provisions, instructions for use
. alterations in contract
. . prescription . . . 52.107
. alterations in solicitation
. . prescription . . . 52.107
. authorized deviations in clauses
. . prescription . . . 52.107
. authorized deviations in provisions
. . prescription . . . 52.107
. clauses incorporated by reference
. . prescription . . . 52.107
. completing provisions and clauses . . . 52.104
. dates of clauses . . . 52.101
. definitions . . . 52.101
. identification of provisions and clauses . . . 52.103
. incorporating provisions and clauses . . . 52.102
. matrix
. . how to use . . . 52.101
. . scope . . . 52.300
. . solicitation provisions and contract clauses . . . 52.301
. modification, defined . . . 52.101
. numbering . . . 52.101
. prescriptions . . . 52.101
. procedures for modifying provisions and clauses . . . 52.104
. procedures for using alternates . . . 52.105
. provisions and clauses prescribed in subpart 52.1 . . . 52.107
. scope . . . 52.100
. solicitation provision, defined . . . 52.101
. solicitation provisions incorporated by reference . . . 52.252-1
. . prescription . . . 52.107

Contract debts
. applicability . . . 32.603
. compromise actions . . . 32.616
. contract clause prescription . . . 32.617
. debt determination and collection . . . 32.606
. deferment of collection . . . 32.613
. definition of responsible official . . . 32.601
. delays in receipt of notices or demands . . . 32.615
. demand for payment . . . 32.610
. examples of debts . . . 32.602

Contract debts—continued
. exclusions . . . 32.604
. general . . . 32.602
. interest charges . . . 32.614-1
. interest credits . . . 32.614-2
. memorandum of pricing agreement with refund . . . 32.609
. negotiation of contract debts . . . 32.608
. responsibilities and cooperation among officials . . . 32.605
. routine setoff . . . 32.611
. scope . . . 32.600
. tax credit . . . 32.607
. withholding and setoff . . . 32.612

Contract delivery or performance
. contract clauses and solicitation provisions
. . commencement, prosecution, and completion of work . . . 11.404; 52.211-10
. . defense priority and allocation requirements . . . 11.604; 52.211-15
. . delivery of excess quantities . . . 11.703; 52.211-17
. . desired and required time of delivery . . . 11.404; 52.211-9
. . government delay of work . . . 42.1305; 52.242-17
. . liquidated damages—construction . . . 11.503; 52.211-12
. . liquidated damages—supplies, services, or research and development . . . 11.503; 52.211-11
. . notice of priority rating for national defense use . . . 11.604; 52.211-14
. . stop-work order . . . 42.1305; 52.242-15
. . stop-work order—facilities . . . 42.1305
. . suspension of work . . . 42.1305; 52.242-14
. . time extensions . . . 11.503; 52.211-13
. . time of delivery . . . 11.404; 52.211-8
. . variation in estimated quantity . . . 11.703; 52.211-18
. . variation in quantity . . . 11.703; 52.211-16

Contract disputes
. alternative dispute resolution (ADR) . . . 33.214
. applicability . . . 33.203
. claims
. . certification requirements . . . 33.207
. . fraudulent . . . 33.209
. . initiation . . . 33.206
. . interest . . . 33.208
. . relationship to PL 85-804 . . . 33.205
. contract clauses and solicitation provisions
. . disputes . . . 33.215; 52.233-1
. . disputes concerning labor standards . . . 33.215; 52.222-14
. disputes (formerly Contract Disputes Act of 1978) . . . 33.202
. . relationship to PL 85-804 . . . 33.205
. contracting officers
. . authority . . . 33.210
. . decisions . . . 33.211
. . duties on appeal . . . 33.212

Contract disputes—continued
. definitions . . . 33.201
. obligation to continue performance . . . 33.213
. policy . . . 33.204

Contract financing
. commercial items
. . administration and payment of commercial financing payments . . . 32.207
. . authority . . . 32.201
. . contract clause and solicitation provision prescriptions . . . 32.206
. . determining financing terms . . . 32.203
. . market research about financing terms, conducting . . . 32.202-3
. . policy . . . 12.210; 32.202-1
. . procedures for contracting officer-specified financing . . . 32.204
. . procedures for offeror-proposed financing . . . 32.205
. . scope . . . 32.200
. . security for government financing . . . 32.202-4
. . statutory authority . . . 32.201
. . types of payments for purchases . . . 32.202-2
. forms prescription . . . 53.232
. funding of contracts
. . architect-engineer contracts . . . 36.609-1
. . contract clause prescriptions . . . 32.705-2; 32.706-1
. . contracts conditioned on funds availability . . . 32.703-2
. . contracts crossing fiscal years . . . 32.703-3
. . general . . . 32.703-1
. . limitation of cost or funds . . . 32.704
. . modifications . . . 43.105
. . policy . . . 32.702
. . requirements . . . 32.703-1
. . scope . . . 32.700
. general
. . applicability of subparts . . . 32.002
. . consideration . . . 32.005
. . definitions . . . 32.001; 32.006-2
. . foreign countries, contract performance in . . . 32.004
. . notification of overpayment . . . 32.008
. . payments . . . 32.007
. . scope . . . 32.000
. . simplified acquisition procedures . . . 32.003
. loan guarantees for defense production
. . application for guarantee . . . 32.304-1
. . asset formula . . . 32.304-3
. . assignment of claims . . . 32.304-5
. . authority . . . 32.302
. . certificate of eligibility . . . 32.304-2
. . definitions . . . 32.301
. . general . . . 32.303
. . guarantee amount and maturity . . . 32.304-4
. . other borrowing . . . 32.304-8
. . other collateral security . . . 32.304-6
. . scope . . . 32.300

Contract financing—continued
. loan guarantees for defense production—continued
. . subcontracts . . . 32.306
. . surety bonds and loan guarantees . . . 32.304-7
. . terminated contracts . . . 32.305
. non-commercial items
. . authority . . . 32.200
. . contract clause prescriptions . . . 32.111
. . customary financing . . . 32.113
. . financial consultation . . . 32.108
. . methods . . . 32.102
. . need for, treatment of . . . 32.107
. . order of preference . . . 32.106
. . payment of subcontractors under cost-reimbursement prime contracts . . . 32.110
. . procedures . . . 32.104
. . progress payments under construction contracts . . . 32.103
. . scope . . . 32.100
. . statutory authority . . . 32.101
. . subcontractor assertions of nonpayment . . . 32.112-1
. . subcontractor requests for information . . . 32.112-2
. . termination financing . . . 32.109
. . unusual contract financing . . . 32.114
. . unusual financing . . . 32.114
. . uses . . . 32.105
. performance-based payments
. . administration and payment . . . 32.1007
. . bases for payments . . . 32.1002
. . contract clause and solicitation provision prescriptions . . . 32.1005
. . criteria for use . . . 32.1003
. . policy . . . 32.1001
. . procedures . . . 32.1004
. . risk of loss . . . 32.1010
. . scope . . . 32.1000
. . suspension or reduction of payments . . . 32.1008
. . title . . . 32.1009
. prompt payment
. . applicability . . . 32.901
. . contract clause prescriptions . . . 32.908
. . contractor inquiries . . . 32.909
. . definitions . . . 32.902
. . determining payment due dates . . . 32.904
. . interest penalties . . . 32.907
. . making payments . . . 32.906
. . payment documentation and process . . . 32.905
. . responsibilities . . . 32.903
. . scope . . . 32.900
. reduction or suspension of payment upon finding of fraud
. . definition of remedy coordination official . . . 32.006-2
. . general . . . 32.006-1
. . procedures . . . 32.006-4
. . reporting . . . 32.006-5
. . responsibilities . . . 32.006-3
. service contracts . . . 37.105

Contract financing—continued
. unenforceability of unauthorized obligations . . . 32.705
. . contract clause . . . 52.232-39
Contract types—see also Multi-year contracting
. agreements
. . basic agreements . . . 16.702
. . basic ordering agreements . . . 16.703
. . scope . . . 16.701
. commercial items acquisition . . . 12.207
. cost-reimbursement . . . 16.301-1
. cost-reimbursement contracts
. . application . . . 16.301-2
. . cost contracts . . . 16.302
. . cost-plus-award-fee . . . 16.305
. . cost-plus-fixed-fee . . . 16.306
. . cost-plus-incentive-fee . . . 16.304
. . cost-sharing . . . 16.303
. . description . . . 16.301-1
. . limitations . . . 16.301-3
. definitions . . . 16.001
. energy-savings performance contracts . . . 23.205
. firm-fixed price
. . application . . . 16.202-2
. . description . . . 16.202-1
. firm-fixed-price, level-of-effort term contracts
. . application . . . 16.207-2
. . description . . . 16.207-1
. . limitations . . . 16.207-3
. fixed-ceiling-price with retroactive price redetermination
. . application . . . 16.206-2
. . contract clause . . . 16.206-4
. . description . . . 16.206-1
. . limitations . . . 16.206-3
. fixed-price contracts, generally . . . 16.201
. fixed-price incentive contracts . . . 16.204
. fixed-price with economic price adjustment
. . application . . . 16.203-2
. . contract clauses . . . 16.203-4; 52.216-2; 52.216-3; 52.216-4
. . description . . . 16.203-1
. . limitations . . . 16.203-3
. fixed-price with prospective price redetermination
. . application . . . 16.205-2
. . contract clause . . . 16.205-4; 52.216-5
. . description . . . 16.205-1
. . limitations . . . 16.205-3
. forms prescription . . . 53.216-1
. incentive contracts
. . cost incentives . . . 16.402-1
. . cost-plus-award-fee . . . 16.405-2
. . cost-plus-incentive-fee . . . 16.405-1
. . cost-reimbursement . . . 16.405
. . delivery incentives . . . 16.402-3
. . fixed-price firm target . . . 16.403-1
. . fixed-price incentives, generally . . . 16.204; 16.403
. . fixed-price successive targets . . . 16.403-2
. . fixed-price with award fees . . . 16.404

Contract types—see also Multi-year contracting—continued
. incentive contracts—continued
. . general . . . 16.401
. . multiple incentives . . . 16.402-4
. . performance incentives . . . 16.402-2
. indefinite delivery . . . 16.500
. . general . . . 16.501-2
. indefinite delivery contracts
. . commercial items acquisition . . . 12.207
. . definite-quantity contracts . . . 16.502
. . definitions . . . 16.501-1
. . emergency acquisitions . . . 18.105
. . general . . . 16.501-2
. . indefinite-quantity contracts . . . 16.504
. . ordering . . . 16.505
. . requirements contracts . . . 16.503
. . scope . . . 16.500
. labor-hour contracts . . . 16.602
. letter contracts . . . 16.603-1
. . application . . . 16.603-2
. . contract clause prescriptions . . . 16.603-4
. . description . . . 16.603-1
. . limitations . . . 16.603-3
. management and operating contracts
. . award . . . 17.605
. . definition . . . 17.601
. . extension . . . 17.605
. . identifying . . . 17.604
. . limitations . . . 17.603
. . policy . . . 17.602
. . renewal . . . 17.605
. . scope . . . 17.600
. research and development contracts . . . 35.006
. scope . . . 16.000
. sealed bidding . . . 14.104
. selection of
. . factors in selecting type of contract . . . 16.104
. . general considerations . . . 16.101
. . negotiating contract type . . . 16.103
. . policies . . . 16.102
. . solicitation provision . . . 16.105; 52.216-1
. solicitation provision . . . 16.105; 52.216-1
. time-and-materials contracts . . . 16.601
Contract work hours and safety standards—see also Labor laws
. administration and enforcement . . . 22.303
. construction contracts . . . 22.403-3
. contract clause prescription . . . 22.305
. liquidated damages and overtime pay . . . 22.302
. requirements . . . 22.403-3
. scope . . . 22.300
. statutory requirement . . . 22.301
. variations, tolerances, exemptions . . . 22.304
Contracting officers
. appointment . . . 1.603-3
. authority
. . approval of contracts clause . . . 4.103; 52.204-1
. . dispute resolution . . . 33.210

Contracting officers—continued
. authority, generally . . . 1.601; 1.602-1; 1.603-1
. certificate of appointment, SF 1402 . . . 53.301-1402
. commercial contract financing procedures . . . 32.204
. contract debt determinations . . . 32.605
. contracting officer's representative . . . 1.604
. corporate administrative contracting officer
. . assignment and location . . . 42.602
. . general . . . 42.601
. . responsibilities . . . 42.603
. disputes
. . authority to decide or settle . . . 33.210
. . contents of decision . . . 33.211
. duties on appeal . . . 33.212
. ratification of unauthorized commitments . . . 1.602-3
. responsibilities . . . 1.602-2
. . classified information . . . 4.403
. . contracts with government employees . . . 3.603
. . organizational conflicts of interest . . . 9.504
. . purchase of economic quantities of supplies . . . 7.204
. . small business subcontracting plans . . . 19.705-1
. selection . . . 1.603-2
. service contracts . . . 37.103
. signature . . . 4.101
. small business subcontracting plans
. . awards . . . 19.705-5
. . determining need for plan . . . 19.705-2
. . general support of plan . . . 19.705-1
. . liquidated damages . . . 19.705-7
. . postaward responsibilities . . . 19.705-6
. . preparing solicitation . . . 19.705-3
. . responsibilities . . . 19.705-1
. . review of plan . . . 19.705-4
. termination of appointment . . . 1.603-4

Contracting-out
. contract clauses and solicitation provisions
. . notice of cost comparison (negotiated) . . . 52.207-2
. . notice of cost comparison (sealed bid) . . . 52.207-1
. . prescriptions . . . 7.305
. . right of first refusal of employment . . . 52.207-3
. definitions . . . 7.301
. policy . . . 7.302

Contractor compliance with environmental management systems
. authority . . . 23.901

contractor compliance with environmental management systems
. contract clause prescription . . . 23.903
. policy . . . 23.902
. scope . . . 23.900

Contractor purchasing system review (CPSR)
. disclosure of approval status . . . 44.306
. extent . . . 44.303
. granting, withholding, or withdrawing approval . . . 44.305-1; 44.305-3
. notification of approval . . . 44.305-2
. objective . . . 44.301

Contractor purchasing system review (CPSR)— continued
. reports . . . 44.307
. surveillance . . . 44.304

Contractors
. annual representations and certifications
. . policy . . . 4.1201
. . scope . . . 4.1200
. . solicitation provision and contract clause . . . 4.1202; 52.204-8
. system for award management (sam) database
. . definitions . . . 2.101; 4.1101
. . emergency acquisitions . . . 18.102
. . policy . . . 4.1102
. . procedures . . . 4.1103
. . scope . . . 4.1100
. . solicitation provision and contract clause . . . 4.1104; 52.204-7
. . solicitation provision and contract clause, maintenance
. certification and disclosure . . . 3.803; 3.103-2; 3.103-3
. conflicts of interest
. . applicability . . . 9.502
. . contract clause prescription . . . 9.507-2
. . contracting officer responsibilities . . . 9.504
. . definition of marketing consultant . . . 9.501
. . evaluation services . . . 9.505-3
. . examples . . . 9.508
. . preparation of specifications or work statements . . . 9.505-2
. . procedures . . . 9.506
. . proprietary information, obtaining access to . . . 9.505-4
. . scope . . . 9.500
. . solicitation provisions . . . 9.507-1
. . systems engineering and technical direction . . . 9.505-1
. . waiver . . . 9.503
. contract clauses and solicitation provisions
. . system for award management (sam) database . . . 4.1104; 52.204-7
. . system for award management database, maintenance . . . 52.204-13
. . certification regarding debarment, suspension, proposed debarment, and other responsibility matters . . . 9.409; 52.209-5
. . protecting the government's interest when subcontracting with contractors debarred, suspended, or proposed for debarment . . . 9.409; 52.209-6
. debarment
. . applicability . . . 9.401
. . causes for . . . 9.406-2
. . continuation of current contracts . . . 9.405-1
. . contract clause prescriptions . . . 9.409
. . debarment scope . . . 9.406-5
. . definitions . . . 9.403
. . effect of listing . . . 9.405

Contractors—continued
. debarment—continued
. . System for Award Management (SAM) . . . 9.404
. . general . . . 9.406-1
. . period of . . . 9.406-4
. . policy . . . 9.402
. . procedures . . . 9.406-3
. . restrictions on subcontracting . . . 9.405-2
. . scope of . . . 9.406-5
. defense production pools
. . contracting with . . . 9.702
. . definition of pool . . . 9.701
. . individual pool members, contracting with . . . 9.703
. documents
. . contract clause prescription . . . 4.303
. . definition . . . 4.301
. . policy . . . 4.302
. . scope . . . 4.300
. evaluation of performance . . . 36.201; 36.604
. first article testing and approval
. . definition of approval . . . 9.301
. . exceptions . . . 9.304
. . general . . . 9.302
. . government administration procedures . . . 9.307
. . risk . . . 9.305
. . solicitation requirements . . . 9.306
. . testing performed by contractor, contract clauses . . . 52.209-3; 9.308-1
. . testing performed by government, contract clauses . . . 52.209-4; 9.308-2
. . use of . . . 9.303
. forms
. . preaward survey of prospective contractor—accounting system, SF 1408 . . . 53.301-1408
. . preaward survey of prospective contractor—financial capability, SF 1407 . . . 53.301-1407
. . preaward survey of prospective contractor—production, SF 1405 . . . 53.301-1405
. . preaward survey of prospective contractor—quality assurance, SF 1406 . . . 53.301-1406
. . preaward survey of prospective contractor—technical, SF 1404 . . . 53.301-1404
. . preaward surveys of prospective contractors (general), SF 1403 . . . 53.301-1403
. . prescription . . . 53.209-1
. incorporation by reference of representations and certifications . . . 52.204-19
. organizational conflicts of interest
. . scope . . . 9.500
. performance evaluation . . . 8.406-7
. performance information
. . general . . . 42.1501
. . policy . . . 42.1502
. . procedures . . . 42.1503
. . scope . . . 42.1500
. personal identity verification of contractor personnel
. . contract clause prescription . . . 4.1303
. . obligation to verify . . . 4.1302
. . policy . . . 4.1301

Contractors—continued
. preference for local area contractor
. . set-asides for local firms during disasters or emergencies . . . 6.207
. qualifications requirements
. . acquisitions subject to . . . 9.206-1
. . changes in status . . . 9.207
. . competition and . . . 9.206-3
. . contract clause . . . 9.206-2; 52.209-1
. . definitions . . . 9.201
. . establishment of qualification requirement . . . 9.204
. . Federal Awardee Performance and Integrity Information System . . . 9.104-6
. . inverted domestic corporation, prohibition . . . 9.108-2
. . inverted domestic corporation, representation by offeror . . . 9.108-3
. . inverted domestic corporation, solicitation provision and contract clause . . . 9.108-5
. . omission from list . . . 9.207
. . performance evaluation . . . 8.406-7
. . policy . . . 9.202
. . prohibition on contracting with inverted domestic corporations . . . 9.108
. . qualification before award . . . 9.205
. . qualified bidders list . . . 9.201; 9.203
. . qualified manufacturers list . . . 9.201; 9.203
. . qualified products list (QPL) . . . 2.101; 9.203
. . removal from list . . . 9.207
. . scope . . . 9.200
. quality assurance responsibilities . . . 46.105
. records retention
. . acquisition and supply records . . . 4.705-3
. . applicability . . . 4.702
. . calculation of retention periods . . . 4.704
. . construction contracts pay administration records . . . 4.705-2
. . financial and cost accounting records . . . 4.705-1
. . policy . . . 4.703
. . purpose . . . 4.701
. . scope . . . 4.700
. . specific retention periods . . . 4.705
. research and development pools
. . contracting with . . . 9.702
. . definition of pool . . . 9.701
. . individual pool members, contracting with . . . 9.703
. responsible prospective contractors, identifying
. . applicability . . . 9.102
. . application of standards . . . 9.104-3
. . certification regarding responsibility matters . . . 9.104-5
. . certification responsibility, solicitation provision . . . 9.104-7
. . definition of surveying activity . . . 9.101
. . determinations and documentation . . . 9.105-2
. . disclosure of preaward information . . . 9.105-3
. . Federal Awardee Performance and Integrity Information System . . . 9.104-6
. . general responsibility standards . . . 9.104-1
. . general standards . . . 9.104

Contractors—continued
. responsible prospective contractors, identifying—continued
. . information regarding responsibility matters . . . 52.209-7
. . obtaining information . . . 9.105-1
. . policy . . . 9.103
. . preaward survey reports . . . 9.106-4
. . preaward surveys, conditions for . . . 9.106-1
. . preaward surveys, interagency . . . 9.106-3
. . preaward surveys, requests for . . . 9.106-2
. . scope . . . 9.100
. . special standards . . . 9.104-2
. . subcontractor responsibility . . . 9.104-4
. . surveys of nonprofit agencies participating in the AbilityOne Program . . . 9.107
. . updates of publicly available information regarding responsibility matters . . . 52.209-9
. suspension
. . applicability . . . 9.401
. . causes for . . . 9.407-2
. . continuation of current contracts . . . 9.405-1
. . contract clause prescriptions . . . 9.409
. . definitions . . . 9.403
. . effect of listing . . . 9.405
. . System for Award Management (SAM) database . . . 9.404
. . general . . . 9.407-1
. . period of . . . 9.407-4
. . policy . . . 9.402
. . procedures . . . 9.407-3
. . restrictions on subcontracting . . . 9.405-2
. . scope of . . . 9.407-5
. team arrangements
. . definition . . . 9.601
. . general . . . 9.602
. . limitations . . . 9.604
. . policy . . . 9.603

Contractor's change of name . . . 42.1205

Contractors performing private security functions outside the United States
. applicability . . . 25.302-3
. contract clause . . . 52.225-26
. contract clause prescription . . . 25.302-6
. definitions . . . 25.302-2
. policy . . . 25.302-4
. remedies . . . 25.302-5
. scope . . . 25.302-1

Contracts for materials, supplies, articles, and equipment exceeding $15,000 (formerly Walsh-Healey Public Contracts Act)
. applicability . . . 22.603
. contract clause . . . 22.610; 52.222-20
. Department of Labor regional jurisdictions, wage and hour division . . . 22.609
. procedures . . . 22.608
. regulatory exemptions . . . 22.604-2
. rulings and interpretations . . . 22.605
. statutory exemptions . . . 22.604-1

Contracts for materials, supplies, articles, and equipment exceeding $15,000 (formerly Walsh-Healey Public Contracts Act)—continued
. statutory requirements . . . 22.602

Contracts performed outside the United States
. contractor personnel in designated operational area or supporting diplomatic or consular mission outside the United States
. . contract clause . . . 52.225-19
. . contract clause prescription . . . 25.301-4
. . government logistical and security support . . . 25.301-2
. . scope of subpart . . . 25.301-1
. . weapons policy . . . 25.301-3

Contributions or donations . . . 31.205-8

Control and compliance procedures
. agency acquisition regulations . . . 1.304

Convict labor
. contract clause . . . 22.202; 52.222-3
. Executive Order 11755 . . . 22.201

Copeland Act
. contract clauses and solicitation provisions . . . 22.407; 52.222-10
. requirements . . . 22.403-2

Copying or printing documents
. contract clause . . . 4.303; 52.204-4
. definition . . . 4.301
. policy . . . 4.302

Copyright—see Patents and copyrights; Right in data and copyrights

Corporations, contract signatures . . . 4.102

Correspondence . . . 42.401

Cost accounting standards
. administration of
. . detailed cost-impact proposal . . . 30.604; 230.605
. . general dollar magnitude proposal . . . 30.604
. . materiality . . . 30.602
. . noncompliances . . . 30.605
. . processing changes . . . 30.604
. . remedies . . . 30.604; 30.605
. . required changes . . . 30.603-1
. . resolving cost-impacts . . . 30.606
. . responsibility . . . 30.601
. . subcontracts . . . 30.607
. . unilateral and desirable changes . . . 30.603-2
. commercial items acquisition . . . 12.214
. contract clauses and solicitation provisions
. . administration of cost accounting standards . . . 30.201-4; 52.230-6
. . cost accounting standards . . . 30.201-4; 52.230-2
. . cost accounting standards—educational institution . . . 30.201-4; 52.230-5
. . cost accounting standards notices and certification . . . 30.201-3; 52.230-1
. . disclosure and consistency of cost accounting practices . . . 30.201-4; 52.230-3

Cost accounting standards—continued
. contract clauses and solicitation provisions—continued
. . disclosure and consistency of cost accounting practices; foreign concerns . . . 52.230-4
. . prescription . . . 30.201-3; 30.201-4
. . proposal disclosure . . . 30.201-3; 52.230-7
. contract requirements . . . 30.201
. . CAS applicability . . . 30.201-1
. . cognizant federal agency responsibilities . . . 30.201-7
. . contract clause prescriptions . . . 30.201-4
. . findings . . . 30.201-6
. . solicitation provisions . . . 30.201-3
. . types of coverage . . . 30.201-2
. . waiver . . . 30.201-5
. disclosure requirements
. . adequacy determination . . . 30.202-7
. . amendments and revisions . . . 30.202-3
. . compliance determination . . . 30.202-7
. . filing . . . 30.202-5
. . general . . . 30.202-1
. . impracticality of submission . . . 30.202-2
. . privileged and confidential information . . . 30.202-4
. . responsibilities . . . 30.202-6
. . subcontractors . . . 30.202-8
. general . . . 30.101
. publication of . . . 30.102
. scope . . . 30.000

Cost contracts . . . 16.302

Cost incentives contracts . . . 16.402-1

Cost of money
. capital assets under construction
. . allowability . . . 31.205-10
. . cost accounting standards . . . 31.205-10
. facilities capital cost
. . allowability . . . 31.205-10

Cost-plus-a-percentage-of-cost system . . . 16.102

Cost-plus-award-fee contracts . . . 16.305; 16.405-2

Cost-plus-fixed-fee contracts . . . 16.306

Cost-plus-incentive-fee contracts . . . 16.304; 16.405-1

Cost principles
. accounting guide, availability of . . . 31.002
. advertising costs . . . 31.205-1
. alcoholic beverages costs . . . 31.205-51
. applicability
. . advance agreements . . . 31.109
. . commercial organizations, contracts with . . . 31.103
. . construction and architect-engineer contracts . . . 31.105
. . educational institutions, contracts with . . . 31.104
. . fixed-price contracts . . . 31.102
. . Indian tribal governments, contracts with . . . 31.107
. . indirect cost rate certification . . . 31.110
. . nonprofit organizations, contracts with . . . 31.108

Cost principles—continued
. applicability—continued
. . objectives . . . 31.101
. . penalties on unallowable costs . . . 31.110
. . scope . . . 31.100
. asset valuations resulting from business combinations . . . 31.205-52
. bad debts . . . 31.205-3
. bonding costs . . . 31.205-4
. commercial organizations, contracts with (see also specific costs, this heading)
. . allocability determination . . . 31.201-4
. . allowability determination . . . 31.201-2
. . applicability . . . 31.103
. . application of principles and procedures . . . 31.204
. . composition of total cost . . . 31.201-1
. . construction and architect-engineer contracts . . . 31.201-7
. . credits . . . 31.201-5
. . direct costs . . . 31.202
. . indirect costs . . . 31.203
. . reasonableness of costs, determining . . . 31.201-3
. . unallowable costs, accounting for . . . 31.201-6
. compensation for personal services . . . 31.205-6
. contingencies . . . 31.205-7
. contributions or donations . . . 31.205-8
. cost of money . . . 31.205-10
. cost of money as an element of cost of capital assets under construction . . . 31.205-10
. definitions . . . 31.001
. depreciation . . . 31.205-11
. economic planning costs . . . 31.205-12
. educational institutions, contracts with
. . applicability . . . 31.104
. . general . . . 31.301; 31.302
. . requirements . . . 31.303
. employee morale, health, and welfare costs . . . 31.205-13
. entertainment costs . . . 31.205-14
. facilities capital cost of money . . . 31.205-10
. fines, penalties, and mischarging costs . . . 31.205-15
. gains and losses on depreciable property . . . 31.205-16
. goodwill . . . 31.205-49
. idle facilities and idle capacity costs . . . 31.205-17
. independent research and development and bid and proposal costs . . . 31.205-18
. Indian tribal governments, contracts with
. . applicability . . . 31.107
. . general . . . 31.601; 31.602
. . requirements . . . 31.603
. insurance and indemnification costs . . . 31.205-19
. interest and other financial costs . . . 31.205-20
. labor relations . . . 31.205-21
. legal and other proceedings costs . . . 31.205-47
. lobbying costs . . . 31.205-22
. losses on other contracts . . . 31.205-23
. manufacturing and production engineering costs . . . 31.205-25
. material costs . . . 31.205-26

Cost principles—continued
. nonprofit organizations, contracts with
. . applicability . . . 31.108
. . general . . . 31.702
. . purpose . . . 31.701
. . requirements . . . 31.703
. notice of intent to disallow costs, contract clause . . . 52.242-1
. organization costs . . . 31.205-27
. other business expenses . . . 31.205-28
. patent costs . . . 31.205-30
. plant protection costs . . . 31.205-29
. plant reconversion costs . . . 31.205-31
. political activity costs . . . 31.205-22
. precontract costs . . . 31.205-32
. professional and consultant service costs . . . 31.205-33
. public relations costs . . . 31.205-1
. recruitment costs . . . 31.205-34
. relocation costs . . . 31.205-35
. rental costs . . . 31.205-36
. research and development costs . . . 31.205-48
. royalties and use of patents costs . . . 31.205-37
. scope . . . 31.000
. selling costs . . . 31.205-38
. service and warranty costs . . . 31.205-39
. special tooling and special test equipment costs . . . 31.205-40
. state and local government contracts . . . 31.601
. taxes . . . 31.205-41
. termination costs . . . 49.113; 31.205-42
. trade, business, technical and professional activity costs . . . 31.205-43
. training and education costs . . . 31.205-44
. travel costs . . . 31.205-46

Cost-reimbursement contracts . . . 16.405
. advance notification requirements . . . 44.201-2
. application . . . 16.301-2
. construction contracts . . . 36.215
. contract clauses and solicitation provisions
. . allowable cost and payment . . . 16.307; 52.216-7
. . allowable cost and payment—facilities . . . 16.307
. . allowable cost and payment—facilities use . . . 16.307
. . cost contract—no fee . . . 16.307; 52.216-11
. . cost-sharing contract—no fee . . . 16.307; 52.216-12
. . fixed fee . . . 16.307; 52.216-8
. . fixed fee—construction . . . 16.307; 52.216-9
. . incentive fee . . . 16.307; 52.216-10
. . predetermined indirect cost rates . . . 16.307; 52.216-15
. . quality assurance, research and development contracts . . . 46.308; 52.246-8
. . quality assurance, service contracts . . . 46.303; 52.246-5
. . quality assurance, supply contracts . . . 46.303; 52.246-3
. cost contracts . . . 16.302

Cost-reimbursement contracts—continued
. cost-plus-award-fee . . . 16.305
. cost-plus-fixed-fee . . . 16.306
. cost-plus-incentive-fee . . . 16.304
. cost-sharing . . . 16.303
. default terminations . . . 49.403
. description . . . 16.301-1
. limitations . . . 16.301-3
. subcontractor payments . . . 32.110
. termination for convenience
. . adjustment of fee . . . 49.305-1
. . adjustment of indirect costs . . . 49.303-4
. . audit of settlement proposal . . . 49.303-3
. . construction contracts, fee adjustment . . . 49.305-2
. . discontinuance of vouchers . . . 49.302
. . final settlement . . . 49.303-5
. . general . . . 49.301
. . partial termination, general . . . 49.304-1
. . submission of inventory disposal schedules . . . 49.303-2
. . submission of settlement proposal . . . 49.303-1
. . submission of settlement proposal (fee only) . . . 49.304-2
. . submission of vouchers . . . 49.304-3
. termination for default
. . completion by another contractor . . . 49.405
. . general . . . 49.403
. . liquidation of liability . . . 49.406
. . surety-takeover agreements . . . 49.404
. transportation . . . 47.104-3

Cost-sharing contracts
. general . . . 16.303
. indirect cost rates . . . 42.707

Covenant against contingent fees . . . 3.405

Criminal penalties, improper business practices . . . 3.104-8

Customs and duties
. exempted supplies . . . 25.903
. policy . . . 25.901
. procedures . . . 25.902
. scope . . . 25.900

D

Damages
. exemplary damages
. . gratuities violations . . . 3.201

Debarment of contractors
. applicability . . . 9.401
. causes for . . . 9.406-2
. continuation of current contracts . . . 9.405-1
. contract clauses and solicitation provisions
. . certification regarding debarment, suspension, proposed debarment, and other responsibility matters . . . 52.209-5
. . contract termination—debarment . . . 52.222-12
. prescriptions . . . 9.409

Debarment of contractors—continued
. contract clauses and solicitation provisions—continued
. . protecting the government's interest when subcontracting with contractors debarred, suspended, or proposed for debarment . . . 52.209-6
. debarment scope . . . 9.406-5
. definitions . . . 9.403
. effect of listing . . . 9.405
. System for Award Management (SAM) database . . . 9.404
. general . . . 9.406-1
. period of . . . 9.406-4
. policy . . . 9.402
. procedures . . . 9.406-3
. restrictions on subcontracting . . . 9.405-2
. scope of . . . 9.406-5
. under Drug-Free Workplace Act . . . 23.506

Debts—see also Contract debts
. bad debts . . . 31.205-3
. taxpayer identification number for debt collection . . . 4.902

Defective certified cost or pricing data
. contract clause
. . price reduction . . . 52.215-10
. . price reduction modification . . . 52.215-11
. contract clause prescriptions . . . 15.408

Defense Acquisition Regulations Council (DAR Council) . . . 1.201-1

Defense of fraud costs . . . 31.205-47

Defense Priorities and Allocations System (DPAS)
. contract clauses and solicitation provisions . . . 11.604; 52.211-14; 52.211-15
. definitions . . . 11.601
. general . . . 11.602
. procedures . . . 11.603
. scope . . . 11.600

Defense production
. loan guarantees
. . application for guarantee . . . 32.304-1
. . asset formula . . . 32.304-3
. . assignment of claims . . . 32.304-5
. . authority . . . 32.302
. . certificate of eligibility . . . 32.304-2
. . collateral security . . . 32.304-6
. . definitions . . . 32.301
. . general . . . 32.303
. . guarantee amount and maturity . . . 32.304-4
. . other borrowing . . . 32.304-8
. . scope . . . 32.300
. . subcontracts . . . 32.306
. . surety bonds and loan guarantees . . . 32.304-7
. . terminated contracts . . . 32.305
. pools
. . contracting with . . . 9.702
. . definition of pool . . . 9.701
. . individual pool members, contracting with . . . 9.703

Defense production—continued
. testing, qualification and use
. . contract clause prescription . . . 34.104
. . definitions . . . 34.101
. . policy . . . 34.102
. . scope . . . 34.100
. . testing and qualification . . . 34.103

Defense Transportation System . . . 47.301-3

Deferred compensation
. fringe benefits . . . 31.205-6

Deferred research and development costs . . . 31.205-48

Definite-quantity contracts . . . 16.502

Definitions
. acceptance . . . 46.101
. accrual of a claim . . . 33.201
. accrued benefit cost method . . . 31.001
. accumulating costs . . . 31.001
. acquisition . . . 2.101
. acquisition planning . . . 2.101
. acquisition savings . . . 48.001
. acquisition streamlining . . . 7.101
. wage and hour division . . . 22.1001
. actual cash value . . . 31.001
. actual costs . . . 31.001
. actuarial accrued liability . . . 31.001
. actuarial assumption . . . 31.001
. actuarial cost method . . . 31.001
. actuarial gain and loss . . . 31.001
. actuarial valuation . . . 31.001
. adequate evidence . . . 2.101
. administrative change . . . 43.101
. administrator . . . 22.001
. administrator, wage and hour division . . . 22.001
. advertisement . . . 5.501
. advertising material . . . 15.601
. advisory and assistance services . . . 2.101
. affected CAS-covered contract or subcontract . . . 30.001
. affiliates . . . 2.101; 19.101; 9.403
. affirmative action programs . . . 22.801
. agency . . . 24.101; 9.403; 3.801
. agency ethics official . . . 3.104-1
. agency head . . . 2.101
. agency head or head of the agency . . . 52.202-1
. agency labor advisor . . . 22.1001
. air freight forwarder . . . 47.401
. allocate . . . 31.001
. allocation . . . 8.701
. allowability . . . 31.205-18
. alternate (clause or provision) . . . 2.101; 52.101
. alternative dispute resolution (ADR) . . . 33.201
. annual receipts . . . 19.101
. applied research . . . 35.001; 31.205-18
. apprentice . . . 22.401
. approval . . . 9.301
. approved purchasing system . . . 44.101
. architect-engineer services . . . 2.101

Definitions—continued
. areawide contract . . . 41.101
. assignment of claims . . . 2.101
. attorney-in-fact . . . 28.001
. authorization . . . 41.101
. authorized individual . . . 13.001
. authorized official of an agency . . . 3.901
. authorized official of the Department of Justice . . . 3.901
. authorized program . . . 11.601
. basic research . . . 2.101; 31.205-18
. best practices . . . 37.501
. best value . . . 2.101
. bid . . . 28.001
. bid and proposal (B&P) costs . . . 31.205-18
. bid guarantee . . . 28.001
. bid sample . . . 2.101
. bidder . . . 28.001
. bill of lading . . . 47.001
. billing rate . . . 42.701
. biobased product . . . 2.101
. bona fide agency . . . 3.401
. bona fide employee . . . 3.401
. bond . . . 28.001
. borrower . . . 32.301
. broad agency announcement . . . 2.101
. building . . . 22.401
. bundled contract . . . 2.101
. bundling . . . 2.101
. Bureau of Land Management (BLM) . . . 8.501
. business partner network (BPN) . . . 2.101
. business unit . . . 2.101
. buying-in . . . 3.501-1
. Canadian end product . . . 25.003
. cancellation . . . 17.103
. cancellation ceiling . . . 17.103
. cancellation charge . . . 17.103
. Caribbean Basin country . . . 25.003
. Caribbean Basin country end product . . . 25.003
. carrier . . . 47.001
. system for award management (sam) database . . . 2.101
. central nonprofit agency . . . 8.701
. certified cost or pricing data . . . 2.101
. change-of-name agreement . . . 2.101
. change order . . . 2.101
. child care services . . . 37.101
. civil aircraft and related articles . . . 25.003
. civil judgment . . . 9.403
. claim . . . 2.101; 33.201
. classified acquisition . . . 2.101
. classified contract . . . 2.101
. classified information . . . 2.101
. clause . . . 2.101
. coercion . . . 22.1702
. cognizant federal agency . . . 2.101
. cognizant federal agency official (CFAO) . . . 30.001
. collateral costs . . . 48.001
. collateral savings . . . 48.001
. commerce business daily (CBD) . . . 2.101

Definitions—continued
. commercial bill of lading . . . 47.001
. commercial carrier . . . 47.001
. commercial component . . . 2.101
. commercial components . . . 52.202-1
. commercial interim payment . . . 32.001
. commercial item . . . 2.101; 29.101; 15.601; 52.202-1
. commercial plan . . . 19.701
. commercial sex act . . . 22.1702
. committee . . . 8.701
. common carrier . . . 47.001
. common item . . . 2.101
. common parent . . . 4.901
. company . . . 31.205-18
. compensated personal absence . . . 31.001
. compensation . . . 3.104-1
. compensation for personal services . . . 31.001
. compliance evaluation . . . 22.801
. component . . . 25.003; 2.101; 52.202-1
. composition and allocation of costs . . . 31.205-18
. computer software . . . 2.101
. concern . . . 19.001
. conditional acceptance . . . 46.101
. connection charge . . . 41.101
. consent of surety . . . 28.001
. consent to subcontract . . . 2.101
. construction . . . 2.101
. construction, alteration, or repair . . . 22.401
. construction material . . . 25.003
. contiguous United States . . . 2.101
. contingency operation . . . 2.101
. contingent fee . . . 3.401
. continued portion of the contract . . . 2.101
. contract . . . 2.101; 3.104-3
. contract action . . . 5.001; 32.001
. contract administration office . . . 2.101
. contract carrier . . . 47.001
. contract clause . . . 2.101
. . prescription . . . 2.201
. . text . . . 52.202-1
. contract clauses and solicitation provisions . . . 52.101
. . definitions . . . 52.202-1
. contract (construction or A-E) . . . 36.102
. contract financing payment . . . 32.001
. contract modification . . . 2.101
. contract quality requirements . . . 46.101
. contracting . . . 2.101
. contracting activity . . . 2.101
. contracting office . . . 48.001; 2.101
. contracting officer . . . 2.101; 52.202-1
. contractor . . . 22.1001; 44.101; 9.403; 22.801
. contractor-acquired property . . . 45.101
. contractor bid or proposal information . . . 3.104-1
. contractor purchasing system review (CPSR) . . . 44.101
. contractor team arrangements . . . 9.601
. contractor's development and implementation costs . . . 48.001
. contribution . . . 15.601

Definitions—continued
. controlled materials . . . 11.601
. controlled substance . . . 23.503
. conviction . . . 2.101; 23.503
. cooperative arrangements . . . 31.205-18
. cost input . . . 31.001
. cost objective . . . 31.001
. cost of capital committed to facilities . . . 31.001
. cost of components . . . 25.003
. cost or pricing data . . . 2.101
. cost realism . . . 2.101
. cost sharing . . . 2.101
. costs . . . 31.205-47
. covered article . . . 4.2001
. covered entity . . . 4.2004
. covered federal action . . . 3.801
. covered personnel . . . 37.201
. criminal drug statute . . . 23.503
. critical nonperformance . . . 46.101
. customary contract financing . . . 32.001
. customs territory . . . 25.003; 2.101
. data other than certified cost or pricing data . . . 2.101
. data universal numbering system +4 (DUNS+4) . . . 2.101
. data universal numbering system (DUNS) . . . 2.101
. day . . . 2.101; 33.101; 15.501; 32.902
. debarment . . . 2.101
. debarring official . . . 9.403
. debt bondage . . . 22.1702
. decision to award . . . 3.104-1
. defective certification . . . 33.201
. deferred compensation . . . 31.001
. deferred IR and D costs . . . 31.205-18
. deficiency . . . 15.001
. defined-benefit pension plan . . . 31.001
. defined-contribution pension plan . . . 31.001
. definitions . . . 32.902
. delegate agency . . . 11.601
. delegated agency . . . 41.101
. delivery order . . . 2.101
. delivery order contract . . . 16.501-1
. delivery payment . . . 32.001
. depreciation . . . 2.101
. deputy assistant secretary . . . 22.801
. descriptive literature . . . 2.101
. design . . . 36.102
. design-bid-build . . . 36.102
. design-build . . . 36.102
. design-to-cost . . . 2.101
. designated agency . . . 32.801
. designated billing office . . . 32.001; 32.902
. designated country . . . 25.003
. designated country end product . . . 25.003
. designated payment office . . . 32.001; 32.902
. desirable change . . . 30.001
. determinations and findings . . . 1.701
. development . . . 35.001; 31.205-18
. deviations from FAR . . . 1.401
. direct cost . . . 2.101
. directly associated cost . . . 31.001

Definitions—continued
. discount for prompt payment . . . 32.902
. domestic construction . . . 25.003
. domestic construction material . . . 25.003
. domestic end product . . . 25.003
. domestic offer . . . 25.003
. drug-free workplace . . . 2.101
. dry bulk carrier . . . 47.501
. dry cargo liner . . . 47.501
. due date . . . 32.001
. e98 . . . 22.001
. earned value management system . . . 2.101
. effective competition . . . 34.001
. effective date (modifications) . . . 43.101
. effective date of termination . . . 2.101
. electronic and information technology (EIT) . . . 2.101
. electronic commerce . . . 2.101
. electronic data interchange (EDI) . . . 2.101
. electronic funds transfer (EFT) . . . 2.101
. electronic funds transfer information (EFT) . . . 32.1102
. eligible offer . . . 25.003
. eligible product . . . 25.003
. employee . . . 22.1702; 23.503
. employment eligibility verification . . . 22.1801
. end product . . . 25.003; 2.101
. energy-efficient product . . . 2.101
. energy-savings performance . . . 2.101
. environmentally preferable . . . 2.101
. EO 11246 . . . 22.801
. EPA-designated product . . . 23.401
. equal opportunity clause . . . 22.801
. estimating costs . . . 31.001
. exception (forms) . . . 53.001
. excess personal property . . . 2.101; 8.101
. Excluded Parties List System . . . 2.101
. executive agency . . . 2.101
. expressly unallowable cost . . . 31.001
. facilities capital . . . 31.001
. facilities capital cost of money . . . 2.101
. facsimile . . . 2.101
. failure to make good faith effort to comply with the subcontracting plan . . . 19.701
. fair market price . . . 19.001
. federal agency . . . 23.1003; 2.101; 3.104-3
. federal agency procurement . . . 3.104-1
. federal helium supplier . . . 8.501
. Federal Power and Water Marketing Agency . . . 41.101
. Federal Reserve Board . . . 32.301
. Federal Technical Data Solution (FedTeDS) . . . 2.101
. federally-controlled facilities . . . 2.101
. federally-controlled information system . . . 2.101
. federally funded research and development centers (FFRDCs) . . . 2.101
. filed . . . 33.101
. final conviction . . . 3.702
. final cost objective . . . 31.001
. final indirect cost rate . . . 2.101

Definitions—continued
. firm (construction or A-E) . . . 36.102
. first article . . . 2.101
. first article testing . . . 2.101
. fiscal year . . . 31.001
. fixed-price contracts and subcontracts . . . 30.001
. flexibly-priced contracts and subcontracts . . . 30.001
. f.o.b. . . . 2.101
. f.o.b. destination . . . 2.101
. f.o.b. origin . . . 2.101
. food donations . . . 26.401
. forced or indentured child labor . . . 22.1501
. foreign construction material . . . 25.003
. foreign contractor . . . 25.003
. foreign end product . . . 25.003
. foreign-flag vessel . . . 47.501
. foreign offer . . . 25.003
. forward pricing rate agreement . . . 2.101
. forward pricing rate recommendation . . . 2.101
. franchise territory . . . 41.101
. fraud . . . 31.205-47
. free trade agreement country . . . 25.003
. free trade agreement country end product . . . 25.003
. freight . . . 2.101
. full and open competition . . . 2.101
. fully CAS-covered contracts . . . 31.205-18
. funded pension cost . . . 31.001
. future unit cost reduction . . . 48.001
. gateway airport abroad . . . 47.401
. gateway airport in the United States . . . 47.401
. general and administrative (G&A) expense . . . 2.101
. general freight . . . 47.201
. government contract quality assurance . . . 46.101
. government costs . . . 48.001
. government-furnished property . . . 45.101
. government or entity of the government . . . 8.701
. government printing . . . 8.801
. government property . . . 45.101
. government rate tender . . . 47.001
. government vessel . . . 47.501
. governmentwide acquisition contract (GWAC) . . . 2.101
. governmentwide commercial purchase card . . . 13.001; 32.1102
. governmentwide point of entry (GPE) . . . 2.101
. guaranteed loan . . . 32.301
. guaranteeing agency . . . 32.301
. hazardous material . . . 23.301
. head of agency . . . 2.101; 52.202-1
. head of the contracting activity . . . 2.101
. high-value item . . . 46.802
. historically black college or university . . . 2.101
. home office . . . 31.001
. household goods . . . 47.001
. HUBZone . . . 2.101
. HUBZone small business concern . . . 2.101
. humanitarian or peacekeeping operation . . . 2.101
. identical bids . . . 3.302
. immediate-gain actuarial cost method . . . 31.001
. imprest fund . . . 13.001

Definitions—continued
. improper influence . . . 3.401
. in excess of $10,000,000 . . . 3.104-1
. in writing or written . . . 2.101
. independent research and development (IR&D) . . . 31.205-18
. independent research and development (IR&D) cost . . . 31.001
. Indian . . . 26.101
. Indian organizations . . . 26.101
. Indian-owned economic enterprise . . . 26.101
. Indian tribe . . . 26.101; 3.801
. indictment . . . 9.403
. indirect cost . . . 2.101
. indirect cost pools . . . 31.001
. indirect cost rate . . . 2.101
. individual . . . 24.101; 23.503
. individual contract plan . . . 19.701
. industry . . . 19.001
. ineligible . . . 2.101
. influencing or attempting to influence . . . 3.801
. information security . . . 2.101
. information technology . . . 2.101
. inherently governmental function . . . 2.101
. inspection . . . 2.101
. inspector general . . . 3.901
. instant contract . . . 48.001
. instant unit cost reduction . . . 48.001
. insurance . . . 2.101
. insurance administration expenses . . . 31.001
. intangible capital asset . . . 31.001
. interagency acquisition . . . 2.101
. interested party . . . 26.101; 33.101
. international air transportation . . . 47.401
. intervention . . . 41.101
. invoice . . . 2.101
. invoice payment . . . 32.902
. involuntary servitude . . . 22.1702
. irrevocable letter of credit . . . 2.101
. Israeli end product . . . 25.003
. issue in controversy . . . 33.201
. item of supply . . . 34.101
. job . . . 31.001
. job class of employees . . . 31.001
. kickback . . . 3.502-1
. labor cost at standard . . . 31.001
. labor market . . . 31.001
. labor-rate standard . . . 31.001
. labor surplus area . . . 2.101
. labor surplus area concern . . . 2.101
. labor-time standard . . . 31.001
. laborers or mechanics . . . 22.401
. latent defect . . . 2.101
. leader company contracting . . . 17.401
. leasing . . . 8.1101
. least developed country . . . 25.003
. least developed country end product . . . 25.003
. legal proceedings . . . 9.403
. life-cycle cost . . . 7.101
. line item . . . 3.302

Definitions—continued
. List of Parties Excluded from Federal Procurement and Nonprocurement Programs . . . 2.101
. List of Products Requiring Contractor Certification as to Forced or Indentured Child Labor . . . 22.1501
. local government . . . 3.801
. maintain . . . 24.101
. major helium requirement . . . 8.501
. major nonconformance . . . 46.101
. major system . . . 2.101
. make item . . . 15.407-2
. make-or-buy program . . . 2.101
. management and operating contracts . . . 17.601
. market research . . . 2.101
. marketing consultant . . . 9.501
. master plan . . . 19.701
. master solicitation . . . 2.101; 14.203-3
. material . . . 45.101
. material cost at standard . . . 31.001
. material-price standard . . . 31.001
. material-quantity standard . . . 31.001
. may . . . 2.101
. Mexican end product . . . 25.003
. micro-purchase . . . 2.101
. micro-purchase threshold . . . 2.101
. minor nonconformance . . . 46.101
. minority institution . . . 2.101
. misrepresentation of fact . . . 33.201
. modified CAS-covered and non-CAS covered contracts . . . 31.205-18
. modular contracting . . . 39.002
. motor vehicle . . . 8.1101
. moving average cost . . . 31.001
. multi-agency contract (MAC) . . . 2.101
. multi-year contract . . . 17.103
. multiple award schedule (MAS) . . . 8.401
. multiple service locations . . . 41.101
. multiple year contracts . . . 22.1001
. NAFTA country . . . 25.003
. NAFTA country end product . . . 25.003
. national defense . . . 2.101
. national security system . . . 39.002
. negative instant contract savings . . . 48.001
. net acquisition savings . . . 48.001
. neutral person . . . 2.101
. no-setoff commitment . . . 32.801
. noncompliance . . . 30.001
. nondevelopmental item . . . 2.101; 52.202-1
. noneligible offer . . . 25.003
. noneligible product . . . 25.003
. nonmanufacturer rule . . . 19.001
. nonpersonal services contracts . . . 37.101
. nonprocurement common rule . . . 9.403
. nonprofit agency serving people who are blind or with other severe disabilities . . . 8.701
. nonqualified pension plan . . . 31.001
. nonrecurring costs (multi-year contracting) . . . 17.103
. nonseverable . . . 45.101
. nonsponsor . . . 35.017
. normal cost . . . 31.001

Definitions—continued
. normal workweek . . . 22.103-1
. notice . . . 22.1001
. novation agreement . . . 2.101
. number of employees . . . 19.101
. off-the-shelf item . . . 46.101
. offer . . . 2.101
. offeror . . . 2.101
. office furniture . . . 47.201
. officer or employee of an agency . . . 3.801
. official . . . 3.104-1
. operation of a system of records . . . 24.101
. option . . . 2.101
. ordering activity . . . 8.401
. ordering office . . . 8.701
. organizational conflict of interest . . . 2.101
. original complement of low cost equipment . . . 31.001
. other work . . . 49.001
. outlying areas . . . 2.101
. overtime . . . 2.101
. overtime premium . . . 2.101
. ozone depleting substance . . . 2.101
. partial termination . . . 2.101
. participating personally and substantially . . . 3.104-1
. party or parties . . . 19.101
. patent defect . . . 46.101
. pay-as-you-go cost method . . . 31.001
. payment date . . . 32.902
. payment information . . . 32.1102
. penal sum or amount . . . 28.001
. penalty . . . 31.205-47
. pension plan . . . 31.001
. pension plan participant . . . 31.001
. performance-based acquisition . . . 2.101
. performance based contracting . . . 37.101
. performance work statement (PWS) . . . 2.101
. person . . . 3.801; 3.502-1
. personal property . . . 2.101
. personal services . . . 2.101
. personal services contract . . . 2.101
. planner . . . 7.101
. plans and specifications (construction) . . . 36.102
. plant clearance officer . . . 2.101
. plant equipment . . . 45.101
. pollution prevention . . . 2.101
. pool . . . 9.701
. possessions . . . 2.101
. postconsumer material . . . 11.301
. power of attorney . . . 2.101
. preaward survey . . . 2.101
. preponderance of the evidence . . . 2.101
. price . . . 15.401
. pricing . . . 2.101
. primary sponsor . . . 35.017
. prime contract . . . 3.502-1
. prime contractor . . . 22.801; 3.502-1
. prime contractor employee . . . 3.502-1
. printing/copying double-sided . . . 4.301
. priority chemical . . . 23.1003

Definitions—continued
. privately owned U.S.-flag commercial vessel . . . 47.501
. proceeding . . . 31.205-47
. procurement list . . . 8.701
. procuring activity . . . 2.101
. professional employee . . . 22.1102
. profit center . . . 31.001
. projected average loss . . . 2.101
. projected benefit cost method . . . 31.001
. proper invoice . . . 2.101
. property . . . 45.101
. property administrator . . . 45.101
. proposal . . . 31.001
. proposal modification . . . 15.001
. proposal revision . . . 15.001
. protest . . . 33.101
. provision . . . 52.101
. publication . . . 5.501
. purchase order . . . 2.101
. qualification requirement . . . 2.101
. qualified bidders list (QBL) . . . 9.201
. qualified manufacturers list (QML) . . . 9.201
. qualified pension plan . . . 31.001
. qualified products list (QPL) . . . 2.101
. rated order . . . 11.601
. rates . . . 41.101
. ratification . . . 1.602-3
. real property . . . 45.101
. reasonable compensation . . . 3.801
. reasonable payment . . . 3.801
. receiving report . . . 2.101; 32.902
. recipient . . . 3.801
. reconditioned . . . 11.001
. record . . . 24.101
. record drawings . . . 36.102
. recoupment . . . 35.001
. recovered material . . . 2.101
. recovered material for paper and paper products . . . 11.301
. recruiting and training agency . . . 22.801
. recurring costs (multi-year contracting) . . . 17.103
. registered in the CCR database . . . 2.101
. regularly employed . . . 3.801
. reinsurance . . . 28.001
. related supplies . . . 8.801
. released or declared value . . . 47.001
. remanufactured . . . 11.001
. remedy coordination official . . . 32.006-2
. renewable energy . . . 2.101
. renewable energy technology . . . 2.101
. required change . . . 30.001
. requiring agency . . . 8.401
. residual value . . . 2.101
. responsible audit agency . . . 2.101
. responsible official . . . 32.601
. responsible prospective contractor . . . 2.101
. sanctioned EU country construction . . . 25.003
. sanctioned EU country end product . . . 25.003
. sanctioned EU member state . . . 25.003

Definitions—continued
. Schedules e-Library . . . 8.401
. scope . . . 2.000
. scrap . . . 2.101
. segment . . . 2.101
. self-insurance . . . 2.101
. self-insurance charge . . . 31.001
. senior procurement executive . . . 2.101
. separate contract . . . 41.101
. service contract . . . 22.1001; 37.101
. service-disabled veteran-owned small business concern . . . 2.101; 19.307
. service employee . . . 22.1001
. service life . . . 31.001
. settlement agreement . . . 49.001
. settlement proposal . . . 49.001
. severe forms of trafficking . . . 22.1702
. sex trafficking . . . 22.1702
. shall . . . 2.101
. sharing base . . . 48.001
. sharing period . . . 48.001
. shipment . . . 2.101
. shop drawings . . . 2.101
. should . . . 2.101
. signature or signed . . . 2.101
. simplified acquisition procedures . . . 2.101
. simplified acquisition threshold . . . 2.101
. single, governmentwide point of entry . . . 2.101
. site of construction . . . 22.801
. site of the work . . . 22.401
. small business concern . . . 19.001
. small business subcontractor . . . 2.101
. small disadvantaged business concern . . . 2.101
. sole source acquisition . . . 2.101
. solicitation provision . . . 2.101; 52.101
. source selection evaluation board . . . 3.104-1
. source selection information . . . 52.101
. special competency . . . 2.101
. special item number (SIN) . . . 8.401
. specified payment date . . . 32.902
. sponsor . . . 35.017
. spread-gain actuarial cost method . . . 31.001
. standard cost . . . 31.001
. state . . . 3.801
. state and local taxes . . . 2.101
. statement of objectives (SOO) . . . 2.101
. subcontract . . . 12.001; 44.101; 15.401; 19.701; 22.801; 52.202-1; 3.502-1
. subcontractor . . . 44.101; 22.801; 3.502-1
. substantial evidence . . . 2.101
. substantially as follows . . . 52.101
. substantially as follows or substantially the same as . . . 2.101
. substantially the same as . . . 52.101
. supplemental agreement . . . 2.101
. supplies . . . 2.101
. surety . . . 2.101
. surveying activity . . . 9.101
. suspending official . . . 9.403
. suspension . . . 2.101

Definitions—continued
. system of records on individuals . . . 24.101
. systems and other concept formulation studies . . . 31.205-18
. tangible capital asset . . . 31.001
. tanker . . . 47.501
. task order . . . 2.101; 16.501-2
. taxpayer identification number (TIN) . . . 2.101
. terminated portion of the contract . . . 49.001; 2.101
. termination for convenience . . . 2.101
. termination for convenience (multi-year contracting) . . . 17.103
. termination for default . . . 2.101
. termination inventory . . . 2.101
. termination liability . . . 41.101
. termination of employment gain or loss . . . 31.001
. testing . . . 46.101
. third party draft . . . 13.001
. toxic chemical . . . 23.001
. trainee . . . 22.401
. unallowable cost . . . 2.101
. unauthorized commitment . . . 1.602-3
. unfair trade practices . . . 9.403
. unilateral change . . . 30.001
. unique and innovative concept . . . 2.101
. unit . . . 48.001
. United States . . . 25.003; 22.1001; 2.101; 22.801
. U.S.-flag air carrier . . . 47.401
. U.S.-flag vessel . . . 47.501
. U.S.-made end product . . . 25.003
. United States (transportation) . . . 47.401
. unsettled contract change . . . 49.001
. unsolicited proposal . . . 2.101
. unusual contract financing . . . 32.001
. USDA designated item . . . 23.401
. utility service . . . 41.101
. V loan . . . 32.301
. value engineering . . . 2.101
. value engineering change proposal (VECP) . . . 2.101
. value engineering proposal . . . 48.001
. variance . . . 31.001
. veteran-owned small business concern . . . 2.101
. virgin material . . . 2.101
. wage and hour division . . . 22.1001
. wage determination
. wage determinations . . . 22.1001
. wage determinations online (WDOL) . . . 22.001
. wages . . . 22.401
. warranty . . . 2.101
. waste reduction . . . 2.101
. weakness . . . 15.001
. weighted average cost . . . 31.001
. whistleblower protections . . . 3.907-1
. women-owned small business concern . . . 2.101
. work . . . 22.401
. World Trade Organization government Procurement Agreement (WTO GPA) . . . 25.003
. writing or written . . . 2.101
. WTO GPA end product . . . 25.003
. year 2000 compliant . . . 39.002

Delays—see also Suspension of work
. contract clauses and solicitation provisions
. . commencement, prosecution and completion of work . . . 52.211-10
. . desired and required time of delivery . . . 52.211-9
. . government delay of work . . . 42.1305; 52.242-17
. . liquidated damages—supplies, services, or research and development . . . 52.211-11
. . stop-work order . . . 42.1305; 52.242-15
. . stop-work order—facilities . . . 42.1305
. . suspension of work . . . 42.1305; 52.242-14
. . time extensions . . . 52.211-13
. . time of delivery . . . 52.211-8
. government delay of work . . . 42.1304

Delivery incentives . . . 16.402-3

Delivery or performance schedules—see also Transportation
. contract clauses and solicitation provisions
. . commencement, prosecution, and completion of work . . . 11.404; 52.211-10
. . desired and required time of delivery . . . 11.404; 52.211-9
. . time of delivery . . . 11.404; 52.211-8
. factors to consider . . . 11.402
. general . . . 11.401
. supplies or services . . . 11.403

Demonstration contracts . . . 34.005-4

Department of Defense—see also Defense production
. forms
. . security agreement, DD Form 441 . . . 53.303-DD
. . security classification specification, DD Form 254 . . . 53.303-DD
. multi-year contracts . . . 17.106-3

Department of Labor—see also Wage determinations
. construction contracts . . . 22.406-12
. employment of veterans . . . 22.1306
. employment of workers with disabilities . . . 22.1404
. forms
. . payroll (for contractor's optional use), Form WH-347 (DOL) . . . 53.303-WH

Depreciation
. allowability . . . 31.205-11
. cost principles . . . 31.205-16

Design responsibility
. funding limitations . . . 36.609-1
. liability for defects . . . 36.608
. redesign . . . 36.609-2
. requirements for registration of designers . . . 36.609-4

Determinations and findings
. advance payments . . . 32.410
. class . . . 1.703
. commercial items acquisition . . . 12.207
. content . . . 1.704
. definitions . . . 1.701

Determinations and findings—continued
. expiration . . . 1.706
. general . . . 1.702
. interagency acquisitions . . . 17.503
. modification . . . 1.705
. scope . . . 1.700
. signatory authority . . . 1.707
. supersession . . . 1.705

Direct costs
. commercial organizations contracts . . . 31.202
. definition . . . 2.101

Disabled individuals
. employees with disabilities
. . applicability . . . 22.1402
. . collective bargaining agreements . . . 22.1405
. . complaint procedures . . . 22.1406
. . contract clause prescription . . . 22.1408
. . Department of Labor notices . . . 22.1404
. . noncompliance actions . . . 22.1407
. . policy . . . 22.1401
. . scope . . . 22.1400
. . statutory authority . . . 22.1400
. . waivers . . . 22.1403
. nonprofit agencies employing blind or severely disabled people
. . allocation process . . . 8.705-3
. . change-of-name and successor in interest procedures . . . 8.716
. . communications with central nonprofit agencies and the Committee . . . 8.714
. . compliance with orders . . . 8.705-4
. . definitions . . . 8.701
. . direct-order process . . . 8.705-2
. . general . . . 8.702
. . optional acquisition of supplies and services . . . 8.713
. . payments . . . 8.709
. . prices . . . 8.707
. . procurement list . . . 8.703
. . purchase exceptions . . . 8.706
. . purchase priorities . . . 8.704
. . purchase procedures . . . 8.705-1
. . quality complaints . . . 8.711
. . quality of merchandise . . . 8.710
. . replacement commodities . . . 8.715
. . responsible prospective contractors, identifying . . . 9.107
. . scope . . . 8.700
. . shipping . . . 8.708
. . specification changes . . . 8.712
. veterans
. . actions because of noncompliance . . . 22.1309
. . applicability . . . 22.1303
. . collective bargaining agreements . . . 22.1307
. . complaint procedures . . . 22.1308
. . definition of United States . . . 22.1301
. . Department of Labor notices and reports . . . 22.1306

Disabled individuals—continued
. veterans—continued
. . policy . . . 22.1302
. . procedures . . . 22.1304
. . scope . . . 22.1300
. . solicitation provision and contract clauses . . . 22.1310
. . waivers . . . 22.1305

Disadvantaged businesses—see also Small business programs
. determining eligibility . . . 19.304
. protesting representation of disadvantaged status . . . 19.305

Disallowance of costs
. after incurrence . . . 42.803
. air transportation, U.S.-flag carriers . . . 47.403-3
. contract clause prescription . . . 42.802
. notice of intent to disallow . . . 42.801
. scope . . . 42.800

Disaster or emergency assistance
. definition . . . 26.201
. disaster response registry . . . 26.205
. evaluation preference . . . 26.202-2
. justification for expenditures . . . 26.204
. local area preference . . . 26.202
. local area set-aside . . . 26.202-1
. scope of subpart . . . 26.200
. solicitation provision or contract clauses . . . 26.206
. transition of work . . . 26.203

Dismantling, demolition, or removal of improvements—see also Construction contracts
. contract clauses and solicitation provisions
. . inspection—dismantling, demolition, or removal of improvements . . . 46.313; 52.246-13
. . quality assurance . . . 46.313; 52.246-13
. . termination for convenience of the government (dismantling, demolition, or removal of improvements) . . . 49.502; 52.249-3
. form prescriptions . . . 36.701
. service contracts
. . bonds or other security . . . 37.302
. . contract clauses . . . 37.304
. . forms . . . 36.701
. . labor standards . . . 37.301
. . payments . . . 37.303
. . scope . . . 37.300

Disputes—see also Contract disputes
. appeal authorities . . . 33.001
. labor disputes
. . construction contracts . . . 22.406-10
. . reporting . . . 22.101-3
. . under service contract labor standards . . . 22.1026

Distribution of contracts
. agency requirements . . . 4.202
. procedures . . . 4.201
. taxpayer identification number information . . . 4.203

Donations . . . 31.205-8

E

Early retirement incentive plans . . . 31.205-6
Earned value management system
. contract clause and solicitation provisions . . . 34.203
. integrated baseline reviews . . . 34.202
. policy . . . 34.201
Economic price adjustment
. as factor in award of contract . . . 14.408-3
. contract clauses and solicitation provisions
. . economic price adjustment—labor and material . . . 52.216-4
. . economic price adjustment—semistandard supplies . . . 52.216-3
. . economic price adjustment—standard supplies . . . 52.216-2
. . economic purchase quantity—supplies . . . 52.207-4
. . prescriptions . . . 7.203; 16.203-4
. fixed-price contracts
. . application . . . 16.203-2
. . contract clause prescriptions . . . 16.203-4; 52.216-2; 52.216-3; 52.216-4
. . description . . . 16.203-1
. . limitations . . . 16.203-3
Economic quantities of supplies
. contracting officers' responsibilities . . . 7.204
. policy . . . 7.202; 14.212
. scope . . . 7.200
. solicitation provision prescription . . . 7.203
Educational institution contracts
. cost principles and procedures . . . 31.104; 31.301
. . general . . . 31.302
. . requirements . . . 31.303
. federally funded research and development centers
. . establishing or changing an FFRDC . . . 35.017-2
. . limitation on the creation of new FFRDCs . . . 35.017-7
. . master list . . . 35.017-6
. . policy . . . 35.017
. . review . . . 35.017-4
. . sponsoring agreements . . . 35.017-1
. . termination . . . 35.017-5
. . use . . . 35.017-3
. indirect cost rates . . . 42.705-3
. research and development contracts
. . broad agency announcement . . . 35.016
. . federally funded research and development centers . . . 35.017
. . general . . . 35.015
Electronic bids . . . 14.201-8
Electronic commerce in contracting
. policy . . . 4.502
. scope . . . 4.500
Electronic funds transfer
. applicability . . . 32.1103
. assignment of claims . . . 32.1105
Electronic funds transfer—continued
. definitions . . . 32.1102
. EFT information submitted by offerors . . . 32.1109
. EFT mechanisms . . . 32.1106
. emergency acquisitions . . . 18.124
. payment by governmentwide commercial purchase card . . . 32.1108
. payment information . . . 32.1107
. protection of information . . . 32.1104
. scope . . . 32.1100
. solicitation provisions and contract clauses . . . 32.1110
. statutory requirements . . . 32.1101
Emergency acquisitions
. available acquisition flexibilities
. . assignment of claims . . . 18.123
. . bid guarantees . . . 18.119
. . system for award management (sam) database . . . 18.102
. . electronic funds transfer . . . 18.124
. . extraordinary contractual actions . . . 18.127
. . Federal Supply Schedules . . . 18.105
. . General Accountability Office protests . . . 18.125
. . HUBZone sole source awards . . . 18.115
. . interagency acquisitions . . . 18.113
. . Javits-Wagner-O'Day specification changes . . . 18.107
. . letter contracts . . . 18.112
. . multi-agency blanket purchase agreements . . . 18.105
. . multi-agency indefinite delivery contracts . . . 18.105
. . oral requests for proposals . . . 18.111
. . overtime approvals . . . 18.119
. . priorities and allocations . . . 18.109
. . proposed contract actions . . . 18.103
. . qualifications requirements . . . 18.108
. . rent-free use of government property . . . 18.126
. . scope . . . 18.101
. . service disabled veteran-owned small business sole source awards . . . 18.116
. . Small Business Administration, contracting with . . . 18.114
. . solicitations from single source . . . 18.110
. . specification changes . . . 18.107
. . synopses . . . 18.103
. . unusual and compelling urgency . . . 18.104
. . use of patent technology under NAFTA . . . 18.120
. . veteran-owned small businesses . . . 18.116
. emergency acquisition flexibilities
. . contingency operations . . . 18.201
. . defense or recovery from certain attacks . . . 18.202
. . emergency or major disaster declaration . . . 18.203
. . incidentals of national significance . . . 18.203
. . major disaster declaration . . . 18.203
. . resources . . . 18.204
. emergency assistance activities
. . contract clause and solicitation provisions . . . 26.206

Emergency acquisitions—continued
. emergency assistance activities—continued
. . expenditure to other than local firms . . . 26.204
. . policy . . . 26.201
. . preference for local area contractors . . . 26.202
. . scope . . . 26.200
. general
. . definition . . . 18.001
. . scope . . . 18.000

Employee stock ownership plans . . . 31.205-6

Employees—see also Labor laws
. classes of service employees . . . 22.1019
. disabilities, workers with
. . applicability . . . 22.1402
. . collective bargaining agreements . . . 22.1405
. . complaint procedures . . . 22.1406
. . contract clause prescription . . . 22.1408
. . Department of Labor notices . . . 22.1404
. . noncompliance actions . . . 22.1407
. . policy . . . 22.1401
. . scope . . . 22.1400
. . statutory authority . . . 22.1400
. . waivers . . . 22.1403
. employment eligibility verification
. . contract clause prescription . . . 22.1803
. . definitions . . . 22.1801
. . policy . . . 22.1802
. . scope of subpart . . . 22.1800
. morale, health, welfare, food service, and dormitory costs and credits . . . 31.205-13
. notification of employee rights under National Labor Relations Act . . . 22.1600
. . complaint investigations . . . 22.1604
. . compliance evaluation . . . 22.1604
. . contract clause . . . 52.222-40
. . contract clause prescription . . . 22.1605
. . definition . . . 22.1602
. . exceptions . . . 22.1603
. . policy . . . 22.1602
. . sanctions for violations . . . 22.1604
. personal identity verification of contractor personnel
. . contract clause prescription . . . 4.1303
. . obligation to verify . . . 4.1302
. . policy . . . 4.1301
. professional employee compensation
. . applicability . . . 22.1101
. . definition of professional employee . . . 22.1102
. . policy . . . 22.1103
. . procedures . . . 22.1103
. . solicitation provision . . . 22.1103
. whistleblower protections
. . American Recovery and Reinvestment Act . . . 3.907
. . contract clause . . . 52.203-15
. . definitions . . . 3.901
. . filing complaints . . . 3.904
. . investigating complaints . . . 3.905
. . policy . . . 3.903

Employees—see also Labor laws—continued
. whistleblower protections—continued
. . prohibition on providing funds to an entity that require certain internal confidentiality agreements or statements . . . 3.909-1
. . remedies . . . 3.906
. . representation by offeror . . . 3.909-2
. . scope . . . 3.900
. whistleblower protections, pilot program . . . 3.908
. . classified information . . . 3.908-8
. . contract clause . . . 3.908-9
. . definitions . . . 3.908-2
. . enforcement of orders . . . 3.908-7
. . filing complaints . . . 3.908-4
. . policy . . . 3.908-3
. . procedures for investigating complaints . . . 3.908-5
. . scope . . . 3.908-1
. whistleblower protections, pilot program
. . remedies . . . 3.908-6

ENERGY STAR . . . 23.203

Engineering, developmental, or research capability
. waiver of competition requirements . . . 6.302-3

Entertainment costs . . . 31.205-14

Environment and conservation programs
. contract clauses and solicitation provisions
. . affirmative procurement of EPA-designated items in service and construction contracts . . . 52.223-17
. . drug-free workplace . . . 23.505; 52.223-6
. . estimate of percentage of recovered material content for EPA designated products . . . 23.406; 52.223-9
. . hazardous material identification and material safety data . . . 23.303; 52.223-3
. . notice of radioactive materials . . . 23.602; 52.223-7
. . ozone-depleting substances . . . 23.804; 52.223-11
. . pollution prevention and right-to-know information . . . 23.1005; 52.223-5
. . public disclosure of greenhouse gas emissions and reduction goals-representation . . . 52.223-22
. . recovered material certification . . . 23.406; 52.223-4
. . refrigeration equipment and air conditioners . . . 23.804; 52.223-12
. . waste reduction program . . . 23.705; 52.223-10
. definition of toxic chemical . . . 23.001
. definitions . . . 23.301
. energy and water efficiency and renewable energy
. . energy-efficient products . . . 23.203; 52.223-15
. . energy-savings performance contracts . . . 23.205
. . policy . . . 23.202
. . scope . . . 23.200
. . statutory and other authority . . . 23.201
. environmentally preferable and energy-efficient products and services
. . application to government-owned or leased facilities . . . 23.704
. . authorities . . . 23.702
. . contract clause . . . 52.223-15

Environment and conservation programs—continued
. environmentally preferable and energy-efficient products and services—continued
. . electronic product environmental assessment tool . . . 23.705
. . policy . . . 23.703
. . scope . . . 23.700
. hazardous material and material safety
. . contract clause prescription . . . 23.303
. . definition . . . 23.301
. . policy . . . 23.302
. . radioactive material, notice of . . . 23.601; 23.602
. . scope . . . 23.300
. ozone-depleting substances
. . authorities . . . 23.801
. . contract clause prescriptions . . . 23.804
. . policy . . . 23.803
. . scope . . . 23.800
. radioactive material, notice of
. . contract clause prescription . . . 23.602
. . requirements . . . 23.601
. recovered materials, use of
. . agency affirmative procurement programs . . . 23.404
. . authorities . . . 23.402
. . contract clauses and solicitation provisions . . . 23.406; 52.223-4; 52.223-9
. . definition of EPA-designated product . . . 23.401
. . policy . . . 23.403
. . procedures . . . 23.405
. . scope . . . 23.400
. . solicitation provision prescription . . . 23.406
. right-to-know laws and pollution prevention requirements
. . applicability . . . 23.1002
. . authorities . . . 23.1001
. . contract clause prescription . . . 23.1005
. . definition . . . 23.1003
. . requirements . . . 23.1004
. . scope . . . 23.1000
. scope . . . 23.000
. sustainable acquisition policy, Executive Order 13423 . . . 23.002
. toxic chemical release reporting
. . applicability . . . 23.903
. . definition of toxic chemical . . . 23.001
. . general . . . 23.902
. . policy . . . 23.902
. . purpose . . . 23.901
. . requirements . . . 23.1005

Environmental Protection Agency (EPA)
. recovered materials, use of
. . agency affirmative procurement programs . . . 23.404
. . authorities . . . 23.402
. . contract clauses and solicitation provisions . . . 23.406; 52.223-17; 52.223-4; 52.223-9
. . definition of EPA-designated product . . . 23.401
. . policy . . . 23.403

Environmental Protection Agency (EPA)—continued
. recovered materials, use of—continued
. . procedures . . . 23.405
. . scope . . . 23.400
. . solicitation provision prescription . . . 23.406

Equal employment opportunity
. affirmative action programs, construction . . . 22.804-2
. affirmative action programs, nonconstruction . . . 22.804-1
. complaints . . . 22.808
. contract clause prescriptions . . . 22.810
. definitions . . . 22.801
. enforcement . . . 22.809
. Executive Order 11246 . . . 22.802
. exemptions . . . 22.807
. general . . . 22.802
. inquiries . . . 22.806
. procedures . . . 22.805
. responsibilities . . . 22.803
. scope . . . 22.800

Equal low bids . . . 19.202-3; 14.408-6

Equipment
. lease or purchase
. . acquisition considerations . . . 7.401
. . acquisition methods . . . 7.402
. . contract clause prescription . . . 7.404
. . GSA assistance . . . 7.403
. repair distinguished from remanufacturing . . . 22.1003-6

Establishing a minimum wage for contractors
. annual executive order minimum wage rate . . . 22.1904
. applicability . . . 22.1903
. contract clause . . . 52.222-55
. contract clause prescription . . . 22.1906
. definition . . . 22.1901
. enforcement of executive order minimum wage requirements . . . 22.1905
. policy . . . 22.1902
. scope of subpart . . . 22.1900

Estimating systems . . . 15.407-5

Ethics
. contractor code of ethics and conduct
. . contract clause, prescription . . . 3.1004
. . definitions . . . 3.1001
. . mandatory requirement . . . 3.1003
. . policy . . . 3.1002
. . scope of requirement . . . 3.1000

Excess personal property
. forms
. . release of lien on real property, OF 90 . . . 53.302-90
. . release of personal property from escrow, OF 91 . . . 53.302-91
. . report of excess personal property, SF 120 . . . 53.301-120

Excess personal property—continued
. forms—continued
. . report of personal property for sale, SF 126 . . . 53.301-126
. information on availability . . . 8.103
. obtaining nonreportable property . . . 8.104
. policy on use as first source of supply . . . 8.102

Excise taxes
. exemptions . . . 29.202; 29.203
. general . . . 29.201

Execution of contracts
. contract clause prescription . . . 4.103
. contracting officer's signature . . . 4.101
. contractor's signature . . . 4.102

Executive Orders
. contract terms and conditions required to implement statutes or executive orders—commercial items . . . 12.301; 52.212-5
. convict labor (EO 11755) . . . 22.201
. energy policy and conservation (EO 11912, EO 13123, EO 13221) . . . 23.201
. equal opportunity (EO 11246) . . . 22.801
. establishing a minimum wage for contractors (EO 13658) . . . 22.1900
. revocation of EO 13201 (EO 13496)

Expert services
. waiver of competition requirements . . . 6.302-3

Extraordinary contractual actions
. contract adjustments
. . contract adjustments . . . 50.103-3
. . contract requirements . . . 50.103-7
. . disposition . . . 50.103-6
. . facts and evidence . . . 50.103-4
. . generally . . . 50.103-1
. . processing cases . . . 50.103-5
. . types of contract adjustments . . . 50.103-2
. definitions . . . 50.100
. delegation of and limitations on exercise of authority
. . contract adjustment boards . . . 50.102-2
. . delegation of authority . . . 50.102-1
. . limitations on exercise of authority . . . 50.102-3
. generally
. . authority . . . 50.101-1
. . policy . . . 50.101-2
. . records . . . 50.101-3
. residual powers . . . 50.104
. . contract clause . . . 50.104-4
. . generally . . . 50.104-2
. . special procedures for unusually hazardous or nuclear risks . . . 50.104-3
. . standards for use . . . 50.104-1

F

Facilities capital cost of money—see also Cost of money
. contract clauses . . . 15.408; 52.215-16; 52.215-17
. idle facility and idle capacity costs . . . 31.205-17

Facilities contracts—see also Government property
. contract clauses and solicitation provisions
. . labor standards for construction work—facilities contracts . . . 22.407

Facsimile bids
. definition . . . 2.101
. general . . . 14.202-7
. solicitation provisions . . . 52.214-31; 52.215-5

Fair Labor Standards Act minimum wage . . . 22.1002-4

Fair market price
. definition . . . 19.001
. determination of . . . 19.202-6
. Section 8(a) program . . . 19.807

Fast payment procedure
. conditions for use . . . 13.402
. contract clause . . . 13.404; 52.213-1
. general . . . 13.401
. preparation and execution of orders . . . 13.403

Federal Acquisition Regulations System
. acquisition-related dollar thresholds . . . 1.109
. acquisition team . . . 1.102-3; 1.102-4
. administration
. . agency compliance with FAR . . . 1.202
. . FAR Secretariat . . . 1.201-2
. . two councils . . . 1.201-1
. agency acquisition regulations . . . 1.301
. agency and public participation
. . definition . . . 1.501-1
. . exceptions . . . 1.501-3
. . opportunity for public comments . . . 1.501-2
. . public meetings . . . 1.503
. . solicitation of agency and public views . . . 1.501
. . unsolicited proposed revisions . . . 1.502
. agency compliance with FAR . . . 1.202
. applicability . . . 1.104
. authority . . . 1.103
. certifications . . . 1.107
. contract clauses and solicitation provisions, numbering of . . . 52.101
. contracting authority
. . appointment . . . 1.603-3
. . authority, generally . . . 1.601; 1.602-1; 1.603-1
. . ratification of unauthorized commitments . . . 1.602-3
. . responsibilities . . . 1.602-2
. . selection . . . 1.603-2
. . termination of appointment . . . 1.603-4
. conventions and interpretation . . . 1.108
. deviations . . . 1.400
. . class . . . 1.404
. . definition . . . 1.401
. . individual . . . 1.403
. . policy . . . 1.402
. . treaties and executive agreements . . . 1.405
. forms prescription . . . 53.201-1
. guiding principles . . . 1.102
. . acquisition team . . . 1.102-3

Federal Acquisition Regulations System—continued
. guiding principles—continued
. . discussion . . . 1.102-1
. . performance standards . . . 1.102-2
. . role of acquisition team . . . 1.102-4
. issuance
. . arrangement of code and publication . . . 1.105-1
. . arrangement of regulations . . . 1.105-2
. . copies . . . 1.105-3
. maintenance of FAR
. . FAR Secretariat . . . 1.201-2
. . two councils . . . 1.201-1
. OMB approval under Paperwork Reduction Act . . . 1.106
. positive law codification . . . 1.110
. publication and code arrangement . . . 1.501-1
. purpose . . . 1.101
. scope . . . 1.000

Federal Acquisition Streamlining Act of 1994—see also Simplified acquisition procedures
. inapplicable provisions and clauses . . . 13.006
. list of laws inapplicable to contracts and subcontracts at or below the simplified acquisition threshold . . . 13.005

Federal Prison Industries, Inc.
. evaluation of performance . . . 8.606
. exceptions . . . 8.605
. general . . . 8.601
. nonmandatory source . . . 18.106
. performance as a subcontractor . . . 8.607
. policy . . . 8.602
. protection of classified and sensitive information . . . 8.608
. purchase priorities . . . 8.603
. waivers . . . 8.604; 18.106

Federal Supply Schedules
. applicability . . . 8.403
. blanket purchase agreements (BPAs) . . . 8.405-3
. coordination requirements . . . 38.201
. definitions . . . 8.401
. description . . . 38.101
. disputes . . . 8.406-6
. emergency acquisitions . . . 18.105
. general . . . 38.101; 8.402
. inspection and acceptance . . . 8.406-2
. limited sources justification and approval . . . 8.405-6
. order placement . . . 8.406-1
. ordering procedures . . . 8.405-1; 8.405-2
. payment . . . 8.405-7
. price reductions . . . 8.405-4
. remedies for nonconformance . . . 8.406-3
. scope . . . 38.000
. Section 8(a) program . . . 19.804-6
. small businesses, ordering from . . . 8.405-5
. termination for cause . . . 8.406-4
. termination for government's convenience . . . 8.406-5
. use of . . . 8.404

Federally funded research and development centers (FFRDCs)
. definition . . . 2.101
. educational institution contracts
. . establishing or changing an FFRDC . . . 35.017-2
. . limitation on the creation of new FFRDCs . . . 35.017-7
. establishing or changing an FFRDC . . . 35.017-2
. interagency acquisitions . . . 17.504
. limitation on the creation of new FFRDCs . . . 35.017-7
. master list . . . 35.017-6
. policy . . . 35.017
. publicizing contract actions . . . 5.205
. review . . . 35.017-4
. sponsoring agreements . . . 35.017-1
. termination . . . 35.017-5
. use . . . 35.017-3

Financial costs . . . 31.205-20

Firm-fixed-price contracts
. application . . . 16.202-2
. commercial items acquisition . . . 12.207
. construction contracts . . . 36.208
. description . . . 16.202-1
. level-of-effort term contracts
. . application . . . 16.207-2
. . description . . . 16.207-1
. . limitations . . . 16.207-3
. negotiating . . . 16.103
. sealed bidding . . . 14.104

First article testing and approval
. contract clauses and solicitation provisions
. . first article approval—contractor testing . . . 52.209-3; 9.308-1
. . first article approval—government testing . . . 52.209-4; 9.308-2
. definition of approval . . . 9.301
. exceptions . . . 9.304
. general . . . 9.302
. government administration procedures . . . 9.307
. risk . . . 9.305
. solicitation requirements . . . 9.306
. use of . . . 9.303

Fiscal year contracts
. funding . . . 32.703-2

Fixed-ceiling-price contracts with retroactive price redetermination
. application . . . 16.206-2
. contract clauses
. . economic price adjustment—standard supplies . . . 16.203-4; 52.216-2
. . price redetermination—retroactive . . . 16.206-4; 52.216-6
. description . . . 16.206-1
. limitations . . . 16.206-3

Fixed-price contracts
. commercial items acquisition . . . 12.207
. consent to subcontract requirements . . . 44.201-2

Fixed-price contracts—continued
. construction contracts . . . 36.207
. contract clauses and solicitation provisions
. . economic price adjustment—labor and material . . . 16.203-4; 52.216-4
. . economic price adjustment—semistandard supplies . . . 16.203-4; 52.216-3
. . economic price adjustment—standard supplies . . . 16.203-4; 52.216-2; 52.216-6
. . inspection of research and development—fixed-price . . . 46.307; 52.246-7
. . inspection of services—fixed-price . . . 46.304; 52.246-4
. . inspection of supplies—fixed-price . . . 46.302; 52.246-2
. . price redetermination—prospective . . . 16.205-4; 52.216-5
. . price redetermination—retroactive . . . 16.206-4; 52.216-6
. cost principles and procedures . . . 31.102
. default terminations . . . 49.402-1
. definition . . . 30.001
. economic price adjustment
. . application . . . 16.203-2
. . contract clause prescriptions . . . 16.203-4
. . description . . . 16.203-1
. . limitations . . . 16.203-3
. firm-fixed price
. . application . . . 16.202-2
. . description . . . 16.202-1
. firm-fixed-price, level-of-effort term contracts
. . application . . . 16.207-2
. . description . . . 16.207-1
. . limitations . . . 16.207-3
. fixed-ceiling-price with retroactive price redetermination
. . application . . . 16.206-2
. . contract clause . . . 16.206-4; 52.216-6
. . description . . . 16.206-1
. . limitations . . . 16.206-3
. general . . . 16.201
. incentive contracts
. . firm target . . . 16.403-1
. . general . . . 16.204; 16.403
. . successive targets . . . 16.403-2
. negotiating . . . 16.103
. prospective price redetermination
. . application . . . 16.205-2
. . contract clause . . . 16.205-4; 52.216-5
. . description . . . 16.205-1
. . limitations . . . 16.205-3
. sealed bidding . . . 14.104
. termination for convenience
. . adjustment for loss . . . 49.203
. . bases for settlement proposals . . . 49.206-2
. . completed end items . . . 49.205
. . deductions . . . 49.204
. . equitable adjustment after partial termination . . . 49.208

Fixed-price contracts—continued
. termination for convenience—continued
. . general . . . 49.201
. . limitation on settlements . . . 49.207
. . profit . . . 49.202
. . settlement proposals . . . 49.206
. . submission of inventory schedules . . . 49.206-3
. . submission of settlement proposals . . . 49.206-1
. termination for default
. . effect . . . 49.402-2
. . government's right . . . 49.402-1
. . memorandum by contracting officer . . . 49.402-5
. . notice of termination for convenience . . . 49.601
. . other damages . . . 49.402-7
. . procedure . . . 49.402-3
. . procedure in lieu of default termination . . . 49.402-4
. . repurchase against contractor's account . . . 49.402-6
. transportation . . . 47.104-2
. warranties . . . 46.707
. with award fees . . . 16.404

Fly American Act . . . 47.403

Foreign acquisitions—see also Buy American
. American Recovery and Reinvestment Act—Buy American statute; construction materials
. . definitions . . . 25.601
. . evaluating offers of foreign construction material . . . 25.605
. . exceptions . . . 25.603
. . noncompliance . . . 25.607
. . policy . . . 25.602-2
. . postaward determinations . . . 25.606
. . preaward determination . . . 25.604
. . scope of subpart . . . 25.600
. . Section 1605 of the Recovery Act . . . 25.602-1
. contract clauses and solicitation provisions . . . 25.1103
. . Buy American Act—construction materials under trade agreements . . . 25.1102
. . Buy American—construction materials under trade agreements . . . 52.225-11
. . notice of required use of American construction materials under trade agreements . . . 52.225-24
. . notice of required use of American construction materials . . . 52.225-22
. . place of manufacture . . . 25.1101; 52.225-18
. . prohibition on contracting for hardware, software, and services developed or provided by Kaspersky Lab and other covered entities . . . 52.204-23
. . required use of American iron, steel, and other manufactured goods . . . 52.225-21
. . required use of American iron, steel, and other manufactured goods under trade agreements . . . 52.225-23
. . violation of arms control treaties or agreements-certification . . . 52.209-13
. contract financing . . . 32.004

Foreign acquisitions—see also Buy American—continued
. contractors performing private security functions outside the U.S.
. . applicability . . . 25.302-3
. . contract clause . . . 52.225-26
. . contract clause prescription . . . 25.302-6
. . definitions . . . 25.302-2
. . policy . . . 25.302-4
. . remedies . . . 25.302-5
. . scope . . . 25.302-1
. customs and duties
. . exempted supplies . . . 25.903
. . policy . . . 25.901
. . procedures . . . 25.902
. . scope . . . 25.900
. evaluating foreign offers—supply contracts
. . application . . . 25.502
. . Buy American Act, example . . . 25.504-1
. . evaluation examples, general . . . 25.504
. . Free Trade Agreements/Israeli Trade Act, example . . . 25.504-3
. . group award basis, example . . . 25.504-4
. . group offers . . . 25.503
. . policy . . . 25.501
. . WTO GPA/Caribbean Basin Trade Initiative/Free Trade Agreements, example . . . 25.504-2
. foreign currency, use of . . . 25.1002
. general
. . applicability . . . 25.002
. . definitions . . . 25.003
. . reporting requirements . . . 25.004
. . restrictions and requirements . . . 25.001
. . scope . . . 25.000
. international agreements and coordination
. . general . . . 25.801
. . procedures . . . 25.802
. prohibited sources
. . certification . . . 25.702-2
. . prohibition on contracting with entities that export sensitive technology to Iran . . . 25.703-3
. . contracting with entities conducting restricted business operations in Sudan . . . 25.702
. . conducting restricted business operations in Sudan; contract clause . . . 52.225-20
. . definition, person . . . 25.703-1
. . definitions . . . 25.702-1
. . further information . . . 25.701
. . Iran Sanctions Act . . . 25.703-2
. . prohibition on contracting with entities engaging in certain activities or transactions relating to Iran, representation and certifications . . . 52.225-25
. . remedies . . . 25.702-3
. . restrictions . . . 25.701
. . waiver, business operations in Sudan . . . 25.702-4
. . waiver, Iran Sanctions Act . . . 25.703-4
. prohibition on contracting for hardware, software, and services developed or provided by Kaspersky Lab
. . contract clause prescription . . . 4.2004
. . definitions . . . 4.2001

Foreign acquisitions—see also Buy American—continued
. prohibition on contracting for hardware, software, and services developed or provided by Kaspersky Lab—continued
. . notification . . . 4.2003
. . prohibition . . . 4.2002
. prohibition on contracting with an entity involved in activities that violate arms control treaties or agreements with the United States . . . 9.109
. . authority . . . 9.109-1
. . certification by offeror . . . 9.109-4
. . exception . . . 9.109-3
. . prohibition . . . 9.109-2
. . solicitation provision prescription . . . 9.109-5
. government property . . . 45.302
. quality assurance . . . 46.406
. trade agreements
. . applicability . . . 25.400; 25.402
. . award of unclassified contracts . . . 14.409-1
. . Caribbean Basin Trade Initiative . . . 25.405
. . definition . . . 25.003
. . excluded acquisitions . . . 18.118; 25.401
. . general . . . 25.403
. . Israeli Trade Act . . . 25.406
. . least developed countries . . . 25.404
. . procedures . . . 25.408
. . solicitations . . . 17.203
. . trade in civil aircraft . . . 25.407
. waiver of right to examination of records . . . 25.1001

Foreign nationals, severance payments to
. solicitation provision and contract clause . . . 37.113-2
. waiver of cost allowability limitations . . . 37.113-1

Formats, contracts and letters
. convenience terminations
. . letter notice . . . 49.601-2
. . telegraphic notice . . . 49.601-1
. delinquency notices . . . 49.607
. granting subcontract settlement authorization . . . 49.606
. release of excess funds under terminated contracts . . . 49.604
. request to settle subcontractor settlement proposals . . . 49.605
. termination for convenience settlement agreements . . . 49.603
. . cost-reimbursement contracts, complete termination, if settlement includes cost . . . 49.603-3
. . cost-reimbursement contracts, partial termination . . . 49.603-5
. . cost-reimbursement contracts, with settlement limited to fee, complete termination . . . 49.603-4
. . fixed-price contracts—complete termination . . . 49.603-1
. . fixed-price contracts, partial termination . . . 49.603-2
. . fixed-price contracts, settlements with subcontractors only . . . 49.603-8

Formats, contracts and letters—continued
. termination for convenience settlement agreements—continued
. . no-cost settlement agreement, complete termination . . . 49.603-6
. . no-cost settlement agreement, partial termination . . . 49.603-7
. . settlement of reservations . . . 49.603-9
Forms
. abstract of offers—construction, continuation sheet, OF 1419-A . . . 53.302-1419A
. . prescription . . . 53.236-1
. abstract of offers—construction, OF 1419 . . . 53.302-1419
. . prescription . . . 53.236-1
. abstract of offers—continuation, SF 1410 . . . 53.301-1410
. abstract of offers, SF 1409 . . . 53.301-1409
. . prescription . . . 53.214
. accounting information schedule, SF 1439 . . . 53.301-1439
. affidavit of individual surety, SF 28 . . . 53.301-28
. . prescriptions . . . 53.228; 28.106-1
. amendment of solicitation/modification of contract, SF 30 . . . 53.301-30
. . prescriptions . . . 15.210; 53.213; 53.214; 53.243; 13.307; 53.215-1; 53.242-1; 49.602-5
. amendment of solicitation, OF 309 . . . 53.302-309
. . prescriptions . . . 15.210; 53.215-1
. annual bid bond, SF 34 . . . 53.301-34
. . prescriptions . . . 53.228; 28.106-1
. annual performance bond, SF 35 . . . 53.301-35
. . prescriptions . . . 53.228; 28.106-1
. application for partial payment, SF 1440
. . prescriptions . . . 53.249; 49.602-4
. architect-engineer contract, SF 252 . . . 53.301-252
. . prescription . . . 36.702; 53.236-2
. architect-engineer qualifications, SF 330 . . . 53.301-330
. . prescription . . . 53.236-2
. award/contract, SF 26 . . . 15.509; 53.301-26
. . prescription . . . 53.214; 53.215-1
. bid bond (annual), SF 34 . . . 53.301-34
. . prescriptions . . . 53.228; 28.106-1
. bid bond, SF 24 . . . 53.301-24
. . prescriptions . . . 53.228; 28.106-1
. certificate of appointment, SF 1402 . . . 53.301-1402
. . prescription . . . 53.201-1
. consent of surety and increase of penalty, SF 1415 . . . 53.301-1415
. . prescriptions . . . 53.228; 28.106-1
. consent of surety, SF 1414 . . . 53.301-1414
. . prescriptions . . . 53.228; 28.106-1
. continuation sheet, OF 336 . . . 53.302-336
. . prescriptions . . . 53.213; 53.214; 13.307
. continuation sheet, SF 25-B (forms 24, 25, 25-A) . . . 53.301-25B
. . prescription . . . 53.228

Forms—continued
. contract award, OF 307 . . . 53.302-307
. . prescriptions . . . 15.509; 53.215-1
. contract security classification specification, DD Form 254 . . . 53.303-DD
. . prescription . . . 53.204-1
. contractor's request for progress payment, SF 1443 . . . 53.301-1443
. . prescription . . . 53.232
. determination, request for and response to, SF 308 . . . 53.301-308
. . prescription . . . 53.222
. excess personal property report, continuation sheet, SF 120-A . . . 53.301-120A
. . prescription . . . 53.245
. excess personal property report, SF 120 . . . 53.301-120
. . prescription . . . 53.245
. general
. . agency forms . . . 53.303
. . computer generation . . . 53.105; 53.111
. . continuation sheets . . . 53.110
. . current editions . . . 53.102
. . definition of exception . . . 53.001
. . exceptions . . . 53.103
. . forms prescribed by other regulations . . . 53.109
. . obtaining forms . . . 53.107
. . optional forms . . . 53.302
. . overprinting . . . 53.104
. . prescription of forms . . . 53.200
. . recommendations concerning forms . . . 53.108
. . requirements for use of forms . . . 53.101
. . scope . . . 53.000; 53.100
. . special construction and printing . . . 53.106
. illustrations
. . agency forms . . . 53.303
. . optional forms . . . 53.302
. . scope . . . 53.300
. . standard forms . . . 53.301
. inventory disposal report, SF 1424 . . . 53.301-1424
. . prescription . . . 53.245
. inventory disposal schedule, continuation sheet, SF 1429 . . . 53.301-1429
. . prescriptions . . . 53.245; 49.602-2
. inventory disposal schedule, SF 1428 . . . 53.301-1428
. . prescriptions . . . 53.245; 53.249; 49.602-2
. inventory schedule A—continuation sheet (metals in mill product form), SF 1427 . . . 53.301-1427
. . prescription . . . 53.245
. inventory schedule A (metals in mill product form), SF 1426
. . prescription . . . 53.245
. inventory schedule B, continuation sheet, SF 1429
. . prescription . . . 53.245
. inventory schedule B, SF 1428
. . prescription . . . 53.245
. inventory schedule C (work-in-process), continuation sheet, SF 1431
. . prescription . . . 53.245

Forms—continued
. inventory schedule C (work-in-process), SF 1430
. . prescription . . . 53.245
. inventory schedule D (special tooling and special test equipment), continuation sheet, SF 1433
. . prescription . . . 53.245
. inventory schedule D (special tooling and special test equipment), SF 1432
. . prescription . . . 53.245
. inventory verification survey, SF 1423 . . . 53.301-1423
. . prescription . . . 53.245
. labor standards interview, SF 1445 . . . 53.301-1445
. . prescription . . . 53.222
. labor standards investigation summary sheet, SF 1446 . . . 53.301-1446
. . prescription . . . 53.222
. modification of contract, SF 30 . . . 53.301-30
. . prescriptions . . . 15.210; 53.213; 53.214; 53.243; 13.307; 53.215-1; 53.242-1; 49.602-5
. offer label, OF 17 . . . 53.302-17
. . prescriptions . . . 15.210; 53.214; 53.215-1
. order for supplies or services, continuation sheet, OF 348 . . . 53.302-348
. . prescription . . . 13.307
. order for supplies or services, OF 347 . . . 53.302-347
. . prescriptions . . . 53.213; 53.251; 13.307; 53.216-1; 53.236-1
. partial payment, application, SF 1440 . . . 53.301-1440
. . prescriptions . . . 53.249; 49.602-4
. payment bond for other than construction contracts, SF 1416 . . . 53.301-1416
. . prescriptions . . . 53.228; 28.106-1
. payment bond, SF 25-A . . . 53.301-25A
. . prescriptions . . . 53.228; 28.106-1
. payroll (for contractor's optional use), Form WH-347 (DOL) . . . 53.303-WH
. . prescription . . . 53.222
. performance bond (annual), SF 35 . . . 53.301-35
. . prescriptions . . . 53.228; 28.106-1
. performance bond, continuation sheet, SF 25-B . . . 53.301-25B
. . prescriptions . . . 53.228; 28.106-1
. performance bond for other than construction contracts, SF 1418 . . . 53.301-1418
. . prescriptions . . . 53.228; 28.106-1
. performance bond, SF 25 . . . 53.301-25
. . prescriptions . . . 53.228; 28.106-1
. performance evaluation—construction contracts, SF 1420
. . prescription . . . 53.236-1
. performance evaluation (architect-engineer), SF 1421
. . prescription . . . 53.236-2
. personal property for sale report, continuation sheet, SF 126-A . . . 53.301-126A
. . prescription . . . 53.245

Forms—continued
. personal property for sale report, SF 126 . . . 53.301-126
. . prescription . . . 53.245
. preaward survey of prospective contractor—accounting system, SF 1408 . . . 53.301-1408
. . prescription . . . 53.209-1
. preaward survey of prospective contractor—financial capability, SF 1407 . . . 53.301-1407
. . prescription . . . 53.209-1
. preaward survey of prospective contractor—production, SF 1405 . . . 53.301-1405
. . prescription . . . 53.209-1
. preaward survey of prospective contractor—quality assurance, SF 1406 . . . 53.301-1406
. . prescription . . . 53.209-1
. preaward survey of prospective contractor—technical, SF 1404 . . . 53.301-1404
. . prescription . . . 53.209-1
. preaward survey of prospective contractor (general), SF 1403 . . . 53.301-1403
. . prescription . . . 53.209-1
. progress payment, contractor's request, SF 1443 . . . 53.301-1443
. . prescription . . . 53.232
. public voucher for purchases and services other than personal, SF 1034 . . . 53.301-1034
. public voucher for purchases and services other than personal, memorandum copy, SF 1034-A . . . 53.301-1034A
. public voucher for purchases and services other than personal, continuation sheet, SF 1035 . . . 53.301-1035
. public voucher for purchases and services other than personal, SF 1034
. . prescription . . . 53.249
. purchase order—invoice—voucher, SF 44 . . . 53.301-44
. . prescription . . . 53.213; 13.306; 13.307
. receipt for cash—subvoucher, SF 1165 . . . 53.301-1165
. . prescription . . . 53.213; 13.307
. reinsurance agreement for Miller Act payment bond, SF 274 . . . 53.301-274
. . prescriptions . . . 53.228; 28.106-1
. reinsurance agreement for Miller Act performance bond, SF 273 . . . 53.301-273
. . prescriptions . . . 53.228; 28.106-1
. reinsurance agreement in favor of the United States, SF 275 . . . 53.301-275
. . prescriptions . . . 53.228; 28.106-1
. release of lien on real property, OF 90 . . . 53.302-90
. . prescriptions . . . 53.228; 28.106-1
. release of personal property from escrow, OF 91 . . . 53.302-91
. . prescriptions . . . 53.228; 28.106-1
. report documentation page, SF 298 . . . 53.301-298
. . prescription . . . 53.235

Forms—continued
. report of excess personal property, continuation sheet, SF 120-A . . . 53.301-120A
. . prescription . . . 53.245
. report of excess personal property, SF 120 . . . 53.301-120
. . prescription . . . 53.245
. report of personal property for sale, continuation sheet, SF 126-A . . . 53.301-126A
. . prescription . . . 53.245
. report of personal property for sale, SF 126 . . . 53.301-126
. . prescription . . . 53.245
. request for authorization of additional classification and rate, SF 1444 . . . 53.301-1444
. . prescription . . . 53.222
. request for determination and response to request, SF 308 (DOL) . . . 53.301-308
. . prescription . . . 53.222
. request for quotations, SF 18 . . . 53.301-18
. . prescription . . . 53.213; 13.307
. schedule of accounting information, SF 1439 . . . 53.301-1439
. . prescriptions . . . 53.249; 49.602-3
. security agreement, DD Form 441 . . . 53.303-DD
. . prescription . . . 53.204-1
. settlement proposal for cost-reimbursement type contracts, SF 1437 . . . 53.301-1437
. . prescriptions . . . 53.249; 49.602-1
. settlement proposal (inventory basis), SF 1435 . . . 53.301-1435
. . prescriptions . . . 53.249; 49.602-1
. settlement proposal (short form), SF 1438 . . . 53.301-1438
. . prescriptions . . . 53.249; 49.602-3
. settlement proposal (total cost basis), SF 1436 . . . 53.301-1436
. . prescriptions . . . 53.249; 49.602-1
. small disadvantaged business participation report, OF 312 . . . 53.302-312
. . prescription . . . 53.219
. solicitation, amendment of, OF 309 . . . 53.302-309
. . prescriptions . . . 15.210; 53.215-1
. solicitation, amendment of, SF 30 . . . 53.301-30
. . prescriptions . . . 15.210; 53.213; 53.214; 53.243; 13.307; 53.215-1; 53.242-1; 49.602-5
. solicitation and offer—negotiated acquisition, OF 308 . . . 53.302-308
. . prescriptions . . . 15.210; 53.215-1
. solicitation/contract/order for commercial items, SF 1449 . . . 53.301-1449
. . prescription . . . 53.212; 53.213; 13.307; 53.205-1
. solicitation/contract, SF 1447 . . . 53.301-1447
. . prescription . . . 53.214
. solicitation, offer, and award (construction, alteration, or repair), SF 1442 . . . 53.301-1442
. . prescription . . . 53.236-1
. solicitation, offer, and award, SF 33 . . . 53.301-33
. . prescriptions . . . 15.210

Forms—continued
. solicitation, offer and award, SF 33
. . prescriptions . . . 53.214
. solicitation, offer, and award, SF 33
. . prescriptions . . . 53.215-1
. standard form 1449, solicitation/contract order for commercial items
. . prescription . . . 12.204
. statement and acknowledgment, SF 1413 . . . 53.301-1413
. . prescription . . . 53.222
. subcontracting report for individual contracts, SF 294 . . . 53.301-294
. . prescription . . . 53.219
. summary subcontract report, SF 295
. . prescription . . . 53.219
. surety, affidavit of individual, SF 28 . . . 53.301-28
. . prescriptions . . . 53.228; 28.106-1
. surety, consent, SF 1414 . . . 53.301-1414
. . prescriptions . . . 53.228; 28.106-1
. tax exemption form, SF 1094 . . . 53.301-1094
. . prescription . . . 53.229
. tax exemption forms accountability record, SF 1094-A . . . 53.301-1094A
. . prescription . . . 53.229
. termination inventory schedule E (short form for use with SF 38 only), SF 1434
. . prescription . . . 53.245
. U.S. tax exemption form, SF 1094 . . . 53.301-1094
. . prescription . . . 53.229

Forward pricing rate agreements . . . 42.1701; 15.407-3

Fraud
. contracting officer's duty to report . . . 33.209
. defense of fraud costs . . . 31.205-47
. definition . . . 31.205-47
. fraudulent claims . . . 33.209
. reduction or suspension of payments for
. . general . . . 32.006-1
. . procedures . . . 32.006-4
. . reporting . . . 32.006-5
. . responsibilities . . . 32.006-3
. termination of contracts . . . 49.106

Freedom of Information Act
. authority . . . 24.201
. policy . . . 24.203
. prohibitions . . . 24.202
. scope . . . 24.000

Fringe benefits . . . 31.205-6

Full-production contracts . . . 34.005-6

Full-scale development contracts . . . 34.005-5

G

Gains and losses on disposition of depreciable property or other capital assets . . . 31.205-16

General Services Administration (GSA)
. equipment lease or purchase . . . 7.403

General Services Administration (GSA)—continued
. Federal Supply Schedules
. . applicability . . . 8.403
. . blanket purchase agreements (BPAs) . . . 8.405-3
. . coordination requirements . . . 38.201
. . definitions . . . 8.401
. . description . . . 38.101
. . emergency acquisitions . . . 18.105
. . general . . . 8.402
. . limited sources justification and approval . . . 8.405-6
. . ordering procedures . . . 8.405-1; 8.405-2
. . payment . . . 8.405-7
. . price reductions . . . 8.405-4
. . scope . . . 38.000
. . small businesses, ordering from . . . 8.405-5
. . use of . . . 8.404
. utilities services areawide contracts . . . 41.204
. utilities services assistance . . . 41.203

Goodwill costs . . . 31.205-49

Government Accountability Office (GAO)
. override of protests for urgent or compelling circumstances . . . 18.125
. protests to . . . 33.104

Government employees
. conflicts of interest . . . 3.601
. . contracting officer's responsibility . . . 3.603
. . exceptions . . . 3.602
. . policy . . . 3.601
. limitation on payment of funds to influence federal transactions
. . certification and disclosure . . . 3.803
. . civil penalties . . . 3.807
. . contract clause . . . 3.808; 52.203-12
. . definitions . . . 3.801
. . exemption . . . 3.805
. . policy . . . 3.804
. . processing suspected violations . . . 3.806
. . prohibitions . . . 3.802
. . scope . . . 3.800
. standards of conduct
. . administrative remedies . . . 3.104-8
. . agency regulations . . . 3.101-3
. . certification . . . 3.103-2; 3.103-3
. . contract clause prescriptions . . . 3.104-9
. . criminal and civil penalties . . . 3.104-8
. . definitions . . . 3.104-1
. . disclosure, protection, and marking of contractor bid . . . 3.104-4
. . disqualification . . . 3.104-5
. . ethics advisory opinions . . . 3.104-6
. . general . . . 3.101-1; 3.104-2
. . gratuities . . . 3.101-2
. . solicitation provision . . . 3.103-1; 52.203-2
. . statutory and related prohibitions, restrictions, and requirements . . . 3.104-3
. . violations or possible violations . . . 3.104-7

Government property
. administrative support
. . prime contractor alternate locations . . . 45.501
. . subcontractor and alternate prime contractor locations . . . 45.502
. . support property administrator findings . . . 45.503
. authorizing use and rental
. . contracts with foreign governments . . . 45.302
. . contracts with or international organizations . . . 45.302
. . use and rental, generally . . . 45.301
. . use on independent research and development programs . . . 45.303
. contract clauses and provisions
. . government property . . . 52.245-1
. . government property installation operation services . . . 52.245-2
. . prescription . . . 45.107
. definitions . . . 45.101
. general
. . agencies . . . 45.103
. . contract clauses . . . 45.107
. . definitions . . . 45.101
. . policy . . . 45.102
. . contractor's system compliance . . . 45.105
. . responsibility and liability . . . 45.104
. . scope . . . 45.000
. . transferring accountability . . . 45.106
. inventory disposal schedules . . . 45.602-1
. liability for loss or damage
. . applicability . . . 46.801
. . definition of high-value item . . . 46.802
. . policy . . . 46.803
. . risk of loss . . . 46.505
. . scope . . . 46.800
. management of property in contractors' possession
. . contractor's management system compliance . . . 45.105
. reporting, reutilization, and disposal
. . abandonment or destruction of personal property . . . 45.603
. . sales procedures . . . 45.604-1
. . disposal of scrap . . . 45.606
. . sale of surplus personal property . . . 45.604
. . interagency property transfer costs . . . 45.602-4
. . inventory disposal reports . . . 45.605
. . inventory disposal schedules . . . 45.605
. . proceeds from sales of surplus property . . . 45.604-3
. . reutilization of government property . . . 45.602
. . reutilization priorities . . . 45.602-2
. . sale of property pursuant to sale or exchange . . . 45.604-4
. . use of GSA sponsored sales . . . 45.604-2
. . scope of requirements . . . 45.600
. . screening . . . 45.602-3
. requirements contracts . . . 16.503
. research and development contracts . . . 35.014
. responsibilities of contractor . . . 45.104
. scope . . . 45.000

Government property—continued
. solicitation and evaluation procedures
. . evaluation procedures . . . 45.202
. . solicitations . . . 45.201
. title
. . contractor-acquired property . . . 45.402
. . government furnished property . . . 45.401
. . performance-based payments and . . . 32.1009
. . protection of government title . . . 32.503-14
. . research and development contracts . . . 35.014

Governmental functions
. applicability . . . 7.502
. definition . . . 2.101
. policy . . . 7.503
. scope . . . 7.500

Governmentwide commercial purchase card
. definition . . . 13.001; 32.1102
. electronic funds transfer . . . 32.1108
. simplified acquisition methods . . . 13.301

Gratuities—see also Prohibited practices
. applicability . . . 3.201
. contract clause . . . 3.202; 52.203-3
. reporting suspected violations . . . 3.203
. standards of conduct . . . 3.101-2
. violations . . . 3.204

H

Hazardous material and material safety—see also Environment and conservation programs
. contract clause . . . 23.303
. definition . . . 23.301
. policy . . . 23.302
. radioactive material, notice of
. . contract clause prescription . . . 23.602
. . requirements . . . 23.601
. scope . . . 23.300

Helium acquisition
. contract clause . . . 8.505; 52.208-8
. definitions . . . 8.501
. exception . . . 8.503
. policy . . . 8.502
. procedures . . . 8.504
. scope . . . 8.500

Historically black colleges and universities and minority institutions
. data collection and reporting requirements . . . 26.303
. general policy . . . 26.302
. scope . . . 26.300
. solicitation provision . . . 26.304; 52.226-2

Historically underutilized business zone (HUBZone) program
. applicability . . . 19.1302
. contract clause prescriptions . . . 19.1309
. definition . . . 2.101
. emergency acquisitions . . . 18.115
. exclusions . . . 19.1304
. general . . . 19.1301

Historically underutilized business zone (HUBZone) program—continued
. limitations on subcontracting, general construction/ special trade . . . 19.1308
. performance of work requirements . . . 19.1308
. price evaluation preference . . . 19.1307
. protesting status as . . . 19.306
. set-asides . . . 19.1305; 6.205
. sole source awards . . . 19.1306
. status determinations . . . 19.1303

I

Identity verification of contractor personnel
. contract clause prescription . . . 4.1303
. obligation to verify . . . 4.1302
. policy . . . 4.1300

Idle facility and idle capacity costs . . . 31.205-17

Imprest funds
. agency responsibilities . . . 13.305-2
. conditions for use . . . 13.305-3
. definition . . . 13.001
. general . . . 13.305-1
. procedures . . . 13.305-4

Incentive contracts
. contract clauses and solicitation provisions
. . allowable cost and payment . . . 16.406; 52.216-7
. . incentive fee . . . 16.406; 52.216-10
. . incentive price revision—firm target . . . 16.406; 52.216-16
. . incentive price revision—successive targets . . . 16.406; 52.216-17
. cost incentives . . . 16.402-1
. cost-plus-award-fee . . . 16.405-2
. cost-plus-incentive-fee . . . 16.405-1
. cost-reimbursement . . . 16.405
. delivery incentives . . . 16.402-3
. fixed-price incentives
. . award fees . . . 16.404
. . firm target . . . 16.403-1
. . general . . . 16.204; 16.403
. . successive targets . . . 16.403-2
. general . . . 16.401
. multiple incentives . . . 16.402-4
. performance incentives . . . 16.402-2
. termination of . . . 49.115
. warranties . . . 46.707

Indefinite delivery contracts
. commercial items acquisition . . . 12.207
. contract clauses and solicitation provisions
. . definite quantity . . . 16.506; 52.216-20
. . indefinite quantity . . . 16.506; 52.216-22
. . order limitations . . . 16.506; 52.216-19
. . ordering . . . 16.506; 52.216-18
. . requirements . . . 16.506; 52.216-21
. . single or multiple awards . . . 16.506; 52.216-27
. definite-quantity contracts . . . 16.502
. definitions . . . 16.501-1
. emergency acquisitions . . . 18.105

Indefinite delivery contracts—continued
. general . . . 16.501-2
. indefinite-quantity contracts . . . 16.504
. leased equipment, tax clause prescriptions . . . 29.401-1
. ordering . . . 16.505
. requirements contracts . . . 16.503
. scope . . . 16.500

Indefinite-quantity contracts
. funding . . . 32.703-2
. general . . . 16.504

Independent pricing certification
. evaluation . . . 3.103-2
. further certification . . . 3.103-3
. solicitation provision . . . 3.103-1; 52.203-2

Indian incentive program
. contract clause prescription . . . 26.104
. definitions . . . 26.101
. policy . . . 26.102
. procedures . . . 26.103
. scope . . . 26.100

Indian tribal governments, contracts with
. applicability of cost principles . . . 31.107
. general . . . 31.601; 31.602
. requirements . . . 31.603

Indirect cost rates
. billing rates
. . definition . . . 42.701
. . establishing . . . 42.704
. certification . . . 31.110; 42.703-2
. commercial organization contracts . . . 31.203
. contract administration . . . 42.701
. cost-sharing rates and limitations . . . 42.707
. documents distribution . . . 42.706
. final indirect cost rates
. . auditor determination procedure . . . 42.705-2
. . contracting officer determination procedure . . . 42.705-1
. . educational institutions . . . 42.705-3
. . establishing . . . 42.705
. . nonprofit organizations . . . 42.705-5
. . state and local governments . . . 42.705-4
. penalties
. . assessment . . . 42.709-3
. . computation of interest . . . 42.709-4
. . contract clause prescription . . . 42.709-6
. . general . . . 42.709-1
. . responsibilities . . . 42.709-2
. . scope . . . 42.709
. . waiver . . . 42.709-5
. policy . . . 42.703-1
. purpose . . . 42.702
. quick-closeout procedure . . . 42.708
. scope . . . 42.700
. terminated contracts . . . 49.303-4

Industrial mobilization
. waiver of competition requirements . . . 6.302-3

Industrial resources—testing, qualification and use
. contract clause prescription . . . 34.104
. definitions . . . 34.101
. policy . . . 34.102
. scope . . . 34.100
. testing and qualification . . . 34.103

Inflation, adjustment for . . . 1.109

Information technology acquisition
. applicability . . . 39.001
. contract clause
. . privacy or security safeguards . . . 39.106; 52.239-1
. definitions . . . 39.002
. electronic and information technology
. . applicability . . . 39.203
. . definition of undue burden . . . 39.202
. . exceptions . . . 39.204
. . scope . . . 39.201
. general
. . contract clause prescription . . . 39.106
. . information technology services . . . 39.104
. . management of risk . . . 39.102
. . modular contracting . . . 39.103
. . policy . . . 39.101
. . privacy . . . 39.105
. scope . . . 39.000

Inherently governmental functions
. acquisition planning . . . 7.500
. definition . . . 2.101

Inspector General
. definition . . . 3.901
. whistleblower investigations . . . 3.905

Insurance
. contract clauses and solicitation provisions
. . agency provisions and clauses . . . 28.311-2
. . cargo insurance . . . 28.313; 52.228-9
. . insurance—liability to third persons . . . 52.228-7; 28.311-1
. . insurance—work on a government installation . . . 28.310; 52.225-5
. . liability and insurance—leased motor vehicles . . . 28.312; 52.228-8
. . vehicular and general public liability insurance . . . 28.313; 52.228-10
. . workers' compensation and war-hazard insurance overseas . . . 28.309; 52.228-4
. . workers' compensation insurance (Defense Base Act) . . . 28.309; 52.228-3
. cost principles . . . 31.205-19
. cost-reimbursement contracts . . . 28.307
. . group insurance plans . . . 28.307-1
. . liability . . . 28.307-2
. definitions . . . 28.001
. fixed-price contracts . . . 28.306
. forms
. . prescriptions . . . 53.228
. . reinsurance agreement for Miller Act payment bond, SF 274 . . . 53.301-274

Insurance—continued
. forms—continued
. . reinsurance agreement for Miller Act performance bond, SF 273 . . . 53.301-273
. . reinsurance agreement in favor of U.S., SF 275 . . . 53.301-275
. loss or damage to government property . . . 28.303
. notice of cancellation or change . . . 28.302
. overseas workers' compensation . . . 28.305
. policy . . . 28.301
. research and development contracts . . . 35.013
. risk-pooling arrangements . . . 28.304
. self-insurance . . . 28.308
. transportation
. . insurance . . . 47.102
. war-hazard insurance . . . 28.305

Integrated baseline reviews . . . 34.202

Interagency acquisitions
. acquisitions by nondefense agencies on DoD's behalf
. . applicability . . . 17.702
. . definitions . . . 17.701
. . policy . . . 17.703
. . scope . . . 17.700
. definition . . . 2.101
. emergency acquisitions . . . 18.113
. general . . . 17.501
. ordering procedures . . . 17.503
. procedures . . . 17.502-1
. reporting requirements . . . 17.504
. scope . . . 17.500
. under the Economy Act . . . 17.502-2
. utilities services . . . 41.206

Interagency acquisitions by nondefense agencies on DoD's behalf
. applicability . . . 17.702
. definitions . . . 17.701
. policy . . . 17.703
. scope . . . 17.700

Interagency fleet management system (IFMS)
. authorization . . . 51.202
. contract clause prescription . . . 51.205
. means of obtaining service . . . 51.203
. policy . . . 51.201
. scope . . . 51.200
. use requirements . . . 51.204

Interest and other financial costs
. advance payments . . . 32.407
. cost principles . . . 31.205-20
. credits . . . 32.614-2
. late payments . . . 32.907
. unpaid contract debt . . . 32.614-1

Internal Revenue Service
. reporting contract information to . . . 4.903
. reporting payment information to . . . 4.904

International agreements—see also Foreign acquisitions; Trade agreements; Treaties
. waiver of competition requirements . . . 6.302-4

Interstate Commerce Act . . . 47.104

Inventories, government property
. disposal reports . . . 45.605
. disposal schedules . . . 45.602-1
. reporting . . . 45.600

Israeli Trade Act
. contract clauses and solicitation provisions
. . Buy American—Free Trade Agreements—Israeli Trade Act . . . 25.1101
. . Buy American—Free Trade Agreements—Israeli Trade Act certificate . . . 25.1101
. . Buy American—Free Trade Agreements—Israeli Trade Act . . . 52.225-3
. . Buy American Act—Free Trade Agreements—Israeli Trade Act certificate . . . 52.225-4
. definitions . . . 25.003
. evaluation example . . . 25.504-3
. general . . . 25.406

J

Joint venturers, contract signatures . . . 4.102

K

Kickbacks, subcontractors—see also Prohibited practices
. contract clause . . . 52.203-7; 3.502-3
. definitions . . . 3.502-1
. general . . . 3.502-2

L

Labor-hour contracts
. description . . . 16.602
. not fixed-price . . . 16.600

Labor laws
. age discrimination
. . complaints . . . 22.902
. . policy . . . 22.901
. basic policies
. . contract pricing and administration . . . 22.101-2
. . federal and state requirements . . . 22.102
. . labor relations . . . 22.101-1
. . overtime . . . 22.103
. . removal of items from contractors' facilities affected by work stoppages . . . 22.101-4
. . reporting labor disputes . . . 22.101-3
. child labor
. . definitions . . . 22.1501
. . policy . . . 22.1502
. . products requiring contractor certification as to forced or indentured child labor . . . 22.1503
. . scope . . . 22.1500
. . solicitation provision and contract clause . . . 22.1505
. . violations and remedies . . . 22.1504
. contract clauses and solicitation provisions
. . affirmative action compliance . . . 22.810; 52.222-25

Labor laws—continued
. contract clauses and solicitation provisions—continued
. . affirmative action compliance requirements for construction . . . 22.801; 52.222-27
. . affirmative action for disabled veterans and veterans of the Vietnam era . . . 22.1310
. . equal opportunity for veterans . . . 52.222-35
. . affirmative action for workers with disabilities . . . 22.1408; 52.222-36
. . apprentices and trainees . . . 22.407; 52.222-9
. . approval of wage rates . . . 22.407; 52.222-16
. . certification of eligibility . . . 22.407; 52.222-15
. . certification regarding knowledge of child labor for listed end products . . . 22.1505; 52.222-18
. . child labor—cooperation with authorities and remedies . . . 22.1505; 52.222-19
. . compliance with Copeland Act requirements . . . 22.407; 52.222-10
. . compliance with construction wage rate requirements and related regulations . . . 22.407; 52.222-13
. . construction wage rate requirements . . . 52.222-6
. . construction wage rate requirements—price adjustment (actual method) . . . 22.407
. . construction wage rate requirements—price adjustment (percentage method) . . . 22.407
. . construction wage rate requirements—price adjustment (none or separately specified method) . . . 22.407; 52.222-30
. . construction wage rate requirements—price adjustment (percentage method) . . . 52.222-31
. . construction wage rate requirements—price adjustment (actual method) . . . 52.222-32
. . contract termination—debarment . . . 22.407; 52.222-12
. . contract work hours and safety standards—overtime compensation . . . 22.305; 52.222-4
. . convict labor . . . 22.202; 52.222-3
. . construction wage rate requirements . . . 22.407
. . construction wage rate requirements—secondary site of the work . . . 52.222-5
. . disabled and Vietnam era veterans . . . 22.1308
. . disputes concerning labor standards . . . 22.407; 52.222-14
. . employment reports on disabled veterans and veterans of the Vietnam era . . . 22.1310
. . employment reports on veterans . . . 52.222-37
. . equal opportunity . . . 22.810; 52.222-26
. . evaluation of compensation for professional employees . . . 22.1103; 52.222-46
. . exemption from application of service contract labor standards . . . 22.1006; 52.222-48; 52.222-51; 52.222-52; 52.222-53
. . Fair Labor Standards Act and service contract labor standards statute—price adjustment . . . 22.1006
. . Fair Labor Standards Act and service contract labor standards statute—price adjustment (multiple year and option contracts) . . . 22.1006

Labor laws—continued
. contract clauses and solicitation provisions—continued
. . Fair Labor Standards Act and service contract labor standards—price adjustment (multiple year and option contracts) . . . 52.222-43
. . Fair Labor Standards Act and service contract labor standards—price adjustment . . . 52.222-44
. . labor standards for construction work—facilities contracts . . . 22.407
. . notice of requirement for affirmative action to ensure equal employment opportunity for construction . . . 22.810; 52.222-23
. . notice to the government of labor disputes . . . 22.103-5; 52.222-1
. . notification of visa denial . . . 22.810; 52.222-29
. . payment for overtime premiums . . . 22.103-5; 52.222-2
. . payrolls and basic records . . . 22.407; 52.222-8
. . preaward on-site equal opportunity compliance evaluation . . . 22.810; 52.222-24
. . previous contracts and compliance reports . . . 22.810; 52.222-22
. . prohibition of segregated facilities . . . 22.810; 52.222-21
. . service contract labor standards—place of performance unknown . . . 22.1006; 52.222-49
. . service contract labor standards . . . 22.1006; 52.222-41
. . statement of equivalent rates for Federal hires . . . 22.1006; 52.222-42
. . subcontracts (labor standards) . . . 22.407; 52.222-11
. . contracts for materials, supplies, articles, and equipment exceeding $15,000 . . . 22.610; 52.222-20
. . withholding of funds . . . 22.407; 52.222-7
. contract work hours and safety standards
. . administration and enforcement . . . 22.303
. . construction contracts . . . 22.403-3
. . contract clause prescription . . . 22.305
. . liquidated damages and overtime pay . . . 22.302
. . requirements . . . 22.403-3
. . scope . . . 22.300
. . statutory requirement . . . 22.301
. . variations, tolerances, exemptions . . . 22.304
. contracts for materials, supplies, articles, and equipment exceeding $15,000 (formerly Walsh-Healey Public Contracts Act)
. . applicability . . . 22.603
. . contract clause prescription . . . 22.610
. . Department of Labor regional jurisdictions, wage and hour division . . . 22.609
. . procedures . . . 22.608
. . regulatory exemptions . . . 22.604-2
. . rulings and interpretations . . . 22.605
. . statutory exemptions . . . 22.604-1
. . statutory requirements . . . 22.602
. convict labor
. . contract clause prescription . . . 22.202

Labor laws—continued
. convict labor—continued
. . Executive Order 11755 . . . 22.201
. definitions . . . 22.001; 22.2002; 22.401; 22.103-1
. disabilities, workers with
. . applicability . . . 22.1402
. . collective bargaining agreements . . . 22.1405
. . complaint procedures . . . 22.1406
. . contract clause prescription . . . 22.1408
. . Department of Labor notices . . . 22.1404
. . noncompliance actions . . . 22.1407
. . policy . . . 22.1401
. . scope . . . 22.1400
. . statutory authority . . . 22.1400
. . waivers . . . 22.1403
. dismantling, demolition, or removal of improvements . . . 37.301
. disputes
. . removal of items from affected facility . . . 22.101-4
. . reporting requirement . . . 22.101-3
. equal employment opportunity
. . affirmative action programs, construction . . . 22.804-2
. . affirmative action programs, nonconstruction . . . 22.804-1
. . complaints . . . 22.808
. . contract clause prescriptions . . . 22.810
. . definitions . . . 22.801
. . enforcement . . . 22.809
. . Executive Order 11246 . . . 22.802
. . exemptions . . . 22.807
. . general . . . 22.802
. . inquiries . . . 22.806
. . procedures . . . 22.805
. . responsibilities . . . 22.803
. . scope . . . 22.800
. establishing paid sick leave for federal contractors
. . applicability . . . 22.2103
. . contract clause . . . 52.22-62
. . contract clause prescription . . . 22.2110
. . definitions . . . 22.2101
. . enforcement of Executive Order 13706 paid sick leave requirements . . . 22.2109
. . exclusions . . . 22.2104
. . multiemployer plans or other funds, plans, or programs . . . 22.2108
. . paid sick leave for federal contractors and subcontractors . . . 22.2105
. . policy . . . 22.2102
. . prohibited acts . . . 22.2106
. . scope of subpart . . . 22.2100
. . waiver of rights . . . 22.2107
. federal and state requirements
. . administration . . . 22.102-2
. . policy . . . 22.102-1
. forms
. . labor standards interview, SF 1445 . . . 53.301-1445
. . labor standards investigation summary sheet, SF 1446 . . . 53.301-1446

Labor laws—continued
. forms—continued
. . payroll (for contractors' optional use), WH-347 (DOL) . . . 53.303-WH
. . prescriptions . . . 53.222
. . request for authorization of additional classification and rate, SF 1444 . . . 53.301-1444
. . solicitation/contract, SF 1447 . . . 53.301-1447
. notification of employee rights under National Labor Relations Act
. . complaint investigations . . . 22.1604
. . compliance evaluation . . . 22.1604
. . contract clause . . . 52.222-40
. . contract clause prescription . . . 22.1605
. . definition . . . 22.1601
. . exceptions . . . 22.1603
. . policy . . . 22.1602
. . sanctions for violations . . . 22.1604
. . scope . . . 22.1600
. overtime
. . approvals . . . 22.103-4
. . contract clause prescriptions . . . 22.305; 22.103-5
. . definition of normal workweek . . . 22.103-1
. . policy . . . 22.103-2
. . procedures . . . 22.103-3
. professional employee compensation
. . applicability . . . 22.1101
. . definition of professional employee . . . 22.1102
. . policy . . . 22.1103
. . procedures . . . 22.1103
. . solicitation provision . . . 22.1103
. project labor agreements for construction
. . definitions . . . 22.502
. . general requirements . . . 22.504
. . notice of requirement for project labor agreement clause . . . 52.222-33
. . policy . . . 22.503
. . project labor agreement clause . . . 52.222-34
. . scope of subpart . . . 22.501
. . solicitation provision and contract clause prescription . . . 22.505
. scope . . . 19.000
. trafficking in persons, combating
. . contract clause prescription . . . 22.1705
. . definitions . . . 22.1702
. . policy . . . 22.1703
. . scope . . . 22.1700
. . violations and remedies . . . 22.1704
. veterans
. . actions because of noncompliance . . . 22.1309
. . applicability . . . 22.1303
. . collective bargaining agreements . . . 22.1307
. . complaint procedures . . . 22.1308
. . definition of United States . . . 22.1301
. . Department of Labor notices and reports . . . 22.1306
. . policy . . . 22.1302
. . procedures . . . 22.1304
. . scope . . . 22.1300

Labor laws—continued
. veterans—continued
. . solicitation provision and contract clause prescriptions . . . 22.1310
. . waivers . . . 22.1305
. wage determinations . . . 22.404-1
. . administration and enforcement . . . 22.406
. . appeals . . . 22.404-11
. . award without . . . 22.404-9
. . correction of clerical errors . . . 22.404-7
. . expiration . . . 22.404-5
. . improper . . . 22.404-8
. . modification . . . 22.404-6
. . posting and notice . . . 22.404-10
. . request procedures . . . 22.404-3
. . requirements . . . 22.404-2
. . solicitations without . . . 22.404-4

Leader company contracting
. general . . . 17.401
. limitations . . . 17.402
. procedures . . . 17.403

Letter contracts
. application . . . 16.603-2
. contract clauses and solicitation provisions
. . contract definitization . . . 52.216-25; 16.603-4
. . execution and commencement of work . . . 52.216-23; 16.603-4
. . limitation of government liability . . . 52.216-24; 16.603-4
. . payments of allowable costs before definitization . . . 52.216-26; 16.603-4
. description . . . 16.603-1
. emergency acquisitions . . . 18.112
. limitations . . . 16.603-3

Letters of credit
. advance payments . . . 32.406

Limitation of cost or funds
. limitation of cost . . . 32.704
. limitation of cost (facilities) . . . 32.704
. limitation of funds . . . 32.704; 52.232-22
. limitation on withholding of payments . . . 32.111; 52.232-9

Line items
. definition . . . 3.302
. policy . . . 4.1001

Liquidated damages
. construction contracts . . . 36.206
. contract clauses and solicitation provisions
. . liquidated damages—construction . . . 52.211-12
. . prescriptions . . . 11.503
. . supplies, services or research and development . . . 52.211-11
. . time extensions . . . 52.211-13
. including clauses in solicitations and contracts
. . policy . . . 11.501
. . procedures . . . 11.502
. . scope . . . 11.500
. policy . . . 11.501

Liquidated damages—continued
. procedures . . . 11.502
. small business subcontracting assistance program . . . 19.705-7
. under contract work hours and safety standards statute . . . 22.302

Liquidation rates
. alternate method . . . 32.503-9
. establishing . . . 32.503-10
. ordinary method . . . 32.503-8

Loan guarantees for defense production
. application for guarantee . . . 32.304-1
. asset formula . . . 32.304-3
. assignment of claims . . . 32.304-5
. authority . . . 32.302
. certificate of eligibility . . . 32.304-2
. collateral security . . . 32.304-6
. definitions . . . 32.301
. general . . . 32.303
. guarantee amount and maturity . . . 32.304-4
. other borrowing . . . 32.304-8
. subcontracts . . . 32.306
. surety bonds and loan guarantees . . . 32.304-7
. terminated contracts . . . 32.305

Lobbying costs . . . 31.205-22

Local contractors, preference for
. set-asides for during disasters or emergencies . . . 6.208

Long-range acquisition estimates . . . 5.404
. announcements . . . 5.404-2
. release procedures . . . 5.404-1

Losses
. contractor liability
. . applicability . . . 46.801
. . definition of high-value item . . . 46.802
. . policy . . . 46.803
. . risk of loss . . . 46.505
. . scope . . . 46.800
. on disposition of depreciable property or other capital assets . . . 31.205-16
. on other contracts . . . 31.205-23
. performance-based payments and . . . 32.1010
. progress payments and . . . 32.503-16

M

Maintenance and repair
. contractor's property management system . . . 45.105
. cost principles . . . 31.205-24

Major system acquisition
. acquisition planning . . . 7.106
. contract clauses and solicitation provisions
. . industrial resources developed under Defense Production Act, Title III . . . 34.104; 52.234-1
. earned value management system
. . contract clause and solicitation provisions . . . 34.203
. . integrated baseline reviews . . . 34.202

Major system acquisition—continued
. earned value management system—continued
. . policy . . . 34.201
. general
. . acquisition strategy . . . 34.004
. . competition . . . 34.005-1
. . concept exploration contracts . . . 34.005-3
. . definition . . . 34.001
. . demonstration contracts . . . 34.005-4
. . full production . . . 34.005-6
. . full-scale development contracts . . . 34.005-5
. . mission-oriented solicitation . . . 34.005-2
. . policy . . . 34.002
. . responsibilities . . . 34.003
. . scope . . . 34.000
. industrial resources—testing, qualification and use
. . contract clause prescription . . . 34.104
. . definitions . . . 34.101
. . policy . . . 34.102
. . scope . . . 34.100
. . testing and qualification . . . 34.103

Make-or-buy programs
. contract clauses . . . 15.408; 52.215-9
. general . . . 15.407-2

Management and operating contracts
. award . . . 17.605
. definition . . . 17.601
. extension . . . 17.605
. identifying . . . 17.604
. limitations . . . 17.603
. policy . . . 17.602
. renewal . . . 17.605
. scope . . . 17.600

Manufacturing and production engineering costs . . . 31.205-25

Market research
. about financing terms . . . 32.202-3
. commercial items acquisitions . . . 12.202; 32.202-2
. contract clause prescription . . . 10.003
. policy . . . 10.001
. procedures . . . 10.002
. scope . . . 10.000

Material safety data sheets . . . 23.302

Materials
. costs . . . 31.205-26
. government provision of
. . definition . . . 45.101

Matrix, contract clauses and solicitation provisions
. clauses and provisions . . . 52.301
. how to use . . . 52.101
. scope . . . 52.300

Methods of contracting—see also specific methods
. selection of method
. . construction and architect-engineer contracts . . . 36.103

Metric system, use of . . . 11.002

Micro-purchase threshold, acquisitions at or below
. emergency acquisitions . . . 18.201; 18.202
. general . . . 13.201
. purchase guidelines . . . 13.202
. unenforceability of unauthorized obligations . . . 13.202

Mission-oriented solicitation . . . 34.005-2

Mistakes
. in bids
. . apparent clerical mistakes . . . 14.407-2
. . general . . . 14.407-1
. . mistakes after award . . . 15.508; 14.407-4
. . other mistakes disclosed before award . . . 14.407-3
. negotiated procurement . . . 15.508

Modifications
. adjustments
. . administration of change orders . . . 43.204
. . change order accounting . . . 43.203
. . cost of performing changed work . . . 43.201
. . releases . . . 43.204
. change orders
. . accounting procedures . . . 43.203
. . administration . . . 43.204
. . authority to issue . . . 43.202
. . constructive change notification . . . 43.104
. . contract clause prescriptions . . . 43.205
. . contractor's statement of release . . . 43.204
. . definitization of . . . 43.204
. . documentation of . . . 43.204
. . general . . . 43.201
. contract clauses and solicitation provisions
. . change order accounting . . . 52.243-6
. . changes . . . 52.243-4
. . changes—cost-reimbursement . . . 52.243-2
. . changes—fixed-price . . . 52.243-1
. . changes—time-and-materials or labor-hours . . . 52.243-3
. . changes and changed conditions . . . 52.243-5
. . notification of changes . . . 52.243-7
. . prescriptions . . . 43.205
. definition . . . 52.101
. forms
. . contract modifications, SF 30 . . . 53.301-30
. . prescriptions . . . 53.243; 43.301
. of bids . . . 14.303; 14.304
. of contracts, generally
. . definition of administrative change . . . 43.101
. . funds availability . . . 43.105
. . notification of changes . . . 43.104
. . policy . . . 43.102
. . scope . . . 43.000
. . types . . . 43.103
. value engineering change proposals . . . 48.103

Motor vehicles
. contract clauses and solicitation provisions
. . condition of leased vehicles . . . 52.208-5
. . marking of leased vehicles . . . 52.208-6
. . prescriptions . . . 8.1104

Motor vehicles—continued
. contract clauses and solicitation provisions—continued
. . tagging of leased vehicles . . . 52.208-7
. . vehicle lease payments . . . 52.208-4
. leasing
. . contract requirements . . . 8.1103
. . definitions . . . 8.1101
. . presolicitation requirements . . . 8.1102
. . scope . . . 8.1100

Multi-agency contracts—see also Interagency acquisitions
. publicizing contract actions . . . 5.601

Multi-year contracting
. applicability . . . 17.102
. authority . . . 17.101
. congressional notification . . . 17.108
. contract clauses and solicitation provisions
. . cancellation under multi-year contracts . . . 17.109; 52.217-2
. . Fair Labor Standards Act and service contract labor standards—price adjustment (multiple year and option contracts) . . . 17.109; 52.222-43
. definitions . . . 17.103
. general . . . 17.104
. options . . . 17.107
. policy
. . objectives . . . 17.105-2
. . uses . . . 17.105-1
. procedures
. . general . . . 17.106-1
. . solicitations . . . 17.106-2
. . special procedures for DOD, NASA and Coast Guard . . . 17.106-3

N

NASA
. multi-year contracts . . . 17.106-3

National Response Plan . . . 18.204

National security—see also Emergency acquisitions
. waiver of competition requirements . . . 6.302-6

Negotiated procurement
. contract clauses and solicitation provisions
. . audit and records—negotiation . . . 15.209; 52.215-2
. . changes or additions to make-or-buy program . . . 15.408; 52.215-9
. . facilities capital cost of money . . . 15.408; 52.215-16
. . facsimile proposals . . . 15.209; 52.215-5
. . instructions to offerors—competitive acquisition . . . 15.209; 52.215-1
. . integrity of unit prices . . . 15.408; 52.215-14
. . limitations on pass-through charges . . . 52.215-23
. . limitations on pass-through charges; identification of subcontract effort . . . 52.215-22

Negotiated procurement—continued
. contract clauses and solicitation provisions—continued
. . notification of ownership changes . . . 15.408; 52.215-19
. . order of precedence—uniform contract format . . . 15.209; 52.215-8
. . place of performance . . . 15.209; 52.215-6
. . price reduction for defective cost or pricing data . . . 15.408
. . price reduction for defective cost or pricing data—modifications . . . 15.408
. . price reduction for defective certified cost or pricing data . . . 52.215-10
. . price reduction for defective certified cost or pricing data—modifications . . . 52.215-11
. . request for information or solicitation for planning purposes . . . 15.209; 52.215-3
. . requirements for cost or pricing data or information other than cost or pricing data—modifications . . . 15.408
. . requirements for cost or pricing data or information other than cost or pricing data . . . 15.408
. . requirements for certified cost or pricing data or information other than certified cost or pricing data . . . 52.215-20
. . requirements for certified cost or pricing data or information other than certified cost or pricing data—modifications . . . 52.215-21
. . subcontractor cost or pricing data . . . 15.408
. . subcontractor certified cost or pricing data . . . 52.215-12
. . subcontractor cost or pricing data—modifications . . . 15.408
. . subcontractor certified cost or pricing data—modifications . . . 52.215-13
. . termination of defined benefit pension plans . . . 15.408; 52.215-15
. . waiver of facilities capital cost of money . . . 15.408; 52.215-17
. contract format . . . 15.204
. . part I—the schedule . . . 15.204-2
. . part II—contract clauses . . . 15.204-3
. . part III——documents, exhibits, and other attachments . . . 15.204-4
. . part IV—representations and instructions . . . 15.204-5
. . uniform contract format . . . 15.204-1
. contract pricing
. . best value continuum . . . 15.101
. . certificate of current cost or pricing data . . . 15.406-2
. . circumstances where certified cost or pricing data not required . . . 15.403-2
. . contract clause and solicitation provision prescriptions . . . 15.408
. . defective certified cost or pricing data . . . 15.407-1
. . definitions . . . 15.401
. . estimating systems . . . 15.407-5
. . forward pricing rate agreements . . . 15.407-3

Negotiated procurement—continued
. contract pricing—continued
. . information other than cost or pricing data . . . 15.403-3; 15.403-5
. . instructions for submission of cost/price proposals . . . 15.408
. . instructions for submission of information other than cost or pricing data . . . 15.403-5
. . lowest price technically acceptable source selection process . . . 15.101-2
. . make-or-buy programs . . . 15.407-2
. . negotiation of . . . 36.214; 15.405
. . policy . . . 15.402
. . prohibition on obtaining certified cost or pricing data . . . 15.403-1
. . requiring certified cost or pricing data . . . 15.403-4
. . scope . . . 15.400
. . should-cost review . . . 15.407-4
. . tradeoff process . . . 15.101-1
. definitions . . . 15.001; 15.401; 15.601
. documentation
. . certificate of current cost or pricing data . . . 15.406-2
. . contents of . . . 15.406-3
. . prenegotiation objectives . . . 15.406-1
. forms
. . abstract of offers—construction, OF 1419 . . . 53.302-1419
. . abstract of offers—construction, SF 1410 . . . 53.301-1410
. . abstract of offers—continuation sheet, OF 1419A . . . 53.302-1419A
. . abstract of offers, SF 1409 . . . 53.301-1409
. . prescriptions . . . 53.215-1
. mistakes, discovery of after award . . . 15.508
. notifications
. . applicability . . . 15.502
. . award to successful offeror . . . 15.504
. . definition of day . . . 15.501
. . forms . . . 15.509
. . notifications to unsuccessful offerors . . . 15.503
. . postaward debriefing of offerors . . . 15.506
. . preaward debriefing of offerors . . . 15.505
. proposal analysis
. . data to support . . . 15.404-2
. . profit . . . 15.404-4
. . subcontract pricing considerations . . . 15.404-3
. . techniques . . . 15.404-1
. protests against award . . . 15.507
. scope . . . 15.000
. solicitation and receipt of proposals and information
. . advisory multi-step process . . . 15.202
. . amending the solicitation . . . 15.206
. . contract clause and solicitation provision prescriptions . . . 15.209
. . contract format . . . 15.204
. . exchanges with industry before receipt of proposals . . . 15.201
. . forms prescriptions . . . 15.210
. . handling proposals and information . . . 15.207

Negotiated procurement—continued
. solicitation and receipt of proposals and information—continued
. . issuing solicitations . . . 44.202; 15.205
. . requests for proposals (RFPs) . . . 15.203
. . scope . . . 15.200
. . submission, modification, revision, and withdrawal . . . 15.208
. . uniform contract format . . . 15.204-1
. source selection
. . best value continuum . . . 15.101
. . decision . . . 15.308
. . evaluation factors and significant subfactors . . . 15.304
. . exchanges with offerors after receipt of proposals . . . 15.306
. . lowest price technically acceptable source selection process . . . 15.101-2
. . objective . . . 15.302
. . oral presentations . . . 15.102
. . proposal evaluation . . . 15.305
. . proposal revisions . . . 15.307
. . responsibilities . . . 15.303
. . scope . . . 15.100; 15.300
. . tradeoff process . . . 15.101-1
. types of . . . 15.002
. types of contracts . . . 16.102
. unsolicited proposals
. . agency points of contact . . . 15.604
. . agency procedures . . . 15.606
. . content of . . . 15.605
. . criteria for acceptance and negotiation . . . 15.607
. . definitions . . . 15.601
. . evaluation . . . 15.606-2
. . general . . . 15.603
. . limitations on use of data . . . 15.609
. . policy . . . 15.602
. . prohibitions . . . 15.608
. . receipt and initial review . . . 15.606-1
. . scope . . . 15.600

Nonpersonal health care services
. contract clause prescription . . . 37.403
. contracting officer responsibilities . . . 37.402
. policy . . . 37.401
. scope . . . 37.400

Nonprofit organizations
. agencies employing blind or severely disabled people
. . allocation process . . . 8.705-3
. . change-of-name and successor in interest procedures . . . 8.716
. . communications with central nonprofit agencies and the Committee . . . 8.714
. . compliance with orders . . . 8.705-4
. . definitions . . . 8.701
. . direct-order process . . . 8.705-2
. . general . . . 8.702
. . optional acquisition of supplies and services . . . 8.713
. . payments . . . 8.709

Nonprofit organizations—continued
. agencies employing blind or severely disabled people—continued
. . prices . . . 8.707
. . procurement list . . . 8.703
. . purchase exceptions . . . 8.706
. . purchase priorities . . . 8.704
. . purchase procedures . . . 8.705-1
. . quality complaints . . . 8.711
. . quality of merchandise . . . 8.710
. . replacement commodities . . . 8.715
. . responsible prospective contractors, identifying . . . 9.107
. . scope . . . 8.700
. . shipping . . . 8.708
. . specification changes . . . 8.712
. cost principles and procedures
. . applicability . . . 31.108
. . general . . . 31.702
. . purpose . . . 31.701
. . requirements . . . 31.703
. federally funded research and development centers
. . establishing or changing an FFRDC . . . 35.017-2
. . limitation on the creation of new FFRDCs . . . 35.017-7
. . master list . . . 35.017-6
. . policy . . . 35.017
. . review . . . 35.017-4
. . sponsoring agreements . . . 35.017-1
. . termination . . . 35.017-5
. . use . . . 35.017-3
. indirect cost rates . . . 42.705-5
. research and development contracts
. . broad agency announcement . . . 35.016
. . federally funded research and development centers . . . 35.017
. . general . . . 35.015

North American Free Trade Agreements—see also Foreign acquisitions; Trade agreements
. emergency acquisitions, use of patented technology . . . 18.120

North American Industry Classification System (NAICS) . . . 19.303

Notices—see also Contract clauses and solicitation provisions
. award of contract . . . 14.408-1
. congressional notification of multi-year contracts . . . 17.108
. delays of . . . 32.615
. employment of veterans . . . 22.1306
. employment of workers with disabilities . . . 22.1404
. improper wage determination before award . . . 22.404-8
. negotiated procurement
. . award to successful offeror . . . 15.504
. . forms . . . 15.509
. . notifications to unsuccessful offerors . . . 15.503
. . postaward debriefing of offerors . . . 15.506
. . preaward debriefing of offerors . . . 15.505

Notices—see also Contract clauses and solicitation provisions—continued
. notification of overpayment . . . 32.008
. of subcontracting opportunities . . . 5.206
. ownership changes . . . 15.408; 52.215-19
. preaward . . . 15.503
. presolicitation . . . 5.204; 14.205
. radioactive material delivery . . . 23.601; 23.602
. rejection of bids . . . 14.404-3
. simplified acquisition procedures . . . 13.106-3
. special notices . . . 5.205
. termination . . . 49.102
. under service contract labor standards statute . . . 22.1010
. service contract labor standards statute . . . 22.1018

Novation and change-of-name agreements
. applicability . . . 42.1204
. definition . . . 2.101
. form prescriptions . . . 53.242-1
. formats
. . contractor's change of name . . . 42.1205
. . novation agreement . . . 42.1204
. processing . . . 42.1203
. responsibility for execution . . . 42.1202
. scope . . . 42.1200

O

Occupational Safety and Health Administration
. hazardous material and material safety . . . 23.302

Occupational safety—see also Environment and conservation programs
. drug-free workplace
. . applicability . . . 23.501
. . authority . . . 23.502
. . definitions . . . 23.504
. . policy . . . 23.504
. . scope . . . 23.500
. . solicitation provisions and contract clauses . . . 23.505
. . suspension of payments, termination of contracts, debarment and suspension actions . . . 23.506
. encouraging contractor policies to ban text messaging while driving
. . contract clause prescription . . . 23.1105
. . contractor policy . . . 52.223-18
. . definitions . . . 23.1103
. . policy . . . 23.1104
. . purpose . . . 23.1101
. hazardous material and material safety
. . contract clause prescription . . . 23.303
. . definition . . . 23.301
. . policy . . . 23.302
. . scope . . . 23.300
. radioactive material, notice of
. . contract clause prescription . . . 23.602
. . requirements . . . 23.601

Office of Federal Procurement Policy Act . . . 3.104-2; 3.104-3

Office of Management and Budget (OMB)
. OMB control numbers . . . 1.106

Options
. buying-in prevention . . . 3.501-2
. contract clauses and solicitation provisions
. . evaluation exclusive of options . . . 52.217-3
. . evaluation of options . . . 52.217-5
. . evaluation of options exercised at time of contract award . . . 52.217-4
. . option for increased quantity . . . 52.217-6
. . option for increased quantity—separately priced line item . . . 52.217-7
. . option to extend services . . . 52.217-8
. . option to extend term of contract . . . 52.217-9
. . prescriptions . . . 17.208
. contract specifications . . . 17.204
. documentation . . . 17.205
. evaluation . . . 17.206
. exercise of . . . 17.207
. in multi-year contracts . . . 17.107
. scope . . . 17.200
. solicitations . . . 17.203
. uses . . . 17.202

Oral presentations by offerors . . . 15.102

Oral solicitations
. requests for proposals . . . 15.203
. simplified acquisition procedures . . . 13.106-3

Ordering agreements . . . 16.703

Organization costs . . . 31.205-27

Organizational conflicts of interest
. applicability . . . 9.502
. contract clause prescription . . . 9.507-2
. contracting officer responsibilities . . . 9.504
. definition of marketing consultant . . . 9.501
. evaluation services . . . 9.505-3
. examples . . . 9.508
. preparation of specifications or work statements . . . 9.505-2
. procedures . . . 9.506
. proprietary information, obtaining access to . . . 9.505-4
. scope . . . 9.500
. solicitation provisions . . . 9.507-1
. systems engineering and technical direction . . . 9.505-1
. waiver . . . 9.503

Overpayment, commercial items acquisition . . . 12.214

Overtime—see also Labor laws
. approvals . . . 22.103-4
. construction contracts . . . 22.406-2
. contract clause prescriptions . . . 22.305; 22.103-5
. definition of normal workweek . . . 22.103-1
. emergency acquisitions . . . 18.118
. policy . . . 22.103-2
. procedures . . . 22.103-3
. uncompensated . . . 37.115

Overtime—see also Labor laws—continued
. under contract work hours and safety standards statute . . . 22.302

Ownership changes, notification of . . . 15.408; 52.215-19

Ozone-depleting substances
. authorities . . . 23.801
. contract clause prescriptions . . . 23.804
. policy . . . 23.803
. scope . . . 23.800

P

Paper documents
. contract clause prescription . . . 4.303
. definition . . . 4.301
. policy . . . 4.302
. scope . . . 4.300

Paperwork Reduction Act of 1980 (PL 96-511)
. OMB control numbers . . . 1.106

Partnerships, contract signatures . . . 4.102

Patent rights under government contracts
. administration of patent rights clauses
. . administration by government . . . 27.305-2
. . goals . . . 27.305-1
. . protection of invention disclosures . . . 27.305-4
. . securing invention rights acquired by government . . . 27.305-3
. contract clauses . . . 27.303
. definitions . . . 27.301
. licensing background patent rights to third parties . . . 27.306
. policy . . . 27.302
. procedures
. . appeals . . . 27.304-4
. . contracts placed by or for government agencies . . . 27.304-2
. . generally . . . 27.304-1
. . subcontracts . . . 27.304-3

Patents and copyrights
. infringement liability
. . contract clauses . . . 27.201-2
. . generally . . . 27.201-1
. patent technology under trade agreements
. . use of patent technology under GATT . . . 27.204-2
. . use of patent technology under NAFTA . . . 27.204-1
. royalty
. . adjustment . . . 27.202-3
. . notice of government as licensee . . . 27.202-2
. . refund . . . 27.202-4
. . reporting . . . 27.202-1
. security requirements for patent applications containing classified subject matter
. . contract clause . . . 27.203-2
. . generally . . . 27.203-1

Payments—see also Advance payments
. commercial items purchases . . . 32.202-2

Payments—see also Advance payments—continued
. contract clauses and solicitation provisions
. . advance payments . . . 32.412; 52.232-12
. . assignment of claims . . . 32.806; 52.232-23
. . availability of funds . . . 52.232-18; 32.706-1
. . availability of funds for the next fiscal year . . . 52.232-19; 32.706-1
. . discounts for prompt payment . . . 32.111; 52.232-8
. . extras . . . 52.232-11
. . interest . . . 32.617; 52.232-17
. . limitation of cost . . . 32.704; 52.232-20; 32.705-2
. . limitation of cost (facilities) . . . 32.704; 32.705-2
. . limitation of funds . . . 32.704; 52.232-22; 32.705-2
. . limitation on withholding of payments . . . 32.111; 52.232-9
. . notice of availability of progress payments exclusively for small business concerns . . . 52.232-14; 32.502-3
. . notice of progress payments . . . 52.232-13; 32.502-3
. . payment by EFT—system for award management . . . 32.1110; 52.232-33
. . payment under communication service contracts with common carriers . . . 32.111; 52.232-6
. . payments . . . 32.111; 52.232-1
. . payments under fixed-price architect-engineer contracts . . . 32.111; 52.232-10
. . payments under fixed-price construction contracts . . . 32.111; 52.232-5
. . payments under fixed-price research and development contracts . . . 32.111; 52.232-2
. . payments under personal services contracts . . . 32.111; 52.232-3
. . payments under time-and-materials and labor-hour contracts . . . 32.111; 52.232-7
. . payments under transportation and transportation-related services contracts . . . 32.111; 52.232-4
. . progress payments . . . 52.232-16; 32.502-4
. . progress payments not included . . . 52.232-15; 32.502-3
. . prohibition of assignment of claims . . . 32.806; 52.232-24
. . prompt payment . . . 32.908; 52.232-25
. . prompt payment for construction contracts . . . 32.908; 52.232-27
. . prompt payment for fixed-price architect-engineer contracts . . . 32.908; 52.232-26
. . providing accelerated payments to small business contractors . . . 52.232-40
. contract debts . . . 32.610
. dismantling, demolition, or removal of improvements . . . 37.303
. due dates . . . 32.007; 32.904
. electronic funds transfer
. . applicability . . . 32.1103
. . assignment of claims . . . 32.1105
. . definitions . . . 32.1102
. . EFT information submitted by offerors . . . 32.1109
. . EFT mechanisms . . . 32.1106

Payments—see also Advance payments—continued
. electronic funds transfer—continued
. . payment by governmentwide commercial purchase card . . . 32.1108
. . payment information . . . 32.1107
. . protection of information . . . 32.1104
. . scope . . . 32.1100
. . solicitation provisions and contract clauses . . . 32.1110
. . statutory requirements . . . 32.1101
. fast payment procedure
. . conditions for use . . . 13.402
. . contract clause . . . 13.404; 52.213-1
. . general . . . 13.401
. . preparation and execution of orders . . . 13.403
. forms
. . partial payment, application, SF 1440 . . . 53.301-1440
. . public voucher for purchases and services other than personal, SF 1034 . . . 53.301-1034
. . public voucher for purchases and services other than personal, SF 1034-A, memorandum copy . . . 53.301-1034A
. . public voucher for purchases and services other than personal, continuation sheet, SF 1035 . . . 53.301-1035
. . receipt for cash—subvoucher, SF 1165 . . . 53.301-1165
. imprest funds and third party drafts
. . agency responsibilities . . . 13.305-2
. . conditions for use . . . 13.305-3
. . definition . . . 13.001
. . general . . . 13.305-1
. . procedures . . . 13.305-4
. notification of overpayment . . . 32.008
. payments to small business subcontractors . . . 52.242-6
. performance-based payments
. . administration and payment . . . 32.1007
. . bases for payments . . . 32.1002
. . contract clause and solicitation provision . . . 32.1005; 52.232-32
. . criteria for use . . . 32.1003
. . policy . . . 32.1001
. . procedures . . . 32.1004
. . risk of loss . . . 32.1010
. . scope . . . 32.1000
. . suspension or reduction of payments . . . 32.1008
. . title . . . 32.1009
. prompt payment
. . applicability . . . 32.901
. . contract clause prescriptions . . . 32.908
. . contractor inquiries . . . 32.909
. . definitions . . . 32.902
. . determining payment due dates . . . 32.904
. . interest penalties . . . 32.907
. . making payments . . . 32.906
. . payment documentation and process . . . 32.905
. . responsibilities . . . 32.903
. . scope . . . 32.900

Payments—see also Advance payments—continued
. reduction or suspension upon finding of fraud
. . general . . . 32.006-1
. . procedures . . . 32.006-4
. . reporting . . . 32.006-5
. . responsibilities . . . 32.006-3
. termination of contracts
. . final payment . . . 49.112-2
. . partial payments . . . 49.112-1
. withholding
. . construction contracts . . . 22.406-9
. . contract debt collection . . . 32.612
. . sureties and . . . 28.106-7
. . under Drug-Free Workplace Act . . . 23.506
. . under service contract labor standards statute . . . 22.1022

Payroll administration
. construction contracts . . . 22.406-6
. contract clause and solicitation provision prescriptions . . . 22.407
. forms
. . payroll (for contractor's optional use), Form WH-347 (DOL) . . . 53.303-WH
. records retention period . . . 4.705-2

Penalties
. civil . . . 3.807; 3.104-8
. cost principles . . . 31.205-15
. criminal . . . 3.104-8
. definition . . . 31.205-47
. indirect cost rates
. . assessment . . . 42.709-3
. . computation of interest . . . 42.709-4
. . contract clause prescription . . . 42.709-6
. . general . . . 42.709-1
. . responsibilities . . . 42.709-2
. . scope . . . 42.709
. . waiver . . . 42.709-5
. interest penalties . . . 32.907
. on unallowable costs . . . 31.110
. prohibited practices
. . limitation on payment of funds to influence federal transactions . . . 3.807
. . procurement integrity . . . 3.104-8
. . safeguards and standards of conduct . . . 3.104-8

Pensions
. adjustments . . . 15.408; 52.215-15
. cost principles . . . 31.205-6

Performance-based service acquisition
. definition . . . 37.101
. general . . . 37.601
. performance standards . . . 37.603
. performance work statement . . . 37.602
. quality assurance . . . 37.604
. scope . . . 37.600

Performance incentives . . . 16.402-2

Personal services
. compensation costs . . . 31.205-6
. contracting for . . . 37.104

Personal services—continued
. cost principles . . . 31.205-6

Plant equipment
. definition . . . 45.101

Plant protection costs . . . 31.205-29

Plant reconversion costs . . . 31.205-31

Political activity costs . . . 31.205-22

Postaward debriefing . . . 15.506

Postaward orientation
. conference arrangements . . . 42.503-1
. conference procedure . . . 42.503-2
. conference report . . . 42.503-3
. contract selection . . . 42.502
. general . . . 42.501
. letters . . . 42.504
. preconstruction orientation . . . 36.212
. scope . . . 42.500
. subcontractor conferences . . . 42.505

Postaward progress payments
. accounting system review . . . 32.503-3
. adjustments for price reduction . . . 32.503-11
. administration of . . . 32.503-5
. application of government title terms . . . 32.503-15
. approval of requests . . . 32.503-4
. establishment of alternate liquidation rates . . . 32.503-10
. initiation of . . . 32.503-3
. liquidation rates—alternate method . . . 32.503-9
. liquidation rates—ordinary method . . . 32.503-8
. maximum unliquidated amount . . . 32.503-12
. protection of government title . . . 32.503-14
. risk of loss . . . 32.503-16
. supervision of . . . 32.503-2
. suspension or reduction of payments . . . 32.503-6

Postretirement benefits—see also Pensions
. contract clause prescriptions . . . 15.408; 52.215-15; 52.215-18

Pre-bid conferences . . . 14.207

Preaward debriefing . . . 15.505

Preaward notices . . . 15.503

Preaward progress payments
. contract clause prescriptions . . . 32.502-4
. contract finance office clearance . . . 32.502-2
. solicitation provisions . . . 32.502-3
. use of customary progress payments . . . 32.502-1

Preaward surveys
. conditions for . . . 9.106-1
. definition of surveying activity . . . 9.101
. determinations and documentation . . . 9.105-2
. disclosure of preaward information . . . 9.105-3
. interagency . . . 9.106-3
. obtaining information . . . 9.105-1
. reports . . . 9.106-4
. requests for . . . 9.106-2

Precontract costs . . . 31.205-32

Prenegotiation objectives . . . 15.404-4; 15.406-1

Prescription . . . 53.222; 53.222
. request for determination and response to request, SF 308 (DOL) . . . 53.301-308
. under service contract labor standards statute . . . 22.1004
. under Service Contract Labor Standards statute
. . cooperation with . . . 22.1024
. . discovery of errors . . . 22.1015

Presolicitation notices
. advisory multi-step process . . . 15.202
. components of . . . 14.205
. synopsis of proposed contract actions . . . 5.204

Price and pricing—see also Indirect cost rates
. antitrust violations reporting requirements . . . 3.303
. as factor in selection of contract type . . . 16.104
. best value continuum . . . 15.101
. . lowest price technically acceptable . . . 15.101-2
. . tradeoff process . . . 15.101-1
. commercial items acquisition . . . 12.209
. construction contracts . . . 36.214
. evaluation of sealed bids . . . 14.201-8
. evaluation preference for historically underutilized business zone (HUBZone) program . . . 19.1307
. Federal Supply Schedules . . . 8.405-4
. forward pricing rate agreements . . . 42.1701; 15.407-3
. independent pricing certification
. . evaluation . . . 3.103-2
. . further certification . . . 3.103-3
. independent pricing certification provision . . . 3.103-1; 52.203-2
. instructions for submission of cost/price proposals . . . 15.408
. labor disputes and . . . 22.101-2
. negotiated procurements
. . best value continuum . . . 15.101
. . certificate of current cost or pricing data . . . 15.406-2
. . circumstances where certified cost or pricing data not required . . . 15.403-2
. . contract clauses and solicitation provisions . . . 15.408
. . defective certified cost or pricing data . . . 15.407-1
. . definitions . . . 15.401
. . estimating systems . . . 15.407-5
. . forward pricing rate agreements . . . 15.407-3
. . data other than certified cost or pricing data . . . 15.403-3
. . instructions for submission of information other than certified cost or pricing data . . . 15.403-5
. . lowest price technically acceptable source selection process . . . 15.101-2
. . make-or-buy programs . . . 15.407-2
. . negotiation of . . . 36.214; 15.405
. . policy . . . 15.402
. . prohibition on obtaining certified cost or pricing data . . . 15.403-1

Price and pricing—see also Indirect cost rates— continued
. negotiated procurements—continued
. . requirements for certified cost or pricing data . . . 15.403-4
. . scope . . . 15.400
. . should-cost review . . . 15.407-4
. . tradeoff process . . . 15.101-1
. prospective price redetermination, fixed-price contracts
. . application . . . 16.205-2
. . contract clause . . . 16.205-4; 52.216-5
. . description . . . 16.205-1
. . limitations . . . 16.205-3
. reasonableness as factor in award of contract . . . 14.408-2
. reductions . . . 32.503-11
. small business considerations . . . 19.202-6
. standing price quotations . . . 13.103
. transportation costs . . . 47.306-1; 47.306-2
. unpriced purchase orders . . . 13.302-2

Printing or copying documents
. contract clause . . . 4.303; 52.204-4
. definition . . . 4.301
. policy . . . 4.302

Priorities and allocations
. contract clauses and solicitation provisions
. . defense priority and allocation requirements . . . 52.211-15
. definitions
. . authorized program . . . 11.601
. . controlled materials . . . 11.601
. . delegate agency . . . 11.601
. . rated order . . . 11.601
. emergency acquisitions . . . 18.109
. general . . . 11.602
. procedures . . . 11.603

Privacy protection
. contract clauses and solicitation provisions
. . Privacy Act . . . 24.104; 52.224-2
. . Privacy Act notification . . . 24.104; 52.224-1
. . privacy training . . . 52.224-3
. definitions . . . 24.101
. electronic funds transfer . . . 32.1104
. general . . . 24.102
. privacy training . . . 24.301
. privacy training, contract clause prescription . . . 24.302
. procedures . . . 24.103
. scope . . . 24.000

Private sector temporaries . . . 37.112

Procurement Integrity Act . . . 3.104-2; 3.104-3

Production engineering costs . . . 31.205-25

Production surveillance and reporting
. applicability . . . 42.1102
. contract clause . . . 42.1107; 52.242-2
. criticality designator . . . 42.1105

Production surveillance and reporting—continued
. general . . . 42.1101
. policy . . . 42.1103
. reporting requirements . . . 42.1106
. requirements . . . 42.1104

Professional employee compensation
. applicability . . . 22.1101
. definition of professional employee . . . 22.1102
. policy . . . 22.1103
. procedures . . . 22.1103
. solicitation provision . . . 22.1103

Profit
. fixed-price contracts terminated for convenience . . . 49.202
. negotiation objectives . . . 15.404-4

Progress payments based on costs—see also Contract financing
. construction contracts . . . 32.103
. contract price as limitation . . . 32.501-3
. customary rates . . . 32.501-1
. forms
. . request form, SF 1443 . . . 53.301-1443
. guarantees, protective terms . . . 32.501-5
. postaward matters . . . 32.503
. . adjustments for price reduction . . . 32.503-11
. . administration of payments . . . 32.503-5
. . application of government title terms . . . 32.503-15
. . approval of requests . . . 32.503-4
. . establishment of alternate liquidation rates . . . 32.503-10
. . initiation . . . 32.503-3
. . liquidation rates—alternate method . . . 32.503-9
. . liquidation rates—ordinary method . . . 32.503-8
. . maximum unliquidated amount . . . 32.503-12
. . protection of government title . . . 32.503-14
. . review of contractor accounting system . . . 32.503-3
. . risk of loss . . . 32.503-16
. . supervision of payments . . . 32.503-2
. . suspension or reduction of payments . . . 32.503-6
. preaward matters . . . 32.502
. . contract clause prescriptions . . . 32.502-4
. . contract finance office clearance . . . 32.502-2
. . solicitation provisions . . . 32.502-3
. . use of customary progress payments . . . 32.502-1
. scope . . . 32.500
. subcontracts . . . 32.504
. unusual payments . . . 32.501-2

Prohibited practices
. agency regulations . . . 3.101-3
. antitrust violations
. . definitions . . . 3.302
. . general . . . 3.301
. . reporting . . . 3.303
. buying-in
. . definition . . . 3.501-1
. . general . . . 3.501-2

Prohibited practices—continued
. contingent fees
. . applicability . . . 3.403
. . contract clause . . . 3.404; 52.203-5
. . definitions . . . 3.401
. . record preservation . . . 3.406
. . scope . . . 3.400
. . statutory requirements . . . 3.402
. . violation of covenant . . . 3.405
. contract clauses and solicitation provisions
. . anti-kickback procedures . . . 52.203-7; 3.502-3
. . cancellation, rescission, and recovery of funds for illegal or improper activity . . . 3.104-9; 52.203-8
. . certificate of independent price determination . . . 3.103-1; 52.203-2
. . certification and disclosure regarding payments to influence certain federal transactions . . . 3.808; 52.203-11
. . covenant against contingent fees . . . 3.404; 52.203-5
. . gratuities . . . 3.202; 52.203-3
. . limitation on payments to influence certain federal transactions . . . 3.808; 52.203-12
. . price or fee adjustment for illegal or improper activity . . . 3.104-9; 52.203-10
. . restrictions on subcontractor sales to the government . . . 52.203-6; 3.503-2
. contracting with inverted domestic corporations
. . definition . . . 9.108-1
. . prohibition . . . 9.108-3
. . relationship with Internal Revenue Code and Treasury regulations . . . 9.108-2
. . solicitation provision . . . 52.209-2
. . solicitation provision prescription . . . 9.108-5
. . waiver . . . 9.108-4
. contracts with government employees . . . 3.601
. . contracting officer's responsibility . . . 3.603
. . exceptions . . . 3.602
. . policy . . . 3.601
. definition . . . 3.501-1
. fraud . . . 33.209; 32.006-3
. general . . . 3.501-2
. government records retention . . . 3.406
. gratuities
. . applicability . . . 3.201
. . contract clause prescription . . . 3.202
. . reporting suspected violations . . . 3.203
. . standards of conduct . . . 3.101-2
. . violations . . . 3.204
. independent pricing certification
. . further certification . . . 3.103-3
. . rejection of bids and offers . . . 3.103-2
. . solicitation provision . . . 3.103-1; 52.203-2
. kickbacks, subcontractors
. . contract clause prescription . . . 3.502-3
. . definitions . . . 3.502-1
. . general . . . 3.502-2
. limitation on payment of funds to influence federal transactions
. . certification and disclosure . . . 3.803

Prohibited practices—continued
. limitation on payment of funds to influence federal transactions—continued
. . civil penalties . . . 3.807
. . contract clause prescription . . . 3.808
. . definitions . . . 3.801
. . exemption . . . 3.805
. . policy . . . 3.804
. . processing suspected violations . . . 3.806
. . prohibitions . . . 3.802
. . scope . . . 3.800
. procurement integrity
. . contract clause prescriptions . . . 3.104-9
. . criminal and civil penalties, and further administrative remedies . . . 3.104-8
. . definitions . . . 3.104-1
. . disclosure, protection, and marking of contractor bid or proposal information and source selection information . . . 3.104-4
. . disqualification . . . 3.104-5
. . ethics advisory opinions regarding prohibitions on a former official's acceptance of compensation from contractor . . . 3.104-6
. . general . . . 3.104-2
. . postemployment restrictions applicable to government officers and employees . . . 3.104-7
. . statutory and related prohibitions, restrictions, and requirements . . . 3.104-3
. . violations or possible violations . . . 3.104-7
. reporting requirements . . . 33.209; 32.006-3
. restrictions on subcontractor sales to government
. . contract clause prescription . . . 3.503-2
. . policy . . . 3.503-1
. safeguards and standards of conduct
. . administrative remedies . . . 3.104-8
. . agency regulations . . . 3.101-3
. . certification . . . 3.103-2; 3.103-3
. . contract clause prescriptions . . . 3.104-9
. . criminal and civil penalties . . . 3.104-8
. . definitions . . . 3.104-1
. . disclosure, protection, and marking of contractor bid . . . 3.104-4
. . disqualification . . . 3.104-5
. . ethics advisory opinions . . . 3.104-6
. . general . . . 3.101-1; 3.104-2
. . gratuities . . . 3.101-2
. . solicitation provision . . . 3.103-1; 52.203-2
. . statutory and related prohibitions, restrictions, and requirements . . . 3.104-3
. . violations or possible violations . . . 3.104-7
. scope . . . 3.000
. voiding and rescinding contracts
. . authority . . . 3.703
. . definition . . . 3.702
. . policy . . . 3.704
. . procedures . . . 3.705
. . purpose . . . 3.701
. . scope . . . 3.700

Prohibited practices—continued
. whistleblower protections for contractor employees
. . American Recovery and Reinvestment Act . . . 3.907
. . filing complaints . . . 3.904
. . investigating complaints . . . 3.905
. . policy . . . 3.903
. . remedies . . . 3.906
. . scope . . . 3.900
. whistleblower protections for contractor employees pilot program
. . scope . . . 3.908-1
. . policy . . . 3.908-3
. . filing complaints . . . 3.908-4
. . procedures for investigating complaints . . . 3.908-5
. . enforcement of orders . . . 3.908-5
. . remedies . . . 3.908-6
. . enforcement of orders . . . 3.908-7
. . classified information . . . 3.908-8
. . contract clause . . . 3.908-9
. . definitions . . . 3.908-2

Project labor agreements for construction
. definitions . . . 22.502
. general requirements . . . 22.504
. notice of requirement for project labor agreement clause . . . 52.222-33
. policy . . . 22.503
. project labor agreement clause . . . 52.222-34
. scope of subpart . . . 22.501
. solicitation provision and contract clause prescription . . . 22.505

Prompt payments—see also Payments
. applicability . . . 32.901
. contract clause prescriptions . . . 32.908
. contractor inquiries . . . 32.909
. definitions . . . 32.902
. determining payment due dates . . . 32.904
. discounts as factor in award of contract . . . 14.408-3
. interest penalties . . . 32.907
. making payments . . . 32.906
. payment documentation and process . . . 32.905
. responsibilities . . . 32.903
. scope . . . 32.900

Proposal analysis, negotiated procurement
. data to support . . . 15.404-2
. profit . . . 15.404-4
. subcontract pricing considerations . . . 15.404-3
. techniques . . . 15.404-1

Prospective price redetermination, fixed-price contracts
. application . . . 16.205-2
. contract clause . . . 16.205-4; 52.216-5
. description . . . 16.205-1
. limitations . . . 16.205-3

Protests—see also Contract disputes
. against award
. . negotiated procurement . . . 15.507
. . sealed bidding . . . 14.408-8

Protests—see also Contract disputes—continued
. against disadvantaged business status . . . 19.305
. against HUBZone status . . . 19.306
. against service-disabled veteran-owned small business status . . . 19.307
. against small business representation . . . 19.302
. contract clauses and solicitation provisions
. . protest after award . . . 33.106; 52.233-3
. . service of protest . . . 33.106; 52.233-2
. court-related authorities . . . 33.001
. definitions . . . 33.101
. emergency acquisitions . . . 18.125
. general . . . 33.102
. protesting firm's status as EDWOSB concern . . . 19.308
. protesting firm's status as WOSB eligible concern . . . 19.308
. protests at Court of Federal Claims . . . 33.105
. protests to General Accountability Office . . . 33.104
. . override for urgent and compelling circumstances . . . 18.125
. protests to the agency . . . 33.103
. scope . . . 33.000

Public interest, waiver of competition requirements . . . 6.302-7

Public Law 85-804
. applicability . . . 32.405
. disputes statute . . . 33.205
. indemnification under . . . 52.250-1

Public participation, solicitation of
. definition . . . 1.501-1
. exceptions . . . 1.501-3
. opportunity for public comments . . . 1.501-2
. public meetings . . . 1.503
. solicitation of agency and public views . . . 1.501
. unsolicited proposed revisions . . . 1.502

Public-private competitions . . . 5.205

Public relations and advertising costs . . . 31.110; 31.205-1

Publicizing contract actions
. American Recovery and Reinvestment Act requirements
. . applicability . . . 5.702
. . definitions . . . 5.703
. . publicizing-post-award . . . 5.705
. . publicizing preaward . . . 5.704
. . scope of subpart . . . 5.701
. architect-engineer contracts . . . 36.601-1, 5
. congressional requests for information . . . 5.403
. definition of contract action . . . 5.001
. disclosure of justification and approval documents for noncompetitive contracts . . . 5.406
. exchange of acquisition information . . . 5.405
. forms prescription . . . 53.205-1
. Freedom of Information Act . . . 24.201
. governmentwide point of entry . . . 5.003
. information dissemination
. . availability of solicitations . . . 5.102

Publicizing contract actions—continued
. information dissemination—continued
. . methods . . . 5.101
. information release
. . general . . . 5.401
. . long-range acquisition estimates . . . 5.404
. . requests from Members of Congress . . . 5.403
. . to general public . . . 5.402
. long-range acquisition estimates . . . 5.404
. . announcements . . . 5.404-2
. . release procedures . . . 5.404-1
. multi-agency use contracts . . . 5.601
. paid advertisements
. . advertising agency use . . . 5.504
. . authority . . . 5.502
. . definitions . . . 5.501
. . procedures . . . 5.503
. policy . . . 5.002
. research and development contracts . . . 35.004
. scope . . . 5.000
. sealed bidding . . . 14.101
. synopses of contract awards
. . announcement of awards . . . 5.303
. . general . . . 5.301
. . preparation and transmittal . . . 5.302
. synopses of proposed contract actions
. . exceptions . . . 5.202
. . general . . . 5.201
. . notices of subcontracting opportunities . . . 5.206
. . preparation and transmittal . . . 5.207
. . presolicitation notices . . . 5.204
. . procedures and response time . . . 5.203
. . special situations . . . 5.205

Purchase orders—see also Blanket purchase agreements
. contract clauses and solicitation provisions
. . invoices . . . 52.213-2
. . notice to supplier . . . 52.213-3
. . prescriptions . . . 13.302-5
. forms
. . purchase order—invoice—voucher, SF 44 . . . 13.306; 53.301-44
. general . . . 13.302-1
. modifying . . . 13.302-3
. obtaining contractor acceptance . . . 13.302-3
. on-the-spot purchases . . . 13.306
. termination or cancellation . . . 13.302-4
. unpriced . . . 13.302-2

Q

Qualifications requirements
. acquisitions subject to . . . 9.206-1
. changes in status . . . 9.207
. competition and . . . 9.206-3
. contract clause . . . 9.206-2; 52.209-1
. definitions . . . 9.201
. emergency acquisitions . . . 18.109
. establishment of qualification requirement . . . 9.204
. general . . . 9.206-1

Qualifications requirements—continued
. omission from list . . . 9.207
. policy . . . 9.202
. qualification before award . . . 9.205
. qualified bidders list . . . 9.201; 9.203
. qualified manufacturers list . . . 9.201; 9.203
. qualified products list (QPL) . . . 2.101; 9.203
. removal from list . . . 9.207
. scope . . . 9.200

Qualified bidders list (QBL) . . . 9.201; 9.203

Qualified manufacturers list (QML) . . . 9.201; 9.203

Qualified products list (QPL) . . . 2.101; 9.203

Quality assurance—see also Acceptance of performance; First article testing and approval; Warranties
. acceptance
. . certificate of conformance . . . 46.504
. . general . . . 46.501
. . place of . . . 46.503
. . responsibility for . . . 46.502
. . risk of loss . . . 46.505
. . transfer of title . . . 46.505
. commercial items acquisition . . . 12.208; 46.202-1
. contract administration office responsibilities . . . 46.104
. contract clauses and solicitation provisions
. . certificate of conformance . . . 46.315; 52.246-15
. . construction contracts . . . 46.312; 52.246-12
. . contractor inspection requirements . . . 46.301; 52.246-1
. . cost-reimbursement research and development contracts . . . 46.308; 52.246-8
. . cost-reimbursement service contracts . . . 46.305; 52.246-5
. . cost-reimbursement supply contracts . . . 46.303; 52.246-3
. . dismantling, demolition, or removal of improvement contracts . . . 46.313; 52.246-13
. . fixed-price research and development contracts . . . 46.307; 52.246-7
. . fixed-price service contracts . . . 46.304; 52.246-4
. . fixed-price supply contracts . . . 46.302; 52.246-2
. . higher-level contract quality requirement . . . 46.311; 52.246-11
. . limitation of liability . . . 46.805; 52.246-23
. . limitation of liability—high-value items . . . 46.805; 52.246-24
. . limitation of liability—services . . . 46.805; 52.246-25
. . research and development contracts (short form) . . . 46.309; 52.246-9
. . responsibility for supplies . . . 46.316; 52.246-16
. . time-and-material and labor-hour contracts . . . 46.306; 52.246-6
. . transportation contracts . . . 46.314; 52.246-12
. contracting office responsibilities . . . 46.103
. contractor responsibilities . . . 46.105
. definitions . . . 46.101

Quality assurance—see also Acceptance of performance; First article testing and approval; Warranties—continued
. general . . . 46.401
. inclusion in solicitations . . . 46.201
. liability for loss or damage to government property
. . applicability . . . 46.801
. . definition of high-value item . . . 46.802
. . policy . . . 46.803
. . risk of loss . . . 46.505
. . scope . . . 46.800
. material inspection and receiving reports . . . 46.601
. policy . . . 46.102
. requirements and inspection
. . acquisitions at or below simplified acquisition threshold . . . 46.404
. . at destination . . . 46.403
. . at source . . . 46.402
. . contracts for commercial items . . . 12.208; 46.202-1
. . criteria for use . . . 46.203
. . foreign governments or international agencies . . . 46.406
. . general . . . 46.201
. . government inspection . . . 46.401
. . government reliance on inspection by contractor . . . 46.202-2
. . higher-level requirements . . . 46.202-4
. . inspection by contractor . . . 46.301; 52.246-2
. . inspection by contractor, government reliance . . . 46.202-2
. . material inspection and receiving reports . . . 46.601
. . medical supplies, food, and seafood . . . 46.408
. . nonconforming supplies or services . . . 46.407
. . single-agency assignments . . . 46.408
. . standard inspection requirements . . . 46.202-3
. . subcontracts . . . 46.405
. . types . . . 46.202
. scope . . . 46.000

Quantity, economic
. contracting officers' responsibilities . . . 7.204
. policy . . . 7.202; 14.212
. scope . . . 7.200
. solicitation provision prescription . . . 7.203

Quantity variation
. construction contracts . . . 11.702
. contract clauses and solicitation provisions
. . delivery of excess quantities . . . 11.703; 52.211-17
. . variation in estimated quantity . . . 11.703; 52.211-18
. . variation in quantity . . . 11.703; 52.211-16
. supply contracts . . . 11.701

Quick-closeout procedure . . . 42.708

Quotations, legal effect of . . . 13.004

R

Radioactive material, notice of
. contract clause . . . 23.602; 52.223-7

Radioactive material, notice of—continued
. requirements . . . 23.601

Rate tenders
. citation of . . . 47.104-5
. contract clause prescription . . . 47.104-4
. cost-reimbursement contracts . . . 47.104-3
. fixed-price contracts . . . 47.104-2
. procedures . . . 47.104-1
. under Interstate Commerce Act . . . 47.104

Real property
. acceptance for bond obligations . . . 28.203-3

Records and recording
. government contract files
. . closeout by the office administering the contract . . . 4.804-1
. . closeout if another office administers the contract . . . 4.804-2
. . closeout of paying office files . . . 4.804-3
. . closeout procedures . . . 4.804-5
. . contents . . . 4.803
. . documentation requirements . . . 13.501
. . general . . . 4.801
. . physically completed contracts . . . 4.804-4
. . scope . . . 4.800
. . storage, handling, and disposal . . . 4.805
. . types of files . . . 4.802
. government property, reporting . . . 45.600
. invitations for bids and bids . . . 14.204
. retention
. . acquisition and supply records . . . 4.705-3
. . applicability . . . 4.702
. . calculation of retention periods . . . 4.704
. . construction contracts pay administration records . . . 4.705-2
. . financial and cost accounting records . . . 4.705-1
. . government contract files . . . 4.805
. . policy . . . 4.703
. . purpose . . . 4.701
. . scope . . . 4.700
. . simplified acquisition procedures . . . 13.106-3
. . specific retention periods . . . 4.705

Recovered materials
. agency affirmative procurement programs . . . 23.404
. authorities . . . 23.402
. contract clauses and solicitation provisions
. . estimate of percentage of recovered material content for EPA designated products . . . 23.406; 52.223-9
. . recovered materials certification . . . 23.406; 52.223-4
. definition of EPA-designated product . . . 23.401
. policy . . . 23.403
. procedures . . . 23.405
. scope . . . 23.400
. solicitation provision prescription . . . 23.406

Recruitment costs . . . 31.205-34

Relocation costs . . . 31.205-35

Remedies—see also Penalties
. child labor violations . . . 22.1504
. cost accounting standards . . . 30.604; 30.605
. Federal Supply Schedules nonconformance . . . 8.406-3
. improper business practices . . . 3.104-8
. postaward disclosure of mistakes . . . 14.407-4
. protests to General Accountability Office . . . 33.104
. reduction or suspension of payments for finding of fraud . . . 32.006-4
. trafficking violations . . . 22.1704
. Whistleblower protections . . . 3.906

Rental costs
. contractor use of government property
. . authorizing use of government production and research property . . . 45.303
. . contracts with foreign governments or international organizations . . . 45.302
. . policy . . . 45.600
. . scope . . . 45.600
. cost principles . . . 31.205-36
. emergency acquisitions . . . 18.126

Reporting requirements
. American Recovery and Reinvestment Act
. . contract clause . . . 52.204-11
. . contract clause prescription . . . 4.1502
. . procedures . . . 4.1501
. . scope of subpart . . . 4.1500
. construction contracts . . . 22.406-13
. general requirements . . . 4.602
. foreign acquisition . . . 25.004
. fraud . . . 33.209; 32.006-3
. government property . . . 45.600
. policy . . . 4.603
. procedures . . . 4.605
. definitions . . . 4.601
. reporting contract information to the IRS . . . 4.903
. reporting data . . . 4.606
. reporting executive compensation and first-tier subcontractor awards
. . applicability . . . 4.1401
. . contract clause prescription . . . 4.1403
. . contract clause . . . 52.204-10
. . implementation . . . 4.1400
. . procedures . . . 4.1402
. reporting payment information to the IRS . . . 4.904
. responsibilities . . . 4.604
. scientific and technical reports . . . 35.010
. scope . . . 4.600
. service contracts inventory
. . applicability . . . 4.1702
. . contract clause . . . 52.204-14
. . contract clause, indefinite-delivery contracts . . . 52.204-15
. . contract clause prescriptions
. . contracting officer responsibilities . . . 4.1704
. . definitions . . . 4.1701
. . requirements . . . 4.1703
. . scope . . . 4.1700

Reporting requirements—continued
. small business participation . . . 19.202-5
. solicitation provisions
. . data universal numbering system number . . . 52.204-6
. . data universal numbering system number maintenance . . . 52.204-12
. . prescriptions . . . 4.607
. . women-owned business (other than small business) . . . 52.204-5
. toxic chemical release reporting
. . applicability . . . 23.903
. . contract clause and solicitation provision . . . 23.903
. . definition of toxic chemical . . . 23.001
. . general . . . 23.902
. . policy . . . 23.902
. . purpose . . . 23.901
. . requirements . . . 23.1004

Requests for information (RFIs) . . . 15.201

Requests for proposals and quotations—see also Bid solicitation
. forms
. . request for quotations, SF 18 . . . 53.301-18
. negotiated acquisitions . . . 15.203
. oral, emergency acquisitions . . . 18.111
. research and development contracts . . . 35.017

Required sources
. contract clauses and solicitation provisions
. . contractor use of mandatory sources of supply . . . 8.005; 52.208-9
. . fleet management system (IFMS) vehicles and related services . . . 51.205; 52.251-2
. . government supply sources . . . 51.107; 52.251-1
. . helium required sources and helium usage data . . . 8.505; 52.208-8
. . motor vehicle lease prescriptions . . . 8.1104
. contractor performance evaluation . . . 8.406-7
. contractor use of government supply sources
. . assistance to contractors . . . 51.104
. . authorization to use . . . 51.102
. . contract clause prescription . . . 51.107
. . ordering . . . 51.103
. . payment for shipments . . . 51.105
. . policy . . . 51.101
. . scope . . . 51.100
. . title to property . . . 51.106
. excess personal property
. . information on availability . . . 8.103
. . obtaining nonreportable property . . . 8.104
. . policy . . . 8.102
. Federal Prison Industries, Inc.
. . evaluation of performance . . . 8.606
. . exceptions . . . 8.605
. . general . . . 8.601
. . nonmadatory source . . . 18.106
. . performance as a subcontractor . . . 8.607
. . policy . . . 8.602
. . protection of classified and sensitive information . . . 8.608

Required sources—continued
. Federal Prison Industries, Inc.—continued
. . purchase priorities . . . 8.603
. . waivers . . . 8.604; 18.106
. Federal Supply Schedules
. . applicability . . . 8.403
. . blanket purchase agreements (BPAs) . . . 8.405-3
. . coordination requirements . . . 38.201
. . definitions . . . 8.401
. . description . . . 38.101
. . disputes . . . 8.406-6
. . emergency acquisitions . . . 18.105
. . general . . . 8.402
. . inspection and acceptance . . . 8.406-2
. . limited sources justification and approval . . . 8.405-6
. . nonmandatory source . . . 18.106
. . order placement . . . 8.406-1
. . ordering procedures . . . 8.405-1; 8.405-2
. . payment . . . 8.405-7
. . price reductions . . . 8.405-4
. . remedies for nonconformance . . . 8.406-3
. . scope . . . 38.000
. . small businesses, ordering from . . . 8.405-5
. . termination for cause . . . 8.406-4
. . termination for government's convenience . . . 8.406-5
. . use of . . . 8.404
. forms prescription . . . 53.251
. general
. . contract clause prescription . . . 8.005
. . priorities for use . . . 8.002
. . scope . . . 8.000
. . use of other sources . . . 8.004
. . use of other mandatory sources . . . 8.003
. helium acquisition
. . contract clause . . . 8.505; 52.208-8
. . definitions . . . 8.501
. . exception . . . 8.503
. . policy . . . 8.502
. . procedures . . . 8.504
. . scope . . . 8.500
. information technology acquisitions . . . 8.001
. interagency fleet management system (IFMS)
. . authorization . . . 51.202
. . contract clause prescription . . . 51.205
. . means of obtaining service . . . 51.203
. . policy . . . 51.201
. . scope . . . 51.200
. . use requirements . . . 51.204
. motor vehicle leasing
. . contract clause prescriptions . . . 8.1104
. . contract requirements . . . 8.1103
. . definitions . . . 8.1101
. . presolicitation requirements . . . 8.1102
. . scope . . . 8.1100
. nonprofit agencies employing blind or severely disabled people
. . allocation process . . . 8.705-3

Required sources—continued
. nonprofit agencies employing blind or severely disabled people—continued
. . change-of-name and successor in interest procedures . . . 8.716
. . communications with central nonprofit agencies and the Committee . . . 8.714
. . compliance with orders . . . 8.705-4
. . definitions . . . 8.701
. . direct-order process . . . 8.705-2
. . general . . . 8.702
. . optional acquisition of supplies and services . . . 8.713
. . payments . . . 8.709
. . prices . . . 8.707
. . procurement list . . . 8.703
. . purchase exceptions . . . 8.706
. . purchase priorities . . . 8.704
. . purchase procedures . . . 8.705-1
. . quality complaints . . . 8.711
. . quality of merchandise . . . 8.710
. . replacement commodities . . . 8.715
. . scope . . . 8.700
. . shipping . . . 8.708
. . specification changes . . . 8.712
. other government supply sources . . . 8.003
. printing and related supplies
. . definitions . . . 8.801
. . policy . . . 8.802
. . scope . . . 8.800

Requirements contracts . . . 16.503

Requirements documents
. contract clause and solicitation provision prescriptions . . . 11.107; 11.204
. customer satisfaction . . . 11.203
. identification and availability of specifications . . . 11.201
. items peculiar to one manufacturer . . . 11.105
. maintenance of standardization documents . . . 11.202
. market acceptance . . . 11.103
. order of precedence . . . 11.101
. service contracts, purchase descriptions for . . . 11.106
. standardization program . . . 11.102
. use of brand name or equal purchase descriptions . . . 11.104

Research and development contracting
. broad agency announcement (BBA) . . . 35.016
. contract clauses and solicitation provisions
. . quality assurance . . . 46.307; 46.308
. contract types . . . 35.006
. contracting methods . . . 35.006
. costs
. . deferred . . . 31.205-48
. . independent, cost principles . . . 31.205-18
. data . . . 35.011
. definitions . . . 35.001; 35.017
. educational institutions . . . 35.015

Research and development contracting—continued
. evaluation for award . . . 35.008
. expanding sources . . . 35.004
. federally funded research and development centers
. . establishing or changing an FFRDC . . . 35.017-2
. . limitation on the creation of new FFRDCs . . . 35.017-7
. . master list . . . 35.017-6
. . policy . . . 35.017
. . review . . . 35.017-4
. . sponsoring agreements . . . 35.017-1
. . termination . . . 35.017-5
. . use . . . 35.017-3
. forms
. . prescription . . . 53.235
. general . . . 35.002
. government production and research property, use of . . . 45.303
. government property and title . . . 35.014
. independent research and development
. . cost principles . . . 31.205-18
. insurance . . . 35.013
. nonprofit organizations . . . 35.015
. policy . . . 35.003
. pools
. . contracting with . . . 9.702
. . definition of pool . . . 9.701
. . individual pool members, contracting with . . . 9.703
. publicizing requirements . . . 35.004; 5.205
. scientific and technical reports . . . 35.010
. scope . . . 35.000
. solicitations . . . 35.007
. subcontracting . . . 35.009
. work statement . . . 35.005

Responsibility of prospective contractors
. applicability . . . 9.102
. award factor . . . 14.408-2
. certificates of competency . . . 19.601
. definition . . . 9.101
. policy . . . 9.103
. procedures for determining responsibility
. . determinations and documentation . . . 9.105-2
. . disclosure of preaward information . . . 9.105-3
. . information regarding responsibility matters . . . 52.209-7
. . interagency preaward surveys . . . 9.106-3
. . obtaining information . . . 9.105-1
. . preaward surveys . . . 9.106-1
. . referral to Small Business Administration . . . 19.601
. . reports . . . 9.106-4
. . requests for preaward surveys . . . 9.106-2
. . surveys of nonprofit agencies participating in the AbilityOne Program . . . 9.107
. . updates of publicly available information regarding responsibility matters . . . 52.209-9
. prohibition on contracting with an entity involved in activities that violate arms control treaties or agreements with the United States . . . 9.109
. . authority . . . 9.109-1

Responsibility of prospective contractors—continued
. prohibition on contracting with an entity involved in activities that violate arms control treaties or agreements with the United States—continued
. . certification by offeror . . . 9.109-4
. . exception . . . 9.109-3
. . prohibition . . . 9.109-2
. . solicitation provision prescription . . . 9.109-5
. small business . . . 19.601
. standards of responsibility
. . application of standards . . . 9.104-3
. . certification regarding responsibility matters . . . 9.104-5
. . certification responsibility, solicitation provision . . . 9.104-7
. . Federal Awardee Performance and Integrity Information System . . . 9.104-6
. . general standards . . . 9.104-1
. . special standards . . . 9.104-2
. . subcontractor responsibility . . . 9.104-4

Responsiveness of bids
. contract clauses and solicitation provisions
. . bid guarantee . . . 28.101-2; 52.228-1
. criteria . . . 14.301
. reasons for rejection of bids . . . 14.404-2
. . all or none qualifications . . . 14.404-5
. . minor informalities or irregularities . . . 14.405

Retroactive price redetermination, fixed-price contracts
. application . . . 16.206-2
. contract clauses
. . economic price adjustment—standard supplies . . . 16.203-4; 52.216-2
. . price redetermination—retroactive . . . 16.206-4; 52.216-6
. description . . . 16.206-1
. limitations . . . 16.206-3

Reutilization and disposal of government property
. abandonment or destruction
. . excess personal property . . . 45.603
. sale of surplus personal property
. . sales procedures . . . 45.604-1
. disposal of surplus property
. . proceeds from sales . . . 45.604-3
. . use of GSA sponsored sales . . . 45.604-2
. . sale of property pursuant to sale or exchange . . . 45.604-4; 45.604-4
. inventory disposal reports . . . 45.605
. inventory disposal schedules . . . 45.602-1
. scope . . . 45.600
. scrap disposal
. . contractor with an approved scrap procedure . . . 45.606
. . procedures . . . 45.606-3

Right in data and copyrights
. acquisition of data . . . 27.406
. . additional data requirements . . . 27.406-2

Right in data and copyrights—continued
. acquisition of data—continued
. . generally . . . 27.406-1
. . major system acquisition . . . 27.406-3
. basic rights in data clause . . . 27.404
. . contractor's release, publication, and use of data . . . 27.404-4
. . copyrighted works . . . 27.404-3
. . inspection of data at contractor's facility . . . 27.404-6
. . limited rights data and restricted computer software . . . 27.404-2
. . unauthorized, omitted, or incorrect makings . . . 27.404-5
. . unlimited rights data . . . 27.404-1
. cospsored research and development activities . . . 27.408
. data rights, generally . . . 27.403
. definitions . . . 27.401
. other data rights provisions . . . 27.405
. . commercial computer software . . . 27.405-3
. . existing works . . . 27.405-4
. . other existing data . . . 27.405-4
. . special works . . . 27.405-1
. policy . . . 27.402
. rights to technical data in successful proposals . . . 27.407
. solicitation provisions and contract clauses . . . 27.409

Right-to-know laws and pollution prevention requirements
. applicability . . . 23.1002
. authorities . . . 23.1001
. contract clause prescription . . . 23.1005
. definition . . . 23.1003
. requirements . . . 23.1004
. scope . . . 23.1000

Royalties
. adjustment . . . 27.202-3
. contract clause prescriptions . . . 27.201-2; 27.204-2
. cost principles . . . 31.205-37
. general . . . 27.204-1
. notice of government as licensee . . . 27.202-3
. refund . . . 27.202-4

S

Salaries and wages . . . 31.205-6

Salvage or scrap
. disposal
. . contractor with approved procedure . . . 45.606
. . procedures . . . 45.606-3

Sanctions
. definitions . . . 25.003
. protests to General Accountability Office . . . 33.104

Sealed bidding
. advance payments . . . 32.405

Sealed bidding—continued
. bid submission
. . disclosure, protection, and marking of bids . . . 3.700; 3.104-4
. . modification or withdrawal of bids . . . 14.303; 14.304
. . procedure . . . 14.302
. . responsiveness of bids . . . 14.301
. competition requirements . . . 6.401
. construction contracting
. . general . . . 36.103; 36.213-1
. . invitation for bids . . . 36.213-3
. . notice of award . . . 36.213-4
. . presolicitation notices . . . 36.213-2
. contract clauses and solicitation provisions
. . amendments to invitations for bids . . . 52.214-3
. . audit and records—sealed bidding . . . 52.214-26
. . bid samples . . . 52.214-20
. . contract award—sealed bidding . . . 52.214-10
. . contract award—sealed bidding—construction . . . 52.214-19
. . descriptive literature . . . 52.214-21
. . evaluation of bids for multiple awards . . . 52.214-22
. . explanation to prospective bidders . . . 52.214-6
. . facsimile bids . . . 52.214-31
. . false statements in bids . . . 52.214-4
. . late submissions, modifications, and withdrawals of technical proposals under two-step sealed bidding . . . 52.214-23
. . late submissions, modifications, and withdrawals of bids . . . 52.214-7
. . minimum bid acceptance period . . . 52.214-16
. . multiple technical proposals . . . 52.214-24
. . order of precedence—sealed bidding . . . 52.214-29
. . period for acceptance of bids . . . 52.214-15
. . place of performance—sealed bidding . . . 52.214-14
. . preparation of bids . . . 52.214-12
. . preparation of bids—construction . . . 52.214-18
. . prescriptions . . . 14.201-6; 14.201-7
. . price reduction for defective certified cost or pricing data—modifications—sealed bidding . . . 52.214-27
. . subcontractor certified cost or pricing data—modifications—sealed bidding . . . 52.214-28
. . submission of bids . . . 52.214-5
. . submission of offers in the English language . . . 52.214-34
. . submission of offers in U.S. currency . . . 52.214-35
. form prescriptions . . . 53.214
. general
. . elements of . . . 14.101
. . limitations . . . 14.103-2
. . policy . . . 14.103-1
. . scope . . . 14.000
. . solicitations for informational or planning purposes . . . 14.105
. . types of contracts . . . 14.104
. minor informalities or irregularities . . . 14.405

Sealed bidding—continued
. mistakes in bids
. . apparent clerical mistakes . . . 14.407-2
. . general . . . 14.407-1
. . mistakes after award . . . 14.407-4
. . other mistakes disclosed before award . . . 14.407-3
. opening of bids
. . classified bids . . . 14.402-2
. . postponement of openings . . . 14.402-3
. . unclassified bids . . . 14.402-1
. receipt and safeguarding of bids . . . 14.401
. recording of bids . . . 14.204; 14.403
. rejection of bids
. . all or none qualifications . . . 14.404-5
. . cancellation after opening . . . 14.404-1
. . disclosure of descriptive literature . . . 14.404-4
. . notice to bidders . . . 14.404-3
. . rejection of individual bids . . . 14.404-2
. two-step sealed bidding
. . conditions for use . . . 14.502
. . general . . . 14.501
. . step one . . . 14.503-1
. . step two . . . 14.503-2
. types of contracts . . . 16.102
. unreadable electronic bids . . . 14.406

Secretariat, FAR . . . 1.201-2

Section 8(a) program
. acceptance of offer . . . 19.804-3
. agency evaluation . . . 19.804-1
. agency offering . . . 19.804-2
. appeals . . . 19.810
. basic ordering agreements . . . 19.804-5
. competitive acquisitions
. . contract negotiation . . . 19.808-2
. . contract preparation . . . 19.811-2
. . general . . . 19.805-1
. . procedures . . . 19.805-2
. . publicizing contract actions . . . 5.205
. . requirements . . . 6.204
. contract administration . . . 19.812
. contract clause prescriptions . . . 19.811-3
. contract negotiation
. . competitive . . . 19.808-2
. . sole source . . . 19.808-1
. contract preparation
. . competitive . . . 19.811-2
. . contract clause prescriptions . . . 19.811-3
. . sole source . . . 19.811-1
. estimating fair market price . . . 19.807
. Federal Supply Schedule contracts . . . 19.804-6
. general . . . 19.800
. multiple awards . . . 19.804-6
. preaward considerations . . . 19.809
. pricing . . . 19.806
. repetitive acquisitions . . . 19.804-4
. selecting acquisitions . . . 19.803
. selecting concerns . . . 19.802
. sole source contracts . . . 19.808-1; 19.811-1

Security—see also Privacy protection
. advance payments and . . . 32.409-3
. dismantling, demolition, or removal of improvements . . . 37.302
. for government financing . . . 32.202-4
. guaranteed loans . . . 32.304-2; 32.304-6

Selection of contractors—see also Contractors
. architect-engineer services
. . collection of qualification data . . . 36.603
. . evaluation boards . . . 36.602-2
. . functions of evaluation board . . . 36.602-3
. . negotiations . . . 36.606
. . performance evaluation use . . . 36.604
. . qualifications of firms . . . 36.603
. . release of information . . . 36.607
. . selection authority . . . 36.602-4
. . selection criteria . . . 36.602-1
. . short selection process . . . 36.602-5
. responsible prospective contractors, identifying
. . applicability . . . 9.102
. . application of standards . . . 9.104-3
. . certification regarding responsibility matters . . . 9.104-5
. . certification responsibility, solicitation provision . . . 9.104-7
. . definition of surveying activity . . . 9.101
. . determinations and documentation . . . 9.105-2
. . disclosure of preaward information . . . 9.105-3
. . Federal Awardee Performance and Integrity Information System . . . 9.104-6
. . general responsibility standards . . . 9.104-1
. . general standards . . . 9.104
. . obtaining information . . . 9.105-1
. . policy . . . 9.103
. . preaward survey reports . . . 9.106-4
. . preaward surveys, conditions for . . . 9.106-1
. . preaward surveys, interagency . . . 9.106-3
. . preaward surveys, requests for . . . 9.106-2
. . scope . . . 9.100
. . special standards . . . 9.104-2
. . subcontractor responsibility . . . 9.104-4
. . surveys of nonprofit agencies participating in the AbilityOne Program . . . 9.107

Selling costs . . . 31.205-38

Service and warranty costs . . . 31.205-39

Service contract labor standards (formerly Service Contract Act of 1965)
. additional classes of service employees . . . 22.1019
. applicability . . . 22.1003
. . administrative limitation, variations, tolerances, and exemptions . . . 22.1003-4
. . examples of contracts covered . . . 22.1003-5
. . general . . . 22.1003-1
. . geographical coverage . . . 22.1003-2
. . questions concerning . . . 22.1003-7
. . repair distinguished from remanufacturing of equipment . . . 22.1003-6
. . statutory exemptions . . . 22.1003-3

Service contract labor standards (formerly Service Contract Act of 1965)—continued
. contract clause . . . 52.222-41; 52.222-49
. contract clause, exemption . . . 52.222-48; 52.222-51; 52.222-52; 52.222-53
. cooperation with the Department of Labor . . . 22.1024
. definitions . . . 22.1001
. delay of acquisition dates over 60 days . . . 22.1014
. Department of Labor responsibilities and regulations . . . 22.1004
. discovery of errors by Department of Labor . . . 22.1015
. disputes concerning labor standards . . . 22.1026
. general . . . 37.107
. ineligibility of violators . . . 22.1025
. notification to contractors and employees . . . 22.1018
. notification to interested parties under collective bargaining agreements . . . 22.1010
. place of performance unknown, procedures . . . 22.1009
. . all possible places of performance identified . . . 22.1009-3
. . all possible places of performance not identified . . . 22.1009-4
. . attempt to identify possible places of performance . . . 22.1009-2
. . general . . . 22.1009-1
. contract clause prescriptions . . . 22.1006
. request for hearings . . . 22.1021
. review of wage determination . . . 22.1013
. revisions to wage determinations . . . 22.1012
. . prevailing wage determinations . . . 22.1012-1
. . wage determinations based on collective bargaining agreements . . . 22.1012-2
. scope . . . 22.1000
. seniority lists . . . 22.1020
. statement of equivalent rates for federal hires . . . 22.1016
. statutory and Executive order requirements . . . 22.1002
. statutory requirements
. . Executive Order 13658 . . . 22.1002-5
. . Fair Labor Standards Act minimum wage . . . 22.1002-4
. . general . . . 22.1002-1
. . wage determinations based on collective bargaining agreements . . . 22.1002-3
. . wage determinations based on prevailing rates . . . 22.1002-2
. termination for default . . . 22.1023
. wage determinations
. . procedures for obtaining . . . 22.1008-1
. . requirements . . . 22.1007
. . revisions to . . . 22.1012
. . 41 USC 6707(c)successorship with incumbent contractor collective bargaining agreement . . . 22.1008-2
. withholding of contract payments . . . 22.1022

Service contracting—see also Required sources; Service contract labor standards
. advisory and assistance services
. . contracting officer responsibilities . . . 37.205
. . definition of covered personnel . . . 37.201
. . exclusions . . . 37.202
. . guidelines for determining availability of personnel . . . 37.204
. . policy . . . 37.203
. . scope . . . 37.200
. contract clauses and solicitation provisions
. . affirmative procurement of EPA-designated items in service and construction contracts . . . 52.223-17
. . commencement, prosecution, and completion of work . . . 11.404; 52.211-10
. . continuity of services . . . 37.110; 52.237-3
. . delivery or performance schedules . . . 11.404; 52.211-10
. . desired and required time of delivery . . . 11.404; 52.211-9
. . identification of uncompensated overtime . . . 37.115-3; 52.237-10
. . incremental payment by contractor to government . . . 37.304; 52.237-6
. . indemnification and medical liability insurance . . . 37.403; 52.237-7
. . payment by contractor to government . . . 37.304; 52.237-5
. . payment by government to contractor . . . 37.304; 52.237-4
. . protection of government buildings, equipment, and vegetation . . . 37.110; 52.237-2
. . quality assurance . . . 46.304; 46.305; 52.246-4; 52.246-5
. . restriction on severance payments to foreign nationals . . . 37.113-2; 52.237-8
. . service contract labor standards . . . 22.1006; 52.222-41
. . service contract labor standards—place of performance unknown . . . 22.1006; 52.222-49
. . site visit . . . 37.110; 52.237-1
. . time of delivery . . . 11.404; 52.211-8
. . waiver of limitation on severance payments to foreign nationals . . . 37.113-2; 52.237-9
. contracting-out policy . . . 37.102
. delivery or performance schedules . . . 11.403
. dismantling, demolition or removal of improvements
. . bonds or other security . . . 37.302
. . contract clause prescriptions . . . 37.304
. . forms . . . 36.701
. . labor standards . . . 37.301
. . payments . . . 37.303
. . scope . . . 37.300
. forms
. . order for supplies or services, OF 347 . . . 53.302-347
. . order for supplies or services schedule, continuation sheet, OF 348 . . . 53.302-348
. . request for authorization of additional classification and rate, SF 1444 . . . 53.301-1444

Service contracting—see also Required sources; Service contract labor standards—continued
. funding . . . 32.703-2
. general
. . competition . . . 37.105
. . contracting officer's responsibility . . . 37.103
. . definitions . . . 37.101
. . extension of services . . . 37.111
. . funding and term of service contracts . . . 37.106
. . government use of private sector temporaries . . . 37.112
. . personal services contracts . . . 37.104
. . policy . . . 37.102
. . quasi-military armed forces for hire . . . 37.109
. . service contract labor standards . . . 37.107
. . small business Certificate of Competency . . . 37.108
. indemnification and medical liability insurance
. . prescription . . . 37.403
. management oversight
. . agency head responsibilities . . . 37.503
. . contracting officials' responsibilities . . . 37.504
. . definition of best practices . . . 37.501
. . exclusions . . . 37.502
. . scope . . . 37.500
. nonpersonal health care services
. . contract clause prescription . . . 37.403
. . contracting officer responsibilities . . . 37.402
. . policy . . . 37.401
. . scope . . . 37.400
. performance-based acquisition
. . definition . . . 37.101
. . general . . . 37.601
. . performance standards . . . 37.603
. . performance work statement . . . 37.602
. . quality assurance . . . 37.604
. . scope . . . 37.600
. scope . . . 37.000
. service contracts inventory
. . applicability . . . 4.1702
. . contract clause . . . 52.204-14
. . contract clause, indefinite-delivery contracts . . . 52.204-15
. . contract clause prescriptions . . . 4.1705
. . contracting officer responsibilities . . . 4.1704
. . definitions . . . 4.1701
. . reporting requirements . . . 4.1703
. . scope . . . 4.1700
. severance payments to foreign nationals
. . solicitation provision and contract clause . . . 37.113-2
. . waiver of cost allowability limitations . . . 37.113-1
. special acquisition requirements . . . 37.114
. uncompensated overtime
. . general policy . . . 37.115-2
. . scope . . . 37.115-1
. . solicitation provision . . . 37.115-3
. value engineering
. . contract clauses . . . 48.201
. . sharing acquisition savings . . . 48.104-2

Service-disabled veteran-owned small business concerns
. definition . . . 2.101; 19.307
. emergency acquisitions . . . 18.116
. procurement program
. . applicability . . . 19.1402
. . contract clause . . . 19.1407; 52.219-27
. . exclusions . . . 19.1404
. . general . . . 19.1401
. . set-aside procedures . . . 19.1405
. . sole source awards . . . 19.1406
. . status determination . . . 19.1403
. protesting status as . . . 19.307
. set-asides . . . 6.206; 19.506

Services directory . . . 42.203

Set-asides
. automatic dissolution . . . 19.507
. class set-asides . . . 19.503
. contract clause and solicitation provision prescriptions . . . 19.508
. economically disadvantaged women-owned small business concerns . . . 6.207
. emergency assistance activities . . . 26.202-1
. Federal Prison Industries, Inc . . . 19.504
. general . . . 19.501, 6
. historically underutilized business zone (HUBZone) program . . . 19.1305; 6.205
. insufficient causes not to set aside . . . 19.502-6
. local firms during disasters or emergencies . . . 6.207
. methods of conducting . . . 19.502-5
. modification . . . 19.506
. multiple award contracts and small business set-asides . . . 19.502-4
. partial set-asides . . . 19.502-3
. rejection of recommendations to set aside . . . 19.505
. requirements for setting aside acquisitions . . . 19.502-1
. service-disabled veteran-owned small businesses . . . 19.1403; 6.206
. total set-asides . . . 19.502-2
. withdrawal . . . 19.506
. women-owned small business program eligible concern . . . 6.207

Setoffs . . . 32.611; 32.612

Severance pay . . . 31.205-6

Should-cost review . . . 15.407-4

Show cause notice . . . 49.607

Signatory authority
. contracting officer's signature . . . 4.101
. contractor's signature . . . 4.102
. determinations and findings . . . 1.707

Simplified acquisition procedures
. actions at or below micro-purchase threshold
. . general . . . 13.201
. . purchase guidelines . . . 13.202
. . unenforceability of unauthorized obligations . . . 13.202

Simplified acquisition procedures—continued
. blanket purchase agreements (BPAs)
. . completion of . . . 13.303-7
. . contract clause prescriptions . . . 13.303-4; 13.303-8
. . establishment of . . . 13.303-2
. . general . . . 13.303-1
. . optional clause . . . 13.303-8
. . preparation of . . . 13.303-3
. . purchases under . . . 13.303-5
. . review procedures . . . 13.303-6
. commercial items acquisition
. . general . . . 12.601
. . streamlined evaluation of offers . . . 12.602
. . streamlined solicitation . . . 12.603
. contract clauses and solicitation provisions
. . invoices . . . 52.213-2
. . notice to supplier . . . 52.213-3
. . prescriptions . . . 13.302-5
. contract financing . . . 32.003
. emergency acquisitions . . . 18.201; 18.202
. fast payment procedure
. . conditions for use . . . 13.402
. . contract clause prescription . . . 13.404
. . general . . . 13.401
. . preparation and execution of orders . . . 13.403
. Federal Acquisition Streamlining Act of 1994
. . inapplicable provisions and clauses . . . 13.006
. . list of laws inapplicable to contracts and subcontracts at or below the simplified acquisition threshold . . . 13.005
. forms prescription . . . 53.213; 13.307
. general
. . definitions . . . 13.001
. . legal effect of quotations . . . 13.004
. . policy . . . 13.003
. . purpose . . . 13.002
. . scope . . . 13.000
. imprest funds and third party drafts
. . agency responsibilities . . . 13.305-2
. . conditions for use . . . 13.305-3
. . general . . . 13.305-1
. . procedures . . . 13.305-4
. methods
. . contract clause prescriptions . . . 13.302-5
. . governmentwide commercial purchase card . . . 13.301
. . obtaining contractor acceptance and modifying purchase orders . . . 13.302-3
. . purchase orders, general . . . 13.302-1
. . termination or cancellation of purchase orders . . . 13.302-4
. . unpriced purchase orders . . . 13.302-2
. on-the-spot purchases . . . 13.306
. procedures
. . award and documentation . . . 13.106-3
. . evaluation of quotations or offers . . . 13.106-2
. . general . . . 13.101
. . promoting competition . . . 13.104
. . solicitation of competition . . . 13.106-1

Simplified acquisition procedures—continued
. procedures—continued
. . source list . . . 13.102
. . synopsis and posting requirements . . . 13.105
. . use of standing price quotations . . . 13.103
. purchase order—invoice—voucher, SF 44 . . . 13.306
. quality assurance . . . 46.404
. test program, commercial items
. . general . . . 13.500
. . special documentation requirements . . . 13.501

Site inspection
. construction contracts . . . 36.210
. contract clauses and solicitation provisions . . . 36.503; 52.236-3

Small and Disadvantaged Business Utilization . . . 19.401

Small Business Administration (SBA)
. agency cooperation with . . . 19.401
. breakout procurement center representatives . . . 19.403
. emergency acquisitions . . . 18.114
. procurement center representatives . . . 19.402
. rejecting recommendations of . . . 19.505
. Section 8(a) program
. . agency evaluation . . . 19.804-1
. . agency offering . . . 19.804-2
. . appeals . . . 19.810
. . basic ordering agreements . . . 19.804-5
. . competitive awards . . . 19.805-1; 19.805-2
. . competitive contracts . . . 19.808-2; 19.811-2
. . contract administration . . . 19.812
. . contract clause prescriptions . . . 19.811-3
. . contract negotiation . . . 19.808-1; 19.808-2
. . contract preparation . . . 19.811-1; 19.811-2
. . estimating fair market price . . . 19.807
. . Federal Supply Schedule contracts . . . 19.804-6
. . general . . . 19.800
. . multiple awards . . . 19.804-6
. . preaward considerations . . . 19.809
. . pricing . . . 19.806
. . repetitive acquisitions . . . 19.804-4
. . SBA acceptance of offer . . . 19.804-3
. . selecting acquisitions . . . 19.803
. . selecting concerns . . . 19.802
. . sole source contracts . . . 19.808-1; 19.811-1
. size standards
. . application . . . 19.102
. . explanation of terms . . . 19.101
. subcontracting . . . 19.707

Small business programs
. awards to economically disadvantaged women-owned small business concern . . . 18.117
. awards to women-owned small business program eligible concerns . . . 18.117
. certificates of competency
. . awarding the contract . . . 19.602-4
. . eligibility determinations . . . 19.601
. . general . . . 19.601

Small business programs—continued
. certificates of competency—continued
. . issuing or denying . . . 19.602-2
. . referral . . . 19.602-1
. . resolving differences . . . 19.602-3
. contract clauses and solicitation provisions
. . equal low bids . . . 19.309; 52.219-2
. . incentive subcontracting program . . . 52.219-10
. . limitations on subcontracting . . . 19.508; 52.219-14
. . liquidated damages—subcontracting plan . . . 19.708; 52.219-16
. . notice of partial small business set-aside . . . 19.508; 52.219-7
. . notice of price evaluation preference for HUBZone small business concerns . . . 19.1309; 52.219-4
. . notice of price evaluation preference for small disadvantaged business concerns . . . 19.1309
. . notice of set-aside of orders . . . 52.219-13
. . notice of total HUBZone set-aside or sole source award . . . 19.1309
. . notice of HUBZone set-aside or sole source award . . . 52.219-3
. . notice of total service-disabled veteran-owned small business set-aside . . . 19.1407
. . notice of service-disabled veteran-owned small business set-aside . . . 52.219-27
. . notice of total small business set-aside . . . 19.508; 52.219-6
. . small business program representations . . . 19.309; 52.219-1; 52.219-28
. . small business subcontracting plan . . . 19.708; 52.219-9
. . small disadvantaged business status . . . 19.309
. . utilization of Indian organizations and Indian-owned economic enterprises . . . 52.226-1
. . utilization of small business concerns . . . 19.708; 52.219-8
. definitions . . . 19.001; 19.101
. emergency acquisitions . . . 18.115; 18.116
. Federal Supply Schedules . . . 8.405-5
. forms prescription . . . 53.219
. historically underutilized business zone (HUBZone) program
. . applicability . . . 19.1302
. . contract clause prescriptions . . . 19.1309
. . emergency acquisitions . . . 18.115
. . exclusions . . . 19.1304
. . general . . . 19.1301
. . price evaluation preference . . . 19.1307
. . set-aside procedures . . . 19.1305
. . sole source awards . . . 19.1306
. . status determinations . . . 19.1303
. policies
. . data collection and reporting requirements . . . 19.202-5
. . determination of fair market price . . . 19.202-6
. . encouraging participation in acquisitions . . . 19.202-1
. . equal low bids . . . 19.202-3
. . general . . . 19.201

Small business programs—continued
. policies—continued
. . locating sources . . . 19.202-2
. . solicitation . . . 19.202-4
. . relationship among small business programs . . . 19.203
. scope . . . 19.000
. service-disabled veteran-owned small business procurement program
. . applicability . . . 19.1402
. . contract clause . . . 19.1407; 52.219-27
. . exclusions . . . 19.1404
. . general . . . 19.1401
. . set-aside procedures . . . 19.1405
. . sole source awards . . . 19.1406
. . status determination . . . 19.1403
. set-asides
. . automatic dissolution . . . 19.507
. . class set-asides . . . 19.503
. . contract clause and solicitation provision prescriptions . . . 19.508
. . Federal Prison Industries, Inc . . . 19.504
. . general . . . 19.501, 6
. . historically underutilized business zone (HUBZone) program . . . 19.1305
. . insufficient causes not to set aside . . . 19.502-6
. . methods of conducting . . . 19.502-5
. . modification . . . 19.506
. . multiple award contracts and small business set-asides . . . 19.502-4
. . partial set-asides . . . 19.502-3
. . rejection of recommendations to set aside . . . 19.505
. . requirements for setting aside acquisitions . . . 19.502-1
. . service-disabled veteran-owned . . . 19.1405; 6.206
. . total set-asides . . . 19.502-2
. . withdrawal . . . 19.506
. size standards
. . application . . . 19.102
. . explanation of terms . . . 19.101
. status determination
. . concern . . . 19.1403
. . determining standard industrial classification codes and size standards . . . 19.303
. . disadvantaged business status . . . 19.304
. . protesting a firm's status as a HUBZone small business concern . . . 19.306
. . protesting a firm's status as a service-disabled veteran-owned small business concern . . . 19.307
. . protesting a representation of disadvantaged business status . . . 19.305
. . protesting a small business representation . . . 19.302
. . representation by offeror . . . 19.301
. . solicitation provisions . . . 19.307

Small business programs—continued
. subcontracting
. . cognizant administrative contracting officer responsibilities . . . 19.706
. . contract clause prescriptions . . . 19.708
. . contracting officer responsibilities . . . 19.705-1
. . definitions . . . 19.701
. . eligibility requirements . . . 19.703
. . Small Business Administration role . . . 19.707
. . statutory requirements . . . 19.702
. . subcontracting plan requirements . . . 19.704

Socioeconomic programs—see also Nonprofit organizations; Small business programs; specific programs
. food donations to nonprofit organizations
. . contract clause . . . 26.404
. . contract clauses and solicitation provisions . . . 52.226-6
. . definitions . . . 26.401
. . policy . . . 26.402
. . procedures . . . 26.403
. . scope of subpart . . . 26.400
. historically black colleges and universities and minority institutions
. . contract clauses and solicitation provisions . . . 26.304; 52.226-2
. . data collection and reporting requirements . . . 26.303
. . general policy . . . 26.302
. . scope . . . 26.300
. Indian incentive program
. . contract clause . . . 26.104; 52.226-1
. . definitions . . . 26.101
. . policy . . . 26.102
. . procedures . . . 26.103
. . scope . . . 26.100

Sole source acquisitions
. documentation requirements . . . 13.501
. emergency acquisitions . . . 18.110; 18.115
. Federal Supply Schedules . . . 8.405-6
. historically underutilized business zone (HUBZone) program . . . 19.1306
. justification
. . approval of . . . 6.304
. . availability to public . . . 6.305
. . content . . . 6.303-2
. . requirements . . . 6.303-1
. leader company contracting
. . general . . . 17.401
. . limitations . . . 17.402
. . procedures . . . 17.403
. negotiated procurement . . . 15.002
. Section 8(a) program
. . contract negotiation . . . 19.808-1
. . contract preparation . . . 19.811-1
. service-disabled veteran-owned small business concerns . . . 19.1406
. waiver of competition requirements . . . 6.302-1

Source selection—see also System for Award Management (SAM) database; Required sources; Selection of contractors
. locating small business sources . . . 19.202-2

Special test equipment
. cost principles . . . 31.205-40

Special tooling
. cost principles . . . 31.205-40

Specifications, standards, and other purchase descriptions
. construction contracts . . . 36.202
. contract clauses and solicitation provisions
. . alternatives to government-unique standards . . . 11.107; 52.211-7
. . availability for examination of specifications not listed in the GSA Index of Federal Specifications, Standards and Commercial Item Descriptions . . . 11.204; 52.211-4
. . availability of specifications listed in the GSA Index of Federal Specifications, Standards and Commercial Item Descriptions . . . 11.204; 52.211-1
. . availability of specifications not listed in the GSA Index of Federal Specifications, Standards and Commercial Item Descriptions . . . 11.204; 52.211-3
. . availability of specifications, standards, and data item descriptions listed in the Acquisition Streamlining and Standardization Information System (ASSIST) . . . 11.204; 52.211-2
. . brand name or equal . . . 11.107; 52.211-6
. . material requirements . . . 11.304; 52.211-5

Standards of conduct
. agency regulations . . . 3.101-3
. certification
. . evaluating . . . 3.103-2
. . need for further certifications . . . 3.103-3
. general . . . 3.101-1
. gratuities . . . 3.101-2
. procurement integrity
. . administrative remedies . . . 3.104-8
. . contract clause prescriptions . . . 3.104-9
. . criminal and civil penalties . . . 3.104-8
. . definitions . . . 3.104-1
. . disclosure, protection, and marking of contractor bid . . . 3.104-4
. . disqualification . . . 3.104-5
. . ethics advisory opinions . . . 3.104-6
. . general . . . 3.104-2
. . statutory and related prohibitions, restrictions, and requirements . . . 3.104-3
. . violations or possible violations . . . 3.104-7
. solicitation provision . . . 3.103-1; 52.203-2

State and local government contracts
. cost principles and procedures . . . 31.601
. . applicability . . . 31.107
. . general . . . 31.602
. indirect cost rates . . . 42.705-4

State and local taxes
. application to federal government . . . 29.302
. application to government contractors and subcontractors . . . 29.303
. exemptions . . . 29.305
. scope . . . 29.300
. special consideration . . . 29.304

State labor requirements
. administration . . . 22.102-2
. policy . . . 22.102-1

Statutory acquisition requirements
. waiver of competition requirements . . . 6.302-5

Subcontracting
. awards
. . contract clause . . . 52.204-10
. . perception . . . 4.1401
. . reporting requirement . . . 4.1400
. commercial items and components
. . applicability . . . 44.401
. . contract clause . . . 44.403
. . policy requirements . . . 44.402
. . scope . . . 44.400
. consent
. . advance notification requirements . . . 44.201-2
. . consent limitations . . . 44.203
. . considerations . . . 44.202-2
. . contract clauses . . . 44.204
. . contracting officer's responsibilities . . . 44.202-1
. . requirements . . . 44.201-1
. construction contracts . . . 22.406-5
. contract clauses and solicitation provisions
. . competition in subcontracting . . . 52.244-5
. . cost or pricing data . . . 15.408
. . certified cost or pricing data . . . 52.215-12
. . certified cost or pricing data—modifications . . . 52.215-13
. . limitations on subcontracting . . . 19.508; 52.219-14; 19.811-3
. . payments to small business subcontractors . . . 52.242-5
. . subcontractors and outside associates and consultants (architect-engineer services) . . . 44.204; 52.244-4
. . subcontracts . . . 52.244-2
. . subcontracts for commercial items . . . 52.244-6
. . subcontracts (labor standards) . . . 52.222-11
. . utilization of small, small disadvantaged and women-owned small business concerns . . . 19.708
. contractor's purchasing system reviews
. . disclosure of approval status . . . 44.306
. . extent . . . 44.303
. . granting, withholding, or withdrawing approval . . . 44.305-1; 44.305-3
. . notification of approval . . . 44.305-2
. . objective . . . 44.301
. . reports . . . 44.307
. . requirements . . . 33.202
. . surveillance . . . 44.304

Subcontracting—continued
. cost-reimbursement contracts . . . 32.110; 44.201-1
. debarment and suspension . . . 9.405-2
. definitions . . . 12.001; 44.101
. Federal Prison Industries, Inc . . . 8.607
. fixed-price contracts . . . 44.201-1
. forms
. . prescription . . . 53.219
. . statement and acknowledgment, SF 1413 . . . 53.301-1413
. . subcontracting report for individual contracts, SF 294 . . . 53.301-294
. kickbacks and . . . 3.502
. loan guarantees . . . 32.306
. nonpayment under contracts for non-commercial items
. . subcontractor assertions . . . 32.112-1
. . subcontractor requests for information . . . 32.112-2
. notices of subcontracting opportunities . . . 5.206
. payment bonds . . . 28.106-8
. payments to small business subcontractors . . . 52.242-5
. performance information
. . contract clause prescription, payments to small business subcontractors . . . 42.1504
. progress payments . . . 32.504
. progress payments based on costs . . . 32.504
. quality assurance . . . 46.405
. research and development contracts . . . 35.009
. restrictions on sales . . . 52.203-6; 3.503-1; 3.503-2
. scope . . . 44.000
. settlement proposals . . . 49.108-1
. small business programs
. . awards involving subcontracting plans . . . 19.705-5
. . cognizant administrative contracting officer responsibilities . . . 19.706
. . contract clause prescriptions . . . 19.708
. . contracting officer responsibilities . . . 19.705
. . definitions . . . 19.701
. . eligibility requirements . . . 19.703
. . liquidated damages . . . 19.705-7
. . Small Business Administration role . . . 19.707
. . statutory requirements . . . 19.702
. . subcontracting plan requirements . . . 19.704
. termination of contracts
. . assignment of rights under subcontract . . . 49.108-8
. . delay in settling subcontractor proposal . . . 49.108-6
. . government assistance . . . 49.108-7
. . prime contractor's rights and obligations . . . 49.108-2
. . recognition of judgments and arbitration awards . . . 49.108-5
. . settlement procedure . . . 49.108-3
. . settlements without approval or ratification . . . 49.108-4
. . subcontractor's rights . . . 49.108-1

Supply contracts—see also Buy American; Required sources
. contract clauses and solicitation provisions
. . delivery or performance schedules . . . 11.404; 52.211-8; 52.211-9
. . quality assurance . . . 46.302; 46.303; 52.246-2; 52.246-3
. delivery or performance schedules . . . 11.403
. evaluating foreign offers
. . application . . . 25.502
. . Buy American, example . . . 25.504-1
. . evaluation examples, general . . . 25.504
. . Free Trade Agreements/Israeli Trade Act, example . . . 25.504-3
. . group award basis, example . . . 25.504-4
. . group offers . . . 25.503
. . policy . . . 25.501
. . WTO GPA/Caribbean Basin Trade Initiative/Free Trade Agreements, example . . . 25.504-2
. forms
. . order for supplies or services, OF 347 . . . 53.302-347
. . order for supplies or services schedule, continuation sheet, OF 348 . . . 53.302-348
. funding . . . 32.703-2
. purchasing economic quantities of supplies
. . contracting officers' responsibilities . . . 7.204
. . policy . . . 7.202
. . scope . . . 7.200
. . solicitation provision prescription . . . 7.203
. records retention . . . 4.705-3
. sharing acquisition saving . . . 48.104-2
. transportation
. . contract clause prescriptions . . . 47.303; 47.305
. . contracting officer responsibilities . . . 47.301-1
. . Defense Transportation System (DTS) . . . 47.301-3
. . determination of delivery terms . . . 47.304-1
. . general . . . 47.301
. . place of delivery, f.o.b. point . . . 47.302
. . scope . . . 47.300
. . shipments from CONUS for overseas delivery . . . 47.304-3
. . shipments originating outside CONUS . . . 47.304-4
. . shipments within CONUS . . . 47.304-2
. . transportation officer participation . . . 47.301-2
. value engineering
. . contract clauses . . . 48.201
. . sharing acquisition savings . . . 48.104-2
. variation in quantity . . . 11.701; 11.703

Sureties—see also Bonds
. corporate sureties, acceptability of . . . 28.202
. definitions . . . 28.001
. forms
. . affidavit of individual surety, SF 28 . . . 53.301-28
. . consent of surety and increase of penalty, SF 1415 . . . 53.301-1415
. . consent of surety, SF 1414 . . . 53.301-1414
. guaranteed loans and . . . 32.304-7

Sureties—see also Bonds—continued
. individual sureties, acceptability of . . . 28.203
. . acceptability of assets . . . 28.203-2
. . acceptance of real property . . . 28.203-3
. . contract clause prescription . . . 28.203-6
. . exclusion of individual sureties . . . 28.203-7
. . release of lien . . . 28.203-5
. . security interests by an individual surety . . . 28.203-1
. . substitution of assets . . . 28.203-4
. irrevocable letter of credit (ILC) . . . 28.204-3
. options in lieu of sureties . . . 28.204
. . certified or cashiers' checks, bank drafts, money orders, or currency . . . 28.204-2
. . contract clause prescription . . . 28.204-4
. . U.S. bonds or notes . . . 28.204-1
. requirements for security . . . 28.201
. scope . . . 28.200
. surety-takeover agreements . . . 49.404

Suspension of contractors
. applicability . . . 9.401
. causes for . . . 9.407-2
. continuation of current contracts . . . 9.405-1
. contract clauses and solicitation provisions
. . certification regarding debarment, suspension, proposed debarment, and other responsibility matters . . . 52.209-5
. . prescriptions . . . 9.409
. . protecting the government's interest when subcontracting with contractors debarred, suspended, or proposed for debarment . . . 52.209-6
. definitions . . . 9.403
. effect of listing . . . 9.405
. System for Award Management (SAM) database . . . 9.404
. general . . . 9.407-1
. period of . . . 9.407-4
. policy . . . 9.402
. procedures . . . 9.407-3
. restrictions on subcontracting . . . 9.405-2
. scope of . . . 9.407-5
. under Drug-Free Workplace Act . . . 23.506

Suspension of work
. contract clauses and solicitation provisions
. . government delay of work . . . 42.1305; 52.242-17
. . stop-work order . . . 42.1305; 52.242-15
. . stop-work order—facilities . . . 42.1305
. . suspension of work . . . 42.1305; 52.242-14
. general . . . 42.1301; 42.1302
. government delay of work . . . 42.1304
. stop-work orders . . . 42.1303

Sustainable acquisition policy
. authorities . . . 23.102

sustainable acquisition policy
. definition . . . 23.101
. exceptions . . . 23.104
. exemption authority . . . 23.105

sustainable acquisition policy—continued
. sustainable acquisitions . . . 23.103

Synopses of contract awards
. award announcement . . . 5.303
. emergency acquisitions . . . 18.103
. general . . . 5.301
. preparation and transmittal . . . 5.302

Synopses of proposed contract actions
. exceptions . . . 5.202
. general . . . 5.201
. notices of subcontracting opportunities . . . 5.206
. preparation and transmittal . . . 5.207
. presolicitation notices . . . 5.204
. procedures and response time . . . 5.203
. publicizing and response time . . . 5.203
. simplified acquisition procedures and . . . 13.105
. special situations . . . 5.205

System for Award Management (SAM) database
. solicitation provision . . . 52.204-7
. contract clause, maintenance . . . 52.204-13
. definitions . . . 4.1101
. description . . . 9.404
. emergency acquisitions . . . 18.102
. policy . . . 4.1102
. procedures . . . 4.1103
. scope . . . 4.1100

T

Taxes
. contract clauses and solicitation provisions
. . domestic contracts prescriptions . . . 29.401
. . federal, state, and local taxes . . . 52.229-3; 29.401-3
. . federal, state, and local taxes (state and local adjustments) . . . 52.229-4; 29.401-3
. . fixed-price contracts with foreign governments . . . 52.229-7; 29.402-1
. . foreign contract prescriptions . . . 29.402
. . foreign cost-reimbursement contracts prescription . . . 29.402-2
. . foreign fixed-price contracts . . . 52.229-6; 29.402-1
. . noncompetitive contract prescription . . . 29.401-4
. . North Carolina state and local sales and use tax . . . 52.229-2; 29.401-2
. . state and local taxes . . . 52.229-1; 29.401-1
. . State of New Mexico Gross Receipts and Compensating Tax . . . 52.229-10; 29.401-4
. . taxes—cost-reimbursement contracts with foreign governments . . . 52.229-9; 29.402-2
. . taxes—foreign cost-reimbursement contracts . . . 52.229-8; 29.402-2
. . taxpayer identification . . . 4.203; 52.204-3
. cost principles . . . 31.205-41
. credit for contract debt . . . 32.607
. federal excise taxes
. . exemptions . . . 29.202; 29.203
. . general . . . 29.201

Taxes—continued
. forms
. . prescription . . . 53.229
. . tax exemption certificate accountability record, SF 1094-A . . . 53.301-1094A
. . tax exemption certificate, SF 1094 . . . 53.301-1094
. information reporting
. . definition . . . 4.901
. . general . . . 4.903
. . procedures . . . 4.904
. . scope . . . 4.900
. . solicitation provision . . . 4.905
. New Mexico gross receipts and compensating tax
. . contract clause prescription . . . 29.401-4
. . definition . . . 29.401-4
. . participating agencies . . . 29.401-4
. problem resolution . . . 29.101
. scope . . . 29.000
. state and local
. . application to federal government . . . 29.302
. . application to government contractors and subcontractors . . . 29.303
. . exemptions . . . 29.305
. . scope . . . 29.300
. . special consideration . . . 29.304
. taxpayer identification number
. . definition of common parent . . . 4.901
. . general . . . 4.203; 4.902
. . reporting contract information to the IRS . . . 4.903
. . reporting payment information to the IRS . . . 4.904
. . scope . . . 4.900
. . simplified acquisition procedures . . . 13.106-3
. . solicitation provision . . . 4.905

Team arrangements among contractors
. team arrangements
. . definition . . . 9.601
. . general . . . 9.602
. . limitations . . . 9.604
. . policy . . . 9.603

Technical data
. commercial items acquisition . . . 12.211

Telegraphic bids . . . 14.201-2

Temporary help . . . 37.112

Termination costs . . . 31.205-42

Termination of contracts
. applicability . . . 49.002
. commercial items acquisition . . . 12.403
. construction contracts . . . 22.406-11
. contract clauses and solicitation provisions
. . contract termination—debarment . . . 52.222-12
. . default (fixed-price construction) . . . 49.504; 52.249-10
. . default (fixed-price research and development) . . . 49.504; 52.249-9
. . default (fixed-price supply and service) . . . 49.504; 52.249-8
. . excusable delays . . . 49.505; 52.249-14
. . failure to perform . . . 49.505

Termination of contracts—continued
. contract clauses and solicitation provisions—continued
. . prescriptions . . . 49.501
. . termination (cost-reimbursement) . . . 49.503; 52.249-6
. . termination (fixed-price architect-engineer) . . . 52.249-7
. . termination for convenience of the government (dismantling, demolition, or removal of improvements) . . . 49.502; 52.249-3
. . termination for convenience of the government (educational and other nonprofit institutions) . . . 49.502; 52.249-5
. . termination for convenience of the government (fixed price) . . . 49.502
. . termination for convenience of the government (fixed-price) (short form) . . . 49.502; 52.249-1
. . termination for convenience of the government (fixed price) . . . 52.249-2
. . termination for convenience of the government (services) (short form) . . . 49.501; 49.502; 52.249-4
. . termination of work (consolidated facilities or facilities acquisition) . . . 49.505
. . termination (personal services) . . . 49.505; 52.249-12
. convenience, cost-reimbursement contracts
. . adjustment of fee . . . 49.305-1
. . adjustment of indirect costs . . . 49.303-4
. . audit of settlement proposal . . . 49.303-3
. . construction contracts, fee adjustment . . . 49.305-2
. . discontinuance of vouchers . . . 49.302
. . final settlement . . . 49.303-5
. . general . . . 49.301
. . partial termination, general . . . 49.304-1
. . submission of inventory disposal schedules . . . 49.303-2
. . submission of settlement proposal . . . 49.303-1
. . submission of settlement proposal (fee only) . . . 49.304-2
. . submission of vouchers . . . 49.304-3
. convenience, fixed-price contracts
. . adjustment for loss . . . 49.203
. . bases for settlement proposals . . . 49.206-2
. . completed end items . . . 49.205
. . deductions . . . 49.204
. . equitable adjustment after partial termination . . . 49.208
. . general . . . 49.201
. . limitation on settlements . . . 49.207
. . profit . . . 49.202
. . settlement proposals . . . 49.206
. . submission of inventory schedules . . . 49.206-3
. . submission of settlement proposals . . . 49.206-1
. convenience terminations, generally . . . 49.301
. cost principles . . . 49.113
. default, cost-reimbursement contracts
. . completion by another contractor . . . 49.405
. . general . . . 49.403

Termination of contracts—continued
. default, cost-reimbursement contracts—continued
. . liquidation of liability . . . 49.406
. . surety-takeover agreements . . . 49.404
. default, fixed-price contracts
. . effect . . . 49.402-2
. . government's right . . . 49.402-1
. . memorandum by contracting officer . . . 49.402-5
. . notice of termination for convenience . . . 49.601
. . other damages . . . 49.402-7
. . procedure . . . 49.402-3
. . procedure in lieu of default termination . . . 49.402-4
. . repurchase against contractor's account . . . 49.402-6
. default terminations, generally . . . 49.401
. definitions . . . 49.001
. Federal Supply Schedules . . . 8.406-4; 8.406-5
. federally funded research and development centers . . . 35.017-5
. formats
. . cure notice . . . 49.607
. . letter notice . . . 49.601-2
. . letter of authorization . . . 49.606
. . notice of termination for convenience . . . 49.601
. . show cause notice . . . 49.607
. . telegraphic notice . . . 49.601-1
. forms
. . inventory disposal report, SF 1424 . . . 53.301-1424
. . inventory schedule A (metals in mill product form), continuation sheet, SF 1427 . . . 53.301-1427
. . inventory schedule B, SF 1428 . . . 53.301-1428; 49.602-2
. . inventory verification survey, SF 1423 . . . 53.301-1423
. . partial payment, application, SF 1440 . . . 53.301-1440
. . prescriptions . . . 53.249
. . schedule of accounting information, SF 1439 . . . 53.301-1439; 49.602-3
. . settlement proposal for cost-reimbursement type contracts, SF 1437 . . . 53.301-1437; 49.602-1
. . settlement proposal (inventory basis), SF 1435 . . . 53.301-1435; 49.602-1
. . settlement proposal (short form), SF 1438 . . . 53.301-1438; 49.602-1
. . settlement proposal (total cost basis), SF 1436 . . . 53.301-1436; 49.602-1
. general principles
. . audit of settlement proposals . . . 49.107
. . authorities . . . 49.101
. . cleanup of construction site . . . 49.105-4
. . duties of prime contractor . . . 49.104
. . duties of termination contracting officer . . . 49.105
. . fraud or other criminal conduct . . . 49.106
. . methods of settlement . . . 49.103
. . notice of termination . . . 49.102
. . release of excess funds . . . 49.105-2
. . responsibilities . . . 49.101
. . scope . . . 49.100

Termination of contracts—continued
. general principles—continued
. . subcontract settlement . . . 49.108-1
. . termination case file . . . 49.105-3
. . termination status reports . . . 49.105-1
. incentive contract settlement . . . 49.115
. loan guarantees and . . . 32.305
. payment
. . final payment . . . 49.112-2
. . partial payments . . . 49.112-1
. purchase orders . . . 13.302-4
. reporting information . . . 49.402-8
. review of proposed settlements . . . 49.111
. scope . . . 49.000
. settlement agreements
. . general . . . 49.109-1
. . government property . . . 49.109-3
. . joint settlement of two or more proposals . . . 49.109-6
. . no-cost settlement . . . 49.109-4
. . partial settlements . . . 49.109-5
. . reservations . . . 49.109-2
. . settlement by determination . . . 49.109-7
. settlement negotiation memorandum . . . 49.110
. subcontract settlement
. . assignment of rights under subcontract . . . 49.108-8
. . delay in settling subcontractor proposal . . . 49.108-6
. . government assistance . . . 49.108-7
. . prime contractor's rights and obligations . . . 49.108-2
. . recognition of judgments and arbitration awards . . . 49.108-5
. . settlement procedure . . . 49.108-3
. . settlements without approval or ratification . . . 49.108-4
. . subcontractor's rights . . . 49.108-1
. under Drug-Free Workplace Act . . . 23.506
. under service contract labor standards statute . . . 22.1023
. unsettled contract changes . . . 49.114

Testing
. emergency acquisitions . . . 18.201; 18.202
. first article testing and approval
. . contractor testing, contract clause . . . 52.209-3; 9.308-1
. . definition of approval . . . 9.301
. . exceptions . . . 9.304
. . general . . . 9.302
. . government administration procedures . . . 9.307
. . government testing, contract clause . . . 52.209-2; 52.209-4; 9.308-2
. . risk . . . 9.305
. . solicitation requirements . . . 9.306
. . use of . . . 9.303
. preaward in-use evaluation . . . 11.801
. special test equipment
. . cost principles . . . 31.205-40

Testing—continued
. under Defense Production Act, Title III
. . contract clause . . . 34.104
. . definitions . . . 34.101
. . policy . . . 34.102
. . scope . . . 34.100
. . testing and qualification . . . 34.103

Third party drafts
. agency responsibilities . . . 13.305-2
. conditions for use . . . 13.305-3
. definition . . . 13.001
. general . . . 13.305-1
. procedures . . . 13.305-4

Time-and-materials contracts
. commercial items acquisition . . . 12.207
. contract clauses and solicitation provisions
. . contract definitization . . . 52.216-25; 16.603-4
. . execution and commencement of work . . . 52.216-23; 16.603-4
. . limitation of government liability . . . 52.216-24; 16.603-4
. . payments of allowable costs before definitization . . . 52.216-26; 16.603-4
. description . . . 16.601
. labor-hour contracts . . . 16.602
. letter contracts
. . application . . . 16.603-2
. . contract clause prescriptions . . . 16.603-4
. . description . . . 16.603-1
. . limitations . . . 16.603-3
. not fixed-price . . . 16.600

Toxic chemical release reporting
. applicability . . . 23.903
. contract clause and solicitation provision prescriptions . . . 23.903
. definition of toxic chemical . . . 23.001
. general . . . 23.902
. policy . . . 23.905
. purpose . . . 23.901
. requirements . . . 23.1004

Trade agreements—see also Foreign acquisitions
. applicability . . . 25.400; 25.402
. Caribbean Basin Trade Initiative . . . 25.405
. definition . . . 25.003
. evaluation examples . . . 25.504-2; 25.504-3
. excluded acquisitions . . . 25.401; 18.118
. general . . . 25.403
. Israeli Trade Act . . . 25.406
. least developed countries . . . 25.404
. procedures . . . 25.408
. trade in civil aircraft . . . 25.407

Trade, business, technical and professional activity costs . . . 31.205-43

Tradeoff process . . . 15.101-1

Trafficking in persons, combating
. contract clause prescription . . . 22.1705
. definitions . . . 22.1702

Trafficking in persons, combating—continued
. policy . . . 22.1703
. scope . . . 22.1700
. violations and remedies . . . 22.1704

Training and education costs . . . 31.205-44

Transportation
. air transportation, U.S.-flag carriers
. . air freight forwarders . . . 47.404
. . availability and unavailability . . . 47.403-1
. . contract clause prescription . . . 47.405
. . definitions . . . 47.401
. . disallowance of expenditures . . . 47.403-3
. . Fly America Act, guidelines for implementation . . . 47.403
. . international air transport agreements . . . 47.403-2
. . policy . . . 47.402
. contracts for transportation or transportation-related services
. . contract clause and solicitation provision prescriptions . . . 47.207
. . definitions . . . 47.201
. . preparation of solicitations and contracts . . . 47.206
. . presolicitation planning . . . 47.202
. . scope . . . 47.200
. . single-movement contracts . . . 47.204
. evaluation of offers
. . adequacy of loading and unloading facilities . . . 47.306-3
. . cost determinations . . . 47.306-1
. . lowest overall cost . . . 47.306-2
. general
. . applicability . . . 47.002
. . definitions . . . 47.001
. . insurance . . . 47.102
. . policies . . . 47.101
. . scope . . . 47.000
. government rate tenders, Interstate Commerce Act sections 10721 and 13712
. . citation . . . 47.104-5
. . contract clause prescription . . . 47.104-4
. . cost-reimbursement contracts . . . 47.104-3
. . fixed-price contracts . . . 47.104-2
. . general . . . 47.104
. . procedures . . . 47.104-1
. ocean transportation, U.S.-flag vessels
. . applicability . . . 47.503
. . construction contracts . . . 47.505
. . contract clause prescriptions . . . 47.507
. . definitions . . . 47.501
. . exceptions . . . 47.504
. . policy . . . 47.502
. . procedures . . . 47.506
. . scope . . . 47.500
. payment and audit regulation
. . contract clause prescription . . . 47.103-2
. . general . . . 47.103-1
. report of shipment (REPSHIP)
. . advance notice . . . 47.208-1
. . contract clause prescription . . . 47.208-2

Transportation—continued
. supply contracts
. . contract clause prescriptions . . . 47.303; 47.305
. . contracting officer responsibilities . . . 47.301-1
. . Defense Transportation System (DTS) . . . 47.301-3
. . determination of delivery terms . . . 47.304-1
. . general . . . 47.301
. . place of delivery, f.o.b. point . . . 47.302
. . scope . . . 47.300
. . shipments from CONUS for overseas delivery . . . 47.304-3
. . shipments originating outside CONUS . . . 47.304-4
. . shipments within CONUS . . . 47.304-2
. . transportation officer participation . . . 47.301-2
. transportation assistance . . . 47.105

Transportation clauses and provisions
. annotation, distribution of shipping and billing documents . . . 47.207-9
. commercial bill of lading notations . . . 47.104-4; 52.247-1
. commodity description and freight classification . . . 47.305-9
. consolidation of small shipments and use of stopoff privileges . . . 47.305-8
. contractor responsibilities . . . 47.207-5
. contracts for transportation and transportation-related services
. . accessorial services—moving contracts . . . 47.207-5; 52.247-13
. . advance notification by government . . . 47.207-8; 52.247-24
. . agreed weight—general freight . . . 47.207-4; 52.247-9
. . capability to perform a contract for relocation of a federal office . . . 47.207-1; 52.247-3
. . charges . . . 47.207-6; 52.247-17
. . contract not affected by oral agreement . . . 47.207-8; 52.247-27
. . contractor liability for loss and/or damage to freight other than household goods . . . 47.207-7; 52.247-22
. . contractor liability for loss of and/or damage to household goods . . . 47.207-7; 52.247-23
. . contractor liability for personal injury and/or property damage . . . 47.207-7; 52.247-21
. . contractor responsibility for loading or unloading . . . 47.207-5; 52.247-15
. . contractor responsibility for receipt of shipment . . . 47.207-5; 52.247-14
. . contractor responsibility for returning undelivered freight . . . 47.207-5; 52.247-16
. . contractor's invoices . . . 47.207-9; 52.247-28
. . discrepancies incident to shipment . . . 47.207-10
. . estimated quantities or weights for evaluation of offers . . . 47.207-6; 52.247-20
. . estimated weights or quantities not guaranteed . . . 47.207-3; 52.247-8
. . familiarization with conditions . . . 47.207-1; 52.247-5

Transportation clauses and provisions—continued
. contracts for transportation and transportation-related services—continued
. . financial statement . . . 47.207-1; 52.247-6
. . freight excluded . . . 47.207-3; 52.247-7
. . government direction and marking . . . 47.207-8; 52.247-26
. . government-furnished equipment with or without operators . . . 47.207-8; 52.247-25
. . inspection of shipping and receiving facilities . . . 47.207-1; 52.247-4
. . multiple shipments . . . 47.207-6; 52.247-18
. . net weight—general freight . . . 47.207-4; 52.247-10
. . net weight—household goods or office furniture . . . 47.207-4; 52.247-11
. . permits, authorities, or franchises . . . 47.207-1; 52.247-2
. . stopping in transit for partial unloading . . . 47.207-6; 52.247-19
. . supervision, labor, or materials . . . 47.207-5; 52.247-12
. . volume movements within the contiguous U.S . . . 47.207-11; 47.207-4
. contracts for transportation or transportation-related services
. . f.o.b. origin, prepaid freight—small package shipments . . . 52.247-65; 47.303-17
. delivery of government-furnished property . . . 47.305-12
. description of shipment, origin, and destination . . . 47.207-3
. destination unknown . . . 47.305-5
. determination of weights . . . 47.207-4
. duration of contract, time of performance . . . 47.207-2
. f.o.b. destination solicitations . . . 47.305-4
. f.o.b. origin solicitations . . . 47.305-3
. government responsibilities . . . 47.207-8
. liability and insurance . . . 47.207-7
. loading responsibilities of contractors . . . 47.305-15
. mode of transportation . . . 47.305-14
. options in shipment and delivery . . . 47.305-11
. packing, marking, and consignment instructions . . . 47.305-10
. qualifications of offerors . . . 47.207-1
. quantity analysis, direct delivery, and reduction of crosshauling and backhauling . . . 47.305-7
. rates and charges . . . 47.207-6
. returnable cylinders . . . 52.247-66; 47.305-17
. shipments to ports and air terminals . . . 47.305-6
. shipping characteristics . . . 47.305-16
. solicitation requirements . . . 47.305-1
. solicitations f.o.b. origin and/or f.o.b. destination lowest overall cost . . . 47.305-2
. submission of commercial transportation bills to the General Services Administration for audit . . . 47.103-2; 52.247-67
. supply contracts
. . bankruptcy . . . 42.903; 52.242-13
. . c. & f. destination . . . 52.247-41; 47.303-13

Transportation clauses and provisions—continued
. supply contracts—continued
. . c.i.f. destination . . . 52.247-42; 47.303-14
. . clearance and documentation requirements—shipments to DoD air or water terminal transshipment points . . . 52.247-52; 47.305-6
. . contractor-prepaid commercial bills of lading, small package shipments . . . 47.303-17
. . destination unknown . . . 52.247-49; 47.305-5
. . evaluation—f.o.b. origin . . . 52.247-47; 47.305-3
. . evaluation of export offers . . . 52.247-51; 47.305-6
. . ex dock, pier, or warehouse, port of importation . . . 52.247-40; 47.303-12
. . exceptions . . . 47.304-5
. . f.a.s. vessel, port of shipment . . . 52.247-36; 47.303-8
. . f.o.b. designated air carrier's terminal, exportation point . . . 52.247-43; 47.303-15
. . f.o.b. designated air carrier's terminal, point of importation . . . 52.247-44; 47.303-16
. . f.o.b. destination . . . 52.247-34; 47.303-6
. . f.o.b. destination—evidence of shipment . . . 52.247-48; 47.305-4
. . f.o.b. destination, within consignee's premises . . . 52.247-35; 47.303-7
. . f.o.b. inland carrier, point of exportation . . . 52.247-38; 47.303-10
. . f.o.b. inland point, country of importation . . . 52.247-39; 47.303-11
. . f.o.b. origin . . . 52.247-29; 47.303-1
. . f.o.b. origin—carload and truckload shipments . . . 52.247-59; 47.305-16
. . f.o.b. origin—minimum size of shipments . . . 52.247-61; 47.305-16
. . f.o.b. origin and/or f.o.b. destination evaluation . . . 52.247-45; 47.305-2
. . f.o.b. origin, contractor's facility . . . 52.247-30; 47.303-2
. . f.o.b. origin, freight allowed . . . 52.247-31; 47.303-3
. . f.o.b. origin, freight prepaid . . . 52.247-32; 47.303-4
. . f.o.b. origin, with differentials . . . 52.247-33; 47.303-5
. . f.o.b. point for delivery of government-furnished property . . . 52.247-55; 47.305-12
. . f.o.b. vessel, port of shipment . . . 52.247-37; 47.303-9
. . freight classification description . . . 52.247-53; 47.305-9
. . guaranteed shipping characteristics . . . 52.247-60; 47.305-16
. . loading, blocking, and bracing of freight car shipments . . . 52.247-58; 47.305-15
. . no evaluation of transportation costs . . . 52.247-50; 47.305-5
. . preference for privately owned U.S.-flag commercial vessels . . . 47.507; 52.247-64
. . preference for U.S.-flag air carriers . . . 47.405; 52.247-63
. . shipping point(s) used in evaluation of f.o.b. origin offers . . . 52.247-46; 47.305-3

Transportation clauses and provisions—continued
. supply contracts—continued
. . specific quantities unknown . . . 52.247-62; 47.305-16
. . standard delivery terms . . . 47.303
. . transit arrangements . . . 52.247-56; 47.305-13
. . transportation factors . . . 47.305
. . transportation transit privilege credits . . . 52.247-57; 47.305-13

Transportation costs . . . 31.205-45

Travel costs . . . 31.205-46

Treaties—see also Trade agreements
. deviations from FAR . . . 1.405
. foreign acquisitions and
. . general . . . 25.801
. . procedures . . . 25.802

Two-phase design-build selection procedures
. phase one . . . 36.303-1
. phase two . . . 36.303-2
. procedures . . . 36.303
. scope . . . 36.300
. scope of work . . . 36.302
. use . . . 36.301

Two-step sealed bidding
. conditions for use . . . 14.502
. contract clauses and solicitation provisions
. . step two of two-step sealed bidding . . . 14.201-6; 52.214-25
. general description . . . 14.501
. step one, requests for technical proposals . . . 14.503-1
. step two, invitations for bids . . . 14.503-2

U

Unit price integrity
. contract clause prescription . . . 15.408; 52.215-14

Unsolicited proposals
. agency points of contact . . . 15.604
. agency procedures . . . 15.606
. content of . . . 15.605
. criteria for acceptance and negotiation . . . 15.607
. definitions . . . 15.601
. evaluation . . . 15.606-2
. general . . . 15.603
. limitations on use of data . . . 15.609
. policy . . . 15.602
. prohibitions . . . 15.608
. receipt and initial review . . . 15.606-1
. scope . . . 15.600

Utility services acquisition
. administration
. . monthly and annual review . . . 41.401
. . rate changes and regulatory intervention . . . 41.402
. applicability . . . 41.102
. contract clauses and solicitation provisions
. . capital credits . . . 41.501; 52.241-13
. . change in class of service . . . 41.501; 52.241-4

Utility services acquisition—continued
. contract clauses and solicitation provisions—continued
. . change in rate or terms and conditions of service for regulated services . . . 41.501
. . change in rate or terms and conditions of service for unregulated services . . . 41.501
. . change in rate or terms and conditions of service for regulated services . . . 52.241-7
. . change in rate or terms and conditions of service for unregulated services . . . 52.241-8
. . connection charge . . . 41.501; 52.241-9
. . contractor's facilities . . . 41.501; 52.241-5
. . electric service territory compliance representation . . . 41.501; 52.241-1
. . multiple service locations . . . 41.501; 52.241-11
. . nonrefundable, nonrecurring service charge . . . 41.501; 52.241-12
. . order of precedence—utilities . . . 41.501; 52.241-2
. . scope and duration of contract . . . 41.501; 52.241-3
. . service provisions . . . 41.501; 52.241-6
. . termination liability . . . 41.501; 52.241-10
. definitions . . . 41.101
. formats
. . annual review . . . 41.702
. . specifications . . . 41.701
. forms . . . 41.601
. GSA areawide contracts . . . 41.204
. GSA assistance . . . 41.203
. interagency agreements . . . 41.206
. policy . . . 41.201
. procedures . . . 41.202
. requests for assistance, requirements . . . 41.301
. scope . . . 41.100
. separate contracts . . . 41.205
. statutory and delegated authority . . . 41.103

V

Value engineering
. contract clauses and solicitation provisions
. . prescriptions . . . 48.201; 48.202
. . value engineering . . . 52.248-1
. . value engineering—architect-engineer . . . 52.248-2
. . value engineering—construction . . . 52.248-3
. definitions . . . 48.001
. general . . . 48.101
. policies . . . 48.102
. processing change proposals . . . 48.103
. relationship to other incentives . . . 48.105
. scope . . . 48.000
. sharing arrangements
. . determining sharing period . . . 48.104-1
. . sharing acquisition savings . . . 48.104-2
. . sharing alternative—no-cost settlement method . . . 48.104-4
. . sharing collateral savings . . . 48.104-3

Variation in quantity
. construction contracts . . . 11.702

Variation in quantity—continued
. contract clauses and solicitation provisions
. . delivery of excess quantities . . . 11.703; 52.211-17
. . variation in estimated quantity . . . 11.703; 52.211-18
. . variation in quantity . . . 11.703; 52.211-16
supply contracts . . . 11.701

Veterans
. equal opportunity
. . definitions . . . 22.1301
. . policy . . . 22.1302
. . scope . . . 22.1300
. . waivers . . . 22.1306
. labor laws
. . actions because of noncompliance . . . 22.1309
. . applicability . . . 22.1303
. . collective bargaining agreements . . . 22.1307
. . complaint procedures . . . 22.1308
. . definition of United States . . . 22.1301
. . Department of Labor notices and reports . . . 22.1306
. . policy . . . 22.1302
. . procedures . . . 22.1304
. . scope . . . 22.1300
. . solicitation provision and contract clauses . . . 22.1310
. . waivers . . . 22.1305

Visits to contractor's facilities . . . 42.402

Voiding and rescinding contracts
. authority . . . 3.703
. definition . . . 3.702
. policy . . . 3.704
. procedures . . . 3.705
. purpose . . . 3.701
. scope . . . 3.700

W

Wage determinations—see also Labor laws
. appeals . . . 22.404-11
. award without required wage determination . . . 22.404-9
. construction contracts . . . 22.406-2
. corrections of clerical errors . . . 22.404-7
. expiration . . . 22.404-5
. general . . . 22.404
. general requirements . . . 22.404-2
. modifications . . . 22.404-6
. notification of improper wage determination before award . . . 22.404-8
. options extending term of contract . . . 22.404-12
. posting and notice . . . 22.404-10
. procedures for requesting . . . 22.404-3
. solicitations issued without wage determinations . . . 22.404-4
. types of . . . 22.404-1
. under service contract labor standards statute
. . procedures for obtaining . . . 22.1008-1
. . requirements . . . 22.1007

Wage determinations—see also Labor laws— continued
. under service contract labor standards statute—continued
. . revisions based on collective bargaining agreements . . . 22.1012-2
. . revisions to prevailing wage determinations . . . 22.1012-1
. . 41 USC 6707(c)successorship with incumbent contractor collective bargaining agreement . . . 22.1008-2
. wage determinations online (WDOL) . . . 22.001

Warranties—see also Acceptance of performance; First article testing and approval; Quality assurance
. authority for use . . . 46.704
. commercial items . . . 12.404; 46.709
. consistency . . . 46.706
. contract clauses and solicitation provisions
. . prescriptions . . . 46.710
. . warranty of construction . . . 52.246-21
. . warranty of services . . . 52.246-20
. . warranty of supplies of complex nature . . . 52.246-18
. . warranty of supplies of noncomplex nature . . . 52.246-17
. . warranty of systems and equipment under performance specifications or design criteria . . . 52.246-19
. criteria for use . . . 46.703
. data . . . 46.708
. duration . . . 46.706
. extent of contractor obligation . . . 46.706
. general . . . 46.702
. incentive contracts . . . 46.707
. limitations . . . 46.705
. markings . . . 46.706
. pricing aspects . . . 46.707
. purposes . . . 46.702
. remedies . . . 46.706
. terms and conditions . . . 46.706

Whistleblower protections for contractor employees
. American Recovery and Reinvestment Act . . . 3.907
. . access to investigative file of Inspector General . . . 3.907-5
. . contract clause . . . 52.203-15
. . contract clause prescription . . . 3.907-7
. . definitions . . . 3.907-1
. . policy . . . 3.907-2

Whistleblower protections for contractor employees—continued
. American Recovery and Reinvestment Act—continued
. . procedure for filing complaint . . . 3.907-3
. . procedures for investigating complaints . . . 3.907-4
. . remedies and enforcement . . . 3.907-6
. applicability . . . 3.902
. definitions . . . 3.901
. contract clause . . . 52.203-17
. definitions . . . 3.908-2
. remedies . . . 3.908-6
. enforcement of orders . . . 3.908-7
. contract clause prescription . . . 3.908-9
. filing complaints . . . 3.904; 3.908-4
. investigating complaints . . . 3.905
. policy . . . 3.903; 3.908-3—3
. procedures for investigating complaints . . . 3.908-5
. remedies . . . 3.906
. scope . . . 3.900; 3.908-1

Withdrawal of bids . . . 14.303; 14.304

Women-owned small business (WOSB) program
. applicability . . . 19.1502
. contract clause prescription . . . 19.1506
. definition . . . 19.1501
. exclusions . . . 19.1504
. general . . . 19.1500
. set-aside procedures . . . 19.1505
. status . . . 19.1503

Workers' compensation insurance
. contract clauses and solicitation provisions
. . insurance—liability to third persons . . . 52.228-7
. . prescriptions . . . 28.309
. . workers' compensation and war-hazard insurance overseas . . . 52.228-4
. . workers' compensation insurance (Defense Base Act) . . . 52.228-3

World Trade Organization Government Procurement Agreement (WTO GPA)
. applicability . . . 25.400; 25.402
. Caribbean Basin Trade Initiative . . . 25.405
. definition . . . 25.003
. evaluation example . . . 25.504-2
. excluded acquisitions . . . 25.401; 18.118
. general . . . 25.403
. Israeli Trade Act . . . 25.406
. least developed countries . . . 25.404
. procedures . . . 25.408
. trade in civil aircraft . . . 25.407